For Reference

Not to be taken from this room

KEN SCHULTZ'S

Fishing Encyclopedia

Worldwide Angling Guide

KEN SCHULTZ'S

Fishing Encyclopedia

Worldwide Angling Guide

Ken Schultz

IDG
BOOKS
WORLDWIDE

IDG Books Worldwide, Inc.
An International Data Group Company
Foster City, CA • Chicago, IL • Indianapolis, IN • New York, NY • Southlake, TX

IDG Books Worldwide, Inc.
An International Data Group Company
919 E. Hillsdale Boulevard
Suite 400
Foster City, CA 94404

For general information on books from IDG Books Worldwide's in the U.S., please call our Consumer Customer Service department at 800-762-2974. For reseller information, including discounts and premium sales, please call our Reseller Customer Service department at 800-434-3422.

For information on a multimedia version of this book, available from Tricom Interactive, Inc., please go to this Web site: intellipedia.com

To contact the author, please visit: www.kenshultz.com

Library of Congress Cataloging-in-Publication Data

Schultz, Ken, 1950–
Ken Shultz's fishing encyclopedia: worldwide angling guide/ Ken Schultz. — 1st ed.
p. cm.
ISBN 0-02-862057-7
1. Fishing—Encyclopedias. 2. Fishes—Encyclopedias. I. Title.
SH411.S38 2000
799.1'03—dc21 99-033719
CIP

Manufactured in the United States of America

04 03 02 01 00 4 3 2 1

First Edition

Trademarks

Table of Contents

Introduction

"Ah, the gallant fisher's life! It is the best of any;
'Tis full of pleasure, void of strife, And 'tis beloved by many."

—IZAAK WALTON

"All men are equal before fish."

—HERBERT HOOVER

WHILE PRODUCING THIS FISHING ENCYCLOPEDIA I SPOKE TO MANY HUNDREDS OF informed anglers. Nearly all of them thought the compilation of all things piscatorial was too overwhelming to contemplate because the angling universe is so enormous and diverse.

Certainly a modern fishing encyclopedia—if it truly provides a full field of knowledge—runs counter to the short and specialized tenets of today's journalism. Yet it is precisely because there is so much to the sport of fishing, plus an increasing profusion of specialized equipment and confusing terminology, that it was necessary to bring order and perspective to all of this in one definitive book.

Ken Schultz's Fishing Encyclopedia &Worldwide Angling Guide has been a long time in the making. I started thinking about it in 1991. Since work began in earnest in 1995, the project became even more expansive than expected, and indeed there were times when it was nearly overwhelming. As a result, the book grew much bigger than originally planned, becoming 50 percent larger than any fishing encyclopedia that has heretofore been published.

As a result, however, this encyclopedia contains the equivalent of thirty standard-length books, meaning that there is ample space to devote to the species, equipment, techniques, locations, and ancillary matters that encompass the angling universe. Consider that nearly one-third of the encyclopedia is comprised of the most comprehensive information on worldwide angling opportunities ever assembled. There is absolutely no place to find these details together; indeed, some elements of the *Worldwide Angling Guide* cannot be found anywhere else at all.

Likewise, the coverage of angling methods and equipment has never been addressed more comprehensively between the covers of any other book. In fact, *Ken Schultz's Fishing Encyclopedia* contains the most modern, illuminating, and extensive discourses on the basic elements of fishing tackle—baitcasting, big-game, conventional, flycasting,

spinning, and spincasting—ever found in one place. Each of these entries undoubtedly contain more than all but the most scrupulous person will want to know.

Great lengths were also taken, however, to make sure that the less obvious subjects in the angling universe were included and reviewed in comprehensive fashion. For example, nowhere else is there a more extensive review of the principles, methods, and pros and cons of catch-and-release—perhaps the most important angling conservation development of the twentieth century.

Topics like fisheries management, angling-related travel, choosing guides and charter boats, and the care and preparation of fish for consumption, which are among many unglamorous subjects taken for granted elsewhere, receive complete explanation and review here. Likewise the otherwise oft-ignored subjects of ethics and etiquette—increasingly important issues as human pressures increase—are included.

Although there's an enormous amount of information in this book, every topic was approached with the intent to take nothing for granted and to present information in straightforward language. Angling is not like nuclear physics, and if it was half as complicated as some people try to make it, no one would enjoy it or have success. The extensive insertion of cross references is thus intended to direct you through a continuing stream of appropriate topics, so you can take any subject as far as you want to go. Some cross references appear within entry text next to topics that are more thoroughly reviewed elsewhere; many cross references apear at the end of entry text, either to direct you to the appropriate subject entry or to note related topics.

We've tried to make things easy to find and to place subjects where you're most likely to look for them, even if you're unsure of the proper terms or spelling. As an example, you'll find rainbow trout under the "T" entries (trout, rainbow) rather than under the "R" entries. Also, at the back of the book is a weights and measures conversion chart; this will be convenient for many readers since there's a liberal mix of metric and U.S. customary weights and measures throughout this book, just as there is at boat docks, fish camps, and tackle shops throughout the world.

Because the text is encyclopedic in format, however, it does not provide a full sense of the joy or spirit of sportfishing—the pleasure that makes it "beloved by many," as Izaak Walton said. Perhaps the accompanying photos help convey this. Photos and line art, incidentally, were planned and selected to reflect the broad, eclectic places and situations that so many anglers experience, as well as to reflect the great diversity of its participants. Angling is a very democratic recreation; as the quotation from President Hoover implies, the fish don't care who hooks them.

It is a special delight to publish this encyclopedia at the close of the twentieth century—a period with the most phenomenal sportfishing growth in the history of mankind—and at the advent of a new millennium. Knowing that the decades ahead will require proper stewardship of aquatic resources—something that anglers in particular have always demonstrated personal and financial support for—this text has been written and edited with sensitivity to conservation issues while also being realistic about the role that humans play as the highest predators and the diverse motivations they bring to angling.

In a sense, the sport of fishing is like a book with as many footnotes as main text. It is full of variables, especially individual skills, weather issues, peculiarities among species, habitat differences, and so forth. You may notice that the words "usually" and "generally" occur often in portions of the text. This isn't meant to be vague; it's because there are often no hard-and-fast rules in catching fish, no matter what you may have heard to the contrary. There are norms, but straying from norms is common for one reason or another, as any angler who has been humbled at a "hot" site at the "best" time of the season can attest.

While there is a wealth of reliable information here, a caveat is in order with regard to the contents of the *Worldwide Angling Guide*. Many of the countries profiled have not in the past provided, or do not currently provide, or may not in the future provide stable travel environments, especially to tourists of certain nationalities. Jungle fishing opportunities are especially among those that may present danger. Angola, Colombia, and Zambia come immediately to mind in this regard. Civil unrest can likewise make travel in certain places dangerous; recent troubles in Kenya, Indonesia, Russia, Uganda, and the Balkans serve as examples. The adventurous angler needs to use good judgment.

Things change the environmental order and aquatic resources, too. Yugoslavia hadn't been wrecked by bombs when that entry was written; Nicaragua and Honduras were leveled by Hurricane Georges right after those entries were written. Environmental changes sometimes radically alter the presence or availability of certain gamefish species, and in the more remote pockets of the world only native people and intrepid explorers are likely to know it.

On a final note, it is tempting to say, as marketers and publicists are wont to do, that this book contains everything an angler will ever need to know about fish and fishing. But new developments in fishing tackle will surely come along, changes in some habitats or in fish populations will alter the techniques and equipment used, and certainly natural changes will take place in some of the world's best angling spots. However, a lot of the fundamentals—the underlying principles of fish behavior, the function of basic equipment, and angling methodology—will be constant, making most of the information in this book relevant to the discerning angler even in years to come.

I expect to add to this body of knowledge in time, so if you think there's something that should have been included, if you have knowledge about fishing in a country that wasn't covered, or if you can suggest an improvement to any aspect of this book, please visit my Web site—www.kenschultz.com—and post a message about it.

Now, turn to any page and become absorbed.

—Ken Schultz

"If I fished only to capture fish, my fishing trips would have ended long ago."

—ZANE GREY

Acknowledgments

PRODUCING A BOOK OF THIS MAGNITUDE REQUIRED THE INVOLVEMENT OF A tremendous number of people and a great array of talents. This encyclopedia would not have gone beyond a mere suggestion, however, had it not been for the endorsement and encouragement of Natalie Chapman, a former publisher at Macmillan General Reference, now IDG Books Consumer Reference, whose confidence and vision made this book possible, and who gave me free rein to produce it as necessary. I'm also indebted to publisher

Marie Butler-Knight, who took this project over in mid-stream, marshaled all the resources, and fervently shepherded the book to completion. Sincere appreciation is also extended to Renee Wilmeth and Kristi Hart, who directed the publisher's nitty-gritty editorial and production work with outstanding dedication and professionalism, plus a reassuring enthusiasm; to Pamela Benner, who paid excellent attention to details in the copyediting process and made good suggestions; and to many other directly involved personnel, particularly Beth Jordan, Faunette Johnston, and Jeanine Bucek.

This book could also not have been completed without the special assistance of my wife, Sandy, and my daughters, Alyson, Megan, and Kristen. They each helped in a variety of ways, especially by being patient. Sandy's assistance with a host of matters was very beneficial, and Kristen was particularly vital, pitching in for a second time during a desperate period with important research and writing assistance.

In order to make this encyclopedia truly comprehensive and of worldwide significance it was imperative to involve a host of contributors with expertise in technical fisheries matters, regional angling opportunities, and specialized sportfishing topics. I'm grateful for their participation and excellent contributions, the bulk of which made up the *Worldwide Angling Guide*. In particular, appreciation is extended to the incomparable Ed Migdalski, who provided technical scientific fisheries advice and vetted all of the fish art.

I'm also indebted to the late, and incomparable in his own right, A. J. McClane. His fishing encyclopedia of 1965 and 1974, though now outdated, was not only a phenomenal reference work, but a monumental achievement in an era before personal computers, electronic mail, fax machines, scanners, laser printers, and the various modern technology that made putting this book together far easier than it was in his time. Unlike me, he was unable to write and edit on a laptop computer in cars, planes, airports, hotel rooms, and other places, or receive electronically transmitted text. More significantly, McClane set a very high bar for what a real fishing encyclopedia ought to be, and provided a template for such a book for the twenty-first century. Without his accomplishment, it would have been much more difficult to plan and publish this book. (Aside to historians: four contributors to this project—Ed Migdalski, George Reiger, Jack Samson, and Bill Scifres—were also contributors to McClane's encyclopedia.)

Just as McClane, the contributors to this book, and the people at IDG Books Worldwide are the best in their fields, so is *Field & Stream* the largest and best fishing and hunting magazine in the world, and I've been privileged to be part of this publication continuously since 1973. I appreciate the confidence and opportunities provided me over that time by its editors. Those opportunities laid the groundwork for this encyclopedia. I'm especially grateful to Editor Slaton White and Managing Editor Mike Toth for allowing me leeway over the last several years that I've been working on this project.

Information, suggestions, encouragement, technical advice, reference paraphernalia, reviews and critiques, and assorted material assistance were received from so many individuals and organizations that some will likely be overlooked in these acknowledgments, for which I apologize.

I'm very grateful to the following individuals:

Blaine Anderson
John Anthon
Dick Ballard
Ron Ballanti
LaVerne Barnes
Cameron Baty
Susan Baumgartner
Gene Bay
Dick Bengraff
Virginia Benoit
Walt Boname
Toby Bradshaw
Eric Burnley

Cyril Calendini
Bill Chapman, Jr.
Jim Chapralis
Larry Columbo
David Cosby
Gary Dollahon
Lou Duarte
Todd DuPuis
Jack Erskine
Mike Fine
Paul Fuller
Riccardo Galigani
Ken Gangler

Guy Geffroy
Lois Gerber
Alessandro Giangio
Barry Gibson
Gary Giudice
Fred Golofaro
Jerry Gomber
George Gowen
Garry Gurke
Judy Hammond
Bill Hilts, Jr.
Bruce Holt
Dr. James Imai
Jimmy Kano
Nick Karas
Glenda Kelley
Gary King
Jason Klein
Bob Lang
Steen Larsen
Mike Leech
Bill Liston
Chun Liu
George Loechl
Paulo Loes
Frank Longino
Jim Matthews
John Mazurkewicz
Tom Melton
Paul Merzig
Ed Mesunas
Bill Miller
Gail Morchower

András Nagy
Andy Newman
Stuart Newman
Donald J. Orth
Tom Pagliaroli
Sheldon Pasternack
Dennis Phillips
Stanko Popovic
Norville Prosser
Jim Reist
Al Ristori
Milt Rosko
Gail Ross
Sharon Rushton
Pat Salimeno
Marty Salovin
Glenn Sapir
Christine Moore Serrao
Vin Sparano
Ron Speed, Sr.
Roy Stiner
Mick Thill
Roger Tucker
Jerry Valentine
Mike Walker
Ben Wechsler
Mark Weintz
Fenner Weller
Jim White
Anthony M. Williams
Dick Wood
Peter Yaskowski

I'm also grateful to the following companies and organizations (and specific people where noted in parenthesis):

American Sportfishing Association (Mike Hayden)
American Wire (Michael Shields)
Arkie Lures
The Atlantic Salmon Federation
Bay de Noc Lure Co.
Bead Tackle (Peter Renkert)
Bear Advertising (Dick Bear, Mark Malkin)
Big Jon (Jerry Livingstone)
Bullet Weights (Douglas Crumrine)
Bushnell Sports Optics (Barbara Mellman)
Cabela's Inc. (Tony Dolle)
Classic Fishing Products (Mike Richards)
C-Map USA (Pam Oldham)
Computrol, Inc.
Cossack Bait Products (Garry Shaw)
Cuba Specialty Mfg. Co. (Craig Osterhus, Dana Pickup)
Daiwa Corp.
Earie Dearie Lure Co. (Helen Galbincea)
EZE Lap Diamond (Donna Long)
Fin-Nor (Niels Stenhoj)
Flambeau Products Corp. (Jason Sauey)
Florida Keys and Key West Visitors Bureau

Flow-Rite of Tennessee (Don Zielinski)
Furuno
Future Fisherman Foundation
Garmin International (Steve Featherstone)
G. Loomis (Gary Loomis, Steve Rajeff)
Gudebrod
International Game Fish Association (Jim Brown)
Hudson River Foundation
Interphase Technologies
K-C Tackle (Raymond Packer)
L. L. Bean (Mary Rose MacKinnon)
L&S Bait Co. (Eric Bachnik)
Lowrance Electronics (Darrell Lowrance, Steve Schneider)
Luhr Jensen & Sons (Phil Jensen, Barry Ternahan)
Magellan Systems Corp. (Don Meyer)
Mann's Bait Co.
Marado Inc.
Old Town Canoe (Jim Kaiser)
O. Mustad & Sons USA (John DeVries)
National Freshwater Fishing Hall of Fame
Nomadic Expeditions (Denise Gogarty)
Normark Corp. (Ron Weber, Craig Weber)
The Orvis Company
Outdoor Technologies
Owner America Corp. (Kat Shitanishi)
Penn Fishing Tackle
Pradco (Joe Hughes, Bruce Stanton)
Scientific Anglers
Shakespeare Fishing Tackle (Mark Davis)
Sheldon's Inc.
Shimano American Corp.
Si-Tex Marine Electronics
Storm Lures (Sharon Andrews, John Storm)
Sufix USA, Inc.
Techsonics Industries
Len Thompson Lures (Richard Pallister)
Top Brass Tackle (Eric Cosby)
Tru-Turn Hooks (Wes Campbell)
Wisconsin Pharmacal
H. D. Wood Advertising
Worden's Lures
The Worth Co.
Wright & McGill Co. (George Large)
Yakima Bait Co. (Rob Phillips)
Zebco Corp. (Jenni Foster)

Gratitude is also due the following government agencies and government-funded programs (and the people noted in parenthesis), which provided research and reference materials, and, in some cases, other forms of assistance:

Alabama Cooperative Extension Service (Richard Wallace)
Alabama Department of Conservation and Natural Resources (Stan Cook)
Alabama Sea Grant Extension Program
Alaska Department of Fish and Game (Jon Lyman)
Alaska Sea Grant College Program (Kurt Byers)
Alberta Department of Environmental Protection

Arizona Game and Fish Department

Arkansas Cooperative Extension Program, Univ. of Arkansas (Nathan Stone)

Arkansas Game and Fish Commission (Keith Sutton)

Auburn University Marine Extension (Richard Wallace, William Hosking, Stephen Szedlmayer)

Brazil Embratur

British Columbia Ministry of Environment, Fisheries Branch

California Department of Fish and Game (A. Petrovich)

Canada Department of Fisheries and Oceans

Canadian Consul General

Cayman Islands Department of Tourism

Colorado Department of Natural Resources

Connecticut Department of Environmental Protection

Delaware Division of Fish and Wildlife

Florida Department of Environmental Protection, Marine Research Institute and Division of Marine Resources (Jim Lewis)

Florida Game and Freshwater Fish Commission, Division of Fisheries (Henry Cabbage)

Georgia Department of Natural Resources (Chris Martin)

Great Lakes Fishery Commission

Guam Department of Agriculture (Gerry Davis)

Hawaii Department of Land and Natural Resources, Division of Aquatic Resources

Idaho Department of Fish and Game (Jack Trueblood)

Illinois Department of Natural Resources

Indiana Department of Natural Resources (Jon Marshall)

International Center for Living Aquatic Resources Management/Food and Agriculture Organization of the United Nations

Iowa Department of Natural Resources (Steve Suman)

Kansas Department of Wildlife and Parks (Mike Miller)

Kentucky Department of Fish and Wildlife Resources (J. Beth Garland)

Louisiana Department of Wildlife and Fisheries

Louisiana Sea Grant College Program

Maine Department of Inland Fisheries and Wildlife (V. Paul Reynolds)

Manitoba Department of Natural Resources, Fisheries Branch (Carl Wall)

Maryland Department of Natural Resources (Eugene Deems, Jr.)

Maryland Sea Grant College Program (Jack Greer)

Massachusetts Division of Fisheries and Wildlife

Michigan Department of Natural Resources, Fisheries Division

Michigan Sea Grant College Program (Martha Walter)

Minnesota Department of Natural Resources (Tom Dickson)

Mississippi Department of Wildlife, Fisheries and Parks (Jim Walker)

Missouri Department of Conservation (John McPherson)

Montana Division of Fish, Wildlife, and Parks

Nevada Department of Conservation and Natural Resources

New Brunswick Department of Economic Development and Tourism

New Brunswick Department of Natural Resources, Fish and Wildlife Branch (Peter Cronin)

Newfoundland Department of Natural Resources

New Hampshire Fish and Game Department (Patricia Fleurie)

New Jersey Division of Fish, Game and Wildlife (Dave Chanda)

New Mexico Department of Game and Fish (Ruth Anderson)

New York Department of Environmental Conservation (Robert Brandt)

New York Sea Grant Program (David MacNeill, Mark Malchoff)

NOAA/Gray's Reef National Marine Sanctuary (Beth Kostka)

NOAA/National Marine Fisheries Service

NOAA/National Weather Service

North Carolina Division of Boating and Inland Fisheries (Fred Harris)

North Carolina Sea Grant

North Dakota Game and Fish Department (Terry Steinwand)

Nova Scotia Department of Fisheries (Murray Hill)

Nova Scotia Department of Lands and Forests (Barry Sabean)

Ohio Department of Natural Resources

Ohio Sea Grant College Program

Oklahoma Department of Wildlife Conservation (Nels Rodefeld)

Ontario Ministry of Economic Development, Trade & Tourism (Tom Boyd)

Ontario Ministry of Natural Resources

Oregon Department of Fish and Wildlife (Randy Henry)

Oregon Sea Grant (Pat Kight)

Parátur, State of Pará, Brazil

Pennsylvania Fish and Boat Commission

Portuguese National Tourist Office (Maria Joáo Ramires)

Prince Edward Island Department of Environmental Resources

Quebec Department of Recreation, Fish and Game

Rhode Island Division of Fish and Game

Rhode Island Sea Grant

Saskatchewan Department of Environment, Fish and Wildlife (Bruce Howard)

South Carolina Department of Natural Resources (Greg Lucas)

South Carolina Sea Grant Consortium (John Tibbetts)

South Dakota Department of Game, Fish and Parks
Spain Ministry of Commerce and Tourism
Tennessee Wildlife Resources Agency
    (Dave Woodward)
Texas Parks and Wildlife (Steve Lightfoot)
Tourism British Columbia
Tourism New Brunswick
Tourism Newfoundland and Labrador
Tourism Nova Scotia (Randy Brooks)
Tourism Prince Edward Island (Carol Horne)
Tourism Quebec (Siegfried Gagnon)
Tourism Saskatchewan (Gerard Makuch,
    Nadine Howard)
Travel Alberta (Peter Gregus)
Travel Manitoba (Dennis Maksymetz, Colette
    Fontaine, Gord Richardson)
University of Connecticut Sea Grant Marine
    Advisory Program (Nancy Balcom)
University of Delaware Sea Grant College Program
University of Florida Cooperative Extension Service
University of New Hampshire and University of
    Maine Sea Grant College Program
U.S. Fish and Wildlife Service
Utah Department of Natural Resources
    (Gerry Schlappe)

Vermont Department of Fish and Wildlife
    (John Hall)
Virginia Department of Game and Inland
    Fisheries (Mitchell Norman)
Washington Department of Fish and Wildlife
    (Nina Carter, James Chandler)
Washington Sea Grant Program (Kris Freeman)
West Virginia Division of Natural Resources
    (Hoy Murphy)
Wisconsin Department of Natural Resources
    (David Kunelius)
Woods Hole Oceanographic Institute
    (Tracey Crago)
Wyoming Game and Fish Department
Yukon Territory Department of Renewable
    Resources (Susan Thompson)

Finally, I'm also grateful to four student interns, whose early work compiling and organizing research materials was of much help—Kristen Schultz of Oberlin College, Alyson Schultz of Boston University, Mathew Kane of Hamilton College, and John Kuhner of Princeton University—and to Megan Schultz of Ithaca College, for Web site development and advice.

—Ken Schultz

About the Author, Artists, and Contributors

PRINCIPAL AUTHOR AND EDITOR

Ken Schultz has been a staff fishing writer and editor for *Field & Stream* since 1973. His feature articles and columns for that publication appear monthly, and he contributes to the magazine's nationally syndicated weekly radio show and to its Web site. Schultz is a frequent author of the outdoors column of the *New York Times*, and he previously was a syndicated newspaper columnist for Gannett. He has authored a dozen books on sportfishing and angling travel topics, has been a featured guest on CNBC, ESPN, and The Nashville Network, and appears regularly in assorted fishing segments for the Outdoor Life Network. A widely traveled angler, Schultz is a former holder of seven line-class world records and was inducted into the Fishing Hall of Fame in 1998. He lives in Forestburgh, New York.

THE ARTISTS

Steve T. Goione is a rising star in the world of fishing and boating art, working in mixed mediums to present his lifelong passion for angling in a dynamic and realistic style. Although he drew the distinctive pen-and-ink illustrations for this book as well as the dust-jacket cover, Goione is primarily a creator of fine art. From his studio in Toms River, New Jersey, he produces commissioned fishing scenes for private collections and limited-edition prints, and he has created original artwork for Sea World in Florida. Goione has also made a mark among boat builders and owners for commissioned renderings of big-game sportfishing craft, and he recently created original artwork for the latest products of Hatteras Yachts. A frequent guest artist on the big-game fishing tournament circuit, Goione appears at exclusive contests each year from Nantucket to Venezuela, and his work is regularly featured at fund-raising events for prominent conservation organizations.

David Kiphuth, whose renderings of fish appear in this book, has had a varied career in the field of art, having been a professional illustrator since 1969. His work has included portraiture, architectural renderings, maps, and book illustration. Kiphuth has created archaeological and scientific book and exhibit renderings for the Yale Peabody Museum, the Yale Department of Anthropology, and Yale University Press. He formerly maintained a studio and gallery in Branford, Connecticut, where he created and sold wildlife and nature art and animal portraits. Since 1989, he has been the staff illustrator

for the *Gazette Newspapers* in Schenectady, New York. He lives in Saratoga Springs, New York.

THE CONTRIBUTORS

Brett Albanese of Virginia is a Ph.D candidate at the Department of Fisheries and Wildlife Sciences at Virginia Polytechnic Institute; he formerly worked at the Mississippi Museum of Natural Sciences.

Ken Allen of Maine is Associate Editor of *Maine Sportsman* and a prolific writer, photographer, newspaper columnist, book author, and guide.

Michael Babcock of Montana is Outdoors Editor of the *Great Falls Tribune*.

Ken Bailey of Alberta is Manager of Field Operations in central Alberta for Ducks Unlimited Canada; he is a prolific writer and President of the Outdoor Writers Association of Canada.

Dick Ballard of Missouri is President of Dick Ballard's Fishing Adventures and a foremost authority on Amazonian angling; he's sent anglers fishing around the world for 18 years, and established the first travel service for Bass Pro Shops.

Scott Bannerot of Pennsylvania and Florida has a Ph.D. in fisheries science and has worked in marine biological research and consulting; he is a photojournalist and a charter boat captain.

John A. Barnes of Bermuda is the Director of Agriculture and Fisheries for Bermuda; he authors a weekly fishing column in the Bermuda *Mid Ocean News*, and is an IGFA representative.

Rob Barraclough of Indonesia and England works in the oil industry and is a charter boat captain and freelance writer.

Carlos M. Barrantes of Costa Rica established the first two sportfishing camps in Costa Rica; he is an IGFA representative and was the first President of the Costa Rican Fishing Federation.

Cody Beers of Wyoming works for the Wyoming Game and Fish Department as Associate Editor of *Wyoming Wildlife* magazine and Editor of *Wyoming Wildlife News and Wild Times*; he is also a freelance writer and photographer.

Bob Berry of California is one of the world's top fish carvers and sculptors, and swept all divisions of the 1986 world championship of fish carving; he is a foremost competition judge, a former professional taxidermist, and author of the book *Fish Carving*.

Mike Bleech of Pennsylvania is a writer and photographer whose work has appeared in most major U.S. fishing and hunting magazines.

Larry Blomquist of Louisiana is Publisher of *Breakthrough*, the world's largest taxidermy trade magazine, and one of the top competition judges in North America; he is a retired award-winning taxidermist, and former President of the National Taxidermists Association.

Fred Bonner of North Carolina is Editor of *Carolina Adventure* magazine; he is also a syndicated newspaper columnist, fisheries biologist, and an IGFA representative.

Judith Bowman of New York has been a foremost sporting books dealer for over twenty years; she produces two sporting book catalogs a year, with special emphasis on fishing.

John Brownlee of Florida is Senior Editor of *Salt Water Sportsman* and a former charter boat captain; he has served on the South Atlantic Fishery Management Council, is former Chairman of the Florida Conservation Association, and is an IGFA representative.

Eric B. Burnley of Virginia is the author of *Surf Fishing the Atlantic Coast* and a radio show host; he is a charter boat captain and Regional Editor of both *Salt Water Sportsman* and *The Fisherman* magazines.

Erwin Bursik of South Africa is Publisher of *Ski-Boat* and *Flyfishing* magazines of Durban, a member of the executive board of the South African Deep Sea Angling Association, and an IGFA representative.

Mac Campbell of Great Britain works for *Angling Plus*, a match fishing magazine, and has previously worked for *Sea Angler*, *Trout Fisherman*, and *Angling Times*.

Jim Casada of South Carolina is the author of many books, including *Modern Fly Fishing*; he is Senior Editor of *Sporting Classics* magazine, and outdoor columnist for the Rock Hill *Herald* and Greensboro *News and Record*.

Göran Cederberg of Sweden has been Editor of several international fact-packed large-format angling books, including *The Complete Book of Sportfishing*; he contributes regularly to north-European publications and has been chief editor of a Swedish sportfishing magazine.

Matthew D. Chan of Virginia is a Ph.D candidate at the Department of Fisheries and Wildlife Sciences at Virginia Polytechnic Institute; he formerly worked as a fisheries biologist for the U. S. Army Corps of Engineers.

Dawn Charging of North Dakota is Outdoors Director for the North Dakota State Tourism Department; she is also a writer and photographer whose family owns a successful fishing resort on Lake Sakakawea.

Homer Circle of Florida has been Angling Editor of *Sports Afield* magazine for 34 years; the dean of American outdoor writers, he is the recipient of numerous media and achievement awards, a former member of the Arkansas Game & Fish Commission, and a renowned television and video host.

Barry Ord Clarke of Norway is a professional photographer and writer and the author of several books on fly fishing and fly tying; he contributes regularly to most European fishing magazines, and is fishing consultant to Norway's largest private sporting estate.

Soc Clay of Kentucky is an accomplished and prolific fishing writer and photographer whose work has appeared in every major outdoor periodical in North America.

Angelo Cuanang of California is a Pacific Regional Editor for *Salt Water Sportsman* and a freelance writer and photographer.

Paula J. Del Giudice of Nevada is Outdoor Columnist for the *Las Vegas Sun*; a freelance writer, photographer, and book author; and former President of the Nevada Wildlife Federation.

Arthur De Mello of Uganda is a representative for the IGFA in Uganda.

Hansjörg Dietiker of Switzerland is Editor of the Swiss Anglers Magazine *Petri-Heil*, and an IGFA representative.

Philippe Dolivet of France is the Chief Editor of the French fly fishing magazine *Plaisirs de la Pêche* and a professional photographer; he is a fly fishing instructor and competitor, an ichthyologist, and an IGFA representative.

Gary Edwards of Wyoming is a longtime fishing guide and a television show host; he is the former Editor and Publisher of *Salmon Fever* magazine, and a former fly rod world record holder.

D'arcy Egan of Ohio has been a sportswriter for *The Cleveland Plain Dealer* for over 20 years; he authored the book, *Guide to Ohio Fishing*, and is host of the American Outdoorsman Radio Network.

Bill Ensor of New Brunswick works for the Fish & Wildlife Branch of the New Brunswick Department of Natural Resources; he was formerly marketing manager of fishing and hunting for the New Brunswick Department of Tourism, and is a longtime fishing guide.

Jack Erskine of Australia is a foremost big-game tackle designer and technical innovator who has helped design many of the modern rods, reels, and drag systems in use today.

Stan Fagerstrom of Oregon is one of the world's best known trick and accuracy casters, and has been featured at sport shows worldwide for half a century; he is also a book, magazine, and newspaper writer.

Jan Fogt of Florida is Editor of *The Bahamas Sportfishing Guide* and was the founding editor of *Bahamas Blue Water Magazine*; she is a contributing editor for *Sport Fishing* and *Marlin* magazines, and is also a book author.

Frank Fry of the Yukon Territory has worked with the Yukon Territory's Department of Natural Resources on various fishing projects.

Mike Garzillo of New Hampshire has been a newspaper columnist for 24 years; he is a regular contributor to various publications and a former regional editor for *Outdoor Life*.

Alessandro Giangio of Italy writes for Italy's premier fishing magazine, *Pesca in Mare*, and has been published worldwide; he has authored five books, is owner and master instructor of the Fishbuster Trolling School and Sportfishing Travel, and has a charter boat in Huatulco, Mexico.

Jerry Gibbs of Vermont is Fishing Editor of *Outdoor Life*, where his career as a staff writer has spanned three decades and made him one of North America's most respected angling authors; he has written several books and has been inducted into the Fishing Hall of Fame.

Barry Gibson of Massachusetts is Editor of *Salt Water Sportsman* and a longtime Maine charter boat captain; he is a former member of the New England Fishery Management Council, and former advisor to the International Commission for the Conservation of Atlantic Tunas.

Jerry Gomber of New Jersey has over twenty-five years of experience in design, development, and marketing of fishing rods and reels; during that period he has been responsible for several successful product innovations.

George Gruenefeld of Quebec and Saskatchewan is Editor of *Canadian Outdoor Publications*; he has written for many magazines in Canada and the U.S., is a book author, and was formerly Outdoors Editor for the *Montreal Gazette*.

Chris Hanks of the Northwest Territories is an anthropologist, freelance writer, and author of the book *Fly Fishing in the Northwest Territories*.

Steve Harper of Kansas is the Outdoors Editor of the *Wichita Eagle* and author of the book *Kansas Day Trips*; in 1995 he was named Conservation Communicator of the Year by the Kansas Wildlife Federation.

Dan Heiner of Alaska is an advertising agency executive and former editor and writer for *Alaska Outdoors* magazine; he is the author of four books on Alaska fishing, including *Fly Fishing Alaska's Wild Rivers*.

Bob Hodge of Tennessee is the Outdoors Editor of the *Knoxville News-Sentinel*; he was named the state's Best Outdoor Writer for 1996-97 by the Tennessee Sportswriters Association.

Grant Hopkins of Ontario is the outdoor columnist for the *Ottawa Citizen*, a frequent contributor to *Ontario Out of Doors*, and retired from the Royal Canadian Air Force.

John Husar of Illinois is the longtime outdoors columnist and general sportswriter of the *Chicago Tribune* and co-host of a Chicago radio show; he has worked for newspapers in Kansas, Texas, and New Mexico, and has covered the last nine Olympics.

Jim Imai of California has a Ph.D in physics and is Professor of Physics at California State University, Dominguez Hills; he is a Consulting Physicist for the Daiwa Corporation, and a leading authority on the design and performance of fishing reels and rods.

James Kano of Ontario is the Marketing Director of Japan Communications in Toronto and Outdoor Coordinator for the Press and Tourism division of the Ontario government; his articles have appeared online and in newspapers, guide books, and magazines.

Nick Karas of New York is the retired outdoor columnist for (New York) *Newsday* and a charter boat captain and ichthyologist; he has written for many national magazines and authored a dozen books, including *The Striped Bass* and *Brook Trout*.

Lee Kernen of Wisconsin is the retired Director of Fisheries for the State of Wisconsin; he is also a writer, fishing guide, and fisheries consultant.

Ronnie Kovach of California is a radio and television show host, educator, magazine writer, guide, and author of five books, including *Bass Fishing in California*, *Trout Fishing in California*, and *Saltwater Fishing in California*.

Steen Larsen of Denmark is one of Europe's leading sportfishing writers and photographers; he is a book author and lecturer, and contributes widely to many European angling publications.

Dick Lewers of Australia is Technical Editor of *Encyclopaedia of Australian Fishing*, author of seven books on angling, a former IGFA representative, 35-year columnist for *Modern Fishing Magazine*, and past President of the Australian National Sportfishing Association.

Bill Loftus of Idaho is the Outdoors Editor of the *Lewiston Morning Tribune* and the author of two guidebooks to Idaho.

Maurice Loustau-LaLanne of Seychelles is the Principal Secretary in the Ministry of Tourism and Transport for the Seychelles, and an IGFA representative.

Carl. F. Luckey of Alabama is a writer specializing in antiques and collectibles; he has authored ten books, including his best-selling, 618-page work, *Old Fishing Lures and Tackle*.

Joe Macaluso of Louisiana is an award-winning outdoors sportswriter/editor for the *Baton Rouge Advocate;* his weekly fishing reports have appeared in Louisiana newspapers since 1976.

Rosanne Macfarlane of Prince Edward Island recently received her Masters degree in Biology at Acadia University; she works for the Department of Fisheries and Environment.

Dennis Maksymetz of Manitoba is Manager of Tourism Marketing for the Industry, Trade and Tourism division of the Manitoba government.

Don Mann of Florida is a longtime contributor to *Florida Sportsman*, a record-holding big-game angler, and book author; his articles and photographs have appeared in many publications.

Al Marlowe of Colorado has written numerous articles for outdoor magazines; he authored a trail guide for the Flat Tops Wilderness area and a fly fishing guide for the Colorado River.

Peter B. Mathiesen of Missouri is Executive Editor and Producer of the *Field & Stream Radio Hour*; he is also a magazine writer, photographer, and video and television show producer.

John McCoy of West Virginia is Outdoors Editor for the *Charleston Daily Mail*, Regional Editor for *Field & Stream*, and a frequent contributor to regional and national magazines.

Tom Meade of Rhode Island writes about the outdoors for the *Providence Journal-Bulletin*; he is the author of *Essential Fly Fishing*, and writes for various magazines.

Ed Migdalski of Connecticut is the retired Director of Yale University's Outdoor Education and Club Sports Programs, retired Ichthyologist for the Yale Peabody Museum, and holder of the current world record for the largest strictly freshwater fish (pirarucu) ever caught on rod and reel.

Kent Mitchell of Georgia has covered outdoor sports for the *Atlanta Journal-Constitution* for three decades; he has received the Communicator of the Year Award from the Georgia Wildlife Federation, and has authored three books on martial arts.

Bill Monroe of Oregon has covered the outdoors for his state's largest daily newspaper, *The Oregonian*, for 18 years.

Gary W. Moore of Vermont is a freelance writer and photographer; he is former Commissioner of the Vermont Fish and Wildlife Department and former Chairman of the Vermont Water Resources Board.

Sam Mossman of New Zealand is Special Projects Editor for *New Zealand Fishing News* magazine; he is the author of three books and hundreds of magazine articles, and has held five world and numerous New Zealand fishing records.

Perry Munro of Nova Scotia is a writer and artist who contributes to *The Atlantic Salmon Journal* and various other magazines; he is also an outfitter, master guide, operator of Maple Mountain Lodge, and a Director of Trout Unlimited Canada.

Iain Nicolson of Angola is an IGFA representative and has a Ph.D. in molecular genetics; he and his family pioneered fishing for blue marlin in Angola and collectively established six world fishing records.

Chris Niskanen of Minnesota is the Outdoors Editor of the *St. Paul Pioneer Press*.

Donald J. Orth of Virginia is a Professor of Fisheries Science in the Department of Fisheries & Wildlife Sciences at Virginia Polytechnic Institute.

Tom Pagliaroli of New Jersey is an advertising agency executive, freelance writer, and photographer whose work has appeared in various regional and national publications.

Ali Pasiner of Turkey is an attorney, the author of two fishing books, and a consultant to the Turkish version of the *Encyclopaedia Britannica*; he is also a writer, editor, and representative of the IGFA.

C. Boyd Pfeiffer of Maryland is a longtime journalist and photographer, a regular columnist for many angling magazines, and the author of numerous books on fishing topics, the latest of which is *Fly Fishing Salt Water Basics*.

Larry Porter of Nebraska has been on the sports staff of the *Omaha World-Herald* for over three decades and their outdoors writer since 1990; he has been named Nebraska Sportswriter of the Year three times, and is a former professional tournament angler.

Steve Price of Texas is a longtime Senior Writer for *Bassmaster* magazine and contributor to a wide variety of national sporting magazines; he is an accomplished photographer and author of several books.

Gareth Purnell of England is Editor of Britain's leading angling magazine, *Improve Your Coarse Fishing*, and former News Editor of *Angling Times*; he has fished annually in the World Freshwater Angling Championships since 1993.

George Reiger of Virginia is Conservation Editor of *Field & Stream* and *Salt Water Sportsman* magazines and the most widely respected conservation writer in North America; he has been a staff writer for *Field & Stream* since 1972, is the author of seven books on angling and marine ecology, and the recipient of numerous honors and awards.

Tim Renken of Missouri has been the outdoors writer for the *St. Louis Post-Dispatch* since 1963; he previously worked for the Nebraska Game Commission.

Len Rich of Newfoundland is the author of two books and many outdoor magazine articles; he operates Awesome Lake Lodge in Labrador, is a former Hunting and Fishing Development Officer for Newfoundland and Labrador, and is a past representative of the Atlantic Salmon Federation.

Tom Richardson of Massachusetts is Managing Editor of *Salt Water Sportsman* magazine, as well as a freelance writer and photographer.

Al Ristori of New Jersey is Saltwater Fishing Editor of the *Newark Star-Ledger*, Regional Editor of *Salt Water Sportsman*, Conservation Editor of *The Fisherman* magazine, and the author of several books; he is also a charter boat captain and has served on the Mid-Atlantic Fishery Management Council.

Jim Rizzuto of Hawaii is Hawaii Editor for *Salt Water Sportsman* and *Western Outdoors*, a longtime columnist for *West Hawaii Today* and *Hawaii Fishing News*, and the author of the books *Modern Hawaiian Gamefishing* and *Fishing Hawaii Style*.

Nels Rodefeld of Oklahoma is an avid angler and hunter who frequently covers Oklahoma's hunting and fishing scene.

Milt Rosko of New Jersey is a writer for *Big Game Fishing Journal* and various other publications and a longtime authority on saltwater sportfishing; he is a photographer, book author, magazine feature writer, and lecturer.

Terry Rudnick of Washington has been writing articles on Northwest fishing subjects for more than 25 years; he is the author of the book *Washington Fishing, the Complete Guide*, and co-author of *How to Catch Trophy Halibut*.

Bob Sampson, Jr. of Connecticut is a writer, photographer, science teacher, and fisheries biologist; his work has appeared in numerous national and regional magazines.

Jack Samson of New Mexico is the retired Editor-in-Chief of *Field & Stream* and a former Associated Press columnist; he is Saltwater Editor of *Fly Rod & Reel* magazine, author of twenty books, and the first angler to catch both Atlantic and Pacific sailfish and all five species of marlin on a fly.

Ray Sasser of Texas is the Outdoor Editor of *The Dallas Morning News* and a freelance contributor to various magazines; he has been writing about outdoor sports for over 25 years.

Carl Werner Schmidt-Luchs of Germany is a contributor to *Blinker*, the largest angling magazine in Europe; he is a photographer, writer, and author of a dozen angling books.

Kristen Schultz of Massachusetts is a writer who recently graduated from Oberlin College; she works for an engineering consulting firm.

Bill Scifres of Indiana has been the Outdoor Editor of the *Indianapolis Star* since 1953; he is a book author, freelance writer, and photographer.

Eric Sharp of Michigan is Outdoor Editor of *The Detroit News*, and was formerly Outdoor Editor of *The Miami Herald*.

Luis Sier of Argentina is a newspaper columnist, a former magazine publisher, and an outfitter who operates several Argentinian fishing camps.

Jeff Simpson of South Dakota is an information officer for the State of South Dakota, a book author and freelance magazine writer, and former project developer for Cowles Creative Publishing.

DeWayne Smith of Arizona is an information officer for the Maricopa County Parks and Recreation Department; he covered the outdoors for over 30 years for *The Phoenix Gazette*.

Ryan Smith of Virginia is a research assistant with the Department of Fisheries and Wildlife Sciences at Virginia Polytechnic Institute.

Michael Snook of Saskatchewan is a freelance writer, conservationist, outdoor educator, and television producer.

Frank Sousa of Massachusetts is a writer for the *Springfield Sunday Republican* and the *Union News*, Editor/Publisher of *Northeast Woods and Waters*, and a freelance writer and photographer.

Vin T. Sparano of New Jersey is Senior Field Editor and retired Editor-in-Chief of *Outdoor Life*, for whom he worked for over three decades; he is a former syndicated columnist for *Gannett Newspapers*, and the author/editor of fourteen books, including *The Complete Outdoors Encyclopedia*.

Vladimir Stakic of Yugoslavia is Deputy Editor-in-Chief of the Yugoslavian angling magazines *Ribolovacka Revija* and *Ribolovacke Novine*, a freelance writer, and the author of three books of short stories.

Bob Stearns of Florida has been the staff boating/saltwater fishing writer of *Field & Stream* for 20 years and is the Electronics Editor of *Salt Water Sportsman*; the author of two books, he is a renowned fly fishing and light tackle expert, and has held two fly rod world records for sailfish.

Larry Stone of Iowa has been a writer and photographer for over three decades, and writes about the outdoors for the *Des Moines Register*.

Keith Sutton of Arkansas is Editor of *Arkansas Wildlife magazine*, a conservation publication of the Arkansas Game & Fish Commission, and a prolific freelance writer and photographer.

Ferenc Szalay of Hungary is Editor-in-Chief of *Magyar Horgász*, Hungary's premier fishing magazine; he is also President of the Hungarian National Committee for Match Fishing and Executive Board member of the Federation Internationale de la Pêche Sportive en Eau Douce.

Allan Tarvid of Texas is a contributing editor for *Sport Fishing* magazine and has authored hundreds of articles on electronics for sporting and commercial fishing and emergency service use; he has been a fishing guide and search and rescue diver.

Rikk Taylor of British Columbia is Editor and Publisher of *British Columbia Sport Fishing* magazine.

Mick Thill of Illinois and England is one of the world's top professional match fishing anglers and the first and only person to medal in the open water and ice fishing World Freshwater Fishing Championships; he is also a prominent float designer, and coach of the U. S. World Championship fishing teams.

Albert A. W. Threadingham of Fiji is an IGFA representative for the Fiji Islands and Governor of the Hawaiian International Billfish Association and the Pacific Ocean Research Foundation; he is a former world-record fish holder.

Raj Tilak of Maryland and India is co-author of the book *Game Fishes of India and Angling*, and author of more than 200 research publications; he is experienced in fisheries and wildlife management, with extensive knowledge of gamefishes and their ecology in India.

Anssi Uitti of Finland works for the Finnish outdoor magazine *Metsästys ja Kalastus*, and his articles have appeared in *Urheilukalastus* (Sportfishing) and *Perhokalastus* (Flyfishing) magazines.

Luis Umpierre of Puerto Rico is a physician, Editor of *Notipesca* (Fishing News), President of the Puerto Rico Sportfishing Association, and advisory member of the Caribbean Fishery Management Council.

Rudy Van Duijnhoven of Holland is a freelance photographer and author; his work appears monthly in *BEET-Sportvissers* magazine, and he is European Correspondent for Fly Fishing in *Salt Waters* magazine.

Carlo Vernocchi of Italy and Zanzibar introduced modern big-game fishing to the Zanzibar archipelago of Tanzania in 1992; he is an IGFA representative and charter boat captain.

Victor Villavicencio of Manila is a representative for the IGFA in the Philippines.

Tsutomu Wakabayashi of Japan is the General Manager of the Japan Game Fish Association; he has written for several Japanese fishing magazines, and is an IGFA representative.

Steve Waters of Florida is the outdoors writer for the *Fort Lauderdale Sun-Sentinel* and occasionally writes for national magazines; he was formerly a newspaper writer and video executive in New York.

Tom Wharton of Utah has been Outdoor Editor of the *Salt Lake Tribune* since 1976; he has co-authored five books, and is past President of the Outdoor Writers Association of America.

Jesse E. Williams of New Mexico is the retired Chief of Public Affairs for the New Mexico Department of Game and Fish, and a former Colorado wildlife manager and environmental education supervisor.

Juergen Willms of the Yukon Territory has worked with the Yukon Territory's Department of Natural Resources on various fishing projects.

Jorge Xifra of Paraguay operates El Pescador, a sportfishing outfitting service; he is a writer, television show host, IGFA representative, and holder of four world fishing records.

Photo Credits

A

ABEAM

A nautical term referring to an object that is to one side of a boat and at a right angle to the fore-and-aft line.

ABOARD

On board a boat; on or within a boat.

ACIDITY

The concentration of acid in water or in a solution as described by the pH *(see)* scale. The neutral value of pH is 7.0; the lower the pH value below 7.0, the greater the acidity. The acidity of a given body of water depends on various natural and man-made influences. Highly acidic water is intolerable to fish, and even moderate levels of acidity may reduce fish populations and adversely affect plants and other animals.

ACTION

"Action" is the term used to designate where a fishing rod flexes along its blank *(see)*.
See: Rod, Fishing.

ADIPOSE EYELID

A translucent tissue partially covering the eyeball of some species of fish.
See: Fish.

ADIPOSE FIN

A small fleshy fin without rays found on the back of some fish, behind the dorsal fin and ahead of the caudal fin. Only a small percentage of fish have an adipose fin; among gamefish these include various trout, salmon, grayling, whitefish, and piranhas.
See: Fish.

AERATOR

An aerator is a device that supplies oxygen to water, usually within a livewell, cooler, or some type of container that holds gamefish or live baitfish. As an item of fishing equipment, aerators are comprised of a pump that brings in fresh (raw) or recirculated water and splashes it onto standing water to both mix and oxygenate the water.
See: Livewell.

AFT

A nautical term meaning at or near the stern of a boat.

AIRBOAT

A flat-bottomed aluminum boat driven by a propeller revolving in the air, an airboat is primarily associated with travel in the swamps and saw grasses of the Everglades, where it is impossible to travel any distance in a quick manner in conventional boats. Some people use them to access hunting and fishing areas, although anglers often leave the boat and wade. Large airboats can accommodate several people and are used by some guides; wearing ear protection is advised, as the motors are extremely noisy.

Airboats have also been used on snow- and ice-covered lakes in the north to facilitate travel to and from places where there is an occasional need to cross (or the possibility of crossing) open water or unsafe ice, especially when the trip cannot be made in a boat sporting a lower unit or would be imprudent with an ATV or snowmobile.

AIRPLANE TEASER

A common term for a bird- or airplane-shaped teaser used in offshore fishing, especially for marlin and tuna.
See: Trolling Lures, Saltwater.

ALABAMA

Anglers looking for diversity, both in fish species and types of water, find it quickly in Alabama. The state has more than a million acres of freshwater open to fishing, including more than two dozen large man-made impoundments, seven major river systems, and 20 smaller state-managed lakes. In southern Alabama, the 400-square-mile Mobile Delta provides brackish water conditions, where freshwater and saltwater fish often swim together; and along the Gulf Coast, Mobile and Perdido Bays offer pier, jetty, and flats fishing as well as quick access to offshore opportunities.

The largemouth bass is easily the state's most popular freshwater species, and specimens over 16 pounds have been recorded. In northern Alabama, particularly in several Tennessee River impoundments, smallmouth bass fishing is rated among the best in the world. Spotted bass, black and white

A

crappie, white bass, several varieties of sunfish, and five species of catfish are present in lakes throughout the state; and in years past, Alabama held world records for both smallmouth and spotted bass. Additionally, striped bass and hybrid striped bass have been introduced successfully to a number of the larger impoundments.

In the brackish water of the delta, as well as in coastal bays, speckled trout, red drum (generally known locally as redfish), and flounder are present, while just offshore at various buoy markers and old oil rig platforms small-boat anglers and charter captains alike chase Spanish and king mackerel, cobia, grouper, amberjack, red snapper, and even an occasional tarpon. Farther offshore along the deep chasm known as DeSoto Canyon and the 100-fathom curve, marlin, wahoo, and sailfish can be taken.

This angling bounty, particularly in freshwater, is primarily the result of Alabama's generally mild weather. Although occasional snow may blanket portions of the state's northern counties, the water temperature remains warm enough to keep the fish active year-round. Additionally, the Tennessee River marks the northern limit of threadfin shad, the smallmouth's favorite prey, and the southern limit of naturally occurring smallmouth. The result is a river system with some of the most consistent trophy smallmouth fishing in the nation.

Freshwater

Tennessee River. With headwaters in northeast Tennessee, the Tennessee River flows southward and enters Alabama just south of Chattanooga. From there the river makes a westward loop through several northern Alabama counties, cuts through a corner of Mississippi, and reenters Tennessee. In Alabama, the Tennessee River has been dammed to form four large reservoirs containing more than 180,000 acres of water. These include Lakes Guntersville, Wheeler, Wilson, and Pickwick.

At 69,000 acres, Guntersville is the largest reservoir in the state. It enjoys an excellent reputation for its largemouth bass and crappie fishing, and during the early 1980s was considered one of America's top bass lakes. This reputation was largely the result of a heavy growth of Eurasian milfoil that infested much of the open water, as well as abundant stump and tree cover. An extensive aquatic vegetation eradication program by the Tennessee Valley Authority in the late 1980s, however, caused a significant decline in the quality of the bass fishery. Fortunately, as the vegetation has slowly regenerated, the fishery is likewise improving.

Wheeler, Wilson, and Pickwick Lakes are famous for their smallmouth bass fishing, particularly in the tailraces below each dam. A then-world record 10.8-pound smallmouth bass was caught in 1950 in the fast water below Wheeler Dam, and today 6- to 8-pounders are regularly caught in these waters each year.

A favorite fishing method in the tailraces is drifting live shad minnows downstream in the current, using spinning tackle, 6- to 10-pound line, and BB-size split shot for weight. The shad are simply hooked through the lips and then kept just above the rocky bottom as the boat drifts with the current. Anglers who learn to read the currents by observing water released from the dam and who steer their boats along the edges where the "slick" calmer water meets the faster flow, are consistently successful.

Other smallmouth techniques for drifting the tailraces include slowly trolling downstream with shallow-running crankbaits, bouncing jigging spoons along the bottom, and casting/drifting small $1/8$-ounce plastic grubs or hair jigs. Largemouth and spotted bass, white bass, catfish, and freshwater drum are also caught this way throughout the year; in winter, jig-drifting techniques often produce excellent sauger catches.

During the summer months, night fishing with spinnerbaits is another productive and popular angling technique for smallmouth. Although the fish remain in relatively deep water during the day, at night they move up on flats and bars less than 10 feet deep to feed. The best flats are those edged by deeper channels, and the most successful technique is usually a slow, steady rise-and-fall retrieve near the bottom.

In spring, channel catfish move onto the flats to spawn, producing excellent opportunities on Pickwick Lake. Most anglers use cut bait and simply anchor at the mouths of tributary creeks or shallow flats, out of the main current flow.

Coosa River. The Coosa River enters Alabama in the northeast corner of the state from Georgia and flows southward for about 175 miles to its confluence with the Tallapoosa River, near the capital city of Montgomery. There the two rivers become the Alabama River, which flows into the Gulf of Mexico.

The Coosa, like all major rivers in the state, has been dammed for flood control and electrical power. The resulting lakes include—from north to south—Weiss, Neely Henry, Logan Martin, Lay, Mitchell, and Jordan. Collectively, they are among the state's most heavily fished waters due to their proximity to Gadsden, Birmingham, and Montgomery. Nevertheless, they continue to provide excellent angling opportunities for Alabama's most popular species: largemouth bass and crappie.

Interestingly, however, three of the lakes have gained nationwide reputations for one particular species. Weiss Lake, especially, has been one of the South's premier crappie lakes for decades, and each spring anglers from as far away as Illinois and Indiana—to say nothing of hordes of locals—converge on the 30,200-acre impoundment to take home coolers full of the tasty panfish.

Live minnows fished under a float are the preferred bait, but many crappie are caught with small bucktail jigs. Crappie are also occasionally caught

by bass anglers fishing small crankbaits. The best places are shallow stump fields throughout the lake, shallow channel drops, wide flats in the tributary creeks, and logjams in the upper Coosa River. Although the majority of fish are caught in water 6 feet deep or less, most anglers use an adjustable float to present baits at different depths until the crappie are located.

While Neely Henry, an 11,200-acre impoundment immediately below Weiss Lake, offers very good bass and crappie fishing, the most well-known largemouth fishing lake on the Coosa chain is the third lake, Logan Martin. Here anglers will find a variety of water conditions, including river current, flats, tributary creeks, and major lake points, that provide year-round opportunities not only for largemouth but also for spotted, white, and hybrid striped bass, as well as for channel, flathead, and blue catfish.

All three fish can be very productive at certain times; spring is undoubtedly the best time, because bass, crappie, and catfish are moving shallow to spawn. Fall fishing is popular and productive as well, with spinnerbaits, crankbaits, and soft-plastic lures the favored choices.

Lake Jordan (pronounced "Jurdan" by many locals) is best known for its spotted bass population. At 6,900 acres it is the smallest of the Coosa River lakes, but it offers excellent combinations of deep and shallow water mixed with abundant rock and stump cover that make it ideal for spotted bass. Local anglers often do well fishing this cover from the shoreline, while others prowl the Coosa's various tributaries, particularly Welona, Weoka, Shoal, and Proctor Creeks.

Both spinning and baitcasting equipment are used for spotted bass, with soft-plastic worms, crankbaits, and spinnerbaits all popular and successful. Spotted bass, especially heavier ones, fight much harder than comparable-size largemouths, making heavier lines and rods somewhat more desirable. These fish tend to stay deeper than largemouths but are often more active.

Chattahoochee River. Along the Chattahoochee River, which forms the boundary between Alabama and Georgia for part of its length, anglers focus on two impoundments: West Point Lake and Lake Walter F. George, also known as Lake Eufaula. Only a small portion of West Point Lake is in Alabama.

After the lake's impoundment in 1974, West Point anglers enjoyed some of the finest largemouth bass fishing in the South, but this gradually changed as the lake's early boom cycle ended. As it declined, however, tens of thousands of hybrid striped bass were stocked in the mid-1980s, and not only did they thrive and create an entirely new sportfishery, their popularity took much of the angling pressure off largemouths.

Today the lake produces excellent catches of both species. Live-bait fishing is popular for both hybrids and largemouths, although artificial lures, especially crankbaits, continue to produce well. West Point does not have the well-defined creek and river channel structure so prevalent downriver on Eufaula, but it does have abundant flats and long, gently sloping points that seem to attract bass whenever water is released through the dam to produce electricity. This makes Carolina-rig fishing with short plastic worms and lizards a popular technique, and places like Wehadkee, Stroud, and Veasey Creeks are well known to every West Point angler.

Lake Eufaula was one of the earliest big-bass lakes in the nation and helped usher in the era of modern bass fishing. It enjoyed a resurgence in its largemouth bass fishing in the mid-1990s, although not quite comparable to its storied heyday of the late 1960s and early 1970s. However, good fishing today—along with many access sites, a national wildlife refuge, and various parks and public-use areas—makes this one of the more popular destinations for anglers from throughout the Southeast and Midwest.

Today, 10-pound and larger bass are caught each spring in Eufaula's tributary creeks, primarily with spinnerbaits and plastic worms. The most notable tributaries include Cowikee, Barbour, White Oak, and Pataula, all of which include different types of stump, brush, and vegetative cover, as well as steep-sided channel drops. Many creeks, coves, points, flats, and other good-looking spots to fish beckon along its 640 miles of shoreline. Crappie, white bass, and other species thrive here too.

This lake is 85 miles long, offering numerous places to explore. The northern sector, above Cowikee Creek, is riverine, whereas the southern sector is typical of impoundments, with wide-open areas. Created in 1963, Eufaula is a substantial hydroelectric and flood control reservoir; almost daily, current is created along the entire lake as power is generated or water is pulled for diversion.

An angler prepares to land a largemouth bass on Lake Eufaula.

Late winter and spring are especially popular with both local and visiting anglers, and are known for large bass. Frequent cold fronts make fishing unpredictable, however, with success dropping off dramatically until several days of stable conditions prevail.

Early in the season, especially when bass are spawning, anglers favor shallow flats, particularly those with stumps, brush rows, and vegetation. Although many of these are in major creeks, some are in the main lake—in the open-water sections—and extend for great distances. Another preferred area is along riprap banks. In mid- to late spring, bass move to river and creek ledges and deeper water, when anglers rely heavily on vertical spoon jigging and worm fishing.

Hybrid striper fishing kicks into gear in the summer, with good fishing in some locales (often the same daily) early and late in the day. Topwater activity is common in the fall, from hybrids as well as white bass and largemouths. The latter move shallower in the fall, and October and November provide good fishing again.

Tallapoosa River. The Tallapoosa includes two significant impoundments, Lakes Harris and Martin, that deserve careful fishing consideration. Harris has become one of eastern Alabama's better-known bass and crappie lakes, while Lake Martin is best known for its spotted bass.

When impounded in 1983, parts of Harris looked like a flooded forest, and it was this flooded timber that provided much-needed habitat for subsequent stockings of Florida-strain largemouths. Overall, the lake retains much of its original winding river configuration, with tributary creeks providing the flooded timber, flats, and backwater areas. Better catches are consistently reported around Fox, Hunter, and Wedowee Creeks, especially with plastic worms, jigs, spinnerbaits, and deep-diving crankbaits.

When viewing Lake Martin for the first time, many people are amazed by how closely it resembles lakes much farther north. The water is clear, and in the lower section there are dozens of tree-covered islands.

Here the spotted bass is king, and anglers work the rocky drops and island points with small plastic worms that require some finesse, and light lines, noisy topwater plugs, and, in colder weather, fast-moving spinnerbaits ripped along steep, rocky bluffs. The latter technique surprises many, yet it lures not only spotted bass but also largemouths up from deep water with vicious strikes.

Tombigbee, Warrior, and Alabama Rivers. These three rivers offer seven reservoirs, perhaps the best known being Lewis Smith Lake on the Warrior River near Cullman. Despite its deep, clear waters, Smith Lake produced a succession of world-record spotted bass, including an 8-pound, 15-ounce fish in 1978. A collection of Smith Lake spotted bass was then introduced into several California lakes, which a few years later produced the first 9-pound spotted bass on record.

Today Smith Lake rarely produces spotted bass larger than 7 pounds. One reason may be the introduction of a now thriving striped bass population. The debate over whether striped bass are eating all the forage formerly enjoyed by the spotted bass, or eating baby spotted bass fry, has raged ever since the stripers were introduced.

To catch big stripers, anglers drift live shad through deep channels, or present jigs and topwater plugs when the fish are surfacing in autumn. Most big spotted bass are caught in February and March as they move shallow to spawn, or at night by anglers familiar with the lake's many rocky coves and points.

The Tombigbee River was dammed and in some places dredged in the late 1970s by the U.S. Army Corps of Engineers to produce the Tennessee-Tombigbee Waterway, designed to open shipping and commerce between rural western Alabama and the Gulf of Mexico. In the process the Corps produced several lakes, including Columbus Lake in Mississippi, and Aliceville, Gainesville, and Demopolis Lakes in Alabama.

These impoundments, especially Aliceville, have produced outstanding bass fishing. Aliceville was stocked with Florida-strain bass in 1980 and nine years later produced two bass weighing more than 14 pounds. All three lakes offer large areas of shallow, weedy, or timber-filled backwater sloughs that provide excellent spawning habitat and are not affected by barge wakes in the main Tenn-Tom navigation channel. Topwater lures, spinnerbaits, and soft-plastic worms and lizards have produced well here, especially in the spring and fall.

Mobile Delta. The vast 400-square-mile Mobile Delta of southern Alabama offers a distinctly different type of fishing, albeit for the same popular species of largemouth bass, crappie, and sunfish. Anglers here, however, can also catch channel bass (redfish), flounder, or speckled trout in the lower portions of the delta, where its freshwater mixes with incoming saltwater from the Gulf of Mexico.

The delta extends approximately 40 miles northward of the Interstate Highway 10 Causeway Bridge. Several major rivers drain into this huge basin, along with numerous smaller streams. The result is a bewildering collection of look-alike waterways, shallow bays, and cypress- and gum-filled swamps. In addition, anglers here must contend with tidal fluctuations that will quickly turn a shallow bay into a mud flat.

Bass anglers in the delta use the same lures and techniques as elsewhere in the state. Notable hotspots include areas with such names as Big Lizard Creek, Twelve Mile Island, Negro Lake, Six Bits Creek, and Squirrel Bayou. Good delta maps are a must for any serious angler.

Public Lakes.   Alabama's public lake program ranks among the best in the Southeast, with nearly

Some fish are capable of changing sex during their lives; some deep-dwelling fish possess both female and male sexual organs.

two dozen small lakes created specifically by the Department of Natural Resources to provide fishing opportunities in areas not readily served by larger reservoirs. They are extremely popular among local anglers, and have been used as models for other state-sponsored public lake programs.

These public lakes are intensely managed for largemouth bass, crappie, flathead catfish, and redear sunfish (shellcrackers). Bass over 13 pounds have been caught in some of the lakes. Most do not allow outboard power, and while small boats may be available for rent, bank fishing has been encouraged by the construction of smooth access areas and piers, as well as special fish attractors within casting distance of the banks. The lakes, none of which is more than 200 acres in area, have a concessionaire on site to sell permits, tackle, and picnic supplies.

Saltwater

With only 5 miles of coastline bordering the gulf, one would expect Alabama's saltwater fishing to be nearly nonexistent, but such is not the case. As previously mentioned, anglers in the Mobile Delta regularly catch flounder, trout, and redfish; in fact, in early spring, bass anglers fishing the lower delta often have to stop using plastic worms because they are so often hit by flounder.

The bays. Alabama's primary saltwater opportunities include Mobile Bay, Perdido Bay, and the Gulf of Mexico. Mobile Bay offers fishing for the same popular inshore species found in the Mobile Delta. The most productive areas are private piers along the shoreline, which produce flounder consistently; and the oil and natural gas rigs, which are located in more open water. Much of the Mobile Bay floor is flat and featureless and doesn't hold many fish.

Plastic grubs like those used by freshwater anglers for bass are excellent for both flounder and speckled trout. Bait anglers use live shrimp or pinfish for both trout and redfish.

Perdido Bay, which is about 20 miles long—with numerous smaller cuts and bayous along its shoreline—runs along Alabama's southeastern tip and opens into the gulf at Alabama Point. The actual entrance to the gulf is quite small, which produces strong tidal currents, and here anglers enjoy some of the bay's best fishing. Redfish, speckled trout, grouper, and even Spanish mackerel and bluefish swim outside this cut; the most productive fishing takes place along both jetties that line the entrance into the bay.

The jetties can be fished on foot or by boat with both artificial lures or live and cut baits. Spoons are effective for both mackerel and bluefish; minnow-imitation jerkbaits catch trout; and redfish hit plastic grubs, especially when the hook is tipped with a piece of shrimp. Live shrimp can be fished under corks to take flounder, grouper, and an occasional redfish.

Gulf of Mexico. For many anglers, piers offer the first and easiest chance to fish saltwater, and there are several along the Alabama coast between the Mobile and gulf shores. The piers are open 24 hours and sell not only bait and tackle, but also refreshments for those who choose to stay longer than just a few hours. Croaker, flounder, and mackerel are taken most often, generally on various types of cut bait with sinker rigs that keep them close to the bottom.

More than 100 artificial reefs and piles of debris are scattered just off the Alabama gulf coast and within easy reach of small boats. These structures have Loran-C identification numbers and are pinpointed on nautical charts, thus offering anglers the opportunity to try for such species as amberjack, red snapper, cobia, and even sharks.

Party boats as well as deep-sea charters are available in each major city along the coast. With charters, anglers can make arrangements to stay inshore to fish the artificial reefs, or venture farther offshore. Inshore charters troll primarily for king mackerel, or work the bottom for red snapper, while offshore boats look for marlin, sailfish, wahoo, swordfish, and dolphin, which are usually present from late spring to early autumn. Generally, party boats and inshore/offshore charters provide all bait and tackle.

ALASKA

It was with good reason that the native peoples named this huge northern landmass *Alyeska*—The Great Land. With 586,412 square miles of total area, and more if the Aleutian Islands are included, Alaska is about one-fifth the size of the lower 48 states combined. Within that area is a bounty of more than 3,000 rivers, more than 3 million lakes, and some 34,000 miles of coastal shoreline—numbers that stagger the imagination, underscore the wealth of opportunities for anglers, and translate into some of North America's premier fishing.

Even though it has now been many decades since "modern" anglers first began exploring the state and probing its waters, much of today's Alaska remains a largely untamed wilderness. With more than 17,500 square miles of inland water alone, it is safe to say that even most longtime residents haven't fished all of what Alaska has to offer.

The Last Frontier, as this state is also known, provides very few roads and/or highway systems, so there is no ready access to many of the state's opportunities. Moreover, much of the state's better fishing is far from populated regions, so it is often necessary to travel great distances.

"Weather permitting," is an expression that holds much meaning for Alaskans, reinforcing the relative inaccessibility of the state's premier fishing locales, especially because so many sites are reached via boat or floatplane.

Anchorage's Lake Hood, the busiest floatplane base in the world, is emblematic of Alaska's

Anglers commonly but carefully share Alaskan streams, and fish, with brown bears.

continuing love affair with, and reliance upon, small, light, float-equipped aircraft. Floatplanes are virtual necessities for transporting anglers to various "bush" destinations. During summers, Alaskan skies are inundated with these small aircraft, a good percentage of which are bound for one of Alaska's premier fishing destinations.

Fortunately, small runways, if not airports, exist in the majority of Alaska's scattered towns and villages, with cities such as Anchorage, Kenai, Fairbanks, Nome, Kodiak, Juneau, and Ketchikan serving as hubs for traveling anglers.

So vast is Alaska that the Department of Fish and Game issues a separate regulations book for each of five regions. A first-time visitor would likely find the task of deciding where to go daunting. There are two ways to approach fishing in Alaska:

- Decide what species you want to fish for, then learn where and when these fish can be found and how to catch them.
- Decide what region you want to visit, then learn what fish are found there and when and where they're usually present.

Five of the six species of Pacific salmon (kings, reds, chums, pinks, and silvers) return to Alaska's freshwater each summer to spawn and are easily the main attractions for most visiting anglers. Substantial populations of rainbow trout, Dolly Varden, arctic charr, lake trout, arctic grayling, and northern pike also draw many anglers, and there are opportunities to catch cutthroat trout, inconnu (sheefish), and steelhead. In saltwater, halibut reign supreme, and Alaska annually produces not only plenty of these flatfish, but also gargantuan specimens. There's also fishing for other bottom dwellers, as well as some effort at catching saltchuck salmon.

Although Alaska has an abundance of waters and freshwater species, the popularity of the relatively few sites that are easily accessed has resulted

in extreme pressures on them, and regulations necessarily have become more restrictive. Likewise, catch-and-release fishing—both voluntary and mandatory—has increased, particularly for rainbow trout and grayling. Most top lodges, guides, and outfitters—of which there are many here—practice and advocate this philosophy.

Anchorage: Highway-Accessible Fishing

Anglers traveling via automobile or motor home and operating on a modest budget can experience fair to excellent fishing via Alaska's limited roads and highways, but it won't be as seductive as the experiences provided by a professional pilot/lodge/guide, unless they're able to get far enough away from Alaska's often crowded, highway-accessible areas. Highway travelers will encounter a much greater number of competing anglers than people who fly into the bush.

In essence, there are two roads leading out of Anchorage. The northern road quickly branches in one direction toward Denali National Park via the Parks Highway, and in the other direction easterly through Glennallen to Tok and then to the Canadian border. The second highway heads south from Anchorage around Cook Inlet's Tumagain Arm and then curves up through the scenic Kenai Mountain Range, paralleling south-central Alaska's Kenai Peninsula.

Although limited camping spots are scattered along Alaskan highways, frequently—and especially during fishing seasons—the number of anglers and vacationers on Alaska's roads can be astounding. These highways, many of which have only two lanes, can become ultracongested with slow-moving motor homes and heavy traffic. On summer weekends these roads can be particularly crowded.

Fortunately for the stalwart angler, many smaller, partially paved, dirt and/or gravel trails of various configuration lead away from Alaska's outlying communities. Obtaining references from residents of such places is one way for auto travelers to discover decent fishing. In fact, float tube and canoe fishing opportunities are not difficult for auto travelers to find, and are more abundant than any individual can experience in a lifetime. Anglers with plenty of time and the desire to explore and search for good near-road fishing will find it.

Kenai Peninsula

Despite its vast number of annual visitors, the Kenai Peninsula, and particularly Alaska's prodigious Kenai River, continues to be one of the Last Frontier's top 20 angling destinations. This river is easily Alaska's best-known and most frequented fishery. The Kenai area is one of few in the state with relatively easy access to excellent, and varied, fishing within a short distance from a highway.

The Kenai River begins at Cooper Landing, at the outlet of picturesque, aqua blue Kenai Lake. It

is approximately two hours by automobile south of Anchorage. All Kenai Peninsula streams and rivers eventually drain into the frigid saltwater of nearby Cook Inlet.

Beginning in late May, anglers find good to excellent fishing on the Kenai for king (chinook) salmon. Late June and early July generally signal the arrival of numbers of sockeye (red) salmon. In late July, pink (humpbacked) salmon appear, especially during even-numbered years, and in mid-August the first silver (coho) salmon enter the river. The Kenai also supports rainbow trout and Dolly Varden, and a smattering of whitefish; one or more of these species are present in many smaller nearby lakes and streams. In the fall, some of the southernmost Kenai Peninsula streams and rivers host a limited number of steelhead.

The Kenai River is suited to two fishing methods, with one method favored in the lower reaches, the other in the upper reaches. The lower Kenai is a large, deep, and somewhat smooth-flowing river—nearly an estuary at its lowermost parts. This region has the largest runs of the world's biggest strain of king salmon. Here, anglers mostly use spinning or conventional tackle while backtrolling (see) from drifting or idling powerboats. In contrast, the upper Kenai is broken and swift flowing, and offers superior rainbow trout, sockeye salmon, Dolly Varden, and silver salmon fishing. These somewhat shallower and swifter currents lend themselves to drift boat and inflatable raft fishing. Anglers typically climb out, secure their craft, and fish from sandbars, or wade. The upper Kenai parallels Sterling Highway in several places, and it's common to see travelers lined up along the roadside, gazing down on inflatable rafts filled with anglers. The waters of the upper Kenai are an unparalleled aqua blue, and owe their distinctive coloration to a blend of ultraclear tributaries with others bearing millions of minuscule particles of silt-laden glacial runoff. There is also a middle section of the Kenai—the area just below Skilak Lake and downstream to Sterling—but it contains difficult-to-negotiate, turbulent areas (especially at and around Naptowne Rapids), where anglers are advised to use a professional guide.

As mentioned earlier, the lower Kenai River is world famous for its strong summer runs of Pacific salmon, particularly for double runs of both king and sockeye salmon, and for outsized kings that haul like a runaway freight train. This is universally the foremost spot for monster king salmon; most of the International Game Fish Association's (IGFA) line-class world records were established here. Each year, especially during June and July, many thousands of visitors arrive from all over to experience this site, some with dreams of breaking its all-tackle 97-pound, 4-ounce chinook salmon record. The majority of those who fish here during the king salmon run are nonresidents, but this trend reverses when the sockeye are in.

At times anglers line the banks of the lower Kenai River in astounding numbers. It's also common to see numerous boats on the Kenai; especially on the lower river during June and July, boat traffic can be bumper to bumper.

Several excellent lakes exist on the Kenai Peninsula. Kenai, Hidden, Crescent, and Jean Lakes are just a few, and they offer reasonably good to excellent fishing. Some Kenai Peninsula lakes are reachable by foot after a few hours of hiking. Anglers with less time or hiking interest can access some lakes by floatplane.

Perhaps a handful of peninsula streams feature good numbers of Dolly Varden, particularly during late summer. One is the famed Russian River, which joins the Kenai where the state ferry crosses. The Russian is considered one of the prettiest flows in all of Alaska. When it is not too crowded with anglers, the river can produce superlative rainbow trout and sockeye fishing. The Moose River at Sterling, and the Swanson River and Lakes system farther south, also offer excellent fishing. Other respected and frequented flows on the Kenai Peninsula are Kasilof River, Deep Creek, Anchor River, and Upper and Lower Russian Lakes.

For saltwater aficionados, the ports of Homer, Seward, and Whittier are departure sites for saltwater salmon, halibut, lingcod, salmon shark, and rockfish angling. All three are commercial fishing centers, and, in season, Dungeness and Alaska king crab may be available here. Halibut is the main interest, however; Homer calls itself the "Halibut Capital of the World," and Cook Inlet has produced monster fish, including line-class world records. Around Deep Creek and Ninilchik, halibut anglers launch in surf to reach the fishing grounds.

The Kenai Peninsula is replete with fishing lodges and services, and several stores and smaller shops that cater to travelers have sprung up along its highways, beginning at Cooper Landing and extending down to Sterling, Soldotna, and Kenai where anglers can procure food, gasoline, lodging, and sundry items, as well as flies, lures, and fishing tackle.

Susitna River Drainage

The mouth of the big, burly, and seemingly always silty Susitna River, which empties into Cook Inlet northwest of Anchorage, is a culmination of several diverse and interesting south-central Alaska tributaries, all of which drain to the ocean via the "Big Su" amidst one of the most awe-inspiring backdrops in Alaska: Mt. McKinley and the majestic, snowcapped Alaska Range. This is easily among the most breathtaking mountain scenery in the state. People commonly refer to the Susitna River as the "Big Su" because it's an unmistakable landmark, especially from the vantage of an airplane. It's one of those rivers you just can't help noticing.

Several miles upstream from where the Big Su meets saltwater, it is fed by the formidable Yentna

When spawning, big Alaskan king salmon turn crimson and seek out shallow gravel bars.

River, which, in turn, is fed by the sizable and swift-flowing Skwentna River. The Skwentna is a paradox in that it is frequently extremely silty, but remains an important and productive south-central Alaska sportfishery.

A few miles upstream are two of this region's jewels. The first of these is the remarkably clear-flowing and lovely Talachulitna River, or Tal, as it's commonly called. This crystalline combination of lovely dry-fly pocket water and cascading riffles plays host to kings, chums, sockeyes, silvers, pinks, Dollies, grayling, and many distinctively spotted rainbow trout. The second is nearby Lake Creek, a virtual twin to the Tal, located across the canyon and downstream a few miles. It yields fair to good numbers of kings, chums, sockeyes, pinks, silvers, rainbows, and grayling, as well as some Dollies.

Extending northeast and northwest from Anchorage, Alaska's Matanuska and Susitna Valleys are dotted with myriad lakes of varying sizes, several of which are suitable for float-tube fishing. Numerous smaller, less-frequented but entirely fishable wilderness streams are scattered throughout this region.

Alexander Lake is representative of several swampy, low-lying areas in the Susitna drainage region where good to excellent northern pike fishing exists. Nearby Hewitt Lake and Fish Lake are other good, fairly easily accessed spots for pike fishing. Other respected waters in this region include Little Susitna River, Theodore River, Deshka River,

Chulitna River, Talkeetna River and its tributaries, and Lake Louise, which is part of the Tyone River system located slightly farther to the east.

Although anglers can reach several Susitna drainage waters by automobile via the George Parks Highway, several others are best accessed via boat or floatplane. Two benefits of fishing in south-central Alaska are the area's mild climate relative to other places across the state, and its proximity to Anchorage. Although they are scattered, frequently rustic, and oftentimes accessible only via boat or floatplane, numerous fishing lodges and services exist along the banks of several of the area's waters.

Katmai Region

Covering an area larger than the state of Connecticut, Katmai is a vast, exceptionally beautiful region, graced with myriad pristine lakes and clear-flowing, untamed rivers and streams.

King Salmon, located about 275 miles southwest of Anchorage, is the gateway to famed Katmai National Park and Preserve and also the Brooks River, easily one of the loveliest, most frequented, and most photographed wilderness flows in all of The Great Land. There are typically many Alaskan brown bears at Brooks Falls—approximately midpoint on the river—attracting well over half of all of those who journey from points around the globe to visit these two sites.

The Valley of Ten Thousand Smokes, which was volcanically active in 1912 when Mount Katmai blew its top and when thousands of steam vents suddenly appeared across the region, is another favorite attraction for visitors, whether fishing is on their agendas or not.

Access to Brooks Camp and the Brooks River is primarily via floatplane, although at least one charter boat operation affords access to Brooks via a two-hour upstream journey against the formidable currents of the Naknek River.

The Brooks River, which connects Brooks and Naknek Lakes, is just $1^1/_2$ miles long. However, with its ultraclear waters, beautiful and lush mountain backdrops, and leaping salmon at picturesque Brooks Falls beginning in July, plus numbers of Alaskan brown bears roaming the banks, the Brooks is not only one of the most scenic rivers in the state, but also one of Alaska's most productive and revered fisheries.

Catch-and-release fishing is largely the name of the game on the Brooks, where rainbow trout, grayling, lake trout, sockeye salmon, and silver salmon are the main attractions. However, of the visitors who experience Brooks Camp each summer, more than half are strictly bear viewers and photographers. The Brooks Camp concession, which is less than half a mile from the river and has operated since 1950, offers visitors buffet meals, hot showers, and limited rental cabins. Two major bear viewing platforms, both of which have been improved and enlarged, are set along the banks.

The region has excellent numbers of lake trout, rainbow trout, Dolly Varden, arctic charr, arctic grayling, and four species of Pacific salmon, available according to season. The numerous fishing lodges in Katmai are at highly commendable sites. One of these is where the Kulik River spills into sizable Nonvianuk Lake, and the other is in the stretch between pristine Colville and Grosvenor Lakes. In season, fishing in these locations can be a virtual panacea, especially for fly anglers.

Other notable waters in the region include American Creek, Naknek Lake's Bay of Isles, and the prodigious Naknek River. Several smaller, lesser-known streams here are excellent in season.

At the northernmost boundary of Katmai National Park is the big, wild, and extremely fertile Alagnak, or Branch, River. This meanders roughly 70 miles across a big, rolling tundra before it eventually joins the Kvichak River (the outlet of Lake Iliamna to the north), some 4 or 5 miles upstream of where the now-combined flow empties into Bristol Bay.

The Alagnak, which drains both Nonvianuk and Kukaklek Lakes, offers excellent fishing with a variety of tackle, and superb fly fishing. The braids of the Alagnak, a wild and varied 25-mile-long mid-section stretch of broken and ribboned water, is an especially sought-after location. Anglers prefer the lower portions of the Alagnak for salmon; trout and grayling anglers venture farther upstream. Of late, overuse on the Alagnak River has spurred greater limitations on drift permits. Accompanying the rise in regulatory efforts are stricter catch-and-release policies as well, but lodges here have not experienced a significant drop in clientele because of this.

Lake Clark/Lake Iliamna Region

With some 20-plus world-class flows all draining into one exceptionally large inland body of water, it's no wonder Alaska's Lake Clark/Lake Iliamna region is famous worldwide, earning a strong reputation as one of Alaska's premier fisheries. Like many of Alaska's preferred sportfishing regions, however, Iliamna's extremely wild, untamed, and remote landscape is largely floatplane country.

Alaska's largest lake, Iliamna covers 1,022 square miles, yet few boats are seen here, in part because of its reputation for sudden and dangerously high winds. Iliamna is so large that it creates its own weather patterns, and with so much big water flowing into it, anglers focus their attention on the rivers.

Iliamna's major tributary, the Newhalen River, drains Lake Clark to the north and ranks as one of the most productive salmon and trout fisheries in all of Alaska. In July, the number of sockeyes in the Newhalen can be astounding, second only to that in the Kvichak River, which is Iliamna's outlet and connects directly to Bristol Bay.

Over the years, such flows as Lower and Upper Talarik Creeks, Gibraltar, Dream Creek, the Copper River, the Iliamna River, the Tazimina River, the Kvichak, and the Newhalen have all received widespread attention, drawing a lot of anglers for excellent trout, grayling, charr, and salmon fishing. A handful of smaller and lesser-known streams in the region are just as productive as the more well-known locations, and these have generally remained anonymous to prevent overcrowding and excessive pressure.

Although a mere 250 miles from Anchorage, this area is wild and desolate, and the weather can be highly unpredictable. Most visiting anglers require lodge, guiding, and outfitting services, which are scattered throughout the region, particularly on Iliamna's northern shores.

Alaska Peninsula

One of North America's last sportfishing frontiers, the Alaska Peninsula easily ranks as one of the most wild, remote, and difficult-to-access fishing regions in all of The Great Land. Although its geographical beginnings lie only several hundred miles southwest of Anchorage, typical weather patterns across Shelikof Strait frequently keep the majority of Alaska's pilots, private and commercial, well at bay.

"The Peninsula," as it is known, has miles upon miles of lonely wilderness rivers and streams to explore. It also has miles upon miles of wilderness beaches, where visitors can discover such things as Japanese glass fishing floats and bleached-out whale carcasses. Aniakchak Crater, which erupted in 1931, thus creating Surprise Lake in Aniakchak National Monument and Preserve, lies in this region.

Few anglers have tread this largely untouched and untamed region, but many of those who have fished here are compelled to return. Imagine a small aircraft secured by ropes against possible rough winds and parked not far from a wilderness stream. The backdrop: arguably the most formidable and rugged mountains on earth. This is the Alaska Peninsula experience, yet only recently have anglers begun to appreciate this undisturbed region of Alaska and the quality of its fishing (it has long been recognized for trophy Alaskan brown bear and moose hunting). The peninsula boasts some of the best charr and Pacific salmon fishing in the state, as well as excellent steelhead angling.

The better waters of the Alaska Peninsula include Becharof Lake, the Ugashik Lakes, Ugashik Narrows, King Salmon River, Painter Creek, Cinder River, Sandy River, Wildman Lake, Meshik River, and Chignik River. There's also good fishing in various streams and rivers extending all the way to Dutch Harbor and Unalaska in the Aleutian Islands, both located at the extreme far end of the Alaska Peninsula and offering outstanding saltwater and estuary angling opportunities.

The Alaska Peninsula is a terrific halibut angling site, and in recent times Unalaska Island has been the focal point of a growing sportfishery. Waters around Unalaska have produced numerous halibut over 300 pounds, including record-class fish of 395, 440, and 459 pounds, the latter an all-tackle world record.

The peninsula is known for severe wind and weather conditions, and only a handful of fishing services and lodges exist throughout the region.

Wood River/Tikchik Lakes Region

This highly respected southwestern Alaska fishery consists of approximately a dozen interconnected lakes and their clear-flowing tributaries, which are primarily accessed via Dillingham. The Wood River, located at the southerly end of this lake system, is the major drainage in the area and connects the lakes to the formidable Nushagak River, which empties into Bristol Bay.

The primary flows include the Agulowak, which links Lake Nerka with Lake Aleknagik; the Agulukpak, connecting Lakes Beverly and Nerka; and the lovely Wind and Peace Rivers to the north. These and numerous lesser-known streams provide exceptional wade and drift fishing amid unsurpassed scenery, including steeply descending, cascading waterfalls in northernmost portions.

While northern pike fishing is excellent in the bays of many of the region's major lakes (spots where anglers rarely probe), the major attraction to the Wood River/Tikchik Lakes Region is the exceptional stream angling, especially dry-fly fishing. This is because of easy-to-wade waters, clear-flowing streams, and plenty of rainbow trout, grayling, arctic charr, and Dolly Varden. Strong runs of Pacific salmon frequent these streams as well.

Some area lakes boast superb arctic charr and Dolly Varden, taken by anglers who drift in boats and cast smolt and streamer imitations on sinking lines. Frequently, swarms of arctic terns and seagulls, which swoop to the surface to snatch an easy meal, best indicate where and when to begin casting to schools of charr.

The famed Togiak River, which meanders to Bristol Bay and partially drains the Togiak National Wildlife Refuge, is known for exceptional rainbow trout and silver salmon fishing. Anglers access the river mainly via flights from Dillingham to the village of Togiak. The Aniak River, which is best accessed by flying directly from Anchorage to the village of Aniak, is another highly respected flow in this portion of the state, and it is great rafting water. Several other lesser-known, smaller wilderness rivers and streams run through this region, many of them difficult to access without a professional guide/pilot.

Fishing lodges are scattered throughout southwestern Alaska and the Wood River/Tikchik Lakes Region.

Western Region

Located about 420 miles southwest of Anchorage, and descending to the saltwaters of Kuskokwim Bay, is the immense, rolling, wilderness region widely referred to as Western Alaska, one of the Last Frontier's better sportfishing destinations.

Two of the main attractions in this difficult-to-access area are the Goodnews and Kanektok Rivers. Both originate high in the vast Togiak National Wildlife Refuge and drain westerly through 80 miles of untouched Alaskan wilderness before eventually meeting Kuskokwim Bay and the Bering Sea—the Goodnews at the native village of Goodnews Bay, and the Kanektok at the native village of Quinhagak. In addition, several smaller, exceedingly difficult-to-access streams entice a small number of adventurous anglers. Rainbow trout, Dolly Varden, grayling, and all five species of Pacific salmon are common to this area.

Western Alaska is a vast, rolling, descending wilderness region that is best experienced from a competent, seasoned lodge/tent camp with the necessary boats and equipment. Their experienced, professional guides are familiar with the territory. Not only have they learned the various and always changing river and stream channels and surrounding terrains, they are also accustomed to interacting with indigenous peoples often encountered here.

Although it may be possible to access this region directly from Anchorage, the normal hub is Bethel.

Kodiak Island

For years Kodiak Island was known for brown bear hunting and commercial fishing, but during the 1990s it earned a well-deserved sportfishing reputation.

This 115-mile-long island is about 275 miles south of Anchorage. Typically, commercial flights from Anchorage transport anglers to the city of Kodiak, an established commercial fishing port on the northeast corner of the island. From there, numerous air services fly anglers to the island's streams and rivers.

A road system leading from the city extends to some half-dozen good to excellent drive-to rivers and streams with the potential for better than decent salmon and charr angling. Among these are Buskin River, American River, Sargent Creek, Olds River, Chiniak River, and Pasagshak River.

Of all the excellent wilderness flows on Kodiak Island, the Karluk River, which drains Karluk Lake and winds some 22 miles to the salt at Tanglefoot Bay, is the island's premier attraction and draws the most anglers, who journey to the Karluk from around the globe.

The river is accessible only by boat or aircraft. There are very few small, scattered trails in this area, although a midriver access point, called Portage, is reachable via a 5-mile hike from Larsen Bay. King, sockeye, and silver salmon, plus steelhead, rainbow trout, and chrome-bright Dolly Varden, are the favored species.

The tidally influenced Karluk is wide, fairly shallow, and relatively easy to wade, making it an

excellent site for fly fishing. Lodging along the Karluk is extremely limited, however. Recently, various native groups have begun charging a per diem fee to Alaskan residents and out-of-state anglers alike.

The Ayakkulik ("Red") River, located about 80 miles southwest of the city of Kodiak, is another highly notable fishery accessible only via floatplane or helicopter. Renowned especially for excellent September silver salmon fishing, the Ayakkulik also receives good numbers of October and November steelhead. In summer, Dollies, sockeyes, and pink salmon are usually also abundant.

The Fraser River (also known as the Dog Salmon River), which empties into Olga Bay at the far southwest corner of the island, is another attractive Kodiak flow with strong runs of red, pink, and silver salmon, as well as a major run of chum salmon.

Brown bears are frequently encountered in many places across Kodiak Island but especially in drainages that host Pacific salmon. Presently, only a handful of scattered small to medium-size lodges and fishing operations exist on Kodiak Island, most of them in the proximity of saltwater coves, bays, and lagoons that also attract commercial fishing ventures. These waters support abundant halibut, with the potential for huge specimens.

Southeast Region

A maze of picturesque and pristine islands, canals, coves, and saltwater bays extends along the southern boundaries of the Tongass National Forest in Southeast Alaska, an area frequently called Alaska's Panhandle. Weather permitting, its waters can be both a freshwater and saltwater angler's delight.

In this immensely forested region, a backpacker—or those anxious to get away from crowds—may easily do so. It is not a do-it-yourself fishing region, however; extreme tidal fluctuations and frequently inclement weather make it prudent to use the services of an established lodge or outfitter, preferably one who resides in the particular area you want to fish.

In good weather, many places in Southeast Alaska can be especially scenic; typically, however, comparatively frequent rains make it far wetter and less inviting than much of the remainder of the state. Temperatures are usually modest in comparison with those in Alaska proper, yet one similarity exists: There are very few roads in this region. Floatplanes and boats provide the majority of access.

The Situk River—a tidally influenced flow featuring kings, reds, silvers, steelhead, and sea-run Dolly Varden—is a few miles from Yakutat, to the north, and is one of the region's better-known and respected fishing sites. However, several less-frequented but excellent wilderness streams and rivers crisscross the region, carving through the thickly carpeted Tongass National Forest to the Gulf of Alaska.

Prince of Wales Island, which lies in the southerly part of the region, across Clarence Strait from Ketchikan, is one of Southeast Alaska's premier locales for those who wish to experience a wide array of angling opportunities using all types of fishing techniques. Several excellent freshwater streams exist on Prince of Wales Island; chief among these are the Thorne, Karta, Klawock, and Sarkar. Chum, pink, and silver salmon, plus steelhead, some indigenous rainbows, sea-run Dolly Varden, and sea-run cutthroat trout make up the island's principal freshwater attractions.

Not to be overlooked throughout this region are saltwater angling opportunities. Halibut, lingcod, and mint-bright, migrating Pacific salmon are the leading marine quarries. Halibut fishing here is unsurpassed. Rich halibut fishing grounds are within easy reach of the Southeast Alaska towns of Ketchikan, Wrangell, Petersburg, Sitka, Juneau, and Yakutat, and many of the biggest specimens, as well as existing line-class world records, have been produced in the region.

Sea-run salmon are caught by boaters drifting or trolling in the coves and bays, and these bright sea lice–fresh fish are as hard-fighting as any salmon an angler will encounter.

Paradoxically, as remote as this area is, Southeast Alaska is easily reached via commercial airliner. Widespread cities extend along the entire southeast and include Juneau, Sitka, Ketchikan, Yakutat, Petersburg, Wrangell, and Craig, all of which are accessible by air and only some of which require connecting flights. There is ferry service to some locations as well. One interesting and popularly accessed site is at Blind Slough near Petersburg, on Mitkof Island.

Southeast Alaska offers exceptional photographic opportunities. The area is replete with scenic splendor, and sightings of bald eagles, whales, sea otters, and myriad sea life are common. Many of the streams here flow cold and crystal clear, so a pair of lightweight gloves and a hat will help maintain body temperature, especially during morning and evening fishing forays. And don't forget rain gear.

Fairbanks Region

A handful of fair to good rivers and streams exist in the Fairbanks region; some of these are accessible via either gravel or paved roads, while others are accessible only via floatplane or boat. Two highways extend northerly from Fairbanks. The Steese Highway, which runs northeast some 140 miles to Circle, parallels the Upper Chatanika River for approximately 70 miles. The Livengood Road, a dirt and gravel road that runs northwesterly, crosses several noteworthy streams, among which are the Chatanika River, Washington Creek, the Tatalina River, the Tolovana, and the Hutlinana. These feature good grayling, decent salmon, and excellent Dolly Varden fishing at various times of the year. Some area waters hold small to medium-size

Interpretations of Egyptian wall paintings indicate that fishing for fun was practiced in the period from 2470–2320 B.C.

sheefish. Minto Flats, a group of stillwater swamps and sloughs about 40 miles northwest of Fairbanks, is reached via the Livengood Road and is one of Alaska's premier sites for northern pike.

All of the streams nearer the road are fairly heavily fished, so hiking in some distance can greatly increase an angler's chance of encountering less human competition. The Livengood Road terminates at Manley Hot Springs, where boats are available for rent to those anglers wishing to pursue northern pike in nearby sloughs.

Two main rivers extend through the city of Fairbanks: the Tanana River, which is a large, deep, glacially influenced flow, and the Chena, which runs clearer and merges with the Tanana. Both are commonly used by boaters from the Fairbanks area. Closer to Fairbanks, the Chena runs slow and deep; its mid- and upper portions, especially the north fork, are much more attractive. A modicum of kings, a smattering of chums, myriad grayling, some burbot, and lots of pike constitute the majority of the Chena's angling opportunities.

Yukon-Tanana Drainage

This enormous region, extending all the way from the Brooks Range in the north to the Alaska Range in the south, and from the Canadian border in the east to the Bering Sea in the west, is among Alaska's least-frequently visited fisheries. Its enormity is blamed for its lack of appeal. Fortunately, however, many of its fishable waters are in the eastern portion, where adequate road access does exist.

Among the overlooked rivers, for example, is the Nation River,—an excellent kayaking flow that joins the Yukon River some 30 miles west of the Canadian border after meandering through prime big-game country (e.g., moose, caribou, Dall sheep, bears, and wolves). It is among the most-respected record arctic grayling water in all of Alaska, yet because of its distance from populated areas, it remains a little-known river.

The mighty Yukon River—which flows westerly for more than 1,300 miles through the state of Alaska to the Bering Sea, where there is an 80-mile-wide delta—does not get significant angling attention. In a state with so many other places that are less foreboding and simpler to fish, and that offer more services, this is easy to understand. Despite its numbers of king, sockeye, and silver salmon, as well as grayling, sheefish, and pike, the Yukon is considered too silty, too deep in many places and too shallow to navigate in others, or simply too wide to be a prime Alaskan sportfishery. A few intrepid anglers do explore portions of the Yukon, however, and it is known that prodigious numbers of pike—some of them huge—inhabit the sloughs and backwaters along the river as well as its large tributaries.

In fact, anglers devote more attention to the Yukon's numerous tributaries. The majority of these are clear-running, and many offer good to excellent angling. The Charley, the Kandik, and the Tatonduk are examples of little-frequented wilderness Yukon tributaries that have excellent grayling, sheefish, and pike fishing. This area is an intriguing, though wild and highly diverse component of the state, where everything from pike in slack water to arctic grayling in ultraclear dry-fly pocket water may be encountered.

Spending a week floating with a professional outfitter down the Yukon from Eagle, Alaska, to Circle would provide ample opportunity to catch various species while experiencing a multitude of river environments and thus employing diverse angling tactics. Such an adventure might afford a glimpse into Alaska's mining history, and particularly its Klondike gold rush days—especially if you ventured into the river's tributaries.

For many individuals, it is the Yukon's salmon that inspire and awe and wonder. Some of these fish struggle more than 2,000 miles upstream, often through extremely strong currents, before they begin to spawn.

Seward Peninsula/Norton Sound

Nome and the Seward Peninsula are storied gold rush country, but this is also a region with superb fishing opportunities. Here, the grayling, chum salmon, silver salmon, and Dolly Varden angling is often excellent. Trophy northern pike abound in many surrounding lakes and at sloughs off several of the main flows.

Although remoteness can easily be found, numerous local mining roads enable fairly easy access to fishing sites scattered about this region's periphery. Three main roads out of Nome provide auto access to many of its waters. One road leads to Teller, another to Taylor, and the third to Council. Excellent area streams include the Nome River, Eldorado Creek, the Pilgrim River, and the Sinuk River; all are home to grayling, pike, silver salmon, and charr.

The vicinity of Norton Sound teems with several Pacific salmon species, but few anglers ever experience these waters due to its remoteness. About 80 miles east of Nome is the Fish River, which drains into Norton Sound at Golovin Bay. Beginning in midsummer, this flowage can be an angler's paradise. Grayling, silver salmon, and charr are the river's leading species, although pinks and chums are generally present, too. Plenty of pike, including trophy specimens, thrive in the weeds near main river channels and also in the many backwater sloughs. The village of White Mountain is not only a favored rest stop for mushers competing in Alaska's annual sled-dog race, the Iditarod, but it is also a jumping-off site for anglers headed to the Fish/Niukluk drainage, as supplies and guides are available there.

Eastward about 40 miles or so are three notable fishing rivers: the Kwiniuk, which has an abundance of salmon, charr, and grayling; the fairly remote Shaktoolik, known for its grayling, charr, pink, chum, and silver salmon; and the usually clear-flowing Unalakleet River, which is largely accessible by boat, originates from the village of Unalakleet, and boasts all five salmon species as well as charr, grayling, and northern pike.

Nome, White Mountain, and Unalakleet provide offbeat, adventurous backcountry angling experiences. Choices of guides and outfitters are typically few and far between, although the native guides generally know the rivers intimately.

Northwest Region

In this lightly visited corner of the state, also referred to as the Arctic region, three of Alaska's major rivers—the Kobuk, the Selawik, and the Noatak—nearly converge as they complete their westward flow and eventually drain into Kotzebue Sound near the village of the same name. All three are premier fishing sites, and wind through largely treeless country on a long, meandering, wilderness journey. The Selawik is a large, deep, typically smooth-flowing drainage best known for big sheefish and pike. The Noatak is known mostly for remoteness, scenery, and substantial numbers of dime-bright Dolly Varden, charr, and grayling. The Kobuk, which features chum salmon, Dolly Varden, grayling, sheefish, and pike, is a bit of a mixture of the other two and is considered one of the state's better sheefish waters.

The Wulik River meets the Chukchi Sea approximately 40 miles north of Kotzebue near Kivalina. This is a premier Alaskan sea-run Dolly Varden river. The region also includes several extremely remote lakes.

Migratory sheefish—or tarpon of the north, as they are called (even though they aren't aerial, as their lofty nickname would suggest)—do at times put up a good thrashing, especially as they come to hand or net. They can grow to more than 50 pounds, but typical sheefish specimens weigh 7 or 8 pounds. Although the official Alaska state record sheefish, caught in 1986 on the Pah River, weighed 53 pounds, natives of the villages scattered throughout this region suggest that a new record inconnu is possible here.

The village of Selawik is an excellent source of local guides, as is Kotzebue, which is located at saltwater's edge. However, finding an experienced pilot who has the appropriate plane and also knows the region (as well as the habits and likely whereabouts of sheefish), might be a challenge, although several air services exist in the Kotzebue area.

As with other regions, the only practical means of transportation is the floatplane, as there are very few roads. Several scattered towns and villages lie along the banks of the wild Koyukuk River, a couple of hundred miles farther inland to the east, as well as on the Kobuk River and farther south on the Yukon. Anglers who fly into the region from Anchorage or Fairbanks rest up and resupply at Bettles, McGrath, Galena, or Kivalina before venturing out to the Kobuk or the Noatak, or to other wilderness fishing sites. For the most part, anglers have most of this wide-open country to themselves, perhaps shared with a grizzly bear here and there and some moose.

The Brooks Range

Of all angling destinations in The Great Land, none is less frequented or more distant from populated areas than the remote Brooks Range, that 700-mile-long, east-west extension of the Rocky Mountains consisting of steep, sparse, scenic mountains and extremely wide-open places. It's a virtually treeless mountain range that separates Alaska's oil-rich north slope from the Yukon River Valley.

Most access to this region is via airplane from Bettles, Fairbanks, or Fort Yukon. Services and facilities are extremely limited. The majority of Brooks Range inhabitants, who are oil company employees, access the region either via the James Dalton Highway or local air-taxi from Barrow. Although summer days are exceptionally long and generally cool, the arctic summer season itself is relatively short, and its harsh weather conditions are notorious.

The Brooks Range is best known for Dall-sheep and caribou hunting, not for fishing, although there's excellent grayling, lake trout, and arctic charr angling in several of the region's remote streams and lakes. Some rivers and streams on the northernmost slopes, which drain to the Beaufort Sea, receive good numbers of sea-run Dolly Varden, as well as a smattering of chum and pink salmon. Anglers will not find king salmon, sockeye salmon, or silver salmon in Alaska's Arctic Slope; however, Dolly Varden, Arctic charr, lake trout, and grayling fishing in this region is often very good and wondrously scenic.

Some notable charr streams in the Brooks Range include the Chandler, Killik, Anaktuvuk, and Hulahula Rivers. Schrader, Porcupine, and Chandler Lakes, plus the Anaktuvuk River Lakes and Etivluk River Lakes, are all known for excellent lake trout fishing. The Jim River, Colville River, and Sagavanirktok produce good grayling fishing, but there are many such waters on either slope.

ALBACORE   *Thunnus alalunga.*

Other names—longfin tuna, long-finned tunny, longfin, true albacore, albacore tuna, albie; German: pigfish; French: *germon;* Hawaiian: *áhi pahala;* Japanese: *binchô, binnaga;* Portuguese: *albacora;* Spanish: *albacora, atún blanco.*

A member of the Scombridae family of tuna and mackerel, the albacore is an excellent light-tackle gamefish. Its profitability and quality as a commercial fish, and its popularity as a gamefish, make it one of the most valuable fish in the United States. Called the "chicken of the sea" because of its white meat, the albacore is commercially harvested in

The Panama Canal, known for inter-ocean boat passage, enabled tarpon to move from the Atlantic to the Pacific, where they previously did not exist but are now established.

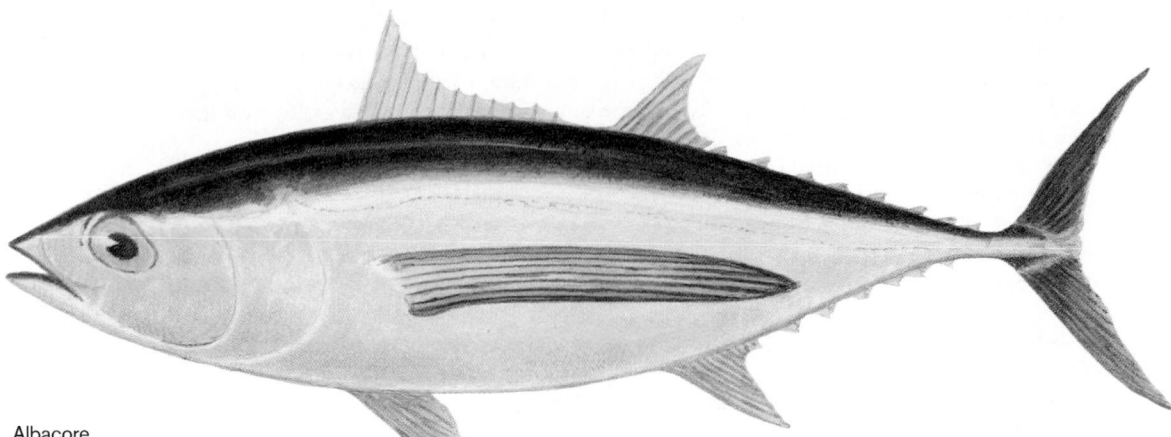

Albacore

large quantities and marketed fresh, smoked, deep-frozen, and canned. It is called true albacore in some places, not to be confused with false albacore *(see: albacore, false)* or little tunny *(see)*.

Identification. Albacore have long pectoral fins that reach to a point beyond the anal fin, as well as small finlets on both the back and the belly that extend from the anal fin to the tail. Albacore are colored dark blue, shading to greenish blue near the tail, and is silvery white on the belly. A metallic or iridescent cast covers the entire body. The dorsal finlets are yellowish, except for the white trailing edge of the tail, and the anal finlets are silvery or dusky. The deepest part of the body is near the second dorsal fin; in other tuna, it is near the middle of the first dorsal fin.

Extremely long, sickle-shaped, black pectoral fins set albacore apart from other tuna; pectoral fins of certain other adult tuna may also be moderately long, but they never extend all the way to the anal fin. This distinction is not as marked in young albacore; in some cases, a juvenile albacore may have shorter pectoral fins than a similar-size yellowfin tuna *(T. albacores)* or a bigeye tuna *(T. obesus)*. The albacore can also be distinguished from other tuna by its lack of stripes or spots on the lower flanks and belly, and by the thin white trailing edge on the margin of the tail fin.

Size. The average weight for albacore is between 10 and 25 pounds. The all-tackle record is 88 pounds, 2 ounces, although commercially caught fish have weighed as much as 93 pounds. The albacore can grow to 5 feet in length.

Distribution. Albacore are found worldwide in tropical and temperate seas, including the Mediterranean, but they also make seasonal migrations into colder zones such as New England, southern Brazil, and the northern Gulf of Mexico. In the western Atlantic, albacore range from Nova Scotia to Brazil, although they rarely range north of New York and are absent from the Straits of Florida; in the Pacific Ocean, they range from Alaska to Mexico. Albacore are abundant in the Pacific but less common in the Atlantic, although in the latter,

larger size classes (31 to 50 inches) are associated with cooler bodies of water, whereas smaller individuals tend to occur in warmer waters. In the North Pacific, they migrate annually between Asia and North America.

Habitat. Albacore favor tropical, subtropical, and temperate waters, commonly in the 60° to 66°F range. These fish seldom come close to shore and prefer deep, wide-open waters.

Life history/Behavior. A schooling fish, the albacore is migratory and pelagic; that is, it lives and feeds in the open sea. It roams widely, varying in location from within a few miles of shore to far offshore, as currents and water temperatures dictate. Its availability can change widely from year to year. Albacore have been described as one of the world's fastest migrant fish, and tagging studies have tracked them across entire oceans. Fish tagged off California, for example, were captured 294 days later off the coast of Japan, nearly 5,000 miles away. This is equivalent to a migration of more than 17 miles a day in straight-line fashion.

Albacore spawn from July through October along the west coast of North America, and in the summer season in the Southern Hemisphere of the mid-Pacific. A single female can shed between 1 and 3 million eggs in one spawning effort.

Food and feeding habits. The albacore diet consists of fish, squid, and crustaceans. Albacore feed in schools, which sometimes consist of other tuna-family members, and these schools are typically found around floating objects such as sargassum. Although they will feed at middle depths, they ordinarily feed close to the surface.

Angling. Anglers avidly pursue albacore wherever these fish occur. In California and Mexico, they are the most prominent tuna and are largely caught between 20 and 100 miles offshore, where the waters are mild and deep blue.

Unless warm currents bring albacore to within a few miles of shore, it is usually necessary to run long distances off North America's coasts to find them. They favor those areas where cooler water interfaces with warmer water. Charter boat captains

sometimes use satellite images of ocean temperatures as a guide, and look for seamounts or the edges of canyons (the latter especially on the East Coast of the U.S., as there are no canyons off the West Coast). Locating these fish is the hardest part of the sport, so anglers invest considerable effort trolling for them. Once a school is found, some anglers stop trolling and immediately begin chumming in an effort to keep the tuna nearby, catching them on live or dead baitfish. Others continue trolling. Charter and private boats, however, usually converge where the albacore are concentrated, so these spots are often a hotbed of activity.

Like all tuna, albacore strike hard and make powerful runs. They are a popular light-tackle quarry (4/0 reels and 20- to 50-pound tackle are standard) and are commonly caught by anglers fishing with such baits as mullet, sauries, squid, herring, anchovies, sardines, and other small fish. In some cases, chunking or chumming with dead bait is preferable; in others, light-lining with live bait is more effective. Fishing with live anchovies is popular on the West Coast. Fly fishing is also possible, usually when a chum slick has been established to attract schools of albacore within casting range.

In the northeastern U.S., trollers fish with both lures and rigged baitfish, and there's a strong preference for using green trolling lures and natural baits (whole ballyhoo or strips) dressed with green skirts. When albacore action is hot and a school is encountered, multiple hookups can occur on a boat with many trolling rigs set out; this can become a wild adventure, with lines tangling, rods bent double, and everyone onboard involved in a pandemonium rush.

See: Big-Game Fishing; Chumming; Chunking; Trolling; Tuna.

ALBACORE, FALSE

"False albacore" is a popular term for little tunny *(see)*.

ALBERTA

The most westerly of Canada's Prairie Provinces, Alberta is in many ways diverse. From the arid short-grass prairie in the south to the aspen parkland farm country of the central region, and from the wild lands of the Rockies to the mixed-wood northern boreal forest, the Wild Rose Province is as varied as it is beautiful. And within each ecological zone is a unique and challenging fishery.

The prairies are a dry, flat landscape dissected by warm, slow-moving rivers that have carved deep scars across the landscape. Walleye, sauger, pike, goldeye, and sturgeon swim the lower reaches of these rivers, while rainbow and brown trout inhabit the upper end, where the prairies meet the foothills. On-stream and off-stream reservoirs, built to store the irrigated water that is the lifeblood of the prairie,

provide underutilized opportunities for growing walleye, pike, and whitefish populations.

For angling, the central Alberta parkland region is the least bountiful sector of Alberta, but it is nonetheless blessed with a few premium locations, especially the Red Deer and North Saskatchewan Rivers. Their tremendous fish populations are the most diverse in the province. The transition zone between parkland and boreal forest is cottage country, with numerous lakes known for their pike, walleye, and perch fishing.

The forested northern half of Alberta contains the majority of the province's 800 fish-inhabited lakes. Northern pike, walleye, and lake trout thrive here, with arctic grayling running some of this vast region's rivers. Much of this part of Alberta is inaccessible by road, but a handful of fly-in lodges offer world-class angling.

The mountains and foothills on Alberta's west side give birth to some of Canada's most pristine creeks and rivers. Originating in the ice pack of age-old glaciers, these sinuous waters harbor cutthroat and brook trout in the cold upper stretches, giving way to highly productive brown trout and rainbow trout waters where the land starts to level out. The city of Calgary sits on this divide, it's heart lanced by the famous Bow River.

The extreme western and southwestern boundaries of Alberta are occupied by Jasper, Banff, and Waterton National Parks. Rainbow, brook, and lake trout are the featured fishing targets in these locations. Visiting anglers can combine pursuit of these species with enjoyment of unparalleled scenery. Neither disappoints either the first-time or the veteran visitor.

The Prairies

Alberta's prairie region lies due north of Montana, bordered on the east by Saskatchewan and on the west by the Rocky Mountain foothills. The Milk River, the only watershed in Alberta that flows south into the United States, parallels the Montana border before sending its water south, eventually linking with the Missouri River. The Milk earned its name from the high silt load that gives it its at times milky-white appearance. The provincial record sauger was taken from the Milk River, and it is this species that attracts most anglers. It is fished in various ways, in pools, eddies, and behind structure. Pike to 10 pounds also cruise these waters.

A little farther north, the lower Oldman and Bow Rivers meet at an area known locally as "the Forks," to form the South Saskatchewan River. Pike, walleye, sauger, and goldeye can all be found throughout much of this water. Any presentation that can get live bait down to the bottom of pools and outside bends is sure to produce. The lake sturgeon, Alberta's largest fish species, can also be found in the South Saskatchewan. A 105-pound provincial record sturgeon came from these waters. Locals

An angler casting on a lake in Banff National Park projects the quintessential idyllic fishing scene.

recommend a three-way swivel setup, using a 2/0 or 3/0 hook baited with worms and enough weight to keep your offering stationary in the current. Summer evenings tend to produce best.

The lower Bow River offers fine opportunities for large brown and rainbow trout between Carseland and the Bassano Dam, though much of this stretch is inaccessible to angling where it passes through an Indian reserve. Fly anglers enjoy tremendous success using streamers, nymphs, or dry flies, depending largely on the season, water conditions, and weather.

The bulk of the remaining quality angling opportunities across Alberta's parched prairie region occurs on the many irrigation reservoirs that provide stock water. Most hold northern pike, walleye, and lake whitefish, with the occasional rainbow trout that's made its way from the Bow or Oldman through the irrigation supply canals.

Travers, Badger, Chin, Stafford, Crawling Valley, and Milk River Ridge Reservoirs, along with man-made Keho, McGregor, and Newell Lakes, have the potential to produce trophy fish. The provincial record pike, 38 pounds, comes from Keho Lake.

These southern reservoirs, despite being relatively featureless and populated with notoriously finicky fish, are quickly gaining a reputation as Alberta's best walleye fisheries. This species grows quickly in the warm, productive waters common here. In recent years more fly anglers have been pursuing trophy pike. They've been wading or drifting in May or June through shallow bays that have an early growth of vegetation.

The Parkland

Alberta's parkland region is a patchwork of native aspen groves and grasslands interspersed with rolling fields of wheat, barley, canola, and hay. A number of pothole-studded moraines created by receding glaciers some 10,000 years ago pockmark the landscape. The predominant rivers here are the Red Deer, Battle, and North Saskatchewan.

The Red Deer River in this region produces pike and walleye to 10 pounds, sauger, Rocky Mountain whitefish to 3 pounds, and goldeye to 2 pounds. Fishing on the bottom with stationary bait is most effective, and casting from shore also yields pike.

In recent years brown trout fishing has increased immediately upstream and downstream of the city of Red Deer. Fly anglers have had good success quietly wading the shoreline in the evening, casting dry flies to rising fish. A number of browns in the 24- to 30-inch range have been taken. Look for a wide variety of mayfly and caddisfly hatches throughout the season. In the lower stretches of the Red Deer the occasional sturgeon have been taken on dead-still live baits.

The Battle is the region's smallest river but is well known locally for producing big walleye. These fish are extremely migratory, so it's always a difficult river to predict. Spring and fall, when the fish stack up in pools, are the most consistent seasons.

Forestburg Reservoir, a hydroelectric impoundment, has yellow perch in addition to pike and walleye. Some big goldeye are caught annually below the reservoir, in the lower reaches of the Battle, mainly on wet flies.

The North Saskatchewan River is arguably Alberta's most productive and underutilized fishery. Running predominantly east-west, and bisecting the capital city of Edmonton, the North Saskatchewan offers quality fishing for walleye in excess of 10 pounds, along with northern pike, sauger, goldeye, burbot, and a few brown trout. Look for fish at creek mouths, above and below islands, on outside curves, and in pools and eddies.

Prior to 1989, the provincial record walleye came from the North Saskatchewan just downstream of Edmonton. During the summer months, fishing with bait rigs, jigs tipped with worms, or bait-tipped three-way rigs is favored, and you never know what to expect on the hook. Lake sturgeon are also common throughout much of this stretch of the river. Stationary bait rigs crammed with worms are preferred for them.

Productive lakes are scattered across the southern portion of the parkland region. Pine Lake, outside Red Deer, yields good walleye, pike, and perch. Sylvan, Gull, Pigeon, and Wabumun Lakes all offer pike, walleye, perch, and lake whitefish. Because of heavily developed water-sports activities on these lakes, they are largely underfished. Pine Lake is the best bet for walleye, while Wabumun gives up pike approaching 25 pounds every year.

These lakes are well known for ice fishing, attracting many winter-only anglers. Lake whitefish are the primary target species, with Gull and Pigeon Lakes the most popular waters. The power plants on Wabumun keep portions of the lake open year-round. These areas attract pike that can be taken throughout the winter months by casting spoons, crankbaits, or flies.

Just outside Edmonton are a number of small, pothole lakes stocked with rainbow trout. Though subject to periodic winterkill, Chickakoo, Eden, Hasse, Cottage, Star, and Black Nugget Lakes are all proven producers. Slow-trolling wet flies and small streamers behind rowed boats or float tubes is popular here, while various baits suspended under a float work well through the ice. East of the city, Hastings and Coal Lakes offer fine perch fishing, particularly in winter.

Within an hour's drive northwest of Edmonton are several lakes with good walleye, pike, and perch populations. Lac St. Anne, Lac la Nonne, Jackfish Lake, and Lake Isle offer good fishing year-round. Another 30 miles farther west, Chip Lake attracts anglers from around the province in search of the burbot that move up from the lake into the Lobstick River in winter. Worms or minnows fished still on the bottom through the ice will almost guarantee a hookup with this tasty table fish.

Within 150 miles northeast of Edmonton is a cluster of lakes known across the province for their walleye, perch, and pike fishing. Though populations of fish are down somewhat from previous years, all still offer fine angling opportunities. Pinehurst Lake near Lac la Biche is probably the best, particularly for walleye; but Touchwood, Spencer, Seibert, Ironwood, Beaver, Moose, and Muriel Lakes are all worth the trip. Look for walleye on sunken reefs and along natural dropoffs during the heat of summer; in spring, fall, and on summer nights search up on the flats. Slow, vertical presentations work best on schooled fish. Perch can be found adjacent to submerged weedbeds, where jigs tipped with minnows will produce. Ice fishing is very popular in this area.

Lake whitefish are found in most of these waters, too. Largely incidental catches in open water, they are more commonly targeted through the ice.

Cold Lake, on the Saskatchewan border, is best known for its lake trout but also has pike, walleye, perch, and whitefish. North of Edmonton, Missawawi, Kinosiu, Mann, and North Buck Lakes are all known for their winter perch fishing. Try small jigs tipped with minnow pieces, fished over sunken weedbeds.

The Boreal Forest

The northern half of Alberta is dominated by mixed-wood boreal forest—a mosaic of aspen poplar, white spruce, and black spruce interspersed with many wetlands of varying sizes. Road access across much of this region is extremely limited, although oil and gas development and its associated roads are opening up more and more of the north each year.

The fishing jewel of this region is Lesser Slave Lake. One of Alberta's largest lakes, it encompasses some 1,160 square kilometers. Located southeast of the town of Peace River, Lesser Slave offers tremendous fishing for walleye to 12 pounds, yellow perch to 2 pounds, and northern pike to 25 pounds. Access to most of the lake is good, with numerous boat launch facilities. The best walleye fishing is in the lake's west basin in spring; the east end picks up after July.

Good pike fishing in Lesser Slave exists wherever deep water is adjacent to forage-fish-holding structure, but the east end of the lake near the town of Slave Lake is a consistent producer. Perch can be found just about anywhere you find walleye, though the mouth of the river, on the lake's extreme east end, has developed a worthy reputation for lots of jumbo perch. Try slow jigging or bait rigging.

Lesser Slave has enviable reputation for terrific ice fishing as well. Anglers travel from afar to tackle trophy pike, walleye, perch, and burbot through the ice. Hilliard's Bay, near the west end, is the most popular winter fishing location. Numerous camping and motel facilities around Lesser Slave Lake cater year-round to anglers.

Other drive-to fishing lakes in the central and western portion of Alberta's north include Utikuma, Peerless, Graham, Cadotte, Fawcett, God's, Sturgeon, Snipe, Iosegun, Baptiste, and Lawrence. Most offer good walleye, pike, perch, and lake whitefish angling all year long. Peerless Lake, a six-hour-drive north of Edmonton, is a notable exception. It offers outstanding lake trout fishing, with 20- to 30-pounders not uncommon. These fish move up shallow in spring and fall, and in summer they congregate in deep cool holes.

Several other lakes in the region offer fine angling opportunities for stocked, but self-sustaining, trout species. The best of these include Dollar Lake, north of Valleyview, which produces brown and rainbow trout to 10 pounds; and Edith and Chrystina Lakes near Swan Hills, which have brook trout up to 5 pounds. Most of the stocked trout ponds are suitable for spinning or fly fishing. On summer evenings it's possible to pick up some nice rising fish on mayfly or caddisfly patterns.

Of the fish-bearing rivers in the northwest, the mighty Peace River is the largest. It is inhabited by pike, walleye, and goldeye in the lower section, and rainbow trout, bull trout, and grayling in the upper stretch. While outstanding at times, and with little angling pressure at any time of year, the Peace is susceptible to carrying high silt loads that leave it unfishable for much of the spring, early summer, and periods following heavy rainfalls.

Southeast of the city of Grande Prairie, the Wapiti, Simonette, and Smoky Rivers all offer quality angling for pike and walleye in their lower sections, and bull trout, arctic grayling, and whitefish in the higher reaches. The best fishing is from late June through October. Concentrate on pools for pike, walleye, and bull trout; work the riffles and slicks for grayling and whitefish.

The Little Smoky River, near the town of Fox Creek, is arguably Alberta's best arctic grayling water. Much of it was designated catch-and-release-only a number of years ago, and the results have been outstanding. Grayling up to 20 inches are not uncommon, although 10- to 16-inch fish predominate.

South of the Little Smoky, the Berland and Wildhay Rivers hold populations of rainbow trout, bull trout, and grayling. Each has innumerable unnamed tributaries that also offer good fishing.

The Athabasca River, which bisects the northern half of Alberta southwest to northeast, offers quality angling wherever there is access. The lower stretches hold big walleye and pike, and the provincial record walleye was taken out of the Pembina River, a tributary to the Athabasca. In the Athabasca's upper stretches look for bull trout, rainbows, grayling, and whitefish.

The eastern portion of northern Alberta, off the Fort McMurray Highway, has fewer accessible waters. The best among them are Wabasca, Calling, Winnefred, and Christina Lakes. All offer year-round fishing for pike and walleye, though the best months are May, June, September, and October.

Though much of scenic northern Alberta is not accessible by road, a number of fly-in camps offer spectacular fishing. Most are accessed out of either Fort McMurray or Fort Smith, the latter a small town on Alberta's border with the Northwest Territories. The best waters serviced by these camps include Andrew, Lealand, Bistcho, Margaret, Island, Gardiner, and Namur Lakes. Trophy northern pike fishing is available at all these, with walleye and/or lake trout also available. The best bet for lakers is Andrew, in the northeast.

None of the fish in these fly-in lakes see many anglers; as a result they are rather unsophisticated. Trolling is very popular, especially with spoons and minnow plugs. Because of the northern latitude of these lakes, the window of opportunity for fishing is relatively narrow. Ice out occurs from late May to mid-June most years, with the lodges shut down by mid-September.

The Rocky Mountains and Foothills

Alberta is probably best known across North America for its trout fishing, a reputation built largely on the magnificent angling available on the Bow River. However, the Bow is just one of many streams and rivers that offer world-class angling and originate in the Rockies.

Another is the Oldman River and its many tributaries, in the extreme southwest. In the upper stretches of the watershed, bull trout and cutthroat trout dominate. As these rivers wind eastward, rainbows and brown trout thrive. This is truly a fly angler's paradise. Cutthroats are aggressive feeders, falling for virtually any well-presented dry fly; high-floating attractor patterns always produce. Bull trout inhabit the deepest pools and are best taken on large leech or Muddler minnow patterns. Rainbows and browns are much more selective feeders here; the prudent angler will try to match the various caddis, mayfly, or stonefly hatches. Hardware anglers will find success with small, in-line spinners. Top tributaries include the Crowsnest, Castle, Livingston, and St. Mary's Rivers.

Moving north along the foothills, the next major system is the famous Bow River. Originating in Bow Lake in Banff National Park, the Bow tumbles and slides its way down and through Calgary. Bull trout, brook trout, and Rocky Mountain whitefish inhabit the higher reaches, while the nutrient-rich lower stretches have rainbow trout and brown trout, the latter being the fish that made the Bow famous.

The most productive stretch of river is between Calgary and the Carseland Dam, some 30 miles downstream. Anglers can expect 20-inch specimens on most floats through this section. Although the river is best known for its dry-fly fishing, anglers must be prepared to fish nymphs and streamers most of the time for optimal results. This stretch can be drifted effectively in two days; access points allow for one-day floats if preferred.

Veterans of the Bow float with two rods: a 4- or 5-weight rigged with floating line for nymphing and throwing dries, and an 8-weight with a high-speed sink-tip line for streamers. Weighted flies are the norm here. Popular patterns include Woolly Buggers, Zonkers, and Muddlers in the streamer class, and a Gold-ribbed Hare's Ear and San Juan Worm for nymphing. The predominant hatches are plenty and varied, so a wide selection of dry flies is required. August on the Bow is tough and unpredictable, but can offer some outstanding hopper fishing.

Continuing north, the Red Deer system is praised for its wonderful brown trout streams. The Raven and North Raven Rivers (Stauffer Creek) are perhaps the best known in the area, but the Prairie, Dogpond, Fallen Timber, Little Red Deer, and the Red Deer proper—and their tributaries—should not be overlooked. These rivers and streams are relatively small, though they have the potential of giving up 5-pound fish in stretches you can leap across. Attractor patterns like the Royal Coachman and H&L variants will turn fish throughout the season, as will leech patterns worked through the deeper pools and runs.

Farther along is the North Saskatchewan River system. The jewels here include the Ram and North Ram Rivers, which are renowned for cutthroat trout. The North Ram is especially productive, due mostly to its catch-and-release designation, with 18- to 20-inch cutts not uncommon. The main stem of the North Saskatchewan harbors browns, cutts, brookies, bull trout, whitefish, and even a few remnant native lake trout. Farther below, as the river slows and widens, pike and walleye dominate. The best places to fish are from shore at creek mouths and deep pools. This river is very turbulent in spots and is best floated by only the most experienced. A number of tributaries in the North Saskatchewan system offer fine angling opportunities for rainbows, cutthroats, and brook trout.

The Athabasca River watershed south of Highway 16 offers anglers easy access to quality grayling and bull trout angling. The late season—August and September—is best. Bull trout hang in the deepest pools, while grayling can be taken from the riffle and slick areas on a variety of spinners or dry flies. The McLeod, Pembina, and Embarras Rivers and their tributaries are top locations.

The entire length of the Rockies is dotted with high mountain lakes that offer virtually untapped angling for stocked cutthroat, golden, rainbow, and brook trout for those capable of the typically arduous hikes required. A horse-pack or helicopter trip allows the high-country angler to bring in a float tube, which is the most effective way to fish these waters.

ALBRIGHT KNOT

A fishing knot used for making line-to-line connections.

See: Knots, Fishing.

ALDERFLIES

See: Dobsonflies, Fishflies, and Alderflies.

ALEWIFE   *Alosa pseudoharengus.*

Other names—herring, sawbelly, gray herring, grayback; French: *gapareau, gaspereau;* Spanish: *alosa, pinchagua.*

A small herring, the alewife is important as forage for gamefish in many inland waters and along the Atlantic coast. It is used commercially in pet food and as fish meal and fertilizer, and it has been a significant factor in the restoration of trout and salmon fisheries in the Great Lakes. The landlocked alewife can at times be a nuisance because of periodic mass die-offs, especially in the Great Lakes; for reasons not fully understood, but believed to be related to the rise in water temperature, landlocked alewives die and drift to shore in the spring and early summer.

Identification.   Small and silvery gray with a greenish to bluish back tinge, the alewife usually has one small dark shoulder spot and sometimes other small dusky spots. It has large eyes with well-developed adipose eyelids. The alewife can be distinguished from other herring by its lower jaw, which projects noticeably beyond the upper jaw.

Size.   Alewives can grow up to a half pound in weight and to 15 inches in length; they usually average 6 to 12 inches in saltwater and 3 to 6 inches in freshwater.

Distribution.   Sea-run alewives extend from Newfoundland and the Gulf of St. Lawrence to South Carolina. Alewives were introduced into the upper Great Lakes and into many other inland waters, although some naturally landlocked populations exist.

Habitat.   Alewives are anadromous, inhabiting coastal waters, estuaries, and some inland waters, although some spend their entire lives in freshwater. They have been caught as far as 70 miles offshore in shelf waters.

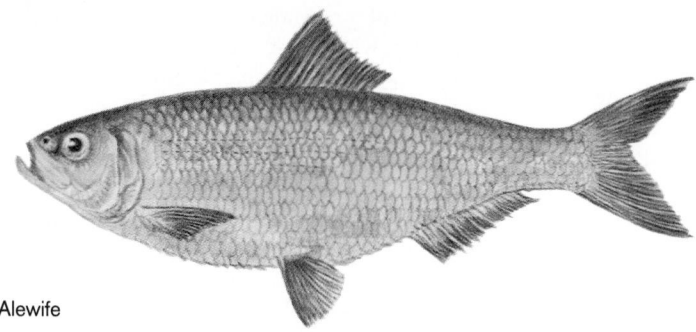

Alewife

A

Life history/Behavior. The alewife is a schooling fish and is sometimes found in massive concentrations detectable on sportfishing sonar. In late April through early June, saltwater alewives run up freshwater rivers from the sea to spawn in lakes and sluggish stretches of river. Landlocked alewives move from deeper waters to nearshore shallows in lakes, or upstream in rivers, spawning when the water is between 52° and 70°F. Saltwater females deposit 60,000 to 100,000 eggs, whereas freshwater females deposit 10,000 to 12,000 eggs. They deposit the eggs randomly, at night, and both adults leave the eggs unattended. Young alewives hatch in less than a week, and by fall they return to the sea or to deeper waters. Adult landlocked alewives cannot tolerate extreme temperatures, preferring a range of 52° to 70°F—the same temperatures they spawn in.

Food and feeding habits. Young alewives feed on minute free-floating plants and animals, diatoms, copepods, and ostracods; adults feed on plankton, as well as insects, shrimp, small fish, diatoms, copepods, and their own eggs.

Angling. Having virtually no sporting value, alewives are almost never deliberately caught by anglers. They may be caught on tiny spoons or jigs or snagged, however, to be used as live baits. They are also used as chum, and as crab and lobster bait. In freshwater, alewives are a popular live bait in trout and salmon lakes, but they are difficult to keep alive and fresh.

See: Bait; Herring.

ALGAE

The term "algae" refers to a large, heterogenous group of primitive aquatic plants that lack roots, stems, or leaf systems and range from unicellular organisms to large networks of kelp. Algae exist in both freshwater and saltwater. They can be blue-green, yellow, green, brown, and red; there are more than 15,000 species of green algae alone. All species of algae photosynthesize.

As the primary or lowest plant forms, algae are important in sustaining marine and freshwater food chains *(see)*. In freshwater, algae occur in three different types often encountered by anglers: plankton, filamentous, and muskgrass. Plankton is a diverse community made up of suspended algae (phytoplankton), combined with great numbers of minute suspended animals (zooplankton). Filamentous algae consist of stringy, hairlike filaments, often erroneously described as moss or slime because of their appearance when they form a mat or furlike coat on objects. Muskgrass, or stonewort, algae are a more advanced form that has no roots but attaches to lake or stream bottoms.

See: Aquatic Plants.

ALGAE BLOOM

An algae bloom is a dense concentration of algae, usually occurring under high nutrient concentrations as one species becomes so abundant that it obliterates other species, making the water appear cloudy (often brown, yellow, or pea-soup green). Sometimes causing scum and odor, an algae bloom is often blown into shallow areas; during a bloom each ounce of water contains millions of microscopic algae cells. Although a bloom may indirectly provide food for fish, it is an indication that a problem exists in the body of water, and to solve it the source of nutrients must be reduced.

Algae blooms occur in both freshwater and saltwater; the most prominent in saltwater is known as a red tide *(see)*. Some algae blooms can be harmful to human health, especially via toxins in seafood, and may cause fish and invertebrates to die; they appear to be occurring more frequently in the coastal zones and estuaries of the United States. The widely reported pfiesteria *(see)*, responsible for killing billions of fish, is an algae bloom.

See: Eutrophic.

ALIEN SPECIES

A species occurring in an area outside of its historically known natural range as a result of intentional or accidental dispersal by human activities. There are also known as exotic or introduced species.

See: Exotic Species.

ALKALINITY

The capacity to buffer or withstand great fluctuations in the pH *(see)* of water. The neutral value of pH is 7.0; the higher the pH value above 7.0, the greater the alkalinity. Fish prefer a pH close to the neutral value. The alkalinity of a lake generally depends on the minerals in its watershed. Watersheds with soils rich in lime and related materials provide more buffering to lakes, whereas those poor in lime, such as bedrock, provide very little buffering and are more susceptible to changes in pH from acid deposition or acid runoff.

ALLISON TUNA

A term for yellowfin tuna *(see)*, mainly used in Bermuda *(see)*.

ALLOCATION

Distribution, by fisheries management agencies, of fishing opportunities among user groups and individuals. This term is often used with reference to the harvest or allowable catch. In saltwater, allocations are made between recreational anglers and commercial fishermen.

See: Fisheries Management.

ALL-TACKLE WORLD RECORD

The largest individual of a given species of sportfish caught on sporting tackle within the parameters established by the International Game Fish Association *(see)*, the certifying organization. An all-tackle world record may also be a line-class world record *(see)*.

See: Records.

AMBERJACK, GREATER   *Seriola dumerili.*

Other names—amberjack, jack, amberfish, jack hammer, horse-eye bonito, horse-eye jack, Allied kingfish (Australia); French: *poisson limon, sériole couronnée;* Hawaiian: *kahala;* Japanese: *kanpachi;* Spanish: *coronado, pez de limón, serviola.*

Sought after by anglers because of its qualities as a gamefish, the greater amberjack is the largest of the jacks, the most important amberjack to anglers, and, like most of its brethren, a strong fighter. Although it is considered a fair food fish, and a substantial commercial fishery for this species exists in some locales, anglers account for most of the catch. The greater amberjack is high on the list of tropical marine fish suspected of causing ciguatera *(see)* poisoning, although this problem may be isolated to certain areas, as greater amberjack are regularly consumed without incident in some places.

Identification. The greater amberjack is greenish blue to almost purple or brown above the lateral line, and silver below the lateral line. A dark olive brown diagonal stripe extends from the mouth across both eyes to about the first dorsal fin; these are commonly referred to as "fighter stripes" and are prominent in live fish, especially when they are excited. A broad amber stripe runs horizontally along the sides, and disappears after the fish dies. The fins may also have a yellow cast. The greater amberjack has short foredorsal fins, a bluntly pointed head, and no detached finlets.

The greater amberjack bears a resemblance in smaller sizes to the bluefish (as well as other jacks), but it can be distinguished by its more deeply concave tail. Also, it has small teeth in bands instead of the large, triangular teeth of the bluefish. The amber stripe sometimes causes anglers to confuse the greater amberjack with the yellowtail, but it can be distinguished by the 11 to 16 developed gill rakers on the lower limb of the first branchial arch; the yellowtail has 21 to 28 gill rakers.

The first dorsal fin consists of 6 or 7 small, fragile spines connected by a membrane; juveniles have an additional detached spine before the first dorsal fin. The second dorsal fin has 1 spine and 29 to 35 soft rays. The anal fin has 3 spines, the first 2 of which are detached, and 19 to 22 soft rays. In adults, the 2 detached spines are sometimes covered with skin. There is a low keel on the caudal peduncle.

Size. Averaging roughly 15 pounds in weight, and commonly ranging up to 40 pounds, the greater amberjack often exceeds 50 pounds and has been reported to attain weights exceeding 170 pounds. The all-tackle record is 155 pounds, 10 ounces. It can reach a length of more than 5 feet.

Distribution. Although greater amberjack range in the Atlantic Ocean as far north as New England, they exist mostly in southern waters. They are known to occur in the Indo-Pacific area around Japan, China, and the Philippines, in the central Pacific off Hawaii, throughout the western Atlantic Ocean (abundant off the coasts of Florida and in nearby Caribbean waters), in portions of the eastern Atlantic Ocean (Madeira and southern West Africa), and in the Mediterranean Sea in tropical and temperate waters.

Amberjack in some waters are resident fish, but others are migratory coastal pelagic fish that swim with the current edges and eddies. Amberjack tagged in the Atlantic off South Florida have been recaptured as far south as Venezuela.

Habitat. Greater amberjack are found mostly in offshore waters and at considerable depths, as well as around offshore reefs, wrecks, buoys, oil rigs, and the like. They can be caught anywhere in the water column, to depths of several hundred feet, but they are mostly associated with near-bottom structure in the 60- to 240-foot range. This trend is due in large part to the habits of anglers. In some locales, they are caught in inshore waters, even as shallow as under 30 feet, but are usually associated with offshore environs.

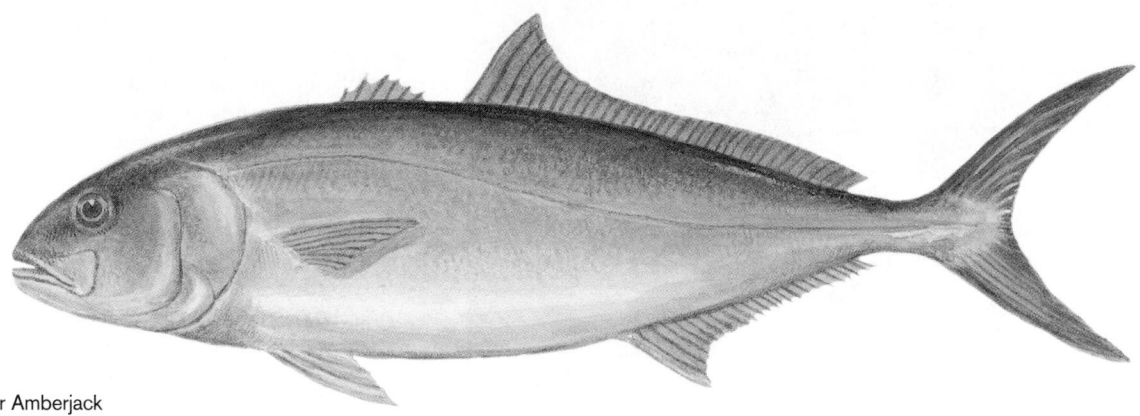

Greater Amberjack

A

Life history/Behavior. The greater amberjack often occurs in schools, but it is not primarily a schooling fish and occasionally remains solitary. Migrations appear to be linked to spawning behavior, which in the Atlantic occurs from March through June. Evidence suggests that spawning may occur in offshore oceanic waters, but few studies have been conducted, although spawning fish are known to congregate over reefs and wrecks. Juveniles have been taken from June through September in offshore waters.

Food and feeding habits. Greater amberjack feed on fish, crabs, and squid.

Angling. With the exception of tuna, amberjack are as hard-fighting a fish, pound for pound, as any found in saltwater. Those anglers who have engaged in a tug of war with a large amberjack know well how their forearm muscles have been strained and how their back and shoulders ache after the duel. Amberjack are especially popular with party and charter boat anglers, as well as those in private boats.

Amberjack are a wide-ranging fish and are likely to be found in various locales, providing good fishing from spring through summer. They are most commonly associated with such intermediate to deep habitats as reefs, rocky outcrops, wrecks, buoys, and other structure. They usually band in small groups, so it is typical to catch an amberjack and have others follow it to the boat. Leaving it hooked or tethered may keep the school around and provide further success.

Amberjack are fast swimmers and voracious predators. Fishing with cut or live baits is very popular, as is vertical jigging with bucktails, jigs with soft-plastic bodies, or metal jigging spoons. Lures are sometimes adorned with a strip or chunk of meat. Popular live baits include herring, menhaden, mullet, and especially pinfish and blue runners. In water under 120 feet, some anglers opt for chumming.

Because these fish take a lure or bait very hard, there is seldom a question that a strike has occurred. When fishing in deep water, it is often critical to muscle big amberjack immediately after the fight begins, as they usually head deep for cover and, if they get to it, will break the line on a rock. It often seems as though the more you pull, the harder the amberjack pulls. With a good-size fish on, using the boat to pull the fish away from a reef or wreck to play it in obstruction-free water can be helpful.

It is a chore to turn a big amberjack immediately and coax it away from cover. Where big specimens lurk, anglers depend on heavy tackle, knowing that these fish make determined runs and fight all the way to the boat, even when brought up from deep water. Many amberjack anglers like stand-up fishing *(see)* with 30- to 50-pound-class outfits and a good harness; a two-speed reel is especially helpful for gaining on these bruisers. Anglers deep fishing for snapper and grouper may find themselves overmatched when an amberjack comes along.

On the few occasions when amberjack are encountered near the surface, anglers can cast baits or plugs, spoons, or flies from a boat or from shore. Trollers use deep-diving plugs when appropriate, and some fish with planers and downriggers.
See: Bottom Fishing; Jacks; Jigging; Reef; Wreck.

Amberjack caught off the Florida Keys.

AMBERJACK, LESSER   *Seriola fasciata.*
Other names—amberjack, jack; French: *sériole babianc;* Spanish: *medregal listado.*

The lesser amberjack is the smallest amberjack, seldom encountered by, and relatively unknown to, anglers.

Identification. The lesser amberjack has an olive green or brownish back above the lateral line and is silver below the lateral line. A dark olive brown diagonal stripe extends from the mouth across both eyes to about the first dorsal fin. It is very similar in appearance to the greater amberjack *(see: amberjack, greater)* but has a deeper body profile and a proportionately larger eye, and eight spines in the first dorsal fin.

Size. Reports on the size of this species vary markedly, from up to 12 inches in length to under 10 pounds.

Distribution. In the western Atlantic, the lesser amberjack ranges from Massachusetts to Brazil; in the eastern Atlantic its range is uncertain due to previous confusion with other species, although it has been found off the Madeira Islands.

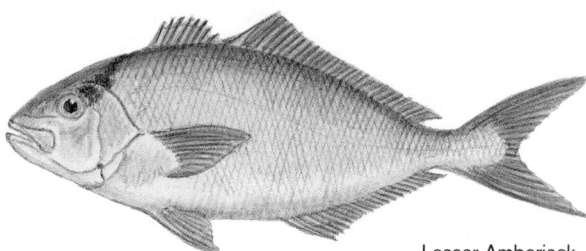

Lesser Amberjack

Habitat. Lesser amberjack are believed to live deeper than other amberjack, commonly in water from 180 to 410 feet deep, and to spawn in offshore waters.

Food and feeding habits. Lesser amberjack feed on fish and squid.

Angling. There is no concerted fishery for this species.

See: Jacks.

AMERICAN SPORTFISHING ASSOCIATION

Known as the ASA, this nonprofit trade association in Washington, D.C., has the goals of ensuring healthy and sustainable fisheries resources and increasing sportfishing participation. Primarily supported by the sportfishing industry, it also has individual memberships, and is involved in education, conservation, promotion, and marketing with regard to sportfishing.

The ASA's educational arm, the Future Fisherman Foundation, was created in 1986. It implements several national sportfishing education programs, including the "Hooked on Fishing—Not on Drugs" campaign in over 500 schools, a national 4-H sportfishing program, and a complete Sportfishing and Aquatic Resources Education program for educators and youth organizations.

The ASA also created and helps to fund the Fish America Foundation, which has directed millions of dollars to volunteer projects, endorsed by state and/or federal natural resource agencies, and is aimed at preserving waterways and enhancing fish populations without regard to geographic location or species limitations. It is the only program of its kind and has operated since 1983.

AMIDSHIP

The center section of a boat, between the bow and stern.

AMPHIPODS

A large group of crustaceans, most of which are small, compressed creatures (such as sand fleas and freshwater shrimp). These may be of food importance to juvenile fish.

AMUR, WHITE

See: Carp, Grass.

ANADROMOUS

Fish that migrate from saltwater to freshwater in order to spawn. Fish that do the opposite are called catadromous.

Literally meaning "up running," anadromous refers to fish that spend part of their lives in the ocean and move into freshwater rivers or streams to spawn. Anadromous fish hatch in freshwater, move to saltwater to grow to adulthood or sexual maturity, and then return to freshwater to reproduce. Salmon are the best-known anadromous fish, but there are many others, including such prominent species as steelhead trout, sturgeon, striped bass, and shad, and many lesser-known or less highly regarded species. Around the world there are approximately 100 species of anadromous fish.

Complicating an understanding of anadromy is the fact that some anadromous species have adapted, either naturally or by introduction, to a complete life in freshwater environments. These species, which include salmon, striped bass, and steelhead, make spawning migrations from lakes, where they live most of their lives, into rivers to spawn. In such instances, these fish are originally saltwater in origin. They remain anadromous when moved into purely fresh water, although they use the lake as they would the ocean. There are also species of freshwater fish that are native to freshwater and that migrate from lake to stream or river to spawn. These are not technically anadromous, but adfluvial.

Fish that originate in saltwater but have freshwater forms are often called "landlocked," whether or not they have a clear path to and from the sea. Sometimes these fish are physically blocked from reaching the ocean. Fish in a reservoir or lake may be unable to leave. Fish in some streams, like those in high-mountain areas, have a clear passageway to the sea but no means of returning because of waterfalls. Coldwater species may be effectively landlocked in the colder headwaters of a stream because temperatures are too high for them in the lowland parts of that stream or in the ocean in that area. Dolly Varden, for example, are landlocked in the southern tip of their range, but anadromous forms are common farther north.

Sometimes the terminology used to discuss the freshwater forms of saltwater fish is confusing. Atlantic salmon that exist in freshwater lakes without access to the sea are popularly called landlocked salmon or landlocked Atlantic salmon. Sockeye salmon that exist in freshwater lakes without access to the sea are often called Kokanee salmon. Other species, like striped bass and arctic char, are called by the same name in saltwater or freshwater.

Another complicating factor in understanding this topic is the fact that some anadromous

A

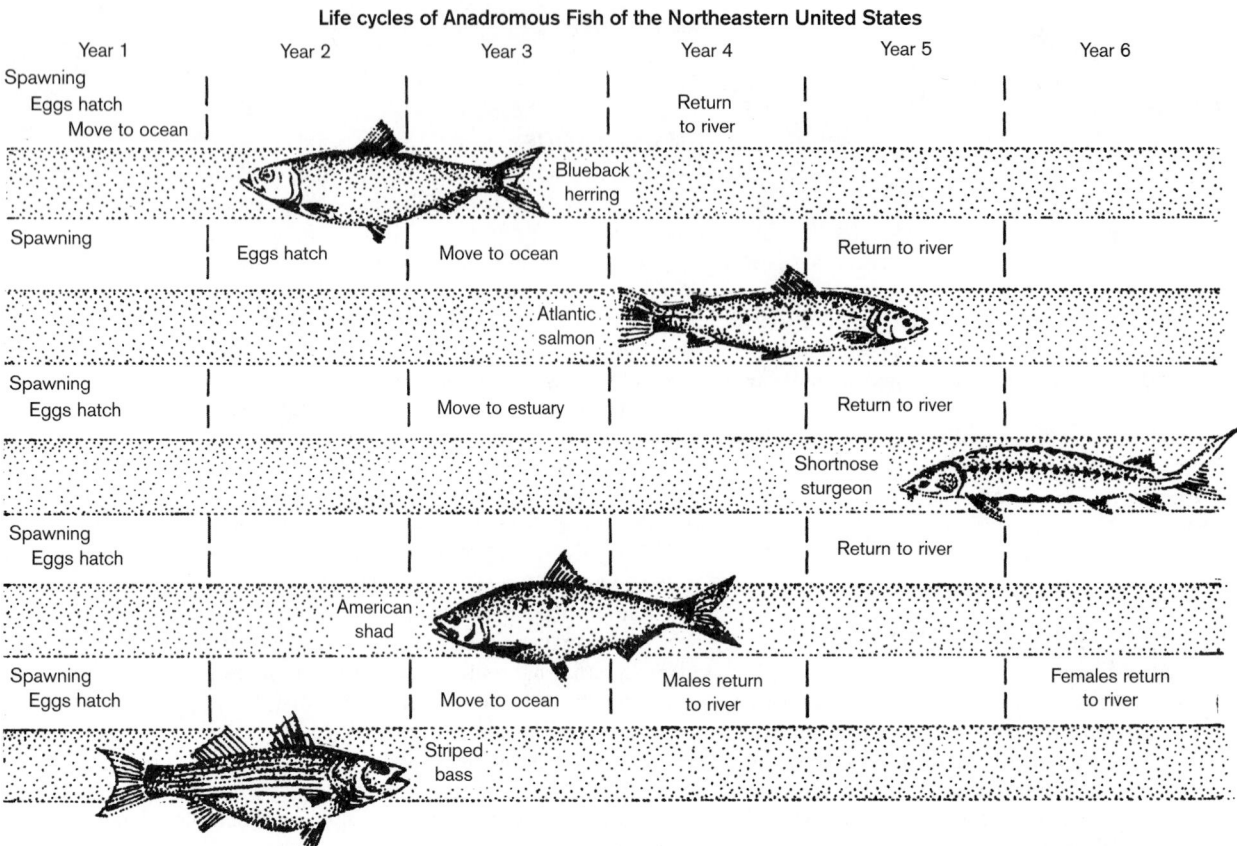

Life cycles of Anadromous Fish of the Northeastern United States

species of fish exercise anadromy optionally. For example, in coastal streams, the young of some steelhead trout may go to sea or may remain in the stream until maturity and then spawn without ever having left freshwater. Trout near the headwaters of a stream are more apt to remain in freshwater. Those that remain are sometimes thought to be genetically different from those that migrate.

Anglers have some difficulty distinguishing by appearance whether an anadromous fish has been to sea. Size is usually an indicator—the large fish having been to sea—but it is not necessarily a determining one. Scientists can tell by aging the fish, often by checking the growth rings on a scale *(see: fisheries management)*. Appearance may be an indicator. Young trout and salmon, for example, undergo a change in appearance before or during their seaward migration. They become more silvery; red colors fade or disappear; and scales get looser. Usually the fish grow so much faster in saltwater that the difference between freshwater growth and saltwater growth is quite apparent on the scales under a microscope. On most subspecies of trout and species of Pacific salmon, the parr marks (large vertical or oval rounded spots on the sides) will gradually disappear whether or not the fish goes to sea. None of these is an infallible indicator. Trout that enter a lake or reservoir, and some of those that remain in large

rivers, will show much the same changes and be difficult to tell from a sea-run individual. When a trout leaves the ocean and reenters freshwater, it will gradually regain some of the appearance of stream trout. In general, the sea-run trout has grown faster and is therefore younger than a stream trout of the same size.

There obviously must be important advantages in living an anadromous existence, or the habit would not have developed independently in such widely differing creatures as lampreys, sturgeon, shad, salmon, and striped bass. The advantages must be great enough to pay for the extra energy and risk involved in the migration from freshwater to saltwater and back again. Greater safety for the eggs in freshwater and a better food supply in the ocean appear to be the chief benefits for many fish, but more favorable year-round temperatures may also be a factor.

Being anadromous has numerous advantages and disadvantages both for the fish and for other animals, as well as for the environment in general. Anadromous fish need to make spawning migrations, which, if they are long, create physical hardship on the fish. And if the hazards of the migratory journey become increasingly great and too few spawners are able to make the trip, the existence of the population can be threatened. This is precisely what has happened to many runs of salmon in the Pacific Northwest. Furthermore, if the quality of their spawning

habitat has been adversely impacted (pollution, thermal variation, flow impediment, etc.), then they are at great risk there as well. The chemical pollution of Atlantic Coast rivers affected the spawning of striped bass and was a major contributor to the collapse of striped bass stocks in the 1970s and 1980s.

Characteristics of anadromous fish. There are varying degrees of anadromy. In the most extreme cases, fish move from hundreds of miles at sea to hundreds of miles up a river. In the least extreme cases, some borderline species move from brackish water a short distance into freshwater to spawn. Anadromous fish stay in freshwater for varying lengths of time, usually dependent upon the species. Young anadromous fish migrate to the ocean for the first time when their growth and development are at a stage that allows them to survive there. The different anadromous species do not all go to the same place(s) in the ocean; each species migrates to the areas that fulfill their own needs for food and growth. The length of time that they stay in the ocean also varies with each species, and may vary within the species as well; this is usually dependent upon the time necessary to reach adult size or sexual maturity.

Most anadromous fish return to the same river in which they were born. However, some stray to other rivers, which may or may not be accidental. How they find their way from great distances in the ocean to the proper river is yet a mystery *(see: migration),* although there are several theories. One is that they use their sense of smell to detect small amounts of certain chemicals coming from their freshwater rivers. Another is that the fish follow ocean currents until they get close to their home river. And another is that they have internal "compasses" like those found in bees and homing pigeons.

Adult anadromous fish build up a considerable amount of fat while they are in the ocean. Their purpose for returning to freshwater is to reproduce, and some species, like the Pacific salmon, have little need to continue eating. They may still strike out of instinct, however, at other animals and at lures or bait. Many anadromous fish die after they have spawned. All Pacific salmon die. The U.S. Fish and Wildlife Service reports that less than 10 percent of all Atlantic salmon live to spawn a second time. However, several species, including striped bass and American shad, spawn several times.

Unique physiology. Anadromous fish are among those species that are able to cope with extreme changes in the salinity of the water they inhabit. Such species are scientifically labeled "euryhaline," which derives from *eury,* meaning broadly, and *haline,* meaning salty. Not all euryhaline species are anadromous; many live in estuaries where tidal action results in rapid changes in salt content. Some flounder, for example, which normally live in a marine environment, have on occasion been known to move many miles into freshwater. Tarpon and some sharks are also euryhaline, but not anadromous.

At some time in their lives, all anadromous fish must be able to move from freshwater to saltwater, and at a later date they must move back again. Most aquatic creatures cannot adjust to any great change in salt content. The bodies of all fish have a higher salt content than that of freshwater, and freshwater tends to be absorbed by their bodies. The amount of freshwater that would enter the body would soon be fatal if there were no mechanism to eliminate it. Freshwater fish cope with this problem by producing large quantities of very dilute urine. This water removal requires energy, which in turn requires additional food.

Most saltwater fish have the opposite problem. Bony fish have a salt content much lower than that of the ocean water, and if there were no mechanism to prevent it, the water in their bodies would permeate outward until the body salt content was in balance with that of the ocean. (In this connotation, the term "salts" includes the sum total of all salts, not just sodium chloride.) Such fish have to drink saltwater to overcome this dehydration and require a mechanism for getting rid of the excess salts. The process is complex and energy consuming; it involves special salt cells in the gills and mouth lining and a kidney that can excrete very concentrated urine. Sharks and hagfish solve the problem differently; their salt content is greater than that of bony fish, and it is naturally in balance with ocean water.

To be able to live in both freshwater and saltwater, a fish must obviously be equipped to cope with either of these two sets of problems and must be able to shift physiological gears as often as habits and circumstances dictate. The requirements are severe, but there are rewards. There is a great deal of estuarine habitat that changes salinity with the tide, and the only fish that can make extensive use of it are those euryhaline forms, which can thrive in rapidly changing salinity. Furthermore, freshwater fish that can withstand an ocean excursion are able to move from stream to stream, and their progeny quickly become established in nearby coastal streams, some of which might otherwise have no fish at all.

Even though an adult fish may be able to adjust to changes in salinity, its eggs and newly hatched young usually lack this ability; thus, the anadromous parents require a freshwater environment at spawning time.

See: Catadromous; Fisheries Management.

ANAL FIN

The median, unpaired, ventrally located fin that lies behind the anus, usually on the posterior half of the fish.

See: Fish.

ANATOMY *(Body, Function, and Relation to Angling)*

Size

Fish range widely in size. On the bantam side of the spectrum are tiny Philippine gobies less than half an inch long, the smallest of all animals with backbones. They are so diminutive that it takes literally thousands of them to weigh a pound, yet they are harvested commercially for use in many foods. At the behemoth end of the spectrum are giant whale sharks 65 to 70 feet long. The largest whale sharks can weigh as much as 25 tons, but they are so docile they may allow inquisitive scientists to pull alongside them with boats and then climb aboard to prod and poke as they give the big plankton-eaters a close examination. Between these extremes are seemingly limitless shapes and sizes among an estimated 21,000 species. This number exceeds the combined numbers of species of all other vertebrate animals—amphibians, reptiles, birds, and mammals.

Another giant of the sea is the mola, or ocean sunfish, which also goes by the name of headfish because its fins are set far to the rear on its broad, almost tail-less body. Molas, which have the unusual habit of basking at the surface, lying on their side as though dead, may weigh nearly a ton but are not a quarry for anglers. Also in saltwater such highly prized game species as bluefin tuna, swordfish, and certain sharks and marlins reach weights of more than a thousand pounds, with some shark and marlin specimens weighing considerably more.

The white sturgeon, one of the largest of freshwater fish, formerly reached weights of well over a thousand pounds in the Columbia and Fraser Rivers, but is now uncommon over 400 pounds. In the 1800s, monstrous sturgeon of over 2,000 pounds were reported, but fishery workers have not verified such legends. European sturgeon, especially along the Siberian coast from the Volga River, also once attained tremendous proportions but no longer do so. Some of the Asian and South American catfish may weigh 100 pounds or more. The arapaima, or pirarucu, found in Peru, Brazil, and Guyana, will reach about 200 pounds. The prehistoric-looking alligator gar of the southeastern United States can attain a weight of 300 pounds.

Fish size is of special interest to anglers. Many anglers aspire to match their skills against the larger specimens of various game species; competitive events often place a premium on large individual catches; and other rewards, both materialistic and intangible, accrue to those who have caught fish deemed to be of large, if not trophy, caliber.

Records for freshwater and saltwater fish caught on rod and reel are maintained by the International Game Fish Association *(see)* based upon specific standards and on weight. Yet, in many cases, fish are known to grow much larger than sport-caught records indicate. Two all-tackle record tarpon taken on rod and reel, for example, each weighed 283 pounds, which is admittedly sizable but much smaller than the 350-pounders that have reportedly been caught in nets. On the other hand, record rod-and-reel catches greatly exceed the average size

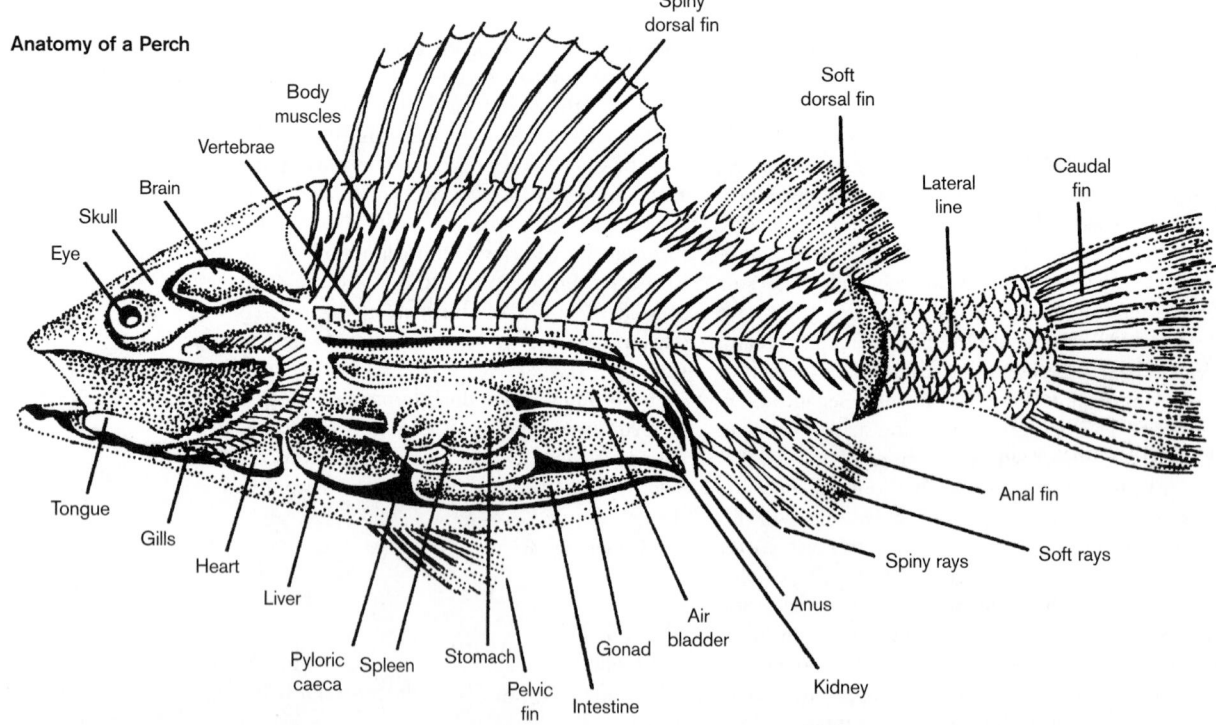

Anatomy of a Perch

Anatomy of a Shark

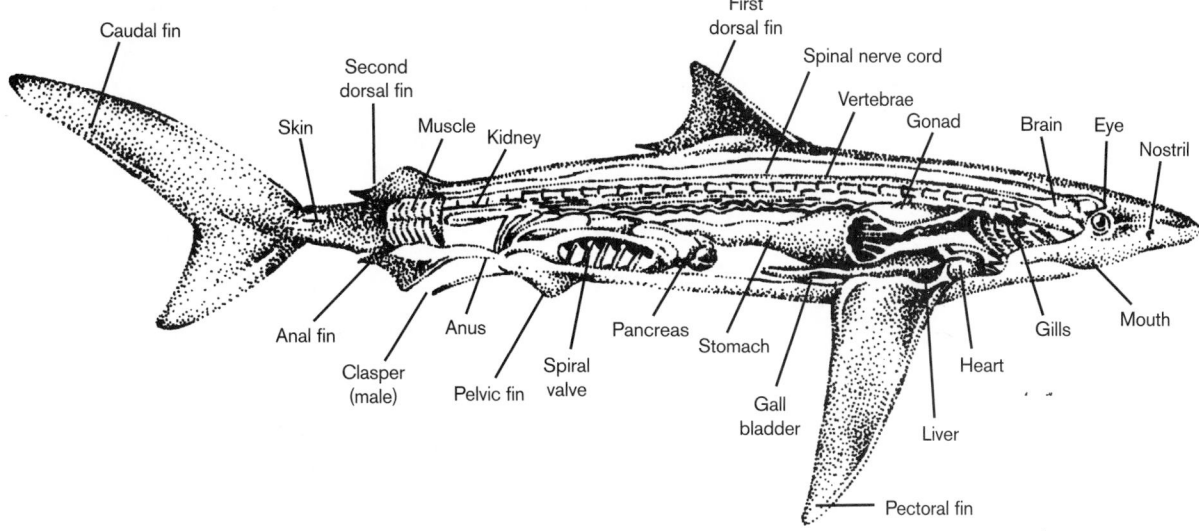

of most species. Most brook trout taken by anglers, for example, weigh less than half a pound, but the sport-caught record for the species is 14 pounds 8 ounces.

A fish does not have to be gigantic to provide fun, however. In this regard, tackle plays an important role. Anglers, using ultralight tackle in ponds and lakes, find it challenging to catch quarter-pound bluegills, rarely if ever hooking one that approaches a pound in weight, let alone the species top record of 4 pounds 12 ounces. Indeed, line-class record categories were long ago established for each species to recognize the angler's fishing skill by virtue of a notable catch for a particular weight of tackle.

Size is a relative issue both in terms of a fish's fighting ability and in its desirability as a catch. Although most larger fish are more difficult to subdue than smaller ones, that is not always the case. Size is also not necessarily comparable between different species; a 10-pound steelhead, for example, provides far better sport than a 10-pound walleye, and a 10-pound bonefish is much more challenging than a 10-pound barracuda. Growing season and geographic location may be a factor as well. A 10-pound largemouth bass in Florida, where a favorable growing season can allow a bass to grow large fast, is akin to perhaps a 6-pound largemouth bass in Minnesota in terms of age and availability within the bass population, the result being that they are catches of similar accomplishment despite being of different size.

Form

The typical fish, such as the yellow perch, large-mouth bass, striped bass, and grouper, has a com-pressed body that is flattened from side to side. In others the body is depressed from top to bottom, as in flounder, rays, and other bottom-hugging types. Still others are spindle-shaped or streamlined, like mackerel, tuna, and trout; and some, such as eels,

have an elongated or snakelike body. All fish fit into one of these four categories, but each form in turn may differ with various adaptations in certain portions of its anatomy.

These differences fit the fish for specific environments or particular ways of life. For example, the streamlined tuna is an open-ocean fish that moves constantly, indulges in long migrations, and pursues fast-swimming schools of smaller fish. Its bullet-shaped body is well adapted for such a life. On the other hand, the flounder's depressed body allows it to be completely undetectable as it lies flat on the sandy or muddy bottom, an adaptation that protects it from enemies as well as allows it to grasp unsuspecting prey. Marlin, sailfish, and swordfish are large fish with a long snout (bill) used as a club to stun prey or as a sword in defense. Eels and cutlassfish have slim, snakelike bodies, enabling them to negotiate seemingly inaccessible areas to hunt for food or to escape enemies.

Among the most unusual fish in shape are those that live in the deep sea. Many have luminous spots or stripes along their body, and fins may be reduced to slim filaments, some bearing bulbous and luminous tips. Many have long barbels around the mouth, with lighted tips that serve as lures for attracting smaller prey within reach of their strong jaws. In some, the tail is long and snakelike. Most have very large mouths and an array of long, dagger-sharp teeth that help in holding their catches. The mouth is generally stretchable, as is the stomach. When the fish has the good fortune to capture a meal in the dark depths where food, as a rule, is scarce, it attempts to devour the prey regardless of size. These deep-sea fish are seldom among the species caught by anglers.

Scales

A typical fish's body is covered with thin scales that overlap each other like the shingles of a roof. They are prominent outgrowths of skin, or epidermis, in

A

Fish Shapes

Anatomical differences among fish are most obvious in general body shape but also include body and tail fins.

which numerous glands secrete a protective coating of slime, often referred to as mucous. The slime is a barrier to the entry of parasites, fungi, and disease organisms that might infest the fish, and it seals in the fish's body fluids so that they are not diluted by the watery surroundings. The slime also reduces friction so that the fish slides through the water with a minimum of resistance; it also makes the fish slippery when predators, including the human variety, try to grab hold. Some fish, such as lampreys and hagfish, give off copious amounts of slime.

As a fish grows, its scales increase in size but not in number. Lost scales may be replaced, however. The ridges and spaces on some types of scales become records of age and growth rate. These can be read or counted like the annual rings in the trunk of a tree to determine a fish's age—the fish's growth slowing or stopping during winter when food is scarce and becoming much more rapid during the warm months when food is plentiful. Experts in reading scales can tell when a fish first spawned and each spawning period thereafter. They can determine times of migration, periods of food scarcity, illness, and similar facts about the fish's life. The number of scales in a row along the lateral line can be used to identify closely related species, particularly the young. Growth rings occur also in the vertebrae and in other bones of the body, but to

study these requires killing the fish. A few scales can be removed without harm to the fish.

Most bony fish have tough, shinglelike scales with a comblike or serrated edge (ctenoid) along their rear margin, or with smooth rear margins (cycloid). The scales of garfish are hard and almost bony, fitting one against the other like the bricks on a wall. These are called ganoid scales. Sturgeon also have ganoid scales, some of which form ridges of armor along portions of their sides and back.

Sharks have placoid scales, which are the most primitive type. These scales are toothlike, each with a central spine coated on the outside with enamel and with an intermediate layer of dentine over a central pulp cavity. The skin of sharks, with the scales still attached, is the shagreen of commerce, widely used in the past and still used today in primitive areas as an abrasive, like sandpaper, or to make nonslip handles for knives and tools.

The scales may be variously modified on different species. Some fish do not have scales at all. Most species of catfish, for example, are "naked" or smooth-skinned. Their skin is very slippery, however, and some of the rays in their fins are modified as sharp spines. Paddlefish and sculpin have only a few scales. The scales of mackerel are minute. Trout also have tiny scales. Those of eels are widely separated and buried deep in the skin.

Scale Types

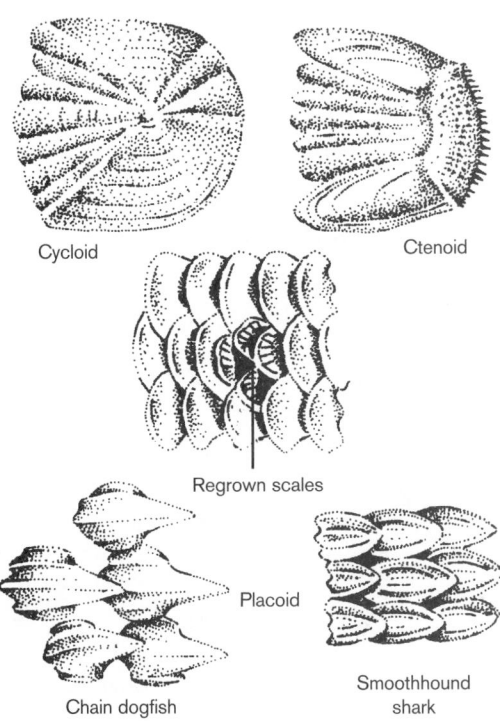

Cycloid

Ctenoid

Regrown scales

Placoid

Chain dogfish

Smoothhound shark

Cycloid scales have smooth rear margins, whereas ctenoid scales have comblike margins; placoid scales, found on sharks, are toothlike. Scales generally are layered, overlapping in rows like roof tiles.

Coloration

The beautiful coloration of fish can be appreciated only when observing them alive, for at death the brilliance and intensity of color begin to fade immediately. Unquestionably, many fish equal or surpass in appearance the most spectacular colored bird or butterfly, and some of the blends and contrasts of body color are impossible to describe with justice.

The color in fish is primarily produced by skin pigments. Basic or background color is due to underlying tissues and body fluids. Iridescent colors are present in body scales, eyes, and abdominal linings of some fish. The rainbowlike reflecting hues of certain kinds of fish are caused by skin pigmentation fragmenting through the irregular ridges of transparent or translucent scales.

All fish are not highly colored, however; the range extends widely from fish with bright colors to species that are uniformly drab in brown, gray, and even pitch-black. In nearly all species, the shades and acuteness of color is adapted to the particular environment a fish inhabits.

In oceanic fish, basic color may be separated into three kinds: silvery in the upper-water zone, reddish in the middle depths, and violet or black in the great depths. Those that swim primarily in the upper layers of ocean water are typically dark blue or greenish blue on the dorsal portions, grading to silvery sides and white belly. Fish that live on the bottom, especially those living close to rocks, reefs, and weedbeds, may be busily mottled or striped. The degree of color concentration also varies depending on the character of the fish's surroundings. For example, a striped bass caught from a sandy area will be lighter in general coloration than one captured from deeper water or from around dark rocks.

The same natural rules apply to freshwater fish. A northern pike, pickerel, or muskie is patterned in mottled greens because its habitat is primarily aquatic plants where it is well camouflaged in alternating light and dark shadows. The bottom-dwelling, dark-backed catfish are almost impossible to detect against a muddy background.

Many anglers are bewildered by the color variances in trouts. Often the same species taken from different types of localities in the same stream may differ in coloration to a startling degree. For example, a trout taken from shallow, swiftly running water over sand and pebbles will be bright and silvery in comparison to a relative that lives under a log in a deep, quiet pool. The steelhead, a sea-run rainbow trout, is another good example of color change. When it leaves the ocean to enter western rivers, it is brilliantly silver; but as it remains in freshwater, the characteristic coloration of the rainbow trout develops: dark greenish blue back, crimson lateral band, and profuse black spots over most of the body.

Regardless of the confusing differences under varying conditions, anglers who know the basic color patterns can easily identify any trout. Each species has recognizable characteristics that do not change. The brook trout, *Salvelinus fontinalis,* for example, always has reticulated or wormlike markings on its back, whereas the under edge of the tail fin and the forward edges of the pectoral, ventral, and anal fins are white.

Most types of fish change color during the spawning season; this is especially noticeable among the trout and salmon tribes. As spawning time approaches, the general coloration becomes darker and more intense. Some examples are surprising, especially in salmon of the U.S. Northwest. All five species are silvery in the ocean, but as they travel upstream to their spawning grounds, they gradually alter to deep reds, browns, and greens—the final colors so drastically different that it seems hardly possible the fish were metallic bright only a short time earlier. Each type of salmon, however, retains its own color characteristics during the amazing transition.

In some types of fish, the coloration intensifies perceptibly when the fish is excited by prey or by predators. Dolphin, a blue-water angler's delight, appear to be almost completely vivid blue when seen from above in a darting school in calm waters.

The color exhibited by most fish is adapted to their particular environments, and a wide range of colors exists, as is evident when comparing the brook trout (top), bonefish (middle), and channel catfish (bottom).

When a dolphin is brought aboard, the unbelievably brilliant golden yellows, blues, and greens undulate and flow magically along the dolphin's body as it thrashes madly about. These changes in shade and degree of color also take place when the dolphin is in varying stages of excitement in the water.

A striped marlin or blue marlin following a surface-trolled bait is a wondrous spectacle of color to observe. As it eyes its quarry from side to side and maneuvers into position to attack, the deep cobalt-blue dorsal fin and bronze-silver sides are at their zenith. This electrifying display of color is lost almost immediately when the fish is boated.

Fins and Locomotion

Fish are propelled through the water by fins, body movement, or both. In general, the main moving force is the caudal fin, or tail, and the area immediately adjacent to it known as the caudal peduncle. In swimming, the fins are put into action by muscles attached to the base of the fin spines and rays. Fish with a fairly rigid body, such as the filefish, trunkfish, triggerfish, manta, and skates, depend mostly on fin action for propulsion. Eels, in contrast, rely on extreme, serpentlike body undulations to swim, with fin movement assisting to a minor extent. Sailfish, marlin, and other big-game fish fold their fins into grooves (lessening water resistance) and rely mainly on their large, rigid tails to go forward. Trout, salmon, catfish, and others are well adapted for sudden turns and short, fast moves. When water is expelled suddenly over the gills in

breathing, it acts like a jet stream and aids in a fast start forward.

A fish can swim even if its fins are removed, though it generally has difficulty with direction and balance. In some kinds, however, the fins are highly important in swimming. For example, the pectoral fins of a ray are broad "wings" with which the fish sweeps through the water almost as gracefully as a swallow does in the air. The sharks, which are close relatives of the rays, swim swiftly in a straight line but have great difficulty in stopping or turning because their fins have restricted movement.

Flyingfish glide above the surface of the water with their winglike pectoral fins extended. Sometimes they get additional power surges by dipping their tails into the water and vibrating them vigorously. This may enable them to remain airborne for as long as a quarter of a mile. Needlefish and halfbeaks skitter over the surface for long distances, the front half of their bodies held stiffly out of the water while their still-submerged tails wag rapidly. An African catfish often swims upside down, and seahorses swim in a "standing up" position.

Many kinds of fish jump regularly. Those that take to the air when hooked give anglers the greatest thrills. Often, however, there is no easy explanation for why a fish jumps, other than the possibility that it derives pleasure from these momentary escapes from its watery world. The jump is made to dislodge a hook or to escape a predator in close pursuit; or the fish may try to shake its body free of plaguing parasites. Some

Caudal (Tail) Fin Types

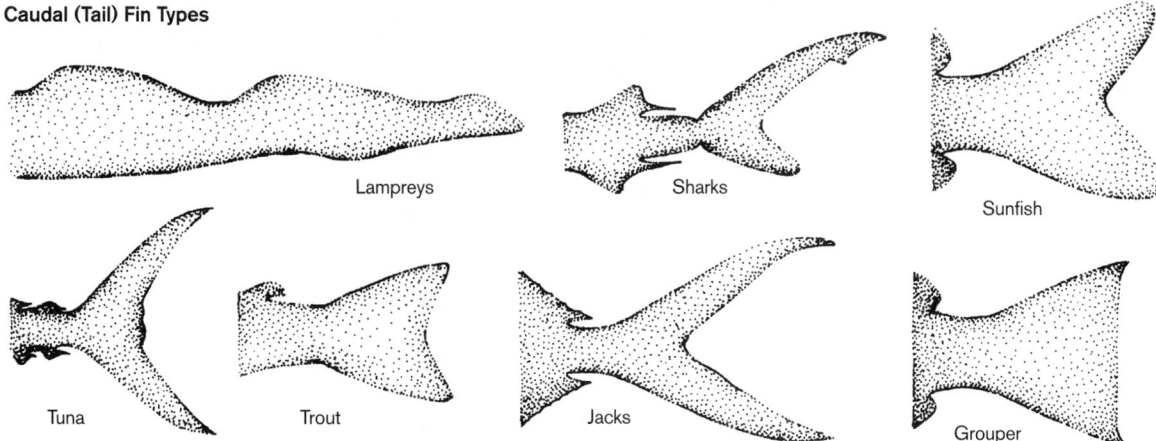

Lampreys

Sharks

Sunfish

Tuna

Trout

Jacks

Grouper

A

species make their jumps by surging at high speed from deep water. Others swim rapidly close to the surface, then suddenly turn their noses skyward and give a powerful thrust with their tails as they take to the air. Sailfish and other high jumpers may leap several feet into the air when hooked, often leaping as many as 20 times before being brought to the boat.

Speed

Fisheries professionals are frequently asked how fast fish swim. This is a difficult question to answer precisely, because fish have a cruising speed, a maximum sustainable speed, and a top speed over relatively short distances.

Statistics for cruising (ordinary travel) speed have been taken mostly from tagged fish released at one point and recaptured at another. For example, some bluefin tuna tagged off Cat Cay, Bahamas, were recaptured in Norwegian waters. Two of these crossed the ocean in less than three months. Another completed the trip in the remarkable time of 52 days. These facts, which contradict the belief that all bluefin tuna migrating from the Bahamas spend the summer in western Atlantic coastal waters, indicate that bluefins swim swiftly, but obviously we do not know whether the recaptured specimens swam a direct course or indulged in detours. Also, ocean currents can be a help or a hindrance.

Maximum sustainable speed, that is, the speed that a fish can maintain for long periods, is almost impossible to judge unless measured experimentally on small fish by determining the length of time they can swim in approximately the same spot when currents of the same velocity are flowing by. Boats traveling alongside big-game fish have clocked their rate of speed. In addition, some anglers have attempted to gauge the speed of gamefish by improvising speedometers on their fishing reels or by using stopwatches to time the runs of hooked fish. The speed of a sailfish has been estimated to be as high as 100 yards per 3 seconds, or 68 miles per hour. All the speeds indicated by such experiments are approximate at best because many factors have to be considered,

including size of the individual, temperature of the water, currents, the area of the mouth where the fish was hooked, physical condition of the particular fish hooked, and so on.

All members of the tunalike fish, such as the bluefin tuna, bonito, and albacore, are also extremely fast. Other species having a reputation for great speed are marlin, wahoo, dolphin, and swordfish. Generally, speeds of 40 to 50 miles per hour are attributed to these fish. In freshwater, the top speed of salmon has been estimated at 14 to 30 miles per hour, and the cruising speed at 8 miles per hour. The top speed for largemouth bass is about 12 miles per hour.

Air Bladder

The air bladder, located between the stomach and backbone, is also known as the swim bladder, which is misleading because the air bladder has no function in the movement of locomotion of fish in any direction. The mixture of gases that it contains is not normal air, so the correct name should be "gas bladder."

The air bladder is present in most bony fish; it does not appear in lampreys, hagfish, sharks, rays, or skates. The air bladder performs several functions. It may be well supplied with blood vessels, as it is in the tarpon, and act as a supplementary breathing organ. The tarpon has an open tube that leads from the upper side of its gullet to the air bladder. (The tarpon also has a set of gills.) Some species of fish use the air bladder as a compartment in which to store air for breathing. The fish falls back on this reserve when its usual supply of oxygen may be shut off. The air bladder plays a part in aiding equilibrium of density between the fish and the water. (It has no function of adjustment of pressure to changing levels.) In other words, the volume of water occupied by the fish should weigh about as much as the fish does. The air bladder is a compensator between them. For example, the pickerel is capable of "floating," its body motionless, anticipating its prey. The catfish, on the other hand, has no air bladder; it spends most of its life on the bottom.

The saltwater flatfish also has no air bladder, and it dives to the bottom swiftly if it escapes the hook near the surface of the water. (A fish does not raise or lower itself by increasing or decreasing the size of the air bladder.) It has also been definitely established that the air bladder is an efficient hearing aid in many types of fish. It is commonly known that the noises some fish make are produced by the air bladder.

Incidentally, there are some exceptions to the general rule, and that includes the primitive lungfish that are represented by five living species. These "living fossils" are found in Africa, South America, and Australia. The African lungfish's air bladder is purely respiratory in function; this fish cannot use its gills for breathing. If the African lungfish cannot reach the surface to gulp air, it soon drowns.

Skeleton and Muscles

A fish's skeleton is composed of cartilage or bone. Basically, the skeleton provides a foundation for the body and fins, encases and protects the brain and spinal cord, and serves as an attachment for muscles. It contains three principal segments: skull, vertebral column, and fin skeleton.

The meat or flesh covering the fish's muscular system is quite simple. All vertebrates, including fish, have three major types of muscles: smooth (involuntary), cardiac (heart), and striated (skeletal). Functionally, there are two kinds: voluntary and involuntary.

In fish, the smooth muscles are present in the digestive tract, air bladder, reproductive and excretory ducts, eyes, and other organs. The striated muscles run in irregular vertical bands, and various patterns are found in different types of fish. These muscles compose the bulk of the body and are functional in swimming by producing body undulations that propel the fish forward. The muscle segments, called myomeres, are divided into an upper and a lower half by a groove running along the midbody of the fish. The myomeres can be easily seen if the skin is carefully removed from the body or scraped away with a knife after cooking. These broad muscles are the part of the fish that we eat. Striated

Superficial Muscles

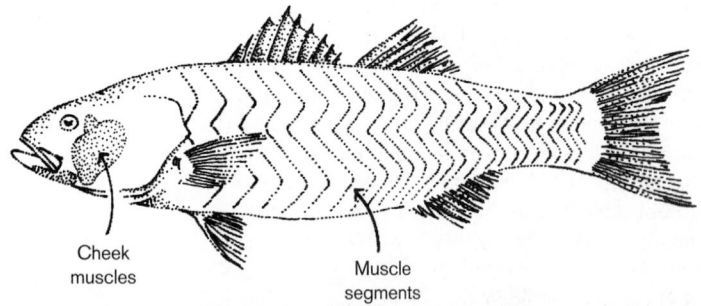

Cheek muscles

Muscle segments

Broad striated muscles make up the bulk of the body of a fish; they run in irregular vertical bands and various patterns, and are functional in swimming.

muscles are also attached to the base of the fin spines and rays, and maneuver the fins in swimming.

Teeth, Food, and Digestion

A tremendous diversity exists in the form and size of fish teeth. The character of the dentition is a clue to the fish's feeding habits and the kind of food it consumes. Of all the fish, some sharks display the most awesome array of teeth: profuse and well structured for grasping, tearing, and cutting. The barracuda's teeth are different from any shark's, but they also draw attention because of their ferocious appearance. They are flat, triangular, closely set, and extremely sharp. Such teeth are ideally adapted for capturing live fish, the barracuda's main diet. Small victims are usually swallowed whole; the larger ones may be cut in two and each piece swallowed separately. The bluefish, well known for its ability to chop up a school of baitfish, has teeth of a similar nature but smaller in size.

Some fish possess sharp, conical teeth (called canine, or dog, teeth); pike, pickerel, and muskies are good examples. Such teeth cannot cut but do a good job of grasping and piercing. Fish fortified with canine teeth generally hold a baitfish until its struggles diminish before swallowing it—a fact taken into consideration by anglers before setting the hook. Anglers must exercise extreme caution when removing hooks from sharks, bluefish, barracuda, pikelike fish, and other fish with dangerous dentition.

The yellow perch, sea bass, catfish, and other species have multiple rows of numerous short and closely packed teeth that resemble the tips of a stiff brush. Such an arrangement meets the fish's need to grasp a variety of food off the bottom or hold prey in a sandpaper-like grip until ready to be eaten.

Some kinds of fish have sharp-edged cutting teeth called incisors located in the forward part of the mouth; some are saw-edged, others resemble human teeth, and still others are variously fused into parrotlike beaks. Parrotfish, for example, have such teeth and thrive on small organisms nibbled from corals, rocks, and reefs. Some bottom-dwelling fish, such as skates, rays, and drum, have molarlike teeth that are well adapted for crunching crustaceans, mollusks, and other organisms.

Many fish, including some of the more common types such as carp, minnows, and suckers, have teeth in their throats. These pharyngeal teeth are sharp in some species, molariform in others, and only remnants in still others. There are fish that have teeth on the roof of the mouth (vomerine and palatine) and on the tongue. Pike, pickerel, and muskies, for example, have vomerine teeth that are profuse and closely packed, whereas other fish, such as certain trout, have comparatively few teeth on these areas. One of the distinguishing features between a true trout and a char (rainbow trout versus brook trout, for example) is the presence or absence of vomerine teeth. The vomerine bone in the center of the char's mouth has only a few teeth, located on its forward end, whereas the vomer of a true trout is much longer and has teeth all along it. Some fish have teeth on the very edges of their mouths (premaxillary and/or maxillary). And many planktonic feeders, such as the menhaden, have no teeth at all; instead, their long gill rakers help in retaining the microscopic organisms they take into their mouths.

Fish are a tremendously diversified group of animals that feed on an extensive variety of foods. Some, when mature, feed exclusively on other fish; others feed entirely on plants. The sea lamprey, a parasitic, highly unattractive eel-like fish, uses its funnel-shaped mouth, lined with radiating rows of sharp teeth, to attach itself to the body of a live fish; then, using its toothed tongue, it rasps a hole in its prey and sucks out blood and body fluids.

In general, the food plan of a fish's life is to eat and to be eaten. Such a scheme involves a food chain. Nutrients in the water nourish various types of free-flowing aquatic plants (phytoplankton) that are eaten by a variety of microscopic animals (zooplankton). A tiny fish feeds on zooplankton, and the bigger fish feeds on the smaller fish. There are many steps in this food chain, as larger fish eat smaller ones until the chain may end with, for example, a bluefin tuna. The tuna eventually expires and sinks to the bottom, where it is eaten by worms, crabs, and other bottom dwellers. Lastly, bacteria return the nutrients to the water in a soluble inorganic form, which the phytoplankton again utilize. The food chain is then complete.

Insects, worms, snails, mussels, squid, and crabs are some of the important larger invertebrates that provide food for fish. Amphibians, reptiles, birds, and mammals, as well as other fish, are also included in the diet of fish. Largemouth bass and muskies, for example, commonly eat frogs and occasionally small turtles or snakes. Gar have been caught that contained bird remains in their stomachs. And goosefish—bottom dwellers with huge mouths—will capture such unusual prey as a diving duck.

Fish also differ in the way they feed. Predators entrap or cut their prey by using their well-developed teeth. Grazers or browsers feed on the bottom. Fish that feed on tiny organisms sifted from the water by using their long gill rakers are known as strainers. Suckers and sturgeon have fleshy, distensible lips well suited to suck food off the bottom and thus are suckers. Some lampreys depend on the blood and fluids of other fish to live; they are categorized as parasites.

Here are a few examples of the structural adaptations of fish that assist them in feeding: catfish and sturgeon have whiskerlike feelers for touching and tasting food before accepting it; sailfish, marlin, and swordfish may stun their prey with their club-like bills before devouring it. The paddlefish employs its long, sensitive, paddlelike snout to stir up the bottom organisms on which it feeds. Gar have elongated snouts filled with needlelike teeth that make a formidable trap for capturing prey. The goosefish, also known as the angler, has a long, slim appendage with a piece of skin at its tip, located on the forward part of its upper snout; this appendage can be wiggled like a worm and acts as a lure to entice prey.

Generally, fish that live in a temperate zone, where seasons are well defined, will eat much more during the warm months than they will during the cold months. In this zone a fish's metabolism slows down greatly during winter. The body temperature of most fish changes with the surrounding environment, and it is not constant as it is in mammals and birds.

The digestive system of fish, as in all other vertebrates, dissolves food, thereby facilitating absorption or assimilation. This system, or metabolic process, is capable of removing some of the toxic properties that may be present in foods on which fish feed.

The basic plan of the digestive tract in a typical fish differs in some respects from that of other vertebrate animals. The tongue cannot move as it does in higher vertebrates, and it does not possess striated muscles. The esophagus, or gullet (between the throat and stomach), is highly distensible and usually can accept any type or size food that the fish can fit into its mouth. Although choking does happen, and has been particularly noticed in pickerel and pike, a fish rarely chokes to death because of food taken into its mouth.

Fish stomachs differ in shape from group to group. The predators have elongated stomachs. Those that are omnivorous generally have saclike stomachs. Sturgeon, gizzard shad, and mullet, among others, have stomachs with heavily muscled walls used for grinding food, just as the gizzard of a chicken does. Some of the bizarre deep-sea fish possess stomachs capable of huge distention, thereby enabling them to hold relatively huge prey. On the other hand, some fish have no stomachs; instead, they have accessory adaptations, such as grinding teeth, that crush the food finely so that it is easily absorbed.

Intestinal structure also differs in fish. The predators have shortened intestines; meaty foods are more easily digested than plant foods. In contrast, herbivores, or plant eaters, have long intestines, sometimes consisting of many folds. Sharks and a few other fish have intestines that incorporate a spiral or coiled valve that aids in digestion. Lampreys and hagfish have no jaws and do not have a well-defined stomach or curvature of the intestine. Lampreys need a simple digestive system because they are parasites that subsist on the blood and juices they suck from other fish. During the long migration from the sea upriver to spawn, the various species of salmon never feed. Their digestive tracts shrink amazingly, allowing the reproductive organs to fill up the abdomen.

Dame Juliana Berners' 1496 pike fishing tip: "Tie the cord to a goose's foot and you shall see good hauling, whether the goose or the pike shall have the better." It is believed the goose was used for trolling.

Gills and Breathing

Like all other living things, fish need oxygen to survive. In humans, the organs responsible for this function are the lungs. In fish, the gills perform the job. However, in some scaleless fish, the exchange of gases takes place through the skin. In fish embryos, various tissues temporarily take up the job of breathing. Some fish are capable of obtaining oxygen directly from the air through several adaptations, including modifications of the mouth cavity, gills, intestine, and air bladder.

A fish's gills are much-divided thin-walled filaments where capillaries lie close to the surface. In a living fish, the gills are bright-red feathery organs that are prominent when the gill cover of the fish is lifted. The filaments are located on bony arches. Most fish have four gill arches. Between the arches are openings through which the water passes. In the gills, carbon dioxide, a waste gas from the cells, is released; at the same time, the dissolved oxygen is taken into the blood for transport to the body cells. This happens quickly and is remarkably efficient—about 75 percent of the oxygen contained in each gulp of water is removed in the brief exposure.

Different kinds of fish vary in their oxygen demands. Trout and salmon require large amounts of oxygen. The cold water in which they live can hold a greater amount of dissolved oxygen than can warm water. Further, many live in fast-flowing streams in which new supplies of oxygen are churned into the water constantly. Most types of catfish are near the opposite extreme; their oxygen demands are so low that they thrive in sluggish warmwater streams and also in ponds and lakes where the oxygen supply is low. A catfish can, in fact, remain alive for a long time out of water if kept cool and moist. Like carp and similar kinds of fish, catfish can be shipped for long distances and arrive at the market alive.

A few fish, such as the various walking catfish, climbing perch, bowfin, gar, gourami, and others, can breathe air. Air-breathers use only about 5 percent of the oxygen available to them with each breath of air. The best-known air-breathers are the lungfish that live in tropical Africa. Their "lung" is an air bladder connected to the lungfish's mouth by a duct, its walls richly supplied with blood vessels. A lungfish gets new supplies of oxygen by rising to the surface and gulping air. It will drown if kept underwater. When the stagnant pool in which it lives dries up, which happens seasonally, the lungfish burrows into the soft mud at the bottom and secretes a slimy coating over its body. It continues to breathe air through a small hole that connects to the surface through the mud casing. When the rains come again and the pool fills, the lungfish wriggles out of its cocoon and resumes its usual living habits.

Lampreys have seven paired gill sacs or bronchial pouches. A lamprey does not take in water through its mouth as other fish do, even when its mouth is not in the act of sucking blood and juices out of its prey. Water, from which the lamprey secures its oxygen, is both taken in and expelled through the gill sacs.

The sea lamprey is a parasitic eel-like creature that exists by sucking out the blood of fish. It attaches itself to the side of its host by means of a funnel-shaped mouth lined with radiating rows of sharp teeth. With its toothed tongue, it rasps a hole in its victim and proceeds to draw out the fish's life blood and body fluids. Surprisingly, fish do not fear the lamprey by sight. The lamprey swims along serenely by the side of a lake trout (or other fish) and simply reaches out, clamping its suction mouth onto the unsuspecting prey. After feasting, it departs and the trout usually dies. If by chance the prey survives, it carries a wound that invites infection.

Rays and skates usually have five paired external gill slits (rarely six or seven) located on the bottom side of the head. Sharks also have the same number of gill slits, but they are located laterally (on the side). In sharks, the water used for respiration is taken in through the mouth and expelled through the gill slits. Rays and skates, however, draw in water through the spiracles located on top, or close to the top, of the head (an excellent adaptation for bottom-dwelling fish). The water flows over the gills and out the gill slits located on the underside of the head.

Because a fish has no opening between its nostrils and mouth cavity as humans do, it has to breathe through its mouth. When the fish opens its mouth, a stream of water is drawn in. During this intake of water the gill cover is held tight, thereby closing the gill opening. Then the fish closes its

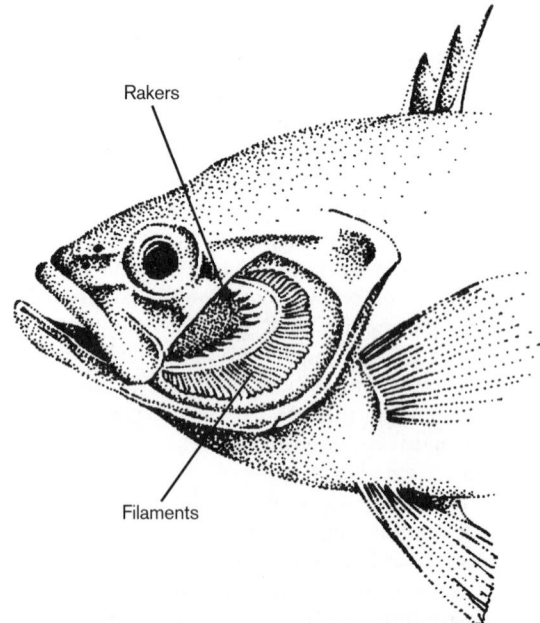

Rakers

Filaments

This cutaway view shows the first gill arch of a sunfish. The rakers, which strain the water, are on the left; the filaments, which transfer dissolved oxygen to the blood, are on the right.

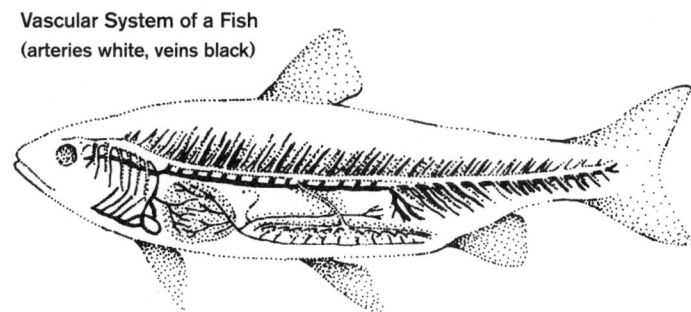

Vascular System of a Fish
(arteries white, veins black)

mouth and drives the water over the gills and out the external openings by using special throat muscles. As the water passes over the gills, the exchange of gases takes place; that is, oxygen (which has been absorbed from the air by water exposed to it) is taken in through the walls of the fine blood vessels in the gill filaments, and carbon dioxide is given off. The blood, well oxygenated, then travels through the fish's body.

The rapidity with which a fish breathes varies with different species. A human in good health under normal circumstances breathes about 20 to 25 times a minute. Some types of fish have a breathing rate as low as 12 a minute, yet others take as many as 150 breaths per minute. If the fish is exerting itself, or if the oxygen content of the water becomes low, the rate of breathing will be faster, and the fish pants like a runner after finishing the mile.

Although gills play a major role in the respiratory organization of a fish, they also serve another purpose. Gill rakers, located along the anterior margin of the gill arch, aid in several ways. By projecting over the throat opening, they strain water that is passed over the gills. Solid particles are prevented from passing over and injuring the gill filaments. Gill rakers may be short and knobby, as in the pickerel, which is primarily a fish-eater. The shad, on the other hand, feeds on minute organisms. Its gill rakers are numerous, long, and thin, and they serve to sieve out the tiny organisms on which the shad feeds. In between these two extremes in size and shape, gill rakers of various sizes can be found in different types of fish. The number of gill rakers on the first gill arch is sometimes used as an aid in identifying or separating species that closely resemble one another.

Blood Circulation

The circulatory system of a fish, which consists of the heart, blood, and blood vessels, carries to every living cell in the body the oxygen and nourishment required for living; it carries away from the cells the carbon dioxide and other excretory products.

In function, the fish's muscular heart is similar to that of other vertebrates, acting as a pump to force the blood through the system of blood vessels. It differs from the human heart in having only two rather than four compartments—one auricle and one ventricle. The fish's heart is located close behind the fish's mouth. Blood vessels are largest close to the heart and become progressively smaller, terminating in a network of extremely fine capillaries that meander through the body tissues. The blood of a fish, like blood in all vertebrates, is composed of plasma (fluid) and blood cells (solid).

A fish's circulatory system is much simpler than that of a human. In humans, the blood is pumped from the heart into the lungs, where it is oxygenated; it then returns to the heart and receives a good thrust to travel throughout the body. In contrast, fish

blood passes from the heart to the gills for purification and then travels directly to all other parts of the body.

Fish are often referred to as "cold-blooded" creatures, but this is not entirely true. Some are "warm-blooded," although they cannot sustain a constant body temperature as humans do. Instead, the fish's body temperature approximates that of its surrounding medium: water. Fish blood is thicker than human blood and has low pressure because it is pumped by a heart with only two chambers. Consequently, the flow of blood through a fish's body is slow. Because the blood flows slowly through the gills where it takes on oxygen, and because water contains less oxygen than air, fish blood is not as rich in oxygen as is human blood. Also, because of the slow flow of blood through the gills, the blood cools and approaches the temperature of the water surrounding the fish.

Senses and Nerves

A fish's eyes are adapted or modified for underwater vision, but they are not very different from human eyes. Fish do not have true eyelids. Human eyelids prevent the eyes from becoming dry and also protect against dirt. A fish's eyes are always covered by water; therefore, they require no lids.

The metallic-looking ring, called the iris, encircling the dark center, or lens, of the fish's eye cannot move as it does in the human eye. The human iris can expand or contract depending upon light conditions. Because light never attains great intensity underwater, a fish needs no such adaptation. The big difference between a human eye and the eye of a fish occurs in the lens. In humans it is fairly flat, or dishlike; in fish it is spherical or globular. Human eyes are capable of changing the curvature of the lens to focus at varying distances—flatter for long-range focusing and more curved for shorter range. Although the eye of a fish has a rigid lens and its curvature is incapable of change, it can be moved toward or away from the retina (like the focusing action of a camera). Scientists note one outstanding similarity between the eye of a human and the fish's eye. In both, six muscles move the eyeball. The six muscles are controlled by the same six nerves and act the same way to provide eye movement.

Although fish have no eyelids, they do sleep. Schooling fish commonly separate periodically to rest. Then they become active again and the schools reassemble. Some fish lie on their sides when they rest; others lean against rocks or slip into crevices. Some kinds wriggle their way into the soft ooze at the bottom to take a nap, and some of the parrot-fish secrete a blanket of slime over the body at night. The preparation of this "bed" may take as long as an hour.

Important to anglers is the fact that a fish can distinguish colors. Experimenters have found, for example, that largemouth bass and trout quickly learn to tell red from other colors when red is associated with food. They can also distinguish green, blue, and yellow. There are indications that some kinds of fish prefer one color to another and also that water conditions may make one color more easily distinguished than others. Although lure action is most important, anglers can increase their chances of taking a fish by presenting lures of the proper color.

Many kinds of fish have excellent vision at close range. This is made especially clear by the archerfish that feeds on insects. By squirting drops of water forcefully from its mouth into the air, it may shoot down a hovering fly or one resting on grass or weeds. As an archerfish prepares to make its shot, it approaches carefully to make certain of its aim and range. An archerfish is accurate at distances up to about 3 feet and is sometimes successful with even longer shots.

The four-eyed fish, one of the oddities of the fish world, lives in shallow, muddy streams in Central America. On the top of its head are bulbous eyes that are half in and half out of the water as the fish swims along near the surface. These eyes function as four eyes because of their internal structure—the lens is egg-shaped rather than spherical. When the fish looks at objects under the water, light passes

Smell receptors are located in the nostrils, and water (carrying odors) is drawn into sacs that are lined with the organs of smell. Olfactory nerves connect the nostrils and brain.

through the full length of the lens, and the foureyed fish is as nearsighted as any other fish. When it looks into the air, the light rays pass through the shorter width of the lens, giving the fish good distance vision.

Fish that live in the dusky or dimly lit regions of the sea commonly have eyes that are comparatively larger than the eyes of any other animal with backbones. Fish that live in the perpetual darkness of caves or other subterranean waters usually have no eyes, but those inhabiting the deep sea, far below the depth to which light rays can penetrate, may or may not have eyes. The reason that most deep-sea fish have well-developed eyes is the prevalence of bioluminescense. Deep-sea squid, shrimp, and other creatures, as well as fish, are equipped with light-producing organs. The light they produce is used to recognize enemies or to capture prey.

Many fish with poor vision have well-developed senses of smell, taste, and touch. Improbable as it may seem, fish do possess nostrils. Four nostrils are located close to the top of the snout, one pair on each side. Each pair opens into a small blind sac immediately below the skin. Water, carrying odors, passes through the sacs, which are lined with the receptors of smell. Some fish, including sharks, possess an extremely acute sense of smell.

Fish have taste organs located in the skin of the snout, lips, mouth, and throat. A fish's tongue, unlike the human tongue, is flat, rigid, and cartilaginous and moves only when the base below it moves; nevertheless, it does possess taste buds that indicate to the fish whether to accept or to reject anything taken into its mouth.

There is a close relationship between the senses of smell and taste in fish, just as in humans. Many types of fish are first drawn to food by its odor. For example, catfish and sturgeon, which are first attracted by food odor, will feel and taste the food with their chin barbels before taking it. These whiskerlike appendages contain taste buds. Some catfish have taste buds all over their bodies; certain kinds can actually taste with their tails.

Although fish obviously do not possess outer ears as humans do, they are still capable of hearing. The human ear is composed of an outer, middle, and inner ear; each part interacts with the other for both hearing and maintaining equilibrium. Fish possess only an inner ear, found in the bones of the skull. Outer and middle ears are not necessary in fish, because water is a much better conductor of sound than air. In many fish, these ear bones are connected to the air bladder. Vibrations are transmitted to the ear from the air bladder, which acts as a sounding board.

The lateral-line system, a series of sensory cells usually running the length of both sides of the fish's body, performs an important function in receiving low-frequency vibrations. Actually, it resembles a "hearing organ" of greater sensitivity than human ears. The typical lateral line is a mucous-filled tube or canal under the skin; it has contact with the outside world through pores in the skin or through scales along the line or in between them. A nerve situated at intervals alongside the canal sends out branches to it. In some cases the lateral line extends over the fish's tail, and in many fish it continues onto the head and spreads into several branches along the outer bones of the fish's skull, where it is not outwardly visible. The fish utilizes its lateral line to determine the direction of currents of water and the presence of nearby objects as well as to sense vibrations. The lateral line helps the fish to determine water temperature and to find its way when traveling at night or through murky waters. It also assists schooling fish in keeping together and may help a fish to escape enemies.

Many fish are noisy creatures. They make rasping, squeaking, grunting, and squealing noises. This came as a great surprise to military forces during World War II when their sound-detecting devices, designed to pick up the noises of submarines, instead were literally jammed by fish noises. Some fish produce sounds by rubbing together special extensions of the bones of their vertebrae. Others make noises by vibrating muscles that are connected to their air bladders, which amplify the sounds. Still other fish grind their teeth, their mouth cavities serving as sound boxes to amplify the noises. Many fish make sounds when they are caught. Grunts and croakers got their names from this habit.

Some fish are capable of generating electricity. To our present knowledge, no other animal possesses organs that can perform such a function. The electric eel can produce an electric current of shocking power. In a properly constructed aquarium, it can be demonstrated that electricity expelled by an electric eel is strong enough to operate light bulbs. The current also stuns enemies and prey, and acts as a sort of radar system. Sensory pits located on the fish's head receive the reflections of these electrical currents from objects close by. The electric ray and electric catfish are also capable of producing electrical currents strong enough to stun prey. South African gymnotids and African mormyrids are among other kinds of fish that produce electric shocks of lesser strength. The electrical field set up around them serves as a warning device to any intruding prey or predator.

Since fish have a nervous system and sense organs, it would appear that they could feel pain. The fish's brain is not highly developed, however. There is no cerebral cortex (the part of the brain in higher animals that stores impressions), and so the fish has little or no memory. It is not uncommon, for example, for an angler to hook the same fish twice within a short time. Many fish are caught with lures or hooks embedded in their jaws. Fish are essentially creatures of reflex rather than action produced or developed by using the brain. In all

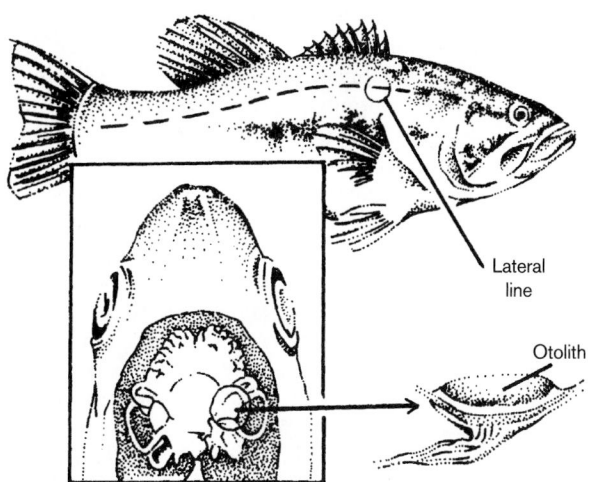

Hearing is accomplished primarily through nerves in the lateral line but also through sound waves detected by the otolith.

probability, physical pain in fish is not very acute, and if any impression of pain is made in the brain, it is quickly lost.

Reproduction

The fish, like most animals, begins life as an egg, and, as in all other vertebrates, the single-cell egg cannot develop unless it is fertilized by a sperm produced by the male. Fish sperm is most commonly referred to as milt.

Eggs may be fertilized either externally or internally. External fertilization takes place when the egg is penetrated by the sperm after the egg leaves the female's body. The vast majority of fish are reproduced by this system. Internal fertilization occurs when the male introduces the sperm into the female's body, where it makes contact with and fertilizes the egg. Some sharks and the live-bearing toothed carp (popular aquarium fish) are ovoviviparous; that is, the egg is fertilized internally and held within the female without attachment to her until it is ready to be extruded alive. In other species, such as some of the sharks and sculpin, a few catfish, and the skate, the egg is penetrated by the sperm inside the female's body, but it does not hatch until some time after being released from the female.

Reproduction and associated activities in fish are generally referred to as spawning. The spawning season, or breeding period, is that time when the eggs of the female and the milt, or sperm, of the male are ripe. This period may last only a few days, as in some warmwater species like the largemouth bass. Or it may extend into weeks and even months in coldwater species such as the whitefish and the arctic char. Fish that live in tropical waters of fairly constant temperature may spawn year-round.

Depending on the species, spawning may take place in a variety of environments. But, regardless of where the spawning occurs, all fertilized eggs require special conditions for successful

development. Sunlight, oxygen, water agitation, salt and chemicals, water temperature, and other factors have an influence on egg development. In the marine environment, spawning may take place in the open ocean or close to shore. In freshwater, spawning may occur in rapidly moving rivers and streams where the parents leave the eggs, or in quiet waters where the fish makes a nest and then protects it. Some fish leave the saltwater to travel up rivers and streams to spawn. Eels leave saltwater to enter freshwater but return to the sea to spawn.

Fish such as mackerel, which travel in the open ocean in large schools, take part en masse in external fertilization. They form huge groups and release their reproductive cells indiscriminately into the water. No attempt is made at pairing. The fertilized eggs are at the mercy of temperature, winds, currents, water clarity, salinity, and other factors. In this open-sea type of spawning, the eggs of most species float freely. In other species, the fertilized eggs sink to the bottom, where they are greedily fed upon by bottom-dwelling species. In either system, the parents show no concern for the eggs.

The striped bass, a popular sportfish, is an example of a fish that leaves the saltwater to spawn in rivers and streams. Its eggs are fertilized more or less freely, and a single female may be attended by as many as 50 males. The nonadhesive eggs are slightly heavier than water and are rolled along the bottom by the current. The parents protect neither eggs nor young.

Six species of salmon, one on the North American East Coast and five along the Pacific, enter freshwater rivers to spawn. Often they travel hundreds of miles before reaching the spawning site. Unlike the striped bass, they pair off and build a type of nest. These nests, called redds, are built in clear water that is well oxygenated and runs over pebbly areas. The eggs sink in between the pebbles of the nest, where they are safe from predators. The parents, however, do not protect eggs or young. If the nest gets covered by silt, the eggs suffocate.

Trout and bass, among the most popular sportfish, have contrasting spawning habits. Bass usually select quiet, sheltered spawning areas, in water 2 to 6 feet deep. The male excavates a depression in the sand or gravel bottom or among the roots of vegetation. The nest averages 2 to 3 feet in width and 6 inches in depth. It is constructed by the male who fans the spot with his tail and transports the small pebbles away in his mouth. Depending on her size, a female largemouth bass usually carries from 2,000 to 26,000 eggs, although there are cases on record of a female carrying as many as 40,000 eggs. The pugnacious male guards the nest, eggs, and young until the school scatters.

In contrast, the female brook trout usually digs her nest in riffles or at the tail end of pools. She turns on her side and with rapid movements of her tail pushes around the gravel, pebbles, and other bottom materials. When the nest, or egg pit, is of proper size and depth, both male and female assume a parallel position over the area; when ready, the eggs and milt are extruded at the same time. Young females may carry 200 to 500 eggs, and larger ones may carry over 2,500.

As soon as the spawning procedure is completed, the female brook trout hollows out another nest a short distance upstream from the first nest. The disturbed pebbles from the second excavation travel downstream, covering the eggs of the first nest with a layer of gravel. Several nests may be required before the female has shed all her eggs.

Time requirements for incubation of eggs depend on the species of fish and the water temperature. For example, largemouth bass eggs hatch in about five days in water about 66°F. The incubation period for brook trout is about 44 days at 50°F, and about 28 days at 59°F. A sudden 10° drop in temperature during the breeding season is usually enough to kill bass eggs or the newly hatched fry.

Attached to a typical newly hatched young fish, called a larva, is an undigested portion of the yolk. This is usually enough food to last until the little fish can adjust to its aquatic world, before it must begin hunting food for itself. Some kinds of fish start to resemble their parents soon after emerging from the egg and may themselves spawn within the year. Others require years of development before they mature.

Young flounder and other members of the flatfish family start life in an upright position, looking like any other little fish. But during the course of development, the skull twists and one eye migrates to the other side of the head until finally both eyes are on the upper side of the fish. Another startling example of differences in appearance between young and adult occurs in the prolific American eel (large specimens deposit 15 to 20 million eggs). The adult eels leave lakes, ponds, and streams to spawn in midwinter in the Sargasso Sea southwest of Bermuda and off the east coast of Florida. In its larval stage, the American eel is thin, ribbonlike, and transparent. Its head is small and pointed; its mouth contains large teeth, although at this stage it apparently takes no food. The larval form lasts about a year. Then it metamorphoses to the elver, at which time the length and the depth of the body shrink but increase in thickness to a cylindrical form resembling the adult eel. The large, larval teeth disappear, and the head also changes shape. The elver, however, does not take on the adult color, and it does not begin to feed until it reaches North American shores. Averaging 2 to $3^1/_2$ inches in length, the elvers appear in spring.

Carp and sturgeon are two of the big egg producers among freshwater fish. When a female sturgeon is full of roe, the eggs may account for as much as 25 percent of her weight. The salted and processed eggs of sturgeons are prized as caviar, as is the roe of salmon, herring, whitefish, codfish, and other fish.

"Like a fish out of water" is a phrase that does not apply to some fish that are very much at home on land; among them are spiny eels, mudskippers, climbing perch, and snakeheads.

Bullhead and many tropical fish lay their eggs in burrows scooped out of the soft mud at the bottom. Gourami make a bubble nest, the males blowing bubbles that rise to the surface, stick together, and form a floating raft. After the nest is built, the female lays her eggs; the male then blows each egg up into the bubbles, where it remains until it hatches. The male stands guard under the raft to chase away intruders.

Male seahorses carry their eggs and also their young in a belly pouch. A female South American catfish carries her eggs attached to a spongy disc on her belly. Sea catfish males use their mouths as brooding pouches for their eggs; once the young are born, the pouches serve as a place of refuge until the young are large enough to fend for themselves.

Many species of fish make nests. Some nests are elaborate, much like those made by birds. The male stickleback, for example, makes a neat nest of twigs and debris and defends it with his life. Other fish simply sweep away the silt and debris where the eggs are to be laid and keep the nest clean and the water aerated until the eggs hatch.

During the spawning season, the sex of most fish is easily discernible. Because of the huge quantity of eggs she carries, the female is usually potbellied compared with the male. As the reproductive apparatus becomes ripe, a slight press on the belly will cause the whitish milt of the male or the eggs of the female to be seen in the vent. When the milt and eggs are in advanced stages of ripeness, they can be forced out by massaging the belly firmly from the head toward the vent. Hatcheries force out the reproductive products in this manner. The eggs are exuded into a pan, and then the milt is forced over them. Milt and eggs are gently mixed, and fertilization takes place. Except in spawning conditions, the sex of many fish cannot be determined unless the belly is dissected and the immature eggs or milt sac is found.

As spawning time approaches, some kinds of fish develop outward signs that make the sexes easily distinguishable. Male trout and salmon acquire hook jaws. Smelts, suckers, and most species of minnows have on their head and snout small horny tubercles that disappear shortly after spawning has finished. Males of many species possess larger fins or extensions on the fins. And color is often different in the sexes. The male may sport much brighter and more intense coloration than the female. Some fish have permanent differences in their anatomy; for example, the male bull dolphin has an extended or square forehead, whereas the female's forehead is rounded. Males of many species develop large fins or extensions on some of the fins. Male sharks, skates, and rays have tubelike extensions of the pelvic fins that function in mating.

Age and Growth

Although birds and mammals cease to grow after becoming fully mature, fish continue to grow until they die, provided food is abundant. Growth is

Scale Annulli

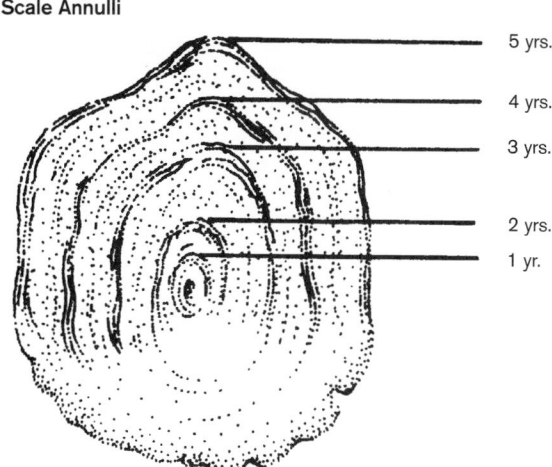

5 yrs.
4 yrs.
3 yrs.
2 yrs.
1 yr.

Annual growth rings from this scale indicate a five-year-old fish.

fastest during the first few years of life and continues at a decreasing rate. It accelerates during warm-weather months when food is abundant. During the cold months, fish do not feed much; their metabolism slows down, and growth is retarded.

Proper determination of age and growth in fish is important in order to regulate the harvest. In both sport and commercial fish, the age and growth rate must be known in order to reap the crop wisely. Fisheries are controlled by rules and regulations based on facts in the life history of fish.

Generally, fish in warm climates reach sexual maturity and grow faster than their cousins farther north, because the growing seasons are longer and the food supply is not shortened by cold weather. For example, a largemouth bass in Florida may spawn after one year; in Wisconsin the same species does not spawn until the third year; and in Canada the largemouth bass may not reach maturity until the fourth or fifth year. Under average conditions, the largemouth bass may attain 3 inches in length in the first five months, 5 to 6 inches in one year, 8 to 10 inches in two years. By the third year, they may be 12 or more inches.

A fish's growth rate is also influenced by its environment. A pond or lake can support only a limited poundage of fish, just as a piece of farmland produces only a limited harvest of vegetables or other crops. In some bodies of water, fish never attain natural size because there are too many of them for the available food supply. Yellow perch are found stunted because only a few, if any, predators, such as bass and pickerel, are present to feed on them. Stunting may also take place because not enough fish are caught, or perhaps because anglers return all the small ones to the water unharmed.

The age of fish that live in temperate climates can be determined fairly accurately from various bony portions of their anatomy, because definite changes in seasons cause annual marks to appear in the bone. These year zones of growth are produced by the slowing down of metabolism in the winter and its rapid

A

increase in the spring. In some species the annual ridges, called annuli, are especially pronounced and easy to read in the scales and cheekbones. In fish with tiny scales, these annuli are difficult to see, even under a microscope. Spines, vertebrae, jawbones, and earbones have to be studied to determine the fish's age. In cross-section, these various bones may show annual rings that appear similar to the rings in the cross-section of a tree trunk.

In tropical areas with seasonal rainfall, the age of freshwater fish can be denoted by seasonal growth marks caused by dry and wet seasons. In uniformly warm waters, such as the equatorial currents, fish demonstrate little, if any, seasonal fluctuation in growth, and age determination is difficult.

Migration

Migration is the mass movement of fish (or any other animals) along a route from one area to another at about the same time annually. This group travel is induced basically by factors of food and spawning. At times, mass movement may take place for other reasons, but such travel should not be confused with migration. Sudden adverse conditions, such as pollution, excessive sedimentation, or water discoloration caused by unusually severe storms, may force large groups of fish to leave the affected area.

Some fish, called "tide-runners," move with the tide to shore and then out again while searching for food. This movement is simply a daily feeding habit and is not considered migration. Some fish remain in deep water during the day and move to shore at night for feeding. In some lakes the entire population of a certain species may move at times from warming shallows to deeper, cooler waters to survive. The lake trout and the walleye are good examples of sportfish that make seasonal movements of this sort.

The bluefin tuna, one of the largest of the oceanic fish, migrates about the same time each year between the coasts of southern Florida and the Bahamas, where it spawns, to waters off Nova Scotia, Prince Edward Island, and Newfoundland. On reaching these far northern waters, the bluefin will find and follow huge schools of herring, sardines, mackerel, or squid in the same localities, year after year. If the temperature rises higher than usual, or other water changes take place, the bait schools will depart from their customary haunts, and the bluefin will follow.

Inshore fish such as the shad and the striped bass may travel varying distances along the coast before arriving in freshwater rivers or brackish stretches that meet the requirements for their spawning activities. Some species do not travel along a coast or migrate north and south; instead, they move offshore into deeper water in cold weather and inshore during warm weather. Others combine a north-south movement with an inshore-offshore migration.

The California grunion, a small, silvery fish, is an example of a unique and precisely timed migration. It spawns at the turn of high tide and as far up the beach as the largest waves travel. This action takes place during that period when the water reaches farthest up shore. The grunion deposits eggs and sperm in pockets in the wet sand. Two weeks or a month later, at the time of the next highest tide, when the water reaches the nests and stirs up the sand, the young are hatched and scramble out to sea before the tide recedes and prevents them from escaping.

Members of the salmon family participate in what may be termed classical migration. All have the same general life pattern. The eggs are hatched in shallow streams; the young spend their early life in freshwater, grow to maturity in the ocean, and then return to the stream of their birth to spawn. The length of time spent in freshwater and saltwater habitats varies among the species and among populations of the same species. All five species of northwestern Pacific salmon die after their first spawning. The Atlantic salmon drops back to saltwater; those fish that survive the hazards of the sea return to spawn again. Salmon migrate varying distances to reach their spawning sites. The chum and the pink salmon usually spawn a few miles from saltwater and often within reach of the tides. The chinook, largest of the salmon family, may cover thousands of miles and surmount many obstacles before reaching its ancestral spawning grounds. And after spending from one to about four years far out to sea, each individual returns to spawn in the river where it was born.

ANCHOR

A heavy object, usually of lead or metal, that is fastened to a chain and/or line and set on the lake, river, or ocean bottom to keep a boat in position.

Although anchor use varies substantially among anglers, every boat should carry one, at least for deployment in an emergency. Many boaters pay little attention to and don't fully understand how to use this device. Indeed, many freshwater anglers, especially those whose techniques involve only casting or trolling, and those who use electric motors for constant boat positioning and manipulation, rarely use an anchor and may even disdain the use of one. An anchor can be an important accessory for anglers, however, as proper anchoring helps ensure that the boat remains in exactly the right spot.

If a boat loses power, and, due to current or wind direction, is in danger—of drifting aground, into shore, onto a reef or shoal, into other boats, over a small dam, or into a weir, among other possibilities—a readily available anchor, quickly placed into the water, can be used to hold a boat in a safe position, or to slow the drift enough to avoid trouble until power is restored or help arrives.

People who stillfish, and those who drift, are among the primary users of anchors, although anglers casting to specific areas may use an anchor to temporarily maintain position until that locale has been thoroughly fished. Anchors may be necessary under windy conditions, to permit more thorough fishing of a certain location or to set up a chum slick in offshore waters. Some river anglers use heavy chains as an anchor to slow their downstream drift and permit sufficient casting while drifting. Some use heavy blocks as a part-anchor/part-drag system, which enables them to slowly drift while stirring up aquatic life on the bottom and presenting some form of live bait in the stirred-up water.

In freshwater, most anglers anchor in fairly shallow water, especially when fishing rivers and small lakes and ponds. Most fish out of small boats and use small anchors. Sometimes these anchors are homemade, serving their purpose mostly because of their weight and a lack of wind or heavy current. Larger boats used in freshwater, and most fishing boats employed in saltwater, have greater anchoring needs. In these scenarios, both the type of anchor and the method of setting and retrieval become critical.

For larger vessels, it is wise to carry a second anchor as insurance against mishaps with the first. If you are forced to break off the first one, it's convenient to have a backup, either when you wish to continue fishing or when you need more holding power in dangerous or emergency situations.

Basic Anchor Types

Of the great variety of anchor types, a relatively small number are used by anglers. Some modern and newly designed anchors are hybrids, and some are slight variations of the standard designs. The weight and/or the design of the anchor usually determine its holding power, but a heavy anchor is not essential for holding a big boat; bottom conditions, sea conditions, anchor design, how the anchor was set, the amount of rode (anchor line) let out, and other factors all play a role.

Improvised. Small-boat owners have used cement blocks, cement- or sand-filled cans and jugs, sash weights, pieces of iron, truck tire chains, and other makeshift and economical dead weights as anchors. Most of these are suitable only for small to medium-size boats, generally under 20 feet in length, and in fairly calm water. They may not hold sufficiently in heavy waves or in current and typically have little ability to grab the bottom and dig in, although they may hold if they snag behind a big object, such as a rock. Large homemade anchors, including blocks and iron chunks, can be used on large boats, but they are not efficient and will bounce and roll in heavy waves; if they fall into water deeper than the rode, they will exert a downward force on the bow, which could be dangerous, and they are also back breakers when retrieved.

Many river anglers use an improvised anchor, especially chain, which functions primarily as a weight to slow their downstream movement. This is

Anchor Types

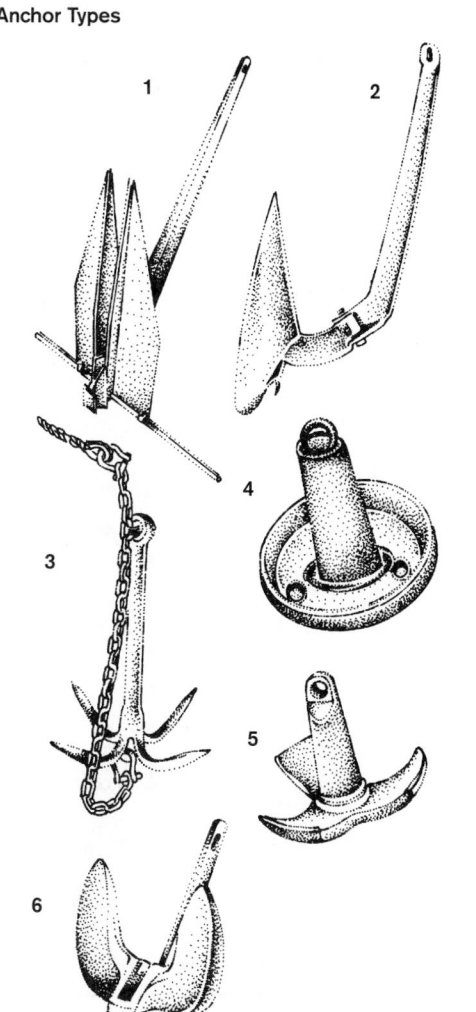

Common anchor types include: Danforth or fluke (1), plow (2), grapnel (3), mushroom (4), river (5), and Navy (6).

particularly helpful in sections of water with riffles, rapids, or shoals. Chains are noisy and may spook fish in some waters; an option is an industrial-strength jug, filled with sand or mud, that bounces along quietly like a piece of wood.

Mushroom. This is a cheap anchor, usually made of lead and sometimes having a vinyl or plastic coating. It has a 360-degree cupped lip and an upside-down mushroom appearance. It is solid, fairly small, and stows easily. It is more popular among small-boat owners in freshwater than in saltwater, and it primarily holds due to its weight (usually 8 to 10 pounds, but some are 15 pounds) rather than any intrinsic grabbing ability. Although commonly carried in boats of 15- to 18-foot lengths, such as bass boats, mushroom anchors are mainly useful under ideal conditions, especially where there is a soft bottom; they are not adequate in fast-moving water and cannot hold a heavy boat well, especially in a marl or hard bottom, unless that bottom has plenty of large rocks. When they settle into a muddy bottom, mushroom anchors are prone to

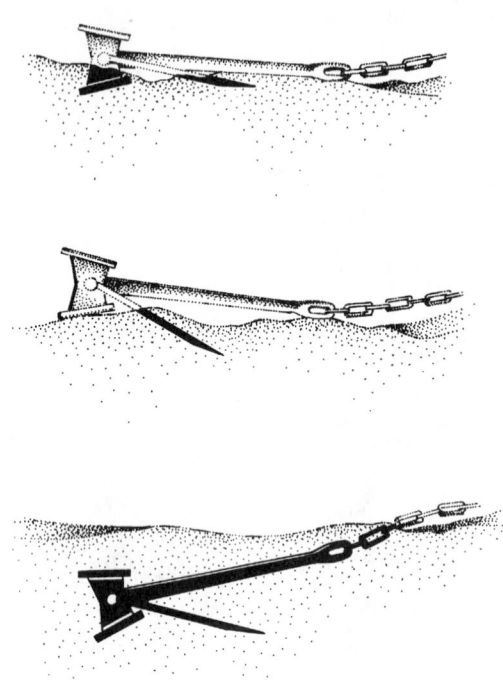

The flukes on a Danforth anchor lie flat when they reach bottom (top), dig in as pressure is applied (middle), then bury the anchor (bottom) for a very secure hold.

bring a lot of the bottom up with them, making for a heavy load to lift out of the water.

Mushroom anchors are regularly used for permanent harbor moorings because they exert a lot of suction once buried into an appropriate bottom. Anglers, who often drop anchor for short periods and mostly when there is wind, wave, and/or current action, do not usually face the ideal conditions that permit mushroom anchors to get a quick and lasting hold.

Danforth.   Also known as a lightweight burying anchor, or a fluke anchor, the Danforth has a high holding-power-to-weight ratio and is a favorite of many boaters. It is easy to operate and folds flat for relatively convenient storage, although the large surface area makes it cumbersome in the smaller compartments of many freshwater boats. Their light weight (3 to 10 pounds) makes deployment and retrieval easy, and most have a trip feature for releasing the anchor.

The Danforth is made of steel or aluminum (the latter being lighter) and features two long, flat, and pointed flukes that dig into the bottom as upward pressure is applied on the rode. It is especially effective in mud, sand, and clay and may actually bury itself if left long enough, as rode pressure forces the flukes deeper. On rocky terrain the flukes may skip over the bottom instead of digging in, and the flukes tend to pick up debris when they're retrieved. They may also be hard to use in extremely soft bottoms with a lot of grass. Some newer aluminum versions feature an adjustable shank that can be changed to suit different bottoms.

Navy.   This design combines movable flukes with a lot of weight. They are made of lead, sometimes coated with vinyl, and feature bulb and pivoting weight design. Navy anchors hold especially well in soft bottoms and are fairly popular, especially in freshwater, but they have a poor holding-power-to-weight ratio. They are manufactured in 5- to 20-pound sizes, the larger of which do not hold as well as much lighter Danforths.

Plow.   This device, which is newer than many of the designs described here, sports a broadhead-like blade and a design that rights the anchor and causes the blade to furrow into the bottom, eventually burying itself if the bottom is soft enough. It has application over diverse bottoms and is especially good in sand and moderate grass. Some versions have a shank that pivots, which reduces the tendency of the anchor to pull out when there's a sharp change in the angle of pull.

These anchors range from 15-pounders, for 25-foot boats, up to 60-pounders. Because they're large, they are hard to store in bow anchor compartments with limited space. For this reason, some boaters fasten them securely to a bow roller.

Grapnel.   This is a metal gang-hook anchor that sports four to six upward-sweeping claws. It has no value on soft bottoms but is excellent on rocky bottoms, as the claws readily catch onto objects. Grapnels are of moderate weight and are manufactured in small versions that serve backup duty or are used to scour the bottom for dropped equipment. Grapnels can get seriously hooked on the bottom, becoming impossible to retrieve. This potential problem can be avoided by attaching a trip line to the bottom of the anchor so it can be overturned. They are slightly bulky for small-boat storage, and the many hooks have a way of snagging things in the boat as well as rubbing against the boat.

River.   This is a lead anchor, usually vinyl coated, with three wide, cupped blades. It is heavy, weighing from 10 to 30 pounds. It has no benefit in soft bottoms but is meant to hold in rocky bottoms and varying current conditions. Other anchor types—including mushroom, twin-fluked lead navy models, and improvised versions—are also used in rivers, and some boaters use a bow cleat to secure these. The anchor cleat is fastened on the bow deck plate, and the rode runs through it, aided by rollers.

Size.   After choosing an anchor style that most suits the types of bottom you'll encounter, you will also have to think about getting the proper size to accommodate your boat. Size should be calculated with potential rough-water conditions (days when it is blowing a lot) or maximum current in mind. Generally, anchor recommendations for boats are based on "working" conditions, that is, rough water and gusty winds in the 20-knot range. Storm conditions short length of galvanized chain—usually 6 to 8 feet long but perhaps greater, depending on the size of the anchor and the manufacturer's recommendations. The chain may be vinyl coated to protect the boat and is attached directly to the anchor.

For boats up to 25 feet long, the line diameter should be no less than $^3/_8$ inch. This size will be more than adequate for most freshwater anglers, especially in smaller craft, and those who anchor fairly shallow. It may be too light for 25-foot boats that run offshore and anchor in deep water, as the line could be subjected to excessive tension. Then, it may be advisable to use $^1/_2$-inch- or $^9/_{16}$-inch-diameter line, which is also easier to handle. Lines that are larger still are recommended for bigger boats.

The necessary length of rode depends on where you will be anchoring and the worst conditions in which you might have to anchor. Small boats usually carry no more than 15 or 20 feet of rode. Although this length is adequate for calm stillwater conditions, it might not be sufficient for the strong current on a river. Generally, the larger the boat, the deeper the water, the more demanding the water conditions, the longer the rode needed. When you have a lot of rode out, however, there is a greater tendency for the boat to swing, especially in wind or current. In some cases a short rode might be adequate, but you would need a heavy anchor to maintain position.

In boating, the term scope is used to describe rode length as it relates to water depth and the height above the water of the anchoring point on the boat. The minimum scope ratio should vary between 5:1 and 10:1, the greater ratio being reserved for rough weather; the U.S. Coast Guard recommends a ratio of 7:1. For example, if the water is 17 feet deep and the anchor point on your boat is 3 feet above the surface (producing a total vertical distance to the bottom of 20 feet), you should let out 140 feet of rode. If the tide rises 3 feet while you are anchored, the ratio would be reduced to 6:1.

Many boaters, especially in freshwater, let out a little more rode than is required for the anchor to contact bottom. In calm waters and protected areas, the boat might remain in position, but this setup will never do in rough water, wind-blown locations, places with current, or emergencies.

Because anchors require a low angle of pull to dig in and to stay in place, scope has a significant impact on efficiency. The less the scope, the higher the angle of pull, and the greater the chance that the anchor will be pulled out of the bottom. In simpler terms, the more parallel to the bottom the angle of the rode becomes, the more an anchor will dig in, especially an anchor with flukes. This tendency is especially true in heavy seas and large swells because they put a great demand on the anchor.

Practical limitations to this do exist, however. Anchoring in 100 feet of water, as is common in

Homemade cement and chain anchors are used with these New Brunswick river guide boats.

require larger sizes. Marine supply stores usually have anchor selection charts that suggest how much holding power is needed for different conditions, and which anchor and corresponding size would be best.

Rode Type and Length

Holding power is determined not only by the design, weight, and size of the anchor but also by the amount of rode you have out. The elements between the anchor and boat, which includes line and chain, are all part of the rode. For many people, particularly freshwater boaters, this is simply known as anchor line. Many boaters in freshwater, and some in saltwater, use only line, without chain, connected directly to the anchor. This is satisfactory for most simple anchoring chores, which depend on light anchor devices and a short rode. Some amount of chain is almost always useful, however, because its weight aids in lowering the angle of pull, it will not suffer when contacting abrasive bottom elements, and it does not get as gritty and dirty as does terminal line.

The vast majority of line used for anchoring is nylon, either twisted or braided. Nylon is preferable to other materials because it resists rot, decay, and mildew if stored out of the sunlight, and its elasticity (between 15 and 30 percent) provides a desirable amount of shock absorption. Twisted nylon is more elastic than braided nylon, but it does not lay as flat and takes up more space. The line is connected to a

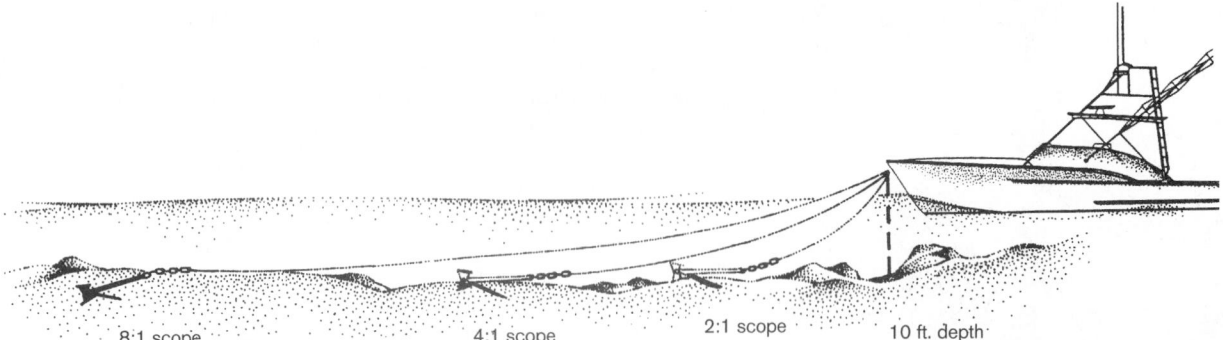

8:1 scope   4:1 scope   2:1 scope   10 ft. depth

Scope is the ratio of the length of anchor rope to depth of the water from an anchoring point, with a 7:1 ratio recommended by the U.S. Coast Guard. In general, the greater the length of anchor rope, the better the anchor can grab and hold. Shorter lengths produce greater upward pull on the anchor. In the scenario depicted, with a bottom depth of 10 feet, deploying 80 feet of anchor rope will achieve an 8:1 scope.

saltwater, requires 500 to 700 feet of rode if the line material is nearly all nylon; to anchor in 300 feet would theoretically require perhaps 2,000 feet of rode, an amount that presents storage problems as well as retrieval difficulty. To overcome this problem, boaters employ a rode comprised of all galvanized chain, or one that has a longer length of chain (15 to 50 feet) combined with nylon line. The chain, which is attached directly to the anchor, sinks rapidly to the bottom, thereby establishing a lower angle of pull. This enables a great reduction in overall rode length.

When you have a lot of rode out, there is more chance of a strong fish wrapping your fishing line around it. In a big boat, it may not be possible to walk around the foredeck to fight the fish, and this could become problematic. For big tuna and sharks caught while chumming at anchor, it may be necessary to maneuver the boat to fight and land the fish. In this case, an anchor ball (also known as a mooring buoy) is clipped to the rode and dropped in the water, and the boat detaches and moves off. This allows the angler to follow the fish, which may help in landing it and will also aid in preventing it from swimming around the rode.

Setting and Retrieving

The following instructions pertain mostly to the temporary anchoring that characterizes most fishing by boat. Additional and more secure measures may be necessary for permanent mooring setups, as in harbors or for overnight stays. Also, in crowded spots the standard scope may be impractical, allowing too much swinging room.

When you're beaching a boat for a short stay, it may be wise to place an anchor on the shore or, at the least, to tie a rope to some object on the shore. Keep in mind that a falling tide could leave the boat stranded ashore. A rising tide would float the boat, potentially causing it to bang against the shoreline. It might be best to anchor near shore, in enough water to float the boat, rather than to beach it, especially if there is an onshore wind or a lot of wave activity. The bow should be facing into the wind or

waves, and the anchor should be set far enough from shore to give the boat room to swing; it may be necessary to tilt the engine up to keep the propeller from dragging. Of course, if the wind direction changes and the boat swings away from shore, you may have to swim out to get into it.

General techniques.   Setting out an anchor is not simply a matter of dropping the anchor overboard and waiting until it grabs. The most important thing is to set the anchor so that the boat is in the position you desire. Precise positioning is sometimes absolutely critical for fishing success, when you anchor in a river and want to cast your lures or bait into the head of a downstream pool, for example, or when you anchor over a ledge to fish immediately below the boat.

First, taking into consideration the effects of wind and current, position the boat reasonably close to where you ultimately want it to rest. Make sure you are not standing on the rode and that it is not likely to entangle with anything as you let it out. Lower the anchor into the water without tossing it; in shallow waters, throwing it in with a big splash is like setting off a bomb, scattering alarmed fish far and near. Pay out the rode through your hands, as this practice keeps the line (and especially heavy chain, if used) above the sinking anchor so that it doesn't wrap around the anchor and foul it. This problem is more likely to happen to anchors with flukes.

If you don't want to drift over the desired fishing spot, at this point, you can set position in two ways. Either pay out the proper length of rode until the scope is right and the boat is where you want it to be; or, drift under power well below the place that you want to anchor, using the boat to help dig in the anchor, then motor forward until the proper position and scope are attained. The latter method assumes you're not anchoring over a desirable fishing spot (as when setting up a chumming drift), as this tactic would spook the fish.

If you're letting out a lot of rode, it's a good idea to pull on it to ensure that the anchor is holding. You can use the boat to help dig in the anchor, and

A plow anchor is retrieved using an anchor ball, which is not visible but attached to the line and ring on this anchor; note the chain and how it is affixed to the anchor.

the bow, back down to the jetty, and then throw a long slender piece of wood (like a green tree branch or a broomstick) into the jetty rocks, where it gets wedged. Attached to the center of the stick is a length of 200-pound-strength fishing line. Then they move the boat the appropriate distance from the jetty, cleat off the bow anchor, and then cleat off the heavy line attached to the stick, all of which helps to keep the boat in the proper position.

Deep-water retrieval. Getting an anchor to the bottom in deep water is usually no problem, but hauling up long lengths (300 to 1,000 or more feet) of rode with a heavy anchor at the end of it would be a most unpleasant chore if you had to do it hand-over-hand.

When an anchor is set extremely deep and is hard to budge, or when it is very deep and it would

in current you can help a dragging anchor grab by motoring slowly forward temporarily so that there is no resistance on the rode.

To retrieve an anchor, do not pull the boat by hand toward the anchor unless it is a small light boat or you don't have far to go. The main reason is to spare your back the strain inherent in this kind of hauling. If you're pulling up to leave a spot, then, using the motor, maneuver the boat over the rode and pull directly upward. If that is not successful in freeing the anchor, motor upstream of it and use the power of the boat, which will easily free many anchors. This is also how you can free anchors that are designed to be tripped with an opposite direction pull. If you plan to continue fishing nearby, using the motor may not be an option, as it could spook the fish.

Another retrieval option is to use a trip line. This is a second line, fastened to the crown of the anchor and used to pull the anchor from the back end. Obviously it has to be attached to the anchor beforehand. A method of setting a trip with a Danforth anchor is to shackle the end of your chain directly to the mud palm of the anchor (you have to drill a hole in it first), run the chain up to the head of the shank and then bind it there with heavy-duty cord so that the line of pull is from the shank, as would ordinarily be. When the anchor is stuck, use the boat to pull it from the opposite direction, which will break the cord and give you a pull from the mud palm.

As mentioned earlier, it may be worthwhile to have a second anchor, perhaps a lighter one, for backup use, or for use when you just want to sit tight for a break; a light anchor for this purpose is referred to as a "lunch hook." Big sportfishing boats should carry a magnum-model anchor for extreme, or storm, conditions. Small-boat owners sometimes use a clever variation of this to anchor and maintain position near a jetty; they set the main anchor off

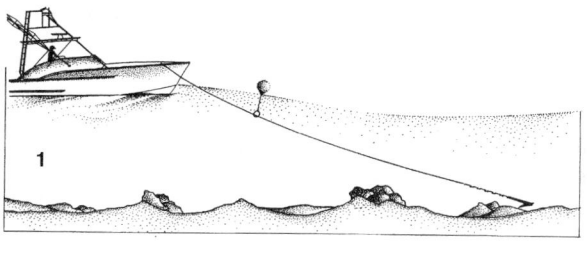

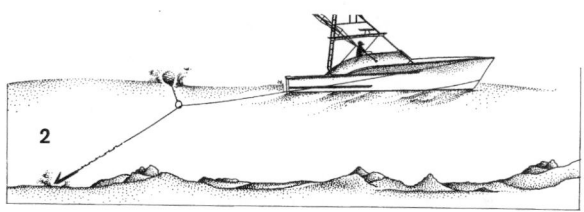

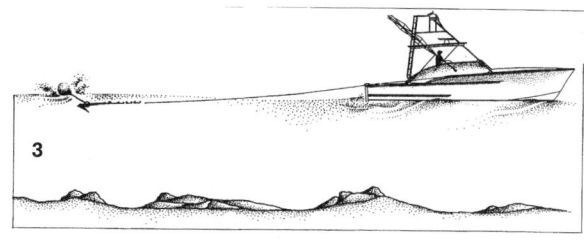

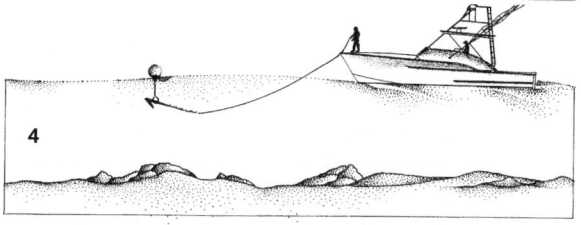

To free a deep, heavy anchor without breaking your back, use a poly anchor ball on a large ring and the maneuver depicted here. Begin by placing the ball so it slides freely on the anchor rope (1). Head directly away from the anchor position, swinging wide so as not to run over the rope (2); the buoyancy of the ball and the movement of the boat will free the anchor. As the boat continues to move forward, the ball will slide down the line to meet the anchor when it is pulled to the surface (3), with the anchor lodging in the anchor ball ring. Slowly head toward the anchor and ball, easily retrieving the rope (4).

A

be an immense strain to raise it completely by hand, the best method is to use a vinyl anchor ball (see), which is also known as a mooring buoy, attached to a short length of line and a spring clip. Fasten the clip to a ring on the cleated rode and drop the ball into the water. Then motor forward, being careful not to run over the rode. Keep moving at a constant speed, which will free the anchor, then pick up speed as the anchor rises and begins to drag the ball. The anchor shank will slide into the ring. Slow the boat and then slowly motor back to the ball while retrieving the rode.

Quick-release anchoring. One of the most useful anchoring techniques for fishing is the quick-release system. This is nothing more than a standard anchor with chain and line; the end of the rode is attached to an anchor ball. A short length of rope from the ball to the boat provides the quick-release feature. The end of the rope can be either looped over a cleat or attached to a boat snap for easy one-handed getaways. This setup is appropriate when you want to stay in a particular spot yet maintain the flexibility necessary to quickly pull away when you hook a large fish and have to move the boat to fight it. When many boats are concentrated in the same area, this system guarantees your position when you return (make sure that your buoy is clearly marked). You'll want a quick release from the anchor to get after a strong fish (like a tuna) and perhaps steer it away from other vessels and their anchor lines. Being able to return to your exact prior spot saves reentering time, of course, but it may also be important in locating fish, especially if you've been chumming. Very often a school of fish will hang around the spot for a good while after the chumming stops. Or, you can tie the chum bag to the ball (if it's not too likely to be eaten by a large shark while you're gone), thus improving the odds that the fish will still be there when you get back.

The ball or buoy used for a quick-release anchor system should be large enough so it won't be dragged under by a strong current, especially if attached to a long rode (rope also has a lot of drag in a strong current). It must be large enough so that you can spot it in choppy seas and thus find it when you return. One of the best devices for this purpose is a plastic-covered, foam-filled boat fender. These come in a variety of sizes and in bright colors for easier spotting.

Freeing a hung anchor. Some methods of freeing an anchor have already been discussed, but what do you do when your anchor is really dug in and the standard methods don't free it? A good anchor is not a cheap item, so before you give up and cut the line or try to break it loose via sheer engine horsepower (which can be dangerous), a few tricks are worth a try.

One option is to pull from several different directions, especially upcurrent and upwind. Start with whichever force is stronger, and use the engine to move the boat as far upstream from the anchor

as the rode length will permit. Then carefully apply a little more power with the rode secured to a cleat. Don't gun the engine; if the line breaks under considerable strain, it could snap back. And pay careful attention to the seas; you don't want to bury the bow or stern while trying to free an anchor that is worth far less than the boat.

If that doesn't work, the next method is almost always successful. Pay out enough rode to obtain a scope that's as close to 10:1 as possible, tie it securely to a sturdy cleat, and put the engine in gear, heading away from the anchor at a slow speed until the rode is tight. Then take up a heading that allows the boat to circle the anchor while maintaining a tight pull on the rode. Increase the power somewhat, but not so much that you place the rode under dangerous strain. Keep up the strain as the boat makes a complete 360-degree circle around the anchor. You might have to make the circle up to a half-dozen times, but almost always the anchor will eventually come free without any damage to it. It's more a matter of technique than brute force, but you can save many anchors of all types by using this method.

Reducing sway. It may be useful at times, especially for precise positioning and to minimize swaying, to deploy two anchors. In relatively protected waters, you can do this by having a bow anchor and a stern anchor, and several companions who can help. Set out the bow anchor first, drifting far back while paying out bow anchor rode; then lower the stern anchor and, while heading forward and simultaneously keeping tension on the stern rode, retrieve bow rode until you get to the desired position.

Another way to use double anchors, and one that is common for larger boats and for positioning over ledges and reefs in saltwater, is by setting the anchors at 45-degree angles off the port and starboard bows. You have to set one anchor first and drop back to where you want the anchored boat positioned, then cleat that rode off and move forward to a point to port or starboard and even with the first anchor, then let out the second anchor, paying out the rode for that anchor until the boat comes taut on the first rode. Tie each rode to a different cleat so that you can release either rode if necessary. You may have to try this more than once to get the correct positioning, but the important thing is to ensure a 45-degree angle of pull; you don't want both anchors set primarily dead ahead.

Reducing sway may be as simple as changing the point where the anchor rode is secured to the boat, usually from the bow to a position somewhere closer amidships. The best way to do this is with a bridle, a length of line slightly greater than the length of the boat. You tie one end to the bow, and the other end to the stern. Then tie the rode to the boat somewhere near the center of the bridle, thus forming a Y, with the centerline of the boat at approximately right angles to the rode. This causes the broad side of the boat to face into the wind

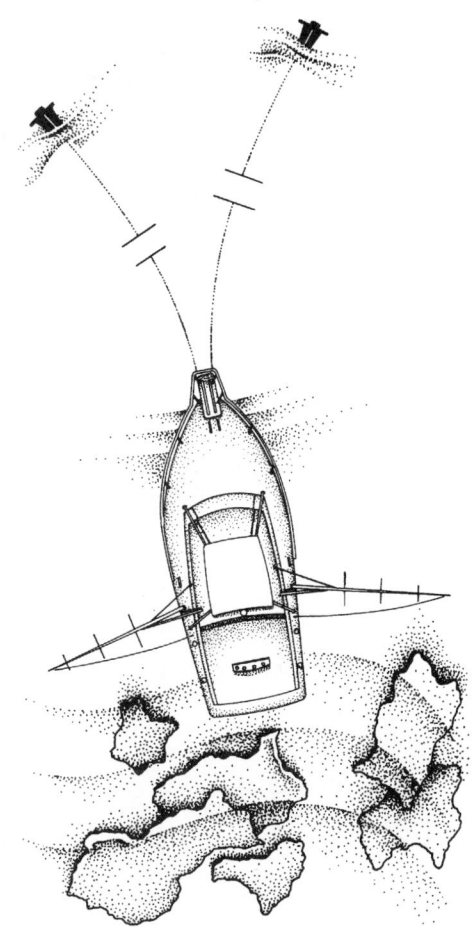

and/or current. You may find it necessary to shorten either the bow or stern section so that the rode itself isn't exactly in the middle. Once you get the hang of this, you can either eliminate boat sway almost completely, or at least reduce it to a level at which you can still fish effectively.

More on positioning. There are ways to change your position once you are firmly anchored. Letting out more rode, for example, is a good way to drop back with the wind or current to cover a greater area. River anglers often lengthen the rode in order to drift farther into a pool, and reef or wreck anglers do likewise to position themselves over different areas. In addition to dropping back when the road is tied to the center of the boat, you can change position by altering the tie-off point. Cleating the rode off-center, usually a few feet down from the bow centerline, you can use the angle of the boat in the water and the direction of the wind or current to bring you to the position you would ordinarily be in if the rode were attached dead-center. This will not work in rough water and heavy winds, but in moderate conditions it can help you spread out horizontally to fish directly over different portions of a ledge, wreck, or reef.

If you have a small boat and primarily fish shallow water, you should still carry ample rode, but in sections rather than in a continuous piece. The main section for shallow water use might be only 25 feet long, but you can carry extra rode in 25-, 50-, and 100-foot lengths. If each section has a loop on one end and a stainless steel snap on the other, the sections can be quickly connected in series to produce a single long line from 50 to 200 feet long. Even if you anchor in just 10 feet of water, this gives a possible scope of 20:1.

The idea behind an extremely long rode is to enable the boat to move forward and backward over a considerable distance by alternately shortening or lengthening the amount of rode, or to deliberately swing the boat back and forth over a wide area with a paddle, electric motor, a pushpole, or even a gas outboard. Silent power is obviously best for the latter maneuver if you're fishing for game that's particularly sensitive to motor noise.

You can, for example, use a long rode to maneuver a boat up and down a river, creek, or canal in which the tide or current is too strong for the electric motor. The idea in this instance is to anchor at the top of a particular productive stretch of water, keeping the rode short at the beginning. Once you've worked the top of the run to your satisfaction, let out just enough rode to reach the next likely productive stretch downstream.

Bit by bit you can continue to work downcurrent, until you reach the end of the rode. At that point, if the current is not too strong and the boat is not too large, you can haul the boat back to the top of the run by hand and work the entire area (or at least the most productive sections) over again, if warranted.

Using two anchors, as depicted for precisely locating the stern of this boat over a reef, is a good way to minimize sideways movement and maintain an exact position.

In stillwater, weak current, and moderate winds, a long rode makes it possible to cover ample water from a quasi-stationary position by deliberately swinging back and forth. Sometimes the wind, like current, can be used to move the boat in one direction. Often, however, swinging the boat over a wide arc requires some source of power. An electric motor enables you to reposition the boat and cast at the same time.

In many situations, fish move up and down shorelines or along shallow depth contours, but not always along precise or relatively narrow underwater pathways. Sometimes you're able to see the fish as they move, or at least detect positive signs of their presence. In other cases, it's just a matter of covering as much of the potentially productive water as possible by blind casting. The large swinging radius of a long rode makes appropriate positioning and repositioning possible, and with stealth.

Safety

Anchor rode should be attached only to the bow of the boat, and to a strong cleat, except under the absolute best of circumstances. It can be extremely dangerous to anchor stern first. Even when the surface of the water is calm, the wake of a passing boat could send a deluge of water over the stern of a boat, causing the boat to capsize. In a river, a boat anchored stern first is susceptible to being pulled down and into the water if another boat should drift into the rode.

In dangerous situations, it may be wise to keep a sharp knife handy in case you have to quickly detach the rode from the boat. And do not coil rode on the bow of the boat. It should be stowed safely away until needed. In heavy seas, rode could be swept into the water and quickly wrapped in the propeller(s), imperiling the boat.

Finally, no matter how much rode you have, always make sure that the end of it is firmly attached to a cleat. People have lost an anchor and all of their rode because it was unattached.

ANCHOR BALL

An anchor ball is a large colorful vinyl ball, also known as a mooring buoy, that is tied to the surface end of anchor line, or rode. This buoy is sometimes used as a fender or for mooring large boats in open water in harbors; in fishing applications, it is used by anglers who anchor in deep water and chum, primarily for tuna or sharks, but also for other species. In offshore chumming, an anchor is set out, and chum and hooked baits drift with the current. When a large fish is caught, it may be necessary to maneuver the boat to fight and land the fish. In this event, the rode is uncleated and the anchor ball, clipped to the rode, is then dropped into the water, enabling the boat to move off. After the fish is landed, the boat returns to the anchor ball (which should be marked for identification) and reattaches to the rode. In this way, the anchor does not have to be hauled in and reset, and proper position in a suitable place is maintained, which can be important when there are many boats in the same area. See: Anchor.

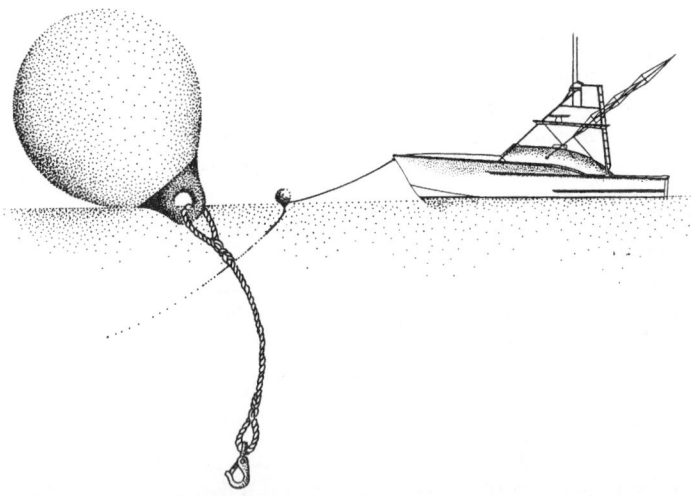

Large boats are often tethered to an anchor ball in a harbor or when fishing offshore, which allows for quickly disengaging from the anchor and easily returning to it.

ANCHOVIES

Northern Anchovy   *Engraulis mordax.*
   Other names—pinhead, North Pacific anchovy, California anchovy, bay anchovy; French: *anchois du Pacifique nord, anchois de California;* Spanish: *anchoveta de California, anchoa del Pacifico.*

Striped Anchovy   *Anchoa hepsetus.*
   Other names—broad-striped anchovy; French: *anchois rayé;* Spanish: *anchoa legìtima.*

Northern Anchovy

Striped Anchovy

Similar in appearance, these anchovies differ mostly in range, although the northern anchovy can be slightly longer. The northern anchovy is one of the most important forage fish in the Pacific and is used as bait for tuna and other large gamefish. A minor percentage of northern anchovies harvested are processed for human consumption, marketed in pickled or salted forms. The striped anchovy is also an important forage fish for game species, although it is too small and fragile to be used often for bait.

Identification.   Anchovies are silvery fish that look like miniature herring. They have overhanging snouts and long lower jaws that extend behind the eyes. The striped anchovy has a ribbonlike stripe along each side and some yellow about the head. Anchovy species are difficult to differentiate, but the fin rays and pattern of pigmentation on the striped anchovy distinguish it; it has 14 to 17 dorsal fin rays, 15 to 18 pectoral fin rays, and 20 to 24 anal fin rays, as well as melanophores outlining all its dorsal scales.

Size.   The northern anchovy can reach 9 inches, although 4 to 5 inches is more common; the striped anchovy can reach 6 inches, but the average length is less than 4 inches.

Distribution.   In the eastern Pacific, the northern anchovy is found from northern Vancouver Island south to Cabo San Lucas, Baja California. Two subspecies are recognized, namely *E. mordax mordax,* which extends from British Columbia to Baja California, and *E. mordax nanus,* found in California's bays. In the western Atlantic, striped anchovies are found from Massachusetts (sometimes Maine or even Nova Scotia) south to Fort Pierce, Florida, but not in the Florida Keys and rarely in southern Florida. They also occur in the northern Gulf of Mexico, the Gulf of Venezuela, and south to Uruguay.

Habitat. Both northern and striped anchovies form dense schools and favor shallow coastal waters, including bays and inlets. Striped anchovies are able to tolerate a wide range of salinities.

Life history/Behavior. Northern anchovies spawn through the year, although they do so mainly in winter and early spring. Spawning occurs in nearshore and offshore environs, predominantly in depths of less than 10 meters and in temperatures of 10° to 13°C. Striped anchovies spawn from April through July in harbors, estuaries, and sounds. The eggs of both species are elliptical and float near the surface, hatching within a few days after being released. The young mature in three to four years.

Food. Both anchovies feed on plankton.

ANGELFISH, QUEEN   *Holacanthus ciliaris.*

Other names—French: *demoiselle royale;* Spanish: *isabelita patale.*

The queen angelfish is not widely sought by anglers, although it is an attractive incidental catch. It has some food value, although it is more popular as an aquarium fish.

Identification. The queen angelfish has a moderately large body that is deep and compressed. It can be distinguished from its nearest relatives, butterflyfish, by its stout spines, blunter snout, and the spines on the gill cover. It has 14 dorsal spines, and the spine at the angle of the preopercle is relatively long.

Most noteworthy about the appearance of the queen angelfish is its coloration. It is speckled yellowish orange and blue, and the amount of blue varies with the individual and differs in intensity. It has a bright blue border on the soft dorsal and anal fins, with the tips of the fins colored orange and the last few rays of them colored bluish black. It also has a yellowish orange tail, as well as a dark bluish black spot on the forehead, ringed with bright blue, which forms the queen's "crown."

The coloring of the young queen angelfish's is dark blue and very similar that of young blue angelfish, but the rear edges of the dorsal and anal fins are not yellow, as they are in the blue angelfish. There are bluish white bars on the body of the queen angelfish, as with the blue angelfish, but these are curved on the queen angelfish instead of straight.

Angelfish in the Caribbean are generally brighter in color than those along the coasts of North and South America.

Size. Although reported to reach a length of nearly 2 feet, queen angelfish probably do not exceed 18 inches, and they average 8 to 14 inches.

Distribution. Queen angelfish are a common to occasional presence in Florida, the Bahamas, and the Caribbean; they are present in Bermuda and the Gulf of Mexico, and south to Brazil, as well as on coral reefs in the West Indies.

Habitat. Queen angelfish inhabit coral reefs in shallow water, although juveniles prefer offshore

Queen Angelfish

reefs, and mature fish sometimes frequent depths of 20 to 80 feet. They often are indistinguishable from the colorful sea fans, sea whips, and corals they swim amongst.

Behavior.   The queen angelfish is usually found alone or in a pair, but not in groups.

Food.   Adults feed primarily on sponges, but also consume algae and minute organisms.

Angling.   Queen angelfish are an incidental but spunky catch for bottom anglers using baits or baited jigs.

ANGLER

A person who catches—or tries to catch—fish for personal use, fun, challenge, and leisure by using sporting equipment, essentially some type of rod, usually but not always equipped with a reel, to which a line and a hook or lure are attached, and by fair and sporting methods that afford the quarry an opportunity to avoid capture. Although the word "angler" is genderless, it is used interchangeably with "sportfisherman." It has a more specific meaning than "fisherman," although both words may connote the same thing when used in reference to the employment of sporting equipment.

See: Angling; Commercial Fisherman; Fisherman; Fishing; Recreational Fisherman; Sportfisherman; Sportfishing.

ANGLERFISH

"Anglerfish" is a common name for the goosefish *(see)*, also called monkfish, bellyfish, frogfish, and sea devil.

ANGLING

The act of catching or trying to catch fish for personal use, fun, challenge, and leisure using sporting equipment, essentially with some type of rod, usually but not always equipped with a reel, to which a line and a hook or lure is attached, and by sporting methods.

Angling is used interchangeably with sportfishing but has a more specific meaning than fishing, although both words may connote the same thing when used in reference to the employment of sporting equipment. The term angling is distinguished from commercial or recreational fishing by virtue of the equipment employed, an implicit understanding of fair chase, and the exercise of sportsmanship. When angling, the equipment used affords the quarry some opportunity to elude capture; thus using a net to encircle and capture fish may be fishing, but it is not angling, and methods that do not have some element of fair play are not truly angling. Angling also implies the intent to keep fish (if fish are kept) for personal use rather than for sale or trade, although some saltwater fish that are caught by sporting means may legally be sold.

What constitutes sport or sporting equipment is open to individual interpretation and encompasses a wide range of equipment and circumstances. Even anglers disagree as to whether certain tactics, tackle, and techniques exclusively used in angling actually qualify as "sport." This is a debate, in part grounded in attitudes and ethical considerations, that defies settlement, and which muddies any attempt at strict definition.

See: Angler; Commercial Fisherman; Fishing; Recreational Fisherman; Sportfisherman; Sportfishing.

ANGOLA

The seventh largest country on the African continent, Angola is well situated along the eastern Atlantic Ocean to provide access to lightly explored saltwater fishing. Bounded by Namibia on the south and the Democratic Republic of the Congo (formerly Zaire) on the north, Angola is larger than Spain and Portugal combined, and has some 1,650 kilometers of coastline that lies between the Equator and the Tropic of Capricorn.

A warm tropical current flows southward along this extensive coastline, from the Gulf of Guinea, whereas the cold Benguela Current sweeps northerly from the South Atlantic. This mixture of currents results in an abundance of forage fish, particularly various species of sardines and scads. The forage fish in turn attract exceptionally large Atlantic sailfish, plenty of dorado, and a still-new fishery for big blue marlin, particularly offshore from the capital city of Luanda.

There is great potential for gamefishing here; however, sportfishing has been limited since the country became independent in 1975 and subsequently endured a lengthy civil war. In the early 1970s the waters off Luanda regularly produced the largest Atlantic sailfish in the world. International Game Fish Association (IGFA) world records were dominated by catches made off Luanda before 1975. Despite advances in angling techniques and equipment, the exploration of other sailfish locations, and a low overall angling effort in Angola in the latter twentieth century, this country still holds the all-tackle world record for Atlantic sailfish, and has produced other existing or former record catches.

In the early 1970s, anglers fished from small speedboats, trolling ballyhoo, mullet, and strip baits. With the arrival of independence, most sailfish enthusiasts fled the country, and recreational fishing for sailfish declined sharply. It was only in the late 1980s that a few people started sailfishing again. However, every passing year sees the arrival of more sportfishing boats and increasing numbers of anglers.

The seas off Luanda are usually calm, as storms are very rare and strong winds virtually unknown. The sea is choppy only in the afternoon, and few days are lost to bad weather. This all makes for comfortable fishing conditions, although the humidity can be high in the rainy season (February through April).

Sea temperatures vary greatly according to season and location along the coastline. Off Luanda, the peak water temperatures of summer (March and April) reach the mid-80s, and in winter (July and August) they drop to the mid-60s. These waters are normally warm from September to June.

Although sailfish are not present in the quantities touted for other hotspots, the size of its sailfish—the largest Atlantic specimens in the world—make Angola (mainly the Luanda area at present) *the* place to pursue this species. The previously mentioned record, a 141-pounder, was caught in February of 1994, and at least a half-dozen fish weighing between 128 and 132 pounds were registered in competitions between 1994 and 1998. These are impressive statistics, as fewer than 80 sailfish overall are known to have been caught during that time. Unfortunately, competitions in Angola as of the late 1990s were still kill events; only one boat opted for catch-and-release angling.

Sailfish are present off Luanda from October to May, but only appear in significant numbers between January and March. The big sails are usually caught in February and March, but this can vary; some years can be very poor, with few sailfish seen or caught due to abnormally cool water temperatures. Inconsistent arrival times from one season to the next also make this fishery problematic. Sails are caught at a distance of 5 to 12 miles from the head of Luanda Bay. A few miles south of Luanda the highly productive 100-meter dropoff is only a couple of miles offshore, whereas due east of Luanda it is 10 miles distant.

Of the few boaters who pursue sailfish here, most troll only lures, or a combination of lures and ballyhoo. The latter are readily available and are caught in nets during the early morning hours; they can be purchased at dawn from local fishermen. Angling with live bait is not practiced here, as it is hard to come by. Schools of ballyhoo are rarely seen offshore, yet flying fish are sometimes plentiful. Although schools of baitfish are often observed offshore, it is rare to see sailfish feeding on them, and bird activity is virtually nonexistent. If the sea gets choppy in the afternoon, sailfish can often be seen tailing; these are usually hunting, and readily attack any offerings put in front of them.

Sailfish are not the only billfish lurking in Angolan waters. The first blue marlin taken here, a fish of about 400 pounds, was boated in December 1990. Since then more than 50 marlin have been caught off Luanda. This figure may seem low at first glance, but in reality it is quite respectable, given that there are few boats with fighting chairs, hardly anyone fishes for marlin, and what little effort is made is concentrated around Luanda, and that many marlin have been raised and lost.

Even more noteworthy is that there are few small marlin around. If small fish (100 to 200 pounds) existed in any quantity, they would have been caught by anglers trolling baits and lures for sailfish. In the late 1990s, the two smallest marlin weighed 175 and 253 pounds, the average was around 490, and the largest two weighed 815 and 943 pounds—the latter caught on 50-pound stand-up tackle in March 1998. Four others over 700 pounds were caught. It is only a matter of time before the first grander is caught.

Most marlin have been taken on lures, and analysis of the captures and sightings of blue marlin shows two definite peaks. The best time is March through May; in April, two to three strikes a day from 500-pounders can be expected. Marlin usually show up in mid-March, but in 1998 four marlin, three over 450 pounds, were caught in three days in late February. April and May peaks coincide with the highest abundance of weed clumps from the rivers and with the appearance of dorado that live under them. Dorado can be extremely plentiful at this time, though large specimens are rare and are sometimes a nuisance to anglers trolling baits for sailfish. They have repeatedly observed marlin attacking dorado and trying to eat hooked dorado.

The second marlin peak usually runs from October to December but varies from year to year. Marlin have been caught each month from September to June, so the season is theoretically very long. For marlin fishing, the calmer the sea the better, and the best time of day in Angolan waters has been between noon and three o'clock. Few marlin are raised on the rare days when the sea is rough.

The marlin sometimes come into very shallow water, and some have been hooked in water that is 60 meters deep. Blue water normally appears within a few miles of the coast, but sometimes green water appears and makes fishing virtually useless. The green water can last from a few days to many months, and during this time the sea appears devoid of life.

There is no structure on which to base a trolling pattern, so most boats concentrate on water between 100 and 150 meters deep, and on current and weedlines. Early and late in the season, offshore fishing becomes a marlin-or-nothing activity, when anglers may troll for days with not so much as a bite from other fish. When a strike finally comes, however, it's usually a big blue.

From December through April the only fish encountered offshore are dorado, sailfish, and marlin. Tuna are rare catches off Luanda, although yellowfins are reputedly abundant farther south and are a favored target of the commercial fishery. Very few people have ever encountered wahoo off Luanda, but a number of large basking swordfish have been spotted during the winter months (mid-May through August). Still, none had been hooked as of 1998.

In his book *Tales of the Anglers,* Zane Grey said, "All experience must be measured as much by what the angler brings to it as by what it gives."

A

Inshore fishing in Angola can be very good, although overharvesting by uncontrolled commercial fishing has taken its toll. The river mouths can provide excellent sport for tarpon, cubera snapper, threadfin, and jack crevalle. Two jack crevalle records—including the all-tackle 57-pound, 5-ounce fish—were set at the Kwanza River, which empties into the Atlantic near Luanda. The Mancha Branca, a shallow area south of Luanda, also produces huge barracuda—many of world-record proportions; a line-class 30.3-kilogram record barracuda was taken there in 1998. There are also cubera snapper to 50 kilograms, and threadfin to 50 kilograms.

The tarpon fishery in the Kwanza River was well developed pre-independence, but afterward—as with offshore fishing—many enthusiasts left the country. Unfortunately, netting has taken its toll in the river; tarpon and other species have decreased over the years. Tarpon to 100 kilograms were reportedly caught in the past.

Tarpon also appear along the coastline around Luanda, and the sportfishery in the Congo River to the north may well be fantastic and untapped. Mussulo Bay to the south of Luanda is a huge, beautiful bay that used to offer a variety of fishing, and has large areas of flats. Tarpon, bonefish, barracuda, and jacks were once available in Mussulo, but relentless local commercial netting has considerably depleted fish stocks. The coast to the far south has other species, including garrick, which reflects the colder waters there.

Unfortunately, the availability of charter boats is extremely limited, and as of 1998 there were no reliable boats for charter at the Kwanza River and only one boat was available for offshore fishing out of Luanda. With positive progress in implementing a peace accord, it is hoped that more boats will be available in time. As facilities improve, more anglers will visit Angola and more records are likely to be established, most likely for sailfish, jack crevalle, and barracuda.

Currently, no freshwater sportfishing exists, although evidently not for lack of fish. Civil strife has long made it extremely dangerous to venture into the bush, and the riverbanks are often mined. Perhaps someday there will be a freshwater fishery to explore. Tigerfish are believed to exist in some of Angola's rivers.

ANTIQUE FISHING TACKLE

Modern sportfishing is viewed by collectors in terms of two distinct periods: pre– and post–World War II. Since that defining event in history, fishing equipment, technique, interest, and knowledge have exploded, with each facet spurring on the other. Angling equipment, in particular, has evolved to advanced levels, a fact evident to even the casual observer and nonparticipant. With the plethora of tackle produced annually, each building technologically upon preceding equipment, it is only natural that some affinity with the tackle of the past was cultivated and that collecting these items became a more active and widely followed pursuit.

Antique tackle collecting was virtually unheard of prior to the 1950s, and even until the mid-1970s it was of minor interest. The few collectors who existed during that period labored in an uncharted field and knew little about each other. In 1976, however, three collectors formed the National Fishing Lure Collectors Club (NFLCC). An organization of more than 3,000 members at the end of the twentieth century, it boasts a continually growing membership.

Although the NFLCC was founded by lure collectors, it has since attracted people who collect all types of fishing tackle, and thus the name is today a bit misleading. Although lures, because of their sheer numbers and prominence in angling, are of foremost interest, all types of old fishing tackle have become popular. Collecting is now a natural extension of the hobby of sportfishing. There are few nonangling collectors of antique fishing tackle and related items.

Because the NFLCC has been promoting antique tackle collecting, the market has undergone some astounding changes both in numbers of collectors and in the prices of collectibles. Fortunately, for the most part, antique tackle has not gone the way of the extraordinary price increases seen in other collecting arenas, as in old hunting decoys, where six-figure prices are not unusual. The values of old fishing tackle remained fairly stable, with moderate growth, for the first 10 years of organized collecting but have realized considerable gains in the 1990s.

Nevertheless, prices have not gone so high in most areas of tackle collecting as to price the average collector out of the market. For example, in 1991 a 1922-vintage South Bend Pike Oreno plug was valued at about $10; today it is valued at $20 to $30. There are some famous aberrations, such as a small metal lure called the Haskell Minnow, which sold for $20,000 at auction, but extremes of this kind are exceedingly rare.

Some reels, on the other hand, are valued extraordinarily high. Early Kentucky reels can sell for $1,500 to $2,500, but there are hundreds of nice old reels available for $20 to $50. Many good contemporary reels will cost more than that at a tackle shop. Likewise, fine old fly rods will bring several hundred, some even thousands, of dollars, but great old casting rods can be found for less than $100, and many nice rods for even less.

Tackle collecting is not limited to lures, rods, and reels. Diverse angling-related collectibles, or ephemera, as some collectors call them, are plentiful. Included as ephemera are all the old manufacturers' catalogs. Some were works of art in themselves, and the market in these is very active. Even colorful old empty lure boxes are sought after; wooden versions are especially prized. Glass minnow traps and buckets, dipnets, calendars, fishing licenses and badges, advertising posters, manufacturer and tackle shop signs, promotional giveaways, metal and wooden tackle boxes, and ice fishing decoys and spears are also among the items collectors fancy.

Fishing tackle made in the United States and Canada from the 1800s into the 1960s is the predominant interest among collectors. Little fishing tackle was manufactured in North America prior to about 1880, other than a few fly rods. Before that, there was little interest in fishing for sport; the passion for angling at that time originated in Europe and most likely spread to the U.S. through European immigrants.

It is thought by some that the limited number of manufacturers over those eight decades resulted in a finite number of potentially available products. Although there is, of course, a finite number, that number is in the millions. Even the smallest lure companies, for example, made lures by the thousands or even tens of thousands. Larger companies, some in business for 50 years, produced millions of items. And many thousands of anglers added to the available collectibles by trying to invent a "better mousetrap" over all those years.

Most lure producers experimented with myriad designs in the continuing quest for the proverbial "secret weapon." There were thousands of these operations, from the one-person shop to the large manufacturer, that came and went during this time. The types of lures produced ranged from the sublime to the ridiculous, from the ineffective to the explosively successful. According to the advertisements of the day, just about every lure was the fabled supreme achievement. In a 1911 advertisement, for example, lure maker Anson (Ans) B. Decker boasted that he could catch more bass over 14 inches with his bait than the reader, and backed this up with a wager of "$1,000 against $500." Considering what a prodigious sum of money that was in 1911, this was a real challenge.

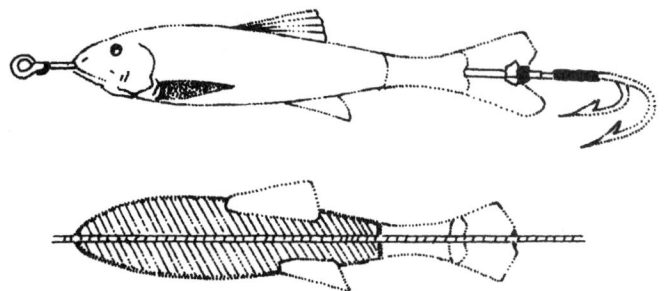

This rendition of the Haskell Minnow is derived from the original patent drawing.

Historical Perspectives

Fishing for food has occurred since prehistoric times, and fishing for recreation is in evidence since at least the late fifteenth century. Research suggests that reels were used by the Chinese as early as A.D. 300 to 400, but there are no clear indications whether this was for food or fun. The modern historical era for angling as recreation begins with a piece of English literature written in 1496. Titled *Treatyse of Fysshynge with an Angle,* it was an essay included in the second edition of *The Boke of Saint Albans.* Thought to have been written by Dame Juliana Berners—a claim since disputed by revisionist historians—it is the first known manual of sportfishing and the first published work espousing angling for recreation.

The development of fishing tackle has its roots in Europe from that point on. It included various methods of storing line on the rod; these setups were, in effect, predecessors of the reel. Single-action reels, whose purpose was primarily storing and secondarily retrieving line, evolved around this time and were used with natural baits or weightless artificial flies. The advancement of the modern fishhook in the seventeenth century (wood, stone, and bone hooks were used by primitive man, followed by copper, bronze, and iron) is credited to Englishman Charles Kirby, who also invented the Kirby Bend, a type of hook still in use today. By 1770, English rods had gained line guides and reel

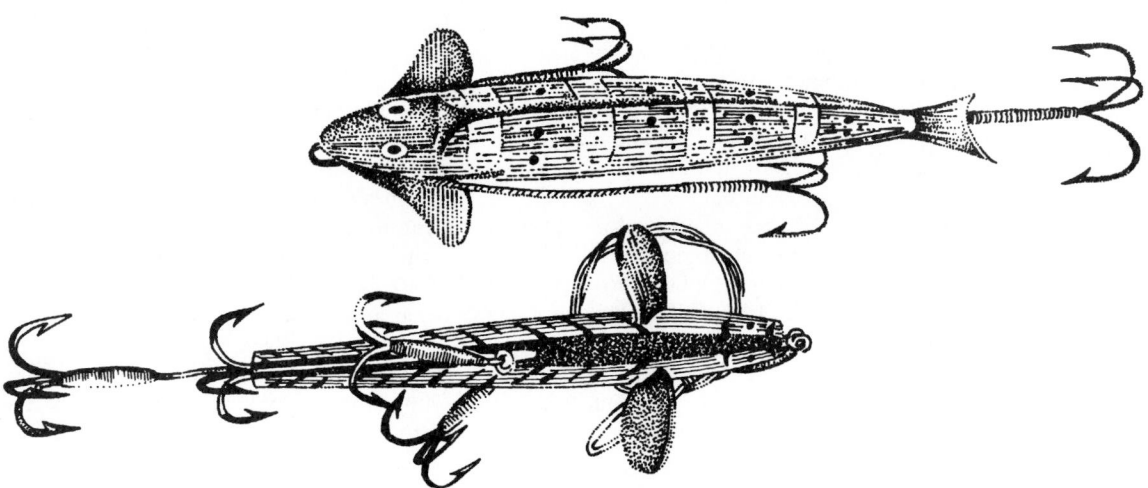

Shown are renditions of the Phantom Minnow (top) and Devon Minnow (bottom).

seats. Numerous artificial lures were developed and widely used in Europe, the most common of which were the Devon lures and Phantom Minnows. These were the primary lures imported and used by a relative few recreational anglers in America. For the most part these lures were made of a combination of hair, metal, and silk.

The modern baitcasting, or multiplier, reel had its origin in England in the latter half of the eighteenth century but did not catch on there. That product, however, was the model for the American craftsmen who fashioned the famous Kentucky reel. Notable among them were Kentucky watchmakers Jonathan Meek and George Snyder, who developed the first baitcasting reels in America around 1800 to 1810. It was at this time that North America joined in the development and manufacture of fishing tackle.

The roots of today's fine baitcasting rods are firmly planted in American soil. In the 1880s, James Henshall invented a new rod that was lighter and shorter than other rods of the time. By contemporary standards, his 8-foot rod was long, but compared to the 10- to 12-footers of the time it was much shorter. When anglers paired it with the Kentucky reel, the combination became extremely popular.

From that point until today, the U.S. has been a major developer, and the foremost consumer, of sportfishing tackle. As a result, the greatest interest in collecting antique fishing tackle revolves around American equipment, especially that produced from the early nineteenth century until about the middle of the twentieth century.

American Sportfishing and Tackle: A General Chronology

1800–10
1. First appearance of the Phantom Minnow in America. Artificial flies and natural baits were the only options heretofore.
2. George Snyder and Jonathan Meek credited with creating the first "Kentucky reels." These were multiple-action casting reels, developed at a time when a single-action revolving-spool reel was the only reel available for sportfishing, and anglers exclusively used natural baits or artificial flies. The single-action reel was primarily employed to store and retrieve line, and had no casting function.

1835–40   The Meeks brothers start the first commercial manufacture of "Kentucky reels."

1844–1925   Development of the "Henshall rod," beginning with Dr. James T. Henshall.

1848   Julio T. Buel begins commercial manufacture of the spoon lure. He actually invented the spoon lure around 1820 by accident, it is said, when a fish struck at a spoon (utensil) he inadvertently dropped from a boat.

1852   Julio T. Buel obtained the first U.S. patent on a spinner.

1859   Riley Haskell received the first known patent for a fishing lure that *mentions* wood as a possible material for the lure body. Haskell's lure was manufactured in metal, and a wooden version has never been found.

1874   First patent granted for an artificial bait that *specifies* the use of wood for the lure body. Patented May 26 by David Huard and Charles M. Dunbar; it is not known if the lure was ever manufactured.

1876   H. C. Brush granted patent for the Brush Floating Spinner on August 22. This is thought to be the first artificial bait actually manufactured that incorporated wood as a major component of the lure.

1880   First known U.S. patent granted for a lure utilizing glass for the body; it was issued to J. Irgens on September 7.

1883
1. Patent for "artificial bait" called the Flying Hellgrammite granted to Harry Comstock, Fulton, New York, on January 30.
2. First patent for the use of luminous paint on an artificial lure granted to Earnest F. Pflueger, founder of the Pflueger Bait Company.

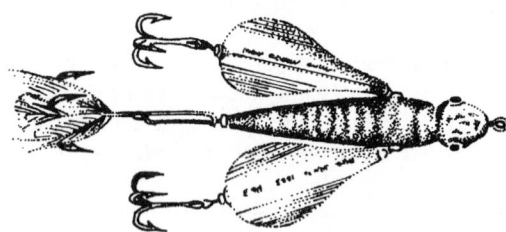

Depicted is a rendition of the 1883 Flying Hellgrammite.

1885   Development of the "Chicago rod," which was 3 feet shorter and more flexible than the 8-foot "Henshall rod." It took a mere five years for it to replace the Henshall product in popularity.

1890s   The beginning of widespread baitcasting in North America. Although the reels had been invented 75 years earlier, it wasn't until this period that lures or plugs were born. James Heddon is generally given credit for inventing the first artificial wooden lure, which is known as the "plug" today. Lore has it that while waiting for a fishing friend, he was whittling on a chunk of wood. He threw it into the water, a bass exploded out of the water striking at it, and an idea was born (see related information later in this entry).

ca. 1900   Theodore Gordon created the first dry-fly patterns appropriate for New World waters around the turn of the twentieth century. Occurring on the Neversink River in the Catskill Mountains of New York, this invention started the American evolution of fly fishing.

1901–2 James Heddon's lure manufacturing company was founded.

1905 First development of the spinning reel. British caster Alfred Holden Illingworth designed and patented a mechanical means of retrieving line and rotating it around a handheld stationary spool. Anglers had previously hand-wound fishing line around stationary objects and used a weight to propel them. This device would not catch on in North America for three decades.

1907 First appearance of jointed wood lures—the "K and K Animated Minnows."

1910 The first widespread use of luminous paint on lure bodies.

ca. 1912 The first "water sonic" plugs appear. The 1912 Bignall and Schaaf "Diamond Wiggler" is thought to be the first of this type.

1913 William C. Boschen catches the first broadbill swordfish (358 pounds) ever taken on sporting rod and reel, using the first internal star drag reel, which he conceptualized and which was made for him by Brooklyn, New York, reel manufacturer Julius Vom Hofe.

ca. 1914 First appearance of fluted plugs. The first was probably the Lockhart "Wobbler Wizard," followed later by the Wilson "Fluted Wobbler" around 1917.

1914 The release of the "Detroit Glass Minnow Tube," thought to be the first commercially available glass lure.

1915 The first appearance of a self-illuminated lure using a battery and bulb—"Dr. Wasweyler's Marvelous Electric Glow Casting Minnow."

ca. 1917 Earliest known advertisement for a lure made of celluloid. This appeared in a May 1917 issue of *National Sportsman* for an Al Foss "Oriental Wiggler," a pork-rind minnow lure. Soon after, his ads began to say "Pyralin," a trade name for celluloid, instead of "celluloid." This may be the first plastic lure.

ca. 1922 The Vesco Bait Company of New York City began advertising artificial baits and spoons made of "DuPont Pyralin."

1932 The Heddon company introduced their "Fish Flesh" plastic lures. The first were the #9100 and #9500 series "Vamps." Soon after, their plastic lures were called "Spooks."

1938 The first spinning reel to be commercially distributed in the U.S., the French-made Luxor was introduced by New York importer Bache Brown. Like the reel developed by Alfred Holden Illingworth in 1905, and unlike other types of fishing reels of the day, it did not use a revolving spool for casting or retrieving line.

1939 The first introduction of nylon monofilament fishing line. Nylon monofilament, also referred to as mono, had a significant impact on rod and reel development, and sportfishing popularity. Synthetic superpolymers were discovered by DuPont research chemist Dr. Wallace H. Carothers in the mid-1930s; nylon was patented by DuPont

in 1937. In 1939, leader material made from nylon was produced by DuPont, becoming the first nylon monofilament fishing line; that same year, nylon stockings were introduced at the New York and San Francisco world's fairs.

1944 Bache Brown designed a spinning reel based on the Luxor and built it in the U.S. Named Airex, it was the first spinning reel made in North America.

1947 R. D. Hull developed the closed-face spinning reel, better known as the spincasting reel. The first production reels, based on Hull's idea, were made in June, 1949, by the Oklahoma-based Zero Hour Bomb Company, later known as Zebco. This reel, which did not use a revolving spool for casting or line retrieval, was very easy to use and gained acceptance in the early 1950s at the same time the spinning reel became popular.

What to Collect

A collection of old fishing tackle can and often does get out of hand. Many collectors devote entire rooms or basements to housing or displaying their wide-ranging collections. Elaborate collections sometimes duplicate old-time bait and tackle shops. While these types of collections are fascinating and fun, most people don't have the resources or space to pursue such elaborate conglomerations. Sooner or later most collectors settle down to a more specialized collection. There are many possibilities.

Specializing in the products of one particular company is a popular concentration. Collecting just old reels is another; these can look like jewels in the right kind of display. An assemblage of all the colors, finishes, and variations that were available on a particular lure can be fascinating and a real challenge. A collection of all metal lures would be of interest. A collection of very old fly rods, fly reels, and flies could be beautiful and even have historical import. In fact, many individual collections have become important enough to tour museum circuits, and some have even become important parts of permanent museum collections. Whatever the area of interest, the hobby of collecting old fishing tackle is not one that is easily abandoned. Collecting becomes a sort of fever, and it is rare that a collector quits. Even those who have disposed of a collection through sale or gift to an institution frequently start anew.

Defining an eclectic collection, at least to a small degree, becomes necessary as it grows. For instance, one might wish to limit a collection to only those items in good to mint condition. This would be difficult, but challenging. However the collection is defined, most collectors, in order to add variety and interest, have a few items from other areas of collectible tackle. Hundreds of accessories are to be found, and many are illustrated in old catalogs and magazine advertisements. The old catalogs and magazines are fascinating and incredibly entertaining to read, not to mention valuable research tools in identifying old tackle.

A

Like humans, whales and porpoises are warm-blooded and breathe with lungs, not gills like fish do; they may have lived on land at one point in time.

An entry in a Marshall Field and Company catalog (ca. 1915) for a "Fishing Alarm Bell" costing five cents and described as "the sleepy fisherman's friend" is a good example of the entertaining aspect of some old catalogs. A 1919 catalog shows that for $1.35 the unlucky angler could obtain a "Line Releaser" complete with a leather carrying case. The copy states in part, "Ever have your fly in a tree? Got mad of course." and goes on to say that the device won't save your temper but will save your line, leader, lure, and possibly even the tip of your rod. It is placed on the tip of the rod, cuts the twig and " . . . down comes twig and your belongings." Where in modern times would one find such a quaint catalog entry?

How and Where to Collect

The four major categories of collectible fishing tackle are Lures, Rods, Reels, and Ephemera. Ephemera is defined as any related material such as tackle catalogs, store displays, pamphlets, and accessories. All share obvious common resources, but ephemera can be found just about anywhere.

Contrary to what some believe, plenty of collectible fishing tackle is yet to be found. The first resource is your own "backyard." Is there an elder in your family who used to fish? Chances are his tackle box is still around. How about your late great-grandfather's tackle box? Look for it. Ask friends and members of your family. Look in the attics, basements, garages, boat houses, well houses, barns, and workshops of not just old family structures, but also newer ones. Many people are loathe to throw out anything that was once treasured by a family member, even if they have no interest in it themselves. An old tackle box is the type of thing that might well have been placed in a dark corner years ago and forgotten.

There are still a few old general stores, hardware stores, and drugstores around; many of these carried tackle, especially lures. Try their storerooms and basements. Many treasures have turned up because someone felt around a dusty top shelf or in the corners of a storage room. Anywhere fishing tackle has been sold for 40 or more years is a good source, although such places are vanishing fast. It could be that present owners or employees may not even know that very old, unsold stock is stuck away somewhere.

Remember trading boards? Some tackle shops still have them. You pay 50 cents or a dollar, put your own lure on the board, and take another of your choice. You might find a collectible lure there. Many tackle shops and repair shops sell used rods and reels. A treasure or two might turn up there too.

Garage sales are particularly good hunting grounds if you're resourceful. Many anglers and most non-anglers don't think of old fishing tackle as particularly marketable and rarely include it in garage or tag sales. Ask if there's any old tackle around. You might be surprised.

Flea markets and junk shops are a source, but not a particularly good one. Dealers have learned that fishing tackle is collectible, and often the prices are way out of line. Most of the time, the tackle is common and/or badly damaged and is offered at grossly inflated prices. Don't ignore this source, however, because anything can happen.

Place a wanted notice on public bulletin boards. Many grocery stores provide them, as do some discount department stores and apartment complexes. Make up a want list with pictures or drawings and pass the list out to friends and relatives. You might even place this on the bulletin boards. Don't use names or numbers. You'll just confuse potential sources.

Don't forget estate sales and auctions. Fishing tackle is often overlooked as significant and just auctioned off as a lot or in a box with other goods not considered important. Sources are limited only by the imagination.

Identifying Old Reels

Many early craftsmen and manufacturers identified their products by engraving or stamping their names and/or patent dates and other information on them. Later, they used decals, hot stamps, transfers, and labels. Many others, however did not bother with any type of identification at all. Identification of these reels can defy even the most knowledgeable of collectors. In addition, many reelmakers furnished jobbers and retailers with their reels but marked them as these quantity buyers wished. This means you might find identical reels of the same vintage with entirely different markings.

The most scarce and valuable reels are those that were handcrafted from about 1800 to 1875. After that, modern mechanized production methods became prevalent. Those early reels were usually signed by the reelsmith and often had beautiful presentation engravings including the name of the craftsman, the recipient, and the date.

Collectors at an auction look over a variety of antique lures.

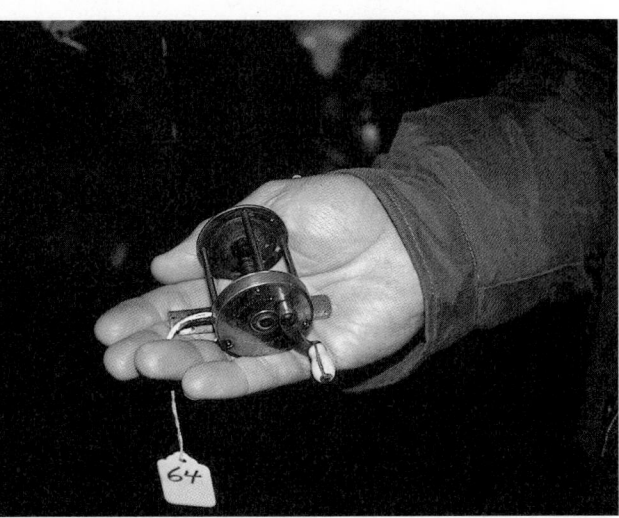

This British-made Ustonson brass winch multiplier reel from approximately the mid–nineteenth century sold for $9,500 at auction in 1998.

George Snyder, the man usually credited with the beginning of the Kentucky reels, made his earliest of brass. All his reels were quadruple multipliers (4:1 ratio). He incorporated jewel pivots and square, steel gears. A watchmaker, Snyder knew that jeweled movements were the most advanced state of pivots at the time. On these early reels, one end of the pillars was riveted to one base plate, and the other end was secured to the other plate by wire. Milam and Hardman improved this later, using screws to secure both ends of the pillars to the base plates. This allowed easier dismantling and reassembly, facilitating lubrication and repairs. The screws on Meek reels made after the period from around 1840 to 1845 were each numbered to match the number stamped at each screw hole. After the Civil War, the reels were made larger, and a double multiplier model was available for the saltwater angler. These early reels are exceedingly rare and valuable.

After mechanized manufacturing began, millions of reels of all shapes, types, and sizes were possible, and the reels found today in the collector market reflect this variety. Experience, a good reference book, and time are necessary for those interested in collecting reels. Start slowly and seek the help of experienced collectors. A good rule of thumb for beginners is if a reel looks good, everything works, and the cost is less than $15, it's probably a good buy.

Identifying Old Rods

Like early reels, most old handmade rods were signed by their makers. The signature is usually found engraved or stamped on the butt cap, but some craftsmen signed them on the shaft, just forward of the handle. If there are no markings at all, check the metal fittings. If the fittings are made of "German silver," the rod is probably an early handcrafted one. German silver (actually not silver at all but an alloy of nickel, copper, and zinc) typically

tarnishes to a dull gray, sometimes tending toward green. There is occasionally a greenish corrosion in crevices or joints. Some of these early rods may also be found with nickel or brass fittings.

Early split cane rods had to be bound at short intervals along their entire length, since the glues and materials used prior to World War I were inferior. After the war, better glues and higher quality cane were used, and the number of wrappings needed was smaller. Often, the binding wrappings were necessary only at the ends of the rods.

The length of an early rod is a good clue to age. Most fly rods made prior to the early 1900s were 10 to 12 or more feet long, while those made afterward are more often found in 6- to 10-foot lengths. In general, baitcasting rods can be evaluated by the same length guidelines, but the collector should be aware that most baitcasting rods are shorter and stiffer than fly rods.

Another, less dependable, method of dating a rod is to examine the hardware, line guides, and handles. Most of the earliest baitcasting rods were made for two-handed gripping. The handles were made of wood and most were ribbed for a better grip. Cork became popular for handles around 1900. Both ribbed and smooth handles continued in wide use, and many were made for single-handed casting. Single-handled rods are often found with a triggerlike addition, which facilitates a more secure grip.

Early line or eye guides were sometimes made collapsible to protect them from damage during transport of the rod. Snake guides and soldered ring or eye guides were developed early on with the snake guide probably coming first. Trumpet-shaped eye guides are also an early development not found on modern rods. The ceramic-type eye guides are not a modern innovation. Many early tackle catalogs illustrate and offer agate eye guides. These are constructed in virtually the same way. The only difference is the use of agate rather than ceramic or some other synthetic material.

The earliest reel seats were simply a place to tie the reel to the rod handle with line. Slide-locking and screw-locking devices followed quickly.

Collectors should be aware that rebuilding rods, changing hardware, and other such replacements, are nothing new, and in the final analysis, identification of an old rod by maker is all but impossible in the absence of a brand name, signature, or other markings.

Identifying Old Lures

Identification of old fishing lures can be easy or very difficult. Identification primarily depends upon who made the plug and how the manufacturer chose to mark his products. Some companies marked them well, some vaguely, and others not at all.

There are some general guidelines for dating and identifying lures. The first thing to do is study the overall appearance of the lure. Most of the older

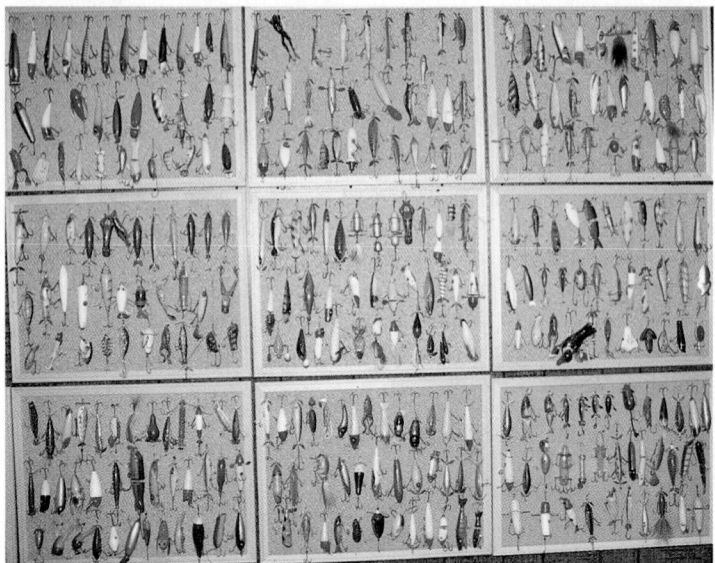

Some antique fishing lures, like those in this collection, are quite valuable.

bass plugs were made of wood and were marvels of craftsmanship, even many that were machine-made in the early days. Most received several coats of high-quality paint. Over time, this paint had a tendency to "check" or "craze," which is the appearance of hairline cracks in the finish. This is a fairly good indication of age; though not all paints on all old lures exhibit this characteristic, some fine finishes did check in just a few years. The collector should also realize that not all the old makers were conscious of quality and that none of them ever gave a thought to their products becoming highly sought collectibles. They most likely would have laughed at the mere mention of the possibility.

The metals used for lure hardware were brass, steel, nickel, and sometimes even gold plate and silver. The earliest hook fastener and line tie hardware was usually a wire passing longitudinally through the body (thru-body), twisted into loops at the front end for the line tie and at the rear end for the tail hook. This made the strongest system. The use of a simple screw eye was the alternative. There were many variations and methods but these two were the most common. The screw eye is the simplest and most common and continues in use today.

The first variation on the screw eye is attributed to the Heddon company circa 1902, when the screw hook was placed in a depression or hole in the body of the lure. This made changing fish hooks easier. Soon after that, Heddon and other companies began using flanges or rimmed metal liners in the screw eye/hook holes to protect the lure. These were soon given bottoms, making them rimmed metal cups. The liners and cups also improved hook presentation. The Creek Chub company used the cup hardware throughout the years they were in business. In 1915, the Heddon company filed a patent for a new hook hanger that collectors call the "L-rig."

Heddon lures have very specific hook hanger hardware progression changes and so are fairly easy

to date. Other companies' hardware progressions are not necessarily so specific, but some have enough to be quite helpful in identification. Pflueger, as a case in point, patented a unique hook hanger called the "Neverfail" in 1911, which helps identify some of their lures.

The type of eye and eye detail is another characteristic helpful to identification. Most earlier plugs didn't have eyes on them at all. Then came a limited use of painted eyes. Glass eyes are common on early lures and a good indication of vintage. There was also the use of plain tacks and painted tacks for eye representation, but it is not possible to tell which came first, the tack eye or the glass eye. It is most likely that they were used concurrently. The tack eye survived long past the glass eye because it was cheaper. The painted eye outlasted the tack eye for the same reason.

The first type of glass eye was slightly rounded, with an opaque yellow iris and a black pupil. The second type was more rounded, with a clear outer section, a yellow tinted iris, and a larger black pupil. These yellow glass eyes vary in size, with the smallest generally being the oldest. The tack eye was one of the latest eye types to be employed before painted eyes became universal. It was a cone-shaped piece of plastic with a hole through the middle for a small tack or brad, which held it on and represented the pupil.

Because they may have been changed one or more times over the years as they were bent or broken in use, types of hooks are usually of no help to identification.

Early plastic lures are quite popular with collectors. In the early days some of the plastic compounds were inherently unstable and subject to self destruction. The earliest plastics were made up of compounds derived from animal and vegetable matter. Many collectors consider these "natural plastics" because of their composition. The first of this genre was created in 1869, when an American named John Hyatt patented a mixture of cellulose, nitrate, and camphor and gave it the trade name celluloid.

In 1910 a completely synthetic plastic was commercially produced. Leo Hendrik Baekelund, a Belgian-born American, invented a dark, thermo-setting resin made of phenol and formaldehyde that was later trade named "Bakelite." Originally available only in a dark brown or reddish color, in 1928 a colorless version that could be tinted any color was invented. Unfortunately, this version was moisture-absorbent until it was refined in 1939. The original dark color was moisture resistant. The famous Al Foss Oriental Wigglers were first made of celluloid in 1917 and later of Bakelite.

Most lure companies didn't get on the plastics bandwagon until the Heddon company introduced their "Spook" series in 1932. This was the beginning of what would later become the widespread manufacture of plastic lures in the United States. Most companies continued with wooden lure production and were still a bit wary of this new material. Although they grasped the versatility of plastics, companies did not begin to widely produce plastic lures until the late 1940s and early 1950s. Many early plastic lures have been found disintegrated after years spent in the darkness of their original boxes. The mixing and ratio of the ingredients was apparently quite critical.

Pricing Collectibles

Pricing collectible tackle is a difficult endeavor. The old adage that "nothin' ain't worth nothin' until somebody wants it" certainly applies to tackle. A fair price could easily be described as what a willing buyer pays a willing seller. That can be quite different from one individual to the next. Price guides are available, but you should choose them with care. Many are written by collectors themselves, and the prices in the guide may or may not be influenced by what the collector/writer wants to buy or sell. Many serious collectors prefer to trade if they can. Members of the National Fishing Lure Collectors Club are able to contact other collectors for buying, selling, and trading through a membership directory. The club has an annual meeting where members display tackle collectibles for sale or trade. Some of these meetings produce over 600 tables. Regional shows may be more convenient in terms of size and geographical location. The meetings and shows are the best venues for the collector. The NFLCC has a very informative quarterly newsletter and a beautiful twice-yearly magazine. Many collectors send for-sale lists to the general membership. All of these publications can be very helpful in determining a value. The NFLCC also has a standard grading system that members use to describe condition and an ethical code for dealing.

Buying, Selling, and Trading Tips

- Knowledge is power. Get and study as much reliable printed data as you can find.
- Handle as much tackle as you can as often as you can. Intimate familiarity with the things you collect can help you avoid mistakes.
- Mutual cooperation builds better collections. Ask for help from knowledgeable collectors and, after you get smart, give an edge to those who helped you in the beginning.
- If you find you have a treasure, don't be greedy; be fair. If you don't deal fairly, you may find your sources drying up.
- If you find that you've made a bad deal, don't worry over it; learn from it. Turn lemons into lemonade by knowing better next time.
- Always make an offer. Nothing ventured, nothing gained. Remember that one person's trash is another person's treasure.
- Honest mistakes are made. If you build a good rapport with, and a good reputation among, collector friends, most mistakes can be rectified painlessly. Keep in mind, however, that it

is not possible to make all deals mutually fair, only mutually acceptable. Don't squawk if you later find the deal wasn't so good after all. You can't win them all.

Tackle Collector Organizations

The National Fishing Lure Collectors Club (NFLCC); HCR #3, Box 4012; Reed Spring, MO 65737. The NFLCC is the premier organization of fishing tackle collectors. It publishes a quarterly newsletter, a full color magazine, and a directory of its over 3,000 members. No one interested in collecting old fishing tackle can do without a membership. The club has a large reference library service, a club shop, fishing tackle collection insurance, and other services.

Old Reel Collectors Association; 849 NE 70th Avenue; Portland, OR 97213. This very helpful organization for collectors of old fishing reels puts them in touch with each other through its newsletter.

Informative Books

Collecting antique fishing tackle is an extremely entertaining pastime, but reading about the history, development, and attendant lore and legend is fascinating, fun, and educational. The best way to master this hobby is to learn as much about it as possible. Dozens of books and publications cover this collecting discipline, and to buy them all represents a significant cash outlay. The following are fundamental references, some of which are periodically updated and revised in new editions.

Old Fishing Lures and Tackle—An Identification and Value Guide by Carl F. Luckey, Books Americana/Krause Publications, Iola, WI. The biggest and most comprehensive reference available on collecting fishing tackle. The main thrust is lures, but it has a fairly large section on reels and a discussion of rods. This book is a must for the lure collector.

Fishing Tackle Antiques and Collectibles by Karl T. White, Holli Enterprises, OK. An excellent and thorough research tool for the lure collector. It illustrates thousands of lures, rods, and reels in color and has value assessments.

Fishing Lure Collectibles by Dudley Murphy and Rick Edmisten, Collector Books, Paducah, KY. A very good full-color book dedicated to the most collectible antique fishing lures, and an excellent identification and value guide.

Antique and Collectible Fishing Reels by Harold Jellison and D. B. Homel, Forrest Park Publishers, Bellingham, WA. A comprehensive guide to the identification, valuation, and maintenance of all types of reels. It is profusely illustrated with

A

detailed photographs, color plates, and historic patent drawings. A must for the old-reel collector.

Lawson's Price Guide to Old Fishing Reels by Stu Lawson, Monterey Bay Publishing, Capitola, CA. The most comprehensive value guide for reels, with over 5,900 reel listings and 103 photo plates of numerous reels.

Antique & Collectible Fishing Rods by D. B. Homel, Forrest Park Publishers, Bellingham, WA. An excellent, authoritative guide to all sorts of rods, including wood, steel, fiberglass, and split bamboo versions. It includes important design patents and the history of rod materials, with close-up photos of ferrules, reel seats, and other distinguishing characteristics. Invaluable for the rod collector.

Fish-Bait: The First Plug

The introduction to Patent No. 696,433, issued on April 1, 1902 by the United States Patent Office to James Heddon, for an invention titled "Fish-Bait," reads as follows:

> *Be it known that I, James Heddon, a citizen of the United States, residing at the city of Dowagiac, in the county of Cass and State of Michigan, have invented certain new and useful Improvements in Fish-Baits, of which the following is a specification.*
>
> *This invention relates to improvements in fish-baits.*
>
> *The objects of the invention are to provide an improved casting or trolling bait which shall be conspicuous, and which shall be effective in presenting the hooks to the best advantage for catching the fish, and which is provided with means for keeping the same one side up, and which is provided with means for producing conspicuous agitation of the water, and which in view of the number of hooks which it carries is quite effective in avoiding weeds.*

Legend has it that one day James Heddon carved a piece of wood into the shape of a fish and tossed it into the water. A bass struck the "plug" of wood, and the idea for fishing plugs was born. That's an oft-repeated, perhaps somewhat accurate, yet hazy condensation of the actions of the man generally credited with devising the genre of lures we call plugs, one of the most historic developments in American angling history.

Heddon was no ordinary whittler. The 1902 patent was one of many he held. And the plug that he carved on the day in question may or may not have been his first. But it was definitely one of the first and a catalyst for millions to follow. The exact

details of when and how his Fish-Bait invention came about are not completely clear.

The father of the casting plug was by trade a bee-keeper. He was also a six-time patent holder and manufacturer of beekeeping equipment, book author, newspaper owner and publisher, and angler. He had been making lures out of wood since approximately 1890. Some accounts say that he gave them to friends and family and that around 1891 or 1892 he started making wooden frogs for bass fishing.

The exact date when Heddon whittled a fish shape and threw it into the water isn't known for certain. It may have been in the early 1890s. Some accounts have it happening in the early 1900s just prior to his 1902 patent. Many have reported that the incident took place on Dowagiac Creek near his apiary; some say it was on the creek pond near the dam that was built to run a nearby flour mill.

The most reliable of the five or more versions of this story may be anecdotal evidence from Larry Bowers, who rowed the boat for Heddon while he fished. In 1962, Bowers told Trig Lund, Dowagiac historical buff and Heddon company employee, that one day James Heddon was waiting by the pond for George Melvin, manager of the flour mill. While waiting he whittled a piece of wood and skipped it along the water. A bass hit it. A week or two later, Heddon made a plug from a corn cob and attached hooks to it. With Bowers rowing for him, Heddon caught seven bass on the corn cob lure. Eventually, though, the cob soaked up water, sunk, and didn't work. A few weeks later Heddon made his first slope-nosed plug from wood. This was the forerunner of the Fish-Bait that he patented in 1902.

At some point, perhaps later in 1902 after his lure was patented and a manufacturing company established, Heddon caught and kept 73 bass on his slope-nosed Fish-Bait, which would later be known as the Old Dowagiac Minnow. One account says the fish were caught in LaGrange Pond, 5 miles east of Dowagiac. The catch stirred up a lot of excitement. A published account states that he sent a photograph to a publication, but the editor replied " . . . if you had followed the usual method of fish hogs and stood beside the string, I should have been glad to print the picture in order that decent men might recognize you when they see you and shun you . . . ."

Another published attribution stated that Heddon's catch, which included a 6-pound large-mouth black bass, had a total weight of 114 pounds and noted, "This wholesale slaughtering of bass has started an agitation which may result in presenting a petition to the legislature asking for passage of a law that will prohibit the use of more than one hook on a bait when angling for bass."

Time has blurred the boundary between fact and fiction in the circumstances surrounding the development of the first plug. It is known for certain, however, that Heddon applied for his slope-nosed Fish-Bait patent on January 9, 1902. It was granted a few months later, on April Fool's Day.

James Heddon started the lure manufacturing company bearing his name sometime between 1900 and 1902. His son Will joined him in the business shortly thereafter. In 1903 the company was called James Heddon and Son. A few years later Son was changed to the plural when son Charles got into the business, and then later to James Heddon's Sons. Will and Charles are credited with much of the company's success. They were both accomplished anglers; Charles was a good businessman, and Will an ardent lure developer.

For a while the company was located and lures were manufactured in James Heddon's house. The plug manufacturing business moved to another building and then to a newly built factory. James Heddon died at his home in Dowagiac on December 7, 1911. That same year Will moved to Florida. Charles took over the tackle business, which would later include fishing rods; he successfully expanded the business, and ran the company until his death in Dowagiac in 1941. The company was later sold several times. It went from being one of the foremost tackle companies and lure manufacturing businesses in the world to an also-ran and then became almost nonexistent. In 1983, it was purchased by Pradco, a large tackle company, which continues to produce a few of Heddon's top lures of the past.

Lures are no longer manufactured in Dowagiac. There is a small historical display on the Heddon business at Southwestern Michigan College in Dowagiac, and a James Heddon Memorial Park at the old mill pond on the East Branch of Dowagiac Creek. It's a typical small lily pad pond with a variety of warmwater species, a lot of fishing pressure, and a sign that proclaims "first artificial fishing lure developed on this site in 1893."

Of course, Heddon did not create the first artificial fishing lure. He may have created the first fishing plug that you could cast and troll with its own built-in action. What he did above all was hook anglers forever.

See: Baitcasting Tackle; Conventional Tackle; Flycasting Tackle; Kentucky Reel; Line; Lure; Spincasting Tackle; Spinning Tackle.

ANTI-REVERSE
A switch that allows the handle and the gears of a reel to be put in reverse by turning it to the off position, or that keeps the reel automatically and constantly out of reverse by turning it to the on position. A reel with such a switch is said to have selective anti-reverse, meaning that the angler has a choice. A reel without such a switch cannot be turned backward, so there is no such choice.

When a reel is in the anti-reverse mode (or if it has nonselective anti-reverse), as the handle is turned forward to retrieve line and then stopped,

or when a fish stops the retrieve by striking, the natural tendency is to pull up on the handle. In older-model reels, and in some lesser-quality current models, there is considerable play in the handle and rotor when the reel stops, and the handle may actually turn backward slightly before stopping. This tendency produces a feeling of sloppiness or instability; too much backward movement of the handle may adversely affect hooksetting and may allow a loop of slack line to appear on the spool in some retrieval motions, which may eventually impair casting. Ideally the reel should engage instantly and firmly, and better reels have features that allow this, which are usually called continuous anti-reverse or infinite anti-reverse. These should keep the drive gear from moving even the slightest bit backward, and most operate silently.

See: Baitcasting Tackle; Big-Game Tackle; Conventional Tackle; Flycasting Tackle; Spincasting Tackle; Spinning Tackle.

APOGEE
The point in the moon's orbit farthest from the earth, producing a lower tidal range.
See: Tides.

AQUACULTURE
The raising of fish or shellfish under some controls, usually for the purpose of commercial sale. Ponds, pens, tanks, or other containers may be used. Feed is often used. This term is applied generically to the raising of fish in either freshwater or saltwater, although it is usually more often associated with the latter because saltwater fish have more commercial interest. The word "fish farming" is often used to describe aquaculture operations, particularly in freshwater (resulting in the term "farm-raised" fish in restaurants), and "mariculture" refers strictly to the raising of marine species. A hatchery is also aquaculture, although hatcheries operated by government agencies usually release fish before commercial harvest size is reached, and usually raise them for the purpose of supplementing gamefish stocks. Private hatcheries may raise fish to be sold for private stocking efforts, or for commercial sale to food processors, fish markets, and restaurants.

As of the late 1990s, over 181 species of fish and shellfish were known to be raised through aquaculture, including trout, catfish, carp, tilapia, scallops, clams, and oysters, although shrimp and salmon dominate international markets.
See: Hatchery; Mariculture.

AQUATIC INSECTS
Aquatic insects spend all or part of their lives in water. They are very diverse and abundant in freshwater, especially in rivers and lakes, where fish feed on their immature and adult forms. So prominent

The Columbia River is not only the largest North American river entering the Pacific; but, together with its tributaries, it is the most important trout and salmon drainage in the world.

A

are aquatic insects in the diet of trout that they form the basis of most fly fishing activities for trout in rivers and streams, and are the object imitated by countless artificial flies.

The most abundant aquatic insects are mayflies, caddisflies, stoneflies, midges, dragonflies, and damselflies. They have varying life cycles, generally a year but ranging from two months to four years. That life cycle encompasses the egg to the immature nymph that emerges on the water's surface, where it hatches into a winged adult. Depending on species, life after hatching lasts only a few hours, days, or weeks; the adults mate, lay eggs on the water, and die. During each of these stages, they are consumed by fish, and artificial flies need to imitate the proper species and stage of the respective aquatic insects. Some anglers develop a great understanding of aquatic insects for both their fly tying and fly fishing endeavors.

See: Caddisflies; Dobsonflies, Fishflies, and Alderflies; Dragonflies and Damselflies; Mayflies; Midges; Stoneflies; Terrestrial Insects.

AQUATIC PLANTS

Most bodies of water support some type and quantity of plant life. Plants are important components of aquatic ecosystems because of their multiple functions. Plants act as a soil stabilizer, trapping sediments from erosion and causing these particles to settle out of the water near shore. In shallow water they protect shores from erosion caused by wave action. They provide nesting materials and sites for various species of birds and fish. They are important nursery areas for young fish, especially many gamefish species. They release oxygen to the water. And, most importantly, they provide food for many organisms that live in the water, as well as for some animals that do not.

Aquatic plants belong to two main groups: algae and flowering plants. Algae *(see)* are the most common and widely distributed of all aquatic plants

and are found in both freshwater and saltwater; kelp *(see)* is a form of algae. Flowering plants, most of which are rooted to the bottom, are also found in both freshwater and saltwater, and are the most conspicuous aquatic plants.

Flowering plants fall into three categories: emergents, submergents, and floaters. Emergents grow along the edges of water, with only short portions of their stems and roots submerged; they are sometimes called marsh plants. Common emergents include arrowhead, bulrush, burreed, cattail, pickerelweed, rushes, and sedges. Many of these have arrow- or spear-shaped leaves. Because of their very shallow or marshy existence, these plants are usually not direct influences on sportfish or on angling, except during high water periods.

Submergent plants grow in deeper water, are usually attached to the bottom, and gain most of their nutrients from sediments; many have a complete underwater existence, like the seagrasses *(see)* of shallow saltwater flats and estuaries, but others flower above the water surface. Common submergents in freshwater include elodea, coontail, milfoil, bladderwort, fanwort, naiad, eelgrass, watercress, hydrilla, and various pondweeds. These are significant aquatic plants for anglers, since many species are attracted to them for shelter and food, and much fishing is done in or around such vegetative forms.

Most floaters are rooted plants, with most of their plant structure, especially leaves, floating on the water surface; they absorb nutrients from the muddy bottom and their flowers are pollinated by insects. Floaters can also be unattached plants that obtain nutrients through small rootlets dangling in the water. These aquatic plants include duckweed, lotus, spatterdock, waterprimrose, watershield, white waterlily, waterlettuce, and waterhyacinth. Floaters also attract many fish species and are important for anglers.

In freshwater, fish rely on aquatic plants to varying degrees. Few actually eat the plants (carp, goldfish, and other cyprinids are exceptions), yet the plants provide food for many organisms that are consumed by fish. Many large and small fish also rely on plants for shelter from light, extreme warm temperatures, and predation; generally, plants with larger leaves provide the best cover and attract larger fish. Dense plant growths, however, can provide so much cover from predators that the prey may become stunted. While aquatic plants are also a vital source of oxygen in the water, they can also deplete oxygen when they decompose and are overly dense.

Aquatic plants are the subject of considerable debate and controversy among various water users. Anglers have seen that increased aquatic plant growth, especially in water bodies that had little or no such life before, has improved fish populations, especially for largemouth bass and sunfish. Yet other water users, and lakefront homeowners, may

Most anglers call them weeds, but aquatic plants are both good and bad for fish and for angling.

be disturbed by the thick wads of plants that grow. As a result, there are many chemical, biological, and mechanical control efforts enacted in water bodies to eliminate or reduce plant communities, and these efforts may have short-term or long-term impacts on the abundance and composition of fish species in the affected water.

Although most aquatic plants are native to their body of water or to the overall region in which they occur, some are not, and many plants have been inadvertently spread to places where they should not be by various means, including transportation on the hulls of boats and on the trailers that carry them. When exotic (nonnative) species of plants are introduced to new environments, they can have serious adverse impacts, and it's important to make sure that they do not get stuck on boats, motors, and trailers prior to leaving that waterway. Another common means of exotic plant introduction is through the dumping of aquarium water that contains nonnative aquarium plants; this should never be emptied into a water body.

Fishing.   The majority of freshwater fishing occurring around aquatic plants is for largemouth bass, although some also occurs for walleye, northern pike, muskellunge, various sunfish, crappie, yellow perch, and bullhead. Anglers find that there are varying concentrations of aquatic plants—which most people simply lump under the umbrella of "weeds"—to contend with, and that the most dense are very hard to deal with. All of it can be fished, though you can't get your boat through the worst of it except by poling. Some types of plants extend through and cover the surface, as well as being submerged several feet, or they can be shallow or deep. You have to adjust to each situation, but certain patterns hold true for all conditions, and some lure types receive prominent usage. Pinpointing the location of the edges, which are called weedlines, is often a crucial element in determining boat position, lure presentation, and fishing technique. Sonar can be a big asset in this situation.

Before fishing in vegetation, it's a good idea to study things a bit to see where the water drops off and to find the plants, plant edges, and perhaps the bait and other fish. Finding plants, of course, is relatively simple, but studying them—determining conformations, edges, and depths—is a little more involved. The objective is to find the better places to spend fishing time.

Density is one element to look for; seek thick clumps as opposed to scattered plants, because the former offer more cover. Clumped plants are the easiest situation to fish. If they are not available, scattered plants become the second choice. Look to see if plants in a given locale grow in different stages or at different levels. Shorter plants in moderately deep water, for example, are often preferred by such fish as walleye over taller plants in the same depth.

Look for the weedline and its depth. An excellent situation to find, though not one as readily fished, is where the plants are thick and the edge is close to a sharp bottom dropoff.

The most obvious, most often used, and most easily managed way to locate fish in vegetation is to work the edges. In large, fairly thick concentrations, for example, many species of gamefish stick close to the outside line, most likely because they can see and ambush prey there. This is especially true if this vegetation is so congested that you can't work any type of lure across the surface without it being fouled up. Milfoil beds are a prime example of this type of cover. Here, you may have to work the edges, with most strikes (from bass) occurring within a foot or two of the edge. Any irregularity in the weedline, such as a protrusion, pocket, and so on, may be an especially significant place to fish.

Frequently the key to unlocking the secrets of catching fish (especially largemouth bass) in sparse vegetation is to fish isolated clumps, small but thick patches that stand off from the main mass (they may be within the main body as well as outside). Take care to identify and fish every likely looking isolated patch. Usually there is a lot of ground to cover, and if you find a spot that is more worthwhile than others, work it thoroughly.

When the vegetation is sparse and partly submerged, you won't be able to find isolated patches such as these. However, if you're using sonar, you may be able to identify the thin and thick sections, as well as dropoffs or holes, by traveling across the area first. If either emergent or submerged plants are thick and you see visible holes, start casting. Clearings are prime fishing locations, and they are easier to fish than the thick spots.

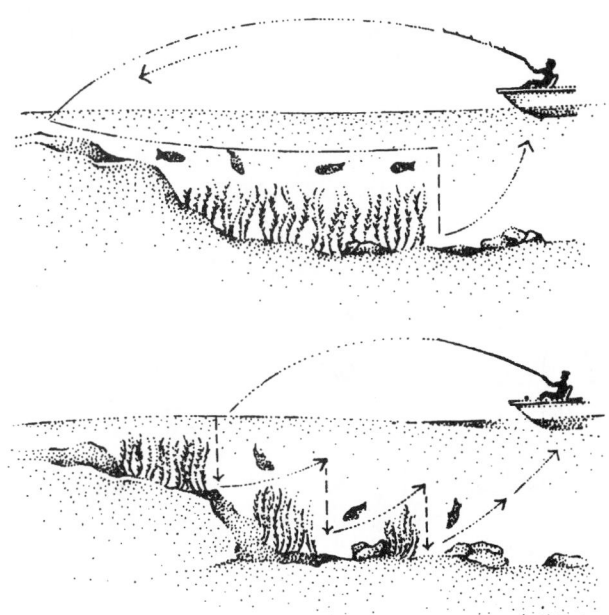

Methods of fishing in, along, and through submerged vegetation vary with type and conformation.

A

The key to the success and enjoyment of vegetation fishing is a weed-free, or so-called weedless, presentation, and your lure naturally plays the lead role. There are relative degrees of weedlessness in lures, just as there are relative degrees of manipulative retrieving skills, but there is no out-of-the-box, guaranteed-never-to-get-stuck fishing lure.

The plastic worm can be one of the most tangle-free lures, although it will hang up if the hook pulls through the plastic body or the sinker gets wedged. The key to using a slip sinker in vegetation is to fish the lightest one that you can toss and that will get the worm down adequately, and also to peg it with a toothpick. In grass or pad stems, or other vegetation, a free-sliding slip sinker pulls off the object, leaving the worm behind. You need to have the two working close together to achieve a proper, natural presentation.

Worms are primarily used for bass. These fish and others may prefer something that moves more enticingly, with a flash of metal. The weedless spoon and pork rind trailer has justifiably been a longtime favorite of bass, pickerel, and pike anglers. In moderately heavy cover, it is fairly tangle-free, and its action is reasonably good when drawn into open pockets from the clustered vegetation. Another popular combination incorporates an in-line spinner, a spoon, and a skirt. There are also good buzzbaits on the market, some of which incorporate a buzzing blade and shaft with a spoon, or spoonlike body; such lures work well over submerged vegetation. For good measure, you can also add a trailer hook to both of these arrangements. The trailer will mean more hooked fish per strike, though it also means more snagging on pad stems, grass clumps, and similar cover.

Spinnerbaits are a particularly effective lure when used near vegetation. When pads and grass are not too thick, as is usual in spring or early summer, a spinnerbait is the best lure for bass and one of the best for northern pike and chain pickerel. For thicker grass and pads, a spinnerbait can be effective when worked on the edges, either fishing parallel along them or fluttering it down vertically along the edges.

Some plugs have merit in and around vegetation, although they must be cast and retrieved judiciously. When fishing over the top of submerged grass, super-shallow-running floating/diving plugs, sonic vibrating plugs, and surface lures are effective. Surface lures will also work in areas that feature openings or channels through which they can be retrieved, and a few are capable of being slithered over the tops of even thick exposed vegetation. A crankbait might be worth using if the plants are not thick; crankbaits are very popular in walleye fishing, for example, but in weedy environs are mostly reserved for earlier in the season. A fine time to catch these fish on plugs is when the first green plants start to show. Jigs might also be worth a try, although they are not usually used in vegetation. A float-and-jig combo works well on windy days in the plants, and straight-lined jigs tipped with bait may also be used if you can maintain a good feel with them.

Bait is fished in and near grass, too. Shiners and worms are fished below bobbers in openings or just above submerged grass, as well as behind jigs and various bait rigs. Of course, attention must be paid to minimizing the fouling of these items. A float with a jig-leech/worm combo is a choice of walleye anglers. Fishing with large live shiners in vegetation is a specialty of many Florida guides, who use these baits in heavily matted saw grass, peppergrass, and hayfields, as well as around floating mats of hyacinths, where the bait can be freelined to swim well back and under this expansive cover.

When vegetation is so thick that you could almost walk across it, and the edges don't produce, you have to deal with fishing deep within, which poses obvious boating dilemmas and presentation troubles, and is primarily a need of largemouth bass anglers. Sometimes there are small holes in the mass that can be readily fished, but more often you wind up making your own hole and dunking in your lure (worm or jig). There is no casting here, just reaching over a hole, dunking the lure up and down, and moving on. You may even use your rod or an oar to poke the hole.

Vegetation fishing usually requires fairly stout tackle. This is not a place for real light line and limber rods, unless fishing for small species. Also, angling in vegetation often seems to be more productive in low-light situations than in bright daylight. Bright days tend to drive fish deeper and further into the vegetation, where they are harder to reach effectively. Dawn, dusk, and overcast days offer the best vegetation fishing conditions. Night is a good time as well.

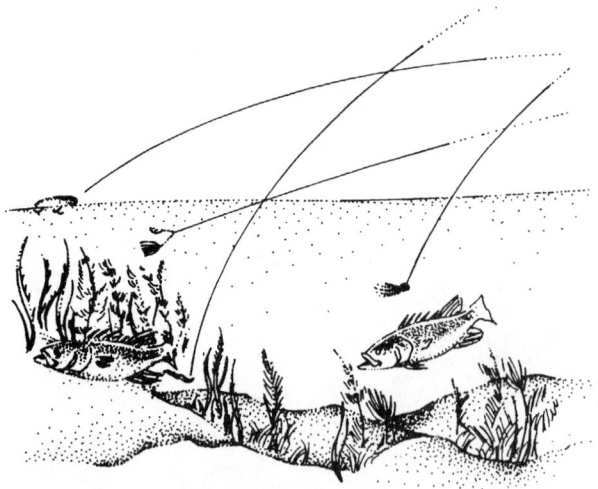

A surface lure, spinnerbait, plastic worm, and jig (left to right) are effective for catching bass around aquatic plants.

Arapaima

ARAPAIMA *Arapaima gigas.*

Other names—piraruçu, giant arapaima, payshi, pirarocou, anatto, lou-lou, warapaima; Portuguese: *piraruçu;* Spanish: *paiche.*

The largest wholly freshwater fish, the arapaima reportedly grows up to 15 feet long. It is fished commercially and is a much-favored food fish in Brazil, usually available in public markets. The arapaima has gained minor familiarity with native anglers and with a few international traveling sportsmen, many of whom know it as piraruçu. Young arapaima are frequently displayed in public aquariums.

Identification. A large-scaled, big-eyed fish, the arapaima has pelvic fins well behind the base of its pectoral fins, most with scales but some with supra-branchial organs capable of breathing air; it also has a highly vascularized swim bladder that functions partially as a lung, and it can absorb oxygen from either water or air.

Size. The average length for arapaima is 6 feet, but it is known to grow up to 8 feet and 200 pounds. Some reports indicate the existence of specimens twice as large and heavy.

Distribution. Found in northern South America, the arapaima is common in the Amazon River and its branches in Brazil and Peru, as well as in freshwater lakes.

Habitat. Mostly inhabiting quiet waters, arapaima are usually spotted drifting or rolling in surface waters.

Life history/Behavior. The arapaima builds a nest about 2 feet in diameter in sandy bottoms among submerged plants. It spawns in April and May, laying about 47,000 eggs and guarding the young. Attracted by a pheromone secreted from glands in the skin of the parent's head, the young gather about the parent's head for protection.

Food and feeding habits. Little has been documented about the feeding habits of arapaima, although they are believed to be omnivorous.

Angling. Arapaima have been known to strike artificial lures, but they are an infrequent rod-and-reel catch. In Brazil they are speared and caught commercially in nets.

See: Brazil.

ARAWANA *Osteoglossum bicirrhosum.*

Other names—aruana, silver aruana; Portuguese: *aruanã;* Spanish: *arahuana.*

A fine food fish, the arawana is also a splendid gamefish as well as a popular aquarium fish in Asia.

Identification. The arawana has large scales, big eyes, and a head protected by a hard bone. Its elongated dorsal and anal fins are located very far back on the body and are barely separated from the tail. Like the arapaima, to which it is related, the arawana has a vascularized air bladder that acts as a lung. It also has two fleshy barbels on its lower jaw that are assumed to have a sensory function. A distinctive and identifying feature is its lower jaw, which slants sharply upward.

Size. The arawana grows to usually less than 2 feet in length, although it is believed to attain at least 3 feet in size. It can weigh as much as 11 pounds.

Distribution. Arawana primarily occur in central and northern South America, mostly in the Amazon drainage of Brazil and Peru.

Habitat. Arawana inhabit the same environs as arapaima *(see)*—mostly shallow, quiet backwaters. They live in marginal lagoons and small tributaries of large rivers during the dry season, and in flooded backwaters during the high-water season.

Life history/Behavior. Not much is known about the life history of this species. The arawana is believed to carry its eggs in its mouth until they have hatched, and to follow and protect its fry by holding them in its mouth.

Feeding habits. The arawana is said to be an opportunistic feeder, lurking on the bottom as well as feeding at middepths and near the surface. It is known to leap high out of the water to take fruit from overhanging branches, and it may be omnivorous. Some observers have reported that it can jump 6 feet out of the water to capture prey.

Angling. The arawana is a popular although unpredictable and infrequent catch for anglers. It is a strong fighter, takes artificial lures, and is usually caught in or near shallow areas in quiet backwaters, usually close to shore and in brushy habitat. Most anglers who encounter arawana do so when using large and noisy lures intended for peacock bass, and

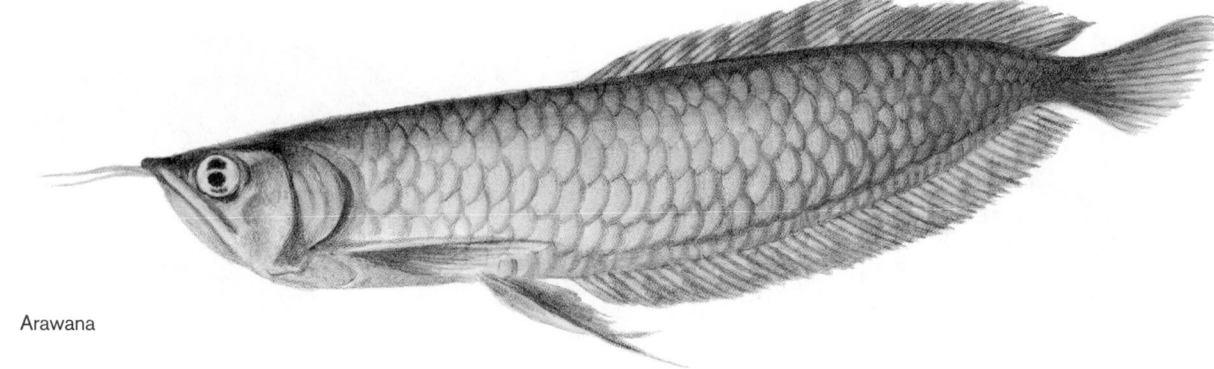

Arawana

it is possible that more refined presentations could produce more of this species. Arawana are netted commercially in Brazil and are commonly found in fish markets there.
See: Brazil.

ARGENTINA

The second largest country in South America (after Brazil), Argentina has a surprisingly modest diversity of gamefish species, especially compared to Brazil, but it makes up for this by offering some of the finest trout fishing in the world, especially in the coldwater rivers of Patagonia and Tierra del Fuego. Saltwater fishing along the lengthy Atlantic coast has little to offer the visiting angler, although sea-run trout in the southern rivers are highly commendable, and dorado fishing in the north is spotty but exciting when at its best. Ironically, Argentina's salmonids are all imports, resulting from fortuitous stockings early in the twentieth century. A good food base and appropriate coldwater lakes and rivers have contributed to a healthy fishery.

This 2,070-mile-long country encompasses more than 2.8 million square miles of land, and its thousands of miles of rivers—some of which contain above-average-size trout—are well spread out. Many of these waters are on the eastern fringe of the Andes, which form a boundary on the west with Chile, and especially in the Patagonian Andes, which seldom exceed 12,000-foot elevations.

Argentina's topography is varied, including mountains, upland areas, and plains. The northwestern mountains boast peaks above 21,000 feet, the highest of which is Aconcagua. At 22,834 feet, it is higher than all other peaks in the world, excluding those in central Asia. The region east of the Andes is largely a flat or lightly rolling plain that slopes gradually from about 2,000 feet to sea level. In the north, these plains are the southern component of South America's Gran Chaco, and are succeeded for nearly 1,000 miles by the pampas—treeless plains that contain Argentina's major agricultural lands. South of the pampas, and roughly below the Rio Colorado, the terrain consists largely of arid, desert plateaus known as

Patagonia. This southern region of Argentina covers about 300,000 square miles and includes the eastern, or Argentine, part of Tierra del Fuego, an archipelago off the southern tip of South America.

Northern Region

The dorado is northern Argentina's main claim to piscatorial fame. This exotic and powerful species has been locally revered, especially along the Paraná River, a mighty flow that courses through the north-central region. The Paraná originates in Brazil, forms the border of Paraguay and Brazil and of Paraguay and Argentina, is joined by the Paraguay River north of the Argentine city of Corrientes, and then heads south and southeast through Argentina and eventually to the Atlantic Ocean at Rio de la Plata. The Paraná and other rivers in this region have been dammed in places, which has ruined some of the best dorado fishing areas and also greatly reduced the likelihood of catching the monsters (50- to 70-pounders) previously taken here.

Today the majority of dorado fishing is concentrated in the northeastern region of Argentina, in an area of Corrientes province roughly enclosed by a border running from Esquina to Corrientes to Posadas to Mercedes and back to Esquina. The Paraná, above its merger with the Paraguay River to south of Posadas, and a large swampy backwater region to the south of this known as Esteros del Ibera, offer prime dorado fishing.

Ibera is a 20,000-square-kilometer region of swamps and grassland with a maze of channels, lagoons, bays, and streams. This region provides water to the Rio Corrientes, which in turn joins the Paraná. Most importantly, it is a clear-water system, which is important for catching the aggressive sight-feeding dorado, and it has a steady flow of water with abundant forage.

In 1996, a lodge was completed on the banks of the Esteros, and anglers explore the region by boat from there. Known for wildlife viewing, the area also hosts surubim catfish, piranhas, pacu, and other Amazonian species. Anglers have success with spinning, baitcasting, and flycasting tackle. The largest dorado caught by angling (larger ones have been speared by natives) in recent years was

reportedly a 42-pounder, but the average fish weighs between 3 and 12 pounds. The dorado in this slow- or stillwater region are good fighters, but not as demanding as those found in fast river currents. The area is accessed from Corrientes or Mercedes, and the best season is reportedly summer, from September through March.

On the Paraná, the town of Paso de la Patria, about a half-hour ride from Corrientes, is the main jumping-off point for big-river fishing. Site of an acclaimed annual dorado festival, Paso de la Patria is a small village with a few hotels and restaurants, mostly geared toward a summer influx of tourists.

The Paraná's strong current and a chance to catch dorado from 30 to 45 pounds dictate big-water tackle and tactics. Sturdy baitcasting reels with long-handled rods and 14- to 25-pound line are the primary tackle. Favored fishing methods include trolling with deep-diving plugs, casting plugs to the shoreline, and drifting with live bait. Cleaner nearby tributaries provide other opportunities, though generally for smaller fish, and other species are available as well. Accommodations exist in Corrientes and Paso de la Patria.

Here, the summer fishing season runs from October through April. Unfortunately, the Paraná, as well as other big area rivers, are subject to fluctuating water levels due to rainfall, and high muddy water does not bode well for big-river fishing.

Patagonia

The northern portion of this region contains the lake region of the Patagonian Andes, and rivers that flow either east toward the Atlantic or west toward the Pacific through Chile. Nahuel Huapi National Park contains the famous lake of the same name, which is an Argentine favorite and certainly a tourist attraction, but not a fishery that attracts many visiting anglers. Visitors are more inclined to cast in the rivers than to troll and fish deep in the lake (something that North Americans can do less expensively, although perhaps in less delightful surroundings, in numerous homeland lakes).

Nahuel Huapi covers 557 square kilometers, with large islands and many peninsulas and deep arms. It is fed by several rivers, including the Espejo, Correntoso, Gallardo, Moreno, Gutierrez, and Frias, and its outlet is the Limay River, which flows eastward. The lake reportedly has depths to 454 meters and contains a variety of species, including introduced brown trout, rainbow trout, and landlocked Atlantic salmon. It has produced huge brown and rainbow trout in the past, and is next to the alpine village of San Carlos de Bariloche, making it readily accessible for even a short visit by anglers headed to the rivers north and south, who might want to try for big browns ascending the tributaries to spawn in the fall. Other lakes of note in the region include Traful, which had the first stocking of landlocked salmon, Correntoso, Espejo, and Gutierrez, but there are many smaller ones as well.

As mentioned, visiting anglers focus their attention on the rivers of this region. Bariloche is the hub of upper-Patagonia trout fishing, and it has many guides. The casual tourist interested in a day or two of angling while traveling in the region can find assistance here, with or without speaking Spanish. Many visitors, however, use outfitters and established camps and lodges with access to specific waters, many of which are on ranches in remote areas and offer less pressured and more private resources. Argentine law permits public access to all streams, provided that such access originates from a public point inside a streambed, which effectively eliminates a lot of areas that are simply too far from public spots to be fished without using the services of lodges (hosterias) that exist on working ranches that range from modest to enormous in size. Some waters are set aside for catch-and-release fishing, and fly fishing is the norm, especially on private sections of rivers.

The Traful River is one of those privately accessed waters. Not far from Bariloche, it is known for big brown and rainbow trout, and landlocked salmon, especially early and late in the season. This is one of Argentina's most hallowed trout waters, and landlocked salmon, which were first imported from Sebago Lake in Maine, migrate up from Lake Traful in March and April to spawn.

North of Bariloche are the rivers and lakes of the San Martin and Junin de Carlos region; these include the Chimehuin, Malleo, Limay, Alumine, Collon-Cura, and Caleuful Rivers, among others. Brown trout and rainbow trout are the mainstays, with some brook trout, and the fish commonly range from 1 to 4 pounds, although much larger trout—including browns to 10 pounds—are possible, especially at the mouths of rivers (bocas). The Alumine, Collon-Cura, and Limay are floatable.

The Limay is a large and well-known trout stream but one that has received much angling pressure for large browns and rainbows in the past. The Chimehuin is a renowned trophy rainbow and

A trout fishing scene on the Carrileufu River of southern Patagonia.

brown river that flows for 60 kilometers from its origin at Lake Huechulafquen to its merger with the Collon-Cura River. Similar to the Chimehuin as classic fly fishing water is the Malleo, which is north of Junin de Los Andes and in the shadow of the Lanin volcano.

South of Bariloche there is excellent trout fishing in various waters within the Esquel region of southern Patagonia. This is the remote and beautiful area visited by Butch Cassidy and the Sundance Kid when they sought refuge in South America. Here, the Arrayanes, Frey, Menendez, Chubut, Carrileufu, and Rivadavia Rivers are all notable brown and rainbow trout fisheries, as is Arroyo Pescado, the region's best spring creek flow. The Rio Grande, accessible by auto and a tailwater fishery from Lake Futaleufu, is noted for its rainbows, and there's good lake fishing, especially in Lago Bueno and Lago Menendez.

Trout season in Patagonia opens in mid-November and extends into April. The Southern Hemisphere's spring months of November and December are very good; high water and light fishing pressure are the norm. The water levels have dropped considerably by the onset of fall in March, and some may not be floatable, but late season has the advantage of fewer anglers again and some fishing for larger spawning-run fish. Peak angling activity occurs in the summer months of January and February. Varied water types and conditions present a smorgasbord of situations and gear requirements, though streamers and nymphs are effective on most waters throughout the season. The fish feed heavily on crabs *(pancoras)*, and fish from 4 to 7 pounds will likely be encountered, although much larger fish are rare.

Opportunities for sea-run brown trout fishing in the southern Patagonia mainland exist, although established outfitters here are slim. Several lengthy river systems flow here. The Rio Gallegos, for example, which is the southernmost Argentine mainland river, has a run of sea trout from October through March, with good average-size trout and big-fish potential.

Tierra del Fuego

Tierra del Fuego, named "Land of Fire" by the explorer Magellan, is an archipelago at the southern tip of South America, separated from the mainland by the Strait of Magellan and jointly part of Chile (west) and Argentina (east). This archipelago consists of the main island of Tierra del Fuego and many smaller islands, with Cape Horn at the southern extremity and bordering the Atlantic, Antarctic, and Pacific Oceans. The northern part of this island is like flat prairie—a desolate, harsh, windswept land of rolling hills with few trees and millions of sheep—while the southern part has densely wooded hills. The eastern, or Argentinian, portion of the main island is an extension of the Patagonian plateau, and contains the Rio Grande and a number of tributaries, which collectively offer what is arguably the world's best fishing for sea-run brown trout.

Brown trout were introduced to the Rio Grande in 1934 and established a resident population, and then an evolved sea-run strain that has continued to improve. Today, large (over 20 pounds) sea-run browns are more common than at any previous time. In some rivers or sections of rivers, 7- to 10-pound fish are the average catch, with smaller fish rare, and specimens from 12 to 20 pounds a real possibility. These are well-fed fish, too, with stocky bodies. Under the best conditions, an experienced angler may catch quite a few trout in a day, and this is a handful of angling, considering that sea-run brown are leaping, thrashing, exciting fish.

Although there are numerous rivers on the main island, the Rio Grande is the most significant and, with its tributaries, receives the lion's share of angling attention. The Rio Grande courses 60 miles from its source in the Chilean Andes of western Tierra del Fuego to the Atlantic Ocean. The middle portions have an average width of 80 feet, and the lower area closer to the estuary widens, although it maintains an average of just over 100 feet. Seventy-foot casts are the norm, especially along the lower reaches, and these are often necessary with a double haul into the wind. Although this does not appeal to some people, it should be noted that some portions of the river are less troubled by wind than others. The wind typically blows from midmorning until evening, and often reaches gale force; it is customary to fish from early morning to midday, then return to camp for an early dinner, returning in the evening to fish (with light available till nearly 11 P.M. in midsummer). Rain occurs frequently, even in summer months, so warm clothes and rain gear are a must.

The Rio Grande has a smooth gravel bed that provides easy wading, and large pools merge into long, wide runs. The water is milky, and seldom permits sighting fish from a bank vantage. Several days of hard rain can make the river unfishable, at least for a day. Water levels generally remain constant during the November through March fishing period, perhaps because of consistent rain on western slopes that face the wind. On the lower Rio Grande, anglers encounter nickel-bright fresh sea-run fish *(plateados),* and these are powerhouses. Some anglers use two-handed rods in this larger water.

Several rivers flow into the middle portion of the Rio Grande; these include the Menendez, Mac Lennan, and Herminita, with the Menendez regarded most favorably. It has the same quality and quantity of sea-run trout as the Rio Grande but is a smaller tributary; 40-foot casts are the norm and easy wading exists.

Sea-run brown move into the rivers in September but they move through in small schools on a staggered basis throughout the season. They do not feed while on their spawning run. January and

Although the large-mouth bass is the most popular single fish in the United States, only four states have designated this species as their state fish.

February—the summer period—is favored by many visitors, but the season runs from November through March. All of the fishing here is controlled by private access through established fishing operations run by various ranches, which own large tracts of land. Most rivers or privately controlled sections are restricted to fly fishing and catch-and-release. Most accommodate only a few people at a time.

Rainbow and brown trout are also caught, in addition to sea-run browns, and other opportunities exist outside the Rio Grande and its tributaries. South of the Rio Grande in the heart of Tierra del Fuego is Lake Fagnano, which has a total length of 115 kilometers (the western tip is in Chile) and various important tributaries. Fagnano is connected to the Pacific Ocean through its outlet in Chile, and it draws in sea-run browns; it also has resident brook trout, brown trout, rainbows, and landlocked salmon. All tackle types are used here, which makes it a good alternative for those unable to wade and flycast in rivers but who still wish to enjoy Tierra del Fuego's angling. The *bocas* here can produce trophy trout, and are especially attractive in late season.

Another southern river, west of Lake Fagnano and some 160 kilometers south of the city of Rio Grande, is the Yrigoyen. This has both sea-run and resident browns, is fly fishing and catch-and-release only, and has a mountain-river character in its upper reaches and a plains character in its lower reaches. Notable tributaries include the Udaeta and Malenguena, the latter reportedly as good as the main river.

See also: Chile.

ARIZONA

Fish and fishing are usually the last images that come to mind when contemplating the state of Arizona, primarily because tourism officials and advertising campaigns have created a finely crafted image of Arizona as "the desert state." When vacationers and newcomers visit or move to the Grand Canyon State, they generally bring their sinuses and their golf clubs. They marvel at the scenery, rejoice in the uniqueness of the desert, exclaim about the warm winters, and can't believe Las Vegas is only six hours away. Fishing rods are at most an afterthought. After all, with respect to fishing, Arizona is never mentioned in the same breath as, say, Florida or Minnesota.

But nearly 600,000 adults annually, plus another 100,000 or so unlicensed youngsters, believe Arizona's sportfish are worthy of pursuit. They do so because fish are in fact as abundant and varied in Arizona as in most states in the country, and thanks to a milder climate, these fish can be pursued pretty much year-round. In fact, as human beings came to depend on fish more for sport than food, the face of Arizona angling changed drastically. Stocking fish became a common practice; the fish, like many of

Arizona human residents, originally come from somewhere else.

The ubiquitous largemouth bass, found in deep, clear reclamation reservoirs across the state's Sonoran Desert midsection and in the giant lakes of the Colorado River, tops the piscatorial menu. Rainbow trout, a put-and-take proposition due to the state's arid personality, are the resident angler's favorite and live mostly in the waters of the pine tree–studded mountains of the north and east. In addition, a variety of other trout, as well as small-mouth bass, striped bass, walleye, northern pike, catfish, crappie, bluegills, and numerous other species are available.

Within the state are distinct zones where certain species predominate. Which fish thrive where is dictated by climate, resulting in equally distinct warmwater fisheries and coldwater fisheries. But there are crossovers.

Catching hefty bass, along with rainbow trout, in a small pond in the 8,000-foot-high White Mountains seems a bit ludicrous. But no more than casting for trout in a desert stream 40 minutes east of the Phoenix metroplex, or trolling for walleye in a saguaro-framed reservoir on the Salt River.

For some anglers, soaking an anchovy for salt-water-transplanted striped bass in one of several Colorado River reservoirs is what it's all about. Others would rather cast flies for storied lunker rainbows in a classic tailrace fishery below Glen Canyon Dam, just before the Colorado River begins its 300-mile journey through the Grand Canyon.

Arizona's sportfishery may not be as plentiful as that of some states, but its uniqueness keeps anglers coming back.

White Mountains

Located in extreme eastern Arizona along the New Mexico border, the White Mountains offer an alpine setting for heat-weary refugees from central Arizona, New Mexico, and Texas during the summer. But anglers view it as a great place to fish for trout, and so they should. This mountainous region held the state's only two native trout species, the Gila and the Apache, discovered when Anglo-Americans began frequenting the 6,500- to 10,000-foot elevations in the early 1800s. Due to pressure from early settlers, both species became nearly extinct around the turn of the twentieth century.

Later, fisheries biologists decided that the Apache—easily recognized by its distinctive overall golden hue mixed with olive on the upper portions, and its unmistakable orange to yellow-orange cutthroat mark—belonged to Arizona while the Gila variety was assigned to New Mexico. A massive recovery program brought the Apache, also known as the Arizona trout, back; currently this unique salmonid is honored as the official state fish.

Apache trout thrive in the West Fork of the Black River and in a few other small impoundments such

as Lee Valley Lake, where it shares the water with Montana grayling. But the largest populations of Apache trout are found on the 1.4 million-acre Fort Apache Indian Reservation, where state fishing licenses aren't needed but special Apache permits are.

Fly and ultralight spinning anglers seek Apache trout up to 5 pounds on Scenic Christmas Tree Lake on the Fort Apache Indian Reservation. This special-fee lake is available to anglers only from the end of May through October, but the results make it worth the effort.

Rainbow, brook, cutthroat, and brown trout, as well as grayling—all of which were imported to the state between 1900 and 1940—reside in the 30-plus man-made lakes dotting the White Mountains. Big Lake, at 9,000-feet in the Apache-Sitgreaves National Forest, is a 450-acre fish factory and gets most of its attention from Arizona Game and Fish Department hatchery trucks, not to mention anglers. Eight- to 9-inch-long rainbow and brook trout are primarily caught here, but carry-over fish are plentiful, making the chances of hooking into a trout up to 20 inches extremely good.

Although flies, lures, and bait work well all year, anglers crowd the shoreline in the fall when brookies are attempting to spawn. Artificial salmon eggs will do the trick, as will the roe stripped from females that have been caught. A hefty brook trout and the changing leaves in the surrounding forest make for an unforgettable autumn outing.

Numerous fishable streams course through the White Mountains, but the Little Colorado River, which eventually joins the main Colorado in the Grand Canyon a half-state away, is the one to visit. It is accessible in the scenic mountain hamlet of Greer, among other places.

And a stop in Greer is a must. In addition to the Little Colorado, anglers have a choice of fishing River, Tunnel, and Bunch Reservoirs, where hefty rainbows have been taken.

North-Central Region

A scant two-hour drive due north of Phoenix is an area that offers perhaps the greatest variety of species and fishing in Arizona. Among other popular waters, it is home to Oak Creek, where the best wild brown trout in the state can be found.

Lakes and streams range in elevation from 7,000 feet in the Flagstaff area, south to 2,500 feet at Camp Verde along the Verde River. Everything from stocked rainbow trout in a variety of small coldwater lakes to largemouth bass, catfish, and other warmwater species are available to anglers who don't mind driving a distance to fish them.

Sharing the billing with the trout are a few species usually associated with similar colder climates at more northerly latitudes. Northern pike and walleye are staples in upper and lower Lake Mary. These two lakes, on the eastern outskirts of

Flagstaff, produce excellent fishing when snow and rain are ample enough to keep them full.

Pike and another upper Midwest species, the yellow perch, make a good combination in Stoneman Lake, southeast of Flagstaff. Considered the only "natural" lake in the state, the tule-ringed 170-acre pond offers a respite from more popular fisheries. Successful anglers present soaked meal worms impaled on the hook of a small jig from a rowboat or canoe. Shore fishing is seldom attempted due to widespread aquatic growth; those anglers who do best position their crafts along the outer edge of the cattails.

Although the perch are small, there is good reason to keep a tight hold of the rod; it's not uncommon for northern pike, some weighing into the teens, to cruise by and take a whack at the offering.

Many trout anglers find their favored catch at Whitehorse Lake, west of Flagstaff and south of the small town of Williams. This 35-acre fishery also supports bass and catfish. Two no-bait waters offering rainbow trout are nearby as well: Perkins Tank and J. D. Dam Lake.

Large fishable streams are at a premium in Arizona, but the Verde River and Oak Creek serve up a diverse fish menu. While wild brown trout inhabit the upper portions of heavily wooded Oak Creek and its West Fork; the larger Verde contains largemouth and smallmouth bass, two kinds of catfish, and a population of smaller fish—from an elevation of 5,500 feet to Horseshoe and Bartlett Lakes just outside Phoenix.

Mogollon Rim

A sharp escarpment that can be traced in varying degrees from New Mexico northwest across Arizona, the 7,000-foot Mogollon Rim is at its most majestic approximately 110 miles northeast of Phoenix, where its rocky face rises above the thick mat of pine trees covering huge canyons and ridges that fall away to lower elevations.

Nowhere in the state is man's trout habitat handiwork more prevalent. Seven lakes, ranging from 200 down to 55 acres, are the result of a massive lake-building spree by the Arizona Game and Fish Department during the 1950s and 1960s. All are located in pine forests at 7,000 feet or higher.

The Mogollon Rim lakes serve as the second most popular destination for trout anglers, a fact not overlooked by state hatchery trucks. Regularly stocked from April through September, the lakes serve up mostly rainbow trout. Anglers looking for something a little heavier seek out Chevelon Canyon Lake for browns, primarily early and late in the season.

Anglers are limited to artificial lures and flies at Chevelon, and must trek three-quarters of a mile to reach their goal. That may not seem far, but the trail is steep and hiking out is more difficult than walking in. This a good spot for an inflatable boat or a float tube.

At 55 acres, Woods Canyon Lake is the smallest of the Rim lakes, but it is the easiest to access, at just 4 miles off the highway along a paved road. Close-by Forest Service campgrounds, a store, boat rentals, and plentiful trout make Woods Canyon an area favorite.

Several local streams are worthy of attention, including Canyon, Chevelon, and Christopher Creeks. Christopher sports a good family campground and stocked trout, and is just off the highway as you head up to the top of the rim. Chevelon is reachable by trail only, and can provide an excellent deep-canyon experience for big fish. Canyon Creek is tucked just under the top of the rim to the south and sports no-kill regulations for fly anglers chasing rainbows and browns.

Central Region

Seven deep, clear reservoirs are within an easy drive of Phoenix and the Valley of the Sun, where the majority of Arizona's largemouth bass fishing is done. Four lakes are on the Salt River, which drains the White Mountains to the east; and two are on the Verde River, which gathers up the watershed runoff from the north-central region.

On the Salt, the chain begins a bit over 100 miles away with Roosevelt, a 13,000-acre lake that was the first water reclamation project in the West when it was constructed in the early 1900s. Formed by the Salt River and Tonto Creek, which pours off the Mogollon Rim, Roosevelt provides excellent year-round fishing for smallmouth and largemouth bass and also attracts crappie hunters by the hundreds in the spring.

Moving west toward Phoenix along the Salt are Apache, Canyon, and Saguaro Lakes. All are under 2,500 acres and not only collect and hold water for the thirsty valley but produce power as well. Each serves up a variety of warmwater species, although with a few surprises. Apache, for example, also contains an excellent walleye fishery, and Canyon harbors decent trout in winter.

Below Saguaro—the last lake in the chain—what's left of the Salt River (before it joins the Verde and is channeled into canals) turns into a top fishery for stocked trout, primarily during the winter months. And it is not unusual to catch fish in 65°F water when the air temperature hits 100°F in the shade.

Bartlett and Horseshoe Lakes on the Verde are less developed than those on the Salt, but they still offer excellent angling opportunities. Bartlett is the best of the two for bass, crappie, and large catfish. The sections of the Verde between the two lakes and below Bartlett produce top bass and catfish action.

On the valley's northwest side is Lake Pleasant, part of the giant Maricopa County regional park system. When full, the 110,000-acre lake serves as a storage facility for water pumped across the desert from the Colorado River. The level fluctuates as much as 100 feet a year, but the up-and-down action gives the fishery a shot in the arm each season. The lake boasts excellent largemouth fishing, and offers white bass and crappie as well.

Although not in the Phoenix area, San Carlos Lake still qualifies as a central Arizona fishery. Located on the Gila River 100 or so miles southeast of Phoenix, San Carlos is on the San Carlos Apache Indian Reservation and, along with Roosevelt, Apache, and Pleasant, rates as one of the top bass fisheries in the state.

State licenses are not applicable at San Carlos, so anglers must purchase a tribal permit to fish this reservoir, which can swell to 17,000 acres after a couple of good rainfall years. Because of its ability to turn out big bass and its easy-to-access shoreline, San Carlos is a favorite of bass clubs during their weekend outings.

Southeast Region

Although not as water-rich as the central, eastern, and northern parts of the state, the southeast offers a milder version of the Sonoran Desert climate. The elevation climbs somewhat and the terrain changes from catclaw, cholla, and saguaro cactus to rolling grasslands.

A collection of small, man-made lakes offering both warmwater and coldwater species keep many southern Arizona anglers happy. Like the rest of the state, this part of Arizona is full of contradictions. Whereas most of the available fisheries are at an elevation of 3,000 to 4,000 feet, Rigg's Flat and Rose Canyon Lakes are nestled atop the region's two highest peaks.

Rose Canyon rests 7,000 feet atop Mount Lemon, just outside Tucson. It is very small and offers catchable trout in summer to Tucson residents looking to cool off. Rigg's Flat, on the 9,000-foot summit of Mount Graham, near Safford, is the region's highest lake and also offers trout if the hatchery trucks can bust through the snow.

Other area lakes are worth a look. Offering a combination of trout, bass, catfish, and panfish is Patagonia Lake, in a state park located between Patagonia and Nogales. Parker Canyon Lake near Sierra Vista, where travelers will find a small motel, rental boats, and other convenient features, has essentially the same species lineup as Patagonia.

Colorado River and Lakes

It's ironic that a state as arid as Arizona features a substantial river as its western boundary. And unlike most rivers in Arizona, which are generally disguised as dry streambeds, the Colorado River is wet all the way.

To say the mighty Colorado has been tamed, however, is an understatement. Not only is it tame, it has been beaten into submission via a variety of dams, both large and small. It seems everyone in the West has a claim to the lifeblood; today, the once giant tributary is a near trickle when it ultimately reaches the Mexican border below Yuma.

The first known artificial fish structure was made in the late 1700s of weighted bamboo frames sunk in 20 fathoms of water by Japanese commercial fishermen.

Fishing opportunities abound in numerous canyons of Lake Powell.

Lake Powell.   Backed by Glen Canyon Dam a few miles southwest of the Utah border, the Colorado begins its life in Arizona as Lake Powell, a huge impoundment formed in the 1960s that backs up for 186 miles, most of it in Utah. It is here that Arizona's most varied sportfishing menu begins with a scenic red rock backdrop. Five marinas serve the public, and houseboats towing fishing boats abound.

Huge schools of striped bass, an introduced species that can be found throughout the system, inhabit the lake, along with largemouth and small-mouth bass, walleye, catfish, and crappie. Although Powell is deep and clear, several hundred canyons, some many miles long, give anglers ample opportunity to fish structure.

Striped bass have become the hallmark of this lake, and they are indeed bountiful. They cluster near Glen Canyon Dam to spawn in the spring, and can be found en masse there again in the fall, offering a chance to cast for surface-busting schools as they chase bait.

Powell—one of the largest man-made lakes in North America—can be intimidating, and it is subject to water level fluctuations; but it is a phenomenal place to fish, cruise, and enjoy beautiful canyon country.

The Colorado flows out of the bottom of Glen Canyon Dam at 50 degrees and transforms the next 14 miles of the river into one of the finest tailwater trout fisheries in the country. Rainbow trout weighing 8 and 9 pounds, plus a smattering of cutthroat trout, are common, with some catches weighing in the teens. Special regulations are in effect, and keeping fish is limited. Techniques include drifting lures from a boat and casting flies into the current while wading sandbars.

From here the Colorado roars into the Grand Canyon and, except for river runners and macho hikers, the next 300 miles doesn't see very much fishing action. Big trout exist. Check the regulations carefully.

Lakes Mead and Mohave. Lake Mead, formed in 1935 by the construction of Hoover Dam, is the next reservoir downstream, and it forms a partial boundary between Arizona and Nevada. Not as large as Powell, but still imposing, Mead is 110 miles long and covers some 162,000 acres.

Lake Mead has been a largemouth bass fishing staple for over a half-century. Bass from 4 to 8 pounds are taken here, in addition to smaller specimens. Las Vegas Bay produces good-size bass because of the available nutrients and forage fish.

Recently, striped bass populations have proliferated, and many people now fish the lake primarily for stripers. Stripers average 2 pounds, but fish in the 20- to 30-pound range have been caught, more commonly in the fall and usually on shad imitations. Beginning in July and continuing through much of the rest of the year, anglers can take striped bass using a variety of topwater lures, often by fishing early and scouting for surface activity.

The best areas to fish for all species in Lake Mead are in Las Vegas Bay, Calville Bay, and the upper Overton; feeder streams and washes at these sites add nutrients to the lake and enhance the production of forage fish. The Overton Arm is a top spot to fish for black crappie, some of which range up to 3 pounds.

Trout return to the menu directly below Hoover Dam. Anglers can catch stocked trout in the Willow Beach area, or below Davis Dam where there's good access for shore fishing.

The water spreads out after this to form 67-mile-long Lake Mohave, which was formed by the creation of Davis Dam in 1951. The upper 15 miles of the reservoir, where trout are stocked, regularly provide the best fishing for striped bass. Most of the stripers in Mohave are small, but a few can weigh from 40 to 60 pounds. The best time is at night or on a slightly breezy day in September through November. Cut anchovies, squid, and large shad-imitating lures work well here.

Largemouth bass up to 9 pounds are present in most Mohave coves that have weedbeds, except the cold upper 15 miles, in the spring. When water levels decline in the fall and weedbeds are exposed, fishing becomes productive again.

Channel catfish up to 15 or 20 pounds are caught throughout the summer on cut bait or stinkbait fished on the bottom. Bluegills are typically caught below the upper 15 miles of the lake.

Below Davis Dam, which backs up Mohave, anglers gamble for more than fish at casinos bordering the west side of the river at Laughlin, Nevada. The river here is essentially a channel. Again, stocked trout as well as stripers, which migrate upriver from Lake Havasu and may reach 20 to 30 pounds, are offered.

Lake Havasu. The river fans out into Topock Marsh and a gorge before it widens at Havasu, impounded by Parker Dam. Topock is a shallow backwater, averaging approximately 15 feet in depth. It harbors largemouth bass, catfish, crappie, and a variety of sunfish; however, anglers are more likely to see canoe campers than fishing boats in this area. At an elevation of 500 feet, Topock is inhospitable in summer due to the intense heat.

It was at Lake Havasu that striped bass were first introduced to the Colorado River in the 1960s, and stripers and largemouth bass have been the main attractions, although the lake also has crappie, channel catfish, bluegills, and rainbow trout. Havasu is 45 miles long and covers 25,000 acres, making it smaller than the upstream reservoirs; however, 450 miles of shoreline provide countless nooks and crannies for angling exploration.

One of the largest freshwater fisheries enhancement programs in North America was instituted here in the early 1990s, and it has resulted in nearly 900 acres of artificial habitat, placed strategically around the lake.

Due east of Lake Havasu on the Bill Williams River is Alamo Lake, another classic desert lake that features an excellent largemouth fishery. Here, Alamo State Park also contains a campground, a store, boat rentals, and other amenities.

Back on the river, California now shares the waterway with Arizona all the way to Mexico, and backwaters proliferate from Imperial Dam south to Yuma. In many places the river looks much as it did before the area was settled.

Large catfish, both in the river and in the backwaters, are popular with the locals. Largemouth bass up to 15 pounds are not uncommon in such backwater lakes as Mittry and Martinez.

Remnants of endangered species—those with such curious names as humpback chub, bonytail chub, razorback sucker, and the Colorado River squawfish—are the subject of recovery programs in the Colorado. It was the taming of this once silty, roaring river that primarily did these species the most harm.

ARKANSAS

Arkansas anglers enjoy exceptional freshwater opportunities and some of the best angling for such prominent species as largemouth bass, striped bass, and brown trout that can be found anywhere. Scattered throughout the "Natural State" are more than 9,000 miles of streams; 600,000 acres of lakes;

and numerous bayous, farm ponds, creeks, and sloughs tailor-made for angling enjoyment.

Plug for largemouths on a huge reservoir, or jig for crappie on a cypress-shrouded oxbow. Sit under a shade tree for some lakeside catfishing, or relax on a fishing pier and dunk worms for bluegills. Cast for schooling stripers in the midst of a timber-laden impoundment, or troll the upper tributaries of a lake for walleye. Float and fish for trout or smallmouth bass on a cool, clear stream in the Ozark or Ouachita Mountains, or adventure down the Mississippi River while fishing for 100-pound catfish and alligator gar.

Mix all this opportunity with great scenery, and you have a state that draws anglers from near and far.

Game and Fish Commission Lakes

The Arkansas Game and Fish Commission owns and operates 35 man-made public fishing lakes covering more than 20,000 acres. It also owns more than 30 natural lakes open to public fishing in wildlife management areas and other locations throughout Arkansas.

At 6,700 acres, Lake Conway is the largest lake ever constructed by a state wildlife agency. Because of its size, central location, and excellent fishing, it has been one of the state's favored angling spots since completion in 1948.

Conway is best known for its seemingly endless supply of bluegills and redear sunfish. Creel surveys indicate these species, known as bream, are not only the most popular fish, they also account for the most poundage taken by anglers. Bass and crappie fans also flock to Conway, hoping to catch the lake's lunker largemouths or big slab crappie. Giant blue and channel catfish are abundant, and Conway is a hotbed for monster flatheads. An east-side nursery pond permits stocking millions of crappie, largemouth bass, and catfish directly into the lake.

White Oak Lake has a well-deserved reputation for producing big fish. This 2,676-acre site produces many 20-pound-class channel cats, numerous 10-pound-plus largemouths, abundant crappie up to 3 pounds, and bream to $1^1/_2$ pounds. The impoundment is actually two lakes in one; Arkansas Highway 387 separates the upper and lower lakes. White Oak's plentiful cover and structure are attractive to fish, and anglers do well probing around dead timber, cypress trees, riprap, lily pad beds, points, islands, and the White Oak creek channel running south to north across the lakebed. Combined with adjacent White Oak Lake State Park and Poison Springs Wildlife Management Area, the lake offers a full complement of outdoor recreation opportunities.

Cane Creek Lake, at 1,700 acres, is a cooperative project of the Game and Fish Commission, the Soil Conservation Service, and the Department of Parks and Tourism. The main merrymakers here are largemouth bass, channel catfish, bluegills, crappie,

A

and redear sunfish. The fishing for all these species is outstanding here, especially in cover along the inundated creek channel and the sloping west-south shoreline. Anglers also catch many rod-bending channel cats. Cane Creek is 3 miles east of Star City in Lincoln County.

Harris Brake Lake in eastern Perry County has cover and structure galore: shoreline brush, sunken timber, cypress trees, underwater islands, creek channel dropoffs, old docks, and more. Visiting anglers land plenty of big bluegills, redear sunfish, crappie, channel catfish, and largemouth bass. Hybrid stripers are also caught here, and when schools are chasing shad, anglers find fast action in open water. The 1,300-acre lake also harbors a host of neglected species like bowfin, bullhead, pickerel, carp, drum, and longear sunfish, which provide exciting sport when other fish have lockjaw.

Lake Overcup, north of Morrilton, is one of central Arkansas' premier angling sites. The bream and crappie are extraordinary, and lunker large-mouths frequently round out the catch. This 1,025-acre lake has forged a place in the hearts of catfish anglers as well, doling out fast-paced action for channel, blue, and flathead catfish. Other popular sportfish inhabiting this fertile lake include hybrid stripers, white bass, chain pickerel, and warmouth. Boat lanes crisscross timbered waters to provide easy access to brushy, stump-laden fish habitat off-shore, while those who prefer bank fishing can relax on the lake's fishing piers or earthen jetty or try for lunkers along the mile-long dam.

Located in the Ouachita Mountains 12 miles west of Waldron, Lake Hinkle offers some of the most diverse fishing opportunities of any Game and Fish Commission lake. In addition to the standard fare of largemouth bass, bluegills, channel catfish, and crappie, this 960-acre impoundment supports white bass, flathead catfish, spotted bass, redear sunfish, saugeye, and other popular sportfish. A south-side nursery pond provides regular stockings of hybrid stripers, crappie, and bass, and a caged fish-rearing operation is a source of catchable-size catfish.

Meandering through the heart of the 16,542-acre Sulphur River Wildlife Management Area, Mercer Bayou is more like a stream than a lake. Indeed, before levees were built on the north and south ends of the lake to maintain the water level, Mercer Bayou was actually an offshoot of the Sulphur River. Although the lake covers only 800 surface acres, it winds 14 miles through the south-west Arkansas bottoms. Largemouth bass, crappie, channel catfish, bluegills, and redear sunfish are the main attractions, but the lake also provides good action for chain pickerel, warmouth, and flathead catfish.

Lake Atkins, which sits in the fertile Arkansas River Valley just south of its namesake town, is best known for crackerjack bream fishing. The water teems with huge bluegills and redear sunfish.

The habit of spinning to tear apart their food is common to eels, whose 6 to 14 spins per second under water is greater than the 5 spins per second achieved on ice by the best skaters.

Visiting anglers also find top-notch fishing for big crappie, largemouth bass, channel catfish, and flat-head catfish. Many anglers consider this 752-acre lake the best small-lake fishery in western Arkansas.

Lake Charles, in the Ozark Mountain foothills of Lawrence County, offers a mixed bag of opportunities. Angling for jumbo largemouth bass, crap-pie, bluegills, channel catfish, and flathead catfish is excellent, and unlike most Game and Fish Commission lakes, 650-acre Charles also harbors good populations of hybrid stripers and white bass. Open water is prevalent, a condition conducive to good hybrid and white bass fishing, but one that makes it difficult to find concentrations of large-mouths, panfish, and catfish. The Flat Creek channel winding through the heart of the lake is a good area to fish, and anglers also do well fishing points, coves, and the area around the dam.

Lake Bois d'Arc, 6 miles south of Hope in southwest Arkansas, is part of Bois d'Arc Wildlife Management Area. Excellent crappie, bluegills, and redear fishing are the main draws for this 650-acre lake, but angling for jumbo largemouth bass and channel catfish is also good. Boaters have ready access to many acres of good timber fishing, and shore anglers can pick a spot along $4^1/_2$ miles of riprap levee on the north, west, and south sides. There's also a man-made peninsula near the lower boat ramp built especially for bank fishing.

Nestled in forested hills atop Crowley's Ridge, 600-acre Lake Poinsett was the first Game and Fish Commission lake built in northeast Arkansas. Fishing is excellent here. Good catches of fat crap-pie are taken year after year, and fish population sampling has turned up state-record-class channel catfish. Redear sunfish, bluegills, and largemouth bass are also found in good numbers and good sizes. During much of the year, anglers concentrate their efforts around the stick-ups and submerged treetops covering the lake's numerous small coves. But the old Distress Creek channel and deeper water around the dam are also productive.

Game and Fish lakes of 500 acres or less include Ashbaugh, Barnett, Bentonville, Bob Kidd, Burnt Cane, Cargile, Cox Creek, Cox Cypress, Crystal, Des Arc, Elmdale, Frierson, Greenlee, Gurdon, Hindsville, Hogue, Horsehead, Kingfisher, Mallard, Pine Bluff, Pullen Pond, Sugarloaf, Tommy Sproles, Tri County, Wilhemina, and Wright.

Corps of Engineers Reservoirs

Sixteen large Arkansas lakes are under control of the U.S. Army Corps of Engineers. These reservoirs, which cover nearly a quarter million acres, provide the angler opportunities to pursue a wide variety of sportfish.

Four of these impoundments—Beaver (28,220 acres), Bull Shoals (45,440 acres), Table Rock (43,100 acres), and Norfork (22,000 acres)—are deep, rocky lakes in the upper White River basin of the Ozark Mountains; Bull Shoals and Table Rock lie partly in Missouri. All offer superb fishing for largemouth and spotted bass, crappie, bluegills, redear sunfish, white bass, and catfish. Walleye reach huge sizes in Bull Shoals and Norfork, and healthy populations of smallmouth bass and stripers thrive in all the lakes except Table Rock. Excellent hybrid striper fisheries exist in Beaver and Norfork.

Greers Ferry Lake is hallowed water for walleye anglers. Few if any lakes have produced as many 20-pound-plus walleye. Large numbers of those monsters have been caught in late winter or early spring in the upper tributaries, although it takes a dedicated angler to have success. This 31,500-acre impoundment on the Little Red River is also one of the country's finest hybrid striper hotspots, having produced a number of record specimens. Other noteworthy angling opportunities exist for bream, catfish, crappie, black bass (including smallmouths), and white bass.

West-central Arkansas encompasses four Corps lakes. Lake Dardanelle (34,300 acres) and Ozark Lake (10,600 acres) are established pools in the McClellan-Kerr Arkansas River Navigation System. Both offer an abundant variety of sportfish, but Dardanelle is best known for producing extraordinary numbers of trophy-class largemouth bass, crappie, and catfish. Ozark is a winter hotspot for sauger. Blue Mountain Lake on the Petit Jean River near Waveland tends to be muddy, but this 2,910-acre reservoir is loaded with big crappie and blue, channel, and flathead catfish. Nimrod Lake, a 3,550-acre impoundment on the Fourche la Fave River, is rightfully recognized as one of Arkansas' top lakes for 2- to 3-pound crappie.

Two of the state's most popular lakes are 40,000-acre Ouachita and 13,400-acre DeGray, both in the Hot Springs area. Lake Ouachita is the largest lake entirely within Arkansas. Trophy striped bass and largemouth bass are common pursuits at Ouachita, but this is also one of the state's top producers of big bream, heavyweight catfish, jumbo white and spotted bass, slab-size crappie, and outsize walleye. DeGray lacks Ouachita's striped bass and walleye, but trophy-size hybrid stripers are common and frequently taken near the dam and midlake islands.

Arkansas' smallest Corps of Engineers lakes—Dierks, Gillham, and DeQueen (1,350 to 1,680 acres)—are grouped at the north end of Sevier County in the state's southwest corner. None offers extraordinary angling opportunities, but all are popular with local anglers seeking largemouth bass, crappie, catfish, and bream. Lake Greeson, a 2,500-acre lake just a few miles east in Pike County, offers similar fishing opportunities, plus a good fishery for 20- to 30-pound striped bass.

Millwood Lake (29,200 acres) near the Arkansas-Texas-Louisiana borders attracts numerous out-of-state anglers. Many consider this shallow, timber-filled impoundment among the South's best reservoirs for trophy largemouths, crappie, and catfish. Panfish anglers work woody cover for abundant bluegills, redear sunfish, and warmouth, and there's fair angling for hybrid stripers and white bass.

State Park Lakes
Scattered throughout the state, Arkansas' 49 state parks offer profuse scenic, recreational, and educational experiences, including excellent fishing opportunities. Several parks are on Corps of Engineers reservoirs and Game and Fish Commission lakes. Seven others provide outstanding public fishing on small lakes within park boundaries.

Lakes Dunn and Austell in Village Creek State Park near Wynne are tiny by most standards (68 and 64 acres respectively), but these two Crowley's Ridge impoundments are among Arkansas' top producers of 10- to 15-pound largemouth bass. Giant blue and channel catfish are also favored here, along with abundant crappie and bluegills. Walcott Lake (31 acres) lacks blue cats but otherwise offers equally good fishing opportunities in Crowley's Ridge State Park north of Jonesboro.

Petit Jean State Park near Morrilton has two lakes: 64-acre Bailey and 11-acre Roosevelt. Visiting anglers enjoy superb bank fishing for largemouths, crappie, bream, and channel cats. Three- to 11-acre lakes in Woolly Hollow, Logoly, and Old Davidsonville State Parks attract campers and other park visitors seeking the same quarry. An 8-acre lake in Devil's Den State Park is the only state park lake where anglers have the opportunity to catch smallmouth bass.

U.S. Forest Service Lakes
The Forest Service owns 18 public fishing lakes within Arkansas' three national forests, all of which cover less than 700 acres each. Anglers can nevertheless expect good fishing for bluegills, catfish, bream, largemouth bass, and other species.

Bear Creek and Storm Creek Lakes are the largest Forest Service lakes, at 625 and 420 acres respectively. Located in St. Francis National Forest near Marianna and Helena, they are among eastern Arkansas' most popular fishing lakes. Many anglers consider Bear Creek Arkansas' top lake for big redear sunfish (shellcrackers), with $1\frac{1}{2}$- to 2-pounders common. Storm Creek is the smallest Arkansas lake stocked with hybrid stripers, and frequently produces 10- to 15-pounders.

Six Forest Service lakes lie within the Ouachita National Forest in west-central Arkansas' Perry County. These are Cove Creek, Dry Fork, Little Bear, Rocky Branch, Site 8, and Sylvia. To the southwest, also within Ouachita National Forest, are Shady and Fenwood Lakes in Polk and Montgomery Counties. Public fishing lakes in the Ozark National Forest include Wedington (Washington County), Shores (Franklin County),

A

Cove (Logan County), Spring (Yell County), Lower Brock Creek (Conway County), and Driver Creek and Upper Brock Creek (Van Buren County). These waters range from 14 to 160 acres, but most cover less than 50 acres.

The Forest Service constructed these lakes for flood control, but each has been stocked with bluegills, channel cats, largemouth bass, and, in most cases, crappie and redear sunfish. Fishing opportunities are superb, but few of the lakes offer a launch ramp suitable for large boats. Lightweight jonboats or canoes that can be carried to the water are preferable.

Mirror Lake in the Blanchard Springs Recreation Area of the Ozark National Forest is the only coldwater lake in the bunch. Fed by clear, frigid waters from Blanchard Caverns, this 7-acre gem is popular for its rainbow trout, with the possibility of an occasional smallmouth bass.

City, County, and Corporate Lakes

Many Arkansas cities, counties, and major corporations own fishing lakes open to the public. Most are small, a few hundred acres at most, but a few are among the largest and most popular in the state.

The largest of these is 8,900-acre Lake Maumelle, owned and operated by Little Rock Waterworks. Just 8 miles west of Little Rock, this water-supply impoundment offers fantastic fishing for largemouths, spotted bass, stripers, white bass, the three major species of catfish, and a wide variety of panfish, including bluegills, redear sunfish, and crappie. Nearly all the timber on the lakebed was cut during the 1957 impoundment, so anglers can't rely much on visible cover like dead snags and brush when trying to pinpoint fish. Sonar is an invaluable aid for locating underwater structure that concentrates schools of fish.

Because it supplies water, Maumelle is governed by many unique regulations. For example, there's a no-fishing zone marked with buoys near the east end of the lake. Anglers should check with the Little Rock Municipal Water Works for details.

Lake Erling, near the Louisiana border in Lafayette County, is owned by International Paper Company. About 85 percent of this 7,000-acre lake's surface is covered with stumps and logs. It offers excellent bream and crappie fishing, but big largemouths steal the limelight. Hundreds of thousands of Florida-strain largemouths have been stocked in Erling, with many growing over 10 pounds. Good fishing areas include dead timber cover; the old Bodcau Creek channel; and shallow flats filled with lily pads, cypress trees, and other thick cover.

Lakes Catherine and Hamilton, two Ouachita River hydroelectric projects owned by the Arkansas Power and Light Company, helped transform the area around Hot Springs National Park into one of mid-America's favorite vacation/retirement areas. Both lakes are adjacent to the city of Hot Springs, providing local citizens superb nearby fishing.

Lake Catherine, 11 miles long and covering 1,940 acres, harbors a surprisingly diverse fishery for such a small body of water. It contains healthy populations of crappie, bluegills, redear sunfish, flathead catfish, channel catfish, blue catfish, striped bass, hybrid stripers, white bass, and even walleye and rainbow trout. Black bass, however, are the main draw for many visiting anglers.

At 7,200 acres, 18½-mile-long Lake Hamilton is much larger than its sister lake, but offers equally good angling for the same diverse sportfish. Black bass and crappie attract most anglers, but Hamilton is also well known for giant striped bass, including two state records over 53 pounds.

For relaxed fishing on less-pressured waters, anglers can investigate scores of smaller city-owned lakes scattered from border to border, including those in Bald Knob, Benton, Booneville, Camden, Charleston, Clarksville, Conway, Dierks, Eureka Springs, Fayetteville, Ft. Smith, Jonesboro, Mena, Nashville, Newark, Newport, Ola, Paris, Pottsville, Prairie Grove, Rogers, Siloam Springs, Van Buren, Waldron, and many other communities.

Oxbows and Other Natural Lakes

Hundreds of oxbows and other natural lakes are open to public fishing in Arkansas, particularly along the Mississippi, White, Arkansas, and Ouachita Rivers, and Bayou Bartholomew in eastern and southern portions of the state.

If fishing for bluegills, channel catfish, crappie, and largemouth bass tickles your fancy, check out Lake Chicot at Lake Village. This 5,300-acre Mississippi River oxbow is said to be the largest in the world. Action for these species is red-hot, and it starts earlier in the year than on most large Arkansas lakes, thanks to Chicot's extreme southern location. The best fishing is around cypress trees, willows, buckbrush, dead timber, and private docks along the shore, unless you're seeking hybrid stripers. Another of Chicot's prized sportfish, these hard fighters are most often taken in open water, where they feed on schools of shad.

Other top-notch Mississippi River oxbow lakes include Horseshoe (2,500 acres), Wapanocca (1,800 acres), Dacus (1,000 acres), and Island 40 Chute (350 acres) in Crittenden County; Midway (1,000 acres) and Whitehall (250 acres) in Lee County; Mellwood (1,000 acres) and Old Town (900 acres) in Phillips County; and Grand (900 acres) in Chicot County. All have a well-deserved reputation for large quantities of big crappie, largemouth bass, bream, and catfish.

More than 200 small (most less than 100 acres) oxbow lakes, are seasonally open to fishing in White River National Wildlife Refuge in southeast Arkansas. Dozens more are in Cache River and Holla Bend National Wildlife Refuges. Several wildlife management areas owned by the Game and Fish Commission also offer excellent oxbow fishing opportunities. These include Henry Gray/Hurricane Lake near Bald Knob, Shirey Bay–Rainey Brake in Lawrence County, and Dagmar near Brinkley.

Along Bayou Bartholomew in Drew and Ashley Counties are four even more popular oxbow fishing hotspots: Lakes Wallace, Grampus, and Enterprise (350 acres each), and Wilson Brake (150 acres). Another natural lake favored by east Arkansas anglers is Big Lake in Big Lake National Wildlife Refuge near Manila. Formed by the New Madrid Earthquake of 1812, this shallow 6,500-acre lake hosts bluegills, channel catfish, crappie, largemouth bass, redear sunfish, warmouth, and white bass.

Coolwater Streams

Scattered throughout the mountain regions of Arkansas are dozens of coolwater streams, where anglers can catch smallmouth and spotted bass as well as various other species that prefer cool water temperatures.

The best known of these is the scenic Buffalo River in the Ozarks. America's first national river, it runs for roughly 150 miles with 95,000 acres of public land along its corridor. The Buffalo is a model smallmouth bass stream with fast, clear, oxygen-rich water, a gravel bottom, and numerous boulder beds. It also harbors plentiful channel catfish, green and longear sunfish, rock bass, and spotted bass.

Another established Ozark stream is Crooked Creek, often described as "the South's best smallmouth fishery." Most recreational use occurs in the lower 50 miles, from Pyatt to the White River, where anglers catch not only smallmouth bass but also several varieties of sunfish, largemouth bass, spotted bass, and channel cats.

The Eleven-Point River is fed by numerous springs, making it an ideal destination for floaters year-round. Rising in the Ozarks of Missouri, this smallmouth haven flows 44 miles through Arkansas to its confluence with the Spring River. The number of smallmouths in these waters is phenomenal; hauling in a pair on a single crankbait isn't unheard of. Anglers also find good action for channel and flathead catfish, spotted bass, and longear sunfish.

Other popular Ozark float-fishing streams include Big Piney Creek, Cadron Creek, Illinois Bayou, Mulberry River, Spring River, Strawberry River, and White River.

The Ouachita Mountains encompass several blue-ribbon smallmouth bass streams. Among the best is the Caddo River, a 40-mile-long stretch of peaceful water that is ideal for family fishing. The most productive smallmouth angling begins near Caddo Gap and ends below Amity. Numerous sunfish are caught in this stretch as well. During spring spawning runs, walleye, white bass, and hybrid stripers ascend the Caddo from DeGray Lake, providing fast-paced fishing for savvy anglers.

The upper Ouachita River above Lake Ouachita offers another 70 miles of smallmouth

The meeting of warm air and cold water causes fog to greet early-morning anglers on the White River.

and spotted bass fishing. The upper reaches are fast and narrow, suitable primarily for wading. But from Oden to the lake, canoeists find lazy pools and sparkling shoals where one can slow the pace and fish the river's rocky bottom thoroughly. In addition to plentiful smallmouths and spotted bass, catches include rock bass, catfish, bluegills, largemouths, and occasional walleye. In the lower reaches just above Lake Ouachita, the spawning runs of white bass attract crowds of springtime anglers.

Many other Ouachita Mountain streams serve up excellent float fishing. These include the Little Missouri River, Mountain Fork River, and the three forks of the upper Saline River.

Trout Waters

To the trout angler, there's just one word that adequately describes Arkansas: Paradise. Since 1945, the Arkansas Game and Fish Commission, through an aggressive stocking program and innovative, intensive management, has developed some of the world's finest trout fisheries. The state features 153 miles of tailwater trout streams.

The upper White River is the state's most famous trout fishery. Some consider it America's best trout river with respect to both size and number of. The most popular section is the Bull Shoals tailwater, a 92-mile stretch from Bull Shoals Dam to Guion. Big brown trout are the main attraction, with 3- to 5-pounders common and 30-pound-plus fish always a possibility. Rainbows are the river's bread-and-butter trout, and at times nearly every cast will produce a 9- to 16-inch fish. Cutthroats and brook trout are also present, thanks to stepped-up stocking efforts.

The Beaver Dam tailwater—another stretch of the White River—also has a reputation for high-quality trout fishing. This 8-mile-long section is stocked throughout the year with rainbow, brown, cutthroat, and brook trout. Rainbows are the

A

predominant species, while browns offer trophy opportunities. The best fishing is in the upper 4 to 5 miles.

The Norfork tailwater, which constitutes 5 miles of the North Fork River, from Norfork Dam to the White River, has produced thousands of 10-pound-plus brown trout, including a 34-pounder and a 38-pound, 9-ounce former world record. Several state-record brook trout came from the North Fork as well, and a significant part of the catch is comprised of rainbows and cutthroats. Anglers fishing here have an excellent chance to catch a grand slam—at least one trout of each species 16 inches or longer.

The Little Red River serves up 29 miles of extraordinary trout fishing below Greers Ferry Dam at Heber Springs. Like the White River, this trout stream is touted as one of the finest in the world. That's partially because it produces big trout, like the mammoth 40-pound, 4-ounce all-tackle world-record brown landed by a local angler in May 1992 (on 4-pound line no less). Rainbow trout are usually just 9 to 12 inches long, but they're abundant enough to satisfy the fishing itch in most anglers. Brook and cutthroat trout are also stocked and commonly reach 13 to 16 inches.

Spring River near Mammoth Spring is unique among Arkansas trout streams. Its cold water comes naturally from a spring rather than artificially from deep within a man-made lake. The river stays cold enough to support a good trout population for 10 miles downstream. One to 3-pound rainbows are fairly common. Brown trout provide a trophy facet to the river's fishing profile. Cutthroat and brook trout are most numerous above Cold Springs.

Although they are limited in size and big-fish potential, short stretches of both the Ouachita and the Little Missouri Rivers provide excellent seasonal fishing for rainbow trout. On the Ouachita, cold-water releases from Blakely Mountain Dam (Lake Ouachita) and Carpenter Dam (Lake Hamilton) allow cool-season fishing for put-and-take rainbows for short stretches below each dam. On the Little Missouri, trout are stocked below Narrows Dam on Lake Greeson, and upstream from Lake Greeson in the Ouachita National Forest near Albert Pike Recreation Area. Stocking begins in late fall and continues through April. Persistent anglers will catch a few trout in summer, particularly below Carpenter Dam.

Warmwater Streams and Rivers

While fast-flowing, cold mountain streams are more popular with visitors, warmwater streams and rivers snaking their way across the delta and coastal plain regions of eastern and southern Arkansas should not be overlooked by serious anglers. These sluggish, flatland waters team with bass, crappie, catfish, bluegills, and a wide variety of other warmwater sportfish. In some areas, bank fishing is popular, while in others a boat is necessary for access to better fishing spots.

The Mississippi River, which runs almost the entire length of Arkansas' eastern boundary, is known nationwide as a phenomenal fishery for warmwater species. One of the state's most popular trophy catfishing areas, Ol' Muddy has produced some of the largest blue cats on record, including a 116½-pounder caught in 1997 near Dermott. Backwater areas and adjacent oxbows give up enormous crappie, bluegills, and bass. Giant alligator gar still turn up occasionally, and it is not uncommon to catch freshwater drum topping 20 pounds, common carp over 30 pounds, and a huge assortment of other rough fish. The Mississippi is also a mother lode of hefty striped and white bass.

The Arkansas River spans the breadth of the Natural State, from Ft. Smith in the west to its juncture with the Mississippi River in the east, some 310 miles in all. In 1971, the U.S. Army Corps of Engineers completed the McClellan-Kerr Arkansas River Navigation Project, which included construction of 12 dams in Arkansas, turning the once untamed river into a series of comparatively tranquil reservoirs. The project not only improved navigation on the river, but the fishing as well.

Largemouth bass brought fame to the Arkansas River among hard-core bass aficionados, partly due to a series of national bass tournaments that produced record weigh-ins. Spotted bass, white bass, and stripers draw the attention of many visiting anglers, too, but these species are just a small part of the overall angling picture. Giant catfish are commonly taken in dam tailwaters, including blues up to 100 pounds, flatheads up to 140 pounds, and channel cats up to 25 pounds. Sauger attract winter fishing fanatics during their January and February spawning runs, and there are plenty of jumbo bream and crappie in river backwaters.

Arkansas has more than a dozen other large bottom-land rivers that offer superb fishing for a wide variety of popular gamefish. Among these are the Black, Cache, Fourche la Fave, St. Francis, lower White, lower Ouachita, lower Saline, L'Anguille, Little, lower Little Missouri, Petit Jean, and Red Rivers, as well as Champagnolle Creek, Bayou Meto, Bayou de View, and Bayou Bartholomew.

ARTIFICIAL FLY

An imitation of a natural aquatic or terrestrial insect, especially one consumed by fish. Because natural flies are rarely used by anglers, imitations are employed and usually referred to simply as flies rather than artificial flies (and fishing with these is simply called fly fishing); in the broadest sense, this is a form of lure.

See: Fly; Fly Fishing; Lure.

ARTIFICIAL LURE

An antiquated term for any nonnatural object with a hook that is used to catch fish.
See: Lure.

ARTIFICIAL REEF

A man-made artificial structure that provides habitat for many kinds of fish. Used in freshwater and saltwater, predominantly the latter, artificial reefs are constructed or placed in structure-less bottom areas to create new and diverse aquatic communities. They provide food, shelter, protection, and spawning areas for fish, and concentrate fish on or close to the structures.

Artificial reefs are made from rock, concrete, ships that are deliberately sunk, auto bodies, railroad flatbed cars, rubber tires, and wood, among many items. Decommissioned oil rigs, cut off well below the water level, have become artificial reefs, and the United States military has a program to recycle old military equipment like tanks, staff vehicles, and heavy equipment, even training their explosives experts to sink these objects.

Newly created artificial reefs are placed at various depths, sometimes to attract specific fish. Many are built as a community effort, with the technical assistance of government agencies, and placed on smooth bottom areas where they won't interfere with navigation and commercial fishing activities and are in relative proximity to launch ramps and marinas. Artificial reefs exist around the world, and are perhaps most used in Japanese waters, where reef development has been a priority of the government for commercial fishing enhancement.
See: Reef

ASP   *Aspius aspius.*

Other names—French: *aspe;* German: *rapfen.*

This strong-fighting European fish is unknown to many anglers and, like its carp and barbel relatives, is a member of the Cyprinidae family.

Identification.   Much like barbel *(see)* in general shape, asp are streamlined and thick-bodied for river and feeding adaptation. They are different from that species, however, in possessing a straight snout without barbels, a lengthier and tapered anal fin, and lighter coloration. They are dark on the back, silvery on the sides, and often have a reddish tint in the fins.

Size.   The all-tackle world record for asp is a Swedish fish that weighed 12 pounds, 7 ounces and was caught in 1993 in Lake Vanern. This species has been reported at twice that weight, however.

Distribution.   Asp are native to northern Europe and have been introduced to the Netherlands. They range from the eastern Netherlands throughout northern and central Europe to the Caspian Sea.

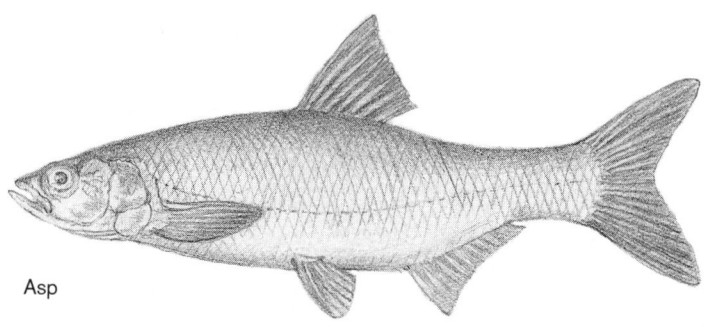

Asp

Habitat.   These fish are primarily residents of the lower reaches of rivers, but they also dwell in lakes and their tributaries. They are particularly fond of pools and may locate around such cover as weirs and bridge pilings. They often occupy midwater sections of pools; in areas where they overlap with barbel, they may frequent similar waters.

Food.   Asp differ from most cyprinids in their food preference, which, rather than being benthic organisms, is small prey fish.

Angling.   Asp are caught on live and dead fish, as well as on some lures, including spoons. Anglers catch them by casting, stillfishing, or trolling. This is a strong-fighting fish.

ASTERN

The direction toward the stern of a boat or beyond the stern of a boat; also the backward movement of a boat.

ATTRACTOR

(1) A type of trolling accessory that uses vibration or visual stimuli to get the attention of fish, especially in midwater to deep water, and draws them to a trailing lure. In freshwater, attractors are usually situated on a fishing line ahead of the lure, and do not themselves have a hook. In saltwater, attractors may be used on the surface in big-game fishing *(see: big-game tackle)* to create noise and motion; they are also called teasers. Here they are used without a hook, as a lure with a hook, or in front of a lure.
See: Cowbells; Dodger/Flasher; Trolling Lures, Saltwater.

(2) Cover, objects, or structures placed in the water that serve to attract prey and predatory fish, and which provide angling opportunities. Brushpiles, artificial reefs, and sunken vessels may all be some form of attractor.
See: FAD; Fish Attractor.

AUGER

A type of drill for boring holes in ice. Augers may be manual or automatic, the latter powered by gasoline. The diameter of the blade determines the size of the hole, usually from 7 to 9 inches in width. (Larger holes are necessary in situations

A

where larger-bodied fish might be caught.) The cutting edge of the blade should be sharp, uniform, and rust-free,

See: Ice Fishing.

AUSTRALIA

Lying between the Pacific and Indian Oceans in the Southern Hemisphere, Australia is the largest island and the smallest continent in the world, yet it is one big country. It has a land area of 7,682,300 square kilometers, and a coastline of 36,735 kilometers. Thirty-nine percent of the total area lies within the Tropical Zone. Made up of six states and two territories, Australia has a population of more than 18 million people, heavily concentrated in its larger cities. From the accessible city of Sydney to the remote city of Perth, and from the state of Tasmania to the "Top End," Australia is virtually equal in size to the continental United States.

Accordingly, Australia offers some of the most diverse fishing imaginable, and angling opportunities galore. No less a figure than the pioneering angler and world-famous author Zane Grey, in his book *An American Angler in Australia,* said that Australia has "fish and fishing which will dwarf all the rest known in the world." Grey based this on his experiences with black marlin and great white sharks, and, though written in 1937, it is quite true even today.

Many of Australia's waters are hard to access, however, and are still lightly explored. While the international saltwater community knows full well about Australia's remarkable billfishing, it actually recognizes only the east coast, especially the Cairns–Lizard Island region. New discoveries of big game are still being made in Australia, but many remain unpublicized. Others that are somewhat known are not even marginally exploited.

Western Australia, which falls into the latter category, has a good but vastly untapped billfishery. Only since the middle of the 1980s have a few anglers sampled blue, black, and striped marlin action off Exmount, some 800 miles north of Perth, and off Dampier, still farther north.

Nationally, some 19 species of freshwater fish are targeted regularly by anglers, the most popular being brown and rainbow trout and barramundi. Trout are not indigenous, having been introduced from England and the United States. They are ample in all states except the Northern Territory and Queensland. Barramundi are a native species, largely confined within the Tropical Zone of Western Australia, the Northern Territory, and Queensland.

Common marine species targeted by anglers number over 30 genera; the most popular gamefish are tuna, marlin, sailfish, sharks, trevally, yellowtail kingfish, cobia, dolphin, and mackerel. Superb saltwater fishing can be experienced from such bases as Cairns and Brisbane (Queensland), Port Stephens and Bermagui (New South Wales), Port Lincoln and Streaky Bay (South Australia), Albany and Broome (Western Australia), and Darwin (Northern Territory). Fishing safaris are popular and are available nationwide. The best opportunities in most areas come in the summer months. Anglers visiting from the Northern Hemisphere need to remember that the seasons are reversed down under. Although the warmer weather commences in September, summer starts in earnest in November and lasts through March.

The discipline of catch-and-release has become widely adopted throughout Australia, with most large angling organizations involved in concerted tag-and-release efforts for scientific research

Queensland
Cairns billfishing.   Sensational gamefishing can be experienced in North Queensland waters, and the most famous area fishing resort is the city of Cairns, the renowned departure point for the best black marlin fishing in the world. Most big-game anglers think of Cairns as the modern-day mecca for black marlin, the Holy Grail for granders, and home of the Great Barrier Reef, which has often been described as the eighth wonder of the world. There is no finer place anywhere to catch black marlin—and unequivocally no greater place to have a chance at catching a 1,000-pounder—than the northwest coast of Australia, along the Great Barrier Reef from Cairns to Lizard Island. In fact, they record granders here by the score—and then some—each season. Among the more sensational occurrences in the past has been the capture of two granders in one boat by different anglers in a single day, and two granders by the same angler in one day.

This region has produced numerous line-class world-record black marlin, including two fish weighing more than 1,300 pounds each—the largest of the two being the 80-pound line-class record holder, a 1,347-pounder taken in 1979.

Black marlin records have been set and surpassed in nearly all categories off the Great Barrier Reef for more than 20 years. Still bigger fish—including the largest specimen recorded by the Gamefishing Association of Australia, a 654-kilogram (1,438 pounds) specimen taken off Cairns—have been reported, and the talk is often about whether a 2,000-pound black might swim in these waters. As with most marlin grounds, there are those who claim to have hooked and lost fish of similar gargantuan proportions off northwest Queensland.

The Great Barrier Reef, of course, is largely responsible for the presence of these billfish as well as so many other species. The seaward side of the reef takes the brunt of ocean swells and currents, and not much farther offshore the bottom slopes quickly into very deep water. Currents and upwelling here serve to push up bait, and marlin have been seen and caught in shallow water not far from the reef.

Some Presidents who were known to enjoy fishing: Herbert Hoover, Grover Cleveland, Jimmy Carter, Chester Arthur, Franklin Roosevelt, George Bush, and Dwight Eisenhower.

A

Cairns has been the jumping-off point for most of this fabulous marlin fishing, with anglers venturing both to the north and south. Because much of the fishing occurs so far from Cairns, however, mother ship operations have evolved to increase fishing time; formerly, runs of 60 miles or more were made in a day. Some anglers pursue the fish for several days at a stretch, overnighting on the same large boat they use for fishing, or staying at a mother ship and using a sportfishing boat for daily trolling.

Exploration north of Cairns has been gradual, resulting in catches around Linden Bank, the Ribbon Reefs, Agincourt Bank, and other shoals, reefs, and passages up to Lizard Island. Lizard is about 150 miles north of Cairns and some 17 miles off the Queensland shore.

Black marlin are fished in various ways, including lure trolling, dead-bait trolling, and live-bait fishing. Live bait is likely to be used on calm-sea days. Dead-bait trolling, using kawakawa, scad, skipjack, rainbow runner, and other baits, is very popular. Some baits weigh 7 or more kilograms, which is more than the weight of an ordinary catch on light tackle when fishing inshore in almost any locale.

The black marlin are here all year long, but the best action, and the biggest fish, occur from September through November and sometimes into December, which is the spring and early summer in the Southern Hemisphere. Smaller fish are reliably caught from August through January; the early and late months are best suited to lighter equipment, although 80- and 130-pound tackle is the equipment of choice at any time. Females (the males are smaller) are targeted in the blue waters close to the Great Barrier Reef. Approximately 90 percent of the marlin caught today are tagged and released.

Striped marlin are among the offshore catch, although they do not show up as frequently as blacks. Sailfish are part of the action, too, although not in the volume experienced farther south, off Cape Bowling Green. Blue marlin primarily remain farther south along the eastern coast, too, but a few monster fish that were tagged and released in Queensland waters and were originally believed to be black marlin were later suspected to have been very large blues. The first blue marlin caught in these waters was a 315-pounder taken off No. 10 Ribbon Reef in late 1988.

The catch-and-release ethic in all of Australia is exemplary. Local anglers were tagging and releasing black marlin long before it was fashionable to do so for pelagic species, and granders as well as near-granders and smaller fish have been tagged and released for many years.

Some anglers have had the good fortune to recapture fish previously tagged on their boats. One fish tagged off Queensland was recaptured almost 4,500 miles away. Obviously, science—not to mention the fish population—has benefited from this practice. In Australia, and in New Zealand, keeping

a marlin is frowned on by local club members, unless it is a potential record.

Incidentally, offshore trollers from Cairns to Lizard Island do catch some other species as well, although outside this area one seldom hears much about this. Trollers take smaller marlin and sailfish, plus dolphin, bonito, wahoo, yellowfin tuna, dogtooth tuna, cobia, sharks, and mackerel.

Facilities for general tourism, accommodations, and charter boat fishing are excellent out of Cairns. The charter boats are superbly equipped and skippered by highly qualified, experienced anglers. Sportfishing tackle within all International Gamefish Association (IGFA) line classes is available for hire.

Great Barrier Reef fishing.   The Great Barrier Reef is just 27 kilometers (14 nautical miles) from Cairns. Extending almost 2,300 kilometers (1,240 nautical miles) along the northeast coast of Australia, it is the longest coral reef system in the world, and the richest in biological diversity. Indeed, it is a coral jungle amidst a cobalt blue sea of striking beauty and remarkable clarity.

Important as the reef may be to big-game anglers, the black marlin is just one of more than 1,400 species of fish found in and around the Great Barrier Reef, many of which are coral denizens with amazing physical characteristics and intriguing behavior patterns. Continually growing and regenerating itself, the reef parallels the Coral Sea's continental shelf for much of its length. Not far from the reef, the ocean bottom drops away from 100 to 1,000 fathoms. Shoals rise and drop here, providing feeding sites for many species.

Anglers use handlines, and rod-and-reel outfits from light sport (to 10 kilograms) to heavy game (to 60 kilograms), and they have an extraordinary variety of fish species—more than 50—to choose from, including marlin, sailfish, giant trevally, barracouta, tuna, wahoo, sharks, queenfish, coral trout, red emperor, cobia, and Spanish mackerel.

Reef fishing methods, as opposed to those for gamefishing, are very ecumenical; no single angling methodology rules. Although 30- to 40-kilogram handlines are still used, however, the major assault is backed by short rods (to 2 meters), fine-tuned revolving-spool reels, lines to 15 kilograms, and leaders to 25 kilograms. Hook sizes vary from 6/0 to 10/0.

Charter boats will take visiting anglers out to productive areas of the reef, but small to medium-size boats, which allow freedom of movement, are preferred by the majority of sportfishing enthusiasts. Australian reef anglers have a great liking for aluminum boats (or "tinnies," as they are called) from 5 to 6 meters long, and they refer casually to offshore fishing trips of 20 to 30 kilometers out to the reef. Sonar is popular for locating fish and identifying the underwater topography.

Tactics atop the reef vary from bottom fishing (known here as bottom bouncing) to lure casting to

A

trolling. Fly fishing is increasing in popularity. Reef anglers have one aversion: sharks, which number in the thousands; they're cursed because of their propensity for attacking hooked fish and leaving only the head. The frustrated angler can only wonder about the size of the whole fish.

Bottom bouncers either catch their own bait, or use frozen pilchards sold by tackle shops. Heavy lead sinkers are essential to counter the current. Two species prized as superb table fish are the red emperor and the coral trout. Lure anglers, using baitcasting or spinning outfits and minnow-imitating lures, work both inside the reef and outside along its edge. Trollers fish the waters around the hundreds of islands and cays, or travel the outer edge of the reef, where they stand a chance of catching mackerel, tuna, black marlin, and other large species.

The best time of the year to fish these waters is from October through December.

Cape Bowling Green.   Cape Bowling Green is in northeastern Australia's Queensland district, and south of Cairns. Accessed from Townsville, it lies along the Great Barrier Reef. Because the reef and continental shelf extend so much farther offshore here than at Cairns, offshore fishing opportunities are seldom sought after, although big marlin no doubt cruise the outer waters. Anglers are typically discouraged by the distance to be covered, often in heavy seas.

The richness of the bay, a mixture of currents, and abundant inshore reefs and shoals attract baitfish and small billfish to Cape Bowling Green. The reefs and shoals along this great coral bed lie in shallow blue-green water (20 to 40 fathoms). Watching for schools of bait and bird activity is a common element of this fishery. Anglers interested in variety, as well as lighter-tackle fishing for billfish (heavy tackle is the norm at Cairns because of the many opportunities for big fish), find the Cape Bowling Green area near Townsville among the finest angling sites in the world.

Sailfishing here has been phenomenal at times, with reported sightings of big schools of these billfish. Fortunately for local anglers and charter boat skippers, really good action can be had here from March through September; thus, they can pass the winter months (June, July, and August) pursuing light action but spend the end of the year farther north, geared up for granders.

Although marlin of several hundred pounds have been caught in this area, as mentioned earlier the fish run much smaller on average (27 kilograms or so—lighter early in the season and heavier later), and the tackle is scaled down to 10 kilograms and less, with 4- and 6-kilogram tackle most popular. Fly-rod tippet records for black marlin have been established off Cape Bowling Green, incidentally, as well as ultralight line-class records. It stands to reason that ample opportunity makes these record catches possible. With the exception of potentially

record fish, virtually all billfish caught here are tagged and released.

Some 125 kilometers east-northeast of Townsville is Myrmidon Reef, a small reef on the edge of an enormous dropoff. It is seldom fished at what is believed to be peak time, in November and December, because of all the big-fish action at Cairns and the problem of accessibility previously mentioned. Blacks over 1,000 pounds have been lost here during the few forays that have been made, and a 989-pounder reportedly was once weighed-in.

Brisbane/Cape Moreton.   In southeastern Queensland the coastal waters are home to more than 30 species of sportfish, including black, blue, and striped marlin; the occasional sailfish; sharks; mackerel; amberjack; yellowtail kingfish; and tuna. Some species appear seasonally, with the warmer summer months (September through March) bringing fish from more tropical waters. Charter boats are available, and should be used wherever possible; entry to offshore waters involves crossing bars, a hazardous procedure best undertaken by experienced boat skippers with local knowledge.

Back in the days of the Tangalooma (Moreton Bay) Whaling Station, Brisbane was the shark fishing capital of the universe. Even today, the eastern coast of Australia—including the waters off Brisbane as well as to the south in New South Wales—ranks among the best. Great whites, blues, makos, hammerheads, and tiger sharks of proportions that would make even Crocodile Dundee blanch have been captured in these waters. The record books are replete with line-class and all-tackle entries from this vast region.

Cape Moreton in particular has achieved fame with its great white sharks, but these days the international angling community's interest leans more toward the billfish, and the waters off Brisbane and Cape Moreton hold all the species. And although the Australian billfishery is generally synonymous with black marlin, Cape Moreton offers perhaps the best chance on this continent of catching blues, and big ones at that, including fish over 800 pounds and possibly to a thousand.

Most of the blue marlin action is for smaller fish, and at times the catch can be extremely good. Reports of double and triple strikes, and even a remarkable tagged-and-released triple-header, have been made, with many fish in the 300- to 400-pound class.

Blues notwithstanding, black marlin, stripers, and sailfish also frequent these waters, sometimes within relatively short range of shore when the east Australian current moves inward. The striped marlin and blacks are small but make good targets for light-tackle fishing efforts. These marlin average 65 to 90 pounds.

The season commences in summer, from October or November through March, with the striped marlin and blacks early and the blues

available from January through June. Seasons can vary, as this fishery is still developing. Sailfish, meanwhile, are extremely popular from February on, and other available species include various tuna and dolphin.

The good fishing around Brisbane/Cape Moreton is not far from the Gold Coast, a popular tourist locale. Although it is not as out-of-the-way as some destinations, as much as a two-hour run separates anglers from the big marlin grounds.

Inshore there is much to be had as well, with cobia, trevally, kawakawa, and the like. Between here and the neighboring waters in New South Wales, almost all of the IGFA kawakawa records have been set.

Fraser Island, north of the capital city of Brisbane, is the largest sand island in the world. It is noted for its beach fishing, especially for bluefish (known as "tailor" in Australia) from July through October. Estuarine waters hold species similar to those in northern Queensland, the barramundi being an exception.

Many inland impoundments and streams in this part of Queensland are stocked with golden perch, Murray cod, Australian bass, silver perch, and saratoga. Both spinning and baitcasting methods are favored for these species. Trout are nonexistent due to high wate temperatures.

Other Queensland locations.   Estuary fishing is popular along Queensland, and hard-fighting species like the mangrove jack, barramundi, threadfin salmon, sharks, trevally (various species), mulloway, queenfish, and long-toms, can provide exciting angling. The mangrove estuaries in the Townsville area are famous for mangrove jack and barramundi. Spinning and plugcasting with lures, fishing with bait, and trolling are practiced, and fly fishing is also an established sport.

Freshwater angling in tropical streams on either side of the Cape York Peninsula is excellent. Access is generally difficult, however, and four-wheel-drive vehicles and trailer boats are a necessity. Excellent guided fishing tours catering to both lure and fly anglers are popular. Species such as jungle perch, sooty grunter, tarpon, barramundi, mangrove jack, freshwater long-tom, fork-tailed catfish, and saratoga are favorites. A world-record 28.65-kilogram barramundi was taken from the Norman River near Karumba on the west coast of Cape York Peninsula. Some impoundments have been stocked with barramundi, and Lake Tinaroo on the Atherton Tableland is well known for its barramundi and sooty grunter fishery.

Precautions.   There are dangers to be aware of when fishing Queensland waters. At the start of a fishing trip, especially to the Great Barrier Reef, visitors should take time to check which species are likely to be poisonous. (This applies to all states, in fact.) For example, the chinaman fish (and a number of other reef fish) of Queensland waters is inedible because its flesh contains a poison that can sometimes cause an incapacitating (and sometimes fatal) condition known as ciguatera *(see)*. The effects of this poison can recur years after ingestion.

Perhaps the most infamous venomous creatures in North Queensland waters are the sea wasp (box jellyfish) and the stonefish, each of which can cause excruciating pain and death. The estuarine crocodile is an ever-present threat to careless humans. The largest reptile in the world, it frequents tropical estuaries, billabongs (backwater areas of rivers), and swamps across the top of Australia.

Sensible precautions such as heeding warning signs (crocodiles), donning long trousers (box jellyfish), and wearing strong footwear (stone fish), are mandatory when wading any waters, or when walking the reef. Anyone interested in the study of mollusks must be extremely careful when handling cone shells, which can inflict a fatal bite. Sea snakes are common, but it is rare for an angler to be bitten. First aid is the same as that for ordinary snakebite. Sand flies and mosquitoes are prevalent.

Regulations.   It is important for visiting anglers to check the angling and boating regulations for both saltwater and freshwater fishing, lest they exceed bag limits for various species, take protected species, or trespass in restricted areas. Details are covered in publications available from most tackle shops. Some areas of the Great Barrier Reef have fishing restrictions; maps of the affected zones can be obtained from the many offices of the Great Barrier Reef Marine Park Authority. Generally, best fishing times are from November through March.

New South Wales

The waters off New South Wales can be fished for more than 30 species of fish, including blue, black, and striped marlin, swordfish, tuna, yellowtail kingfish, albacore, greater amberjack, cobia, dolphin, mackerel, bluefish, sharks, trevally, and snapper.

The gamefishing bases of Sydney, Port Stephens, and Bermagui are world famous for their excellent facilities, while sport anglers of every persuasion can find something to interest them in bay, estuary, beach, rock, and inland fishing. Along the north coast are many outlets to coastal fishing, but only experienced boaters should attempt to cross the bars.

Rock and beach fishing opportunities are excellent; land-based sportfishing was pioneered in this state. Records include a 34.4-kilogram yellowtail kingfish, a 110-kilogram black marlin, a 26.2-kilogram cobia, and a 77-kilogram yellowfin tuna—all taken from the ocean rocks. Tackle consists of two-handed rods, 3 to 4 meters long, fitted with sidecast, surf-spinning, or surf-casting reels, and lines appropriate to the species sought. Surf-caught species include mulloway, bluefish, Australian salmon (kahawai), and sharks. Captures of marlin, yellowtail kingfish, and big tuna from the rocks are common, although conditions can be hazardous when seas are high. Visitors should be

The Great Lakes contain about 6 quadrillion gallons of water, enough to cover the lower 48 United States 10 feet deep.

A

accompanied by an experienced rock angler. Angel rings (life buoys), thrown to anglers washed into the sea, have been placed at angling black spots along the coast, and have saved a number of lives.

Estuary, bay, and coastal lake fishing from small boats, jetties, and shore, using light spinning and plugcasting tackle, is excellent for smaller species such as bream, flathead, whiting, bluefish, and mulloway. Access points are plentiful, as are boat ramps, and boats can be hired in most places. Sydney Harbour and Botany Bay are two of the better-known estuarine waters.

An offshore location worth noting is that of Lord Howe Island, which is southeast of Brisbane and some 435 miles northeast of Sydney. The waters in the vicinity of Lord Howe feature rocky pinnacles, immense depths, and sheer dropoffs. There has been almost no fishing pressure here until the late 1980s, but impressive catches of blue marlin, sailfish, wahoo, yellowfin tuna, and yellowtail have been registered, and some monstrous blues have been sighted. Many more species are available.

The freshwater fishery in New South Wales is superb, with brown and rainbow trout being the most targeted species. Large Lake Eucumbene and its smaller neighbor, Lake Jindabyne, in the Snowy Mountains region of the Eastern Highlands, are the prominent trout waters on the mainland; specimens in excess of 4 kilograms are not uncommon. Bait, lure, and fly fishing from shore or boat are accepted techniques, and captures of trophy fish are not uncommon, whichever method is adopted. Lake fishing is permitted year-round, but the warmer months from September to March, when the insect life is more active, are the most popular.

There are many excellent trout streams in New South Wales, the majority of which are suitable for spinning and fly fishing. Other fine trout fisheries are found in the New England and Hunter regions, and the Central Highlands, with both rainbow and brown trout averaging 1 to 2 kilograms.

The Australian bass, which can grow in excess of 5 kilograms, is the second most popular freshwater species in New South Wales. It can be found in most streams that flow into the Pacific Ocean from southern Queensland to Victoria, and large numbers have been stocked in several big impoundments throughout the state. Bass plugs are the best lures to use in impoundments, while fly fishing with Muddlers, hair bugs, and streamers, is a favorite stream tactic. Redfin to 2 kilograms are prevalent in many of the inland dams and lakes, and they will respond to spinners and bass plugs. West of the Great Divide, in streams and lakes, there is an important recreational fishery that includes golden perch, Murray cod, silver perch, redfin, and catfish. European carp exist here, too, but are considered a pest and efforts are made to eradicate them.

The summer months, which last from November to March, are the best for most angling activities. During this time the main danger is snakes, the deadliest ones being the tiger snake and the brown snake. Encounters stream-side are not uncommon. Access to many streams can be difficult, but a considerate approach to landholders will rarely meet with a refusal.

Saltwater and freshwater angling and boating regulations exist, and visitors can approach fishing tackle shops for applicable printed material.

Victoria

While lacking the publicity given to the northern states, Victoria offers some excellent sportfishing in ocean waters off its eastern coast, from the New South Wales border to Port Phillip Bay. Southern bluefin tuna, yellowtail kingfish, marlin, striped tuna (skipjack), albacore, and sharks can be taken. Surf fishing from superb beaches, such as Ninety Mile Beach, will produce sharks, Australian salmon, mulloway, and bluefish. Tackle consists of surf rods to 4 meters in length, fitted with sidecast, surf, or spinning reels spooled with nylon line to 10-kilogram-strength nylon line. Baitfishing is the most popular angling method here.

Estuary fishing in the southeastern region is extensive, with a chain of lakes and bays holding smaller species such as bream, flathead, mulloway, garfish, and whiting. Light spinning and plugcasting tackle is appropriate. Hire boats (unguided rentals) are available in most areas, but extreme caution should be exercised if approaching dangerous entrances to the open ocean.

Port Phillip Bay is heavily fished for snapper, flathead, and whiting, and the entrance is famous for its large yellowtail kingfish. To the west of Port Phillip Bay, the coastline is less accessible, but surf and rock fishing can still be pursued, and there is some offshore fishing for tuna and sharks.

Victoria has a wealth of inland streams and large waterways that contain a surprising variety of fish species, the most notable being trout—both brown (to 4.6 kilograms) and rainbow (to 5.27 kilograms). Renowned fishing waters are found in the central region, where major lakes—such as Lake Eildon—and rivers provide excellent angling for trout, Murray cod, redfin, and golden perch. Some lakes have been stocked with chinook salmon, the largest of which registered 6.6 kilograms. The eastern and western regions also fish well for trout, golden perch, and redfin. Australian bass can be found in some of the eastern streams that flow into the Tasman Sea.

Angling methods include spinning, plugcasting, trolling, and fly fishing, and general angling services are available in all areas. Fly anglers can rely on nymphs and dry flies, and spinners and plugs can usually be cast or trolled successfully. Access to most waters is by car, although it may be necessary to ask landholders for permission to enter their properties.

There are some protected species and waterways; details on this are covered in regulations and boating rules available from tackle shops, and the offices of the Department of Conservation and Natural Resources throughout the state. The best fishing months are November through March.

Tasmania

This largely mountainous island state, situated at the most southerly part of the Australian continental shelf and bordered by the Indian, Southern, and Pacific Oceans, has an international reputation for providing some of the finest trout fishing in the world, and a less-widely known, big-game fishery along its east coast. The warm East Australian Current flows its length, and this brings within reach such larger saltwater species as southern bluefin tuna (the world record of 106.5 kilograms was caught here), skipjack, albacore, yellowtail kingfish, sharks, and striped marlin.

Coastal fishing includes offshore, estuary, rock, and beach fishing, and the preferred waters are those along the north and east coasts. Two Bass Strait islands, King to the west and Flinders to the east, offer excellent bay, beach, and rock fishing for Australian salmon, flathead, yellowtail kingfish, sharks, trevally, tuna, and snapper. Charter boats for offshore fishing are available.

Most of these species can be found along the north coast of Tasmania where boat, rock, and beach fishing are popular. Angling in offshore waters fronting Bass Strait should be attempted only in charter boats with experienced skippers, as the conditions are often windy and stormy. Estuarine waters are safe, and rental boats can be hired to fish for many species, including snapper, bluefish, trevally, flathead, whiting, and Australian salmon. These species, plus barracouta, are also taken by rock and beach anglers using rods to 4 meters in length and sidecast, spinning, or surf reels spooled with lines to 10-kilogram breaking strength.

The inland fishery is chiefly for trout, although redfin inhabit some waterways. Brown trout were introduced in 1864 from England, with a later introduction of rainbow and brook trout from the United States. The famous Salmon Ponds hatchery on the Plenty River now raises thousands of trout each year.

The central highlands region is most renowned for its trout fishing, with a number of major waterways, especially Great Lake, Little Pine Lagoon, Arthurs Lake, and Lake Sorell, acclaimed for their superbly conditioned brown and rainbow trout. The region is accessible by car, with ample lodging available. Both lure and fly fishing are popular, and boats can also be hired. Nearby, is the "Land of 3,000 Lakes," where thousands of smaller stream-fed lakes hold wild brown trout and a lesser number of rainbows. Access can be difficult, however, and visitors should be prepared to walk to most waters. Care should be exercised to avoid tiger snakes, which are common in many of these areas.

In the west coast region of Tasmania, Lakes Pedder, Burbury, and Gordon are the most popular. Easily accessible by car, they fish well for brown trout. A record brown trout of 8.25 kilograms has been recorded from Lake Pedder. To the north, the Leven, Henty, and Mersey Rivers have a reputation for good stream fishing, with sea trout also being taken in their lower reaches. In northeast Tasmania, the famous Brumby's Creek fishes well, and the Esk system of rivers is acclaimed for its excellent stream fishing. The southern region has a number of streams and lakes that hold both trout and redfin. Most are within a couple of hours drive from the capital city of Hobart.

Fishing with spinning tackle and lures like the locally made Tasmanian Devil, or bladed spinners, is permissible in most waters, although some, like Little Pine Lagoon, is a fly-fishing-only water. Fly anglers can stock up with both wet and dry flies, but local advice should be sought as to patterns. Mudeyes, the larvae of the dragonfly, are a deadly bait; they can be found under submerged rocks and logs, or bought from some tackle shops. However, some waters are closed to bait use.

Regional regulations and boating rules exist. Details are obtainable from the Marine Resources Division of the Department of Primary Industry, tackle shops, and all tourist centers.

South Australia

Situated between Western Australia and Victoria, South Australia's main angling claim to fame is its fishing for shark, southern bluefin (with a world record of 33.5 kilograms), Australian salmon, and snapper. There's a lesser trout fishery for brown and rainbow trout, while other freshwater species present include redfin, Murray cod, and golden perch.

Kangaroo Island, lying off the tip of Cape Jervis, allows rock, beach, and bay fishing for a variety of species, including Australian salmon, snapper, flathead, King George whiting, barracouta, and yellowtail kingfish. Charter boats operating offshore will take anglers out to where they can catch sharks, southern bluefin tuna, and yellowtail kingfish. The winter months—May to October—are best for southern bluefin tuna.

Spencer Gulf and Gulf St. Vincent waters provide some excellent fishing for both shore-based and boat anglers. Big snapper, King George whiting, sharks, Australian salmon, flathead, mulloway, and bream are some of the available species. Charter boats can also be hired within these areas, and pier fishing for bream, salmon, and King George whiting, with light tackle, is popular throughout the year. It was in these waters that famous gamefisherman Alf Dean landed a then-world record white shark of 1,208.38 kilograms in 1959.

The southeast region of South Australia extends from Victor Harbour to the Victorian border. It's here that the beaches of the Koorong, a chain of salt lagoons that run for more than 140 kilometers

A

behind the ocean shoreline, provide some of the best beach fishing on the continent for Australian salmon, flathead, bream, sharks, and mulloway. Huge mulloway to 40 kilograms have been taken from the mouth of the Murray River; fishing is best after dark. Beach rods to 4 meters; sidecast, spinning, and surf reels; and lines of 10 to 15 kilograms are used. Access is by four-wheel-drive vehicles.

The inland fishery in South Australia is small because it is the driest of the states, there's an absence of large rivers, and many of the streams dry to a series of pools during the summer months. Both the Onkaparinga River and the Broughton River rely on stocking for their brown and rainbow trout fishery, and golden perch and redfin are present in the Onkaparinga River. Spinning and fly fishing are practiced here. The freshwater reaches of the Murray River, which cuts across the southeastern corner of the state, hold Murray cod, golden perch, redfin, and catfish.

For angling and boating regulations, look for detailed information at tackle shops and Fisheries offices throughout the state. The best fishing is during the summer months, from November through March.

Western Australia

The largest of Australia's states, with an area of more than 2.5 million square kilometers (975,100 square miles), Western Australia includes some of the best rock, beach, offshore, estuary, and bay fishing in the world. Indeed, in its northern waters it surpasses North Queensland for abundance of angling species. Unfortunately, access to its remote angling areas is usually difficult, requiring large or small boats and four-wheel-drive vehicles driven by experienced anglers with a sound knowledge of the terrain and the climate. In addition, temperatures in excess of 40°C are not uncommon in the north during the summer months.

In the Albany region to the south and southeast of the capital city of Perth (said to be the most remote city in the world), there is excellent beach and rockfishing for Australian salmon, big bluefish, groper (grouper), sharks, large silver trevally, snapper, mulloway, Westralian jewfish, and samson fish (*Seriola hippos*). Rods to 4 meters, and sidecast, spinning, or surf reels equipped with lines of 10- to 15-kilogram breaking strength are used here. Also present in these waters are big yellowfin tuna.

Estuary and bay fishing for bluefish, mulloway, flathead, and King George whiting is very popular. Tackle consists of light to medium spinning and plugcasting outfits. Generally, both access and facilities are good, but some four-wheel-drive vehicles are needed to reach a number of good fishing spots.

In the Perth/Fremantle region lies the Swan River estuary, where Australian salmon, mulloway, flathead, bluefish, bream, and trevally are commonly taken. Anglers fish the beaches and rocks immediately north and south of Perth, with conventional beach/rock tackle, target bluefish, mulloway, Australian salmon, silver trevally, and snapper. The reefs surrounding Rottnest Island to the west are favorite fishing grounds for Spanish mackerel, yellowfin tuna, dolphin, and yellowtail kingfish, while still farther west is the Rottnest Trench, which is fished for blue marlin.

To the north, from Shark Bay to the Northern Territory border, exists fishing that most anglers only dream about. This is the Kimberley region, where high temperatures, rugged country, big seas, saltwater crocodiles, and cyclones can challenge even the most adventurous. Species to excite any angler thrive here, and include sailfish (a world record 77.95-kilogram Pacific sailfish has been taken here), amberjack, barramundi, cobia, dolphin, Spanish mackerel, black marlin, queenfish (including a 10.5-kilogram world record specimen), mulloway, samson fish, sharks, snapper, bluefish, giant trevally (a 39.5-kilogram world record fish came from these waters), yellowfin tuna, wahoo, and yellowtail kingfish.

Land-based angling in the area is famous among anglers nationwide, and cannot be bettered anywhere in the world. Because of the area's remoteness, however, it is strongly recommended that guided fishing tours (from Broome and Kununurra) be undertaken by those attempting this sport for the first time.

Offshore fishing is superb, and boats to work the waters for sailfish, wahoo, mackerel, and tuna can be chartered from Denham (Shark Bay), Exmouth, Port Hedland, and Broome. Gamefishing tackle in appropriate line classes is recommended, even for land-based fishing where rock fishing tackle may be considered unsuitable. This area is also famous for its excellent saltwater fly fishing, especially for sailfish, which abound. Smaller species can be fished with spinning or plugcasting tackle, and small-boat skippers will find wonderful angling in the complex of waterways for snapper, mulloway, flathead, bream, and whiting. The wet season (December through March) renders most of the Kimberley area inaccessible, but the dry season (June through September) is not only cooler, it opens up the country.

Inland fishing is confined largely to the Perth/Albany region in the south, and to freshwater sections of rivers like the Fitzroy and impoundments such as Lakes Argyle and Kununurra in the north. In the south, redfin are plentiful, and streams and dams are stocked with brown and rainbow trout, which are usually pursued with spinning, plugcasting, and fly fishing methods. The northern waters are renowned for their barramundi and sooty grunter fishery. These species are taken on both spinning and plugcasting tackle using lures. Lines from 7 to 10 kilograms are favored.

Regulations and boating rules exist for most areas, and copies can be obtained from Fisheries offices and most tackle shops. Potential dangers, mainly in the north, include saltwater crocodiles, cyclones, and big seas, plus heat that can be oppressive in the extreme. Sand flies can also be a nuisance.

Northern Territory

Constituting one-sixth of the landmass of Australia and located in the Tropics at the "Top End" of Australia, the Northern Territory is sparsely populated and replete with world-class sportfishing potential. Tourism here is rapidly growing, and it seems like more of that potential will be enjoyed by visiting anglers in the near future, for a variety of opportunities.

The upper end of the Northern Territory abuts the Timor Sea on the northwest, the Arafur Sea on the north, and the Gulf of Carpentaria on the east. Nhulunbuy is an aboriginal preserve that sports a bauxite mine, and provides a jumping-off point for fishing north of the Gove Peninsula, around its barren and desertlike islands. Bathurst Island is accessed by plane from Darwin, with fishing primarily concentrated on barramundi in the creeks and lagoons. Many of the rivers, estuaries, and lagoons to the east and west of Darwin have notable barramundi fishing as well, and there is a growing offshore fishery.

The capital city of Darwin is the base for guided fishing tours to all worthwhile parts of the hinterland, and to some exciting offshore gamefishing for black marlin, sailfish, Spanish mackerel, sharks, giant trevally, northern bluefin tuna, queenfish, and barracouta. Small-boat anglers have a wonderful playground to explore in the many bays and estuaries, which are within easy reach. In these waters they can catch barramundi, black jewfish, trevally, mangrove jack, threadfin salmon, queenfish, and many other species. A camera or camcorder is well worth carrying, to record what are almost certain to be memorable fishing moments in an unusual part of this continent.

Inland fishing in the Northern Territory is mainly for barramundi, sooty grunter, and saratoga, with mangrove jack, threadfin salmon, and fingermark bream being taken from the brackish waters that can extend for many miles upstream. Spinning, plug-casting, and flycasting are widely used.

Outside Australia, the Top End is most known for barramundi; specimens in excess of 27 kilograms have been recorded, not to mention various line-class world records. This cover-streaking hard-fighting leaper is caught in the estuaries and rivers that abound throughout the Northern Territory, and although these fish exist in various parts of Australia, they are nowhere as abundant as here.

Unquestionably, barramundi fishing in the Northern Territory is a true angling adventure, offering opportunities that are rare today. For one thing, this is the land of Crocodile Dundee fame—sparsely populated, wild, and sometimes dangerous.

Fishing takes place in remote areas in junglelike habitat. Mangrove-lined rivers and tropical lagoons and estuaries are the angling grounds, and casters fish amidst heavy cover, including vegetation and mangrove roots. The struggle to keep larger barramundi from reaching sanctuary once hooked is formidable. A lot of tackle gets tested to the maximum by these fish, and many a lure is lost. The fishing, to say the least, is challenging.

Perhaps as challenging is the fact that good barramundi fishing waters are frequented by saltwater crocodiles, which are aggressive, known man-eaters and highly respected by anglers. Signs warn against swimming, and boaters do not venture close enough to risk an encounter.

Barramundi fishing demands an ability to play the tides, which can fluctuate severely here. The best fishing time is during low tide because it draws barramundi out of the mangroves in creeks, lagoons, and other spots and concentrates them in holes, channels, and the like, making them more accessible. Trolling and casting are both popular, using diving and rattling plugs on baitcasting tackle. Fishing is primarily done from small skiffs, 12 to 15 feet long.

Bathurst Island has some excellent fishing for relatively large barramundi, but the bulk of angling for this species takes place around Darwin, in jungle rivers and mangrove-lined lagoons. The Daly River to the southwest of Darwin, and the Mary River to the east, are among the top locations.

Both Bathurst and Melville Islands to the north are controlled by the Aboriginal Land Trust, and permission to travel on them must be obtained. They are well known for their good bay, beach, creek, and estuary fishing, with some excellent offshore angling for larger species. Some other areas on the mainland are designated aboriginal areas, and permission must also be obtained to enter and fish them.

The remote northern region of the Northern Territory has billfishing in two distinctly different

Anglers try to extricate a hooked barramundi from a snag on the Daly River.

The coast of the Northern Territory along the Sea of Arafura has lightly explored angling opportunities.

locales, neither of which received more than an occasional visit by ardent billfish anglers before the late 1980s. The easternmost of these locales is some 50 miles north of Darwin in the waters around Bathurst Island, and some remarkable catches of sailfish and black marlin have been made here.

The other billfish possibility exists off Gove Peninsula, more than 350 miles to the east. There, black marlin have been caught off Truant Islands and the English Company's Islands, reportedly in sizes over 500 pounds, as well as many sailfish. A few charter boats have worked this area from Nhulunbuy, and reports are that light-tackle fishing starts in March, with plenty of sailfish action at that time, and that larger blacks show up in October and November.

Both of these locales sport opportunities for other fish, either around island reefs or while trolling the offshore environs. The islands off the Gove Peninsula are especially a potpourri of opportunities for light-tackle angling for willing, aggressive fish. In the Gove region along the east coast of Arnhem Land, the fishing is largely untouched. Besides black marlin, other species include giant trevally, golden trevally, queenfish, mackerel, cobia, barracouta, Spanish mackerel, and northern bluefin tuna. Access is by plane to the remote mining town of Nhulunbuy, and facilities range from elaborate to austere.

Most of the coast of the Northern Territory bordering the Arafura Sea from Gove Peninsula east has seen little if any sportfishing ventures, and there are many bays, lagoons, reefs, and islands that could provide virgin fishing if there were access and if the fishing wasn't as good elsewhere. There is little motivation to explore this region. In any event, these are aboriginal lands, and access permits are required.

Guided tours for anglers visiting the Northern Territory are strongly recommended, especially in the wet season (October to April), when most roads are impassable. The fishing range is extended during the dry season (May to September), when many places can be accessed by four-wheel-drive vehicles. The best fishing for barramundi is during the months of April and May, which is the crossover period between the wet and the dry seasons.

The chief danger to anglers is the big saltwater crocodile that can move well up into the freshwater reaches of most waterways. Fishing from shore is inadvisable, as is fishing from a canoe. Wading could be a suicidal pastime! Heed all warning signs; they are empirically based. Sand flies and mosquitoes also exist, and can be an annoyance.

The tidal range is exceptional in Northern Territory waters, sometimes exceeding 7 meters. Anglers who hire their own boats for self-guiding will find that tide charts are essential; they can generally be obtained from tackle shops or the Darwin Port Authority. Regulations and boating rules exist, and copies of the "Northern Territory Fishing and Boating Guide" are available from tackle shops and the Department of Primary Industry and Fisheries.

AUSTRIA

With most of its 83,859 square kilometers of land in the eastern Alps, Austria is a central European country noted for stunning scenery and clear, clean waters that originate in the high peaks, offering good trout and grayling fishing before flowing into larger waters and coursing through broad valleys. Austria's high-quality mountain waters offer fishing as good or better than that found in most other European countries, particularly for salmonid species.

Roughly the size of the state of Maine, this predominantly mountainous country, with an average elevation of 3,000 feet, contains portions of the Danube, Europe's second largest river, and such prominent tributaries to the Danube as the Rivers Inn, Traun, Enns, and Ybbs. The high country is studded with small rivers and streams, as well as assorted lakes and reservoirs of varying size, plus a pair of large border lakes. Among the latter are the Bodensee, which forms the western border with Liechtenstein and Switzerland (see); also known as Lake Konstanz, it is part of the Rhine River, covering 544 square kilometers, reaching depths of more than 250 meters, and serving as an important commercial fishery for whitefish and pike. The largest lake entirely within the country's borders is the Attersee east of Salzburg, which is a major all-around recreation site for Austrians.

The cool rivers and streams and associated smaller lakes are really where the fishing action is for the majority of resident and visiting anglers. European grayling and brown trout, both native species, are abundant and vie for the distinction of most popular species, and are also found in the lakes. The largest brown trout are caught in lakes; a lake-resident brown trout here is known as a *seeforelle,* whereas a river- or stream-resident brown trout is known as a *bachforelle.*

Confusion over terminology exists when referring to brown trout in rivers versus those in lakes. In Europe, the Western term "lake trout" actually refers to a *seeforelle;* though published literature may indicate that lake trout exist in various waters, the species referenced is actually *seeforelle.* The species that Westerners refer to as "lake trout" *(Salvelinus namaycush)* is actually in the charr family, and the type of fish referred to in central European nations as "lake char." This is important to understand, because some of the largest brown trout in the world have come from European lakes, but they are still considerably smaller than the largest *Salvelinus namaycush* caught in North America. Few traveling anglers from the West would visit Europe to fish for *Salvelinus namaycush,* but they might try to catch a trophy *seeforelle* in its native environment (brown trout in the West are an introduced species).

Other salmonids are also found in many of the cool flowages and lakes in Austria. These include brook (speckled) trout, rainbow trout, lake charr, huchen, and whitefish.

Some of the deeper lakes contain two-story fisheries for various salmonids, usually brown and rainbow trout, plus warmer-water denizens like native pike and zander (pike-perch), as well as assorted coarse species. The latter can be found in many of the shallower and warmer ponds, lakes, canals, and rivers. Large specimens of wels catfish are in a few waters, and a number of lakes are reported to contain black r bass.

The River Traun, which flows northerly to the Danube, is one of the premier trout and grayling flows in the country. Other notable and larger rivers for these species include the Enns, Erlauf, Lammer, Salza, Traisen, and Ybbs.

Most fishery resources are privately managed and controlled. A system of fishing private waters (rivers, streams, ponds, lakes, and canals) exists through packages offered by a great many resorts and lodges, many of whom cater to angling visitors, some of them offering fly fishing schools.

Nearly all trout streams and rivers are restricted to fly fishing only, and without the use of shot or added weight. Barbless hook requirements exist at many prime sites as well. Lure fishing with spinning tackle is generally permitted in large waters; live bait is mainly prohibited, but some forms of bait are allowed for coarse fishing.

Selected Venues

This brief review of opportunities at some venues reflects a diversity in species and water types, and is generally representative of the broad array of fishing found at hotels and vacation sites throughout Austria. Many fishing sites are easily reached by auto, although those close to dense population centers are heavily pressured. The more distant and reserved waters tend to offer the best fishing overall, and most are managed via regulation and annual restocking.

Southern region. The southernmost portion of Austria contains the whole gamut of Austrian fishing experiences. Most of the rivers contain brown trout, rainbow trout, and grayling.

In the southernmost Carinthia district near the Slovenia border, the River Drau (Drava) is known for monster wels. This river is a mountain torrent in its upper reaches, then moderates on its way to the Danube, with the region near Völkermarkt being a place to do battle with big catfish. Large huchen, incidentally, have come from the Drau; 32- and 34-kilogram world records were caught in the Drau in the early 1980s.

Nearby Drau Reservoir is a narrow 25-kilometer-long impoundment of the Drau River that contains pike, zander, and catfish that may only be caught on artificial lures. The Gösselsdorfer See in the vicinity is a small lake with pike, carp, and tench, and area rivers possess brown and rainbow trout, which are governed by a barbless-hook fly fishing requirement. There are other small impoundments on this long river, some containing trout.

Farther west, and to the southeast of Villach, is the Faaker See, perhaps Austria's preeminent whitefish lake. One of the country's southernmost lakes, and a deep one at the foot of the Karawanken Mountains, it not only contains large and plentiful whitefish (which prompts an international whitefish competition each September), but counts brown trout, pike, and carp among its prominent species, and also contains lake charr, rainbow trout, zander, and black bass. Live bait is prohibited here, but all types of fishing methods are allowed.

Still farther west, and closer to the East Tyrol region of Austria, is Carinthia's highest altitude lake, the Weissensee. Outboard motors are prohibited on this premier lake nestled between mountains northwest of Villach, but various angling methods are allowed, and species include brown trout, rainbow trout, lake charr, zander, pike, whitefish, and coarse species. Pike to 16 kilograms have been caught here in the 1990s, and the lake has produced a former European record 21-kilogram *seeforelle.*

To the north of Villach, another mountain lake, Ossiacher See, is the third largest lake in this region. At more than 2,700 acres it has wels catfish, zander, pike, numerous coarse species, and black bass. Various fishing methods are allowed, but live bait and sonar are prohibited.

Central and northern regions. This central mountain region of Austria features some of the finest river trout fishing in the country as well as in Europe. The headwaters of the Traun system originate here in the Salzkammergut district, and such flowages as the Altausseer, Grundlseer, Kainischer, Koppentraun, and countless small streams and tributaries in the upper watershed provide opportunity for brown trout, rainbow trout, speckled trout, and grayling. There are countless small lakes and ponds in the region as well, many with brown trout, lake charr, and rainbow trout, and some with pike, zander, coarse species, and also bass.

Some of the finest river fishing for trout and grayling exists in the Traun below Traunsee Lake, from the town of Gmunden downstream. Rainbow and brown trout from 1 to 2.5 kilograms are abundant here, and specimens of both species exceed 4.5 kilograms annually. The Traun is considered one of the top trout rivers in Europe; it provides relatively easy wading and is restricted to barbless hooks and fly fishing. A number of fishing-oriented hotels are located here.

South of this area to the east and west is the River Enns and many tributaries to that long flow. Brown and rainbow trout and grayling are the mainstays, with the area from Gröbming to Radstadt of special note and with various hotels catering to anglers. Some of the streams here also have speckled trout and charr, and the lakes have most of the same species as noted elsewhere in Styria. A few have large *seeforelle* as well as large pike; some, like 655-acre Fuschlsee near Halbach, produce pike to 14 kilograms.

In the western Salzburg Province, Hohe Tauern National Park near Mittersill features more than 100 kilometers of trout and grayling streams, in a barbless-hook fly-fishing-only area that was formerly a haunt of the Austrian aristocracy a century ago. The Hohe Tauern is noted for the Grossglockner, the highest peak in Austria at 3,797 meters, and one of Europe's largest glaciers, the Pasterze.

Permits

Anglers need two types of permits to fish in Austria. One is the *amtliche Fischerkarte,* an Official Fishing License issued by the respective local government office (in Upper Austria and Vienna by the local fishing authority; in Tyrol and Vorarlberg by the owner of the fishing rights). This is a document with a photograph valid for one to three years throughout the province concerned. In all provinces except Upper Austria and Vienna, a temporary fishing authorization, *kurzfristige Fischergastkarte,* valid only for a specific fishing preserve, is issued by the owner of the fishing rights (in Burgenland only by the local government office). In some federal provinces, one-day tickets are issued.

The other necessary permit is the *private Fischereierlaubnis,* a Private Fishing Permit of the local owner. This is in addition to the Official License, and obtainable from the fishing water's lessee or proprietor for a fixed sum. A limited number of Private Fishing Permits may be issued for certain fishing preserves, as some waters are rationed as to the number of anglers who can access them at a given time. Permits for private waters are issued for varying periods of time, and

are usually accompanied by regulations regarding catch limits, size limits, catch-and-release, angling methods, baits and lures, and so on.

AUTOMATIC REEL
A type of flycasting reel that retrieves line automatically.
See: Flycasting Tackle.

AUTOPILOT
A hands-free navigational instrument used for steering large boats on a preselected bearing. It is occasionally used by trollers.
See: Steering Device, Remote.

AXILLARY PROCESS
A fleshy flap, which is usually narrow and extends to the rear, situated just above the pectoral or pelvic fins on some fish.
See: Fish.

AYU   *Plecoglossus altivelis altivelis.*
Other names—sweetfish, ayu sweetfish; Japanese: *ayu, koayu.*

The only member of the Plecoglossidae family, the ayu—more commonly known in English as sweetfish—is a prized species in Japan and a unique salmonid of economic importance. Fishing for ayu is very specialized.

Identification. The ayu has an olive brown body with a pale-yellow blotch on its side. Its fins, including the expanded dorsal fin, are reddish. There are 10 to 12 rays on the dorsal fin, 9 to 17 rays on the anal fin, 5 or 6 branchiostegal rays, and usually 59 to 64 vertebrae. When the ayu spawns, its fin colors are enhanced (the fish is then known as *sabi,* meaning "rusty"), and both sexes are covered with tubercles. The male does not develop a kype, but its upper jaw shortens; the female's anal fin expands during this time.

Size. The ayu attains a maximum size of roughly 12 inches.

Distribution. An anadromous species, ayu occur in the western North Pacific, from western Hokkaido in Japan southward to the Korean Peninsula, Taiwan, and China.

Ayu

Habitat/Life history.   Adult ayu inhabit the upper reaches of rivers, where they mature before migrating downstream to spawn. Spawning occurs in the lower reaches, and most ayu die after spawning. Breeding occurs in the fall, and the fish begin to show their spawning colors during summer. The adhesive eggs hatch in three weeks, and the larvae move out of the river and into the sea when they are about 1 inch long. They overwinter in the sea and return in spring, when they are about 3 inches long, migrating upstream in huge numbers.

Food and feeding habits.   Ayu have a peculiar but highly evolved mouth and dentition. When reentering freshwater, they develop a series of comblike teeth that lie outside the mouth; these replace the conical teeth they used to catch small crustaceans at sea. In freshwater, these fish feed on algae. The tip of each jaw features a bony pointed process that fits into a corresponding recess on the opposite jaw when the mouth is closed. It is believed that adult ayu eat algae from rocks by grazing, using their snout and teeth to scrape off the algae.

AZORE ISLANDS
See: Portugal.

BACK BOUNCING

See: Backtrolling.

BACK CAST

The backward motion of the rod and line in flycasting.

See: Flycasting Tackle.

BACKING

Reserve line that is connected to the main line on the spool of a reel for situations when greater line lengths are necessary. Backing is normally of a different type or strength than the main line and is most commonly used on flycasting reels, where it is attached to the fly line, since it is practical to cast only a certain amount of fly line. Backing may be employed with other forms of tackle, although in these it is most common to use a continuous length of the same line to fill the spool.

See: Flycasting Tackle.

BACKING DOWN

A boat manipulation tactic primarily used in offshore fishing (see) to help an angler gain line when hooked up to a large and strong fish. The boat is driven in reverse, with its stern facing in the direction of the fish and the line. The angler winds line on the reel while the boat backs (often swiftly) toward the fish. The boat captain backs down instead of turning and heading toward the fish so he can see the line and the position of the fish. This prevents the boat from interfering with the fish and also prevents slack from developing in the line.

This fish-fighting strategy may be necessary when a fish has taken an exceptional amount of line and the angler is in danger of losing all the line on the reel. It may also be used where significant boat traffic or obstructions could enable a fish to break the line. Because anglers have more control over a fish on a short length of line than a long one, backing down will narrow the distance to the fish and possibly help prevent its loss. This tactic may be put to use unfairly by anglers employing light tackle in open water (often when fishing during a contest or for the sake of establishing a light-line record). By lessening the effect of a long length of line on light tackle and reel drag, the angler can bring a fish to capture more quickly than would have been possible otherwise.

See: Playing Fish.

BACKLASH

The tangle of line that develops on the spool of a revolving spool reel as a result of the differential between the speed of the line moving through the rod guides and the amount of line being made available to follow the lure by the spin imparted to the reel spool. In essence, the spool moves faster than the line can depart, causing the spool to overrun the line and pile up line on the spool. The causes and preventions for this are discussed in other entries (see: baitcasting tackle; conventional tackle).

One way to attempt to remove a backlash in a revolving spool reel is to put the reel in gear, tighten the drag so it doesn't slip, press the thumbnail of your rod-holding hand on the snarl to flatten and relax the coils, take two or three turns of the reel handle, put the reel in gear, and pull out the line. This does not tighten the coils and should allow you to get all but the worst backlashes out in a few seconds. Make sure you reset the drag.

Many people pick at the backlashed loops of line with their fingers. To do this, put the reel in freespool with your thumb on the spool. Carefully pick away at the leading loops to remove tightening overwraps until you get to the loop that is dug in the worst; then pull it out. Get all snarled line segments out before rewinding the line on the spool, and do not wind over any loops.

See: Casting.

BACK-REEL

The activity of turning the handle on a reel backward. This is possible on reels with direct drive, and also on baitcasting, spincasting, and spinning reels that have a selective anti-reverse, in which the user can elect to turn the anti-reverse mechanism off, thus allowing the drive gear to move either forward or backward, as well as the handle of the reel to turn forward or backward.

In the past, when reel drags were poor and often unreliable, anglers felt more comfortable when playing a strong fish if they could reel backward to let line out to play the fish. Many were accustomed to doing this with baitcasting, or levelwind, reels, which initially had direct drive and had to be back-reeled, or wound backward, when a strong fish put a lot of pressure on the reel.

The trouble with back-reeling is that rarely can you reel backward quickly enough to keep up with a rapidly turning handle when a strong fish speeds off; therefore, you have to let go of the handle, which usually spins wildly and may cause a snarl, backlash, or overrun upon completion of the swift back-reeling. When you try to grab the rapidly turning handle, it often smacks your fingers, a result that caused the old reels to be called knucklebusters.

Another problem is that you have to gauge the action of the fish in order to reel quickly to keep up with it. Although it is possible to back-reel small fish, like 2-pound bass, as long as the drag is a good one and properly set; it is better to keep the anti-reverse engaged, especially for stronger and harder-fighting fish.

Today, reel drags are quite reliable and efficient, especially when properly set; and there is no reason to back-wind, even if a reel has the ability to do so. Today's baitcasting, spincasting, and spinning reels do not really need selective anti-reverse, but most of them have it to give anglers—especially competitive bass anglers who insist on cranking the drag tension up high—the option of using it. Probably the only time that the average angler uses this feature is when line is accidentally wound around inner or outer parts of the reel and needs to be worked free.

See: Baitcasting Tackle; Spincasting Tackle; Spinning Tackle; Playing Fish.

BACKTROLLING

"Backtrolling" refers to two freshwater fishing techniques primarily used by walleye, steelhead, and salmon anglers. In both methods, the angler uses a small boat and precise boat-handling methods to manipulate the boat while presenting a lure or bait behind the boat in a systematic way, making a thorough, slow, and careful presentation. A backtroller can maintain position along specific depths, nearly hover over selected spots, and maneuver the boat using wind direction to ensure that the following bait remains in the proper place. This is especially vital when a school of fish is packed into one small spot.

In one form of backtrolling, the angler runs a small boat stern first, and the boat is typically outfitted with transom-mounted splash guards to keep wave action from dumping water into the boat. Using a tiller-steered outboard motor in reverse, or a transom-mounted electric motor (with the lower unit turned so that the stern goes backward when the motor is technically in a forward position), the angler maneuvers the boat very slowly to maintain precise position around points, reefs, weedlines, sandbars, and along dropoffs. Favored by walleye anglers, this was once an extremely popular technique but has become less so.

A more common method of maintaining precise boat control and efficient lure or bait placement—one that is often used in rivers—is achieved by floating, drifting, or trolling slowly backward downcurrent. In some places this is called backtrolling or back bouncing, but in others it is called hotshotting (a derivative of the West Coast technique of using a tight-wiggling, deep-diving

trolling plug) for river steelhead and salmon, or pulling plugs. In still other places, it is called slipping. In Europe, it is called harling *(see)*.

Whatever you call it, the idea is to have the bow of your boat pointed upstream, using the motor or oars to control the downstream progression of the boat. The boat moves very slowly—it actually drifts—downstream and at times remains stationary in the current (some boaters anchor in the spot where they catch a fish) as lures are fished at varied distances (from a few feet to 75 feet) behind the boat. The benefit of this technique is that the lures essentially dangle in front of fish that the boat has not yet passed over; in upstream trolling, the boat passes over the fish and alerts them to your presence and probably spooks them. Additionally, lures that are backtrolled downstream approach the head of fish instead of coming from behind and swimming past their head. Anglers usually fish these lures in the channels and deep pools where bigger fish lie, and the lures waver in front of the fish much longer than they would if cast and retrieved or if trolled upstream and away from the fish. Overall, this technique is highly effective in river fishing because the presentation is more natural (resembling, for example, a small fish struggling against the current and being slowly swept downward toward the fish) and because the fish are less likely to be disturbed by the lures before they see them.

In most downstream backtrolling, the angler uses diving plugs for fish that take them. Some fish, such as shad, don't take plugs; in that case, the preferred offerings are a shad dart (a type of jig) or tiny spoons fished behind a torpedo shaped beadchain sinker. Others respond well to bait; winter-run steelhead, for example, are caught with pencil lead-weighted spawn sacks, single-hook salmon eggs, or worms. Many different attractions, including plugs, spoons, spinners, flies, and baits, are used as conditions and location dictate. Plugs are most often flat-lined with or without a sinker, and some form of sinker is always used with baits. If a plug is to be effective, it must run straight and dive to the bottom; if it doesn't, then it has to be tuned *(see: tuning lures)* to run properly.

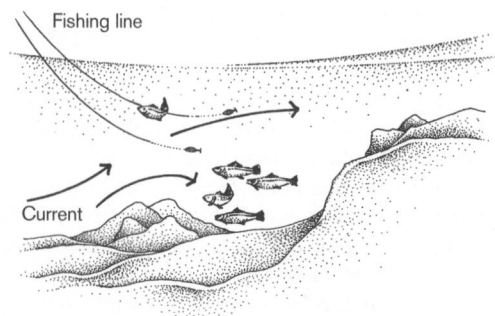

Depicted is the tail of a river pool and two lures that are being backtrolled downstream to approach fish facing upstream.

When backtrolling, skilled boat maneuvering is a prerequisite to precise lure positioning. The location and depth of the offering is critical to successful river fishing. The lure must be on or close to the bottom, and only the appropriate amount of weight or lure design will achieve this.

Pools and deep runs are the areas in which backtrolling is most favored. Often, the boat must be positioned far enough upriver so the lure works slowly from the head of a pool, or runs down through the tail of it; it's not sufficient to maneuver downstream to a spot and then hold position, as the fish you seek may be at the head of that location. When working from side to side across the river, realize that it takes awhile for a trailing lure to catch up to the boat's position. When you sweep close to a bank, for instance, hold that position momentarily, allowing time for the lure to work its way over too. If you sweep in and out quickly, the lure won't get as far to either side as you might like.

Be sure to troll backward in a slow, controlled fashion. When you stop rowing or throttle back the motor, a floating plug rises, a spinner doesn't spin, weights sink, and so forth. This is caused by the sudden lack of pressure against those objects. Slow, controlled backward movement keeps lures working best and draws more strikes. Boat control is maintained with oars, especially in rafts, jonboats, and river drift boats (McKenzie River–style dories), or with a small tiller-steered outboard motor. The bow of the boat is headed upstream and always above the area to be fished. It is important to row or run the motor just fast enough to hold even with the current.

Once in position and keeping pace with the current, if fishing a plug you should freespool or strip out line until the plug is the appropriate distance behind the boat; many plugs are fished 50 feet back. If you use several lures or several plugs, they should all be set out the same distance to avoid tangling and to thoroughly work the area downstream. The lure will dive when line movement stops; the stronger the current (and the lighter the line), the deeper the lure will dive, so keep constant pressure on it. After a few minutes, the boat operator can slowly decrease forward momentum so that the boat always runs downstream at a slower pace than the river's natural speed.

Under these conditions, the fish can see the plug, or bait, or other lure coming and can anticipate its arrival. Bear in mind that fish view these objects, especially lures, as territorial invaders; consequently, they may move away, move downstream, or stay and strike them. When they do strike, it is usually suddenly and aggressively. If an object is fished too quickly, however, fish will view it with less alarm and usually ignore it, or they will decide that it is moving too quickly to waste effort chasing it. By drifting slower than the natural current, the slowly moving object is available longer and is more threatening and provocative, or simply an easier meal.

Oregon anglers backtroll through a river pool for salmon.

If necessary, in order to get lures into the right spots and to fish a hole without moving the boat over the entire run, anglers use a tactic called back bouncing. To do this, slowly lift the rod tip upward and feel the lure working, then drop it down till it hits bottom. Then either reel up a bit or lift and bounce back the plug or bait with the current flow as you drift. As it is alternately dropped back to hit the bottom and then lifted, the offering is always worked back toward the fish.

It can be hard to get the hang of backtrolling and back bouncing, but anglers must remember to maintain contact with the bottom and constantly watch their rod tips for a strike and for the proper working action of a lure. Many anglers know how fast to run their boat by watching the action of their rod tips, especially when using hard-pulling plugs. A constantly pulsating rod tip, incidentally, indicates that a lure is working properly. In deeper holes, the fish will not come up much for a lure, so it must be kept on or near the bottom. In shallower water, fish will rise to the lure. Some fish are caught almost under the boat, so they do not fear it. This is not the case when a river is low and very clear.
See: Flatlining.

BACKWATER
A quiet, still pool, lagoon, or pondlike body of water on the side of a stream channel or river. Backwaters are often stagnant, shallow, and heavily vegetated or filled with such cover as stumps and timber; in large river systems they are often created or greatly enlarged during periods of high water.
See: Oxbow.

BACTERIA
Unicellular organisms that lack a distinct cell nucleus. They are different from plants and animals, and are important as the bottom rung of the food chain (see) in most aquatic systems.

BAG LIMIT

Synonymous with creel limit, bag limit means the quantity or number of fish of a species or group of species that may be taken, caught, or killed during a specified period. That period is usually one day, from 12:01 A.M. to midnight, and it may be identified as a "daily bag limit" or simply "daily limit." Bag limits may apply universally to many waters or may be site-specific. A bag limit is a legal game regulation established by the fisheries agency that has jurisdiction over the location being fished, and is enforced by fish and wildlife conservation officers.
See: Fisheries Management; Regulations.

BAHAMAS

When it comes to sportfishing, the 700-island Bahamas chain pretty much has it all, from the drama of Atlantic blue marlin and bluefin tuna to the singular thrill of silvery bonefish and the line-stretching adventure of grouper, snapper, and other reef dwellers.

Located as close as 50 miles from the continental United States, the Bahamas have been one of the world's most popular sportfishing destinations since the mid-twentieth century. Each year, tens of thousands of anglers travel to the Bahamas in search of 10-pound bonefish, 20-pound permit, 30- to 100-pound tarpon, 200- to 1,000-pound blue marlin, 20- to 60-pound dolphin, 40- to 120-pound wahoo, 300- to 1,000-pound giant bluefin tuna, 100-pound yellowfin tuna, and myriad bottom fish.

The Bahamas offer a potpourri of tropical angling opportunities but are especially known for big-game fishing—blue marlin in particular—and flats fishing, especially for bonefish. Bonefish range throughout the Bahamas, and some of the world's largest have been recorded at Bimini. Excellent flats guides and good boats are available at all the better-known resorts. Just about anyone who lives in the Bahamas can point you to a good flat where you can pursue bonefish and possibly other flats denizens as well.

Unlike many nations, the Bahamas has become a strong advocate of marine conservation. In the mid-1980s, the government established daily bag limits for recreational anglers and commercial fishermen. In an effort to conserve and preserve breeding stocks, it passed laws limiting overly effective commercial gear, including longlines. Pressure also was brought on tournament organizers to promote tag-and-release. The Bahamas is a popular site for big-game tournaments, and most of these now employ a combination of tag-and-release and limited killing of fish; minimum weights of 300 to 400 pounds for big-game fish to be brought to dock have been established. Inshore species such as bonefish have always been released. These efforts and more continue to make the Bahamas a popular, affordable, easy-to-reach, year-round destination for anglers in search of quality flats and big-game fishing.

Anglers are blessed with many choices in the Bahamas. In addition to hiring offshore charter boats and guides with flats boats, they can hire professional local guides at an economical price to accompany them on their boat, or they can use published charts and sportfishing guides to explore and fish the Bahamas on their own. Either way, the Bahamas is an angling oasis.

Bimini

Often called the birthplace of Atlantic big-game fishing, Bimini is among the world's most famous sportfishing destinations.

It was here off Alice Town that author Ernest Hemingway developed the aggressive fishing style that enables anglers to catch giant bluefin tuna before plentiful sharks can maul them. The first lever-drag big-game reel, a Fin-Nor, was tested off Bimini. Sitting around the docks at night, mates and captains developed important components of offshore fishing—like the Haywire Twist, ballyhoo rigs, and the Bimini Twist knot—that are widely used by big-game anglers to fish Bimini's waters.

Geologically, Bimini is a series of coral atolls. The two largest are the safety-pin-shaped North Bimini, where the main settlement of Alice Town is located, and the sparsely inhabited island of South Bimini. North Bimini is only 7 miles long by 150 yards wide, but it has the area's only road, the single-lane King's Highway. The rectangular-shaped South Bimini lies roughly east to west and is just 3 miles long; it has a 5,000-foot paved airstrip and a 281-foot radio tower. Cat Cay lies 10 miles south; the landmark Great Isaac Lighthouse is 19 miles north.

Bimini's ultimate appeal is due largely to the ambiance created by the friendly native population and to its close proximity to the United States; Bimini ranks as the easternmost of the 700 Bahamian islands. It lies 47 miles east of Miami along a deep-water drop in the Florida Straits, a migratory highway for bluefin tuna, blue marlin, and other big-game species. In this same area lies a 300-foot rectangle of large hand-hewn rocks that many experts believe is the lost city of Atlantis. Radioactive tests suggest these rocks were indeed situated above the water about 5,000 years ago. Scientists have theorized that the stones could be remnants of a highway system, built by a highly advanced culture.

Bimini is very accessible. By seaplane, it is only a 25-minute flight from Miami, and it doesn't take much longer to get there by boat. In calm weather, powerboats can make the trip in two to three hours. Fishing for snapper and grouper is a year-round sport off Bimini. The island also enjoys seasonal runs of giant bluefin and yellowfin tuna, monstrous wahoo, king mackerel, blue and white marlin, and sailfish.

Big-game fishing. The Bahamas' only 1,000-pound blue marlin was taken off Bimini. Although blue marlin are caught here year-round, the peak run is from late March through early May—when the fish are migrating north from their spawning grounds in the Caribbean and Gulf of Mexico through the Florida Current (Gulf Stream), which brushes against the western edge of the Bahama Banks. This is the eastern edge of the Gulf Stream, an area where depths go from 60 to 600 feet in a matter of yards. This 100-fathom curve runs 2 miles offshore of Bimini, between nearby Ocean Cay and Great Isaac Lighthouse, then turns sharply north into the Northwest Providence Channel.

In addition to marlin fishing, Bimini enjoys an excellent run of large wahoo from September through December. The action centers west of Bimini in 10 to 25 fathoms, just inside the 100-fathom line, from Great Isaac to North Pines Beach. Early in the season wahoo average 30 to 40 pounds. It often takes little effort to catch 8 to 10 a day. The fish get bigger as the season peaks in late November and December. Wahoo fishing is best on the outgoing tide, when bait delivery runs from the grassflats and inshore reefs to deeper water. A north or northwest wind is most favorable for wahoo here. Locals fish for them using barracuda strips, rigged mullet, and ballyhoo, as well as chrome-headed offshore lures with a green or black-and-red skirt.

At one time Bimini enjoyed a tremendous influx of giant bluefin tuna migrating along the offshore edge of the Bahama Banks between mid-April and May. Those fish still come, but in far fewer numbers and over a much less dependable period of time. Instead of hundreds of dark football shapes, you might see a dozen fish in a matter of weeks. The best tuna fishing at Bimini these days is not for bluefins as in the past, but for yellowfin tuna, which migrate by here between late February and April. Most fish are caught by trolling medium-speed blue-water trolling lures, or rigged baits with green-and-yellow skirts, across the edge of the Gulf Stream to the bank.

Spring delivers the best dolphin action. Bigger 50- to 70-pounders are caught in April and May, but as summer wears on, 10- to 20-pounders predominate. Schoolies are thick in August. Fall and winter are the seasons for mackerel on spoons and white feather jigs. Grouper and snapper are consistent year-round, with hogfish, lane and gray snapper, and good-eating margates plentiful everywhere along the dropoff of the continental shelf and among the numerous shipwrecks along the reef between Bimini and Great Isaac. Larger fish are found in 90 or more feet of water. At 30 to 80 feet, 8- to 15-pounders are consistently available in the fall and winter months.

Light-tackle fishing.   When it comes to fishing for bonefish, tarpon, and permit, Bimini has produced its share of records, among them a 15-pound bonefish for golfing legend Sam Snead in February 1953. That was beaten a few years later by a 16-pounder that also came off the flats at Bimini.

Bonefish are caught year-round off Bimini's shallow east shoreline, and in the harbor in the fall, late spring, and early summer. Spring brings the biggest schools. Fall is when reel-stripping 8- to 12-pounders attract serious fly anglers. Bonefish are bottom feeders that hunt shrimp and crabs on the marl flats around Bimini. The fish bite best on the morning and evening incoming tides. You can also find them on the grass flats lying directly opposite the harbor and along the offshore edge of the islands dotting South Bimini.

The top areas for permit are along the tip and elbow of North Bimini in 12 feet of water. They are also caught on the bonefish flats.

Live shrimp is the best bait for bonefish, followed by small live crabs (which are best for permit) and fresh-cut conch. Fly anglers do best on shrimp-like flies in pink, brown, and white.

A popular nighttime attraction at Bimini is the tarpon that appear each summer in the harbor. Although this is not a predictable fishery, 60- to 100-pound fish are sometimes taken by drifting live bait around the docks.

Walker's Cay/North Abacos
Located roughly due east of Vero Beach, Florida, and 150 miles northeast of Fort Lauderdale, Walker's Cay is a lush 100-acre outpost situated at the top of the Abacos Wall. A one-time anti-submarine base, Walker's Cay is a pure fishing resort—one often labeled as idyllic, peaceful, and secluded—and a frequent inclusion in listings of top-10 angling getaway destinations.

Walker's has as diverse a fishery as one could expect in the Bahamas, and has been the location for notable catches (including various world records), with its offshore fishing and reef bottom fishing most acclaimed.

Big-game fishing.   Walker's is considered one of the best blue marlin areas in the Bahamas because of the island's northernmost location at the end of the Abaco Wall as well as its proximity to the Florida Current. Prodigious numbers of blue marlin are caught here year-round.

Blue-water fishing is so consistent here because off Walker's is not only the 100-fathom line but also a 1,000-fathom curve 12 miles offshore to the northeast. In addition, Walker's lies on the northeast point of the barrier reef that is the Abaco Wall. Deep water begins less than a half-mile offshore, plummeting from 60 to 90 feet and then from 200 to 600 feet. Just north of the 1,000-fathom curve, the bottom becomes even more irregular over a series of canyons dropping to 2,500 feet in places.

These seamounts, in concert with the ever-present easterly current, combine to create upwellings that force bottom water to the surface. The upwellings provide nutrients for small organisms that become prey to baitfish that in turn attract such pelagic species as blue marlin, white marlin, sailfish, giant bluefin tuna, hordes of

B

yellowfin tuna, huge 100-pound-class wahoo, and scads of dolphin.

Weather permitting—and it usually does thanks to the protection offered by the Bahama Banks to the west of the island—good blue-water action for some of these species is available 12 months out of the year. Winter and spring, however, deliver the best blue-water fishing, when giant wahoo and white marlin are present, followed by blue marlin at their most active.

White marlin show up from January through March and roam the same 1,000-fathom drop where blues are found. Most whites weigh 50 to 75 pounds, but fish as large as 125 pounds have been caught here. The best offshore months overall are March through May, when yellowfin tuna and dolphin are most abundant. The dolphin can be big; an existing line-class record 80-pounder was taken here. With an advantageous north-northeast wind, it's not unusual for anglers to raise two or three blue marlin a day.

Reef and flats fishing.   Walker's Cay is least heralded for flats fishing for bonefish, but depending on who you consult, it's either good here or just so-so. The latter description is typical of a bonefish fanatic looking for miles of flats, lots of opportunities, and big fish, especially for shallow-water tailing fish. But since most folks don't fit that category, they'll find the bonefishing pretty good here, and an interesting diversion from reef and offshore angling.

Flats are not extensive at Walker's, but bonefish are available year-round, mainly just past the marina by the airstrip, and over at Grand Cay and Double Breasted Cay. The flats also produce barracuda and sharks.

Although most anglers come to Walker's Cay for offshore fishing, there is also fast and furious bottom action here. When it comes to reef fishing, there's no better site in the Bahamas. The coral edges nearby and offshore in the deep-water reefs are the favored spots.

Light-tackle anglers revel in the expansive flats of the Bahamas.

On the ocean side of Walker's the coral quickly drops off into 40 feet of water , and this provides action for both small red grouper and red hind (strawberry grouper), as well as Nassau, yellowfin, and black grouper. These species are present all the way out to depths of 150 feet or more, and although light-tackle fun can be had in shallow water, the larger fish frequent the deeper water, with 130 to 200 feet the range usually fished by deep jiggers. The fish they look to tempt in the deeper reef waters include the aforementioned species, plus the occasional African pompano, shark, amberjack, barracuda, and wahoo, among others.

Stout tackle is preferred because these fish can reach heavyweight sizes, and make vigorous efforts to escape by powering back into the rocky habitat. Twenty-pound grouper, especially Nassau and yellowfin, are common, and 40- to 50-pounders are possible. Red grouper may hit the 15-pound mark, and black grouper can be in the 40- to 60-pound class or larger; some over 100 pounds have been caught here.

Reef fishing is productive all year long at Walker's. Jigs tipped with curly soft plastics or with bait are the hot ticket, especially on a moving tide. Anglers usually work close to the bottom for grouper and up the water column to attract other species.

Generally, the northern Bahamas possess many varieties of snapper and grouper. The most common grouper are the red, Nassau, and black varieties, plus a fish Bahamians call yelloweye. Deep-water fish with small heads and big bodies, yelloweye taste a little like a yellowtail snapper. Most are caught on wire lines and electric reels in depths of 300 feet or more.

Of the three most common snapper species— mutton, mangrove, and yellowtail—mutton are the most prized catch because they are the biggest and wariest. Thus the most effective way to fish for snapper here and elsewhere in the Bahamas is to lure the fish in by chumming. The choicest chum are scraps left over from commercial conch fishing ventures, which often operate from major marinas throughout the Bahamas. Lacking a conch fisherman, you can easily catch or buy fresh conch to use for bottom bait and combine that with frozen blocks of pilchard, frozen glass minnows, menhaden, or leftover fish scraps.

When fishing for mutton snapper, fresh pilchards can be used both as chum and chunk baits to take quality 20- to 30-pound fish. Pilchards are easily gotten via cast nets tossed around marina docks early in the morning or late in the afternoon, when the light is low.

In the northern Abacos, the best snapper fishing is found in areas where there is grass around coral heads.

After you've set up a good chum line, patience becomes the order of the day. Mutton snapper are curious animals; they may not bite on the first go-around but will usually come back for a second look. Normally it takes 20 to 30 minutes of chumming for the fish to bite. The bite begins with 2- to 5-pounders, which are soon replaced by 10- to 20-pounders. Don't strike a fish as soon as you feel it pick up the bait. Count to 5 before setting the hook.

When fishing for yellowtail snapper, always use small pieces or strips of bait, and bury the hook in the bait. Good choices include shrimp, conch, and pilchards. For yellowtail, drift the bait back into the chum line with no leader and little or no weight, to spook the fish. Bahamian yellowtail average several pounds, and 5-pounders are sometimes caught here.

With so few landmarks and the water looking pretty much the same throughout the Bahamas, it can be difficult to pick a good spot to bottom-fish. Charts and a color fathometer can be helpful. Dive charts are better yet because they contain all the wrecks and ledges.

Berry Islands/Chub Cay

Chub Cay is part of the Berry Islands, a bank of small cays that is 20 miles long and situated at the northern end of the Tongue of the Ocean. A short distance from Andros and Nassau, it is 90 miles east of Bimini.

Chub Cay is one of the most prolific big-game fishing areas in the Bahamas. The term "grand slam" for capture of a sailfish, white marlin, and blue marlin in one day was coined at Chub, which remains one of the few places in the world where grand and even double grand slams are regularly caught. Although most blue marlin here are relatively small (75 to 250 pounds), there are plenty of them. Three-fish days are almost routine at Chub during the peak months of May and June. These are also the months most likely to produce a slam. The billfish season runs from March through August, with white marlin usually more abundant in the spring and blues more abundant afterward. June has produced blue marlin in the 700-pound range and is considered a prime month.

The unique features of this area of the Bahamas is evident when looking at a navigational chart. A dogleg-like alley of water comes from the Atlantic Ocean and runs south of Little Bahama Bank, through the Northeast Providence Channel. It turns southeasterly below Chub Cay and parallels Andros Island, running up onto Great Bahama Bank. This strip is called the Tongue of the Ocean.

An area known simply as "the pocket"—a V-shaped notch where the Tongue of the Ocean and the Northwest Channel converge—is Chub's billfishing mecca. The best action is along the contour, from Joulter Cay on the south to Rum Cay on the north end of the edge. To the south, Morgan's Bluff can be good for big fish. "Yellow bar," between the lighthouse at Chub Point and Number Cay, produces some of the island's biggest fish. This is understandable because the water drops off precipitously into a virtual abyss a few yards from the reef.

Southeast breezes, which blow the bait into the pocket—where it gets trapped in the corner—are best for blue marlin. West, southwest, and northwest winds bringing dirty water are not conducive to good fishing.

Most anglers troll high-speed lures and rigged natural baits like 10-inch mullet, ballyhoo, or Spanish mackerel. They work from deep to shallow, back and forth across the edge, looking for color edges, weeds, and current eddies. The top of the outgoing tide, when the water is coming off the banks, brings small food that flyingfish and little tunny feed on. This is the ideal time for marlin here and elsewhere in the Bahamas. Fish also tend to bite best on the dark of the moon and up to four days before and after.

Some large dolphin are taken from April through June as well, although smaller specimens are readily caught in the winter months. The smaller dolphin hit trolled baits well, but they offer great sport on lighter casting tackle. Chub Cay produced some former line-class world-record dolphin, including a 76-pounder. Wahoo, sharks, barracuda, and other species round out the lineup, plus assorted reef species.

With most attention focused on big-game angling, the area's excellent flats fishing remains relatively unheeded. Bonefish are the mainstay, but permit are here as well. Although the majority of bonefish are small, some 8- to 10-pounders grace these waters, and larger specimens have been sighted. Ambergris Cay and the flats north of Chub are the prime locales, but it is often worth the trip over to Joulter, north of Andros, where large bonefish are a possibility.

Andros

Andros is the largest island (2,300 square miles) in the Bahamas, yet it is lightly populated and has only a few fishing camps. The eastern edge fronts extremely deep water, whereas the western edge fronts the shallows of the Great Bahama Bank. Andros is bisected, offering good angling in the middle reaches around the North and Middle Bights, along extensive flats and mangrove-lined swamps. Tidal passes or creeks, plus flats, exist on the east and west shores, and offer various species. At Andros the fishing is good no matter what kind of wind develops.

Among the large variety of fish available at Andros are small tarpon, ladyfish, barracuda, permit, various snapper and grouper, and blacktip sharks. The east-shore flats are more likely to harbor permit, probably because they edge deep water, although this species is also found elsewhere. The tidal passes on the east shore are best for tarpon, and the catch can be in the 60- to 70-pound range. These locales, referred to as "creeks," possess diverse opportunities on both shores, and light spinning tackle or flycasting tackle produces equally well.

Bonefish are the main quarry here, however, and they are both plentiful and large, sometimes traveling in vast schools. The best area for these fish is in the bights—the mangrove-studded cays and shores in the island's midsection—but good opportunities exist on the east and west sides as well. Bonefish at Andros average from 3 to 5 pounds, with larger fish to 10 pounds a common catch. Some 14- and 15-pounders have reportedly been caught, and still bigger fish have been seen. One of the known spots for big fish is Cabbage Creek, on the western edge and above the North Bight.

Middle Abacos/Treasure Cay/Boat Harbour

As a group of islands, the Bahamas are certainly well known and well visited. Certain islands are heavily trafficked by tourists and equally heavily publicized for their fishing opportunities. It stands to reason that a few less-publicized and/or out-of-the-way laces exist, including those that offer good but not heavily pressured fishing. Several such locales are in the northern Bahamas, in the central Abacos, and near Grand Bahama.

One such locale is Deep Water Cay, at the eastern end of Grand Bahama Island and separated from it by Rummer Creek. Found on few maps, this 2-mile-long island is reportedly home base for some 200 square miles of flats replete with various typical, finny creatures, but most especially bonefish and permit. The bonefish here average 5 pounds, but fish weighing up to 10 pounds are seen fairly often. Specimens of up to 14 pounds have been caught and are present year-round. Permit, too, roam the local waters, in sizes ranging from a few pounds to 25 pounds, and some up to 20 pounds heftier still. Burroughs Cay, a one-hour run, is a particularly good permit locale. Fly fishing is especially productive here.

Another destination situated in excellent bone-fish country is Green Turtle Cay, midway along the ocean side of Great Abaco. Fish here are not large, but they are plentiful year-round, with good-size schools of bonefish spotted by wading or boating

anglers. Poling in search of cruising fish, and stalking tailing feeders, are possible along flats devoid of people. A run up north to Little Abaco Island may be worthwhile (also from Deep Water Cay), where larger bonefish are sometimes found in the vicinity of Cooperstown and Fox Town.

Three miles across Abaco Bay from Green Turtle is another locale worthy of note, although not without regular patronage—mainly from the big-game crowd. This is Treasure Cay, which has a lot of small bone-fish. The angler looking for a respite from the big water or hoping to get that first bonefish will find the skinny water near this island worth investigating.

All of these locales boast other flats species of note, as most Bahamian waters do, including bar-racuda, lemon sharks, blacktip sharks, and mutton snapper, as well as the usual assortment of bottom fish on the reefs adjacent to the flats.

Treasure Cay is the only one in this area, however, that has significant blue-water fishing. This part of the Abacos has the bottom structure and deep water necessary for great marlin fishing. The barrier reef just offshore drops quickly; only a few hundred yards east is the 100-fathom edge, and just beyond that, depths quickly reach 300 fathoms.

Local captains regard the week following or preceding the full moon to be best for marlin. While dark, clean blue water, current edges, and working birds are good signs, what you really want to look for when fishing for marlin here is bait down deep on sonar. Off Treasure Cay, that bait is likely to hold the small tuna that are the preferred forage of big blue marlin.

At Elbow Cay the island-hugging current makes its sweep offshore, a condition that contributes to tide boils and an ever-present bait supply. The depth at the tip of the point is 300 fathoms, but within a few feet it drops to more than 2,000 fathoms. A north current and wind are the most favorable conditions for targeting marlin and yellowfin tuna during the peak runs from April through June.

Boat Harbour routinely produces some of the largest blue marlin caught in the Bahamas. While blue and even white marlin action is consistent from spring to early fall, Boat Harbour is a good spot for dolphin, wahoo, and yellowfin tuna. Like Treasure Cay, deep water lies just offshore of the area's three natural inlets: Tillhoo Cut, North Bar Channel, and Man of War.

The best time to fish for marlin is when yellowfin tuna and dolphin are abundant, from March through June. A north-northeast wind is advantageous. Early in the season, marlin fishing is best in 300 to 900 feet of water; from spring through summer it's best in 1,000 to 6,000 feet.

Other Areas

certainly, notable fishing opportunities exist in the southerly cays and islands of the Bahamas archipelago on the Atlantic side of the Great Bahama Bank,

Sportfishing boats sit ready in their berths at a yacht club in the Abacos.

including Exuma, Long Island, Crooked Island, and Eleuthera. This is predominantly flats country fishing, although in some places good reef- and/or offshore fishing are available.

Eleuthera is farthest north and closest to Providence and is one of the southerly Out Islands known for big game. The northern end of this 100-mile-long island abuts the deep water of Northeast Providence Channel and is on the pathway of migrating billfish and tuna, so it merits attention from the trolling enthusiast. At the southern tip of Eleuthera, a ridge between that island and Cat Island to the south also provides trolling action.

Bottom fishing is particularly good for grouper here, and bonefishing is fair to good, depending on where one looks. Perhaps the most notable location for bones are the flats around Harbour Island, at the northeastern tip—where 5- to 7-pounders are possible and fair-size schools may be encountered—and St. George's Cay at the northwestern tip.

Moving south, Great Exuma has miles of small cays and flats that provide exciting bonefishing. According to local lore, the Exumas represent God's calendar: The 90-mile-long chain numbers exactly 365 islands, one for each day of the year. The Exumas are also green-water country—in other words, shallow. Thus, many people consider the Exumas to be the center of the bonefish universe. And at the heart of this shallow-water fishing mecca is the charming hamlet of George Town. Originally a sponge market, George Town has become the "in" spot for serious fly anglers the world over who come to stalk the gray ghost.

Overall, the Bahamas quite likely rank as the world's greatest bonefish habitat. In truth, all it takes to catch these fish is a shallow flat, which accurately describes the greatest part of the Exumas. Just about anywhere in the Bahamas there is superb bonefishing to be had from skiffs or by wading. In many places you won't see just a few tailing and rooting fish but, as in the case of the Exumas, schools upon schools of silvery shadows that keep coming in a seemingly endless parade. Some large bones are periodically encountered, but for the most part 3- to 5-pounders are the catch. Should bonefishing get too monotonous here, the reefs offer good deep jigging opportunities.

East-southeast of the Exumas, Long Island is one of the prettiest of the Bahamian Out Islands and a locale that has abundant bonefish and an opportunity for varied adventures. Narrow and 60 miles in length, Long Island can provide lee fishing when necessary. Bonefish, mostly small, range along the entire coast, and in large schools on 15 miles of easy-to-wade flats. Some bones up to 10 pounds cruise the shallows, and permit are a possibility. Long Island also offers good reef jigging for assorted species.

Still farther to the southeast, Crooked Island has seldom-explored bonefish flats, with the bonus of small tarpon. The latter are found up to 50 pounds, and the bonefish are on the small side but abundant. The flats in all of these areas also sport snapper, sharks, barracuda, the occasional permit, and the ever-present chance of spotting a huge school of silver streakers.

BAIL

An arm on a spinning reel, also known as a pickup bail, that gathers line for winding onto the spool. The bail must be opened to release line for casting, and is closed automatically or manually for line pickup and retrieval.
See: Spinning Tackle.

BAIT

(1) In the most strict, narrow, and accurate sense as used by anglers, the term bait refers to any natural or processed food that is used to catch fish; this is distinguished from a lure, which, through popular usage, has come to mean any man-made object that represents or imitates food.

Natural bait *(see)* is any live or dead organism that occurs in nature; examples include worms, crickets, assorted fish, shrimp, eels, leeches, frogs, fish eggs, squid, crabs, and clams. A review of this occurs separately.

Processed bait is food that does not occur naturally in aquatic environments; examples include bread, dough, cheese, cubed meat, seeds, and vegetables. Processed bait is often used when angling for coarse fish *(see)*, and in association with chumming *(see)*, and is reviewed in more detail in those entries and elsewhere *(see: float)*.

Generally, food that is normally eaten by a particular fish is preferred by anglers as hooked bait for that fish, but on some occasions natural bait may include organisms that are rarely part of the diet of fish. A field mouse or a lemming, for example, is not an everyday food item for predatory freshwater fish, but these do occasionally occur in the water and are consumed by some species. These would represent an uncommon natural bait and one that, when in the water, attracts fish because of its movement. In a much different vein, a piece of chicken liver, which falls under the category of processed baits, is often an effective bait for catfish, which are attracted to it through their senses of smell and touch.

(2) In a broad sense, the term "bait" is used with reference to any object—natural, processed, and artificial—that is used to catch fish. In a confusing twist of language, the application of the word "bait" to lures (which in essence are "artificial baits") is primarily a U.S. phenomenon, where many types of lures are widely used in freshwater. Thus, the terms crankbait, spinnerbait, jerkbait, and so forth have become standards for very specific types of lures, and many anglers (especially those who fish for

B

bass) refer to a lure as a "bait" even though it is strictly artificial. Lures *(see)* are reviewed elsewhere.

BAIT-AND-SWITCH

A saltwater angling tactic in which a trolled hookless teaser (usually an offshore lure or daisy chain) that has attracted a fish (usually a billfish) is quickly removed from the water while a hooked lure, bait, or fly is simultaneously presented. The substitute offering is usually one that—either because of its size or because of the light tackle being employed—could not be trolled at high speeds or would not create enough attraction to bring the fish in. The teaser does the work of bringing the fish close to the real lure. Bait-and-switch is used in particular with very light tackle, and for casting a lure or fly to a big-game fish.

See: Big-Game Tackle; Trolling Lures, Saltwater.

BAIT BUCKET

A round container to hold live bait; also, in saltwater, a term for a milk crate or chum pot *(see)* used for holding chum *(see)* in the water alongside the boat. Bait buckets may hold fish, frogs, crickets, eels, crayfish, or other items; large buckets used for containing baitfish may be equipped with portable aerators for oxygenating the water. For baitfish, common buckets are made of steel or plastic and have a perforated insert pail that contains the bait and can be easily removed to facilitate water changing; another common version is a floating plastic bucket with a spring-loaded door, which is kept in the water when the boat is at rest or when it is slowly trolled.

See: Bait Container.

BAITCASTING TACKLE

Baitcasting tackle is a type of light- to medium-light multipurpose fishing equipment characterized by a reel with a revolving spool that turns to dispense and retrieve line. The spool rotates like sewing thread, with the line moving perpendicular to the spool axis.

This equipment is related in general characteristics to conventional tackle *(see)*, which sports a larger revolving spool reel, has a greater ability to deal with strong fish, and holds more line. It is distinctive from spinning tackle *(see)* and spincasting tackle *(see)*, which both feature a stationary spool around which line is wound.

Baitcasting tackle ranks first in sales revenue in North America, where it is widely used, and third in sales volume (behind spincasting and spinning tackle), but it is not commonplace outside North America. Baitcasting reels are sometimes called levelwinds because all such reels have a feature that automatically distributes the line evenly across the spool as it is retrieved.

This tackle is not relegated to use with natural bait *(see)*, as its name implies; it can be used with natural bait and for trolling, but it is most likely to be employed in casting artificial lures. It can be used for light saltwater activity but is principally a freshwater fishing tool. It is especially popular in angling for largemouth bass and is widely used for most of the major species when fishing with heavier lures and terminal rigs.

Baitcasting reels predate spinning and spincasting reels. They were once notorious for being difficult to learn to use without incurring a backlash, or spool overrun, in which a bird's nest of line had to be painstakingly untangled. As a result, anglers flocked to the easier to use stationary spool products when they were introduced in the 1940s and 50s. Modern reels have greatly reduced this backlash problem. Meanwhile, the advantages of baitcasting tackle continue to be accurate lure placement in casting, superior cranking power, and control over strong-fighting fish.

Today, this equipment is vastly different, more angler-friendly, and compatible with diverse fishing methods. Appropriate baitcasting tackle may be used for virtually all fishing methods, including casting, trolling, and fishing with bait.

Reels

As a revolving spool product, the baitcasting reel has the same origins as the conventional revolving spool reel. The development of both has been intertwined since the nineteenth century. Baitcasting reels originated in Kentucky between 1800 and 1810, when a single-action revolving-spool reel (essentially a fly reel) was the only reel available for sportfishing, and anglers used only natural bait or artificial flies. The single-action reel was used to store and retrieve line and had no casting function. To present natural baits at any distance, anglers stripped an appropriate length of line off a single-action reel and either looped the line and laid it aside or coiled it in the noncasting hand. Using a wooden rod, they made a sideways motion to propel the bait and carry the stripped-off line. This was done because the bait and any weights used could not overcome the inertia of the single-action spool.

Between 1800 and 1810, George Snyder, a Kentucky watchmaker, and reputedly president of the Bourbon Angling Club, invented a reel with a delicate spool that would pay out line during the cast and that revolved several times for each turn of the crank handle. Thus was born the multiple-action reel, to be called the multiplier or multiplying reel, as well as a spool capable of dispensing line during a cast. The line of that day was raw silk, and there were no lures; for decades multiplying reels were small and because they were exclusively used for tossing natural baits, they were called baitcasting reels.

For most of the nineteenth century, such reels were made by hand. Various modifications and improvements were made, including the addition of a mechanism to distribute line evenly on the spool (called levelwind), better gears, and the addition of external drag. What had developed as a tool for freshwater fishing, primarily for bass, became available in large sizes for situations where greater line capacity and mechanical strength was needed.

These reels were soon used for really powerful fish in saltwater. The lack of an internal drag mechanism, however, meant the fish didn't have to work for the line it took off. To offset this, anglers applied pressure to the reel spool with their thumbs (which was ineffective for large fish and sometimes painful to the angler) or with a leather thumb pad attached to the reel frame.

William C. Boschen, a member of the legendary Catalina Tuna Club of California, is credited with originating the concept of the first internal star drag on revolving spool reels, a handy threaded knob adjustment that internally regulated spool pressure. A prototype of a reel with such a device was reportedly made for Boschen by Brooklyn, New York, reel manufacturer Julius Vom Hofe. Boschen used it to catch the first broadbill swordfish (358 pounds) ever taken on sporting rod and reel. That catch was made in the summer of 1913 off Catalina Island Later versions of this reel were named B-Ocean.

This product was the predecessor of modern revolving-spool reels. The star drag mechanism provided an internal friction adjustment mechanism, or brake, that provided greater resistance against strong fish and slowed the rate of line being pulled off the reel. This mechanism was incorporated in all types and sizes of revolving-spool reels in later years. Today all conventional or baitcasting reels feature a star drag. A baitcasting reel is essentially a small revolving-spool reel with a levelwind line-guiding mechanism and star-spoked wheel drag adjustment.

The largest baitcasting reel is about the size of the smallest conventional reel. Most modern baitcasting reels are used primarily for cast-and-retrieve angling (with lures rather than natural bait) and are likely to be fished with heavier lures and weights than spinning or spincasting reels. They're all suitable for casting, but the larger models are not comfortable for continuous casting. Some light models, however, are used with very light lines and lures, some heavier and large-capacity models are used in very demanding situations, and trolling and baitfishing are eminently feasible in addition to casting.

Gears, cast control, and drag are the most critical components of baitcasting reels. The cast control and gears are especially important because they significantly affect casting and retrieving functions. The main problem with a baitcasting reel is that, when casting, it is tough for the user to control the movement of the spool making it difficult to avoid a backlash. When control is mastered, however, the angler can be extremely accurate when casting with this equipment. Gears are of special concern when it comes to line recovery and cranking power. Many baitcasting reel users seldom use the drag feature; others, use it only occasionally, but when they do use it, it is important to them. Drag tension is not easily or readily adjustable to known levels, however, during the fight of an especially strong fish, a weakness that is seldom a problem for anglers who know how to use their tackle well.

General Operation

Baitcasting tackle basically works like all tackle except flycasting: A weighted object at the end of the line pulls line from the spool. The spool of a baitcasting reel revolves as line pays out during the cast and as it is retrieved when the handle is turned. When the gears are disengaged and line is dispensed from the reel, a backlash, or spool overrun, can occur when the revolving spool turns faster than the line is leaving the spool. Applying light pressure to the spool can prevent this.

The baitcasting reel has a spool release clutch in the form of a button or bar that activates or deactivates the gears; this takes the reel into or out of freespool. With the reel on top of the rod handle and facing toward the angler, the rod-holding hand's thumb is placed on the spool to keep the line in check, and the free hand is used to depress the spool release, which disengages the gears and puts the reel in freespool. When thumb pressure is relaxed, line flows off the spool and out through the rod guides, carried by the weight of the object at the end of the line.

A few baitcasting reels (wide-spool versions) feature a click ratchet that signals when line is being taken off the reel; this can be used when a reel is not handheld or when it is left unattended. To retrieve line, the gears are engaged by turning the handle forward, which winds line onto the reel. A levelwind mechanism automatically distributes it back and forth across the spool.

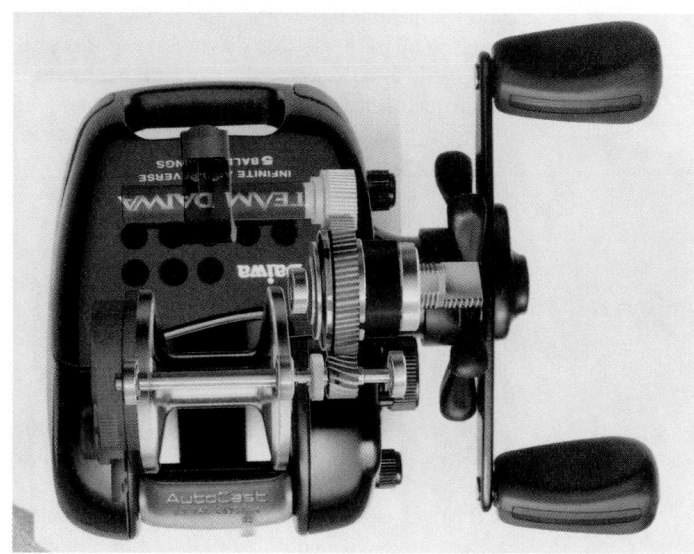

The components of a Daiwa baitcasting reel and their interrelationship are evident in this composite image.

Every baitcasting reel has an adjustable drag mechanism, which is activated by turning a star wheel on the drive gear. This is located on the sideplate under the handle. The drag tension is set to the desirable level at the beginning of each day's fishing and relaxed at the end of the day.

These are the basic elements of operating a baitcasting reel. Some models have cast control and anti-reverse features; the size of the spool, the materials used, and the designed application of each product are also relevant.

Casting/Line Release Features

Controlling the flow of line off the spool is an important and basic element of use in all baitcasting reels and in all means of fishing.

Freespool.   Disengaging the gears of a revolving spool reel so that its spool can freely turn backward and dispense line is known as putting the reel into freespool. When using a baitcasting reel, the angler simply depresses the line release clutch, which is also known as the freespool switch and is in the form of a button or bar. When the clutch is depressed, the pinion gear is disengaged from the spindle, which it drives. The reel is then in freespool; the gears are still intact but not the drive mechanism.

To permit quick, one-handed operation, the clutch is conveniently placed on the front (facing the angler) of most reels. This may be a contoured bar over the spool that bridges the sidewalls, or a switch that is recessed in the sidewall and permits the thumb to slide onto the spool. On some new reels and many older ones, the clutch is a button that is located away from the spool; you hold the reel in one hand and use your noncasting hand to depress the button.

A clutch bar (also called a thumb bar) is generally more convenient than a recessed switch. A bar gives you constant control of the spool because the tip of your thumb is on the spool while the heel of your thumb pushes the bar down. As long as the bar is properly situated, you only have a slight chance of accidentally hitting it and inadvertently putting the reel into freespool, which could result in disaster while playing a hard-fighting fish. (Incidentally, baitcasting reel manufacturers report that premature engagement of the clutch while the spool is still rotating at high speed during a cast is the single most damaging action to these reels.) A large-capacity reel that might be used for big fish and for trolling more often than for casting, and one where you might apply thumb pressure as extra drag, is better suited, however, to a side button.

When you depress the clutch of some reels, the levelwind line guide moves back and forth as line goes out. Others have a curtain line guide made of two bars that separate; this is no longer common, as it is prone to malfunction. The line guide of most reels remains in position until the handle is turned.

Spool revolution.   When putting the reel into freespool, you must apply finger pressure to the spool to prevent line from paying out prematurely or haphazardly. Without this pressure, and assuming that a lure or weighted bait is tied to the end of the line, the weight at the end of the line would cause the spool to turn the moment the reel was placed into the freespool position, which could cause an instant backlash on the spool.

It is therefore necessary to place the thumb of the rod-holding hand on the spool so the spool can't turn; this is done instantaneously when the reel has a thumb bar or recessed switch because the thumb of the casting hand contacts the spool as it depresses this clutch. You must use both hands if the reel has a clutch button, keeping the thumb of the noncasting hand on the spool while you press the button with your other hand. The line can then be released by easing the tension or, in some instances, by casting.

Spool braking/control.   When releasing line without casting, thumb pressure is lessened on the spool to pay line out at a controlled rate; the objective is to let out the desired amount of line at a rate that doesn't make the spool turn so fast that it causes a backlash. This is important because a revolving spool can gather speed quickly and an uncontrolled spool can lead to a serious backlash in an instant. The backlash not only impedes immediate fishing effort because of the time required to undo it, but can also cause damage to the line.

This situation becomes even more acute when you use the reel for casting because the activity of casting builds up greater spool speed (spool speed in casting has been measured as high as 20,000 rpms). Casting requires very precise control of the revolving spool. In either application, it is necessary to brake the spool to slow its speed. The three means of controlling the spool when line is flowing off the reel during casting are mechanical, magnetic, and manual.

Manual spool braking is done by applying thumb pressure to the moving spool when casting. This is an action learned through trial and error and perfected with experience; it requires the application of different degrees of braking tension, depending on the weights on the line, distances being cast, and types of rods and reels being used. Although you can learn to use a baitcasting reel without applying thumb pressure, you cannot fish without some manual control all the time and with all reels, so it is something you must learn.

Mechanical spool braking is done by using centrifugal brakes (also called weights) to apply pressure to the moving spool. Reels with centrifugal brakes have blocks that must be engaged to effect spool braking. These blocks are usually found on the left side of the reel. They are accessed on some reels by removing the entire sideplate and on others by unlocking a quick-release bayonet cover.

On the spindle of the spool is a cross pin with a centrifugal brake block on either side (some reels have a wheel-spoke system with four to six brake blocks). To be employed, these brake blocks must be moved out toward the spool flange and snapped into a notch. In this position they rub against the flange and apply centrifugal pressure to slow the spool and help avoid a backlash. The harder you cast (greater spool rpms), the harder the brakes work.

The centrifugal braking system varies with different products and manufacturers. Accessing this area is easy with most reels. Read the instructions that come with the product because some are supplied new with the brakes in the off position and some with the brakes in the on position.

These centrifugal brakes are used in conjunction with operating the spool tension knob. This device is a knurled knob or bearing cap on the sideplate where the handle is located, and it is adjusted by hand. Tightening this device puts tension on the spindle of the spool, but it is not purely a spool-braking device, as many people think. Its purpose is to control excessive end play, or sideways movement, of the spool, and its value in controlling spool braking is limited.

If the spool tension on a reel is too loose, there will be too much movement in the spool, and line could get behind it. If the engineering mechanics of a reel are correct, line should not get behind the spool; you should be able to loosen the spool tension knob completely and, although there will be excessive end play, you will not be able to pull the flange of the spool out of the centering ring of the sideplate.

As the spool tension knob on baitcasting reels is tightened, an interior wear plate rubs against the spool spindle. Tightening is usually accomplished

The sideplate of this Marado baitcasting reel shows the spool tension control knob and the switch for a click ratchet, the latter being found on only a minority of such reels.

in a clockwise motion, and the knob should be adjusted so that there is barely any perceptible sideways motion of the spool. Place your thumb on the middle of the spool and move it back and forth to see if you can move the spool. For general use, adjust the spool tension to a tight but not immovable tolerance.

Spool tension needs to be adjusted according to the weight of the object being cast; in theory, if you switch frequently to lures of different weights, you should reset the tension each time. To do this when the reel is on the rod with line attached to a lure, hold the rod out and dangle a lure from the tip, place your thumb on the spool, and put the reel into freespool. Decrease thumb pressure and allow the lure to fall. Adjust the spool tension knob so the lure slowly descends to the ground when thumb pressure is relaxed. The spool should stop revolving at the instant the lure hits the ground. For continued long-distance casting, you may want to decrease spool tension and (if your thumb is well educated) put the centrifugal brake blocks in the off position.

Experienced casters tighten or loosen the adjustment knob, and employ this level of control in conjunction with an educated thumb. Newcomers to a baitcasting reel should start with a tighter adjustment at the outset to provide some assistance with spool braking, or they will be picking backlashes out with every cast. This tension can be gradually lightened as you become more proficient with thumb control.

Magnetic spool braking is a completely different system. It is common on the majority of reels from many manufacturers. Magnetic spool braking systems use a magnetic field to place variable degrees of force on the spool. A series of small disklike magnets are located in the interior of the sideplate opposite the handle. When an exterior magnetic control knob is turned, it changes the distance of the magnets from the metal spool; when the magnets are closer, more force is applied, and when they are more distant, less force is applied. Lower settings enable longer distance casts; higher settings help prevent backlash under adverse conditions, such as when casting into the wind.

While these systems are touted as "eliminating backlash," they are not foolproof, and if magnetic spool braking reels aren't used correctly, they will still backlash. They are, however, excellent for those who are learning to cast with this equipment when the proper settings are selected. Beginners should use a higher tension setting when they start; this will cut down on the distance achieved, but it is better to cast a shorter distance at first than to be frustrated by backlashes. With a little practice you can ease off on the tension and keep learning until you become comfortable with less tension.

Some of the newest magnetic spool control systems are very sophisticated and have the ability to alter magnetic force according to the speed of the

Removing the sideplate of this Zebco Quantum baitcasting reel allows spool changing and reveals the spool control magnets.

spool during the cast. This is different from most systems and is significant because spool speeds vary from extremely high rpms at the outset to lower rpms near the end of the cast. Variable-force magnetic systems automatically apply pressure according to the speed of the spool, which is essentially what an educated thumb is supposed to do. This type of system actually allows a spool to maintain its speed longer, meaning that it will result in longer casts. While a longer cast sounds good, the best benefit of this system is avoiding backlash without sacrificing accuracy. Thus, with some practice and experience, and with proper setting of the magnetic spool control on better reels with a variable magnetic control system, it is possible, strictly by using the magnetic control, to cast without having a backlash.

It should be noted, however, that no matter how sophisticated these magnetic anti-backlash systems are, many expert anglers are very comfortable with, and continue to use, baitcasting reels without this feature. The late 1990s saw a resurgence in high-end premium baitcasting reels, very few of which had a magnetic spool control feature. If you only use a baitcasting reel for noncasting activities, you don't need magnetic spool braking; most saltwater anglers who use baitcasting tackle do not use reels with magnetic controls because of the likelihood of corrosion.

Incidentally, baitcasting reels usually do not have both centrifugal and magnetic cast control systems. It's one or the other. In both systems, however, you still use the spool tension adjustment in conjunction with the centrifugal or magnetic spool braking.

To set up a reel with magnetic spool control for casting, begin by adjusting the spool tension knob as previously detailed, starting with the magnetic control at the lowest setting. Once the mechanical tension knob is adjusted, turn the magnetic setting from zero to an appropriate level, make a few medium-intensity casts, and adjust the magnetic control up or down as necessary before you start serious casting. Slight thumb pressure on the spool is advisable when starting with low magnetic control, but you can apply less pressure than you would if using only mechanical braking. Complete

beginners should set the magnets at maximum level until they get proficient at releasing the lure and applying thumb pressure.

A more detailed explanation of the entire backlash issue, especially the phenomenon that causes it, is contained later in this entry.

Flipping feature.   Many baitcasting reels have a selectable switch that automatically engages the pinion. This is known as the flipping switch because it is primarily used in this method of bass fishing, which requires specialized short-distance casts *(see: flipping)*. It can also be employed, however, by anglers who use bait and need to let a fish run when it takes the bait offering.

With this switch on, the reel is out of gear only when the thumb is kept on the freespool bar. When you release thumb pressure, the reel is instantly in gear. The advantage is that you don't have to turn the handle to put the reel in gear. Because the reel is already in gear when a fish takes or when the line tightens, no time is wasted setting the hook. The kind of fishing and the techniques you use really determine whether this feature is necessary.

Retrieving/Line Recovery Features

Line pickup.   To be in a position to set the hook and to return line to the spool, some drag tension must be established and the gears must be engaged. Line is retrieved by rotating the handle, which drops the pinion gear onto the spindle and engages the drive mechanism. As long as there is some drag tension in effect, turning the handle will revolve the spool, bringing line onto it.

Left/right retrieve.   The great majority of baitcasting reels are set up only for right-handed retrieve and are not convertible. Although right-and left-handed anglers have been using this system for many decades, it favors the minority of people who are left-handed. A few reels are available with left-handed retrieve, but these are not nearly as accepted in the marketplace as right-retrieve reels.

Despite the fact that right-handed anglers have become accustomed to fishing backward with baitcasting reels, it is theoretically beneficial for people who are right-handed to reel with their left hand and for lefties to reel with their right hand, so that the dominant hand is the one that holds the rod and is used to play the fish or direct the retrieve. This is especially significant when frequent casting is involved, as is usually the case with baitcasting tackle. The dominant hand is used to cast the rod, so there is no need after casting to take further action to start using the reel; the other hand is immediately placed on the reel handle grip and turns the handle. This lack of time delay is important in some fishing situations.

Making a well-executed cast and getting the lure precisely on target, for example, is often not the end of the casting action. When angling in some places and using lures that sink, you have to be able to start fishing them the instant they hit the water, or they'll get tangled or snagged on objects in the water. A spinnerbait worked very shallow is an example of a lure that should "hit the ground running."

Left-handed baitcasters who retrieve with their right hand and right-handed baitcasters who retrieve with their left hand will have little trouble if they thumb the spool properly and get cranking the instant the lure touches down. Such anglers are in the minority, though; most users both cast with their right hand and retrieve with their right hand, meaning that they switch the rod and reel from right to left hand at some point.

Most good casters become adept at making this transfer while the lure is in flight, taking their right thumb off the spool just as the lure touches the water and then quickly grabbing the reel handle and cranking before the lure has a chance to get deep. This takes fine timing and is an oft-overlooked aspect of baitcasting technique. You must master this (or learn to cast with your other hand) in order to effect the best possible retrieve under certain circumstances.

As mentioned, there are some left-retrieve baitcasting reels. Most of these are flip-flopped copies of right-retrieve reels, although at least one company has recently produced a distinctive left-retrieve reel that has a rearward handle (instead of forward on all other reels) and a top-mounted line release that are meant to reduce the awkwardness of right-handed casting and left-handed reeling.

If you are new to baitcasting and are right-handed, you should consider getting a left-retrieve reel because you don't have old habits to break. If you're already accustomed to casting a spinning outfit with your right hand and reeling with the left, this is the same principle. Many new right-handed baitcasters have found it worthwhile to start out with a left-retrieve reel and continue with it (left-handed anglers can simply use the many standard right-retrieve reels).

Many experienced right-handed baitcasting users, who are already used to reeling right-handed, have found it difficult to make the transition to left-retrieve reels, however, especially when fishing with various outfits during a day. From a practical usage standpoint, owning both right- and left-retrieve baitcasting reels becomes more gear-intensive than most people like or can afford. The obvious answer is a convertible reel, but none are presently available.

Line winding/levelwind.   Line is wound directly onto the spool of a baitcasting reel, but it is not necessary to manually level or disperse that line across the spool. All baitcasting reels have a mechanism known as a levelwind that automatically disperses line evenly across the spool. The levelwind may be gear-driven by the spool or by the main gear; it turns whenever the spool revolves, both forward and backward. It is located in a carriage that spans both sides of the reel. Inside is a nylon idler

gear that turns a worm gear and catches a pawl that moves the line guide back and forth across the spool to distribute the line evenly, which helps eliminate line buildup.

Most winding lays line on the spool evenly in side-by-side wraps, but some reels use a cross-wrapping wind. The cross wrap helps with some lines, especially slick thin-diameter microfilaments, which have a tendency to dig deep into side-by-side wraps when subjected to severe tension.

Virtually all mass-produced baitcasting reels have featured a levelwind mechanism for many years. Only competitive tournament casters are likely to have a small revolving-spool reel without a levelwind, and that for distance events.

This brings up an interesting issue. The levelwind line guide contacts the line when it is cast and when it is recovered. Although a levelwind has great merit for constant cast-and-retrieve fishing, it has some drawbacks that most people do not realize. One of these is that it reduces casting distance. The reduction may be slight for the average angler, and is compensated for by the use of less resisting materials on the line guide. Levelwind line guides are made from many different materials. Some, and especially the old standards and large-spool models, have a long open metal guide; in others, the guide opening is narrow and made of ceramic, titanium, or aluminum oxide.

Line speeding off the spool on a cast contacts the spool by one of several methods. On a few baitcasting reels, the levelwind guide moves freely back and forth in its carriage when the line is outgoing (high friction); this is preferable to others where it does not move at all when line is outgoing or moves to a center position and stays there (both of which cause more friction when line comes off the edges of the spool).

The other drawback is that the carriage is prone to getting grit, dirt, and sand in it, which can hamper smooth use or cause the carriage to malfunction. Many saltwater anglers are skeptical of the levelwind and view it as a likely problem, if not because of sand then because of corrosion. Proper care and washdown of a reel should minimize this problem in good quality reels.

Gears.   The most basic part of the operation of every reel is the gear set. In baitcasting reels, this is generally stronger and more efficient than that of a stationary or fixed-spool reel because the gear set operates on a parallel axis.

In a baitcasting reel, a large gear, the main or drive gear, engages a smaller gear, the pinion. The drive gear is linked to the reel handle, and the pinion gear connects to the spool. This system provides the multiplying gear ratio for ample line retrieval rates with a small spool and still delivers substantial cranking power. It also allows for the use of heavy lines.

Most baitcasting reels have pinion and main gears that are made from the same material, such as

In March of 1882, an estimated 1.4 billion tilefish were found dead on the Atlantic Ocean surface, covering an area 25 miles wide and 170 miles long.

B

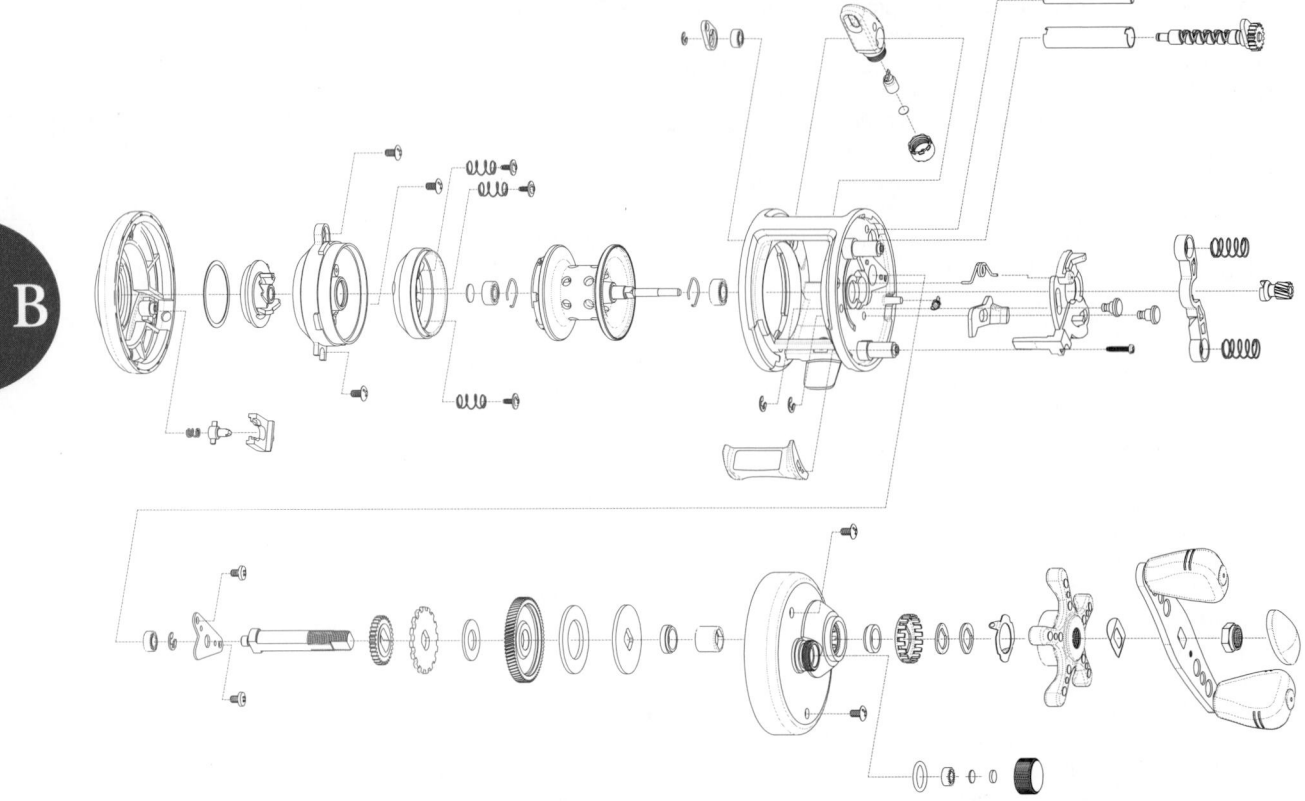

Shown are all the parts of a Quantum baitcasting reel, which includes a one-piece aluminum frame, centrifugal brake, three ball bearings, and continuous anti-reverse.

a hard brass. Some of the better quality baitcasting reels have dissimilar materials, such as a bronze pinion and a brass main gear. Very few have a stainless steel pinion gear and a bronze main gear (which is common on conventional reels). Unless one gear is slightly softer than the other, problems can arise.

In almost any simple gear set, one gear material should be different from the other. Use of the same materials tends to cold weld, or "gall" together; dissimilar metals nearly always offer the lowest coefficient of friction. The presence of an oil film helps to reduce friction. Use of dissimilar metals and an oil film ensures that gears run smoothly for a longer period of time.

The best situation is for the main drive gear material to be slightly softer than the pinion gear for wear characteristics, especially in reels that are used often for demanding applications, and where the gear ratio is high. In a multiplier reel (such as a baitcasting or conventional reel), one tooth of the pinion gear contacts its mating teeth on the main gear the same number of times as the gear ratio. That is, in a 5:1 ratio reel, each tooth on the pinion gear is activated five times more often than its counterpart on the main gear. Therefore, it is subject to five times the wear and needs to be harder simply to survive. Use of harder materials on the pinion gears produces a hardness differential that favors the smaller diameter pinion gear and provides longer life.

Gears are made to work in a given way with respect to each other, so there must be a certain distance between the two to match up; otherwise the gears will feel tight. Naturally, the gear teeth must be machined as precisely as possible to assure smooth operation and long life. Some reels, especially those with a higher gear ratio, have helically milled gears. This means that each gear tooth is spiral or curved, rather than straight, on the gear circumference. Helical milling results in increased contact area, greater strength, a thicker cross section, and a high degree of inherent smoothness, particularly for smaller gear teeth. The major benefit is that, unlike straight-milled gears where only a single gear tooth is fully engaged at one time, helical gears allow at least partial engagement of several gear teeth at all times, spreading the load and potential wear. This is mainly an issue where the gear teeth are small, as is found on higher ratio models, and there is less surface to make contact.

The high-stress cranking that is experienced when using baitcasting reels with some methods of fishing (such as using hard-pulling lures and landing strong fish), requires a rigid support system, so that under great duress there is no flex to affect the inner workings of the reel. The use of heavy line, and cranking large fish in extreme conditions, can put tremendous stress on all components. Both the material and construction of the frame and shaft supports are what keep the gears precisely located and delivering long life.

Gear ratio.   Because the drive gear is linked to the reel handle and the pinion gear is engaged with the spool, the basic numerical ratio of the drive and pinion gears in a baitcasting reel merely establishes the number of revolutions made by the spool per turn of the handle. That number is determined by counting the gear teeth on the larger drive gear and dividing that by the tooth count of the smaller pinion gear. In a gear set consisting of a 53-tooth drive gear and a 10-tooth pinion gear, the ratio is calculated at 5.3:1, because the pinion will turn 5.3 times for each full rotation of the drive gear.

Gear ratios are generally categorized as high (fast) or low (slow), but this is relative to the type of reel and application. Furthermore, the size of the spool may be such that a low gear ratio reel actually recovers more line per full turn of the handle than a high ratio reel with a smaller spool. Typical low gear ratios for a baitcasting reel are about 3.8:1, and typical high gear ratios are from 6:1 to 7:1; most high gear ratio baitcasting reels are between 6:1 and 6.3:1. If numerical ratio were the only factor of comparison, what is low or somewhat low for many baitcasting reels would be high for nearly all conventional reels. In a baitcasting reel, a high gear ratio may be preferable for cast-and-retrieve fishing with lures that do not pull hard, but a low (or at least lower) gear ratio reel is preferable for hard-pulling lures. What is gained in retrieve speed is lost in cranking power.

The higher the ratio, the greater the potential for stripping gears under severe strain. On a high gear ratio reel, the individual teeth become narrower because more teeth are fitted into a given area and they are weaker. An inexperienced angler is more likely to do damage on a high gear ratio reel when he puts the smaller gear teeth under a heavy load. Fishing with a high gear ratio reel requires using the rod a lot, pulling it back and then winding line onto the spool quickly on the downstroke. This is necessary because, with high gear ratio reels, the smaller tooth configuration does not have sufficient cranking strength. This is a factor in all reels but obviously of more concern with reels that get a heavy load.

Cranking power.   Gear ratio and cranking power are inextricably linked in all reels, and most affect how easy or difficult it is to retrieve a heavy weight or an object that offers a lot of resistance. Reels that can easily handle a heavy load are said to have a lot of cranking power. There are various factors that affect this.

The length of the handle has a bearing because length is a factor in the amount of leverage you can put on the handle. The longer the handle, the more leverage, and the easier it is to retrieve a set load. If you make a handle longer, you reduce the force at the knob. It is essentially the same principle as having a long-handled wrench; it's easier to loosen nuts with a long-handled wrench than with a short-handled one. So a longer handle equates to greater power (although your hand and arm must describe a larger circle to operate the reel).

The gear set itself is also a big factor with regard to cranking power. If you have a baitcasting reel with a gear ratio of 3.8:1, then it's easier to retrieve a load because this is a low gear ratio. If you have a baitcasting reel with a gear ratio of 6.2:1, which is high, it's much more difficult to retrieve a load, although you get more speed. If you're retrieving something that offers very little resistance, the high gear ratio is okay. You need a lower gear ratio, however, for something that offers more resistance. Thus, the lowest gear ratio reels have the greatest cranking power, and the highest gear ratio reels have the least cranking power.

Naturally, there are times when you want the best of both extremes. Some baitcasting reels have two-speed operation: in essence, the ability to switch between a higher and a lower gear ratio. In these two-speed baitcasting reels, gears are changed by moving a knob or lever. Most people who use these wind up doing nearly all of their fishing with the high-speed mode (6:1) because the low speed (3.5:1) is just too slow for retrieving most lures.

Regardless of the gear ratio, the evaluation of a reel's ability to retrieve line should boil down to something engineers call Inches Per Turn of the handle, or IPT. This is the amount of line recovered per turn of the handle or, simply, line recovery, which is a better measurement of retrieval ability than gear ratio. Line recovery is determined by spool diameter, which is a key dimension for any reel and which sets the circumference of the line level on the spool and the amount of line wound onto the spool with each turn of the reel handle.

When the level of line on a spool is low, as it might be when a strong fish takes a lot of line, less line is recovered per turn of the handle than it would be when all of the line is on the spool. Similarly, the amount of line recovered per turn of the handle of a fully spooled 4:1 ratio reel that has a small spool is less than the amount of line recovered per turn of the handle of a fully spooled 4:1 ratio reel that has a large spool.

Thus, the amount of line recovered is the measurement an angler should be most interested in. Yet anglers cannot quickly determine line recovery when evaluating a reel they might purchase because specifications on the circumference of the spool are seldom provided on the reel or in the packaging materials. You may know, for example, that in a 4:1 ratio reel one revolution of the handle puts four wraps of line on the spool, but if you don't know how much line is gained with each complete wrap, you don't know the actual recovery. (In a reel that you own, of course, this can be determined by marking the line and then measuring it.)

For a greater discussion of this subject, *(see: gear ratio)*. Although most people have a notion that

B

Wild freshwater fish with low levels of fat and calories include yellow perch, walleye, pickerel, and crappie; high levels belong to chinook salmon, rainbow trout, and lake trout.

gear ratio is of primary importance in retrieval and some think that the higher the ratio the better, other factors are involved, and line recovery is a major one. Remember, however, that reels with a low gear ratio do better under heavier loads, whether those loads are due to the size of the fish or the type of equipment being used (heavy weights, deep-diving lures, and so on).

This issue is most critical in baitcasting reels that are used in hard or heavy duty applications. Chances are, the bigger the reel the more likely it is that a heavy load will be placed on it. The larger the reel, the more noticeable the effect of a high gear ratio, so you'll feel that load a lot more.

Handle. The length of the handle affects cranking power, so the distance from the center of the gear stud to which the handle is attached to the handle knob is a key element in retrieval. A long handle equals power, yet many people have the misconception that a long handle also equals speed—that the longer the handle, the faster it can travel. The opposite is true. The longer the handle, the greater distance the cranking hand must travel with each turn. The shorter the handle, the quicker it can be turned, but there's less power, so there's a trade-off either way. You can't get power and speed simultaneously. All baitcasting reels have dual-grip handles, which provide a counterbalancing effect and easy grabbing of the handle without having to look at it. A baitcasting reel grip or knob is mainly grasped with the fingertips and operated by wrist motion, and is not affected by the presence of a second handle knob. There are various styles of grips. Most have a contoured, textured, paddlelike surface with grooves, which is quite comfortable; many are round, which is traditional. The size of the knobs and the handle is often a problem for many people who have long fingers and large hands. The smaller baitcasting reels seem designed for small hands and are not comfortable in a large hand when used for a considerable period of time.

Ball bearings/bushings. Bearings and bushings provide a way to minimize friction on rotating shafts. Bushings don't spin as freely as ball or roller bearings, which are typically viewed as durable and reliable and a way to add rotational freeness to the retrieval system. A bushing can deliver as smooth a retrieve as a ball bearing under low load conditions, but under heavy loads, ball bearings are vastly smoother and more durable.

One to four stainless steel ball bearings are used on many baitcasting reels, primarily on both ends of the spool shaft and on the crankshaft. Some reels have only one ball bearing and a bushing on the end of the spool shaft. It is possible to have up to 11 ball bearings in a reel, including one on the cap area of the shaft, one on each end of the worm gear, and two on each handle knob. They are unnecessary in most of these places, however, and drive the cost of the reel up; the most that baitcasting reels have is six or seven ball bearings. The most noticeable value

Six stainless steel ball and roller bearings from a premium baitcasting reel.

of ball bearings is the smooth operation of the spool. Ball bearings are, or should be, of the highest grade to provide the most benefits. For a more detailed review of ball bearings and bushings, *see: Reel, Fishing.*

Warning click. Known simply as a click or clicker, this is a ratchet device that is primarily intended to let an angler know that line is going out. It is only found on a small number of baitcasting reels, usually the larger wide-spooled models.

The warning click is generally used when a rod and reel have been placed in a rod holder (for instance, when trolling or baitfishing) and is not handheld. In some situations, as when fishing with bait, the reel is placed in freespool with the warning click on so that, if a fish picks up the bait, the line is free to move with minimal resistance yet without risking a spool overrun. In other situations, such as when trolling, the gears are engaged and the warning click is employed so that it instantly alerts an angler (or mate or boat captain) to a strike and to the fact that a fish is on and taking line off the reel.

The click itself features a spring-loaded tongue that moves back and forth against ratchet teeth to make this sound. It is activated by moving a small off-center button on the sideplate (usually the left sideplate). The click is intended for part-time rather than full-time use, and the click button should be disengaged when retrieving. Continued use of the click causes premature ratchet wear. Some people view leaving it on as a sign of an inexperienced angler, although some charter captains like it to be left on because the sound lets them know what a customer's fish is doing; when the clicking sound speeds up, for example, the fish is taking line. Some captains have even asked manufacturers for different types of sounds in the click. (This is especially prevalent in the Great Lakes, where the clicks are always used for trolling.)

Drag Features

The purpose of the drag function on any reel is to let line slip from the reel at varying pressures when force is applied to the line. It serves as a sort of clutch, or shock absorber, and is especially important when using light line, when playing large and strong species, and when fish make strong and sudden surges while being landed. If an angler never catches large fish, only uses heavy strength line, and is content to wind fish in, then it is conceivable that the drag will never be used.

Many people who use baitcasting tackle do not use the drag very often. Many bass anglers, who are major users of this tackle, seldom use the drag, or they tighten it down so that they cannot use it. This is not a good idea, however, as it defeats the purpose of this feature altogether. Those who do use the drag on baitcasting reels are anglers who generally fish with lighter strength line; those who catch big steelhead, salmon, catfish, pike, muskies, and stripers; and those who use baitcasting tackle for various saltwater species.

Catching large fish, which weigh more than the actual breaking strength of the line or that can apply extreme pressure on the tackle, requires some finesse rather than sheer strength. This means that the drag will come into play because if it doesn't, the force will exceed the strength of the line and the line will break.

When the drag comes into play, it allows the fish to continue applying force but at a pressure that is less than the breaking strength of the line. When the force reaches a certain level (usually a specific percentage of the line's breaking strength), a properly set drag mechanism turns the spool and allows line to slip from the reel under tension. In essence, this means that a fish can run instead of engage in a tug of war. The fish must work for the line it takes off the reel, however, which tires the fish and helps the angler subdue it.

Many people mistakenly think that they need to set the drag very tight for effective hook setting. When you have 20 yards of line out, and you have rod flex, line stretch, and the dampening effect of the water to contend with, you don't need very much drag force at the reel. You cannot exert the maximum pressure when you set the hook. When you set the drag pressure at or near maximum force, once the fish is close to the boat and less contribution is made by line stretch, rod flex, and water, having the drag locked down may mean that the line cannot absorb the sudden shock of a quick run, even from a fish whose weight is less than the breaking strength of the line. People are often amazed that a 15-pound fish can break 20-pound line, but that doesn't happen if the drag is set properly and the washers are allowed to slip freely when necessary.

In typical fishing with baitcasting reels, anglers set the drag at 25 to 30 percent of the breaking strength of their line. Some people measure this with a short length of line on a straight pull off the reel. Others measure it with line running through the rod guides and the rod flexed as it would be in fishing circumstances. Most people use the "feels good" method of establishing drag tension by pulling line off the reel and adjusting the star wheel until the tension feels right. The most precise way to measure drag tension is by using a reliable scale and attaching it to the line. No matter what method is used, the objective is to adjust the drag so that the line will not slip until the appropriate amount of tension is applied. Understanding how to use and set drag is one of the most important aspects of sportfishing; it is thoroughly reviewed in detail elsewhere *(see: conventional tackle; drag)*, so that information will not be repeated here.

This drag stack from a top-quality baitcasting reel has three friction washers interspersed between three metal washers, the latter keyed into the main gear and gear stud.

It should be noted, however, that on baitcasting reels the drag is located on the main gear and is usually a multi-element system with washers that are keyed together to increase the working surface area. Different materials are used in the friction washers; a popular one in some better reels now is graphite-impregnated Teflon. Drag tension is increased or decreased by turning a drag star (radial-arm star wheel), which is located under the handle on the sideplate. The drag star threads onto the gear stud or drive gear, which is connected to the handle, so it rotates concurrently with the handle without affecting the setting.

Turning the drag star clockwise or forward increases tension; turning it counterclockwise or backward decreases tension. When spool friction exceeds the tension on the line, the reel handle turns the main gear and the spool, and allows line to be recovered. When tension on the line exceeds friction on the spool, the spool revolves against handle pressure, and line can be pulled off the spool. The handle is prevented from turning backward by a dog and ratchet, which is known as an anti-reverse.

This system eliminates the possibility of line twist due to turning the handle when line is flowing off the spool, which is a major contributor to severe line twist in fixed-spool reels. On a baitcasting reel, twist isn't possible if you're cranking the reel handle and the drag is slipping at the same time. There is no line twist unless it comes from the lure use or you put it on when the spool is filled.

The range of drag tension adjustment is somewhat more limited on baitcasting reels than spinning reels, although it looks like more because of the star wheel knob. With these products, it is often the case that a smooth drag and the ability to fully lock down the reel (so the spool cannot turn backward) are not compatible, although better baitcasting reels do have good drag systems with a wide range of adjustment.

Anti-Reverse Features

The anti-reverse component of reels is an element that restricts backward movement of the handle. In most baitcasting reels a dog and ratchet mechanism provides a variable amount of backward handle movement; this is a multi-stop anti-reverse. The amount of this movement is decided by the number of ratchets for the dog to catch. In some reels it is a one-way roller bearing that allows no backward movement and which is called continuous or infinite anti-reverse.

This feature is especially relevant to cast-and-retrieve applications and to some styles of bait-fishing, primarily because it is relative to how the reel operates when the forward-turning motion is stopped. There is a natural tendency to pull up on the handle when not reeling, whether to set the hook or to momentarily stop while retrieving. If there is considerable play in the handle and drive gear when the reel stops, the handle may actually turn backward slightly. This produces a feeling of sloppiness or instability, and too much backward movement of the handle may adversely affect hook-setting. Ideally, a reel used for casting should engage instantly and firmly. Many of the better baitcasting reels have a continuous anti-reverse that keeps the handle and drive gear from moving even the slightest bit backward.

The number of ratchets in the system is one factor that governs how quickly the drive gear engages in a reel with multi-stop anti-reverse. The ratchets are little stops for a dog; as you turn the handle, this part slides over a ramp, and when the dog stops moving, it slides backward and engages a ratchet. The greater the number of ratchets, the quicker it engages; 10 ratchets, for example, mean 10 stops per turn of the handle. More ratchets also mean finer teeth, which are easier to break or clog.

In theory, more ratchet stops could pose a strength problem because you're depending on more ratchets with less material backing to stop the force of the hookset. This seems as if it could be a problem when using low-stretch lines and when using line that is overmatched by strength for the reel. Fewer ratchet stops, however, may be worse because that provides perhaps an extra 4 or 5 inches of rod tip movement when you set the hook before you take up the slack and engage the dog. With a hard hookset using strong low-stretch line and a tight drag, you can develop a lot of force and strip the dog and ratchet system when there is this much rod tip movement.

In a trolling application, where baits or lures are always set out under a fair load, when you have a strike you are already in a position to respond without any backward movement of the handle regardless of the number of ratchets. So in this application there is no relevance. In a casting application, where it is undesirable to have backward travel of the handle when you set the hook, more ratchet stops are advantageous for quick hooksets. A one-way roller bearing, which provides continuous anti-reverse, however, is most desirable. Some baitcasting reels have an optional anti-reverse feature, which means that the anti-reverse can be disengaged so the handle and the spool can be turned either forward or backward. This is accomplished by moving a small spring-loaded lever on the sideplate (usually the right sideplate or handle sideplate). This may be referred to as a direct drive feature, although it is actually a mechanism for disengaging the anti-reverse.

This feature is often preferred for specific fishing applications when anglers want a direct feel of the line for strike detection, for instance, when they are drift fishing and putting the reel in and out of gear frequently, or when they are live-lining bait and want to let line out frequently to follow the movement of the bait. After casting, engage the gear by turning the handle, then disengage the anti-reverse. When a fish takes and runs off, flip the anti-reverse lever into the on position and set the hook. If you leave the anti-reverse disengaged, the reel handle will be free to move wildly backward as line comes off the spool, which could cause trouble. Make sure to keep your hand on the handle if you have the anti-reverse disengaged, or you'll have a runaway handle.

Other Features

Spool. Many people believe that narrower baitcasting spools are easier to cast and to attain distance with than wider ones, but this is a function of many reel elements and not an absolute determination. It is reasonable to believe that there is less friction on the line from the levelwind line guide during a cast because the line comes from less of a side angle when it's at the ends of the narrow spool. Narrow spools are smaller and also lighter, requiring less effort to get them moving, and they are very suitable for lightweight lures. Narrow spools also have less capacity, however, and when there is a lot of line out, it takes more work to recover line when the handle is turned. Wider spools also tend to be used with heavier lures, which provide more momentum in a cast, thus allowing for good distance, all other things being equal.

For a time there was a trend toward narrow V-shaped spools in baitcasting reels; very few of these are still produced because they tend to bunch the line, which impeded smooth outward line flow. Nearly all spools today are level from edge to edge, and capacity is determined by the width as well as the depth.

Many anglers do not need significant line capacity on a baitcasting reel, and most have more line capacity than the average caster needs, even with a thicker diameter line. Some hold just 100 yards of 10-pound test, but most hold about 150 yards of 12-pound line, and some large models hold more than 200 yards of 20-pound line. Naturally, this is relative to line diameter, which means a reel that holds 100 yards of conventional-diameter 10-pound line might also hold 100 yards of 17-pound line that has the diameter of a conventional 10-pound line *(see: line)*. Although not all reels have this feature, line capacity information, provided on the sideplate of many reels, is very helpful.

Incidentally, baitcasting reels are primarily used with 10- to 20-pound strength line. Some high-quality light models are suitable for use with 8-pound line and possibly with 6; some sturdier models are used with 25- to 40-pound line for special situations.

A recent trend is toward a shallower arbor on a wide baitcasting spool. The smaller depth means that the reel holds less line overall, but because these have less mass in the core region, they are lighter; this means it takes less effort to move the reel on a cast, so they cast very well. For use with light lures and special short-casting situations (bass anglers like this for pitching, *see*), this can be beneficial. Some spools are also perforated to decrease their weight. This also helps because, in general, a lighter spool requires less momentum to start turning, plus it doesn't have the inertia to keep it going, so it's easier to handle, especially for casting light lures.

Spools are primarily made of aluminum. Some of the best and higher priced reels have aircraft grade aluminum, and some of the lower end reels have graphite spools. Though lightweight, graphite spools are of dubious value for hard-core fishing with baitcasting reels. They are uncommon in conventional reels, which take much more punishment than the average baitcasting reel because they are frequently broken when subjected to extreme tension and the use of heavy line. A greater discussion about revolving-spool materials and properties is contained with the entry on conventional tackle *(see)*.

One other thing worth noting is that the spools of modern baitcasting reels are very easy to access for changing or to adjust the centrifugal brake shoes. Many reels now feature bayonet-style access to the spool; this is flush to the exterior sideplate that is opposite to the handle, and hands-down the quickest system for spool changing. Such a design is one of the best creations of manufacturers and eliminates the protruding finger-grip screw heads that exist on other reels. Actually, the majority of reels still feature relatively quick access via two or three screw heads that are located on the handle sideplate and which, when completely loosened, detach the entire opposite sideplate or (most commonly) the handle sideplate to provide spool access.

Because spool changing is not that common, most people never use this feature, although they may need it for easy access to the spool for adjusting the centrifugal brake. Rather than changing spools to use their outfit with different strength line (which means derigging and rerigging the same outfit), most anglers simply have multiple baitcasting outfits.

Frame. The weight, material, and construction of the frame can make a difference after many hours of use, and especially depending upon the severity of use in casting, retrieving, and playing fish.

The materials used in the frame and sideplates vary widely. They include one-piece forged aluminum spools on premium reels, as well as one-piece die-cast or machined aluminum and one-piece graphite models. One-piece frames provide superior strength and precision alignment of the spool and other components. One-piece aluminum frames are especially favored for heavy-duty applications; baitcasting reels used for lighter applications may have a multi-piece frame.

A one-piece aluminum frame on baitcasting reels has strength and torque-free advantages, and provides the best possible gear alignment.

Multi-piece frames are also made of aluminum, graphite, and even plastic. Plastic frames are not durable enough for serious use. Graphite frames are generally adequate for most casting activities; graphite has weight and corrosion advantages over aluminum, but even the latest grades of graphite do not yet have the strength of properly manufactured aluminum, so it is not quite as resistant to torque or flexing. Thus, subjecting a graphite reel to a great deal of pressure could result in deterioration in the gears. This is why some reels have a graphite sideplate and an aluminum frame and spool; the weight of a reel with a multi-piece frame can be reduced if the sideplates are graphite, and these do not have much effect on overall strength. Only one sideplate on a reel has a one-piece frame; this is the handle sideplate and it is made of the same material as the frame.

All frames have a reel foot attached to them; this component sits in the reel seat of a rod and may be integral to the frame or riveted on. Riveting is less preferable because rivets can get loose and can't be tightened.

Ergonomics. The shape and weight of baitcasting reels is especially important because these products are either frequently or exclusively used for casting by many anglers. Baitcasting reels were once entirely round in design, but they are now ergonomic, with low profile and teardrop designs very common in addition to round models. Teardrop reels are especially favored by anglers who tend to palm the reel, so a smooth sideplate that cups neatly into the palm of the rod-holding hand is quite popular.

Although weight is a major concern of manufacturers, this is (or should be) subordinate to having strength and durability. The majority of baitcasting reels weigh between 9 and 12 ounces. Some are between 7 and 9 ounces and mini versions with plastic bodies may weigh less, while large-spool versions may weigh up to 21 ounces. Light weight can make a difference after many hours of use, but so can comfortable styling. A comfortable shape may be more important than overall weight, especially if just fractions of an ounce are involved. If you do not palm the reel when holding it, however, lower weight is probably preferable to shape.

Manufacturers would like to make lighter baitcasting reels, but have not completely figured out how to do it without making disadvantageous sacrifices and compromises. Furthermore, light and ultralight versions of these products have not caught on as well as larger versions, which dominate the market.

Cosmetics, or appearance, has nothing to do with function and doesn't have practical use implications. Handles do have a bearing on comfort and ease of use. Some people like bigger handles than are supplied by the manufacturers and some prefer smaller, and these can be changed. The other aspects of handles relative to speed and power were discussed previously.

Lastly, an overlooked item of convenience, or in many cases inconvenience, is that of threading line from the spool out the line guide or spooling it onto the reel for the first time. It's difficult to put line on many modern baitcasting reels because of the number of bars, narrowness of the spool area, and presence of a reel hood. Many hoods pop up to provide access to the spool for putting line on or for picking out a backlash, but these hoods are more of a nuisance than a help. Round reels with an open metal line guide and medium-width spool are the easiest to handle when putting line on, getting it through the line guide, and picking out a backlash.

Rods

As with most types of rods other than spinning and flycasting, baitcasting rods have guides that mount over the axis of the rod and are placed on top of it, with the reel sitting on top of the handle rather than under it. This arrangement, which is necessary because of the nature of baitcasting reels, is especially well suited to fighting and controlling a fish, as well as for retrieving lures. In a general sense, fighting fish is what this tackle does particularly well; therefore, since the load of a gamefish on the line applies both a crushing downward force on the guide ring and frame, and a simultaneous tendency to torque or twist the rod, guides have to be of top quality and properly spaced and placed.

Guide rings on baitcasting rods have a smaller diameter than those on spinning rods; this is a double-foot guide.

The rings on baitcasting rod guides are smaller than they are on most other tackle because they don't have to accommodate large spirals of line coming from the reel when casting (as in spinning), the line is fairly close to the rod blank when it leaves the reel, and the line is not prone to twisting and coiling on baitcasting reels. Guides may be single- or double-foot versions, with the latter more likely to be used along the entire blank on heavy-action rods or just in the position of the first guide or guides (closest to the reel), and the former generally preferred because it improves rod action and slightly lessens the weight.

Reels mount close to the handle in the reel seat, which makes it fairly comfortable to palm the reel and rod. They are secured in the seat with a locking foregrip that screws down on the reel foot or by a locking ring that screws up on the reel foot.

Baitcasting rod handles are straight or have a pistol grip design, the latter usually found on smaller models. All baitcasting rods that are used for casting have a trigger grip on the underside of the rod, opposite and at the lower end of the reel seat. When you hold the rod, this trigger grip rests under either the middle or ring finger. Rods designed for trolling, which have a long handle, usually do not have a trigger grip so they can fit onto rod holders.

Handle length and overall rod length vary widely according to application, ranging from $5^1/_2$-foot models to 9-footers for steelhead and salmon fishing. Most rods used for casting are in the 6- to $7^1/_2$-foot range.

Baitcasting rods are available in one- and two-piece models. Most of the better rods up to $7^1/_2$ feet long are one piece, although longer models may have a telescoping butt in which the upper section slides into the lower for storage. There are very few travel or pack models among baitcasting rods, but a few excellent ones exist in two-piece versions with a telescoping butt section.

Action, taper, and material construction vary considerably. Baitcasting rods are commonly made of graphite and a mix of graphite and other materials, and many models are specifically tailored to special uses and styles of fishing.

Unlike reels, many of the issues pertaining to baitcasting rods—functions, materials, and

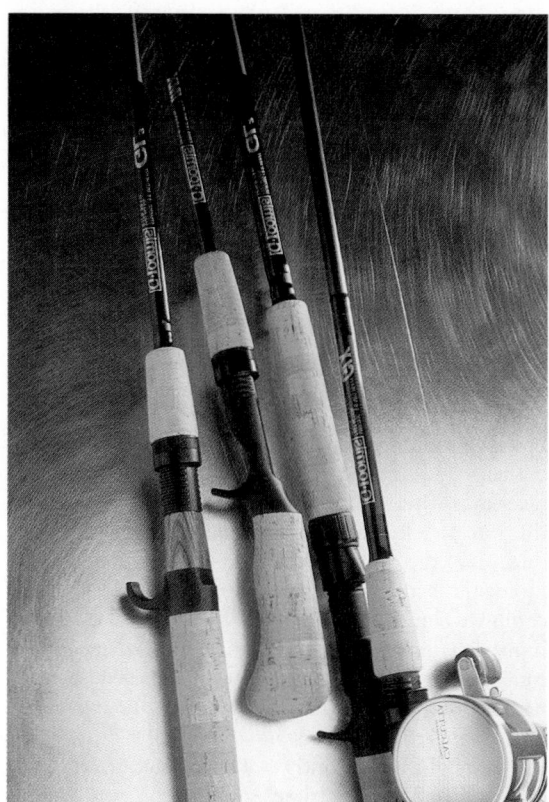

These G. Loomis rods exhibit typical baitcasting rod handles and cork grips.

components— are similar to those of other rods; these are more fully detailed elsewhere *(see: rod, fishing)*.

Using Baitcasting Tackle

Line.   As mentioned, 10- through 20-pound line strengths are most commonly used with baitcasting tackle. Fishing line is not prespooled onto baitcasting reels, although when a reel is purchased from some tackle retailers, it may be spooled by the dealer with the brand and strength of line you desire using a line winding machine. Most people fill the reel with line themselves, primarily with nylon monofilament, but also with braided or fused microfilament lines. Line coiling is not much of an issue on revolving-spool reels, so suppleness may not be much of a factor in line selection. Most baitcasting reel users are especially concerned with abrasion resistance in their line, and in line diameter, especially since diameter affects the working of many lures.

Filling/refilling the spool.   The various aspects of properly filling a reel spool are detailed elsewhere *(see: line)*. Putting line on a baitcasting reel spool is not complicated, but it should be done under tension. In brief, the spooling process entails mounting the reel on the rod and running line from a service spool through the rod guides beginning at the top of the rod, and then through the levelwind line guide of the reel. Tie the line to the arbor of the spool, snip off the tag end excess, and reel the line on under tension. It is important to avoid or at least

minimize twisting of the line during the spooling process, as detailed elsewhere *(see: line)*. Fill the spool to within no more than $3/16$ inch of the lip.

Line twist.   Line twist is not an inherent problem in baitcasting reels. With other types of tackle, twist is often caused when the angler turns the handle against a slipping drag. Twist isn't possible on a baitcasting reel if the handle is turning and the spool is simultaneously slipping. When the drag mechanism is activated on such a reel, the spool rotates and line unwinds in an untwisted manner. There is no line twist unless it comes from lure use or it is incurred through improper filling of the reel spool.

Matching and selecting.   As with any type of fishing tackle, the issue of pairing the right reel to the right rod is an important one, but today it is a relatively easy one. Some baitcasting reels and rods are packaged in combination, but tackle retailers can match rods and reels for you. Usually, a reel is purchased separately from a rod. Matching these up used to be referred to as balancing, and properly paired outfits were referred to as "balanced tackle." This simply meant that the rod and reel felt right when used together; the outfit was not overly butt heavy due to a large reel paired with a lightweight rod, or tip heavy due to a small reel paired to a medium or heavy action rod.

Fishing rods are virtually all labeled by line classifications and by weight of objects to be used, which practically assures that you don't put a light-duty reel, for example, on a medium-heavy rod.

Baitcasting reels are occasionally classified according to specific use, or species of fish, but this is no absolute matter. Reels might be classified as high speed or heavy duty, but the exact definition of such categorizations can differ from one manufacturer to the next and, in any event, is determined by the line capacity, features, and components.

When selecting baitcasting tackle, as well as matching a rod and reel, you must take into consideration the applications for it. A beginning angler may be unsure what to select without any prior fishing experience. Guidance from a knowledgeable salesperson is very helpful; such a person is more likely to be found in a specialized store (a sporting goods dealer or bait and tackle shop); a knowledgeable salesperson will not be found with a mail-order supplier and seldom in a mass merchandise mart. Lacking such a person, or in addition, you might seek guidance from an acquaintance or relative who has experience with this type of equipment and some knowledge of the fishing that a beginner is likely to do.

In a general sense, selecting baitcasting tackle starts with a determination of the size of fish that you will likely catch and evaluating the conditions under which you'll be fishing. The larger and stronger the fish, the stronger the tackle necessary for beginners, until you get the experience to use lighter gear. Fishing where there are a lot of obstructions usually requires medium or heavy grades of this type of tackle. Most selection starts with a

B

determination of the line strength necessary for the conditions, and having the rod and reel appropriate for this. You should also pay attention to line capacity so that you have an appropriate amount of line on the reel for the application (this is especially relevant where trolling is done).

Holding the rod and reel. This issue was detailed previously when reviewing the right- and left-retrieve features of baitcasting reels. When casting, anglers must keep their thumb on the reel spool and control the spool revolutions; their casting hand is positioned around the handle so that the index or middle finger simultaneously grabs the finger knob at the back of the handle. The palm may or may not cradle the sideplate of the reel depending upon user preference.

Many baitcasting outfits are held by palming the reel, with the fingers wrapped around the trigger grip underneath the rod handle. Another method is to move the hand slightly toward the butt, with most of it cradling the rod handle, although still with fingers wrapped around the trigger grip.

When retrieving, the same grip is made with the rod-holding hand (which may be the noncasting hand). Some people cast with two hands, in which case the hand that does not operate the reel is wrapped around the lower butt of the rod and used for leverage.

Casting technique. How to cast with baitcasting tackle is described in detail in a separate entry *(see: casting),* but it's worth reviewing a few key points here.

Before you cast, you must make sure that the drag control has been properly set, that the spool tension knob has been adjusted, and that the centrifugal or mechanical spool control has been set as applicable.

Many anglers attempt to use baitcasting gear without realizing that you don't cast it with the reel facing you as it rests atop the rod handle. Instead, do this: Depress the freespool button or bar and, with casting thumb on the spool, turn the reel sideways so the sideplate is facing you. Your wrist will be in the same position as if you were writing with a pen or tossing a dart. It stays this way throughout the cast. Release thumb pressure on the spool as the rod arcs forward, and you're in business.

If you lob or toss a lure with baitcasting gear, you're not really casting and you are inviting backlash trouble, although a lob can be desirable when casting some forms of bait so it doesn't tear off the hook. You can make this soft type of presentation more readily with a spinning reel, but in baitcasting with lures, you really want to make the rod do what it was designed to do, and employ its arc and power

in both backward and forward cast motions. You can only do that if you're confident about your ability to control backlashes.

Although perhaps half a dozen casts are employed in baitcasting, the basic overhead style is by far most common. Here, the wrist and forearm do the work. The cast should begin with the rod low and pointed toward the target. Bring the rod up crisply to a point slightly beyond vertical position, where flex in the rod tip will carry it back; then, without hesitating, start the forward motion sharply, releasing the lure roughly halfway between the rod's vertical and horizontal positions.

The entire casting action should be a smooth, flowing motion; you are doing more than just hauling back and heaving. Remember that your thumb takes over with delicate spool feathering the instant the lure is released, and that the thumb clamps down on the spool to stop spool rotation the moment the lure reaches its target. Realize, too, that casting technique may vary a bit depending on numerous factors, including length and action of rod, weight of lure, distance to be achieved, and nature of cover, and that some modifications and adjustments may be necessary accordingly.

Although the majority of people cast with one hand most of the time, some people use two hands, especially when learning and where large or heavy lures are used, wind is encountered, or long distances are necessary. Some people cast two-handed with all kinds of baitcasting equipment the majority of the time, except for short distances. The result is crisp low-trajectory casts, improved distance, and increased accuracy.

Maintenance and repair. Many people do very little, if anything, to maintain their baitcasting reels. This may be alright if the reel is only used occasionally. Common sense dictates that if the reel has any loose part (most likely a sideplate screw) it should be tightened as soon as you notice it, and that you should rinse any reel that has encountered sand, dirt, mud, or saltwater. Clean the reel as soon after use as possible, using a fine spray of freshwater rather than a hard stream. There is nothing wrong with dipping a reel in freshwater if you must cleanse it of dirt or sand; after all, it is likely to be exposed to wet and rainy conditions while fishing. Just don't make a habit of it, give the reel a chance to dry out completely, and keep it lubricated.

Details on reel maintenance are discussed elsewhere *(see: tackle—care/maintenance/repair).* Manufacturers recommend that infrequently used reels be cleaned and relubricated annually, and that reels that are used several times a week be attended to monthly. Periodic maintenance means lightly oiling and greasing accessible parts. Check with the manufacturer's literature on the specific lubricant to use because this differs with certain parts and among manufacturers. Some reel manufacturers, for example, do not recommend lubricating their drag washers. Some reels come with small oil or grease tubes, and these can be purchased from tackle suppliers or obtained from the manufacturer. A thorough cleaning requires disassembling most of the reel, scrubbing or rinsing most of the gunk from the parts, drying, and then relubricating and regreasing. Do not apply excessive grease or oil.

Backlash Demystified

A backlash on a baitcasting reel is the tangle of line that develops on a spool during an imperfectly executed cast. Backlashes range from minor tangles that are easily undone to major bird's nests that require a lot of time to unravel, if indeed they can be unraveled. The tendency of baitcasting reels to develop backlashes has intimidated anglers for many decades. The fact that a backlash often occurs at inopportune times, such as when the fish are turned on and are willing to hit any bait presented to them, makes their occurrence all the more troublesome.

Cause. In designing and developing fishing reels and their mechanisms, manufacturers have made detailed studies of the effect of, and, more importantly, the physical cause of, this phenomenon, which is sometimes referred to, either politely or scornfully, as a "professional overrun."

Through many years of research and the creation of a variety of mechanisms specifically intended to control backlashes, some reel manufacturers employed a variety of means to observe the birth and evolution of backlashes during a cast. A great deal of empirical research has been conducted to learn how to deal with this unique phenomenon.

One manufacturer of modern high-performance reels used stroboscopic-flash photography to attempt to track the way a backlash starts in order to design a foolproof means of eliminating it completely. Through this study, the researchers discovered that the precursor to even the slightest backlash was that the top loops of line on the rotating spool would rise up above the line level before traveling through the levelwind and rod guides. Depending on numerous other factors, the line could relax back down to the spool for a problem-free cast or progressively snarl into a tangled mess.

Another manufacturer employed high-speed motion photography to create a super-detailed, slow-motion examination of every stage in the development of some of the worst backlashes ever observed. This film record provided a motion analysis showing that several causes contribute to a backlash, with each offering its own possible design solution. The slow-motion film proved that one form of backlash, usually the worst, occurs almost instantly at the start of the cast.

Basically a backlash results from a differential between the speed of the line moving through the rod guides behind the cast lure and the amount of line being made available to follow the lure by the spin imparted to the reel spool.

Although the end result may be the same— a backlash—there is more than one kind and more than one cause. Backlashes usually occur at the beginning or at the end of the cast and are respectively called an overrun or an overflow. Overrun backlashes have many causes: a jerky casting technique; lures with a great deal of air resistance, which begin to slow down right from the start of the cast; a rod that is too stiff to properly load with the lure weight being cast; casting directly into the wind, which slows down the lure; a line with a high percent of stretch; multiple thumb contact with the spool during the cast; and overly heavy line. Fewer causes contribute to overflow backlashes, but they include: late spool release by the thumb, which produces a short downward cast and a fast lure impact; striking an object such as a tree branch or dock before the lure has reached it target; and, most commonly, allowing the lure to hit the water without thumb control to stop the spool.

In order to help avoid or solve each of these problems, you should know what constitutes a proper cast. Technically, the perfect cast consists of a dynamic blend of optimum energy management. With the reel in freespool and the thumb holding the spool stationary, energy is transmitted from the casters' arm muscles and wrist flex to the rod, causing the rod to move forward in the direction of the cast. This movement creates an inertial lag in the rod and lure that causes the rod to bend or load, thus storing the transmitted energy to cast the lure. At a point in the forward movement, thumb pressure on the spool is relaxed and arm movement is stopped, unloading the energy stored in the rod and allowing the lure to travel in an arc through the air to its target. When the spool is released, the built-up kinetic and centrifugal energy in the rod and lure is translated to rotational energy in the spool, which suddenly begins to spin as a result of the fast initial lure movement. Spool spin releases the line, which travels through the line guides and follows the flight of the lure.

This spool spin is the critical factor in causing or preventing a backlash. Under ideal conditions, the spin imparted presents just enough line from the spool to follow the lure without creating any drag as it travels. It is almost as if a "zero gravity" effect is created; the line on the spool neither pushes nor drags the lure but merely appears behind it as a link to the reel. This lack of drag on the lure is the reason baitcasting and conventional reels can outcast all other designs. Casters have long recognized that their lures travel farthest when the line breaks and there is absolutely no line drag to stop their lure from heading to the horizon.

It is only when the spin rate of the spool, the speed of the line, and the travel of the lure through the air are all in balance that the cast is faultless.

Controls. Reel manufacturers have created several reliable designs to control or eliminate backlash. One of the earliest, and still most commonly used, is the mechanical spool control. This is usually a screw-down-cap device on the handle side

B

Caught by relatively few anglers, the colorful Arctic charr has the most northerly distribution of any freshwater fish; it is also one of the hardest fighting and finest eating species.

B

of the reel that applies pressure to the ends of the spool axle. The resulting friction slows the spin of the spool. As described earlier, this mechanism is typically adjusted to control spool tension for the weight of the lure in use at any given time. Because it is friction-controlled, it is wear- and lubricant-sensitive. By over-controlling (tightening too much) the spool with this mechanism alone, all overrun backlashes can be eliminated, as well as most overflow backlashes. However, all casts made at such an adjustment require much more energy input from the caster in order to achieve distance, and it can cause the mechanism to wear prematurely.

The centrifugal brake system was another of the early backlash control designs; it was first introduced by Garcia in 1953. That it was successful is attested to by recent modifications to improve its versatility and its inclusion on some of the most expensive high-performance reels now made. In this mechanism, multiple friction weights are freely suspended on radial shafts attached to the spool. The free ends of the weights are allowed to run against the inside surface of a highly polished circular drum or raceway. Depending on the size, number, and the material of the brake weights, a varying amount of friction is created between the weight and drum as the spool spins during the cast. High spool speed creates greater centrifugal force and, therefore, greater friction and braking action. Although the highest spool speed and braking takes place at the start of the cast, the centrifugal brake mechanism has some effect at all but the slowest spool speeds.

Centrifugal brakes have been designed to allow as many as six individual weights to contact the drum at once. Braking force can be fine-tuned by eliminating some or all of the weights from the system. In some large-weight designs, it is possible to exercise fine control by shaping the free end of the brake weight to change the amount of contact surface each weight presents to the brake drum. Finally, the performance and life of the brake weights can be extended by placing a thin coating of light machine oil on the raceway contact surface.

At one time, some reel manufacturers used a unique spool design—the V-shaped spool—to attempt to control both forms of backlash. This shape was created on the theory that, as the cast progresses, the line level drops deeper into the V-shaped spool arbor making less line available. With less line available to backlash, there was, theoretically, less likelihood of a backlash occurring. This was not one of the most popular or successful control attempts because not only was less line available for backlashing but also for extreme-distance casting, general fishing applications, and battling far-running gamefish. Additionally, as the line level on the spool was reduced, the spool spin rate had to increase as the cast progressed. This caused increased line drag on the lure, shortening casts or requiring much more energy input from the caster to achieve sufficient distance.

Magnetic spool controls were popularly introduced by several manufacturers in a variety of designs in the early 1980s, and first introduced by Daiwa in 1981. These designs offered an easily adjustable, nonwearing, friction-free spool control that would have an effect throughout the entire cast. The physics of this control are based on electromagnetism or, more specifically, eddy current braking. When a metal object is passed through a magnetic field, it creates an electromagnetically induced current, which causes resistance to the movement of the metal through the magnetic field, slowing its passage. This is known as eddy current braking.

This is used to control backlash in baitcasting reels by mounting a series of small but powerful rare earth magnets to the body of the reel with their magnetic fields aimed at the reel spool or at a drum attached to the spool flange. The magnets are mounted with alternating poles facing the spool: North-South-North, etc. The alternating poles reinforce the magnetic field of the adjacent magnet, intensifying the total magnetic coercive force and focusing the fields more closely to the magnet surfaces. This allows the resulting shallower, more powerful field to be adjusted, usually through a dial mechanism, by bringing the magnets closer or moving them away from the metal spool or drum. At the farthest setting, typically represented by a zero on the adjustment dial, the magnetic fields are theoretically far enough away from the metal that there is no resistance applied and no drag on the spool.

For use in baitcasting reels, the strength and life expectancy of these magnets are permanent. Because no parts come in contact in this control, there are no wear or lubrication concerns. Proper adjustment in use should allow for minimal spool control to a strong eddy current resistance.

Physical laws state that, for any of the available magnetic control adjustments, the eddy current resistance increases as the speed of the metal (spool) passing through the magnetic field increases. A spool spinning at high speed at setting X encounters greater resistance than when spinning more slowly at the same X setting. In this way the magnetic design "self adjusts" during the cast to control overrun at the start of the cast as the spool spins fastest and as the spool slows throughout the remainder of the cast.

Perhaps the most important and effective anti-backlash control is the caster's thumb. In the decades before the advent of the mechanical devices just described, it was only the "educated thumb" that stood between the caster and disaster. It is still the best and most reliable option available. Once trained to do its job, the thumb can deliver all of the necessary control inputs throughout the entire cast to eliminate both overrun and overflow backlashes.

The only way to train your thumb to control the spool is through practice, preferably away from water. Trying to learn to cast and to fish at the same time results only in frustration. A good idea is to go

The genealogy of fishing line includes the use of vines in pre-history, horsehair in the Middle Ages, silk in freshwater around 1900, and linen in saltwater around 1900.

B

into the backyard or to a local park or ballfield and practice casting using a $1/2$-ounce practice plug.

Over-control the reel at the start by tightening the mechanical control, using all of the centrifugal brake weights, or dialing the magnetic spool control to its maximum setting. This helps minimize any tendency for the reel to backlash during a properly executed cast. Over-control with the thumb is also in order, by keeping a slight but constant drag on the line level of the spool, throughout each cast. Distance is not yet the goal. Timing of thumb release and line control is important at this point. As the rod moves forward, release the thumb pressure on the spool to allow the plug to be cast at an upward and outward angle. Monitor the spool spin with slight thumb pressure through the cast, and stop the plug before it lands on the water. This combination will provide full control of overrun and overflow backlashes.

Repetition teaches the thumb how to react, and sensory feedback from the thumb allows the brain to learn just how much control to input at any time. After some confidence-building practice, the reel can be de-controlled by reducing the various adjustable settings to allow a more freely spinning spool. This permits longer distances on the cast without requiring greater energy input. Eventually, the level of casting proficiency achieved permits use of the reel at minimal control settings for effortless casting. Adjustments are needed only when using very air-resistant lures, heavy lines, and when deliberately casting into the wind.

Clearing a backlash. To clear a backlash, put the reel in gear, tighten the drag so it doesn't slip, press the thumbnail of your rod-holding hand on the snarl to flatten and relax the coils, take two or three turns of the reel handle, put the reel in gear, and pull out the line. This does not tighten the coils and should allow you to get all but the worst backlashes out in a few seconds. Make sure to reset the drag.

Many people pick at the backlashed loops of line with their fingers. To do this, put the reel in freespool with your thumb on the spool. Carefully pick away at the leading loops to remove tightening overwraps until you get to the loop that is dug in the worst; then pull it out. Get all snarled line segments out before rewinding the line on the spool, and don't wind over any loops.

Other issues. Baitcasting gear is remarkably free of the line twisting troubles that are associated with spinning and spincasting tackle, so in a sense, it is more trouble-free. You can minimize casting problems and potential backlashes by soaking your line before casting. This is particularly beneficial when old line is on a reel or where the line is of high strength and heavily coiled. Dip the reel in freshwater or pour water on the spool before first use, or soak the spool in lukewarm water after putting new line on.

One source of much baitcasting trouble, via backlashes, comes from anglers trying to cast great distances. Anglers equipped with long rods with two-handed grips, thin-diameter lines, and deep-diving

plugs that can cover a lot of territory, are often inclined to "air it out." The extra power required to send an ordinary lure an extraordinary distance with baitcasting tackle often overwhelms calculated thumb pressure, and the result is trouble.

Any time you get a little line overlapped on the spool or sense impending backlash trouble, make a medium-force cast in a nonfishing direction (downwind is best) to clear the spool, and then wind the line back on under pressure. It may help at such times to put your nonwinding hand on the rod shaft ahead of the reel and run the line through thumb and index finger as you quickly spool it back on. You should do this anyway when filling the reel with line.

Wind is the bane of many baitcasting tackle users, more so than spinning gear because of a heightened chance of backlash when casting into the wind. When casting with the wind, everyone looks like a champ. When you have to cast into the wind with baitcasting tackle, you should try low trajectories (use a low sidearm cast, if possible, and/or release the lure a little later than you ordinarily do), increase magnetic spool control and/or thumb pressure, and use more aerodynamic lures. You will probably have to use more force to achieve normal distance in a strong wind, so greater thumb pressure, in addition to increased magnetic force, will likely be necessary.

See: **Conventional Tackle; Reel, Fishing; Rod, Fishing; Spincasting Tackle; Spinning Tackle.**

BAIT CONTAINER

Devices to hold bait take many forms and rank fairly high on the list of accessories used by anglers who fish with bait. For baitfish, some form of steel or plastic bucket, including some with a perforated insert pail, which contains the bait and which can be easily removed to facilitate water changing, or floating plastic buckets with a spring-loaded door, are the primary models. The latter can be kept in the water and are especially useful for slow trolling. Both can be used for other bait, such as leeches, crayfish, or salamanders. Worms, however, are usually kept in small plastic or fiber containers, or simply in the Styrofoam container that small quantities are sold in. Larger bait, especially that used in saltwater, is kept in boat livewells (see: livewell) or large storage containers. For some species, particularly shad, alewives, and herring, the containers must be round; rectangular containers pile such fish up in the corners and they die quickly.

BAIT DROPPER

A device lowered on a rope or fishing line to drop bait on the bottom of a water body. These are tube-like with a flap that opens when the device contacts the bottom; the speed and force of the descent keeps the flap closed on the drop.

See: **Chumming.**

BAITFISH

A generic term used by anglers for any fish species that are forage for predators, although it often specifically pertains to smaller fish; this term also references fish that are used in live bait angling.

BAITHOLDER HOOK

A hook with mini-barbs on the shank.
See: Hook.

BAIT RIG

Technically, an arrangement of any type of natural bait with other terminal tackle for fishing, the term bait rig has become synonymous with methods of fixing whole fish, partial fish, and strips of fish for saltwater trolling activities. Three of the most important basic such rigs are detailed here.

Rigging a strip bait. Strip baits are about the easiest trolling bait to rig and are very effective. Strip baits are made from various fish, with such species as bonito, small tuna, and dolphin preferred for their durability.

To fashion a strip bait, cut an appropriate length from a fish's belly (a) and trim it as illustrated (b). With wire leader partially rigged to the hook, leave a long tag end that faces the barb (b) and insert that leader end into the bait close to the forward section; then insert the hook in the middle of the tail section (c). The strip should be flat, not pinched or curled, to skip properly without being destroyed in short order. Wrap the end of the wire around the leader several times (d). Cut off excess but leave enough tag end available to rerig when it's time to change baits.

Rigging a balao. To rig a balao, which is one of the most popular baits for sailfish and white marlin, start with a hook that has been prepared with wire leader using a Haywire Twist (1), and wrap in a length of light copper wire at the base of the pin. Keep about an inch of tag end protruding

Rigging a strip bait

Rigging a balao

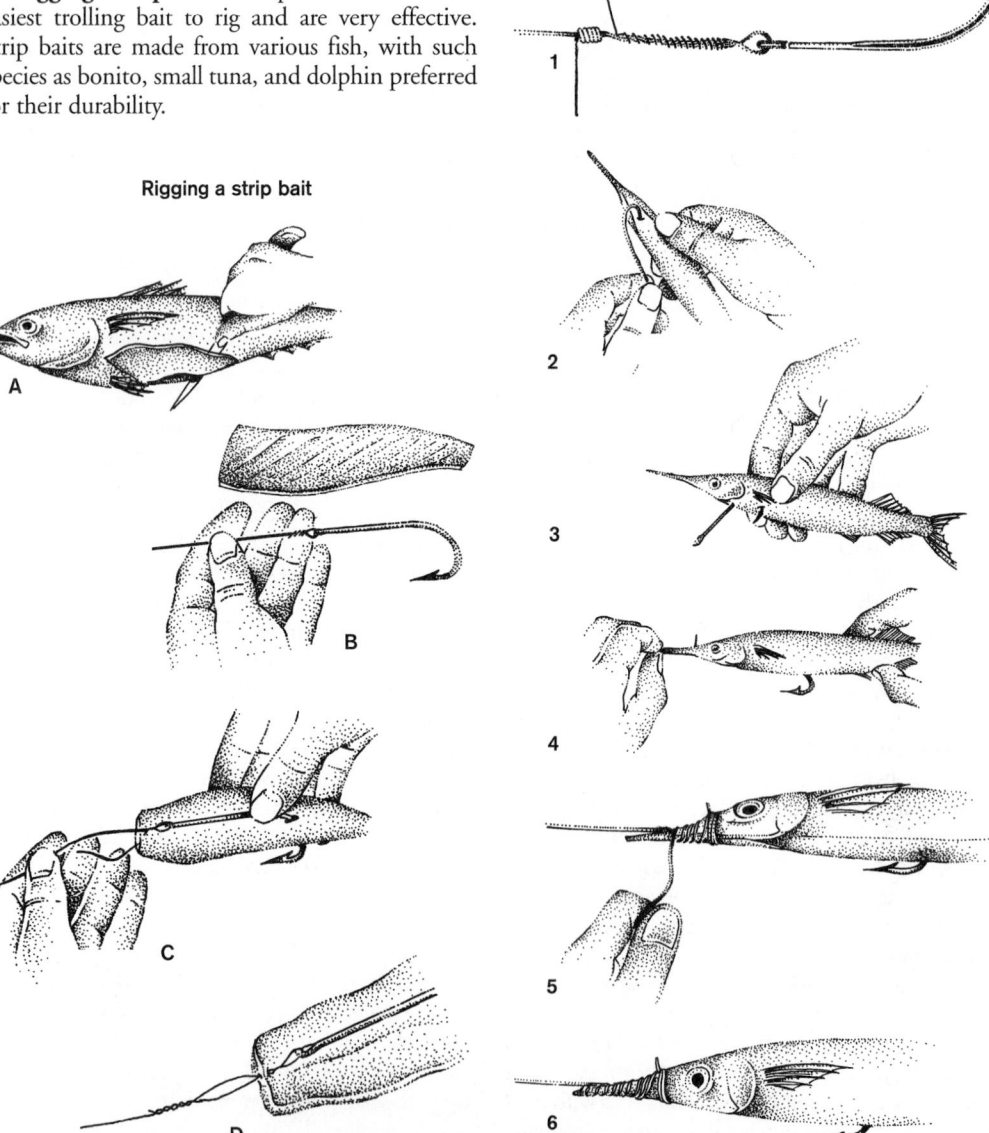

from the wire pin as shown, making sure it is in the opposite direction of the bend of the hook. Insert the hook by lifting a gill plate and sliding the hook point into the cavity (2), working it through by moving the hook and bending the bait (it may need to be softened first for this). Guide the point of the hook around and out the bait (3), and then slide the hook eye under the gill plate and push the protruding tag end of wire up through both of the jaws (4). The hook should align with the bait; if the bait is curved or hooked, it will spin and not troll properly. Hold the leader wire firm under the balao and wrap the copper wire twice around the head behind the pin (5). Then loop the remaining wire around the head in front of the pin and halfway down the bill; snap the bill off close to the jaw (6).

Rigging mackerel. Follow these procedures to rig a mackerel for offshore trolling.

Begin by slitting the belly of the fish, gutting it, and removing the anal fin. Taking care to locate the dead center of the nose, use a pick to punch a hole through the nose just forward of the eyes, then cut a small hole dead center under the mouth. Measure the belly length for a double-hook rig; then prepare the rig and place it in the fish coming from the cavity. Push the wire leader through the head and lead hook eye, and make a loop that does not bind; then form a Haywire Twist to finish the leader. Using waxed thread or dental floss and a heavy duty needle, sew the bait's mouth closed, then the gill flap and body cavity, ending just beyond the rear hook.

See: Natural Bait.

BAIT TRAP
See: Trap.

BAITWELL
A containment device for keeping bait alive.
See: Livewell.

BALAO
See: Halfbeaks and Balao.

BALLAST
Additional weight placed low in a boat to improve stability.

BALLOON
Using small balloons when fishing with live bait is a crafty but little-used idea, though one that can be employed by freshwater and saltwater anglers alike. Instead of fishing live bait under a float *(see)*, it is fished below a colorful 4- to 5-inch-diameter balloon. The balloons are inflated and tied around the fishing line, take up no space before and after use, can readily be popped off a fishing line, and are easily moved up and down the line to change the distance to the bait swimming below. They are also easily observed when fished 40 to 60 feet away from the angler.

Balloons can be employed when drifting, at anchor, and when slowly trolling (the latter is popular with freshwater striped bass anglers in the

Rigging mackerel

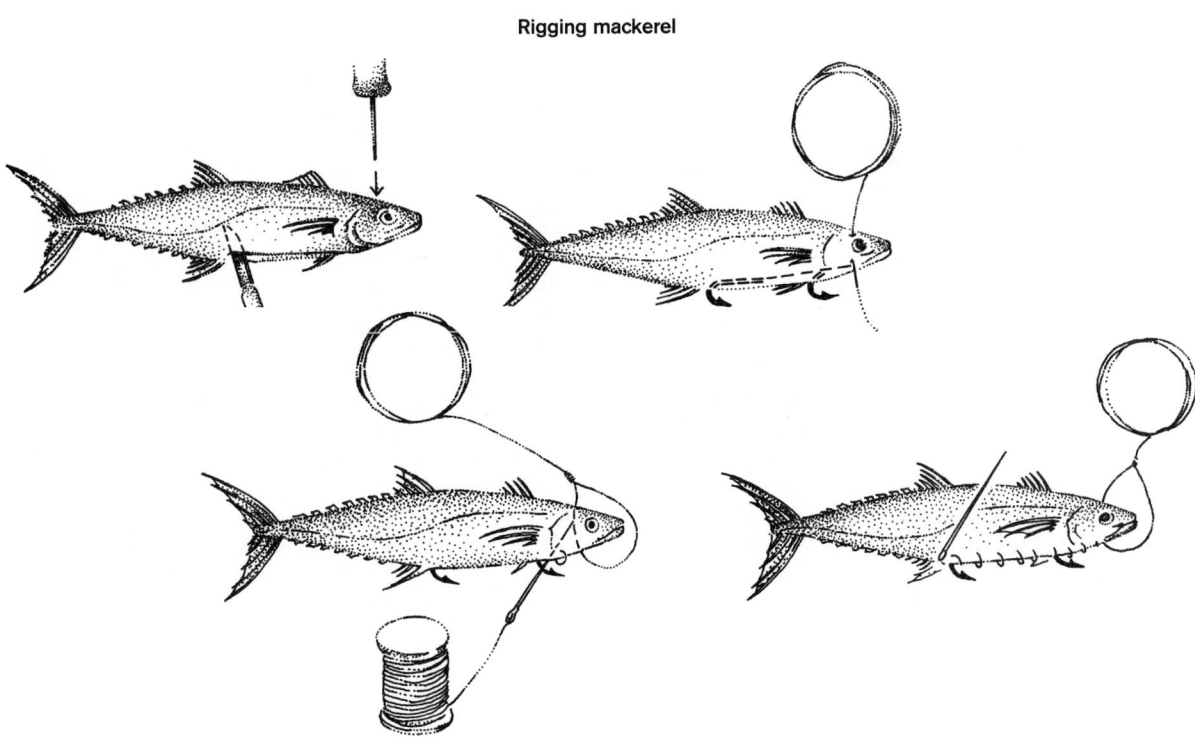

fall). Generally reserved for use with large baitfish (a big shiner, shad, or herring), balloons not only keep the bait from finding a place to hide, but also indicate a possible strike as it reflects the agitated bait below.

BALLYHOO

"Ballyhoo" is a common name for balao, which are widely used as trolling baits in big-game fishing.
See: Halfbeaks and Balao.

BAMBOO ROD

A fishing rod made of split and glued strips of bamboo, mounted with a handle, reel seat, and guides. Split-cane bamboo rods were favored for fly fishing and baitcasting prior to the development of synthetic rod materials, particularly fiberglass, and the perfection of rods manufactured from those materials.

Once a primary rod construction material, bamboo is today in extremely minor use for rod construction, limited to custom rod builders and relatively light-duty freshwater fly fishing application. Some older bamboo rods, created in certain periods and by some well-known makers, are collectibles.

Long bamboo poles with attached fixed-length line may be used for stillfishing, primarily for panfish species. These are simply long bamboo stalks unaccompanied by reels or rod components, and are used for making short-distance (the length of the pole, which is 10 to 15 feet) presentations, primarily of bait; they are not cast.
See: Antique Fishing Tackle; Pole; Rod, Fishing.

BANK

(1) A shallow elevation of the bottom of a body of water, often in a river or estuary (see), that has shifting composition and may be hazardous to navigation, such as a sandbank or gravelbank. It is also known as a bar (see).

(2) An elevation of the sea on a continental or island shelf. Depths may range from 60 feet near an island to perhaps 600 feet on a continental shelf (see), such as George's Bank in the North Atlantic, Hurricane Bank in the Pacific off Mexico, or Hannibal Bank off Panama.

(3) The land abutting either side of a river or stream; also the shore of a lake. In freshwater, land alongside flowing water is called the bank while land alongside a lake or pond is called the shore, but increasingly the word "bank" is associated with lakes and ponds as well, and used interchangeably with "shore."

Rivers have a left bank and a right bank, which is determined by facing in the direction in which the water is flowing.

BAR

A shoal of sand, mud, rocks, oyster shells, or other debris. Bars are commonly located at the mouths of rivers and at harbor entrances but may also be found on the bends of rivers, in impoundments, and in natural lakes. Bars may be impediments to navigation, especially at low tide or during periods of low water, and may cause boaters to run aground. Often they are desirable angling locations, especially the edges that drop off to deep water. Fish that cruise shallows may be attracted to the flat areas atop a bar.

BARB

The sharp projection behind the point of a hook that impedes the hook's backward movement.
See: Hook.

BARBADOS

See: Lesser Antilles.

BARBEL

(1) A whiskerlike feeler on the snout of somefish that contains taste buds and is used for touching and tasting food before ingesting it. One or more barbels may be present on either side of the mouth of fish that are primarily bottom feeders and attracted by food odor. Catfish (see), carp (see), and sturgeon (see) are among the species with such appendages.

(2) *Barbus barbus.*
Other names—French: *barbeau fluviatile;* German: *barbe;* Italian: *barbo;* Spanish: *barboderio.*

This is a popular European river fish unknown to most North Americans and, like carp, a member of the Cyprinidae family.

Identification. This fish derives its name from a signature characteristic of four barbels (also called *barbules* by the British), two on each side like carp, that are intrinsic to its bottom-feeding behavior. It has a downturned mouth and fleshy lips that also make it especially efficient at scrounging for food.

Otherwise well adapted to swift waters, the barbel has a long and rather streamlined body with a flattened belly; it is much more sleek and trim than its fellow cyprinids, especially carp. Its coloration is a brownish gray on top, and brown to bronze on the sides, tapering to a whitish or light-gray belly. It often has a reddish cast, particularly on the fins. Juveniles may have speckled flanks and an olive green tint.

Size. Barbel are commonly caught up to 5 pounds; 16- and 17-pounders have been recorded, and 20 pounds is believed to be the maximum weight.

Distribution. This fish ranges throughout western and central Europe, excluding the Italian, Greek, and Iberian Peninsulas.

Habitat.   A denizen of the upper reaches of clean and relatively swift-flowing rivers, barbel mainly live in the deeper parts of pools but will move into shallower waters, sometimes at night in heavily fished locations, and sometimes to slack waters. They may also feed at the surface among weeds on summer nights but are rarely caught at such times. In pools, they may hold behind objects that offer feeding advantages.

Spawning behavior.   Barbel spawn in late spring or early summer after migrating upriver, the female laying eggs over rocky gravel and the male fertilizing them. The eggs are broadcast, not deposited in a nest; they adhere to the bottom and are poisonous to humans.

Food and feeding habits.   Barbel are bottom feeders that eat a wide range of invertebrates, as well as algae, nymphs, worms, crustaceans, and eels. They root along the bottom, using their mouths like sucking tools, and are able to suck organisms off stones and from under rocks. They are extremely effective at vacuuming whatever they are after from the bottom and digging out their food. Their four mouth barbels have taste and touch cells that are important to feeding, allowing the fish to inspect probable food.

Angling.   Because barbel run larger on average than many other commonly pursued European species (most referred to as "coarse fish"), and are a strong fish, they are a popular catch. Their fight, although not showy, is determined, and their perseverance has been favorably compared to that of carp and salmon.

Barbel fishing principally requires bottom presentations (called "legering" in Europe) with an assortment of prepared, processed, and natural baits, often in conjunction with groundbait *(see)* chumming. Maggots, corn, worms, cheese, bread, grubs, seeds, meat cubes, pastes, and other items are used, especially those commodities that have been employed in prebaiting or chumming if the fish have been conditioned to that food. Hooked baits may be fished with a float and drifted, but drifting with a hand-held tight line to sense light strikes is especially favored.

Anglers try to observe the fish and their movements if possible. In order to make an appropriate presentation fast to the bottom, anglers must be familiar with the bottom terrain. Barbel sometimes take a bait and head directly downstream, resulting in an unmistakable and forceful strike. Often, however, they just pick up the bait without moving, or move slightly upstream with it. British anglers use up to 12-foot rods, 6- to 10-pound-test line, and No. 8 to 12 bait hooks.

The depth of the pool and the severity of current will dictate fishing choices, although sometimes these fish move shallower, especially if the river is high and muddy. Daytime and nighttime locations often vary, and some areas produce best in low-daylight or overcast conditions.

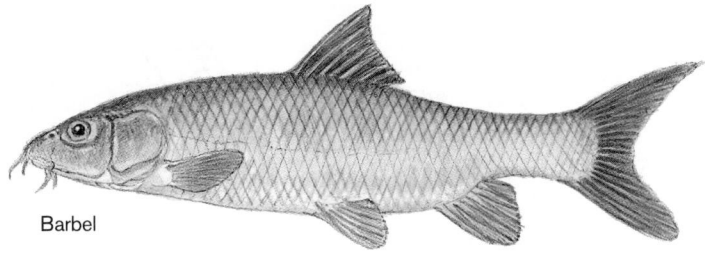

Barbel

BARBLESS HOOK
A hook that is manufactured without a barb behind the point, or whose barb has been pinched or filed down to render it inoperative.
See: Catch-and-Release; Hook.

BARNACLE
A barnacle is a saltwater crustacean sometimes thought to be a mollusk because of its "shell." Although some species of barnacles are enclosed in calcareous plates, other species lack this modification. There are over 800 species of barnacles; some are parasites, but others are commensal or independent organisms, living in communities attached to marine animals. Barnacles feed by using their feathery cirri (slender feet) to strain food from the water and beat it into their stomachs. Most have both male and female reproductive organs, and they grow in large colonies in marine environments. They are responsible for extensive damage done to ships, piers, and offshore structures.

BARRACUDA, GREAT   *Sphyraena barracuda.*
Other names—'cuda, sea pike, giant sea pike; French: *barracuda, brochet de mer;* Hawaiian: *kaku, kupala;* Japanese: *onikamasu;* Portuguese: *barracuda, bicuda;* Spanish: *barracuda, picuda.*

A ferocious fighter and an excellent gamefish, the great barracuda is considered potentially dangerous because of its tendency to strike at flashing objects (which it mistakes for fish) and its ability to inflict serious harm, in or out of water, through its prodigious teeth. The great barracuda has been known to attack waders, swimmers, and divers, but such incidents are uncommon. It is also a dangerous fish to eat because it leads a list of marine fishes that cause ciguatera *(see)* when eaten, although small fish are apparently not poisonous. Not every barracuda causes ciguatera, but there is no safe or reliable way of recognizing toxic fish.

Identification.   The great barracuda is long and slender with a large, pointed head, resembling a freshwater pike in body shape. It also has large eyes. The dorsal fins are widely separated, and the first dorsal fin has five spines, whereas the second has 10 soft rays. In a large underslung jaw, the great barracuda has large, pointed canine teeth. It also possesses a bluish gray or greenish gray

Great Barracuda

B

body coloration above the lateral line and a silvery white belly. A few irregular black blotches are usually scattered on the sides of the body, especially toward the tail; it is the only species of barracuda that has these blotches. The young have a dark stripe down the side, which mutates to become the blotches as the fish grows. The great barracuda also occasionally has 18 to 22 diagonal dark bars above the lateral line. It grows much larger, in general, than its relative the Pacific barracuda.

Size. Known to reach a weight of 106 pounds and a length of $6^1/_2$ feet, the great barracuda averages 5 to 20 pounds in weight; larger specimens are rare. The all-tackle world record is an 85-pounder.

Distribution. Great barracuda occur in all tropical seas except the East Pacific and range in the United States from Massachusetts to Brazil, although not in abundance from the Carolinas northward. They are caught mainly around Florida, in the Florida Keys, the Bahamas, and throughout the West Indies.

Habitat. Young barracuda live in inshore seagrass beds, whereas adults range from inshore channels to the open ocean. They are also found in bays, inlets, lagoons, and the shallows of mangrove islands, as well as around reefs, wrecks, piers, sandy or grassy flats, and coastal rivers where saltwater and freshwater mingle. They prefer shallow areas and appear to move inshore in summer, and offshore in fall and winter.

Life history/Behavior. Spawning behavior is triggered by a rise in water temperature; mating takes place between late spring and September, when the water temperature rises above 70°F. Young barracuda under 3 pounds usually inhabit shallow waters, such as harbors and coastal lagoons, until they become adults and live farther offshore, sometimes far out to sea. Smaller barracuda will occasionally school, but the large ones are typically solitary. Curiosity is a trait of all barracuda, and they will follow waders or divers as a result.

Food and feeding habits. The great barracuda eats whatever is available in its habitat, and needlefish, small jacks, and mullet are among the mainstays. They are attracted by shininess or flashes and movement, feeding by sight rather than by smell.

Angling. Barracuda often won't be around when an angler wants to catch one, but they can be a nuisance when he's looking for something else. On the other hand, many a blue-water troller has ventured a little too shallow inshore and been rewarded with a barracuda when seeking other game. Nonetheless, barracuda are able battlers that often strike savagely, and they frequently jump out of the water when hooked. The barracuda remains an underrated saltwater gamefish despite these qualities.

When holding in shallow waters close to shore, barracuda linger around such locales as mangrove edges, bridges, and jetties. When far from shore, they favor reefs, wrecks, oil rigs, coral heads, and the edges of dropoffs.

For a fish with a ferocious reputation, barracuda can actually be shy. They are alert to the presence of anglers and boats, eventhough they have been known to closely approach divers. They will follow a lure for quite a distance, but they'll scoot off as the lure nears a boat. For this reason, fairly distant casts, beyond the fish, are recommended. This gives it a chance to follow and strike the lure without being alarmed.

Barracuda are best caught on flashy, erratically worked items such as plugs, spoons, and surgical-tube lures. Fly anglers take them on big streamers. Flies and surface plugs, or shallow-running minnow plugs, are sometimes the best offerings, as they do not grab in the grass that is prevalent on so many shallow flats. A quick retrieve is favored, however, regardless of lure. Barracuda often follow a lure that is worked at a slow or moderate speed but refuse to strike it, or will ignore a lure that stops altogether, whereas an increase in speed, even if it means working it fast and then faster, can be provocative.

Casters often ply the shallows and flats looking for barracuda, most of which lie motionless, waiting to pounce on unsuspecting prey; they can be difficult to spot when still, despite their length. Light- to medium-action spinning, bait-casting, or flycasting tackle provides the best sport. Many anglers troll for these fish, too, although usually with heavier tackle and while simultaneously pursuing other fish. Their arsenal includes plugs, spoons, trolling feathers, and rigged baits.

Barracuda have a prodigious array of teeth and should be handled with care; it's best to use wire leaders with lures.
See: Barracuda, Pacific; Flats Fishing.

BARRACUDA, PACIFIC   *Sphyraena argentea.*
Other names—California barracuda, barry, snake, scoots, scooter; French: *bécune argentée.*

The Pacific barracuda is the best known of the four types of barracuda found in Pacific waters. It has always been one of California's most prized resources, both commercially and to sportsmen, and it continues to be an important market fish and sportfish.

Identification. The Pacific barracuda is slim-bodied, has a tapered head, a long thin snout, and large canine teeth in a lower jaw that projects beyond the upper jaw. It also has a forked tail, large eyes, and short, widely separated dorsal fins with five dorsal spines and 10 dorsal rays. The anal fins have two spines followed usually by nine rays. Grayish black on the back with a blue tinge, shading to silvery white on the sides and belly, it has a yellowish tail that lacks the black blotches on the sides of the body that are characteristic of other barracuda. Large females have a charcoal black edge on the pelvic and anal fins, whereas the male fins are edged in yellow or olive.

Size/Age. The Pacific barracuda is shorter than the great barracuda *(see: barracuda, great).* It reportedly can grow to 5 feet but has been recorded only to 4 feet; it rarely weighs more than 10 pounds, and although specimens of about 12 pounds have been captured, most of the fish caught by anglers are much smaller. They live for at least 11 years, and the females grow larger than the males; most fish over 8 pounds and all fish over 11 pounds are female. The growth rate is similar in both sexes until the fourth year of life, when the females begin to grow a bit faster.

Distribution. Pacific barracuda occur along the Pacific coast of North America from Alaska to Magdalena Bay, Baja California, although their common range is between Point Conception, California, and Magdalena Bay. The Pacific barracuda is the only barracuda found along the Pacific coast of North America.

Habitat. Pacific barracuda prefer warmer water. Only caught off California during the spring and summer, they are caught in Mexican waters throughout the year, reflecting a northerly spring migration and a southerly fall migration.

Life history/Behavior. Spawning takes place off outer Baja California in the open ocean, peaking in June but extending from April through September. The eggs are pelagic, and once they hatch, the young come inshore and stay in the shallow, quiet bays and coastal waters while they grow. By July, fry spawned in early spring grow to 4 inches and average roughly 16 inches in length a year later. A few males spawn in their first year, and all do so by their second year, whereas most females spawn in their second year and all have spawned by their third year. When small, they travel in schools, although adults are normally solitary. They are naturally curious and attracted to shiny objects.

Food and feeding habits. The Pacific barracuda feeds by sight rather than smell, and eats small anchovies, smelt, squid, and other small, schooling fish.

Angling. Pacific barracuda, one of the most popular of the small gamefish in Southern California, are most abundant during the spring and summer, from close to shore to about 7 to 8 miles out. They are caught by anglers trolling or casting with $1/4$- to 1-ounce feather jigs, strip bait, or live bait.

The primary means of taking Pacific barracuda is with a live bait such as a sardine, queenfish, or anchovy fished at or near the surface. Many anglers simply tie their line directly to a nickel or silver hook and freeline it with or without a small bit of split shot for weight. Be sure to set the hook a few seconds after the strike so the fish doesn't swallow the bait and cut the line.

Larger Pacific barracuda have a greater tendency to attack lures than do smaller specimens, and they also have a tendency to hold in deeper water. Thus, a jig is a good lure for larger fish. Jigs can be cast and retrieved in a stop-start fashion, but sometimes it's necessary to fish it deeper and work it vertically.

BARRAMUNDI   *Lates calcarifer.*
Other names—silver barramundi, giant perch, cock-up, barra, anama, barramundi perch, Asian sea bass, giant sea perch; French: *perche barramundi;* Japanese: *akame;* Spanish: *perca gigante.*

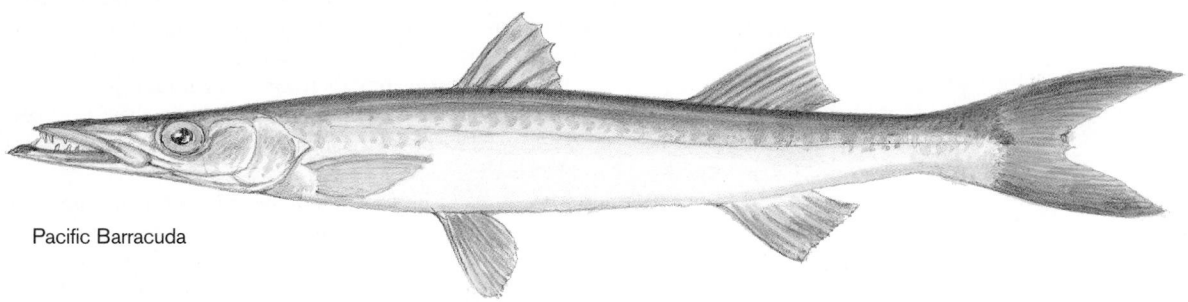
Pacific Barracuda

B

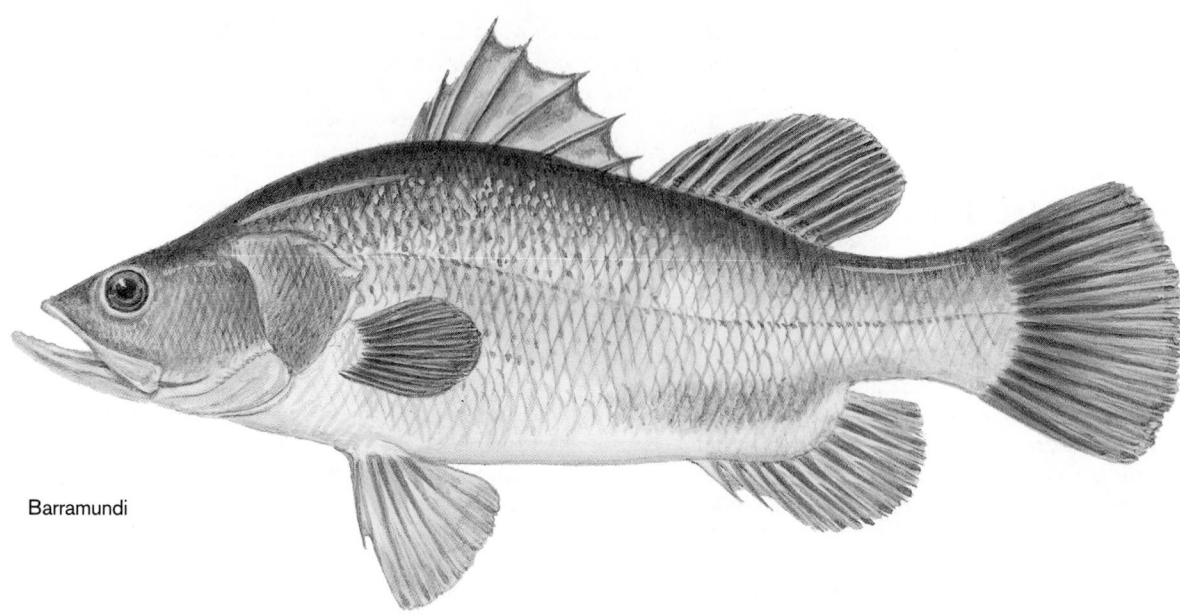

Barramundi

Excellent eating, the barramundi draws high prices in markets as a gourmet-quality fish. It should not be confused with an Australian species by the same name but of the genus *Scleropages,* which is a strictly freshwater species; nor should it be confused with a saltwater fish of the genus *Cromileptes* called "barramundi cod." It is one of Australia's most important and highly prized game-fish, and perhaps the one fish most synonymous with freshwater angling on that continent.

Identification.   The body of the barramundi is more or less elongated, and the head is relatively long and flattened on top, which accounts for a noticeable resemblance to its relative the snook *(Centropomus undecimalis; see: snook).* It is also closely related to the huge Nile perch *(Lates niloticus; see: perch, Nile).* The forehead is concave and the back is rounded; the maxillae of the huge mouth extend back beyond the eyes. The smooth tongue distinguishes it from the much smaller but closely related sand bass *(Psammoperca waigiensis),* which is often confused with the juvenile barramundi.

The gill flaps are particularly sharp-edged and will readily slice through fishing line and nets. The two dorsal fins are set close together. The tail is more or less rounded (convex), in contrast to the snook's forked tail, and the lateral line is highly developed. The sides of the body are silvery, and the back has a greenish gray tint. Startling pinkish red eyes, which glow brilliantly at night and even reflect in sunlight, are a striking characteristic of the barramundi.

Size.   Fish of about 120 pounds and 5 feet in length are the largest officially recorded, although unverified accounts of barramundi up to 595 pounds exist. In Australian waters, barramundi of 50 pounds or more are considered unusually large; the average size caught by most anglers is in the 11- to 22-pound range. Barramundi weighing 20 pounds or less are preferred for eating. The all-tackle world record is 63 pounds, 2 ounces.

Distribution.   Barramundi occur from Queensland, Australia, and southern Papua New Guinea to the Philippines, in southern Japan and southern China, and around the coasts of eastern India to the eastern edge of the Arabian Gulf.

Habitat.   Found in marine, brackish, and freshwater environments, barramundi are catadromous fish, maturing in freshwater and moving downstream at the beginning of the summer monsoon season in October to spawn in the mouths of estuaries and on mud flats in water of about 2 to 3 percent salinity. As a result, they commonly stay close to shore, lingering in clear to turbid water, and prefer temperatures between 26° to 29°C.

Life history/Behavior.   Barramundi are hermaphrodites, starting their lives as males and then becoming females around their second year when they weigh about 11 pounds.

Only fish that have access to the sea can initially spawn, although flooding during monsoons allows previously landlocked fish to spawn, accounting for a second spawning peak. Although spawning ordinarily ends in November, larvae have been found as late as January, and in one case, February. Each female can produce more than a half million eggs.

Newly hatched larvae are initially distributed by the flow of the tide but soon search out sheltered habitats in lagoons, swamps, and saltwater mangrove creeks. The young begin migrating back upstream after about six to eight months and enter freshwater streams by the end of their first year. They spread throughout rivers and estuaries during their second year.

With the return of the monsoon rains, most barramundi go downstream with the help of the tidal flow, and mature fish will spawn. A few barramundi may act contrary to this general pattern and swim upstream against the tidal flow, whereas others may remain in salt- or brackish water year-round. Though it was once believed that fish seen swimming upstream would eventually spawn, barramundi will not spawn in freshwater.

Food and feeding habits. The barramundi prefers live mullet, minnows, barra frogs, and prawns. It is not an open-water feeder; instead, this fish waits under cover along the banks, swiftly ambushing prey as it comes within range, inhaling it into a huge mouth before swallowing.

Angling. As a sportfish, the barramundi is somewhat like a snook, somewhat like a large-mouth bass, and somewhat like tarpon, embodying several of the best characteristics of these premier gamefish. Australians, who possess the most known barramundi fishing, have become increasingly enamored with this species, and many international anglers have been eager to seek it out as well because it grows large, jumps madly, swims with the fearsome saltwater crocodiles, and tests the tackle and techniques of light-tackle anglers.

In Australia, barramundi, or "barra" as they are frequently called, are primarily caught along the Northern Territory coast, in scenic and rugged areas subject to extreme tidal fluctuations and in locales that vary from flood-plain rivers to rain forest creeks. Although some anglers pursue these fish in pure saltwater, most angling for barramundi occurs in brackish water or freshwater, much of it in billabongs—lakes and ponds that feed creeks and rivers but become landlocked some time after the rainy season ends. Depending on tides, and creek and river flows, barra water runs from brackish to completely salt-free.

Some anglers fish for barra from shore, but most chase their quarry from boats, as mobility is of great importance. This fishery occurs mostly where smaller flows converge with other creeks or with major rivers. Barra fishing is heavily influenced by seasonal weather. The wet season begins in October in northern Australia and extends through March. The dry season starts in April. The wet season sends great volumes of water out of the billabongs, allowing fish that have been trapped in still, fresh waters and swamps since the previous dry season to escape. It also concentrates small fish and baits (prawns and mullet). In coastal creeks the same thing occurs, although the tidal influences send saltwater up small creeks (called gutters) and pull it out on a falling tide. These changes attract barra to such spots.

The barramundi can be an elusive and difficult fish to catch, in part because it is a strong fighter and in part because it favors habitat that is challenging to anglers. Most of these places are in thick cover, which Australians call snags. Fishing in and near these snags is an important element of the barramundi chase. Tides play an critical part in barra location and fishing technique. Barramundi enthusiasts must do a great deal of casting around

A barramundi from Australia's Daly River.

mangroves in coastal waters and around fallen trees in rivers, especially near gutters an hour before and after a low tide. Neap tides are particularly desirable periods. High tidal fluctuations, which can be up to 7 meters in the extreme, are harder to fish. When the tides are up, certain rivers and creeks experience the rush of a wall of water that quickly changes the flow direction of the river and repositions the fish. A fair number of anglers troll for barramundi, concentrating on water from 3 to 4 meters deep.

Whether trolling or casting, anglers primarily use baitcasting or spinning tackle and 2- to 6-kilogram lines, including sections of double lines and up to 50-pound-test leaders. Some anglers use heavier tackle, but sport-minded Australian anglers prefer the challenge of light gear. This is indeed light tackle, as the fish frequent extremely snag-infested locations, put up a vigorous extended fight, and can range to 40 and 50 pounds. Excellent results are possible with fly tackle, particular on streamers, and sometimes this can be more productive than tossing the standard offering of a swimming plug or a jig.

Although some fish are caught by casters, in large rivers and where there is considerable flow, the predominant activity is trolling with large mid- to deep-diving plugs. Anglers flatline these at varying distances behind the boat. Shallow runners are preferred by anglers casting with plugs in the backwaters. Surface plugs are extremely popular, especially because in the often turbid water, the fish zero in on the disturbance.

See: Australia.

B

BASIN

(1) A depression of the sea floor of an ocean (North Atlantic Basin); the bottom of a large inland lake (Western Basin of Lake Erie); part of a continent (Mississippi River Basin) of usually considerable extent.

(2) A series of watersheds *(see)* that drain into a large body of water; also known as a drainage basin.

BASS

Many species of fish, in both freshwater and saltwater, are referred to as "bass." Some are truly bass and some are not, but all have a physique and profile that is generally similar. Three of the most prominent freshwater sportfish with this name include the largemouth bass *(see: bass, largemouth)* and smallmouth bass *(see: bass, smallmouth),* both of which are actually sunfish *(see),* and the peacock bass *(see: bass, peacock),* which is actually a cichlid.

True bass are members of the Serranidae family of sea bass *(see),* which in freshwater includes the white bass *(see: bass, white)* and yellow bass *(see: bass, yellow),* and in saltwater includes the black sea bass *(see: sea bass, black),* striped bass *(see: bass, striped),* giant sea bass *(see: sea bass, giant),* kelp bass *(see: bass, kelp),* and many other species that do not carry the name "bass."

BASS, AUSTRALIAN

Macquaria novemaculeata.
Rated as one of the three most popular freshwater sportfish in Australia (alongside trout and barramundi), the Australian bass is a member of the Percichthyidae family of temperate bass and an indigenous species to that continent. Although the fish has an excellent flavor, it is sought more for its tough fighting tactics and explosive surface strikes than for its culinary appeal. It should not be confused with the American smallmouth or largemouth bass, to which it is not related.

Identification. The Australian bass is sometimes mistaken for the estuary perch *(Macquaria colonorum),* which is rarely found in freshwater. However, the more rounded and streamlined head-and-body profile of the bass, and the whitish leading edge and tips of its anal and pelvic fins, readily distinguish it from the perch. The back and sides of the bass are dark green, whereas the perch is silvery and has a slight hump on the head just behind the eye.

The tail is forked, and the deeply notched dorsal fin almost forms two separate dorsal fins. The edges of the gill cover are very sharp and should be avoided, and the opercular, anal, and ventral spines can inflict a painful wound that may be sensitive for several hours. It has large eyes and a big mouth, the maxillae extending to about the center of the eye.

Size. Unverified reports of bass to 8 kilograms exist, although it is rare to catch specimens exceeding 4 kilograms. They're commonly taken at 1 kilogram, and specimens of 100 to 200 grams are abound in nuisance numbers. Australian bass stocked in impoundments grow bigger than their counterparts in streams; captures of 2-kilogram fish are unremarkable.

Distribution. Wild Australian bass inhabit nearly all streams that flow into the ocean along the eastern seaboard, from southern Queensland to the Gippsland region of southeast Victoria. Hatchery-reared fish have been stocked in a number of large inland impoundments in both New South Wales and Queensland.

Habitat. In its home waterway, which may be a river, feeder creek, or lagoon open to a nearby stream with access to the sea, the Australian bass usually lies concealed under sunken logs, in submerged tree branches and roots, in and on the edges of weedbeds and reed gardens, under rock ledges and undercut banks, or in clefts in the shoreline. Its

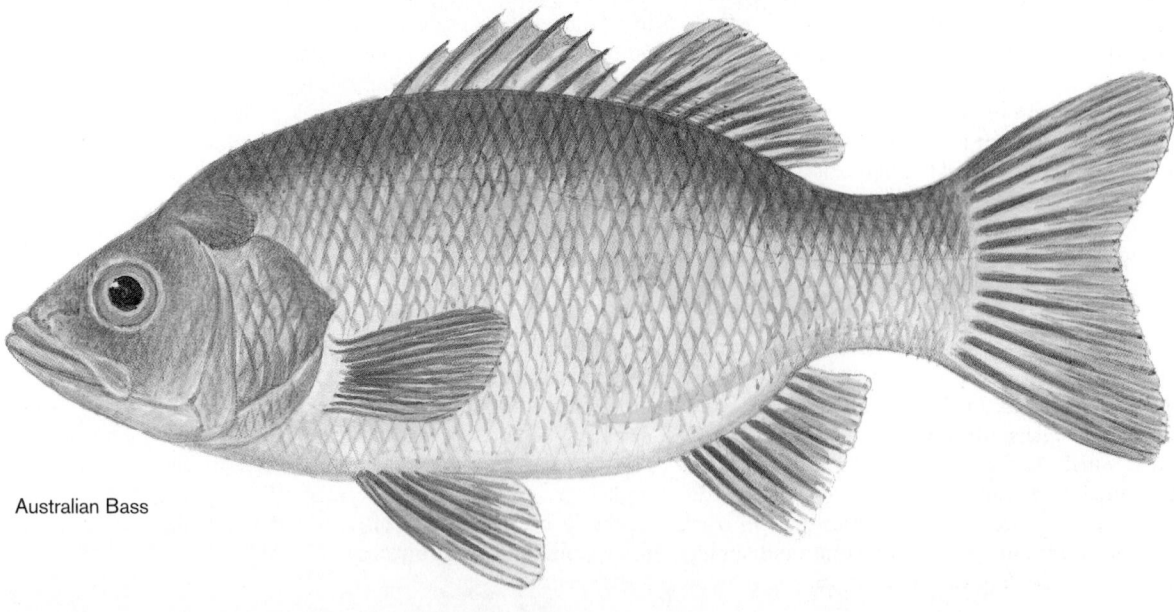

Australian Bass

ideal temperature range is 18° to 20°C, and the pH should lie between 6.5 (acid) and 8.5 (alkaline). A euryhaline fish, it can tolerate fluctuations in salinity from freshwater to seawater. In impoundments, it seeks out the mouths of creeks, patches of dead trees, rocky shores, submerged weedbeds, and other underwater structure, where it lies in wait for food to enter its feeding zone.

Life history/Behavior. The Australian bass is crepuscular, becoming more active during twilight hours and from just before dawn to a couple of hours afterward. A catadromous fish, it moves into brackish water and saltwater to spawn during the winter months (June through September). In dry winters, bass range from the mid- to lower reaches of the estuary; when significant flooding occurs, they move down to the mouth of the estuary to seek out the correct salinity. Eggs are fertilized immediately after release, and the egg's shell becomes tough and rigid. They float on the surface of the seawater, or become neutrally buoyant, as determined by the water's salinity. Fecundity is high; a bass weighing 1 kilogram can spawn a half million eggs about 1 millimeter in diameter.

When the eggs hatch, the larvae are at the mercy of the elements and predators. In spring and summer, the survivors move into freshwater beyond tidal influence and take up residence in streams and lagoons, where they remain until the urge to procreate takes them back to the brackish water or saltwater in which they were born.

Bass that become landlocked or exist in an impoundment never spawn. Females can be full of roe, but the eggs are never shed and are converted into body fat. Successful artificial breeding of the Australian bass has been achieved at the Australian Bass Hatchery at Lower Mangrove in New South Wales.

Food and feeding habits. Australian bass will feed on anything small enough to eat, and any type of insect, fish, crustacean, or animal that falls into the water. Cicadas, fish, crayfish, lizards, baby birds, and other prey are readily taken. These fish are gluttons and will stuff themselves until their prey is literally hanging from their mouths. Small wonder, then, that they will attack a lure regardless of its size. During daylight hours, they lie in ambush, attacking prey that comes within their feeding zone, and by night they roam farther afield.

Angling. Anglers land Australian bass in streams, lagoons, and impoundments, using baitcasting, spinning, and flycasting tackle; casting, trolling, and baitfishing are preferred techniques. Ninety percent of them work from small to medium-size boats on large waterways, and from canoes and punts on lagoons and small feeder streams. Shore fishing is rare because access to most areas is difficult. Many craft use electric motors to control fishing position. The favored technique is to slowly drift within casting distance of home-based structures while casting lures as close as possible to the bass's strike zone.

Bass anglers pay careful attention to weather changes and plan their trips around the barometer, preferring the period prior to summer thunderstorms. The summer months provide the best fishing, especially after dark. Warm evenings, which induce active insect life, stimulate feeding, and bass embrace the cover of darkness to feed. Mid- and deep-diving lures are preferred during daylight hours, and surface poppers (also popular during the twilight and very early morning hours), are pivotal to successful fishing after dark. Floating/diving lures are favorites.

During the winter months, when bass have moved into the estuaries to spawn, some anglers troll using baitcasting and spinning tackle with mid- to deep-diving lures and concentrate on weedbeds and rocky shorelines. Most anglers prefer to toss lures in these situations, however, using deep-diving plugs that can cover the deeper water. Specimens taken in estuary environments are usually breeding adults weighing up to 2 kilograms. Most anglers voluntarily practice catch-and-release or do so to comply with legal requirements, as these fish are subject to catch limits.

Fly fishing is a well-established method, and No. 6 or 7 floating and sinking lines with 1X through 3X tippets are favored. All white or all black Muddler Minnows and Matukas take fish, but better results are gained with poppers, or clipped deer-hair frogs and bass bugs. Although small trout flies will take bass, they also attract 10- to 15-centimeter-long freshwater herring, so preferred hook sizes are Nos. 2 to 6.

Impoundment bass tend to grow faster and heavier than do wild bass, and they are eagerly sought. Anglers target patches of drowned trees, rocky shorelines, and the mouths of small creeks or streams. Many anglers use sonar to locate fish and identify underwater structures. Baitcasting and spinning with heavier lines (to 7 kilograms, to cope with cover-seeking fish) and deep-diving plugs are favored methods, but baitfishing with worms, crayfish, and crickets is frequently adopted.

BASS, BLACK

"Black bass" is a common name for all species and subspecies of the genus *Micropterus*, which belong to the Centrarchidae family of sunfish *(see)*. These include largemouth bass *(see: bass, largemouth)*, smallmouth bass *(see: bass, smallmouth)*, redeye bass *(see: bass, redeye)*, spotted bass *(see: bass, spotted)*, Suwannee bass *(see: bass, Suwannee)*, and Guadalupe bass *(see: bass, Guadalupe)*. Black bass are strictly freshwater species, and they are more elongated and generally larger than their family relatives.

The term should not be confused with the various sea bass *(see)* that are members of the Serranidae family of saltwater fish, some of which have a physique similar to that of species in the genus *Micropterus*.

B

B

BASS BOAT

The term "bass boat" has evolved through common usage to refer to a type of boat that is popular for largemouth and smallmouth bass angling, but which is simply a good fishing boat that is particularly functional where a lot of casting is required and where presentation and boat positioning are especially important. So-called bass boats are also used for fishing for many other species, primarily in freshwater or in brackish bays and rivers.

Bass boats have evolved over several decades from narrow flat-bottom craft with raised seats to comfortable glittery high-performance machines. The most common example of a bass boat today is a craft that averages 17 feet in length, is made of fiberglass (though many are aluminum) and sports a six-cylinder outboard powerhouse, high-speed bow-mounted electric motor, console and bow sonar devices, livewells, rod locker, platform decks with pedestal seating, plus other accessories, and is usually stored on a trailer for transport to and from the water. These boats, or scaled-down versions, have become standard vehicles for freshwater fishing situations where casting is the primary, if not exclusive, technique, where the majority of fishing requires the use of an electric motor for maneuvering, where it is often necessary to travel a good distance from one place to another, and where the water conditions encountered are generally mild to moderate (although the better and deeper-hulled bass boats are used in huge waters that can get very rough, even though they may not provide comfortable fishing under extreme conditions).

Almost any boat can be used for bass fishing, though some suit particular situations better than others. In general terms, the most popular types of boats used for bass fishing are fiberglass V- or semi-V-hulls, aluminum V-hulls, flat-bottom rowboats (jonboats), and canoes.

Fiberglass or aluminum bass boats are well-outfitted, comfortable vessels with lots of room. A V-hulled, fiberglass version is especially suitable for large lakes, ponds, and rivers, where rough water dictates sturdy craft and where a big boat with a lot of engine muscle can help cover a lot of distance quickly. Aluminum bass boats can also be used under these conditions, but the flat-bottomed models do not handle rough water well. V-hulled aluminum boats take rough water better, but still not as well as a fiberglass boat. They sit up higher in the water, and because they are lighter are more susceptible to being blown around in the wind, making electric motor control a little more difficult.

The larger fiberglass and aluminum boats are generally preferred by people who do a lot of bass fishing and who need room in their boats for an abundance of gear (no one beats a bass angler for owning equipment). Storage is an important factor, as is room to move about within the boat (especially important if three people will fish in it). Dual consoles, once touted for all-around use as bass boats, are unacceptable to hardcore bass anglers because they cramp occupants and gear.

The larger bass boats may be 20 feet in length and propelled by outboard motors with between 200 and

18 ft. Bass boat

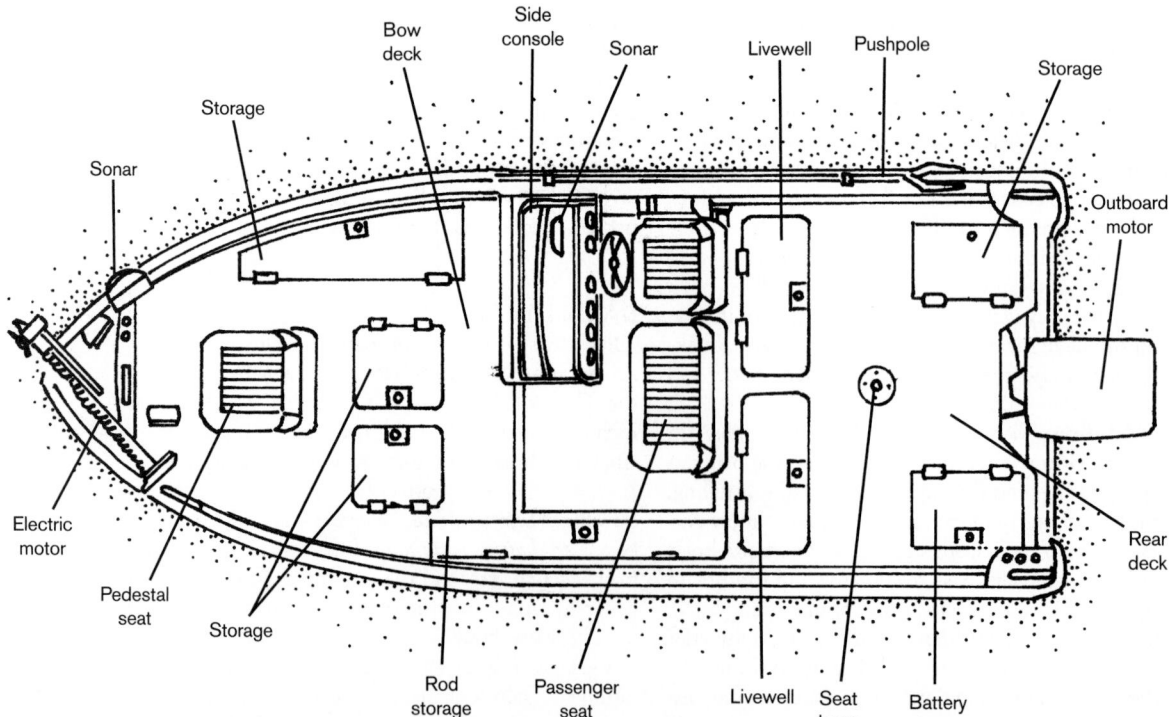

A bass boat provides a stable, comfortable platform for anglers who do a lot of casting.

250 horses of power. This seems extraordinary for freshwater fishing applications, but such craft are used in guiding applications and big-water fishing, especially in huge western reservoirs, as well as by tournament anglers for whom maximum speed and gear storage are big concerns. This notwithstanding, a 17- or 18-foot fiberglass boat equipped with a 150 hp motor is a common bass fishing tool on medium to large lakes and big river systems.

A smaller aluminum or flat-bottom bass boat is very functional for fishing on small lakes, rivers, and ponds, where it isn't necessary to cover a huge territory and where adverse conditions are seldom present. Many anglers use jonboats on small bodies of water where either outboard motors are not allowed or the sight of big boats might create ill feelings with local residents. Small aluminum V-hulled boats can be used in the same manner, except that they are less suitable for small river fishing than a jonboat and more suitable to moderate-size lakes, owing to their deeper draft design (meaning that they draw more water, which makes them less suitable for shallow, rocky water, such as rivers, but more suitable to small lakes).

Canoes are used primarily by bass anglers in small bodies of water, and on shallow rivers. As a vehicle for bass fishing, where constant casting and positioning are required, they are generally deemed too unsteady and too difficult to position. Canoes are influenced by current, the force of wind, or even the working of some lures, and if two people are fishing, one must be regularly paddling to position the canoe for the other. Canoes become moderately useful for bass fishing when used with an electric motor. They have the virtue of silent operation, however, as well as extreme shallow-water maneuverability.

Safety is the most important consideration in buying and using a bass boat, especially a high-performance model, many of which can fly in excess of 60 (even 70+) miles per hour. Speed is important primarily to tournament anglers and race jockeys, and is of less importance to the recreational angler. High performance bass boats are some of the fastest and most powerful vessels on the water, however, and they must be properly maintained (steering, propeller, etc.), and should be driven sensibly. Accidents involving bass boat operators have resulted from excessive speed, and speed limits have been enacted on some waterways for all boaters. If you have a modern bass boat, make certain that the now-mandatory ignition safety cutoff switch is always attached to the operator when the boat is under outboard power, and that life preservers are worn during high-speed operation.

Newcomers to bass boating face an array of choices and need to carefully evaluate the types of places they will be fishing and determine what they really need. They should also consider the type and quality of access facilities; bigger heavier boats are not as easy to launch in shallow and unimproved access spots. First-time purchasers should also

A bass boat provides a stable, comfortable platform for anglers who do a lot of casting.

consider the weight of the boat and rig and the ability of their vehicle not only to tow it, but to pull it out of a (sometimes steep) launch ramp.

Much of the dissatisfaction that people have with their bass boats stems from anglers themselves as a result of their not knowing what they really needed when they first purchased and equipped their boat. Like other boaters, many bass boat owners started small and worked their way up to more sophisticated and more costly equipment through several trade-ins and purchases, when they needed the latter all along. If they had correctly judged their needs in the first place, they would have saved money and time by selecting properly initially. The converse is also true. Many bass anglers have far more boat and engine than is practical for their needs.

See: Boat; Motor, Electric; Motor, Trolling; Sonar; Trailer.

BASS BUG

A type of floating fly, or bug, tied with deer hair and primarily used in bass fishing.

See: Fly.

BASS BUG TAPER

A specially designed type of weight-forward fly line for casting large flies, deer hair bass bugs, and fly-rod poppers.

See: Flycasting Tackle.

B

BASS, CHEROKEE
"Cherokee bass" is a term for hybrid striped bass.
See: Bass, Striped; Hybrid.

BASS, EUROPEAN   *Morone labrax.*
Other names—scientific: *Dicentrarchus labrax;* simply called "bass" in Europe, also white salmon, sea bass, European sea bass or seabass; Danish: *bars;* Dutch: *zeebars;* French: *bar européen;* Gaelic: *doingean;* Italian: *perchia;* Norwegian: *havaborre;* Portuguese: *robalo.*

The European bass is regarded by many European saltwater anglers, especially British anglers, as their best gamefish. It is a prominent species for commercial as well as recreational fishermen, and has been subject to overexploitation and varied abundance. It is sold both fresh and smoked in markets.

Identification.   The European bass has a broad, extended body that is bluish gray on its back, silver on the sides, and a silvery white on the belly. On each gill cover there is a black mark, and other dark markings emphasize the lateral line. The fins are dark gray and deepen in color each year, whereas the anal fins remain tinged with white. A young bass, or "school bass," is usually lighter with a bit of olive or spotted coloring on its back, but older fish may be slightly brown or yellow. It has a large mouth that holds many teeth—including teeth on the roof of the mouth and the tongue—soft and spiny rays on its fins, and dorsal fins that are completely separated.

The European bass bears a resemblance to the striped bass *(Morone saxatilis);* although it lacks stripes, it has a similar body shape, leading some scientists to believe that it should be classified in the same family (Percichthyidae) as the striped bass instead of in the Serranidae family.

Size/Age.   Although it can grow to more than 30 pounds, the common weight of a European bass is between 2 and 9 pounds. It can live up to 15 years in the wild and 30 years in captivity.

Distribution.   European bass are an eastern Atlantic species restricted to the European coast, ranging from Norway to Morocco and northern Africa, the Canary Islands, Senegal, the Mediterranean Sea, and the Black Sea.

Habitat.   Found in fresh, brackish, and saltwater, European bass prefer warm and temperate marine environs. They usually favor the strong surf of inshore waters in the intertidal zone, often lingering in less than a foot of water. They are also common in estuaries, lagoons, and sometimes rivers. Like the striped bass, they can live in freshwater, but they prefer turbulent and well-oxygenated habitat. When the surf cools, European bass move offshore, preferring waters that remain between 8° and 24°C. They are often nocturnal in shallow waters.

Life history/Behavior.   When the inshore waters begin to cool in late October and November, European bass migrate out to sea to spawn in groups. They then return sometime between February and May, when the inshore waters warm again. Some schooling bass, particularly those in river estuaries, do not leave the inshore waters to spawn; those bass that do leave tend to be the first to return in the spring.

Evidence shows that even though European bass don't spawn inshore, the eggs are not shed during a fixed spawning time; instead, they may be shed over the period of time spent in the offshore waters to which the fish migrate. This pattern has been observed in mackerel as well. European bass eggs are buoyant, smooth, and round.

Food and feeding habits.   A well-known voracious predator, the European bass will eat a wide variety of creatures, including mollusks, crabs, prawns, shrimp, razor clams, squid, and other small fish. Schooling bass feed on smaller crustaceans or fish fry.

Angling.   Most angling for European bass occurs from shore; surf fishing on protected and unprotected beaches is particularly popular. Bass are found in the surf, in the troughs near beaches, on rocky shoals, and in channels. Most anglers offer them some type of bait, primarily worms, crabs, squid, clams, shrimp, and fish. These fish are also caught by boaters drifting with baits under floats, casting with spools and plastic eels, and trolling.
See: England.

BASS, FLORIDA LARGEMOUTH
Micropterus salmoides floridanus.
The Florida largemouth bass, also known as Florida bass, is a subspecies of the largemouth bass *(see: bass, largemouth),* which in turn is often called a northern largemouth. This fish occurs naturally in Florida. Mixtures of it and northern largemouth are called intergrades, as they are neither pure Florida nor pure northern strains. These fish occur from northern Florida to Maryland.

Florida bass grow to trophy size more readily than do northern largemouth bass. They have been stocked in many states, including California, which has produced near world record 22-pounders from transplanted stocks, and in Texas, which has completely transformed its big-bass potential by stocking this fish.

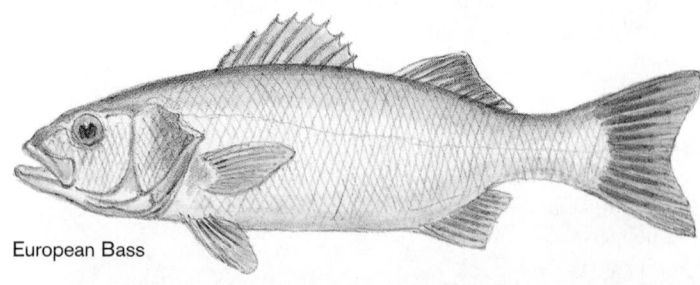
European Bass

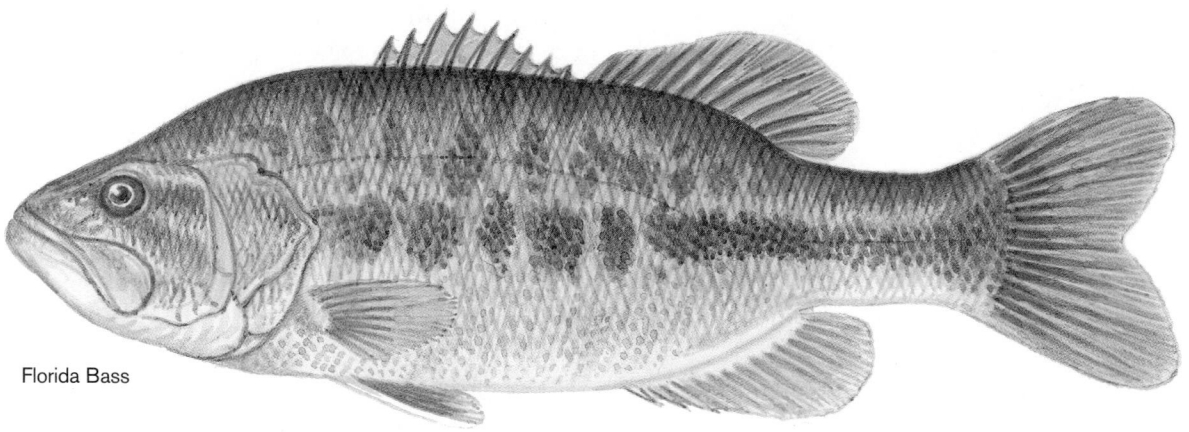

Florida Bass

BASS, GUADALUPE *Micropterus punctulatus.* The Guadalupe bass is a member of the Centrarchidae family and is similar to spotted bass *(see: bass, spotted)* in appearance. It has 10 to 12 dark bars along its sides, which are less distinct in older fish; it usually has 16 pectoral rays and 26 to 27 scales around the caudal peduncle. It can grow to almost 16 inches and usually weighs less than a pound. The all-tackle world record is a 3-pound, 11-ounce Texas fish taken in 1983.

In North America, Guadalupe bass are restricted to the Edwards Plateau in the Brazos, Colorado, Guadalupe, San Antonio, and upper Nueces (where introduced) River drainages in southern Texas. It occurs in gravel riffles, runs, and flowing pools of creeks, as well as in small to medium rivers.

See: Bass, Black.

BASS, KELP (Calico) *Paralabrax clathratus.* **Other names**—calico bass, California kelp bass, rock bass, rock sea bass, sand bass, bull bass, kelp salmon, cabrilla; Spanish: *cabrilla alguera.*

One of a large number of sea bass found in the eastern Pacific, the kelp bass is one of the most popular sportfish in Southern California as a mainstay of party boat trips to the northern Baja. Because it is a powerful fighter and an excellent food fish, it is highly sought by anglers. Its popularity and nonmigratory status put kelp bass populations at risk from overfishing.

Identification. A hardy fish with the characteristic elongate and compressed bass shape, the kelp bass has a notch between its spiny and dorsal fins. The longest spines in the first dorsal fin are longer than any of the rays in the second dorsal fin. It is brown to olive green, with pale blotches on the back and lighter coloring on the belly.

Kelp bass are easily distinguishable from various sand bass by their third, fourth, and fifth dorsal spines, which are about the same length; sand bass have a third dorsal spine that is much longer than the fourth and fifth dorsal spines. Kelp bass also superficially resemble freshwater black bass, except that their dorsal spines are longer and much heavier, and their overall appearance is rougher.

Size/Age. Kelp bass grow slowly, taking 5 to 6 years to reach a length of 12 inches, when they are capable of spawning. Fish weighing 8 to 10 pounds may be 15 to 20 years old. The largest kelp bass are said to exceed 15 pounds, although the largest fish caught was only 14 pounds, 7 ounces. They can grow to $1^1/_2$ feet in length.

Guadalupe Bass

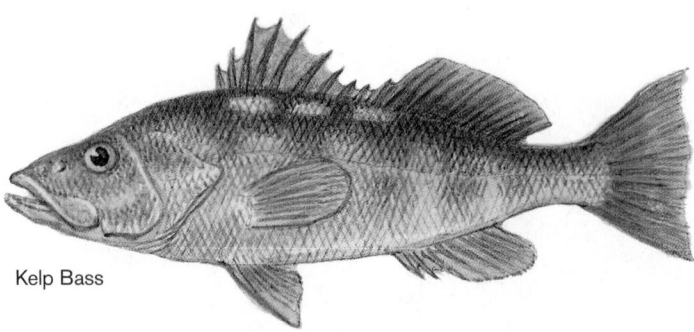

Kelp Bass

B

Distribution. Primarily found along the central and southern California coast and northeastern Baja, kelp bass range from the Columbia River in Washington to Magdalena Bay in Baja California.

Habitat. Kelp bass typically linger in or near kelp beds, over reefs, and around rock jetties and breakwaters or structures in shallow water; larger fish hold in deeper water, to roughly 150 feet.

Life history/Behavior. Spawning occurs from May through September and peaks in July. Kelp bass do not migrate and instead tend to be territorial.

Food and feeding habits. An omnivorous feeder, kelp bass favor assorted fish and small shrimp-like crustaceans when young. Adults consume anchovies, small surfperch, and other small fish.

Angling. Kelp bass are a popular light-tackle fish caught from breakwaters in bays, or around kelp beds by anglers trolling, drifting, or stillfishing from anchored boats. Live baits such as anchovies, sardines, queenfish, and mackerel squid are popular, as are a variety of artificial lures, particularly a metal jig and whole squid, as well as streamer flies fished on a sinking shooting-head line. Chumming is often done in combination with baiting and jigging, and larger calicos are often caught at small patches of kelp away from the larger kelp beds. The best fishing is summer to fall, although kelp bass are caught year-round in some areas.

BASS, LARGEMOUTH
Micropterus salmoides.
Other names—black bass, largemouth, bigmouth, linesides, Oswego bass, green bass, green trout, Florida bass, Florida largemouth, southern largemouth, northern largemouth; French: *achigan à grande bouche;* German: *forellenbarsch;* Italian: *persico trota;* Japanese: *okuchibasu;* Portuguese: *achiga.*

The largemouth bass is the biggest and most renowned member of the Centrarchidae family of sunfish and its subgroup known as black bass *(see: bass, black).* As the result of widespread introductions throughout North America, it has become available to more anglers than any other species of fish. Its adoption of varied environments and its penchant for aggressive behavior have helped make it the most popular sportfishing target in North America.

Classified as a warmwater species, the largemouth bass thrives in relatively fertile bodies of water, primarily inhabiting reservoirs, lakes, ponds, and large slow rivers with quiet backwaters. In all of these environments, it is one of the top predators. It has a wide-ranging diet and seeks numerous forms of weed, rock, or wooden cover, which it uses to ambush prey. These characteristics make it suitable for a plethora of fishing techniques, thus also endearing it to manufacturers of fishing equipment. A species tailor-made for casting, it has probably spawned more artificial lures—and variation upon variation of lures—than all other freshwater sportfish combined. And its short-lived but action-packed fight, replete with aerial maneuvers and explosive bursts for cover, keep anglers coming back.

The largemouth bass is not actually a bass, as are the various members of the temperate bass family of fish, which include striped bass and white bass. It is a large sunfish, related to such other popular sunfish as the bluegill *(see)* and crappie *(see: crappie, black; crappie, white),* as well as to fellow members of the *Micropterus* genus. The word "bass" derives from the Middle English *basse,* which is either a corruption of the Old English *baers,* meaning bristly or spiny, or of the Dutch word for perch, *barse.*

Whether appropriately or inappropriately named, the largemouth is the one species that people in North America think of when they hear the word "bass," and this generic term has also come to be used in reference to boats, rods, reels, lures, and other gear specifically employed in pursuit of these fish.

Although largemouths are popular throughout their range, they are not as popular with some people as their close relative, the smallmouth bass *(see: bass, smallmouth),* even though the largemouth grows considerably larger on average. This is because smallmouths have an even friskier disposition when hooked and are more likely to be repeat acrobats. Smallmouths alternately jump and bear down for the depths, whereas largemouths head for the jungle, looking to break the angler's line on the nearest obstruction. The largemouth is more the kick boxer than the pugilist.

Largemouth bass have not always been atop the popularity chart in North America, although they have always been widely appreciated. The rise of levelwind tackle in the mid- to late 1800s, and the development of early lures, spinners, spoons, and plugs, helped move all forms of North American fishing from the cane-pole-and-bait approach, or the fly rod, into a different element that was perfect for bass.

Bass fishing arguably got its biggest boost in the mid-twentieth century when scores of dams were erected on rivers, creating large reservoirs that allowed populations of baitfish and predators to explode. With these changes came fast fishing and an explosion of opportunity.

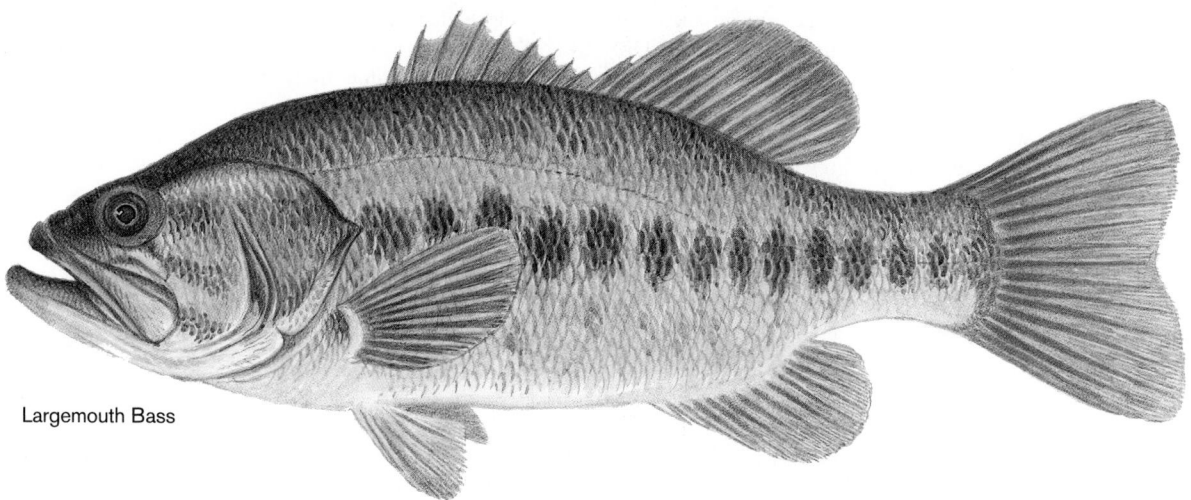

Largemouth Bass

B

Today bass fishing is an entrenched activity in North America, and largemouths (and their black bass relatives) are the only species that see a widespread and high level of club activity and competition. They have benefited from intensive fisheries management and special regulations, and there is no commercial fishing for or sale of these species in the United States or Canada (although there is some in Mexico). Some populations have declined due to environmental and fishing pressures, however, and habitat alterations have played a part in the changing nature of some fisheries as well.

The bass fishing culture is such today that most avid bass anglers release every bass they catch, including trophy specimens. Many have a replica taxidermy mount prepared instead of keeping the fish. Largemouth bass are of fairly good table quality, especially the smaller specimens and those from clear-water environments; their white, flaky, and non-oily flesh is generally mild and not unlike larger specimens of other sunfish. Those taken from more turbid and weedy waters tend to be less flavorful.

The largemouth bass is sometimes confused with the smallmouth in places where both species occur, and also with the spotted bass *(see: bass, spotted)*. One subspecies, the Florida largemouth bass *(see: bass, Florida largemouth)*, *M. salmoides floridanus*, is capable of attaining large sizes in appropriate waters but is otherwise similar.

Identification. The largemouth bass has an elongate and robust shape compared to other members of the sunfish family; this shape has come to define species that are called bass, whether they be true bass *(see: bass)*, true black bass *(see: bass, black)*, or merely look-alikes. It has a distinctively large mouth compared with other family members, as the end of its maxillary (jaw) falls below or beyond the rear margin of the eye; the dorsal fin has a deep notch separating the spiny and soft rays; and the tail is broad and slightly forked.

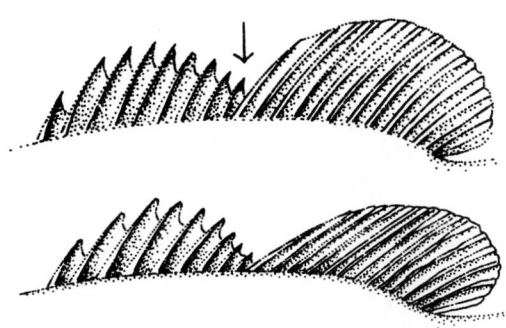

The separation between first and second dorsal fins is less in smallmouth bass (top) than in largemouth bass (bottom), a difference that aids in differentiating these species.

Although coloration varies greatly and is especially dependent on biological factors and host environments, the largemouth bass generally has a light green to light brown hue on the back and upper sides, white lower sides and belly, and a broad stripe of diamond-shaped blotches along the midline of the body. This stripe particularly distinguishes it from its close relative the smallmouth bass, as does the upper jaw, which in the smallmouth does not extend past the eye.

There are patches of dark scales above and below the lateral stripe, three dark bars on the sides of the head, and a complete lateral line. There are no scales on the base portion of the soft-rayed second dorsal fin of the largemouth bass, a characteristic unlike those of other black bass. The largemouth lacks a tooth patch on the tongue, which helps distinguish it from the spotted bass. Coloration can range from pale green or nearly silvery to extremely dark and near black on the upper sides and back. The lateral line, stripe, and other markings may be indistinct—all are dependent on the clarity and color of the water. The most distinctively marked fish tend to come from the clearest waters.

Size/Age. Although the largemouth bass can live up to 15 years, the average life varies; these fish seldom live more than 10 years. Throughout their range, largemouth bass encountered by anglers average 1 to $1^{1}/_{2}$ pounds (10 to 13 inches) but are commonly caught up to 5 pounds and less commonly from 7 to 10 pounds. In northernmost waters, a largemouth bass over 5 pounds is uncommon, due to slow growing seasons. Fish exceeding 5 pounds are common in good lakes in southern regions, where fish can grow faster and enjoy a longer growing season. A 10-pounder is a trophy anywhere, and, with few exceptions, is harder to come by in modern times.

The maximum size attainable for largemouth bass may be 25 pounds, but this has not been proven, and only about a dozen bass in the 20-pound class are known to have been caught. The largest specimen is the all-tackle world record of 22 pounds, 4 ounces, caught from Montgomery Lake, Georgia, in 1932. This is one of the longest-standing freshwater records and certainly the most coveted of all sportfishing records. Although Florida once had the best chances of producing record-threatening largemouth bass, that distinction has moved west with transplanted fish (Florida strain) to California. Texas also boasts many large specimens today, and Cuba is another candidate for producing the biggest largemouths.

Distribution.   The largemouth bass is endemic only to North America, and its native range was generally the eastern half of the U.S. and southernmost Ontario and Quebec in Canada. It occurred roughly from Iowa south to Texas and northeastern Mexico, and east to the South Atlantic coast and to western New York and western Pennsylvania; it was absent from most of the Appalachian and Ozark Ranges, most of the northeastern U.S. from Maryland to Maine, and easternmost Canada.

Since the late 1800s, its range has been expanded to include major or minor portions of every state in the U.S. except Alaska, and most of the southern fringes of Canada, as well as numerous countries in Europe, Asia, Africa, South America, Central America, and the Caribbean.

Habitat.   In capsule summary, the largemouth bass is typically described as a fish that frequents the weedy sections of ponds and lakes. In reality, the largemouth is highly adaptable to many environments and to many places within various types of water. They inhabit creeks, ditches, sloughs, canals, and many little potholes that have the right cover and forage, but they live principally in reservoirs, lakes, ponds, and medium to large rivers, and not always in the weedy sections.

More specifically, however, they orient toward cover in those environments and find most of their food in or near some form of cover, whether it is visible in relatively shallow water or existing beneath the surface out of sight. Favored haunts include logs, stumps, lily pads, brush, weed- and grassbeds, bushes, docks, fencerows, standing timber, bridge pilings, rocky shores, boulders, points, weedline edges, stone walls, creekbeds, roadbeds,

ledgelike dropoffs, humps, shoals, and islands. Although much bass cover is nearshore, some bass do spend time away from shore, especially in unvegetated lakes.

Largemouth bass are most active in waters ranging from 65° to 85°F; the lower 70s is likely optimum. Yet they do well in temperatures much higher and lower, including waters that touch the 90°F mark as well as frozen lakes that dip to the mid-30s. They can and do thrive in waters that are clear, as well as in those that are highly turbid.

Life history/Behavior.   Largemouth bass spawn from late winter to late spring; the timing depends on latitude and temperature. Southern populations spawn earliest, and most northern populations latest. They begin to spawn about the time the water temperature reaches 60°F. Fish of about 10 to 12 inches are mature enough to reproduce for the first time. Males select and prepare the nest site, a circular bed usually in 1 to 4 feet of water, often positioned near or including some type of object along the shoreline. The female is nudged to the nest site by the male, deposits her eggs, and leaves; the male guards the eggs, which hatch in a few days, and then guards the young fry for a short period.

Largemouth bass do not undertake extensive migrations and are essentially cover-oriented homebodies. The pattern of their lives is fairly simple: hide, ambush, eat, and eat some more. This is oversimplified, but bass do have "home areas" that they seldom range far from unless environmental changes require it. The larger the fish, the larger its home area; the more vegetation, the smaller the home area. They are susceptible to changes in water levels and temperature, and may change behavior based on food abundance or availability. They usually favor shallow-water living (1 to 20 feet), but when temperature, falling water, abundance of deep baitfish, or other conditions dictate, they may move to deeper water.

Growth rates for largemouth bass are extremely variable, influenced as they are by broad geographical location (north versus south), the specific body of water they inhabit within a particular region, and individual differences even within the same population. Despite these influences, bass are capable of growing quickly under the right circumstances.

Food and feeding habits.   Adult bass predominantly eat other fish, including gizzard shad, threadfin shad, golden shiners, bluegills and other sunfish, small catfish, and many other small species, plus crayfish. They are extremely opportunistic, however, which explains why anglers like them so much, and they may consume snakes, frogs, salamanders, mice, and other creatures. They swallow their food whole instead of biting off pieces, which limits the size of the prey they can consume. Any prey having a body depth less than the diameter of the largemouth bass's mouth may be consumed, usually headfirst.

As aggressive predators, bass primarily are ambush feeders, but they may pursue fish in open water, where there are no ambush opportunities. In normally warm waters, digestion occurs fairly quickly; however, at extreme warm or cold temperatures digestion actually slows, causing the bass to feed less frequently and making them less susceptible to anglers.

Bass are well known for their ability to locate prey in turbid water and at night. Although they are primarily sight feeders when water clarity permits, they otherwise use their highly developed lateral line to detect vibrations and locate prey. They can also detect odors, but their senses of smell and taste are poorly understood by scientists, and evidently used less for feeding than sight or hearing.

Angling. A particular charm of angling for largemouth bass is that bass lures needn't closely imitate specific forage. As a result, there is probably no other freshwater gamefish for which there is such a wide range of lure types, sizes, colors, and actions.

Spring is the most popular time to pursue these fish in most areas (a few states have seasons on bass and there is little or no spring fishing), as the bass are spawning and hold relatively shallow and close to shore. Water temperature, which varies according to geographical location, is a big factor in fish activity in the spring. Small lakes and ponds are best for early-season bass fishing because they warm up quickly. On large lakes, the shallow flats, coves, feeder creeks, and tributary areas are generally warmer than the rest of the lake in the early season and thus hold more fish.

Various lures are effective on spring bass, but few are more consistently effective than spinnerbaits and crankbaits. Of the latter, the best type to use depends on a number of variables. If the water is very cold, a lure that gets down 5 to 10 feet and is worked around points, steeply sloping banks, and shores with a breakline (a distinct dropoff into deeper water) may be best. In shallow lakes with many stumps, flats with cover (preferably vegetation that just starts to emerge), and the like, a shallow- or intermediate-running crankbait is best. As the water warms and the cover—which may be grass, milfoil, hydrilla, or cabbage weeds—begins to grow higher, an angler can use the same crankbaits to skim the edges and tops of that cover, perhaps varying only the speed of retrieval. Crankbaits are especially productive in places with a lot of deep water and where submerged creek or river channels meet the shore.

Spinnerbaits are generally fished close to the surface and within sight in the spring. Relatively snag- and weed-free, they work particularly well around moss, lilies, milfoil, and other forms of vegetation, and around stumps, standing timber, fallen trees, and docks.

Bass are generally harder to catch in the summer than in the spring, in part because anglers as a whole

A plastic worm lured this hefty largemouth bass from a Florida phosphate pit.

are not as persistent, and in part because bass become less accessible, going deeper or becoming more ensconced in thick cover that is difficult to fish.

Generally, such surface lures as plugs or buzzbaits work best early and late in the day in the shallows. Plastic worms are the preferred offering otherwise, and jigging spoons or weedless spoons are also of value.

On lakes with ample cover, focus on the heaviest cover that a bass could hide in. The water probably won't be especially deep, but the cover provides bass with security, comfort, and many opportunities to ambush unsuspecting prey. With heavy cover, an angler often has to get into the midst of it to be successful, plodding along, working spots deliberately, and probing carefully.

The most obvious, most frequently employed, and most easily managed method of catching summer bass is working the edges of vegetation. In large, fairly thick concentrations of vegetation, the easiest fish to catch are those close to the edges, especially where the perimeter is readily observed. Pinpointing the edges of submerged weedlines, however, is not as easily done. Nevertheless, this can be a critical area, especially in clear northern waters, as much vegetation does not grow above the surface. A plastic worm, rigged with a slip sinker, is the main vegetation lure. Sometimes a lure that moves more enticingly, such as a weedless spoon with a plastic skirt or pork chunk, or a weedless surface product, is a better bet.

B

On big bodies of water with little vegetation, the midsummer trick is to locate deep water (15 feet or more) that holds largemouths, fish the edges of those areas, and present lures in a precise way. Look for submerged humps, long points, and old roadbeds well away from shore.

Bass are often found in flooded timber in the summer, and here, plastic worms, jig-and-pork combinations, and occasionally deep-diving crankbaits are the ticket. The junction of two old channels, the outside bend of a channel, clumps of timber, and timber adjacent to boat lanes where there is a depth change are all good locales. If bass suspend in the midsection limbs, a jigging spoon, worked vertically, is the lure of choice.

Don't overlook fishing at night during the summer, which may be especially beneficial on clear-water lakes that get copious daytime traffic. Surface plugs, spinnerbaits, and plastic worms are good nighttime lures.

In fall, bass are coming off their summer behavior and gradually moving shallower as the water cools. Temperature and habitat conditions vary greatly by geographic area, and far southern bass waters experience favorable conditions for a longer period of time than northern ones. Ponds and small lakes are especially worth fishing, although they cool off quickly after a succession of cold fall nights. Shallow and nearshore environs become worthy of greater attention in the fall, but anglers should not be averse to working deeper water if shallow prospecting fails to bring dividends. Spinnerbaits, crankbaits, jigs, and surface lures have merit at this time.

Because pinpoint presentations are more important in largemouth bass angling than in many other forms of freshwater fishing, and as boats equipped with an electric motor are in wide use among bass anglers, it is important to position the boat in ways conducive to accurate casting and proper presentation. The first cast to a likely bass hole is often the most important one, so it pays to make each cast count. Make casts to all sides of likely cover, and learn to feather your casts so that lures don't crash into the water like a bomb.

Serious bass fishing involves a range of angling conditions, lure styles and sizes, and fishing methods. Most anglers, however, are partial to baitcasting rods, particularly when using crankbaits and worms, fishing in heavy cover, and fishing for very large bass. Baitcasting tackle offers good casting control and favors big lures. Ten- or 12-pound-test line is the standard, although lighter or heavier line is used when appropriate.

Some anglers use spinning gear for largemouth bass, but they opt for lighter line and generally don't seek out areas with heavy cover where lures and fish are likely to get hung up. Fly tackle is also of merit at times, especially when fishing with deer-hair bugs and poppers for shallow fish.

See: Bass, Black.

BASS, NEOSHO SMALLMOUTH
See: Bass, Smallmouth.

BASS, NIUGINI   *Lutjanus goldiei.*
Other names—Papuan black bass, Papuan black snapper; French: *vivaneau de Papua;* Malay: *ilkan merah;* Spanish: *pargo de Papua.*

Popularly nicknamed the Niugini bass and Papuan black bass, this species is actually a snapper that inhabits freshwater and brackish water. Known only to Papua New Guinea, it is a member of the Lutjanidae family of snappers and one of the world's toughest yet least-known fish found in freshwater.

Identification.   The Niugini bass is a stocky fish with a deep, compressed body; it looks somewhat like a cross between a mangrove snapper and a largemouth bass, with large fanlike pectoral and pelvic fins. The first dorsal fin is spiny rayed and separated from the soft-rayed second dorsal fin. The body is silvery to steely gray, darker on top and lightening on the belly, and has large scales. Larger fish are darker. It has two canine teeth on the upper jaw, and smaller teeth on the lower jaw.

Size.   The maximum size attainable is uncertain, although it can reportedly grow to at least

Neosho Smallmouth Bass

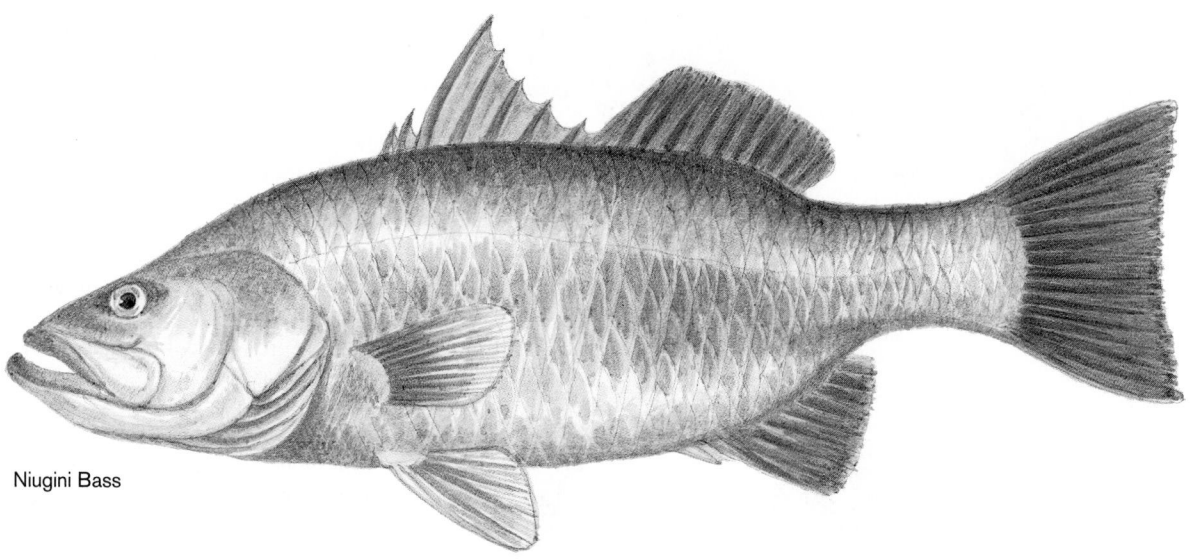

Niugini Bass

40 inches in length. Average weights are from 10 to 20 pounds, but fish weighing up to 30 pounds are common. Despite its great sporting virtues, the Niugini bass is not currently listed with the International Game Fish Association (IGFA), and no world-record weights have been established.

Distribution. The Niugini bass is known only in southern Papua New Guinea between the Port Moresby district and the Fly River. It may occur in rivers in Irian Jaya (the western half of the island of New Guinea).

Habitat. This fish inhabits large freshwater jungle streams and tributaries. It has not been reliably reported from marine habitats, but it may occur in estuaries. Little is known about the life history of this species; angler experiences suggest the fish favors cover, usually holding tight to the thickest snags and deadfall cover along riverbanks, where it waits to ambush prey. Deforestation and changes in jungle river environments may threaten sizes and populations.

Angling. The Niugini bass is a heavyweight jungle brawler, caught in locations full of snags and presenting extreme challenges for casting and for landing fish. Casting with surface plugs, and shallow- and medium-running plugs, is the primary practice, with emphasis on accurate lure placement very close to cover. Some plug trolling is done in main channels, where Niugini bass, as well as other species, may be encountered.

Owing to the fierce close-quarters battle of these fish, and the snag-infested nature of the jungle environs in which they are found, heavy baitcasting tackle is mandatory. Australians who have fished a good deal for this species use a minimum of 30-pound line, prefer 40, and will use 50-pound line. They use short, powerful rods and favor reels with top-quality drags. Like largemouth bass, Niugini bass are heavyweight short-term brawlers, and the key to catching them is stopping their freight-train-like bursts for cover.

Niugini bass are tough on tackle, and only lures with saltwater-quality hooks and the strongest connections will do; scarred and crushed lures and bent hooks are standard occurrences, and many fish are lost due to cover or when the angler is outmuscled. Very few anglers have encountered this excellent gamefish.

See: Papua New Guinea.

BASS, PEACOCK

Peacock bass are among the world's hardest fighting freshwater fish, and species that perform much the same as largemouth bass and can be caught using similar methods. Native to South American jungle or rain forest rivers and reservoirs, peacock bass have become popular with anglers as fishing opportunities in South America have increased and as these fish have been introduced in appropriate North American waters through stocking efforts, most notably in canal systems in southern Florida and warmwater reservoirs in Texas. They are valued in their native range as table fare, but their willingness to take lures, strike hard, and provide a strong and exciting fight make them primarily of interest to anglers.

The Name Game

The term "peacock bass" is a misnomer in nearly all respects, but it is a name that has good marketing value and one that has stuck in the English-speaking world. Species that are called peacock bass in English are formally known as *pavón* in Spanish-speaking South American countries and as *tucunaré* in Brazil.

The actual number of species that masquerade under the name "peacock bass" is unclear, as extensive scientific and taxonomic evaluations and reports have been lacking, especially in the English language and in the native range of these species. Because peacock bass are broadly referenced in

A dark, male peacock bass (note the humped back) from Guri Lake, Venezuela.

scant literature as fish of "the Orinoco and Amazon River basins"—which make up two of the world's greatest watersheds, thousands of tributaries, six or more relatively undeveloped countries, and probably half of an entire continent (much of it roadless)—it is not hard to understand that the exact number of different species and their ranges and life histories is barely known. In fact, more has been learned about one or two species due to their introduction to nonnative waters (as in Hawaii and Florida). It is known, however, that the biggest species and specimens have been caught in lakes and rivers in Brazil, Venezuela, and Colombia.

Like many other fish that are called bass, peacock bass are not true bass. Their body shape is generally basslike, however. All known species of peacock bass have a prominent black eyespot, surrounded by a gold ring (ocellus), on their tail fin. At some time North Americans saw the physical similarity between this fish and the largemouth bass, observed that it was readily taken on similar fishing tackle and techniques as largemouth bass, noticed that the eyespot was like that of the eyelike spot on the plumage of a peacock, and dubbed it a "peacock bass." This unofficial nickname turned into a fortunate stroke of public relations genius, and as more became known about the sporting attributes of this species, it kindled interest. Ironically, there are other species of South American fish that are also admirable but little known because of their less-familiar names and less-extensive range.

These include payara *(see)*, bicuda *(see)*, matrincha *(see)*, trahira *(see)*, and arawana *(see)*.

Peacock bass probably would have become a star attraction under any name, and deserve their great reputation. They are stronger, harder fighting, jump more and higher, and are generally much meaner than a largemouth bass or most anything else that swims in freshwater. Some species of peacock bass grow much larger, or are found on average in larger sizes, than largemouth bass. They also hit surface lures like no other fish, and destroy lures, line, equipment, and the thumbs of anyone foolish enough to lip-lock them.

Species

As noted, the number of peacock bass species is unknown and most, including the more prominent ones, have not been thoroughly identified and described. Brazilian biologists at the Instituto Nacional de Pesquisa Amazonia in Manaus, reported in 1996 that there were "eight, maybe more" species of *tucunaré*.

Whatever the actual number of species, they are all cichlids, members of the Cichlidae family. Well known to aquarium hobbyists, this family includes the popularly collected oscar *(Astronotus ocellatus)* and angelfish *(Pterophyllum scalare)*, as well as the important food fish tilapia *(see)*. Cichlids are the third or fourth largest family of bony fishes, numbering approximately 1,300 species (with 105 genera), and are widely distributed in Africa, Central and South America, Syria, southern India, Sri Lanka, Madagascar, and Iran. Many cichlids are colorful species, which is a main reason for their popularity with aquarium hobbyists. Most have bodies that are moderately deep and compressed; this is especially so for peacock bass, which, although similar in shape to largemouth bass, are more sleek and appear more muscular, without the sagging belly that big largemouths develop.

It is estimated that 300 cichlid species are native to South America, primarily in rivers; the various peacock bass species are among the largest and most predatory of these. As with piranha *(see)*, many terms have been used to name the different peacock bass species, and the term "peacock bass " (also *pavón* and *tucunaré*) is often used by anglers and nonscientists generically to refer to any of these fish, regardless of their particular characteristics, appearance, or species.

In addition to being superb gamefish, peacock bass are excellent table fare, and larger species and individuals are important commercially. All known peacock bass have a similar shape and a particularly distinguished coloration; some are especially brilliant, and, individually or as a group, peacock bass are among the most colorful of all sportfish in freshwater or saltwater.

The three species currently recognized by the International Game Fish Association (IGFA) for record-keeping purposes are the speckled peacock, butterfly peacock, and blackstripe peacock.

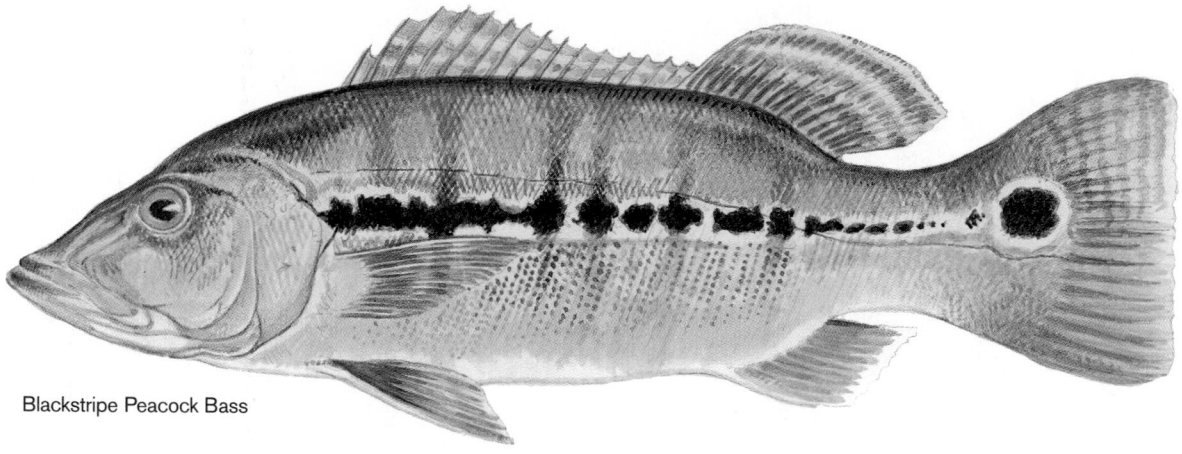

Blackstripe Peacock Bass

B

Blackstripe peacock bass (*Cichla intermedia*). The blackstripe peacock is also known as royal pavon, royal peacock bass, *pavón real*. It is limited to the Orinoco watershed in Venezuela south of San Fernando, making it a less frequent encounter for anglers.

The blackstripe peacock bass has an irregular black stripe that runs laterally along the full length of the midsection of the fish and is crossed intermittently by a series of six to eight fainter black oval bars. This is the only species of peacock bass that has more than three black vertical bars. It rarely weighs more than 10 pounds, although 12-pound specimens have been caught. Some consider it the toughest species pound for pound.

Butterfly peacock bass (*Cichla ocellaris*). The butterfly peacock is also known as peacock cichlid, tucunare, tuc; in Spanish as *pavón mariposa, pavón amarillo, pavón tres estrellas, marichapa;* in Portuguese as *tucunaré-acu;* and in Hawaiian as *lukanani.* The full extent of its range in tropical South America is undescribed scientifically, although it occurs in the Orinoco and Amazon drainages and in the upper reaches of these systems in several countries *(see: Brazil).* It was introduced in Hawaii (where it is primarily known as tucunare) from British Guyana in 1957, and in Florida in

1984 and 1986; it has also been stocked in Puerto Rico, Panama, Guam, and the Dominican Republic.

Butterfly peacock bass possess great variation in color. They are generally yellowish green overall, with three dark, yellow-tinged blotches along the lateral midsection; these blotches intersect with faint bars, which typically fade in fish weighing more than 3 to 4 pounds. The iris of the eye is frequently deep red. A conspicuous hump exists on top of the head in breeding males, and spawning fish have an intensified yellow coloration. They are distinguished by the absence of black markings on the opercula and are believed to attain a maximum size of 11 to 12 pounds; the all-tackle world record is a $10^1/_2$-pound individual from Río Branco in Brazil.

Speckled peacock bass (*Cichla temensis*). The speckled peacock bass is also known as speckled pavon, painted pavon, striped tucunare; in Spanish as *pavón cinchado, pavón pintado, pavón trucha,* and *pavón venado;* in Portuguese as *tucunaré-pacu.* As with the butterfly peacock bass, the full extent of this species' range in tropical South America is undescribed scientifically, although it occurs widely in the Orinoco and Amazon basins. It was introduced to Florida in 1985 and has reportedly been stocked in other countries.

Butterfly Peacock Bass

B

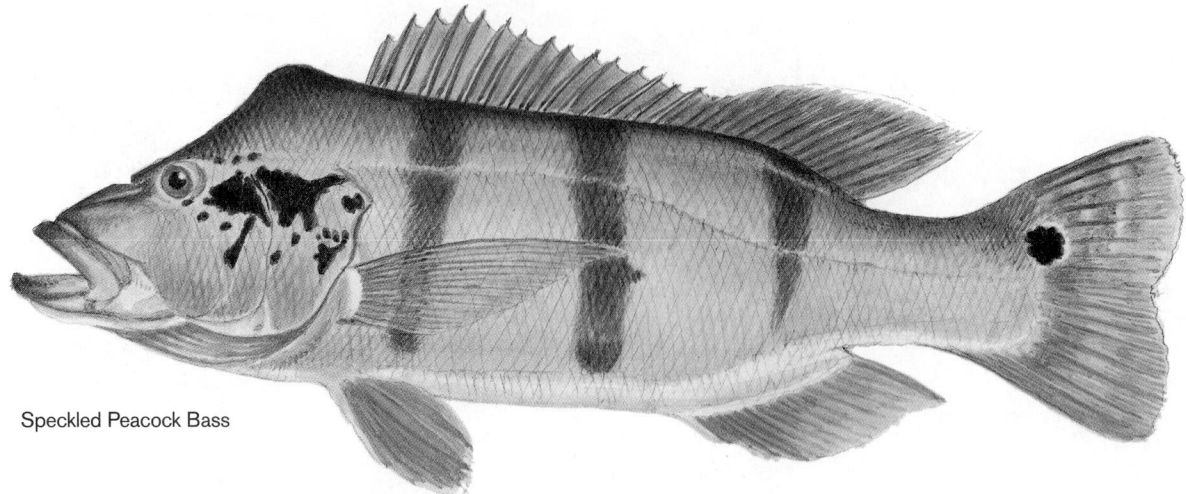

Speckled Peacock Bass

Speckled peacock bass have dark blotches on the opercula and three distinctive vertical black bars on the body; these may become more pronounced with age, although this does not appear to be absolute. There are light or faint spots on the dorsal and caudal fins, and a conspicuous hump exists on top of the head in breeding males. Some individuals (described as another color phase) may have four to six horizontal rows of light-colored dashes or spots along the sides and speckling over the rest of the body and fins; these fish are called "spotted peacock bass" by many anglers and were previously thought to be a distinct species.

It is the only peacock bass that has broken longitudinal lines and spots on the head, opercula, and caudal and dorsal fin regions, resulting in a speckled appearance. Many speckled peacock bass, however, especially the largest specimens, do not exhibit this speckling along their flanks.

Speckled peacock bass exhibit many color variations, the adults being lighter than the juveniles. Generally, they are dark green to black along the back, golden to yellow or light green along the flanks, and lighter on the belly. The pelvic, anal, and lower half of the caudal fins are often reddish in color, sometimes yellowish green. These colors are general conformities, however, and significant variations exist, especially in intensity (some have an orange or bronze tinge), which may or may not be due to season or habitat.

This species attains the greatest size of all the peacock bass. The current all-tackle world record is a 27-pound speckled peacock bass from the Río Negro in Brazil, but fish of 30 pounds and better reportedly have been speared, netted, or handlined. Speckled peacock bass up to 10 pounds are the norm in many waters; however, specimens exceeding 10 pounds are common in some places, and fish over 15 pounds are considered trophies. Some waters consistently produce individuals from 18 pounds to more than 20 pounds.

Due to its size, the speckled peacock bass is an important commercial species, especially in the larger rivers of the Amazon and near population centers. Overall, owing to its wide distribution and large size, it is the most important species to visiting anglers, and the main object of angling interest throughout the Amazon and Orinoco watersheds.

Angling
Like other fish of the rain forest regions of South America, peacock bass are primarily river fish,

Spotted Peacock Bass

although they are sought by anglers in the flooded backwaters and in the still areas of lagoons. They are seldom found in swift current but have adapted to impoundments. Anglers often land them among flooded timber or along the edges of timber, and they occasionally take them in open water.

Peacock bass are categorically described as schooling species, and they are often encountered in schools; catching many fish from a school, however, is not a likely possibility, and it is not uncommon to catch single fish from various locations. Although they may become active as a school and chase baitfish, there are only occasional opportunities to spot a feeding school and to fish for them. When an active school is present, however, one strategy for keeping them around involves one angler catching a fish and letting it swim along, hooked near the boat, while a companion casts to following fish. Peacock bass will often follow a hooked companion to the boat, just as in some places hooked peacock bass will be attacked by a school of piranhas.

The life history and food preferences of peacock bass are not fully understood, although it is clear from their behavior that they are voracious predators and aggressive fish. They obviously consume other fish, although their favorite prey, if any, are unknown in their various native environments. The sizes of lures successful in taking these fish indicate that both small and large fish are their targets. In Hawaii, butterfly peacock bass are known to consume threadfin shad, tilapia, bluegills, and mosquitofish. Spawning is believed to occur in 80°F waters, and before the flood season; these fish build shallow nests and guard their young.

The chief concern for visiting South American anglers in catching either numbers or sizes of peacock bass is being in the types of waters that contain large fish and being present in the appropriate season *(See: Brazil)*. Because the rainy season greatly raises water levels and floods the rain forest, it disperses all fish populations and makes the job of locating peacock bass prohibitively difficult. The dry season usually results in receding waters, which concentrates fish in backwater regions (lakelike areas off main rivers or tributaries, also called lagoons). These seasons vary in different areas of South America, and, in some years, unusual weather patterns disrupt the norm.

Anglers in Brazil typically catch peacock bass by casting and trolling. Natural baits are almost never employed by visiting anglers, and live baitfish are generally unavailable or cannot be maintained in most jungle fishing situations. Casting is preferred over trolling, although in periods of slack activity, especially in the heat of midday, or when high water makes locating fish difficult, trolling can be effective. Peacock bass are often more active in shallower water early and late in the day, evidently moving deeper in midday.

A brilliantly colored peacock bass from the São Francisco River, Brazil.

Peacock bass strike a variety of flashy diving, shallow-running, and surface plugs, as well as jigs and large streamer flies and fly-rod poppers. They nearly always strike hard, and their explosive strike on surface plugs is savage if not heart-surging, especially if the fish is large.

Shallow-running floating/diving plugs are excellent lures in backwater cover and catch peacock bass and other species; blue-and-silver, chartreuse, and green-and-white work well. Lipless rattling crankbaits are favored by many anglers, especially in open-water fishing. Blue-and-silver is highly recommended, but a host of flashy colors will do. Shallow-and mid-diving crankbaits that have good action and noise will do the job in open water as well. Surface lures include large walking, popping, and buzzing models. Large plugs with fore-and-aft propellers, which make a lot of commotion, are good for big fish, and can be effectively trolled as well as cast; the former being a rather unique method of freshwater fishing but one that points up the value of making noise to attract fish.

Spinnerbaits produce some strikes but are greatly outfished by plugs, and they do not hold up to abuse. Weedless spoons are good in cover, and heavier nonweedless spoons are good in open water. A 4- or 5-inch heavy-body spoon in a five-of-diamonds pattern is especially effective when trolled.

Be prepared to have lures mangled, crushed, and stripped of their paint if the action is hot; standard freshwater lures for bass or walleye withstand abuse from peacock bass (and other ruffians in the same waters). These fish, and the angling circumstances, are tough on equipment. Heavy-duty hooks and connections are necessary on lures, as lightweight hooks will be bent and crushed. Replace treble hooks with sturdy singles for lures that will work as well in this manner. It's smart to fish with barbless hooks, as there are dangerous moments in close-quarters jungle fishing, with its shallow water, close-to-boat strikes, and thrashing fish. Lures often fly back at you, and the potential for being impaled is high.

Peacock bass jump often, make repeated powerful short runs, do not give up at the sight of the boat, and try to run for the security of heavy cover. In tight quarters and heavily obstructed areas, it takes a lot to stop them. Baitcasting gear loaded with 17- and 20-pound-test line is considered the minimum for dedicated peacock bass anglers, and some use 20- to 40-pound gear, including low-stretch microfilament lines. Spinning gear will do if it is heavy-duty, and lures can be cast very accurately with it. Lighter tackle may be appropriate in some situations, usually in open areas and where there are smaller fish. Casting accurately among heavy cover is often necessary, and this is much harder to do with spinning tackle than with baitcasting gear. Good-quality line and reels with an excellent drag are important, although line capacity is not critical. Short wire leaders of at least 20- to 30-pound strength are very useful for these and other species, and they don't seem to hinder the fish in most of their habitats.

BASS, REDEYE   *Micropterus coosae.*
Other names—black bass, coosa bass, shoal bass, Flint River smallmouth.

There are two widely recognized forms of this member of the black bass group of the Centrarchidae family: the Apalachicola, which is called a shoal bass, and the Alabama, which is generally referred to as the redeye bass or the true redeye. The shoal bass has yet to be described fully or

given a distinct scientific name, and there is some confusion over the two. A scrappy fighter, the redeye bass often jumps when hooked and is hard to catch. Its white, flaky meat is of good table quality, similar to that of other black bass.

Identification. As its name indicates, the redeye bass is characterized by the considerable amount of red in its eyes. It is bronze olive above with brownish to greenish sides and yellow-white to blue below, usually with dark vertical bars on the flanks. The bars on the caudal peduncle are diamond shaped with light centers. There is a prominent dark spot on the gill cover, and rows of dark spots on the lower sides, as well as white upper and lower outer edges on the orange-tinged tail. The upper jaw of its large mouth extends to the rear portion of the eye but not beyond, and there is usually a patch of teeth on the tongue. The redeye has redder fins than do other black bass; the first and second dorsal fins are connected, and the second dorsal and caudal fins and the front of the anal fin are brick red on young fish. There is a dusky spot on the base of the tail, which is darkest also on young fish. There are 12 dorsal rays and 10 anal rays.

The shoal bass can normally be distinguished from the redeye bass by a prominent spot immediately before the tail and another on the edge of the gill cover, which is generally indistinct on the redeye. The shoal bass also lacks white outer edges on the tail, has smaller scales, and lacks the patch of teeth on the tongue. It has 12 to 13 dorsal rays and 10 to 11 anal rays.

Size/Age. The redeye bass grows to $18^1/_2$ inches and about 3 pounds, although some reach more than 8 pounds and live as long as 10 years. The shoal form grows faster, although it generally reaches about 15 inches in length. The all-tackle world record is an 8-pound, 12-ounce fish taken in Florida in 1995.

Distribution. Redeye bass are found in North America in the Alabama, Savannah, Coosa, Chattahoochee, and Warrior River systems in Georgia and Alabama, and in southeastern Tennessee (Conasauga drainage). It has been

Redeye Bass

introduced to a limited degree in California, Puerto Rico, and Kentucky's upper Cumberland River drainage, as well as into other river systems near its native range.

Shoal bass occur in the Apalachicola River system in Florida and in the Chattahoochee, Chestatee, and Flint Rivers in Georgia.

Habitat. Inhabiting the rocky runs and pools of creeks and small to medium rivers, redeye bass prefer the cold headwaters of small streams. They seldom exist in natural lakes, ponds, or reservoirs, and they prefer water temperatures in the mid-60s. Shoal bass are most likely to thrive in main-channel habitats.

Spawning. Spawning occurs in spring, when water temperatures are between 60° and 70°F, usually over coarse gravel at the head of a pool. Males build the nest and guard the eggs and fry.

Food. Redeye feed primarily on terrestrial and larval insects, crayfish, and small fish.

Angling. Due to their limited range and small size, redeye bass are not known to many American anglers. There is little concerted angling effort targeting them.

Fishing tactics are similar to those for black bass, especially smallmouths in rivers.

See: Bass, Black.

BASS, ROANOKE *Ambloplites cavifrons.*

The Roanoke bass is a sunfish and a member of the Centrarchidae family, similar in body shape to a rock bass *(see: bass, rock)* or warmouth *(see)*. It can be identified by its unscaled or partly scaled cheek and the several iridescent gold to white spots on its upper side and head. It is olive to tan above, has a dark and light marbling on the side, and often sports rows of black spots and a white to bronze breast and belly. It is also distinguished by the 39 to 49 lateral scales, 11 anal rays, and 27 to 35 scale rows across its breast between the pectoral fins. The all-tackle world record is a 1-pound, 5-ounce fish taken in Virginia in 1991.

Growing to a maximum of 14$^{1}/_{2}$ inches, the Roanoke bass occurs in North America in the Chowan, Roanoke, Tar, and Neuse River drainages in Virginia and North Carolina. It inhabits the rocky and sandy pools of creeks and small to medium clear rivers.

See: Sunfish.

Roanoke Bass

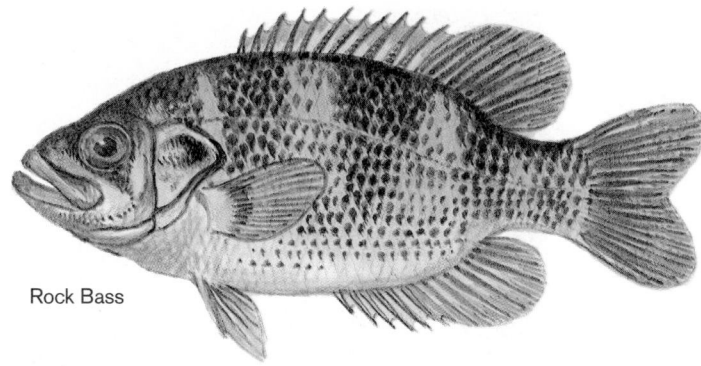
Rock Bass

BASS, ROCK *Ambloplites rupestris.*

Other names—black perch, goggle-eye, red eye, rock sunfish, goggle-eye perch: French: *crapet de roche.*

The rock bass is actually a member of the sunfish family and is not a true bass. Rock bass are fun to catch because they can be caught on many types of baits and lures and they put up a decent fight on ultralight tackle. Its meat is white and firm and makes good eating. Because rock bass prefer protected waters, however, they can have a muddy flavor or host numerous parasites. Rock bass are known to overpopulate small lakes, making population control measures necessary.

Identification. Although it looks like a cross between a bluegill and a black bass, the rock bass is actually a large and robust sunfish with a deep body; it is less compressed than most sunfish and is more similar to a black bass in shape. The back is raised, and the large head is narrow, rounded, and deep. The mouth of the rock bass is also large, especially in comparison to other sunfish; the upper jaw reaches beyond the beginning of the eye but not to the back of the eye. It has two connected dorsal fins, five to six anal fin spines, and large eyes.

The rock bass is olive brown or bronze on the back and sides, with faint lines of tiny dark marks; the centers of the scales below the lateral line also have dark markings that form 11 or more rows and give the fish a striped appearance. In some rock bass, the coloring is lighter but consistent underneath, whereas others are silver, gray, or white on the belly. The vertical fins have pale circular spots, and all fins are usually darker at their margins, although the edges of the anal spines are white, the tips of the pectoral fins are clear, and the pelvic fins sometimes have a white edge. A distinguishing characteristic is the bluish black blotch found on the tip of the gill covers. The young and breeding adults have a striking "checkerboard" pattern of squarish blotches; during spawning, some males become almost black. Rock bass can develop an overall bluish tinge in some waters.

Rock bass are frequently confused with the warmouth *(Lepomis gulosus; see: warmouth)*. Warmouth have teeth on their tongue, whereas rock bass do not. There are also six spines in front of the anal fin of a rock bass as opposed to the three spines in the

B

A large rock bass from Balsam Lake, Ontario.

silt. Young rock bass are frequently found in vegetation. Rock bass tend to frequent the same habitats as do smallmouth bass.

Life history/Behavior. Rock bass are able to reproduce once they are two years old or 3 to 5 inches long; spawning occurs from midspring to early summer, when water temperatures range from 60° to 70°F. Males move into the shallows three to four days prior to the females arrival, to establish territories. They begin building round nests in gravelly or sandy areas near weedbeds or other protection such as submerged tree trunks, using their pectoral, anal, and caudal fins to fan the gravel for the nest.

Spawning occurs during the day, usually in the morning. The females spawn at least twice, moving from nest to nest and laying from 3,000 to 11,000 eggs in total. The adhesive eggs are released and fertilized in short intervals over a period of about one hour; they hatch in three to four days at temperatures between 69° and 70°F. The males guard the nest until the eggs hatch and the young swim away, and many males nest a second or even a third time. After spawning, the adults leave the nesting area for more protected habitat.

Rock bass are a schooling fish and often cluster with other sunfish and smallmouth bass.

Food and feeding habits. Young rock bass feed on minute aquatic life when young, then on insects and crustaceans as they grow. Adults eat mostly crayfish, as well as minnows, insects, mollusks, and small fish. This diet varies with season and location. They can consume relatively large specimens because of their large mouths. Some evidence shows that they feed during the day and that feeding peaks in late afternoon; other evidence supports the claim that they feed both day and night. Rock bass generally feed on the bottom but may occasionally feed near the surface.

Angling. Rock bass are scrappy fighters, but they tire quickly. There is no need to use anything but light or ultralight tackle for these fish. Because they often travel in schools, anglers frequently catch several or many from the same location. Sunken logs or tree stumps are prime places to find these fish, as are deep-water rocky ledges, quiet, still pools along riverbanks where large rocks are present, deep-water gravel beds where a large weed structure begins, and beneath overhanging willows along a river or lake shoreline.

Traditionally, rock bass have been caught by cane-pole anglers using live baits. Many are still caught by live-bait anglers using garden worms, nightcrawlers, small crayfish, and small minnows. The most common tactic is placing a small worm on a short-shanked No. 4 hook with a few small split shot above it and stillfishing with a float or bobber, allowing the bait to sit about 6 inches above the bottom. Among artificials, small crankbaits, spinners, and spoons may work, as will fly-rod poppers or bugs. Light grub or curl-tail jigs and very light spinnerbaits are perhaps even more effective.

warmouth. Rock bass may also resemble the mud sunfish *(see: sunfish, mud);* rock bass have a forked tail and rough scales, whereas mud sunfish have a rounded tail and smooth scales.

Size/Age. The most common size for rock bass is about 8 ounces, although they have been known to reach 3 pounds. Often rock bass in a particular lake will weigh around a pound, with a few fish exceeding 2 pounds. As with most sunfish, however, size is extremely variable, and rock bass living in streams are often stunted. The International Game Fish Association (IGFA) all-tackle record is a 3-pound Canadian fish. Rock bass can reach a length of 12 to 14 inches but are usually less than 8 inches long. Although aquarium fish have lived for 18 years, those in the wild live 10 to 12 years on average.

Distribution. Native to the northeastern United States and southeastern Canada, rock bass range from southern Manitoba east to Ontario and Quebec, and southward through the Great Lakes region and the Mississippi Valley to the Gulf of Mexico as far as northern Alabama and northern Georgia. They have been introduced into other states including some in the western U.S.

Habitat. Rock bass prefer small to moderate streams with cool and clear water, abundant shelter, and considerable current; they are plentiful in shallow, weedy lakes and the outer edges of larger lakes, as well as in thousands of smaller lakes and ponds. Rock bass almost always hold over rocky bottoms (resulting in the name "rock" bass) where there is no

These should all be retrieved very slowly. Fishing techniques for rock bass are similar to those for sunfish, especially bluegills.

See: Bluegill; Sunfish.

BASS, SHOAL

See: Bass, Redeye.

BASS, SMALLMOUTH   *Micropterus dolomieui.*
Other names—black bass, smallmouth, bronzeback, brown bass, brownie, smallie, redeye; French: *achigan à petite bouche;* German: *schwarzbarsch;* Japanese: *kokuchibasu.*

The smallmouth bass is the second largest member of the Centrarchidae family of sunfish and a North American original. To anglers it is one of the most impressive of all freshwater fish and is coveted for its fighting ability. This is the fish to which the famous Dr. James Henshall quote, "inch for inch and pound for pound the gamest fish that swims," of the 1800s is ascribed. Henshall was probably not acquainted with some saltwater fish, or he might have restricted this praise to freshwater species, but it is certainly true that the smallmouth has spunky fighting habits and an appreciated willingness to take a variety of lures and baits.

It is less tolerant of very warm environs and is not as widely distributed as its close relative, the largemouth bass *(see: bass, largemouth).* Because most of the smallmouth's abundance occurs in the northern states and southern Canadian provinces, many avid freshwater bass anglers, especially in extreme southern U.S. states, have not made this fish's acquaintance.

The smallmouth is not actually a bass but a sunfish, and its mouth is only small in comparison to that of some other black bass relatives. It is naturally a fish of both clear rivers and lakes, and has been widely introduced to other waters outside its original range. Smallmouths that reside in small to intermediate streams do not grow as large, on average, as those from lakes or reservoirs, although fish from big rivers, and especially those with tailwater fisheries, can attain large sizes. River smallmouth are even spunkier than their lake-dwelling brethren, however, and tend to be more streamlined and to lack a drooping belly.

Although smallmouths have been popular with most anglers throughout their range, they were not well appreciated in the northeastern region of North America, where Atlantic salmon and brook trout were esteemed and bass were trash fish, until the early 1980s. There was once even a commercial fishery for smallmouths early in the twentieth century, although they are strictly a gamefish today wherever they are found, and are usually subject to careful management and regulations.

Unlike some members of the sunfish family, which are coveted for their tasty flesh, smallmouths are not sought for food by most people, and there's a high degree of catch-and-release fishing for them. This has not always been the case but has evolved in the latter decades of the twentieth century, as their value for recreation has become more important to avid anglers. Smallmouth bass are good to eat, however, particularly specimens from cool waters; their white flesh is similar in taste to that of other sunfish, and better than that of the largemouth bass but not as tasty as the walleye *(see),* both of which sometimes inhabit the same waters as the smallmouth.

The smallmouth bass is occasionally confused with the largemouth where they both occur, and also with the spotted bass *(see: bass, spotted)* and redeye bass *(see: bass, redeye).* They have been known to hybridize with spotted bass. Two subspecies are often recognized: the northern smallmouth, *M. d. dolomieui,* and the Neosho smallmouth, *M. d. velox.*

Identification.   The smallmouth bass has a robust, slightly laterally compressed and elongate body, a protruding lower jaw, red eyes, and a broad and slightly forked tail. Its pelvic fins sit forward on the body below the pectoral fins; a single spine is found on each pelvic fin and on the front of the anal fin. The two dorsal fins are joined or notched; the front one is spiny and the second one has one

Northern Smallmouth Bass

spine followed by soft rays. Its color varies from brown, golden brown, and olive to green on the back, becoming lighter to golden on the sides and white on the belly. Young fish have more distinct vertical bars or rows of spots on their sides, and the caudal, or tail, fin is orange at the base followed by black and then white outer edges.

The smallmouth is easily distinguished from the largemouth by its clearly connected dorsal fins, the scales on the base portion of the soft-rayed second dorsal fin, and the upper jaw bone, which extends only to about the middle of the eye. The coloration is also distinctive, being usually more brownish in the smallmouth and more greenish in the largemouth. The smallmouth has faint bars on the body (prominent in the young), whereas the largemouth has a fairly wide streak of oval or diamond-shaped markings or blotches down the midline of the sides. In either species, the colors may vary, and the markings may be inconspicuous or absent in individuals based on time of year and various biological factors. Generally, the smallmouth has bars radiating back from the eyes, and although similar bars may be present in individuals of other species, including the largemouth, they seem to be more prominent and more consistently present in the smallmouth.

Size/Age.   The average life span of the smallmouth bass is 5 to 6 years, although it can live for 15 years. Most smallmouths encountered by anglers weigh between 1 and $1^{1}/_{2}$ pounds and are from 9 to 13 inches long; fish exceeding 3 pounds are considered fairly large but not uncommon. Most anglers have caught few, if any, smallmouth bass over 5 pounds, although some waters do produce 5- to 8-pound specimens annually. The largest smallmouth known, and the presumed maximum weight, is the Tennessee state record, a fish that weighed 11 pounds, 15 ounces when caught from Dale Hollow Lake in 1955. It measured 27 inches in length and 21.7 inches in girth. The Canadian record was caught in Ontario in 1954 and weighed 9.84 pounds.

The Neosho subspecies, which is more slender than the smallmouth, occurs in the Neosho River and tributaries of the Arkansas River in Missouri, Kansas, Arkansas, and Oklahoma.

Distribution.   The smallmouth bass is endemic only to North America, and its original range was from the Great Lakes and St. Lawrence River drainages in Canada south to northern Georgia, west to eastern Oklahoma, and north to Minnesota. It has since been widely spread within and beyond that range, across southern Canada west to British Columbia and east to the Maritimes, west to the Pacific coast states, and into the southwestern United States. It has also been introduced to Hawaii, Asia, Europe, and Africa. Although it has been nearly as widely dispersed as the largemouth bass, it has more specific habitat requirements, and within this broad range it is not as widely abundant or distributed as the largemouth

bass. The biggest smallmouth populations occur in cool northern waters, but a greater number of big smallmouth are caught in the southern portion of their range.

Habitat.   Smallmouth bass prefer clear, quiet waters with gravel, rubble, or rocky bottoms. They live in midsize, gentle streams that have deep pools and abundant shade, or in fairly deep, clear lakes and reservoirs with rocky shoals. Although they are fairly adaptable, they are seldom found in murky water and avoid swift current.

In the typical river, smallmouth bass predominate in the cool middle section where there are large pools between riffles, whereas trout occupy the swifter and colder upper section. In stillwaters, smallmouth bass may occupy lakes, reservoirs, or ponds if these waters are large and deep enough to have thermal stratification, and they are usually located deeper than largemouth bass once the surface layer warms in spring or early summer.

Life history/Behavior.   Smallmouth bass spawn in the spring (or early summer in most northern waters), when the water temperature is between 60° and 65°F. The male builds a nest in water that ranges from 1 to 12 feet deep depending on the environment. The nest site is often over a gravel or rock bottom but may be over a sandy bottom in lakes, and it is usually near the protection of a log or boulder. In waters cohabited by both smallmouth and largemouth, the largemouth bass will spawn a little earlier, as their shallower nesting sites, chosen in protected areas with emergent vegetation, warm to the optimum temperature sooner than the deeper, rockier sites chosen by the smallmouths.

Females usually produce 5,000 to 14,000 eggs, depending on their size. They stick to stones in the bottom of the nest. The young are about 5.8 millimeters long when they hatch in 4 to 10 days, depending on the temperature. Hatching success can vary a lot. Sudden changes in temperature or water level can cause the eggs to die from shock, or they can cause the male to abandon the nest, leaving it open for predators. The male protects the young as they absorb their yolk sac and continues to guard them for three to four weeks until they begin to leave the nest. Young fish tend to stay in quiet, shallow areas with rocks and vegetation.

Older bass prefer rocky, shallow areas of lakes and rivers and retreat to deeper areas when water temperatures are high. They tend to seek cover and avoid the light, and generally do not inhabit the same types of dense, weedy, or wooded cover that largemouth bass prefer. They hide in deep water, behind rocks and boulders, and around underwater debris and crevices, preferring water temperatures between 66° and 72°F. Most bass do not travel great distances, and those in streams spend all season in the same pool. As temperatures fall, they become less active and seek cover in dark, rocky areas. In the winter, they cease feeding, remain inactive on the bottom, and stay near warm springs when possible.

Smallmouth bass generally mature when they are about 10 to 11 inches long. Males usually mature a year earlier than females.

Food. These highly carnivorous and predatory fish will eat whatever is available, but they have a clear preference for crayfish and small fish. In lakes, this includes small bass, panfish, perch, and assorted fingerling-size minnows in lakes. In rivers, it includes minnows, crayfish, hellgrammites, nymph larvae, and leeches. Juveniles begin feeding on plankton and switch to larger prey like water insects, amphibians, crayfish, and other fish as they grow.

Angling. In lakes, ponds, and reservoirs, smallmouths prefer a rocky bottom, cool water, and crayfish. Crayfish make up an important part of their diet wherever these creatures are found. In lakes, smallmouths are mainly located around rocky points; craggy, clifflike shores; rocky islands and reefs; and riprap banks, preferring small rocks but also favoring boulders. In flowing water, smallmouth bass concentrate around boulders, smaller rocks, gravel, stone, shale, and various obstructions (fallen trees, bridge pilings, and the like) that offer holding and feeding benefits.

In rivers, anglers primarily tend to fish below structures or objects, which is fine in spring and during high water flowage. Later in the season, areas above these places are also productive. Anglers should work with the current to imitate the natural movement of fish in a river. This doesn't mean always retrieving downstream, however, except when fly fishing on the surface. Most casts should be made upriver at a 45° angle, and offerings should be retrieved across and down. In smaller flowages with less midriver structure, working the undercut banks, sunken logs, stumps, and rock walls is best.

Fishing for smallmouths with live crayfish, especially the soft-shelled variety, is particularly popular among bait anglers. Another good natural bait is a nightcrawler. Live crayfish and worms can be worked behind various bottom-bouncing rigs in flowing water, and on floats in stillwater.

Crayfish-imitating crankbaits are a popular river and lake lure for smallmouths. These look and act a bit like a crayfish, and can be productive all season if smallmouths aren't too deep; they are especially worthwhile in the spring. Bottom scratching is critical most of the time with these. Another good smallmouth lure is a floating/diving plug, worked by twitching it on the surface or by a stop-and-go underwater retrieve.

Surface lures have most merit in the springtime, and early and late in the day in the summer. Poppers, wobblers, and the aforementioned plugs are of most merit, and fly fishing with bugs and poppers is also effective when the fish are fairly shallow. Streamer flies and dry flies may also work in flowing water.

Perhaps the best all-around smallmouth bass lure, however, is a jig. Hair-bodied, soft-plastic, and

A scrappy battler, the smallmouth bass has to be tired out before it can be hand-landed.

rubber-legged jigs are tantalizing and very effective in the hands of a good angler. Rocky banks and sharply sloping shorelines are suitable for jig fishing, although it is critical to get the jig down and working along the bottom. Dark jig colors, such as black and brown, are good, but many anglers have success with yellow and white jigs with soft-plastic curl-tail bodies.

In many lakes and reservoirs, smallmouth bass are fairly deep in summer when the water warms up. Fishing vertically with jigs or jigging spoons is necessary, and in some environs trolling with deep-diving plugs or with assorted lures run behind downriggers or off planer boards is the favored method.

Spinners are a good flowing-water lure for smallmouths at times, incidentally, especially in the spring. They may also be effective when fished on a slow-and-deep retrieve in the spring on lakes along rocky shores where bass are staging prior to spawning. Spinnerbaits can sometimes produce good smallmouth action as well, although they are not universally appealing. When bass are shallow and aggressive, especially early in the season, spinnerbaits are extremely effective (and better than a multihooked plug for releasing fish unharmed), but later, as these fish move deeper and become warier, spinnerbaits don't produce unless you want to spend time fluttering single-blade models off deep ledges.

Light- and medium-duty spinning gear will handle the majority of smallmouth bass fishing situations. Light (6- and 8-pound) and ultralight (2- and 4-pound) lines are practical, even desirable, because smallmouths are residents of open water for the most part; when hooked, they do not have to be muscled from obstacles other than the bottom, as is common with largemouth bass.

In many places, smallmouths inhabit relatively clear, deep lakes and are wary, so delicate presentations involving light, thin-diameter line, small lures, and corresponding rod and reel combinations make light and ultralight tackle a fundamental part of smallmouth fishing success. Using heavier gear, including baitcasting tackle, is usually overkill, although some plugs and large jigs are worked a little better on these outfits.

See: Bass, Black.

BASS, SPOTTED   *Micropterus punctulatus.*
Other names—Alabama spotted bass, black bass, Kentucky bass, Kentucky spotted bass, lineside, northern spotted bass, redeye, spot, Wichita spotted bass.

Often mistaken by anglers for largemouth bass *(see: bass, largemouth)*, the spotted bass is a lesser-known member of the black bass group of the Centrarchidae family than either the largemouth or smallmouth *(see: bass, largemouth; bass, smallmouth)*, but this is a spunky and distinguished-looking species that no angler is unhappy about catching, even if the majority are encountered by accident.

The general term "spotted bass" really incorporates three recognized subspecies: the northern spotted bass *(M. p. punctulatus)*, the Alabama spotted bass *(M. p. henshalli)*, and the Wichita spotted bass *(M. p. wichitae)*; the last was previously thought to be extinct and is still rarely encountered.

Spotted bass are scrappy fish whose fight is often compared to that of the smallmouth, although they jump less frequently. Their average and maximum sizes are smaller than those of the largemouth, and they are seldom encountered over 4 pounds. They are more likely to utilize and suspend in deep water, even moving about in deep water in loose groups rather than schools. Spotted bass have white, flaky meat with a good flavor, similar to that of other black bass. Most are released by anglers.

Identification.   Spotted bass have a moderately compressed elongate body with coloration and markings that are similar to those of the largemouth bass; both have a light green to light brown hue on the back and upper sides, white lower sides and belly, and a broad stripe of diamond-shaped blotches along the midline of the body. Like all black bass except the largemouth, the spotted bass has scales on the base portion of the second dorsal fin, its first and second dorsal fin are clearly connected, and its upper jawbone does not extend back to or beyond the rear edge of the eyes. Spotted bass have a distinct patch of teeth on the tongue, which largemouth do not, and there is a large spot on the point of the gill cover.

The spotted bass differs from the smallmouth bass in that it lacks the vertical bars that are present on the sides of the body in the smallmouth. It also has small black spots in alternate rows below the lateral line (the rear edges of certain scales are black), unlike either the largemouth or the smallmouth. Reportedly, spotted bass and smallmouth bass have hybridized in nature, which could make identification of some specimens where both species are known to occur even more difficult. Juvenile spotted bass resemble juvenile smallmouths in having a broad band of orange at the base of the tail, followed by a broad black band and white edge.

The Alabama spotted bass has a dark spot at the base of the tail and on the rear of the gill cover, and 68 to 75 scales along the lateral line. The northern spotted bass also has a spot on the tail, but the spot on the gill cover is not as distinct, and there are only 60 to 68 scales along the lateral line.

Size/Age.   Spotted bass seldom exceed 4 to 5 pounds and are rarely encountered up to 8 pounds. The all-tackle world record is a 9-pound, 7-ounce fish taken in California in 1994 (it was transplanted from Alabama spotted bass stock), which may or may not be the largest attainable size. Because of the difficulty in recognizing the species, it is probable that larger record-size specimens of spotted bass have gone unnoticed. The life span of about seven years is much shorter than that of the smallmouth or largemouth, and the growth rate is intermediate between the two.

Distribution.   Spotted bass were once primarily found in the lower to central Mississippi River

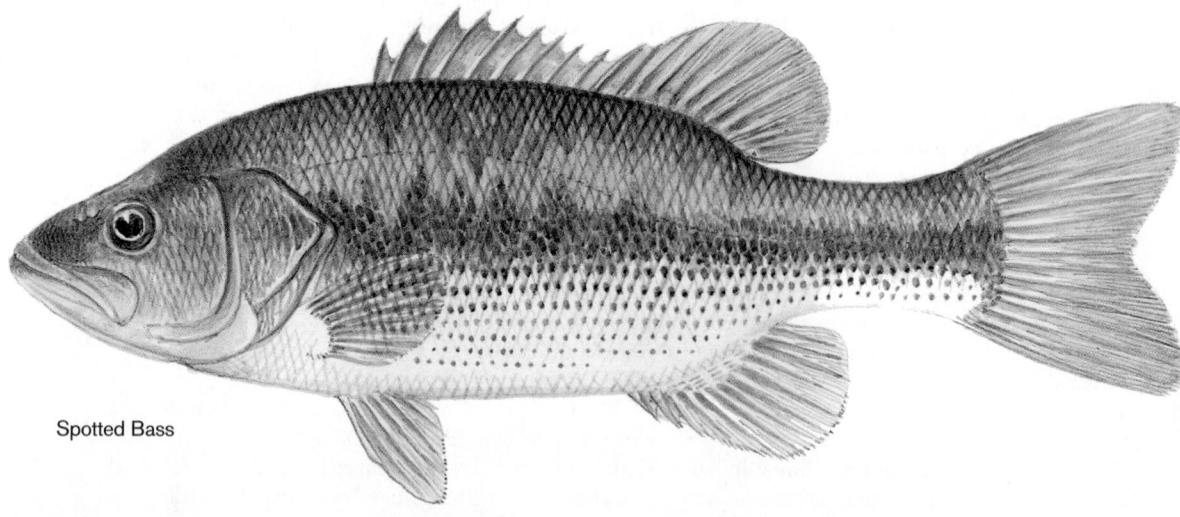

Spotted Bass

drainages of North America, but their range has expanded greatly. They are now found throughout the central and lower Mississippi basin, from southern Ohio and West Virginia to southeastern Kansas and south to the Gulf of Mexico (from Texas to the Florida Panhandle), including the Chattahoochee drainage in Georgia, Alabama, Tennessee, Kentucky, and other nearby states where it occurs naturally or has been introduced. Spotted bass have been introduced as far west as California, where some of the larger specimens are now found, and outside North America, including South Africa, where the species has become established in several bodies of water.

The infrequently encountered Wichita spotted bass appears to be limited to West Cache Creek, Oklahoma. The Alabama spotted bass is native to Alabama, Mississippi, and Georgia.

Habitat. The natural habitat of spotted bass is clear, gravelly, flowing pools and runs of creeks and small to medium rivers; and they also tolerate the slower, warmer, and more turbid sections that are unlikely to host smallmouth bass. They are seldom found in natural lakes but have adapted well to deep impoundments, which were created by damming some of their natural rivers and streams. In reservoirs they prefer water temperatures in the mid-70s and are especially suited to deep, clear impoundments. Typical habitat is similar to that of the largemouth bass, although the spotted bass prefers rocky areas and is much more likely to inhabit and suspend in open waters; it may hold in great depths (between 60 and more than 100 feet) in some waters. Rocky bluffs, deep rockpiles, and submerged humps are among its haunts.

Life history/Behavior. Spotted bass spawn in spring at water temperatures of about 63° to 68°F. Males sweep away silt from a gravel or rock bottom to make the nest, generally near brush, logs, or other heavy cover. The males guard the eggs, and then guard the fry after they leave the nest. Fry are extremely active, much more than either the largemouth or smallmouth.

These fish tend to school more than any other member of the black bass family and are often encountered chasing shad in open water.

Food and feeding habits. Juveniles feed on small crustaceans and midge larvae, whereas adults eat insects, larger crustaceans, minnows, frogs, worms, grubs, and small fish. Crayfish are usually the most important item in the diet, followed by small fish, and larval and adult insects.

Angling. Most catches of spotted bass are incidental to attempts for other black bass. Fishing tactics in rivers are similar to those for smallmouth bass, and in impoundments to those for large- and smallmouth bass. They are likely to be found in groups, so more than one can be caught in specific places. Lures that imitate crayfish, as well as small jigs with grub or other soft-plastic bodies, are especially productive. In summer, deep fishing over planted brush piles, especially near a major creek or river channel, can be especially effective.
See: Bass, Black.

BASS, STRIPED   *Morone saxatilis.*

Other names—striper, rock, rockfish, striped sea bass, striper bass, linesider, squid hound, and greenhead; French: *Bar rayé;* Spanish: *Lubina estriada.*

An excellent sportfish that attains large sizes, the striped bass is a member of the temperate bass family (often erroneously placed with the sea bass family). It has been considered one of the most valuable and popular fish in North America since the early 1600s, originally for its commercial importance and culinary quality, and in more recent times for its recreational significance. Striped bass have been successfully transplanted to landlocked freshwater environments and crossbred with related species. Both sea-run and landlocked stripers provide important angling opportunity in North America, and are among the most valued and prized species.

There have been great fluctuations in abundance of stripers in modern times, particularly in saltwater and on the East Coast, and many disputes among commercial and recreational interests. In California, the striped bass has been designated solely a gamefish since 1936, meaning that it cannot be harvested commercially from the wild, although it may be farmed. Gamefish designation has been sporadic and resisted on the East Coast, however, where stripers have historically been a mainstay of commercial fishing and where abundance has been threatened by overfishing, pollution, and other factors.

Since the late 1980s, due to restrictive measures and environmental cleanup along the East Coast, striped bass numbers, which are primarily dependent on the Chesapeake Bay and secondarily the Hudson River, rebounded from a near-endangered status to exceptional abundance. The sportfishing catch has been estimated as several times that of the commercial catch, although federal statistics indicate that up to 90 percent of the sport-caught stripers are being released alive, by choice or edict.

The striper's pleasant and almost-sweet white flesh has made it desirable table fare, and striped bass were long one of the most important market fishes along the East Coast. That market shrank to virtually nothing when Atlantic populations crashed and is still only a fraction of what it once was. Many of the striped bass presented in restaurants today, in fact, are farmed, but anglers are able to harvest enough fish to provide fine dining.

Identification. A large fish with a large mouth, the striped bass is more streamlined than its close relative, the white bass. It has a long body and long head, a somewhat laterally compressed body form, and a protruding lower jaw. Of the two noticeably separate dorsal fins, the first one has 7 to 12 stiff spines, usually 9, which make this fin quite

B

a bit higher than the second; the second dorsal fin has one sharp spine and 8 to 14, ordinarily 12, soft rays. The striped bass also has a forked tail and small eyes.

These fish are mostly bluish black or dark green above, fading into silver on the sides and white on the belly. On each side of its body, there are seven or eight prominent black horizontal stripes that run along the scale rows that are the distinctive markings of the striped bass; one of the stripes runs along the lateral line, and the rest are equally divided above and below it. The stripe highest up on the side is usually the most noticeable, although on some fish, one or more of the stripes is interrupted. Most of the fins are a dusky silver, with the exception of the white pelvic fins. The young of less than 4 inches long as well as the breeding adults have 8 to 10 dark vertical bars that are more apparent than the horizontal stripes. The vertical bars disappear as the fish mature.

In freshwater, the striped bass has been crossed with the white bass to create a hybrid called the whiterock bass *(see: bass, whiterock)* or sunshine bass *(see: bass, sunshine)*. Striped bass differ from hybrids in the regularity of their stripes, whereas the hybrid usually has interrupted stripes. The narrow body of the striped bass also distinguishes it from the white bass.

Size/Age. Growing rapidly in early life, striped bass average 5 to 10 pounds, although they often reach weights in the 30- to 50-pound range. The maximum size that a freshwater striped bass can achieve is unknown, although the largest sport-caught freshwater striper weighed 59 pounds, 12 ounces. The all-tackle record for the species—78 pounds 8, ounces—belongs to a saltwater fish, although larger ones have been reportedly taken commercially. Striped bass normally live 10

to 12 years, although most fish more than 11 years old and more than 39 inches long are female. The largest striped bass ever reported was a 125-pounder believed to be between 29 and 31 years old.

Distribution.   On the Atlantic coast of the United States, the striped bass commonly occurs from the St. Lawrence River south to the St. Johns River in northern Florida. It has also ranged along the coasts of Florida, Louisiana, Alabama, and Mississippi in the Gulf of Mexico. Some fish migrate north from North Carolina, Virginia, or Maryland during the summer and return during the fall. Others living in estuarine river systems such as the St. Lawrence, the Santee-Cooper, or the Savannah are nonmigratory.

Striped bass were introduced to San Francisco Bay in 1879 and 1882; today, along the Pacific coast, they are abundant in the bay area and extend from Washington to California; some California fish migrate north to Oregon and are occasionally found off the west coast of Vancouver Island.

Striped bass need rivers with long stretches of freshwater and brackish water for spawning. Only a few places meet that criteria; the Hudson River in New York and the Chesapeake Bay in Maryland are the most prominent spawning grounds and are inexorably linked to the abundance, distribution, and future of saltwater stripers.

Habitat.   Striped bass inhabit saltwater, freshwater, and brackish water, although they are most abundant in saltwater. They are anadromous and migrate in saltwater along coastal inshore environs and tidal tributaries. They are often found around piers, jetties, surf troughs, rips, flats, and rocks. A common regional name for stripers is "rockfish," and indeed their scientific name, *saxatilis,* means "rock dweller," although they do not necessarily

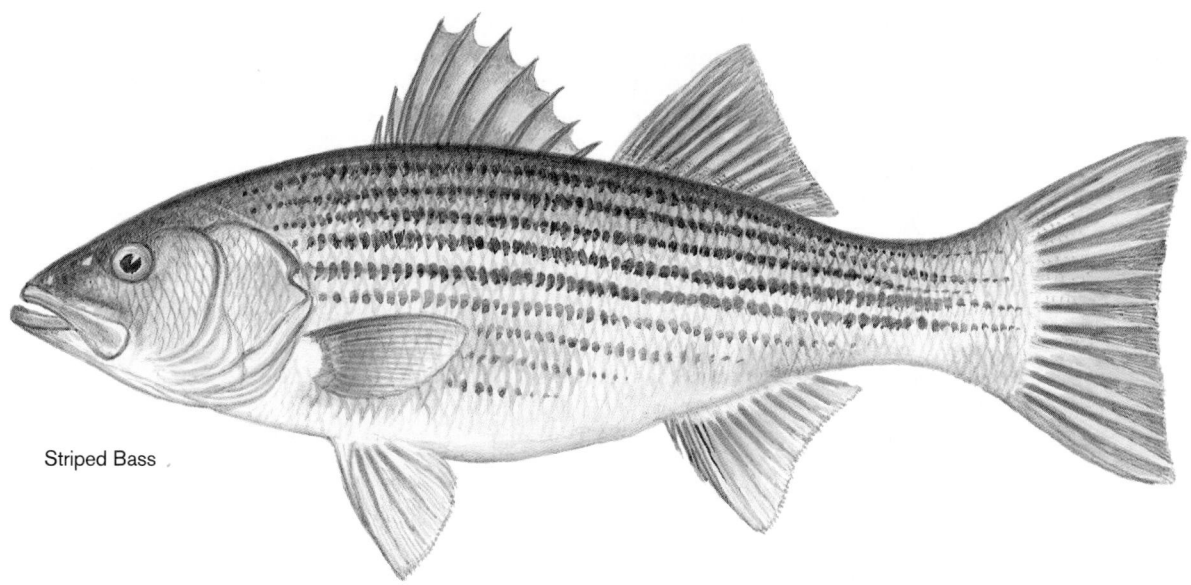

Striped Bass

spend most of their lives in association with rocks. They run far upstream during spawning runs and are also found in channels of medium to large rivers at that time. The striped bass is entirely a coastal species off the coast of the Carolinas and southward, never ranging more than a few miles offshore; along the entire Atlantic coast, they are rarely caught more than a short distance from shore except during migration.

Most striped bass along the Atlantic coast are involved in two types of migrations: an upriver spawning migration from late winter to early spring, and coastal migrations that are apparently not associated with spawning activity. Coastal migrations can be quite extensive; striped bass tagged in the Chesapeake Bay have been recaptured in the Bay of Fundy. Coastal migratory behavior appears to be limited to stocks north of Cape Hatteras and is related to sex and age.

Striped bass were introduced into freshwater lakes and impoundments with successful results. In some freshwater populations, striped bass were not introduced but landlocked, due to man-made barriers that blocked their return to the sea. In freshwater, stripers are commonly found in open-water environs, or in the tailrace below dams. They are seldom found near shore or docks or piers, except when chasing schools of baitfish.

Life history/Behavior.   Striped bass males are sexually mature by their second or third year, whereas females are sexually mature sometime between their eighth and ninth years; males measuring at least 7 inches, and females as small as 34 inches, are known to spawn. Spawning occurs in fresh or slightly brackish waters from mid-February in Florida to late June or July in Canada, and from mid-March to late July in California, when the water temperature is between 10° to 23°C; peak spawning activity is observed between 15° and 20°C. They prefer the mouths of freshwater

tributary streams, where the current is strong enough to keep the eggs suspended.

Females can carry 180,000 to 4.5 million eggs, depending on their size. When mating, each female is accompanied by several smaller males. The spawning fish swim near the surface of the water, turning on their side and rolling and splashing; this display is sometimes called a "rock fight." The semi-buoyant eggs are released and drift with the current until they hatch two to three days later, depending on the water temperature.

The young move downstream to the estuarine portions of rivers in the late summer or early fall. As young and as adults, striped bass move in schools, except for larger fish, which either travel alone or with a few others of similar size. Most striped bass along the Atlantic coast are involved in two types of migrations: an upriver spawning migration from late winter to early spring, and coastal migrations that are apparently not associated with spawning activity. Coastal migrations can be quite extensive; striped bass tagged in the Chesapeake Bay have been recaptured in the Bay of Fundy. Coastal migratory behavior in the Atlantic appears to be limited to stocks north of Cape Hatteras and is related to sex and age.

Food and feeding habits.   A voracious, carnivorous, and opportunistic predator, the striped bass feeds heavily on small fishes, including large quantities of herring, menhaden, flounder, alewives, silversides, eels, and smelt, as well as invertebrates such as worms, squid, and crabs. Young striped bass feed on zooplankton and quickly graduate to freshwater shrimp and midge larvae. Freshwater striped bass prefer shad, herring, minnows, amphipods, and mayflies. There has been controversy over the effect of freshwater stripers on other gamefish, most notably largemouth bass, but bass and other popular sportfish do not appear to be important components in the diet of freshwater stripers.

B

Feeding times vary, although many anglers believe that stripers are more active nocturnal feeders and that they are more effective at catching them in low-light conditions and after dark. Stripers are unlike some anadromous fish during their spawning run in that they will feed while migrating to their spawning grounds, although they reportedly cease feeding shortly before spawning.

Angling in saltwater. Striped bass are omnivorous feeders; in other words, they will eat almost anything in their environment that swims, crawls, wiggles, or slithers, and even some things that don't. They also have another unique feeding characteristic: They will usually feed on only one kind of food at a time when they are in an eating mood. Scientists still haven't determined how striped bass are able to communicate their menu of the day to other striped bass in a river or bay, but when they elect to feed on sandworms, they refuse such dependable baitfish as eels or bunker (menhaden) until the next dinner call. It's anyone's guess as to what will be on the new menu.

It is these two characteristics that often makes it difficult for both novice and experienced anglers to catch striped bass whenever they wish. But the feature that separates a pro from a novice is that he knows what striped bass like to eat and will begin trying all their favorite foods until he finds what they will take. In reality, it is not as difficult to determine what striped bass will feed on in saltwater because the choices can be narrowed down to three or four favorites.

Unlike other species of marine fishes that are most often caught using just one, two, or three fishing techniques, striped bass are caught by all the fishing tactics known to anglers. They can troll live baits, rigged baits, spoons, plugs, tube lures, and just plain hardware. Or they can use spinning, baitcasting, or conventional equipment to cast plugs and spoons, or live, rigged, or cut baits. These fish can be taken from an anchored boat by anglers using casting equipment or conventional equipment to fish on or near the bottom or at different levels in the water column, with or without chum attraction. They can be taken from boats drifting with the tide or pushed by the wind as anglers bounce bucktail jigs off the bottom, drag live eels or bunker near the bottom, or even use chunks of cut baits. Striped bass succumb to the fly rod, on streamers or artificial replicas of real baitfish, in every environment in which they swim.

Those environments are particularly varied in saltwater. Stripers linger off open beaches; in rips where tidal streams flow into bays or open water; off rock jetties or concrete walls; under docks, piers and bridges; or around pilings where baitfish naturally congregate. In other words, where there is something to be eaten, striped bass will at some time be there to feed upon it. The only time striped bass might be found in waters lacking food is when they migrate north in spring along outside beaches

to their summering grounds, in fall when they move south to their wintering grounds, or in early spring when en route to their spawning grounds. But even at these times, they often migrate when their foods are also on the move, so baitfish are never really far away.

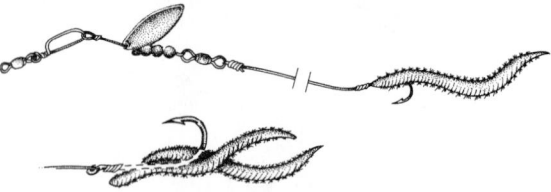

A shallow-water sandworm rig is productive in slow-trolling for stripers.

One of the most enjoyable ways to catch striped bass is from the beach. On the East Coast, surf casting for this fish has developed a devoted following, a highly social camaraderie of anglers who are in the suds both day and night. Long, one-piece rods are in order here, and plugs—either surface swimmers, poppers, or shallow divers—are the favorite enticements. The only drawback to surf casting is that too often the fish work surface waters just out of reach of an angler's longest cast.

The most effective way to fish for striped bass is from a boat, and another dedicated cadre of bass anglers takes bass only by plugging from a drifting boat. Many of these anglers work just outside the surf, and outside the range of surf casters, and plug toward the beach to pull bass from the surf.

The deadliest method for taking striped bass is by drifting live eels from a moving boat. Eels are the favorite food of striped bass, ahead of either bunker or mackerel. Here, the eels are hooked through both jaws and attached to a three-way rig. The hook is attached to a length of monofilament, which in turn is tied to one eye of a three-way swivel. The main line is attached to another of the swivel eyes. And the other eye sports a foot-long piece of lighter monofilament attached to a sinker. The sinker keeps the eel on the bottom; if it hangs up, the weaker leader breaks before the eel and hook are lost.

In many fishing ports, the favorite striped bass lure of charter boat skippers is the umbrella rig. This trolling setup does resemble the metal skeleton of an umbrella, and often four to six cross arms are used with small tube lures that contain hooks on the outer arms. The rig was designed to look like a small school of baitfish, and although it certainly fools the fish and can produce lots of them, many anglers scorn these rigs because they can snare more than one fish at a time and because the cumbersome umbrella rig must be used with very stout tackle.

Large single tube lures, often more than an inch in diameter and up to 18 inches long, are popular among trollers for trophy striped bass. These lures are mounted on leadheads that impart a swimming action to the lure, which is designed to duplicate a swimming eel. Because the tubes are so large, small fish are discouraged from striking them.

Fly fishing for striped bass in saltwater is not a new sport, as it has been practiced for more than a century. It has undergone a rapid expansion in the last decade, however. Historically, anglers who took their fly rods to saltwater looking for striped bass usually carried big, heavy, cumbersome tackle intended for salmon. The development of better rods from stronger materials, and the evolution of reels capable of handling 40- and 50-pound bass, have made fly fishing for striped bass in saltwater not only possible but efficient.

Flies have distinct advantages over plugs and baits when stripers are in shallow water. For example, it is otherwise impossible to avoid spooking a school of stripers when casting a plug into 2 to 3 feet of water along a clear, sandy beach at high noon. With a fly rod, the splash of a small streamer or other artificial is no more than that of a small spearing or silverside jumping out of the water to avoid a predator. This experience can be closely akin to bonefishing on tropical flats. When fishing in deep water, or when it is necessary to cover a lot of ground, however, anglers opt for other forms of fishing.

One of the hottest fishing techniques for striped bass, trolling with sandworms, is also one of the oldest. The lowly sandworm has made a great comeback as a striped-bass producer and the manner in which it is being fished—trolled as slowly as possible behind a small boat in shallow water—is one of the more pleasant ways to fish.

Although the sandworm is a natural bass food, over the years it has fallen from favor as a bass-producer, overtaken by a constant array of new plugs, spoons, tubes, and soft-plastic eels and worms that have flowed from the minds of innovative anglers. Although the new products work at times, they've clouded the picture for those new anglers and even old-timers who have abandoned marine worms.

Those who still favor the sandworm use the following productive technique: two or three long sandworms (the longer the better; see below) are skewered through their heads onto a hook and then trotted a hundred or so feet behind a boat, in shallow water close to shore. The ideal boat is a small aluminum or "tin" version pushed by about a 15-horsepower outboard. The aluminum craft easily bounces off whatever boulders it might strike, causing little or no damage. This low-horsepower motor is ideal because it can push the boat at a snail's pace but move out at a hurried dash when traveling to and from the fishing area.

Big, long worms are vital. Most sandworms bought at a bait station range from 6 to 12 inches. If you can convince the bait dealer to save his "bass worms,"—those on the longer side of the spectrum—for you, the better your chances of catching a big striper. Although the size of the worm is an important factor, the key to the rig's success is the terminal tackle that accompanies it. The proper rig first appeared in the angling literature in the early 1930s, when striped bass were making a reappearance in waters along the northeast coast of the U.S. after a hiatus of more than 50 years. Outboard engines were rare then, and a pair of oars and strong arms provided the power, pulling the rig slowly through the water.

A good shallow-water sandworm rig starts with a 5/0 or 6/0 hook, heavily dressed with either natural white or dyed red bucktail hairs. The worm is impaled on the hook, which is then tied to a 12- to 14-inch piece of 30-pound-test monofilament line. Ahead of the hook as an attractor is a Cape Cod spinner (a willowleaf-like blade), three or four 8-millimeter round red beads, then a size 6 hammered Colorado or Indiana spinner blade mounted on a size 4 folded clevis. Ahead of this clevis are three more red beads, then a size 5 blade of the same style, also on a clevis. To the end of the rig is added a 75-pound-test black barrel swivel. This terminal setup is connected via the barrel swivel to the main line by a snap swivel. A ³/₈-ounce in-line beaded lead drail is added 2 feet ahead of the rig on the main fishing line. To avoid twisting, which can occur with spinners, use the smallest available ball-bearing snap swivel, which is 60-pound test. When bluefish are mixed with schools of bass, substitute 30-pound-test black nylon-coated stranded (braided) wire leader for the monofilament.

Enthusiasts troll this rig along the beaches, working the shallows. It is most effective where large numbers of glacial boulders dot the shore, even at high tide. These are ideal places for striped bass to feed. The best time to fish such areas is during the last hour of the flood and throughout the ebb, or until you run out of water. The best winds are those that create a lee for your boat. Most of this kind of fishing occurs in 5 to 10 feet of water. With the worms well astern of the boat, engine noise doesn't seem to bother the fish. The biggest problem you'll encounter in catching striped bass by this method is locating exceptionally big sandworms.

Naturally, tides play a role in all striper fishing methods and locations. Many anglers hold fast to beliefs in specific tides, some preferring the ebb, others the flood. More than likely, however, there is no single best tide during which to fish for striped bass. Actually, it is the fish itself that determines which tide it prefers. Striped bass are drift feeders, preferring to lie in wait and let the tidal currents bring food to them rather than exert energy in searching for it. This is especially true of larger bass, fish exceeding 15 to 18 pounds, which are less prone to schooling than are smaller bass.

In certain places and at certain times, however, striped bass do show a preference for feeding on one or the other tide. When an ebbing tide drains a bay, tidal estuary, or river, emptying water from the area,

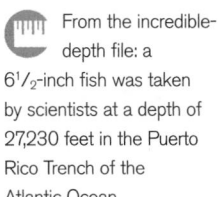

From the incredible-depth file: a 6¹/₂-inch fish was taken by scientists at a depth of 27,230 feet in the Puerto Rico Trench of the Atlantic Ocean.

B

baitfish become wary of being stranded. They therefore exit with the flow of the ebb. So, if any one state of the tide is in fact better, it is most likely the ebb. As a result, many anglers who consistently catch bass will begin fishing during the last hour of the flood and then fish through the first two to three hours of the ebb.

Striped bass feed most often when the ambient water temperature is to their liking, that is, between 57° and 68°F. When it is colder, they become lethargic and don't feed for days, remaining in a semidormant state. In summer, when water temperatures rise above 70°F, striped bass stop feeding and search out cooler waters. Water temperatures that exceed 70°F for anything but a short period are lethal to striped bass. Because of these temperature preferences, the best seasons for catching striped bass are in late spring and mid- to late fall along the Atlantic coast.

Spring feeding is spurred by a return to an active life after the winter hiatus. Spawning also occurs at this time, but unlike most fish species, striped bass do not quit feeding during their spawning run, except for a day or two while the act takes place. In fall, striped bass feed with a renewed frenzy after the August doldrums. Striped bass along the northeast coast of the U.S., anticipating the long migration ahead, feed ravenously to prepare for the southward journey that may require long passages through areas where baitfish can be difficult to find.

To most bass anglers along the northeast coast of the U.S., the two best periods to catch striped bass are during and around the months of June and October. Farther south, the better periods are April and May, then November. On the Pacific coast, because the relatively narrow continental shelf and deep, cold water are always near, the best months are July and August. Along the Gulf of Mexico coast, the winter months offer the best fishing.

Angling in freshwater.   Stripers are predominantly nomads in freshwater, so locating these fish is sometimes a more formidable task than catching them. They are vigorous predators, however, just as in saltwater, and their habitats are usually blessed with abundant forage populations, primarily gizzard and threadfin shad. Because they do a lot of eating, they are a good target for various angling techniques.

The methods of catching freshwater stripers include using live baits, jigging, casting, and trolling. Casting is done to schools of fish that are ravaging large pods of baitfish near the surface (observed by watching for bird activity), and to fish in the tailrace waters below a dam. Live baits are stillfished while the boat is at anchor or slowly adrift, using a fair amount of weight to keep the bait at the proper depth and immediately below the spot where you have positioned it. Cut bait, in the form of chunks or strips, is sometimes effective, but fresh, lively baitfish are usually preferred.

Jigging is primarily done when stripers are holding in deep water in a defined area, using $^1/_2$- to 2-ounce bucktail jigs and jigging spoons. Trolling may be practiced the most, either flatlining or downrigging, using plugs in a range of sizes and colors.

Long rods, in the $8^1/_2$- and 9-foot categories, are popular for casting, trolling, and bait fishing, especially if large fish might be encountered. Baitcasting reels with large line capacity, a solid drag, and a freespool clicker are popular. Most anglers prefer 17- or 20-pound line, although lighter line and other light tackle, including fly rods, are used in appropriate circumstances.

Stripers migrate up tributaries (if they exist) in the spring to spawn, usually when the water temperature is around 55°F. Fishing on channel bends is popular during the spring. After spawning, stripers scatter, migrating back to the lake and often following the path of channels and streambeds into deep water. They may locate over old creek beds and channels, near sunken islands, along ridges with quick dropoffs, at the deep end of points, near bridges and adjacent causeways, and near any natural funneling point for baitfish. In the fall, they move into shallow, flat areas and chase schools of baitfish. In winter, they stay deep and favor many of the same places they prefer in summer, although they travel less.

For freshwater striper fishing it is generally important to have some type of sonar to find the places that attract stripers, to locate catchable fish, or to determine the depth at which stripers are located so you can place your lures or baits at the right level.

Because stripers wander a good deal and exist in open-water environs on lakes, many anglers spend a lot of time trolling, flatlining a diving plug or using assorted lures behind downrigger weights. When stripers are within 25 feet of the surface, most trollers flatline by tradition; plugs, spoons, flies, and jigs can be used for shallow fishing, but only plugs have merit from 10 to 25 feet, unless sinkers or weighted lines are used.

Fishing with live baits is also extremely popular, especially in the spring and fall. The primary baitfish used are gizzard and threadfin shad, herring, bluegills (where it is legal to do so), alewives, shiners, and assorted minnows. Which one is preferable depends on which species is present naturally and whether it is available. Live baits are stillfished while the boat is at anchor or slowly adrift. Depending on the depth to be fished, the size of the bait, and whether there is current or wind, you'll need from $1^1/_2$ to 4 ounces of lead in the form of a bead-chain weight to keep the bait at the proper depth and right below the spot where you have positioned it. The weight should be about 2 feet ahead of the bait. Use a 2/0 or 3/0 hook for small baitfish like threadfin shad, and 4/0 to 6/0 hooks for larger baits. Hook them through the top of the back so

A bucktail jig with soft trailer is a top striper lure.

anywhere, and the key to finding it is observation. The popular tactic is to race to the site of the commotion, glide to the outer edge of it, cut the motor, and cast into the melee with jigs, spoons, surface plugs, or flies, trying not to force the fish into the depths and trying not to lose which direction they're moving in.

B

BASS, SUNSHINE   *Morone saxatilis x Morone chrysops.*

Other names—whiterock bass, wiper, hybrid striped bass, hybrid striper, hybrid bass, striper.

A hybrid striped bass resulting from the breeding of a male pure-strain striped bass and a female white bass, and a term used primarily in Florida. See: Bass, Whiterock.

they can swim freely if they are large, or through the top of the nose if they are smaller (while using smaller hooks). Sometimes it is best to keep the weight just off the bottom, but when you already know where the stripers are, keep it slightly above the depth at which you've pinpointed them. Keeping baits fresh and lively is extremely important; this is difficult with alewives, herring, and threadfin shad. Circular livewells are used for those. Cut baits are also effective in some places.

Although casting lures for open-water stripers is seldom done, except when the fish are schooling, a fair amount of jigging takes place, usually once you have located stripers holding in deep water in a defined area, or when fishing submerged humps or mounds visited by feeding stripers. Metal and slab-sided jigging spoons are almost exclusively used for this, and both standard and speed jigging techniques are employed.

In many locales in the summer and fall, striped bass, hybrid stripers, and white bass chase and consume pods of baitfish (usually threadfin or gizzard shad) and roam over a wide area as they keep up with the baitfish and maraud them. Often this phenomenon is best observed in early and late daylight hours. With stripers it may happen

BASS, SUWANNEE   *Micropterus notius.*

The Suwannee bass is similar in bodily appearance to the smallmouth bass *(see: bass, smallmouth)* and in markings to the redeye bass *(see: bass, redeye),* except that it is generally brown overall, and the cheeks, breasts, and bellies of large males are bright turquoise. It, too, has a large mouth, with the upper jaw extending under the eye, and possesses a patch of teeth on the tongue, a spot at the base of the tail, and blotches on the sides. It is further identified by its 59 to 64 lateral scales, 16 pectoral fin rays, 12 to 13 dorsal fin rays, and 10 to 11 anal fin rays.

Growing to just over 14 inches and weighing generally less than a pound, the Suwannee bass is a small species. The all-tackle world record is a 3-pound, 14-ounce fish taken in Florida in 1985. A member of the Centrarchidae family, it has the smallest range of any black bass *(see: bass, black),* occurring in North America, commonly in the Suwannee River drainage in Florida and less commonly in the Ochlockonee River drainage in northern Florida and Georgia. Limited range and small size make this species of minor angling interest, but it is an aggressive species found in rocky riffles, runs, and pools and is typically caught around rocky structure and along steep banks.

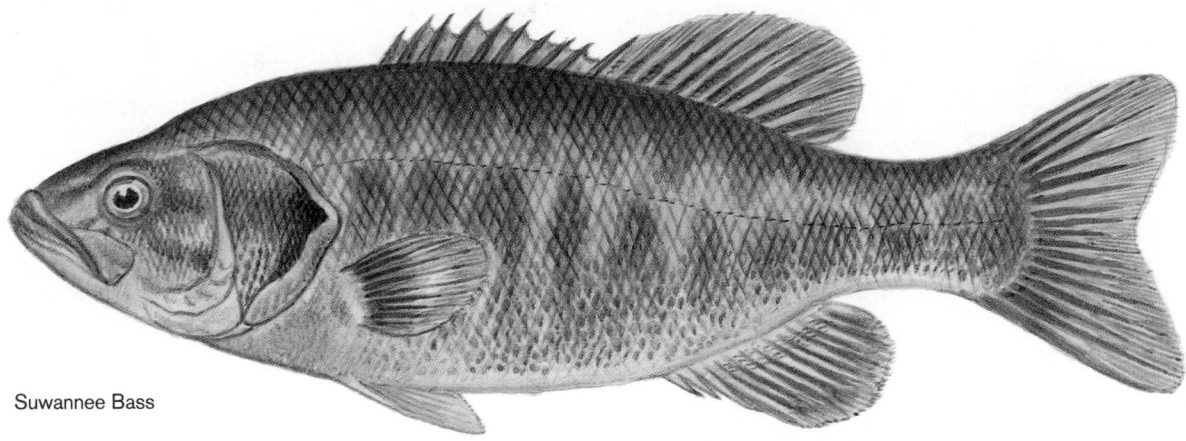

Suwannee Bass

B

BASS, WHITE   *Morone chrysops.*

Other names—white lightning, barfish, striped bass, silver bass, striper, stripe, sandbass, and sandy; French: *Bar blanc.*

A member of the temperate bass family, the white bass is a freshwater fish known for its spunky fighting ability and its prolificacy, as well as its merits as an excellent eating fish. White bass are a popular, important gamefish in many regions of North America, particularly south of the Mason-Dixon line and in large river systems. Because of its small size, it is often considered as a panfish *(see)*. White bass usually travel in schools and can provide a lot of action, making them highly desirable among light-tackle enthusiasts and for fishing with family and youths. Generous bag limits and fine-tasting flesh encourage large take-home catches where the fish are abundant.

Identification.   The white bass has a moderately deep and compressed body which is raised behind the small head and large mouth, deepest between the two dorsal fins. It also has 11 to 13 rays on the anal fin and one to two patches of teeth at the back of the tongue. The coloration is mostly silvery with a dark grayish green on the back, and anywhere from 4 to 10 dark horizontal stripes running along the sides. It also has a yellow eye, clear to dusky dorsal and caudal fins, and clear to white pectoral and pelvic fins.

White bass are sometimes confused with other members of the temperate bass family. It resembles the striped bass *(M. saxatilis)* by possessing the same silver sides and black stripes; it is shorter, though, than the striped bass and has a smaller head, a deeper body, a humped back, and dorsal fins that are closer together. White bass are also similar in appearance to yellow bass *(M. mississippiensis)* but are more silvery in color and have unbroken stripes

as well as a projecting lower jaw (in yellow bass, the jaws are about even); the white bass has separate spiny and soft portions of the dorsal fins, whereas those of the yellow bass are joined at the base. These two species sometimes occur in the same waters and are similarly colored.

The white bass also thrives in some waters inhabited by white perch *(M. americana)*, particularly in the Great Lakes and tributaries. Due to similar size and coloration, these fish are often confused, although these species are members of different families. The white bass can be distinguished from the white perch by the lack of distinct stripes on the sides of the body of the white perch, although stripes are occasionally found on the young of that species. Closer examination reveals other distinguishing characteristics, especially with regard to fins, as noted in the accompanying illustration.

Size/Age.   White bass average between $1/2$ pound and 2 pounds but may weigh as much as 3 to 4 pounds; the all-tackle world-record white bass is 6 pounds, 13 ounces. They can grow up to $17^3/4$ inches long, averaging 10 to 12 inches, and can live at least 10 years, but few make it past age 4. Females grow faster and probably live longer than males. Cold water and a lack of shad in the north, and warm water and abundant gizzard and threadfin shad populations in the south, account for regional growth differences.

Distribution.   White bass have a wide distribution extending throughout river systems in the Mississippi Valley (including Texas, northwest Florida, and Louisiana), the Ohio Valley, and the Great Lakes. Native in the east from the St. Lawrence River, in the north from Lake Winnipeg, and in the west from the Río Grande, white bass are found from Canada to the Gulf of

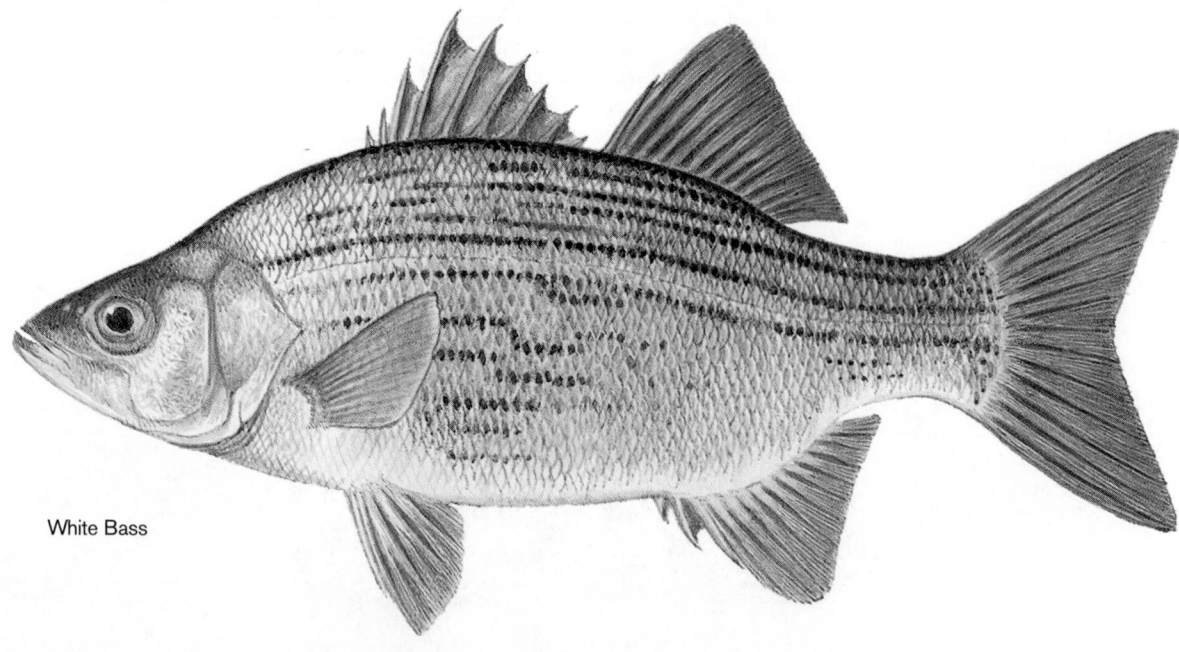

White Bass

Mexico. They have been stocked within and outside their natural range and transplanted into various states, including California.

Habitat.   The white bass is most abundant in clear, cool lakes, reservoirs, ponds, and pools of small to large rivers. White bass prefer lakes exceeding 300 acres and with considerable stretches of water at least 10 feet deep.

Life history/Behavior.   White bass are potadromous, which means they migrate within freshwater rivers to spawn, specifically 40 miles or less. Two-year-old sexually mature males reach the spawning grounds about a month before the females, moving into the same spawning grounds every year; they arrive sometime between February and June, depending on when the water temperature rises above 45°F. As with the striped bass, several white bass males gather around a female in 6 to 7 feet of water and push her to the surface, where she releases between 62,000 and 1 million eggs that are quickly fertilized. Settling on rocks and vegetation in shallow water, the tiny, adhesive eggs hatch in 45 hours at 60°F. The adult fish do not protect the eggs or the young, and as a result, very few fish survive their first year. Adults move to deeper water once they have spawned, where they swim in compact schools, often close to the surface. By the end of their first summer, young white bass have grown rapidly to reach 4 to 5 inches in length, and then they follow the adults into open water.

Food and feeding habits.   White bass feed on shad, silversides, crustaceans, yellow perch, sunfish, insects, crayfish, and their own young. Although they stay mostly in deep waters, they usually come to the surface to feed on schools of small shad or other minnows and often make a great commotion that is noted by observant anglers; this normally occurs early or late in the day, or on overcast days.

Angling.   Because white bass are a schooling fish, it is common to catch quite a few in one location. This ample action is one of the things that makes these small fish a popular species. This can be a misleading phenomenon, however, as white bass are often very fickle. Even when they are abundant in large schools, they may not be aggressive.

Light tackle is highly suitable for these fish, which are aggressive, tugging fighters. Spinning or spincasting rods loaded with 4- to 8-pound line are ideal, although a fly rod can be used at times as well.

White bass feed primarily on small shad, smelt, alewives, or minnows. Lures that correspond to the size and likeness of these baitfish are best. This includes small crankbaits, bucktail or marabou jigs, silver jigging spoons, spinners, sinking lures, and tailspinners, but also small stickbaits and buzzbaits. Some anglers troll for these fish, and in northern environs where anglers use plugs off planer boards for walleye, they accidentally catch a slew of white bass. Jigging, casting, and live baits account for the most success, however.

White bass from Norfolk Lake, Arkansas.

In the spring, white bass run up tributaries to spawn and provide a lot of action. Spring white bass runs are renowned on many large lakes and river systems, and this movement seems to generally take place once the water temperature in the tributaries exceeds 55°F. Late in the summer and into fall, anglers enjoy exciting angling for schools of white bass that feed near the surface on shad. There are many fish in such schools, and they are literally frenzied while tearing into the baitfish. Many boats follow these schools and enjoy fast jump fishing, similar to that experienced for striped bass. Often when one is hooked, another, or others, will follow along as it is played in, and angling companions can catch the followers. In the fall shallow, windblown, gravelly points are also a prime white bass locale. In rivers, look to those areas where streams enter, where bridge pilings disrupt current flow, above wing dams, along riprap, downstream from lock-and-dam structures, and on rocky points.

Because white bass are on the move so much, an angler who relies on one spot may be disappointed. In lakes and reservoirs, it is wise to pick out a dozen or so areas where white bass have been caught before and return to each one when you are pursuing these fish specifically (many anglers catch whites while fishing for other species, such as largemouth bass or stripers). At other times, look for riprap on shorelines, rocky points, reefs off islands, old river channels, sandbars, sudden dropoffs, and stony flats where the depths hold constant at a level between 10 and 16 feet.

White, yellow, or chartreuse marabou jigs are favored among casters, who usually swim them just off the bottom. Crankbaits can also be good for fish suspended in open water, however, especially if they are near humps. Some anglers use a small minnow for baitfishing, often with a popping cork ahead of it to make a surface commotion via twitching; the cork gets a fish's attention, and the nervous minnow several feet below draws the strike.

For surface lure action a small propellered floating plug twitched like a wounded baitfish is favored, especially when white bass are schooled and chasing small baits. Virtually overlooked, however, is the effectiveness of a $^1/_8$-ounce white or chartreuse buzzbait with a plastic blade; this is a killer off rocky points in the fall. Windblown points and adjacent shorelines are the best spots then, as they often have schools of baitfish, which in turn attract the whites.

Anglers should remember that except for the spawning period, white bass in a reservoir or river are constantly on the move. They often seem to prefer deep, open water but venture near the surface when vigorously pursuing baitfish. A school of white bass may slash into minnows or shad one minute, then vanish, traveling anywhere from a hundred yards to a mile before reappearing, in the process of plundering baitfish again. They may not reappear at all, or they may resurface out of sight.

This tendency leads to jump fishing, which is the activity that most white bass anglers, especially in big lakes and reservoirs, associate with this species. In those waters, anglers watch the horizon for circling, feeding sea gulls, which are attracted to surface-busting white bass because they often get an opportunity to snatch baits or pieces of fish from the melee. When you spot working birds, rush toward them, throttle the motor back upwind, shut the motor off, and drift to the school of surfacing fish, casting surface or shallow-running lures in their midst. This can go on for hours under the best of circumstances, although most schooling/feeding eruptions last only a few minutes, followed by a period of inactivity, and then a recurrence of action.

Jump fishing action is often a late-in-the-day or early-morning proposition, especially in late summer and in the fall. This activity can occur with striped bass or hybrid stripers, and occasionally the species will mix. When a striper takes, it becomes apparent very quickly, as they are usually larger and peel more line off the reel.

See: **Jump Fishing.**

BASS, WHITEROCK   *Morone saxatilis x Morone chrysops.*

Hybrid striped bass have become one of the most popular introduced fish in freshwater. Hybrid stripers are the progeny of one pure-strain striped bass parent and one pure-strain white bass parent. When the cross is between the female striper and

Hybrid Striped Bass

the male white bass, the result is primarily known as a whiterock bass; in some places it is referred to as a wiper, and in some simply as a hybrid striped bass. When the cross is between the male striper and the female white bass, it is called a sunshine bass (primarily in Florida), or simply a hybrid striped bass.

These fish, which usually look like stockier versions of pure-strain stripers, are an aggressive and hard-fighting fish that provide great sport. The fact that they are so strong and grow fairly large rather quickly endears them to anglers, not to mention that they can be a more ambitious lure and bait consumer than pure stripers.

Hybrid stripers do not occur in saltwater; they are strictly a freshwater phenomenon. In freshwater, whiterock or sunshine bass may crossbreed naturally in the wild, although this is not the norm. Most hybrid stripers existing in freshwater lakes and rivers are the result of state fish-stocking programs.

The first stocking of hybrid stripers was in Tennessee's Cherokee Lake in 1965, and they have since been widely distributed by fisheries managers, not only to provide additional angling opportunity but also to take advantage of abundant baitfish populations. In southern states this is essentially threadfin and gizzard shad, and in northern states it may include alewives as well as shad. In many waters these hybrids fill an ecological niche. They do not relate to nearshore structure, as so many popular warmwater gamefish do, and because they forage in open water for nomadic baitfish, they can help keep predator-prey balances in check, especially in waters where the balance of the biomass is composed of nonsport forage fish. Additionally, hybrid stripers, when they achieve certain sizes, are also a predator for large baitfish, particularly gizzard shad, which would be underutilized by other species.

Although very popular with the general angling public, whiterock and sunshine bass have been criticized by ardent largemouth bass anglers who fear that competition for forage or possible consumption by the more aggressive striper will adversely impact the universally appealing largemouth bass. This has not proven to be the case, however; hybrid striped bass (as well as their parents) tend to roam open water for bait schools and stay away from shallow cover, so they do not threaten largemouth populations.

Like both of its parents, the whiterock or sunshine bass is good table fare, and its flesh is virtually indistinguishable from that of the parent fish.

Identification.   This fish looks like a stockier version of striped bass, usually having a shorter length and greater girth, but with very similar coloration. The primary means of distinguishing the whiterock or sunshine bass is by the less-distinct and interrupted or broken lines along its sides. The lateral lines of the parent fish are unbroken. Hybrid stripers (and pure-strain stripers) can be distinguished from white bass by the tooth patterns on their tongues. The white bass has a single broad U-pattern while the striper has two distinctive elongated tooth patches.

The accompanying illustration shows the distinguishing characteristics. It is important to learn the differences between these fish when angling in waters that may contain all three species, as regulations regarding them may differ.

Size/Age.   Whiterock and sunshine bass have an extremely fast growth rate in their early stages. Specimens that have been stocked as inch-long fish have grown to 4 inches in just one month, and 15 inches by their second summer, so they quickly attain sizes of angling interest. When 18 inches long, a hybrid striper will weigh at least 3 pounds and possibly as much as 5 pounds.

Their maximum attainable size is uncertain, although they grow much larger than a white bass and are much smaller than a pure-strain striped bass. The all-tackle world-record hybrid striped bass is a 25-pound, 15-ounce Alabama fish.

Distribution.   Hybrid striped bass distribution is limited to freshwater and to places with a good population of baitfish, principally members of the herring family. Nevertheless, stocking programs have resulted in plantings of these fish in lakes and reservoirs in more than 30 states, from California to New York and from Nebraska to Florida. The greatest concentration is throughout the southern half of the country, and the most fishing opportunity is in the southeast.

Habitat.   Whiterock and sunshine bass inhabit the same freshwater habitats as their parents, primarily large lakes and reservoirs, but they also thrive in midsize to large rivers and occasionally in small lakes or ponds. They are largely nomadic in those environments and are found in the same places as their parents, sometimes commingling with them, mostly in open-water environs or in the tailrace below dams. They are seldom found near shore or docks or piers, except when chasing schools of baitfish.

Life history/Behavior.   These elements are essentially the same as for the parent species, including spring spawning runs, open-water migrations, schooling, and baitfish-pillaging tendencies. One difference with whiterock and sunshine bass is that when planted in lakes with no other related species with which to interbreed, they can be controlled entirely through stocking programs. Unlike many hybrid fish, which are sterile, these specimens are fertile fish, but they can reproduce only if they cross with a pure-strain parent. But in lakes where neither pure-strain stripers nor white bass are present (usually in northern states), fisheries managers have stocked hybrid striped bass with the comfort of knowing that the fish wouldn't expand beyond the numbers stocked. Thus, if the fish proved detrimental to baitfish or other game species, they could be eradicated by discontinuing stocking.

Food and feeding habits.   The food preferences and feeding habits of these fish are similar to those of freshwater striped bass and white bass.

Angling.   Prodigious eating habits can mean that hybrids are vulnerable to angling, especially if stocked in sizable numbers. This is good news to anglers but does not guarantee success.

In general terms, the methods of fishing for whiterock and sunshine bass are akin to those for striped bass and for white bass. However, these fish often exist where there are no pure-strain striped bass, and sometimes in places where there are no white bass; thus, anglers may be unfamiliar with the other species.

The most popular season for whiterock and sunshine bass fishing is in the spring, although good success is possible in all seasons if one spends a lot of time on the water and can track the movements of these fish. In spring, hybrids attempt to spawn in tributaries when the water temperature reaches the mid- to upper 50s. They usually are right on the heels of white bass, and just before pure-strain stripers, although in many of the lakes where hybrids are stocked, one or both of the parents do not exist.

A hybrid striper from Boone Lake, Tennessee.

B

Hybrids travel in schools. When located, it's often possible to catch more than one or two. The most exciting fishing for them is the frenzied jump fishing that occurs early and late in the day from late summer through fall, when hybrids locate a school of baitfish, pin them against the bank, a sandbar, or the surface of the water and rip into them.

When jump fishing, casting with assorted lures (spoon, spinner, fly, jig, surface lure, and the like) is obviously effective. If surfacing schools are not apparent, trolling becomes the preferred method, both as a means of fishing and in order to locate the fish. Trollers will jig vertically for them once located, or in areas they are likely to visit.

Whiterock and sunshine bass are primarily sight feeders. Lures that work well for them are those that imitate small baitfish, especially if they have white, silver, chrome, and clear or translucent finishes. Live baits, of course, are also effective, particularly herring and threadfin shad.

Places to locate whiterock and sunshine bass include gravel and sandy bars, points, tailrace runs below dams, spillways, the mouths of rivers and creeks, between submerged or visible islands, along dropoffs, and above humps or levees. They are often found above humps, ledges, and points in the summer; and, in some really warm waters, hybrids will gather at roughly 20 to 22 feet—around the thermocline.

Hybrids congregate in the tailrace water below dams which provides shore and boat fishing opportunities. Near the dams, most action occurs on the side of the river that is opposite the locks, and low-light hours are prime.

See: Bass, Striped; Bass, White.

BASS, WIPER   *Morone saxatilis x Morone chrysops.*
See: Bass, Whiterock.

BASS, YELLOW   *Morone mississippiensis.*
Other names—barfish, brassy bass, stripe, striped bass, streaker, yellowjack, jack, streaks, gold bass.

A popular light-tackle quarry and usually lumped into the category of panfish *(see),* the yellow bass is a scrappy fighter and provides good sport on light tackle. With white, flaky flesh, it is also a good food fish, on a par with or exceeding white bass and compared by some to the yellow perch.

Many anglers are unfamiliar with this member of the temperate bass family because it is largely restricted to the middle portion of the United States and is smaller than its relatives; a true bass, the yellow is related to striped bass, white bass, and white perch. Those fishing with larger lures and baits for largemouth bass or stripers are likely to encounter only the occasional, and larger, yellow bass specimen, although they can be caught with great frequency where they are abundant and by anglers using light tackle.

Identification.   The body shape of the yellow bass is very similar to that of the white bass: moderately long and stocky, with the deepest part between dorsal fins, as opposed to round and compressed. It has a small head, a large mouth, and connected dorsal fins. Its coloration is a brassy, silvery, or bright yellow, sometimes with a grayish olive on the back, and it has clear to blue gray fins that are particularly blue when the fish is in water. Five to eight distinctively dark horizontal stripes line the sides, and the lower stripes may be irregularly interrupted and offset above the anal fin; these markings are different on either side of the fish.

The yellow bass can be distinguished from the white bass by its golden coloring and broken stripes. Also, the second spine of the anal fin is longer and thicker than the third on the yellow bass; in the white bass it is noticeably shorter. The yellow bass has even jaws, whereas the white bass has a projecting lower jaw.

Size/Age.   Yellow bass are smaller than the largest bluegills, and the usual size caught by anglers ranges from 4 to 12 ounces. They can grow to 2 pounds and 18 inches, although few are seen over a pound; the all-tackle world record is a 2-pound, 4-ounce Indiana fish caught in 1977. These fish grow slowly after becoming juveniles and rarely achieve the size of white bass, perhaps because they are extremely prolific and often become stunted. In some places, their small size and bait-stealing tendency brands them a nuisance. They have a short life expectancy of about four years on average, and may live to age 7.

Distribution.   Yellow bass inhabit the Lake Michigan and Mississippi River basins from Minnesota, Wisconsin, and Michigan south to the Pearl River drainage in Louisiana, the Galveston Bay drainage in Texas, the lower Coosa and Mobile Bay drainages, east to western Indiana and eastern Tennessee, and west to western Iowa and eastern Oklahoma. Found mostly in the central Mississippi Valley area, they have been stocked only within their native range and transplanted to nearby states, and have been generally unsuccessful elsewhere. They are scattered within this range and vary in abundance from lake to lake.

Habitat.   Yellow bass thrive in quiet pools, ponds, backwaters of large streams, small to large

Yellow Bass

rivers, large lakes, clear to turbid waters below lakes, and reservoirs; they are somewhat tolerant of weedbeds, more so than white bass, and are fond of warm water.

Spawning.   Yellow bass spawn in the spring and move into tributary streams when the water temperature reaches the upper 50s. They spawn on shoals and abandon their nesting site without protecting the young.

Food and feeding habits.   Yellow bass feed on insects, minnows, small shad, and small sunfish. Insects and insect larvae constitute a good portion of their diet, especially in smaller sizes. Similar to white bass, they will maraud baitfish in schools, although with less of a tendency to do so on or near the surface. Yellow bass are more active in shallow and nearshore environs early and late in the day, and roam deeper open-water expanses during the day.

Angling.   Yellow bass are one of those species that are ignored in favor of largemouth bass, crappies, bluegills, and other popular fish, but they are as sporting and spunky on rod and reel as any of these other fish, even though they are smaller. In some waters they are very abundant, and can provide day-long light-tackle fun. They may even be a secondary quarry when other species fail to cooperate. In the spring, when they are in large schools, fast action is possible.

Like white bass and other panfish, yellow bass are caught on various lures, including small jigs, spinners, spinnerbaits, and spoons, as well as streamer and wet flies. Minnows and worms, usually fished on a float and near the lake bottom, whether drifting or anchored, are common. Some anglers locate schools of yellow bass by trolling or when fishing for other species, then stop and set up for more deliberate action. Light and especially ultralight tackle in the 2- to 6-pound-test range, is just right for these frisky fish, which typically fight stubbornly enough to convince an angler that a much larger specimen has been hooked.

BATFISH

Members of the Ogcocephalidae family, batfish are mostly small fish comprising nearly 60 similar species. These peculiar-looking fish are closely related to anglerfish and employ the energy-saving tactic of luring instead of hunting for their food. This method is valuable in deep-sea environments, where food is scarce and thinly distributed.

Identification.   The head and trunk of the batfish are broad and flattened, having either a disc or triangular shape, and its body is covered with broad spines. The long pectoral and rodlike pelvic fins enable batfish to "walk" on the sea bottom. There is a protuberance, the rostrum, on the front of the head between the eyes, which can be long or short. Under the rostrum hangs a small tentacle that acts like a lure. The mouth is small but capable

Shortnose Batfish

of opening broadly. Batfish are usually heavily armored by bony tubercles and hairlike cirri, with the exception of the gill opening on the pectoral fin. Coloration varies among individual species; for example, pancake batfish *(Halieutichthys aculeatus)* are yellowish with a net design, whereas polka-dot batfish *(Ogcocephalus radiatus)* are yellowy white with small black dots. Most are camouflaged according to their surroundings.

Batfish can be distinguished from goosefish and frogfish by the reduced fins on their head.

Size/Age.   Batfish can be between 2 and 20 inches long, but the average length is 7 inches.

Distribution.   Most common in the Gulf of Mexico and southern Florida, batfish inhabit waters from North Carolina to Brazil. They are also found in Jamaica. In warm Atlantic and Caribbean waters, it is most common to see the longnose batfish *(Ogcocephalus vespertilio),* which is often camouflaged in the sand by its warty, brownish body.

Habitat.   Most batfish are found along reefs, dwelling anywhere from the water's edge out as far as 1,500 feet. Some species prefer shallower water, but most batfish remain in deeper waters between 200 and 1,000 feet. Shallow-water species frequent clear water, mostly in rocky areas or around the bases of reefs; deep-water species prefer more open, muddy or clay bottoms.

Behavior.   Batfish partly hide by covering themselves in sand or mud during the day, and swim at night.

Food and feeding habits.   Mostly feeding on polychaete worms and crustaceans, batfish also eat other fish. Prey are attracted by the vibrations of the batfish's lure; if a smaller fish swims close enough, the batfish explodes from its hiding spot and engulfs the prey. Batfish reportedly produce scented secretions that entice prey with their odor. Batfish are capable of swallowing fish nearly as large as themselves by suddenly opening their mouth very wide, creating a suction effect.

Angling.   Batfish have no angling value, but anglers occasionally observe them in shallow waters, and, infrequently, they may catch one.

B

BATTERIES
See: Motor, Electric.

BAY
A bay is an extensive area of a large lake or the ocean that extends into the land, being enclosed on three sides. Bays are prominent for inshore fishing (see) in saltwater and also for varied fishing activities in freshwater, in part because of their generally shallow nature, often the presence of current, and the fact that some (especially in saltwater) are part of estuary (see) systems. In small lakes an area that would otherwise be classified as a bay may be called a cove.

BEACH BUGGY
A term for any four-wheel-drive vehicle used by surf anglers for accessing coastal beaches.
See: Surf Fishing.

BEAD HEAD
A term for an artificial fly weighted with a bead head.
See: Fly.

BEAM
The width of a boat at its widest point.

BEAR
To move or point in a given direction. In nautical terms, when a boat bears toward an object, it is heading directly toward that object.

BEARING
The direction or position of an object relative to one's own position, usually related in degrees or points of a compass, and sometimes in relation to the hour hand of an imaginary clock (the bow being 12 o'clock).

BELGIUM
Belgium is a small country of just 30,519 square kilometers, but it has a little diversity in its fisheries thanks to distinctive coastal plain, central plateau, and highland regions. It borders the Netherlands (Holland) and the North Sea on the north, Germany and Luxemburg on the east, and France on the south, and has numerous canals, rivers, and streams with sportfishing opportunities, although this seldom attracts visiting anglers except for match competitions. About half of the Belgian population speaks French, the other half Vlamish/Dutch.

The coast is a low-lying area with fine sandy beaches and slight inclination, with polders (sections of land reclaimed from the sea and protected by dikes), behind which is flat pasture land drained by canals. Various flatfish species, as well as eels and cod, are the primary interests here.

Inland, the central plateau is slightly more elevated and features wide fertile valleys and many waterways, most of which are slow and warm, and productive for coarse and warmer-water species. The Ardennes highlands, a densely wooded and generally rocky region in southeastern Belgium, has numerous peaks ranging between 300 and 700 meters, and is popular with hikers, canoeists, campers, and anglers. Trout, found in many rivers and tributaries, are the mainstay of this region.

Freshwater
The freshwater resources of Belgium can be generally characterized according to major river watersheds, which in a broad sense host coldwater species in their cooler and swifter upper flows, and warmwater species in their warmer and slower middle and lower reaches. Trout and grayling are the primary coldwater catch; perch, eels, carp, roach, bream, and other coarse species are the primary warmwater attractions.

Pollution has taken a high toll in many of the public waters of Belgium. The numbers of fish are down compared with the same types of waters in Holland, for instance, and the size of the fish often leaves much to be desired as well. Water quality is improving, however, although slowly. Zander and pike are still rare in the rivers and canals of Belgium; to find these species, Belgian anglers usually go to Holland.

The major Belgian rivers are the Schelde and the Meuse, which originate in France and are essentially navigable throughout Belgium. The Schelde is Belgium's principal waterway, and hosts the ports of Antwerp, Brussels, and Ghent. Its primary tributaries are the Lys, Dendre, Senne, Dyle, Gette, Demer, Great Nèthe, Small Nèthe, and Rupel Rivers.

The Schelde basin is situated entirely in the lower and middle regions of Belgium. The main river and its tributaries possess various coarse species, as well as perch, eels, and smelt, in the lower tidal section; but heavy traffic, pollution, and muddy water have hurt the fishing. Many canals connecting to the Schelde have been formed in lower Belgium, particularly in the areas of Flanders, Campine, and Brabant-Hainault.

The Meuse River basin in Belgium is a more important system for fisheries, and its highland tributaries are trout and grayling water, while its slower reaches are home to chub, perch, eels, carp, and various coarse species. Most of the rainfall in the Ardennes is transported to the Meuse, the remainder toward the Rhine River.

The Sambre and Ourthe Rivers are the principal tributaries of the Meuse, but others include the Ton, Semois, Viroin, Hermeton, Lesse, Lomme,

Bocq, Molignée, Hoyoux, Amblève, Vesdre, Berwinne, Geer, Vierre, and Rulle. The Semois, Ourthe, Lesse, Lomme, and Amblève rivers are familiar to many European trout anglers.

Early in the season, when the water is cold and running high, the rivers and creeks of the Ardennes are fished with worms and baitfish for brown trout. Later, wet flies, nymphs, and dry flies are cast over the same water.

There are a few catch-and-release stretches on these rivers, mainly on the Ourthe, but for the most part anglers are allowed to keep their catch, and many do so, enjoying cooking it over a campfire. Because of this, once the fishing season is a few months old, the better part of the trout population on large stretches of the aforementioned rivers has disappeared. Those that remain are wary and respond only to very small nymphs and dry flies, fished on very fine tippets. The better fishing is likely to be in the least accessible locations.

During the day the traffic from passing canoeists can be a problem, but in early morning and late evening anglers have the water to themselves. Brown trout are the major angling interest here, but European grayling and chub come to a well-presented fly just as readily. Wading is not allowed on these waters until June 1 each year, a measure imposed to protect the eggs deposited by trout and grayling.

The Meuse, Schelde, and many other rivers and canals in Belgium are frequented by coarse anglers. The long pole is still the number one tool of the trade; Belgium has a long and rich tradition of fishing with this method—the tip of the float antennae rests just barely over the water surface. Where allowed, bloodworms are the finest bait for local pole anglers, with maggots, casters, and worms following in productivity.

More than 150 years of organized coarse fishing events, and the last 30 years of practicing catch-and-release for these species, has resulted in educating Belgium's most sought-after coarse species—roach and bream. This has made ultra finesse a necessary element of catching these fish consistently.

Anglers, especially those in match fishing competitions, thus use small, specialized floats carefully balanced so that all bites are detected. This method, involving a take-apart (multisection) pole from 2 to 12 meters long, was developed on the Belgium/France border around the city of Roubaix, and became known throughout Europe as *roubaisienne*. Belgians have won numerous world-match fishing titles, making them one of the leading countries for this style of fishing.

Other noteworthy angling opportunities in Belgium deserve mention here. In southeast Belgium, trout and grayling frequent the headwaters of the Süre and Our Rivers, which flow to the Rhine, and black bass are reportedly present in the Semois River. Private ponds abound in Belgium. These small lakes, owned mostly by fishing clubs, are regularly stocked with bream and roach, and they host fishing matches nearly every weekend. These matches typically impose a restriction on the length of the rod and line, and the float should be capable of carrying the weight used on the line. Here, fine and concentrated fishing is necessary to gather a good catch.

Many small ponds, called reservoirs, in Belgium are stocked with rainbow trout; a water the size of a backyard swimming pool may be a designated trout fishery. This practice continues to exist because trout waters are in great demand in Belgium. As a result, Belgian reservoir fly anglers are among the best competition anglers in Europe. There are a few first-class trout reservoirs in Belgium, and these are managed by fly fishing clubs. Here, because at least part of the catch is usually released again, a fly angler should be able to handle all techniques.

Licenses and permits. Fishing licenses are a complicated matter in Belgium. The state sells regional fishing licenses, obtainable at post offices. To fish in the Flemish and French districts, plus the area around Brussels, an angler needs three different regional licenses. Each of these is also sold as a license to fish from the bank, from a boat, while wading, etc.

For nonnavigable waters, especially in the French region, an extra license from the owner of the water or the local fishing club is also necessary. On many small ponds, all that is necessary is a license from the owner or the fishing club that rules over the water; regional licenses are not required here.

There are closed season and special regulations for different species as well.

Saltwater

Saltwater fishing has been developing along the Belgian coast over the past few decades. It largely consists of fishing for various flatfish, but other species are present as well.

The Belgian coast is only 60 kilometers long and has few obstructions or islands, making it different in this respect from neighboring Netherlands. This coast is protected by immense breakwaters sunk deep into the sea, especially from Zeebruges to the Dutch border. Fishing along the breakwaters produces eels and sea perch, and cod through the winter. The fine sandy beaches of the coast are primarily places for catching plaice, sole, flounder, and turbot. European bass, mackerel, and garfish are also among the catch, these species taking lures as well as bait.

In the east, the Zwyn Gulf is noted for surf fishing, and produces rays and various flatfish from the beach. The breakwaters from Lekkerbeek to Knock-le-Zoute are known for sole, eels, cod, and ray.

West of there, Zeebruges Harbor produces a host of species, and is noted for conger eels. There is a 1.5-kilometer-long pier here that is extremely

In early America, much of the economy revolved around the exportation of salted fish; 1 bushel of salt was required to cure 100 pounds of fish.

B

popular with shore anglers, and produces conger eels among its rocky footings. Farther west, various flatfish and cod are caught at the pier and jetty at Blankenberghe. The east jetty at Ostend is popular for sole and eels, and the same species, as well as cod, are caught in the estuary environs of Newport.

Although there's a good deal of shore-based fishing along the Belgian coast, small seaworthy boats are seen more frequently of late and some boaters cross the British Channel on calm days and fish wrecks near the UK for cod, pollack, coalfish (pollock), whiting, conger eel, and ling. Larger party boats leave for a day's fishing for either mackerel (summer) or cod (colder months) from all larger harbors along the coast.

In general, cod are prevalent from September through March, eels from May through September, whiting from October through January, plaice from October through June, and sole from May through October. Flounder are available year-round.

BELIZE
Place-names like Orange Walk, Pulltrouser Swamp, Monkey River, and Double Head Cabbage may not sound like inviting fishing locales, but the country that contains such sites has a name that no one can positively explain either: Belize.

It is speculated that *Belize* is a derivation of the Mayan word *belix,* which means muddy river. Belize definitely has muddy waters among its plentiful creeks and flooded mangroves, but it also offers beautifully clear water out on the reefs and around its various islands and keys (islets known locally as *cays*). Muddy or clear, the water of Belize hosts almost as diverse a fish population as its jungle rain forest does birds.

That rain forest was part of the route of the Maya in pre-Columbian times, and it is virtually inconceivable that one hour from the Belize border, at Tikal in Guatemala, there was once a jungle community that was home to 55,000 people in the ninth century. One wonders what sort of fish they encountered.

The impact of the Mayan civilization can be seen even out on the water while fishing. Some of Belize's highly respected flats fishing takes place around a spit of land that should have been part of Mexico. Ambergris Cay was once connected to the mainland as a small peninsula on the Yucatan, but a thousand years ago the Maya built a canal there to circumvent the site's coral reef, making Ambergris an island and eventually part of what would become Belize.

Mexico's loss was Belize's gain because that location is one of many in this country that have earned Belize its sterling reputation for fine light-tackle angling for the fastest and toughest fish of inshore waters and shallow flats. This not only includes such obvious gamesters as bonefish, snook, tarpon, and permit, but also cubera snapper, jack crevalle, and mutton snapper.

One of the least-known freshwater sportfish is the sheefish, or inconnu; these members of the whitefish clan are found in Alaska, the Northwest Territories, and Siberia.

Belize is situated between Guatemala and Mexico's Yucatan Peninsula, along the western Caribbean. The shoreline is relatively undeveloped; flats and inshore fishing predominate along the coast, in and around river mouths, and in the creeks, inlets, bays, and other environs. Mangrove-covered keys, islands, and shores are plentiful. An outstanding coral reef, which attracts many divers, extends along the coast, and reefs exist offshore as well. The Turneffe Islands and Ambergris Cay are a short distance from the Belize coast, and the former comprises numerous keys within a barrier reef. Sharp dropoffs to extremely deep water exist close to the inshore and offshore reefs.

The Belize coast is predominantly mangrove-lined. There are many creeks, rivers, canals, and overgrown backwaters that provide great habitat for snook, small tarpon, and snapper. The Belize and Sibun Rivers, in central Belize and not far from Belize City, and their many tributaries and backwater lagoons and sloughs, were especially notable in the past, with snook up to 20 pounds and numerous small to midrange tarpon. Most fishing for these species, however, now takes places along the coastline and at various river mouths.

Snook up to 20 pounds and small tarpon are prominent here, and most are caught along the mangrove shores and in the creeks and canals and inlets rather than on the plentiful flats, although some larger tarpon—from 50 to 100 pounds—are found cruising the flats in front of the Belize River, usually in small schools. Sight fishing is possible here when the water is calm and clear, which is most likely from April through July and sometimes even through summer until early October (March is often very windy). The coastal shores provide excellent opportunity when bad weather or heavy winds make the reefs and flats impossible.

Bonefish are plentiful on the various flats along the coast and around the keys. They run small as a rule, with the average catch being a few pounds. Some weigh up to 6 pounds (although few larger), which is typical of this region as a whole. Numerous flats along the coast host these fish, as well as permit, which are often sighted daily and in large numbers; flats near Dangrigia, Placentia, and the Monkey River—all in the south—are especially good for permit. Permit have become more abundant throughout Belize, making it one of the best places to catch this species on light tackle or a fly rod. Some are taken to 25 pounds.

Some of the finest flats fishing in Belize is at the Turneffe Islands, offshore and about 20 miles east of Belize City. Here a grand slam—taking a bonefish, a tarpon, and a permit on a single day—is very possible, and wading and sight fishing for schools of bonefish are run-of-the-mill experiences in the right conditions. Here, too, the fish average several pounds, although anglers occasionally encounter much larger specimens.

The palm-studded Turneffe Islands lie within a barrier reef that extends more than 30 miles and include many mangrove-covered keys. The bonefishing, for which these islands are most noted, as well as the permit fishing generally occur on the eastern shore. Out at Lighthouse Reef, some 12 miles to the east, anglers enjoy bonefishing, with particularly good angling around Long Cay. The reef is more than 20 miles long and offers shallow fishing for other species as well.

There is an abundance of reef opportunity off the Belize coast, in fact. A string of coral reefs, flats, and atolls is just offshore and extends all along the coast; it is part of the world's second longest barrier reef (which extends northward along the Yucatan Peninsula as well). The usual flats fish are found here, too, along with barracuda, grouper, and snapper.

Out at Turneffe, on the southwestern side of these islands, the water spills from a reef to very deep water, and this edge is a great place for jigging or trolling. The usual reef dwellers live here, plus king mackerel and wahoo. Anglers who have devoted serious efforts to jigging the reefs have landed jack crevalle, amberjack, Nassau grouper, cubera snapper, and a host of other species. Between these and the various flats species, at least two dozen types of fish can be hooked. Wahoo are said to be extremely abundant in these offshore waters from November through March, and they provide reef trollers with plenty of action, sometimes with several dozen in a day. Wahoo up to 70 pounds have been taken here, but 20-pounders are the norm.

Offshore fishing for billfish is still relatively ignored, although when conditions are right, the areas around Turneffe and Ambergris Cay are worth exploring. Tarpon and bonefish are the most sought after species at Ambergris. Flats that hold tarpon are found a short run from the island, and this species can be sight-fished here year-round. Bonefish are plentiful, and run small for the most part; they can be caught by wading or fishing from a skiff. Permit are also available here, especially on the northern outside flats; jack crevalle and barracuda are common flats catches; and other opportunities wait inside the reefs.

Although there is only offshore trolling here, it makes sense that pelagic species would be present, given the proximity to deep water and the Cayman Trench. Anglers pursue sailfish, tuna, dolphin, wahoo, and king mackerel , mostly in April and May. White and blue marlin have been caught here in the past; these were generally small, yet some of the latter ranged to 400 pounds. The marlin arrive a little earlier than the sailfish. The minimal effort expended for these fish—when compared to the deference accorded light-tackle flats action—implies that less is known about offshore opportunities. On a few occasions, however, local boats have experienced spurts of blue marlin activity. Good offshore sites are in the remote waters and

atolls beyond the barrier reef, and around Glover Reef, Lighthouse Reef, and Turneffe Islands; the water around each of these drops off steeply.

Several lodges cater to anglers along northern Belize, with at least a pair at Turneffe and one at Ambergris. A lodge on the mainland not far from the airport runs a mother-ship operation that cruises the inner reef and keys and the coastline, towing fishing skiffs behind. There are also several fishing lodges in southern Belize, in the vicinity of Placentia. Good guiding services are also available.

BELL BUOY
An aid-to-navigation sound buoy with a bell that rings as the waves move it.
See: Buoys.

BELLY BOAT
A term for oval-shaped self-propelled float tubes.
See: Float Tubes.

BELT, FISHING
See: Rod Belt; Waders.

BENTHIC
The bottom layer of the marine environment and the fish or animals that live on or near the bottom.

BERLEY
Australian term for chum (see).

BERMUDA
Rising off the floor of the Atlantic is the remains of a volcanic pedestal, which gives rise to two underwater pinnacles and one shallower platform on which rests the group of about 150 islands collectively known as Bermuda. Situated solitarily in the North Atlantic—at 32° north, 64° west—and some 600 miles from Cape Hatteras, North Carolina, Bermuda comprises a total landmass of about 21 square miles, surrounded by reefs and shallows.

Best known for beautiful pink sandy beaches and crystal clear waters, Bermuda also offers plenty of angling opportunities for both the casual angler and the most dedicated record hunter.

The Gulf Stream to the west of Bermuda serves as an effective temperature buffer for cold fronts coming off the North American continent. This moderating effect is most pronounced in the winter months and ensures that water temperatures seldom drop below 62°F, making Bermuda the site of the northernmost coral reefs in the world.

Although mild, the winter months are unfortunately unreliable from an angler's standpoint; blustery conditions often prevail. From about mid-April through November, however, the same climatic system provides conditions favorable to those inclined toward piscatorial pursuits.

Devoid of freshwater, Bermuda nonetheless offers both variety and quality in its fishing. The shoreline, sandy beaches, flats, the reef platform and dropoff, and the open sea offer some of the most challenging action to had anywhere. Perhaps unexpectedly, given Bermuda's proximity to the coast of North America, such popular game species as bluefish and striped bass are absent. The reason for this is that well over 90 percent of Bermuda's marine fauna is derived from the Caribbean region, making the Bermuda experience more tropical than temperate.

Bermuda fishing is usually classified by shore, reef, and offshore opportunities, although there are areas of overlap and certainly many of the fish don't recognize any such artificial boundaries.

Shore Fishing

The shore-bound angler will find that docks and jetties offer a surprising variety of fishing opportunities. Gray snapper, Bermuda chub, small yellowtail snapper, several species of grunts, and bream (an endemic member of the porgy family) are all commonly encountered. This sort of fishing is often best pursued in darkness, particularly if the preferred quarry is the super-smart gray snapper, but there is action virtually all day long. In spring, night fishing produces sennet, a small member of the barracuda family, readily taking both bait and lures.

Casting artificial lures from the beaches will entice palometa, a tough member of the pompano family that seldom exceeds 4 pounds but more than makes up for its lack of size with sheer determination to avoid the landing net. Barracuda cruise these same gin-clear waters during the summer, and although they offer absolutely no danger to swimmers, they will take a variety of lures, including spoons and tube lures. Streamer flies can also be productive. Fishing the bottom off the beaches will

occasionally produce a bonefish, although bonefishing is of itself a bit of a specialty.

The sandy shallows and grassy areas harbor bonefish that are larger than in most places. The fish move inshore when the water warms up in April, and continue to be readily available well into October. Averaging better than 6 pounds, this species may be sought from shore, by wading through picturesque sandy coves, or from a boat on the grass flats farther offshore. Although their scarcity makes them seldom deliberately sought after, a few tarpon and the odd permit frequent waters favored by bonefish.

Spinning tackle with fresh bait or proven artificial lures has long been the preferred equipment for catching the gray ghost of the shallows in Bermuda, but more recently it has been demonstrated that a well-placed fly is also an effective tool. There are more than enough bonefish to ensure multiple opportunities for hookups. Best of all, the tendency toward catch-and-release means that many individuals of this relatively lightly fished species are significantly larger than average here, and there can be little doubt that some record candidates cruise Bermuda's shallows.

Reef Fishing

Leaving the coastline and moving offshore a few hundred yards provides the transition from shore fishing to reef fishing. The diversity of the reef environment makes for a number of different habitats, each of which offers its own particular type of fishing action.

In the shallower waters overlying muddier bottoms such as ship channels, the most commonly encountered species is the gray triggerfish (locally called turbot) and whitewater snapper (actually lane snapper). Although neither species attains more than a few pounds, both can occur in large schools, and it is not unusual to catch many of these after just a few hours of fishing.

Just about anywhere over the reef, anglers can expect action from Bermuda chub, a species of little food value but exceptionally game on light tackle—so much so that in years gone by lobster was used as the preferred bait. This species occurs inshore, but the largest schools are found in 12 to 20 fathoms of water.

Over coral areas, catches are likely to be far more varied, often including species that are more usually encountered in blue water. Chumming, which has been raised to a fine art form in Bermuda, will see false albacore rocketing through the slick at the surface, while amberjack, Almaco jack (locally "horse-eye bonita"), and yellowtail snapper can be lured off the bottom. The gwelly, a relatively poorly known species related to the jack family, is also common and is a powerful game fish well suited to light tackle. All of these species reach record proportions in Bermuda, and all are avidly sought game species.

The Bermuda surf is worth prospecting for an assortment of species.

Dropping a line down to the bottom will tempt some of the smaller grouper species such as the coney, red hind, or barber (Creole fish). Porgy, wrasse, snapper, and triggerfish are all likely candidates as well. There are also seven other grouper species, ranging from the brightly hued 1-pound mutton hamlet to the hundred-plus-pound black grouper (rockfish), which is all but unstoppable on anything other than the heaviest gear.

Night fishing over the reefs during the summer offers the best chance for a haul of gray snapper and, as the season progresses, yellowtail snapper are more than willing to please in a big way at night. Deeper fishing produces red snapper and misty grouper along with other obscure species.

For the most part, reef-fishing tackle is conventional gear in the 16- to 30-pound-test range, with anchovy, cut fish, or squid as bait, although many anglers prefer to use spinning gear. The latter is generally used for bait fishing, although most standard lures can be productive.

Offshore Fishing

The offshore fishing scene draws the most angling attention and supplies the real glamour. The opportunities range from top-flight light-tackle action to working the abyss in search of a record-class heavyweight blue marlin. As Bermuda is surrounded by the reef platform, it is necessary to travel past the so-called inner bottom out to the dropoff, where it quickly becomes apparent that the island is anchored out in the middle of the open ocean.

Fishing from the eastern end of the island means the shortest run to the "Bermuda Edge" (the colloquial name for the 30-fathom curve), and there is plenty of potential along both the northern and southern fringes of the reef platform. It is the western end, however, that offers access to the greatest variety of fishing grounds. These include the famed Challenger Bank, which is 15 miles southwest of the island, and Argus Bank, which is a farther 10 miles offshore.

A normal daylong excursion will include fishing the southwestern edge before moving off to one or both offshore banks. In recent years, the very deep water between the Bermuda Edge and the banks has been exceptionally productive for blue marlin.

Trolling is the main means of offshore fishing. Although trolling produces year-round, the best sporting action starts in late April and runs through early June, and then picks up again in late August and continues into October.

The tackle aboard most charter boats tends to be 50-pound class or heavier, but, with few exceptions, lighter gear in the 20- or 30-pound classes is better suited to most Bermuda game fish. Virtually all local angling tournaments are restricted to line classes ranging from 8- through 30-pound-test, and most of the world records set in Bermuda waters have been on the lighter line classes. Opportunities

for the ultralight line classes are plentiful as well—for those who are proficient enough.

Standard trolling baits are in common use, with garfish (ballyhoo) and flying fish the preferred naturals, whether used in combination with a skirt or other artificial. It is not unusual for a troller's spread to include artificials on the outriggers, and bait combinations on the downriggers.

Downriggers are an essential part of Bermuda fishing. It has been determined that speed is the key to catching fish in blue water, and it has the added advantage of allowing anglers to cover 100 or more miles of water during the course of the fishing day.

The wahoo is the most sought-after blue-water gamefish in Bermuda, and there can be no doubt that Bermuda is a premier destination for anglers seeking this particular challenge. With their lightning strike, high speed, and often erratic runs, these sleek, handsome fish are particularly challenging when an angler is trolling with light tackle.

The wahoo's speed, keen vision, and razor-sharp powerful jaws often enable it to cut off baits without giving any indication that they have done so. For this reason, trolling speeds in Bermuda are considerably faster than in most other places, even when rigged baits are being fished exclusively. Although wahoo are present year-round, the largest fish (to well over 100 pounds) tend to be caught outside the summer months, when schoolies in the 12- to 25-pound bracket are most common.

There is a minor run in the late spring/early summer and a major autumnal run that gets underway in late August or early September. This latter run often coincides with an influx of juvenile false albacore, which makes for some of the fastest, finest live-baiting to be had anywhere.

Trolling also catches yellowfin tuna, locally referred to as "Allison tuna." These never-give-up battlers range from just a few pounds to 200 pounds or more. Large tuna tend to be caught early and late in the season, with the middleweights dominating from June through early August. There are, however, plenty of exceptions to this rule.

Blackfin tuna, another very worthy opponent, commonly take trolled offerings, while barracuda, dolphin, false albacore, rainbow runner, and oceanic bonito (skipjack) are all likely to help round out a mixed bag from a day's trolling.

As the height of the summer approaches, attention shifts from trolling and focuses on chumming on the banks, or right on the dropoff at anywhere from 30 to 90 fathoms. During extremely calm weather, drifting is also an option; but either way, plenty of fast action can be expected. This is an extremely effective means of fishing and, although the primary target is yellowfin tuna, the chum slick can rustle up everything from an ocean robin (a live bait par excellence) to a blue marlin.

The chum can consist of anchovies, hogmouth fry, or other small baitfish that are ladled overboard with great precision. The action often starts almost immediately with false albacore and brightly hued rainbow runners flitting in and out. It has been recently discovered that blue marlin is the ultimate chum bait, with the tuna going berserk when diced chunks are tossed overboard. With the clarity of the water and this method of fishing, it is actually possible to select an individual fish to which to toss the bait and, if the bait is marlin, there is little doubt that the fish will inhale it. However, locals do not encourage killing marlin for bait.

Chumming is often combined with kite fishing using either dead, rigged flyingfish—which are especially effective on tuna—or live baits, usually robins or false albacore.

The school-size yellowfin tuna generally range from 20 to 60 pounds, although considerably larger fish have been taken while chumming. These fish offer optimum sport on light tackle, with 8- and 12-pound lines the choice of local anglers. This method of fishing also lends itself to the use of both spinning and fly tackle, with the tuna readily taking both flies and an assortment of artificial lures.

The blackfin tuna's fighting spirit more than makes up for its lack of size when compared to the yellowfin. Many a record blackfin tuna has been caught in Bermuda, and even an average fish in the 15- to 18-pound range gives an exceedingly good account of itself.

Catches of tuna are often exceptional, and there is an increasing tendency to tag and release fish. As a result of this conservation effort, it should be noted that tuna are sometimes recaptured here within days of having been released.

Most other blue-water species will invade a chum line. Wahoo commonly take up residence, and barracuda can become positive nuisances, often attacking smaller fish that are hooked. Dolphin, skipjack tuna, and even billfish have been drawn to within a few feet of the transom of a chumming boat, thereby providing the added excitement of a visual thrill prior to the hookup.

Working the waters nearer the bottom while chumming will not only produce a selection of fish similar to those found over the deeper coral reefs, but also invite the attention of large amberjack (to well over 100 pounds) and Almaco jack. Despite the latter's slightly smaller size, both these species offer a great challenge on suitable tackle.

The remnants of an offshore rig remain submerged on Argus Bank, and this wrecklike structure is a veritable fish bowl. Large barracuda and a tremendous variety of jack species can be lured to the surface in such numbers that the water actually becomes discolored—a splendid opportunity for fast action.

Although not highly regarded as gamefish by most local anglers, sharks provide plenty of sport. Commencing over the reef areas and extending out to the offshore banks, various shark species offer sporting action. The most common species is the Galapagos shark (closely related to the dusky), but tigers are numerous; the pelagic sharks thrive in good numbers out toward deeper water. Blue sharks are abundant but not sought after, and large hammerhead sharks are commonly encountered. During the early summer, mako sharks occasionally attack hooked wahoo and tuna, and each year sees a few makos brought to gaff. These range from fish less than 100 pounds to the full-size versions weighing in at 800 pounds or more.

White marlin are never truly abundant, although they occur pretty much year-round. They are most often raised during the early summer, when trolling is the preferred fishing method. In May or June there is frequently a period of two weeks or so when they are relatively common, before giving way to the prevalence of blue marlin.

The exception to light-tackle fishing in Bermuda is the blue marlin. Bermuda blues run big and, although seasonally available, the action is top class. Peak season for blues is from about mid-May through September. There seems to be a rough pattern to the blue marlin. Early-season fish tend to be females. Smaller fish, probably mostly males, predominate later in the season, when numbers also seem to be greater.

It is not unusual to raise several fish in a day, and as many as seven blue marlin have been caught in a single day. The average size of the fish is close to 300 pounds and, in recent years, the use of 130-pound tackle has revealed that granders are very real possibilities. Indeed, quite a few have been caught; the Island record is more than 1,300 pounds, with reports of huge fish every season.

It is noteworthy that, with few exceptions, most marlin are released, and there is heavy emphasis on tagging programs to help promote billfish research.

Sailfish and spearfish are also taken incidentally, usually when anglers are trolling for wahoo or tuna. Other rarely encountered species of interest are bigeye tuna, bluefin tuna, cobia, and kingfish.

Evidence of other undeveloped fisheries resources exists. Commercial longliners and exploratory sportfishing efforts have revealed the presence of both albacore and swordfish around Bermuda. Each year sees a few albacore taken, usually by trolling early in the morning or at dusk, and the extremely limited effort directed toward swordfish has been surprisingly successful. The application of different techniques in the future may well mean even more varied fishing opportunities.

BICUDA   *Boulengerella ocellata.*
Other names—pike-characin; Spanish: *picudo, per lápiz.*

Although "bicuda" refers to the barracuda in Spanish and Portuguese, a number of fish that thrive in the tropical freshwater drainages of South America are known in English as bicudas. In Brazil, the species referred to as bicuda and shown in the accompanying photograph is extremely popular in those places where it is encountered. In shape, it looks somewhat like a barracuda and also somewhat like a North American pike.

Bicuda, in fact, are pike-characins and members of the family Ctenoluciidae. They belong to the American pike-characin branch of the family and are distant relatives of African pike-characins. They are freshwater fish of tropical origins; juvenile specimens are generally regarded as aquarium candidates. Other known species of bicuda include *B. lateristriga* (striped), *B. lucius* (golden), and *B. maculata* (spotted).

Information about the different bicuda and their behavior and life history is fairly slim, but the frisky behavior and energetic leaping ability of *B. ocellata* make it a welcome catch and an admirable sportfish.

Identification. Color patterns differ according to the species. The Brazilian bicuda encountered most by anglers are silvery gray, slightly darker on top and lighter on bottom, but may have tinges of yellow on the lower half of their body, particularly around the gills and fins, with yellow orange coloring on the tail. They have a dark spot at the base of the caudal fin.

Bicuda are slim and elongate with a long, pointed snout. The upper jaw extends beyond the lower, and the tip of the upper jaw is slightly rounded and bulbous. They possess a small adipose fin, and their dorsal and anal fins are situated along the posterior end of the body. The tail fin is broad and slightly rounded.

Size. The larger species of bicuda can reach up to approximately 40 inches in length and reportedly may weigh up to 13 pounds.

Distribution. Bicuda are found in tropical South America, primarily in the Amazon basin and adjacent areas.

Habitat. The primary habitat of bicuda is evidently flowing water, and they generally favor the moderate-flowing sections of rivers, especially in pools, and the mouths of lagoons and bays that empty into rivers.

Food and feeding habits. Bicuda are carnivorous and are usually present in small schools. They attack forage fish aggressively, although it is unknown which species, if any, they have a preference for.

Angling. Larger bicuda will attack assorted lures, leap out of the water frequently when hooked, and fight hard on light tackle. They are not endurance battlers, nor are they prone to streaking off with large amounts of line, unless caught on very light tackle. They are aggressive, however, and may repeatedly strike a lure. Most anglers who encounter bicuda do so by accident, usually while fishing for peacock bass and using fairly stout tackle, although bicuda do not inhabit the same cover-laden backwaters as peacock bass. They may be nearby, however, and sometimes are caught when anglers turn their attention from the shore and areas with cover to ply the more open reaches of water.

A bicuda from Brazil's São Francisco River.

Spoons, spinners, and an assortment of plugs—including large surface plugs that walk, pop, chug, and make a commotion—are effective on bicuda. See: Brazil.

BIG GAME

A general term that refers to large and strong saltwater sportfish that are customarily caught in offshore *(see)* waters and with medium- to heavy-duty conventional tackle *(see)* or big-game tackle *(see),* even though some of these species, or smaller specimens, may be caught with other equipment. Historically they were pursued with heavy equipment, primarily by trolling or drifting, and the term has stuck.

The principal big-game species include all of the billfish (marlin, sailfish, and swordfish); most sharks; the larger tuna (bigeye, bluefin, dogtooth, and yellowfin); and wahoo. Dolphin do not grow as large on average as any of these fish, but they are caught in the same offshore waters and via the same methods, and are generally lumped into this designation as well. Tarpon are considered big game by some because of the heavy-duty tackle sometimes used for them, they are often caught as large (100 pounds) as many of the aforementioned species, and they are very active when hooked. See: Offshore Fishing.

BIG-GAME FISHING

See: Big-Game Tackle; Offshore Fishing.

BIG-GAME LURES

See: Big-Game Fishing; Trolling Lures, Saltwater.

BIG-GAME TACKLE

Big-game tackle is a type of high-performance saltwater fishing equipment characterized by heavy-duty revolving-spool reels equipped with a lever drag mechanism. It is related in a general way to conventional tackle *(see)*, although the hallmark of big-game tackle is reels that feature superior drag performance and durability.

Big-game tackle may also be referred to as offshore tackle, trolling tackle, or lever drag tackle, and it is almost exclusively used in saltwater. Although some extremely large and stubborn freshwater fish might lend themselves to angling with small-size big-game equipment, 99 percent of big-game tackle usage is in marine environs, and the vast majority of that by big-water boaters. This tackle is most often associated with blue water trolling or bait-fishing for billfish, tuna, and sharks, but smaller models are suitable for some types of reef and inshore fishing, and some may also have limited casting application.

This tackle has evolved a lot in recent decades. With the advent of smaller reels, improved drag materials, reels with greater line capacity, and new rod designs, the uses for big-game tackle have expanded greatly. Though more expensive than similar purpose conventional tackle, big-game tackle has become very popular, especially among anglers likely to encounter the largest and most gear-punishing saltwater species, largely because of its ability to endure extreme pressures and to subdue tough fish quicker than would otherwise be possible. For this reason, line capacity, gears, and drag are the most critical components of big-game reels.

Appropriate versions of big-game tackle can be used in applications ranging from giant marlin trolling offshore to baiting tarpon in bays, and to such in-between uses as reef fishing for big groupers, live-baiting for cruising sailfish, and employing light thread for assorted large species at times when fish become "line shy." Appropriate models of big-game reels with corresponding rods—classified by the intended line strength—may be used for various tasks, although specific outfits are best suited to particular applications.

Big-game reels, such as this group, are premium products in price, features, and performance.

Smaller and lighter versions of this tackle, especially those with two-speed gears, have been popular for lighter-duty uses, displacing some conventional gear and being used in such diverse applications as fishing for large cobia and striped bass around bridge and buoy structures, school tuna in open water, and deep bottom-hugging halibut. These are likely to become increasingly popular and more widely used.

Lever Drag Reels

The origin of big-game tackle is intermingled with that of conventional tackle, and, indeed, the term "big-game tackle" was once used to refer solely to rods equipped with large-capacity revolving-spool reels that sported star drag mechanisms. The first revolving-spool reel with a star drag was used in 1913; prior to that time, reels did not have an internal drag mechanism. Pressure on the reel spool—to make a fish work for the line it took off—was applied by putting the thumb on the line (which was ineffective for large fish and sometimes painful to the angler) or by a leather thumb pad that was attached to the reel frame.

The star drag mechanism provided an internal slip clutch to help pressure strong fish and slow the rate of line being pulled off the reel. It was incorporated in all types and sizes of revolving-spool reels in later years. All products that are today categorized as conventional reels feature a star drag; this also includes baitcasting *(see)* reels.

The large-capacity star drag reel of the early twentieth century was a big advance for its time and has been greatly improved to this day. Arguably, the biggest improvement has been in the area of drag performance, due to advances in drag washer materials. Nevertheless, early conventional reels, and to some extent their modern counterparts, often provided insufficient drag performance when used to strike and fight large, powerful fish. It should be noted that large, powerful fish are not necessarily the biggest and toughest specimens; a 50-pound Atlantic sailfish caught on 12-pound-test line can do some furious greyhounding through the water, possibly overheating a reel in the process. Therefore, size and strength in a fish is relative to the class of tackle and strength of line employed.

The problem with conventional reels is that drag tension is not easily or readily adjustable to known levels. Turning the star wheel adjusts the drag tension, which is usually set to a predetermined level before fishing. If that wheel is deliberately or accidentally turned later, especially while playing a fish, drag tension is changed and may be too little or too great for the circumstances. Once the tension is changed, it cannot be recalibrated with absolute certainty while playing a fish. Furthermore, it may be desirable to deliberately increase or decrease drag tension while playing a fish (usually a very large and powerful one for the tackle), but doing so means making an adjustment to a "guesstimated" level of tension, and being unable to return to a known pre-set tension level later on.

Experienced anglers can make adjustments to the preset tension of a star drag reel and be reasonably close to the tension level necessary for the circumstances, but most anglers cannot do so, and may have a high degree of error when making adjustments by feel under difficult and pressured angling circumstances, which can have harmful results. This is most significant when fishing for the toughest species, when using light lines, and in circumstances where a lot of line is taken from the reel.

This drawback, which was originally of greatest significance to big-game anglers fishing with fairly unsophisticated conventional reels, lead to the development of the lever drag revolving-spool reel by Fin-Nor in the mid-1930s. For several decades, this product was available in limited supply in large-capacity heavy-line models that were very expensive and tailored to the elite offshore angler. In 1966, Penn Reels, a major conventional reel manufacturer, produced its first two models of lever drag reels; these were more affordable than existing products, and in ensuing decades, this entire genre of tackle improved exponentially. Lever drag reels came to be known as offshore reels because the first applications, with large models, were geared to billfish and tuna. It later became known as big-game tackle, although it should be noted that many heavy-duty, large-capacity conventional reels are used to catch big-game species.

In lever drag reels, the drag adjustment mechanism is separate from the reel handle and doesn't turn with the handle as the star wheel on a conventional reel does. This, plus the fact that the position of the drag lever is constantly visible, means less chance of inadvertently changing drag tension, and always being certain of the level of tension applied. Lever drag reels also have several (at least Strike- and Full-drag) tension settings, which permit preset tension at one level for setting the hook and at another level for bringing maximum pressure to bear on a stubborn fish. This is a significant difference from conventional reels, which can only be preset to one drag tension setting and whose tension adjustment cannot be reliably changed to precise levels during use. Lever drag reels also feature a device to limit the drag-setting range, and the drag is capable of being fine-tuned.

Essentially, a big-game reel today is one with lever drag operation. It does have overlapping features with conventional reels, and in some instances, the same rods can be used with either type of reel. Categorically, however, these reels are generally more expensive, more durable, and heavier than conventional reels that hold a comparable strength and amount of line. Models with two-speed gearing are wholly unlike conventional reels, and have special application for catching tough fish.

Big-game reels are rarely used for casting and are almost entirely used for trolling lures or bait and for fishing at various depths with sinking lures or bait, both of which call for paying line off the reel rather than casting. However, a growing interest in varied methods of fishing has caused some modern big-game reels to be used for casting either lures or natural bait, as well as for other types of fishing, despite their comparatively large size and greater weight.

The two-speed gear components of a Fin-Nor Ahab big-game reel are evident in this composite image; quick one-step gear shifting is possible with this reel.

A common characteristic of all big-game reels is that they do not possess a level line-winding mechanism. When using them, the angler must manually direct the placement of line on the spool to produce an even line lay. This can be a problem for inexperienced anglers or those who are unfamiliar with this action. When line is not wound evenly, it bunches and may prevent either retrieval or dispensing, as well as contributing to the binding of line wraps. Manual line leveling can seem even more burdensome when combined with the fact that big-game reels, which sit on top of the rod facing the angler, are heavy and, for some people, awkward to hold.

Being heavy is a double-edged sword, however. The weight is a result of the size necessary for adequate line capacity, and a result of the sturdy components necessary for the frame, spool, and gears, which, in addition to the drag, are the elements that make these reels capable of subduing fish that can instantly peel a lot of line off and need backbone to land.

General Operation

In the most basic sense, big-game tackle works much like all other tackle except flycasting in that a weighted object at the end of the line pulls line from the spool. The spool of a lever drag reel revolves when you turn the handle as line pays out and when line is retrieved. When the reel is placed in freespool and line is dispensed from the reel, a backlash *(see)* or spool overrun can occur if the revolving spool turns faster than the line is carried off that spool. Applying light pressure to the spool prevents this and may be accomplished in several ways.

The big-game reel has a lever that applies various amounts of drag tension on the spool; the greater the tension, the more force it takes to pull line from the spool. Completely releasing tension allows the spool to turn most freely (freespool). In use, the reel sits atop the rod and faces toward the angler; the rod-holding hand thumb is placed on the spool to keep the line in check, and the free hand is used to move the drag lever backward to minimum tension, which places the reel in freespool. When thumb pressure is relaxed, line flows off the spool and out through the rod guides, carried by the weight of the object at the terminal end of the line. Big-game reels feature a click ratchet, also called a warning click, used to signal that line is being taken off the reel; this may be employed when a reel is not held or left unattended.

To retrieve line, the drag lever is moved forward to apply some degree of tension on the spool, and the spool is turned by rotating the handle, which winds line onto the reel. When line is wound onto the spool, the user must level the line manually for even line distribution.

The adjustable drag mechanism is activated by moving a lever that is located on the same sideplate as the handle. Unlike other reels, this equipment

When recovering line on a big-game reel, it's necessary to guide the line evenly onto the spool with your thumb.

has dual drag settings, usually referred to as Strike and Full, which are preset to the desirable level at the beginning of each day's fishing and relaxed when the day is concluded. These are the basic elements of operating a lever drag reel.

Line Release Features

The vast majority of lever drag reels, and most large models, are not used for casting, but primarily used for trolling or for drift fishing with bait, generally in situations where a modest amount of line is let out. Nevertheless, controlling the flow of line off the spool is an important element of usage.

Freespooling. Technically, there is no such thing as freespool on a lever drag reel, although the term is universally used and is a carryover from other types of revolving spool reels, where the gears are disengaged to achieve freespool. In lever drag reels, the gears are always engaged, and the drag mechanism drives the spool. To achieve freespool—in this case meaning a state where there is no tension on the spool and line can flow off without resistance—disengage the drag by moving the adjustment lever fully backward. This disengages the clutch parts while leaving the gears intact. Moving the drag lever forward applies tension to the spool and allows a return to a known, preset level, as will be explained shortly.

Spool revolution. Before putting the reel into freespool, you must apply finger pressure to the spool to prevent line from paying out prematurely or haphazardly. Without this pressure, and assuming that a lure or weighted bait was tied to the end of the line, the weight of either object would cause the spool to turn the moment the reel was placed into the freespool position, which could cause an instant backlash on the spool.

It is therefore necessary to place the thumb of the rod-holding hand on the spool so the spool can't turn, and then move the drag lever fully backward. Now the line can be released by easing the tension. Thumb pressure is lessened on the spool to pay line out at a controlled rate; the objective is to let a sufficient amount of line out for the fishing circumstances at a rate that doesn't cause the spool to turn so fast that it causes a backlash. This is important because a revolving spool can gather speed quickly and an uncontrolled spool can lead to a serious backlash in seconds. The backlash not only impedes immediate fishing effort because of the time required to undo it, but can also cause damage to the line.

Tension releasing. Line can also be released from lever drag reels under moderate tension. This is often done by anglers when lengthening the amount of line already out while trolling, or feeding more line to bait that is drifting with current. This is accomplished by turning the warning click on and backing the drag lever off to a point between the Strike setting and freespool, where line can be pulled off easily yet without causing an overrun.

Line can then be paid out in intervals as necessary, generally by pulling it from the tip-top guide or directly from the reel. When enough line has been deployed, the drag lever is returned to its original setting (usually the Strike position).

Retrieving/Line Recovery Features

Most factors that affect line retrieval with lever drag reels are similar to those for other revolving-spool reels, although because of the applications of these products, some elements, particularly gears, are very significant.

Line pickup. To be in a position to set the hook and to return line to the spool, some drag tension has to be established. In the most basic sense, with the drag lever moved forward so that some level of drag tension is in effect, turning the handle revolves the spool, bringing line onto it. When there is sufficient resistance from a fish, the mere act of turning the handle, even with tension applied to the drag washer, may not place line on the spool, which causes other actions—increased drag tension, methods of playing the fish, boat manipulation, etc.—to be used to aid line recovery.

Left/right retrieve. Lever drag reels are manufactured in right-handed cranking versions and cannot be converted by the angler, as a spinning reel can, although some lever drag reels (as well as conventional reels) may be converted to or even originated in left retrieve by custom shop operators. The reason for this is that applications with big-game reels are very demanding, the outfits are generally heavy, and most people are right-handed, meaning that it is normal to want to use the dominant hand for the hard cranking work that is often an element of lever drag reel use. Lever drag reels are especially used for landing big fish, and it is common to attach these reels to a harness, which relieves the rod-holding arm. If a person is right-handed, all of the heavy-duty cranking of the reel is done with the stronger hand, which in theory is better for anyone who is right-handed, although not as desirable for a lefty.

Lefthanders complain about this to reel manufacturers, but the problem is basically economic on two levels. If there was enough demand, manufacturers would make left-handed lever drag reels. But there aren't enough left-handed anglers (or not enough of them have complained) to make it worthwhile for manufacturers to undertake the costs necessary to produce two versions of every lever drag reel. Furthermore, from a practical usage standpoint, owning both right- and left-handed retrieve models of expensive lever drag reels becomes more gear-intensive than most people would like or can afford. This is especially true for party boat operators, charter captains, or private boat owners, who take customers, friends, and family fishing. It is simply easier to have everything that works the same way (right-retrieve), especially since most people are right-handed.

With his thumb controlling spool speed, this angler lets line out on a big-game outfit; note the full set of roller guides on the rod.

Line winding. Line is wound directly onto the spool of lever drag reels, but they do not have a mechanism for leveling or dispersing that line across the spool (called a levelwind). This leveling must be done manually. The hand that holds the rod (usually the left hand) must be situated in such a way that the thumb can be used to direct the line back and forth onto the spool as it is retrieved. This means holding the rod at the foregrip ahead of the reel, and extending the thumb to the right to catch the line with both sides of the tip of the thumb, moving it to the left and right to disperse the line. (An alternate method when using a harness is to run and direct the line between the fingers while the rod hand is held over the reel.) This leveling has to be done whenever the handle of the reel is turned and line is recovered onto the spool.

Failing to disperse the line by hand results in bunching on the spool. If the line bunches severely enough, it may jam at the frame crossbars and prevent retrieval of additional line or inhibit outflow of line when the reel is placed in freespool. Bunching also causes wraps to bind among each other, impeding the free flow of line off the spool; and makes it more likely to incur a spool overrun; a horrific tangle that will have to be painstakingly picked apart.

The reason these reels have no levelwind mechanism (also the case on many conventional reels), is that really big, powerful fish can strip line extremely fast off a reel. The line guide cannot keep up with the swift back and forth movement of the departing line, necessarily putting friction and more tension on the line, which might cause the levelwind to fail or the line to break. Furthermore, the levelwind, which is always exposed to the elements, might break due to the corrosive effect of saltwater, even when carefully cleaned and maintained, or a really powerful fish might be lost due to friction on the line.

Gears. The most basic part of the operation of every reel, and one of its most significant attributes,

B

is the gear set, which in a lever drag reel is as heavy duty as reel gears get.

In a lever drag reel, a large gear, the main or drive gear, engages a smaller gear, the pinion. The drive gear is linked to the reel handle, and the pinion gear connects to the spool. This system provides the multiplying gear ratio for ample line retrieval rates with a small spool and still delivers substantial cranking power. It also allows for the use of heavy lines.

Top quality lever drag reels have stainless steel main and pinion gears. In some products these are the same grade; in others one grade of stainless steel is slightly stronger than the other.

In almost any simple gear set, one gear material is normally different from the other. This is because use of the same materials would tend to cold weld, or "gall" together; dissimilar metals nearly always offer the lowest coefficient of friction. The presence of an oil film helps to reduce friction. The result of using dissimilar metals and an oil film is that gear runs smoothly for a longer period of time.

The best situation is for the main drive gear material to be slightly softer than the pinion gear for wear characteristics, especially in reels that are used often for demanding applications, and where the gear ratio is high. In a multiplier reel, one tooth of the pinion gear contacts its mating teeth on the main gear the same number of times as the gear ratio. That is, in a 5:1 ratio reel, each tooth on the pinion gear is activated five times more often than

its counterpart on the main gear. Therefore, it is subject to five times the wear and needs to be harder simply to survive. Lever drag reels, however, generally have low gear ratios and a greater tooth configuration that doesn't produce such problems.

Gears are made to work in a given way with respect to each other, so there must be a certain distance between the two to match up; otherwise the gears will feel tight. Naturally, it is important that the gear teeth are machined as precisely as possible to assure smooth operation and long life. Due to the high-stress cranking that is experienced with lever drag reels, it is also important that they have a rigid support system, so that under great duress there is no flex to affect the inner workings of the reel. The use of heavy line, and cranking large fish in extreme conditions, can put tremendous stress on all components, and both the material and construction of the frame and shaft supports are what keep the gears precisely located and deliver a long life.

Gear ratio/single and dual speeds. Since the drive gear is linked to the reel handle and the pinion gear is engaged to the spool, the basic numerical ratio of the drive and pinion gears establishes the number of revolutions made by the spool per turn of the handle. That number is determined by counting the gear teeth on the larger drive gear and dividing that by the tooth count of the smaller pinion gear. In a gear set consisting of a 53-tooth drive gear and a 10-tooth pinion gear, the ratio

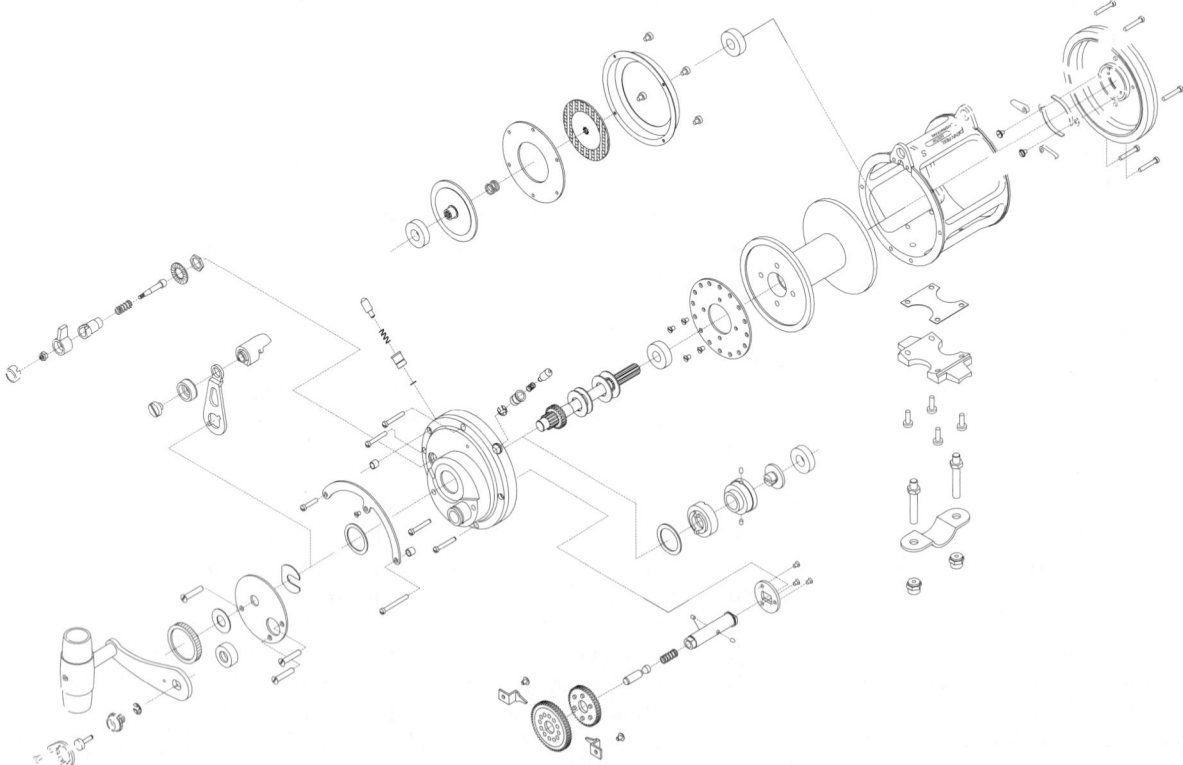

All of the parts of a Penn International II big-game lever drag reel are shown here; this product features quick-changing two-speed stainless steel gears, a carbon-fiber friction drag, and a machined one-piece frame.

would be calculated at 5.3:1 because the pinion will turn 5.3 times for each full rotation of the drive gear.

Gear ratios are generally categorized as high (fast) or low (slow), but this is relative to the type of reel and application. Furthermore, the size of the spool may be such that a low gear ratio reel actually recovers more line per full turn of the handle than a high ratio reel with a smaller spool. If numerical ratio were the only factor of comparison, what is high for many lever drag reels would be low for other revolving-spool reels. Low gear ratios for lever drag reels range from 1.2:1 to 1.8:1 and high gear ratios range from 2.2:1 to 4.5:1

In general terms, the higher the ratio, the greater the potential for stripping gears under severe strain. On a high gear ratio reel, the individual teeth become narrower because more teeth are fitted into a given area, and they are weaker. An inexperienced angler is more likely to do damage on a high gear ratio reel when he puts the smaller gear teeth under a heavy load. Fishing with a high gear ratio reel requires using the rod a lot, pulling it back and then winding line onto the spool quickly on the downstroke. This is necessary because, with high gear ratio reels, the smaller tooth configuration does not have sufficient cranking strength. This is a factor in all reels, but obviously of more concern with reels that get a heavy load, such as conventional and lever drag reels.

In the past, most lever drag reels were single speed, meaning that they had one fixed gear ratio. Today, there are lever drag reels with dual-speed operation, meaning that they can operate at two gear ratios, one of which is classified high and the other low. Shifting from one gear to the other is simple, generally done by pressing a button on the handle. Although more expensive, two-speed lever drag reels have become very popular and may account for half of all lever drag reels sold (aftermarket conversions installed by reel technicians can convert some single-speed reels to dual-speed models).

There is a good reason for this popularity. Having two-speed operation permits shifting from high ratio, which would be used for most purposes, to low ratio for the extra cranking power necessary for demanding situations. Low is used for power, and high is used for speed. If you have to clear lines quickly, for example, you do this in high gear; there is little resistance, and you can crank away quickly. Being able to instantly shift from high to low speed provides benefits for various situations, including out-muscling a big fish that has sounded directly below you, or pulling a large grouper away from its craggy bottom hole.

When you're using high gear to fight a fish, and it gets to be a tough fight, you can switch to low gear and make the work easier. In principle, less line is recovered per turn of the handle in low gear, so you theoretically spend more time when using this gear. You'll find it easier, however, to get a strong fish's head, turn it, and be in control, when using low gear. If you were using a high gear ratio to battle a stubborn fish, it might actually take more time, since it is harder to turn the handle, and thus you actually have to work harder with the fish.

Having both gears provides opportunity to employ either one on the same fish as circumstances warrant. The greater power of the low-speed mode, when used in combination with high speed (gaining line quickly, for example, when a fish runs toward you) can have the benefits of reducing fighting time overall, which is clearly helpful for releasing fish in good health, as well as diminishing angler fatigue, which can otherwise lead to mistakes and prolonged battles.

High and low are relative terms when discussing gear ratio, and categorization is relative to the size and diameter of the reel. A 2.2:1 gear ratio might actually be a "high" gear ratio on a large line capacity lever drag reel (like a 130-class model), and would provide a lot of line recovery compared to a smaller diameter reel that had a numerically greater gear ratio.

Cranking power. Gear ratio and cranking power are inextricably linked in all reels, and most affect how easy or difficult it is to retrieve a heavy weight, or an object that offers a lot of resistance. Reels that can easily handle a heavy load are said to have a lot of cranking power. Various factors affect this.

The length of the handle has a bearing because length is a factor in the amount of leverage you can put on the handle. The longer the handle, the more leverage and the easier it is to retrieve a set load. If you make a handle longer, you reduce the force at the knob. It is essentially the same principle as having a long-handled wrench; it's easier to loosen nuts with a long-handled wrench than with a short-handled one. So a longer handle equals greater power (although your hand and arm must describe a larger circle to operate the reel).

The gear set itself is also a big factor with regard to cranking power. If you have a reel with a gear ratio of 2:1, it's easier to retrieve a load because this is a low gear ratio. If you have a reel with a gear ratio of 5:1, which is high, it's a lot more difficult to retrieve a load, although you get more speed. If you're retrieving something that offers very little resistance, the high gear ratio is okay. You need a lower gear ratio, however, for something that offers more resistance. Thus, the lowest gear ratio reels have the greatest cranking power, and the highest gear ratio reels have the least cranking power. Obviously, there is an advantage to having dual-ratio reels, so the best of both reels can be employed as necessary while angling.

No matter what the gear ratio is, the evaluation of a reel's ability to retrieve line should boil down to something engineers call Inches Per Turn of the handle, or IPT. This is the amount of line recovered

The earliest written account of fishing reels appeared in England in 1651 in *The Art of Angling* by Thomas Barker; the earliest visual depiction of a reel appeared in a Chinese painting from the mid–twelfth century.

B

per turn of the handle, or, simply, line recovery, which is a better measurement of retrieval ability than gear ratio. Line recovery is determined by spool diameter, which is a key dimension for any reel and which sets the circumference of the line level on the spool and the amount of line wound onto the spool with each turn of the reel handle.

When the level of line on a spool is low, as it might be when a strong fish takes a lot of line, less line is recovered per turn of the handle than would be when all of the line is on the spool. Similarly, the amount of line recovered per turn of the handle of a fully spooled 4:1 ratio reel that has a small spool would be less than the amount of line recovered per turn of the handle of a fully spooled 4:1 ratio reel that has a large spool.

Thus, the amount of line recovered is the measurement an angler should be most interested in. Yet anglers cannot quickly determine line recovery when evaluating a reel they might purchase because specifications on the circumference of the spool are seldom provided on the reel or in the packaging materials. You may know, for example, that in a 4:1 ratio reel one revolution of the handle puts four wraps of line on the spool, but if you don't know how much line is gained with each complete wrap, you don't know the actual recovery. (In a reel that you own, of course, this can be determined by marking the line and then measuring it.)

For a greater discussion of this subject, *(see: gear ratio)*. Although most consumers have a notion that gear ratio is of primary importance in retrieval, and some think that the higher the ratio the better, other factors are involved, and line recovery is a major one. Remember, however, that reels with a low gear ratio do better under heavier loads, whether those loads are due to the size of the fish or the equipment being used (heavy weights, deep-diving lures, and so on).

This issue is critical in lever drag reels because of their basic size, capacity, and applications, which often result in a heavy load being placed on them.

Handle. The length of the handle affects cranking power, so the distance from the center of the gear stud to which the handle is attached to the handle knob is a key element in retrieval. A long handle equals power, yet many people have the misconception that a long handle also equals speed, that the longer the handle, the faster it can travel. The opposite is true. The longer the handle, the greater distance the cranking hand must travel with each turn. The shorter the handle, the quicker it can be turned, but there's less power, so there's a trade-off either way. You can't get power and speed simultaneously. The handles supplied by manufacturers with lever drag reels are fairly similar and have a moderate length suitable for most tasks.

Lever drag reels have a single handle grip, or knob, which is what you hold to turn the handle. These are barrel- or torpedo-shaped, and tend to be grasped by the whole hand rather than by just the thumb and index finger.

Some users of lever drag reels, especially those with single speed versions, opt to replace their handles with aftermarket products, some of which may be adjustable so you can change the distance from the crankshaft connection to the handle knob and thus affect power and speed to best suit the physical build of the angler. Some aftermarket handles sport a grip that is angled farther outward than factory grips, which are said to be more ergonomic.

Ball bearings/bushings. Bearings and bushings provide a way to minimize friction on rotating shafts. Bushings don't spin as freely as ball or roller bearings, which are typically viewed as durable and reliable and a way to add rotational freeness to the retrieval system. Ball bearings, rather than bushings, are imperative on lever drag reels because they are vastly smoother and more durable under heavy loads, and most use sealed versions of the highest quality. The main ball bearings are placed on both sides of the spindle, and others are located on the drag stack and the gear stud. On the biggest lever drags reels, there are also two ball bearings on the handle. For a more detailed review of ball bearings and bushings, *(see: reel, fishing)*.

Warning click. Known mainly as a click or clicker by most anglers, this is a ratchet device intended to let an angler know that line is going out. All lever drag reels have this, and it is generally employed when a big-game outfit has been placed in a rod holder and is not handheld. In some situations, as when fishing with bait, the reel is placed in freespool with the warning click on so that if a fish picks up the bait, the line is free to move with minimal resistance, yet without risking a spool overrun. In other situations, such as when trolling, the drag is set to the Strike position and the warning click is employed so that it instantly alerts an angler (or mate or boat captain) to a strike and to the fact that a fish is on and taking line off the reel. On some lever drag reels, the click is adjustable so you can go from a soft to hard clicking sound. The soft click is preferred for drifting bait when minimal resistance is desired, while the hard click is preferred for trolling when you want a loud sound.

The click itself features a spring-loaded tongue that moves back and forth against ratchet teeth to make this sound. It is activated by moving a small off-center knob on the sideplate (usually the right sideplate). The click is intended for part-time rather than full-time use, and it should be disengaged when retrieving. Continued use of the click causes premature ratchet wear.

Drag Features

The hallmark of lever drag reels is their drag mechanism; how it is employed and how well it does its job are the elements that separate these reels from all others. Because drag function and performance are so essential to big-game fishing, it is important to review the basic principles of drag and the factors that are especially influential in big-game fishing.

Overview. The purpose of the drag function on any reel is to let line slip from the reel at varying pressures when force is applied to the line. It serves as a sort of clutch, or shock absorber, and is especially important when using light line, when playing large and strong species, and when fish make strong and sudden surges while being landed. If an angler never catches large fish, only uses heavy strength line, and is content to wind fish in, then it is conceivable that his drag might never be used. This is not the case with lever drag reels and big-game tackle, which is expressly meant for catching large fish and dealing with tough conditions.

Nevertheless, catching large fish, which weigh more (usually far more) than the actual breaking strength of the line or which can apply extreme pressure on the tackle, requires some finesse rather than sheer strength. This means that you cannot simply winch a fish in when using sporting grades of line; the drag will come into play, because if it doesn't, the force will exceed the strength of the line and the line will break.

When the drag comes into play, it allows the fish to continue applying force, but at a pressure that is less than the breaking strength of the line because when the force reaches a certain level (usually a specific percentage of the line's breaking strength), a properly set drag mechanism allows line to slip from the reel under tension by turning the spool. In essence, it means that a fish can run instead of engage in a tug of war, but it has to work for the line that it takes off the reel, which is tiring to the fish and helps the angler subdue it.

In typical fishing with lever drag reels, anglers set the drag at 25 to 30 percent of the breaking strength of their line. This is measured by some people with a short length of line on a straight pull off the reel. It is measured by others with line running through the rod guides and the rod flexed as it would be in fishing circumstances. When using other types of tackle, many people use the "feels good" method of establishing drag tension by pulling line off the reel and adjusting the drag mechanism (the star wheel for other revolving spool reels) until the tension feels right. The most precise way to measure drag tension, however, is by using a reliable scale and attaching it to the line. No matter what method is used, the objective is to adjust the drag so that the line does not slip until the appropriate amount of tension is applied.

Understanding how to use and set drag is one of the most important aspects of sportfishing, and is also reviewed elsewhere *(see: drag),* but needs special consideration with lever drag reels due to the applications that these reels face. Because a lot of line is often taken from lever drag reels and because big-game fish have to be battled for sometimes long periods, the buildup of heat, and the dissipation of that heat, are critical issues, and it is essential that

the drag pressure remain relatively stable. Furthermore, big-game fishing techniques, especially offshore trolling, benefit from having one preset drag tension for striking and playing fish and another for maximum pressure.

Big-game fishing issues. As noted, the drag system on a fishing reel is meant to allow line to slip smoothly from a reel before the line's breaking strength is surpassed by the load placed on it by a fish. The ideal drag system for big game is one that is fully adjustable and provides consistent performance over a wide range of tension settings. This is of most importance when fishing for large, strong fish, and when using light tackle. In big-game fishing the drag is of particular importance not only because of the size and strength of the fish, but because some of the lines used have very little stretch, which puts the full fighting load on the rod and reel drag. A line with sufficient stretch would act a bit like a shock absorber and be more forgiving, but only up to a point *(see: line).*

While it has always been the goal of reel designers to produce the ideal drag system, in the wide range of big-game reels available today, few drag systems actually meet this criteria and only a few have recently come close to meeting this criteria when new and fresh out of the box. Many anglers, especially big-game aficionados seeking large fish and record specimens on light line, have taken manufactured reels to specialists to overhaul, fine-tune, or improve the drags on their reels. This is especially true for reels using lever drag systems.

In big-game fishing, the lever drag reel is the main workhorse. With the latest generation of drag materials in use, the lever drag reel is capable of delivering the degree of drag performance that both light- and heavy-tackle anglers demand. A modern lever drag reel meters out line under precisely controlled resistance that forces a hooked fish to overcome that preset pressure before it can take line. The physical effort it takes to overcome drag resistance during the fight should quickly tire the fish and lead to its capture or release.

Whether they are on spinning, baitcasting, fly, conventional, or big-game reels, drag systems share a few common problems. One of the most significant of these is start-up inertia, which is the increased effort required to start a spool turning from a dead stop. Another is acceleration, or surge, which is the difference in effort required to turn the spool at various speeds. In big-game reels, the spool and line have significant mass, which is difficult to start in motion and, once moving, has to be controlled by the drag. Resistance can vary considerably between slow-speed and high-speed running drags, and thus have a big impact on fishing effectiveness.

The performance provided by any reel drag system is the end result of the composition and design of the system and the materials used, including the friction disc(s), metal drag disc(s), backing plates, heat sinks, and thrust mechanism; the surface

B

The Guinness Book of Records reports that more than 300 people were killed and eaten by piranhas in 1981 when an overloaded boat capsized and sank at the Brazilian port of Obidos.

finish, heat dissipation ability, and thermal stability of these items are especially significant. The primary factors that ultimately dictate the performance of any drag design are the amount of friction of the drag material; the amount of surface contact with suitable metal disc(s); and the amount of mechanical pressure or thrust applied to these components to determine the drag tension. Other variables that influence drag performance include heat buildup, conductivity, expansion, distortion, glazing, galling, and the amount of line on the spool at any given time during the fight of a fish. When the line level changes, it affects performance. Drag resistance increases as spool diameter is reduced, which is what happens when a fish takes line off a reel. The less line on the reel, the greater the drag pressure.

All of these factors add to the complexity of designing an efficient drag system. They may be unknown to the average angler, who is usually only concerned with determining the ideal static drag setting for the reel in relation to the breaking strength of the line. He then sets the drag and goes fishing. Understanding what actually happens to the drag when fishing is useful, however, for knowing what problems exist and understanding what the limitations of the reel are in order to adjust accordingly and ensure that there is not a tackle-induced loss of fish.

The principle behind a drag system is the conversion of mechanical energy into heat energy through friction This is accomplished by the discs and washers spinning against one another. How smoothly this friction can be controlled is the difference between an average drag and a really great drag. When a fish makes a long run against a substantial drag tension setting, a tremendous amount of heat is generated; in simulating this on machines to test their reel's components, some manufacturers have gotten reels so hot that water boils on top of them.

Heat buildup can drastically change the amount of friction between drag washers and discs, and can cause major problems if not efficiently conducted away from the drag washers. In general, heat expansion increases the amount of pressure between the parts of the drag, resulting in greater friction. To eliminate or reduce this pressure, heat must be transferred away from the drag washers and discs to other surrounding components of the reel. The components of the reel, including the main gear (which may act as a heat sink) and the frame, help to do this. If the pressure is long enough and intense enough, however, you reach the maximum ability of the components to dissipate heat, and the drag friction material has to handle the pressure.

One sign of a superior drag system is its ability to conduct heat away from friction-generating surfaces as quickly as possible through the washers, spool, spool shaft, and housing, where it is dissipated. If a drag washer's surface is damaged by extreme heat, it becomes unreliable and produces erratic

performance, often with disastrous effects. If this heats builds up quickly and is not dissipated, or not dissipated fast enough, there is a major problem brewing—a reel seizing and the drag pressure becoming too great for the breaking strength of the line.

Clearly, the materials that are used in the drag system are critical to proper performance, more so with this type of tackle than with any other. Yet, because the friction coefficient of various materials is not constant—it also depends on whether the material is operating dry, lubricated, or partially lubricated—and because the friction washer is asked to do nearly opposite jobs—slip freely and also create a high amount of pressure—finding the perfect friction lining material has been difficult. Thus, the design of big-game fishing reel drag systems and the use of different materials has been a calculated compromise to meet varying applications.

Older drag-lining materials, made of asbestos and other elements, expand when hot and actually increase drag pressure. Because the expanding parts have nowhere to go, they're trapped and therefore exert greater force on each other; this continues to compound the tension problem, and when the pressure builds too much, the line breaks. Various older materials (including Teflon, which is slippery, and cork, which is jerky when it gets wet) were also employed and proved to be quite a challenge when used in long and hard battles with fish.

In the development of drag systems, titanium-impregnated washers evolved and helped greatly to counter the problem of heat buildup. They are still in use today but, unfortunately, are greatly affected by water intrusion or condensation, which produces acceleration problems. Some manufacturers of reels with titanium drag washers try to address this by offering alternative drag setting recommendations.

The use of modern materials, as well as continuing research and development, has been aimed at achieving the best possible drag performance, and utilizing materials with a coefficient of friction that is stable over a wide range of temperature changes. Today, the heat problem has been greatly reduced through the use of drag materials made of carbon fiber, which can withstand extreme heat without distortion, and through more efficient heat-conducting designs to cool the drag system.

Heat and thrust affect carbon-based washers differently than other materials used in the past. One of the physical properties of carbon fiber is that it has a natural slipperiness to it. Another is that drag friction decreases with heat; as it gets hot, the carbon fiber actually gets slicker. However, this can be a problem when the washer's drag coefficient decreases too much under heat, thus resulting in less drag tension than would theoretically be desirable (although you have to remember that other factors, like spool diameter and water resistance, are also at work and may compensate).

This may be better than having more tension, and is not the perfect answer, but it's the best one yet known (although some repair specialists who install drag washers that are made with a silicone-impregnated zinc and rubber compound rate this very highly). To deal with this aspect of carbon fiber washers, one manufacturer developed a self-compensating oil-filled expansion piston in the spool of their lever drag reels; this expanded with heat, theoretically compensating for drag drop-off by automatically applying additional thrust to maintain a stable setting. Reel designers continue to argue the pros and cons of such a system, but it illustrates the lengths to which they will go to create a drag system that is as consistent as possible.

In addition to heat buildup, there's the problem of controlling acceleration differences, a phenomenon known by anglers as "surging," and common in all of the myriad combinations of drag frictional materials and metal friction discs. This is exemplified by the varying speed at which line may be pulled from the reel, as occurs when fighting a powerful fish.

Acceleration differences are more clearly evident in some reels than in others, and anglers should check this. Some brands of reels have more problems with surging than others, and those that are seriously deficient should be modified by a skilled big-game reel technician; if not, it is necessary to make a careful tension setting to compensate for variations in drag performance at low and high running speeds.

You can illustrate this phenomenon yourself with the following test:

Take a lever drag reel fully loaded with line and mounted on a rod; tie a loop in the terminal end of the line and pass it through the guides. Using a good quality drag scale (or force gauge), hook it to the loop and have someone use the scale to pull line from the reel with the drag preset to 25 percent of the breaking strength of the line at the Strike position (i.e. 12.5 pounds for 50-pound-test line). This will simulate the drag temperature of a reel that may have been standing for some period in a rod holder. Do this at least 10 or 12 times before taking any readings to ensure that friction surfaces are mated correctly, slightly warm, and maintaining full surface contact.

Pull 10 or 15 feet of line from the reel by walking backwards at a reasonably slow rate. Do this at least six times, taking readings from the scale after each pull, and carefully rewinding the line. Add the scale readings together and divide by the number of pulls to obtain a mean average drag setting for all the test pulls. This should still be 25 percent of the breaking strength of the line.

Then, secure the rod and reel well and have someone pull line from the drag by taking a few steps at normal speed and then actually running for a short distance. Do this at least six times, then compute the mean average for the high-speed pulls

and compare the two mean averages against each other. The differences in drag friction at the two speeds is probably quite different. If it is low, like 2 to 3 pounds, this is acceptable and should not pose a problem in actual fishing. That is often not the case, however, and there can be as much as a 50 percent increase in drag resistance between slow- and high-speed tests for some reels. These differences, and the range of speeds that are encountered under fishing circumstances, are what have to be offset with a properly functioning running drag.

If the difference is high, you should probably take the reel to a competent big-game reel technician to modify the reel and correct the problem. Correcting the problem is cheap insurance against the possibility of losing the fish of a lifetime because the reel malfunctions and the line breaks.

The acceleration problem is generally less troubling than the start up inertia problem, where a cool drag system must immediately go from idle to speeds in need of braking control. Difficulties here can be responsible for breaking off fish on the strike or at the very beginning of a fish's first hard run. Experiments to correct excessive start-up inertia or the so-called "sticky drag" have included treating carbon fiber drag washers with various forms of synthetic lubricants, a subject which is also debated by engineers.

The friction value of carbon fiber is low compared to other types of brake materials, and it requires running against suitable metal pressure plates. The choice of material, the flatness (as flat as possible is important), and the surface finish of such metal plates has a great effect on the overall performance. Some manufacturers have opted for carbon fiber materials treated with synthetic lubricants, running on highly polished stainless steel pressure plates. Others recommend no lubrication, and install their carbon fiber washers dry. While lubrication in general reduces start-up inertia problems, it also causes a reduction in the amount of desirable or necessary friction—which is needed to create drag resistance. This, in turn, requires much higher thrust pressure to attain the ideal drag performance of 25 percent of the line's breaking strength in the Strike position and 50 percent at the Full position.

When all is said and done, fine-tuning drag systems on big-game reels has become a cottage industry and a job that is more than the average reel repair technician can handle (most small tackle shop repair people cannot). Out of a need to service and correct drag problems in older big-game reel drags, a new breed of technicians with machine shops arose. Many of these are fine reel specialists, all trying to develop the ultimate drag either by reworking existing reels or by designing complete aftermarket systems.

Using a master big-game reel technician is also beneficial for addressing other issues with reels, and these specialists can fine-tune a reel for absolute maximum performance, particularly for the

B

IGFA-class line that you may be using (especially important for record-setting efforts). Fine-tuning factory big-game reels is analogous to Grand Prix racing. There, many production cars prove very successful, although they have been rebuilt and modified to achieve winning results.

Nevertheless, by working with different mediums and approaches, today's manufacturers have come closer to solving the problems that exist in the high-tech world of big-game fishing reels. They will likely be improving these reels further by mating even better synthetic materials with improved surface finishes and exotic metals for drag discs.

Water resistance and line level. There are two very important factors affecting drag pressure that anglers must deal with when fighting big fish. The first is the effect of water resistance on line being dragged through the water by a running fish.

Not only does water resistance increase drag on a straight-away run, but many times the fish will turn, which forms a giant belly in the line and magnifies the problem greatly. Even when an angler does nothing more than just hold on, without pumping and reeling, a gamefish can break the line with nothing more than the pressure created by water resistance if the angler and captain allow a large belly to occur. This situation can only be overcome through angling skill and good boat handling. The person on the rod has to understand when to reduce drag settings to compensate for the problem that exists when a large belly develops. The captain has to work the boat to try to prevent a large belly from forming.

The second issue is increasing drag tension due to lower line levels. As previously noted, more line is recovered per turn of the reel handle when the diameter is greater than when it is smaller. So it is easier to retrieve line when the diameter of the spool is high. Where the drag is concerned, as line is

x/z = 1/2 = 2 times force needed to move spool

As shown in this mathematical representation, when line on a reel spool is reduced to half of its full level, twice the amount of force is necessary to move the spool at the reduced level than at the full level. This has significant implications for reel drag performance if a large fish takes a great amount of line off a reel.

pulled off the spool and the diameter decreases, the leverage that the line has on the spool diminishes, so it takes more effort to move the spool against the drag. So, drag tension increases as the level of line on the spool decreases; it starts out at one level when the spool is full of line, but increases when the diameter of the spool is smaller due to a fish having taken plenty of line. Depending on the diameter of the spool, when the line level is reduced to half capacity, the drag pressure usually increases by almost double the original setting. If the line level decreases further, the drag pressure could increase to triple the setting that was established when the spool was full.

This is a matter of physics and an unchangeable one, but it's important for anglers to recognize. When spool diameter has decreased and drag tension increased, it is all the more important to have a smooth drag and a friction washer that maintains top performance. Because of the dynamics of carbon friction washers, drag tension remains on a more even level with heat buildup, rather than increasing as line is lost; these washers do not make it easier to pull line off when the level of line on a spool decreases, but it does make the drag tension more consistent, meaning that more even drag pressure is maintained.

Despite this, and especially for older reels that do not have carbon friction washers, the angler should be prepared to compensate when a fish runs a lot of line off the reel. He must know when to compensate for this mechanical increase in drag pressure during the fight by backing off on drag tension.

Drag system components. The drag mechanism on lever drag reels is comprised of an adjustment lever that is rotated in circular fashion and located near the handle and on the same sideplate of the reel as the handle (usually the right sideplate). The metal part that denotes drag lever position may be referred to as a quadrant, and may sport numerical markings correlated to tension settings. Moving the adjustment lever along this arc changes the tension settings.

Internally, most lever drag reels feature a large-diameter single friction washer that is affixed to a drive plate and driven by the spindle (some two-speed models have two washers that sandwich the metal disc). The adjustment lever is eccentric and keyed to cams so that more or less pressure is brought to bear on the spool by the friction washer. Moving the lever completely backward (toward the angler) totally removes spool pressure, resulting in a drag-free condition that is commonly called freespool. Moving the lever forward from this position gradually applies pressure to the spool over a varied range of tension settings. When spool friction exceeds the tension on the line, the reel handle turns the main gear and the spool, and allows line to be recovered. When tension on the line exceeds friction on the spool, the spool revolves against handle pressure, and line can be pulled off the spool. The handle is prevented from turning backward by a full-time nonselectable dog and ratchet, which is otherwise known as an anti-reverse.

Whereas other revolving-spool reels have multiple friction washers and multiple metal washers, lever drag reels have either single-plate or multiplate clutches. Many have just one friction washer, so there is low inertia start up, but the size and material of that washer is critical. As noted previously, the drag in any reel should ideally operate smoothly, without hesitation. In other words, it will start immediately when needed and maintain a constant rate of tension as line flows continuously off, as well as keep the same level of tension as is periodically called for during the time it takes to play and land a strong fish. The less variation there is in the performance of the drag, the better.

The friction washer is asked to do something very difficult—slip freely but also create a high amount of pressure. Thus, you're looking for two opposite attributes. Most modern lever drag reels have a woven carbon fiber friction washer, referred to by some as graphite, which does an excellent job of addressing these demands.

Positions. Although they may be labeled differently in some reels, the primary drag settings in lever drag reels are referred to as the Free, Strike, and Full positions. The Free position, as noted, is zero drag tension, or freespool. In some reels, it is obtained by moving the adjustment lever fully backward; in others, the adjustment lever is moved backward until it hits a stop button (to prevent accidentally achieving freespool), which is pushed in to allow the lever to be moved from a minimal drag tension to zero tension. This is used whenever line has to be paid out.

The Strike and Full settings, also known as Strike Drag and Full Drag, have to be preset to desired levels of tension that correspond to a percentage of the breaking strength of the line being used. The Strike and Full positions receive most attention by anglers, but the whole range of tension from just above Free to Full is available. Starting at the Free position and moving the adjustment lever forward gradually increases drag pressure until you are up at the preset Strike position (which is usually 25 to 30 percent of the breaking strength of the line); manually overriding the button brings you to the preset Full position.

The Strike position is the one used for most fish-fighting activity, and most anglers will fish or troll with the drag set at, or slightly below, the Strike position. When drifting with bait, where it may be necessary to let a fish take and run with the offering momentarily, anglers may place the drag in the Free position with the warning click on, or just barely over the Free position with the click on. There is a button at the Strike position that must be pressed to move the drag adjustment lever forward and apply more pressure, as well as to reach the Full position.

The Full position is designed so that once you get up close to a big fish (in big-game fishing that is likely to be when the double line comes onto the reel), you can apply a few extra pounds of pressure. The Full position does not signify a tension setting that is equal to the breaking strength of the line, nor does it signify lockup, in the sense that no line can be stripped from the reel; it signifies the maximum tension that has been preset, which is likely to be 50 percent of the breaking strength of the line, or some factor between 25 to 30 percent and 50 percent. It is not a good idea to use the Full setting for normal fighting of a fish because drag tension becomes that much greater as the line diameter of the spool decreases due to a large fish taking a lot of line.

Setting drag. Drag-setting procedure is a hotly debated subject among highly skilled anglers, and there are varying opinions on how to do this with a lever drag reel. The following recommended method is generally accepted as being applicable for most, if not all, fishing situations, particularly for lines under 80-pound class (37 kilograms). You can use it for 80- and 130-pound-class reels, although some anglers increase the Strike drag setting to 33 percent for these heavy line categories.

The base point of reference for all drag settings begins with a reel that is filled to capacity with line. As previously noted, drag pressure increases when the amount of line on a spool decreases, so the starting point for drag-setting considerations on any type of reel must be determined on a reel that is fully loaded.

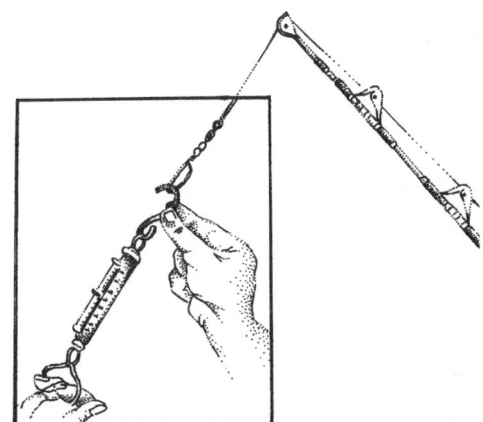

A top-quality spring scale, especially one with an easily read gauge (inset), can be used to accurately measure reel drag tension.

To set the drag, mount the reel on a rod, tie a loop in the terminal end of the line and thread it from the reel spool through the rod guides and attach it to an accurate drag scale with calibrations suitable for the line class and drag setting. Brass barrel scales with a weight indicator for drag-setting purposes are in standard use for this purpose.

Pull the drag lever all the way back into the freespool position, which should allow the spool to turn with no resistance from the drag washers. If there is any drag on the spool in this position, adjust the preset knob to eliminate it. Push the drag lever to the Strike position. Most reels have a built-in safety stop that requires the angler to push a button to go past the Strike setting. Pull some line off the reel to seat the washers and warm them up before proceeding, or have someone hold the line and turn the reel handle with the lever at Strike for a minute to accomplish the same thing.

Have someone draw on the scale to pull line from the reel. There is some disagreement among anglers and manufacturers as to whether this is best done with the rod tip pointed directly at the scale, or with the rod angled up so that it applies tension on the line. The general principle of how to set the drag is the same, although the tension effects may differ.

The following describes how to set the drag without rod tension: With the rod tip pointed directly at the scale, read the drag resistance on the scale in pounds after each pull. If the setting is too light or too heavy, back off the lever to the freespool position and increase or decrease the thrust pressure by turning the preset knob. Never adjust the preset knob with the drag engaged. Repeat this procedure until you reach the desired drag pressure in the Strike position. If the reel is in good operating condition and being used for the line rating it was designed for, it should offer a no-resistance freespool setting, a light running drag setting, a 25 percent Strike drag setting, and approximately a 50 percent Full drag setting.

The most accurate way to measure reel drag tension is with a scale and by pulling line off a fully loaded rod from a greater distance than is shown in this compressed depiction. Measuring with the rod at a high angle (top) produces greater drag resistance due to friction from rod guides. Pointing a rod directly at a fish or at the scale (bottom) results in line being pulled straight off the reel, producing the least amount of drag tension.

If you do this with the rod tip pointed directly at the scale, you will obtain a completely static setting—the absolute minimum pressure possible. When the setting is obtained this way, it eliminates any additional drag tension caused by the pressure of the loaded rod. Therefore, percentages of drag refer to a straight pull off the reel. When you measure drag on a loaded rod, with the line pressing on the rod guides, there can be variations in drag setting achieved because of variations in the amount of drag created due to many different rod-and-reel (and guide) designs, and because rods differ in their loading characteristics. In all line classes the 25 percent value compensates for these other variable and incalculable values, but it is still true that as rod arc increases, line tension multiplies. When you are always using a particular reel on the same rod, setting the drag on a loaded rod gives you an indication of what the pressure is when the rod is flexed, and many anglers like this method because they reason that the rod is always flexed when a fish is on. However, setting drag tension without rod flex gives you the lightest possible scenario. If your reel experiences significant variations in drag force when accelerating, and in light of the many factors that can affect drag performance, it is probably wise to err on the light side and measure it by taking line directly off the reel.

Strike drag. This is the basic fish-fighting drag pressure. Most people fish with the drag lever set at or slightly below the Strike position. This may depend on the method of fishing, however. When a rod is sitting in a holder and anglers are chumming *(see)* and/or chunking *(see)*, anglers will often put the reel in freespool with the warning click on, or keep it just barely over freespool. For other fishing, especially trolling, the drag lever should be placed in the Strike position, and this should be calibrated to 25 percent of the breaking strength of the line. Thus, if the unknotted wet breaking strength *(see: line)* of a line is 50 pounds, a 25 percent Strike drag setting would produce a straight-pull drag resistance measuring 12.5 pounds.

Since the Strike drag is the most critical setting, it is important to get it right, so take your time and double-check the finished setting before you start fishing. If your drag system has been properly designed and calibrated for a specific IGFA line class, it should come very close to obtaining the other desirable settings (depicted in the accompanying graph) automatically when you set the Strike drag at 25 percent of the breaking strain.

Drag Quadrant in Straight Plane

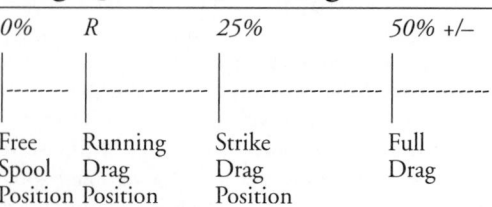

0%	R	25%	50% +/–
Free Spool Position	Running Drag Position	Strike Drag Position	Full Drag

There is an exception to the 25 percent ratio that some anglers call into play with 80- and 130-pound line classes. They prefer to increase the Strike drag setting to 33 percent with this gear. If you do this, remember that it reduces the margin of error when fighting big fish and that other variables, like spool diameter, become even more critical during the fight. Remember, you can always increase your drag setting above Strike if you need more pressure on a fish. That's why most people prefer to use the 25 percent ratio for Strike drags in almost all instances.

Running drag. With the Strike drag properly set, you should have a slight "Running" drag when the lever is initially engaged just above the freespool position to prevent backlash problems from occurring when an outfit is left in a rod holder. When a fish grabs a trolled offering, especially a live or rigged natural bait, the Running drag allows line to slip from the spool freely without backlashing the reel. Anglers can grab the rod, let the fish take the bait for a few moments, then move the lever to the Strike position and set the hook. A good Running drag will allow this to happen without backlashing line on the spool or causing tension on the fish that causes it to drop the bait.

Some reels have a hard time accomplishing the correct Strike drag setting while still maintaining a workable Running drag or even attaining full freespool capabilities. If this is the case, the reel is ready for some serious drag maintenance or refinement.

Full drag. The Full drag setting is not really full in the true sense of lockup. Full is the highest recommended setting above Strike for a specific strength of line. Full drag is the position of last resort in a battle. It is designed so that once you get the fish close to you and double line is on the reel, you can apply a few extra pounds of pressure. You could also use the Full setting to apply a few more pounds of pressure during the initial stage of a fish's run, then back it off, but this is a gamble that not many anglers want to take, especially with monster or record-class fish. It is also not advisable to keep the drag tension at the Full setting for fighting the fish, as this would be too much pressure when you take into account the effects of decreasing line on the spool.

The maximum or Full drag setting should be approximately 50 percent of the line's breaking strength. Rarely is this much drag used on any size reel, except in certain circumstances when 80- and 130-pound-class tackle is being used to fight very big fish from a chair. A bucket harness and curved butt rod are needed to capitalize on such a high drag setting.

A properly operating reel will offer a smooth transition from the Strike position on up through the Full position so that you can get more than Strike resistance but less than the maximum. Some savvy anglers will mark one or two additional drag positions on the reel housing with a marker or tape.

This is used to apply more pressure to a fish while still maintaining control of the amount of drag pressure throughout the fight. If you do this, mark each additional setting so you know just how much pressure you're putting on the fish at any given time.

Other considerations. It's a smart idea to allow reels to reach the outside ambient temperature before setting the drag. Don't make the mistake of taking your reels straight from the storage area in an air-conditioned cabin or house and then setting the drags. Once you've done that, and the reels sit in the sun, the drag setting can increase due to heat expansion of the parts. In extremely hot climates, particularly with larger reels, it is advisable to check the drag settings several times during the day's fishing.

As mentioned, the drag should be "preheated" before the Strike drag setting is adjusted. This can be done by engaging the drag, holding the spool, and turning the reel handle to create friction, or by having someone pull line against the drag as you turn the reel handle. This process should be repeated at least 15 or 20 times, which ensures that everything is up to operating temperatures and that any lubricants have dispersed and thinned to a workable consistency on the drag surface.

Be aware that you run the risk of having problems with reels, especially with the gears and drag mechanism, when bumping up line strength over the manufacturer's rating. Putting 80-pound-test line on a 50-pound-class reel has obvious ramifications for line capacity (depending on diameter), but not-so-obvious ones for internal parts that may receive more punishment than they were designed to take.

Water intrusion in drag systems can also be a major problem. If you run the boat with your outfits in rod holders in the cockpit exposed to a lot of spray, it is of major importance that the drag systems be fully engaged to keep any water that may enter the reel from getting into the drag washers. Reel covers or even a plastic shower cap placed over your reels will help greatly. When cleaning reels after use, position the lever at Full drag and spray them using light water pressure. Only after a reel is completely dried off should it be put in the freespool position and the ratchet or clicker engaged to prevent line tangles in storage.

Water can cause many problems, even condensation, which can collect inside a reel when it is taken from an air-conditioned room to the outside. It can affect drag performance or your drag settings, which is another reason to use the drag warm-up procedure outlined previously.

When storing lever drag reels between uses, the golden rule is to back the drag lever to the freespool position. This removes any pressure and allows the washers to relax. This also ensures that the drag components won't fuse and become bonded to the pressure plate, resulting in a frozen drag. When doing this, back the drag completely off, turn the reel handle while holding the spool, and crank for 10 to 20 seconds. This ensures that the washers are all totally free and clear of each other.

The care and checking of your lever drag reels should be something that you do religiously. There is nothing as final as a line broken on a good fish; understanding and proper use of your reel's lever drag system will greatly reduce this problem.

No twist. Because of the revolving-spool nature of lever drag reels, no twist is imparted to the line when an angler reels at the same time that line slips off the spool via the drag. This is a common problem with spinning *(see)* and spincasting *(see)* reels. Twist isn't possible on a lever drag reel if the handle is turning and the spool is simultaneously slipping. When the drag mechanism is activated, the spool rotates and line unwinds in an untwisted manner. There is no line twist unless it comes from lure use or you put it on when the spool is filled.

Other Features

Frame/spool materials. Because lever drag reels are used in saltwater and susceptible to extreme stresses and fishing conditions, construction and materials must be of the highest caliber.

The one-piece frame (left) and lever drag system shown here are from a Penn International big-game reel.

One-piece frames have been standard on better models for nearly two decades because they are more resistant to torque and twist, providing superior strength and precision alignment of the spool and other components. These frames, which also help dissipate heat, are usually made from the highest grade of extruded marine alloy aluminum, although some are made of graphite.

The spools are aluminum, and may be extruded, machined, or forged, and sideplates are usually machined aluminum. The finish is anodized, an aesthetic and corrosion-inhibiting feature that doesn't affect performance. Other materials, incidentally, include aircraft quality stainless steel ball bearings.

Clamps/lugs/braces. Lever drag reels all have clamps to secure the reel to the rod, lugs for attachment to a fighting harness, and, on some versions, a brace for additional support.

Older reels used to have metal rod clamps, which were fastened around the rod with exposed wing nuts. These could get in the way of grabbing or lead to scratching. They've been replaced by

molded synthetic clamps with recessed screws; there is no protrusion to get in the way, and they allow easier handling or even palming of smaller models.

The harness lugs are situated on the top of the reel because when fighting a large fish, the angler is likely to wear a shoulder or kidney harness *(see)*, which is attached to these lugs. Forward and rear braces on the largest models are used to provide torsional stability on rods.

Preset drag lock. Some large lever drag reels have a preset drag lock that is tamperproof and meant to keep the preset drag adjustment from being accidentally altered. You must purposely press a button to override the lock; this is mainly an advantage to charter captains out for big marlin and tuna, who don't want an itchy fingered client to accidentally turn the drag adjustment button and thereby cause the loss of a prized fish.

Reel designations. Lever drag reels are classified by the strength of line that they are designed for and the capacity they hold. Unlike conventional reels, which use an "O" (or ought) designation from decades ago, lever drag reels conform to well-established line classifications from 12- through 130-pound strengths, with corresponding capacity and drag system capability. These classifications are usually specified as being IGFA class, which means that they conform to established parameters of line breaking strength for world-record consideration. Thus, a 30-pound IGFA class lever drag reel is intended for line that will break according to IGFA record-testing specifications; in this case, that would be 15 kilograms, or 33 pounds *(see: line)*.

Naturally, the diameter of the line has a bearing on the capacity, and the reel can be spooled with line that is heavier or lighter than the rating. Many anglers do use a different strength of line with some models than what they are designated for. They might use a lighter line (say 20-pound on a designated 30-pound reel) to get more of that strength on a reel, or they might use heavier line (say 50-pound on a 30-pound reel) to get the benefits of heavier line with a smaller and lighter reel. Increasing the strength of line can have ramifications for the drag and freespool, however.

Some manufacturers have models with differing spool widths but meant for the same strength line, to allow for capacity concerns. Certain wide-spool models may hold up to 200 yards more line than a standard-spool reel, and the greater capacity provides an extra dose of confidence that you won't be spooled out. But even the wide-spool models have been fished with heavier lines than they were intended for (especially by long-range party boat anglers) to get greater capacity of heavier line.

The largest lever drag reels, the 80- and 130-pound class versions, are used for the biggest game, such as monster billfish and tuna. The 30- and 50-pound reels have been more popular for wide-ranging offshore applications, but greater interest in light-tackle and stand-up fishing *(see)* has increased the popularity of 12-, 16-, and 20-pound reels. Line capacity is way up there, of course, for all of these products. The 80- and 130-pound-class reels hold about 1,000 yards of line; lighter models hold between 500 and 900 yards of line, but this varies with wide-spool versions and according to the diameter of the line used.

Ergonomics. Lever drag reels are large, generally cumbersome, and heavy. There are few points to be made about their ergonomic nature other than weight and rod clamps, which have been discussed, and handles. Cosmetics, or appearance, has nothing to do with function.

Some people like bigger handles and some smaller, owing to application and interest in power versus speed. Handles can be changed, and aftermarket accessories are available for this. The barrel shape is fairly uniform on handle grips; this is deemed necessary because it is easier to put an entire hand on such a grip, and the whole hand is needed to fight big fish with this equipment.

Rods

Big-game rods used with lever drag reels, also called offshore rods, tuna rods, billfish rods, and, less commonly, deep sea rods, have some overlap with rods used with heavy-duty star drag conventional reels, and are generally short, stiff, heavy-action products that have to be more solidly built than other rod types and extremely dependable. The stress and torque put on these products is extraordinary, which requires that components and construction processes be of the highest caliber.

At one time, big-game rods were all $6^1/_2$ to $7^1/_2$ feet in length, featuring detachable wooden, aluminum, or fiberglass butts and a long slow-curving tip section. New rod manufacturing technology and changing needs have shortened many big-game rods and resulted in one-piece products with shorter butts and lighter tips that bend into the foregrip, resulting in an ability to put a lot of pressure on a fish for quicker and easier landing, especially for stand-up fish fighting. Big-game rods today range from 5 to $7^1/_2$ feet in length, with the majority being $5^1/_2$ to $6^1/_2$ feet long, and the butts are largely aluminum or graphite composite.

These workhorse rods have long, beefy two-handed handles and heavy-duty reel seats that securely accommodate lever drag reels, and they have a cushioned foregrip large enough for two-handed use when fighting and lifting heavy-duty fish. The butt of all these rods has a gimbal for insertion into a gimbaled rod holder or kidney belt.

Heavy-duty roller guides are used on most big-game rods and all of the top line-class models. These are mounted (with two feet) on top of the rod like the reel. This is because these rods are mainly used for fish fighting (as opposed to casting, retrieving, or detecting strikes), and the load of a gamefish on the line applies both a crushing downward force on the guide ring and frame, and a simultaneous tendency

to torque or twist the rod, so guides have to be of top quality and properly spaced and positioned. Most big-game rods feature a full complement of roller guides, and some have tip and butt-end (stripper) roller guides. Graphite, fiberglass, and composites of the two are used in their construction.

All big-game reels are designated according to line strength based upon the IGFA record classification; this ranges from 6- through 130-pound test and coordinates with both the reel and line strength that the product was designed to handle. However, there is some latitude in this, and anglers will go up or down (usually up) one line size, using a 50-pound IGFA class rod, for example, with a wide-spooled 50-pound lever drag reel filled with 80-pound line.

Unlike reels, many of the issues pertaining to rods used with big-game reels—functions, materials, components, etc.—are similar to those of other rods, and these are more fully detailed elsewhere *(see: rod, fishing).*

Using Big-Game Tackle

Line. Although various line strengths from 12 through 130 pounds can be employed with the appropriate big-game or lever drag gear, 20- through 80-pound lines are the most commonly used strengths. Application dictates use, and one of the things that is frequently done by lever drag reel users is stepping up to a higher strength line, which may not be what the reel is designed for. As noted previously, often anglers use a wider spool version of a particular model to step up in line strength while maintaining capacity. Some may step down in line strength to get a greater amount of a lighter line on the reel (i.e. putting 12-pound test on a 20-pound reel).

Fishing line is not prespooled onto lever drag reels, although it may be spooled at some shops that cater to offshore anglers. Proper spooling of line—under tension and with proper manual leveling—is essential to this equipment and is covered in the following section.

Nylon monofilament is the primary choice of line type for lever drag reels; there is some use of microfilament line and braided Dacron lines. Since line coiling is not much of an issue on these large-spool reels, suppleness may not be much of a factor; abrasion resistance and stretch are high priorities in line for many lever drag reel users. Basic strength—the rated strength of the line when tested in a wet condition—is critical for many (if not most) lever drag reel users because of the possibility of catching a record fish, and because the reel drag is finely tuned and set to specific standards based on knowing the absolute breaking strength of the line. This is why IGFA class lines are the only type of line used by many lever drag reel users.

Obviously lever drag reels hold a lot of line. The range is from approximately 500 to 1,000 yards with conventional diameter nylon monofilament line, and this is often understated by manufacturers. Using line that has the strength of conventional diameter nylon monofilament but a thinner diameter allows for greater capacity; in other words, a 20-pound-class lever drag reel holds more thin-diameter 20-pound class line than it will conventional diameter 20-pound-class line. Using a heavier strength line with conventional diameter results in less capacity; in other words, putting a conventional-diameter 30-pound line on a lever drag reel designed for 20-pound line results in less line being spooled on the reel. Using a lighter strength line with conventional diameter results in greater capacity; in other words, putting a conventional-diameter 12-pound line on a lever drag reel designed for 20-pound line results in a greater length of line being spooled on the reel.

Generally, it is best to keep within the recommended line strengths when filling a reel. For the most part, you can take a lever drag reel and not have a problem going 10 or 20 percent over the recommendations. Remember that when a manufacturer recommends using 30-pound line with a particular reel, that recommendation is based upon a standard 30-pound line with a conventional diameter. You can probably use conventional diameter 25- and 40-pound line as well, but it would not be worthwhile to use much heavier line. Not only is spool size and capacity an issue, but this reel may not be able to handle the greater stresses that might be generated with much heavier line, as noted previously. So, for example, putting 50-pound line on that reel could be problematic (although manufacturers and technicians do modify reels to cope with this).

However, and this is where things get tricky, there are 50-pound lines that have the diameter of a conventional 30-pound line, so you can get just as much of it on the spool. Nevertheless, it is still line with a 50-pound breaking strength (and may actually break much higher); this may be capable of overpowering the reel frame or spool. If the rod is

up to handling a lot of stress, and the line is rated to break at a minimum of 50 (often more) pounds, and the reel is meant for up to 30-pound line, then the forces generated on the reel by maximum pressures could be harmful.

On the other hand, you might use a 30-pound line with a diameter of conventional 17-pound line, and achieve much greater line capacity on the reel at a line strength that the reel is rated for. Or, you could "cheat" a little bit and use 40-pound line that has a diameter of conventional 20-pound line, if that benefited your fishing situation (see: line). This is a grossly misunderstood aspect of reel usage that has largely been brought about by the emergence of thin diameter lines (nylon monofilaments, braids, and microfilaments). However, most lever drag reel users, especially those who fish tournaments and who fish for records or who want to be certain of qualifying for a record if the circumstance arises, stay within the manufacturer's rated strength of the reel.

Filling.   There is no form of fishing in which it is more important to fill a reel properly than big-game fishing; in a nutshell, the key here is packing new line on tightly. If you fish with a big-game reel that has been loosely packed with monofilament line, there's a good chance of losing a terrific fish.

When a truly big fish rips line from a reel on its initial sizzling run, there is enormous tension on the line. If the line is not tightly packed on the reel, it can bind into itself, hanging up deep in the line mass or even digging all the way down to the spool arbor. That's usually enough to cause it to break off at the reel. When the line breaks there, it does so with a sound as sharp as the crack of a rifle shot; the sudden realization of what has happened is enough to make an angler feel sick.

Most often, such binding happens when new line is spooled onto the reel under little or no tension. You may have seen anglers spooling new line on their reels from a filler-spool bouncing about the cockpit deck. It's the easy way, and it may be suitable for lighter tackle and less demanding species, but it can cost you the fish of your lifetime when a big tuna or billfish is using its power to stream away.

The solution is simply to spool new line by packing it tightly under tension. This should be done with the reel's drag set to the Strike position and a slight bend in the rod. Two people can do this with one seated in a fighting chair or on the floor at home with a shoulder harness snapped to the reel lugs and the rod butt nestled on a pillow on the floor. In either case the line should be run through all of the rod guides. The helper stands a short distance away, holding a dowel placed through the middle of a bulk filler spool (often one holding about 2,400 yards of line). The helper should wear heavy gloves and hold small towels against the ends of the filler spool to create enough friction to cause tension on the rod as the person holding the rod in a holder cranks line onto the reel. Keep the rod bent

An angler holds on as a fish takes line from a big-game stand-up outfit.

slightly while cranking so there is enough tension to lay the line on the spool tightly. As you put the line on, crisscross it every five or six turns to help prevent binding. Fill the spool to within $1/4$-inch of the edge of the spool flange.

Any similar method for creating tension on the line as it's spooled will do the trick. Although the job of cranking the reel is tough, it's well worth the effort when the first fish is on the new line. While it might be argued that a normal fight with a fish creates enough tension to pack the reel tightly, that is true only if the line doesn't bind and break in the process of playing that first fish. Playing a fish under tension does pack a reel tightly, but only if the line has been packed properly to start, so that the underlying line does not allow the respooled line to dig in. You have to get it right for the first fish.

Incidentally, the same binding and breaking problem that occurs when line is loosely spooled onto a reel can occur when line is allowed to mound in one place on the spool of the reel. Mounding occurs when the line is not properly leveled by hand when being retrieved. Obviously, whether the reel is packed tightly or not, line must be fed back and forth onto the spool as it's being packed.

When it comes to retrieving line under tension, as when fighting a fish, realize that the power of nylon monofilament under a heavy load (as is generated by hard-cranking the line under the great pressure of a big fish) has caused spools to break, popping the flange by spreading the spool. This has occurred with some of the best reels when a big fish has been fought for hours. When line with compounded stretch is retrieved onto the spool and then compacts, it can cause tremendous pressure. Be aware that a large amount of lighter strength monofilament can do more damage than a smaller amount of heavier monofilament. There are more layers of the lighter line and in total a greater stretch factor, so you can get more stretch out of lighter nylon monofilament lines. Manufacturers have turned to forged spools to help eliminate this problem, and spreading the line properly onto the spool helps as well.

De-spooling.   When seeking trophy fish with big-game tackle, line must be changed regularly. Sometimes that means after every trip or after each protracted fight with a large fish, especially if the line has been stretched and dragged through the sea for great lengths of time, where debris can abrade it in the process. Sargassum weed can be very abrasive, as can the junk that often floats along in weedlines. Your next big fish should be fought with fresh line with no risk of cutoff due to damage from previous fishing activity.

When you're taking old line off a big-game reel it must be completely emptied from the reel and properly discarded. This is a lot of line to deal with, as these reels have great capacity. To de-spool, simply pull the line from the reel against minimal drag

while holding the butt of the rod down with one foot. It's a tedious process, but it avoids littering the ocean with discarded tangles of line.

An easier method than pulling it off by hand is to employ an electric drill with a dowel inserted into the bit clamp. Wind the line over the dowel, turn the drill on, and empty the reel quickly. Although there are a number of battery-powered devices for pulling line from reels, most are engineered for lighter line and don't handle heavy offshore trolling sizes.

Refilling the spool.   Line on a lever drag reel is often replaced because it's been used severely rather than because it gets low on the spool. Extreme pressures, as when fighting tough fish, put a lot of stress, especially stretch, on the line. Many anglers replace the entire spool of line, even though it is a lot of line and costly, rather than replace a portion of it.

With most other reels, when the line is suspect and needs replacement, or when the line gets low on the spool, you have the option of completely refilling the spool, or refilling only part of the spool. Although economically it seems to make sense to refill these large-capacity spools with just 120 or 180 yards of line rather than the full complement of 500 or 900 yards, that may not be a good practical decision.

When you partially refill the spool, you have to tie a line-to-line knot *(see: knots, fishing)*. The weakest portion of a line is usually the knot, so this connection must be a good one to maintain the basic strength of the line, should that knotted section come under severe pressure. This is especially important when angling for large and strong fish. However, the problem with making a line-to-line knot for most lever drag reel filling is that the line used is fairly heavy with a thick diameter, and the line-to-line knot is bulky and obtrusive on the reel spool. Furthermore, it may get caught on a rod guide when departing under extreme pressure and cause a break off or spool overrun. This disadvantage is a deciding factor when it comes to refilling lever drag reels, and thus, most anglers do not tie line-to-line knots on the reel, but completely respool with new unknotted fresh line.

Matching and selecting.   As with any type of fishing tackle, the issue of matching the right reel to the right rod is an important one, but in these times, it is a relatively easy one, as big-game rods are designed and classified for specific line strengths. Thus, a 30-pound IGFA-class rod is matched with a 30-pound lever drag reel.

When selecting big-game tackle, as well as matching a rod and reel, you must take into consideration the applications for it, and determine the size of fish that you will likely catch, and evaluate the conditions under which you'll be fishing. The larger and stronger the fish, the stronger the tackle necessary for beginners (which is why heavier gear

B

is most often used on offshore charter boats), until you get the experience to use lighter gear. Most selection starts with a determination of the line strength necessary for the conditions, and having the rod and reel appropriate for this. You should also give a lot of attention to line capacity so that you have an appropriate amount of line on the reel for the application.

Holding the rod and reel. Lever drag reels are too large for palming and not conducive for usage like a baitcasting reel, so they are usually held by putting the left hand on the rod foregrip. This is obviously the hold for placing the butt in a belt gimbal or into a harness. Holding the foregrip with the left hand also helps with guiding the line on the spool in a level manner.

Backing off the drag. Before any on-the-water use of a big-game reel, it is vital to set the drag to the proper amount of tension. Issues pertaining to setting drag were reviewed earlier in this section, and using and setting drag is covered in more detail elsewhere *(see: drag).*

At the end of each day of fishing, and after a reel has been washed and dried, it is a good idea to back the drag tension off to relieve pressure on the drag washers. This is not quite as important for lever drag reels with carbon fiber drag washers, as they resist compression better than washers made of other friction material; nevertheless, releasing tension is still a good idea. This is done by moving the drag lever back to the freespool position and making sure that the clicker is engaged so the spool does not spill loose line. It's a good practice to keep pressure off the washers, and it also allows internal parts to dry out if necessary.

Maintenance and repair. Maintenance is an ongoing issue for big-game tackle users. Rods and reels must be washed down every time they are taken on the water, even if not used, because they are likely to be exposed to salt spray. Use a fine but ample spray of freshwater, rather than a hard stream, to clean the reel and remove salt deposits, and do so as soon as possible after you return to the dock or launch site. Use soap and a scrub brush to remove any hardened matter. Warm water is best if available, and make sure not to use a hard stream, which could drive salt deposits into the internal mechanisms. Dry off excess freshwater on the reel and lubricate exposed areas, perhaps with a pressurized spray oil. A light coating of oil with a rag can also be applied to exposed metal parts. Give the reel a chance to dry out completely, and store it in a cool, dry place, not in a bag that is wet or which will promote condensation. Be sure to keep the drag tension set when washing to help keep unwanted moisture out of internal parts, especially the drag washers. Some reels have a special internal collar to help keep moisture and dirt out, but you should keep maximum drag tension on anyway until the reel has been wiped down

and is ready for storage. Then back off the drag pressure completely.

Make sure to periodically examine screws and fittings. If the reel has any loose part, which is most likely to be a sideplate screw, it should be tightened as soon as you notice it. Do not excessively lubricate reels, which may cause harm if oil or grease get on parts that don't need, or shouldn't have, the lubrication. That includes carbon fiber drag washers. Using the wrong kind of lubrication is also a problem. Follow the manufacturer's recommendations for the type of lubrication to use, the locations, and the frequency, as this will vary with different brands.

If you are mechanically minded, you can carefully strip down and examine and clean the reel yourself. Pay special attention to the drag components and to the drag friction washers. If the drag has been underperforming, it may be due to (excessive) lubrication. You may be able to alleviate some of the problem by washing the friction washer in white spirit or dry cleaning fluid (do this in a well-ventilated area and wear a mask to avoid breathing fumes) until all traces of the lubrication have been removed. Allow it to dry thoroughly. You can relubricate the friction washer lightly if recommended by the manufacturer and only with the suggested lubricant, or, in the case of carbon fiber washers, do not lubricate it. Carefully reassemble the parts (you did save the manufacturer's manual with schematic diagram, didn't you?). Although some people try polishing the metal friction disk or drag pressure plates to improve performance, manufacturers say that polishing can cause an uneven surface, so they recommend replacement.

Details on general tackle maintenance are discussed elsewhere *(see: tackle—care/maintenance/repair).* Manufacturers recommend that lever drag reels be overhauled at least once a season, perhaps more if used vigorously. Periodically oil and grease moving parts, but don't overdo it, and only use the type of oil and grease recommended by the manufacturer. A thorough cleaning requires disassembling most of the reel, scrubbing or rinsing most of the gunk from the parts, drying, and then relubricating and regreasing. If you are unsure about doing this yourself, have a reel service and repair shop do it, or send it to the manufacturer for servicing.

Lever drag reels, as previously noted, are subject to maintenance and repair work by very specialized master technicians. These are the finest high-tech fishing instruments in the world, so it makes sense to have maintenance done in the off-season by professionals, as well as to have them look at fine-tuning operational features, especially the drag.

BIGHT

A bay formed by an indentation or curve in a coastline.

BILGE

(1) The lowest part of the interior of a boat.

(2) Rank water collected in the bottom of a boat.

BILHARZIA

See: First Aid.

BILLABONG

An Australian term for a backwater or pond connected to a river; it is derived from the aboriginal words "billa," meaning river, and "bong," meaning dead. Billabongs have vegetation and fallen or flooded trees (snags), and they drain during the dry season. During and after rainy periods, billabongs are usually flush with water and may host gamefish, especially barramundi, amidst profuse cover. During the dry season, billabongs may dry up, or they may develop into a stagnant pool cut off from the main stream, at which time they are likely to support only carp.

BILLFISH

The term "billfish" refers to members of two families of marine fish: Xiphidae, which has only one genus and one species, the swordfish; and Istiophoridae, which numbers 11 species in three genera and includes marlin, sailfish, and spearfish. Of the latter family, the term "marlin" is used for the larger species, "spearfish" for the smaller species, and "sailfish" for the species with a high dorsal fin. All are good sportfish, and some—especially swordfish, blue marlin, and black marlin—are among the largest and most coveted angling quarries.

Billfish are characterized by a long spearlike or swordlike upper jaw or beak that may be used to stun prey during feeding; although this bill has been employed in apparent aggression to spear objects, including boats, it is not deliberately used to spear prey. These species are pelagic, migratory, and found in all oceans. They are related to tuna *(see)* and mackerel *(see)* and, like those fish, are able to swim at great speeds; the sailfish is considered the fastest of all fish, having been clocked at 68 miles per hour over short distances. Billfish also have complex air (or swim) bladders that enable them to compensate rapidly for changes in depth and thus can move without difficulty from deep water to the surface.

Billfish grow fairly rapidly and feed on various pelagic species. When alive, they are generally ocean blue above and silvery below. They spawn in the open sea and are usually solitary or travel in pairs or small groups. Sportfishing interest in these big-game species is high, although due to their migratory and pelagic nature they are seldom accessible to large numbers of anglers, and rarely

A Pacific sailfish from Huatulco, Mexico.

to those who fish from small boats and inshore. Fishing in offshore blue-water environments is the norm.

Most billfish, particularly swordfish, have good to excellent food value and are of significant commercial interest. As a whole, and especially in certain parts of their range, billfish stocks are overexploited and have seriously declined due to commercial longlines and gillnets. Sportfishing has not adversely impacted billfish stocks; only a small percentage of the world's billfish are caught by recreational anglers, and a still smaller percentage of those are killed. Angler tagging of released billfish has contributed significantly to scientific knowledge about this species. Nevertheless, worldwide, commercial fishermen kill millions of billfish annually. The Billfish Foundation, a research and conservation organization, reports that more than 500,000 billfish in the Atlantic Ocean alone were killed each year from the 1970s through 1990s by longlining. Furthermore, their data show that for every porpoise killed by commercial tuna fishermen, 10 tons of billfish were killed during the same period. Although efforts to save porpoises from commercial destruction have been widely reported and awareness has triggered some success, no organized international effort has emerged to prevent the commercial overharvesting and destruction of the world's billfish stocks.

See: Marlin, Black; Marlin, Blue; Marlin, Striped; Marlin, White; Sailfish; Spearfish; Swordfish.

BILLFISH ON FLY TACKLE

Although offshore fishing has long been the domain of big fish and beefy tackle, a surge has occurred in the number of people who pursue what some consider the ultimate light-tackle challenge: billfish on a fly rod. Although there are practical limits to what can be done with a fly rod—the real heavyweights are beyond its capabilities—the envelope of achievement in this arena has been steadily pushed forward for the last few decades.

In the early 1960s, attempting to catch sailfish or marlin on a fly rod would have been thought virtually impossible, or merely a stunt. A few pioneers were convinced it could be done even then and set about trying to prove it. Lee Cuddy caught the first record billfish on a fly—an Atlantic sailfish of 47 pounds, landed off Florida on June 4, 1964. Stu Apte caught the first Pacific sailfish of record on a fly (on 12-pound tippet) at Pinas Bay, Panama, on June 25, 1965. Lee Wulff landed a fly-caught striped marlin of 148 pounds at Salinas, Ecuador, in May 1967, and accomplished a record that still stands; but Floridian Doc Robinson caught a 145-pound striped marlin off Baja California in 1965, establishing him as the first to catch a marlin on a fly. After those feats, the pursuit of billfish on a fly became more serious, and people took it up for the general fun and achievement as well as in an attempt to establish records. South Carolina's Billy Pate was the first to set saltwater fly-rod records in all the marlin and sailfish categories except Pacific blue marlin. And by the 1990s, Jack Samson had become the first to catch both Atlantic and Pacific sailfish, as well as all five species of marlin, on a fly rod, achieving a "super grand slam" of billfish.

Since the late 1980s, catching large ocean fish on a saltwater fly rod has been an established niche game. Although bonefish, tarpon, bluefish, and striped bass are still the most popularly sought saltwater species among fly anglers, sailfish and marlin are now pursued by a growing legion of enthusiasts.

Fly-tackle dealers on all coasts are catering to neophyte fly-rod billfish anglers in search of the proper gear and more information on this growing sport. Thanks to more information, better equipment, and the accomplishments of earlier anglers, catching some of the ocean's most spectacular fish on a fly rod is a realistic goal, particularly for experienced anglers. For those who are less experienced, sailfish, white marlin, and striped marlin are reasonable targets, as these species do not attain the monster weights of their blue and black marlin brethren. Due to their size and availability, however, sailfish are the primary billfish for saltwater fly rodders.

Fish size is a bit of an issue, and a limitation, where fly rodding is concerned, especially for marlin. Unlike conventional big-game anglers, fly rodders are generally limited to billfish up to about 400 pounds. The largest fly-caught marlin record to date is a 260-pound Pacific blue marlin caught on 20-pound-class tippet. No one knows how many larger marlin have been caught by anglers who don't care about records and release their fish without fanfare, although it seems likely that extremely few have accomplished such a feat. It seems possible that larger fish can be caught, and perhaps some will. For an experienced angler, it is no problem holding billfish below 200 pounds. The biggest fly-caught sailfish in the record books weighed 136 pounds—caught in 1965 on a 12-pound tippet; but again, perhaps some bigger sailfish have been caught by fly rodders who prefer not to kill their quarry and instead turn it loose.

Today's billfish angler is limited mainly by skill and luck, mostly the latter. The rods, reels, lines, leaders, and flies exist to catch larger billfish. Some anglers who have specialized in this type of fishing, however, have been after bigger fish for many years and haven't landed them. So this particular sport is definitely not an easy one.

Technique

The technique used to take a big striper out of the surf won't work on a striped marlin, and the 7-weight rod and line used to catch big bonefish would be like a child's toy if used for sailfish. Furthermore, the game of stalking and casting for shallow-water and inshore species is nonexistent for pelagic species.

As many conventional big-game anglers know, sailfish and marlin generally are taken from a trolling boat underway. This is because the ocean is big, a lot of ground has to be covered, and the fish have to be attracted to your offering. This is all true in fly fishing for billfish, but the resemblance ends there. In general terms, an angler could theoretically troll a fly, but the chances of catching a billfish on a trolled fly are fairly slim, and this technique would not meet International Game Fish Association (IGFA) requirements for establishing a record, should the fish be large enough to qualify. Because it is never known when a record fish might be

A fly-hooked sailfish clears the water close to the boat, forcing the angler to point his rod directly at it to minimize drag.

caught by offshore anglers (those using big-game tackle or flycasting tackle), most ardent anglers follow accepted procedures that guarantee they will be within record-setting guidelines whenever and wherever they are fly fishing.

IGFA world-record rules state that a fly can be cast to billfish only while a boat is out of gear (not trolling and moving forward). The original rules, set up by early saltwater fly rodders, make a lot of sense on closer examination. The boat is taken out of gear partly to ensure that an angler casts rather than drags a trolled fly, but it is primarily done to ensure precise presentation of a fly that will land close to a billfish searching for food. Billfish come up and strike baits, lures, and flies with their bills; they stun the object so they can turn and then take it. If the fly is moving at the same speed as the boat, and directly forward of a fish swimming immediately behind the boat, it is almost impossible to position the lightweight fly inside a billfish's mouth at a spot where you can set the hook.

Billfish must be attracted up behind the boat by trolling baits and teasers. Veteran billfish fly rodders generally agree that big, gaudy teasers run off outriggers or on flatlines behind the transom, and dead baits rigged without hooks and trolled 30 to 50 feet behind the boat, work best to attract billfish in an effort to present a fly to them. There is considerable leeway in this. Some veterans like to troll a daisy chain of squid as teasers, and others like trolling live baits without hooks. Most experts prefer trolling a rigged dead bait on a long, whippy teaser rod so they can retrieve it rapidly when a billfish appears or strikes it.

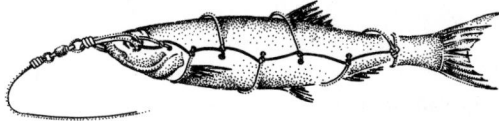

A durable sewn teaser bait is used for bringing billfish into casting range.

Whatever the choice of attractor, when a billfish comes up to eat it, it is imperative that the trolled offering be pulled rapidly toward the boat ahead of the searching billfish, until it is possible to cast a fly to it. At that time, the boat is taken out of gear, the bait is rapidly yanked from the water, the fly is cast, and the billfish is allowed to pursue the fly. The aim of this tactic, often referred to as bait-and-switch (see) is not only to get the billfish to take the fly, but for the angler to set the hook in the corner of the billfish's mouth as it makes a turn with the fly. Most successful billfish flies today are tied in tandem, one hook riding point up and another point down, in order to increase the chances of getting a hook into tough cartilage. It should be set either in the corner of the mouth or in the soft top of the mouth. If the hook is sharp enough, clamping down on the line with the thumb and forefinger should set the hook

firmly, but yanking hard on the rod will certainly help set the hook better.

Once the billfish is hooked, it is important to make sure that the rest of the fly line, the running line, and the backing is free to run out through the rod guides as the big fish makes its first run. For that reason, when casting to billfish most anglers keep that line in a large plastic bucket at their feet. Snagging on the least obstruction in the cockpit, or stepping on the line, will cause a tippet to part.

More about teasing.   Perhaps the most critical aspect of fly fishing for billfish is the act of attracting, or teasing, a fish and exciting it so much that it is willing to strike the fly. This activity requires teamwork from a crew, usually a minimum of three people, which includes the angler, captain, and mate.

The items used to attract billfish are hookless trolling lures *(see: trolling lures, saltwater)* and hookless rigged baits. These are all referred to as teasers because they are used to attract a fish and perhaps draw a strike but are not meant to be consumed or grabbed and held by the fish. They are usually skipped across the surface rather than fished below it. The number of people in the boat available to reel in lines when a fish appears determines the number of teasers used. The lures may be run off a line attached halfway up one outrigger, as well as on transom flatlines. Some anglers prefer to use lures on the outside and longer trolling lines, primarily those with a soft head that are easy to retrieve quickly. A lure or bait (usually the latter) is attached to a long sturdy rod (9 feet or longer) and trolled off the transom. The bait is a completely sewn mullet, mackerel, ballyhoo, or flyingfish, but it could be other items, as well as strips of bait if whole fish are unavailable; these are often adorned at the head with a colorful plastic skirt. The long rod is necessary to exert control over the teaser when it is close, and to quickly yank the teaser out of the water. If 9 feet of line, measured from the rod tip, is let out, and the rod holder stands flush against the transom, a 9-foot rod allows for placement of a teaser approximately 18 feet behind the boat, yet the teaser is still capable of being instantly lifted out of the water. The object is to get the fish just behind that close-range teaser and pursuing it excitedly.

When a fish comes into the spread, the captain reels in the outrigger teaser lure and then watches the fish while preparing to adjust speed. The mate(s) retrieves the other lures while maintaining the interest of the following fish. The billfish may switch from one teaser to another, but it is important to attract it to within 20 to 25 feet of the boat in pursuit of the teaser attached to a teaser rod. The person holding the teaser rod tries to maintain the interest of the fish without letting it firmly grab the teaser, generally trying to keep the fish a few feet behind the moving teaser. If the job is done well, the billfish will keep slashing at the teaser, trying to stun it and appearing to have missed it. This game

B

B

is a bit different for some species than for others, or may differ by location, requiring faster or slower boat speeds, for example, to sustain the interest of the pursuing fish.

Assuming the fly angler is right-handed, the best casting scenario is for the angler to stand in the port transom corner of the boat, with excess fly line and backing in a tub or bucket at the feet. There should be no nearby obstructions that could snatch the line, and the port outrigger should be in a vertical position so the angler has plenty of room for a back cast. The person doing the teasing tries to keep the teaser lure or bait to the starboard side of the whitewater boat wake, and the angler gets the fly in the water and about 20 to 25 feet back. The fish is allowed to touch the teaser, and the captain is told to put the boat in neutral; with the boat in neutral, the angler picks up the fly line and casts behind and to the right of the billfish. The teaser is yanked away, the fly is stripped into view, and the fish turns toward the fly, putting itself into position for a good set should it immediately strike the fly. The same tactic is used if the angler is left-handed, except that the angler would stand in the starboard corner and the fish would be teased to the port side.

Generally, slower boat speeds make for better teasing, although this method may not raise or excite fish. Fish that are really excited and aggressive are most likely to take the fly. And if the fish doesn't take the fly after a careful effort and perhaps a second cast and retrieve, then it may be necessary to resume trolling with the teasers to re-attract the fish.

Fighting and Landing

After the billfish has made its initial runs, landing it is usually simply a matter of maintaining control until the fish is tired and can be brought to the boat. A fight with a billfish on fly tackle can last hours, depending on the class of leader tippet, the weight of the fish, and the experience of the angler.

It takes a sturdy rod and reel and well-tied knots to withstand the pressure of battling billfish on fly tackle.

Fighting big fish on a fly rod takes some physical strength, but not so much as to prevent women from enjoying the sport as much as men. Although you can power-fight a billfish, it takes considerable strength to tire a billfish in the first few minutes of a battle. It is better to let the parabolic curve of the big saltwater fly rod do its work, which it will certainly do in time.

When a billfish is making its first runs and jumps, it's best to almost freespool the big saltwater reel. In this way, the pressure of the shooting head passing rapidly through the water does not put undue strain on the class tippet. The sailfish or marlin will eventually tire and will settle down to a stubborn fight. At this point, the angler can increase the reel drag and begin to take up line while the skipper backs down slowly in the direction of the fish.

Some billfish elect to stay near or on the surface for the duration of the battle, which makes life easier for the angler, but others may head for the depths. This is where the size and construction of the fly rod becomes important. Many 12- and 13-weight fly rods are simply not constructed to lift big billfish from the depths; they either break or do not put sufficient pressure on the fish to budge it. Manufacturers have lately been making 14-weight rods to compensate, and the relatively new breed of "lifting" fly rods, which are strong 15- to 18-weight models, can bring up a stubborn billfish from the depths when no other fly rod would work.

As the billfish begins to close in on the transom for landing, the crew becomes all-important. These strong fish often make sudden thrashing moves at the last minute and can inflict injury. Billfish anglers must be able to anticipate violent moves by the fish and make sure to grasp it properly. It is not necessary to sink large gaffs into a billfish to get it alongside the boat. Many times the fish can be led alongside with a small bill gaff; now and then a tail rope may be slipped over the tail. A crewmember can grasp the bill with a gloved hand, and the fish can be released at the boat or brought in over the transom briefly for photographs before being released.

A beginning fly rodder can use any strength leader to take billfish, but if angling for records, IGFA stipulates seven leader tippet categories: 2, 4, 6, 8, 12, 16, and 20 pounds. For the novice, and for general fishing purposes, a 20-pound tippet makes the most sense. Because most billfish are released, using a heavier tippet usually ensures a shorter fight, which is generally better for the fish than one that is long and drawn out. If you have no concerns about records (although if you're fishing with established charter boat captains, they usually are very attentive to this), you could choose a tippet size that exceeds IGFA regulations but still ensures a good fight. With some experience under your belt, you can move down in tippet size.

The lightest tippets are very difficult to use for billfishing, however, and this is evident from existing fly-tackle world records. Several of the light-tippet categories for sailfish are still vacant, and for the five species of marlin, most of the categories under 12-pound tippet are vacant. The light-tippet categories for marlin are vacant because few anglers have hooked marlin on a fly, even on the heavier tippets. Although it's possible to land billfish on light tippets, years of experience are generally necessary before even the best of anglers can handle a billfish on such fragile leaders.

Fortunately, almost any size boat can be used to catch billfish on a fly. It is no longer necessary to use the big, expensive sportfishing boat common to conventional big-game angling. Today, small, fast, compact, and maneuverable boats are taking billfish off all North American coasts. They transport fly rodders out to the billfish grounds fast and are able to return home in a hurry. Although small boats provide a degree of angler maneuverability that big yachts may not, the distance offshore to the billfish grounds, the potential sea conditions, and the skill of the captain are all factors that impact boat selection.

The vast majority of those who use fly tackle for billfish do it for the thrill of the sport and release most if not all of the billfish caught *(see: catch-and-release)*. The exception might be for fish that are potential records, although anglers should make every effort to evaluate the size of their catch quickly *(see: measuring fish)* and determine if it's large enough to be a potential record. If there is any doubt, the fish should be quickly released. In most cases, a photograph of the fish, plus its measurements, should be enough to establish the record.

Tackle

Sailfish and marlin require a different set of tools than do other fish sought with flycasting tackle: strong fiberglass and graphite rods in the 12- to 16-weight class, reels capable of carrying 400 to 600 yards of line and backing, and sinking shooting-head lines in 12- to 16-weight categories. These fish also demand strong leader material and a set of knots that will not part under enormous strain; these are knots that most fly anglers have never had occasion to use.

Flies that imitate the many species of ocean baitfish need to be tied on hooks that will not break and will resist the constant effects of corrosion from exposure to saltwater. These hooks must be filed to points sharp enough to penetrate the tough mouth cartilage of billfish, which is no small task.

The beginner has plenty of excellent rods, reels, and lines to choose from, as the major line companies have spent a lot of time researching and developing lines that will stand up to rough treatment in saltwater. Leader material has come a long way in the past few decades, and many brands are available. Although one can have a custom rod made, first-class billfish fly rods are being manufactured today by various companies, primarily in 10- to 14-weight models for smaller fish, and 14- to 16-weight for larger fish.

Large, bright streamer flies, some with popping-style heads, are standard for billfish.

The most import aspects of a big-game fly reel are the line capacity and the drag. Today's big-game fly reels are machined from solid blocks of aircraft-quality aluminum and stainless steel bar stock. The drag systems use stainless steel bearings and multiple-disc surfaces of metal, Teflon, and cork; the spools are also machined from the same high-quality aluminum. These fast-spinning spools are counterbalanced to within a few grains of weight.

To handle strong and far-running billfish, a big, saltwater fly reel must have a capacity of at least 400 yards, preferably 600 or more yards, including 30-pound Micron or Dacron backing plus 100 feet of nylon monofilament running line (optional) and 25 to 30 feet of 15-weight sinking shooting-head fly line. A reel just for sailfish, particularly the big Pacific sailfish that run in excess of 100 pounds, should have a total capacity of 350 to 400 yards. For marlin, a fly reel should carry no less than 600 combined yards of fly line and 30-pound backing; many of the best have a capacity of 800 to 900 yards.

Although beginning fly rodders might use a floating fly line, it is better to have a sinking line. The floating line is easier to pick up off the water for casting (or recasting, as it were), but its bulkiness becomes a drag problem when a billfish has steamed off with a lot of line and then turns, creating a huge bow in the line, which increases drag. Experts use a 30-foot head of fast-sinking line and a short total fly-line length (under 60 feet) to reduce drag. The angler and captain need a brightly colored backing in order to see where the fish is and how far out it is, especially if it becomes necessary to follow the fish.

With big billfish-class fly rods, it isn't necessary for an angler to be in a casting class with the best distance flycasters—these rods are so heavy, it's difficult to heave line far, and very few casts per day are required in billfishing. Under ordinary circumstances, it's unnecessary to cast a big billfish fly any more than 30 to 40 feet.

B

Critical knots. It is absolutely essential that saltwater fly rodders, especially those intent on catching billfish, learn to tie knots well. Knots are the most important element of terminal tackle. The backing is fastened to the running line by back-to-back Nail Knots. The running line is connected to butt leader sections with Loop-to-Loop or Double Surgeon Knots. Leaders and tippet sections utilize Bimini Twist Knots or Spider Hitches, and leader sections are connected to 80- to 100-pound shock tippets by Albright Knots or modified Nail Knots. The shock tippet may be fastened to the fly by a three-turn Improved Clinch Knot *(see: knots, fishing)*. Most of these knots are difficult to learn and harder to tie, but they are absolutely necessary to hold fish in the 100- to 300-pound category when traveling at great speeds.

Some anglers aren't knot aficionados, and even though they may use such knots as the Albright, the Surgeon's Loop, and the Spider Hitch, they prefer metal connector sleeves when forming certain connections. These connector sleeves are used to fasten the fly to 100-pound-test shock leader and also to make loops in the ends of the shooting-head fly line, which are fastened to either butt leader or mono running line with loop-to-loop connections. These sleeves may not be as pretty as knots, but they are very strong and don't slip when used properly.

Some anglers use a Spider Hitch Knot rather than the hard-to-tie Bimini Twist. The Spider Hitch is simple to tie and is every bit as strong as the Bimini in lines below 30-pound test, which are applicable for nearly all saltwater fly fishing.

Where to Go

For the specialized game of fly rodding for billfish, knowing only where billfish will be at any time of the year is not sufficient. You also must know where the right size billfish will be. Thus, for practical reasons, anglers hoping to land billfish on a fly must seek these species in sizes that average from under 100 pounds up to 350 pounds, and this prerequisite somewhat limits the selection of locations.

There would be little sense, for example, in fishing with a fly rod off Cairns, Australia, in October or November for black marlin, when 1,000-pound blacks are cruising and the average black ranges from 500 to 600 pounds. On the other hand, if you wanted to catch a nice fly-rod black marlin, it would be wise to fish off Townsville, Australia, which is inside the Great Barrier Reef, in August or September. The blacks there average 50 to 100 pounds then. Though most fly rodders think the only place one can find small black marlin is off Australia, there are small black marlin off Panama in January, February, and March. Off the mouth of Pinas Bay they run in the 300- to 500-pound range during those months and are caught on a regular basis by conventional big-game and light-tackle anglers.

White marlin almost never grow much larger than 100 pounds, so during for most of the year you can fish for them almost anywhere. They are caught all up and down the Atlantic coast, from late spring until late summer. To find them in great numbers, however, serious anglers head for Venezuela in October and November. A month later, they appear in concentrated numbers off Brazil.

Places to catch small Atlantic blue marlin are few, but possibilities include Jamaica in February and March, St. Thomas later in the spring and summer, and Venezuela in October, November, and early December. The channel that runs between the island of Cozumel and the east coast of Mexico, close to Cancún, is a great spot to pursue Atlantic blue marlin from February through May.

Finding small Pacific blue marlin is a tough one to call. Unfortunately, there is really no one place in which one can be certain of finding smaller sizes of this fish in great numbers at any one time. Pacific blue marlin exist off Hawaii and a number of Pacific islands, but their size renders them impractical for a fly rodder. The best place to try for small Pacific blue marlin might be off Cabo San Lucas. El Niño notwithstanding, the best time to pursue them off Baja would be from late spring up through November. Although there is no guarantee that they would be the right size for fly anglers, the catch records indicate that more blue marlin in the 200- to 400-pound category are caught there than anywhere else. Some blues in the 60- to 70-pound class have been caught there, which indicates that they migrate past that port at a fairly early age.

Atlantic sailfish congregate off Florida's East Coast, particularly in the winter off such areas as Jupiter Inlet and Palm Beach. But they are usually also plentiful off the Florida Keys at that time and later in the spring. Cozumel in March is a fine spot for Atlantic sails, as well as white marlin and small Atlantic blue marlin through May.

Pacific sailfish range all the way up the west coast of Central and South America to Baja and the Sea of Cortez. The best place to catch Pacific sailfish at any one time might be Panama in April and May, particularly at Pinas Bay. Also worth considering are Bahia Pez Vela on the upper coast of Costa Rica and Flamingo in the spring. During the winter months, when the winds make fishing almost impossible in those northern areas, Golfito in extreme southern Costa Rica, and Quepos, where a barrier range of mountains keeps the winds down and the seas calm, are good candidates.

In Mexico, Mazatlán is the top Pacific sailfish location, especially from May through October. But that is on the mainland—off Baja there are plenty of sails in the late spring and summer months, from an area south of La Paz all the way up to Loreto and Mulege.

The acrobatic Pacific striped marlin is a natural for fly rodders. It seldom exceeds 150 pounds in weight, which is just right for most fly anglers. The East Cape of Baja, from about La Paz down to Cabo San Lucas, is prime striped marlin territory from May through October. Another excellent spot for striped marlin is off Ecuador in the spring out of the port of Salinas, although it is a difficult place to reach. Striped marlin are caught regularly off Panama and Costa Rica, but they don't seem to congregate in any one spot at any one time. Striped marlin are also found resting on the surface in small pods off Mazatlán from February through April.

Striped marlin in the 250-pound class are regularly taken in New Zealand, although not on a fly. Since the records for striped marlin in New Zealand on conventional tackle are impressive—from 271 pounds to nearly 500 pounds—this fishery seems to offer possibilities for fly rodders as well.

BILL-WRAPPED
The wrapping of the bill of a marlin or sailfish with the leader or fishing line. This occurs occasionally during the fight of a fish. It may cause the line to be chafed and cut or may inhibit the behavior and fight of the fish.

BIMINI TWIST
A double-line knot primarily associated with saltwater fishing, especially the use of heavy leaders and big-game angling.
See: Knots, Fishing.

BIOLUMINESCENCE
The emission of visible nonthermal light by chemical reaction in living organisms. Bioluminescence is a highly developed characteristic of species in the deepest parts of the ocean, and a less highly developed characteristic of many near-surface ocean creatures, including species of bacteria, phytoplankton, metazoans, marine invertebrates, and fish. It occurs when luciferin, a compound found naturally in the luminescing organism, combines with oxygen and the enzyme luciferase to form oxyluciferin, water, and energy. Thus, chemical energy is transformed into light energy, and the resulting light is often used to attract prey. Some species have daily light cycles; others have seasonal ones. Individual luminescing organisms are difficult to see, but a large population of organisms glowing together becomes visible in darkness.

Saltwater anglers who fish at night, and boaters traveling at night, sometimes observe an eerie glow in the water caused by luminescent organisms being displaced by the movement of the boat.

BIOMASS
The total weight or volume of a stock or of a component of a stock. Also referred to as standing stock.

Spawning stock biomass is the total weight of all fish in a stock that are old enough to spawn.

BIRDS
Birds are a good indicator of fish in saltwater, although less so in freshwater. In freshwater environments, anglers are likely to see such fish-eating birds as herons, kingfishers, loons, mergansers, and cormorants, as well as seagulls. Herons are shorebirds usually found where there are many small fish in shallow water. Mergansers and most other diving ducks are seldom of much assistance to anglers, although actively feeding loons and cormorants may indicate the nearby presence of baitfish schools. Seagulls are seldom of much fish-locating value, except when they are actively following schools of surface-feeding striped bass in impoundments.

The situation in saltwater is quite different, however, because there are more birds and more surface food to attract birds. In the marine environment, noticing birds, learning to recognize them, and following them, can help find gamefish. Knowing which ones to follow and when is a skill that comes from experience. When to follow them is usually dependent on whether they are searching, actively feeding, or flying by. When birds are searching, their flight path is straight, graceful, and relaxed. Once they spot a food source, they speed up; their turns become sharp, and eventually they begin swooping down to the water. An increased level of excitement is obvious from loud chattering, which is meant to attract other birds. Take particular notice of whether birds seem afraid to sit on the surface. If so, bluefish are probably present, and the birds have good reason to fear having their feet bitten off. Pelicans, though, will actually dive into the water and feast on smaller bluefish.

The number of birds that you see is not necessarily an indication of the number of fish below

When diving to pluck baitfish, seagulls and terns often indicate the presence of feeding gamefish.

B

them. A single large billfish might push up a large ball of bait and attract many birds, yet only a few birds may be observed at a site where there is a school of other gamefish. And not all birds are reliable fish indicators; examples in saltwater include cormorants and albatrosses. Here is a synopsis of birds commonly observed at sea, and their general significance.

Terns. Terns are a wide-ranging bird, with long, slender wings, straight beaks, and forked tails. Smaller than seagulls and known for their flitting, dive-bombing activity, terns are good indicators of fish location. Within a few miles of shore, they are great indicators of baitfish—information that is helpful when you're catching bait. Offshore, they often provide an excellent clue that schools of baitfish are being worked over just beneath the surface. If terns are swooping but not touching the water, they may be positioned over patches of algae—and often big dolphin. If terns are tightly bunched, the fish are probably small. If the flock is moving quickly from one spot to another, the baitfish are likely being run by schools of king mackerel, tuna, or bonito. In inshore waters, they can be indicators of mackerel, bluefish, tarpon, snook, and kingfish.

Frigate birds. The most reliable offshore fishfinders are frigate birds, also known as man-o'-war birds. They're easily recognized from a distance by their wide wings and long, deeply forked tails. High-flying frigates are known for helping anglers find big blue-water gamefish (and floating objects), including bull dolphin, marlin, and sailfish, by shadowing their movements from above. They'll follow large, solitary predator fish in anticipation of diving quickly to the surface to grab fleeing baitfish. Closer to shore they may be found in groups of two dozen or more but are more solitary farther offshore.

Shearwaters. These pelagic seabirds are similar in appearance to gulls. They often beat their wings several times, then glide low to the water. Shearwaters will swim underwater to catch bait, at times feeding so heavily they struggle to fly. Offshore, look for them on top of kelp paddies; their presence helps you spot paddies from long distances, and their movements tip you off to the direction in which the fish are headed. They are often associated with tuna and less commonly with billfish.

Boobies/gannets/pelicans/jaegers. Boobies can be found in huge groups numbering in the hundreds and can be visual aids for leading anglers to baitfish and gamefish. Gannets are high-diving birds that plummet into the water for food and are noticeable from a long distance. Pelicans are sometimes an indicator that such offshore gamefish as billfish and sharks are feeding, and may be present where mackerel and anchovies are balled up. Jaegers look like dark-colored seagulls with erratic, flared-tail flight, but their sharply bent wings and long central tail feathers distinguish them from gulls. These food thieves tend to follow other birds that have found fish.

Seagulls/petrels. Some saltwater anglers do not find seagulls very useful, although others do. Inshore, seagulls can be terrific indicators of fish activity along the beach, especially for mackerel, bluefish, tarpon, snook, and kingfish. They do not dive but pick up scraps off the surface, as well as wounded baitfish on the surface, which could be an indication of feeding gamefish in the area. Offshore, seagulls are perhaps the least reliable seabird because they have a tendency to get excited about picking at floating garbage. Many anglers do not find petrels useful, but others find them helpful for locating tuna.
See: Finding Fish; Sight Fishing.

BIRD, TROLLING

A common term for a bird- or airplane-shaped teaser used in offshore fishing, especially for marlin and tuna.
See: Trolling Lures, Saltwater.

BITE

(1) The strike of a fish, especially common to natural bait usage.

(2) An expression for hot sportfish activity, as in, "There was a good walleye bite on spinners yesterday."

(3) A point of measurement on a hook *(see)*.

BITE INDICATOR

Any small object, usually one that floats, which is used to indicate a bite, or strike, by a fish on some form of bait. All floats *(see)* and bobbers *(see)* are types of bite indicators, although not actually called bite indicators. In Europe, the term bite indicator is used for a small object that may be attached to the rod tip or to the line when fishing groundbait *(see)* without a float. Bite indicators are more sensitive than rod tips.
See: Float; Legering; Strike Indicator.

BIVISIBLE

A highly visible, high-floating, and generally light-colored type of dry fly *(see)*.

BLACKFISH

"Blackfish" is the common or regional name for black sea bass (see: sea bass, black), bowfin *(see)*, luderick *(see)*, tautog *(see)*, and tripletail *(see)*.

BLACK SALMON

A term for kelt *(see)*, or overwintering sea-run Atlantic salmon.
See: Salmon, Atlantic.

BLACKMOUTH

A term used in the Pacific Northwest for immature, resident chinook salmon *(see)*, derived from a black gum line that helps distinguish them from other salmon species.

BLADE BAIT

A lipless sinking lure with a thin metal body.
See: Spoon.

BLANK

The shaft of a fishing rod. This refers both to the newly fabricated product unadorned with components (guides, wrapping, handle, and reel seat), and to the shaft of a completed rod. The exterior of most rod blanks is fitted with guides to assist in dispensing and retrieving line; however, line passes through the interior of some completely hollow blanks. The material of the blank is most commonly fiberglass, graphite, or a composite of these materials.
See: Rod, Fishing.

BLIND CASTING

Fishing in circumstances in which the fish cannot be seen, and lures or flies are presented without firm knowledge that the quarry is present.

This term is most often applied to stalking saltwater species (including tarpon, permit, and bonefish) in shallow water and in circumstances in which the fish are casually observed and cast to even though the water conditions (depth or turbidity) prevent visual sighting and exact presentation. In all but clear-water conditions, however, or when fish are actively feeding in an observable manner, most casting in fresh- and saltwater is done in a "blind" manner, that is, the angler relies on knowledge of the water and the quarry to make a presentation in the right place and in the right manner.
See: Finding Fish.

BLOOD KNOT

A fishing knot for line-to-line connections.
See: Knots, Fishing.

BLUE DUN

A gray blue color of hackle preferred for fly tying, and also called iron blue dun.

BLUEFISH   *Pomatomus saltatrix.*

Other names—blue, tailor, elf, chopper, marine piranha, rock salmon, snapper blue, snapper, Hatteras blue, skipjack (Australia), shad (South Africa); French: *tassergal;* Japanese: *amikiri;* Portuguese: *anchova, enchova;* Spanish: *anjova, anchova de banco.*

The only member of the Pomatomidae family, the bluefish is an extremely voracious and cannibalistic saltwater fish. A fierce opponent, it has gained a reputation among marine anglers as the hardest fighter per pound. These fish put up a long battle, even though they are typically caught in the 5- to 12-pound range. True to their scientific name (*saltatrix* means "leaper"), they will also jump if not caught on very heavy tackle. Schooling bluefish are particularly aggressive, often rampaging through a pod of baitfish. They have distinguished themselves as an occasional menace to bathers, and have attacked and lacerated bathers. They have also been known to run up on the beach when frenziedly chasing baits in the surf wash.

Bluefish are an important commercial fish, noted for a strong but delicious flavor; the flesh becomes soft if not eaten fresh and does not keep well if frozen for a long time.

Identification.   The body shape of a bluefish is fairly long, stout, and compressed, with a flat-sided belly. The mouth is large and has extremely sharp, flattened, and triangular teeth. The first dorsal fin is low and short and consists of six to eight spines, whereas the second dorsal fin is long and has one spine and 23 to 28 soft rays; the anal fin has two spines and 25 to 27 soft rays. Both the second dorsal fin and the anal fin are covered with small, compact scales. The coloring is greenish or bluish on the back, and silvery on the sides; a distinguishing characteristic is a dark blotch at the base of the pectoral fins. The tail is dusky and deeply forked,

A bluefish caught on a party boat near Cape May, New Jersey.

B

Bluefish

and, with the exception of the whitish pelvic fins, most of the fins are dark.

The bluefish is distinguished from the greater amberjack *(Seriola dumerili)* by the spine in the second dorsal fin, the absence of markings on the head, and the lack of a space between the dorsal fins. The absence of finlets easily distinguishes bluefish from mackerel.

Size/Age. Bluefish can grow to about 45 inches in length and more than 44 pounds in weight. They average 1½ to 2 feet and 3 pounds, although it's not uncommon for a fish to weigh around 11 pounds. The rod-and-reel record is a 31-pound, 12-ounce fish. They live for about 12 years.

Distribution. Found worldwide in most temperate coastal regions, bluefish inhabit the eastern Atlantic from Portugal, Madeira, and the Canary Islands southward along the African coasts to South Africa, including the Mediterranean and Black Seas. They are also present in the western Atlantic from Nova Scotia and Canada to Bermuda and Argentina, as well as in the Indo-West Pacific, but are absent from the eastern and northwestern Pacific. They are also rare between southern Florida and northern South America.

Habitat. Favoring temperate to tropical waters, bluefish range along rocky coasts and in deep, troubled waters, although they are known to be sporadic, if not cyclical, in occurrence and location. The young are often found in bays and estuaries. Adults migrate along coastal areas and are caught from the beach by surf anglers, on shoals and rips inshore, or farther offshore.

Life history/behavior. Atlantic coast bluefish spawn mainly in the spring in the South Atlantic Bight and during summer in the Middle Atlantic Bight. Recent studies suggest that fish from the two spawning seasons mix extensively on the fishing and spawning grounds and probably constitute a single genetic stock. At breeding time, bluefish migrate out to open sea to spawn, anywhere from 2 miles offshore to the continental platform. The eggs are released and drift along with plankton in surface waters, hatching about 48 hours after fertilization. As adults, bluefish are commonly found in schools, especially when foraging on schools of baitfish—

menhaden in particular. Along the U.S. Atlantic coast, bluefish migrate northward in the spring and southward in the fall.

Food and feeding habits. Insatiable predators, bluefish feed on a wide variety of fish and invertebrates but target schools of menhaden, mackerel, and herring. These fish have earned the nicknames "marine piranha" and "chopper" because they feed in large groups, viciously attacking schools of smaller fish. This feeding frenzy destroys everything in their path, including their own young. A bluefish may continue to attack its prey even when it is no longer hungry. These creatures are said to consume twice their weight in one day.

Anglers must use care when landing and handling these fish; even when a bluefish has been taken out of the water, an angler can lose a finger if not wary. Most bluefish enthusiasts use a dehooking tool to steer clear of the snapping dentures of this fish.

Angling. Historically, bluefishing has been a feast or famine pastime for East Coast anglers, and in recent years these fish have been overexploited, in part because bans on commercial fishing for striped bass set a higher priority on bluefish. Nevertheless, recreational anglers have been responsible for more than 80 percent of the catch in the past decade. Blues have long been a favorite among party boat ventures, and in the past party boat anglers have caught and kept copious (indeed excessive) numbers of this species when they encountered a lot of fish.

Availability and abundance are somewhat unpredictable, however. Bluefish roam widely, at times staying well offshore and at other times venturing up into the surf. They are sometimes caught in marshes, brackish rivers, and estuaries, although these are usually small fish, called snapper.

Birds working a slick are a dead giveaway to bluefish plundering schools of baitfish. Casting, jigging, and trolling on the perimeter of the slick are standard tactics. At other times, however, blues are a little harder to locate; they often favor deep water, tide rips, and unruly water, particularly inshore on a moving tide. Bluefish feed on a wide range of small fish, usually preferring whatever is most available, but they can be selective feeders and will also scrounge the bottom for sandworms and eels.

Bluefish succumb to a host of angling techniques and terminal tackle, in large part due to their aggressiveness. This is true for boat and shore anglers alike. Trolling may be the most employed boating technique, using diving plugs, thick-bodied spoons, and surgical tubes; a fast speed is preferred. Drifting and jigging are popular where bluefish are known to linger; metal jigging spoons and bucktails, sometimes tipped with a piece of meat, are preferred offerings. Live baits work better than dead baits, but some anglers chum for blues and successfully drift hooked pieces of cut bait amidst the chum. Casters use a variety of plugs, as well as streamer flies, when the fish are thick. Shore, surf, and pier anglers can stillfish with baits in current, or cast surface or diving plugs and squid-imitation spoons. There should always be movement to the offering, as still lures or baits go untouched. Some anglers, incidentally, "sniff out" bluefish by smell, searching for a fresh-cucumber odor where blues have been plundering baitfish.

Tackle varies widely, from heavy boat rods for trolling and deep jigging to light spinning tackle and fly rods. The reel drag should be of good quality, and anglers should use a gaff for fish that are to be kept. It bears repeating that bluefish have extremely sharp teeth; great care is a necessity when handling these fish. Many an angler has been scarred, or worse, when unhooking a lively blue.

BLUEGILL *Lepomis macrochirus.*

Other names—bream, brim, sun perch, blue perch, blue sunfish, copperbelly, blue bream, copperhead bream, red-breasted bream, bluegill sunfish, roach.

At times easily caught by novice and experienced anglers alike, bluegills are among the most popular panfish species in North America. This notoriety is the result of their vast distribution, spunky fight, and excellent taste. Commonly referred to as "bream," bluegills are the most widely distributed panfish and are found with, or in similar places as, such companion and related species as redbreast sunfish, green sunfish, pumpkinseeds, shellcrackers, and longear sunfish, all of which are similar in configuration but different in appearance.

Despite their abundance and popularity, bluegills are not heavily targeted in some waters and are thus underutilized. Bluegills are so prolific that their populations can grow beyond the carrying capacity of the water, and as a result many become stunted; these stunted fish are regarded as pests, and waters containing them must often be drained and restocked. There are three subspecies of bluegills in existence, although stocking has intermingled populations and subspecies.

Identification.   The bluegill has a significantly compressed, oval or roundish body, a small mouth, and a small head, qualities typical of members of the sunfish family. The pectoral fins are pointed.

Its coloring varies greatly from lake to lake, ranging from olive, dark blue, or bluish purple to dappled yellow and green on the sides with an overall blue cast; some fish, particularly those found in quarry holes, may actually be clear and colorless. Ordinarily, there are six to eight vertical bars on the sides, and these may or may not be prominent. The gill cover extends to create a wide black flap, faint in color on the young, which is not surrounded by a lighter border as in other sunfish. Dark blue streaks are found on the lower cheeks between the chin and gill cover, and often there is a dark mark at the bottom of the anal fin. The breeding male is more vividly colored, possessing a blue head and back, a bright orange breast and belly, and black pelvic fins.

Size/Age.   These fish range from 4 to 12 inches in length, averaging 8 inches and reaching a maximum length of $16^1/_4$ inches. The largest bluegill ever caught was a 4-pound, 12-ounce specimen taken in 1950. The growth of the bluegill varies so much that estimates of age as it relates to size are at best inexact. Bluegills are estimated to live for 10 years.

Distribution.   Native to approximately the eastern half of the United States, the bluegill's range extends southward from the St. Lawrence River through the Great Lakes and the Mississippi River basin, eastward from New York to Minnesota and draining south from the Cape Fear River in Virginia to the Río Grande in Texas, including states as far east as Florida and as far west as New Mexico. Also found in a small portion of northeastern Mexico,

A bluegill from a Georgia farm pond.

B

Bluegill

the bluegill has been widely introduced elsewhere in North America as well as in Europe, South Africa, Asia, South America, and Oceania.

Habitat. Although mainly lake fish, bluegills inhabit sluggish streams and rivers, vegetated lakes and ponds, swamps, and pools of creeks. They prefer quiet waters and may hold in extremely shallow areas, especially early in the season and during spawning time, although when the surface and shallow water temperature is warm in summer, they may go as deep as 30 or more feet. They occupy the same habitat as their larger relative, the largemouth bass.

Life history/Behavior. The age of sexual maturity varies with environment and locale, although most bluegills reach spawning age when two or three years old. Spawning occurs between April and September, starting when water temperatures are around 70°F.

The males build shallow, round nests in water up to 6 feet deep over sandy or muddy bottoms. These nests occur in colonies of up to 500 along the shoreline, densely concentrated and easily spotted by anglers. Females may lay between 2,000 and 63,000 eggs, which hatch 30 to 35 hours after fertilization. It is common for fish to spawn many times, with a particular fish laying eggs in several nests and a single nest containing eggs from more than one female. Males guard the eggs throughout the incubation period and stay to protect the hatched young. Having reached lengths of $1/4$ to $1/3$ inch, the young leave their nests for deeper waters. Bluegills travel in small schools typically made up of similar-size individuals.

Food and feeding habits. A variety of small organisms serve as food for bluegills, including insects, crayfish, fish eggs, small minnows, snails, worms, and sometimes even plant material. The young feed mostly on crustaceans, insects, and worms. Adults will feed at different depths depending on temperature, so they obtain food on the bottom as well as on the surface. Active mostly at dusk and dawn, the larger bluegills move inshore in the morning and evening to feed, staying in deeper water during the day.

Angling. Bluegills are highly respected fighters even though they are diminutive fish. They are most commonly pursued in the spring and early summer while spawning in shallow water and where their round, clustered nests are readily visible along the shoreline of ponds and lakes. Vegetation is a prime place to seek bluegills, followed by stumps, logs, and fallen trees.

Many anglers pursue bluegills and other sunfish with live worms and bobbers in relatively shallow water, although the bigger fish are usually found deep. Because sunfish don't have large mouths, a long-shanked No. 8 or 10 hook is best, unweighted or with just a small split shot. Other baits include crickets, tiny minnows, and mealworms. Small jigs are a fine lure, and small spinners and spinnerbaits can be productive. A slow retrieve is best. Bluegills (and other sunfish) are popular in winter, too, taken on small jigs, flies, and mealworms.

The tackle used for these panfish needn't be stout. Light spinning or spincasting outfits are more than adequate; in many areas, anglers use long cane poles without reels to dabble baits into selected pockets for various sunfish species. Four- to 8-pound-test line is ample. Fly fishing is also an excellent way to pursue bluegills and other sunfish species, especially when they are in shallow water in the spring or during the summer when the surface is relatively calm. Floating and sinking flies, small streamers, and poppers are the terminal items.

See: Panfish

BLUE HOLE

Dark blue spots that are distinguished from surrounding bottom covered with sand or vegetation. Found in the Caribbean, these are submerged limestone caverns or sinkholes of ancient lineage, with powerful currents moving in and out.

BLUE RIBBON STREAM

A term used to describe highly rated or highly productive trout streams, especially in the western United States.

BLUE TANG   *Acanthurus coeruleus.*

Other names—blue tang surgeon; French: *chirurgien bayolle;* Portuguese: *acaraúna-azul;* Spanish: *navajón azul.*

A member of the surgeonfish family that has distinctive coloration and is occasionally encountered by anglers, the blue tang is sometimes used as an aquarium fish and is also marketed fresh.

Identification. The oval, deep-bodied, and compressed blue tang is more circular than other surgeonfish. Its coloring is almost entirely blue, ranging from powdery to deep purple, and it has many dark or light blue horizontal stripes running down the sides and blending into the background. The dorsal and anal fins have a bright blue border, and there is a white or yellow spine on the base of the tail. Juvenile blue tang are colored bright yellow, whereas intermediate fish have blue heads and bodies and yellow tails. The yellow of the tail is the last to change to blue, and some fish are found with yellow tails. The change from juvenile to intermediate to adult coloration does not depend on size; some blue adults are smaller than yellow juveniles.

Size. Blue tang average 5 to 10 inches in length and may grow to 15 inches long.

Distribution. In the western Atlantic, the blue tang is most commonly found in Bermuda, and from Florida to the Gulf of Mexico and Brazil. In the eastern Atlantic, it inhabits the waters off Ascension Island.

Habitat. Blue tang favor inshore grassy and rocky areas, and shallows above coral reefs.

Life history/Behavior. In the fry stage, the pelvic, second dorsal, and second anal spines of some fish are venomous and cause a painful sensation like a bee sting. This venomous quality is lost once they reach the juvenile stage. Blue tang

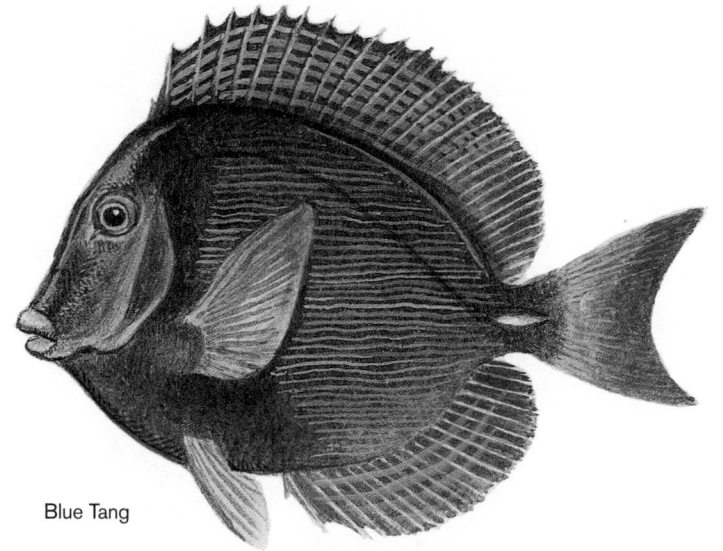
Blue Tang

form schools that may include surgeonfish and doctorfish.

Food and feeding habits. Blue tang feed entirely on algae, mostly during the day.

Angling. Blue tang are of little significance to anglers. Most are incidental catches by bottom anglers, although divers do take them with spears.

BLUE WATER

That portion of the open ocean that is blue in color and usually many miles from shore. Blue-water fishing is synonymous with offshore fishing *(see)*.

The water in the open ocean appears deep blue in a manner similar to the blue color of the sky. Particulate matter in the open ocean is relatively scarce, and marine life has a low concentration in comparison with coastal waters, causing the water to appear blue due to the size of the water molecules and the fact that they disperse solar radiation in such a way as to mostly scatter wavelengths for blue light. Coastal waters are usually greenish in color, partly because of yellow-green microscopic marine algae in coastal waters but mostly because they have more large particulate matter, dispersing solar radiation so as to mostly scatter wavelengths for greenish or yellowish light.

BOAT

In simplest terms a boat is a floating object propelled by oar, sail, or motor. It is a vital accessory for anglers who want to be highly mobile and find fish that aren't accessible from the bank or surf or pier, or by wading. Without a boat, anglers are restricted to areas that can be accessed by walking, and to covering only water that can be reached by the length of a cast.

Because many species of fish roam widely in their environments, and because much fish habitat is located away from shore or at great distances from the areas accessible by land, boats extend the range

B

Anglers take to the water in a variety of boats, as this fall salmon-fishing scene on New York's Black River attests.

of anglers as well as pare the time necessary to reach desired locations. Boats also enable anglers to carry and store extra fishing equipment and accessory gear, and they provide for the storage and maintenance of fish and bait.

Each year a high percentage of people who purchase boats (and motors) list fishing as a primary or secondary intended use for that equipment. Some boats are designed purely for fishing, some are for specific angling situations, and some have general recreational use, including fishing.

Many factors influence the choice of a fishing boat. These include the size of the body of water; extreme conditions that might be encountered; distance to be traveled; type of fishing; equipment needed; number of anglers; preferred boat length, hull design, or method of propulsion; and funds available. In many cases, anglers go to places or boat in conditions that are seldom visited or experienced by nonfishing boaters.

Boats for saltwater fishing are larger because of the influence of tide, current, waves, weather, and the size of fish. Long, broad-beamed fiberglass sportfishing boats *(see)*, also called offshore boats, are the pride of the angling fleet, used for distant big-game forays. Eighteen- to 25-foot fiberglass V-hulled boats fill the bill for most inshore saltwater anglers. Center console models are preferred in warm weather climes and where a variety of casting, jigging, and drift fishing by several anglers is done. For shallow water flats fishing, most aluminum or fiberglass shallow draft boats, many with bow casting and aft poling platforms, get the nod.

In freshwater, a V-hulled fiberglass boat is especially suitable for large lakes, ponds, and rivers, where rough water dictates sturdy craft and where a big boat with a lot of engine muscle can help cover great distances quickly. Aluminum boats can also be used under these conditions, although flat-bottomed models do not handle rough water well. The V-hulled aluminum boats take rough water a little better, but still not as well as fiberglass boats; they sit up higher in the water and, because they are lighter, are more susceptible to being blown around in the wind. Sixteen- to 25-foot boats, aluminum and fiberglass, are used in a wide range of freshwater fishing, with those over 20 feet generally reserved for the largest inland waters.

A smaller aluminum flat-bottom boat (jonboat) is very functional for fishing on small lakes, rivers, and ponds, where covering a lot of territory is not necessary and where adverse conditions are seldom present. Small aluminum V-hulled boats can be used in the same manner; their deeper draft makes them less suitable for small river fishing and more suitable to moderate size lakes. Canoes and canoe-like craft are popular in small lakes and ponds and in flowing water, although they are unsteady vessels for the inexperienced and are highly susceptible to positioning problems.

This overview is necessarily generalized. Other types of craft are used for fishing, such as pontoon boats and inflatables, and some standard boat hulls are useful in both freshwater and saltwater, although the interior configurations are greatly different.

A fishing boat is a tool that gets you where the fish are. It must weather the best and the worst water conditions. It must be reasonably comfortable to allow you to put in long hours. It must be versatile enough to handle a variety of angling pursuits. It must be designed and/or modified to allow you to fight and land fish (especially big fish). And it should have readily available accessories.

Fishing boat designs and interior configurations have changed a great deal in the past few decades because of manufacturing advancements, changes in propulsion systems, and the evolving styles and interests of anglers. Virtually all of the changes in fishing boats, be they flats skiffs, walleye boats, bass boats, or offshore boats, have evolved to meet the particular needs of anglers in the places they fish and in the manner they fish. The more popular types of fishing boats are reviewed in more detail in their respective entries, as are methods of propulsion, but the following information generally applies to all fishing boats.

Types of Fishing Boats

Anglers use nearly anything that floats as a means of getting to and from desired fishing locations. Among smaller vessels, that includes such generally manually operated craft as canoes *(see)* and canoe-like boats such as pirogues and kayaks *(see)*, folding boats, inflatable boats *(see)*; and float tubes *(see)*, which are also known as belly boats and aren't really boats from a navigability standpoint. Fishing boats might include such "incidental" craft as sailboats or jet-propelled personal watercraft *(see)*, and such specialty items as pontoon boats, houseboats, and one- or two-man cartoppers for ponds.

Among midsize craft, popular fishing boats include a jonboat *(see)*, bass boat *(see)*, flats boat *(see)*, and walleye boat *(see)*, and any number of aluminum and fiberglass vessels that have been designed for fishing but have not come to be associated with a species or style of fishing. Larger fishing boats include center console, cuddy, and walk-around versions of outboard- and inboard-powered offshore boats, which may be called sportfishermen or sportfishing boats *(see)*, and inshore boats.

Hull Styles

Because a boat must not only float, but move through varying water conditions, hull configurations differ. Depending upon the size of the body of water you fish, the hull can be more important to an angler than the overall size or the interior layout of a boat. Categories of hulls are displacement and planing. Displacement hulls include canoes, jonboats, and flat-bottomed dories or skiffs, and are noted for slow speed; they push through the water rather than ride on top of it.

Planing hulls include V-bottoms and are noted for faster speed and quicker steering response; speed is largely a function of engine power, and most of the hull is raised out of the water while running.

The standard types of these hulls on fishing boats include flat, semi-V, modified-V, deep-V, and cathedral. Some other hulls, such as tunnel, and catamaran also exist.

Flat-bottom hulls are probably the oldest hull style in existence and are of primary use in small streams, shallow rivers, ponds, and small lakes. They are easy to control by oar, paddle, or electric motor, but are unstable in lengths under 12 feet. Flat-bottom hulls are not advisable for heavy loads or for use in rough water unless they are large, broad-beamed, and properly powered. Anglers who like to cast from a standing position may find these boats a bit tippy, especially in the shorter lengths and narrower beams. Flat-bottom hulls are easy to row, paddle, or pole in shallow water and perform well with an electric motor; they tend to pound the water when underway, and the (lighter) bow may slap the water when it is choppy, which can be alarming to fish.

V-bottom boats can be primarily separated into deep-V, modified-V, or semi-V versions, with the latter sometimes described as round. Some type of V-hull is preferred over a flat-bottom in places where the water gets rough, so they are a very popular fishing hull. The difference between them is primarily in deadrise, which is the angle formed at the transom by the V and determined by the amount of the V that is carried from the bow through the transom. Boats with a transom deadrise over 19 degrees are considered deep-Vs, but this is a general rather than absolute indicator. Because deep-V-hulls carry their shape all the way to the transom, they ride better in rough water than modified-V-hulls; some deep-V boats handle poorly off-plane at slow speeds, but modifications to the chines and stern have changed this in more recent hulls. The greater the deadrise at the transom, the more water a V-hull draws, meaning that it is less suitable for shallow operation (how shallow depends on the size of boat and the depth of water). A deep-V-hull requires more horsepower to attain top and cruising speeds than hulls with less deadrise need. That means more expense in the cost of the engine(s), and greater gas consumption.

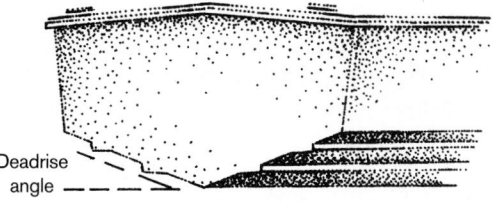

The angle between the dotted lines shown is the boat's deadrise.

Hull Types

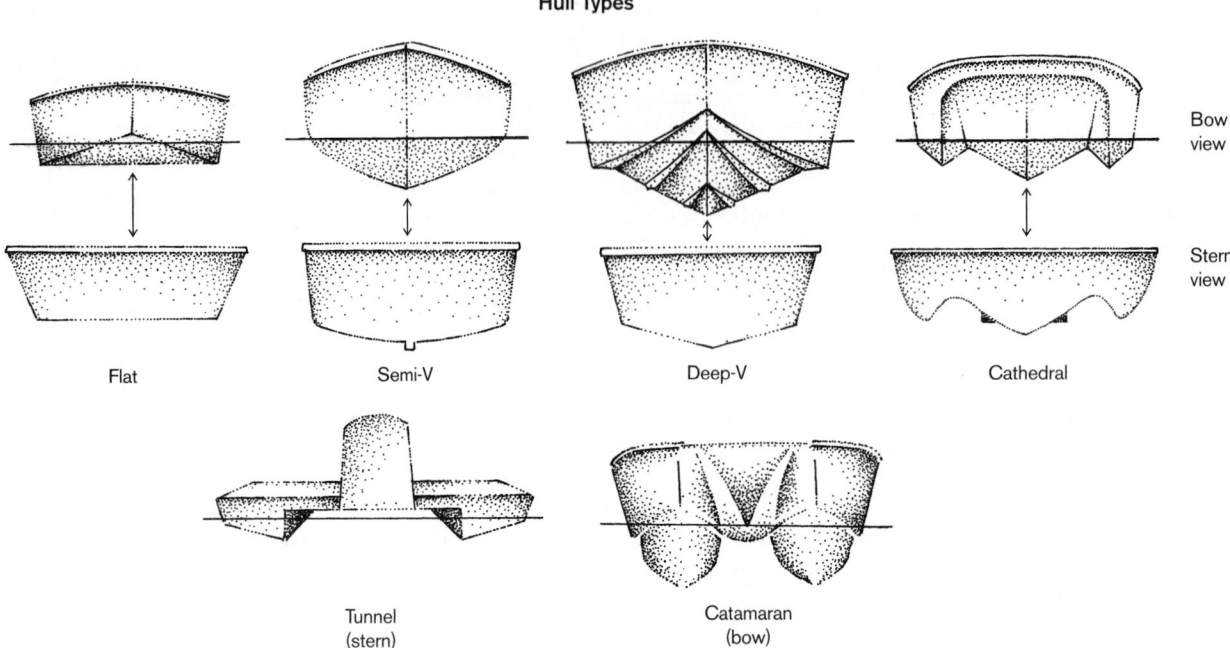

Bow view

Stern view

Flat   Semi-V   Deep-V   Cathedral

Tunnel
(stern)

Catamaran
(bow)

Some type of modified-V-hull is a favorite with many freshwater anglers in boats under 18 feet long, and with many inshore saltwater anglers. Recent versions of these, called variable-V or progressive-V-hulls, have a deadrise that is greater toward the bow and less at the stern. The original deep-V-hulls carried the same deadrise at the transom quite a bit forward (some as much as two-thirds the distance) before it began to increase significantly. The newer versions begin that increase ever so slightly in the beginning, from almost immediately forward of the transom. Thus, you can find a 20-foot boat, for example, whose deadrise progresses from 18 degrees at the transom to almost 40 degrees at the stem, and which has longitudinal bottom strakes that provide lift, eliminate the tendency to plow that would otherwise be typical of having so much deep-V forward, and still produce a fast (40 mph) speed with just a single outboard.

Within this category are also flat-bottom and V-bottom hybrids. For example, some high-performance bass boats have a modified-V-hull with a flat pad on the transom; this produces great speed in calm water or small waves, but a tooth-jarring ride in sloppy conditions and a spine-pounding ride in rough water.

The cathedral hull, also known as a tri-hull, has faded in popularity but had a following in small boats into the 1980s, especially in freshwater and for inshore saltwater use. Cathedral-hull boats are stable, roomy, wet, and slow. They ride poorly in rough water, but well in flat water or small waves. They do have the advantage of ample interior space, largely because of their essentially rectangular shape, but their general disadvantage is that they have the same basic horsepower requirements as a deep-V-hull because they run on more wetted surface.

The catamaran hull is one that is now contending with deep-V-hulls. These have been used with increasing popularity in the seas of Australia and South Africa, where the water is usually anything but gentle, and have been forging into the North American marketplace. Catamaran, or cat, hulls are faster than deep-V-hulls when weight and horsepower are the same. Nothing beats the catamaran's stability at rest in a nasty beam sea, which is a factor that anglers can easily appreciate when drift fishing. A steep deep-V-hull tends to snap roll miserably when drifting in a rough sea, and other boats usually can't take it at all.

The so-called tunnel hull is similar to a squashed down version of the catamaran hull. It is not intended for long stretches of very rough water, but it is faster for the same horsepower. Its big advantage to anglers is that the engine can be mounted far higher on the transom than normal, which allows the boat to jump quickly on plane in bare inches of water. It's a very popular design among the thin-water redfish and sea trout crowd along the Texas Gulf Coast, where it performs superbly.

These are the general characteristics of common fishing boat hulls, but evaluating a hull is not always simple. Many manufacturers use the same terms to mean different things (like calling a semi-V model a deep-V). Hybrid hulls and nuances to certain basic hull types, plus the use of other terms also confuse the situation.

Many prospective fishing boat buyers spend more time looking at the interior of a boat than they do evaluating the hull and determining whether it is the right type for their intended use. Clearly, an angler who spends a lot of time on the ocean, especially offshore, or on big lakes, and who needs to travel long distances with the likelihood of encountering rough water, requires a deep V-hull. Anglers who primarily spend their time in shallow areas, such as on flats or in moderately protected bays, can use a boat with little draft. If, however, they must cross water that is sometimes rough to get to those shallow places, a compromise may be necessary. The trick is to find a happy medium between riding comfort and hull efficiency.

Keep in mind that any boat's comfort and riding ability, as well as it's aptitude for certain water conditions, may have to be tempered with fishability. Big fish in skinny water, for example, like bonefish, permit, tarpon, redfish, striped bass, largemouth bass, and northern pike, are among the many gamefish sensitive to noise, and even if the draft of a boat is shallow enough to get you there, a hull that slaps or thumps in that environment is like a hunter wearing fluorescent orange in a duck blind while standing up and waving both arms. In some areas there's been a trend toward "stealth" hulls, with slightly rounded chines that may give up some dryness but don't telegraph the boat's presence before you're close enough for an easy cast.

To select the best hull shape for your type of fishing, analyze your goals and needs carefully, then go looking. Ask others who already do the type of fishing you want to do, and get out with someone who experiences that type of fishing. Spend a day or two aboard as many boats that fit your profile as possible, especially when conditions are less than favorable. Have a seller, including a new boat dealer, take you out for a serious test ride. And remember that all boats behave well when the seas are flat.

Picking the Right Boat

Usually, if you're a serious angler you already know how you intend to use a new boat, and this guides your choice. Inexperienced anglers and first-time boaters, however, often make the mistake of getting a boat that isn't right for their needs (especially for developing needs as they get into different types of fishing and wider-ranging activities). This means either replacing the boat or making some significant modifications to its interior. The old homily about not being able to make a silk purse out of a sow's ear was never more true than when applied to boat hulls. If the basic hull is unsuitable, there's nothing you can do to make it right, no matter how extensive the interior modifications. So, if you plan to do any serious angling from your boat, choose carefully.

Picking a fishing boat starts with knowing what kind of fishing you'll be doing—taking it everywhere, just to small lakes, or just on the ocean—and under what conditions you'll be doing it—only on fair weather days, whenever you have the chance, or any time they're hitting. Then come the other considerations, such as whether you will tow the boat and how much weight your vehicle can handle, how much space you'll need for stowing gear and carrying passengers, and whether the boat can accommodate all the accessories you need.

Consider carefully the size boat you need. You don't want to select "not enough" boat; being caught out in rough seas in a too small boat could get you in serious trouble. On the other hand, buying "too much" boat because you're unnecessarily worried about potentially rough seas could make the vessel almost completely unfishable. Every boat is a series of compromises, and choosing size is the first of many decisions you'll have to make.

If you don't have a solid idea regarding the boat you want, get friendly with someone who has a lot of experience in the type of fishing you have in mind. Get out on boats with others who have had experience, and learn as much as you can. Spend time prospecting various boats before you buy. That time will be repaid a hundredfold if you do your homework properly.

After you decide what type of boat (or actual brand and model) you want, it's a question of buying new or used. If you're considering buying a used boat from its current owner, take someone with you who has experience with that particular model (and also the engine, if possible). Such a person might help you avoid some pitfalls. You should have an experienced mechanic take a look at the engine of any used boat and, if possible, run it in the water. Put the entire boat in the water and run it for awhile as well. Once you buy a used boat—and there are plenty available—you're stuck with it, so make sure you cover all bases, just as you would if you bought a used automobile from a private party.

If you're planning to buy a new rig, try to select a good dealer. Sometimes you can't choose the dealer unless you're willing to do a lot of traveling because many dealers of the same brand boats are (deliberately) not close to each other. Don't sign anything or put any money down, until you've had a test ride in the exact model, with the same horsepower engine you plan to use. Be almost as careful about selecting the dealer as you are in selecting the boat. Ask around before you sign any purchase contracts. Check with reliable boating friends and perhaps the local Better Business Bureau, and don't be pushed into buying extra equipment that you don't need.

Unfortunately, no one ideal boat suits all fishing needs and interests, no hull type handles all conditions, and no interior configuration meets every angler's desires. Some boats have multi-species or multi-water applications and suit varied angling; anglers who do only one type of fishing, however, prefer a boat that is especially suited to that activity, like a flats boat *(see)* or a bass boat *(see)*.

Be especially careful about trying to get a boat that will serve many needs other than fishing. While it seems good to have a boat that the family can use for general boating, cruising, and skiing, multi-purpose boats seldom make serious anglers happy. Runabouts—boats that are primarily meant for general boating—are seldom suitable for serious fishing, although many people in freshwater and saltwater go fishing in them.

B

When you've selected the hull you feel is best suited for your angling interests, the next step is to choose the proper power for it. In some cases you won't have much choice among the types of power due to the model or design of boat or because the entire rig is assembled at the manufacturer's plant. If you have time to wait for a custom-ordered boat, a dealer can order some models with different types of power. If it's simply a matter of changing the existing outboard motor to one with a different horsepower, they can usually do that without a long wait. For more information on power and selection, see the appropriate motor entries.

In small and midsize boats, a major selection issue is the material used in constructing the boat. Fiberglass is the most widely used material for boats over 16 feet long because it is strong, easy to work with, and cost effective in construction. Aluminum is still the lightest material, though used more often on smaller boats, and Kevlar (an aramid fiber used for radial tire cords and bulletproof vests) is close behind in weight, though stronger. Wood is still being used to build simple craft, but it is barely a factor in the new powerboat field, and some plastics are being used for specialty lightweight boats, but not in fishing boats.

Aluminum boats are most common in freshwater and for fishing on rivers, where there may be obstructions, and on smaller bodies of water. Aluminum is lightest and fiberglass heaviest. Aluminum boats are easier to tow, which is a big consideration for many freshwater anglers, but fiberglass generally tracks better and, without rivets to pop loose, is less likely to need maintenance. Aluminum, however, is more forgiving for regular contact with the bottom, like scraping over rocks

and beaching. Aluminum is ideal for boats under 16 feet long because it produces a light and easily portable boat, and is cost effective for both builder and buyer. It's major drawback is that it is noisy, but that can be improved upon with interior modifications, such as platforms and carpeting. It is not used as much for boats over 16 feet, although it can be and there are some large aluminum boats. Generally, as boat length increases, and the size of the water fished grows, most anglers choose fiberglass.

Some choose Kevlar as an alternative to fiberglass. Kevlar is more expensive than fiberglass but stronger and lighter. That lightness can translate into significant fuel economy when a Kevlar boat is powered, for example, by a 75-horsepower engine and gets better performance than an identical fiberglass boat with a 115-horsepower engine. It can also translate into greater top-end speed when the same boats with identical engines are compared. The material is far more resistant to impact damage and to flexural fatigue (which is the reason why most fiberglass hulls fail).

When choosing a larger boat (either trailerable or permanently moored), after you reach a decision on hull type and overall boat size, the most important item of consideration is usually the amount of usable deck and cockpit space. This is of much greater concern to anglers than it is to people who ski, cruise, or enjoy general boating. Anyone who has been cramped into the tight quarters of a boat primarily meant for cruising or skiing understands how unacceptable these craft are for storing gear, using accessories, fighting fish, and getting out of the way of fellow anglers. It is surprising how many people try to adapt a runabout or ski boat to serious

25 ft. Saltwater Sportfishing Boat

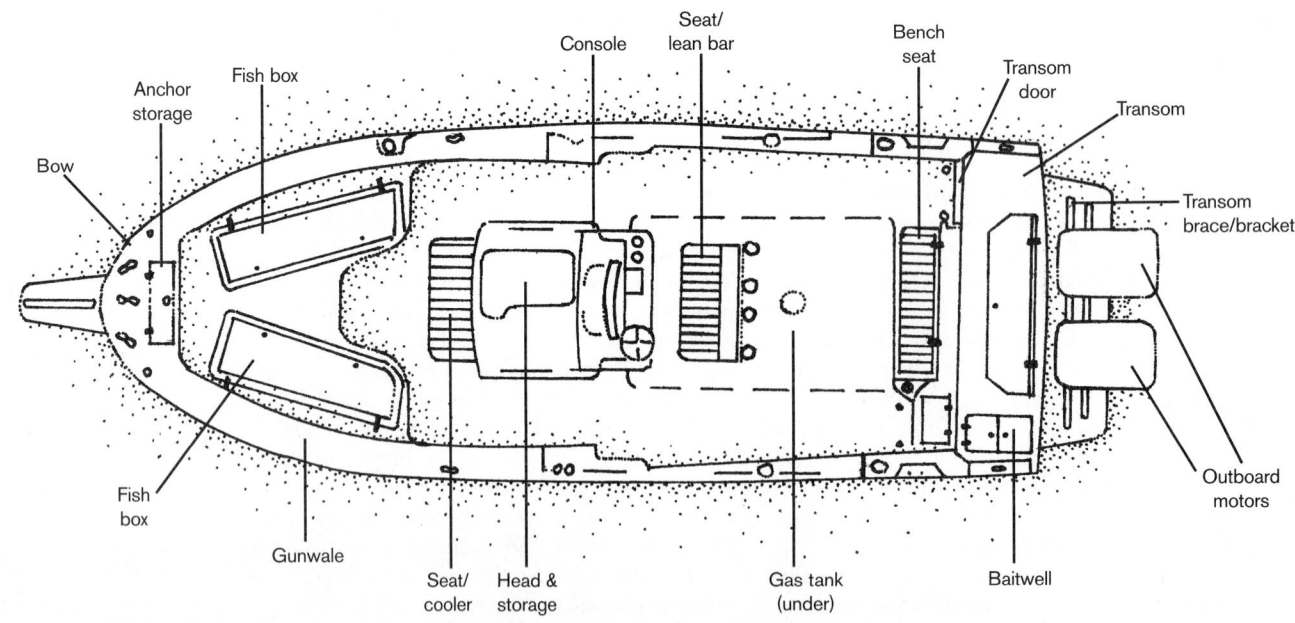

fishing, although the usable space for gear and mobility within such boats is seriously lacking. Space in a fishing boat, whether for moving around to fight a big fish, or being able to keep myriad gear out from underfoot, is a big concern. Check the layout of the boats you review for uncluttered and usable inside space. Remember that you might want to add some accessories, such as downriggers, to the boat, and will need appropriate and accessible places to do so.

As a general rule, a boat that is to be used primarily for casting needs to have open space on raised decks or platforms, definitely in the bow and preferably both bow and stern. The boat should provide enough room to stand or to sit, and storage space beneath the anglers. For fly fishing, a clean deck with nothing to catch loose fly line, and possibly a thigh-high bow brace or rail, are special considerations.

In bigger boats, which are used for big-water fishing, storage space should be in a cabin, under or alongside a console, or below decks, and in large boats, it is a combination of these. The bigger the boat, the more fishing action that takes place from amidship to transom, so this area has to be clutter-free. It is important to make sure consoles have ample space for mounting all electronic devices.

Storage is one of the most important items to consider. You need both tackle storage and incidental storage, and while some boats look great, they suffer from a lack of proper storage area when in use, especially if the boat can accommodate three or four (or more) people. Anglers tend to quickly clutter a boat with fishing paraphernalia and accessory items, so pay attention to the storage that a boat has. Look for dry storage if you need to keep various things under cover.

As for tackle storage, first consider rods. Good rods are expensive and should not be left to bounce or tangle in a heap; be sure that they can be properly restrained when the boat is running on the water and when it is in tow. Check that rod storage areas will hold the length and style of rod that you use most often, or can at least be customized to adapt to your special needs. Make sure they are easy to access and, preferably, lockable. Rod holders, for storing rods while the boat is underway or when trolling or baitfishing, are also a common consideration.

As for tackle boxes, only you know what storage you need in this regard, though most avid anglers carry more than they need or can use. Tripping over tackle boxes, having them slide around, and not being able to get them out of the way for fishing action, are common troubles that can be avoided. Look for a boat that meets your needs in this area while fishing as well as running, and which provides storage while wasting a minimum of space.

In addition to tackle storage, remember that boats must be equipped with proper life preservers for every person onboard, so these must be kept somewhere accessible, and you need a place to store an anchor and rode. Add these, plus foul weather gear, spare parts, a first-aid kit, a fire extinguisher, and possibly an external cooler for food and beverages, and you can pile a lot into a boat.

Do you keep fish or bait alive while angling? If so, you'll need some type of livewell or baitwell. Long-term storage and boating great distances usually demand built-in systems, with adequate aeration. A system that brings water in from outside, rather than recirculating the same water, is infinitely better. Recirculation is especially undesirable when the water is warm. Systems that don't operate, or operate minimally, when the boat is traveling at high speed (because of poor water intake), may kill fish, so it is important to have a high circulation raw water system that pumps a constant flow of highly oxygenated water on the fish to keep them perky.

On larger boats, don't overlook the (possible) need for fishboxes or ice chests, a transom door for bringing big game into the cockpit, and fuel capacity.

In new trailerable boats, the consolidation of motor and boat manufacturers and the desire to market ready-to-go items have made packages the rule rather than the exception. The majority of these are targeted at anglers. Whether you're thinking new or used, prepackaged or mix-and-match, you should take a critical look at all aspects of the boat you buy for fishing, and not be swayed by appearance (although, chances are if you don't like the appearance, you won't buy it anyway).

In addition to appearance and interior appurtenances, the motor and the propeller are important considerations in the selection of a proper fishing rig. With the wrong items, and depending on boat and hull type, fuel efficiency can be drastically lowered. As a general rule, the motor on a boat should be no less than 80 percent of the boat's rated maximum horsepower. Underpowering a boat is a common problem. A boat that doesn't seem to run properly may actually have the wrong propeller. The wrong propeller causes a boat to labor to get on plane and to fail to reach proper rpm. Be careful also about putting excessive horsepower on a boat, especially if you're are buying a used boat and a motor from different sources. Every boat has a capacity plate that specifies its maximum horsepower rating. Exceeding this may be illegal, and may void your insurance if an accident occurs.

Lastly, many boats need a trailer that is suited to the specific hull type and length of boat *(see: trailer, boat).*

Rigging for Fishing

Many new boats come with most, if not all, of the accouterments that an angler needs for fishing, but others need modification to suit angling styles. Many things can be done to rig a boat for fishing, or to make it more angler-friendly.

The hull usually gets little attention in this regard, although trim tabs can be added to improve

Minnow is a word applied to many small fish; in scientific terms the minnow family, with more than 1,600 species, is one of the largest in the world.

B

rough water performance and splash guards can be added to the transom if you backtroll. Ditto for the motor, although on some outboards, boaters add a hydrofoil to improve planing ability, or a trolling plate to slow boat speed for trolling.

The interior of the boat is where most rigging attention is focused. Anglers address all of the following issues, and more: rod storage, fore and aft platforms, livewells, baitwells, tackle and dry gear storage, downriggers, trolling boards, outriggers, planer retrievers, rod holders, towers, Bimini or T-tops, electric motors, remote steering devices, seats, fighting chairs, and assorted electronic devices. In small boats, especially aluminum models, anglers commonly add carpeting to their boats to deaden noise, as well as nonskid paint or adhesive strips.

Self-rigging, especially of small and midsize fishing boats was a bigger issue in the past, but the advent of factory-rigged boats, sold as a package, has made it a bit less of an issue today. Some anglers, however, still make many modifications to their boats for fishing purposes. The selection and location of rigging items requires a lot of attention, as does the setup that has been pre-designed by manufacturers.

When evaluating a boat that is already rigged for fishing, or when deciding how you will modify or rig a boat yourself, your foremost concern should be how it will improve your fishing. Sonar, for example, must be placed so that it can be viewed easily from wherever you'll be sitting or standing (in some cases both). Every item used for fishing and boating must be readily accessible, so some things that look nice (like a curved console that does not provide a sonar or GPS mounting surface) can be problematic.

Maintenance and Storage

Constructed primarily of aluminum or fiberglass, modern fishing boats need less care and maintenance than did the wooden boats of decades ago. Most maintenance needs arise from accidents, from being towed on poor-fitting trailers, or from striking underwater objects or running aground. A leak may be caused by a loose rivet, insufficient caulking around installations on the transom, or a crack. Clearly, it pays to inspect the hull periodically, especially after an unusual occurrence (nicking a rock or wedging atop a submerged piling, for instance). Small aluminum repairs can be made with an epoxy-based aluminum putty, or by melting an aluminum repair stick onto the affected area, but larger problems require heliarc welding. Larger problems with fiberglass boats require a dealer's attention, but gel coat repairs can be made easily enough with the proper paste and polish.

Accessories should be routinely checked. Boats that are used in big waters and run at high speeds can take a severe pounding, as can boats that are trailered often, and it is not unusual for fittings to loosen. Bolts and screws especially need periodic surveillance and tightening. If they are not of the highest marine quality, mechanical and electrical equipment are subject to malfunction when exposed to the elements. Some sonar and radio equipment can run underwater, but not all marine electronics are so blessed, and anglers should protect those items that need it, especially in a saltwater environment. Boats that are used in brackish water or saltwater should be rinsed with freshwater after every use. A washdown is also necessary if a boat has gotten especially dirty, slimy, or bloody from fish or bait. Once slime, blood, bait parts, and the like get baked onto a boat from the sun, they are particularly hard to remove, so it can be good to

17 ft. Multipurpose Freshwater Boat

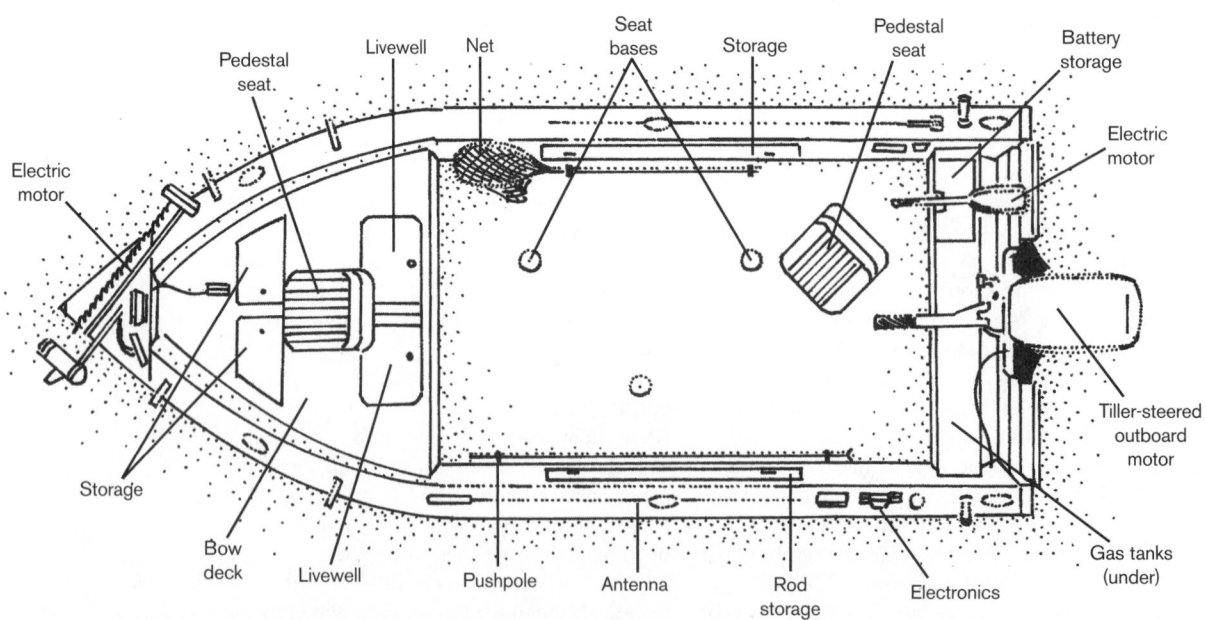

make a preliminary washdown while on the water and a final scrub back at the dock or at home.

Boats can be stored in the water at a dock or a slip, on a trailer at a marina or at home, and on the ground or on supports in a yard. Storage at docks or boat slips requires sufficient bow and aft lines and a knowledge of proper knots for mooring to the dock, the use of boat fenders to keep the boat from rubbing against the dock or pilings, and consideration of the effect of waves, storms, and tidal fluctuations. Many a boat has been damaged or sunk at docks or boat slips because the boat operator did not take proper steps for its storage. Trailer storage requires the use of a trailer that is appropriate for the length and weight of the boat. Smaller boats and trailers may fit into a garage or under a carport. This is especially good as it keeps the boat and trailer protected from the elements and lessens trailer rust and boat fading. Boats on trailers do not have to be covered, but fitted covers or tarps do protect them from sun, rain, and snow, and from road grit while trailering; covers are especially useful for boats that are stored outdoors through the winter and for long periods without being used. Small boats that can be carried by one or two people generally are not covered, but are often turned over, either resting directly on the ground or preferably propped on supports.

In places where the water freezes, a boat is usually taken out of the water for the winter, although electric water bubblers can be used to move the water around a dock or slip and keep ice from forming. This is only useful if larger floes of ice cannot be pushed into the dock or slip when the wind shifts during spring. For winter storage, the drain plug should be removed and the boat propped up in the bow so that water and melting snow or ice drains to the stern. The bigger the boat, the more attention to winter preparation it needs, including cleaning the hull of algae, fungi, and barnacles, and thoroughly cleaning and drying all parts of the boat. Remember that some ventilation is important to evaporate condensation.

Boat Handling

General Issues.   Handling a boat looks very simple to the inexperienced and to those who view that operation in open, unobstructed water. Although it is not generally difficult, some situations and factors make handling a boat very different from driving an automobile, and not all boats handle the same way due to hull design and/or propulsion system. Learning to handle a boat properly comes from on-the-water experience.

Speed and direction are the basic factors to be controlled in all boating, complicated by the fact that, unlike automobiles, a boat has no brakes to slow it down or stop it. Rowing, paddling, or using an electric motor are the simplest methods of moving a boat, and the least troublesome in most situations because only minor speed is attained. Boating under power, however, where

A boat that is overloaded in the front (top) will plow and may dig into an oncoming wave; one that is overloaded in the rear (middle) will be hard to steer and perilously low in the stern. One with passengers and gear well distributed (bottom) is safest and will handle best, since it is properly trimmed fore and aft.

significant speed is possible, and where boats of varying size are employed, is a different matter.

Most power boats are directed by a steering wheel located on a console. Some midsize boats, and most small boats, are directed by a tiller handle on the motor. The throttle, or accelerator, is located on the handle of small outboard motors, and by the steering wheel in larger boats. Some boats, especially bass boats, are fitted with after-market foot-control throttles for high-speed boat operation with two hands on the steering wheel, but there are obvious drawbacks to this, and it is not a widely used option.

Because boats are pushed from the rear by a motor, they steer by the stern. When the motor is turned to the left, the thrust of the propeller drives the stern to the left and the bow to the right. This is of special significance in heavy traffic, when trying to run the boat over a specific bottom contour (as when trolling), when faced with current or wind, and when negotiating tight spaces such as a dock or boat slip in a marina. The motion of a boat is stopped when the engine is put into neutral and its natural drift ceases. This is often aided by placing the engine into opposite gear (reverse when the boat is moving forward), but only at slow speeds.

All boaters are required to observe established rules of the road. These exist in freshwater as well as saltwater, although boaters in saltwater and on large navigable waterways are generally more cognizant and observant of these rules than their counterparts

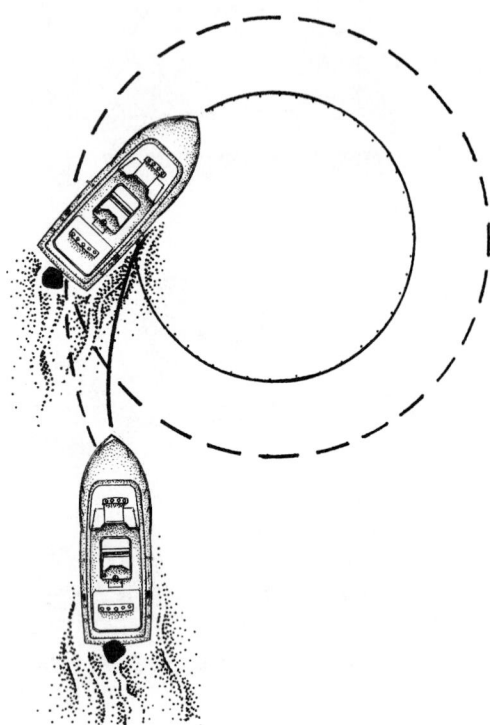

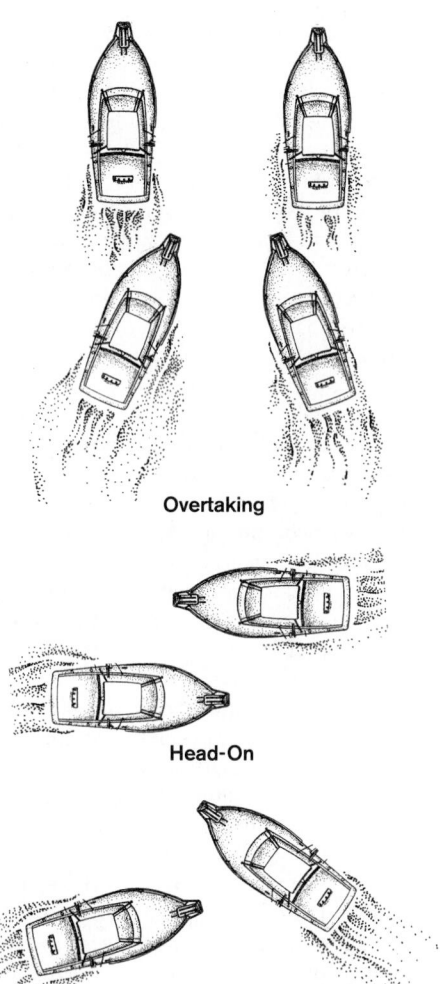

Steering a boat is not like steering a car. As this illustration shows, in a turn, the stern of a boat follows a different and larger path (dotted circle) than the bow (solid circle).

Overtaking

Head-On

Crossing

Depicted are three of the most common boat-to-boat encounters. When one boat is overtaking another from behind (top), it may pass on either side, but should slow down while passing. When boats approach head-on (middle), each should stay to the right. When paths cross (bottom), the boat that is coming from the starboard side of the other boat has the right of way.

in freshwater. These rules cover most circumstances, including which vessels have the right of way when meeting, crossing, or overtaking one another; signals to be issued to declare intentions; actions to avoid collision; and so forth. The United States Coast Guard publishes navigation rules, which apply to navigable waterways. State and local regulations apply to landlocked bodies of water. Boat operators are legally responsible for knowing these rules and abiding by them, and may be liable for not adhering to them. Because waterways are more open than the roads traveled on land, and because there is less law enforcement presence on waterways, it is a fact that many boaters knowingly or unknowingly violate established rules of the road. This is particularly so in freshwater, and among nonfishing boat operators.

Some general rules that anglers should be aware of include:

- Boats under manual power (paddling or rowing), have the right of way over power boats.
- Sailboats, if propelled by sail and not auxiliary motor, have the right of way over power boats (including fishing boats that are slow trolling).
- Boats approaching each other head-on should stay to the right.
- A boat overtaking (passing) another boat can pass on either side but should slow down.
- In a crossing situation, a boat that is off the starboard of another boat, from a dead-ahead point to a position just aft of amidship, has the right of way.

- Boaters must undertake a safe speed at all times; safe speed varies with visibility, traffic, maneuverability, prevailing weather and water conditions, and other factors.
- Navigating in a no-wake zone means no wake; note: an off-plane speed, though slow, may still produce a wake.
- Give way to boats that are heading with the current, as in a river; boats with a following current have less maneuverability than boats headed into the current.
- From sunset to sunrise, boats are required to use navigational lights in order to avoid collision. Commonly referred to as "running lights," these must include red and green sidelights on the bow centerline (red to port, green to starboard), and a single white sternlight visible over a 135-degree arc.

One of the most commonly violated rules or laws by all boaters regards the safe distance to be maintained from other boats, swimmers, water-skiers, docks, and shore. In most places that distance is 100 feet. Some precautions or unwritten rules are more an adherence to common sense than established laws. Anglers who are boating on a river, for example, should slow down and leave no wake when passing people who are wading, even if they are a safe or legal distance from those individuals. A power boat should always be operated slowly near people, docks, marinas, and the like, and should idle away from, or into, these situations in complete and safe control. Lastly, no boat should be operated under the influence of alcohol or drugs.

Rough water handling. Rough water and changing conditions are a fact of life for anglers virtually all year long. Anglers are often on the water in boats when conditions change, perhaps starting the day in calm seas and later facing big waves. They may get caught miles offshore or away from their launch site in a sudden squall, or they may simply need to cross a severely wind-blown section of lake to get to a back bay or creek. There are certainly times when a small boat does not go forth, and times when it is prudent for even a large boat to stay at the dock. But when you must venture into rough water—because the forecast is for improving conditions, or you know that it will be better at your ultimate fishing destination—or when conditions change and you have to face worse seas than you started out in, it is important for health and safety that you do so in the right manner.

Nothing can take the place of experience in handling rough water. You have to do it and be in it to fully learn how to handle a boat properly.

"Rough water" and "heavy seas" mean different things, of course, depending on the body of water and the boat. Five-foot waves are extremely rough and very dangerous on large lakes, but it can be a lot worse than that on the ocean. In a small boat, genuine two-footers are rough. Furthermore, "rough" is different depending on whether a boat is in shallow water or deep water. Large shallow lakes, for example, provide some treacherous boat operating conditions when powerful winds whip it up, since the waves are spaced closer together and the danger of running the boat or motor aground while in a trough also exists. On a deeper body of water, that same wind may create big waves with large swells, but be much easier to negotiate.

Before you commence running under difficult conditions, it is necessary to take certain precautions. All loose items in a boat should be put away. Anything that is not lashed down or properly stored could be washed overboard, bounced overboard, broken while banged around, or become an impediment to safety. Bilges should be

pumped dry, not only because the extra weight affects boat operation, but also because spray and waves often bring water into the boat when it is rough, and you may need to work the bilge pumps often to discharge incoming water. Life preservers should be available for those in large boats, and worn by all occupants of smaller boats. In a large boat, where anchor rope may be laid on the foredeck, stow the rope away; if it gets washed overboard and grabs in the propeller, the boat will be dangerously impaired.

Wind direction, wind velocity, and current are key factors in how to handle rough water. Here are some general guidelines for operating under heavy seas:

- Plan your approach to minimize discomfort if possible. If you can run along a protected shoreline for a while, even if it takes you slightly out of your way or is longer than a straight-line approach, it may be advisable to do so to lessen rough-water running. Take a course across the troughs for a while, if that is easy running, before turning to run straight into the sea or directly with the sea.
- Match boat speed to the sea conditions. A lot of people take an unnecessary beating because they operate the boat too fast, so it pounds or slams down. Freshwater anglers have hurt a lot of backs this way. Slow down to a speed that allows you to make headway, holding the bow at a 45-degree angle to oncoming waves if possible. If you go too slow, however, the water controls the boat.
- Try tacking or quartering with the waves, much as a sailboat operates. Ride the edge of the

Quartering into a Head Sea

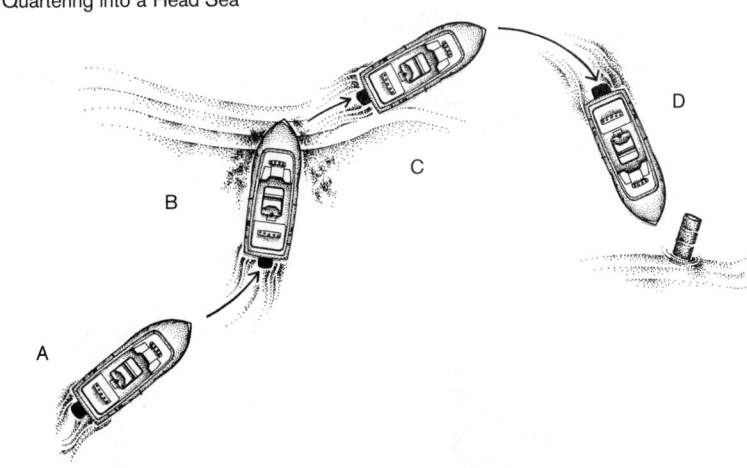

When you need to reach a position (the buoy here) that would require quartering into a head sea, which would be a rough, rolling ride, a safer and smoother-riding alternative is to (A) head directly into the oncoming waves (B) until you're upwind of the desired position (C), then turn and head directly downwind with the following sea to that position (D).

B

B

waves and then head into the waves or with them, so that you are only briefly in the trough. Then ride at a 45-degree angle again for as long as you can, either zigzagging to stay straight ahead, or moving more in one direction according to destination.

- Adjust the trim on your motor, and, if necessary, adjust the weight distribution in your boat. When heading into waves, if the boat is not adjusted properly or has too much forward weight, the bow will stay down and may plow through a wave rather than ride over it.

  If you have too much weight aft, however, the boat will ride back with a wave. Generally, however, it is preferable to keep the bow up.

- Vary the speed to ride the waves, throttling up and down as necessary to time big swells or waves. This can be done by increasing speed to reach the crest of a wave, then throttling back at the peak to ride smoothly down the back of the wave and repeating this for the next wave. Small boats can do this just as well as large boats; however, small boats used in freshwater are more likely to encounter waves that are closer together, and not as easy to vary speed on.

- Head straight into a really large wave to minimize the possibility of it catching you sideways and broaching the boat.

When you are fishing in rough water, rather than running through it, you must handle a boat similarly, although the slow speed of fishing can lead to a boat being sideways to the waves often, which can be dangerous in some craft. In drifting, some motor positioning is required to keep the drift from being too rapid or to keep the boat in proper relation to oncoming waves. Landing a fish, especially a large one, can be a problem, especially if the boat operator has to abandon the wheel to assist. Essentially, the boat has to be steered into the waves when landing a fish (especially a large one); steering with

the waves can cause the boat to be lifted up and crash down uncontrollably and may lead to capsizing (capsizing is the third most common reason for boating accidents). With three people, one holds the boat into the waves; with two people, the operator steers into the waves until the fish is right at the boat, then leaves for a quick assist, returning immediately to the wheel to maintain control.

Motor in, bow low, boat plows

Motor out, bow high, boat pounds

Proper trim, smooth ride

How a motor is trimmed affects the planing action and the ride.

Safety

Proper handling of a boat means safe handling, of course, and boating anglers should bear in mind some safety concerns. Some of these are common to all boating, but anglers need to be extra careful because they handle hooks, knives, gaffs, and thrashing fish. Being careful with fish, especially large and toothy ones, is a safety issue, too. Some anglers have found themselves hooked to a lure that was in turn hooked to a powerful fish that was thrashing on the floor of their boat. A life-threatening medical emergency can arise in a moment.

Boat Operation Directly into a Head Sea

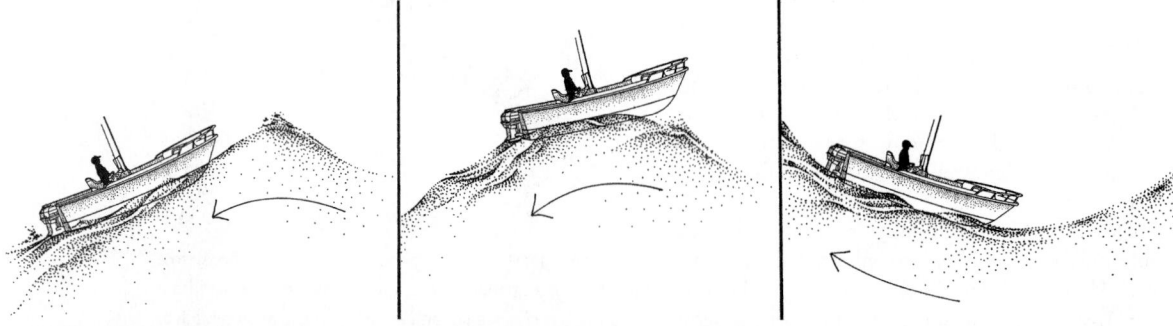

When running into a head (coming toward you) sea, trim the boat so the bow is up and doesn't dig into an oncoming wave. Increase speed to climb the face of the oncoming wave (left), decrease speed as you reach the top of the wave (middle), coast down the back of the wave (right), then speed up to climb the next wave.

Boat Operation with a Following Sea

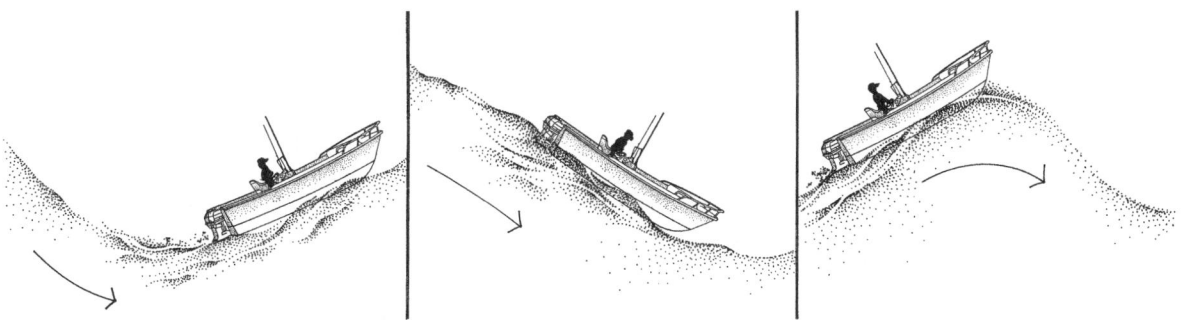

When running with a following sea, maintain position on or near the back of a wave (left) by constantly adjusting boat speed. When a following wave starts to overtake you (middle), increase boat speed to regain position on the back of the preceding wave.

Pre-trip.   A pre-trip check should ensure that you have all legally required equipment as well as optional equipment. If a fishing license is required (it is not in some coastal waters), it must be with you on the boat. Although it is not a safety item, boats must be registered with appropriate authorities, and proof of either registration or documentation should be carried onboard; in some states it is not necessary to register a nonmotorized craft, like a canoe or rowboat. Carry proof of insurance as well.

Make sure that you have ample fuel. Be careful about fueling the boat, especially if it is done at a marine dock or if filling external tanks; make sure that no one smokes at the fuel pump. Because unforeseen events do occur on the water, it's advisable to top off your fuel tank, especially if you'll be ranging far and spending a long time on the water. Be attentive to the fuel level, not only to prevent running out of gas, but to avoid it happening at a critical time (heading toward swift water on a river, for example, or negotiating a rough inlet).

When boarding small boats, be careful to step into the middle of the boat and keep your body low and along the centerline, holding onto the gunwales to help steady the boat. Do not step on the gunwales or jump into the boat. Pass heavy objects in if there is another person onboard. Be seated when someone else is boarding, and keep the boat as steady as possible. If entering from a beach or shore, come in over the bow. Have a companion go to the rear to weight the stern of the boat to make it easier to push it away from the shoreline. Although few people actually fall out of a small boat while boarding, many lose their balance and fall inside the boat, sometimes hurting themselves or doing damage to fishing equipment.

In larger boats, entry is usually from a dock. Do not jump in, but step down. Wear proper footwear with soles that will not scuff the boat and which will grab the deck when it is wet and when you are bouncing in waves.

With large boats that will be traveling some distance, it is recommended that a float plan, detailing destination, route, and other information, be filed with a friend or family or marina in case of an emergency. This may not be a bad idea for anyone, even small boaters, especially if you're headed into some backcountry area. Make it as detailed as possible, including information on your trailer and tow vehicle, as well as expected launching site; this could help narrow the search for you considerably.

Before you depart, it's a good idea to check on the weather forecast so you can be aware of any predicted weather patterns that might adversely affect fishing and boating. This is especially important on large bodies of water, and for people who are traveling long distances to fish, with a lengthy return later in the day. The best forecasts for marine purposes are usually obtained from The National Weather Service. These forecasts are available on handheld marine radios as well as marine VHF radios; they should be checked occasionally during the day. Storms, lightning, water spouts, heavy rain, and fog are some obvious natural phenomena that deserve respect and attention on the water. These may or may not be forecast, but they do require evasion or special navigational consideration. If you can identify weather signs, you have a good chance of avoiding potential trouble. Give yourself plenty of time to avoid a thunderstorm or squall; many anglers have run into trouble by waiting too long to make their move. Be aware of the changes in wind speed and direction, and the changes in wave height. On small bodies of water, once whitecaps start appearing on the waves, you should be thinking of heading to port, especially if you're in a small boat.

Before departing, it is wise to check with passengers to determine their physical limitations and/or swimming proficiency so you are aware in case something unforeseen happens. You should also orient them to the boat and to the location of all safety and emergency equipment, including first-aid items.

Equipment and emergencies.   Basic safety equipment should be carried on boats, and is required on most. These include personal flotation devices *(see),* or life preservers, for each passenger, fire extinguisher, lights, horn or whistle, flares (for larger boats), paddle or oars, visual distress signals, and in some places a bilge pump or bailer. As a practical as well as a safety matter, the following items may also be carried: compass, boat hook, fenders or bumpers, EPIRB (Emergency Position Indicating Radio Beacon), flashlight or searchlight, anchor, sonar or lead sounding line, extra rope, tool kit and spare parts (especially fuses), and a VHF marine radio or handheld weather radio. Some other items that may come in handy include: a cellular phone, rain gear, warm clothing, an extra hat, flashlight, emergency signal mirror, binoculars, extra fishing pliers, emergency food rations, insect repellent, sunscreen, lip balm, extra eyeglasses or sunglasses, matches in a waterproof bag, seasickness remedy, and anti-diarrhea tablets.

From a survival standpoint—should your boat break down and you have to spend a night or more on the water—you should at least have raingear and warm clothing, perhaps a change of clothes as well; enough fresh water for at least 24 hours afloat; a little bit of food; some type of signaling device or flares; some means of electronic communication; a signal mirror; and a waterproof flashlight with good batteries.

Communicating when you need help. A VHF marine radiotelephone is standard for communicating on the water, but its range is limited. You might reach 40 miles over open water with a 25-watt unit and a good antenna under ideal conditions, but in wooded backcountry it could reach only 10 miles or less. Handheld VHFs rarely make it past 5 miles, but they can still help.

Cellular telephones can offer more help options if an antenna site is close enough. Sometimes you're in a fringe area where signals are there but hard to get. Try just a slight change of position in the boat, or move the boat just a little by whatever means available to get as far from trees or other tall vegetation as possible. Or get as high as you can. Sometimes just elevating that antenna by three or four feet is all it takes.

If these don't work and you have an EPIRB, this can save your bacon. Don't overlook flares. You are required by law to carry both day and night Coast Guard-approved visual distress signals if your boat is over 16 feet in length and you are operating on waters more than 2 miles wide. You must also have them aboard any size boat if you operate after dark. Only flares, hand/fuse type or aerial, meet both day and night requirements. Aerial flares can be seen at far greater distances, and their meaning is unmistakable. Aerial flares come in shells for a pistol, and hand-launched in self-contained tubes (you must carry at least 3 day/night signals). For small boats the hand-launched variety makes a lot of sense because they take up so little space and are easy to carry.

With a flashlight you can signal for help from dusk to dawn. The international distress signal is three short, three long, three short (Morse code for SOS). If you don't already know this, it should be committed to memory or permanently etched onto the flashlight. During daylight hours a small mirror can do the same job if the sun is bright enough to make a distinct shadow. To flash sunlight at a target, such as a passing boat or aircraft, hold the mirror under your master eye and extend your other arm with the thumb up, like the front sight on a rifle. Position your thumb just below the target, and flash the sunlight back and forth across its tip in the SOS sequence. Ready-made signal mirrors are unbreakable plastic, small, inexpensive, and have a built-in sight. They also come as part of many compact flare kits.

Overloading and overpowering.   Overloading boats, especially small ones, is a common occurrence and a major cause of mishaps. Anglers should know the capacity of their boats. This information is displayed on a certification label affixed to the boat (for boats that must comply) by the manufacturer. It is illegal for anyone to remove or alter this certification label, which provides maximum capacity information as well as maximum horsepower rating.

Proper distribution of weight in a boat is important for personal safety as well as boat handling.

Exceeding these ratings by overloading and overpowering can be dangerous and may draw citations from law enforcement authorities. Maximum capacity standards were developed for boats by the United States Coast Guard because most boats, especially small ones, can accommodate more people and gear than they can safely carry. Inexperienced boaters run the risk of overloading a boat. Overloading reduces the freeboard and makes the boat more likely to swamp in bad weather or from the wakes of other boats. Overloading can have adverse effects on the stability of a boat and make it hard to control, particularly if the weight is unevenly distributed or moves about suddenly.

The capacity information on the label or plate is a guide and not an absolute. Two capacities are listed: the maximum persons capacity and the maximum weight capacity (which is the total weight-carrying capacity of the boat). The persons capacity is the most prominent information; persons capacity is referred to as "live load," which can move around the boat and affect stability. Generally, the persons capacity is less than the maximum weight capacity, except on very small boats where the persons capacity and maximum weight capacity may be the same.

The maximum persons capacity is shown on the label both in terms of the number of people and the total number of pounds. Total pounds is the controlling figure. The number of persons is a convenient and approximate guide. If you subtract the persons capacity from the maximum weight capacity, you get a figure that represents the total weight of portable gear (which on small boats could include an outboard engine, portable fuel tanks, and coolers) that can be brought aboard. If you want to bring aboard more portable gear than is allowed, you'll have to carry fewer people to compensate.

Bear in mind that the capacity of a boat, either in weight or number of people, is largely a measure for calm to moderate water conditions; heavy loading of a boat, even though it may still conform to the manufacturer's recommendations, may be dangerous in rough water.

As to overpowering, a boat with an engine that exceeds the certification label rating is dangerous. Too much power can make a boat difficult to control. As the power of an engine increases, so does the weight. Overpowering of an outboard boat can produce a stability problem due to excessive weight on the stern. This decreases freeboard at the stern and increases the chance of following seas or wakes coming over the transom, possibly swamping or capsizing the boat. In addition to being unsafe, overpowering may be illegal, and overpowered boats may not be covered by insurance policies or covered by the warranties of boat manufacturers.

Obviously, operating a boat at safe speeds—which vary with seas conditions, localities, and traffic—is of great importance. Do not operate a boat with a passenger in a bow pedestal seat, or sitting on the bow deck (legs dangling over the edge).

PFDs. Safety also applies to standing up in a boat, and being careful not to fall out. Most anglers prefer to stand up in a boat to aid casting, retrieving, fish playing, hook setting, and vision. This necessarily entails some problems, primarily in small boats, since standing changes the center of gravity. It has long been recommended that boat occupants wear PFDs, but the fact is that few do, unless they cannot swim and are afraid of the water, or unless they are young and are obligated by elders to wear them. Some people do wear PFDs while moving at higher speeds in a boat, and this has saved some lives. Striking a submerged object or losing control of a fast-moving boat has thrown small-boat operators and passengers out of their vessel; in such a situation, a careening boat makes a clockwise circle back toward its passengers due to the rotation of the propeller and literally can run the passengers over. Someone who falls out of a boat in this manner may need a good PFD to save them from drowning, especially if they are rendered unconscious by striking the boat. Some people who were not wearing a PFD when this happened were killed.

Anglers occasionally fall out of boats that are not under power, often by losing their balance from a raised platform. For many this has not been a problem, but if they fall on top of a submerged tree stump or rock or piling, they could receive serious injury. If they panic, struggle, and get tangled in vegetation, they could drown. In fact, some people drown this way every year, not necessarily as the result of falling, but more likely diving in to cool off. A common cause of drowning, not necessarily of anglers, is men who fall overboard while relieving themselves. Often this type of accident is alcohol related, but in any event, it is best to do this in a kneeling rather than standing position, or to use a bail bucket.

Even anglers who wear a PFD when a boat is underway usually take it off when the boat is at rest or when actually fishing, whether trolling, drifting, casting, or stillfishing. It is more comfortable to have the PFD off (unless it is the inflatable suspender type), and this is generally regarded as acceptable by most anglers. Common sense is the key here. If you can swim well, if the water is warm, if there are no objects nearby, and if the boat is not likely to run you over or be bounced on top of you, then you probably have little to worry about. Standing up is more likely to be a problem in small boats, in tipsy boats, in boats with raised casting platforms, in boats with slippery platforms or decks, and when the water is rough enough to bounce a boat around. It is less likely to be a problem in large boats, especially those with high gunwales and plenty of freeboard.

If you are ever in doubt about your own safety, concerned about existing conditions, or encounter troubles with your boat under adverse conditions, put on your PFD if you're not already wearing it, and have your passengers do the same. If your boat should swamp or capsize, stay with it unless your life is threatened. Rescuers will be better able to find you if you stay with the boat. Obviously, there are conditions that would mitigate this advice (such as if you are very close to shore), and in some cases, it may not be possible to stay with your boat (a capsized canoe in rough water is hard for several people to hang onto, or your boat might even have sunk).

Most outboard boats manufactured since August 1, 1978 (as well as manually propelled boats less than 20 feet long) are required by law to have level (also called upright) flotation to make it easier for people to stay with a boat that has been swamped or capsized. This requirement does not apply to canoes, kayaks, inflatable boats, and some other specialty craft.

B

B

Coast Guard accident statistics suggest that many drownings could be prevented after a capsizing or swamping accident if the occupants stayed with the boat rather than trying to swim to shore. Thus, the Level Flotation Standard, as it is called, requires the manufacturer to provide enough flotation material in a boat so that, if the boat is holed or swamped, the fully loaded boat will float the passenger carrying area at or just below the surface of the water, providing a survival platform for the occupants until help arrives. Even if the boat capsizes, the overturned hull must still float basically at the surface so the occupants can get out of the water by climbing onto the hull.

Most inboard and inboard-outboard boats manufactured since August 1, 1978 are required by law to have basic flotation. The Basic Flotation Standard has a lesser degree of flotation performance than the Level Flotation Standard because swamping and capsizing accidents are not as prevalent with inboard boats and because it would require large and costly amounts of flotation material to compensate for the heavy inboard engines. To satisfy this requirement, the manufacturer must provide enough flotation to keep any portion of the boat above the surface of the water after swamping or capsizing so that passengers can hang on until helps arrives. This requirement also does not apply to canoes, kayaks, inflatable boats, and some other specialty craft.

Alcohol and drugs. Operating a boat while under the influence of alcohol or drugs is no less a concern than it is for vehicular driving. Many boating related accidents are due to impaired judgment as a result of alcohol or drug use, especially the former. This applies not only to those who operate a boat, but also to those who are passengers. Accident statistics show that more than half of all the people who drown in boating accidents had consumed alcohol prior to their accident. Several hours of exposure to sun, glare, wind, boating, noise, fishing, and the various elements that make up a day on the water are in themselves fatiguing without introducing alcohol or drugs. Sometimes, just a couple of beers is enough to seriously impair the judgment of an angler or boat operator. People who are tipsy are more likely to fall overboard—an oft-cited government statistic is that many of the alcohol-influenced men who have drowned after falling out of a boat had the fly to their trousers unzipped. Alcohol reduces the body's ability to protect against cold water, so if you are under the influence and fall into cold water, you may have less time to call for help or swim to safety. And a drunk person can actually get disoriented in the water.

Furthermore, operating a vessel while intoxicated (Boating Under the Influence or BUI) has been a federal offense since 1988. Operating a boat under the influence of alcohol or drugs may be considered negligent operation subject to civil or criminal penalties, so, in addition to practical safety issues, there are civil and criminal issues associated with boat operation while under the influence.

This entire section can be summed up with the proviso: Always be careful, no matter where you go, no matter what the conditions are, and no matter what type of boat you go fishing in.

See: Bass Boat; Canoe; First Aid; Flats Boat; Jonboat; Navigation; Motor, Electric; Motor, Trolling; Outboard Boat; Personal Flotation Device; Sonar; Sportfisherman; Trailer; Walleye Boat; Weather.

BOATHOOK
A pole with a hook at the end, used for picking up or retrieving objects, especially rope, and for fending off or holding onto a dock or other boat.

BOAT LAUNCH
An access site, usually with a paved ramp, for getting boats off a trailer and into the water. Boat launches may be at parks, marinas, fishing camps, concession docks, and other places. They may be improved, with long paved ramps that extend far enough into the water to allow for water level fluctuations, or they may be unimproved, without pavement and possibly with gravel, sand, or mud that may impede access efforts. Usually a fee is charged to launch a trailered boat at privately owned ramps, and there may be a fee at publicly owned and maintained facilities, but some locations, such as those provided by the Corps of Engineers on inland waters, are free.

A boat launch is commonly referred to as a boat ramp, and most have ample parking nearby for trailer and tow vehicles. Boat launches are also used by anglers with smaller boats not carried on trailers, including cartop boats and inflatables.
See: Launching.

BOBBER
A North American term for a lightweight surface-floating device that is attached to fishing line and indicates the subsurface bite or strike by a fish. Sometimes referred to as a "dobber," this form of bite or strike indicator is more properly known as a float *(see),* and the types and fishing methods are discussed under that entry.

BOBBIN
A small tool that delivers the thread used to tie flies.
See: Fly Tying.

BOBBING
A term for ice fishing *(see),* commonly used in the Midwest where bobhouses *(see)* are utilized.

BOBHOUSE
Shack or shanty used for ice fishing *(see).*

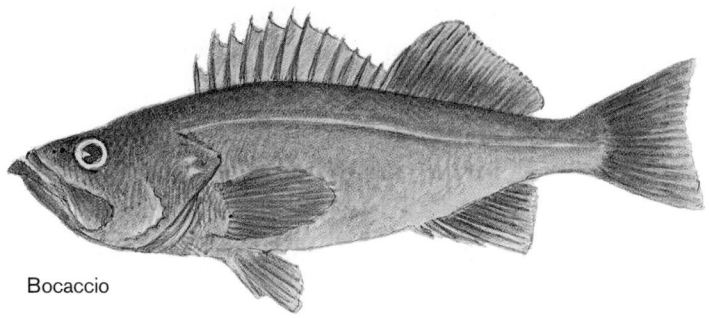
Bocaccio

BOCACCIO   *Sebastes paucispinis.*

Other names—salmon grouper, mini-grouper (juveniles), red snapper, Pacific red snapper.

Abundant off the central and southern coast of California, the bocaccio is one of the most commercially important rockfish in that region. It is also a well-known gamefish in its range and a good eating fish with soft and juicy white meat. Anglers should be cautious when handling the bocaccio, because it has venomous first dorsal and anal spines.

Identification. Although its elongate and compressed body form is less bulky than that of most fish in the scorpionfish family, the bocaccio has a large mouth. The upper jaw extends farther back than the eye; the lower jaw extends past the upper one considerably. The first dorsal fin has spines and is deeply notched, and there are usually nine soft rays in the anal fin. Bocaccio are variably colored olive or brown on the back, reddish on the sides, and pink or white on the belly. Young fish are generally light bronze with speckling over the sides and back. As they mature, their color generally becomes darker and the speckling gradually disappears.

Size/Age. Bocaccio can grow up to 3 feet and 21 pounds and can live for 30 years.

Distribution. These fish inhabit waters from Punta Blanca, Baja California, to Kruzof Island and Kodiak Island, Alaska.

Habitat. Adults dwell in waters over rocky reefs but are also common in deeper water. Young bocaccio live in shallower water and form schools; they are caught more frequently than adults, especially in rocky areas.

Life history/Behavior. One- or two-year-old bocaccio travel in loose schools and move into shallow water where they may be captured in quantity. With increasing age, they seek deeper water and move from near the surface to near the bottom. Adults are commonly found in waters of 250 to 750 feet over a somewhat irregular, hard, or rubble bottom. They are known to dwell in depths as great as 1,050 feet.

Females start maturing when they are 17 inches long. As with all rockfish, fertilization is internal, and development of the embryos takes place within the ovaries of the female until they are ready to hatch. A 28-inch female was estimated to contain 1.5 million eggs. The main hatching period runs from December through April.

Food. Bocaccio feed mainly on fish, including other rockfish. Their diet comprises surfperch, mackerel, sablefish, anchovies, sardines, deep-sea lanternfish, and sanddabs, as well as squid, octopus, and crabs.

Angling. Almost any rocky or rubble bottom at depths of 250 to 750 feet will yield bocaccio. The usual rig is made up of three to six hooks above a sinker that is heavy enough to take the line to the bottom on a fairly straight course. Because of the extreme depths fished, a lot of weight and a lot of line are required to fish bocaccio. The bait should be sufficiently firm to stay on the hook while being chewed upon by bocaccio; for this reason, squid are a common bait choice.
See: Rockfish.

BOILIE

A small ball of processed protein bait made from assorted ingredients (milk and animal proteins, eggs, soy flour, wheat germ, coloring, and flavoring) that have been rolled together and boiled. It has a crusty shell that retards small fish pecking. This is a European term and innovation primarily used in carp fishing.
See: Carp.

BOLIVIA

One of only two South American countries without access to the sea, Bolivia is the fifth largest country of that continent, and strongly influenced by two ranges of the Andes Mountains. It contains a portion of Lake Titicaca, the largest lake in South America, which has no currently known sportfishing significance *(see: Peru),* and numerous rivers, most of which flow to the north through plains and rain forests and into Brazil, eventually meeting the Madeira River and flowing to the Amazon River. The many rivers and fishing opportunities here are described in the Amazon review under Brazil *(see).*

BOLT RIG

A European term for a shore-based baitfishing setup for carp utilizing a heavy sliding sinker, a rod and reel in a fixed holder, and a taut fishing line, which results in a fish hooking itself.
See: Carp.

BOMBORA

An Australian term for a rocky reef, usually found near shore, that is submerged at high tide and exposed at low tide. The reef may be obvious because of crashing waves, or it may be hidden to boaters, especially in calm midtide conditions. Bomboras attract certain fish species.

B

BONEFISH   *Albula vulpes.*
Other names—banana fish, phantom, silver ghost, ladyfish, grubber, silver streak, tenny; French: *banane de mer, sorte de mulet;* Hawaiian: *o'io;* Japanese: *soto-iwashi;* Portuguese: *juruma;* Spanish: *macabí, zorro.*

Although the bonefish was previously thought to be the only member of the Albulidae family, there are now five recognized species. The bonefish is the only significant sportfish among them, however, and is one of the most coveted of all saltwater gamefish. In keeping with its scientific name, which means "white fox," it is indeed a wary, elusive creature, one that usually must be stalked with stealth and that bolts with startling speed when hooked or alarmed.

Although bonefish have little food value to anglers and virtually all are released, they are a subsistence food in some locations. It is generally believed that bonefish are not good table fare, but some gourmands maintain that bonefish flesh is firm and tasty and the roe a delicacy.

Identification.   The bonefish has armor plates instead of scales on its conical head and is distinguished from the similar ladyfish by its suckerlike mouth and snout-shaped nose, which are adapted to its feeding habits. It also has a single dorsal fin and a deeply forked tail. The coloring is bright silver on the sides and belly with bronze or greenish blue tints on the back; there may also be yellow or dark coloring on parts of the fin and snout, and sometimes there are dusky markings on the sides. The young have bronze backs and nine narrow crossbands.

Size.   Although the average bonefish weighs between 2 and 5 pounds, bonefish weighing up to 10 pounds are not uncommon. They can grow to 41 inches in length, averaging 1 to $2^{1}/_{2}$ feet long. The all-tackle world-record catch is a 19-pound fish.

Distribution.   Bonefish are found worldwide in tropical and subtropical waters. Around North America, they are most bountiful in the Florida Keys, the Bahamas, and the Caribbean, more so in winter than in summer; they are also somewhat abundant in Belize, Panama, and other Central American countries.

Habitat.   Occurring in warm coastal areas, bonefish inhabit the shallows of intertidal waters, including around mud and sand flats as well as mangrove lagoons. They are also found in waters up to 30 feet deep and are able to live in oxygen-poor water because they possess a lunglike bladder into which they can inhale air.

Life history/Behavior.   The particulars of bonefish reproduction are not well known, although it is thought that bonefish spawn from late winter to late spring, depending on locale. With a small head and a long, transparent body, the young bonefish looks like an eel until it undergoes a leptocephalus larval stage. It grows to about $2^{1}/_{2}$ inches long during this period, then experiences a metamorphosis that shrinks the young bonefish to half that size. The fins begin to appear during the shrinking, and in 10 to 12 days it attains the adult bonefish body form, only in miniature size. This growth process is similar in tarpon and ladyfish development. The young migrate out to the open sea to live on plankton, returning as juveniles to live in the shallows.

Generally, bonefish are a schooling fish; smaller specimens are seen traveling in large numbers on the flats, whereas larger ones prefer smaller schools or groups of 5 to 10 fish.

Food and feeding habits.   Bonefish feed on crabs, shrimp, clams, shellfish, sea worms, sea urchins, and small fish. They prefer feeding during a rising tide, often doing so near mangroves. They root in the sand with their snout for food and are often first detected while feeding with their body tilted in a head-down, tail-up manner, with all or part of the tail fin protruding from the surface. These are referred to as tailing fish. Bonefish also sometimes stir up the bottom when rooting along, which is called mudding; this can be a telltale indicator to the observant angler.

Angling.   Although some bonefish are caught accidentally in deep water, the primary habitat

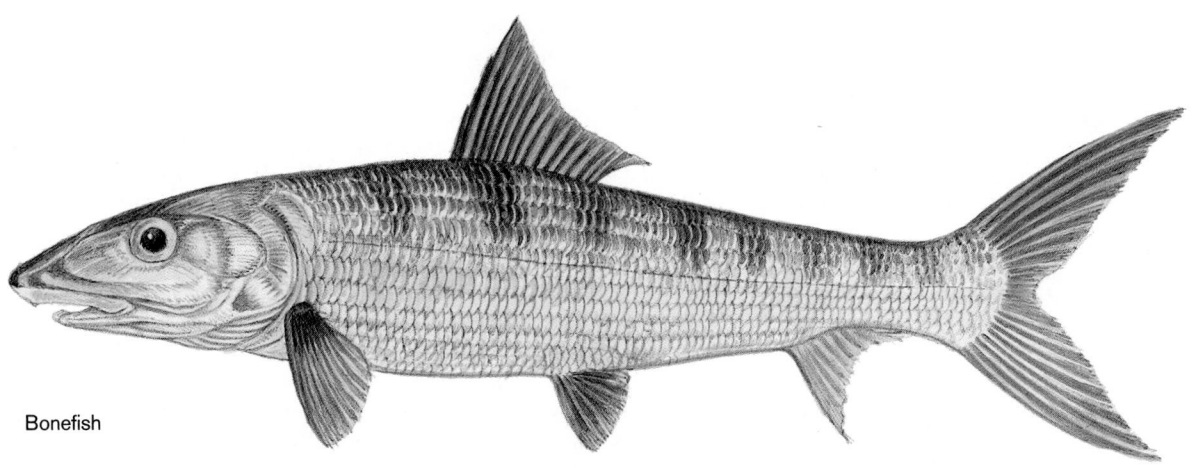

Bonefish

explored by anglers is shallow tidal flats and shoals. Bonefish feed on these flats, scouring the bottom for small clams, crabs, worms, and shrimp. The shallow flats, which range from less than a foot to as much as several feet deep, leave the fish most vulnerable, so bonefish have good reason to be skittish. Engine noise will send the fish scattering, so boaters prefer to pole silently along in search of fish, staking the boat and fishing from the boat or by foot when bonefish are spotted. Waders walk on hard bottoms and carefully approach feeding fish.

Bonefishing is primarily sight fishing, so this species, in effect, is stalked. Unless their tails are poking through the surface, the silvery form of a bonefish can be surprisingly difficult to see, even in the shallowest water. Polarized sunglasses aid through-the-water vision and are virtually a necessity. Calm water and bright sun help visibility as well. When bonefish are spotted, the angler maneuvers into position to intercept the fish with a judicious cast.

If the terminal tackle lands on top of the fish or a school, the fish will dart away. So the lure, fly, or bait should be cast 6 to 10 feet ahead of feeding or cruising fish.

At the strike and hookset there is an explosion in the water, and the bonefish instantaneously streaks across the flats toward the security of deep water. It is not uncommon for a bonefish to strip 80 to 100 yards of line off the reel in a scorching run, and the angler must have the drag set properly and keep the rod tip high so the line avoids mangrove roots, grass, and other flats objects that could cut the line or leader.

Bonefishing is primarily done with fly or light spinning tackle, using a 6- to 7-foot spinning rod or a 9-foot fly rod and a reel with adequate line capacity. Six-pound nylon monofilament line is just right for spinning gear.

Small streamers or a weighted fly pattern like the Crazy Charlie and epoxy flies work best in light browns and yellow; jigs are the primary artificials, in pink, white, and yellow; and shrimp, clams, and conch meat are popular baits. Shrimp is the best natural offering for bonefish. They are particularly attracted to the scent of fresh shrimp, so break off the tail and two of the four fans and thread the shrimp on the hook. A piece of conch or crab will also catch bonefish. Chum slicks are equally effective. Some bonefish anglers anchor or stake their boat and chum with crushed shrimp.

The end of an ebb tide and the beginning of a flood tide are usually best for the sake of spotting shallow fish (bonefish coming in over the flats on a rising tide are not half as wary when the tide starts to fall), but a slack flood tide can produce for anglers who fish waist-deep water by casting blindly with small jigs. Seldom do bonefish feed on shallow flats when the water temperature falls much below 70°F; they stay in deeper water then.

A bonefish is released near Islamorada, Florida.

B

The main secret to catching bonefish is in the presentation. Bonefish spend most of their time probing for food and tend to pounce on any tidbit that looks tasty. Thus, if you can get a fly, lure, or natural bait in front of the fish in a natural manner, you should get a strike.

Bonefish arrive on the flats with the incoming tide, working higher on the shoal as water depth increases. Receding water forces them to retreat to deep holes or channels until the tide returns. These eating machines are opportunistic feeders, constantly in search of crustaceans and small baitfish. With their hard nose, and eyes set high on the head, they are built to dig. In skinny water, you'll see them standing on their noses, their tails waving in the air as they ferret out dinner. Thus, the best way to catch a bonefish is to get the bait, lure, or fly down on the bottom.

Bonefish need to see, hear, or smell the bait, lure, or fly. Blessed with an incredible sense of smell, acute hearing, and terrific eyesight, they can do this easily. A bonefish can hear a fly or a shrimp "splat" on the water some distance away. To utilize their sense of smell, feeding bonefish work into or across the current. They expect their food to be carried by the tide, which means that it's best to make a presentation upcurrent from the fish. When fishing natural baits, this is critical if you expect your quarry to get a whiff of your offering.

Regardless of tackle, aim your cast so the lure lands in front, but not too close to the fish. If the bait goes astray, the fish won't see it; but drop even the tiniest fly too close and every fish in the school vanishes. Always position your offering in front of the fish and beyond its path of travel. If the cast is not perfect, retrieve it quickly until the lure lies directly in the path of the fish. Then, start a stripping retrieve. When fishing artificials, the idea is to "take" the lure away from the predator. The lure must be moving away from the fish, not toward it. With natural baits, cast upcurrent and let the bait lie on the bottom a short while, so the fish can get the scent.

There is little point in keeping a bonefish for eating or mounting. Replica taxidermy mounts are readily available, and the meat of a bonefish, although better than most anglers believe, is still not the equal of many other species. Bonefish can fight until so exhausted that it may be necessary to carefully revive them after capture.

See: Flats Fishing.

BONITO, ATLANTIC   *Sarda sarda.*

Other names—common bonito, katonkel, belted bonito; French: *bonito à dos rayé, boniton, conite, pélamide;* Japanese: *hagatsuo, kigungegatsuo;* Portuguese: *cerda, sarrajão, serra;* Spanish: *bonito del Atlántico, cabaña cariba, cerda.*

The Atlantic bonito, a relative of the tuna, has a reputation as a tough fighter and a tasty fish. This combination makes it highly popular among anglers. In the eastern Atlantic, this species has moderate commercial value, although it is of limited importance in the western Atlantic, specifically off southern Brazil, Argentina, Venezuela, Mexico, Martinique, and Grenada. The light-colored meat is served dried, salted, smoked, and canned.

Identification.   The Atlantic bonito has a completely scaled body (some types of bonito have only a partially scaled body), a noticeably curved lateral line, and six to eight finlets on the back and belly between the anal fin and the tail. The caudal peduncle—the narrow muscular area connecting the body and the tail—has a lateral keel on either side with two smaller keels above and below the main keel. It also doesn't have a swim bladder or teeth on its tongue. The back is blue or blue green, fading to silvery on the lower sides and belly; a characteristic feature of the Atlantic bonito is the dark lines that extend from the back to just below the lateral line. It can be distinguished from the tuna by its slimmer body, a mouth full of teeth, and dark lines on its back rather than its belly.

Size.   The Atlantic bonito averages 2 to 10 pounds, although it may attain a weight of 20 pounds and a length of 36 inches. Smaller fish are often used as trolling baits for big-game fish. An 18-pound, 4-ounce specimen holds the all-tackle world record.

Distribution.   As implied by its name, the Atlantic bonito inhabits the Atlantic Ocean, from the tropical and temperate waters around Nova Scotia to Argentina in the western Atlantic, and from Norway to South Africa in the eastern Atlantic. In the United States, it is most abundant from southern New England to New Jersey. The Atlantic bonito is rare in the Caribbean and the Gulf of Mexico; it is absent in the West Indies, although it is frequently found in the Mediterranean and Black Seas. In the Pacific Ocean, other members of this family take the place of Atlantic bonito.

Habitat.   Atlantic bonito occur in brackish water and saltwater, particularly in tropical and temperate coastal environs. Schooling and migratory, they often inhabit surface inshore waters.

Life history/Behavior.   In coastal waters, spawning occurs from January through July, depending on locale (June and July in the western Atlantic). Bonito reach sexual maturity at about 16 inches in length. Spawning usually takes place close to shore, in warm coastal waters. By the end of the first year, females will sometimes spawn, although many wait until the end of their second year of life. They release 450,000 to 6 million eggs, depending on size. Growth is rapid.

Food and feeding habits.   Living in open waters, the Atlantic bonito feeds primarily at or near the surface in schools that are often 15 to 20 miles offshore, but are also found close to shore. Adults prey on small schooling fish and will also eat squid,

Atlantic Bonito

B

mackerel, menhaden, alewives, anchovies, silver-sides, and shrimp; they also tend to be cannibalistic. Atlantic bonito larvae feed mostly on copepods but eat larvae of other fish as well, as do juveniles.

The Atlantic bonito is an athletic swimmer and a ferocious feeder, occasionally leaping out of the water in pursuit of its quarry. Young bonito develop this killer instinct as soon as they become able to feed. Adults and young alike feed during the day but are especially active at dawn and dusk.

Angling.   Bonito are often caught by anglers trolling with baits or lures for larger quarry. When caught on the heavier tackle used for that sport, the fish are understandably overmatched. When caught on light tackle, however, they are a robust battler—diving, surging, running, and generally doing their best to stretch the fishing line. They typically streak away after a smashing strike, making tremendously swift runs, and then head deep, where they may stay until whipped.

Some anglers keep light tackle handy for use while trolling, in case they encounter a school of bonito (when bigger baits are retrieved and light rods—equipped with a jig, spoon, or plug—are used). They sometimes employ light tackle when drifting and live-bait fishing or when chumming and using live or cut baits. A light- to medium-action spinning rod, 7 to 8 feet long, with 10- to

15-pound line, is about right. Still lighter tackle will ensure more of a battle.

When trolling deliberately for bonito (as well as skipjack and small tuna) a fast boat speed is usually best, as are trolling plugs and feather jigs. The fish are primarily caught near the surface and aren't put off by the wake of a boat or engine noise, so flatline length can be relatively short.

In some areas of the northeastern U.S., bonito are caught near shore and may be pursued deliberately by casters using various tackle and catching these fish on assorted lures and flies, either from boats or from beach and jetty. Metal jigs, long minnow plugs, and streamer flies that imitate sand eels and spearing are used; 12-pound line on spinning or baitcasting tackle provides great enjoyment, as do 9- or 10-weight fly outfits with a weight-forward or sink-tip line.
See: Bonito, Pacific.

BONITO, PACIFIC   *Sarda chiliensis.*
Other names—California bonito, eastern Pacific bonito, bonehead, Laguna tuna, striped tuna, ocean bonito; French: *bonite du Pacifique;* Japanese: *hagatsuo;* Spanish: *bonito del Pacífico.*

The Pacific bonito is an important gamefish, often caught from party boats and from shore. It is valued more for sport than for food, as is the Atlantic bonito. The flesh is light colored and tasty; commercially caught fish are mostly canned and sometimes sold fresh or frozen. They are less valuable in the commercial market than are tuna family members and cannot be labeled as "tuna," even though they are related.

Identification.   Similar in size and pigmentation to the Atlantic bonito, the Pacific bonito is distinguished from most other bonito by the lack of teeth on its tongue and the possession of a straight intestine without a fold in the middle. The Pacific bonito has 17 to 19 spines on its first dorsal fin and is the only tunalike fish on the California coast that has slanted dark stripes on its back. Like other bonito, its body is cigar shaped and somewhat compressed, with a pointed and conical head and a large mouth. It is dark blue above, and its dusky sides become silvery below.

An Atlantic bonito caught near Montauk, New York.

Pacific Bonito

Size/Age. The Pacific bonito can grow to 25 pounds and 40 inches, although they are usually much smaller. The all-tackle world record is 14 pounds, 2 ounces. Fast-growing fish, bonito will be 6 to 10 inches long by the early part of their first summer, weighing 3 pounds by that fall and 6 to 7 pounds the following spring.

Distribution. Pacific bonito occur discontinuously from Chile to the Gulf of Alaska. Their greatest area of abundance occurs in the Northern Hemisphere in warm waters between Magdalena Bay, Baja California, and Point Conception, California.

Habitat. Bonitos live in surface to middle depths in the open sea and are migratory. Older fish usually range farther from the coast than juveniles. Bonito may arrive off the coast in the spring as ocean waters warm, but they may not show up at all if oceanic conditions produce colder than normal temperatures.

Life history/Behavior. Pacific bonito form schools by size; at two years old, they reach sexual maturity. Spawning occurs sometime between September and February. Although spawning is usually successful each year in the southern part of their range, it may not be successful each year farther north. The free-floating eggs require about three days to hatch at average spring water temperatures.

Food and feeding habits. Pacific bonito prey on smaller pelagic fish as well as on squid and shrimp, generally in surface waters. Anchovies and sardines appear to be their preferred foods.

Angling. Fishing methods for Pacific bonito are similar to those for Atlantic bonito. These include trolling at or near the surface, as well as casting, jigging, or live-bait fishing with small fish, squid, cut or strip baits, or with any of a variety of small artificial lures.

Pacific bonito are excellent fighters, and their hearty appetites make them willing to strike many lures and baits. Once a school is aroused, they will take almost any bait or lure anglers toss their way. Most Pacific bonito are taken by a combination of trolling and live-bait fishing. Anglers locate the schools by using trolling feathers, and live anchovies or squid pieces bait the fish once located. Most fishing for Pacific bonito takes place offshore over a bottom depth of 300 to 600 feet, but it can occur next to kelp beds when the fish are near shore.

Anglers usually catch 3- to 12-pound bonito. Activity tapers off in the fall as the water cools, but good fishing is still possible around warmwater outflows associated with power plants.
See: Bonito, Atlantic.

BONY FISH
Fish that have a bony skeleton and belong to the class Osteichthyes. Basically, this includes all fish except sharks, rays, skate, hagfish, and lampreys.
See: Fish.

BOOK COLLECTING *(Rare/Out-of-Print Fishing Books)*
The literature of angling, certainly in terms of quantity, and most probably in terms of quality, surpasses the literature of any other sport or pastime engaged in by civilized men and women.

The first English language book, *The Treatyse of Fysshynge Wyth an Angle,* was printed in 1496 and was reputedly authored by a nun, Dame Juliana Berners. Izaak Walton's *The Compleat Angler* (1653) is said to be the third most reprinted book in the English language after the Bible and *Pilgrim's Progress.*

Serious collectors and bibliographers were active as early as the late eighteenth century, their heyday in England being the nineteenth century. During the mid-nineteenth century, a new era of increased prosperity and leisure time began to develop in America, and the first American fishing books started to appear. Some of the important books were *Natural History of The Fishes of Massachusetts, Embracing a Practical Essay on Angling* by Jerome V. C. Smith (1833); *Schreiner's Sporting Manual* by William Schreiner (1841); *The American Angler's Book* by Thaddeus Norris (1845); *The American Angler's Guide* by John J. Brown (1845); *Fishing in American Waters* by Genio C. Scott (1869); *Favorite Flies and Their Histories* by Mary Orvis Marbury (1892); and the numerous works by Frank Forester (who used the pseudonym of Henry William Herbert).

Since the late nineteenth century, and particularly since the growth in sportfishing after World War II, the number of fishing books published—and the interest in collecting books about and related to sportfishing—has grown. Book collecting has become a small hobby for some, and a major one for others. Usually but not always, collectors are people who partake in the sport, their focus is rare and out-of-print works.

Starting a Collection
The most important consideration in building a quality fishing book library is to buy titles that appeal to your interests. Buy wisely, buy books in the best condition you can afford, and take good care of them. Try to buy first editions; if a book was originally published with a dust jacket, try to buy it with the dust jacket.

Study bibliographic material to learn the values of fishing books. Alfred B. Maclay, Henry A. Sherwin, Dean Sage, Daniel B. Fearing, and John Gerald Heckscher, among others, amassed some of the finest angling collections during the late 1800s. Most of these collections were sold in the mid 1900s, and their auction catalogs have become important references for some of the very rare books they owned. For more recent values, study the auction catalogs of Col. Henry A. Siegel, Harry and Elsie Darbee, Joseph D. Bates, Jr., Rudolphe Coigney, and Charles B. Woods III.

An important bibliography by Henry P. Bruns, *Angling Books of The Americas,* is still available from many out-of-print book dealers. Most sporting magazines carry ads of book dealers who specialize in fishing books; write and subscribe to their catalogs. Those with detailed bibliographic information will become valuable references.

Make friends with experienced collectors and pump them for all the information you can get. Once you have done all of this, don't worry when you still make a mistake. It happens to the best.

The Focus

Forming a library exclusively of American fishing books is no small achievement. Collecting the early American fishing books can be expensive and challenging. Since the mid-twentieth century, a veritable avalanche of fishing books has been published, making it a necessity (unless you have unlimited resources) to focus your collection on a particular area of personal interest.

One possible subject area is books on a particular species, such as tarpon, brook trout, black bass, striped bass, salmon, and muskie, to name a few popular ones. If you enjoy fly tying or tackle collecting, buy books on tying freshwater and/or saltwater flies, lure making, tackle, rods, and trade catalogs.

Many people collect all the books by their favorite author, such as Roderick Haig Brown, Zane Grey, Joseph Bates, or Charles Brooks, or a group of authors who all knew each other, like George LaBranche, Edward Ringwood Hewitt, Emlyn Gill, Preston Jennings, and Eugene V. Connett. Many collect fishing books published by a particular press, such as Derrydale Press, Knopf/Borzoi, Penn, or Van Nostrand; others collect every bibliographic book available.

Some people collect beautiful fine-leather bindings bound by famous binders of the period. Favorites among collectors are books signed by the author or signed presentation copies; the best of these, of course, is a book signed by the author to another well-known fishing writer or to a spouse.

You can have fun with children's fishing books or fishing humor. Fishing club histories and mysteries with fishing plots are two fascinating new areas for exploration. Collectors with a scientific bent buy ichthyology, fisheries, and conservation titles.

One popular area is books about a person's favorite type of fishing as practiced in a certain part of the country or world: surf casting, saltwater fly fishing, big-game fishing, carp on a fly (it exists!), trout fishing in Montana or Chile or South Africa, salmon fishing in Norway or Scotland or Canada, western steelhead fishing, etc. Another focus might be books covering a specific locale or river and maybe your home state, province, or country: the Catskills, the Rockies, the Florida Keys, Montana, Maine, Texas, British Columbia, Michigan, New Zealand . . ... The list can be as endless as your imagination.

Valuations

Older fishing books have continued to hold their value very well. Fishing has become a popular sport, and the demand has increased greatly, especially with the classics. For example, a fine copy of the 1892 first edition of Mary Orvis Marbury's *Favorite Flies and Their Histories* sold for $300 in 1993; now, when one can be found, it will bring $500 or more.

An interesting trend over the past several years is the influx of younger collectors with an avid interest in the history and literature of angling. This influx has caused a surge in the reprint market. Many classic fishing titles are being reprinted at modest prices, and some of the reprinted books have started to climb in value if they are well cared for. For example, Haig Brown's *Fisherman's Winter,* first published in 1954, was reprinted in 1975 at $7.50; a fine reprint copy now sells for $40. Not a dramatic increase, but it sure beats bank interest rates.

Recently published books can produce some real bargains if you're astute and lucky enough to choose the right author. John Gierach's *Sex Death and Fly Fishing* was published at $19.95 in 1990 and now sells for $200. All of Dana Lamb's limited editions published by Barre Press in the 1960s were issued at $15 to $20, and all now sell for over $150. Art Lee's *Fishing Dry Flies for Trout on Rivers and Streams* was $19.95 in 1982 and now sells for $85. Norman Maclean's *A River Runs Through It* was $7.95 in 1976; now a pristine copy of the first printing sells for $1,000. What a movie can do for a book! Harry Middleton's untimely death increased the prices of his first printings tenfold. These books were all published by different publishers, and all had very small first printings. In some cases, when a paperback and hardcover are issued simultaneously, as was the case with the Gierach and Lee books noted, the hardcover printing will be quite small, sometimes as low as 1,000 copies. That's almost a limited edition, and the hardcover version becomes an instant collectible.

Where to Buy Books

There are many sources for collectible rare and out-of-print fishing books. The best sources are reputable booksellers specializing in out-of-print

B

works, but they usually know the value of what they sell. You won't find too many bargains, but you can depend on them for quality. They may also be able to locate particular titles that you want to add to your collection.

Auction houses that specialize in selling books have some sales featuring out-of-print fishing books. Other, more chancy, sources are used bookshops, local library sales, tag or estate sales, and flea markets. When you start buying from these places, your own storehouse of knowledge is important. Many general bookshop owners grossly overprice very common books, and the condition of books at flea markets can be appalling. Keep digging and trying all sources; part of the fun of book collecting is the treasure hunt.

Care of the Collection

Ideally your books should be kept in a climate-controlled room. This can prove difficult. At best, the room should be air-conditioned in hot, humid weather. Store normal-size books upright on a bookshelf, never too tightly packed, but tight enough that all the books stand up straight. Make sure there is normal air flow around the books to prevent mildew. Place tall or heavy books flat on the shelf.

If you look closely at any book, you'll notice that the cloth covers are slightly larger than the printed book block. When you stand it on the shelf, the weight of the book block pulls against the binding. This may create broken hinges and loose bindings.

If possible, locate your bookshelves on a wall that does not get direct sunlight. Sunshine is the cause of many a faded spine. Once a year, take your books off the shelf and dust them. If the book has a dust jacket, take it off and wipe the book with a soft cloth. Dust collected along the top of the book will mix with the acids in the air and permanently darken it. Wrap the dust jackets in Mylar covers to prevent tearing or chipping. These can be purchased from any library supply house (like Brodart Office Supply, Williamsport, PA).

Did you see your favorite author's obituary in the newspaper? Don't put it into his book! Newsprint is the most acid paper there is and will leave a permanent brown spot. First, encase it in clear plastic wrap, then lay it in the book. Writing your name in pencil on the first blank page is acceptable, but never use an embossing stamp. Never store books in boxes in the basement or the attic. Boxed books don't receive the needed air flow; basements are often damp; and hot, airless attics can turn paper brown and brittle.

This sounds like a lot to do, but not when you've spent a lot of time and money collecting your books. Taking good care of them will only help to maintain their value. Most importantly, read and enjoy your books. If over the years your books increase in value, enjoy that too.

Did you know there was a right and left bank to every stream or river? It's determined by facing in the direction in which the water is flowing.

Selective Bibliography

Biscotti, M. L. *The Borzoi Books for Sportsmen.* Madison, OH: Sunrise, 1992. Lists all the books published by this high-quality publisher, and includes Penn Publishers.

Bruns, Henry P. *Angling Books of The Americas.* Atlanta: Privately printed, 1975. Over 18,000 annotated and cross-indexed entries with outdated price values. Available from many specialist dealers at $165.

Carter, John. *ABC for Book Collectors.* New York: Knopf. Seventh edition still available at $25. A valuable book to understand the bookman's language.

Coigney, Rudolphe L. *Izaak Walton: A New Bibliography 1653–1987.* New York: Cummins, 1989. The latest bibliography of all the editions. Covers in detail over 525 editions and their variations. Out of print but if your interest is Walton, worth the search for a copy.

Drury, Clyde E. *Books of the Black Bass, fourth edition.* Tacoma, WA: 1991. Privately printed. An exhaustive bibliography based on Drury's own collection and all other information he dug up.

Gingrich, Arnold. *The Fishing in Print.* New York: Winchester Press, 1974. Out of print but worth the hunt for a copy. It's not hard to find and usually sells for around $50.

Goodspeed, Charles E. *Angling in America.* Boston: Houghton Mifflin, 1939. Limited to 750 signed copies. Long out of print but copies do turn up in specialist's catalogs.

Heckscher, John Gerald. Merwin Clayton Auction House, New York, 1909. This is a listing from the auction house; Heckscher had one of the largest privately owned libraries to be auctioned at that time. It contained over 2,320 lots.

Oinonen Book Auctions. Sunderland, MA. Specializes in books and has held many angling auctions over the last 10 years (Darbee, Bates, Siegel, etc.).

Sage, Dean. Parke-Bernet Auction House, New York, 1942. This listing from the auction house is an excellent reference to American fishing books, as over 2,000 volumes collected by Sage were included in the auction.

Sherwin, Henry A. Parke-Bernet Auction House, New York, 1946. Sherwin's huge collection of over 5,000 volumes sold in two parts by this auction house.

Siegel, H. A. et al. *The Derrydale Press: A Bibliography.* Goshen, CT: Angler's and Shooter's, 1981. May still be available from the publisher.

Westwood, T. and Satchell, T. *Bibliotheca Piscatoria.* First published in England in 1883. Numerous reprints have added a supplement covering books published up to 1901. This is the best bibliography of older British fishing books. A reprint edition was published in New York in 1996.

Wetzel, Charles M. *American Fishing Books.* First published in 1950 and since reprinted. All reprints are out of print, but the most recent one, published by Meadow Run Press, still turns up.

Zack, Stanley S. *The Muskellunge: A Bibliography.* Rhinelander, WI: Fishing Hot Spots, 1986. Another based on the author's collection.

BOOT FOOT WADERS
See: Waders.

BOOTS, WADING
See: Waders.

BORON ROD
A rod that uses boron in conjunction with another material, usually graphite, in the construction of the blank. Though some rods may be labeled "boron" rods, they have a small percentage of boron fiber content, and the material of the rod is not solely boron. Boron fiber is stronger than graphite but also heavier.
See: Rod, Fishing.

BOTSWANA
Roughly the size of Kenya, this landlocked country in southern Africa has some of the last unspoiled wilderness in Africa, game reserves roamed by large herds of wild animals, spectacular wildlife and birdlife, and excellent angling for tigerfish in the world's largest inland delta.

The waterless Kalahari Desert, in the central and southwestern regions, constitutes two-thirds of Botswana. In the north lies one of Africa's prime fishing grounds and most pristine wildlife regions, the Okavango Delta, a vast marshland that covers 15,000 square kilometers of lush subtropical islands, waterways, and crystal-clear streams.

The headwaters of the delta begin more than 600 miles away in central Angola. Rainwater falling in this region flows slowly southward in the Okavango River, through varying geographical regions and into northwestern Botswana, until it finally reaches the Kalahari and transforms the desert into one of Africa's wildlife wonders. The

Okavango's waters spread out through a labyrinth of channels and shallow basins; almost all of the water evaporates in the delta, where there is extensive aquatic vegetation. The volume of water fluctuates with the wet and dry seasons, the greatest amount arriving from upriver in March.

In the best fishing areas, the Okavango is clear and bilharzia-free. More than 75 species have been documented, but sportfishermen focus on tigerfish and bream (tilapia), the latter valued for table fare as well.

To fully appreciate the Okavango, anglers should experience its three geographical areas: the perennial waters comprised of fast-flowing rivers and large lagoons, the seasonally flooded plains, and the islands and woodlands, which also possess the best game viewing. The perennial waters offer the most sought-after fishing spots, but anglers must be willing to travel to fish for the biggest tigers. The northern Okavango and the Chobe River boast the largest of the species, which reach up to 15 pounds; the larger bream can reach 8 pounds.

Accommodations in the Okavango are generally best in the small tented lodges. Botswana doesn't feature many of the large, impersonal Kenya-style hotels. The tented lodges, which typically serve a maximum of 16 guests, offer the atmosphere and excitement of a camping trip with the comforts of a hotel, with activities tailored to the guests. There is an assortment of these that cater to tigerfishing. Each has standard fishing gear and boats.

The best fishing is generally from September through May, when the waters are at their warmest. The peak months are October and November. This is also when the famous "barbel run" takes place, as thousands of small catfish swim up the main rivers to their breeding areas. Predator species are attracted to these small fish, and one can actually see and hear the waters boil and bubble when the barbel run passes by.

Most fishing is done from 18-foot aluminum boats, but the more adventurous can also try fishing from *mekoros* (dugout canoes). All lodges supply fishing tackle and standard rods, except fly fishing equipment. Dedicated anglers should plan to bring their own gear. Most anglers use lures, with very few people using live bait. Both tilapia and tigers take lures quite readily.

Although lightly populated, Botswana has been prospering, in large part due to diamond mining. Tourism is geared to attract the discerning visitor, and mass tourism is discouraged. The emphasis is on quality; service and the personal touch are more in evidence here than in most African countries.

BOTTOM
(1) A common term used by anglers to refer to the floor underneath a body of water, although not necessarily the deepest part of that body of water. A bass angler in a lake retrieves his or her jig slowly

over the "bottom," for example, in 15 feet of water, although the maximum depth of the lake is 65 feet. Describing fish as being "on the bottom" usually means that they are on, or quite close to, the lake, river, pond, or ocean floor.

Technically the bottom is the bed of a body of water, such as the lakebed, riverbed, or seabed; it is also known as the substrate *(see)*.

(2) That portion of a boat from the waterline to the lowest part of the hull.

BOTTOM BOUNCER

A bent wire-armed weighted bottom rig for trolling or drift fishing with bait or lures. The lower extension of a bottom bouncer features a wire arm with a cylindrical weight about midway along the arm; the extended wire minimizes hangups while the rig ticks along the bottom. The crook of the wire arm attaches to the fishing line, and the other wire extension features a snap swivel, to which a leader containing natural bait, a small floating/diving plug, or other lightweight lure, is attached. Worm spinner harnesses are especially popular with a bottom bouncer.

The rig is especially useful in rocky areas, which is why it is preferred for some walleye and smallmouth bass fishing efforts. Its jerky, stumbling motion can be helpful in imparting some realism to the action of the trailing bait or lure. It is important to set out just the right amount of line to reach bottom and keep the rig at a 45-degree angle. Fishing with a rig of the right weight (they vary from about $1/2$ ounce to 3 or 4 ounces) is essential, so you may have to change rigs until you get it right.

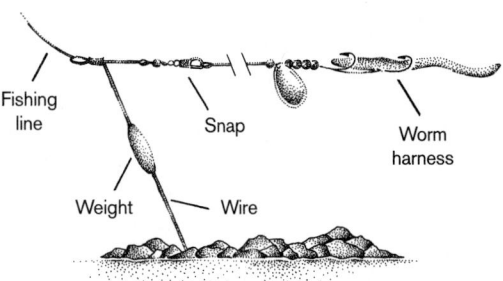

Depicted is a bottom bouncer rig, used to fish a nightcrawler on a spinner-worm harness along the bottom.

These rigs, in different weights, are homemade by some anglers, or purchased in tackle shops. Some similar bottom-walking rigs, incidentally, do not have the long wire arm, but are a keel-like weight at the end of a shorter wire arm. These are also used for some lighter current situations.

BOTTOM BOUNCING

The deliberate manipulation of bait or lures along the bottom of a body of water, aided by current or the movement of a boat. This practice is also called bottom bumping. Some form of weight is usually employed and must be heavy enough to keep in contact with the bottom, but not so heavy as to invite snagging or unnaturally slow the drift.

See: Back Bouncing.

BOTTOM FISHING

Fishing on the bottom of a body of water, usually with stationary baits presented on or just above the substrate, but also with baits that are drifted.

See: Chumming; Drift Fishing; Float; Inshore Fishing; Surf Fishing.

BOTTOM RIG

Any type of weighted terminal tackle configuration for fishing a bait, lure, or fly along the bed of a waterway. Most bottom fishing rigs are used with some type of live or dead natural bait *(see)* or a processed bait *(see);* they are especially used in freshwater for walleyes, catfish, and panfish in lakes and rivers, as well as coarse fish *(see),* and in saltwater for a variety of inshore and reef species.

See: Drift Fishing; Float; Inshore Fishing; Surf Fishing.

BOUNCE CAST

A cast made with spinning or baitcasting tackle in which a lure is made to bounce or skip over the surface to reach an object or area to be fished. This requires horizontal rod movement, usually with the rod or rod tip held low to the water; is mostly done with a soft lure like a plastic worm or grub; and is generally employed where there are overhanging objects (tree branches, dock, boathouse, and the like) that have to be avoided to reach a targeted area. A bounce cast is usually a short-distance cast and requires skill to avoid both hitting and hanging up on the overhead object, as well as creating a backlash or snarl on the reel.

See: Casting.

BOW

The forward part of a boat.

BOWFIN   *Amia calva.*

Other names—dogfish, freshwater dogfish, blackfish, mudfish, western mudfish, mud pike, cabbage pike, shoepike, griddle, grindle, spottail grindle, grinnel, lawyer, scaled ling, speckled cat, cypress trout, cypress bass, cottonfish John A. Grindle; French: *choupiquel, poisson de marais.*

Described as a living fossil, the bowfin is the only existing member of the Amiidae family, a group of fish that originated in the Cretaceous period more than 100 million years ago. Of little commercial value because of their poor-tasting

Bowfin

flesh, they are excellent fighters and are caught by anglers wherever they are abundant, although mostly unintentionally. When not abundant, they are a rare catch, and many anglers are unfamiliar with them. Although it is sometimes considered a pest or a nuisance by anglers seeking other quarry, the bowfin is helpful in constraining otherwise large, stunted populations of smaller fish.

Identification. An ancient fish in design, and described by some as looking more like a serpent than a fish, the bowfin has a rounded tail and a considerable amount of cartilage in its skeletal system. Underneath its head is a large, bony gular plate, with several other bony plates protecting the skull. Distinctive qualities include a large flattened head with tubelike nostrils and long, sharp teeth, as well as a long, spineless dorsal fin that extends almost the entire length of the body. Another interesting feature of the bowfin's anatomy is a modified, lunglike air bladder, in addition to gills; as in the gar, which possesses a similar organ, the bowfin is able to breathe surface air and, consequently, live in water too polluted or stagnant for most fish.

Its long, thick, cylindrical body is covered with large olive-colored scales, although it occasionally has a brownish or gray cast that fades to white or cream underneath. The male has a dark spot on the upper tail with a yellowish orange rim around it, and the female has a less-conspicuous spot without a rim.

Size/Age. The bowfin can grow to up to 43 inches in length but averages 2 feet. The world-record bowfin weighed 21 pounds, 8 ounces, although the average weight is in the 2- to 5-pound range. The male is smaller than the female, and they survive up to 12 years in the wild and 30 years in captivity.

Distribution. Bowfin occur only in North America, from the St. Lawrence River and Lake Champlain drainage of Quebec and Vermont west across southern Ontario to the Mississippi drainage, from Minnesota south to Texas and Florida.

Habitat. Bowfin are generally a big-water fish and inhabit warm and swampy lakes with vegetation, as well as weedy rivers and streams. With a significant tolerance for high temperatures and a modified air bladder, the bowfin is able to live in stagnant areas by taking in surface air.

Life history/Behavior. When bowfin are three to five years old, they reach sexual maturity. They spawn between early April and June, when water temperatures are between 60° and 66°F. Males move into the weedy shallows after dark, before the females, and build bowl-shaped nests of plant material among tree roots or under fallen logs. A single male may try to mate with more than one female, and sometimes several pairs of bowfin will use the same nest.

The male is left to protect the eggs, which hatch in 8 to 10 days. The newly hatched bowfin use an adhesive organ on their snouts to attach themselves to the bottom of the nest as they grow to about $^1/_2$ inch long. Once they reach this length, the fry school and follow the male, which guards them for several weeks against potential predators. Adult coloration appears when they are about $1^1/_2$ inches long, and the young begin to protect themselves at this stage. They stop schooling entirely when they reach 4 inches in length.

Bowfin swim slowly along the bottom, although they can move very quickly if disturbed or when in pursuit of prey.

Food and feeding habits. Bowfin can be extremely ravenous and eat a large variety of food, including crayfish, shrimp, adult insects and larvae, small fish, frogs, and large amounts of vegetation. Scent is as important as sight in obtaining food, and bowfin have the habit of gulping water to capture their prey. Although bowfin are always ready to feed, they are most active in the evening.

Angling. Although bowfin strike viciously and provide hardy action, they are generally considered a nuisance by anglers. They are seldom deliberately pursued, but a small minority of anglers will sight-fish for them in the shallows in the spring. At that time, they typically linger in very soft mud bottoms that can be impossible to wade. Bowfin are difficult to land and release, and anglers must be careful when unhooking them. They habitually snap their jaws and can do serious damage to fingers. Bass anglers are particularly likely to catch bowfin, especially when angling in shallow, murky backwaters, as these fish are susceptible to many bass lures. They are caught occasionally on surface lures, as well as on diving plugs, and assorted live or dead baits. Bowfin nibble bait rather than inhale it; thus they are harder to land on baits. They are also caught in southern locales on baited commercial trotlines.

BOWFISHING

Hunting for, and shooting, certain species of fish with archery equipment. Also called bow and arrow fishing, it is practiced by bowhunters who convert regular bows into fishing bows by attaching a reel directly in front of the grip. The reel is spooled with 70- to 100-pound line, tied to the head or the shaft of the arrow. The line spools off the reel after a shot, and the fish are pulled in by hand. Bowfishing arrowheads have large wire barbs that hold fish as they struggle to escape.

Some bowfishing enthusiasts wade into the water; others use shallow-running boats with raised platforms for shooting. Bowfishing boats also feature floodlights for finding fish at night, a time when many of the species sought are active.

The act of bowfishing is regulated by fisheries agencies; usually requires a fishing license; is subject to seasons; and is often practiced for rough or coarse species, primarily carp, gar, chub, buffalo fish, and suckers. Bowfishing is prohibited for designated gamefish species, and may or may not be permitted with a crossbow. It is popular with some archers and bowhunting enthusiasts but is not widely practiced. Where legal, it is considered a form of recreational fishing, but it is not treated as sportfishing by the general angling community. The topic is rarely addressed in sporting publications.

BOWING

Leaning forward, lowering a fishing rod to horizontal or near-horizontal position, and pointing the rod toward a tarpon to give it slack line when it jumps clear of the water. This is known as "bowing" or "bowing to the fish." It is mainly done so that the tarpon, which shakes its head violently when jumping, cannot use line tension to rip the hook from its mouth. The instant that the fish falls back to the water, the angler resumes high rod tension and a tight line.

BOWLINE KNOT

See: Knots, Boating.

BRACKISH WATER

Water that is somewhat salty, but its salinity is not as high as the sea; water that contains too much salt to be drinkable. Habitats characterized by a mixture of freshwater and saltwater—particularly marshes, estuaries, and wetlands—are said to be brackish, as is a certain portion of tidal rivers and streams.
See: Salinity.

BRAIDED LINE

See: Line.

BRAZIL

Occupying almost half of the South American continent, and the fifth largest country in the world, Brazil can boast of its overall stature among international and Brazilian anglers alike. With thousands of fish species in its freshwaters alone, and with incredible water resources in general, Brazil can rightly assert itself as one of sportfishing's superstars. Its reputation continues to grow despite its poorly developed infrastructure for angling tourism and both because and in spite of the fact that many of its top waters are remote and very difficult to access; it is subject to seasonal extremes in water levels; and its rivers and tributaries are incomprehensibly vast.

Of Brazil's waters, the Amazon River receives the most angling attention, and this is well deserved; the northerly Amazon basin encompasses more than a third of the country. Many parts of the tropical rain forest in this basin have been little explored, making any report on fishing opportunity a partial one at best. The Brazilian Highlands, which encompass most of the southeastern half of Brazil and are closer to its largest cities, are themselves comprised of extensive forested tracts and a network of lesser-known but commendable rivers and tributaries, especially the Plate and São Francisco systems.

Still less known, and hardly encountered by visiting anglers, is the saltwater opportunity along 4,650 miles of Atlantic Ocean coast.

Freshwater

With 3,286,488 square miles of terrain and seemingly countless rivers and tributaries, Brazil ostensibly has the largest hydrographic network in the world, which is a bit hard to describe in simple terms. Much is yet unknown about the full breadth of freshwater fishing opportunities, but much has happened since the late 1980s. As mentioned, interest in sportfishing has been growing rapidly within Brazil, and international visitors increase each year, although the majority head for the large peacock bass waters of Amazonia. To make an overview of Brazil's freshwater fishery comprehensible, one can look at the country's principal hydrographic basins, which are those of the Plate, the São Francisco, and the Amazon.

The Plate basin of southwestern Brazil is the second largest in the country and is predominantly made up of the Paraná and Paraguay Rivers, which flow into Paraguay, Argentina, and Uruguay. The main course of the Paraná has been impounded for hydroelectric purposes in several places, altering the composition and sizes of the native fish species.

The main rivers of this basin include the Paraibuna, Grande, Tietê, Paranapanema, Paraná, Paraguay, Iguaçu, Teles Pires, Cuiabá, Taquari, and Coxim. The lower reaches flood during the rainy season, from November through April. Major fish species include peacock bass, payara, pacu, curimbata, traíra, corvina, piapora, piraputanga (a relative of matrinxã), dorado, and some catfish.

The São Francisco basin of southern and eastern Brazil consists of the primary São Francisco, Preto, Jequitinhonha, das Velhas, and Grande Rivers. It is the only basin that originates and stays within the country. In the highland headwaters these rivers are clear, but the main São Francisco eventually becomes sediment laden. There are a number of hydroelectric impoundments here, and the species vary according to rivers and impoundments, with prominent fish including matrinxã, curimbata, piapora, payara, traíra, piranhas, peacock bass, catfish, and dorado.

The Amazon basin is so vast, and includes so much water, that the best way to detail it is to include with it the Orinoco watershed of Venezuela, and consider both with respect to their species and fishing possibilities.

Falls and swift water on the São Francisco offer opportunity for payara.

Amazon and Orinoco Watersheds

Two great South American rivers, the Amazon and Orinoco, and their watersheds are the arteries of life for much of the South American continent. The region that these rivers encompass extends from the Andes Mountains to the west, the Guiana Highlands to the north, the Brazilian Highlands to the south, and the Atlantic Ocean to the east. This vast and essentially roadless area is equivalent in size to the western two-thirds of the United States. Most of this is comprised of the Amazon basin, referred to as Amazonia, and the entire region is one of the few places on earth that offers a combination of plentiful prized gamefish, few people, fewer anglers, and ample opportunity to enjoy fishing in remote, pristine waters surrounded by abundant and exotic wildlife.

The Amazon River is the world's largest by virtue of its watershed area, number of tributaries, and volume. It is second only to the Nile in length, flowing about 3,900 miles from its headwaters in the high Andes in Peru to the Atlantic Ocean in northeastern Brazil, where it forms a delta maze that is more than 150 miles wide. Half of the Amazon's 2.3-million-square-mile drainage area is in Brazil, the remainder being in Peru, Ecuador, Bolivia, and Venezuela.

The Amazonia watershed encompasses the largest and wettest tropical plain in the world. It experiences periods of heavy seasonal rainfall, which affects the width, speed, and volume of the entire system. Nevertheless, the Amazon proper is navigable for ocean freighters to Manaus, a distance of 1,000 miles, and for smaller ships to Iquitos, Peru, a distance of 2,300 miles. Small steamers and houseboats can navigate at least 100 of the larger tributary rivers. A dozen tributaries of the Amazon are larger than both the Mississippi and the Missouri Rivers in North America.

The Orinoco River flows for 1,590 miles from its source in the Guiana Highlands in southeastern Venezuela, on the border of Brazil, to the Atlantic Ocean in northeastern Venezuela, where it forms an enormous delta. An arm of the Orinoco becomes the Casiquiare River, which heads south for 180 miles and merges with the Río Negro, a prominent tributary of the Amazon River. The main river is joined by numerous tributaries as it winds through Venezuela and along its border with Colombia. The Guaviare, Meta, Apure, Caura, and Caroni Rivers are among the major tributaries; the main river is navigable for oceangoing vessels for 260 miles to Ciudad Bolívar; the delta begins about 120 miles from the ocean.

The thousand-plus tributaries of the Amazon and Orinoco watersheds make up the most biologically diverse region on earth. Freshwater gamefish abound here, as do thousands of plant, insect, and animal species. Categorizing the fish species and angling opportunities, however, is complicated by the size of the rivers and the extent of land area, the relatively unexplored nature of some parts of this landmass, the nature of the waters, and the significance of the wet and dry seasons.

Most of the region's fishing waters are in Brazil, but many waterways extend into Venezuela, Colombia, Ecuador, Peru, Bolivia, and Guyana. Political boundaries tend to be obscured in such remote areas; the population density ranks among that of the world's least inhabited lands. Some native tribes still have little or no contact with civilization. Major population centers along the Amazon are Iquitos in Peru, and Manaus and Belem in Brazil. Only these three Amazon cities have direct flights from North America. Caracas is the preferred city for travelers to and from Venezuela.

Seasons and water levels. The equatorial rain forests of South America have only two seasons: wet and dry. These seasons occur at different times of the year in three general regions of the Amazon and Orinoco basins. The wet season corresponds with high water levels, and the dry season with low water levels. Periods of low water and low rainfall are the prime sportfishing seasons. With high water and

B

high rainfall, the rivers may rise as much as 40 feet, flooding all but the highest grounds in the rain forest and scattering fish over thousands of acres. Low water concentrates fish in rivers, lakes, and lagoons.

The rainy season in the southern third of this region generally starts in November in the Brazilian Highlands and the Andes, and the water levels rise and flow north to the main channel of the Amazon River. These rains usually end in April each year. Southern-tributary water levels rise greatly during this period, receding in April or May and continuing until the rains fall in November. The lowest water level and best fishing in this region is normally from June through October.

The rainy season in the northern third of this region, in the northern Andes and Guiana Highlands, generally begins sometime in April or May, with corresponding high water levels from May through October. By November, water levels are low enough to permit good fishing, with ideal conditions usually present, from Venezuela's state of Amazonas to the Río Negro and Río Branco region of Brazil, from December through March. The rainy season begins again around April.

The central third of this region is essentially the flood plain of the Amazon River. This huge area is impacted by rain and subsequent flooding from an enormous number of northern and southern tributaries. The only respite from this constant torrent of water usually occurs around August and lasts until late November. During this period, anglers will find low water levels and good sportfishing in waters just north and south of the Amazon River. The natural lakes here (mostly lagoons or oxbows) adjacent to the Amazon are extremely large, compared to other Amazon basin lakes. Some are more than 40 miles long and up to 10 or 12 miles wide. Constant flood waters along the main Amazon channel have resulted in lakes at the mouth of the Xingu and Tapajos Rivers that are nearly 100 miles long and more than 5 miles wide.

Sportfishing in this region usually takes place in the smaller tributaries of the major rivers, and in lakes and lagoons adjacent to these tributaries during the low water period. The larger rivers and lakes are fished by commercial fishermen for a variety of species. Anglers may fish the larger lakes, but most are inhabited by local villagers who may practice both subsistence and commercial fishing with gillnets and other devices.

Access.   This is a very big region overall and access has been largely limited to using the rivers as highways. When rapids and falls are encountered, anglers portage around the obstacle if the boat can't navigate the hazard. Big boats can only go so far, which is partly why the native dugout canoe is still the vehicle of choice among natives. A shallow-draft aluminum fishing boat works well for the rest of us, but most anglers are in more of a hurry than the native with a dugout and a paddle. The Amazon native doesn't mind sleeping under the stars along the way. Nor does he mind a journey of a few days or weeks.

Small charter planes have improved accessibility to the interior of these watersheds. Flights can be expensive, however, and landing strips are few and far apart. The region does have a few floatplanes, but almost all are too small to carry more than two to three anglers with gear.

All of this, plus other factors, has limited sportfishing access to this region somewhat, but a great variety of facilities are nevertheless still available to the Amazon angler, including fixed lodge facilities, houseboat based operations, outpost camps, tent camps, floatels, and progressive float-trip operations with mobile tent camps. Sometimes it is necessary to give up creature comforts to access the most productive, remote fishing spots. Sometimes you can have comfort *and* great Amazon fishing. The possibility of being the first outsider to cast a lure to fish in a remote Amazon stream still exists.

Many parts of the Amazon have been set aside as national parks or reserve areas, or restricted to nonfishing and nonhunting refuges. Native Indian lands are often off-limits to all but the natives and a few government agencies. Many villages have established nearby waters as private fishing areas for personal use.

Commercial fishing in a large part of Amazonia is very common, and since this tends to center around populated areas and local communities, it usually diminishes fish populations nearby and often requires some travel from established areas by anglers to reach areas that are productive. Some remote areas are indeed accessible to those willing to make the effort.

Water types and colors.   Understanding the complex nature of this region and tapping its great sportfishing potential require a knowledge of when and where to fish a number of distinct geographic zones for a variety of species. A knowledge of various water types and what each may provide in the way of species variety, numbers, and size is extremely important to the guide or outfitter in this part of the world, and helpful to the visitor. Waters and their sportfishing attributes can be classified according to their color and flow characteristics. There are white-, brown-, black-, and blue-water rivers in the region. All but whitewater occur throughout the Amazon and Orinoco watersheds, but each is predominant in one particular region.

Whitewater rivers.   These are clear, swift-flowing waters in the higher elevations of the Brazilian Highlands, Guiana Highlands, and Andes Mountains. They are devoid of the warmwater gamefish that are especially prized and highly sought in the Amazon and Orinoco watersheds. Whitewater rivers are insignificant as a fishery for coldwater sportfish when compared with the great trout waters found in the more temperate climates of Patagonia and Tierra del Fuego. In the Andes region of the Amazon basin, these waters carry heavy sediment and nutrient loads into the basin, forming brown-water rivers.

Brown-water rivers. These coffee- and cream-colored waters of the upper Amazon basin are rich in sediments and nutrients washed from the high Andes. As these waters settle into the flood-plain basin of the upper Amazon, their flow is greatly slowed by a nearly flat topography with a level just above that of the Atlantic Ocean. Surprisingly, these are not great fishing waters for giant specimens of the most prized gamefish of the Amazon, like peacock bass and payara. Payara grow to giant proportions in other areas, but not in these slow, off-colored waters. Peacock bass are found primarily in black-water lakes and oxbow lagoons located adjacent to the rivers, or in the black-water creeks or channels that often connect the lakes and rivers.

Peacock bass do not grow to giant proportions in this upper watershed region, even though it is rich and fertile. They are found in abundance, however, and generally range in size from 3 to 6 pounds, with a maximum weight of about 13 pounds. Most anglers catch peacocks of 10 pounds or less, and smaller butterfly peacock bass predominate.

The major brown-water tributaries are the Napo in Ecuador and Peru, the Maranon and Ucayali in Peru, the Putumayo in Peru and Colombia, the Japura in Brazil (called the Caquetá in its upper reaches in Colombia), the Yavari in Peru (known as the Javari in Brazil), and the Jaruá and Purus in Brazil. The Madre de Dios, Beni, and Mamore rivers in Bolivia are also major brown waters, and they form the giant Madeira in its upper reaches in Brazil. The Madeira is the largest brown-water tributary of the Amazon. The Amazon itself, called the Solimões above the city of Manaus, is the largest brown-water river. The Mamore is called the Guapore in Brazil, and it is a blue-water river in its headwaters.

Blue-water rivers. The rivers of the southeast region of Amazonas flow down from the Brazilian Highlands into steep and beautiful lush green valleys in their upper reaches, creating topaz-colored rivers. These are lovely watersheds that abound with rapids, waterfalls, narrow gorges, boulder-strewn river bottoms, and beautiful white-sand beaches. The Brazilian Highlands are extremely old formations and carry a low sediment and nutrient load into these crystal-clear rivers as they snake their way through the verdant carpet of the rain forest.

A great variety of gamefish exists here, more so than in any other region of the Amazonas. It is common to catch nearly a dozen different species during a week's stay on one of these waters. In the swift, upper stretches of blue-water rivers, payara grow to 20 pounds or more, and in the lower parts of these basins, peacock bass can often grow to 15 pounds, although fish of less than 10 pounds are far more common. Black-water lagoons often occur here, along with larger lakes, but neither are as common here as in regions that exhibit flatter flood

Peacock bass are Brazil's major gamefish attraction; this colorful specimen was caught on the southerly Cururu River.

plains. Consequently, anglers are forced to spend more time fishing in the river channels and creeks, which results in catches of a greater variety of species. Anglers in these waters who concentrate on lakes and lagoons only for peacock bass will frequently catch just a few other species. If they make an effort to also fish the rivers using a variety of lures and lure sizes, they can catch a great many species.

The major blue-water tributaries are the Tapajos, Xingu, and Araguaia-Tocantins. A large hydroelectric dam and reservoir, the Tucurui, now exists on the lower Araguaia-Tocantins. This lake is more than 100 miles long and more than 12 miles wide. Terms like "large reservoir," "big lake," and "major tributary" are inadequate to describe an area in which everything seems to be monumentally huge, and where such "tributaries" are larger than the biggest rivers in North America.

Black-water rivers. For the most part, these rivers originate in the Guiana Highlands on the Venezuelan-Brazilian border, in the northernmost reaches of Amazonia. Several brown- and blue-water rivers are also found here, but black water is predominant. The Vaupes and Guiana Rivers originate in the Andes of southern Colombia, and both flow into the upper Rio Negro near the Colombian borders with Venezuela and Brazil. The lower part of Venezuela's mighty Orinoco is coffee and cream brown; it becomes stained by other rivers from the Colombian Andes, which flow through that country's Llanos region (comprised of plains or grasslands).

The most important fishing waters in this region are all black-water tributaries, and this area produces the very largest of the peacock bass and payara in Colombia, Brazil, and Venezuela. Natives call these rivers "starvation rivers" due to the absence of nutrients and biomass in the black waters. They are so acidic that mosquito larvae cannot survive and propagate. Population density is

A houseboat carrying anglers lies at rest on the Trombetas River, near its confluence with the Rio Negro.

very low on these rivers, which are all in remote areas with no roads, with poor soil for farming or grazing, and with little commercial fishing efforts or prospects. Why peacock bass grow to more than 25 pounds and payara to more than 35 pounds in these places remains a mystery. The color of the water is also a puzzle, but most believe that tannic acids leach out of the rain forest and into the flood waters during the six months each year when the forest is inundated by river waters.

The significant black-water rivers of this region all merge with the Orinoco or the Amazon. They include the Paru, Jari, Trombetas, Uatuma, Jatapu, Río Negro, and Río Branco in Brazil; Vaupes, Guaviare, Meta, and Vichada in Colombia; and the Cinaruco, Capanaparo, Ventuari, Casiquiare, Apure, Caura, Paragua, and Caroni in Venezuela.

The Casiquiare is a unique river because it diverts part of the upper Orinoco into the Guainia River on the Colombian border, forming the upper Río Negro, which flows south into the Amazon at Manaus, thus connecting the Orinoco with the Amazon.

The Caroni and Paragua Rivers are at the head-waters of Guri Reservoir and Dam in Venezuela. Guri is another 100-mile-long reservoir. The upper headwaters of the Caroni cascade from atop the mesa-like mountain Ayán Tupui, also known as the mile-high waterfall, Angel Falls. The tailwaters below Guri Dam, and three other dams on the Caroni, flow into the Orinoco at the city of Puerto Ordaz. Guri Lake, the Caroni River, and the Paragua River are important fishing waters for pea-cock bass and payara.

The Uatuma in Brazil was also dammed, creat-ing Balbina Reservoir, but Balbina received heavy commercial fishing pressure from the time it was completed. Sportfishing in Balbina has been disappointing.

Gamefish species.   The total number of fish species throughout the Amazon and Orinoco

Basins is still unknown, but it numbers many hundreds, including aquarium species and some of the largest and most fearsome specimens in freshwater. Of these, relatively few fish species are the targets of anglers, and only a few others are caught incidentally.

The Amazon is generally thought to have an extreme abundance of fish, and although that may be true to some extent—especially in some waters—it is also a fact that much has changed since the 1960s, when there was almost no sport-fishing by anyone and when local fishing was largely subsistence netting and spearing.

The growth of some cities and other population centers, the accompanying pollution, and a greater diversification in commercial fishing activities have led to diminished fisheries in accessible areas, as well as a reduction in the size of some of the larger species of fish. Recreational fishing by residents is growing rapidly in some South American countries, especially Brazil, but it is not a major factor in over-all pressure on resources, except perhaps in a few isolated locations. Subsistence fishing in remote areas, and commercial fishing (especially gillnet-ting), are prominent activities.

Nevertheless, the Amazon and Orinoco water-sheds region is one of the last great frontiers of sportfishing, boasting lots of fish and relatively few anglers. Peacock bass remain the single most highly pursued freshwater species, although many other fish have been only lightly—if at all—targeted by serious anglers. The size and remoteness of the watersheds have ensured a slow growth in sustained fishing tourism. There is virtually no tourism infra-structure in these countries, however, and that is unlikely to change in the near future, given the challenges posed by seasonal water levels, equip-ment, personnel, logistics, and myriad other mat-ters. Thus, sportfishing development has largely been at the hands of individual entrepreneurs.

There are few lodges or camps relative to the size of this region, and most operators use houseboat-like river vessels (some fairly primitive) for accom-modations and as a means of reaching distant waters, towing aluminum skiffs for fishing with them. Since the mid- to late 1980s, there has been a sharp growth in peacock bass fishing excursions—especially based out of Manaus, Brazil, and in the less risky areas of Venezuela such as at Guri Reservoir and its tributaries; only a small number of outfitters are conducting sportfishing operations, yet the places they visit are largely unexplored by nonfishing tourists. Virtually all fishing opportuni-ties throughout these watersheds are managed by one of these operators, fishing in boats they provide and with local guides who are usually more naviga-tor than guide. Self-guided fishing is impractical and a rarity, due in part to language barriers and in part to the lack of facilities and equipment.

Most Amazon fish can bite, slash, or sting, so it's best to let the guide handle and release fish, and to be very careful (use a gripping tool) if you do this yourself. Guides won't use nets for some species, such as payara, trairão, and piranha because they chomp through the net bottom. In this region, for most species, traveling anglers will need stronger rods, reels, lines, baits, hooks, split rings, knots, and other terminal tackle than they are likely accustomed to at home, as well as a strong heart for the topwater strikes of certain species. Surface strikes by peacock bass in particular are explosive.

Peacock bass.   This fish is not a bass at all, but a cichlid. In Spanish it's called *pavón,* and in Portuguese (the language of Brazil) it is *tucunaré.* North Americans saw the similarity between this fish and the largemouth black bass and observed that it was readily taken on the same lures and stackle and by utilizing similar methods. Someone dubbed it a "peacock bass" due to the round spot on its tail. This nickname was a fortunate stroke of public relations genius; as word spread north, anglers flocked to South America in search of this new kind of "bass."

The peacock really did not need to be hyped because it has made and deserved its own great reputation. This one species has put the Amazon on the world's fishing map, and established itself on the most wanted list of many anglers. The peacock bass is bigger, stronger, harder fighting, jumps more and higher, and is generally much meaner than a largemouth bass or most anything else that swims in freshwater. It also hits surface lures like no other fish, and destroys lures, line, equipment, and the thumbs of anyone foolish enough to lip-lock it.

Although peacocks exist in a few places outside this region, all of the big specimens—and all of the world records—have been caught in lakes and rivers in Brazil, Venezuela, and Colombia.

Payara.   This is the Spanish name for this so-called saber-toothed, silver salmon, which is also known as *cachorra* in Brazilian Portuguese. There is no English name for this toothy fish, and there is certainly nothing like it in North America. The payara is extremely strong and acrobatic, and found in rivers and reservoirs, especially in Brazil and Venezuela. In rivers, payara often frequent the swiftest water and hold near the largest boulders. In reservoirs they are a less predictable catch, sometimes caught by deep jigging. A specimen of more than 20 pounds will make several long runs and spectacular jumps. Its long canine teeth are very sharp and frequently puncture plastic and wooden lures. A strong steel leader and snap swivel, the stronger the better, are necessary for fishing. Large, tough, diving minnow plugs, lipless crankbaits, heavy spoons, and heavy-duty jigs are the lures of choice. Heavy-action rods, with baitcasting reels capable of holding 100 yards of 30-pound-test line, are commonly used. The current world record is 39 pounds.

Traíra/trairão.   Known as *traíra* (trairão is a larger specimen) in Brazil, this species is called

imara in Venezuela and *guabina* in Colombia. It resides in lakes and rivers, especially in shallow cover and in low-oxygen environs. It looks like a bowfin (mudfish). In the Amazon it grows to more than 40 pounds and strikes artificial lures, including topwater plugs. A trairão of 25 or 30 pounds may fight for more than 15 minutes before coming to the boat, after you've towed it around for awhile. This fish has a nasty set of teeth and is mean and ugly. The same tackle that is used for peacock bass and payara is useful for this fish.

Bicuda.   This fish has a hard birdlike beak and a pikelike body. It hits a variety of baits, including topwater tackle. The bicuda runs like a barracuda and makes spectacular jumps. It may stay airborne for most of the battle. Bicuda seldom exceed 12 to 13 pounds, but such a fish will test heavy tackle. Pound for pound, it compares very favorably with a northern pike. Bicuda are always found in rivers.

Matrinxã.   This species looks and fights like a hefty American shad and can grow to 11 to 12 pounds. A close cousin, the *jatuarana,* may weigh as much as 17 pounds and is usually caught in the Pantanal region, just south of the Amazon range of the matrinxã. Most matrinxã in the Amazonas run from 3 to 6 pounds. Small spoons, in-line spinners, and jigs are very productive, with lighter spinning tackle, 6- to 10-pound line, and steel leaders recommended. This fish is very acrobatic, and its silver-scaled sides flash through the water when it runs and in the sunlight when it jumps, which it does often. A matrinxã smoked on an open fire is as tasty as any salmon. It is a resident of clear-water rivers.

Piranhas.   These notorious, toothy critters are found throughout the Amazon and Orinoco watersheds; specimens of 3 to 8 pounds are great sport. Piranhas, like almost all sportfish of this region, are great table fare, and close cousins of pacu and tambaqui, which can grow to more than 30 pounds. That's big enough and strong enough to make you think about cutting your line after a 10-minute battle and no sign of surrender (from the fish). The biting strength of all three can crush nuts, shells, and bones. Small spoons, jigs, and lipless crankbaits are effective for these species, with a steel leader advisable. There are dozens of species of piranhas (the morocotto variety of the Orinoco is a close relative of the tambaqui), and some are vegetarians. These are all river species, but they can adapt to lakes. Piranhas are commonly found in rivers, lakes, and lagoons in most watersheds.

Arawana.   Called *aruanã* in Portuguese and *arahuana* in Spanish, and also known as the "monkey fish," this acrobatic performer with a snakelike body can leap many feet into the air to get food. The arawana grows to 11 pounds or more and leaps repeatedly when hooked, or thrashes its body on the surface. This fish also takes a variety of lures, including topwater plugs. It is most often caught in lakes and lagoons or in backwater areas of rivers.

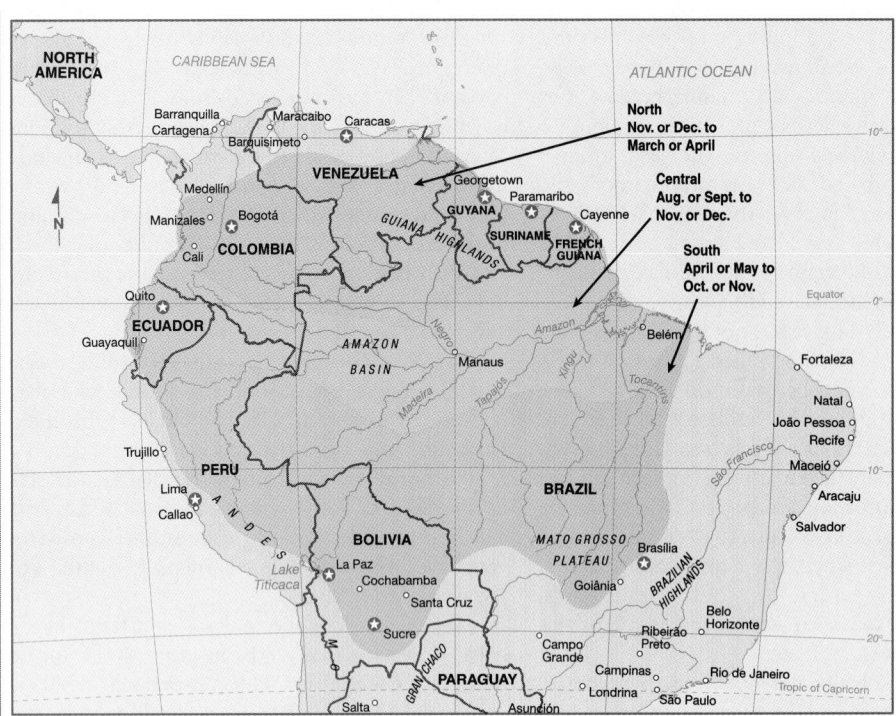

Amazonas—Region by Fishing Season (Dry Season)

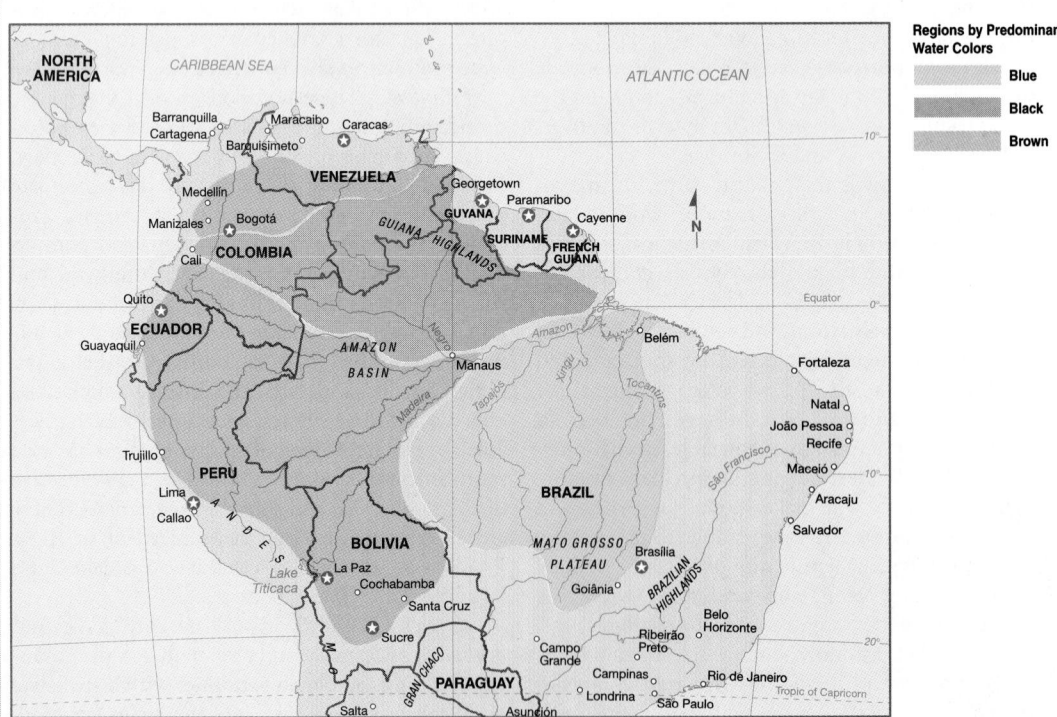

Sportfishing Regions of South America's Amazonas

B

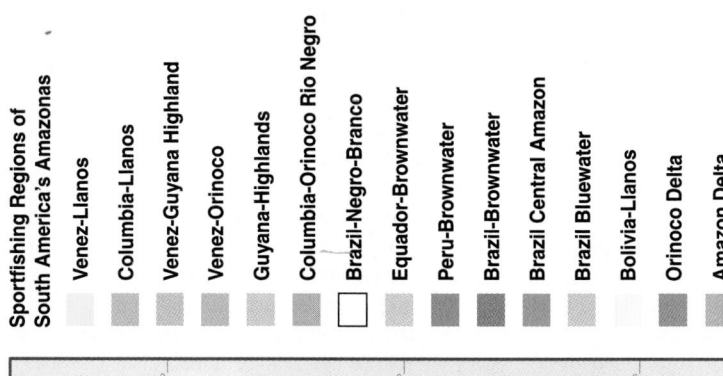

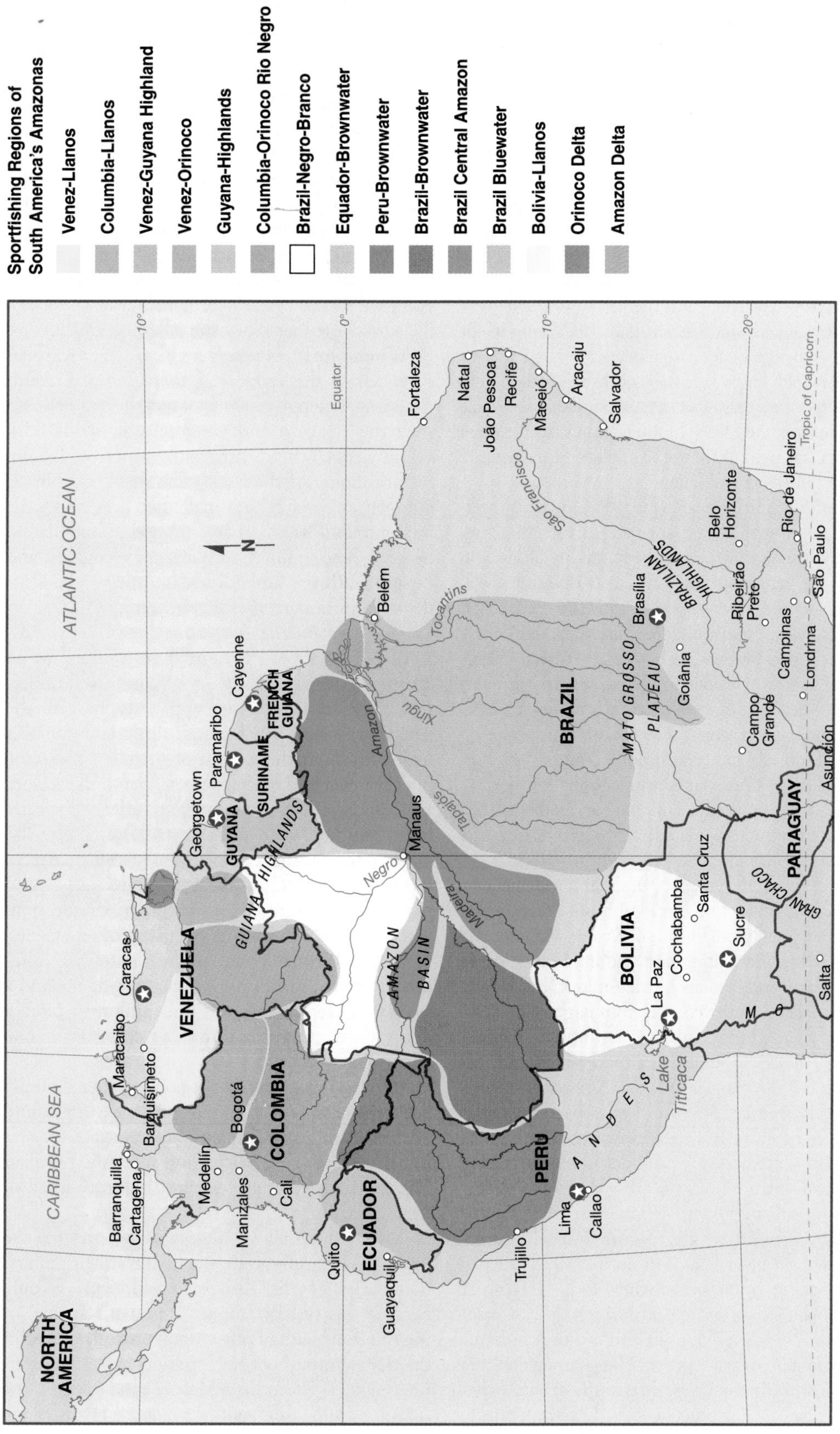

Sportfishing Regions of South America's Amazonas

- Venez-Llanos
- Columbia-Llanos
- Venez-Guyana Highland
- Venez-Orinoco
- Guyana-Highlands
- Columbia-Orinoco Rio Negro
- Brazil-Negro-Branco
- Equador-Brownwater
- Peru-Brownwater
- Brazil-Brownwater
- Brazil Central Amazon
- Brazil Bluewater
- Bolivia-Llanos
- Orinoco Delta
- Amazon Delta

Regions by Predominant River Water Colors

B

B

Sardinata.   Found in the Orinoco watershed of Venezuela and Colombia, this "leaping maniac of the Orinoco" looks like a small tarpon, grows to 15 pounds, and frequently fights more out of the water than in it when hooked. Small surface plugs, spoons, and lipless crankbaits are effective. The sardinata is frequently caught in lakes, lagoons, and river backwaters.

Pirarucu.   This giant-scaled fish can grow to several hundred pounds and is occasionally hooked by an Amazon angler, resulting in Moby Dick–like tales. Natives shoot them with bow and spear, with a strong rope attached, and the fish tows the native's dugout canoe around for hours before giving in, or tries to sink the boat. A machete is at the ready to cut the rope. These fish frequently tail-walk across the surface in rivers, and the sight of this spectacle is awesome to behold. The huge scales from a large pirarucu are used as files or sandpaper. Pirarucu are at home in rivers and lakes.

Catfish.   Sorubim and pintado are two shovel-nosed, tiger-striped, or spotted catfish that frequently strike spoons, crankbaits, diving plugs, and jigs. Both get very large (40- to 80-pound specimens are not uncommon), and they are great fighters. Most Amazon catfish are great table fare, and these two battlers are very tasty as well. Many visiting anglers consider these two species gamefish because they are often enticed into taking artificial baits and give a great account of themselves in battle. Both are more commonly caught in rivers but frequently cruise lakes and lagoons for food.

Jau, dourada, pirarara, piraiba, and other catfish may be encountered by anglers. Some catfish species in the Amazon, such as bagre, valenton, and dourada, grow to several hundred pounds and can be seen hanging like sides of beef in local fish markets. These catfish are usually caught by stillfishing with bait and heavy tackle. Big catfish are seldom found in the smaller lakes and lagoons of the Amazon but are frequently taken from rivers and from larger lakes, such as those adjacent to the main Amazon River channel.

Other species.   Some other species are frequently encountered by anglers in the Amazonas region. One of these is apapa, a freshwater herringlike fish that is comparable in size, appearance, and fighting ability to white bass; a 6-pounder is very large. The pescada-do-piauí, or corvina, is a drum or croaker-like fish that can grow to 17 pounds; when schools of these are found, it's great fishing fun. The curimbatá is a silver-scaled, bottom feeder frequently caught on jigs and spoons, which fights very much like a white bass or hybrid striper; it can reach weights of nearly 17 pounds and is a double handful of trouble in swift waters. The jacunda could be compared to the rock bass of streams in the United States. The smaller peacock bass, like the butterfly and royal varieties, could be compared to smallmouth bass. Almost without exception, these South American counterparts of prized North American gamefish are bigger, stronger, and meaner.

Most all of the species found in the Amazon and Orinoco watersheds are also found in the swamplike Pantanal region and River Plate region, both located just south of the Amazon Basin in Brazil. It has been reported that the infamous golden dorado has also been taken in the Amazon Basin, but this is not substantiated and it would be a rare catch.

A great many more species, some very colorful and unusual looking, are taken occasionally on rod and reel, and certainly by locals using nets. The numbers, varieties, sizes, beauty, and fighting abilities of these species—combined with the natural, unspoiled beauty of their environs—certainly make this one of the world's premier sportfishing destinations.

When and where to fish.   A seasonal approach is the right way to plan for a South American fishing adventure, and the best way to view the Amazon and Orinoco watersheds is to acknowledge their various distinctive fishing regions. Some of these are established by political boundaries, some by seasonal differences, and some by limitations to access due to physical boundaries. Most of these regions have a few knowledgeable and capable outfitters and guides. In others there is little or no infrastructure for sportfishing.

Southeast Brazil's blue-water region.   By mid-April the rivers of this area have dropped to an acceptable level, and the dry season is well underway. Beginning in the upper reaches of the Araguaia, Xingu, or Tapajos, you could fish this region through the month of October, prospecting the lower end of these rivers later in the season. You can expect to catch a great variety of species here, but not huge peacock bass or trophy-size payara. Ten-pound peacocks are a realistic expectation, however, and there are some 20-pound payara with a rare larger specimen. In addition, you will surely catch a good many other species, including bicuda, pacu, matrinxã, trairão, piranhas, corvina, sorubim, pintado, curimbatá, and a variety of catfish. It is not uncommon to catch a dozen different species during a week's stay on one of the rivers here.

Local gateways to this region are Alta Floresta, São Felix do Araguaia, São Felix do Xingu, and Tucurui. International gateways are Belem and Brasilia. These rivers, all flowing out of the Brazilian Highlands, are among the most beautiful in all of Amazonia.

Many Amazonia references do not include the Araguaia-Tocantins watershed within their defined boundaries of the Amazon basin. This is only because this system empties into a subchannel of the Amazon south of huge Marajo Island, located in the deltaic mouth of the Amazon. The flow from the Araguaia-Tocantins passes Belem as it enters the Atlantic from this southern route. Hydrologists consider the Amazon channel to be the channel that is routed north of Marajo Island, entering the Atlantic Ocean at that point. If the southernmost channel were included in the full length of the

Amazon, then it would be not only the world's largest river by volume, but also the longest. Actually, the Araguaia is in every way a true Amazonas river, with a typical Amazon rain forest watershed.

The lower Araguaia-Tocantins has been dammed to provide hydroelectric power, forming huge Tucurui Lake. Like Guri Lake in Venezuela, it is an important fishery for peacock bass and even for payara in its upper reaches. Unlike Guri, there is a large, well-organized commercial fishing operation here on a year-round basis, which has severely impacted sportfishing results.

Due to the large number of rapids and waterfalls on the Tapajos and Xingu, and many of their tributaries, this remote and sparsely populated region remains cut off and isolated. There are also a number of Indian reserves here, with little or no access to these reserved lands and waters. There are a few outfitters in the region, however, and they have hosted a number of international anglers.

Brazil's central Amazon basin. The dishpan-like central Amazon flood plain has its gateway in Manaus at a crossroads where the largest tributaries of the Amazon come together. The Río Negro flows southward past Manaus, where it joins the muddy Solimões rolling down from the Andes of Peru. At this point, the mighty river is called the Amazon, and several miles east of Manaus that great brown-water river of southern Amazonia—the Madeira—joins the Amazon.

This central Amazon basin is impacted by seasonal runoff from huge tributaries on almost a continual basis, so the fishing season in this region is short. Water levels in the tributaries and lakes in this area are low enough to provide excellent fishing from about mid-August to mid- or late November. Although many of the larger rivers hold brown water, black-water tributaries like the Uatuma, Jatapu, Trombetas, Nhumanda, Marmelos, Tupana-Maderinha, Jari, and Paru provide excellent fishing for peacock bass, along with most other Amazon species.

Blue-water rivers also run here, and black-water tributaries of the Manicore, Aripuanã, Abacaxis, and Maués provide excellent fishing in season. Peacock bass can reach 20 pounds but are most frequently encountered in the teens. Good-size payara can be had in the upper reaches of those black-water rivers coming out of the Guiana Highlands from August through November, and from the lower Xingu and Tapajos Rivers during the fall fishing season. More and larger payara, however, come from areas north and south of this central flood plain. Arawana, piranhas, and many species of catfish are frequently caught in this region.

Manaus hosts a number of houseboat-based fishing operations that are highly mobile and may travel north, south, east, and west to reach good fishing waters in season in the Central Amazon basin. However, they can and do extend their season by moving up the Río Negro to the north, accessing those tributaries from November through April in the Río Negro's black waters near the equator.

Brazil's black-water region. From November through April, this area of northwest Brazil provides some of the greatest peacock bass fishing the Amazonas has to offer in tributaries of the Río Negro and Río Branco. The Vaupes, from Colombia, also enters the Río Negro here in Brazil, as does the Branco. The largest black-water river on earth, the Río Negro flows south to the Amazon. The Branco is actually tinged brown for most of the year, but like the Orinoco to the north in Venezuela, most of its tributaries are black-water rivers.

The current 27-pound world-record peacock bass was caught in a tributary of the Río Negro, and tributaries of the Branco have yielded a 26-pounder and numerous fish over 20 pounds in the late 1990s. The Vaupes in Colombia has a reputation for giant peacocks, too, as does the upper Río Negro and the Casiquiare. There is no question that this region is home to giant peacock bass.

This sparsely populated region is beautiful, remote, and contains more than a dozen species of the most sought after gamefish species. Payara grow large here, but sportfishing operations have concentrated on the big peacock while largely ignoring the swifter, boulder-strewn rapids of the region's rivers, where huge payara lurk. Local gateways here are Barcelos and Boa Vista, and international access is through Manaus. Boa Vista may also be reached through Caracas.

Venezuela's black-water region. The tributaries of the mighty Orinoco in Venezuela are predominantly black-water rivers. These are the Ventuari, Sipapo, Atabapo, Conorochito, Pasimoni, Pasiba, and the Casiquiare and its tributaries, all in the Venezuelan state of Amazonas. World-record-class peacock bass, payara, and many other species are routinely taken from these waters. The Pasimoni produced the largest peacock caught on a fly rod, a fish of $25^1/_2$ pounds. A 31-pound payara caught in the Orinoco near Puerto Ayacucho was the all-tackle world record for many years, and the Orinoco in that area continues to produce world-class payara.

The season here is from November through April, and these black waters are almost a mirror image of those in the Brazilian black-water region. They are located just south of the Guiana Highland mountain range, which separates the two countries, leaving similar terrain on either side of the range. The renowned and primitive Yanomami Indians consider the lands on both sides of the mountains and borders their homeland, and tribal families are located in both Venezuela and Brazil.

The Brazilian and Venezuelan black-water regions are connected by the Casiquiare, which runs from the Orinoco into the Guainia to form the

 A layer of natural barnacle cement $^3/_{10,000}$ inch thick over 1 square inch will support a weight of 7,000 pounds.

B

headwaters of the Río Negro, which in turn flows into the Amazon at Manaus, connecting two giant watersheds. Puerto Ayacucho is the local gateway, and Caracas the international gateway. These waters are home to sardinata, morocotto, imara, piranhas, and numerous giant catfish, in addition to peacock bass and payara.

Colombia's black-water region. Here the Orinoco is fed by the Tomo, Vichada, Mataveni, Guaviare, Inirida, and Guainia Rivers on the Venezuela border (which is the Orinoco River) and the Vaupes eventually feeds the Río Negro in Brazil. These are the black-water rivers of Colombia, and they are full of trophy-size peacocks and payara and all of the other species common to the neighboring Venezuela-Orinoco tributaries.

This area in Colombia and Venezuela contains all the speckled, spotted, butterfly, and royal varieties of peacock bass in its rivers. The Mataveni produced a previous 26-pound world-record speckled peacock, and Colombia's side of the Orinoco produced the previous 31-pound record payara. This region, unfortunately, has had no sportfishing operations for international anglers for some time because of safety concerns due to illegal drug production and trafficking, and frequent kidnappings. This is truly a blow, because the remote, productive, lightly populated, and beautiful rivers, lakes, and lagoons here provide great fishing from November through April. Gateways are Puerto Correño locally, and Bogota for international access.

Venezuela and Colombia's llanos regions. Brown-water rivers flow toward the Orinoco basin from the Andes of northern Colombia and through the llanos of central Colombia and Venezuela. In Venezuela these rivers are the Apure, Arauca, Capanaparo, and Cinaruco. In Colombia they are the Meta and Bita. The smaller tributaries, lakes, and lagoons contain black water during the dry or fishing season (November to April), but for most of the year these rivers color the lower Orinoco a very brown hue. This llanos area has never produced the giant peacocks and payaras found just south in the black-water Amazonas, but great numbers of teen-size and smaller fish have been consistently found in rivers like the Cinaruco and Bita.

Unfortunately, drug trafficking, kidnapping, and plane hijackings have taken their toll on this area, and sportfishing camps in Colombia have all closed. In Venezuela, they remain open with caution and extreme safety measures in force. Many roads, ranches, and private river camps are now located in this area. The fishing remains very good, but a very real threat to the safety of tourists in the area exists. Local gateways are Puerto Carreño in Colombia, and Puerto Ayacucho and San Fernando de Apure in Venezuela. International gateways are Bogota and Caracas.

Venezuela's Guiana Highlands. Angel Falls cascades from the mile-high top of Ayán Tupuy Mountain in east-central Venezuela, and the stream

below cuts through the Guiana Highlands and Gran Sabana region of Venezuela to the Caroni River. The Caroni flows north toward the Orinoco River and is joined in this highland valley by the Paragua River. These are the headwaters of Guri Lake, a huge impoundment dammed for hydroelectric power production at Guri Dam and by three more dams near the boom towns of Puerto Ordaz and Ciudad Bolívar.

Huge Guri Lake has been an important sportfishing destination since the mid-1980s for peacock bass and payara. While 15- to 20-pound peacocks are still caught, and payara of 20 pounds are caught on occasion in the lake, the world-record-class payara in the Paragua River are now the main attraction in this area. The 39-pound all-tackle world-record payara, and most of the line-class records, were set on the Paragua and its falls in the upper river, above the lake. There are still a number of camps on the upper end of the lake near the two rivers. The season is from November through April. Access is via Caracas to Puerto Ordaz, or Ciudad Bolívar.

Brown-water regions (Peru, Brazil, Ecuador, and Colombia). By late May or early June, the rainy season has ended in the upper Amazon rivers flowing out of the Andes in Ecuador and Peru. These nutrient-rich and chocolate brown rivers include the Napo and Pastaza in Ecuador and Peru, the Maranon and Ucayali in Peru, the Putamayo and Caquetá in Colombia, the Yavari and Jupurá in Brazil, and several more that join to form the Solimões in Brazil. The Juruá, Purus, and Madeira also add to this great brown massive river, which then becomes the Amazon.

From June or July until the November rainy season, it is fishing time in the upper Amazon's brown-water tributaries. Anglers concentrate on the black-water tributaries, lakes, and oxbows off the large rivers. (It is worth noting that throughout the Amazon, commercial fishermen and native subsistence fishermen ply the area year-round, in all kinds of waters and at all water levels, for all kinds of fish. Keep that in mind when asking locals about the best times and places to catch fish.) In this region, many of the lakes become landlocked in the dry season, and it may be necessary to leave the river and portage into the lakes, where small boats or dugout canoes have been placed for the occasion. Thick vegetation at the mouths of lakes may also make access difficult. Vegetation growth on these sand and mud bottoms, as well as dead fall trees may be the keys to locating peacock bass and other species.

These are usually slow, sluggish rivers (the tributaries), and in the dry season the absence of swift current and rocks is accompanied by an absence of swift-water species like payara, morocotto, sardinata, and matrinxã. You may find sabalo, however, in moving black-water rivers and creeks. This species is related to the matrinxã.

The earliest known success at facilitating anadromous fish passage in America was the 1882 construction of a pool-type fish ladder at Willamette Falls, Oregon.

These waters generally hold piranhas, payara, pirarucu, arawana, butterfly peacock bass, and many catfish species, including sorubim. Peacocks do not exceed 13 pounds, most won't reach 10 pounds, and the norm is 3- to 6-pounders. The number of peacocks can be very good in lakes that are not fished by locals or commercial fishermen, but finding those waters can be difficult.

Iquitos is the gateway to this region in Peru, and there are a couple of sportfishing outfitters in the area. Most operations cater to the ecotourist, which is seldom suitable for the avid angler. In Quito, Ecuador, you may find someone to organize a fishing expedition into Amazonas, but you should be prepared to rough it and do a lot of exploration. As in Peru, peacock bass are not big in Ecuador.

In Brazil, tour operators have largely ignored the brown-water region, because of the much smaller peacocks and the existence of many villages along most of the more productive fishing waters. It costs the same to fish for small peacocks as it does to fish for big ones, and the big ones are on more attractive and remote rivers. The access to these Brazilian brown-water rivers is through Manaus to Tabatinga, Coari, Tefe, or Fonte Boa. In Colombia you may try to find an outfitter in Leticia.

Another Peruvian sportfishing destination is the Manu National Rain Forest, near Puerto Maldonado in southern Peru. Nearby Cusco and Machu Picchu are popular tourist attractions. Rivers here are the Manu, Madre de Dios, Piedras, and Tambopata, with the latter boasting large payara. There may be an outfitter in Puerto Maldonado who will guide an exploratory float-fishing/camping trip in the area for peacocks, piranha, sabalo, and/or payara. Efforts at sportfishing here have been a hit-or-miss proposition.

Guyana's highland rivers. The Rupununi, Essequibo, and New Rivers in Guyana harbor plenty of peacocks, payara, pirarucu, catfish, and piranhas, but there is no infrastructure for sportfishing in the remote upper-watershed rivers. Finding someone in Georgetown, Guyana, who knows fishing in these rivers may be difficult, but that's the place to start. Presently there are no outfitters offering fishing expeditions into this region. An angler looking for a real adventure may want to take a chance in Guyana. The fish are certainly still there and waiting.

Bolivia's llanos region. The rivers in this region originate in the Bolivian and Peruvian Andes and flow through hundreds of miles of plains and grasslands before forming the headwaters of the Río Madeira in Brazil at Abuna. These tributaries are the Guapore, Mamore, Beni, Abuna, and Madre de Dios. Most are brown-water and some are black-water rivers.

This Llanos area is a huge, saucerlike depression with north-flowing rivers. The Madeira, strengthened by combined waters, cuts through the highland here as it rushes north to the Amazon. Some large lakes have formed in this vast and relatively flat topography, and many are full of small peacock bass. Payara thrive in some of the swifter streams, and also catfish and piranhas. During floods in the rainy season, these waters mix with those of the swampy Pantanal area, resulting in a common pool of many species.

The fishing season here is from May or June through October. Gateways in local areas are Vilhena, Porto Velho, and Guajara-Mirim in Brazil, and Cobija, Trinidad, and Riberalta in Bolivia. International flights into this region are through Santa Cruz and La Paz in Bolivia, and Manaus and Brasilia in Brazil.

Delta regions of Brazil and Venezuela. The delta regions of both the Orinoco and the Amazon contain peacock bass and other freshwater species, but very little is known about freshwater fishing in the many channels and lagoons in these two areas. Outfitters in both have tried to establish fishing operations for tarpon and other salt-/brackish-water species, but not for peacock bass. These two frontiers require further exploration.

Travel suggestions. The Amazon is not the hostile environment pictured in some B movies. You will not be eaten by snakes or jaguars, speared by natives, or caught up in a revolution (although there is some danger, as noted in and near Colombia). Deadly diseases are extremely rare among tourists here, and the cities and villages of these regions are more crime-free than most cities inhabited by North Americans.

Probably the biggest concerns will be protecting skin from intense equatorial sun and the bite of tiny insects. Immunization and preventative medication against yellow fever and malaria are recommended but not required. Sun dehydration is prevented by consuming lots of bottled water during the fishing day and with meals. Tourists visiting this region for the first time may experience an upset stomach and diarrhea.

Traveling here is really no different than traveling to any other part of the world, although more patience may be required at certain times and places. Those journeying to remote areas anywhere should be in reasonably good health, as medical facilities may be difficult to reach in a reasonable period of time during an emergency.

Saltwater

Brazil's saltwater sportfishing has been called a sleeping giant at least since the mid-1970s, and it seems to continue that way, despite an enormous coastline and a wide range of species. The main reason is that relatively few Brazilians (the majority of whom reside in just a few areas, mostly Río de Janeiro) have large sportfishing vessels, and charter operations have been almost nonexistent. That's not to say that there has been no fishing, as private boats have plied offshore waters for marlin and sailfish regularly; but it can still be said that the

B

offshore environs of Brazil constitute a virgin or near-virgin big-game fishery, and that only minimal effort has been generated in just a few areas.

Given the size of the country, the amount of water to cover, and the lack of boats to cover it, this relative lack of interest is not difficult to understand. Nevertheless, efforts to increase the interest of serious anglers in the blue marlin, white marlin, and sailfish here—especially blues—has slowly boosted charter operations, and today it is possible to find commercial sportfishing ventures in a few locations.

Most of this activity occurs from Río de Janeiro north to Ilhéus, a distance of more than 600 miles, with activity concentrated out of Río, Victoria, and Comandatuba Island south of Ilhéus. Vitoria has produced at least seven world-record white marlin, including an all-tackle fish of 181 pounds, 14 ounces, and in 1992 it saw the capture of an all-tackle world-record blue marlin that weighed 1,402 pounds and 2 ounces. Nearby seamounts, a strong southerly current flow, and sharp dropoffs—especially near Vitoria—are key factors, but conditions may be even better farther north, from Salvador to Natal and beyond, and offshore from Natal to such structures as Atol das Rocas and the 21-island archipelago of Fernando de Noronha, a former penal colony that rises 13,000 feet from the ocean floor.

Wahoo, dolphin, yellowfin tuna, and king mackerel are also among the offshore seamount catch, and there were once many sightings of broadbill swordfish. The wahoo and dolphin can get large, and the sailfish average 60 to 65 pounds. The spring and summer seasons here—from October through February—are the primary time for billfish, with northern areas getting the early burst and southern areas the later one. Río de Janeiro, for example, sees its best sailfishing from November through February, usually peaking in December and January. Blue marlin arrive in mid-October, beginning some 60 to 70 miles south and west. White marlin are uncommon at Río but bountiful off Vitoria; sailfish, on the other hand, are rare off Vitoria.

A smorgasbord of other species is available along the coast and inshore, almost none pursued by visiting anglers. Tarpon, snook, jack crevalle, various snapper and grouper, bluefish, weakfish, mackerel, drum, pompano, amberjack, and many others frequent these waters. Large bays, estuaries, and various river deltas with lagoons and lakes exist, and inshore opportunities—sometimes well up tidal rivers—should be present, although boats and operators to exploit them may not be; recent information about these areas is lacking.

BREACHING
The free jumping of an unhooked fish in offshore waters.

BREAKAWAY LEADER
A light leader, branching from a heavier main line, that usually extends to a sinker or other weight and is intended to break free if it gets snagged. This is intended to save the lure, bait, and other terminal tackle on the main line.

BREAKERS
Waves reaching their highest point in shallow water; usually refers to waves that crest into foam on a beach.

BREAKING FISH
Fish that are chasing baitfish, usually in open water, and herding them to the surface while feeding, with the result that the bait and/or the pursuing fish erupt on the surface in such a manner as to be visible from a distance. This event is often accompanied by active birds who hover over the melee, trying to pick up stunned or injured baitfish.

BREAKING STRENGTH
The amount of pressure, expressed in pounds or kilograms, that must be applied to an unknotted line before the molecules part and the line breaks. This may also be expressed as breaking strain.
See: Line.

BREAKLINE
Where the sloping bottom of a body of water changes distinctly from one contour level to the next, as determined by observation of a sonar device or contours on a hydrographic map or chart. Most often used with regard to lakes, this term generally references a place where the bottom moves more sharply from one depth level to the next. Depending on depth, species, and presence or absence of other underwater features, the breakline may be a place to find fish, especially during warm weather.
See: Dropoff.

BREAKOFF
To end a fight with a fish by breaking the line. Occasionally this term refers to losing a fish because the hook pulls out, but the primary meaning is losing a fish through line breakage. An unintentional breakoff occurs when the line is cut or is stressed beyond its breaking point. An intentional breakoff occurs when an angler deliberately applies more tension to the line than it can stand in order to end a fight. This is usually done by increasing the drag on a reel, applying pressure to the line on a reel spool, pointing the rod directly at the fish, and holding tight when it surges away.

BREAKWATER

A man-made barrier to break the impact of waves and/or current at the mouth of a harbor or inlet, in front of a marina, or in front of a boat launch or other access site. A breakwater is usually detached from the shoreline, and may be parallel to the shore or at an angle to it. It is built up from the ocean or lake bottom and usually protrudes above the surface, at least to average wave height, except under extreme water conditions; it may or may not have navigational aids. A breakwater serves essentially the same function as a jetty *(see);* when it extends directly from the shore, the terms are interchangeable.

A breakwater for a harbor is usually made of concrete or stone, and anglers may be able to fish directly from it. For those fish not accessible to anglers by foot, trolling, casting, or drifting nearby may be worthwhile.

Breakwaters may exist in noncoastal locations, such as in large inland lakes and reservoirs, where they are usually intended to diffuse wave action and protect marinas. They may be fashioned from various materials, including auto tires, and are seldom accessible or fished from.

See: Jetty Fishing; Surf Fishing.

BREAM

Many species of both freshwater and saltwater fish around the world are referred to as bream, particularly in Australia, the United Kingdom, and the United States. In the U.S., "bream" (pronounced "brim") is a colloquial expression for various freshwater panfish species, particularly sunfish *(see)* and especially bluegills *(see)*.

In Europe, the bream pursued by anglers are members of the Cyprinidae family and are relatives of carp *(see)*, barbel *(see)*, and tench *(see)*. These primarily small or midsize fish (less than 8 pounds) are bottom feeders and are widely distributed. They are also a popular coarse fish *(see)*. The primary quarry is the bronze bream *(see: bream, bronze)*, which is also known as the common bream or carp bream.

In saltwater, various members of the Sparidae family are known as sea bream, and are related to porgies *(see)*. Sea bream *(see: bream, sea)* occur in temperate and tropical waters worldwide.

BREAM, BRONZE   *Abramis brama.*

Other names—bronze bream, common bream, carp bream, skimmer (small fish) bream; French: *bréme;* German: *brachsen brasse;* Italian: *brama.*

This popular coarse fish *(see)* is a member of the Cyprinidae family and a relative of carp *(see),* barbel *(see),* and tench *(see).* It is the largest-growing and most abundant member of the bream clan and is pursued for sport and food, having local commercial value in some parts of its range.

Identification.   The bronze bream has a comparatively small head and a deep body that produces

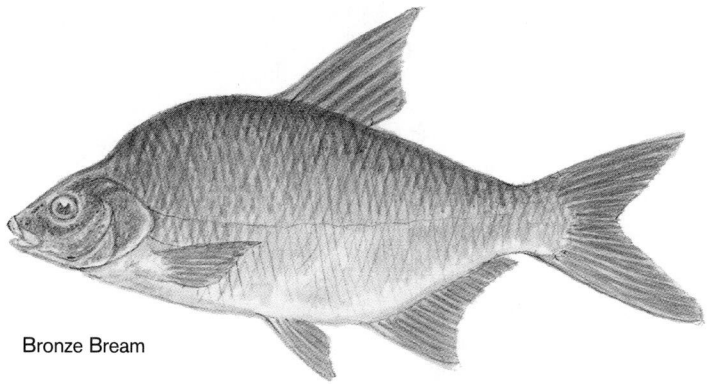
Bronze Bream

a broad girth. The laterally compressed body is punctuated with a humplike appearance on the back, just ahead of the dorsal fin, and tapers sharply to the caudal peduncle and a deeply forked tail. The back is dark brown, and the sides are golden brown, fading to a grayish white on the belly. It has a long and tapered anal fin, and the fins may have a light reddish tint. The scales are small, and the body is covered with thick mucus.

Juveniles are lighter in coloration, being silvery with black fins; these young fish are confused with a similar-looking silver bream *(Blicca bjoerkna),* which is found in many of the same waters but is much smaller at maximum weight (about 1 pound) and slender.

Bronze bream with light broad stripes inhabit parts of Ireland, where they are referred to as Irish bream, and can grow to 10 pounds. Bream may breed with roach *(see)* and produce a hybrid fish that is a bit lighter, slightly less humpbacked, and with a shorter anal fin. The anal fins are a distinguishing difference, with 14 to 19 rays in the hybrid and 23 to 29 in the parent bream.

Size.   The all-tackle world record for bronze bream is a Swedish fish caught in 1993 in Lake Vanern that weighed 12 pounds, 7 ounces. Bream have been reported to twice that weight, however, and commonly weigh 3 to 7 pounds.

Distribution.   Bronze bream range from Ireland eastward throughout most of Europe and into central Asia.

Habitat.   Stillwaters and deep, slow-flowing rivers are the primary preferences of bronze bream. Their wide distribution includes lakes and canals, and they locate in places with rich bottom life, usually over a mud bottom.

Life history/Behavior.   Bream spawn in late spring and early summer, usually in weedy shallows, broadcasting numerous adhesive eggs rather than constructing a nest; this activity is usually accompanied by an obvious splashing and rolling commotion. The fry stay in schools and gather in large congregations. Bream are one of the most intensive schooling of all cyprinid species, and they gather in large groups when smaller, tapering to small schools of a few of the oldest individuals. These schools (called shoals) generally consist of similar-size individuals.

Schools of bream wander and feed, often in habitual patterns or paths of travel. Their route is frequently discernible due to the roiling, muddying, or bubbling of the water caused when numbers of these fish feed by rooting among plants, sediment, and soft bottom. They also have a tendency to roll on the surface prior to or during feeding, another indicator of their presence.

Food and feeding habits. Bream eat insect larvae, worms, mollusks, crustaceans, algae, and other bottom organisms. They occasionally feed in midwater, perhaps when the school is thick and stirring up food, and less occasionally on the surface, but the bulk of activity occurs on the bottom. Bream assume a more angular, rather than horizontal, position when feeding on the bottom, and their tail is pointed up as the mouth, used like a sucking tool, is positioned to pick food off the bottom. They are extremely effective at vacuuming up what they are after, blowing on the bottom to wash out food and then sucking up what has been uncovered. By alternately sucking and blowing several times, they wash their food and remove sand from it.

Like tench, bream are low-light feeders and are more active at night, dawn, and dusk, and on dark days. They are active in temperatures up to 68°F and relatively inactive in water below 45°F. Because they are a schooling fish, when active they may sometimes be caught in good numbers in a given location.

Angling. Bream are tenacious although not spectacular fighters, but they are a popular fish for many Europeans, especially British anglers. Fishing for bream is similar to fishing for tench and other coarse fish, although more bream may be available in a given spot.

Bottom fishing with assorted baits is the favored technique for bream. This involves intensive prebaiting or chumming, using groundbait *(see)* and an assortment of prepared, processed, and natural baits. Baiting may be done for long periods in advance of fishing, and is considered necessary to acclimate a school to a location and to keep them there while angling. Sometimes a school of bream come through and stay only long enough to scour the bait before moving on.

As with other coarse fishing, maggots, corn, worms, cheese, bread, pastes, and other items are used, particularly those commodities employed in prebaiting or chumming (although in areas where fish have repeatedly been caught with the same bait, they become conditioned to avoid that item).

Hooked baits may be fished with a float or without one, but many bream anglers prefer a bolt rig *(see)* and a bottom feeder (a device for precise-location chumming). Anglers use rods from 11 to 14 feet in length, line from 4 to 10 pounds in strength, and No. 6 to 14 bait hooks.

Most bream anglers fish from the bank or from shore, and often at distances of more than 60 feet from the water's edge. Where possible, fishing from an anchored boat, with the ability to move to new locations, seems beneficial.

BREAM, SEA

Numerous members of the Sparidae family that are found in temperate and tropical waters are referred to as sea bream, or seabream. They are related to porgies *(see)*, have moderate to important significance commercially (depending on abundance and geography), and are commonly caught by inshore anglers. These fish are tough, dogged fighters that are commendable on appropriate light tackle, and they rate as excellent table fare. The more commonly distributed and popular species are noted here.

The red seabream *(Pagellus bogaravero)* is an important food and recreational fish found in the eastern Atlantic Ocean, from Norway through the Strait of Gibraltar and into the western Mediterranean Sea, including Cape Blanc in Mauritania, Madeira, and the Canary Islands. It has red fins and a reddish tint on the back and sides, lightening to the belly, with a large dark spot above the pectoral fin and behind the gill cover. It is also known as the blackspotted seabream and common seabream. Other names include, in Danish: *blankensteen;* Dutch: *zeebrasem;* Finnish: *pikkupagelli;* French: *dorade rose;* German: *meerbrasse, seekarpfen;* Italian: *rovello;* Norwegian: *flekkpagell;* Portuguese: *besugo, esparidoes;* Spanish: *besugo, bogarrabella;* Swedish: *fläckpagell.*

The black seabream *(Spondyliosoma cantharus)* is an important food and recreational fish found in the eastern Atlantic Ocean from Scandinavia south to northern Namibia, including the Strait of Gibraltar, the Mediterranean Sea, and, rarely, in the Black Sea, as well as in Madeira and the Canary and Cape Verde Islands. It is a silvery gray color with a dark back and six or seven bars on the flanks. Other names include, in Danish: *lavrude;* Dutch: *zeekarpfen;* Finnish: *meriruutana;* French: *dorade grise, griset;* German: *seekarpfe, streffenbrassen;* Italian: *tanuta;* Norwegian: *havsruda;* Portuguese: *choupa;* Spanish: *chopa;* Swedish: *havsrusa;* Turkish: *sarigöz.*

The black bream *(Acanthopagrus butcheri)* is a popular recreational catch found in the western Pacific Ocean in Australia, from southern New South Wales to Victoria, Tasmania, South Australia, and as far north as Shark Bay in Western Australia; it is possibly found in New Zealand. The black bream's body color can vary with its habitat from a silver, bronze, or olive brown dorsally, to a whitish belly, and dusky gray to black fins. It is also known as sea bream, eastern black bream, and southern black bream.

The silver bream *(Acanthopagrus australis)* is also a popular recreational catch found in the western Pacific Ocean, occurring in Australia from southern New South Wales to northern Queensland, and also reported in Taiwan. The silver bream's body is silvery to olive green dorsally, shading to a whitish belly, and its ventral and anal fins are splashed with a bright to dull yellow. Its pectoral fin has tinges of yellow in it, and there is a dark spot at the base; the caudal fin is distinguished by a distinct black trailing edge. It is also known as yellowfin bream, sea bream, eastern black bream, southern bream, golden bream, and, in Japanese, as *ósutoraria-kichinu*.

The river bream *(Acanthopagrus berda)* is a prominent commercial and recreational catch that is wide ranging in the Indian and western Pacific Oceans, occurring from South Africa to Japan and northern Australia, and appearing in the lower Zambezi and Lucuara Rivers in Zimbabwe and South Africa respectively. It is also known as pikey bream (Australia), black bream, black porgy, black seabream, dark-finned porgy, sly bream. Other names include, in Arabic: *shaami*; Cantonese: *hak lap*; French: *pargo picnic*; Japanese: *nanyóchinu*; Malay: *bandan, kuku, kapas-kapas.*

The western yellowfin bream *(Acanthopagrus latus)* is a prominent commercial and recreational catch that is wide ranging in the Indian and western Pacific Oceans, occurring from the Persian Gulf through India to the Philippines, north to Japan and south to the northwest coast of Australia; it also appears in Djibouti.

The sea bream *(Archosargus rhomboidalis)* appears in the western Atlantic Ocean from the northeastern Gulf of Mexico to Argentina, including the Caribbean and West Indies. Its bluish back is streaked with gold, the belly is silvery, and there is a black spot on each side just above the pectoral fins.

Size. Most of these sea bream can reach a maximum weight of between 3.5 and 4.5 kilograms, but on average they weigh between 0.5 and 1 kilogram. The sea bream of the western Atlantic is rarely more than a foot long.

Habitat. Some sea bream are abundant in estuaries, and some are found in deeper, offshore waters. Some move up into brackish water but not into freshwater. The black bream, however, which rarely ventures beyond its estuary confines, ranges well upstream in freshwater. The silver bream can be found in estuaries and also in offshore waters, especially in the vicinity of reefs, in the corners of beaches, along surf beaches, and off rocky headlands. It also moves upstream into brackish water but seldom extends to the freshwater reaches. As adults, red and black seabream are found in deeper continental slope waters (the latter from 50 to 300 meters and the former from 400 to 700 meters). Coastal and offshore sea bream are found over a wide variety of bottoms. In the estuarine environment, bream frequent seagrass beds, underwater reefs and rocks, bridge pilings that grow mussels, and oyster beds.

Spawning behavior. Red seabream spawn from January to June depending on location, and

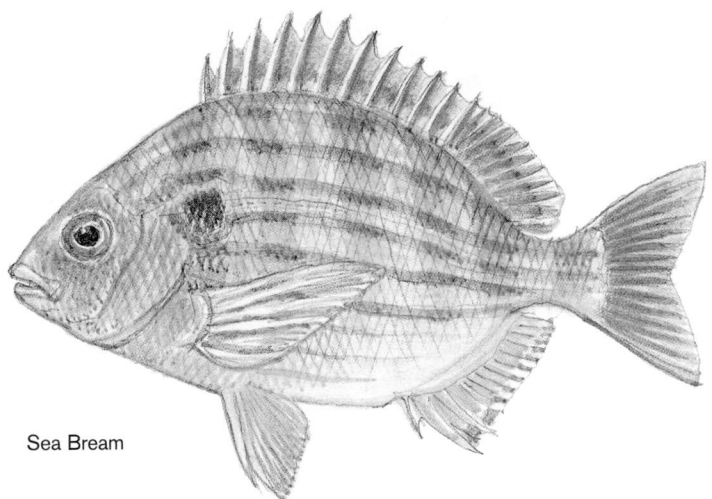

Sea Bream

black seabream spawn from March to May in their northern reaches. Both are hermaphroditic.

Along the east coast of Australia, silver (yellowfin) bream spawn close to river entrances during February in southern New South Wales, and progressively later through to August the farther north they are found (in July and August in Queensland). Black bream start spawning from October through early December within estuaries in Victorian waters, from November through January in South Australia, and between July and November in Western Australia. Each species is thought to produce from 300,000 to 3 million eggs during the spawning season. The eggs of the silver bream are planktonic, as are the larvae that hatch after about two days. After a month, the larvae are carried into the estuaries by flood tides and settle into seagrass beds. The eggs of the black bream are pelagic and hatch after about two days, and the larvae also settle into and over seagrass beds.

Food. Bream are largely omnivorous and feed on crustaceans; crayfish; mollusks, including oysters and mussels; small fish; worms; and algae. Some will also eat bread, chicken gut, mullet gut, cheese, and meat, all of which are sometimes used for baits.

Angling. A spirited and determined fighter and an excellent table fish, the ubiquitous bream responds readily to many natural baits, as previously noted, plus pieces of pilchards, garfish, tuna, squid, and other baitfish. It will also take small plugs, spoons, soft plastics, spinners, and flies in prawn, shrimp, or streamer patterns.

Tackle varies with location; 5- to 7-kilogram lines are generally used, and 5- or 6-weight outfits are favored for fly fishing. Handlines to 7 kilograms are popular with estuary anglers. Hook sizes to 3/0 in the surf, and to 1/0 within estuarine waters, are best and, where practical, the lightest-weight sinker, or none at all, is recommended.

Depending on species, sea bream are taken from surf beaches, ocean rocks, and estuaries by shore anglers, and from estuaries, bays, and deeper offshore reefs from a boat. The best fishing generally occurs early in the morning and late in the afternoon and into the night. Baits should be kept moving across the bottom using a slow rate of retrieve. Strike timing is especially important. Close inspection of the bream's mouth reveals a series of tough, crushing molars that hooks are often unable to penetrate, so the bream must be allowed to swallow a bait before striking to set the hook. Chum and bait mixtures are extremely important, and usually consist of minced fish flesh, prawn scraps, soaked wheat, tuna oil, and bread.

Lure anglers wade over sand flats and cast to seagrass beds or deep channels during daylight hours. Sight fishing is sometimes possible but is more the exception than the rule. Bass plugs are popular in Australia for black bream, which are often taken by anglers plying freshwater and brackish-water reaches for Australian bass. Many anglers there make their own bream lures, often tying a bunch of yellow plastic hair to the shank of a No. 1 hook, and crimping a split shot over the binding just behind the hook eye; this rig is bounced across the bottom.

Very sensitive and timid, bream are easily frightened away from a bait by sudden noise or, at nighttime, by flashing lights.

BRIDGE FISHING

Bridges span many bodies of water, especially canals, marshes, and bays where there is either one-way current from upstream flows or two-way current from tidal action. In freshwater, bridges range from large structures that cross over large rivers to small-roadway bridges that pass water through a culvert. In saltwater, they range from bay bridges that are miles in length to small culverts to narrow passageways connecting sections of a marsh. Nearly all bridges offer some ready and accessible fishing opportunities that should not be overlooked by anglers, whether they fish on foot or from a boat.

Bridges provide current breaks and ambush opportunities for many varieties of opportunistic fish.

Smaller bridges obviously form a narrowing of water that slows the upstream section and then shoots it through the downstream section (this works both ways in tidal situations, which would be uptide or downtide). This action scours a hole on the downstream side and may cause full-blown eddies or minor countercurrents on the downstream edges, as well as slackwater pockets, if the situation is conducive. Similarly, culverts will have a deep hole where the greatest force of water emerges, and possibly a small backcurrent to the sides of this. All of these areas may hold fish, especially the bottom of the hole or edge areas where little or no current has to be overcome by the fish and where they can grab food as it drifts by. Eddies on the upstream side of a narrow bridge, along the shore and created by funneling, may also hold fish.

Larger bridges crossing bigger rivers have bridge pilings or pylons for support. Pilings are pillars, whereas pylons are larger and more islandlike support structures. Pilings create downstream pockets of holding water; pylons may do likewise, and may also create eddies or even a dead area directly ahead of the structure on the upstream side. Changing current or tide flows may alter the position of fish here, and in slow or slack water cause them to move about more. Larger bridge supports can be trolled, cast with leadhead jigs, or fished with live baits. When casting, the first step is to find a position that will enable proper presentation. The offering must sweep across the face of the bridge supports and swim toward them; one doesn't start at the supports and work away from them.

Fishing from above and sweeping, however, often sends the bait or lure down the middle of the current chute. To avoid this scenario, it may be necessary, especially in confined areas, to do some creative casting in addition to finding the right spot from which to cast. Bounce casts, short flips, lob casts, and casting to shore and then dragging your lure into the water may be necessary to achieve a productive effect.

Shade, which varies depending on the angle of the sun, and shadow lines created by overhead lights must also be factored into this type of fishing. Fish favor locations that take advantage of the dark/light interface.

Be aware of some problems inherent to bridge fishing. Fishing from the road-surface areas on bridges can be dangerous due to vehicular traffic; in some cases it may be illegal. Bridges that experience boat or canoe traffic can be difficult to fish, especially if you anchor and sit in the main channel. And the current funneling through some bridges is more powerful than inexperienced anglers or waders realize; it is possible for wading anglers to lose their footing and be swept into a swift current.

Bridge fishing is also discussed in pier fishing (see).

BRIGHT FISH

A term for fresh, migratory anadromous fish that have recently entered and are ascending a tributary. Such fish are still silvery from their life at sea (or perhaps in large lakes), and do not yet exhibit their spawning coloration and markings. In the case of sea-run Atlantic salmon, a bright fishery is one for fresh-run specimens, as opposed to those that have overwintered, which are called kelts *(see)*.

See: Salmon, Atlantic.

BRILL *Scophthalmus rhombus.*

Other names—Danish: *slethvarre;* Dutch: *griet;* Finnish: *silokampela;* French: *barbue;* Italian: *rombo liscio;* Norwegian: *slettvar;* Portuguese: *rodovalho;* Spanish: *rémol;* Swedish: *slätvar.*

The brill is a left-eyed member of the Scophthalmidae family of flatfish *(see)* that has been commercially significant for European markets and is mainly caught by commercial trawlers. Like other flatfish, it undergoes a unique maturation from egg to adult in which the eyes migrate to one side of the head.

Identification. The body of the brill is oval; the eyed side is grayish to greenish brown with variable-color patches, and the blind side is white.

Size. This species grows to 30 inches and is reported to reach 16 pounds, but it is commonly 12 inches long.

Distribution. The brill occurs in the northeastern Atlantic along the coast, in the Mediterranean and Black seas, and from Morocco to about the 64° latitude.

Habitat. Brill are located over sandy and mixed bottoms in depths between 100 and 300 feet.

Spawning behavior. Spawning occurs from March through August; males reach maturity at 14 inches, and females at 13 inches.

Food. The diet of brill consists primarily of various fish and larger crustaceans.

Angling. Brill are primarily caught from party boats by anglers fishing with heavy weights and natural baits, or heavy metal jigs.

See: Drift Fishing, Flatfish, Inshore Fishing.

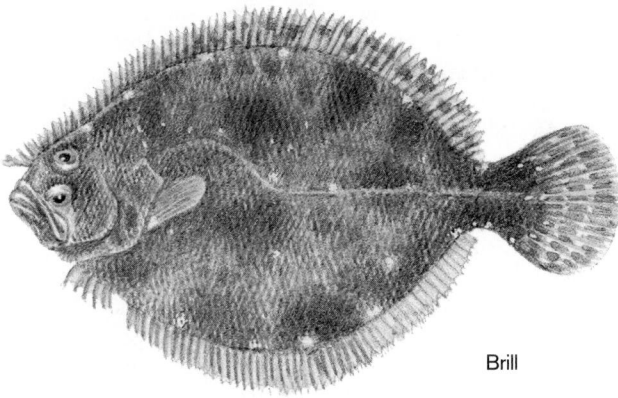

Brill

BRITISH COLUMBIA

Spectacular by nature is what some say of British Columbia. Beauty is its birthright say others. Indeed, this Pacific Northwest province can justifiably flaunt its inland and coastal attractions. There may well be no prettier place to wet a hook than the high mountain lakes and rivers of British Columbia's interior, or the tranquil coves along its northern coast, where there are enough inlets and straits and river mouths to explore that an entire summer could be spent delightfully cruising and fishing.

British Columbia's 1,600-mile-long coastline serves up a daily menu of salmon, halibut, lingcod, and some 14 species of rockfish. Almost every beach yields shellfish, Dungeness crab, king crab, and sometimes the prized box crab. There is plenty of drive-to angling in the lower portion of the province, but because so much of British Columbia's coast is remote, saltwater fishing adventures are enjoyed as packaged trips at more than 150 saltwater lodges and resorts. These provide guides, gear, and fish care. Almost every fly-in lodge is situated in a serene wilderness location, and each day's fishing is punctuated by encounters with such marine wildlife as orca, gray, and humpback whales, porpoises, sea lions, bald eagles, and, on a few occasions, black or grizzly bears.

Bald eagles, egrets, blue heron, assorted waterfowl, bears, wolves, cougars, moose, and goats live in almost every mountain watershed, where rivers run from snow-capped mountains to the Pacific Ocean. All contain sustaining runs of sea-run salmon, and many also have steelhead.

Several hundred campgrounds and a like number of lake lodges, many with outpost camps and licensed guides, exist within this 1.3 million-square-mile province. Provincial fisheries managers maintain a huge annual stocking program on thousands of lakes and hundreds of rivers, which supplements abundant native resources. The more northerly and interior of these see few if any anglers in a season, if not a lifetime.

Saltwater

Five species of salmon and multiple species of bottom-dwelling fish are indigenous to the coastal waters of British Columbia. Although there are some area and seasonal closures, chinook, coho, chum, pink, and sockeye salmon can all be taken from these waters. Of course, salmon are the prime drawing card for both visitors and residents. Considerable interest in other species exists as well, however, especially lingcod, yelloweye rockfish, and halibut.

The beautiful white fillets of the lingcod are favored by many anglers over all other fish. When properly filleted, yelloweye rockfish are equally praised. Lings are minty green when hooked from depths up to 150 feet, whereas a sharp blue cast covers the pearl white meat of a deep-caught fish.

B

There is no difference in taste, however. All of the really large lings (more than 15 pounds) are female; some can reach weights of 70 to 100 pounds.

A huge British Columbia population of halibut almost matches the quantity of salmon. This popular white-fleshed species of fish-and-chips fame can attain weights of more than 400 pounds and can be found in ocean depths to 3,000 feet. Most anglers are limited to catching "chicken"-size halibut in waters less than 200 feet deep, but the really large "barn-door" brutes move into these shallower depths at certain times of the year.

British Columbia's most productive halibut grounds are on the north coast and along the rises west of Vancouver Island. Halibut baits range from plain jigs to herring and octopus. Strong halibut rods must have full spools of 70- to 90-pound line, and anglers can count on an arm-tiring battle in bringing larger halibut to the boat.

The main angling quest is larger chinook, known by the native Indian word *tyee,* which refers to any specimen 30 pounds or better. Early-run fish are locally called "spring" salmon. Chinooks are distinguished from other salmon by their black mouth and gums, and from coho by virtue of the spots on both the top and bottom of the tail fin (the coho sports these on the top only).

Also highly sought in British Columbia waters is any size of the flashy, acrobatic coho, especially the aggressive late-season kype-nosed specimens called "northerns." In general, coho are also referred to as "silver" salmon. These sleek fish may not grow as large as chinooks, but they lack nothing in the way of excitement at the end of a fishing line. Known for repeated acrobatics, swift runs, and jolting strikes, coho are the darling of light-tackle enthusiasts. They commingle with chinooks and can be caught at the same time, but the angler who targets coho would do well to scale down offerings, use lighter tackle, and focus on later seasons when these fish are most abundant.

Both chinook and coho are anadromous fish, spending their lives in the ocean and returning to their rivers of birth to spawn, after which they die. In the ocean for several years, they wander great distances and feed prodigiously. Most of the salmon are caught relatively close to shore and in the nearshore vicinity of offshore islands, especially where there is deep water and the influence of currents.

Most British Columbia anglers prefer to catch salmon by mooching *(see),* keeping the weighted line and rigged bait at a 45-degree angle by utilizing a slow boat speed. For spring salmon, the optimal depth to hold the rigged bait is 3 to 5 feet off the bottom. Coho are usually in the upper depths. Use of downriggers to troll either bait or plugs is on the increase.

By far the greatest saltwater lure for salmon is dead natural herring or anchovy. Herring are fished whole or cut plug style; anchovies are fished in a rig referred to as a baitholder. Both are sometimes accompanied by a dodger. Plugs are fished both with a dodger and by themselves.

In the Queen Charlotte Islands and along the west coast of Vancouver Island, anglers and salmon are not finicky about their bait hookups; anything works fairly well there. Along the midcoast, near Bella Coola, Hakai, and Rivers Inlet for example, success comes to anglers who can cut and rig their baits to present either a slow roll for chinooks or a fast roll or spin for cohos.

Downriggers and long, light rods are popular along the north coast and in the inside waters of the Strait of Georgia to achieve the depths of the returning salmon. Mooching with 6- to 12-ounce weights is the normal style at Rivers Inlet or along the western fiords of Vancouver Island. Plugs and hoochies behind a dodger, which are the main lure of commercial trollers, are also top producers for anglers all along the coast on certain runs at certain times. Many anglers have also achieved good success with jigging baits, spinning gear, herring strips, hoochies, and spoons.

Using a fly rod to quickly fish a lightly weighted bucktail in the wake of a boat is one of the most exciting techniques for catching northern coho in the fall. Tackle consists of an $8^{1}/_{2}$- or 9-foot fly rod for 6- or 8-weight line, with a long extension handle and a salmon fly reel that will hold 600 yards of 8-pound-test monofilament. A streamer fly (with or without a weight) is trolled on or just below the surface. When the fly is fished on top, watch for a big wake from a large charging fish.

Southern region. Most of the fishing emphasis in the southern region is along the mainland coast, between the mainland and the eastern perimeter of long Vancouver Island. The western part of Vancouver Island, however, has excellent fishing and less crowded conditions. From early May through late September, large numbers of migrating Canadian and American chinook salmon are available at such popular west coast destinations as Kyuquot Sound, Nootka, Clayoquote, Tofino, Ucluelet, Bamfield, and Sooke. A good run of northern cohos move down the coast in the fall, and the rivers provide trout and steelhead fishing, which supplements the ocean fishing and is especially enjoyed on those afternoons when conditions become uncomfortable. Halibut are also a common catch here, with larger fish caught on offshore banks. These sites are accessed direct by floatplane, or by road from locations on the island.

Campbell River, at the midpoint of Vancouver Island, has justifiable reason to proclaim itself Canada's Salmon Capital, as more than 50,000 anglers annually fish here for the hordes of salmon that return through the narrow tidal surges and rapids en route to their spawning rivers. The largest of these, the Fraser, has historically been one of the world's most important salmon rivers.

Carp were imported by the U.S. Fish Commission in 1876 with high praise as gamefish; the value of carp decreased considerably as they began to take over American waters and crowd out other fish.

British Columbia is not a place one associates with crowds, yet when fish are plentiful, on any summer night hundreds of fishing boats are scattered throughout the Campbell River area. Moreover, when the action is particularly hot, several thousand boats—each with two to four anglers—will be within a few miles of that river, most tightly packed into two or three locations. As a result, in peak season, Campbell River is home to 500 guides, and a mecca for small-boat salmon fishing, especially using live bait or cut plugs.

This is due in large part to the salmon, of all sizes, that filter past Campbell River in prodigious numbers. The waters in the Discovery Passage between Vancouver Island and the mainland are like a funnel for Pacific salmon stocks. A high percentage of all salmon migrating to or by British Columbia go through the passage, some headed to Vancouver Island rivers, others farther south or north. The passage is to salmon as Times Square is to New Yorkers. En route this way and that, any fish coming inside Vancouver Island passes by.

Unlike most other prominent sportfishing destinations, which are of relatively recent discovery, the Campbell River area has more than 100 years of sportfishing tradition. In October 1896, British angler Sir Richard Musgrave wrote in *The Field* of his experiences fishing for tyee with an Indian guide out of a dugout canoe off the mouth of the Campbell River. His largest catch was a 70-pounder; a model of it, which was once proclaimed as the largest salmon ever taken on hook and line, is still on display in the Natural History Museum of South Kensington, London.

Musgrave attracted others, who attracted others, and in 1924 the now-famous Tyee Club—analogous to the Catalina Tuna Club—was founded, for the purpose of standardizing the sport of salmon fishing in British Columbia. The club formulated many sportfishing guidelines, most of which are in force for members to this day. These include fishing with only light tackle and artificial lures (spoons or plugs) with a single hook, trolling from a boat powered only by oars, and fishing with no help from the guide other than netting.

Nowadays, in the inky predawn blackness Tyee Club members tow their rowboats to the fishing grounds, anchor the towing vessel, and row off in fiberglass skiffs, hoping to tempt an early-morning salmon in either Tyee Pool or Frenchman's Pool. The "Tyee Angler of the Year" title is awarded each year to the angler with the largest catch. A ruby lapel button is awarded to those who land a tyee of 70 or more pounds, a diamond pin for a fish in the 60s, a gold pin for a fish in the 50s, silver for a fish in the 40s, and a bronze button for any fish over 30 pounds. Fewer than 100 members are inducted into the select club each season.

The rowers, of course, are vastly outnumbered by powerboaters, who are more mobile and more efficient; but sometimes sportfishing isn't about efficiency or success ratios.

Not that there isn't plenty of success for both chinook and coho salmon anglers in these rich waters. There is so much success, in fact, that people come from all over the world to try to pluck some bounty from the intricate tidal currents of Discovery Passage.

The premier salmon fishing spot, not only here but probably worldwide, is the gigantic back eddy in front of the lighthouse where the Strait of Georgia and Discovery Passage meet. It is here that 600 to 700 boats often fish at a given time, with thousands upon thousands of salmon annually falling to the hook. When the run is on, boats routinely have doubles and triples; all across the eddy, nets are waving and rods are bending.

Another extraordinary spot, although not as conducive to heavy traffic or to boaters with a weak heart, is Seymour Narrows. Here, when the tide is high the current can flow as fast as 16 knots, and there may be 50- to 60-foot-wide whirlpools. At 10 knots it is estimated that 1 million gallons of water move by per second; nonetheless, this dangerous water draws salmon.

And those salmon can be quite large. Several 60-plus-pounders are accounted for every season, although it isn't every day that fish of 40 pounds or more are garnered. Hereabouts the emphasis is on sportsmanship, especially with the larger lodges and their guides, so a good deal of fishing is done with relatively light tackle—swift waters notwithstanding.

This is especially true for coho salmon, which are abundant in this locale. When there is a good run of cohos on, 30 to 40 can be caught in a day. The sizes run smaller than they do farther north, but light line, long rods, and fly tackle are popular among anglers fishing for coho, so a scrappy bout is virtually ensured. An excellent spot for coho is Whilby Shoal on the extreme southern tip of Quadra Island. A substantial shoal bed of kelp runs from green to red buoy and from point to point, and it supports thousands of fish, especially coho, which feed on massive pods of tiny shrimp.

Although salmon are the main attraction, some river fishing for sea-run cutthroat trout and for steelhead occurs here. The latter enter the area in the fall and winter and provide good river fishing, although it doesn't get the attention that is directed toward king salmon.

Because of its protected location, this region is fishable year-round, no matter what direction the wind is from. This is another good reason for its popularity and makes it a good place to hold tournaments, of which there are many. Here anglers can book a trip well in advance and be assured of meeting fishable conditions.

Guides are numerous, not only because of the numerous lodges in the area, but also because these waters are tricky. Both boat handling and technique are complicated by these complex waters.

B

B

For example, the tide is important here. When it is low, fish don't move and are widely scattered, causing some places to produce better than others. The new and full moon phases produce higher tides and are better times to fish. The depth to work varies as well, although for tyee the lure or bait must generally be just off the bottom.

Mooching with herring is extremely popular for salmon; lighter tackle, smaller hooks, and smaller bait are used for coho. A fair number of anglers, however, fish with artificials and light outfits, and trolling and jigging are also practiced.

Campbell River is one hour from Vancouver and is accessed by floatplane (with water taxi service) or wheeled aircraft from the mainland. Anglers with boat in tow can ferry to Victoria and drive north.

August is prime tyee season, when the big fish, preparing to spawn, are around. The best time for bigger cohos is September and October. For pure numbers, June is tops, with May also a good bet because there are fewer grilse (2-year-old salmon) around. When the grilse are abundant, you can catch 50 in a morning. Other coho average 5 to 6 pounds, with bigger northern coho in the 6- to 12-pound range in the fall.

Midcoast. The midcoast region of British Columbia is inaccessible by road and thus available only to those who access seasonal lodges and camps, or to those who have a large boat capable of long-distance cruising and overnight voyaging. The latter are few, and the former are relatively few, at least when compared to areas to the south. The result is that there is a lot of water to fish but not many anglers to fish it. Channels, inlets, and islands abound in this large area, portions of which comprise part of the Inside Passage, a 1,600-kilometer waterway extending along the Pacific Northwest from Seattle to Skagway.

Shearwater and Bella Bella in the northern portion of this region are good fishing destinations. Anglers take salmon, halibut, red snapper, and

Big chinook salmon, like this one from Rivers Inlet, are British Columbia's main coastal draw.

lingcod in the remote waters of Seaforth, Spiller, and Return Channels; from Idol Point to Cape Swain; and in Milbanke Sound south to Cape Marks.

Chinook over 40 pounds are caught in these areas, and barn-door halibut can be found in the offshore depths. Anglers have particular success with coho in Lama Pass, between Denny and the Campbell Islands.

South and east, Hakai Pass is a good place for big chinooks, as some world records have been established here, including an 85-pound line-class specimen. Forming the northern entrance to Fitz Hugh Sound, Hakai enjoys a clustering of fish as they funnel through coastal islands. Early runs of spring salmon occur here in March and April and compete at the same time with a flood of halibut. The first cohos appear by midsummer, with late July and August being tops for an abundance of northern coho. Larger chinook are available in late summer and early fall; popular spots include Odlum, The Gap, Kelpie Point, Bayley Point, and Spider Island.

Farther south, the most prominent area of the midcoast is Rivers Inlet, east of Fitz Hugh Sound and protected from the northwest by Calvert Island. Forty miles long and 7 miles wide at its entrance, Rivers Inlet is situated at the southeast corner of Queen Charlotte Sound, just north of Cape Caution. The cape is a funneling spot for large numbers of chinook and coho salmon. Fish migrating northward, having come from the Strait of Georgia between Vancouver Island and the mainland, land right at the doorstep of Rivers Inlet. Salmon migrating southward along the coast, having come from the Hecate Strait and Queen Charlotte Sound, swim right by as well. Some of these fish are not just passing through; they are returning to spawn in one of the four major rivers that empty into the inlet. The result is that from mid-June through September the action is continuous.

Chinook are the main attraction, and large specimens have been caught here in the past. An 82$^1/_2$-pound chinook, taken in 1951 at Rivers Inlet, stood as the all-tackle world record for three decades until surpassed by an Alaskan fish, and that was eclipsed locally by an 84-pound fish caught at Rivers Inlet in 1986. Other 80-pounders have been caught since. At some point years ago a chinook of 126 pounds was caught in a commercial net at the mouth of the inlet. While the monsters aren't always predictable, 50- and 60-pounders are sure to be caught every year. These are impressive-looking fish, deep-bodied and with thick girth.

King salmon aren't the only catch at Rivers Inlet. Silver salmon, some weighing up to 25 pounds, come into the Inlet in two different runs; and chum, sockeye, and pink salmon are seasonally available as well.

Salmon fishing at Rivers Inlet has actually been improving in general, due in part to a hatchery at the head of the inlet that was started in 1985 and is operated by the lodges in the area (40-pounders have already been produced from hatchery stock), and in part to less pressure. In the 1960s there were many canneries in Rivers Inlet, and lots of traffic. Virtually all of the canneries are now gone.

The salmon fishery starts in mid-June at Rivers Inlet, when there is an early run of big kings. July is the month for unadulterated action, when small coho show up as they follow baitfish schools. Coho get larger as the season progresses, with northern coho available in late August and September. September is generally the best time to catch a large coho.

Pink and chum salmon show up in mid- to late July. The run builds in late July and peaks in early August. Chinook salmon fishing is good from the beginning of the season through the end of August, with the biggest fish usually being caught in late July and the first three weeks of August.

One of the best locations for all salmon species at Rivers Inlet, especially for large chinook, is a spot known locally as "The Wall," west of Goose Bay along the southern shore. Here the water drops sharply by a cliff into 90 feet, and is 180 feet deep a short distance offshore; it then drops to 400 feet around 100 yards offshore. Fish congregate in this spot.

Early morning and late afternoon are preferred times for catching fish at The Wall, with some importance attached to having lines in the water at first light. Many a large salmon is hooked before the sun pokes over the mountains and filters through the fog that wafts up the valleys. It is cold then, without the sun; even in summer the water temperature is in the upper 40s. But salmon that have come into the inlet during the night are more agreeable before boat traffic increases and before the brighter light sends them deeper.

Rivers Inlet has plenty of deep water and many places worth fishing. The inlets of minor tributaries—back in secluded bays hemmed in by spruce and hemlock—are particularly appealing; at times one easily forgets that this is saltwater fishing, not angling in a pristine mountain lake or deep in a fiord. And at Drainey Narrows, on a good tide, water rushing out of Drainey Inlet produces a 6- to 8-foot waterfall. Out in open water, however, the sight of a breaching whale serves as a reminder that this is indeed saltwater.

Northern region.   For a long time the waters of northern British Columbia, both along the main coast and on the offshore Queen Charlotte Islands, were simply too remote for all but a handful of people to access. And with good and closer fishing elsewhere in the province, this northern bounty went unrecognized. But that changed as salmon, halibut, and lingcod fishing declined in southern waters; now a half-dozen luxurious lodges exist around what have become the fabled waters of the Queen Charlottes, as well as a few at Portland Canal, practically a stone's throw from Alaska. Langara Island on the northwest corner of the Charlottes, and Dundas Island at Naden Harbour to the east, are now fished by many people from May through September. Anglers take barn-door halibut and massive tyees here every year, accessing the region via charter flights from the South Terminal at Vancouver Airport, and also via floatplane from Prince Rupert.

The Portland Channel can be excellent for chinook and halibut fishing, with little competition from other anglers, but the focal point of the northern region is the Queen Charlotte Islands. Roughly 150 islands make up the Queen Charlottes. Located between the 52nd and 54th latitudes, they form the western boundary of Hecate Strait north of Queen Charlotte Sound. The most noted fishing occurs at Langara Island, which is the northernmost point of the Queen Charlottes and is actually closer to the Alaska Panhandle than to mainland British Columbia, and near Rennell Sound on the western end of Graham Island.

Since the mid 1980s or so the Queen Charlottes, especially the northern tip in the Langara area, have become a coveted place for tyee. Taking a cue from the popularity of mainland floating resorts that moved from hotspot to hotspot, entrepreneurs at first devised a mother-ship approach for exploring the Queen Charlottes, using large boats that could be moved to accommodate changes in fish distribution and that could be secured in a protected moorage, complete with a fleet of small sportfishing craft. These continue, but now land-based lodges exist as well.

The Charlottes are truly 60-pound salmon country. It takes a 50-pounder to raise eyebrows, and 40-pounders are routine. In fact, these fish are so fat and chunky that newcomers routinely underestimate the size of their catch, later learning that the fish they thought was 35 pounds was nearly 50. Quite a few fish 70 pounds or better have been caught here, so there are obviously some real leviathans to be had.

As with other British Columbia salmon grounds, there are generally two times when the biggest salmon are more prevalent. One is early in the fishing season, which in the Queen Charlottes is from mid-May through June, and the other is through the month of August. It is uncertain whether this phenomena is due to two different runs of fish, and, in fact, big fish do appear throughout the summer. They are more prevalent in some years (although which years usually isn't predictable) than in others.

The Queen Charlottes experience some truly nasty weather, with rain and mist almost a surety in the course of a short visit. Westerly and northwesterly winds frequently pound the archipelago, and some days fishing is possible only in sheltered locales, if at all. Good foul-weather gear is a must here, to protect against both wind and rain, and is provided by outfitters.

B

B

When the weather is more hospitable, however, anglers are able to get in long days of fishing, with first light coming as early as 4:30 in the month of June and lasting well past 9 in the evening. It is common for many anglers to fish the morning and evening periods and to rest during midday.

King salmon aren't the only fish here, although they certainly are the most coveted. Plenty of coho swim among the Queen Charlotte Islands. Cohos become increasingly abundant as the season advances. Small fish appear early, with 10- to 15-pounders becoming available through the summer; northerns of 20 pounds and more are present from late August into October.

Halibut are abundant in sections of the Queen Charlottes, and have been known to occasionally rise to take the trolled herring presentations of salmon anglers, which is unusual behavior for these bottom dwellers. Taking a 60-pound halibut and a 60-pound king salmon in the same day, let alone the same trip, is a possibility, and many over 100 pounds are landed. The larger halibut, however, are generally caught by anglers deliberately pursuing this species rather than catching them accidentally. Lingcod and snapper, incidentally, are also caught here.

Because of the difficulties in establishing a fishing operation, it isn't likely that the Queen Charlottes will get overrun with anglers. If commercial fishing operations and other influences don't decimate salmon stocks, and if anglers moderate their take of trophy kings, there will be outstanding tyee fishing in the Queen Charlottes for a long time.

Resource Issues

The future of salmon in British Columbia is a complicated one, and centers around the fish, federal regulators, 6,000 unionized commercial fishermen, native Indians, and more than 400,000 saltwater anglers. The federal Department of Fisheries and Oceans (DFO) administers the salmon resource, although there is also a provincial Fisheries Ministry. Commercial fisheries include unionized seiners, gillnetters, and trollers. Native Indians have been allocated rights to a number of fish from each run.

Overfishing by the commercial fleets, habitat loss, and pollution have taken their toll of the salmon resource in British Columbia. A prime example of this loss is on the Fraser River, which is still the world's greatest salmon producer and one of the three top salmon rivers (along with the Skeena and Nass) in the province.

For more than a century, sockeye salmon have been the economic basis of commercial salmon fleets and the salmon processors. Sockeye leave saltwater in the fall to head upriver to their spawning grounds. En route, they are targeted by in-river gillnetting and native harvest. In 1996, the Federal Fisheries Ministry introduced a reduction plan for the commercial fleet that cut 800 (of 6,000) licenses in the first year. However, 90 percent of the fisheries allocation management plan still goes to commercial fishermen, while natives and recreational anglers each take about 4 percent of the resource, with only the remaining 2 percent allowed to spawn and to repopulate. Not surprisingly, a limited number of British Columbia salmon farms are raising and selling more salmon each year than the total catch of the commercial fleets.

The net effect of the fleet cutbacks has been to reduce the number of seine and gillnet boats. But because of electronics and efficiency, the catch taken by commercial boats now equals the amount taken prior to the cutbacks. These same boats compete for herring stocks for the export of herring roe.

Urban growth and chemical discharges from the Lower Mainland and the Fraser Valley threaten the lower Fraser's tributaries below Hope, the area currently responsible for rearing 90 percent of the river's chum salmon, 80 percent of the chinook, and more than half of the pink and coho salmon stocks.

Biologists report that a third of the streams in the Fraser Basin were devoid of salmon in 1998. Since the early 1980s, sportfishing salmon limits have been reduced from 16 fish a day to only 4. Some runs, particularly the sockeye run on the Horsefly River, which was devastated in the early 1940s to less than 1,000 fish, have now responded with 10 million returning spawners. Anglers hope for similar success with enhancement projects on chinook and coho.

Freshwater

If wilderness in large doses, breathtaking scenery, solitude interrupted by the cry of a loon, and plenty of fish to catch are your requisites for trout fishing, then British Columbia has the goods. Rainbow trout and Kamloops trout are the dominant quarries for almost 400,000 anglers who fish British Columbia's rivers and lakes each year, yet in the north the province also offers opportunities to catch whitefish and charr, and in the southeast, bass. There's also brown trout, lake trout, and, of course, some of the finest steelhead rivers in North America.

Steelhead. In British Columbia, steelhead come in two sizes, big and bigger; and in two seasons, summer and winter. Although most large steelhead are historically found in the larger rivers (Nass, Skeena, and Fraser), there are dependable runs in smaller rivers in the Queen Charlottes, Vancouver Island, and most coastal fiords that lead to river systems. These bright fish are sought by a special breed of anglers who willingly endure wading in icy water.

In order to avoid crowding and overfishing a limited resource, a classification system is in effect on some of the top steelhead waters. This requires a non-resident to buy a special license, fish with a guide, and pay a premium price for each day's fishing. Two-thirds of these restricted waters are on tributaries of the Skeena River in northern British Columbia.

Summer-run steelhead are taken from June through October. Winter-run fish are more numerous and are caught from mid-November through March.

Major steelhead waters on Vancouver Island are the Big Qualicu, the Cowichan, Englishman, Campbell, Gold, Nanaimo, Oyster, Quinsam, Somass, Sproat, and Stamp Rivers. On the Lower Mainland, large numbers of steelheaders find success on the Vedder, Capilano, and Squamish Rivers. The greatest runs, size, and diversity of steelhead are found in the northern part of the province on the Bulkley, Kispiox, Morice, Kitimat, and Skeena Rivers. In the interior, the famous Thompson River is the only major steelhead water, whereas in the Cariboo Coast region, action is found on the Dean and the Bella Coola, the former being one of the more highly publicized fisheries.

The lower Dean affords first opportunity for strong, silvery fresh-run fish, although it is not an intimate experience because it's accessible to the public and has numerous campsites. The salmon run peters out on the Dean by late June, when the steelhead are just starting. Steelhead numbers are best here in summer and fall, when the water is low, but by late August the river is so crowded with pink salmon that it's hard to hook steelhead.

Southwest and Vancouver Island. There's a wide variety of lake and river fishing for trout, salmon, and steelhead within two hours of Vancouver. The Vedder and Capilano Rivers are located here, too, and provide steelhead and coho salmon fishing.

The Fraser River courses through this region as well and, in addition to salmon, harbors white sturgeon—one of the world's largest and oldest freshwater fish. There is no commercial fishery for Fraser sturgeon, and in the late 1990s the sport-fishery was on a strict catch-and-release basis while biologists sought to find the cause of mysterious deaths by many large sturgeon in 1994 and 1995.

The lower Fraser River is wide, shallow, and slow moving. From Mission to Hope, the majority of sturgeon anglers fish for the giants, which spawn in the creeks and beaches of tributary rivers and lakes. Above Hope, the river narrows and plows through a narrow channel, foaming through white rapids. Between the rapids each sand-bottomed pool offers ideal sturgeon water. There is a good, active catch-and-release fishery for large sturgeon at Lillooet.

Hooking and playing sturgeon is a matter of practice and luck. Gear is usually strong 11-foot rods with conventional reels filled with 60- to 80-pound nylon monofilament. Sturgeon are bottom feeders, and they are attracted to odors. Eels soaked in garlic—plus shrimp, meat scraps, and fist-size

Fishing in interior British Columbia offers great trout action among fabulous scenery.

worm balls—are all presented, along with fresh salmon roe. Fishing is either aboard stout river boats or from sandbars. When landed, each sturgeon is tagged and measured for report to fisheries managers. Most fish these days are between 18 inches and 10 feet. Few records were kept in the early glory days, but a mammoth specimen of 1,387 pounds was pictured hanging above railway cars in New Westminster in 1897.

On Vancouver Island, there are various species of fish, although rainbow and cutthroat trout take precedence. Brown trout, brook trout, kokanee, Dolly Varden, charr, and smallmouth bass are also present in some locales. The southern part of the island contains bass in Elk Lake, and brook trout in Spectacle Lake, but it experiences greater angling pressure than the other areas due to a higher population. The northern part of the island has the least fishing pressure.

Some brown trout grow to double-digit weights in the Cowichan River on Vancouver Island. This river is a terrific fishery in every respect, and also has coho salmon, steelhead, cutthroat trout, and rainbows. This is a short (two-day drift) river that flows from its headwaters lake to Georgia Strait; every pool is named, and each reach holds fish.

Okanagan, Kootenay, and Rockies. The Okanagan Valley has a different texture than other regions of the province, and its fisheries reflect that. Most opportunities are associated with various lakes and focus on trout, although bass exist in the region as well. The big Okanagan, Kalamalka, and Skaha Lakes are good spring and fall fisheries for large rainbow trout, plus lake trout and kokanee salmon (landlocked sockeyes). Wood Lake, at the southern end of Kalamalka, has produced exceptionally large kokanee in the past. Excellent Kamloops fishing is available in many high-elevation lakes on both sides of the valley; better-known ones include Tepee, Hatheume, Oyama, Postill, Swalwell, Beaver, Bolean, Pinaus, Spa, Arthur, and Aberdeen Lakes. These are easily accessible waters.

B

The Kootenay region boasts the unique Gerrard strain of huge rainbow trout, which can rival a tyee salmon in size and spirit. Guide boats on the large Kootenay lakes can lead anglers to these giants, which have been introduced to more than 30 lakes in central British Columbia. The largest sport-caught Gerrard came from Kootenay Lake and weighed 35$^1/_2$ pounds.

The larger lakes of this region, incidentally, are also the best places to find burbot, a freshwater fish likened to saltwater lingcod, and gaining in winter fishing popularity. This includes places like Slocan Lake and Upper and Lower Arrow Lakes, which also have Dolly Varden and rainbow trout.

To the east, the lake-dotted Rocky Mountain Trench has good opportunities for cutthroat and rainbow trout in the upper lakes, plus whitefish and Dolly Varden in the valley lakes. There's a smattering of smallmouth bass in the lower lakes as well.

Central interior. The areas known as the Cariboo Chilcotin and High Country regions have tremendous resources of rainbow and Kamloops trout. Both regions boast of providing "a lake a day, as long as you stay." The city of Kamloops has excellent surrounding lakes with abundant weed-beds to provide forage for trout, and the result is terrific fly fishing opportunity. Kamloops trout have inspired multiple high-country lodges to band together under the "Rainbow Capital" banner. The lakes around Kamloops open early; three—Roche, Tunkwa, and Paul—were a past venue for the World Championship of Fly Fishing.

At the towns of Sicamous and Salmon Arm lies enormous Shuswap Lake, which has 1,000 miles of shoreline and is undeniably the houseboat capital of British Columbia. Trophy Kamloops, as well as Dolly Varden, kokanee salmon, and whitefish, are found in Shuswap.

In the southern Cariboo region, between 100 Mile House and Little Fort, Highway 24 travels through a lake-rich plateau known as The Interlakes. This is one of British Columbia's famous collections of very fishable high-altitude lakes.

In the northern Cariboo region, Williams Lake is the jumping off point for a great variety of opportunities for fly fishing, big-lake trolling, and salmon, steelhead, and trout fishing on the Dean, Atnarko, Bella Coola, and Blackwater Rivers. Likewise, the town of Anahim Lake provides interior access as well, especially to Moose Lake and its exceptional trout fishing on the Blackwater River.

Moose Lake is near the Coast Mountains—which include the tallest peaks in the province—and on the eastern bush-country fringe of Tweedsmuir Park, the largest provincial park in British Columbia. The surrounding area is full of rugged wilderness terrain, from boggy meadows and glacial rock formations to unending forests and brim-full lakes whose shallows bear the crisscrossing tracks of moose.

Dapping, the practice of dancing a dry fly on the surface of the water, is the oldest form of fly fishing.

It is just remote enough to have been spared from extensive logging and access roads, and probably not much changed since Alexander Mackenzie first explored this region 200 years ago. Having already traveled the great Arctic river that bears his name, Mackenzie struck westward from the Northwest Territories in 1793 searching for an overland route to the Pacific for the fur-trading North West Company. He ultimately found a low pass to the sea near Bella Coola. Today, parts of the Mackenzie Trail are accessed by horseback and floatplane from Moose Lake.

The Blackwater is one of the finest rainbow trout flowages in the province—and a small, swift, brush- and tree-lined gem. There are other flowages like this here, however, as well as a variety of remote turquoise lakes with easy trout pickings and no identification on the maps.

Northern region. In the northeastern sector of the province, the area known as the Peace River Alaska Highway region includes the cities of Dawson, Fort Nelson, and Chetwynd, and covers vast stretches of lightly fished wilderness. Charr, arctic grayling, whitefish, Dolly Varden, and rainbow trout are on the angling menu, and anglers can choose from hundreds of rivers to pursue these species. At least two dozen of these and a half-dozen lakes are easily accessible along the Alaska Highway.

The coastal northwest region has the steelhead and salmon runs previously noted, and also some interior lakes and remote small rivers that are often overlooked. Some of the coastal rivers are reached via helicopter, an exhilarating experience but a rather common one inland in northern British Columbia. The mountains here form a divide that separates Pacific and Arctic watersheds, so that rivers on one side flow northerly, and on the other side flow southwesterly through Alaska.

Inland, perhaps 40 miles from the town of Atlin and accessed only by floatplane, is one of the finest lakes in western Canada. This is Hall Lake, a narrow 12-mile-long body of water that features numerous rocky shoals and a fair number of islands. It has barely been fished but compares extremely favorably with its better-known neighbors—Atlin, Teslyn, and Gladys Lakes.

From early June until early September, the attraction is lake trout, including 15- to 20-pounders; pike up to 20 pounds; and a nonstop parade of grayling. Couple a visit here with a wild river salmon experience, and you simply have the best that the Pacific Northwest has to offer.

BROACHING

Also known as broach to, this nautical term refers to the unplanned, sudden turning of a boat so that it is broadside to the waves and wind and in danger of capsizing or swamping.

BRUSH

A collective term in freshwater for flooded bushes and small trees, the tops of large trees that have fallen into the water, and isolated piles of material that have been placed in the water to attract fish. The latter is called a brushpile *(see: fish attractor)*, which is a small tree or group of small trees bundled together, weighted, and strategically placed on the bottom of a lake.

Brush can provide excellent fishing opportunity for largemouth bass, and sometimes other species, depending on the depth and location. Bushes are a common characteristic of many reservoirs, where they exist on flats, along tributaries, and in shallow locations subject to flooding during high water. It includes buckbrush, small willows, and assorted shrubs, most of which can thrive when flooded as well as when dry. Fallen treetops exist in all types of waters, but obviously near shore. This usually means that they are in shallow water, although in some places the bottom drops sharply away from a wooded shore and the water can be up to 20 feet deep where a treetop has fallen.

Where there is a lot of fishing pressure, as occurs on most lakes and reservoirs, it is important to develop a system for approaching these places and fishing them properly.

Brush and bass.   Bushes or small trees showing in the water usually mean that the water level is high. High water causes more food in newly flooded areas for small fish—and thus more small fish for predators like bass. Bushes offer ambush cover to bass and draw food.

In natural lakes, bushes may grow along shorelines or around the shore of islands. Bushes along mainland shorelines usually indicate that there is a couple of feet of water near the shore, and perhaps an undercut bank. The bass are close to the edge here because these bushes don't extend very far into the water. Usually they are just temporarily flooded. When fishing shore-based bushes, you may be able to get close if the water is turbid; but when it is clear, you have to stay a reasonable casting distance away. If you can get close, it pays to pitch a jig or plastic worm to the cover. If you have to stay back because of water clarity, a surface lure, especially one with subtle motion that doesn't move too far too fast, is a good bet.

If the fish are not aggressive and/or the water is clear, try a slow-moving lure like a soft jerkbait or Texas-rigged worm. These should be cast parallel to the cover rather than perpendicular to it because it is unlikely that a bass will come far out of the cover to get it. Therefore, you need to work the lure as close to the cover as possible, for as long as possible; casting parallel accomplishes that.

Much of the same is true for bushes that are around an island or marshy hummock, although water may extend farther into this brush and thus bass may get back into this cover. Focus attention on the points of the island brush cover and on the pockets that indent the island. If the bass are not aggressive, perhaps because of cold water, a front, or angling pressure, they are likely to be deeper in this cover and tougher to coax into striking. Pinpoint presentations, and perhaps low-light approaches, may be necessary.

In reservoirs, bushes and small trees are usually found in patches near or away from the shoreline. High water often means a lot of bushes; the trick is figuring out which ones to fish. Bushes on points are an obviously important place to concentrate, and so are bushes along creek channels, in shallow bays, along flats, and in small coves or pockets. Isolated bushes are likely to have fish, as are bushes that stand out from others because they are on the points of a cluster or the edge of an opening; large bushes frequently harbor bigger bass.

Bushes may hold fish from springtime, when the water starts warming, through the fall. In midsummer, however, when the water is low and very warm in the shallows, the shallowest bushes are unlikely to be productive. On the other hand, shallow bushes may be very productive in the spring when the water is warming and bass are preparing to spawn. Thus, in spring, bushes in backwater areas are likely to be better than bushes along a mainland shoreline, but the reverse would be true later in the season. Bushes located along creeks would also be good in the summer.

Fallen treetops and bass.   Fallen trees are a common bass cover, particularly on natural lakes and ponds, and in many places they remain as cover for a long time, regardless of water levels. They usually fall nearly perpendicular to the shoreline, or on enough of an angle from the shore to put all the

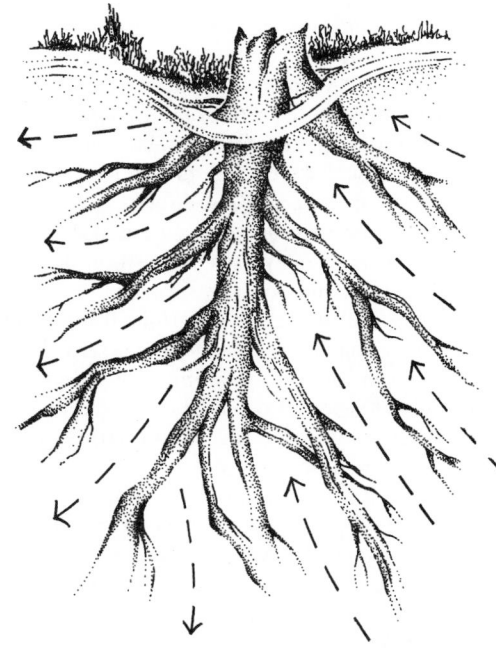

When fishing for bass among the snaggy cluster of a fallen tree, you must retrieve your soft worm, weedless jig, or spinnerbait through lanes and parallel to the limbs.

B

High water, common to reservoirs in spring, often floods brush; this is a scene at Lake Eufaula, Alabama.

upper branches into the water. These branches, limbs, and trunks provide cover for bass to ambush prey; in time these objects collect organisms that attract small fish, which attract other fish, and soon a food chain has developed around the tree.

Fallen treetops are obvious spots to fish for large-mouth bass, and they do see a lot of lures. Some trees attract numerous bass; others may hold just one or two. Those holding only one may hold the king of the pond. A fallen treetop on a point would be an exceptional place to find bass, but that seldom happens, although a tree close to the point or just around the corner can be just as attractive. Fallen treetops near a creek channel, in a location also having other cover (like lily pads or grass), in flooded backwater areas, and on rocky shorelines or banks with riprap, are especially worthwhile. If the water is extremely shallow, the tree is unlikely to hold bass, except in spring at spawning time and in late fall. With a few feet of depth or more, and preferably some shade, the tree could attract bass throughout the season.

Not all fallen treetops are alike; some are much thicker than others. Recently fallen ones may be full of leaves, which offer cover and shade. Bass may be suspended in the limbs, underneath them in the deeper water, or back up near the trunk in the thickest part of the tree.

Proper approach. Whenever you're fishing brush, you should approach it strategically for several reasons. First, the cover may hold a number of catchable fish. Second, you don't want to spook the fish. Third, heavy cover like bushes and small trees means a lot of limbs and roots that can snag a hook and around which a bass will charge once it has your lure. The fewer snags you incur the better, and if you're ready to muscle a fish away from cover, you've got a better chance of landing it.

The clarity of the water and the depth will influence how you approach brushy cover. Generally, bass are spooked if you bring your boat into very shallow water, especially if you make noise. Also, if the water is clear, you shouldn't bring your boat too close to the cover. A lot of bass waters, especially in the south and in reservoirs, are fairly turbid, especially in spring and early summer. Turbidity means you can get closer. Many waters in northern locations, and also natural lakes, are quite clear throughout the season. When the water is clear, you cannot get too close to fish or their cover without alarming them. Within reason, you can get closer if the brushy cover is thick and has depth to it. But if it is shallow and sparse, you cannot.

These are generalities, but the point is that conditions should dictate how you approach the cover; you can always change if you find things different from what you expected. For example, if bass are feeding heavily on minnows in the shallows, as they often do in the fall, then you might be able to get close to thick cover even in shallow, clear water because the fish are aggressive.

Fishing close to brush entails pitching and flipping jigs or worms, or short-casting spinnerbaits. Longer casts allow the use of these lures as well as surface or near-surface lures and sometimes crankbaits. Shorter casts and closer presentations are generally preferable because accuracy is better, less time is spent casting and retrieving, more presentations to the cover can be made, and you likely will fish deeper in the cover, which is often where the fish are. Longer presentations make it difficult to get lures to deeper cover and to work effectively in it.

Whether you're approaching brush from a distance or close by, first cast to the edges rather than to the heart of it. This may pick off a fish on the fringes, or it may bring a fish from the interior of the brush to the edge to strike your lure. Casting around the edges of brush may pick up aggressive fish without lessening your chances of drawing a strike from other fish in this cover. The reverse is not true; if you cast into the middle of the cover and catch a fish and then have to battle it out, chances are any other fish in that cover will be too disturbed to catch for a while.

Larger bass, however, are likely to occupy the thicker and deeper part of the cover. If you are specifically targeting larger fish, you may not want to fish the fringes of cover, but go right for the whole enchilada. Also, when the sun is out, target your approach to the shaded areas, keeping in mind that the thickest limbs or trunks provide the most shade.

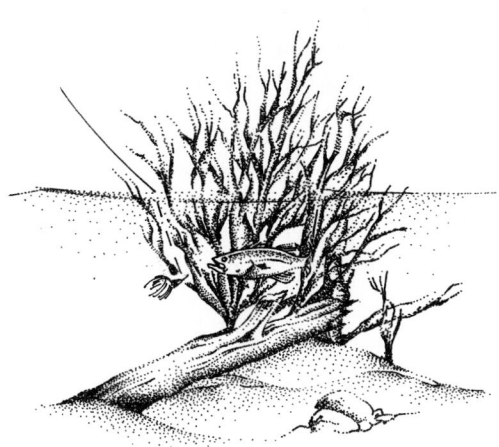

When fishing a jig for bass that are lurking in a bush, get the jig directly on the edges and in the midst of the bush.

Since you want to fish in, around, and through this type of cover, you must make accurate presentations and avoid getting hung up. Often, the first cast to a bush or fallen treetop is the one that gets rewarded with a strike, so if an errant first cast snags a limb in or out of the water and you have to jerk it free or go over to liberate it, you can usually kiss that cover goodbye.

It is also important to make strategic casts so that the path of retrieve goes with the flow, so to speak. You don't want to retrieve a lure crosswise to a series of limbs, but rather lengthwise with one limb. If you're going to dabble a jig into a fallen treetop, try to get over the top of it, or extend your rod tip over the top of it, so that the presentation is vertical in the brush and thus less likely to snag. Presenting the jig from a distance, where it has to crawl over a succession of limbs, is more likely to cause a snag.

So fish the edges first to draw out bass; then probe the inner sanctum with casts that fish the right places in the right direction.

Lures for bass in brush.   Clearly it is beneficial to use weedless or relatively snag-free lures in bushes and treetops, especially if they are thick. You can certainly use lures with exposed hooks around the edges of this cover and over the top of the submerged portion.

A spinnerbait, which is a relatively snag-free lure even though it has an exposed hook, is a favorite for brush fishing. That hook is a single one, and it rides up rather than down, so it doesn't hang up that readily. Additionally, vibration, flash, and ability to be worked through cover make a spinnerbait dynamic for fishing bushes and fallen treetops. The flashes mimic the look of small baitfish in the water, and the vibration makes it detectable by fish, even when they cannot see it very well. This is a lure for drawing aggressive fish, however, and out of necessity it is fished on a steady retrieve. When fish are active, a spinnerbait can be fished fairly quickly; but if not, it has to be slowed down.

Large spinnerbaits cast well but are not always the ticket, especially if the local food comprises very small baitfish. You may not know what the food is, but if a large spinnerbait, say $5/8$-ounce, fails to produce, then you try dropping down in size, either to a $3/8$-ounce or perhaps even to a $1/4$-ounce. A spinnerbait with tandem blades, especially a rounded Colorado blade followed by a willowleaf, is a good bet for brush, but don't overlook using a lure with a single large round blade for extra vibration. Tandem blades stay up better in the water, and when it's necessary to fish slowly, these are a better choice. Both styles can be fished through the tops of brush on a steady retrieve, but they should be worked through lanes in this cover if any exist, and rolled over limbs as well as bumped into trunks, limbs, and the like before being rolled over or around them. This draws strikes from some fish that are close to the cover and not chasing.

To help make a spinnerbait more snag-free, do not put a trailer hook onto it, and bend the overhead arm closer to the lower body.

The primary lure for close-quarters flipping is a lead jig with a rubber skirt, weedguard-protected hook, and trailer. Most anglers use a pork trailer, but a plastic lizard, eel, or other adornment can be used, and the dressing on the shank can also be bucktail instead of rubber tentacles. These lures are very unobtrusive and are fished slowly, which makes them excellent for sluggish bass and bass deep in cover, not to mention larger-on-average fish.

Many anglers tend to fish a jig too fast in brush because there is a lot of it and they want to cover as much ground as possible. However, if the fish are not aggressive, then it may take a couple of presentations to a good-looking bush to draw a strike. It may be necessary to work the jig down through the limbs as well. Bass that are suspended will take a jig before it gets to the bottom, but those on the bottom usually do not come up into the brush for it. Pay attention to whether you catch fish up or down, so you can repeat this effort as you move from bush to bush. If bass are suspended in brush, then it might pay to use a light jig, which will not fall through the cover as quickly.

Worms can also be flipped, or cast from moderate distances. Rigged Texas style, and with the slip sinker pegged so that it doesn't slide, a worm will ride through limbs without snagging, although sinewy curl-tail worms tend to grab onto wood like an opossum. A jerkbait worm, however, which is rigged without a sinker and fished in a slow stop-and-go manner and through the cover, can be very effective. Sometimes fish will take these worms when they are cruised through the top of the cover, and other times when they settle down into the midsection.

Surface lures are always a candidate for fishing over and near cover, and their commotion, especially if it can be generated with slow tantalizing retrieval, can draw explosive strikes. Surface lures present some problems around brush and fallen treetops, however. They are usually of necessity fished around the fringes, which means they have to appeal to an active or aggressive fish. Many anglers try this because it isn't too difficult, and the fish may wise up to this. Also, a multi-hooked surface lure can snag on the brush when a fish grabs it and dives for his inner sanctum, so the chances are greater of losing a fish that strikes such a lure because it gets into the cover, than they are with single-hook lures. Nevertheless, poppers, minnow-style stickbaits, walking stickbaits, and sometimes propellered plugs or a buzzbait, can produce around this cover.

It is also possible, incidentally, to use a crankbait near brush or over submerged brush. A suspending plug, for example, can be effectively worked through the tops of a bush or fallen tree limbs. Also, some buoyant diving lures can avoid snagging limbs with a stop-and-go retrieve, but they are usually best for brush in deeper water rather than for bushes and fallen treetops in shallow environs.

Panfish in brush.   It is common to find panfish around brush. Shallow flooded bushes provide spawning habitat in the spring for crappies, and fallen treetops can be a place to catch crappie, bluegills, and other panfish, especially if the treetop is thick and there is 5 to 10 feet of water at the end of the tree. These species are seldom fished in the same manner as bass in bushes or treetops, although large panfish will occasionally strike a spinnerbait or plug. This is rare but may be indicative of the presence of fish of similar size.

If the water is turbid, panfish anglers can quietly get close to brush and sit near or on top of it. Small jigs fished plain or tipped with a piece of worm, or such live bait as minnows, crickets, and worms, are the top choices. Hooks should be light wire so that they can be straightened if they snag on the cover and freed (they can be rebent for continued use), and both jigs and bait can be fished beneath a small float or bobber. Fishing vertically is best to minimize snags, and if you can't get close enough to the cover to do this, it may be necessary to use a long (perhaps cane or telescoping) pole for precise presentation.

In deeper water, submerged brush is often a target of anglers who seek panfish, and a lot of hidden brush in lakes and reservoirs is planted by anglers specifically for this purpose. Similar tactics, as well as the use of vertically fished jigging spoons, work in these places.
See: Fish Attractor; Flipping.

BRUSHGUARD
Synonymous with weedguard, a piece of plastic, metal, or rubber that covers a fish hook to help prevent snagging in cover.

BRUSHPILE
A tree, treetop, or group of small trees bundled together, weighted, and strategically placed on the bottom of a lake to attract fish. Many brushpiles are made of cedar trees or various Christmas trees, and placed near private docks on large lakes and reservoirs for crappie and bass fishing.
See: Fish Attractor.

BUBBLE
See: Casting Bubble.

BUCK
A mature, male fish in spawning mode; this term is usually applied to anadromous *(see)* spawners.

BUCKTAIL
(1) A type of streamer fly, tied with hair or other fur.
See: Fly.

(2) A jig dressed with hair.
See: Jig.

(3) A large in-line spinner featuring a single or treble hook dressed with hair, used in casting for muskellunge and northern pike.
See: Spinner.

BUFFALO, BIGMOUTH   *Ictiobus cyprinellus.*
Other names—buffalofish, common buffalo, lake buffalo, slough buffalo, blue buffalo, baldpate, bullnosed buffalo, brown buffalo, stubnose, pug.

A member of the Catostomidae family of suckers, the bigmouth buffalo is so called because of its humped back. Its body form resembles that of the carp. A fairly important commercial species, the bigmouth buffalo has white flesh of excellent quality. It is seldom caught by anglers, although it may be hooked by accident on occasion. These run-ins provoke high expectations by the angler, owing to the fish's size and pulling power.

Identification.   The robust and deep-bodied bigmouth buffalo has a large head with a big, distinctively oblique, and toothless mouth. This terminal, thin-lipped cavity angles downward when closed, although the edge of the upper lip is practically on a level with the eyes. The sickle-shaped dorsal fin is characterized by a taller lobe at the middle of the back that tapers off into a shorter lobe; the whole fin extends to the caudal peduncle. A comparison between the bigmouth and smallmouth buffalo reveals that the smaller mouth of the smallmouth buffalo is nearly lateral when closed, and subterminal—angled downward—as is more typical of suckers. It is the only member of the

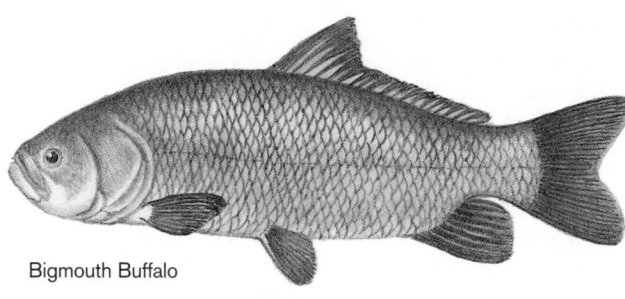

Bigmouth Buffalo

sucker family with its mouth directly in the front of the head.

The color of the bigmouth buffalo may be gray or coppery olive brown or slate blue on the back, and the sides are yellowish olive, fading to a white belly; all the fins are blackish in tint. Although the bigmouth buffalo resembles the carp, the latter can be recognized by its lone serrated spine at the front of the dorsal fin, whereas the former possesses only soft rays.

Size/Age. The largest of all the suckers, the bigmouth buffalo is said to grow to 80 pounds, although the all-tackle rod-and-reel record is a 70-pound, 5-ounce fish. It typically weighs between 3 and 12 pounds, and it has been known to grow as long as 40 inches. Most fish will live only six to eight years and grow to 20 pounds.

Distribution. Found only in North America, bigmouth buffalo occur in the Nelson River drainage of Hudson Bay, the lower Great Lakes, and the drainages of Lake Erie and the Ohio and Mississippi Rivers, from Ontario to Saskatchewan and Montana south to Louisiana and the Gulf of Mexico. They have also been introduced in Arizona, California, and Cuba with success.

Habitat. Bigmouth buffalo have a preference for pools and backwaters of small to large rivers and are found in lakes and impoundments.

Life history/Behavior. At about three years of age, adults spawn in April or May, waiting for water temperatures to reach the 60° to 65°F range. During their runs in the shallows, adults seek weedy areas in 2 to 3 feet of water to lay their eggs. The randomly scattered eggs stick to vegetation and hatch in 10 to 14 days without the protection of the adults. Young bigmouth buffalo stay in the shallows until the end of their first summer. They travel in schools throughout their lives and are capable of tolerating temperatures of up to 90°F in waters with little dissolved oxygen.

Food and feeding habits. Roughly 90 percent of the food a bigmouth buffalo eats is small crustaceans. It may feed on plant matter and algae as well, but insects, insect larvae, fish, and other bottom organisms are a very small part of its diet.

Angling. The bigmouth buffalo does not take ordinary baits or artificial lures and is seldom caught by anglers. There is virtually no dedicated fishing by anglers specifically in pursuit of this species. Most bigmouth buffalo are taken accidentally by anglers using some form of bait, especially a worm or doughball, or a small jig. Some are inadvertently snagged on the hook of an artificial lure. These large fish, which are often confused with carp, are strong and present a challenging fight, especially if hooked on light tackle. Like carp, they are overlooked for their sporting virtue, playing second fiddle to species that have historically received better press. Their rich flesh has made them an important commercial species, particularly along the Mississippi River.

See: Buffalo, Smallmouth; Suckers.

BUFFALO, SMALLMOUTH   *Ictiobus bubalus.*

Other names—razorback buffalo, roachback, thick-lipped buffalo, channel buffalo, humpbacked buffalo, high-back buffalo, river buffalo.

The smallmouth buffalo is second only to the bigmouth in the sucker family in terms of size and commercial importance, although it has a better reputation as a food fish than its larger relative. The smallmouth buffalo, however, is less abundant and subsequently less commercially important. Limited abundance contributes to its lack of significance as a sportfish, caught only occasionally or accidentally by anglers.

Identification. A deep-bodied and compressed fish, the smallmouth buffalo has a small conical head, a high-arched back, and a long dorsal fin. It also has a small, thick-lipped mouth with distinct grooves on the upper lip; the upper jaw is considerably shorter than the snout. Usually lighter in coloration than other buffalo, it is gray, olive, or bronze on the back, black to olive yellow on the sides, white to yellow on the belly, and it has an olive bronze sheen. The pelvic fins are olive or grayish black, and the other fins are indistinctly dark.

It bears a noticeable resemblance to the bigmouth buffalo, but it can be distinguished by a more compressed body and a more steeply arched back. It also possesses a smaller, subterminal mouth that lies laterally; the bigmouth buffalo's mouth lies at a slant. Characteristic of all suckers, the mouth extends downward, a noticeable feature when the smallmouth buffalo is feeding.

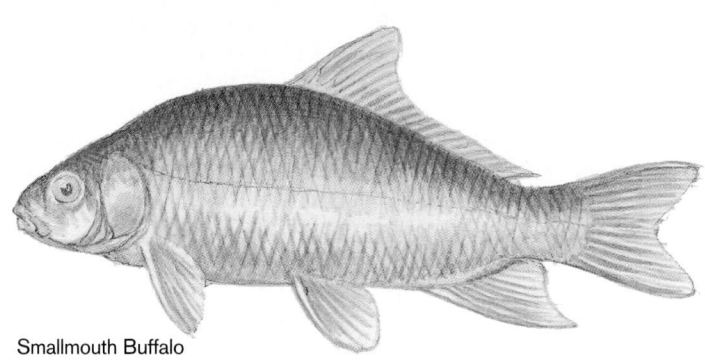

Smallmouth Buffalo

B

Size. Growing slower than the bigmouth, a smallmouth buffalo can reach 36 inches in length. The average commercially taken fish are in the 2- to 10-pound range, although some specimens weigh 15 to 20 pounds. The all-tackle world record for a smallmouth buffalo is 68 pounds, 8 ounces.

Distribution. Found only in North America, the smallmouth buffalo has a range similar to that of the bigmouth buffalo. It occurs in the Lake Michigan drainage and the Mississippi River basin, from Pennsylvania and Michigan to Montana and south to the Gulf of Mexico, and from Mobile Bay, Alabama, west to the Rio Grande in Texas and New Mexico. It is also found in Mexico and was introduced in Arizona. It is most abundant in the central states.

Habitat. Smallmouth buffalo inhabit pools, backwaters, large streams, main channels of small to large rivers, as well as warm lakes and reservoirs. They prefer slightly cleaner and deeper waters than do bigmouth buffalo, an explanation for relatively smaller numbers.

Life history/Behavior. Spawning and schooling habits are similar or identical to those of the bigmouth buffalo.

Food and feeding habits. Smallmouth buffalo feed on shellfish and algae, grinding it with the bony plates in their throats designed for that purpose; they eat more insects and bottom organisms than bigmouth buffalo do.

Angling. As with its bigmouth cousin, there is little concerted angling effort for this species.
See: Buffalo, Bigmouth; Suckers.

BUG
A type of floating fly.
See: Fly.

BUG TAPER
A specially designed type of weight forward fly line for casting large flies, deer hair bass bugs, and fly-rod poppers.
See: Flycasting Tackle.

BULKHEAD
An embankment or retaining wall along the waterfront, often made from wood but sometimes from metal or masonry. Bulkheads parallel the water and shoreline, and keep the water from eroding the shore behind it. They also serve as a buffer to boats and may be similar to a seawall. The water is usually moderately deep alongside a bulkhead, although this varies with tidal extremes. Bulkheads can be attractive to some species of fish and may be worth fishing along their length and at the corners.
See: Pier Fishing.

BULK SHOT
A number of split shot grouped at the same point on a fishing line.
See: Float; Sinker.

BULLHEAD, BLACK   *Ameiurus melas.*
Other names—catfish, black catfish, yellow belly bullhead, horned pout; French: *barbotte noire.*

A smaller member of the catfish family, the black bullhead is very popular due primarily to its fine culinary appeal. It is often stocked in farm ponds and raised commercially. An excellent table fish, the black bullhead has flavorful white meat that is marketed by some as a delicacy. It is sold either fried, broiled, or smoked.

Identification. Although the name would imply something else, the "black" bullhead may actually be yellowish green, dark green, olive, brown, or black on the back, bronze or green on the sides, and bright yellow or white on the belly. The entire body possesses a lustrous sheen. Only the young and spawning males are truly black.

Distinguishing the black bullhead from brown or yellow bullhead can be done by noting the rear edge of the pectoral fin in the latter two, which have a spine that is serrated with numerous sharp, thorny protrusions; those found on the spine of the black bullhead's pectoral fin are much less prominent and may be absent altogether. The black bullhead has dark chin barbels that may be black-spotted, whereas the yellow bullhead has lighter ones. Also, the black bullhead has a chubby body that is deeper than the body of both the brown and yellow bullhead. Another distinguishing feature is the squarish tail, which contrasts with the distinctly forked tails of the channel catfish, white catfish, and blue catfish.

Size/Age. Black bullhead reportedly grow to $24^1/_2$ inches in length, but they are most common at 6 to 7 inches and are seldom larger than 2 pounds. The maximum life span for black bullhead is approximately 10 years, although most live only 5 years. The world-record rod-and-reel fish was an 8-pounder.

Distribution. The black bullhead is found from southern Ontario west to Saskatchewan and throughout the Great Lakes, Hudson Bay, St. Lawrence, and Mississippi River basins, extending to New York in the east, the Gulf of Mexico in the south, and Montana in the west. Introduced populations exist in Arizona, California, and other states.

Habitat. Black bullhead inhabit pools, backwaters, and slow-moving sections of creeks and small to large rivers; they also inhabit impoundments, oxbows, and ponds. They have a preference for muddy water and soft mud bottoms, and are able to tolerate polluted water better than other catfish do. They prefer water in the 75° to 85°F range and tend to avoid cooler, clearer water.

Spawning behavior. Spawning takes place in May, June, and July, usually at water temperatures between 66° and 70°F. In weedy sections, the female clears away debris and silt to prepare the nest. When the male joins her, the two proceed to butt and run their barbels over each other's bodies, after which the male wraps his tail around the female's head as she lays the eggs. Spawning up to five times an hour, the female releases roughly 200 eggs each time, fanning the eggs in between spawning. Both parents fan the eggs until they hatch, and guard the fry, which leave the nest in compact schools.

Food and feeding habits. Adults feed primarily at night, whereas the young are most active at dawn and dusk. Young black bullhead feed on immature insects, leeches, and crustaceans; adults eat clams, snails, plant material, and fish.

Angling. Bullhead are a frisky but not especially strong fish at the end of line; they tend to spin when landed and may be problematic to subdue. The spines at the base of the dorsal and pectoral fins can "lock" into an erect position, which evidently helps protect the fish from predators by making it much harder to swallow. When handling bullhead, anglers must be careful to grasp the fish by positioning the finger behind these fins to avoid being painfully stuck by these sharp protrusions.

Bullhead are not held in great esteem from a sporting standpoint and are primarily pursued for their table virtues. Thus, most bullhead that are caught are kept for consumption. This influences angling methods to some degree, as does their primarily bottom-scrounging nature. Most targeted bullhead fishing is done with some form of bait, either by bank and shore-based anglers, or from small boats in backwater environs.

Bullhead are disdained by many anglers for several reasons: Like all catfish, bullhead are rather ugly; they are not a dainty insect feeder like trout but a scrounger; the spines of their pectoral and dorsal fins can inflict painful wounds that heal slowly; they tend to swallow bait and be caught deep, making unhooking difficult; and they are very tough to clean for the table.

Many fish, in addition to bullhead, have to be handled carefully to minimize injury. If you intend to keep a catfish for consumption, then it doesn't matter if it is hooked deeply; if you don't want to keep it, then you have to detect a "strike" early on and set the hook sooner to avoid hooking the fish deeply. And once you learn how to properly clean a small catfish, and do it a few times, that chore won't seem so onerous.

Bullhead are a willing fish for anglers early in the season in northern climes as soon as the ice goes out. The best early-season angling is usually at the mouth of small tributaries to lakes and ponds. If the flow is moderate, bullhead will ascend creeks and streams and can be quite abundant. In the spring, when the water is warming, bullhead are caught all day long. Later, in the summer or when the

Black Bullhead

water has warmed sufficiently, bullhead become nocturnal and are best caught after dark.

Bullhead and other small catfish are caught by anglers stillfishing with all sorts of baits. Nightcrawlers are the top natural baits for bullhead, and it is often worthwhile to put two on a hook, as bullhead possess a large mouth and a hefty appetite. Use a float or bobber on a bottom rig, with split shot and a long-shanked No. 1 or 1/0 hook, and get the bait just on or near the lake bottom. If fishing without a float or bobber, use a bell sinker with a couple of hooks spaced above it; some shore-based anglers use this setup for handlining because it can be cast a fair distance.

Bullhead are susceptible to a variety of other offerings, including many aimed at their larger catfish cousins and possessing scented characteristics. These include rancid cheese, doughballs, liver, fish, chunks of meat or fish, chicken entrails, congealed chicken blood, and an endless array of items that fall under the category of "stinkbait" *(see).*

For the purposes of sport, most light to medium tackle is suitable, including 5- to 6-foot rods of light to medium action; 6- to 8-pound-test line is the norm. For purely food-procuring purposes, and where legal, bullhead and other catfish are caught on handlines, setlines, and trotlines.

See: Bullhead, Brown; Bullhead, Yellow; Catfish.

BULLHEAD, BROWN *Ameiurus nebulosus.*

Other names—bullpout, horned pout, brown catfish, mudcat, common bullhead, marbled bullhead, squaretail, minister; French: *barbotte brune.*

With its firm, pink flesh of excellent quality, the brown bullhead is an exceedingly popular species, sometimes included in the panfish category. Of moderate commercial importance, it is frequently stocked in farm ponds and can be prepared and cooked in many different ways.

Identification. The head of the brown bullhead is large for its round and slender body, and the skin is smooth and entirely scaleless. The coloring of the brown bullhead is not always brown, as the name would imply, but it may actually range from yellowish brown or chocolate brown to gray or olive with brown or black scattered spots; the belly is yellow or white. The young are jet-black and are

Brown Bullhead

often mistaken for black bullhead, and adults sport darker pigmentation during the breeding period.

The brown bullhead is distinguished from the yellow bullhead by its mottled coloring (the yellow fish has an even coloring) and its dark brown to nearly black chin barbels (the yellow bullhead has yellowish or white chin barbels). Color does not necessarily distinguish the different species of bullhead from one another. Instead, an inspection of the pectoral spine on the pectoral fin of brown and yellow bullhead reveals sharp, toothlike serrations, whereas the black bullhead shows very weak serrations or the absence of them. Also, the tail of brown and black bullhead is squarish or somewhat notched; the tail of the yellow bullhead is more rounded.

Size/Age.   The average weight of the brown bullhead is less than a pound, and although fish in the 2- to 4-pound range are occasionally caught, this species seldom exceeds 3 pounds in weight. A 5-pound, 11-ounce fish was the largest ever caught on rod and reel. Brown bullhead can grow to 21 inches in length, although they are most commonly 8 to 14 inches long. Their life span is six or seven years.

Distribution.   Brown bullhead range from Nova Scotia and New Brunswick to Saskatchewan, from North Dakota to Louisiana in the west, and from Maine to Florida in the east. Native to the eastern United States and southern Canada, they have been widely introduced elsewhere.

Habitat.   Brown bullhead inhabit warm and even stagnant waters as well as sluggish runs over muddy bottoms. They occur in farm ponds, pools, creeks, small to large rivers, lakes, and reservoirs. Unlike other bullhead, they are found in large and deep waters, although they are able to withstand low oxygen concentrations and are known to bury themselves in mud to survive such conditions.

Spawning behavior.   Spawning takes place in April and May. Nests are made by one or both sexes by fanning out dish-shaped hollows in mud or sand. The pair engages in a ritual of caressing each other with their barbels, facing opposite directions as they finally settle over the nest to spawn. Between 2,000 and 10,000 adhesive eggs are released in cream-colored clusters, hatching in six to nine days. The eggs are guarded by one or both parents, although some fish have been said to eat them. Young brown bullhead are jet-black and resemble tadpoles, forming large schools that swim in surface

waters. The male continues to guard the young until they reach 2 inches in length and are able to protect themselves.

Food and feeding habits.   Brown bullhead feed mainly at night on immature insects, worms, minnows, mollusks, crayfish, plankton, and offal.

Angling.   See: Bullhead, Black.

See: Bullhead, Black; Bullhead, Yellow; Catfish.

BULLHEAD, YELLOW   *Ameiurus natalis.*

Other names—yellow cat, creek cat, white-whiskered bullhead, greaser.

Although the least commercially important of the catfish, the yellow bullhead can provide decent angling and is a good food fish. The meat of this small catfish has been described as cream-colored and one of the best tasting of all panfish, but it is subject to quick deterioration if not iced immediately after the catch.

Identification.   A moderately slim fish, the yellow bullhead has leathery skin without scales. The coloring ranges from yellowish olive to brown or almost black on the back with yellowish olive or brown sides, yellow or white on the belly, and dusky fins. Juveniles are dark brown or jet-black, making them difficult to distinguish from the young of black or brown bullhead.

The rounded tail helps to distinguish the yellow bullhead from other bullheads, which have squarish or truncated tails. On the back edge of the spine at the top of the pectoral fins, yellow and brown bullhead have sharp, toothlike serrations, whereas in the black bullhead the spine is only weakly serrated, if at all. Also, the chin barbels of the yellow bullhead are white, yellow, or pale pink, unlike the dark barbels of black and brown bullhead.

Size/Age.   Yellow bullhead usually weigh less than a pound, although they sometimes reach a weight of 3 pounds. The most common length is between 7 and 11 inches, and they can be as much as 18.3 inches long. Because they have less of a tendency to overpopulate than do black bullhead, they are less likely to be stunted. The world-record fish is a 4-pound, 4-ounce specimen. They can live up to seven years.

Distribution.   Yellow bullhead inhabit most of central and eastern North America, ranging in the east from New York to Florida and in the west from southern Quebec to central North Dakota and south to the Gulf of Mexico. As with other

Yellow Bullhead

bullhead, this fish has also been introduced outside its original range and is most common in the center of its range.

Habitat. With a preference for clear waters, gravel or rock bottoms, sluggish current, and heavy vegetation, yellow bullhead are found in pools, ponds, streams, small to large rivers, and small, shallow lakes. In comparison to the brown bullhead, they are more common in smaller, weedier, and shallower bodies of water. They are also more tolerant of polluted water and low oxygen levels than most other types of bullhead. They are most abundant at water temperatures between 75° and 80°F.

Spawning behavior. In May and June, sexually mature fish of 3 years and older move into shallow water at temperatures in the upper 60s or low 70s. After finding a suitable site, one or both of the parents constructs the nest, which consists of either a shallow depression in an open area or a 2-foot-deep burrow in the bank in a protected area. Clusters of cream-colored adhesive eggs, numbering from 2,000 to 6,000, are released and fertilized. The male guards the eggs and the fry hatch in 5 to 10 days, after which the young continue to be protected by the male in a tight group until they are able to protect themselves.

Food and feeding habits. Yellow bullhead are nocturnal scavengers that feed by smell and taste. They eat crustaceans, immature aquatic insects, snails, small fish, dragonfly nymphs, crayfish, mollusks, and bits of aquatic vegetation.

Angling. See: Bullhead, Black.

See: Bullhead, Black; Bullhead, Brown; Catfish.

BUMPER, ATLANTIC

Chloroscombrus chrysurus.

Other names—French: *sapater;* Spanish: *casabe.*

The Atlantic bumper and its Pacific relative (*Chloroscombrus orqueta),* are two of the smaller members of the jack family. Both species have not been greatly studied, and there is some speculation that they may be the same.

Identification. Although the bumper doesn't have a high back, it has an extended belly and a very thin body. With an overall silvery coloring, it has greenish tints on the back and yellow highlights on the sides and the belly. It also has a yellowish tail. There is a black spot on each gill cover and a black saddle on the base of the tail.

Size. Bumper rarely weigh more than half a pound and can reach a length of 10 inches in the western Atlantic or 12 inches in the eastern Atlantic.

Distribution. In the western Atlantic Ocean, Atlantic bumper are found north to Massachusetts, off Bermuda and south to Uruguay, as well as in the Caribbean Sea and the Gulf of Mexico. In the western Atlantic they range from Mauritania to Angola.

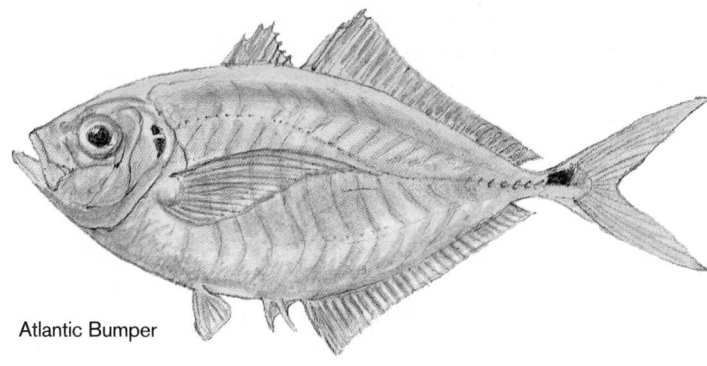
Atlantic Bumper

Bumper are said to be absent from the Bahamas and the Caribbean. The Pacific bumper ranges from Peru to California.

Habitat. Inhabiting brackish and saltwater, bumper occur over soft bottoms in shallow water. They are common in bays, lagoons, and estuaries.

Life history/Behavior. Small bumper have been observed in offshore waters, but they frequently range along sandy beaches. They travel in extensive schools, and juveniles are often found in association with jellyfish.

Angling. This fish is only an occasional and incidental catch by anglers. When caught, the bumper often emits a grunting noise.

See: Bumper, Pacific.

BUMPER, PACIFIC *Chloroscombrus orqueta.*

Other names—French, *sapater;* Spanish: *casabe.*

The Pacific bumper ranges from Peru to California and is a very similar species to the Atlantic bumper.

See: Bumper, Atlantic.

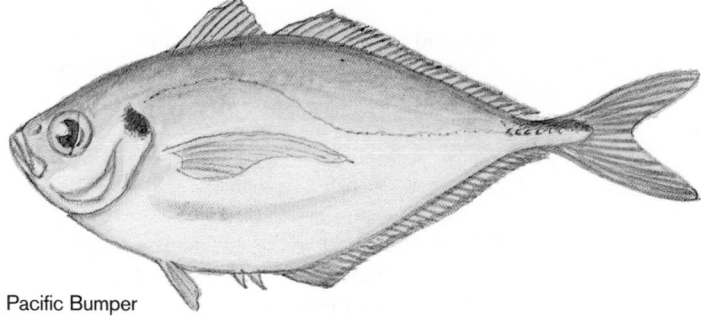
Pacific Bumper

BUNKER

A term for menhaden *(see).*

BUOY, MARKER

See: Marker Buoy.

BUOYS

Buoys are the principal daytime aids to navigation encountered by boaters. These are man-made objects strategically placed on navigable waterways by the United States Coast Guard and by appropriate state agencies on waters within the state boundary and without access to the sea. Buoys mark hazards, denote location, define routes, and conform to a standard color and numbering system. Most unlighted buoys are of the "can" or "nun" variety; some have lights, and some also have bells or gongs.

In many waters, buoys mark reefs, shoals, channels, and bars, and can be significant in helping to identify fishing areas depending on the species sought. In northern waters where ice may be encountered, buoys are removed for the winter and may not be returned until midspring; anglers who are on the water in late fall and early spring must proceed cautiously.

Other aids to navigation encountered by boaters include daybeacons, which are fixed structures; minor lights, which are the equivalent of lighted daybeacons; lighthouses; and channel markers. Channel markers are the least formal of all aids and may or may not have lights or painted signs.

Fishing around buoys. Some species of saltwater fish are attracted to buoys and channel markers, no matter how small the object or structure and its foundation or anchoring means might be. Cobia are often caught around these, as are tripletail, drum, snapper, amberjack, and, on occasion, other species.

Boaters should approach buoys and channel markers slowly, shutting the outboard motor off at a distance and allowing the boat to drift past the object or within reasonable casting distance of it. The shallower the water the more this is true. Engine noise will likely drive fish away. Consider the direction of wind and current in order to position the boat for a proper drift, and work the surface and near-surface water first, trying to draw an eager fish away from the buoy or marker. If you don't catch a fish immediately, try another drift or two, and try getting a little deeper, probably with a bucktail jig. If the water is deep and the current is too swift to make a good deep presentation while drifting, you may have to drop anchor well upcurrent to position the boat right next to the structure. Then you can fish a jig or bait.

Often, when the tide or current runs hard, there is little action at these locations. Keep trying. Sometimes buoys and channel markers produce fish when there is little or no water movement.

See: Navigation.

BURBOT *Lota lota.*

Other names—eelpout, pout, ling, cusk, lawyer, lingcod, gudgeon, freshwater ling, mud blower, lush (Alaska), maria (Canada); French: *lotte, lotte de riviére;* Spanish: *lota.*

The only freshwater member of the Gadidae family of codfish found in North America, Europe, and Asia, the burbot is often caught accidentally by anglers fishing for other species. Although it is a popular food fish in Europe, its ugly appearance makes it unappetizing to a fussy majority of Americans. It is mainly sold in salted form for ethnic consumption in North America, but is also a source of oil and is processed into fishmeal; the liver is high in vitamins A and D and is sold smoked or canned in Europe.

Identification. The elongate shape of the burbot resembles an eel or a cross between an eel and a catfish. It has been mistaken for a catfish, and in some places it is called an eel, although it is neither. It also looks like a smaller and slimmer version of the saltwater cod. Other distinctive features include tubular nostrils, a single chin barbel, and a rounded tail. The soft-rayed fins are also noteworthy in appearance: The pectoral fins are large and rounded, the first dorsal fin is small and short, and the second dorsal and anal fins start near the middle of the body and continue to the tail. It has a wide head, small eyes, and small, embedded scales that produce a slick skin.

The burbot has a mottled appearance, due to a dark brown or black pattern scattered over a yellow, light brown, or tan background; there may be regional color variations, including light brown, dark brown, dark olive, or even yellow. The anal fins have a dark edge to them.

Size/Age. Full-grown fish average 15 inches in length and less than a pound in weight. Burbot that are caught by anglers usually weigh several pounds and are occasionally in the 8-pound class, although they can grow much larger. An 18-pound, 11-ounce fish holds the all-tackle world record, but Alaska has produced larger fish, at least one of which was reportedly almost 60 pounds. Some are able to live for 20 years.

Distribution. The burbot is common throughout the circumpolar region above 40° north, especially in Alaska, Canada, the northern United States (including the Missouri and Ohio River drainages), and parts of Europe. It is absent from Scotland, Ireland, the Kamchatka Peninsula, the west coast of Norway, extreme western British Columbia, Nova Scotia, and the Atlantic Islands.

Habitat. Occurring in large, deep, cold rivers and lakes, the burbot are found in depths of up to almost 700 feet. It inhabits deep water in summer and moves shallower during summer nights.

Spawning behavior. By the time it is three years of age, the burbot is sexually mature. It is one of the few species that spawns in mid- or late winter under ice, doing so at night in shallow bays in 1 to 4 feet of water over sand or gravel; occasionally it will spawn in rivers in 1 to 10 feet of water. Burbot may produce more than a million spherical, amber eggs at one time, although the average amount is half that number. Without a nest or parental protection, the eggs hatch in four to five weeks.

Food and feeding habits. Young burbot feed on plankton and insects, graduating to a diet made up almost entirely of fish, especially perch, cisco, and whitefish. They will also eat mollusks, fish eggs,

Burbot

plankton, and crustaceans. Rocks and other indigestible items have been found in their stomachs.

Angling. Most burbot caught by anglers deliberately fishing for them are taken in the winter under the ice. Many are caught incidentally by ice anglers fishing for lake trout. Jigging spoons tipped with a minnow tail, and leadhead jigs tipped with a minnow, are the top producers. Applying luminescent paint on lures to make them glow in greater depths may be helpful. A dead minnow fished on the bottom also catches burbot in the winter. In early spring and late fall, when the water is cold, burbot remain shallow, and can be caught on a slowly worked lure. Some anglers in northern locales use cutbaits to stillfish for burbot in rivers on summer nights. Generally, however, they are deep and beyond the reach of most anglers once the water is warm.

Burbot are slow swimmers, and they don't chase after swiftly moving lures, which possibly explains why they are held in low regard by many anglers. Another explanation is their looks and a tendency to roll their eel-like tail around while squirming when an angler attempts to unhook them. Nevertheless, burbot are an excellent food fish, and some anglers find them preferable even to walleye. Their flesh and liver are held in high esteem in Europe, and the roe is consumed as well in Scandinavian countries.

See: Cod and Hake.

BURPING
A technique, usually used by fisheries professionals and occasionally by anglers, for relieving the pressure that has built in the air bladder of a fish that has been retrieved rapidly from deep water and is to be released. Burping is performed only on species that have a pneumatic duct connected to the air bladder, which allows them to expel air and make more extensive vertical movements; it is primarily used for lake trout and salmon.

See: Catch-and-Release.

BUTT CAP
The end covering at the base of a fishing rod. In fly rods this is often removable, covering a portal for the optional placement of a butt extension or fighting butt (see).

BUTTERFISH   *Peprilus triacanthus.*
Other names—American butterfish, Atlantic butterfish, dollarfish, pumpkin scad, sheepshead; French: *stromaté fossette;* Spanish: *palometa pintada.*

The fatty and oily quality of the meat of the butterfish does not detract from its reputation as an excellent food fish. It is sold fresh, smoked, and frozen and may be prepared in many ways; the meat is white, tender, moist, and contains few bones. The fat content of the flesh varies greatly over time, at its minimum in August and its maximum in November.

Despite its culinary significance, the butterfish's importance to anglers is as a live or dead bait for larger saltwater gamefish and as natural forage for assorted species. The shape of the butterfish resembles that of some members of the jack family.

Identification. An oval fish, the butterfish has a very thin and deep body and a blunt head. The anal and dorsal fins are equally long. Butterfish are silvery fish with pale blue coloring on the back and upper sides, which often have irregular dark spots and usually possess 17 to 25 large pores directly underneath the dorsal fin.

Size/Age. The butterfish grows quickly, although it rarely exceeds more than 1 pound in weight or more than 12 inches in length. It is usually a short-lived fish, although it is thought to be capable of living longer than four years.

Distribution. Inhabiting the western Atlantic Ocean, butterfish occur in waters off eastern

Butterfish

Newfoundland and the Gulf of St. Lawrence in Canada, ranging down the North American coast to Palm Beach, Florida. They are also found in the Gulf of Mexico.

Habitat.   Butterfish live and feed in large, dense schools along the coast in near-surface waters less than 180 feet deep and in the 40° to 74°F range. They may also inhabit brackish waters and in the winter may move into deeper water. Juveniles are usually associated with floating weeds and jellyfish.

Life history/Behavior.   Sexual maturity is reached when butterfish are two years old and close to 8 inches in length. Spawning occurs once a year from May through August in offshore waters. The eggs float freely until they hatch within two days; juveniles enter coves or estuaries to conceal themselves in floating weeds and among jellyfish tentacles for protection from predators.

Food and feeding habits.   Feeding primarily on jellyfish, butterfish are one of very few fish that eat such low-nutrition foods. Their diet also consists of assorted small worms, crustaceans, squid, shrimp, and fish.

Angling.   The butterfish species is of no direct value to anglers other than as a baitfish. It is caught commercially in trawls along with squid, hake, scup, flounder, and skate, primarily in the spring and summer, when large schools migrate inshore and northward.

BUTTERFLYFISH   *Chaetodontidae.*

There are 114 species and 10 genera that are classified under Chaetodontidae, although the entire family is better identified by its two main subfamilies, the butterflyfish and the angelfish (Pomacanthinae). These differ in size, the former

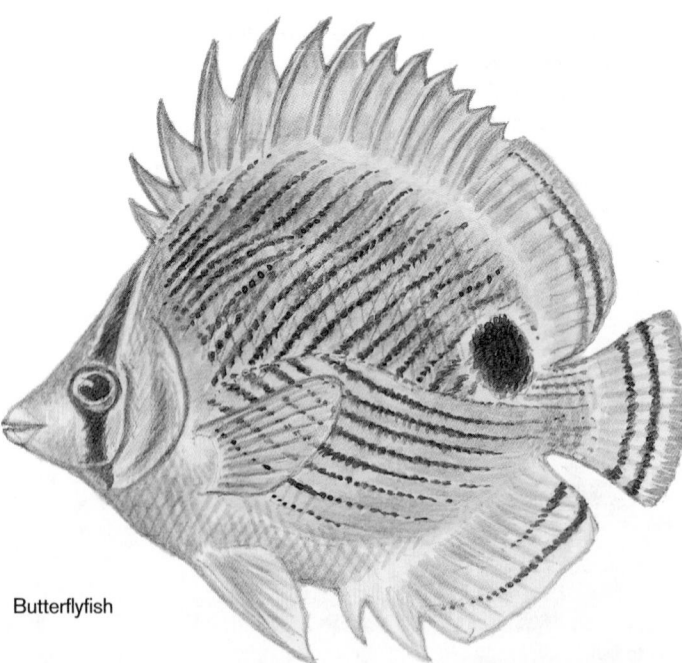

Butterflyfish

being small, swift swimmers; the latter being larger and slower swimmers. Butterflyfish can also be distinguished from angelfish by their lack of spines, found on the preopercles of the angelfish.

Butterflyfish are brightly and strikingly colored, making them among the most beautiful fish in the sea and in aquariums. They earned the common name "butterflyfish" from their graceful movements and from their coloring; the scientific name *chaetodont* comes from the bristlelike teeth common to all family members.

Common shallow-water species include the foureye butterflyfish (*Chaetodon capistratus*), the spotfin butterflyfish (*C. ocellatus*), and the banded butterflyfish (*C. striatus*). Deeper-water species include the reef butterflyfish (*C. sedentarius*), the Caribbean butterflyfish (*C. guyanensis*), the bank butterflyfish (*C. aya*), and the longsnouted butterflyfish (*Prognathodes aculeatus*).

Identification.   Conspicuous and brightly colored, butterflyfish are small, compressed fish that have disk-shaped bodies. They also have rounded to emarginate tails and densely scaled dorsal and anal fins. Among the butterflyfish is a variety of jaw sizes and shapes specially suited to different feeding methods. They have small mouths and lines of small, bristlelike teeth. Butterflyfish larvae have bony plates or armor that cover the entire region of the head.

Butterflyfish have several methods of protecting themselves from potential predators. Of note is the "eye spot" found near the tail on many species. The true eye is often camouflaged by a dark band to trick predators; some fish have even been seen swimming backward, which further confuses predators as to which end is the head. Also, the deep bodies and the dorsal and anal spines make them difficult for predators to consume, and their narrow width lets them slip into crevices.

Size/Age.   Butterflyfish range from $3^1/_2$ inches to 12 inches, although most are less than 6 inches long.

Distribution.   Found in the Atlantic, Indian, and Pacific Oceans, the majority of butterflyfish inhabit the Indo-Pacific region.

Habitat.   Occurring in marine and brackish environments, these reef fish are found in tropical, subtropical, and warm temperate waters. Coral reefs and rocky bottoms are preferred habitats for butterflyfish.

Life history/Behavior.   Butterflyfish have a prolonged larval stage that lasts two months or longer. The larvae have thin bony plates instead of head bones, which vary considerably in shape and design between butterflyfish. These fish ordinarily travel alone or in pairs, the pairs being described as nearly inseparable and thought to be exclusive throughout their lives.

Food and feeding habits.   They are usually active by day, feeding on an assortment of crustaceans, small invertebrates, fish eggs, and algae;

some butterflyfish have more specific diets. The ornate butterflyfish is an example of one type of butterflyfish that has short jaws, used to pinch off pieces of coral polyps. The long-nosed butterflyfish *(Forcipiger flavissimus)* has a different type of mouth with elongated jaws that act as forceps and pick food from crevices in coral. Some species pluck parasites off larger fish, living in symbiosis with them.

Angling. Butterflyfish are an incidental catch for bottom anglers.

BUTT EXTENSION

See: Fighting Butt.

BUZZBAIT

See: Surface Lure.

BYCATCH

The portion of a commercial catch that is not targeted and is either economically undesirable or is governmentally regulated and, therefore, cannot be landed. Sometimes referred to as incidental catch, bycatch is discarded at sea and often results in nearly 100-percent mortality. The size of fish caught as bycatch is directly related to the shape and size of the mesh used for the targeted species. One example of the extent of the problem: In the Southeast and Gulf of Mexico shrimp fishery, trawls with small mesh are used to retain shrimp, causing as many as 10 pounds of undersize finfish bycatch to be taken for each pound of shrimp.

Although the impact of bycatch-induced mortality on stock recruitment is unknown, the unhealthy condition of many of the world's saltwater fisheries has focused attention on factors contributing to the decline of desirable stocks. Efforts have been intensified by the public to bring about a reduction in bycatch as a conservation measure, and in some cases by the commercial fishing industry as a means to avoid more restrictive regulations because bycatch caps are set for certain species. When the caps are met, the fisheries are closed even if the target species quota has not been landed.

Bycatch can include protected marine mammals, such as porpoises that get caught and killed by commercial tuna fishermen; smaller fish than can be harvested or marketed; and a host of assorted marine life that is not part of the target catch, such as small prey fish scooped up into shrimp nets. These are all incidental. Species that cannot be kept or that have no economic value at market are discarded, usually with total mortality. Coastal anglers have seen the dead small-fish bycatch of commercial trawlers littering the surface of the sea for great distances. In some places, recreational anglers buy or barter bycatch discards from shrimpers to use for their own angling purposes, or these anglers fish closely around shrimp boats because the discarded

All of these small fish on the surface were discarded by the trawler on the horizon.

bycatch draws various species and sometimes provides good angling opportunity.

Bycatch can have serious implications to the food chain. Since each species has a role in the community, the removal of an important food item through bycatch could adversely affect species that eat that item. However, predators often eat a variety of food items. Reduction in the numbers of a single prey species may lead to an increase in another prey species that the predator will readily consume, although bycatch of prey species may lead also to the reduction in numbers of multiple prey species. It is generally thought that less bycatch, rather than more bycatch, is more desirable for maintaining a balance among the various species in a community.

Research on selective gear has caused changes in some commercial fishing practices. The development of a shrimp separator trawl used in North Atlantic waters, for example, reduces bycatch of small groundfish. As a result, many New England states have passed shrimping regulations requiring separator trawls to be used in state waters. However, a lot more must be done to reduce bycatch in these and other fisheries.

Relation to angling. For anglers, bycatch is a mixed blessing. On the one hand, it can contribute to the decline of some desirable fish stocks. On the other hand, the bycatch can be used to greatly assist angling. On balance, the former should outweigh the latter.

B

The most pernicious bycatch problem occurs with commercial shrimpers. Shrimp trawlers rake in a lot of bycatch. They are prevalent in the inshore and coastal waters frequented by anglers, some of whom habitually use and depend upon shrimp-boat bycatch for use in their daily angling activities, especially when fishing for tuna, shark, kingfish, and reef fish.

From a conservation standpoint, and for reasons previously noted, it is desirable to eliminate bycatch entirely and to avoid wasting important marine resources. When anglers use bycatch, they are indeed using something that would otherwise go to waste (discarded in the ocean), but they are also helping to support and subsidize commercial fishing, and even helping to make it more difficult to get bycatch reduced or eliminated. The ethics of using bycatch (usually as chum) are therefore muddy ones. Some people feel that it is more important to stop buying trawled shrimp so that there is no market for trawling, buying farm-raised shrimp instead. Others advocate catching your own bait or buying frozen bait rather than taking the shortcut of using bycatch.

See: Fisheries Management.

CADDISFLIES

Caddisflies belong to the scientific order Trichoptera, a term derived from *tricho,* meaning hair, and *ptera,* meaning wing, owing to the fact that hairs cover the wings. They are a large group of hardy organisms that have adapted to many types of aquatic environments. Their life cycle is different from that of mayflies *(see)* and stoneflies *(see)* since they have no nymph form; it consists of egg, larva, pupa, and adult stages, with most of the cycle being in the wormlike or grublike larva stage. Typically, caddisflies have one generation (hatch) per year, but many have several overlapping generations annually.

Many caddisfly larvae construct cases or houses out of a variety of different materials, including rocks, sand, gravel, twigs, leaves, or other debris, using a gluey substance secreted from their back end. The short, sticklike case is dragged along with the larva as it searches for food on the bottom of a stream or lake. Often, the methods and materials a caddisfly uses to construct its case can be helpful in identifying its taxonomic group. Certain caddisflies (family Hydropsychidae) are also known to spin webs for trapping food from flowing water. Fish eat the larva, case and all.

When it is time to mature, the caddisfly larva develops into its preadult stage, the pupa, in which the larva changes form inside the now-sealed cocoon-type case. The pupating period takes several weeks; then the pupa emerges, quickly migrates to the surface, and hatches into a winged adult. The appearance on the surface is brief, because most caddisflies appear suddenly, bounce a few times, and fly off, looking much like moths. The adults do not hold their wings upright at rest like mayflies, but fold them over their abdomen in tentlike fashion. The brief period of emerging pupa and winged adult provides quick foraging opportunities for fish.

Caddisfly

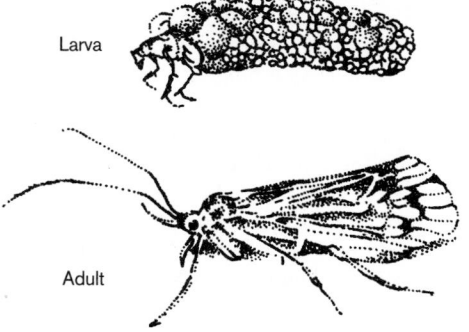

Larva

Adult

Caddisfly adults live from several days to several weeks depending on species. They mate in flight. Some females deposit their eggs on the water, alternately drifting and bouncing across the surface; yet other species land on the surface and swim to the bottom to deposit their eggs. Both behaviors provide significant feeding opportunity for fish, even more so than for other aquatic insects during the egg-laying period. The mating flights usually occur in the afternoon and evening, and may appear as a swarm. Hatches of caddisflies are drawn out well over the season.

Caddisfly larvae are up to $1\frac{1}{2}$ inches long and are mostly distinguished by these characteristics: three pairs of segmented and usually hooked legs on the upper middle section of the body; two small fleshy extensions at the end of the abdomen that may have a hairy or feathery appearance and end in a single hook; filamentous gills that may be present on the underside or end of the abdomen; and no antennae, or antennae that are very small and inconspicuous. They also have a characteristic motion, known as the caddisfly dance, of wiggling back and forth and then up and down in the water.

Caddisfly larvae may be confused with the larvae of dobsonflies, fishflies, alderflies, beetles, or aquatic caterpillars. Caddisfly larvae can be distinguished by the presence of single hooks on the end of each leg and at both tips of a slightly forked abdomen; dobsonfly and fishfly larvae have a forked tail with two distinct hooks on each fork, and similar beetle larvae have four hooks extending from a single point on the end of the abdomen. In addition, caddisfly larvae do not have long pointed tails (like alderfly) or caterpillar-like legs (like aquatic caterpillars or watersnipe fly larvae).

Like dobsonfly larvae, the caddisfly larvae may have fluffy gills on the underside (along the belly), but caddisflies do not have the fleshy or hairlike appendages protruding from the sides of the abdomen that are characteristic of dobsonfly, alderfly, fishfly, or certain beetle larvae.
See: **Aquatic Insects.**

CALIFORNIA

California is an angler's paradise. How could this not be the case in a state that covers nearly 159,000 square miles, has 2,674 square miles of inland water, and spans 3,400 miles of shoreline? California leads all of the states in numbers of

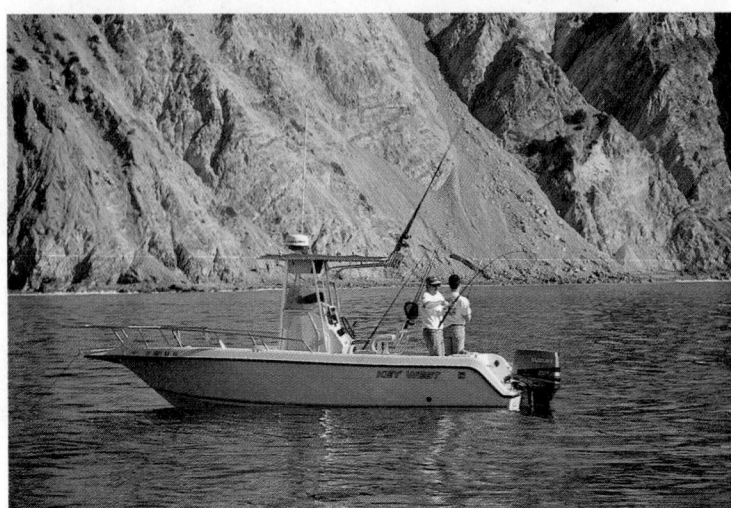
Yellowtail anglers enjoy a double hookup off Catalina Island.

C

licensed anglers, with more than 2 million, and it's small wonder. With thousands of lakes, and with people on the eastern boundary only 220 miles from the ocean, there is a plentiful and accessible array of fishing opportunities in the Golden State, almost all of them available year-round.

Near the Mexican border, anglers can experience sizzling saltwater action not only in the ocean, but also at an inland waterway, the Salton Sea. San Diego's city lake chain is home to world-class double-digit-size largemouth bass, and around the Los Angeles metropolitan area, Catalina Island and other offshore areas provide enviable opportunities for a variety of species, particularly yellowtail and huge white seabass. At nearby tiny Irvine Lake, trout anglers catch more trophy rainbows than anywhere else in the state.

Along the central coast, diversity in the salt extends from schools of albacore tuna to king and silver salmon, and in freshwater, from numerous bass lakes to trout streams. Farther inland, some of the finest mountain trout fishing in the country exists on both slopes of the majestic High Sierra.

Fishing is equally varied in Northern California. Large waterways like the Sacramento River Delta and San Francisco Bay yield striped bass, sharks, and sturgeon, while freshwater sites range from large Lakes Tahoe and Shasta to numerous small lakes and wild trout streams and rivers.

Getting a handle on the breadth of California's fisheries is a challenge, but separating the state angling opportunities into three broad segments—trout and salmon, warmwater/bass, and coastal and offshore fishing in saltwater—makes that challenge less daunting.

Trout and Salmon

Trout are the most popular gamefish species in both freshwater and saltwater in the Golden State, and California's wide range of trout waters is guaranteed to satisfy anglers, no matter how they fish or what means they use.

Numerous man-made impoundments in Southern California are within an hour's drive of many of the cities and towns between San Diego and Los Angeles. These lakes have unfairly received the reputation of being simply put-and-take reservoirs, but innovative stocking programs at many have resulted in annual catches of numerous trophy trout over 5 pounds.

Deeper Southern California lakes, including those in the San Diego reservoir system, sustain a trout population all year long. Many planted rainbows hold over through the winter and grow to healthy proportions. These trout lazily feed on abundant threadfin shad and are not restricted by short seasonal growth periods, as are trout in the colder and higher regions of the state.

In the northern part of Southern California, the complexion of the trout fishery changes somewhat. Trout in lakes such as Casitas share an important permanent niche in the lake ecology with warmwater species. These lakes have strong trout populations providing year-round sportfishing.

Trout are the primary sportfish in the midsection of California, through the Central Valley and into the High Sierra. Their dominance increases with elevation. Some High Sierra lakes, including Crowley, Bridgeport, and Twin, are renowned for their excellent trout fisheries. Many large rainbow and brown trout are consistently taken from these mountain lakes.

In Northern California, many small creeks, streams, and larger rivers sustain great trout fishing. Hotspots like the Owens, Truckee, and Walker Rivers have long been bonanzas for California fly anglers. This type of water is distinctly absent in the southern portion of the state.

Northern California possesses many semi-alpine lakes, such as Trinity and Shasta, that support warmwater species, including bass and trout. The Upper Sacramento River, Hat Creek, the McCloud River, and the Fall River are among the great trout waters, and thousands of pristine mountain lakes and streams are available throughout the region. Not to be overlooked are outstanding trout angling opportunities and extraordinary scenery in the far northeastern corner of the state.

Southern California. More trophy-size rainbows are taken from Orange County than from anywhere else in California. Irvine Lake, in particular, has an astonishing track record. Lake managers plant magnum-size hatchery-raised rainbows here. Although Riverside County has only a few trout lakes, they offer quality fishing. Lake Skinner is the top trout lake in this region, producing 1- to 2-pound fish nine months a year. San Diego County generates excellent winter and early spring fishing. Trophy-size trout are rare here, but the volume of fish at Poway, Jennings, and Cuyamaca is outstanding.

Lake Cuyamaca. Little-known Lake Cuyamaca is stocked with rainbows year-round, but the fishing is best in winter. Both bank and shore fishing are productive, especially along the log boom and the west shore. This is a scenic alpine fishery, where temperatures can drop to well below freezing during colder months.

Dixon Lake. Dixon is a small lake stocked with large quantities of pan-size rainbows from November through May. Trout in the 10-pound range add spice to the standard small plants.

Irvine Lake. A small reservoir in the foothills of Orange County, Irvine is a premier trophy trout fishery. Seasonal plants by the state are augmented with commercially raised rainbows that reach lunker size in a short time. Irvine has two trout seasons, one that starts in the fall and another that coincides with the High Sierra opener. It is estimated that more trophy-class fish over 5 pounds are caught at Irvine's spring opener than in all of the High Sierra lakes combined. Trout fishing is prime here from fall through late spring.

Lake Jennings. Covering only 85 acres, Lake Jennings has some of the best trout fishing in the region. It is regularly stocked from winter through early spring. Most trout are small, but a few 6- to 8-pounders are caught each year. Bank fishing is truly exceptional at Jennings. Boaters like to stillfish the deeper water near the dam.

Lake Miramar. Miramar excels in late winter and early spring, and produces quantities of trout following weekly plants. Trollers should try a flat-line approach in the early part of the season. Bank fishing at Miramar can be highly productive, especially during midweek, when there's less pressure.

Lake Poway. A stellar trout lake lately, Poway is loaded with chunky rainbows, many caught from November through May. Most of the fish are under 2 pounds, but 5- and 6-pounders exist. Weed growth is heavy here, so it's necessary to keep your offering above the bottom.

Lake Skinner. Another notable trout impoundment, Lake Skinner doesn't have lunkers, but weekly plantings of 10- to 14-inch rainbows keep anglers busy. The prime spot is near the spillway, especially if the water is flowing over the dam, which churns up the bait and stimulates the bite. Sheltered coves in the east and south ends of the lake, and long rocky points, are also good trout-holding spots at Skinner.

Lake Wohlford. From January through the end of May this small Lake Wohlford steadily produces small rainbows. Shore anglers should try the boat docks as well as Oakdale and Willow Coves. Boaters like the buoy line by the dam and the cove across from the docks. Salmon eggs, marshmallows, and nightcrawlers are standard trout baits.

Los Angeles area. Trout fishing in the Los Angeles area can be challenging. The key to success is timing, with late winter through early spring best. Most trout here are planted pan-size rainbows; however, commercial stocking augments the state's program and provides larger specimens up to 10 pounds.

Two unexpected treats a short drive from the heart of Los Angeles are the West Fork of the San Gabriel River and the Upper Sespe Creek. These are bona fide wild trout rivers offering some of the most spectacular angling in the state.

Fly anglers should consider exploring the three major streams of the San Bernardino Mountains: the Santa Ana River, Bear Creek, and Deep Creek. Each has its own unique brand of fishing and all are excellent destinations for the angler seeking isolated waters in crowded Southern California.

Big Bear Lake. Big Bear is the largest lake in the San Bernardino Mountains and is considered the best of all Southern California trout lakes. This mountain reservoir has year-round angling, including ice fishing in the winter, with best results from late spring through fall.

Floating baits are particularly good here since they suspend above the weedy bottom. Shore casting is productive in the deep water at the west end of the lake. And trollers do well during the height of the season, with flatline and lead-core strategies excellent options.

Fly fishing can be spectacular at Big Bear during the summer. Both shore casting and fly trolling with traditional fly fishing gear work well. Bubble and fly rigs give bank anglers and waders an excellent opportunity to take quality 1- to 3-pound rainbows.

Lake Casitas. Casitas is one of the most popular recreational destinations in Southern California. In spite of the crowds, the lake produces some quality angling for rainbow trout, which are stocked from October through May. Trollers generally catch the larger fish.

Lake Piru. Piru provides considerable angling activity from December through March, when rainbows are planted. The trout fishing at Piru seems to be unaffected by changes in water levels, which can fluctuate seasonally. Shore anglers should focus on the west shore. Trollers have the greatest success in the summer.

San Gabriel River. The West Fork of the San Gabriel River, in spite of its proximity to downtown Los Angeles, has some of the finest wild trout waters in the West. Good options are the area past the Rincon Ranger Station, and the section below the second bridge where Bear Creek converges with the West Fork. Ultralight spinners and dry flies produce in this river. Spring and fall are best for fly fishing, although it may be necessary to scale down all the way to tiny size-26 dry flies for clear shallow areas.

Bay Area/Central Coast. The San Francisco Bay area has a wealth of sites that offer surprisingly good trout fishing. Some are small urban lakes, whereas others—such as San Pablo near Berkeley—approach 1,000 acres. San Pablo Lake experiences excellent fishing for trout in the 3- to 6-pound range.

At other bay-area lakes, such as Parkway or Del Valle, weekly trout plants during colder months produce outstanding shoreline action for stocked rainbow trout. Occasionally these metropolitan lakes are also stocked with huge 8- to 10-pounders—the fish of a lifetime for many people—just a few minutes from downtown San Francisco.

Southern Sierras. Trout fishing can range from terrific to tough in the waters of the Southern Sierras. Huntington Lake can be a standout in the early season. The Kern River also has remarkably good fishing for the stream angler.

Huntington Lake. Rainbows, browns, kokanee, and a few wayward brookies abound at Huntington Lake. There is some good boat and shore activity for 12- to 16-inch trout, as well as larger holdover fish. The angler on foot has some 14 miles of shoreline to explore. Early May can be an outstanding time to fish Huntington.

Kern River. The Kern is one of the most popular fishing holes in the state. Some of the best fishing is in the area above Lake Isabella, starting at Kernville. Early in the season, many small rainbow trout frequent these waters. Some anglers may encounter a lunker brown or jumbo rainbow using artificials. The higher up you travel, the better the chance of tying into a trophy specimen, especially on dry or wet flies.

Central Sierras. This area has sensational angling with minimal pressure. The lakes in the Carson Pass offer exciting trout fishing. Backpackers can select from scores of lakes in this region of the Sierras, and only a handful of hikers each season visits these remote alpine lakes, which are teeming with rainbows, browns, and brookies.

Emigrant Wilderness Area. There's a wealth of lakes in the 100,000 acres of pristine Emigrant Wilderness Area, which is located about 30 miles west of Sonora in the western Sierra Nevada. The forested terrain varies from rolling hills to ridges and granite domes. The best angling is at the lakes in the southwestern portion of this wilderness. Fly fishing is the best strategy, especially for native brown trout; natural baits are also a good choice. Hikers might consider packing-in a small inflatable boat.

Anglers venturing into this region to find some of these high-country lakes should carry a good topographic map and a compass, and perhaps a GPS unit. Many are not on marked trails, and some rock scrambling may be necessary. Be sure to file a trip itinerary with the local ranger's office and obtain required permits before heading into this remote wilderness.

Mokelumne and Merced Rivers. The Mokelumne and the Merced offer excellent fishing. The Merced River from below Crocker-Hoffman Dam to Merced Falls has a solid population of small rainbows. Both dry and wet flies produce on this river, especially for anglers willing to wade.

Numerous prime runs along the Mokelumne River are worth trying. This river is best fished by wading, or from a boat when the water is high. Dry-fly fishing can be outstanding from late spring to early summer. Although plenty of legal-size rainbows are planted along the Mokelumne each

A trout fishing scene in the western Sierras.

season, 16-inch-class fish can be found in the quiet, less-accessible deep pools.

Lake Tahoe. A magnificent crystalline body of water, Lake Tahoe is the jewel of the Central Sierras and home to gigantic mackinaw trout. Submersible research vessels have observed schools of these fish in the 40- to 50-pound range. Anglers trolling for mackinaws use a variety of methods; deep fishing with large jigs tipped with minnows can be successful at times.

There are also considerable numbers of rainbows, kokanee salmon, and even brown trout at Tahoe. Near-surface trolling, especially in the fall, is often successful. Locals prefer plugs that mimic rainbow trout or have dark finishes, and they tend to troll fast in this clear water, to give rainbows and browns less opportunity to study the lure.

Baitfishing is best from a boat at the mouth of Emerald Bay and at Logan Shoals. Fishing from shore is difficult but is most successful after a big wind, when the surface water is churned up with forage baits and other food.

Yosemite National Park. Trout fishing at Yosemite means getting out of the valley and up into the high country. The Tuolumne Meadows area off Highway 120 is easily fished. The Dana Fork area holds larger trout, as does the Lyell Fork area along John Muir Trail, south of the meadows. This beautiful trout stream meanders through the Upper Tuolumne Meadows and offers good brook trout fishing in the morning and evening. Plan on a four-hour hike.

Backpackers can choose Edith, Wilmer, or Tilden Lakes out of the Hetch Hetchy Dam area. These lakes hold both brookies and goldens. More than 300 significant lakes grace the Yosemite high country, but there is good fishing at only about one-third of them.

Eastern Sierras. The Eastern Sierras get more angling pressure than any other part of the Golden State. Two of California's most majestic rivers, the Walker and the Owens, tumble through this region and are known for trophy brown trout. In addition, both Bridgeport and Twin Lakes hold brown trout exceeding 30 pounds. Many lunker hunters spend long hours at these lakes in quest of the fish of a life-time.

In the western U.S., there is perhaps no event that comes close to the excitement of the Lake Crowley Opener. This occasion signals the opening of the High Sierra season and is an essential part of the fishing year for hundreds of California anglers who visit the lake in quest of their first trout of the spring. The Eastern Sierras also hold dozens of other fine trout lakes and streams scattered throughout the magnificent wilderness lands of Inyo and Mono Counties.

Lone Pine, Independence, Big Pine area. The southernmost locales of the Eastern Sierras offer a series of fine mountain trout fisheries off access roads from U.S. Highway 395. There are creeks loaded with planted trout as well as trail heads into the wilderness areas. The high country provides good fishing opportunities at lakes ranging in size from 4 to 25 acres, at altitudes of 10,000 to 11,000 feet. Both rainbow and brook trout inhabit these lakes. The best months are June through September.

Bishop area. Bishop is one of the centers of Eastern Sierra fishing. The elevation of lakes in this area varies from 7,000 to 9,000 feet, although the higher-elevation lakes are accessible only in the warmer months. Bishop Creek, and the lake at its headwaters, are planted regularly and generate good angling. A few excellent trout lakes in this area are accessible by car. The headwaters of Bishop, Pine, and Rock Creeks are also good starting points for wilderness pack-in trout trips.

Lower Rock Creek, which runs from Tom's Place along Route 395 to Pleasant Valley Reservoir, is a very special trout stream. It holds both wild and planted fish, including large browns and rainbows. The upper reaches of this stream are accessible by a good trail and produce many wild brown trout. The last mile of Lower Rock Creek, before it empties into Pleasant Valley Reservoir, has an entirely different character. At the Los Angeles Department of Water and Power plant, Lower Rock Creek joins Pine Creek and the Owens River Aqueduct system to create a large river. Anglers catch many trophy browns and rainbows in this converging water. Pleasant Valley Reservoir is a highly underrated trophy trout fishery. There's a healthy population of medium-size rainbows in this impoundment, but the real treat is tackle-busting giant brown trout. There are a number of 20-pound-class fish here. Be prepared to do some serious rock hopping in order to get around the rugged shoreline. No boats are allowed, so all the hotspots must be approached along the bank. Early and late in the season are the best times, and it's good to use an outfit that permits long casting, as well as heavier line. Big spinners and spoons are a good choice, and magnum minnow plugs in rainbow trout finish are popular with lunker hunters.

Crowley Lake. As mentioned, there is probably no greater California fishing spectacle than the traditional opening-day extravaganza at Crowley, which is usually in mid-April and inaugurates trout season in the Sierras. Trout anglers from all over the West converge on this lake for the event. It is planted with hundreds of thousands of small rainbow trout each summer, and by the following season opener, these average almost a pound each. Trolling is the best method for catching larger rainbows and browns in the early season.

From August through October, a second (no bait) season goes into effect, as anglers gear up for trophy rainbows and browns. At this time of year, a legion of dedicated float tubers visit Crowley and work the weedbeds using flies that replicate small Sacramento perch, an important forage food for bigger trout.

The Owens River. The Owens produces many trophy-size trout. The two runs of the Upper Owens, from Benton Crossing and from Big Springs, are prime spots. The Owens Gorge below Lake Crowley also has a reputation for quality fish.

The Upper Owens River, which feeds Lake Crowley, is a meadow stream with open banks and excellent fly fishing water. Concentrate on the undercut banks in late evening. Good-size browns hold in these areas, and the section downstream out of Benton Crossing is especially good in the early spring for rainbows coming up from Lake Crowley to spawn. Excellent fly fishing here generates a lot of excitement.

Convict Lake. Located north on Route 395 a short distance above Crowley Lake, Convict Lake is one of the most beautiful spots in the Eastern Sierras, with rugged peaks surrounding clear, cold waters. Fishing for rainbows and lunker browns is generally best in late spring and early fall, but can also be good in summer months. It's possible to hike from Convict to about six small mountain lakes and numerous streams to find fishing and spectacular scenery.

Mammoth Lakes. Long recognized as a mecca for Southern California snow skiers, the Mammoth Lakes basin excels as a trout fishery in summer. This area is only a short distance off Route 395 above Crowley Lake. The town of Mammoth Lakes is a jumping-off point for a variety of good trout fishing experiences, including lake, stream, day-hike, and pack-in angling. There's a wide assortment of winding creeks and secluded mountain lakes in the immediate area.

One of the most popular local destinations is Twin Lakes, which offer good fishing for brookies, browns, and rainbow trout. Most are pan-size but can range up to 6 pounds. Lakes Mary, Mamie, Horseshoe, and George are accessible by car and provide good fishing using a variety of techniques.

The June Lake loop. Like Lake Crowley, the June Lakes area is a favored destination during the annual trout opener. June, Gull, Silver, and Grant Lakes offer sensational early-season limits and trophy trout. In general, bigger fish come from Gull and June. The best bank fishing is at Silver, and the largest volume of browns come out of Grant. Each has its own unique personality, but all offer great fishing as well as spectacular scenery.

Rush Creek. One of the most popular spots in the Sierras is Rush Creek in the June Lake Loop. The hottest stretch is just above Silver Lake. This creek is stocked weekly, so it usually has an ample supply of small rainbow trout. Rainbows and browns over 5 pounds are a realistic goal for the talented angler. The area between Silver and Grant Lakes is best for taking trophy fish.

Tioga Pass. The eastern gateway to Yosemite National Park, Tioga Pass is just north of the June Lake Loop. Ellery and Saddlebag Lakes along this road provide excellent fishing for the weekend angler. Ellery Lake holds quantities of rainbows, and almost all standard bait offerings produce. Saddlebag has rainbows, brookies, and some Kamloops; baitfishing or trolling are the best tactics here.

Twenty Lakes Basin offers excellent high-elevation fishing within a one-day hike from the Saddlebag area. Rainbows, brook trout, golden trout, and even cutthroats frequent Greenstone Lake. Shamrock, Odell, Lower Twin, and Potter are good for goldens. Leave prepared baits at home and try natural offerings.

Bridgeport Reservoir/Walker River. Bridgeport Reservoir is one of the most prolific waters for trophy brown trout in the state. Rainbows and browns from 1 to 4 pounds are common here; planted fish grow fast because of the abundance of food. Veterans start the season by trolling big trout-colored plugs for trophy browns; fan casting bigger spinners and spoons can also be productive. Early-season rainbows are caught by trolling; baitfishing is an excellent technique later in the summer.

The East Walker River flowing out of Bridgeport Reservoir is known for trophy brown trout; browns of 14 to 18 inches are common. Waders work the river in chest waders, using spinning or flycasting gear. Heavier tackle may be advisable, as it's possible to tie into a 20-pound brown.

Twin Lakes. The modest Twin Lakes are an excellent brown trout fishery, with specimens up to 25 pounds and tactics similar to those at Bridgeport. Bank fishing and trolling work particularly well. Most of the lunker trout landed at Twin Lakes are caught in windy, inclement weather or close to dusk, or both.

Northern Sierras. The Northern Sierras offer some of the most consistently good angling in California and experience limited angling pressure. For the person with time, these lakes provide an excellent alternative to the heavily pressured lakes elsewhere.

Lake Almanor. Trophy-size browns, rainbows, and king salmon (an experimental program that has been fairly successful) exist at Almanor, a lake with plenty of shoreline access as well as great fishing for boaters. Stillfishing with baits, and trolling—both around underwater springs—can result in a stellar catch. As water temperatures increase, trollers fish deep with flashing blades ahead of a nightcrawler.

Feather River. The North Fork of the Feather River flows along Route 70, between Lake Almanor and Lake Oroville, through the Feather River Canyon. Where accessible, the main river is good trout water. Perennial hotspots include the convergence of the North Fork with the East Branch of the North Fork, and the mouth of Yellow Creek, which are both just above the town of Belden. The Feather River has excellent fly fishing, and the North Fork supplies good baitfishing.

The Middle Fork of the Feather River is accessible along Routes 70 and 89 between Sloat and Portola. The annual stonefly and caddisfly hatch create good fly fishing opportunities. Tributaries out of Portola generate quality rainbows and browns early in the season.

Gold Lake Basin. Gold Lake is the most important trout fishery in this area. It is by far the largest lake and holds the biggest trout of all waters in this basin, including some mackinaws topping the 20-pound mark. Veteran anglers troll for these macs down to 100 feet during the summer months, and there are some bank fishing spots.

Truckee River. The Truckee River originates at Lake Tahoe and tumbles along Highway 89 toward the town of Truckee, then northeast along Interstate 80 to Nevada. The waters from Tahoe to Truckee possess pan-size rainbows and large native brown trout. Live baits account for some lunker browns here. Bigger browns and rainbows roam the 1-mile section below the Truckee lumber mill between Hirschdale and Floriston. The stretch of fast-flowing water that parallels Interstate 80 northeast of Truckee produces the best fly fishing action, and is one of California's finest fly fishing sites.

Yuba River region. Collins, Bullards Bar, and Englebright Lakes are located in the lower region of the Yuba drainage system, about 90 minutes northeast of Sacramento. These three reservoirs are fewer than 20 miles apart and provide fine trout fishing.

Collins is a 1,000-acre lake with an underrated trout fishery; it has ample populations of rainbows and browns supported by an expansive spring planting program. Bullards Bar is loaded with rainbows and kokanee salmon, mostly caught by trolling, with shallow action beginning in early February. Later in the season, kokanee range anywhere from 40 to 140 feet. Englebright Lake is another option for serious trollers; it has rainbows and browns, plus kokanee fishing that is frequently excellent.

North Coast. The North Coast is one of the most overlooked trout fishing areas in the Golden State. Trinity, Lewiston, and Whiskeytown Lakes are superb fisheries, and many different techniques work here. In the backcountry, Trinity Alps and the Trinity Divide are remote alpine lakes teeming with hungry trout. Even more remote is the Marble Mountain Wilderness, with scrappy brookies, rainbows, and browns. Trout fishing is restricted in this region to protect juvenile migratory fisheries.

The North Coast is home to most of the great steelhead and salmon streams in California. These include the Eel River, south of Eureka, and—farther north toward the Oregon border—the Mad, Redwood, Klamath, and Smith Rivers. These have legendary runs of steelhead and salmon, varying from late spring through early winter.

Lake Berryessa and Putah Creek. Lake Berryessa offers many opportunities for the angler, with rainbows that average 14 inches, trophy browns, and feisty Eagle Lake–strain rainbow trout. Trout season lasts from Memorial Day through mid-November. Baitfishing and flatline trolling are preferred methods at this lake.

The Trinity Alps Wilderness. More than 55 fishable lakes are located in these spectacular mountains northwest of Trinity Lake. Some are accessible by automobile; others require a multiday pack trip. Most are at elevations between 5,000 and 7,000 feet and hold brookies, rainbows, and browns. Live baits produce best in this area, with fly-and-bubble rigs a popular option.

Trinity Lake. A beautiful alpine lake, Trinity is on the southern edge of Trinity Alps, north of Redding. Trinity is heavily planted with 9- to 13-inch rainbows, and produces fish up to 20 inches that hold over each year. There is a smaller population of browns. Trolling generates good results at Trinity, especially in the dam area; stillfishing is productive in the west coves and the mouths of the feeder streams; and fly fishing is also an excellent option. Substantial numbers of kokanee salmon exist at Trinity; areas near the feeder streams are good later in the year for these fish.

Northeast Corner. *Pit River.* There's a natural fishery of 12- to 15-inch trout in the Pit River, with some up to 4 pounds. Fishing here requires caution while wading or shore fishing, because currents resulting from hydropower generation can be swift; watch for deep, hidden holes as well.

Lower Sacramento River. An excellent fishery for large native rainbows, the Lower Sacramento is often overlooked. Salmon can be caught from September through December, and fat rainbows are taken all year long. Anglers work The Lower Sacramento primarily in drift boats, from Redding to Red Bluff. Drift anglers who drag lures catch rainbows consistently. From late April through mid-September, the Lower Sacramento offers exciting fly fishing opportunities, especially for 10- to 22-inch rainbows.

Upper Sacramento River. One of California's premier trout waters, the Upper Sacramento has plenty of 10- to 14-inch fish, including wild rainbow and brown trout. There's the occasional brook trout here, among them trophy-size fish. The river's many deep pools are excellent for bait anglers, and the deeper pockets and tail-out areas provide good lure action; overall, however, these waters are known for outstanding fly fishing. Traditionally the best hatch has been from late July through early October.

Lake Shasta. Shasta's year-round fishery has one of the foremost trout populations in the state. Its 30,000 surface acres hold rainbow and brown trout, as well as Kamloops. Fishing is best in the early spring, when near-surface feeding peaks. Flatline trolling is particularly productive at this time. As water temperatures increase, the trout actively begin to pursue schools of threadfin shad; casters can score when they push the bait to the surface.

Warmwater/Bass

California is the most populous state in the nation and is also home to equally impressive numbers of bass, including northern- and Florida-strain largemouth bass, smallmouth bass, and some spotted bass. Since the 1970s, California has enjoyed a reputation for producing monster and near-world-record largemouth bass due to the cultivation and stocking of transplanted Florida-strain bass. Several 20-pound or better largemouths have made headlines, and anglers maintain an intense pursuit of both trophy and record-breaking fish in waters with big-bass potential. The Golden State's multitude of warmwater lakes and impoundments also feature outstanding angling for redear sunfish, bluegills, and black crappie. In addition, many reservoirs are home to popularly sought bullhead and channel catfish, as well as trophy blue catfish and striped bass.

Most California reservoirs are 1,000- to 3,000-acre impoundments, but some, like those on the Lower Colorado River and Lake Shasta, are expansive and complex fisheries. All receive a great deal of fishing attention, and the smaller ones, particularly near metropolitan areas, get very crowded. The following information is a brief summary of the top warmwater lakes.

San Diego Area. *El Capitan Reservoir.* El Capitan is one of the smallest big-bass fisheries in the state. At its maximum capacity, which is rarely reached due to seasonal water demands, the lake has only 1,100 surface acres and a bare 15 miles of shoreline. It is among the reservoirs in the famous

Stories of sea monsters may have been based on surface sightings of the dorsal and caudal fins of two or more basking sharks—which grow to 50 feet—swimming one behind another as they often do.

San Diego City Lakes group managed especially as a trophy fish factory. March and April are the choice times to fish for bass, and the first few weeks after the lake opens can be sensational.

El Capitan has an excellent population of 2- to 3-pound black crappie, which are best fished in the early spring in shallow, brushy flats. The lake also features giant channel and blue catfish in the 15- to 30-pound range.

Lake Henshaw. At only 1,100 acres, Henshaw is another relatively small lake. Located in northern San Diego County, it is flat and has minimal visible shoreline; when looking across the lake, you might feel as though you were fishing on a flooded meadow. Anglers catch northern-strain large-mouths here in modest numbers, and the lake receives little fishing pressure. The wind can howl across this unsheltered area and chill things down, even during the summer.

Henshaw is open and produces bass all year long. Spring is the best time, when the fish move shallow to the bank and are easiest to catch. The lake also has a solid population of pan-size black crappie, as well as bullhead and channel catfish.

Lake Hodges. Lake Hodges recurrently appears at the top of the list of best bass lakes in California. Many largemouths over 8 pounds are regularly caught from this 1,100-acre impoundment. Early in the season, the weekend crowds can be huge, with more than a thousand people sometimes waiting in line to get on the water.

Hodges is a premier flipping lake. In high-water years, miles and miles of tules line its shores. When the bass have moved up into the banks, tules almost anywhere on the lake hold some fish. Numerous coves and steep banks have excellent bass cover. Early spring, from March through May, is the best time to take a lunker-class fish. Fall action, using a variety of methods, can bring success.

Fishing for bluegills and crappie can be excellent at Hodges during the summer. In these warmer months, the lake produces limits of 3- to 5-pound channel catfish.

Lake Morena. Morena is a fine low-pressure alpine lake. It has been a true sleeper among Southern California bass fishing enthusiasts. Many Florida-strain largemouths between 7 to 10 pounds are caught here each year.

Winds can whip through this high-elevation lake, and it may get quite chilly. In good weather, however, the bass fishing is sometimes sensational, and just about every imaginable structure exists here. Morena turns on from late spring through summer. The water temperature—along with the bass bite—drops dramatically from late fall through winter.

Lower Otay Lake. Otay is one of the premier big-bass lakes in the world, and may be the best lake in the San Diego City system for early-season fishing. Otay annually yields a bumper crop of 8-pound-plus Florida-strain bass and is rivaled perhaps only by Lake Hodges for big fish. It's also legendary for immense catfish; both channel and blue catfish thrive here, and many double-digit specimens are landed from spring through fall.

Like most San Diego lakes, Otay is open only at certain times of the year. It is a tough lake in the hot summer months. For overall bass population, as well as trophy fish, the best time is in the spring and especially immediately after the lake opens in late January or early February.

Lake Sutherland. One of the smallest lakes in the San Diego chain, Sutherland has only 500 surface acres. This lake is also the most difficult to reach, stashed away in the hills outside the little hamlet of Ramona, about 45 miles northeast of San Diego. From late spring through summer, Sutherland is famous for its surface-busting Florida-strain largemouths, which can literally keep acres of water churned up for hours. The lake has an impressive population of these fish, and spring and summer are also good angling times.

Lake San Vincente. San Vincente is a famous impoundment in the San Diego City Lakes system. It has produced monster largemouths in the past, and there's an excellent possibility that a world-record bass swims in this lake. This canyon lake has only 1,000 surface acres and limited visible shore-line cover. Water clarity varies, ranging from very clear to stained. The fishing can be tough, however. Many anglers scale down to 6- or 8-pound-test line and learn to fish a variety of subtle baits. Mid-April through mid-May is the best period for sustained action. This is just before the spawn, when these Florida-strain fish move into shallower waters.

Los Angeles and Orange Counties. *Castaic Lake.* Castaic is one of the most popular fishing lakes in the state. Located 45 miles north of metropolitan Los Angeles, it hosts bass anglers from all over the West.

Castaic is comprised of two sections, the main lake and the after bay. The main lake covers about 2,500 acres, divided into two arms. Fishing is permitted in both arms, but water-skiing is allowed in only one arm—in the designated ski area. The after bay covers only 180 acres, with no powerboats allowed, but it has some of the best fishing at Castaic.

Weather permitting, this can be an outstanding bass lake, particularly for Florida bass, many of which are caught in double figures each year. Because the lake is heavily stocked with rainbow trout—a favorite big-bass delicacy—largemouths over 15 pounds are common.

Depending on fluctuations in water level, Castaic may have excellent shoreline brush or a lot of rocky banks. The bass hang around the steeper rocky walls, particularly those in the water-skiing area in the early morning and late afternoon. The longer rocky points and ledges in the fishing arm always seem to hold some bass, as does the buoy area at the far end of the ski arm. During the colder months, bass frequently move up from deep water during the day, particularly in the fishing-only arm. On this lake, the banks of coves traditionally are good during the spring spawn.

Lake Castaic also has a thriving striped bass fishery, and a number of fish from 15 to 20 pounds are registered each year.

Lake Irvine. Located almost in the center of suburban Orange County, Irvine has only 700 surface acres at peak water level. In the summer, it is heavily stocked with channel catfish and is open to night fishing. Many trophy blue catfish topping the 50-pound mark have been caught at Irvine. The lake has a solid population of black crappie as well as a small number of large white sturgeon. The bass fishing at Irvine can also be remarkably good. Many of the fish are 2- to 3-pounders.

Spring through fall is a good season for bass. Summer nights are also productive, especially during a full moon. Deep-water methods at this metropolitan lake can be effective too. Visit during midweek to avoid the heavy weekend pressure.

Pyramid Lake. A small impoundment north of Los Angeles, Pyramid has some of the best small-mouth fishing in Southern California, and modest populations of largemouth bass and striped bass. Although striper numbers aren't high, these fish can be good sized; 20- to 30-pounders are frequently caught. Spring and fall are the prime periods for bass; the stripers action runs throughout the year.

Riverside and San Bernardino Counties. *Big Bear Lake.* A longtime favorite of western anglers, Big Bear is $7^1/_2$ miles long and more than a mile wide, with more than 22 miles of shoreline.

The bass fishery is primarily comprised of largemouths, but smallmouths are also present. The bass are commonly found along numerous weed lines scattered throughout the lake. Anglers can target bass near docks and boulders, as well as at the dam on the western end. Fishing excels from late spring through fall.

This mountain lake frequently freezes in midwinter. It can be windy and chilly even in midsummer. Big Bear also has a great black crappie population, which can produce terrific fishing from spring through fall.

Lake Elsinore. Elsinore is a relatively small body of water. It has had a diverse history, as the water levels vary greatly with local rainfall. The lake has considerable submerged structure, lots of shoreline brush, and groves of trees. The northern-strain bass are ample; catches include many 2- to 3-pound fish. Fishing is hampered by endless ski wakes and heavy pleasure-boat traffic from late May through September; however, the lake excels in November and December as well as in the early spring, when the water is cool and boaters are few.

Perris Lake. Perris was once home to world-record spotted bass, but this species is a rare catch now. Perris does have one of the most dynamic largemouth fisheries in the state, however, producing many bass over 10 pounds annually. There's also excellent panfishing here for redear sunfish, bluegills, and black crappie.

There are few prime fishing spots, so anglers must slow down and work with diligence and patience. The dam, submerged islands, and the brushy east shore are favored. Largemouths can be caught all year here, including midwinter. Spring is the best time for overall action.

Lake Silverwood. A small alpine lake of a little over 1,000 acres, Silverwood is a major recreational playground for weekenders throughout Southern California. Located in the mountains north of San Bernardino, Silverwood has year-round largemouth bass fishing, with lunkers topping 17 pounds.

The canyon lake can be miserably cold in this mountain setting, however, generating some rough wave action. An anchor might be necessary when the electric motor struggles; there are few places to take cover. Late spring is preferred for bass, as they spawn later here than at lower elevations. Striped bass numbers are not great, but 25- to 35-pound fish are always a possibility.

Lake Skinner. Skinner is one of California's truly underrated bass lakes. It covers only 1,200 acres when the water level is at its highest. It has somewhat unimpressive terrain—gentle sloping banks, a few rocky points, some mud flats—but a fair amount of tule growth when the lake is up. It is populated with pure-strain largemouths.

Skinner is an excellent summer lake. Many bass anglers prefer to fish it from June through September, when the fish are feeding actively on threadfin shad. The spring action is fair, but if the water level is up, look for some nice fish in the tules. Late fall and winter are also good for slower presentations and deep-water fishing.

Skinner also features a large population of small striped bass, but some fish over 30 pounds exist here. Most striper activity is in open water. The lake is open all year long and receives greatest angling pressure when rainbow trout plants start in late fall.

Ventura and Santa Barbara Counties. *Lake Cachuma.* For sheer scenic beauty, it's hard to beat the mountain setting of 7-mile-long Lake Cachuma. It has more than 3,200 surface acres, and most of the shoreline is accessible. Northern-strain largemouth bass and smallmouths are available here, although the former are most common. Largemouths over 10 pounds have occasionally been caught, usually on live crawdads. The coves at Cachuma always seem to hold some fish, and have good moss and aquatic plant growth during the summer and fall.

Cachuma can be productive year-round. Summer is toughest due to the heat and increased boat traffic. Spring is good, and there is usually a prolific bite in the fall. Bass are landed here in the dead of winter, particularly with deep-water tactics.

Lake Casitas. Scenic Lake Casitas may well be the most heavily used body of water in California,

Competitive casting began in the 1860s at the same time as organized baseball was starting; it preceded both professional basketball and football.

and draws bass anglers from all over the West. Just 78 miles from Los Angeles, it is the first choice for weekend anglers and campers. Casitas lures serious bass anglers in quest of a world-record largemouth. It has a thriving rainbow trout fishery that bulks up these Florida-strain bass in a matter of years. Numerous fish over 10 pounds are caught each spring.

It is a large lake by Southern California standards, with more than 30 miles of shoreline and nearly 3,000 acres of water at its highest level. With its gin-clear water, however, Casitas can be a very difficult lake to fish. The most successful bass anglers are proficient with light line and subtle baits and techniques. An excellent population of redear sunfish resides at this lake. Panfish anglers target redears all year, although early spring is best.

Casitas is an exceptionally good lake in late winter and early spring, especially from the first few weeks of February through the first week of April. It is particularly tough in the summer and then picks up again in late fall. Those seeking the bass of a lifetime should try to fish the lake when the first warm rains fall in the early spring. The rain stimulates feeding activity, and big female bass move up from deep water to feed on the shallower points and ledges.

Lake Piru. Piru is a 1,000-acre lake about 50 miles north of Los Angeles. The northern bass bite can be fantastic at times, and these fish are not as difficult to catch as largemouths in other waters. Many anglers rate it highly for deep-structure angling in the cold winter months. Piru's bass usually eat well from December through February. The more obvious choice is March through May, when the bass spawn and move up shallow. Piru is a tough summer lake.

Colorado River. *Lake Havasu.* Lake Havasu is an immense and varied waterway lying between California and Arizona on the Colorado River. It spans more than 45 miles, from Davis Dam to the north to Parker Dam to the south.

It was at Lake Havasu that striped bass were first introduced to the Colorado River in the 1960s, and stripers and largemouth bass have been the main attractions here, although the lake also has crappie, channel catfish, bluegills, and rainbow trout. Havasu covers 25,000 acres, making it smaller than the upstream reservoirs; however, 450 miles of shoreline provide countless nooks and crannies for angling exploration.

One of the largest freshwater fisheries enhancement programs in North America was instituted here in the early 1990s, resulting in nearly 900 acres of strategically placed artificial habitat around the lake.

Havasu's largemouth bass frequent the main body of the lake, which has a lot of structure, as well as in the main river arm. There are sheltered coves, steep canyon walls, broken rock, moss beds, reefs, rocky points, and some trees and deadfalls in the lake proper. Out in the main river heading north, there are many coves, endless tule banks, deadfalls, sandbars, and some steep walls. Sometimes, the "bite" can be good in the lake and off in the river and vice versa.

Havasu is literally a year-round fishery. Spring is always popular for more aggressively feeding fish. However, fall and winter are good in both the main lake and river. Summer can be a little tough, but if you can find sanctuary from heat, day cruisers, and skiers, the bass can be caught.

Lower Colorado River. The immense lower Colorado comprises one of the most unique bass fisheries in the Golden State. Situated along the California border at the southernmost portion of the state, the section of the Colorado River from Parker Dam to Mexico is especially fertile. The river snakes for endless miles, and the banks are sometimes lined with massive tule growth, at other times with thick brush and deadfalls. Occasionally there are steep canyon walls to cast to, along with hidden lakes or backwater pockets, plus numerous small coves off the main river channel.

The lower portion of the river has excellent all-around fishing during the fall and the early spring. Because the water doesn't get that cold this far south, look for good action as early as January or February, when the bass hold tight to the shallow cover. For consistently outstanding catches of northern bass, however, it is hard to beat this area in the fall.

Navigation can be dangerous along this stretch of the Colorado River, with the current and sandbars posing tricky boating. The Lower Colorado also has excellent channel catfish and monster flathead catfish, the latter sometimes weighing more than 30 pounds. Black crappie and bluegills are caught in the calmer backwaters.

Central California. *Lake Isabella.* Lake Isabella is the premier trophy bass lake of Central California. It has more than 11,000 surface acres, and people speculate that this might produce a world-record largemouth someday. The lake annually produces many Florida-strain largemouths over 10 pounds and has an excellent population of both northern- and Florida-strain bass. Isabella's winds are notorious, however, and can make fishing impossible; it is also a tough lake through much of the summer.

Lake Isabella is also one of the top black crappie fisheries in California. Anglers catch hordes of these panfish every year, fishing the shallow flats, particularly in the spring and summer.

Lopez Lake. Lopez has minimal angling pressure for largemouths or smallmouths. It covers only 950 acres but has more than 22 miles of shoreline. The banks of this canyon lake are steep, and most shorelines are rocky. There is little visual structure and few flats. Good dropoffs, many rocky points, and some good submerged structure do exist here. A thriving smallmouth fishery has blossomed, and more of this species is showing up in the catch.

Lopez is good in the spring and fall, but summer is tough.

Lake Nacimiento. Nacimiento has more than 5,000 surface acres and 165 miles of shoreline. Smallmouths outnumber largemouths by about three to one, which is understandable with the predominantly rocky shoreline. Bass are sometimes hard to come by, however, because the water level fluctuates dramatically. Just when the angler has the lake figured out, the water might be drawn down almost 100 feet. Nacimiento is an excellent winter bass lake from November through March. Anglers will find some decent activity in the spring, more so on largemouth than smallmouth bass.

Nacimiento has a prominent white bass fishery, too. These panfish generate terrific sport for hours at a time when they're chasing schools of bait. The summer months become especially tough between hot days and widespread water-skiing.

Lake San Antonio. San Antonio is a 16-mile-long, 5,500-acre lake on the edge of California's Central Valley. It boasts a thriving northern and smallmouth bass fishery. When the lake level is up, there is a wealth of shoreline and structure to fish, compatible with a wide range of approaches. The lake is divided into two distinct parts: The western arm has shallows and flats, with numerous coves and minor points. The eastern arm has deeper cover, steep rocky walls, and long, extended points. The bass are typically biting in either one half of the lake or the other, but usually not both. Spring and fall can be excellent periods to fish San Antonio for both smallmouth and largemouth bass, but summer suffers due to heavy boat traffic.

San Antonio also offers excellent striped bass fishing. Although the stripers are primarily small, anglers catch many of double-digit weight each year.

North-Central Lakes. *Lake Berryessa.* One of California's largest lakes, Lake Berryessa is more than 25 miles long, up to 3 miles wide, and drops to 275 feet. Spanning some 20,000 surface acres, Berryessa produces about an equal catch of northern-strain largemouths and smallmouth bass, with some of the former having been caught at 10 pounds. A few jumbo-size Florida bass thrive here, as well some spotted bass. Midspring and fall offer the best fishing; smallmouths move shallow in the early spring, sometimes feeding around the smallest streams that enter the lake. By late spring, these fish—along with the largemouths—move into the larger creek arms to spawn.

Clear Lake. Stretching out over 100 miles of shoreline, Clear Lake is the largest natural lake in California. Located about three hours north of San Francisco, it has one of California's finest bass fisheries. Anglers annually catch many largemouth bass between 5 and 7 pounds, and 10-pounders are common in spring and fall.

Clear Lake is not particularly deep, but it has rocky, brushy banks, extensive tule growth, and many grassy areas. Some anglers compare the terrain of Clear Lake to that of typical lakes in the southeastern United States.

Indian Valley Reservoir. A 4,000-acre lake that is somewhat off the beaten path, Indian Valley nevertheless has a good population of northern-strain largemouth bass. It is about 90 miles from Sacramento and a short distance from Clear Lake, and is loaded with structure. March and April are the best months overall, but the lake produces good catches from midsummer through late fall.

New Melones. A fairly large lake covering 12,000 acres and spanning up to 8 miles across, New Melones has a large contingent of northern-strain largemouths and has become a popular spot for avid Northern California bass anglers. Loaded with structure, it excels as a late-spring bass lake, yet fishing is consistently good from summer through early fall. Those who know the lake take a share of winter bass with deep-water techniques.

Pardee Lake. Pardee has a terrific population of both northern-strain largemouth and smallmouth bass. Largemouths over 10 pounds have been recorded, as well as smallmouths between 3 and 5 pounds. The lake covers more than 2,000 surface acres and has 43 miles of shoreline, with a lot of action taking place along rocky banks. The better areas for both species are the south arm of the lake, where the Narrows are formed, and the rocky points and coves where the river runs into the lake. The channel arm with the rocky shoreline around Shad Gulch and Cave Gulch can also be productive.

Pardee's bass fishing is remarkably good year-round, with May and June best. Angling pressure is very light. The bass bite can be outstanding during the first few weeks in February when the lake reopens.

Sacramento River Delta. A complex waterway, the Sacramento River Delta can be an outstanding bonanza at times. Both largemouth and striped bass frequent this river system. The key to fishing both is to monitor tidal flow and current. Its many smaller fingers, eddies, tules, sandbars, and backwaters make the delta an intriguing place to fish. This large river system also requires some knowledge of navigation, as ocean-class freighters and large big-wake-generating vessels share the water on a continuous basis.

Western Sierra Lakes. *Lake Camanche.* Resting in the heart of mother lode country, Camanche has over 7,600 acres and 60 miles of shoreline to fish. Largemouths and smallmouths lurk in its many grassy areas. It also has a small population of spotted bass, which often prefer slightly deeper water. April and May are excellent months, with summer tougher, and fall again productive.

Folsom Lake. Folsom is one of the largest reservoirs in Northern California. Covering nearly 12,000 acres, it offers a variety of opportunities for both northern largemouth and smallmouth bass, which are divided between the two major forks of the lake. Smallmouths primarily thrive in the north fork, and largemouths in the south fork. Two- to

The cement that barnacles use to attach themselves to objects will not melt at temperatures above 6,000°F nor crack at −380°F.

C

4-pound largemouths are common; smallies run much less. Folsom is open all year but becomes a tough proposition in summer and winter. Anglers using deep-water tactics at the latter times. The best months are from April through June.

Lake Don Pedro. Don Pedro is one of Northern California's largest bodies of water, spanning nearly 13,000 surface acres at full capacity and offering in excess of 160 miles of shoreline. More than 26 miles long, this riverlike lake has numerous winding coves and creek inlets. It harbors an abundance of northern largemouths, with a few Florida-strain bass and a smattering of smallmouths mixed in. Most anglers pursue the fish from boats, and there is a wealth of good sites and cover. Although they make for tough fishing, March and April are the best bass months.

Lake Oroville. Lake Oroville lies behind one of the largest dams in the United States, and encompasses more than 15,000 acres in a deep canyon. The lake has primarily largemouths and smallmouths, but it holds a few spotted bass as well. Spring provides the best fishing at Oroville for northerns and bronzebacks, with summer tough, and fall good.

Northern Mountain Lakes. *Lake Almanor.* Lake Almanor offers fantastic smallmouth fishing. Like many California lakes, Almanor is a reservoir formed by a dam, in this case on the Feather River. A shallow lake, Almanor is about 13 miles long and up to 6 miles wide, and offers a magnificent view of nearby volcanic Mount Lassen from almost any place on the water. The smallmouth bass at Almanor are usually found in rocky areas or shallow flats, especially along the dam and the eastern shore. Smallmouth fishing is best from late spring through summer.

Lake Amador. Amador is a very small lake, with only 400 surface acres and a little more than 13 miles of shoreline, yet it is a genuine trophy bass fishery. Florida-strain largemouths were stocked initially at Amador in 1970, then again in 1973. From this initial plant, a quality hybrid population has emerged. Fish over 6 pounds are common, and a few top the 10-pound mark. The lake has a series of long, steep-sided arms and lots of underwater brushy structure. It is supplied only by runoff from surrounding creeks, so water temperatures vary widely with the seasons. The best fishing is during the spring spawn, when the water is clean.

Lake Shasta. With more than 30,000 surface acres and numerous coves, arms, and inlets, Shasta constitutes one of the largest and most varied inland waters in the West. The lake sports a year-round fishery and offers one of the state's finest smallmouth fishing opportunities. It also includes a thriving largemouth population; some of these bass have topped the scales at more than 10 pounds.

Spring is the best time overall to fish both bass species here. By April, the largemouths usually move to the backs of coves for the annual spawn.

Smallmouths can also be caught in the middle of winter, which is a good time for a visit, especially with diminished crowds.

Trinity Lake. With more than 17,000 acres, 145 miles of shoreline, and some of the prettiest scenery in California, Trinity is one of the premier smallmouth fisheries in the state. It also has a thriving northern largemouth bass population that is sometimes overlooked with all the attention given to bronzebacks. April through mid-May is the best time for big bass of both species; action is also good from spring through October.

Saltwater Fishing
The Pacific coast of California has some of the finest saltwater angling in the world and is enjoyed year-round. Marine species range from marlin to salmon and from tuna to rockfish, and strategies to catch the various and diverse saltwater fish in Southern California are as unique as those used along the central and Northern California coasts.

Naturally, many marine gamefish are pelagic or migratory by nature, and follow currents. Migrtory patterns greatly impact gamefishing opportunity along the coast from year to year. Whether large numbers of yellowtail, for example, are caught off San Diego depends largely on water temperature and coloration. When conditions are ideal, large quantities of bait species such as anchovies, smelt, sardines, and squid move offshore. If the water is too cold or too dirty, there is no bait and thus no yellowtail. Likewise, changing temperatures— as happens with the well-documented El Niño phenomenon—may spread the range of some species, or curtail it, in a given year. Similar ecological relationships govern the albacore tuna and salmon fisheries in the central and northern sectors. Not all saltwater fish are pelagic, however. The surf fishes, such as corbina and spotfin croaker, usually stay in the shallow-water zones all year along southern beaches.

Similarly, the many rockfish species popularly found around the Monterey Peninsula are permanent residents. Water temperature is the critical ingredient for activity. This is especially true near Point Conception above Santa Barbara and heading north. The coastline here is rugged and exposed to prevailing northwest winds, which tend to work with the current to bring up colder water from the depths. This action displaces the otherwise warmer surface layer. The process of wind and current "upwelling" typically occurs in the spring, so the inshore area remains cold year-round, in contrast to offshore waters that warm in summer along the southern coast. Thus the central and northern regions can sustain large populations of nonmigratory coldwater dwellers. The fishery in this part of California is stable; rockfish, lingcod, eels, and so forth are always available. On the other hand, Southern Californians are more dependent on optimal movements of warm, bait-laden currents for

Fishing is mentioned often in *The New Testament*, albeit for food not sport; the fish that fed the biblical 5,000 is thought to have been tilapia.

banner catches of such gamefish as bonito, barracuda, yellowtail, albacore, and bluefin tuna.

Surface-feeding pelagics such as tuna, yellowtail, and dorado have a tendency to aggressively strike fast-moving baits and lures. A combination of swimming metal jigs, spoons, and soft-plastic trolling lures produces consistently for these fish. In contrast, coldwater bottom dwellers like lingcod, salmon, grouper, and sheepshead are more inclined to strike slowly retrieved artificials, sometimes bounced off the bottom, or natural baits fished dead and deep.

When all of the variables—including water temperature, wind exposure, offshore topography, and proliferation of forage are considered—a very complex portrait of the California marine fishery emerges. The picture becomes even more intricate when lure selection and application are considered. As a result of all these elements, California offers one of the most dynamic and challenging saltwater fisheries in North America.

San Diego/Imperial County Area. Numerous sandy beaches that lie to the north and south of San Diego Harbor offer outstanding surf fishing. Torrey Pines, noted for its famous golf course, is also a good local barred perch spot. The Silver Strand, Ocean Beach, and Imperial Beach are similarly good perch and corbina stretches and experience minimal angling pressure.

The sportfishing catches of San Diego and Mission Bay often sample the offshore bite along these coastal waters. The Point Loma and La Jolla kelp beds are important fisheries for pelagic species.

In Ocean Beach, the short rocky spit near the pier can be a real hotspot. Few surf anglers try it, but the perch bite is phenomenal here at times.

The Point Loma kelp is a popular spot for the San Diego party boat fleet. Barracuda and bonito, as well as calico and sand bass, are found here, sometimes throughout the year. Yellowtail are another strong option in this kelp bed. Sheepshead, sculpin, shallow-water rockfish, and a few white sea-bass round out the catch.

Coronado Islands. The four rocky outcroppings of the Islas de los Coronados are technically in Mexican waters. They are about 7 miles off the Baja California coast and 10 to 12 miles south of San Diego Harbor. Sportfishing boats from all San Diego landings make runs to these islands, which are the yellowtail capital of the Southern California sportfishing fleet. Numerous other species abound off these desolate islands. South Island is the largest of the Coronados, and two smaller outcroppings to the north—Middle Ground and North Island—are also prime fishing targets.

San Diego Harbor and Mission Bay. Both San Diego Harbor and Mission Bay provide year-round angling opportunities. Anglers fish these bays either from shore or in small boats. Fish are abundant in the quiet waters. Species include halibut, bonito, barracuda, sharks, rays, mackerel, croaker, and perch, as well as sand and spotted bay bass. The deep edges of the main ship channel in San Diego Bay are excellent places to drift both lures and live baits. The areas near Harbor Island and Shelter Island Pier are noted hotspots. Fishing near the Coronado Bridge can be equally productive.

In Mission Bay the Ventura Bridge offers both bass and halibut action. Fish the pilings slightly north of this bridge. The seasonal weedbeds are prime territory for sandies and spotted bay bass. Fiesta Island is one of the premier spotfin croaker fisheries in the state when the run is on (usually a falling tide). The Quivara Basin has sporadic flurries of mackerel, bonito, and small barracuda. For bat rays, head to Mariners Point inside Mission Bay.

The Salton Sea. A unique inland sea, Salton lies in the middle of the Mojave Desert. It was formed when the Colorado River overflowed its banks at the beginning of the century. The Salton Sea has a higher salinity level than the Pacific Ocean, yet a number of saltwater species thrive here.

The prized gamefish is the orangemouth corvina, which can grow to more than 30 pounds. Both boat and shore anglers catch these fish all year long. Fishing can be best in midsummer using both lures and bait. The Salton Sea also has a modest population of sargo, small gulf croaker, and tilapia. Strong desert winds can kick up severe wave action, so boaters must be cautious.

Oceanside Area. Numerous interesting and varied opportunities exist around Oceanside. Landings inside Oceanside Harbor provide half-day and full-day excursions to the Barn Kelp and offshore islands for rockfish in the winter. A variety of pelagic species live here, including yellowtail, calico bass, sand bass, mackerel, white seabass, and halibut, as well as many bonito and barracuda.

Carlsbad Lagoon is an excellent source of spotfin croaker, big bat rays, halibut, and even a rare white seabass. Encino Lagoon and Oceanside Harbor are also worthwhile spots to try.

The Barn Kelp is one of the most prolific kelp beds for gamefish on a year-round basis. Farther north, the waters off the San Onofre nuclear power plant have been excellent sand bass territory when the spawning run is in full swing.

Orange County. *San Clemente Island.* San Clemente Island is an incredible bonanza for the saltwater angler willing to make the five-hour run from the Southern California mainland. Both party boats and private charters make full-day excursions to this isolated island.

Pyramid Head and China Point are favorite spots on the island's southeast end. The kelp beds are thick and provide sanctuary for big calicos. Bonito and barracuda also move along this kelp line. Yellowtail recurrently cruise the kelp, and it's a good place to catch live squid for bait in the winter. The White Rock sector on the middle of the eastern side of the island is another potential yellowtail stretch.

Opportunities for serious bass fishing exist at the isthmus on the far west side of Clemente. Bird Rock and Castle Rock on the outside are potential hotspots for calicos. The windward southwest side is an area to work for bluefin tuna. Shark hunters looking for blues, makos, and threshers can scout the channel between Clemente and Catalina Islands. Striped marlin are also a possibility.

Santa Catalina Island. Santa Catalina is the most popular of the offshore islands off the California coast. Located roughly 26 miles from the mainland, Catalina is 22 miles long and 7 miles wide. An abundance of saltwater gamefish can be caught around the island throughout the year.

Most private and party boat captains prefer to fish the leeward side of the island facing the mainland. The windward side can become rough from gale-force winds, with swells crashing into the rocky shoreline. The tip of the West End inside the floating kelp stringers is a favorite hotspot for big calico bass. Yellowtail, bluefin tuna, bonito, and barracuda breeze through this area.

Emerald and Cherry Coves, and the isthmus near the center of the island, are good areas for yellowtail. Halibut drifting occurs from Goat Harbor to the beaches north of Avalon. Bonito, barracuda, and some small shallow-water rockfish are also possibilities in this area. At the East End, near The Slide, yellowtail, bonito, and barracuda can be found cruising within a mile of the bank.

Rock-codding for deep-water species is best at both ends of Catalina. Striped marlin are possible in these areas. The West End and The Slide are also traditional hotspots for marlin.

Dana Point Harbor. Dana Point is one of the most diverse angling havens in Southern California. Gamefish—including halibut, sand bass, spotted bay bass, spotfin croaker, bonito, halibut, mackerel, and corbina—abound in the harbor basin. Along the outside rocks and jetties are sheepshead, opaleye, calicos, sculpin, sharks, and rays. To the north of the jetty, the rocks and kelp of South Laguna are prime calico bass haunts. In the offshore kelp, yellowtail, and a seasonal flurry of bonito and barracuda, can be found. Anglers working the sandy beach near South Laguna can also nail corbina, barred perch, croaker, and, occasionally, halibut.

Newport Harbor. One of the most interesting fishing sites in the region is Newport Harbor. This shallow bay sports a prominent population of spotted bay bass, sand bass, halibut, croaker, corbina, mackerel, bonito, barracuda, sand sharks, rays, and an occasional striped bass. Halibut can usually be found on the hard mud and sandy bottoms. Drift or troll the main channel for sandies and bay bass. The areas around the various boat docks and in front of the Balboa Pavilion are good spots for bass, perch, croaker, and the occasional halibut. Striped bass, in limited numbers, are landed in the Back Bay. Spotted bay bass are abundant in Newport Bay. Key-in on the dock pilings and under moored

boats. Look for signs of eelgrass and places where currents converge. Spotted bay bass gravitate to this type of water. Corbina are frequently taken in the surf line or along Balboa Pier. Newport and Balboa Piers also have occasional runs of halibut and bonito.

Huntington Beach to Seal Beach. The Huntington Beach Pier is frequently invaded by schools of mackerel and small bonito. Most of the action here is on surfperch, a few halibut, tomcod, herring, and queenfish. At times there can be outstanding bonito action off this pier, as well as keeper-size halibut, yellowfin, croaker, and sargo. Seal Beach operates a sportfishing landing, and private craft can launch from Huntington Harbor. The beach below the bluffs to the north of Huntington Beach are good for barred perch. Windy Bolsa Chica State Beach between Huntington and Sunset Beaches is another barred perch stretch.

The beach around Surfside can produce a variety of fish ranging from sharks and halibut to corbina and yellowfin croaker. Small flounder, halibut, and turbot are taken in Huntington Harbor. For shallow-lagoon species, investigate the area around the Pacific Coast Highway bridge connecting Surfside and Seal Beach. The San Gabriel River Channel north of Seal Beach is another good spot for small bonito. The Huntington Flats and offshore oil platforms have been a favorite run for sportfishing and private boats. Halibut, bonito, and barracuda frequent the flats. The big news occurs when sand bass move in to spawn. The offshore oil rigs provide sanctuary for large yellowtail, as well as calico bass, bonito, and mackerel.

Los Angeles Area. *Long Beach Harbor and Palos Verdes area.* In the Long Beach harbor, fishing opportunities abound at jetties, piers, breakwaters, and even offshore oil islands. Anglers land bonito and mackerel off the Belmont Pier and outside the jetty and breakwaters. Spotted bay bass, sand bass, and calicos are popular species in the harbor. Halibut, croaker, perch, sharks, and rays are other possibilities. Spring is the best time for bass and halibut. However, the harbor can provide steady action throughout the year. The federal breakwater can be outstanding at night during the winter.

To the north, anglers can experience excellent surf casting for big calicos off the rocks on the Palos Verdes Peninsula. Sheepshead, surfperch, and opaleye are also available off these jagged bluffs.

King Harbor to Marina del Rey. King Harbor in Redondo Beach offers a variety of saltwater angling opportunities. Fish the breakwaters for bonito and mackerel as well as perch, opaleye, halibut, tomcod, smelt, and the occasional sand bass. The warm water inside the harbor yields bonito, barracuda, mackerel, and even yellowtail. Bonito fishing is outstanding from the pier. Outside the harbor, boaters can sample the pelagic gamefish that migrate into the area following schools of anchovies. To the north, Hermosa and Manhattan Beach Piers have excellent winter runs of barred surfperch. Good shallow-water surf fish can be found at 18th, 19th, and 26th Streets, especially for quality halibut.

Marina del Rey. There's good fishing inside Marina del Rey Harbor. Spotted bay bass, sand bass, and halibut are all possibilities. Other areas to work are the short breakwater and the long jetty. Big calicos and sand bass are good targets for night fishing; other species include tomcod, queenfish, small calicos bass, sand bass, halibut, bonito, and barracuda. Fish for bonito and barracuda on the ocean side of the jetty and toward the end. The sandy beach adjacent to the north of the jetty occasionally has some 1- to 3-pound corbina.

Santa Monica Bay to Malibu. This scenic stretch of coastline runs from the Santa Monica Pier to Bass Rock below Oxnard. The Santa Monica pier itself intermittently produces bonito, halibut, a stray calico or sand bass, mackerel, sharks, and rays. The Malibu Pier is on parity with Santa Monica for species variation and overall quality of fishing.

Beaches accessible from this point northward offer some other intriguing possibilities. Calico bass, halibut, cabezon, leopard sharks, barred perch, sargo perch, yellowfin croaker, and shallow-water rockfish are within a cast from the beach. Kelp beds and submerged reefs dot the public-access beaches from Malibu to Oxnard. Look for barred perch action at small rocky outcroppings. The larger rocks inside the bay near the Santa Monica Pier are outstanding for nighttime bass fishing. These rocks can be reached only by carefully maneuvering a small boat close to shore.

Private boats and sportfishers explore Santa Monica Bay for surface-feeding action. Skiff and party boat anglers sometimes get into hot bluefin tuna action in this bay. Here is also some of the best halibut fishing in the region, with anglers drifting over predominantly sandy bottoms. Coral Beach north of Malibu is an excellent spot for surf casting to offshore kelp beds. The surfer's reef to the right of the Malibu Pier is a legendary haunt for big calicos. Night fishing with heavy-duty tackle produces the best results. Other good fishing spots for barred perch, halibut, cabezon, sand bass, and calico bass are Latigo Canyon, Paradise Cove, and Leo Carrillo Beach.

Ventura and Santa Barbara Areas. *Ventura and Oxnard.* A wealth of kelp beds line this part of the coast. Ventura Harbor has good numbers of smelt, perch, and tomcod, as well as a few sand bass and halibut. Channel Islands Harbor has plenty of warmwater species, including sand bass, spotted bay bass, and a few calicos on the outside rock walls. Anglers pursue halibut extensively inside this harbor.

Halibut and barred perch are frequently caught along the windy beaches. Work below the naval base south of the pier. Offshore kelp beds are loaded with calicos, sand bass, barracuda, halibut, and even white seabass. Salmon activity also occurs in this area in late winter or early spring.

Channel Islands. The islands of the Santa Barbara Channel offer tremendous variety for anglers venturing out of Oxnard, Ventura, or Santa Barbara. Private and party boats fish Santa Cruz, San Miguel, Santa Rosa, or Anacapa Islands. Surface fishing in warmer months can be sensational here for calico bass, bonito, barracuda, yellowtail, white seabass, and sometimes migrating schools of albacore. These islands also offer excellent shallow-water lingcod and rockfish, and deep-water rock cod action. Winter and spring runs of both silver and king salmon also occur in the channel itself, as well as in the areas around San Miguel and Santa Rosa Islands.

Santa Barbara. This quiet seacoast city has a lot to offer the saltwater enthusiast. Private fishing boats and party boats ply the Channel Islands or One Mile and Naples Reefs to the north for some of the best shallow-water rockfishing on the coast. Surf casters can sample good perch and corbina action along the sandy stretches from Santa Barbara to Point Conception. Stearn's Wharf and the breakwater rocks are great spots for pier anglers and jetty jockeys.

The kelp south of Santa Barbara and Carpinteria is a hotbed for pelagic species. Bass, barracuda, white seabass, and assorted rockfish are local residents. Ledbetter Beach, Thousand Steps, Goleta, Shoreline Park, Refugio, El Capitan, and the Rincon Stretch are strong candidates for steady surf-casting action. Perch, halibut, corbina, sharks, bass, and cabezon can be caught from the beach. The harbor and breakwater are good places to look for perch, sand bass, and halibut. The water off Goleta Pier is a prime spot for both calicos and halibut on the drift.

Central California. *San Luis Obispo to San Simeon.* It is estimated that only about 10 percent of the beachfront area above Santa Barbara is ever fished, yet it can produce great fishing. Notable are rock cod and late-season albacore in the 30- to 50-pound range out of Avila Bay. Inside Morro Bay try for smelt, halibut, mackerel, or sand bass. Outside Morro Bay, rockfish are plentiful; these include blue, gopher, and copper rockfish, and also lingcod and cabezon. North of Morro Rock is a beach with excellent barred perch potential. Try the blowhole near Morro Rock for fork-tail and barred perch, as well as cabezon and starry flounder.

At Pismo Pier, fish for barracuda, halibut, corbina, and mackerel, plus barred, fork-tail, and walleye perch. Avila Pier and San Luis Pier are best for tomcod, shiner perch, and jack smelt. Offshore waters can sustain a good run of both king and silver salmon at times.

Cayucos, Moonstone, Sandstone, and San Simeon Beaches have great perch action. San Simeon Pier has barred, walleye, rubberlip, and piling perch, plus halibut and jack smelt. From Cayucos to Piedras Blancas, shallow-water rockfishing can be sensational for small-boat anglers.

The Nile perch of Africa is one of the largest gamefish in the world; its only North American relative is the wary, strong, and acrobatic snook.

Lingcod, cabezon, halibut, flounder, petrale sole, and even salmon can be caught off the nearshore reefs.

Monterey and Carmel Bays. Because of the broad variation in ocean conditions contained within this unique bay, Monterey-area fishing ranges from shallow-water rockfish to deep-water pelagics. The many piers, landings, beaches, rocks, and sloughs of the Monterey Bay area hold a variety of coldwater treasures, among them salmon, striped bass, perch, sanddabs, halibut, petrale sole, flounder, lingcod, cabezon, greenling, kelp and grass rockfish, sculpin, jack smelt, sablefish, and sharks. Party boaters, skiff anglers, surf casters, and rock hoppers alike can share in the bounty.

Rock anglers can also find abundant inshore rockfish. Greenling; olive, grass, and blue rockfish; cabezon; lingcod; and surfperch are all within casting range at 17-Mile Drive and Asilomar State Beach. Smelt, perch, and shallow-water rockfish are taken off the pier at the eastern end of Monterey Harbor. Occasional striped bass also show up here. Skiff operators can target rockfish, lingcod, and sanddabs inside both bays. In warmwater periods, bonito and barracuda can be an unexpected treat.

Salmon frequent the bay from early spring through fall. One good area is the mouth of the Salinas River. Albacore can occasionally be located in late summer as close as 10 miles offshore.

San Francisco Area. *Moss Landing to Santa Cruz.* Rockfish, perch, greenling, cabezon, lingcod, halibut, sanddabs, smelt, salmon, and striped bass are all landed in this area. The jetty and the beaches south of Moss Landing are excellent surfperch territory. Elkhorn Slough is famous for its shark and bat ray fishing, as well as sole and starry flounder.

The beaches north of Aptos range from sandy to rocky. Fish for cabezon, jack smelt, perch, and shallow rockfish from the shore and at Capitola Pier. Santa Cruz Pier also features lingcod, boccaccio, sculpin, sole, and starry flounder.

Numerous shallow reefs outside the Santa Cruz small-craft harbor sensational lingcod and rockfish populations. Other popular reefs lie off Soquel Point and Capitola.

Half Moon Bay. Pillar Point Harbor at Half Moon Bay is one of the most diverse fisheries in Northern California. Boats out of this harbor can fish the nearby reefs for copper, olive, yellowtail, black, canary, olive, and blue rockfish, as well as cabezon and lingcod. Salmon, striped bass, flounder, sanddabs, sculpin, perch, and jack smelt are sought too. Shore anglers can try their luck off the breakwater or pier for rockfish, perch, and sometimes salmon, lingcod, or striped bass. Poke-polers (anglers who use 12- to 16-foot telescoping rods to fish cut baits in rocky crevices) can work the adjacent rocky areas for rockfish, cabezon, and eels.

Fish the reefs outside the harbor for rockfish and lingcod. The stretch from Pillar Point to Moss Beach is a good area to prospect for bottom fish. Pier anglers can fish inside Pillar Point Harbor for perch, smelt, rockfish, sanddabs, and sculpin. Shore anglers can fish the jetties for surfperch, greenling, rockfish, cabezon, and lingcod, as well as flounder, sanddabs, and perch.

San Francisco Bay. Light-lining inside San Francisco Bay can be excellent for perch, smelt, flounder, shallow-water rockfish, and kingfish. The prized gamefish are striped bass, halibut, salmon, and sharks. Smelt and perch dominate catch totals at the Berkeley Pier. Jack smelt can be red-hot along the Burlingame shoreline. Wharves and piers on the San Francisco waterfront also yield starry flounder, smelt, and perch. An excellent perch bite often occurs on the stretch of shoreline from Coyote Point to San Francisco's airport. Other popular sites for perch include the Alameda Estuary and East Fort Baker under the Golden Gate Bridge on the Marin side.

The deeper channels around Marin—west of Angel Island, the Bay Bridge, and Hunter's Point—are longtime favorites for shark hunters. Anglers probe the waters off the greenhouse south of Sausalito, and the main channel between the Dumbarton and San Mateo Bridges in South San Francisco Bay. Leopard, soupfin, smoothhound, dogfish, and six- and seven-gill sharks can be taken almost anytime. Look for seven-gill sharks in spring and fall, and soupfin in spring and summer. Shark fishing is usually best at the top or bottom of a moving tide. The same holds true for halibut and sturgeon catches in this area.

Striped bass fishing is a seasonal event in San Francisco Bay. The best places to fish include Sausalito, Berkeley, Emeryville, Richmond, and the City of San Francisco. Stripers can be reached from shore as well as from boats. Fish Coyote, Oyster, and Hunter's Points, Candlestick Park, Mission Rock and Baker's Beaches, the Berkley flats, Alameda Rocks, the Raccoon Straits, Alcatraz, and Treasure and Angel Islands for major striped bass action.

San Francisco Bay produced this fine California halibut.

Farallon Islands. The Farallon Islands are 35 miles west of the Golden Gate and generate some of the finest bottom fishing in the West. Sportfishing and charter boats from Angler's Wharf, Berkeley, Sausalito, Pillar Point, and Emeryville fish these rocky outcroppings. King salmon and lingcod are additional quarries here. Be prepared for rough water and miserable weather at any time of the year.

Bottom fish taken from the islands include copper, blue, yellowtail, chili, golden eye, vermilion, and blue rockfish. Cowcod and lingcod round out the catch. Salmon are taken in the gulf between the islands and the mainland. Some of the largest lingcod caught in California are landed during the fall spawning period at these islands. Troll, drift, and mooch between Duxbury Reef and the Farallons in spring. Move from the San Francisco light buoy to Duxbury Reef in late summer through fall.

Northern California to the Oregon Border. Above San Francisco are numerous sandy beaches, docks, bays, piers, and rocky shorelines that host coldwater species. Tomales Bay, for example, is renowned for its shark population. Skiff anglers also enjoy some limited action on striped bass, salmon, perch, and starry flounder. Surfperch are the number one catch from the beach. Poke-polers target rockfish. Catch greenling, cabezon, and lingcod off the rocks and in outside waters all the way to the Oregon state line.

Bodega and Tomales Bays. Surf and jetty anglers as well as boaters can fish for schools of king salmon and quality rockfish north of San Francisco. Target the Cordell Banks for lingcod and rockfish. The Whistle Buoy off Bodega Bay is prime for chinook salmon. Fish the Bodega Bay wharf for smelt and perch. The rocks at Doran Park are excellent for shallow-water greenling, cabezon, and assorted rockfish. Carmel and Dillar Beaches are perfect for poke-polers. Wright's, Goat, Salmon Creek, and Portuguese Beaches are key places for smelt and surfperch. Lawson Landing at the mouth of Tomales Bay is the hotspot for striped bass, leopard sharks, and halibut. Hog Island is best for perch.

Fort Ross and Timber Cove areas. For excellent bottom fishing, try the reefs at Salt Point, Ocean Cove, Seal Rocks, Stillwater Cove, and Timber Cove. Look for big lingcod in the shallows in the winter. Target salmon from late April through the summer.

Crescent City. This quiet stretch of shoreline offers both salmon and bottom fishing. Rockfish specialists should try the St. George and South Reefs outside the harbor, and the 5-fathom curve from Three Sister Rocks to the harbor entrance for bottom fish. The catch includes black, blue, vermilion, China, and boccaccio rockfish. Pier anglers can catch flounder, perch, smelt, and greenling off Citizen's Dock. Lingcod, rockfish, and cabezon are year-round favorites in this cold water. Smaller silver salmon are caught in June, whereas August is best for king salmon. Poke-polers can fish the rocky

outcroppings for rockfish, perch, and greenling. Surf casters can fish all year long here.

Eureka and Humboldt Bay. Four-mile-long Humboldt Bay has a solid population of walleye and redtail perch for surf anglers. Fish for shallow-water lingcod, black snapper, and greenling from the jetties. King salmon are also a possibility here, even from the rocky breakwaters.

Shelter Cove is a rockfish haven, especially for lingcod. The reefs off Ft. Bragg are excellent haunts for rockfish and salmon trolling. Prime targets include greenling, rockfish, cabezon, perch, and lingcod.

CALIFORNIA CURRENT

The California Current is an easterly offshoot of the North Pacific Current that flows southward and a bit eastward off southern Canada and the Pacific Coast of the United States to Baja California, Mexico, where it turns sharply westward into the North Equatorial Current. This is a flow of colder water, and it is slow and not as well defined as the Gulf Stream *(see)*, which is a warm northerly flowing current affecting the Atlantic Coast of North America.

See: Currents.

CANADA

Specific fisheries and angling opportunities in Canada are detailed elsewhere. Please refer to the individual province or territory listing. This entry provides an aggregate overview of sportfishing in Canada.

Like the United States, Canada has excellent sportfishing, but unlike any other country it has thousands of bodies of water that are far removed from population centers. With a larger landmass than the United States and less than one-tenth its population, most of which is concentrated in the southern portion of the country, Canada is a dream-come-true for anglers who want to fish in seclusion. Access to the most remote and roadless areas is not easy to afford or accomplish with limited time, however, and the open-water seasons are fairly short for most of the country.

Canada's abundant sportfishing opportunities range from the water-rich frozen tundra of the Arctic barrens to the wolf-inhabited boundary wilderness lakes on the U.S. border, from fiordlike Pacific coast bays with whales and salmon to tidal maritime island streams with sea-run brook trout, and from Great Lakes rich with trout and salmon to bush lakes rich with walleye and northern pike. Surrounded by three oceans, and covered with spruce forests, taiga, and tundra, Canada offers bass fishing in the shadows of metropolitan skylines, lake trout fishing in the company of caribou, salmon that are likely to be snatched by an eagle if left on a boat dock, and trophy walleye angling in central, drive-to rivers.

Pike, Lake Trout, and Walleye

By far the greatest overall angling effort in Canada is devoted to freshwater fishing, in part due to geography, as most provinces are located far from marine environments, and in part due to abundance, because there is more diversity inland. Lake trout, northern pike, and walleye are the top freshwater attractions. Certainly these fish are most widely distributed and available across the interior provinces and territories; pike and lake trout are favorites certainly of American visitors, who cannot do as well in their home states for these species as in Canada. Americans cannot find consistently fast pike action in most of the United States; and trophy pike are increasingly rare. In the U.S., a 15-pound pike or lake trout is a large specimen, but not one found regularly or with much certainty. Not so in Canada.

Except for the Maritime Provinces and British Columbia, all of Canada offers pike fishing. Pike are as plentiful in some waters as bluegills are in American lakes. In many of the former you can count on having lots of action, and in some of the more conservation-oriented waters you can catch and release your personal best.

The bigger pike generally come from the remote northern lakes in the heartland provinces of Manitoba, Saskatchewan, Ontario, and, to a lesser degree, northern Quebec, although some big pike are caught in the southerly reaches of the Northwest and Nunavut Territories, too. There's also good pike action in some of the bigger rivers and lakes within big-river systems, but the majority of the best fishing is in lakes, especially big lakes and places that aren't readily accessible from roads.

This is almost always a casting fishery rather than a trolling one. You seldom fish in big open-water areas, although you may have to cross large expanses of lake (which can sometimes be rough) to get from place to place. Pike fishing often takes you to some of the northern lakes' prettier locations: weedy back bays, meandering marshes, nooks and crannies. And there's a more visual element to the fishing. You see a lot of pike, whether they're cruising the shallows or chasing a lure. And, because the fish are fairly voracious, you sometimes get to see a cavernous mouth open and inhale your lure. It's an active game.

Anglers can have great action early in the season, especially for lots of fish. When northern lakes melt, the shallow bays and backwaters are the first to open and warm up, and pike cluster in these places, sometimes resting in water barely deep enough to cover their backs. You can do a lot of sight casting then. Weeds are sparse at best, and the water is ultraclear. You can also catch large fish, but because pike spawn in late winter or early spring, the early-season pike are not as hefty as they will be later, and the real monsters seem to be elusive.

On good pike lakes there is usually no bad time for pike. Later in the season, when the weeds are thick, most pike will be off the shoreline and in the weeds, and sight fishing opportunities are greatly reduced. Pike will have been feeding well and many will have better girth.

Lake trout are generally doing well in many parts of Canada, and with more emphasis on conservation of these old and slow-growing fish the future looks good. The better lake trout angling is usually in the upper half or upper third of the southern provinces, as well as throughout the Northwest and Nunavut Territories. Northern Manitoba and northern Saskatchewan provide some of the best opportunities for big fish, but the eastern and central tundra waters, as well as Victoria Island, are equally notable.

In the far north, rivers offer exciting lake trout fishing by casting, but seldom big fish; however, larger fish will prowl the turbulent inlet. In lakes, these trout are often structure oriented, and migrate to reefs, shoals, and islands to feed. They also cruise the shorelines. In lakes that warm up and create a thermocline, lakers will go to cool water below the thermocline in large open-water bowls. This is where their primary food, cisco and other lake trout, is found.

A lot of Canadian lake trout fishing is done in the upper 30 feet of water, and these fish are scrappy. The smaller ones, which sometimes thrash and roll wildly near the boat, can be a spunky nuisance. More than one angler, fishing in prime waters, has hooked and played a tenacious and drag-pulling laker for an hour or more.

In those far-north places where the water stays cold all season, you can catch lake trout in the upper strata all year long. In places that warm up in the summer and where the surface water reaches the 60s, the trout will positively go deep. It is late in the season that some of the heaviest fish are caught and the fewest anglers are out. Few far-north lodges stay open late in August or into September because of hostile weather and airplane delays. But those who do cater to knowledgeable, hearty anglers searching for trophy fish.

The busiest time for most lake trout lodges is the first few weeks of the season. Camps are usually full. Most bookings are made 8 to 12 months in advance, prior to knowing what the winter will serve up. A severe winter and/or a long, cold spring will delay ice out and possibly limit the places you can fish if you're scheduled at a lodge during the first or second week. But many anglers take that chance.

From big fish to lots of action, Canada's got whatever suits your walleye interests. Big and small lakes and big and small rivers, of which there are plenty in southern Canada, provide ample angling opportunity. Quebec, Ontario, Manitoba, and Saskatchewan lead the field, particularly the mid- to southern regions of those provinces.

You don't necessarily have to visit remote waters to find great walleye fishing. Although there's some fine walleye (called pickerel in many parts of Canada) angling in distant spots, seldom are the

To many people, angling in Canada is synonymous with remote wilderness, such as this scene at secluded Hunt Falls in northern Saskatchewan.

biggest fish found in those places. A 6-pounder, which is a good-size walleye, is relatively rare in most northern waters. The biggest fish may be closer to the border; such waters as Lake of the Woods, Rainy Lake, the Detroit River, Lake Erie, the St. Lawrence River, and the Bay of Quinte on northeastern Lake Ontario produce 8- to 10-pound or larger walleye and good overall numbers of fish.

For most of the season, from late spring through summer and into fall, walleye are located on rock reefs, sandbars, points, weed edges, and the like. In big lakes some walleye suspend in open water where there are schools of baitfish.

Lots of people fish walleye in near and far Canadian waters, from Labrador to Saskatchewan, and much of it is fish-on-your-own angling, either piloting a boat by yourself at a resort, or towing your own fish-catching machine to the designated site. The entire gamut of walleye tackle and techniques is employed, with fishing ranging from difficult to find in hard-fished waters to cast-after-cast easy in some remote fly-in lakes. The latter usually also offer good pike fishing, so there's good combination angling available.

There's a big rush in Canada when the spring walleye season opens, which varies by province and by district within provinces. Walleye have usually spawned by the time the opener occurs, but not necessarily. The angler rush subsides after the walleye disperse and migrate to summer grounds, becoming temporarily harder to locate.

Salmon, Charr, and Trout

To find Canada's other most heralded fish—salmon and charr—in their naturally occurring state, you have to migrate to all four extremities of the country. Salmon and charr are intensely popular in the coastal regions where they occur, but the anadromous coldwater species native to those areas are not available to the vast majority of Canadians without incurring substantial travel; this is even more so for charr than for salmon.

Atlantic salmon have been under tremendous pressures due to various factors, especially excessive commercial harvest in the North Atlantic. Naturally occurring Atlantic salmon are found in maritime Quebec, Newfoundland, New Brunswick, and Nova Scotia, all of which have well-known and storied rivers. Quebec's Gaspe Peninsula is easily accessed and has a significant amount of opportunity, but here and elsewhere the fish are subject to seasonal conditions and ocean events that cause fluctuations in the numbers and size of fish returning each year.

Angling for Canada's Atlantic salmon is almost entirely restricted to fly fishing, although land-locked populations exist (in Labrador and Quebec) and these can be pursued by various methods, including casting spoons with spinning tackle and trolling with various tackle types.

Overharvesting has had some impact on naturally occurring stocks of Pacific salmon (coho, chinook, sockeye, and chum salmon) off British

C

Columbia, but a greater impact has come from environmental changes, especially damming of rivers, and water-quality issues, some due to extensive logging. These fish, as well as sea-run rainbow trout (steelhead), however, are caught in rivers and coastal tidewaters, and the chinooks and cohos may range to large sizes, with the larger individuals usually caught in tidewater at the mouths of significant rivers.

Major runs occur at different times, and occasionally this can be adversely affected by commercial activities. British Columbia has 27,000 kilometers of coastline and more than 1,500 spawning rivers, so there's a lot of opportunity here, although the majority of resident and nonresident salmon anglers fish in the salt for the brightest, hardest-fighting, and best-tasting fish—so fresh they still carry sea lice. Anglers primarily mooch (a form of slow-trolling with cut-herring baits) or troll baits and lures with downriggers.

It is often forgotten that some of the most prolific salmon fishing in Canada occurs on its interior border with the U.S., in the Great Lakes, where Lakes Michigan, Erie, and Ontario in particular produce good numbers and sizes of chinook salmon, as well as cohos and steelhead. These fish have been introduced by Canadian and American wildlife agencies and are largely sustained through annual stocking, but provide ample opportunity throughout the year. Being close to major population concentrations (salmon and steelhead can be caught in view of Toronto skyscrapers) makes these fish accessible to a greater number of Canadians, even if they aren't native to that region.

Salmon, steelhead, and some trout are caught near shore in spring and late summer and in deeper offshore water later in midsummer, as well as in tributaries in late summer and early fall. Steelhead are caught through the winter in tributaries.

In northernmost Canada, fresh from the Arctic Ocean, naturally occurring sea-run arctic charr are perhaps the most exotic major Canadian sportfish, a species that relatively few anglers have caught, available for a limited midsummer period, and accessed almost entirely by fly-in air service.

Arctic charr inhabit many isolated interior lakes and most of the coastal rivers and streams that rise from lakes that can support spawning. The majority of charr are caught in rivers; however, the larger specimens are primarily caught in the lower stretches closer to the salt. Arctic charr rivers flow into the Arctic Ocean, Hudson Bay, and the Atlantic coastlines of Nunavut.

Charr do not run huge distances inland like Pacific salmon, and it is usually small specimens that are in the lakes. The charr that are caught early in the season are very bright fish, looking in coloration like a steelhead or fresh-run salmon, but they develop remarkable colors, and the later-season fish can possess beautiful shades of red and orange, plus spots. Nonspawning fish, especially the sea-run forms, tend to be silver.

The largest known arctic charr taken by anglers have come from the Tree River in the Nunavut Territory. The Tree River stock and related runs from the Coppermine and others rivers have consistently produced big fish. Chantrey Inlet in Nunavut also produces big charr, although it has a very small window of opportunity at ice out. More reliable are various rivers on Victoria Island, which have produced assorted line-class world records over the years. Although there are plenty of charr in the various rivers of Baffin Island, these waters have not been known for large specimens, and fish over 15 pounds have not been common there.

Various trout are available across Canada, from plentiful rainbows and cutthroats in British Columbia to brown trout in Alberta to brook trout in the eastern provinces. The best place in North America for large brookies is in Labrador; although some large fish occasionally come from northern Quebec waters. Brook trout, actually a charr and native to the continent, are favored by many eastern river and stream anglers, and sea-run brookies, or salters, are found in some of the maritime rivers.

Other Species

Other species with some following include bass, muskie, grayling, tuna, and halibut.

Both largemouth and smallmouth bass are found in Canada, with smallmouths more abundant and providing good fishing in southern Ontario, southern Quebec, New Brunswick, and Nova Scotia waters. One or both species are prominent in large and small inland lakes across this region, and smallmouths are prevalent in such large waters as Lake of the Woods, Georgian Bay, Lake Erie, eastern Lake Ontario, and the St. Lawrence River.

Muskies are likewise present in southern Ontario and Quebec, with especially large fish in Lake Huron/Georgian Bay and tributary waters, in the Ottawa River, and in the St. Lawrence River in both Ontario and Quebec.

Grayling are widely present in northern rivers and streams and are generally unavailable without making a fly-in trip. Few anglers make northern expeditions exclusively for these fish, which average $1\frac{1}{2}$ pounds, but they are popularly sought on light spinning and fly gear, as an adjunct to other fishing activities in the north. Halibut are just the opposite of grayling in almost every respect. They are caught off the northern British Columbia coast, primarily as a diversion to salmon, albeit in large sizes and with very stout tackle.

Bluefin tuna of enormous sizes are caught off Nova Scotia and Prince Edward Island. This fishery declined for a while but recovered in the late 1990s, with a federal quota placed on the total commercial and recreational catch. Although this species is generally in poor shape internationally, giant bluefins from 500 to 1,000 pounds are caught annually in the northwestern Atlantic under the quota system in late summer and early fall, and a portion of these

Cold-weather anglers can avoid life-threatening hypothermia by staying dry, eating high-energy snacks, covering extremities, and staying out of the wind.

are caught by anglers fishing out of charter boat from Nova Scotia or Prince Edward Island ports.

Related Topics

Visitors to Canada will find no lack of guides, charter boats, and services catering to anglers, especially in the well-known and well-publicized areas. Most lodges and camps have guides *(see)*, and charter boats *(see)* can be found in major inland waters and on the coasts. Lodges, camps, and other facilities dedicated to serving anglers are plentiful and are widely advertised in major outdoor publications in both Canada and the U.S. Outfitters exist who cater to canoe-camping and fishing trips, houseboat vacation and fishing trips, horse or foot pack trips, and so forth *(see: travel)*.

Canada is so large, and has such a plethora of angling opportunities, that it can be a bit bewildering for visitors from other countries who want to do some fishing. Prospective anglers therefore need to focus either on the region they plan to visit (perhaps on vacation) to discover the opportunities available and the common means of angling, or to focus on the species they wish to catch and then decide where to go to catch either many of that species or large specimens (at some places it is possible to do both).

Sportfishing in Canada is most popularly pursued from early spring through fall, but ice fishing has a large constituency, with perch, whitefish, and lake trout the major interests. Huge Lake Simcoe in Ontario bills itself as the "Ice Fishing Capitol of the World" and attracts up to 5,000 anglers per weekend in the height of the season.

There are regulations that restrict sportfishing by season, usually to protect spawning fish or fragile populations, and these are in place for most species of freshwater fish. For the most part, regulations regarding seasons, methods of fishing, catch limits, and licensing are determined by provincial and territorial governments. There is no national or federal sportfishing license in Canada, although each of the 14 provinces and territories requires a license issued by their government, which is valid only in waters within that jurisdiction, and in none is there a test or examination required to obtain a sportfishing license. Any person, whether resident or nonresident, can purchase a fishing license, although the nonresident fee is higher. Licenses can usually be purchased for varying time periods (a full year, a week, three days); they are most commonly acquired at stores selling fishing tackle, but are also obtained at some government offices, marinas, lodges, and camps.

Various provinces and territories are likely to have region-wide or water-specific regulations pertaining to the manner of fishing. Manitoba, for example, mandates the use of barbless hooks throughout provincial waters. These and other issues are addressed in a brochure or booklet provided when you purchase a fishing license.

Although some are not as productive as in the past, many of Canada's waters still provide good fishing. In some places, however, drive-in access has resulted in extraordinary fishing pressure. More logging roads have increased access to places few could previously reach in the summer, and these have gotten hammered.

Overfishing is one of the reasons why travelers who are able to fish without the convenience of having their own boat journey to fly-in locations, whether main lodge or outpost, to be assured of a high-quality Canadian experience. At such places there is a growing emphasis on catch-and-release (except small fish for lunch), including trophy specimens; using barbless or de-barbed hooks; using single-hook lures; and prohibiting fishing with bait to minimize injuring fish.

New owners, new customers, and a quality resource, have contributed to the acceptance and success of these policies. Younger and progressive owners have stepped in at many fly-in lodges across Canada. They have refurbished or built new deluxe or near-deluxe accommodations and made an enormous investment in the resource; most have exclusive outfitting rights. Aside from offering a good service, they must sink or swim with that resource. They, and most of their customers, recognize the resource is finite. People used to think there was no limit to the number and size of fish they could keep, even in lightly angled wilderness waters, and that there was no harm from fishing pressure. Now they know better.

Resource-protection changes have been well received by most conservation-oriented visitors. Considering the cost of such trips, no amount of killing fish, trophies or otherwise, would be of comparable worth, so quality of experience becomes the real issue. And the quality of experience is surely enhanced where there is enjoyable fishing opportunity.

CANARY ISLANDS

See: **Spain.**

CAN BUOY

A cylindrical buoy, usually green, used as an aid to navigation.

See: **Buoys.**

CANDIRU

The candiru is a small parasitic South American catfish.

See: **Catfish.**

CANDLEFISH

See: **Eulachon.**

CANE POLE

An inexpensive long pole, usually cut from a stalk of bamboo, unaccompanied by a fishing reel or rod components, and used for making short-distance presentations, primarily of bait. Cane poles are usually from 10 to 15 feet in length; they are not cast, and have a fixed length of line attached to the tip. The line is no longer than the length of the pole, and the hooked bait, often with float or bobber, is usually lobbed or swung into the water.

Cane poles are used for stillfishing, primarily for panfish species, and hooked fish are retrieved by being jerked or lifted out of the water. Other materials may be used to make a "cane" pole, but the principal of operation remains the same.

CANINE TEETH

Pointed canine teeth are found in some carnivorous fish; they are usually larger than the surrounding teeth. **See: Anatomy.**

CANNONBALL

See: Downrigger.

CANOE

Canoes are popular boats, widely used for fishing in flowing waters and in smaller lakes and ponds, and for accessing shallow backwaters and places where most other craft cannot be taken. Their popularity in part stems from the fact that they are relatively inexpensive compared to other fishing boats, eminently portable due to their light weight, easy to store and maintain, and durable. However, they are also more subject to capsizing because they're less stable than most other craft, although it is usually operator misuse or misjudgment, rather than the craft itself, that contributes to tipsiness or instability.

Canoes range widely in size, from mere one-person 10-footers to 24-foot models; the common lengths used by anglers are in the 15- to 17-foot range, although the longest canoes (which are heavy,

Canoes are very popular for river fishing, although many places are best fished by getting out of the canoe and wading.

broad-beamed, very stable, and commonly called "freighter" canoes) are used by anglers in some northern lakes, where they are also a primary means of transport for native people and wilderness residents.

Canoes are primarily open-interior craft with no closed storage compartments. The typical canoe tends to be narrower than other boats, and with limited leg room in the bow. The majority of canoes are double-ended, meaning that both the bow and stern are pointed; some models, however, have a square stern for the attachment of a small motor. Double-ended canoes are mainly paddled, but they can be poled or rowed with special attachments. They must be fitted with a near-stern cross-gunwale bracket to be used with a motor. Square-sterned canoes are propelled in the same manner.

Most canoes used with motors are operated with low-horsepower models, with the exception of freighter canoes. Electric motors are very useful on standard canoes, and can be attached to a square stern, a bracket, or in some cases to the gunwale. An electric motor moves a canoe along very nicely, and is a big aid for positioning while fishing, but it does nothing for portability. The heavy battery needed to power the electric motor negates portaging, and the same weight problem holds for gas motors.

Anglers have mixed feelings about canoes for pure fishing purposes. On the plus side, a lightweight canoe can be portaged over short, medium, and long distances to fish waters that other craft cannot reach. They are also easy to manipulate in shallow environments and in backwater spots that most other boats cannot access. If handled properly by paddlers, they are very quiet. They're also very good in shallow rivers and streams, and if you traverse whitewater.

On the minus side, canoes are highly susceptible to maneuvering problems, especially when paddling and when there's a wind. Many people who fish out of canoes spend more time paddling, positioning, maneuvering, and repositioning, than they do fishing, which means that they are not very effective anglers. This is especially so for anglers fishing alone, for those who do not care to anchor, or for those whose fishing is not helped by anchoring. Even when two paddlers fish out of a canoe, a little bit of wind or current means one angler must keep working the canoe while the other fishes. When anglers are guided from canoes, however, the guide does all of the critical maneuvering and position maintenance.

Another problem for many anglers is that it is unwise or at least risky to stand up in many canoes. Anglers see better, cast better, set the hook better, and play fish better when standing, but only the biggest, broadest, and most stable canoes permit this. The feeling of instability and of being pushed or pulled around by wind, current, or even the working of some lures, makes canoes a non-choice, or least-favored choice, for some anglers.

Canoes, especially smaller models and those propelled manually, are not good vessels on big waters, or in places where conditions can change suddenly into large waves and rough water. Although they can be paddled long distances, possible exposure to bad weather, heavy winds, and large waves restricts their useful practical range.

Materials and shapes. Canoes are made of aluminum, fiberglass, Kevlar, and various plastic composites. Aluminum has long been a favored material because it is light, durable, and maintenance free. But aluminum canoes tend to catch on rocks and are noisy and shiny, which can be detrimental to fishing in the very backwaters that a canoe is meant to access. Fiberglass canoes are less susceptible to being blown around because of greater weight and, in general, are less tipsy than aluminum. They are also durable and quiet, but their weight makes them tougher to portage long distances and harder for some people to lift, transport, or cartop by themselves. Kevlar canoes are expensive but lighter than fiberglass and also quiet, while plastic composites are moderately heavy but quiet and very durable. There are also wooden or wood/canvas canoes, which are expensive and require high maintenance, but are quiet, durable, and aesthetically appealing.

The length, width, and hull shape affect how a canoe paddles and maneuvers, and how much weight it can carry. Shorter canoes are generally lighter and

Canoe Features

Keels

Straight/no rocker

Straight/slight rocker

Curved/high rocker

Hulls

Flat

Round

Modified-V

Semi-V

Sides

Flare

Tumblehome

Straight

more maneuverable. Longer canoes track better (stay in a straight line) and can hold more weight. Double-enders are easier to paddle than square-stern models.

Hull shapes are roughly analogous to the hulls on conventional boats *(see):* flat, round, or some form of V, and with similar characteristics. Flat-bottoms are fairly stable, especially in flat water, but do not track very well unless they have a keel, which also aids turning; round hulls are unstable for the average user; V-shaped hulls (there are variations) are stable in rough water and track well. The keel line of the boat varies with the rocker, which is the degree to which the keel is straight or curved. A canoe without any rocker is considered to have a straight keel; it has more surface in the water and turns more slowly. A canoe with a lot of rocker turns quickly but is poor at tracking; it is more suitable to fast water than to flat water. Most canoes for fishing have a slight rocker, so they turn and track adequately.

For fishing and general outdoor use, a width or beam of between 32 and 39 inches is preferred; this is measured at the widest spot from the interior rather than at the gunwales because there are different designs to the sides of canoes. Sides that flare outward help keep water out but can be harder to reach over for paddling; sides that flare inward, called tumblehome, are easier to paddle but not as good at keeping water out. Straight sides are a blend of these and have less outward flare.

Canoe handling and loading basics. Canoes are paddled primarily with straight or bent-shaft paddles, the former preferred for general use because of versatility. A canoe usually turns away from the side the stern is paddled on, so direction is maintained by the stern paddler using a hook motion that twists the paddle through most of the stroke. It moves straight ahead when two paddlers keep their paddles vertical and pull straight back parallel to the keel line. To change direction, a paddler swings the paddle out in an arc; this is called a sweep, and the canoe will head in the opposite direction of the stroke. A solo paddler may find it best to sit in the bow seat facing aft, paddling stern-first as it were for better balance and control.

For some people, getting in and out of a canoe is often harder than controlling it. Canoes are meant to carry a load in the water, so they are weak and unstable when one end is on shore and the other unsupported. If you must get into a canoe that is partially on shore, keep your weight and center of gravity low, step in the center and keep hands along both gunwales; this can be aided by a companion who straddles the bow of the canoe and helps support it. Approach shore bow-first in still water and maintain stability for the bow occupant to get out, pull up the canoe slightly, and then straddle it for the rear paddler to exit. In flowing water, point the bow upstream when coming ashore to keep it from being swept into the current.

Canoes have a carrying capacity as do other boats, and this is identified on a capacity label in the canoe. Remember that this weight includes paddlers. Be sure to situate the load so that there is a low center of gravity in the canoe, and evenly distribute the load for normal travel. When headed into a strong headwind, adjust weight to keep the bow down and stern high to achieve better directional tracking. You can move cargo forward or simply kneel in front of your seats to accomplish this.

Canoeists are well advised to wear properly fitting personal flotation devices (see). Because canoes are more susceptible to capsizing than other craft, you have a greater chance of needing a PFD; water conditions, temperature, and other circumstances affect the situation, but be aware that a canoe can get away from paddlers pretty quickly in some situations, and a PFD that isn't on may not be accessible when needed. Be careful about making sudden moves in a canoe or shifting weight or cargo around. If you have to shift weight or change position, paddle to shore and make changes there. Be particularly careful where you are likely to encounter sudden waves from the wake of boats, and where there is current. In some situations it may be necessary to lash cargo to the canoe, and/or to use watertight bags for storing gear.

Anglers use canoes in both flowing and stillwaters and encounter different natural elements that can cause problems. In stillwater, waves, wind, and storms are likely to pose a threat, especially if you're laden down and traveling a far distance. Do not take unnecessary chances, and try to avoid problems (like heading for the lee shore when the wind starts to pick up, even if it means you have to paddle farther and it's less direct). In flowing water, you must know how to handle your canoe, and how to read a river for best navigation. An upstream V, for example, suggests rocks at the apex of the V; a downstream V suggests a gap between rocks. You may also need to scout ahead; where conditions are beyond your skill level (rapids, dams, fallen trees, whitewater) get to shore and portage or rope the canoe down. Remember that heavy rains or water releases can change a river's flow quickly. You should stay off water that is at or near flood stage.

One of the biggest problems with canoeing in rivers is that you are likely to encounter other anglers, including those who are wading or fishing from shore and have established their position. As an angler, you should be able to appreciate that the passage of a canoe over rising trout in a pool is going to put down those fish for quite a while, or that running right through the casting and fishing range of an angler is an uncaring if not hostile act. So make it a point to paddle behind an active angler, or to float by as far away as seems reasonable, or to ask if it's okay to move through the area the angler is fishing.

Canoes are perhaps the most frequently capsized craft, and for anglers, this not only poses obvious safety concerns, it can lead to the loss of a lot of gear. Anglers usually carry a fair amount of tackle, either in a box or satchel, and frequently leave it

Follow the depicted procedures to right a capsized canoe; helpers should apply their weight to the gunwale of the emptied canoe (bottom) to allow a capsizing victim to enter from the opposite side.

open. Be aware that if you capsize in this state, you can kiss just about all of your gear goodbye. It might be a good idea when fishing from a canoe to secure anything that you are not currently using. If all of your gear is in a closed tackle box, for example, you stand a better chance of getting the whole box (unless the water is really deep) and contents back, albeit soaked; if the box is open and you tip over, you'll lose a lot.

Regarding capsizing, if this happens in moving water, stay on the upstream side of the canoe to avoid being pinned against some obstacle. Hold onto the canoe unless you can increase your safety by letting go. When you reach a place where you can stand, bring the boat into the shallows to get the water out. In a lake or pond, a capsized canoe can be refloated by pulling it over the midsection of another, upright, canoe, but getting back into it without getting into the shallows is very difficult for many people.

If someone else is around, say in another canoe, they can help the capsizing victim refloat his canoe by pulling it, gunwales down, over the gunwales of their own canoe. The helpers can pull while the person in the water pushes. It may be necessary to rock or twist the capsized canoe to overcome suction. Once the bow and stern of the capsized canoe are out of the water, turn it over and ease it back into the water alongside the assisting canoe and preferably downwind. A light, athletic, and strong-armed person can get into the canoe by boosting in while the person(s) assisting lean on the opposite gunwale to help stabilize it. See: Boat.

CANYON

A narrow, deep underwater valley with steep slopes, usually found far offshore in the ocean beyond the continental shelf. This underwater structure is often situated amidst powerful currents and attracts pelagic prey and predator fish, making it attractive to anglers who are able to reach such an area. In the northeastern United States, sportfishing the various Atlantic Ocean canyons is virtually an industry unto itself.
See: Offshore Fishing.

CAPE

The feathered skin of a chicken, from neck to the base of the back, which provides hackle for fly tiers.
See: Fly Tying.

CAPELIN   *Mallotus villosus.*

Other names—Danish/Dutch/German/Norwegian: *lodde;* French: *capelin atlantique;* Japanese: *karafuto-shishamo.*

A member of the smelt family, the capelin is an important food fish for cod, pollock, salmon, seabirds, and whales. It has commercial value; females are prized for their roe, and the meat is used as animal feed and fish meal. Like other smelts in flavor and texture, it is an excellent table fish, marketed canned and frozen and prepared by frying and dry salting.

Identification.   The capelin has a large mouth with a lower jaw that extends below the eye. Males have larger and deeper bodies than females; also, the male has an anal fin with a strongly convex base, whereas the female has a straight anal fin base. Both sexes possess a single dorsal fin and extremely small scales. The body is mostly silver, and the upper back is a darker bluish green.

Size/Age.   Capelin may reach a size of 9 inches, although they are usually less than 7 inches long.

Distribution.   Capelin are found in the North Atlantic, especially in the Barents Sea up to Beard Island; in the White and Norwegian Seas; off the coast of Greenland; and from Hudson Bay to the Gulf of Maine. In the North Pacific, their range extends from Korea to the Strait of Juan de Fuca between Vancouver Island, Canada, and Washington, USA.

Habitat.   Inhabiting saltwater, capelin are pelagic and live in the open seas.

Life History/behavior.   Between March and October, capelin move inshore in large schools to spawn in shallow saltwater areas over fine gravel or on sand beaches; however, some may spawn at great depths. Spawning occurs more than once, and each female produces between 3,000 and 56,000 eggs; these are released at high tide and hatch in two to three weeks.

Food and feeding habits.   Capelin feed primarily on planktonic crustaceans.

Angling.   Capelin have no angling value, although they are used as food in some areas and are mostly caught in cast nets and dipnets.

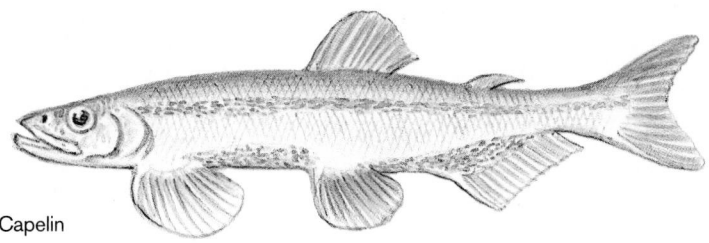
Capelin

CAPTAIN
See: Charter Boat Captain.

CARBON FIBER
A term for graphite.
See: Reel, Fishing; Rod, Fishing.

CAROLINA RIG
See: Soft Worm.

CARP

Although many freshwater anglers have a distinct affinity for certain species of fish, they often have a clear dislike or indifference for others, and in North America carp usually top the list of the latter. Carp, which are nonnative or so-called exotic species *(see)* in the United States, Mexico, and Canada, get little respect and have been the subject of intense, and unsuccessful, eradication measures. When considered in terms of weight (biomass), however, they are among the most abundant fish in North America, especially in the U.S.

Modern-day fisheries managers, whose predecessors were largely responsible for the ill-advised introduction of carp, mounted campaigns in the mid-1980s to encourage angling for these fish. Although a small carp following currently exists in North America, promotional efforts have produced little change in the appreciation of, or effort spent on, these fish. This trend continues despite the existence of large specimens in many bodies of water and despite the fact that when hooked, carp are among the strongest fish in freshwater.

Due to a small constituency, minor media attention, and plenty of other angling options, the methods of fishing for carp in North America lag behind those in Europe, where carp fishing is popular. Interest among North Americans may slowly increase, and methods become more focused, if populations of other important freshwater fisheries seriously decline. The abundant carp might then be more attractive. This is relatively unlikely, however, given the ingrained predispositions of anglers to certain styles of fishing. Meanwhile, because carp are abundant, relatively large on average, and overlooked by most anglers in the U.S. and Canada, these areas have relatively untapped potential for those who are interested in these species.

Scores of big carp mill near a marina at Lake Mead, Nevada

Species

Carp belong to the Cyprinidae family of freshwater fish, a large grouping of about 2,000 species that is abundantly represented in Europe, Asia, and North America but has no native species in Australia and South America. Cyprinids lack teeth in the mouth, although many have pharyngeal (throat) teeth for crushing hard foods and chewing plant material. Feeding habits vary; in many species, the mouth is somewhat protractile, or suckerlike, for feeding on the bottom, and many have sensory barbels on the chin or lips. Typically, the rays in the fins are soft, but in some (carp and goldfish) the first ray is spinelike. Most cyprinids are 6 inches or less in length, but they are highly important ecologically as food for larger fish; these include many species of minnows *(see)*, chub *(see)*, and others. Many of these smaller fish are used as bait. The few larger species provide sport for anglers or are harvested as food fish.

Types of Carp. The largest member of the minnow family, and a significant species to anglers, is *Cyprinus carpio.* Of the three varieties of *C. carpio,* foremost is the familiar and profusely scaled type that is primarily referred to as the common carp *(see: carp, common),* which is also popularly referred to as the king carp or scaled carp. A second type is a scaleless version called the leather carp, sometimes referred to as the nude carp. The third type is one with a haphazard placement of a small number of oversize scales that is known as the mirror carp. The mirror and leather carp are actually domesticated, or cultivated, versions of the common carp as well as its predecessors. A related fish of increasing prominence is *Ctenopharyngodon idella,* the white amur, or grass carp *(see: carp, grass),* an Asian species that is particularly adept at feeding on aquatic vegetation.

The above-mentioned fish are the ones people most commonly refer to when speaking of carp. Confusing terminology and identifications stew the pot somewhat, however, and fishing and scientific literature is full of references to fish that are, and are

not, different from these. Mirror carp, for instance, generally have a smattering of scales, but may also appear with a full lateral representation of scales, or completely scaled, making these variants appear to be something other than mirror carp. The mirror carp with linear scales has two full rows of scales on each side, one running along the lateral line and the other below and alongside the dorsal fin. The fully scaled mirror carp is completely covered with scales of varying sizes and shapes, and is fairly rare. Mirror carp are scarce in North America, and it believed that no leather carp exist there; thus, common carp and grass carp are the major carp species on the continent.

The forerunners of the common carp in Britain are called wild carp, or wildies. This is not a separate species, as wild carp—like the common, leather, and mirror varieties—are designated *C. carpio,* but they are reportedly natural descendants of the original strains of common carp introduced to Britain. These slow-growing fish are smaller than common carp and possess a fully scaled body that seldom exceeds 10 pounds in weight. There is, however, a species called crucian carp *(Carassius carassius)* that is small, deep-bodied, and more closely related to the goldfish; it can reach a weight of $5^1/_2$ pounds and is of European and Asian distribution. Many carp are rather like goldfish; some of the carp cultivated in the Orient have gold-tinged scales, showing the close relationship of this species to the goldfish.

In addition to these fish, numerous other variations of common carp exist. They may be called European carp, German carp, Israeli carp, French carp, Italian carp, silver carp, snail carp, and bighead carp—all with some variation in color, body shape, or scale pattern.

Common carp average less than 5 pounds in weight through most of their range. A 10-pounder is ranked as a big fish in most places, but they can grow much larger. In North America, there are many carp in the 15- to 25-pound class; a relative lack of fishing pressure and low harvest suggest the possibility of many monster fish.

The all-tackle world record for common carp is a 75-pound, 11-ounce fish caught in France in 1987. How large these carp can grow is generally unknown; an $83^1/_2$-pounder was reported from South Africa earlier in the twentieth century. A 74-pound carp from Mississippi in 1963 is the largest reported North American state record, but it is unknown if this is the largest carp ever captured there. There are at least 14 state-record carp that weighed 50 pounds or better, and many states annually yield carp in the 25- to 40-pound range, and an occasional 50-pounder, some obtained through sportfishing and some through bowhunting or spearing. A few of these are grass carp and some are common carp. A 65-pound, 14-ounce grass carp taken in Arkansas in 1995 is the all-tackle world record for this species, and their ultimate size is unknown. Alabama and Arkansas have produced other 60-pound grass carp, and some states have produced 50-pounders.

The age that carp can attain is somewhat uncertain as well. An 1805 account of carp in a garden pond in Cambridge, England, mentioned a fish that had inhabited that pond for more than 70 years. A sixteenth-century Swiss naturalist cited a fish that was 150 years old. It is believed that the average longevity of carp in the wild is 15 years, and the life expectancy is much greater for those in cultivated ponds or aquariums. Large carp can clearly live 30 years, and perhaps as many as 50 years.

Carp are of primarily Asian origin and were widely transported and cultivated over centuries and broadly introduced in North America. In their native Asia, carp once graced the private fish ponds of emperors and were harvested only on festive occasions. Carp were among the first species of fish to be "farmed" as a means of controlling or increasing the population. European explorers transported carp to their continent, where these big minnows became choice fare on royal menus and were intensively raised in food ponds. In England, Izaak Walton, the ex officio patron saint of anglers and an oft-cited source by trout and fly fishing devotees, selected the carp as a favorite, calling it "the queen of rivers: a stately, good and very subtle fish" in his classic book *The Compleat Angler.*

Carp are sometimes reared in flooded paddies. In this way, protein and starch are produced simultaneously on the same acres, an important technique in overpopulated, protein-poor countries. Carp are often kept in special fattening pens before being sent to market; they can be shipped alive because they are hardy and will survive long periods out of water, as long as they are kept cool and moist.

Although their food value is underexploited and underappreciated in North America, carp are an important food fish elsewhere in the world. Its culinary popularity is due in small part to catches for personal consumption and in large part to commercial production and harvest. Carp are commonly used, for example, as an ingredient in gefilte fish, a favorite Jewish preparation, and they are valued in restaurants throughout Europe.

Many North Americans—anglers and non-anglers alike—turn their back on carp as a food fish, ostensibly because its flesh is tainted by the muddy or polluted waters in which it lives. In some situations, this may be true, but carp taken from many locations taste fine, whether consumed immediately or kept in cold, clean water for a while to eliminate muddiness (and firm up the flesh) prior to consumption. Carp can be prepared in a virtually unlimited number of ways, and in the U.S., where they are abundant, increased consumption would be appropriate not only for culinary reasons but also for environmental reasons, as they overpopulate many places.

North Americans' distaste for these fish stems in part from the carp's feeding habits and lifestyle. They subsist on tiny plants and animals, which they obtain by rooting along the lake or river bottom, often but not exclusively in mud. They draw-in the rich organic ooze with their suckerlike mouth and spit out or excrete bottom sediments. When spawning, they wallow in the mud and roil the water, sometimes causing stifling clouds of silt to settle over the nests and spawn of bass and other prized gamefish. Carp may also accidentally suck in the eggs or newly hatched young of these fish. The clouding of the water prohibits sunlight penetration, which in turn reduces plant and algae growth. This is not an attractive scenario, but then many people are fond of domestic pork even though the habits of pigs are not exactly regal. Moreover, catfish are prolific and omnivorous bottom feeders, known to eat dead fish even, yet they are appreciated by a large segment of the sportfishing public (although also unappreciated by some who are swayed by appearance and feeding behavior).

In addition to rooting around for food in turbid shallow environs, carp mate there and bring forth bumper crops of their own. A large female broadcasts her eggs over a wide area of shallows as she swims along, laying perhaps more than a million eggs in a season (a 20-pounder reportedly can produce 10 million eggs). The males fertilize the eggs by releasing clouds of milt in the areas where the eggs are laid. Neither the eggs nor the young get attention from the parents, but the carp population spirals upward because of the quantity of eggs and young produced. As a result, large populations of these fish exist in some waters, especially big lakes, reservoirs, and rivers.

The senses of carp are extremely well developed, more so than those of many other species. Their

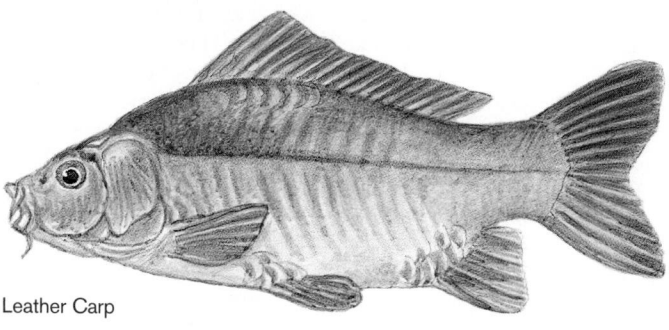

Leather Carp

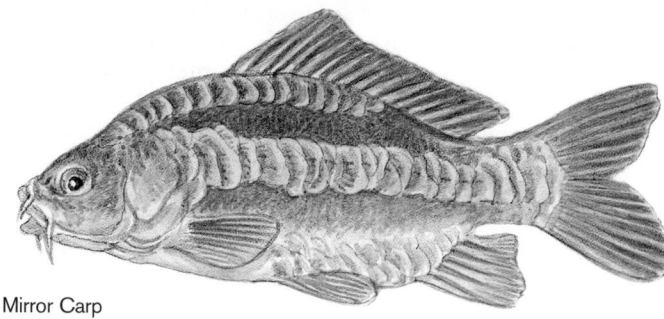

Mirror Carp

C

senses are in part responsible for their ability to adapt so well to so many environments, including areas that inhibit other species. Carp have a keen sense of smell, which explains why so many anglers offer them flavorful baits and lure them with advance chumming. Carp are reportedly capable of distinguishing one type of shellfish from another. They also have a highly developed sense of taste. Biologists report that carp have specialized taste buds in the skin of their snout, mouth, lips, and throat that are connected to the brain by nerves. Tests have shown that carp can differentiate between salty, bitter, and sweet substances, as well as between many extracts of fish skin and other fish tissues. They detect most of their food, especially in murky waters, by scent and then sample it with their barbels or lips. Sometimes curious, they will pick up a possible food item and taste it before ingesting it. They are also cautious and wary, however, and know when to avoid suspect items.

One seldom-addressed aspect of carps' acute senses is widely known by European anglers but is rarely detailed in the North American angling literature: carp (and some minnows) are supposedly capable of being alerted to danger through their sense of smell. Their skin possesses large cells that release sensory chemicals, called allomones, into the water when their skin is damaged by a predator. The scent of these allomones evokes a survival response in other similar fish, which scatter and possibly also seek cover. Does this imply that when a captured fish has been handled and then released, it alarms other fish? Some folks believe this is so, but there's no conclusive proof.

Goldfish.   The goldfish *(Carassius auratus)* vies with carp in fame and for the length of time it has been associated with humans, although it has no significance in sportfishing and is primarily affiliated with aquarium collection. This cyprinid has been kept in ponds and aquariums in the Orient for many centuries.

Goldfish in the wild resemble carp in shape and sometimes in color, but they lack barbels under the chin. Those goldfish that escape captivity or that live in large outdoor ponds revert in only a few generations to their original natural greenish or black colors. They also grow to large size, weighing 2 pounds or more. For aquariums, they have been bred to produce a variety of shapes and colors, including rich black, red, yellow, and spotted, as well as the conventional gold. Some have bulging or telescopic eyes; others have tremendously enlarged fins. Goldfish are extremely hardy, which accounts for their ability to survive in small bowls and in poorly tended aquariums. When properly cared for in aquariums, they can live for more than 10 years.

Ecologists caution against the release of goldfish, intentionally or by accident. Although they will not breed in small aquariums, they will spawn and produce prodigious numbers in the wild. They can soon become so abundant that they crowd out native species. Because of this threat, in some areas there are laws prohibiting the sale of goldfish for bait (although carp minnows are used, deliberately or accidentally, for bait).

History, Attitudes, and Image

Carp present perhaps the greatest anomaly among freshwater species that exists in all of angling. When a species is abundant, hard-fighting, and respectable table fare, people will typically pursue it feverishly. Witness, for example, the historically recent introduction of Pacific salmon in the Great Lakes, which brought hordes of anglers out and spurred all manner of changes and evolution in equipment and fishing methods. But not so with carp in North America. Despite the abundance of carp and the large sizes attained—they reach heavier weights than most freshwater fish—they are largely ignored on this continent, to the bewilderment and envy of European devotees.

In the latest U.S. government surveys of angling participation, when respondents were asked what single type of fish they pursued most often, carp were not even represented among the 27 categories of response, which accounted for 98 percent of all replies. As mentioned earlier, in the U.S. the carp is generally more cussed than caught. By contrast, in Europe carp are less widely available yet far more highly valued. They are revered by many anglers and pursued with great devotion and fervor. And most of the carp caught are released. An evaluation of the history of carp and angling preferences may put attitudes and image into perspective.

Carp were native to Asia and known to both the ancient Greeks and Romans. They were apparently introduced to Great Britain in the mid-fifteenth century, although there are many different dates ascribed to this event. British writers have long attributed the spread of carp in England to their cultivation in monastery ponds, called stews or stewponds.

According to a report on exotic fish by the Sport Fishing Institute, carp "were apparently brought to the United States from Europe in 1831 and 1832 by a private citizen." The New York Department of Environmental Conservation reported that carp were first introduced into New York in 1831. The general introduction of carp in the U.S. occurred in May of 1877, when German fish culturist Rudolph Hessel arrived in New York with 227 leather and mirror carp, and 118 scaled carp for the U.S. Commission of Fish and Fisheries. These fish were first distributed by request to the constituents of congressmen in 1879, and by 1882 some carp had been distributed to every state and territory in the U.S. except Montana. A groundswell of complaints arose, and by 1896 federal carp stockings were discontinued. But the fish were then virtually everywhere, in many cases crowding out native species and spreading unhindered, with few enemies to keep them in control.

As the Sport Fishing Institute and many others have written, the introduction of the common carp to U.S. (and other North American) waters was a monumental mistake. Ironically, however, at the same time that carp were being distributed across the U.S., so were brown trout (also imported from Germany). And both American shad and striped bass were being moved from the East Coast, where they were indigenous, to the West Coast, where they were not indigenous. Today, the shad, striped bass, and brown trout exotic introductions are not looked upon with disfavor, at least by the general angling public.

Obviously there is some bias against the carp that cannot be ascribed to the mere fact that it is not indigenous to North America. This should evidently be attributed to the collective North American sense of what constitutes a sporting, or game, species. Although carp are not the sluggish fish that some people think, they are not an aggressive species in the same manner as many freshwater fish, and their diet is one that provides minor inspiration for people who like to cast lures or flies (that overwhelmingly imitate fish, aquatic insects, or terrestrials).

As Izaak Walton himself pointed out in *The Compleat Angler*, "if you fish for carp, you must put on a very large measure of patience." And in North America, unlike Europe, where there is an abundance of species of good size to pursue (several types of trout, salmon, and bass, plus pike, muskies, walleye, striped bass, catfish, and others), there has been little incentive to exhibit patience for a spooky, light-biting species that does not eat other fish, often scrounges for food, consumes vegetation, is considered by many an overgrown aquarium species, and primarily responds to odd bait preparations and oftentimes intensive chumming.

Europeans do a great deal of chumming (called feeding) for carp, and yet in North American freshwaters chumming is lightly, if at all, practiced for any species. It is illegal in some places, and at the very least it is viewed with disdain in others. Saltwater sportfishing enthusiasts in North America, on the contrary, rely heavily on some form of bait to catch fish, and chumming is the favored means of attracting many species of fish to a hooked bait. Granted, chumming in saltwater is largely done with ground, chunked, or whole fish, whereas chumming in freshwater (at least for carp) is accomplished with assorted prepared exotic, and some not so exotic (like corn), foods that are nevertheless not normally found in the water.

Naturally these attitudes, disparities, and contradictions provide a great deal of fodder for comparisons with fishing in Europe, where there are fewer prominent, large, and abundant freshwater species, and where angling traditions and attitudes differ. In England, not only are attitudes about carp and carp fishing more reverential, but there is great zeal about releasing the fish. Among the English, it is

practically criminal to even think about keeping a carp because these fish are much less abundant. Carp farmers breed the fish for live sale to sporting syndicates; a 30-pounder might be worth more than $10,000. Yet in North America, carp anglers would not be questioned about keeping a carp (other than why they would want to eat it), and there is even a constituency for stalking and shooting carp with an arrow (legal in many places). This practice commonly occurs when the fish hold in the shallows and often when they spawn.

It is perhaps ironic that carp in Europe, especially in England, have been released so often that it is very difficult to recatch those fish, especially the old, large ones. They are either evidently crafty or become more so after being caught and released. One of the most intriguing footnotes with regard to carp surrounds the capture of the former British record, a fish of 44 pounds caught in 1952 and kept alive in the London Zoo Aquarium for 20 years after capture. The fish was visited and fed by Richard Walker, the angler who caught it. It would eat various baits, but never took the type of bait— reputedly a ball of bread paste—that Walker originally used to catch the fish. If this is indicative of the intelligence of these creatures, then it is no wonder that large specimens are very tough to catch on heavily fished European waters. Moreover, if carp in general are perceived to be hard to catch, requiring, as Walton said, a lot of patience, plus a lot of still-fishing, then it is little wonder that North Americans, having an abundance of more aggressive species with higher popularity quotients, do not warm to the different angling methods required to catch carp.

In North America, carp are not presently as difficult to catch as they are in Europe. Some anglers have terrific success in terms of numbers of fish, and many large ones are caught each year. So there is some question as to whether carp are as difficult to catch as many people believe, or whether they are just not well understood.

It will likely be a long time before carp are widely embraced by North American anglers, and before carp fishing is broadly recognized as an appealing sport. But for anglers with an open attitude, a follow-their-own-path mind-set, and an interest in pursuing a challenging and hard-fighting fish, the carp is a worthy quarry.

Angling for Carp

Whether you like their looks, food preferences, spawning habits, or other characteristics, carp are certainly a desirable fish to have on the end of a fishing line. They don't jump the way some popular gamefish do, but then the prized bonefish of saltwater also don't jump, opting instead to make blistering runs. Similarly, the hallmark of a fight with a carp is a streaking dogged run, the severity of which will depend on the size of the fish, the strength of your tackle, and perhaps whether the

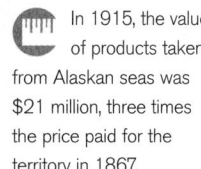

In 1915, the value of products taken from Alaskan seas was $21 million, three times the price paid for the territory in 1867.

environment is a river or lake. Big carp can take a lot of line off a reel in a hurry, and offer a lot of resistance throughout the fight, so there is little chance of horsing-in the large bruisers. And they fight until every last inch of line is retrieved. With a powerful sweep of its broad tail, this bronzed battler is off on a surging run that will test the finest tackle and overcome inferior equipment. Several determined runs and many minutes after being hooked, the fish may roll on its side to be led in. But that's not the end. Carp have a knack for rolling and flapping violently just as the net is swooping toward them, and many a good fish has escaped at this moment.

Hooking the fish, or, more appropriately, getting it to take your offering, is the biggest problem. Carp are not impulsive predators or ambush strikers. For the most part, they are not chasers or stalk-and-attack hunters. They are unlikely to strike a surface lure or diving plug, or, for that matter, most lures that are worked in a swimming manner and at a relatively fast (from their perspective) pace. When a lure is cast near them, they depart instantly. On occasion and where they are abundant, carp will strike a slow-moving jig, and either a weighted fly or a dry fly. Speed of movement is an issue but obviously not the major one. With all of the soft lures popular in North America, and especially with all the various types of soft worms and wormlike lures, one would expect plenty of accidental encounters with carp when using these items. In reality, however, there are darn few. So an angler who used plugs, spoons, spinners, surface lures, and most soft lures deliberately and exclusively for carp could cast or troll the paint off them, and then some, before realistically having a chance of catching carp in a natural environment. Nevertheless, carp are caught by anglers fishing for other species, mostly with some type of bait and looking for "whatever bites."

Deliberate fishing for carp requires a focused, not haphazard, approach, a good deal of patience, a knowledge of the habits of these fish, and slightly

A float angler fishes for carp on a New York pond.

different equipment and tactics than are used for most popular freshwater species. As mentioned, many European anglers rank carp among the most difficult to catch of all freshwater fish. This is partly because carp are not exceptionally abundant, because there is intense pressure on them, and because of the natural cunning and wariness of the species. In the Old World, this sport is engaged in with a craftsman's care and with a degree of stalking and refined presentation that is uncommon among North American anglers. On the North American continent, with its bounty of big waters and variable species, anglers are not as refined in their approach or equipment, but they are moving in that direction.

Tackle.   Tackle for carp varies. Ten-pound line is adequate strength, but if you want great sport and don't mind losing a fish or two, 4- to 6-pound line on an ultralight outfit will do nicely, especially if you're fishing unobstructed open water. Where carp in the 10- to 20-pound or better range might be encountered, it is important to have a quality line and a reel with a smooth-working drag. For big carp in waters with snags and a lot of thick grass or pad cover, it might be necessary to use heavier line, from 12 to 20 pounds in strength. Thin-diameter line is especially useful in carp fishing because it is less detectable yet has the strength of conventional-diameter line. A line with good abrasion resistance is also important.

Spinning, spincasting, and baitcasting tackle are all used to land carp, but spinning is probably the most functional method. The drag on many spincasting reels is often suspect, and if you hook a big fish, you must be able to apply pressure to it and count on a drag that is smooth and sturdy. Although most baitcasting reels are adequate in this respect, they are tough to use with light gear and might not be suitable for presenting the lightest terminal rigs and baits. Casting, as in cast-and-retrieve angling, is not a prominent aspect of carp fishing (except in some fly fishing and jig fishing situations), although casts are routinely made to put a bait into position; in many cases, this is more of a flip or toss than an actual cast. Where larger objects and weights are used, baitcasting reels will do the job, and they are certainly capable of handling the fight of a fish. Best to use a model with a flipping feature and, for large fish, one with a clicker.

Spinning gear, however, is a good choice for making all types of presentations, and midrange models with ample line capacity and a good drag are universally employed. Some anglers prefer spinning reels with a baitfishing or quick line-release feature.

Rod length is a matter of technique and preference. Lengthy rods with long handles are used by shore anglers, who prop these into rod holders while waiting for their bait to be picked up, and who need length when fishing close to shore for finicky fish. Using a long rod helps keep a close bait in precise position and minimizes line interference—from the rod tip to float *(see)* or terminal rig. When targeting spots at a long distance, however, a long rod does not offer a significant holding advantage, although it does enhance distant bait placement and is more forgiving on light line strengths. Some anglers prefer them for controlling and playing a fish as well.

A long rod to most North Americans is 7 feet, but something in the 9- to 10-foot range might be more appropriate; 11- to 13-footers are common among European carp anglers. Many boat anglers can use their normal walleye and bass fishing gear, which includes rods that are in the 6- to 7$\frac{1}{2}$-foot range and of light to medium action, but when specifically looking for big carp, it's necessary to gear up as one might for striped bass and to use a medium-heavy outfit.

Whatever length you settle on, look for a rod with a sensitive tip that will readily detect strikes, and a powerful butt for fighting the fish. A stiff rod might be useful for heavier fish, but casting soft baits with it will be more difficult, requiring more of a lob action than a cast; a softer rod with more flex will be easier on making bait presentations but also less punishing on a strong fish.

For those few who give fly fishing for carp a go, the primary needs are an 8- or 9-weight rod, a corresponding reel with ample backing capacity and an adjustable drag, and primarily a floating weight-forward line. A sink-tip line can be useful on occasion, but most fly anglers pursue visible, shallow fish, and a weighted fly will reach them without the benefit of a sink-tip fly line.

Bait. In North America, carp have been caught on an assortment of bait, primarily doughballs, corn, worms, processed baits, and commercially prepared baits, usually without chumming, although more anglers are using chum nowadays. They are also caught, although generally less often and more likely in Europe, on a variety of items that most anglers would find strange fishing items: cheese, beans, potato and carrot cubes, peanuts, rice, bread chunks, dog biscuits, cat food, and luncheon meat.

Doughballs are the most popular item used specifically for carp; these homemade concoctions are prepared from such ingredients as cornmeal, flour, syrup, anise oil, vanilla extract, among other offerings, and rolled into a ball. Much as been made by anglers about the various doughs and flavored concoctions that should be used for carp, and plenty has been said about favorite recipes for strange concoctions that are necessary to take carp (cornflakes mixed to a paste with strawberry soda is an overdone but popular example). Some sweet and flavorful product is almost always an ingredient. These concoctions are primarily items that produce a lot of scent and are meant to attract a wandering fish quickly. They are somewhat randomly effective but have taken a lot of carp, in part simply due to

the abundance of unsophisticated fish. In Europe, such a bait is seldom used.

Many anglers who specifically target carp realize that the European style of attracting carp through elevated levels of chumming (which they call feeding or prebaiting) is much less of a hit-or-miss means of angling. In Europe, this chumming may be done for lengthy periods, perhaps several days, prior to actually fishing a location. In North America, few anglers do this. As previously noted, the legality of chumming in North America varies, not to mention that it is viewed with disdain by some anglers. Most of those who can legally chum do so while they are fishing, and a minority chum for a short period (perhaps a few hours or half a day) beforehand. A study of carp chumming by Nebraska fisheries personnel reportedly found that baiting drew carp within 6 hours and held them for about 24 hours. Of course, the effective time may depend on the type of water, where you place the chum, and the abundance of carp.

The chum used is often the same item that will be fished on a hook, although some chumming is done with groundbait. Groundbait is essentially made from crushed bread crumbs or stale bread, the latter being soaked, mixed into a paste, and stiffened with bran or cornmeal. These items are made into balls and tossed into the water, clouding and flavoring it. Other highly preferred chum, as well as hooked baits, are corn and boilies. "Boilie" is a British term for a small ball of processed bait made from assorted ingredients (milk and animal proteins, eggs, soy flour, wheat germ, coloring, and flavoring) that have been rolled together and boiled. They have a crusty shell that retards pecking by small fish. Corn is used straight from a can, but canned corn is usually soft, doesn't last, doesn't cast as well on a hook, and is taken by other nontarget species. Carp prefer corn that has a bit more crunch to it. Anglers take hard-kernel field corn (maize), boil it long enough to soften it a bit (or let it sit in water for several days), and add sweetener. The result is a corn with more consistency than the canned version; it stays on a hook, is not attractive to other fish, and carp pick it up and try to crush it with their throat teeth.

When chumming, anglers distribute these baits over an area where carp are likely to move and feed, if necessary using a slingshot (catapult) or other throwing device to help reach the right locations. The hooked bait (called hookbait by the British) is fished among the chum. Corn, of course, is fished when corn has been used as chum, and bread or boilies are used with groundbaits. Anglers must strike a fine balance between overfeeding the fish, which could cause them to gorge and shut down; feeding too little, which can cause the fish to move on; and chumming just enough to attract them and trigger their interest. Overfeeding is not as much of a problem in North America, where there are more fish and more big waters, as it is in Europe. One of the keys to the success of these items is that they do not attract, or are not consumed by, other species of fish, particularly pesky panfish and perch.

Hook size varies with the size of the bait. Many anglers use treble hooks for carp, especially with doughballs, but it's better to use single hooks. They're less likely to snag, are smaller and less obtrusive to finicky fish, and may make it harder to hook a fish, even though they seem to offer more points for hooking. A sharp and strong single hook, usually in size 6 or 8 but ranging from sizes 10 to 12, is the best bet.

Techniques.   Many people believe that carp are strictly bottom feeders, but that is not the case. Although they primarily feed on the bottom, they also feed on or near the surface as well as at midlevels. Another popular misconception is that carp fishing is strictly a sit-and-wait affair. Although it is true that carp fishing is mostly a waiting game, anglers can opt to take a more aggressive approach and hunt for carp, stalk them, and cast to visible fish. Admittedly, these methods require care and stealth.

Because carp inhabit all types of environments, it is unnecessarily restrictive to expect predictable behavior or to limit one's pursuit to a single fishing method. In clear-water environs, for example, carp may depend very heavily on sight when feeding. In this case, they may be more susceptible to certain colors of baits, to striking jigs or flies that are cast ahead of them, and to using their vision in conjunction with smell or taste as a means of foraging. On the other hand, in muddy waters it is likely that they rely exclusively on smell or taste; vision then either plays an extremely limited role, or not at all.

Sight fishing for carp is not currently popular, because few anglers realize it is possible. Once it is recognized as a legitimate and potentially productive tactic, it might become more appealing. It is most likely to gain interest, possibly out of necessity, in waters that are experiencing a significant improvement in clarity, making sight fishing for carp routinely possible.

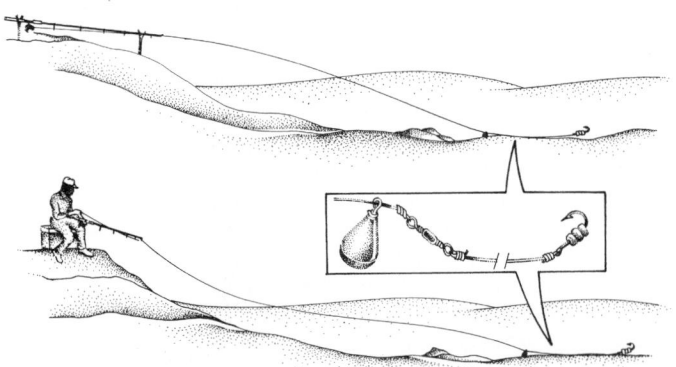

As described in the text, techniques for carp fishing from shore involve a tight-lined fixed bolt rig, depicted here in a rod holder (top), and ledgering, depicted here with a handheld rod (bottom). In both instances, the hook is baited with corn, and the area has likely been chummed.

The great majority of carp anglers, however, stillfish with baits, primarily from shore but also from boats. As previously noted, they employ an assortment of baits, and chum selected areas. Most shore anglers rest their fishing rod in a holder or otherwise prop it up (with the classic forked stick), and pay close attention to the rod tip, the line, a float if in use, and to any strike-indicating device.

Given the carp's proclivity for warmth, backwaters, slow current, and a tendency to root food out of the mud or rocks and suck it up, finding carp and learning where to concentrate one's efforts is not particularly difficult. Carp primarily inhabit shallow water in lakes and reservoirs, knowing that they can find baits better on a sand or gravel flat than in thick weeds. In backwaters, anglers work narrow, open areas between deep-water locales; carp funnel through these while feeding. They like weedbeds, if not for the plants then for the snails and other food items found under or within them. And they like shady spots, such as those found under overhanging trees and bushes. Well-aerated water and a choppy surface during windy weather are said to encourage feeding.

The favorite hangouts in rivers are at the head of pools, in eddies and slow-moving slicks, beneath undercut banks, and near banks beneath snags. They also hold along bottom structures where there is some relief from the current. In big rivers, they gather en masse below dam structures where eddying currents rotate against lock-and-dam walls or gate ends.

Carp usually scour the bottom when feeding, sometimes uprooting aquatic plants in the process. They consume much vegetation, as well as insect larvae, crustaceans, and small mollusks. They tend to hold in shallow areas, clustering in groups of fish that are akin to small schools. In ponds, lakes, and reservoirs, they seldom stay in one spot, preferring to roam in search of food. This tendency explains the popularity of chumming, as it helps attract and concentrate fish that would otherwise be on the move.

Many times these fish can be observed or intercepted in clear or murky shallow water near banks, as this is where much of their favorite food happens to be. In some places, such as municipal and community ponds where people feed ducks along the shoreline, carp hang out right under this frequent food supply.

In some nearshore muddy waters, carp create streaks of mud as they root along the bottom when feeding. They may also release trapped gas from the bottom. This appears on the surface as bubbles, perhaps in a trail, and is another giveaway that carp are present. Carp have a tendency to lie on the surface, seeming to bask in the sun, even in the middle of the day.

Fishing the edges of ponds and lakes, called margin fishing by European anglers, is a primary method of landing carp. Always fishing from the

shore (they do not employ boats to the extent that North Americans do) with long rods, European anglers pursue the fish quite close to the shoreline. In sight fishing, this technique may entail dappling the surface with a bait to attract cruising or basking fish. For example, they may dapple a soaked piece of bread to a fish that is consuming small morsels of bait on or close to the surface. This is a game in which the bait is out of the water more than it is in it, and the angler watches intently for opportune moments to lightly deposit the bait on the surface, unencumbered by a weight or by line drag. Margin fishing sometimes encompasses bottom fishing.

Carp spawn in shallow bays, stream tributaries, or flooded fields and marshes from mid- to late spring or early summer. They are quite noticeable then as they thrash about and disturb the water. Often their backs are exposed, providing an obvious target for spear anglers or bowhunters. At other times of the year they frequently leap out of the water or roll or fin in shallow water or near the surface. Despite their sometimes obvious appearance in the water and their clearly raucous behavior when spawning in the shallows, carp are one of the most cautious of fish, and their wariness should not be underestimated.

When the water is clear, it is impossible to get close to carp without spooking them; casting overhand or waving a rod, or plopping a bait or float on the water close to a fish, is likely to immediately alarm it and send it scurrying. When the water is murky, anglers can maneuver closer, but they must still make a delicate presentation.

Bait presentations are usually made at varying distances from the angler, but seldom in water that is more than 10 feet deep, and often in depths of 3 to 6 feet. Once the bait is in the water, the angler places the rod in a rod rest, positioning the rod so that is pointed in the direction of the bait, preferably parallel to the water, and also pointed at the fish. Many people who watch the line or the tip indicator for a strike, angle the tip of the rod upward to observe the strike more easily. Europeans refer to these bait presentation styles as legering (called ledgering among North Americans).

A variety of bait rigs are used in this technique. For untutored carp in waters where they are abundant, some split shot placed a short distance from the bait might be sufficient. This rig is fished on the bottom, and the hook is set as soon as a pickup occurs. But most carp are more cautious than many unsuspecting anglers realize, and it is generally best to use a method that encourages the fish to pick up the bait but not sense the presence of bait or line. Bottom or near-bottom rigs intended for wary carp, therefore, are best embellished with a sliding sinker. This setup enables the fish to pick up the bait and perhaps move with it—a situation that is ideal in theory but not always possible in practice.

A common way to do this is with a bell or dipsey sinker that slides on the main line and is stopped by a barrel swivel. A leader is attached to the barrel swivel and a hook to the leader. An angler can hold the rod while keeping the reel in the freespool position (with the bail open) and guiding the line between thumb and forefinger, feeling for a strike on the taut line; or, the rod can be left in a holder. The bait is allowed to lie on the bottom or to float just a few inches above the bottom; a small piece of foam (or other commercially available item) is ideal for flotation. Theoretically, a carp venturing into a chummed area will see the higher bait first and take it before rooting on the bottom. Anglers who can legally fish two rods sometimes employ one of each setup.

Another favorite rig of carp anglers is a tight-line setup with a heavy sinker, known in Europe as a fixed bolt rig. This is similar to the rig described above in that a sliding sinker and bottom or raised bait are used, but the sliding weight is heavy, usually 2 or 3 ounces, and the main fishing line is kept tight to the reel, without slack. Here, the carp is expected to pick up the bait, instantly feel the tension of the weight, and bolt, thereby hooking itself.

Although hooks can be imbedded in bait, they can also be fished free of but close to the bait. The way to do this is with a so-called hair rig.

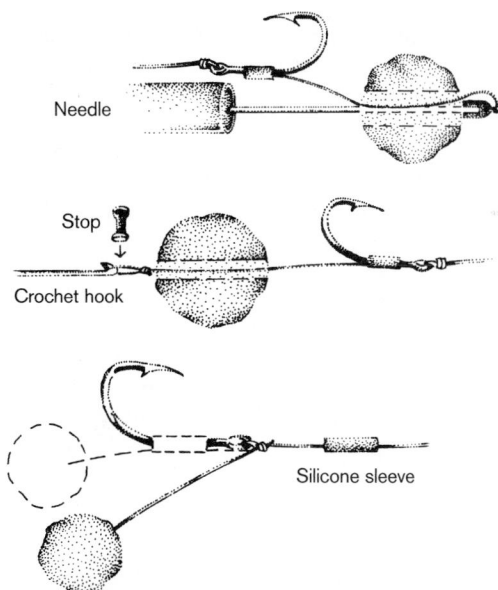

There are several ways to form a hair rig. The bait can be attached by tying line to it with a bait needle (top); by tying line to it via a crochet hook and a jamming stop (middle); or by pinning it with a silicone sleeve moved over the shank of the hook (bottom).

This sophisticated setup, originally tied with hair but nowadays constructed with fine monofilament or microfilament line, is also a self-hooking method of rigging. The fine line is tied to the eye of a hook and slid to the midpoint of the shank via a rubber stopper; threaded to the fine line is a boilie or corn kernels. A bait needle is necessary to thread the bait onto the fine line. The accompanying illustration shows this setup, but it's important to understand that the fine line should emanate from the shank of the hook for the best results. This placement allows the hook portion to enter the carp's mouth first but also ensures that if the rig is ejected by the fish, the hook will exit the mouth eye-first, greatly increasing the chance of a hookup.

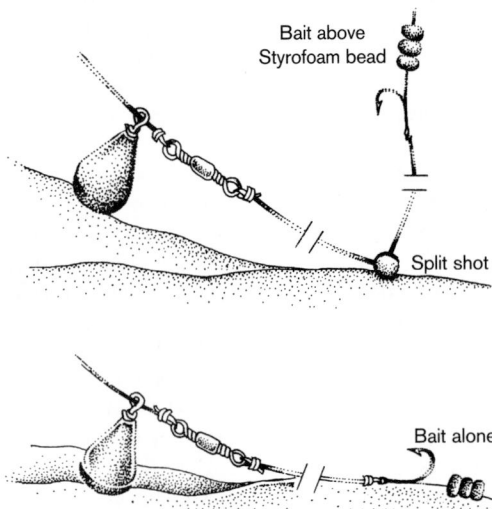

Bait above
Styrofoam bead

Split shot

Bait alone

The bait on a bottom hair rig for carp can be raised slightly off the bottom (top) or lie directly on it, as circumstances warrant (bottom).

In current, or when the fish are not holding on the bottom, it may be necessary to use a float and also split shot that will force the bait downward yet be light enough to keep it drifting naturally.

With all of this emphasis on bait rigs and bait fishing, it seems odd to segue to fly fishing. Certainly not a mainstream tactic, fly fishing can nevertheless be productive for carp. The purists among trout and salmon fly anglers may balk at the thought, but sometimes flies make a lot of sense for carp; pursuing carp on fly tackle may be comparable to fishing for bonefish with flies (except the carp are bigger on average). Wherever carp are abundant, they often cruise along shorelines, singly or in small groups; if they happen to be slurping insects on the surface, a dry fly may catch them. Otherwise, a weighted fly (tied with the hooks riding up to avoid hangups) is the ticket.

Stalking and spotting, followed by careful casts, are the secrets to fly fishing for carp, a method that is sometimes extremely rewarding and sometimes not. If you think about it, a fly cast far enough ahead of the fish and resembling an insect or small crustacean has the potential to be a better lure than any other artificial and even most bait. As mentioned, however, these creatures spook easily, not unlike some more hotly pursued species. The challenges of presenting a fly without slapping the line on the water, or retrieving the line too fast and thus pulling the fly away from the quarry, can make fly fishing for carp as interesting as highly touted fishing methods aimed at species less widely available than carp (like bonefish).

CARP, COMMON   *Cyprinus carpio.*

Other names—European carp, French carp, Italian carp, German carp, Israeli carp, leather carp, mirror carp, king carp, koi, sewer bass, buglemouth; French: *carpe, carpe commune;* German: *karpfen;* Japanese: *koi;* Spanish: *carpa.*

One of the largest members of the minnow family and a close relative of the goldfish, the common carp was also one of the first fish whose populations were regulated to increase production. Propagated for centuries and distributed widely, common carp are both beloved and despised. In North America, they are abundant but among the least-favored targets of freshwater anglers.

Three varieties of common carp exist, including the scaleless leather carp, the partially scaled mirror carp, and the fully scaled common carp, which is the most abundant of the three. In Europe and

Common Carp

Identification. The common carp has a deep body form and a heavy appearance. Distinctive features include a short head, rounded snout, single long dorsal fin, forked tail, and relatively large scales. The mouth is toothless and suckerlike, adapted to bottom feeding, and the upper jaw projects slightly past the lower one. As in the goldfish, to which it is related, the common carp has a single serrated spine at the front of the dorsal and anal fins. Unlike the goldfish, however, the common carp has two pairs of fleshy barbels on either side of its mouth.

The pigmentation of the common carp ranges from gold to olive to brown with a yellowish coloring on the lower sides and belly and a reddish tint to the lower fins. Each scale on the upper sides of the fish has a concentrated dark spot at its base and a conspicuous dark rim. Juveniles and breeding males are usually a darker green or gray with a dark belly instead of a yellowish one, and females are lighter. Males develop tiny tubercles (temporary epidermal projections that help the male remain in contact with the female during spawning), which are found in a random pattern on the head and the pectoral fins. The common carp superficially resembles the bigmouth buffalo (*see: buffalo, bigmouth*).

Size/Age. Growing quickly and to moderately large sizes, the common carp is said to reach weights in the 80-pound range, although the average fish is considerably smaller. The all-tackle rod-and-reel record is 75 pounds, 11 ounces. The maximum life span is disputed but may be a half century; the average carp seldom exceeds 15 years of age.

Distribution. The common carp was one of the first species to be introduced into other countries. Its native range was restricted to temperate Asia and the rivers of the Black Sea and Aegean basins in Europe, specifically the Danube. At some point, the carp found its way to England, and in the nineteenth century it was brought from Germany to the United States. Today it is also found in South Africa, Australia, and New Zealand.

Habitat. Common carp are incredibly hardy and flexible in their preferences for living conditions. Primarily bottom-dwelling fish, carp like quiet, shallow waters with a soft bottom and dense aquatic vegetation. Although they favor large turbid waters, they also thrive in small rivers and lakes. They can live in low-oxygen environments and can tolerate temperature fluctuations and extremes, with the ability to survive in 96°F water for 24-hours. They tend to monopolize some of the bodies of water they inhabit.

Most of the time carp prefer to hold in quiet, shallow places with a muddy or sandy bottom, which they browse over. In some northern waters where the fish are abundant and such terrain is lacking or offers no food, carp will cruise over shallow, rocky flats and shoals, browsing along the rubble bottom. They are often observed during the day in

A common carp from Lake Oahe, South Dakota.

Asia, these carp have always been thought of as premier sport and food fish. In North America, however, the introduced common carp has wreaked economic and biological havoc. It was proclaimed a miracle fish for its economic benefits when it was first introduced across the continent in the 1870s, but then it began to crowd out native fish by reproducing too rapidly, damaging entire habitats, and exhibiting destructive feeding habits. It was soon regarded as a first-class pest and a hazard to natural ecosystems.

This view generally persists today, even though carp have not overcome most populations of other, more highly regarded, species. As a result, carp are harvested in huge quantities for commercial reasons, especially to curb their infestation of gamefish waters. In fact, many methods have been used and efforts made to rid American waters of common carp, including poisoning. Despite the favorable European outlook on carp, the effects this fish on waters in the New World is destined to remain a classic example of the problems that can result from introducing exotic species into new habitat.

Nevertheless, with eradication in North America virtually impossible, common carp exist in good supply and in relatively large sizes (compared to most other species), and provide an underutilized resource for anglers, not to mention an ample source of protein. In some circles carp are highly regarded as a food fish and can be prepared in many ways. The roe of the female has some food value and is often canned.

protected areas, sometimes adjacent to deep water, although they are seldom caught in deep water.

Life history/Behavior.   By their second year, males are able to reproduce, whereas females are able to do so once they are three years old. Carp spawn in spring and summer, depending on latitude, becoming active once temperatures rise to the 60°F range. During the day or night, several males will accompany one or two females to shallow, vegetated waters and splash and thrash as the eggs are released and fertilized. A large female can carry millions of adhesive eggs, but the average amount is 100,000 eggs per pound of body weight.

The eggs go unattended, hatching in 3 to 10 days. The fry are born with an adhesive organ that they immediately use to adhere to bottom vegetation; after the first day, they must go to the surface and gulp air to survive. Common carp fry carry a large yolk sac, which they initially absorb for sustenance, later graduating to algae and plankton. They are quick to grow and may reach about 9 inches in length during the first year of their lives, if they escape the hungry jaws of their primary predators, which include northern pike, muskellunge, and largemouth bass. Juvenile carp make good baitfish, but their use is forbidden in some areas where trout are the main species.

Food and feeding habits.   Omnivorous feeders, carp favor predominantly vegetarian diets but will feed on aquatic insects, snails, crustaceans, annelids, and mollusks. Aquatic plants and filamentous algae are the most popular food groups of the common carp. Their feeding habits are noteworthy, because they grub sediments from the bottom with their suckerlike mouths, uprooting and destroying vegetation and muddying the water. They have done severe damage to habitats by causing the loss of large quantities of plant life. This has proved detrimental to native fish populations and other animals.

Carp primarily spend their lives in small groups and are inclined to roam for food. They can gain several pounds a year in rich fertile environments but may remain smaller in those that are less fertile and where there is overcrowding.

Angling.   The sporting value of carp is an issue that has been, and will continue to be, subject to much disagreement among the majority of anglers on both sides of the Atlantic, with most in the West devaluing it and most in the East, especially in Europe, extolling it. In the Old World, the carp has long been within ecological balance, seldom displacing the native fauna, so it has achieved a desirable status there. Because carp primarily eat aquatic plants, and not other fish, they are less receptive than many other species to the most commonly practiced methods of fishing in North America. Nevertheless, they are strong fish and hearty battlers, capable of stretching a fishing line and testing the skills of most anglers.

For more information and a detailed review of angling for carp, *see: Carp.*

CARP, GRASS   *Ctenopharyngodon idella.*

Other names—white amur, amur, carp; French: *carpe amour, carpe herbivore, amour blanc;* German: *graskarpfen;* Japanese: *sogyo.*

A large member of the minnow family and an aquaculture species of worldwide importance, the grass carp is used for weed control because of its aggressive and herbivorous feeding habits. In the United States, where it was introduced in the early 1960s, it has become an extremely controversial species because of the biological damage it inflicts in the process of eliminating vegetation. In fact, there is growing concern that the introduction of the grass carp into nonnative waters will be as disastrous as was the introduction of its close relative, the prolific and destructive common carp. This species is called the grass carp by critics, whereas supporters often refer to it as the white amur to avoid the negative connotations associated in North America with the name "carp." It is commercially caught by seines in large quantities and prepared in a host of ways.

Identification.   The grass carp has an elongate and fairly compressed body, a wide and blunt head, a very short snout without the barbels found on common carp, a short dorsal fin, and a moderately forked tail. The terminal and nonprotractile mouth has thin lips and sharp pharyngeal (throat) teeth especially suited to its feeding habits. The grass carp is covered with large scales; the ones on the upper sides of the body have a dark border and a black

Grass Carp

spot at the base, and give the fish a cross-hatched appearance. It is colored gray or green on the back, shading to white or yellow on the belly, and has clear to dark fins.

Size/Age.   The grass carp grows quickly and to large sizes, some have been reported at 100 pounds in native waters. It can add 3 to 5 pounds a year to its weight under favorable conditions. The largest fish taken by rod and reel was a 65-pound, 14-ounce Arkansas specimen.

Distribution.   Found originally in China and eastern Siberia, specifically in the Amur River basin from which it gets its name, the grass carp has been widely introduced to more than 20 countries. Only those in certain areas have been able or allowed to reproduce naturally; these places include the Danube River in central Europe, the Mississippi River in North America, and Russia and southern Africa. In the U.S., it was first stocked in Arkansas waters in 1963 and intentionally released in 35 states, although it has subsequently spread to other bodies of water where it was unwanted. In fact, many states have made it illegal to stock grass carp within their borders, unless a permit issued by the appropriate fisheries management agency has been obtained.

Habitat.   Occurring in freshwater, grass carp inhabit lakes, ponds, pools, and backwaters of large rivers, with a preference for slow-flowing or standing bodies of water with vegetation. They are able to withstand temperature variation, extreme salinity, and low oxygen concentrations.

Life history/Behavior.   Spawning takes place once a year over gravel bottoms in rivers, between April and September according to temperature; adults will migrate upstream to find acceptable spawning sites. The round eggs of the grass carp are semibuoyant and amber colored, hatching in 24 to 30 hours without the protection of the parents. After they absorb the nutrients in their yolk sacks in the first two to four days of their lives, the larvae feed on microplankton in quiet waters. The young hide in deep holes in riverbeds during the winter.

Food and feeding habits.   Primarily vegetarians, grass carp have earned their name by eating aquatic plants and submerged grasses, adding the occasional insect or invertebrate. With the help of teeth on the pharynx, they tear off vegetation with jerking motions. Unlike common carp *(see: carp, common)*, grass carp do not muddy the water with their browsing, but their aggressive feeding habits cause other problems. Grass carp tend to break off the upper portions of grasses, leaving the roots to grow, so they are not as useful in eradicating vegetation as they are supposed to be. Also, grass carp cannot digest all the plant matter they take in, so instead of eliminating a vegetation problem, they make it worse by excreting plant material and distributing it to new areas. In addition, they contribute to increased water turbidity and to eutrophication. Finally, heavy browsing may stimulate faster than normal growth in certain kinds of plants.

Triploid grass carp.   A technique that consists of exposing fertilized eggs to heat shock was invented by researchers in 1981 to produce sterile grass carp. This method creates nonreproducing fish of both genders. They are called triploid grass carp because they have three sets of chromosomes instead of the usual two sets (those fish are called diploid). They are as hardy as the ordinary variety of grass carp, but they have the benefit of not being able to overpopulate their habitats. They look like large creek chub, flourish in warm water, and may reach weights of 25 pounds or more. Triploid grass carp are useful in controlling unwanted aquatic plants, but the water clarity may deteriorate due to the substantial passing of plant material as fecal matter.

Angling.   Grass carp are not a highly regarded species by a majority of North American anglers, for largely the same reasons as the common carp. However, they are strong fish that put up a tenacious fight, and they are known to jump. Where they are pursued by anglers, techniques are analogous to those for common carp, although these fish are known to feed on or near the surface, especially in locations where they have pared down the vegetation.

For more information on angling for carp, *see: Carp.*

CARP, LEATHER
The leather carp is a scaleless variety of the common carp *(see: carp, common)*.

CARP, MIRROR
The mirror carp is a partially scaled variety of the common carp *(see: carp, common)*.

CARRYOVER FISH
Stocked fish, usually trout, that survive at least one winter in the wild; also known as holdover fish.

CARVING
See: Fish Carving.

CAST
To throw an object that is connected to a rod via fishing line; also, the distant placement of an object via line and rod in the water, as in, "make a cast toward those lily pads."
See: Casting.

CASTER
A person who casts.
See: Casting.

CASTING

A fundamental element of many types of angling, casting is the act of throwing an object that is connected to a fishing rod via line. It is critical to some types of fishing but marginal or nonessential to others, and it may be enjoyed as a game or contest unto itself. The object cast is usually a lure or bait with hook(s), but it may be a hookless weighted object used for practice casts.

From an angling standpoint, the objective of casting is to present a lure or bait at some distance away from the caster's position, and to place it where it will be attractive to the species sought. In many instances, anglers cast to specific habitats, or targets, where fish may be present, or to roaming fish that must be intercepted; in such cases, accuracy—and possibly distance—are vitally important. Often, however, anglers cast blindly, seeking fish whose presence or precise location is unverifiable; in such cases, accuracy may have little or no significance, and distance may or may not be a factor.

Casting is done at close range in some situations, and at great distances in others. Some forms of angling require repeated, or continuous, casting throughout the day, whereas others require occasional or moderate amounts of casting. The weight of the objects cast varies with the species sought, the tackle, and the circumstances; thus, anglers must be adaptable and possess tackle suited to the conditions.

With few exceptions, casting is not difficult, and in some cases it can be an art form. Although a basic component of angling, it is one that many anglers do not master fully. Yet mastery is virtually guaranteed to contribute to success, if not greater enjoyment of sportfishing. In fact, many anglers prefer types of fishing that involve casting, especially those that require skillful casting (that is, accurate placement), because it is a measure of overall proficiency and an enjoyable activity in itself.

Two diametrically opposed principles govern casting. One requires the use of a weighted line to cast a nearly weightless object. This is the principle involved in fly fishing; a fly line carries a fly or fly-like object that is virtually weightless although not necessarily small or wind-resistant. This is a specifically focused activity that is detailed in the entry on flycasting tackle (see).

Arguably 90 percent of all sportfishing activity does not involve fly fishing; instead, a light or virtually weightless line is used to cast a weighted object. The weight of the object cast varies, but it is the terminal weight that carries the line forward or backward. This form of casting will be discussed in detail here—including the use of spincasting, spinning, and baitcasting tackle—although specialized forms of casting such as flipping (see) and pitching (see) are reviewed elsewhere.

Becoming Proficient

The majority of casters use spinning tackle (see) and spincasting tackle (see), and a significant number use baitcasting tackle (see). A few use conventional tackle (see). For the most part, casting requires placing a lure or bait at a moderate distance, generally from 30 to 60 feet in freshwater. It does require some competency to cast unerringly, particularly when circumstances are problematic—for example, when the wind is blowing, the boat is turning, or the current is changing your position. Often, and especially when lures are used, proficiency is necessary because the first cast made to a targeted location is most critical to success.

Many people do not take the time to fully master their equipment. As a result, they are able to cast well enough to get a lure or bait into the water, but not well enough to put it where they want it whenever necessary. This is never more obvious than when two people are together in a situation that demands the ability to put a lure in a specific spot. The one who can catches the fish; the one who cannot lags far behind. In some angling situations, this means not just being able to get your lures close to where you want them to go; it means pinpoint placement. Often, species of fish that live or forage in heavy cover—largemouth bass, peacock bass, and snook are examples—will not chase a lure that doesn't land in its dining area. Placing a lure or bait at the dining room door is often not close enough. Therefore, obtaining accuracy is a main element of casting proficiency.

Practice. Accurate casting is a function of experience. For most anglers, especially those who are new to fishing or to using a particular type of tackle, achieving proficiency, and especially accuracy, is derived from practice. Ironically, although casting is obviously important to many types of fishing, few anglers practice.

People accept practice as a part of almost every kind of participatory recreation, but few seem to relate the concept of practice to casting, with the exception of fly anglers. Yet, improving casting accuracy with spinning, spincasting, and baitcasting tackle through practice is essential to increasing success. Nothing can be done about many things that influence angling success, especially such variables as air temperature, wind direction, wind velocity, and water temperature, yet you can control your ability to put a lure on target by using quality, balanced equipment and by practicing. Beginners especially should not wait until they go fishing to learn to cast but should practice before they get near the water. Casting at targets in your yard or in a neighborhood park is good for everyone.

Targets. The best targets to start with are brightly colored plastic hoops or children's wading pools. They stand out well on yard grass and are about the right size. When you're learning to cast, you should set a pair of these out at 25 and 30 feet. Don't try to throw a foot farther until you can hit these targets consistently. You'll hit them often enough not to be totally frustrated, and you'll also be surprised how often you miss. Forget about distance and concentrate on accuracy. Resist the trap that most casting beginners fall into: putting a choke hold on their rod and winding up as if they were in the Olympic hammer-throwing competition. The objective is not to see how far you can cast.

Concentrating on accuracy is extremely important in the learning process. Physical strength has little to do with good casting. What does count is developing timing and coordination through practice. If you concentrate on accuracy until you're hitting those targets 8 times out of 10, then greater distance will come as a fringe benefit. If you do it the other way, by putting the emphasis on distance, you'll be in trouble from the beginning.

Casting weights.   Practicing in the yard must be done with hookless objects known as casting weights or casting plugs. These are available in several sizes and in round or flat-sided versions, although they're not always easy to come by. Manufacturers should include them with their merchandise to foster practice, but none do. Some tackle shops don't carry them, although they might be able to order them. You may have to order them from a catalog merchant, and you may not have a choice of versions. It may be difficult to find the heavier weights (like the $^5/_8$-ounce size, which are better for baitcasting).

If you have a choice, flat versions are preferable to round for yard casting. On a hard surface the flat-sided weight is retrieved without much line twist. That's not true of the round type, which roll and spin and can cause twisted line. You don't need that, especially when learning.

If you practice much, the line tie at the end of your casting weight will eventually wear out and break. To repair this, get a small screw eye, like those used for hook hangers on lures, and screw it into the head of the plastic casting weight. If you're not successful in finding flat-sided $^5/_8$-ounce casting weights (or others for that matter), you can make them yourself by hollowing out the base of a $^3/_8$-ounce casting weight, adding sufficient lead shot, and covering the hole with epoxy.

Weight size varies with the tackle used. Once you've gotten some confidence by practicing at the learning distances, try using more targets and setting them at varied ranges. In actual fishing, you will be making one cast to an object that is 20 feet away, then to one that is 50 feet away, and then to another that is 35 feet away, perhaps from the same shore or boat position, with each cast separated by only a few seconds. You must be accurate at all distances at any given time, so position the targets at varied ranges. You might make a game of it, awarding yourself points for successful casts and setting some point goals, or you might cast with a companion in a friendly competition. Also try to make the targets more challenging as well. They might be plates, cups, tires, and the like. Finally, by changing the weight of the practice plugs, you can make the activity completely different. Not every lure cast will be the same weight nor, for that matter, as aerodynamic as a practice plug.

Spincasting

The spincasting reel is enormously popular because of its ease of use. No better reel exists for the child or adult who wants to enjoy fishing without working too hard at learning how to cast. Although it is fairly easy to cast a country mile with a spincasting reel, it is unfortunately the most difficult reel with which to learn accuracy unless you know the right technique. The problem centers around the pushbutton line-release device.

To operate a spincasting reel, you must depress the pushbutton and hold it in until you're ready for the casting plug to fly out. Many people unfortunately think they must press that button in again to stop the plug; even some manufacturer's manuals recommend this practice. As you'll discover the first time you try it, if you depress the pushbutton while the casting plug is airborne, the plug stops with a jerk and lurches back several feet. But if you don't stop the plug somehow, it flies too far and winds up in the brush or nearest tree, and if you've put much power into the cast while fishing, when you clamp down on the pushbutton again, the lure (and hooks) may come hurtling back at you. That could hurt.

To avoid this and thereby cast accurately, use the forefinger on your noncasting hand (the left forefinger for most people) to control the line.

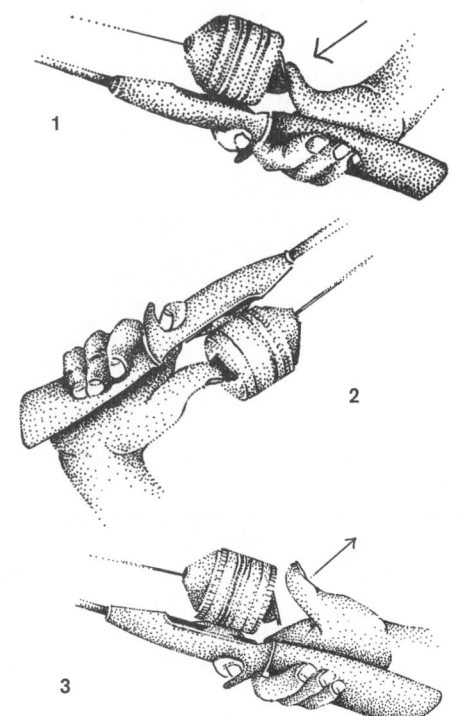

Casting with a spincasting reel begins by pressing the pushbutton with your thumb (1) and holding it throughout the backcast (2); release the pushbutton at the optimum point of rod flex in the forward motion of the cast (3).

C

Casting with a spincasting reel is essentially accomplished by pressing the pushbutton with your thumb (or the trigger with your forefinger) and holding it throughout the backcast, then releasing it at the optimum point of rod flex during the forward motion of the cast. When the button is released, line flows off the spool, through the opening in the reel cover, and out through the guides, carried by the weight of the object at the terminal end of the line.

Before making a cast, you should set the drag to the proper amount of tension (this is most critical) and adjust the position of the plug at the rod tip. The plug (or lure or bait, when fishing rather than practicing) should hang a few inches below the rod tip. You can get it to this position by reeling in the line until the lure is a few inches from the tip guide; if the reel is right at the tip, then pull a few inches of line off the reel drag, which will cause the lure to hang a few inches below the tip.

If you're right-handed, place the rod and reel in the palm of your left hand so that the handle of the reel is up and facing you. Extend the left forefinger to trap the line against the opening of the spool. Depress the pushbutton with your right thumb and point the rod tip at your intended target. Lift the rod back toward you swiftly, using your wrist and forearm (not the whole arm), and allowing the weight of the plug to flex the rod. In a continuous and unhesitating motion, and still using the wrist and forearm, bring the rod forward in an accelerated motion. Release the line and the pushbutton at the same instant during the forward stroke to cast the plug toward the target. While the casting plug is in the air, the line should flow across the tip of your left forefinger. To put the plug right where you want it, increase upward pressure with the left forefinger. With a bit of practice you will learn at what exact point in the forward stroke to release the line and the pushbutton, which is a major element in attaining the proper trajectory for accurate placement. Casting is the same for left-handed anglers, although hand positions are reversed.

Although these instructions belabor the act of casting, it is really a simple technique that almost anybody can master quickly. You'll quickly learn to feather the line with your left forefinger so that the plug drops right where you want it. Although spincasting does involve the use of both hands, your right hand still executes the casting stroke. The only function of the left hand is to get your left forefinger out where it needs to be to control the line. (Again, this text assumes a right-handed angler.)

When you are learning, and whenever striving for accuracy, get the rod and reel out in front of your body with both hands and make the rod follow an imaginary line from your nose to the target. Remember that the most important single phase of the spincasting technique is to have the line flowing over your forefinger while the plug is in the air. Once you get the feel for the control you have over the lure by simply lifting the forefinger slightly up against the line, you're on the way to accurate casting.

Proper casting, of course, is made easier with equipment of good quality. Some spincasting reels are junk. No one, especially a young beginner, can learn good casting with worthless equipment. Excellent spincasting reels are available in different sizes, and they come prespooled with line of appropriate strength. For beginners, a smaller size filled with 8- or 10-pound line is fine for starters. A smaller reel is easier for youngsters as well as for adults with small hands, to use in two-handed casting. It will be much easier to grip, and it lets them get their left forefinger out where it needs to be to achieve casting accuracy.

As for casting weight, use $3/8$ ounce. You can also use a $1/4$-ounce version, but a $3/8$-ounce weight is easier to work with, especially in the beginning. A 6-foot light or medium-light action rod is a good choice for use with spincasting reels, but it may be too large for youngsters. Choose a shorter one accordingly. Spincasting rods with an offset handle used to be common but aren't now, so you'll probably have to use a straight-handled rod. The reel sits up higher on such a rod and is not as easy to grip as it is on a rod with an offset handle, which places the reel lower in the seat. This is especially true with a larger reel. An offset handle is helpful when you use the two-handed technique, but you can manage otherwise.

Spinning

Spinning tackle started out as equipment for casting lightweight objects and for light angling applications. Today its foremost use is still in this area, although spinning gear that spans nearly all angling applications is available. Nevertheless, most casting with this equipment involves tackle on the lighter end of the spectrum, and tossing objects that weigh less than a half ounce (and in many freshwater applications at least half of that). Proper casting with spinning gear, especially when accuracy is required, involves more than just heaving. Although spinning tackle is easy to use, many people exhibit poor form when casting, especially inexperienced anglers. It is common to see many casters hold a spinning rod behind them and then throw their lure or bait forward, as if they were tossing a javelin or operating a catapult. It's not pretty, it's not effective for distance or accuracy, it may be dangerous to yourself or companions, and it can be a detriment to angling success. Effective casting starts with learning the basics properly.

One of the criticisms of spinning tackle, especially from freshwater bass anglers, is a lack of accuracy when fishing in tight quarters or when pinpoint accuracy in heavy cover is essential. If you have ever seen master casters exhibit their abilities at sport shows, you know that it's possible to be as accurate with spinning gear as with any other tackle; accuracy may not be as easy, but it is possible.

As with all casting equipment, accuracy with spinning tackle requires that you stay in touch with your line while the practice weight is in the air. Spinning reel users usually do this by dropping the right forefinger to feather the line as it comes off the spool, which is moderately, but not superbly, effective, even in the hands of experts. There are other techniques you can utilize, and they will be described shortly.

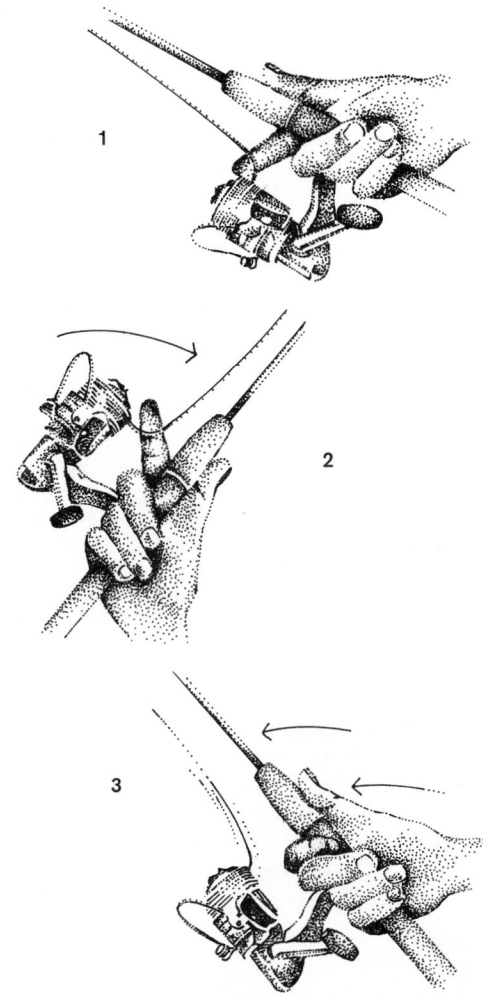

To cast most spinning reels, open the bail and use the tip of the forefinger to grip the line (1); then bring the rod back (2). As the rod comes forward, release the line (3) when the rod tip is pointing above the target.

Another criticism of spinning tackle is its tendency to produce twisted line or loose coils or loops on the spool. These will certainly adversely affect casting distance and accuracy. Line twist and how to avoid it are discussed in detail elsewhere (see: line; spinning tackle). Recommendations for eliminating spool loops are given there.

Be attentive to the level of line on your spinning reel spool, especially when filling it up. Overfilling is a common mistake, and it contributes to loops and errant coils that lead to tangles and that hinder casting. Having too little line is better than too

much when you are spinning, although you reach a point where too little line can impede achieving distance.

As with other kinds of equipment, every minute you spend practicing pays dividends when the time to fish actually comes. Practicing absolutely leads to increased fishing success. When practicing with spinning tackle, use $1/4$-ounce casting weights to start, and rods loaded with 6- or 8-pound-test line. You can change tackle components as your skills sharpen.

Basic casting technique. The basic method of casting with spinning equipment involves the following steps: Begin with the reel under the handle and facing away from you. Adjust the drag to the proper tension level. Hang the casting weight (or lure or bait when fishing) from 3 to 6 inches below the tip of the rod, and turn the handle to bring the bail roller close to the reel stem. If the weight is not in this position, reel it up to the tip and strip line off the reel by pulling on the line above the reel. Pull just enough line off the spool that the weight is the right distance below the rod tip, while at the same time bringing the bail roller close to the reel stem and extended index finger. The bail roller must be properly positioned to allow the finger to easily grab the line and to touch the lip of the spool.

To open the bail manually, grab the line at the roller with the tip of your forefinger and flip up the bail with your other hand. To open the bail automatically, depending on the reel, either extend your forefinger over the roller and grab both the line and the trigger, or simply grab the trigger.

Keep tension on the line with your finger; the tension will be released at the optimum point of rod flex in the forward motion of the cast. When this tension is released, line flows off the spool and out through the guides, carried by the weight of the object at the terminal end of the line.

To execute the cast, the reel should face away from you and you should be looking at the back of your hand. Point the rod tip at and slightly above your intended target. When you are learning, and whenever you're striving for accuracy, get the rod and reel out in front of your body and make the rod follow an imaginary line from your nose to the target. Bring the rod back sharply, using your wrist and forearm (not the whole arm) and allowing the weight of the lure to flex the rod. In a continuous and unhesitating motion, and still using the wrist and forearm, bring the rod forward in an accelerated motion, releasing the line with your forefinger during the forward stroke when the rod tip is pointing above the target.

The degree of flex in the rod will depend on the rod design and material; pure graphite rods require only a short hammering type of stroke, whereas more-parabolic composite or fiberglass rods require a back-and-forth motion. With a bit of practice, you'll learn what adjustment to make for the rod action as well as for different lure weights, and you'll learn at exactly what point in the forward stroke to release the line, which is a major element in attaining the proper trajectory for accurate placement. If the lure goes too high in the air, the line was released prematurely; if the lure lands a short distance in front of you, the line was released too late. It shouldn't take long to get the hang of it, which is one of the benefits of using this type of tackle.

The released line can be moderately controlled during a cast by allowing it to brush against an extended index finger from the rod-holding hand; the finger should be held near the spool lip. This is called feathering and is the most common method of controlling line that is cast from a spinning reel, although it is only moderately effective at achieving accuracy.

Better accuracy can be obtained by allowing the outgoing line to brush against the forefinger of the noncasting hand, although the open bail wire may make this difficult. To do this, the front of the reel has to be in the palm of the other (usually left) hand; extend the left forefinger out and press it against the lip of the reel's spool, keeping it there during the casting motions. When the cast is made and the weight released, keep the left hand in place and control the line by applying slight pressure on it with the left forefinger. This method puts your left forefinger on top of your line as it peels off the spool during the cast.

On some reels, the location of the open bail arm makes this two-handed method of line control a little difficult, but it can nevertheless be done. An improvement is removing the bail arm, as described later.

In lieu of feathering the line in either of these manners, many spinning reel users simply stop the cast altogether either by pressing the extended index finger against the spool, by closing the bail, or waiting for the end of forward momentum when the lure or weight reaches its target. Abruptly pressing a finger against the spool and closing the bail may cause the plug to stop abruptly and even lurch back toward you; allowing the lure to stop when it loses its own momentum is suitable only for open-water situations and cannot be used when obstructions are present or when pinpoint accuracy is necessary. These acts are not conducive to pinpoint casting, although they may be acceptable in situations where exact placement of a lure or bait isn't required.

Several options to the basic casting motion need to be pointed out. Although casting is often accomplished with one hand holding the rod and making the backward and forward motions, many people find it more comfortable and more secure to use two hands on the rod; they are able to attain greater distance and/or straight-line casts by using two hands. Two-handed casts are made by placing the secondary hand on the lower part of the rod handle and using both forearms and wrists to execute the proper motions; the secondary hand can be released

from the rod while the casting weight is airborne, and moved up to the reel if desired. Many anglers use two hands for nearly all casting with spinning rods; when using large tackle and heavy lures, it is virtually mandatory.

Lowering your casting weight, lure, or bait a short distance below the rod tip is a necessary component of casting, but exactly how far is variable. You can put it too far or not far enough. This depends to some extent on the rod you're using as well as the weight of the object being cast. When using spinning gear, leave a longer drop from rod tip to practice plug than you would with a baitcasting outfit; timing on the cast seems to work out better if you do. Usually, the lighter the object you're casting, the longer drop you'll want between it and the rod tip. Practice will determine what works best for you. Try letting out different amounts of line between your rod tip and the plug. When you find out what you like best, stick with it.

An alternative to releasing the line with your forefinger after you've opened the bail is simply to drop the forefinger straight down to trap the line against the side of the reel's spool. When you cast, release finger pressure; then use the same forefinger to feather the line while the plug is in the air.

Line loops that form on reel spools often occur because of slack line that is momentarily present after a cast. To minimize slack line, don't crank the handle right away after a cast. Instead, reach out and manually close the bail arm with your left hand; then grab the line ahead of the bail roller with your left hand and pull off a few inches. Raise your rod tip at the same time. If you discipline yourself to do this after each cast, you'll eliminate a lot of problems; however, this technique obviously is not applicable in situations where you must begin retrieving the instant that your lure hits the water.

No-bail casting.   To stay in touch with your line and improve accuracy while casting lightweight lures, consider removing the bail wire and learning

Spinning tackle is relatively easy to cast; with it you can cast light lures a significant distance.

to control the line with the forefinger of your non-casting hand, which then has unobstructed access to the reel and line.

The bail arm on a spinning reel is not an absolute necessity; in fact, early models did not have them, and many surf casters remove the bail arms on their reels to avoid malfunctions. The bail arm does nothing that your fingers can't do as well or better if you invest some time in training them.

Removing the bail arm gives you better control of your line by making it easier for your noncasting hand to access and feather the line for accuracy. Removal also eliminates many of the difficulties associated with spinning tackle, the most significant of which is the loop of line that forms occasionally on the spinning reel spool when you're using a bail. When you have a loop on the spool but don't realize it's there, the next cast will often result in a gob of line jamming up between the reel and the first guide of the rod. You'll lose time and patience untangling it, and you may have to cut the line. Since the bail contributes to the formation of that loop, you nearly eliminate that problem with a bail-free spinning reel.

When you take off the bail arm, leave the line roller in place, because the line roller is necessary for winding line on the spool. On some reels, the line roller and bail arm are integral and cannot be separated, in which case you cannot detach the bail arm without also removing the line roller.

To cast with a bail-less spinning reel, and assuming that you are right-handed, begin by holding the rod and reel with your right hand and palming the reel in your left hand. Extend your left forefinger and press it against the lip of the reel's spool. Flip the line off the line roller with your right forefinger; then trap the line against the front of the reel spool with your left forefinger.

Keep pressure on the spool while both of your hands raise the rod and flex it into motion. On the forward stroke, release the line with your left forefinger, keeping the left hand in place so that the forefinger can control the outflowing line as necessary.

Every second that the practice weight is in the air—and this is the real key to accuracy with a spinning reel—you must control the weight by applying slight pressure on the line with that left forefinger. This method puts your left forefinger on top of the line as it peels off the spool during the cast. The line is under your forefinger just as the line is under your thumb when using a baitcasting reel. If you practice this enough, you'll find that you can achieve a degree of accuracy with a spinning reel that comes close to the hallmark accuracy of baitcasting equipment.

Since the reel no longer has a bail that automatically picks up the line and directs it to the line roller, you must use your finger to put the line on the line roller. Once the cast is complete, simply reach down with your right forefinger and catch the line that is above the reel. Pull it up against the base of your rod and slightly back toward your body, then cradle it in the line roller as it comes around when you turn the reel's handle.

As you can see, in this procedure your fingers have simply replaced the bail. If you train them properly, they will work as well or better than the bail arm. Once you get the hang of this procedure, you won't even have to glance down to do it. It becomes almost automatic, and is accomplished in half a heartbeat. Always remember to pull up the line against the base of the rod with your right forefinger and slightly back toward your body before you crank.

It helps when using this method to raise your rod tip and put tension on the line as you get the line back on the spool. That little bit of tension helps prevent a spool loop from forming.

Baitcasting

Baitcasting tackle has a Jekyll and Hyde reputation. On one hand, it shines at providing accuracy, particularly where anglers need pinpoint lure placement; on the other hand, it gets rapped for being difficult to learn, being prone to spool overruns that produce horrible line snarls known as backlashes, and not being useful for casting lightweight objects. Some anglers still have a love-it or hate-it attitude toward baitcasting (also commonly referred to as levelwind tackle), despite the fact that the modern equipment has vastly improved.

Like all forms of tackle, baitcasting gear is a tool, and one that has an important place in angling. It is true that a person who has never used a baitcasting reel cannot pick one up and become an accurate or effective caster in a few minutes. However, if the rod and reel are of good quality and set up properly, and if a new user follows proper instructions and is willing to practice, he or she will soon be reasonably accomplished. Furthermore, that angler will be on the path to great proficiency as well as successful fishing with a form of tackle that is often preferable to spinning or spincasting.

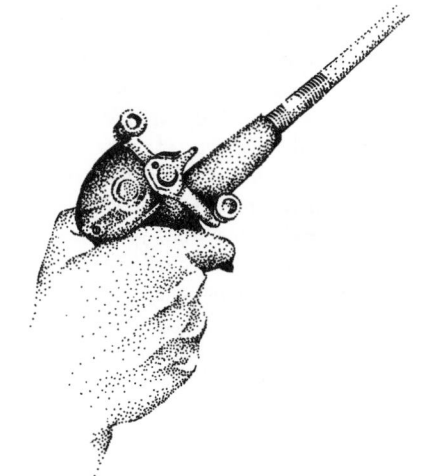

This is the common way to hold baitcasting tackle; turn your wrist so that reel handles face upward when casting.

Although baitcasting tackle is available for a range of fishing applications, its foremost use is in casting objects that weigh upward of $^3/_8$ ounce. Largemouth bass anglers, for whom baitcasting tackle is the preferred equipment choice, routinely cast lures weighing from $^3/_8$ to $^5/_8$ ounce, and some anglers use baitcasting gear for tossing lures and bait that weigh up to 2 ounces. Obviously, different models of rods and reels accommodate different applications, but effective casting, whether for distance or accuracy, always involves proper technique.

Baitcasting reels are noted for accuracy because they feature revolving spools that can be controlled constantly by the user's thumb. They are considered problematic because learning to apply appropriate thumb pressure to the spool in order to control it takes practice, and failure to control the spool produces an annoying overrun. To simplify casting, reel manufacturers have developed braking devices that apply tension to spools to prevent, or at least minimize, overruns, although not all reels have them and not everyone is benefited by them. Users must learn to cast without the aid of these devices so that they will be able to use any type of baitcasting reel under any circumstance.

Practicing with baitcasting tackle is as important, or more so, than with other gear, and practice does lead to increased fishing success. When practicing with baitcasting equipment in a yard or park, use a heavier weight than you would with other gear; a $^5/_8$-ounce weight is best for new users and helps achieve a feel for the game. You can practice with lighter weights after you've achieved a comfortable level of proficiency. Eventually you should practice with different casting weights because you'll be using a range of lure weights on the water, often switching between them.

No matter what you cast, you need good-quality equipment capable of doing the job. For beginners, a $5^1/_2$- to 6-foot graphite rod of medium-light or light action is a good choice, accompanied by a reel spooled with 12-pound line. For a starting setup, avoid an overly large or heavy reel as well as a stiffer rod. This setup should provide a semblance of the balance needed when beginning to practice. Later you'll want different equipment for various fishing applications, but for learning, this is the best type of outfit.

The easiest line to cast with a baitcasting reel is the braided variety, because it is supple and lays nicely on the reel spool. But, if you aren't going to use braided line for your actual fishing—and the majority of people do not—then you might as well learn with the lines you'll actually be fishing with on the water. Many of the top-quality nylon monofilament lines available today have excellent casting qualities. Avoid bargain basement line, and seek a product that is reasonably limp and not overly elastic (see: line). When you put line on the spool, don't overfill it; overfilling can cause loose wraps that might catch each other. Don't underfill it either,

because underfilling can adversely affect distance. If the ends of the spool have markers showing the maximum line capacity, put on enough line to stay even or slightly below them. Don't reel on so much that you cover up the markers.

Basic casting technique.   Assuming that you are right-handed, the basic cast starts with holding the outfit in your right hand with your thumb on the spool. The drag should be adjusted for angling conditions, and the casting weight should be adjusted to the proper position at the rod tip. The weight (or lure or bait when fishing) should hang a few inches below the rod tip. You can get it to this position by reeling in the line until the lure is a few inches from the tip guide; if the reel is right at the tip, then pull a few inches of line off the reel drag, which will cause the lure to hang a few inches below the tip. With the weight in position, depress the freespool button or bar with your thumb and then rest it on the spool to secure the line.

To cast, take a relaxed stance with your rod and reel out in front of your body. Rotate your wrist to the left so your knuckles and the reel handle are up. This unlocks the wrist joint. The wrist does almost all of the work in a well-executed cast. When the wrist is turned so that the knuckles face up, the joint has greater flexibility and can work the rod so that the tip comes up far enough to provide the necessary casting power. Wrist action along with a slight upward movement of the right forearm is all the effort needed to cast properly.

To make the casting weight go where you want, draw an imaginary line from your nose to the target. Make your rod move back and forth along this line as you cast. The entire casting stroke should be executed out in front of your body; do not let the rod tip come back over your shoulder. If you keep your rod and reel out in front of your body as you cast, and your rod moves back and forth along this imaginary line, there's no way you can be off to the right or left of your target. You'll be off in depth in the beginning, but not to the left or right, and depth perception will improve with practice.

Casting in this manner keeps you from making the mistake of letting the rod tip come way back over the right shoulder. If you do that, your arm will be doing the work of the rod, and you won't be able to make the rod travel along that imaginary nose-to-target line that is helpful for achieving accuracy. Keeping the rod in front of your body forces it to work for you. There is tremendous strength in the modern baitcasting rod, but you have to load it up and put a bend in it so it will fire the casting weight where it needs to go. If you bring your rod back over your shoulder, you might as well have a broomstick in your hand.

With practice you'll develop and hone timing and coordination, which are the keys to casting success. Don't expect to knock the center out of your targets in the beginning. A good casting stroke is like flipping an apple off the end of a stick, or like hitting a nail right in front of your nose with a hammer. You release thumb pressure on the reel's spool at the same exact instant that you would smack the nail. Then you must be sure that your thumb stops the rotating spool as the practice plug lands.

Don't expect everything to come together for you within the first 10 minutes of practice. That's unlikely. As your skill develops, you'll find that you never completely remove your thumb from the reel except at the instant you let the practice weight fly out. You lift the thumb so that the spool can start, but you maintain contact to keep the line flowing smoothly and to slow the spool and drop the lure neatly into the target. This constant contact with the line as it pays out is what enables the expert caster to obtain pinpoint accuracy and, in some situations, a soft landing.

Although casting with baitcasting tackle is usually accomplished with only one hand holding the rod and making the backward and forward motions, many people find it more comfortable and more secure to use two hands on the rod, and are able to attain greater distance and/or straight-line casts by using two hands. Two-handed casts are made by placing the secondary hand on the lower part of the rod handle and using both forearms and wrists to execute the proper motions. This is easiest to accomplish on rods with a long, straight handle. Short pistol-grip handles are harder to use with two hands because of their short length and the bulb at the base; but if you take a knife and whittle down the bulb, then run sandpaper over it, you can make it two-hand friendly. Some anglers use two hands for almost all their baitcasting; when you're using big outfits and heavy lures, two hands are virtually mandatory.

Tension controls.   Preventing an overrun by screwing down every tension control device on your baitcasting reel is indeed possible, but it is not a good idea, even for beginners. The key to becoming proficient and really accurate with baitcasting reels is to practice. Timing, coordination, and a trained thumb are developed through practice. Don't depend on mechanical features to eliminate your backlashes.

The best exhibition casters, who are able to unerringly put a casting weight into a cup at 40 feet by using a baitcasting outfit, find it unnecessary to use the magnetic antibacklash device or spool tension adjustment. They set the magnetic tension at or near zero and the spool tension so loose they can feel the slightest side-to-side movement in the spool if they use their thumb to push it back and forth. This kind of free-wheeling allows a baitcasting reel to perform at its best and enables accuracy with minimum effort—provided you practice.

This doesn't mean that you shouldn't use these controls at all as you learn. Read what the manufacturer has to say about tension controls in the manual supplied with the reel. But no matter what the best of these reels promises, realize that you will lose casting efficiency when you rely entirely on those controls.

A baitcasting tackle user shows good form by keeping his rod directly in front of him to help direct and follow a lure toward its target.

Most reel manufacturers suggest setting your controls so that a casting weight drops slowly when you take your thumb off the spool, and the spool stops turning as soon as the casting weight hits the ground. This technique is all right for starters, but strive to train your thumb so you can depend on it to control the spool.

First spooling.   The following advice about putting on line arose from difficulties that were posed by baitcasting reels with V-shaped and semi-V-shaped spools. However, this advice has proven useful with all baitcasting reels and is an aid to effective casting, especially for people who are new to this equipment. Instead of putting new line on the reel by using the levelwind mechanism to guide the line back and forth, bypass the levelwind, tie the line onto the spool, and then carefully guide it onto the spool with your fingers as you reel. After you've filled the reel, run the terminal end of the line back out through the levelwind guide. You still use the levelwind guide when casting and retrieving; you just don't use it when you first fill the spool with line.

By doing this, you avoid a buildup of line along the sides, or edges, of the spool. Such a buildup leads to loops of loose line at the end of a cast, no matter how careful you are in thumbing the spool. Those loops will cut down on your efficiency and may cause a snarl or backlash. If you put on the line in a way that avoids edge buildup, you can minimize the likelihood of this happening.

Types of Casts

The basic casting information provided here for spincasting, spinning, and baitcasting tackle applies to all types of casts. The example used is the most common and straightforward situation, known as the overhead cast or the straight-ahead cast because the rod tip is raised vertically and the line is projected directly in front of the caster, whose eyes pick up the flight of the line and the cast object immediately. There are many situations, however, when it is not possible, or beneficial, to cast in this manner, either because of the nature of the cover in which some species are found or because of the necessity for accurate lure placement. Such situations give rise to a side cast, underhand cast, lob cast, and flip cast, which will be discussed shortly, and to such specialized procedures as flipping *(see)*, pitching *(see)*, and making bounce casts *(see)*, which are detailed separately because they are more involved.

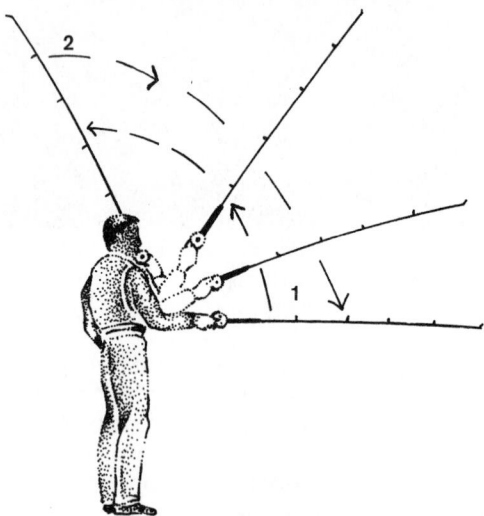

Shown is the basic overhead casting motion for spincasting, spinning, and baitcasting tackle. Note that the process starts with the rod aimed at the target and that the back cast (1) extends no further back than an imaginary 11 o'clock position before the forward cast (2) begins.

To recap the overhead cast, the wrist and forearm do all the work, using the top section of the rod for thrust. The cast begins with the rod low and pointed at the target. The rod is brought up crisply to a point slightly beyond vertical position, where flex in the rod tip will carry it back; then, without hesitation, the forward motion is started sharply, the lure being released halfway between the rod's vertical and horizontal positions. The entire casting action is a smooth, flowing motion; you are doing more than just hauling back and heaving.

The side cast, or sidearm cast, uses essentially the same motion as the overhead cast, except that it features horizontal movement. It begins with the rod low and pointed slightly outward. The wrist and forearm are used to flex the top section of the rod back and then forward, releasing the line just before the rod tip is pointed at its target, and following

through with the forward motion after line release in order to bring the rod in front of you.

Getting the timing down, especially the proper moment to release the line, is a little more difficult and requires some practice, as does achieving accuracy, and accuracy is affected by the fact that the line, lure, and rod are not immediately aligned with the caster's eye and the lure is not as quickly picked up as it heads toward its target, although it does have a much lower trajectory than the overhead cast.

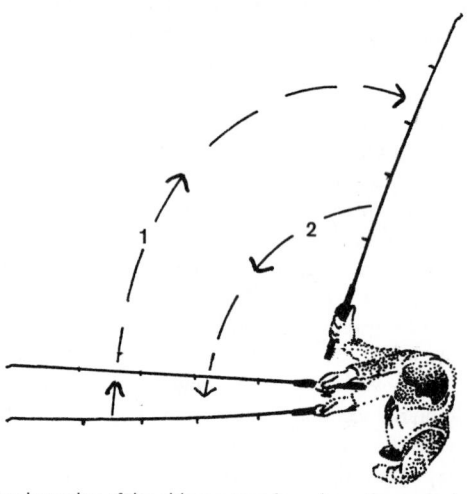

The dynamics of the sidearm cast for spincasting, spinning, and baitcasting tackle are the same as those for the overhead cast. The process starts with the rod aimed at the target, and the back cast (1) extends slightly past a perpendicular position before the forward cast (2) begins.

You can modify the conventional side cast into a side lob cast by starting with the rod tip pointed low toward the water and raising up the tip on the forward motion; this action raises the trajectory but produces a soft landing, which is good for shallow water. The same thing can be achieved by reaching across your body and sending the lure out with a backhand motion.

The conventional side cast is advantageous when overhead cover (like an overhanging tree limb) has to be avoided, or when there is a lot of wind; keeping the line and lure low to the water minimizes drifting off course and is a good way to deal with a blow. This cast is not very effective when distance has to be achieved, and it can be dangerous if performed next to another angler in a small boat, so you must be mindful of the position of your companions at all times.

To make an underhand cast, hold the rod waist-high, angled halfway between vertical and horizontal positions and pointed at the target. The rod must be flexed up, then down, then up again to gain momentum for the lure through the flex of the rod; on the second upward flex, the line is released.

This cast has very little arm movement but plenty of wrist action and can be useful when other casting motions are severely restricted. Many rods, however, are too stiff to permit this kind of casting.

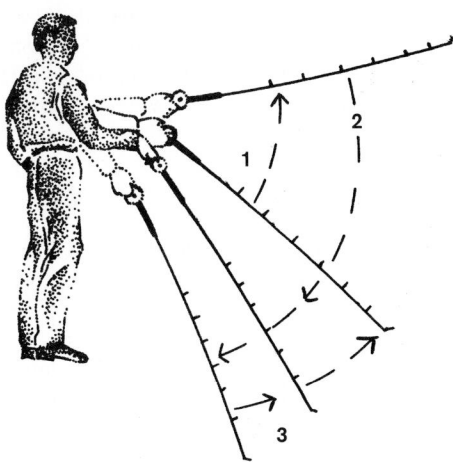

The underhand cast starts with the rod held waist-high, angled halfway between vertical and horizontal positions. From this attitude the rod must be flexed up (1), then down (2), then up (3) again to gain momentum for the lure through the flex of the rod; on the second upward flex, the line is released.

The flip cast is another cast used in special situations. Employed in tight quarters or for short ranges, the flip cast is a cross between the sidearm and underhand casts (different from flipping). It starts with the rod horizontal to your side, but you bring it backward only a short distance and then make a loop with the tip so that the tip springs around in a 270-degree arc and flips the lure straight out and low. This cast is used for short-distance (under 20 feet) work in areas where you can't bring your rod up or back for a conventional cast. It is a very efficient and very accurate cast when mastered but is almost impossible to accomplish while sitting down in a boat.

Another cast is the bow-and-arrow cast, which is a short-distance cast used with a limber rod in tight quarters. In this cast, you hold a lure by its rear hook in one hand and simultaneously release the hook and line from a freespooled reel. This cast is rarely used in actual angling situations, since many rods, especially graphite baitcasters, are not limber enough for it, and a flip cast will do just as well. Obviously you have to be careful about holding the hooks if you try this cast.

Casting Distance Issues

What angler, seeing a fish rise or break water just out of normal casting range, hasn't reached back and heaved a lure that extra distance to get the offering closer to the quarry? What person hasn't tossed a lure farther than normal to avoid spooking wary fish? What angler, caught up in the flow of casting and intrigued with testing his or her skills, hasn't "let one fly," especially downwind?

In football, a quarterback is said to "air it out" when he makes an extremely long pass. A long pass usually doesn't occur play after play in a game. However, a lot of anglers do "air out" their casts

routinely. Unlike the quarterback, whose job is over when the ball leaves his fingertips, the angler has much to do until the lure or bait being cast returns to the tip of the rod. The distance of the cast has a substantial impact on fishing efforts.

Although surf anglers and people fishing in special situations, like casting to schooling (see) fish, have always had to make long casts, in recent decades the emphasis on achieving distance in casting, especially with the use of spinning, spincasting, and baitcasting tackle, has increased.

One reason is that most tackle manufacturers tout products whose chief virtue is achievement of distance. This claim is especially prevalent in spinning reels where spool design, line-wrapping systems, and spool rim materials have been modified to make it easier for line to flow off the spool. Rods, too, have had more attention with respect to enhancing distance, particularly guides and products that are part of a matched system. Baitcasting rod manufacturers started producing longer models for ordinary fishing years ago, mostly at the prompting of bass anglers, partially because longer rods help anglers cast greater distances.

The burgeoning of thin-diameter/conventional-strength lines as well as high-tech microfilaments (see: line) has intertwined with the distance-casting game. Better-quality lines have proven to be slick, limp, and eminently castable, and they improve ability to achieve distance.

Another, but lesser, factor, was an emergence of truly deep-diving plugs for freshwater fishing. To take advantage of the diving capabilities of these plugs, anglers must make long casts so that the lures run at the desired depths for the greatest amount of time possible in a cast-and-retrieve circumstance (this dovetails with longer rods). Thin-diameter lines allow lures to dive even deeper; combined with long rods and improvements in reels, they help the caster toss a lure almost as far as a quarterback can throw a football. And that's a long way.

So, casting a great distance with all forms of casting tackle except fly gear is now easier to accomplish than ever. But is it necessary? There is no correct answer; fishing success is influenced by too many different variables and situations/waters/lures/etc. Many anglers tend to think only in terms of the main advantages to casting greater distances: getting lures to fish they wouldn't have reached otherwise and covering more ground than otherwise possible to attract more fish.

Long casts are of course achievable, though perhaps not necessary. With some species of freshwater fish, and in some types of water, seldom do anglers need to cast great distances. Most walleye, largemouth bass, pike, and panfish anglers, for example, do not need to routinely make long casts because of the nature of the fish, the cover they inhabit, and the fishing techniques used.

The clarity of the water is one criterion for distance. Generally, fish in clear water are spookier

C

than those in turbid water. The more difficult it is to see the lure as you drop it in the water, the murkier the water is; this is an indication that you can probably get fairly close to your quarry.

A prime benefit of getting close is simply the ease with which you can achieve accuracy. This is especially true when fishing in heavy cover, such as timber, or in places where casting is difficult, such as a small brushy creek. The effect of wind is also minimized at shorter distances; when using bait-casting gear, a shorter distance means that the chance of a backlash is lessened.

Backlashes occur in baitcasting reels when the spool turns faster than the line departs the spool; even highly experienced casters get backlashes when they give extra punch to their forward casting stroke in order to get a lure farther out. The best magnetic spool braking reels often cannot prevent such misfortune, although they are suppose to.

With practice and with continued long-distance casting in actual fishing conditions, you can lessen the chance of backlash and also increase accuracy. If you start long-distance casting efforts by not shooting for the moon at the start, but by building up to greater distances gradually (which is hard to do when a fish breaks water just a bit beyond your normal range), then you will overcome this problem.

One of the drawbacks to long-distance casting with any type of tackle is the loss of fish; at long distances, more fish that strike lures and get hooked are lost before being landed than fish that strike lures and are hooked at shorter ranges. How many more are lost cannot be known, but it is likely quite a bit. There is a good reason for this occurrence, though, and it is one that many anglers don't realize but can do something about.

The key here is hooksetting *(see)*. Anglers are more effective at setting the hook at short and midrange distances than they are at long distances. Most people simply do not set the hook well when a fish takes their lure a long distance away.

This angler gains casting leverage by using his left hand on the butt of the rod to propel a large lure a long way from the beach.

Sometimes the reason is that they don't detect strikes as well, and this may be a function of their attentiveness or their savvy, or more likely the tackle they are using. Not all rods are the same, for example, and it is possible to receive a strike but not feel it because the rod is soft and the fish nip the lure rather than slam it. With more appropriate tackle, such a thing won't happen. Nonetheless, certain types of lures are still hard to fish when cast long distances. Lures that you work by feel, which are generally made of soft material, and where you have to know what the lure is doing as you fish it, may not be struck the same way as other lures, so you have to be fully tuned into a long-distance strike when using these types of lures.

A noted fishing film once showed a largemouth bass swimming up behind a quickly moving diving plug, engulfing it, and then expelling it, all the while the lure kept swimming forward. The angler working that lure, which had two sets of treble hooks, reported that he never felt the strike. How could that be possible? As already mentioned, the reason could be that the rod wasn't sensitive enough, but it could also be that his line was too elastic. Elasticity, or stretch, in fishing line is an element that works against anglers where long-distance strike detection and hooksetting are concerned. In this particular instance, the fisherman used a nylon monofilament line that had 25 to 30 percent stretch, and the stretch had to be a factor in not detecting the filmed strike.

The stretch feature of line has been reviewed in detail elsewhere *(see: line),* but it should be remembered that some lines stretch more than others; the greater the stretch, the more problem with lures (or hooks) that are a long distance away. The simple act of retrieving a hard-pulling plug can stretch some lines a little. Setting a hook and playing a fish, especially a large or strong fish, stretches some lines much more. It is harder to counter the effect of stretch when setting the hook if you have a long length of line. At short distances, you can generate more force and be more efficient at setting the hook.

You don't have to be an engineer to appreciate this fact. Take the hooks off a plug sometime, and with the help of a friend try a simple test. Soak the fishing line so that it absorbs water and you have simulated its condition when being fished. Have your buddy hold the rod as if retrieving a lure. Take a practice casting plug or hookless lure 40, 80, and 120 feet away, grasp it firmly in your hand at waist level, and tug on it to have your friend set the hook at each distance. Can you feel a difference in the force your friend applies? The force is more obvious if you use a scale or force gauge, because you're likely to measure a high percentage of loss from the shortest distance to the longest.

To counter the effect of line stretch, an obvious solution is to use a line with little or no stretch, provided that it offers the other characteristics that you need. Using such a line may remove or reduce one of the problems associated with long-distance casts and long-distance fishing.

However, you also need to pay greater attention to the fine points. A super-sharp hook can make all the difference in landing or losing a fish that strikes a long distance away. Most long-distance fish are lost because the hook slipped out or was thrown when the fish jumped. A super-sharp hook penetrates easier and increases your chance of landing a fish. Sharpening your hook (see: hook sharpening) is a fundamental, but mostly overlooked, fishing technique.

Sharp hooks, of course, won't eliminate line stretch, but combined with a lower stretch line, they can make a big difference. You should also pay close attention to what you're doing. Be alert. Anticipate strikes at all times so you can react properly and swiftly. If you are casting surface lures, for example, make sure that slack is always out of your line.

The position of your rod, and your body, is important as well. The rod should be held at a low level; when setting the hook, you should be reeling and striking all in one motion, keeping the pressure on constantly and not yielding unless the fish is strong enough to pull line off the drag. Good hook-setting technique is never more important than when long distances are involved, and the same is true for fish-playing tactics (see: playing fish). Fish that are a long distance off are harder to control than those up close. It is more difficult to keep a strong fish away from an obstruction when it is 125 feet from you than when it is 40. When fishing from a boat, you may have to maneuver the boat in order to change the angle of pull on a large fish and steer it away from obstructions. You have to anticipate and react quickly, however, to do this.

Rather than casting long distances as a matter of habit, you might try making a stealthier approach to fish. Wading river anglers know that it is possible to get fairly close to rising trout or to salmon in their lie by going slowly and as unobtrusively as possible, by not making excessive above-water motions, by keeping movement to the barest minimum in the fish's direct viewing window, and by being patient and not casting until achieving the most advantageous position for making the best possible presentation.

Pond and lake anglers, whether boaters or bank casters, should do likewise. Most lake and pond anglers are impatient; they want to cover lots of water, and in doing so they often don't make the best possible presentation. Certainly this statement isn't applicable where schooling fish are chased, but it is in most other circumstances.

Achieving distance isn't always necessary or advantageous, but when it is, there is more to being effective than just being able to air out a cast. You have to bring many elements together. However, when you do, you are usually on top of your game, and that means more success and enjoyment.

See: Baitcasting Tackle; Spinning Tackle; Spincasting Tackle; Surf Fishing.

CASTING BUBBLE

A small plastic float (see), often transparent, used as an aid to casting and fishing with lightweight objects (like flies, tiny jigs, or unweighted natural bait) with spinning or spincasting tackle.

CASTING REEL

A term for baitcasting reel.
See: Baitcasting Tackle.

CAST NET

A circular net with fringe weights that is thrown for collecting baitfish. Cast nets come in various sizes and are used by anglers for collecting live bait. Shad, herring, and mullet are among the most common cast netting targets, and they are usually netted in shallow waters, although some netting takes place in the ocean in deep water, where large schools of baitfish are attracted to the surface with chum and then netted. In use, when a cast net is thrown, the full net opens as it hits the surface of the water, the weights carry it down quickly, the bottom of the net closes around fish, and the net is retrieved via a long connecting polypropylene line.

Using a cast net is the quickest way to catch a supply of bait in a short period of time, assuming that bait is plentiful and that you know where to find it. In some situations where live bait is necessary, anglers may spend a considerable amount of time trying to collect bait, even with a cast net, but the cast net is still most effective.

It takes practice to learn to throw a cast net properly, as it is usually necessary to cast the net to a specific place and to have it open fully to capture the greatest number of fish. You should practice throwing a net on a windless day and in shallow water. Face 90 degrees from where you want the net to land, place your weight on your back foot, and keep the net close to the water when throwing it. It takes a good back motion as well as a forward one to throw a cast net properly. Many cast nets come with 25-foot-long handline, but a 50-foot handline is better for deep-water use, current, and the inevitable problem situations. Don't wrap the handline around your wrist, and do not cast it over a rocky bottom, which invites hangup.

Cast nets come in different mesh sizes, different diameters, different weights, and with different strengths of mesh. They are commercially made and custom made, the latter preferred by people who gather bait professionally and by guides or charter boat captains who routinely use a cast net. Heavier weights and larger diameters are needed for deeper water use. The smallest cast nets have a 6-foot diameter and $1/2$-inch mesh, and weigh 10 pounds. They should be stored in a tall bucket when not in use, preferably one with large holes to allow drying and prevent rotting, and kept out of

C

With a portion of the net clenched in his teeth and the retrieval line wrapped around his right wrist, a guide uses a cast net to capture mullet. Getting the net to open fully is essential (3).

the sun; rinse the net in freshwater after use, and when it hasn't been used for awhile, soften it in warm water with fabric softener.

Using a cast net in freshwater and in some coastal or tidal waters may be illegal, or may require a permit. The overall diameter of the net may be restricted as well, and in some places there are regulations as to the number of nets that can be carried aboard a boat.

CATADROMOUS

Fish that migrate from freshwater to saltwater in order to spawn. Fish that do the opposite are called anadromous, and are more numerous. Freshwater eels are typical of catadromous fish; they are born at sea, migrate upstream to live and grow to adulthood, and then return to the sea to migrate to their spawning grounds.

See: Anadromous.

CATCH

(1) To capture a fish (usually by legal and sporting means in the recreational sense). A fish has been caught once it has been brought close enough to the angler to be secured and is restrained for unhooking, whereupon it may be kept or released.

See: Catch-and-Release; Landing Fish.

(2) The total number or poundage of fish captured from an area over some defined period of time. This includes fish that are caught but released or discarded, as well as those that are kept. With respect to saltwater fisheries, catch differs from "landings," a term referring to the number or poundage of fish unloaded at a dock by commercial fishermen or brought to shore by recreational anglers.

See: Fisheries Management.

CATCH-AND-RELEASE

"Catch-and-release" is a term that refers to the practice of catching gamefish by sporting methods and with sporting equipment and then releasing them alive. It is a concept rooted in angling ethics and tradition, and an action that has long been voluntary on the part of the angler—who chooses to release a fish that could be captured and retained for consumption. In the voluntary sense, catch-and-release is a personal, if not moral or ethical, judgment, and some practitioners believe that the spirit of catch-and-release has special meaning only when it is done voluntarily, especially with respect to fish that are notable for their size or scarcity. However, what was once primarily a voluntary action has increasingly become a legally mandated action for certain sizes, numbers, and species of fish. Thus, catch-and-release has become both personal philosophy and governmental policy.

Nevertheless, whether personal belief or management tool, catch-and-release has taken a long time for large numbers of people to embrace. It is widely debated by anglers and fisheries managers, and it is still evolving as more is learned about the factors affecting the survival of sport-caught fish that have been released, and as anglers learn and practice the proper methods of landing, handling, and releasing their catches.

Evolution of Laws

The notion of releasing fish that are not needed for consumption and that legally can be kept developed as a result of the actions of several groups of anglers: experienced anglers who had kept enough fish of a certain size or species that they didn't need to keep more, anglers who wished to extend their angling enjoyment by not keeping a legal limit and thus being able to continue fishing, and enlightened anglers who, perhaps most importantly, recognized that the removal of more fish of a certain size or species would be detrimental to a given water and fish population and might adversely impact future angling.

The modern-day genesis of catch-and-release angling advanced from a matter of individual conscience and choice into a movement as the result of a boon in angling participation in the latter half of the twentieth century, particularly through the 1960s and 1970s; other factors were the development of sophisticated sportfishing equipment, improved knowledge about fish, and the resulting increased pressure on fisheries populations. Many popular fisheries resources in North America were diminished or depleted in the decades following World War II. Although numerous factors contributed to this, and in varying degrees, the primary ones were water and air pollution, habitat destruction or alteration, commercial fishing, and sportfishing.

Sportfishing efforts in both freshwater and saltwater have long been targeted at selective species that have favorably appealed to the angling psyche. Bass, trout, salmon, crappie, and walleye, for example, have been leading freshwater favorites; striped bass, redfish, tarpon, tuna, and billfish are among the more popular saltwater species. Before pressure on these and other popular gamefish intensified, and before there was a more widespread collective modern-day sense of the need for conservation, anglers usually kept nearly all the fish that they caught in accordance with what were then very liberal limitations. Eventually, regulations regarding seasons, bag or creel limits, length limits, and methods of fishing were either enacted or made more encompassing and more restrictive.

At one time, anglers, as well as the general public, believed that recreational angling did not harm populations of fish, especially in freshwater where commercial fishing was generally less of a factor than it was in saltwater. Today it is recognized that this is not so; indeed, enough skillful anglers can decimate nearly any fish population over time if unchecked, with or without the contribution of other factors (pollution, commercial fishing, etc.). In some situations, skillful anglers can do this in a fairly short period of time, even while behaving according to legal limitations. Even if they do not decimate the entire population, they are still capable of changing population dynamics by selectively fishing for and keeping certain species or certain sizes (usually the biggest) of gamefish. An intense effort at catching, and then subsequently keeping, huge lake trout in northern Canada, for example, destroyed or gravely depleted many populations of slow-growing trophy fish from the late 1950s into the 1970s.

In response to changing situations, and in many cases at the request of various anglers' organizations,

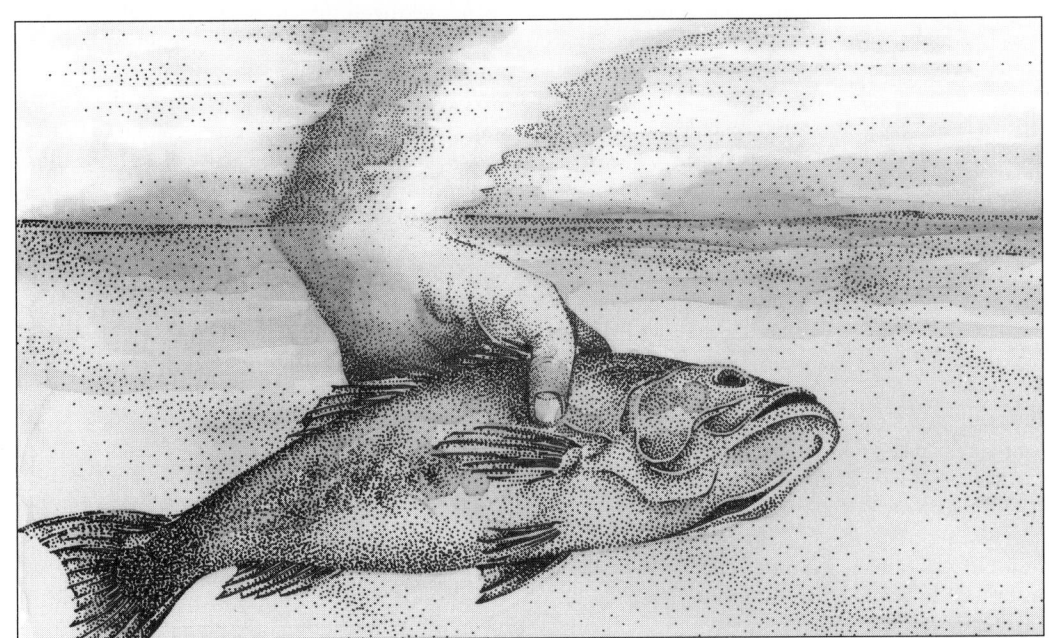

fisheries managers took action by implementing size or bag limits where there had previously been none, creating seasons, decreasing existing size or bag limits, specifying the terminal tackle that could be used, and taking other measures, such as creating slot limits, to maintain or improve specific resources.

Many fisheries management regulations pertaining to size, numbers, and seasons were established to allow young fish the opportunity to mature and to spawn. This is especially true in freshwater, and to a lesser extent in saltwater. Some regulations were established to achieve a specific objective, such as making available more trophy specimens of a certain species in a certain lake; releasing the larger members of a fish population is viewed as a way to foster the propagation and availability of larger specimens. Other regulations were established for what may seem an opposite reason: to address an imbalanced population of fish. In an unexploited, balanced population of fish, there should be many size groups (also called age classes), with fish in the medium ranges making up the bulk of the population, and with a good number of both small and large specimens. But where a fish population is exposed to angling, the usual result is that fish of all sizes are caught but the larger specimens are intentionally and disproportionately removed, which in time will significantly alter the structure of the population. It may lead to unbalancing it, with fewer size groups and fewer adult fish to reproduce.

Thus, by law, recreational anglers must release fish that they inadvertently catch out of prescribed seasons, or that do not meet size criteria, or that exceed the total number of fish allowable for a particular species. There are other reasons that fish must legally be released as well. For example, in certain places some species may not be kept if they are foul-hooked. This is a regulation based on sporting ethic rather than on biological management principle.

Indeed, some of the regulations concerning size and bag limits have more to do with social concerns—managing people—than with fisheries resources; although catch-and-release as a general principle has become more accepted, the extent to which it is accepted remains a dividing line between some groups of anglers. In fact, length-limit laws have actually had the unintentional effect of making larger fish more subject to exploitation. If anglers have to release all fish under a certain size, say bass under 15 inches, for example, some of them are much more likely to not release a legal fish after catching many "shorts."

Issues

To the nonangler, releasing a fish seems like a dubious decision—considering the expense that might be involved, the general uncertainty of achieving success, and the rejection of a fresh source of healthy food—unless it must be done to satisfy legal mandates. In terms of consumption, releasing fish that have been captured, regardless of the "sporting" means, runs contrary to mankind's long harvest tradition. Indeed, in most cultures of the world today, fish that are caught by rod and reel are almost always kept for consumption.

If you have been to some of those places, especially in freshwater, you might sarcastically say that this is why their fishing is not particularly recommendable, certainly not in comparison with the extent of the resources that exist in North America. Perhaps they needed to practice some measure of catch-and-release a long time ago.

Anglers who voluntarily release fish that they might otherwise keep do so for a variety of reasons. Some actually don't like to eat fish and don't even think about keeping them. Some like to eat fish but release them because of health advisories about consumption. Most, however, voluntarily release fish as a matter of conscience and because they are interested in seeing the fish they've just caught, and the population that it came from, continue to prosper.

Individual anglers, and some organizations representing anglers, advocate catch-and-release as a means of improving or maintaining the density of fish in a certain body of water, or the composition of the population, whether or not there are regulations in effect for this purpose. Although a high density, or number, of fish is not a guarantee of fishing success, it often translates into better fishing, especially for skillful anglers; greater numbers of fish are widely perceived as providing more opportunity for success and are therefore conducive to a good experience. Many anglers feel that voluntarily releasing all or most of the fish they catch in a given place helps ensure more fish for future fishing. Studies do back up this fact, although it may not be universally true. In some freshwater lakes and rivers, fish populations are sustained largely or entirely through stocking efforts. The fish that are voluntarily released in such places may not contribute to expanding the future population in those water bodies, although they may have the opportunity to grow into a much larger specimen that someone will have the pleasure of catching in the future. Nevertheless, anglers consciously choose to release their catches to foster the objective of ensuring more fish for future fishing, hoping that if enough other anglers do likewise, they will have a positive impact.

Most anglers who have fished for a long time and caught many fish of a particular species simply feel it is unnecessary to keep more of them, or more than what the anglers currently need to eat. In the early evolution of catch-and-release, this thinking became the basis for the motto: Limit your kill; don't kill your limit. Keeping only what they need, rather than taking the limit that the law allows, is probably the primary motivation today among knowledgeable and well-rounded anglers who voluntarily practice catch-and-release. When this motivation is combined with the rationale of choosing fish to keep based upon their condition, their size in relation to the fish population, or their species, an angler may be making the most intelligent decision. In other words, when an angler chooses to keep a fish, the angler can fine-tune the choices, perhaps choosing to keep a fish that has been wounded and has less chance of survival, instead of one that is in better shape, or perhaps keeping a fish that is smaller rather than bigger, when there are plenty of small fish available but few big ones. Perhaps the angler will choose to release a healthy spawning female fish so that its genes remain in the population pool or perhaps will choose to keep a specimen from an abundant species, rather than one from a species that is either less abundant or less intensively pursued.

Unfortunately, catch-and-release fishing has been touted by some as a panacea for improving fishing. This is simply not true for all species and in all situations. Moreover, some have preached this concept so aggressively that one could get the impression that keeping any fish is wrong, even if the law allows otherwise. Some newcomers to angling, particularly fly fishing, have embraced total catch-and-release out of a sense of being politically correct; this thinking puts them at odds with the many anglers for whom having a meal of freshly caught fish is appropriate not only for nutritional reasons, but also for the satisfying conclusion to an angling experience that it represents.

Some anglers deem it morally reprehensible to keep a particularly large fish. Others who rarely keep fish would however keep a particularly large

Most fish can be released quickly after capture, but it's always best to do so gently; this angler is releasing a bonefish.

one to send to a taxidermist. The former group needs to recognize that keeping or releasing a fish should remain a matter of choice and that, in some circumstances, it is not only acceptable but the right thing to do (when the fish is injured, for example; more on this issue later in the entry). The latter group needs to know that replica taxidermists *(see: taxidermy)* can produce fish mounts from fiberglass molds that are as good as skin mounts—and longer lasting; thus, in the case of trophy fish, it is possible to have the unique pleasure of releasing one of the rare members of a fish population and still have a representation to hang over the fireplace.

Compounding the acceptance of catch-and-release is the fact that regulations vary widely, and what is acceptable on one body of water is not on another. In certain situations, biologists have the challenging chore of convincing anglers to release small fish of a certain species at one lake, and then keep them at another. In some situations, regulations are applied unilaterally to many bodies of water, even when local conditions warrant having regulations uniquely tailored to fit the specific place or fish population.

Besides the sometimes confusing application of regulations, other factors enter into the issue of catch-and-release. For example, some species of fish, especially in saltwater, are available only seasonally because of migratory patterns. An angler who fishes for two days during that seasonally abundant period and keeps a legal limit of fish—say five fish—is not a game hog, yet someone who does this every day for 10 straight days is surely a game hog. However, if the latter angler kept just one fish a day for 10 days, the angler would have the same seasonal take as the angler who fished for only two days. On the other hand, an angler could fish for 10 days and not catch an average of a legal fish per day, but a more skillful angler could conceivably catch (and keep or release) a legal limit every day.

As the preceding examples have shown, the amount of fishing done by individual recreational anglers varies widely, and the skill level and success among anglers varies from novices to professionals. Thus, the amount of fishing that an angler does, and the amount of success that the angler experiences, has to be part of the equation in developing a personal catch-and-release ethic.

Anglers who fish often and with a high degree of accomplishment are the most likely to have an entrenched interest in catch-and-release, if they accept the fact that populations of fish can be harmed by excessive harvest. Yet many anglers who fish often take a holier-than-though approach to their sport, especially if they release all or most of their catch. A person who fishes 50 days a year, who enjoys good success, and who releases 95 percent of the catch, does not have a higher moral standing than the person who fishes only 5 days a year, who has relatively modest success, and who keeps most of the legal catch to eat. Furthermore, as will be

C

illustrated in the following section, there is undoubtedly some mortality among the fish that are released by all anglers; even anglers who live-release every fish that they catch cannot claim to have no effect on the resource.

Of course, much of the effect that anglers have is very tightly focused. Many of the gamefish sought by anglers are among the top predators in their environment, yet they are also a small segment of the total food pyramid. There are approximately 22,000 species of fish in the world, but only a couple hundred are the quarries of anglers, and only a few dozen each in freshwater and saltwater are aggressively and intensively pursued by anglers. No wonder that things can get out of whack. However, this situation is all the more reason to take steps to ensure that those targeted species remain a renewable resource for the sake of biodiversity, recreation, and food.

Although anglers can have a serious impact on fisheries populations, and in some cases the most serious impact, they are just one of many influences. In the natural world, even in a perfectly balanced population not exposed to angling, a given number of gamefish, including specimens of catchable size, will die from natural causes every year. They are caught by predators (including each other), and they die of old age and disease. The percentage that is lost to natural causes varies in each situation, but they are annually replaced by new fish. When angling is introduced, some fish will be lost to angling-related mortality, and some, although fewer than previously, will be lost to natural causes. If the number lost to angling is in balance with the number lost to natural causes, so that the same percentage of overall mortality is achieved, the population will maintain itself, all other influences being equal. If angling-related mortality is negligible, there will be no net loss. But if angling-related mortality is equal to or greater than the natural mortality that would have occurred without angling, then the population will decline. Thus, it is desirable to keep angling-related mortality to acceptable levels. Fortunately, fish can be recycled, and they are a natural resource that can be enjoyed without being destroyed.

The rub is that simply releasing a fish that is breathing is not an assurance that the fish will survive. So to effectively practice catch-and-release, whether by choice or by mandate, anglers must know how to properly release fish, and they must understand what factors contribute to unintended angling-related mortality.

Survival Generalities

The most logical question to ask about releasing fish is whether they will survive after being hooked, played, landed, handled, unhooked, and returned to the water. The answer is that many, but certainly not all, will survive, and that survival depends on many factors.

Some fish, like this large Saskatchewan pike, need to be held stable in the water for a while until they can swim off on their own.

Many anglers have personally caught or seen fish caught that were undeniably previously landed and released by other anglers. Whether the fish had identifiable markings, cut-off hooks, or tags, it obviously survived previous capture. A small minority of anglers have had an opportunity to personally tag and release fish, and they or others have recaptured some of the tagged fish, a few of them many times. One angler reported in a letter to a popular periodical that a tagged bass in his pond had been recaptured over 20 times, and at least once it had been caught twice on the same day.

More significantly, numerous studies have been conducted by professional fisheries researchers on the survival of fish that are caught and released by anglers. Researchers have been evaluating this issue since the 1930s, long before catch-and-release became popular. Such studies have been done in controlled situations and with respect to most, if not all, of the most favored species of fish, particularly in freshwater. Trout and bass, being the most popular and prominent sportfish, have been especially well studied, and continue to be.

Although scientifically valid studies have proven conclusively that fish released by anglers can survive, the studies have not produced identical results or percentages of survival. In some cases, the methodologies were criticized—especially when released fish were confined to holding areas—and few attempts have estimated the survival of fish that are repeatedly caught and released (which may happen more often than is realized, and which is known to happen in "no-kill" sections of trout rivers). Moreover, many studies have specifically focused on hooking mortality to determine the effects of terminal gear. The effects of other factors, especially playing and handling the fish, are more difficult to assess; the general issue of stress has been less extensively studied, although the effects of stress on fish are fairly well established. The results of myriad scientific studies have been reported in many technical and popular publications. One of the most frequently quoted results is from a study of the heavily fished Buffalo Ford section of the Yellowstone River (devoted to only barbless flies and lures), where research indicates that cutthroat trout survived 9 to 10 catch-and-release occurrences per season.

Nevertheless, some general conclusions stand out in the collective body of scientific studies, chief among them that using bait is more detrimental to fish than using lures or flies, that barbless hooks cause slightly lower mortality than barbed hooks, that bleeding fish are unlikely to survive, and that deeply hooked fish are at much greater risk than fish caught around the edges of the mouth.

Injury and Stress

Fish primarily die before and after being released because of injury and stress. Some weakened or struggling fish may also die as a result of predation by other fish, birds, and some reptiles and mammals; this seldom accounts for a high mortality, although injury or stress may be an indirect factor. Death that occurs after release, usually out of sight of the angler and without the angler's knowledge, is called delayed mortality. Many fish that die from injury or stress do so within 24 hours after being released, the vast majority within 48 hours. Anglers can eliminate or reduce fish injury and stress, but to do so they should understand the physiological factors at work.

A general understanding of the biology of fish is contained in the anatomy *(see)* entry. Following is a synopsis of the key parts of the anatomy that play an important role in injury and stress.

Mucus.   This is the protective coating of a fish that is a barrier to the entry of parasites, fungi, and disease organisms; it also seals in the fish's body fluids so that they are not diluted by the watery surroundings.

Air bladder.   Located between the stomach and backbone, the air bladder performs several functions. Some species of fish use the air bladder as a compartment in which to store air for breathing; the fish falls back on this reserve when its usual supply of oxygen is shut off. The air bladder plays a part in aiding the equilibrium of density between the fish and the water.

Digestive system.   The tongue, located just inside the mouth, is flat, rigid, and cartilaginous, and moves only when the base below it moves; the esophagus, or gullet (between the throat and stomach), is highly distensible and usually can accept any type or size of food that the fish can fit into its mouth; the stomach varies in shape and in most gamefish is elongated but may be saclike; and the intestines are generally shortened.

Gills.   Fish breathe through their mouths and receive oxygen through the gills, which are much-divided thin-walled filaments where capillaries lie close to the surface. As the fish opens its mouth, a stream of water is drawn in and the gill cover is held tight, thereby closing the gill opening. Then the fish closes its mouth and drives the water over the gills and out the external openings. As water passes over the gills, oxygen is taken in through the walls of the fine blood vessels in the gill filaments and carbon dioxide is given off. The blood, well oxygenated, then travels through the fish's body. Gill rakers, located along the anterior margin of the gill arch, project over the throat opening and strain water that is passed over the gills; they also prevent solid particles from passing over and injuring the gill filaments.

Circulatory system.   Fish blood passes from the heart to the gills for purification and then travels directly to all other parts of the body. The heart, blood, and blood vessels carry oxygen and nourishment to every living cell in the body and carry away carbon dioxide and other excretory products. The fish's heart is located close behind the fish's mouth. Blood vessels are largest close to the heart and become progressively smaller, terminating in a network of extremely fine capillaries that meander through the body tissues.

Pain.   Since fish have a nervous system and sense organs, it would appear that they could feel pain; however, a fish's brain is not highly developed. There is no cerebral cortex (the part of the brain that stores impressions in higher animals), so the fish has little or no memory. Fish are essentially

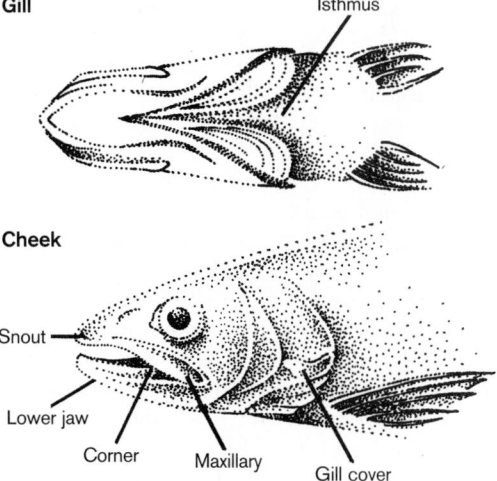

Gill   Isthmus

Cheek

Snout

Lower jaw

Corner   Maxillary   Gill cover

The least harmful hooking areas are the jaw, snout, corners of the mouth, maxillary, and cheek. The most harmful hooking areas are the eye, tongue, isthmus, and gills.

Transplanting fish
was a common
practice through the
nineteenth century; as early
as 1810, northern pike
were transplanted to Maine
and New Hampshire.

C

creatures of reflex rather than of action produced or developed by the brain. In all probability, physical pain in fish is not very acute, and any impression of pain in the brain is quickly lost.

Responses to capture. When a fish is hooked, it resists the capturing efforts of the angler. This struggling can cause stress. Where the fish is hooked and how it is landed, handled, and unhooked can cause injury, which may compound stress. How the fish is played by the angler, the length of time involved, how the fish is revived, and how it is released may cause injury and further stress.

The response of fish to these injury and stress factors varies widely between different species, and even between fish of the same species. In a general sense, some species are more resistant to rough-handling stresses than others, and such variables as water temperature, season (spawning), and even size of the fish make a difference in how fish react to the process of being caught and released. Thus, although one particular action may be identified as being harmful to a fish, or as causing stress, or as causing mortality, a number of actions may be collectively responsible.

However, much of the stress-related problems center around the gills, the respiratory system, and the circulatory system.

Gills. The gills are an especially sensitive area of a fish. Bleeding can come from even a slight nick, and bleeding in itself is a high-stress factor. A fish cannot breathe out of water; it gets oxygen from the water that is passed over the gills. Keeping a fish out of the water, whether to unhook it, photograph it, or weigh it, increases the stress load. When oxygen is low, fish breathe faster, trying to pass more water over the gills. If held out of the water for too long, a fish can suffocate. How long is too long? There is no stopwatch answer for this. The size and species of the fish, the temperature, and even humidity all play a role. However, lifting any fish by its gill flap, as many anglers do, is definitely harmful; it exposes the gill tissues to air and can result in tearing of the filaments. Touching and grabbing the gills can be very harmful. To reduce stress, anglers should minimize exposure of the gills to air, avoid touching them, and avoid grabbing a fish by the gills or lifting it by the gill cover.

Lactic acid buildup. As with most animals, vigorous physical exertion causes lactic acid to accumulate in the fish's muscles. This buildup occurs when the muscles are deprived of oxygen and the body incompletely metabolizes glucose. The same thing occurs in humans after strenuous exertion, and it produces the "oxygen debt" that long-distance runners and other athletes experience. When the exertion is over, if all other systems are functioning properly, the body metabolizes the lactic acid and restores the oxygen to appropriate levels. But this may not happen immediately; the more severe the lactic acid buildup, the longer it takes to return to normal.

Ordinarily, the metabolic process operates at a continuous balanced level, but there are natural times when lactic acid builds up in a fish. Chasing or escaping from predators, for example, is likely to temporarily build up lactic acid. The rigors of migration can produce moments of buildup; a fish that migrates up a river, like salmon or shad, may experience lactic acid buildup after it endures the hardships of running through a particularly difficult section of water, perhaps a falls that the fish must hurdle. After passing that difficult section, the fish will usually rest in a pool above that spot and recoup its energy, moving on when it has regained strength and when other factors tell it to do so.

As noted, the accumulation of lactic acid in a fish's muscles can lead to blood acidification and temporary disruption of many metabolic processes. If a captured fish is able to restore its blood acid (pH) level to normal or pre-stress levels, normal physiological processes return and the fish may survive after being released. If the blood chemistry balance is not restored, the fish will probably die. The volume of lactic acid generated is directly proportional to the duration of muscular activity.

In freshwater, most species of fish are landed fairly quickly, even on light tackle, by the average angler. There are some exceptions, such as salmon and big trout. In saltwater, more species attain large size and have a lot of strength, so there are more fish able to extend the battle with an angler. No matter what the environment, extended battles promote lactic acid buildup. The issue of playing fish so as to minimize lactic acid buildup is dealt with in more detail later in this section, but in general it is advantageous to land a fish quickly if you intend to release it, unless it has been hooked in very deep water. Playing the fish until it is exhausted, or "belly up," may lead to lactic acid poisoning and death. This eventuality may be prevented not only by playing a fish quickly, but also by unhooking it carefully and releasing it as quickly as possible.

Experienced anglers know that lactic acid buildup and the resulting stress work differently in fish. A rainbow trout, for example, will put up more struggle than a bullhead catfish. The coolwater trout is more likely to build up lactic acid than the warmwater bullhead; and the trout will not last long if kept out of the water, whereas the hardier bullhead may last a surprisingly long time. Anglers become acquainted with the fighting characteristics of the different species and should be able to recognize when certain fish need to be landed quickly and given more attention in the revival and release process. Some fish are so stressed after being landed (as well as handled for release), and their lactic acid level so high, that they have a greatly increased need for oxygen. This condition makes them harder to revive, and they may need more time to recover before they regain equilibrium and can swim off on their own.

Stress is the factor that initiates lactic acid buildup and this is compounded by injury, either because of where the fish is hooked or how it is handled later on. Bringing a fish to boat quickly, for example, while generally recommended, can have a drawback if the fish is so frisky that the angler, in efforts to unhook and release it, causes internal or external injury. Putting a stressed fish into a livewell may not be helpful either, if the well doesn't have sufficient aeration. In that case, the fish will struggle to get the oxygen it needs, thereby creating more stress rather than less. If the livewell is uncrowded, is properly aerated, and/or the water has been treated with conditioning agents, then stress can be reduced.

Thus, in the various stages of contact with a sport-caught fish, anglers may compound or mitigate stress, and it is important to have an understanding of the impact of all actions.

How a Fish Is Hooked

The catch-and-release experience starts with the angler becoming connected to a fish via rod, reel, line, and, of course, hook. A determining factor in the survival of a fish after release is where it is hooked. Where it is hooked is often a function of the angling technique, the terminal tackle employed, and the skills of the angler.

Many studies have proven that fish caught with bait suffer a much higher rate of mortality than fish caught with lures or flies. The studies differ in the percent of mortality of bait-hooked fish, but they agree that the use of bait generally results in deeply hooked fish and a significantly higher mortality. An analysis of the findings of studies conducted on lake- and stream-dwelling trout and salmon species showed an average mortality rate of 31 percent for bait-hooked fish, 4.9 percent for lure-hooked fish, and 3.8 percent for fly-caught fish.

While this is an alarming difference, it should be pointed out that the manner of fishing also effects deep hooking. Trolling with a lure or fly, for example, is unlikely to cause a deep-hooked fish. If an angler lets a fish run with either live or dead bait, and waits to set the hook, the likelihood is great that the fish will swallow the bait, and swallowing the bait will probably result in the fish being hooked deeply, especially in the esophagus or stomach. Removing a hook from these areas is usually difficult; it often cannot be done without taking the fish out of the water and hook removal in this instance may cause internal damage. If the hook is swallowed so deeply that it punctures the heart, which is just behind the mouth, or the liver or kidney, the fish is going to die.

Although such deep hooking is often a result of fishing with bait, it can also happen with lures Some lures, like plastic worms, for example, may be swallowed by fish if they are allowed to run with them, and deep swallowing of the lure can cause the same degree (if not more) of hooking mortality as bait swallowing. Indeed, some studies have shown

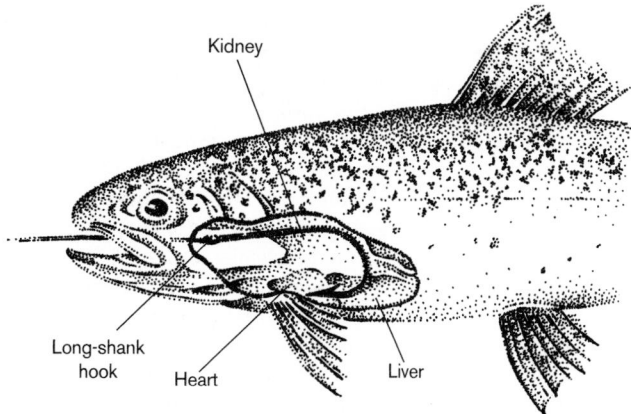

The kidney, heart, and liver are all vulnerable when a fishhook is lodged within the throat of a fish.

that live bait has caused no significant difference in mortality over certain types of lures that were likely to be taken deep. A study of live bait use compared with the use of Carolina-rigged plastic worms on largemouth bass, for example, showed a slightly higher mortality for the worms. This type of rig often is taken deeply, and anglers usually wait to set the hook *(see: hooksetting)*.

Obviously, one way that anglers using bait can reduce harm to fish is to set the hook quickly after a pickup or strike, rather than waiting for the fish to inhale it and then set the hook. This action is helpful, since most fish can inhale a bait item in an instant; however, it does not work for all species, and its success may depend on the type of bait used or species sought—pike and muskie, for example, will often hold a bait before consuming it rather than simply inhale it. Not all fish crush a bait and then turn it around to inhale; for those species, deep hooking can be avoided by being alert to a take and quickly reacting properly. Incidentally, some baitfishing with treble hooks is actually better than baitfishing with single hooks, since the trebles are harder to swallow (although the bait may act less naturally with the treble and the fish may detect a treble hook sooner than a single one). In some saltwater fishing, the use of circle hooks *(see: hook)* has gained popularity for baitfishing (especially for tuna) because these hooks usually catch in the corner of the mouth, causing less injury to a fish that will be released.

Most lures or flies are far less likely to be taken deep than bait hooks, in part because they are usually moving and anglers naturally react fairly quickly to a strike. As a result, most fish caught on lures or flies are hooked in body locations where the hook does not severely damage the fish. The lowest mortality of fish occurs when they are hooked in the jaw, the snout, the corners of the mouth, the maxillary, and the cheek. Hooking in the eye, the tongue, and the isthmus are a little more serious.

Being hooked in or near the gills is bad news because the hook may damage the gill filaments, either as a result of being hooked or as a result of

C

hook removal. This type of injury causes bleeding and decreases the fish's chance of survival. Occasionally a single hook, whether used with bait or on lures or flies, will get into the gill area, but it is more common when a multihooked lure is used.

Studies have shown that fish caught on flies have a slightly lower mortality rate than those caught on lures, but the difference is so small that it has virtually no impact on the overall mortality picture. This negligible impact is the reason why special-use regulations established by fisheries managers generally prohibit the use of bait but permit the use of lures and flies, or specify single-hook lures and flies. Nevertheless, a belief persists among some anglers, primarily fly anglers, that people using lures, or hardware as it may derisively be called, cause more harm to the resource. Assuming that proper care is taken to unhook and release a fish, this is not so.

The use of treble hooks versus single hooks is another issue hotly debated. Here, too, some advocates of catch-and-release maintain that more harm is caused by trebles than singles. This is a split issue. Studies comparing the two have varying results. However, an evaluation of all studies on this issue concluded that there was no significant relationship between mortality and the number of hook points. This conclusion stands to reason in view of the slight difference in mortality between the use of lures and the use of flies (since nearly all flies have just a single hook). However, treble hooks on average are more difficult to remove from fish, which means that removing a treble hook usually takes longer than removing a single hook. A lure with multiple treble hooks, such as many plugs, may have two or three sets of treble hooks. Fish are often impaled by two or three hook points on multiple-treble-hooked lures; unhooking them may take longer, or one hook may cause no damage (in the corner of the mouth, for example) but another may damage a vulnerable area (such as the eye or the gill). Therefore, a reasonable conclusion is that the probability of injury to a fish is greater when a lure with multiple treble hooks is used.

In certain places, especially remote waters of northern Canada, the use of single hooks is either mandated by law or required as lodge or outfitter policy; and in some cases, those hooks must be barbless as well (barbed hooks have been banned throughout Manitoba since 1990). If an angler has a banned treble hook rather than the approved single hook, the guide will actually cut two of the points off the treble hook and pinch the barbs down on the hook before allowing fishing to start. These policies are in effect in waters where few fish—usually just one per person per day for shore lunch—are kept. The purpose of such policies is to minimize injury and permit quick release; these actions in turn help to maintain a large population of fish, all of which are slow-growing, and to increase the likelihood of big fish getting bigger. More comments on treble hooks versus single hooks follow later in this section.

As for barbless hook-related mortality, some older studies report no significant difference in mortality of fish caught on barbed versus barbless hooks; whereas some more recent ones show that fish caught on barbless hooks suffer lower hooking mortality than those caught on barbed hooks. Concerns that barbless hooks may cause deeper hook penetration, and thus facilitate injury, have proven groundless, and anglers who frequently, or exclusively, use barbless hooks do not report any findings that support these concerns. In fact, barbless hooks have the benefit of being easier and quicker to remove from fish, and this fact may contribute to a quicker release of the fish and less time spent out of the water.

With regard to some of these issues, it is reasonable to ask if mountains are being made out of molehills. For example, what is the difference if a barbless hook is removed in 18 seconds versus a barbed hook removed in 23 seconds, assuming that neither removal causes an injury? Or, is a 1 percent difference in fish mortality for barbless flies over barbed flies really important? Does it matter if fish-hooking mortality with a treble-hooked lure is 5 percent versus 4 percent for a single-hook lure? Maybe the differences are negligible if the fish is striped bass, the legal limit is one fish, and millions are around. But, maybe the differences are significant if the fish is a cutthroat trout in a special-regulation section of river that gets pounded by thousands of anglers.

A key issue in all these situations is the percentage of fish mortality. Studies of trout show mortalities of less than 5 percent for fish caught on lures and flies, and the percentages decrease from there with single and barbless hooks. But all of this has to be kept in perspective, because a fish that is caught on a barbless hook may still be mortally wounded if the angler rips out the hook, squeezes the fish hard while holding it for release, drops the fish on the ground or boat floor, and so forth. The hooks used and the location of hooking are just part of the picture. How the angler plays, lands, handles, and releases fish is also very important.

Playing Fish

The technical aspects of how to play a fish are discussed in detail in another entry (see: playing fish). The intent here is to spotlight the effects of playing techniques upon fish that are to be released.

It was once axiomatic that the safest way to catch a fish was to play it until it was exhausted and then land it. That was in the days when many, if not most, fish that were caught were kept. It is true that an exhausted fish is less likely to thrash about and is easier to land and handle, and thus safer to the angler. But it is also true that an exhausted fish is more likely to be severely stressed.

As fishing tackle improved over the past half-century, the sport of fishing took on newer dimensions with an increasing interest by anglers in catching large fish by using light tackle. Devotees, in fact, advocated light tackle in part to "give the fish a chance." The challenge of using light gear and employing above-ordinary angling skills created an interest in light-tackle usage that still runs strong today (see: light-tackle fishing). However, as more was learned about the physiological factors that affect hooked fish, the clearer it became that there is a correlation between stress in fish and the length of time that they're played, and that light-tackle use may cause some fish to be played for such a length of time that it affects their ability to survive when released. Ironically, although the use of light tackle may give the fish a better chance to avoid capture, it may give the fish less of a chance to survive the catch-and-release experience.

But the issue is not quite this clear-cut, and the solution to this dilemma is not necessarily to disavow the use of light tackle. Indeed, capable anglers can catch some fish quicker on light tackle than other anglers can catch them using heavier equipment. In fact, while it is hard to dispute the effects of lactic acid buildup over an extended playing time, what constitutes a long time and how much of a factor it is in causing mortality of fish varies widely among species and is complicated by the location of the hook in the fish, the temperature of the water, the size of the fish, environmental factors (like current), and other influences.

In general terms, large fish tend to have more difficulty with lactic acid buildup, and in some studies they have experienced a higher mortality rate than smaller fish. This fact, too, is ironic, because the larger fish are often the ones that many catch-and-release practitioners desire to see survive. In freshwater, most of the fish that are caught by anglers are landed in a relatively short period of time, either because of the skill of the angler or the type of equipment employed, or because most freshwater fish are small (1/2 pound to 2 pounds) and able to recover from lactic acid stress fairly quickly if they are not otherwise injured or mistreated. The scenario is a bit different in saltwater, where the average size is larger and where many sport-caught fish reach greater sizes than their freshwater brethren. Many species of saltwater fish are simply tougher than freshwater fish; and even on an equivalent-size basis, and assuming the use of identical equipment, they will be harder to subdue, which means landing them will take longer.

So how long is too long for large or strong fish? There is no guaranteed timetable, and no good way to measure the time. Where species in freshwater or saltwater are concerned, how you play a large or strong fish may be the most important factor of all. This is probably more important than whether you use a barbed or barbless hook or whether you use a lure instead of a fly. In some cases it may also be more important than whether you caught the fish on bait or not.

This issue of how you play the fish is central to what constitutes an exhausted fish, and it is admittedly a gray area. On the one hand, fish played to complete exhaustion may not survive. The key words are may not. If complete exhaustion meant certain death for a fish, then it would mean death for every animal that exercises itself to exhaustion, including long-distance runners and racehorses. Obviously, exhaustion cannot equate entirely with death. Some large and strong fish that are played to exhaustion can be revived and set free. Some cannot.

Indeed, the way that a fish is played may be the critical element. Playing a fish aggressively is more likely to result in breaking its spirit and saving its life. A tug-of-war can last longer and result in a "stubborn" fish that will not give up and cannot be resuscitated after capture. Fish of identical sizes can be played to identical times with different outcomes; one may be played aggressively by an experienced angler using light tackle and be successfully released, and the other fish may be played by an inexperienced angler using heavier tackle and be incapable of revival.

If you take the fight to the fish, no matter what the tackle, you often can convince the fish to give up. Anglers who fish for such powerful bruisers as tuna and billfish experience this frequently. If you are in a river playing a large fish, the battle might be prolonged if you move or lunge after the fish; whereas, by remaining motionless, you could actually fool it and make it feel less threatened, despite being on the end of your line (remember that you know what this means, but the fish doesn't), and you may land it quicker than you would have otherwise.

This gray area is evidently a psychological one. It is definitely an aspect of playing large and tough fish that many anglers give no thought to.

Landing and Handling Fish

The technical aspects of how to land a fish are discussed in detail in another entry (see: landing fish). The intent here is to spotlight the effects of landing and handling upon fish that are to be released.

One of the critical areas affecting the well-being of fish to be released is how they are treated once they are caught. Mishandling results in injury and stress, and is an aspect of catch-and-release that every angler can do something about.

Whether or not a fish is tired, its chance of survival is best if it never leaves the water, a feat that few anglers practice often enough. In some instances, frisky and obviously unharmed fish can be shaken off at boatside by leaving some slack in the line and jiggling the rod tip. This is especially true if single-hooked and barbless lures are used. An angler who is having great success and catching many fish while using multihooked lures should consider using lures with a single hook or pinching the barbs, rather than continuing to catch fish on the original lures, especially if the fish are repeatedly small and frisky.

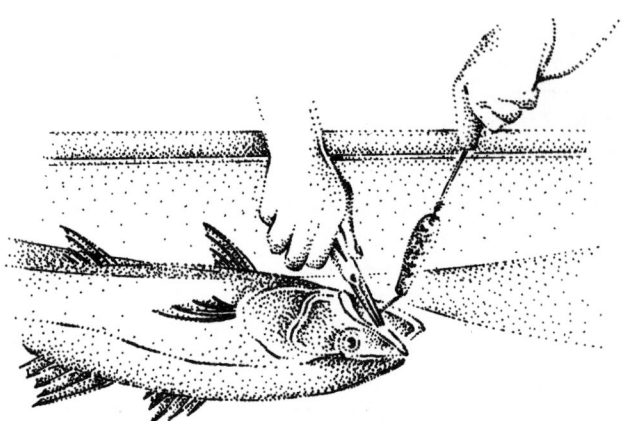

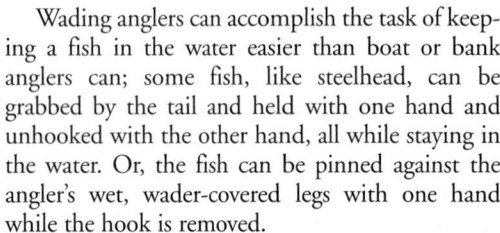

When fishing from a boat, you can easily release some fish without handling them by keeping the fish in the water at boatside and using pliers to free the hook.

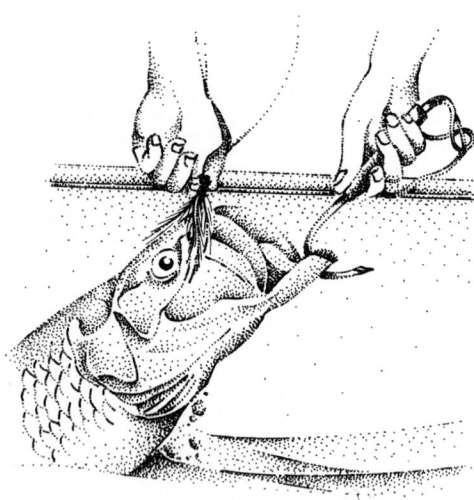

Lip-gaffing is one way to unhook a large fish without harming it. This may be a two-person operation, as depicted here, where one person lip-gaffs the fish and the other frees the hook.

Wading anglers can accomplish the task of keeping a fish in the water easier than boat or bank anglers can; some fish, like steelhead, can be grabbed by the tail and held with one hand and unhooked with the other hand, all while staying in the water. Or, the fish can be pinned against the angler's wet, wader-covered legs with one hand while the hook is removed.

Some fish can be unhooked in the water without handling. To do this, grasp the hook with needle- or long-nosed pliers and, without touching the fish (which may cause it to thrash about), quickly pull back and up on the point (in the opposite direction from which it is embedded) to free it. Once you have hold of the hook with the pliers, unhook the fish instantly in a quick wrist-twisting motion. This is usually, but not always, a two-person operation; one angler is holding the rod while the other reaches over (possibly holding the line lightly to steer the fish to an advantageous position) and, while the fish rests at the surface, uses pliers to quickly grab and free the hook. This is about as simple and as good a no-touch release as you can get. Unfortunately, this release method isn't always possible because of the size or behavior of the fish, the number of hooks or how the fish is hooked, the distance from water to gunwale of the boat, or other factors.

When you can't release the fish in the water, you have to land it by grabbing the fish by hand, netting it, cradling it, or gaffing it.

Gaffing.   Gaffing *(see)* is usually a method for landing a fish that you intend to keep, because the gaff point snares the fish through its flesh. A fish landed this way is almost certainly a goner, so you can't gaff a fish that will be released. You can, however, safely gaff some species through the lower jaw with a short-handled lip gaff; these species are usually fairly large fish that are difficult to subdue for unhooking.

Tarpon, red drum, and striped bass are commonly landed in the lower jaw with a hand gaff and then freed by slipping the gaff hook point back out. These fish have fairly large mouths, and it is not difficult to bring the gaff down through the skin behind the lower jaw. There are no organs to damage here, so gaffing will not be fatal to the fish if it is done carefully, and this method is preferable to bringing the fish into the boat or trying to hold onto it.

Netting.   Netting *(see)* can be harmful to fish and is a practice that probably should be reserved for fish that will be kept, but as with so many other aspects of catch-and-release fishing, this dictum is not absolute. A stream trout, for example, caught on a fly, can be landed and briefly held in a net without harm. A large salmon, caught on a multi-hooked plug, may pose a problem the instant that the hooks snare the side of the net as it is being raised around the fish. It's a situational thing.

Conventional round- or oval-shaped nets with deep mesh bags can damage the eyes and the jaws of fish and, possibly, the mucous coating. Cotton mesh nets are softer and don't seem to hurt the fish as much, but hooks are harder to get out of cotton mesh nets, and the nets are not as widely available today as nylon or rubber nets. One of the biggest problems in using a round or oval net is not actually the net itself, but the damage done to fish that are netted when a multihooked lure is used to catch the fish. The hooks inevitably grab the webbing of the net, and the fish thrashes and rips itself while pulling violently against the embedded hooks. If the fish rolls in the net with treble hooks, as pike and lake trout frequently do, then untangling becomes a real problem, and a good deal of time is lost before the fish can be unhooked. The situation is bad all around; some species may go into the net in good shape but come out with ripped skin, jaws, or eyes and be much worse off.

Cradling.   Perhaps the best method of netting a fish that will be released, and one that deserves more attention, is to use a type of net called a cradle, or release cradle. This is not a net in the traditional handle-and-dipping sense, but it has similarities

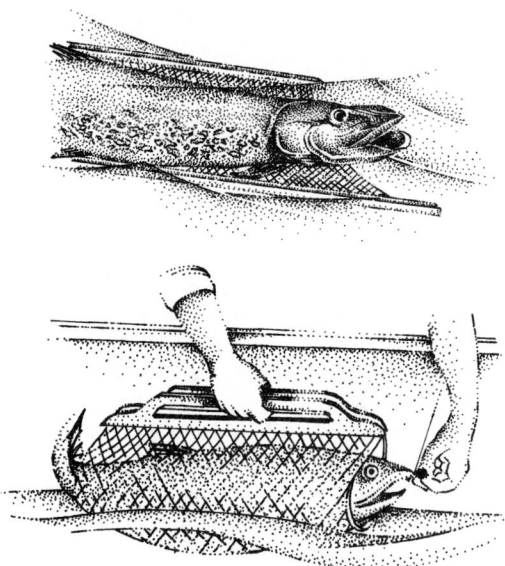

Cradles are an excellent way to handle some species of fish; a release cradle (top) provides optimal support for a long fish.

and is a benign way of landing and subduing a large or long fish so that it can be unhooked and released.

The most popular release cradles have two long narrow wood boards that are connected by $1/4$-inch soft-mesh knotless netting that is closed at the ends and that droops into the water to envelop a fish. The cradle is laid alongside a boat, and the netting droops into a trough below. The angler leads a captured fish alongside the boat and over the netting, and the net is folded up like a purse to enclose the fish, which remains full-length and in the water. Perhaps most importantly the cradle supports the full body of the fish in a horizontal position. Another version, usually homemade and intended for shorter fish, is smaller, with open ends and open-grip handle. In both cases, the fish stays relaxed in the net while the hook is removed, and the fish can be released without having to be handled. Moreover, you can rig the cradle up so that it's possible to weigh the fish and cradle while providing excellent horizontal support for the fish. It is very difficult to use a cradle when fishing by yourself, however; in that case, avoid a cradle or net altogether if possible and try to unhook the fish while it is in the water.

Release cradles, especially the larger ones, are more common among pike and muskie anglers, and are mostly a Midwest item, but the idea has broad application for landing freshwater fish and has some application in saltwater (although it is almost unknown there, perhaps because many saltwater boats have a high freeboard). If you can find a source for strong fine-mesh netting in 4- to 5-foot lengths, you can make your own cradle in both long and short lengths.

Hand-landing.   When you land a fish without a net or gaff, you have to hold it somehow. Big fish

are difficult to hold, and when brought into a boat, they are liable to be dropped or to squirm out of your hands and fall. Some fish, like a sailfish or big tarpon, might have to be held by two people in order to be properly subdued, supported, and unhooked. Nevertheless, large and small fish are often brought into boats to be released, and therefore are handled. In fact, in some cases, there is no other choice. In a big-water boat, for example, the freeboard makes it difficult, and unsafe under some conditions, for someone to lean over and attempt to hold and/or unhook a fish, especially if the boat is rolling with waves. In a low-freeboard craft, like a flats boat, bass boat, or jonboat, it is much easier and safer to get to a fish that is in the water.

Yet, even in these low boats, anglers regularly bring fish aboard for unhooking and release. Bass anglers, for example, often bring a fish into the boat, many by swinging it in because the fish is small and the line and tackle heavy enough to permit this. If they grab the fish by the lower jaw without letting it hit the floor or objects, then there's no problem. But if they swing it in and plop it on the floor, then pounce on it to unhook it, there is a problem.

The problem with physically handling a fish, as well as with letting a fish flop on the deck or floor of a boat or on the shore, is that the protective mucous coating may be removed, and the possibility increases of an infection that eventually may become grotesque and life-threatening. In addition, if the fish flops about while still hooked to a lure, the hooks on the lure may catch on some object (it might even be someone's leg or arm, which can be extremely serious) and cause further injury to the fish, which may also lead to infection. Such injury or exposure is likely more serious for freshwater fish than for those in marine environments because of the composition of saltwater; nonetheless, minimizing injury and exposure is always advisable whether the fish is in freshwater or saltwater.

Don't let a fish flop onshore or in a boat if you intend to release it. Wetting your hands before you hold a fish may help prevent removal of that protective mucus; however, many anglers maintain that wet hands make it harder to hold the fish, meaning that they have to grip it tighter. Using a sure-grip cotton glove that has been wetted is a good idea, and more anglers are using one to get a firm grasp

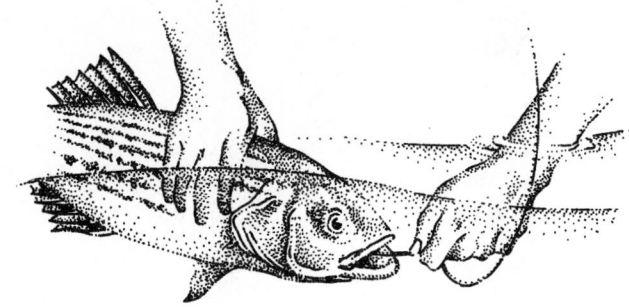

Lacking pliers, you should wet one hand before grasping the body of a small fish; keep the fish in the water while you free the hook with your other hand.

on a fish and to minimize harm. However, don't grasp a small fish tightly around the middle of the body during unhooking, because you may cause internal damage. Admittedly, it's a fine line between holding a fish tightly enough to keep it from squirming free, but not so tightly that the internal organs are compressed. These organs are concentrated behind the mouth and the head, exactly beneath the "neck" or nape where many fish are likely to be held. Obviously, the smaller fish, with less meat at the nape, are more easily hurt by holding tightly there. Big freshwater fish, and many saltwater fish, can be held in that location without harm; for many, it is the best place to do so.

When holding and subduing larger fish, try placing a wet cloth or towel over the fish, at least over the head. This action usually has a calming effect and is especially useful for fish that may be held for a longer period, such as the extra few moments needed when tagging a fish or when unhooking a particularly hard-to-unhook fish.

Some fish have a handle that you can grab to facilitate holding, especially in the water. In a very few species that handle is the bill; mostly it is the tail. The tails of some fish are rigid enough to permit grabbing by placing your hand over the caudal peduncle just ahead of the tail fin. You can grab a jack or a tuna that way, and you can grab large salmon and pike by the tail. Smaller fish usually can't be grabbed that way, and the tails of many fish are not rigid enough to permit this. You can't grab a big

A good gripping tool such as this helps keep hands away from fish and hooks, and facilitates unhooking for release.

largemouth bass securely enough by the tail, nor can you grab most trout (except really large ones) this way. You can hold bass by the mouth, however, and there are a few species whose mouths, lack of teeth on the jaws, or size may permit this. Bass are held by inserting the thumb inside the lower jaw and pinching the jaw against the bent forefinger, which is outside and pressing against the lower jaw. Some anglers wear a leather thumb guard for this, especially if they will be handling a lot of fish. However, larger and stronger fish that can be held by the jaw (anglers often call this the lip) are best secured by keeping the thumb outside and below the jaw, and putting the other four fingers inside the jaw, preferably (although not often) with a wet glove on.

Most fish cannot be hand-held by the mouth, usually because of teeth. One way to hand-land and hand-hold species by the mouth is with one of various jaw-gripping tools. These tools clamp over the lower jaw to secure the fish without requiring that the fish be touched by hand, and do no harm to the fish, although many models work best on smaller fish. For some species, a small lip gaff can be used to hold the fish for unhooking, although it should not be employed to lift the fish out of the water in such a manner that all the weight is placed on the jaw.

Many fish cannot, or should not, be supported by the lower jaw whether you are holding the jaw by hand or with a gripping device, but they can be gripped there while they are still in the water or while the rest of the body is being supported. Lifting fish up may or may not be a problem. The longer and heavier the fish, the more inappropriate lifting seems; yet lifting and briefly carrying fish, either headfirst or tailfirst, has been unharmful to many fish. Atlantic salmon have been tail-lifted, unharmed, by experienced anglers, although it's not something that ought to be done for very long.

In water, a fish maintains its equilibrium and balance, and body parts don't move around, but out of water, especially when held vertically, more pressure is brought to bear on internal organs and connective tissues. This is not necessarily harmful, although it can be, especially to larger fish (such as billfish) and/or fish that have already been severely stressed (don't forget that while you're lifting the fish vertically the fish is in need of oxygen). Therefore, keeping fish in a horizontal position, in or out of the water, is more in their best interests than lifting them vertically.

Smaller fish are less likely to be harmed when held vertically. Largemouth bass, which have been much studied, are commonly held vertically by anglers for unhooking and do not suffer from this position. However, most largemouth bass are small, and holding a 2-pound largemouth this way is not comparable to holding a 40-pound striper this way.

Holding fish under the gills, as previously discussed, is not appropriate, nor is putting your fingers in their eye sockets. It was once fairly common to grab some species by the cavity of their eye sockets, but this sorry practice has become almost universally abandoned unless a fish is going to be kept. This practice causes obvious injury to the fish, and it may lead to infections.

One technique that anglers find helpful is turning a fish over and holding it upside down (out of the water with small fish and in the water with larger ones). This technique doesn't appear to cause problems for the fish and seems to tranquilize it. Some small fish, largemouth bass included, can be gently lifted with a hand placed under the belly.

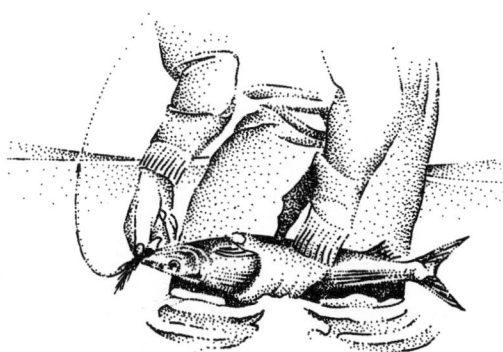

Before you unhook a small, frisky fish, try turning it upside down to tranquilize it.

This may be a good alternative for the angler when a fish has been caught on a lure with multiple hooks; however, it is really a technique for small fish, because proper balance cannot be supplied to larger fish this way, and a lot of pressure would be brought to bear on the internal organs.

When you do have to touch and hold fish, keep in mind that a minimum amount of handling is desirable in all cases, particularly in warm water. If fish must be taken out of the water, as previously explained, be conscious of their inability to breathe and of the length of time that they are forced to forego oxygen while being unhooked. Many of the fish that are held by anglers in the photographs in this book were released, even though they were held briefly out of water to take the photograph. When photographing fish, be prepared to take the photo quickly by having your camera available and ready to shoot (in other words, don't hold the fish out of water while you find your camera and load film into it). Of course, it helps if the fish are caught quickly and the water is cool.

The length of time that you hold a fish out of water—for unhooking, admiring, photographing, weighing, etc.—is one that has no set limit. For some exhausted fish, every second counts. For some hardy fish, a couple of minutes is no problem. If the fish has been landed pretty quickly, you should be able to tell its condition and whether there is a sense of urgency to the handling. Taking photos of a fish can put a fish in danger that is otherwise in fair to good condition. Not only is the fish held out of the water longer, but it is subjected to extra handling, sometimes by a couple of people, and this is often

when fish get dropped or damaged. Photographing the fish without harming the fish is possible, although it is easier for people who have more experience in handling fish. In all cases, have unhooking tools, loaded camera, and other supplies at the ready. Dousing the fish with water is also a good idea; some saltwater anglers in large boats use a washdown hose to keep running water on a fish that is being unhooked and prepared for photographing prior to release.

As for weighing, lifting up a fish to weigh it is certainly not beneficial to the fish, and it prolongs the time spent out of water. Weighing occasionally leads to injury when a fish gets dropped, or when its gills are damaged from being touched or from the way the fish is hoisted for weighing. There are methods of estimating the weight of a fish (see: measuring fish), and some grippers and nets have built-in scales so that the fish does not need further handling. If you absolutely have to weigh a fish, do it quickly, preferably with the assistance of someone else, and place the hook of the scale through the membrane behind the lower jaw, not under the gills or gill cover. Remember to be careful for your own sake as well as that of the fish, since some fish are especially difficult to handle, like a thrashing dolphin, and some are simply dangerous, like a bluefish, northern pike, or shark.

Unhooking Fish

A hook should be removed carefully, not in a jerking or ripping manner that might cause injury. Tugging at a hook could rip the flesh inside the mouth or on the cheek or other location, which could prompt bleeding or lead to infection. Ripping out a hook could also tear the jaw or the maxillary. So the best action is to try to remove the hook without damaging the fish. Removal is usually easier with barbless hooks than with barbed ones, and in both cases it means backing the hook point out rather than just grabbing and pulling, which is sometimes difficult. Of course, hook removal should be done quickly for the sake of the fish but also carefully to avoid hooking yourself.

If you are removing the point of a hook from a fish by using your fingers, be very careful; should the fish move or slip from your grasp, the potential

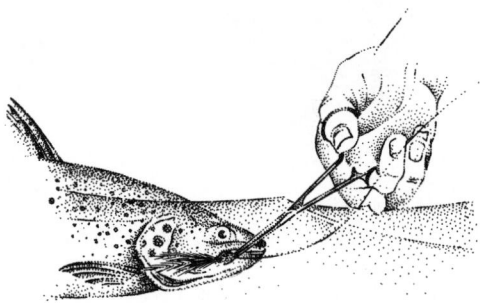

For small fish caught with a fly hook, use a hemostat to free the hook; the fish can remain in the water and often doesn't need to be handled.

for hooking yourself is great. People have been hooked in this manner, and one of the worst scenarios that you can imagine is getting a finger stuck on a hook that is still connected to the fish; this is definitely a possibility when a multihooked lure or a treble hook is used. Whenever you're unhooking a fish or otherwise handling it, whether with your fingers or with some tool, be careful not to hurt yourself, since the gill covers, fin spines, and teeth are some of the body parts that can cause a nasty cut, which may become infected.

For grabbing and freeing many hooks, the most popular tool is a long-nosed, or needle-nosed, plier. It is especially useful for midsized hooks and treble hooks on lures, which make up the bulk of hooks used by anglers. With a tapered head, it fits well into a fish's mouth, or fairly deep into the mouth. For strictly small hooks and for flies that anglers would prefer not to crush (or to tear the dressing) during removal, a standard or angled-head hemostat works fairly well.

These tools may not be adequate for fish with big mouths and large or sharp teeth, but other unhooking devices, usually with long arms and a trigger to secure the grip on a hook, are available. Jaw spreaders, which keep the mouth of toothy fish open for unhooking work, help a lone angler unhook fish, but you have to use the proper size for the circumstances and be careful not to rip the fish with the ends.

Still another tool is one that is used in saltwater by anglers fishing with fairly heavy line or leader, and is simply called a hook puller by many.

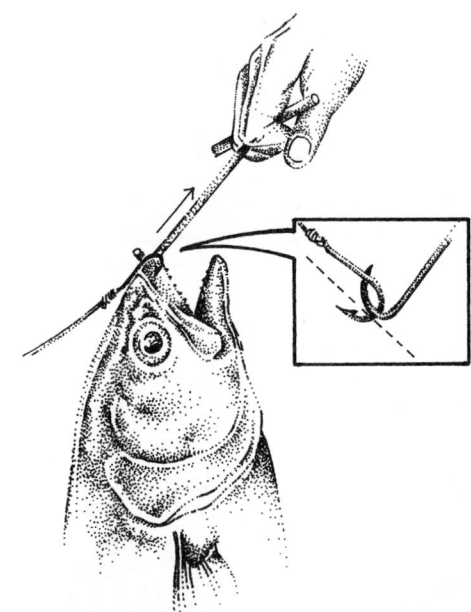

Small and intermediate size fish, especially in saltwater, are often unhooked with a hook puller, a tool with a crooked end. When a fish is lifted up with heavy line or leader, the hook puller is looped over the bend of the fishhook (inset), the fish is quickly raised up, and the fishhook point is pulled in the opposite direction, allowing the fish to fall back into the water.

It looks a lot like an old hauling tool for ice blocks, except the business end is hooked and is used to grab around the bend of a hook when a fish is lifted up with a heavy line or leader. With one hand on the line close to the hook and with the hook puller looped over the bend of the hook, the angler quickly raises up the fish and pulls the hook point in the opposite direction. This works best when the hook is embedded within a few inches of the jaws, and when the fish is not so large that it can't be lifted by the line or leader.

Perhaps the most contentious aspect of catch-and-release is whether to remove the hook from a fish that has been deeply impaled. This has primarily been a baitfishing issue, and for a long time the standard advice was to cut the line or leader off and leave the hook in the fish rather than to try to remove it and risk causing internal injury and bleeding. Many studies have found greatly increased rates of survival—sometimes two and three times better—if the hook is left in. However, hooks do corrode (depending on the type of hook, and they corrode faster in saltwater), and sometimes the hooks are passed through the anal vent. Although leaving in a hook may indeed be preferable to pulling it out, nevertheless a deeply swallowed hook that is well into the stomach may puncture vital organs; even if the fish is released, the damage is done. A hook left in the throat above the gills or the esophagus is not as serious.

Some recent studies contradict the cut-the-line advice, thus casting a cloud over the entire subject. They find that the survival of deeply hooked fish is good, or better, when the hooks have been removed. Whether or not to cut the line is usually a decision that anglers make based on circumstances at the exact moment and also based on such factors as the condition of the fish, the length of the fight, and the tools available for unhooking.

Sometimes the difficulty of unhooking a deeply caught fish is increased because of the size of the fish's mouth, the strength of the fish, the presence of teeth, and other factors. If two anglers work on a fish, one holding and controlling the fish and/or keeping its mouth open and the other working to free the hook, the unhooking time can be shortened and the need for resuscitation lessened. So, where a difficult situation exists, an angler should try to involve an extra pair of hands.

Where a difficult fish is concerned—a dangerous, toothy, or extremely active specimen—it may be helpful to place a wet rag or a wet cloth over the head of the fish to cover its eyes, and/or also to rest the fish on a soft surface (like an old and clean foam cushion). Saltwater anglers are more likely to do this, particularly with bluefish and small tuna, and it often has a calming effect.

The Release

With the hook out, it's time for the final act. In many cases, especially with small fish and with fish that have been landed quickly, simply putting them back in the water and letting go is all that has to be done; the fish is lively, makes a thrust with its tail, and disappears. Many anglers release fish rather cavalierly. They may be standing in a boat and, after unhooking the fish, just toss it back in the water. For the most part, this does not seem to hurt a fish, but it can't be good for them. Some people who have witnessed bass anglers on television do this repeatedly (as well as showing the fish off in a manner that some complain must be hurting its jaw) have written to major magazines complaining about this action, and it does seem to demonstrate indifference or to send a conflicting message, especially when anglers talk about what a great deed they are doing by releasing the fish. So it does not seem to be asking too much for anglers to bend over and release fish into the water more gently.

If a fish has been kept out of water for a while, if it has struggled mightily, and if it is stressed, then just returning the fish to the water may not be enough, no matter how gently it is done. A stressed released fish often turns over on its side or back, being too weak to maintain its equilibrium.

If you release a fish that seems to be okay but then turns over, retrieve it quickly, if possible, and hold it in an upright position in the water. Some released fish drift off and then turn over out of the angler's reach, or turn over when too deep to be retrieved. Therefore, you shouldn't let a fish go until it is clearly able to swim off under its own power. The fact that a fish is breathing doesn't mean it can do that. In fact, as noted previously, a stressed fish will breath more frequently in an effort to force oxygen over its gills because it is deprived of oxygen. Breathing just means that the fish isn't dead. You have to be patient.

To revive a fish, you need to keep it upright in the water. If you are in a river or a place with current, the fish should be headed into the current, not facing away from the current. You should not let a stressed

In a river, be sure to face a fish upstream so that water flows into its mouth forcing oxygen over its gills; a chinook salmon is being released here.

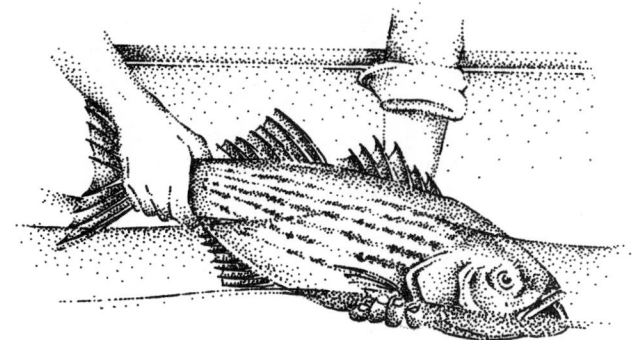

Before some fish can be released, you may need to revive them; this requires careful handling and moving the fish forward to pass oxygenated water over their gills.

fish free in a swift current, even after it has been revived, because it may not have the strength to resist the current, which could carry it away and bounce it on the bottom or against objects. In a river, a stressed fish should be taken out of strong current and released where the current is less. Sometimes, a fish released in the shallow backwaters of a river will rest there for a short while before moving, and it should not be rushed out before it is ready.

When you are reviving a fish, you can get oxygen to it by moving it forward to force water into its mouth and over the gills. Most instructions on this subject, including that provided by many fisheries agencies, advise moving the fish back and forth in the water to accomplish this. There is a minority viewpoint that advises against moving the fish backward, which makes more sense, but which may be subject to debate. The fact is, however, that a fish takes water into its mouth and forces it over the gills and out the external opening to take oxygen into the blood. The fish does not do this by swimming backward or by facing downstream. If you hold a fish facing downstream long enough in a strong current, it will die. That seems to indicate that moving water backward over a fish may not be helpful.

Moving a fish back and forth, to increase its oxygen intake, evidently does no good half of the time—when the fish is moving backward. Could a wading angler stir up sediment and induce suffocation from backward movement? Maybe. Could a person move the fish backward so quickly and abruptly as to do harm? Maybe.

Moving a fish forward only is admittedly harder to do for fish that cannot be held by the mouth by hand; however, with the right gripping tool, it may be possible. Mouth-gripped fish can be led forward in a circular or figure-eight pattern, especially if they are not big, but other fish, and large individuals, are harder to lead like this. Boat anglers can aid some fish by moving the boat slowly forward under outboard or electric motor power, but such fish have to be held by the head, or supported by the head and forward part of the body. You can seldom hold a fish by the tail alone and move the boat forward, because the fish gets turned sideways or backward.

If you hold a fish by the tail, you can usually move it forward and backward—an action that is easier to do and is at least somewhat helpful to the fish. Most of the time, such as when you're in clear open water, moving a fish backward and forward does not appear to be harmful, especially if you do not move it backward with the same vigor that you might move it forward. Even just moving it side to side may be helpful.

Cradling the fish with both hands is an alternative if you cannot move the fish forward. One hand holds the caudal peduncle, and the other supports the belly close to the pectoral fins. Hold the fish upright and keep it steady, perhaps moving it sideways if possible, until the fish recovers and can swim off on its own.

No matter what you do, the key is keeping the fish upright and supporting it, and giving it time. Devote whatever time is necessary to reviving a fish and getting it to the point where it can swim off on its own. It is not uncommon to devote 20 minutes to reviving a large fish, and some people have devoted an hour to a successful effort.

A fish is usually ready to go off on its own when it uses its tail muscles to try to swim. If it does this forcefully enough, you may let go of the tail immediately and the fish will dart off or swim slowly but assuredly away. It sometimes helps to poke the fish in the tail; this action provokes the fish into a short flight away and forces a burst of water and oxygen into its system, perhaps also giving it a boost in its recovery. If the fish swims off well on its own, this isn't necessary, but if it sits in one place and looks like it could be vulnerable to a predator's attack, then a slight poke with a rod tip, boathook, net handle, oar, or paddle might be worthwhile. Keep an eye on the fish as it swims off until you can no longer see it.

Finally, think about why the fish had to be revived in the first place. If you had played it better, could the fish have recovered quicker? What could you have done to decrease the stress before the fish was landed? Perhaps the fish needed revival because you held it out of the water too long for photos. Or perhaps it needed revival because you did not play it well enough. Ideally, you should be able to play a fish, no matter what the gear used, so that it is capable of swimming off immediately after you land and unhook it. Perhaps you need to improve your fish-fighting techniques to minimize the need for reviving fish.

Special Circumstances
Certain aspects of releasing fish and of catch-and-release in general deserve special consideration and more detailed evaluation.

Releasing deep-water fish. A general rule when releasing some fish and keeping others is to keep the ones that are caught in deep water rather than those caught in shallow water. Fish caught in deep water are usually harder to revive than those caught in shallow water, so being thoughtfully selective makes sense. However, if you do have to release deep-water fish, they should be appropriately cared for, since the deep water may cause a problem that is not experienced when shallower fish are released.

When some species of freshwater and saltwater fish are brought up from very deep water, they suffer a condition that is equivalent to what people know as "the bends," because pressure increases about 15 pounds every 33 feet in the water. This pressure has to be relieved; if it is not, the air bladder expands within the abdominal cavity, and the expansion may cause the stomach to protrude from the mouth. A fish in this condition, which is compounded by a sometimes drastic change in water temperature, will turn belly up if released and cannot recover until it has been "degassed."

Some species are able to belch the pressure away during retrieval, but in others it builds. Those in which it does not build have a pneumatic duct connected to the air bladder, allowing these fish to expel air and make more extensive vertical movements. Such fish include the various trout and salmon species, as well as carp and catfish. Those in which pressure builds are without this duct and cannot expel air; adjustment to pressure is slow, meaning that these fish cannot make rapid vertical movements. These species include largemouth and smallmouth bass, spotted bass, walleye, yellow perch, panfish species, striped bass, snapper, grouper, cod, hake, and black sea bass. Other fish, including lake trout and salmon, that have been brought up too quickly for their bodies to naturally adjust to the pressure changes, may still experience a problem, even though they have the natural means to overcome it.

How deep is deep enough to cause this depressurization? This is hard to say, but over 40 feet is generally thought to be deep enough to cause it in snapper and grouper, over 30 feet for walleyes, and over 60 feet for lake trout.

To relieve this pressure in trout and salmon, especially in lake trout, the fish can be "burped." Salmonids have an opening between the air bladder and esophagus that allows them to expel the air that bloats the air bladder. Burping is accomplished by holding the fish on its side or back and massaging or kneading the belly from the anal vent toward the head. This is sometimes difficult and may require a more active effort, actually squeezing the fish. A sound is made when the air is expelled. When the fish is ready to be released, hold it in the water at the surface with the head in the water, moving it forward or from side to side until it is fully recovered. To release it, there are two options. For fish that are large and too heavy to hold well, give the tail a quick squeeze to stimulate a vigorous dive. For fish that aren't so large and hard to hold, give the fish a vigorous shove or push headfirst and straight toward the bottom for a solid head start back down to the pressures and temperature from which it was taken. This thrusting tactic may also be helpful with other fish.

A large electric ray may have as many as a million generating units in its two special electric organs and can give an initial shock of more than 200 volts.

Burping is not suitable for other species because the air pressure cannot be naturally vented. It can still be expelled, however, using a technique that is called puncturing or venting by fisheries professionals and "fizzing" by some laypeople. Puncturing entails the insertion of a sharp object, usually a long needle, through the body wall of the fish to let the pent-up air escape through the puncture hole. The proper type of needle is a 16- to 20-gauge hypodermic needle obtained from medical or veterinary supply stores; a larger needle may be needed for very big fish. Where the needle is inserted into the fish may vary with the species. For walleye, the location is on either side of the fish approximately 1 inch above the anal vent; for snapper and grouper, it is just behind and above the base of the pectoral fin. The needle is inserted on a 45-degree angle under, not through, the scales, preferably when the fish is in a livewell. Hold the fish with its head slightly down and stroke the abdominal area to force air out. A sharpened pump needle also works, perhaps better because the air is quickly released through the hollow tube. If done correctly, the fish will be able to right itself in the livewell, and it then can be returned to the water.

A more detailed explanation of how to do this, and an illustration of location and technique, have not been provided here because this is a controversial topic still subject to testing and evaluation, although the California Dept. of Fish and Game, Ohio Dept. of Natural Resources, Florida Sea Grant, and the Southeast Office of the National Marine Fisheries Service have information on this subject available to the public. In general, puncturing is not recommended by most fisheries professionals because of concerns about inexpert handling by untrained anglers. The extra length of time that a fish would be held out of the water (where a livewell is not used) and the possibility of improper technique and perhaps further internal damage to the fish are other reasons why fisheries managers discourage the general public from this practice.

There is no direct evidence that puncturing or burping is effective against delayed mortality, and some research has indicated that untreated fish left on the surface of the water do recover on their own and return to deep water—unless they are discovered by sea gulls. Those who would attempt puncturing should probably practice first on deep-caught fish that would be kept for eating anyway. The difficulties inherent in releasing fish caught from deep water lend some credence to the belief that catch-and-release is primarily a shallow-water proposition, although the definition of deep and shallow is open to vastly different interpretations.

Anglers can take two other courses of action to help a deep-dwelling fish survive. The first is to play a deeply caught fish on a moderate and steady retrieve, rather than trying to bring it in as quickly as possible. A fast retrieve, which is the usual recommendation in most situations, does not give the

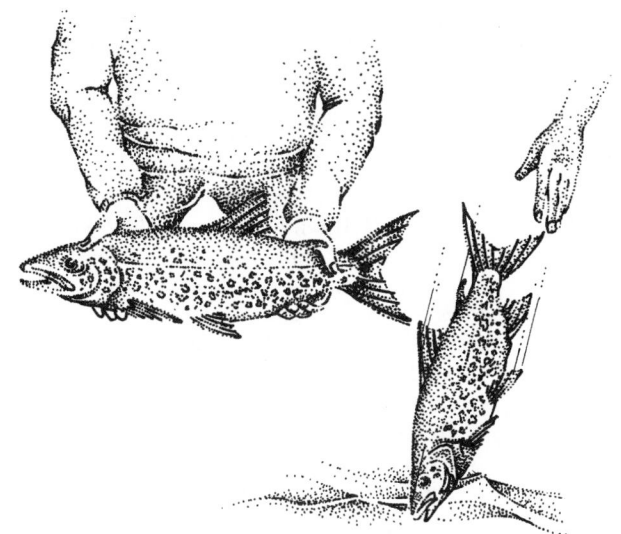

A fish caught in deep water may benefit from a deep-thrust head-first release action; support the fish horizontally until unhooked, and then quickly turn it head-first and plunge it into the water.

fish time to adjust to changes in pressure naturally. Avoiding a fast retrieve may make the fish more suitable for release without degassing efforts. On the other hand, following this advice increases your chances of losing a fish because of the extra playing time, and there is no clear guide regarding how long a fish needs to adjust internal pressure. Moreover, in saltwater, bottom-dwelling fish, once they are initially hooked, often have to be played aggressively to keep them from diving into cover and cutting the line, and this aggressive fight carries through into the rest of the playing action.

The second course open to anglers is to give the fish a good head start by thrusting it headfirst into the water when they release it. This is especially useful with lake trout or salmon, and is also useful for releasing tuna and amberjack that are small enough to be hand-lifted. To propel the fish forward, lift it by the tail and then thrust it headfirst into the water and as far as you can reach, as if you were stabbing a spear deep into the water. This quickly propels it downward.

Bleeding fish.   Another general rule when releasing some fish and keeping others is to keep a fish that is bleeding rather than one that is not; bleeders, particularly those hooked in the gills, are less likely to survive than unharmed fish. This is not an absolute, however. In professional studies, and in the results of tag-and-release efforts of anglers, some fish that were bleeding when released have survived and been well enough to live for a long time and be caught again. Cuts or tears in flesh that cause a minor amount of bleeding may not be fatal; many anglers have caught fish that had been recently attacked by other predators, enough to create an open wound with some signs of bleeding, and the fish survived.

Fish that are bleeding from the gills, however, receive an extra dose of stress, and this is most

likely to be critical. If there is a lot of bleeding, regardless of the cause, the appropriate action is to keep the fish if you can legally do so, rather than to cause it to become a mortality statistic that doesn't serve a meal purpose (although it may be food for other aquatic creatures).

However, the biggest dilemma is what to do when you land a fish that is bleeding but cannot legally be kept. Some anglers feel that keeping such a fish is an ethically appropriate act, but good intentions are hard to prove when confronted by law enforcement officials. If you don't release a fish that is bleeding, it will surely die, but if you have to release one that is bleeding, it might just recover.

Replacing treble hooks with singles.   Suppose that you catch a large energetic fish on a plug. The fish is impaled by a barbed treble hook in the mouth. It flops over and over, hooking itself near the gills with another treble. When headed into the net, the fish rolls; the hooks catch in the net webbing. The net becomes a tangled mess, and some of the hook points are twisted out of shape; the flesh of the fish is ripped. You want to release it, but because the fish has been gashed and has been out of the water for so long during unhooking, it may succumb shortly to exhaustion or later to infection, or be easy prey.

Now imagine that you've cast a surface plug to heavy or close-to-shore cover. You lower the rod tip, take up slack line, and a fish strikes. You react reflexively and try to drive the hook into the fish, but it misses the lure. In a heartbeat, the tight-lined plug springs from the water toward you. Some people react fast enough to turn from this multihooked missile, but many take it in the arm, the chest, the hat, or even the face.

Similar things may happen when fish jump and throw lures, or when fish are close to the surface near the boat and the hook pulls out under extreme pressure. An accident may happen when you're trying to release a fish and it buries a hook into you.

You can't completely avoid these difficulties, but you can minimize the chance of them happening, especially when using plugs, almost all of which are supplied by manufacturers with multiple sets of treble hooks. To ensure individual safety and the well-being of fish that are released, use plugs with single, rather than treble, hooks. A detailed review of how to accomplish this is contained elsewhere (*see: plugs*).

Single-hook use is required in only a few places in North America, so using a single hook is mostly a personal choice. By choice some anglers don't use live bait. Some won't troll. Some won't angle for various species during the spawning period. The issue of single hooks over treble hooks is also an individual choice, one that is based on your attitude. You don't have to take the treble hooks off all your lures, but there are times when a single hook is more appropriate than a treble for safety, fishing effectiveness, and the benefit of the resource.

Confining fish.   Fish that are to be released should not be kept on a stringer or cooped up in a warm, poorly oxygenated container or well; you're reducing their survival chances significantly by doing this. In a well or container, cool water and abundant oxygen are vital. Don't cull unless you are keeping an injured fish and releasing a healthy one. Culling is replacing a fish on a stringer or in a well with another. In some places, once you have taken possession of a fish by confining it, culling by returning that fish to the water is illegal.

Generally a fish that has been confined is not as suitable for release as one that has been freshly caught. Livewells are very popular in freshwater and are especially geared for confining bass and walleye, although they are sometimes used to retain other fish. Although it is seldom beneficial to keep fish in these so-called livewells for later release (as opposed to instant, on-the-spot release), many people do this in freshwater. Most bass and walleye tournaments are based on the weight of fish caught, which are supposed to be kept in properly functioning livewells. That is the primary reason why livewells have proliferated in freshwater fishing boats. If you have to keep fish in a livewell, pay special attention to the water temperature and to the fish's need for frequent and ample aeration. In closed systems, the use of a stabilizing chemical, which decreases the fish's need for oxygen consumption and fights fungus infection and mucus loss, is beneficial. Using ice, noniodized salt, and some drugs (available from aquarium supply stores) are other measures that can be taken to aid fish that are detained for a long period prior to release, though this is something that relatively few anglers other than tournament anglers need to be concerned with.

General Guidelines for Releasing Fish

Plan in advance if you're going to keep or release a fish. This not only makes a difference in how you land the fish, but also helps you decide which fish you might keep that day and which ones you might release. For example, if you've made a decision to keep one or two fish, and you catch one early in the outing that is deeply hooked and/or bleeding, you might immediately decide to keep it since it is one that could have trouble surviving. If you haven't decided about keeping or releasing a fish until one is on the line, don't bring the fish into the boat and then decide, unless the fish has to be measured to see if it meets specific length requirements. The best course of action is to make the decision when the fish is in the water so that you can take proper steps from the start.

The major aspects of releasing fish have been detailed and explained throughout this section. In summary, to release a fish in good shape:

- Do not freespool a fish that has struck live bait.
- Set the hook quickly to keep bait or lures from being taken deep.

Like this walleye, many fish can be grasped behind the gills without injury, provided they aren't squeezed tightly.

- Play and land the fish quickly, unless it is taken from very deep water.
- Do not confine fish that will be released.
- Avoid netting; keep the fish in water whenever possible.
- Hold the fish firmly but gently; a wet hand, glove, or towel might help.
- Do not let the fish flop around.
- Keep fingers and objects out of the gills and eyes.
- Use a long-nose pliers or other tool for extracting hooks.
- If a fish is hooked in the esophagus or stomach, cut the line.
- Revive a tired fish by holding it upright and moving it forward or from side to side.
- Return the fish to the water gently and headfirst.

When you do keep a fish, be discriminating. The decision can be based on the condition of a fish or its size in relation to the fish population. You can choose to keep a species that is plentiful rather than one that is scarce. You can choose a nonspawner, a bleeder, or a small fish rather than one of the prime specimens.

Lastly, remember that even if you return all the fish you catch to the water, you're still having an impact. If the average delayed mortality rate for fish that are released after being caught is only 5 percent, and if you catch and release 60 fish in a few days or a week, chances are good that at least 3 of those fish will die. If the average delayed mortality

is 10 percent, then 6 of those fish will die. And if you keep some of your catch, then the total impact you have is the number that you kept, plus a percent of those that died after release.

Considerations for Releasing Bass

Because largemouth and smallmouth bass are the most popular of all gamefish species, fishing pressure for them in many places is very intense, and there is a great deal of interest in, and adherence to, catch-and-release. Fortunately, largemouth and smallmouth bass, as well as their family cousins, are fairly hardy fish. Except under unusual circumstances, bass do not put up an extremely long fight, and they are fairly easy to land. They are not too disturbed by moderately respectful handling. They can be grasped without harm to fish or angler—in fact, you have a greater likelihood of injury than the fish because of the sharp points of multihooked lures. But bass are not immune to problems, and it is wise to avoid excessive or rough handling and excessive time held out of water. Try to minimize injury from multiple hooks, and avoid or minimize netting. Take special care of bass that are confined in livewells. Probably no fish are subjected to livewell containment more than largemouth bass, particularly by competitive anglers who retain the fish until weigh-in and then release them. Good handling, adequate water temperature, and ample oxygen are keys to their survival in livewells.

Bass are often hooked lightly and it is sometimes possible to free them from the hooks simply by letting them idle near the surface, lowering the rod tip, and putting slack in the line. You might try jiggling the rod tip. If this doesn't free the fish, then try freeing it while in the water using long-nosed pliers. If bass are not released in the water, it's best to grab them by the lower jaw. This hold provides the least possible physical contact and does the least damage. Few other species of fish can be grasped so handily. This landing technique requires caution, however, since a bass is usually hooked in a corner of the mouth, and the hooks are often exposed. If the lure has many hooks, the bass should be well subdued before a lip-landing attempt is made; an alternative in this situation might be to land the fish under the belly.

Soft plastic lures, especially worms, salamander and crayfish imitations, and grubs—many of them scented in part to encourage bass to hold onto them longer—are a prominent part of the bass angler's arsenal. However, some of these products or methods of using them could result in deep-hooking. The same is true, of course, for live bait. The manner in which bait or soft plastic lure users set the hook in a bass is a factor in the fish's survival later on. Waiting to set the hook should be avoided where possible.

Considerations for Releasing Trout

If proper care is taken of trout that will be released, the survival rate is very high; many studies have put it in the 95 to 97 percent range for stream trout when caught on lures and flies. The survival rate of trout that are released after being caught on live bait is about three times better if the hook is left in than if it is extracted. Thus, anglers should snip the line and not try to extract a small hook. If bait is used, a larger hook is less likely to get caught in the stomach than a small one. Most lure- and fly-caught trout are hooked in the jaws and the edges of the mouth, a few on the tongue, so it is relatively easy to get the hook out. On those occasions when a lure or fly hook is swallowed or manages to lodge in the gills, don't even bother with a token attempt unless the job looks easy; snip the line or tippet as close to the lure or fly as possible.

The less you handle trout, the better, but that is not always possible. Small stream trout squirm like eels, and often the hook cannot be removed without grasping the fish to keep it still. Here you can keep the fish in the surface water, but grab it around the body by gripping it behind the head and between the dorsal fin, trying to keep finger pressure off the soft belly and avoid squeezing it. Small fish can be completely encircled with a wet hand. Turning the fish upside down seems to have a tranquilizing effect. Only larger stream trout should be netted, usually when wading in deep rivers or fishing from a floating boat; if a net is used, keep it in the water with the fish and work the hook out while the fish is in the net and not struggling.

Make sure that you are not releasing the fish in swift current. Moving to the edge of the current is a good idea for releasing a large and tired fish, but take care not to stir up the shallows so much that it adds to the fish's breathing hardship.

Bigger trout, like lakers, are easy fish to injure in the landing and handling stages at all sizes. The big ones are fragile, and the small and medium-size ones have a notorious habit of wiggling and spinning. If they are captured in a net and the net lifted out of the water, the fish may continue to spin and cause itself problems because of the net and the lure. Large trout may be brought alongside a boat and held upright in the water for hook removal. They should not be brought into the boat if you are going to release them, although the cold water that lakers inhabit does help in preventing the onset of infection from the unintentional loss of their protective coating during handling. Methods of dealing with the release of lakers taken from deep water were previously described.

Considerations for Releasing Atlantic Salmon

Many of the advisements previously issued also apply to Atlantic salmon, but a few things are slightly different. Most Atlantic salmon fishing is with flies, by law or by custom/preference, so there isn't much at issue regarding deeply hooked fish. Salmon are fairly easily released if they haven't been played too long, so anglers should be able to achieve a high degree of survival for released fish.

Atlantic salmon are taken in rivers, virtually all by wading anglers who should move to a quiet location if possible to play and land the fish. By using a tippet of medium to heavy strength, an angler should be able to land a fish fairly quickly. The Atlantic Salmon Federation recommends breaking the leader on a fish that is not landed in 15 to 20 minutes, and not using a tailer to land a fish that will be released. When being released, the salmon should be kept in the water, held gently in a supported horizontal and upright position, and revived gently facing upstream. Give the fish plenty of time to recover.

Considerations for Releasing Marine Offshore Species

The National Marine Fisheries Service Game Fish Tagging Program advises anglers to simply tow such species as sharks and tuna slowly headfirst alongside the boat for tagging and before release. The forced flow of water over the gills will help revive the fish. The leader should be cut with cutting pliers as close to the hook as possible, allowing the revived fish to swim off. These fish can also be released by using a gaff as a dehooking tool. The technique requires the use of a V-notched stick or other device to depress the leader. The gaff hook is slipped over the hook, and simultaneously the leader is pressed down while the fish hook is popped back and out.

The same can be accomplished for billfish, although these species can be grabbed by the bill by one person while being tagged and unhooked by another. Holding the bill allows you to control the fish, which is very important. If you can reach far enough overboard (difficult if not impossible on many large sportfishing boats), hold the head of the billfish under the water, which in itself has a calming effect. When you grab the bill, place your hands so that the thumbs face each other; this position makes it easier to push the fish away if the fish thrashes. There are tools to slip over the bill for facilitating handling and hook removal.

CATFISH

Catfish comprise a large group of predominately freshwater fish that are distributed around the world. Some accounts peg the total number of catfish species worldwide at more than 2,200. South America is especially rich in quantity and species of catfish, and has some of the largest freshwater specimens. Many of the world's significant river systems are home to at least one species of catfish, and in most cases these fish rank among the largest fish of the river system. The same applies to large lakes, especially in reservoirs that are impoundments of large rivers. Many catfish are important for commercial and recreational purposes.

Angling for catfish is one of the most popular freshwater fishing activities, second only to bass fishing in some surveys, especially in the midsection of the United States. Despite high levels of participation, fishing for catfish is somewhat maligned, largely by omission, in most of the major outdoor media. Catfish, like some other species, are viewed with condescension in deference to other species with (subjectively) higher pedigrees and greater sporting virtues. In some U.S. locations, catfish are designated as gamefish by state fisheries agencies. They may be lumped in the negative-sounding category of "rough fish" *(see)* and treated to only incidental management. Catfish are the subject of (sometimes intense) commercial pursuit, and most of them are certainly short on color and beauty.

It is true that catfish lack some of the sporting attributes appreciated in other species. They almost never jump out of the water when hooked. Their fight is more bulldogging and bottom digging than sudden streaking; when hooked, a 20-pound river catfish does not fire 100 yards downriver the way a 20-pound salmon or steelhead would (although a 60- to 100-pounder might). They live in deep holes, often in turbid water, and their feeding habits are less than regal. Most people tend to fish for them in a laid-back, forked-stick, bait-on-bottom, wait-till-something happens manner. When you put all this together, it adds up to a fish that is relatively abundant but without a great deal of glamour and sex appeal.

Some of the perceived deficiencies of catfish might also be applied, incidentally, to other popular freshwater fish, especially panfish and walleye. Critics point out that stream trout and largemouth bass, most of which are rather small on average, are overhyped as gamefish and that the catfish deserves greater appreciation and better press than it gets. Indeed, looking at the abilities and habits of catfish, one finds an impressive fish that has adapted especially well to its niche in the environment, and one that is probably worthy of greater public attention. It is unlikely to get more respect, however, until it starts rising to the surface to take dry flies and/or aggressively attacks spinnerbaits and then cartwheels out of the water. Don't hold your breath. But don't ignore these fish simply because they lack the characteristics of other species.

Indeed, more Americans angle for catfish than they do for trout. There is arguably more national effort expended on catfish in a single week than in an entire year of Atlantic salmon fishing or bonefishing. This is partly because catfish are so abundant; the vast majority of anglers have access to some species of catfish. This attention is partly due to their importance as a food source; most species of catfish rank very highly as table fare, and people who catch catfish overwhelmingly tend to keep them, a practice that within reason is not harmful to most populations of catfish and is encouraged by fisheries managers. Another important reason for their popularity is that they are a fairly willing fish that are generally not too difficult to catch in smaller sizes; they don't require much sophistication in technique, tackle, or presentation methods. Like other species, most of the catfish caught are on the smaller side, certainly under 2 pounds, but on the right tackle they have spunk, and the bigger specimens can be a challenge to land, even if they don't provide the drama of some other species. Although their fighting virtues are short on style, the larger specimens are long on strength and rod-bending drama, not unlike many of the bottom-dwelling bruisers of saltwater.

As with other types of fishing, you can make angling for catfish as intricate as you like. But anyone can enjoy this activity, without special casting skills or highly sophisticated methods, and generally from almost any type of craft as well as from shore, so they clearly deserve a high popularity quotient.

Species

The majority of catfish are scaleless, but some are armored with heavy scales. They vary in size from tiny versions that are popular for aquarium use, the smallest of which grow no larger than $1/2$ inch, to huge specimens, the largest of which has been recorded at more than 600 pounds. Most catfish prefer the sluggish localities of lakes and rivers; some do best in fairly swift waters. Tenacious fish, they can stay alive out of water for a considerable time, especially if kept moist. They are characterized by having a single dorsal fin and an adipose fin; strong, sharply pointed spines in dorsal and pectoral fins; and whiskerlike sensory barbels on the upper and lower jaws. The head and mouth are generally broad, and the eyes small.

North American freshwater catfish. Members of the family Ictaluridae, North American freshwater catfish are distributed from Canada to Guatemala and contain about 50 species. These bottom-loving fish are important commercially; and many millions are harvested annually, some from natural environments and some from aquaculture or fish-farming operations.

Thousands of anglers pursue these fish, employing a wide variety of methods to catch them. All species obtained from fairly clear waters are delicious on the table. Many fish farms specialize in raising and marketing catfish. All members of this group have scaleless skins and a stiff, sharp spine at the leading edge of the dorsal fin and pectoral fins. Just in front of the tail, on the dorsal surface, is a fleshy adipose fin. Their eight barbels are sensory structures that help them to locate food.

Nearly all North American catfish live in sluggish streams or in the quiet waters of lakes and ponds. They are bottom feeders, taking both live and dead foods. They are typically active at night—although some are more active during the day than others—and on dark, overcast days or in roiled, murky water. Catfish spawn in spring and early summer, fanning a nest area in the sand or mud. One or both parents stand guard until the eggs hatch and then shepherd the young until they are large enough to fend for themselves.

Odor-eliminating soaps will rid your hands of the smell of fish; rubbing baking soda, vinegar and salt, or lemon juice will also do the trick.

C

Perhaps the most abundant and best-known members of the clan of about a dozen species of the genus *Ictalurus* are the three principal species of bullhead: brown bullhead *(I. nebulosus; see: bullhead, brown)*, black bullhead *(I. melas; see: bullhead, black)*, and yellow bullhead *(I. natalis; see: bullhead, yellow)*.

Bullhead abound in freshwater from coast to coast in North America. In some regions they have been introduced by humans, either accidentally when a bait bucket containing a few baby bullhead was emptied, or intentionally when an angler stocked bullhead in his private pond. Settlers from the East carried bullhead over the Rockies to stock the waters with their familiar favorite. Until then, bullhead were not found west of the Rockies. Nature's way of moving bullhead into new habitats is more unique. The bullhead travel on the feet of wading birds that unknowingly carry the adhesive eggs with them from place to place. The eggs wash off as the birds wade, and in this way a new population of bullhead becomes established.

These catfish can survive in water that is so low in oxygen that the bullhead must come to the surface from time to time to gulp air. In these emergency conditions, the air bladder acts as an auxiliary lung. In the confinement of a pond in which conditions are initially favorable, bullhead may soon multiply beyond the food capacity. The result is an overpopulation of stunted, freakish fish—weird-looking creatures with oversize heads and shrunken bodies. Some years ago, biologists in Wisconsin poisoned a 9-acre pond that seemed crowded with bullhead. It contained nearly 250,000. The pond was supporting about 1,500 pounds of fish per acre, but not one bullhead was big enough to grace a skillet.

East of the Rockies, all three species are in abundance. Most common—and the species that has been introduced most widely—is the brown bullhead. In their original distribution, the black bullhead was the most widely distributed. In habits and flavor, the three species are scarcely distinguishable.

Also of commercial and recreational importance in some areas are the channel catfish *(I. punctatus; see catfish, channel)*, blue catfish *(I. furcatus; see: catfish, blue)*, white catfish *(Ameiurus catus; see catfish, white)*, and flathead catfish *(Pylodictus olivaris; see catfish, flathead)*. The largest is the blue catfish, which may tip the scales at more than 150 pounds. The record caught on rod and reel weighed 109 pounds. A 25-pound catch is considered large, however. Slate blue above and white below, this big catfish ranges throughout the large streams of the Mississippi River system but is most abundant by far in the deep, warm waters of the South. Small blue catfish are most easily confused with channel catfish. Both have forked tails, but the latter is more likely to have dark spots; they can be positively distinguished by anal fin ray count.

The channel catfish's maximum weight is uncertain, although a 58-pounder has been recorded; the average is less than 5 pounds. A young channel catfish has black spots over its bluish body, and its fins are also margined with black. The black becomes subdued or is absent in older fish. Of all the catfish, the channel cat shows the greatest preference for clear, flowing waters, but it does equally well in lakes and ponds. Because of its strong fight at the end of a rod and line, it rates favorably with anglers. It is stocked regularly in farm ponds to provide fishing fun as well as food and is a principal fish stocked in pay-as-you-fish ponds (white catfish are also popular here). The channel catfish is also the species most commonly used in catfish farming enterprises.

The white catfish lives primarily in streams feeding into the Atlantic, ranging southward from New England to Florida. Until the introduction of the channel catfish, it was the largest catfish inhabiting these waters. It reaches a known maximum size of about 22 pounds, but the average is less than 3 pounds. Growing much larger than the white catfish, the flathead catfish has a broad, flat head, and the lower jaw projects beyond the upper. It is known to reach weights exceeding 100 pounds; the average size caught by anglers weighs less than 5 pounds, although 20-pounders are not especially rare.

The foregoing North American catfish are not finicky about what they eat. They will accept almost anything offered for bait, although some are more finicky than others, and this is not to imply that they will strike anything at any time, only that they have eclectic tastes. Biologists have found strange collections of debris in the stomachs of catfish. But avid catfish anglers are especially likely to use a foul-smelling concoction called a stinkbait *(see)* for luring catfish. Most catfish, in fact, have taste glands located over much of their body, although these glands are concentrated in their long, sensory whiskers. Among the favorite stinkbaits are soured clams, ripened chicken entrails, coagulated blood, and a variety of cheese and doughball mixtures—all allowed to cure until they acquire a potent odor. A good catfish bait will attract some species from a long distance.

Finally, the North American freshwater catfish family includes the various madtoms *(see)*, about two dozen of which are in the genus *Noturus*. All are small, most of them less than 5 inches long. Madtoms are recognized by their unique adipose fin. Non-madtom catfish have a fleshy fin protruding from their back just ahead of the caudal fin. The adipose fin of a madtom is continuous with their caudal fin. Madtoms possess stinging venom in their dorsal and pectoral spines. The venom originates from cells of the skin sheath over the pectoral fin. The toxicity of the venom varies but approximates that of a bee sting, causing stab wounds to swell and become extremely painful. Some madtoms inhabit the fast waters of streams, living in the rapids or riffles; others prefer slow-moving streams or the stillwaters of ponds and lakes, much like other members of the catfish family.

The stonecat *(N. flavus; see: stonecat)*, is one of the largest of the madtoms, sometimes attaining a length of 12 inches, although it is usually less than half this size. It is found in the rubble and boulder riffles and runs of creeks and small to large rivers over most of the U.S. and southern Canada, from the St. Lawrence River system southward to Florida, westward to Oklahoma and across the northern tier of states to Wyoming, and north to Manitoba. It is occasionally caught by anglers and is of some importance as forage for game species. The tadpole madtom *(N. gyrinus)*, seldom more than 3 inches long, occurs in much the same range but prefers sluggish waters. The freckled madtom *(N. noctumus)* is also small and has numerous black specks over its body. It is sometimes found in swift waters but may as frequently inhabit weedy, quiet waters. Some madtoms are fairly common, but most are rarely seen by anglers. A number of madtom species are on lists of protected fish.

South American freshwater catfish.   There is enormous diversity of catfish throughout South America, especially in the Amazon and Orinoco basins, and they are members of several different families.

The names of these fish are sometimes confused among different languages, including native Indian, Portuguese, and Spanish, as well as English. The following general information concerns a few of the more notable catfish of South America. Most catfish there, especially the larger-growing specimens, are heavily valued for commercial distribution. Recreational fishing for most South American catfish is of some value for food but is a small part of the overall harvest. Until the late 1980s, many of

the larger-growing species were substantial in size, but relentless commercial pressures have steadily lowered the average size of these fish, and the upper-end specimens are either nonexistent or far fewer in number.

The largest family of freshwater catfish in South America is Pimelodidae, which range from Mexico southward through South America except for the cold southern regions. These fish are reportedly the most abundant predators of other fish in the river channels and undertake upstream migrations to capitalize on prey that becomes concentrated during spawning runs or low-water periods. When these fish spawn, their young offspring drift or swim downstream to their nursery estuary. They are distinguished from other catfish mainly by their very large adipose fins. All have scaleless skins. The caudal fin is forked, and the medium-size, spined dorsal fin is high and located far forward on the body. The pectoral fins are also spineless. Typically, there are three pairs of long barbels that stretch back halfway or more along the body. Some of the numerous species in the more than 20 genera in the family are favorites with fish hobbyists.

Among the South American catfish encountered by anglers are various shovelnose catfish of the *Pseudoplatystoma* genus, which are called sorubim or (incorrectly) surubim by anglos or by an assortment of other names.

The tiger sorubim (listed as *Pseudoplatystoma tigrinum* and *Sorubim tigrinum*) and the barred sorubim *(Pseudoplatystoma fasciatum)* are among the species, but there is confusion between them. The shovelnose catfish is so named because its flat head is projected into a ducklike snout. The mouth projects down under the snout, conveniently located for picking up food rooted from the bottom.

The tiger sorubim of Brazil is known as *cachara* and *caparari* in that country and in Spanish as *tigre zúngaro*. The barred sorubim is listed as *doncella* and *rayao* in Spanish, and may also be called the tiger shovelnose catfish. The differences between these species are uncertain, although they have a zebralike pattern of vertical stripes, with dark spots on the back, flanks, and fins. They inhabit lagoons, narrow channels, and flooded forests and are more likely to strike lures than other Amazonian catfish. The *cachara* of Brazil is said to reach weights exceeding 20 kilograms and a length of more than 1 meter.

An apparently related fish, with spots but no stripes, is a shovelnose catfish known as *pintado* in Brazil *(Pseudoplatystoma coruscan)*.

This fish, which may also be called the spotted sorubim or polka dot catfish, is a strong and tasty fish that is said to reach 80 kilograms in weight and nearly 2 meters in length. It sports a bluish gray color and black spots. It is found in river outlets, lagoon mouths, and channels, under floating plants, and along riverbanks, and is primarily caught at night.

A sorubim from the Trombetas River, Brazil.

Blue Catfish

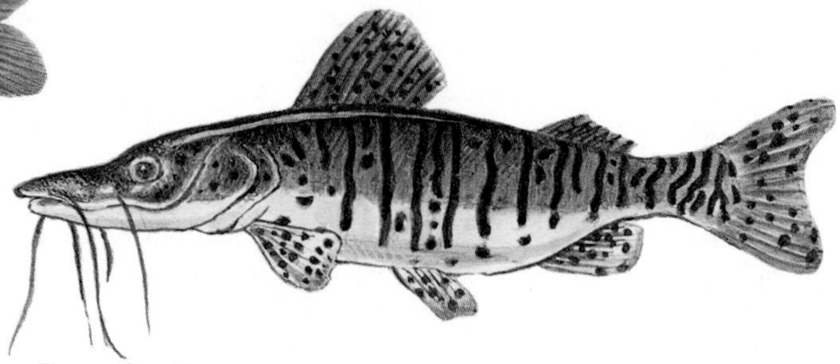

Barred Sorubim

Channel Catfish

Pintado

Flathead Catfish

Jurupoca

White Catfish

Dourada

C

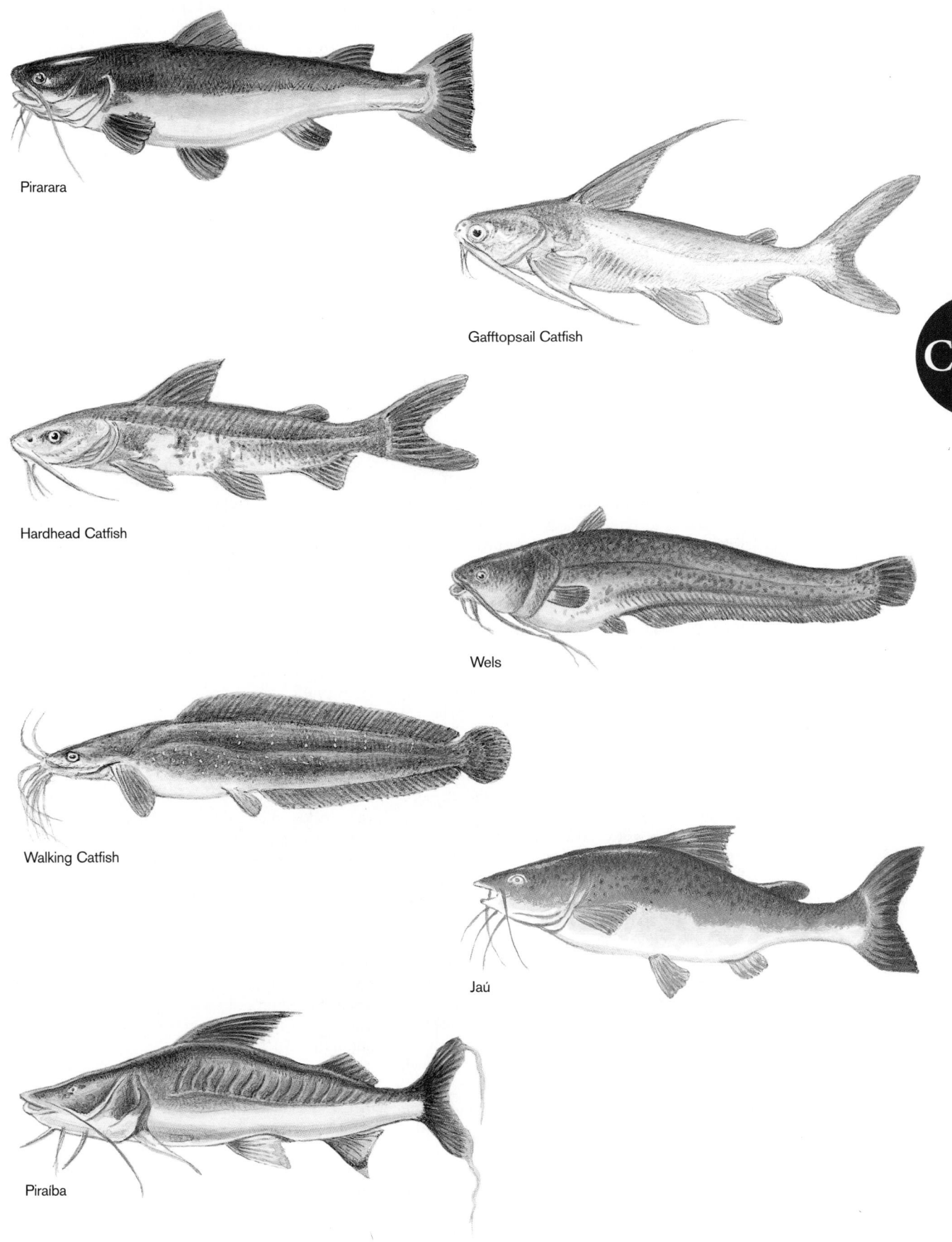

Pirarara

Gafftopsail Catfish

Hardhead Catfish

Wels

Walking Catfish

Jaú

Piraíba

A slightly different fish, reaching just 10 kilograms, is the *jurupoca (Hemisorubim platyrhyncos)*; it has a different mouth shape, with a lower jaw that extends past the upper and turns up.

Two prominent and large catfish are members of the *Brachyplatystoma* genus. The smaller of these, growing to 40 kilograms and nearly 5 feet in length, is known as *dourada* in Portuguese *(Brachyplatystoma flavicans)* and has been an especially important commercial species—one that has been heavily pressured.

Exhibiting a dirty gold color, it is easily distinguished and is also known as the golden catfish, although this terminology, as well as its Portuguese name, has caused it to be confused with the highly popular and sporty dorado *(Salminus maxillosus)*, which is also golden.

A larger cousin, *Brachyplatystoma filamentosum*, is called *piraíba*, a Tupi-Guarani Indian word that means "mother of all fish." Appropriately, the *piraíba*, which attains a reported weight of up to 300 kilograms (660 pounds), is the largest of South American catfish and one of the largest freshwater fish in the world.

This grayish catfish lacks the color of the *dourada* and is reputedly not valued for food in large sizes owing to hosting parasites. In pursuing this fish, some native Brazilians bait a small fish with a hook and tie that to a rope attached to the bow of their canoe. When a large *piraíba* is hooked, it may drag the canoe for several kilometers. Today a large specimen is one weighing more than 200 pounds.

Another member of this genus, incidentally, is the commercially valuable *piramutaba (Brachyplatystoma vaillantii)*. This light gray species, which reportedly grows only to 20 pounds but is especially valued for its flesh, has been heavily exported from Brazil.

Two other significant South American catfish are the *pirarara (Phractocephalus hemeliopterus)*, a colorful and hard-fighting species, and the deep pool-dwelling *jaú (Paulicea lutkeni)*.

The *jaú* grows to 100 kilograms and 1.5 meters, and ranges from a soiled yellow to solid black in color. It is a strong species that prefers rocky bottoms and quiet water below falls and rapids. The *pirarara's* colors blend yellow, brown, and deep red, and it is noted for producing a startling snort when it is taken out of the water. This fish has a short, stout body and a broad head with a thick bony plate. The broad-tailed *pirarara* is a strong fighter that has been reported to 125 pounds and is desirable table fare.

These catfish are primarily predatory carnivores; when deliberately pursued by anglers, they are caught on whole or cut fish for bait. Some other South American catfish, presumably those seldom encountered by anglers, are herbivores. The armored catfish of the Amazon, for example, eat fleshy fruits, leaves, and mollusks, especially when the forests are flooded.

Sea catfish.   Although the vast majority of catfish inhabit freshwater, some live in the ocean. Sea catfish of the family Ariidae are best known for the remarkable way they incubate their eggs. The male picks up the eggs as the female lays them and holds them in his mouth until they hatch. With 50 or more pea-size eggs, this can be a mouthful. More astonishing, when the eggs hatch, the male continues to serve the needs of his progeny by permitting them to use his mouth as a place of refuge. Up to a month may pass before the swarming mass of black baby catfish set off on their own. By this time, six or eight weeks have passed since the male has had a meal. Once his appetite is triggered, he does not hesitate to gobble up even his own offspring if they foolishly swim too close.

Sea catfish are found in tropical and subtropical seas throughout the world, sometimes straying into temperate waters that are warmed in summer. The sea catfish common in the Gulf of Mexico and along the southern Atlantic coast of the U.S. is *Arius felis*. Known as a hardhead catfish or hardhead sea catfish *(bagre gato* in Spanish), it reportedly ranges as far north as Massachusetts.

About 12 inches long and rarely weighing as much as 2 pounds, this greenish sea catfish has two barbels on its upper jaw and four on the lower. The tail is deeply forked. It is generally abundant, traveling in schools of a hundred or more. It frequents estuaries, and in some areas it enters freshwater. It is most often caught from bridges and piers in passages and inland waterways. Although edible, it is not generally consumed.

The gafftopsail catfish *(Bagre marinus)* occurs in much the same range as the sea catfish but is more abundant southward through the Caribbean and off northern South America, evidently extending as far as Brazil.

This species, also known as the gafftopsail sea catfish *(bagre cacumo* in Spanish and *bagre-fita* in Portuguese) grows larger than the hardhead catfish, usually twice the size. The gafftopsail has only two barbels on the lower jaw, is bluish above and silvery white below. The gafftopsail's most distinguishing feature is its high dorsal fin, the first ray drawn into a long, slim filament. The pectoral fins also end in long filaments. As does the sea catfish, the male carries the eggs, which may be as much as an inch in diameter, in his mouth until they hatch.

Other members of the sea catfish family, consisting of roughly 40 species in all, occur in warm seas throughout the world, but the family is notably absent from European waters. Sea catfish in Brazil, generally called *bagre,* are reported to attain a maximum size of 15 kilograms.

Other catfish of note.   Among the numerous catfish, there are many odd species, including some that are armored, some that are parasitic, some that are dangerous, and so forth. This section briefly reviews a few species that have some angling significance, and a few that have no angling significance but are notable for their unusual characteristics.

One of the largest of all freshwater fish, which belongs to the Siluridae family of Eurasian catfish,

According to a U.S. Fish and Wildlife Service survey, 35.2 million people fished in 1996; they spent $37.7 billion on trips and equipment.

is the wels *(Silurus glanis)*. The wels is said to exceed 12 feet in length and weigh up to 700 pounds, although the largest reported specimen was 3 meters long and weighed 200 kilograms.

Known also as the Danube catfish, it is found in eastern Europe and northern Asia, primarily in large lakes and rivers, although it has been known to enter brackish water in the Baltic and Black Seas. It inhabits deep-water environs but is reported to feed at night on ducks, voles, crayfish, and smaller fish. Typical of the family, its body is scaleless, the anal fin is long, and there are only two pairs of barbels, one on the upper jaw and one on the lower.

Fish hobbyists know the Siluridae family best for the glass catfish *(Kryptopterus bicirrhus)*, a 4-inch species native to southeastern Asia. The body is so "glassy" that it reflects light in glittering rainbow hues and is transparent enough so that, particularly in young fish, the internal organs are visible. The dorsal fin consists of a single small ray, but the exceptionally long anal fin may contain as many as 60 rays. Unlike many catfish, this species thrives on the companionship of others of its kind. In nature, it lives in small schools.

Another large catfish is *Pangasius gigas* of the Pangasiidae family. Known as the giant catfish, this species is native to Indochina and the Mekong River basin, but is now listed as rare due to overexploitation. The giant catfish is said to weigh more than 250 pounds and exceed 7 feet in length. It has a deeply forked tail, a small adipose fin, a very long anal fin, a short but high dorsal fin, and a bristling of barbels (two or three pairs) around its mouth.

Catfish of the Clariidae family are unique in possessing an expanded, lunglike cavity in front of the gills and extending along each side of the spine as a much-branched or labyrinthic structure that is well supplied with blood vessels. As a result, these catfish can breathe air, enabling them to remain out of water for long periods if their bodies stay moist. They typically inhabit fouled or stagnant water that no other fish can tolerate. This auxiliary breathing apparatus makes the front of the body thick; the tail portion is thin, flat, and, in some species, almost ribbonlike. Both the dorsal and anal fins are long and spineless, and most species do not have an adipose fin. The body is scaleless, but the skin is thick and covered with mucus, an additional feature that makes possible its long exposure to the air.

The famed walking catfish *(Clarias batrachus)* is a member of this family. A native of southeastern Asia, it was imported to the U.S. as an oddity for fish hobbyists.

Some were either set free or escaped captivity in southern Florida. With snakelike movements and by using their pectoral fins as "legs," these catfish literally walk on land. When attempts were made to poison bodies of water to kill them, the walking catfish simply moved out of the undesirable water and traveled overland to a new home, leaving the native species to die.

Similarly, when ponds dry up during the dry season or in periods of drought, walking catfish keep moving to find pools with water. As a last resort, they bury themselves in the mud at the bottom of a pool of water where, like lungfish, they manage to survive until rains come again. Aggressive, reaching a length of about 8 inches, they do not hesitate to attack fish larger than themselves. There are about a half-dozen other species of walking catfish, some from Africa and some from Asia.

Among the smallest of all catfish, the few members comprising the parasitic Trichomycteridae family have a fearsome reputation. The species most responsible for this is the candiru *(Vandellia cirrhosa)*. Only about 2 inches long, this little South American catfish enters the gill cavity of larger fish to suck blood. It has been known to enter the urethra of waders or bathers urinating under water; presumably it mistakes the urea for water exhausted from gills. Once inside, it erects its spines and lodges itself. The pain is agonizing, and the fish can be removed only by surgery. The candiru burrows in sandy bottoms and when disturbed from its natural hiding place, seeks any orifice or protective situation. It is native to the Orinoco and Amazon River basins in northern South America.

Another unusual and harmful tropical species is the electric catfish *(Malapterurus electricus)*, an aggressive fish of the Malapteruridae family, sometimes exceeding 3 feet in length and weighing as much as 50 pounds. It is fearless, attacking and feeding on other fish. A large electric catfish can reportedly deliver a shocking 300 to 400 volts to kill small fish or stun large ones. The initial jolt is generally followed by a series of smaller ones. In addition to serving as a weapon of defense or as a means of overcoming prey, the electrical impulses may act as a sonar of sorts for navigation in the murky tropical waters where the electric catfish lives. The electric organs are located just under the skin along the full length of the body and tail. They are derived from glandular cells in the epidermis rather than from muscle tissue as in other fish capable of generating electricity. In polarity, the electric catfish is negative toward the head and positive toward the tail; this pattern is reversed in the electric eel.

The electric catfish holds among roots and rocks in sluggish or standing water in tropical Africa along the Nile (except Lake Victoria and the rivers of East Africa north of the Zambezi River), in Lake Tanganyika, in the lower Zambezi, Pungwe, and Lower Save Rivers, and throughout the Zaire system.

Catfish senses. It is no coincidence that catfish can thrive in diverse habitats and in waters that get extremely warm and stagnant, or that they are attracted to some vile-smelling concoctions offered as angling baits. Catfish are opportunistic feeders, similar to largemouth bass, and they are especially adaptable due to exceptional sensory abilities.

Catfish are believed to primarily rely on smell, taste, and hearing to feed, but this is only partly true. Some species and populations live in clear-water environments and are capable of being effective sight feeders. If you have observed catfish in an aquarium, you have probably noticed how their eyes move and follow things that get their attention. Some species, including channel catfish, may be susceptible to lures where the water permits reasonable visibility. Generally, catfish can see fairly well, but in many of their environments, especially large rivers and reservoirs, turbid water is common if not continuous and their vision is extremely limited. In these waters, hearing, taste, and smell play more important roles than vision in locating food, and these faculties may even be aided by taste and touch.

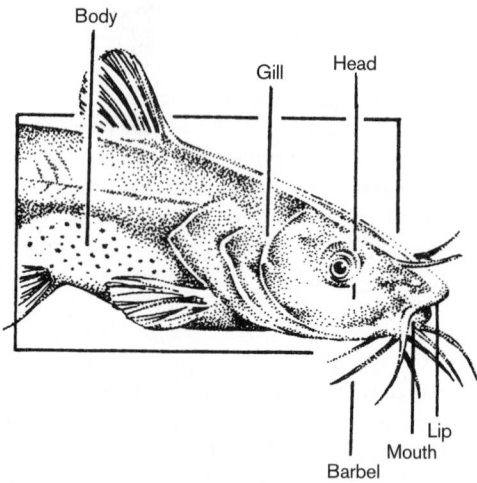

The catfish's exceptional external sensory faculties exist in each of the areas depicted above. The greatest sensitivity is in the barbels and lips.

Channel cats, blues, whites, and flatheads all have a finely developed sense of smell; bullhead have a less developed sense of smell than these species, but it is nevertheless better than that of most other fish. And like other fish, catfish smell as water enters their nares (nostril-like openings on the snout) and contacts an olfactory sac with many folds (catfish have more folds than do most other species). Catfish are first attracted by food odor; smaller fish will often feed, and taste the food, with their chin barbels before taking it. These whiskerlike appendages contain taste buds. Some catfish have taste buds all over their bodies—certain kinds can actually taste with their tails. The external taste buds greatly outnumber the internal ones, although the highest concentration of taste buds exists in the gills, barbels, and mouth. The combination of these intense senses allows catfish to be very aware of objects that produce odor, particularly prey fish, other predators, and other catfish. The distance at which they can detect odors is debatable, but some veteran catfish anglers believe that some catfish have the ability to follow a scent trail from up to 200 feet away. This may be more likely where there is current than in stillwaters.

Catfish also have excellent hearing ability. The otoliths in the inner ears are found in the bones of the skull, and these "ear bones" are connected to the air bladder. Vibrations are transmitted to the ear from the air bladder, which acts as a sounding board, allowing catfish to have greater detection of high-frequency sounds than that of many other species, including trout and bass. Low-frequency sounds are detected through the lateral-line system, a series of sensory cells running the length of both sides of the fish's body. The fish utilizes its lateral line to determine the direction of currents of water and the presence of nearby objects, as well as to sense vibrations both near and afar.

The highly developed senses of catfish work in combination to make these fish extremely adaptable and very capable of foraging effectively in places and conditions that inhibit other fish.

Angling for Catfish

As the profiles of the various bullhead and catfish indicate, these species inhabit a wide range of waters and locations. Channel catfish probably receive the greatest attention of the North American species, with proportionately less attention given to bullhead and blue catfish, followed by flathead and white catfish. Some aspects of angling for these species are uniform to all of them and some are different. One common but misunderstood element is that not all catfish are caught only on rotten baits. And not all catfish anglers smell bad, wear dirty overalls, and chew snuff. Today, catfish anglers might well fish from sleek and well-appointed boats instead of bare and battered jonboats powered by small old outboards, or they might spend considerable time wading and probing small rivers instead of lounging on the bank.

The diversity among catfish extends from species to their environment. Large catfish are generally the product of big waters, and the gargantuan specimens tend to be in the biggest river systems and in big lakes and reservoirs, especially those with abundant forage fish and in warm locales. Nevertheless, much catfishing occurs in smaller waters, particularly ponds, especially for bullhead and stocked white and channel catfish.

On the whole, anglers spend as many hours working these species after dark as they do during daylight hours. In the south, night fishing is a common practice; in the north, more anglers work this fish during daylight. But don't overlook fishing at night, as well as at dawn and dusk, when these fish are likely to be active.

Unlike most other freshwater species, catfish are the target of three distinctly different means of recreational fishing. These are noodling, setline fishing, and angling with rod and reel.

Noodling *(see)* involves taking fish directly by hand, which is an interesting and unique activity but not an element of sportfishing in the true sense. In setline *(see)* fishing, people use a line that is

Anglers use a cane pole and a fly rod for small catfish on a Georgia pond.

especially channel cats, are abundant, some cast-and-retrieve fishing, especially using diving plugs or jigs tipped with baits, has merit. The tactile nature of catfish, and their general behavior, however, lends itself primarily to more passive presentation methods.

Tackle.   Although in some circumstances and locations catfish are caught on flies, flycasting gear is rarely used for deliberate catfishing. Small fish in well-stocked ponds are an exception. Light spinning and spincasting tackle is particularly appropriate for the majority of catfish, especially bullhead and white catfish. For fish up to a couple of pounds, light-action outfits, short rods, and 2- to 8-pound lines are more than adequate. For variety, and in anticipation of midsize and some larger fish, light- and medium-action spinning or baitcasting gear, with 8- to 14-pound line and rods of $5^1/_2$ to 7 feet, is suitable.

The possibility of encountering large catfish (more than 15 pounds) in waters beset with thick cover, snags, and objects that a powerful fish can swim under or through and that enable it to break off, require heavier-duty tackle. For big cats, a sturdy light-duty conventional reel or medium- to heavy-duty baitcasting reel, spooled with a minimum of 17-pound line, is necessary. This should be coupled with a medium- to heavy-action rod; a shorter rod, in the 6- to 7-foot range, will suffice if there is little need for casting and you're using heavy line, but for regular casting and for cushioning light line, try a 7- to 9-footer. Line strengths used by big-cat anglers are often between 25 and 40 pounds, and some spool this onto heavy-duty levelwind reels with ample capacity.

Although this may seem like overkill, one does have to take into consideration the environment. A reservoir loaded with stumps and deadfalls and timber is a poor place to out-muscle a large catfish with light gear. And the biggest of catfish are individuals that can steam off with all of the line on a reel. Similarly, when fishing from shore in the wide environs of a tailrace, it may be necessary to use a surf casting outfit to propel a heavy weight out the necessary distance while having the line capacity to deal with the demands of proper presentation and playing fish.

Bait.   If a researcher investigated all the articles ever written about the stuff that is used to catch catfish, they would probably include most of the items commonly found in a grocery store. No doubt everything from sardines to soap to pizza dough would have a recommendation and, indeed, catfish have eclectic taste. Anglers disagree greatly on which bait best attracts various species of catfish. On each sector of major waterways, there is someone who makes a home-brewed concoction that native catfish anglers swear by. Generally these contain cheese, anise oil, sour mash, ground corn, crushed shad, and sometimes a bit of rotten chicken liver. Most homemade bait works, but fresh

anchored at one point but is not connected to a hand-operated mechanical reel; it might be a trotline *(see)* or a simpler line attached to a limb, log, or jug, often not under the direct view and control of the person placing the line and not an instrument of sportfishing.

Fishing with rod and reel can run a gamut from cane poles for small specimens to heavy-duty levelwind reels and stout saltwater boat rods for big bruisers. For the majority of catfishing activities, anglers overmatch their tackle to the standard size of fish expected. Sometimes this is because a lot of catfishing requires bait-on-the-bottom presentations, using a heavy enough weight to keep the offering in place, and sometimes it is because of the possibility of hooking big and strong catfish in snag-laden habitat.

Catfish do not lend themselves to traditional trolling as a routine means of fishing, and very few catfish are caught in this manner. Their general bottom-hugging nature, the types of cover they are often associated with, and their general lack of midwater roaming and aggressive pursuit of forage are all unconducive to this method. In this respect, they are somewhat similar to largemouth bass. This is not to say that catfish cannot be aggressive; it is simply that trolling does not lend itself to most catfish environments. Stillfishing and drift fishing, however, are the general methods of catfishing in all of their habitats, whereas casting is generally ineffective. On occasion, and in places where some species, bait is usually are more productive. Items used to attract and catch the various catfish fall into these general categories: cut bait, which are pieces of dead fish; live baits; prepared bait, which includes dips, pastes, and various concoctions labeled stinkbaits; and miscellaneous bait, which include animal meat, cheese, blood, and sundry offerings.

Cut bait can include parts of various species of fish, often but not exclusively those that are present and abundant normally in the catfish's environment. Sometimes a whole dead fish is used for bait, especially in locations where there may be periodic die-offs of some species (like shad, which often happens in cold weather). Usually chunks and pieces of dead bait are used, and fished until they lose their freshness; fastidious catfish chasers with access to a lot of bait may re-arm with a new cut bait every time they reel in to check it. Fish used for cut bait include (but are not limited to) herring, gizzard shad, threadfin shad, mullet, suckers, chub, carp, shiners, smelt, and panfish, although in some locations it may not be legal to use certain of these species (particularly panfish). Dead shrimp and clams are also used for bait.

Cut bait is seldom used for bullhead, although small chunks might be tried where there are large individuals. Fresh cut bait is generally preferred, and a serious day of fishing for bigger catfish requires an ample supply of fresh cut baits (preferably just killed and not water-logged-soft and mushy).

Live bait runs a wide gamut of offerings but primarily includes fish and worms. Nightcrawlers, or even little wigglers or angle worms, are the main live bait for small catfish, especially bullhead. Most of the same fish used for cut baits are also live-bait candidates, where legal, especially herring, gizzard shad, shiners, mullet, suckers, and panfish, as well as goldfish. These bigger offerings are menu items for flatheads, blues, and channel cats. Other live bait that are used for catfish includes catalpa worms, leeches, crayfish, shrimp, hellgrammites, grasshoppers, crickets, and even frogs (a channel cat delicacy at times). Although many catfish anglers use treble hooks for live-bait fishing, a single hook (sized according to bait and fish, but running from 1/0 up to 6/0) does a good job. Preferences vary from a straight eye to an upturned eye and from a straight to an offset barb. Both the upturned eye and the offset barb help when the hook is set by presenting the hook's point at an offset angle in the fish's mouth. Although generally foreign to catfish angling, tuna circle hooks that have become popular for many saltwater bait applications may have merit.

"Prepared bait" is a pleasant and general term for a diverse bunch of doughs, pastes, dips, and general goop, some of it manufactured and sold commercially and much of it devised in repulsive home-kitchen experiments. Generally these odoriferous preparations are called stinkbait. Some are simply chunks of fish that have been marinated in some type of liquid long enough to turn them unbearably rancid; these are the crudest of preparations.

Most stinkbait is dip or moist preparations the consistency of paste or dough and can be molded and formed into shape on a hook. Dips may be between sour cream and cream cheese in consistency and include all types of smelly foods (cheese, ground chicken liver, ground oily fish, and the like) mixed with various liquids and fillers (like meal). A hooked sponge is thoroughly immersed in the dip, or a short soft-plastic ringed worm can be used as a dip holder. Paste-style stinkbait is like a dip that has been mixed with more filler and bonding agents so they can be formed into balls; pastes are fished with single or treble hooks buried in them. Stinkbait that is too loose to hold by themselves on a hook, but too firm to be a dip, can be fished in a net sack similar to the egg or spawn sacks used by river steelhead and salmon anglers, although it may be necessary to contain the bait in a small piece of plastic kitchen wrap, then poke holes in the wrap after the hook and net are secured.

All of these produce an odor that offends human beings, with pastes usually being less odiferous and rancid fish chunks being most offensive. These are especially effective on smaller catfish and are better for channel cats than blues or flatheads.

Miscellaneous bait is a catchall categorization for any of the catfish concoctions that people use that don't fit the prior molds. Perhaps the foremost of these is chicken liver, which has long been a popular offering. Frozen, rather than unfrozen or rotten, chicken liver is a popular bait for channel catfish, partly for its effectiveness and partly for its availability and general ease of use, as it lacks much preparation. Frozen liver holds well to a single hook, much longer than unfrozen new or aged liver; as it thaws, it exudes much more scent, making it more attractive. Use one section of liver (not both parts) and thrust a single hook in and out one time while the liver is still frozen.

Natural bait, whether cut or live, usually seems to be the best offering because it is what is normally found in the catfish's environment. Stinkbait, chicken liver, and assorted nonnatural items are not resident food, although it is possible in heavily fished locations that catfish can be conditioned to such foreign items if enough people use them. For larger fish (and obviously "large" varies with the locality and species), natural bait is generally a better item, although many catfish aficionados have distinct preferences for one of these categories over the others. It is disputed whether the more aromatic offerings are best in current or stillwater; in the latter environment, chumming is another scenario entirely. Dead bait is usually fished without a float, whereas live bait is fished either way. In big reservoirs, fishing a lively bait deep with a slip float is recommended. Natural bait should be changed often to be most effective, and live bait should indeed be lively.

According to Chinese legend, in the third century Tao Tzu Ming was fishing on a lake when a dragon surfaced from the water and carried him away to a sacred mountain.

Bullhead and small catfish tend to mouth and nibble bait, whereas larger fish may take it more readily. Blue and flathead catfish take bait more forcefully than do channel and white catfish, sometimes really nailing it.

Techniques.   For the most part, fishing on or close to the bottom with some form of bait is the most reliable way to hook catfish. They will take artificials, but not nearly as well as some anglers might like, and lures are much less effective than baits. Flatheads are fairly susceptible to lures, and crankbaits are most productive. Channel cats are often caught by anglers who have tipped a jig with a minnow or a lively piece of nightcrawler. Some largemouth bass anglers, fishing with a jig-and-pork combo, have latched onto catfish. In big impoundments, anglers will catch some catfish while trolling plugs or while using jigging spoons or bucktail jigs, usually when seeking striped bass. Cats have even been known to run down schools of shad or river shiners just like walleye. Anglers are often surprised to land a channel catfish on a minnow-style plug while angling for bass or walleye. These are generally incidental catches; success seldom comes from deliberately casting lures for catfish. Stillfishing and drifting with some form of bait is the way to go.

As for bottom fishing, catfish will suspend, as mentioned earlier, and are more likely to roam at night to actively feed. This activity can take them away from the bottom. Catfish have been known to chase schools of bait (blues do this occasionally), but for the most part they are a less aggressive and more deliberate bottom or near-bottom feeder. To have continual success with these fish, they must be sought near or on the bottom of rivers and lakes.

A great deal of catfishing occurs in rivers, the natural habitat of most catfish species. Other popular locations include reservoirs, ponds, small lakes, and the backwaters connected to rivers, so strategies vary according to habitat. Bullhead fishing, for example, which focuses on small waters and stillfishing with worms, is a fairly straightforward

bait-and-wait affair, but angling for channel cats is different. There are overlapping tactics and strategies, however.

In rivers, look to current cuts, stream mouths, gravel and rock bottoms, deep-cut riverbanks, shallow riffle areas with a hard bottom, river channels, and pools below riffles.

Deep holes or pools present good river catfishing opportunities. Channel cats work up into shallow water to feed, and move back into deeper water. Although some channel catfish are caught during daylight hours directly from within a hole itself, they are best caught as they move into the shallower areas upstream from the hole. This movement, throughout most of the season, occurs just prior to sundown and lasts for an hour or so after dark.

Flatheads, on the other hand, may refrain from feeding throughout the day and then begin foraging at dark. Unlike channel cats, flatheads venture only partway out of the deep hole to feed. If hole depth is 20 feet and the upstream area is 12 feet, a flathead may work only into 16 feet of water to feed, whereas a channel cat will work into the shallowest upstream point.

Obviously, holes and pools differ from place to place. Some are much longer than others, some deeper, some have more cover. Catfish are generally not found in the runs below a pool, and some pools taper so gradually into a run that it is hard to tell where the run actually starts. Cover, especially boulders near the head of the pool, is a likely place for catfish. Cover includes logs and fallen or sunken trees, which are likely places to get snagged but which frequently harbor catfish. If these and other objects slow fast current and provide a comfortable holding spot for catfish, they will probably serve as feeding stations, especially in deeper water. When fishing holes or pools, start at the end of a riffle and the top end of the pool; be careful to fish the head of the pool first, especially if there's cover. Then move down through the pool to the tail end, fishing any cover or snags as you get to them.

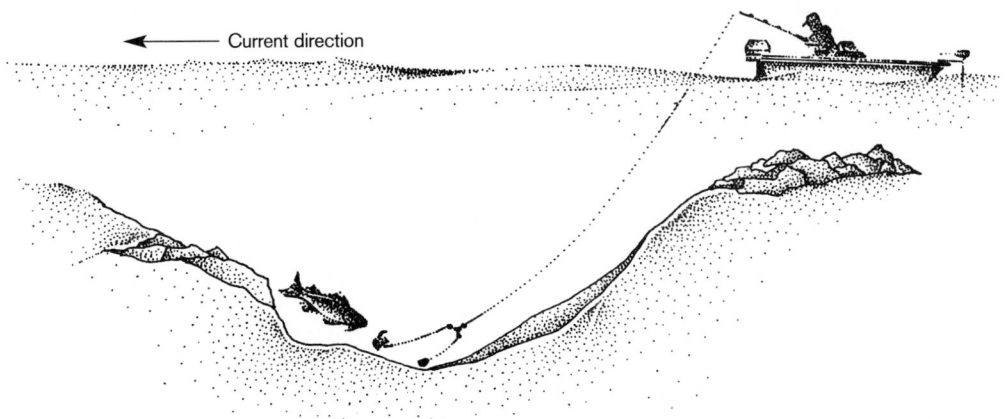

Catfish in rivers typically linger in deep holes and are best approached from upcurrent. A three-way bait rig is a good choice for this situation.

Sluggish rivers provide a multitude of wing dams and navigational structures, and catfish—especially flatheads—prefer to hold below these areas. Wing dams, in particular, are a favorite place for young individuals. Older, larger fish are more apt hold below a dam, lingering below open, churning gate waters, where dead, stunned, and mutilated fish are easily snatched up by the waiting fish.

In rivers with wing dams, anglers can harvest many channel and flathead catfish around riprap near these structures. In spring, they are found directly below the structure and close to it. Later, in warm weather, catfish will move up and around the wing dam and position themselves upstream from it.

Wing dams are man-made structures placed in large river systems to divert current flow toward the center channel. They consist of broken rock and are formed like a solid rock dock bed. In most cases, water runs over wing dams all the time, being deeper in the spring. On all wing dams, one end is anchored to the shoreline. Channel cats and large flatheads feed at these wing dams immediately after sundown. The sides of these hard structures are literally alive with crayfish and baitfish at sunset and during the first hour thereafter.

Catfish hold downstream from hydro dams where there is a dugout area followed by a hump. Constructed of hard material forced downstream with the current, the hump provides an ideal staging area for gamefish. The hump may come within 6 to 10 feet of the surface before falling off into the depths downstream; there the water may be 45 to 65 feet deep. Most of the channel catfish will be found in this area, as will trophy blue and flathead catfish. The hump will vary in form, but most are oval or egg-shaped. Look for channel cats to hold along the upstream sides. Flatheads and blue cats hold downstream from the hump.

Below many hydro dams, there is also an area of shoreline riprap that attracts catfish, which spawn here in small pockets and swirling eddies. Here, in early summer, along the outer edges in 5 to 8 feet of water, catfish feed on crayfish when they shed their shells.

Along this riprap you can catch catfish by walking from shore along the riprap structure downstream while your float and baits drift with the current. Use a slip float to keep the bait 3 to 4 feet deep; for bait try a black leech (spawning catfish love leeches) on a No. 8 hook, with BB-size split shot 6 inches above the hook. The leech hangs 3 to 4 feet below the bobber while drifting just off bottom. In some areas, where riprap literally runs for miles, an angler will walk his bobber three to four blocks before returning to his starting place to repeat the procedure. Later in the season, catfish move deeper off the riprap. Eventually they hold at a point where rock riprap and soft river bottom meet. Here they are best caught using standard fixed-place methods of bottom fishing.

When fishing areas other than the tailrace section of rivers, it's the mobile catfish angler who has the best chance of producing. Sitting on a hole and waiting for catfish to come and take a bait may deliver some success, and is a common means of catfishing, but there's no reason why catfish anglers shouldn't take a page out of the bass, stream trout, and walleye angler's book of methods by fishing likely places more intensively and aggressively, then moving on to look for more likely places. This enables an angler to cover a lot of ground and to look for fish rather than sitting and waiting for the quarry to get active or to come calling.

Keep in mind that river and stream catfish always feed into the current, and take advantage of their keen sense of smell, approaching them from above. Detecting a strike is a key to success, especially with smaller fish and with the particularly adept bait-nibbling channel cat. It's best to position yourself directly upstream of the area to be fished and to cast your offering directly downstream to the target. Once the rig rests on bottom in proper position, reel in slack line. This affords direct contact between sinker, trailing bait, and rod tip. Current-flow shifts will lessen and increase pressure on the rod tip at times. Keep constant pressure evenly distributed between the rod tip and bait by lifting and lowering the rod tip as pressure decreases and increases. When a catfish picks up the bait and moves slightly forward with it, a small vacuum around the bait is created in its mouth. The rod tip will slack off dramatically as the catfish crushes down. At this moment, drop the rod tip, reel hard, and set the hook.

Naturally, when some fish, including bigger ones, take the bait forcefully and move off, you should just point the rod at the fish, engage the gears, reel quickly, and set the hook. But, many times you need to detect that almost imperceptible pickup that creates slack line. Many people don't notice the slight slack in the line when the fish has food in a closed mouth and is confirming taste, and miss their opportunity because the fish then moves, detects something (the point of the hook or line tension), and then opens its mouth while the angler is just then setting the hook. In effect, the angler feels the "strike" when the fish is just letting go of the bait, and sets the hook when its mouth has opened.

If you simply cannot get the hang of strike detection (which many people cannot, because a common complaint in catfishing is missing strikes), and you've been hiding your hook inside bait, then fish with the hook more exposed. Catfish aren't dainty or ultrasensitive feeders and may not discern the hardness of a small light object like a hook (although the hook point is a different story). So try fishing your bait with the hook exposed; run it once through a cut bait, for example, rather than burying it inside, and make sure the point is exposed when any bait is impaled. This may induce more snags and lost terminal gear, but it also could produce many more landed fish, especially if you focus on setting the hook soon after getting a pickup.

Many anglers use egg sinkers on their bait rig, which allow catfish to run with the offering. There is some merit to this, as slow-water cats will pick up a bait and move sideways with it, mouth it a number of times before swallowing, and stay there. This presents good conditions for using an egg sinker. But where there is any significant current flow, and when fish are especially finicky, a bell sinker on a slip rig or three-way rig, or a bottom-walking sinker, may work better. Sinker weight will vary, depending on water conditions, from $5/8$ ounce to 2 ounces. Some conditions may require still heavier weight. The deeper and faster the flow of water, the heavier the sinker needed.

You may need to experiment with the length of leader from weight to bait, as well as with the distance fished behind the boat. Many people fish fairly close to the boat because of the general turbidity of water, but a longer length of line (120 to 150 feet) presents a different angle of line-to-bottom bait, and may be more effective at drawing pickups.

In lakes, reservoirs, and ponds, tactics vary a bit. Naturally, in big impoundments there is likely to be good catfishing in the tailrace water below the dam, and in the river (or rivers) that feed the reservoir. Current flow may vary with seasons and with demand for water, and levels and flow can change as water is stored or released, so these factors have an impact on fishing, although methods are generally similar to those already noted.

In big impoundments, places to focus your efforts are varied, but old riverbeds and channels are especially important. In these places, concentrate on the curves, bends, and deepest holes, and especially where two channels come together. Ledges, or any place where the lake bottom drops off to deep water out in the main lake, also produce catfish, as do humps that drop fairly abruptly to deep water. Flats may have catfish earlier in the season when the water is warming, and points are also worth trying but are often sporadic producers. The area near the dam, especially the face of it (if fishing there is permissible—many are cordoned off), and the riprap and boulders along the face can concentrate fish, including spawners.

Catfish are regularly caught at the mouths of tributaries, including small feeder creeks, and at the mouths of coves, backwater ponds, sloughs, and other areas that provide a funneling point for travel. Some anglers blanket the mouths of such areas with multiple baits to ensure getting the attention of cruising fish. Steep rocky timbered banks, especially in coves, and the back of coves, sloughs, and backwater ponds where there are stumps and timber along a sharply sloped bank, merit fishing effort.

Bullhead and small catfish favor soft-bottom backwaters and ponds with ample submerged vegetation. In ponds or small lakes where there is a weedline, bullhead are likely to be found along the deeper edge of the weeds, but in many places there

Big catfish are often found on the bottom of turbulent water below dam tailraces, such as this one on the Red River in Manitoba.

is no such delineation, and most weeds are thick and submerged in varying depths of water. In this case, look for them in the deeper portions, fishing your bait right above thick bottom-hugging weeds or on the bottom amidst sparser weeds. An inlet is a good place to concentrate efforts, as is the deep water near a dam if there is one, and also any areas that might funnel fish.

Fishing in ponds for catfish is often a sit-and-wait situation; in nonstocked ponds it usually takes time for cats to get to your bait. When fishing from shore, the question is whether to use a float with a bottom rig. Where there are bottom weeds, you'll probably need to use a fixed- or slip-float rig. When fishing from a boat, there is the added question of whether to drift or anchor. In stillwater, especially big impoundments, drift fishing is attractive to fish that are active and aggressive, and tends to produce more smaller fish; anchoring does not allow an angler to cover a lot of water, but it may help produce a bigger fish. In ponds, live baits (like nightcrawlers for small fish) are the main offering for bullhead; cut baits and stinkbaits are popular for catfish and blues. In impoundments, however, live or cut baits (shad or herring mostly), fished off the bottom, are the main tickets, and these can be fished on various rigs.

Of the various rigs used to pursue catfish in both rivers and lakes, certainly the most common ones are the slip rig and the three-way rig. The latter features a three-way swivel with a 5- to 8-inch drop line tied to a bell sinker, and a bait line of varying length tied to a hook. A slip rig usually employs a barrel or egg sinker (sometimes a sliding bell sinker), which slides on the fishing line above a swivel, and a variable-length leader attached to the lower end of the swivel. The slip rig gives the fish some slack line so it doesn't detect trouble when it picks up the bait. These rigs differ in one important way: The slip rig lets a fish run with a bait, whereas the three-way does not.

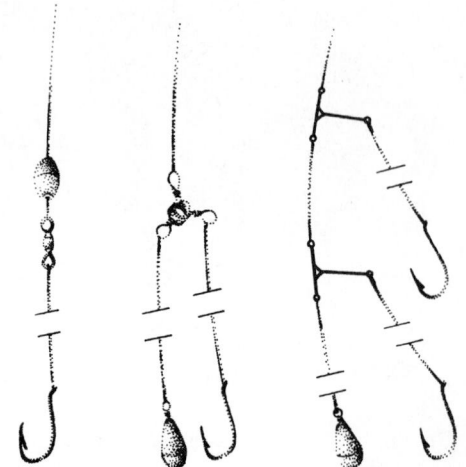

Shown from left to right are three common baitfishing arrangements used for catfish: the slip rig, the three-way rig, and the double-bait (or high-low) rig.

If you're paying attention, there's no need to let a catfish run with the bait, nor is it necessary to delay setting the hook. In fact, by waiting you are likely to hook the fish too deep, which makes hook removal more difficult (and may make rerigging necessary); in most cases, a deeply hooked fish won't survive (which is fine if you intend to keep it but not if you don't or can't). For this reason, a three-way rig seems better; it seems even more useful when you consider that it doesn't snag in current as frequently as a slip rig.

A commonly employed third rig is a simple baited hook with a split shot placed roughly 8 to 15 inches above the hook on the fishing line. Fished like this, it's a snag getter in current, but when fished under a float—in both rivers and lakes—it has merit for drifting. You can also double-up on bait with a two-bait rig; in this setup, a bell sinker is used, and the baits are separated—one on the bottom and the other above the bottom—to avoid tangling.

The length of leader used in these rigs, or the length from shot or weight to hook, is subject to conditions, current, flow, and the angler's preference. Often the choice is a matter of habit. Many anglers stick with a midrange length of 10 to 15 inches, whereas some use leaders up to 3 feet long. Others prefer a leader that is just a few inches long. In heavy current, the greater the distance from weight to hook, the more the bait is likely to move, so this arrangement could produce more hangups than it would in lighter current. When a live baitfish is positioned on or close to the bottom, the bait's movement is enhanced and proper depth is achieved with a moderate length of 10 to 18 inches between the weight and the hook.

Although extensive information about handling and landing fish *(see)* is contained elsewhere, it is worth mentioning here that an angler must be careful when handling catfish, especially small ones that wriggle continuously. Catfish have sharp pectoral and dorsal spines that can inflict pain and cause

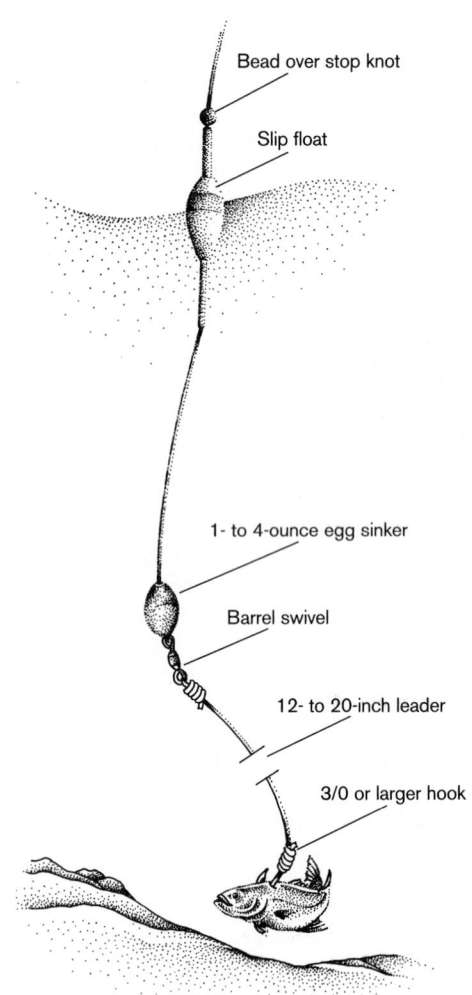

A live-bait float rig for large catfish.

wounds that can easily become infected. To avoid any chance of sticking yourself, approach small fish from their underside, placing your thumb against the back side of one pectoral fin and your index or middle finger against the back side of the other pectoral fin. Grasp the fish firmly with your palm across its stomach. The fish will be securely held and can be safely unhooked.

CATFISH, BLUE   *Ictalurus furcatus.*
Other names—catfish, chucklehead cat, white catfish, forktail cat, Mississippi cat, Fulton cat, blue Fulton cat, great blue cat, silver cat, blue channel cat, highfin blue cat.

This is a popular species within its range and valued for its flesh as well as sporting value. The blue catfish is a strong, stubborn fighter. It can grow quite large, which enhances its appeal. It is considered good table fare and is widely pursued by commercial fishermen for the market. Its flesh is white, delicate, and tender, especially in smaller specimens.

Identification.   Blue catfish are generally blue gray or slate blue and possess no spots or other markings, although they may be almost pale blue or silvery; their flanks taper in color to the belly, which is light gray or white. They have a deeply forked tail, and the anal fin has a straight margin. They resemble channel catfish (see: catfish, channel) and when small are most easily confused with that relative. Larger blue cats have a distinct humped-back appearance, with the hump occurring at and in front of the dorsal fin; their head is generally larger than that of a channel cat, and their body is less sleek. They can be distinguished from channel cats by their longer and straight-edged anal fin, which has 30 to 35 rays. In smaller specimens, a distinguishing characteristic is their lack of black body spots. Internally, the blue catfish has three chambers in the swim bladder, whereas the channel cat has two.

Like the channel catfish and the little-known yaqui catfish of Mexico, the blue cat has a deeply forked tail, a characteristic that distinguishes these three from the flathead catfish and bullhead, and to some degree also from the white catfish (see: catfish, white), which has a moderately forked tail. As with other catfish, channel cats have heavy, sharp pectoral and dorsal spines, as well as long mouth barbels.

Size/Age. Blue cats are capable of growing to gargantuan sizes but are rarely found at the upper limits of their capabilities. Most anglers catch blues in the 5- to 20-pound range. Fish in the 20- to 50-pound class are not uncommon in waters with a good population of fish, but blue catfish in that range are infrequently caught and specimens exceeding that size are rare. The all-tackle world record for the species is a 109-pound, 4-ounce fish caught at Santee Cooper in South Carolina in 1991. A 116-pounder caught on a trotline was reportedly taken at Lake Texoma, Texas, in 1985, and in 1879 a 150-pounder from the Mississippi River near St. Louis was found at a local market and shipped to the U.S. National Museum. Historical accounts describe 100-pounders at the turn of the twentieth century, and individuals between 200 and 400 pounds have been reported but undocumented, perhaps being more lore than likelihood.

There is similar haziness concerning the blue cat's growth and longevity. Several scientific reports indicate that these fish grow up to 14 years of age, and they have been reported to live to 21 years, but greater longevity for the biggest specimens is evidently possible.

Distribution. Blue cats are native to the Mississippi, Missouri, and Ohio River basins in the central and eastern United States, extending north into South Dakota and south into Mexico and northern Guatemala. Dams and commercial harvest are among the factors that have affected their population and perhaps their size in some parts of their native range. They have been introduced with good success into some large river systems outside of that range, most notably in the Santee Cooper waters of South Carolina. They are now most abundant in the deep, warm waters of the South.

Habitat. Blue catfish inhabit rivers, streams, lakes, reservoirs, and ponds but are primarily a fish of big rivers and big lakes/reservoirs. They have been introduced into smaller lakes and ponds but seldom attain large sizes in such places. This species prefers the deep areas of large rivers, swift chutes, and pools with swift currents. Like the channel catfish, they prefer locations with good current over bottoms of rock, gravel, or sand.

Spawning behavior. Blue catfish spawn in the spring or early summer when the water temperature is between 70° and 75°F. Nests are constructed by one or both parents, usually among crevices and holes under logs and trees and in undercut banks. Secluded and dark places are often preferred.

Food and feeding habits. Blue catfish evidently eat most anything they can catch; their diet includes assorted fish, crayfish, aquatic insects, and clams. Herring and gizzard shad are part of their diet, especially when the catfish are larger and in places where these are abundant. Blue cats primarily feed on or near the bottom, and they are principally nocturnal foragers.

Angling. Blue cats are primarily caught by anglers bottom fishing with live or dead baits and with assorted stinkbaits. They are a strong fish that digs in; in larger sizes they are seldom immediately subdued. For in-depth angling details, see Catfish.

Blue Catfish

Channel Catfish

CATFISH, CHANNEL   *Ictalurus punctatus.*
Other names—catfish, river catfish, fiddler, blue channel catfish, Great Lakes catfish, willow catfish, spotted catfish, forked-tail catfish, lady catfish.

The most widely distributed of all freshwater catfish, the channel cat is a significant component of recreational angling efforts as well as a mainstay of commercial fishing; its tender, white, and nutritious flesh is highly valued as table fare. It has been stocked widely in lakes and ponds, and provides the backbone of catfish farming activities. In some states, the sporty channel cat is ranked at or near the top among all species in angling popularity. Channel catfish have the potential to attain large sizes, although less gargantuan than other species, but their general willingness to strike baits, their wide distribution, and their high food esteem primarily account for their popularity.

Identification.   Channel catfish are often recognized at a glance, owing to their deeply forked tails and small irregular spots on the sides. The spots may not be present in all specimens but generally are obvious in smaller individuals. These pigmented spots are most noticeable on younger fish, and obscure on older ones. Blue catfish *(see: catfish, blue)* also have a forked tail, but no spots, and the same is true for the yaqui catfish (*Ictalurus pricei;* a species in the Yaqui River drainage of Mexico). Channel cats are more slender than other catfish, perhaps owing to their native riverine existence, and they have a relatively small head. They are distinguished from white and blue catfish by their 24 to 29 anal fin rays.

The body of a channel catfish is pale blue to pale olive with a bit of silvery tint, but the color variation is subject to location and water conditions. Male channel cats during the spawning season may be entirely black dorsally, and other channel cats may be dark blue with little or no spotting, or uniformly light blue or silvery like the blue catfish *(see: catfish, blue)* or white catfish *(see: catfish, white).* Another feature distinguishing them from a blue catfish is the anal fin; this is shorter and more rounded on a channel catfish than on a blue catfish.

Like other catfish, channel cats have heavy, sharp pectoral and dorsal spines, as well as long mouth barbels.

Size/Age.   The maximum age for these fish varies by latitude; some fisheries sources report a maximum longevity of 15 to 20 years, although it is believed it can exceed 20 years. Those commonly caught weigh from 1 to 7 pounds; fish exceeding 15 pounds are infrequent, and a 20-pounder would be considered extremely large. The all-tackle world-record specimen, a fish caught in 1964, weighed 58 pounds.

Distribution.   Channel cats exist in freshwater throughout most of the United States and parts of southern Canada and northeastern Mexico. In the U.S., they are most abundant in the central region east to the Appalachian Mountains, and sparser on

A channel catfish from the Assiniboine River, Manitoba.

the West and East Coasts, where they are present mostly through introduction.

Habitat. The channel catfish inhabits rivers, streams, lakes, reservoirs, and ponds. Of all the catfish, the channel cat shows the greatest preference for clear, flowing waters, although it does equally well in lakes and ponds. It prefers clean bottoms of sand, rubble, or gravel in large lakes and rivers. Although it tolerates some amount of current, it is more likely to inhabit warm, quiet, slow-moving areas.

Spawning behavior. Channel catfish spawn in the spring or early summer when the water temperature is between 70° and 85°F. Nests are constructed by one or both parents, sometimes over open bottom but more likely among crevices and holes under logs and trees and in undercut banks. Secluded and dark places are often preferred. The male guards the eggs and aerates them, and has been reported to eat some of the eggs during incubation, although it guards the young until they disperse. Ten-inch females may lay only 2,000 eggs, whereas fish over 30 inches long may lay 20,000 eggs.

Food and feeding habits. Channel catfish are primarily but not exclusively bottom feeders. They are omnivorous and consume insects, crayfish, clams, snails, crabs, fish eggs, and assorted small fish, including sunfish, darters, shiners, and gizzard shad, plus a variety of plants.

Angling. The vast majority of channel catfish are caught by bottom anglers, but these fish sometimes linger on or near the surface, as well as at mid-depths. They are strong and provide a good fight on light tackle, although the smaller specimens are often overwhelmed by heavy-tackle users. Most anglers use some form of bait, and many find that channel cats prefer live baits over dead baits. For in-depth angling details, *see Catfish.*

CATFISH, FLATHEAD   *Pylodictus olivaris.*
Other names—mud cat, muddy, shovelhead, shovelnose, yellow cat, appaloosa, goujon, johnnie cat, pied cat, Morgan cat.

A common and large-growing species, the flathead is one of the ugliest members of the freshwater catfish clan. Nevertheless, large specimens are commonly caught, and the fish provides a good struggle on hook and line. It is important both for commercial and recreational use, and produces good table fare when taken from clean environments.

Identification. The flathead catfish is distinctive in appearance and not easily confused with any other species. It has a squared, rather than forked, tail, with a long body and large flattened head. Medium to large specimens are rather pot-bellied and have wide heads and beady eyes. With their distinctly flat-looking oval shape, the eyes accentuate the flatness of the head, and the lower jaw further accentuates this trait by protruding beyond the upper jaw. Compared to that of other catfish species, the anal fin of the flathead is short along its base, possessing 14 to 17 fin rays.

Flathead color varies greatly with environment, and sometimes within the same environment, but is generally mottled with varying shades of brown and yellow on the sides, tapering to a lighter or whitish mottling on the belly. As with other catfish, flatheads have heavy, sharp pectoral and dorsal spines, as well as long mouth barbels.

Size/Age. Flathead catfish are a large and fairly quick-growing species, especially in the southern and warmer parts of their range. Most anglers encounter flatheads weighing from several pounds to 10 or 15 pounds; fish up to 20 pounds not uncommon, and fish to 50 pounds are a possibility in better waters. Many of the state records for flathead are in the 60- to 80-pound range, and the all-tackle world record, established in Kansas in 1998, is a 121-pounder. Flatheads do grow larger, however; Texas produced a 122-pounder caught on a trotline, and Arkansas has reported flatheads up to 139 pounds. The upper limits are generally unknown, although this species reportedly does not reach the maximum size of the blue catfish *(see: catfish, blue).* The chances of catching a really big flathead are better than those of catching a blue catfish, as the former species has a wider range and because more large flatheads seem to be available.

Flatheads have been reported to attain 30 pounds at less than 10 years of age, and presumably the largest specimens are 20 to perhaps 30 years old, although there is scant information on their absolute longevity. A Texas flathead that was tagged

Flathead Catfish

Food and feeding habits. Like its brethren, the flathead is omnivorous and opportunistic, and consumes diverse and available foods. Flathead catfish are primarily but not exclusively bottom feeders and consume insects, crayfish, clams, and assorted small fish, including sunfish, shiners, and shad. Adults consume larger prey, including bullhead, gizzard shad, and carp, and reportedly some terrestrial animals that have the misfortune of finding themselves in the water. Live fish are popular baits for flatheads, more so than other catfish species, as these fish are more reluctant to consume old and smelly bait. Although not exclusively nocturnal, flatheads are more active at night and may spend the day inactive in deep water or under cover. At night they may move shallower and feed at different levels.

Angling. Flatheads are popular with catfish anglers in large lakes and rivers and provide a strong and stubborn deep-digging fight. It takes time to subdue larger individuals, which are pursued with heavy tackle, especially because they exist in snag-filled environs. Bottom fishing with some form of natural or prepared baits is widely practiced, although live baits are very popular, especially for larger specimens. For in-depth angling details, *see Catfish.*

A flathead catfish from Lake Marion, South Carolina.

at 1.76 pounds was recaptured many years later when it weighed 31 pounds; analysis showed it to be 12 years old.

Distribution. Flatheads are native to the lower Great Lakes and the Mississippi, Missouri, and Ohio River basins from southern North Dakota to western Pennsylvania and south to northern Mexico, reaching as far east as the western tip of the Florida Panhandle. They are widely dispersed within that range and have been transplanted successfully well beyond this.

Habitat. This species is primarily found in large bodies of water, especially reservoirs and their tributaries, and big rivers and their tributaries. In rivers, they prefer deep pools where the water is slow, and depressions or holes, such as those that exist in eddies and adjacent to bridge pilings. They are also commonly found in tailraces below dams. Their chosen habitat often has a hard bottom, sometimes mixed with driftwood or timber. In large reservoirs, they are usually found deep, often in old river beds, at the junction of submerged channels, and near the headwater tributary.

Spawning behavior. Flathead catfish spawn in the spring or early summer when the water temperature is between 70° and 80°F. Nests are constructed by one or both parents, usually among crevices and holes under logs and trees and in undercut banks. As with other catfish, secluded and dark places are often preferred, and there is often a log or tree or other object at the nest site. The male guards the eggs and aerates them, and then guards the young until they disperse.

CATFISH, GAFFTOPSAIL   *Bagre marinus.*

Other names—bandera, sailboat cat, gafftopsail sea catfish, gafftop cat, tourist trout; Portuguese: *bagre-fita;* Spanish: *bagre cacumo.*

This sea catfish is a common catch by both commercial fishermen and recreational anglers in the Gulf Coast, especially between April and August. Its dark, tender, lean meat is popular as table fare and has a moderate flavor.

Identification. The gafftopsail catfish has a steel-blue dorsal fin, silvery ventral fins, and a robust body with a depressed broad head featuring a few flattened barbels. The dorsal and pectoral fins have greatly elongated spines.

Size/Age. Mature gafftopsails grow to 36 inches and 10 pounds. Average small fish weigh less than a pound to $1\frac{1}{2}$ pounds and are 17 inches long. The maximum age is unknown.

Distribution. These fish range along the western Atlantic coast from Cape Cod to Panama and throughout the Gulf of Mexico, being abundant along Louisiana and Texas. They are absent from most of the West Indies and Caribbean

Gafftopsail Catfish

Islands but are present in western Cuba, and extend to Venezuela and possibly as far south as Brazil.

Habitat.   Gafftopsails prefer deeper channels, particularly brackish water in bays and estuaries with sandy bottoms of high organic content. They prefer water temperatures between 68° to 95°F.

Life history/Behavior.   Gafftopsail catfish move in large schools and migrate from bays and estuaries to shallow open waters of the Gulf of Mexico in winter. This movement and migration in gulf coastal and estuarine waters is related to spawning activity and environmental conditions. Spawning takes place in the waters of inshore mud flats between April and July, and has some unusual characteristics.

Gafftopsails reach sexual maturity at the age of two and are between 10 and 11 inches in length at the time. They have low fecundity, producing just 20 to 64 eggs per female; their eggs are believed to be the largest of all eggs produced by bony fish. Males carry the eggs and young in their mouths for 11 to 13 weeks until they are about 3 inches long; as many as 55 young have been reportedly carried in this manner at a time.

Food and feeding habits.   Crabs, shrimp, and various small fish make up their diet, but like all catfish, gafftopsails have broad dietary interests.

Angling.   Gafftopsail catfish are caught by some for their food value and by others as cut baits for angling for other species. They are primarily caught on live and cut baits, and occasionally on lures, including jigs and plugs.

For more angling information, *see Catfish.*

CATFISH, GOLDEN

The golden catfish is a South American catfish, also known as *dourada.*
See: Catfish.

CATFISH, HARDHEAD

The hardhead catfish is a sea catfish.
See: Catfish.

CATFISH, SEA

See: Catfish.

CATFISH, TIGER

The tiger catfish is a shovelnose catfish of South America, also known as sorubim.
See: Catfish.

CATFISH, WALKING

A walking catfish that uses its pectoral fins as "legs," which enables it to walk on land.
See: Catfish.

CATFISH, WHITE   *Ameiurus catus.*

Other names—catfish.

White catfish are a common and popular fish with more limited range than other catfish species, and with commercial as well as recreational value. They have been successfully stocked in pay-to-fish ponds and are also cultivated for commercial bulk harvest. Their flesh is white and fine, and they make excellent eating, especially when caught from clean environments.

Identification.   The white catfish looks somewhat like a cross between a channel cat *(see: catfish, channel)* and a bullhead *(see),* owing to its slightly forked tail, broad head, and squat body. Midsize specimens are often thought to be huge bullhead. The white catfish has a moderately forked tail, which distinguishes it from flathead catfish *(see: catfish, flathead)* and bullhead, whose tails are not forked. Its anal fin is rounded along the edge and has 19 to 23 fin rays, fewer than in either the blue catfish *(see: catfish, blue)* or channel cat. Without close inspection, it could be confused with other catfish, although it doesn't possess the spots seen on young channel catfish. This fish is olive gray or slate gray on the head, and bluish gray or slate gray on its backs and sides, tapering to a white belly. As with other catfish, the white cat has heavy, sharp pectoral and dorsal spines, as well as long mouth barbels; its chin barbels are white.

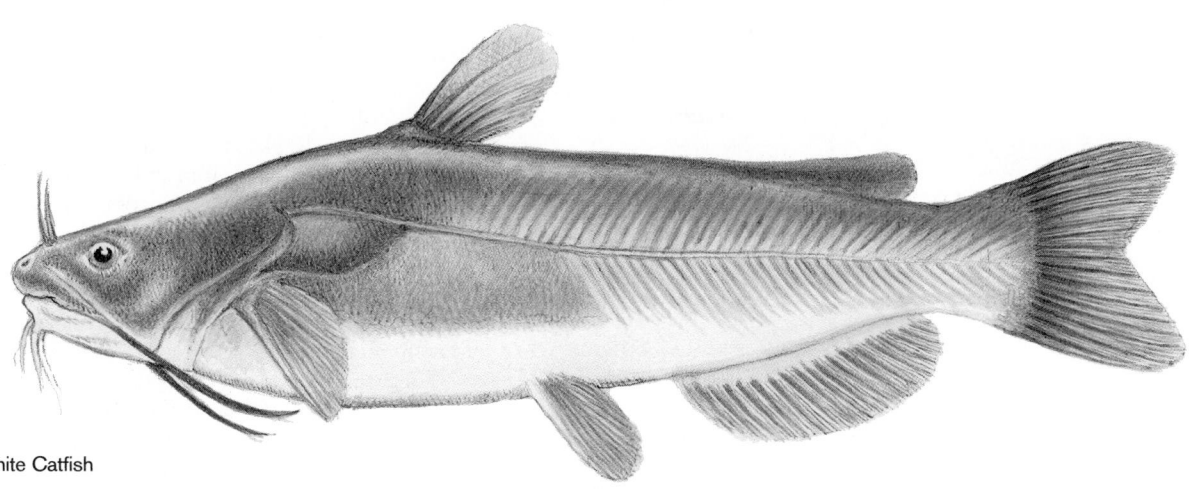

White Catfish

Size/Age. White catfish are smaller than their blue, channel, and flathead brethren, but may grow larger than bullhead. The all-tackle world record for this species is a Florida fish that weighed 18 pounds, 4 ounces, but a 22-pounder has been reported from California. These are the known upper limits for this species, but it may grow larger. Most white catfish are small, averaging 10 to 14 inches, and are often confused with bullhead. They are a relatively slow-growing fish, reaching sexual maturity at three to four years. They have been reported to live 14 years but may get older.

Distribution. The native range of white catfish is freshwater and slightly brackish water of rivers along the Atlantic coast from southern New York to Florida. It exists along the Gulf Coast from Florida to Texas, and has been introduced to some inland waters in the eastern and western parts of the United States, including several New England states, plus Oregon and Nevada; it is well established in California.

Habitat. White catfish inhabit the silty bottom areas of slow-moving streams and rivers, as well as ponds, lakes, and the low-salinity portions of tidal estuaries. They generally avoid the swift water of large rivers and do not thrive in weedy or muddy shallow ponds.

Spawning behavior. This species spawns in spring and early summer depending on latitude, and its spawning behavior is generally similar to that of the bullhead. The parents build a nest on sand or gravel substrate, usually near shore and often in places associated with some form of sheltering cover; spawning occurs when the water reaches approximately 70°F, and the parents both guard the eggs and young.

Food and feeding habits. White catfish have a broad appetite and consume aquatic insects, crayfish, clams, snails, mussels, fish eggs, assorted small fish, and some aquatic plants. Adults primarily feed on fish and are active at night, although they are less nocturnal than other catfish.

Angling. Where they exist, white catfish are fairly abundant and aggressive, making them good targets for anglers, particularly bottom fishing enthusiasts. These fish produce a good fight on light tackle, although the smaller specimens are often overwhelmed by heavy-tackle users. Most people fish with some form of weighted bait. For in-depth angling details, *see Catfish*.

CATHODE-RAY RECORDER
A sonar device using a cathode-ray tube.
See: Sonar.

CAUDAL FIN
The tail fin, or the fin at the rear of the fish. The fleshy section connecting the caudal fin to the end of the body is called the caudal peduncle *(see)*.
See: Fish.

Carp were brought to America from Europe; in 1831 carp stocked in a pond in Newburgh, New York, escaped and became established in the Hudson River.

CAUDAL PEDUNCLE
The fleshy tail end of the body of a fish between the anal and caudal fins. On some fish the caudal peduncle is rigid and provides a convenient "handle" of sorts for holding fish.
See: Caudal Fin; Fish.

CAYMAN ISLANDS
Just a one-hour flight from Miami, Florida, and well out in the western Caribbean, the three-island Caymans nevertheless remain relatively obscure to most big-game and inshore anglers. Yet the Caymans offer excellent light-tackle big-game fishing, plenty of flats with bonefish and tarpon, and reef fishing for numerous species, all on a year-round basis.

Perhaps the general lack of sportfishing attention given to the Caymans—which consist of Grand Cayman Island and the much smaller Little Cayman and Cayman Brac Islands—is due to their proximity to Cuba; Cayman Brac is less than 100 miles from Cuba's south shore islands, and Grand Cayman is about 200 miles away. Private boaters from the United States don't just run here for short periods, as they do out in the Bahamas.

The Caymans are not without visitors, however. With at least one beach classified among the best in the Caribbean, they attract many sunbathers and water-sports enthusiasts. And with outstanding reefs and tropical waters, the Caymans are explored underwater by thousands of divers each year.

The divers know well what some big-game anglers have learned by watching their sonar equipment: The bottom of the ocean drops off a long, long way just outside these islands. In fact, the word *dropoff* doesn't begin to explain what happens here, because these islands are mountains rising from the sea, part of the Cayman Ridge and a range of submarine mountains that extend all the way to the Misteriosa Bank.

Described as a "layer cake of life zones," the trenchlike dropoff outside Grand Cayman Island is known as The Wall. Here, the inshore reef plummets to 800 feet a few hundred yards from the island, and slopes to 3,000 feet within 3 miles. Beyond that it drops below 20,000 feet into the Cayman Trench, which is the deepest hole in the Caribbean.

If this sounds like the makings of big-game country, especially blue marlin and tuna, it is. With the blue water of the Windward Passage enveloping these islands en route to becoming the Yucatan Current, and year-long tropical water conditions, the stage is set for blue marlin. These fish are available here year-round and peak in abundance from May through July.

These aren't big blues; the island record to date is a 584-pounder, which is nothing to sneeze at but it is far short of the possibilities elsewhere in the Caribbean, especially out in the Indies. Blues here are said to average 150 pounds, which makes this grounds for males (the smaller fish) and juveniles and for light-tackle efforts, including fly tackle. White marlin and sailfish are occasional catches during the year as well.

Yellowfin, blackfin, and skipjack tuna are also on the Caymans' offshore scorecard, as are dolphin and wahoo. Yellowfins are the most prominent tuna, average 30 to 40 pounds (the local record is 189 pounds), and are caught year-round. They are most abundant from April through August. Blackfins are more spotty, but opportunities to land them increase in July and August. Skipjacks are prominent from October through January and average 12 pounds.

Dolphin average 10 pounds here but run much larger in the period of peak abundance, from April through September. The wahoo fishing has been excellent in the past; these are very plentiful but lightly pursued, especially from December through March, sometimes very close to shore at Grand Cayman. These species are all caught close to Grand Cayman, of course, as well as at the Cayman Banks, which is a large shoal area about 10 miles west of Grand Cayman. Deep peaks and valleys here affect the currents, and both attract and hold baitfish schools.

Inshore, there is fishing for bonefish, tarpon, permit, pompano, and barracuda, although, again, for relatively small fish. Loads of baby tarpon exist in the mangroves and inland brackish waters of Grand Cayman and also at Little Cayman. Five- to 15-pound fish provide phenomenal action to light-tackle casters in shallow waters along the coasts and throughout the year; the fishing occurs along the mangrove shores, in the ditches on Grand Cayman, and in a popular brackish lake at Little Cayman. Larger fish are in the area, too, but are seldom caught by anglers. Fifty- to 100-pound tarpon appear at dinner time, to be fed by tourists at the Grand Cayman waterfront in George Town, the capital city; and divers frequently see large tarpon in deeper water off the reefs, but virtually no one fishes for them.

Bonefish are found near all three islands, with the most opportunity existing around Little Cayman and Cayman Brac. They run from 2 to 6 pounds on average and are plentiful. The flats at the sister islands (which are 5 miles from each other and 89 miles northeast of Grand Cayman) are pristine, with turquoise water. The lightly populated islands (with lodges) are remote enough that one is truly away from it all.

Anglers land bonefish year-round in the Caymans, but the better fishing exists in the summer, from May through July, when winds are light; winter months can be good if winds don't drive the fish to slightly deeper water, although big schools are present then, and sight or blind casting with light jigs is likely to be effective. Some fishing from a boat can be had for bonefish in the deeper water

of the North Sound at Grand Cayman, but the prime places for flats stalking are at the northwest end of the island, in the South Sound, from Pirate's Lair to Red Bay; in Frank Sound, from Betty Bay Point to Cottage Point; and on the eastern end at Colliers Bay. Some mangrove flats on Grand Cayman have been set aside for protection.

Permit and pompano are also available on the flats but are less frequently encountered. The local record for permit is 36 pounds. Barracuda frequent the shallows and provide good light-tackle sport. Anglers also land them around the reefs.

Reef fishing here is likely to produce Nassau grouper, jack crevalle, mutton snapper, yellowtail snapper, and other species, although it is lightly pursued in favor of flats and offshore action. Some angling visitors combine a trip inshore or offshore with a dive on the reefs.

The Caymans offer many facilities, including well-equipped and experienced charter boats and guides on all three islands.

CEDAR JIG
An old-time saltwater trolling lure used for schooling fish.
See: Trolling Lures, Saltwater.

CELLULAR TELEPHONE
See: Communications.

CENTREPIN REEL
A revolving-spool single-action reel with a large arbor, used in Europe for fishing with a float *(see)*. Also known as a float reel, and similar in appearance to a fly reel, this item always has two handles and a 3- to 4-inch diameter, and a very sensitive and free-spinning spool.

CHAFING GEAR
A wrapping of tape, cloth, canvas, tubing, or other material over line or boat rigging to prevent wear.

CHAIR, FIGHTING/FISHING
See: Fighting Chair; Sportfishing Boat.

CHALK STREAM
See: Limestone Stream.

CHARR
The term charr (or char) is used to describe five members of the genus *Salvelinus*. They are members of the Salmonidae family, which also includes trout, salmon, whitefish, and grayling, all of which are endemic to the temperate and cool regions of the

C

A silvery Arctic charr caught in the ocean along the coast of Victoria Island, Nunavut Territory.

Charr as a group are among the most distinguished-looking and prettiest fish that appear in freshwater. Some are especially colorful, particularly in spawning mode. All have distinctive body markings, although there are great variations depending on their environments. The lake trout found deep in one of the Great Lakes, for example, is rather bland compared to the lake trout caught in more sterile waters of the far north.

Most members of the Salmonidae family are in some way associated with cold, often rushing waters and high oxygen demands. Some, including two of the charr, are also tied to the sea, spending a portion of their lives there. All members of the family spawn in freshwater, and most require cold running water. Members of some of the sea-running species, including at least arctic charr, have become accidentally or deliberately landlocked, living and reproducing successfully entirely in freshwater without ever taking a journey to saltwater.

Some charr species, especially arctic charr and lake trout, are of great historical, cultural, and food significance to native peoples of the Arctic or near-Arctic and to settlers, and they have had—and to some degree still have—both subsistence and commercial value. All native charr have rich, red flesh and are excellent eating, primarily when fresh or smoked. They are all highly valued sportfish, although the limited range or remoteness of arctic charr, Dolly Varden, and bull trout make them less encountered by, and less known to, anglers. The poorly named lake trout and brook trout are among

Northern Hemisphere but have been introduced widely outside their native range.

The charr group includes only one species that is actually called a "charr" in the English language, the arctic charr *(Salvelinus alpinus)*, which is also referred to in some scientific texts as the "*S. alpinus* complex," because in modern times it has come to represent many fish that were previously thought to be separate species or subspecies. The arctic charr's four cousins include two of the most prominent species that are referred to as "trout," the lake trout *(S. namaycush),* and the brook trout *(S. fontinalis),* and two less widely known species, the Dolly Varden *(S. malma),* and the bull trout *(S. confluentus).*

Charr and other members of the Salmonidae family are primitive fish; their fossil remains date to more than 100 million years ago. Evidence indicates that many of the more advanced or specialized families of modern-day bony fish have ancestral stocks closely resembling these primitive fish.

The most clearly evident primitive feature of the group is the lack of spines in the fins. Most of the soft rays in the fins are branched. The pelvic fins are situated far back on the body—in the "hip" region where the legs of amphibians articulate with the body. This position differs from the location of the pelvic fins in many other species, including largemouth bass *(see: bass, largemouth)* for example, which are so far forward they are almost directly beneath the pectoral fins. Other indications of their primitive nature are an adipose fin and a crude type of air bladder.

A colorful brook trout from the English River, Labrador.

the most valued North American game species. Both have been extensively cultivated in hatcheries and have been widely planted to supplement existing stocks, to reintroduce the species to waters where natural populations were extirpated, or to introduce them to waters where they did not previously exist.

Like virtually all members of the Salmonidae family, charr have suffered from changes wrought by humans. These include overfishing (especially of lake trout in the largest waters via commercial efforts, and in some remote waters from sportfishing), pollution, habitat alteration, factors that have caused a warming of waters, hatchery impacts, and competition from exotic species.

Some populations of the various charr have declined dramatically, and most are not what they were decades ago, in terms of overall size as well as in number of large individuals. In addition, some landlocked forms with limited distribution (blueback trout, Quebec red, and Sunapee trout) have become extinct, their loss in some cases hastened by stocking of nonnative salmonids. Commercial fishing for lake trout and arctic charr has been stopped or greatly reduced by quotas in many places, although in the far north subsistence netting by native peoples continues at varying levels.

The subject of the proper spelling of this group—charr or char—has generated spirited debate in the scientific community. The original and historical spelling is reportedly Celtic (from *ceara,* meaning blood red), and became charre in seventeenth-century England, then charr. The general public, especially the popular media, today predominantly use "char," and this spelling is recognized in several prominent U.S. authoritarian lists. Many Canadian ichthyologists, who arguably have a greater claim to the group because of their abundance of these species and studies of them, use "charr." At least one pundit has noted that "char" means "to burn," as in char-broiled steak, and is confusing, implying that "charr" is unambiguous. Another has noted that such other accepted words of Celtic derivation, redd and parr, would be inappropriate if the second *d* or *r* was dropped. Usage of

the word char, however, will not be the first instance in which the wrong spelling of a word becomes the accepted one through common expression, and it has happened with other fish species.
See: Charr, Arctic; Dolly Varden and Bull Trout; Trout, Brook; Trout, Bull; Trout, Lake.

CHARR, ARCTIC   *Salvelinus alpinus.*
Other names for the seagoing fish—char, red charr; Cree: *awanans;* Danish: *fjeldørred;* French: *omble chevalier;* German: *saibling;* Greenlandic: *eqaluk;* Icelandic: *bleikja;* Inuit: *iqalugaq, iqaluk, ilkalupik, ivisaaruq, kisuajuq, majuqtuq, nutiliarjuk, situajuq, situliqtuq, tisuajuq;* Japanese: *iwana;* Norwegian: *arktisk roye, royr;* Russian: *goletz;* Swedish: *röding.*
Other names for the landlocked fish—blueback charr, blueback trout, Sunapee trout, golden trout (Sunapee), Quebec red.

Although the majority of anglers are unfamiliar with arctic charr and have not even been close to catching one, this species is technically among the most widely distributed salmonids, and the most northerly ranging member of the Salmonidae family. It is one of five species that are actually classified as charr *(see),* including the more familiar lake trout *(see: trout, lake)* and brook trout *(see: trout, brook).* The arctic charr varies so greatly in coloration throughout its North American, Asiatic, and European ranges that up to 26 varieties, many thought to be species or subspecies, have heretofore been identified, resulting in a great deal of confusion and a tremendous problem for taxonomists. This confusion extended to anadromous and nonanadromous forms, the latter including three New England charr—the blueback trout, Sunapee trout, and Quebec red trout, which were once separately recognized species but which were all reclassified and folded under the highly inclusive umbrella *S. alpinus* in 1974.

The arctic charr exists in anadromous (migrating annually to the sea) and nonanadromous (landlocked or living entirely in freshwater) forms. Because of plentiful food resources in the ocean, the

Arctic Charr (sea-run phase)

Arctic Charr (spawning phase)

anadromous version tends to be larger than the landlocked one and of more importance to commercial and sport fisheries. The landlocked charr is blocked from the sea by some physical barrier. It is found everywhere that the sea-run charr exists but also occurs in smaller numbers much farther to the south. Thus, the arctic charr is known as a glacial relict in cold, deep lakes as far south as New England, Switzerland, and Britain.

Some anglers consider sea-run arctic charr the equal of Atlantic salmon, because both are strong battlers that make long runs and thrilling aerial jumps when hooked. The charr are perhaps more prone to furious spinning and head-twisting gyrations. Although charr may be caught in river pools like Atlantic salmon, most arctic rivers are more turbulent and swift than salmon rivers, and fishing concentrates at the head of pools and where swift runs empty into open areas. Arctic charr are also schooling fish and are likely to be present in small numbers in a given location.

Arctic charr have long been a staple in the diets of native peoples (and their dogs) in the far north, and in North America they have been an object of commercial fishing since the 1860s off Labrador, as well as commercial interest in Newfoundland and in Nunavut Territory and the Northwest Territories at Rankin Inlet, Cambridge Bay, Pelly Bay, and Nettilling (Seal) Lake on Baffin Island. They are primarily taken with gillnets.

The flesh of sea-run charr is deep orange red and an Epicurean delight, although it can spoil quickly. Depending on diet and location, some charr may have lighter colored, or white, flesh.

Arctic charr is marketed mainly fresh and frozen as whole dressed fish and steaks. A small quantity is canned. Red-fleshed fish command the highest price.

Like other salmonids, arctic charr have felt the impact of human encroachment, mainly increased development and overfishing, and some stocks have declined in overall number and average size. Sportfishing has also had some impact in a few places, especially when numbers of the largest specimens were removed, as these are fairly slow-growing fish. Other than humans, the arctic charr has few enemies. Gulls and loons prey on small fish, and a few seagoing charr may succumb to seals and white whales, but the greatest effect may be predation by other fish.

Identification. Like all members of the *Salvelinus* genus, the arctic charr has light-colored spots on its body, including below the lateral line, and the leading edges of all fins on the lower part of the body are milk white. It is a long and slender fish with a small, pointed head, an adipose fin, an axillary process at the base of each pelvic fin, and a slightly forked tail that almost appears squared. It also has very fine scales, so deeply embedded that the skin has a smooth, slippery feel. Unlike the trout, it has teeth only in the central forward part of its mouth.

Coloration is highly variable among seagoing and landlocked forms, and can change even within individual stocks; those migrating to one coastal system may appear different from those migrating to another, as also happens with salmon and trout. In a general sense, however, the arctic charr is silvery in nonspawning individuals, with deep green or blue shading on the back and upper sides, and a white belly. Spawning males exhibit brilliant red or reddish orange coloration on the sides, underparts, and lower fins; their backs are muted, sometimes without the blue or green coloration or possibly with orange to olive hues. Spawning males of some populations develop a kype, and some have a humped back. Spawning females are also colorful, although the red is less intense and present only on the flanks and belly; the back remains bluish or greenish.

The tremendous variation among arctic charr (which leads some scientists to view different stocks as subspecies) makes it almost impossible to make a clearcut identification based on coloration, especially if other charr exist in the same area. Lake trout, Dolly Varden, and bull trout *(see: Dolly Varden and bull trout)*, for example, may overlap with arctic charr, and whereas lake trout are readily discerned due to their bodily patterns, the other species are not. Color, for example, is not a factor that distinguishes the arctic charr from its close relative the Dolly Varden, which is the species most often confused with the arctic charr.

Often it is virtually impossible to distinguish between the two species except by laboratory analysis, and even today there are few scientists who know how to make a positive identification. Much incorrect information has been published concerning the distribution of each species, and consequently anglers and scientists alike have made many false identifications based on the mistaken belief that only arctic charr or only Dolly Varden occurred in a given area, lake, or river (especially in Alaska). An individual who is familiar with both species may be able to make an identification based on the size of the spots, which are larger on the arctic charr. Fish returning from the sea are often silvery with no spots at all, however, making external identification all but impossible. Gill raker counts are helpful. On Canada's Victoria Island, charr have about 25 to 30 gill rakers on the first left gill arch. Dolly Varden have 21 to 22 gill rakers. Arctic charr have 40 to 45 pyloric caeca (wormlike appendages on the pylorus, the section of intestine directly after the stomach), whereas Dolly Varden have about 30.

Size/Age. How large arctic charr can grow is uncertain, but some may live up to 30 years and grow to 3 feet in length. Sea-run charr grow much larger, and the all-tackle world record is a 32-pound, 9-ounce sea-run fish that was caught in 1981 in the Tree River of Canada's Northwest Territories. It has been reported that a 15.4-kilogram (33.8 pounds) charr was caught at Novaya Zemlya in Russia.

In most places sea-run arctic charr range up to 10 pounds and average 7 pounds; landlocked fish normally weigh a few pounds. A sea-run arctic charr weighing more than 15 pounds is a trophy in most waters, although such fish are not uncommon to streams entering Coronation and Queen Maud Gulfs in north-central Canada, and emanating from Victoria Island. These waters are especially notable for arctic charr that range from 15 to 20 pounds, and sometimes higher.

Distribution. As the name suggests, the arctic charr is circumpolar in distribution, occurring in pure and cold rivers and lakes around the globe, from the northeastern United States north and west across northern Canada, Alaska, and the Aleutian Islands, and from northern Russia south to Lake Baikal and Kamchatka, as well as in Iceland, Great Britain, Scandinavia, the Alps, and Spitsbergen, among other places. The most northerly ranging fish, it has been reported above the eightieth parallel from Ellesmere Island's Discovery Harbour, some 800 kilometers below the North Pole.

In North America, they occur from Alaska around the Bering Sea and along the Arctic coast to Baffin Island, along the coastline of Hudson Bay, and from the northern Quebec coast easterly and southerly to Maine and New Hampshire. Except in larger rivers, they seldom range far inland here, although there are a few pockets of landlocked charr. In the Northwest Territories and Nunavut

Territory, where they are especially known, charr distribution includes most coastal rivers, some coastal lakes, the streams of the high-Arctic islands, and several islands in Hudson Bay.

Habitat. In their ocean life, arctic charr remain in inshore waters; most do not migrate far. In rivers, they locate in pools and runs. The lakes inhabited by anadromous and landlocked charr are cold year-round, so the fish remain near the surface or in the upper levels and may gather at the mouths of tributaries when food is plentiful.

Life history/Behavior. The charr spawns in September or October in colder regions and later if it lives farther south; a water temperature of around 4°C is preferred. The spawning female seeks out a suitable bed of gravel or broken rock. It will choose a stretch of river or lake bottom deep enough to keep the eggs safe from the winter ice, or it will choose the bottom of a rapid, where ice does not form.

Using her fins, the female scoops out a nest, or redd, in the loose gravel. The nest is little more than a shallow depression about the length and width of the female's body. Here, she releases some of her 3,000 to 7,000 eggs as the male releases milt. Then, the female lightly fans the gravel over the fertilized eggs, usually in the course of digging another nest nearby. This process is repeated until the female is spent.

The eggs hatch sometime in the first week of April, although the timing depends on light and water temperature at the specific location. Temperatures above 8°C at any time will kill the eggs. The alevin remain hidden in the gravel for many weeks, emerging as free-swimming fish or fry only when the food reserves are used up. This occurs around the time of ice breakup, which may be as late as mid-July in the most northerly regions, when their emergence coincides with the renewed growth of plankton.

The anadromous charr lives in its birth river for at least four years and is about 15 to 20 centimeters (6 to 8 inches) long when it migrates to the sea for the first time. Spring comes, the rivers break free of ice, and the four- or five-year-old charr makes its first trip down to the ocean. It will return anywhere between mid-August and late September, before the ice begins to form again. The larger fish return first, even as soon as mid-July in some cases. Unlike other salmonids, all arctic charr leave the sea and overwinter in rivers and lakes, although not all are spawners; some go back and forth several times before they first spawn.

The charr matures sexually around its 10th year in the Arctic, when it has reached a length of about 65 centimeters, although maturity comes a couple of years earlier in Labrador, and at a shorter length. After that, the fish spawns every second or third year. Often it does not migrate to the sea during its reproductive years.

It is not known what mechanisms control migratory behavior, but it is thought that hormonal changes are touched off by changes in light intensity. Once in the sea, it is clearly the availability of

C

food that governs movement. When food is plentiful, the fish tend to remain near the mouth of the river from which they emerged. In times of scarcity, however, they move into offshore waters, sometimes traveling long distances. Tagged charr are frequently recovered 30 to 50 kilometers from their river of origin, and some fish have made recorded journeys of up to 600 kilometers; the record is 1,000 kilometers.

While in the sea, charr from many different rivers meet and mingle, but when the time comes to return upriver, they tend in most cases to separate and return to the parent stream. In some instances, they even return to the exact spawning site of previous years.

The cold northern waters are not conducive to rapid growth. Even with its flexible eating habits and its fine adaptation to a cold environment, the charr grows slowly, which makes it vulnerable to excessive exploitation. At the age of one year, when scale development begins, the charr is often less than 5 centimeters (2 inches) long. Growth rates vary greatly among individual fish within a given habitat. It is usual, however, for a charr to reach full growth at 2.5 to 3 kilograms, or at about age 12.

Nonanadromous or landlocked charr tend to reach maturity when they are smaller and younger. They have the same lifestyle as their anadromous brethren.

Food. Insects, mollusks, and small fish constitute the diet of arctic charr. Ninespine sticklebacks are important forage in some places. The charr often does not eat in winter, when its metabolic rate slows in tune with a cooling environment. Rather, it lives on the fat it has accumulated during the summer, and growth is accordingly limited during the cold months, and greatest when at sea.

Angling. The magnificent coloration of spawning fish, the excellent quality of the flesh, its terrific fighting spirit, and its relative inaccessibility combine to make the arctic charr a highly desirable quarry for those relative few who have the time and means to venture to the far north. They are as royal a fighting fish as is found in freshwater, known for blistering runs and salmonlike leaps, especially in river environs, and great tenacity in swift rivers.

Sea-run arctic charr are the main interest of anglers, although landlocked charr are caught in lakes, usually incidental to fishing for lake trout or when they are the only sportfish present. Most of the better fishing for larger charr occurs far north and in a very limited time window, mainly in mid- to late summer. Some areas have just a six-week season before the weather becomes cold and possibly snowy. The end of this period, however, is usually when the largest and most colorful spawning fish are available, although this varies with location.

Arctic charr angling can be a feast-or-famine affair. Charr sometimes are clustered so thickly that a river seems full of these fish, or they can be scarce. Although the fishing is sometimes fast, with continuous action, these fish are easily spooked; when a school is alarmed (as can happen when one or more of its members are caught), it will move off, and the spot has to be rested for an hour or two.

River fishing is more dependable than lake fishing, with the charr often holding at the head of a pool. Where current drops over a gravel bar and dumps into a deep pool is a particularly good location. In swift, high water it is necessary to use heavy-bodied spoons, which sink below the surface turbulence; a touch of red or orange on the spoons is helpful. Weighted spinners and some plugs may also do the job, and heavily dressed flies on fast-sinking lines are necessary for fly anglers. Fly fishing is better when the water level is lower; many different wet flies and streamers are appropriate, also with some bright color for appeal, and dry flies may catch fish when there is a hatch (often mosquitoes) in progress.

Anglers do very little fishing for charr in the sea or in nearshore ocean waters, because of a lack of suitable boats in far northern locations, because of the dangerously cold temperature of the water, and because enough fish are usually available in nearby rivers. Arctic charr range along coastal shorelines and estuaries in summer prior to migrating upriver, however, and can provide some excellent action. Shore-based anglers usually find it necessary to wade out on extensive, shallow, nearshore flats to make long casts with heavy-bodied spoons into deeper water. Long spinning rods and light line are

A large, colorful Arctic charr from a river on Victoria Island, Nunavut Territory.

well suited to this, and the fish that are caught are chrome-bright, faintly spotted, and very vigorous. It is not possible to sight-cast to these charr, so blind casting is the norm.

In lakes, anglers concentrate on inlets, where the river dumps into a lake. Early in the season, charr in lakes can be seen and caught as they wander along the edges of ice floes that are breaking up; a spoon, jig, or streamer fly will take them.

Light to medium spinning tackle are best for arctic charr, and 6- to 10-pound line is the standard. Fly anglers need a reel with ample backing, and usually fast-sinking or sink-tip 7- to 9-weight outfits.

See: Charr.

CHARTER BOAT

A sportfishing boat available for hire and capable of taking a limited number of anglers aboard on an exclusive basis, nearly always by advance reservation. Most charter boats exist in navigable waters and are piloted by captains certified by the U.S. Coast Guard. Charter boats are primarily found in saltwater and on large lakes and rivers, and are usually craft in the 25- to 50-foot range with broad beams, deep-V hulls, and the ability to run great distances and endure rough conditions if necessary. They typically take four anglers for a day of fishing, but may take between one and six anglers depending on the size of the boat. In some places, primarily in freshwater, 20- to 25-foot cabin or center console boats are also chartered for fishing, taking fewer passengers, and generally angling in less demanding situations. The term charter boat is sometimes erroneously applied to smaller boats for hire, such as 18- to 20-footers that accommodate two anglers and an operator; these are actually guide boats (see), even though the "guide" may have a captain's license.

Charter boats are usually hired for the day, but may be engaged for several consecutive days, a week, or longer. In some places a charter boat may be hired for half a day. In most situations, charter captains are assisted by a mate (perhaps two on the largest offshore big-game sportfishing boats) who is responsible for setting and rigging lines and baits, assisting customers, netting or gaffing fish, cleaning fish, and associated chores. Some smaller charter boats in freshwater do not use a mate, and the captain serves both functions, usually having one of the passengers steer the boat while he takes care of rigging.

Charter boats supply all of the customary fishing equipment unless some specialized angling is preferred. Anglers usually bring only their own food, beverage, and personal comfort items (sunglasses, sunscreen, foul weather gear, etc.), and are expected to wear appropriate footwear (nonscuff boating shoes or sneakers). The majority of people who fish on a charter boat are relatively inexperienced, or at least unaccustomed to the style of fishing or the species pursued by that boat in that location. Many charter boats use fairly heavy tackle to compensate for their customer's lack of experience, particularly in freshwater when fishing for trout, salmon, and muskies. However, some charter boats specialize in certain techniques or species, and market themselves to anglers with specific interests or abilities. An increased interest in light tackle fishing has caused some charter boat operators, particularly in saltwater, to specialize in using light spinning, baitcasting, or fly tackle.

Hiring a charter boat is a great way to set up good odds for a rewarding fishing experience, and it is also one of the best ways to learn more about sportfishing. Although it may be expensive on a per trip outing, it may, in fact, be an economical means of fishing if several people share expenses, and if you are otherwise limited in the number of times that you are able to go fishing. If, for example, you owned your own boat, but could only use it ten times per season for fishing, the cost of equipment, fuel, amortization, insurance, dockage, and other items might annually be greater than it would if you chartered a boat ten times, especially if you pooled the cost with others. Not to mention that you would have to find and catch your own fish instead of being with a professional who does it day in and day out.

On the other hand, chartering is a terrific way of learning about boats, fishing methods, equipment, locations, and other issues, as a prelude to getting your own boat and being your own skipper. Many people have plunged deeply into some facet of sportfishing (and boat and equipment ownership) after having booked a few charters and gotten a yen to run their own boat and find and catch their own fish. So it works both ways.

General Fishing Issues

Taking turns.   There is great diversity in the types of fishing and species pursued on charter boats. When jigging or drift fishing, and especially when drifting bait in a chum slick, anglers may hold a rod or be assigned a rod to watch and all or many of the anglers on the boat can be active simultaneously. However, when trolling, which is a primary charter boat activity, there may be many rods in play, only one of which actually gets a hookup, and a fair system has to be worked out to determine who gets to fight the fish. Many customers will ask the mate or captain what to do, but they will usually leave it up to their customers to decide.

One way to do this is to assign each angler to a rod, but since some rods inevitably get more strikes than others, this is the least acceptable and least fair method. After all, the fish are primarily attracted to strike due to the trolling efforts of the captain and mate, not the angler. The angler is there to play the fish and bring it to the boat. Most anglers simply take turns "up," like batters coming to the plate on a baseball team. When a fish strikes, it's somebody's turn, and he catches the fish and then yields to whoever has the next turn, and so on. A variation of

Around the world, charter boats are the means for visitors to enjoy a day of offshore fishing.

this is to establish a time limit on each turn, usually 30 minutes. If there are no strikes in that time, it's the next person's turn. Of course, the timing of a strike has nothing to do with the angler, and this system takes on more of a lottery-like scenario.

The key thing is to establish some order before you actually get fishing; don't wait until a fish strikes and someone—usually the person who is quickest, most eager, or closest—grabs the rod. Drawing straws is a fair way to get turns established. It might happen that with four anglers on the boat, only two fish are caught, and the anglers who have the first two turns are the ones who get to battle them.

Another thing that should be addressed is whether a "turn" is ended if an angler plays and loses a fish without landing it. Time limits make this a moot issue if it is determined that whatever strikes in a given time period occur to the person who has that block of time. If not, does a person who has had an opportunity to play a fish lose his turn if the fish breaks off or otherwise escapes the hook? If they don't lose their turn, what if they play and lose another fish, and another? Some charter groups adopt a three-strikes-and-you're-out attitude, which may rankle some of the people onboard, and which may work for dolphin fishing when there's plenty of action, but not marlin or sailfish when there's relatively few opportunities.

This may seem like nitpicking issues to some, but when you've been part of a group chartering a boat for between $300 and $1,000 for a single day

of fishing, you'll appreciate the establishment of a system that is agreed upon and which tries to offer everyone opportunity.

Etiquette.   Despite the fact that you're paying someone to take you fishing when hiring a charter boat, you must remember that it's not your boat; it's the captain's or his employer's. The captain is in charge and presumably knows what's best in the maintenance and operation of his craft, as well as the most effective fishing techniques in his backyard.

No matter what your level of fishing expertise, it is rude and presumptuous to flaunt your knowledge or demean that of the captain or crew. There is no better way to get off on the wrong foot and diminish the day's fishing experience than to play "know all" with people who sportfish for a living every day. If you spot a crewman doing something flagrantly wrong, it will not help the mood of the day to point it out to him, especially in an arrogant manner.

Realize that what you're paying for is the crew's superior knowledge of the particular area and species sought, and what it takes to catch fish in their local water. One of the primary reasons for hiring a charter boat is to learn, especially if you have your own boat, and hopefully to take what you learn and apply it yourself. The more varied your charters and locales, the more varied will be your store of techniques. When chartering, just remember that the people you are fishing with are your teachers. If the mate is doing something (like rigging baits) in an unfamiliar manner, watch

carefully; it just might be a technique you could learn and use elsewhere. So take their advice and counsel, and ask about the things you do not know.

If you do wish to provide input, do so in a way that's not overbearing and offensive. A pet peeve of charter mates the world over is hearing the comment, "That's not the way we do it back home." Naturally, when they hear this they think, "Then why didn't you stay home?" or "This isn't home." It's not rude to make gentle suggestions, which will be better received than criticism or confrontational demands. An offer of your own equipment that you deem more effective will hardly be turned down. Granted, there are times on charters, especially in Third World countries, where the latest in modern equipment and techniques have not yet arrived or boats cannot run up to adequate lure trolling speed, when you may have little choice but to politely insist on doing things your way.

Occasionally, of course, you may actually know better. For example, if the mate has not sharpened old hooks, why not pull your sharpener from your bag and simply begin sharpening hooks yourself? Any mate worth his salt will instantly pick up the clue and gladly borrow and use your file for the balance of the day; there's no need for you to shout orders to do so. He will usually watch you sharpen the first several hooks and imitate your technique thereafter, or will simply thereafter hand you hooks to sharpen yourself. Most good mates in hot fishing areas know how to earn good tips, and anything that may contribute to lost fish will be avoided.

Many misunderstandings aboard charter boats can be avoided by a friendly discussion as you step aboard, especially if you want to "do your own thing." A quick and early examination of the condition of the natural baits, for example, on an off-shore charter boat trip, might prompt you to prefer using artificial lures all day. The time for such a suggestion would be early on, not as a complaint later in the day.

Setting the hook and rod handling.   Another thing you need to address is the matter of setting the hook yourself, or allowing the mate or captain to do it. Many anglers will not take a rod and fight a fish if someone else has first set the hook and then attempted to hand them the rod. They feel that it's unfair, and that the person who set the hook should play the fish. If one person sets the hook and then hands the rod to someone else, and the fish turns out to be a world record candidate, that action would be judged unfair and would disqualify the catch from record consideration, according to the rules established by the IGFA. Most big-game anglers are familiar with this but the vast majority of anglers are not.

If you have any concerns or interests regarding establishing a record *(see)* catch, then no one else should touch your rod. If you feel strongly that it is unfair to have someone set the hook and hand you a rod, then you should not allow it when it's your turn. You may have to make your feelings on this issue known to the captain or mate, or have a discussion about it with them before the moment of truth arrives. In foreign countries, especially those in the Third World, charter boat crews are unfamiliar with the rules for establishing records, and unless they are instructed (politely and pleasantly) about what is expected at the beginning of the day, it is likely that someone from the crew will grab a rod (especially when trolling for billfish) before the angler can get to it.

Many charter boats in saltwater, especially those who fish for big-game species and participate in tournaments, are ever-conscious of records and of following the sportfishing regulations established by the IGFA in regard to the tackle used, and in regard to leader lengths, method of fishing, and manner of landing the fish, so they are well attuned to the issue of who sets the hook and handles the rod. If he is concerned about the abilities of a customer, a captain will allow that customer to set the hook, but then actually aid his efforts by increasing the throttle greatly when the actual hook setting occurs and immediately afterward, in order to help drive the hook into the fish. Should they really be doing that? And who really set the hook? It's a debatable point.

The hook-setting issue is of particular concern on charter boats, because in many situations the mate actually grabs a rod when a fish strikes, then sets the hook. Part of the reason for this is that with some species, it is necessary to do more than just set the hook. The line may have to be paid out under freespool for a short while so that the fish gets a good hold of the bait; then the reel has to be put into strike mode, the hook set, and perhaps the drag adjusted for playing the fish. Anglers unaccustomed to doing this often inadvertently strike too soon, apply too much pressure on the line when the fish is actually swallowing the bait, or do other things that cause the fish to drop the bait or to avoid being hooked. If these missed opportunities happen repeatedly, the mate and captain (and other anglers waiting their turn), may get testy. Charter boat skippers are very concerned with their productivity, which translates into the number of fish actually caught. Fair or not, it's a measure of their ability, a competitive thing amongst the charter fleet, and a means of securing other customers. To ensure that customers actually catch fish (whether they're kept or released), they like to get solid hookups and, if they're worth their charter fees, they know how to do it well.

If you need instructions on the proper manner of setting the hook for the species being pursued or the method being employed, the mate and captain should be able to give you instruction and coach you through this. However, charter boat captains universally agree that many of their customers, especially men, and especially people with some fishing experience, do not listen to their instructions or do not follow them fully, while inexperienced anglers and most women pay greater attention to instructions and to the execution of them, resulting in better success.

If you have no qualms about being handed a rod, and no concerns about records (the chance of catching a record fish is usually slim), then this is a nonissue. Most mates and captains simply want their customers to catch fish, and because they're on the water every day, they are on top of their game while most of the customers are not. The majority of anglers, especially in freshwater, don't have any problem with taking a rod that someone has handed them, but most of them also don't understand the ramifications. In saltwater fishing, especially for big-game species, this is a major issue.

Other Matters

Ownership of the fish. If you have caught and kept fish on a charter boat, who do they belong to? Logic says they belong to the angler who caught them. In freshwater, this is almost always the case. Freshwater sportfish throughout North America are also designated as gamefish and cannot be sold. In saltwater, that is sometimes different; sportfish may not be designated as gamefish in certain places, and may legally be sold. In those places, some charter boat captains seek to sell all or part of the day's catch to enhance their earnings or to subsidize their costs.

Customers may give their catch to the mate or the captain if they don't want them (although there is an ethical question: Why not release them if you didn't want them?), or to other customers. But some saltwater fish have a lot of market value, and in some places they may be sold, with or without a special permit or commercial license. There is special interest in tuna, mako shark, dolphin, swordfish, other billfish, and certain other species, and a good sport catch can have monetary value. Tuna are especially valuable, and giant bluefins can be worth in the tens of thousands of dollars. The cost of fishing on a deluxe charter boat is expensive, especially if a lot of fuel is expended in offshore runs, so some charter boats claim ownership of their catch, or a portion of the catch. Customers should be advised of this up front, in fact prior to making a reservation. If you have a problem with this, you should resolve it before the boat leaves the dock. Many people don't have a problem with this, but should. And some don't become aware of it until they're out fishing or headed back to the dock with the day's catch.

In foreign countries, language barriers or local custom sometimes cause a problem with regard to ownership of the fish, or especially with regard to fish that a customer wants to release immediately unharmed but which the captain or crew expect as food. In these cases, especially in Third World countries, your wish to release all or certain species caught must be established at the start of the day, perhaps by an agreement that you will pay an extra tip for this (representing the amount the crew would probably earn for the fish at the market). This decreases the chance of unpleasant shouting matches when desirable fish are caught. In Third World countries it might help to pay some tip in advance for expected services, provided that you are sure that you can communicate what is expected.

Limits. There's a temptation on charter boats (as there is in other group fishing activities, but especially so on charter boats, perhaps because of expense) for anglers to pool their fish or for more successful anglers to contribute more than their allowable share to the overall pot. Four anglers on a charter boat sometimes may catch the legal limit of a particular species that would apply to six people, figuring in the mate and captain, who did not actually fish but who possess licenses (if licenses are required). Then they divvy the six-limit catch among the four anglers at the end of the day. Except it's illegal. And tough to police.

In most places the legal limit for sport-caught fish applies to one day's catch and to each individual angler, who is responsible for catching those fish himself. One person can give another angler the fish that he caught, but may not catch more than his own legal limit. In other words, if the limit is five fish, you can't legally catch six and give one to someone else. Some charter boats encourage this or look the other way when it happens because they don't want to anger possible repeat customers. On the Great Lakes, you can hear charter boat captains talking all the time on their VHF radio about "filling the box up," which usually means by hook or by crook and by whomever.

While few reputable charter boat skippers will exceed limits in aggregate, sharing like this is fairly common in freshwater and saltwater. Captains should discourage it and work to make sure that people who don't catch as many fish as others get help, but customers need to recognize that this activity is unethical and illegal; if they're caught, there are legal ramifications.

In some waters, there are no limits, or extremely generous limits, on all or certain species of fish, and in the midst of frenzied action some boats have loaded up. The customers have gone home with coolers full of fish, and then they've rotted in the garbage or freezers later on. This has happened on charter boats as well as party boats and private fishing boats, and there really is no justification for it. Many a saltwater angler who has helped plunder fish on great days has later whined about the absence of fish, never associating his own excesses with that absence.

Where there are no limits, a charter boat captain should establish a reasonable boat or per-person limit and cut the anglers off when they've reached it. It's more than shameful to participate in this excess, it's unethical. Customers should keep only those fish that they can eat in a reasonable period of time, and not every fish they catch. The idea of never-ending bounty, irrespective of some days in which the water seems full of fish, was debunked long ago, and some people argue further that anglers should not give their catch away to others, who may not have licenses or in any way contribute to the maintenance of natural resources. Another debatable issue.

Tipping. It is customary to give a cash tip to the mate on a charter boat at the end of the day. This will vary depending upon the activities, the efforts of the mate, and whether there have been some exceptionally good (or bad) things happen. The customary tip for the mate is usually about 10 percent of the cost of the charter, or slightly more to be split between two mates (if the boat has two mates, although it might be split to give more to the primary mate and less to the secondary mate, who is usually someone learning. A lesser tip might be in order if you've had major problems, or a larger tip if the day is truly spectacular or extra services (like a lot of fish cleaning) are rendered. The captain is not generally tipped. It is customary in saltwater big-game fishing to generously reward the mate (and perhaps the captain) when you've caught a record fish, achieved a significant milestone, won a tournament, earned cash from a calcutta pool, and so forth.

Finding and Hiring a Charter Boat

Standard procedures. As with most good products or services, the best advertisement for a good charter boat captain is a happy customer, so if a friend, relative, or acquaintance has a strong recommendation for a charter boat to hire, consider it seriously. Otherwise, you must do some homework, checking out ads, asking people, reading fishing publications, and possibly talking to some references given by the charter boat captain.

Be wary of extreme claims. There cannot be outstanding success or big fish every day. Be wary of captains who guarantee fish, promising a refund if nothing is caught. It's a good-sounding strategy, but some guarantee-fish operators, near the end of a day spent unsuccessfully seeking certain species, will ease out to places where they are sure to find a few nontarget fish that will technically result in a "catch." On the Great Lakes, for example, some skippers will drag the bottom to catch a few lakers (often a sure thing) when they've been unable to get salmon.

Be prepared to pay a deposit in advance to secure your reservation, and to lose it if you don't cancel early enough to allow your date to be filled. Charter boats do have peak seasons and it's not always possible for them to get stand-in customers on short notice, so when they lose parties in prime time, they may not be able to recoup.

If bad weather cancels a booking, the captain should apply your deposit to another date or refund it to you. If bad weather or unusual circumstances adversely affect your day of fishing, some captains will give you a credit or reduction toward another booking. People who book the same charter boat frequently, several or more times a year, usually get a rate break, as well as date preference.

If you can inspect a charter boat before reserving it, that may be helpful; in vacation spots this is often possible. Talking to people at the docks, the marina, or local tackle shops can be very helpful. If you can, get to a dock in the afternoon when the boats come in and talk to customers who have just returned from a day with a charter captain; they'll usually talk freely.

The condition of a charter boat is sometimes an indication of the ability of the skipper and sometimes not. Not every good captain spit-polishes his boat at the end of each day. And not every new and sparkling boat is better than an older weathered one. Do your homework, ask questions, and make sure to tell a prospective captain exactly what you want.

When booking charters in distant places, especially a foreign land, start with a booking agency that specializes in fishing trips, rather than general travel agencies. Such organizations can give advice on numerous destinations and create complete travel packages. The larger and better agencies keep tabs on current fishing conditions all over the world and many have personal experience with both the local areas and the charter boats and crews. Their recommendations are generally reliable.

When planning a trip with a booking agent, it's wise to pose a number of questions in advance of paying a deposit. Things you should know in advance might include many of the issues previously

A lot of factors are involved in selecting a charter boat.

C

mentioned regarding setting your own hook, releasing fish, the type of tackle supplied and condition (you may wish to bring your own), extra costs, the name and phone number of someone who fished with the charter captain (or camp) the same time last year; if the crew speaks English or there's an interpreter, and other issues germane to visiting a foreign country or a lodge with fishing services. Confirm everything in writing to avoid misunderstandings. And never accept, "No problem," as a satisfactory or complete answer to any of your questions; get details.

Make-up charters.   An angler who would like to fish aboard a charter boat but doesn't have the money to hire one alone, or doesn't have enough people to share the expense, sometimes has an alternate option. Many charter boat captains will work up what are commonly referred to as "make-up charters." As the name implies, anglers call and have their names added to a list, and as soon as sufficient anglers are available, usually four to six people on the average-size charter boat, everybody can be accommodated.

There are some operators at major fishing locales who specialize in make-up charters. This is especially true in tourist areas, and often you can talk with the concierge of a hotel adjacent to a fishing area; they will be pleased to work with you to get you aboard a quality boat with a captain and crew capable of putting you into a good day's fishing. Keep in mind that it is often to their benefit to direct you to a professional, qualified captain. In many instances they receive a referral commission, but equally important is that as a result of your being a guest in their establishment, it is in their best interest to provide the best service possible.

Another source of make-up charters is often a local marina, especially those with large fleets of charter boats. Frequently there are boats without regular, full-boat charters, and the captains advise the marina office that they are available. Occasionally you may luck out and get a captain who's anxious to be on the water and who will sail even if he only has two or three anglers, paying only a portion of the regular charter price. While it may seem like a losing proposition on the surface, the income may at least pay for boat costs, and it keeps the captain and his crew active. They also stay with the pulse of the fishing, which is an important consideration in chartering.

What's especially nice about make-up charters is that they bring together a group of people who essentially have the same problem: They want to go fishing, but don't have anyone to go with. You'll usually find that conversation is spontaneous, and many friendships develop, with a camaraderie that is typical among outdoor enthusiasts.

Other matters.   Some people have unreasonable expectations with regard to hiring a charter boat, and it's important to remember that this is fishing, not an exact science, and that things can change from day to day. This makes it unpredictable as to whether on a given day you can expect to catch a certain size or number of a particular type of fish. Do not be disappointed if your day doesn't live up to the catch of the previous day, and don't expect to get a break on the charter cost for this unless there have been extenuating circumstances.

You should recognize that although this is a fun outing or vacation day trip for you and your companions, it is also a job for the captain and the mate. Help out where you can if that is feasible, and be grateful for their assistance and for good results. Recognize that the length of the charter doesn't mean the amount of time that you will necessarily be fishing; an eight-hour charter almost always means that you are back at the dock eight hours after you left, even if you had to spend two hours to get to and from the fishing grounds.

Finally, don't be upset with the captain if you move off a place that has been producing good action, such as a reef or wreck. Once you've caught a reasonable amount of fish from a known structure like this, the captain may move to another area to avoid overfishing that spot. This is not unreasonable. Both you and he would like to return to that place again sometime and have good results, but that won't happen if the structure is beaten to death every day.

See: **Fishing Lodge; Fishing Regulations; Guide Boat; Party Boat.**

CHARTER BOAT CAPTAIN

A licensed skipper of a charter boat *(see)*.

CHART, NAVIGATIONAL

Also called a nautical chart, this is a precise and accurate aid to navigation printed on durable paper and used by mariners. Navigational charts are primarily used in boating applications because they detail water areas, but also have great value to anglers who use them to identify depths, habitats, and underwater features relevant to specific fish species.

See: **Maps.**

CHART PLOTTER

Electronic navigation equipment featuring maplike or chartlike detail in electronic cartographic form, used in conjunction with GPS.

See: **GPS.**

CHART RECORDER

Also known as a graph recorder, this is a sonar device using a roll of paper upon which the images of fish, objects, and underwater terrain are displayed.

See: **Sonar.**

CHILE

Chile has an excellent fishing reputation, yet it is an angling enigma. This 2,650-mile-long country is entirely bounded on the west and south by the Pacific Ocean, but its long coastline is currently not a hotspot for visiting saltwater anglers. The topography of Chile is dominated by the Andes Mountains, and the country is highly regarded for its freshwater trout fisheries. Yet brown and rainbow trout are not native here. The primary angling action for trout occurs in the country's southernmost 1,000 miles. Despite its many lakes and rivers, Chile is not noted for diversity in its freshwater species, although this doesn't bother trout anglers, as it has plenty of diversity in its trout waters.

Because Chile's most popular trout waters are in the Southern Hemisphere, they can be enjoyed when most visiting anglers from the Northern Hemisphere are experiencing cold weather at home. This advantage—coupled with terrific scenery, friendly and hospitable Chileans, and trout that are eager and large on average—makes for an inviting situation.

Bordered on the north by Peru, on the northeast by Bolivia, and on the east by Argentina, Chile has an average width of under 110 miles and is fringed by the Andes along the entire eastern region. The Andes are widest in the north and include broad plateaus and many peaks over 20,000 feet. Northern Chile, which is arid, also features low coastal mountains on the west; between these and the Andes is a plateau region. This area has few freshwater resources, but the northern coast has garnered historical billfishing significance.

In central Chile, which has a Mediterranean climate (somewhat akin to northern California), the plateau region becomes the fertile Central Valley, which is about 600 miles long, between 25 and 50 miles wide, and the most heavily populated area of the country. This is Chile's main agricultural area. The Andes in central Chile are narrower and lower, but they have the most important passes. The central coast has Chile's finest natural harbors.

Southern Chile has a temperate climate (similar to the Pacific Northwest in the United States) and is without an interior valley. The Andes here are mainly under 6,000 feet, and the coastline is markedly indented with fiords. Archipelagoes extend along the southern coast from Chiloé Island to Cape Horn, and are actually the peaks of submerged coastal mountains. These include the Chonos Archipelago, Wellington Island, and the western portion of Tierra del Fuego. The central and southern regions contain the greatest freshwater fishing opportunities, with numerous deep blue lakes and hundreds of rivers and streams that are relatively short and flow from the western slopes of the Andes toward the Pacific Ocean.

Large portions of Chile are considered geologically unstable and are subject to earthquakes and volcanic activity. These events have affected some freshwater resources over the years.

Freshwater

Although it has been visited by intrepid anglers since the late 1940s, and despite its size and abundance of waters, Chile has relatively few fishing camps. Many operators have come and gone over the years, and possibly two dozen in total exist today, perhaps half of which have opened since the early 1990s. That may reflect a new interest and growing popularity in Chilean fishing, but it also implies an abundance of wilderness water that is rarely visited.

For the trout angler, Chile offers wading or drifting in rivers under a backdrop of snowcapped peaks, and dozens of trout daily, all in the 1- to 3-pound range and some that press the 5- to 8-pound mark. The fishing isn't always that good, and some rivers have better-size fish than others, but good numbers of quality fish combined with gorgeous scenery is the reason anglers travel to Chile.

Chilean rivers are relatively short, generally rising in the Andes and flowing west to the Pacific; some originate in Argentina, and most are fed primarily by the perpetual snow cover of the Andes. Brown trout and rainbows are the mainstays, although some brook trout exist as well in certain streams. The browns were introduced from Germany in 1905, while the rainbows and brookies came from the United States.

The "Lake Region" of Chile has gained a lot of attention in the past, and is well known among traveling trout anglers. Situated about 500 miles south of the capital city of Santiago and located in an area extending roughly from Temuco to Puerto Montt (the southern part of Chile's central region), the Lake Region includes Lakes Villarrica, Ranco, Rupanco, Panguipulli, Riñihue, and Llanquihue—all of which are connected to rivers and in the past have supported the bulk of Chilean angling. Among the rivers of note are the Cumilahue, Calcurrupe, Petrohue, Tolten, San Pedro, Trancura, Liucura, Furaleliu, Nilahue, and Carran. Many of the region's larger waters, such as the Petrohue, are floated in drift boats, as well as waded.

The southern region, however, has some of the less-accessible and more undisturbed fishing, with excellent angling for brown and rainbow trout. The arrival of camps in the area has focused increased attention here. The region is sometimes referred to as the Chilean Patagonia, because the Patagonia region of South America once included the southern parts of both Argentina and Chile. Local lakes include Paloma, Yelcho, Pollux, and others, which likewise are amid rivers and generally known for larger trout on average. Significant rivers include the Paloma, Azul, Balboa, Simpson, Desague, Sin Nombre, Nireguao, Futaleufu, Palena, and Cisnes. There are many more, including tributaries, and other lakes. Some are floated as well as waded.

Although trout are the almost exclusive quarry of visiting anglers, steelhead, chinook salmon, and coho salmon also flourish in southern coastal rivers.

 Among the most primitive of gamefish, tarpon are long-lived; a tarpon held at Chicago's Shedd Aquarium lived an estimated 60 years.

These have become established over the years as a result of escapes from pen-rearing farm operations along the coast. Sea trout exist in the southernmost region of Tierra del Fuego *(see: Argentina)*.

Trout fishing in southern Chile consists almost exclusively of fly fishing, primarily because local lodge operators want it that way. Various methods produce, so an assortment of fly-line types are necessary; 6- to 8-weight rods are suitable. Flies vary widely, but it's worth knowing that a common trout food item in many Chilean rivers is a small freshwater crab called the *pancora*. Felt-soled waders are necessary for mossy rocks, and light chest waders are best. Good sunglasses are necessary, especially when sight fishing for trout, which is sometimes possible in low clear waters.

The trout season in southern Chile is the opposite of what visitors from the Northern Hemisphere are accustomed to. Spring and summer extend from October through April, and trout fishing generally takes place from November through early April Some anglers prefer to fish early and late in the season, but in some locations this may have no bearing. Later in the season, however, larger browns often move out of the lakes and into rivers prior to spawning. Early-season fishing can be productive during periods of high cold water due to runoff.

Saltwater

Approximately 3,100 miles of Pacific coastline should offer opportunity for exceptional saltwater fishing, but Chile has not developed this resource; boats, guides, information sources, and the like are almost nonexistent in most areas. Their availability has fluctuated a good deal over time, in part due to offshore current shifts, in part to commercial activities.

Chile has a great number of beaches, coves, bays, fiords, and the like from which to fish, and Chileans primarily fish from the shore or surf for corvina and flounder. Some boat fishing exists near shore for these species, as well as other bottom fish and mackerel, but offshore fishing is nearly nonexistent. The reasons for this are many: Boats and tackle are unavailable or too expensive, the water can be rough, and recreational angling is of minor interest and is not a tradition among Chileans. A host of other factors influences this trend

Perhaps ironically, Chile is engraved in the historical annals of broadbill swordfish angling. This is because the northern coast was once a hotbed for this species. The northern ports of Antofagasta, Tocopilla, Iquique, and Arica, were jumping-off points for offshore expeditions for swordfish, black marlin, striped marlin, dolphin, and tuna, with Iquique being the most prominent site. In the early 1950s, Iquique had a few sportfishing boats, and expeditions here by renowned anglers S. Kip Farrington and Michael Lerner were well chronicled. Many broadbills, and numerous large fish, were caught here, and sight fishing for these bruisers became legendary. The current all-tackle world record—a 1,182-pounder—was registered at

There are no crowds to compete for the trout on the Rio Baker.

Iquique in May of 1953, and, in light of the world-wide depressed state of swordfish, seems like an untouchable accomplishment. Two other record swordfish, 759 and 772 pounds, were also caught during this period.

This great fishery existed thanks to the course of the cold, rich Humboldt Current and its upwelling nature near shore, but the fishery for broadbills and marlin declined as a result of commercial fishing, the vagaries of El Niño, shifts in the Humboldt Current, political changes within the country that made angling forays less likely, and perceived problems related to the collapse of anchovy stocks off Peru. As a result, there was almost no offshore fishing effort for decades, until the mid-1980s. Swordfish of 533 and 657 pounds were caught in the late 1980s at Algarrobo, about 50 miles south of Valparaiso, which is much farther south from Iquique. These established new line-class records and they, as well as other fish caught and observed around the same time, proved that big fish still existed. This did not result in a rush of anglers, however, in part because the entire coast is devoid (or nearly so) of recreational boats, there is no infrastructure for salt-water angling tourism, and hot billfisheries exist elsewhere. Also, with most swordfishing being a sight-and-bait affair, it's necessary to have calm conditions. A preponderance of rough weather here from January through May can mean a lot of down time, not to mention cold-weather fishing.

Nevertheless, the central coast is one that might be viable in the future should a number of conditions change. It could well be the place for catching record swordfish in the future.

CHINA

Covering nearly 3.7 million square miles of Asian territory, China is the third largest country in the world, yet it is virtually anonymous to anglers. With no known history of fishing for sport, with a great dependence on inland and marine fish as protein, and with no infrastructure for angling-related travel, China has been virtually off the world angling radar screen for most of the twentieth century. This is likely to be unchanged in the near future, although the country has enormous water reserves and the world's longest history of fish cultivation and propagation. There are rainbow trout in China as well as a smattering of largemouth bass, plus the mother lode of carp; pelagic species are reportedly caught sporadically off Hong Kong. There are no reports of commendable opportunity, however, although the exotic nature of travel within China is in itself meritorious and compelling.

To comprehend why there is so little opportunity in such a large country with a lot of water, and also why it might have potential in the future, it is helpful to understand the overall nature of the country, its natural resources, and the needs of its people.

China has a diverse landscape, not unlike the United States. Its higher elevations are generally in the west and include some of the world's highest mountain ranges and plateaus; mountains take up more than 40 percent of the country, mountain plateaus more than 25 percent, and basins and plains the remainder. Climate varies from subarctic to tropical, with alpine and desert regions, and there are broad water resources.

China's population of more than 1.4 billion people constitutes more than 20 percent of the world's population. Obviously, fish are an important food resource today, but they have been so for thousands of years. China's Fan Li is believed to be the first person to breed and raise fish (reportedly common carp); this occurred more than 2,400 years ago in the eastern part of the country, at Wushi in Kiangsu Province. Fan Li wrote the first known document on fish culture, a book entitled *Fish Breeding,* in 473 B.C.

The Chinese have almost exclusively viewed fish as an integral part of farming. Fish culture in China exists in ponds, reservoirs, and lakes. Chinese farmers and scientists have become masters of integrated fish farming. They have long utilized cut grasses to feed pond carp, for example, and now use animal manure (treated to kill parasites and bacteria) for fertilizing the ponds where fish are raised.

They have also mastered fish production in rice fields (paddy culture). Rice has always been the number one grain crop in China, and relics unearthed from the mid-Eastern Han Dynasty (A.D. 25–220) have shown that even at that time farmers placed excess carp fry from cultivated ponds in their rice fields. This cultivation practice was evidently reserved for carp until the middle of the twentieth century, but since then has included other species, among them tilapia, catfish, and rainbow trout (in the north). Rice-fish farming has become much more refined in recent decades and is now an important component of the national drive to increase food production.

Commercial sea fishing and inland fish farming have been vitally important to the Chinese, both for national consumption and export. Taken together, these constitute an annual fisheries harvest that has ranked China first among all nations since 1990. Sea harvests have been decreasing, however, particularly in local waters, and aquaculture efforts—especially inland—have intensified with the encouragement of the Chinese government. China has 192 fisheries research institutes with nearly 30,000 specialists. Five fisheries institutes have 9,000 students. Virtually all of this effort is focused on food production and not on fisheries development or management that provides recreation. As a result, China's food-fish harvest since 1985 has increased at roughly 10 times the annual rate of increase in the rest of the world. The production of inland aquaculture ranks first in the world, and 75 percent of it occurs in ponds.

This success has not been without some problems, including reduced water quality, water needs that exceed supply in some areas, fish diseases, and declining inshore saltwater fishery resources. Concurrent with this are problems with regard to pollution of major rivers and deforestation. The objective of fisheries managers in China in the late 1990s was to increase aquaculture production by 60 percent. This would seem to leave little room for predatory species favored by anglers, given that the benefit and revenue from whatever tourism is so generated would be dwarfed by commercial activities.

The major fish species for inland aquaculture today are grass carp, black carp, silver carp, bighead carp, common carp, crucian carp, Chinese bream, mud carp, and tilapia. Marine aquaculture in China is mostly operated in shallow seas, shoals, and bays, with cultured species including shrimp, oysters, mussels, scallops, various clams, abalones, red porgies, black porgies, grouper, and crabs.

Freshwater Resources

The major rivers, and more than 50 percent of China's watershed, drain to the Pacific. Rivers account for nearly 40 percent of China's water resources. The most well-known rivers include the Yangtze, Yellow, Lujiang, Lancangjiang, Yarlung Zangbo, Heilongjiang, Liaohe, Haihe, Huaihe, Xijiang, Tumenjiang, Yalujiang, Qiantangjiang, Minjiang, and Oujiang. Although these rivers are large, some are nearly or virtually dry at their mouths due to upriver needs and usage, and many are extremely dirty.

Lakes contribute more than 42 percent of China's water resources. The most prominent freshwater lakes are Boyanghu, Dongtinghu, Taihu, Hulunci, Hongzehu, Chaohu, Weishanhu, Xingkai, Qinghai, Dalai, Namucuo, Qilincuo, Nansi, Boshiteng, Aibi, and Zarinanmucuo; reportedly, more than 130 of China's lakes cover more than 100 square kilometers. Large saline lakes include Qinghaihu, Namujiehu, Zhalinghu, and Bositenghu.

The remaining 18 percent of China's water resources are contained in tens of thousands of reservoirs (one source pegged the number at 38,600, although there are conflicting reports), and many tens of thousands of ponds. The majority of reservoirs and ponds are in the east, mostly in the vicinity of the middle and lower reaches of the Yangtze Valley. The overall water area is increasing as the Chinese dam rivers and create new reservoirs and ponds. Many of the reservoirs, and reportedly some of the lakes, are subject to extremes in fluctuation. Bighead carp are the most prominent species in reservoirs, and grass carp the most prominent one in ponds, which are heavily eutrophic.

According to a report by the Food and Agriculture Organization (FAO) of the United Nations in 1977, China has more than 500 species of freshwater fish; these are dominated by cyprinids (carp), and of these some 200 are suitable for table use. According to a 1981 report, China has 709

freshwater fish species and 58 subspecies, excluding 64 species that migrate between sea and inland waters.

The FAO characterized China as "having fewer native species of freshwater fishes than in North America, and many fewer than in South America or Africa. The Asian species are more typically riverine. Thus, the natural or spontaneous fish fauna of lakes and reservoirs does not encompass the variety of feeding habits that is typical of the faunas of most African water bodies. Mollusks, detritus, phytoplankton, and plant feeders, and even zooplankton feeders adapted to open water, are often missing."

There are evidently only a few native predator species in China, and it is unclear what these are, although a couple have been reported to be similar to popular Western species. The evidence, however, is mainly anecdotal. In 1982 some anglers spent several days fishing large Jingpo Lake in southeastern Heilongjiang Province, which is in northeast China. The lake, which covers about 90 square kilometers and is 45 kilometers long, produced a fish locally called *Ao Hua Yu*, or "number one fish," which was described as basslike with tiger marks (striations) on its side. These fish were said to average 7.5 kilograms in the lake and reach up to 15 kilograms, but this has not been verified. However, it may have been a species referred to by the FAO in its 1977 report as mandarin fish *(Siniperca chautsi)*, although it appeared to resemble a large white bass in body shape and could be a member of the Percichthyidae family (which includes white bass, yellow bass, and striped bass). The gringos called it a "China tiger bass," although there is no such recognized nomenclature, and its exact taxonomic classification is uncertain. The species was reportedly a game battler, however.

These anglers and their local guide also suggested that the lake, which has depth to 180 feet, held lake trout and muskellunge, but these species were not caught or personally verified. Whether there are lake trout, or a different species of lake-dwelling trout or landlocked char, here or elsewhere is unknown, and the probability of true muskellunge is remote, although the existence of a pike- or muskielike fish (perhaps the so-called pikehead of Southeast Asia) is plausible. The anglers fished from old rowboats, from narrow 30-foot-long motor launches, and also from shore.

A traveler to the middle of mainland China in 1997 reported seeing largemouth bass in a restaurant aquarium, and was told that they existed up to 5 kilograms in one lake in the region. The presence of largemouth bass in China has also been reported by a Canadian fisheries authority and by an independent resource organization, although specific locations and sizes in China have not been confirmed, nor is it known if they exist in any waters that are accessible for public recreation.

It is believed that largemouth bass, and also walleye, have been brought to China for cultivation

---

Anglers often cast to the wake of a cruising fish. The wake indicates where the fish has been; you need to determine where the fish is headed and then cast ahead of it.

C

purposes and to assess their prospects as farmed fish. Reportedly there is a fish similar to the walleye in Chinese waters (it has the similar opaque and reflective eye), although where and how widespread is unknown. Native predator fish have been expunged from natural lakes and reservoirs when local water authorities determined that the body of water should be domesticated and used for food-fish production. If predators are found in existing or created lakes and reservoirs, the body of water is often poisoned to remove the predators and then stocked with filter-feeding species.

The FAO reported just two favored species of predatory fish in China in its 1977 report, which was based on a visit by a professional fisheries team. One was the basslike species previously noted; the other was a snakehead *(Ophiocephalus argus)*, or murrel, which is a bowfinlike species, some of which are barred along the flanks and may be known as striped snakehead or chevron snakehead. Although possibly growing to 2 or more feet in length, this fish would be of little interest to visiting anglers.

Other species, although in unknown quantities and distribution, that have been reported in China's freshwaters—according to an independent resource organization in 1997—include various sturgeon, catfish (including channel catfish in aquaculture and wels catfish), and tilapia; copper and putitor mahseer; barramundi; and white-spotted charr (also known as Siberian charr and which may be the species referred to as salmon in some literature).

While rainbow trout are farmed in the cooler areas of northern China, aquaculture reports from Chinese agencies indicate that salmon (species unidentified) are also produced, but it is unknown if there are any wild or naturally occurring trout or true salmon in this country, with the exception of Tibet. Brown and rainbow trout are known to exist in the high mountain lakes of the Himalayas, and they may exist in some waters of Tibet near the border with Bhutan, Nepal, India, or Pakistan, but this is speculative. Many of the lakes in the Tibetan Plateau of southwestern China are saline, but the headwaters of many major Chinese and south-Asian rivers originate in the mountain and plateau region.

Saltwater

On the east, China borders the Bohai, Yellow, and East China Seas; and on the south it borders the South China Sea. The coastline is 18,000 kilometers long, and the more than 6,500 islands along it form numerous bays.

There are reportedly more than 3,000 marine species in the region, and coastal resources have been pressured for a very long time, especially in more recent times. The economically important species caught commercially in local waters, according to Chinese scientists, are various croaker, chub mackerel, scad, Pacific herring, Spanish mackerel, Chinese herring, pomfrets, flounder, butterfish, porgies, red snapper, cod, sardines, sharks, and anchovies. Cuttlefish, squid, octopuses, mussels, oysters, clams, abalones, and scallops are among the mollusks taken, with shrimp and crabs among the shellfish. Aquaculture is practiced in the tidal inshore areas.

Little, if any, angling takes place, as it is inconceivable to fish for any purpose other than securing food, although reports indicate some sportfishing for pelagic species at several oil platforms 60 to 90 miles offshore from Hong Kong. Small black marlin are said to be available here—plus wahoo, yellowfin tuna, barracuda, and rainbow runners—from April through October. Sailfish were reported in the past but not in recent times. There were reportedly 6,500 pleasure boats in Hong Kong in 1998, but only two were rigged for sportfishing.

Other species, although in unknown quantities and distribution, were reported in China's brackish and marine waters by an independent resource organization in 1997. Among them were various sharks, trevally, tuna (including bigeye and bluefin), snapper, grouper, and flounder; dolphin; barramundi; kawakawa; cod; steelhead; blue marlin; and oxeye or Indo-Pacific tarpon. As with inland species, there is apparently little, if any, sportfishing effort for these species.

Ninety miles from mainland China, the island of Taiwan reportedly has recreational fishing for grouper, snapper, jack crevalle, sea bass, trevally, mackerel, corvina, barracuda, needlefish, and ladyfish, mainly from rocky shores and surf. Swordfish, marlin, sailfish, wahoo, yellowtail, albacore, and dolphin were reported in the late 1980s in offshore waters, mainly some 42 miles southeast of Taiwan at Lanyu (Orchid) Island, although the present status of fisheries there is speculative.
See: Mongolia.

CHINE

The longitudinal strake between the upper portion of a boat above the waterline, and the bottom; the meeting spot of the bottom of a hull and the sides.

The angle of a hard chine is very precise whereas the angle of a soft chine is rounded or curved. A hard chine typically benefits speed but sacrifices comfort in heavy seas; a soft chine does not permit as much speed as a hard chine, but takes big waves more softly. In fiberglass fishing boats, manufacturers may modify these two basic chines to create a style that improves the performance of a particular hull, often with the added objective of producing a dry ride by deflecting spray.
See: Boat.

CHIRONOMID

Insects of the genus *Chironomus*.
See: Midges.

C

CHOCK

A block or wedgelike object set behind the wheels of a tow vehicle at a launch ramp to keep the vehicle from sliding backward while a boat is being launched or loaded; also a fitting that controls a rigging or mooring line.

CHRISTMAS ISLAND

See: Kiribati.

CHUB

In North America, the term chub is used to describe many unrelated fish, all of which are members of the largest fish family in the world, minnows *(see)*. Although the word minnow is commonly applied to many small fish, to scientists the minnow family is a large and old group of bony fish, Cyprinidae, which includes river chub as well as countless species of shiners *(see)*, dace *(see)*, and carp *(see)*.

Confusion about the chub branch of this family exists nevertheless; this is particularly evident when one sees "smoked chub" on a menu or in a fish market. This is actually a fish-market description for species of whitefish *(see)* or cisco *(see)* from the Great Lakes, which are not cyprinids. True chub are rather bony and do not make admirable table fare.

Species and habitat. Twenty-six minnows merit the name chub and inhabit waters from the Appalachians to the Pacific Coast. The larger, primitive chub of the genus *Gila* inhabit western North America. The most familiar chub may be the creek chub *(see: chub, creek)*, an inhabitant of creeks and lakes throughout eastern and central North America. Also well known are the various river chub, which are members of the genus *Nocomis* and famed architects of the fish world.

River chub are olive-colored minnows with stout bodies, large scales, and light yellow to red orange caudal fins. The seven *Nocomis* species are identified by unique patterns and the size of the tubercle spots on the head and snout of males. Female and young chub lack tubercles.

The largest river chub are bull chub and bigmouth chub, and the largest males range from 12 to 15 inches. Bull chub and bigmouth chub are rivaled in size only by the fallfish *(Semotilus corporalis; see fallfish)*, the largest native eastern minnows. The closely related creek chub *(Semotilus atromaculatus)* rarely reaches 12 inches in length.

River chub are widely distributed in streams of eastern and central North America, although some have restricted distribution: redspot chub in eastern Oklahoma and parts of Kansas, Missouri, and Arkansas; redtail chub in the highland rim of the Cumberland River drainage of southern Kentucky and north-central Tennessee; bigmouth chub in the New River drainage of North Carolina, Virginia, and West Virginia; and bull chub from parts of Virginia and North Carolina.

Other species (hornyhead, river, and bluehead) are more widely distributed. The hornyhead is a common baitfish, often called redtail chub. The wide distribution of chub stems from past geologic events, such as glaciation and changing river courses.

Chub often occur in schools with other minnows, particularly stonerollers, in runs and pools of clear, moderately sloping gravel and rock-bottomed streams and rivers. It is not unusual to see young smallmouth bass swimming and actively feeding near chub. Chub and young bass may be eating the same prey, but older smallmouth bass readily consume chub. Bluehead chub, redspot chub, and redtail chub more commonly inhabit smaller streams, whereas river chub, bull chub, and bigmouth chub are more common in main stems and large tributaries.

Chub are primarily sight feeders, taking small invertebrates from the bottom or from the drift. Although they have small barbels, they may not be useful for feeding, more likely being a trait retained from a primitive ancestor. Chub primarily eat immature insects, although they also eat aquatic worms, crustaceans, mollusks, water mites, small fish, and aquatic plants. Chub prefer to feed in the swifter-flowing sections because more food is available there, but to avoid sapping their energy, they usually stay within 4 inches of the streambed, often behind larger stones.

Spawning. Chub spawn in spring when water temperatures are between 60° and 75°F. During the breeding season, males develop large hornlike tubercles and spectacular coloration—pink, rose, yellow, orange, and blue, depending on the species. The "bluehead" name comes from the intense slate blue head of the spawning male.

Colors and tubercles signal spawning readiness to nearby ripe females. Male river chub, bigmouth chub, bull chub, and bluehead chub in breeding colors also have a swollen head, or "nuptial crest." Female chub do not grow as large as males and lack tubercles, presumably because females play no role in building or defending the nest.

Large body size and tubercles help the male repel other males that invade his territory. Fights can be vicious, and the nuptial crest cushions blows to the head from other males. Tubercles may play a role in stimulating the ripe female, but probably the tubercle patterns help female chub recognize the correct species for breeding.

All species of *Nocomis* chub construct gravel mounds, as do the tongue-tied and cutlips minnows (genus *Exoglossum*). Fallfish and creek chub build a similar, although more ridge-shaped, mound. The gravel nests of chub are truly impressive in size.

The male chub first picks up pebbles with his mouth or pushes them with his head to remove them from the nest site, forming a depression 2 to 4 inches deep. He then fills that depression with pebbles to form a platform, and adds pebbles to the platform to make a circular mound.

Males collect pebbles from areas within 20 feet of the nest, but sometimes they gather material from as far away as 80 feet. The geometric shape of the mound suggests that the architect understands fluid mechanics. The mound actually creates an eddy behind the nest and slows the current in the spawning trough where eggs and sperm are deposited.

Often the male is spooked before an observer encounters a nest, leaving no clues to the builder's identity. As water levels recede, some chub mounds are left "high and dry," resembling castles. Early ichthyologists thought that children or crayfish built the mounds.

Bigmouth and bull chub build the largest mounds, up to 50 inches in diameter and 15 inches high. The usual pebble used in mound construction is 1 to $2\frac{1}{2}$ inches in diameter, which is quite a mouthful, yet some are as large as 4 inches in diameter. The largest stones must be pushed or dragged to the mound. It has been estimated that a male chub spends 20 to 30 hours building his gravel mound and may travel up to 16 miles during his many short forays to collect pebbles.

To indicate readiness to spawn, the male expels pebbles from the spawning trough, positions himself over the trough, and quivers his anal fin and lower body, as if fanning the spot intended for eggs. The female then approaches and swims beneath the male. The male quivers his caudal fin and embraces the female as eggs and milt are shed in the spawning trough. The brief spawning act is repeated dozens of times in rapid succession with one or more females. The male then collects more pebbles to cover the fertilized eggs and repeats the process; he tends the nest for up to two weeks after spawning.

Spawning may be interrupted when male chub from other nests attack the spawning male. Hornyhead chub have been observed diving head-first into the spawning trough of another male and dislodging some eggs, which are quickly eaten by other chub. After such bold affronts, the fight is on.

Perhaps as a means of sizing up each other, males sometimes align themselves and swim upstream with strong tail swings, head butting, or heads pressed together in a fish version of locking horns. At other times, the nesting male and his challenger swim in a circular pattern over the nest, not unlike wrestlers moving around the ring, planning their next move.

Chub use these displays to avoid fights they can't win. Fights usually occur between similar-size males. In later spring, one might find dying males with head wounds, suggesting the heavy toll of breeding behavior.

Egg-eating predators, which are common in streams, occasionally invade the chub's nesting territory. Male chub charge and head-butt intruding suckers that are easily five times heavier. Sometimes a group of male chub simultaneously attack the intruder, an effective signal for a sucker to move on.

Building a large gravel mound is an enormous undertaking that must be worth the investment or the habit never would have evolved and persisted. The mound protects eggs and larval chub from predators, current, temperature variation, and siltation. The gravel mound also provides greater aeration and water flow.

Community nests.   Chub mounds become hotspots for spawning by other minnows as well, often resembling "minnow orgies" as hundreds of minnows in breeding color are attracted to these mounds. It has been reported that at least 13 minnow species have reproduced on a bluehead chub nest. Several species of minnows may spawn on a single chub mound, and the male does not chase the minnows away, even as he continues to spawn. Minnows spawn most often on chub mounds regularly attended by a male chub; abandoned mounds are inferior.

This relationship may be obligatory for some minnows; yellowfin shiners, for example, do not display reproductive colors or behaviors unless spawning bluehead chub are present. Apparently, yellowfin shiners are stimulated by the spawning activity of chub. These and other nest associates benefit from a clean, protected nest site, tended by the diligent male chub. Chub may also benefit from the association because chub embryos and larvae represented only 3 percent of the young reared in these "co-op" mounds. So the more numerous young yellowfin shiners diluted predation on young chub.

As builders and tenders of the spawning habitats for numerous species, river chub are what biologists call "keystone species." In other words, removal of chub from a stream would be more detrimental than the removal of other species. One researcher discovered that chub nests were possibly the only suitable spawning gravel for common and rosyface shiners in a small creek. Chub concentrate gravel that otherwise would be scattered over unsuitable nesting substrates, thereby enhancing minnow reproduction.

Chub watching and angling.   Chub nests can often be spotted by the observant angler, beginning when water temperatures first exceed 60°F. Concentrate a search for nests in knee-deep water with noticeable current and patches of gravel. If you're wading, use polarized glasses to reduce surface glare. For a closer view, don a face mask and gradually move through likely areas such as transitions between riffles and pools, where surface turbulence is slight.

The most obvious benefit anglers derive from chub is using them as bait when fishing for such top predators as smallmouth bass, spotted bass, catfish, walleye, and sauger. These fish are all adaptable predators that normally take advantage of locally abundant chub and minnow populations.

Chub do not have a devoted following of anglers and are not considered a gamefish, but some people

 A six-month growth of barnacles on a ship's hull can result in having to burn 40 to 45 percent more fuel to maintain cruising speed.

C

do angle for them with light tackle; there is plenty of enjoyment to derive from this sport, especially since it is easy to find unfished populations. Small chub can be caught by fly fishing with small nymphs or by drifting a bit of worm. Larger chub are more prone to streamers, standard-size nymphs, and spinners. Chub stay close to the streambed, so it's important to get and keep your offering in the chub's domain.

Threats. Like other stream fish, chub are threatened by large-scale alterations of native habitats. Chub populations have been locally reduced or eliminated by excessive sedimentation, daily flow fluctuations that obliterate mounds, deep-release dams and associated cold tailwaters, gravel mining, and nonnative fish predators. Good land management practices that restore or protect streamside vegetation and natural stream meandering benefit chub and the rest of the fish community. None of the chub in the genus *Nocomis* are federally threatened or endangered. Some are, however, listed as species of special concern due to their limited distribution or recent declines in distribution or abundance.

CHUB, BERMUDA   *Kyphosus sectatrix.*
Other names—Bermuda sea chub; French: *calicagère blanche;* Spanish: *chopa blanca.*

A member of the Kyphosidae family of sea chub, the Bermuda chub is a commonly encountered species, although not one that is aggressively sought by anglers. It is often caught in clear-water harbors and around reefs. Most individuals are reportedly good table fare, but their flesh spoils quickly and should be eaten soon after capture.

Identification. The Bermuda chub has an ovate profile with a short head and small mouth. A yellow stripe, bordered in white, runs from the edge of the mouth to the edge of the gill cover. The body is compressed and generally steel or blue gray with muted yellowish stripes. The fins are dusky, the tail forked, and the scales are usually edged with blue. It may occasionally have white spots or blotches. A less common, very similar, but larger-growing relative is the yellow chub (*K. incisor*).

Size. Bermuda chub commonly weigh $1^1/_2$ to 2 pounds and measure 10 to 12 inches in length.

Bermuda Chub

Reported maximum lengths and weights vary widely; the all-tackle world record is a 13-pound, 4-ounce Florida fish.

Distribution. In the western Atlantic, the Bermuda chub occurs from Massachusetts and Bermuda south to Brazil, including the Gulf of Mexico and the Caribbean; in the eastern Atlantic it occurs south of Morocco to the Gulf of Guinea, and rarely in the Mediterranean or off Madeira.

Habitat/Behavior. Like most other sea chub, the Bermuda chub is a schooling species that moves quickly and is often abundant in clear water around tropical reefs, harbors, and small ships.

Food and feeding habits. Bermuda chub mainly feed on benthic algae, and also on small crabs and mollusks. Because of its small mouth, it nibbles food and is regarded by anglers as an accomplished bait stealer.

Angling. Although Bermuda chub are numerous in some areas and very energetic and scrappy fighters, there is no concerted angling effort for them. They are primarily caught in clear-water harbors around docks, and incidentally on reefs. They are not aggressive feeders like most predators, and patient anglers using light tackle catch them on small hooks baited with pieces of shrimp, crab, or cut bait. Because they nibble food, it's necessary to set the hook quickly the instant that one gnaws on the bait.

CHUB, CREEK   *Semotilus atromaculatus.*
Other names—horned dace, common chub, brook chub, mud chub.

The creek chub is one of the largest chub and a member of the minnow, or Cyprinidae family, making it a distant relative to carp *(see)*. Occurring in great abundance in North America, it is important forage for sportfish, often competes with those larger predators for food, and, because it is hardy and lively, is also a prominent bait used by anglers.

Identification. The snout of the creek chub is pointed and its mouth large, with a single small barbel in the corner of each jaw, sometimes hidden between the maxillary and the premaxillary. The body is stout, colored olive brown on the back, silvery on the sides with shades of iridescent purple, and whitish on the underside. Both adults and juveniles have a blackish stripe along the back and a black caudal spot, although these become faint or absent on adults. There is a large black spot at the front of the dorsal fin. Breeding males take on an orange hue, also gaining 4 to 8 large, thornlike tubercles (thus the name "horned dace") on their opercles, body scales, and fins. The creek chub may occasionally appear to be speckled with black sand, but this is the result of being heavily covered with the parasite that causes black spot disease (which is harmless to the fish and is not transmittable to humans), and not as a result of natural coloring.

Other characteristics include a complete lateral line with 47 to 65 scales, 8 anal fin rays, 8 dorsal fin rays, and a pharyngeal tooth count formula of 2-5-4-2 (2 teeth in minor rows and 4 or 5 teeth in major rows).

The creek chub can be distinguished from the pearl dace *(Semotilus margarita,* a k a *Margariscus margarita),* by its larger mouth. The fallfish *(Semotilus corporalis; see fallfish),* is a strikingly similar fish to the creek chub, but with larger scales, larger eyes, and without a black spot on the dorsal fin.

Size/Age.   The creek chub can attain a maximum length of between 6 and 12 inches, depending on environment; the average 4 to 6 inches long. Adult males grow faster than females, and the largest creek chub are usually male. They can live up to seven years.

Distribution.   Creek chub are found from the Maritime Provinces of Canada west to Montana and south to Texas and northern Georgia. Their distribution extends throughout the eastern half of southern Canada and the central and eastern United States. They occur in the Atlantic, Canadian (of New Mexico), Great Lakes, Gulf Coast, Hudson Bay, and Mississippi drainages.

Habitat.   These fish prefer cool, clear water in the gravel-bottomed pools and runs of creeks and streams. In dry weather and during low water, they can survive in isolated pools. They are seldom found in lakes. Some ichthyologists refer to the creek chub as "king of the headwaters" because they are often the largest fish found in very small streams. Deeper pools usually contain the largest individuals. Creek chub are tolerant of some pollution and can be abundant in urban streams.

Spawning behavior.   Creek chub are pit-ridge spawners that build their gravel nests in runs and the downstream sections of pools. Nest building and spawning occurs between March and June in water temperatures ranging between 12° and 20°C. Creek chub have an interesting spawning ritual, which begins in spring when the male digs a pit in the stream bottom by removing bits of gravel with his mouth. He carefully guards the pit where the spawning occurs and attracts a female. Adult males are territorial during the breeding season and can be observed swimming in parallel, chasing each other, and ramming their tuberculate heads against each other. Some males attempt to spawn over the nests built by other males. Spawning occurs when the male wraps his body around the female and eggs are released over the nest. A single female can produce more than 7,000 eggs, but only a portion of these are released during a single spawning event. Females are often observed floating belly up for a few seconds after spawning. They quickly recover and can spawn again.

Food.   Creek chub are omnivores that feed on a variety of foods, including zooplankton, aquatic and terrestrial insects, crayfish, mollusks, frogs, and fish. Adult creek chub have been shown to primarily consume fish, including the young of their own species.

Creek Chub

Angling.   Although sometimes caught for recreation, often by stream netting, the creek chub does not support much angling effort; however, most captured fish are used as baits. Although edible, it is usually not eaten due to a multitude of tiny bones. **See: Chub; Minnow.**

CHUB, EUROPEAN   *Leuciscus cephalus.*
Other names—chub; French: *chevaine;* German: *aitel;* Italian: *cavedano;* Spanish: *cacho.*

The European chub, which is primarily known simply as chub in Europe, is an important coarse fish *(see)* that is widely sought by anglers and the subject of minor commercial interest. It is a member of the large Cyprinidae family, which includes minnows *(see)* and carp *(see),* and is a darker and larger-growing relative of European dace *(see: dace).* One of the warier coarse fish, it is pursued with varied baits and some lures, and by stalking as well as by stillfishing.

Identification.   European chub have a stocky and somewhat cylindrical body, a blunt snout and large wide mouth, slightly forked tail, and an erect dorsal fin. The scales are dark-edged, which produces a grille-like appearance. The back is dark and the sides golden brown tapering to a white or gray belly; the fins are tinged with pink coloring in young fish and are darker in older fish. Young chub may be confused with dace *(Leuciscus leuciscus);* fin coloration is different, however, as is shape. The chub has convex dorsal and anal fins, whereas those of the dace are concave.

Size/Age.   This fish is commonly caught in the 1- to 3-pound class, and any specimen over 5 pounds is a good one. The all-tackle world record is under 6 pounds, but this is not indicative of its potential, as the European chub is reported to attain a maximum of 16 pounds. Chub exceeding 7 pounds are rare, however.

European Chub

Distribution.   The European chub is widespread in inland waters from Portugal east to the former Soviet Union and Turkey.

Habitat.   Creeks and fast-flowing rivers are the principal domain of this chub, although it also enters brackish water in the eastern Baltic and has been introduced into some lakes. The upper reaches of flowing water are primary habitat, but it may compete in those environs with salmonids and be viewed with disfavor by anglers.

Behavior.   During spawning season male chub develop large hornlike tubercles like their smaller North American relatives *(see: chub).* They spawn in the spring in rocky shallows, and the young form schools, or shoals, and feed eagerly; these schools dissolve by maturity, however. Adult chub are not a school fish, but they are nearly so. There may be a collection of chub in one place, and these may be of similar or disparate sizes, but this is a loose collection rather than a school. Only when alarmed do chub seem to act as one, and otherwise the fish behave singularly.

Food and feeding habits.   The omnivorous European chub has a general-purpose appetite, which is one of the reasons why it is an amenable fish for anglers. It consumes aquatic insects, invertebrates, crayfish, snails, assorted small fish, lamprey eel larvae, and other food items, and may feed at all levels of the water column. Its powerful pharyngeal teeth (throat crushers) allow it to cope with various forage, some quite large.

Unlike most other cyprinids, these chub are prone to feeding throughout the day, rather than principally in low-light conditions, and they are not as averse to cold water. In warm water, they are likely to feed aggressively and may then be easily caught. Yet they are also discerning and sometimes take a hooked bait without offering any strike indication.

Angling.   Like many other coarse fish, chub are tenacious but not spectacular fighters. Fishing for chub is similar to fishing for other coarse fish, although there may be more of them available in a given spot than of other species.

Most chub fishing is done from the bank or shore, with people fishing river runs that are from within 2 to 6 feet deep. Bottom fishing with assorted baits is the primary tactic, and this involves intensive prebaiting or chumming *(see),* using groundbait *(see)* and an assortment of prepared, processed, and natural baits. Maggots, corn, worms,

cheese, bread, pastes, slugs, and other items are used. Hooked baits may be fished with or without a float. Anglers use rods from 11 to 14 feet in length, line from 3 to 6 pounds in strength, and No. 8 to 20 bait hooks.

Although chub are mostly taken on baits, it is very possible to use other methods, especially fly fishing. Weighted nymphs are especially popular, followed by wet flies, terrestrial imitations, and dry flies dappled on the surface.

Chub are sometimes sought by sight fishing, rather than by angling in known chub-holding runs or pools. This requires spotting fish and using stealth to approach them, as chub spook readily.

CHUB, HORNYHEAD   *Nocomis biguttatus.*
Other names—redtail chub.

The hornyhead chub is a member of the large Cyprinidae family, and a fairly common stream and river resident; smaller specimens are used as bait by anglers.

Identification.   The body of a hornyhead chub is slender with a rounded snout. The mouth is large, almost terminal, with a small barbel above the jaws, and it has pharyngeal (throat) teeth. Hornyhead chub have dark-edged scales, a complete lateral line, and seven anal rays. Their coloring is bluish olive on the back, yellowish with iridescent green on the sides, and whitish on the underside. On the adult male, there is a bright red dot behind the eye; on the female the dot is brassy colored. Yellow iridescent stripes run along the back and the sides. There is a dark caudal spot, which is darkest on juveniles, around the snout. Breeding males are colored pink with pinkish orange fins and have many tubercles on the head.

The hornyhead chub can be distinguished from a bull chub *(Nocomis raneyi)* by its shorter snout, larger eyes, and red dot behind the eye. The bluehead chub *(Nocomis leptocephalus),* although strikingly similar, has no red dot behind the eye, and it has a large loop on the right side of its intestine, distinguishing it from the hornyhead.

Size.   The average size for a hornyhead chub is 8 inches, although some can grow to up to 10 inches.

Distribution.   The hornyhead chub is found from New York west to Wyoming and Colorado and south to northern Arkansas; in its easternmost range in New York, it can be found in the Niagara River and several streams in the Mohawk River system, but it does inhabit the Susquehanna, Delaware, and Hudson Rivers.

Habitat.   This species lives in small to medium-size rivers and streams. It prefers warm, clear waters with a moderate to sluggish current, especially with a sandy, gravelly bottom and aquatic vegetation.

Spawning behavior.   The spawning season for hornyhead chub is from late May through June, when the male develops tubercles on the head. The male builds a nest from pebbles *(see: chub).* Other kinds

Hornyhead Chub

of fish use this nest for spawning, but the male hornyhead will ward off other fish of the same species.

Food. The hornyhead chub is omnivorous, feeding primarily on insect larvae but also consuming small crustaceans, earthworms, and algae.

Angling. As with other chub, the hornyhead presents minor sportfishing value, although it is occasionally caught on small jigs, flies, and spinners fished close to the streambed. The greater interest is in smaller specimens as bait for predator species.
See: Chub.

CHUB, SEA

Sea chub are members of the Kyphosidae family, which are distributed in the Atlantic, Indian, and Pacific Oceans. Some 50 species are among this group, and most are usually found near shore. Some are primarily algal feeders, others are primarily carnivorous. Most are medium-size schooling species and are abundant in clear water around tropical reefs, harbors, and ships. The most commonly known member is the Bermuda chub *(see: chub, Bermuda).*

CHUBSUCKER

Chubsuckers are members of the sucker *(see: suckers)* family, Catostomidae. They are divided into three separate species: the creek chubsucker *(Erimyzon sucetta)*, the lake chubsucker *(Erimyzon oblongus)*, and the sharpfin chubsucker *(Erimyzon tenuis)*. All species are extremely similar and are interchangeably referred to as "suckers" or "mullet" in different locales.

Chubsuckers are of little importance commercially and are predominately ignored for sportfishing. When taken from cold water, however, chubsuckers have good-flavored, firm flesh. Because of their abundance and their large size, suckers often account for the greatest biomass in streams and lakes, making them important forage for predator species.

Identification. Chubsuckers are characteristically defined by their small, protruding, suckerlike mouths and thick fleshy lips. Creek, lake, and sharpfin chubsuckers are similarly colored a greenish bronze, without a lateral line. There are usually 10 to 12 dorsal rays and 7 anal rays. The scales are dark-edged, and, on the creek chubsucker, accompanied by dark blotches. Young chubsuckers have a concentrated black band from the tip of the snout to the tail, on top of which is a yellow band. Breeding males are dark with a pink orange tint and several tubercles on each side of the snout. The creek chubsucker has a chubby body, whereas the lake and sharpfin chubsuckers are slightly more elongated.

All suckers excepting the chubsucker have a fully developed lateral line.

Size/Age. Chubsuckers can grow to 13 to 15 inches, but they rarely exceed 10 inches in length. The average age for a chubsucker is 5, although one can live up to 8 years.

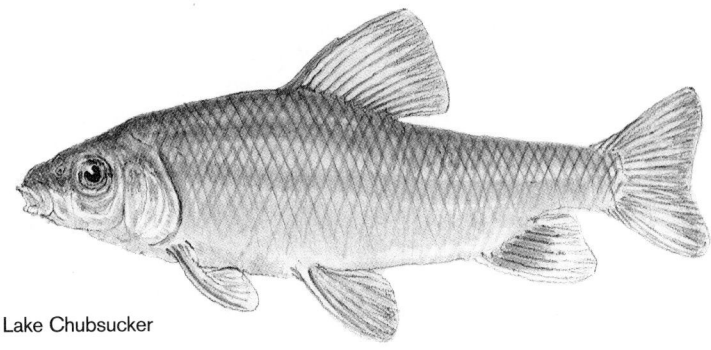
Lake Chubsucker

Distribution. Creek chubsuckers inhabit waters from the Great Lakes and the Mississippi River drainages south to Georgia and gulf slope waters. Lake and sharpfin chubsuckers inhabit waters similar to those favored by creek chubsuckers, including waters as far west as Oregon and as far south as Florida.

Habitat. Lukewarm, clear waters of creeks, small rivers, lakes, ponds, and swamps, or other waters without turbidity, are favored environments. Chubsuckers are seldom found in streams, favoring the depths of still, calm waters. As bottom dwellers, chubsuckers prefer sand, gravel, or silt bottoms with abundant vegetation.

Life history/Behavior. Spawning occurs in early spring in small tributary waters. Sometimes the male builds a nest, but the eggs are usually scattered randomly over sand, gravel, or vegetation bottom and left to hatch unattended.

Food and feeding habits. Chubsuckers are bottom feeders, consuming insect larvae, aquatic plants, and small crustaceans.

CHUGGER

A term for a popping plug.
See: Surface Lure.

CHUM

Various types of food and attractants used to interest, hold, and concentrate fish. Chum is generally used in quantity, most often for bottom-feeding or pelagic species of fish; it is most frequently employed in conjunction with the use of a hooked bait (hook bait), but may also be used to bring fish into the range of anglers who cast a lure or fly. Chum may include live baitfish; whole dead baitfish; chunks of fish; a ground-up hashlike mixture of fish, various aquatic organisms (including mollusks and crustaceans), worms, or sundry other foods; bread *(see: groundbait)*; grains; and processed foods. Chum may be dispensed by hand or in some type of containment device. It may be made and prepared by anglers or purchased ready-to-use from vendors; some items used as chum (shrimp boat refuse and bycatch, for example) are acquired from commercial fishermen and prepared for angling use.

Anglers who make their own fish-based chum primarily use the carcass of fish that they have kept and removed the meat from, or assorted forage fish that they have caught (usually by netting), perhaps mixed with mollusks or crustaceans, and mash these up using a heavy-duty meat grinder. Freshwater anglers have made creative soupy chums, particularly using worms, with kitchen blenders. Most mashed chum for saltwater fishing is purchased at bait stores, and shark anglers, who are especially likely to use chum, buy this by the bucket-load.

Chum is mostly used when anchored, and sometimes when drifting, but almost never employed for trolling. The use of chum is an integral part of many types of saltwater fishing. It is a small element of most freshwater fishing in North America, but an important one for certain species, in certain locations, and with some presentation methods, and is more popular in other parts of the world. In North America, the use of chum in freshwater is illegal in some localities, and a freshwater angler who wishes to use any type of chum should check on this, as well as what foods or baits are defined by the regulating agency as chum.
See: Chumming.

CHUM BAG

A mesh bag or sack filled with chum and lowered into the water next to a boat to attract fish.
See: Chum; Chumming.

CHUM LINE

The continuous underwater trail of chum and chum particles that is carried away from a boat by tide and or current.
See: Chum; Chumming.

CHUMMING

An effective technique for attracting, holding, and concentrating fish so that they will be available and susceptible to the angler's offerings. In chumming, various foods, called chum *(see)*, are put into the water to draw fish. The chum may include live baitfish; whole dead baitfish; chunks of fish; a ground-up hashlike or souplike mixture of fish, various aquatic organisms (including mollusks and crustaceans), worms, or sundry other foods; bread; grains; and processed foods. In saltwater, the items used for chum are most often endemic to the area, such as anchovies, herring, menhaden, or other forage fish, and are ordinarily favored by the species sought. Giant bluefin tuna, occasionally weighing more than a thousand pounds, will readily circle through a chum line, picking up chunks of herring, a fish they naturally consume. However, chum is not necessarily limited to the food on which fish normally feed. Bread is often an effective chum for some fish, as is whole kernel corn, neither of which exists in the normal food chain. A river carp, weighing just a few pounds, will eat both of these nonnatural items, as well as assorted processed baits. In saltwater, more anglers are experimenting with chum that includes oatmeal, cornmeal, and bread; and some use flavored dog food in bags or containers.

Chumming is most often done from a fixed position, such as an anchored boat, but chum may also be utilized in nearshore areas by a bank-, beach-, or pier-bound angler, and may be used while drifting in a boat. It is not employed when trolling but may be used to attract fish into casting range for both lure and bait presentations, although most chumming is coincidental with the offering of hooked bait.

Nearly every saltwater fish, and many freshwater species, will respond to some type of chum. However, chum is most practical for pelagic, or roaming, species, and for bottom-feeding fish. For sharks, chumming and fishing with bait is the major means of angling *(see: shark)*. It is also more practical for fish that rely on their sense of smell and taste more than vision, especially in freshwater. When one considers the energy expended as fish search for a meal, it's easy to understand why they will readily move toward the source of food, which in many cases is carried along by current. This may ultimately be their undoing, of course, when they encounter a piece of bait with a hook in it drifting or laying with the unhooked chum.

Dispersing chum in the water and then placing a hooked bait among it seems, at first glance, an easy technique and one that would guarantee successful angling, but this is not necessarily the case. There is an art to chumming, as well as to fishing in places where chum has been established. You must plan and work at it to be successful. Although chumming isn't always essential for a good day's catch, sometimes it does make the difference between success and failure. Moreover, chumming is not only used in conjunction with fishing a hooked bait, but often used in conjunction with lure or fly fishing. Saltwater fly anglers, for example, often chum on flats and in offshore waters to draw fish close enough to cast a fly to them.

When chumming, the route to achieving consistent success and minimizing failure is experience. Knowing where to anchor, whether to anchor or drift, how frequently to dispense the chum, when to add weight to your line to take the bait deeper, when to use a float to keep it at the right level, and other issues is possible only with experience. Even then, successful chumming may simply be trial and error. But, since so much of angling is finding and attracting fish, chumming is a technique that deserves consideration by every serious angler.

Saltwater Chumming

Chumming is an important element of catching fish in saltwater, yet this technique varies from area to area and for each species sought. There are literally scores of variations, and the following sampling is representative of the most popular. Chumming in saltwater should be in every angler's arsenal of options; keep in mind that although most saltwater chumming takes place from boats, it may also be practiced from jetties, beaches, bridges, piers, and bulkheads.

Because saltwater is affected by tides and current (plus wind), chum is dispersed according to the movement of water. It may be dispensed by hand or from some type of container that is lowered into the water, or via a combination of both approaches, plus some innovative spot methods (like sand balls mixed with chum, which disperse as they lower). Putting chum into some type of dispenser is common. Devices used to contain various types of chum include a pot, bucket, mesh bag, wire basket, plastic crate, and an assortment of similar commercial or homemade devices. The overall size of these, and the size of holes or mesh, will vary with the bait used. There are also commercially available chum logs (made of zooplankton and menhaden oil). Most objects are hung from a transom cleat and lay in the surface of the water aft of the boat. Some chum baskets or cages may be lowered to various depths or near to the bottom, with a heavy weight. Long-distance placement of chum is made via quick-release arrangements.

In chumming, the tide or current moves the pieces or particles away from the place where they are dispensed, and they form an underwater trail called a chum line. A visible surface indication of the presence and movement of the chum is called a slick. A chum slick is the oily surface of the water above a chum line, and it is also carried away from the boat and may or may not extend as far back as the underwater trail of chum. Usually the chum particles sink deeper as they are carried away from the initial drop point, and the slick portion of surface water dissipates at some distance from the boat.

Where the current is substantial, the chum line may extend a long distance, and particles may not sink very deep. In slack water, the chum line has much less distant movement and more vertical sinking. Many saltwater species are fish that move in and out of areas or move widely in search of food, so if they are present in the area you chum, they will eventually detect the chum line. However, in some locations, particularly in shallow backwaters and marshes, and on reefs, the fish are more resident and wander less, and may require more concentrated chum rather than a long trail.

Maintaining the chum.   To be successful at chumming, you must maintain a delicate balance. You want to attract the fish you're seeking so that they will respond to a baited hook or to an artificial lure that is fished in the chum line or in the area being baited. However, if you chum too heavily, the fish will often settle well back in the slick, gorging on your offering. On the other hand, if you chum too sparingly or fail to maintain a consistent flow of chum, the fish will show little interest and will often move off. Maintaining that perfect balance is something that isn't difficult, but it comes with experience. A good rule of thumb is to drop pieces of chum into the water at regular intervals. When fishing with a group of anglers, and especially aboard a boat, one person should be assigned the responsibility of maintaining the chum line because, in the excitement of catching fish, the chumming is often forgotten, only to be remembered too late, after the fish have moved out of the area.

Offshore, eastern Atlantic canyons.   Anglers seeking bigeye tuna, yellowfin tuna, and albacore in the offshore canyons and shelf areas of the eastern Atlantic often use a combination of chunks of fish and ground fish with excellent results. Boats either are anchored or drift along with the wind or current, usually along the edges of the dropoff, where an upwelling of currents causes baitfish to congregate and the larger gamefish to feed.

Forage species, such as butterfish, mackerel, and herring, are cut into pieces, usually about the size of your index finger. Five or 6 pieces from a butterfish, and 8 or 10 from a mackerel or herring, is about right. This is usually done before leaving for the fishing grounds to save the chore of doing it on the water. The chummer tosses three or four chunks into the water and watches as they drift away. When the chum is 30 to 40 feet from the boat, more pieces are tossed over.

Chum needs to be dispensed at a consistent rate to keep a steady stream in the water column, but without providing too much free food.

After a dozen or more chunks have been deposited into the sea, a ladle full of "soup," which is a mixture of ground menhaden, mackerel, or herring and equal parts seawater, is deposited into the ocean. This mixture disperses in a cloud and is carried along with the current. As fish detect the scent of the soup drifting along, they move toward its source, picking up tiny pieces of the ground fish and also the chunks. It's not unusual to attract a school of tuna and see the fish moving ever closer to the boat, as the fish vie for the offering drifting along.

As the chummer goes about the task of attracting the fish, anglers must work their lines so as to present the bait in a natural drift. Terminal rigging is very basic. Some anglers just tie a size 4/0 through 7/0 O'Shaughnessy, beak, or circle style hook directly to the ends of their lines. Because the members of the tuna clan are often line-shy, many anglers use fluorocarbon leaders. The hook is tied directly to the end of a fluorocarbon leader that is 5 or 6 feet long, and the leader is attached to the monofilament line using a Surgeons Knot.

A half or a whole butterfish is an effective bait in the chum line. Some people favor the head section of butterfish because it is more durable, and others prefer the tail section. The choice evolves from experience as to which works for you.

Because squid are abundant in offshore and canyon waters, as are mackerel, some anglers will obtain a live bait and work that in the chum slick with excellent results. A live bait in distress will often immediately attract tuna. If your boat has a livewell *(see),* you can keep fresh bait in it. Live spots or porgies, 6 to 7 inches long and caught from coastal rivers and bays, also make an effective bait in a chum line.

Once hooked, the bait should be permitted to drift back with the chum unimpeded. Keep no tension on the line, letting it drift along with the chum until it is a hundred or more feet from the boat. Then reel in and repeat the procedure. As a rule, the angler who works at keeping the bait moving along with the chum will catch far more fish than the angler who locks the reel in gear and keeps it in one position. If you let the line hang in a fixed position, the current pushing against the bait will often push it toward the surface and spin it in a manner that is not as attractive to the fish as a drifting bait.

Make sure the hooked bait drifts with the chum; this may require adjustment from time to time. When there is little or no current, the chum will sink directly beneath the boat, as will your bait. With a moderate current, the bait and chum will usually flow together, and this is easily observed in the clear offshore water. If you see the chum settling deep and the current carrying your line near the surface, attach a rubber-cored sinker to your leader about 5 feet from the bait. Select a sinker size that will keep the bait drifting at the proper depth.

At times, even with a light current carrying the chum, the bait may tend to sink too deep. You can counter this by inserting a tiny piece of Styrofoam into the bait to give it a bit of buoyancy.

Another possibility is using a 4-inch block of Styrofoam with a slit cut into it; place your line in the slit, adjusting it so the bait will be suspended at a desired level as you let it drift back in the chum line. This may prove effective at keeping the bait just 10 feet beneath the surface or 50 feet deep. Catching fish beyond the latter depth is generally not a result of fish feeding on the chum, although some anglers do set one or two lines to depths of even 200 feet for the tuna and occasional swordfish feeding at those levels. An inflated toy balloon may also be used as an effective float.

This is an overview of offshore chumming, and elements may be modified as conditions warrant. Some anglers rely especially heavily on the use of chunks of bait, which has come to be called chunking. This term refers to the use of pieces of fish meat, often in 2- to 3-inch cubes, especially for chumming yellowfin and bluefin tuna. The procedure is essentially the same as that described earlier, although heavy pieces sink deeper and faster than smaller chum and particles, so you have to be constantly attentive to the location and condition of your hooked chunk.

In fact, you have to be alert at all times in this type of fishing. As you permit your line to drift in the slick, the fish will move up and inhale your bait and swim off with it in an instant. It will take longer to read this sentence than the reaction time needed to set up on the fish. A good rule is to always keep your rod pointed in the direction the line is drifting, with ever-so-light pressure on the line to keep it from overrunning. As the fish moves off, lock your reel in gear, lift the tip smartly to set the hook, and the fight is on.

Inshore, eastern U.S.   Chumming for inshore species, such as bluefish, striped bass, bonito, school bluefin tuna, Spanish mackerel, king mackerel, and little tuna, is similar to offshore chumming. Basically, tackle is scaled down from the 50- to 80-pound outfits used offshore to more appropriate 15- to 30-pound-class tackle. Likewise, hook sizes from 1/0 through 5/0 are more in order. Even the chunks of bait used as chum are smaller—usually about the size of your

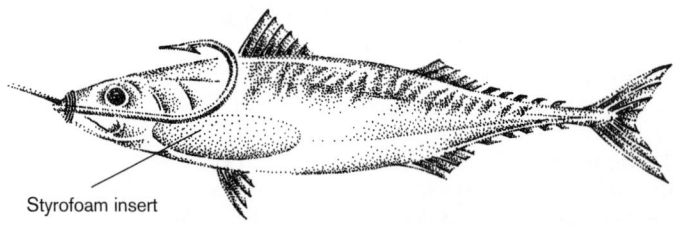

Styrofoam insert

To give a bait the buoyancy that it needs to drift along with chum, insert a piece of Styrofoam into the stomach cavity, forcing it down the mouth; then insert the hook and sew the mouth closed. This method is typically used with whole mackerel or herring when offshore canyons are being fished for various tuna.

thumbnail or slightly larger—as are the baits. Small mullet, spearing, sand eels, and killies are all effective in attracting strikes when drifted back in a chum line, and chunks or strips of butterfish, mackerel, croaker, bluefish, spot, and menhaden are popularly used.

Menhaden is the preferred chum substance; it is commonly purchased in frozen blocks by private and charter boaters. A few operators, including some party boat operators, have large electrical grinders to mince fresh menhaden onboard—an operation that is noisy and messy. Some inshore menhaden chummers will ladle out chum; others like to put the frozen chum in a covered plastic 5-gallon bucket that has been riddled with 1-inch holes, hanging it alongside the boat with a rope that has been run through a hole in the side and the top. Fifty pounds of chum is recommended for a full day of fishing, especially if the water is warm and the currents swift.

Arrive at your designated fishing spot before the top or bottom of the tide, and allow some time to anchor and get the chum line going. Use the frozen material for chumming, but bait up with fresh fish pieces. Fresh bait, which has not been previously frozen, works best and does not become as mushy on the hook. Although at times any piece of bait works well, strips may be more effective in moderate current and chunks in heavier current.

One slight modification in terminal rigging is essential when the targets are bluefish and king mackerel, both of which have extremely sharp teeth. A 6- to 12-inch-long piece of No. 8 or 9 coffee-colored stainless steel leader wire, connecting the hook on one end and a tiny barrel swivel on the other, prevents these fish from biting through the monofilament. If you don't want to use a wire leader, which can be a detriment when the fish are leader shy, try a directly tied long-shanked hook, although now and then when a fish takes the bait deep it will still gain its freedom by biting through the monofilament.

Inshore/offshore, western U.S. Anglers on the West Coast of the U.S. enjoy exciting chumming for a wide variety of species when they're able to obtain live anchovies as chum. Southern California boats that fish the inshore kelp beds, along with long-range boats that head far to sea for albacore and those who head off the Baja Peninsula for yellowfin tuna, rely on the anchovies to bring gamefish within range.

Boats sailing from ports such as San Diego, Long Beach, and Newport Beach take on dipnets, popularly called "scoops," full of anchovies from bait barges anchored in coastal harbors. The anchovies are kept in livewells with circulating seawater to keep them in perfect condition until the fishing grounds are reached.

When inshore fishing at the kelp beds, boats anchor just off from the kelp, which is massive and looks like a willowy tree growing up from the sea

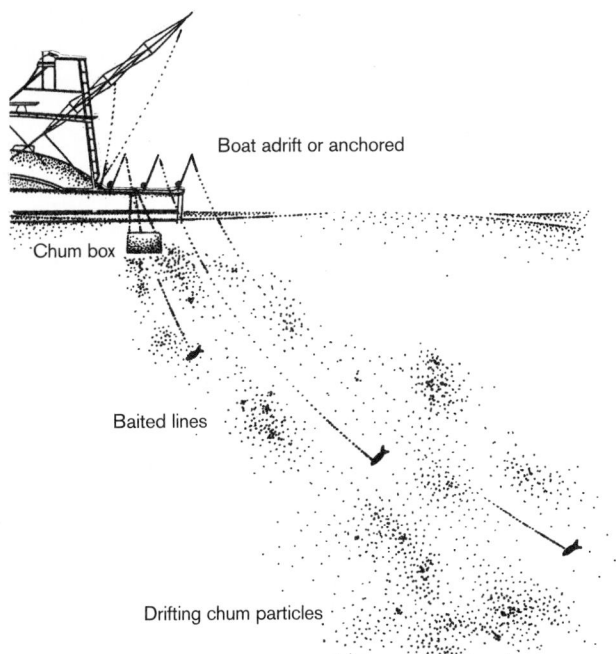

This is a typical ocean chumming scene; chum particles drift with the current, and hooked bait is allowed to drift at different levels amidst the chum.

floor. Its density makes it impenetrable to a boat, but the baitfish seek sanctuary there and gamefish roam nearby, occasionally making sorties into the kelp for a meal.

It takes patience and skill to coax fish from the kelp. A small dipnet is used to remove several anchovies from the livewell, and the chummer tosses these into the air so they land midway between the boat and the kelp. The excited anchovies either seek the sanctuary of the kelp or hurriedly swim back to the boat to seek shelter beneath its stern. Gradually the anchovies get the gamefish excited, and it's not unusual to have yellowtail, white seabass, bonito, barracuda, and kelp bass vying for them.

The most popular technique is to tie a tiny hook, such as a No. 3 or 4 O'Shaughnessy, Beak, or Claw style hook directly to the end of the line. Gently hook a lively anchovy under the gill collar. Anchovies are only 3 to 5 inches long, and too large a hook will restrict the movement of the live baitfish. While the collar-hooking method is most popular, some anglers hook the bait through the lips or the eyes, or place the hook into the back just ahead of the dorsal fin.

The bait is cast away from the boat, using either conventional or spinning tackle, and live-lined. An active anchovy will often swim about excitedly, and when gamefish are plentiful, the strikes come fast and furious. Always keep your rod tip pointed in the direction the line is moving; when a fish picks up the bait and moves off, lock your reel in gear and lift back smartly to set the hook.

Anchovies are also a popular chum on the Pacific's offshore grounds, as are several small species of mackerel and jacks. Long-range boats

C

usually sail with a supply of chum in the tanks but often stop on productive banks where anglers onboard fish to fill the live tanks with a supply of fish that can be used as live or dead chum.

In some cases, boats anchor over productive banks and kelp beds. Albacore anglers often troll until either albacore or bluefin tuna strike the trolled lures; while the trolled fish are being fought, the chumming begins and holds what is usually a school of albacore at the boat. The techniques used with other types of chumming are essentially the same. Maintain a chum line of the anchovies, but don't feed the fish. When done properly, you can actually see the albacore picking the anchovies right off the surface (called a "boil") and being teased ever closer to the boat by an experienced chummer. Keeping the bait drifting back unimpeded is very important.

Tackle and hook size must be tailored to the species sought. When huge 250- to 300-pound yellowfin tuna are targeted by long-range boats, short stand-up outfits are favored, along with fluorocarbon leaders. Tailor the hook size and style to the bait being used, with the smaller bends ideal for anchovies and the larger for mackerel and jacks as hooked baits.

While anchovies are popular Pacific Coast chum, the use of chunk bait has become more popular, following the lead of Atlantic Coast offshore anglers, as mentioned earlier. Some of the largest yellowfin tuna are now caught by chunking, using pieces of mackerel, rainbow runners, jacks, or other common fish, burying the hook inside the pieces so that the point is buried and does not penetrate the skin. The most common hooks for this are 8/0 and 9/0 sizes, usually connected to a 150- to 200-pound-strength fluorocarbon leader, which in turn is connected to the fishing line via a 4/0 to 6/0 black barrel swivel.

Hooked chunks are changed frequently and observed closely as they drift with unhooked bait. Strong current and no current require a little more attention and finessing, the former keeping the bait up and the latter permitting it to sink. When chunks sink for two minutes, they should be retrieved and redropped.

More on chumming with live fish.   As West Coast anglers who use live anchovies to chum fish know, there is a lot of merit to chumming with live fish as bait. In many cases, however, this is a specialized affair with several requirements: a means to store and keep the fish lively, the ability to obtain or find copious amounts of the proper baitfish, the ability to catch large numbers of live baitfish in a short time period, and sometimes gamefish that are concentrated or visible.

Livewells or baitwells with ample capacity and constant seawater replacement are standard today on many sportfishing boats, so it is possible to keep many small fish alive and frisky for a day of angling. The baitfish used are generally small and are located in inshore waters. Species will depend on locale but may include herring, anchovies, menhaden, mullet, and pilchards, to name some of the more abundant and popular ones. These are caught by using a net, in most cases a cast net *(see),* and this method takes energy and effort, and is dependent on finding ample schools of baitfish, usually in fairly shallow water.

In south Florida, charter boat captains developed a technique of using live pilchards for offshore fishing, especially dolphin and sailfish. They start by finding schools of pilchards via sonar in inshore environs. Softball-size balls of sand are readied and tossed in the water where pilchard schools are located, usually within 20 to 30 feet of the surface. When the balls are pitched into the water, they sink and disperse in a cloud, which draws the pilchards. A large cast net is thrown on top of the spot where the ball was pitched; if it sinks fast enough and the schools are large enough, a bunch of pilchards will be captured and quickly deposited into a livewell. This is repeated until at least 100 to 200 baits are garnered. Then the boat runs 15 to 20 miles offshore.

From a tower, the skipper can see cruising sailfish or dolphin that are clustered near weedlines or flotsam. The skipper searches for fish and, upon finding them, idles the boat while the mate pulls out a dipnet of live pilchards and tosses them individually in the vicinity of the dolphin or sailfish. Often this sudden presence of frisky bait gets the dolphin or sailfish to attack; the angler casts a hooked live pilchard amid the activity and in short order is into a fish. This type of live-bait chumming is repeated as long as there are fish around; then the boat moves and looks for more fish elsewhere.

This live-bait chumming is very exciting; it may also be used to draw gamefish close enough to the boat to take a cast offering of an artificial, usually a fly. It is a technique that should work well for some other species, inshore as well as offshore, although its success is hindered by a frequent inability to find ample live baitfish.

Bays, rivers, and estuaries.   In protected bays, rivers, and estuaries where striped bass, weakfish, spotted weakfish, and summer flounder reside, you may continue to use essentially the same techniques previously described, selecting as chum the foods most often found in these inshore waters. Common grass shrimp measuring 1 to 2 inches in length are plentiful in inshore waters and constitute a major portion of the diet of these species. Also very plentiful and a major source of food are the many species of crab, most notably the blue crab, calico crab, and sand crab. Both the grass shrimp and various crabs are very effective as chum and hook baits.

Grass shrimp may be obtained using a seine worked in coastal marshes and around pilings and along bulkheads. A couple of quarts are all that are needed to fish a tide. Crabs may also be seined or caught in traps. Since crabs are larger, they are often cut into small pieces. Some anglers prefer eating the crabs and saving the discarded pieces for later use as chum. Both the grass shrimp and crab pieces may be frozen and used as chum as the need arises.

The preferred method of fishing is to anchor along the edge of a channel where these species are known to move with the tide as they search for a meal. The same consistent chumming is all that is needed to attract them to your boat, just dribbling a few shrimp at a time overboard or a nominal amount of crab, or a combination of the two. The crab gills, stomachs, and swim fins offer a great attraction in the chum line; they are small enough that they do not feed the fish but still get them to the hooked baits.

Because the shrimp are so small, No. 1 through 4 Claw or Beak bait holder hooks are preferred. A tiny rubber-cored sinker is often used if the current is swift, sometimes in conjunction with a float, keeping the bait at a desired level. In many bay and river waters, you'll be fishing in depths of just 6 to 12 feet, so the float and sinker combo works well. Just let the bait drift out a hundred feet or so; reel back in and repeat the drift so that the bait moves along with the chum.

The techniques outlined for using grass shrimp and crabs as chum work well when fished from piers, bulkheads, docks, and bridges. In each type of platform, the key is positioning yourself so you can dispense the chum and have it carried away by the current, along with your baited rig. The float and sinker combination often proves deadly. It's not unusual to see the fish move up into the chum line, especially when you are fishing night tides from bridges, piers, and docks that have bright lights.

Chumming for bottom feeders. Bottom-feeding fish, such as winter flounder, sea bass, and porgies, also respond to a chum line, but for these fish the chum must be on the bottom. To accomplish this, anglers use a chum pot. The most popular size chum pot is 4 to 5 inches in diameter by 8 to 10 inches in height. It is made of a lead bottom, hinged metal top, and 1/4-inch galvanized wire mesh. The pot is filled with ground chum, and the chum pot is then eased to the bottom via a piece of cord. As the chum thaws, it oozes from the pot and is carried along the bottom, and the fish move toward the source of the free meal.

Many kinds of ground chum are effective when used in a chum pot. Ground menhaden, mussels, clams, conch, grass shrimp, and sea worms all have their devotees. A combination of these ingredients often works extremely well. If you have a little spare time, make up several batches of chum and keep them in your freezer. The chum is easy to make and stores well in the freezer, and you will have a supply on hand and ready to go.

After a strong storm, you can often go to the beach and collect a 5-gallon bucket of big sea clams that have been washed up by the storm. Remove all the clam meat from the shell; grind it up with a grinding head that produces pieces small enough to be carried from the chum pot's 1/4-inch mesh. You can also grind up the meat from sedge, black mussels, and conch. Be attentive to local regulations with regard to shellfish harvest, since some states prohibit collecting shellfish in certain waters.

Once you've ground the ingredients, add an equal quantity of boiled white rice to the same quantity of whole kernel corn. Mix all three ingredients together, and place the chum in paper cups of a size that will fit into the chum pot. Then freeze the cups of chum.

Chum Pot

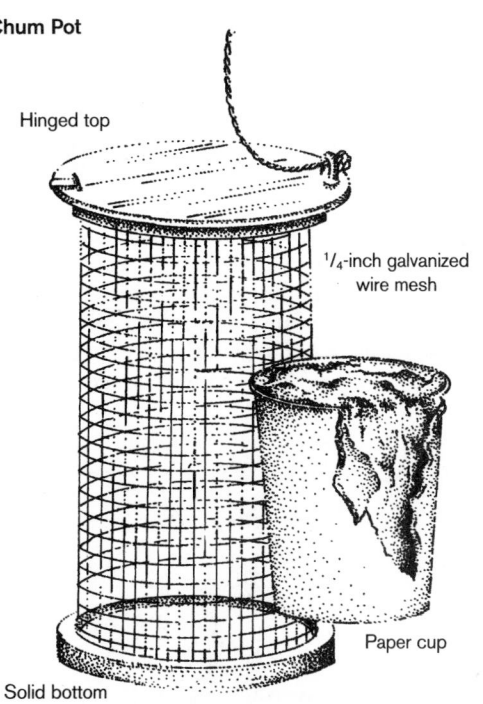

Hinged top

1/4-inch galvanized wire mesh

Paper cup

Solid bottom

Tear away the paper cup that contains the pre-frozen chum, place the frozen chum into a mesh pot, and lower it by heavy line into the water.

Upon arriving at the fishing grounds—which could be a mud flat or dock for flounder or a reef for sea bass, porgies, and tautog—peel off the paper cup from the frozen chum log and insert it into the chum pot. Ease the pot to the bottom via a piece of cord, and let the current carry the chum to the fish. You can use the same bottom rig for winter flounder that you would use if you were not chumming, usually a pair of No. 8 or 9 Chestertown hooks baited with bits of clams, sandworms, bloodworms, or mussels. In the case of sea bass, porgies, and tautog, a high-low rig, with hook size tailored to the fish in residence, works fine. Sizes 2 to 6 Beak or Claw hooks snelled to 8 to 12 inches of leader material are ideal. Strips of squid and pieces of clam and conch work well with sea bass and porgies; fiddler crabs and pieces of blue or green crabs are perfect for the tautog, popularly called "blackfish" or "white chins" in some areas. Occasionally it pays to give the cord holding the chum pot a good yank, especially if there is little current around slack tide; this will send a cloud of chum streaming from the pot.

Although all these species are fun to catch on light tackle, some anglers often attach a baited rig to the chum pot. This action often gets a couple of bonus fish for the pan and proves that the chum pot attracts them. Further proof of the chum's effectiveness is evident when you clean your catch; whether you've caught tuna in the canyons or flounder in bay waters, they will invariably have chum in their stomachs.

Still another trick to attract winter flounder in particular is to stir up the bottom by using a long pole with a plumber's toilet plunger or a garden cultivator attached to the end of it. Stirring the bottom creates a cloud of mud that is carried off by the current. The mud, in turn, attracts flounder to the area, where they often find sea worms, crabs, and shrimp that have been stirred up out of the mud.

Whole sea clams, conch, and mussels are used by many middle and north Atlantic Coast bottom anglers to attract codfish, pollock, sea bass, porgies, flounder, and a host of other bottom feeders. The clams, conch, and mussels are crushed with a hammer, and the combination of shell and clam meat is dispensed overboard to settle to the bottom around the boat.

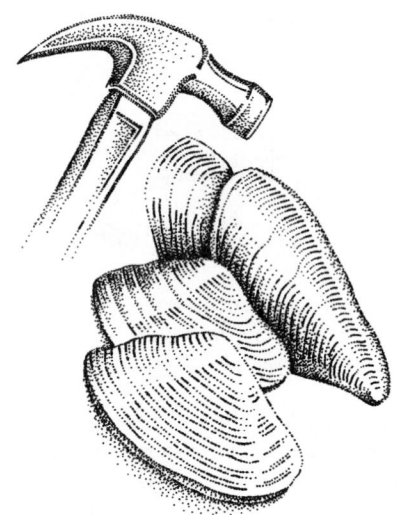

Use a hammer to break up whole clams and mussels; then drop the shells and meat overboard to attract a variety of bottom feeders.

When bottom-feeding fish pick up the scent of the chum, they move to the source and pick away at whatever meat they can obtain from the crushed shells. When they spot a piece of clam on a hook, they're onto it in a flash.

Reefs and wrecks. Chumming is very effective for reef- and wreck-dwelling fish. In Florida and along the Gulf Coast, many party boat captains who fish reefs and wrecks wouldn't think of leaving the dock without a good supply of chum onboard (roughly 5 pounds of chum per half hour of fishing). Their chumming techniques are quite productive and worth noting for the benefit of large- and small-boaters alike.

These skippers find a specific reef and then use sonar to determine where on the reef the fish are located. Then they position the boat and place an anchor in sand bottom just off from the reef, easing back and using sufficient anchor line to place the boat at the edge of the reef.

The act of ladling out chum and selecting appropriate devices and equipment to use for chumming is a big part of this technique. However, it can all go for naught if you are not positioned properly to fish with the chum or if the chum does not get where it needs to be to attract fish. Simply putting chum in the water, even if near an appropriate reef or wreck, does not guarantee that the chum will act like a fish magnet. Whether you anchor or drift, how you position the boat to set up your chum line is very important. The better boat captains may reposition themselves frequently until they get into the right position, since being just off the spot may sometimes make all the difference.

Chumming always takes place with the boat positioned upcurrent of the chummed location. When you are trying to attract fish from a deep location, such as a reef or a wreck, you must assess the flow of the current and the distance to your target area in order to determine where you need to be. A strong current will keep bait up, and a slow current will allow it to sink deeper, so you may need to position the boat farther away when the current is strong than when it is weak.

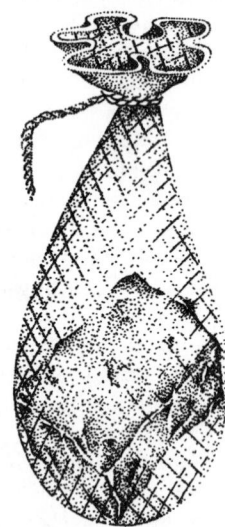

Place a 5-pound block of frozen ground fish chum in a cloth mesh bag, and hang it over the side of the boat so that it gradually thaws and oozes through the bag.

In many areas, and including Florida, reef chumming begins with frozen ground fish chum that is supplied in 5-pound cardboard boxes. The cardboard is pulled away from the frozen block of chum, which is placed in a mesh bag and hung over the side. As the chum thaws, it oozes from the mesh bag.

The deckhands then begin to dispense a separate chum concoction that was previously prepared. It is composed of thawed chum, rolled oats, and play sand in equal parts, with just enough water added to enable the chum to be molded into what are commonly referred to as "meatballs."

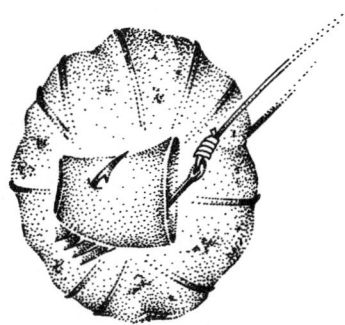

A chum meatball consists of ground chum, rolled oats, and beach sand, with a bait hook placed inside; a leader is wrapped around the meatball to hold it together while it settles to the bottom.

The chum is molded into a meatball the size of a tennis ball and dropped overboard around the boat. The weight of the sand in the chum mixture immediately takes the meatball to the bottom, where it crumbles and is carried along the bottom.

To get bigger pieces of chum to the bottom, "depth charges" are employed. These are made by using two small brown paper lunch bags. A layer of sand is placed in the bottom of one bag and then a layer of cut-up fish. Any fish will do, such as mullet, pilchards, balao, or scraps from fish that have been cleaned. On top of this is added a layer of rolled oats. This bag, which when filled will weigh about 2 pounds or more, is placed inside the second bag so that the package doesn't fall apart on its descent to the bottom. The bags are loosely twisted closed and dropped overboard near the bow of the

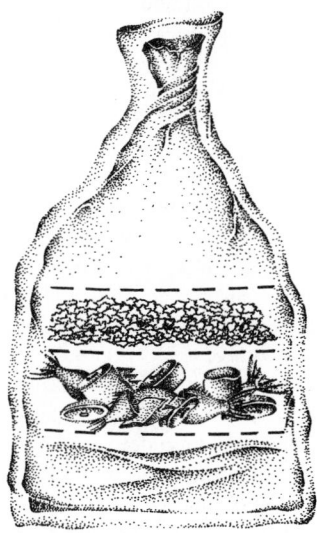

A chum depth charge can be made by placing one paper bag inside another and then layering the interior with sand on the bottom, pieces of bait on top of the sand, and rolled oats on top of the bait pieces. Twist the bag closed.

boat. When the depth charge reaches bottom, the paper bag quickly disintegrates. The oats and pieces of fish are carried along the bottom by the current, attracting the fish from the reef to a point beneath the boat.

Once the chum area has been established via the three sources of chum, fishing begins in earnest. Some anglers fish with a regular bottom rig; others employ a meatball rig to entice strikes.

The favored bottom rig is fairly simple. Slip an egg-shaped sinker of appropriate weight, usually 1 to 4 ounces, onto your line and tie a tiny barrel swivel to the terminal end to secure the sinker. Then tie a 24-inch piece of monofilament leader material to the other eye of the barrel swivel, and a Beak or Claw style hook to the end of the leader. The hook is often 1/0 size but may be smaller if small yellowtail snapper are the only target; the hook could be up to 6/0 size if big black grouper, Nassau grouper, or mutton snapper are in residence. Baited with live shrimp, pieces of squid, chunks of bonito, mullet, or other fish, the rig is lowered to the bottom. Now it's a waiting game until the reef dwellers are attracted by the chum in the depth charges, and eventually find your bait.

The baited meatball rig is another effective method of combining chum and bait. It works in Bermuda, the Bahamas, Florida, the Gulf Coast, and wherever reef dwellers are found. The rig is made up of the same mixture described for meatballs (the consistency should be suitable for forming into balls).

To make it, tie your hook directly to the end of the monofilament line. Leaders are seldom used, unless very heavy grouper or snapper are around. Bait the hook with a pilchard or a piece of cut bait. Mullet, balao, or a piece of bonito are very effective. Bury the bait carefully inside the chum, and make a complete offering that is the size of a tennis ball. Next wrap the monofilament line around this ball, much the same as you would wind up a ball of yarn, making two wraps and then a turn, for a total of about 10 wraps. Then firm up the ball so it stays together.

To fish it, strip off a sufficient length of line to reach the bottom. Toss the meatball away from the boat underhanded so that it lands 10 to 20 feet from the boat; let it settle unimpeded to the bottom. Keep the bail of your spinning reel open, or keep a conventional reel in freespool. While the meatball and bait are settling to the bottom, the meatball begins to disintegrate and creates its own mini-chum slick. In just a minute or so, the meatball will disintegrate and be ravaged by the first fish to reach it. By watching the line, you'll quickly know that the fish has it. As the fish moves off with the bait, keep your rod pointed in the direction of the line and close the bail or engage the spool; lift back smartly, and you're apt to be hooked to anything from a 2-pound yellowtail snapper to a 60-pound black grouper. The key is always having

sufficient line stripped from your reel so that the meatball reaches bottom unimpeded. If there is any drag whatsoever, the meatball will disintegrate completely on the way down, leaving the bait at midlevel and losing its effectiveness.

The meatball rig differs from other chumming tactics in that it is a self-contained chum-and-fish arrangement. You might call it in-line chumming. Another way to accomplish the same thing is to tie small bags filled with chum loosely on your line. Cut a paper grocery bag into 5-inch squares, and fill each square with up to a dozen pieces of freshly cut $1/4$-inch chunks of bait. Twist together the ends of the paper square and secure with two half hitches of light line/leader that extends from your bait rig. Bait a hook with the same chunks, and lower the whole thing to the bottom; give a quick jerk on the fishing line and the half hitches unravel, depositing a burst of bait right where your hook is. This technique can be used at mid-depths, too; some swordfish anglers put a baited bag pocket on their rig below a light stick and then yank the line to free the bait at the desired depth.

Other methods of deep chumming are also worth noting. In addition to frozen blocks of chum, options include shrimp bycatch, chunks, and live bait. Usually a mesh bag of chum is hung over the side in conjunction with other types of chum or bait usage. In some places, a bit of fishing effort may produce some species that can be used as fresh cut bait or as live bait; these include balao, bonito, and mackerel.

If the chum in the upper water column draws many small fish, you may want to get down deeper with the chum. Several innovative tactics make this possible. One is to secure a heavy (10 pounds or so) weight on the end of a strong line and place small mesh bags at various spots along the line. To draw fish from deep areas, you might try lowering live bait in a container with a trip line or trip mechanism. The container is heavily weighted, and the opening mechanism is tripped to free the bait. This can be repeated at higher levels in the water column, the object being to draw fish up from the bottom.

When reef and wreck angling, remember that fish may sometimes be found away from the objects. This is especially true with wrecks, where species like yellowtail, barracuda, and bonito may be 50 to 100 yards away on the downcurrent side when that current is strong. You may have to either reposition an anchored boat to approach these fish or strip-line your bait a long way to get to those fish. Also, for some types of fish, it can be advantageous to chum the entire water column, which may require a multiple-method approach to chumming.

Shrimping bycatch. Shrimp trawling is a major business, especially from the Carolinas to Florida and along the Gulf Coast. Shrimpers trawl mostly at night and anchor during the day, culling their catches and tossing overboard huge quantities of refuse, which is referred to as trash or bycatch.

The trash consists of literally dozens of species of small fish, squid, crabs, and crushed or broken shrimp. When dropped into the sea, this smorgasbord attracts hordes of gamefish in quantities that sometimes defy description. At times, hundreds of fish gather to feed on this chum line from the shrimp trawlers.

Anglers who know the shrimp trawler owners or captains may get permission to tie up to the stern of the shrimper and take advantage of the chum slick that is established as the trash is shoveled over. Others often pull up to a shrimper and for a few dollars or some horse trading take aboard a couple of containers filled with trash. Some shrimpers retain the trash and sell it when they return to port.

The approach used when chumming with shrimp trash is to cut small fish into several pieces and then dispense them overboard to attract a multitude of species, most notably yellowfin and blackfin tuna, bonito, dolphin, wahoo, amberjack, and even the occasional sailfish and white marlin. The trash chum also accounts for many fine catches of cobia and tarpon along the Gulf Coast. In offshore waters, the trash and cut fish are used essentially as previously described in the section on offshore chumming.

In inshore waters, the shrimp boat trash is regularly used to attract tarpon and permit to hooked baits. There is an extensive fishery for these great gamefish in the waters adjacent to Key West, Florida, for example, where the tarpon and permit follow regular patterns, moving with the tide as they feed. The accepted manner of chumming for them there is to anchor in an area they frequent; the anchor rope is attached to a quick-release floating red buoy so that you can get off the anchor quickly to chase a hooked fish.

Once positioned on anchor, small pieces of trash are dropped overboard and carried away with the tide. Light 20-pound-class tackle is most often employed on these fish, for the permit average 15 to 35 pounds and the tarpon range from 50 to 100 pounds or more. A size 6/0 O'Shaughnessy hook is used by many guides and tied directly to the monofilament leader, which is 50-pound test or stronger. Most baitfish are silvery and because of their reflective qualities are favored for tarpon, although most anything removed from the trash, including crabs, shrimp, or squid, will bring strikes. If permit are the target, a large manta shrimp is an excellent bait choice.

The key, as in all chumming, is keeping the bait moving with the chum. If there is no pressure on the line, the bait will drop deep as it moves along in the swift current with the chum. It's not unusual to pay out 125 feet of line. If a strike isn't received, the bait is reeled back in and the step repeated. Even though both tarpon and permit are big, their strikes are often subtle, and you have to be alert and set back quickly and hard, especially with tarpon because they have bony mouths that are difficult for a hook point to penetrate. Make your hooks needle sharp; sharpness often determines whether a hook penetrates or pulls out of a tarpon's mouth at the time of the strike.

Chumming bonefish on flats.   Many anglers feel that the only way to catch bonefish is to hunt for them by observing them tailing and then casting to them. However, wind conditions sometimes make it impossible to pole the flats; also, tidal conditions or a storm can roil the flats and make visual contact virtually impossible. Under such conditions, chumming is an effective way to attract bonefish within range.

Veteran bonefish anglers will stake out their skiffs on a promising flat or thoroughfare that is known to be frequented by bonefish at a particular stage of the tide. They prefer a spot that has a patch or two of open sand bottom within easy casting range of the skiff, usually 25 to 35 feet. They take live shrimp from the livewell and break them into two or three pieces. These pieces are tossed out and targeted to land on the sandy bottom. Then it becomes a waiting game.

Bonefish have fixed patterns of movement as they search for a meal and thus can often be seen approaching the area. They soon get the scent of the shrimp chum resting on the sand. It is then that anglers make their casts, with just a single live shrimp on a size No. 1 or 1/0 Beak or Claw style hook tied directly to the monofilament line. Many anglers have caught their first bonefish using this approach. Once you've mastered casting to these cautious fish, you can advance to casting tiny bucktail jigs to them or even employ a fly rod to present a shrimp fly or crab fly after the bonefish have been coaxed within range using the shrimp chum.

Chumming giant bluefin tuna.   Giant bluefin tuna are those weighing in excess of 300 pounds and at times achieving a weight over 1,000 pounds. These world travelers are classified by many as the strongest, hardest-fighting fish in the ocean. A single fish requires huge quantities of food each day to sustain it, so when large schools of giant tuna move into an area, they need an enormous quantity of forage on which to feed. These giants usually roam the sea from June through October from New Jersey north to the Canadian Maritimes, settling into areas where mackerel and herring, their staple foods, are abundant. Although mackerel and herring constitute the bulk of the giant bluefin's diet, tuna are not adverse to feeding on the abundance of squid, bluefish, red hake, and silver hake that are found in the area, along with most any fish they encounter.

This search for food and voracious appetite make tuna a natural for chumming, and the bulk of the summertime fishery is done by private and charter boats who anchor in choice locations and use huge quantities of forage species as chum. A single boat may dispense several hundred pounds of chum overboard in a day.

Catching these giants is a challenge requiring the finest quality tackle and a crew working as a single team. With 130-pound-class tackle, which is the standard for these bruisers, there is no room for error.

Anglers have learned that giant bluefin tuna usually follow a pattern of moving along the coast searching for food. Some feel that a tuna may travel a hundred miles in a day, making a massive sweep of an area. Chummers position their boats by anchoring in known tuna travel spots. Aboard are two plastic trash containers filled with either mackerel, herring, or menhaden, usually obtained directly from a local dragger. Chumming begins by taking a whole fish and cutting it into three or four pieces. If the mackerel or menhaden are small, they may be used whole or in halves.

Some chummers use what is popularly called "cod guts" as both chum and bait. These are the carcasses of fish that have been filleted by commercial fishermen. Sometimes the carcasses are cod, hence the name, but pollock, haddock, hake, bluefish, and other species are used. It's not unusual to have huge tuna swarm into this type of chum, gorging on what were 5- to 10-pound fish, which, even without the fillets, still weigh a couple of pounds with the head, body, and entrails remaining.

As with all chumming, steady maintenance of the chum line is essential. Often these big fish are spotted on sonar. They swim through the chum line, moving in a big circular pattern, picking up pieces as they go. At times when they move near the surface, you can actually toss three or four pieces, at 5-foot intervals, and the fish will draw in each piece of chum as it steadily swims along.

There are many ways to rig the basic 130-pound-class tackle to present a bait in the chum line. The standard approach is to employ 130-pound-test Dacron line, with a 150- to 200-foot-long piece of 250-pound-test monofilament spliced into the Dacron. Some anglers snell or crimp the hook directly to the monofilament. Others use a ball bearing swivel and a 10- or 12-foot-long fluorocarbon leader, to which the hook is snelled or crimped.

A wide range of giant tuna hooks are available, and opinions vary on which is best. Some anglers prefer a size 7/0 or 8/0 forged offset hook, reasoning that the small hook is more easily concealed in the bait; others prefer the extremely strong forged size 12/0 and 14/0 Martu models. Circle hooks have also come into vogue after their successful use in the Hatteras, North Carolina, winter giant tuna fishery.

Tuna anglers often bait up with a whole mackerel or herring, but some use half a fish so that the bait looks like the chum being employed. Fillets from a bluefish also bring strikes. When using dead baits, many anglers insert a small piece of Styrofoam into the bait; the Styrofoam makes the bait more buoyant and it drifts along in the chum much the same as a piece of chum.

 New Zealand is noted for its rainbow trout fishing, but rainbows are not a Kiwi native; they were shipped to New Zealand from the United States in 1883.

Live bluefish, which sometimes may be caught on the tuna grounds, are also an excellent bait. Often tuna anglers will bottom fish for silver hake or red hake, popularly called ling, to use as live bait. Live baits are hooked through the fleshy part of the back, just ahead of or behind the dorsal fin.

The most effective way to fish baits in a chum line for giant tuna is to work the bait, paying it out with the chum and then pulling it back in and repeating the procedure. Many people prefer to coil 100 feet of the fishing line in a plastic trash bucket, and pay line out hand over hand into the slick. This keeps the line from getting tangled, but safety should be observed so that your feet don't get hung up in the line as a giant takes the hooked bait and runs off with it.

The normal procedure is to pay out the line by hand with the rod positioned in a rod holder (usually in a fighting chair) and ample line in a bucket. When a strike is received, the fish is struck by hand by the person holding the line; then the line is quickly dropped and permitted to flow from the bucket until the hooked fish takes all the free line and then it is tight to the rod and reel.

For these big fish, it's not unusual to fish with 40 or 45 pounds of drag pressure, using a fighting harness (see: harness, fighting) with safety line attached to the chair, to assist in fighting the fish. As soon as the fish is hooked, the boat is released from the anchor line buoy, and the fish is followed by the boat, positioning the angler so maximum pressure

Frozen butterfish are thawed and cut into chunks, to be used for chumming tuna and sharks.

may be brought to bear. The objective is to boat the fish as quickly as possible, and some experienced big-game anglers can boat a fish in less than a half-hour, although individual fish may be fought for six hours or more.

During the early 1990s, a large school of medium and giant bluefin tuna were located in the waters adjacent to wrecks off Hatteras, North Carolina. This discovery resulted in the development of an exciting chumming fishery that takes place during January through April. During the day at that time, tuna travel from wreck to wreck or to wherever there are heavy concentrations of forage. Boaters locate them on sonar and then chum with half or whole menhaden, called bunker or moss-bunker, as the boat idles along above where the fish are spotted. This provides exciting fishing as the tuna boil to the surface, often snatching the bunker as quickly as they are tossed over.

Once the fish are boiling, the angler gets into the fighting chair, or attaches and hooks up a shoulder and belt harness if using stand-up tackle. As several pieces of chum are tossed, the Circle hook baited with a whole menhaden is tossed over and permitted to settle with the chum. When the fish are actively feeding, two or more tuna may zero in on a single bait.

Federal regulations limit a boat's catch to one medium tuna per day, which keeps down the take. The season on giants over 300 pounds is closed at this time, and the fish are usually brought to boat-side quickly and released. The Circle hooks are often lodged in the corner of the tuna's jaw, and release is easily accomplished, especially if using the proper hook remover.

Chumming sharks.   Chumming is the primary method of angling for sharks and is discussed in more detail elsewhere (see: shark). However, a few words about shark chumming are appropriate here, whether the purpose is to attract sharks to hooked baits (mostly the case) or to lures, especially streamer flies, that are cast, and particularly because some of the tactics employed primarily for sharks may have merit in other fishing.

It is true that most of the chumming activities previously mentioned will attract sharks, especially smaller sharks, and some techniques—like chunking with large pieces of fish or whole fish in conjunction with an established line—may have merit for the larger and more desirable species. However, sharks are especially sensitive to smell, so the approach is a bit different.

In shark fishing, a long trail of scent may be necessary to attract the shark, and even under favorable conditions this method can take a long time. Some shark veterans use a method referred to as power chumming or super chumming to jump-start the action. They do this by leaving a scent and chum trail along a quarter to half mile of water while en route to the primary fishing destination. The boat slows from cruising speed to trolling speed, and chum is dispensed continuously in the water. One method is to drag a milk-container crate of chum behind the boat; the crate is closed with mesh netting and is attached to a 40-inch poly ball, which keeps it on the surface. Another method is to use the washdown hose to spray overboard some chunks and pieces from a frozen block or can while the boat is underway at trolling speed; the can or block is placed in the splashwell or by the scuppers to permit quick washing into the water and the formation of a long trail. In both cases, once the preferred site is reached, the boat is anchored or allowed to drift, and the standard method of washing the chum through a mesh bag, perforated bucket, or crate is used.

Most shark chumming is aided by a good current and a slight breeze. When the wind is strong, the amount of chumming should be increased in order to keep the shark chum line in good order. This may require ladling additional chum overboard to supplement the chum that is already in a bucket or bag. It may be necessary to use a sea anchor to slow the boat's drift and to establish a thicker chum line. With the wind heavy, shark anglers may also have to weight the hooked bait (which is usually fished on a float) to get it to the right level, or to fish it unweighted if not using a sea anchor and drifting quickly. Running a live bait under a downwind kite is another tactic for high-wind drifting. When the seas are becalmed and current is slack, the chum sinks; some shark anglers take this time to move under power, slow-trolling and spreading their chum trail higher in the water column. In this case the baited lines must be kept spread apart to avoid tangling.

Casting lures amidst chum. Remember that the main purpose of chum is to attract and concentrate fish. Although much chumming includes fishing with hooked bait, it is entirely possible to use assorted lures—including plugs, spoons, jigs, and flies—for catching fish when a chum line has been well established and fish are abundant and aggressive. Competitiveness seems to draw many fish from the end of the chum line to the front of the chum line and causes them to vigorously pursue tidbits of food; when this happens, there is definitely potential for presenting an artificial lure fairly close to you, and it can be very exciting.

Surface plugs, of course, are one possibility. Plugs that pop or chug usually work best, and it helps if they can spit water out and work quickly to look like bait splashing and being hounded over the surface. These lures should be balanced so that they do not tumble forward and foul the line, especially when being fished fast or in rough water. Spoons are a good choice for some species because they can be cast well, and far if necessary; they sink quickly and roll in the process; and they usually have enough flash when being retrieved to draw attention and look vulnerable. Jigs are a chum line possibility at times, usually when possessing a bucktail

hair body but also with a soft plastic body. These jigs can also be cast quickly and far if some action is noticed, and they can be drifted down below in the event that some fish are feeding at the bottom depths of the chum line. Flies are usually streamer versions, although poppers catch some chummed fish; the former can be fished on a sink-tip line when it is necessary to get them away from the boat or deep.

Lures should generally be cast beyond and in front of fish, and retrieved properly in front of them. Ditto for flies, although many anglers will drift a fly back in the current and chum line and then jerk it or strip it in quick bursts, rather than repeatedly casting it. Don't be afraid of fishing blind in the chum with a lure, especially a surface plug or a fly. Blind strikes are not uncommon and are usually quite a surprise, so you'd better be holding your rod tightly.

Another chumming technique, practiced by some inshore anglers who ply the tight areas of mangrove backwaters, is to use copious amounts of small live minnows, obtained from baiting and cast-netting, to trigger gamefish into feeding. They toss live baitfish, often with the aid of a handheld tube-style launcher, to a structure that might hold snook and redfish. When the predators start feeding on the dazed live bait, a hooked bait or streamer fly is cast to the same place.

See: **Bait; Baitfish;** *and individual species.*

Freshwater Chumming

Chumming in freshwater is not as widely practiced for a range of species as it is in saltwater, although it is a major component of fishing for carp, somewhat of a component for catfish and bullhead fishing, and of minor practice for other species, including panfish and trout. In Europe, however, it is a major component of fishing for coarse species *(see: coarse fish)* such as roach, barbel, tench, rudd, and various carp.

To some extent outside Europe, and especially in North America, chumming is a minor technique

A river angler prepares chum for coarse fishing.

because of traditional attitudes and practices. A general abundance of fish and the relative availability of fish to anglers make it theoretically less necessary to "resort" to the use of feeding or chumming. To some extent, a low reliance on chumming in North America is due to the nature of the fish species or the aquatic conditions; sight-feeding, cover-relating fish like bass and pike, for example, would seem a less desirable target for chumming, although this is not an absolute. To some extent it is also due to attitudes; some freshwater anglers, for example, believe that chumming is either undignified or unfair. The low use of chumming is also due to laws; chumming is illegal in some places in North America. There are no general bans on chumming in Europe, with the exception of certain trout waters that are restricted to the use of artificial lures or flies.

One of the most glaring differences between freshwater fishing in North America and in Europe is the heavy reliance on chum in the Old World, and the general lack of reliance on it in the New World. Several important differences contribute to this. European fisheries are not as diverse as those in North America (or South America), where there are many major species that are aggressive territorial sight feeders and easier to catch. These fish have also not been exploited and pressured for nearly as long as the fish in Europe. This is a bit of an over-simplification, but it is true that many European fish, especially coarse fish, which would not be of significant angling interest in North America, are caught and recaught so often that they are extremely wary and require extensive baiting (chumming), and even pre-baiting (baiting well in advance of actual fishing effort), to concentrate and fool with a hooked offering.

However, as a result of these circumstances, freshwater chumming has been highly refined in Europe. North Americans by comparison have barely scratched the surface of freshwater chumming techniques. They may not have to in the near future if fisheries resources are well maintained; but for some species (especially those that rely heavily on their sense of smell), and in isolated locations where fishing pressure is intense, chumming, if legal, may take on more significance in the angler's bag of options.

Freshwater chumming is much different than saltwater chumming. There are few opportunities to obtain, by purchase or catch, large amounts of fish to use as ground-up chum, so chum availability is an inhibiting factor in many places. However, some rivers and large reservoirs support big populations of alewives, gizzard and threadfin shad, smelt, or herring, which conceivably could be used for chum if they could legally be obtained and retained in necessary quantities. Therefore, partially by default, and partially owing to the nature of some of the species that are most susceptible to chumming, most freshwater chumming is done with foods that are not naturally found in the water, or with commercially prepared attractants. Freshwater chumming as practiced in Europe is greatly different, and far more refined, than it is in North America or in many other parts of the world.

History.   For over 500 years, anglers in Europe have been practicing the art of chumming for such species as roach, dace, chub, and bream, all of which are nervous schooling fish that can be spooked by just one scared member in their school. Intense fishing pressure and a century of catching and releasing these species have educated these and other fish to all kinds of chumming, especially on venues that are fished regularly in competitions, which are very popular. Thus, European anglers have long been searching for a magical chum (called groundbait in England) that always catches fish. Every kind of bread, grain, seed, spice, oil, blood, alcohol, and more have been mixed and blended trying to find the infallible chum, and the search continues.

Chums and chumming tactics have taken many forms over the centuries. The most unbelievable fish attractant is attributed to James Chetham who, in his 1681 book *The Angler's Vade Mecum,* recommended a chum that consisted of 1 ounce of human fat (found in the surgeries of London), 1 ounce of feline fat, 3 drams of powdered mummy, 1 dram of cumin seed, 6 drops of anise oil, 6 drops of spike, 4 grains of camphor, and 2 grains of civet. This amazing mixture was to be spread on 8 inches of line directly above the hook! Chetham also had a favorite powder, made from human bones, that was to be sprinkled on the moss where the angler kept his worms.

In his 1653 book *The Compleat Angler,* Izaak Walton noted that the addition of honey to bread paste (dough bait) was irresistible to carp. He also mentioned that tar was a deadly additive to bait that would always catch tench.

North American Indians chummed in at least two ingenious ways. One was to gradually crawl alongside a stream so that grasshoppers would jump away into the flowing water; after the fish became preoccupied with this form of loose feeding, the Indians would carefully place a grasshopper with a hook in front of active fish. Another method was to tie a dead animal in a tree above a stream; within a week flies would lay their eggs and the maggots would simply drop off the carcass, providing free food to fish that lined up downstream. The food concentrated the fish and, after the meat was gone, they could easily be caught.

In Victorian England in the late 1800s, fashionable men and women had gudgeon (a small goby) parties along streams in the summer. These exciting parties began with the men rolling up their trousers and the ladies carefully lifting up their skirts, and both walking around on the gravel runs. This stirred up the mud and all kinds of insects that were hiding there; hundreds of gudgeon would immediately swim into the mud cloud looking for food.

The men and women retired to the shoreline and used little red worms with tiny hooks under a very small float to catch many dozens of fish, which they would immediately behead, dress, and quickly fry in butter as a delicacy.

Techniques. As with saltwater chumming, all the elements of freshwater chumming are mastered only after much experience; the angler must know a great deal about the targeted fish, including where it lives throughout the year and its feeding habits. Also like saltwater chumming, freshwater chumming aims to keep fish in the area you're fishing, or attract them to it, and then get them feeding on the bait you have on the hook. After you start catching fish, you have to keep them interested; be careful not to underfeed or, worse, overfeed the fish in that area. This is something that only experience can teach.

After much experience, you will develop an instinct for knowing how much and when to feed; the best advice in this respect is to chum little and often. By chumming modestly at the start, you will not overfeed; the worst thing that can happen when you are chumming is to see your chances ruined by a nearby angler who throws in a lot of chum (like a full can of corn). An abundance of chum discourages the fish from picking up your baited hook.

How you chum depends on whether the fish you seek are sight feeders or smell and/or touch feeders. Sight feeders include such species as bluegill, crappie, perch, bass, trout, walleye, etc. Smell and/or touch feeders include catfish, carp, drum, suckers, etc. Chumming also varies by the type of waterway. Stillwaters and flowing waters are very different environments, and each affects the behavior of fish differently. Flowing-water fish, for example, can be drawn upstream hundreds of yards by scent, or by following particles upstream to where they are being introduced. Even stillwaters (especially larger bodies of water) have gentle current that moves in the opposite direction of any prevailing wind; it is possible that targeted fish could be above, below, or ahead of any chum drift you have created. Furthermore, targeted fish can literally be yards away from your scent trail, so they have no way of sensing that your bait is so close to them, unless they feel (via their lateral line) or hear other fish activity near them, or if the wind changes.

Stillwater chumming. There are two methods of stillwater chumming: loose feeding and throwing in balls of chum, which is called balling.

Loose feeding is simple and inexpensive. Corn, chopped worms, or maggots are thrown into the water by hand for close fishing. For chumming at greater distances, anglers use a flat mesh pouch catapult (a special type of slingshot) to get loose feed 30 to 40 yards away, depending on the wind.

Loose feeding is a highly effective way to fish because the idea is to attract fish with the same chumming bait that is used on the hook. Loose

Competition anglers line a canal in Finland, using groundbait to chum the area being fished.

feeding of maggots is generally the best technique for bluegills, crappie, perch, catfish, carp, and shiners.

The balling method of chumming uses ground dried breadcrumbs, which have been carefully blended with water into a ball. The ball does not contain chunks of chum but is fine and unclogged. The best way to mix this chum is in a large bucket or bowl so that any chunks that form can be broken up and mixed in; the end result should be an evenly mixed, damp, fluffy bowl of breadcrumbs.

The basic chum mixture is rolled into a ball in two ways. One is by gently squeezing a ball of chum with one hand so that it just holds together; when this ball is lobbed gently into stillwater, it will explode and drift downward through the water in a cloud. This cloud is extremely attractive to many species of very small fish. In turn, the activity created by the small fish will attract larger species, such as bluegill, crappie, and others, and begin a literal chain reaction of feeding excitement. Since there is nothing of any substance to fill up the larger fish, they will be excited and looking for food, so a hook-bait that is cast into the cloud produces action.

Balls of this chum can be thrown even farther than what is possible using loose feeding and a catapult. Balls can be thrown as far as the angler can reach; if greater distance is needed, special catapults with cup pouches can fire chum up to 80 yards away.

The other way to feed the same stillwater mix of breadcrumbs is to squeeze it into a hard ball. When pitched into the water, the hard ball goes directly to the bottom with very little of it breaking off. Corn, chopped worms or minnows, maggots, or liver can be added to the hard ball of chum and will be carried directly to the bottom. This is a good idea for targeting such species as catfish, carp, buffalo, and drum.

Flowing water chumming. In flowing water, a heavier mix of chum is necessary to get to the bottom quicker. This can be achieved by adding cornmeal and breadcrumbs that are much larger and coarser than stillwater cloud chum.

Mixing chum for flowing water takes more time than it does for stillwater. You must slightly overwet the chum mixture so it is very damp, but it must not clog up. The wet and mixed chum must be left for at least 30 minutes so that all the moisture is absorbed and it is very sticky. When you're ready to make a ball, mix in your chosen hookbait; the addition should never be more than 40 percent of the entire ball, or the ball will break up when it is thrown or when it hits the water. Squeeze the chum into a hard ball, and throw it a couple of yards upstream so it lands directly in front of you on the bottom.

Hundreds of baits and chums are successful for catching catfish and carp. A well-known favorite is Wheaties cereal soaked in strawberry soda; it makes a fantastic dough bait for carp and buffalo. There are dozens of effective stinkbaits that catch catfish, but a favorite when the fishing is really tough because of weather extremes is thin slivers of half-frozen liver; the chum here is the blood that leeches out and is carried downstream to those sensitive barbels of the catfish.

The major ingredients for most commercial chums and mixes made by professional European competition anglers are breadcrumbs, cornmeal, and peanuts, although you can experiment with every other type of grain and seed to find a personal favorite. However, most angling activities (at least in North America) only require different textures of breadcrumbs and cornmeal. In places having a lot of stocked fish (usually trout), ground-up fish pellets will be a very good attractant, because the fish will know the smell.

Only with experience will you learn how to correctly blend, wet, squeeze, and feed the chum in a precise spot.
See: Charter Boat; Drift Fishing; Inshore Fishing; Party Boat; Pier Fishing.

CHUM POT
A galvanized wire mesh basketlike pot with a hinged lid that is filled with ground chum and lowered into the water to attract fish. It is often placed on the bottom to interest bottom-feeding fish.
See: Chum; Chumming.

CHUM SLICK
The oily surface of the water above a chum line. The term chum slick is often used synonymously with chum line (see), but a slick is merely the obvious smooth section of the surface, which is made by oil from the dispensed chum sitting on top of the water. The slick is carried away from the boat by tide and/or current, and it may or may not extend as far back as the underwater trail of chum. Usually the chum particles sink deeper as they are carried away from the initial drop point, and the slick portion of surface water dissipates at some distance from the boat. If chum particles stay close to the surface,

some feeding fish may actually be visible as they move near the surface and swim through the slick.
See: Chum; Chumming.

CHUNKING
The use of pieces of fish to chum in offshore fishing, primarily for yellowfin and bluefin tuna. Most chunks are pieces of fish meat, in 2- to 3-inch cubes, that are dispensed piecemeal alone or in conjunction with ground chum. The term originated with Atlantic offshore tuna anglers, primarily in the Northeast.
See: Big-Game Fishing; Chum; Chumming; Tuna.

CIGUATERA
Poisoning caused by eating the flesh of fish toxic to humans. Found in many tropical reef fish, ciguatera is caused by a toxin found in certain algae eaten by reef fish. The poison accumulates when reef fish are eaten by larger fish and then by humans. There is no visual clue identifying a fish that contains the toxin, and any reef fish can carry it.

Ciguatera is unpredictable and causes sickness that may last for days, weeks, or months; it is sometimes fatal. It occurs in the Pacific and Caribbean, and is known in the western Indian Ocean only at Mauritius and Reunion Islands. It is a serious problem in some areas, including Hawaii. Symptoms include weakness; diarrhea; muscle pain and joint aches; numbness and tingling around the mouth, hands, and feet; nausea; chills; itching; headache; sweating; and dizziness.

To avoid ciguatera poisoning, health experts advise that anglers know the most common types of reef fish that carry the poison; know if and where cases of ciguatera fish poisoning have been reported in the areas they fish; clean the fish very well; eat only small portions of large fish that might have the poison; and not eat the roe, liver, head, or viscera because they have higher levels of poison.

If ciguatera fish poisoning is suspected, contact a doctor immediately, as well as health or fisheries authorities; save any uneaten portions of the fish for testing. Barracuda, amberjack, mullet, surgeonfish, and moray eel, as well as some jacks, snapper, and grouper, are all fish that may carry the ciguatera toxin.

CIRCLE HOOK
A pattern of hook popular for use with bait in tuna fishing due to its excellent holding virtue.
See: Hook.

CISCO   *Coregonus spp.*
Other names—gray back, tullibee, lake herring, whitefish.

There are a number of similar species under the *Coregonus* genus, which is classified as a member of the Salmonidae family and generally acknowledged as a subfamily of whitefish *(see)*. Whitefish and cisco inhabit many of the same waters, and may be confused, although cisco are generally smaller. One of the most common of these is *Coregonus artedii*, simply referred to as cisco. This species is often portrayed as the only cisco because the differences between species are only minor variations in body or snout shape, depth preference, or number of eggs. However, there are, or were, perhaps as many as 11 species of cisco, some of which were primarily very deep-dwelling fish.

Overfishing by commercial interests, predation, pollution, and habitat degradation have caused some cisco to be listed as endangered or threatened; these include the longjaw cisco *(C. alpenae)* and the kiyi *(C. kiyi)*. The shortnose cisco *(C. reighardi)*, may be extinct. It was the only cisco species that spawned in the spring and was last observed in 1985 in Lake Huron. The deepwater cisco *(C. johannae)* is listed as extinct in Canada.

In the Great Lakes, cisco have evidently suffered from competition with more aggressive plankton feeders (like alewives and smelt), and from predation by salmon and sea lampreys, all of which were nonnative species. The bloater *(C. hoyi)* has suffered the least of the Great Lakes species. Bloaters do not support any sportfishing effort, as they dwell far from shore and have a mouth too small for ordinary baits. They are efficient feeders, however, and grow more on less food than do alewives.

Bloaters, as well as other Great Lakes cisco, are commonly called "chub." The bloater, in fact, is also known as a bloater chub. These small, soft-fleshed, and oily fish are tasty table fare and are popular for commercial smoking, usually bearing the name "smoked chub."

Cisco provide some sportfishing opportunity, especially for ice fishing, and are important forage fish for other species, particularly northern pike, walleye, perch, and rainbow trout. They are especially significant to lake trout.

Identification. Characterized by an adipose dorsal fin and forked tail, cisco have a terminal mouth (lower jaw projecting slightly beyond upper jaw). The body is elongate and slender with less than 100 scales in the lateral line. The pelvic axillary process, or daggerlike progression, is well developed. Its coloring is dusky gray to bluish on the back, silvery on the sides, and white on the underside. All fins are relatively clear, although the anal and pelvic fins may be milky on adults.

As a group, cisco (and whitefish) are quickly differentiated from other species by the presence of an adipose fin. Cisco can be differentiated from lake whitefish *(Coregonus clupeaformis)*, which inhabit the same deeper waters, by their pointed snout, terminal mouth, and lack of teeth; the cisco's mouth is at the end of the head, whereas the whitefish's mouth is behind and under the snout. They are differentiated from lake trout *(Salvelinus*

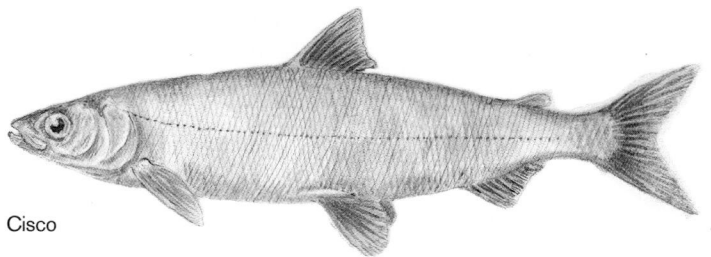

Cisco

namaycush), by having larger scales, a bigger mouth, and lack of teeth.

Size. Cisco can vary in length from 6 to 25 inches, the average size being between 10 and 14 inches and $1/2$ pound; the all-tackle world record is a Manitoba fish *(C. artedii)* that weighed 7 pounds, 6 ounces. The average life span is eight years. In some lakes, the cisco population may be stunted, and most fish are small.

Distribution. Cisco are primarily inhabitants of Canada, where they range from roughly east of the Mackenzie River through Ontario and north throughout the Northwest Territories, as well as throughout much of Quebec. They inhabit the Great Lakes and its tributaries (including the St. Lawrence River). They are found in some lakes of states bordering the Great Lakes, including the Finger Lakes in New York, and in upper Mississippi River drainages.

Habitat. Coldwater lakes are the favored dwelling places of cisco. They may be near the surface when the water is cold, or at depths of several hundred feet, but they generally remain below the thermocline in lakes where this stratification occurs. They tend to school in midwater and move into shallower areas when the water cools in the fall. Water temperatures ranging above 60°F are lethal to cisco, and as the surface waters warm, these fish move deeper. Many swim close to the surface during the winter, providing opportunities for ice fishing.

Life history/Behavior. Cisco are schooling fish that spawn in large congregations in late fall after moving into shallow water roughly 3 to 10 feet deep, often on reefs, and when the water temperature is about 4° to 5°C. Females can lay up to 30,000 eggs on the lake bottom, usually over gravel or stones. The eggs are given no parental care and hatch within four months. Nearly all cisco reach maturity by their fourth season. Some, such as the least cisco *(C. sardinella)*, are anadromous but do not stray far from river mouths during migration.

Food and feeding habits. Plankton is the main food source of cisco. During early spring, which is their most active (and shallow) feeding season, they may also consume minnows, crustaceans, and mayflies.

Angling. There is some open-water fishing for cisco, but this is generally confined to spring, when the fish are abundant and near the surface, perhaps feeding on mayflies. Use ultralight spoons and

spinners, a tiny jig, and flies, fished on fine line or tippets. Most angling for cisco occurs in winter, through the ice, using tiny jigs and ice flies, perhaps tipped with a mealworm or grub and lowered to a depth of from 10 to 30 feet below the ice with an appropriate-size split shot. Small minnows may work also. Fine line, from 1- to 4-pound test, is necessary, and it's wise to use sonar to search for schools of roving fish.
See: Ice Fishing.

CLASS LINE
See: Line.

CLASS TIPPET
A 15-inch-long tippet on a fly fishing leader that conforms to exact breaking strength standards for world record purposes.
See: Tippet.

CLEANING FISH
See: Fish Preparation—Cleaning/Dressing.

CLEAT, BOAT
A small object, usually aluminum or stainless steel, with projecting ends, primarily used for fastening mooring lines on a boat.

CLEATS, WADING
See: Surf Fishing; Waders.

CLICKER
A term for the click ratchet on fishing reels that is used to signal that line is being taken off the reel. It is also known as the warning click.
See: Big-Game Tackle; Conventional Tackle.

CLINCH KNOT
Also called "cinch" and a precursor to the superior Improved Clinch Knot, this is a fishing knot for terminal connections, and a common term for the popular and widely accepted Improved Clinch.
See: Knots, Fishing.

CLIPPERS
A commonly used small tool for trimming knots and cutting fishing line; these may be fingernail clippers or a similar device.

CLOSED-FACE REEL
A spincasting reel.
See: Spincasting Tackle.

CLOVE HITCH
See: Knots, Boating.

CLUTCH
A component of fishing reels and downriggers.
See: Baitcasting Tackle; Big-Game Tackle; Conventional Tackle; Downrigger; Flycasting Tackle; Spinning Tackle.

COARSE FISH
A British term for freshwater species that are not considered gamefish. This is a vague and loose-fitting term referring to such species as bream (see), roach (see), and tench (see), but it has also been used to include carp (see). It is only partly analogous to the American term "rough fish" (see), since coarse species are regularly sought and appreciated by many European anglers.

Most coarse fishing is done with chum (see), particularly groundbait (see), by using various types of generally small baits, and while fishing from shore.

COASTER
A brook trout (see: trout, brook) that leaves its natal stream and spends part of the year in large, deep clear lakes, cruising close to the shore. This occurs in the Great Lakes, and is akin to the activity of salters (see).

COBIA   Rachycentron canadum.
Other names—ling, cabio, lemonfish, crab-eater, flathead, black salmon, black kingfish, sergeant fish, runner; French: mafou; Japanese: sugi; Portuguese: bijupirá.

The only member of the Rachycentridae family, and with no known relatives, the cobia is in a class by itself, and a popular food and sportfish for inshore anglers in areas where it is prominent.

Identification.   The body of a cobia is elongated with a broad, depressed head. The first dorsal fin consists of 8 to 10 short depressible spines that are not connected by a membrane. Both the second dorsal fin and the anal fin each have one to two spines and 20 to 30 soft rays. The adult cobia is dark brown with a whitish underside and is marked on the sides by silver or bronze lines. Young cobia, possessing alternating black and white stripes and speckled with bronze, orange, and green, are more colorful than adults.

A cobia's shape is comparable to that of a shark, with a powerful tail fin and the elevated anterior portion of the second dorsal fin. It can be distinguished from the similar remora (Remora remora), by the absence of a suction pad on the head.

Size/Age.   Cobia can grow to a length of 6 feet and a weight of 90 pounds, the average size being 3 feet and 15 pounds. Females are slightly larger than males. They generally live 9 to 10 years, and some reports indicate greater longevity. A 9-year-old fish can weigh close to 100 pounds. Scientific reports say that cobia can reach a maximum weight of 150 pounds, but that has not been the case in U.S. waters. The all-tackle rod-and-reel record cobia weighed 135 pounds, 9 ounces.

Distribution. Found worldwide in tropical and warm temperate waters, cobia inhabit the western Atlantic from Cape Cod to Argentina (being most abundant in the Gulf of Mexico), the eastern Atlantic from the coast of Morocco to South Africa, and Indo-West Pacific waters from Japan to Australia and the East Indies.

Habitat. Adult cobia prefer shallow continental shelf waters, often congregating along reefs and around buoys, pilings, wrecks, anchored boats, and other stationary or floating objects. They are found in a variety of locations over mud, gravel, or sand bottoms, coral reefs and man-made sloughs, and at depths of up to 60 feet.

Life history/Behavior. Although juveniles are sometimes found in schools, adult cobia often swim alone or among small schools of other cobia or sharks. Fish in these schools may vary considerably in size. They are believed to spawn in the offshore waters of the northern Gulf of Mexico during late spring and summer, between April and May, and the larvae migrate shoreward. Males reach sexual maturity when they are two years old and 24 inches long, and females at age 3 and 36 inches in length. An adult female cobia may lay 6 to 7 million eggs at one time. Juveniles are abundant in summer along coastlines after the spawning season.

Cobia migrate from offshore to inshore environs as well as inshore from east to west and vice versa. Little about their movements has been confirmed, although it is known that in winter some fish move from shallow to deeper water, or laterally to warmer areas. A tagged cobia migrated 1,300 nautical miles from west of the Mississippi River to Daytona Beach, Florida, in an eight-month period. In the western Atlantic, cobia migrate as far north as Cape Cod in the summer and then south again to tropical waters in the fall.

Food and feeding habits. Cobia feed mostly on crustaceans, particularly shrimp, squid, and crabs (thus the name "crab eater"), as well as on eels and various small fish found in shallow coastal waters.

Angling. With cobia populations having improved in the Gulf of Mexico and along the South Atlantic coast, this species has become especially favored and hotly pursued from spring through fall by boaters, in part because it often offers sight fishing opportunities, making it a species that anglers can cast lures and baits to, and in part because it is fairly predictably found around such structures as bridges, buoys, channel markers, and oil rigs. Cobia are fairly aggressive a good deal of the time, readily striking plugs, jigs, and flies, and are sometimes caught handily on baits. They are usually not afraid of boats and often come to a boat and mill around. In addition to being good fighters on the line, they are known for thrashing about after being boated, which requires caution.

In the Gulf of Mexico, the greatest cobia action occurs from March through May in shallow near-beach waters, when migrating fish are hunted by cruising anglers. Working from boats, they search for shallow, near-the-surface swimming cobia, sometimes close to the beach but as far as a half mile from it. Anglers use jigs or lures, often on spinning tackle with 12- to 25-pound line (using the heavier strength when really big fish are possible), casting 60 to 80 feet to the brown-backed cobia. Live baits are also cast, although positioning is more of a concern because the baits cannot be cast as accurately for long distances. The same is true for fly fishing, although sometimes live baits are used to draw cobia closer to a boat for fly presentation. These fish move offshore on wrecks and reefs in summer and fall.

Live baits for cobia depend on geographic location and availability, but there's a range of choices. Peeler crabs, spot, and eels are favored in some areas, whereas mullet, pinfish, and grunts are used in others, in addition to pieces of squid. Lures include bucktail jigs, tube lures, and assorted swimming plugs.

Some anglers pursue cobia by trolling and by drifting over deep structure, but many carefully approach buoys, channel markers, and oil rigs, where lone or grouped cobia may be present. The quiet approach is an effort to keep the fish from approaching the boat; many anglers gauge current and wind direction and set up to drift by such places, freelining bait or making repetitive casts.

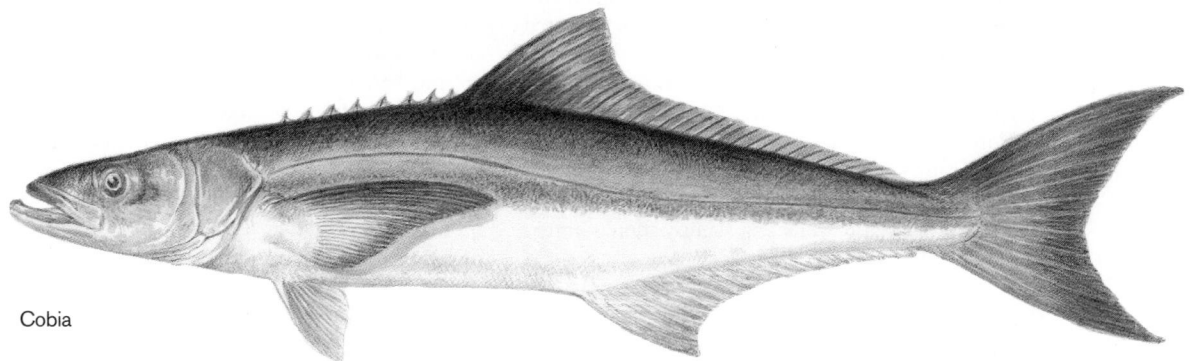

Cobia

C

COD AND HAKE

The various cod and hake are all members of the Gadidae family of codfish. All codfish live in cold waters of the Northern Hemisphere, some in the Atlantic and some in the Pacific. Most of the species are harvested commercially, although some have been in serious decline.

All members of the cod family have spineless fins. The pelvic or ventral fins are located far forward, commonly ahead of the pectorals. The body is elongated, and there is a single barbel on the chin. Most species have two dorsal fins, some have three, others only one.

Codfish and other pelagic species in the family produce prodigious numbers of eggs. A 20-pound female may lay 4 to 5 million eggs in a season, and a specimen of 75 pounds may produce more than 9 million eggs. Males spread their milt in the sea around the eggs and fertilize them. The eggs float freely, as do the newly hatched fish. The young are about an inch long before they are strong enough to swim well, and the few that survive manage to get into shallow enough water for them to find refuge, feed, and grow. By the time they are three years old, they weigh roughly 5 pounds. Cod are mainly bottom dwellers, feeding on small fish, mollusks, crabs, sea worms, and similar creatures.

Cod have been important in both commercial fishing and sportfishing, although their significance in both areas has diminished markedly. Some cod are sold fresh, but most of the catch is now processed as frozen fillets. In the early days, cod were preserved mainly by salting. Oil from the cod's liver was the main source of vitamin D.

The Atlantic cod (*Gadus morhua; see: cod, Atlantic*) occurs off both the European and North American coasts in cool waters and from near the surface to depths of a thousand feet or more. Smaller fish are generally closer to shore, larger ones remain in deeper water. Cod like cool waters and may sometimes follow cool currents out of their normal range. In winter, for example, they are found as far south as North Carolina.

The Atlantic cod has three dorsal fins and two anal fins. The light lateral line against its dark sides is a distinctive feature. The snout is rounded or cone-shaped on top, the upper jaw projecting slightly beyond the lower. The tail is almost squared or is slightly concave. There are two principal color phases, gray and red; in both, the sides are covered with dark dots.

The Pacific cod (*G. macrocephalus; see: cod, Pacific*) is found on both sides of the Pacific. Off the North American coast, it occurs from Oregon northward, only occasionally straying southward. The Pacific cod is almost identical to the Atlantic cod, differing only in having slightly more pointed fins. It is somewhat smaller on average.

Closely related, and sometimes placed in the genus *Gadus,* is the haddock (*Melanogrammus aeglefinus; see: haddock*), found off both the North American and European coasts in the Atlantic. Haddock, like cod, travel in large schools. Today the catch has declined drastically because of overfishing. Most of the catch is filleted and frozen. Some is smoked, which is called finnan haddie. The largest haddock fishery historically has been off the Grand Banks of Newfoundland and in Europe, in the North Sea south of Spitsbergen.

Haddock are bottom feeders, usually found in greatest numbers in water 100 to 500 feet deep. The two most common of the several color variations are grayish green with a dark lateral line and golden brown with a yellow lateral line. Like the cod, the haddock has three dorsal and two anal fins, but it lacks spots on its body. The first rays on the leading dorsal fin are exceptionally long. Just above and behind each pectoral fin is a large, dark blotch.

The pollock (*Pollachius virens; see: pollock*), has been the most popular of the cod family with anglers. Averaging 4 to 10 pounds in weight (but with some catches weighing more than 30 pounds), the pollock is found on both sides of the Atlantic in cool to cold waters, usually close to shore but commonly netted at depths of 400 to 500 feet. The pollock's snout is pointed, the lower jaw projecting beyond the upper; the chin barbel is very small or lacking. The broad caudal fin is forked. Because the back and sides are a greenish brown, another name for the pollock is green cod. There are no spots, however, and the lateral line is white.

Pollock are active feeders, preying mainly on small fish but also taking crabs, mollusks, and other small animals. Anglers catch them principally by trolling, using jigs or spoons, but the smaller fish are known also to take artificial flies along inshore waters. They are strong fighters.

The Atlantic tomcod (*Microgadus tomcod; see: tomcod, Atlantic*) and its close relative, the Pacific tomcod (*M. proximus; see: tomcod, Pacific*), also have three dorsal and two anal fins, which are rounded, as are the long caudal fins. The pelvic fins extend into long filaments that may be sensory in function. These fish are generally olive brown above and lighter below, the sides heavily blotched with black. Tomcod average less than 12 inches in length, and only occasional individuals weigh more than a pound.

Hake differ from cod in having the second and third dorsal fins joined to make one large fin that typically is indented or notched where the two are joined. Directly below is an indentation on the anal fin. The lower jaw projects beyond the upper, and the chin barbel is either very small or absent. The caudal fin is shallowly forked. Hake are predators, feeding on smaller fish and squid. They travel in schools, generally at the edge of the continental shelf or below, down to 2,000 feet. Their eggs contain oil droplets so that they rise to the surface and float in the open sea until they hatch. Compared to cod, the flesh of hake is soft, and thus generally less appealing. Hake have nevertheless been harvested commercially in large quantities.

Grayling were once abundant in Michigan's Manistee River and even had a town named after them, but grayling haven't been seen in that state since 1932.

The South African hake *(Merluccius capensis)* is considered the most valuable commercial fish netted off the African coast. It sometimes reaches a length of 4 feet but averages 2 feet or less. The European hake *(M. merluccius),* which is similar in size, ranges from Norway southward to Africa and occurs also in the Mediterranean.

The common species off the Atlantic coast of North America, from Newfoundland south to the Bahamas, is the silver hake *(M. bilinearis; see: hake, silver),* which is regionally known as whiting and quite popular. In the Pacific, the only representative is the Pacific hake *(M. productus; see: hake, Pacific).*

The white hake *(Urophycis tenuis; see hake, white),* ranging from Newfoundland to North Carolina, is a slender fish that may exceed 3 feet in length and weigh more than 30 pounds. The average is about half this size. As in the hake of the genus *Merluccius,* the second and third dorsal fins are joined. The first ray of the first dorsal is extended into a slim filament, and the caudal fin is rounded. There is a small chin barbel, and the pelvic or ventral fins are reduced to long filaments. The back and sides are reddish, grading into yellowish gray below.

The red hake *(U. chuss; see: hake, red)* occurs in the same general range as the white hake. The filament of its first dorsal fin is much longer, and the sides are mottled. The maximum size of the red hake is 8 pounds; the average is about 2 pounds.

Several other species in the genus *Urophycis* are all about the size of the red hake or smaller. These include the southern hake *(U. floridanus),* which averages a pound in weight. It has dark spots above and behind the eyes and also on the gill covers, and the first ray of the dorsal fin is of normal length. There are round white spots at regular intervals along the black lateral line. The southern hake occurs in the Gulf of Mexico and is sometimes caught on hook and line, particularly in winter.

The spotted hake *(U. regius)* also lacks the long filament on the first dorsal fin, and its scales are larger than in other hakes of the genus *Urophycis.* The slim pectoral fin is exceptionally long, extending to the anal fin. The spotted hake is the most common species in the mid-Atlantic region. It is seldom fished for but is caught accidentally on hook and line. Commercial fishermen also catch these hake from time to time, but the fishery for hake is not large or well developed.

The common species in European waters is *U. blennoides,* which is much more fat-bodied and blenny-like than other species of the genus. About a dozen other rare or commercially unimportant hake and cod inhabit northern waters.

Only one species of the cod family lives exclusively in freshwater—the burbot *(Lota lota; see: burbot),* which is found in deep, cold lakes and streams, sometimes in great abundance, from Alaska southward throughout Canada and in the northern portion of the United States. It occurs also in the cold regions of Europe and Asia. Other common names

for the burbot are ling, lawyer, eelpout, and freshwater cod. It is sometimes mistaken for some kind of catfish. Its scales are so small that the burbot appears to be naked, like a catfish, and beneath its chin is a single long barbel. The pelvic fins are located far forward, ahead of the pectorals, directly under the throat. There are two dorsal fins. The first is short, the second long and nearly matched in length by the anal fin below. The caudal fin is small. The burbot is white or yellowish orange, mottled with black, but the coloration depends greatly on the chemistry of the water in which the burbot is living. It is not unusual for the burbot to reach a weight of 5 or 10 pounds and to measure 3 feet in length.

Burbot are active predators. In most places they are considered trash fish that are destructive to populations of more desirable species, but there has been some increased interest in sportfishing for them, particularly among ice anglers.

COD, ATLANTIC *Gadus morhua.*
Other names—cod, codfish, codling, scrod; French: *morue de l'Atlantique;* German: *dorsch, kabeljau;* Italian: *merluzzo bianco;* Japanese: *madara, tara;* Norwegian: *torsk;* Portuguese: *bacalhau;* Spanish: *bacalao del Atlántique.*

The Atlantic cod has historically been one of the world's important natural resources, and the waters of the North Atlantic once teemed with this fish. The Basques fished the Banks off Newfoundland for cod centuries before Columbus discovered America, and cod bones have been found in coastal dwelling sites dating from the Mesolithic period. Overstating the cod's value as a food fish to the New World would be difficult. So important was the cod in colonial America that it even appeared in the state seal of Massachusetts, a reflection of the fact that cod fishing was that colony's first industry and the source of early fortunes.

In earlier times, the cod catch was split, salted, and dried. Salt cod, once a staple food on both sides of the Atlantic, was one of the first export items from American colonies, and it was an important fish during Lent. Today, however, no salted cod is produced in the United States. Improvements in fishing gear, the transition to steam and diesel engines, and technological changes in handling the catch (both at sea and ashore) made it possible to bring the fish to market more rapidly. Quick freezing and filleting resulted in a more popular market form: boneless fillets ready for the pan. Domestic landings now are primarily filleted or steaked and sold fresh or frozen. Most of the fish once used in the production of breaded fish portions and fish sticks was cod, when still in great abundance. The term "scrod," incidentally, is fish market terminology for a small (to 3 pounds) cod with the head on.

Commercial fishing for cod has long been conducted year-round; otter trawls and gillnets have been the primary gear. Today, the commercial catch

Atlantic Cod

of cod is far below its historical levels, and cod are generally in a collapsed or near-collapsed condition, having been overexploited by commercial fishermen even though the U.S. commercial and recreational fisheries for cod are managed under the New England Fishery Management Council's Multispecies Fishery Management Plan. The 1990s experienced record-low commercial catches; older fish have been almost nonexistent, and incoming year classes have been relatively weak. With recruitment extremely poor and spawning stock biomass at unprecedented low levels, there is enormous concern for the future of this species.

Identification.   The Atlantic cod has three dark dorsal fins and two dark anal fins, none of which contain any spines. The body is heavy and tapered, with a prominent chin barbel, a large mouth, and many small teeth. Its snout is rounded on top, and the tail is almost squared. There is a characteristic pale lateral line. The coloring is highly variable on the back and sides (ranging from brownish or sandy to gray, yellow, reddish, greenish, or any combination of these colors), gray white on the underside, and with numerous light spots covering the body.

The Atlantic cod can be distinguished from its relative the pollock (see) by its barbel and projecting upper jaw, and from the haddock (see) by its pale lateral line. It can also be distinguished from the Pacific cod (see: cod, Pacific) by the less pointed fins. The tomcod (see) is similar, but the caudal fin is rounded; in the Atlantic cod it is squared.

Size/Age.   Young fish ages 2 to 5 generally constitute the bulk of the recreational (and commercial) cod catch, with the average size being from 4 to 15 pounds. Larger sizes in New England are not unusual, some with a length of 30 to 40 inches. When they were more abundant, cod were caught in the 55- to 75-pound range. The largest cod known weighed 211 pounds, 8 ounces, and was taken off the coast of Massachusetts in May of 1895. The all-tackle fishing record is 98 pounds, 12 ounces. Atlantic cod can live up to 22 years.

Distribution.   Atlantic cod occur in subarctic and cool temperate waters of the North Atlantic from Greenland to North Carolina, including the Hudson Strait, and from Novaya Zemla, in the former USSR, to the northern reaches of the Bay of Biscay, including the Baltic and North Seas and Iceland. They have generally been most abundant in the Gulf of St. Lawrence, off Newfoundland. In U.S. waters, cod are assessed as two stocks, the first being that of the Gulf of Maine, and the second being that of Georges Bank and southward.

Habitat.   These fish are found primarily off the coasts along the continental shelf. They prefer cool water of 30° to 50°F and may reside in depths of up to 200 fathoms. Adults are generally found in water over 60 feet deep, whereas juveniles may be found in shallower water; both move deeper during the summer. Growth rates differ between the two stocks. It has traditionally been slower in the Gulf of Maine than on Georges Bank.

Spawning behavior.   The spawning season is during winter and early spring, in December and January off the Mid-Atlantic Bight and from February through April farther north. The transparent eggs hatch, after floating, within 50 days at 32°F, and in 17 days when the surface temperature is 41°F.

Food and feeding habits.   Omnivorous feeders, cod are primarily active at dawn and dusk. Many unusual items have been found in the stomachs of adult cod, including an oil can, a rubber doll, finger rings, clothing, and some very rare deep-sea shells that were previously unknown to science; however, their diet is invertebrates and assorted fish. Very young cod feed on copepods and other small crustaceans while at the surface, and, after dropping to the bottom, small worms or shrimp.

Angling.   Recreational fishing for cod occurs year-round, although the peak activity is during the late summer in the lower Gulf of Maine, and during late autumn to early spring from Massachusetts southward. A cold winter may cause spring and early summer water closer to shore to be cold, and this may produce cod in shallower waters.

Traditionally, cod fishing was practiced over rough bottoms, but most Atlantic cod fishing today takes place on wrecks. Those far offshore tend to

A group of Atlantic cod, headed for the kitchen.

produce the better fishing and larger specimens. Far offshore, off Georges Bank for example, is the province of long-range party boats, some of which run for five hours to reach desired areas.

In the shallow nearer water, the early fishing—when the cod first show up and are aggressive and abundant—is productive on 10-ounce diamond jigs. This tactic may be useful into the winter if there's plenty of live bait around, but baitfishing is the typical winter strategy. In shallower waters, 8 to 16 ounces of lead are best, as these heavier weights are necessary in the strong tide conditions. Anchoring is possible when there's less current, but most of the time anglers will drift. Skimmer clams are the primary baits, usually fished on high-low rigs and sometimes combined with a tube bait or hooked soft-plastic bait. Jigs are also sometimes combined with a second, upper, lure (plastic or small bucktail), which is especially worth doing when small sand eels are present.

In deeper water, heavier jigs and weights are necessary; live-bait sinkers running up to 32 ounces are the norm, and all fishing is done via drifting. Bottom depths vary from 120 to as much as 200 feet. Fresh baitfish is a necessity. Skimmer clams are the main item, but squid is also used. Bait is provided on party boats, but private boaters must have an ample supply of their own. Some cod anglers will shell a bushel or two of skimmer clams a day before going cod fishing and then salt them in buckets overnight to toughen them so they will stay on the hook.

Because cod are bottom fish, the trick is getting and staying in the right places. The angler must find the weight that will position the rig on the bottom in the given conditions while keeping a little slack in the line. This method enables the angler to detect a strike while the bait is drifting. Jigging does not have to be done right on the bottom, with the jig bouncing off it, but the jig should be fairly close to the bottom. Given the weight of jigs used and the depths attained, many cod aficionados prefer low-stretch lines. Dacron line was favored in the past, but these days the newer thin-diameter microfilaments are popular. Conventional tackle is the standard gear, and 4/0 reels are the norm.
See: Cod and Hake.

COD, MURRAY   *Macullochella peeli.*
Other names—cod, codfish, goodoo, and ponde; also known as *Macullochella peelii peelii.*

Endemic to Australia, the Murray cod is the largest of that continent's freshwater species, and one of the world's biggest entirely freshwater fish. A member of the Percichthyidae family of temperate bass, it is a fine table fish in its early growth stages, although its flesh becomes coarse and more oily as the fish ages. It is closely related to, and often confused with, the trout cod (*Macullochella macquariensis),* and the eastern freshwater cod (*Macullochella ikei).* A small commercial fishery for Murray cod exists in southwestern New South Wales; these fish are for domestic consumption.

Identification.   The general body coloring varies from brown or olive green above, and yellow green with a mottling of pale green on the lower sides and fin bases. The belly is white. The caudal fin is convex and may have white margins on the upper and lower tips, as may the soft dorsal fin and the anal fin. The head is broad and depressed, with a rounded snout, and the forehead profile is concave. The upper and lower jaws are usually of equal length.

Size.   Reported to grow to more than 1.8 meters and 113 kilograms, the Murray cod commonly reaches 60 to 70 centimeters and up to 5 kilograms when mature, at about five years of age. Anglers fishing waterways such as Lake Mulwala on the Murray River frequently take specimens to 20 kilograms. The average size runs to about 8 kilograms; at that size, they are considered excellent eating. Regulations exist to limit the tackle used as well as the size and number of fish caught and kept.

Distribution.   Murray cod were once found throughout the Murray-Darling system from Queensland to South Australia, but wild stocks have declined in recent years and the species is considered rare in many Victoria streams. The decline is largely attributed to the clearing out of underwater cover, and the construction of weirs and dams along major rivers. Murray cod are now successfully reared in numerous hatcheries, and their decline has

Murray Cod

C

been checked somewhat; stocks have been introduced to many inland streams and impoundments in Victoria, New South Wales, and southern Queensland.

Habitat. The Murray cod, which are found in a wide range of habitats, shows a surprising tolerance to water that ranges from clear to muddy. They favor sheltered areas away from strong currents and like to station themselves on the downstream side of underwater boulders and submerged logs and tree roots, where swirling back eddies carry food to them. In the still waters of impoundments and billabongs, they will establish themselves in areas of weeds, dead trees, and warm backwaters.

Life history/Behavior. Murray cod spawn from spring through early summer (September through October) as water temperatures increase. If spawning coincides with flooding, the larvae will not only have more food available, improving their chances of survival, but the flood waters will also distribute the larvae to feeder streams and billabongs (backwater area or pond connected to a river) downstream.

Spawning takes place when the fish reach 4 years of age. The eggs, which are 3 to 4 millimeters in diameter and demersal, can number to 90,000. They are also adhesive, and stick to hollow logs, rocks, and other hard surfaces. Hatching takes place within 7 to 10 days, and the larvae grow rapidly. They are mature when 4 to 5 years old, at which time they weigh about 5 kilograms. At 15 years of age, they might weigh in excess of 20 kilograms.

Murray cod are territorial and may spend most of their lives within a short (10 kilometers) stretch of a stream.

Food and feeding habits. The huge mouth of the Murray cod enables it to feed on small fish, crayfish, shrimp, freshwater mussels, grubs, worms, frogs, birds, mice, rodents, and any other small creatures that fall into the water. Feeding activity increases during the summer months and is largely nocturnal.

Angling. Although it is one of the largest freshwater fish in the world, the Murray cod is not highly regarded as a sportfish. It is capable of putting up a stubborn fight, but there is nothing spectacular about its struggles when hooked. Complacency, however, can be dangerous when a large specimen takes a bait or lure, as this bulky fish is strong and unlikely to surrender until totally exhausted.

Many anglers using rod and reel, or handlines, resort to such live baits as small fish, yabbies (crayfish), shrimp, worms, and grubs. The most popular grub is the barti grub (the burrowing larva of a large moth), which is extracted from its hole in the ground by a 1-meter length of piano wire with a sharp-pointed corkscrew twisted into one end. The wire is pushed down the hole until the soft body of the grub is felt, screwed into it, and withdrawn.

Bait anglers seek out deep holes away from the main current, or toss their baits into back eddies where the cod rests up. Experienced cod anglers fish along the riverbank, rather than into the main stream, knowing that after dark the cod roams along the sides of the stream seeking out crayfish that burrow in the banks and emerge after nightfall. Anglers favor hook sizes to No. 7/0, and handlines of 15- to 50-kilogram strength.

In those streams where the water runs clear, casting with small diving lures and spinners is highly successful. Where the waters are turbid (common in western streams), rattling lures and large, noisy, bladed spinners take over. Most fishing on impoundments is done from boats, and trolling around, or casting to, patches of dead trees is preferred. Night fishing with surface lures is also worthwhile. Baitcasting and spinning tackle with up to 10-kilogram line are used for trolling and casting. Fly fishing has been successful but is not widely practiced.

COD, PACIFIC   *Gadus macrocephalus.*

Other names—cod, gray cod, true cod; French: *morue du Pacifique;* Italian: *merluzzo del Pacifico;* Japanese: *madara;* Portuguese: *bacalau-do-Pacifico;* Spanish: *bacalao del Pacifico.*

Extremely similar to Atlantic cod, and a member of the Gadidae family, the Pacific cod is an excellent food fish and a good sportfish. It is harvested commercially for fish sticks and fillets and is usually sold frozen. In British Columbia, it is the most important trawl-caught bottom fish, with millions of pounds landed there alone.

Identification. Characteristic of the cod family, the Pacific cod has three separate and distinct dorsal fins, two anal fins, and one large barbel under the chin. Its body is heavy and elongated, with small scales, a large mouth, and soft rays. Its coloring ranges from gray to brown on the back, lightening on the sides and belly. Numerous brown spots speckle the sides and back. All the fins are dusky, and the unpaired fins are edged with white on their outer margins.

The Pacific cod can be distinguished from the Atlantic cod, which is almost identical, by its smaller body and the pointedness of its fins.

Size. The average size is less than 3 feet, with a weight of 15 pounds or less. The all-tackle record is 30 pounds.

Distribution. The Pacific cod inhabits waters along the U.S. Pacific coast from Santa Monica,

Pacific Cod

California, to northwestern Alaska; and in Asia from the Chukchi Sea to the Yellow Sea and Lushen (Port Arthur), China. It is common in the U.S. northwest waters of Oregon, Washington, and Alaska.

Habitat. Although primarily a coastal bottom-dwelling fish, the Pacific cod can be found from shallow waters to depths of nearly 800 feet. It prefers rocky, pebbly ground or sandy bottoms in cold water.

Spawning behavior. The spawning season for the Pacific cod is winter and early spring. The eggs are pelagic, or free-floating. It generally lays great quantities of eggs; depending on the size of the fish, a female may release between 1 and 9 million eggs.

Food and feeding habits. The Pacific cod is mainly omnivorous. The adult feeds dominant food organisms, especially herring, capelin, sand eels, sardines, pollock, and other cod. Its habits are similar to those of the Atlantic cod.

Angling. *See: Cod, Atlantic.*
See: **Cod and Hake.**

COELACANTH *Latimeria chalumnae.*
Other names—latimeria; Afrikaans: *seelakant.*

The coelacanth is not a species of interest to anglers, but it is one of the greatest curiosities of the seas and an important link to the evolutionary past. It is the only known species in its genus and family, Latimeriidae, and is considered an endangered living fossil.

A sensational zoological discovery was made in December 1938 when a coelacanth was netted from the depths of the western Indian Ocean off the Comoro Islands along the coast of South Africa. Before then, coelacanths were known only from fossil records of the Devonian period, considered to be more than 360 million years ago. These fish, ancestors of present-day vertebrates, were believed to have become extinct many millions of years ago. The first specimen captured was sent to a taxidermist, who saved only the skin and not the organs. Scientists considered the decision a disaster. Since then, through a reward program to commercial

anglers in the area, other specimens have been made available to scientists and studied in detail.

Coelacanths have been caught in depths of between 75 to 200 fathoms at rocky areas with steep gradients. They evidently also exist in deeper water, but they are bottom fish and cannot be taken easily because ragged rocks prevent commercial fishing nets from reaching them. Very few have been taken by noncommercial fishing methods, although a specially outfitted Japanese expedition caught two specimens, one of 1 meter in length and the other 1.77 meters long (weighing 85 kilograms), in late 1981 using computerized electronic fishing equipment; these were exhibited in February 1982 at the Tokyo Fishing Show.

The maximum size the coelacanth can obtain is not known. They are a slow-moving species, found in caves. They may travel up to 8 kilometers in a night while foraging. They are an ovoviparous fish; that is, the eggs are retained inside the fish, and the young are born alive.

Coelacanth are not handsome fish. They are bulky in form and have shades of brown toward the belly. The scales are large, and the fish is well marked with irregularly shaped whitish or creamy splotches. They are predacious creatures, feeding exclusively on other fish. The fin structure is the coelacanth's most unusual external feature. The second dorsal, pectorals, and pelvics are supported by a stalklike arrangement or lobes—thus the name lobefins (or lobefin fish)—that appear limblike. The fins are supported by their own skeleton and are fortified by an elaborate system of muscles, enabling the coelacanths to move in a wide range of positions.

The value of living coelacanths is their great antiquity; they are by far the oldest vertebrates alive today. Whereas dominant animals such as dinosaurs disappeared from the earth, the coelacanth has remained unchanged throughout the ages. This has been proven by imprints in geological strata and by the paleontologists who reconstructed these fossils before the first coelacanth was taken alive. In addition, coelacanths are the only survivors of the large group of crossopterygians, the focal group from

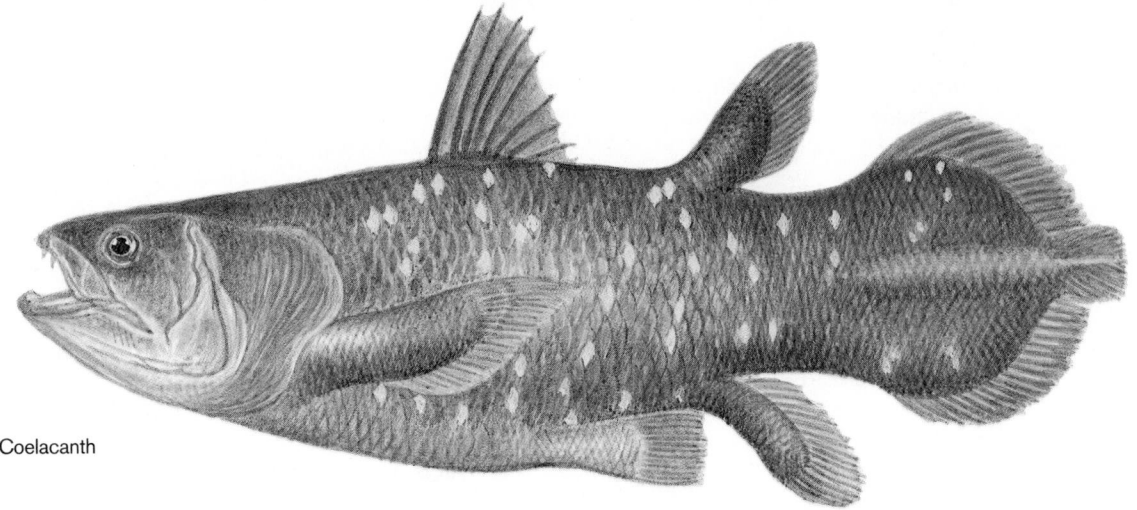

Coelacanth

which evolved the entire lineage of air-breathing vertebrates up to humans.

The causes for their survival over the ages and their peculiar restriction to the north of the Mozambique Channel between Madagascar and Africa remain a mystery.

COLDWATER FISH

A term for freshwater species whose optimum environment contains cold and well-oxygenated water, usually under 60°F, throughout the season; trout, salmon, grayling, whitefish, and cisco are among this group. They inhabit coldwater streams and generally infertile lakes; in lakes their deep environs must have cold, well-oxygenated water through the summer.

See: Coolwater Fish; Warmwater Fish.

COLLECTING

See: Antique Fishing Tackle; Book Collecting.

COLOMBIA

The only South American country with coasts on both the Caribbean Sea and the Pacific Ocean, Colombia offers fine sportfishing possibilities; unfortunately, these largely hang under a dark cloud of suspicion due to safety concerns. Well-publicized problems with crime exist here for tourists, depending on their nationality and the passport they carry. Although this may not be true for all areas of the country, Colombia's reputation as a dangerous country has largely curtailed sportfishing development and exploration.

In the mid-1980s, developing opportunities in the interior of Colombia—in waters that flow to the Orinoco River—were providing what was at the time arguably the world's best fishing for peacock bass and payara, plus outstanding opportunities for other species. The region in which these fisheries existed was a haven for illicit drug activities, however, and caused travel here to virtually shut down. Although coastal fishing is reputedly less risky, infrastructure remains limited, and interest—especially from North Americans—has been greatly dampened by safety concerns, resulting in little to no recreational angling in many places.

Freshwater

Colombia's principal river is the Magdalena, which flows between mountain ranges from south to north for a distance of 960 miles, emptying into the Caribbean near Barranquilla. A significant tributary to the Magdalena is the Cauca River, which flows for some 200 miles. Sportfishing opportunities and major species in these large waterways have been unreported in recent times. Rainbow trout reportedly existed in the 1960s in mountain waters, and in Lake Tota near Bogota and Lake Cocha near Pasto,

although no recent information is available at this writing.

A vast area of eastern Colombia consists of plains, rain forest, and tropical lowlands. It is lightly populated, and traversed by numerous rivers. These flow from the Bolivian Andes to Brazil and Venezuela, contributing respectively to the Amazon and Orinoco Rivers. The many rivers and fish species here are described in the Amazon review under Brazil *(see).*

Saltwater

Colombia has 1,090 miles of Caribbean coastline and 900 miles of Pacific coastline, the latter between Panama to the north and Ecuador to the south, with many inlet rivers and few harbors. Significant species known to exist along these coasts include sailfish, blue marlin, striped marlin, black marlin, wahoo, amberjack, roosterfish, dolphin (dorado), yellowfin tuna, tarpon, and snook.

Most of these are found on the Pacific side, the species being similar to those found in Panama *(see)* waters. In the mid-1990s, anglers were fishing from Solano Bay on the northwest coast, where deep water is 20 to 50 miles from shore, and fish prowl a series of dropoffs. Fishing for sailfish and striped marlin was reportedly best from April through June, for other marlin from June through August, for tuna from April through July, and for dolphin from December through August. The Cabo Marzo area to the north of this has a good reputation but is difficult to reach. A number of significant rivers in Colombia enter the Pacific, but no information about their fisheries—at the mouth or upriver—is known, although snook are likely found here.

The Caribbean coast is also reported to have sailfish, marlin, tuna, dolphin, wahoo, and the like in offshore environs, as well as tarpon and snook inshore; although here, too, there are no current reports on abundance, seasonal availability, fishing camps, or charter services. The deltaic mouth of the Magdalena River covers a large expanse of lagoons, lakes, and estuarine area; in the past, tarpon were reportedly caught as far up the Magdalena as El Banco, and up the Cauca River to Ayapel.

COLORADO

You would expect a state that covers more than 104,000 square miles and includes 54 peaks that exceed 14,000 feet to have a lot of flowing water and plenty of trout. And, indeed, Colorado does, with approximately 10,000 miles of streams and more than 2,000 natural lakes and reservoirs, which together cause about 750,000 licenses to be sold annually to resident and nonresident anglers. Moreover, it is a headwater state with the unique distinction that every stream within it originates from the Rocky Mountain region.

The Centennial State lies within three geologic areas. The Eastern Plains covers the eastern third of the state from the Front Range to the Kansas-Nebraska line; here, in the southeast, is the state's lowest elevation of 3,500 feet. The Colorado Plateau covers much of the western third, and this includes the Colorado River, which exits midstate into Utah. The Rocky Mountains extend south from Wyoming to New Mexico through the central area, where they are bifurcated in the south by the San Luis Valley.

The central area is responsible for all of the state's water. Here, the Rockies quickly rise from just over 5,000 feet to more than 14,000 feet along and near the Continental Divide. Glaciers formed the present landscape on both sides of the divide and left behind countless small streams fed by alpine lakes and snow melt. These waters contain native species of cutthroat trout: the greenback cutthroat is natural to the East Slope, the Rio Grande cutthroat originates from the Southern Rockies, and the Colorado River cutthroat is indigenous to the Colorado River drainage. The native greenback cutthroat, a species once believed extinct and recovered in the 1990s, is Colorado's state fish.

Although trout are the primary species sought by anglers, the Colorado Division of Wildlife (CDOW) has significantly expanded the number of game species available. In addition to the three native cutthroat trout, anglers have the opportunity to fish for such other coldwater species as Snake River cutthroats, golden trout, brown trout, rainbow trout, brook trout, lake trout, splake, Dolly Varden trout, mountain whitefish, arctic grayling, and arctic charr in coldwater lakes and streams. Anglers also can catch such warmwater denizens as largemouth bass, smallmouth bass, striped bass, hybrid stripers, white bass, northern pike, tiger muskies, walleye, sauger, saugeye, crappie, perch, bluegills, catfish, and bullhead.

The general fishing season runs year-round, although the winter months are limited to fishing tailwaters for trout, and ice fishing for all species. Anglers who prefer to fish streams for trout pursue their sport beginning in March or April. Most rivers below 8,000 feet will be open by then, and pre-runoff angling is often exceptional. Open streams correspond with rainbow spawning, and egglike fly patterns are extremely productive then for rainbows and browns.

The timing of the runoff depends on the snowpack, late-spring storms, and warming temperatures. On average, snow at the middle elevations (7,000 to 9,000 feet) begins to melt in April or May. Lakes and reservoirs at these elevations begin to open, offering excellent angling during the short ice-out period. Runoff normally peaks in early June and begins to subside by mid-June, about the time the high lakes (to 10,000 feet) become ice free. In July the higher elevations (above 11,000 feet) open, although a few alpine lakes may not open until August.

Prime stream fishing follows the runoff. Summer also brings the majority of insect hatches, and excellent angling continues into October. Fly anglers use a variety of patterns to imitate mayflies, caddisflies, stoneflies, midges, and terrestrials, whereas those using other gear are successful with small spinners and spoons, or bait where legal. The fall is often preferred by the more dedicated angler because of decreasing numbers of people. Winter trout fishing on tailwaters is primarily done using flies, mainly very small midge and mayfly or caddisfly nymphs. The most used nymphing rig consists of a leader with a fine tippet, a small amount of weight, and a strike indicator.

On the Eastern Plains, warmwater reservoirs are normally open by March or April. Spring is a prime time to fish these reservoirs because of mild temperatures, cool water that makes the fish more accessible, and increasing fish activity. Summer angling is best early and late in the day.

Colorado was hit hard in the 1990s by whirling disease *(see: diseases and parasites),* an organism that destroys cartilage in trout fry. The disease is usually fatal to young trout. It affects rainbow trout most severely, and caused a significant reduction in spawning success on some of the state's coldwater rivers. Both hatcheries and streams were infected. In some cases, the loss of rainbow trout was offset by an increase in the brown trout population.

The Colorado Division of Wildlife classifies trout water as Gold Medal and Wild Trout. The Gold Medal designation is given to streams, lakes, and reservoirs that have high-quality aquatic habitat, a high percentage of trout 14 inches or longer, and the potential for trophy trout fishing and angling success. Wild Trout Water designates streams and lakes in which the trout population is self-sustaining without stocking.

Angling behavior and attitudes in Colorado have changed in recent decades, and catch-and-release fishing is more prevalent for both coldwater and warmwater species. Artificial flies and lures have become increasingly popular as anglers attempt to minimize the impact on the state's fisheries. Many anglers in Colorado rate their fishing on the quality and aesthetics of the experience rather than on the total number of fish caught.

Colorado's water is completely allocated. The juggling of a scarce resource requires constant monitoring to meet all of the state's needs and, at the same time, keep water in the rivers. Because most of Colorado's water originates on public lands, the U.S. Forest Service requires that streams on forest lands maintain minimum flows, thereby preventing dewatering of these streams and thus providing fish habitat.

About one-third of Colorado's land is in the public domain and under the jurisdiction of federal and state agencies. Federal lands are administered by the U.S. Forest Service, the Bureau of Land Management, and the National Park Service. State lands include CDOW properties, State Trust properties, and lands administered by the Colorado

A 2,704-pound Russian sturgeon captured in 1924 yielded 541 pounds of caviar, which was worth $300,000 in 1995 market value. Guinness lists this as the world's most valuable fish (commercial).

State Forest Service. This opens many miles of streams and numerous lakes to the public. A majority of the state's high natural lakes are within designated wilderness areas. Access to these waters is restricted to foot and horseback travel. The majority of Colorado's high lakes (above 10,000 feet) were once barren; by planting native (to elsewhere in the state) and exotic species, management agencies made fishing possible, and today they maintain the fishery through periodic stocking of fingerlings.

Despite Colorado's wealth of public land, it has only a small number of legally navigable streams. These waters are rivers can be floated without trespass. Where streams flow through private property, a landowner not only owns the land along the stream, he also owns the stream bottom and can legally prevent access, both for wading and boating. The fish, however, belong to the state. On the navigable-stream sections of the Colorado, Arkansas, Roaring Fork, Gunnison, Animas, and Yampa Rivers, anglers can float and fish through private property as long as they remain in the boat and do not set foot on the private property.

In some cases anglers can fish private property by joining private clubs. A few of these club-managed waters offer angling for better-than-average-size fish, both cold- and warmwater species. Naturally, private waters are available through leasing arrangements to individuals or clubs, and outfitters and guides take clients to excellent waters that may not be accessible to the public.

In addition to the many fishable waters on public land, the Division of Wildlife has developed both coldwater and warmwater fisheries in many Colorado cities. Perhaps every city and town of any size has at least one lake or pond to fish.

Northeast Region

The South Platte River originates near Fairplay, about 100 miles west of Denver. Three reservoirs on the upper river—Antero, Spinney Mountain, and Elevenmile—produce large, fast-growing rainbows, browns, and Snake River cutthroats. The latter two reservoirs also have large northern pike, some of which are taken on flies. Spinney Mountain Reservoir is a designated Gold Medal site. Fifty miles southwest of Denver, the Platte offers world-class tailwater angling in Cheesman Canyon for particularly selective rainbows and browns. The Platte also has close-to-home stream fishing for rainbows and browns in Waterton Canyon.

In the Denver Metro area, Cherry Creek and Chatfield Reservoirs—both contained in state parks—plus Quincy, Aurora, and Bear Creek Reservoirs provide close-in angling for trout, walleye, yellow perch, hybrid striped bass (called wiper), crappie, largemouth bass, and smallmouth bass. Most city-park lakes in the Metro area are stocked with a variety of the same species.

The South Platte River flows northeast from the Denver Metro area to Nebraska. Irrigation reservoirs in the drainage offer a significant and varied warmwater sportfishing resource. The majority of these privately owned reservoirs are open to the public through arrangements with the CDOW. East of Denver along Interstate 76, Barr Lake, Jackson, Prewitt, Sterling, and Jumbo Reservoirs offer angling for bass, crappie, yellow perch, wipers, and walleye. Barr Lake has trout in addition to these species.

The Cache la Poudre River west of Fort Collins, and the Big Thompson River west of Loveland, are both tributaries of the South Platte and offer angling for brown trout, rainbow trout, and whitefish. Between Fort Collins and Denver near the Front Range, some irrigation reservoirs are open through the CDOW and provide fishing for largemouth and smallmouth bass, walleye, wipers, catfish, sunfish, yellow perch, trout, and kokanee salmon. Reservoirs open to angling include Horsetooth, Carter, Boyd, Horseshoe, Boedecker, Lon Hagler, Lonetree, and Boulder. Tiger muskies were stocked in Lon Hagler Reservoir. Along Interstate 25, Barbour Ponds and Big Thompson Ponds State Wildlife Areas offer warmwater fishing.

In and around Colorado Springs are reservoirs that provide fishing for warmwater species. Rainbow trout, Snake River cutthroats, Pikes Peak cutthroats, and mackinaw (lake trout) in the Pikes Peak region are found at Rampart Reservoir and at North and South Catamount Reservoirs. Bison and Skagway Reservoirs are open in state wildlife areas.

Bonny Reservoir, about 15 miles west of the Kansas line on the Republican River, is the only important fishery between the Platte and Arkansas Rivers. Part of the state park system, this large reservoir holds bass, tiger muskies, saugeye, crappie, walleye, wipers, and catfish.

Southeast Region

The Arkansas River originates in Twin Lakes near Leadville. The lakes hold rainbow, cutthroat, and large mackinaw trout. The river is an excellent brown trout fishery, with many miles of public access through Brown's Canyon and the Salida and Granite areas. The river is famous for its Mother's Day caddis hatch.

Downstream, in Pueblo Reservoir, the largemouth and smallmouth bass fishing is so good, tournaments are held there. It also has walleye and wipers. The tailwater below Pueblo Dam has brown trout. The Runyon/Fountain State Wildlife Area in Pueblo offers both warmwater and coldwater angling. East of Pueblo, Lake Meredith, Lake Henry, Horse Creek, Adobe Creek, and John Martin Reservoirs are the primary warmwater fisheries.

North of Lamar, near the southeast corner of the state, Nee So Pah, Nee Gronda, Nee Noshe, and the two Queens Reservoirs are open as state wildlife areas. The lakes have wipers, saugeye, crappie, catfish, and white bass.

Northwest Region

North Park in Jackson County is known for lakes with brook, brown, cutthroat, and rainbow trout. The three Delaney Buttes Lakes, as well as Lake John and the Big Creek Lakes, have good forage, and trophy fish are not unusual. The North Platte River originates here and flows north into Wyoming. Fly fishing in the summer for browns and rainbows is excellent on the North Platte. Other trout streams in North Park include Norris, Roaring, and Grizzly Creeks, the North Fork of the North Platte, and the Michigan and Illinois Rivers.

The Colorado River is fed by every stream heading on the West Slope. It begins in Rocky Mountain National Park, where anglers may catch but not keep brook, brown, and rainbow trout. Shadow Mountain Reservoir and Lake Granby are heavily stocked with these species. Granby also has kokanee salmon and large mackinaws. Anglers sometimes catch fish between the two reservoirs.

Between Granby and Glenwood Springs more than one-third of the Colorado River is open to fishing for browns, rainbow-cutthroat hybrids, and rainbows. Downstream from Gore Canyon near Kremmling, more than 60 miles of the Colorado can be floated, with the opportunity to catch large brown trout. The Fraser, Williams Fork, Blue, Eagle, Roaring Fork, and Fryingpan Rivers are prime fisheries that join the Colorado. The Fryingpan is noted for its July green drake hatch, while a mid-April caddis hatch occurs on the Roaring Fork and Colorado. Between Glenwood Canyon and Rifle, the Colorado is too large to wade, but fishing from the bank or a raft can be good for cutthroat and rainbow trout. From Rifle to the Utah line, the river turns into a warmwater fishery. Endangered species—squawfish, humpback chub, and razorback suckers—could seriously reduce sportfishing opportunities in this section.

Both the North and South Forks of the White River begin in the Flat Tops Wilderness Area. From their headwaters downstream to Buford, where they merge, these waters offer angling for brook, brown, cutthroat, and rainbow trout, plus whitefish in the lower stretches as well as in the White River between Buford and Meeker.

The Yampa River is formed by the confluence of Bear River and Chimney Creek at the town of Yampa. From there, the river runs north into Stagecoach Reservoir, completed in 1989 and containing rainbows and northern pike. From the reservoir, the Yampa is a free-flowing river to its confluence with the Green. Anglers catch northern pike along with trout in the river around Steamboat Springs.

The Taylor and East Rivers merge at Almont in the Central Rockies to form the Gunnison River, 10 miles north of Gunnison. The Taylor has a half-mile stretch of tailwater angling for very large rainbows that are measured in pounds. West of Gunnison, Blue Mesa and Morrow Point

Fishing for trout on a tributary of the Yampa River.

Reservoirs flood much of the river. Both have trout and kokanee, while Blue Mesa also produces large mackinaws. Good rainbow and brown trout fishing on the Gunnison River is available to anglers via rugged foot access in the Black Canyon section of Gunnison National Monument.

The Uncompahgre River joins the Gunnison River at Montrose. About 20 miles south of the town, Ridgeway Reservoir provides trout fishing in the lake and in the tailwater below the dam.

Southwest Region

The Rio Grande begins its long journey to the Gulf of Mexico high in the San Juan Mountains of southwest Colorado. It has good brown and rainbow trout fishing from Rio Grande Reservoir downstream to Del Norte. Fly fishing is best in June and July when stonefly and mayfly hatches dominate the trout's diet. The section from South Fork to Del Norte provides an opportunity to catch trophy brown trout and northern pike. Much of the river is privately owned, but public access is available on state leases.

The San Juan is the main stream in southwest Colorado, collecting the flows of all other southwest Colorado rivers. Because of limited public access, although, the Piedra, Pinos, Florida, and Animas Rivers provide the most stream-fishing opportunities. The Animas offers excellent trophy fishing within the city limits of Durango.

McPhee Reservoir and dam turned the Dolores River from a fair fishery into a very good tailwater

C

that holds brown trout and Snake River cutthroat trout. The reservoir has both coldwater and warm-water species. Below McPhee, about 30 miles of the Dolores is open for wade fishing and float fishing. The San Miguel is the main tributary, although nearly every stream in the region also offers trout fishing.

High-Mountain Lakes and Streams

Throughout the Rockies, countless small streams, some only 3 feet wide, provide angling opportunities primarily for small brook and cutthroat trout. Many of these streams have beaver ponds that hold fish averaging 6 to 10 inches, but they are eager to strike. Favorable conditions can grow 12- to 18-inch trout in the ponds, but this is rare. In most high-mountain lakes, the cutthroats can be temperamental, feeding only when weather conditions and insect activity are optimal. In many cases, headwater streams are rarely visited, offering a combination of solitude and fast fishing.

The Colorado State Forest along the Jackson-Larimer County line offers a rugged landscape with scattered alpine lakes, and at least one has golden trout. The Grand Mesa National Forest in western Colorado is dotted with roughly a hundred small reservoirs, which are maintained by stocking. The Mesa offers angling for rainbow, brook, splake, brown, and cutthroat trout. Most are accessed by road or a short walk.

About 75 percent of Colorado's high lakes are within wilderness areas. This gives the adventurous angler an opportunity to backpack, or use horse or llama to reach remote lakes for extended periods. Those who journey into the backcountry can expect to find less-crowded settings than they would in easily accessible areas. A few high-altitude lakes might be visited by only a dozen anglers in a season. Because of harsh conditions, the fishing season above the timberline (11,500 feet) might be as short as six to eight weeks. Anglers will find an assortment of species including cutthroat, rainbow, brook, golden, and mackinaw trout, and grayling. Wilderness lakes at the higher elevations rarely have conditions conducive to spawning. When this is the case, the state periodically stocks them with fingerlings. Alpine conditions are severe enough to slow growth rates.

Wilderness areas that have consistently good angling include Rocky Mountain National Park; the Comanche Peak and Rawah Wilderness Areas in Roosevelt National Forest; Indian Peaks, Eagles Nest, Never Summer, and Mount Evans in Arapaho NF; Mount Zirkel in Routt NF; Flat Tops, Holy Cross, Maroon Bells, and Hunter-Fryingpan in White River NF; La Garita and West Elk in Gunnison NF; and South San Juan and Weminuche in the San Juan NF.

COLUMNARIS
See: Diseases and Parasites.

Legends persist of 100-pound muskellunge, but the largest sport-caught muskie was a controversial St. Lawrence River fish that weighed 1 ounce shy of 70 pounds when taken in 1957.

COMMERCIAL FISHERMAN
A person who catches fish and shellfish for the purpose of sale. In a general sense, this includes all people who sell their catch, regardless of the capture methods used. It is usually inferred that a commercial fisherman is one who uses harvesting equipment, such as seines and nets, designed to capture numbers or volume; however, this term may include those who capture fish individually on rod and reel, and sell them. Theoretically, a commercial fisherman and a sportfisherman (an angler) are distinguished by methods and intent, but in saltwater the distinguishing line can be blurred in places where anglers who use a rod and reel, and as such are counted as recreational anglers, sell some or all of their rod-and-reel catch. Furthermore, some people harvest fish for their personal consumption without the use of "sporting" equipment; these people are not commercial fishermen or anglers, but they would be considered recreational fishermen because they do not sell their catch.
See: Angler; Recreational Fisherman; Sportfisherman.

COMMERCIAL FISHERY
The entire process of catching and marketing fish and shellfish for sale. This includes fisheries resources, commercial fishermen, and related businesses directly or indirectly involved in harvesting, processing, or sales.
See: Commercial Fisherman.

COMMUNICATIONS
Until the advent of cellular telephones, most electronic voice communications in sportfishing boats were made via fixed-mount or portable VHF (Very High Frequency) radios, and some with fixed-mount CB (Citizen's Band) radios. CB radios are rarely used in boats, in part because there are so few other boaters with these devices, and in part because there is no channel monitoring by marine authorities or channels set aside for marine purposes, particularly the transmission of weather information and contact with the Coast Guard. VHF radios are the standard communications tool on boats, primarily for boat-to-boat communications, although for the sake of a backup and for privacy purposes (anyone with a marine radio can overhear communications if they are tuned into the same frequency and within range), cellular phones have become very popular. Those who can afford them may also use satellite communications devices.

VHF Radio
Very High Frequency (VHF) radios are the standard for marine communications, particularly for communication between boats and for emergency purposes. These radiotelephones are the prescribed method of marine ship-to-ship and ship-to-shore communications; they are limited by law to 25

watts output power and are required to be licensed. Available in fixed-mount and handheld versions, VHF radios are standard equipment on virtually all charter boats and inshore saltwater guide boats. Many private boats possess a VHF radio as well, especially if they navigate waters within the jurisdiction of the Coast Guard, which monitors certain frequencies (channels). Various channels are set aside for specific marine purposes. All distress calls, for example, must be made on channel 16. Receive-only channels are designated for weather broadcasts, which are available on a full-time basis.

Fixed-mount VHFs. Fixed-mount VHF radios are the most common tool for small-boat anglers. VHF radios are used rarely by some anglers and too frequently by others. In some locations, the amount of chatter—most of it mindless—on the radio causes anglers to keep their VHF off except to get a current weather report, call for help, or check in with a friend at pre-arranged times. Some anglers rarely talk on their radios, but leave them on to intercept fishing reports between others in the area. The purpose here is to find out what other anglers are doing (either in terms of success or places they fish) as an aid to their own fishing efforts. This may produce useful information, but it may lead (sometimes deliberately) to a wild goose chase. A great deal of misinformation is passed around on VHF radios by anglers, and the whole psychology of this aspect of fishing is an interesting one, but not worth delving into in this book. Suffice it to say that fishing information obtained or overhead on the radio from anonymous sources is on a caveat emptor basis. However, a group of anglers working together can use the radio (overtly or covertly, usually the latter) to share information that is useful to them all. This usually quid pro quo action pays off for them all over time.

VHF radios range widely in price and features. They are capable of transmitting up to 25 miles on a line-of-sight basis, depending on the height of the transmitting and receiving antennas, but their range is usually less due to other factors. Most VHF radios list their output power as the legal maximum of 25 watts, but many do not actually put out 25 watts when used, which may greatly affect performance. Heat buildup in a VHF causes output to drop unless the unit can dissipate the heat or otherwise overcome the output drop. Radios encased in metal, rather than plastic, have a greater ability to dissipate heat. Output is also related to the voltage level of a battery, which supplies the power. A fully charged battery should produce 25 watts of radio output, but that output lessens when a battery is weaker. Better radios produce more output (although less than 25 watts) than others when the battery voltage is low. Most units are said to be water-resistant, but some are much more so than others. Some are said to be waterproof, but there's a big difference between that and being water-resistant (waterproof means it can be submerged; water-resistant means it can be splashed).

Most of the time, fixed-mount VHF radios are installed inside a console and away from the weather, because even the best models cannot indefinitely survive a constant hosing, especially of saltwater. Often the console is crammed with other electronics, like sonar and navigation gear, and finding a good place that separates these items adequately can be a problem.

More of a problem is the antenna. The best radio is only as good as its antenna, and this is where small-boat anglers have trouble because they like a small antenna that doesn't get in the way of casting. A longer antenna, like a typical 8-footer, provides good range. It can be mounted on the gunwale via a bracket that allows it to lay flat when not in use. But on many of today's more popular rigs, that gunwale is kept open and clear for other uses, so this is acceptable only when you aren't casting. If the antenna is down, however, this means that the unit is off and possibly not being useful. Yet, if it sits atop the console, it is not only in the way of just about everything, especially fly rods, but its close proximity to other electronics (and even the VHF transceiver itself) can create a whole new set of problems.

If the antenna is placed too close to other electronic devices, when you key the mike it produces interference with other devices and may blow fuses. Those who are willing to sacrifice some range to get away from long antennas resort to smaller, more compact antennas, like a 3-foot whip with a short fat loading coil at the base. Generally, however, shorter antennas mean much shorter transmitting range.

If the VHF transceiver and antenna are placed too close together, it can cause feedback, usually in the form of a squeal when the mike is keyed, so you need to separate these by a reasonable distance. A foot should be enough most of the time. No matter how close the unit and the antenna, keep at least 6 feet of coaxial cable between them; it's better to coil up the extra footage than to cut it too short. To get rid of the feedback squeal, disconnect the antenna cable from the back of the VHF, tie a very loose figure-eight knot in it, then reconnect. You might have to change the size and location of that knot a few times to get it right, but this quick fix usually works.

A VHF radio should be separated a greater distance from a GPS receiver, perhaps 10 feet, or when the radio is used it will cause the GPS to lose its satellite signal; it can reacquire that within seconds after the radio is used, but that can be, at the very least, a nuisance, especially if the signal is lost repeatedly in a back-and-forth radio conversation. It may also be necessary to mount some items higher than others for best performance. Some manufacturers recommend putting a GPS receiver 2 feet higher than the VHF radio to avoid interference.

If you don't use your VHF often, you can determine if it's transmitting properly when you do turn it on with a small meter that fits in-line between the VHF and the antenna. It can be mounted inside the console where you can see it, so when you use the VHF for the first time in months, you can see at a glance if it's working.

Hand held VHFs. There are times when the ability to quickly and easily communicate with another boat is important and would not be possible without hand held VHF radios. These are often relegated to small boaters but may be useful in any size boat when traveling to foreign-language speaking countries, to places where there are no (or few) radios, as a backup for a fixed-mount unit, and for use when away from a larger boat with a fixed-mount unit.

Size and portability is the primary advantage for hand held VHFs, but significantly less range is a primary disadvantage. Hand held units have limited (5-watt) output power and integrated antennas; this combination limits their effective range under the best of conditions to 4 to 5 miles (more or less depending on height). Furthermore, although they are diminutive enough to be easily portable, their small keypad is harder to use, the small speaker inhibits audio quality, and their usefulness is limited to battery life.

Extension antenna. It is possible to considerably extend the range of a fixed-mount or hand held VHF by using any sort of long pole to raise an antenna to an elevation that's 12 or more feet higher. If the antenna disconnects easily from the mounting and the cord is long enough, use the antenna cord usually hooked up to your fixed-mount radio for this. If not, you need a separate antenna. This is also true for hand held radios. Any good 3- to 4- foot sailboat masthead VHF antenna works fine. Using 25 feet of the proper coaxial cable, and the necessary connectors for your VHF, rig the antenna to one end of a long pole. A pushpole is perfect for this. Place the pole in a rod holder or lash it to something that will keep it vertical, connect the cable to the VHF, and go on the air. In many cases you'll more than double your effective range, especially if you're far from land, in a backcountry creek, or other remote area. Keep an emergency antenna stowed in a plastic tube, complete with the necessary coax cable, where it is out of the way but quickly available.

Cellular Telephone

Cellular telephones have become common on sportfishing boats, and may be the best communication tool in an emergency, provided that the user can get a signal and is within range of a transmission tower. Though not a marine radio, the cellular phone is nonetheless a prominent communications device. A cellular telephone has the technical advantages of theoretical access to and from all land-based telephone systems, easy and familiar use, and no licensing requirement. For anglers the biggest advantage is a practical one of privacy; you won't be telling the whole world where you found the fish when you pass that information

along to someone else. That is often not the case when using a VHF radio.

A cellular phone, however, is not truly a marine radio, there are charges associated with each transmission, and it does not provide instant marine information. Therefore, cellular telephones are generally used fairly close to population centers for transmission purposes, and as an adjunct to a VHF radio. Usually a cellular phone's working distance over the water is ten times that over land, but it won't do well in the midst of tall trees and other obstacles, as in fishing tidal creeks and inland bays. Sometimes elevation is the cure for that; standing on top of the poling platform or in a tower may make a difference. Moving the boat far from trees or high banks may also be helpful.

Satellite Communications Devices

Although not as widely used as cellular telephones, and far more expensive, satellite communications devices are available, and they offer the ability to communicate anywhere in the world. Some not only offer voice communications, but also fax and data transmissions. The number of satellites servicing these devices has been expanding and will eventually be numerous enough to provide full-time (24-hour) service anywhere in the world. Some systems can be interfaced with GPS, or are part of a combined GPS/communications unit. This aspect of communications will become a more integral part of the big-water boater's equipment.

COMPASS

An instrument used for showing direction, a compass features a free-swinging magnetic needle that points to magnetic north. A compass is marked with points of direction and sometimes degrees of a circle. It is used for navigation *(see)* and is important to many anglers who use boats or visit backcountry waters.

Anglers who boat on large bodies of water, who fish at night, or who may encounter conditions that would obscure their vision (fog or severe weather), should have some type of compass. Boaters using a fixed-mount marine compass should be aware of the need to zero-in the compass for accuracy and to mount it away from metal, magnetic, and electrical influences, which may be difficult in the confined console area of small boats.

Using a compass on a boat for basic purposes is fairly straightforward, especially when there's a clear path of travel from one position to another. It can become more involved when great distances are traveled and navigational charts have to be referenced. Using a compass on land, of course, is very different, and is often done in conjunction with a topographic (topo) map. For backcountry anglers, especially those who seek high-elevation lakes and ponds, a compass may be a very important piece of equipment. For anglers who visit remote areas

(South American rivers, for example, or northern Canada lakes), a compass should be a main or adjunct navigational accompaniment.

In the current age of electronic products, too many people, boaters as well as remote and back-country land travelers, have a tendency to rely on devices (mainly GPS) that may fail for lack of power (especially small batteries), which can be an obvious impediment to navigation. Therefore, it's important to keep a compass in your pack or emergency kit, and to have a basic understanding of how to use it. If you are ever placed in a survival situation, especially if lost in a remote area, having and using a compass could be critically important; thus, the following information is provided with respect to land-use of a compass (in conjunction with a topographic map), although general principles of use apply for big-water situations.

Compass basics.   A compass contains a magnetized steel needle that points toward magnetic north. The end of this needle will be black or red, stamped with the initial N, or shaped like an arrow.

The force that attracts this magnetized needle is the earth's magnetism. The earth is similar to a tremendous magnet, with one pole in the north, the other in the south. Compass needles always point toward magnetic north when at rest. The magnetic North Pole is about 1,400 miles south of the true North Pole. That means that there are two north directions to deal with: true north as is shown on a map, and magnetic north as it is found with the compass.

There are conventional and orienteering compasses. Conventional versions are of watch-case, pin-on, or wristwatch design. Orienteering compasses have a protractor and ruler as well as a magnetic needle, a revolving compass housing, and a transparent base plate. In some situations it is useful to have both, a pin-on model for quick reference and an orienteering compass for cross-country traveling while referencing a map.

A compass and topographic map are not difficult to use. Finding your way with one on land is known as orienteering and is easy to learn. Topo maps contain a wealth of information. Some topos have a scale of 1:24,000, which means that 1 inch on the map equals 24,000 inches (or 2,000 feet) in the field. It may be easier to visualize the area covered by such a map if the scale is translated as $2^5/_8$ inches equals 1 mile.

Topo maps usually show manmade structures, water, vegetation, and elevation. Each is represented in a distinct color. Manmade features include roads, trails, and buildings. All are depicted in black except some major highways, which may be red. Water features are printed in blue, vegetation in green.

Elevation is represented by thin brown contour lines. A contour line is an imaginary line on the ground along which every point is at the same height above sea level. Follow a brown line on the map, and you'll find a number. If the number is 100, for example, everything on that line is 100 feet above sea level. If the line next to it reads 200, then you have a rise of 100 feet and a contour interval of 100 feet (generally, the contour interval is 20 feet). This information is noted at the bottom of topographic maps.

Finding bearings.   To find a bearing with an orienteering compass, face the distant point toward which you want to know the direction. Hold the orienteering compass level before you, at waist height, with the direction-of-travel arrowhead pointing straight ahead.

Orient your compass by twisting the housing (without moving the base plate) until the needle lies over the orienting arrow on the inside bottom of the compass housing, with its north part pointing to the letter N on the top of the housing. What you've done is make your compass show actual field directions.

Read the degrees of your desired direction, which is the bearing, on the outside rim of the compass housing at the spot where the direction line, as an index pointer, touches the housing. That's all there is to it.

Following a bearing.   Suppose you're standing in a field and decide to travel cross-country to a distant hilltop. Set your orienteering compass for the direction of the hilltop by holding the compass in your hand with the direction-of-travel arrowhead pointing to your destination. Twist the compass housing until the north part of the compass needle points to the letter N on the housing rim. Proceed in the direction in which the direction-of-travel arrowhead points.

If you lose sight of the distant hilltop, hold the compass in front of you, orient it, and sight a nearby landmark in the direction in which the arrowhead points. Walk to that point, then take a similar reading to another landmark, and so on until you reach the destination.

You can forget about degrees and figures when you use an orienteering compass. Your compass is set. Just orient it and proceed.

Returning to original location.   Let's suppose that you've reached your destination and want to return to your original location. Your orienteering compass is already set for the return journey.

When you went out, you held the compass with the direction-of-travel arrowhead at the front of the base plate pointing away from you toward your destination. The back of the base plate was in the opposite direction, pointing backward toward the spot from which you came. Make use of this fact.

Hold the compass level in your hand but with the direction-of-travel arrow pointing toward you instead of away from you. Orient the compass by turning your body (don't touch the compass housing) until the north end of the compass needle points to the N on the compass housing. Locate a landmark, and head for your original starting point. Your compass is set—use it backward.

According to the United Nation's Food and Agricultural Organization, the world's leading fishing nation, as measured in weight of commercial catch, is China.

C

Using compass and map. The difference or angle between magnetic north and true north is called declination, and it varies according to your geographic location. The degree of declination is indicated on topo maps. Fortunately, magnetic north is also indicated on topo maps, and you can use it to avoid the whole problem of declination and adjusting map bearings.

Instead of compensating for declination, simply draw magnetic-north lines on your topo map. By using these lines instead of the true-north lines of the regular meridians, you make your map speak the same language as your compass. The settings you take on your compass using these lines do not require resetting to compensate for declination—the declination is already taken care of.

To provide your map with magnetic-north lines, draw a line up through the map on an angle to one of the meridian lines corresponding to the degrees of declination given on the map. Then draw other lines parallel to this line, 1 to 2 inches apart.

With your combined knowledge of map and compass, you can now travel from point to point. This is done with three easy steps:

1. On the map, line up your compass with your route. Place the orienteering compass on the map with one long edge of its base plate touching both your starting point and your destination, and with the base plate's direction-of-travel arrow pointing in the direction you want to go. Disregard the compass needle.

2. On the compass, set the housing to the direction of your route. Hold the base plate firmly against the map. With your free hand, turn the compass housing until the orienting arrow on the bottom of the housing lies parallel to the nearest magnetic-north line drawn on your map, with arrow-point to the top. Disregard the compass needle. The compass is now set for the direction to your destination. By using the drawn-in magnetic-north line, you have compensated for any compass declination in the territory covered by your map.

3. In the field, follow the direction set on the compass. Hold the compass in front of you, at waist height, with the direction-of-travel arrow pointing straight ahead. Turn yourself, while watching the compass needle, until the needle lies directly over the orienting arrow on the bottom of the compass housing, with the north end of the needle pointing to the letter N on the housing. The direction-of-travel arrow now points to your destination. Raise your head, pick a landmark, and walk to it. When you've reached it, again check the direction with your compass (be careful not to change the setting). Ahead is another landmark, and still another until you reach your destination. When it's time to return to your starting point, repeat this step, but keep the direction-of-travel arrow pointing toward you. Your compass is already set; simply use it backward to return home.

Applying compass use to high-country fishing situations is not difficult. If you can follow a bearing, you can easily travel across strange terrain to a remote lake you've found on a topo map. When it's time to head back, simply let your compass lead you safely back to camp. With a little practice, you'll be able to travel in unfamiliar territory with complete confidence.

See: GPS; Maps; Navigation; Survival.

COMPETITIVE FISHING

Contests that pit anglers against each other as well as against the fish—called tournaments, derbies, rodeos, or matches—exist for a wide range of species and purposes, with varying importance, prizes, and notoriety, not to mention viewpoints as to their merits and demerits.

More fishing tournaments are held for freshwater bass than any other single species, especially considering all the fishing clubs that hold small-scale competitions for their members. Counting these, the many big-game fishing tournaments, and even the contests run by local sporting goods stores, there are many thousands of events annually in North America alone, plus many more in other countries. In Europe, the primary competitive events are called matches, and match fishing is a specialized, highly competitive activity targeting coarse species.

Competitions focus on the weight of overall catch, on the basis of the largest specimen(s) of a given species, and on whether the effort is an individual accomplishment or that of a team of people (usually two to four). There are many different aspects to the competitions, and they may be one-day or multiple-day events, and sometimes season-long.

Some competitions, especially offshore saltwater events, have large purses and individual prizes.

In the modern era, many prominent fishing competitions are catch-and-release events. This is especially true for bass, and tournaments for these fish have fostered improvements in boat design and livewell construction and performance to help ensure that captured fish (which are usually brought alive to a central weighing point and then released) are returned to the water in good shape, although there is often some level of mortality. (Critics question the delayed mortality, which is when death occurs at a later and unobserved time, of fish that are retained and later released away from their capture sight after boat rides and handling.) Some tournaments, such as those for tarpon and bonefish, are conducted on a point basis for fish that are caught and released immediately at the site of capture. The killing of billfish and sharks in tournaments has been greatly curtailed or has been restricted to fish over a certain size, although some big-game events still result in the death of fish. Many contests on a lesser scale, particularly for stocked species like trout and salmon in the Great Lakes, do not have provisions for the release of any fish entered in the event.

In North America, fishing competitions are lightly regulated by some state fisheries agencies but not at all by others. Few saltwater tournaments have oversight. The level of attention to honesty and sportsmanship in competitions varies widely, although in today's organized events with high entry fees and major purses, and in events run by many well-organized clubs, officials take great steps to ensure that the events are above question. This was not always the case in the past.

Since the 1970s, fishing tournaments have created a new category of people who fish: professional anglers. Technically anyone who pays the entry fee for a fishing tournament and wins something of monetary value is a professional angler, but in common usage this term is attributed to those who fish in competitions as an occupation. This especially applies to bass and walleye tournament competitors, but there are also professional tournament anglers in saltwater, including some who compete in king mackerel events.

Large prizes are at stake in an increasing number of tournaments, including some in the six-figure range for winners of certain events; others feature calcuttas that may double the take-home purse. Many local competitions have modest prizes, perhaps just a trophy or inexpensive fishing merchandise. A lot of competitions are organized to provide funds to charity and even conservation causes.

COMPOSITE ROD

A composite rod is commonly understood to mean one that is constructed of multiple material fibers. This would primarily include a rod that blended fiberglass and graphite, or graphite and boron, in the fabrication of the rod blank. The percentage amounts of the different fibers vary widely, and there is no uniformity among manufacturers; thus, a rod whose fiber materials consisted of 5 percent graphite and 95 percent fiberglass might be marketed as a "graphite" rod, although it would likely be termed a "graphite composite rod."

To some degree, however, all rods, even those made from one material, are composites. Each rod blank consists of a strength or stress element, typically a fiber, and a bonding element, typically a resin. The stress element stores and transmits energy by elastic deformation, and the bonding element both fixes the location of the stress element and prevents the failure of one fiber from directly propagating to another. The material cannot function without being bonded, thus making the rod at the very least a composite of resin and fiber, and subject to evaluation as to percentages of each.
See: Rod, Fishing.

CONEY   *Cephalopholis fulva.*

Other names—French: *coné ouatalibi;* Spanish: *canario, cherna cabrilla, corruncha, guativere.*

The coney is a member of the Serranidae family of grouper.

Identification.   Because the coney experiences numerous color phases, it is inadvisable to try to identify this fish by color. These phases range from the common phase in which the fish is reddish brown, to a bicolor period in which the upper body is dark and the lower body is pale, to a bright yellow phase. The body is covered with small blue to pale spots, although the spots are uncommon in the bright-yellow phase. There are often two black spots present at the tip of the jaw and two more at the base of the tail, as well as a margin of white around the tail and the soft dorsal fin. The tail is rounded, and there are nine spines in the dorsal fin.

Size.   The coney weighs about a pound, although occasionally it can weigh as much as 3 pounds. The average length is 6 to 10 inches, and the maximum length is 16 inches.

Distribution.   In the western Atlantic, coney extend from Bermuda and South Carolina to southern Brazil, including the Gulf of Mexico and Atol das Rocas; they are commonly found in the Caribbean and less commonly in southern Florida and the Bahamas.

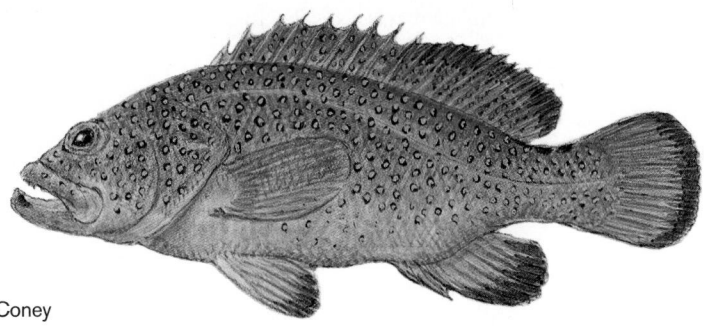

Coney

Habitat. In the Gulf of Mexico, coney occur in clear deep-water reefs, and in Bermuda and the West Indies they spend the day in caves and under ledges, preferring shallower water the rest of the time. Coney tend to drift immediately above the bottom or rest there in 10- to 60-foot depths, remaining in close proximity to protected areas.

Life history/Behavior. As with many grouper, coney females transform into males, usually when they reach 20 centimeters in length. They are gregarious fish, and the males are territorial.

Food. Coney feed mainly on small fish and crustaceans.

Angling. Like other grouper, anglers primarily catch coney by fishing at the right depth over irregular bottoms.

See: Grouper; Inshore Fishing.

CONNECTICUT

The word "variety" best describes the mix of fishing opportunities in the Nutmeg State. Although small in land area, Connecticut is well endowed with waters ranging from deep tidal rivers to pristine brook trout streams, including man-made impoundments, deep coldwater lakes, boglike ponds, and kettle holes left behind by glaciers. Within Connecticut's borders are an amazing total of 6,000 lakes and ponds and 8,400 miles of rivers and streams, although there are 209 principal lakes, 124 principal rivers, and 169 small streams—ample opportunity for anglers to fish for freshwater species within a short drive from literally anywhere in the state.

Those species include such typical and long-established fish as largemouth and smallmouth bass, chain pickerel, crappie, and assorted panfish, as well as walleye and northern pike. Among coldwater species, brown trout are by far the mainstays, but there are brook trout, rainbow trout, and Atlantic salmon here, in addition to opportunities for shad, sea-run brown trout, and tidewater striped bass.

Six of Connecticut's lakes are classified as bass management areas, and 11 streams as trout management areas (generally using some form management strategy such as no-kill, reduced creel limit, or increased size limit). Eleven rivers, primarily along the coast, are open to fishing year-round. In addition, 26 areas are designated as youth-only fishing, 29 lakes and rivers have handicapped fishing access, and there is a 1,000-foot-long fishing pier in East Lyme that is accessible to the handicapped.

Heavily stocked public fishing ponds are available at the state's Quinebaug Valley Hatchery, and hundreds more small private ponds and lakes can be fished with the permission of landowners. A growing number of private pay-to-fish areas are scattered around the state.

Anglers who like a challenge will enjoy fishing for surplus adult brood-stock Atlantic salmon weighing 4 to 14 pounds on average, occasionally stocked in state waters. And, during the winter and

early spring, hearty and reclusive anglers fish a half-dozen coastal rivers that sport remnant populations of sea-run brown trout, some of which reach 8 pounds or more.

Connecticut's saltwater fishery is every bit as compelling as its freshwater opportunities, yet when most anglers from outside southern New England think of great saltwater fishing, the state of Connecticut seldom comes to mind. Even the Dutch, the first Europeans to explore this coast in 1614, passed it by.

Connecticut boasts 253 miles of coastal shore-line, with outstanding opportunities for inshore and coastal species from Byram Point in the west to Pawcatuck Point next to Rhode Island. Connecticut shares this water, of course: half of Long Island Sound with New York, and part of Little Narragansett Bay with Rhode Island. New York and Rhode Island have a border in common, near the entrance to Lords Passage, just off the eastern end of New York's Fishers Island—in effect enclosing Connecticut's marine environs. These aquatic boundary lines hold little meaning for Connecticut anglers, who regularly fish such well-known grounds in New York as Plum Gut, The Race, Fishers Island Sound, and the numerous seaward passages between New York and Rhode Island.

Saltwater angling is an important element of recreational fishing among Connecticut anglers. Nearly one-third of the state's 3.75 million residents live along the coast. At most, it is an hour's drive for the remaining inland anglers bent for the sea. There, the major interests include striped bass, blackfish, flounder, fluke, bluefish, weakfish, mackerel, porgies, and black sea bass.

Freshwater

Ranking 48th in land mass among U.S. states, Connecticut is understandably not noted for big bodies of water. Man-made Lake Candlewood, Connecticut's largest, covers just 5,420 acres, which in most other states would be considered small. Its most significant waterway is the Connecticut River—the longest in New England. Even so, less than one-quarter of it crosses Connecticut en route to Long Island Sound. Inland fishing opportunities, therefore, are best viewed in terms of the Connecticut River and Lake Candlewood, and then by the major species available elsewhere.

The Connecticut River. The Connecticut River, which bisects the state and flows roughly 90 miles from Massachusetts to Long Island Sound, supports the best overall fisheries resource in the state. The river holds tremendous populations of largemouth and smallmouth bass, northern pike, white perch, yellow perch, black crappie, sunfish, white catfish, channel catfish, carp, shad, and striped bass. It even holds Atlantic salmon, produces an occasional walleye, and on rare occasions yields a sturgeon. As mentioned, the Connecticut

Fishing for shad on the Connecticut River.

River is by far the state's biggest, best, most accessible, and most varied fishery resource, and there are numerous shore-based and launch access sites all along the river.

Largemouth and smallmouth bass are especially prominent in the Connecticut River, and although some may disagree, this is likely the state's greatest fishery for those species. Both largemouth and smallmouth bass are caught from Hamburg Cove, which is just 6 miles north of Long Island Sound, all the way to the Massachusetts border in Enfield. Smallmouths are more prevalent north of Hartford and in the deep ledges and narrows around Portland and Middletown. Largemouths tend to dominate the slower-flowing backwater sloughs of the river. Places like Chapman's Pond in East Haddam, and Wethersfield Cove in Wethersfield, are year-round hotspots for bass.

Lake Candlewood.   Anglers will find unrivaled lunker trout fishing in Lake Candlewood, located near the western border with New York State. Like many Connecticut lakes, Candlewood has a quality two-story fishery for both bass and trout.

Candlewood is famous for its population of trophy brown trout. Maintained by a huge forage base of landlocked alewives, brown trout in Candlewood gorge themselves to large proportions; 7- to 10-pound brown trout are caught every year. Anglers land most of these large trout by jigging, trolling, deep-fishing with crankbaits or baitfishing in open and deep water around suspended schools of herring, locating them with sonar.

Along the shoreline, anglers will find both largemouth and smallmouth bass in abundance, mixed in with the usual variety of panfish. Largemouth bass fishing is especially productive here, as the lake contains every conceivable type of habitat, from deep rocky ledges to shallow weedbeds. The bass run to good size here, and the lake draws bass anglers from neighboring states, especially early in the season. Candlewood is also known to produce some monstrous white perch of 2 pounds and larger.

Trout waters.   For the most part, trout are sustained in Connecticut waters through hatchery plantings. Some of the better waters and those with excellent trout habitat are designated as Trophy Trout Lakes or Trout Management Areas and are subject to special regulations.

The state angling guide issued with licenses lists all of the lakes and streams in Connecticut that are stocked with trout, and the town of their location. Most of the lakes listed in that guide have free public access (and launch) areas. A few of the deeper lakes, such as Gardners Lake in Bozrah, Rogers Lake in Lyme, Beach Pond in Voluntown, East Twin Lake in Salisbury, Lake Waramaug in Kent, and Crystal Lake in Ellington thermally stratify and therefore hold trout throughout the summer, as do some of the other deep-water lakes. Smaller ponds and shallow lakes usually reach the upper limits of the trout's temperature tolerance by June, and therefore do not hold trout through the summer.

Likewise, most of the state's streams do not hold many trout through the summer, although most provide good trout fishing opportunities through mid- to late June. The state's best year-round trout rivers are the upper reaches of the Housatonic River north of Cornwall, and the Farmington River above Burlington, which has cold tributaries and enough summer habitat to hold fish all year.

To the east, anglers will experience great spring, and decent fall, trout action on the Yantic River in Lebanon/Bozrah, the Nachaug River in Chaplin, the Shetucket River from Scotland to Baltic, the Salmon River from Colchester to Haddam, and the Quinebaug River and its major tributaries from Canterbury to the Massachusetts border. The Shetucket and Quinebaug Rivers provide "big water" fishing conditions and some fabulous hatches during the spring and early summer.

Bass waters.   The aforementioned Lake Candlewood is probably the state's most noted bass water, in large part due to its size. Another larger lake, by local standards, is Pachaug Pond. At 830 acres this is the largest lake in eastern Connecticut. A shallow, weed-filled, heavily fished body of water, it traditionally exhibits fast-growing largemouths and produces its share of jumbo bass each year.

Connecticut is blessed with many small but productive largemouth bass lakes. Among the more notable of these are Winchester Lake in Winchester, Moodus Lake in Moodus, Lake Zoar in Oxford, Rogers and Uncas Lakes in Lyme, Powers Lake in East Lyme, Lake Waramaug in Kent, Lake Saltonstall in New Haven, and Mashapaug Lake in Union. Mashapaug is the site of Connecticut's state-record 12-pound, 14-ounce largemouth. Moodus Lake is known for its huge bass and has given up more than its share of largemouths of 8 pounds or better.

All of the state's waters that formerly contained only smallmouth bass have been contaminated with largemouths over time, so many waters have both species. This situation has often not worked to the benefit of resident smallmouths. The most notable lakes for smallmouth now include Lake Candlewood in Danbury, Shenipsit Lake in Ellington, Mashapaug Lake in Union, Saugatuck Reservoir in Easton, Waumgumbaug Lake (Coventry Lake) in Coventry, Wyassup Lake in North Stonington, Middle Bolton Lake in Bolton, Bashan Lake in East Haddam, West Hill Pond in New Hartford, and Lake Waramaug in Kent.

Survey work done throughout the state indicates the oldest and largest smallies are found in Wyassup Lake, Middle Bolton Lake, and Shenipsit Lake (site of the state-record $7^3/_4$-pound smallmouth).

Some good smallmouth bass fishing is available in rivers and streams, including a few of the trout streams that have shriveled up in midsummer. The Housatonic River is regionally famous for smallmouth fishing. The Connecticut, Norwalk, Saugatuck, and Upper Quinnipiac Rivers also sport fishable populations of smallmouth bass. In eastern Connecticut, the Shetucket River is the main big-stream smallmouth bass fishery; however, the Quinebaug, Yantic, Natchaug, Willimantic, and Salmon Rivers all come to life with smallies throughout the summer in a small-stream setting. Most of these little smallmouth rivers can be fished by wading, and are nearly 100 percent fishable with sneakers, shorts, and insect repellent. They are ideal for tiny fly rods and ultralight spinning gear with tiny jigs, spinners, and 2- to 3-inch-long soft-plastic jerkbaits.

Northern pike.   The Connecticut River is also the state's best fishery for northern pike, yielding fish up to 15 pounds every year. Bantam Lake in the town of Litchfield runs a close second. A managed fishery, Bantam has been greatly enhanced by pike spawning marshes. The Connecticut River's natu-rally spawning population of pike is used as a source of juvenile pike, which have been released at Mansfield Hollow Lake in Mansfield/Willimantic. Incidental pike are caught in the Quinebaug River system; these fish drop down from sources in the state of Massachusetts. Aspinook Pond, an impoundment on the Quinebaug River, regularly yields pike each year.

Walleye.   Connecticut has also experimentally stocked walleye in four lakes around the state. In the west, bordering on Candlewood Lake, Squantz Pond appears to be producing the largest, most numerous, but hardest to catch walleye in the state. Rogers Lake in Lyme, and Gardners Lake in Bozrah, seem to have fewer, smaller, but more catchable walleye. In addition to walleye, Gardners Lake has excellent fisheries for trout, largemouth and smallmouth bass, and panfish. Walleye have recently been stocked in Lake Saltonstall, a New Haven water-supply reservoir.

Panfish.   Connecticut has a small but avid group of anglers who pursue white perch in the Connecticut, Thames, Niantic, and Pawcatuck

Rivers each spring. Beginning sometime after ice out, the perch move upriver into spawning areas, where they concentrate in huge schools that provide some of the fastest action of the spring fishing sea-son. Hamburg Cove, Lieutenant River, Salmon River, and Connecticut Yankee's power plant out-flow on the Connecticut River are popular and pro-ductive spots. However, white perch, mixed with yellow perch, can be caught in any backwater of the river during the late winter and early spring. In the Thames River, Poquetanuck Cove and the Shetucket River above Norwich provide the most consistent white perch catches.

Black crappie, locally known as calico bass, reach their largest proportions in Pachaug Pond and Winchester Lake. Lake Lillinonah in Brookfield, Lake of Isles in North Stonington, Glasgow Pond in Voluntown, Highland Lake in Beach Pond, and the Connecticut River all contain healthy populations of calicos as well. Patagansett Lake in Old Lyme, which produced a 4-pound state-record calico in 1974, is always listed among top waters but has dropped off considerably in productivity over the years.

Shad.   The Connecticut River sports one of the premier American shad runs on the East Coast. Shad enter the lower river in early March and begin showing in anglers' creels north of Hartford by late April and early May. The most productive shad spots on the river are the rapids below the Enfield Dam, the mouth of the Farmington River, and the Windsor Locks Bridge. Anglers also pick up shad behind bridge abutments, islands, rocks, and other obstructions. The fish collect in the lee of such objects in order to rest during their upstream migration.

There is a secondary yet productive American shad fishery in the Thames River, located in south-eastern Connecticut. The potential of this run is enhanced by a fish-passage facility at the Greenville Dam, which opened during the spring spawning run of 1997.

All the major coastal rivers—the Housatonic, Connecticut, Thames, Niantic, and Mystic—sup-port fishable runs of hickory shad that are often mixed in with schoolie striped bass during the spring. These fish show up sporadically along the coast during the summer and move into coastal estuaries again during the late summer and fall, cre-ating excellent light-tackle opportunities. In the spring, the timing and location of hickory shad is neither as consistent nor as predictable as it is with American shad. The lower Connecticut River appears to develop the largest hickory shad run dur-ing both spring and fall fishing periods.

River and winter striped bass.   Although technically not a freshwater species, the fabulous spring (and to a lesser degree fall) striped bass runs provide excellent fishing in all major coastal rivers. Action is primarily from school stripers, although fish up to and occasionally exceeding 50 pounds are caught every year. Each spring, as hordes of striped bass migrate through Long Island Sound, they are

Ever heard of the sweetfish? Growing to 12 inches long, it is abundant and popular in streams in Taiwan and Japan, where it is caught with some very specialized methods.

C

drawn into the Connecticut, Housatonic, and Thames Rivers by migrating schools of herring, shad, and other forage species. The bass chase bait up to the first major dam or obstruction, where they gorge themselves till the herring runs subside and/or warming waters push them back out to sea, sometime in late May or June.

To a lesser degree the Saugatuck River in Fairfield County; the Hammonassett River in Middlesex County; the Quinnipiac River in New Haven County; and the Pawcatuck, Mystic, and Niantic Rivers in New London County also draw feeding runs of striped bass well upstream from Long Island Sound. Any angling north of Interstate 95 or Route 1, which is the freshwater demarcation line along the Connecticut coast, requires a freshwater license, regardless of species sought.

During the spring striper run, fishing action in these rivers can be exceptional. The novelty lies in the often "trout river" atmosphere in which these fish may be caught. In the shallows of these coastal rivers, anglers can catch striped bass on a variety of gear, including flies and light spinning tackle. For example, in the stretch of the Shetucket River (a major tributary to the Thames) north of Norwich and below Greenville Dam, in the waters below the Derby Dam on the Housatonic, or at Enfield Dam on the Connecticut River, anglers can wade the shallows and catch stripers when the tides are right, or fish for trout, panfish, black bass, and shad when stripers don't cooperate.

The reverse occurs during the fall runs, although at this time stripers do not run as far upstream, nor do they spend as much time in these rivers as they cool down for winter. The prime exception is the Thames River, which, due to its unique fiordlike qualities, draws and holds a huge population of striped bass throughout the winter. The fish tend to settle in the upper third of the Thames, as far north as Norwich Harbor, but move around to some degree in response to rains, snowmelt, and temperature changes throughout the winter. They school very densely, creating fabulous catch-and-release fishing on school fish averaging 14 to 24 inches, although occasional jumbos exceeding 30 pounds are caught throughout the winter.

Salmon.   There is a seasonal fishery for discarded brood-stock Atlantic salmon ranging from 2 to 15 pounds or more in the Naugatuck and Shetucket Rivers. In the Naugatuck, salmon are released between Union City and the Thomaston Flood Control Dam, and in the Shetucket between the Scotland and Occum Dams. The salmon are stocked after they've been spawned out in hatcheries in November. They remain in these rivers throughout the winter and spring, but they unfortunately do not tolerate summer temperatures and thus perish. If an angler wishes to keep a salmon, it must be caught on fly fishing tackle; those fish caught incidentally on spinning tackle must be released unharmed.

Anglers fishing the Connecticut River may catch wild sea-run Atlantic salmon while fishing on the main stem or its tributaries. These fish must be released immediately. Efforts to restore Atlantic salmon to the Connecticut River and some tributaries continue but are slow-going. Success is in part dependent on the return of mature adult fish, which can be used by fisheries managers for propagation, and in part upon having large numbers of young salmon (smolts) survive and migrate from the river to the ocean.

A smattering of kokanee (landlocked sockeye) salmon live in three lakes in Salisbury: East Twin Lake, West Hill Pond, and Lake Wononscopomuc. It is unknown how the kokanee got here, but they supported fisheries of varying abundance since at least the 1940s, with a significant population in East Twin and a lesser one at the other lakes, until alewives appeared in East Twin and out-competed the kokanee for food. Brown trout were introduced in order to control the alewives and restore the salmon fishery. At present, there are minor kokanee fisheries on these waters.

Sea-run brown trout.   In the 1960s, Connecticut established sea-run brown trout populations in Latimer Brook, the headwaters of Niantic River; Whitford Brook, the headwaters of the Mystic River; Shonnock Brook, a tributary to the Pawcatuck River in North Stonington; and in the Thames River. Historically, anglers caught sea-run trout up to 10 pounds between November and May each year. Stocking of fingerling sea-run browns ended in the late 1970s, but remnant populations of these fish remain in the Niantic, Mystic, and Thames systems. The best fishing is between December and March. Flies and lures are used for these aggressive, hard-fighting, and elusive fish, but most successful anglers employ live killifish.

Hatchery fishing.   The Quinebaug Valley Hatchery has ponds open to the public for fishing on a first-come, first-served basis between March and May. Anglers may reserve spots to fish by calling the hatchery prior to fishing, or they can show up and hope there are slots available.

Saltwater

While some anglers catch fish from Connecticut's marine waters throughout the year, for most it's a nine-month season that begins in early March with flounder and ends in late November with blackfish, known locally by the Indian name tautog. Throughout this long season, in addition to these two species, anglers take mackerel, fluke, porgies, black sea bass, striped bass, bluefish, and weakfish.

Connecticut has some great striped bass fishing, and its coastal rivers and inshore reefs produce fish from April through November; many of those stripers are monsters. The existing state-record striped bass, although not accepted by IGFA, is a 75-pound, 6-ounce specimen, which was the third-largest striper caught in the twentieth century on rod and reel. Various world records have been established in Connecticut in the past, including line-class world records for blackfish, weakfish, and striped bass.

Connecticut anglers also have one anadromous species that only a few other Atlantic coastal states offer, American shad. The Connecticut River, which begins almost at the Quebec/New Hampshire border and flows 407 miles south to enter Long Island Sound at Old Saybrook and Old Lyme, is arguably the best shad river on the coast; angling for these fish, however, takes place in the upper reaches of this freshwater flow, not in the salt.

Connecticut's larger freshwater rivers that flow into Long Island Sound are unique in that they have fairly large tidal or brackish sections that provide good habitat for striped bass and flounder. Not as large as the Connecticut River, but also productive, is the lower section of the Housatonic River, which enters Long Island Sound at Stratford; the smaller Quinnipiac River, which enters The Sound near New Haven; the Pawcatuck River; and the rather substantial tidal section of the Thames River at New London.

The lower Housatonic River provides excellent fishing for striped bass, bluefish, flounder, and fluke in season. The town docks in Stratford, Stratford Point, and Milford Point Jetty, provide good, fishable shore-based access to the lower river.

Connecticut's shore along the north side of Long Island Sound differs vastly from that of Long Island, a sandy terminal moraine created 20,000 years ago by glaciers. Instead, it is rocky, highly irregular, and pocked with hundreds of small, rocky islands or outcroppings, all not far from shore. Blackfish and striped bass find such environments just to their liking. The rivers and irregular shore also have created numerous inlets and harbors, and these give anglers great access to Long Island Sound. Their marinas harbor a large armada of recreational craft, and there are nearly a dozen public boat launching ramps.

Some of the best fishing in Long Island Sound is a bit farther out, over numerous reefs and ledges just off the shore. From west to east, these include the Norwalk Islands, the Goose and Falkner islands complex, Madison Reef, Kimberley Reef, Long Sand Shoal, and Hatchett and Bartlett Reefs. A plethora of fishing reefs, shoals, ledges, and islands exist in Fishers Island Sound, and these are shared with New York. There is also a unique geological feature in mid–Long Island Sound, but wholly under the aegis of Connecticut: Stratford Shoal, alias The Middle Grounds. The shoal rises from some of the deepest water in Long Island Sound to depths of 8 to 10 feet. It is capped by a lighthouse on the shallowest part. The shoal extends northeast for a mile and produces some of the summer's best bluefishing.

Because most of the Connecticut shoreline is privately owned, surf fishing spots are few and far between. In Fairfield, anglers can fish the jetty and, in the off-season, the beaches at Sherwood Island State Park. Pennfield Reef, a near-mile-long spit that emerges and sinks with each tide, is one of the premier shore fishing sites in the western half of the Connecticut coast. Access is via a tiny right-of-way at the end of Reef Road in the town of Fairfield.

In Milford, Charles Island State Park is a productive shore fishing location that becomes accessible via a long sand spit that is dry at low tide and covered at high tide. Milford Harbor itself, although small, draws bait, bass, and blues in and out with the tides when in season. Its protected waters also provide habitat for winter flounder, fluke, and snapper bluefish in season.

At New Haven, on the harbor's west side, anglers can wade-fish Sandy Point, a long sand spit that juts into the harbor. To the east, Light House Point Park provides good shore access.

In Madison, Hammonassett State Park provides anglers with a mile-long beach with fishing access jetties at either end. Meggs Point Jetty, at the park's east end, juts into the waters that drain Clinton Harbor, making it one of the most productive shore fishing spots in the middle portions of the Connecticut shoreline.

The lower Connecticut River is one of the state's best marine fisheries resources, but access is limited. Anglers can fish off the Interstate 95 state launch in Saybrook; off the causeway that crosses South Cove; and by walking the rocks (a little more than 1 mile) out to Cornfield Point from Castle Inn, to the west of Saybrook Light House. The best lower-river access is a 1,000-foot anglers' access and observation pier built along the shoreline from the headquarters of the Department of Environmental Protection in Old Lyme to the mouth of the Lieutenant River. The site not only provides good handicapped access to some great waters, it is also an excellent observation point for ospreys that inhabit Great Island. Small-boat anglers can find great striped bass and bluefish action along the shoals at Great Island by launching at the Great Island state launch off Route 156 in Old Lyme.

You'll also find a jetty and beach at Rocky Neck State Park in Old Lyme. This provides seasonally good fishing for striped bass, bluefish, fluke, and winter flounder. West of this location, Hatchett Reef and east Black Point are two top gamefishing spots for those who fish from boats.

Perhaps the best-kept surf fishing secret in the state is Harkness Memorial State Park, in the town of Waterford. This beach has no swimming, so it is open to fishing year-round. Its rocky shoreline and inflowing tidal stream provide excellent habitat for all marine species. Harkness is locally famous for excellent striped bass and bluefish catches, but its rocky shore also harbors blackfish, porgies, fluke, and winter flounder. Bartletts Reef, off the coast and to the west of Harkness, is one of eastern Connecticut's

In 1992, a 715-pound bluefin tuna was sold in Tokyo for a then-record price of $67,500, or $94.40 a pound.

C

best fishing destinations for stripers, bluefish, porgies, and blackfish when these species are present.

In Groton, Bluff Point State Park provides a wide variety of fishing habitat. This mile-long peninsula is bounded by Poquonnock River (a long tidal estuary) to the west and Mumford Cove on the east, with a rocky beach on the seaward side. The cove provides exceptional flounder fishing beginning in midwinter, and attracts striped bass in good numbers throughout the season. Its rock-bound beach is good for stripers, bluefish, and blackfish. Offshore is Seaflower Reef, a locally famous area for fluke.

Access to the Mystic River is mostly over private property, with the exception of the Noank Town access and Six Penny Island. Upriver, where Interstate 95 crosses, is a seasonal shore fishing and small-boat access that is productive for blue crabs, winter flounder, tomcod, and an occasional sea-run brown trout during the late winter and early spring. Off the mouth of Mystic River lies Ram Island and its namesake reef, both sporadically hot striper fishing grounds. To the west of the river mouth, boat anglers can fish the Spindle at Groton Long Point, or move across Fishers Island Sound to the West, Middle, and East Clumps, a series of rocks off Fishers Island, New York, all of which provide excellent rips and currents favored by striped bass.

On the eastern Connecticut border with Rhode Island, inside Little Narragansett Bay and bounded on the seaward side by Sandy Point Island, is Barn Island State Park. The park itself doesn't provide much fishing opportunity, but the launch site at the park is a small-boat owner's best access to fishing the excellent waters of Fishers Island Sound, Fishers Island itself, the southern Rhode Island beaches, and the famous Watch Hill/Fishers Island reef complex.

See: New York; Rhode Island.

CONTESTS

See: Competitive Fishing.

CONTINENTAL SHELF

The shallow area of an ocean that is closest to a continent; it gently slopes near the low-water line and more abruptly slopes around the edge of the continent. The area between the low-water line and the continent margin averages 45 miles in width and deepens as it extends seaward, averaging a depth of about 400 feet. At the shelf break, where the shelf descends sharply to the deeper ocean floor, there is a marked change in fauna, with an abrupt cutoff of species that do not extend past the cliff or slope. Often there are canyons (see) that cut deeply into the shelf.

CONTOUR MAP

See: Maps.

CONVENTIONAL TACKLE

Conventional tackle is medium- and heavy-duty fishing equipment characterized by a reel with a revolving spool that turns to both dispense and retrieve line. It is called "conventional" tackle in part because the spool rotates in a normal manner, just like sewing thread, with the line moving perpendicular to the spool axis. It is related in general characteristics to baitcasting tackle (see), which sports a smaller reel that is more limited in its ability to deal with the strongest fish and with situations requiring a lot of line.

Conventional tackle is particularly popular and widely used in saltwater, in part because of the differences in conditions, techniques, and size of fish when compared to freshwater. While conventional gear was once relegated to specific applications, like offshore trolling, bottom fishing, or surf fishing, it now has a wide range of functions, and appropriate versions of conventional tackle can be used in applications ranging from flounder fishing inshore to shark and marlin fishing offshore, and to such in-between uses as deep grouper and cod fishing, casting to tarpon and wahoo, trolling for Great Lakes salmon, and bottom fishing for big catfish and sturgeon. Appropriate models of conventional reels with corresponding rods may be used for casting, trolling, and bottom fishing, but many outfits are best suited to specific tasks, and the factors that go into the selection and use of this or any type of fishing tackle are many and varied.

Reels

The conventional revolving spool reel evolved from the same origins as the baitcasting reel, and the development of both has been intertwined since the nineteenth century. Baitcasting reels originated in Kentucky between 1800 and 1810 at a time when a single-action revolving spool reel was the only reel available for sportfishing, and anglers exclusively used natural bait or artificial flies. The single-action reel was used primarily to store and retrieve line, and had no casting function. To present natural baits at any distance, anglers had to strip an appropriate length of line off a single-action reel and lay the loops down or coil them in the noncasting hand. Using a wooden rod, they made a sideways motion to propel the bait and carry the stripped-off line. This was done because the bait and whatever weights were used could not overcome the inertia of the single-action spool.

In 1810 or sometime during the preceding decade, George Snyder, a Kentucky watchmaker and reputedly president of the Bourbon Angling Club, invented a reel with a delicate spool that would pay out line during the cast, and which revolved several times for each turn of the crank handle. Thus was born the multiple-action reel, to be called the multiplier or multiplying reel, as well as a spool capable of dispensing line during a cast. The line of that day was raw silk, and there were no

C

lures; for decades multiplying reels were small, and because they were exclusively used for tossing natural bait, they became popularly known as bait-casting reels.

For most of the nineteenth century, such reels were made by hand. There were various modifications and improvements, including the addition of a mechanism to distribute line evenly on the spool (called levelwind), better gears, and the addition of external drag. What had developed as a tool for freshwater fishing, primarily for bass, became available in large sizes for situations where greater line capacity and mechanical strength was needed.

Multiplier types of revolving spool reels for saltwater use were being made in the late 1800s, but they lacked an internal drag mechanism. To offset this, anglers applied pressure to the reel spool with their thumbs (which was ineffective for large fish and sometimes painful to the angler) or with a leather thumb pad that was attached to the reel frame.

William C. Boschen, a member of the legendary Catalina Tuna Club of California, is credited with originating the concept for the first internal star drag reel, a handy threaded knob adjustment that internally regulated spool pressure. Reportedly a prototype of a reel with such a device was made for Boschen by Brooklyn, New York, reel manufacturer Julius Vom Hofe, and used by Boschen to catch the first broadbill swordfish (358 pounds) ever taken on sporting rod and reel. That catch was made in the summer of 1913 off Catalina Island, and later versions of the reel were named B-Ocean.

This product was the predecessor of the modern conventional fishing reel. The star drag mechanism provided an internal friction adjustment mechanism (or brake) to help pressure strong fish and slow the rate of line being pulled off the reel. It was incorporated on all types and sizes of revolving spool reels in later years. All products that are today categorized as conventional reels feature a star drag; all baitcasting reels also feature a star drag. Other

aspects of these reels evolved and improved over time, particularly drag washer materials, gears, and component materials.

A conventional reel today is essentially a medium- or large-size revolving spool reel, and is usually a product that does not have a levelwind line guiding mechanism (although there are exceptions). In modern marketing parlance, conventional reels are called many things, particularly boat, bay, surf, trolling, bottom fishing, and ocean reels. Categorically they are distinct from baitcasting reels, as well as from big-game or lever drag reels *(see: big-game tackle),* although there are overlapping features.

Conventional reels are larger than baitcasting reels. They have a star-spoked wheel drag, are likely to be used with heavier lures and weights, and may or may not have a line-leveling mechanism. Some models may be cast, but many are used for bottom fishing and trolling. In saltwater, they are extremely popular for diverse usage; in freshwater, they are mainly used for the most-demanding applications. Conventional reels differ from lever drag reels, which are essentially a big-game fishing tool with a different method of achieving freespool and applying drag tension (using cam rather than threaded adjustment).

Most conventional reels of the modern era are more elementary in design and features than contemporary baitcasting or spinning reels, primarily because they are used for more demanding fish and in more punishing circumstances. Unlike contemporary baitcasting reels, which are primarily used for cast-and-retrieve angling activities (with lures rather than with natural bait), modern conventional reels are less frequently cast.

Many conventional reels are never used for casting, but exclusively used for trolling lures or bait and for fishing at various depths with sinking lures or bait, both of which call for paying line off the reel rather than casting. An ever widening interest in varied methods of fishing, coupled with a need for greater line capacity than even the largest baitcasting reels can provide, has resulted, however, in demands to use some modern conventional reels for casting either lures or natural bait. This requires some models to have features appropriate to the demands of frequent casting and retrieving. Thus, some conventional reels are used for casting as well as other types of fishing, despite their comparatively large size and greater weight.

One of the most distinguishing differences between a conventional reel and a baitcasting reel is that the latter have a level line-winding mechanism and the majority of the former do not. Thus, when using most conventional reels, the angler must manually direct the placement of line on the spool to produce an even line lay.

Manually leveling line on a spool is the biggest drawback to using conventional tackle, and often a problem for inexperienced anglers or those who are

Assorted conventional reels and rods are displayed at a sport show.

unfamiliar with this action. When line is not wound evenly, it bunches and impedes retrieval or dispensing, and contributes to binding of line wraps. Manual line leveling can seem even more burdensome when combined with the fact that conventional reels, which sit on top of the rod facing the angler, are heavy and, for some people, awkward to hold.

Being heavy is a double-edged sword, however. The weight is a result of the size necessary for adequate line capacity, which ranges from about 275 yards in smaller models to over 1,000 yards in the largest models, and a result of the sturdy components necessary for the frame, spool, and gears, which is what makes these reels capable of handling tough fishing.

Line capacity, gears, and drag are the most critical components of conventional reels. One of the problem areas with conventional reels in the past was a drag that became erratic when heavy pressure was intense and sustained or as a result of long-term compression of friction washers during storage. Modern conventional reels have improved, particularly the drag systems, which have become smoother due to modern friction materials, and which better resist compression and the effect of heat.

Conventional reels do have a drag-related drawback where striking and fighting large, powerful fish is concerned. Drag tension is not easily or readily adjustable to known levels. Turning the star wheel adjusts the drag tension, which is usually set to a predetermined level before fishing. If that wheel is deliberately or accidentally turned later, especially while playing a fish, drag tension is changed and may be too little or too great for the circumstances. Once the tension is changed, it cannot be recalibrated with absolute certainty while playing a fish. Furthermore, it may be desirable to deliberately increase or decrease drag tension while playing a fish (usually a very large and powerful one for the tackle), but doing so means making an adjustment to an uncertain level, and being unable to return to that preset level if necessary later on, as well as possibly exceeding the limits of the tackle. This drawback—which is primarily related to big-game fishing *(see)*—is one that lead to the development of the special purpose lever drag big-game reel *(see: big-game tackle)*.

Experienced anglers can make adjustments to the preset tension of a star drag reel and be reasonably close to the tension level necessary for the circumstances. But most anglers cannot do so, and may have a high degree of error when making adjustments by feel under difficult and pressured angling circumstances, which can have harmful results.

This, of course, is most significant when fishing for the biggest and hardest-fighting species, and when using lighter lines. For the majority of angling circumstances involving conventional reels, adjusting the star drag while playing a fish is seldom necessary, and preset tension is maintained throughout the fight.

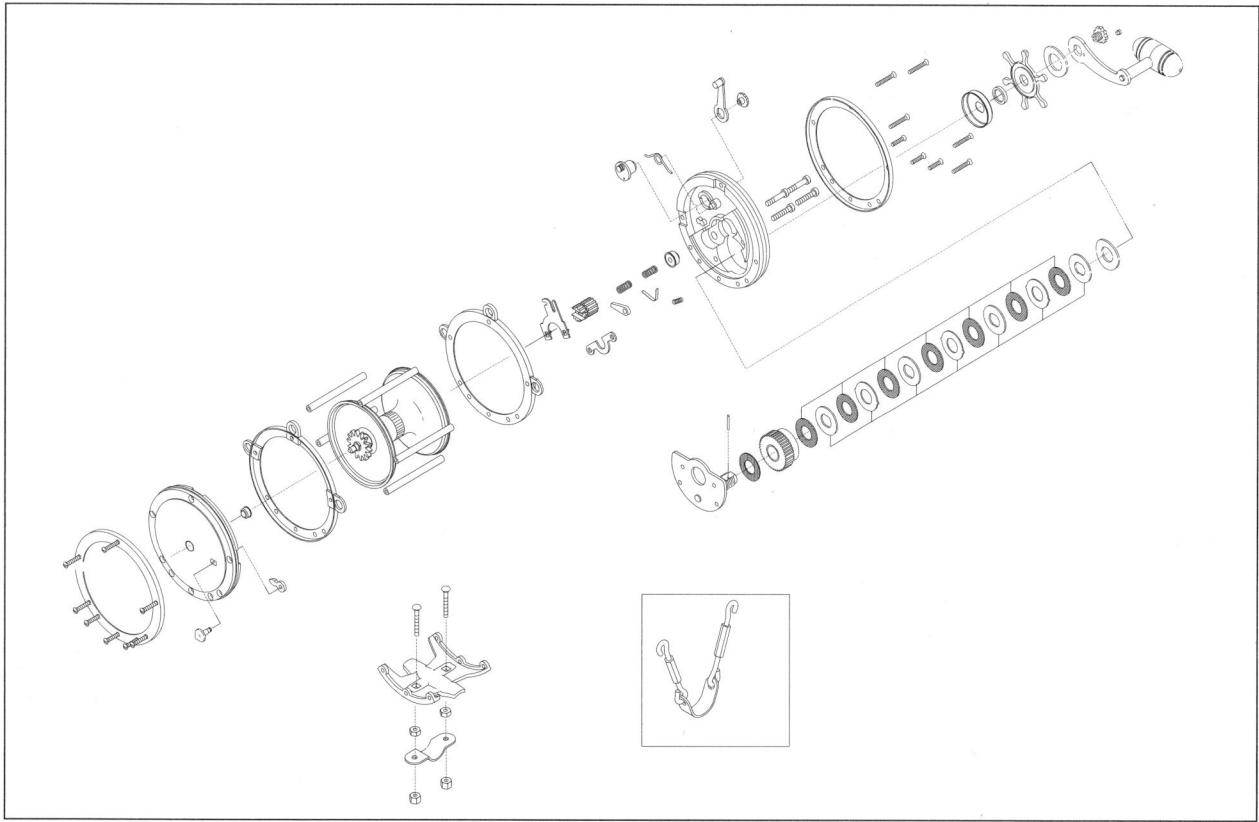

All of the parts of a Penn Senator conventional trolling reel are shown here; this product features a multi-disc star drag system.

C

General Operation

In the most basic sense, conventional tackle works like all other tackle except flycasting in that a weighted object at the end of the line pulls line from the spool. The spool of a conventional reel revolves during the cast, as line pays out and when line is retrieved, when you turn the handle. When the gears are disengaged and line is dispensed from the reel, a backlash *(see),* or spool overrun, can occur if the revolving spool turns faster than the line is carried off that spool. Applying light pressure to the spool can prevent this, and it may be accomplished in several ways. One of these is with finger or hand tension, another is with a lever-operated clutch, which can be engaged or disengaged as in a car.

The conventional reel has a lever that activates or deactivates the gears and essentially takes the reel into or out of freespool. In use, with the reel on top of the rod handle and facing toward the angler, the rod-holding hand thumb is placed on the spool to keep the line in check, and the free hand is used to move the gear lever backward, which disengages the gears and puts the reel in freespool. When thumb pressure is relaxed, line flows off the spool and out through the rod guides, carried by the weight of the object at the terminal end of the line. Conventional reels feature a click ratchet, used to signal that line is being taken off the reel; this may be employed when a reel is not held or when it is left unattended.

To retrieve line, the gears are engaged by moving the lever forward, and the spool is turned by rotating the handle, which winds line onto the reel. When line is wound onto the spool, the user generally must level the line manually for even line distribution, although some lighter-duty conventional reels have a levelwind mechanism that automatically distributes the line back and forth across the spool.

Every conventional reel has an adjustable drag mechanism, activated by turning a star wheel on the drive gear. This is located on the sideplate under the handle. The drag tension is set to the desirable level at the beginning of each day's fishing and relaxed when the day is concluded.

These are the basic elements of operating a conventional reel. In some models cast control and anti-reverse features come into play; the size of the spool, the materials used, and the designed application of each product also have relevance to its use.

Line Release/Casting Features

The vast majority of conventional reels, and virtually all large models, are not used for casting. Some smaller-size reels are used for casting as well as for other applications. In all models, controlling the flow of line off the spool is an important element of use.

Freespool.   Disengaging gears to enable a reel to freely turn backward and dispense line is known as putting the reel into freespool. This is accomplished in conventional reels by moving the eccentric lever that is located on the sideplate and extends just beyond the edge of the plate. This lever is actually a gear shift lever but may be known as the freespool lever or freespool clutch. It should not be confused with the lever that controls drag tension on a lever drag reel, although they are both in similar locations. A similar mechanism is used on baitcasting reels but is in the form of a button or bar, which is more convenient; a lever is used on conventional reels for positive engagement and strength, and because casting is less prevalent.

Under the sideplate, the pinion gear, which drops down on the spindle and drives it, is cradled in a yoke. When the eccentric lever (clutch) is moved to the freespool position, which is usually backward or toward the holder, it moves a shifter that pushes a ramp in, lifting the pinion off the spindle to disengage it. Now the reel is in freespool mode. In this method of achieving freespool, the gears are still intact but not the drive mechanism; this is different from lever drag reels, where pulling the drag lever back into the freespool position keeps the gears intact but disengages the clutch parts.

This is the basic method used in conventional reels to achieve freespool. Some reels achieve this in a circular fashion, where there is a ramp on either side of the yoke to lift the pinion, although this is more common in smaller reels (and baitcasting products) and necessitated by a smaller area under the sideplate.

This is a very straightforward operational method. Some conventional reels, especially those with a pair of eccentric springs, provide more decisive and forceful shifting in both directions, but all are reasonably fail-safe.

Spool revolution.   Before putting the reel into freespool, you must apply finger pressure to the spool to prevent line from paying out prematurely or haphazardly. Without this pressure, and assuming that a lure or weighted bait is tied to the end of the line, the weight of either object causes the spool to turn the moment the reel is placed into the freespool position, which could cause an instant backlash on the spool.

Therefore, it is necessary to place the thumb of the rod-holding hand on the spool so the spool can't turn, and then move the eccentric lever into the freespool position. Now the line can be released by easing the tension or, in some instances, by casting.

When releasing line without casting, thumb pressure is lessened on the spool to pay line out at a controlled rate; the objective is to let a sufficient amount of line out for the fishing circumstances at a rate that doesn't cause the spool to turn so fast that it causes a backlash. This is important because a revolving spool can gather speed quickly, and an uncontrolled spool can lead to a serious backlash in seconds. The backlash not only impedes immediate fishing effort because of the time required to undo it, but can also damage the line. This situation becomes even more acute in those conventional reels that are used for casting applications, because the activity of casting builds up greater spool speed.

Casting requires precise control of the revolving spool. In either application, it is necessary to brake the spool to slow its speed. For more details about the cause and cure of backlash, *see: Baitcasting Tackle.*

Spool braking/control. The majority of conventional reel users employ thumb pressure to brake the spool, because most do not have any other means of controlling spool revolution. Applying thumb pressure is an action learned through trial and error and perfected with experience; it requires the application of different degrees of braking tension for the weights on the line, distances being cast, and types of rods and reels being used.

There are also magnetic and mechanical ways of helping to control revolving spool speed. In function, magnetic spool breaking systems employ a magnetic field to place variable degrees of resistance on the spool. Magnetic spool braking is seldom used on conventional reels and rarely in saltwater applications. It is popular for baitcasting reels used in freshwater and described in more detail in the baitcasting tackle *(see)* entry.

Some conventional reels have a mechanical means of controlling spool braking via centrifugal brakes. Those with it have blocks that must be engaged to effect spool braking. These blocks are usually found on the left side of the reel, and accessed by removing the left sideplate. Underneath the click ratchet and next to the spool flange is a cross pin with a centrifugal brake block on either side. To be employed, these brake blocks must be moved out toward the flange and snapped into a notch. In this position they rub against the flange and, due to centrifugal pressure, exert the greatest force at lightest speeds, and slow down the spool to help avoid a backlash.

This system is common on baitcasting reels but uncommon for conventional reels, although models with this feature are used for specific saltwater casting applications, especially in long-range party boat *(see)* and kingfish angling, and some bluefish and tuna angling. The centrifugal casting system is an extra feature that makes reels so equipped more expensive than comparable models without the feature.

Spool tension control. Some people view the adjustable screw tension mechanism found on most conventional reels as a means of controlling spool braking, although its value in this regard is limited. This device is sometimes the knurled knob or bearing cap on the nonhandle sideplate (usually on the left sideplate, but it may be on the right sideplate), which is adjusted by hand. In some reels it may be a slot that is adjusted with a screwdriver or coin. Tightening this device does put tension on the spindle of the spool, but its real purpose is to control excessive end play, or sideways movement, of the spool.

If the mechanical spool control on a reel is too loose, there is too much movement in the spool and line could get behind it. If the engineering mechanics of a reel are correct, line should not get behind the spool; you should be able to loosen it completely and, though there will be excessive end play, still not be able to pull the flange of the spool out of the centering ring of the sideplate. Even if you lose the adjusting screw, this should not happen.

On conventional reels, a small piece of rubber or a dished spring lies on the sideplate fronting against a brass or bronze wear plate. As the adjustment knob is tightened, the wear plate rubs against the stainless steel spindle. Tightening is usually a clockwise motion, and this should be adjusted so that there is barely any perceptible sideways motion of the spool. One manufacturer recommends that the sideways motion be no more than the thickness of a hair; ascertaining this by sight is dubious, but it provides a clue as to the acceptable level of end play. To see how much play there is, take both thumbs and put them on either side of the spool and press back and forth to see if you can move it. Adjust it to a tight but not immovable tolerance.

Do not fully tighten the spool tension adjustment mechanism; this can damage or cause premature wearing (and failure) of the right and left side bearings. The rubber should provide some cushion for a better range of adjustment, and in the event that something wears out, it will preferably be the wear plate and not the spindle.

In reels that are not employed for casting, the tension control mechanism is seldom used after any sideways movement has been eliminated. Most people don't use this adjustment much. Experienced anglers who cast often with a conventional reel will tighten or loosen the adjustment knob, and employ this level of control in conjunction with an educated thumb. People who are unfamiliar with casting a revolving spool need a tighter adjustment for some assistance with spool braking, however, or they will be picking backlashes out with every cast. This tension should gradually be lightened as they become more proficient with thumb control.

Retrieving/Line Recovery Features

The elements that affect line retrieval with conventional reels are similar to those for all other reels, although because of the applications of these products, those elements are very significant. They especially include gear components, gear ratio, spool diameter and capacity, and the handle.

Line pickup. To be in a position to set the hook and to return line to the spool, some drag tension must be established and the gears must be engaged; the latter is accomplished by moving the eccentric lever from the freespool position to the retrieve position. These positions may or may not be labeled on a given reel, but this is usually accomplished by moving the lever upward or forward (clockwise if looking at a reel from the side). This action drops the pinion gear onto the spindle and engages the drive mechanism.

With the eccentric lever forward, and some drag tension in effect, turning the handle revolves the spool, bringing line onto it. Turning the handle

Dolphin *(mahimahi)* are an incredibly fast-growing yet short-lived fish; one-year-olds will be about 13 pounds, and soon-to-die four-year-olds 70 to 80 pounds.

without moving the eccentric lever forward does not engage the gears in most conventional reels. The operation of others is more like a baitcasting reel, with the lever moving to the retrieve position automatically when the handle is turned forward. More mechanics are involved in such reels, however, and they are generally less favored for saltwater application.

Left/right retrieve. With a few exceptions, the majority of conventional reels today are only set up for right-handed retrieve and are not convertible. Some conventional reels are made in left-retrieve versions. The left/right retrieve situation with these products is akin to that for baitcasting, and it mostly favors people who are right-handed.

With regard to catching smaller fish and using lighter gear (like baitcasting), it is beneficial for people who are right-handed to reel with their left hand and for lefties to reel with their right hand, so that the dominant hand is the one that holds the rod and is used to play the fish or direct the retrieve. This is especially significant when frequent casting is involved. Because the dominant hand is used to cast the rod, no further action is required after casting to start using the reel; the other hand is immediately placed on the reel handle grip and starts turning the handle. This lack of time delay is important in some fishing situations.

However, because less casting is done with conventional reels, applications are more demanding, the outfits are generally heavy, and most people are right-handed, the right-retrieve aspect of most conventional reels is not the problem that it is in baitcasting products. Large conventional reels especially are used for big fish, and it is common to attach these reels to a harness, which relieves the rod-holding arm. If a person is right-handed, all of the heavy-duty cranking of the reel is done with the stronger hand, which, in theory, is better for anyone who is right-handed, although not as desirable for a lefty.

A minority of conventional reels have a levelwind feature, and this model also sports a digital line counter.

Left-handed people complain about this to reel manufacturers, and although a few left-handed retrieve conventional reels are available, there aren't enough to suit people who prefer to reel with their dominant left hand. From a manufacturer's perspective, changing retrieve comes down to the gearing. It can be done, but the engineering isn't just a simple matter of reversing things. Conventional reels that feature a levelwind are even more problematic. Completely new tooling, including a new frame or sideplate, is necessary to produce a left-retrieve levelwind product, which is obviously much more expensive.

The problem essentially is one of demand. Manufacturers would make such reels if there were enough demand. There aren't enough left-handed anglers (or not enough of them have complained) to make it worthwhile for manufacturers to undertake the costs necessary to produce two versions of every conventional reel. Finally, from a practical usage standpoint, owning both right- and left-handed retrieve models of conventional reels becomes more gear-intensive than most people would like or can afford. This is especially true for party boat operators, charter captains, or private boat owners, who take customers, friends, and family fishing. It is simply easier to have everything that works the same way (right-retrieve), especially because most people are right handed.

Line winding/Levelwind. Line is wound directly onto the spool of a conventional reel, but most conventional reels do not have a mechanism for leveling or dispersing that line across the spool. For such reels, this leveling must be done manually. The hand that holds the rod must be situated in such a way that the thumb can be used to direct the line back and forth onto the spool as it is retrieved. This means holding the rod at the foregrip ahead of the reel, and extending the thumb to the right to catch the line with both sides of the tip of the thumb, moving it to the left and right to disperse the line. This has to be done whenever the handle of the reel is turned and line is recovered onto the spool.

Failing to disperse the line by hand results in bunching on the spool. If the line bunches severely enough, it may jam at the frame crossbars and prevent retrieval of additional line or inhibit outflow of line when the reel is placed in freespool. It also causes wraps to bind among each other, impeding the free flow of line off the spool. Bunching also makes it more likely to incur a spool overrun; a horrific tangle must be painstakingly picked apart.

Some conventional reels have a mechanism, known as a levelwind, to automatically disperse line evenly across the spool. This does not require any hand or thumb movement to accomplish. Conventional reels that have a levelwind mechanism are the same in every other way as conventional reels without this mechanism.

In conventional reels, the levelwind may be gear-driven by the spool or by the main gear and turn whenever the spool revolves, both forward and backward. The mechanism is located in a carriage that spans both sides of the reel. Inside is a nylon idler gear that turns a worm gear and catches a pawl that moves the line guide back and forth across the spool. This mechanism distributes line evenly on the spool, which avoids line buildup.

Although a minority of conventional reels feature a levelwind, this feature has been growing steadily in popularity among conventional reel users, perhaps as a spillover effect from the freshwater use of baitcasting reels. Virtually all mass-produced baitcasting reels have featured a levelwind mechanism for many years. Only competitive tournament casters are likely to have a small revolving spool reel without a levelwind, and that for distance events.

In this area of conventional reels, there is disagreement among users, especially between saltwater and freshwater anglers. The average saltwater angler looks at a conventional revolving spool with a levelwind as an item for neophytes and views the mechanism as an accident waiting to happen. The average freshwater angler looks at a conventional revolving spool reel that doesn't have a levelwind mechanism and asks why not.

For saltwater anglers who cast with conventional reels, like surf anglers, the levelwind is disliked because it reduces casting distance. How much it reduces distance is debatable, but it does reduce it some because there is friction on the line when it flows off the spool and contacts the line-winding guide during a cast. Achieving distance is often important in surf fishing (see), as well as in other saltwater casting applications.

More important for saltwater anglers is the possibility of the levelwind, which is always exposed to the elements, malfunctioning. This can be caused by the corrosive effect of saltwater or the levelwind trapping sand particles from the line, even when it is carefully cleaned and maintained. Added friction on the line can also cause the loss of really powerful fish. Generally, saltwater anglers like to simplify things because of the corrosive environment they constantly deal with. Enough goes wrong without adding more to worry about, and the levelwind is viewed as another potential point subject to breakage. Furthermore, really big, powerful fish can strip line extremely fast off a reel. The line guide cannot keep up with the swift back and forth movement of the line, necessarily putting friction and more tension on the line, which might cause the levelwind to fail or the line to break. For this reason, no large conventional reels have a levelwind mechanism.

Although veteran saltwater anglers spurn conventional reels that possess a levelwind, the use of these reels in saltwater is increasing, and they are considered essential in freshwater applications. This may be partly due to more people with freshwater fishing experience venturing into saltwater, and partly due to minor improvements in levelwind reliability, but mostly due to application. Levelwind conventional reels are being used more in lighter saltwater applications, such as inshore fishing, bottom fishing for flounder, and casting for bluefish and striped bass. They are being used in all places where there is less likelihood of pressure-related levelwind problems provided that the reel is cleaned properly after every use. Some saltwater charter boat captains are using levelwind reels more because they're tired of having problems with inexperienced angling customers who forget to manually distribute the line on non-levelwind reels.

A few levelwind-style conventional reels have a line counter for determining the amount of line that is off the reel. This is of primary use in freshwater trolling, in drift fishing with bait for suspended fish, or in bottom fishing at specific depths, and may be mechanical or electronic.

Gears.   The most basic part of the operation of every reel is the gear set, which, in a conventional reel, is universally heavy-duty and more efficient than that of a stationary or fixed spool reel because the gear set operates on a parallel axis.

In a conventional reel, a large gear, which is the main or drive gear, engages a smaller gear, which is the pinion. The drive gear is linked to the reel handle and the pinion gear connects to the spool. This system provides the multiplying gear ratio for ample line retrieval rates with a small spool and still delivers substantial cranking power. It also allows for the use of heavy lines.

Most better conventional reels have a stainless steel pinion gear and a bronze main gear. In a few reels both are stainless steel, and in some bargain-priced reels both may be brass, but unless one gear is slightly softer than the other, this can cause problems.

In almost any simple gear set one gear material is normally different from the other. This is because use of the same materials tends to cold weld, or "gall" together; dissimilar metals nearly always offer the lowest coefficient of friction. The presence of an oil film helps to reduce friction. The result of using dissimilar metals and an oil film is that gears run smoothly for a longer period.

The best situation is for the main drive gear material to be slightly softer than the pinion gear for wear characteristics, especially in reels that are used often for demanding applications, and where the gear ratio is high. In a multiplier reel, one tooth of the pinion gear contacts its mating teeth on the main gear the same number of times as the gear ratio. That is, in a 5:1 ratio reel, each tooth on the pinion gear is activated five times more often than its counterpart on the main gear. Therefore, it is subject to five times the wear and needs to be harder simply to survive. The predominance of stainless steel pinion gears and bronze main gears in conventional reels produces a hardness differential that favors the smaller diameter pinion gear to provide longer life.

These are low-speed (left) and high-speed gear sets from different conventional reels; both feature a stainless steel pinion gear and bronze alloy main gear.

Gears are made to work in a given way with respect to each other, so there must be a certain distance between the two to match up; otherwise the gears will feel tight. Naturally, it is important that the gear teeth are machined as precisely as possible to assure smooth operation and long life. Some conventional reels, especially those with a higher gear ratio, have helically milled gears. This means that each gear tooth is spiral or curved, rather than straight, on the gear circumference. Helical milling results in increased contact area, resulting in greater strength, thicker cross section, and a high degree of inherent smoothness, particularly for smaller gear teeth. The major benefit is that, unlike straight-milled gears where only a single gear tooth is fully engaged at one time, helical gears allow at least partial engagement of several gear teeth at all times, spreading the load and potential wear. This is mainly an issue where the gear teeth are small, and there is less surface to make contact, as is found on higher ratio models.

The high-stress cranking that is experienced with conventional reels requires a rigid support system, so that under great duress there is no flex to affect the inner workings of the reel. The use of heavy line, and cranking large fish in extreme conditions, can put tremendous stress on all components. Both the material and construction of the frame and shaft supports are what keep the gears precisely located and delivering long life.

Gear ratio. Because the drive gear is linked to the reel handle and the pinion gear is engaged to the spool, the basic numerical ratio of the drive and pinion gears in a conventional reel merely establishes the number of revolutions made by the spool per turn of the handle. That number is determined by counting the gear teeth on the larger drive gear and dividing that by the tooth count of the smaller pinion gear. In a gear set consisting of a 53-tooth drive gear and a 10-tooth pinion gear, the ratio would be calculated at 5.3:1, since the pinion will turn 5.3 times for each full rotation of the drive gear.

Gear ratios are generally categorized as high (fast) or low (slow), but this is relative to the type of reel and application. Furthermore, the size of the spool may be such that a low gear ratio reel actually recovers more line per full turn of the handle than a high ratio reel with a smaller spool. What is high for many conventional reels would be low for nearly all baitcasting reels, if numerical ratio was the only factor of comparison. Typical low gear ratios for conventional reels are 2:1 to 3:1 and typical high gear ratios are 3.5:1 to 5:1, although they range both higher and lower. In a conventional reel, a high gear ratio may be preferable for cast-and-retrieve fishing, but a low gear ratio reel may be preferable for deep bottom fishing. What is gained in retrieve speed is lost in cranking power.

The higher the ratio, the greater the potential for stripping gears under severe strain. On a high gear ratio reel, the individual teeth become narrower because more teeth are fitted into a given area, and they are weaker. An inexperienced angler is more likely to do damage on a high gear ratio reel when he puts the smaller gear teeth under a heavy load. Fishing with a high gear ratio reel requires using the rod a lot, pulling it back and then winding line onto the spool quickly on the down stroke. This is necessary because with high gear ratio reels the smaller tooth configuration does not have sufficient cranking strength. This is a factor in all reels, but obviously of more concern with reels that get a heavy load, such as conventional and lever drag reels.

Cranking power. Gear ratio and cranking power are inextricably linked in all reels, and most affect how easy or difficult it is to retrieve a heavy weight, or an object that offers a lot of resistance. Reels that can easily handle a heavy load are said to have a lot of cranking power. Various factors affect this.

The length of the handle has a bearing because length has to do with the leverage that you can put on the handle. The longer the handle, the more leverage and the easier it is to retrieve a set load. If you make a handle longer, you reduce the force at the knob. It is essentially the same principle as having a long-handled wrench; it's easier to loosen nuts with a long-handled wrench than with a short-handled one. So a longer handle equates to greater

power (although your hand and arm must describe a larger circle to operate the reel).

The gear set itself is also a big factor with regard to cranking power. If you have a conventional reel with a gear ratio of 2:1, it's easier to retrieve a load because this is a low gear ratio. If you have a conventional reel with a gear ratio of 5:1, which is high, it's much more difficult to retrieve a load, although you get more speed. If you're retrieving something that offers very little resistance, the high gear ratio is okay. But you need a lower gear ratio for something that offers more resistance. Thus, the lowest gear ratio reels have the greatest cranking power, and the highest gear ratio reels have the least cranking power.

No matter what the gear ratio is, the evaluation of a reel's ability to retrieve line should boil down to something engineers call Inches Per Turn of the handle, or IPT. This is the amount of line recovered per turn of the handle, or, simply, line recovery. That is a better measurement of retrieval ability than gear ratio. Line recovery is determined by spool diameter, which is a key dimension for any reel and which sets the circumference of the line level on the spool and the amount of line wound onto the spool with each turn of the reel handle.

When the level of line on a spool is low, as it might be when a strong fish takes a lot of line, less line is recovered per turn of the handle than would be when all of the line is on the spool. Similarly, the amount of line recovered per turn of the handle of a fully spooled 4:1 ratio reel that has a small spool would be less than the amount of line recovered per turn of the handle of a fully spooled 4:1 ratio reel that has a large spool.

The amount of line recovered is the measurement an angler should be most interested in. Yet anglers cannot quickly determine line recovery when evaluating a reel they might purchase because specifications on the circumference of the spool are seldom provided on the reel or in the packaging materials. While in a 4:1 ratio reel, for example, you know that one revolution of the handle puts four wraps of line on the spool, if you don't know how much line is gained with each complete wrap, you don't know the actual recovery. (In a reel that you own, this can be determined by marking the line and then measuring it.)

For a greater discussion of this subject, *see: Gear Ratio and Line Recovery.* Although most consumers have a notion that gear ratio is of primary importance in retrieval and some think that the higher the ratio the better, other factors are involved, and line recovery is a major one. Remember, however, that reels with a low gear ratio do better under heavier loads, whether those loads are due to the size of the fish or the equipment being used (heavy weights, deep-diving lures, etc.).

This issue is critical in conventional reels because of their basic size, capacity, and applications. Chances are the bigger the reel, the more

likely it is that a heavy load will be placed on it. The larger the reel, the more noticeable the effect of a high gear ratio, so you'll feel that load a lot more.

Handle. The length of the handle affects cranking power, so the distance from the center of the handle to the handle knob is a key element in retrieval. A long handle equals power, yet many people have the misconception that a long handle also equals speed, that the longer it is, the faster it can travel. It's just the opposite. The longer the handle, the greater distance the cranking hand has to travel with each turn. The shorter the handle, the quicker it can be turned, but then there's less power, so there's a tradeoff either way. You can't get power and speed simultaneously.

Some conventional reel handles are equipped with two center holes so you can change the distance from the crankshaft connection to the handle knob and thus affect power and speed to best suit the physical build of the angler. For others, it may be possible to purchase a convertible handle as an accessory.

Some conventional reels sport a counterbalanced handle: one handle knob and an opposing counterbalance weight. This is usually found on medium-size reels (up to about 4/0) used in applications where there is a lot of retrieving. The counterbalance gives the reel a more solid feel with a better cadence to the retrieval action, which is important when you're casting frequently and regularly using a quick retrieve. In some situations, like casting plugs for wahoo, you can't retrieve too fast for the likes of the fish. With a bigger reel, you wouldn't feel such rapid retrieving because of the mass of the reel, but then speed of retrieval is seldom an issue on larger reels, which is why they don't have a counterbalanced handle. Power is the main issue with larger reels, and this is consistent with their lower gear ratio.

Nearly all conventional reels have a single handle grip, or knob, which is what you hold onto to turn

The cranking power of conventional reels makes them preferable to some surf anglers, especially for catching large fish.

the handle. This is contrary to baitcasting reels, where nearly all handles have dual grips. While a single handle grip would look out of place on a baitcasting reel, a dual handle grip would look out of place on a conventional reel, where the grips are fairly large and two of them would seem garish. It is worth noting that the way these reel handles are held and turned has some bearing on this design. A baitcasting reel knob is mainly gripped with the fingertips and operated by wrist motion, and is not affected by the presence of a second handle knob. Larger conventional reel knobs are gripped with more of the finger and operated with the arm and elbow, which would be affected by a second knob.

Conventional reels have various styles of grips or knobs, and size is usually commensurate with the size of the reel. Small and medium reels have a soft nonslip handle grip with a large and comfortable surface area. Many reels, particularly larger models, have barrel or torpedo shaped grips, which tend to be grasped by the whole hand rather than just the thumb and index finger.

Ball bearings/Bushings. Bearings and bushings provide a way to minimize friction on rotating shafts. Bushings don't spin as freely as ball or roller bearings, which are typically viewed as durable and reliable and a way to add rotational freeness to the retrieval system. A bushing can deliver as smooth a retrieval as a ball bearing under low load conditions, but under heavy loads, ball bearings are vastly smoother and more durable. Two to four stainless steel ball bearings are used on many conventional reels, primarily on both ends of the spool shaft and on the crankshaft. These are (or should be) of the highest grade, and some manufacturers claim to use aircraft quality stainless steel ball bearings on certain reels. For a more detailed review of ball bearings and bushings, *see: Reel, Fishing.*

Warning click. Primarily known simply as a click or clicker by most anglers, this is a ratchet device that is primarily intended to let an angler know that line is going out. It is generally employed when a rod and reel have been placed in a rod holder (as when surf fishing, trolling, or bait fishing) and is not handheld. In some situations, as when fishing with bait, the reel is placed in freespool with the warning click on so that if a fish picks up the bait, the line is free to move with minimal resistance yet without risking a spool overrun. In other situations, such as when trolling, the gears are engaged and the warning click is employed so that it instantly alerts an angler (or mate or boat captain) to a strike and to the fact that a fish is on and taking line off the reel.

The click itself features a spring-loaded tongue that moves back and forth against ratchet teeth to make this sound. It is activated by moving a small off-center button on the sideplate (usually the left sideplate). The click is intended for part-time rather than full-time use, and the click button should be disengaged when retrieving. Continued use of the click causes premature ratchet wear. Leaving it on is viewed by some people as a sign of an inexperienced angler, although some charter captains like it to be left on because the sound lets them know what a customer's fish is doing; when the clicking sound speeds up, for example, the fish is taking line. Some have even asked manufacturers for different types of sounds in the click (this is especially prevalent in the Great Lakes, where the clicks are always used for trolling).

In older reels, if the click wore out you needed a whole new sideplate, but in newer models the configuration allows for replacing the subassembly but not the whole sideplate. Thus, excessive wear is not as big or costly a problem as in the past.

Drag Features

The purpose of the drag function on any reel is to let line slip from the reel at varying pressures when force is applied to the line. It serves as a sort of clutch, or shock absorber, and is especially important when using light line, when playing large and strong species, and when fish make strong and sudden surges while being landed. If an angler never catches large fish, only uses heavy strength line, and is content to wind fish in, it is conceivable that his drag will never be used. This is not the case with conventional tackle, however, which is expressly meant for catching large fish and dealing with tough conditions.

Nevertheless, catching large fish, which weigh more than the actual breaking strength of the line, or which can apply extreme pressure on the tackle, requires some finesse rather than sheer strength. This means that the drag will come into play, because if it doesn't, the force will exceed the strength of the line and the line will break.

When the drag comes into play, it allows the fish to continue applying force, but at a pressure that is less than the breaking strength of the line, because when the force reaches a certain level (usually a specific percentage of the line's breaking strength), a properly set drag mechanism allows line to slip from the reel under tension by turning the spool. In essence, it means that a fish can run instead of engage in a tug of war, but it has to work for the line that it takes off the reel, which is tiring and helps the angler subdue it.

Many people mistakenly think that they need to set the drag very tight for effective hook setting. Once you have 20 yards of line out and you have rod flex, line stretch, and the dampening effect of the water to contend with, you don't need very much drag force at the reel. You cannot exert the maximum pressure when you set the hook. But when you set the drag pressure at or near maximum force, once the fish is close to the boat and there is less of a contribution made by line stretch, rod flex, and water, having the drag locked down may mean that the line cannot absorb the sudden shock of a quick run, even from a fish whose weight is less than the breaking strength of the line. People are

These are stainless steel ball bearings (left) and a series of carbon friction and stainless steel washers, both found on better conventional reels.

often amazed that a 15-pound fish can break 20-pound line, but that doesn't happen if the drag is set properly and the washers are allowed to slip freely when necessary.

In typical fishing with conventional reels, anglers set the drag at 25 to 30 percent of the breaking strength of their line. This is measured by some people with a short length of line on a straight pull off the reel. It is measured by others with line running through the rod guides and the rod flexed as it would be in fishing circumstances. Most people use the "feels good" method of establishing drag tension by pulling line off the reel and adjusting the star wheel until the tension feels right. The most precise way to measure drag tension is by using a reliable scale and attaching it to the line. No matter what method is used, the objective is to adjust the drag so that the line will not slip until the appropriate amount of tension is applied. Understanding how to use and set drag is one of the most important aspects of sportfishing, and is reviewed in detail elsewhere (see: drag).

The drag mechanism is an especially important characteristic of a conventional reel due to the applications that these reels face. For years manufacturers employed various types, combinations, and numbers of drag washers, which produced mixed results when tested by powerful fish. Better materials, however, have greatly improved the drags of these products, and many contemporary models have very good drag systems. Moreover, because of the nature of revolving spool reels, no twist is imparted to the line when an angler reels at the same time that line slips off the spool via the drag. This is a common problem with spinning and spincasting reels. Twist isn't possible on a conventional reel if the handle is turning and the spool is simultaneously slipping. When the drag mechanism is activated on a conventional reel, the spool rotates and line unwinds in an untwisted manner. There is no line twist unless it comes from lure use or you put it on when the spool is filled.

Drag system. On conventional reels, the drag is located on the main gear and is usually a multi-element system with washers that are keyed together. The main gear is hollowed out, which decreases weight and increases space, and a stack of washers is located ahead of this, with all of these fitting over a threaded gear stud. The washers are alternately stainless steel and friction material, interleaved to increase the working surface area.

Drag tension is increased or decreased by turning a drag star (radial-arm star wheel), which is located under the handle on the sideplate. The drag star threads onto the gear stud or drive gear, which is connected to the handle, so it rotates concurrently with the handle without affecting the setting. Turning the drag star clockwise or forward increases tension; turning it counterclockwise or backward decreases it.

Turning the drag star forward causes it to spiral around the threads of the gear stud and compress a tension spring washer, which compresses the drag washers. The stainless steel washers are keyed separately to the gear shaft and the main gear to prevent slippage; without keying, all washers would slip and there would be no drag since the interleaving would be inoperative. Washers that are alternately keyed off both the shaft and the main gear transmit power from the handle into the gear via the drag material itself by relying on the friction between those oppositely keyed parts to drive the gear. The more pressure on them, the more friction that is applied to the spool.

When spool friction exceeds the tension on the line, the reel handle turns the main gear and the spool, and allows line to be recovered. When tension on the line exceeds friction on the spool, the spool revolves against handle pressure, and line can be pulled off the spool. The handle is prevented from turning backward by a dog and ratchet, which is known as an anti-reverse.

Variation/Force. Variation is an important aspect of drag function. If you set the drag to create 4 pounds of tension on the line, it should stay at 4 pounds. If it varies to 5 and 6 pounds, that is not good. Influencing factors include how fast you pull on the line, and where you set the drag. If you have

30-pound line and you set the drag at 4 pounds, you'll have less variation than if you set it at 10 pounds. With lower force, it is easier to control variation.

Another aspect is maximum drag force. For most fishing, the drag on conventional tackle should be set at 25 to 30 percent of breaking strength. For a 30-pound line, that would be between $7^1/_2$ and 9 pounds. If you could only set it at 6 pounds, it would probably not be enough for some fishing situations, meaning that the maximum tension for that reel is less than what is desirable for ordinary fishing. So you should check the maximum force you can obtain on the reel before using it to make sure that it will be adequate for your needs. With most conventional reels, this is not a problem, and maximum drag force usually exceeds the strength of line for which the reel is rated. But this can be a problem on an older or poorly maintained product.

Some anglers are very interested in being able to readily get maximum force, which locks the reel down and completely prevents the drag from slipping. This is more common for smaller reels used in freshwater. However, this maximum force is seldom beneficial for most fishing activities, including playing large or strong fish, unless you're using very heavy line. Where it is most likely to be useful, however, is when a lure or hook gets snagged and cannot be freed; this situation may require you to lock the reel down, point the rod directly at the snag, and pull back to free the hook or break the line *(see: unsnagging)*. If the drag cannot be locked down completely, line will slip off, and it may be harder to free the hook.

Range. Another important aspect of drag function is range of adjustment, or how many revolutions you can turn the control mechanism on the reel to achieve the desired result. Most star wheels have a lot of latitude in revolutions from the point where the wheel cannot turn backward any further to the point where it cannot turn forward any further.

Range actually starts the moment you've got some drag tension, not from the point where the star wheel is completely backed off. Sometimes you can make two revolutions from the fully backed off position before achieving resistance. This does not affect the drag tension. To avoid this, manufacturers may put a spacer of varying size inside the mechanism to cut down on the turns of the star wheel necessary to produce tension. Although anglers generally dislike making these extra turns, having this provides some leeway for the manufacturers in case the drag materials differ in thickness from the norm. Thicker materials take up more space; if a spacer is placed in the mechanism, it may not be possible to completely back off the drag tension, so this adversely affects range. In a situation requiring ultralight drag tension, it may not be possible to back the drag all the way off to get that light amount of tension.

The wider the area from the point where line slips under no load to where it doesn't slip at all, the finer the tension adjustment. A wider area makes setting drag tension easier, especially for the more experienced angler. For conventional reels, a good range of drag adjustment from initial tension to maximum tension should require one and a half to two revolutions of the star wheel. This is an arguable point, however, and personal preferences vary. The problem with adjustment range comes from conflicting demands. Some anglers want a wide range of adjustment while others want to quickly get to maximum force, or lockdown. Satisfying these differences requires tradeoffs in design elements. There's a point where smoothness and lockdown become incompatible. Nevertheless, how many rotations it takes to get to the lockdown point is important. Ideally, a conventional reel drag should have a wide range of adjustment from initial tension to about 50 percent of the line's breaking strength, and then quickly jump to the maximum point; the lockdown mode is then achieved quickly in case you have to break off, pull on a snag, or have the greatest possible tension for special circumstances.

One factor that contributes to range as well as overall performance is the material of the friction washers; a material with a relatively high coefficient of friction helps a lot. Another factor is the size of the thread on the stud or main gear. If a reel has a post with heavy pitch thread, just half a turn could take you from initial tension to maximum tension. If a reel has a post with very fine pitch thread, it may take three turns to go from initial tension to maximum tension. So a finer thread provides a better range of adjustment no matter what the materials or components are. Having a conical washer with the crown up also provides range as the washer collapses.

Friction washers. The material of friction washers is critical to the operation of any reel, especially conventional reels used for rugged fishing. Ideally, the drag in any reel operates smoothly, without hesitation. In other words, it starts immediately when needed and maintains a constant rate of tension as line flows continuously off, and it keeps the same level of tension as it is periodically called upon during the time it takes to play and land a strong fish. The less variation there is in the performance of the drag, the better. Some of this performance is affected by the capable range of adjustment, as previously noted. Some is affected by the number and material of the friction washers.

One of the problems with friction washers is that they are asked to do something which is very difficult. It is desirable to have a drag that slips freely and yet can create a high amount of pressure. It has to be able to slip, yet also to sustain a high load, perhaps even a complete no-slip lockdown load. Thus, you're looking for two opposite attributes in a friction washer to accomplish these needs.

Friction washer materials in conventional reels, like those in other reel types, have evolved over the years. They've been made of many materials in the past, including felt, leather, asbestos, and Teflon. Most contemporary conventional reels use a washer made of woven carbon fiber. Penn Reels, which was the first manufacturer to discover this material and use it in the 1980s, calls their carbon fiber friction washer HT 100, because in their initial test, they ran it under tension for 100 miles and it was as good after that as before, with no appreciable wear on the friction material (although some on the metal washers). This synthetic material was first used to brake F-16 jets.

This woven carbon fiber compresses slightly, and that little bit of give contributes to excellent drag range. A bigger factor, however, is that the carbon fiber doesn't change characteristics when it heats up, because it is, in effect, already "cooked." With other friction materials, as heat builds up, the material changes and there is more friction. Other materials become inconsistent after they are heavily worked. The carbon fiber doesn't build up friction as it heats up.

Heat dissipation is obviously an important element that complements, or constricts, the action of the friction washers. As mentioned previously, the metal washers in the drag stack help disperse heat buildup from the action of the friction washers. The heavy main gear containing the drag acts as a heat sink, and takes out heat for all or part of most initial runs by a fish. However, these cannot dissipate the tremendous heat built up by the lengthy and sustained run of a really huge fish, and it is possible to overheat a reel to where the drag becomes paralyzed. The carbon fiber friction washer resists that type of problem better than other materials.

The carbon fiber is also especially good when applying maximum tension, or deliberately locking down the drag tension as far as it will go. Some friction washers, such as Teflon versions, can't be locked down enough on a conventional reel that is used for large fish; they still slip even when the drag star is turned as tight as possible. Bearing down on a big grouper so you can just pull the fish up out of the structure is a type of situation where you might need real lock-down power. The carbon fiber permits that type of lockdown; by comparison, asbestos and Teflon friction washers are slippery and, when compressed fully, may still give.

Carbon fiber friction washers also resist sustained compression as well as contamination from water, salt, dirt, grease, and oil. Although other materials are used in friction washers, many conventional reels now possess this material.

In most conventional reels, and especially better quality models, carbon fiber friction washers are used with stainless steel washers. The number of combined friction and metal washers in a drag stack varies; some manufacturers have between seven and thirteen elements, the greater number being on bigger reels, in each case alternating friction washers with metal ones. More friction washers increases the total drag surface area. This interleaved stack is topped with a tension spring washer for range and compression purposes, and might also have a spacer and a ball bearing, the latter providing a smooth feel without any load.

If the stainless steel washers are removed for maintenance, care should be taken when replacing them. These are stamped parts, and one side is slightly concave and the other slightly convex. Find out which side has a slight bow (use a straight edge), and put the bow side up. This way, when the drag is tightened, surface contact is made at the very end, and then flattens out and spreads over the full area of the friction washer.

The drag performance of most conventional reels is good to excellent, which it must be for the strenuous applications they endure. A majority of conventional reels sold are used for saltwater use, where the drag is frequently employed and often tested, so it has to be of high quality.

Spool diameter. Due to the normal usage of conventional reels, capacity is an important aspect. Capacity is linked to diameter, and the diameter of the spool at any given moment can also be a factor that affects drag. More line is recovered per turn of the reel handle when the diameter is greater than when it is smaller, so it is easier to retrieve line when the diameter of the spool is high. Where the drag is concerned, as line is pulled off the spool and the diameter decreases, it takes more effort to pull it off. So drag tension increases as the diameter of the spool decreases; it starts out at one level when the spool is full of line, but increases when the diameter of the spool is smaller due to a fish having taken plenty of line. Fortunately, with some lines the increased stretch of the longer length being fished tends to compensate for this.

This is a matter of physics and an unchangeable one, but it's important for anglers to recognize. When spool diameter has decreased and drag tension increased, it is all the more important to have a smooth drag and friction washers that maintain top performance. Because of the dynamics of carbon friction washers, drag tension remains on a more even level with heat buildup, rather than increasing as line is lost; these washers do not make it easier to pull line off when the level of line on a spool decreases, but they do make the drag tension more consistent, meaning that more even drag pressure is maintained.

Anti-Reverse Features

The anti-reverse component of reels is an element that restricts backward movement of the handle. In most conventional reels, it is a dog and ratchet mechanism that provides a variable amount of backward handle movement; this is a multi-stop anti-reverse. The amount of this movement is decided by the number of ratchets for the dog to catch. In some reels, it is a one-way roller bearing that allows no backward movement and is called continuous or infinite anti-reverse.

This aspect of conventional reels is of most significance to cast-and-retrieve applications and to some styles of baitfishing, primarily because it is relative to how the reel operates when the forward-turning motion is stopped. There is a natural tendency to pull up on the handle when not reeling, whether to set the hook or to momentarily stop while retrieving. If there is considerable play in the handle and drive gear when the reel stops, the handle may actually turn backward slightly. This produces a feeling of sloppiness or instability, and if there is too much backward movement of the handle, it may adversely affect hooksetting. Ideally, a conventional reel used for casting should engage instantly and firmly. The few models that have a continuous anti-reverse keep the handle and drive gear from moving even the slightest bit backward.

One thing that governs how quickly the drive gear engages in a reel with multi-stop anti-reverse is the number of ratchets in the system. The ratchets are little stops for a dog; as you turn the handle, this part slides over a ramp, and when the dog stops moving, it slides backward and engages a ratchet. The more ratchets there are, the quicker it engages; if there are ten ratchets, there will be ten stops per turn of the handle. More ratchets also mean finer teeth, which are easier to break or clog. Therefore, the number of ratchets varies on conventional reels depending on their designed usage. Infinite anti-reverse reels use a cam-operated roller and are self cleaning. This property may be more important to some anglers, like surf casters, for example, than any other.

In theory, having more ratchet stops could pose a strength problem, because you're depending on more ratchets with less material backing to stop the force of the hookset. This would seem like it could be a problem when using low-stretch lines and when using line that is overmatched by strength for the reel. However, having few ratchet stops may actually be worse, because that will provide perhaps an extra 4 or 5 inches of rod tip movement when you set the hook before you take up the slack and engage the dog. With a hard hookset using strong low-stretch line and a tight drag, you can develop a lot of force and strip the dog and ratchet system when there is this much room to move.

In a trolling application, where baits or lures are always set out under a fair load, when you have a strike you are already in a position to respond without any backward movement of the handle, no matter how many ratchets there are. So in this application, there is no relevance. In a casting application, where it is undesirable to have backward travel of the handle when you set the hook, more ratchet stops are advantageous for quick hooksets. A one-way roller bearing, which provides continuous anti-reverse, however, is most desirable.

Some conventional reels have an optional anti-reverse feature, which means that the anti-reverse can be disengaged so the handle and the spool can be turned either forward or backward. This is accomplished by moving a small spring-loaded lever on the sideplate (usually the right sideplate or handle sideplate). This may be referred to as a direct drive feature, although it is actually a mechanism for disengaging the anti-reverse.

This is a feature preferred for specific fishing applications, often when anglers want a direct feel of the line for strike detection, as when fishing with bait in the surf, or when they are drift fishing and putting the reel in and out of gear all the time, or when they are live-lining bait and want to let line out frequently to follow the movement of the bait. After casting, engage the main gear by moving the eccentric lever from the freespool position to the retrieve position, and then disengage the anti-reverse. When a fish takes and runs off, flip the anti-reverse lever into the on position and set the hook. If you leave the anti-reverse disengaged, the reel handle is free to move wildly backward as line comes off the spool, which could cause trouble. Make sure to keep your hand on the handle if you have the anti-reverse disengaged, or you'll have a runaway handle.

Other Features

Frame/spool materials. Because conventional reels are predominantly used in saltwater, and because they are susceptible to extreme stresses and fishing conditions, construction and materials must be of the highest caliber, and not only suitable for the marine environment but for withstanding severe usage. This is especially true in the larger models meant for heavy lines. One-piece aluminum frames are especially favored for heavy-duty applications; conventional reels used for light applications may have a multipiece frame. One-piece frames provide superior strength and precision alignment of the spool and other components. These may be of extruded anodized aluminum in top contemporary models and graphite in others (some older reels can be retrofitted with a one-piece frame through a conversion kit). At the present time, a graphite frame on a midsize reel is pushing the limits of graphite for use in saltwater. When newer grades of materials emerge, graphite may be used in heavier reels, which will lower weight and increase corrosion protection (it is essentially corrosion-proof). Graphite does not yet have the strength of properly manufactured aluminum; the newest generation of graphite material has greater strength than previous generations, and is more resistant to flexing, but it is still not up to aluminum. That is why bigger contemporary reels have aluminum frames and the smaller ones, meant for under 50-pound-test line, have graphite.

One of the problems that occurs in using midsize reels with graphite frames is that aggressive

The unheralded, disdained, and toothy gar can trace its genealogy back over 70 million years; the alligator gar species can grow to 300 pounds.

anglers fish them with heavier line than they are rated for, punishing both the spool and frame. A graphite-frame reel that is meant for 30-pound line, when used with 50- or 80-pound line, may break or become deformed.

Conventional reel manufacturers all strive for products with lower weight, but these items still tend to be heavy, and some brands a little heavier than others. The use of various materials has a bearing on weight, of course, but also on strength. There's always a balance. While anglers prefer lightweight equipment, they also need performance for battling bigger fish; doing this requires heavier materials and sturdy construction.

Aluminum spools, for example, are common on most top conventional reels, while a few also have chrome-plated cast bronze spools. You cannot get by with graphite spools on large saltwater conventional reels; they'll be broken left and right, especially when used with heavier line than the reel is intended for. You can use graphite spools on lightweight reels meant for either saltwater or freshwater use, but when these models are heavily used, they may not hold up to extreme pressure.

The manufacturing process for spools (and other components) has improved greatly and is one reason why today's reels are much better than yesterday's. Aluminum spools may be diecast, forged, or machined, which have different strengths and advantages. It is a lot cheaper to diecast, in which the metal is melted down into a mold. In forging, the metal is softened and banged into shape. In pure machining, a form is cut out of a solid block of aluminum; this is more labor intensive and expensive. Different uses and price points of reels dictate what process manufacturers use. The most demanding applications require forging because the molecules are compacted closer together in the forging process, which makes them stronger. However, it is not the process alone that accounts for strength; some aluminum alloys are much stronger than others, reacting differently to these processes.

Other manufacturing features include injection-molded sideplates and stamped stainless steel exposed parts. Sideplates used to be compression-molded, which meant taking the material in a mold and closing it. Most sideplates are now molded by injection methods, which results in superior strength. Environmental concerns have made the multi-step chrome-plating process used for exposed parts less desirable, so stamped stainless steel parts have become more prevalent.

Clamps/Lugs/Braces. Larger conventional reels used in saltwater may have clamps to secure the reel to the rod, lugs for attachment to a harness, and on some versions a brace for additional support.

Older conventional reels used to have metal rod clamps which were fastened around the rod with exposed wing nuts. These could get in the way of grabbing or lead to scratching. They've been replaced by molded synthetic clamps with recessed screws; there is no protrusion to get in the way, and they allow easier handling or even palming.

Reels meant for 30-pound line and up sport harness lugs on the top of the reel because they are often used for bigger fish. The angler is likely to wear a shoulder or kidney harness *(see)*, which is attached to these lugs. Forward and rear braces on the biggest models are used to provide torsional stability on rods.

Reel designations. Conventional reels are generally classified by the strength of line that they are designed for and the capacity they hold. Some have long been characterized by an "O" (or ought) designation that was created many years ago, and which has been gradually fading in common parlance. However, some conventional reels for saltwater use have been labeled from 1/0 to 14/0 sizes, the latter meant for 130-pound-test line. The most popular sizes in this categorization system have been the 2/0, 4/0, and 6/0 models, which are respectively meant for 20-, 30- and 50-pound line. It is more likely to see contemporary reels designated by manufacturers according to the product series name, accompanied by some combination of model numbers and letters; these may or may not have an obvious connection to the intended line strength or line capacity.

Ergonomics. Conventional reels are by nature large, generally cumbersome, and often heavy. There are few points to be made about their ergonomic nature other than weight and rod clamps, which have been discussed, and the sideplates and handles. Cosmetics or appearance has nothing to do with function.

A smooth sideplate on the noncranking side of the reel (which is the left side for most conventional reels) is preferable for general comfort and use, especially in smaller versions that may be palmed. Bearings on the sides are not good for gripping; they used to be on the left side of some reels, but have generally been moved to the right, where they are also more secure. Likewise, some conventional reels now have a contoured cutout on the back of the frame for more thumb contact on the spool.

Some people like bigger handles and some smaller, owing to application and interest in power versus speed. Handles can be changed, and aftermarket accessories are available for this. The torpedo shape of many handle grips is still available on some conventional reels, but is dated and likely to disappear altogether on smaller products. Most small and midsize conventional reels have a soft grip handle, which has a large surface area and comfortable nonslip material. Generally, smaller reels have counterbalances and soft grips. Reels from 4/0 on up generally have torpedo grips and no counterbalance, and the largest reels have a barrel knob, because it's necessary to have a bigger grip that can be worked with a full hand.

Rods

Rods that are used with conventional reels may in general terms be called "conventional rods," but this is misleading because a vast array of rods falls under this oversimplified categorization. Some products in that array, in fact, may be called ocean rods, deep sea rods, boat rods, bay rods, pier rods, trolling rods, bottom fishing rods, live-bait rods, wire line rods, saltwater rods, downrigger rods, and so forth.

They are generally stiff, heavy-action products, with longer ones used in pier and bridge fishing and downrigger trolling and shorter ones in such boat work as casting, jigging, and bottom fishing. Special attributes exist with some models for particular applications, such as standup fishing (see).

For the most part, these are workhorse products with long, beefy two-handed handles that securely accommodate either level- or free-winding conventional reels, primarily the latter. Virtually all models have a long cushioned foregrip, large enough for two-handed use, for heavy-duty fish fighting and lifting, and the butt of many handles has a gimbal (sometimes with detachable butt cap) for insertion into a gimbaled rod holder or belt.

Heavy-duty double-foot rod guides are used with such rods and are mounted on top of the rod like the reel. This is because fish fighting is what such tackle does best, and the load of a gamefish on the line applies both a crushing downward force on the guide ring and frame, and a simultaneous tendency to torque or twist the rod, so guides must be of top quality and properly spaced and placed. Some rods feature a full complement of roller guides or tip and butt-end (stripper) roller guides. The guide rings are generally small, because little casting is done with most such rods (although it is done with some versions).

Lengths and materials vary, although fiberglass and composite materials are used with greater frequency in many more such rods than in other types, and few are exclusively made with graphite. Graphite may be used in some reel seats, however, all of which are extremely rugged; a few rods also feature trigger grips.

Unlike reels, many of the issues pertaining to rods used with conventional reels—functions, materials, components, etc.—are similar to those of other rods, and these are more fully detailed elsewhere (see: rod, fishing).

Using Conventional Tackle

Line. Although various line strengths from 6 through 130 pounds can be employed with the appropriate conventional gear, 20- through 80-pound lines are the most commonly used strengths in saltwater, and 12- through 30-pound lines are common in freshwater. Application dictates use, and one of the things that is frequently done by conventional reel users is stepping up to a higher strength line, which may not be what the reel is designed for. Often, anglers use a wider spool version of a particular model to step up in line strength while maintaining capacity. Some reels that are rated for 30-pound line are used by just as many people with 50- and 80-pound line on it as 30; such users may also tighten the drag way down for big bottom fish, and this type of action may be too much for the reel. There are implications to doing this, especially for the reel in terms of the frame and spool material, and drag tension adjustment, and these are discussed earlier in this section.

Fishing line is not pre-spooled onto conventional reels, although when purchased from some tackle retailers it may then be spooled by the dealer with the brand and strength of line you desire using a line winding machine. Because capacity is great, this can be beneficial for first-time conventional reel users, especially since it is important that the line be distributed properly on the reel and with ample tension. When you spool line on yourself, you should use a large bulk filler spool.

Nylon monofilament is the overwhelming choice of line type for conventional reels; there is some use of microfilament line, and on certain models (usually with narrow spool), wire line, lead core, and braided Dacron lines are employed. Because line coiling is not much of an issue on these large-spool reels, suppleness may not be much of a factor; abrasion resistance is a high priority in line for many conventional reel users, especially those

Using a fairly substantial conventional reel and rod equipped with wire line, a fisherman plays his catch with the butt of the rod in a seat gimbal.

who fish on the bottom and around wrecks and reefs. For casting applications, however, there is more of a need for a line with balanced properties, including less stiffness.

Obviously, conventional reels hold a lot of line. The range is from 275 to 1,000 yards with conventional diameter nylon monofilament line, and this is often understated by manufacturers. Using line that has the strength of conventional diameter nylon monofilament but has a thinner diameter allows for greater capacity, and using a heavier strength line with conventional diameter results in less capacity.

Generally, it is best to keep within the recommended line strengths when filling a reel. For the most part, you can take a conventional reel and not have a problem going 10 or 20 percent over the recommendations. Remember that when a manufacturer recommends using 30-pound line with a particular reel, that recommendation is based upon a standard 30-pound line with a conventional diameter. You can probably use conventional diameter 25- and 40-pound line as well, but it would not be worthwhile to use much heavier line. Not only is spool size and capacity an issue, but this reel may not be able to handle the greater stresses that might be generated with much heavier line, as noted previously. So, for example, putting 50-pound line on that reel could be problematic.

However, and this is where things get tricky, there are 50-pound lines that have the diameter of a conventional 30-pound line, so you can get just as much of it on the spool. Nevertheless, it is still line with a 50-pound breaking strength (and may actually break much higher); this may be capable of overpowering the reel frame or spool. If the rod is up to handling a lot of stress, and the line is rated to break at a minimum of 50 (often more) pounds, and the reel is meant for up to 30-pound line, then the forces generated on the reel by maximum pressures could be harmful.

On the other hand, you might use a 30-pound line with the diameter of conventional 17-pound line, and achieve much greater line capacity on the reel at a line strength that the reel is rated for. Or, you could "cheat" a little bit and use 40-pound line that has a diameter of conventional 20-pound line, if that benefited your fishing situation (see: line). This is a grossly misunderstood aspect of reel usage that has largely been brought about by the emergence of thin diameter lines (nylon monofilaments, braids, and microfilaments).

Filling/refilling the spool. The various aspects of properly filling a reel spool are detailed elsewhere (see: line). Putting line on a conventional reel spool is not complicated, but it must be done evenly and under tension. If you are an inexperienced angler or new to the use of conventional reels, the fastest and easiest way to fill a reel is to have it wound on by a linewinder, which is a professional machine. Many tackle dealers offer this service to their customers, although that service is seldom available from a mail order supplier or mass merchant.

In brief, the spooling process entails mounting the reel on the rod and running line from a service spool through the rod guides beginning at the top of the rod. Tie the line to the arbor of the spool, snip off the tag end excess, and reel the line on under tension. It is important to avoid or at least minimize twisting of the line during the spooling process, as detailed elsewhere (see: line). Fill the spool to within no more than $3/16$-inch of the lip.

When the line gets low on the spool, or when it is old and needs replacement, you have the option of completely refilling the spool, or refilling only part of the spool. If a conventional reel holds 450 yards of line, it makes sense economically to refill with just 120 or 180 yards of line rather than the full 450, but that may not be a good practical decision.

When you partially refill the spool, you must tie a line-to-line knot (see: knots, fishing). The weakest portion of a line is usually the knot, so this connection must be a good one to maintain the basic strength of the line, should that knotted section come under pressure. This is especially important when angling for large and strong fish. However, the problem with making a line-to-line knot for most conventional reel filling is that the line used is fairly heavy with a thick diameter, and the line-to-line knot is bulky and obtrusive on the reel spool. Furthermore, it may get caught on a rod guide when departing under extreme tension and cause a breakoff or spool overrun. Depending on your application, this disadvantage may be a deciding factor; most conventional reel users do not tie line-to-line knots on the reel, but spool up with new unknotted fresh line.

Line twist.   Line twist is not an inherent problem in conventional reels. With other types of tackle, twist is often caused when the angler turns the handle against a slipping drag. Twist isn't possible on a conventional reel if the handle is turning and the spool is simultaneously slipping. When the drag mechanism is activated on a conventional reel, the spool rotates and line unwinds in an untwisted manner. There is no line twist unless it comes from lure use or is incurred through improper filling of the reel spool.

Matching and selecting.   As with any type of fishing tackle, the issue of matching the right reel to the right rod is an important one, but in these times it is a relatively easy one. Conventional reels and rods are usually not packaged in combination, but there are some, and tackle retailers can match rods and reels for you. Most of the time a reel is purchased separately from a rod. Matching these used to be referred to as balancing, and properly paired outfits were referred to as "balanced tackle." This simply meant that the rod and reel felt right when used together; the outfit was not overly butt heavy due to a large reel paired with a lightweight rod, or

C

tip heavy due to a small reel paired to a medium or heavy action rod.

Fishing rods are virtually all labeled by line classifications and by weight of objects to be used, which practically assures that you don't put a light-duty reel, for example, on a medium-heavy rod.

Conventional tackle is often classified by the manufacturers as being in a certain category and for a certain use, such as jigging or bottom fishing or trolling. Reels, for example, might be classified as high speed, or heavy-duty, or casting, as well as levelwind, but the exact definition of some of these categorizations can range from one manufacturer to the next, and in any event is determined by the line capacity, features, and components.

When selecting conventional tackle, as well as matching a rod and reel, you must take into consideration the applications for it. A beginning angler may be unsure what to select without any prior fishing experience. Guidance from a knowledgeable sales person is very helpful; such a person is more likely to be found in a specialized store (a sporting goods dealer or bait and tackle shop); guidance will not be found from a mail order supplier and seldom in a mass merchandise mart. Lacking this, or in addition to it, might be advice from an acquaintance or relative who has experience with this type of equipment and some knowledge of the fishing that a beginner is likely to do.

In a general sense, selecting conventional tackle starts with a determination of the size of fish that you are likely to catch and evaluating the conditions under which you'll be fishing. The larger and stronger the fish, the stronger the tackle necessary for beginners, until you get enough experience to use lighter gear. Fishing where there are a lot of obstructions usually requires medium or heavy grades of tackle; in saltwater, it is often necessary to turn or move a deep- or bottom-dwelling fish soon after it strikes to keep it from getting into cover, and this may take a lot of pressure and tough tackle.

Most selection thus starts with a determination of the line strength necessary for the conditions, and having the rod and reel appropriate for this. You should also give a lot of attention to line capacity so that you have an appropriate amount of line on the reel for the application.

Holding the rod and reel. Few conventional reels come in left-handed retrieve models, so most require left-handed holding and right-handed retrieval. This is akin to the use of baitcasting tackle, and it obviously favors people who are right-handed. Because less casting is done with conventional reels, applications are more demanding, the outfits are generally heavy, and most people are right-handed, however, the right-retrieve aspect of most conventional reels is not the problem that it is in baitcasting products. Large conventional reels especially are used for big fish, and it is common to attach these reels to a harness, which relieves the rod-holding arm. If a person is right-handed, all of the heavy-duty cranking of the reel is done with the stronger hand, which in theory is better for anyone who is right-handed, although not as desirable for a lefty.

Clearly, when casting with conventional tackle, right-handed anglers must keep their thumb on the reel spool and control the spool revolutions, then, after the cast, switch the rod into the left hand to reel with the right hand. Most conventional reels are too large for palming and are not conducive for usage like a baitcasting reel, so they are usually held by putting the left hand on the rod foregrip. This is obviously the hold for placing the butt in a belt gimbal or into a harness; for bait and jig fishing, the butt is tucked into the armpit and between the left arm and body, with the hand on the foregrip and the rod held level or pointed slightly down. Holding the foregrip with the left hand also helps with guiding the line on the spool in a level manner, and with feeling the line by keeping your fingers on it.

Casting technique. The actual method of casting with conventional tackle is similar to that for baitcasting tackle, although the former is heavier and the objects cast are usually much heavier, so the casting motion is more one of throwing than casting, with the exception of conventional tackle used in surf fishing *(see)*.

Setting up the centrifugal casting control is necessary for those reels that possess this component, and the drag should likewise be pre-adjusted. To cast, begin with the reel facing upward and toward you. Adjust the drag for fishing. Hang the lure or weight from 4 to 8 inches below the tip of the rod and place the thumb of the rod-holding hand on the spool so the spool can't turn; then move the eccentric lever into the freespool position.

The vast majority of conventional reel users employ thumb pressure to brake the spool because most do not have any other means of controlling spool revolution. Applying thumb pressure is an

An angler plays a fish on conventional tackle, being careful to use his thumb to evenly lay the line on the reel as it is retrieved.

action learned through trial and error and perfected with experience; it requires the application of different degrees of braking tension for the weights on the line, distances being cast, and types of rod and reel being used.

Keep tension on the line with your thumb; this will be released at the optimum point in the forward motion of the cast. When this tension is released, line flows off the spool and out through the guides, carried by the weight of the object at the terminal end of the line. Applying too much pressure results in a cast that is short, and applying too little pressure results in a backlash.

Accuracy is often not an issue with conventional tackle because anglers do a lot of open-water casting with this equipment; however, it can definitely be an issue when casting bait to visible, quickly moving, or feeding fish. Achieving distance is an issue for some conventional tackle users, especially surf anglers (see: casting).

Setting/checking drag. Before any on-the-water use of a conventional reel, it is vital to set the drag to the proper amount of tension. Issues pertaining to drag in conventional reels were reviewed earlier in this section, and using and setting drag is covered in more detail elsewhere (see: drag).

Briefly, however, in typical fishing with conventional reels, drag tension is increased or decreased by turning a drag star (radial-arm star wheel), which is located under the handle on the sideplate. The drag star threads onto the gear stud or drive gear, which is connected to the handle, so it rotates concurrently with the handle without affecting the setting. Turning the drag star clockwise or forward increases tension; turning it counterclockwise or backward decreases tension.

Anglers set the drag on conventional reels at 25 to 30 percent of the breaking strength of their line. This is measured by some people with a short length of line on a straight pull off the reel. It is measured by others with line running through the rod guides and the rod flexed as it would be in fishing circumstances. Most people use the "feels good" method of establishing drag tension by pulling line off the reel and adjusting the star wheel until the tension feels right. The most precise way to measure drag tension is by using a reliable scale and attaching it to the line. In any method, the objective is to adjust the drag so that the line will not slip until the appropriate amount of tension is applied.

If a reel is used infrequently, it is a good idea at the end of each outing to back the drag tension off to relieve pressure on the drag washers. This is not quite as important for conventional reels with graphite drag washers because they resist compression better than washers made of other friction material; nevertheless, releasing tension is still a good idea. When starting a day of fishing, you should check and adjust the drag tension setting before starting to fish. Many an angler has neglected this and found upon hooking the first fish of the day that the drag was so weak it impaired hook setting, or so tight that it adversely affected fish playing.

Maintenance and repair. Maintenance is an ongoing issue for conventional tackle users, especially saltwater anglers. Rods and reels must be washed down every time they are taken on the water, even if not used, since they are likely to be exposed to salt spray. Use a fine but ample spray of freshwater, rather than a hard stream, to clean the reel and remove salt deposits, and do so as soon as possible after you return to the dock or launch site. Use soap and a scrub brush to remove any hardened matter. Warm water is best if available; make sure not to use a hard stream, which could drive salt deposits into the internal mechanisms. Dry off excess freshwater on the reel and lubricate exposed areas, perhaps with a pressurized spray oil. A light coating of oil with a rag can also be applied to exposed metal parts. Give the reel a chance to dry out completely, and store it in a cool, dry place, not in a bag that is wet or which will promote condensation.

Make sure to periodically examine screws and fittings. If the reel has any loose part, which is most likely to be a sideplate screw, it should be tightened as soon as you notice it.

Many people tend to excessively lubricate conventional reels, which may cause harm if oil or grease gets on parts that don't need, or shouldn't have, the lubrication. That includes graphite drag washers. Over-lubrication can be especially problematic for a reel employed for casting. Some older conventional reels used to have built-in lubrication points with spring loaded balls, which worked great when they were used right, but people had a tendency pump too much oil in there and it got into other parts of the reel. Using the wrong kind of lubrication is also a problem. Follow the manufacturer's recommendations for the type of lubrication, the locations, and the frequency, as this will vary with different brands.

Details on tackle maintenance are discussed elsewhere (see: tackle care/maintenance/repair). Manufacturers recommend that conventional reels be overhauled at least once a season, perhaps more if used vigorously. Periodically oil and grease frictional parts, but don't overdo it. Some reels come with small oil or grease tubes, and these can be purchased from tackle suppliers or obtained from the manufacturer. A thorough cleaning requires disassembling most of the reel, scrubbing or rinsing most of the gunk from the parts, drying, and then relubricating and regreasing. If you are unsure about doing this yourself, have a reel service and repair shop do it, or send it to the manufacturer for servicing.

COOK ISLANDS

The Cook Islands are a group of 24 coral atolls and volcanic islands in the South Pacific Ocean, flanked

C

on the west by Tonga and Samoa and on the east by Tahiti. The group is about the same distance south of the equator as Hawaii is north of it. Originally a New Zealand protectorate, the Cook Islands became independent in 1965 but exist in free association with New Zealand, which provides considerable assistance to these islands.

Named for the English explorer Captain James Cook, the island group has a total population of approximately 19,000 friendly and good-hearted people of mostly Polynesian descent. Nearly all speak English in addition to Cook Island Maori, and there is little crime.

The capital of the group and site of an international airport is Rarotonga, a high volcanic island and the most developed one in terms of quality accommodation. The main town is Avarua. Light aircraft make regular flights from Rarotonga to most of the other islands in the group, regularity depending on demand.

Currency in the Cook Islands is the New Zealand dollar, supplemented by coins and notes minted for local use that are not negotiable outside the Cook Islands but are sought after by collectors. This is one of the few places in the world where you can get a $3 bill.

Several 28- to 38-foot charter boats work out of Rarotonga, as so several smaller open boats, but they are not of international quality. Serious anglers should bring their own tackle. With little in the way of offshore structures, most boats troll around the edge of Rarotonga or target the fish-attracting device off the airport. Catches are mostly yellowfin and skipjack tuna, wahoo, and mahimahi (dolphin); some marlin, mostly blues and some blacks, are also caught.

Fishing success is a little spotty, with more wahoo from June through September (the cooler, drier winter) and the other species more common from December through March, which is the warmer, wetter time of year, with occasional cyclones (hurricanes), and temperatures from 22°C to 30°C.

Shore fishing centers on several reef passes, Muri lagoon, or the town wharf. Lures or baits are used. All manner of tropical reef species can be caught, with bluefin and giant trevally the most sought-after gamefish.

A popular sportfishing destination in the Cook Islands is the picturesque atoll of Aitutaki (pronounced a-to-tark-ee). One of the most scenic spots in the Cooks, it has 13 islands (called *motus* locally) and a ring reef 45 kilometers in circumference, which encloses a magnificent lagoon.

The atoll is about 8 kilometers long and 4 kilometers wide, and has a population of approximately 2,000 people. An hour by light plane north of Rarotonga, Aitutaki has accommodations that range from full hotel to guest house. There are some enthusiastic anglers here, and visiting anglers are advised to join the local fishing club on arriving.

There are two 30-foot charter boats at Aitutaki, which are probably the best available in the Cook Islands, although isolation makes maintenance difficult. As in Rarotonga, visiting anglers should bring their own tackle. Of the numerous small open boats, some are of dubious quality.

Trolling outside the reef produces barracuda and wahoo in the colder months, and mahimahi, yellowfin tuna, skipjack tuna, and blue marlin during the warmer months. Blue marlin over 200 kilograms have been caught here from small boats. Flying fish are a popular trolling bait and are caught at night under lights.

Deep jigging with metal lures on the reef dropoffs has produced such tough customers as dogtooth tuna and bigeye and black trevally, as well as a wide range of reef fish. Anglers fish the reef by casting inward from a boat or, more interestingly, by wading out to the reef on the lee side. It is plate coral and easy to walk on, but anglers need to beware of any large swells.

During warm months, heavy (15-kilogram) casting tackle and large surface lures or spoons can see giant and bluefin trevally action in the surf breaks. At any time of the year, lighter tackle (4 kilograms) and smaller minnow lures, spoons, and soft-plastic lures can produce a lot of fun around the reef and inside the lagoon. Common species are smaller trevally, longtoms (needlefish or houndfish), queenfish, a wide range of colorful wrasses, reef snapper, and small grouper. Many of these species are adept at diving under coral heads for shelter, so anglers should use abrasion-resistant leaders.

The lagoon itself is extensive and up to 15 meters deep in places. There is excellent fishing inside for a wide variety of fish, including barracuda, bonefish, and several species of trevally.

The bones here average 3 to 4 kilograms and are found in reasonable numbers. As yet, however, no one has located an area that produces classical flats fishing. Most bonefish seem to be located in an area of the lagoon called *vehu,* which roughly translates as "milk water." It appears to be a giant "mud"—an area of bottom disturbed by feeding fish. Unfortunately, it is too deep and dirty for sight fishing, and most bonefish here are taken on bait.

Many of the other islands in the Cook group can be reached by light aircraft from Rarotonga. These include Atiu, Mangaia, Mitiaro, Mauke, Manihiki, Pukapuka, and Penrhyn. All of these have some form of accommodation, be it only in guest houses or private homes.

No formal charter boats exist in these places, but often a local fisherman can be persuaded to take a visiting angler out. In addition, nearly everywhere you go, good sport can be had casting small lures off the shore. Soft plastics and small metal baitfish imitations are best.

These outer islands are ideally suited to the adventurous angler who is prepared to take things

as they are; there's no five-star service here. The people are kind and friendly, however, and if this is reciprocated by the visitor, they will often go out of their way to help.

A great many fishing stories have come from the outer Cook Islands. Some of the more reliable ones include the capture of a wahoo in excess of 80 kilograms, and an 11.5-kilogram bonefish speared from a school that included even bigger fish in one remote lagoon. Difficult access to some areas has been the main barrier to further exploration of fishing opportunities in the outer Cook Islands. Nevertheless, this region may have some rewarding angling surprises in store in the future.

As in many Pacific islands, Sunday is a day of rest in the Cook Islands, and Sunday fishing is frowned upon. The intensity of this prohibition varies from island to island, so ask the locals before wetting a line. When interacting with Cook Islanders, visitors should be aware that time means little here, and punctuality is not a strong point. You have to go with the flow. Dress is informal, but revealing clothing should not be worn when visiting towns and villages.

COOLWATER FISH

An occasional term for freshwater species whose optimum environment is water of intermediate temperature, approximately from 60° to 70°F; northern pike, muskellunge, yellow perch, walleye, and smallmouth bass are among this group. They inhabit cool to moderately warm rivers and lakes of moderate fertility, often existing in waters that also accommodate species preferring colder and warmer temperatures.

See: Coldwater Fish; Warmwater Fish.

COPEPODS

Minute crustaceans at the bottom of the food chain (see) that consume phytoplankton (see).

CORAL REEF

A coral reef is a complex colony of individual animals called polyps. These produce limestone skeletons cemented together by blue-green algae, resulting in massive but surprisingly fragile formations.

Polyps are filter feeders that trap floating plankton in their tentacles and eat it. As polyps die, new ones expand the reef by growing on their remains. Polyps enjoy a mutually beneficial relationship with algae (see) living inside them. This efficient symbiosis makes coral reefs rich with an incredible diversity of animal and fish life. Smaller fish on coral reefs attract larger predators; thus, anglers may find it advantageous to fish near them or along their perimeter.

In the coral reef environment, life has evolved elaborate strategies for exploiting every available niche.

The sea's nutrients are extracted and redistributed, and shelter from predators is provided.

Coral reefs have existed for millions of years and are as ancient as rain forests. They grow in tropical waters where sea temperatures are more than 70°F all year. They occur only off the east coasts of the world's continents, seldom farther north or south of the equator than 22°, in clear water with maximum light penetration, and rarely at depths exceeding 200 to 250 feet. Optimum growth occurs within a few yards of the surface.

Boat anchors destroy a lot of coral reef, so they should never be dropped directly on a reef but rather in the sandy patches found between coral formations. (The water over a reef appears dark; sandy areas are light.) Only anchors that will hold in sand should be used, and at least four times as much line as the water depth should be laid out. Boats should navigate slowly and carefully in all reef areas to avoid the possibility of striking projecting reef formations, and should not be navigated through shallow formations.

See: Reef.

CORBINA, CALIFORNIA
Menticirrhus undulatus.

Other names—California whiting, surf fish, sucker.

The California corbina belongs to the family of fish Sciaenidae (croaker and drum) and is a member of the whiting group. But because it lacks a swim bladder, it cannot make the croaking or drumming noises characteristic of the croaker family. This bottom fish is popular with surf and pier anglers, and has excellent table value; it should not be confused with the corvina (see).

Identification. The body of the California corbina is elongated and slightly compressed, with a flattened belly. Its head is long and the mouth is small, the upper jaw scarcely reaching a point below the front of the eye. The first dorsal fin is short and high, the second long and low. Coloring is uniformly gray with incandescent reflections, and with wavy diagonal lines on the sides.

This croaker and the yellowfin croaker (*Umbrina roncador; see croaker, yellowfin*) are the only two of the eight coastal croaker present in California waters that have a barbel on the lower jaw. The California corbina can be distinguished from the yellowfin croaker by the presence of only one weak spine at the front of the anal fin; the yellowfin croaker has two strong spines.

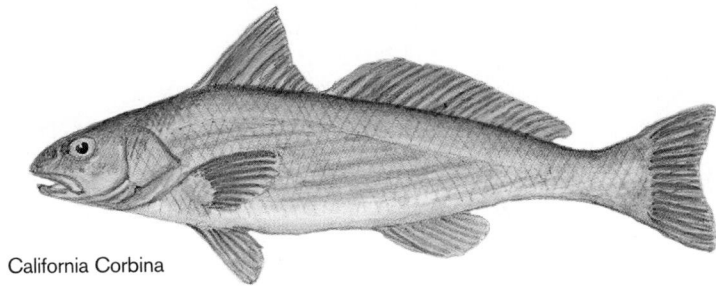

California Corbina

Size. The average corbina weighs 1 pound. The all-tackle record is 6 pounds, 2 ounces, but corbina are reported to grow to 8 pounds.

Distribution. California corbina occur from the Gulf of California in Mexico to Point Conception, California.

Habitat. Preferring sandy beaches and shallow bays, the California corbina is a bottom fish appearing along the coastal surf zone.

Life history/Behavior. Males mature when two years old, at a length of 10 inches; females mature at age 3, at 13 inches long. Spawning occurs from June through September, although it is heaviest in July and August, and takes place offshore. California corbina travel in schools or small groups, although large individuals often solitary.

Food and feeding habits. A fussy feeder, the California corbina primarily consumes sand crabs and spits out bits of clam shells and other foreign matter; they also consume small crustaceans and marine worms. Corbina scoop up mouthfuls of sand and separate the food by sending the sand through their gills. Adults are sometimes seen feeding in the surf, occasionally in water so shallow that their backs are exposed.

Angling. Surf and pier anglers use bottom fishing rigs to catch corbina on small crabs and worms.

CORDAGE

A nautical term for rope or line.

CORK

(1) A cork-bodied float *(see)*.

(2) A common material used for the grip and handle of a fishing rod *(see: rod, fishing)*.

CORVINA

Members of the Sciaenidae family (drum and croaker), corvina inhabit the Pacific Ocean and are known for the noises they make. These fish are often called corbina as well as corvina, and both words appear in the Spanish and Portuguese languages for common names applied to various drum and croaker.

They are typically referred to as croaker by some anglers and as weakfish by others, and inhabit tropical and temperate seas. Almost all are inshore

Orangemouth Corvina

bottom-feeding fish usually found over sandy bottoms, either in schools or in small groups. Corvina are generally Pacific species, primarily inhabiting the Gulf of California and waters south of the gulf; they are likely to inhabit the surf line and to hug the near shoreline, feeding on crustaceans, worms, and small fish. They generally have a silver sandy coloration that blends with this environment. Most if not all are good to eat.

Species that may be encountered include the orangemouth or yellowmouth corvina *(Cynoscion xanthulus)*, which occurs throughout the Gulf of California in Mexico and south to Acapulco, as well as in the Salton Sea in Southern California, and can grow to 36 inches; the Gulf corvina *(Cynoscion othonopterus)*, a resident of the upper Gulf of California that grows to 28 inches; the shortfin corvina *(Cynoscion parvipinnis)*, a surf fish also in the Gulf of California and south to Mazatlán that grows to 20 inches; the yellowfin corvina *(Cynoscion stolzmanni)*, ranging from the Gulf of California to Peru and growing to 35 inches; the striped corvina *(Cynoscion reticulatus)*, ranging from the Gulf of California to Panama and growing to 35 inches; and the totuava or totoaba *(Totoaba macdonaldi)*, a white seabass *(see: seabass, white)* look-alike that was once abundant and is now endangered. It inhabits the middle and upper Gulf of California and once grew to 6 feet and 300 pounds. The totuava is the largest of all croaker and was slaughtered in great numbers in the early 1900s for its air bladder, which was used as a soup base, and then later for its meat.
See: Corbina, California; Croaker; Croaker, Yellowfin; Drum; Queenfish (Croaker); Weakfish.

COSTA RICA

Costa Rica means "rich coast," an appellation bestowed in the sixteenth century by Spanish conquistadors seeking gold. They didn't find that precious metal, but traveling anglers today find a different sort of treasure in this peaceful and scenic country. That treasure has fins, grows large, fights hard, comes in varied denominations, and is plentiful. Offering a stable democratic government, an excellent overall tourism base, an emphasis on ecotourism, a favorable climate, and easy access from the United States, Costa Rica has become one of the most popular destinations for the traveling angler.

Facing the Caribbean on its east coast and the Pacific on the west, Costa Rica can offer exciting action for the premier gamefish swimming in both environs. In particular, anglers land tarpon and snook in the Caribbean, and sailfish and marlin in the Pacific; dolphin, wahoo, cubera snapper, amberjack, jack crevalle, roosterfish, grouper, barracuda, cobia, yellowfin tuna, and a plethora of other species in offshore and inshore waters. And that's just in the oceans. A few lakes and countless miles of inland rivers and estuaries produce rainbow trout, guapote, machaca, and other species.

This is indeed a lot for a small country, and there is no lack of lodges and charter operations for visitors. Many camps specifically devoted to angling exist on both coasts. Most have excellent equipment and boats and are easily reached by connecting through the capital city of San José.

Caribbean Coast

Big fish, lots of fish, arm-wrenching action, more fish jumps in one week than most people see in a lifetime, double hookups—these are just some of the reports that regularly filter out of experiences on the Caribbean side of Costa Rica. This is one of the premier places in the world to fish for tarpon and snook. It is *the* place for the angler who prefers relatively light tackle and the resulting muscle-match with fish that are tough and big, but not so big that they require special tackle and tactics. Something on the order, say, of a 20-pound snook or a 70-pound tarpon. You can catch a few other species for diversion as well. Guapote, machaca, mojarra, and mangrove snapper are small but plentiful fish that provide fun in the creeks and tidal rivers. Fishing the coastal rivers, lagoons, and nearshore open water here is sure to delight all but the most jaded angler.

A particularly fine aspect of this fishery is the jungle treks to and from fishing spots. Anglers can enjoy the flora and fauna, which include rich vegetation and plentiful birdlife, not to mention assorted monkeys.

Along Costa Rica's largely unindented Caribbean coast, the main rivers include the Colorado, Parismina, and Tortuguero, each with many tributaries and lots of jungle atmosphere, some in or close to extensive wildlife refuges. Irrespective of tide, the rivers flow well, but during the rainy season they are swollen and muddy, and are not fished. Lodges are located near the mouths of these rivers and can be reached via a short flight from San José.

Other areas of the coast have little access. Some remote waters in the north near the Nicaragua border have been accessed in recent years via a mobile houseboat operation, fishing lagoons, rivers, and nearshore waters in both northern Costa Rica and southeastern Nicaragua. Tarpon and snook headline the fishing here, but great variety of species, especially in the lagoons and including the likes of sharks and huge sawfish, also thrive here.

Tarpon. Tarpon, or *sabalo,* are the premier attraction in Costa Rica's Caribbean waters. Although tarpon grow bigger elsewhere, they are nowhere more numerous or less finicky. Tarpon in the 50- to 100-pound range are caught all along the Caribbean coast. Some bigger fish are possible, and 75-pounders are about average. In the past, much of the angling took place in rivers and at river mouths, but netting and increased boat activity have gradually changed this. Today more action is available in the ocean, off the river inlets, where there are big fish and also schools of them.

A tarpon takes to the air along the Costa Rican coast near the Parismina River.

While in the ocean, the tarpon travel in great schools, then move individually into the freshwater lagoons and rivers that characterize the Caribbean coastline. More a mating rendezvous than spawning grounds, these beautiful jungle rivers and backwaters used to offer the kind of sport people dream about. Not long ago, in the early morning hours one could often see hundreds of tarpon rolling on top. This has not been a staple of recent years, but it could happen again if efforts to prohibit commercial netting near the river mouths hold up.

Thus, the tarpon are mostly sought in the ocean, water conditions permitting. In rough weather, going to sea can be an adventure due to bars at the river mouths. At some camps, however, oceangoing fishing boats have evolved from small jonboats to rugged center-console V-draft fiberglass vessels. This not only increases accessibility, but it also improves the fishing; when the water is rough, angling can be difficult or unproductive in a small boat.

Anglers practice both sight and blind casting for tarpon in the nearshore waters off the river mouths, depending on locale and water clarity. It is easier and more enjoyable to search out and cast to roving pods of fish, the method favored when and where the water is clear and fairly calm. This is the most preferred form of fishing, and under favorable conditions opportunities to cast to pods of fish with flycasting, baitcasting, and spinning gear abound. Flycasters use 12-weight fly rods, fast-sinking lines, and large streamer flies.

This is not flats fishing, and the boats cannot be poled to intercept fish. When the schools are observed, boats attempt to move into position to intercept them, trying to drift where possible, as motor noise will spook the fish. Although spotting and casting are preferred, when storms have dispersed the schools and colored the water, there is likely to be little sight fishing. Then fish can be caught by deep jigging with heavy metal jigs.

Tarpon are available in the Costa Rican Caribbean all year, but the best fishing is usually from mid-January through June, when the heavy rains start. After June the bulk of the tarpon move out; although some fish are around, they are not as concentrated. Action is also good, however, from late August to mid-October, when the ocean flattens and anglers can more readily position themselves outside the river mouths. At that time, offshore adventurers often find schools of jack crevalle, kingfish, tripletail, barracuda, and occasional cobia, sailfish, yellowfin tuna, and wahoo, although the offshore environs and species are usually pursued only by anglers who have caught plenty of tarpon and look to do something different offshore for a day.

Snook. Although tarpon receive a great deal of attention, snook are an equally formidable resource in Costa Rican waters and, unlike tarpon, are found on both coasts. Several species of snook inhabit the Caribbean coast, including the fat snook (locally called *calba*).

The best fishing for snook is from July through October, when the bigger fish are available. During that period it is possible to encounter a surf run of 20-pounders, and even bigger fish have been landed. Among the many world-record snook taken from Costa Rica's Caribbean waters are a 53-pound, 10-ounce fish that holds the 20-pound line-class and all-tackle world records. That fish was caught in October at Parismina, and shows the size potential of these fish. Generally, a big snook from these waters would weigh more than 25 pounds. When small snook are abundant, it is possible to catch dozens in a day. Snook fishing is concentrated both in the rivers and in the frothing surf at the river mouths, with the latter producing the biggest specimens.

When the rain begins in late November and December, the region also gets a run of fat snook that average about 4 pounds, seldom more than 7. Pound-for-pound they fight as well as their big brothers, and catches of dozens or more a day are not uncommon on ultralight tackle.

Pacific Coast

A volcanic mountain landmass separates the eastern and western coasts of Costa Rica, and even though the distance between oceans varies from just 75 to 180 miles, the gap might as well be a lot farther, as the coasts differ greatly from one another. Costa Rica's 275-mile-long Pacific coastline is a narrower lowland region broken by a number of bays and is much more developed. Sportfishing has progressed significantly in the past two decades. From Nicaragua on the north to Panama on the south, there's an incredible number and great variety of fish, an almost year-round season, easy accessibility, and a well-established infrastructure.

For light-tackle offshore anglers in particular, this has been something of a mecca. The world-record books are cluttered with fish caught in these waters, especially Pacific snook.

Sailfish are the mainstays of the fishing here, but blue, black, and striped marlin are all part of the mix, not to mention dolphin (dorado) and yellowfin tuna, and a host of inshore species headlined by roosterfish, cubera snapper, and amberjack.

Well-developed facilities exist at many places along the coast, including Quepos, Flamingo, Guanamar, Tamarindo, Golfito, Ocotal, and Drakes Bay. The hot ports have differed over the years, as billfish availability and water temperature changes have varied. Quepos, which has also become a popular tourism town, is generally regarded as the leading sportfishing port on the southern Pacific coast. In recent years, however, some operators have become more mobile, and mother-ship operations even exist, to take anglers to less accessible or more active areas. This has paid off for some such operators, particularly in the 1990s when El Niño affected billfish areas, making the northerly waters much more active than the southerly ones.

At the centrally located Quepos, the top billfishing time is usually from November through May, when the weather is also at a peak and dry, with seas fairly calm. January through March is peak—a time when the area is crowded with sportfishing boats, requiring arrangements well in advance. It is typical in this region to land between 5 and 10 sailfish on an ordinary day; when conditions are right, several times that number are possible. With plenty of in-season sailfish action, few boats venture farther offshore for attempts at marlin, wahoo, and tuna.

Sailfishing normally takes place within 30 miles of port. Trolling with rigged baits, usually mullet, is standard procedure. The presence of many sails, however, presents light-tackle opportunities, making this area ripe for bait-and-switch strategies, using teasers to draw the fish in for fly presentation.

In normal years the prime sailfish season is a bit different in the waters fished from Flamingo and nearby Guanamar and Tamarindo. May through September has historically been the hot period, when the seas here are calm. Conversely, in the rough-water period, from November through March, the marlin are most likely to be present, although they can be caught at other times. It was just out in front of the Guanamar Sportfishing Resort at Playa Carrillo in May of 1991 that Costa Rica's 13th Annual International Sailfish Tournament posted the highest score in tournament history with a phenomenal 1,691 sails caught and released in four days. May has varied as a good month, however, in years since that event. Traditionally, December through June has been the most productive season, with April and May considered peak.

One of the most productive fishing areas here is Guardian Bank, 120 miles west of Punta Guiones. Rising 1,700 fathoms to 15 or 20 fathoms in the blue water, it has been widely fished by commercial tuna boats. But immense concentrations of bait, particularly squid, make the bank a playground for huge marlin and swordfish, as well as locomotive-size tuna and other species.

The northern Pacific coastal area above Punta Guiones is handicapped by heavy winds that usually blow from late November through March or early April, and some operators in that area move south during the northerlies.

Although the winds and resultant heavy seas don't make for particularly pleasant fishing, it doesn't mean the fish aren't there, and increasingly larger and more seaworthy boats have made it possible to enjoy what is often the best season for big marlin, with a liberal sprinkling of sails, dorado, roosterfish, and tuna at that time.

In the northwest at the long, wide Gulf of Papagayo, anglers run offshore to the deep water or fish around the Bat Islands. These islands have been productive for billfish and other species, as have the grounds offshore at the 100-fathom mark, and off of Catalina Island.

This is a bait-rich area, due in part to the easterly North Equatorial Current, which washes into the gulf in the summer months, drawing small-game species and larger ones. The black marlin, which have averaged 300 pounds in the past but have also been much larger, usually arrive in the gulf in May. Blue and striped marlin follow, although they are not as populous.

Although the emphasis is on billfish along the Pacific, these certainly aren't the only attraction. Dolphin are sometimes a nuisance, bouncing a bill-fish bait as fast as it hits the water. They are thrillers on light tackle, however, and the long-standing International Game Fish Association (IGFA) all-tackle record dolphin (an 87-pounder) came from Costa Rica.

When the billfishing is slow, or for extra diversity, there is plenty of opportunity for catching varied reef and bottom species by trolling, casting to rocky shorelines, or jigging or baitfishing in inshore water. Roosterfish from 20 to 70 or more pounds are possible, as are similar-size cubera snapper in some locales. The inshore waters have produced numerous world-record cuberas. Amberjack, snapper, grouper, jack crevalle, dogtooth snapper *(pargo)*, and other species are on the menu as well, although species and sizes may vary by locale.

With so much boat fishing for various species, visiting anglers pay little attention to the shoreline. But at least four species of snook frequent the Pacific coast, including the large-growing Pacific black snook. An all-tackle world-record 57-pound, 12-ounce black snook was caught at the mouth of the Río Naranjo, accessed from Quepos. A 69-pounder was caught in the 1960s at the mouth of the Tarcoles River, and a 72-pounder was caught at an unidentified site in 1992.

As with fishing in the Caribbean, most snook are caught at or close to river mouths. They can be caught year-round on this side of the country, but big fish are more likely in December, January, May, and June.

Conservation is a major consideration in Costa Rica, as it is in many Central and South American countries. It must be if the Pacific coastal fishery is to survive. Commercial longliners have been hurting sailfish and other billfish; tuna have been under a lot of pressure; and netting in estuaries and at river mouths has impacted tarpon and snook. The Costa Rican government has had some success with regulating these activities.

Inland

The San Juan River, which flows along the border with Nicaragua and forms the Colorado River, has recently become a more prominent site. Tarpon are said to be up the river nearly all year, but the dry months of March and April are best. Good fishing can also be expected in September and October when the tarpon reach as far upriver as Caño Negro Lagoon, 40 miles south of Lake Nicaragua but within the confines of Costa Rica. The rapids are perhaps the best location on the river, and there are two on the San Juan—one close to El Castillo on the upper river not far from San Carlos, and the other about 10 miles upriver from the confluence with the Río Sarapiquí.

Snook are also available in this region, and October and November are the best months. They move up through the Colorado River into the San Juan and all the way to Lake Nicaragua and the Río Frío in Costa Rica. Fish from 10 to 15 pounds linger around small tributaries to the main river.

Guapote have grown into a popular freshwater prey throughout Costa Rica. Dubbed "rainbow bass" because their iridescent shadings are reminiscent of rainbow trout, they are fished similar to largemouth bass. Also a popular food fish, guapote are extremely strong fighters, seldom breaking the water surface, although they do take surface lures viciously and pounce on trolled lures.

In the rivers, guapote favor deep pools and cuts, and generally calm water. They inhabit all of the rivers draining to the Caribbean or following a northerly course to the San Juan basin (on the Pacific side, guapote are present only in rivers north of Puntarenas).

The favorite guapote site in Costa Rica, however, is Lake Arenal. Guapote became landlocked here when the dam was finished, and they flourished into a great freshwater fishing attraction. Surrounded by lush, green mountains and dairy farms, Arenal provides a high percentage of the nation's hydroelectric power and is a popular overall recreation area. In addition to guapote, the lake also has machaca, a high-jumping silvery fish that readily takes a fly or surface popper. Its acrobatic leaps, scaled sides, and bone-hard mouth have caused locals to refer to the machaca as the little tarpon.

Arenal Volcano stands at one end of the lake and is one of the most active volcanoes in the world, bellowing towers of lava that create an incredible pyrotechnic display at night. Guide service is available locally, a few lodges exist at the lake, and there

Wild saltwater sportfish with low levels of fat and calories include sea bass, red snapper, and halibut; high levels belong to flounder and mackerel.

C

are campsites nearby. A number of the rivers that feed Lake Arenal from the high mountaintops have reputedly been stocked with rainbow trout.

Among the many Costa Rican rivers popular among anglers is the Teffaba, in the southern part of the country. It can be waded for more than 50 kilometers of its length, from the Brujo Bridge to Palmar Norte. It is muddy about half the time during the rainy season, but during dry months it is a beautiful stream.

A combination of fast water, deep and shallow ponds, and a broad estuary where the Teffaba flows into the Pacific provide a shot at both freshwater and saltwater species. Snook, red snapper, and occasionally jacks work well up the river, but big snook are found among the hundreds of square kilometers of estuaries that wind through the mangroves.

Rivers flowing east into the Caribbean and north into the Río San Juan offer Costa Rica's best bobo fishing. The bobo is a variety of mullet that occasionally grows to 12 pounds and favors fast water. Most are taken on a variety of natural bait, and some on spinners. The bobo also frequents Panama and Nicaragua, but only in Costa Rica, and among local anglers, are they highly regarded as a sportfish. They head for fast water when hooked, and use the current to good advantage. They are an excellent table fish. These rivers also harbor machaca, croaker, and other species that are great on ultralight tackle.

The San Carlos, Sarapiquí, Reventazón, and Rio Frío are the most popular rivers with local anglers, not only for the fishing but also because of their beauty and clear, clean waters during the dry season. They are muddy during the rainy period, especially in the late afternoons, but even then they usually begin to clear by midmorning, as most of the rain comes in the late afternoon.

Although these streams carry a great volume of water, they can be waded for 75 percent of their length, and most can be reached within a two-hour drive from San José.

COUNCIL
See: Fisheries Management Council.

COUNTERSHADING
A scheme for coloring fishing plugs that contrasts with nature by placing the most visible color on the underside, or belly, of the lure and the least visible color on the top, or back.
See: Lure.

COUNTING DOWN
A method of determining the relative depth to which a lure has sunk by counting each second that it is sinking. The sink rate of a lure varies with its weight, material, and shape. To determine relative depth, start counting every second once the lure enters the water until it strikes bottom and the line goes limp. If you counted to 10, then the next time you let out the lure you know that counting to 5 puts that lure halfway in the water column, and counting to 9 brings it just above the bottom.

By measuring the line, you can be more precise and determine the sink rate. If it took a count of 10 to put the lure on the bottom in 20 feet of water (measured from the surface), the lure falls at a rate of 2 feet per second under existing conditions; therefore, to fish it precisely at 16 feet, count to 8 before engaging the reel and retrieving (or jigging). By knowing the sink rate, you can cast a sinking plug, for example, a long distance away, count it down to a certain level, and then begin retrieving to keep the lure at a specific level. A jig can be fished at a certain level vertically by counting it down from the instant it enters the water by the boat; jig it upward and then count it down to a different level. By repeating this action, you can fish through the water column at known levels, and return to levels where strikes have been received.

COVER
Any natural or man-made object that provides shelter and feeding opportunity to fish, and which fish use as a place from which to ambush prey. Some species, like largemouth and smallmouth bass, northern pike, muskie, walleye, crappie, and sunfish, are largely cover-oriented, whereas salmonid species are not. Shallow cover-oriented species of fish are usually more conducive to casting than to trolling. In saltwater, snook are shallow-water fish that prefer cover, while groupers are deep-water fish that use reef bottoms for cover.
See: Finding Fish.

COWBELLS
Cowbells are a form of attractor featuring multiple in-line blades and used in trolling to simulate a group of baitfish. They usually feature a series of lightweight spoons, or blades, spaced at intervals over a short to medium length of braided-wire line. There are many versions; some feature a rudder at the head, to which the fishing line is attached, and all feature a swivel to prevent line twist. A short leader (6 to 24 inches) and lure is attached to the end of the rig. Usually a spoon or streamer fly is attached to cowbells, but sometimes a shallow-swimming plug or strip of bait is used.

The shape and size of the blades vary widely. Shapes include willowleaf, Colorado, and Indiana; lengths may be $1^{1}/_{2}$ to 5 inches, although only a few anglers use the larger sizes. Blades are predominantly silver, but they can be painted or taped with colors.

Cowbells are used mainly for deep lake trout trolling. A few anglers use them with downriggers, but traditionally they have been fished on wire or

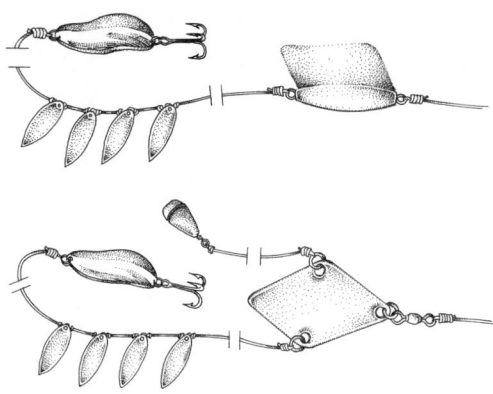

Two versions of cowbell rigs, both with a rudder and a series of spinning blades, are depicted here, each followed by a spoon.

lead core line, or on lines weighted with a heavy sinker. A novel deep fishing presentation is a string of large bladed cowbells snapped to a downrigger weight, with a lure running slightly above and behind them and attached to a line release located on the downrigger cable just above the weight.

CRADLE

Also known as a fish cradle or release cradle, this device is used to land a fish that is intended for release, and which supports the full body of the fish in a horizontal position. The most popular version features two long narrow wood boards that are connected by 1/4-inch soft-mesh netting that is closed at the ends and which droops into the water to envelop a fish as if it were slipped into a purse. The cradle is kept in the water while the fish is unhooked and then released. Another version, for shorter fish is smaller, with open ends and open-grip handle.
See: Catch-and-Release; Landing Fish.

CRANEFLIES
See: Midges.

CRANKBAIT
A term that has reached popular usage in North America, "crankbait" refers to various small and midsize treble-hooked diving and sinking plugs that have a built-in, vibrating, wiggling, swimming action. The term originated from the fact that the simplest and most practiced way to fish such a lure after casting it is to crank the reel handle steadily to bring it in on a nonstop retrieve. This is not the only way to use this lure, nor is it necessarily the best, but the mere "throw it" nature of this plug has resulted in the name.

Crankbaits are staple lures in bass fishing, and have a following in walleye fishing as well. Although most plugs used for these activities are commonly known as crankbaits, they are, in actuality, plugs and are useful for a wider range of angling activity. For this reason, these lures are covered in greater detail under the plug entry.
See: Plug.

CRAPPIE, BLACK *Pomoxis nigromaculatus.*
Other names—speckled perch, calico bass, grass bass, speckled bass, strawberry bass, oswego bass, sacalait, barfish, crawpie, bachelor perch, papermouth, shiner, moonfish; French: *marigane noire.*

Crappie are like that Chinese dog called a Shih Tzu. Most people don't say the name of that dog in a way that sounds flattering. Ditto for the poor crappie. If its name were pronounced by more folks as if it contained the letter *o* instead of *a*, as in "crop," we would all be better off. No matter how you pronounce the name, both the black crappie and the white crappie *(see: crappie, white)* are the

Black Crappie

most distinctive and largest members of the Centrarchidae family, which includes sunfish and black bass. Both species are considered excellent food fish and sportfish, and have white flaky meat that makes for sweet fillets. In many places crappie are plentiful, and creel limits are liberal, so it does no harm to keep a batch of these fish for the table.

Identification. The black crappie and the white crappie are similar in color—a silvery olive to bronze with dark spots, although on the black crappie the spots are irregularly arranged instead of appearing in seven or eight vertical bands as they do on the white crappie. Both species are laterally compressed and deep-bodied, although the black crappie is somewhat deeper in body, and it has a large mouth that resembles the mouth of a largemouth bass. It also has distinct depressions in its forehead, and large dorsal and anal fins of almost identical size. The gill cover also comes to a sharp point, instead of ending in an earlike flap. The best way to differentiate the two species of crappie is by counting the dorsal fin spines, as the black crappie usually has seven or eight, the white crappie six. The breeding male does not change color noticeably, as it does in the white crappie species.

Size/Age. With lengths of up to 13 inches, the black crappie can weigh up to 5 pounds but usually weighs less than 2 pounds and is commonly caught at a pound or less. It is thought to live to 10 years of age. The all-tackle world record is a 4-pound, 8-ounce fish taken in Virginia in 1981.

Distribution. Black crappie have been so widely introduced in North America that the native range is uncertain, although it appears to start at the Atlantic slope from Virginia to Florida, the Gulf slope west to Texas, and the St. Lawrence–Great Lakes and Mississippi River basins from Quebec to Manitoba, Canada, south to the Gulf of Mexico.

Habitat. Black crappie prefer cooler, deeper, clearer waters with more abundant aquatic vegetation than do white crappie. This includes still backwater lakes, sloughs, creeks, streams, lakes, and ponds. Because they form schools, an angler who comes across one fish is likely to find others nearby. They are especially active in the evening and early morning, and remain active throughout the winter. An abundant species, black crappie occur in smaller concentrations than do white crappie.

Life history/Behavior. Spawning occurs in early spring and summer in water temperatures between 62° to 68°F. These fish spawn over gravel areas or other soft material and nest in colonies. The males excavate the nests, and the females lay the eggs, sometimes in several of these. The eggs incubate for three to five days, and the young mature sometime between their second and fourth years.

Food and feeding habits. Black crappie tend to feed early in the morning on zooplankton, crustaceans, insects, fish, insect larvae, young shad, minnows, and small sunfish. Small minnows form a large part of the diet of adults; in southern

Crappie are among the panfish species that are especially well suited for young anglers.

reservoirs, gizzard or threadfin shad are major forage, and in northern states, insects are dominant. Crappie also consume the fry of many species of gamefish. They continue to feed during the winter and are very active under the ice.

Angling. In the spring, when water temperatures reach about 60°F, crappie move shallow to build nests and spawn, and this is a particularly favorite time for angling. Most crappie enthusiasts pursue these fish around some form of wood or brush. The behavior of spawning crappie is reasonably predictable, making them easy to catch. After spawning, they move to deeper water and gather in schools, congregating tightly in sunken weedbeds, dropoffs, offshore brushpiles, river-channel drops, shoreline riprap, flooded timber, and sunken cribbing. Many crappie are caught in 10 to 15 feet of water among tree limbs in standing timber. During the hottest part of the day, they hold on the cool, shaded side of such structures. Other shaded areas that may attract these fish, although not necessarily in large numbers, include bridges, piers, docks, and the bases of old tree stumps. Massive schools of crappie may form at different levels of the lake, and usually are spread horizontally rather than stacking vertically.

In the fall, crappie may move into deeper water to gather around underwater structures such as old channels, rocky ledges, or weedbeds. Although they will move around a bit, they generally remain in deep water until spring. Crappie also offer a prime opportunity for winter fishing, and many northern ice anglers make these fish their number one pursuit.

In many bodies of water without timber, especially large reservoirs, anglers plant brushpiles (where it is legal) to attract and hold crappie, as well as other fish. Where this practice is allowed, anglers may plant many brushpiles, often in places known only to them and sometimes in front of their own docks or boathouses, and will visit them often.

Although some anglers troll for crappie, the vast majority drift or anchor, and either jig or stillfish with minnows. A greater number of crappie are caught using live minnows than on any other baits; other good baits, however, are grasshoppers, crickets, and worms. Unquestionably, the favored artificial crappie catcher is a small, fine-wire jig. Marabou or soft-plastic bodies (grubs especially) are favored. White and yellow are the standard colors, but silver, green, chartreuse, and multicolored tinsel versions are productive. These should be small—the $1/8$-ounce size is perhaps most useful—but slightly lighter or heavier weights are used as depth and wind warrant. A small, single-bladed spinnerbait, with a plastic grub or curl-tail body, is another good crappie taker, as is a small jig tipped with a tiny minnow (hook it from the top of the head through the mouth). Crappie have tender mouths, and strikes are often delicate; the most regularly successful anglers are those who develop a fine jigging motion and a subtle feel.

Crappie don't usually strike a large minnow or lure, although this does happen occasionally, especially where these fish are abundant; $1^1/2$- to $2^1/2$-inch-long offerings are best for jigs, spinnerbaits, and plugs. Few small crankbaits will dive very deep unaided, although they can be fished deep with the assistance of bottom-walking sinkers. These can be cast or trolled.

These fish are not prone to striking fast-moving baits. You have to get down to their level (usually bottom) and work your offering slowly. Many anglers work lures too quickly for crappie, even though they think they're retrieving at a reasonable speed. Anglers also have a tendency to go too fast when jigging. It's essential to put some effort into maneuvering the boat properly over crappie structures and fishing carefully. Rather than fight wind, many anglers tie off to brush or stumps, or they simply drift. A moderate wind will move a boat along at a speed conducive to drifting, especially when an electric motor is used to control location and rate of drift. With the right wind speed and direction, you can drift slowly over deep-water channels, weedbeds, or dropoffs, or through timber, using a slow lift-and-drop method with jigs, spinnerbaits, or plug-and-sinker combinations.

Crappie anglers primarily use ultralight spinning or spincasting reels equipped with 4- or 6-pound-test line and 5- to $5^1/2$-foot-long rods. Fly rods, telescoping fiberglass rods, and cane poles are popular as well. Cane poles or telescoping glass rods play a large, traditional role in crappie fishing. Boat anglers favor 8- to 12-foot poles, but bank anglers prefer 16- to 20-footers. The line is seldom longer than the length of the pole. Live baits are used, and dabbled in place after place.

See: Panfish.

CRAPPIE, WHITE   *Pomoxis annularus.*

Other names—crappie, speckled perch, speckled bass, calico bass, sacalaitt, papermouth, bachelor perch; French: *crapet calicot.*

Members of the Centrarchidae family, which includes sunfish and black bass, white crappie are usually thought of in the same breath as black crappie. Both species are considered excellent food fish and sportfish, and have white flaky meat that makes for sweet fillets. In many places, crappie are plentiful, and creel limits are liberal, so it does no harm to keep a batch of these fish for the table.

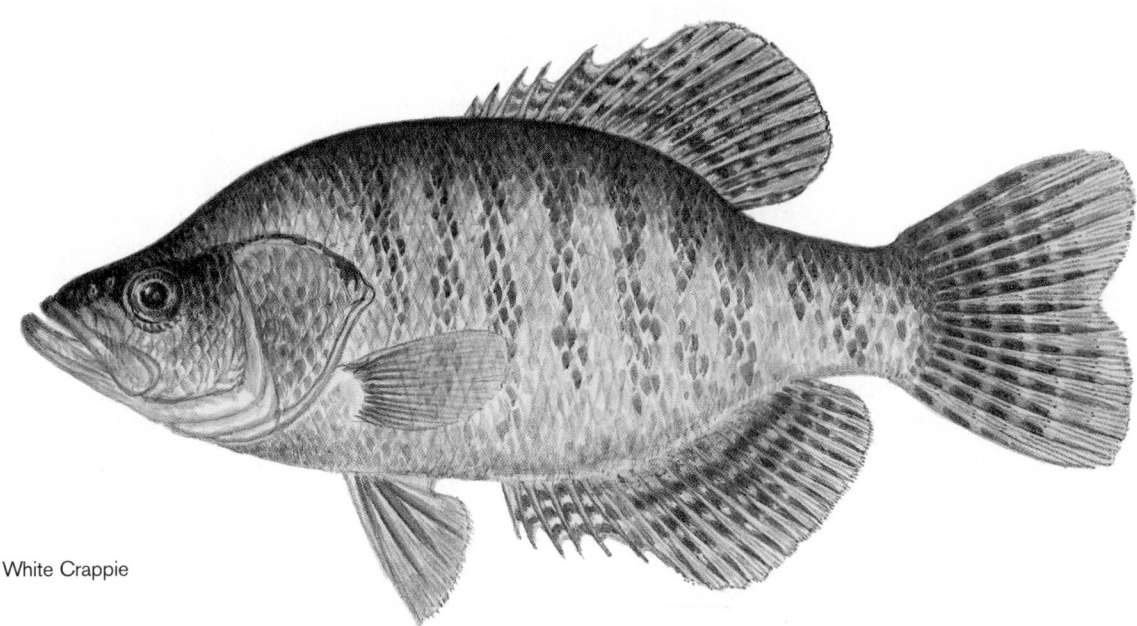

White Crappie

Identification. The white crappie and black crappie are essentially the same color, a silvery olive to bronze with dark spots, although the white crappie is somewhat paler; in the white crappie the spots are arranged in seven or eight vertical bands on its sides, whereas in the black crappie the spots are scattered. Deep-bodied and laterally compressed, the white crappie has a large mouth, an upper jaw that extends under the eye, and a lower jaw that seems to protrude. It also has distinct depressions in its forehead, and large dorsal and anal fins of almost identical size. The best way to differentiate these fish is by counting dorsal fin spines, as the white crappie has six, and the black crappie usually has seven or eight. The white crappie is also the only sunfish with the same number of spines in both the dorsal and anal fins. The breeding male grows darker in color and is often mistaken for the black crappie.

Size/Age. The white crappie can reach a weight of 5 pounds but usually weighs less than 2 pounds and is commonly caught at a pound or less. The all-tackle world record is a 5-pound, 3-ounce fish taken in Mississippi in 1957. White crappie live for a maximum of 10 years.

Distribution. Widespread in North America, white crappie are found in the Great Lakes, Hudson Bay, the Mississippi River basins from New York and Ontario west to Minnesota and South Dakota and south to the Gulf of Mexico; they also inhabit the Gulf of Mexico drainages from Mobile Bay in Georgia and Alabama to the Wueces River in Texas. They have been introduced widely elsewhere.

Habitat. White crappie occur in creek backwaters, slow-flowing streams, sand- and mud-bottomed pools, small to large rivers, and lakes and ponds. They prefer shallower water than do the black crappie and can tolerate warmer, more turbid, and slightly alkaline waters. They are usually found near dropoffs, standing timber, brushy cover, or other artificial cover. Because white crappie school in loose groups, when an angler catches one, others are likely to be around. They are especially active in the evening and early morning, and remain active throughout the winter.

Spawning behavior. Spawning occurs in early spring and summer in water temperatures between 62° and 68°F, and during that time the male grows dark on the sides of its head, lower jaw, and breast. Spawning takes place in sandy, muddy, and weedy areas, and the fish nest in colonies. In moderately deep water, males brush away sediment to form a shallow nest and guard the 27,000 to more than 68,000 eggs. The eggs incubate for two to four days, and the young white crappie mature in two to four years.

Food and feeding habits. White crappie feed on small crustaceans, zooplankton, insects and insect larvae, minnows, young shad, small sunfish, and other small fish. Small minnows of many species are probably the most common food item for adults.

Angling. *See: Crappie, Black; Panfish.*

CRAWLER

A nightcrawler.
See: Natural Bait.

CRAYFISH

Freshwater crayfish are common stream and lake inhabitants of the order Decapoda and in the Astacidae or Cambaridae families. Over 200 species occur in North America, most of which live for approximately two years, although certain species may live up to six or seven years. They often hide under rocks by day, and forage on stream or lake bottoms at night.

Resembling lobsters and also known as crawfish, crayfish grow by molting, or shedding their shell. After shedding their hard covering, they have a very soft shell, and they hide from predators while waiting for it to harden. They may grow to 6 inches, have five pairs of walking legs, including two large claws, and possess eyes that stand out from the body. They are usually red, orange, brown, or dark in color.

A favorite food of many gamefish, crayfish are widely imitated with hard and soft lures, as well as flies, and are fished in both hard- and soft-shelled forms as live bait. Crayfish tails or pieces of tail meat are used to tip some lures.

CREEL

(1) A basket, bag, or pouch for holding a mobile angler's fish. The traditional creel was a well ventilated wicker basket, which was lined with moist grasses or ferns, and primarily used by bank or wading stream trout anglers, the latter of whom carried it around the back via a strap. Such creels are very rarely used today, in part because of greater emphasis on catch-and-release *(see)*, and in part because other devices made of modern and easy to clean materials (some with insulating properties) are available. Pouches to retain fish are also incorporated into many fishing vests or can be added to them.

(2) To keep or retain a fish for personal use instead of releasing it upon capture, regardless of the method of retaining the fish.
See: Creel Limit; Creel Survey.

CREEL LIMIT

Synonymous with bag limit, creel limit means the quantity or number of fish of a species or group of species that may be taken, caught, or killed during a specified period. That period is usually one day, from 12:01 A.M. to midnight, and it may be identified as a "daily creel limit" or simply as a "daily limit." Creel limits may apply universally to many waters or may be site-specific. A creel limit is a legal game regulation established by the fisheries agency having jurisdiction over the location being fished, and enforced by fish and wildlife conservation officers.
See: Fisheries Management; Regulations.

CREEL SURVEY

A fisheries management tool for estimating anglers' catches, usually by a sampling program involving interviews and inspection of individual catches. Creel surveys may be conducted wherever anglers are found (on the water, at access points, at fish cleaning stations, etc.) and are not necessarily dependent upon fish actually being creeled, or physically possessed, by anglers.
See: Fisheries Management.

CREEPERS

Spiked-soled footwear used for walking on jetties.
See: Jetty; Surf Fishing.

CRIMPING PLIERS

A pair of heavy-duty pliers designed for crimping metal sleeves.
See: Leader.

CROAKER

Members of the Sciaenidae family (drum and croaker). The common name "croaker" is derived from the voluntary deep croaking noises made when the fish raps a muscle against its swim bladder. The sound resonates and is amplified, and the resulting drumming noise can be heard from a far distance. These fish are generally good to excellent table fare, mostly of smaller sizes, and common along the Atlantic and Pacific coasts.
See: Croaker, Atlantic; Croaker, Spotfin; Croaker, White; Croaker, Yellowfin; Drum; Queenfish (Croaker); Spot.

CROAKER, ATLANTIC

Micropogonias undulatus.
Other names—croaker, crocus, golden cracker, hardhead, king billy; Japanese: *ishimoki;* Portuguese: *corvina;* Spanish: *corbina, corvinón brasileño.*

The Atlantic croaker is a member of the Sciaenidae family (drum and croaker). The common name "croaker" is derived from the voluntary deep croaking noises made when the fish raps a

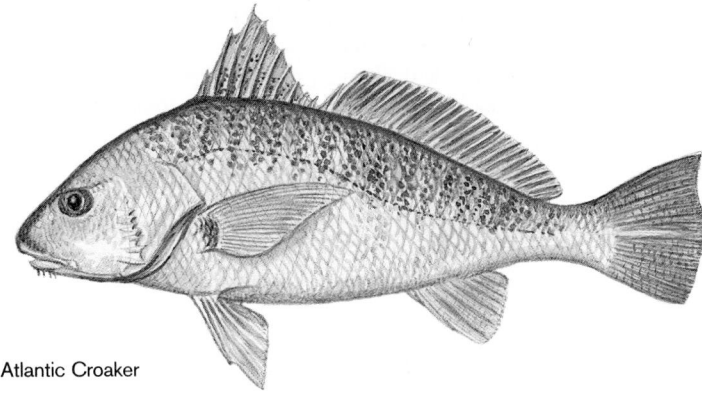
Atlantic Croaker

muscle against its swim bladder. The sound resonates and is amplified, and the drumming noise can be heard from a far distance.

The sciaenids as a group are among the most important food fish in the world because nearly all species are good to eat and are harvested commercially. The Atlantic croaker, a bottom fish, is one of the most frequently caught estuarine and near-shore marine fish along the eastern coast of the United States, although in recent years stocks have dwindled in the northern part of its range. It is a good table fish, having lean white meat with a firm texture, often substituted for pompano or mullet in dishes. Commercially, the croaker is sold whole or in fillets.

Identification. The Atlantic croaker has a small, elongated body with a short, high first dorsal fin and a long, low second dorsal fin. There are 6 to 10 tiny barbels on the chin and 64 to 72 scales along the lateral line, and the preopercular margin has three to five spines. The middle rays of the caudal fins are longer than those above and below, creating a wedgelike appearance. Its coloring is greenish above and white below, with brownish black spots and a silver iridescence covering the body. There are dark, wavy lines on the sides. During spawning, the Atlantic croaker takes on a bronze hue (thus the nickname "golden cracker"), and its pelvic fins turn yellow.

It can be distinguished from its cousin the spot *(Leiostomus xanthurus; see: spot)* by its convex tail, which is unlike the spot's concave caudal tail. Its unique coloring and spotted patterns also help distinguish the Atlantic croaker from its other relatives.

Size/Age. The average fish is 12 inches long and weighs $1^1/_2$ pounds, although the species may grow to 20 inches. The all-tackle record weighed 3 pounds, 12 ounces. The Atlantic croaker, like most fish in its family, can live up to five years.

Distribution. The Atlantic croaker is found along the Atlantic coast from Cape Cod to the Bay of Campeche. While it is abundant off the entire coast of the Gulf of Mexico, the croaker periodically becomes most common in Louisiana and Mississippi waters; it may also be found in southern Brazil and Argentina.

C

Habitat. Atlantic croaker are a bottom-dwelling, estuarine-dependent fish that become oceanic during spawning. They prefer mud, sand, and shell bottoms; areas around rocks; waters near jetties, piers, and bridges; and surf. Juveniles inhabit both open and vegetated shallow marsh areas. Adult croaker can occupy a wide range of salinities, from 20 to 75 parts per thousand, and temperatures of 50° to 96°F. Large fish are not found at temperatures below 50°F. Larvae and juveniles, however, are more tolerant of lower temperatures and can be found in waters ranging from 33° to 96°F.

Life history/Behavior. Spawning occurs at sea in winter and spring (the peak month is November), when the Atlantic croaker migrates to deeper, warmer water. In the southerly range, it is assumed that all croaker spawn in the open Gulf of Mexico, near the mouths of various passes that lead into shallow bays and lagoons. Large females may release up to 180,000 eggs, which will drift shoreward after hatching. Croaker larvae are abundant on soft bottoms with large quantities of detritus.

Atlantic croaker grow rapidly at approximately 6 inches per year. Males reach maturity at the end of their second year (10 inches), and females at the end of their third (14 inches). Adults migrate in schools or small groups to the bays in the spring and leave the marsh in the fall to enter deep gulf waters. To the north in the Chesapeake Bay area, the post-larval and juvenile fish migrate into the estuaries and return to the ocean as yearlings.

Food and feeding habits. Larval and post-larval fish subsist mostly on zooplankton; detritus is a major part of their diet as they grow. Adults feed on detritus as well, but they also consume larger invertebrates and fish. Sensory barbels allow the Atlantic croaker to find food on the bottom.

Angling. Atlantic croaker are caught in large numbers from March through October on such natural baits as shrimp, soft-shell or shedder crabs, clams, worms, and cut fish, and with artificial lures such as small jigs and weighted bucktails. Light tackle and small hooks are best, and although some fish are caught during the day, angling after dark is often better. Fishing is also often best just before, or right after, a hide tide in channels or deep holes.

CROAKER, SPOTFIN   *Roncador stearnsii.*
Other names—spotty, spot, golden croaker.

A member of the Sciaenidae (drum and croaker) family, the spotfin croaker is a small North American Pacific Coast fish caught by bay, surf, and pier anglers and highly valued as table far. The common name "croaker" is derived from the voluntary deep croaking noises when the fish raps a muscle against its swim bladder, which acts as an amplifier.

Identification. The body of the spotfin croaker is elongate but heavy forward. The upper profile of the head is steep and slightly curved, and abruptly rounded at the very blunt snout.

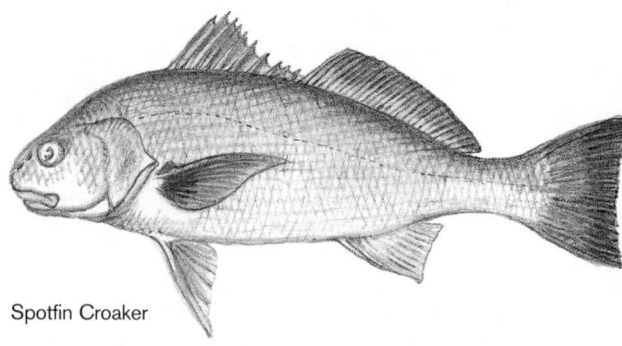

Spotfin Croaker

The mouth is subterminal, being underneath the head. The color is silvery gray with a bluish luster above and white below. There are dark wavy lines on the sides, and a large black spot at the base of the pectoral fin.

The pectoral fin spot, subterminal mouth, and absence of a fleshy barbel distinguish the spotfin croaker from other California croaker. Small specimens may be confused with small white croaker *(see: croaker, white),* although dorsal fin counts differ. The spotfin has 11 or fewer (usually 10) dorsal fin spines; the white croaker has 12 to 15. Large male spotfins in breeding colors are known as "golden croaker."

Size. The average spotfin croaker is small to medium in size, and most weigh roughly a pound. The largest caught on rod and reel in California was 27 inches long and weighed $10^1/_2$ pounds.

Distribution. Spotfin croaker range from Mazatlán, Mexico, to Point Conception, California, including the Gulf of California; in California they are most abundant south of Los Angeles.

Habitat. Spotfins are found along beaches and in bays over bottoms that vary from coarse sand to heavy mud and at depths varying from 4 to 50 or more feet. They prefer depressions and holes near shore.

Life history/Behavior. Spotfin croaker travel considerably but with no definite pattern, moving extensively from bay to bay, usually in small groups but sometimes in groups numbering up to four dozen. Males are sexually mature at 9 inches in length and about two years of age; most females mature at three years and about $12^1/_2$ inches in length. Their spawning season is from June through September, and spawning evidently takes place offshore, as no ripe fish are caught in the surf, although 1-inch juveniles do appear in the surf in the fall.

Food and feeding habits. Spotfin croaker have large pharyngeal teeth that are well suited to crushing clams, which make up a major portion of their diet; crustaceans and worms are also eaten extensively.

Angling. Although some spotfins are caught throughout the year, the better angling period is late summer, after the fish have spawned and return to the surf line. When a large number of fish have moved into an area (called "running"), there is generally good activity in the bays, and at piers and beaches. Clams and worms are the main natural baits, fished on bottom rigs; relatively light tackle is best for sporting value.

CROAKER, WHITE   *Genyonemus lineatus.*

Other names—kingfish, king-fish, king croaker, shiner, Pasadena trout, tommy croaker, little bass; Japanese: *shiroguchi.*

A member of the Sciaenidae family, the white croaker is a small North American Pacific Coast fish. The common name "croaker" is derived from the voluntary deep croaking noises made when the fish raps a muscle against the swim bladder, which acts as an amplifier. The resultant distinctive drumming noise can be heard from a far distance.

Although the flesh is edible, the white croaker is considered a nuisance, being easily hooked on most any type of live bait. Like its cousin the queenfish *(Seriphus politus; see: queenfish),* many white croaker are caught accidentally by anglers.

Identification.   The body of the white croaker is elongate and compressed. Its head is oblong and bluntly rounded, and its mouth is somewhat underneath the head. A deep notch separates the two dorsal fins. Its coloring is iridescent brown to yellowish on the back, becoming silvery below. Faint, wavy lines appear over the silvery parts. The fins are yellow to white.

The white croaker is one of five California croaker that have subterminal mouths. They can be distinguished from the California corbina *(Menticirrhus undulatus; see: corbina, California)* and the yellowfin croaker *(Umbrina roncador; see: croaker, yellowfin)* by the absence of a barbel. The 12 to 15 spines in the first dorsal fin serve to distinguish white croaker from all the other croaker with subterminal mouths, as none of these has more than 11 spines in this fin.

Size/Age.   The average weight is 1 pound. It is believed the white croaker can live up to 15 years, although most live far fewer years.

Distribution.   White croaker range from Magdalena Bay, Baja California, to Vancouver Island, British Columbia, but are not abundant north of San Francisco.

Habitat.   Preferring sandy bottoms, white croaker inhabit quiet surf zones, shallow bays, and lagoons. Most of the time they are found in offshore areas at depths of 10 to 100 feet. On rare occasions, they are abundant at depths as great as 600 feet.

Food and feeding habits.   White croaker consume a variety of fish, squid, shrimp, octopus, worms, small crabs, clams, and other items, living or dead.

Angling.   Easily hooked and caught on almost any type of live baits, white croaker provide little angling excitement. Fishing is good for this species throughout the year from piers or jetties in sandy or muddy areas.

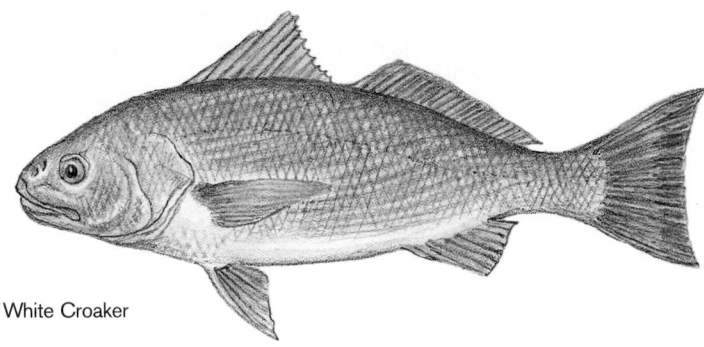

White Croaker

CROAKER, YELLOWFIN   *Umbrina roncador.*

Other names—Catalina croaker, yellowtailed croaker, golden croaker, yellowfin drum.

The yellowfin croaker is a member of the family Sciaenidae (drum and croaker), known for the drumlike noises they make when they rap a muscle against their swim bladder. The resulting distinctive drumming sound is amplified by the swim bladder and can be heard at some distance.

The sciaenids are one of the most important food fish in the world because nearly all species are good to eat and are harvested commercially. Found along the Pacific coast, the yellowfin croaker is a popular catch for light-tackle surf anglers.

Identification.   The body of the yellowfin croaker is elliptical-elongate; the back is somewhat arched and the head blunt. Its coloring is iridescent blue to gray with brassy reflections on the back diffusing to silvery white below. Dark wavy lines streak the sides. The fins are yellowish except for the dark dorsal fins. It has a small barbel on the chin tip and two strong anal spines; the barbel and heavy anal spines distinguish the yellowfin from other California croaker.

Size.   The average weight for a yellowfin croaker is less than 1 pound. The all-tackle record is 2 pounds, 11 ounces.

Distribution.   The yellowfin croaker is found from the Gulf of California, Mexico, to Point Conception, California.

Habitat.   These fish inhabit shallow parts of bays, channels, harbors, and other nearshore waters over sandy bottoms.

Life history/Behavior.   Yellowfin croaker are sexually mature at 9 inches in length. Their spawning season is in summer, when this species is most

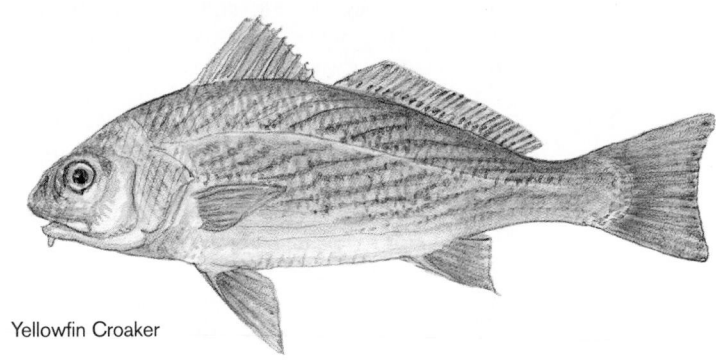

Yellowfin Croaker

common along sandy beaches. They move into deeper waters in winter, traveling in schools or small groups.

Food and feeding habits. Although the yellowfin croaker primarily consumes small fish and fish fry, it also feeds on small crustaceans, worms, and mollusks.

Angling. These fish are mostly caught in shallow sandy areas by surf anglers. Sand crabs, mussels, clams, cut pieces of fish, and worms are used as baits, preferably on small hooks and light tackle.

CRT

A recorder with a cathode-ray tube.
See: **Sonar.**

CRUSTACEAN

A group of freshwater and saltwater animals having no backbone, with jointed legs and a hard shell made of chitin. In saltwater this group includes shrimp, crabs, lobsters, and crayfish, all of which may be used as bait when angling but are not targeted by anglers or deliberately sought with sporting equipment. Freshwater crustaceans also include crayfish, as well as scuds *(see)*, sowbugs *(see)*, and shrimp.

CUBA

Surrounded by the Gulf of Mexico, the Atlantic Ocean, and the Caribbean Sea, Cuba is the largest island in the West Indies and a location coveted for both freshwater and saltwater fishing. Nevertheless, little of Cuba's fishery is currently known to many anglers. Once a playground for American travelers, Cuba was considered a hunting and fishing paradise in the 1950s; it was famous for blue marlin in the Gulf Stream off the north coast near Havana, bonefish off the south coast on the flats at Isle of Pines, and largemouth bass inland at Treasure Lake. Since 1960, however, American anglers, among the most voracious in the world, have looked upon Cuba as the forbidden fruit.

Although travel to this country for nearby Americans was temporarily relaxed in the late 1970s and early 1980s—allowing numerous expeditions inland for bass fishing and modest saltwater efforts—Cuba's waters have been lightly sportfished for decades, except by a modest number of Canadian anglers and very few Europeans, although some Americans have fished its coastal waters for big-game species. The island lacks a developed tourism infrastructure, reliable and modern equipment, and the means to mount sustained expeditions to explore coastal regions along its 2,500 miles of coastline. Consequently, reports on angling are few, but some have been positively glowing for inshore and bass fishing. It is generally

accepted that Cuba has some of the best largemouth bass fishing, and some of the biggest specimens, to be found anywhere; likewise, it is still considered a utopia for light-tackle flats fishing for various species, especially bonefish and small tarpon.

As is common in poor, underdeveloped countries, pollution, commercial fishing, and subsistence fishing have lessened the quality of some of the formerly stupendous fisheries. It remains unclear, however, to what extent these have been affected, as well as which areas may not be affected.

Given Cuba's proximity to the United States, if normal travel becomes a reality, and outside investors provide the means to comfortably fish the varied nooks and crannies of Cuba, a rush to explore its fertile flats, canals, keys, and lakes will ensue, and much will be written about the opportunities. In saltwater, this will be especially likely if private boats are allowed in. If not, visitors may find themselves in mother-ship operations in Cuba's distant backwaters.

Saltwater
Offshore. Cuba's offshore environment is not particularly far from land, especially along the northeast coast. It has been said that you can virtually cast from Cuba's northern shore and wet your hook in the Gulf Stream. Not quite, but the Great Blue River, as Ernest Hemingway called it, does pass surprisingly close to the walls of the now run-down Malecón in Havana, where the water is 100 fathoms deep within 100 yards of land, and the 1,000-fathom curve lies just a short distance beyond.

Today that once beautiful seaside boulevard features local anglers casting for bottom fish with handlines, with the line wrapped around a circular *carrete* and using old spark plugs for weights and a chunk of meat for bait. They fare pretty well, too. But then, so did the Old Man.

Not much in this Caribbean country is as it was in 1960, not long before Papa rode the *Pilar* out to the edges of the blue for the last time. The Stream still flows easterly, however, as it has for thousands of years, coursing through the Yucatan Channel into the Florida Straits, curving around Cabo San Antonio and hugging the shoreline past Havana, then past the small fishing village of Cojímar, which provided the setting for what is arguably the greatest story of the sea ever written.

Each hour the Stream brings with it some 10 cubic miles of tropical water. Hemingway, who considered this the greatest fishing stream in the world, made Havana a port with big-game status through his pioneering exploits here, and there is a museum dedicated to him at San Francisco de Paula, his old estate, where the *Pilar* rests. In tribute to Papa, each year anglers go forth in the spring to ply the edge of the Stream in the Hemingway Tournament, an event that was a national competition for many years but has had some measure of

international participation over the past several decades. One of the early winners of that contest, incidentally, was Fidel Castro. In 1960 Castro personally boated three marlin to capture the silver cup by virtue of overall weight.

Indeed, the edge of the Gulf Stream on the north shore does attract billfish, although the tournament seldom produces earthshaking results. Certainly, these are lightly fished waters, and with travel restrictions on many would-be visitors (primarily Americans), meager local tackle and big-game fishing skills, and the likely adverse effect of localized commercial fishing operations, this fishery remains a question mark. Despite the proliferation in angling communication in recent times, and despite the extensive search for new grounds by many anglers, Cuba's blue-water fishing remains an enigma. This is true on the north and south coasts as well as at the extreme ends of the island.

In the past, the best marlin grounds were deemed to be on the north coast, with most effort concentrated at Bahía de Cabañas, 40 miles west of Havana, in front of Havana itself, and 60 miles east at Matanzas. Blue marlin were caught from July into October, with the best fishing for this species, locally called "Cuban black marlin," in August and September. White marlin were present from April through August, and sailfish were reportedly available year-round. Wahoo, tuna, and large dolphin were also caught.

Inshore. Even more enigmatic than the blue-water fishing is Cuba's virtually untapped and even less heralded inshore light-tackle fishing. Although this is believed to exist predominantly on the south side of the island, particularly at the eastern end, Cuba's irregular shoreline is indented by numerous gulf and bays (reportedly 200 bays of varying size), with a vast amount of wetlands and mangroves. Bonefish and tarpon headline the species found in some of these places, and they probably exist in more areas than is generally realized outside Cuba. In fact, Cuba's inshore waters may be one of the few remaining fishing frontiers, even though it is likely that records for weight will probably not be threatened if and when modern exploration resumes.

Very few tourists have visited much of the inshore coast in decades, although in bonefishing circles the flats around Isle of Pines are remembered for their renowned bonefish, which roamed in great schools. Isle of Pines, which was also infamous for its penal colony, has since been renamed Isle of Youth. Reports suggest that commercial fishing around the island has wiped out the bonefish (*macabi* here), although this is uncertain. Few if any anglers have fished the waters nearby, but numerous expeditions have been made to flats and keys some 250 miles to the east, where even today the bonefish are sometimes clustered in schools measuring in the hundreds.

These are small fish, for the most part ranging between 2 and 5 pounds. These weights are characteristic of Cuba's population of this species. Bigger bones do not group like this and appear to be scarce; modern reports of sightings of 10-pound bonefish exist, and the Cuban national bonefish record pre-1960 was reportedly 14 pounds.

Those anglers who have encountered massive bonefish schools have been able to hook scores of them per day, making this a tremendous place for light tackle and for anglers new to bonefishing. Although bonefish have the reputation of being wary and difficult to stalk, it is possible to take several from a single large school on the Cuban flats, to have several bones rush to your offering, and even to allow a hooked fish to swim back and rejoin the school. These are all unusual occurrences and seldom happen in well-trafficked waters. The best time for bonefishing is said to be from November through February, but this is uncertain.

One area that has seen occasional fishing—via bargelike shrimp boats converted into floating hotels and towing small skiffs—is near the province of Ciego de Avila. There is an archipelago known as Garden of the Queens on maps but commonly referred to as Last Paradise Keys, which also attracts divers for its black coral, dropoffs, and walls with diverse life. Huge numbers of bonefish have been landed here, and small tarpon are abundant.

In fact, these waters are rich in many forms of aquatic life. Barracuda, permit, red snapper, jack crevalle, and yellowtail snapper are some of the inshore species, with the likes of amberjack, grouper, and other fish in deeper water off the edge of the flats. Locals talk of 25-pound permit (*palometa*) and 30-pound barracuda (*picua*), although this hasn't been proven. Snook are believed to be along this coast and in some of the lower rivers; snook from 20 to 30 pounds have been reportedly caught in one of the rivers here.

Tarpon in this region are all small, running from 10 to 25 pounds and occasionally to 50 pounds, but they are numerous, and some anglers have jumped several score in a day. Some tarpon (*sabalo*) have reportedly been seen to 100 pounds. The tarpon are said to be present year-round, either in the canals and among the mangrove keys, or out in deeper water, with only the smaller fish reportedly up in the turtle-grass-covered shallows.

Tarpon up to at least 70 pounds roam the freshwater confines of Treasure Lake, once a renowned largemouth bass environment in the Zapata Swamp, not far from the infamous Bay of Pigs. How the tarpon got there remains a mystery, although some locals allege that an underwater passage exists from lake to salty flat. Whatever the explanation, it is quite likely that large tarpon do exist in Cuban waters.

Big tarpon were reported in some of Cuba's larger bays in the 1950s, including those at Havana and Matanzas, and smaller tarpon were known along the north coast, even in some of the rivers that empty into the Atlantic there. Little had been

The deep-dwelling tilefish of the Atlantic was first discovered and named in 1879; it was nearly exterminated in 1882 by a Gulf Stream shift that exposed these fish to excessively cold water.

C

confirmed about modern tarpon fisheries along that coast, although the extensive Sabana Archipelago east of Cárdenas Bay seems worthy of exploration. It is rumored that large bonefish are in this area, and that snook roam these waters as well.

Freshwater

About a quarter of Cuba's landmass is mountainous or hilly and the rest is flat or rolling terrain, with low-lying coastal areas. Its rivers are relatively short, but there are more than 100 significant lakes (many of them man-made) and many hundreds of small lakes. The latter are mostly of fairly recent construction. They range from shallow mangrove swamp lakes to deep high-mountain lakes.

Largemouth bass exist throughout the country and have been widely transplanted. Their numbers exploded in many of the newly constructed lakes, as often happens, but the overall size of Cuban bass was exceptional in the early 1980s.

Many lakes produced extraordinary numbers of 8- to 10-pounders in the late 1970s and early 1980s. Anglers have landed quantities of fish from 12 to 15 pounds, and some in the 18- to 20-pound class have been verified. Reports indicate that some bass over 22 pounds have been caught illegally, and the possibility certainly exists that a new all-tackle world record could be landed in one of a number of Cuban lakes in the future. Lake Redonda yielded a sport-caught 21-pounder some years ago, and Lake Buffalo a 20-pounder more recently. Lake Hanabanilla, a mountain lake fished extensively in

A big largemouth bass comes to the net at Lake Hanabanilla.

the early 1980s and known for trophy fish, reportedly produced an 18-pound fish in 1996.

The premier lake of old in Cuba was swampy Treasure Lake, which was turned into a popular vacation resort by the time visiting anglers first fished it in 1977. It is no longer fished, but a succession of lakes, including Zaza, Hanabanilla, Redonda, and others, were fished into the early 1980s. Sportfishing was severely limited after that, with sporadic angling at a number of newer waters.

In the late 1990s, Cuba enacted regulations protecting bass lakes for sportfishing, and various lakes are expected to be fished on a rotational plan, all on a catch-and-release basis. A limited number of anglers, including Americans who were visiting to bring humanitarian supplies, have fished some lakes in the latter 1990s. Among the more recently opened bass lakes are Guananeo, Cubano Bulgaria, Porvenir, Granizo, Chambas, Calbario, Versalles, Laguna de la Leche, and Munoz. Bass are also present on lakes on the Isle of Youth.

CULLING

The replacement of a fish that has been caught or confined (in a basket, in a livewell, on a stringer) with a freshly caught fish. A fish that is culled is taken from confinement and returned to the water, usually in order to comply with regulations pertaining to the maximum number of fish that may be kept.

In many locations, once a fish has been reduced to possession, it may not be culled; returning it to the water is illegal. In some locations culling is not illegal, and in others, special allowances let participants in fishing tournaments cull fish that have been kept in a properly aerated livewell. In some locations, once a legal limit of fish has been kept, it is illegal to continue fishing.

Tournaments notwithstanding, anglers should not cull unless they are keeping an injured fish and releasing a healthy one. Fish that have been kept in confinement, especially on a stringer, are usually highly stressed and more likely to experience delayed mortality than fish that are released immediately after unhooking. Fish that have been kept in properly aerated livewells, where the water temperature is appropriate for the fish and the water has been treated with stabilizing chemicals, have the best chance of surviving when culled.

See: Catch-and-Release.

CUNNER   *Tautogolabrus adspersus.*

A member of the Labridae family of wrasses *(see)* the cunner is related to, and occurs even farther north than, the tautog *(see),* ranging from Chesapeake Bay to Newfoundland. Where their ranges overlap, the two species are often found together. They are similar in general body shape, but the cunner is slimmer and has a much lower head profile. Further, the cunner has scales on its gill covers and only about 40 scales in a count along its lateral line.

Cunner are smaller fish, averaging only about a quarter of a pound and only rarely exceeding 2 pounds. Anglers catch cunner more by accident than by choice. The fish is a superb bait stealer, but if one is hooked, its spiny fins make it a formidable creature to take off a hook. On very light tackle, this species can be sporting, however, and is generally considered a good table fish.

CURRENTS

Defined as horizontal movements of water, currents are an everyday part of fishing for virtually all salt-water anglers, for freshwater anglers who fish in rivers or streams, and for some freshwater anglers who fish in large lakes with major sources of inflow and outflow.

The most visually obvious influence of current is in rivers and streams, whose character and aquatic life are molded by the velocity of water, from trick-ling runoff in the headwaters to the silted and expansive delta. The types, sizes, and even shapes of fish and aquatic life vary greatly from small, shal-low, fast waters in the hills to wider, deeper, and slower waters downstream, possibly even affected by tides *(see)* in the most downstream reaches. Within the different sections, there are variations in current; narrow, constricted areas cause a swifter flow than wider and deeper areas. Nevertheless, cur-rents flow slower near the banks than in the center of the river, except along the outside bank of a sharp bend.

Currents may exist in large lakes and impound-ments but are usually less visually obvious. In some impoundments, when there is high and regular demand for water, usually in summer for power generation, the drawdown of water creates a current that astute anglers can observe around points, around bridge and roadway supports, and along some shores. Since it is intermittent, it is less likely to be a major influence on the composition of aquatic life, although it may influence the behavior, especially feeding, of some species, particularly striped bass. Continual current, which may exist at subsurface levels in some of the Great Lakes, is unlikely to affect fish behavior, but it can affect the behavior of lures and influence fishing patterns when strong, although many anglers are unaware of its existence.

Tides and major oceanic currents are, of course, very well known and observed. Most anglers and boaters in coastal areas are affected by tidal currents, and the world is well acquainted with surface ocean currents, which circle the ocean basins on either side of the equator. These are vastly different na-tural elements than currents in freshwater.

Surface circulation in the oceans is caused by wind patterns that sweep across the earth in

Anglers in the Straits of Georgia in British Columbia fish for salmon among some of the swiftest currents in the world.

different latitude zones. The general pattern of surface currents is modified by physical factors and the effects of friction, gravity, the sun's heat, the shape of land masses, local winds, and the earth's rotation. Several factors may interact to com-plicate the general flow. For example, the earth's rotation helps form huge circular water masses that move clockwise in the Northern Hemisphere and counterclockwise in the Southern Hemisphere (known as the Coriolis force). As the sun heats the ocean surface in the tropics, the warmed water tends to flow toward the poles to displace colder, heavier water that, in turn, flows toward the equa-tor in subsurface currents.

These great ocean currents are known as "rivers of the sea," and the ones of greatest interest in North America are the Gulf Stream *(see)* of the Atlantic, and the California Current *(see)* of the Pacific. South of the equator in the Pacific, the Humboldt Current, which moves along the west coast of South America, is one of the richest fish-producing currents in the world, and it is this current that is disturbed by the periodic El Niño *(see)* phenomenon.

There are also subsurface currents in the ocean, although these are generally very slow and the result of deep-water circulation. This is a vertical move-ment that is the result of cold water from the polar regions sinking. Another vertical movement of ocean water is an upwelling *(see)*, which occurs when deep current meets the shelving bottom or submerged banks. A persistent blow of wind can also bring about a form of upwelling by pushing surface waters outward and turning colder deep waters toward the surface.

Tidal currents exist in all the oceans and are mostly observed in coastal areas as water flows into and out of bays, increasing and decreasing in speed; dangerous, turbulent currents may form where rivers meet the sea, and several currents mix. Tidal currents also exist in offshore waters, usually

C

observed with little change in speed, but slowly and steadily changing direction. Lastly, local currents may also be set up by wave action along the shore or beach, creating undertows as water rushes back into the sea from the beach.

Currents are an obvious influence—and sometimes hazard—to boating, and are clearly a factor in the presence of fish and in fishing efforts.
See: Boat; Finding Fish.

CURVE CAST
An in-air technique for presenting a fly or mending a fly line.
See: Mending.

CUSK
(1) A term for burbot *(see)*.

(2) *Brosme brosme.*

The saltwater cusk (also known as tusk) is a deep-water relative of cod in the Lotidae family. It is found in rocky, hard-bottom areas in a temperature range of 0° to 10°C, and is generally solitary or travels in small groups. It occurs in the western Atlantic from New Jersey to Newfoundland and in the eastern Atlantic off Iceland, in the northern North Sea, and along the Scandinavian coasts to the Murmansk coast. In its western range, it prefers waters between 150 and 450 meters deep, and between 18 and 550 meters in its eastern range.

Relatively slow growing and late maturing, the cusk is a highly commercial species caught by trawlers and longliners; it is an incidental catch for anglers. It can attain a maximum size of 47 inches and 65 pounds, but grows to 35 inches and 20 pounds in the western Atlantic, where it is believed to be overexploited.

CUT BAIT
A chunk, slice, or other piece of fish used as bait.

CUTLASSFISH
Other names—cutlass fish, ribbonfish, Atlantic cutlassfish, Pacific cutlassfish, largehead hairtail; Japanese: *tachinouo, tachiuo, tachuo;* Portuguese: *lírio, peixe-espada;* Spanish: *espada, pez sable, sable, savola.*

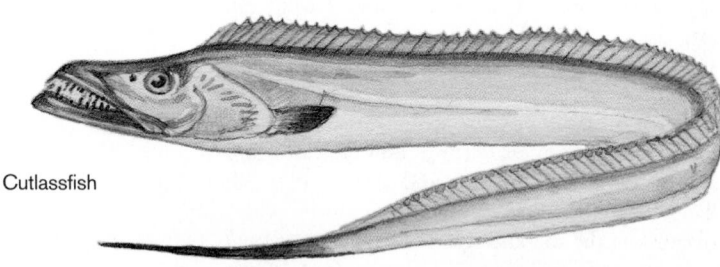
Cutlassfish

Cutlassfish are members of the family Trichiuridae, encompassing nearly 20 species. They are swift swimmers that generally dwell on the bottom. Used as baits for larger gamefish in the United States, cutlassfish are a valued food and commercial species in many other countries, especially Japan, where they may be used for sashimi. They are also marketed salted/dried and frozen.

Identification.   Characterized by their long, compressed bodies that taper to a pointed tail, cutlassfish are also commonly known as ribbonfish. The head is spear-shaped, and the fish has sharp arrowlike teeth in a large mouth. Its coloring is silvery, the jaws edged with black.

Size/Age.   Cutlassfish can reach up to 5 feet in length and 2 pounds in weight. The average length is 3 feet. The all-tackle record for Atlantic cutlassfish *(Trichiurus lepturus)* is a 7-pound fish caught in South Africa in 1995.

Distribution.   These fish are found in the Atlantic, Indian, and western Pacific Oceans. In North America, the Atlantic cutlassfish commonly ranges from Massachusetts to Argentina and throughout the Gulf of Mexico, especially Texas. In the Pacific, cutlassfish inhabit waters from Southern California to northern Peru.

Habitat.   Preferring muddy bottoms in shallow water, cutlassfish gather large numbers in bays, estuaries, and shallow coastal areas.

Food and feeding habits.   Cutlassfish feed on anchovies, sardines, squid, and crustaceans. Adults usually feed on pelagic prey near the surface during the daytime and migrate to the bottom at night. Adults and small juveniles do the opposite.

Angling.   Although occasionally encountered by anglers and used as baits, cutlassfish are not considered sportfish and there is no genuine angling effort for them.

CUTPLUG
A wooden or plastic trolling plug *(see)* with a large scooped out face, lipless head, and body that tapers to a point at the tail. Primarily used in salmon fishing, it is so named because it's similar in appearance to the cut herring natural bait rig commonly employed in mooching *(see)*. Cutplugs have an erratic swimming and darting motion, and are primarily fished deep with weights or downriggers.

CUTTYHUNK LINE
A handlaid, twisted linen fishing line formerly used by saltwater anglers.
See: Line; Linen Line.

DABBLING
A term for flipping *(see)* and pitching *(see)*.

DACE
Dace belong to the largest family of freshwater fish, Cyprinidae, which includes assorted minnows *(see)* and carp *(see)*. These are small and extremely hardy fish. Some dace species in North America are not pursued by anglers, and a prominent variety exists in Europe and Asia that is the source of much angling effort despite its small size.

(1) In North America, dace are distributed widely in small streams, lakes, and ponds, providing an important food source for many species sought by anglers. They inhabit colder, moving, clear water that runs over gravel or pebbles. Adults generally inhabit deep water, and juveniles hold in shallow water closer to shore.

Commonly referred to in North America by the all-encompassing generic term "minnows," dace are small (2 to 3 inches in length) and have slender bodies. Most dace species have terminal barbels. On the pearl dace *(Semotilus margarita margarita)*, the barbel is sometimes hidden or even absent. The *Clinostomus* species has no barbels.

Dace are greatly valued as baits for larger gamefish; the blacknose dace *(Rhinichthys atratulus; see: dace, blacknose)* is preferred for trout and salmon, whereas the longnose dace *(R. cataractae; see: dace, longnose)* is highly popular for bass. Dace can survive in very crowded or stagnant waters, like any other member of the minnow family, due to low oxygen demand, so anglers who want lively and sturdy baits value this kind of resilience. Some dace are also valuable for insect population control. The longnose dace, for example, primarily consumes blackfly larvae and is a major factor in the control of the blackfly population.

Identifying and distinguishing between the different species of dace is difficult. Although not all dace are identical, the variations are minor, such as a slightly longer snout. The coloring is extremely similar on all dace: olive green fading to white on the belly, with silvery overtones. The small scales are pronounced and have dark patterns that can change not only from species to species, but also among individual fish. The best way to identify the different dace species from each other, and from other similar fish like chubs or minnows, is by their breeding attributes. *Rhinichthys* dace acquire a rusty tinge on their fins during breeding season, whereas *Clinostomus* dace turn iridescent pink. The pearl dace develops bright-red flanks. All dace, especially males, have well-developed tubercles on the body, primarily around the head and snout. These tubercles, also called pearl organs, are used for nest building, in fighting and courtship rituals, and for maintaining contact with the opposite sex during spawning.

Eggs are given little or no parental care after spawning, and the young feed on zooplankton and phytoplankton for the first several months of life. Adults feed on insect larvae, worms, and algae.

(2) *Leuciscus leuciscus.*
Other names—common dace, Eurasian dace; French: *vandoise;* German: *hasel, hasile.*

The Eurasian dace is one of the smallest coarse fish *(see)* sought by anglers. It is a silvery, slim-bodied fish with concave dorsal and anal fins and a moderately forked tail, commonly caught at 6 to 8 ounces in weight and growing to a maximum of little more than twice that size.

Eurasian dace are widespread throughout northern Europe and northern Asia but are not found below the Alps or Pyrenees. They have been introduced in Ireland. These dace are common in the upper reaches of moderate-flowing rivers and in clean, cold lakes but reportedly enter brackish water in the eastern Baltic. They feed on crustaceans, insects, and plants, and are caught on small bits of natural or processed baits, as well as on flies. Anglers land them at all depths and often throughout the day.

DACE, BLACKNOSE   *Rhinichthys atratulus.*
Other names—eastern blacknose dace, brook minnow, potbelly, redfin dace, chub.

A member of the Cyprinidae family of minnows *(see)* and carp *(see)*, the blacknose dace makes excellent bait due to its small size and hardiness, and, like many small minnows, provides excellent forage for

Blacknose Dace

predator fish, especially bass and trout. It is not sought by anglers but may be netted for use as bait.

Identification.   The blacknose dace has a long slim body with a slightly protruding snout. The barbels, which are characteristic of most minnows, corner both sides of the mouth. The coloring is silvery, with dark olive gray fading to white on the belly. A dark lateral line runs along either side onto the head. It can be distinguished from the longnose dace *(Rhinichthys cataractae)* by its shorter snout.

Size/Age.   Blacknose dace generally live two to three years, and have an average size of 2 to 3 inches.

Distribution.   The range of the blacknose dace spans from North Dakota to the St. Lawrence drainage and south to Nebraska and North Carolina.

Habitat.   These fish are commonly found in rapid, clear streams, and the rocky runs and pools of small rivers; they can survive in stagnant summer waters and tolerate crowded conditions.

Spawning behavior.   Blacknose dace spawn in spring, starting in late May or early June. They build no nest; the fertilized eggs are dropped over the gravel bottom. The male, however, is known to defend spawning territories. Females release approximately 750 eggs, and little or no parental care is given to them.

Food and feeding habits.   Blacknose dace feed on insect larvae, small crustaceans, small worms, and plant material.

See: **Dace.**

D

DACE, LONGNOSE   *Rhinichthys cataractae.*
Other names—dace; French: *naseux de rapide.*

A member of the Cyprinidae family of minnows *(see)* and carp *(see),* the longnose dace has many valuable functions. Easily obtainable, small, and extremely hardy, it is prized as exceptional bait and is especially significant for bass fishing. Primarily feeding on blackfly larvae, it is also valued for its control of the blackfly population. And, like many small minnows, it provides excellent forage for predator fish, especially bass and trout. It is not sought by anglers, but may be netted for use as bait.

Identification.   The longnose dace is a distinctive minnow with a long fleshy snout, a subterminal mouth, and a deep caudal peduncle. The head and nape slope downward from its cylindrical body, giving this minnow a streamlined appearance. Pigmentation is widely variable; the dorsum can be greenish, brown, or reddish purple, and the lower sides and venter may be silvery, white, or yellow.

The sides are sometimes marked by darkened scales, a lateral stripe, and a blotch near the tail. The longnose dace can quickly be distinguished from most other minnows by the presence of a frenum, a small fleshy bridge between the snout and the upper jaw. It can be distinguished from other species of *Rhinichthys* by its long snout. Other characteristics of the longnose dace are small barbels in the corner of the mouth, small scales, a complete lateral line with 48 to 76 scales, and eyes that are situated near the top of the head. Breeding males have red coloration on the head and fins, and develop small tubercles on the head, body, and ventral fins.

Size/Age.   Adults can reach lengths exceeding 6 inches, but most are less than 4 inches long. They have been known to live up to five years.

Distribution.   The longnose dace has the widest distribution of any minnow in North America and is an important forage species where it is abundant. Several subspecies are recognized, but further study may reveal the occurrence of unique populations or additional subspecies. The distribution of the longnose dace spans the entire continent, ranging throughout the southern half of Canada and the northern United States. It extends southward to Georgia within the southern Appalachian Mountains and into northern Mexico through the Rocky Mountains. Its northern limit is the Mackenzie River drainage, Canada, which lies within the Arctic Circle.

Habitat.   Longnose dace occur in a wide variety of habitats. They are found in the riffles, runs, and pools of creeks, streams, and rivers. Within lakes, they are usually prefer areas around rocky shorelines. These streamlined fish are well adapted to fast-moving waters. Their species name, *cataractae,* means "of cataracts" and is appropriately descriptive of the habitat longnose dace often prefer.

Spawning behavior.   Longnose dace mature within two years but may live up to five years. Females often grow larger and live longer than do males. Reproduction occurs between late spring and early summer. Interestingly, an eastern subspecies spawns during the day, whereas a western subspecies spawns at night. Longnose dace are categorized as broadcast spawners, scattering their eggs in shallow, fast-flowing areas and over chub nests. Males aggressively defend spawning areas, but more than one male may line up next to the female during spawning. Spawning occurs on the stream bottom and may result in the burial of eggs within the substrate. The female deposits between 200 and 1,200 eggs during spawning.

Food and feeding habits.   Longnose dace feed on aquatic insects (especially midges and blackfly larvae), worms, small crustaceans, mites, algae, and plants. They have taste buds on their ventral fins, lower head, lips, and snout, which may enable them to find food along the stream bottom.

See: **Dace.**

Longnose Dace

DACRON LINE
See: Line.

DAISY CHAIN
(1) A combination of natural or artificial teasers rigged together in-line and used in offshore fishing, especially for marlin and tuna.

(2) The observed behavior of schools of tarpon swimming near the coast in a circular, rotating motion, prior to their departure for offshore spawning grounds.
See: Tarpon; Trolling Lures, Saltwater.

DAM
See: Lowhead Dam; Tailrace; Wingdam.

DAMSELFLIES
See: Dragonflies and Damselflies.

DANFORTH
A steel or aluminum anchor with two long, flat, and pointed flukes, also known as a lightweight burying anchor, or a fluke anchor.
See: Anchor.

DAPHNIA
A freshwater crustacean that moves along the water's surface with sudden leaps; also called water flea.

DAPPING
Dancing a dry fly on the surface of the water with leader and line held out of the water. The oldest form of fly fishing, dapping can be very tantalizing to fish, especially trout; the term was coined by Izaak Walton.

In general, dapping can be done with any rod to which a light monofilament line is tied and attached at the terminal end to a dry fly; this includes a cane pole, standard-length fly rod, or extra-long fly rod or pole. The shorter the rod or pole, however, the closer the fly must be fished to the angler, and the less likely a fish is to strike, since the fish is likely to see the angler or the boat (if there is one).

In a small, brush-lined creek, where making casts is very difficult, an angler can use a conventional fly rod, kneel behind or beside a streamside bush, extend the rod over the water, and dap the fly over the surface as if it were a natural insect depositing eggs in the water or struggling to stay out of the water.

Dapping is most practical, however, in open areas with the use of long poles. Irish and Scottish anglers dap for trout from boats, using poles that are 14 feet long or longer. In England, dapping poles range from 20 to 30 feet long. The long pole not only provides outward reach in open areas but also allows for a good length of line from the pole to fly. The long line is able to catch any breeze and move the fly around in a manner that cannot be replicated with conventional casting and recasting; the surface of the water remains undisturbed, except when a fish fiercely strikes the fly. When a strike occurs, the angler pauses for a moment to let the fish turn away with the fly and then lifts up the rod to set the hook.

British anglers use a length of silk floss (untwisted silk thread) above a fine tippet to catch the breeze, with a shorter length for breezier conditions and a longer length for calmer conditions. Heavily hackled flies are good for getting the attention of fish. The technique works on small waters in either a strong or a light breeze, but it can be frustrating in places where shoreside cover or trees tend to snag an errant fly or line. In a boat, an angler can avoid shoreside snags and can dap while at anchor or while drifting.

DARTERS
Darters are an incredibly diverse and colorful group of freshwater fish that rival saltwater fish in brilliance. They are actually small representatives of the perch family (Percidae) and are closely related to yellow perch and walleye. The darter group is comprised of approximately 160 species, all of which are restricted to North America. As such, they represent 20 percent of all fish in the United States.

Distribution. Darters range from northern Mexico into Canada and from the eastern coastal plains west to the Continental Divide. Only one species, the Mexican darter *(Etheostoma pottsi)*, occurs west of the Continental Divide, in northern Mexico. Darters are most diverse in the southern Appalachian Mountains of Tennessee and Virginia and the Ozark plateau of northern Arkansas. The johnny darter *(Etheostoma nigrum)* is the most widely distributed, followed by the orangethroat darter *(Etheostoma spectabile)* and perhaps the logperch darter *(Percina caprodes)*.

Identification. Three genera of darters are recognized: *Percina*, which includes roughly 40 species; *Etheostoma*, which includes roughly 112 species, and *Ammocrypta*, with 7 species. The genus *Percina* contains the largest darters. Most are rather drab and cryptic in coloration, although the males of some species exhibit impressive spawning coloration. The genus *Etheostoma* is diverse in the shape and coloration of its representatives. The

Johnny Darter

D

bodies and fins of many of these darters are painted with shades of red, blue, yellow, green, and orange interspersed with black blotches. Members of the genus *Ammocrypta* are dull and sand-colored. This camouflages them from predators in the large, sand-bottomed rivers they inhabit.

Darters can reach a length of 12 inches (*Percina lenticula,* the freckled darter), although most are only a few inches long, even as adults. The smallest is the fountain darter *(Etheostoma fonticola),* which reaches an adult size of only $1^1/_2$ inches. Darters have two dorsal fins, the front with hard spines and the rear with soft rays. The caudal fin is usually rounded or emarginate. Many darters are sexually dimorphic, and the males are usually larger and brightly colored. Males also develop thickened body tissues, fleshy knobs on the dorsal fin rays and spines, and breeding tubercles during spawning. The showy appearance of courting males is thought to attract females during spawning and accounts for the large amount of angling interest in this group.

Habitat. Darters are found in all types of freshwater habitat. They may inhabit small streams, large rivers, spring seeps, ponds, lakes, or reservoirs. They are most frequently found in fast-moving water, however.

Life history/Behavior. As a group, darters are well adapted to life in fast water and on the stream bottom. Their rounded bodies and slightly flattened head regions are especially hydrodynamic. In addition, most members of the group have completely absent, or poorly developed, swim bladders. They use their enlarged pectoral fins to perch on rocks, allowing them to remain on the stream bottom out of the current. Their body style is suited to the unique swimming manner for which this group as a whole is named. Darters do not swim in the same way that most fish do; instead, they leap from one spot to another with short jumps or "darts."

Darters display much variability in reproductive strategies. Most produce few, relatively large eggs and provide some degree of parental care. Most members of the genus *Etheostoma* are cavity spawners and lay adhesive eggs on the underside of medium-size rocks, usually in fast water. Males of this genus are often brightly colored to attract females to nest sites that they have prepared for egg laying. Members of the genera *Percina* and *Ammocrypta* spawn in a simpler manner. Two or more individuals group together in fast-water areas over sand between larger rocks. Males and females align their bodies next to each other, then simultaneously release sperm and eggs into the substrate and bury them. This protects the eggs from predation and floods.

Most darters spawn in spring to early summer. Several species are believed to spawn multiple times per year. Darters are not a long-lived group. Most species live less than five years. Sexual maturity is usually attained between one and three years.

Food and feeding habits. Darters primarily feed on bottom-dwelling organisms, mostly small insects, worms, and snails. However, as a group they exhibit a diversity of feeding strategies that correspond to morphological differences. Large darters feed on insects on top of rocks or pick them out of sand and gravel. Shorter, more flexible darters often feed on clinging insects between and underneath rocks. As a result of these different feeding strategies, several darter species can coexist in the same area of a stream.

Darters as bait. Although darters are not a sportfish group because of their small size, they may be taken incidentally by anglers fishing for other species. Incidental landings are not common because these fish primarily inhabit fast riffles, that is, areas not frequently fished by anglers. Darters are often used as baits, however, most often when anglers collect their own baitfish with minnow seines or other less-discriminating gear. Their effectiveness as baits is likely related to their role as prey for piscivorous gamefish. Many fly fishing streamer patterns and some small jigs imitate darter species, and anglers would be wise to remember the movements of these fish when trying to imitate them.

Darter watching. Darter watching requires careful observation. Because they are small, hide under rocks, and move about quickly, darters are hard to follow and not commonly observed by anglers. Because of their striking coloration and impressive diversity, however, darters are often watched by snorkelers in warmwater streams. The majority of darter species are most colorful during spawning in late spring and early summer, so this is the best time to observe them.

Threats. Most darters survive best in clean and clear water. Because of this, they are good indicators of water and habitat quality. Due to the specific habitat requirements of many darters, the nature of impacts on aquatic systems can be judged by which darters are impacted.

Many darters are declining or are already threatened or endangered. Declines are due to a number of factors, including habitat alteration, pollution, and the introduction of additional competitors and predators. Because many darters require clean substrate for spawning, sedimentation from poor land-use practices can negatively affect their reproduction. Alteration of a stream channel as a result of such disturbances can also eliminate adult and rearing habitats. Because many darters have naturally small populations, one impact can wipe out a whole species. Because of this, anglers who collect baitfish should take care to not remove many darters from a single area. They should also inform themselves of any endangered or threatened species that may be present in areas where they are collecting bait.

DAYBEACON

An unlighted aid to navigation that is a fixed structure on shore or in the water close to shore, used for shallow water and channel marking.

A bull shark reportedly journeyed 1,700 miles up the Mississippi River in 1937; another bull shark was found 2,500 miles up the Amazon in 1972.

DAY BOAT
A term for party boat *(see)*.

DEAD BAIT
Whole dead fish or other natural organisms used to catch predatory fish, especially bottom scroungers. This term is also spelled as "deadbait."
See: Bait; Chumming; Natural Bait.

DEAD DRIFT
Another term for drag-free drift *(see)*.
See: Mending.

DEAD RECKONING
Dead reckoning is a nonelectronic method of calculating a boat's position, especially on a navigational chart *(see)*, using speed through the water, course steered, and time traveled from a known location. A dead reckoning is done without any adjustment for current, wind, waves, or steering error. It has nothing to do with visual observation of landmarks.
See: Navigation.

DEBONER
A tubelike tool for removing the backbone of a moderate-sized fish that will be used as offshore trolling bait. The tube cuts around and extracts the backbone out of an otherwise intact fish, making it more pliable for better trolling action when properly rigged.

DEBONING
See: Fish Preparation—Cleaning/Dressing.

DECALS, BOAT
A relatively new concept, boat decals are adhesive-backed imitations of small baitfish and squid that are applied to the entire hull of a boat to look like a school or ball of forage and to attract gamefish.

DECOY
Fish-shaped objects used under the ice to lure large species to a baited hook or, more often, within range of a spear. Decoys are not commonly used in standard ice fishing today. Antique ice fishing decoys are collectibles.
See: Antique Fishing Tackle; Spearing.

DEEP-SCATTERING LAYER
A layer of marine organisms in the open ocean at depths greater than 660 feet that produces a scattering effect detectable by sonar. The sonic difference results from an echo produced by gas bubbles within the animals in the layer. More than one deep-scattering layer may be present at any particular place, with the layers moving up in daylight or bright moonlight and descending at night or on heavily overcast days. The movement follows that of schools of small fish, squid, and larger crustaceans.

DEEP-SEA FISHING
A term widely used to refer to ocean fishing. Commonly used by tourism interests, deep-sea fishing usually refers to angling on charter and party boats, especially for bottom-dwelling species, and is distinguished from fishing in shallow waters near or close to shore, or fishing from smaller boats, such as skiffs or guide boats.
See: Inshore Fishing; Offshore Fishing.

DELAWARE
A small state with no large lakes or large rivers, Delaware nevertheless holds its own in sportfishing opportunities. Much of that is in the salt because the Delmarva Peninsula constitutes nearly 95 percent of the state and offers 381 miles of tidal shoreline. The western and southern fringes of this South Atlantic state drain west toward Chesapeake Bay, while the others flow to the Delaware River, Delaware Bay, or the Atlantic Ocean.

In the salt chuck, the First State boasts excellent bottom fishing for weakfish, flounder, and croaker, as well as sea bass and tautog on offshore wrecks; big bluefish, tuna, dolphin, king mackerel, blue marlin, and white marlin; and striped bass, bluefish, weakfish, king whiting, and flounder for surf and jetty anglers. The interior offers impressive smallmouth bass fishing in the northern part of the state; big largemouths in the old millponds and tidal rivers below the Chesapeake and Delaware Canal (also known as the C & D Canal); and good action in various waters for catfish, carp, pickerel, crappie, and sunfish. This isn't too shabby for a state that is smaller than some Texas counties.

Freshwater
New Castle County. In the early part of the eighteenth century, the DuPonts were attracted to Brandywine River and harnessed its power to turn their mills. The mills are long gone, but this waterway is still beautiful and provides excellent light-tackle smallmouth bass fishing.

One of the more enjoyable ways to fish the Brandywine, which has shallow water and moderate current flow, is from a canoe. Anglers launch from the bank near the Delaware-Pennsylvania line and paddle downstream to Rockland. The dam left over from an old paper mill at this location requires a portage before heading downstream again. Another dam, Hagley, at the site of DuPont's first gunpowder plant, marks the end of the line for fishing from a canoe. Smallmouths are pursued in the rocky waters below this point from shore or by wading.

Largemouth bass also thrive in the Brandywine, but they are larger and more common in the ponds of the southern part of this county. Lums Pond, which is the largest impoundment in New Castle County, is one such site; it's located between Routes 896 and 301 just north of the C & D Canal. Another is Becks Pond. This small waterway produces big bass and is located between Route 72 and Salem Church Road.

Delaware doesn't have a population of native trout, but each spring the Department of Natural Resources (DNR) stocks several streams in New Castle County with rainbows. White Clay Creek holds most of these and receives most of the angling pressure. Located near Newark, this stream has a fly-fishing-only section at the north end, but assorted baits are favored along the rest of the waterway.

Tidal streams and the C & D Canal provide good catfish angling. The canal has several fishing piers with easy, safe access. In the tidal streams, bank anglers typically favor the waters around bridges. Augustine Beach has a boat ramp and beach fishing access.

Kent County. Delaware's middle county has a network of small streams and ponds. The streams hold little angling interest, but the ponds offer excellent fishing opportunities for bass, bluegills, crappie, and pickerel.

Many large bass have been landed in the so-called Milford chain, three ponds located near Milford in the southern part of the county. Blairs Pond, Silver Lake, and Haven Lake in the chain produce big bass on a regular basis. Those who expect big bass to live in big water will be surprised to find that these ponds cover a small area. They are old millponds, as are most of the freshwater impoundments in Delaware, and were built on the headwaters of the Mispillion River.

These ponds would have filled in over the years, but the DNR has managed them for the benefit of anglers. Delaware's pond-management program is a model for similar programs in other states. All three are accessible from shore; Silver and Haven Lakes offer boat ramps.

Another noteworthy pond in the county is Killen, which has bass, catfish, sunfish, and pickerel. Located in Killen Pond State Park, it has a boat ramp and camping area and is located close to other good fishing sites in Kent and Sussex Counties.

Sussex County. The overwhelming favorites of freshwater anglers in this part of Delaware are Nanticoke River and Broad Creek. The two waterways join at Phillips Landing, where there is an excellent boat ramp. Largemouth bass are the primary target, but pickerel and stripers are fished here as well.

This is tidal water, so the bass do not grow to exceptional size, yet they strike and fight harder than their larger local pond cousins. The environment here is hard on bass, which must be on the move to overcome tidal currents and keep away from a wider array of predators than are found in sheltered waters.

Fishing on the Nanticoke River and Broad Creek requires working with the tides. As a general rule it's best to start downriver at the Delaware-Maryland line and work upriver toward Seaford or Laurel on a falling tide. As the water washes out of the tidal marshes and creeks, bass set up ambush sites to intercept the baitfish. Anglers cast toward and around shore cover with spinnerbaits, crankbaits, and plastic worms.

Elsewhere in the county, Trap Pond State Park has a unique setting as well as good fishing. Trap Pond drains into Cypress Swamp, the only cypress grove north of the Mason-Dixon line. Here, anglers fish from canoes for bass and pickerel, amid beautiful scenery.

Saltwater

New Castle County. Saltwater fishing in this county is restricted to the southern sector, except during dry spells in late summer, when saltwater intrusion works as far north as the Delaware Memorial Bridge. The jumping-off place for upper Delaware Bay and the lower Delaware River is Augustine Beach off of Route 9, just south of the C & D Canal. A boat ramp is available, and it is also possible to fish from the beach.

Anglers catch small blues and weakfish here in the summer, and striped bass in the spring and fall. Small bucktails tipped with peeler crabs, shrimp, or squid work well on the weakfish and blues. Bucktails are also effective on striped bass, but bloodworms are the first choice for these fish.

Structure, like that found near Reedy and Pea Patch Islands or around the wrecks and lighthouses, holds the best angling potential. On occasion, schools of bluefish or striped bass chase baits to the surface, where diving gulls will mark the location. This activity is more likely to occur early or late in the day.

Kent County. Kent County contains the entire 28 miles of Delaware's Atlantic coastline, plus access to both the upper and lower regions of Delaware Bay.

Fishing upper Delaware Bay out of Woodland Beach produces more consistently than does working the waters near Augustine Beach. The bottom close to shore is covered with the remains of old oyster beds and holds a variety of baitfish and gamefish. Farther out, the edge of the channel provides deeper water where weakfish, flounder, and bluefish stage, particularly at low tide. Bottom fishing with peeler crabs and squid is the most popular technique here, but anglers also find success casting bucktails and plastic grubs. The best bite is almost always at dawn and dusk.

Port Mahon is another launch site for anglers who fish the upper bay. Bowers Beach has a launch ramp and a fleet of charter and head boats; this fleet specializes in bottom fishing for weakfish, flounder, blues, and croaker. There's nothing fancy to this activity, which mainly involves soaking baits, but the action can be fast when schools of fish frequent the shoals or deeper sloughs.

Slaughters Beach is the site of the most impressive run of big weakfish ever recorded during the 1980s, but this might not be seen again. Weakfish are still the most important species here, but they now average less than 5 pounds rather than 15. Brandywine Light, 14 Foot Shoal, and the Coral Beds drew anglers from all over during the banner years, and they still hold good numbers of weaks, plus flounder, bluefish, and croaker. Cut squid, peeler crabs, and live minnows are favored bait offerings, with bucktails and grubs employed by lure users.

Roosevelt Inlet, in Lewes, empties into the lower Delaware Bay, with access to the Atlantic Ocean. Charter and head boats running from this port fish for everything from croaker and weakfish to tuna and marlin. A public launch ramp in town provides access for the private boater. The Lewes Breakwater, a long rock jetty near Cape Henlopen, provides excellent fishing for tautog. Spring and fall are prime, and most fish are taken on fresh-cut crabs.

Surf fishing in the fall is especially good along the beach from Cape Henlopen down to Navy Beach. Big blues and striped bass are the primary targets, with king whiting and weakfish mixed in the catch.

Indian River Inlet, south of Rehoboth, is home to a large fleet of private and charter boats that work the inshore and offshore waters of the Atlantic Ocean. Anglers travel 70 to 80 miles or more from this site to the canyons in search of dolphin, tuna, wahoo, and marlin. Closer to shore, the wrecks provide good fishing for sea bass and tautog. Trollers working over wrecks and seamounts catch big blues, little tunny, king mackerel, and bluefin tuna.

Behind the inlet, Indian River and Rehoboth Bays host hoards of small boaters who target summer flounder, weakfish, and blues. The shallow, sheltered waters of these bays are ideal for family excursions, and pontoon boats are popular craft.

The surf from Rehoboth to Fenwick Island is open to fishing and supports a large number of anglers and their beach buggies. Fishing is best in spring and fall, but summer action can sometimes be good early or late in the day, perhaps depending on tide stage.

DELAYED MORTALITY

A term for the instance when a fish that was caught by an angler and released alive dies at some later time, usually because of injury or stress.
See: Catch-and-Release.

DELTA

A fan-shaped, low-lying plain at the mouth of a river, created by deposited sediment. Formation of a delta depends on the rate of sedimentation, volume of river flow, and the currents of the sea; a strong sea current can prevent formation of, or can erode, an existing delta. The local coastline in a delta is constantly changing as sediment is moved and rearranged.

Deltas are often rich in aquatic life and are especially likely to host nearshore species of gamefish that utilize or tolerate lower levels of salinity. Such species as snook and tarpon are common inhabitants of warm deltas.

DEMERSAL

A term used for fish or animals that live on or near the seabed or water bottom. Examples include flounder and croaker. Demersal is often used synonymously with groundfish.

DENMARK

Situated in northwestern Europe, Denmark is the southernmost Scandinavian country. It is a low-lying nation best known in angling circles for its exceptional sea trout (sea-run brown trout) fishing. Bordered on the south by Germany, Denmark's mainland, known as Jutland (Jylland), is a 400-kilometer-long peninsula bounded on the west and north by the North Sea, and on the east by the Baltic Sea. The country includes more than 500 islands, 100 of which are populated; most of these lie to the east, directly in the outlet of the Baltic.

The largest Danish island is Zealand (Sjaelland), which contains the capital city of Copenhagen. The second largest is Funen (Fyn). Denmark also contains the Faeroe Islands, located almost midway between the Shetland Islands and Iceland in the North Atlantic.

Though small in area at 43,000 square kilometers, Denmark has good fishing opportunities in the ocean, brackish water, and freshwater. Some of the Atlantic's best cod fishing takes place here; sea trout fishing is well developed along much of the coastline; pike and perch fishing is good along the brackish inner islands; rivers contain resident and sea-run populations of trout; and small interior waters hold good fishing for coarse species.

Freshwater

Freshwater fishing in Denmark's rivers for brown trout, sea trout, grayling, hatchery-escaped rainbows, and a few salmon is the favored pursuit among anglers. All of the important rivers are on the Jylland peninsula. A lowland area (the average elevation is about 30 meters), it has no falls or rapids, and the rivers run with good speed.

Only a handful of Danish rivers originally held salmon. Except for the easterly flowing Gudenå, all

Dr. James Henshall is noted for his classic 1881 book on bass fishing, but he also developed fishing tackle and, while in Montana, was the first to breed grayling artificially.

Trout fishing on the Gudenå in Denmark.

the salmon rivers enter the North Sea. They are the Storåen, Skjernå, Snerumå, Vardeå, Kongeåen, Ribeå, and Vidåen. Some of these rivers, especially the Skjernå, once had excellent populations of big salmon. A 60-pounder was caught in the Skjernå in 1956. Agricultural pollution, habitat alteration, and dams wiped out the salmon, however. Today, significant effort and money is being expended to increase or to reintroduce them.

Almost all Danish rivers, from the largest rivers in Jylland to the smallest brooks on Bornholm Island, have runs of sea trout. Quite a few of these, mainly the smallest streams, still contain original strains of wild fish.

Among the better sea trout rivers are the Karupå, Kongeåen, Ribeå, Gelså, Vejleå, and Koldingå. The most prolific sea trout river is the Karupå, where the spring run begins as early as the end of April. The largest Danish sea trout was taken in the Karupå and weighed 14.6 kilograms; it was also the world record for many years.

Fresh sea trout enter the Karupå until spawning occurs in November and December. In many of the medium-size rivers, the first fresh trout enter in July and August. In the smaller rivers, fish enter when a good autumn rain facilitates upstream movement. From January through April, rivers experience another popular season, with a run of mainly sexually immature sea trout weighing between .5 kilogram to 1.5 kilograms.

Brown trout thrive in all suitable rivers and streams. They are commonly caught to 1 kilogram, and the summer months of June through August have the best hatches. Grayling inhabit a few rivers, all of them on the west coast of Jylland and in the Gudenå on the east. The official open-river season is from mid-January through mid-November, but in many rivers the season is shorter.

In addition to salmonids, most rivers also support populations of pike, perch, eels, whitefish, and other species in their lower reaches. Some rivers hold large perch—of 1 to 2 kilograms—that enter

from the sea to spawn. The most well known is the Tryggevaeldeå, which is 40 kilometers from Copenhagen.

Pike, perch, zander, bream, rudd, tench, whitefish, eels, roach, and carp inhabit most larger lakes. A few lakes hold brown trout, whitefish, and burbot. Apart from this natural fishing, several hundred small put-and-take lakes or ponds dot the country. These are regularly stocked, mainly with rainbow trout from 1 to 10 kilograms, but they also have brown trout, brook trout, salmon, and hybrid trout.

No professional fishing guides are available, but tackle shops can provide assistance, and most Danes speak English. Day tickets can be bought for particular stretches on most rivers.

Anglers require a state-issued license to fish in natural waters in and around Denmark and can obtain one at any post office. Short-term tourist licenses are available. Fishing rights on natural lakes, rivers, and streams are nearly always private, but they are often leased to local angling clubs. These clubs issue daily or weekly permits, which are available from tourist offices. In some locations anglers can rent a boat with fishing rights included.

Saltwater

In addition to facing the North Sea on its west, Denmark is bounded on the north by the Skagerrak, which is an arm of the North Sea, and on the east by the Kattegat Sea and the Øresund Strait, which links Kattegat to the Baltic Sea. On the south it is bounded by the Baltic Sea and Fehmarn Strait.

Because the Baltic Sea is the largest brackish water in the world, most inner and southern islands in Denmark are surrounded by water that holds both freshwater fish like pike and perch and saltwater species like cod. Above the narrow channels where most of the islands are located, the water turns more saline until reaching full salinity at the Kattegat Sea.

The influence of the tides is minimal around most of Denmark. At the most southern part of the west coast of Jylland, the maximum fluctuation is 2 meters. In the channels, the tides range between 12 and 15 centimeters; around the island of Bornholm in the lower part of the Baltic Sea, the difference is visible only when there is no wind.

With more than 7,500 kilometers of coastline in Denmark, saltwater fishing is the country's largest angling resource. All fishing in saltwater is public; and all that is necessary to enjoy the resource is an inexpensive state license. Fishing from the shore or wading in the surf are favored pursuits. The shallow, and in many places well-sheltered, coastline offers excellent fishing for sea trout. A large food supply is available here, as is good shelter for smaller fish.

Thanks to a temperate maritime climate, saltwater fishing for sea trout is a year-round enterprise in Denmark, except for the rare winters when the sea

D

freezes. The main months are March, April, and October, when the fish are moving to and from the rivers. The summers mainly offer night fishing along the open coast; winter fishing occurs predominantly in sheltered bays, where the water is less saline, and on the open coast south of channels, where the water is more brackish. The average sea trout weighs between 1 and 2.5 kilograms; a few are larger, and every year a number of trophy fish are in the 7- to 10-kilogram range.

The main technique for sea trout fishing does not change much throughout the year. Most anglers prefer spinning tackle, using 8- to 10-foot-long rods, light line, and long-casting spoons or plugs. Because 90 percent of the fishing occurs in 1 to 3 meters of water, and long casts are essential, the typical Danish coastal trout lure is not a fast sinker. Shore anglers often wear waders. The technique is simply to cover water by moving between each cast, using casting distances of between 45 and 80 meters. Reefs and areas with tidal current are fished more intensely. A bubble float used with a fly or a bait is also highly effective.

Fly fishing for coastal sea trout is popular, too. Fly anglers use 7- to 10-weight floating weight-forward or shooting-head lines and a 9- to $9^{1}/_{2}$-foot-long rod. There's a great variety of food available for the trout, so the fish are normally not picky. Most flies are streamers or shrimp patterns.

Other species commonly encountered from the shore or surf include cod, flounder, and eels; in season, garfish, herring, mullet, and mackerel are pursued. South of the channels, the fiords might hold perch and pike.

Fishing on the open waters is popular and offers a great variety of fish. Winter fishing for big spawning cod in Øresund Strait between Sweden and Denmark is a particularly popular fishery. In winter, large cod gather in this area to spawn. Big specimens are fish over 10 kilograms; individual catches may exceed 20 kilograms. This is one of the best places in Europe for large cod, especially from January through March. In the 1960s it was also a prime place for bluefin tuna.

Most of the year, ocean fishing charter boats pursue cod, flounder, garfish, mackerel, and other common saltwater species, but they might get into 2- to 5-kilogram sea trout. In Kattegat and the North Sea, the list of fish is much longer, and includes catfish, haddock, conger eels, tope, and many more species. Bottom fishing is the primary angling method.

Trolling is a relatively new saltwater tactic in Denmark. Since the early 1990s, a hidden potential has been found by trollers; many larger sea trout feed mostly off the coastline and out of reach of shore-based casters, but trolling can produce these fish. Around Bornholm in the Baltic Sea, a developing trolling sportfishery for Atlantic salmon is underway. The best season is spring, and salmon are in the 7- to 12-kilogram range. In the spring of 1998 the record was broken twice, first with a fish of 19.65 kilograms, then a few weeks later with one of 20.74 kilograms.

Faeroe Islands

Located in the North Atlantic, between Iceland, Norway, and Scotland, are 18 small, beautiful, rugged and windy islands covering just 1,373 square kilometers, populated by 45,000 people and 100,000 sheep. A self-governed territory of Denmark, the Faeroe Islands are accessed via daily flights from Copenhagen, or twice-weekly flights from Iceland. During the summer a weekly ferry crosses from Iceland and Denmark.

There is no reliable river angling here, as only after a good rain will fish be able to swim upriver. Sea trout can be fished outside all streams when there is just a slight chance that they might be able to swim upriver. When it does rain, rivers that contain lakes along their system usually have excellent sea trout fishing. An example is Sandsvatn on Sandoy Island.

Salmon also inhabit the Faeroes but are more plentiful in lakes, such as Saksun and Leynarvatn on Streymoy Island and Skálabotnur on Eystoroy Island. Salmon normally range from 2 to 5 kilograms, and sea trout from 1 to 3 kilograms.

All Faeroe lakes—from the largest, which is Sørvágsvatn at 7 kilometers long, to the tiniest little ponds in the mountains—hold small brown trout. Only a few hold larger fish. The most southern island, Suderoy, has the most lakes. A few lakes offer arctic charr in the 1- to 3-kilogram range. Lowland lakes with sea access might offer good fishing for eels.

All around the islands—that is, anywhere the steep and indented coast permits access—anglers can pursue pollock, flatfish, and red cod. Escaped salmon and rainbow trout are sought after near fish farms. There is potentially good offshore bottom fishing for the likes of cod, pollock, and halibut, but the wind-whipped sea is often rough, making it difficult to find a charter.

No permit is required for saltwater fishing. Freshwater fishing requires a permit or permission from the landowner.

DENTEX   *Dentex dentex.*
Other names—common dentex, dentice, denton, dente; French: *denté commun;* Spanish: *dentón.*

A member of the Sparidae family, the dentex is a popular eastern Atlantic gamefish and an esteemed table fish.

Identification. Dentex have an oval, deep body with a smoothly rounded head. Exceptionally large individuals have a profile with a slight frontal hump. Both jaws have well-developed caninelike teeth, plus several rows of smaller teeth of similar shape. The dorsal fin has 11 spines and 11 or 12 soft rays, the spines increasing in length from the first to the fourth or fifth then subequal. The lateral

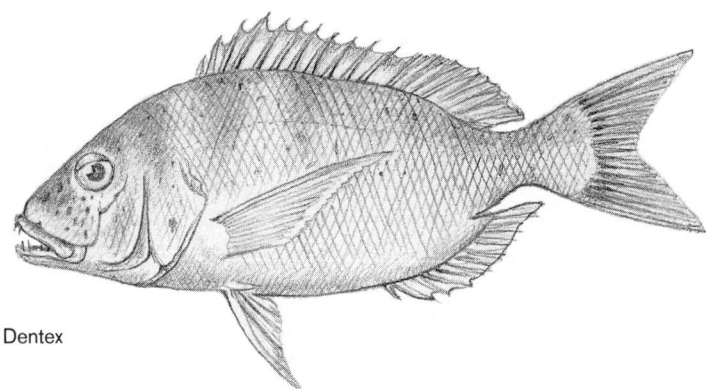

Dentex

line has 62 to 68 scales. Their coloration is variable, but young dentex are grayish, spotted with black on the back and upper sides, becoming pinkish with sexual maturity. Older individuals are grayish blue with spots becoming more or less diffuse with age. Some have a yellow tinge behind the mouth and on the gill cover.

Its dark spots can distinguish the dentex from other similar species, as can the several rows of canine-like teeth. Other species have more than one type of teeth, or incisor-like teeth.

Size.   The all-tackle record is 21 pounds, 11 ounces, which was caught in Italy in 1993, but dentex reportedly grow to 33 pounds.

Distribution.   The dentex occurs in the Mediterranean Sea and the Atlantic Ocean from the Bay of Biscay to West Africa north of Cape Blanc, Mauritania, and Madeira. Occasionally, the dentex ranges as far north as the British Isles and as far south as Senegal.

Habitat.   Although they inhabit hard bottoms (rock or rubble) down to 650 feet, dentex are more commonly found between 50 and 165 feet.

Life history/Behavior.   In summer dentex approach the shore, but in winter they migrate to deeper water. Adults are generally solitary, and juveniles travel in schools.

Food and feeding habits.   Dentex are active, predatory fish that feed on fish, mollusks, and cephalopods (octopuses, cuttlefish, squid).

Angling.   Fishing methods include trolling with bait and lures, generally in water from 35 to 165 feet, and bottom fishing in these and greater depths with live or dead baits. Angling prerequisites for the canny dentex include light leaders and small hooks.

DEPTHFINDER
See: Sonar.

DEPTH SOUNDER
See: Sonar.

DERBY
A fishing contest, usually open to the general public, and usually one in which a nominal entry fee is charged. Derbies are often associated with events for children or families, and where there is a high number of participants.
See: Competitive Fishing.

DESIGNATED WATER
A term used in some Canadian provinces for waters where Atlantic salmon are considered the primary species pursued by anglers as of a specified date, and where nonresidents must be accompanied by a guide, regardless of target species. Most such waters are also scheduled (see).

DETRITUS
Waste from decomposing organisms, which provides food for many other organisms.

DGPS
An acronym for Differential GPS.
See: GPS.

DIADROMOUS
Fish that migrate between freshwater and saltwater.
See: Anadromous; Catadromous.

DIAMOND JIG
A metal lure with four sides, wide at the middle and tapered to a point at either end. A diamond jig is a common lure in saltwater for bottom fishing and vertical jigging, and it is used on bluefish, striped bass, cod, pollock, and many other species. It is not a jig in the sense of leadheads, but since it has no inherent built-in action, it must be manipulated in a jigging manner to be effective and is actually a type of jigging spoon. Diamond jigs come in various weights and lengths and with single or treble hooks, which are attached to the base of the lure with a sturdy O-ring.
See: Inshore Fishing; Jig; Jigging; Spoon.

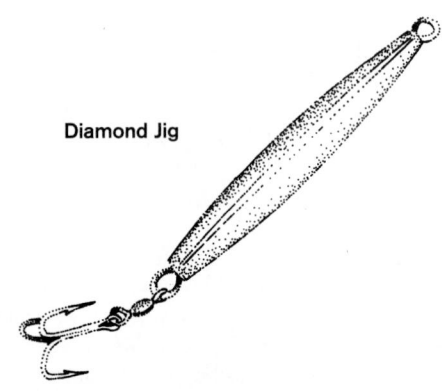

Diamond Jig

DINGELL JOHNSON ACT
See: Federal Aid in Sport Fish Restoration Act.

DINOFLAGELLATE

Unicellular microscopic organisms, classified as plants or animals depending on the presence of chlorophyll or the ingestion of food, respectively. Found in two main groups, armored and naked, dinoflagellates have flagella (whiplike extensions) that provide locomotion, and move vertically in response to light. Many dinoflagellates are phosphorescent, and some greatly increase in number periodically, occasionally resulting in toxic red tides (see). Some dinoflagellate blooms are toxic to shellfish and can cause gastroenteritis in the organisms that feed on them, including humans. As a component of phytoplankton (microscopic organisms that photosynthesize), dinoflagellates are an important basis for marine life.

DIPNET

Any small handheld net, with rigid support about the mouth, used for landing fish. Generally, dipnet refers to a small-mesh net that is used for hand-gathering baitfish and/or some nongamefish species and that is subject to specific regulations. A small net used to land gamefish, such as trout or bass, is also referred to as a dipnet, but it should not be confused with the act of dip-netting baitfish or nongamefish. **See: Landing Net.**

DIRECT DRIVE

A term for fishing reels without a gear set, in which one revolution of the reel handle produces one revolution of the reel spool, meaning that there is a 1:1 ratio in line retrieval. This is the simplest and most powerful reel, but also one with slow line recovery, especially when the level of line on the spool is reduced. **See: Big-Game Tackle; Conventional Tackle; Flycasting Tackle; Gear Ratio.**

DISC DRAG

A term for reels with disc drag systems; also the disc-shaped washers that are used in reel drags. **See: Baitcasting Tackle; Big-Game Tackle; Conventional Tackle; Flycasting Tackle; Spincasting Tackle; Spinning Tackle.**

DISEASES AND PARASITES

Like all other living creatures, fish are capable of harboring parasites or contracting diseases. From a consumption standpoint, these are usually more damaging to the angler's sense of aesthetics than they are to the fish itself, although certain parasites can be harmful to humans, and many diseases are harmful to fish. With proper preparation, most infected fish can be eaten without concern.

Diseases are fairly commonplace in fish populations. Parasites and bacteria are a natural part of the ecosystem in which fish live. Lake fish are especially susceptible because of warmer water temperatures and the abundance of other organisms through which disease may be transmitted. Saltwater fish are not immune, however.

Most parasites spend only part of their lives in fish. Birds, snails, plankton, and even mammals may host a parasite at different stages of its life. Parasites go through as many as six different stages from egg to adult.

Anglers may notice that some symptoms follow seasonal patterns or other cycles. This situation is especially noticeable when parasites are passed to fish through migrating birds.

Most fish disorders are classified as parasitic, bacterial, or viral. Anglers are more likely to come into contact with fish affected by parasites or bacteria than by viruses. Viral infections are usually detected at hatcheries while fish are at the fry stage. Wild or stocked fish with viral infections are generally small, weak, and unlikely to strike at anglers' offerings; natural predators usually catch these fish before anglers do.

Evidence of parasites or infection in an occasional gamefish doesn't automatically point to an unhealthy environment or poor water quality. It also doesn't mean that every fish in the area will be affected the same way. However, some diseases are more insidious than others, and result in the death of significant numbers of fish. Whirling Disease (see), a parasitic infection that attacks the cartilage of young trout and salmon, is such a case. Pfiesteria (see), which is a toxic algal bloom (though many people think of it as a disease), is a mass killer.

Internal Parasites

Internal parasites are found in the muscle tissue, eye, under the skin, and in or around the internal organs. Some of the more common ones include the following.

Yellow grub (*Clinostomum marginatum*).   One of the most common North American fish parasites, yellow grub infests a variety of freshwater fish, though it is rarely found in trout species. The $1/4$-inch-long grub is flat and encased in a cyst just under the skin in the muscle where it forms a wart-like bump. These bumps are often visible at the base of the fins and tail, or may be found on the gills.

Black spot or black grub (*Uvulifer ambloplitis*). Larvae of black grubs are most noticeable in fillets of fish that have white meat. Infection from the larvae creates small, raised black spots, which look like pepper in the skin and flesh. The tiny larvae are white, but the fish produces a black pigment that surrounds the thick-walled cysts. Skinning an infected fish will remove most grubs, since the majority of cysts occur in the skin.

Eye fluke (*Diplostomum spathaceum*).   Eye flukes seem to be most abundant in rainbow trout but also occur in other species of trout and in bass, bluegills, and other warmwater species. The fluke

D

occurs in the lens and fluid portion of the fish's eye. A popeyed effect is sometimes created from accumulation of fluids in the eyeball. In advanced cases, the eye becomes opaque white and the fish becomes partially or totally blind.

Bass tapeworm *(Proteocephalus ambloplitis)*. The bass tapeworm can be very damaging to freshwater fish but is not transmissible to humans. Largemouth, smallmouth, and rock bass are the most susceptible species. Although the adult tapeworm looks serious, with lengths up to $2^1/_2$ feet, the larvae actually do the most damage to the fish. Larvae invade reproductive organs and can cause sterility in the fish. Bass tapeworms are most evident in the fish's intestine. In heavy infestations, internal adhesions may be so great that the intestines, liver, spleen, and reproductive organs are bound into a single mass by a mat of connective tissue.

Trout tapeworm *(Diphyllobothrium spp.)*. The larvae of this tapeworm appear as white cysts in the abdominal organs and body cavity of trout. When heavily infested, the trout becomes listless and swims lazily near the surface. Only fish host the larvae of this parasite. Adult trout tapeworms are found in birds, dogs, cats, and bears. Several species are infectious to people.

Seatrout tapeworm *(Poecilancistrium caryophyllum)*. This tapeworm and a similar one in black drum are known as spaghetti worms. They are white, 1 to 3 inches long, and are parasitic tapeworms of sharks, which use the trout and drum as an intermediate host. Usually one to two worms exist in a fish, and they are harmless to humans.

Spiny-headed worm *(Acanthocephala)*. Various species of these small worms are found in just about all freshwater fish. Spiny-headed worms, usually no longer than $^3/_8$ inch, are most often found imbedded in the fish's intestine. These worms are easily identified by their round bodies. They can be white or pale yellow but are often a bright orange color. Their tubelike snout is covered with spines, which are used to attach to the fish.

Roundworm *(Nematode)*. Roundworms can be identified by their round elongated bodies and lack of segmentation or suckers. Most roundworms pose little danger to humans, but the kidney roundworm, found in bullhead and northern pike, may be transmitted to humans, as may the herring worm *(Anisakis simplex)* and cod or seal worm *(Pseudoterranova decipiens)*, which are marine nematodes. The latter nematodes can be found in all marine fish, not just herring or cod, as their common names suggest. Researchers have found these worms in cod, herring, tuna, mackerel, flatfish, anchovy, pollock, rockfish, salmon, halibut, and squid, to name just a few. Thorough freezing and/or cooking will greatly reduce the possibility of parasite transmission; not doing this, however, poses a serious risk for humans of getting an intestinal disease known as Anisakiasis. Commercial processors candle white-fleshed fish (by illuminating fish portions over a bright backlit table) to see and remove this parasite from the muscle tissue.

Red roundworm *(Eustronglydes sp.)*. Red roundworm is one of the most common nematodes, or roundworms. This parasite is found in many species of fish, including largemouth and smallmouth bass, walleye, sunfish, rock bass, crappie, yellow perch, pickerel, and eels. Redworm larvae are found in the fish's flesh and internal organs and are easily recognized by their deep red color. Occasionally, their infestation is so great the fish can't be salvaged to eat. They are infectious to people.

White roundworm *(Philonema sp.)*. These small, white, threadlike worms are 1 to $1^1/_2$ inches long. White roundworms are found in the air bladder or free in the body cavity of various trout species.

External Parasites

External parasites are most often found attached to the outside of the skin, fin, or gills of fish. Copepods, which are part of a large group of tiny aquatic crustaceans, are common external parasites that are abundant in both freshwater and saltwater and form an important part of the food chain for fish and plankton-eating marine animals. However, some copepods have turned the tables and adapted to life as parasites. Two of the most commonly seen parasitic copepods are fish lice and anchor worms.

Fish lice *(Argulus spp.)*. The 17 known species of fish lice have been found in almost all warmwater and anadromous fish. At first glance, fish lice look somewhat like scales, but they are actually saucer-shaped. The lice sometimes have jointed legs and two disk-shaped suckers, which are sometimes mistaken for eyes. The lice, usually $^1/_8$- to $^1/_4$-inch long, can creep over the surface of the fish and are found attached to the skin, fin, or gills.

Anchor worm *(Lernea spp.)*. When anglers complain of "wormy-" or "grubby-looking" fish, they're often referring to an infestation of anchor

Sea lice, shown here on a pink salmon, are one of the most common and harmless fish parasites.

worm. The parasite is about the size of a grain of rice, is yellowish white, and is found primarily in the gills, mouth, or fins of trout. The head of this copepod is buried in the flesh, with the remainder of the worm hanging from the wound. When the copepod dies and falls off, an inflamed wound may be left.

Other external parasites include the following.

Leeches *(Hirudinea spp.).* Leeches are sometimes found attached to freshwater fish. They somewhat resemble flukes but are actually segmented and have suckers at the head and tail. Leeches have no effect on the quality of the meat.

Ich *(Ichthyophthirius multifilis).* Ich is most common among warmwater species but can be found on salmon and trout. Pinpoint grayish-white swellings or elevations on the body and fins are prominent signs of ich infection. The swellings are usually well defined but in cases of heavy infection may appear as irregular, light-colored patches. Similar lesions may occur on the gills, but these are harder to see.

Fungal Diseases

Fish fungi *(Saprolegnia sp.).* Physical injury or infection stemming from invasion of other parasites usually provides the initial foothold for this fungus. The fungi appear as cottony patches, $1/3$ inch or longer, white or off-white in color, growing on or out of the fish. Threads of the fungus may appear gray or brown if the water is muddy. Fish fungus can occur both internally and externally, usually growing in small patches but spreading in later stages.

Bacterial Diseases

In most bacterial infections, affected areas can be cut away and the rest of the fish eaten after thorough cooking or freezing. However, if the infection is extensive or the fish has a puffy body and swollen eyes (dropsy), the meat should not be eaten.

Furunculosis. In 1894, furunculosis became the first bacterial disease of fish to be scientifically described. The bacteria attack salmonids, with brown and brook trout particularly susceptible. The most common symptoms of furunculosis are ulcers and boils around the dorsal fin. The ulcers may be tinged with blood, and larger ones may contain a sticky, dark-reddish pus. Hemorrhages may also be seen in the eyes and on the fins. Gills may be white or pale pink, and occasionally soft, blisterlike lesions filled with blood form just beneath the skin. Internally, there may be bloody fluid or inflammation around the heart, and red spots in the body cavity.

Columnaris. Columnaris is widespread among freshwater fish, affecting spiny ray species and catfish as well as trout. Outbreaks occur most often when water temperatures are above 55°F. The disease shows up as gray-white spots on the head and fins, although gills and sides of the body may also be affected. As the disease progresses, the spots grow into small circular lesions and the fins become frayed. Yellowish slime may cover tissue exposed by the lesions.

Precautions for Consumption

Most common North American fish parasites are not harmful to humans, but there are a few parasites, including some tapeworms, flukes, and roundworms, that can be troublesome. It never hurts to wear gloves when cleaning fish, or at least protect any cuts, and wash your hands thoroughly after handling fish. Extra care should always be taken when handling fish that have a disease or parasite. In all but the most severe cases, proper freezing and/or cooking will make the catch safe to eat.

Completely remove all viscera and wash the body cavity, taking care to remove all visible parasites. Most importantly, thoroughly cook or freeze your catch before you eat it.

Freezing. Commercial fish-processing procedures, such as canning and freezing, inactivate parasites. As a result, illness from consuming commercially caught fish containing live parasites is very low in the United States.

Although freezing will kill parasites, it is necessary to reduce the product temperature to −35°C (−31°F) and hold it there for 15 hours, or −18°C (0°F) for 24 hours, to kill such parasites as herring worm and cod worm. According to experiments conducted by the Food and Drug Association, five days in a home freezer set at −4°F killed roundworms in rockfish. Home freezers often do not freeze fish as low as −4°F. For these freezers, it is recommended that fish be frozen for five to seven days to kill the parasites. When the fish is wrapped well and frozen while still fresh, the quality of the meat won't suffer.

Freezing alone isn't an absolute guarantee that all forms of parasites will be killed. However, when used in conjunction with cooking, hot smoking, salting, kippering, or marinating, chances of parasite survival are greatly reduced.

Cooking/smoking/salting. Cook the fish until all translucency is gone and the fish flakes completely. This method is not necessarily the best way to cook fish, but using previously frozen fish will alleviate worries about fish on the rare side.

Contrary to popular opinion, smoking does not preserve fish. "Light-smoked" fish can carry the same risks as raw fish. However, most parasite larvae and bacteria are destroyed when the internal temperature throughout the meat reaches 180°F. The meat must be 140°F throughout the fish, particularly the thicker portions, to kill parasites and must reach 180°F to kill any bacteria. You can still light-smoke fish safely if the fish has been frozen first at −4°F for seven days.

You can't count on the safety of salted or marinated fish unless the meat has been frozen first. Use previously frozen fish in raw and marinated fish recipes.

D

If the meat smells bad or if the flesh is obviously affected throughout, don't take a chance. Dispose of the fish, and be sure that the carcass will be secure from scavenging pets or wildlife.
See: Fish Preparation—Care.

DISPLACEMENT HULL
One of two broad categories of boat hulls that includes canoes, jonboats, and flat-bottomed dories or skiffs. Displacement hulls are noted for slow speed; they push through the water rather than ride on top of it.
See: Boat.

DISTRESS SIGNALS
The boating community has devised many recognized ways of communicating the fact that a vessel is in distress. On large boats, recognized distress signals include radiotelephone communication, marine radio communication (especially the well-known expression of "mayday" for a boat that is in imminent danger, particularly of sinking), activation of an EPIRB, firing of a flare, and continuous sounding of a horn. Smaller boats may be equipped with a horn or spotlight to signal for help. A person who holds his or her arms out to the side and repeatedly raises and lowers them is signaling for help. Continuous noise-making, be that blowing a whistle or horn, is an accepted means of signaling for help, and any action will do in a life-threatening situation.

DIVING PLANER
See: Planer, Diving.

DOBSONFLIES, FISHFLIES, AND ALDERFLIES
These three groups of insects are members of the scientific order Megaloptera, a term derived from *megalo,* meaning large, and *ptera,* meaning wing, owing to the large wings of these species. Their life cycle consists of egg, larva, pupa, and adult stages, with most of this being in the larva stage.

The larvae of dobsonflies, fishflies, and alderflies are aquatic and carnivorous and may bite if handled. The larval stage generally lasts less than a year but may last up to three years. Larvae leave the water and pupate on shore for several weeks, after which the adult insect emerges. The adult dobsonfly has four large wings that are folded back tentlike over the abdomen. They, and fishflies, are most active at dusk or night; alderflies are active during the day. All become abundant in and around the shoreline.

The larvae of these insects are all found in streams and rivers, and they have common traits that distinguish them from other insect larvae. All

Dobsonfly, Alderfly, and Fishfly Larvae

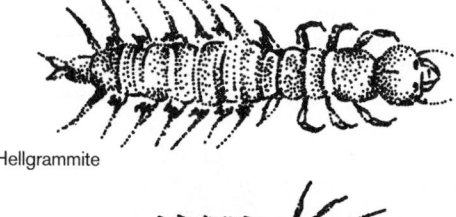
Hellgrammite

Alderfly

Fishfly

have three pairs of segmented legs (six legs total) on the middle section of the body, with tiny pincers at the end of each. The abdominal segments have many fleshy, filamentous (strandlike) appendages extending from each side, and they have large, chewing pincerlike mouthparts.

Dobsonfly larvae are known as hellgrammites and belong to the Corydalidae family. They have paired, cottonlike or filamentous gill tufts under their abdominal appendages; the back end is forked with two short fleshy tails, and two hooks on each tail; they are usually 1 to 4 inches long, and are dark brown to black in color. Although eaten by various fish, they are a preferred live bait (or artificial imitation) for smallmouth bass, and they in turn consume the larvae of smaller aquatic insects, including caddisflies *(see).*

Fishfly larvae belong to the Corydalidae family as well. They have a smooth abdomen (no gill tufts); the back end is forked with two short fleshy tails and two hooks on each tail; they may be light colored; and their breathing tubes, which may be retracted and not visible, extend from the top of the abdominal surface.

Alderfly larvae are members of the Sialidae family. They have a smooth abdomen (no gill tufts), have a single branched tail filament extending straight back, and may be light colored. Both alderfly and fishfly larvae are much smaller than hellgrammites.

A few species of beetle larvae (especially whirligigs) are sometimes confused with dobsonfly, fishfly, or alderfly larvae because they may have similar fleshy filaments along the sides of the abdomen and also may have four hooks at the back end. On beetle larvae with these characteristics, the four hooks come from a single short projection (point) rather than having a pair of hooks on each of two fleshy extensions like fishfly and dobsonfly larvae. In addition, beetle larvae do not have a single filamentous tail like alderflies.

Caddisfly *(see)* larvae are sometimes mistaken for dobsonfly, fishfly, or alderfly larvae, but caddisfly larvae do not have fleshy filaments (which look like spikes) extending out from the sides of their abdomen and have only two abdominal hooks.
See: Aquatic Insects.

DODGER/FLASHER

These devices are attractors used exclusively in trolling and primarily in freshwater to get the attention of deep fish (especially trout and salmon species).

Both dodgers and flashers are thin metal objects, oblong and rounded at the ends, usually 2 to 3 inches wide and 5 to 10 inches long. Dodgers sway from side to side and do not rotate unless they are being run too fast; flashers rotate but don't sway. Both have swivels at each end, come in various sizes and colors, and can be altered in appearance with the application of prism tape. Dodgers are more widely trolled than flashers.

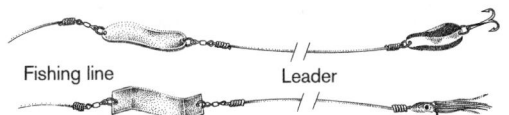

Fishing line   Leader

Typical dodger (top) and flasher (bottom) trolling rigs.

Plugs, spoons, flies, and imitation squid are fished behind dodgers and flashers. Flies and squid are the most popular trailing lures, particularly for steelhead and coho salmon, and are run 12 to 18 inches behind the attractor. Plugs (primarily cut plugs) and spoons are run 18 to 30 inches back. There is no need to use long leads; short leads make netting fish easier.

These attractors don't have any built-in weight, so they are usually fished behind a downrigger, but they also are used in conjunction with diving planers and heavy sinkers. The distance from the planer or sinker to the attractor is 2 to 6 feet; a short lead improves its action. When attractors are trolled with a downrigger, it's important to have a moderately tight tension setting on the line release because attractors pull fairly hard and may pull the line out of a lightly set release.
See: Trolling.

DOGFISH, SPINY   *Squalus acanthias.*
Other names—dogfish, dog shark, grayfish, Pacific grayfish, Pacific dogfish, spinarola, California dogfish, blue dog, common spiny fish, spiny dogfish, picked fish, spiky dog, spotted spiny, spurdog, white-spotted dogfish, Victorian spotted dogfish; French: *aiguillat;* Italian: *spinarolo;* Japanese: *aburatsunozame;* Portuguese: *galhudo;* Russian: *katran;* Spanish: *galludo.*

The spiny dogfish may hold the record for most English-language aliases among saltwater fish. It is the most prominent member of the Squalidae family of dogfish sharks, which includes 18 genera and 72 species, among them the smallest sharks in the world. Dogfish sharks are widely distributed in the Atlantic, Pacific, and Indian Oceans. Some live in relatively shallow water close to shore, and others inhabit great depths. They vary widely in length, and one of their chief anatomical characteristics is the lack of an anal fin.

The spiny dogfish is possibly the most abundant living shark. Commercial fishermen view these fish with mixed feelings (when large schools invade fishing grounds, they mutilate other species caught in nets or by hooks), and anglers generally consider them a nuisance. Most anglers catch this species incidentally (and release it) while fishing for other bottom dwellers. Commercial fishermen principally use otter trawls and gillnets to land dogfish. Although they are frequently taken as bycatch and are discarded during groundfish operations in some waters, spiny dogfish are of moderate importance in other fisheries where a good market for this species exists. They are used for human consumption, liver oil, leather, fertilizer, and other purposes.

The U.S. commercial fishery for spiny dogfish is similar to that of European fisheries in its selection of only large individuals (exceeding 5 pounds and 33 inches), which are mainly mature females, to meet processing and marketing requirements. Smaller individuals, however, consisting of both mature and immature males as well as immature females, are also taken as bycatch and discarded. In the Atlantic, these stocks are fully exploited.

Identification.   The body of the spiny dogfish is elongate and slender. The head is pointed. The color is slate gray to brownish on top, sometimes with white spots, and fading to white below. It has spines at the beginning of both dorsal fins; these spines are mildly poisonous and provide a defense for the spiny dogfish.

Size/Age.   Spiny dogfish are common at 2 to 3 feet in length; the maximum size is about 63 inches and 20 pounds. In California waters, a large fat female will be roughly 4 feet long and weigh 15 pounds. In the northwestern Atlantic, maximum ages reported for males and females are 35 and 40 years respectively.

Distribution.   Spiny dogfish occur in temperate and subtropical waters. In the western Atlantic, they range from Greenland to Argentina; in the eastern Atlantic, they range from Iceland and the Murmansk coast of Russia to South Africa, including the Mediterranean and Baltic Seas. In the

Spiny Dogfish

western Pacific, they range from the Bering Sea to New Zealand, and in the eastern Pacific they range from the Bering Sea to Chile.

Habitat. This species is common in near-shore waters along some coasts and may be found in enclosed bays and estuaries; it generally inhabits waters up to 1,200 feet deep, although spiny dogfish have been taken at depths of 2,400 feet. It reportedly enters freshwater but cannot survive there for more than a few hours. It typically favors the bottom. In temperate waters during spring and fall, spiny dogfish can range into coastal waters, heading more northerly in summer. In winter, they are distributed primarily in deeper waters along the edge of the continental shelf.

Life history. Spiny dogfish tend to school by size and, for large mature individuals, by sex. Females are larger than males and produce from 3 to 14 young at a time in alternate years. The species bears live young, and has a gestation period of about 18 to 22 months. Spiny dogfish are long lived and nonmigratory; heavy commercial fishing pressure in a given area will rapidly lower populations of this slow-growing, low-reproductive species.

Food and feeding habits. The spiny dogfish is voracious and feeds on practically all smaller fish, including herring, sardines, anchovies, smelts, and even small spiny dogfish and crabs. They have been known to attack schools of herring and mackerel, as well as concentrations of haddock, cod, sand lance, and other species.

Angling. Assorted baits fished on bottom rigs will catch spiny dogfish. When present in abundance and striking baits meant for other species as soon as those baits reach the bottom, they can be extremely disruptive to angling efforts. This behavior can make it impossible to catch such desirable fish as cod, pollock, and flounder.

Spiny dogfish squirm greatly when captured, and it's necessary to take great care in handling them, as they often stab human flesh with their spines. The mild toxin that is released with the stabbing can cause infections, and the wounds are slow to heal.

DOLLY VARDEN   *Salvelinus malma.*
AND BULL TROUT   *Salvelinus confluentus.*
Other names for Dolly Varden—Dolly.
Other names for bull trout—bull charr, western brook trout, Rocky Mountain trout, red spotted salmon-trout, red spotted charr.

The Dolly Varden and bull trout are members of the charr *(see)* group of the Salmonidae family and close relatives of arctic charr *(see: charr, arctic).* Early studies described these two fish as a variant of the arctic charr and as one distinct species, and for a long time the bull trout was considered just a localized version of the Dolly Varden. Today many fisheries scientists believe that Dolly Varden and bull trout are two distinct species that look amazingly similar. As a result of this early confusion, much of the scientific literature on the Dolly Varden is based in part or in whole on the bull trout.

Found in lakes, rivers, and small headwater streams, sometimes migrating back and forth between freshwater and saltwater, and sometimes not, these fish have puzzled fisheries biologists and ichthyologists since they were first discovered. About the only thing everyone agreed on was that they were charr, although somehow the incorrect name "trout" stayed with the bull trout, when the species should have been called bull charr.

Why it is called bull, in fact, is unclear. The Dolly Varden, according to legend, received its moniker because its unique coloration was associated with the colorful clothing of a character in the Charles Dickens novel *Barnaby Rudge.*

Like the arctic charr, the Dolly Varden is an anadromous species, although some populations are landlocked. Its Arctic coastal range overlaps with that of the arctic charr, and its Pacific coastal range overlaps with the bull trout's, which is generally described as a strictly freshwater-dwelling species, although Washington State biologists have found bull trout in Puget Sound.

As gamefish, the bull trout and the Dolly Varden are not as highly rated as most other salmonids, but they do have considerable sporting and food value and are gaining esteem. It was once thought that

Dolly Varden

their predatory nature posed a threat to other salmonids; people attempted to eradicate them, and loggers even dynamited pools where bull trout and/or Dolly Varden congregated. The state of Alaska once offered a bounty on them. Of course, salmon and steelhead managed to survive for thousands of years despite the predatory habits of the bull trout and Dolly Varden.

Not all populations of these species have managed to survive, however; some runs are now extinct, and populations of both species have been steadily declining in much of their range, especially in western lower 48 states, and the bull trout there is generally, although unofficially, considered endangered. Habitat loss, overfishing, rising stream temperatures, stream siltation, and hybridizing with (nonnative) brook trout have all contributed to this decline. Historically, sportfishing regulations were liberal for bull trout and Dolly Varden, but in recent years more restrictive regulations have been imposed.

The flesh of both species is pink and firm and good to eat, and there has been some commercial value for Dolly Varden in parts of its range.

Identification.   These two charr, as well as the arctic charr, are difficult to distinguish from external characteristics alone, even for specialists. Due to past misidentification of species in various locales and lack of scientific knowledge, much of the available literature on these species is either misleading or incorrect, and some disagreement as to their distribution still exists among scientists.

In general, the Dolly Varden and the bull trout can be distinguished by their size and habitat. The Dolly Varden is usually a coastal species, whereas the larger bull trout inhabits inland waters, namely large, cold rivers and lakes draining high, mountainous areas. Although both can grow large, they seldom do. Dollies are typically smaller and tend to have a more rounded body shape. Bull trout have a larger, flattened head and a more pronounced hook in the lower jaw.

The color of both varies with habitat and locality, but the body is generally olive green, the back being darker than the pale sides; cream to pale yellow spots (slightly smaller than the pupil of the eye) cover the back, and red or orange spots cover the sides; and the pectoral, pelvic, and anal fins have white or cream-colored margins. The male in full fall spawning dress sports a dark olive back, sometimes bordering on black, an orange red belly, bright-red spots, and fluorescent white fin edges, rivaling fall's spectacular colors. Sea-run Dollies are silvery, and the spots can be very faint.

Bull trout and Dolly Varden can be distinguished from the eastern brook trout (also a charr) by the absence of vermiculations on their back. In addition, the eastern brook trout's red spots are surrounded by blue halos. Bull trout and brook trout have been known to spawn together, and their hybrid offspring can have features of both parents.

Bull Trout

(Hybridization can be a serious problem in some areas, resulting in the dilution or destruction of the gene pool of the native bull trout.)

A much greater problem arises in trying to distinguish the Dolly Varden from the arctic charr. Much published information on the distribution of these species is incorrect, and it often presupposed that only one species or the other occurred in areas or rivers where it is now believed both species may occur. The two are outwardly almost identical in every respect, and to complicate matters, significant variations occur in both species. The spots on the Dolly Varden are usually smaller than the pupil of the eye, whereas on the arctic charr they are larger than the pupil. When returning from the sea, both species are silvery and lack spots. Arctic charr on the average have more gill rakers on the first left gill arch (25 to 30 as opposed to 21 to 22 in the Dolly Varden) and more pyloric caeca (40 to 45 as opposed to roughly 30 in the Dolly Varden), but fish with intermediate counts are not uncommon in either species.

Fish that don't clearly "fit the pattern" will almost certainly have to be examined in a laboratory to determine their identity, a matter that is of real concern only if a large and possibly record-setting specimen is caught. Because the problem of identification was only very recently diagnosed, at present very few scientists are qualified to make a positive identification on an unusual specimen.

Size.   Sea-run Dolly Vardens generally range from 1 to 3 pounds, and freshwater specimens seldom weigh more than 8 pounds. The all-tackle world record is an 19-pound, 4-ounce Alaskan fish. Bull trout are larger growing than Dollies, although the typical fish weighs between 2 and 5 pounds. The all-tackle world record is a 32-pounder that was $40^{1}/_{2}$ inches long and was caught in Lake Pend Orielle, Idaho, in 1949.

Distribution.   Varden occur from the Sea of Japan, throughout the Kuril Islands to Russia's Kamchatka Peninsula, throughout the Aleutian Islands, and around Alaska and the Yukon Territory to the Northwest Territory, as well as in the northwestern United States. In North America, they are especially abundant in Alaska and parts of British Columbia.

The bull trout is endemic to the Pacific Northwest and inhabits most of the significant drainages on both sides of the Continental Divide. It seems to prefer large, cold rivers and lakes draining high mountainous areas, and tends to frequent

D

D

the bottoms of deep pools. It has been recorded in northern California, Oregon, Washington, northern Nevada, Idaho, western Montana, Alberta, and British Columbia.

Habitat/Life history. Bull trout and Dolly Varden prefer deep pools of cold rivers, lakes, and reservoirs. Streams with abundant cover (cut banks, root wads, and other woody debris) and clean gravel and cobble beds provide the best habitat. Their favored summer water temperature is generally less than 55°F, but they nevertheless tolerate temperatures less than 40°F. Spawning during fall usually starts when water temperatures drop to the mid- to low 40s. Cold, clear water is required for successful reproduction.

Bull trout and Dolly Varden have complex but similar life histories. Anadromous (seagoing) and migratory resident populations (for example, lake-dwelling stocks and main-stem rearing stocks) often journey long distances in summer and fall to spawn, migrating to the small headwater streams where they hatched. Mature adults with these characteristics are generally four to seven years old and 18 to 22 inches in length when they make their first spawning run, although they may be older in some populations.

The adults can undergo some impressive journeys on their spawning runs. Fish in Washington's Skagit River system may travel more than 115 miles from the river mouth and ascend to an elevation of more than 3,000 feet. The spawning area may be upstream of areas used by other anadromous species.

Logjams, cascades, and falls that are barriers to the chinook's brute strength and the steelhead's acrobatic abilities may be only minor obstacles to the cunning and guile of Dolly Varden and bull trout. Although these charr can jump remarkably well for fish their size, as much as 7 or 8 vertical feet under good conditions, they are just as likely to maneuver around a difficult spot. At a potential barrier, they sometimes seem to be actively seeking alternative ways around it.

Bull trout and Dolly Varden use headwater areas that typically are in pristine environments. Spawning begins in late August, peaks in September and October, and ends in November. Fish in a given stream spawn over a short period of time, two weeks or less, making redds in clean gravel.

Almost immediately after spawning, adults begin to work their way back to the main-stem rivers, lakes, or reservoirs to overwinter. Some of these fish stay put, others move on to saltwater in the spring, evidently not wandering far. Some survive the perils of the river to spawn a second or even a third time. Kelts (spawned-out fish) feed aggressively to recover from the stress of spawning. In parts of their range where steelhead are also present, this also happens to be when many anglers are searching the river for winter steelhead. Steelhead anglers must learn how to identify these charr and safely release them.

Newly hatched fish emerge from the gravel the following spring. Those that migrate down to the main rivers, reservoirs, and saltwater normally leave the headwater areas as two-year-olds. But further complicating the picture are resident stream populations that exhibit limited movements, living their entire lives in the same stretch of headwater stream. These fish may not mature until they are age 7 to 8, and rarely exceed 14 inches in length. Biologists have observed these local residents spawning side by side with their much larger anadromous kin.

Food. Bull trout and Dolly Varden are opportunistic feeders, eating aquatic insects, shrimp, snails, leeches, fish eggs, and fish.

Angling. Both species are fairly easy to catch and do not display the leaping tendencies of more admired salmonids like arctic charr or steelhead (see). Anglers cast spoons, spinners, and flies to Dollies and bull trout in river pools. Some troll deep in lakes, as they do for arctic charr and various salmon.

DOLPHIN, COMMON   *Coryphaena hippurus.*

Other names—dolphinfish, common dolphinfish, mahimahi, mahi mahi, dorado; Chinese: *fei niau fu, ngau tau yue;* French: *coryphéne commune;* Italian: *lampuga;* Japanese: *shiira, toohyaku;* Portuguese: *doirado, dourado;* Spanish: *dorado, dorado común, lampuga.*

The common dolphin is the larger of the two extremely similar species in the family Coryphaenidae, both of which are cosmopolitan in warm seas. This fish is one of the top offshore gamefish among anglers, as it is an excellent, hard-fighting species that puts on an acrobatic show once hooked. It routinely leaps or tail-walks over the surface, darting first in one direction, then another. This fish is a superb light-tackle quarry, although it is frequently caught on heavier gear meant for larger offshore species.

The flesh of the common dolphin is considered gourmet fare, and it is prepared in a variety of ways. It is usually presented in fish markets and restaurants under its Hawaiian name, *mahimahi.* The common dolphin is often referred to as the "dolphinfish," to distinguish it from the so-called dolphin of the porpoise family, which is an unrelated mammal and not sought by anglers.

Identification. The body is slender and streamlined, tapering sharply from head to tail. Large males, called bulls, have high, vertical foreheads, whereas the females' foreheads are rounded. The anal fin has 25 to 31 soft rays and is long, stretching over half of the length of the body. The dorsal fin has 55 to 66 soft rays. Its caudal fin is deeply forked, there are no spines in any of the fins, and the mouth has bands of fine teeth.

Its coloring is variable and defies an accurate, simple description. Generally, when the fish is alive in the water, the common dolphin is a rich iridescent blue or blue green dorsally; gold, bluish gold, or silvery gold on the lower flanks; and silvery white

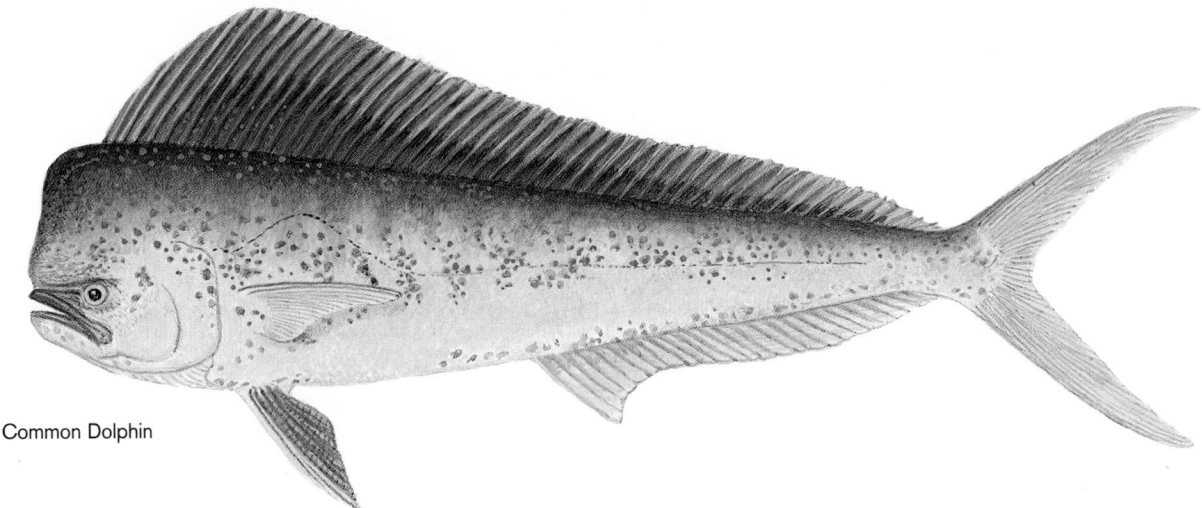

Common Dolphin

or yellow on the belly. The sides are sprinkled with a mixture of dark and light spots, ranging from black or blue to golden. The dorsal fin is a rich blue, and the anal fin is golden or silvery. The other fins are generally golden yellow, edged with blue. Dark vertical bands sometimes appear when the fish is attacking prey. The color description of dolphin is difficult because the fish undergoes sudden changes in color, which occur in an instant, often when it is excited.

When removed from the water, however, the colors fluctuate between blue, green, and yellow; the brilliant colors apparent when in the water fade quickly. After death, the fish usually turns a uniform yellow or silvery gray.

The common dolphin is so distinctive in body color and shape that it cannot be mistaken for any other fish. The pompano dolphin (see: dolphin, pompano) is the only related species and is considerably smaller and lacks a high forehead. Female and young dolphin are often confused with pompano dolphin.

Size/Age. The average size is 5 to 15 pounds, although larger catches up to 50 pounds are not uncommon. The all-tackle world record is an 87-pounder caught in Costa Rica in 1976, and it has been rumored that fish up to 100 pounds have been caught by commercial longliners. The maximum length is reportedly 82 inches.

Dolphin are fast growing and short lived. Few common dolphin live longer than four years, and most live just three years. Males grow larger than females and are capable of growing to 60 pounds in just two years, although this rate of growth would be exceptional and the result of consistently favorable warm temperatures and abundant food.

Distribution. The common dolphin is found worldwide in tropical and subtropical waters of the Atlantic, Indian, and Pacific Oceans. The greatest concentrations are believed to be in the Indian Ocean and the western Pacific. In the western Atlantic, it occurs in areas influenced by the warm waters of the Gulf Stream, and has been caught as far north as Prince Edward Island and as far south as Río de Janeiro; in the eastern Atlantic it is known from the Canary Islands to Angola. In the eastern Pacific, it ranges from Peru to Oregon.

Habitat. Common dolphin are a warmwater pelagic fish, occurring in the open ocean and usually found close to the surface, although in waters of great depth. They sometimes inhabit coastal waters and occasionally areas near piers, but in the open ocean they often concentrate around floating objects, especially buoys, driftwood, and seaweed lines or clusters. The young commonly frequent warm nearshore waters in sargassum beds or other flotsam. In developing countries, commercial fishermen may place floating bundles of bamboo reeds, cork planks, and the like in the water to concentrate dolphin before seining or gillnetting commences.

Life history/Behavior. The common dolphin is a prolific spawner and grows rapidly, meaning

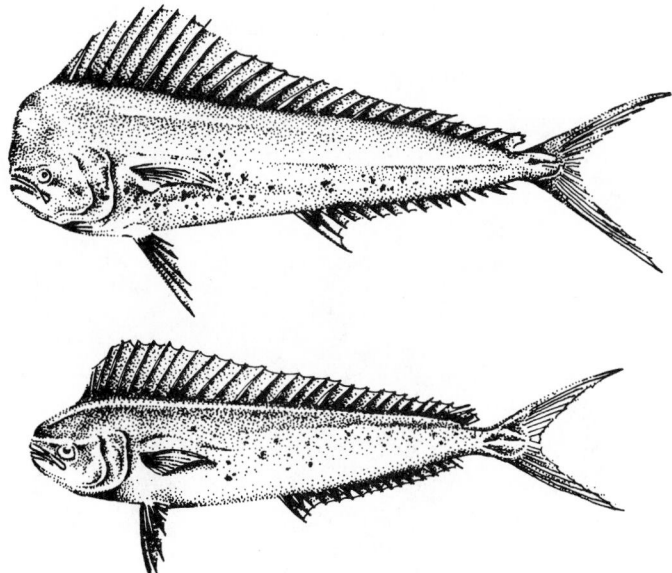

Although both male (top) and female (bottom) common dolphin have a streamlined, tapered body, the male, or bull, is distinguished by a high, vertical forehead.

that it must by nature be an eating machine. Spawning season begins primarily in spring or early summer and lasts several months in warmer waters. Dolphin reach sexual maturity in the first year of life and produce a large volume of eggs.

Dolphin are a schooling fish and often congregate in large numbers, sometimes in the thousands. They are almost always between the surface and 100-foot depths, but anglers encounter them on or just under the surface. They are probably the most surface oriented of all big-game fish. This characteristic, as well as their propensity for feeding by sight and thus primarily foraging in daylight, helps endear them to anglers. Offshore enthusiasts frequently encounter packs of dolphin and are able to elicit strikes from several fish in quick order.

These fish are evidently also migratory. It is believed that dolphin in both hemispheres migrate away from the equator in the spring and summer and toward the equator in fall and winter.

Food.   Common dolphin are extremely fast swimmers and feed aggressively in pairs, small packs, and schools, extensively consuming whatever forage fish are most abundant. Flyingfish and squid are prominent food in areas where these fish exist, and small fish and crustaceans around floating sargassum weed are commonly part of their diet, especially among smaller dolphin.

Angling.   Dolphin inhabit blue-water environs and, although they roam the unobstructed near-surface waters of the open ocean, are commonly found around objects. Floating debris, buoys, weeds, and even boats can attract and hold these fish, and such objects are searched by anglers specifically looking for dolphin.

Dolphin up to 8 or so pounds, which are called chicken or peanut dolphin, are especially found around floating debris, which offers both protection and feeding opportunity. Fish from 8 to 20 pounds or so gather in schools, often segregated by size and/or sex, and they may also be found around debris, especially extensive lines of weeds and tidal

rips. Larger dolphin, called slammers by many charter boat captains, are more likely to travel in small packs, usually with one or two bulls and a few cows. These fish are more likely to be ocean roamers rather than object ambushers. They are consequently harder to deliberately target.

Most dolphin are located by trolling, usually by anglers fishing for other blue-water species, primarily marlin and sailfish. Rigged trolling baits on large hooks are usually used, and flyingfish, squid, mullet, and balao are the common offerings. Offshore trolling plugs and feathers are popular as well. Because dolphin are very fast swimmers, a quick trolling speed is optimal. Primarily because it is necessary for larger quarry, heavy big-game tackle is the norm. Although big dolphin fight well even on this tackle, anglers will enjoy the fight much better when pursuing these fish on light big-game outfits or spinning or flycasting equipment.

Trollers often keep spinning and fly tackle handy in case they encounter a school of dolphin while trolling. When this happens, they stop and cast to the fish, using surface or diving plugs, bucktail jigs, spoons, and streamer flies. Live baits are also used. Dolphin run hard and leap often and rather spectacularly, sometimes tail-walking across the surface. This fight is especially enjoyable when a fish has been caught on light tackle and played from a drifting boat. A 7-foot spinning rod and 6- to 12-pound line is ideal, as most of these fish don't weigh more than 20 pounds. The strike, when casting or trolling, is usually savage.

Sometimes anglers keep a hooked dolphin on the line near the boat to encourage a group to stay around, and this may result in catching several or all of the fish out of a group. To keep the fish in the vicinity, some anglers chum once they've found a school, or they use sand chum balls to attract deeper fish to hooked baits.

In some areas, anglers deliberately fishing for dolphin, and casting to them either with live natural baits or lures or flies, cruise offshore areas as the captain searches the waters from the tower and heads toward debris, observed schools, birds, and the like. When the boat gets in casting range of observed fish, the captain instructs the mate and anglers as to their position. Unhooked live baits are thrown to tease the fish close to the boat, and then hooked baits, lures, or flies are cast to the school of dolphin as individuals come close and weave in and out. It is not uncommon for several anglers to hook up at the same time, causing an epic melee of jumping fish, crossed lines, and scrambling anglers.

Not all fishing for dolphins is fast and easy. Sometimes, the friskiest live pilchards, mullet, menhaden, and others don't do the job, and it's necessary to switch to the type of fish the dolphin are preying on around the weedlines. Or, it may be necessary to change tactics entirely, offering other lures or other types and colors of lures, or fishing deeper. **See: Big-Game Fishing; Offshore Fishing.**

A big bull dolphin caught offshore from Islamorada, Florida.

Pompano Dolphin

DOLPHIN, POMPANO *Coryphaena equiselis.*
Other names—mahimahi, blue dolphin, small dolphin, dolphinfish, pompano dolphinfish; French: *coryphéne dauphin;* Japanese: *ebisu-shiira;* Portuguese: *dourado;* Spanish: *dorado.*

The pompano dolphin is the smaller of the two Coryphaenidae family species and is often confused with the females and young of its larger relative the common dolphin *(C. hippurus; see: dolphin, common).* Like its relative, it is caught commercially and by anglers, and it is an excellent food fish. The pompano dolphin is usually presented in fish markets and restaurants under its Hawaiian name *mahimahi.* This species, and its relative, are often referred to as "dolphinfish" to distinguish them from the so-called dolphin of the porpoise family, which is an unrelated mammal and not sought by anglers.

Identification. This species is almost identical to the common dolphin in coloring and general shape, although it has greater body depth behind the head than the common dolphin, and a squarish rather than rounded tooth patch on the tongue. There are fewer dorsal rays on the pompano dolphin—48 to 55 versus the common dolphin's 55 to 65.

Size. The average size is 20 to 24 inches and 4 to 5 pounds, although it reportedly grows to 50 inches.

Distribution/Habitat. The pompano dolphin is found worldwide in tropical seas; in the United States it is most commonly encountered in Hawaii. The pompano dolphin reportedly prefers surface temperatures above 75°F. It is considered more oceanic than the common dolphin but may enter coastal waters.

Life history/Behavior. Little is known of the life history of the pompano dolphin, other than that it is a schooling tropical water species, prone to near-surface feeding and attracted to objects. This fish is similar to common dolphin in most behavioral respects.

Food. The pompano dolphin's diet consists of small fish and squid.

Angling. See: *Dolphin, Common; Offshore Fishing.*

DOODLESOCKING
Doodlesocking, also called yo-yoing, is the activity of repeatedly raising and lowering a jig or worm in an opening made in heavy cover. Using a pole or paddle, the angler makes a small clearing in a clump of thick moss, milfoil, or other grass and drops in a jig or worm to fish for largemouth bass, crappie, and/or panfish.

DORADO
(1) The Spanish word for "dolphin" *(see: dolphin, common).*

(2) *Salminus maxillosus.*
Other names—South American salmon; Portuguese: *dourado;* Spanish: *dorado, dourado, picudo.*

A member of the Characidae family and a relative of the piranha and the tigerfish, the dorado is one of the finest freshwater gamefish, yet it is little known to most anglers. This is due in part to its limited mid–South American range. There are reportedly four species of fish within the genus *Salminus,* but information about the other species is scant, and the taxonomic classification of all four is uncertain. They are believed to be among the most primitive of characins. A related "salmon" of the genus *Catabasis* has been identified from a specimen captured in 1900 but is believed extinct. Smaller dorado may be confused in Brazil with a similar-looking species, piraputanga *(Brycon orbygnianus),* a fish that grows to 3 kilograms.

Large and strong, the dorado is an aggressive fish known for hard strikes, frequent aerial displays, and bulldog tenacity, but its population has suffered through habitat alteration. It has long been an important food fish within its native range, where it is held in great esteem; dorado festivals have been held in various river communities, especially in northern Argentina, in celebration of this species.

Identification. In overall body shape, the dorado somewhat resembles a salmon, although it is unrelated. The fins have the same position and shape as those of salmon. There is an adipose fin after the

D

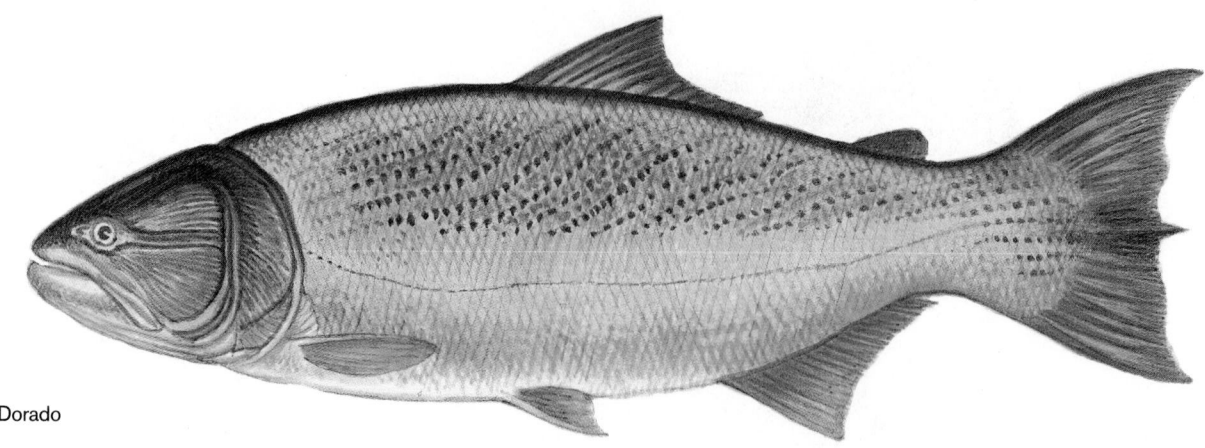

Dorado

dorsal fin, an axillary process, and the tail is some-what scalloped. The head is tapered and streamlined, predominantly gold with bluish or dark highlights. The powerful lower jaw, which is stout and strong, contains a double row of teeth, the outer row consisting of strong canines. True to the meaning of its name (golden), the dorado has a golden body, with blue, orange, and yellow overtones or highlights, and a dark splotch or strip in the center of the tail. The fish change colors, turning bright golden with a dark back in clear waters when they spawn in swamps, or into a hazy gold with a greenish back when in tea-colored waters. In all cases their fins are orange red.

Size.   The all-tackle world record for dorado is 51 pounds, 5 ounces. Dorado of 60 to 75 pounds and up to 40 inches in length have been reported by anglers in the past. A dorado in excess of 30 pounds is presently an exceptional fish, and fewer such specimens have been reported in recent years.

Distribution.   Found solely in South America, the dorado occurs in Brazil, Paraguay, Uruguay, and Argentina, essentially in connected watersheds that flow southward through these countries. Small specimens have been reported by anglers in the Magdalena River system of Colombia, but modern evidence of dorado there has been lacking, and species identification remains unclear.

The native range of dorado has been the Plate River basin, largely made up of the Paraná and Paraguay Rivers and their many tributaries. The main course of the Paraná from southeastern Brazil to Argentina has been impounded for hydroelectric purposes in several places, which has altered native fish species, including dorado.

The native range also includes the São Francisco River basin of southern and eastern Brazil; this system has many tributaries, originates and stays within Brazil, is clear in the headwaters but sediment laden downstream, and also has a number of hydro-electric impoundments.

Neither the Plate nor the São Francisco systems flow into the Amazon River. Dorado have been widely reported from the Amazon and Orinoco basins, but this has not been observed in recent times, and the capture of one from either of these watersheds would be rare.

Habitat.   The dorado is primarily a fish of rivers and fast-moving runs. It also occurs in slower tributary waters and in backwater swamps, although larger dorado do not move into tributaries until spawning time. The dorado is often present in groups and moves frequently in search of food; whether this is a migration or not is uncertain, although the dorado do migrate into spawning tributaries. In spite of a similarity in behavior to salmon, the dorado is not an anadromous species and are seldom found in the brackish waters of the Río de la Plata estuary between Argentina and Uruguay.

Food and feeding habits.   Dorado feed on other fish and are aggressive predators. Small sábalo, a schooling species, is a significant food item, and dorado follow this bait. They are likely to occur where a quick ambush is possible, including along banks, but especially in the swift runs of rivers and ahead of rocks and other structures.

Angling.   Several characteristics of dorado fishing especially endear them to the relatively small number of anglers who have caught this species. The first is that they strike with exceptional speed and savagery. Another is that they not only fight long and with great vigor (often running wildly downstream), but they also repeatedly leap high out of the water, perhaps 8 to 10 times during a battle, and thrash wildly in an effort to throw the hook. Their strength also applies to the viselike gripping power of their jaws, which can crush some lures and mangle hooks.

Big spoons, spinners, and swimming or diving plugs—lures normally associated with striped bass and muskie, and equipped with the best hooks and hardware—are the artificials of choice, especially for large specimens. Trolling is the most common method of fishing in many rivers, usually running at fast speeds, but dorado are also caught by anglers casting lures and drifting with live baits. Most fish are taken on or near the bottom, especially in large rivers. Medium- and heavy-duty baitcasting tackle is the best overall equipment for this species, using lines from 14 to 25 pounds. Fly fishing and lighter tackle are possible in certain situations, especially in smaller rivers, although it is usually important to still use lures or flies with a large body size.

Clear-water environments are best for the largely sight-feeding dorado; silted and roiled waters do not produce as well. Fluctuating water levels and changed water conditions, therefore, can adversely affect success. A heavy rainfall can hurt the fishing, and variable increased releases from upstream reservoirs can also be detrimental. If silt isn't the problem, then scattered baitfish due to increased water area is likely to also disperse the dorado.

In major rivers, dorado are particularly found near sandbars and rocks. They prefer fast water and strong current. Sometimes a school will chase baitfish into the air.
See: Argentina; Paraguay.

DORSAL FIN
A median fin along the back, which is supported by rays. There may be two or more dorsal fins, in which case they are numbered with the fin closest to the head called the first dorsal fin.
See: Anatomy; Fish.

DOUBLE
(1) Two anglers who simultaneously each hook a fish, a feat not uncommon when schools of certain species are encountered or when there is a lot of action in a specific place. In some cases, a triple is possible.

(2) Two fish simultaneously caught on one lure. This occurs when the fish are impaled on the front and rear hooks, respectively, of a given lure, as a result either of both attacking the lures simultaneously or of one trying to take it from the other. This kind of double usually occurs only with very aggressive fish; it is more likely with largemouth bass, smallmouth bass, and peacock bass than with such species as trout or salmon.

DOUBLE ENDER
A canoe with a pointed bow and stern. Double enders are easier to paddle than square stern canoes, which have a square stern for the attachment of a small motor.
See: Canoe.

DOUBLE-FOOT GUIDE
A guide with upper and lower attachment points to the blank of a fishing rod. A double-foot guide is advantageous for fish fighting, and is primarily found on baitcasting and conventional rods, where it is placed on the top of the rod.
See: Rod, Fishing.

DOUBLE HAUL
An element of flycasting in which the line is accelerated on backward and forward casts for better control or greater distance.
See: Flycasting Tackle.

DOUBLE HOOK
A hook with two points.
See: Hook.

DOUBLE LINE
The terminal section of a fishing line that is doubled for extra strength and abrasion resistance. A double line is most commonly used in saltwater by big-game anglers fishing for very large and strong species, but it may be used in any circumstance where the target fish are large compared with the lighter line being used and/or where the conditions (especially an abrasive bottom or fish with sharp teeth or abrasive skin) dictate having the extra insurance that a double length of line can provide.

The doubled section is made from the actual fishing line that comes off the reel, and a Bimini Twist or Spider Hitch Knot is used to convert a certain length from one strand into two strands of equal length. Although a double line may be any desired length, for practical reasons it must be short enough to stay off the reel when used in casting applications, yet not so long for trolling or bottom fishing that it affects the action of the lure or bait. To qualify for world records, international standards established by the International Game Fish Association (IGFA) mandate that a double line in freshwater can be no longer than 6 feet for any type of tackle; in saltwater it can be no longer than 15 feet when used with up to 10-kilogram tackle, and no longer than 30 feet when used with tackle over 10 kilograms. In some circumstances, a leader may be attached to the doubled line; for records, the length of this leader must also conform to certain length standards.
See: Knots, Fishing; Line.

DOUBLE TAPER LINE
A fly line that has the same taper at both ends and a section of level line in the middle.
See: Flycasting Tackle.

DOUGH BALL
A popular fishing bait for carp (see) and sometimes catfish (see), these homemade concoctions are prepared from cornmeal, flour, syrup, anise oil, vanilla extract, etc., and rolled into a ball. Carp devotees prepare various flavored dough balls, and many recipes exist for their preparation. For carp, some sweet and flavorful product is almost always an ingredient; for catfish, the concoctions might be

sweet, or might be rather vile. Their purpose is to produce a lot of scent and attract roaming fish, and they are fished both on single and treble hooks, although single hooks in general are better.

DOURADA

A South American catfish, also known as golden catfish.
See: Catfish.

DOWNRIGGER

A downrigger is a device that is used primarily for trolling (and sometimes for deep fishing with live or dead bait) and that offers controlled depth presentation of a lure, bait, or fly. This device originated on the Great Lakes for trout and salmon fishing, and then spread inland for muskies, stripers, and walleye, and later to saltwater.

Downriggers are among the best gear ever to have hit the trolling scene. They've revolutionized deep trolling since the early 1960s by making it more sporting and fruitful. In the pre-downrigger age, deep trolling consisted of assorted methods that suffered from imprecise depth control—anglers often were unsure exactly how deep they were fishing—or the use of extremely long lines and tackle heavy enough to tow a submarine. Until the creation of downriggers, getting deep nearly always required deep trollers to use lead weights, weighted lines, or diving planers, all of which were fastened directly to the fishing line.

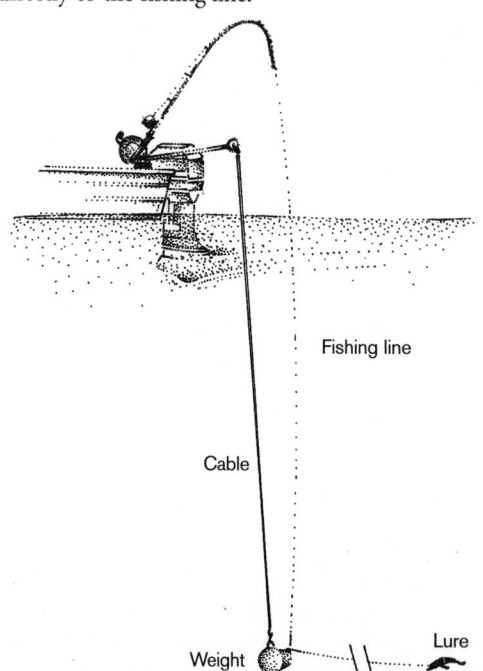

Fishing line

Cable

Weight   Lure

The general concept of fishing with a downrigger is very simple. Fishing line is attached via a release clip (not shown) to a weight, which in turn is attached to a heavy cable. When a fish takes the lure that is on the fishing line, the line is released by the clip.

Downriggers take the burden of getting a line to a specific depth away from the fishing line and put it on an accessory product, meaning that they can be used with light and ultralight tackle that tests angling skills and provides extra enjoyment.

A downrigger is not a complicated device. Components include a reel, cranking handle with clutch, boom, cable, and pulley. A heavy lead weight attaches to the end of the downrigger cable, and a line-release mechanism is located on or near the weight or at any other place along the cable.

A lure attached to your fishing line is placed in the water and set at whatever distance you want it to run behind your boat. The fishing line is placed in the release attached to the downrigger cable. The downrigger weight is then lowered to the depth you want to fish. When a fish strikes the lure, the fishing line pops out of the release and the fish is played on your fishing line, unencumbered by a heavy weight or strong cable.

Downriggers are made in manual and electric models. Manual downriggers include small versions that clamp onto the transom or gunwale, or fit into the oarlock; larger versions can be mounted permanently. Some are available in either right- or left-crank versions. Manual downriggers are always hand-cranked up; some older manual models are cranked down, too, though for most you can release clutch tension to lower the weight. Many small-boat owners use manual downriggers because they are less costly.

Electric downriggers are raised and lowered by flicking a switch. They're generally made for permanent and sturdy mounting locations. Electrics are considerably more expensive than manual downriggers and require power hookups, often through an auxiliary battery. Because they can be easily retrieved through an automatic "up" switch, electric downriggers are invariably preferred by busy veteran trollers.

The length of the boom, or arm, which carries the cable from the spool to a pulley, can vary from 1 foot to 8 feet, depending on the boom's location on the boat and the need to spread out weights over the greatest possible horizontal range of water. The length of the boom also depends on the size of your boat and your ability to move freely around in it to rig lines and set weights. The length of the boom on some downriggers can be changed, and some allow an extension to be bolted on.

As a rule, as boat size increases and the vertical distance from gunwale to water surface increases, the length of the downrigger arm increases. On 12- to 17-foot craft, it is most common to use just two short-armed downriggers. On large boats, such as those with an 8- to 10-foot beam, as many as four 2- or 3-foot-boom downriggers may be spaced equally across the transom, with two longer-boomed downriggers on the gunwales.

In boats with adequate room, the arms can be swiveled in to retrieve the weight or line release and

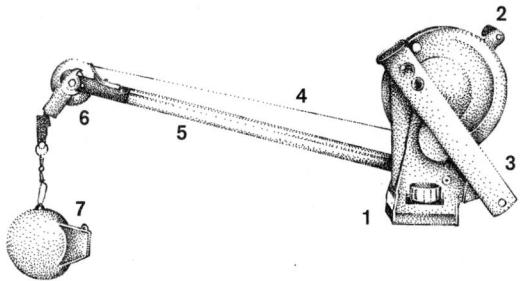

Components of a manual downrigger are: base (1), handle (2), rod holder (3), cable (4), boom (5), pulley (6), and weight (7). Not shown but also near the handle is a counter that indicates the depth of the weight by virtue of the amount of cable in the water.

to set the fishing line in the release. Preferably, the cable can be pulled inward via a free-sliding pulley on the cable that is attached to a lanyard.

At the outer end of a downrigger boom is a pulley that guides the cable downward to the water. This pulley should pivot from side to side because the cable usually extends back rather than down when the boat is moving forward. Some type of cable guard should be mounted on the pulley to prevent the cable from jumping off. Some downriggers sport a hook on the underside of the spool frame, which is convenient for hanging the downrigger weight or a just a snap at the end of the cable, which is useful for in-transit storage. If you are moving from place to place and have the weight stored this way, you can simply unhook it and drop it in the water instead of having to reattach the weight to the snap.

Downriggers utilize 150- to 200-pound strength braided steel cable that does not stretch; the depth on the line counter will conform exactly to the length of cable let out. Spools are filled with approximately 200 feet of cable, though more can be used provided it is unspliced. Cable has a tendency to coil or kink and can be weakened when it does. It can also be weakened in places where line releases have been set repeatedly or where the cable has been nicked because of collision with some object.

It's a good idea to check the cable periodically for signs of fraying or crimping and to cut off the affected length so that you don't lose a downrigger weight and terminal hardware. Be sure to carry tools in your boat or tackle box to remake connections. Keep a supply of connector sleeves, snubbers, large (No. 10) stainless steel snap swivels, and U-shaped cable supports with you. A pair of crimping pliers will help secure the sleeves tightly.

If you lose a weight and terminal hardware and don't have replacement materials, you can still jury-rig an arrangement by running the cable through a heavy-duty snap swivel (or directly to the weight if you don't have a snap; however, you can't take the weight off readily when you do this) and tying a series of jam knots in the cable. Test the holding

strength of this arrangement, be careful not to hang the weight on bottom, and re-rig properly at the first opportunity. To minimize fraying and stress at the end of the cable, you can use a rubber snubber that fits over the wire.

Downriggers have a line counter to measure the length of cable that comes off the spool. It's important to account for the length of cable between the pulley and the surface of the water; the counter should read zero when the weight is just below the water surface. If you don't adjust it in this fashion, the weight will run 1 to 3 feet shallower than the counter shows.

The size of lead weight used in downrigging varies, although 10- to 12-pound weights are the norm. Heavy weights are needed to keep the cable directly below the boat, or as close to it as possible, for precise depth determination. This is especially important when you're using a wide-angle sonar transducer (so you can see the weights on your screen or gauge), when there is current, and when you are trolling fast. Heavy weights are also necessary for fishing in very deep water (50 feet or more). In relatively shallow water (20 feet or more), in places where there is no current, and when you are trolling slowly, you can use a 7- or 8-pound weight. A 2-pound weight is used on some small downriggers, but it can be difficult to calculate the actual running depth of a light weight.

Weights are often referred to as cannonballs because the earliest models, and many current ones, are shaped like a round ball. A round ball with a stabilizing fin on the back is the most popular shape, although there are various configurations. Weights shaped like a fish or a torpedo are fairly popular; a favorite with some anglers is a "pancake" weight with a slender head and a broad fin.

Some weights have a thick rubber or vinyl coating. Coated weights don't mar your boat when they hit the side or when they're dropped on the gunwale

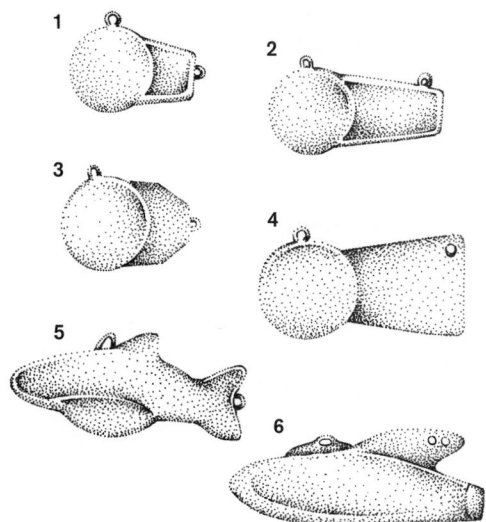

Common styles of downrigger weights include: cannonballs (1, 2, and 3), pancake (4), fish (5), and torpedo (6).

or deck, and they're easy to handle. They are no more efficient than uncoated weights, however, although their coloring lasts indefinitely; painted lead weights lose their color over time. Manufacturer-supplied weights are available in white, black, chartreuse, green, orange, and red. Fish are often attracted to the trolled downrigger weight, possibly because of the color but most likely because of the vibration.

Rod holders *(see)* are critical to downrigging, and some downriggers come with integral holders or can be fitted with them as accessories. Mount one or two rod holders on the downrigger itself or locate them nearby. Place rod holders strategically and allow for more holders than you expect to need when fishing—the extra holders come in handy to store rods out of the way when landing fish, rigging, running, and so forth.

Line release. A line release mechanism is also critical to the downrigging system and presents a lot of room for experimentation, as well as problems. The line release must free the fishing line when a fish strikes or when the angler chooses to detach the line in order to retrieve it (otherwise, the weight must be brought in to manually release the line).

Line releases can be attached to the weight, to the downrigger cable at the weight, and to the cable at any location above the weight. In all line releases, the fishing line is clamped into it under variable pressure. Some feature a trigger that pops open and that can be set to release under greater or lesser tension. Some feature spring-loaded jaws capped with rubber pads; how far into the pads you set the fishing line determines the tension.

If the line has been placed properly, when a fish strikes, the line immediately pulls free of the release, which remains attached to the weight or cable. To free a fishing line from the boat, take the rod out of its holder, point the rod tip toward the water, and reel up slack; then pop the rod tip upward as if

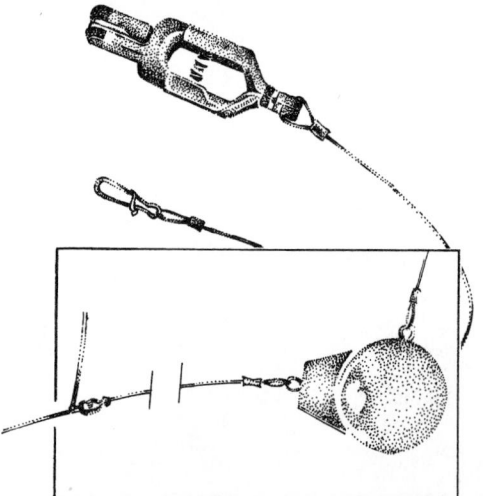

Depicted is a spring-tension release attached to a downrigger weight by a short cable (inset); fishing line is placed inside the forward pad of the release.

setting the hook. If this procedure doesn't free the fishing line, it was not properly set in the release or the tension on the release was set too high.

Easily adjustable tension settings are important in line releases, and setting the right tension is critical for catching fish. Most fish that take a lure trolled behind a downrigger weight impale themselves with the hook(s) of that lure when they strike it and pull the fishing line out of the release. A release set too loosely will provide little resistance to help set the hook; if it is set too tight, a small fish may strike the lure and not pop the line out of the release, causing the fish to be dragged for some distance before the problem is discovered. Also, a tight release often cannot be freed by an angler while in the boat when the angler wants to change lures.

There is a proper middle ground that varies, depending upon the strength of the fishing line used and the type of lure trolled. When using light line, you have to set release tension fairly light so that the line isn't broken if a big fish strikes the lure. When using lures that are heavy or that create a lot of resistance when pulled through the water, such as large deep-diving plugs or a dodger *(see)*, you must set the release tension high enough that the fishing line stays in the release and doesn't pop out without a fish striking, especially in rough water.

If you frequently lose fish, either because the hooks pull out or the fish strike the lure and pop the release but fail to get hooked, try tightening the tension on the release and shortening the length of line between the lure and the release. Missed strikes can occur when fish are slapping at the lure or when the release is set too light.

If you want to get technical, conduct the following experiment on dry land: Take a top-quality spring scale and attach it to the end of a fishing line. Set the line in your release, using a tension setting that you judge to be just right. Have someone watch the release and holler at the moment the line snaps out of the release. Watch the scale as you pull on the line to see the weight indicated at the moment your companion hollers. By doing this, you'll get a relative idea of how much pressure it takes to free the release at your chosen setting. Conduct the same experiment with different tension settings, with different lengths of fishing line between the scale and releases, and with different strengths of line. Although this is not quite the same as using line in the water (because stretch and breaking strength of wet line differ), it is a reasonable comparison and may lead you to a better understanding of the tension settings that increase your strike-to-hook ratio.

For some releases, you should twist the fishing line before putting it into the release. Twisting is necessary because the line will slip freely through the release if it is merely snapped into place. If this happens, (1) the lure might swim up to the weight and stay right behind the weight when you set the weight down; (2) a fish may not have enough resistance at the release to trip it properly, which could mean you'll lose the fish; and (3) you can't trip the release from above because the line might simply slide through the release. To avoid these problems, take the fishing line and make six or seven twists with it after the lure has been set back, and then insert the twisted line or the loop into the release. Although a few anglers complain that twisting weakens fishing line, this practice is generally effective.

Some anglers don't use commercial releases at all but employ rubber bands for this purpose. No. 14 or 16 rubber bands (available in quantity at office supply stores) are preferred by many. These are attached to fishing line via a half hitch and then connected to a large snap affixed to the downrigger weight.

When a fish strikes a line that is attached to a rubber-band release, it must stretch the rubber band to its breaking point to disconnect the fishing line and downrigger cable. Occasionally you'll catch a fish that is small and can't break the band, and the fish will be inadvertently trolled for a long time. Sometimes it will be hard to snap the rubber band from above to retrieve the lure; at other times you'll get broken pieces of rubber band wrapped in your fishing reel, which can be messy when they melt or adhere to the line. Rubber bands left in the sun will lose their strength. A drawback to using even fresh rubber bands is that they may have inconsistent breaking strength.

Setting lines. To use a downrigger and set out a trolled line, begin by opening the bail or pushing the freespool button on the reel and letting the lure out to whatever distance you think it should be swimming behind the downrigger weight. Keep the reel in freespool—with the clicker on if it's a level-wind reel—and either loosen the drag or keep the bail open with a spinning reel. Bring the downrigger weight and line release close to the boat so that you can reach them without stretching far over-board. Grab the fishing line at the top of the rod and place it in the release, twisting the line first if necessary. Set the weight back overboard or swing the boom arm back to its outboard position so that the weight can be lowered. Take the rod in one hand, and make sure that the line is not fouled at the tip and that it will freely come off the reel spool. Use your other hand to lower the weight, either by depressing the down switch on an electric downrigger, by releasing clutch tension lightly, or by back reeling a manual downrigger. Stop the weight when it reaches the depth you want, as indicated on the line counter. Set the rod in a holder, and reel up slack so that the rod tip is bowed in a sharp C position.

Other than changing the length of line between release and lure or altering the depth to fish, you will go through this same procedure every time you set out a lure with a downrigger.

Because you lose touch with how your lures are working once you have lowered them on a

An angler attaches fishing line to a release on the downrigger weight.

downrigger weight, it's important to put them in the water and watch them swim before you set them out and before you attach the line to the downrigger release. Also, don't cast a lure out from the boat—it may become fouled. Place the lure in the water next to the boat so that you know it's working right, and then strip out the correct length of line. If there is a lot of surface debris, don't let the lure snag on debris before it is lowered with the weight.

Acquire the habit of scanning your downrigger rods and watching for signs of action; you'll often see a rod straighten the moment a fish strikes and pulls the line out of the release. When this happens, you should get to the rod fast to set the hook and play the fish. You'll also know when a fish has hit the lure but hasn't been hooked by noting how the rod suddenly dips without springing up. If the rod tip surges, it may be an indication that there is a small fish (baitfish or gamefish) on, even though the release hasn't tripped.

See: Downrigger Fishing; Trolling.

DOWNRIGGER FISHING

Fishing with downriggers is all about making a controlled presentation, whether in deep water, as is usually the case, or in shallow water. With downriggers, you can be versatile enough to cover a broad range of trolling situations, including river fishing, drifting, and live-bait fishing. Proper employment of downriggers begins with their installation on a boat.

Downrigger Placement

Downriggers are primarily located on and across the transom, or near the transom on the gunwales. Transom-mounted downriggers extend straight back, perpendicular to the stern. The booms should be long enough to clear any trim tabs or swim plat-form and to enable the cable to clear the propeller (especially for an auxiliary outboard) when seas are

With two lines attached to the downrigger behind him, a troller watches his sonar to avoid running the weight too deep.

rough or when tight turns are made. A four-downrigger setup would have one unit on each corner, perpendicular to the gunwale, and one on each side of the motor, facing aft, to give a good horizontal spread to the weights and trolling lines. A six-downrigger setup would have a unit on each gunwale a few feet ahead of the stern, perpendicular to the gunwale, and four properly spaced downriggers on the transom (including two on the corners), all of which would face aft. Long booms would be used on the gunwale riggers to increase horizontal spacing.

On small boats, downriggers can be located wherever they are most convenient, especially if only one or two are used and it is easy to get to them. Place them as close to the stern as possible. If downriggers are mounted amidship and used for shallow fishing, the trailing line may be cut by the propeller in tight turns.

Whether you use pedestal mounts, swivel bases, trolling boards, or the like depends on the interior arrangement of your boat, the amount of freeboard it has, your budget, and your personal taste. On small boats, and on some midsize and larger vessels as well, a cross-transom trolling board is a great way to go. On small boats, it offers versatility and portability for other types of fishing. Swivel bases are handy for gunwale-mount and long-boom downriggers, since the swivel lets you turn the boom inward for docking and trailering as well as for setting lines.

Some downriggers can be mounted in flush-mount rod holders and on rails, but look at such options carefully; some of these don't have the strength to support a downrigger. You could be inviting trouble when trolling in big seas, when using the heaviest weights, or when a weight hangs on the bottom. A handrail would not provide enough support, for instance, and a thin gunwale may not be adequate, even for small, clamp-on downriggers. However, you can reinforce a thin aluminum gunwale with a long, strong piece of metal or wood.

Boaters who use their vessels for many types of fishing, including conventional casting or stillfishing, might want to use downriggers or rod holders for occasional trolling but wouldn't want permanent mountings or drilled holes in a boat that they might not keep more than a few seasons. By fastening downrigger plates to the appropriate transom areas, you can take them on and off with ease. However, a trolling board (see) system might be better.

Fishing Depth

The depth that is trolled with downriggers can vary from just below the surface to as deep as the cable on your spool will allow. Determine desired fishing depth by checking temperature levels to see where the thermocline (see) or preferred temperature of your quarry, or its bottom habitat, can be found. You can also pick what seems like an appropriate depth temporarily and wait until you find fish on sonar (see) before making changes.

Sonar equipment is essential for downrigger fishing. Use it to find baitfish or gamefish and the levels at which they are located, as well as to determine the depth at the lake bottom or ocean floor and other aspects of the underwater terrain. Without sonar, you're just guessing, and you also run the risk of hanging up your weight if the depth gets shallower.

Many downrigger anglers like to use a wide-angle (32 to 50 degrees) transducer to see their weights on sonar screens. This wide-angle view can be valuable, but it can also give false impressions. The angle of view is very large at deeper levels, and sometimes the fish you see with a wide-angle transducer may not be directly below your boat. Nonetheless, a wide-angle display allows you to see more of what is around you.

Be aware that just because your downrigger line counter reads 50 feet, your lures may not be running at exactly 50 feet for several reasons. One of these is swayback.

Cable swayback is the tendency of downrigger cable to angle toward the stern of the boat. It becomes more pronounced if you increase boat speed, encounter underwater current, or fish in fast-flowing rivers. Astute big-lake trollers can tell when they've encountered underwater currents by the increased angle of the cable as it enters the water. With swayback, the weight is not running directly below the boat or at the level indicated by the depth counter, and you must allow for this.

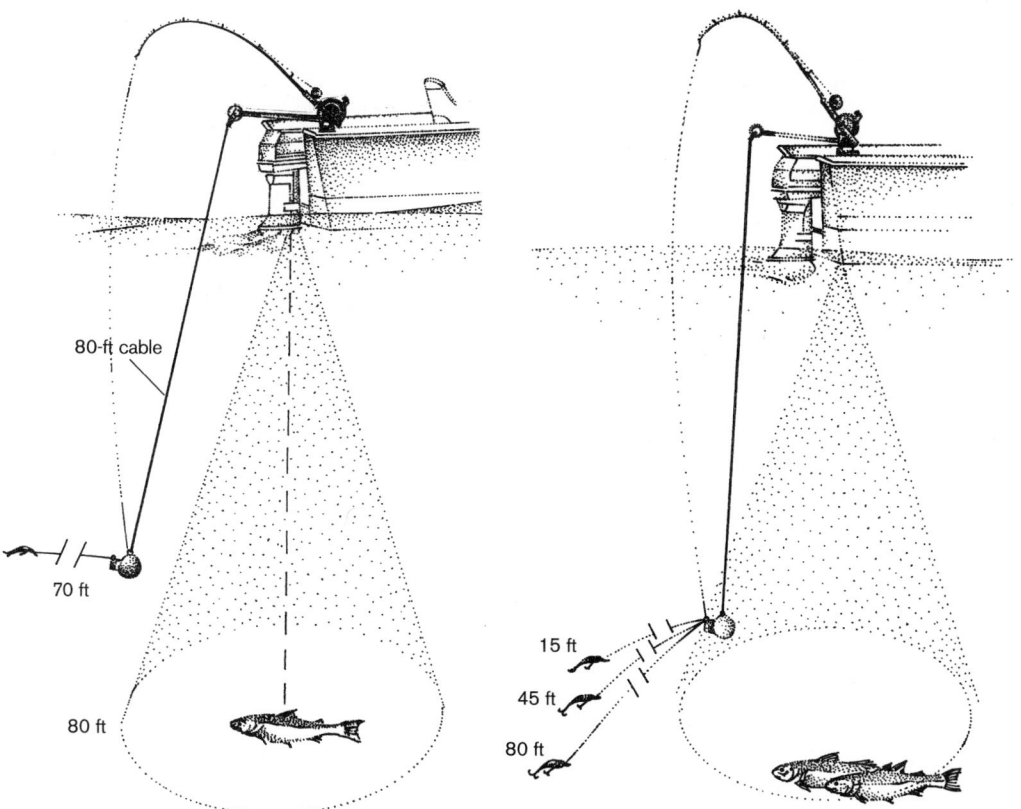

Because of certain conditions, a downrigger weight may not be at the vertical depth indicated on the cable counter. For example, if you set out 80 feet of cable to reach a fish that is 80 feet deep, the effects of swayback may cause the weight to be at the 70-foot level instead. Swayback has to be figured in setting the weight properly to put the lure in front of fish. This means letting out more cable, especially if the lure runs at the same depth as the weight.

Lures should swim just above fish rather than below them or far above because most fish attack prey from below. When you are trolling a diving plug behind a downrigger weight, the depth at which the lure will run actually depends on the distance it is set behind the weight as well as the design of the lure's lip. Thus, when you detect fish on sonar, the placement of the downrigger weight should take into account the diving ability of the lure.

Many anglers attach temperature- and speed-sensing probes to downrigger cables. These are usually part of lightweight, torpedo-shaped tubes set just above the weight. Such devices can present more drag and increase swayback; using heavy, 12-pound weights can help minimize this. Such devices also make sonar readings a little confusing because, in concert with the weight directly below them, they make a formidable streak across the screen that can obliterate fish or bait marks that may be at the same level. You can adjust the sensitivity of your sonar unit to reduce this problem, however.

As with swayback, you must account for the extra depth achieved by diving plugs when you troll them behind a downrigger weight. If, for example, you want your lure to run at 20 feet and you set a diving plug at the 20-foot level as indicated on the counter attached to the downrigger, that lure will be below the indicated level and will probably not be successful. If a diving plug runs 5 to 6 feet deep at a given speed and at the distance you have set it behind the downrigger weight, you must set the weight until the line counter reads 13 or 14 feet, no more.

Lure Distance/Setback

How far back from the weight to set your lures varies from a few feet to 200 feet, depending on the depth being fished and the species being pursued. As a general rule, the deeper you fish, the less distance you need to have between weight and lure; the shallower you set the weights, the farther back you put the lines. This is only a general guideline, because at times some fish can be caught shallow on short lines. Determining the proper setback requires experimentation and analysis of different conditions. It is advantageous, though not always effective, to fish with the shortest setback possible (depending on water clarity, species, depth, and so forth), because a shorter line increases hooksetting efficiency, minimizes possible conflicts with other boats in heavy traffic areas, and makes boat maneuvering easier.

To determine the length of line paid out, you can use one of several systems. With levelwind reels, you can count the number of "passes" that the levelwind guide makes across the top of the reel. Measure the amount of line that comes off the spool for one pass; then multiply that amount by the number of passes to arrive at an approximate setback distance. Some reels have built-in line counters that calculate distance; these are preferred by many charter boat captains and big-water boaters.

Another method, used with levelwind reels possessing a line guide that locks in an open position, and with spinning and fly reels, is to count "pulls." Start with the lure or fly in the water, hold the rod in one hand, and grab the line just ahead of the reel with your other hand. Pull off line in set increments, either as far as your arm will reach or in 1- or 2-foot strips. Count the number of pulls to arrive at setback length.

A third method is to "sweep" by putting the lure in the water, pointing the tip at the lure, and sweeping the rod toward the bow of the boat for a measured length. As the boat moves ahead, bring the rod tip back and then sweep forward again. If your sweep is 6 feet, multiply that by the number of sweeps you make to approximate setback length. Sweeping is a bit less accurate than using pulls or passes.

You can estimate setback distance by sight when surface lures are fished. But rough water, glare, and hard-to-see lures make this tough, and sometimes inaccurate. Many people are not good at judging even short distances, however, and often grossly overestimate the distance that they have set a lure behind the boat; this misjudgment can sometimes be detrimental to angling success.

Line-Setting Patterns

The way you mount downriggers and the number you use determine the horizontal spread that can be achieved with lures presented on downriggers. If you troll with only two downriggers, you needn't be too concerned with line-setting systems other than to keep the weights at different levels; also, try to vary setback lengths and to maximize your opportunities per line or per downrigger. The more 'riggers you employ, however, the more you should employ patterns or systems of operation, not only to cover the water well horizontally and vertically but also to facilitate landing fish, to minimize line crossing and tangling, and to make a better appeal to the fish.

Boaters who fish large open waters with four to six downriggers can employ some variation of V patterns in terms of the depth of the weight and lure setback; such patterns will help prevent inconsistent, possibly confusing, and perhaps troublesome lure and line placement.

Regarding depth, a V-down pattern will have the inner weights set deepest, the weights adjacent to them set shallower, and the outside weights set shallowest. A V-up pattern is just the reverse. An equal-depth pattern will have all the weights set at the same level.

Regarding line-to-lure setback, a V-in pattern will set the inner lures closest to the weight, the lures next to them farther back, and the outside lures farthest back. A V-out pattern is the reverse. An equal-length setback will have all lures set at the same distance behind the downrigger weight.

V-down

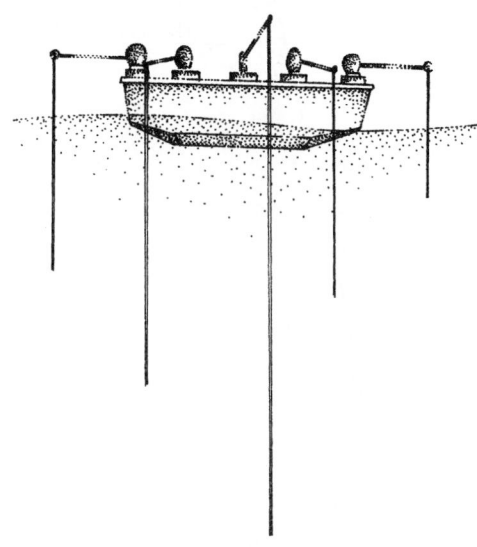

V-up

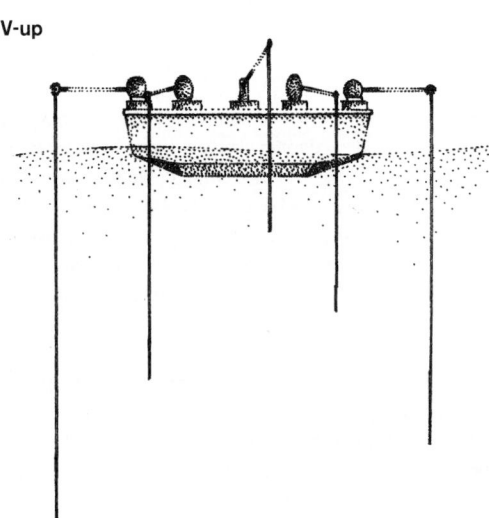

When using many downriggers on a large boat, set the weights in a pattern in order to scour different depths and help minimize tangling. In a V-down pattern, the deepest weights are set in the middle; in a V-up pattern, the deepest weights are set on the outside.

A V-down depth system is preferred by many trollers because the deepest lines are directly below the boat; shallower lines are out of the boat's direct path, perhaps where fish that are spooked by the boat or the inner downriggers may have moved. The V-up system might be the best approach when you're after fish that are attracted to boat noise or prop wash. An equal-depth presentation may be useful when fish are being caught only at a specific level—such as when they occupy a narrow band near the thermocline—or when you don't need to scour all depth levels.

Regarding setback lengths, there is seldom much reason to use a V-out setback. The V-in pattern is favored for the different downrigger depth settings and also for flatlining *(see)* and planer-board trolling *(see)*. When fish are falling regularly to lures trolled at a fairly specific midrange distance behind downrigger weights (especially when depths are nearly the same), there is little reason to stagger them much, so equal-length setbacks can be used. With the V-in system, the inner lures will run under the outer ones in turns, and fish directly below the boat may move up and out toward the lures set farther back. When used in combination with either the V-down or V-up depth settings, this setback system helps avoid line tangling when a fish strikes and pulls a deep line from the release.

Naturally, you have to experiment with these patterns and see which is best for your type of fishing and boat. (When you fish only one or two downriggers, this is all academic.) Such patterns are most useful when fishing in mid- to large-size boats; the most common pattern is a V-down/V-in combination.

Keep in mind that depth and setback distances are relative. A V-down system could set the shallowest depth trolled at 12 feet, the intermediate depth at 18, and the greatest depth at 24, which are not significant variations, or it could set the same progression at 20, 40, and 60 feet. The same is true for setbacks. There are no limitations.

The reason to use some type of pattern is to always know relatively where your weights and lures are, and the more rigs you troll, the harder it is to keep track of things. When a good fish strikes and lines are cleared, you can easily forget which weight the successful lure was on, how deep that weight was, and how far the lure was set behind the release. When you use a pattern, you know these facts, and you can re-rig immediately in a similar fashion. To fish with downriggers at various depths and setback lengths and to change them while trolling invites haphazardness; you won't have adequate control, and you may spend unnecessary time fixing problems.

Because outside lures speed up and inside lures slow down on a turn—and because the effects vary with the type of lure used (floating plugs rise while spoons and sinking plugs descend)—it is important to minimize the possibility of lines crossing and tangling. Some anglers troll for hours without checking their lures, only to find that they've been dragging a tangle for who-knows-how-long. This happens not only when downriggers are used but also when flatlines are trolled. The potential for problems is magnified by the effects of tide and current. To avoid tangling lines, you can employ two other solutions: never turn, or make only very slow, wide turns. Unfortunately, both are impractical and often fail to stimulate fish.

When setting out lines, try to keep the boat running straight, even if you're temporarily headed in a direction you don't want to go. A straight course while rigging minimizes line crossing and tangles.

More than one fishing line can be used with a single downrigger cable and weight, with the second or third lines set at various distances above the weight. This process is called stacking *(see)* and is particularly useful for covering different depths when you're unsure how deep to troll. Another way to cover different depths is to use a slider rig *(see)*, which lets you fish with more than one lure on a trolled line.

Boat Manipulation and Lure Behavior

Unlike casting, where a lure is retrieved by the angler, trolling is a matter of using the boat to work the lures; and in downrigger fishing, once you get the lures set where you want them, you have to make sure that they cross paths with fish and stimulate them. This is not just an issue of locating fish and driving the boat straight ahead, although that does work many times. Unfortunately, it doesn't work all the time, and some fish are not as aggressive as others, meaning that you must try to make the trolled offerings more appealing.

Line placement, lure presentation, and boat control are absolutely critical for sustained trolling success, and they work together. Downrigger fishing is usually combined with sonar use to locate fish or suitable habitat, primarily the former. Many of the fish caught by downrigger trollers have not been spotted first on sonar, which means that the fish were out of the boat's path of travel and that the fish came to the lures, instead of the lures being swum past their noses.

Creative and intelligent boat maneuvering can bring lures into the range of fish that are out of the boat's path. To regularly alter the lure's course of travel, you can turn the boat, steer in an S-shaped pattern or other irregular way, or change the boat speed. A good tactic is to sweep in and out from shore and to plan strategic approaches to points, sandbars, islands, shoals, channels, and the like. To be successful in some situations, you must cover a lot of territory and make versatile presentations; in other situations, you need to keep covering the same area or keep following the fish.

One reason why maneuvering in irregular patterns is a good tactic for trollers is because it imparts varying actions to lures, and these changes in a lure's behavior can precipitate a strike. Do whatever you can to make your offerings more attractive. Turning and altering speed are two basic activities and are aspects of successful trolling that are overlooked. Both alter lure behavior.

When you turn, some lures sink, some rise, some stay at the same level, some slow down, and some speed up, depending on the kind of lure and which side of the boat they are used on. Outside lures tend to speed up, and inside lures to slow down, depending on the sharpness of the turn. When lures are set a short distance behind downrigger weights, it's possible to make very sharp turns; wider turns are necessary when many lures are

Until the politically correct mid-1990s, the state fish of Colorado was the nonnative rainbow trout; it is now the rare but native greenback cutthroat trout.

D

D

trolled and when they are set further back, primarily to prevent them from tangling with each other.

Changing boat speed is a tactic to try when you locate fish but don't catch them, or when you are pursuing species that are known to be curious (lake trout, for example, may follow a lure for great distances before striking or swimming away). Speeding up is often more effective than slowing down, perhaps because it gives the impression of prey trying to flee.

Another way to alter a lure's behavior is by raising and lowering the weight periodically. Some electric downriggers can be programmed to oscillate automatically. It's worth doing this on your own, however, when fishing is slow and you want to trigger a strike from a fish that you've just spotted on sonar. Simply raise or lower the downrigger weight quickly to just above the level of the fish. If that doesn't work, wait a few moments for the lure to pass the fish; then take the rod out of its holder and pop the fishing line out of the release. Let the lure flutter down for a few seconds; then jig it once or twice. If nothing happens, retrieve the lure and reset the line. Often you'll catch fish in some stage of this operation.

Clearing Lines

You've got a whole bunch of lines set and you hook a fish. Do you keep moving? Do you pull in all the lines and raise all the weights?

Many big-boat trollers, particularly charter boat captains who fish a lot of lines, do not stop—they may slow down, but they don't really want to re-rig everything and they hope to catch another fish in the same area. They try to maneuver the boat to land the fish without crossing lines, messing up the rigging pattern, and pulling everything in and resetting. Small-boat trollers with only a few lines out don't have that problem and can usually pull in without too much trouble. Most anglers interested in sport don't like to keep moving, especially for good-size fish. After determining how large the fish is, they may clear everything, or may clear just one side of the boat and work the fish to that side for netting. This depends on the boat handler's skills, the angler's fish-playing abilities, the size of the fish, and the amount of gear in use. With big fish, it's usually best to clear everything, put the boat in neutral, and maneuver the boat as necessary to maintain a desirable position on the fish. There is no question that you get more sport and satisfaction out of playing a fish from a still boat than from dragging it in while the boat is moving.

Rods and Reels

A long rod, preferably having a long handle for insertion in a rod holder and an action that is not overly stiff, is optimum for downrigger use. This primarily means 8- to 10-foot rods, although you can use shorter ones. The stiffer the rod, the harder it is to get a bow into it when rigging and the more likely the tip will be unforgiving in rough water; a stiff rod will often cause a false release when the boat does a lot of rocking and rolling. Longer rods, including the 12-foot and greater noodle rods (see) preferred by some ultralight-tackle anglers, can be used with downriggers. Long rods used in steelhead fishing can be adapted for downrigger use but aren't quite as accommodating as more "parabolic" action downrigger rods.

Reels used in downrigger fishing run a wide gamut, but, in general, when fishing deep water, using long setbacks, or fighting strong fish capable of stripping off a lot of line, you need a reel with plenty of line capacity and a good drag. Levelwind products are more functional for downrigger fishing (and all trolling) if they have a clicker.

When you place the downrigger-set rod in a rod holder, it's important to do several things. Reel in all the slack; then pull on the line near the first rod guide while you turn the reel handle to bring the line as tight as possible, without pulling it out of the release. The rod should be well arched if properly set. Also check the reel drag for proper setting. The clicker should be on, so that if a fish strikes and takes line before someone spots the rod tip bouncing, the clicker will alert you that a fish is on and taking line off the reel.

See: **Downrigger; Stacking; Trolling.**

DOWNRUNNER

A term for shad that have spawned and are migrating downriver to return to the sea. Unlike pre-spawn shad, downrunners do feed and can be caught because of their hunger; however, they are less energetic than pre-spawn shad.

See: **Shad, American.**

DOWNSTREAM FISHING

Facing, casting, and fishing downstream in flowing water. This is the opposite of most river and stream fishing activities for fly anglers who wade and fish dry flies, since it is normally advantageous to face upstream and cast up, or up and across. However, some situations don't permit an upstream presentation. For lure users and fly anglers fishing wet flies and streamers, downstream fishing is less problematic and is standard procedure; dry fly anglers must mend line to get a proper drift or must be content with a very short drift, which requires an accurate cast to the right spot to start with.

See: **Upstream Fishing.**

DRAFT

The depth of water required to float a boat, often referred to as the amount of water that a boat "draws," and determined by the vertical distance from the waterline to keel, or from the waterline to the lowest point on the boat (including propeller, skeg, etc.).

DRAG

(1) Drag is basically an adjustable friction clutch that allows line to slip outward from a reel spool when a strong fish cannot be readily hauled in and swims the other way. Without drag, the line may break, the hook may straighten or rip out, or other bad events may occur. The drag essentially allows an angler to wear down and land a fish whose overall weight and strength outmatch the breaking strength of the line. It's an important function of a fishing reel, especially when light line is being used, when large and strong fish are being played, and when fish make strong and sudden surges while being landed.

The drag mechanism on a fishing reel allows line to slip outward by turning or revolving the spool, and it is controlled by the amount of friction applied, primarily by drag washers, to the spool. The amount of friction, or drag tension, is increased or decreased by turning a knob or wheel.

Drag tension ideally should be set before fishing and should not be adjusted during a fight—unless it has been improperly set to start with—because most anglers can't tell by a quick feel whether too little or too much tension has been applied, and the wrong decision is likely to hinder efforts to land a fish.

Most people set the drag via the "feels good" method—pull a little line off the reel, fiddle with the drag adjustment, and pull a little more until it feels "about right." The most precise way to set drag tension is to use a calibrated scale and measure the tension. The drag should be adjusted to the point where it slips at between 30 and 50 percent of the wet breaking strength of the line. That would be 3 to 5 pounds of tension for a 10-pound line. Most people are better off in the 30 to 35 percent range.

There are two methods to measure drag tension, both using a line that is run through the rod guides and tied to a calibrated scale (a good spring scale will do). One way is to hold the rod parallel to the ground and pointed directly at the scale, pulling on the scale so that there is no tension on the rod; adjust drag tension until it takes 30 percent of the line's breaking strength to make the drag slip. This is the least amount of pressure you can apply when fighting a fish, assuming that when a big fish steams off you point the rod directly at it until it stops running and then raise the rod up again to fight it.

In the other method, hold the rod at a 45- to 60-degree angle as if you were fighting a fish, and use the scale to pull on the line so that tension is applied to the rod as it would be in many fishing situations. Adjust drag tension until it takes 30 percent of the line's breaking strength to make the drag slip. In either case, you can apply judicious supplemental tension by placing your palm or fingers on the spool.

Once you have set drag tension in either manner, you'll readily appreciate the difficulty of getting a precise setting by the "feels good" method and, more important, the inadvisability of changing tension in the midst of battle. If you unintentionally

up the ante to 70 percent of breaking strength, for example, you're flirting with disaster. If you don't think so, just set the tension at 50, 65, or 80 percent, walk off about 30 feet, and try pulling on the line attached to a scale.

How well the drag operates when it's needed most is the real issue, and that encompasses the following considerations:

- **Variation.** Does it retain its original setting, or does it stray from that setting? Straying is bad.
- **Maximum drag force.** Can the drag be set so that it doesn't slip at all (lockdown), should that be necessary? This is useful but not critical to many situations.
- **Range of adjustment.** How many revolutions can you obtain by turning the control mechanism on the reel? Ideally you should be able to get up to that 30 percent number with just a short adjustment, then have a lot of adjustment from 30 to 50 percent, and finally ramp up very quickly to full lockdown. The force required to start up the drag is an element of this as well, and it can be hampered by a drag that has been tightened and left to sit for several days, which puts a "set" in the drag washers. For this reason, you should relax the drag tension after every trip.
- **Drag washer size.** Are the drag washers large enough for the most severe tests? The most efficient drag washers are those with a large inside diameter as well as a large outside diameter to best cope with heat dissipation.

Much more can be said about the technical aspects of reel drag; these aspects are reviewed under the respective tackle categories.
See: Baitcasting Tackle; Big-Game Tackle; Conventional Tackle; Flycasting Tackle; Lever Drag Reel; Spincasting Tackle; Spinning Tackle.

(2) Drag is the influence of current on a fly, inhibiting the fly from drifting freely. The movement of some flies (mainly dry flies and nymphs) as a result of current is unnatural and is likely to make them unattractive to fish; to counter this, accurate casts *(see: flycasting tackle)* and mending *(see)* of the fly line is necessary.

DRAG-FREE DRIFT
Presenting a fly in current so that it drifts naturally and without the movement that is created by fly line.
See: Mending.

DRAGONFLIES AND DAMSELFLIES
These two groups of insects are members of the scientific order Odonata, a term derived from *odus,* meaning tooth and owing to the large mandibles of these species. They are common inhabitants of silty

areas of aquatic environments and usually have a generation time of one year, but many may have life cycles up to four years. Their life cycle consists of egg, nymph, and adult stages, with most of this being in the nymph stage, which is also the stage that is of significance as fish prey. The adults are readily observed along the shore but are not significant food for fish.

Dragonfly and Damselfly Nymphs

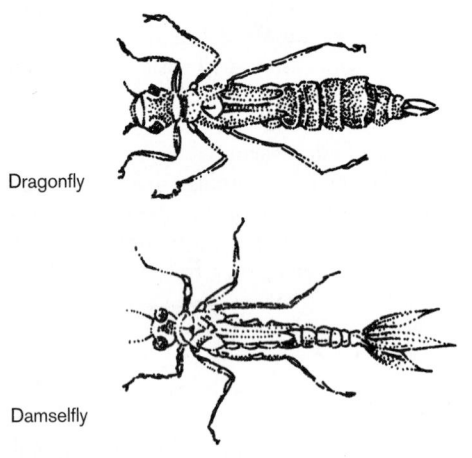

Dragonfly

Damselfly

Dragonfly and damselfly nymphs are large and highly predacious insects who favor hiding and feeding among algae or aquatic plants, especially in lakes. They are 1 to 2 inches long, and have large eyes, three pairs of long segmented legs on the upper middle section (thorax) of the body, and a large scooplike lower lip that covers the bottom of the mouth. There are no gills on the sides or underneath the abdomen.

Damselfly larvae have a narrow body with three oar-shaped tails (gills) extending in a tripod formation. Their legs are long and spindly, and the body is thin and narrow. Dragonfly larvae have a wide oval or round abdomen that may end in three wedge-shaped extensions. They both capture other insects and small crustaceans with a double-hinged lower lip that is armed with spines.

Damselflies may be mistaken for mayflies (see) because of the presence of three tails, but the tails of damselflies are broad and fan shaped and extend from the body in a tripod formation. Mayfly larvae have three (sometimes two) filamentous tails extending from the body parallel to the ground. In addition, mayfly larvae have platelike or feathery gills extending from the sides of their abdomen. Dragonfly larvae are easily distinguished by their wide oval or round (sometimes flattened) abdomen and their large bulbous eyes.
See: **Aquatic Insects.**

DRAINAGE
The region or area drained, usually by a river.
See: **Basin; Watershed.**

DRAWDOWN
The deliberate lowering of water in an impoundment, usually as a result of hydroelectric or irrigation needs. This may cause a current to exist in a body of water that is usually without significant current and, if large enough, may quickly change the nature of the shallows of the affected impoundment. Severe drawdowns can affect gamefish behavior and location (sending some species to the security of deeper water where they are harder to locate and catch) and may create navigational hazards.

DRESSED WEIGHT
The weight of a fish after the viscera (or entrails), and sometimes the head and other body parts, have been removed.

DRESSING
(1) The coating or treatment that is used to help float a dry fly or fishing line, or to clean a fly line.

(2) The materials that, when tied on a hook, form the appearance, or pattern, of an artificial fly.
See: **Fly.**

(3) A term for cleaning fish, especially the act of scaling and eviscerating.
See: **Fish Preparation—Cleaning/Dressing.**

DRESSING FISH
See: **Fish Preparation—Cleaning/Dressing.**

DRIFT BOAT
(1) A term for party boat (see), primarily used in saltwater.

(2) A particular type of manually propelled flat-bottomed boat used for floating rivers bow-first; it draws very little water and is extremely stable and maneuverable. Drift boats are especially employed by trout, salmon, and steelhead fishing guides.

Design and components. Drift boats are designed after the East Coast ocean dory, with two obvious differences: They are keel-less, and they have a wide flat bottom to create minimum draft while providing maximum stability and maneuverability. Both the bow and the stern are sharply upswept; the bow comes to a point and faces downstream when the boat is rowed, whereas the stern is usually slightly squared, primarily as an anchor support, and faces upstream when the boat is rowed. The oars are located in the center of the craft, making it easy to pivot from the rowing seat. The gunwales vary from about 10 to 20 inches in height depending on the turbulence of the water that the boat will be used in. The bottom is disproportionately wide compared with the length. A typical 16-foot drift boat, for example, will have a 54- to 60-inch-wide bottom, while a 20-foot boat will have a 60-, 66-, or even a 72-inch-wide bottom, making these craft uniquely stable.

Seating arrangements vary depending on the intended use on any given waterway. The rowing seat, which generally is made out of braided rope or nylon straps (somewhat like a lawn chair), often has no back for several reasons. On most waters, the operator doesn't have to overexert while rowing a drift boat, since drift boats, when properly balanced, row quite easily. However, in rough current with obstacles such as rocks and overhanging limbs, the operator may need to really put some backbone into the rowing and pivoting process. Not having a back on the rowing seat facilitates hard rowing; a back to the seat would get in the way. Most drift boat users choose a rowing seat without a back to make it easier to move from one end of the boat to the other.

The rowing seat is generally attached to a bench that is connected to both gunwales. A popular option is for the bench to have a lift-up lid for stowing gear. Passenger seats are typically mounted to another storage-type bench on a sliding track and are located in front of the rower. The reason for the sliding track is to allow the passengers' weight to be balanced. It is of paramount importance that a drift boat be balanced port to starboard, or the rower will have a most difficult time of rowing and maneuvering the craft.

Another popular seating arrangement, especially for fly anglers, is to have two pedestal seats, one fore and one aft. This gives both anglers the most casting room. This seating arrangement usually incorporates a leg brace located in front of both seats so that when anglers stand up they can secure their legs in the braces. With the braces, the anglers can stay balanced while casting when the boat is drifting through rough water.

Most commercially made drift boats are constructed of either aluminum or fiberglass. However, a few companies still make wooden boats. Wooden boats are most popular among the do-it-yourself crowd, and numerous designers and manufacturers sell blueprints for those that are so inclined. All three materials have pros and cons when it comes to use. Fiberglass is generally the most buoyant; aluminum is most durable; and wood, without doubt, has the most eye appeal.

Operation. Since drift boats draft very little water (draft is the amount of water that a boat needs to float), usually not more than a few inches, they offer excellent river fishing opportunities and have an equal ability to navigate deep or shallow environs. The wide, flat bottom of a drift boat also offers excellent stability in rough whitewater.

A typical 16-foot drift boat has 8-foot-long oars made of wood, fiberglass, or a combination of plastic and metal. Some rowers prefer even longer oars,

up to 10 feet in length. Located amidship, the oars make it possible to turn a drift boat on a dime, so to speak. This excellent maneuverability not only allows the rower to position anglers in the best fishing water, but also makes it possible to quickly avoid potential hazards.

When rowing a drift boat, remember that these water craft, unlike other boats, are designed to be rowed forward by pushing on the oars, or backward by pulling on the oars; in other words, with the bow pointed downstream, which is the same direction that the rower faces, when the rower pulls backward on the oars, the stern of the boat heads upstream. The human physique allows the rower to put more strength into pulling oars than into pushing them, so the most critical maneuvering is done by pulling on the oars to position the boat. When approaching a bend in a river, or any other potentially dangerous rowing situation, always point the stern away from the potential hazard so that the rower can pull hard with the oars, backing away from the hazard.

When the boat is running whitewater, the rower must be vigilant and ready to respond on a moment's notice. Despite the apparent stability of a drift boat, it is still possible to upset and sink one. Interestingly, most drift boats do not have any built-in flotation. Therefore, if you sink one, it's going to the bottom.

When rowing downstream, the rower should always keep the boat parallel with the current; getting sideways and hitting a rock is the surest way of sinking a drift boat. A good rule of thumb that drift boat operators live by is: If you have to hit a rock, hit it straight on and hit it hard. Generally, if you hit a rock straight and hard, the drift boat will slide over the rock. Fiberglass drift boats tend to slide easily over rocks and gravel, whereas wood and aluminum boats tend to hang up. Therefore, most drift boaters cover the bottom of a wood or

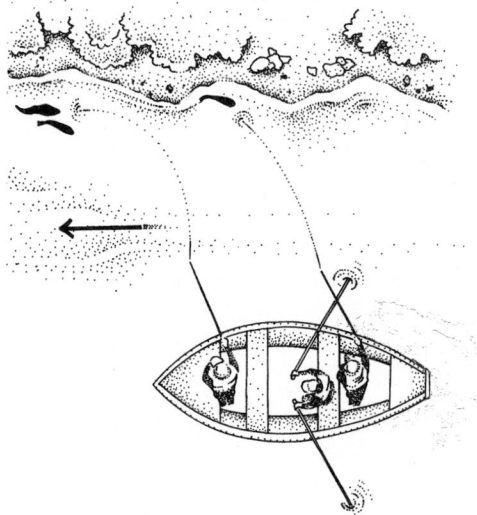

With bow facing downstream, a drift boat operator rows upstream to slow the drift or maintain position, while bow and stern anglers cast to likely fish lies.

aluminum boat with a thin ¹/₄-inch sheet of plastic, or they apply several coats of marine epoxy to the bottom, in an effort to both protect the bottom and ease the boat's passage over objects.

One downside to the keel-less, flat-bottomed, and high-sided design of drift boats is that they can catch a lot of wind. They can be difficult to control on big open water like a lake or bay. Installing a stern-end anchor is helpful for times when a boat has to be kept in a specific position; without the anchor, the rower would have to constantly keep rowing to maintain position, which is either tiring or impossible in swift current. Many anchors can be raised and lowered from the operator's midboat position.

Fishing from a drift boat. Fishing from a drift boat offers many unique opportunities, as well as sometimes challenging circumstances. For example, anglers accustomed to wading in a river generally cast upstream to virgin water. In a drift boat, however, the virgin water lays ahead of the angler downstream. And, unless the boat is anchored, or the rower is holding the boat still, the angler and the water are constantly moving, which can create one of several interesting casting scenarios. Depending on the position of the boat in relation to the current, and the position of the water where you want to cast, you will be moving at the same speed as the water, moving slower than the water, or moving faster than the water. Each of these situations can feel quite foreign and awkward to the inexperienced drift boat angler.

When the boat is moving faster than, or at the same speed as, the current, you should cast downstream approximately at a 45-degree angle. If the boat is moving slower than the current, you should cast perpendicularly to the boat. When the boat is anchored, cast upstream, as you would do when wading.

When you are casting flies from a drift boat, it is important to get the most out of each cast and drift, rather than trying to achieve constant accurate casts. A lot of mending (see) can be done to keep a fly in the right position. Leave it in the right position until the fly, or strike indicator, starts to drag and then mend the line. Keep mending until you cannot do so any longer; then cast again. The longer you have to cast, the more the belly of the line is swept up in the current, and the faster the flow, the more frequently you may have to mend line. A good drift boat operator will work the boat into such a position as to keep casting distances down and help even novice anglers get a good drift from each cast. Some circumstances allow a drift boat to get fairly close to the desirable fishing areas, but others do not.

With fly anglers casting from both ends of a drift boat, there are many opportunities for lines to get fouled during casting. To avoid this, the stern angler should be especially mindful of the activities of the bow angler and should try to develop an alternating rhythm to casting; this can be done by casting after the bow angler has cast and laid line on the water and also by either or both anglers saying "casting" when they are about to pick their fly lines off the water. An equitable solution may be to alternate positions.

Both anglers—especially the bow angler—should always be mindful of where the boat is headed and what aspects or features of the river are about to come up, so that they are ready to make a presentation to an especially likely spot. Upcoming objects, current seams, and rising fish may provide a good opportunity, and your offering should be in the water and drifting or swimming properly before you come upon the site, rather than as you draw even with it. Casting back at a site that you are floating by is rarely productive. Obviously the rower is instrumental in positioning and presentation, and the speed of the current is also a critical factor.

Although drift boats can cover a lot of territory, some of which may not be otherwise accessible or often fished, it may be advantageous in some situations to beach the boat temporarily and fish a particular area thoroughly by wading. Trespass considerations may have to be taken into account, however, and in some waters you can fish and float through in a boat but not get out of the boat. A guide should know what is legal in the particular waterway.

Because drift boat anglers, unlike wading anglers, have miles of river at their disposal, it is very important to remember stream etiquette and give wading anglers a wide berth when passing through their area, even though this is sometimes difficult. It may, in fact, be preferable to go behind a wading angler in the area that is not being fished, rather than float through and disturb the area that is being fished. Some wading anglers do not understand that you are doing them a favor by coming behind them, so be courteous and ask for their preference before you float by.

It is also proper etiquette to give other drift boats a wide berth. When approaching another boat in a tight spot, yell ahead to the other boaters, letting them know that you are coming through. If possible, pass them on the side that they request you to pass on.
See: **Backtrolling.**

DRIFT FISHING

Who hasn't seen television commercials showing an angler sitting in a boat with feet propped up and a line dangling over the side, waiting to get lucky. Although some anglers are indeed like this, others who look laid-back will fool you. These anglers seem to be doing little or nothing, yet they often have an uncanny knack for achieving success. Drift fishing from a boat appears to be about as lazy a fishing method as you can find, but there

Bronze, blue, nickel, and gold hooks begin to corrode after 3 to 4 days in freshwater and within 36 hours in saltwater; they'll take 2 to 3 weeks to break down in freshwater and 2 days in saltwater.

is more to it than meets the eye. In fact, drifting with bait or lures is sometimes more advantageous than moving under electric or outboard motor power; for example, when the fish appear to be spooked by motor noise, drift fishing is actually a smart strategy.

Drift fishing can be either haphazard or calculated. The haphazard drifters, who pay little regard to how deep they are fishing, where they are headed, and what they are using, are not likely to be as effective as those drifters who use carefully selected tackle and make calculated approaches that take into account careful boat positioning.

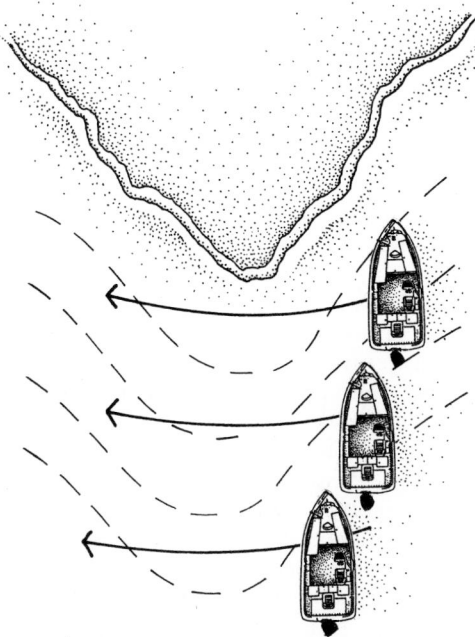

This fishing boat is using the wind to drift across an extended underwater point (note angle of motor to aid drift); several drifts are made to cover the water from shallow to deep.

One of the keys to calculated drifting—deliberately drifting over a specific location—is setting up your boat for it. Because of its design, the weight inside, the hull configuration, and a variety of factors, every boat has a tendency to move off a straight line even though wind direction would seem to dictate a certain path as long as you start at the right spot. To determine how your boat drifts, do it in a controlled situation with the outboard motor in the water and aligned straight with the keel. To counter the tendency to move off a straight line, turn the motor in the direction that the boat wants to head; the motor will act like a rudder and keep the boat in a proper attitude with the wind.

Freshwater

Drifting in freshwater occurs in both lakes and rivers; it is usually a deliberate activity but sometimes can be forced upon anglers. Anglers on a lake may have to drift if the wind is too severe or if their source of power is lost (especially a dead battery on an electric motor). Really strong blows make it impossible for bass anglers to control their actions unless they drift, and anglers in small to midsize boats may be unable to troll without being bounced around.

Whether drifting is forced upon you or deliberately chosen, certain factors affect success and make drifting less likely to be an aimless hit-or-miss activity.

When drift fishing with bait, for example, pay attention to the type of bait rig that you use and to the weight *(see)*, or sinker. Bank, dipsey, pencil lead, and split shot sinkers are commonly used in bait drifting. Split shot are often used for suspending bait at specific depths; the others are essentially used for keeping contact with the bottom and are good in deep water and cast well. Split shot are preferred for light tackle. Dipsey sinkers are also used with light to medium tackle and where bait is suspended off the bottom above the sinker.

A very popular freshwater baitfishing rig, used for drifting as well as for trolling, is a spinner rig, which features a small spinner ahead of a worm, with a fixed sinker or sliding sinker above it; a spinner rig is especially useful for perch, walleye, and bass. Another popular bottom-drifting bait rig features a three-way swivel with one lead going to a sinker and the other to a bait hook.

Bass anglers will find that a Carolina rig *(see)* is a very good worm rig for bottom drifting. You need the right size weight to keep the worm down, of course, which will depend on wind and depth.

Some anglers who cast lures use a wind-aided drift to their advantage, in combination with occasional electric motor use, to help maintain a desired position. In fishing for bass, for instance, anglers can successfully work an open weedy area this way with a variety of lures. Plastic worms are especially good for some slow drifting work and can be fished on a slow retrieve that is combined with a drift. Crankbaits are a good drifting lure because they stay down and generally swim well at varied speeds of retrieval. Generally, however, the best lure to use when drifting is a jig, either with a soft-plastic attachment or with a strip of live or dead bait.

If you cast while drifting, you should cast ahead of the boat to cover the area you are approaching, especially when drifting over weeds. However, a fast wind-aided drift does not allow for proper retrieval of some lures that are cast downwind and retrieved upwind, and some strikes are missed because of decreased sensitivity. When jigging and worm fishing, you are better off fishing on the upwind side of the boat, letting the lures cover ground at the same pace as the boat. It is hard to fish jigs that drift underneath the boat, as they would when fished on the downwind side of the boat. This is especially necessary in deep water.

D

If the wind is pushing you at such a clip that you cannot maintain contact with the bottom, you may need to use a heavier weight, or periodically reel in and lower the jig or worm right beside the boat until it hits bottom. Another option is to cast it to the side and slightly ahead of the boat; this action gives the lure (or bait) the opportunity to reach the bottom by the time the boat is directly overhead, increasing the effective time that it stays in the likely area before swinging upward and having to be retrieved.

To properly drift over a particular stretch of water, you must plan the approach properly, taking wind and current into consideration. Preferably the boat is broadside to the wind, but this is not possible with some boats, although on smaller craft the use of a sea anchor *(see)* can assure this. Note where you start a drift and have success so that you can return and redrift over productive stretches; also drift to the sides in order to cover all of a particular area. The longer you drift and the more the wind shifts, the harder it will be, especially in open water environs, to return to the proper place or to achieve the desirable drift.

When making a long drift, you'll usually find that fish are caught sporadically rather than in one tight spot, but this may depend upon the species. Repeat this drift and focus on adjacent waters for similar drifts. Although the places to drift vary with species pursued, points are a universal possibility. Submerged weeds are good drifting locations for

Controlling the path and speed of a drift, as these walleye anglers are doing, is usually essential to success.

bass and pike, provided the weeds have enough depth and density.

If you have an electric motor, use it sparingly to keep you in the right position or to slow the drift speed. One of the benefits of drifting, especially in shallow water and near shore, is that you are not creating noise, so try to use the motor sparingly.

River drift fishing is popular, too, and there is little that is haphazard about this. Using electric motors, outboard motors, or oars, boaters try to effect a downstream boat movement at a pace much slower than the speed of the current. The slowed movement allows them to cast lures and baits and work them better or longer (or present them more often) in likely places. This drifting method is especially effective for salmon, steelhead, trout, bass, and walleye.

The most critical aspect of river drift fishing is proper bait or lure presentation through boat control. Slipping, which is a form of backtrolling *(see),* is the best way to achieve success in river drift fishing. It entails moving slowly backward downstream while in complete control of your craft, in such a way that you and the passengers can fish at ease. To do this, point the bow of your boat upstream and accelerate the outboard motor in forward gear. With the bow placed into the current, throttle down the motor to a point where your boat has begun to move backward downstream. The thrust of the motor is not enough to keep you going forward, and your boat slowly drifts backward, stern first. The boat moves very slowly, sometimes almost imperceptibly, and you have precise control over your position and rate of descent.

With the motor at a steady forward thrust, the boat backs downstream with ease as you cast and retrieve. Cast upstream and retrieve slowly downstream. Upstream casting allows you to present lures in a manner similar to the movement of natural bait in current. The bow of the boat is always pointed into the current. It is a position easily held, providing you don't allow eddies and backwaters to entrap your boat, and you can readily move across current as necessary.

A similar outcome can be produced in moderate- to slow-flowing rivers by using an electric motor to position the boat face into the current and wind, and then by drifting with bait or jigs. Maintaining pace with the current allows for a vertical presentation that aids hooksetting and gives the fish less of a chance to detect the offering. It also permits the use of lighter jigs, which are often more likely to be taken than a heavier product.

Most river anglers who fish from shore are drift fishing. The standard procedure for casting to nearly every river species, regardless of whether you're using lure, fly, or bait, is to cast across and upstream and then allow the offering to drift or swim naturally in the current.

Saltwater

Drift fishing in saltwater takes place in coastal bays, tidal rivers, and the open ocean, with movement caused by tide and wind. Because of tide, these places can be completely devoid of fish or activity at one stage of the tide, yet provide sterling action just hours later. Thus, it's important to study each place you plan to fish, and determine how different wind and tide conditions affect the area. Above all, study coastal charts of the area, so you know the bottom conformation.

Canal drifting.   Canals are a favorite drifting spot because they are usually narrow, clearly defined, and rather restricted, with extremely swift currents, especially during moon tides. Their bottoms may be irregular, including flat areas, shallow spots, sandy areas, rocky areas, and deep holes. The water may run swift and silent in some spots or noisily with large waves in others. Each hour presents a different set of circumstances; by carefully studying the conditions, you can quickly adjust to the changing conditions, movements, and feeding habits of the fish, which can include a wide variety of species. Incidentally, many canals are best fished at night because of daytime boat traffic; dusk and daybreak when the tides are right are also good.

A light popping or spinning outfit is ideal for this type of waterway. Monofilament line in the 10- to 15-pound-test range is preferred, because it is fine enough for employing a variety of terminal rigs and lures, yet sufficiently heavy if you have to pull off an obstruction or shell beds.

If the canal has swift current, flounder will bury themselves in the sand bottom sections; as the current slows, they begin to move about searching for food. They are most active from an hour before the change in tide to an hour after and readily take a bait drifted along the bottom. A good bait rig for flatfish uses a three-way

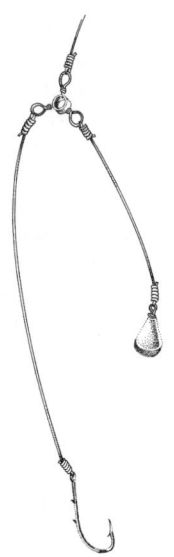

This is a common bait rig for drift fishing.

swivel with one arm sporting a short piece of 8- or 10-pound-test monofilament with a loop in the end, which is used for attaching a $1/2$- to 1-ounce dipsey sinker. The light mono-to-sinker connection permits you to easily break free if the sinker fouls bottom, and the lightweight sinker doesn't drag bottom but stays down and bounces along while drifting. The rig is completed with 18 inches of 10-pound line and a No. 8 or 9 hook. Next tie a dropper loop into the leader, and tie in a 6-inch leader with a second hook. Bait up with a 3-inch-long piece of sandworm, bloodworm, clam, or mussel, and focus your drifting efforts on either side of slack water.

Another place to catch flounder, especially summer flounder or fluke, is where the canal meets with a bay. The current carries plenty of food; on the flood tide it flows toward the bay, and fishing is productive where the waterway widens and empties into the bay. A three-way drift rig is very effective here, and small live bait, like mummichog, hooked through the lips, are good. You can also add a thin strip of squid to the hook, which flutters when the bait swims. Wait a second or two after feeling the strike, and lower the rod tip to give the fish slack and time to mouth the bait. When you feel a firm pull, slowly reel; this often causes the fluke to bite down securely on the bait, resulting in a hookup. This technique works better than striking quickly at the first sign of a pickup.

If a canal has bulkheads, you may find species like sea bass, blackfish, and porgies close to the bulkheads, feeding on grass shrimp and mussels. Drifting a sinker along close to the bottom often results in snagging on debris, especially in the rocky bottom areas, so use a float rig that keeps the hooked bait just off the bottom yet within range of feeding fish.

Check your sonar to determine the depth of the water where you'll be drifting. Tie a knot in your line at a distance a foot shorter than the water depth. Slip a bead or button onto the line, and then slip a plastic float with a hole in the middle onto the line so that it slides freely. Tie on a No. 4 or 5 Claw or Beak style hook, and finish off the rig by placing a small rubber-core sinker onto the line, about a foot from the hook. The sinker helps hold the entire rig perpendicular to the bottom as you drift along. Live grass shrimp are a good bait to use, but a tiny fiddler crab, small piece of clam or mussel, bloodworm, or sandworm, all work well.

This rig enables you to reel to the sinker, with the plastic float sliding on the line. As you let it back out, the sinker takes the baited hook to the desired depth just a foot or so off the bottom, and the bead and float slide up the line, stopped by the knot, which holds the rig in just the right position. Because the fish stay close to the bulkhead, the best tactic is to drift close to the bulkhead, holding your rod tip as close to it as possible.

D

Keep in mind that some species (like stripers and weakfish) avoid swift tidal flow and may stack up in deep holes. As the tide slows, usually an hour before, during, and after the change, they fan out searching for food. Live bait is good for these fish and is often very effective when drifting.

To rig up with live bait for drifting, tie a 2-foot-long loop in the end of your line using either a Bimini Twist or a double Surgeon's Knot. Then use a double Surgeon to tie a 36-inch-long monofilament leader material to your double line. Tie your hook to the leader. Bait up with sandworms for stripers and weakfish, using No. 1, 1/0, or 2/0 Beak-style hooks with a baitholder shank. Slip the hook point into the worm's mouth, and bring it out about $^3/_4$ inch from the head. The baitholder shank holds the worm securely, and it will swim enticingly as you drift along. For larger baits like live eels, herring, spot, or other small baitfish, a 4/0 through 6/0 hook is more appropriate.

With live bait, drift along with the current, paying out 40 to 50 feet of line. When the current is running fast, you may have to add a rubber-core sinker to the line to take the bait down, but as the tide slackens no weight is needed. Fish the reel in freespool; as a fish picks up the bait, let the fish move off to ensure that the bait is well within the fish's mouth.

Open ocean.   Drift fishing on the open expanse of ocean is totally different from that experienced in a confined area like a canal. On the surface the water is all the same as far as the eye can see. There is a difference on the bottom, however, because depressions, peaks, ridges, rocks, and reefs contribute to where bait will congregate. Where the bait congregates is where you'll find larger game, so it's important to know the bottom conformation and the direction that your boat will drift, whether as a result of wind or tide. Through careful planning, your boat will drift over the area most likely to be populated by feeding fish.

Sharks are a common drift fishing catch, and the best way to score with them is while chumming and drifting, which is reviewed elsewhere (see: sharks). Anglers should position their drift so that tide or wind carries them across known wrecks, reefs, or irregular bottom conformations where fish known to attract feeding sharks are found. If you're well positioned, the drift can carry you several miles, with the chum leaving a shark-attracting trail behind the boat. It may take minutes or hours, but if you cover the grounds, chum correctly, and have your baits set at various depths, you'll have a great chance to score.

Bottom-feeding fish like snapper and grouper are also a common drift fishing catch, located over rock and coral bottom. At intermediate depths around reefs and rocks, you may catch dolphin, king mackerel, Spanish mackerel, barracuda, wahoo, and little tunny. This combination is ideally suited to deep jigging from a drifting boat.

Favored jigs are leadheads with either bucktail or plastic bodies. Depending on the depth of the reef and the swiftness of wind or current, use hook sizes ranging from 4/0 through 7/0, with heads weighing from $^1/_2$ ounce through 3 ounces, the latter where swift currents or 100-foot depths dictate.

The key to successful deep jigging is being intimately familiar with the bottom conformation. This can be accomplished by carefully studying charts of the area and then using sonar to view the reef, wreck, or ridge. The sonar lets you determine where the peaks and valleys exist and where the fish are holding. Then it's a matter of determining the direction of drift. If wind is lacking, you'll be moved by the tidal flow; if wind is present, it may overpower you and move you against the current.

Once you've made this determination, move to the high bottom spot and drop a marker buoy, moving farther away from the marker on each succeeding drift. The buoy allows you to bracket the area and also alerts you to avoid drifting from deep water into the peaks of the reef—where the line may snag and where a hooked fish may escape by diving into the coral and breaking off.

The most effective method is to move up to the marker buoy and shut down the motor. Allow the jig to settle all the way to the bottom. As soon as it touches down, lock the reel in gear promptly, lift back smartly with your rod tip, and begin reeling. Grouper and snapper cruising along the bottom often view the plummeting jig and then excitedly charge it as it leaps off the bottom and heads to the surface.

While retrieving, you can jig with your rod tip, smartly lifting it, which causes the jig to dart upward and then falter; keep repeating this until the jig reaches the surface. Many bottom feeders often strike the jig deep; intermediate cruisers will strike at midlevel, sometimes just as you're about to lift the jig from the water.

When you receive a strike, set back firmly and quickly attempt to get a few turns on the reel, lifting back smartly to get the fish away from the sharp coral. If you've positioned the drift properly, the movement of the boat away from the peaks of the reef will help put more distance between the fish and the bottom. In shallow water the positioning of your drift isn't as critical as it is when fishing offshore reefs.

Still another type of open-water drift fishing that enjoys tremendous popularity is fishing for the various members of the flatfish clan, which typically inhabit a sandy, soft, or mud bottom. Flatfish spend a lot of time almost completely buried, using their fins to flip sand or mud over their backs, with just their eyes exposed. They will do this when storms occur, roiling the water, and particularly when there is a quick drop in water temperature. Sometimes they use this vantage to wait for unsuspecting food to be carried by with the current. When water clarity and temperature are to their liking, they vacate the sand bottom and move about aggressively searching for a meal.

A black marlin tagged at Australia's Great Barrier Reef was recaptured two and one-half years later off New Zealand, some 2,000 miles away.

D

As flatfish move about, they may move along the perimeter of rocky bottom, or where wrecks or artificial reefs litter the bottom. They'll often move to a broad expanse of relatively flat bottom, punctuated by a series of hills or lumps that rise to the surface, because forage is most plentiful here. A similar rig to that used in shallow canal or bay waters is used, although heavier weight is necessary to hold bottom. This may be a 6- or 8-ounce bank sinker, or even much heavier if the drift is fast and the depth greater. Using heavier sinkers is often better than using lighter ones, since a fast drift makes it hard to stay on the bottom with lighter sinkers. It may be necessary to keep adjusting by replacing a light sinker with a heavier one to stay on the bottom.

Open-water drift fishing opportunities exist in many bays, rivers, and creeks, where weedbeds can be fished for seatrout. This can be fine light-tackle sport, using a light popping rod or a spinning outfit with 10-pound line. Natural baits and artificials are both effective.

Perhaps the most relaxing tactic is using the time-tested popping cork and shrimp bait combination, which is designed to float a bait just off the bottom or above the weedbeds, or occasionally at intermediate levels. As such, you must know the prevailing depths over which you'll be drifting. A popping cork is slipped onto the line and held in position with a stopper that slides into the bottom of the cork. The popping cork is tapered at the bottom end, and is blunt and hollowed out at the other end, which is positioned facing the rod. Thus, when you pull back smartly, the cork gurgles and pops; the seatrout is attracted to the area, at which time it observes and takes the bait, which can be any variety of live or dead shrimp, as well as a sandworm, or live spot. Casting and retrieving lures, especially jigs with plastic shrimplike tails, is also a possibility.

Leisurely drifting and chumming on a broad expanse of offshore water may bring great rewards. With modern electronics you can cruise known haunts of pelagic species. Once a favorable temperature break is located, you'll often see schools of squid, mackerel, herring, and other types of forage. This can be exploited by shutting the motor, drifting, and establishing a chum line to attract the targeted species. Fishing may include jigging, fishing with live bait, or drifting dead bait or strips in the chum.

While you're drifting along, if you stream a bait out 100 feet or more, the current will push it toward the surface; adding a rubber-core sinker to the leader will keep the hooked bait drifting along at the same depth as the chum. Conversely, in minimal current or wind, you may have to add an inflated balloon, cork, or Styrofoam float to the line to suspend the bait at the desired level. Otherwise, it might sink directly to the bottom while the light, partially suspended chum particles drift off at intermediate levels.

The suspense and excitement generated in far offshore waters comes as a result of not knowing just which of the world's greatest gamefish will strike your bait. It may be a small yellowfin tuna or a blue marlin that normally dines on small tuna.
See: Bait Rig; Bottom Fishing; Drift Boat; Inshore Fishing; Jigging; Party Boat.

DRIFTING
(1) A manner of fly fishing in moving water, especially using nymphs, and resulting in a drag-free presentation.
See: Mending.

(2) A manner of fishing from boats, using current or wind.
See: Drift Boat; Drift Fishing.

DRIFT NET
A long net that is set in the sea (or a large inland lake) by commercial fishermen (see) and that passively catches anything swimming into it.

DROPBACK
A tactic used in offshore fishing, especially for marlin and tuna, in which a lure or natural bait, usually the latter, is fed to an interested fish that has been raised into a spread of trolled lures or baits, or that is following or attacking a teaser in the spread. The dropback is simply a maneuver in which the rod is held high above and behind the angler's head with a firm two-handed grip. When the fish grabs the bait or lure, the rod tip is instantly lowered to a position pointing at the fish, thus feeding the bait into its mouth. Then, the rod tip is immediately raised hard several times in a stabbing motion to set the hook. If the hook pulls free, the lure is rapidly reeled back to the surface and the procedure is repeated.
See: Big-Game Fishing; Trolling Lures, Saltwater.

DROPOFF
A place where the bottom of a body of water changes abruptly downward and the depth is significantly greater. Dropoffs are often places to locate gamefish, both in freshwater and in saltwater. In the latter, offshore canyons, seamounts, and shelves have the most extreme dropoffs, which actually cause an upwelling (see) of water toward the surface because of current action; there are often dropoffs along the edges of banks, islands, reefs, and the like. In freshwater, natural lakes and impoundments have dropoffs at various places and levels, especially where old channels or river beds once existed or where there are steep underwater ledges or cliffs.

Dropoffs are usually precisely located by observing sonar but may be generally located by reviewing detailed nautical charts or underwater contour maps. Depending on depth, species, and presence or absence of other underwater features, dropoffs

may be good places to fish, especially during warm weather.
See: Breakline.

DROPPER FLY

An auxiliary fly, attached on its own tippet, to a fly fishing leader ahead of the principal fly. Droppers can be used in nymph, wet fly, and streamer fishing, and in combination with dry flies. A dropper can be affixed to the leader simply by leaving a few inches of overlap hanging down from the Blood or Uni Knot used to connect different strengths of leader material. Tie a dropper fly to the protruding tippet, and the main fly to the end of the leader. The accompanying illustration shows how this is done by using a dropper on a short tippet.

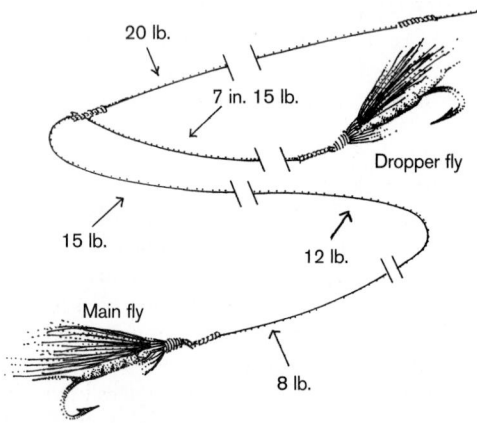

Shown are the latter stages of a knotted tapered leader, with a short length of line extending from one knot to a dropper fly.

Although two different patterns of the same fly type can be fished simultaneously, like two wet flies or two streamers, it is common to use a nymph on the dropper in conjunction with a dry as the main fly. In some cases, the dry fly acts as a strike indicator for the nymph. This is often a good ploy when prospecting and when there is no visible insect activity, or before a hatch occurs. If two fish in a row strike the dry fly, it's a simple matter to clip off the nymph. A dropper fly can also be fished with a lure, incidentally, especially a small spoon or spinner.

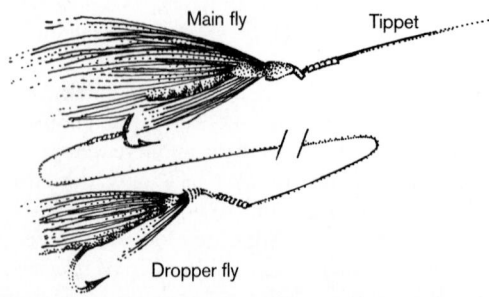

One method of using a dropper fly (in effect a second fly) is to tie it via a short length of line to the main fly.

Fishing two flies is also possible when the flies are not technically droppers in that the auxiliary fly is fished behind the main fly instead of ahead of it. More of a tandem arrangement, this is accomplished via a short leader attached to the eye of the main fly hook, or to the bend in the main fly hook. Tying to the eye is generally better for nymphs, and tying to the hook is better for streamers, provided the main hook has a definitive barb. These placements have the advantage of less tangling than if a dropper setup were used.

DROPPER LOOP RIG

A bottom fishing rig used for drifting with live or cut bait. Primarily employed in saltwater, a dropper loop rig features a bank sinker that is just heavy enough to touch bottom and one or two baits fished 18 to 35 inches apart. The baits are attached to the main line with 6- to 12-inch-long dropper loops, the lower of which is at least a foot above the sinker. This can be fished with one or two loops (baits) and minimizes the chances of hanging up with the hooks while drifting along the bottom. In obstructed waters where the sinker may get hung, a breakaway leader can be employed, attached via a swivel to the main (heavier) fishing line.
See: Inshore Fishing.

Dropper Loop Rig

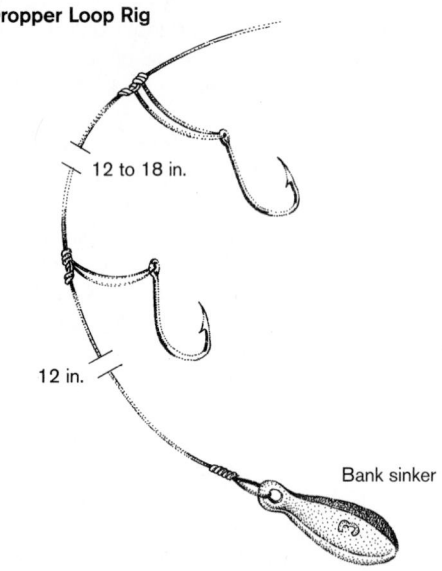

DRUM

Members of the Sciaenidae family (drum and croaker), these fish are known for the noises they make. Most drum have a muscle close to the swim bladder, and when that muscle is vibrated, the bladder acts as a resonator and amplifier for the sound. These noises can sometimes be heard from a far distance. In some species, only the male can make a noise; in others, both sexes can drum or croak. A few do not have a swim bladder and make no noise.

Drum of about 200 species inhabit tropical and temperate seas. Almost all are inshore fish usually found over sandy bottoms, either in schools or in small groups. Only one species, the freshwater drum, inhabits freshwater. Most if not all are good to eat, and some grow to large sizes.

See: Corvina; Croaker; Drum, Black; Drum, Freshwater; Drum, Red; Meagre; Perch, Silver; Seabass, White; Seatrout, Sand; Seatrout, Silver; Seatrout, Spotted; Totuava; Weakfish; Weakfish, Acoupa.

DRUM, BLACK   *Pogonias cromis.*

Other names—drum, sea drum, common drum, banded drum, butterfly drum, gray drum, striped drum, sea drum, oyster drum, oyster cracker; French: *grand tambour;* Japanese: *guchi, ishimochi, nibe;* Portuguese: *corvina;* Spanish: *corvinón negro, corbina, corvina negro, corvina, roncador.*

The black drum is the largest member of the Sciaenidae family (drum and croaker). The common term "drum" refers to the loud and distinctive "drumming" noise that occurs when the fish raps a muscle against the swim bladder. The noise is voluntary and is assumed to be associated with locating and attracting mates, and it can sometimes be heard from a good distance, even by people above the water.

The black drum is a popular sportfish in much of its range, and a common market fish that has been in greater demand since tighter restrictions were placed on the commercial catch of red drum. They are bottom feeders, with a strong liking for oysters and an equally strong propensity for destroying oyster beds. Larger fish are typically caught by anglers who bottom fish in surf and bay areas.

Small drum, between 10 and 15 pounds, are good eating, but they are frequently infested with parasites. Infected areas are circular and milky. The parasites are not harmful to humans and can be eliminated by cooking, but they detract from the fish's appeal. Larger black drum are likely to have a greater concentration of parasites. The flesh is coarse, but tender and delicately flavored. Black drum roe is a highly prized delicacy. The large, silvery scales, which are hard and difficult to remove, are often used in fish jewelry.

Identification.   The black drum has a short, deep, and stocky body with a high arched back and a slightly concave tail. The lower jaw sports numerous barbels, or short whiskers. There are large pavementlike teeth in the throat, and the mouth is low. The dorsal fins have 11 spines, 20 to 22 dorsal rays, and 41 to 45 scales along the lateral line, which runs all the way to the end of the tail. There are 14 to 16 gill rakers on the lower limb of the first arch. Its coloring is silvery with a brassy sheen and blackish fins, turning to dark gray after death. Juveniles have four or five broad, dark, vertical bars on the body.

The black drum can be distinguished from the red drum *(see: drum, red)* by the absence of a dark

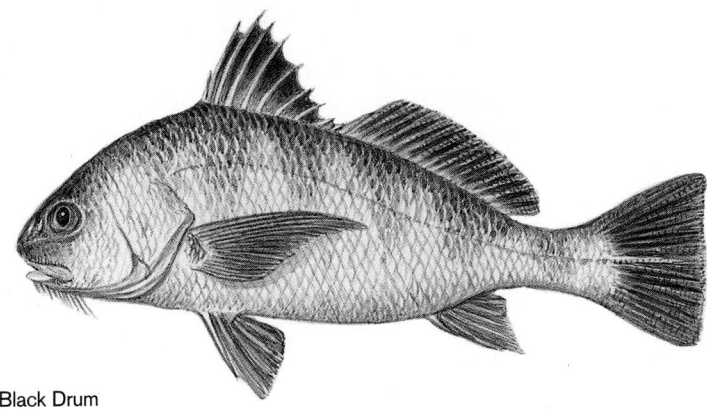

Black Drum

spot on the tail base, by the lack of dark streaks along the scale row, and by the presence of chin barbels. An unusually large spine in the anal fin and many barbels set the black drum apart from other similar species.

Size/Age.   Average small drum weigh 5 to 10 pounds, whereas large specimens commonly weigh 20 to 40 pounds; in Delaware Bay between New Jersey and Delaware, fish from 40 to 70 pounds are fairly common in the spring. The all-tackle record is a fish that weighed 113 pounds, 1 ounce. It was caught in Delaware in 1975. Black drum live up to 35 years, although most of the fish caught are 10 years old or younger.

Distribution.   Black drum are found in the western Atlantic Ocean, from Massachusetts to southern Florida and across the Gulf of Mexico to northern Mexico. They rarely occur north of New Jersey in this region. They also inhabit South America, ranging from southern Brazil to Argentina.

Habitat.   An inshore bottom fish, the black drum prefers sandy bottoms in salt or brackish waters near jetties, breakwaters, bridge and pier pilings, clam and oyster beds, channels, estuaries, bays, high marsh areas, and shorelines. Juveniles are commonly found over muddy bottoms in estuaries. Larger fish often favor shoal areas and channels.

Black drum can survive wide ranges of salinity and temperature. The small fish inhabit brackish and freshwater habitats; the adults usually prefer estuaries in which salinity ranges from 9 to 26 parts per thousand and the temperature ranges from 53° to 91°F. They are susceptible to low temperatures and do not survive long at temperatures below 37°F.

Life history/Behavior.   Black drum reach sexual maturity at the end of their second year at 14 inches in length. Adults form schools and migrate in the spring to bay and river mouths for the spawning season; in the Gulf of Mexico this is from February to May. A female can lay up to 6 million eggs; the larger the fish, the more eggs it will lay. Larval black drum remain in shallow muddy waters until they are 4 to 5 inches long; then they move near shore.

D

The drumming noise characteristic of the drum family is largely associated with spawning behavior. It is used to locate and attract a member of the opposite sex. The drumming of the males is particularly loud, and that of the females is softer.

Food and feeding habits.   Larval black drum feed on zooplankton, and young drum feed on small crustaceans and marine annelids. Adult black drum feed on crustaceans and mollusks with a preference for blue crabs, shedder crabs, shrimp, oysters, and squid. They locate food with their chin barbels and crush and grind shells with their pharyngeal teeth.

Angling.   Fishing for black drum is a different proposition than fishing for red drum. Most larger fish are caught by standard bottom fishing methods used in surf fishing *(see)* and inshore fishing *(see)*. In the mid-Atlantic, where the greatest number of larger black drum are encountered (40- to 80-pounders), bottom rigs with baits—especially clams—are the predominant offering. This method is often combined with chumming *(see),* typically with a clam and crab chum mix. Shrimp, crabs, squid, and cut fish are the most common natural baits in the Gulf of Mexico, where some fish are also caught on spoons and jigs. Spoons, plugs, and flies can produce in conditions favorable to artificials.

Black drum mouth a bait, so anglers need to wait a few seconds before setting the hook when using natural baits. These fish are strong battlers and require stout tackle; bigger blacks are fished with 30- to 40-pound line and heavy terminal gear. They are caught throughout the year along the Gulf coast but are most common along Texas and Louisiana; in the mid-Atlantic, there is a strong bay fishery for large black drum in the spring, but fish are caught all year. The region from southern New Jersey to North Carolina provides the most opportunity.

DRUM, FRESHWATER   *Aplodinotus grunniens.*
Other names—sheepshead, croaker, grunt, drum, silver bass, thunder pumper; French: *malachigan.*

The freshwater drum is the only North American freshwater representative of the Sciaenidae family, which includes the croaker,

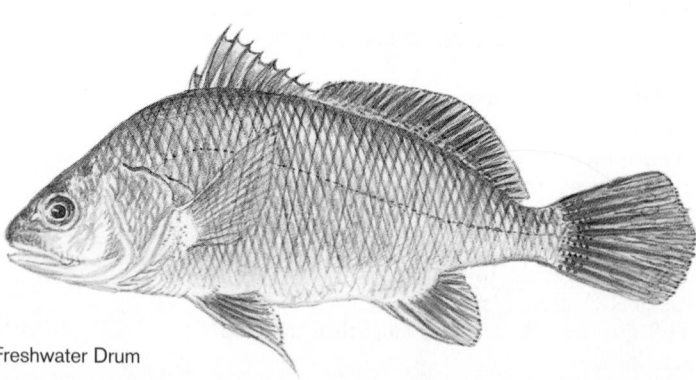

Freshwater Drum

A large freshwater drum from Lake Winnipeg, Manitoba.

drum, corbina, and seatrout, among others. It also has the greatest range of any North American freshwater fish, is highly adaptable, and is an excellent battler on light tackle, although it is extremely underrated and underutilized as a sportfish.

A unique feature of the freshwater drum is its oversize otolith—a flat, egg-shaped "ear bone" used for hearing and balance. It is surrounded by fluid and has a white, enameled surface with alternating light and dark bands that can be used to determine the age of the fish. They are often kept as good luck charms or made into jewelry. Excavated from Indian village sites, huge otoliths from freshwater drum indicate that at one time they grew as large as 200 pounds.

Although a strong fighter with some commercial value, the freshwater drum is not generally highly sought as either a sport or a food fish. It is deliberately sought by some anglers in the southern and midwestern regions of the United States, although it is mostly caught accidentally by anglers. The freshwater drum is often confused with carp in both appearance and taste, although on close examination it does not look like a carp. The drum's flesh is white with large, coarse flakes. It has been described by some as being of low quality, but this determination is inaccurate. Often found in clear waters, it is a relative of saltwater drum and croaker, which are highly valued as food. The freshwater drum, too, is fine table fare. Perhaps 5 to 10 million pounds are taken annually for commercial purposes, mostly from Lake Erie, and mostly for animal feed.

Identification.   The body is deep with a humped back, a blunt snout, and a subterminal mouth adapted for bottom feeding. A set of powerful teeth are in the pharynx. It has two dorsal fins, the first having eight to nine spines. The anal fin has two spines, the second of which is long and extremely stout. The caudal fin is bluntly pointed. Its coloring is green to gray on back with silvery overtones and a white belly. The large, silvery scales are rough to the touch.

The freshwater drum's two dorsal fins and rounded tail distinguish it from the carp and the buffalo. Also, the first dorsal fin of the freshwater drum is composed of eight to nine spines, whereas the carp has only one spine at the beginning of its single soft-rayed dorsal fin, and the buffalo has no spines at all. The freshwater drum can be distinguished from all other freshwater fish by the lateral line, which extends to the tip of the tail and is characteristic of sciaenids.

Size/Age.   The average size of a freshwater drum is 15 inches and 3 pounds, although they can grow to 50 pounds. The average commercial catch usually weighs 1 to 5 pounds. The all-tackle record is 53 pounds, 8 ounces. They can live up to 20 years.

Distribution.   The freshwater drum occurs over much of the U.S., between the Rockies and the Appalachians southward throughout eastern Mexico to Guatemala's Río Usumacinta system and northward through Manitoba, Canada, all the way to Hudson Bay. It also occurs in some areas of Ontario, Quebec, and Saskatchewan.

Habitat.   Although it prefers clear waters, the freshwater drum is adaptable and can withstand turbid water better than many other species. It is commonly found in large lakes and in the deep pools of rivers. It favors deep water, staying at the bottom but moving shoreward at dusk. The drum is rarely found in small streams or small lakes.

Spawning.   The freshwater drum spawns in spring when the water temperature reaches 65° to 70°F. The eggs are released over shallow gravel and sandy stretches near shore. They stick to pebbles or stones on the bottom and hatch within two weeks. Neither the eggs nor the young receive parental care.

Food and feeding habits.   Young drum feed on minute crustaceans. Adults consume mollusks, insects, and fish. Using their snout, they slowly move small rocks and other bottom materials to find food. Their pharyngeal teeth crush snail or clam shells, and they spit out the shell and swallow the soft body.

Angling.   Freshwater drum, or sheepshead as they are commonly known, can be taken on artificial lures or live baits, almost always fished near the bottom. Earthworms fished on bottom rigs or simply with enough split-shot weight to get to the bottom are effective, and small crayfish may also be used. Although small spinners, spoons, and sometimes plugs can catch drum where they are plentiful, jigs are the most reliable lures. Small marabou jigs or leadheads with plastic trailers are generally best, and they can be tipped with a piece of bait as well.

Sheepshead are generally easier to target in rivers than in lakes. In rivers, freshwater drum favor deep holes, tailrace pools below dams, eddies, deep riprap areas, the area outside bends, and similar places. In lakes, they are likely to be around rocky areas, including boulder and riprap banks, but they are not found where there is vegetation.

As with other drum, the flesh of the sheepshead can deteriorate quickly, so it is best to eat it soon after capture, rather than to store it for a long time. This fish can be prepared in many ways.

DRUM, RED   *Sciaenops ocellatus.*
Other names—channel bass, redfish, rat red (schooling juveniles less than 2 pounds), bull red (more than 10 pounds), puppy drum (under 18 inches), drum, spottail bass, red bass, red horse, school drum; French: *tambour rouge;* Spanish: *corvinón ocelado, pez rojo, corvina roja, pescado colorado.*

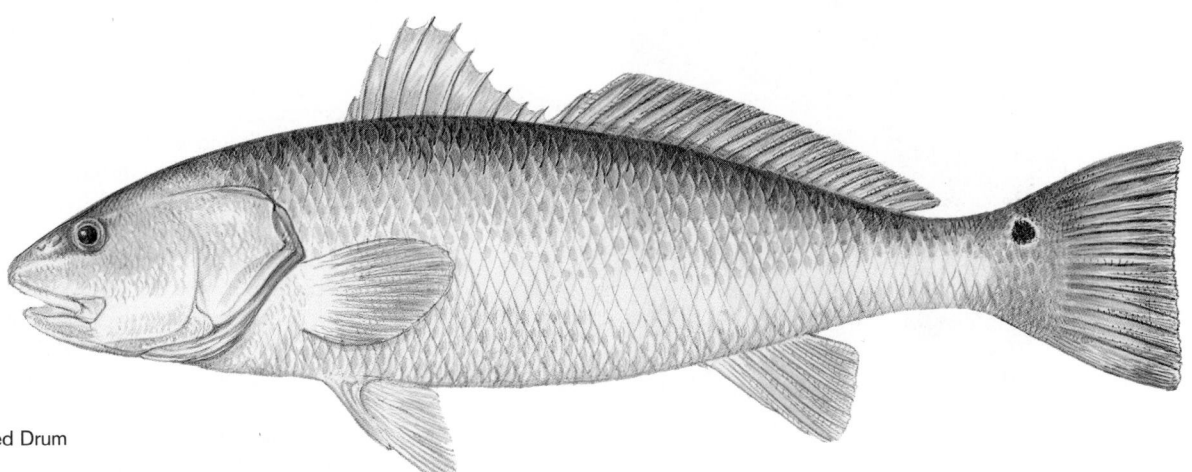

Red Drum

Commonly known as a channel bass and red-fish, the red drum is second only to black drum (see: drum, black) in size among members of the drum family, Sciaenidae, but probably first in the hearts of anglers. The common term "drum" refers to the loud and distinctive "drumming" noise that occurs when the fish raps a muscle against the swim bladder. The noise is voluntary and is assumed to be associated with locating and attracting mates, and it can sometimes be heard from a good distance, sometimes even by people above the water.

Red drum have been in great demand in recent decades. They were intensely harvested by commercial fishermen until fishing restrictions or outright bans were enacted, and the great popularity of blackened redfish as a restaurant menu and fish market item was a significant factor in the collapse of redfish populations, especially due to netting in the Gulf of Mexico. A ban on netting, however, resulted in a dramatic comeback of gulf populations and caused exceptional growth in light-tackle inshore fishing. Today the red drum is one of the most popular coastal species in the U.S.

The management of redfish is complicated by the biology of the fish. The younger fish are found in state waters and thus are subject to state regulations, whereas the larger fish and schools are found either in offshore state waters (from shore to 3 miles out) or federal waters (from 3 to 200 miles offshore). Most coastal states have length and bag limits for red drum.

A large red drum from Cape Hatteras, North Carolina.

As mentioned, red drum are excellent food fish—one of the most desirable in the Gulf of Mexico. It is still commonly used in the popular dish known as blackened redfish. Larger specimens can be coarse and stringy, but smaller fish are quite good. The flesh is white, heavy, and moist, with a fine texture and mild flavor.

The red drum is also a popular surf fish, often caught under classic surf conditions. Although it isn't a flashy fighter, it is stubborn and determined, persistent on heading for the bottom. Large red drum, which are primarily found in the mid-Atlantic states, are powerful, premier coastal sportfish.

Identification. The red drum is similar in appearance to the black drum, although its maximum size is smaller and it is more streamlined. The body is elongate with a subterminal mouth and blunt nose. On adults the tail is squared, and on juveniles it is rounded. There are no chin barbels, which also distinguishes it from the black drum. Its coloring is coppery red to bronze on the back, and silver and white on the sides and belly. One black dot (also called an eyespot), or many, are found at the base of the tail.

Size/Age. The average adult red drum is 28 inches long and weighs roughly 15 pounds. Although red drum can attain enormous sizes, they seldom do so. A 30-pounder is generally rare south of the Carolinas or in the Gulf of Mexico, although fish weighing up to 60 pounds are caught in offshore locations. Thirty- to 50-pound fish are most prominent in the mid-Atlantic, principally in North Carolina and Virginia; these sizes are considered trophies.

Red drum can live 50 or more years. They are reported to live to at least 40 years in the Gulf of Mexico, and the all-tackle record, a North Carolina fish of 94 pounds, 2 ounces, was reportedly 53 years old.

Distribution. Red drum are found in the western Atlantic Ocean from the Gulf of Maine to the Florida Keys, although they are rare north of Maryland, and all along the Gulf coast to northern Mexico.

Habitat. An estuarine-dependent fish that becomes oceanic later in life, the red drum is found in brackish water and saltwater on sand, mud, and grass bottoms of inlets, shallow bays, tidal passes, bayous, and estuaries. The red drum also tolerates freshwater, in which some have been known to dwell permanently. Larger red drum prefer deeper waters of lower estuaries and tidal passes, whereas smaller drum remain in shallow waters near piers and jetties and on grassy flats.

Red drum can survive wide ranges of salinity and temperature. Smaller drum prefer lower salinity levels than do larger ones. Optimum salinity levels range from 5 to 30 parts per thousand, optimum temperatures from 40° to 90°F.

More big reds and fewer small ones exist in a fairly short stretch of the mid-Atlantic because of its downturned mouth, to locate forage on the bottom through vacuuming or biting the bottom. Juveniles consume copepods, amphipods, and tiny shrimp. In summer and fall, adults feed on crabs, shrimp, and sand dollars. Fish such as menhaden, mullet, pinfish, sea robin, lizardfish, spot, Atlantic croaker, and flounder are the primary foods consumed during winter and spring. In shallow water, red drum are often seen browsing head-down with their tails slightly out of the water, a behavior called "tailing."

Angling. Red drum are a democratic fish in that they are susceptible to a variety of methods, lures, and baits, in clear as well as turbid waters, and along beaches, at inlets, on grassflats, in marshes, in deep channels, and around shoals. Sight casting with lures or flies, bottom fishing with baits, and surf fishing are popularly enjoyed in various locations. They can be very easy to catch at times, and spooky and difficult at others.

Sight casting is probably the most favored method, and takes the form of spotting nearshore roving schools along beaches, or stalking shallow-water tailers as the feed. The former is more likely along the Atlantic coast, and the latter in gulf marshes. Shallow-water stalking is especially conducive to fly fishing, using Clouser Minnows, Deceiver patterns, and crab or bunker imitations. Eight- to 10-weight fly rods are fine for quiet back-country conditions, but 10- to 12-weight outfits are necessary for the bigger fish found in surf and beach conditions.

When fishing for larger schools, anglers in boats try to get a high vantage point and cruise along beaches and inlets looking for dark masses of fish just under the surface in water that varies from a few feet to 20 feet deep. Sunny conditions are generally necessary for this, and the clear water of spring makes for the best visibility.

Blind casting along the edges of marshes on an outgoing tide is a standard practice. It is likely to produce generally smaller fish but is excellent for light-tackle and small-boat anglers.

Red drum are more likely to take lures than are black drum, and casting spoons, surface plugs, swimming plugs, and jigs are productive for these fish. The smaller fish of gulf waters are commonly caught on leadhead jigs fished with soft trailers. When the water is off-colored or turbid, rattling plugs and poppers can be effective. Smaller fish in estuaries and flats are suited to many of the same lures that catch largemouth bass in freshwater, as well as similar fishing tackle, namely, medium to light spinning and baitcasting outfits. Ten- to 15-pound lines are generally adequate. Live bait such as crab, shrimp, and finger mullet are effective but often unnecessary where the population of reds is good.

The bigger red drum of the Atlantic surf are a different story, however, and they generally require sturdier tackle, bigger lures, and heavier line. Bait is

An unusual redfish, with four spots, from Aransas Bay, Texas.

the rich feeding opportunities. This is said to keep the fish from migrating southward each fall, as they prefer to move offshore to warmer continental shelf waters until spring.

Life history/Behavior. Males are mature by four years of age at 30 inches and 15 pounds, females by five years at 35 inches and 18 pounds. The spawning season is during the fall, although it may begin as early as August and end as late as November. Spawning takes place at dusk in the coastal waters of the northern Gulf of Mexico, near passes, inlets, and bays, and is often tied to new- or full-moon phases. Right before spawning, males change color and become dark red or bright bluish gray above the lateral line. Both males and females, hours before mating, chase and butt each other, drumming loudly. Females may release up to $4^1/_2$ million eggs, although very few survive to adulthood. Currents and winds carry the larvae into estuarine nursery areas.

Adult red drum form large schools in coastal waters, an activity presumably associated with spawning, although it occurs throughout the year. Anglers often see them at the surface or moving under schools of blue runner and little tunny. Sight casting to schools is a favored activity.

Drum are known generally to remain in the waters where they were hatched, although some populations migrate seasonally, and large reds may move offshore as previously noted.

Food and feeding habits. As a bottom fish, this species uses its senses of sight and touch, and

often preferred, with cut mullet being especially favored, although various other bait works also. Red drum frequently mouth a bait before running off with it, so you need to adapt accordingly.
See: Surf Fishing.

DRY FLY
A floating artificial fly that represents an aquatic or terrestrial insect in freshwater.
See: Fly.

DUN
A post-nymphal but immature aquatic insect or fly (subimago); also, a grayish artificial fly that imitates this.

DUNCAN LOOP KNOT
A loop-type terminal fishing knot, inferior to a Non-Slip Loop Knot.
See: Knots, Fishing.

D

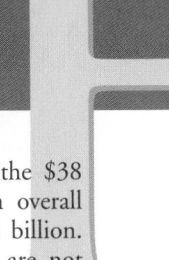

EARTHWORM

A worm that lives and burrows in the ground. It is estimated that 5,000 species of earthworms inhabit the world, living in all environs except the desert and continually frozen tundra. The most common forms of earthworm are the nightcrawler, which is usually 6 to 8 inches long, and the redworm, which is usually 3 to 4 inches long. Worms are highly popular and effective freshwater bait.

See: Natural Bait.

EBB TIDE

Outgoing, or falling, tide.
See: Tides.

ECHO SOUNDER

See: Sonar.

ECOLOGY

The study of living organisms in relation to each other and their environment; the entire network of associations between living organisms and their environment.

See: Ecosystem.

ECONOMIC VALUE (Sportfishing)

Although sportfishing is a traditional pastime, it has an important economic value, especially in North America and particularly in the United States. Many local and regional surveys of the economic benefits of sportfishing have been done, and in some cases they have been instrumental in increasing or adjusting governmental or private tourism expenditures, increasing or adjusting wildlife resource agency expenditures, affecting the buyout of commercial fishing operators, and otherwise reflecting the importance of healthy aquatic resources.

In the United States, the only national measure of the total economic impact of sportfishing comes from a national survey conducted every five years by the U.S. Fish and Wildlife Service (see). The most recent survey, conducted in 1996, determined that recreational anglers (35.2 million aged 16 or older) in the United States spent $38 billion directly on freshwater and saltwater angling activities and equipment. According to an analysis by the American Sportfishing Association, the $38 billion spent at the retail level had an overall ripple-through economic effect of $108 billion. Comparable figures for other countries are not available.

ECOSYSTEM

An intricate community of interaction among animals (including humans), plants, microorganisms, and the physical and chemical environment in which they live. Ecosystems are everywhere—from exotic tropical rain forests to small urban parks, and from oceans to farm ponds—and, obviously, the earth is the largest ecosystem. A lake or pond is an ecosystem. Every river has its own ecosystem. And all of these are subsystems of larger ecosystems (a lake drains into a stream, which flows to a river, which flows to an estuary, which meets with the ocean), which means that an impact on any given element may influence other elements.

ECUADOR

One of the smaller South American countries, the equator-straddling Ecuador is on the northwestern coast of that continent, bordering Peru, Colombia, and the Pacific Ocean. About one-fourth of the country is coastal plain, one-fourth takes in two ranges of the Andes Mountains, and one-half (the eastern region) is rain forest.

A boat trolls for roosterfish off Punta Elena.

Saltwater

The fertile waters off Ecuador's brief coastline offer among the finest offshore fishing opportunities available worldwide. Most of this originates at the seaside resort town of Salinas, only a two-hour drive through desert flats from the airport arrival city of Guayaquil. Salinas is not far from the once revered black marlin grounds of northern Peru, and just $2^1/_2°$ south of the equator. At Salinas, vacationing city dwellers and villagers from the higher elevations to the east come to enjoy the cool waters of the Pacific and the long, narrow beaches. Here, too, is a fleet of fishing boats available for charter, and thus the opportunity to experience one of Ecuador's major overlooked attractions.

Salinas (and Manta, about 45 miles to the north) is strategically located to benefit from a mix of formidable ocean currents. Just a few miles offshore from the beaches of Salinas and the tall condominiums nearby, an eddy of the cold Antarctic Humboldt Current sweeps by, bringing with it acres and acres of baitfish and a host of predatory species, particularly black marlin, Pacific blue marlin, bigeye tuna, and striped marlin. Stripes are the foremost attraction to the many anglers who come here annually. It isn't the record potential that does it (although Salinas was the site of two long-standing fly rod records for striped marlin). It is the sheer number of fish to be encountered, and the excitement of stalking and baiting them, that turns everyone on.

A typical day begins with a short ride by dinghy from the beach to nearby charter boats. The run offshore travels by Punta Elena, a tall, rocky promontory that serves as a shoreside reference point during the day's fishing. Within an hour, lines are dropped into the water and all eyes are scanning the sea for marlin tails. This is a unique method of fishing for marlin: Here you usually see your quarry before the strike.

Observing and stalking the quarry sounds like hunting, or like fishing on tidal flats for bonefish—not like something you would do in the wide-open ocean over deep, indigo water. In the offshore salt, this would be rather dull if there were very little to see. But because there's a lot to see in the Pacific off Salinas, this pastime is not only exciting, it has transformed the area into one of the world's most renowned spots for big-game fishing.

Salinas is one of few places where anglers deliberately and continuously sight-fish for marlin. Although skirted ballyhoo baits are trolled behind the boat at all times, most fish are first sighted and then deliberately baited. The captain races the engines and maneuvers the boat ahead of the fish to present the baits within its field of view. Often two, or four, or even up to a dozen tails are sighted at once. Pods of marlin are often seen surfing down the long, rolling Pacific swells, and when such a bonanza occurs, the odds for a hookup or two greatly increase.

A minority of striped marlin actually charge one of the baits. Some move off immediately, whereas others look over the various *baits* and follow for several minutes before drifting off. The watching, waiting, and anticipating make for some anxious but enjoyable moments in themselves, especially because up to 20 fish might be spotted in the course of a day. Although great-size blue and black marlin are occasionally seen, their tails visible above the surface of the water, these larger fish usually crash the bait or lure from below without warning. It's hard to say which is more exciting, a blind strike or an anticipated one from a tailing fish, but either way, a marlin strike is for many the experience of a lifetime.

The boats off Ecuador's coast have at times averaged a billfish a day year-round, so even the novice can expect a good chance to tangle with one or more of these magnificent gamefish. This makes Ecuador a superb place for the novice big-game angler to hook that first billfish. Striped marlin are not only abundant, they average 100 to 150 pounds and tire themselves through spectacular greyhounding performances across the ocean surface.

Black and blue marlin in this area, of course, average considerably larger than striped marlin—500-pounders not uncommon. A former world record Pacific blue marlin weighing 1,014 pounds was taken in 1985 off Manta, about 45 miles by boat from Salinas. La Plata Island, between Salinas and Manta, has become a hotspot for blue marlin. The record-size fish swimming in these waters contribute in no small part to Ecuador's angling fame; giant bigeye tuna and blue marlin, in particular, feed offshore from Salinas and nearby Manta, and the constant anticipation of encountering such monsters simply adds to the experience.

Ecuador is blessed with such activity in part because of the interaction of the powerful currents mentioned earlier. The most prominent current along the western coast of South America is the Humboldt Current, a cold northerly flowing stream of water that moves toward the west as it nears the equator. The Equatorial Current at the equator produces eddies that spin off and head back toward Ecuador's coast. These eddies of warm tropical water force the colder Humboldt waters offshore, and they contain baitfish and gamefish species. Additionally, some 10 to 12 miles offshore there's a sharp drop in the ocean floor, which rises back again before plunging into great depths. An abundance of baitfish in this area causes the striped marlin to skim the surface waters, and accounts for all the sightings.

Of course, other marlin are present here, too, perhaps not in the same numbers as stripes but with no less interest from anglers. Black marlin are more prevalent inshore than striped marlin, whereas blue marlin are likely to be farther out over deeper water.

The billfish here are sometimes thrown a whammy by El Niño, creating great concern for the commercial longline fishery. Yet, monster blue marlin have been taken by anglers (longliners have reportedly taken numerous granders). In May 1985, an International Game Fish Association (IGFA) 80-pound line-class world record Pacific blue marlin of 1,014 pounds was caught off Manta, and several 800- to 900-pound fish followed in later years.

Black marlin aren't typically that large, although 500- to 700-pounders have been hooked. These fish are on average in the 350-pound class, and the median weight for blues is about 400 pounds.

That's good, especially because the blue marlin are available year-round. May through January is the better period. The optimal time for blacks is April and May and again in the fall. Prime time for striped marlin is usually October through January, although El Niños can foul up that timetable; many anglers like variety and opt for September through November, when the overall options are at their best.

Bigeye tuna represent another notable fishery here. These fish average in the heavyweight division, and several records have been set in Ecuadorian waters, including a 341-pounder on 80-pound-test line. Off Ecuador, January through March is a peak time for these bruisers.

Numerous other species inhabit these waters, including swordfish. Anglers seldom attempt to land swordfish, however, which are longlined in fair numbers here and are occasionally seen on the surface. During the late 1970s anglers did put some effort into baiting swordfish. These were spotted fairly regularly on the surface about 30 miles south of Salinas.

Trollers encounter sailfish and dolphin (dorado) here too. Dolphin used to be so abundant that boats ran from them in pursuit of striped marlin. The capture of at least one dolphin for lunch was a sure thing. Dolphin species have been heavily impacted by longlining, however, which started in the 1980s.

Sailfish are a common year-round trolling catch. They often build up in the Ecuadorian winter (July through September) and usually average more than 100 pounds. When an occasional current shift alters the water temperature and turns the billfish bite off, which happens periodically, the do-or-die angler can opt to try casting or trolling coastal rocks for the feisty roosterfish or corvina, or troll a nearby close-to-shore seamount for wahoo.

The commercial fleet that operates here has long raised conservation concerns among sporting anglers, as longliners and gillnetters have been abundant. Even among sportfishing boats in the past, the catch belonged to the crew, and was often sold to local Ecuadorians, for whom the fish is an important food source. Increasing numbers of anglers interested in catch-and-release have helped conservation efforts.

Most anglers need not bring fishing tackle to experience the billfish action, as the seasoned offshore fleet here have first-rate 50- and 80-pound-class tackle. Costs for a one-day charter run less than the fee for a day's big-game fishing at most of the world's angling hotspots.

Galápagos Islands

This fabled group of islands (13 major, 6 minor, and 42 islets with names plus many unnamed rocks and islets) is owned by Ecuador but located about 600 miles off the coast and serviced by flights from Guayaquil into the islands of Baltra and San Cristóbal, as well as by cruise ships. It was here that Darwin formulated his theory of evolution during the famous 1835 journey of H.M.S. *Beagle.*

The only element common to all the Galápagos, a strictly controlled national park, is the friendly nature of its animals and birds, which have lived largely free from predation. Otherwise, the islands, which are spread over about 800 square miles, range from desolate and volcanic to lush, and from cool to semitropical. Although the equator passes through the islands, the Humboldt Current has a cooling influence.

Fishing possibilities are unlimited but have been sampled primarily by large private boats. At this writing, attempts are underway to set up charter operations. An exceptional striped marlin fishery has been discovered on the Cristóbal Banks, north of San Cristóbal. The all-tackle world record Pacific sailfish was caught off Santa Cruz Island on February 1947, but no one has located other such outsize sails since.

Unlike the reptiles and resident birds, which are almost all unique to the Galápagos, fish found around the islands are familiar game and food species, including yellowfin tuna, cubera and mullet snapper, bonito, black skipjacks, dolphin, grouper, wahoo, amberjack, California sheepshead, and many types of sharks. The colorful leather bass isn't a common species in the eastern Pacific but is found around other offshore islands. Most surprising is the abundance of snook in Tortuga Negra Cove on Santa Cruz, opposite the airfield at Balta.

Freshwater

Ecuador has traditionally offered few freshwater fishing opportunities for traveling anglers, but waters in the highlands reportedly have been stocked with trout, and largemouth bass have been stocked in the lagoon at Otavalo. Good fishing for trout reportedly existed in high-mountain waters, at altitudes over 10,000 feet, in the late 1970s and early 1980s, but recent news of this has been scant.

The steep mountains of Ecuador produce many streams; those that flow west from the Andes in Ecuador are relatively short and might be accessible from Quito. The Rio Napo, which originates in the north-central mountains, is the country's major river, but many others flow westerly into Peru and then to the Amazon River. Some of the rivers and fishing possibilities in Ecuador are described in the Amazon review under Brazil *(see).*

EDDY

A counter current forming on the side of or within a main current. Eddies occur in air and water, are markedly different from the general movement of a large mass of the main current, and usually move in a circular path. They develop where main currents encounter obstacles or where two currents flow past one another. The number and velocity of eddies increase as the velocity of the surrounding mass (air or water) increases. More eddies and faster-moving ones spin off in rapidly moving water than in a more sluggish stream. If water moves around an obstacle, an eddy may form at some critical velocity (this depends on the nature of the obstacle) on the leeward side of the obstacle because the pressure of the fluid is reduced at that point by the rapid movement of the flow. If the velocity of the main current is great enough, a vortex or whirlpool will form. Whirlpools are permanent eddies.

In freshwater, eddies appear in rivers and occasionally in streams or creeks, varying in size and velocity. Many eddies are along the edges of a flowage but may be present where there are large rocks and bridge pilings. Because food, including insects and fish, may utilize or be swept into eddies, predatory fish will use them for feeding opportunities, sometimes stationing themselves in the eddy facing downstream (which is actually facing into the upstream-flowing portion of the eddy), or in the confused water of the seam where the main current and the eddy meet. Eddies of sufficient speed can create tricky casting and presentation situations.

Eddies seldom occur in lakes, although in large inland bodies of water they may be present in a grand and slow-moving scale where there is sufficient current. Eddies are present in the oceans, where they are spun off wind activity, upwellings, or waves encountering an obstacle, and also by the convergence of large current systems. In the latter case, they may be enormous sections of water that do not provide visible clues to direction, although a drifting boat with navigational devices will be able to detect movement that is related to eddies and not wind or wave action. The edges of these eddies may trap minute food organisms and thus attract pelagic baitfish and, in turn, larger predators. The Gulf Stream is a prime example of an eddy-creating ocean system.

EELS

More than 20 families form a large group, or order—Anguilliformes—of jawed fish called eels. They share a number of features that make them unique among fish. All have spineless fins and long, slim, snakelike bodies that lack ventral fins. In most, the dorsal, caudal, and anal fins are joined to form one continuous fin over the rear of the body. Except in a few species, there are no visible scales, although microscopic examination will reveal numerous very tiny scales—100 or more to the square inch. Most eels are palindromic, that is, they have the unusual ability to move equally well forward or backward forcefully. This serves them well not only for burrowing purposes, but for pulling, twisting, and spinning when tearing apart prey that is too large to be consumed whole.

All the different families of eels are marine except the family Anguillidae. Some eels have important commercial significance and are valued food fish; a few are caught by anglers. Not to be confused with eels are the eel-like lampreys *(see),* which do not have jaws or pectoral fins, and are commonly but erroneously called "lamprey eels."

Freshwater Eels

The Anguillidae family of freshwater eels includes such better known species as the American eel *(Anguilla rostrata),* European eel *(A. anguilla),* Japanese eel *(A. japonica),* Indian eel *(Phisodnopsis boro),* and about a dozen other species that live in the Indo-Pacific region. Freshwater eels are curiously absent from the eastern Pacific and South Atlantic, presumably due to their higher salinity.

These eels have been prized as food since ancient times and have been caught in eel traps or pots, in nets, or on hook and line. Little was known about their life history until the late 1800s. All sorts of stories were told about how eels came into being, including a persistent tale that they came from horse hairs that fell into the water and somehow came to life. A Danish scientist finally unraveled the strange true story.

The American eel and the European eel both spawn in the same area of the Atlantic Ocean, in deep water at the northern edge of the Sargasso Sea. There, each female lays as many as 10 to 20 million eggs, which the males fertilize. The adults then die. The eggs float slowly to the surface and soon hatch into slim, transparent leptocephali, or larvae, commonly called glass fish.

The baby eels begin drifting and swimming in the ocean currents. Their swimming motions help keep them directed toward their ultimate home waters. Baby American eels travel toward North America, and baby European eels swim toward Europe. How they know which way to go when neither has ever seen its "home" is unknown. For the American eels, the trip is about 1,000 miles; the journey requires about a year. European eels travel 3,000 miles or more, their trip taking nearly three years. It is equally astonishing that the growth rate of each type differs, so that each has developed to about the same size when it reaches its destination. By this time they have metamorphosed from the leaflike leptocephalus stage and have become thick-bodied little eels (also called elvers).

Male eels stay near the mouths of rivers, but the more venturesome females continue to swim upstream into the headwaters. Or sometimes they slither through dewy grass to move from one body of water to another. Eventually they find a place that suits their needs and settle there to feed and grow. The female may reach a length of 3 feet; males rarely grow more than a foot long. After several years, the females lose their greenish color, becoming almost black. They begin their downstream journey to the sea, where they are joined by the mature males, who swim with them to the spawning area. Eels that have established themselves in ponds or lakes without tributary streams do not move out even after maturing. They remain landlocked, living in these waters for 50 years or longer and never spawning.

The adult American eel and the adult European eel are so similar in appearance that they can be distinguished only by counting their vertebrae. An American eel has 103 to 111 vertebrae; the European, 110 to 119. Both have sharp snouts and numerous teeth. Some scientists believe the two are really one and the same species.

In Europe and Japan these eels rank as delicacies. They are less favored in America, even though they're delicious when fried, grilled, roasted, smoked, or pickled. In sportfishing, eel skins and whole live eels are used as bait for striped bass and other marine fish, and artificial eels made of soft plastic and other substances are commonly used.

See: Eel, American; Eel, European.

Moray Eels

The Muraenidae family of morays is the most infamous group within the order Anguilliformes. They constitute a family of more than 80 species occurring in greatest abundance in tropical and subtropical waters, but with a few species straying into waters of temperate regions during warm months.

Morays live primarily in coral reefs or in similar rocky areas. The typical moray's body is flattened from side to side, pectoral fins are lacking, and the scaleless skin is thick and leathery. The dorsal and anal fins are low, sometimes almost hidden by the wrinkled skin around them. The gill opening is small and round, and the teeth are large. Most morays are large, reaching a length of 5 to 6 feet. Some are as much as 10 feet long; a few are less than 6 inches long.

A moray will anchor the rear half of its body in coral and rocks, allowing the front of its body to sway with the current. In this position, with its mouth agape, it is ready to grasp any prey that comes close. This gaping stance appears menacing, but it is an adaptation suited not only to foraging but also to respiration, allowing the eel to pump water across its gills. Morays have vicious tempers, as divers will attest, and it is unwise to torment them. This temper is shown when provoked; spearing morays or reaching blindly into holes where they live can cause an attack. Their bites are not poisonous, as many believe, but a large moray can make multiple deep wounds that not uncommonly become infected and are slow to heal. Deaths have resulted from encounters with morays. Normally, morays are nocturnal, but they never miss an opportunity to appear from their rocky lairs when a meal is in the offing. They feed on small fish, octopus, crustaceans, and mollusks.

Morays themselves are captured and eaten in many parts of the world and have been esteemed

E

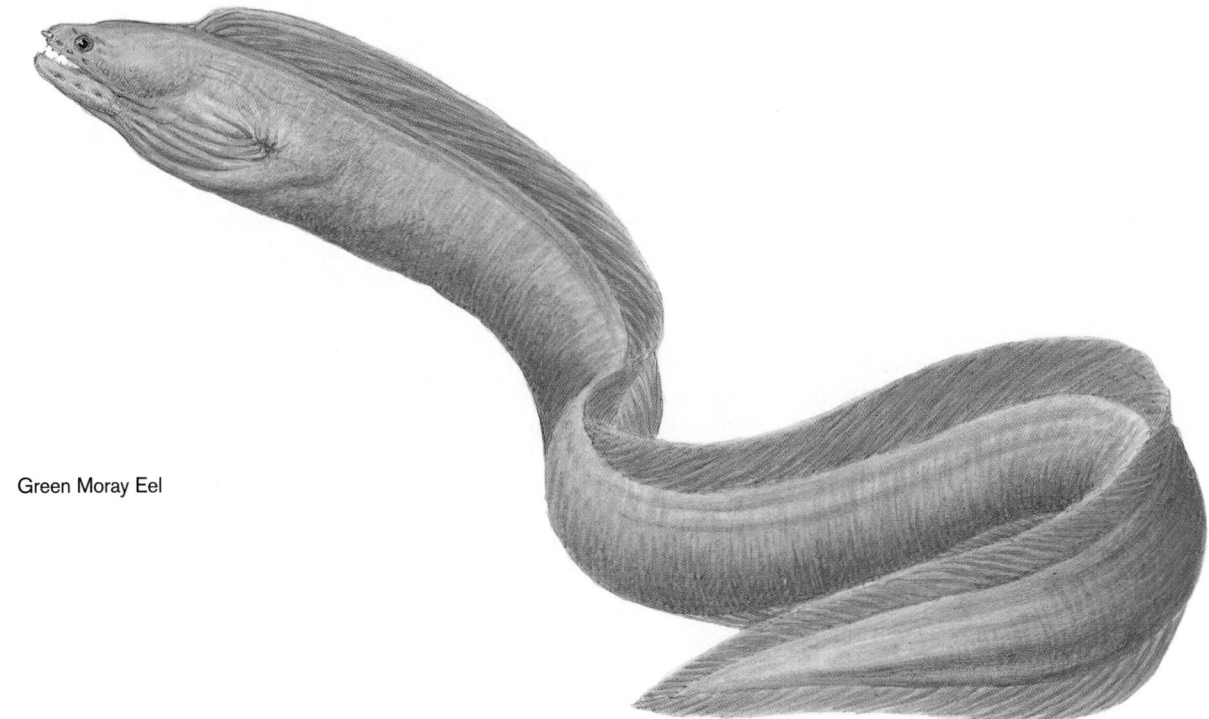

Green Moray Eel

food since Roman times. However, the flesh of some morays is reputed to cause debilitating ciguatera *(see)* poisoning.

Many morays are attractively colored. The green moray *(Gymnothorax funebris),* which lives in tropical and subtropical waters of both North and South America, is an unusual brownish green due to a yellow slime that covers the eel's blue body. Although most green morays are less than 5 feet long, occasional reports of 10-footers exist. The green moray inhabits coral reefs, sometimes going into deep water to prowl for food.

The spotted moray *(G. moringa)* occurs in the same range as the green moray. Smaller, it almost never exceeds 3 feet in length, and it has prominent dark spots or a chainlike pattern of dark lines on its usually yellowish body. The basic body color commonly matches the eel's surroundings, however, and may vary from white to dark brown.

Off the Pacific coast, the California moray *(G. mordax)* is similar in appearance and habits to the spotted moray; it grows to a length of 5 feet. It is found in waters between 2 and 65 feet deep and may live more than 30 years. The blackedge moray *(G. nigromarginatus),* prevalent in the subtropical Atlantic, the Caribbean, and the Gulf of Mexico, is of similar size, but the black pattern is more pronounced, with black margins on the dorsal and anal fins.

The puhi-paka *(G. flavimarginatus),* which grows to 4 feet long, is common in Hawaiian waters and elsewhere in the western Pacific. Its fins are bordered with bright green. Also prevalent in the same area is *G. eurostus,* growing to 2 feet long.

Morays of the genus *Echidna,* most abundant in Indo-Pacific waters, are among the most striking eels in their bright colors and patterns. The zebra moray *(E. zebra)* is marked with vertical bands or rings of white the full length of its dark, brownish yellow body. The chain moray *(E. catenata),* found in the warm Atlantic from Florida to South America, is marked with a black chainlike pattern over a yellowish background. Many of the Indo-Pacific morays of this genus have flattened molars for crushing the shells of mollusks and the hard outer skeletons of sea urchins, crabs, and other sea creatures.

The dragon moray *(Muraena pardalis)* of the western Pacific, is one of several attractive species in its genus, distinguished by its curiously elongated, tubelike nostrils, the posterior pair of which is located far back on the head, just in front of the eyes. In some species, the nostrils are large and leaflike. The dragon moray has irregularly shaped red and white spots on a dark background.

Among the smallest of the morays are *Anarchis* species, including the pygmy moray *(A. yoshiae)* of the Atlantic coast of North America, all measuring less than 8 inches in length.

Another widely distributed species in the Indo-Pacific region is the $1\frac{1}{2}$-foot *Lycodontis petelli,* marked with alternating, broad light and dark bands.

Conger Eels

The small Congridae family of conger eels are marine eels distinguished from the morays by having pectoral fins and by the black margin on their dorsal and anal fins. Conger eels inhabit temperate as well as tropical seas and sometimes shallow inshore waters, where they may be mistaken for the American or the European eel. Conger eels are scaleless, however, and the dorsal fin originates over the tips of the pectorals. Some conger eels live only in deep water. Nine species are found off North America's coasts, eight in the Atlantic and one in the Pacific.

The best-known species are the European conger eel *(Conger conger)* and the American conger eel *(Conger oceanicus),* which are respectively widely distributed in European and North American waters. The former can reach 10 feet in length and more than 140 pounds. The most common species in Japanese waters is *Astroconger myriaster.* The Catalina conger *(Gnathopis catalinensis)* is a small species, growing to 16 inches and possessing a large pectoral fin; it is found from Southern California to the Gulf of California in Mexico.

Snake Eels

The Ophichthidae family of snake eels have long, cylindrical, snakelike bodies and can move backward extremely effectively. The tail is stiff and sharp rather than broad and flat, as it is in morays. It is used like an awl to burrow tail-first into sand or mud. The nostrils are located in two short, stout barbels on top of the nose, which the eels use to probe into crevices and cavities as they search for food. Compared to morays and most other eels, snake eels are docile creatures, commonly seen crawling over the bottom like snakes.

In most snake eels, the dorsal fin extends almost the full length of the body, beginning just behind the head but stopping short of the tip of the tail. The anal fin is only about half as long, also stopping before the tip of the tail. Pectoral fins are lacking or very small. Only a few of the profuse species reach a length exceeding 3 feet; most of them are less than a foot long. They are typically brightly colored and are generally strikingly marked with bands, spots, or both. Snake eels are found throughout the world in subtropical and tropical seas, a few ranging into temperate waters.

One of the several dozen species in the Atlantic and Caribbean is the spotted snake eel *(Ophichtus ophis),* averaging 2 feet in length and occasionally growing to 4 feet. Its yellowish body is covered with large brown spots. The yellow snake eel *(O. zophochir)* is a similar species that lives in the Pacific.

Another genus represented by numerous species is *Myrichthys,* which includes the sharptail eel *(M. acuminatus),* in the Atlantic, and the tiger snake eel *(M. tigrinus),* in the Pacific. In Indo-Pacific waters, *M. maculosus* is marked attractively with dark bands that bracket round spots.

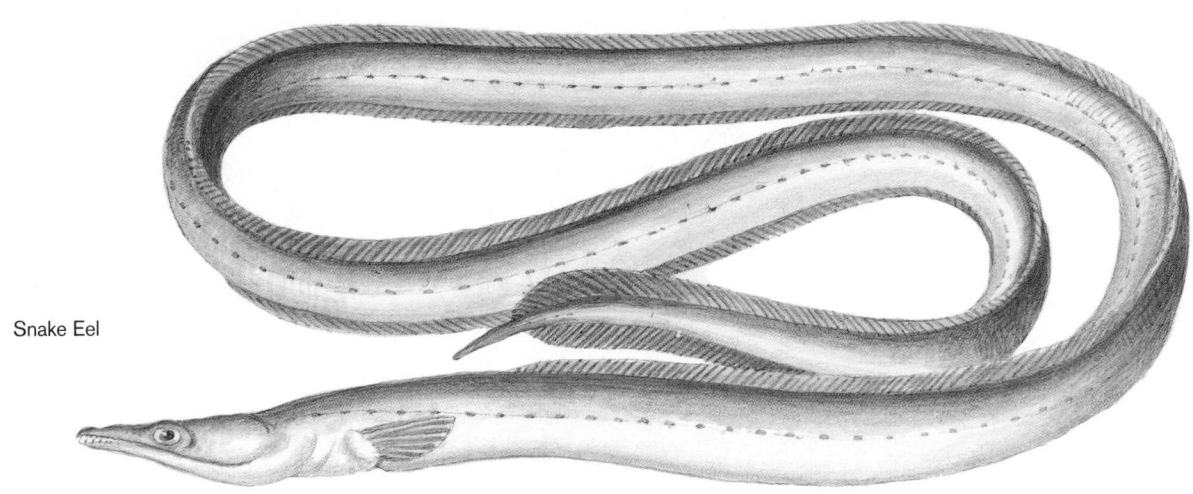

Snake Eel

EEL, AMERICAN *Anguilla rostrata.*
EEL, EUROPEAN *Anguilla anguilla.*

Other names for American eel—silver eel, Atlantic eel, common eel, yellow-bellied eel, freshwater eel, bronze eel, water snake, whip; Dutch: *amerikaanse aal;* Finnish: *amerikanankerias;* French: *anguille d'Amerique;* Italian: *anguilla americana;* Japanese: *unagi;* Portuguese: *enguia-americana;* Spanish: *anguila, anguila americana;* Swedish: *amerikansk ål.*

Other names for European eel—silver eel, common eel, yellow eel, freshwater eel; Dutch: *aal;* Finnish: *ankerias;* French: *anguille, anguille d'Europe;* Italian: *anguilla;* Japanese: *unagi;* Portuguese: *eiró, enguia;* Russian: *retschnoi ugor;* Spanish: *anguila, anguila europea;* Swedish: *ål.*

American and European eels are members of the Anguillidae family of freshwater eels. They are common and have been the object of many wild tales speculating on the nature of their existence. Aristotle was convinced they rose spontaneously from mud, whereas Roman scholar Pliny the Elder believed young eels came from bits of skin that adult eels rubbed off on rocks. Italian anglers believed that eels mated with water snakes. The most common hypothesis was that eels arose spontaneously from horse hairs that fell into the water. These many ancient theories likely occurred because of the mystery and complexity surrounding both fish; their spawning habits and many diverse growth changes are among the most unique among freshwater fish.

These eels are preyed upon by many species at different stages of their existence. They are important forage for such larger offshore predators as sharks, haddock, and swordfish; for inshore species like striped bass; and for many species of birds, including bald eagles and various gulls. Their greatest predators, however, are likely humans.

American and European eels have been prized as food since ancient times and are caught in eel traps and nets, as well as by hook and line and spearing.

They are intensively sought commercially in many places and considered a delicacy, especially in Europe and Japan. Eels of all sizes are desirable for consumption, although larger individuals, having spent many years on the bottom of lakes and rivers and being high in fat content, may be especially susceptible to elevated levels of contaminants in areas that are highly polluted.

Larger individuals (10 to 16 inches or so) are used as bait by anglers, especially those seeking big striped bass, and they may be sold as bait in coastal shops. Smaller individuals are also sold by commercial interests for consumption and have been known to fetch many hundreds of dollars per pound. Increased coastal netting of small eels (elvers) due to rising market demands has raised concerns about the exploitation of these fish. European and Asian stocks have been especially diminished, and North American stocks have likewise been under severe pressure. Elvers have been harvested for use in pond culture and aquaculture operations. They have also been caught and transplanted to inland waters to boost or establish eel stocks.

Identification. The body is elongate and snakelike with a pointed head and many teeth. It is covered with thick mucus, hence the phrase "slippery as an eel." The large mouth extends as far back as the midpoint of the eye or past it. There is a single gill opening just in front of the pectoral fins. There are no pelvic fins, and the soft-rayed dorsal, anal, and caudal fins form one continuous fin. There are no visible scales. Coloring changes with maturity, as described later in this text.

The American eel and the European eel are almost identical; they can be distinguished only by counting vertebrae. The adult American eel has 103 to 111 vertebrae, whereas the European has 110 to 119 vertebrae.

Size/Age. American eels grow to 50 inches and 16 pounds. The average size for adult females is

American Eel

about 3 feet, whereas adult males are considerably smaller, rarely growing more than a foot long. They can live longer than 9 years in rivers, streams, and lakes. European eels can achieve similar size and age but are usually smaller on average.

Distribution.   The American eel occurs from southwest Greenland to Labrador, south along the North American coast to Bermuda, the Gulf of Mexico, Panama, and the Carribean islands. Within this region, inland it occurs from the Mississippi River drainage east, and northeast to the Great Lakes and to the Atlantic Ocean.

The European eel occurs in drainages feeding the North Atlantic, Baltic, and Mediterranean Seas, and along the east coast of Europe from the Black Sea to the White Sea. It has been introduced to Asia and South and Central America but has not reproduced.

Habitat.   These eels are catadromous, spending the majority of their life in freshwater and returning to saltwater to spawn. They prefer to dwell in heavy vegetation or to burrow in the sandy bottom. Their physical structure is such that they can easily swim backward and dig tail first into soft bottom sediments.

Life history/Behavior.   When it comes time to spawn, the males and females stop feeding, change in color from olive to black, and move out to sea. Both the American eel and the European eel spawn in the same area of the Atlantic Ocean, in deep water at the north edge of the Sargasso Sea. There each female lays as many as 10 to 20 million eggs, and both sexes die after spawning.

The eggs float to the surface and soon hatch into slim, transparent larvae (glass eels). The sex an eel becomes is thought to be partly determined by environmental conditions such as crowding and food abundance, but it is not determined until they are about 8 to 10 inches long and living in their freshwater habitat.

The larvae drift and swim for one year (American) or three years (European) with ocean currents toward river mouths. Males stay near the mouths of rivers, whereas females travel upstream, mostly at night. Eels can absorb oxygen through their skin as well as their gills and are known to travel overland, particularly in damp, rainy weather.

Balls of intertwined eels have been seen rolling up beaches in search of freshwater for overwintering.

Distinctive terms are used to identify the size, coloring, and behavior of these eels at different life stages. They are as follows:

Glass eels are those in the young larval stage called leptocephalus; they are shaped like willow leaves and have ribbonlike transparent bodies with a distinct black eye. These range from approximately 1 to $2^1/_2$ inches in length and are attracted to coastal estuaries and freshwater, where they are the target of intense commercial fishing interest.

Elvers are small eels in the stage of adapting to freshwater. They range from $2^1/_2$ to $3^1/_2$ inches in length and are darker in color than glass eels, being fully pigmented and ranging from gray to greenish brown. Mass upstream migrations of elvers have been observed. Although inconspicuous as they swim along river bottoms, they are especially visible when they encounter obstructions like dams and waterfalls.

Yellow eels are growing eels that exist in freshwater. Some biologists refer to them as adults, whereas others call them subadults. In any event, they are sexually immature, and yellowish to olive brown on the back and lighter on the belly. They swim freely along river bottoms, through shoreline rock crevices, and into silty lake bottoms in search of prey.

Silver eels are sexually mature adults that are dark with a bronze black hue on the back and silver on the underside. Many have enlarged eyes, which is believed to give them better vision in the ocean. These fish are ready to migrate, or they are in the process of migrating, out of freshwater to their ocean spawning grounds, a process that is believed to last three to five months during the fall and winter.

Food.   The diet of the nocturnal feeding American and European eels includes insect larvae, small fish, crabs, worms, clams, and frogs. They also feed on dead animals or on the eggs of fish, and are able to tear smaller pieces of food that are too large to be swallowed whole.

Their feeding habits are rather unusual with respect to large quarry. These eels have relatively weak jaws that are mainly suited to grasping, yet they possess many small, round, and rather blunt teeth. Because they are palindromic—that is, they can move equally well forward or backward forcefully—they are able to pull, twist, and spin when tearing apart prey that is too large to be consumed whole. The habit of spinning, which also occurs when they are caught by anglers (with some consternation about line twist and grasping), deserves explanation.

Spinning habits. When food cannot be consumed whole, or when it cannot be broken into morsels for swallowing by jerking and pulling, an eel spins at a dizzying rate. Researchers have recorded a rate of 6 to 14 spins per second (Olympic ice skaters can spin five times per second). The purpose of this is to break apart food into edible pieces; what is edible is determined by the width of its mouth, which is said to seldom exceed 2 inches. It also serves the purpose of gaining access to interior portions of food items, such as entering the body cavity of a dead fish to consume its eggs.

The habit of spinning, however, is also one that brings attention to the eel itself. Eels may spin several times in succession for a protracted period, during which they are less alert to predators and more vulnerable. This tendency may in part account for the effectiveness of wavy and spinning lures and bait rigs in sportfishing applications.

Angling. Fishing for these eels is more popular in Europe than in North America, perhaps owing to less overall diversification in fisheries opportunities and also to a greater cultural inclination toward eel consumption. In North America, these fish are not considered game species and are seldom the deliberate target of anglers using lures, flies, and most conventional sportfishing techniques. They are captured, however, by design and accident, by anglers bottom fishing with natural baits. Worms, small dead fish, pieces of fish, and some aromatic processed and natural baits are used on bottom rigs. They are also taken in freshwater by spearing or gigging, where legal, as well as on trotlines and in eel weirs, eel pots, fyke nets, and the like for commercial purposes.

Using eels as bait. Live eels are a popular bait for striped bass fishing in estuaries, rivers, and along the coast, and are often responsible for larger catches. These are universally fished on the bottom and may be employed by anglers drifting or stillfishing from an anchored boat or a fixed shore position. Enthusiasts use fixed and sliding sinkers, heavy enough to stay on the bottom, usually with a 2- to 3-foot length of leader from hook to sinker.

Eels are hooked through the lips from bottom to top, using 4/0 to 6/0 hooks. They may be kept in a cold cooler, which renders them less active for handling and hooking; they regain energy in the water. When there's a pickup, it's best to have the reel in freespool mode and to let the fish take the eel. Once the fish starts to move off steadily, it's time to set the hook.

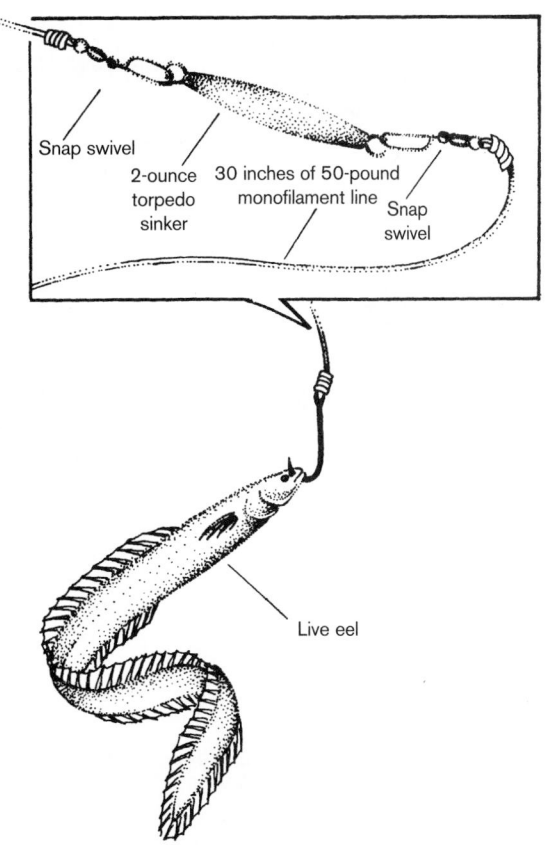

Snap swivel

2-ounce torpedo sinker

30 inches of 50-pound monofilament line

Snap swivel

Live eel

This is one of various rigs used for fishing live eels.

Skinning an eel. The skin of an eel can be removed by tying a strong line or string around the head and also to a secure object like a well-fastened nail. Cut the skin around the fish just below the head. Peel the skin back enough to get a grasp on it with a pair of good-gripping pliers, then quickly jerk the skin back and down the entire length of the eel. The skin may be used over certain lures or metal bodies; this was more common in the past before eel-like soft bodies were available.

To further clean the eel, cut the head off, cut the eel open and clean it out, then use scissors to remove the fins. Use it as is for cooking, smoking, and so on, or fillet it by cutting through the flesh on both sides of the backbone.

See: Eels.

EEL, AMERICAN CONGER *Conger oceanicus.*
EEL, EUROPEAN CONGER *Conger conger.*
Other names for the American conger eel—conger, dog eel, sea eel, silver eel; French: *congre d'Amerique*; Spanish: *congrin americana.*
Other names for the European conger eel—conger, sea eel; Dutch: *congeraal, kommeraal*; Finnish: *meriankerias*; French: *congre d'Europe*; Italian: *grongo*; Norwegian: *havål*; Portuguese: *congro, safrio*; Russian: *morskoi ugor*; Spanish: *congrin americana*; Swedish: *havsål.*

E

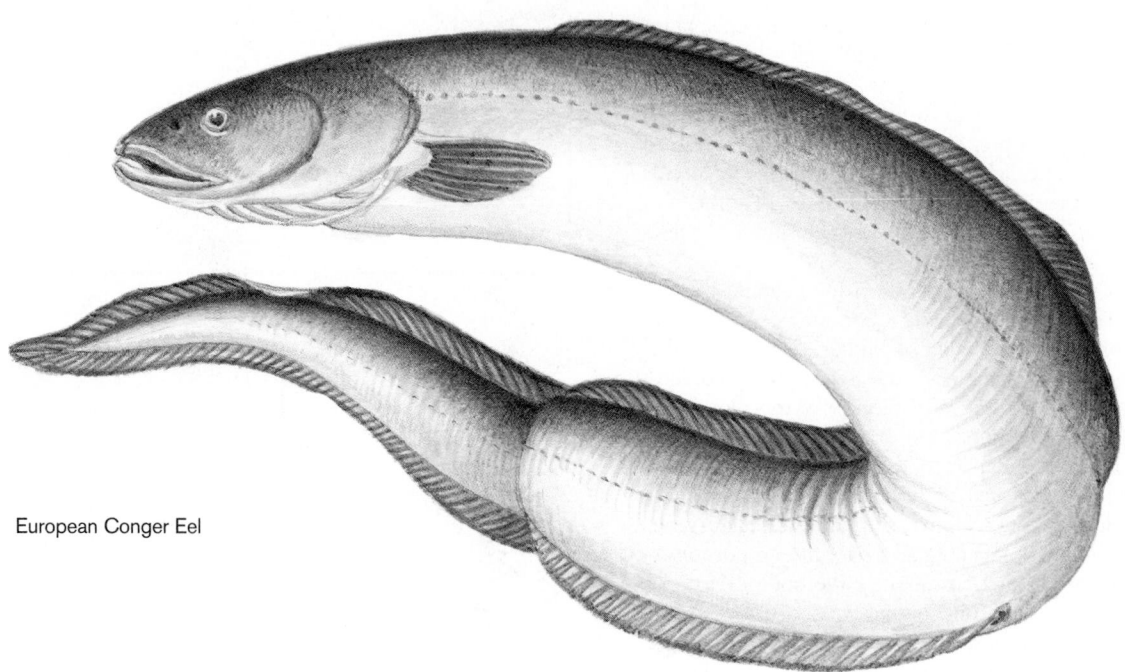

European Conger Eel

Conger eels are widely distributed members of the small Congridae family of marine eels that inhabit temperate and tropical waters.

Identification.   Conger are distinguished from moray eels by having pectoral fins (morays have none) and by the dark or black margin on their dorsal and anal fins. Conger eels are scaleless, and the dorsal fin originates over the tips of the pectorals. They grow much larger than American and European eels *(see: eel, American; eel, European)*, with which they are sometimes confused in inshore environs.

Size/Age.   The American conger is reportedly capable of growing to $7^1/_2$ feet and 87 pounds, although it is most frequently encountered at 10 to 20 pounds and 5 feet in length. The European conger is capable of growing to nearly 10 feet and 142 pounds, although most are under 50 pounds. Females grow larger than males.

Distribution.   The American conger occurs in the western Atlantic from Cape Cod, Massachusetts, to Florida and in the northern Gulf of Mexico. The European conger occurs in the eastern Atlantic from Norway and Iceland to Senegal, including the Mediterranean and western Baltic Sea.

Habitat.   Both species range widely from shallow inshore waters, occasionally in brackish environs, to waters hundreds of feet deep. They usually suspend over rocky or broken bottoms. Shallow-dwelling fish may linger around wrecks, piers, pilings, and jetties.

Life history.   The life history of these fish is similar to that of the American eel, although these fish enter freshwater or spawn in one place. Sexual maturity occurs between 5 and 15 years of age, and spawning fish migrate seaward, spawning in summer in water that may be more than 1,000 feet deep.

Food.   The diet of the nocturnal feeding conger eels includes fish, shrimp, small shellfish, and crustaceans.

Angling.   Anglers use stout tackle to take conger, which are strong fish that have to be muscled away from rocks and obstructions so they don't wrap their powerful tails around them and hold on. Heavy weights and bottom fishing rigs for natural baits (squid, crabs, cut or whole fish) are employed. This fish is difficult to remove from the hook, so anglers must take care to avoid being caught in its powerful snapping jaws. Fish brought to boatside often resort to furious spinning, a maneuver that often gains them freedom by pulling the hook or causing some item of terminal tackle to fail.
See: Eels.

EELPOUT
See: Burbot.

EGG FLY
A small, bright, artificial fly imitating a fish egg or eggs, usually made from yarn and used in fishing for Pacific salmon, steelhead, and some trout species.
See: Fly.

E-GLASS
A term for alkalai borosilicate glass, a type of high-tensile modulus fiberglass used in fishing rod construction.
See: Rod, Fishing.

EGYPT

Although some opportunity likely exists for pelagic species in the Red Sea and its arms—the Gulf of Suez and the Gulf of Aqaba—as well as possibly in the Mediterranean, virtually nothing has been reported in the Western world about the present status of saltwater sportfisheries off the 1,520-mile-long Egyptian coast and the availability of sportfishing boats. Historically, visiting anglers, mostly European, have paid more attention to freshwater fishing in Egypt, although news is scant in this regard as well.

Nile perch are known to populate the Nile River and its lakes throughout Egypt and neighboring Sudan. Lake Nasser, formed by the Aswan Dam, is 300 miles long and up to 10 miles wide, with its upper third in Sudan; it contains huge Nile perch, huge vundu catfish, and tigerfish, as well as tilapia and numerous other species.

Anglers have caught Lake Nasser tigerfish to 12 pounds, and vundu to 74 pounds, although vundu over 100 pounds reportedly exist. In late 1997 a 213-pound all-tackle world record Nile perch was caught by angling in Nasser; reports also indicate that a larger fish, unweighed but estimated at 250 pounds, was landed by a visiting Indian angler some years before. The latter fish boasted a length of 6 feet, 2 inches and girth of 4 feet, 11 inches. Shore anglers have hooked Nile perch over 100 pounds, although the larger ones had to be landed from a boat. The lake record is purportedly a 392-pound Nile perch, although it is unknown if this was caught by a commercial or a recreational angler. These larger perch greatly exceed all existing International Game Fish Association (IGFA) world records for the species.

Trolling is the most common method of catching the biggest specimens, and safari operators select overnight shore campsites for shore fishing opportunity. There are few organized freshwater sportfishing operations in Egypt, however, and little is presently known about opportunities elsewhere, particularly along the rest of the Nile (which covers more than 960 miles in Egypt alone), in other inland lakes such as Birkat, and in brackish lakes near the wide and rich Nile Delta.

EL NIÑO

El Niño is a disruption of the ocean-atmosphere system in the Equatorial Pacific due to unusually warm ocean temperatures. It has important consequences for weather around the globe, among them being drought, sometimes associated with devastating brush fires; and increased rainfall in certain areas, some of which has caused destructive flooding.

For anglers, El Niño is one of the most prominent natural global phenomena that can have beneficial or adverse implications for sportfishing in saltwater or freshwater. Floods, droughts, and changed ocean temperatures impact the presence and availability of many species, not to mention the conditions under which they are sought. Its harmful effect can be seen when heavy flooding raises the levels of rivers or impoundments to such extremes that gamefish are widely scattered and nearly impossible to locate, assuming that it is even safe to be on such waters. A beneficial effect occurs when warmer-than-usual currents bring pelagic fish closer to shore than normal or extend their northerly range; this happened in 1997 off California.

In normal, non–El Niño conditions, the trade winds blow toward the west across the tropical Pacific. These winds pile up warm surface water in the western Pacific, resulting in the sea surface being about one-half meter higher at Indonesia than at Ecuador. The sea surface temperature is also about 8°C higher in the west, with cool temperatures off South America, because of an upwelling (see) of cold water from deeper levels. This cold water is nutrient-rich, supporting high levels of primary productivity, diverse marine ecosystems, and major fisheries. Rainfall is found in rising air over the warmest water, and the eastern Pacific region is relatively dry.

During El Niño, the trade winds relax in the central and western Pacific, leading to a depression of the thermocline in the eastern Pacific and an elevation of the thermocline in the west. This reduces the efficiency of upwelling to cool the surface and cuts off the supply of nutrient-rich thermocline water to the euphotic zone (the upper layer where photosynthesis occurs). The result is a rise in sea surface temperature and a drastic decline in primary productivity, the latter of which adversely affects higher trophic levels of the food chain and hurts commercial fisheries in this region.

The weakening of easterly trade winds during El Niño means that rainfall follows the warm water eastward, with associated flooding in Peru and with drought in Indonesia and Australia. The eastward displacement of the atmospheric heat source overlaying the warmest water results in large changes in global atmospheric circulation, which in turn force changes in weather in regions far removed from the tropical Pacific.

El Niños have been experienced in the periods 1986–87, 1991–92, 1993, 1994, and 1997–98. It is unusual for El Niños to occur in such rapid succession as they did between 1991 and 1994. They are sometimes followed by La Niña, which is unusually cold ocean temperatures in the Equatorial Pacific. Global climate impacts from La Niña tend to be opposite those of impacts from El Niño. In the tropics, ocean temperature variations in La Niña tend to be opposite those of El Niño. Different La Niña and El Niño events vary in strength; the 1997–98 El Niño, for example, was unusually strong.

E

El Niño means the little boy or Christ child in Spanish. This name was used because of El Niño tended to arrive around Christmas and because the phenomenon was originally recognized by fishermen off the Pacific coast of South America. La Niña means the little girl; it is sometimes called El Viejo, or simply "a cold event" or "a cold episode."

At higher latitudes, El Niño and La Niña are two of the factors that influence climate, and their impacts there are most clearly seen in wintertime. In the continental United States during El Niño years, temperatures in the winter are warmer than normal in the North Central States, and cooler than normal in the Southeast and Southwest. During La Niña years, winter temperatures are warmer than normal in the Southeast and cooler than normal in the Northwest.

See: Current.

EL SALVADOR

Sportfishing in El Salvador has been virtually nonexistent in recent times due to the country's politics and economics and to the availability of other opportunities along the Pacific coast of Central America. The effect of commercial fishing and netting is uncertain, but it seems reasonable that El Salvador should have many of the same species found in bordering Guatemala and Honduras.

The smallest country in Central America, El Salvador is well situated along the coast to support pelagic species, and the excellent sailfish population found not far up the coast in Guatemalan waters is likely to be reflected to some degree offshore from El Salvador. Densely populated and mountainous, El Salvador has several small rivers and one larger one, the Lempa, that flow into the ocean. A few lakes and reservoirs (on the Lempa) exist, with unknown species and potential. The coastal area around the mouth of the Lempa, especially eastward to El Cuco, is distinguished by an extensive network of bays and estuaries, and snook may be present.

ELECTRIC MOTOR

See: Motor, Electric.

ELECTROFISHING

A method of biological survey in which waters are electrified with special equipment to temporarily incapacitate fish, which can then be gathered for quantitative and qualitative data. This method can be used to build a baseline of biological data trends and has been used to monitor fish, especially to determine the effect of length limits and habitat change. Electrofishing, which is also called electroshocking or shocking, is carried out only by trained biologists and technicians. Anglers are prohibited from using an electrical device to stun fish.

Electrofishing has been a preferred method of taking a census, or survey, of fish since the 1940s. For fisheries managers, electrofishing has long been preferable to such other survey methods as gillnet sampling, which is ineffective in many places and for some species, or rotenone (chemical) poisoning, which kills all fish captured. Electrofishing is quicker and more economical than angler surveys, which also don't produce sublegal-size fish or prey species. Biologists generally believe that electrofishing produces more reliable information than other sampling methods, especially angler surveys. It is not without some controversy, however, and can have adverse effects on fish. Some states have limited or prohibited their use of electrofishing, especially in trout waters and where there are fragile or threatened species.

Electrofishing is done from boats and from the bank, and portable backpack devices may be used. Alternating current (AC) was used originally, but that has given way to safer direct current (DC), which provides variable levels of electricity to probes in the water. Fish in the vicinity experience a muscle contraction and are temporarily stunned, whereupon they are immediately captured in a long-handled net. They are usually measured and weighed, and a scale sample may be taken; then the fish are released, or held briefly in a holding tank before release.

Studies have shown that certain fish may be susceptible to injury, stress, and fatigue, and that some delayed mortality may occur, particularly when the equipment is adjusted too high. Trout are more susceptible to problems than other species. Concern has been voiced that electrofishing can harm fish eggs or impact spawning, or drive fish out of the sampled area, particularly since a lot of electrofishing takes place in spring and/or when fish are shallow. In some situations, especially lakes and along deeper water shorelines, only a portion of existing fish are sampled, and nests are not affected. The effect on spawning or fish eggs has been hard to measure definitively, but some agencies have adopted a policy to avoid electrofishing in spawning areas containing eggs or larvae.

Some biologists feel that only a small portion of an overall population is available or vulnerable to electrofishing at any given time, and that the potential loss of a small number and small percentage of the overall population is not cause for concern, especially in light of the natural and angler-related mortality that is annually experienced, and because of the need to obtain reliable information to monitor management programs. In many places, electrofishing work has been successfully used to create or refine management regulations that have resulted in reduced angler mortality, increased numbers and sizes of fish, and development of trophy fishing and catch-and-release waters.

See: Fisheries Management.

ELECTRONICS

In a boating sense, the primary electronic accessories of interest beyond those associated with the operation of the engine include navigational devices such as GPS *(see)* and Loran *(see),* various types of sonar *(see),* remote or automatic steering devices, marine radios and other communications instruments, radio direction finders, and radar. For many people with mid- to large-size boats, or who navigate on large inland waterways or in marine environs, having sonar, a VHF radio, and some type of electronic navigational instrument (mainly GPS) is essential.

In a fishing sense, the primary electronic accessories of interest also include sonar and GPS, as well as electric motors, electric downriggers, temperature sensors, and speed gauges. There are other devices that might be used, primarily by freshwater anglers; these include oxygen meters, pH meters, and light meters. All of these devices are discussed in more detail in their respective entries. To most anglers who fish from a boat, and to all avid anglers, some type of sonar instrument is indispensable. To freshwater anglers who cast and seek fish that are oriented to structure, an electric motor *(see)* is close to being indispensable. To anglers who seek roaming fish, a temperature gauge *(see)* is extremely important; the same is true of speed gauges to trollers and electric downriggers to big water boaters and freshwater charter boat captains.

Electronic accessories have been a major part of the angling and boating scenes for decades. The primary emergence of electronic accessories started in the 1960s with the blossoming of both the electric motor and the fishfinder, which are arguably the two most important fishing accessories and certainly the most prevalent electronic devices. Fish-finding sonar was first developed by Carl Lowrance in 1957 and was a major milestone in the development of sportfishing equipment; it had a profound influence on angling technique, and it unarguably made anglers more effective. Today, the use of sportfishing sonar is taken for granted, and many boats contain two or more such devices.

The creation of that first lantern battery-operated fishfinder was nevertheless one in a long line of important advancements that helped open new eras in fishing. Similarly significant innovations included the modern hook, the outboard motor, the fiberglass rod, and the spinning reel.

Electronics, however, as a group of products, have moved forward faster and quicker than others, in keeping with general technological advancements. The advent of microprocessors, liquid crystal displays, and digitizing have helped rush electronic accessories to levels that were previously unimaginable, and that will continue. Whereas many electronic accessories were viewed with suspicion in the 1970s and 1980s—because of the introduction of products that did not live up to manufacturers' claims or that were sold to the

This protected center console contains the key electronics instruments used by anglers: VHF radio, navigational devices, and sonar.

public before being perfected—the contemporary era has seen a more uniform level of quality in this arena, befitting the high cost of research and development as well as relatively high retail prices. Electronic accessories for sportfishing have a better contemporary reputation and are being used by ever more people for increasingly diversified applications.

Questions have been raised about the effects of using electronic equipment for sportfishing, especially about the impact on fisheries resources. Obviously most of the same technology used in electronics sold to anglers is also in the electronics employed so effectively by commercial fishermen. Sonar, in particular, was once the target of some governmental entities, which unsuccessfully sought to ban them for recreational fishing.

These efforts failed for the logical reason that sonar is just one of myriad factors that contributes to increased pressure and effectiveness on the part of the recreational angler. Some other factors include the four-wheel-drive or all-terrain vehicle that allows a person to access a remote spot; the state-of-the-art graphite rod that makes hooksetting more effective; the swift boat that permits rapid coverage of expansive waterways; the high-tech fishing line that makes strike detection easier; the publication that details the characteristics of every pool on a given river and enumerates all of the fly hatches and all of the access spots; and so on. So who is to say what is and what is not fair, and where the line is to be drawn?

As always, anglers need to concentrate on quality fishing experiences, sportsmanship, and catch-and-release *(see)* efforts. There is no doubt that some electronic accessories, when skillfully used, can lead to greater and quicker success. Some of the devices help educate anglers so quickly that it almost seems unfair when compared with the education that pre-electronic-era anglers earned only after years and years of trial-and-error experience.

Nevertheless, these devices cannot lead to success unless anglers have a good idea of what they are doing. Although these devices can provide you with increased confidence and can show you where the fish are or help you locate the places where they should be, they still cannot make the fish strike. Electronic wizardry does not equate with automatic sportfishing success, as any guide or charter boat captain whose clients have not been able to catch the fish that are plainly shown on a sonar screen can affirm.

Furthermore, having a boatload of electronic accessories has the potential for overdosing on technology and either losing some of the simple charm of angling or neglecting to use your own wits and knowledge to figure out where the fish are, what they are doing, and how to attract them. There is a likelihood that some anglers, especially novices, could become mere technicians manipulating a lot of sophisticated paraphernalia, who wouldn't know what to do if they didn't have sonar to tell them the depth, GPS to direct them to the hotspot, a gauge to tell them the temperature or the speed, and so on.

Yet, for many people, electronic devices have not only increased their effectiveness but added to their understanding and appreciation of aquatic environments, particularly by providing them with a lot of information. And if nothing else, as charter captains, guides, and big-water boat operators have found out, some of this electronic stuff is very entertaining to the passengers onboard, especially when the fish aren't biting.

See: Downrigger; Light Meter; Navigation; Oxygen Meter; pH Meter; Radio; Radio Direction Finder; Speed Gauge.

EMERGER

An aquatic insect evolving from the larval (nymph) to adult form on the water's surface; also an artificial fly (nymph) that represents this surface-emerging insect.

See: Aquatic Insects; Fly.

EMPEROR, RED   *Lutjanus sebae.*

Other names—sea perch, government bream, king snapper, red kelp, redfish, emperor red snapper, emperor snapper; Arabic: *hamra;* French: *bourgeois, empereur rouge, pouatte;* Japanese: *sen-nendai;* Malagasy: *zazamanango;* Malay: *merah, jenehak;* Thai: *pla kapong dang.*

This fine sportfish, a member of the Lutjanidae family of snappers, is also a highly rated table fish that is much prized. In Australia, it is especially favored by anglers who fish the Great Barrier Reef, where they are a common target using handlines or traps baited with pilchards or other oily fish. Red emperor are not known to carry the toxin ciguatera, though caution should be exercised where large specimens (over 10 kilograms) are

taken, and this poison is known to occur in other related snappers.

Identification.   Red emperor are deep pink with three, bright red, crosswise bands across the stout, compressed body. These bands are the reason for the fish being called the government bream in Australia, as they bring to mind the shape of the Government "broad arrow" that was once worn by convicts in early Australian history. All the fins are pink, the caudal fin is emarginate, and there is a distinctive preopercular notch.

Size.   This fish is known to reach a weight in excess of 32 kilograms, and specimens commonly weigh from 1 to 6 kilograms.

Distribution.   The red emperor occurs in Indo-Pacific waters from the southern Red Sea and East Africa to New Caledonia, north to southern Japan, and south to Australia. It is found along the East Coast of Australia from Sydney to the Great Barrier Reef, and across the top of Australia to the coastal waters of western Australia as far south as Shark Bay. The principal recreational fishery in Australia is along the Great Barrier Reef and, in particular, the Cairns region.

Habitat.   The habitat of red emperor ranges from reefs, coral reef lagoons, shale bottoms, and sand flats, in waters from a few meters to 180 meters deep. As they grow, they move to deeper water where they tend to form into schools that prefer fast-flowing currents in channels around reefs. They will often move into shallow water during winter months.

Life history/Behavior.   Red emperor are highly fecund, with large females producing at least five to seven million eggs during a season; both the eggs and the larvae are pelagic. On the Great Barrier Reef, spawning usually takes place at night during the summer, between October and April. In Northern Territory waters, spawning takes place throughout most of the year. By the time red emperor are a year old, they have reached a fork length of 20 to 21 centimeters. They reach a maximum length of about 115 centimeters and are said to live for at least 10 years.

Food and Feeding Habits.   The red emperor is a carnivore, feeding mainly at night as it forages for fish, crustaceans, octopus tentacles, and squid. It can also be fed cut fish baits of tuna, trevally, and shark.

Angling.   Although red emperor can be caught during daylight, fishing usually takes place at night from a boat anchored in up to 50 meters of water. Knowledge of reef conditions and locations is imperative, lest weather blow up to make the outing dangerous; a quick getaway at those times can be lifesaving. Tackle is heavy, with short, stout boat rods fitted with revolving spool, spinning, or sidecast reels holding 15- to 30-kilogram line rigged with 6/0 to 9/0 extra-strong hooks. Handlines in excess of 40 kilograms are common and are used with gloves to prevent line burns. Sinkers must also be heavy to cope with currents. Baits of fresh-cut fish flesh, squid, and pilchards, are fished close to the bottom. When hooked, the red emperor quickly demonstrates its strength, and a major league tug of war ensues.

See: **Snapper.**

ENDANGERED SPECIES

In the United States, a species is classified as endangered if it is in danger of extinction throughout all or a significant portion of its range. Elsewhere, a species is classified as endangered if the factors causing its vulnerability or decline continue to operate, as defined by the International Union for the Conservation of Nature and Natural Resources (IUCN).

See: **Threatened Species.**

ENGLAND

Angling is a popular activity in Britain. Of the officially estimated 3.5 million anglers here, most pursue specific disciplines. About half of these are bank fishing coarse anglers; the remainder equally comprise sea anglers and people who pursue game fish (trout and salmon). The majority of the coarse anglers are English, and certainly England can lay claim to the most renowned angling writer of all time in Izaak Walton. His book, *The Compleat Angler*, written in 1653, illuminated his fishing exploits in the seventeenth century on such rivers as the Thames, Dove, Lea, and Test, and served not only as a guide to the techniques of the time but also as a chronicle of rural life and contemplative sport. He famously likened angling to poetry, and his words inspired millions to cast a line. But Walton would not recognize much of the angling sport in England today, which is like big business in many respects.

The majority of freshwater fishing is controlled by profit-making individuals or by nonprofit clubs. Season or day tickets (permits) must be purchased either in advance or on the bank and, in addition, anglers must buy a national fishing license, the proceeds from which go into a national fund. That fund is used to maintain the quality of freshwater fishing throughout England and Wales, fight pollution, and provide law enforcement. Daily and weekly licenses are available for the short-stay or holiday visitor, and discounts are granted to certain age groups.

Angling is strongly divided in the United Kingdom into coarse, sea, and game fishing, with many divisions within each branch. Coarse anglers use floats or leger fish with baits for nonpredatory species, and fish lures or baits for predators (coarse fish that are piscivirous such as pike, perch, and zander). Coarse fish are targeted for the sport only and are almost always returned alive. The rules governing when you can fish vary from region to region. As a general guide, you can fish most still

An angler fishes for trout on the Itchen, one of England's classic chalk streams.

waters (in a broad sense anything that is not a river, stream, or tributary) year-round, whereas on rivers there is a closed season from March 15 through June 15 inclusive.

The many man-made canals and drains that crisscross the industrial areas and farmlands of England create a complex fishery. Coarse anglers can fish for species such as carp, bream, roach, chub, and barbel with baits such as maggots, worms, and luncheon meat, all of which can be bought in the hundreds of tackle shops that dot the country. Interestingly, many thousands of anglers are happy just to fish for bites from small or large fish rather than targeting only big fish, and as a result a thriving match fishing circuit has built up. During match competitions, anglers fish for five hours and then weigh in their catch, which is kept alive during the match in a keepnet with a mesh fine enough to prevent even a minnow from escaping. The winner takes the spoils (including money), and fishing can be so hard that some matches in winter are won with just a few ounces of total catch.

So accomplished are the English in this field that England is broadly recognized as one of the world's top three match fishing nations (with France and Italy). The English have secured more team and individual world championship medals than any other nation, with one Cambridgeshire angler taking the individual title a record-equaling three times.

There are no freshwater bass in Britain, the main predators being pike, perch, and zander, which are caught by using lures, live bait, or dead bait. The country's largest native predator is the pike, which grows to more than 40 pounds. With the opening of large artificially stocked trout fisheries for seasonal pike angling, many pike over that mark have been landed, including several British record fish. Zander, which are very similar to walleye, grow to around 18 pounds, and perch up to 5 pounds.

The biggest native coarse fish of all, growing to more than 50 pounds, is the carp. Regarded as a pest in some countries, in England carp are all but revered as intelligent and hard-fighting fish that quickly become wise to anglers' techniques and baits. So respected are carp—they are never taken for food—that a thriving Carp Society has evolved, as well as a weekly newspaper and several monthly magazines dedicated purely to techniques for catching this species.

Small carp have been the driving force behind a wholesale change in coarse fishing in Britain. Artificially stocked coarse fishing waters have sprung up all over as the perceived general standard of river fishing has declined. Anglers can fish small, manageable venues (sites) knowing big fish lie before them waiting to be caught. These venues are often heavily stocked with carp from 1 to 10 pounds, and virtually all are run as a business. For the price of their day ticket, anglers benefit from high stocking levels and comfortable fishing (plat-forms are created for ease of fishing), they can often hire tackle on site, and they can buy lunch at some locations. Purists, however, wouldn't be seen dead at such venues, preferring to fish for what they regard as "wild" river coarse fish.

English coarse anglers, more than those from any other European nation, arguably have a strong tendency to specialize in one branch of the sport. The Carp Society is far from the only single-species group; societies for anglers who like to concentrate on catching zander, perch, chub, barbel, catfish, eels, and tench also exist. Members pay an annual fee, hold regular meetings, and publish newsletters to ensure familiarity with the latest techniques and catches. The level of devotion and sophistication is high.

The one element that joins all coarse anglers is a respect for their quarry. Coarse anglers almost never kill and eat the fish they catch and, outside the match fishing scene, fish are usually returned quickly and carefully to the water. The challenge is in the catching, and size is not everything. Catching a 3-pound roach would be a much more meritorious accomplishment than, say, catching a 20-pound pike.

As coarse fishing methodology has evolved, especially over the past few decades, it has brought this sport to an extremely sophisticated level. English anglers in Sheffield pioneered long-distance float fishing with rod and reel in the 1800s, and this became known as the Sheffield, or fine and far off, style. Float fishing on fast-flowing rivers was developed in Nottingham on the River Trent and became known as the Nottingham style. A third prominent style—called tight-lining, or London style, in England and known throughout Europe as *Peche Anglaise* (the same as *roubasiane* in France)—developed more recently. These styles have been adopted throughout Europe and have become known in North America only since the late 1980s.

More expensive licenses are required for game fishing in England and Wales, although there is no license requirement for either coarse fishing or game fishing in Scotland, which is the best bet for quality salmon experiences. In general, salmon fishing is only allowed from March through October, and in Scotland, tradition prohibits salmon and sea trout fishing on Sundays, although coarse fishing and brown and rainbow trout fishing are allowed.

The majority of English fly anglers concentrate on artificially stocked put-and-take trout stillwaters, where rainbow and brown trout up to and over 20 pounds are stocked. There is no season for rainbow trout, as they are not believed to breed in England, but there is a closed season on taking brown trout in the winter.

Sea fishing around Britain, including the offshore islands of the Hebrides, Orkneys, and Shetlands, plus the Isle of Man in the Irish Sea and the Isle of Wight off the south coast, is among the most varied in the world, considering the size of the fishery. The Gulf Stream, which flows north from the Atlantic Ocean, brushes the southwestern corner of England and continues north through the Irish Sea, past the Welsh coast, up past Lancashire and the world-famous seaside resort of Blackpool, and along the western coast of Scotland. This has a warming effect on the sea temperature, and often brings with it strange, exotic species from the tropics.

In contrast, the eastern coast of England and Scotland is bordered by the colder North Sea, and tends to offer both shore and boat anglers different species than those encountered on the western coasts, although some species are common to both areas, and global warming appears to be making the differences smaller each year. The seasons vary considerably because of the changeable weather, and some summer species are never caught in winter. Since the 1980s, however, global warming appears to have considerably changed the pattern of fish movements, whereas other changes have doubtless been brought about by overfishing—especially following the huge influx of commercial fishing boats from the rest of Europe and Russia, which have been allowed to fish all around the coast.

The most striking example, however, concerns the overfishing of herring after World War II. Tunny used to follow the herring shoals north from the Bay of Biscay along the eastern coast of England, and were regularly caught off Scarborough, where there was a big trade for them. Tunny numbers peaked in the 1930s, but after the war they declined rapidly as the herring shoals declined. Despite a total ban on herring fishing for decades, the species has never properly recovered, and tunny fishing is now extinct around England, although the odd tunny has been reported off southern Ireland in the Gulf Stream, mainly taken in nets.

The result of general overfishing of species like mackerel and cod, as well as sand eels—which formed a major part of the diet of many other fish—has been a definite decline in fish populations, and a resultant decline in the numbers of fish caught on rod and line. Sea fishing is still a big industry all around the coast, however, with hundreds of charter boats dedicated to taking out parties of anglers, usually up to 12 at a time, and considerable numbers of shore-based clubs, as well as some clubs dedicated to private boatowners who own seaworthy fishing dinghies powered by outboard motors.

The rocky nature of the continental shelf around the mainland offers a certain amount of shelter from commercial netters in many localized areas, and the charter boats know where these marks (sites) are. The seas around the mainland are among the most dangerous in the world, and extreme caution is urged at all times; drownings of both boat anglers and those fishing from the shore are not uncommon. Due to increased safety regulations, the standard of charter boats is quite high compared

with many other countries. There are several charter boat associations, and they will not accept members who do not meet certain minimum requirements. Virtually all charter boats have sonar equipment for locating fish.

In summer, many charter boats offer fishing trips that last about three hours; frequently these cater only to holiday makers who are content to fish with handlines. The more serious trips last longer. Some modern charter boats are fast, with planing hulls, but most boats have displacement hulls, which ride deeper in the water and give a better ride in choppy seas but are much slower. Charter boats advertise in the many angling journals, although the very best skippers rarely advertise, because they are fully booked in advance. The best advertisement is word-of-mouth.

There is no true American-style sportfishing in England, but blues, porbeagles, and the very occasional mako sharks do frequent these waters. Methods of sea fishing here differ considerably from those in America. Sea conditions and the lack of big-game fish rule out downriggers and outriggers, and fish are generally pursued on or near the bottom. The main boat methods are downtiding (putting a bait overboard to the bottom and fishing it downtide), uptiding (casting uptide and out from the boat and allowing a bow to develop in the line), and drifting with heavy pirks (from 50 grams to 1 kilogram) that are either baited or unbaited. With 12 anglers on a boat, it's almost impossible for everyone to use different styles, so anyone who wants to fish a particular style—drifting, downtide baitfishing, or uptiding—should always check with the skipper first.

To get the best day's fishing by boat, it's often better to book with a small party who have agreed to fish the same method; this is more expensive but likely to be more productive. Bait, at extra cost, is usually provided by the skipper, who will ask whether you need any when you make a reservation. Shore fishing is free and no license is needed. There may be an entrance fee for piers and jetties. Britain tends to observe size limit rules to a greater extent than any other European country, and these rules are strictly enforced in matches. In addition, it is an unwritten rule that all tope, common skate, and sharks are returned alive; most skippers now insist on this. Some skippers expect, though, to keep part of the catch of other sizable species such as cod, which they sell to defray their costs. The size limit for bass (European sea bass) is also strictly enforced, and many anglers return all bass. Other catch limits are introduced from time to time.

On boats, tackle up to 80-pound rating is used on the deep-water wrecks, with 20-pound to 30-pound rating sufficient for most inshore marks. Few Britons bother to chase International Game Fish Association (IGFA) line-class records, so there is scope for the visitor who fancies beating some of these.

Norman and Breton fishermen are believed to have fished for cod off Newfoundland as early as 1504.

E

Coarse Fishing

Probably the top English coarse river is its longest: the mighty, powerful River Severn, which rises in Wales before flowing east into England, then turns south and empties into the Bristol Channel. Virtually every species of coarse fish thrives here, with superb summer barbel fishing around the Bewdley area in particular.

Barbel are regarded as the hardest fighting of all the river coarse fish. They are not native to the Severn, but have bred and grown so successfully since being stocked in 1956 that the river boasts a British record barbel of more than 16 pounds. Another nonnative fish that has thrived in this river is the zander. These were first stocked into the drains of eastern England but have quickly spread across the country. The Severn also lays claim to a record zander of more than 18 pounds from Upton.

Much of the River Severn is controlled by Britain's biggest angling club, the Birmingham Anglers Association, which has more than 20,000 members. Other top areas to try include Arley and around Worcester and Tewkesbury. The majority of specimen (large or trophy) fish are caught from Bewdley downward.

Another great river is the Avon, which joins the Severn near Tewkesbury. Scenic and fruitful angling with floats can be enjoyed in and around Stratford and Evesham. Pegs behind the theater at Stratford are noted for excellent roach sport. Luddington, Twyford Farm, and Offenham Weir are other noted roach spots, and anywhere below Pershore is good for plentiful big bream, with 80-pound catches possible.

Farther north, the most famous coarse angling river is the Trent, which starts life north of Birmingham and flows north, meeting the sea at the Humber estuary. For years this venue was fed by warm water from several power stations situated along its length, which led to sensational fishing all year for bream, roach, and chub. Such quality fishing is harder to come by now that these stations

have closed, and the river is known more as a summer venue, with good fishing to be found in and around Nottingham.

The rivers of northeastern England are mostly spate (rain-induced) rivers that are not controlled by reservoirs and therefore rise and fall quickly in flood conditions. Flows are swift and the water clear, conditions the barbel in particular enjoy. The rivers Ure, Swale, and Wharfe all hold excellent barbel and chub stocks. Famous fishing spots include Boroughbridge (Ure), Topcliffe (Swale), and Ulleskelf (Wharfe).

Quality river coarse fishing is not easy to come by in the northwest, with better sport on the canals. Big barbel and chub can be caught from the River Ribble, however. In the south, the Hampshire Avon and the Dorset Stour still offer the kind of fishing Izaak Walton would have written of, with specimen barbel, chub, pike, roach, and dace thriving in crystal clear water. Much of the fishing is privately controlled, but anglers can enjoy excellent day-ticket fishing around Ringwood in Hampshire, where there is a first-class tackle shop. The more famous River Thames is at its best outside London, and excellent localized fishing can be enjoyed around Oxford.

Closer to the capital, Teddington Lock holds plenty of fish, including big river carp. Quality fishing is localized toward the east of England. Huge barbel are caught on the Great Ouse around Newport Pagnell. Specimen chub are worth targeting on the River Wensum in Norfolk. Good fishing for pleasure is available on the River Nene around Peterborough, on the River Welland around the scenic town of Stamford, and on the River Yare around Norwich.

Many of the big cities are also home to a network of canals used during the Industrial Revolution to transport coal and goods. These once-polluted waterways have been transformed, and where once there was no sign of life there are now thriving fish populations. South Yorkshire's Sheffield Canal, for instance, was once one of Europe's most polluted waterways, yet it is now full of fish. And the nearby River Don, which was also once devoid of life, now remarkably holds trout.

Generally speaking, canals are places to catch a lot of small fish, usually with fishing poles, and top venues include Regents Canal (London), Bridgewater Canal (Manchester County), Erewash Canal (Nottingham), Exeter Canal (Devon County), Grand Union Canal (Buckinghamshire County), and Oxford Canal (Oxfordshire County). Most canals can be fished on a day ticket.

In East Anglia more than 1,000 miles of man-made drains were built from the 1600s onward to drain water off farmlands to The Wash, and these have become excellent fishing venues, particularly for predator species. It was here that zander first thrived in England, and during the 1970s venues such as the Forty Foot Drain, the Middle Level Drain, and the Relief Channel became known as England's pike

Portions of the Thames are known for coarse fishing.

angling Mecca, where a 20-pounder was quite easily attainable and a 30-pounder possible.

It can take plenty of legwork to find the predators on these long, straight, featureless bodies of water. Fish are localized, but once found they are generally easy to catch, and you can land one after another. Artificially stocked lakes are plentiful throughout the country, and a chat with the local tackle dealer will put you onto the in-form venue.

Gravel pits are another form of stillwater angling that warrants mention. Once mining has been completed, gravel pits are flooded, creating deep, clear venues. Fish thrive in these conditions and, because stocking densities are usually low, they grow to outsize proportions. This has resulted in a growing army of anglers (known as specimen hunters) who target gravel pit complexes. Many of Britain's record coarse fish, including carp, bream, and tench, were taken from gravel pits. Pike also thrive in such complexes and have been known to achieve 20 pounds in just six years.

Gravel pit complexes exist all over England, but sites famous for consistently producing specimen fish include those around Oxford, those close to the west side of the M25 motorway near Heathrow Airport, and the South Cerney complex near Cirencester, Gloucestershire.

Game Fishing

Trout.   The majority of game fishing in England is for trout, mainly rainbow trout and the indigenous brown trout. This sport is largely pursued in the hundreds of commercially operated stocked stillwater fisheries that sprang up in the 1970s. These vary in size from perhaps half an acre up to 40 acres or more, with a few dozen much bigger reservoirs and lakes, such as the famous Rutland Water (3,000 acres), or Blagdon, which is the oldest stillwater brown trout fishery in the UK. These fisheries vary greatly in configuration, from recently dug barren holes in the ground to beautifully landscaped waters or natural lakes surrounded by forests and hills or mountains. The number of trout that may be taken is always limited, and a report form (return) showing the number of fish landed must be filled in, to enable restocking of fish and thereby maintenance of the population.

Some waters specialize in stocking considerable numbers of very big fish, and these tend to be more expensive. If you are content to catch smaller fish—those up to 2 pounds—the cost is less. Most waters give you the option of purchasing a less-expensive ticket, allowing you to take fewer fish. Some allow catch-and-release, which is usually cheaper. After having been caught a few times, these fish can become very wary, but then the pursuit becomes a rewarding challenge for the angler.

It is possible to find rainbows over 20 pounds at a considerable number of these fisheries, and brown trout over 15 pounds at a few. These have all been bred artificially, although in any case rainbows rarely breed naturally in the UK.

On many of these waters it is possible to obtain instruction, and rent tackle; some outfits have their own tackle shops on site, with food available either on site or in a nearby public house. Offerings include weighted flies (banned on some waters) like Dog Nobblers and Tinheads, and smaller, more natural patterns such as Damsel flies, Hare's Ears, various buzzers, various Pheasant Tail Nymphs, and floaters like Adams, Shipman's Buzzers, and sedge and olive patterns.

Rental boats are available on larger reservoirs and lakes, and advance booking is advisable. Match fishing for trout is big in the UK, and these events take place largely on the bigger reservoirs, mainly by boat; hence, most of the boats might be booked in advance on a particular day. Boobies fished on a sinking line are a favorite early-season pattern, followed by various lures, with smaller flies like Shipman's Buzzers working well when fish start rising in summer, and fly patterns from August onward. Otherwise, fly patterns are very similar to those used elsewhere.

Wild brown trout inhabit some rivers in England and are quite small; a 2-pounder is considered a good fish. But the thrill of catching a wild brown of any size makes trout fishing a popular activity. Rivers with wild brown trout include the upper reaches of the Severn, Tamar, and Fowey in the west; the Hampshire Avon and its tributaries; the Dove (where Izaak Walton started fishing) in the Midlands; the Wharfe, Yorkshire Derwent, Ribble, Swale, Nidd, Coquet, Wear, Derwent, and Tees in the northeast; the Lune and Eden in the northwest; and the Dart in the southwest.

The fishing is controlled either by private owners (often estates), who may or may not allow fishing, by syndicates who do not normally allow outsiders to fish except as guests of members, or by local clubs who will frequently allow outsiders to fish after paying a fee. The local tackle shop or post office is a good starting point for information.

The two most famous chalk stream trout fisheries in the world, the Test and the Itchen, have been stocked with rainbows and bigger brown trout, and some stretches can be fished. Costs vary enormously, corresponding roughly to the density of fish in the water. Other rivers have been artificially stocked also, and some of these are run in conjunction with a stillwater fishery; with easy access, you just show up and pay (advance booking is advisable on the smaller waters).

Grayling thrive in most of the rivers that hold wild brown trout, and there is a growing interest in restocking these fish into the waters from which they have gradually disappeared. Baitfishing for trout is allowed on very few fisheries; otherwise, the rule is flies only, and many sites limit the size of the fly.

On trout rivers there may be some restrictions as to methods allowed. The English place great store on tradition, and some purists still would not

E

dream of casting downstream or using a wet fly. For up-to-date information, the best bet is to telephone one of the many angling magazines that have access to the latest publications, and indeed may even publish some. The staff are invariably anglers themselves and will be only too pleased to help.

There is no closed season for rainbow trout, which can be fished year-round. There is a closed season for brown trout, and where a stillwater is attached to a river there may be a general closed season. All the big reservoirs have a closed season for brown trout. The big reservoirs close in winter, for commercial reasons, but some small stocked stillwaters are open year-round, some including Christmas and Boxing Day, when special festivities take place. Hard winters, which cause small stillwaters to freeze over, will bring trout fishing to a halt.

There is a closed season on all rivers; the approximate dates of the trout season are April 1 through September 30, but these vary from area to area. The grayling season is generally June 16 through March 13 inclusive, but local rules may apply.

Salmon and sea trout. Salmon and sea trout fishing are far less popular in England than in Wales and Scotland. Main English rivers include the Lune, Ribble, Eden, and Cumbrian Derwent in the northwest; the Tyne, Tees, Wear, Coquet, and Yorkshire Esk in the northeast; the Hampshire Avon and Test in the south; and the Camel, Tamar, Torridge, Exe, and Severn in the southeast. Atlantic salmon were reintroduced to the Thames in the 1980s, but there is no significant run up the river yet. Other rivers have odd salmon and sea trout runs, but these are insignificant compared with the ones mentioned.

Although the odd spring fish is caught, stocks of Atlantic salmon have dwindled since the 1960s. From August to the end of the season (which is roughly September, although seasons vary), however, the autumn runs of salmon can offer superb sport, with fish in excess of 20 pounds.

Although the traditional method of catching salmon and sea trout is by fly, certain waters allow fishing with spinners, worms, and, in some cases, prawns. Prawns are such a deadly bait, however, that they are banned on the majority of such waters.

Salmon flies include Willie Gunn, Stoat's Tail, Thunder & Lightning, Munro Killer, Garry Dog, Hairy Mary, and Ally's Shrimp (one of the most effective). Variations of these patterns tied as weighted tube flies will allow you to cope with any river conditions. A 15-foot double-handed salmon rod rated for a 10- or 11-weight line will be necessary to fish the majority of these waters. Chest waders are also advisable.

Sea trout fishing is best at night. Flies for sea trout include Teal Blue and Silver, Lethal Weapon, Silver Butcher, Peter Ross, Black Pennell, and tube flies based on these patterns.

The majority of salmon and sea trout fishing is privately owned. Fishing is available by booking a private beat, or it is controlled by an association that allows daily or weekly tickets. For details contact local tackle shops or purchase one of the national trout and salmon magazines for latest details and some contacts.

Sea Fishing

In northeastern England, fronting the North Sea, the area from Berwick on Tweed southward to Newcastle offers codling (small cod) to 5 pounds to shore anglers in winter, flounder and silver eels (not conger) most of the year, and red codling in among the kelp on rocky shores in summer. Expect to lose a lot of terminal tackle in the rocks here, but the fishing is great fun.

Small sea bass started to appear here in numbers in the late 1980s, and they always turn up on the same beaches, mainly in summer, when small turbot—one of the most prized British flatfish—may also appear. Charter boats take mainly codling and haddock over inshore rough ground, with ling and cod to 30 pounds–plus from deep-water wrecks, using heavy pirks to beat the strong North Sea currents. The main charter ports are Berwick on Tweed, which is on the border with Scotland, and Tynemouth.

From Newcastle down to The Wash, the main summer shore species are mackerel and small coalfish, taken from piers and jetties (there's exceptional fishing around South Shields), codling from rocks and cliffs, and flounder from open sandy beaches. The flounder linger near estuaries during winter. A winter run of codling is also available. Crabs are a popular bait for codling and flounder, as they can be gathered locally. The main charter ports are Hartlepool, Whitby, Scarborough, and Bridlington, and boats here produce huge catches of codling and cod if conditions are right. Deep-water wreck fishing produces cod over 30 pounds and ling over 20 pounds, both of which are invariably taken on baited pirks.

The bulge of East Anglia, south of The Wash, used to produce huge catches of codling for shore anglers, but these have dwindled dramatically, although codling are still taken in numbers as soon as the sea is fishable after a good easterly blow. With few rocks in this area, soft-backed crabs are rare, so the popular baits are lugworms (available fairly easily from tackle shops or local bait diggers) and ragworms, which are a little scarcer. Whiting appear in September, codling in November and again in March, and bass are found year-round, although many are undersize. The sole and dab fishing can be quite exceptional from May through Christmas, and long casts are not needed.

These beaches are almost invariably shallow. For codling, casts of 100 yards are usually needed, so this area has produced many casting champions. Some can cast distances approaching 300 yards over grass without bait, which equates to 180 yards with bait. Yarmouth and Lowestoft are the charter ports;

no ports exist to the north because there are so few estuaries.

Essex County, just north of the Thames estuary, sees fantastic sport with thornback ray, tope, smoothhound, and bass, and excellent charter boats offer opportunities around the small port of Bradwell on Sea in the Blackwater estuary, and at Southend. The best skippers are always booked on weekends, often for years ahead, so a midweek trip is the visitor's best bet. Shore fishing can be good from the various sea walls, and in the many creeks and inlets, but access can be long and tortuous as much of this area is marshland.

South of the Thames estuary, the Kent County coast is one of the codling hotspots, and anglers land these fish all winter, although not in the fantastic numbers of the 1970s, when 20 codling per angler per night was not uncommon. The famous Dungeness Beach is still a favorite mark, as it offers deep water close to shore. Numerous easily accessible marks are available on the various seaside parades in Kent coastal towns. A top mark is Dover breakwater, which can be reached only by the daily boat service (details are available at Dover Harbour). Fishing by boat in the Thames estuary is brilliant for bass upward of 10 pounds, tope, and thornback ray, and these are found around the entire Kent coast. The area's main charter ports are Ramsgate, Deal, Dover, Folkestone, and Hastings.

The whole south coast, from Eastbourne west to Lyme Regis on the Dorset/Devon County border, offers highly varied fishing, with whiting, flounder, and codling available in winter from the shore, plus the chance of ray and hard-fighting triggerfish, which now appear in numbers. Mullet are extremely popular here; go at first light or at dusk to the marinas, where the fish can be seen cruising between boats until disturbed. Anglers land them on bread bait, or small scraps of worm, often by using floats. Most common is the thick-lipped mullet, found in saltwater; the scarcer thin-lipped mullet inhabits a few rivers.

Notable shore marks include rocks below the famous Beachy Head cliffs, where bass are taken; Poole Harbour, which is a flounder hotspot; the Hurst Castle shingle bank at Milford on Sea; and the 18-mile-long bank of shingle known as Chesil Beach, which offers a host of species, including mackerel in August, triggerfish in summer, and codling in winter.

Boat fishing appeals most to anglers here, however, with some of the best sport around the Isle of Wight. All of the south coast of the island regularly produces cod to 30 pounds as well as a host of other species, including thornback ray, conger eels over 50 pounds, tope and smoothhound in summer and autumn, blonde ray over 20 pounds, plaice to 7 pounds–plus, big bass, and many other species. Black bream inhabit these coasts, favoring certain localized reefs in summer and autumn. Shore

fishing on the Isle of Wight is excellent; ask for details at tackle shops on the island.

Anglers can easily reach the Isle of Wight via regular crossings from Lymington, Southampton, and Southsea. Mainland charter ports are Eastbourne, Newhaven, Brighton, Littlehampton, Hayling Island, Poole, Weymouth, and the little town of West Bay. The bigger ports offer some of the most modern, fast charter boats in the country, and some travel on three-day or five-day trips to the Channel Islands, where huge cod, ling, and conger are taken. There are several charter ports on the Isle of Wight also.

Devon and Cornwall Counties, in the southwest corner of the mainland, offer particularly easy shore fishing. Anglers land mackerel, as well as wrasses and mullet, from the dozens of piers and rocks. Casting and float fishing are productive. Long-distance casters pursue several species of ray, big bass, and plaice. The best flounder fishing in the country exists in the mouths of the Teign and Exe Rivers, and there's excellent flounder action in most of the other estuaries, plus some cod mainly on the northern coasts. Summer shark fishing is again becoming popular here after the peak in the 1950s and 1960s, when every blue shark caught was slaughtered. The policy of releasing them is paying dividends now. Plymouth, Mevagissey, and Looe are the main ports, with Padstow and Boscastle the prime sites for porbeagles, which are caught off the west coast.

Cornwall and Devon offer probably the most varied boat fishing in the UK, and anything can turn up, although the area is perhaps best known for the huge conger eels taken by Plymouth charter boats; fish over 100 pounds are not uncommon, but it's tiring work winching them in. There's also excellent pollack and coalfish to be had, and big bass shoals, which don't get much publicity to limit leaks of their whereabouts to commercial fishermen. Also expect thornback ray, blonde ray, and the biggest turbot in the country. The main charter ports are Dartmouth, Plymouth, Falmouth, Rock, Padstow, Ilfracombe, Lynmouth, Porlock, and Minehead.

The English coast north of Wales is known as the North West, and the main boat species here are cod, mackerel in season, thornback ray, tope, plaice, and bass, plus conger, ling, and pollack over the wrecks. Gurnard are more prolific here than in most other areas of the country, and anglers land spurdog and haddock in season in some areas. The main charter ports are Fleetwood, Barrow, and Maryport. Several large small-boat clubs are in the area, particularly around Blackpool. Shore anglers tend to focus on flounder, dabs, and eels; the Dee and Ribble estuaries, Arnside in the Kent estuary, and Silloth on the south bank of the Solway Firth are quite outstanding at times. As winter approaches, the quarry changes to whiting and codling, although along the rocky edges of Cumbria, pollack, coalfish, and conger are taken from shore. Crabs are a popular bait along this coast, as they are easily found in certain estuaries.

 Sixty percent of the world's 3.4 billion people lived within 60 miles of a coastline in 1997; 75 percent of a projected world population of 6.3 billion is expected to do so in 2025.

E

This area also includes the Isle of Man in the Irish Sea, which offers fine and little-explored fishing. Tope to 40 pounds are taken from its northwest coast; wrasses, pollack, mackerel, coalfish, conger, bass, and plaice, among other species, are regularly taken from shore. Contact the helpful Isle of Man Tourist Board, which is keen to promote sea fishing on the island. Charter boats operate here, with Peel the main location, or you can make arrangements with one of many small-boat owners.
See: Scotland; Wales.

ENTOMOLOGIST

A person who studies the forms and behavior of insects. Some stream trout fly anglers become so engrossed in fly tying and fly fishing that they become amateur entomologists.

EPILIMNION

The upper and warmer layer of water in a lake or pond that is stratified; the layer of water above the thermocline (see).
See: Stratification.

EPIRB

Acronym for Emergency Position Indicating Radio Beacon. Used in emergency situations and carried primarily by large boats and by anglers who venture far offshore, this transmitter issues a constant signal on a distress frequency; the activated signal indicates a distress situation and allows rescuers to determine the boat's position.

There are several classes of EPIRBs. The class A version is at the top of the list in both cost and function. It sends a homing signal on 121.5 MHz and communicates directly with satellites on 406 MHz frequency. The class A version is encoded with an identifier that is unique to the owner, so authorities can not only pinpoint your location anywhere in the world, but also tell who is in trouble. The class A EPIRB turns itself on automatically as soon as it gets wet, but it is bulky, expensive, and best for those who spend a lot of time far offshore.

The class B version requires manual activation, is cheaper, less bulky, and is preferred by most small boaters. It comes with a six-year lithium battery and a continuous operating life of at least 48 hours. Both A and B operate on 121.5 MHz and 243 MHz, and their signals are picked up by aircraft and shore stations that monitor their frequencies.

You can test a class A or B EPIRB yourself by holding it close to an AM radio and turning it on for just a few seconds. There will be a warbling tone through the radio's loudspeaker.

Federal regulations require that all EPIRB tests be as brief as possible and that they be conducted only during the first five minutes of each hour.
See: Boat.

ESTIMATING WEIGHT

See: Measuring Fish.

ESTUARY

In simplest terms an estuary is a body of water where freshwater from rivers and streams meets the saltwater of the sea. It may be called a bay, a sound, or a lagoon. Most estuaries are partially enclosed by islands, beaches, and the mainland; they may get freshwater from one large river, from several large rivers, or from hundreds of small rivers, streams, creeks, canals, and even springs. In addition to inlets and incoming freshwater sources, estuaries may contain barrier islands that protect estuary mouths, open water areas, oyster bars, salt marshes, mangrove forests, submerged seagrass beds, and mud flats. Much sportfishing is done in or near estuaries.

In an estuary, freshwater draining from incoming sources dilutes the saltwater to varying degrees. In a positive estuary, more freshwater meets the sea than evaporates; in a negative estuary, more freshwater evaporates than enters; and in a neutral estuary, evaporation and inflow are about the same. Freshwater is also diluted by tides, which push saltwater upriver to varying extents depending on the strength of the tide, geologic formations, offshore currents, and the quantity of freshwater entering the estuary.

The mixture of saltwater and freshwater in estuaries provides a plentiful supply of food that supports abundant plant and animal life. Tons of nutrient-rich materials washed from the uplands accumulate to make estuaries among the most productive natural systems known. In many coastal states and countries, 80 to 90 percent of all marine species of fish and shellfish spend some portion of their lives in estuaries. For many, these are nursery areas. Estuaries also provide homes for huge numbers of birds, protect the mainland by absorbing the force of storms from the sea, and provide an outlet for flood waters from the land.

Estuaries have been adversely impacted in many places because of pollution, siltation, and habitat loss through development.
See: Inshore Fishing.

ETHICS AND ETIQUETTE

Before delving into the murky waters and sometimes hot button issues of angling ethics and etiquette, it is necessary to provide some definitions, which are quoted from Webster's New World Dictionary and re-stated (in parentheses) in synonymous general terms and concepts.

Ethics: "The system or code of morals of a person, group, religion, profession, etc." (Moral principles and/or rules of conduct.)

Etiquette: "The forms, manners, and ceremonies established by convention as acceptable or required in social relations, in a profession, or in official life." (Rules, conventions, protocol, ceremony, formalities, custom, decorum, manners, politeness, courtesy, civility, and seemliness.)

Sportsman/sportswoman: "A person who can take loss or defeat without complaint, or victory without gloating, and who treats opponents with fairness, generosity, courtesy, etc."

Sportsmanship: "Qualities and behavior befitting a sportsman." (Fair play, fairness, honesty, honor, probity, scrupulousness, integrity, uprightness, justice, justness.)

Although etiquette is technically different from ethics, both are often discussed interchangeably, especially regarding matters pertaining to manners and courtesy. The definition of ethics is especially important because it establishes that ethics are different from laws *(see: regulations)*. What is legal may not be viewed by a majority of people as ethical, or may not fit an objective view of the proper behavior of a sportsman or sportswoman. Sportsmanship is essential to any discussion of ethics because it is the notion of fair play, and angling by sporting means, that should separate the recreational angler from the commercial fisherman *(see: angler; angling; commercial fisherman; recreational fisherman)*.

As George Reiger, North America's foremost fishing and hunting conservation writer, notes: "We're at a crossroads in angling today—a fork in the evolution of sportsmanship made all the more perilous by the fact that few anglers can define angling ethics. Most assume it's the same as law. The law, however, involves public obligations; ethics involve personal ones. Breaking the law entails public expense; the only cost—but it's a significant one—of betraying an ethical standard is the damage it does to one's soul. This confusion between ethics and law provides fertile ground for the agenda of groups who oppose angling."

"Any culture that allows law to become the arbiter of all human behavior runs the risk of losing its soul. Back about the time Pericles was refining a legal system for ancient Athens, a Chinese philosopher by the name of Kung Futzu (alias Confucius) was developing a social system based on personal conscience and peer pressure for every imaginable activity, including angling. Confucius believed that legalistic societies eventually fall apart because people come to believe that whatever isn't specifically forbidden by law is condoned by it. That's why he resisted the idea that an institution or the state should arbitrate personal behavior. Rules of conduct agreed on by the majority should be enforced by peer pressure, not the police. But all activities should have peer-pressured rules."

In angling today, and especially in North America, there is a lack of spoken and written attention to ethics. Many people, particularly fly anglers, believe that they adhere to a generally understood but seldom expressed code of ethics; most often this revolves around the act of harmlessly releasing fish (the catch-and-release ethic) or around the methodology (casting and/or fishing exclusively with flies or artificial lures, for examples, as ethics unto themselves).

Ethical Issues

The purpose of this entry—which is unfortunately rare in books about sportfishing—is to raise awareness of some of the major ethical issues that exist. Some, though certainly not all, of those issues are briefly noted here.

Casting. As mentioned, casting with artificial lures (which includes flies) is a sportfishing methodology especially favored by many anglers, in some cases to the exclusion of various forms of bait presentation. In Europe, a clear distinction is made between coarse fishing *(see)*, in which some form of bait is used in a still manner, and gamefishing, which primarily means the act of casting with artificial lures, especially flies, for trout and salmon.

Many people who cast artificial lures believe that doing so is more challenging, or more interesting, or more sporting, than fishing with any form of natural or processed bait or fishing by means of trolling; this view is derived from centuries of tradition of fishing with flies in streams, mainly for trout.

There is little doubt that the vast majority of anglers prefer to catch fish by actively casting and retrieving an artificial lure and by always holding the rod in their hand. However, it is not feasible to fish exclusively by casting with artificial lures for all species and for all sizes of fish in all places where they're found (rivers, big lakes, ocean reefs, blue water, and so forth), although one can certainly argue that the means are more important than the results. Some environments and some species clearly lend themselves to casting, making a personal casting ethic for those species one that is also practical and not counterproductive.

Artificial lures. The ethical issue of using artificial lures in lieu of natural or processed bait likewise involves the subject of practicality and incorporates questions about releasing fish, which are discussed in detail in the entry on catch-and-release *(see)*. Many people who use only artificial lures (especially flies) assume moral superiority because of this, which is not necessarily justified. The artificial lure versus bait issue is one of many ethical concerns that has been addressed in specific instances by laws.

Fishing for spawners. One of the few ethical issues that is raised from time to time is that of angling for spawning largemouth and smallmouth bass, which are vulnerable to detection and catching when on their large and easily observed shallow nests in the spring. The effect of deliberately or incidentally catching (and in many cases releasing) spawning bass has triggered a few scientific studies, and

Estimates have it that 50 million plastic worms are produced annually. Most popular size: 6 inches. Top colors: black and purple.

E

perceived potential negative effects from fishing during the spawning season are the main reason why a minority of fisheries agencies close the angling season (especially for trout, bass, walleye, pike, and muskellunge) during the spawning period. Such closures, however, are inconsistent among fisheries agencies, some with neighboring jurisdictions, which logically raises questions about validity.

Although the personal ethic of some anglers is that it is unsportsmanlike to deliberately angle for spawning bass, many anglers do so (it is legal in most states). Curiously, questions regarding the propriety and sportsmanship of angling for other species when they are spawning or specifically on their spawning migration—such as salmon, steelhead, trout, charr, striped bass, shad, and tuna—is almost never raised, perhaps because of their generally fleeting availability.

Fishing/catching to excess.   The propriety of keeping a limit or excessive number of fish each time an angler goes fishing, even if legal to do so and even if the fish will be consumed, raises ethical questions. Many anglers have done this, whether for bluefish in saltwater or crappie in freshwater, and this practice long ago gave rise to game hog and other derisive terms ("game hog," incidentally, was coined by publisher George O. Shields in editorials in his magazine *Recreation* in the 1890s). Likewise, continuing to catch and release high numbers of fish when the angling is very good is viewed by some people as excessive, somewhat like running up the score in a lopsided athletic contest or piling onto the ball carrier in a football game.

Assistance.   Ethical concerns exist with the very act of setting the hook on a fish and playing it. The International Game Fish Association *(see)* long ago established ethical rules for catches that were acceptable as world records *(see)*. Anglers who do not set the hook themselves on a potential record catch, for example, and/or who allow someone else to handle their rod while playing or landing that fish, cannot receive a record, no matter how stupendous the fish is. Although the wisdom of this is widely supported, similar mandates do not exist in many state record programs and most anglers are generally unfamiliar with these principles. Many other aspects of the equipment used and means of fishing are covered by these record establishing rules.

Foul hooking.   Although it is generally addressed in laws and agency regulations, foul hooking of fish is another area that raises ethical questions and has caused a lot of controversy. Unfortunately, it does not raise ethical concerns for enough anglers, as some are willing to keep a gamefish that has been accidentally foul hooked, which many people view as unsportsmanlike.

The legal foul hooking of fish, known as snagging *(see)*, is another matter entirely, and one that is still supported by some fisheries agencies (previously for salmon and, in many if not all cases, for paddlefish).

Its adoption by a significant number of people, and advocacy by some fisheries agencies (New York, for example, until the early 1990s) has fostered a great deal of such activity, legal and illegal, especially for salmonid species in Great Lakes tributaries. This has lead to atrocious behavior by people who are unconscious of fair play ethics, and disapproval by a small number of anglers, with the vast middle ground of the sportfishing fraternity being silent.

Mismatched tackle.   Many anglers fish with tackle that is either too light or too heavy for the intended species or common size of the species they seek. This includes rods and reels but especially the breaking strength of line used. With modern fine-diameter lines, it is possible to use a product that has 25-pound strength but the diameter of a conventional 10- or 12-pound line; the fairness of using this for 1- and 2-pound largemouth bass, for example, is extremely dubious. Many situations exist where anglers use heavy tackle on the off chance that they'll hook a huge fish, thereby ensuring that there is little contest in landing the much more plentiful smaller specimens.

On the other hand, using extremely light tackle for some species, especially those that are hard, strong fighters, is also unfair if the fish will, or must, be released, because it is likely that the fish will have a harder time recovering and/or escaping its other predators when released. Fair play is again the main issue here (although there is a question of the well-being of the fish and its ability to escape predators as well), and in their zeal to use productive methods in the right places, anglers may overlook this.

Selling fish.   Some saltwater sportfish (especially tuna and dolphin) are legally sold by people using recreational angling methods to capture the fish. The lack of ethics in this is pretty obvious, not to mention the fact that commercial fishermen are rightly accused of overexploiting most ocean fisheries resources (particularly tuna) by the angling community at the same time that some of their own brotherhood are selling fish that have been caught on rod and reel.

Killing fish.   The subject of killing fish that are kept for personal consumption is poorly addressed by the outdoor sports media, although it has been covered elsewhere in this book *(see: fish preparation—care)*. Anti-angling groups object to catch-and-release fishing because fish "are only let go to be hooked and tortured all over again," and the criticism is that even when fish are kept, most are not killed immediately; they're put in boxes where they slowly suffocate. Although British sporting magazines recommend that anglers carry a "priest," or club, to kill fish instantly and humanely, North American writers rarely broach the subject. Perhaps many people feel that the growing popularity of catch-and-release fishing is proof of its moral superiority, or that what isn't actually written into law is ethically acceptable.

Pollution. It is ironic that anglers—who have a lot to gain from clean environments and healthy fish populations—number amongst themselves people who discard trash on the shore or into the water. Used fishing line, for example, is especially harmful, as it can entangle birds or other animals, but there are many examples of ways in which some anglers (albeit a small minority) despoil the environment through their personal behavior, both while fishing and not fishing.

Competitions and equipment. Competitive fishing events are commonplace and raise ethical concerns that are rarely addressed because many of these events are important business and tourism tools. Concerns include the use of public resources for private gain, the philosophy of angling, methodologies used by competitors, the handling and disposition of fish, interfering with and/or usurping the rights of the general public, the well-being of fish that are caught/transported/handled/released, and more. Many competitions, especially catch-and-release events for bass and walleye in freshwater, cause anglers to temporarily break the law and certainly abrogate ethical standards when they cull (*see*) a limit of fish in a livewell.

The kinds of equipment employed in recent decades has mushroomed enormously, and much of it is profiled in some way within this book. Electronic developments have lead to some attempts to curb or eliminate by law their use; these have been unsuccessful but included proposed bans on using sonar equipment and underwater viewing cameras. The use of some of these items has raised regionally isolated ethical debates.

In a related sense, the amount of fish-finding equipment used, and how it is used, is questioned by some people, among them George Reiger, who notes: "Confucius believed that the 'true angler' must fish with only one hook and line at a time and never use a net, not even to help land a fish. The measure of an angler's worth is in how he captures a fish, not in what he does with it once it's in hand. An angler who fishes with more than one hook and line, or uses a net, tips the balance of the sport in his favor and, thereby, reduces the ethical value of its experience.

"Confucius believed that while we're all born with conscience, it must be cultivated to serve us and society. Neglected or corrupted by false standards of fair play, conscience grows rank and unwanted like a weed. Since Confucius believed he was only articulating what everyone intuitively knows to be true, he called himself 'a transmitter, not an originator' of the precepts he codified. What makes his teachings so remarkable is that 2,500 years later, his disciples are still practicing what Confucius preached—including fishing with only one hook and line at a time.

"Even as recently as a century ago in the United States, anglers held themselves to a number of standards higher than those we accept today. A commercial fisherman might fish more than one line, but never a sportsman. In addition, many 1890s anglers felt it was unethical to fight a fish sitting down (unless the angler were in a canoe), wear a harness, or accept assistance of any kind while the fight was going on, unless he were handicapped, a novice, or—forgive those Victorian gentlemen—an 'anglerette.'

"In 1894 off California's Catalina Island, General Charles Viete hooked and fought for two hours a giant sea bass that eventually took refuge in a kelp bed. Determined to win the battle, the general tightened up his line and tied it to the rod. He then lashed the rod to an empty oil drum and left it adrift while he went back to the island for lunch. When he returned some hours later, he brought a grapnel and succeeded in tearing away the kelp without breaking the line. After another half-hour of stand-up combat, the 227-pound sea bass was gaffed and hauled over the side. It was a remarkable victory, but was it a fair catch?

"'Of course not,' the general replied. 'I had lunch; the fish didn't.'

"When big-game fishing came into vogue in the 1910s, some anglers—including most charter operators—thought it too much to ask the average angler, especially newcomers to the sport, to hold a rod all day and then fight a tuna or billfish standing up. Yet in 1913, William C. Boschen did precisely that when he landed the first broadbill swordfish (a 358-pounder) ever taken on rod and reel. He subsequently caught dozens of billfish single-handedly, without a harness, and all standing up.

"Another member of the Catalina Tuna Club, J. A. Wiborn, was so fearful he might accept assistance if it were available, he fished by himself and earned the sobriquet, 'Lone Angler.' A number of anglers, such as 89-year-old Frank Mather, keep this tradition alive today. Mather does so less because he's too proud to accept assistance than because he can find few younger men willing and able to maintain his pace in pursuit of giant bluefin tuna and billfish. He has caught, tagged, and released dozens of such big fish single-handedly.

"Why do we no longer teach the ethical validity of fishing only one line per big game angler and then fighting fish unassisted and standing up?

"The answers involve money and competition in a legalistic society. Right from the outset in what was called 'deep-sea fishing,' guides—not sportsmen—set ethical standards based on minimal levels that would enable even the most inexperienced or inept anglers to catch records 'according to the rules.' Four, six, up to a dozen lines at a time were trolled for half as many anglers aboard a boat. While it may be too much to expect a greenhorn to tackle his first tuna standing up, it also belittles the skill of an expert to establish standards that put him on a par with the greenhorn. Even worse, big game trolling has become a team sport in which the skipper and mate play roles that are as or more important than the angler.

Bluefin tuna have been known to make journeys in the western Atlantic Ocean exceeding 4,000 miles in less than two months.

"What's allowed in charter fishing has gradually become the standard in most fishing. The goal is to capture the largest or the greatest accumulated poundage of fish under the most rudimentary rules of sportsmanship. There are notable exceptions, of course, but increasingly the moral 'hows' of angling have been overwhelmed by the amoral 'how-tos.' And whereas competition was once seen as a corrosive influence on good sportsmanship, even conservation groups now use angling contests as a means of raising money and publicizing their cause.

"Writing in the September, 1922, issue of the Izaak Walton League's *Outdoor America,* 'Lone Angler' Wiborn spoke for a now forgotten generation's view of the matter when he noted that 'competition creates a false standard of sportsmanship. The best interests of conservation are debauched by prize contests. The joy of a day a-stream, or a-field, often is deadened by false desire to be number one.'

"A century ago, our angling forefathers thought they could best perpetuate the sport by giving certain species 'gamefish' status, thereby putting them off-limits to commercial exploitation. Trout and bass were soon followed by other freshwater fishes, and, in recent years, coastal states have begun doing the same for certain marine species. At the same time, however, recreational fishing is increasingly haunted by a different kind of commercial enterprise (and an oxymoron) called 'tournament angling' in which the most successful (meaning 'richest') anglers depend on corporate sponsorship to provide their fortunes.

"They're more like golf pros than recreational anglers. Fishing for them has lost its innocence and much of its charm. It's a job. Yet it's precisely these jaded pros who their corporate sponsors encourage us to emulate, not the ethical champions of the past. But unless we find ways to offset the increasing commercialism of recreational fishing with a revival of ethical standards, angling will not only lose the moral high ground to groups who oppose this activity, but the sport as a sport will die, and

we'll have lost one of our species' best ways to immerse ourselves in nature while reinforcing the one ingredient that separates us from nature: our conscience."

Etiquette

In the modern era in which few people hold doors open for others, where a decreasing number say "thank you," and where people fight over street and mall parking spaces, it is no surprise that recreational fishing (and boating) has its share of issues pertaining to manners and courtesy.

Because there's no Emily Post or Miss Manners for the sportfishing world, there is no established guide to proper conduct on the water for anglers, many of whom are also boaters. There are certain conventions that are followed in some places and by some groups of anglers, however. For example, many North American Atlantic salmon anglers gather at a river pool and take turns rotating through the pool, fishing from the head of the pool to the run-out, with following anglers entering the water only when their predecessor has moved sufficiently downstream, depending on the size of the pool. This is one of the more civilized forms of angling behavior on crowded water, made bearable in part by a general lack of fish.

On the other hand, the presence of large numbers of fish has a tendency to bring out some of the worst behavior in people. A large school of chinook salmon in a small river, a huge school of surface-busting stripers or white bass in an inland reservoir, and a mass of bluefish rampaging in the surf along a beach are just a few examples of incidents that can draw a flock of wide-eyed people in a desperate bid to catch fish, often with the result that they get in the way of other anglers, cut off fish that are hooked by others, do things that cause the fish to be spooked, or act in ways that are unsafe or may cause harm.

Although the number of people who might be called "slobs" are a minority, their actions are detrimental to the way in which all anglers may be perceived. Some are simply anglers who don't know what is good etiquette on the water because they don't understand enough about the sport or the particular circumstances.

Trespass is probably the number one problem in freshwater and needs little explanation. If it isn't yours and isn't clearly public, then it's private. You must obtain permission to fish on private waters, to cross private property to access public or private waters, and, in some cases, even to stop briefly on private property while wading or navigating through public waters.

Trespass, of course, is a legal matter, but courtesy and manners are not, and they apply to all aspects of angling. For example, if you're fishing a small stream and come upon an angler working a pool, you should pass that pool up or wait until the angler fishing it departs. Likewise, when fishing in

Anglers crowd a New York river during the fall chinook salmon run.

a lake or reservoir, it is bad form to come into an area that another boat occupies. Allow a reasonable amount of space, and assume that they are, and will continue, working the area and not just the immediate spot where they're located. Crowded waters, however, make breaches of such reasonable etiquette too frequent. So do competitive fishing events.

Although common sense prescribes that proper behavior is necessary when sharing waters with others, this becomes complicated when anglers don't realize the extent of the circumstances. For example, a person fishing along a saltwater flat by poling and stalking fish will generally be heading downtide to spot and cast to fish that will be moving or facing uptide. Another person who runs by downtide or who pulls up to start fishing downtide, even within a hundred yards, is more than inconsiderate; this action is likely to spoil a careful stalk by spooking fish. In such an instance the pre-positioned angler should be given a very wide berth by a passing boat, should be allowed its original course by the newly arrived angler moving uptide (like the Atlantic salmon river anglers), or should be asked by the newcomer where he can fish (only after approaching quietly from uptide or via radio communication) without interfering.

Most examples of proper etiquette involve common sense. For example, trollers shouldn't run their boats too close to other trollers or anchored boats to avoid cutting or hooking lines, and should stay well away from shore anglers; well away is out of casting range. Boaters who cast along a shoreline should swing away from shore anglers (or swimmers) and leave this area completely to their less mobile counterparts.

Boating anglers should always give the right of way to a boat that has a fish; pull in your own lines if necessary and swing far away from their area. Sometimes in crowded situations this requires quick action.

Most boating anglers don't think of themselves as being a problem for non-boaters, although they're very aware when they are on the receiving end of poor conduct by water-skiers, some pleasure boaters, and many operators of personal watercraft. However, the wake of fast-moving fishing boats (bass boats in particular), especially in narrow places like canals and near-shore areas, can cause people in a small boat to grip the gunwales while the boat rocks, and does little to engender goodwill. Idling away from shore, observing no-wake zones and speed limits, and giving a wide berth to shores (100 to 150 feet is the minimum and a legal requirement in some waters), especially where there are homes and docks, are examples of good etiquette.

Boating anglers should be aware of others in a variety of not so immediately obvious ways. For example, boaters greatly interfere with duck

When waters are fringed with docks and boathouses, as this Ontario lake is, anglers should be mindful of private property and steer clear of those in use.

hunters in the fall by getting anywhere near an active blind; sometimes it's difficult to know which blinds are currently in use, even if decoys are on the water, but boating or angling activity may too easily destroy the duck hunter's already limited chance of success.

Fishing around docks and boathouses, which are popular fishing targets for bass anglers, requires common sense courtesies as well. Those who don't have pinpoint casting control should avoid fishing around these objects, as owners do not appreciate having lures and hooks bounce off their property, get tangled in dock lines, or stuck on foam dock supports. Do not fish docks when they're being used, and leave the area politely if asked to do so, even though the surrounding water is public.

Boating anglers should also make sure that they spend minimal time launching and loading a boat from active or crowded access sites. Boat preparation for fishing, and unloading, should take place away from the launch ramp and the public dock. When fish are kept, they should never be cleaned on the beach or shore; do so in designated fish cleaning areas at a launch site, or at home.

Kick boaters who fish flowing waters, as well as drift boaters and anglers fishing while floating in canoes, kayaks, jonboats, or other craft, need to steer clear of wading anglers. Sometimes this is not possible, and they wind up floating right in front of anglers and over the pool they're fishing. Where possible, it's best to go behind a wading angler, or directly in front of that person (if it is too shallow behind them) so as to minimize your impact on the pool or run. You may have to explain your intentions as you approach.

These are just a few examples of ways in which common sense dictates courteous behavior. The golden etiquette rule should always be do unto others as you would have them do unto you.

E

Eulachon

EULACHON   *Thaleichthys pacificus.*
Other names—candlefish, hooligan; French: *eula-chon, eulakane.*

The eulachon is a member of the smelt family, Osmeridae. It is one of the largest members of this family of small, Pacific coast fish, and has been important to the Chinook Indians. High in oil content (15 percent of body weight), eulachon used to be dried and fitted with a wick for use as a candle.

Like other smelts, the eulachon is important as forage food for Pacific salmon, as well as marine mammals and birds. It is also harvested or caught commercially and is a highly esteemed seafood by Native Americans from California to Alaska. Although some are hard-salted, these surf smelts are too delicate to be preserved and are generally smoked.

Identification.   The eulachon is a small slender fish with a stubby adipose fin just in front of the tail. The lower jaw projects slightly beyond the tip of the snout. Its coloring is bluish black on the back, fading to silvery white on the belly. Smelts are so similar in appearance that it is difficult to differentiate among species. Its larger size, however, helps distinguish the eulachon from its relatives.

Size/Age.   The eulachon can reach up to 12 inches. It generally lives two to three years.

Distribution.   This fish is common throughout cool northern Pacific waters, with a range from west of St. Matthews Island and Kuskokwim Bay in the Bering Sea, and Bowers Bank in the Aleutian Islands to Monterey Bay in California.

Habitat.   This fish is found near shore and in coastal inlets and rivers. It spends its life at sea prior to spawning.

Spawning behavior.   Eulachon spawn between March and May when they enter freshwater tributaries from Northern California to the Bering Sea. They mature when they reach two to three years of age, and die following spawning.

Food.   The eulachon feeds on planktonic crustaceans.

EUTROPHIC
In a lake, high nutrient levels and a natural aging; an increase in the rate of nutrient supply to a water body, characterized by an abundance of nutrients.

A eutrophic lake is one that is old, with a soft mucky bottom. Rooted plant growth is abundant along the shores and out into the lake, and algae blooms are not unusual. The water is often colored, with suspended and organic matter reducing its clarity; oxygen is limited or absent in the hypolimnion, especially during the summer. Eutrophic lakes support only warmwater fish such as perch, catfish, panfish, and bass, plus coarse species.

Lake aging goes through a process from oligotrophic *(see)* to mesotrophic *(see)* to eutrophic. Lakes age at different rates depending on natural and human-influenced factors. When plant growth is accelerated, particularly the growth of algae, and when the water body receives little or no flushing, the lake undergoes eutrophication, a hastening of the aging process. If this continues unabated, dense mats of algae choke off the surface and block the water column's access to sunlight. The algae below the surface begin to die for lack of light. The resultant decaying mass deoxygenates the water as it decomposes and makes the water unfit for anything to live in. There is a rapid die-off of many species; eventually the water may become clean again, but unless it is restocked, it will not exhibit the same populations it once had. If it does not come clean, it may simply fill in and die.

Eutrophication is most often associated with freshwater lakes and ponds, but can occur in fairly constricted saltwater bays.

See: Algae Bloom.

EXOTIC SPECIES
Organisms introduced into habitats where they are not native are called exotic species. They are often the agents of severe worldwide, regional, and local habitat alteration. Also referred to as nonindigenous, nonnative, alien, transplant, foreign, and introduced species, they can be the cause of biological diversity loss and can greatly upset the balance of ecosystems.

Exotic species have been introduced around the world both intentionally and accidentally; occasionally exotic species occur in new places through natural means, but usually the agent is some action of humans. That includes transportation of fish or larvae via the ballast of ocean freighters and the bait buckets of small-boat anglers, passage of new species via newly constructed canals, the introduction of plants by using them in packing shellfish that are shipped transcontinent, the dumping of aquarium plants and fish into local waterways, the experimental stocking of predator and prey species by scientists and nonscientists, and many other means. Exotic species can be transported by animals, vehicles, commercial goods, produce, and even clothing.

While some exotic introductions are ecologically harmless, many are very harmful and have even caused the extinction of native species, especially those of confined habitats. Freed from the predators, pathogens, and competitors that have kept their numbers in check in their native environs, species introduced into new habitats often overrun their new home and crowd out native species. In the presence of enough food and a favorable environment, their numbers explode. Once established, exotics rarely can be eliminated.

Sometimes the introductions of exotic species have generally beneficial results. Anglers consider the importation of coho and chinook salmon from the Pacific Ocean into the Great Lakes, for example, to be a highly successful introduction of a non-native species. Certainly in terms of providing recreation, this is true. The same can be said for brown trout, first imported from Germany to the United States in the 1880s, and also spread to many countries on others continents. But the same cannot be said for carp, imported in the late nineteenth century and spread throughout North America, resulting in the destruction of spawning habitat for other species and the alteration of many environments into which they were placed. Likewise, the introduction of Nile perch into Lake Victoria in Africa is generally viewed as one of the most destructive exotic introductions of all time, having resulted in the apparent extinction of hundreds of small native tropical species.

Exotic species include other aquatic animals and plants as well as fish. These include such organisms as zebra mussels, hydrilla, the spiny water flea, purple loosestrife, and watermilfoil. Many exotic plant

Clusters of zebra mussels cling to the stalks of vegetation.

introductions have been especially harmful. Several examples from the Great Lakes reflect this.

The zebra mussel *(see)* invaded the Great Lakes from its native habitats in Europe and has become a nuisance by clogging the intakes of water pipes and outboard boat engines. It has received much attention because it can be common in shallow water near shore and is large enough to be easily seen. During the 1980s, the 1-centimeter-long zooplankton called spiny water flea *(see)* entered the Great Lakes, and may have as profound an effect on the ecosystem as a larger invader. The sea lamprey *(see)*, aided by overfishing in the early to mid-1900s, decimated lake trout, which used to reproduce naturally in all the Great Lakes, and now reproduce naturally primarily in Lake Superior, with isolated occurrences in the other lakes.

Prevention. Anglers and boaters have an obligation to make sure they do not assist in transplanting any organisms to places where they don't belong. This pertains to the known problem exotics and also to not so obvious ones (like yellow perch being introduced into a small trout pond). This prevention starts with not deliberately planting or stocking species from one environment to another, which may also be illegal *(see: regulations)*. However, since many introductions are accidental, and many of the organisms moved are so small they cannot be readily seen (like larvae), anglers must be diligent at all times. These are some of the precautions to take:

North American Exotic Species

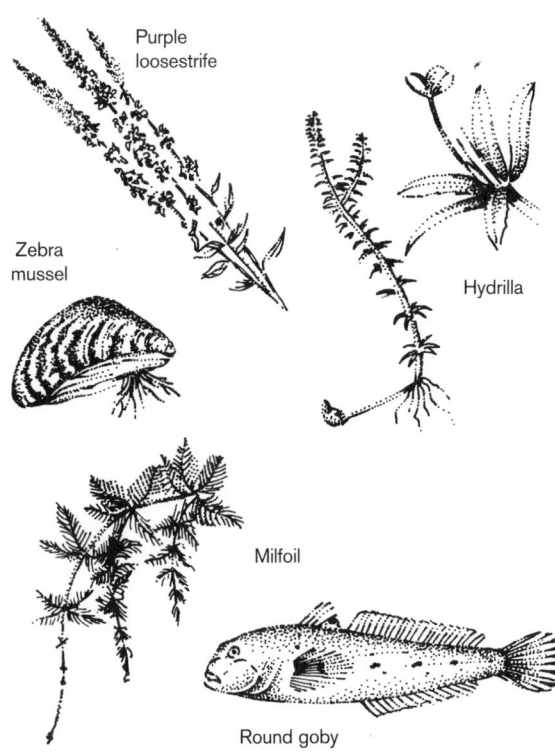

Purple loosestrife

Zebra mussel

Hydrilla

Milfoil

Round goby

- Empty a bait bucket on land before leaving the water; do not transport bait from one water body to another.
- Inspect the boat, the motor, all parts of the trailer, and any boating equipment that gets wet, and remove any plants and animals that are visible before leaving the water body.
- Drain livewells, bilge water, and transom wells at the access site before leaving the water body.

- Where zebra mussels and spiny water fleas are known or suspected, wash and dry your boat, tackle, trailers, and other equipment with hot water when you get home. Flush water through the motor's cooling system and other parts that get wet. If possible, let everything dry for at least three days before transporting the boat to another water body. Flushing with chlorinated tap water may be helpful.

E

F

FAD

Acronym for Fish Attracting Device.
See: Fish Attractor.

FAEROE ISLANDS

See: Denmark.

FALKLAND ISLANDS

Located about 600 kilometers east of the southern tip of South America, the Falkland Islands lie in the South Atlantic Ocean and encompass more land than most island groups. There are about 200 islands in this self-governing British dependency, but East and West Falkland Islands cover most of the group's 16,000 total square kilometers and are separated by Falkland Sound. The Falklands are one of the most spectacular and remote places in the world.

The visitor may be surprised to find that these islands offer fishing for resident and sea-run brown trout. These trout were introduced to a few rivers here in the 1950s and acclimated well. Today they inhabit many rivers and streams, and some migrate to and from the sea. Several larger lakes exist on rivers with sea access, but it is uncertain whether they support trout fisheries.

The average sea trout in rivers weighs around 5 pounds, but much larger specimens exist here. A 22-pound sea trout was reportedly caught in the San Carlos River. The main rivers on East Falkland Island are the San Carlos, Malo, and Murrell; on West Falkland they include the Warrah and Chartres.

A trout is hooked on the Chartres River on West Falkland Island.

Freshwater fishing rights in the Falklands are privately owned. On West Falkland, a fishing lodge in the Port Howard settlement provides access to the Warrah and the Chartres Rivers, as well as smaller streams and brooks, with a 4-wheel-drive vehicle. On East Falkland, a road runs from the capital city of Stanley, which holds about half of the Falklands' 2,300 residents, across the northern part of the island to Port San Carlos. The road passes several small streams and estuaries, all of which hold trout but require access permission from local farmers. Near its end the road passes the San Carlos River, where local farmers offer bed-and-breakfast accommodations and fishing.

The trout fishing season here extends from September through April. Spring (September/October) and autumn (March/April) are best for river fishing.

Saltwater fishing is accessible to the public. Sea trout can be fished in saltwater along the open coast and especially outside the river mouths year-round. Along the coast, anglers also catch Falkland mullet, which can reach 20 pounds. These mullet, which are strong fighters, are primarily fished near the bottom with flies, bait, and lures. Near- and offshore fishing opportunities are unknown but could be minimal due to climate and wind.

The climate is often harsh, and summer temperatures are relatively cold; rain and high humidity are frequent. The islands are so windswept that the countryside is treeless. Despite this, the Falklands possess varied wildlife, including more than 200 species of birds, and several of these are rare outside the islands; the Falklands also host five species of penguins, as well as sea lions and seals, and the enormous elephant seal.

FALLFISH *Semotilus corporalis.*
Other names—windfish, silver chub.

The fallfish is a member of the Cyprinidae family, the largest family of freshwater fish, which also includes minnows *(see)* and carp *(see)*. Often confused with the creek chub *(see: chub, creek),* the fallfish is the largest in its minnow clan, and is a common catch for anglers. Rather than the result of targeted effort, these landings are typically accidental, and there is little constituency for these fish from an angling standpoint. The fallfish is likewise seldom used as table fare, but it is important forage for larger fish.

Identification. The body of the fallfish is slender with a bluntly pointed head. There is a

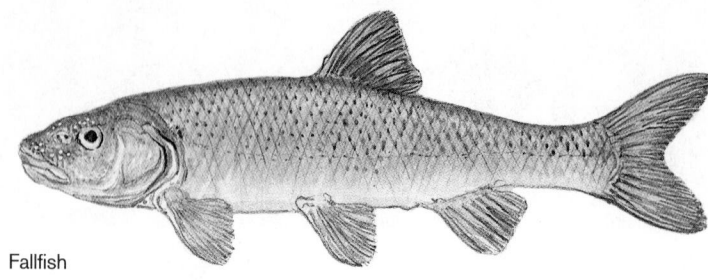

Fallfish

single, long dorsal fin. On adults, the scales are arranged in a pattern of dark, triangular black bars. The mouth is terminal and has barbels—which are characteristic of cyprinids—that are sometimes hidden. Its coloring is olive on the back, silvery on the sides, and white on the belly. Breeding males have tubercles on the snout and a pinkish coloring. Juveniles have a dark black line along the sides. The fallfish can be distinguished from the creek chub (*Semotilus atromaculatus*) by the absence of a black spot at the base of the dorsal fin.

Size/Age. Fallfish may grow to 16 inches or more in length. In smaller streams, they are more likely to be smaller, averaging 10 to 15 inches. A common weight is 1 to 2 pounds. Fallfish have been known to live as long as 10 years.

Distribution. These fish are commonly found from eastern Canada into the James Bay drainage, and south on the east side of the Appalachian Mountains to Virginia.

Habitat. Fallfish inhabit the gravel- and rocky-bottomed areas of cold, clear streams, as well as the edges of lakes and ponds. In rivers and streams, adults prefer deeper, quieter waters, whereas juveniles often frequent swifter, shallower water.

Spawning behavior. The spawning season is from spring through summer, beginning in early May when the water warms. The male builds a pit-ridge nest out of small stones and pebbles in shallow areas or quiet pools over a clean gravel bottom. The nest can reach 6 feet in length and 3 feet in height. It can weigh up to 200 pounds, due to the volume of pebbles, and is the largest stone mound nest built by any fish. The male repeatedly spawns over one nest with several different females. Each female releases roughly 2,000 eggs. The eggs become adhesive after fertilization and are then covered by the parent with gravel. They hatch within 138 to 144 hours.

Food. Adult fallfish consume aquatic and terrestrial insects (such as mayflies, beetles, wasps, and ants), small crustaceans, small fish, and algae. Juveniles feed on zooplankton and phytoplankton.

FALSE CAST

An element of flycasting in which the fly line is cast forward and back without allowing line or fly to touch the water. It is achieved by making a new back cast as soon as the loop of a forward cast has rolled out and before it has a chance to fall on the water. Repeated false casting is done to dry out a fly for better flotation, or to lengthen or shorten the overall length of line being fished without disturbing the surface. When you are ready to stop false casting, simply stop the forward motion and lay the line down on the water.
See: Flycasting Tackle.

FAMILY

A group of closely related species *(see)*.

FAN CASTING

A method of fully covering the water in front of an angler by casting in an arcing pattern. Whether in a boat, fishing from shore, or wading, the angler starts casting with a lure or fly in one spot and makes successive casts clockwise or counterclockwise from the original starting point until the full range of water has been covered. If no strikes are received, casting may be repeated with a different lure or fly, or the angler can move and start anew from a different position, covering new water that has not been previously cast over. The objective is to systematically and thoroughly cover all likely fish-holding water.

FANWING

A type of dry fly *(see)* with matching wings that stand upright and are curved outward to help the fly fall gently on the water, hook down.

FATHOM

A common nautical measurement in the Imperial system, equaling 6 feet, or 1.83 meters.

FATHOMETER

Antiquated term for sonar.
See: Sonar.

FAUNA

The animal life of any particular area or of any particular time.

FEATHER

To use a thumb or fingers to apply light pressure on the line of a reel to help achieve accuracy when casting *(see)*.

FEATHERING

A manner of controlling line to help achieve accuracy during a cast with spinning, spincasting, and baitcasting tackle.

On a spinning reel, line can be feathered by placing the index finger of the rod-holding hand near the lip of the spool and allowing the line to brush against it. This slows line flow and shortens distance to help place a lure at a given target. The same effect can also be accomplished by allowing the outgoing line to brush against the palm or finger of the noncasting hand. On a spincasting reel, line can be feathered by using the thumb and forefinger of the noncasting hand to apply varying degrees of pressure to the outgoing line.

On a baitcasting reel, feathering is accomplished by applying pressure from the thumb of the rod-holding hand onto the revolving spool, rather than touching the outgoing line. This is a better means of obtaining accurate lure placement and is also necessary to help prevent a spool overrun, or backlash *(see)*. See: Baitcasting Tackle; Casting; Spincasting Tackle; Spinning Tackle.

FEATHERS

A type of weighted trolling lure.
See: Trolling Lures, Saltwater.

FEATHERWING

A fly tied primarily with hackles instead of with fur (which is a hairwing).

FEDERAL AID IN SPORT FISH RESTORATION ACT

Established by Congress in 1950 and also known as the Dingell-Johnson Act, this legislation captured the funds from a manufacturer's excise tax on fishing rods, reels, creels, and artificial lures that had been established as a luxury tax during World War II. The law required a state match of 25 percent on project funding and was intended to provide capital for sport fishery restoration, management, or enhancement projects. It also protected anglers' license fees by prohibiting their diversion to other than approved purposes. It was, and still is, administered by the U.S. Fish and Wildlife Service in partnership with the states.

In 1984, the Wallop-Breaux Amendment of the Federal Aid in Sport Fish Restoration Act was passed and allowed for expansion of the tax base to include essentially all items of fishing tackle, electric (trolling) motors, and flasher-type sonar devices; plus motorboat fuel taxes and import duties on fishing tackle and boats. This amendment changed the program from a small but valuable source of funding for state fisheries agencies to a significant portion of their fisheries management budgets, and it broadened the constituency base within the angling and boating communities. In 1990, the act was expanded again by an additional increase in the federal excise tax on gasoline, and also by deposit of the federal tax on gasoline from small nonhighway engines into the program (although millions of dollars of boater-paid taxes have annually been diverted by Congress for federal deficit reduction).

Funds may be used for almost any type of sport fishery restoration, management, or enhancement projects; and the Wallop-Breaux Amendment mandated that each state spend at least 10 percent for boat access projects, and that each could use up to 10 percent of its apportionment for aquatic resource education. The required portion for boating improvements was increased to 12.5 percent in 1992.

An annual apportionment of these monies is made available to each state. Forty percent of this amount is based on the state's land and water area in relation to the total land and water area of the United States. Sixty percent of this amount is based on the number of paid sportfishing license holders in each state in relation to all the paid sportfishing license holders in the United States.

The funds in the Federal Aid in Sport Fish Restoration Program have come under frequent attack from Congress, particularly as a means to reduce the federal deficit and to support omnibus budget bills. Many anglers are unaware of the nature of this program or of the impact that it has had on fisheries management and the creation of fishing and boating opportunities in the United States.

The Federal Aid in Sport Fish Restoration Program, particularly through the Wallop-Breaux Amendment, was designed to bridge a growing gap between the needs of state fishery programs and the funding available. In other words, the state programs were (are) costing more to run than the user base could (or will) provide through license, stamp, and permit fees to run them. In addition, as state government budgets have tightened, general appropriations for conservation programs (including fisheries management) have declined. Not only has the program provided much-needed state funding, but it has been matched with state dollars that have partly come from increased license fees, and it has spurred increases in funding from nonfederal sources.

The Federal Aid in Sport Fish Restoration Program has been responsible for important programs and access projects in all states, and many hundreds of millions of "user-pay" dollars are annually channeled to the states for fisheries management, fish production and stocking, state university research activities, boat access improvements, and other undertakings. The program has specifically been responsible for:

- Acquisition of tens of thousands of acres for access
- Development of thousands of boating and fishing access sites
- Production of several billion fish for restoration or maintenance projects
- Work on habitat enhancement projects at over 2,000 stream sites
- Work on habitat enhancement projects at over 2,300 lakes and reservoirs
- Review of hundreds of thousands of public projects

- Technical assistance to hundreds of thousands of private landowners
- Surveys of thousands of fish populations
- Investigation of thousands of habitats
- Aquatic education courses to several million students

Funding has allowed states to seize fisheries enhancement opportunities that might otherwise have been missed, and to undertake large projects that might otherwise have been unfunded, such as hatchery construction or rehabilitation, or acquisition of important habitats. All of these efforts translate into more sport fishery conservation efforts and more angling opportunity.

See: Fisheries Management.

FELT SOLE
See: Waders.

FENDER
An object hung over a boat to cushion it from impacts with docks, piers, or other boats. In big-game fishing, large polyfenders are sometimes used as teasers *(see)* to attract marlin from the depths. These are spray painted to look like bait or other pelagic fish (like dolphin), rigged with a weighted trailing skirt, and towed on a weighted line (egg weights crimped to the line at the nose), which allows them to kick up a greater disturbance than conventional attractors.

FERRULE
The mating sections of a rod blank, which are joined to form a complete fishing rod. In the past, these sections were produced by cutting a rod blank and joining the sections with separate metal fittings or ferrules, which produced multipiece rods but hampered the action. The majority of rods today are joined with integral ferrules. The sections of multipiece rods are manufactured as separate blanks with ferrules integral to the blanks; if properly designed and manufactured, the ferrules allow the rod to perform as if it were a one-piece rod.

The receiving end is called the outside or female ferrule, and the other the inside or male ferrule. The outside ferrule is a bit larger so that the inside section slides into it. The joint is ground with a precision taper, and the friction fit is sufficient for a secure grip.

Many anglers lubricate this joint with beeswax both to increase the grip and to promote smoother assembly and disassembly. Do not apply wax excessively, or it will trap abrasive dirt particles; always wipe a ferrule before assembly. For disassembly, hold the rod firmly at both ferrules and turn each in opposite directions while gently pulling each away from the other.

See: Rod, Fishing.

FIBERGLASS ROD
A fishing rod that uses fiberglass material in the construction of the blank. The evolution of fiberglass proved the demise of steel rods *(see)* and eventually bamboo rods *(see)*, although some limited fabrication of split-cane bamboo rods is still practiced by custom rod builders. Uniform quality of production was the key to the success of early fiberglass rods, and several processes evolved, using different types of fiberglass, particularly today E-glass *(see)* and S-glass *(see)*.

Modern rods are primarily made of fiberglass material, especially those having lower cost and offering certain performance distinctions (durability and softer recovery); graphite material; and, increasingly, a blend of fiberglass and graphite.

See: Rod, Fishing.

FIELD DRESSING
A method of cleaning fish that involves the removal of the entrails, gills, and kidney.

See: Fish Preparation—Cleaning/Dressing.

FIGHTING BELT
See: Rod Belt.

FIGHTING BUTT
An extension to the base of a fly rod handle. Because fly reels sit at the base of most fishing rods, it is awkward, if not inhibiting, to fight strong fish by jamming the rod and reel into the angler's midsection. A fighting butt, which is from 2 to 6 inches long, improves leverage and places the reel and its handle far enough away from the angler's body to allow unimpeded cranking.

A fighting butt may be an integral part of a fly rod, and not removable, or it may be an optional extension of the reel seat, employed by removing the butt cap and inserting it into the portal at the base of the reel seat. An optional extension is useful on a rod that sees varied fishing activities, since the extension can be removed when the angler is casting for small fish. When a fighting butt is used, the rod-holding hand is placed at the top of the handle, or often above the handle on the blank, for fighting leverage. The end cap of the butt is usually rounded to ease its effect on the body, although a prolonged battle with a fish will leave a bruise on the body where the fighting butt has been jammed, unless something buffers it (like heavy clothes or a rod belt).

FIGHTING CHAIR
Also known as a fishing chair, this specialized chair is used on sportfishing boats and is designed to give anglers an advantage when fighting large fish. Fighting chairs used for smaller species are usually free-standing, resting on four legs. These chairs

have the advantage of mobility, since they can be placed wherever desired in the boat.

Larger fighting chairs are mounted atop fixed pedestals, and they turn on some sort of bearing so that the angler can keep the rod tip pointed toward the fish at all times. Pedestal chairs usually have footrests for leverage and have rod holders in the arms of the chair.

Rod gimbals are normally mounted on the front of a fighting chair and allow the angler to pump the fishing rod in a fore-and-aft motion for leverage and to gain line. These gimbals swing in one direction only and contain a receiver with locking mechanism to receive the rod butt.

See: Sportfishing Boat.

FIGHTING FISH

See: Playing Fish.

FIGHTING GRIP

The foregrip on the handle of a fishing rod (see), located ahead of the reel and used by an angler for gripping when applying pressure to strong, deep, and hard-pulling fish.

FIGURE EIGHT

A motion made when a muskie, and sometimes a northern pike, follows a lure (especially a bucktail spinner) to the boat, in order to induce a strike. This is done from a standing position by keeping the lure a few inches from the rod tip, pointing the rod tip close to the water's surface, and quickly making a series of wide figure-eight motions to try to get the following fish excited enough to pounce on it. A figure eight works only occasionally, but it is better than removing the lure from the water and casting again quickly, especially for muskies.

FIJI ISLANDS

Fiji consists of about 332 islands, which vary in size from 10,000 square kilometers to tiny islets a few meters in circumference. One-third of these are inhabited, and they spread over thousands of square kilometers of ocean in the heart of the South Pacific. Although distant and exotic to many people, Fiji has become a crossroads of air and shipping services between North America, Australia, and New Zealand. Travelers and international vessels enter the country via the international airports at Nadi or Nausori, or the natural harbors at Suva and Lautoka—all located on the largest island, Viti Levu. The second largest island, Vanua Levu, is about 60 kilometers from Viti Levu, and together they constitute 85 percent of Fiji's landmass.

Fiji enjoys a tropical maritime climate without great extremes of heat or cold. It lies in the area occasionally traversed by tropical cyclones. They occur mostly between November and April, with greatest frequency around January and February. On the average, some 10 to 12 cyclones per decade affect some part of Fiji, and 2 to 3 do severe damage.

In all seasons the predominant winds over Fiji are the trade winds, blowing from the east to southeast. On the western and eastern sides of Viti Levu and Vanua Levu, however, daytime sea breezes blow in across the coast.

Temperatures at low elevations are usually fairly uniform. Because of the influence of the surrounding oceans, the changes from day to day and season to season are relatively small. Sunshine duration is relatively high in the northwestern area, especially in winter. Southeastern coastal areas and the high interior often experience persistent cloudy, humid weather.

Rainfall is highly variable. It is usually abundant in summer (particularly January)—especially over the large islands—but in winter and spring it is often deficient, particularly in the dry zone on the western and northern sides of the main islands. The dry season is from May through October, and the wet season from November through April. In the drier half-year, from May through October, the heaviest rainfall occurs on the windward (southeast) sides of the larger mountainous islands.

Some of the first attempts at gamefishing here were made from the old capital, Levuka, on Ovalau Island in 1918. These efforts were followed in later years by angling in the area between Ovalau, Wakaya (which has wild deer and where the German raider Baron von Luckner was captured during World War II), and Makogai Islands; Makogai was a leper colony and, with the eradication of that disease, is now a government station.

Tropical gamefish species are abundant in the waters around Fiji, and angling exists year-round for some; billfish, tuna, dolphin, wahoo, barracuda, and narrowbarred mackerel are most prominent. World records have been established here for Pacific

F

Although most fishing in the Fiji Islands is for big-game species, the shallow waters also provide diverse opportunities.

sailfish, dogtooth tuna, wahoo, kawakawa, and giant trevally. There are no long coastlines in Fiji to monitor fish migration; however, pelagic species, especially billfish, migrate through these waters, providing year-round fishing activity as they move through and back again.

Because of Fiji's geographic location, it is difficult to know whether the fish caught were migrating north or south, or visiting to feed in one particular area. Local anglers have made observations about this, drawn from trends in neighboring countries. It is known from participation in New Zealand tournaments that Fiji's winter months—June, July, and August—are likely to produce the best catches of striped marlin. Fiji appears to be too distant from other significant marlin species' territories, such as Cairns in Australia and Kona in Hawaii, to monitor or have knowledge of the movement of black or blue marlin through the Fiji Islands, as both species are taken almost year-round here.

Many very large specimens of blue marlin have been hooked and lost. The local records for marlin (all marlin are known to Fijians as *sakuvorowaqa*) are 447 kilograms for blue (caught in January 1997), 184.6 kilograms for black, and 133 kilograms for striped.

Pacific sailfish, known here as *sakulaca,* appear to be present throughout the year, with captures every month. The recent local best was a 77.11-kilogram fish, but an 85.72-kilogram line-class world record, which still stands, was caught in 1967.

Wahoo are Fiji's main species and usually appear in early May, but the length of the wahoo season has been erratic of late. They are best caught from May through July. A 63.8-kilogram specimen is the local record.

Tuna species include yellowfin, bigeye, dogtooth, skipjack, kawakawa, and Pacific bonito. Tuna are locally known as *yatu,* and island records for the larger species include a 111.5-kilogram yellowfin, a 74.3-kilogram dogtooth, and a 64.8-kilogram bigeye.

Yellowfin occur from November through March and migrate back through the island group from May through August, occurring in schools with skipjack and kawakawa. Large bigeye tuna are less available to anglers and are usually caught deep, on live bait, when the angler is pursuing yellowfin or marlin. Fish up to 20 kilograms are caught in schools, sometimes mixed with yellowfin. Dogtooth tuna are fished in deep water, using downriggers or drop lines along dropoffs and over seamounts, with dead or live bait.

Skipjack occur in large schools and are usually easily caught. Used as live or dead bait, they are occasionally cut into strips for trolling or to enhance plastic trolling lures. They are available in most months, with the middle of winter producing the largest specimens.

Kawakawa occur mainly around passages and in the large areas of lagoons, often in less than clear water, where they feed on herring, squid, and crustaceans. The best time is November through May. Bonito occur in schools and are sometimes mixed with skipjack, but are not recorded often.

Mahimahi (dolphin) are abundant in almost all months. The largest average approximately 19 kilograms. Known here as *ika narokaveisau,* these fish are caught to 26.76 kilograms and take almost all known baits and lures; many have been caught on Fiji's traditional *viavia* lure, fashioned from a plant. This has a shiny silver texture similar to onion flesh. It is rolled around the hook and trace, and cut to desired shape—Kona head or bullet-nosed, according to preference. This type of lure has caught many other species as well, although modern lure technology has caused a marked decline in its use.

Barracuda, in particular great barracuda and pickhandle barracuda, occur throughout the year. Some very large barracuda (called *ogo*) have been known to attack anglers and divers in Fiji, and some attacks have been fatal. The largest recorded great barracuda here was over 45 kilograms (100 pounds), and many have been taken over 23 kilograms. A 28.3-kilogram line-class world record was established in Fiji at Serua in 1988.

Narrowbarred mackerel, known as *walu,* are an important local species. This fish bears a high price in Fijian markets and is the basis of *kokoda,* the traditional raw fish delicacy of Fiji. Apart from being a prominent food source, mackerel are sought by anglers and occur here mainly from February through July, and weigh an average of 18 kilograms. From July through September, however, schools appear off the north coast of Vanua Levu, where it is believed they spawn, and some large specimens from this area have weighed more than 47 kilograms.

The most successful rig for this species is a specially designed and shaped lead weight created by an avid local angler. Aptly named after its designer, the Houng Lee rig consists of a short trace attached to the lead, and two hooks that are rather short but still in accordance with International Game Fish Association (IGFA) rules. A small baitfish, known locally as *salala* and similar to scad, is attached to the hook. The best speed for trolling this rig simulates the speed of the swimming rigged bait; the size of the bait determines the speed at which the bait swims. A rigged bait trolled at the correct speed looks so lifelike that a novice would mistake it for a live fish.

Many species of trevally are regularly caught in Fijian waters. Giant trevally to 68 kilograms have been landed here, although the most common size is from 13.5 to 23 kilograms, and all species are taken when casting from beach, pier, wharf, or boat. As with other pelagic species, trevally *(saqa)* school and hunt for herring *(daniva),* which occur in great schools.

Also common are rainbow runners, which range to 10 kilograms. Other species include Pacific crevalle jack and horse-eye jack. Permit have not been caught on rod and reel, although they are here in numbers. Also present but not generally caught by anglers are African pompano and a variety of small inshore species, some of which are used as whole trolling baits. Swordfish are caught commercially by longliners, although none have been recorded on rod and reel.

In freshwater, largemouth bass have been introduced into Vaturu Dam, the main water supply for Nadi. Sportfishing techniques have recorded these fish up to 2 kilograms.

FILLET BOARD

In a commercial sense, a fillet board is a narrow wooden or plastic board for cleaning and filleting small fish, usually with a spring clip at one end, that holds the fish in place while it is being dressed. A homemade fillet board or cleaning board often lacks the clip but is larger and wider. In saltwater, a fillet board may be constructed with a back and sides and lower dimensions that allow it to fit over the gunwale of a boat; the board is used for cutting up fish for chumming, chunking, or bait use, as well as for cleaning the catch.

See: Fish Preparation—Cleaning/Dressing.

FILLET KNIFE

See: Fish Preparation—Cleaning/Dressing.

FILLETING

Cutting the sides of a fish lengthwise, parallel to and free from the backbone, accompanied by removal of the rib cage.

See: Fish Preparation—Cleaning/Dressing.

FIN

An organ on different parts of a fish's body that may be used for propulsion, balance, and steering.

See: Anatomy; Fish.

FINDING FISH

Successful fishing is the result of many activities, the foremost of which is finding fish. The act of finding fish involves a combination of elements, including visual observation, intensive searching, an understanding of the habits of fish and their preferred habitat (which varies from species to species), and savvy and good judgment to realize how these elements relate to one another and how they can be taken advantage of.

Visual observation is one factor in selecting places to fish and in looking for signs that indicate the presence of fish (see: sight fishing). In a stream, trout may indicate their presence by rising to the surface to capture insects. In a lake, a school of bass chasing shad may force their prey to the surface, and the resulting commotion allows anglers to pinpoint a group of fish and perhaps readily intercept

Learning to read the flow of rivers, such as this one in Labrador, will help keep you fishing in the most productive places.

them. In saltwater, the frenzied activity of a distant group of birds (see) may indicate a school of bluefish that is ripping into bait. And on a grassy flat at low tide, the exposed tail of a bonefish or redfish that is scrounging the bottom may give away its presence to the stalking angler. In all these instances and in many others, the problem of locating a fish—which is just one element of the game of catching them—has been solved because of the activities of the quarry and the observance of the angler. Most of the time, however, fish are not readily found by observation, and anglers must search for them by other means.

It is important to realize that fish are not found everywhere in a given body of water; they inhabit specific places, primarily for food, cover, and temperature reasons. The extent to which they inhabit specific places or prefer certain habitat varies with the species and may be influenced by seasons, spawning, water conditions, and other factors. Clearly, many variables influence the location of fish.

For anglers, the question of where to fish—presumably in a place where the quarry is or will be—can become a big issue when the fishing location is new or unfamiliar. The answer, in the modern fishing era, is increasingly supplied by sophisticated electronic equipment. Some of this equipment has become important, if not almost indispensable, to many ardent anglers, satisfying their desire and need to learn more about the places they fish. Sonar devices and temperature-sensing units are chief among these and are truly instrumental in helping boat anglers unlock the secrets of the places they fish. Using sonar (see) to locate fish has become one of the foremost facets of fishing from boats in the modern era. But sonar does not tell you where to look for fish; it only tells you if they are where you are, and then it does not assure you that the fish you find are the species you want to find.

So you have to evaluate the place that you're fishing, observing water conditions to determine where fish may be and how to present lures or bait to them. This skill is referred to as "reading water" and can be practiced in all types of environments, especially in freshwater. It is sometimes easier in rivers than in stillwaters (ponds, lakes, reservoirs) because many elements are more obvious. For example, in current, any sizable obstruction (boulder, bridge footing, pier, etc.) creates a slack pocket where fish can lie without exerting much effort and watch for food; these are readily located. Stillwaters especially pose problems for many anglers, particularly in places that they do not know well, and for the obvious reason that the surface usually gives no indication of what is below.

Lakes, ponds, impoundments, bays, oceans, and other bodies of water are all quite different, so the type and the size of a body of water play a role in what you do and how you do it. The species available and/or desired is another consideration; obviously the more you know about fish behavior and habitat, the better. Gamefish are usually found in certain places for specific reasons, and the better you understand the relationship between their depth, cover, temperature, food needs, and other requirements, the better you are able to put the pieces of the underwater puzzle together while employing electronic equipment.

The pieces of that puzzle can be filled in by making preparations before you get on the water. You can get a head start (especially on unfamiliar water) by simply talking to those who know something about it. Visit local tackle shops (several if possible), and talk to the people there as you purchase bait, license, lures, etc. Talk to people at the launching ramp and marina. Ask specific questions and be observant. Look at the products being sold in the stores to see what the most popular lures and colors are.

Obtaining and studying charts and maps *(see: maps)*, particularly those with underwater contours and with depth and channel markings, can be a key factor. At the very least, they will familiarize you with the general layout of the place and its characteristics, but they also may detail some very specific structures (such as rock reefs, rips, shoals, flats, old roadbeds and culverts, sunken weeds, etc.) that may be important to fish. Such maps are not available for all waters, unfortunately, or the ones that are available may not be as detailed as you'd like. Even the best maps often fail to pinpoint certain underwater features that attract gamefish. Such features might include a nearshore trough that is created by wave action, or a slight pinnacle, mound, or hump that rises high enough off the lake or ocean floor to attract baitfish and thus predators, but not enough to be highlighted on a map. So don't let maps be the last word. In any event, you still have to put your boat in the water and wet a hook.

Picking a spot to fish and immediately wetting a hook, however, is often not such a good idea. Everyone wants to get fishing right away, but you are wise to do some cruising first, looking over the water with your electronics as you go. Sonar study is especially important, but at certain seasons a temperature evaluation may be equally so.

A typical freshwater lake scenario. To illustrate how an initial exploratory trip might be carried out, let's take a freshwater scenario and assume that you're on an unfamiliar lake. You leave the ramp or dock, and the first thing you do is check for surface water temperature. This is a matter of habit, like making the bed in the morning, and something that is more important at some times than at others. Spring is a season when evaluating surface water temperature is of utmost value.

If it is spring, you may want to seek the warmest locales on the lake first. Often that is along the north or northwest shores, where tributaries enter (especially after a warm rain), or in coves, bays, and sloughs. Many freshwater gamefish, and/or baitfish, spawn sometime in spring, often near shore or in and near tributaries; and water temperature is a triggering factor. By finding spots that have favorable temperatures, or temperatures warmer than other areas in the lake, you may locate either the places where fish are congregated or the places where fish are most likely to be active.

As full-time guides and charter boat captains can attest, angling for inactive fish is very tough;

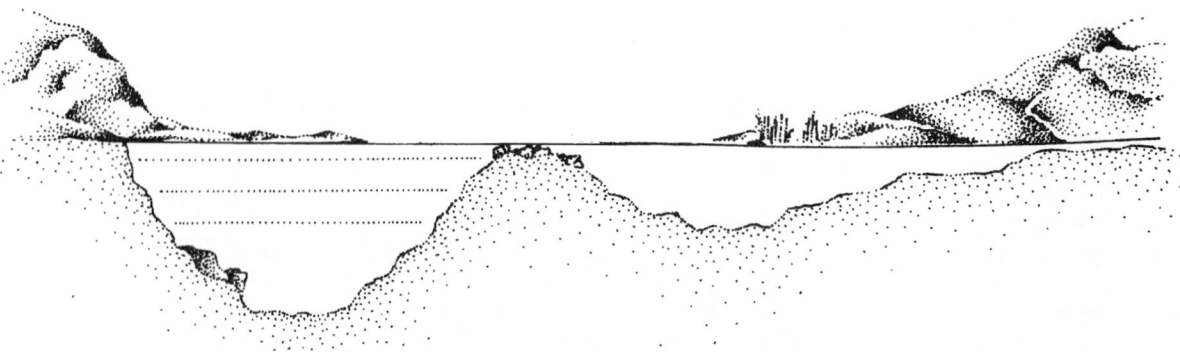

This cross-section view of a lake, with a tributary entering at far right, helps put into perspective the underwater characteristics that are not visible to the eye above water, though they are detectable with sonar.

obviously, fishing where they aren't is a waste of time. Therefore, monitoring a surface temperature gauge (available as a self-functioning unit or as an option with sonar instruments) in the spring is an important adjunct to the business of casting or trolling.

As you move out on the lake, you also watch your sonar instrument. That, again out of habit, was turned on right after you started the motor and will stay on until you stop fishing (unless it is a portable, battery-operated unit). For the moment, let's assume that you're trying to unlock the secrets of this lake in the summer. What you'll look for depends largely on the species of fish you intend to catch, but let's say you have an interest in all game-fish and thus need to consider all of the variables.

You could begin simply by looking for fish on the sonar unit. When you know your quarry well, you may be able to identify the species you see on sonar, but most of the time specific identification is uncertain. Knowledge of the habits and locales preferred by certain species of fish makes them easier to identify on sonar, but there is a lot of gray area here.

In some cases, the level at which concentrations of fish, especially large ones, are found is an important clue to the depth at which you should be fishing. This information is especially pertinent in midlake open-water situations, in trolling, and in seeking such species as trout, salmon, suspended walleye, and striped bass. In other cases, finding schools of bait and knowing their preferred depth can point you to the depth to fish. Looking for fish, then, is something that is often best accomplished while simultaneously learning the lake and looking for suitable places to cast or troll for targeted species.

Observe general depths and underwater contours as you move around the lake. In certain waters, such observations are one of the most interesting aspects of unlocking the secrets of a lake. People who seldom use sonar may have no idea how deep the water is in a chosen spot, meaning that they often fish less efficiently.

Attend to the slope of the shoreline, to the depth near shore, and also to the depth as you move away from shore, especially if there is rock, wood, or vegetative cover. This information can be gauged to some extent by visual observation of the land formation onshore. A gradual slope on land usually indicates a flat and gently sloping terrain under adjacent water, whereas a sharp slope onshore indicates a quick dropoff underwater. However, the particulars aren't as readily discerned without sonar. In the spring, certain species of fish, such as bass, might be more attracted to a shallower shoreline area (which would warm up faster) than to one that dropped off quickly. The reverse could be true later in the year, especially if the steep shoreline was protected from late-day sun.

If you will be fishing in open water (well away from shore), check not only for basic depth but for the presence of such features as shoals, submerged timber, and old creekbeds or channels. Many types of warmwater and coldwater fish are attracted to a shoal because of the proximity to deep water and the ability to find prey there. When you find a shoal (or hump, mound, or reef), glue your eyes to the sonar and motor all around it; watch the conformation on all sides, noting how quickly it drops off and whether bait or larger fish are hanging along the dropoff to deeper water. Scour the shoal with your underwater eyes first; don't just motor over it, but rather stop at the shallowest spot and start fishing. Use the sonar to learn about the shoal first; it takes only a few moments.

Sonar is also helpful in checking out timber and the tops of submerged trees—an important fishing location. When those trees are 30 or more feet below the surface, sonar allows you to stay in the right position. Clearly you need to study the sonar to know about the timber before fishing, as well as watch the sonar closely while fishing. You also should be looking for fish (striped or white bass, in particular). You might use marker buoys to define the edges, channels, and other key features.

One of your main tasks is to check out any points in the lake. A point is a place where the land juts out in the water away from the shore and where the bottom terrain underwater continues to taper down and off. Some points are very obvious, and others are subtle; some taper very gradually and extend (almost like a bar) a long way out into the lake, yet others end abruptly and drop quickly to deep water.

Points are important lake features for many species of fish, so you will use the sonar to do several things: look for fish in the immediate vicinity of well-defined points and on the breaklines (the distinguishable drops to greater depths), establish the contours of points in order to fish them most effectively, and look for less obvious points while otherwise fishing or cruising. Some of the best places to fish in many freshwater environments are points that are not readily detected by looking at the shore, but that are found by accident while fishing along a shoreline and watching sonar.

Vegetation is another important lake feature, especially for walleye, bass, pike, and muskies. It may consist of lily pads, cabbage weeds, milfoil, hyacinths, or other aquatic plants. Look over the vegetation carefully, with and without sonar, if you seek the aforementioned species.

If vegetation appears in shallow water and you're fishing for largemouth bass or pike, use sonar mostly to monitor depth while casting, since you can visually find the places that you should fish. But when the vegetation lies in deeper water, tapers from shallow to deeper water, and/or is submerged, the sonar is helpful for precise positioning and depth monitoring, and it becomes much more important to your fishing.

Initially, slowly cruise along the edges of the vegetation. Try to define its contour, establish the depth at which it ceases growing (which is the weedline and which often appears in 12 to 14 feet of water in northern lakes), look for clusters of isolated weeds or

Fisherman James Heddon, father of the casting plug, ran one of the largest apiaries in the United States, held six patents for beekeeping equipment, founded a newspaper, and was Mayor of Dowagiac, Michigan.

F

for open patches amidst thick weeds, and generally get to know what lies below.

Because fish are often close to the bottom in the weeds or are deep in the vegetation, you may not see fish on the sonar while scrutinizing the weed edges. However, it is possible to see fish amidst scattered weeds, and sometimes you will do so. Primarily, though, you're trying to establish an underwater picture of what you might see with your eyes if the weeds were on the surface. This picture will point you to the places (edge, irregular features, pockets, etc.) to concentrate your angling efforts.

As you use your electronic equipment to learn about this body of water, try to determine whether the bottom composition—soft as in sandy or hard as in rocky—in specific places is noteworthy; this information may be a clue that the species of fish you seek are in that area. The thermocline, which can be a summertime clue to locating certain fish, is identifiable on some high-quality sonar units.

Once you've spent a little time familiarizing yourself with this lake or with selected areas of it—you don't try to survey the whole lake at one shot—you can stop to fish. How you will do so depends, of course, on what species you seek, the time of year, and the depths or techniques involved. Suppose your sonar shows fish at 30 feet along the dropoff of a point. It won't pay to cast a crankbait into shallow water and crank it back; a better move would probably be slow-trolling with a bottom-bouncing sinker rig or with a lure behind a downrigger; another option is jigging.

You also might employ buoy markers, incidentally, to help identify the places checked on sonar and to act as reference points. These are typically used, for example, to mark the deep sides of shoals, the breaklines on either side of a long point, the location of a cluster of fish or a pile of brush or a road bridge, the meandering of a submerged weedline, or the course of a channel.

Observing features. Although the preceding scenario emphasized the use of electronics as an aid in exploring and learning about a body of water, much can be learned simply by observing the shoreline and surrounding topographical features. If the shore is sandy or rocky, the bottom of the body of water nearby will likely be similar. When the land declines steeply down to the water level, the lake there will drop off sharply into deep water, but where the shore slopes gradually, the lake near shore will do likewise. This is particularly true in man-made bodies of water and in times of high water.

As already noted, points are an important land form in fishing. Many points extend underwater well out into a lake before dropping off abruptly into deep water. This feature can attract both migratory and nonmigratory species of fish and can be worth exploring, although by looking strictly at the water's surface you seldom have a clue that anything unusual is below and near the point.

Perhaps more obvious are such features as rock walls, fence posts, and roadbeds, which are typically

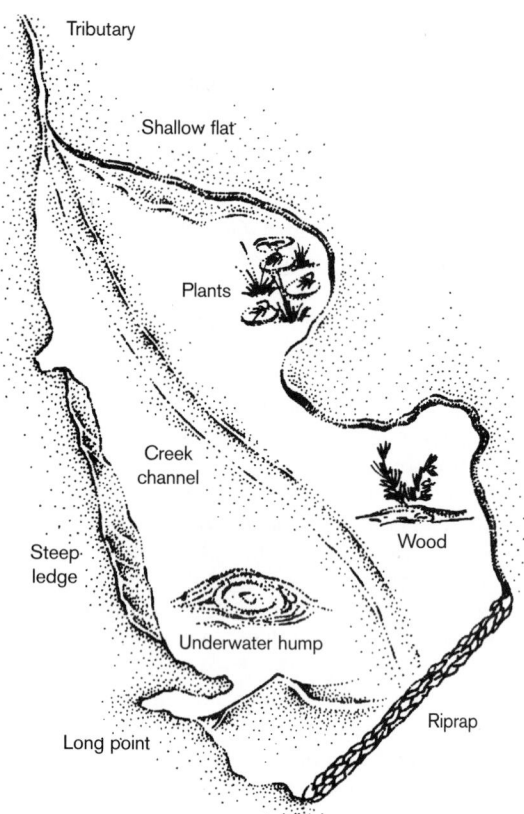

This simplified view of an impoundment depicts many different features that may be relevant to fishing efforts.

found in bodies of water that have been artificially made or enlarged, and which extend from shore into the water and provide cover for some species of fish.

Even more obvious, of course, is vegetation, stumps, timber, docks, and the like, which provide cover and attract bait and smaller prey fish. Some species of fish are especially attracted to various forms of cover, and you should look for emerged and submerged cover, especially if it is near deep water, because it may hold the type of fish you seek. By judiciously fishing these objects (and in the case of vegetation, seeking the pockets and edges within), you can enhance your opportunities for catching fish.

Big water considerations. Many anglers enjoy fishing in streams, ponds, rivers, inlets, marshes, and small lakes because of their relatively small size, not only from an accessibility or boating standpoint, but because the options are narrower. A big body of water, with miles and miles of shoreline or a maze of islands, can be intimidating.

Big waters have abundant populations of major gamefish, in many cases species and sizes of fish unknown or rarely found in small waters. To enjoy these bounties, you must solve the problems posed by fishing big water and not be overwhelmed by them.

In big lakes and river systems, tributaries play a critical role in gamefish behavior and therefore fishing success. This is especially true in the spring when many predator and prey species enter tributaries to spawn, or when they come into the near-shore areas influenced by tributaries because of the presence of food and more comfortable conditions.

Tributaries, whether they are major rivers, small streams, the outlet of upstream dams, etc., are the lifeblood of big water. In the spring, they bear the rain and the runoff from snowmelt that helps open up the lake, then the warm water that ultimately raises the temperature of the cold main lake. A warm rain is a blessing for a big body of water that is influenced by a major tributary, because the warmth will stimulate activity, feeding, and possibly spawning, though it sometimes takes two or three days for a heavy warm rain to have an impact on a big lake system. This phenomenon is most evident in large mid-South impoundments hosting stripers, white bass, black bass, and walleye.

However, the area where a tributary intersects a lake is an edge that attracts bait and major gamefish. Water that is a few degrees warmer than the main lake temperature flows into the lake and mixes with it, encouraging fish activity. A distinct mudline, the result of stained or muddy spring runoff, is often created around tributary mouths. On some waters, this mudline attracts gamefish because there is usually a thermal break here as well, with the inner edge being warmer and the mudline itself being attractive to bait and prey species.

Water temperature is certainly a key to gamefish behavior. In the Great Lakes, for example, early-season fishing primarily occurs in fairly shallow water close to shore. Trout and salmon seek warm water there, as do the alewife and smelt that they feed on. Sometimes the way to get action is to find the warmest water along the shore.

Elsewhere, however, the upper layer of water may warm up a bit on a mild, sunny spring day and act as an attracting edge, where fish may be caught very shallow. This is especially so for bass, for example, which will eventually make nests in warm shallow water, or for trout or salmon, which will be attracted to pockets of warm water or vertical separations of different-temperature water away from immediate tributary areas. Such areas may be in the vicinity of a warmwater discharge or may simply be the phenomenon of water movement and mixing. Nonetheless, surface temperature variants can be edges.

Perhaps the most extraordinary example of this phenomenon is that of the so-called thermal bar that exists in mid- to late spring on the Great Lakes, where there is a sharp surface distinction between temperatures offshore at a time when nearshore environs are relatively warm and theoretically in a temperature range that should attract trout and salmon. Nevertheless, colder offshore water on a distinct surface thermal break is the better place to be looking for fish, particularly salmon and steelhead.

Temperature remains a factor after spring for many fish species. Water stratification sends cold- and coolwater fish to deeper freshwater locales in the summer. Thus, when you fish open-water areas, you must know the preferred temperature of the

species you seek, attempt to find out the depth at which this temperature is found, and try to relate this to prominent areas that would attract your quarry (such as long sloping underwater points, submerged creek channels, sharp dropoffs, and so forth).

The thermocline is usually a fairly narrow band of water, but it is found where temperature drops off sharply, often averaging a drop of .5° to 1°F degree every foot. Sometimes it is only 10 feet wide and 15 to 20 feet below the surface; usually it is a bit wider and begins deeper. To locate the thermocline, lower a thermometer on a rope or fishing line, checking it every 5 feet or so. Give the thermometer enough time at checked depths to register the proper reading.

Most lakes that stratify like this have a good deal of deep water. Shallow lakes don't stratify, since they become uniformly warm with too little variation from top to bottom. Fewer southern lakes stratify than northern ones; many lakes display the same patterns from year to year.

In lakes with clearly defined thermoclines, you can identify the thermocline on a good sonar instrument. Try to fish in and around the thermocline because it will have the best combination of food, oxygen, and temperature. But keep in mind the temperature preferences of the fish you seek, since the actual temperature of the thermocline will vary by locale and the fish may be just above or below it.

A thermocline usually lasts until the fall, or when there is a trend toward cool air temperatures. When the surface water cools off enough, a body of water mixes and the thermocline dissipates. This is often referred to as the "fall turnover."

Big waters are slow to warm up in the spring and slow to cool off in the fall. This fact means that small bodies of water may be better to fish in the earliest part of the season—until the larger waters warm up—and that big waters may sustain good fishing for a longer period of time in the fall.

Other places offering warmth are bays and coves, especially if they are shallow and contain the type of cover preferred by the species you seek. Bays are especially good places to fish in the spring on natural lakes that are not fed by major tributaries; bays may also be productive in sprawling man-made lakes that do have tributaries. Bays with a north and northwest exposure (or sections of a bay with such an exposure) get the most sun in the day. They also benefit from southerly winds, which stack warm surface water up on their shores. Thus, they tend to warm up fast and may attract certain species if the habitat is right.

Grass, weedbeds, and other forms of vegetation may also be important fishing areas of big lakes, but this habitat may not be readily observable or may not be found in all sectors of a lake. Bays, coves, islands, and shoals are usually good places to start the search for vegetation, which is as likely to be submerged in moderate depth water as it is visible and close to shore.

A good tactic for anglers apprehensive about where to begin fishing is to approach big water as if

 Mako shark (*Isurus oxyrinchus*) fossils have been dated to the Miocene epoch 25 million years ago; a prehistoric relative of that era, *Isurus hastalis,* may have reached 6 to 8 meters long.

F

it were several smaller bodies of water, and focus on one section at a time. Some anglers become familiar with big lakes by zeroing in on prominent points. Some fish use points as full-time domiciles because they offer frequent opportunities to ambush prey. Others migrate by them often, or they leave deep-water haunts temporarily to visit points for feeding.

When you are solving the mysteries of where to fish and what to look for in a big body of water, your knowledge of fish habits and seasonal habitat requirements will prove a great ally. In freshwater, for instance, if lake trout are your quarry, you should be looking for rocky shoals, reefs, and islands near deep water, since lakers come in from deeper water to such areas, feed, then leave. In contrast, open-water salmon don't orient much to underwater features; thus, when they aren't close to shore in spring or fall, you have to fish specific temperature zones (mostly in deep water) and aggressively search for them and for baitfish. Stripers, too, are often nomadic and follow schools of bait, although they do seek out impoundments, where the tops of submerged timber, old river channels, and other identifiable underwater terrain give them a place to find food. Largemouth bass and pike orient strongly toward various forms of cover, usually near shore, so they present different demands upon the angler. Draw upon your knowledge of a species when deciding where to go and what to do.

Also, think in terms of edges. Fish, like most animals, are attracted to some type of edge, whether one of structure or temperature. Think about the type of edge—for example, a long sloping underwater point, a reef or shoal, or even a rocky versus sandy bottom—that may appeal to your target species for reasons of comfort, security, or feeding.

A prominent edge lair might be a shoal or reef. Underwater mounds or islands, sandbars, and gravel bars are similar. These locations may be rocky or boulder-strewn, or they may be sandy with moderate weed growth; in any case, they attract small baitfish, which in turn attract predators. Often, there is deep water on one side.

How you fish such places is almost as important as the fact that you do fish them. When trolling the perimeter of weeds, sandbars, shoals, and so forth, for example, you might have a shallower running lure on the side of the boat nearest the edge, and your deepest running lure on the opposite side. If fishing two lures off the same gunwale, put a deep runner on the inside rod on a short- to medium-length line and a shallow runner on the outside position but on a longer length of line (it might get as deep as the other lure but be further back to avoid tangling and to aid in fish playing and hooksetting). Or, use a lure on a short line behind a downrigger and use a diving lure on a longer flatline.

The deep-water/shallow-water interface near islands can be similarly thought of as an edge, as can a sharply sloping shoreline. These are places to

which bait migrates naturally, and logically they present feeding opportunities.

Current is also a factor. Locales where a strong current retards the movement of weak, crippled, or wounded fish, or brings bait washing by, are possible fishing spots. Back eddies, slicks, tidal rips, and current edges are more good spots. In rivers, where a secondary tributary meets a major flow is also a promising intersection, especially in summer when the secondary tributary may be dumping cooler and more oxygenated water into the main flow.

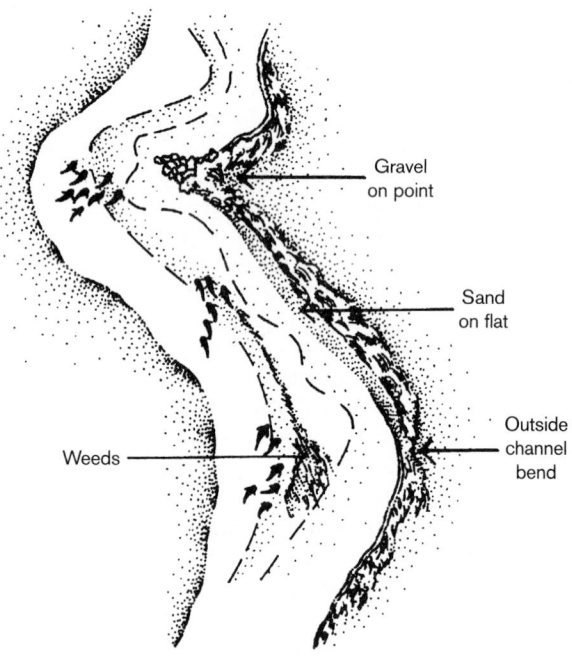

This compressed view depicts some of the common characteristics of a river.

Knowing which types of edges appeal to which species of fish makes a difference when fishing in current. For example, the inside bend of major tributaries is often a hotspot to troll or cast for stripers in the spring. Stripers like a point where water rushes by, so they hold on the inside bend of a channel and use this spot to ambush whatever comes around. Walleye are known for locating along an edge, particularly along a deep-water breakline. Walleye commonly move shallower in the evening to the fringes of a bar or a rock or gravel point that breaks sharply to deep water. One successful fishing tactic here is to use plugs that dive to 8 or 10 feet and troll from deep water to the point; then go along one side and work along the edge.

Some fish are known for congregating in or along the edges of vegetation. Weeds attract small baitfish and larger fish in the food chain, and they also offer protective cover. Working submerged weed lines, where the weeds end and the bottom begins to drop off to deeper water, is not only possible, but an especially effective fishing method.

Many fish use the edges of vegetative cover or other structures to hide and to ambush prey. They lurk in or by places where food is abundant and where they can lie relatively concealed to pounce on appropriate-size forage. Some anglers refer to such feeding stations as ambush points, and they like to be as close as possible to deep water, dropoffs, shelves, ledges, creekbeds, channels, and the like. Whether you angle for species that prefer the confines of cover or the vastness of open water, be aware of the subtle borders and margins of these habitats and seek and fish those places.

Much of the preceding information also applies to flowing water, especially large rivers. The reading of water is most obviously practiced by anglers who fish in smaller rivers and creeks, where some boating is done, but most fishing is by wading or angling from the bank. Current in rivers and creeks is a premier influence on where and how fish are situated, both for resting and for feeding purposes. Fish face flowing water, so lures must generally come down-current toward them in a natural manner.

In flowing water, the deeper places are the ones that often hold fish and are sought by anglers. Slow-moving water is a sign of depth. Water is deepest where the current comes against the bank; years of this action have gouged the bank and bottom, resulting in deeper water. Shallow water is found on the inside of a bend. In many places the bank is much steeper on the outside of a bend than on the inside, and this is another clue to the location of the deeper and shallower portions. This information is important not only for angling but also for navigating a boat or wading safely.

When current strikes an object, it may cause less turbulence in front of, or behind, that object. Fish may locate here because they don't have to work as hard to resist the flow and also because it may be a good place to find food. Boulders are the most common objects in currents, but small islands or shoals also exist; in high water, stumps and fallen trees are objects that can attract fish.

Saltwater tides and current. Many of the same factors that apply to finding fish in freshwater also apply in saltwater, one major difference being that saltwater involves a much broader expanse of water and not as many forms of cover. However, in saltwater, finding fish is influenced by tide *(see)*, current *(see)*, and weather *(see)*. The effect of weather can sometimes be greater than either tide or current. For example, murky water caused by severe storms stirring up the water in inshore areas can temporarily impact bottom fishing adversely.

Tides and current have a major impact not only on where fish may be found, but on whether they are likely to be feeding. There are exceptions, but many saltwater fish, particularly species inhabiting inshore areas, bays, and brackish water, are more active when the tide is moving than when it is slack. The effect of tide can be more pronounced in certain places than others, and underwater structures (like rips) or differing bottoms (like flats) may present good feeding opportunities when a tide is

Shallow-draft boats and poling platforms are used to search Gulf Coast waters for redfish and seatrout.

falling, rather than when it is rising. Tides act much like a river current in many places, especially in bays and estuary areas.

Currents are more pronounced in offshore waters, and fishing where main warmwater currents exist is important for certain species, although eddylike pockets of ocean currents may hold pelagic species.

Obviously, changes in tides affect much of the inshore, nearshore, estuary, and marsh environment. Jetties that might be good to fish just before and after a high tide are probably not worth fishing at the other end of the tide range. Some flats, mangrove islands, marshlands, and the like will be dry or nearly so on a low tide. And yet, in some instances (for example, when you are stalking bonefish), the low water is best because it makes the fish easier to spot. So the places that you fish in high water and low water may be greatly different. And this difference is more profound during a high or new moon.

Tide, current, and weather affect more than just your target species; they also affect the availability of bait and the behavior of different species, and these factors should be considered when deciding where to fish.

FINESSE BAIT

A bass fishing term for a small lure, especially a soft tube lure or light jig, used on light line for heavily pressured fish, especially in clear deep water. Finesse fishing is a term often used to refer to the use of light or ultralight tackle and appropriately sized lures. See: Jig.

FINFISH

An alternative collective term for all species of fish, used to separate true fish from crustaceans and mollusks, which are collectively termed shellfish. The term is rarely used in reference to freshwater species

F

but is commonly used to refer to saltwater and anadromous fish, particularly by fisheries managers.

FINGERLING

A young fish about 2 to 4 inches long.

FINLAND

A northern European country with strong ties to sportfishing, Finland is situated on the northern side of the Baltic Sea, northwest of Russia and east of Sweden and Norway. Renowned for its many lakes and ponds, Finland is called the "Land of a Thousand Lakes"; in actuality, there are more than 62,000 lakes here.

Comprising an area of 130,085 square miles, Finland spreads over 600 miles from south to north, and its geography is as varied as the country is long. Southern Finland is flat; the rivers flow slowly for short distances, and the lakes are typically shallow and warm. Hardwood like birch, aspen, and alder are present in the forests, although softwood, pine, and spruce are dominant. Central and eastern Finland have some longer rivers and extensive lake formations, the largest of which is the Saimaa lake system. Farther north are extensive spruce forests, low wetlands, and longer rivers. Near the Arctic Circle, the forests and the soil get drier, and pine is the dominant tree. Even farther north lies Lapland, the land of the reindeer, the dwarf

A pike comes to hand in Baltic waters among Finland's Åland Islands.

birch, and the midnight sun. In general, Lapland is a country of smallish lakes, rivers, and brooks, although huge Lake Inarinjårvi breaks the rule.

Finland's lakes, combined with its numerous rivers and streams and more than 2,760 miles of Baltic shoreline, offer fine and varied opportunities for anglers. Trout are the most sought-after sportfish in Finland, and there's also great enthusiasm for salmon and charr; however, northern pike, European perch, zander, bream, and many lesser members of the carp family offer opportunities for good sport.

The Baltic Sea and Åland Islands

The northern Baltic Sea has an extremely low saline content and thus a peculiar saltwater fishery; one can catch many common freshwater fish in the brackish coastal waters of the Gulf of Bothnia and the Gulf of Finland. Northern pike and sea-run brown trout (sea trout) are at the top of the list, and some specialists troll for Atlantic salmon. In some areas of the Gulf of Bothnia it is even possible, and productive, to cast flies for big grayling in the sea. This is truly exotic fishing of a sort available almost nowhere else in the world.

Casting for sea-run browns is a Scandinavian specialty and a particularly popular form of sportfishing in Finland. Trolling for these fish is also popular, especially in the summer, when trout cruise in deeper water. A limited number of people cast flies for them.

The favored tackle for sea trout consists of a sturdy, but not too stiff, rod and a reel that can hold at least 100 yards of 10-pound nylon line. Long, slim spoons in sizes of $1/2$ to 1 ounce are the most popular bait, but minnow plugs and larger spinners also produce results.

Handmade Finnish minnow-spoons are a local specialty and were originally developed for this fishery, which is often practiced in very shallow water. They might not be readily available in Europe or North America, but they can be bought from most tackle dealers in the coastal towns of Finland. Several skilled local artisans here make fine minnow-spoons.

The best seasons for sea trout are early spring and late fall, when air and water temperatures chill and trout swim closer to shore, but some fish can be caught at any time of the year. A boat is almost essential for success, however. In larger towns professional guides are available to assist the visiting angler. These silvery fish are worth a lot of trouble; when fresh from the sea, they are almost always in top condition, and their average size lies around 3 pounds, with double-digit fish not a rarity. During the best seasons, especially in the fall, the weather may get rough, and the air temperature falls well under 0°C, so it is very important to dress accordingly and have a flotation aid of some sort; a flotation suit is best.

Northern pike can be caught along the entire coastline, but the most popular and productive fishing is in the archipelago between the town of Turku and the Åland Islands. The latter is an autonomous province of Finland and can be reached from the mainland by boat or plane. The sportfishing in Åland is well organized, and several skilled professional fishing guides operate in the area. Pike can be caught almost year-round, but spring and fall offer the best opportunities for big fish. The sea trout fishing in Åland is also very good, and as the top seasons for both species overlap, it is possible to fish both species successfully during the same day.

Åland pike are rarely exceptionally large; the average fish is 5 to 10 pounds, but specimens up to 35 pounds are caught every year. Fishing methods include casting and trolling. Standard pike spoons work well in these waters, but there are local favorites. Anglers after truly large pike prefer trolling with enormous plugs, especially deep-diving versions. Excellent fly fishing for pike exists in the Åland Islands and has been gaining in popularity. Large streamers are the standard offerings.

The perch is a humble inhabitant of these waters; nevertheless, it is valued for its fine table quality. In Baltic waters these fish grow well, and 2-pounders are regularly caught. Spinning tackle, small spinners, and various jigs are effective.

Southern Region

The lakes of southern Finland are mostly shallow and warm. The most popular fish species in these waters are northern pike, pike-perch (zander), and European perch. Pike and perch are common everywhere. Zander inhabit many larger lakes and, although not great fighters, they are highly regarded for their tasty fillets. Trolling is the most popular way to catch zander, and minnow-type plugs are the preferred lures. The best time to fish for zander is July, and the average size is around 2 pounds.

Perch are the most common fish in Finnish lakes and ponds. This species is found practically everywhere and is caught year-round. It grows well in larger lakes, which produce bigger fish on average than those found in smaller waters. Many small ponds hold an enormous population of dwarfed perch. This is the standby, and most important, species for ice anglers. Ice fishing competitions are popular, and perch are normally the only qualified species.

Southern Finland offers many coarse fishing opportunities. The European bream and ide are the most sought-after species. Anglers typically use earthworms or bread as bait, but stream-dwelling ide also take small spinners and artificial flies. Roach are fairly common, but due to the severity of the winters, carp exist in only a few lakes and ponds in southern Finland.

Some southern rivers have runs of salmon and sea trout. One of these, the Vantaa, flows on the outskirts of Helsinki, but only the river Kymijoki near the town of Kotka is a true salmon river. This fishery is detailed later. Most trout streams in the south are small, but several streams and brooks, as well as some trout lakes within a one-hour drive from Helsinki, are available. Although they are not untamed wilderness waters, they do offer nice fishing near the capital. These waters mainly hold stocked rainbow and brown trout; some have brook trout, and the smallest brooks hold native wild brown trout.

Eastern and Central Regions

Looking over a map of eastern and central Finland, it is easy to see why these regions are popular among anglers: There seems to be more water than land. Some area lakes are large and deep. Lakes Pielinen and Saimaa in the east are good examples, and both are prominent for lake trolling.

Brown trout and Saimaa salmon, a landlocked form of the Atlantic salmon, are the most important species. The latter is a relic form that has inhabited these waters since the Ice Age. It was earlier found only in the lakes of the Saimaa watershed but has lately been introduced into many other lakes as well. The average fish is smaller than its sea cousins, but 10-pounders are caught every year; larger fish are caught occasionally. The average brown trout in these lakes is about the same size as the Saimaa.

The trout streams of eastern and central Finland are mostly short links, called rapids (koski), between lakes. For many Finnish fly anglers, the rapids of central Finland are the true classic brown trout waters of the country. Although they are short—some only a hundred yards long—they offer fine fishing; the lakes constantly produce trout and grayling, which run into these rapids for feeding.

The water is often deep and fast flowing, so a pair of good felt-soled waders and a wading staff are a must for effective fishing. Many of these rapids are stocked regularly with catchable-size brown and rainbow trout, whereas others yield only native fish, and if any stocking is carried on it is done with fingerlings.

The rapids are exciting waters to fish, both with fly and spinning rods. The average trout caught weighs about 2 pounds, but 4- to 6-pounders are not rare. Smallish plugs are popular, but spinners and spoons produce, too. Fly anglers use streamers, nymphs, and dry flies. Caddisflies dominate during the high season (June through August), so their imitations are preferred, and they may be quite large, too. The larval and pupal imitations of caddisflies are deadly. High-floating deer-hair patterns are effective as well. A 9-foot, 5- to 7-weight rod with enough backbone for long casts and windy conditions is a good choice. Floating line covers most situations, but it is wise to have a sink-tip or a full-sink line for high-water conditions and the deepest pools.

There are hardly any no-kill areas here, but almost all rapids have a small limit—usually two or three trout a day—and a large minimum size for brown trout. Day tickets for the very best waters are usually limited, so it is advisable to book in advance.

Some of the best stream fishing for brown trout in eastern and central Finland occurs near the towns of Viitasaari, Rautalampi, and Heinävesi.

F

Northeast Region

The northeastern corner of Finland, particularly the area around Kuusamo, includes vast spruce forests and several great rivers. The Kitka, Oulanka, and Kuusinki—Kuusamo's major rivers—all have their source in Finland and flow across the border into Russia. These are famous as world-class brown trout fisheries, and the World Fly Fishing Championships took place on these rivers in 1989.

The major attraction of these waters is the so-called Russian brown trout, which has a life cycle similar to that of Atlantic salmon. They spend their early life in the headwaters, then migrate downstream into several large lakes in Russia. There they feed on small fish, grow to very respectable size, and return (normally in midsummer) to the rivers to spawn.

These browns may not be numerous, but they are big. Specimens under 4 pounds are rare, and the average size is around 6 to 8 pounds. Trout up to 15 pounds are caught every year, occasionally even bigger ones. Russian browns are fished with various tackle. Plugs are reliable lures, but many locals use traditional Devon minnows successfully. Fly fishing is also popular. Streamers and special local trout flies that resemble smaller salmon flies are standbys, but even dry flies and nymphs take their share of large trout.

Although these three famous rivers are in a class of their own, many smaller streams and a variety of lakes in the area offer fine fishing for trout and grayling.

Lapland

Known as The Land of the Midnight Sun, Lapland is a prime place for anglers who enjoy solitude and wide-open space, and who don't mind blackflies and mosquitoes. An ample supply of bug repellent is a necessity when fishing here.

Except for salmon anglers, Lapland is not a place for those after trophy-size fish. This doesn't mean that one couldn't catch the trout of a lifetime, but most of the fishing is on smaller streams, and small lakes and brooks. Winters are tough, and trout grow slowly. A 2-pounder is a very good fish, except in the few stocked waters. Trout in smaller brooks are usually in the 10- to 12-inch class. They are nevertheless fine, wild fish and full of fighting spirit.

Grayling are an important gamefish in Lapland. They are present almost everywhere and grow well in all but the smallest streams. In bigger rivers they reach 2 pounds and more. The largest fly-caught grayling, those over 4 pounds, are usually taken in western Lapland, with the Låtåseno watershed on the top of the list. The salmon rivers of northeastern Lapland—the Teno and Nååtåmö—however, have enormous grayling populations, and the fish tend to be good sized.

The northernmost lakes and streams of Lapland hold arctic charr. These little jewels are highly prized by Finnish anglers. Charr are fished with flies and small artificial lures. Ice fishing is also popular, especially in the late "winter" months of April and May, when sun warms the angler.

Arctic charr are seldom big, usually under two pounds, but backpacking anglers are ready to walk miles through rough terrain for them. Some of the larger lakes have bigger charr, and trolling with downriggers is the way to get them. The most popular trolling water in Lapland is the vast Lake Inarinjårvi. In the 1980s this lake produced a charr of almost 20 pounds. Inarinjårvi also has brown trout, grayling, landlocked salmon, and even some stocked lake trout.

Most anglers visit Lapland for trout, charr, and salmon only, but for more broad-minded anglers there is good fishing for large whitefish, big pike, and perch.

Atlantic Salmon

Finnish salmon fishing has declined from its former glory, but significant improvements have been made in recent times. In Finland, an angler can't have an exclusive salmon beat, as occurs elsewhere. Fishing rights are not sold this way. Some fisheries might have rod limits, but day tickets are available for everyone on a first-come, first-served basis. Day tickets are available for all salmon rivers and are inexpensive given the quality of the fishery. Theoretically, it would be possible for a group of anglers to buy all-day tickets for a river with a rod limit and then have it all to themselves, but this rarely happens.

The most classic salmon river in Finland is the massive river Teno (Tana in Norway), which forms the northernmost border between Finland and Norway and flows to the Arctic Sea. This may very well be the greatest salmon river in the world. Harling (see: backtrolling) with flies, plugs, and spoons is the most popular fishing method, even though strict regulations make fishing from boats a bit difficult for the visiting angler nowadays. The same applies to spinning and baitcasting from shore. There are some very good places for the wading fly angler, however, and as the regulations treat fly fishing more freely, this method is recommended for visitors. The most popular place is by the swift rapids of Alaköngås.

The Teno is a wide river, where long double-handed rods are the norm. On the upper river (from the village of Karasjoki upstream), the stream is narrower and one can fish it effectively with a single-handed rod. Many traditional and modern salmon patterns are used on the Teno; this includes flies like the Green Highlander, Black Doctor, Thunder & Lightning, and a wide variety of hairwings. The same flies are used in harling, but they are tied very sparse and slim. Many popular Finnish salmon patterns have been devised on the banks of the Teno, and various plugs are popular there, too.

The salmon run normally starts in late June and continues through late August. Early in the season

the run consists of smaller groups of large fish. Later, the river is filled with grilse. Teno salmon are big; the average size is about 20 pounds, and every year the river yields at least a fish or two in the 50-pound class. Teno also has a good stock of European grayling, and the river is a world-class grayling fishery, with specimens over 2 pounds common.

The only other Finnish salmon river flowing to the Arctic Sea is the Nåårämö, which is a genuine wilderness river, as there are no roads or people living nearby. The Nåårämö River rises from the northeastern corner of Lapland, flows across the border, and runs some 10 miles through Norway before it reaches the ocean.

To visit this site, one has to get to the small village of Sevettijärvi, situated on the northern shore of Lake Inarinjärvi. From this village one can trek to the Näätämö (about 6 miles) or hire a helicopter. Chopper pilots are locals, who can give good tips regarding the best fishing places and camping areas. On the upper river there is a fly-fishing-only area.

Näätämö salmon are, in general, smaller and less numerous than those of the Teno, but they are nevertheless well worth the effort. Näätämö also has a good stock of grayling, which are often large.

On the Baltic side are two notable salmon rivers: the river Tornionjoki, which forms a natural border between Finland and Sweden, and the river Kymijoki in the south.

Like Teno, the Tornionjoki is a huge watercourse. It is hundreds of miles long and boasts almost unlimited possibilities. Just a few years ago, Tornionjoki (also called Tornio) was a beautiful, free-flowing river, but there were practically no salmon in it. The closure of commercial netting in the river mouth and increased stocking efforts have brought salmon back, and today the river is almost as good as it was in the late 1940s. Harling with plugs and spoons is the most common fishing method, but some areas offer good possibilities for spinning and fly fishing from shore and by wading. The salmon run starts in mid-June, with July and August the best months. The average salmon is around 15 pounds. Accommodations are easy to find, boats are available in many places, and access is easy, as a road runs parallel to the river along the length of the main fork.

The Kymijoki, or Kymi, is the southernmost salmon river in Finland. It flows to the Gulf of Finland near the town of Kotka, about 100 miles east of Helsinki. Only a few sections are open to anglers, and some of them don't have rod limits. They can get fairly crowded when the run is in. At special areas, however, like the short Langinkoski rapids near the river mouth, the number of day tickets is limited. These rapids are seldom crowded, because the area is fly-fishing-only and a little more expensive than others. The Kymijoki is a beautiful place, and on its bank stands the former fishing lodge of Russian emperors, built in the late 1800s and today a museum.

There are two reasons for the popularity of this river: It is situated in a metropolitan area, and the salmon are especially large. Some seasons the average weight is well over 20 pounds, and every year the river produces some 40- to 50-pound fish. The salmon run starts in mid-July and continues through the fall. Sea-run browns arrive in larger numbers in October, and there is another smaller run in the spring. Trout are not plentiful, but their size is impressive; 6- to 10-pound fish are the norm, and some twice as large are caught occasionally. Day tickets for Kymijoki are reasonably priced.

Licenses and Regulations

Most fishing waters in Finland are privately owned; the Finnish Forest and Park Association administers state (national) fishing waters, the majority of which are in northern and eastern Finland. There are closed seasons for some species, particularly salmonids, and restrictions and regulations on private waters are often more severe than prescribed by national Fishing Acts.

Licensing requirements are complicated for the visitor to comprehend, and they vary considerably across the country. To practice sportfishing in Finland, other than angling with an ordinary baited hook or ice fishing, a visiting angler over 18 or under 65 years of age must pay a state fishing management fee, available in seven-day or calendar-year options. This is not a fishing license, and it can be obtained at banks or post offices on weekdays, as well as through a self-service payment machine or through home computer.

In addition to this, one must have the permission of whoever owns the fishing rights to each body of water, and/or one must purchase a daily permit or day ticket to access specific sites. The fee for this varies, and may depend on the manner of fishing (with lures or bait), the type of water, or the species present.

A newly enacted license is called a "Lure Fishing Fee," which government literature says "opens new opportunities for trolling, fly fishing, or fishing with other types of lures in addition to the lure fishing permits available from water owners, fishing corporations, etc. Paying a lure fishing fee entitles you to practice lure fishing within a single province, using one rod, reel, and lure."

Outfitters and fishing agents usually have these matters sorted out for clients, but visitors traveling on their own must seek permits from local fishing associations, hotels, holiday villages, and the like. Tourist offices may be able to provide information and direction, as will tackle suppliers and local fishing associations. Separate fee arrangements exist in the province of Åland, which has its own Fishing Act.

Finland has only about 5 million inhabitants, so there is plenty of water for everyone to fish. Angling tourism is developing, and many new fisheries are opening every year.

"All Americans believe that they are born fishermen. For a man to admit a distaste for fishing would be like denouncing mother love and hating moonlight."
—John Steinbeck, 1954

F

FINNING

A fish that is basking near the surface with dorsal and/or tail fins protruding from the water is said to be finning. This action is most often observed in saltwater, particularly with such large creatures as billfish and sharks. When fishing on the open ocean, big-game skippers often look for finning fish in order to intercept them and bring a trolled bait or lure in front of them.

The exposed portions of the dorsal and tail fins of marlin (top), swordfish (middle), and shark (bottom) help distinguish them from each other when they are spotted finning on the surface.

Experienced anglers are able to identify marlin, swordfish, and sharks on the surface by the characteristics of the visible portions of their fins, as depicted in the accompanying illustration. The marlin's tail fin is rigid and pointed; its dorsal fin is folded into a groove and not extended unless excited. The swordfish's tail fin is rigid and pointed; its dorsal fin sickle shaped and rigid, and it cannot be folded into a groove. The shark's tail fin is flexible and rolls when moved; its dorsal fin is more rounded than pointed and stays fixed in position.

FIRST AID
Treatments and Preventions

Knowledge of basic first aid, as well as advanced aid for the treatment of such serious problems as burns, sprains, fractures, broken limbs, shock, poisoning, bleeding, and heart failure is certainly at least as useful in the field as at home. Nevertheless, it is beyond the scope of this book to thoroughly document and illustrate these issues. Instead, this section will be devoted to the first aid, or medical, issues that are most common to sportfishing activities and that are most likely to be encountered owing to the nature of angling and the places visited by anglers. This includes a discussion of preventions as well as treatments.

First aid situations include exposure to the sun, heat, cold, and wind; insect bites and stings; cuts, bruises, and punctures, including those of fish hooks; and waterborne ailments, such as giardia, dengue, and others. Seasickness *(see)*, an inner ear problem, is detailed separately.

Insect Bites and Stings

Anglers come into contact with creatures that bite or sting more often than most people who spend time outdoors. Some of these are aquatic insects that have food value to small fish and are not harmful to humans, but many are flying or crawling bugs that bite or sting and can be harmful or annoying to varying degrees. Bees, horseflies, deerflies, mosquitoes, blackflies, and no-see-ums are the common airborne pests; and ants, spiders, tarantulas, scorpions, and centipedes are among the common terrestrial pests. Encounters may occur from the tropics to the Arctic.

Many insects bite or sting and can cause itching, but few cause serious symptoms by themselves unless the person bitten or stung is allergic to them. However, some insects transmit diseases. For example, certain types of mosquitoes transmit malaria, dengue, yellow fever, and other diseases; certain types of ticks transmit spotted or Rocky Mountain fever or Lyme disease; and certain types of biting flies transmit tularemia or rabbit fever.

Occasionally, stinging or biting insects that have been feeding on or have been in contact with poisonous substances can transmit this poison when they sting or bite. People who have experienced serious reactions from previous insect bites should secure any possible immunization or have an antidote readily available to prevent more serious reactions from future insect bites and stings.

The stings of bees and the bites of many insects usually cause only local irritation and pain in the region stung or bitten. Moderate swelling and redness may occur, and some itching, burning, and pain may be present.

First aid includes:

The sting area should be inspected to determine whether the stinger is still in the body. If it is, remove it in order to prevent further injection of toxin. The stinger should be carefully scraped off the skin, rather than grasped with tweezers, so that toxin is not squeezed into the body.

Application of ice or ice water to the bite helps to slow absorption of toxin into the blood stream. A paste of baking soda and water can also be applied to the bite.

The victim should be observed for signs of an allergic reaction. For people who are allergic, maintain an open airway and get the victim to medical help as quickly as possible.

Prevention.   Many insects are attracted to dark colors, so wearing light-colored clothing can be helpful. Covering exposed areas prevents many problems with flying insects, and tucking pant cuffs into socks or boots is good for keeping out ticks. Even with long-sleeved shirt, long pants, and a hat, there are still exposed areas, so using an insect repellent will probably be necessary.

Choice of insect repellent depends to some degree on the level of problem that has to be dealt with. Some anglers encounter situations with enormous concentrations of mosquitoes or heavy outbreaks of blackflies, and only the most potent repellents will do. Such repellents are also necessary in places where there are known disease problems associated with biting insects (malaria, dengue, encephalitis, etc.). The most effective insect repellents contain the chemical DEET, which has been subject to some health concerns, but which has proven safe when used according to label instructions. The use of products with DEET is recommended by the World Health Organization and the Center for Disease Control and Prevention when traveling to countries where insect-borne diseases are prevalent.

The concentrations of DEET vary within specific products, ranging up to 95 percent. Lotion products with the maximum concentration of DEET have proven to be most useful to anglers where mosquitoes and fly numbers are heavy. Products with lesser concentrations (typically under 30 percent) have shorter terms of effectiveness and are meant for use where infestation is light. Lotion, spray, and ointment products are available; lotions cost more but are viewed by many people as being more effective and longer lasting per application, especially when compared with sprays, unless a spray is applied to the hands and then rubbed on.

When using repellents, always follow the label instructions and keep the repellent away from your eyes and mouth. After application, wash the palms of your hands before touching other objects, especially food. Keep repellents off fishing equipment, plastics, and clothing. Be especially careful with children; repellents without DEET are best for them.

An alternative to repellent use is to wear a mesh jacket that can be sprayed with repellent, or wear a mesh headcover. The headcover may impair vision and is uncomfortable for many people, but it is effective.

Sun

Anglers are exposed to a lot of sun in all seasons of the year. Over time this exposure can lead to problems—melanoma and nonmelanoma skin cancer, immune suppression, cataracts, and premature skin aging—that require medical attention. This is more of a preventive issue than it is first aid treatment, although a sunburn does require minor first aid attention. Preventions are especially important today because skin cancer cases have grown dramatically in recent years.

Problems are caused by ultraviolet (UV) radiation, most of which is screened out by the ozone layer. UV radiation that penetrates the ozone layer also penetrates the surface of the skin. Factors that affect UV levels and degrees of exposure include the condition of the ozone layer (thinner is poor), time of day, time of year, latitude, altitude, and weather conditions.

Minimizing exposure.   To protect your eyes, wear sunglasses *(see)* that block 99 to 100 percent of UV radiation. For the sake of reducing glare and improving your through-water vision when fishing, the sunglasses should also be polarized. Many anglers prefer sunglasses with side protection as well. In terms of eye care, the proper sunglasses reduce sun exposure that can lead to cataracts and other eye damage.

Wearing a hat, especially one with a wide brim, helps shield your face, ears, nose, and neck, which are vulnerable areas prone to sun overexposure. Exposed skin should be covered with clothing to protect it. Light, tightly woven clothing is best, and this includes long pants and long-sleeved shirts.

Skin that is directly or indirectly (like your face that is shielded by a hat) subject to UV radiation should be protected by sunscreen with at least a Sun Protection Factor (SPF) factor of 15, preferably one that guarantees "broad spectrum" protection. This blocks most harmful UV radiation. People with red or blonde hair, fair skin, and light eyes should consider sunscreens with a higher SPF factor, which goes up to 50. Sunscreen should be applied liberally, and as frequently as recommended by the manufacturer. Make sure to reapply it when you towel off perspiration or water. Apply especially well to the nose, ears, neck, wrist, and the back of the hands.

Bear in mind that the most recent medical research on sunscreens indicates that they alone do not prevent skin cancer. A combination of sunscreen use and wearing protective clothing and a wide-brimmed hat is recommended by dermatologists. Furthermore, prevention of overexposure to sun should start in childhood, since the greatest exposure to sun and potential damage is incurred by the age of 18.

Heat

Extreme heat can require first aid because of the reactions that some people incur. Medical problems resulting from heat exposure are less well known than those from cold exposure, but more deaths and injuries are caused by summer heat than are caused by all kinds of storms. Heat is actually only one part of the problem; high humidity increases heat stress.

Heat stroke.   Heat stroke is a sudden onset of illness from exposure to the direct rays of the sun or from too high temperatures without exposure to the sun. Physical exertion and high humidity definitely contribute to the incidence of heat stroke.

The most important characteristic of heat stroke is the high body temperature caused by a disturbance in the body's heat-regulating mechanism.

 Coelacanths, which can manipulate their pectoral and pelvic fins independently like four-legged animals, are related to extinct species that scientists say are closest to amphibians, the earliest land animals.

F

The affected person can no longer sweat, and this causes a rise in body temperature. The elderly are very susceptible to heat stroke, as are alcoholics, obese persons, and those on medication.

The signs and symptoms of heat stroke include:

- The skin is flushed, very hot, and very dry; perspiration is usually absent.
- The pulse is usually strong and rapid, but it may become weak and rapid as the victim's condition worsens.
- The respirations are rapid and deep, followed by shallow breathing.
- The body temperature can reach 108°F.
- The victim rapidly becomes unconscious and may experience convulsions.

Care should be centered around lowering the body temperature as quickly as possible. Failure to do this will result in permanent brain damage or death. The care for heat stroke is as follows:

1. Maintain an open airway.
2. Move the victim to a cool environment.
3. Remove all clothing.
4. Wrap the victim in a cool, moist sheet and use a fan to cool the victim.
5. Immerse the victim in cool water if the preceding treatment is not feasible.
6. Use cool applications if neither of the previous treatments is feasible.
7. Transport the victim to the hospital as rapidly as possible, continuing cooling en route.

Heat exhaustion. Heat exhaustion is brought about by the loss of water and salt through sweating. This loss of fluid will cause mild shock.

This illness occurs most commonly in persons unaccustomed to hot weather, those who are overweight, and those who perspire excessively. The signs and symptoms of heat exhaustion include:

- The skin is pale and clammy.
- The skin shows evidence of profuse perspiration.
- Breathing is rapid and shallow.
- The pulse is rapid and weak.
- The victim may complain of nausea, weakness, dizziness, and/or headache.

First aid for heat exhaustion is as follows:

1. Move the victim to a cool and comfortable place, but do not allow chilling.
2. Try to cool the victim by fanning and/or wiping the face with a cool, wet cloth.
3. Loosen the victim's clothing.
4. If fainting seems likely, have the victim lie down with feet elevated 8 to 12 inches.
5. Treat the victim for shock.

Heat cramps. Heat cramps affect people who work in a hot environment and perspire. The perspiration causes a loss of salt from the body; if replacement is inadequate, the body will suffer from cramps.

Signs and symptoms of heat cramps include:

- The presence of profuse perspiration is evident.
- The victim complains of muscle cramps, painful spasms in the legs or abdomen.
- The victim may feel faint.

First aid for heat cramps is as follows:

1. Move the victim to a cool environment.
2. If the victim is conscious, give sips of cool salt and sugar water (1 teaspoon of salt plus as much sugar as the person can stand, per quart of water) or commercial electrolyte solution.

Prevention. The first rule for avoiding thermal shock is to slow down and don't try to do too much, especially in the first few days of exposure; this is especially important for anglers who visit hot (and humid) places when they are unaccustomed to these conditions. Stay in cool, shaded places during the worst part of the day if possible. A midday siesta may be a good idea for those who are older or whose physical condition is below par.

Proper clothing will help you stay as cool as possible. Light-colored garments that fit loosely and are light in weight are best; a hat, preferably one that shades all of your face and neck, is important. Sunglasses are also necessary, if only to save stress on your eyes. Using a sunscreen is important for avoiding burns; sunburns not only damage your skin but make your body work harder to dissipate heat.

In extreme heat and high humidity, it is essential to replenish fluids lost through perspiration. Do this with nonalcoholic drinks. Cold water, juices, and sports drinks with high glucose content are good choices. Pay more attention to drinking fluids than to eating.

Cold Weather

People who are exposed to the cold, whether on land, on the water, or in the water (falling overboard, capsizing, etc.), run the grave danger of becoming hypothermic. Conditions that may induce hypothermia include being on the ice in winter, being in a boat exposed to strong winds blowing across the water in spring, or being caught lightly clothed during a backcountry storm in the fall. Everyone should know what to do when someone falls into cold water, and this circumstance is covered under survival *(see)*. How to care for a victim of cold is discussed here. Prevention is mostly a matter of common sense, primarily wearing appropriate warm clothing and layering it, and covering your head and neck. Outerwear should be suitable for conditions and should keep out water and wind.

In olden times, Scottish law required commercial fishermen to wear a gold earring, which would be used to pay for funeral expenses if they drowned and washed ashore.

F

Hypothermia.   Hypothermia is a general cooling of the entire body. The inner core of the body is chilled so that the body cannot generate heat to stay warm. This condition can be produced by prolonged exposure to low air or water temperatures or to temperatures between 30° and 50°F with wind and rain. Also contributing to hypothermia are fatigue, hunger, and poor physical condition. Exposure begins when the body loses heat faster than it can be produced. When the body is chilled, it passes through several stages.

The initial response of a victim exposed to cold is to build a fire and to voluntarily exercise in order to stay warm. The fire can also signal rescuers if the victim is lost.

As the body tissues are cooled, the victim begins to shiver as a result of an involuntary adjustment by the body to preserve normal temperature in the vital organs. These responses drain the body's energy reserves.

The symptoms of hypothermia are:

- Cold reaches the brain and deprives the victim of judgment and reasoning powers.
- The victim experiences feelings of apathy, listlessness, indifference, and sleepiness.
- The victim does not realize what is happening.
- The victim loses muscle coordination.

Cooling becomes more rapid as the internal body temperature is lowered. Eventually hypothermia will result in a coma. The victim will have a very slow pulse and very slow respirations. If cooling continues, the victim will die.

The victim of hypothermia may not recognize the symptoms and may deny that medical attention is needed. Therefore, it is important to judge the symptoms rather than what the victim says. Even mild symptoms of hypothermia need immediate medical care.

First aid for a victim of hypothermia is as follows:

1. Get the victim out of the elements (wind, rain, snow, cold, etc.).
2. Remove all wet clothing.
3. Wrap the victim in blankets. Be certain the blankets are under, as well as over, the victim.
4. Maintain the victim's body heat by building a fire or placing heat packs, electric heating pads, hot water bottles, or even another rescuer in the blankets with the victim. Do not warm the victim too quickly.
5. If the victim is conscious, give warm liquids to drink.
6. If the victim is conscious, try to keep the victim awake.
7. CPR is indicated if the victim stops breathing and the heart stops beating.
8. Get medical assistance for the victim as soon as possible.
9. Remember to handle the victim gently. In extreme cases, rough handling may result in death.

Frostbite.   Frostbite results from exposure to severe cold. It is more likely to occur when the wind is blowing, rapidly taking heat from the body. The nose, cheeks, ears, toes, and fingers are the body parts most frequently frostbitten. As a result of exposure to cold, the blood vessels constrict. Thus, the blood supply to the chilled parts decreases and the tissues do not get the warmth they need.

The signs and symptoms of frostbite are not always apparent to the victim. Since frostbite has a numbing effect, the victim may not be aware of it until told by someone.

The beginning stage of frostbite is called frostnip. The affected area will feel numb to the victim, and the skin becomes red, then white. Treatment consists of placing the hand over the frostnipped part, and placing frostnipped fingers in the armpit.

The second stage is called superficial frostbite. As exposure continues, the skin becomes white and waxy. The skin is firm to the touch, but underlying tissues are soft. The exposed surface becomes numb. Treatment requires removing the victim from the cold environment and applying a steady source of external warmth.

Do not rub the affected area. Cover it with a dry, sterile dressing (when dressing the foot or hand, pad between the toes and fingers). Splint the area if dealing with an extremity, and transport the victim to the hospital. As the area thaws, it may become a mottled blue color, and blisters will develop.

The most advanced stage is deep frostbite. If freezing is allowed to continue, all sensation is lost, and the skin becomes a "dead" white, yellow-white, or mottled blue-white. The skin is firm to the touch as are the underlying tissues. Areas affected with deep frostbite should be left frozen until the victim reaches a hospital. Dress, pad, and splint frostbitten extremities (when dressing the injury, pad between the fingers and toes), and transport the victim to a hospital.

If there is a delay in transport, rewarming may be done at the site. Place the affected part in a water bath of 100° to 105°F. Apply warm cloths to areas that cannot be submerged. An extreme amount of pain is associated with rewarming. Rewarming is complete when the area is warm and is red or blue in color, and remains so after removal from the bath. Do not rewarm if there is a possibility of refreezing.

General rules for treating frostbite are:

- Apply loose, soft, sterile dressings to affected area.
- Splint and elevate the extremity.
- Give the victim warm fluids containing sugar to drink if he or she does not have an altered level of consciousness.
- Do not rub, chafe, or manipulate frostbitten parts.
- Do not use hot water bottles or heat lamps.
- Do not place the victim near a stove or fire; excessive heat can cause further tissue damage.

F

- Do not allow the victim to smoke; nicotine constricts the blood vessels.
- Do not allow the victim to drink coffee, tea, or hot chocolate; these substances will cause the blood vessels to constrict.
- Do not allow the victim to walk if the feet are frostbitten.

Cuts and Punctures

Anglers are subject to minor cuts, lacerations, and skin punctures when fishing, mainly as a result of landing, unhooking, and cleaning fish, but also from the use of knives and hooks. Wounds produced by a sharp cutting edge are smooth without bruising or tearing. If such a wound is deep, large blood vessels and nerves may be severed, and bleeding may occur freely and be difficult to control. This not a common problem, but it is a possibility. Minor cuts are common in fishing, many caused by the sharp teeth of fish.

Puncture wounds are produced by pointed objects passing through the skin and damaging tissues in its path. The small number of blood vessels that are cut sometimes prevents free bleeding. The danger of infection in puncture wounds is high because of this poor drainage. There are two types of puncture wounds. A penetrating puncture wound causes injured tissues and blood vessels whether it is shallow or deep. This type is most common in the fingers, often occurring when the angler is fishing, and is caused by contact with hooks and the spiny fins of fish. A perforating puncture wound has an entrance and an exit wound. The object causing the injury passes through the body and out to create an exit wound, which in many cases is more serious than the entrance wound. This type of puncture wound is not common, except in some rare cases where a hook is deep and has to be pushed through skin.

Hook removal. When a hook becomes embedded in human flesh, the first consideration is whether it's safe to attempt removal. If the hook can be moved gently and doing so does not increase the pain, then the injury is most likely in a soft tissue area and hook removal can be attempted. Single hooks or a single point of a treble hook that is lodged in fleshy exposed skin are good candidates for removal.

If moving the hook gently causes greater pain, tingling, or numbness, it is likely near a tendon, bone, or nerve, and you should head to the nearest doctor's office. If more than one point of a treble hook is embedded in the skin, you should leave removal to a doctor as well, since removing one point may drive the other one deeper. A hook that is anywhere near the eye should be left to medical experts.

There are two ways to remove a hook in the field, the first being the push-through method. To do this, first cut the hook from the lure or line; then get a firm grip of the shank with a sturdy pair of

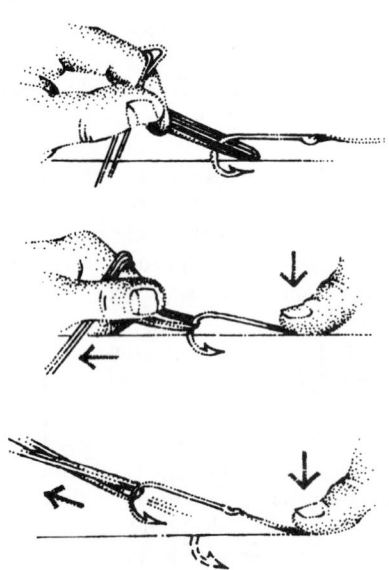

To use the line-pull method of fishhook removal, take a doubled length of strong line and run it behind the bend of the hook (top). Apply thumb pressure to the eye or lower shank of the hook, pressing it toward the skin (middle). Pull sharply backward on both ends of the doubled line.

pliers. Push the hook point forward, following its natural curve, until the barb is free of the skin. Cut off the barb with the cutting edge of the pliers; then back the hook out the way it went in.

The other way to remove a hook is the line-pull method. To do this, first cut the hook from the lure or fishing line; then take a 36-inch length of heavy line (20 pounds or greater) and double it to make an 18-inch piece. Run this behind the bend of the hook; use a thumb to apply pressure to the eye or the lower shank of the hook, pressing it toward the skin. This frees the barb from the soft tissue under the skin and provides a path for removing the hook.

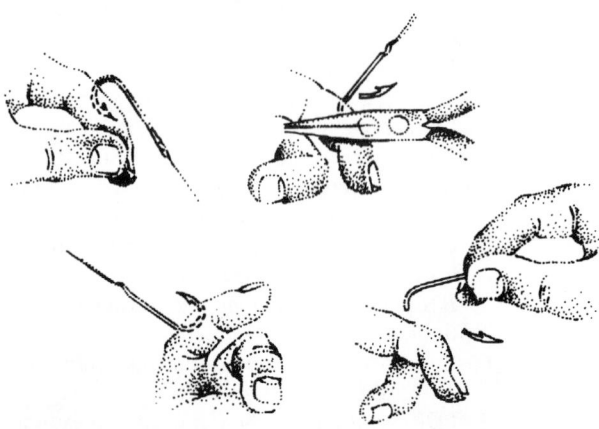

To use the pull-through method of removing a fishhook whose point is near the skin (left, top) or protruding through the skin (left, bottom), get a firm grip of the shank with a sturdy pair of pliers and push the hook point forward, following its natural curve, until the barb is free of the skin. Cut the barb off, then back the hook out the way it went in.

Grab both ends of the doubled line and pull sharply backward. If this doesn't work with one quick jerk backward, do not attempt it again.

When the hook is out, cleanse the wound. Soaking it in clean water is a good idea, and an antibiotic ointment should be applied under a bandage. If an infection occurs, see a doctor. A tetanus shot may be in order.

Waterborne Ailments

Traveling anglers should not overlook the fact that drinking water, and even just coming into contact with it (as in swimming or wading wet), can be harmful in some places.

Schistosomiasis, for example, is a tropical disease caused by a freshwater parasite *(see: diseases and parasites)* that enters the skin through direct contact with infected water. It is also known as bilharzia. Acute symptoms are flulike and include fever, chills, cough, diarrhea, weakness, and headache. It requires treatment by a doctor, and the prevention is staying out of water that may be infected.

More common for most people is giardiasis, known as giardia and "beaver fever," which can be contracted anywhere in the world and has been especially prevalent in Russia. There are several types of giardia and similar parasites; some of these are not killed by freezing or chlorination, and have been known to infiltrate public water supplies. Giardiasis results in chronic diarrhea and can lead to dehydration. Prescription medicines are used to treat it. The best preventive is to boil water for at least 3 minutes and then let it cool slowly; this also will purify water that might contain viral pollution.

Any water to be consumed should be boiled, since it is often unknown which water source may have the problem (even in the cool, clear waters of high-mountain country), and the problem is widespread. The alternative is to carry bottled water with you, an option not practical for backcountry-camping anglers. Some chemical water purifying treatments (which use iodine) will remove many but not all potentially harmful items in the water. The ones that have Environmental Protection Agency approval will remove nearly all the bad bacteria and parasites that might be encountered.

FISH

Usage 1   As a noun, the word "fish" is commonly used by anglers for both the singular and the plural form and is used in a generic sense without regard to species. Anglers might say, "Tuna are the strongest fish" or "We caught three fish this afternoon." It is uncommon for anglers to employ the word "fishes," although "fishes" is a required usage by scientists and in technical literature, especially when referring to two or more kinds or species. The compound word is also used similarly; the plural of catfish is "catfish," not "catfishes." However, scientists would say, "South America is home to many catfishes," distinguishing between species as opposed to overall numbers. This book generally uses the common form rather than the scientific.

Usage 2   As a noun, the word "fish" is used to refer to the flesh of a fish used as food.

Usage 3   As a verb, the word "fish," as in "He fishes every evening," is the act of catching, or trying to catch, fish. It has a general meaning with no explicit distinction between commercial or recreational action or, in the latter case, the techniques or equipment employed. The words "angle" and "sportfish" are often used interchangeably with the word "fish," although they refer solely to the recreational activity and the implied usage of sporting equipment. *See Angler; Angling; Sportfisherman; Sportfishing.*

Defined

The term "fish" is applied to a class of animals that includes some 21,000 extremely diverse species. Fish can be roughly defined (and there are a few exceptions) as cold-blooded creatures that have backbones, live in water, and have gills. The gills enable fish to "breathe" underwater, without drawing oxygen from the atmosphere. This is the primary difference between fish and all other vertebrates. Although such vertebrates as whales and turtles live in water, they cannot breathe underwater. No other vertebrate but the fish is able to live without breathing air. One family of fish, the lungfish, is able to breathe air when mature, and actually loses its functional gills. Another family of fish, the tuna, is considered warm-blooded by many people, but the tuna is an exception.

Fish are divided into four groups: the hagfish, the lampreys, cartilaginous fish, and bony fish. The hagfish and lampreys lack jaws, and as such they form the group called jawless fish; the cartilaginous fish and the bony fish have jaws. The bony fish are by far the most common, making up over 95 percent of the world's fish species. Cartilaginous fish, including sharks, rays, and skate, are the second largest group, numbering some 700 species. There are 32 species of hagfish and 40 species of lamprey.

Overview

Body of the fish.   The body of a fish is particularly adapted to aquatic life. The body is equipped with fins for the purpose of locomotion. Scales and mucous protect the body and keep it streamlined. The skeleton features a long backbone that can produce the side-to-side movements needed for forward propulsion in water. Since water is 800 times more dense than air, fish must be extremely strong to move in their environment. Fish respond to this condition by being mostly muscle. Thus, muscles make up 40 to 65 percent of a fish's body weight. Many fish have air or gas bladders (sometimes called swim bladders), which allow them to float at their desired depth. Fish also have gills, their

F

underwater breathing apparatus, located in the head. Most fish have only one gill cover, although some, like sharks, have gill slits, some as many as seven. The gills are the most fragile part of the fish; anglers should avoid touching the gills on fish that they plan on releasing.

The limbs of fish come in the form of fins. A fin is a membrane that extends from the body of the fish, and is supported by spines or rays. Because the number of rays is usually constant within a species, a ray count is often used by scientists to determine the species of a fish. Each of the fins on a fish has a name. Since these names are used in almost all descriptions of fish, and are used in this encyclopedia, it is worthwhile to become familiar with the different fin names.

Moving from the head toward the tail, the first fins are the pectoral fins. The pectoral fins are used for balance and maneuvering in many species, and in a few are used for propulsion. Further down the underside of the fish are the pelvic fins, located beneath the belly and used for balance. On the back of the fish is the dorsal fin. Some fish have more than one dorsal fin; in this case the dorsal fins are numbered, with the fin closest to the head called the first dorsal fin. Behind the dorsal fin on the top part of the fish there is occasionally a smaller, fleshy fin called the adipose fin. Back on the underside of the fish, behind the pelvic fins and the anus, is the anal fin. The final fin, usually called the tail, is known scientifically as the caudal fin. The caudal fin is the most important fin for locomotion: By moving it from side to side, a fish is able to gather forward momentum.

The scales of a fish form the main protection for the body. Fish scales are kept for the entire life of a fish; as a fish grows, the scales get larger rather than growing anew. Scales are divided into several types. The majority of fish have ctenoid or cycloid scales. Ctenoid scales are serrated on one edge and feel rough when rubbed the wrong way (largemouth bass have such scales). Cycloid scales are entirely smooth, like the scales of trout. More rare types of fish have different types of scales: Sharks have more primitive placoid scales, which are spiny; sturgeon have ganoid scales, which form armor ridges along parts of the body. Some species, like catfish, have no scales at all. Fish scales can be used to determine the age of a fish. A fish scale will develop rings showing annual growth, much like the rings of a tree.

Many fish also have a covering of mucous which gives them a slimy feel. This covering helps streamline their body and prevent infections. The mucous covering will rub off onto a person's hands (this is the slimy substance that you can feel on your hands after handling a fish). Since the loss of mucous is detrimental to the fish, it is better to wet your hands before handling a fish which will be released to minimize the amount of mucous removed, being careful not to harm a fish by holding it too tightly *(see: catch-and-release)*.

The skeletal and muscular systems of fish work together to maximize swimming power. The serially repeated vertebrae and muscle structure work together to create the shimmering, undulating muscle movements that allow a fish to move forward quickly. This structure is particularly evident in a filleted fish, where the muscles show themselves in their interlocking pattern. The muscular nature of fish is the reason why fish make such good eating, and also is a factor in making fish a high-yield food source.

Bony fish have developed an organ called an air bladder, which acts as a kind of flotation device. A fish's body is naturally a bit more dense than water, but the air bladder, filled with gas, increases a fish's ability to float. Fish can change the depth at which they float by varying the amount of gas in their air bladder. This allows a fish to float at any depth it desires without expending any effort. Fish that do not have air bladders, such as sharks, must continually move in order to prevent sinking.

Like virtually all animals, fish need oxygen to survive. However, a fish can get all the oxygen it needs from water by use of its gills. Water entering through the mouth of the fish is forced over the gills, and oxygen is removed from the water by the gills. In order to breathe, fish must constantly have water passing over their gills. However, in order to get enough oxygen, certain fish must either move continually or live in water with a strong current.

Although most fish are referred to as cold-blooded creatures, this is mostly but not entirely true. Some species are called warm-blooded, yet they cannot sustain a constant body temperature as humans do. Instead, the body temperature of fish approximates that of its surrounding medium—water. Certain types of fish, such as tuna, by their constant vigorous propulsion through the water, sustain high muscular flexion that creates heat associated with rapid metabolism. Through built-in heat conservation measures, the fish is capable of maintaining a warmer body temperature than the medium that upholds it; for example, a bluefin tuna's fighting qualities are not impaired physically when it suddenly dives from surface waters where it was hooked down to the colder depths.

Fish Shapes

Fish shapes have also uniquely evolved to suit the needs of their aquatic life. The body shapes of fish fall into general categories: Some are narrow, with bodies that are taller than they are thin, like sunfish, largemouth bass, or angelfish. Some are flat, with bodies that are shorter than they are wide, like flounder. Some are torpedo-shaped, like tuna or mackerel. Some are tubular and snakelike, such as eels.

Shapes tend to be related to a fish's habits and habitats. Narrow-bodied fish are extremely maneuverable, and tend to live in reefs or densely weeded ponds where the ability to maneuver between rocks or plants is essential. Flatfish tend to live on the bottom, where their low profiles prevent recognition. Torpedo-shaped fish are built for speed and are found either in open water or in strong currents where less-streamlined fish would be swept away. Tubular fish often live in small crevices and areas that are inaccessible to other animals, rather than in wide-open ocean waters.

Fish Color

The amazing variety of colors that fish display clearly demonstrates the importance of color in the fish world. Most fish are colored for purposes of camouflage. When viewed from above, fish tend to be dark in order to blend in with the dark bottom of the water. When viewed from below, they look light in order to blend in with the sky (this is called countershading). Fish have developed a huge variety of colors and markings that allow them to escape detection in their own environments. Color is also used for mating purposes. Certain fish have special breeding colors, usually brighter than normal colors. Many reef fish have brilliant colors year-round. The wide variety of colors of reef fish helps to differentiate between the many species that live on the reef.

Fish Senses

An angler should understand the way a fish's senses work. Knowing what a fish is sensitive to helps an angler approach the fish without scaring it. Although some fish rely more on certain senses than on others, there are statements about senses that apply to all fish.

Fish hear very well. Sound travels five times faster in water than in air, and fish are quite sensitive to loud noise (which is why you should not tap on fishtank glass). Fish can be scared off by the noise from people banging around in a boat, loud talking, and motors. Although fish do not have external ears, they do have internal ears. These internal ears, set in the bones of the skull, hear very well. The role of sound in the lives of fish is not entirely understood, but many fish are known to be noisy; fish have been recorded grunting, croaking, grinding teeth, and vibrating muscles. The importance of these sounds is not yet fully known; but what is known for certain is that hearing is an important sense for fish.

A fish's sense of smell is often very good, but the importance of this sense varies widely among species and may be subordinate to other senses, especially vision. With olfactory nerves in their nostrils, fish can detect odors in water just as terrestrial animals can detect odors in air. Some fish use their sense of smell to find food, detect danger, and perhaps also to find their way to spawning areas. There is evidence that a salmon's keen sense of smell contributes to its ability to return to its birthplace. Certainly a salmon's sense of smell must be considered incredible: Salmon can detect one part per billion of odorous material in water. They may refuse to use fish ladders if the water contains the smell of human hands or bear paws. Salmon will panic if placed in a swimming pool with one drop of bear-scented water. With the apparent importance of smell to many fish, removing human scents from fishing tackle is something that anglers should consider, although the extent to which this is useful varies widely with species, and is considered important by some anglers and irrelevant by many others.

Sight varies in importance for fish. Most fish are nearsighted; although they can see well for short distances, their vision gets blurry past three feet or so. Some fish are exceptions to this rule; brown trout, for instance, have excellent vision. An important fact to realize about most fish is that they can see almost 360°; the only space they cannot see is a small patch directly behind them. Fish can also see color. In laboratory experiments, largemouth bass and trout have been able to identify red, green, blue, and yellow. Some fish have demonstrated preferences for certain colors, and red has long been considered a foremost attraction, although this is subject to a host of variables as well as disagreements among anglers.

The sense of taste does not seem to be as important to fish as other senses; taste buds are not as well developed, although there are exceptions, especially among bottom-scrounging fish. Some species, like catfish, use taste to find food and utilize this sense much more than other species of fish. Catfish even have taste buds on their barbels, and certain species have them on the underside of their body.

Fish have an additional sensory organ called the lateral line. Visible as a line running along the length of the body of many fish, the lateral line is used to detect low-frequency vibrations. It acts like both a hearing and a touch organ for fish, and it is used to determine the directions of currents, the proximity of objects, and even water temperature. The lateral line is sensitive to water vibrations and helps fish escape predators, locate prey, and stay in schools.

The senses of fish are more highly developed than most people realize; this is a chinook salmon.

Reproduction

Fish reproduce in many different ways. Most lay eggs, but some bear live young; most eggs are fertilized after they are released from the female's body, but some are fertilized inside the female's body. Since almost all gamefish are egg layers (sharks being the main exception), the reproductive habits of egg-laying fish are the most important to the angler. Mating, called spawning in egg-laying fish, usually occurs once a year at a particular time of year. Each species has its own spawning habits, which have a great influence on behavior. Some fish do not eat when they are in a spawning mode; others are voracious prior to spawning. Some migrate; some build visible nests, and others have no nests; some move to the deep water, and some move to shallow water. Once a site is chosen for spawning by fish, or the time is right, they begin to mate. Sometimes the mating is an elaborate ritual; sometimes it merely amounts to the female scattering the eggs and the male fertilizing them. After the eggs are fertilized, some fish guard and care for the eggs, and some do not. The eggs hatch fairly quickly, at times in as little as 24 hours, although the time is influenced by such factors as water temperature, turbidity, sunlight, salinity, and current. The young fish just out of the eggs are called fry. Fry are usually so much smaller than their parents that they are not recognizably similar. Fry live on microorganisms in the water until they are ready for larger food. In certain species, each spawning pair can produce thousands of fry, but only a few grow to adulthood. Most fall victim to predation; fry are eaten by many predators, including other fish and, in some species, their own parents.

Certain types of fish spawn in habitats other than their normal ones. Some fish that live in the ocean spawn in rivers, and some fish that live in rivers spawn in the sea. Fish that live in the ocean yet spawn in freshwater are called anadromous. The most prominent examples of such fish are salmon. Fish that live in freshwater and spawn in the sea are called catadromous. The most prominent examples of such fish are eels.

Fish Food and Feeding

Fish have evolved to fill almost every ecological niche. Many fish are strictly herbivores, eating only plant life. Many are purely plankton eaters. Most are carnivorous (in the sense of eating the flesh of other fish as well as crustaceans, mollusks, and insects) or at least piscivorus (eating fish), and some—like the great white shark or the piranha—are among the most feared predators in the world by humans, although their danger to humans is oversensationalized. Almost all species that are considered gamefish are predators because their eating habits and aggressive behavior lead them to strike bait or lures that essentially mimic some form of natural food. Many predaceous fish eat other fish, but they also eat insects, worms and other invertebrates,

and other vertebrates. Some fish will eat almost anything that can fit in their mouths and is alive. Some fish are scavengers, and will consume dead fish or parts of fish. Many fish fill only specific niches and have very specific diets. As a result, knowing the natural food of a gamefish can be important for anglers.

Fish Growth

Growth in fish is affected by many factors; especially important are heredity, length of growing season, and food supply. Although each species can be expected to reach a predetermined size, the length of time required to reach this size is extremely variable. The growing season is the time during the year when a fish will actively feed and grow. Generally, fish living in northern latitudes and colder waters have a shorter growing season than fish living in southern latitudes and warmer waters. If all other growing factors remain the same, the fish with the longer growing season will reach a greater size over a given time period.

Additionally, a fish that has optimum food and space conditions will grow more rapidly than one that must compete more heavily for food and space. This in part explains why fish of the same species in the same latitude and growing seasons, but in different bodies of water, may have different rates of growth.

The Diversity of Fish

Fish are the most diverse class of vertebrates. There are more fish species than all other vertebrate species combined. Their sizes can vary from the Philippine gobies, no more than a third of an inch in length (the smallest of all vertebrates), to whale sharks that can reach 60 feet in length and can weigh 150,000 pounds. Fish live in almost every aquatic environment in the world, from lakes 14,000 feet above sea level to 36,000 feet beneath the ocean surface. Fish are found in desert pools that are over 100°F and in Antarctic waters that are only 28°F (water freezes at less than 32° there because of the salinity; the fish do not freeze because they have a special biological antifreeze in their bodies). Some fish can survive for entire summers out of water by hibernating; others can glide out of the water for several hundred feet; a few can produce their own electricity or their own light. Some can achieve speeds of 50 or 60 miles an hour, and some live immobile, parasitic lives. In terms of biological and habitat diversity, no group of animals can outdo fish.
See: Anatomy.

The Evolution of Fish
Ostracoderms.   Fish are the most ancient group of vertebrates. Fossil records indicate that they first appeared in the Ordovician period, more than 400 million years ago. The earliest types were covered with several kinds of armor, from which the name

Ostracoderms

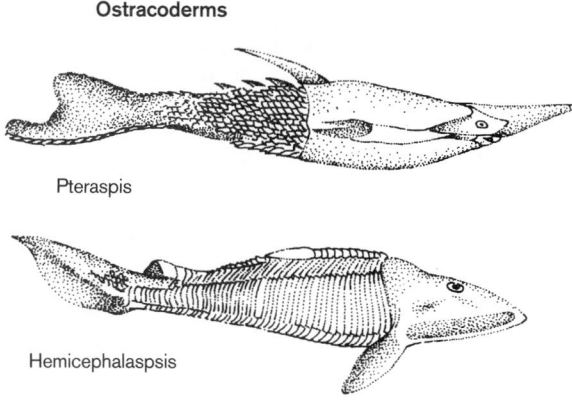

Pteraspis

Hemicephalaspsis

The extinct Ostracoderms are the oldest known fish. They were armor-plated; lacked a well-defined head; and had no scales, jaws, or paired fins.

"ostracoderms," or shell-skinned, is derived. The oldest positive remains were found in rocks from Colorado and other western states. The nature of the sediments involved suggested that the ostracoderms lived in inland waters, supporting an early theory that vertebrates were of freshwater origin. Analyses of the habitats of early fossils by paleontologists, however, have led to the conclusion that, as a group, the invertebrates were originally marine.

Ostracoderms are now extinct. Their living relatives are the Agnatha, or Cyclostomes (hagfish and lampreys), which are the most primitive of the present-day fish. Generally eel-like in shape, cyclostomes lack a well-defined head and have no scales, jaws, or paired fins. Outwardly, in bodily outlines and in the presence of hard skeletal parts, the ostracoderms appear to be more remote from the cyclostomes; yet both are characterized by the absence of jaws and by the absence or weak development of paired fins. Other resemblances in structural features also exist with the two groups.

Placoderms. In the Devonian period of the geologic time scale, often called the "Age of Fish," the placoderms, or plate-skinned fish, were the most abundant forms. This group of fish, peculiar in structure, consists of several types now long distinct.

The various fossil groups have been assigned to many different positions in the classification system, and there is no complete agreement about their arrangement.

Chondrichthyes. In the evolutionary order, the ostracoderms and placoderms are followed by the sharks and their relatives, which extend to the era of modern types of jawed fish. Here the jaws are highly developed, and the fins and general body structure resemble a more familiar design. These types of higher fish forms are easily divided into two definite groups that may have evolved in a separate but parallel fashion from placoderm ancestors. They are the cartilaginous, jawed fish (sharks, skates, and rays) called Chondrichthyes, and the higher bony fish called Osteichthyes.

Bone is completely absent in the Chondrichthyes, and the internal skeleton is entirely cartilaginous. The principal advancements in these fish over earlier types are scales, paired fins, and well-developed jaws on a definite head. Some of their chief or distinguishing characteristics include five to seven pairs of gill clefts, all opening separately to the exterior; dorsal fin or fins and also fin spines, which, if present, are rigid yet not erectile; spiracles present or absent; skin covered with many placoid scales, or "dermal denticles"; and numerous teeth. In bottom-dwelling types of skates and rays, where the mouth is on the underside, water enters through a pair of spiracles on the top of the head and is expelled through the gill clefts, located on the underside of the head. In males, the pelvic fins bear projecting clappers that aid in internal fertilization. Development is oviparous (the eggs are laid before hatching), ovoviparous (the eggs hatch and embryos develop within the mother but without placental attachment), or viviparous (born alive, embryos are attached to the uterine wall of the mother by a yolk-sac placenta).

Osteichthyes. The archaic fish that preceded the bony fish in the evolutionary scale were prominent in older geologic periods, but they diminished in later times. In contrast, the Osteichthyes, or the

Placoderms

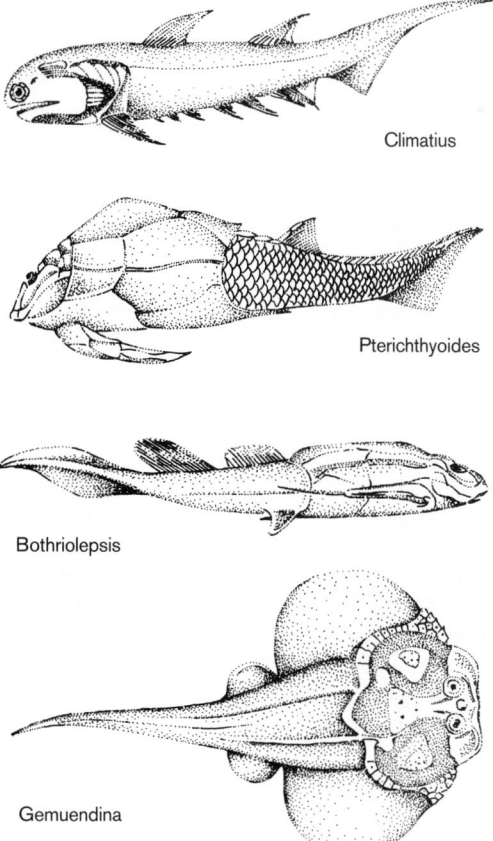

Climatius

Pterichthyoides

Bothriolepis

Gemuendina

The extinct but once abundant Placoderms were plate-skinned fish.

F

higher bony fish, became more abundant and more prominent and eventually dominated lakes and streams. This group, at present, includes all freshwater fish and the great majority of marine types.

The chief characteristics of the bony fish are skeletons of bone; a single gill cover or operculum over the cavity containing the gills; fins strengthened by spines or soft rays; and scales that partially or completely cover the body, or which may be absent entirely. Today the bony fish far outnumber the cartilaginous fish. The most reliable estimates indicate that Osteichthyes include more than 20,000 species, in contrast to approximately 550 species for the Chondrichthyes.

FISH AMERICA FOUNDATION

Formed in 1983 for the purpose of assisting the enhancement of water quality and fish populations, the Fish America Foundation funds grass-roots projects in the United States and Canada. It helps create partnerships that involve industry, private citizens, foundations, and governments, and funds such hands-on fishery enhancement projects as shoreline restoration, plantings, artificial reef/habitat construction, fish rearing/stocking, and fishery education. It has supported over 450 such projects in 47 states and five provinces.

The Foundation especially works with angling and conservation groups to produce self-sustaining projects, most of which rely on volunteer manpower. All are funded only after receiving the endorsement of the appropriate governmental resource agency.

The Foundation is financed through the cooperative efforts of a coalition of sportfishing and boating manufacturers, and is unusual in that it has the ability to overcome the political and bureaucratic obstacles that often prevent small volunteer groups from receiving government assistance for conservation projects.

Fish America Foundation, 1033 North Fairfax Street, Suite 200, Alexandria, VA 22314; phone: 703-548-6338.

FISH AND WILDLIFE SERVICE

Founded in 1871 as part of the United States Commission of Fish and Fisheries, the U.S. Fish and Wildlife Service (USFWS) is the federal agency that is charged with managing and maintaining fish and wildlife and their habitats, with major responsibility for migratory birds, endangered species, certain marine mammals, and freshwater and anadromous fish.

The agency is part of the Department of the Interior, where it was placed in 1939 when it was called the Bureau of Fisheries. It became the Bureau of Sport Fisheries, and then the U.S. Fish and Wildlife Service in 1974. One of its primary responsibilities is managing the National Wildlife Refuge System, the world's largest and most diverse

collection of lands set aside specifically for wildlife. Another is the conservation of over 800 species of migratory birds, the regulation of migratory bird hunting, and implementation of the North American Waterfowl Management Plan. Another is helping to save endangered species (more than 700 species are currently on the Interior Department's official "List of Endangered and Threatened Wildlife and Plants").

It is also charged with restoring nationally significant fisheries that have been depleted by overfishing, pollution, or other habitat damage. Major efforts are currently directed at lake trout in the upper Great Lakes, striped bass of the Chesapeake Bay region and the Gulf Coast; Atlantic salmon of New England; and the major salmonid species of the Pacific Northwest. As part of this program, nearly 80 national fish hatcheries produce some 60 species of fish, totaling over 200 million fish annually.

The Fish and Wildlife Service also enforces federal wildlife laws that protect endangered species, migratory birds, certain marine mammals, and fisheries. It undertakes activities designed to deter illegal trafficking in wildlife, and employs a nationwide network of special agents and inspectors who help enforce wildlife laws and treaty obligations.

Two federal laws administered by the Fish and Wildlife Service—the Federal Aid in Wildlife Restoration Act and the Federal Aid in Sport Fish Restoration Act (see)—have created some of the most successful programs in the history of fish and wildlife conservation. These programs provide federal grant money, which is derived from excise taxes on equipment and certain fuel sales, to support specific projects carried out by state fish and wildlife agencies.

The Fish and Wildlife Service is not involved with the management of strictly saltwater fish, which falls under the jurisdiction of respective state fish and wildlife agencies and the National Marine Fisheries Service (see), which is part of the Department of Commerce.

FISH ATTRACTING DEVICE

A man-made fish attractor, also known by the acronym FAD.
See: Fish Attractor.

FISH ATTRACTOR

Many fish are found close to structural objects of some kind, be they natural or man-made. The construction and planting of artificial habitat has become a very popular activity over the last few decades by groups and individuals as well as by state agencies, specifically to attract fish for angling. These structures, called attractors, provide shade, shelter, and food. They concentrate small plant and animal life that attracts the intermediate-size fish which larger fish prey upon. Thus, they may also concentrate

F

Coelacanths are rare, living fossil fish that date to nearly 250 million years ago; once thought extinct, the first living specimen was found in 1938 off South Africa.

sportfish and become good places to angle throughout the year, and especially in the summer.

Freshwater

Through the planting of brushpiles in some lakes, ponds, and reservoirs that are largely devoid of cover, individual anglers have created habitat that attracts warmwater species and offers open-water angling opportunities. Channel catfish, bluegills, largemouth bass, and crappie are particularly concentrated by the existence of brush and automobile-tire attractors.

In some freshwater locales, large attractor structures planted by fisheries agencies or sports clubs are well marked and known to the general public. But many anglers plant their own. Private and commercial dock owners, for example, often plant brushpiles to provide fish habitat at arm's length. Some guides and avid anglers plant their own brushpiles to have "secret" fishing holes that often are very productive places. These are unmarked and located at sites known only to those who do the planting.

Types. Brush shelters are the oldest and most commonly used types of attractors. Virtually any type of woody brush can be used, but hardwoods resist decay longer than do softer pines. Discarded Christmas trees, for example, generally last only a few years, whereas scrub oak may be almost as resilient five years after being planted. A variety of brush shelter designs can be made, including crescents, pyramids or tepees, rings, and horizontal bundles. Those that are spread out generally prove more useful in shallow water, whereas taller structures are better in deeper water. However, providing variation within each attractor is probably the most important single characteristic for success. The most successful shelters usually contain areas of sparse, moderate, and thick brush cover, and use a variety of brush diameters.

Another successful shelter is an attractor made from bundled and weighted old automobile tires. Cement blocks or cement poured into a portion of the tire cavity is used for weight, and holes can be drilled into the tires to allow air to escape. Often, five or six tires are bundled together, although they can be piled at a site. Bundles may follow different patterns and bottom arrangements like brush shelters.

While brush and tires are the primary materials for attractors, some are made out of rubble, including broken bricks and cement blocks, slabs from demolition projects, and rocks. Large piles of rubble are not that efficient, since the major volume of rubble is covered by outer objects, but when it is spread out, more surface area is exposed. Another possible attractor is a stake bed. This is made from shafts of 1 × 2 lumber that is 4 to 6 feet long and which are driven into the lake bottom about 1 to 2 feet apart. In deep water where the stakes cannot be driven into the bottom, they are nailed to a 2 × 4 lumber frame. These cover an area that is a few feet wide and 4 to 6 feet long.

A pile of brush, attached to a block and located near a submerged stump along a sloping bottom, provides cover and food for different species of fish.

Planting. If you have a notion to create your own hotspot, check first to make sure that it is legal to do so. Planting brushpiles or any structural attractor is prohibited in some places. In some bodies of water, you must first check with the controlling agency (municipal water supply, Corps of Engineers, etc.); a permit may be required, and attractors may be prohibited from specific navigational channels where they might obstruct boat operation (especially in times of low water).

Shallow flat areas, large sandy bars, the backs of creeks, and ledges adjacent to dropoffs are popular sites for planting attractors. These usually are placed in locations that are devoid of structure or cover, as there is seldom a need to supplement existing cover with more. Some anglers place brushpiles a good distance away from a creek channel or breakline because they feel it is less likely to be spotted (on sonar) by other anglers.

Small trees and an accumulation of brush and limbs are the most favored attractors for individual planting. This is true for a few reasons. They're economical and readily available. They aren't as unsightly as other materials, in the event that low or clear water makes them visible. They pose less of an environmental concern.

Hardwood trees last longest and are preferable for durability. However, discarded Christmas trees (which are softwoods) are widely used because of their abundance, especially for crappie shelters. Trees can be planted singly or in clusters, which are usually better; they must be weighted and tied down. Cinder blocks work well for weights. Tying should be done with nylon rope or nylon-coated wire.

If the objective of planting a brushpile is to attract panfish, it's a good idea to spread out a lot of brush. But a room-size area of brush isn't necessary to attract bass. Placements of single trees or treetops or small amounts of brush can be just as effective for attracting good-size bass, and by placing a number of these in good places, you can create a host of private hotspots. The smaller groupings, incidentally, are also harder for other anglers to detect with their electronics.

In northern areas, brushpiles can be constructed on the ice and left to sink when the ice melts, although you can't be sure that they'll land exactly where or how you want them to unless they are heavily weighted so that they sink straight and don't glide. Elsewhere, you must put the brush or trees on a boat (pontoon boats can be good for this), bring them to the site, and then plant them. On lakes where the water level is lowered in the late fall or winter, you may be able to affix an attractor to a stump or rock that is exposed and that will be well covered by spring. Or you may be able to physically plant the brush on the bottom that you can walk or wade to, although this defeats the purpose of secretiveness.

Don't plant in places where navigation may be impeded or where motors may strike the structure. Attractors are usually planted 3 to 20 feet deep, but depth is relative to the situation. In water that usually stays turbid, 10 feet may be enough. If it is in the intermediate-clarity range, then 15 to 17 feet is about right. Clear, deep lakes may require deeper positioning, perhaps around 30 feet. Most brushpiles in reservoirs are planted on sloping banks and laying down, but in places with constant water levels they can be placed on a flat in a standing-up position with a super-heavy trunk weight and by slowly lowering them down with a rope.

On large bodies of water, you should use the sonar on your boat to precisely pinpoint the place to set the attractor, and use permanent landmarks as reference points to line you up when you want to return unerringly to the attractor without having to do a great deal of searching.

When you plant brushpiles, it is worthwhile to take the time to do it in a way that also aids future fishing efforts. Trimming bushy branches and stripping them of leaves may make it easier for your lures to avoid snagging. Also, planting the brush so that it lays at the right angle may be helpful. For instance, consider planting a small tree so that the trunk faces shore and the top lays down facing away from shore. Since you will usually cast to it from back to front, your lure works in the same direction as the limbs extend, which causes fewer hang-ups than if your lure runs against the grain.

Saltwater

In saltwater, attractors are much larger and more substantial in material. They are usually called artificial reefs *(see),* which result from the deliberate sinking of large vessels in strategic locations. There are also smaller attractors, commercially made fish attracting devices (FADs) that are placed in the water (free-floating or anchored) to help attract small baitfish and larger gamefish. The more extensive these are and the farther they extend into the water from the surface, the more they are likely to be effective and to attract diverse species. Less-substantive but portable and temporary attractors can be made by spreading newspapers, cardboard, old bed sheets tied to floats, and so on, over the surface to provide shady cover for baitfish. Even a drifting boat sometimes act as an attractor by providing shade that brings in baitfish.

Fishing

As for fishing attractor sites, jigs are a hands-down favorite lure. In saltwater, lead jigs with bucktail or plastic bodies, and heavy jigging spoons are the primary lures, but assorted bait or strips of fish can also be used depending on what you're fishing for. In freshwater, small light-wire jigs (the hook can be bent to work free when it is hung) are tops for crappie and other panfish around brushpiles in relatively shallow water, and live minnows and crickets fished on floats are also popular. Plastic worms, spinnerbaits, and crankbaits are top bass producers, but in deeper water, a jigging spoon is also effective and may catch white bass or stripers as well.

FISH BOX

A compartment for storing fish. On many larger boats, a fish box is integral to the interior layout of the boat and provides storage for fish that are to be

An insulated box, complete with crushed or cubed ice, keeps fish fresh. (Fish should be completely covered.)

kept and not released. Unlike a livewell, it is not meant for the containment of live fish or bait; the fish box is readily accessible and provides a compartment where fish can be stored off the floor of the boat and out of coolers that would take up cockpit space.

The fish box is located either beneath the cockpit sole of a boat or in a transom wall, and dimensions are dependent upon the size of the boat and the game to be pursued. It drains overboard either directly or through a macerator pump, but not into the bilge; this drainage system facilitates cleaning and permits the removal of blood and debris while fish are being stored. A fish box can also be a removable large ice chest or cooler. Fish that are kept in fish boxes should be iced down, especially in warm weather and on hot sunny days, to keep their temperatures low and to stay fresh.

See: Fish Box; Sportfishing Boat.

FISH CARVING

Fish carving is one of the fastest-growing areas of decorative carving. Fish are good subjects for wood reproduction in exacting detail, and an expertly carved and painted fish is often thought to be an outstanding taxidermy mount or fiberglass reproduction. In fact, the best fish carvers consider their art form far ahead of taxidermy, and the commissions received by the world's top fish carvers, which rival those of wildlife painters, reflect this judgment of fish carving as an art form.

Although there are carvers who are masters of this art form and carve fish professionally, there are many home workshop carvers who replicate fish in wood for their personal enjoyment. Like all crafts or expressions of art, fish carving can encompass a wide range of styles and interpretation, from a simple folk-art style to the finest highly detailed and realistically painted contemporary wood sculptures that can be made. Competitions for carvers reflect the sophisticated level to which this art form has risen, and the competitions are held nationally in conjunction with taxidermy competitions. Many people who create wooden carvings of fish are, or once were, taxidermists; and some sculpt fish out of materials other than wood.

Individual carvers have personal preferences in the types of wood they use. The most commonly used woods are tupelo, jelutong, and basswood. Sugar pine, alder, and cedar are also used. Carvers who specialize in interpretive natural finish carvings prefer hardwoods with color, figure, and character to enhance their work.

The carving tools and supplies for fish carving are the same as those used for all other types of carving, and primarily consist of a few knives, chisels, and rasps. As carvers develop experience, their tools may become more sophisticated. Modern, high-speed, flexible-shaft machines that cost hundreds of dollars are used by some.

Noted carver Bob Berry created this decorative 24-inch rainbow trout.

As fish carving has developed through the 1990s, specialized tools have been invented or designed especially for this type of work. The most commonly designed and altered tools are ones for making lifelike scales. These generally consist of wood burning tips, which are implements for pressing in scales or are rounded chisels that cut in and lift an edge of wood to resemble a scale. Since fish come in all sizes and shapes, their scales do also. Fish carvers are constantly trying to come up with a perfect tool for a particular fish scale pattern and size.

The actual carving of a fish from wood is sometimes the best part of the overall project. Not all wooden fish carvings are crafted entirely from a single piece of wood. Some carvers do a few or all of the fins separately, and may cut off and later reattach the top of the head to provide extensive inner mouth detail. The presentation of the fish on accurate habitat is often more tedious and intricate than creating the fish itself. Many of the best pieces blend the habitat in exquisite composition and design that complement and complete the carving of the fish. This is essential for submissions in competitions but certainly not necessary in the majority of fish carvings. Simply mounting the carved fish on a piece of driftwood that nicely complements the carving is often enough.

However, as fish carvers progress and strive for the best possible work they can do, they usually find that attaching a nicely carved and painted fish to a piece of driftwood is not satisfying enough. They become more observant of details and accuracy. The best carvers leave nothing to chance. They carve, texture, and paint every part of their piece in realistic detail. This level of craftsmanship generally happens only with carvers whose years of experience in combining carving and painting skills have developed into an artistic style that accurately depicts the carved fish and the entire setting.

Accuracy is something that the top carvers work hard at, and they use plenty of reference materials—from photos in magazines and books to their own photos of the actual subjects—to re-create the fish and the habitat properly. The painting of the piece, especially the fish, is an art form in itself; advanced carvers may employ dozens of steps in completing complicated projects.

Some of the most difficult parts of a carving that includes habitat are aquatic plants. Most, being leafy and delicate, pose major problems to the carver. Carving realistic rocks and driftwood can also be very time-consuming. Many smaller elements that are often included in a carving to set the theme—like a minnow or group of minnows, a snail, or a crayfish—can take as long as carving the fish itself.

The matter of water is always difficult for beginning carvers to overcome. The best carvings imply the water surface with floating plants such as lily pads. Splashes with jumping fish are quite difficult to imply. Although these elements can be conveyed through the use of cast resin or Plexiglas, and might be suitable to some people, this technique is generally not acceptable in fish carving competitions.

Fish carving is a good fit with the catch-and-release *(see)* fishing ethics commonly practiced today, and to some people it is preferable to a taxidermy mount or a fiberglass reproduction. An angler needs only a good photograph and a length measurement for a skilled carver to re-create a particular fish. A highly detailed, accurate depiction of the angler's fish is usually appreciated by everyone who sees it.

Recreating actual fish, however, is just one facet of fish carving. There are not many limits on a fish carver. An angler's fish of a lifetime, caught many years before, can be re-created; rare, endangered, protected, and world-record species can be depicted; many such carvings are done, in fact, with amazing accuracy for display in museum exhibits or nature centers. Scale can be easily adjusted; large fish can be miniaturized, and small fish enlarged.

Nor is the fish carver limited to species caught by anglers. Tropical reef fish are a favorite of many carvers. They are relatively small and have exceptional colors and patterns that can be a challenge to re-create accurately. Their coral reef habitat, with its extreme variety of life, offers limitless possibilities.

FISH CLEANING
See: Fish Preparation—Cleaning/Dressing.

FISH CULTURE
See: Hatchery.

FISH EGGS
See: Natural Bait.

FISHER
An archaic and non-gender-specific version of the word "fisherman," and one that may refer to an individual engaged in sportfishing, commercial fishing, or recreational fishing. Fisher is receiving increased current use in an attempt to employ politically correct terms; however, the word "angler" is used in this book not only because it isn't gender-specific, but because it cannot be confused with commercial fishing or non rod-and-reel recreational fishing.
See: Angler; Commercial Fisherman; Fisherman; Recreational Fisherman; Sportfisherman.

FISHERIES
All the activities involved in catching a group of species; the places where a group of species are caught. This term is used interchangeably with fishery *(see)*.

FISHERIES MANAGEMENT
Recent decades have seen an increase in the number of regulations pertaining to the sport of angling, in both freshwater and saltwater, for the purpose of managing fisheries resources. However, such regulation and management are not new. One of the earliest laws regulating the taking of fish was implemented in 1678 when Virginia banned the use of lights to attract fish.

In the eighteenth and nineteenth centuries in North America, several factors—an abundance of fish, a relatively small population of people, and unsophisticated means of harvesting fish for food or catching them for sport—meant that fisheries resources were seldom threatened. In time, some resources were adversely impacted, largely because of the alteration of the landscape through timber harvesting, and pollution caused by burgeoning industry and population concentrations. Anglers and hunters, who were the early conservationists and forerunners of today's environmentalists, clamored for regulations that would foster fish (and game) conservation, the establishment of public parks where natural resources could flourish, and the creation of government agencies to conduct resource management and research. Indeed, American fisheries research first began in 1871 at Woods Hole, Massachusetts, with the establishment of the United States Commission on Fish and Fisheries, and 10 states had established fisheries commissions prior to that year.

Eventually all states and the United States government became responsible for the oversight and management of fisheries resources. A similar situation evolved in Canada. In time, that management became not only an issue of doing what was best for the betterment or maintenance of fisheries resources, but also an issue of managing other natural resources and, perhaps most importantly, managing people and their divergent needs and interests.

Hundreds of years ago, European community leaders observed that when a resource was owned by the people, no one took responsibility for maintaining the resource. Human nature being what it is, each person tended to use the resource to the maximum extent. There was little incentive to conserve or invest in the resource because others would then benefit without contributing to the welfare of the resource. In the case of common (public) grazing areas in England, grass soon disappeared as citizens put more and more sheep on the land held in common. Everyone lost when "the commons" were overgrazed, and this situation became known as "the tragedy of the commons."

To prevent "the tragedy of the commons," most common property resources are held in trust and managed for the people by government agencies. Fish living in public waters are such a common property resource. In the United States, state and federal governments have the responsibility of managing the fish for the benefit of all citizens, including those who do not fish. In order for all to benefit from this renewable resource, the fish are supposed to be managed on the basis of scientific principles.

Managing public fishery resources is ultimately the responsibility of elected officials. Elected officials, however, have delegated much of that responsibility to resource agencies that employ people trained in the sciences of fishery biology, economics, and natural resource management. The National Marine Fisheries Service (NMFS) *(see)* is the federal government agency in the United States with primary responsibility for managing marine fish from 3 to 200 miles offshore. Coastal states are responsible for inshore waters and offshore waters out to 3 miles (9 miles on the Florida west coast and off Texas). State agencies are responsible for freshwater resources within their state.

In an idealistic and theoretical sense, the purpose of fishery management is to protect and maintain fish resources, but in a practical sense the purpose is to satisfy the desires and needs of people. Those desires and needs are varied but primarily include outdoor recreation and food. Therefore, this entails fishery (and water) management based on scientific principles to provide continued sustained utilization of those resources for maximum public benefit. It also entails dealing with social, political, and economic issues.

Biological Principles

Renewable resources like fish and shellfish are living things that replenish themselves naturally and can be harvested within limits on a continuing basis

Managing people, such as these on a Washington river, is a major element of modern fisheries management.

without eliminating them. The scientific principles behind this renewability are well known and provide the basis for fish and game management. To understand these principles, it is helpful to know that, in fish resource management, "species" refers to a group of similar organisms that can freely interbreed; a "population" is a group of individuals of the same species living in a certain area; "stock" means a harvested or managed unit of fish; and "fishery" encompasses all of the activities involved in catching a species of fish or group of species.

Survival

All animals produce more offspring than survive to adulthood as a kind of biological insurance against natural calamities. Actually, for a species to maintain itself, each pair of fish has to produce only two offspring that in turn survive to reproduce. However, most individual fish and shellfish produce tens of thousands to millions of eggs. Most of their eggs do not survive to become juveniles, and even fewer live to become adults. This extra production, together with the effects of harvesting fish, can result in surplus or sustainable production.

Surplus production. The theory of surplus production goes something like this: In an unfished, or unexploited, population, the biomass (total weight) of fish in a habitat will approach the carrying capacity (maximum amount that can live in an area) of the habitat. This population will have a lot of older, larger fish compared to a fished, or exploited, population. These older fish dominate the habitat, and their presence prevents all but a small percentage of the young fish produced each year from surviving to become old fish. When fishing begins (this includes recreational, commercial, and personal subsistence fishing), many large, older fish are removed. Removal of these older fish, as well as other fish, reduces the biomass below the carrying capacity and increases the survival chances for smaller, younger fish. Thus, the unfished population can be viewed as a relatively stable population with moderate production.

The fished population, on the other hand, is a dynamic population with a higher turnover of individuals as the older fish are replaced by younger, faster-growing fish. Some of this new production must be allowed to survive and reproduce to maintain the population. The remaining, or surplus, production is available for harvest.

Surplus production, however, is a complex biological process that is influenced by several factors, particularly carrying capacity and habitat loss. Carrying capacity can be thought of as the amount of fish an area of habitat will support. Habitat that historically supported a certain amount of fish is unlikely to support a lot more or a lot less unless conditions change. If the amount or quality of habitat is reduced, carrying capacity will likewise be reduced.

Human activity has obviously altered, and in some cases reduced, fish habitat. Water pollution, loss of wetlands and seagrasses, destruction of spawning areas, thermal changes, and changes in freshwater flows are some of the many factors that have led to habitat reduction. Unfortunately, fishery managers and anglers have had little influence on, or control over, habitat alterations. Fishery managers have to manage the fish populations that the habitat can support at the present time, not the fish populations that past habitat conditions supported.

Furthermore, carrying capacity changes as environmental conditions change from year to year. When environmental conditions are good in a given year, there is more suitable habitat and more young survive. When environmental conditions are poor in a given year, there is less suitable habitat and fewer young survive. The biological principles that cause surplus production are the natural methods that a species uses to increase the population when environmental conditions are favorable.

Harvesting

The basic goal of fishery biology is to estimate the amount of fish that can be safely removed, or harvested, while keeping the fish population healthy. That estimated amount is called total allowable catch, and it may be modified by political, economic, and social considerations. Overly conservative management can result in wasted fisheries production because of underharvesting, whereas too liberal or no management may result in overharvesting and severely reduced populations. Harvesting fish lowers the population below the carrying capacity of the environment. Continued harvest depends on the ability of the population to produce enough offspring to move toward the maximum carrying capacity. Variations in natural conditions can alter the carrying capacity, resulting in good years and bad years for survival of young.

Populations and Stocks

Ideally the various populations of a species would be the units that are managed. In freshwater environments, a population would be the entire group living in that body of water, and it is usually managed as a whole. Freshwater environments are relatively small in area and in volume when compared with the sea (even a large lake is small compared with the ocean), and they are essentially treated as closed systems. The number of species in freshwater is smaller than in saltwater, and their interrelationships are different.

It is rarely practical in saltwater to manage the population of a species as a unit. There, fishery biologists often refer to stocks rather than populations. For example, Spanish mackerel occur from Maine to the Yucatan Peninsula in Mexico. For purposes of management in the United States, Spanish mackerel are divided into two stocks. Fish from one stock migrate from Florida northward along the East Coast of the United States, and the others migrate from Florida into the Gulf of Mexico. The two stocks may represent one or several populations that make up the species. However, current knowledge about harvesting and migration patterns dictates that they be managed as two stocks. Sometimes more than one species is included in a stock because they are harvested together as though they were one species. In other cases, different species may be managed together for convenience.

Because so many saltwater species are targeted by commercial fishermen, and many are targeted by recreational anglers, management of stocks necessarily takes into account the efforts and results of both groups. In freshwater in the United States, commercial activity is very limited, especially for game species; thus fishery management efforts are primarily focused on the impacts of recreational anglers on populations, and on the impacts of habitat loss or change.

Management in Freshwater

(*Note:* Because there is overlap in principles and methodology, not all aspects of freshwater fisheries management have been discussed in the following section, and likewise in the saltwater management section. Readers are urged to review both sections for the most complete view of these issues.)

Freshwater fishery management in North America has had an interesting evolution in terms of angling interests and attitudes, and in terms of management activities.

Because fishery management (research, regulation, and resource manipulation) has always been geared to the needs and interests of people, it has had an erratic and sometimes conflicting development. For example, at the same time late in the nineteenth century that fishery research in the United States was started, fish culturists were eagerly importing, shipping, stocking, and tinkering with fish species in freshwaters all over North America.

Some of that turned out to be beneficial; some turned out to be disastrous.

Procuring fresh food has been, and continues to be, a strong reason for fishing in freshwater, but fishing purely for recreational fun has also become an increasingly important reason in itself. Other motivators, including the act of fishing as a means of enjoying the outdoor environment, also exist. Selective effort aimed at specific species—most of them at the top of the food chain—and the increasing embrace of catch-and-release (see) have been more recent influences on management. Thus, an evolution in attitudes, in addition to increasing demands and influences on natural resources, has resulted in changing and primarily reactionary management activities.

With commercial fishing largely nonexistent in freshwater, competition for the fish is strictly between recreational anglers. Commercial fishing is permitted only for those species and in those locations where there is little or no interference with the recreational fisheries (although in some waters there is competition with native treaty fishing). Thus, the major focus of management activities has been on preserving or enhancing habitat, sustaining or increasing fish populations, and managing angler activities. The objective is to produce abundant and diverse fish life and enhance fish populations so that they are accessible to anglers in desirable quantity, variety, and size range. Accomplishing this takes a knowledge of fisheries science and aquatic ecology, and an understanding of socioeconomic factors, including angler attitudes.

Optimum yield. Optimum yield is the harvest level for a species that achieves the greatest overall benefits, including economic, social, and biological considerations. This is different from the traditional biological concept of maximum sustainable yield, which is the largest average catch that can be taken continuously and which considers only the biology of the species and the production of protein.

The concept of optimum yield has long been used in freshwater fishery management, and it comprises the sometimes intangible factor of "quality." Angling quality includes considerations of species, sizes, and quantity of fish involved; situations in which they are found; and methods of capture. Optimum yield management requires establishing and maintaining ecological supplies of some species in order to sustain other desired species or merely to assure diversity of abundant life forms. It also requires establishing safety factors in the total allowable catch to moderate effects of unanticipated disasters and human errors.

Biology

In the broadest sense, fisheries management activities are predicated upon knowledge of the species, which requires extensive and time-consuming research. From the late nineteenth century until after World War II, research at all levels was probably the foremost activity of fishery scientists. Understanding the life history of a given species is the underpinning of biological efforts, and it includes knowledge of spawning habits and early development, age and growth, food and feeding, migration and movements, diseases and parasites, predators, subpopulations, and physiology and behavior.

Much is known about the biology of many primary freshwater species, while less is known about the biology of others. The biology of most of the species of interest to anglers is by now fairly well understood, and there has been a lot of research on the dynamics of predator-prey relationships. Nevertheless, the biology of some nontargeted species and some prey fish is less well understood, and an understanding of the dynamics between all species is still being explored.

Methods. Freshwater fisheries management involves a number of methods. These include: hatcheries and stocking of popular game species; establishment and enforcement of regulations to prevent overfishing; management and enhancement of streams, lakes, and reservoirs to stabilize populations; surveys to determine angler needs and wants; allocations to user groups, primarily for sport and recreational use and occasionally for industry, farming, and commercial purposes; and research to address specific fisheries management problems and issues.

Since fisheries management encompasses all action that protects, enhances, improves, or maintains fisheries and fishing areas, methods include such diverse activities as protection of a woods or forest serving as a buffer zone to prevent agricultural runoff; institution of unique slot limits or catch-and-release regulations; protection of certain species and sizes of fish; and creation of regulations limiting water use by some groups in order to protect the resource.

Hatcheries and Stocking

Early attempts at raising fish for food date to the Orient and early Roman times, but fish culture for sport purposes began in Europe prior to 1850. At that time, fish hatcheries could be found for a number of species, even though, at the same time, breeding and hatching trout in North America was still a novelty.

Hatcheries might seem to be the solution for all fishing problems, since stocked fish from hatcheries theoretically could be raised to fill every angler's needs and wishes. In the early days of stocking, that is how they were viewed, and there are still some anglers who feel that stocking is the absolute answer to population abundance problems, which it often is not.

Hatcheries and stocked fish can be expensive and are not always practical or possible. At one time, shad hatcheries abounded all along the East Coast, but their minimal replenishment of the species and high expense doomed them. There are very few hatcheries for saltwater species, although

Bycatch is the term for the unwanted fish that are commercially netted along with targeted species; these fish often are dumped back dead into the sea. The ratio of bycatch to intended catch can be as high as 4 to 1.

F

Atlantic salmon are raised in this New Brunswick hatchery.

vary with each species and situation, but usually fish 6 to 8 inches or longer will have low mortality if handled carefully. Obviously, larger fish are more expensive. Adult fish can be economical or expensive, depending upon the species. Rainbow trout are generally less expensive than muskies.

There are problems associated with rearing fish in hatcheries. Under the crowded conditions of a hatchery, cannibalism can cause large losses. The fish also become trained to feed on hatchery food and need time to make the transition to wild conditions. In addition, the opportunity for disease or fungus to develop is greater, and serious problems can be caused when diseased fish or fry are released in the wild. Another problem, though not a biological issue, is the fact that hatchery-raised fish seldom taste as good as their wild counterparts, especially if they are caught soon after release. Although hatchery managers have learned to control most of the biological problems, there are still occasions when things go wrong.

The majority of anglers prefer the stocking of adult fish, especially trout, since these fish can be readily and immediately caught. However, the costs are high. Stockings of smaller fish may be more cost-effective and may be accepted by the fishing community, especially if time and conditions for growth in the wild are provided.

In states, hatcheries and the numbers of fish stocked depend upon funding, which is largely derived from the revenues obtained from angling license fees or stamps. The federal government also operates fish hatcheries to restore certain major and indigenous fisheries or to mitigate the effects of federal water development projects. Some federal stockings are allocated to the states annually. Other federal-hatchery fish go to federally managed lands or to such interjurisdictional waters as the Great Lakes or the Columbia River. Many states have species-specific stamps in addition to the standard fishing license; these help pay for species-specific stocking and management programs.

It should be repeated that stocking has had some beneficial results and some notably harmful ones, and that it is still controversial in current times as a management method for certain situations. Many of the harmful results came early in the days of fish culture and fisheries management. The widespread and indiscriminate stocking of carp across North America, for example, which were imported from Europe, is generally regarded as the most disastrous hatchery-raising and stocking effort ever accomplished in freshwater. On the other hand, the raising and stocking of striped bass in freshwater impoundments, and the stocking of steelhead and salmon in the Great Lakes, have been extremely successful from the perspective of anglers. Stocking, however, especially of nonnative species, can be, and in some cases has been, harmful to other populations of fish and the cause of multiple changes in assorted aquatic resources.

technical difficulties in raising marine species are beginning to be overcome; red drum, snook, and sea trout are among the species now being raised successfully.

Even in freshwater, the costs, food needs, possible cannibalism, and habitat requirements of different species make some difficult to raise. Muskellunge, for example, are very difficult to raise, since they tend to be cannibalistic; and satisfactory foods and (economical) feeding systems are still being developed. Trout, including rainbow, brown, and brook, are easier. They can be kept in large areas, exhibit little cannibalism, and eat food pellets. Trout also are easy to strip (remove the eggs and milt from spawning adults), fertilize, and produce from eggs. However, even the trout species differ in cost effectiveness. Rainbow are the easiest and cheapest (and thus most heavily stocked by most states); brown and brook trout are more difficult and costly.

The size of the fish stocked also determines the ultimate cost, and thus reflects the number of fish stockings that can be made with a given amount of money. The smallest fish, called fry, are less than finger length and are generally inexpensive to produce. Little time, money, manpower, or food is allotted to them, although their natural mortality is high when released.

Fingerlings, which are 3 to 5 inches long, or a finger's length, are more expensive but may still be economical with most species. The mortality will be less with these fish than with fry, but higher than with adult fish. The optimum size for stocking will

Regulations

Many populations of popular game species in freshwater would be in danger of rapid depletion without regulations attempting to control their harvest. Fishing regulations cover a variety of issues but are most typically associated with size and creel limits. Size limits usually state the minimum legal size for specific species, the rationale being to prevent small fish from being kept and to allow fish to spawn at least once. Some biologists feel that this simple designation places too much emphasis and fishing pressure on larger fish. Slot limits, where anglers can keep fish only above and below a certain specified size, and catch-and-release areas have become popular in some waters for population management reasons and because of expressed angler interest.

Creel limits regulate the number of fish that can be taken daily. They are usually based on an aggregate number, although some specify limits for fish of a certain large size within that number. Possession limits are similar to creel limits but specify the number of fish that can be in one's possession. Possession limits are usually equivalent to a two- or three-day creel limit, and thus they prohibit anglers from repeatedly catching creel limits and storing them for future use. Creel limits attempt to distribute the catch among more people over a greater time period.

Slot limits allow harvesting of fish of only a certain size and prohibit the taking of fish smaller or larger than that size. Many biologists believe that this is a better way to limit catches, since it protects not only the smallest of the species but also requires release of trophy fish. These trophy fish can then theoretically be caught another day, and their return to the water helps to repopulate the species during spawning season and to maintain predator-prey balance.

Some regulations restrict catches on specific waters to only one large trophy fish, thus ensuring that many will be left to replenish the species. Some fishing camps or lodges or managers of privately controlled waters impose regulations that are more restrictive than government-imposed regulations. They realize that their continued success depends upon constant catches of fish and angler satisfaction.

Catch-and-release fishing is popular in certain areas and is a method utilized by some agencies to limit harvest. An increasing number of anglers practice partial or total catch-and-release on a voluntary basis, but catching any fish in any water that does not meet regulations for harvest requires release, so there are various forms that this concept can take. Specific total catch-and-release fishing by regulation is usually limited to certain waters, and this method requires the immediate release of every fish that is caught. Variations of this are "lure fishing only" or "fly fishing only" and other regulations in which certain types of equipment (lures but no bait or traditional flies only) are allowed. Some fly-fishing-only regulations are also accompanied by other regulations regarding equipment, particularly the use of barbless hooks, and some catch-and-release area regulations also prohibit the use of bait or barbed hooks.

Other regulations prescribe the fishing seasons for selected species. Usually the closed seasons are those in which the fish are spawning. This prevents too many from being taken and permits adequate replacement, although there is not uniform agreement among fisheries biologists as to the need for closed seasons; some states have them and others don't. For similar reasons, other regulations prohibit night fishing for some species, or establish off-limit areas on certain waters.

Regulations that prohibit the use of certain types of bait are enacted to prevent the entry of undesirable species into streams and lakes. Thus, a common regulation is one that prohibits the use of goldfish, carp, or species not bought from a bait shop. Other regulations unilaterally prohibit any use of baitfish. The reason for such prohibitions is that it is possible to adversely affect predator or prey species in a certain location by the deliberate or inadvertent release of these undesirable fish. Similarly, transferring game species from one body of water to another is prohibited by most agencies to protect existing populations of fish. The deliberate or inadvertent transferring of yellow perch, for example, to lakes and ponds with trout, has been detrimental to trout because the perch prey on the young trout and eventually overtake the trout.

(For more information about special regulations, see that section later in this entry.)

Habitat Management

Habitat management involves the protection, restoration, control, or enhancement of lakes, ponds, streams, rivers, and other habitat areas. In some cases, habitat management or improvement is accomplished with the help of fishing clubs, scout troops, community groups, and the like under the direction of state or federal fisheries personnel.

Stream improvements can be accomplished by building small dams to raise pool levels, reinforcing banks with rock or logs, and creating cover from log and brush cuttings. On lakes and ponds, the planting of structure such as weighted brushpiles and Christmas trees, cutting and chaining shoreline logs for cover, planting water weeds, and building small reefs to hold fish can improve fish habitat.

Artificial reefs are an important way to improve some fisheries and increase available fish. Reefs can be as simple as a Christmas tree weighted with concrete blocks or as complex as the sinking of large scrap freighters (largely a saltwater phenomenon) or the sinking of wired tires and concrete block and rubble. While artificial reefs connote a bottom structure, there are commercially available reefs that are anchored to the bottom but are mid-depth structures to attract fish.

F

Reefs are important in two different ways. Reef structure will hold, foster, and develop algae, weeds, invertebrates, crustaceans, and other flora and fauna, which are the bottom of the food chain and the basis of life for larger prey and predator species. The structure provides comfort, safety, and food. Also, reefs help to gather and hold fish. Fish species that seek structure will not stay in areas with plain flat bottoms. The presence of structure in these areas gathers those species and improves fishing.

In freshwater, the quality of the water is part of the habitat concerns, and the acidity of an environment is one water-quality issue that can have a large influence on fish. Water pH within certain narrow ranges close to a neutral pH of 7.0 is important for the maintenance of fish life. A pH of 7.2 to 8.3 is typical, a pH of 6.0 to 9.0 is acceptable, and a pH of 5.5 to 9.5 is generally tolerable. However, fish prefer neutral (pH 7.0) or slightly alkaline (up to pH 7.9) water. Acid rain, acid mine runoff, and acid industrial pollution make pH abnormally low and kill fish life. Some pH control is possible, either by using crushed limestone (alkaline) in affected streams and lakes or by releasing limestone slurry in careful doses to counteract any acid influx into the water. However, pH control is temporary, expensive, and needed most in those waters that naturally are least productive.

Another habitat concern, and one with many resource-user conflicts, is aquatic vegetation. Weeds or aquatic plants are important in most waters. They provide a basis for the food chain and protection for fish, and convert carbon dioxide to oxygen. However, uncontrolled vegetation growth can be bad, since some aquatic plants can choke waterways, make boat traffic impossible, and begin the eutrophication (overenrichment) process of small lakes and ponds. In some areas, artificially introduced plants such as hydrilla have become serious problems. There is no simple answer for aquatic plant control, although cutting, poisoning, uprooting, and introducing other species to eat or destroy

the plants have all been tried, with varying results. In some cases, the eradication of certain aquatic plants has had major adverse impacts on fishing for certain species, especially bass.

Temperature is the most important factor affecting the species in a given body of water. All species have a range of preferred temperatures. Warm waters are best for the so-called warmwater species such as sunfish and bass; cold waters are best for coldwater species such as trout and salmon. Watershed protection will help maintain a cool temperature for trout streams. Temperature can be controlled in streams running from dam outlets by controlling the level of the outlet from a dam. High-level outlets, which take water from on or near the surface, result in downstream flows with higher water temperatures; low-level outlets, which take water from deeper levels, result in downstream flows with colder water temperatures. Since most dams are on fast-flowing streams, a low-level outlet for cold water is preferred for trout habitat. However, low outlets often result in water with little or no oxygen, and baffles leading from the outlet to the stream are often used to aerate and oxygenate the water.

Watershed maintenance involves everything from watershed protection to clearing of hazardous snags or obstructions. All waterways need a suitable buffer zone of forest land around them to protect them from rapid runoff; muddying of the water; and runoff of pesticides, herbicides, insecticides, and fertilizers from nearby agricultural areas; also necessary is adequate natural shoreline to protect against erosion. Good agricultural practices, control of urban development, and pollution control are vital components of watershed management.

Surveys

Management surveys provide information on the needs of anglers, the fish harvest, and the condition of fish populations. They can include angler surveys, biological surveys, and tagging surveys.

Angler surveys are conducted at points of access or on a roving basis. Access-point surveys are usually accomplished at dockside to compile information; roving surveys are done on the water. Fishing success, rate of catch, catch per unit of effort (hours, days, trips, etc.), number and size of catch, equipment used, locations fished, and similar information is recorded. This information can then be used to determine the need for creel or size limits, seasons, or stocking programs.

Biological surveys usually involve electrofishing (or electroshocking), poisoning, or netting. In shocking, waters are electrified with special equipment to temporarily incapacitate the fish, which can then be gathered for quantitative and qualitative data. This may be used to build a baseline of biological data trends, including information on the habitat and the food chain. Poisoning, using selective chemicals that pose little danger to

New York fisheries technicians sample a lake by netting.

humans, is generally reserved for very specific purposes. In addition to being used in surveys, poisoning may also be used to renovate or reclaim some bodies of water (usually small), killing all fish to permit restocking with other species more desirable or appropriate. Chemicals are also used in some control situations; the lampricide TFM, for example, is an effective, selective poison used to control sea lampreys.

The survey method of tagging involves placing a tag or mark on fish. Fish are marked through a clipped fin to obtain general information. However, this often does not provide data on fish growth (other than general data), since specific fish cannot be identified and measured without expensive tracking mechanisms (see: tagging). Using various types of tags, placed in different locations on the body of the fish depending on the agency or the species of fish, allows biologists to obtain important information on growth rates, migrations and movements, species health, weight increases, and similar data when the fish are recaptured later. Comparing data taken at the time fish were released with similar data gained upon capture gives fisheries biologists important information.

Allocation

Water is basic to human life in a host of ways. Besides personal uses, it is necessary for manufacturing, trade (shipping lines), housing developments (thus increased prices for shoreline property), farming, and recreational interests. There is a constant demand for water from a variety of users, all vital in a way, but all in a way destructive to the natural waterway. The great amount of water needed for the production of aluminum might affect water usage in that area. Water utilized and released in chemical and steel production will pollute waterways if not monitored and treated. The damming of a stream for flow control or irrigation may deplete water flow downstream, affecting habitat and fisheries. A reservoir formed for recreation might be applauded by swimmers, water-skiers, sailors, boaters, and lake anglers but might ruin the favorite recreation of river canoeists, stream anglers, and whitewater rafters.

Constant water monitoring is required along with adequate controls to ensure that the quality remains high. When there are conflicting areas of water usage, a balance must be met to make sure that industry, farming, commercial, and recreational needs—including boating and many forms of fishing—are all treated fairly.

Since most freshwater commercial species such as trout and catfish are raised in ponds, and most freshwater commercial fishing is concentrated on species other than those sought by anglers, conflicts about fishing use, such as those experienced in saltwater between commercial fishermen and recreational anglers, seldom occur. Allocations based on economic issues with regard to freshwater fisheries

usually focus on maintaining the fisheries or enhancing them to sustain or improve sportfishing participation, which is unarguably of significant economic importance, especially since it involves expenditures made for fishing and boating equipment, gasoline (for boats and for cars to reach the area), incidentals at convenience and grocery stores, lodging, dining, guide and charter boat services, boat rentals, and much more. Many billions of dollars are affected nationally by recreational angling, and economic considerations are among the factors affecting fisheries management.

Problems

In theory, fisheries management seeks to avoid problems through preventive measures, but in reality many of the practices of fisheries managers are in response to public needs or interests and in response to problems that develop with fisheries. Nevertheless, control measures and ongoing management can revitalize some fish habitats and fish populations, and such practices do prevent the occurrence of some problems or prevent existing problems from worsening.

Some common issues facing all fisheries managers include overharvesting, the depletion of genetic strains of fish, and loss of habitat. Habitat loss is by far the greatest danger, since it is generally out of the hands of anglers and fisheries biologists. Housing developments, shopping malls, industrial plants, human consumption, irrigation, loss of buffer zones, and natural disasters and environmental changes (like storms or changing weather patterns), and other factors can alter, reduce, or completely eliminate habitat areas or cause loss of natural waters.

Controlled size and creel limits and constant monitoring and surveys by fisheries biologists can prevent or curtail overharvesting. When it becomes a danger, emergency regulations usually allow for closure of an area, pending a more detailed survey and analysis.

Biologists can carefully control species so that hearty, viable strains are produced in hatcheries. A problem can develop when a hybrid is introduced in an area in which one of the parent species is still present. A dilution of genes or a loss of the original species can occur if the hybrid proves to be more adept in adapting to the environment, or if it proves to be a more dominant strain than the original stock.

Management in Saltwater

Marine fish have had a long history of importance for humans. This was always rooted in fish as a food source. Accounts of vast shoals of saltwater fish in the New World helped draw colonists, and fish were the first items exported. But even then, fluctuations in abundance were noted, and catches were found to be variable. From the early days until the late nineteenth century, virtually all saltwater fishing was of the commercial, or fish-for-food, variety,

F

Commercial fishing is often at odds with recreational fishing; this is a scene along the British Columbia coast.

and it was not until well into the twentieth century that fishing for recreation and food became a component of the utilization of marine resources.

Eventually, recreational angling would become a significant part of total marine fishing effort, although recreational anglers target a more limited number of fish species and do not target shellfish in volume. In time, recreational fishing evolved from being almost entirely a catch-and-keep endeavor to a more selective type of harvest, either by personal choice or by regulation. Some popularly sought saltwater species, like tarpon and bonefish, have negligible food value either to commercial fishermen or to recreational anglers and are primarily released by anglers. But such instances are in the minority. Nevertheless, when marine fishery resources are managed, both recreational and commercial uses and interests must be considered, even as the economic value of, and participation in, these activities change.

Stock assessment.   Stock assessment encompasses all of the activities that fishery biologists undertake in evaluating the conditions or status of a stock. The result of this assessment is a report on the health of that stock and recommendations for maintaining or restoring it. These assessments often consist of two nearly separate activities. One is to learn as much as possible about the biology of the species in the stock. The other is to learn about the fishing activities for the stock. Historically, the demand for assessment has come after a stock is already declining. When the assessment begins, there may be little or no information on the biology of the species or the fishery. Meanwhile, there is pressure to complete some kind of assessment so that the stock can be managed. This leads to preliminary assessments that form the basis for initial management recommendations until more information is available.

Catch and effort.   One of the simplest assessment methods requires almost no knowledge about the biology of the stock. However, good information about the fishery is required. In an assessment based on catch and effort, managers look at the history of landings for the stock and the effort expended to catch the stock. The key word here is effort. Data alone are not very useful for landings, the amount of fish caught and landed (kept) per year. Landings can fluctuate up and down for a variety of reasons. A trend of decreased landings may be a cause for concern, but the amount of effort made to catch the stock tells the real story.

Effort is calculated in various ways, including days or hours of fishing time. To account for effort, fishery biologists divide the yearly landings by the fishery effort; this gives the catch-per-unit effort. The catch-per-unit effort is directly related to the amount of fish in the stock. A decline in catch-per-unit effort usually indicates a decline in the stock.

A number of fisheries have followed a pattern in relation to the catch-per-unit effort. At the beginning of a new fishery, the catch-per-unit effort is high and the effort is low. As interest in the fishery grows, the effort increases, the catch increases, and the catch-per-unit effort usually levels off or declines. Finally, as more effort is applied, the catch declines and the catch-per-unit effort declines even more. A decline in both the catch and the catch-per-unit effort indicates that the stock is probably overfished. This means too much effort is being applied for the stock to maintain itself. Landings decline despite increasing effort. The obvious solution is to reduce the amount of fishing until the catch-per-unit effort returns to the earlier stages of the fishery.

This seems simple enough, but there are a number of reasons why assessments based on catch and effort aren't used or are not used more often. These include: insufficient landings data, insufficient effort data, and the use of new technology that makes it hard to compare the effort today with the effort of several years ago.

Adequate landings data are often available, but the effort data are usually missing, incomplete, or unusable. Another problem is that by the time there is a clear decline in catch-per-unit effort, stocks may be well overfished, even to the point of collapse.

If fishing effort is too high, the cause is usually too many boats in the fishery. Fishery managers call this overcapitalization, meaning that more money (capital) has been invested in boats than the fishery can support. Overcapitalization can also refer to the ability of fishermen to increase effort without increasing the number of boats. If no new boats are added to a fishery, but each boat doubles its fishing power through newer equipment or new technology, the resulting effort can be more effective and have the same result as doubling the number of boats.

Biology/spawning assessment.   When little is known about the biology of a fish stock, one of the first questions asked is, At what age do the fish spawn? The second question is, What proportion of the fish caught are one year, two years, and three years old? If some of the fish spawn when they are two years old, and all spawn at age three, and most of the fish caught are two years old, then there is a danger that too many fish may be caught before they can spawn and replace themselves. This is called recruitment overfishing.

Harvesting some fish before they spawn does not automatically doom the stock, but the practice needs to be evaluated. Declining landings, greater effort to catch the same or smaller amounts of fish, or declines in average size of fish are all signs of possible problems. Determining the age of spawning and caught fish is one step toward management.

When fishermen appear to be catching fish before they have a chance to spawn and other signs of trouble exist in the fishery, the usual management response is to protect small fish. Protection most often takes the form of length limits or gear restrictions that favor the catch of larger fish. In commercial fishing, minimum limits on the mesh size of gillnets is a gear restriction that allows smaller fish to escape.

Unfortunately, protecting small fish does not necessarily address the larger problem of overfishing. Recruitment overfishing occurs when more fish are being removed than can replace themselves; even when the remaining small fish are protected, it can still occur because small fish produce fewer eggs than large fish.

Anglers sometimes suggest a closed fishing season during the period when a stock is spawning. This would seem logical, but marine biologists usually reject the idea. A fish caught before, during, or after the spawning season is still not available to spawn the next year. As a result, biologists prefer to focus more on protecting fish until they're old enough to spawn and then determining how many fish can be safely removed without harming the stock. Exceptions to this approach are cases where spawners gather in certain locations and are very vulnerable to being caught in unusually large numbers.

Other assessment information. Few fish stocks, if any, have been fully assessed. Fishery biologists and managers always wish they knew more about the fish and the fishermen. Full assessment would include some of the following information:

- The kinds of fishermen in the fishery (longliners, netters, recreational, etc.)
- Pounds of fish caught by each kind of fisherman over many years
- Fishing effort expended by each kind of fisherman over many years
- The age structure of the fish caught by each group of fishermen
- The ratio of males to females in the catch
- How the fish are marketed (preferred size, etc.)
- The value of fish to the different groups of fishermen
- The time and geographic area of best catches

Full biological information would include:

- The age structure of the stock
- The age at first spawning
- Fecundity (average number of eggs each age of fish can produce)
- Ratio of males to females in the stock
- Natural mortality (the rate at which fish die from natural causes)
- Fishing mortality (the rate at which fish die from being harvested)
- Growth rate of the fish
- Spawning behavior (time and place)
- Habitats of recently hatched fish (larvae), juveniles, and adults
- Migratory habits
- Food habits for all ages of fish in the stock

When the previous information is collected by examining the landings of fishermen, it is called fishery-dependent data. When the information is collected by biologists through their own sampling program, it is called fishery-independent data. Both methods contribute valuable information to the stock assessment.

Even in the best stock assessments, rarely is everything about a stock known. Assessments proceed with the assumption that the best available information (data) will be used. Fishermen often disagree with this assumption when they are adversely affected. Fishery managers respond that they are obligated to protect the stocks, and, in the case of federal fishery management, they are mandated by law to use the best available data.

The principle of best available data may create a conflict for fishermen. In the past, when managers have asked for more and better data from fishermen (primarily commercial fishermen), the result has usually been more regulations. From the fishermen's point of view, the data appear to have been used against them. From the managers' point of view, the data were used to ensure that the fishery could continue. When fishermen don't provide good data, then the fishery must be managed on the data available, which may be incomplete. This can result in overly restrictive management, which is wasteful, or in continued overfishing and declining catches. In either case, fishermen are the losers. It is in the long-term interest of fishermen to provide the best data possible.

Age, Growth, and Death
Any reliable information about the fishing process or the biology of the stock contributes to the stock assessment. Among the basic biological information that fishery biologists find most useful are the age structure of the stock and the relation between fish length and age. Once this is known, important characteristics of the stock, such as growth rate and death rate (mortality), can be determined. This information is used to create a picture of the stock that describes its current status.

F

Aging fish.   Basic biological data are the foundation on which all assessments of fisheries resources are built. These include parameters such as the size and age composition of the population and catch (both landed and discarded), growth rates, and maturation. The most thorough and reliable assessments include age-specific estimates of stock biomass, mortality rates, and predictions of future stock conditions, for which knowledge of the size and age composition of the catch is essential. Rates of growth, mortality (due to natural causes and fishing), and reproduction can be calculated only if age-specific time vectors exist. Fish age is also a critical component of many biological and pathological processes.

Samples of fish for aging are collected from recreational anglers and commercial fishermen, as well as from the research activities of biologists or fisheries technicians. In saltwater, unbiased estimates of the age composition of a fish population are obtained by analyzing samples from surveys made by research vessels. These surveys are conducted several times each year in order to monitor the abundance of the species and to follow the seasonal progression of growth and maturation. Samples are also collected from commercial and recreational fisheries in order to estimate the age composition of the fish that are removed from the population. These samples are collected both from the docks (the landed portion of the catch) and directly from fishing vessels (to estimate the age composition of the discarded portion of the catch). Many fish may be aged in the course of a year; the Fishery Biology Investigation staff of the Woods Hole Oceanographic Institute, for example, ages up to 30,000 fish per year.

Age and length data are then utilized in models that allow assessment scientists to estimate the biomass of fish populations and to examine the potential effects of continuing removals from those populations. The choice of an age determination method for a given species involves deciding on an appropriate aging structure (scales, otoliths, vertebrae, spines, etc.) and processing method (impressions, thin sections, etc.) for that structure. The next step is validation, in which the marks used to age fish are verified to occur once per year and at approximately the same time each year. Common validation techniques include direct methods, such as tag/recapture studies and marking with chemicals; and indirect techniques, such as back-calculation, marginal increment analysis, edge progression analysis, length-frequency/year-class progression analysis, radiometric/isotope analysis, and elemental analysis.

To age a fish, one must identify the annual growth marks (annuli) on the structure chosen. You cannot tell the age of a fish by looking at it. There are too many differences between species and within a species. In temperate waters, fish growth is fast during the summer months when water temperatures are warm, and slow during the cold winter months. A year of growth is defined as one summer zone plus one winter zone. These zones are identified on scales as areas of wide (summer) and narrow (winter) circulus spacing.

Otoliths provide the most definitive biological information, including history, spawning, and environmental influences, plus age and growth. Otoliths are the layered stonelike buildups of calcium carbonate in the fish's inner ear, and are also called ear stones. On otoliths, the zones of growth are identified as alternating opaque and translucent bands when viewed microscopically. Once it is established that each zone, or ring, truly represents a year, then the age of a fish can be determined.

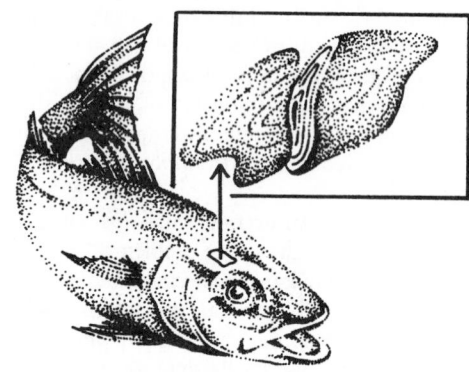

The age and environmental history of fish can be documented by examining a cross section of the otolith (inset).

After the fish have been aged, the length and weight are compared to the age of the fish. This results in a length-at-age key in which the age of a fish can be estimated from its length. Also, by looking at the change in length and weight from a one-year-old fish to a two-year-old fish etc., the growth rate can be estimated. The more fish that are aged, the better the picture of the stock. However, in the case of long-lived fish, growth usually slows in the older fish, and past a certain point the age cannot be readily assumed by the length. In these cases, it is better to age strictly on analysis of the bony parts rather than by length.

When enough fish have been aged, either directly or indirectly, a picture (catch curve) of the age structure of the stock may be drawn. The age structure of a stock is like an historic picture, revealing something about the current status as well as the past. Usually that picture will reveal that younger fish are more numerous and that there are fewer fish at each subsequent age owing to various causes. If younger fish are not being caught in proportion to their abundance, the reason may be that they are not as abundant in the same areas as the older fish, or they may not be caught by the fishing gear, or they may be caught but released. A fish that is readily harvested in a fishery during the first year is referred to as a recruit. Younger fish that are not being caught in proportion to their abundance are termed "not fully recruited" to the fishery, and those that are being caught in proportion to their abundance are considered to be "fully recruited."

A fishery assessment using the abundance of each age group is based on the portion of the stock that is fully recruited to the fishery. It would be desirable to know more about the unrecruited stock between the time of egg fertilization and the age of recruitment, but for many species there is little that management can do that would affect this part of the population. For other species, management could affect water quality, the amount of suitable habitat, or even the death rate to promote greater survival of young fish before they reach harvestable size (are recruited to the fishery).

Mortality and spawning potential. In order to determine the amount of fish that can be safely harvested from a stock, biologists must first determine how many fish in a stock can die (mortality) and still allow the stock to maintain itself. If 1,000 fish are alive at the beginning of the year and 200 fish die, then the annual mortality rate is 20 percent and the survival rate is 80 percent. Each year some fish die whether they're harvested or not. The rate at which fish die from natural causes is called natural mortality, and the rate at which they die from fishing (both commercial and recreational) is called fishing mortality.

Several methods are used to determine each mortality rate. For example, fishing mortality can be estimated from a tagging study. After many fish from a stock are tagged, the percentage of tagged fish that are caught and reported is an estimate of the fishing mortality. Natural mortality is then calculated by subtracting fishing mortality from total mortality. Sometimes there is no available estimate of fishing mortality for a stock. However, fishery biologists may have a good idea of what the natural mortality might be from studying other similar stocks. In this case, natural mortalities (or a range of possible natural mortalities) can be subtracted from total mortality to get fishing mortality (or a range of possible fishing mortalities).

Biologists often attempt to define a rate of fishing mortality that, when added to the natural mortality, will lead to the rebuilding of a stock or the maintenance of a stock at some agreed-upon level. The level being used in many coastal fishery management plans is based on the spawning potential ratio, which incorporates the principle that enough fish have to survive to spawn and replenish the stock at a sustainable level.

Spawning potential ratio is the number of eggs that could be produced by an average recruit over its lifetime when the stock is fished, divided by the number of eggs that could be produced by an average recruit over its lifetime when the stock is unfished. In other words, spawning potential ratio compares the spawning ability of a stock in the fished condition to the stock's spawning ability in the unfished condition.

As an example, imagine that in a fished population 10 fish survive the first two years of life and are now large enough to get caught. Four are caught before they spawn (no eggs produced), 3 others are caught after they spawn once (some eggs produced), and the last 3 live to spawn three times (many eggs produced) before dying of old age. During their lifetime, the 10 fish produced 1 million eggs, and the average egg production was 100,000.

Now take an unfished population in which 10 fish also survive for two years as before. Three die from natural causes after spawning (some eggs produced), and the other 7 spawn three times (very many eggs produced) before dying of old age. During their lifetime, these 10 fish produced 5 million eggs, and the average egg production was 500,000.

The spawning potential ratio is then the 100,000 eggs produced by the average fished recruit divided by the 500,000 eggs produced by the average unfished recruit, and is equal to 20 percent. Spawning potential ratio can also be calculated using the biomass (weight) of the entire adult stock, the biomass of mature females in the stock, or the biomass of the eggs they produce.

In a perfect world, fishery biologists would know what the appropriate spawning potential ratio should be for every harvested stock, based on the biology of that stock. Generally, not enough is known about managed stocks to be so precise. However, studies show that some stocks (depending on the species of fish) can maintain themselves if the spawning stock biomass per recruit can be kept at 20 to 35 percent (or more) of what it was in the unfished stock. Lower values of spawning potential ratio may lead to severe stock declines. If the spawning potential ratio is below the level considered necessary to sustain the stock, then fishing mortality needs to be reduced.

Growth overfishing. Growth overfishing occurs when the bulk of the harvest is made up of small fish that could have been significantly larger if they had survived to an older age. The issue here is that the fishery can produce more weight if the fish are harvested at a larger size. The question biologists must answer is how much bigger or older should the fish get before they are harvested.

Typically most fish grow rapidly in the first few years and grow more slowly in later years. One approach to getting the most out of a stock of fish would be to harvest them near the point where the growth rate begins to level off. However, this approach is too simple because all the while the fish are growing, their numbers are decreasing from mortality.

There are two opposing forces at work in a stock of fish. Growth increases the weight of fish, whereas mortality reduces the number of fish. Biologists can calculate the harvest (also called yield) that can be expected from different combinations of harvest rates and the age of the fish when they are first captured.

Another type of overfishing occurs when commercial fishermen catch fish before they reach their

From the duplicate name file: You say you're going yellowtail fishing? Is that for the flatfish (yellowtail flounder), the snapper (yellowtail snapper), or the jack (California yellowtail)?

F

maximum price per pound. The idea here is that the catch will have a higher value if the harvest is delayed when a premium is paid for larger fish.

Management aimed at growth overfishing has more to do with getting the most benefit out of a stock than ensuring the renewability of the stock. This may be a legitimate goal for fishery management as long as recruitment overfishing is not a problem.

Virtual population analysis. At times, fishery biologists have more information available than what is provided by the snapshot of the age structure. Sometimes the number of fish caught from a single year class (the group of fish born in the same year) is known for each year that the year class is fished. Using the number caught each year from a year class and the mortality rate, the size of the year class can be reconstructed. The reconstructed year class can then be tested with different rates of fishing mortality to see what the effects might be, or the information can be used in other calculations, such as determining the spawning stock biomass.

Indices. Fishery biologists sometimes employ an index to help assess the general state of a stock. The index is an indirect measure of the stock and is taken the same way at the same time over many years. The index can be compared with the catch in the fishery or other data to see if there is a relationship between the index and the health of the fishery.

One of the better known fishery indices is the juvenile striped bass index. Since the 1950s, biologists have sampled streams surrounding Chesapeake Bay where striped bass spawn and have counted the number of recently hatched fish caught with standardized methods. The index closely follows the decline in the striped bass fishery with a three-year lag (striped bass do not appear in the fishery until they are three years old). An increase in the index is assumed to indicate improvements in the stock. Other indices use number of eggs, number of larval fish, or actual counts of fish through aerial, underwater, or acoustic (fish finder) surveys.

When an index is based on the early life history of a fish, it must be remembered that many things can happen to the fish before it is large enough to harvest. Despite some drawbacks, indices are usually easy to understand and can be useful indicators of changes in a fish stock.

Bycatch. Bycatch is all the animals that are caught but not used during the act of fishing. In the sense of catching untargeted species, it can be applied to recreational fishing but is seldom a factor there. Almost all commercial fisheries have an associated bycatch. When the bycatch includes endangered species or protected mammals, then regulations are made to reduce or eliminate the bycatch as required by federal laws. When the bycatch includes species that are targeted by other fishermen, the bycatch may be included in the overall quota for that species; in this case, the bycatch is simply a part of the total allowable catch for that species.

A more difficult problem with bycatch occurs when the bycatch contains undersized fish of economically desirable species. The undersized fish may be of the same species that the fishermen are targeting but have no economic value at the smaller size. Alternatively, the undersized fish can be the target species for other fisheries when they reach a harvestable size. In these cases, the effects of the bycatch on the stocks are often unknown. However, it is generally accepted that catching large amounts of a stock before it is old enough to spawn or before it has economic value is wasteful and possibly harmful to the stock. Fishery managers try to account for bycatch in their stock assessment because bycatch may be an important cause of mortality.

The bycatch of species that have no current economic value presents problems that traditionally have not been addressed by fishery managers but that can have serious implications to the food chain.

Since each species has a role in the community, the removal of an important food item (such as prey species) through bycatch could adversely affect other species (predators) that eat the item. However, predators often eat a variety of food items. Reduction in the numbers of a single prey species may lead to an increase in another prey species that the predator will readily consume, although bycatch of prey species may lead also to the reduction in numbers of multiple prey species. In moving down the food chain (big fish eat little fish, which eat smaller fish, etc.), the link between prey species in the bycatch and important predator species gets weaker and the relations less clear.

Understanding all of the relations among predator and prey species may be impossible. However, it is generally thought that less bycatch, rather than more bycatch, is more desirable for maintaining a balance among the various species in a community. Furthermore, the waste of bycatch by commercial fishermen is often viewed negatively by the public, and it may present a problem that exceeds biological issues.

Allocation. When the harvest of a stock is restricted by management, the different groups of fishermen using that stock often find themselves in conflict. The conflict occurs because each user group realizes it could harvest more fish if the other group didn't exist or if the other group were restricted even further. These disagreements occur among different kinds of commercial fishermen or between commercial fishermen and recreational anglers.

The decision as to how much each group gets to harvest is called allocation. From a strictly biological viewpoint, there is no fair or unfair allocation. It doesn't make any difference who catches the fish as long as the total allowable catch is not exceeded.

Allocation is a political, social, and economic decision usually made by elected or appointed officials, particularly the latter. In federal fishery management, the decision is made by regional fishery management councils (combination of managers

F

and appointees). Similar boards or commissions are often responsible at the state level.

Allocation decisions are often made on the basis of historical catches. If Group A normally caught 60 percent of the landings and Group B 40 percent, then the fish are allocated on that basis. Disputes often arise over the accuracy of historical records, particularly when poorly documented fisheries are involved, and particularly as the amount and economic value of recreational fishing increases.

The determination of total allowable catch and the allocation decisions have not always been separated as described, and have often been tilted excessively to commercial fishing interests on the basis of prior activities or industrial economic concerns. Theoretically, fishery biologists determine the total allowable catch based on the scientific information available, but in reality many decisions are not made that way. In theory, the biological decision would not be modified by other considerations, but the regulations and allocations to achieve the target catch in fact often have been.

Critics charge that greed, not science, has dominated marine harvest allocation decisions in the past and continues to do so. And even though marine fishery resources still support substantial fishing by commercial and recreational interests, and provide important food resources to the fishing and non-fishing public, most of the major fish stocks have fallen to levels far below even the poor times. Many species have been heavily exploited, primarily by domestic and foreign commercial fishermen; and as popular or easily accessible fish stocks have been depleted, the focus has shifted to other, formerly less favorable, species. Management, despite its principles and capabilities, and in spite of the methodology previously outlined, cannot overcome human greed over a resource held in common.

Government management structure and federal law. The National Marine Fisheries Service (NMFS) is part of the National Oceanographic and Atmospheric Administration (NOAA), which in turn is part of the United States Department of Commerce. The NMFS is the federal agency with primary responsibility for managing marine fish from 3 to 200 miles offshore. Coastal states are responsible for inshore waters and offshore waters out to 3 miles (9 miles on the Florida west coast and off Texas).

The legislation that directs how NMFS manages the nation's fisheries is the Magnuson Fishery Conservation and Management Act, also known as the Magnuson Act. The Magnuson Act created eight regional fishery management councils to advise NMFS on fisheries management issues. The voting members of the councils include a representative from each state fishery management agency, a mandatory appointee from each state, at-large appointees from any of the states in the region, and the regional director of NMFS. The councils produce fishery management plans (FMPs), with public input, that describe the nature and problems of a fishery along with regulatory recommendations to conserve the fishery; in other words, they define overfishing and spell out steps to prevent or correct overfishing. After approval by the Secretary of Commerce, regulations that implement management measures in the FMP become federal law and are enforced by NMFS.

Although some recreational anglers are aware of this process, the majority are not, and are ill-informed about this federal legislation, the councils, and the management plans. It is imperative that coastal anglers become involved, attend public hearings, review management plans, and voice their opinions, in order to be part of the process of determining how marine fishery resources are both managed and allocated.

Special Regulations, Trends, and Funding

Special regulations. Fisheries scientists define special fishing regulations as those that differ considerably from the regulations that apply more broadly, usually across a state or province. This is a generic definition that can apply at any point in time. The regulations that were standard, or conventional, in 1990 were at one time considered special regulations, and the so-called special regulations that apply today will no doubt be conventional at some future time.

Initially, special regulations were meant to let fish have enough spawning opportunities to continue self-perpetuating populations and to protect fish with high growth potential so they could attain larger size. These regulations were not very effective and were generally very liberal until the latter half of the twentieth century when angler numbers and effectiveness increased substantially and at the same time the quality of many habitats began to deteriorate. Special regulations came into much wider use in recent decades; they have been effective in some cases and ineffective in others, and many anglers inappropriately view them as a panacea for reversing declining fisheries.

Special regulations, or regulations that are particular for certain species or locations, proliferate today. They may be used to maintain or protect a unique, threatened, or endangered fishery; to reserve a fishery for specific angler activities; to permit harvest of underutilized or highly productive populations; to improve or maintain fishing quality; and for other reasons. Sometimes these regulations are not clearly understood or clearly defined, and confusion exists.

Special regulations can be appropriate tools for fishery management if based upon scientific principle, but they are often set in place as a result of socioeconomic considerations. Improper use of special regulations by fishery managers can result in negative angler perceptions, continued decline of fishing quality, loss of managerial credibility, and unrealistic angler expectations.

The American Fisheries Society, an organization mainly comprising accredited fishery professionals, in a position statement on special regulations, urges anglers and scientists to consider the following:

- Development of realistic and attainable goals and measurable objectives for a fishery. The fishery manager should ensure that the goals of a special regulation are compatible with broader, ecological management objectives. The goals of the regulation should be clearly defined and well-stated so they are easily understood by anglers. The regulation should include quantitative objectives that can be measured within a specified time frame, allowing for proper assessment of the regulation.

- Involvement of the angling public in all phases of planning, development, and implementation of a special regulation to help ensure public acceptance, support, compliance, and effective enforcement once the regulation is in place. The rationale for the regulation should be communicated to peers, associates, enforcement officials, and the public. Effective communication among all user groups minimizes conflict arising as a result of different expectations. Social conflicts stemming from different definitions of angling quality may be minimized if well-defined goals are developed and agreed on early in the process.

- Assessment that includes recognizing fiscal and temporal constraints. Evaluation techniques should be peer-reviewed to anticipate and minimize possible shortcomings, which reduce the credibility of the resource agency and its fishery managers. Natural fluctuations often influence population parameters for a short time and, consequently, short-term studies could indicate that a regulation was a success or failure when observed changes were actually a result of natural fluctuations. Replicates or use of reference waters may prove invaluable in accounting for natural fluctuations during an evaluation period. Additionally, lack of angler compliance could result in regulation failure even if biological considerations were correct.

- Recognition of unforeseen problems that arise during implementation and evaluation of special regulations to further the understanding of site-specific special regulations. For instance, special regulations may concentrate fishing pressure on particular waters or on certain segments of a fish population, or the value of catch-and-release regulation may be negated by high hooking or handling mortality. Compensatory responses such as reduced growth rates or increased natural mortality may produce unanticipated results. Angler behavior may change and also confound the evaluation process. For example, the increasing popularity of voluntary catch-and-release on a reference water could confound evaluation of a nearby special regulation. Angler use may initially decrease when a special, more restrictive regulation is applied. Several years of increasing use may then follow as anglers become accustomed to the new regulation.

- Communication of evaluation results to the public and to the professional community through news media, agency reports, peer-reviewed publications, and appropriate public and professional presentations. Successes and failures of a particular special regulation or modifications of the proposed special regulation must be reported because they can provide valuable guidance to other fishery managers. Agencies should strive to make the best use of special regulations as a fishery management tool. Well-developed goals and objectives, public participation in the process, adequate evaluation, and ongoing communication will contribute to successful use of special fishing regulations in fisheries management. To meet the challenge of appropriate use of special regulations, fisheries professionals must make a deliberate, planned effort to create long-term changes for the benefit of fisheries resources and user groups.

Trends in management and regulations. Making predictions about future management activities, the state of fishing in the future, and regulations that will exist to manage resources and people, is risky and foolish. However, in the near term, based on current and evolving attitudes and regulations, it is not so risky to suggest that some of the special regulations existing today will be even more prominent in the future, and that more restrictions will be placed on recreational anglers in both freshwater and saltwater, especially the former.

In those places where fishing seasons are identifiable, they will likely be extended, offering more opportunity; in general, however, limits will become more restrictive, probably with decreased bag limits and increased size limits. Bag limits may incorporate multiple species rather than apply on a species-by-species basis. In other words, a limit of five fish per day may be imposed regardless of species, or with restrictions on how many of the five may be of a certain species or size. This limitation already exists in the Great Lakes and in some Canadian waters, and may spread further in both freshwater and saltwater.

More restrictions on the equipment used by anglers could be imposed. Barbless hooks, and hooks that will rust or decompose more quickly, may be mandated in certain situations. The province of Manitoba was first (in 1990) to prohibit the use of barbed hooks, and more provisions mandating the use of barbless hooks are likely to be implemented. There may be further attempts to reduce the use of lead in terminal fishing tackle (lead weight for fishing has been banned in

England for some time), and a greater interest in the environmental effects of some types of lures, especially soft plastics, which could eventually lead to attempts to control their use. Chemicals or substances that give (or are perceived to give) anglers an unfair advantage could be regulated. The use of nets and gaffs, or the type used, may come under more scrutiny and regulation. The number of rods used by anglers could be decreased. Throughout Canada, anglers are allowed to use one rod or line at a time in open water, but in the United States anglers are allowed to use two rods in most places and more in some others (ice fishing regulations may vary). If the number of rods or lines is not regulated, then the number of hooks used on a rod or line could be decreased.

In the future, more places in freshwater will probably be designated as trophy or complete catch-and-release waters, with correspondingly restrictive regulations. Some waters will likely be specifically managed for extensive harvest, such as designated panfish lakes. And more attention will be paid to the harvest of wild versus hatchery fish, especially in salmonid species, and to identifying and protecting wild fish.

In time, people may need to take an aquatic education course in order to receive a sportfishing license, similar in some respects to the hunter safety training course mandatory for all new hunters. Aquatic or fishery education courses are required in some European countries. Such courses might review the basics of aquatic ecology, fisheries management principles, local and regional regulations, ethics and etiquette, safety and first aid, and, of course, angling methods and equipment.

No courses, regulations, restrictions, or laws will protect or enhance resources without adequate enforcement. If a substantial number of anglers do not believe in and support the evolving ethics required to protect and maintain fishery resources, and if the number of law enforcement personnel is inadequate, then any new or special regulations will be problematic and likely ineffective. Furthermore, the usefulness or need for these regulations may be affected by factors such as the impact on fishery resources by an increasing or decreasing number of anglers, and increased demands on all natural resources because of population growth.

Funding. Most recreational fisheries management activities are funded by user taxes and fees. Hence the funding comes either directly or indirectly from those who use the resource.

The primary avenue of funding is license fees and special-use stamps. Usually license revenue provides funding for general fisheries management and for operation of a state fisheries department (or in cooperation with hunting licenses in a combined department). Special-use stamp revenues are allocated to specific programs or activities. In some instances, general fisheries management (and law enforcement) is partially subsidized from the general fund of state tax coffers, but this avenue is an uncertain and politically risky one that does not assure consistent levels of funding. However, one state, Missouri, funds conservation programs, including fisheries management programs, from a percentage of the revenue received from annual state sales taxes.

Additional money for fisheries management and conservation comes to the states from the Federal Aid in Sport Fish Restoration Act *(see),* which levies an excise tax on the sale of certain fishing and boating equipment and motorboat fuel. These funds are apportioned to the states based on a formula weighted 40 percent on the basis of land and water area, including coastal and Great lakes waters; and 60 percent on the basis of paid fishing-license holders. No state receives less than 1 percent of the available money nor more than 5 percent. Approximately 6 percent of the funds are utilized for administration, and over 100 million dollars is annually available for use by the states.

The funds may be utilized for sportfish restoration and enhancement activities, including lake construction, motorboat access, fisheries management and research, and aquatic resource education. This highly effective program is administered by the federal government.

See: Catch-and-Release; Ecology; Regulations.

FISHERIES MANAGEMENT COUNCIL

Also known simply as a council, and as a Regional Fisheries Management Council, this is a group established by the Fishery Conservation and Management Act to develop fishery policy for managing those species most often found in federal waters.

See: Fishery Conservation and Management Act; Fisheries Management.

FISHERMAN

A person who catches, or tries to catch, fish. "Fisherman" has a general meaning with no explicit distinction between commercial or recreational action or, in the latter case, between the methods, techniques, or equipment employed. The words "angler" and "sportfisherman" are often used interchangeably with the word "fishing," although they refer solely to the recreational activity and the implied usage of sporting equipment. Thus, a person who sets a net in saltwater and one who uses a trotline in freshwater are both fishermen. The former is commercial fishing and the latter recreational fishing, but neither is an angler or sportfisherman. However, the words "angler," "sportfisherman," or "fisherman" could describe a person using a rod and reel to catch fish for personal use.

Although "fisherman" has a masculine gender, it is used in a generic sense throughout the recreational and fisheries management communities, the sportfishing equipment industries, and the boat and motor manufacturing industries to imply

A 30-foot basking shark weighing 6,580 pounds, taken off Monterey, California, had a liver weighing 1,800 pounds, 60 percent of which was oil.

females as well as males. That generic usage occasionally appears in this book (although preference is given to the word "angler") because of its overwhelming idiomatic dominance, and also because the alternative, "fisher," which is an archaic although non-gender-specific version of "fisherman," may also refer to an individual engaged in commercial or recreational activity.

See: Angler; Commercial Fisherman; Recreational Fisherman; Sportfisherman.

FISHERY

In a biological sense, all the activities involved in catching a species of fish or group of species; the place where a species or group of species is caught. In common usage by the general public, fishery also refers to fishing opportunity or species availability in either a recreational or a commercial sense, as in "the fishery for coho salmon does not commence until the annual migration run." This term is used interchangeably with fisheries.

FISHERY BIOLOGIST

An individual trained in the biological study of fisheries and who manages fisheries resources. This term is distinct from "ichthyologist," a person who studies fish, but practically synonymous with "fishery manager" and "fishery scientist." A fishery biologist undertakes all of the activities necessary to manage fisheries. Those activities include learning the biology and life history of fish (and also usually other aquatic organisms), gathering data, analyzing data, offering management options, and evaluating the status of the fishery, all of which are natural resource issues. A fishery biologist must deal with relevant social, economic, and political issues, none of which have to do with biological matters, but all of which have a great impact on effective fisheries management.

See: Fisheries Management.

FISHERY CONSERVATION AND MANAGEMENT ACT

Also known as the Magnuson Act, or the Magnuson-Stevens Fisheries Conservation and Management Act, this federal legislation directs how the National Marine Fisheries Service (NMFS) manages the nation's marine fisheries. This act empowered the federal government to regulate fishing from 3 nautical miles offshore (9 miles off the Florida Gulf Coast, Texas, and Puerto Rico) out to 200 nautical miles. This area is sometimes referred to as federal waters or the Exclusive Economic Zone. A main purpose of the act was to eliminate foreign commercial fishing while developing the United States commercial fishing industry.

This act created eight regional fishery management councils to advise NMFS on fisheries management issues. The voting members of the councils include a representative from each state fishery management agency, a mandatory appointee from each state, at-large appointees from any of the states in the region, and the regional director of NMFS. The councils produce fishery management plans (FMPs), with public input, that describe the nature and problems of a fishery and give regulatory recommendations to conserve the fishery; in other words, they define overfishing and spell out steps to prevent or correct overfishing. After approval by the Secretary of Commerce, regulations that implement management measures in the FMP become federal law and are enforced by NMFS.

In 1996, reauthorization of this act included an amendment that also required councils to identify all essential fish habitats including "those waters and substrate necessary for fish for spawning, feeding, or growth to maturity." Known as the Sustainable Fisheries Act, it is especially significant because it mandates not only the management of the harvest of commercial species, but also their environment. This act is thus a new legislative approach to environmental management.

See: Fisheries Management.

FISHFINDER

See: Sonar.

FISHFINDER RIG

A bottom fishing bait rig used in surf fishing *(see)*.

FISHFLIES

See: Dobsonflies, Fishflies, and Alderflies.

FISH HATCHERY

See: Fisheries Management; Hatchery.

FISHHOOK

See: Hook.

FISHING

The act of catching, or trying to catch, fish. The word "fishing" has a general meaning with no explicit distinction between commercial or recreational action or, in the latter case, the methods, techniques, or equipment employed. The words "angling" and "sportfishing" are often used interchangeably with the word "fishing," although they refer solely to the recreational activity and the implied usage of sporting equipment. Thus, a person who sets a net in saltwater and one who uses a trotline in freshwater are both fishing. The former is commercial fishing and the latter recreational fishing, but neither is angling or sportfishing.

However, the words "angling," "sportfishing," or "fishing" could describe a person using a rod and reel to catch fish for personal use.

See: Angler; Angling; Commercial Fisherman; Fisherman; Recreational Fisherman; Sportfisherman; Sportfishing.

FISHING CHAIR
See: Fighting Chair.

FISHING GUIDE

A person hired to take people fishing, usually by boat, sometimes on foot, in freshwater and saltwater. A guide is distinguished from the captain of a charter boat (see) by the size of the boat used and the number of people involved. Guides usually take one or two people fishing rather than a group. Although charter boat captains are commonly referred to as guides, charter boats are larger, capable of taking a group of people, and normally used on waters that require the comfort and security of a big vessel.

The types, abilities, and services of fishing guides vary as greatly as the species of fish, the conditions of fishing, and the nature of human beings. A guide may be associated with a fishing camp, lodge, or marina, or may be unaffiliated with any business. A guide may fish one body of water exclusively or many bodies of water; the guide may keep a boat on a trailer for mobility, starting each day wherever necessary, or the guide may keep a boat at a certain dock or marina and start each day from the same location. A mountain-country guide may use a canoe, jonboat, or inflatable that is hauled atop a truck and driven to whatever location is necessary. A guide may also accompany river, bank, or beach anglers by walking, wading, and fishing from shore or in the water. The possibilities are as broad as the fishing options.

The majority of fishing guides are found in freshwater by virtue of the number of opportunities, the differences in species and habits, and fewer charter boats (except in the Great Lakes). The craft that a freshwater guide uses includes canoes, jonboats, bass boats, walleye boats, and multipurpose craft, most accommodating two people in addition to the guide, and a few large enough to contain a third angler.

When a guide takes people for hire on navigable water under the jurisdiction of the Coast Guard, the guide must be certified by that agency and pass a rigorous examination to receive the mandatory captain's license. Even if that person operates a boat only on a bay, nearshore flats, or tidal river, and even if the person is called a "fishing guide," a captain's license is still required.

In all other cases, a guide is usually not required to have a captain's license, and the level of training, certification, and licensing varies greatly. In a few states, people who want to call themselves guides and hire out their services can do so without any

Guiding activities vary as widely as angling opportunities; these guided anglers are mooching for salmon in British Columbia.

formal process. In some states, the only requirement for being a guide is paying a fee to the appropriate government agency. In many Third World countries, there is usually no requirement for guiding, unless imposed by a lodge operator or outfitter. There, as well as in some North American locations, so-called guides are really boat drivers (although a boat driver with local waterway knowledge is important in many places).

Many states and Canadian provinces have a formal program established for guide certification. These vary but may include taking a written test(s) on fishing knowledge, game laws, water safety, and boating safety; demonstrating some level of in-field proficiency (this is rare); and completing basic first aid and cardiopulminary resuscitation (CPR) courses.

Formal training and government certification does not in itself make a person a good fishing guide. Many guides have been around boats, the water, and fishing all or most of their lives, and they don't need a government endorsement to be competent. On the other hand, plenty of people have become state certified to guide but are nevertheless not proficient at finding and catching fish. And no amount of training will help someone who just isn't good with people.

One thing that is especially worth remembering is that in many cases there is a lot of responsibility, above and beyond catching fish, involved in a day of guiding. Traveling at high speeds in relatively small open boats (like bass boats and flats boats) can pose a risk if something goes wrong, such as snapping a steering cable (unusual) or striking some hidden obstruction (much more likely). A cold body of water can be life-threatening if you get tossed into it as the result of an accident. Some places present dangers like alligators, crocodiles, piranhas, and snakes. Exposure to storms and high winds, getting stuck with a hook, and injury from a thrashing fish tethered to a multihooked lure are other possibilities. There is a practical necessity for cautious behavior and attention to everything that is going on. A reckless and careless individual should not be a guide.

Guides are most often hired by the day but may be hired for longer periods, a common practice at fishing lodges or camps. Fishing guide work is seasonal in many locations, year-round in a few; many fishing guides also work as hunting, rafting, hiking, and/or camping guides. Some guides provide a shore lunch service; this is especially common in northern lodges and camps and is a very pleasant experience, although one that can take a good chunk of fishing time out of the day.

Guides who do wilderness trips may be responsible for more than just fishing, especially if camping, canoeing, and portaging are involved. Guides who strictly take people fishing generally work 8 hours but may work 10 or 12, usually starting early in the day, although hours and times of day vary. In midsummer in some places, it is common to fish with a guide for several hours in the morning, break for midday when the sun is scorching, and resume in late afternoon. In places with limited runs of seasonally available fish, guides may have an 8-hour trip starting at dawn and then take another party on a 3- or 4-hour pre-dark trip as well.

Usually guides are reserved in advance for specific dates, with a deposit, and during peak seasons they may be fully booked in advance. In places where guides are numerous, it may be possible to hire a guide on the spur of the moment for a day (through a lodge, hotel, or booking service). Hiring a guide is generally an elective activity, although in some places (parts of Canada especially) the law mandates that a nonresident angler be accompanied by a guide; this is mostly a government employment issue rather than a practical matter or one of demonstrated necessity. Some lodges or camps require guide use as policy or as part of the total package they provide, and anglers are assigned a guide rather than being given the option of selecting one, although repeat clients may be given the option of reserving a specific guide.

A river guide rows a drift boat for steelhead anglers in Oregon.

General Issues

The benefits of a guide.   Hiring a guide doesn't brand you as someone who cannot catch fish on your own or who is deficient as an angler. Even if you have your own boat, or have plenty of fishing experience, there are times when you can benefit from using a guide. For some methods of fishing, or for species that you are unfamiliar with, or for locations that are tricky and foreign to you, a guide is an especially good idea.

It may, for example, be your intent to fish on your own for a week at a certain place. Hiring a guide for the first day of your week, learning the water, understanding the current conditions from the guide's perspective, seeing what the guide does, and more will improve the time spent on your own. Having the benefit of the guide's expertise for a day could save you a week of futility or at least a few days of blundering around figuring things out on your own. This is especially true if you don't fish that often or if you are completely new to that place and fishing.

Perhaps you need a guide because of tricky waters. Some places have dangerous sandbars, swift channels that have to be traversed, or other special conditions that not every person is able to handle equally well alone. In some northern Canada locations, for example, you have to use a guide because the waters are loaded with shallow rock reefs that will eat an outboard's lower unit or a boat hull, not to mention maybe putting you in a dangerous situation; the guide knows how to navigate here and has the responsibility that you may not want.

And, of course, in the most common scenario, a guide is someone that you can learn from. You're thinking of buying a certain type of boat? What better way to get acquainted with that model than to actually use it while fishing with a guide who has one? If you want to learn fly fishing for a particular species, then fish with a guide who specializes in this and tell the guide that you're there for instruction and education as much as, if not more than, fish-catching. Many guides are really good at teaching—about the body of water, about technique, about the habits of a certain species, etc. Unless they think that you're there to steal their spots, they'll explain the hows and whys to you, and the day not only will be a learning experience but also will produce fish as a bonus.

Although hiring a guide may be expensive on a per trip outing (with fees for two people in a boat costing from $150 to $450 a day, depending on guide, season, type of fishing, location, etc.), guide fees may be economical if you are otherwise limited in the number of times that you're able to go fishing. If, for example, you have a boat but can use it only 10 times per season for fishing, you might find that the cost of equipment, fuel, amortization, insurance, dockage, repair, gas, and other items is annually greater than if you hired a guide 10 times, especially if you pool the cost with someone else—not to mention that using your own boat means finding and catching your own fish instead of being with a professional who does it day in and day out.

If you really do want to do your own thing, then hiring a guide(s), like hiring a charter boat, is a terrific way of learning about boats, fishing methods, equipment, locations, and other issues, and is a practical prelude to going off solo. Many people have plunged deeply into some facet of sportfishing (and boat and equipment ownership) after having hired a few guides and have acquired a yen to do it all themselves (some becoming guides as a result).

Selecting. What makes a good guide? Ability to interact well with clients is foremost. That is closely followed by knowledge of the waters and fishing experience but also includes boat-handling ability and willingness to work to achieve success.

Naturally, a guide with a few years of experience, either on that particular water or on other waters, is preferred over someone who is guiding for the first time as a summer job. Someone who is inexperienced on that water will probably be fine if the person has had significant guiding background elsewhere or if you are otherwise assured of the person's guiding skill. Although there is no substitute for experience, a lot can be said for hustle and effort when combined with fishing acumen, and many young guides make up for their shorter guiding experience by having good judgment, willingness to experiment and adapt, and energetic effort. If you are especially interested in learning about a certain type of fishing, try to find a guide who specializes in that type. More guides today focus on light-tackle and fly fishing, for example, or on certain species.

In some places, you need a guide less to show you what to do than to get you to the right places. In distant waters, the concern you should have is not just one of being able to navigate properly in tricky places, but one of knowing where to fish when the obvious spots aren't producing.

The more traveling and fishing experiences that you have, the better you'll be able to satisfy yourself when hiring a guide. Some guides advertise in various media, exhibit at shows, and have brochures or information available. Some do little if any of this. Word-of-mouth referral is the number one factor in hiring guides, as it is in selecting fishing lodges. People who are satisfied with guides they've used are good sources of information. If you are considering a particular guide but have no recommendations, then ask the guide you're considering for references and follow up by speaking to those references.

While word-of-mouth is helpful, it isn't essential. Clearly you have to first learn of the existence of a guide from some source. That process includes reading articles, attending sport shows, looking at advertisements and television shows, attending lectures, etc. If possible, try to visit a guide at a sport show, lecture hall, or other location. Speaking face to face is the best way to get direct answers to specific questions and also to see if you connect with this person and could establish a rapport in a day (or more) together on the water. This is also a prime opportunity to go beyond obvious questions and into details.

Articles in newspapers and magazines reflect the experiences of someone who has been there. Seldom are articles published about bad guides or locations. Sportswriters who review angling destinations and fish with guides focus on the positive. One of the drawbacks of most newspaper or magazine articles is that they place too much emphasis on exceptional catches and outstanding days. A result can be that a reader's expectations are easily raised too high. This is even more acute with television fishing shows; most people fail to realize that 23 minutes of constant video fishing action may have taken one or two weeks to actually experience and film. Seldom do all those TV lunkers fall cast after cast in real life, although it seems like they do on the tube. Every guide should have that kind of success on a daily basis! So, consider the reliability of these sources of information, and look through them with a careful eye to search for the details that are most important to you.

When you talk to a guide, find out if the person guides full- or part-time. Some part-time guides are excellent, but there is no substitute for being on the water daily. This is more critical in some types of fishing than others, and guides who fish every day usually don't have to spend much time on each outing figuring things out, especially when conditions change frequently and when pursuing species that move a lot.

Most guides that are booked in advance require a deposit, which is customarily refunded if you have to cancel. Inquire about cancellation policies and payment procedures, extra costs (bait or unusual gas consumption), etc. If you have special medical concerns, or any ailments or disabilities, you should discuss them. This is not as obvious an issue as it seems. You may, for example, have to get down to a boat from a high dock at low tide; if you are weak-legged that may prove too difficult or dangerous. Or, you may need to cross a few miles of potentially rough water in a small boat to get to the sacred fishing grounds; the pounding of the boat on rough water could aggravate a back condition. Often the guide can work around these issues, but you should bring them up.

Communication. Although many guided fishing trips go well and many first-time clients become repeat clients (in fact, repeat business is the backbone of a guide's success), some guided trips do not go as well as people would like. Changing weather and water conditions often cause this, and a conscientious guide will let you know if you should expect a problem. A good guide will cancel a trip if conditions are unsafe or if the fishing has been so poor that the guide knows you'll be wasting

F

your time. It is much better for a guide to be honest and upfront about things and reschedule you at another time than to take your money in the face of a hopeless situation (which the guide may recognize but you probably won't).

Often, however, dissatisfactions with a guide or a day of guided fishing have to do with the client's failure to communicate. You have to tell your guide right at the beginning of the day, or maybe even when you book a trip, what you want and what you are particularly interested in. Most guides are very accommodating. In some cases, you must let a guide know in advance about your interests so that the guide can be prepared (with the right tackle, required bait, and so forth) ahead of time and not have to waste potentially important early fishing time.

If you have a particular interest in mind, as many experienced anglers do (this might include how far you travel by boat during the day, how long you stay in a certain place, whether you would prefer to have an in-boat lunch instead of a shore lunch, etc.), let your guide know. If you don't care for a certain kind of fishing or situation (like traveling a great distance for remote fishing only to be bunched with a group of other boats in the same place), tell your guide. But you'll get much further if you do this in a pleasant rather than confrontational manner or by barking like a general. You may be a big shot on the home front, and you are paying for the guide's services, but most guides are independent types who will tolerate a jerk for only so long.

Communication problems may occur with guides in foreign countries, especially when there is a language barrier. The client has to be the one to try to overcome this. Many native guides are very willing to please but don't always understand what the client wants, particularly regarding the fishing method (casting versus trolling, for example) and location selection. If you will be departing a camp or houseboat in the morning for a day of fishing, it's wise to construct your own plan before you leave and discuss it with someone at the base camp who can relay your interests and desires to the guide; if you don't do this, at least find out ahead of time what the guide is planning on doing so that you know what to expect during the day. Otherwise, you may think or assume that the guide understands you and then find yourself taken to some place you didn't want to go to (perhaps the same area that you fished the day before) and doing something that you didn't want to do. When this happens, typically the client gets mad and starts shouting, the guide doesn't understand the problem but knows the client is unhappy, and things deteriorate.

Many non-English-speaking guides try to learn to speak the client's language, but there is no guarantee that a passing acquaintance with English will lessen communication problems. Smart traveling anglers try to compile a list of key words and phrases in the local language (mostly Spanish, and Portuguese in Brazil) so that they can convey, however crudely, what they want (such as, "Can we move closer to shore," "I'd like to fish shallower," "Let's move to another spot," etc.). When there is a language barrier, it does not pay to get mad at the guide. Better to try to involve the guide in the pursuit, politely show the guide what to do (such as handling and releasing the fish more carefully), and give sincere praise or thanks where due. Treat the guide fairly and like an equal. The guide will be happier with you and will try much harder, even if you're unable to speak in complete sentences to each other.

When you can communicate with your guide, by all means ask plenty of questions; guides are used to this, although they do get tired of the same questions over and over again. A guide who is sullen and uncommunicative is not much fun to be with, but the person may make up for this by producing a great fishing experience. Many native guides in northern Canada have been criticized for monosyllabic responses, for a lack of communication and effort, and for ignoring the wishes of clients, but this is not a universal occurrence. Cultural differences and other issues are at play here, so you may need to dig into your motivational grab bag to get somewhere. On the other hand, some guides are truly unique and interesting characters but spend more time gabbing, telling jokes, and entertaining than working to produce fish. Storytelling is nice, but not if it's the sum result of a day mostly spent sitting on a hole waiting for something to happen. Obviously the ideal guide is someone interesting and perhaps entertaining to be with, yet one who really knows fishing and works at it to produce good results.

Fishing Issues

When in Rome. From the guide's perspective, the ideal client is someone who is a decent person to be with, a reasonably able angler, a person who can follow instructions, and someone who knows that fishing is not magic. Many clients do not understand that at times no one catches fish, or that even the best efforts can fail to produce, or that the lack of production is due to the inabilities of the angler rather than the guide. It is not always the guide's fault when you don't have a successful day; the fact that most inexperienced anglers do not understand this, or expect that paying a guide ensures success, is very frustrating to a guide.

You don't have to be a world-traveled angler to impress a guide. In fact, you shouldn't try to impress a guide with your knowledge and experience. If you're good, the guide will know soon enough. Many guides are shocked and pleased to find clients who can tie their own knots and unhook their own fish, and will let clients do so if they wish. Most people who talk a good line can't produce, and a guide finds this out fast. In fact, many guides recognize that the clients dressed in the latest brand-name outdoor wear are more fashion savvy than fishing savvy.

No matter what your level of experience, until you've developed a rapport with a guide, yield to the guide's direction and ways. In many types of fishing, there is a bit of a knack to doing certain things (hooking a bait, for example, or jigging method, or retrieval technique), and the guide would not do a certain thing unless the guide thought it was best. After all, the primary object is catching fish, and whether or not you catch fish is often the yardstick for measuring a day's success. A good guide wants to produce results and wants to do what will best accomplish that. Yield to the guide's discretion when reasonable; the guide should know best and, most of the time, does know best. That doesn't mean that some technique or lure or approach that you have in mind isn't worth trying or suggesting. Some experienced anglers know things that some guides have yet to learn, and you might teach the guide something (but don't do it by insulting the guide) that will benefit both of you.

Guides, however, are often frustrated by anglers who don't pay attention to what they are told and who do things their way rather than the guide's way. Some anglers have just enough fishing experience to think they know a lot, and these people are among the worst offenders because they already have developed habits and methods, whereas inexperienced anglers have not. Many guides say that greater success is achieved by children and women with little or no fishing experience, rather than by men with considerable experience, because the former follow instructions and pay better attention. There's a lesson here.

In instances where there is a knack to setting the hook, or a preferred method of doing so for a particular species and the way it strikes (like steelhead and salmon), many guides say that they have problems with people who are avid bass anglers. These anglers have a tendency to reel down and rear back ferociously on the hookset, sometimes ripping the hooks out of fish. So, listen to the guide, and if the guide says that you just have to lift up and keep a tight line, then do it that way.

Does the guide fish?   This is an important issue to inquire about. In most types of guided fishing, the guide does not fish unless invited to by the client or unless the guide has to show the client how to do something. In some types of fishing, especially bass fishing, it is common for a guide to fish as much as or more than the client. Bass guides who have fully equipped bass boats and strictly cast lures are particularly likely to do this. Such guides run their boats from the bow and usually get first presentations at most cover; inevitably they catch a lot of fish during a good day. In effect, the clients are subsidizing the guide's fishing habit. A guide should fish only if there is prior agreement. If you have strong feelings about a guide fishing, then you should discuss the issue beforehand. But be forewarned that you are likely to meet resistance from bass guides, since this practice has become common.

In some cases, having several lures in the water will maximize your opportunities, and the lure or tactic that the guide is using may prove best. However, while the guide might show you this technique or strategy, the real object of a day of guided fishing is to get the client(s) to catch fish. In muskie fishing, for example, where the opportunities to catch fish are few and far between, a desirable outcome is not one in which a guide fishes and catches a muskie while the clients do not. If you merely wanted to see a muskie you could go to an aquarium. However, if the action on a given day or at a certain time/place is plentiful, then letting the guide fish is generous and appropriate, as long as boat handling and other chores are not neglected.

Hooksetting and rod handling.   Although hooksetting and rod handling are more of an issue when you are fishing on charter boats than when fishing with a guide, on some guided fishing occasions the guide still hooks a fish and hands the rod to a client or takes a rod out of a holder, sets the hook, and then hands the client the rod. The reason that the guide does this is to ensure that the fish is well-hooked and to increase the chances of it being landed. For most people, especially in freshwater, such an action is not a problem. However, a few anglers will not take a rod and fight a fish if someone else has first set the hook and then attempted to hand over the rod. They feel that it's unfair and that the person who set the hook should play the fish. If one person sets the hook and then hands the rod to someone else, and the fish turns out to be a world-record candidate, that action, according to International Game Fish Association (IGFA) rules, would be judged unfair and would disqualify the catch from record consideration, much to the consternation of the person who caught the would-have-been record fish. Most big-game anglers, and many light-tackle saltwater anglers, are familiar with this rule but the majority of anglers are not.

If you have any concerns or interests in regard to establishing a record *(see)* catch, then no one else should touch your rod. If you feel strongly that having someone set the hook and hand you a rod is unfair, then you should make your feelings known to the guide or discuss it with the guide before the moment of truth arrives. There is, after all, something to be said for feeling the strike and setting the hook by yourself, since that is one of the intrinsically appealing aspects of sportfishing.

If you need instruction on the proper manner of setting the hook for the species being pursued or the method being employed, the guide should be able to instruct you; most guides are patient while you are trying to get the technique right. After all, it's your fishing trip.

If you have no qualms about being handed a rod, no concerns about records (the chances of catching a record fish are usually slim), and no deep feelings about setting the hook yourself, then these concerns are a nonissue. Most guides simply want

The first of the 10 plagues of Egypt, described in *The Bible's* book of Exodus, may be one of the earliest recorded instances of a red tide (" . . . and all the waters that were in the river were turned to blood. And the fish that were in the river died; and the river stank. . . . ").

F

their customers to catch fish, and since the guides are on the water every day, they are on top of their game while most of the customers are not. The majority of anglers, especially in freshwater, don't have any problem with taking a rod that someone has handed them, but most of them also don't understand all of the ramifications.

The best-time dilemma. The best times (or those perceived to be the best) are usually booked first by anglers-in-the-know, many of whom are repeat clients. How honestly a guide deals with this issue will tell you a lot about how the person conducts business. Ideally, any time in a given season will be a good time to visit; in a few cases this may be true but usually it is not. The best guides will tell you that this is so, and they will squarely lay out your options and explain to you how things differ at nonprime times. They will also tell you that conditions may not be the same from year to year on given dates and that weather (cold, excessive rain, excessive heat, storms) and other forces beyond their control can affect your success, even at those times that are usually reliable.

It is entirely possible to be somewhere at what is ordinarily the "best" time, with one of the best guides in the business, yet have terrible fishing. Experienced anglers know this happens. But many people who visit good fishing spots are not skillful or experienced anglers and do not understand this point.

Tackle and other gear. Although charter boats supply all customary fishing equipment unless specialized angling is preferred, a guide may or may not furnish equipment. For some types of specialized fishing (drifting egg sacks or pulling plugs for big salmon and steelhead, for example, or drifting with bait for striped bass), the fishing outfits and all terminal rigging will be supplied by the guide. Some guides, like those who fish on saltwater flats, provide tackle but invite you to bring your own if you choose; they'll check your equipment to see if it's suitable for the anticipated action. Some guides do not provide any fishing equipment other than bait or terminal rigs, and they expect you to bring your own; this is true for most bass fishing guides. Guides at distant locations (the Canadian wilderness, the South American interior, etc.) rarely have any tackle for you, although a lodge may supply some loaner equipment or sell lures and terminal items. Here, you usually are expected to bring whatever you'll need, and the guide provides no tackle (and may not have any in the boat either).

Naturally, guides who do not provide equipment should charge less than those who do. You should inquire about the equipment issue beforehand; when you are bringing tackle, ask the guide for recommendations. The majority of people who fish with a guide are relatively inexperienced, or at least unaccustomed to the style of fishing or the species pursued by the guide in that location. Many guides thus use fairly heavy tackle to compensate for their customers' lack of experience. An experienced angler who is skilled at light-tackle use will probably be disappointed most of the time when using the standard gear supplied by a guide, because it is in the medium to heavy range for durability. However, some guides specialize in certain techniques or species, and they cater to anglers with these interests or abilities, so they will have the corresponding tackle and their gear will be high quality.

Anglers who fish with guides are expected to bring their own food, beverages, and personal comfort items (sunglasses, sunscreen, foul weather gear, etc.). Anglers are expected to wear appropriate footwear for some types of boats; nonscuff boating shoes or sneakers are good for most situations, although in cold locations and in the far north a pair of warm waterproof boots may be necessary. Where a license is required, it is usually the client's responsibility to obtain it, but a good guide will check for one or assist in obtaining one if necessary. Sometimes guides are able to obtain licenses in advance for clients who are arriving too late to get the licenses themselves, or guides may get licenses required by bordering states/provinces, for which guides should be reimbursed.

It's a good idea to bring extra food, drink, or treats to share with the guide. The matter of beverage is left to personal discretion, but it is poor form for a guide to consume any alcoholic beverage while on the water, and clients shouldn't offer any. Some lodges and outfitters prohibit the consumption of alcohol by guides and request that anglers not give or offer any to their guides, either on the water or as a gratuity. Generally it is a good policy for anglers not to consume any alcohol while fishing for obvious practical reasons *(see: safety)*. Water and juice are the best cold beverages, especially under hot conditions.

Tipping. Tipping a guide is customary, and the tip, of course, varies depending upon the activities, the effort the guide has made, and whether any exceptionally good (or bad) things have happened. The customary cash tip for a guide is usually $15–20 per person per day for most fishing ($30 to $40 for a pair of anglers); a lesser tip might be in order if you have had major problems and more if the day is truly spectacular or extra services are rendered. Some guides will clean fish that are kept, but others do not; those that do, deserve something extra for this service. If you catch a record or contest-winning fish with a guide, then a suitable bonus is appropriate.

Sometimes anglers give tips in the form of merchandise, including fishing tackle, in lieu of, or in addition to, a cash tip. In distant locations where good equipment is costly or hard to obtain, fishing tackle (reel, tackle box, spools of line, etc.) may be especially appreciated by the guide for personal use or for its trading value. In poor countries, clothing items in addition to the cash tip are very welcome; you'd be surprised how much a T-shirt with a fish design on it is appreciated.

In distant places, however, you should check with the outfitter or lodge manager to see if it is appropriate to give a guide fishing equipment. In some Mexican bass lakes, for example, lodge managers discourage this, fearing that such tackle will wind up being used by someone for commercial fishing, and thus have a negative impact on the resource. See: Fishing Lodge.

FISHING LICENSE
See: Regulations.

FISHING LODGE

A loosely used term that applies to facilities of various quality levels that cater to anglers (sometimes hunters and other recreationists) and that are either on or close to desirable angling waters. A lodge may provide only accommodations, food, and proximity to fishing spots; or it may also provide guides, boats, instruction, dockage, launch ramp, equipment, or some combination thereof. Accommodations may range from deluxe five-star resort quality with matching cuisine to a spartan main house with tent-frame cabins and family-style dining. Fishing lodges are sometimes referred to as camps, although camp usually signifies a facility with humble, if not rugged, accommodations, perhaps even of a temporary or tent nature. Lodges may house just a handful of people at one time or 50 to 60. Some popular lodges in the Pacific Northwest can accommodate more than that.

Fishing lodges exist in remote as well as readily accessible locations. They advertise in various media, exhibit at shows, and may be represented by booking agents and outfitters who specialize in outdoor travel. The better ones are usually booked well in advance, especially during peak fishing times. Most operate seasonally, although some are open year-round and others for a very limited time because of weather and water conditions; far-northern Canadian lodges have only a six-week season.

Selecting. Many lodges are too remote for people to visit personally before booking a stay, and since there are so many lodges, most with attractive brochures and rather generous claims, it can be difficult to select one that meets your interests, abilities, and budget.

The more traveling and fishing experiences that you have, the better you'll be able to satisfy yourself when selecting a fishing lodge. Astute lodge owners and their representatives make this chore a little easier by anticipating the kinds of things that you might want to know about and by providing you with those particulars in their literature to help you make a decision.

That decision-making starts with how you learn about a prospective lodge in the first place. Word-of-mouth referral is the number one factor in getting people to a fishing lodge that they've never visited

The ideal setting, such as this one in coastal British Columbia, is remote and beautiful.

before. The recommendation of satisfied customers, especially if they are serious anglers, is important, and you should talk to anyone that you know who has been to a lodge that you're interested in.

While word-of-mouth is helpful, it isn't essential. Clearly you first have to learn of the lodge's existence from some source. That process includes reading articles, attending sport shows, looking at advertisements and television shows, attending slide lectures, checking direct mailings, soliciting booking agents, and so forth.

If you can visit a lodge owner at a sport show, you should do so. Shows include many exhibits by lodges and outfitters whose booths are usually manned by owners and/or their families and employees. Speaking with these people is the best possible way to get direct answers to specific questions. This is a prime opportunity to go beyond obvious questions (When is the best time to visit? or What lures should I bring?) to the most intricate matters (Are there reefs and shoals in the lake? If so, how deep are they and do you need sonar to locate them? Do they hold walleye throughout the summer?). Answers to such specifics will help an ardent angler make up his or her mind as well as plan ahead. Sometimes, booths are manned by people who are filling in for the lodge owner, and who cannot answer the most detailed angling questions; that doesn't mean the place is unsuitable, but you will have to dig deeper for information.

Articles in newspapers and magazines reflect the experiences of someone who has been there. Seldom are articles published about bad lodges. Be aware, however, that sportswriters who review angling destinations focus on the positive and may omit negative comments about places that are otherwise commendable. The sportswriters usually receive red carpet treatment, visit at the best times, and are hosted to some extent by the lodge, so it is easy to accentuate the positive and bypass some of the things that are not as notable.

Many fishing lodges are known for good food; this is the dining area of a lodge in Pará, Brazil.

Not all of the things that interest or concern you will be mentioned in any article, and reading a very positive article doesn't prevent you from asking probing questions. In fact, it ought to help focus your questions. Photographs accompanying an article may be helpful in establishing the setting and the kind of place it is, but often the photos are too few or of people holding fish and little is seen of the other aspects of the lodge, the locale, or the body of water.

Keep in mind that most newspaper and magazine articles place too much emphasis on exceptional catches and outstanding days. They fail to note that every day was not fabulous and did not produce a monstrous fish, or that only one behemoth was caught all week even though there were 15 people at the lodge, or that it took a particularly skillful angler to really do well. A glowing account may raise readers' expectations too high, and when people do not attain the same level of achievement, they feel that the author of the article lied or that some special circumstances were at work. They're disappointed when they do not experience what the author experienced. This problem is even more acute with television fishing shows; most people fail to realize that 23 minutes of constant video fishing action may have taken one or two weeks to actually experience and film. Seldom do all of those TV lunkers fall cast after cast in real life, although it seems like they do on the tube.

It's important to note that the skill level of the angler who wrote an encouraging article about a good fishing locale may be quite different from the skill level of most other anglers. Of course, some readers will be better anglers and may find even better fishing than the author described, but many readers will be much less proficient and may be inadvertently set up for disappointment. Make sure that you ask the lodge staff whether you can expect to have the same kind of experience or whether you need special skill levels to do so.

One of the first things you'll do is look over the lodge's literature, usually a brochure, obtained from the lodge or its agent. This will range from a black-and-white photocopy to a glossy color folder. Be wary of the former and of literature that appears to have been hastily slapped together; that may reflect on the rest of the operation as well. Don't be too expectant based on the photos either. In the best brochures, the boats, rooms, facilities, and scenes seldom look as impressive in person as they do when the photographs were taken from the best possible angle, in the best possible light, with a telephoto or wide angle lens, and under the best of circumstances. Some lodges also offer videotapes, which give you a better feel for the type of water, boats, and facilities, as well as the area in general. Many also have Web sites, and the same issues apply to these as to literature.

Many lodge brochures and Web sites give good details about accommodations, food, and services but are less specific about actual fishing information, which is described in general and glowing terms, although there are certainly exceptions. Ardent anglers usually want as many particulars as possible about the fishing (boats, angling styles, equipment needs, etc.). If the lodge has guides, the brochure or other information may say that the guides will help you achieve success, but that may not be enough if success depends on casting extremely accurately but you cannot, or having the proper equipment for a technique but you don't. Lodges that are really fishing-oriented put together a seasonally detailed description of angling activity.

Most brochures and Web sites depict large fish, especially camp-record fish, but sometimes these are very old photos of fish taken years ago. What have you done lately? is a good question to ask. Be wary of photos that show strings or piles of dead fish; lodges that appeal to meat hogs tend to emphasize that aspect more than others. Many people aren't pleased to be at a place where the major interest of the staff and guests is in poundage and full coolers.

Look for a commitment to resource conservation and to the continuation of quality fishing. Far more lodges and outfitters are interested in advocating this today than in the past, because the clientele has matured into one that recognizes the value of sportsmanship and conservation. A lodge whose policy allows keeping only one trophy fish of a particular species, or total catch-and-release other than for a shore lunch meal, is one that is not attracting the meat hog element and is interested in having quality angling for the future. This kind of lodge plans to be around in the future rather than trying to make a quick buck, and it will be a place worth returning to.

Speaking to someone who has been to the lodge or the waters in question is an excellent idea, and some places encourage this and will gladly supply a few references. If a lodge doesn't volunteer this, ask. Certainly a lodge is only going to refer you to someone who has had a positive experience, but in speaking to such a person you can learn some valuable things. Among other questions, ask what the angler would do differently if he or she were to return (a different time of the season, different gear, things they wouldn't do, etc.). Ask for a guide, cabin, or room recommendation.

Here are some other topics to consider:

Distance to fishing grounds.   Here's a subject many people don't inquire about. Great Bear and Great Slave Lakes in the Northwest Territories are excellent examples because they have good fishing, but much of it takes place considerable distances from the lodges. It is not uncommon to boat daily between one and two hours each way to get to the favored spots on these huge lakes. A lot of potential fishing time is spent riding. Maybe the time is worth it if you're assured of catching a big lake trout; but since such assurances cannot realistically be made, you may find the long boat rides unappealing.

Long boat rides may be worth taking once during a week's stay, especially if you can pick the right day. When it's calm, the ride can be quite nice, but when the wind picks up and you have to venture in rough open water for a great distance in a small boat with aluminum seats, little or no rump padding, and no back support, it can be uncomfortable (and wet) for many, and intolerable for those with back problems.

The distance issue is also relative to getting to the boats. Find out how far it is from the lodge to the boats, and how rugged the walk is.

How rigorous will the activities be? Some distant fishing adventures require getting in and out of high-sided boats and airplanes, assisting with portages, toting gear, trekking through rugged terrain, and so forth. They may entail enduring cold weather, extreme heat and humidity, exposure to biting insects, encounters with dangerous animals (bears especially), or exposure to other dangers. The personal safety and medical implications here seem quite obvious. Some lodges and outfitters will properly detail the nature of things and forewarn clients. But this is not always the case. When the client asks, "Why didn't you tell me?", the response may be, "You didn't ask." So ask.

The guides.   A guide can make or break a trip. Not all guides are good, not all guides have been guiding very long, and in some places anyone can hang out a "guide shingle." What makes a good guide? Ability to interact well with clients is foremost. That is closely followed by knowledge of the waters and fishing experience but also includes boat handling ability and willingness to work to achieve success.

Everyone wants to get the lodge's top guide, which is impossible. It is reasonable to ask how many guides there are, how many years they have guided on the waters you will be fishing, if some specialize in certain techniques (fly fishing, trolling, etc.), and other questions. Better to be with someone who has a few years of experience on that water than with someone who is guiding for the first time

as a summer job. Someone who is inexperienced on that water might be fine, however, if the person has had guiding experience elsewhere, or if the lodge owner assures you that the person is skillful. The concern here is not just being able to navigate properly in tricky places, but knowing where to fish when the obvious spots aren't producing. If you are especially interested in learning about fishing techniques, ask if you can be placed with a guide who is able and willing to communicate and show you how things are done.

Boats, motors, PFDs.   Although this maxim is not carved in stone, it's generally better to be at a place where the motors and perhaps the boats are replaced fairly often. Most lodges replace their motors on a two-year cycle, sometimes annually. Motors are the lifeblood of many remote fishing experiences, and they have to work like a clock. In many places they are put through their paces all season, being run a lot and also abused, so it's a good investment for a lodge to change them frequently.

Boats don't need replacing as frequently, but it is not reassuring to arrive at a lodge where the boats are obviously old and battered. But if they are functional and, most importantly, don't leak, it may not matter. On the White River in Arkansas, a lot of older flat-bottomed boats are in guide use, but these are specialized craft and well cared for, so a newer boat is not always a necessity.

Safety equipment is a necessity, however, and personal flotation devices (PFDs) are the foremost concern. Some lodges don't put PFDs in the boats or may supply inadequate ones (a 200-pound angler isn't well served with a medium adult vest or a skimpy Type I orange neck-wrapper). Ask what they have. A top-quality lodge should have Type III upright flotation PFDs. You may want to bring your own. There is no harm in asking about the age of any lodge's boats and motors and about the availability of PFDs. Your life could depend on them.

Clothing and gear needs.   Most lodges will advise clients what to bring; some provide more detailed and specific advice than others. Foul weather gear is always important but often underappreciated by novice travelers, who may not know what good rain gear and truly nasty weather are. Remember to ask whether you'll need waders and whether they should be lightweight models or the heavier (and bulky to pack) neoprene versions. In some places, you may need to bring a survival suit or snowmobile suit.

Specific advice about tackle needs (fly rod length and fly line size, for example) is never unwelcome. Experienced anglers can give themselves latitude, but the inexperienced need very explicit instructions. A lodge that will provide you with these details is one that is looking out for your best interests in all aspects of the experience.

The best-time dilemma.   The best times (or those perceived to be the best) are usually booked first by anglers-in-the-know, many of whom are repeat clients. How honestly a lodge owner or agent deals with this issue will tell you a lot about how he or she conducts business. Ideally, any time of a given season will be a good time to visit, and in a few cases this may be true, but usually it is not. The best lodge operators will tell you that this is so, and they will squarely lay out your options and explain to you how things differ at nonprime times. They will also tell you that conditions may not be the same from year to year on given dates and that weather (cold, excessive rain, excessive heat, storms) and other forces beyond their control can affect your success.

It is entirely possible to visit at what is ordinarily the "best" time, yet the fishing is terrible. Experienced anglers know this happens. But a lot of people who visit good fishing spots are not skillful or experienced anglers and do not understand this point. Many lodges don't warn people about this, perhaps because they fear losing a prospective customer, but it's better to be forewarned than to learn after the fact when disappointment and frustration have set in.

Of course, there are other concerns regarding the selection of a fishing lodge, including deposit, cancellation, and final payment policies; extra costs (such as fly-out trips); travel routing (including overnight stays); special food concerns; language barriers, particularly with guides; availability and cost (usually high) of tackle at the lodge; and so forth. Ask.

The agent route.   Some booking agents represent fishing lodges all over the world. If they have visited the places that they represent, they can give you a first-hand evaluation or direct you to another place within your means, interests, and abilities. They should be able to refer you to people who have been there if they have not. They probably know the best air routes to take and what to advise in terms of scheduling. It should not cost any more to use an agent, whose fee is derived from a percentage of the overall package cost, than to make the booking yourself.

See: Charter Boat; Guide.

FISHING PRESSURE

The amount of fishing effort generated is called fishing pressure. Effort is the time, expressed in number of people, boats, hours, days, and other units of measurement, as well as some combination of these, that is applied to one species or group of species. Biologists calculate effort for management purposes, especially through surveys or through landings (see) that have been reported. Anglers broadly refer to the number and frequency of people fishing as fishing pressure.

Excessive sportfishing pressure or effort in freshwater and saltwater may not reduce populations but may result in more difficult angling and a lower success rate. When combined with harvesting for personal or commercial purposes, the result may be overfishing (see).

In freshwater, the more popular species of fish, and those at the top of the food chain, are especially likely to be subject to heavy, and perhaps excessive, fishing pressure. In saltwater, some species (such as tarpon) are only targeted by anglers, and the effect of fishing pressure varies. Many saltwater fish are sought by commercial as well as recreational interests, and fishing pressure combines effort and landings. A different level of harvest is achieved and may result in overfishing.

See: Fisheries Management.

FISHING REGULATIONS

See: Regulations.

FISHING TACKLE

See: Tackle.

FISHKILL

The die-off of fish, usually in numbers. Fishkills may occur as the result of chemical pollution, especially from pesticides in agricultural runoff, but most often happen as a result of insufficient oxygen in the water.

A winter fishkill occurs when ice and snow cut off the transfer of oxygen from the air to the water; the oxygen in the water gets used up, and fish die. This does not happen if there is enough oxygen in the water to last throughout the winter until the ice and snow melt.

A summer fishkill usually occurs when inadequate amounts of oxygen exist in the water during extended periods of hot, calm, and cloudy days. Warm summer water temperatures, high demands for oxygen, and days with no sunlight or wind to mix the surface water may lead to oxygen demands exceeding oxygen production. When this happens, distressed fish may be seen as they rise to the surface and gasp for oxygen, and dead fish may be seen floating on the surface.

FISH LADDER

See: Fishway.

FISH POISONING

See: Ciguatera.

FISH PREPARATION—CARE

There are no apologies here for killing and keeping *some* fish to eat. Indeed, surveys reveal that one of the primary purposes of sportfishing—and a chief benefit—is getting fish for the table, especially fresh fish. This includes numerous species that are not available in supermarkets or fish markets, species that are available only seasonally, and species that command very high prices commercially.

Many species of fish that are classified by state agencies as gamefish *(see)* cannot legally be sold in the United States, meaning that to enjoy them you have to catch them, or someone else has to catch them and share with you. If species classified as gamefish are available in markets, they have probably been imported from distant places where they can legally be sold, or they have been raised through aquaculture. Connoisseurs who know the difference will affirm that most species of farm-raised fish are not fully comparable to the same species from the wild.

Most species of freshwater fish taken from the wild cannot be sold. Even trout offered by the finest restaurants is not from the wild; those restaurant fish are raised in hatcheries, and although they seem good to many patrons, they rarely compare favorably in appearance or taste to a wild, native trout.

Eating the fish that you or friends and family catch is nearly as satisfying as catching a fish on a lure of your own making. In a world where most of the flesh from living creatures comes to us in sanitized pressure-wrapped packaging, having been killed and prepared by others, catching, cleaning, and eating your own fish is a direct reminder of the connection and dependence that human beings have always had upon these creatures. Of course, fish have a high nutritional value and, if properly cared for, are delicious when prepared in many different ways.

The key to enjoying fish isn't necessarily having a good recipe or using a certain method of preparation. Once the fish is in the kitchen, you can increase or decrease its palatability, but to enjoy its fullest taste and nutrition, you must give it proper attention from the moment you catch it until the moment you prepare it for the table. The advantage that anglers have over people who buy commercially caught fish is that anglers get their food as fresh as it can possibly be found, and they alone control its preparations and treatment. The foundation for enjoying fish and for having good-tasting fish is the treatment that this product receives after it is caught, the care that is given to transporting it from where it is caught to where it will be stored or consumed, and the storage that it receives between cleaning and preparing for consumption. The end results will be only as good as you want them to be, and as good as you make them.

There may be no other food that loses its freshness as quickly as fish. The flesh of a fish does not improve with aging, so it is literally true that the best time to eat a fish is immediately after it has been caught. Such a gastronomic utopia can be realized on big boats with galleys, in locations where a shore lunch is possible, and in situations when you are camping on or near the water or can head to the house immediately after catching a fish. Most of the time, however, eating a fish soon after catching it is not possible or feasible, or happens only occasionally.

Therefore, to avoid spoilage and to keep fish as fresh as possible, you should begin caring for it as soon as you've finished taking photos and congratulating yourself on your accomplishment. Unfortunately, many anglers, after devoting a lot of energy, time, and perhaps money to sportfishing, take fair to poor care of their catch, because of either ignorance, expedience, or lack of planning. Their fish may lose freshness even before it gets to the place of cleaning or storage. You can tell when a fish has lost its freshness because it looks dried and shriveled, it smells, the eyes are glossy, the skin is bleached, the flesh is soft, and so on. Fish that exhibit these conditions may be edible, but the manner of handling has contributed to some loss of freshness and therefore tastiness. Incidentally, a fish exhibiting these conditions is not necessarily unfit for consumption; the fish is simply not as fresh as it could be for maximum benefit. Many people take minimal care of their fish, yet still find them delicious. Clearly, some people are not as discriminating as others, and the purpose of the following information is to make you more discriminating so that you enjoy the fullest benefit and taste from your catch.

There are three main aspects to proper care: what you do after catching, what you do after cleaning, and how the fish is transported if more than just a short period of time is involved. Each of these is important and is linked to the others. It does no good to properly care for a fish until you get it home and then store it improperly for later consumption. On the other hand, if you've let a fish become stale in the hours after catching it, it will not improve in flavor no matter how well you later wrap and store it.

Many anglers recognize that fish are good to eat, but strangely enough they do not equate taste with proper handling. They, their spouses, or friends may spend more time looking up a recipe for the fish than caring for it in the first place.

Start out with plenty of ice to help keep your catch in great shape.

Spoilage Facts

Changes take place in a fish after it is caught because of its biological composition and its environment. These changes begin when a fish is hooked, and they continue after it dies.

When a fish is hooked, it is engaged in a struggle for its life. It gets energy for this struggle from the glycogen in its muscles. (Glycogen is the animal kingdom's version of starch.) The longer the fish struggles, the more it depletes its energy reserve. This depletion can cause physiological changes. The fish's flesh may lose some of its natural sweetness, and metabolic products that can affect its flavor and texture begin to accumulate. These changes begin even before the fish is landed. Thus, a fish that will be used for food should be landed quickly.

As soon as a fish dies, an irreversible spoilage process begins. This process occurs through the activity of enzymes and bacteria. Enzymes that normally regulate a fish's metabolism can work unchecked after it dies. Digestive enzymes may begin to digest the fish itself, causing belly burn or softening of the flesh around the gut. This is especially likely if a fish is caught while feeding, since its digestive enzymes will already be active. Other enzymes in fish muscle can also begin to affect the flavor and texture of the fillet. These enzymes work rapidly at warm temperatures.

Fish are also subject to bacterial degradation after death. Natural barriers that protect fish while they are alive break down when they die. Bacteria from the environment and the gut can grow and multiply in fish tissue. This activity diminishes fish quality and eventually causes spoilage. Bacteria also grow rapidly at warm temperatures.

Finally, the highly unsaturated fat in fish is also affected by oxygen in the air. Oxygen reacts with this fat to produce the odors and flavors associated with rancidity. Fat oxidation can be a serious problem if the fish is to be frozen or stored for very long. This is one reason why fattier fish (like bluefish) do not remain in good condition during frozen storage as long as leaner fish (like flounder).

After the Catch

Preparations for taking care of your catch should really begin before you head to the water. In other words, before you go fishing, give some thought to whether you want to keep any of the catch and then to how you will store and transport it to maintain maximum freshness. If you catch a fish that you want to keep and have to ask "Now what?" you haven't planned properly. If you catch a fish you want to keep and you just toss it aside in the boat until you head for home, shame on you.

Let's say you've caught a good fish and it's been unhooked. Where are you going to put it? On the floor of the boat? On the pier? In a tub or bag? That's what a lot of people do, and this is okay if the weather is very cold, if the sun isn't shining on it, if it will be there for only a short time, or if you don't particularly care what it will taste like.

The worst thing you can do is pay no attention to fish you've just caught. Leaving fish exposed to air and sun for a long time is undesirable, as is leaving fish undressed overnight. Unaerated livewells, livewells filled with warm water, and stringers that are overcrowded or trolled or hung in warm surface water do not enhance the edibility of fish. Yet that's what so many people do with their catch. Not surprisingly, the result is a reduction in quality and taste of the catch.

Ideally you should clean or dress fish immediately after they've been caught *(see: fish preparation—cleaning/dressing)* and then put them on ice. But that isn't always practical. Maybe you can't clean fish at the place where you catch them (this is seldom the case in saltwater but is often the case in freshwater). Or you simply don't want to stop fishing to do so. Or you don't have ice or a knife with you. Do, however, clean and dress the fish as soon as possible. If you've planned ahead, you have a cooler or ice chest and ice to keep the fish cool.

Air and water temperatures are partial keys to good fish care. The warmer the air and temperature, the harder it is to keep fish alive and/or fresh until you are ready to clean and store them, and the sooner you need to begin preparations. Although some angling takes place in conditions that allow freshly caught fish to stay cool naturally, these situations are usually the exception. Do whatever you

Keeping her crappie alive in the water in a wire basket has helped ensure that this angler will have fine eating.

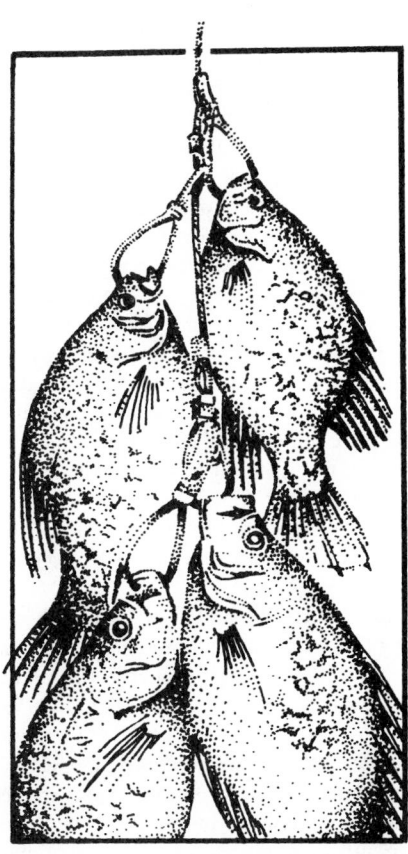

A stringer should be used only to retain fish that will be kept for consumption; the clip-on style, depicted here, is best for small fish and prevents overcrowding.

can to keep fish protected from heat and warmth. At the very least, that may mean putting them in the shade, stopping fishing after a reasonable length of time to clean them, covering them with a wet cloth, or taking care to keep them alive in a protected, cool environment.

Containing fish alive. Many boats are equipped with a livewell (see), which can be used for keeping small- to medium-size fish alive. Livewells work better for some species than for others. Freshwater bass, for example, are fairly easy to keep alive in a well, whereas most species of trout are not, unless the water is cold and well aerated.

A good livewell will not only aerate the water and provide plenty of oxygen, but also circulate the water to keep the temperature down and bring in fresh outside water. Livewells in saltwater boats are usually meant for bait storage but can accommodate some species of saltwater fish. Larger livewells are necessary for long fish and species that grow large, and are usually not practical for most small- to medium-size fishing boats. If you have a livewell, however, and can keep the water temperature down, this is a desirable way to store fish until you can get to the dock (or home in the case of trailered boats) and clean them. If fish die while they are in the livewell, remove them and place them on ice. Many livewells are not large, so

watch out for overcrowding, particularly with large specimens.

People without livewells, which include those who fish from shore or from small boats, need some other method of retaining fish. One way to keep fish alive without a livewell is to use a wire or net mesh basket. This collapsible basket is commonly used for panfish and is hung over the side of the boat in the water. Fish need to have enough room to move around in the basket, so it can't handle larger fish and great numbers. Be sure to pull the basket out of the water when moving, and don't keep the fish out of the water long when you do move.

A stringer or rope is the most common way to contain whole fish until you can bring them home or to the landing site—and it is one of the poorest methods of retention. The fish inevitably become stressed and bruised while on a stringer, especially if they get dragged around a lot or taken in and out of the boat often. For fish, a stringer or rope is usually a means of dying slowly. Nevertheless, using a stringer is better than just laying fish on the floor of the boat, exposed to sun and dirt. And some species, such as panfish and catfish, do better on a stringer than other species.

If you must string fish, make sure they are allowed to breathe so they stay alive. A metal or plastic clip stringer is better than a rope stringer for small fish because it doesn't crowd them, but rope is better for large and lively fish. Don't run a rope stringer through the gill. Put it through the lower jaw (and in the case of big fish or weak stringers, put it through both jaws). Try to keep the stringer away from gasoline in the water or any other substance that might affect the flavor of the fish. Take the stringer out of the water when the boat is underway at full speed, and avoid leaving it out of the water for a long time. If you're going a long distance, stop for a minute and put the stringer back in the water or put the fish in a pail of water while

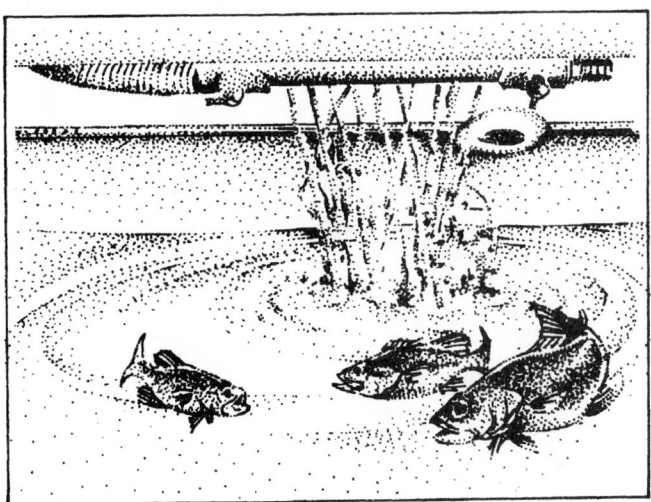

In a livewell, shown here in an interior view, the water streaming in from above is a significant help with aeration.

you move. The more time that fish spend out of the water, the worse it is for them.

Whether the stringer is in the water or on the boat, keep it in a shaded locale. And always make sure that it is fastened to some solid object. Many anglers have lost their stringer when it slipped or pulled off an unsecured spot. Recognize that stringers can attract other creatures. In coastal waters a string of fish trailing from the belt of waders may bring in interested sharks. Snapping turtles, snakes, and even alligators in freshwater have found stringers of fish attractive, although this is not a regular occurrence.

If a fish dies on a stringer or in a basket, dress it and put it on ice or in a cool, shaded spot. Although this is not possible or practical on some occasions, be aware that once a fish dies its flesh starts to deteriorate, and deterioration happens more rapidly in the water than out of it.

Killing.   There is merit to killing some fish immediately, even if you have the option of keeping them alive. On the other hand, some fish are better if kept alive. Fish that die slowly, struggling and bruising themselves in the process, won't taste as good as they might if they were simply dispatched with a couple of quick blows to the top of the head and stored temporarily in an appropriate environment. Still other fish are pretty hardy; if you have the option, for example, of keeping them alive in cool water rather than dead under a cloth on the floor of the boat, opting for alive may enhance the food value. You have to make this decision based on the circumstances. The bruises that fish receive, or the discoloration that results from the way they are stored or from their contact with other fish, is more likely to be an aesthetic default rather than one affecting edibility. If appearance matters to you (and it may to some family members or for the sake of artistic presentation in a recipe), then keep dead fish separated from each other and out of contact with objects.

If ice is available, the best option is to kill the fish after you've caught it, field dress it quickly, and then put it on ice. However, cleaning a fish on the water may not be legal in some places; in certain

From the northern-most sportfish file: Arctic charr have been reported at 82' 34" degrees North on Ellesmere Island, about 497 miles south of the North Pole.

freshwater lakes, this practice is prohibited and may result in a fine. In this situation, you can still dispatch the fish and ice it down, and then clean it later at a fish cleaning station or at home. Killing a fish immediately after catching it and then cleaning it, even if legal, is not always practical. In the midst of promising activity, few anglers want to stop to deal with a fish they've caught when more or larger fish await. If that is the case, stop to take care of the catch as soon as you have a break in the action.

The actual act of killing a fish is a delicate subject in this modern era of heightened sensibilities, and one that is rarely addressed in most books and educational literature on fishing. Few, if any, laws address the manner or timeliness of killing a sport-caught fish, nor would it be reasonable or practical to have such laws. Similarly, there are no laws regarding the killing of the hundreds of millions of fish (and shellfish) that are taken by commercial fishermen every year.

From a practical standpoint, as already stated, killing a fish soon after capture may be best for the preservation of the meat if proper storing and chilling are available. That in itself should be reason enough to dispatch a fish as soon as the decision is made to keep it. This also seems reasonable from a humane standpoint, the purpose being to prevent death through a slow and presumably painful process.

Two questions must be raised: Is it inhumane to let fish die slowly, say by bleeding, by stringing or by placing in a basket or well; and what is the best method of dispatching a fish? The answer to the first question is best left to the sensibility of the individual angler, especially since the question of pain and suffering in fish is one that is prone to anthropomorphic assertions and there is practically no scientific information on the extent to which fish experience pain.

Some people feel that putting a live fish on ice, which slows the metabolism and produces numbing, is the most innocuous way to let a fish die, and many people do so. (Do, however, put the ice under, around, and on top if you can rather than just laying the fish on ice.) Many anglers allow a fish to die of its own accord, with or without ice, although others dispatch it with a quick blow or series of blows to the top of the head and just behind the eyes with a club—referred to as a priest (as in dispensing last rites) by some anglers. Striking a fish may or may not kill a fish immediately, but it does stop the fish from thrashing and flopping. The cessation of activity prevents the flesh from being damaged and ensures better and more attractive table fare. It also has advantages for your fishing gear and the cleanup. If you do crack a fish on the head, be careful not to hit yourself in the process; strike the fish in the right spot so that you accomplish your objective without ruining the meat.

Another method of killing a fish is pithing. A small pick is inserted into the back of the head from the top, scrambling the brain. Pithing is fairly easy to

To dispatch a fish quickly and humanely, use a heavy club (top) in saltwater or a lighter club (bottom) in freshwater, or use a pick.

accomplish for some species and for small fish, but not for others, especially if they are lively and large.

In fact, some large species are customarily killed in ways that seem odd to those who don't know better or who are accustomed to catching only small fish. Huge Pacific halibut are a good example. These monsters can do a great deal of damage if brought alive into a boat, even though they have already been mortally impaled with a flying gaff. Their powerful and still beating tail could literally rip a boat apart. Therefore, big specimens are shot.

Many anglers dispatch fish just before cleaning or dressing them while the fish are alive, though seldom lively. Before using a knife or skinning tool, these anglers either pith the fish with a pick or knife blade, rap them on the head, or, in the case of some small species, snap their heads to sever the spinal cord.

Storing with and without ice. Once fish are dead, the flavor and texture of the flesh will start to deteriorate without proper care. As previously noted, deterioration is caused by many factors, chief among them being the presence of spoilage bacteria, blood, and normal digestive fluids. Thorough evisceration and cleaning will help remove these problems, combined with immediate icing to lower the temperature of the fish. Obviously it is important to slow down the natural deterioration that takes place. The factor that is easiest and the most important to control is temperature, and that can be handled with ice.

But what if you don't have ice? Avoid placing whole dead fish in a plastic bag unless they are in an unsealed bag in an ice-filled cooler; without air circulation, fish or fillets placed in a nonporous bag and kept outside will deteriorate quickly. On the other hand, if you fillet the fish immediately, place the rinsed fillets in a bag (sealable is okay now) and then place the bag on ice. If you have a paper towel or napkins, place the rinsed fillets on the paper towels and then put both towel and fish in the bag so that the towel can absorb moisture. Try to keep the fillets or the fish from soaking in water. Wicker creels, once a mainstay of stream and wading anglers, are less commonly used today, although they do provide reasonable air circulation. Layered with moss or grass or ferns, wicker creels are adequate for short-term storage (a few hours) of small fish and are preferable to canvas bags or other nonporous retainers.

If no conventional containers are available, you can improvise. A burlap bag, a mesh fruit or potato sack, wet newspapers or towels, or other objects that would allow fish to cool and allow air to circulate can be employed. Where necessary, you should rinse or clean them first. Keep the wrapping moist and shaded. If you add grasses, ferns, or other natural growth to the holding device to help air circulation, make sure that they are not aromatic; otherwise, the fish may develop that flavor.

If you have to hike to your fishing place, you may not have the luxury of bringing a cooler with ice. Consider taking a small amount of ice in a clean burlap bag. Put the bag in the shade (or bury it in moist sand if you are surf fishing) to keep the ice from melting for as long as possible. When ice is not available, use table salt and a burlap or similar type bag. When you catch a fish, eviscerate it and wash it. Rub about one tablespoon of salt for each pound of fish into the cavity, and then lightly salt the skin. Put the fish and enough wet seaweed to surround it into the bag. Keep the bag in the shade or bury it in moist sand. If you are at a suitable place, like the beach while surf fishing, and no container is available, bury the fish in moist sand near the waterline. To avoid losing your fish, mark the location carefully and watch the tide.

Pounds of Ice Required to Chill and Store Fish at an Ambient Temperature of 80°F

Fish Weight (in lbs.)	Hours on Ice			
	6	12	18	24
10	4.1	8.3	9.5	10.7
20	6.8	12.9	14.8	16.6
30	9.3	17.1	19.6	22
40	11.8	21.1	24.1	27
50	14.2	25	28.4	31.9
60	16.7	28.8	32.7	36.5

If you're not keeping fish alive, dispatch them right away and place them in an ice-packed food or beverage cooler for later cleaning. Separate the fish from food and beverages by placing the latter in bags. You can leave undressed fish on ice all day and clean them at the end of the day without sacrificing freshness or taste. Plan for this by obtaining ice before going fishing. For short-term storage, cube ice is better than block ice because you can cover fish fully with it, touching all parts. The best, however, is crushed, chipped, or shaved ice; unfortunately it's seldom conveniently available. Notice that a good fish market or supermarket always displays its fish and shellfish on crushed or chipped ice with good drainage. That's the best you can do.

When anglers talk about icing down fish, they often say they are putting fish "on ice." What is really best, though, is putting fish *in the ice*. To quickly cool the entire fish, including the core, use a cooler to surround the fish with ice cubes or crushed or flaked ice. If the fish have been eviscerated, store them in the ice with the belly facing down so that meltwater does not accumulate in the cavity.

Periodically drain the water from your cooler (or tub or fish box or whatever you hold the fish in) to eliminate standing water; dead fish are stored better on ice than in water, even if that water is ice cold. This is because the flesh becomes soft in water, and once softened it is very unappealing. Be especially careful to keep fillets out of water and keep the cooler top tightly closed when not in use; open and close it quickly just as you would a freezer door in warm weather.

If you have any doubts about the necessity or benefits of icing down fish, take a page from

F

commercial fishermen. If their fish spoil, they don't make money. So commercially caught fish are processed immediately. They are usually dressed and placed on ice as soon as possible after they come onboard. In some cases, they are flash frozen.

If you're really fastidious about fish care, then you need to pay even closer attention to icing and to temperature control. Ideally, try to keep the internal temperature of fresh, unfrozen fish as close as possible to 32°F (the temperature of melting ice). The best way to do this is to pack fish in ice. Ice cools fish from the outside, and it can take considerable time for the center of a large fish to reach 32°. Make an effort to store fish on ice as soon as possible for complete and rapid cooling.

Placed in contact with the fish, the melting ice cools it, washes bacteria from its surface, and keeps it from drying out. Crushed or flaked ice is best because a greater amount of ice surface is contacting the fish and maximum cooling can occur. Large pieces of ice can also crush, tear, or bruise fish more easily than smaller pieces. Large pieces of ice, however, are better than no ice at all. If possible, break or crush large cubes or blocks before using them. Food technologists differ as to how much ice is necessary to maintain fish properly, but the general recommendation is 1 pound of ice to 3 pounds of fish for several hours. But it's better to have more ice than not enough. The preceeding table, prepared by Michigan Sea Grant, makes a more generous recommendation, and puts the storage-on-ice question into perspective for longer periods.

Pack fish in ice made from clean, potable water if at all possible. Commercial ice and ice made at home work equally well. Use saltwater ice only if it is clean. The freezing point of saltwater is lower than 32°F. Although saltwater ice will cool fish faster, it can also stick to the skin and cause surface discoloration. Therefore, it's best to use saltwater ice in a slush or slurry. Chilled seawater, or slush, is a mixture of seawater and crushed or flaked ice. Making chilled seawater requires clean seawater, ice, and an insulated bucket, cooler, or tank. Partially fill the container with ice and add clean seawater. A mixture of 8 pounds of ice to 1 gallon of seawater makes a good slush. More ice may be needed on very warm days.

Wintertime—care on the ice. Speaking of freezing, how you care for fish caught on the ice in winter is a different story. Most anglers, because the air is cold and the lake frozen, simply drop their fish on the ice or snow and leave them there until it's time to go home. Naturally the fish freeze. If the fish are transported inside a heated vehicle, they warm up on the way home. Or they warm up later at home when it's time to clean them. If they are going to be consumed immediately or within a few days, this thawing may be fine, but it may not be fine if the fish (or fillets) are to be refrozen for longer-term storage. And in any event, the rapid change in temperature advances spoilage, so you would be wise to avoid premature thawing, especially

since fish caught from cold winter waters have such firm and delicious meat. Although fish should not be frozen more than once, fish that have been frozen and then thawed and smoked can be frozen again.

The best way to keep fish caught on open ice is to make an ice-water tub in the area you're fishing. A little effort on your part is required. Chip out an area of ice that is large enough (maybe 2 by 3 feet) to hold a reasonable number of fish, poke a small hole in the bottom with a spud, and let the tub fill with water. Then put freshly caught fish in the tub, where they will remain alive until it's time to go home. Make sure the fish can't escape through the bottom—and they will if the ice is thin and you've made your initial hole too large and it has increased in size during the day. To avoid this problem, you can locate the tub near your fishing hole and chip a narrow channel from the fishing hole to the tub to import water. Or you could use a chain saw to nick a sliver at the bottom of the tub. The tub works well when the temperature is relatively mild, but when the temperature is less than 20° and/or the wind is blowing, the tub may freeze up.

An alternative is to bring a cooler with you, fill it with cold water, and put your fish in that, although the lack of aeration may cause the fish to expire after a while. You could always put your catch directly in the cooler with some shaved ice collected from around your fishing holes. If there is snow on the ice, you might be able to use that for insulation around a bucket, and place the fish in the bucket with a cover over the top.

Remember that the size of the fish affects whether it freezes or not. A 10-pound lake trout will not freeze as readily as a 10-inch perch; the former might be just fine if covered with snow. If you fish in a heated shanty, the fish may stay cold but not freeze if you keep them in a pail or bucket placed on the ice in a corner of the shanty. If you leave them on the ice, they will probably freeze. If the shanty is really toasty, make sure that the temperature of the fish does not rise significantly—unless the temperature is rising because you're putting the fish in the skillet, in which case the eating is as good as it ever gets.

Bleeding and Eviscerating

To ensure the quality of fresh fish, the commercial fishing industry bleeds and eviscerates (guts) many species. These practices enhance the appearance, shelf life, and overall quality of some commercially important fish. Although the beneficial effects of bleeding are still undocumented for many species, it is reasonable to assume that anglers can also use this technique to maximize the quality of the fish they catch. You will have to decide whether this practice makes a difference. Some anglers bleed their fish all the time, some never do, and some bleed only certain species (like bluefish and tuna).

Removing the blood from fish does, however, retard deterioration in several ways. It decreases the

In 1991, as a demonstration, U.S. National Long Distance Casting Champion "Big Lou" McEachern cast a 5¼-ounce weight 750 feet over the roof of the Houston Astrodome.

F

cooling time, since the fish loses heat from bleeding. It also gets rid of waste products and removes oxygen; rancidity, caused by the oxidation of fats in fish flesh, is an important consideration if fatty fish are to be stored for several months. Fish that have been bled also tend to have lighter colored fillets with fewer bruises, blood spots, and other defects.

Before bleeding a fish, you may want to stun it to make the fish easier to handle. If you do not kill it, more blood will flow out if the heart keeps pumping, although not killing it may run contrary to your views on humanely dispatching the fish, as noted earlier in this section.

To bleed a fish, make a tail and/or throat cut or eviscerate the fish. Make a tail cut about an inch from the caudal or tail fin, across the caudal peduncle. Slice across the tail until the knife touches bone. To ensure maximum bleeding in some species, such as dogfish, cut the tail completely off just behind the anal fins. However, the tail portion of the fillet may spoil faster when the entire tail is removed unless the fish is kept clean and iced down quickly. On some species, cutting the tail may not produce significant or quick bleeding, but it will serve to keep a lively fish from flapping, since the muscles and tendons connected to the tail will be severed.

The throat cut minimizes the risk of bacterial contamination to the edible part of the fish. Make a single cut, severing the main artery that runs from the gills to the heart. Do this by slicing through the flesh just behind the gill cover. Make sure the cut is ahead of the heart, which must be undamaged if it is to continue pumping blood. Eviscerating, or gutting, a live fish will cause significant bleeding through the internal organs and intestinal cavity. For large fish that have a lot of blood to circulate, it may be best to let the heart pump all the blood out and then shortly afterward eviscerate.

The fish should be bled for 10 to 20 minutes. Bleeding will be more effective if you immerse the fish in clean water or seawater after making the cut. The water you use should be as clean and as cold as possible. Use a bucket, cooler, or tub, and change the water in the bleeding container frequently. If containers are not available, hang the bleeding fish over the side of the boat in a mesh bag. If this method is not practical, the fish can be bled without a container. Pour water over it from time to time to remove the blood before it coagulates.

Eviscerate a fish as soon as possible after it has been bled or after you catch it. Keep the entrails intact if possible when eviscerating. The stomach and intestines contain enzymes and bacteria that can contaminate the edible part of the fish and accelerate spoilage, so try not to puncture them. Bile from the gall bladder will also taint any part of the fish it touches, and it is very difficult to wash away. Rinse the cavity to remove blood, slime, and bits of viscera, and rinse the exterior as well.

Keep your work area clean and avoid contaminating other fish with eviscerated matter. Wash your work area and knives after each eviscerating operation. Finally, do not allow your fish to become tainted by coming into contact with oily or dirty areas of a boat, workstation, or dock.

After Cleaning

Once you've cleaned the fish (see the following section), they must be stored properly, most likely in a refrigerator or freezer. If you're traveling and many days from reaching home, this storage may be a cooler. Obviously your catch will at times exceed what can be consumed in one sitting; then you will want to store the extra fish for later consumption, perhaps when the season is past. The length of time that you plan on storing the fish determines the type of storage.

Cold storage. How long fish will stay fresh in cold (unfrozen) storage once they've been cleaned will depend not only on storage temperature but on the fish and how you've treated them. Some delicate species, like stream and river trout, do not lend themselves to many days of cold storing, even under the best of conditions. Bluefish, with their strong flavor and oily texture, do not keep well for more than a day after cleaning. Lean fish, however, may keep well for several days. And some fish can be kept for up to a week if they are ultrachilled. It is possible to keep fish that are whole but eviscerated in good condition for up to five days if they are kept on crushed ice that is drained regularly and in a container that is seldom opened.

Obviously the colder the storage temperature, the longer you can hold fish. Thirty-four degrees is better than 50°F. If fish are kept in an iced cooler for a long period, the ice should be checked every few hours, and the drain should be opened every time that the cooler is checked to release any liquid. Avoid opening the cooler any more often or longer than necessary; make sure that the lid fits snugly. You may have to tilt the cooler to drain it completely; if it is clogged, push something long and thin into the drain hole to unclog it.

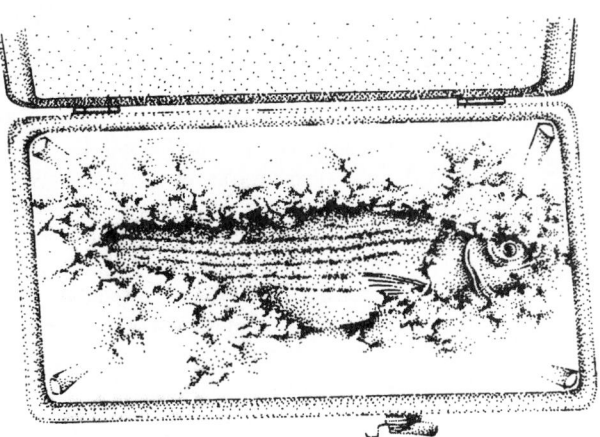

The best method of keeping fish in top condition is to put them on crushed ice in a cooler.

If you have to hold fish for a long time, they can be ultrachilled by using a 20:1 mixture of crushed ice (chipped ice will work if you can't find crushed ice) and coarse salt. Spread half of the mixture on the bottom of the cooler. Place the fish, enveloped securely in a plastic wrap, on the mixture and then cover with the other half. This should bring the temperature down below 32°, making it cooler than a refrigerator but not as cold as a freezer.

If you plan to store dressed fish, steaks, or fillets in the refrigerator for several days, temperature control is critical. Because many home refrigerators operate at 40°F or higher, fish can spoil fairly rapidly. It's good to pack dressed fish on ice in the refrigerator. Seal fillets or steaks in plastic bags or containers and then cover them with ice in trays or pans. The vegetable bins in the lower part of the refrigerator make convenient containers. Empty the meltwater regularly and add more ice as necessary. Fillets take up less room in the refrigerator or freezer and cool more quickly. If the fillets will be used right away, prepare them as soon as possible. If, however, you plan to use fresh fillets several days later, and if you have room to refrigerate the whole fish, wait and cut the fillets just before they're needed.

For fish that will be consumed immediately, rinse thoroughly in cold water and pat dry with paper towels. Put a double layer of paper towel on the bottom of a plate or tray and place small fish, fillets, or chunks of fish on the towel and then cover tightly; plastic wrap is the first covering choice, aluminum foil second. Make sure the wrapping is tight and holds. Uncovered fish can dehydrate quickly and lose flavor even if you're going to cook them in a few hours. For large pieces of fish or whole fish, rinse and pat dry, wrap tightly in plastic wrap, and wrap tightly in freezer paper. Take the fish out of the wrapping only when you are ready to prepare it for consumption; don't leave it lying out on the kitchen counter for a long period of time.

Frozen storage.   Before detailing the methods of home-freezing of fish, it is worth reiterating that if fish have been poorly handled before freezing, it will not be possible through freezing to get good results. Freezing only protects the quality of the fish at the time it was frozen. Airtight packaging and proper temperatures are critical to achieving this protection, however, and it is important to understand what happens when you freeze fish.

Although freezing prevents the growth of microorganisms, it only slows down the enzymatic and chemical reactions that cause flavor, color, and texture deterioration. As the temperature is lowered, these reactions occur more slowly; thus, frozen foods, including fish, should be stored at the lowest possible temperatures, and preferably in the coldest part of a freezer. Rapid freezing at the outset is very important for good long-term storage. Home freezers are primarily designed for storage, not for rapid freezing. A home freezer can properly freeze 1 to 2 pounds per cubic foot in 24 hours.

Don't overload the freezer. Fish will freeze faster if uncrowded, so don't bunch together pieces or whole fish or pans of fish when you first place them in the freezer. For the fastest freeze, place packages in direct contact with the freezer floor or walls until they are frozen. If the packages take more than 5 to 6 hours to freeze, they are too large. Store packages at a temperature of 0°F or colder, where the temperature doesn't fluctuate. The farther away from the freezer door, the more stable the temperature.

Properly packaged fish can be kept for a long time, although how long varies with the type of fish and with the method of freezing. Frozen fish can generally be kept for up to one year, but this is merely a guideline for shelf life in a freezer rather than an indication of whether the fish will still be appetizing after such a long period. It is probably a very generous advisement, except for frozen smoked fish, which can last more than a year, and even longer if vacuum-sealed. If your freezer allows for really low temperature, you may be able to freeze fish longer than someone whose freezer temperature is barely below 32°F. Thus, if you have a separate freezer, it is better to store fish in that than in

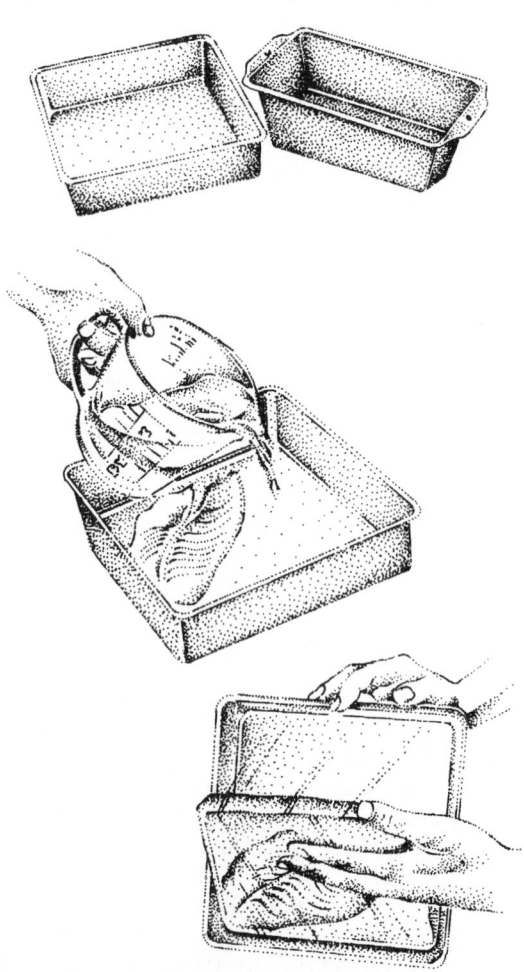

Place small fish and fillets in a pan, and cover them with water; after freezing, remove the block.

the freezer compartment of your refrigerator, which is subject to frequent opening and closing.

Large fish typically last a little longer than small fish, and whole fish last a little longer than steaks or fillets because they retain more moisture. Oily fish are best thawed and consumed within one to two months after initial freezing, and lean fish in three to six months. These are general guidelines, however; you can keep some fish, especially lean species, for longer periods, especially if frozen in blocks of ice. Taste varies among individuals, but seafood technologists advise that the best flavor in frozen fish is enjoyed in the first two months.

Regardless of these time frames, it's wise to eat fish as soon as possible. By labeling and dating packages, you can consume stored fish on a rotational calendar basis, using the older fish first.

Many of the undesirable flavor and color changes in fish are caused by oxidation of the unsaturated fats, oils, and color pigments in fish. This is a chemical reaction that cannot be stopped once started. Oily fish, like salmon and bluefish, are highly susceptible to oxidation. However, airtight packaging, especially if it is accomplished on a

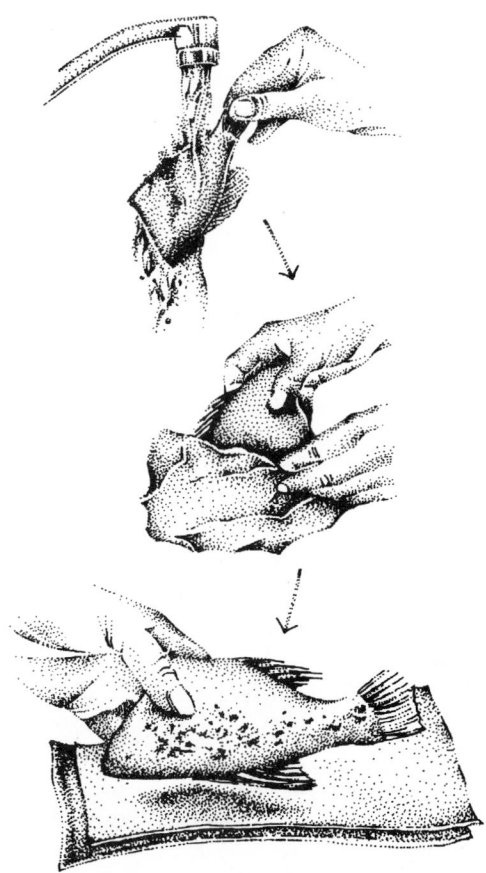

One way to freeze fish is to dip them in water (top), place them in a plastic bag (middle), and then put them in the freezer, where they will freeze with a glaze coating. Dip and reglaze a few times before covering in freezer wrap or foil (bottom).

freshly caught fish, can help prevent oxidation, more so for some fish than for others.

Another benefit of airtight packaging is the prevention of water evaporation from the flesh of fish during freezing. When water evaporates from food, it causes the food to become dry and tough; this effect is called freezer burn. Freezer burn promotes oxidation and is always accompanied by substandard flavor, color, and odor. By packaging and freezing properly, you can entirely eliminate freezer burn.

If space is at a premium in your freezer and/or you'll be eating newly caught fish very soon, then you can simply double- or even triple-wrap small fish, steaks, and fillets using plastic wrap, aluminum foil, and/or freezer paper. Plastic or cling wrap should be used first for prewrapping, and it should be tight to the flesh of the fish; two wraps may be a good idea, folding and pressing the wraps against the skin to remove air. Over this, you can use an outer wrap to help protect the fish in the freezer. The delicatessen wrap, in which the ends of foil or freezer paper are brought over the fish to meet one another and then are folded together several times, ensures a reasonably good final seal over the initial plastic wrapping. This method is suitable only for short-term freezing, however, since it is very difficult without Cryovac sealing to eliminate all air. As best as possible, eliminate air pockets, which contain oxygen and space for moisture to be withdrawn from the flesh. Do not use plastic bags, and use freezer wrap only as an outer protective wrap over an inner wrap.

A larger fish that is drawn or dressed is more difficult to wrap and to protect from oxidation. It should be dipped in water, placed temporarily in an unsealed plastic bag, and frozen as is. Once frozen, take the fish out of the bag and dip it in cold water, then put it back in the bag and return it to the freezer. You might repeat this a few times to form a thick glaze over the entire fish, and check it every few weeks to reglaze.

For longer freezing, and for best overall results, freeze fish in a block of ice; the ice seals out air and preserves the quality of the product.

This method is especially recommended for fillets and for small, whole dressed fish. Trays, pans, cut-down beverage cartons or gallon jugs, plastic food storage containers, and similar items all make good storage containers for frozen fish as long as the containers are washed thoroughly and are deep enough to hold the fish and a covering of water. Make sure that the containers bear no odor from previous usage, and fill them with ice water, leaving room at the top for expansion. Be wary of using chlorinated tap water, although you can use good-quality untreated well water from the faucet or bottled spring water.

After the fish have frozen, remove the block from the container; wrap it with aluminum foil or freezer paper; label the contents for species, portion,

F

and date of storage; and then put the block back in the freezer. If you leave the frozen fish in the container, it may be good to add a little more water on the top of the block.

Smaller fish can also be glazed before wrapping for longer storage. Glazing builds up a thin layer of ice around the fish. To glaze, freeze the fish in a plastic bag. After it is frozen, remove it from the bag, dip it in ice water, return it to the bag, and place the bag back in the freezer. Repeat several times; the glaze can be as thick as a quarter of an inch. The plastic bag protects the glaze from evaporation and prevents wet pieces from freezing together or from freezing onto the shelf or other objects. An ice glaze will evaporate in the freezer, so you may need to renew it in a month. Cover the glazed fish tightly with plastic wrap and then foil.

Be sure to pack fish in large enough quantities for a single meal, whether for yourself or your family and friends; if you place freezer wrapping paper between the frozen fish or fillets, they will be easier to separate and thaw. Fish that are frozen separately will defrost more quickly than fish frozen together. Also, label each package by writing on the outside with an indelible marker, crayon, or grease marker (or put a piece of masking tape on the package and label that). Label the package with the date, type of fish, and number of servings or pieces. You can also keep a log that lists the contents of the freezer and possibly the section of the freezer where particular packages are stored. The purpose of the log is to help you locate packages quickly, so that the rest of the freezer contents don't warm up.

Thawing.   How you thaw fish is important to their quality as table fare. The poorest choice is using hot water; never thaw fish in warm or hot water. Also poor is thawing the fish at room temperature, which hastens surface spoilage. The best option is to thaw fish gradually over an extended period. Japanese sushi chefs—known for their delicate, fresh, and finely prepared fish—use a controlled method of raising the temperature gradually over an extended period to thaw the fish and retain maximum taste and texture. This method is seldom possible in the home, but if you plan a day or two ahead of time, you can thaw a meal of frozen fish somewhat gradually in the refrigerator. A 24-hour period should be enough for smaller fish, pieces, and fillets that are separated; large fish can take longer.

Most people do not plan this far ahead and like to speed up the process. Some accelerate the thawing process via a microwave oven; microwaves have excellent thawing capability for most foods but require careful attention where fish are concerned. Whole fish, or pieces of fish, do not have uniform thickness, so a thinner section will defrost faster and may actually cook a little when thawed quickly in a microwave. If this happens, which it can easily, you would defeat all of your previous efforts to ensure a good-tasting fish.

Frozen fish or pieces that are not in a block of ice can be placed in a sealed (watertight) plastic food storage bag and then placed in a bowl of cold water to accelerate thawing. Fish stored in a block of ice can be defrosted fairly quickly if necessary by holding the block under cold running water or by immersing the block in a bowl of cold water until the block melts enough to separate the fish. Then pat the fish dry with paper towels, line a plate with fresh paper towels, cover the plate with plastic wrap, and put it in the refrigerator. In both methods, try to keep the fish out of stale melted water while defrosting, don't let it contact warm or hot water, and finish the thawing while the fish is covered in the refrigerator.

When thawing vacuum-sealed fish, open them immediately after thawing to allow air to enter the package. To help avoid botulism, never leave smoked or kippered fish in a tightly wrapped or vacuum package after it has thawed.

Storing for Transportation

Sometimes you must transport fish a considerable distance or for a long period of time before you can permanently store them. Examples of this situation would be while driving, boating, or flying back from a distant location. Refer to the earlier discussion of cold storage methods for information on keeping fish in good condition during transportation. Ultra- or superchilling, as described, is one method. Get a large supply of crushed ice, or if that is not available, get cubed ice; you will need a lot of ice, especially if the weather is warm. If dry ice is available, and your cooler is large enough, place the dry ice in the cooler surrounded by crushed or cubed ice. If you can't get dry ice but can get regular ice in block form, put the block ice in a cooler surrounded by crushed or cubed ice with the fish mixed in.

Don't let the fish lie in melted water, which usually has blood and bacteria in it. Keep the drain open if weather and conditions permit, or periodically open the drain and let out accumulated water. This is not possible in a cooler transported by air carrier,

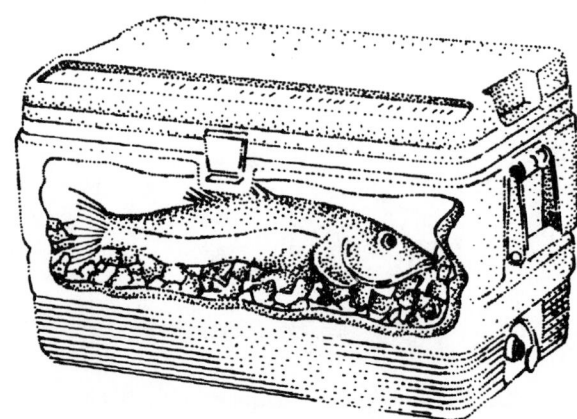

For long-term transportation, place fish on crushed ice in a cooler and open the vent to let water escape, so that the fish doesn't lie in the water. Add more ice as necessary.

since the cooler is out of your control for a long time; so proper packing is essential. If the cooler is transported in a vehicle, position the cooler so that it is accessible and can be drained. If the fish cooler is buried amid luggage and gear, you won't want to make the effort to get to it and drain it.

If you're transporting fish by air, as checked luggage, be advised that some carriers may not allow the shipment of a container with dry ice or may require notification that it contains dry ice. A non-crushable heavy-duty cooler is the best container for shipping; the lid should be completely secured with duct tape. Write the word perishable on the tape in several spots; a kindly baggage handler might put it in the shade if it has to sit on the tarmac, or might give it other considerations that will help.

At some remote camps and lodges, your fish can be frozen and then packed and shipped. The fish are usually shipped in a well-packed cardboard box. Unfortunately, the cardboard box isn't as good as a cooler. If the shipped fish is delayed in transit, the frozen contents could begin thawing and you may have to prepare and consume the fish at once upon reaching your final destination. In a worst-case scenario, the fish could be lost altogether, or misrouted for several days, and thus spoiled. If the fish haven't been frozen but have been packed in ice well, then a delayed trip may not adversely affect them as long as the ice holds up. If the ice does not hold up, the fish may spoil. How far you have to travel, whether an overnight stay is involved, and how much faith you have in the air carrier are factors in deciding whether or not to freeze.

If you are a traveling angler, especially one visiting the far north, you may have an overnight stay between leaving the fishing site and flying home. If this is the case, you'll need to make storage arrangements. If the outfitter or expediter doesn't make arrangements for you (they usually do), you'll have to fend for yourself. The situation may be difficult if you arrive late and leave early and haven't planned for this in advance. Many people no longer bring back fish from distant locations because of the hassle, the extra baggage charge, the possibility of spoilage, and the preference for catch-and-release, so storage arrangements may not be a concern. Also, some fishing places do not permit anglers to take fish home; thus storage is not even a consideration.

When you do transport fish, you must follow appropriate laws. The laws may require you to leave on the skin, or a patch of skin, for identification purposes; or to keep the fish whole after evisceration (to determine legal size); or to apply a tag to it until it reaches its permanent storage; or to identify the contents on the outside; or to follow some other procedures established by state and provincial authorities. Do not assume that following the laws of your home state or province will suffice when transporting fish from other places. And remember that it is your responsibility to find out what the law is.

See: Regulations.

FISH PREPARATION— CLEANING/DRESSING

Preparing a fish for the table or for storage is usually referred to as cleaning or dressing. It is not a difficult chore. Those with plenty of experience can do it quickly and in difficult circumstances. The native guides of northern Canada fillet big fish on the blade of a paddle before starting a shore lunch. Experienced anglers have been known to clean fish atop rocks and boulders when no suitable place was available. Some anglers are adept at cleaning small fish right in their hands. But cleaning can be a difficult chore for those who don't know what to do or who find the job distasteful.

Once the fish is killed, it becomes a food product. It can eventually be as appetizing and aesthetically pleasing as any well-wrapped, sanitized, store-bought food item if you treat it right.

For many people, even those who love to eat fish, the job of cleaning them is a distasteful or repulsive one because of the sight, smell, and feel of the dead fish and its body parts. This problem can be overcome if you have fresh air, running water, and a clean workstation to minimize exposure to the objectionable elements. If you like to eat fish, then keep in mind that cleaning them is the price you pay for having good table fare; so you might as well learn to clean the fish properly and safely, plus as enjoyably as possible. Think about how good the fish are going to taste later on.

A dislike for the cleaning process, or pure ineptitude, can result in unattractive table fare or, worse, the wastage of potentially fine food. If you can't learn to clean fish properly, then you probably shouldn't keep them in the first place, or you better find someone who can do it for you. Learning to clean fish simply takes a knowledge of what to do (either by watching someone else or following written instructions), the right tools, and a willingness to practice and be patient. Patience is necessary because cleaning fish can be exasperating when you're learning, and it helps to go slowly, despite the fact that the natural inclination is to hurry up and get it over with.

First Steps

Knives.   If you've tried to clean fish and found it difficult, you're probably using the wrong knife or a dull knife or you're unfamiliar with using a knife *(see)*. Not everyone is adept at using a knife for things other than buttering bread and cutting a morsel of steak. That's why some people don't have a clue about carving a roasted bird. Such simple things as how you hold the knife, whether you cut in one direction instead of another, and when to use finesse instead of force, are aspects of knife wielding that you become familiar with only after you've used a knife often and for different tasks. So if you're a stranger to knives, your first fish-cleaning efforts are likely to be disappointing.

A dull knife defeats nearly all fish-cleaning efforts, whereas a sharp knife helps you do a

From the muddled names file: Don't confuse the California sheephead, a member of the wrasse family, with the sheepshead, which is a member of the porgy family and also a common term for freshwater drum.

F

Guides prepare salmon at a fish-cleaning station, where there is proper disposal of entrails.

professional job. A sharp knife keeps you from hacking away at a fish and losing meat or making it unattractive. Some people think you can have a fish-cleaning knife that's too sharp, but this is untrue. Although extremely sharp knives can cause people to make mistakes, the real problem is that they are not using the knife properly or are rushing. If you're cleaning a lot of fish, or filleting big fish with many large bones, you may have to stop during the process and resharpen the blade.

Despite the fact that someone who is experienced at fish cleaning can make do in a pinch with almost any blade if it's sharp, the perfect knife for all fish-cleaning tasks does not exist. A thin 6-inch blade is universally popular, especially for filleting most freshwater fish. A longer blade, in the 9-inch range, is necessary for larger fish, particularly many saltwater species. A small knife with a 3- to 4-inch blade is fine for dressing most small panfish and trout. You do not have to spend a fortune on knives for cleaning fish, but you should have the right one for the job.

Although a 6-inch blade does work when you're eviscerating (gutting) small fish, you don't have enough control over it unless you're especially careful; you have more control over a shorter blade. With the shorter blade, you are less likely to poke the blade too deeply into the stomach or to cut through the belly too far. A pocket knife with a narrow and pointed blade is adequate for the simple act of field dressing; it's portable and easily accessible.

For filleting fish, you need a blade that is slightly flexible and thin and that tapers to a sharp point at the tip. Many good filleting models sweep up slightly at the tip as well. The length is a function of the size of the fish. A filleting knife is slightly different than the knives found in most kitchens. The blade should be long enough to cut both the belly and the back with the same stroke; if the blade is just a bit short for that, you can cut the belly first and then the back and rib cage section before sweeping through the tail area (see the discussion of filleting, later in this section). On larger fish it may be more difficult to cut through the tough rib cage with a light knife, although if you fillet without slicing the rib cage, such a knife will be fine.

Additionally, a broad heavy-duty blade may be needed for steaking fish, since you're cutting through the backbone. You can easily dull a regular fillet knife by trying to saw through a thick backbone unless you get lucky and happen to find the spot between vertebrae. A large inflexible knife with a less tapered point, or a cleaver if you have one, makes a neat instant steak.

If you have a regular fish-cleaning station, keep your cleaning tools and a knife sharpener handy. If you clean in different places, bring your tools along so you can do the job right. A knife sharpener *(see)*, whether it's whetstone, steel, or ceramic, is a necessity for putting an edge back on your knife. The more fish you do at one sitting and the tougher their skin, bones, and scales, the quicker the knife seems to lose an edge. A knife that is hard to sharpen quickly will be a hindrance when you're filleting more than one or two fish. Blades made of soft steel will sharpen quickly, although they may lose their edge a little faster than hard steel knives. A thin knife with a tapered rather than a beveled edge will cut best, so try to hold the blade at a low angle when you sharpen it.

Electric knives are popular with some anglers, especially older ones whose grasp and dexterity isn't as firm as it used to be. These knives are particularly useful when filleting or cleaning a lot of fish, and many public fish-cleaning stations provide electrical outlets for them.

Location. There's little doubt that the best time to clean a fish is as soon as possible after catching it, or before leaving the water to head for home, especially if it will be a while before you get the catch to your final destination for cleaning *(see: fish preparation—care)*. If you're going to clean the fish on the water or on the shore, make sure that it's legal to do so and find out the extent to which it is legal (for example, you may be able to eviscerate the fish but not fillet it, or you may have to leave the skin intact).

On saltwater, you can generally clean fish on your boat, perhaps while headed back to port of it's not a rough ride, or just before you finish fishing for the day. Many large boaters improvise a removable wooden work board for fish cleaning, perhaps one that fits over the gunwale or sits in a rod holder.

A striped bass is cleaned at dockside, where remains discarded in the water become food for crabs.

Such a board should have back and side stops to keep fish from sliding off, and should be large enough for the usual size of fish. Cleanup on the boat is easy, provided you have a washdown hose or at least a bucket and scrub brush. The offal gets flipped overboard and winds up feeding gulls, crabs, eels, and other scavengers.

Many marinas, launching sites, camps, and other public places have fish-cleaning stations or houses (in warm areas a screened site helps keep the bees and flies away). Some have waist-high aluminum tables with backstops for the cleaning chores; these are good for cleanup and don't absorb refuse, but they can be very slippery and tough on knife blades. Others have a wooden table, which is less slippery and easier on knives but not as clean for the less fastidious angler. If you have and can put a clean board down on an aluminum fish-cleaning table, you should be in good shape.

A board, incidentally, is useful for cleaning all fish anywhere, and you can often improvise. Some anglers like to use a commercially made board with a large spring clip at the head; the clip holds the head or tail of the fish in place. Some anglers use a board with a large nail driven into it at an angle. The head of a fish (via the gill and mouth) is placed over the nail to keep the fish in place while working on the body.

Most public facilities have a water supply at the fish-cleaning station for rinsing fish and also have electrical outlets. Some have a central pit for disposal of offal, and others grind the remains for appropriate disposal (disposal is a big benefit because it's one less thing you have to do at home). If you can use these facilities, you should do so; after cleaning your fish at a public facility, be sure to store them properly and keep them iced before heading home.

If a public fish-cleaning facility isn't available to you, it's best to do the cleaning outside, especially if you'll be scraping the scales off the fish. Dry scales may fly all over the place, and they can be a nuisance indoors, not to mention an obstruction in the kitchen drain. If you have to scale fish inside, then wet the fish thoroughly to moisten the scales and remove them under running cold water. This will minimize scale dispersion, but it will clog the sink strainer (which you did remember to put in the sink, right?).

When cleaning outside, make sure you cover the surface of the work area; cleanup will be a lot easier. You can put a clean board over the location, covering it with multiple sheets of newspaper; the paper is also good for small fish that are cleaned indoors on a countertop. Newspaper grabs the fish well and helps hold it in place, as well as soaks up moisture. When you're working on newspapers, periodically bundle up the soiled paper and fish remains and put them in the garbage. This gives you a clean surface to work on and avoids a large pile of repulsive refuse at the end. Keep the cleaned fish off the newspaper to avoid picking up ink or sticking to the paper.

If you have no source of running water, fill a deep bowl or clean bucket with ice cold water for rinsing the fish. Two such bowls are better, because one can be used for rinsing and the other for a final clean-water bath. In the ideal scenario, you have a helper who rinses the fish thoroughly after you clean them and then places them on paper towels. If you are working solo, you can put the fish aside after you clean them and rinse them afterward, but waste matter, especially blood, will harden and be much more difficult to rinse off even a short time later, especially if it's on the flesh instead of the skin. If you're doing all this fun work alone, you have two choices: You can stop and rinse each fish after you've cleaned it, which many people don't want to do because their hands are constantly getting dirty and then wet, or you can place the fish in a bowl of water (ice cold is best) and rinse them all at once after you're finished. Putting chunks of fish and fillets in water for long periods is not desirable, especially if the water is not super cold.

A final reminder: Wherever people congregate for fish cleaning, flies and bees seem to follow. If young children are around, watch out for bees that may have congregated in the garbage container where fish carcasses are disposed.

Methods

How you clean a fish depends on the size of the fish and what will be done with the end product. Small fish, for example, are seldom stuffed and baked but are often pan-fried. Very large fish are hard to cook evenly throughout, so steaking them, or the thickest parts of the body, is a good idea. Scaled fish that will be presented whole need to be eviscerated and the scales removed. Fish that will be filleted do not need to be eviscerated, and so on. In broadest terms, the complexity of cleaning is determined by the degree to which skin, bones, and scales must be removed. Novices attempting their first cleaning job may find it helpful to review the anatomy *(see)* of a fish, especially to become familiar with the basic skeleton. Knowing the layout of the skeleton is helpful when you are cutting through and removing bones, many of which are small and pliable; it also acquaints you with the names and location of fins.

Since fish cleaning involves the use of sharp knives, you obviously should be very careful when handling knives, especially when you're cleaning fish in cold weather and when your hands are cold. Gloves made of a high-tech material that resists knife piercing and slicing are available; they also give you a good grip on the fish and protect your hands from spiny fins, sharp gill covers or gill edges, and teeth. If you will be doing a lot of fish cleaning, you should consider using a pair. Holding fish properly and working at a moderate and careful pace will prevent a sore mishap. Finally, be careful if others are helping you clean the fish; they should not reach into the work area when the fish cleaner is cutting.

Field Dressing. The cleaning of small fish, such as stream trout and panfish, is referred to as field dressing. In field dressing, freshly caught fish are killed soon after their capture, eviscerated, and the bodies spread in well-ventilated wicker creels lined with grass to facilitate cooling. Field dressing requires the removal of the entrails, gills, and kidney. It is sometimes also referred to as gutting, although gutting usually refers to larger fish and basically implies the removal of just the intestines.

Field dressing small trout and salmon, head intact. Small trout and salmon are the simplest fish to field dress. They don't have to be scaled, and, once eviscerated and cleaned, they are ready for cooking. After you have learned to field dress a fish and have practiced a few times, field dressing takes only 30 seconds.

To field dress a small trout or salmon, begin behind the lower jaw by sticking the tip of your knife through the tissue that connects the lower jaw to the gills and slitting this tablike section free. This is actually the tongue that is being freed. Then insert the point of the knife into the vent (the anal opening); slit through the skin and up the center of the fish's belly in a straight line to the gills, stopping before you get to the V-shaped spot behind the jaw.

Try not to puncture the intestines as you make the slit. Put the knife down and hold the fish by the head with one hand. With the other hand, grab the tongue and pull down on it toward the tail; this will

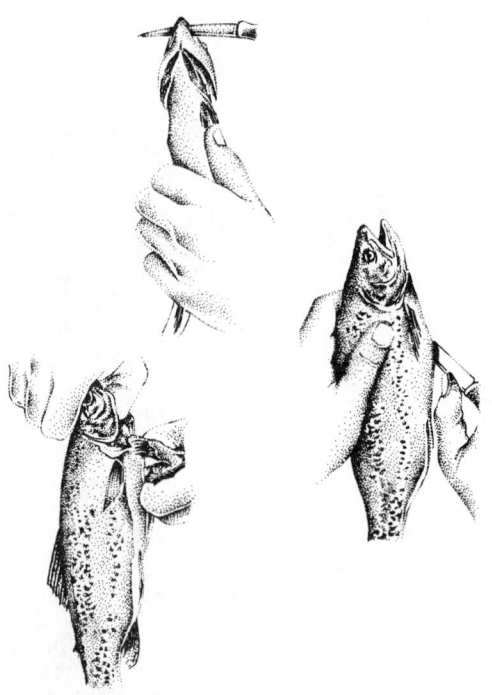

To eviscerate a small whole trout with head intact: slice the lower jaw away from the gill membrane (top); insert the knife blade into the anal vent and slice up to the gills without puncturing the intestine (middle); then place your thumb into the throat and pull down to remove the gills and entrails (bottom). Clean the body cavity thoroughly. This process can be done in the field with a small sharp knife.

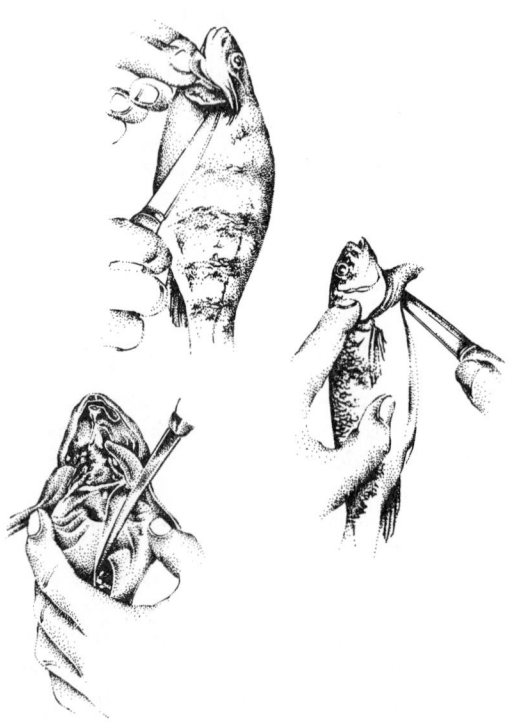

To eviscerate a small whole perch with head intact: slice the gills from the throat (top); insert the knife blade into the anal vent and, without puncturing the intestines, slice up to the gills (middle); remove gills and entrails, and scrape out the bloodline (bottom). Clean the body cavity thoroughly.

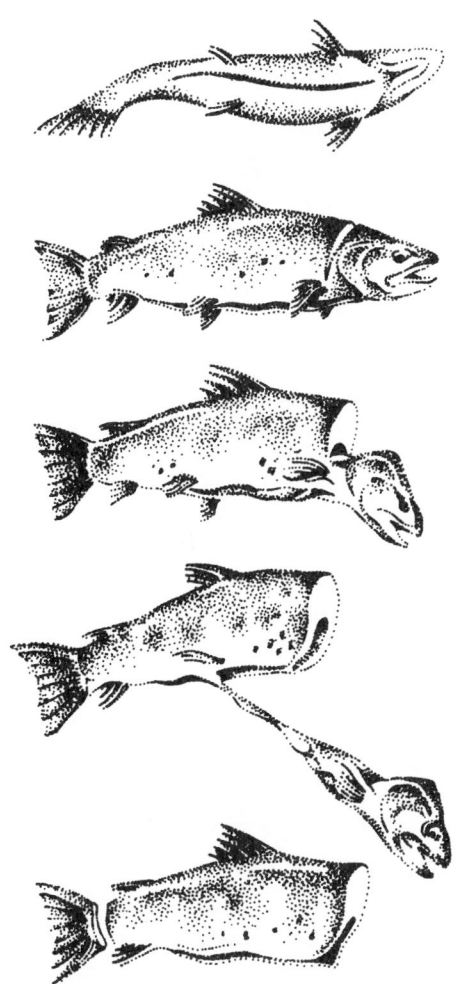

To eviscerate a whole fish while also removing the head: insert the knife blade into the anal vent and, without puncturing the intestines, slice up past the pelvic fins to a spot between the gill covers; cut downward behind the head and through the backbone; pull the head away from the body to remove both the head and the entrails. Clean the body cavity thoroughly. Cutting off the tail is optional.

free the gills and the entrails. Remove the kidney, which is the bloodline along the backbone, with your fingers or a knife or spoon; then rinse the cavity with cold water and dry it with a paper towel or napkin.

Field dressing small trout and salmon, head removed. This procedure is one to follow when you don't want to leave the head on the fish (and are not restricted by laws). The process begins by inserting the point of the knife into the vent (the anal opening) and then slitting through the skin and up the center of the fish's belly in a straight line to the gills, stopping before you get to the V-shaped spot behind the jaw. Try not to puncture the intestines as you make the slit. Place the fish belly down and make a cut behind the head down through the backbone until it is severed, stopping after severing it and without cutting the head entirely free. Put the knife down, hold the body in one hand, and with the other hand grasp the head and pull it away from the body. This will remove the entrails and the head. Cut off the tail if you

wish; then remove the kidney by the backbone, rinse, and pat dry.

Field dressing other fish. Most small to medium fish can be field dressed by following the previous directions, with some minor changes. Species like bluegills or perch, for example, must be scaled first. Do not field dress and then attempt to scale the fish. Also, be aware that the belly skin of some fish is tougher than others and requires more careful slitting. The belly skin of a trout is soft and easy to cut with a sharp knife; the belly skin of a yellow perch is tougher. Field dressing some fish (including perch) requires the additional step of cutting away the gill connections in order to remove the entrails and gills in one motion. To do this, pull up on the gill covering and slice under the gill to free it from the body; do this for each gill; then slit the tongue and the belly, and remove everything in one pull.

Of course, for any fish you can simply cut off the head, slit the belly from the anal opening on up, and then grab the entrails and remove them. The disadvantages of this method are that it is usually messier than the other methods, requires more scraping and pulling to remove the contents of the cavity, and some of the innards contact the flesh (an action you should try to avoid). After cleaning a fish this way, make sure you rinse it immediately and thoroughly.

Pan Dressing. Small fish that are unsuitable for filleting or that are to be cooked whole by various methods can be prepared in a manner called

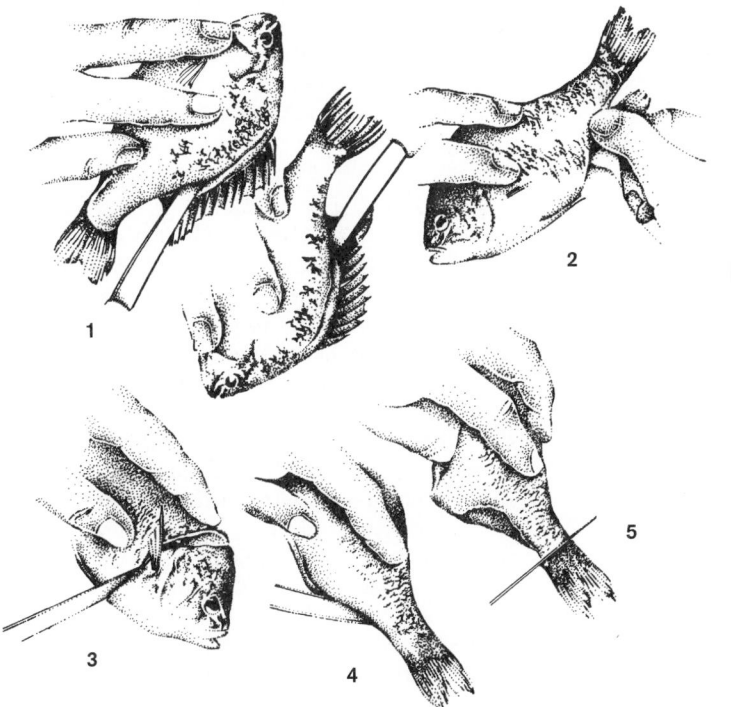

To pan dress a small whole panfish with skin and ribs intact: cut the top of the fish along both sides of the dorsal fin (1) and remove the fin; cut along both sides of the anal fin and remove it (2); cut off the head at an acute angle (3) and remove it; slice along the belly to the anal vent (4); as an option, cut off the tail (5). Clean the body cavity thoroughly.

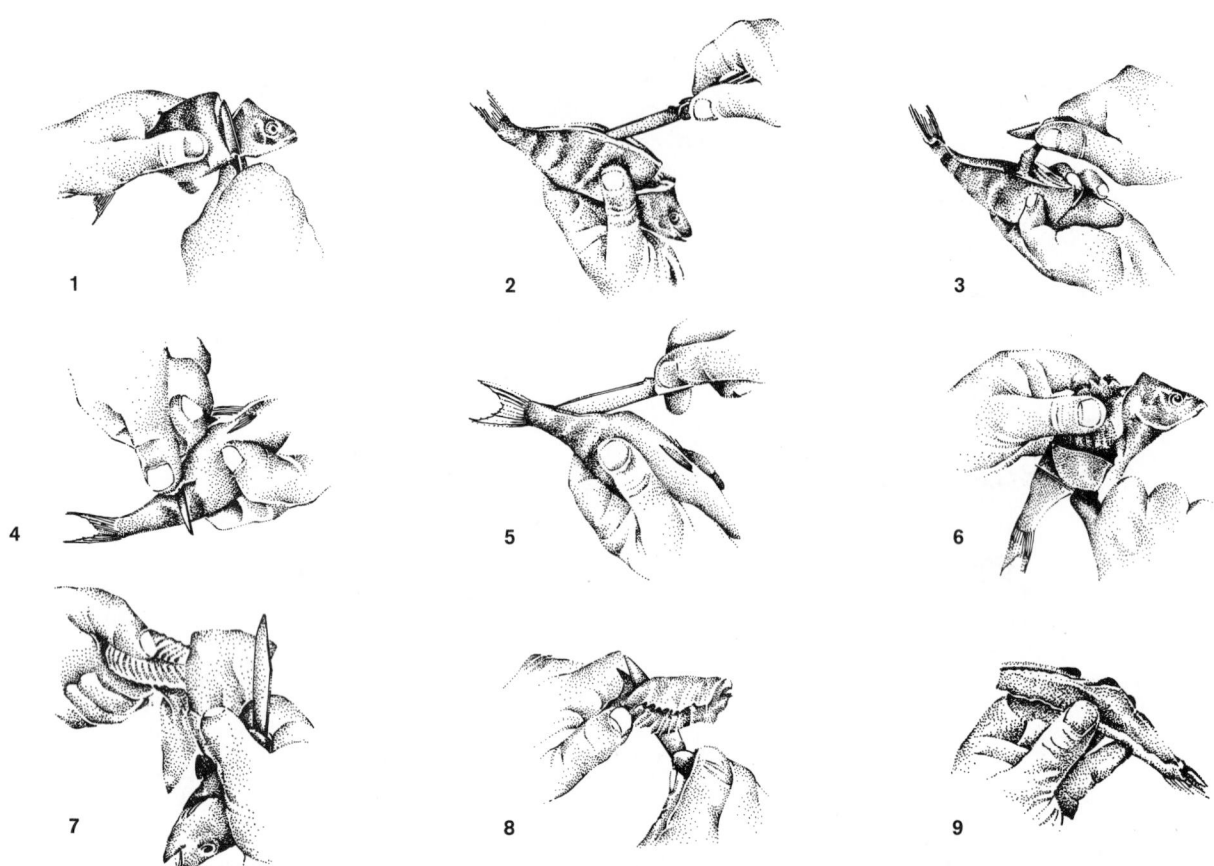

To efficiently dress a small whole perch in a manner that produces a skinless fish with maximum meat: Cut down through the backbone without severing the head (1); cut the skin along each side of the dorsal fin (2); pinch the forward end of the fin between thumb and knife blade and pull it toward the tail, removing it and attached bones (3); turn fish over, cut under the anal fin until the blade meets the supporting fin bone, pinch the anal fin between thumb and blade, and then twist away the bone and fin (4); slice the belly skin between the anal fin and (5); turn the fish over, grip a corner of upper back skin between thumb and blade, peel back the skin along the flank, and repeat for the other side (6); holding the partially skinned body in one hand, grab the head and skin in the other hand and pull them toward the tail in order to remove these items plus entrails in one piece (7); hold skinned fish as shown, bring knife blade up from belly behind the rib cage to the backbone, and then slice forward to separate the rib cage from the backbone (8). The final result (9) is a skinned, beheaded, eviscerated fish with just backbone.

F

pan dressing. The standard and most common method leaves the skin and ribs intact, but a more involved method allows for their removal. Both methods remove the head, entrails, and fin bones. Small fish should be pan dressed with a narrow knife having a short blade and a pointed edge, as opposed to a standard fillet knife having a longer, flexible blade.

Pan dressing, skin and ribs intact. Start by laying a scaled fish on one side and slicing along the dorsal fin on both sides. Then pull out the fin. Do the same thing for the anal fin. Do not cut these fins flat because you'll leave bones in the meat.

Cut off the head as close to the gill cover as possible, angling the knife over the top of the head to maximize the amount of meat. Slit the belly and remove the entrails; cut off the tail if desired and then rinse quickly in ice-cold water and pat dry.

Pan dressing, skin and ribs removed. Start by laying a fish with scales intact belly down on a cutting board. Make a cut over the top of the head and close to the gills, and continue cutting down through the backbone without completely severing the head. Slice the skin along each side of the dorsal fin from the head to the tail, making the slice as shallow as possible. Grasp the dorsal fin between your thumb and the fat part of the knife blade and pull it free; this will remove the dorsal fin bones. Turn the fish around and slice along both sides of the anal fin; pull the fin free to remove the anal fin bones. Now make a shallow slice from where the anal fin was to the tail. Turn the fish over again, and position the knife blade under the upper fold of skin near the back; pinching that fold between the knife blade and your thumb, peel the skin halfway down the body. Repeat on the opposite side. Then grab the partially skinned carcass in your left hand and the head and skin in your right hand, and pull both apart; this will liberate the head, skin, and entrails in one piece. Finally, hold the skinned carcass belly up, and slice off the rib cage by cutting from behind the first rib down to and then along the backbone. Rinse quickly in ice cold water and pat dry.

This method produces a fish with only the backbone, which easily parts from the meat after cooking. It also saves more meat than filleting.

Scaling. Removing the scales on a fish is referred to as scaling. You do not need to remove the scales on a fish if it will be filleted with the skin removed or if it is from a species that has no scales (bullhead) or has extremely small scales (small trout). Species that have large, loose scales and that will not be skinned should be scaled before field dressing. If you do not do this, and even if you have no intention of eating the skin, loose scales will almost certainly find their way into the food, which is unpleasant and shows carelessness.

Scaling can be performed on fish that have been eviscerated, but this is more difficult and could lead to tearing of the meat and an incomplete job. Scaling, therefore, is best accomplished on a whole fish, in the round, that can be scraped and pulled freely while still intact.

Scale removal can be accomplished with various devices. A knife blade is commonly used and is effective, provided you're careful and can handle the knife skillfully enough to avoid slicing into the skin. Using a knife for scaling will dull the blade, however. Many anglers like to use scaling tools, usually called scalers, which have serrated edges; others prefer a thin-metal spoon for scaling small surface areas. The spoon can also be handy for scraping the bloodline out of the cavity.

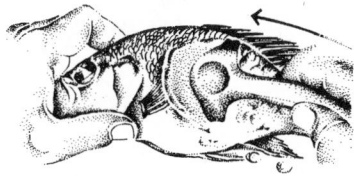

When scaling, run tool from tail toward head.

Always scale against the grain, moving from the tail of the fish toward the head. Working against the grain can be a messy process, sending scales everywhere, but you can minimize the mess by wetting the surface of the fish before scaling, or scaling under the running water of a faucet. If you have a hose with a high-pressure nozzle and you're working outside on fish that have been kept wet, you can scale them quickly by holding them about 6 inches from the high-pressure water stream; it's effective, but it sends scales flying. The hosing method works better for loose-scaled species like bluegills and crappie than for tight-scaled species like yellow perch or walleye. In general, the longer a fish has been left dry and out of water, the harder the scaling process. If you have to scale in a kitchen, you can immerse the fish in a sink of cold water and ice, pin the fish against the bottom of the sink, and scale it. The scales stay in the water and should be caught in the strainer when the sink is drained.

Filleting. Generally the quickest method of cleaning fish is to fillet them. Filleting means cutting the sides of a fish lengthwise parallel to and free from the backbone, accompanied by removal of the rib cage. A fillet is typically a boneless piece of fish, and it may or may not have the skin removed. When correctly done, filleting causes little loss of meat, is accomplished easily with the proper instrument, and, most important, removes all the rib cage bones that anguish many reluctant fish-eaters. The word "fillet" is properly pronounced "fill-lay," not "fill-it."

Basic filleting, version 1. Place the fish on one side, and make an angled cut behind the pectoral fin down to the backbone, being careful not to sever the backbone. Reverse the direction of the blade so that it is facing the tail and lying flat on the backbone, and slice back toward the tail along the backbone. A smooth cut, rather than a stop-and-go sawing motion, is best. If the fish has been scaled, cut through the skin at the tail.

If the skin is to be removed in the filleting process, do not cut through the tail but slice

Basic Filleting, Version 1

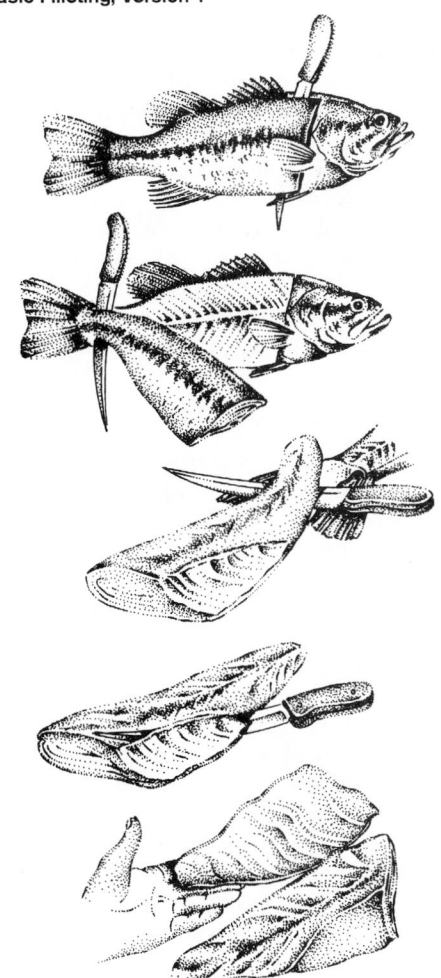

This is the most popular method of filleting. The same process is followed for both sides, with slicing the rib cage away from the fillet being the final step.

to the end without severing, and flop the meat backward.

If the fish has a thin skin that is easy to slice through, make sure you leave plenty of it attached to the caudal peduncle so that it grabs there and makes the skinning process easier. Angle your knife through the meat to the skin; then slice along the skin, separating the meat while exerting pressure on the skin with your free hand. If you accidentally cut through the tail, freeing the fillet from the carcass, you will find that removing the skin is a little more difficult. In this case, press the thumbnail of your free hand on the tail of the fillet (or use a fork), and cut between the skin and meat with your knife hand. You can use a sawing motion here and aid the effort by pulling on the tail of the fillet in the opposite direction of the cut.

Now, with either scaled or skinned fillet, cut behind the rib cage, slicing the whole section away. Use the same procedure for the other side of the fish. Rinse fillets quickly in cold water and pat dry. This filleting technique can be used on many fish, except those with additional Y-shaped bones. They require a few more steps (see the later section on filleting to remove extra bones).

Basic filleting, version 2. Place the fish on one side, and make an angled cut behind the pectoral fin down to the backbone, being careful not to sever the backbone. Slice the skin along the backbone from the head toward the tail, running the knife along the top of the rib cage but not cutting through it. Push the knife through the flesh at a point opposite the anal vent, and continue cutting, running the knife along the backbone until the blade slices the flesh away at the tail. A smooth cut, rather than a stop-and-go sawing motion, is best.

Lift the top of the fillet up to expose the rib cage; with smooth, measured strokes, flesh the meat away from the ribs, skimming the bones to procure as much meat as possible. Slice the fillet away from the carcass at the stomach. Turn the fish over and repeat on the opposite side, concluding with two boneless fillets with skin attached. If you have previously descaled the fish, the job is complete except for rinsing and patting dry. If not, you can remove the skin by pressing a fork or the thumbnail of your free hand on the tail of the fillet; cut between the skin and the meat with your knife hand. You can use a sawing motion here and aid the effort by pulling on the tail of the fillet in the opposite direction of the cut.

The second version is generally used less often than the first, but it has some benefits. It does not dull the knife as quickly since there is no cutting through rib bones. It produces slightly more meat than the first version, and it is better for use on larger fish. Large fish would be those for which the blade of the knife was not long enough to reach the top of the back and the bottom of the belly. For really large fish and those with thick bones, you may need a bigger, sturdier knife; it must, of course, be sharp. It's easy to lose meat on large fish when filleting if you don't do the job right. A heavy-duty blade will easily cut through the rib cage so that you don't have to hack at the fish; this is a big consideration if you're using the first filleting version. If you don't have a larger knife, you can still fillet with a smaller one by using version two and slicing in small sections while folding back the side of the fish to allow deeper penetration and continued slicing. To cut off the skin with a smaller knife, cut the skinned fillet in half lengthwise and then take off the skin as previously described.

If you make a mistake when filleting, try to correct the error rather than continuing with the mistake. The biggest problem when filleting, especially when the fish are small and you're using a sharp knife, is inadvertently cutting through the backbone. If this happens, withdraw the knife and come back at another angle until you strike the backbone; then lay the blade down and make the stroke along the backbone. Another common mistake is cutting

Basic Filleting, Version 2

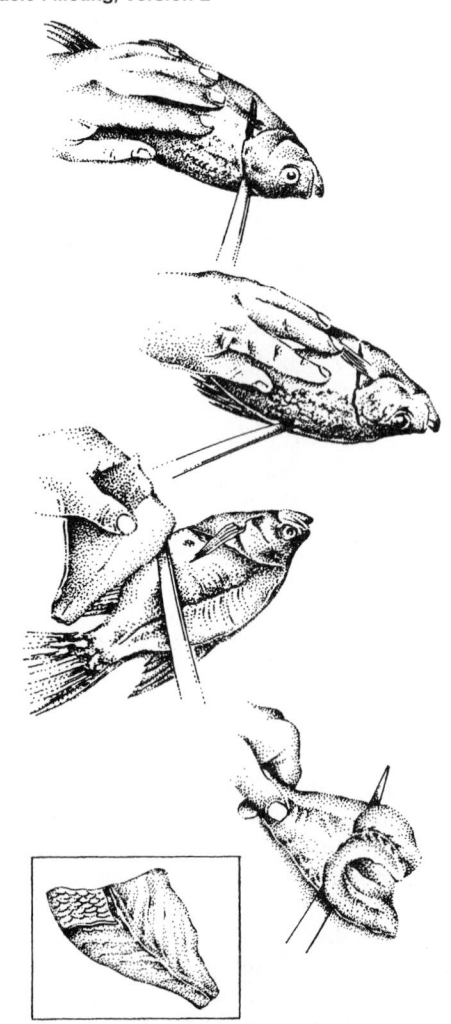

This is a good method of filleting; it requires a sharp knife and produces the maximum meat. The same process is followed for both sides. Leaving a patch of skin on a fillet (inset) may be necessary for legal identification purposes.

through the skin when you're trying to remove the skin from the fillet. If this happens, go to the head of the fillet, angle the blade through the flesh to the skin, and then start skinning from that direction.

Butterfly filleting. If you keep the skin attached to the sides of the fish while filleting and leave them joined at the belly, you can achieve a double fillet. This has some panache from a presentation standpoint. This method is used for smoking or planking fish, as well as for baking when stuffed. The skin helps hold in the juices for baking.

To butterfly a fish, first scale it if the species or your presentation demands it (planked fish do not need to be scaled since the meat is flaked away), and then cut off the head. With the belly away from you and the tail to the left, run the knife along the backbone, slicing through the rib bones and continuing through the tail, taking care not to cut

Butterfly Filleting

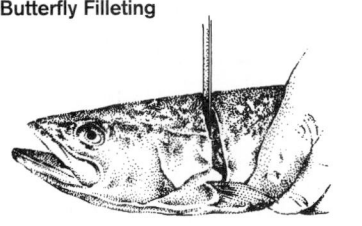

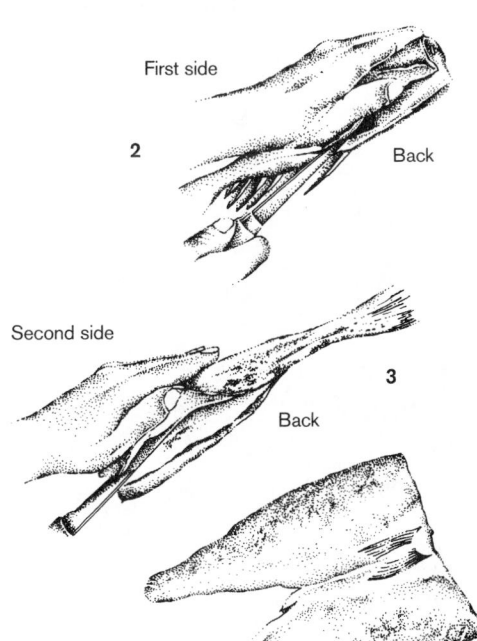

To create a butterfly fillet, first cut off the head (1); with the tail to the left and the belly up, slice along the backbone, cutting through the rib bones and continuing through the tail without cutting through the belly skin (2). Turn the fish over so that the tail is to the right and the belly is up, and cut from the tail toward the ribs (3), slicing the meat through the tail and then close to the backbone, continuing through the ribs, again not cutting through the belly skin. Remove entrails and backbone, and trim away whatever remains of the rib bones (not shown), creating a double fillet (4).

through the skin at the belly. Turn the fish over and around so the tail is to the right and the belly is away from you; this time work from the tail toward the ribs, slicing the meat through the tail and then close to the backbone, continuing through the ribs and again taking care not to cut through the skin at the belly. Remove the entrails and backbone, and lay the double fillet skin-side down and open. Trim away whatever remains of the rib bones; then rinse in cold water and pat dry.

Filleting to remove extra bones. Some fish have more than the usual number of bones, and these cannot be removed through standard one-cut filleting. Such species include pike, pickerel, and muskellunge, all of which have additional intermuscular, or floating, Y-shaped bones. To deal with this, you can fillet the fish as previously described in version 1 and remove the skin. The Y bones are located on the fleshy back portion of the fillet above the ribs and run lengthwise to a point equal with the ventral opening. Locate the lower edge of the Y bones just above the midsection of the fillet, and cut through the flesh beneath them all the way to the tail. Then guide the knife blade along the upper edge of the Y bones, scraping

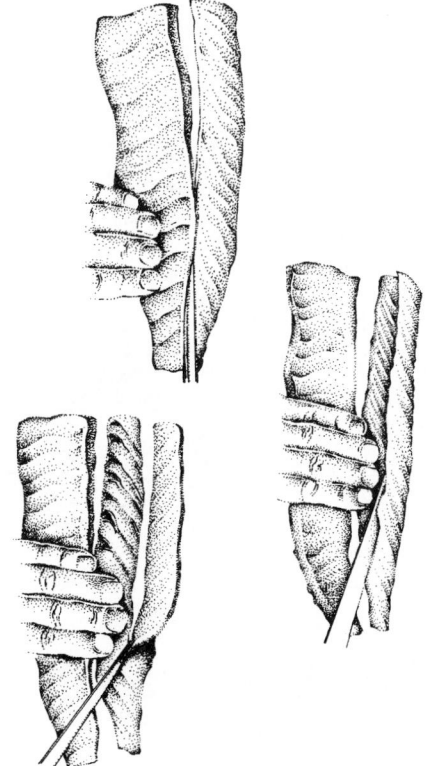

To remove Y-shaped bones from a skinless fillet of pike, pickerel, and muskellunge, locate these bones just above the midsection of the fillet and cut through the flesh beneath them all the way to the tail (top). Run the knife blade along the upper edge of the Y bones (middle), scraping gently against the bones and slicing down and away to the tail (bottom). Discard the middle piece, leaving two boneless segments.

F

gently against the bones and slicing down and away to the tail. The upper and lower portions will be free of bones and can be rinsed in cold water and patted dry.

Some meat is obviously lost in this process, but a safer and more enjoyable fillet results. If you use the bony fillet for fish stock, and use a fine strainer, the bony strip does not have to be wasted. An alternative is to leave the strip of Y bones in the fillet, cut the skinless fillet into chunks, and run the chunks through a food grinder with fine blades, after which you can create patties or a fish loaf.

Filleting flatfish. Flatfish such as flounder are among the most popular of inshore saltwater species. Although they have a different body shape from most other fish, they are not difficult to clean, especially if you use a sharp knife with a long, slightly flexible blade.

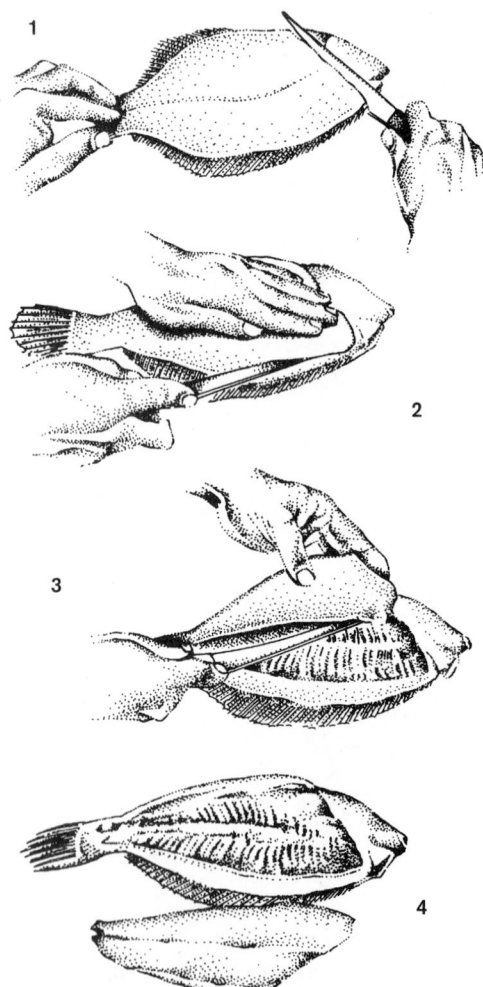

To fillet a flatfish, cut across the body just behind the head and down to the backbone (1) and then slice the length of the fish from head to tail, scraping the blade along the backbone (2). Continue this cut down to the other side of the fish, lifting up the fillet as necessary (3) and slicing the entire fillet free (4). Remove skin if desired.

To fillet a flounder, slice the meat across the body just behind the head and down to the backbone; then slice the length of the fish from head to tail, scraping the blade along the backbone. Continue this cut down to the other side of the fish, lifting the fillet up as necessary and slicing the entire fillet free. Lay the fillet skin down, and remove the skin by pressing a fork or the thumbnail of your free hand on the tail of the fillet; cut between the skin and the meat with your knife hand. You can use a sawing motion here and aid the effort by pulling on the tail of the fillet in the opposite direction of the cut.

Steaking.   Steaking fish for frying or broiling is a good way to handle large specimens. To steak a fish, scale and eviscerate it first; then make a slice on both sides of the fins and pull them free. If the fish is firm or partly frozen, and you have a good cleaver, cut off the head and tail and make the steaks from three-fourths to one-inch thick, starting from the head and working toward the tail. You may find it easier to leave on the head and steak the fish from the tail toward the head, grasping the fish by the head. Trim the belly fat and any obvious bones from the steak; then rinse each steak quickly in cold water and pat dry. When you get to the tail section where no more steaks are available, fillet it.

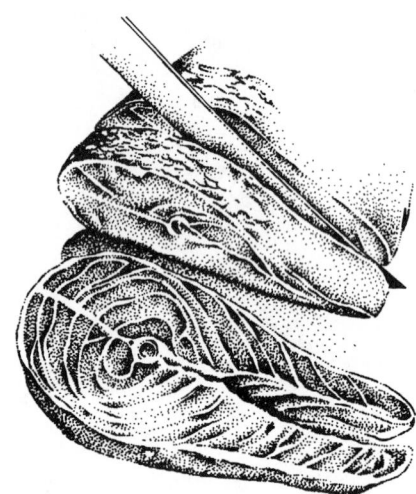

Steaks are created from a beheaded, eviscerated carcass by making equal-diameter cuts across the body and through the backbone.

A fillet knife won't do an adequate job of steaking fish. Steaks should be neatly cut, not ragged and hacked. Use a butcher's knife or a cleaver for steaking. Don't use a serrated knife or one that is likely to grind the backbone; fine pieces of ground backbone may get in or on the steaks. Fish that are very cold or partially frozen will steak better than those that are soft and fleshy, so if your knife isn't super sharp or you're making do with a less rugged blade, it might be good to chill or partly freeze the fish before steaking.

F

Skinning. Most fish skinning takes place during the filleting process, with the skin being separated from the flesh as a next-to-last step. However, some people like to have a whole fish without the skin and certain fish—like dolphin, for example—do not yield their skin very well when their sides have been cut away from the whole body. If you think that the skin may leave an objectionable flavor in the flesh, remove it; removing the skin also helps spices or sauces penetrate the flesh better. If the fish is slimy (some freshwater species have more abundant and more offensive-smelling mucous than others), the skin should be removed. Wiping with a cloth doesn't seem to remove slime unless you have a lot of clean cloths available. You can try placing the fish in a solution of one part vinegar and three parts water to help remove the mucous. You can also rub the fish with generous amounts of salt and then rinse with cold water.

Small fish can be skinned by following the procedure described earlier for pan dressing, with skin and ribs removed. Large whole fish can be skinned by making three shallow cuts: along the back and past the dorsal fin from just behind the head to just ahead of the tail; diagonally across the body, meeting with the forward end of the dorsal cut; and along the belly from the end of the diagonal cut past the anal fin to the tail. At the cut corner behind the head, pry up a small strip of skin with the knife; then grab this with your fingers or a pair of pliers and peel the skin back. Repeat this on the other side, and finish the fish by any method you choose.

If you have already eviscerated a fish but want to keep it whole without the skin, then cut the skin around the tail and head (behind the pectoral fins) and along the back. Pry up a small strip of skin at

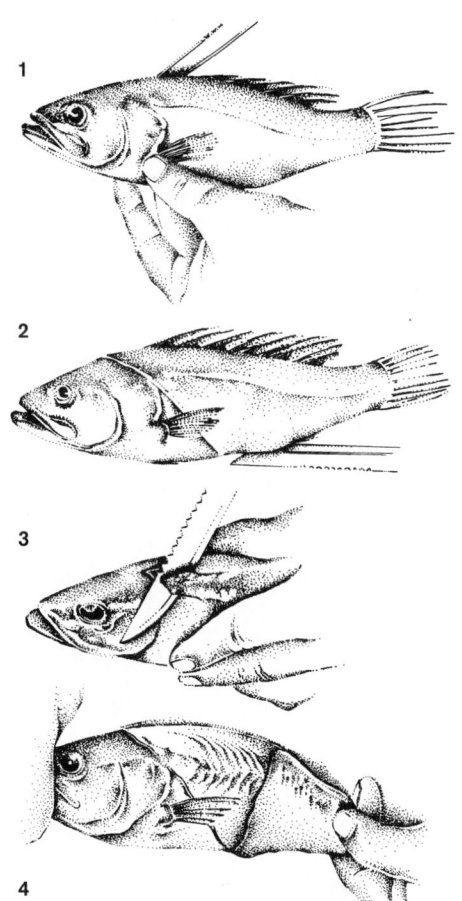

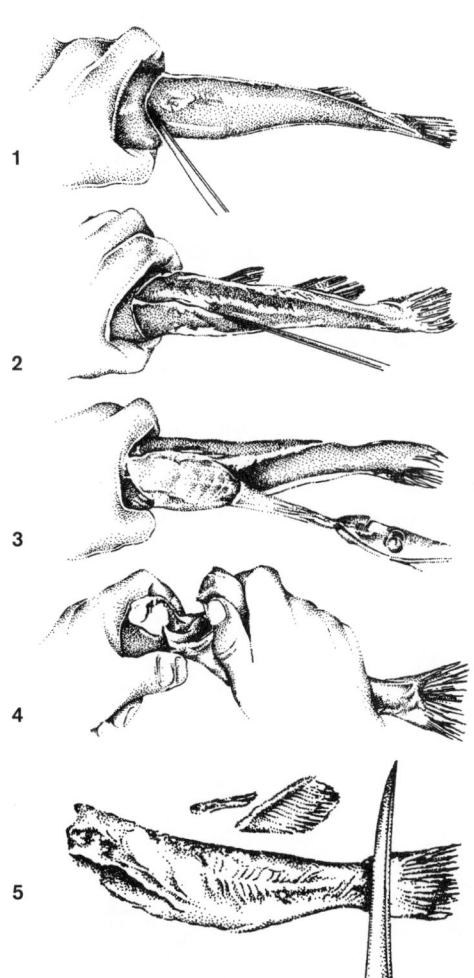

To skin a large whole fish, make shallow cuts along the back and past the dorsal fin from just behind the head to just ahead of the tail (1). Then cut diagonally across the body, meeting with the forward end of the dorsal cut (2), and cut along the belly from the end of the diagonal cut past the anal fin to the tail. At the intersected cuts behind the head, pry up a small strip of skin with the knife (3); grab this strip with your fingers or a pair of pliers and peel back the skin (4).

To skin and eviscerate bullheads and small catfish, hold them carefully at the head with your fingers pinning the sharp pectoral fins; make a shallow cut of the skin around the entire head of the fish (1) and also along the backbone from the dorsal fin to the adipose fin (2). With pliers, grab the skin at the back and pull it to the tail (3); repeat on the other side. Holding the fish as shown, bend the head down to break the backbone (4), and then pull the head away from the fish toward the tail, removing skin and entrails in the process. Cut off the tail and rinse the fish.

the tail, grip this with pliers, and peel back the skin while holding the tail firmly.

Skinning small catfish.   Bullheads and small catfish pose cleaning problems for many anglers, yet these fish can be dressed easily with proper treatment. They have a tough skin that is thin and slippery, and it cannot be removed like other fish. To skin and eviscerate bullheads and small catfish, make a thin slice on the top of the fish from behind the adipose fin up to the dorsal fin, and continue with a vertical cut from the dorsal fin down to the backbone. Put the knife aside, grab the head with one hand and the body with the other, and bend the head down to break the backbone. Hold the body portion firmly, with your finger over the broken backbone, and pull the head away from the fish toward the tail, removing skin and entrails in the process. Cut off the tail and rinse the fish.

With larger catfish, it's best to slice the perimeters of the skin. Hold the head firmly. Slice completely around the fish behind the pectoral fin. Slice along the top of the fish and around both sides of the adipose fin; then slice along the belly and around both sides of the pectoral fin. Use a pair of snub-nose pliers to grasp the skin near the pectoral fin, and pull back firmly toward the tail to remove it. Repeat on the other side. Sever the head and tail and remove the entrails. You can now fillet the fish, keep it as is, or steak it.

Trimming for Health and Taste Reasons

Some fish contain a dark lateral line that has a different flavor than the rest of the meat. If you fillet these fish and remove the skin, you can slice away this dark flesh (which is not detectable by taste, incidentally).

Many fisheries agencies advocate trimming away the fatty parts from fish, as well as removing the skin to reduce the intake of certain environmental contaminants. We are not talking about the taste or the flavor of fish flesh here. This is about the hidden and tasteless elements with such foreboding

To remove fatty flesh that may contain contaminants, trim the flesh from the back and belly and also along the lateral lines (inset); then remove the skin.

names as mirex, PCBs, dioxin, and chlordane. These contaminants have a long residual life in the aquatic environment and work their way through the food chain into the flesh of food and sportfish.

A high percentage of contaminants is found in the fatty portion of fish, so the best policy is to trim away the fatty area of the back, belly, and lateral line. A study that evaluated untrimmed brown trout fillets versus trimmed fillets found that trimming resulted in an average reduction of 62 percent in fat content and 45 percent in contaminants.

Researchers note that cooking trimmed fillets in a way that allows the remaining fat to drain out and away from the flesh will further reduce levels of contaminants. Some studies suggest that baking or broiling on a rack will result in further reduction in fats and the contaminants stored in them, although the exact percentage varies.

Depending on where you fish and what you keep for consumption, you can lessen potential health risks simply by carefully cleaning your catch.

Market Definitions

Although the terms used in this book are generally understood by anglers, supermarkets and fish markets may use slightly different terms. Here's a partial guide to the common terms used there.

Whole fish.   An unprocessed fish exactly as it comes from the water, complete with head, scales, skin, and entrails. Another common term is "in the round." Whole fish are usually found at dockside.

Drawn fish.   A fish with only the entrails removed. It may need to be descaled or filleted, or to have the head cut off, etc.

Dressed fish.   A fish that has been descaled and eviscerated, with the head, tail, and fins removed. "Whole dressed" means that the head and tail are left on.

Steaks and fillets.   Generally the same as the meaning used by anglers, although stores may offer different cuts of steak depending on the size of the fish and the location that the steak came from.

See: Regulations.

FISH SCALER

A tool for removing the scales from a fish.

See: Fish Preparation—Cleaning/Dressing.

FISH SCENT

See: Scents.

FISH SHELTER

See: Fish Attractor.

FISHWAY

A man-made passageway that allows fish to move around a dam in a river system or to migrate into a collected in the hopper and lifted to an exit channel at the top of the dam, from which they swim out into the river.

Incorporated into most fishways or ladders are facilities that allow for counting and identifying fish; in some places they include public viewing rooms with glass sidewalls.

FIZZING
See: Puncturing; Catch-and-Release.

FLARE
A bright light used as a distress signal, usually pyrotechnic; also the outward curvature of the top-side of a boat.

FLASHER
(1) A type of sonar with a flashing light that indicates depth on a circular dial.
See: Sonar.

(2) A type of attractor used in trolling to get the attention of deep fish.
See: Dodger/Flasher.

FLAT
A long, level, and shallow part of a body of water adjacent to deeper water and/or channels. In freshwater, flats exist in rivers, lakes, and reservoirs and along tidal rivers; and in saltwater, flats are found in bays, estuaries, and marshes, as well as atop reefs and atolls and around islands. Some expansive shallow areas along a mainland coast or beach may also be considered flats.

The bottom composition of a flat may be mud, sand, gravel, rock, grass, or a combination of sand and aquatic vegetation. In many cases, flats having hard bottoms and shallow depths are suitable for wading, and may have enough water to float shallow-draft fishing boats, some of which are called flats boats *(see)*.

Flats, and the edges of flats, provide feeding opportunity for various species of fish as the fish move on and off them, migrate through them, and reside in them for varying periods. Flats with grass or other vegetation are among the best for fishing, since they offer cover for some species and food for smaller and larger fish alike. Mud and sand flats are not as productive, although those with cover, such as flooded bushes or stumps (in an impoundment, for example), may be used by such object-oriented fish as largemouth bass. The term "flats fishing" is usually specific to saltwater and to wading/poling/sight fishing activities, especially for tarpon, bonefish, permit, redfish, and seatrout. Angling for these species is discussed under their respective entries.
See: Sight Fishing.

This fishway for salmon and steelhead is a series of stepped pools leading to a fish hatchery.

fish hatchery. Also called fish ladders, fishways are primarily used by migratory (anadromous) species to continue natural migrations in a river system. Fishways have been constructed to help rebuild or reintroduce fish stocks that have suffered from the construction of dams; a dam may prevent the upstream movement of fish to natural spawning areas, and the downstream movement of out-migrating adults or juvenile fish. Fishways are also located below fish hatcheries so that fish can move into hatchery facilities.

Fishways are permanent fish passage devices. Ladderlike fishways are passive flume-type structures that are inclined and equipped with a series of baffles or weirs, which interrupt the flow of water and create ascending pools. They reduce water velocity so fish can navigate up them in a ladderlike progression at their own pace, just as they would negotiate natural rapids. One such style, the Denil, is suited to small to medium rivers having relatively consistent flows, is designed to pass small populations of fish, and is limited by large water depths. Another, the vertical slot, is suited to medium to large rivers having dramatic flow fluctuation, is designed to pass large populations of fish, and has a moderate slope.

Another fishway is the mechanical lift, or elevator, which is used at high hydroelectric dams. Here, attraction flows draw fish into a pool area equipped with a large hopper. At fixed intervals, a gate is used to crowd fish into a confined area. The fish are

FLATFISH

The term "flatfish" broadly refers to a group of more than 500 species of unique, compressed fish that have developed special features for living on the bottom, the most interesting of which is that both eyes are on one side of the head. They are capable of excellent camouflaging and are widespread, ranging from cold, boreal habitats to warm, tropical environments. The flatfish group includes among the world's most important commercial, recreational, and food fish, such as sole, flounder, halibut, dab, plaice, and turbot—names that often apply to species in different families.

External Characteristics of Flatfish

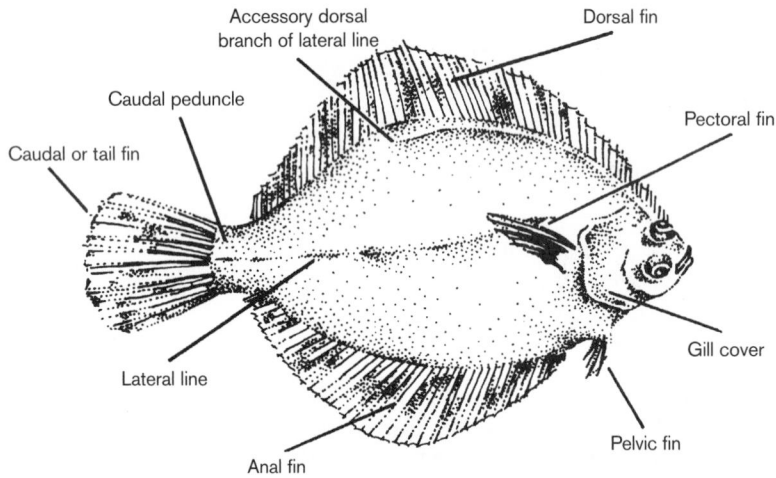

Accessory dorsal branch of lateral line

Dorsal fin

Caudal peduncle

Pectoral fin

Caudal or tail fin

Lateral line

Gill cover

Anal fin

Pelvic fin

Characteristics

Flatfish represent an unusual form of piscine engineering; as mentioned, they are unique in that the skull is asymmetrical with both eyes on the same side of the head. Nonflatfish species are typically streamlined, possess intricately carved fins and tail, and are adorned with neat, symmetrical coloration. Flatfish, however, look more like a squashed footballs or a large decaying leaves. Whereas one side of their body appears translucent or milky white, depending on the species, the other is a mottled assembly of muddy browns, reds, whites, and greens,

which aids in camouflaging. The simple fins make an even fringe around the body, and a loosely shaped tail seems to have been tacked on. Oddest of all are the two beady eyes perched much too close together on the flatfish's brown side, adding the pièce de résistance to an already grotesque appearance.

Flatfish actually begin life like symmetrical fish, with an eye on each side of the head. A few days after hatching, their bodies flatten, one eye begins to migrate, and soon both eyes are close together on one side. At this time, the flatfish begins to swim and lies on its blind side. If the right eye migrates to the left side, the flatfish is left-eyed (sinistral). If the left eye migrates to the right side, the fish is right-eyed (dextral). Flatfish spend the rest of their lives on or near the bottom with the eyed side facing up.

In general, flatfish have a highly compressed body, which gives rise to the name "flatfish." Their dorsal and anal fins are usually long, the adults do not have a swim bladder, and they can change the color of their skin as well as the intensity of its coloration. This last trait of most flatfish takes advantage of their existence on the bottom, allowing them to match their background or sometimes bury themselves in the sediment and lie in wait for unsuspecting prey. If, for instance, a dark, pebbly patterned flounder settles on a light-colored, sandy bottom, the fish's skin will rapidly shift to a sand color, usually in less than a minute.

The lack of pigmentation on a flatfish's blind side has a purpose, too. Although this white half often rests against the bottom, where complex designs would be of no value, the absence of markings aids the fish when it swims high in the water (which some species do more often than others). Because of light reflecting off the surface, any flatfish predator looking upward sees a uniform whitish cast in that uppermost region; a flatfish passing through this light will be well concealed.

Flatfish also have a wide range in maximum size. Both Atlantic halibut and Pacific halibut have been reported to reach 700 pounds, although the largest specimens caught by anglers weighed 255 pounds and 459 pounds respectively. The smallest is probably the pygmy tonguefish *(Symphurus parvus)*, which reaches its maximum size at 3 inches.

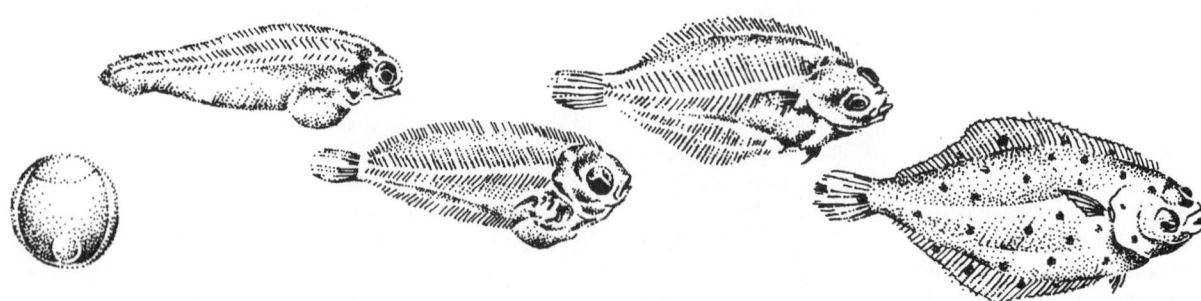

The amazing transformation of flatfish begins after the egg develops into a symmetrical fish with an eye on each side of the head. A few days after the fish hatches, the body flattens, one eye migrates to the opposite side of the body so that both eyes lie close together, and the flatfish begins to swim and lie on its blind side.

The Eye Development of a Right-Eyed Flatfish

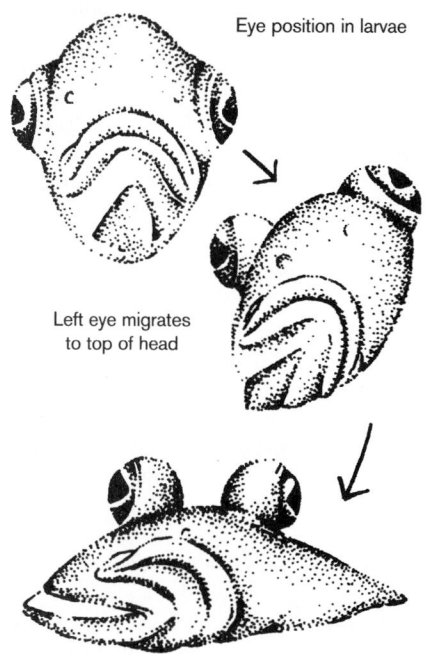

Eye position in larvae

Left eye migrates
to top of head

Both eyes on right side

Flatfish resemble a fly carpet or a flying saucer as they ripple and glide through the water. The smaller inshore species found over sandy bottoms, especially flounder, glide to the bottom, flip sand over their backs, and become almost invisible except for their protruding eyes. When a small fish or other prey is spotted, they squirt water from the underside gill and quickly propel themselves outward in pursuit. As a result of their tendency to bury and camouflage themselves, flatfish are often tough for divers to spot with an untrained eye.

Flatfish make delicious eating. They have firm, white delicate flesh that adapts well to a variety of preparation methods. Because many flatfish are found in shallow estuaries and bays, however, they, and other bottom-dwelling species, are particularly susceptible to pollutants, especially those that gather in bottom sediments. As a result, in some locations, they may be covered by consumption advisories.

Classification

Flatfish as a whole are in the order Pleuronectiformes (sometimes called Heterosomata). Worldwide there are more than 500 (estimates say 520) species of flatfish, in six or seven families. Flatfish include flounder, sole, turbot, halibut, sanddabs, plaice, and tonguefish. These names do not indicate that a fish belongs to a specific family; for example, species referred to as sole occur in the Bothidae, Pleuronectidae, and Soleidae families. Flatfish found in North American waters fall in two broad categories; one includes the families Bothidae and Pleuronectidae, and the other includes the families Cynoglossidae and Soleidae.

The Bothidae is a very large family that contains more than 200 species. This family is called the left-eyed flounder because the eyes and dark color typically are on the left side. In some fish, like the California halibut *(see: halibut, California),* however, the eyes can be on the left side or the right side. Bothidae family members are closely related to those in the Pleuronectidae family.

The Pleuronectidae family is composed of right-eyed flounder, with the eyes and dark color usually on the right side. This family includes about 100 species, many of which are found along the North American coast. One, the starry flounder, regularly has the eyes on either the left or right side of the head. The Pacific halibut occasionally breaks the rule and is left-eyed.

The Cynoglossidae family comprises roughly 100 species of tonguefish. Their eyes are on the left side, and the dorsal and anal fins are joined to the pointed caudal fin. Cynoglossidae species are closely related to Soleidae (sole); the latter includes species with the eyes on the right side and a distinct caudal fin that is not pointed. True sole are members of the Soleidae family, but the word "sole" has been widely used to refer to some flatfish that actually belong to other families, such as petrale sole.

True sole are right-eyed flatfish. Species referred to as sole in North America are rarely seen by the recreational angler but are more common in cold European waters, where they are taken by both commercial and recreational anglers. In the Gulf of Mexico, sole are frequently caught in commercial or bait trawls. The lined sole *(Archinus lineatus),* is sometimes sold in aquarium stores as "freshwater flounder" because of its ability to tolerate freshwater or saltwater. The European sole *(Solea solea)* has been heavily marketed, and the term "fillet of sole," which was once specific to the European sole, is now applied to many other sole and indeed to many nonsole flatfish.

In North America, flatfish range along almost every coastline. Prominent or significant along the Pacific coast are the giant Pacific halibut, California halibut, Pacific sanddab, longfin sanddab, starry flounder, and petrale sole. Prominent or significant along the Atlantic and Gulf coasts are winter, summer, southern, windowpane, and gulf flounder, plus the endangered Atlantic halibut.

Some flatfish live along the continental shelf and slope, whereas others come into shoal and inshore waters, and are found in bays and estuaries. A good deal of diversity exists among the species, and some are even tolerant of brackish water. Along the northern Gulf of Mexico, for example, the southern flounder is found in waters of lesser average depth than the waters favored by the gulf flounder, and the southern flounder frequently occurs in low-salinity environs or even in freshwater. The gulf flounder rarely enters waters of reduced salinities, and it is usually caught outside Mobile Bay.

F

For specific species information, *See Brill; Halibut, Atlantic; Halibut, California; Halibut, Pacific; Flounder, Gulf; Flounder, Southern; Flounder, Starry; Flounder, Summer; Flounder, Windowpane; Flounder, Winter; Plaice, American; Plaice, European; Sanddab, Longfin; Sanddab, Pacific; Sole; Sole, Gray; Sole, Petrale; Turbot.*

Angling

Although many anglers do not consider flatfish, especially the smaller varieties, as glamorous as red drum, bluefish, or striped bass, some flatfish do take artificial lures and most are game fighters. Fishing for flatties, as the shallower inshore flatfish are commonly known, does have its advantages. For instance, flatfish do not school, so they are found over a wide area; this is conducive to drifting with the tide and/or wind over bay and estuary flats, for example. Also, many species are easily caught in shallow, protected areas that are accessible in small boats. In temperate and warm waters, certain species are caught year-round, including times when other more glamorous sportfish are unavailable.

Angling techniques for these fish are noted in some species entries and are generally discussed in greater detail under other entries. For more information *see: Drift Fishing; Inshore Fishing.*

FLATHEADS

Dusky Flathead   *Platycephalus fuscus.*
    Other names—estuary flathead, black flathead, mud flathead, lizard.
Sand Flathead   *Platycephalus bassensis.*
    Other names—slimy flathead, southern sand flathead, bay flathead.

Members of the Platycephalidae family, flathead species number about 55 throughout marine and brackish Indo-Pacific waters. Of the many species found in Australian waters, the dusky flathead and the sand flathead are the two most highly regarded by anglers for their table qualities. There is a valuable commercial market for each species, the dusky flathead being taken by gillnets from estuaries and coastal bays, and the sand flathead from trawlers netting open coastal waters. There is a small, inshore, recreational fishery for a third species, the tiger flathead *(Neoplatycephalus richardsoni),* which is a target for anglers in Tasmania, Victoria, and New South Wales.

Identification.   As the name implies, the flathead has a depressed or flattened head and a moderately elongate and moderately depressed body with a truncated to slightly convex tail. The eyes are set on top of the head, which carries two large preopercular spines. Pectoral fins are large. Its body colors are variable, from sandy to dark brown, and are influenced to a degree by the bottom upon which the flathead lies. There is a distinct black spot on the upper lobe of the tail of the dusky flathead,

and one or two dark spots on the lower lobe of the sandy flathead's tail. Spinous and dorsal fins are separate.

Size.   Dusky flathead can grow to at least 15 kilograms (an Australian record is 7.72 kilograms), and sandy flathead to at least 3 kilograms (the Australian record is 2.58 kilograms).

Distribution.   Dusky flathead occur along the East Coast of Australia from Cairns in Queensland to the Gippsland Lakes in eastern Victoria. Sandy flathead range from northern New South Wales along the southern coastline to just north of Perth in Western Australia.

Habitat.   The dusky flathead inhabits sheltered estuaries, bays, and inlets, and can range well into river systems, frequently being taken in freshwater reaches by lure anglers chasing the Australian bass. The sandy flathead also inhabits estuaries and bays but is more often taken from coastal waters over sandy bottoms. Both species are bottom dwellers living mainly over sandy, gravel, or mud bottoms, and in seagrass beds.

Life history/Behavior.   Dusky flathead spawn during the warmer months (September through March) but at different times, depending on their geographic location. Sandy flathead spawn from August through October. Fecundity details are not known. Both species tend to be solitary.

In winter, they tend to spread upstream or move into deeper water off the coast. In summer, they gather in the lower parts of estuaries and along ocean beaches, where spawning occurs.

Food and feeding habits.   Flatheads are carnivores and live on small fish (e.g., whiting, mullet), crustaceans (e.g., prawns, crabs), worms, squid, and octopuses. To capture these, they lie in ambush, concealed in the sand or mud with only their eyes protruding. Any of these are used for bait, as are, among others, cut baits of tuna, bonito, and whole pilchards.

Angling.   The most popular angling method is bottom fishing while drifting in a boat. Shore, jetty, and beach fishing are also practiced. Boats rods are used, but handlines are common because they allow the angler to better feel the relatively timid bite of the flathead. Line strengths range from 3 kilograms to 7 kilograms, and hook sizes vary from 3/0 to 7/0. Ganged rigs—constructed by joining three, four, or more hooks, eye to bend, and baited with cut fish or whole pilchards—are especially popular. Live baits are favored over dead baits.

Movement of the bait across the bottom is very important for attracting the fish's attention. Jigging (known as yo-yoing in Australia) has a high priority as a handline method because it tempts the fish to leave its ambush position and take the bait in a more positive manner. Flatheads are sluggish fighters when taken on bait; when lures are used, their behavior is much more aggressive and challenging.

This fish will respond quickly to a lure fished close to the bottom. Small to medium diving minnow-type lures that have a lively action at a slow retrieve rate, soft plastics, spinners, and spoons are all used. Soft plastics should be allowed to sink, then bounced along the bottom to disturb the sand and attract the fish. Fly fishing is also effective, using No. 7 or 8 sinking lines and streamer flies; best results are had when fishing over sandy bottoms in water up to 2 meters deep.

Hooked flathead have a bad habit of fighting sluggishly to the side of the boat, then getting energized when about to be netted, which enables many to escape. When handling the fish, anglers should exercise care to avoid a painful wound from the preopercular spines.

FLATLINING

Trolling a lure or bait on an unweighted fishing line is known as flatlining. This is a popular technique for angling in relatively shallow water (1 to 25 feet), because the depth achieved is primarily dependent on the weight or diving ability of the object being trolled. Flatlines are used in freshwater and saltwater angling for a variety of species, and often in conjunction with planer boards or sideplaners.

Running a flatline is the simplest kind of trolling. Flatlines are set straight out behind the boat; there are no heavy sinkers, downrigger weights, diving planers, or other devices that influence the depth attained by the lure. Flatlines are sometimes referred to as high lines, usually when trolled in conjunction with some type of deep-diving lure. Anyone with a rod, reel, line, and lure can run a flatline. Most people who do some trolling in the course of their fishing run a flatline, usually for hours on end without regard to technique.

The keys to flatline trolling productivity are the length of line and how you maneuver the boat to position the lures or bait. Generally, in freshwater the clearer the water, the shallower the fish, the spookier the fish, and the more boat activity there is, the longer the line you need. Long lines are particularly important in inland, clear-water trout and salmon fishing, where it is not uncommon to troll lures 200 to 300 feet behind the boat. Long lines have also become more common in Great Lakes walleye trolling because of the increasing water clarity. If you're used to casting 50 or 60 feet to catch fish, trolling distances of 200 to 300 feet seem outlandish. They're not.

Trolling a line for seemingly endless hours is boring, unimaginative, and unproductive. You have to alter the lure's path regularly by turning, by steering in an S-shaped pattern or other irregular way, or by altering the speed of the boat. These changes enhance your presentation by altering the speed and action of the lure and making it appear less "mechanical."

In making a flatline trolling presentation, you must consider where the fish are and how to get your lures close without alarming them. Fish in shallow water near shore, or close to the surface in open water, characteristically move out of the boat's path because they are especially wary, perhaps even nervous. With few exceptions, you can't motor through the shallows and expect fish to stay around or to be receptive to your offerings. This is one reason why you seldom see fish in less than 15 feet of water on sonar: Fish swim off to one side of the boat as it approaches and thus are well outside the cone angle of the sonar's transducer.

After the boat has passed, the fish may continue to swim away, they may stay where they are once they have moved, or they may return to their original location. If your lure is trailing directly behind a straight-moving boat, the fish in the first two

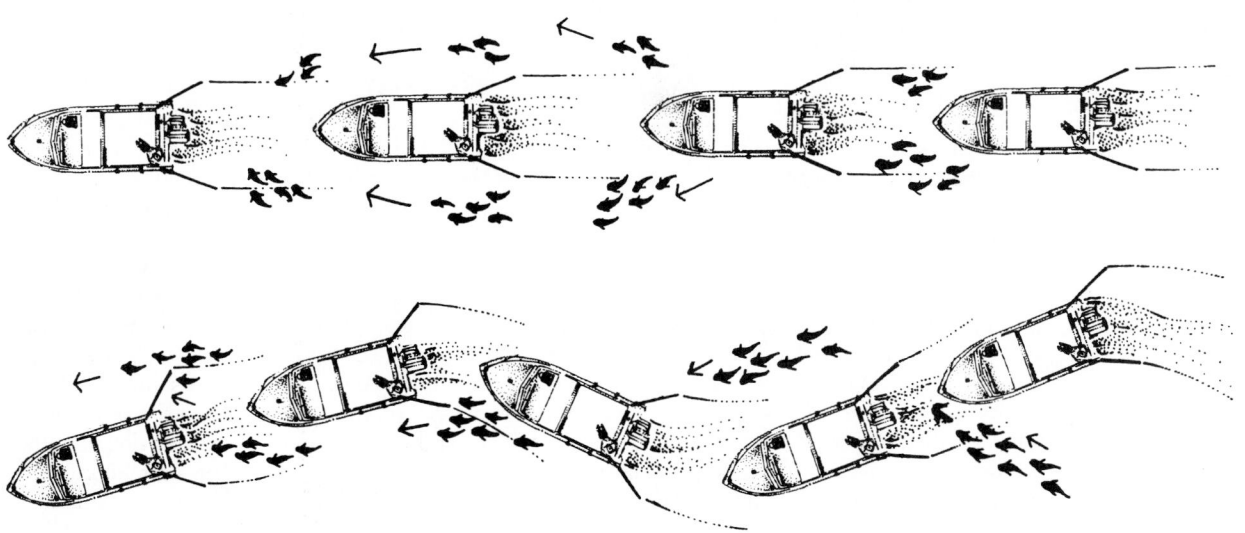

When using a long line (200 to 300 feet) in flatline trolling, you may intercept fish that move off and then return after the boat has passed by (top, right to left). It is often more productive to vary your course by making moderate or exaggerated S-turns, which allow lures to pass fish you might have missed otherwise (bottom, right to left).

instances may never see your lure. If your line is too short, fish in the third instance may not see it if they are slow to return to their position, or they may see it but associate it with the boat. This illustrates why a lure should be fished on a long line for some types of fish and how proper boat maneuvering can bring lures into the range of fish that may not have been in the boat's path or that may have moved out of it.

A lot of shallow-holding fish can be caught by trolling, particularly in the spring, when fish are most likely to be shallow. Correct line placement, lure presentation, and boat control are critical for shallow flatline trolling success. The true test of shallow flatline trolling is to make your presentations in tight areas. Near shore, around reefs or shoals or islands, along grass lines and weed edges, and so forth, are hard places to troll effectively because maneuverability is limited. Consider, for example, a lakeshore that drops off fairly sharply and has boulders or stumps submerged just under the surface. If you bring your boat too close to shore, your motor may hit these structures. You could try using an electric motor and steering around them, but this doesn't always work; and if the wind or current isn't favorable, you would go nowhere. The only way to deal with this problem when flatline trolling is to sweep in and out from shore and plan strategic approaches to points, sandbars, islands, shoals, channels, and the like. You may have to troll by these structures more than once and from different directions to cover the location effectively.

Flatline trolling is not just for shallow-water fishing, however; many anglers flatline both large and small deep-running plugs. When fishing deep water, though, you must know how your lures dive with various lengths and strengths of line, and you must pay attention to the depth beneath you and to the lures behind you while trolling. This applies equally to trolling weighted lures and medium- or deep-diving plugs. Learn to evaluate the depth that your trolled lures or bait actually attain to avoid haphazard flatlining and sporadic success.

When flatlining, either place lures or bait on a direct path behind the boat or place them to the side of the boat via sideplaners or outriggers (see). Those that are set off to the side are connected via releases (see) to the line that is towing the sideplaner or extended along the outrigger. Those that are run directly behind the boat are often not placed in any release, so the line extends directly from the rod tip to the trailing lure or bait. For some situations, this latter method may be adequate; adjusting the position of the rod is important for avoiding tangles or getting lures deeper in the water. Tangles are more likely when the line rides high and when it is windy.

The higher the rod tip, the more the lure or bait tends to ride toward the surface; if you want it to get deeper, you may need to position the rod tip closer to the water (by angling it to the side of the gunwales). To get the lines lower or to aid in setting the hook upon a strike, you can use a release clip that is attached to a low position on the transom of the boat. One way to do this is by securing a release to a stern cleat or to a transom eye bolt; after the lure or bait is placed the appropriate distance back, the fishing line is secured in the release, and the line from rod tip to release is tightened.

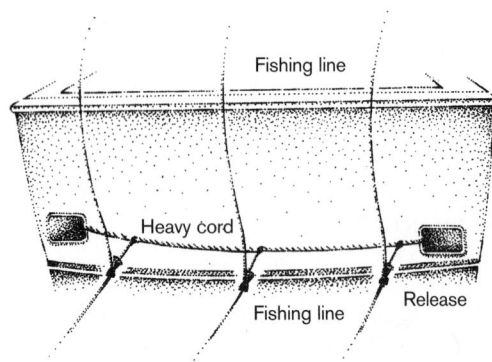

To increase hooksetting effectiveness when flatlining, attach fishing line to a release that is fixed to the transom of the boat.

Another way to accomplish the same thing is to run a heavy-strength fishing line, parachute cord, or other thin but strong line across the outside of the transom of an inboard boat. The line can be high and extend from one transom eye bolt to the other, or it can be lower by running through the scuppers. In the latter, connect the line to one stern cleat on the inside gunwale; run it out the scupper, across the outside of the transom, through the other scupper; and connect it to the stern cleat on the other inside gunwale. Leave some slack in the line for retrieval. Connect two or three releases to the outside lines, and you're ready to put trolling lines in them.
See: Planer Boards; Sideplaners; Trolling.

FLATS BOAT
A flats boat is not a flat boat. It's a shallow-draft fishing-only boat that was originally designed for use on saltwater flats, where the method of angling entailed poling in shin-deep water for shallow and often spooky fish, and where it was necessary to have a boat that drew little water, provided a stable standing and casting platform, was easy to pole, and was tough enough to cross long stretches of not-so-flat open sea in order to reach the flats. The concept of a boat that could do these things, provide plenty of storage, speed to the good spots, and not be a bear to ride in bad water has been evolving since the late 1960s. In some ways, the flats boat is analogous to a high-performance bass boat, which is also intended for the specific activity of casting and which includes high-speed travel and some contact with rough water in the mix.

Known originally as a flats skiff or flats boat, and originating in the Florida Keys, these 16- to 20-foot fishing vessels have become popular outside of Florida in many coastal locations, and have a small following in freshwater, partly with anglers who occasionally fish inshore in saltwater and want a boat for both. Thus, they are not a flat hull, but a modified-V hull with sharp water entry.

Owing to design and construction materials, flats boats sit high in the water. They are light, draw only a small amount of water, and have plenty of beam. Although at casual glance a flats boat looks somewhat like a bass boat, most flats boats actually have higher freeboard, which is flared to help deflect spray and keep the interior dry when running in rough water (though there are limits to how much can be deflected). The hull is also a little more V-shaped, which contributes to a gentler ride.

Flats boats draw roughly 6 to 12 inches of water depending on the particular boat, and this gets them into the skinny water of flats, bays, marshes, and the like, where not only bonefish and redfish prowl, but also sea trout, striped bass, and in some places largemouth bass and snook. Flats boats intended for the skinniest of water differ from those intended for general bay and shoreline fishing in more open and sometimes rougher water.

Although a flats boat is one that can float in mere inches of water, it also must be able to ride as comfortably as possible in the sometimes rough stretches of water between the various flats. It takes a lot of V in the hull to produce a good ride in a stiff chop, and the greater the V, the greater the draft. It's possible to make a 17-footer that rides like a dream at 30 mph in 3-foot seas, but unfortunately that same boat could not be poled in much less than 18 inches of water.

The first flats boats drew 13 to 14 inches, which was too much for many flats situations. But builders learned that by reducing the V to a modified form with between 12 and 14 degrees of deadrise at the transom, getting rid of as much weight as possible via lightweight hull materials (like Kevlar and/or carbon fiber composites), using a lighter and lower-horsepower engine, and leaving unnecessary junk ashore, that same boat would float in an honest 9 or 10 inches instead of 13 or 14. By adding a set of hydraulic trim tabs to the transom, they got back a lot of the soft (and drier) ride that can otherwise only be provided by a lot more V in the hull.

Nowadays if you're really serious about skinny water flats fishing, the issue is the number of inches in draft. However, not all flats boats are used in the shallowest water, and since different situations require different draft capabilities, flats boats have evolved up and down to meet specific conditions.

Bonefishing in thin water is what drove the creation of the genuine flats boat, and many flats boats today are still targeted directly at this activity. Decades ago, bonefish flats were reached with 16-foot flat-bottom wood skiffs powered by a 10- to 15-hp outboard. This produced a long, slow, and wet ride between flats, but the boats floated in 6 or

A typical flats boat is poled across Florida Keys shallows.

7 inches of water. Today's modified-V-hulled boats get to the next flat much faster, smoother, and dryer, but if the boat draws too much water it is not truly a bonefish boat. You can catch bonefish (and redfish) by using boats that draw 13 to 14 inches of water, mostly by parking the boat and wading whenever the water is too shallow, though a soupy bottom precludes wading. And of course you can't follow or intercept moving fish as well on foot as you can in a boat. So the right boat is critical for several reasons.

If you're serious about flats fishing for bonefish, skip any boat that draws over 10 inches. Also, consider length, hull weight, and horsepower. Less total weight translates directly into easier poling. Wide boats are harder to pole; a long skinny boat pushes a lot easier than a short, beamy craft. Consistently successful bonefishing calls for precise boat maneuverability, even (especially) on windy days, so you will really appreciate a boat that is easy to pole.

Hull noise is a major factor in flats fishing. Bonefish, permit, redfish, snook, and sometimes tarpon are all affected by noise. There is a huge difference among hulls when it comes to noise. Boats with large reverse chines, which are downturned for a dryer ride, make noise in even the slightest ripple, and most of the time this noise alerts a bonefish long before you're within casting range. Manufacturers are working on making these boats stealthier, and some boats are much better at being quiet. Many anglers who have otherwise reasonably quiet hulls even refuse to have spray rails added to them because of the extra noise the rails make on the flats.

Some boats that are inherently noisy can become a lot less so by poling them from the bow. Aluminum hulls, especially jonboats, certainly fall into this category, but poling could be difficult with wide hulls.

No one boat can do it all. The quiet poling in super-thin water so essential to bonefish anglers is not critical in other flats boat applications, nor is the minimal draft. A 12-inch draft is not too much

F

for chasing striped bass or bluefish on deeper northern flats, for example. You can get by with 14 inches in that environment and at the same time have a bigger boat to make the ride across miles of open water a lot easier. Plus you'll often fish in open water and/or around tide rips, where shallow draft is not an issue. Most anglers in this situation opt for an 18- to 20-footer, with 130 hp or more to get the desired cruising speed. Such a rig is big and heavy by southern flats standards, and it will pole like a dump truck, but mostly you'll be using the pushpole to control your drift with wind and tide. You could use the same rig for flats tarpon fishing, although the loss of pushpole mobility would be a little irksome.

At the other end of this spectrum are the superthin flats where redfish shimmy into water so shallow that every inch of draft counts. A boat that draws 10 inches can be way too much here, although it can be used very successfully on the deeper flats and around the edges of the really thin stuff whenever the fish are found there.

A number of somewhat specialized boats have evolved for this fishery; these are not specifically flats boats in the high-tech modern sense, but they have a similar principle. For many years, the "scooter" was very popular in Texas because it drew only a few inches and planed like a jet boat. The original version was extremely plain, like a sled with handle bars built to carry one angler and powered by 10 hp or less. From a distance, it looked just like an old Cushman motor scooter, hence the name. The more modern versions are bigger, can carry two or three anglers, and have much larger engines. But they still can get into rather skinny water, even if they're not really popular elsewhere on large bodies of open water for obvious reasons.

Others who want that super-shallow capability turn to durable, thick-aluminum 15- to 17-foot jonboats. Versions with a shallow V that starts in the bow and runs almost to the transom ride far better than completely flat-hulled types, although they draw perhaps an inch more of water. A 16-footer that weighs about 250 pounds reaches 30 mph with a 25-hp engine and two anglers aboard, and it poles almost as easily as a canoe in just 5 inches of water. Some anglers custom-outfit these rigs very economically, with flooring and carpet as well as reinforced-top fore and aft deck coolers for mini-platforms.

Because casting is the only object with flats boats, and because they are geared for light tackle and especially fly tackle use, manufactured versions have a lot of fore and aft deck space. These decks are open and flush casting platforms with ample storage underneath, no pedestal seats, and no cluttering accessories. The large deck area, coupled with a wide beam, makes for living-room-like stability, and even when you get into one of these boats from a dock you'll notice how they don't lean to one side. Some newer flats boats, especially those intended for northern-water use, have a beam up to 8 feet, although most others fall into the 6- to 7-foot range. A wider beam makes for even more stability but a tougher boat to pole; those who would not be poling, either primarily drifting or using an electric motor, and those fishing in more open and thus rougher water, might opt for a boat with greater beam.

As noted, poling is the standard means of moving these boats along the shallows, and most flats boats are equipped with a transom poling platform, a feature relatively unique to this type of fishing boat and its signature characteristic. From the elevated high-above-the-outboard-motor transom platform, you gain the near and distant visibility advantage that extra height affords, and by using an 18-foot fiberglass or graphite pushpole, you can maneuver the boat appropriately to follow a contour, drift properly over a flat, or move to intercept a feeding fish, all while keeping a good lookout. This platform is also useful for sitting and casting, and it can be used in conjunction with a remote-controlled transom-mount electric motor. Many saltwater anglers are averse to using electric motors on flats boats, however, because of the added equipment, the battery needs (unless you run it off the main engine battery and use a recharge system), and the opinion that the motor noise may scare shallow clear-water fish.

Another characteristic of flat boats is the capacity to store plenty of fishing rods. Wide gunwales permit storage of six or more racks per side, with some allowing for full-length storage and having enclosed tip protectors. Livewells are featured on these boats as well, and most sport a center console and three-person bench seat arrangement; the center console on some is spartan, but the placement allows anglers who tangle with big or tough fish on light tackle to quickly run around the boat as necessary when fighting it.

Unlike bass boats, conventional flats boats aren't carpeted; they do have nonskid surfaces, but anglers need to wear shoes or sneakers with boat soles that grip well. In a flats boat, anglers spend most of the time standing and looking or casting; the only time they sit is when moving quickly to and from fishing areas or when stopping to eat lunch. However, some flats boats are equipped with a bow casting platform that elevates the angler 15 to 20 inches above the deck and that can double as a seat, and a few are outfitted with a thigh-high railing to lean against in rough water.

Flats boats are light enough for towing, and many are kept on fitted or customized boat trailers for mobility.

There are options to using flats boats in shallow-water fishing. Some bass boats, especially lighter ones, and some flat-bottom aluminum boats, draw little water. If you can access the necessary fishing areas without having to cross rough-and-tumble water, and if you can get by without flat and uncluttered casting platforms, these may do well. The absence of a poling platform will affect visibility but not necessarily maneuverability.

Certainly canoes offer shallow-water access, but they do not have the stability or casting advantages of other fishing craft. However, there are some places where fish go that even shallow-draft flats boats cannot. Filling this void are some canoelike fiberglass boats, with a pointed bow and square stern for a small outboard, that draw even less water than flats boats, are pretty stable, are far lighter (making them easier to maneuver with a pushpole or electric motor), and are much less expensive. These backwater boats are compromises of a sort for shallow-water use, but compromise is a factor in every fishing boat.

See: Boat; Trailer.

FLATS FISHING

See: Flat; Flats Boat; Sight Fishing.

FLIP CAST

See: Casting

FLIPPING

Flipping is a fairly simple, controlled short-casting technique used in close quarters for presenting a moderately heavy jig or plastic worm in a short, quiet, accurate manner to cover that cannot be properly worked by a lure cast from a long distance away. Some form of flipping has been around for years and was called dabbling or pitching until the marketing wizards latched onto this term. Flipping is a premier close-to-cover fishing technique almost exclusively used by bass anglers standing up in a boat. The basic principle of flipping, however, can be useful when fishing for other species and when wading, fishing from shore, or fishing from a float tube. It is best when there is thick cover, when the water is turbid, and when a jig or weighted worm is used, but flipping can be employed at times with other lures and in other circumstances.

The main purposes, however, are making a quiet presentation in close quarters for largemouth bass and putting the lure in places where other lures cannot be reached with conventional casts. To understand, imagine that you're looking at a bank with a sharply sloping shoreline. Within half a foot of the bank are some bushes, the bases of which may be in 2 feet of water. Any plug pitched at such a target will land directly in front of it and will be on its way without getting very near the fish. A worm might do the trick, but the first cast would have to be extremely accurate; most likely the worm will fall too far in front of the bush to entice the bass to come out. The advantage of flipping is that you can position your boat 15 to 18 feet from the bush and use a long rod to swing a jig or worm so that it lands in the most opportune place without smashing down noisily on the water's surface. Flipping is a surefire way of getting a lure literally in front of a

This thick fallen cover on Missouri's Truman Lake could not be fished properly by casting from afar.

bass in such thick cover as brush, standing timber and stumps, logjams or debris-filled flotsam, heavy lily pad and vegetation clusters, steep craggy ledges, docks, and boathouses.

The tackle required is a long rod, heavy line, and a jig or worm. The rod should be between 7 and 8 feet long, with a long, straight handle. It must be stout because bass are often violently jerked out of heavy cover on a short length of line; and the bigger the bass, the greater the stress and the greater the degree of difficulty. Flipping rods are one-piece, with an upper section that telescopes down into the handle for easy transportation and storage. Most flipping is done with baitcasting tackle, but some anglers prefer spinning gear. The same rod features, however, are applicable. Flipping takes a toll on arm muscles if done for a long period of time; because of this, a graphite rod, weighing considerably less than fiberglass, is desirable.

The reel used on a flipping rod can be the same that you use for other bass fishing applications, but it is best if the reel has a narrow spool (line capacity is not a factor) and is light. It should also have a clear sideplate (no knobs sticking out on which to catch line). A reel that allows one-handed operation is preferable. A so-called flipping feature, which allows the line to be stripped out without having to disengage and re-engage the free spool, makes a difference in convenience when flipping, since you often have to strip off more line but don't have to take time to crank the handle to engage the gears.

When flipping, many anglers use 25- to 30-pound-test nylon monofilament line because it takes a lot of effort to get it to stretch, abrades less, and is suitable for muscling big fish out of thick cover. You can use lighter line, however, although you have to be sensible. Braided and fused super lines, with their high strength and low diameter, are good candidates for flipping. Their low stretch improves strike detection, but because of the close sudden struggles that characterize flipping, you'll have to be careful that you don't overload your rod.

Black or brown jigs, primarily in $^1/_2$-ounce sizes, but also a little lighter and a little heavier, are the most popular flipping bait. These should have fiber weedguards when used in all but rocky ledge areas and should sport a "living rubber" type of skirt and a large hook. They are adorned with all manner of enticements, including worms, curl-tail grubs, pork strips, and the like, but black or brown pork chunks are the most popular.

You can also flip a plastic worm. Use a 7- to 8-inch worm on a 5/0 hook and a heavy ($^3/_8$- or $^1/_2$-ounce) slip sinker that is pegged to prevent it from sliding up the line. This seems to get hung up less frequently than a jig, and when you have a strike, you can hesitate for the slightest moment to get a firm hookset. Try a worm with a paddle or beaver tail when flipping, although curl tails work also if they aren't so sinewy that they grab onto every limb.

To flip properly, remember that the goal is to make a pinpoint bait presentation to a particular object within 10 to 20 feet of the boat and to do so in a quiet, splash-free manner. Seldom are you able to flip while sitting down; this is a technique that requires stand-up work, occasionally with two anglers close together in the bow of a boat (as when working every nook and cranny of a stump- and blowdown-filled stretch of shoreline). To begin flipping, let out about 7 to 8 feet of line from rod tip to lure; the rule of thumb is to let out about an amount equal to the length of the rod. Strip line off the reel until your free hand and rod hand are fully extended away from each other; this will give you 5 to 7 feet of line in your free hand. If you have a $7^1/_2$-foot rod, you're now able to reach a target about 20 feet away.

To flip your bait out, hold the flipping rod at about a 45-degree angle and pull on the line with your left hand to get the bait moving backward. Now drop the rod tip, and start bringing it up to move the lure forward. Practice so you can speed the lure forward to its target with just a slight flexing of your wrist. Let the extra line you're holding in your left hand slide out through the rod guides. Move your left hand forward as the line flows out. Do it right, and the practice plug should go out in a low trajectory and land accurately and softly on its intended target. Extend your rod arm if necessary to reach the target, although you're too far away if you have to do this.

Do not hold onto the line in your hand once it reaches the target. As a flip cast is completed, let

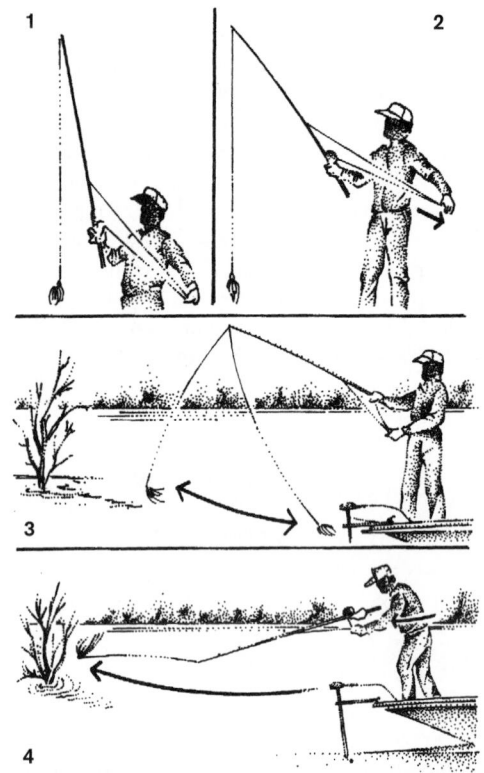

To flip, let out about 7 to 9 feet of line from rod tip to lure; strip line off the reel and hold it in your left hand (1). Point the rod tip up and out, and swing the jig forward (2). The bait will come back toward you; when it reaches the top of its pendulum-like swing, direct it toward the target (3). Lower the rod tip, and let line flow through your free hand; extend your rod arm if necessary to reach the target, and keep the line in your hand (4).

your left hand move forward as the extra line you've been holding in it slides out through the guides. It's natural and easy to make this movement. You should wind up with your left hand up close to the rod and just in front of the reel. At that point, position your thumb and the forefinger of the left hand on top of the rod. The other three fingers of the left hand should go under the rod. Make sure the line coming from the reel runs under your thumb and over the forefinger of your left hand. Having the line in this position lets your thumb and forefinger feel every little bump as the lure you're using works through cover. Having your left hand out there also permits you to grip the rod in two hands at the strike, making for a stronger, more solid hookset. Then you may play the fish in the conventional manner, with one hand on the reel handle and the other on the rod handle, and work it out of the cover.

An angler who holds the line in the left hand away from the rod is likely to struggle when a strike occurs, especially if it's from a big fish. There isn't time to grab the tackle conventionally, so you strip the free line back, jerk the rod tip up sharply, and hope you have hook penetration but can yank the fish out, all in the same motion. It doesn't always happen, and a lot of good-size fish are lost this way. Even when holding the rod with both hands, you have to work fast and try to muscle the fish through the cover as best as possible. At times you'll hook a small fish and yank it out of the cover, but when you hook a big bass while flipping, you'll have an excitingly fast and furious bulldog scrap.

When you retrieve the lure to move it to another spot, lower the rod tip and point it toward the lure; grab the line between the reel and the first guide with your free hand and strip it back while lifting up on your rod (similar to the hauling technique used by fly casters). Swing the lure out and back, and send it forward again to the next object.

When the lure is in the water, you may jig it up and down or crawl it along after it has fallen freely to the bottom. Climb it up, over, and through all of the cover. Closely watch the line for the slightest movement, and be attentive to the softest strike. Don't keep it in any one place long, and try to nudge it through cover instead of ripping it.

Practice is every bit as important in learning how to flip as it is in developing mastery of any casting technique. Even so, you'll see anglers trying to flip who obviously don't know how to go about it. An hour of practice on dry land would ease their problems and make them far more effective when the chance to fish comes along.

FLOAT

A lightweight surface-floating device attached to fishing line for indicating a subsurface bite or strike by a fish, primarily on some form of bait and occasionally on an ultralightweight jig or fly. Technically a float is the most prominent form of bite indicator (see) or strike indicator (see) although it is not actually referred to as either of these. In North America such a device is primarily called a bobber, sometimes a cork, and occasionally a float, but it is only known as a float in Europe, where such devices originated hundreds of years ago. Modern floats are primarily made of balsa wood or hollow plastic.

Modern float designs, rigging, fishing tactics, and control techniques are part of a highly effective fishing system that is an art form and a science in the hands of diligent anglers. Float fishing methods have evolved in recent years and have expanded opportunities to catch many species of fish, especially in freshwater lakes and rivers.

Until recently, floats and float fishing had changed little from their first recorded existence in the fourteenth century until the first modern-era reel development in the mid-nineteenth century. This development allowed anglers to make bigger floats that could be cast farther and also to control their floats at greatly increased distances to reach fish that had previously been out of range before with just a pole. Progress remained stagnant again until spinning reels became popular in the mid-twentieth century and caused casting distance to

An assortment of balsa floats for varied types of fishing.

advance again. In recent decades, floats and float fishing have also benefited from high-tech rods, reels, and lines that have dramatically extended distances, depths, and current speeds.

Thinner, stronger nylon, combined with long-distance casting spools on spinning reels and ultralightweight rods, permits a perfect natural bait presentation in many situations. You can, for example, cast a 13-inch float nearly 80 yards from the bank and place a baited hook or jig 20 to 40 feet deep to unsuspecting walleye, catfish, or trout; cast a $1^1/_2$-inch float to panfish in 12 inches of clear water 30 yards away; and tempt catfish or stripers with a live shad just off snaggy, rocky bottom in powerful flowing water below a dam.

A range of float designs can be bought or made, allowing you to literally fish anywhere at any time and to precisely and naturally present a hooked bait as the fish would expect it to behave and, in most cases, with the fish unaware that you are anywhere near.

There are three major styles of float fishing: fishing with a pole on stillwater and slow-flowing water, fishing with a rod and reel on stillwater, and fishing with a rod and reel on flowing water. Each of these styles employs specific float designs, balancing patterns, casting techniques, and control techniques.

Some Basics

Presenting a hooked bait naturally is an important concept in all types of fishing and especially when using floats. Many species of fish, particularly those that live in stillwater environments, inhale their food most of the time; this begins when they are tiny and start inhaling zooplankton for food. Many fish—most panfish, for example—feed this way their entire lives. Thus, when they suck in a bait that is attached to a float, they are acutely aware that something is very wrong if the bait doesn't move readily when they inhale it.

Anglers should remember that fish have different feeding states. For a small portion of their time they are aggressive, for a larger portion they are

F

neutral, and for the greatest amount of time they are negative; some people estimate that the respective percentages for these behaviors are 10, 30, and 60. Whatever the percentage might be, these behaviors vary according to many factors, especially weather changes and fishing pressure.

When fish are in an aggressive mood, they will attack and consume a bait even if something is wrong with it. But they are especially likely to immediately reject a suspicious bait if they are in a neutral or negative mood. As a result, anglers have to use methods and equipment that will not alarm even the wariest fish.

A major factor in making an unalarming presentation is the float. In places where fish are not very astute or when fishing for aggressive species, a float that has a lot of buoyancy (such as the round bobber that is very common in North America) may be used with success often enough to overlook its deficiencies. However, such buoyancy acts as a drag on hooked bait and is a dead giveaway to light-biting fish. So it's better to fish with a float that is designed to avoid alerting fish and is still sensitive enough to alert the angler to a bite.

Correct float selection is dependent upon knowing the depth of the water at the fishing place. In a boat, depth is readily determined by using sonar; without sonar, and for shore fishing, it is necessary to use some type of weight attached to the line (called a plummet in Europe) to plumb the depth.

Using highly specialized tackle and the most delicately balanced floats, a match angler fishes the 1992 World Championships at the River Erne in Northern Ireland.

Determining depth in this manner is known as plumbing. This activity also is meant to determine the composition of the bottom (mud, gravel, weeds, etc.), the location of stumps or other snags, and changes in depth so that the angler can create a mental picture of the area and visualize where the fish might be.

A major factor in float usage is balancing the float properly. This balancing is also known as shotting, since small split shot or a jig, or a combination of both, is added in just the right amount and placed so that only a minimum amount of the float tip is above the surface and visible to the angler depending on the circumstances. It is always best to have the least possible weight to get the float in a balanced position.

When casting modern floats, always lob the float upward slowly and smoothly. Never snatch it or cast it quickly, which causes tangles. When a float starts to lose momentum, feather the line as it comes off the spool; this pulls the float back so that the baited hook passes over the float before it hits the water.

Float Fishing with a Pole

Float fishing with a pole on stillwater and slow-flowing water is the oldest and simplest way to fish, and it is ideal for children or beginners of any age. Perhaps the earliest illustration of any type of angling is a hieroglyphic from about 2000 B.C. that depicts an Egyptian angler with a pole catching a fish. The use of a float with a pole was known to be practiced in the late 1300s, if not before.

Anglers learned by trial and error in the hundreds of years following the fourteenth century that it was vital to use the smallest possible float that was carefully balanced by lead shot. These floats were made from crow, goose, swan, or porcupine quills (cork bodies were used when extra weight was needed and pear-shaped cork floats were used for pike), and with proper balancing only a fraction of the quill's air chamber was above the surface. This was vital, since it gave the float an almost neutral buoyancy and meant that the most discriminating fish, or even a tiny specimen, could suck the bait into its mouth and simultaneously pull the float under, signaling the angler to set the hook.

This is exactly how the most famous angling writer of all time, Izaak Walton, fished his beloved River Lea, and his book *The Compleat Angler*, written in 1653, described how he used this technique to hook that river's famous, nervous, and difficult-to-catch roach. Even earlier, in 1496, the first English language essay to teach the art of angling, *A Treatyse of Fysshynge with an Angle* by Dame Juliana Berners, illustrated an angler using a 16-foot pole to catch a fish from a river. While Berners graciously credited several earlier angling writers with teaching the fundamentals, both she and Walton noted that the golden rule was always to use the smallest float possible for the conditions and to carefully balance it with lead split shot.

Poles. There are actually two styles of poles: one-piece or telescopic versions that are 9 to 20 feet long, and multipiece (or take-apart) poles that are 18 to 60 feet long. These are both useful in any type or speed of water, but since they do not have a reel, the distance from the angler and the depth of water that can be fished are limited to the length of the pole. Longer poles have the advantage of allowing anglers to reach out to distant locations (such as a weedbed) from a bank or boat and carefully lower a float and bait into small pockets that would be impossible to cast into (or to cast into delicately) with a rod and reel. As a rule, the length of the line from the tip of the pole to the hook should always be shorter than the pole; use 12 feet of line, for example, for a 14-foot pole, and 18 feet of line for a 20-foot pole.

The main tackle component in pole fishing for the average angler is a 10- to 14-foot-long pole, which may be as simple and inexpensive as a cane pole; fiberglass or graphite poles, however, though more expensive, are deadly for anglers who are serious about catching more and bigger panfish.

Floats. For pole fishing in shallow water from 6 inches to 4 feet deep, mini-floats (called a mini shy bite by some) in several sizes from 1 inch to $2\frac{1}{2}$ inches long are perfect and are not likely to scare fish when they are presented in the water because of their smaller shape and lesser splash. These floats are easy to make or find in stores. In essence to make one, take a 1- to 2-inch piece of a thin dried tree branch ($\frac{1}{8}$-inch to $\frac{3}{16}$-inch thick), varnish it, and paint one end with a highly visible color (often red). In use, this is balanced with one or two small split

shot. Such an all-balsa float is available in many sizes from stores; it is capable of being fished with up to four BB-size shot (one shot weighs about $\frac{1}{64}$ ounce).

For pole fishing in intermediate and deep water from 4 to 18 feet, a simple crow or porcupine quill float, or a balsa-bodied float on a thin dowel stem (called a shy bite by some and about 7 inches long in several sizes), is extremely sensitive and deadly for all panfish, catfish, and small carp. Because these floats have longer stems, they are more stable in the wind. Even the wariest old crappie, perch, or bluegill can easily suck these floats under when they are balanced to sit just $\frac{1}{2}$ inch or less above the surface.

Both of these styles are attached to the line and held in place by two silicone sleeves (which are first slipped onto the line before it is tied to the hook), one at each end, which allows the angler to interchange floats if the conditions or the location changes. Each time the float is changed, however, it has to be balanced either by adding or subtracting split shot. These floats are especially deadly for crappie fishing with small minnows.

Since these floats are attached to the line and held in place by silicone tubes at each end of the float, only the length of the pole limits the depths that can be fished.

Multipiece pole use. Multipiece, or take-apart, poles are used by professional tournament anglers in major match fishing events, including national and world championship events, and exist in lengths from 18 to over 60 feet long. These poles allow the angler to fish any depth of water, from as shallow as 8 inches to the length of the pole minus 24 inches from pole tip to float. For example, to catch crappie 2 feet deep and 30 feet away from your position under a dock or trees, simply place the float rig precisely where you want it. With just 6 inches of line between the float and pole, you can place or push the float into tight places.

To land fish with a multipiece pole, you push the pole behind yourself until the section where the pole is joined (about 5 or 6 feet) is reached and then take the sections apart to land the fish. After rebaiting, the pole is put together again and the float rig is placed anew.

These are very expensive graphite poles, however, and not necessary in normal angling situations; only when there are lots of anglers and spectators do these poles become important. There is also an entire range of pole floats that are specially designed for use with the long take-apart poles; these, too are very expensive and much more fragile than other floats, and are not necessary unless competing in bank-fishing events where the presence of competitors and spectators makes the fish much more difficult to catch.

Float Fishing with Rod and Reel

The techniques and float designs for float fishing with a rod and reel on stillwater and flowing water are completely opposite to each other and were

Pole Floats

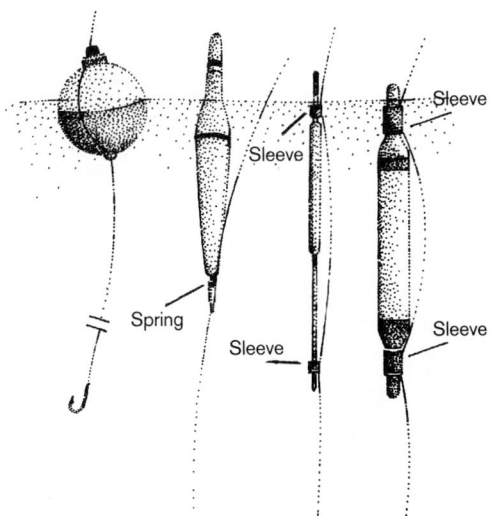

Shown are common floats used with poles. The two versions on the left typify highly buoyant floats that are not sensitive enough to depict light bites and the action of small fish; the two floats on the left, if balanced with the proper amount of weight, are very sensitive and able to indicate lift bites and the immediate bite of even small fish.

English centrepin reels used for float fishing.

bottom and, even though floats are used on the surface, the baits are fished on or near the bottom. On a straight section of a trout stream that is 4 feet deep, for example, the flow just off the bottom will be approximately 20 to 25 percent slower than the surface speed. On a river that is over 20 feet deep, there will be very little current near the bottom, even if the surface speed is swift. These variations mandate that a float be controlled with the rod top and that the angler be stationary.

Even if you know the exact speed just off bottom, the fish may want the hookbait faster or slower. These factors can and do change every day, and learning them is part of the mystery and magic that continuously challenge anglers.

Floats on flowing water. The type of float used varies with the flow speed. Among fixed floats shown in the illustration above, the classic bulblike Avon style (A), for example, is used for medium flows, whereas a more buoyant float (B) is needed for fast and more turbulent water, where bait must be dragged along the bottom without being pulled under easily. These and other fixed floats stay on the line at a preselected position, usually being held in place by silicone sleeves at both the top and the bottom of the float.

There are two eyes on all flowing water slip floats—on the top and the bottom of the float. These floats slide on the line, with depth setting controlled by attaching a stop to the line. Smaller-bodied versions (C) are good all-around floats for any species when using small- to medium-size bait; larger and more buoyant versions (D) are good for big bait and big fish. A float stop and a bead must be used for both of these.

developed in England in the 1850s. Anglers learned to drift floats in Nottingham by carefully controlling the float with the rod tip, so that the baited hook moved at the same speed as the slower flowing water near the bottom, where most fish feed. The improvement of the smooth-running centrepin reel (a single-action two-handled reel that is also called a float reel and features a large-diameter arbor) in England was the main contributor to this advancement.

About the same time around the major steel town of Sheffield, where there were slow-flowing rivers and drains (canals) and some 2,220 angling clubs, intense fishing pressure made it very difficult to catch fish close to the angler, especially in big competitions. Anglers were forced to find several ways to cast their floats across the drains and rivers in order to reach the wary, nervous fish that were scared off by the vibrations and movement of anglers, spectators, and people strolling the river banks. This method of float fishing was called the original Sheffield style and also known as Fine and Far Off, and today is known as waggler fishing.

Flowing water principle. In flowing water with a rod and reel, it's necessary to fish a controlled float that is connected to the fishing line on the top and bottom of the float, whether of a fixed or slip variety. When fishing a float in flowing water, the angler must be stationary in order to find the correct float speed that catches fish at that moment (this means anchoring when fishing from a boat). The reason is that stream flows vary from top to

Floats for Flowing Water

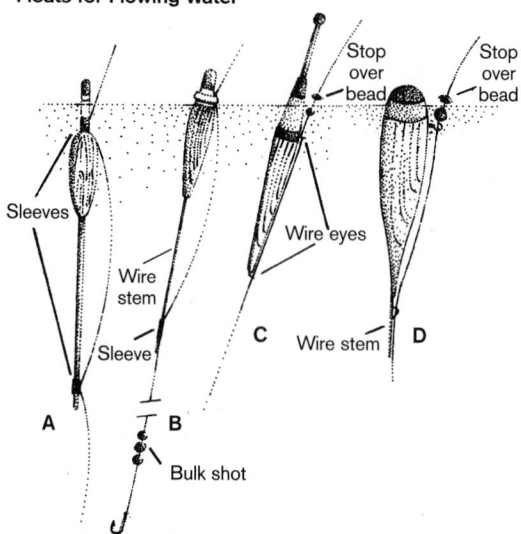

Shown are common balsa floats used in flowing water. The two on the left are fixed in place with silicone sleeves, with one being used in medium-speed flows (A) and the other in faster flows because of greater buoyancy (B). The two on the right are slip floats (C and D), in which line passes through wire arms, with a stop knot used for positioning.

The simplest and often the best weight placement for balancing in flowing water is a bulk pattern. Place all the shot together a few inches in front of the hook if you want the bait to be just above, or just on, the bottom; or place the shot 18 inches from the hook if the bait is to be dragged along the bottom. In smooth-flowing water, shot can be spread out evenly from float to hook. In Europe this is called the equidistant or shirt button shotting pattern. There are many other ways to place shot, these being the most basic.

Stillwater principle. An important element of fishing a float with a rod and reel in stillwater is to cast a relatively long distance (in some places close to the far bank) with floats that are attached only at their bottom (called waggler style in Europe), then push the rod top as deeply under the water as possible, and wind in quickly. This sinks the line and prevents the wind from affecting the float. If anglers will do this, they can master float fishing in windy and wavy conditions. This is the general method that was originally developed in Sheffield.

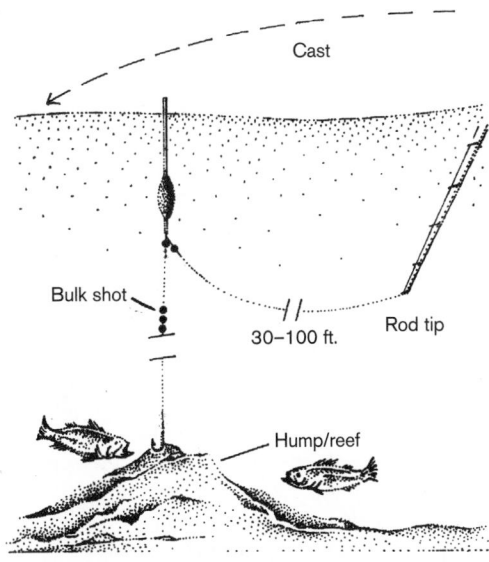

To bury the line so that wind and wave action don't move the float and baited hook away from a given position, cast beyond the target fishing area, place the rod tip under the surface, retrieve some line to get the float and bait where you want it (in this case over a hump or reef), then let the float settle on the surface. Keep the rod tip in the water so the line to the float remains submerged.

Floats on stillwater. The floats that have been developed for fishing with rod and reel in stillwater are called wagglers in Europe; they are used for fishing at any distance and at any depth, and may be used as slip or fixed versions. They are attached to the line only at the bottom, and because of their aerodynamic shape (bulbous at the bottom and long-stemmed at the top) they cast very well, infinitely better than any round type of float (such as a bobber).

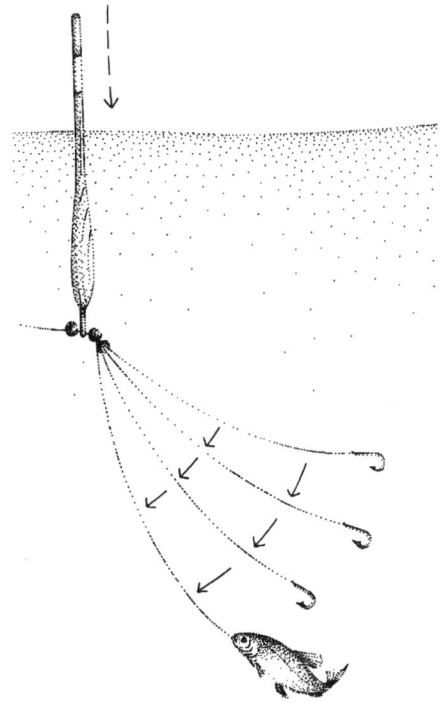

When a fixed float is cast in stillwater, the baited hook drifts down as depicted and the tip of the float settles down in the water. However, if a fish takes the baited hook while it is falling and before it reaches a vertical position, the tip of the float remains high in the water. This is a subtle but sure indication of a bite, and reason for the angler to set the hook.

When such floats are correctly balanced in the water, their shape is hydrodynamic, meaning that they slide through the water (with less drag than a round-shaped float) when a fish bites. When using these floats, you can catch fish as your bait falls through the water—fishing on the drop—and see bites if the fish moves up in the water as it takes the bait.

Generally the float settles in the water after the hookbait has fully dropped into position; when a fish takes the hookbait, the float lifts up in the water, indicating a strike. This is known as a lift bite. The angler sets the hook upon observing this, and since the float folds over when the hook is set (because the float is attached at the bottom only), the angler gets a better hookset. Always strike sideways with the tip near the surface, and after the fish is felt, lift the rod back up to normal playing position.

There are small and low-profiled balsa-bodied wagglers for casting to shallow water along the bank or up to 30 yards away, with larger models for windy conditions or longer casts. Deep fishing or very windy conditions require long peacock quills, some with and without a balsa body, to present the hookbait correctly on most windy days. Some of these models are up to 13 inches long.

As a general guide for balancing, fixed wagglers should have at least 60 percent of the total lead shot positioned to lock the float in place, with the rest of

F

it being drop shot (lower and closer to the hook or jig head). For slip wagglers, start with a bulk pattern, and for a rest shot place two smaller shot 4 feet from the bulk shot, which helps minimize tangles.

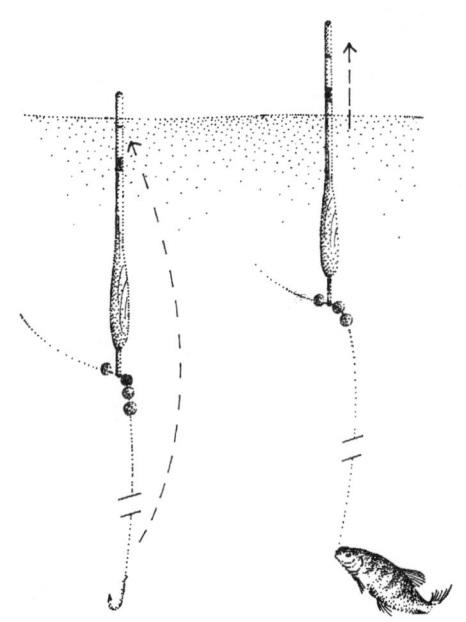

When a fixed float is balanced and positioned properly, the tip of the float is just below the surface (left). When a fish takes the baited hook and moves down, the float disappears, which is very obvious; but when the fish takes and moves upward, it is less obvious because the tip of the float moves up (right). This latter scenario is known as a lift bite, because the action of the fish lifts the float.

Stillwater Fixed Floats

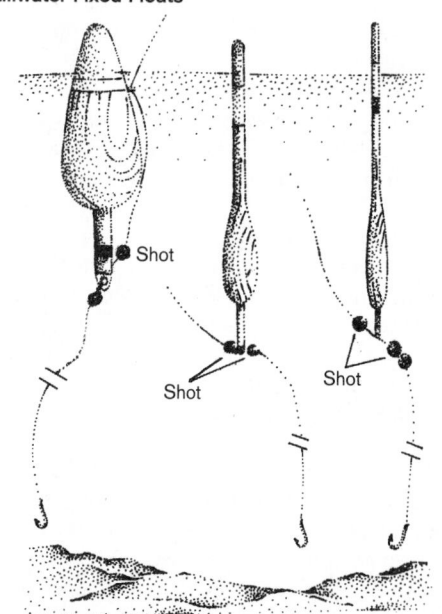

Shown are common fixed floats used for making distant casts when fishing in lakes and ponds. Although not drawn to scale here, they depict how split shot is used to fix various floats at given positions. The length of line below the float determines the level of the baited hook.

FLOATANT

Dressing applied to a fly to help it repel water and float.
See: Fly.

FLOATING/DIVING PLUG

See: Plug.

FLOATING LINE

The fly line that is designed to float on the surface of the water.
See: Flycasting Tackle.

FLOATING LURE

See: Plug; Surface Lure.

FLOATING/SINKING LINE

A fly line with a floating body and a sinking tip section, also called a sink-tip or sinking-tip line.
See: Flycasting Tackle.

FLOAT TUBES

Also known as belly boats, kick boats, personal inflatables, and U-tubes, the diverse category of fishing (and boating) accessories known under the generic umbrella of float tubes includes a broadening and evolving type of equipment used by anglers primarily to access ponds, small lakes, protected sections of bigger waters, secluded waters, and small to moderate streams and rivers. This new equipment is manually propelled, mostly inflatable, and is loosely called watercraft but is not actually recognized as boats in the formal sense, as in requiring state registration and meeting industry safety certification. However, the more complex and sophisticated models, and those that can be fitted with motors, may be recognized as boats and fall under established watercraft guidelines.

Float tubes for fishing purposes have been increasing in popularity since the 1980s, starting with inflatable inner tubes wrapped in a cover with seating support and propelled by fins or other devices. These evolved as alternatives to conventional boats and have matured into designs that feature high-placed seating and rowing.

Most float tubes have expediency as their primary virtue. They are light and easily stowed in a small car or a closet. They can be packed into a remote location and then inflated. They are quiet, relatively unobtrusive, and inexpensive in comparison with most conventional boat options, although comparably priced with canoes.

Float tubes are not only easy to transport, but also provide transportation. In rivers, tubes allow anglers to float downstream to fish selected places, rather than walking along trails or over often rocky and slippery river bottoms. In lakes, they allow anglers to drift along shorelines while casting, fishing farther from shore than they might if restricted to casting from shore. Tubes also make access and passage simpler; portaging—past swift water, over obstructions, or to nearby or connected bodies of water—is pretty easy. They even provide some security for waders in case they slip; anglers can wade conventionally while ensconced in tubes, knowing that they won't fall in and get wet because the tube will cushion the effects of a misstep.

Float tubes have their drawbacks, of course. Although some anglers use them in big lakes and quick waters, they aren't meant for places that can get rough, or where current or wind can overcome the power of foot propulsion. They can be effective under appropriate conditions for fishing, but they cannot cover ground in the timely and effective way that a small boat equipped with an electric motor can. Nevertheless, for anglers who don't have a boat and boating-related accessories, they provide a good way of reaching otherwise unreachable spots, and they invite a simple, different, and pleasurable experience attuned to a slower, more thorough pace of fishing.

The general scenario for fishing out of these devices is that an angler floats on or in a tube, wearing chest-high waders and a pair of fins on his or her feet. The waders are usually neoprene, but lighter materials work in warm waters at appropriate seasons. The float tube is propelled backward by leg power, which theoretically frees the angler's hands for casting and allows for constant positioning adjustments.

Float tube types. The first inflatable float tubes adapted for fishing were oval, like a donut with a hole. The oval shape, which created a lot of drag in the water and was hard to get in and out of with fins on, is now outdated, yielding to versions with the entry end open and the opposite end squared or pointed. Most of these have what is called a U shape, but some have a wedge or V shape for cutting through the wind and waves better. Remember that anglers in float tubes propel themselves backward and face the opposite direction of movement.

Early oval float tubes, which were commonly called belly boats, were essentially inner tubes covered with canvas or nylon cloth. Newer tubes have an open end that permits easy entry and exit, and better models have a stabilizer to keep the open end from collapsing on itself. The open ends also help propulsion by allowing operators to raise their legs more horizontally for increased thrust and to raise legs to pass over obstructions, which is especially useful in current.

Whereas oval float tubes had one interior tube, U-shaped versions have separate arm and back bladders, which raise the level of the angler. The lower the angler sits, the less visibility and the harder it is to cast with certain tackle, so sitting higher is

A float tube angler lands a hefty rainbow trout.

desirable if it does not adversely affect stability. The tubes or bladders are inflated by mouth (tough for many to do), foot pump, or compressor.

The better float tubes have a high back support, adjustable seat, an apron or lightweight basket for catching fly line or laying objects while rigging, and a lot of watertight zippered pockets for gear storage.

Float tubes are sometimes a bit awkward to maneuver and turn. With the angler's legs hanging down, they tend to get caught in weeds, brush, and logs, and to bump on rocks and other objects. They also don't provide a lot of thrust, and operators struggle to buck strong current, heavy wind, and wave action. They should always be worn with a PFD *(see)*.

Kick boats/pontoon tubes. Pontoon-style float tubes have evolved from the desire to make self-propelled watercraft more maneuverable and raise the angler to a higher, or at least an adjustable, position. These craft are primarily called kick boats, and the majority feature two inflatable pontoons, pointed at the ends, bridged by a frame with a seat. Some feature noninflatable molded hard-plastic pontoons. These were primarily set up for kicking with the feet, but many so-called kick boats now have oars and perhaps should be called row tubes.

These craft take longer to assemble than conventional float tubes, weigh two to three times as much in total, and cost more, but they are versatile, easier to maneuver, and faster. They have improved thrust when used with oars, and because so little of the angler is actually in the water, they offer more control. They also allow a little more gear to be carried than what a float tube allows, and they keep more of the anglers body out of the water. Some models can be disassembled and toted as a backpack.

Accessories. A good pair of swim fins is as important to using float tubes or kick boats as the boats themselves. Some anglers use paddle pushers in lieu of fins; these are devices that strap around the boot heel and have a paddle that allows you to go forward by moving your legs as if you were walking. Swim fins are preferred, however, because they provide quicker movement from point to point if your leg muscles are in good shape. You must move backward in fins virtually all the time to get anywhere, and they are tough to walk in on land or on a murky lake bottom. For beginners, paddling and traveling backward is a bit like walking backward.

Popular fins for tubes and kick boats are shorter than fins used for swimming and diving, and should have more rigidity. It's best if they float and also have a lanyard so that they can be readily retrieved if they fall off.

Many options are available for float tubes and kick boats today, especially with the increasing popularity of the latter. Most are involved with boating rather than fishing, and if you get too loaded up with the options, you might wonder why you didn't get a canoe or a jonboat in the first place.

Remember that tackle selection with many float tubes has to be a little conservative. You generally have only one rod with you, and you can't take a full tackle box of equipment, though with a fishing vest or suitable storage compartments on the float tube, you can still bring a fair amount along. Always be attuned to safety with these devices, and wear some type of PFD. Inflatable PFDs are a lightweight option.

See: Boat.

FLOOD TIDE

Incoming, or rising, tide.

See: Tides.

FLORIDA

Florida is justifiably called a sportfishing mecca. Millions make angling pilgrimages to the Sunshine State each year, many of them in search of the fish of their dreams, especially big largemouth bass, bonefish, tarpon, and sailfish. But these are just the most storied species. With tens of thousands of fish-filled inland waters, and 1,350 miles of coastline bounding the Atlantic Ocean and the Gulf of Mexico, the abundance of Florida's angling opportunities is rivaled only by their diversity.

The fabled St. Johns River, which empties into the Atlantic at Jacksonville, holds everything from largemouth bass and stripers to shad and seatrout. In the shadow of the space center at Cape Canaveral, anglers consistently catch huge red drum. Palm Beach, where the warm north-flowing waters of the Gulf Stream come closest to the United States, provides anglers with the chance to catch and release double-digit numbers of sailfish in a single day.

The Florida Keys, at the extreme tip of the peninsula, are perhaps the most hallowed destination in the state, offering saltwater aficionados everything from bonefish to blue marlin. The state's most remote waters are within Everglades National Park, home to a vast array of wading birds as well as snook, redfish, tarpon, and seatrout. Those four species are also found along the Gulf Coast. In the Panhandle, the seatrout is king, but anglers also target cobia in nearshore waters, and snapper and grouper on wrecks and artificial reefs. And so it goes, with ample interest for such other Florida saltwater species as barracuda, sharks, swordfish, spearfish, wahoo, white marlin, dolphin, amberjack, blackfin tuna, yellowfin tuna, bluefish, little tunny, flounder, permit, pompano, sheepshead, king mackerel, Spanish mackerel, and cero mackerel.

In freshwater, Florida is synonymous with big largemouth bass because of the year-round growing season and abundance of food. Lake Okeechobee, Lake Kissimmee, and Lake Seminole are among the best bass waters in the country, but the chances of catching a trophy are just as good in any number of Florida's ponds, lakes, and canals. In addition to largemouth and peacock bass, Florida also has white bass, sunshine bass, bluegills, black crappie (also known as speckled perch, or specks), redear sunfish (a k a shellcrackers), spotted sunfish, warmouth, catfish, bullhead, chain pickerel, gar, bowfin, oscars, and tilapia.

Saltwater

Florida Keys. The Keys consist of 42 islands, connected by bridges, that stretch 100 miles from Key Largo to Key West, the southernmost point in the continental United States. Unlike other parts of Florida, the Keys have severely limited development, which contributes to the area's exceptional inshore and offshore fishery.

The flats on both the Atlantic Ocean and Florida Bay sides of the Keys are best known for big, silvery bonefish. Islamorada, the self-proclaimed Sportfishing Capital of the World, is the most popular bonefish destination. It is ideally located for running north to the flats of Key Largo or south to the flats of Marathon.

Keys bonefish can top 15 pounds but typically run 7 to 9 pounds. They can be caught year-round, but the best fishing is usually in late spring and early fall, when water temperatures are neither too cold nor too hot. During the summer, bonefish are on the flats early in the morning, when temperatures are relatively cool; then they seek the comfort of deep water before returning to the flats late in the afternoon. In winter, bonefishing is best a few days after a cold front, when the water has had a chance to warm.

The bass are always in the grass at Lake Okeechobee.

Also known as the gray ghost of the flats, bonefish come onto the shallow flats to feed, rooting in the grassy bottom for crabs, shrimp, and other crustaceans. Anglers most commonly pursue them with light spinning tackle (6- to 12-pound line) and live shrimp, crabs, or jigs. Bonefish also are a favorite of fly anglers, who pursue these fish with 8- and 9-weight outfits. Extremely wary, bonefish will flee at the slightest hint of danger, such as a boat, or a cast that comes too close.

An effective way to catch bonefish is to anchor or stake a boat on the edge of a flat, put out pieces of shrimp as chum, then cast out a live shrimp and wait for a bonefish to swim through and eat it. Most experienced anglers prefer to sight-cast for bonefish. Typically, the angler stands at the bow of a flats skiff, which can float in just a few inches of water, while a guide or friend propels the boat forward with a pushpole from a poling platform at the stern of the boat. They scan the flat for signs of bonefish: shaky or nervous water, caused as the bonefish swim against the current; muds, created by bonefish as they root up the bottom; bonefish themselves, which most often appear as dark shadows; and tailing bonefish, who give themselves away in shallow water when their tails break the surface as they feed.

Casts must be on the mark, neither too close nor too far; too close and the bonefish will spook, too far and the bonefish will never find the bait, lure, or fly. A successful cast will result in an electrifying run, which is the event bonefish anglers live for, with the bonefish ripping out 100 or more yards of line as it streaks across the flat.

In addition to bonefish, Keys flats also have tarpon and permit. Tarpon fishing is best in the spring, when the fish migrate north through the Keys. From early March to late June, tarpon and tarpon anglers position themselves all along the flats, as well as at bridges.

As with bonefish, fishing for tarpon is most exciting when sight-casting. The spring migration finds tarpon on flats throughout the Keys, and the chance to hook a 150-pound fish in 3 feet of water is enough to make a veteran tarpon angler's legs shake. Fly fishing with a 12-weight outfit is effective, as is the use of 20- or 30-pound spinning tackle and live shrimp, crabs, and baitfish such as pilchards. Tarpon are most commonly found around openings in banks (raised areas on the flats), where they ambush baitfish as they are swept through the openings by the tide.

Tarpon also concentrate around bridges. Among the best bridges in the Keys are the Seven Mile Bridge and Bahia Honda Bridge, south of Marathon. Tarpon also frequent the channels that run through the bridges and in Key West Harbor. The standard technique is to anchor a boat and fish a live bait under a cork float. Mullet, pinfish, and crabs are the most popular bait.

Permit is the third member of the flats grand slam and usually the hardest of the three species to catch. Warier than bonefish, permit run a lot bigger, averaging 15 to 20 pounds and sometimes exceeding 40 pounds. These larger relatives of the pompano frequent many of the same flats as bonefish, but typically at high tide, when the water is deep enough to accommodate their wide, platter-like bodies. Permit also inhabit holes, channels, and rockpiles, with Key West and the Content Keys ranking among the best permit spots. A live crab is by far the best bait for permit. Tackle is the same as that used for bonefish.

Another common, but overlooked, Florida Keys flats inhabitant is the barracuda. These sharp-toothed predators take live bait, lures, and flies with gusto and produce sizzling runs when hooked. A variety of sharks—including bull, blacktip, bonnethead, hammerhead, lemon, and nurse species—also cruise the flats.

From Marathon, located in about the middle of the Keys, to Key West, anglers have ready access to Florida Bay and the Gulf of Mexico. Some of the best fishing is on shallow wrecks for cobia, permit, jacks, sharks, grouper, and snapper.

The Keys' inshore fishing is rivaled only by its offshore fishing. From one end of the Keys to the

F

One of Florida's top saltwater draws is fishing the Keys' flats, as here near Islamorada.

other, anglers encounter amberjack, blue marlin, sailfish, dolphin, wahoo, cobia, king mackerel, snapper, grouper, and blackfin tuna as the fish migrate through the area.

Winter is prime time for sailfish, blackfin tuna, and king mackerel. Sailfish show up in November as they seek warm waters, and usually stay until late spring. Fishing is often best in December and January. Trolling lures, live bait, and dead bait is productive. When sailfish are especially abundant, many anglers run offshore and look for sailfish chasing bait or swimming down-sea. Then they use 12- to 20-pound spinning tackle to cast live bait in front of the fish. Catches of 10 or more sailfish in a day are not uncommon under those conditions.

Blackfin tuna are staples of the Keys in winter and early spring, especially around offshore humps, where the ocean bottom rises significantly and attracts huge concentrations of bait and fish. Blackfins, which range from 15 to 40 pounds, will hit trolled lures and bait, but live pilchards are preferred. Typically, charter boats will go offshore with 500 to 1,000 of the little baitfish. Upon arriving at a hump, two or more lines baited with live pilchards are put out, then the mate starts chumming by throwing handfuls of pilchards into the water, attracting the tuna.

Yellowfin tuna run much bigger than blackfins—50 to 150 pounds—but aren't nearly as abundant or easy to target. Key West has the best run of yellowfin, with ideal fishing typically in December.

The Keys get both Atlantic and gulf king mackerel as the fish head south for the winter. Kingfish, as they are known, are found along the edge of the coral reefs that run the length of the Keys. Some of the best fishing is south of Key West, where boats catch kings up to 40 or more pounds. The most common technique is to slow-troll with live or dead bait. Some anglers prefer to anchor their boats and, as with blackfin tuna, chum with live pilchards. When the kingfish show up—they'll often skyrocket behind the boat—they can be caught on everything from live bait to jigs to flies.

By March, amberjack begin concentrating at the humps as they prepare to spawn, and remain there through May. These hard-fighting fish can easily top 50 pounds. Anglers typically fish a live bait near the bottom in 200 or more feet. Thirty- to 50-pound tackle is needed to wrestle an amberjack to the surface.

One of the most popular species in the Keys, dolphin generally make their appearance in April and remain abundant for much of the summer. These colorful, acrobatic fish often travel in schools anywhere from 10 to 30 miles offshore. Depending on their size, they can be caught on everything from fly tackle or light (8-pound) spinning tackle to 30-pound conventional outfits. Schoolie dolphin run anywhere from 5 to 10 pounds, with the size of the school ranging from a few fish to more than 100. Gaffer dolphin, which are big enough to require the use of a gaff to get them in the boat, run up to 20 pounds. Fish bigger than that are known as slammers, and they can top 70 pounds. Typically, the bigger fish are farther offshore.

Most anglers locate dolphin around floating debris and weedlines or under frigate birds. The weeds and debris attract baitfish, which attract the dolphin. Frigate birds will follow dolphin in the hopes of picking up scraps when the fish feed.

Trolling dead ballyhoo or squid is the most common tactic for catching dolphin. When there are no signs of dolphin, blind trolling can produce fish in the middle of nowhere. When weeds, debris, or birds are located, trolling in the area often produces dolphin. Many anglers employ a run-and-gun technique, cruising in their boats until they come across dolphin. Then they cast jigs, live bait, or chunks of bait to the fish.

Blue marlin show up soon after the dolphin arrive and often are found in the same places. One of the best spots in all of Florida is The Wall, 19 miles south of Key West, where the ocean bottom drops off sharply. The fish range from 100 pounds to more than 500 pounds.

The coral reefs provide excellent fishing for a variety of snapper and grouper year-round, with the best fishing from spring to fall. Most anglers target yellowtail snapper, which run up to 5 pounds, and mutton snapper, which can top 20 pounds. The favored method is to fish dead bait on the bottom. Heavy chumming can bring yellowtail to the surface, where they can be landed on small jigs, dead bait, live bait, and flies.

Florida Bay/Ten Thousand Islands.   In addition to great fishing, the southern end of Florida's mainland offers anglers an opportunity to experience Florida the way it was before hordes of people and condos arrived. This is true wilderness, and more than one angler has spent the night after getting lost in the maze of mangrove islands scattered throughout the vast area.

Much of Florida Bay is contained within the 1.5-million-acre Everglades National Park, which was created in 1947. Access is via boat from the Keys, but a favorite jumping-off point is Flamingo, an isolated outpost at the tip of the mainland. In addition to boat ramps, Flamingo has a marina with food, fuel, bait, tackle, rental boats, canoes, and a motel. Once you leave the dock, you're on your own. You have a choice of fishing out front in Florida Bay or heading north into what is known as the backcountry.

The backcountry features a tangle of mangrove islands separated by rivers, creeks, and rivulets. Anglers who venture here must remember the precise route they took if they plan to return to the dock the same day.

To successfully fish the backcountry, one must think of Florida Bay as a shallow body of water that simply floods and drains. When the water is high, fish forage for shrimp and crabs on the flats. When the level is low, they are forced to feed in deeper water, such as channels. At the edge of a channel intersecting the flats, predators ambush smaller fish carried from the shallows by the falling tide. That's where anglers can ambush the predators—primarily snook, seatrout, baby tarpon, and redfish, but also croaker, jack crevalle, ladyfish, mangrove snapper, catfish, and pinfish. The best fishing is during the spring and fall, when temperatures are tolerable for both fish and anglers. Spinning rods spooled with 8- to 20-pound line, and 8-weight fly-rod outfits, can handle just about everything an angler will encounter.

Whitewater Bay, near Flamingo, is one of the largest backcountry bodies of water. It has sea trout, redfish, jacks, snook, and tarpon. The fish typically aren't as large as those found in Florida Bay, but in the Whitewater area, Lake Ingraham, East Cape Canal, and other sheltered waters offer good fishing and protection from wind, even when it's blowing 15 to 20 mph.

Everglades National Park possesses several no-motor areas, such as the West Lake and Bear Lake canoe trails, where only hand-propelled vessels are allowed. Few anglers have the desire or stamina to paddle a canoe or row a boat into the remote interior of the park, which results in excellent fishing for seatrout, snook, redfish, black drum, snapper, jacks, and baby tarpon. Go far enough north and you can catch snook and largemouth bass on consecutive casts.

Given the challenges of navigating the interior of the park, it's no surprise that most anglers who depart from Flamingo fish out front around the channels, grassflats, and mangrove islands in Florida Bay.

Seatrout inhabit the grassbeds, where the standard tactic is to fish a live shrimp under a foam bobber, known as a popping cork. The bobber suspends the shrimp just over the grass and is jerked hard to gain a trout's attention. Flies and jigs also catch trout.

Redfish are commonly found on the flats near the islands in Florida Bay as well as in Snake Bight and Garfield Bight, two popular spots east of Flamingo. Fishing is typically best during a rising or falling tide, early or late in the day.

Although redfish can be caught by a variety of methods, the most exciting way is to creep up on tailing fish on the flats and cast with a fly rod or a light spinning rod. Redfish favor weedless spoons as well as jigs and live shrimp and mullet.

Snook frequent the same areas but prefer the mangrove shorelines, where they can ambush baitfish swept past by the tides. Flies, topwater plugs, jigs, live pilchards, mullet, and shrimp are all favorites of these hard-fighting fish. Tarpon, which can be seen rolling on the surface in channels and around mangrove islands, will hit the same offerings.

The large tripod markers that border Everglades National Park are helpful reference points on a run to the Flamingo area. During the fall and winter they also provide a focal point for schools of cobia ranging from 30 to 80 pounds. A brief stop at each marker is sufficient to discern whether cobia are present. If the cobia are home, hook a live grunt on a light or medium plug rod and troll it slowly past the marker.

Moving around the southwest tip of Florida, anglers encounter several rivers—Shark, Lostmans, Chatham, and Lopez—that offer good angling for snook, redfish, seatrout, and tarpon, especially at the mouths.

The Ten Thousand Islands are at the western end of Everglades National Park and are just as remote. Access is best from Everglades City and Chokoloskee Island, with the option of fishing the backcountry, the mangrove islands out front, or the Gulf of Mexico.

Most people primarily fish the rivers and bays of the backcountry for snook and redfish. Fishing around the islands out front produces snook, reds, seatrout, and Spanish mackerel, and sheepshead are commonly caught in the channels. The wrecks and artificial reefs in the Gulf of Mexico hold snook, cobia, and permit.

Pavilion Key and Rabbit Key, south of Chokoloskee, are among the more popular islands. Armed with flies, plugs, and live bait, one can work around the oyster bars for redfish, over the grassflats for seatrout, and along the shorelines for snook. From either island, it's a short hop to the gulf, where some anglers have created their own artificial reefs to attract fish. Anglers must watch their sonar closely, because the location of those reefs is seldom divulged.

East Coast

The majority of Florida's population lives on its eastern coast, from Jacksonville to Miami. Despite a population in the millions, sportfishing can be surprisingly good and is often excellent.

The Intracoastal Waterway, which runs the length of the state, offers much of the best inshore fishing along the coast for species such as snook, seatrout, and redfish. Offshore anglers target resident species such as snapper and grouper, as well as migratory species, including king mackerel, sailfish, tuna, and dolphin.

The St. Mary's River is the border between northeastern Florida and southeastern Georgia. St. Mary's Inlet, where the river empties into the Atlantic Ocean at Fernandina Beach, offers good fishing for seatrout, redfish, and sheepshead. Striped bass are usually in the river in late winter.

The north-flowing St. Johns River meets the Atlantic at Jacksonville. The brackish waters of the river and the numerous tidal creeks that join it are home to redfish, seatrout, and flounder. At the mouth of the river and along the beaches there are sheepshead, whiting, and black drum. Winter is the prime season to catch striped bass at

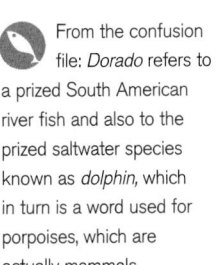

From the confusion file: *Dorado* refers to a prized South American river fish and also to the prized saltwater species known as *dolphin*, which in turn is a word used for porpoises, which are actually mammals.

F

the mouth of the St. Johns, with morning and late afternoon best. Crankbaits, jigs, and live eels are the favorite baits. During the summer, stripers run up the St. Johns to spawn. Shad run up the river in winter.

Grouper can be found offshore, along with dolphin, wahoo, sailfish, and blue marlin, but the king mackerel is the lord of offshore species. Kingfish, as they are also known, migrate through the area starting in May and running through the summer. Trolling or drifting with live or dead bait and 20- to 30-pound tackle is the preferred strategy to take kings, which can range from 5-pound "snakes" early in the season to 50-pound "smokers" when the migration is at its peak.

St. Augustine is the oldest city in the country. No doubt its first settlers took advantage of the bluefish, Spanish mackerel, cobia, flounder, whiting, and pompano that still patrol the city's beaches, and the redfish and seatrout that swim in its inshore waters. A 50-mile, or longer, run to the Gulf Stream puts anglers in dolphin territory. Fifteen miles to the south is Matanzas Pass, which harbors redfish, tarpon, flounder, and sheepshead. Whiting and pompano lurk in the surf.

The Halifax River in Daytona Beach is home to redfish and sheepshead. Trout and snook show up in early spring. The river can be fished from a boat or from any numbers of piers. South of Daytona is Ponce de Leon Inlet. Flounder hang out near the inlet during winter. Seatrout and redfish start biting as the water warms. Sheepshead, mangrove snapper, and black drum also visit the inlet. In spring and summer, anglers run offshore in search of blue marlin and kingfish.

At Ponce Inlet, the Indian River begins to trickle south. Stretching all the way to Stuart, the Indian River is a fish factory. Name an inshore species, and chances are that the river has it; but the area here is best known for snook, redfish, seatrout, and tarpon.

The Mosquito Lagoon, part of the Indian River just north of the Kennedy Space Center, offers the best fishing for big redfish in Florida. The 20-mile-long lagoon is bordered by mangroves and features acres of grassbeds and clear, shallow water. Redfish inhabit the lagoon all year, but the best fishing is in fall and early spring, when water temperatures are neither too hot nor too cold. Seatrout also frequent the flats at those times.

Anglers in shallow-draft boats can sight-cast to schools containing a hundred or more reds. The biggest redfish run from 30 to 50 pounds. The standard offering is a weedless spoon or a live crab fished with an 8- to 20-pound spinning outfit. Fly fishing with an 8- to 10-weight outfit is also popular.

The Indian River broadens as it flows past Titusville and Cocoa. Anglers fish the flats from boats or shore, or by wading for snook, redfish, and "gator" seatrout weighing 8 or more pounds. The big trout are on the flats during warm weather, and in the holes and channels bordering the flats when the water cools. Seatrout hit flies, live shrimp, and jigs tipped with shrimp.

Canaveral National Seashore offers good surf fishing in a beautiful locale. Pompano, a favorite of beach anglers and gourmet cooks, bite best in winter, along with bluefish and whiting. In spring, cobia, Spanish mackerel, and even king mackerel come close enough to be caught from the beach.

Offshore anglers go out of Port Canaveral. Close to shore, there's bluefish and flounder in the winter, and snook, Spanish mackerel, and cobia in the spring. In May, anglers head for the Gulf Stream in search of dolphin and blue marlin.

Sebastian Inlet offers great fishing from boats, jetties, bridges, and beaches. Doormat flounder and bluefish bite during winter, then Spanish mackerel and cobia move in. Snook fishing picks up in early spring and remains excellent through early fall. Ladyfish, Spanish mackerel, king mackerel, jacks, and redfish are caught in and around the inlet.

At Fort Pierce Inlet, anglers enjoy similar fishing. They catch snook, redfish, tarpon, seatrout, and snapper on the inside, and pompano and bluefish in the surf. Cobia migrate along the beaches starting in early spring, when grouper and snapper begin congregating on reefs—both inshore and offshore. Sailfishing can be outstanding during the winter and early spring, especially when these fish are in close balling bait. At those times, it's not unusual to catch 10 or more sailfish in a day.

The Indian River meets up with the St. Lucie River in Stuart. Fishing on the flats inside St. Lucie Inlet is excellent for snook, redfish, trout, and tarpon, as there's usually plenty of baitfish to keep the predators around. The flats can be fished from a boat or by wading. An 8-weight fly rod or an 8-pound spinning outfit with a live shrimp, mullet, pilchards, or a baitfish imitation will catch whatever is on the flats. Stuart is the heart of Sailfish Alley, the stretch from Palm Beach to Fort Pierce where the Gulf Stream comes within a few miles of shore. Closer to shore there are bluefish, Spanish mackerel, and cobia. Bluefish and Spanish mackerel hammer silver spoons. Cobia prefer live bait such as pinfish and blue runners.

Jupiter Inlet is a favorite of snook anglers, especially during late spring, summer, and early fall. That's when snook concentrate at inlets as they prepare to spawn. Fifteen- to 30-pound snook are caught in the inlet itself, as well as along the beaches to the north and south. Diehard snook anglers typically go out with 500 to 1,000 baitfish (pilchards, croaker, or herring) and attract the snook by live chumming. When the snook show up, anglers toss out live bait on light spinning outfits, or cast flies. The Intracoastal Waterway offers shelter in windy weather, as well as the opportunity to catch snook, seatrout, jacks, and ladyfish. Surf anglers catch bluefish, Spanish mackerel, pompano, and jacks from beaches north and south of the inlet.

Lake Worth Inlet, at the north end of Palm Beach, harbors huge permit, African pompano, and jacks, which anglers catch by bouncing a jig off the rocky bottom. Inside the inlet, in Lake Worth, are 30-pound tarpon and snook as well as jacks and ladyfish. Anglers catch tarpon by drifting from a boat with live shrimp. The snook prefer live sand perch and pilchards, and are fished from boats and bridges.

Offshore reefs have a variety of snapper, including yellowtail, mangroves, and muttons, as well as opportunistic barracuda. King mackerel patrol the edges of the reefs, and sailfish are just outside in 100 to 200 feet of water. Drifting with live bait or slow-trolling with dead or live bait—most commonly ballyhoo and mullet—produces both species. Wahoo lurk in 100 to 500 feet. Dolphin fishing is best in spring and summer, and anglers routinely run up to 30 miles offshore to encounter a school.

There are four inlets between Palm Beach and Miami: Boynton Beach, Boca Raton, Hillsboro in Pompano Beach, and Port Everglades in Fort Lauderdale. Fishing opportunities are about the same at all four. Natural coral reefs as well as an abundance of artificial reefs in 40 to 400 feet provide consistent fishing for snapper and grouper, as well as for pelagic species.

Thanks to catch-and-release efforts, sailfish are a year-round species, but the best fishing is from November through April. King mackerel migrate through in fall and spring, with the biggest fish—20 or more pounds—typically showing up in early spring. Cobia migrating through the area swim along the beaches. Amberjack up to 50 pounds move onto artificial reefs in 200 to 250 feet in spring to spawn. Dolphin generally appear in March, along with blackfin tuna.

In summer, little tunny show up in force. When nothing else is biting, anglers will target this hard-fighting species, known locally as bonito. A popular technique is to anchor near a wreck in 100 or so feet and chum heavily with either live or dead bait. When the bonito show up on the surface behind the boat, they can be caught on bait, jigs, plugs, and flies. Fishing picks up with the cooler temperatures of fall. Mutton snapper spawn on reefs and wrecks, and kingfish start to head south. Spanish mackerel, which are caught from boats, beaches, and piers, show up in force a little while later, followed by sailfish and pompano.

Inshore opportunities center around snook and tarpon. Snook congregate at inlets in spring and summer. After spawning, they move back inshore, into canals off the Intracoastal Waterway. Snook lurk around bridge pilings and docks, waiting for unsuspecting baitfish to swim past. Most anglers use live bait, but deep-diving plugs trolled parallel to bridges, and jigs bounced along the bottom, are both top-notch snook producers.

Tarpon move inshore during winter in search of warm water. One of the best tarpon spots is near the power plant in Port Everglades, where water used to cool the plant's electricity-generating turbines is discharged into a canal. When cold fronts hit South Florida, tarpon flock to the area. The fish, which range from 50 to 150 pounds, eat live shrimp and mullet either slow-trolled or drifted up and down the canals.

Other tarpon hotspots include the two inlets that serve the Miami area, Haulover Inlet and Government Cut. Both inlets have significant runs of shrimp during the winter. Tarpon that routinely top 100 pounds wait at the inlets for the floating feast, which occurs from December through March. The best fishing is usually at night, when the shrimp run. Fishing for tarpon is as easy as drifting or slow-trolling a live shrimp on a 20-pound conventional outfit in and around the inlets. When shrimp aren't running, live mullet and live crabs will catch fish.

Like neighboring cities to the north, Miami has natural and artificial reefs that offer good fishing for bottom dwellers. Sailfish, kingfish, dolphin, pompano, Spanish mackerel, amberjack, and wahoo also are pursued by offshore anglers. Unlike its neighbors, Miami offers excellent flats fishing in Biscayne Bay, which extends from downtown Miami to the upper end of the Florida Keys.

The upper reaches of the bay hold snook, tarpon, jacks, and barracuda. During winter, seatrout frequent the bay's grassflats. South of Key Biscayne, but within sight of the Miami skyline, bay anglers catch bonefish. The farther away from Miami one goes, the better the fishing. South Biscayne Bay is known for its big bonefish, in the 10- to 12-pound class, and also has permit and tarpon. Most of the flats fishing is done within Biscayne National Park on both bay and ocean flats. Tarpon tend to hang out in the channels and on the edges of the ocean flats. Fishing techniques are the same as those employed in the Keys.

West Coast

Although it is bordered by the Gulf of Mexico, Florida's west coast is best known for its inshore fishing opportunities, primarily for snook, tarpon, redfish, and seatrout. Most of the effort is concentrated around mangrove islands, beaches, flats, and river mouths.

At the southern end of the coast, Marco Island and Naples feature bays, passes, and acres of mangroves, which are home to the aforementioned species, as well as to jacks and sharks. Tarpon migrate up the coast starting in early spring, making for exciting fishing off the beach. Live pinfish or crabs are fished from the surf or from boats.

Snook fishing turns on in late spring. The fish move out of the backcountry during the summer as they prepare to spawn. Angling is best in the passes and along the beaches using live bait or baitfish-imitating lures. Bridges and docks also are snook hangouts, with the best bite typically at night.

F

Other species that visit the area include sheepshead, Spanish mackerel, whiting, and pompano. The best fishing is in late winter and early spring. Cobia head north a little later. Gulf reefs and wrecks attract king mackerel, grouper, snapper, amberjack, and barracuda.

The Fort Myers area offers outstanding inshore fishing. There, the Caloosahatchee, Peace, and Myakka Rivers empty into a relatively small area, creating a prolific aquatic environment.

The Peace joins with the Myakka to form Charlotte Harbor, which—along with nearby Pine Island Sound—has an abundance of redfish, seatrout, small tarpon, and snook. Most anglers browse around the mangrove shorelines and grassy flats.

Charlotte Harbor feeds into the gulf at Boca Grande, which has a storied tarpon fishery. From mid-April to mid-July, Boca Grande Pass might hold 20,000 or more tarpon. At times, it seems almost as many boats are in the pass fishing for them. Traditional tarpon anglers use only live bait, such as crabs, squirrelfish, pinfish, and pilchards, fishing them at the bottom of the holes in the pass where the tarpon gather. Jigs work especially well. The rigs consist of a circle hook with a plastic grub. A round lead weight is attached to the hook with a tiewrap. The jig is fished just off the bottom from a drifting boat. When a tarpon hits, the weight breaks free.

Nearshore and offshore species in this region include cobia—which migrate along the gulf edge of barrier islands—sheepshead, sharks, permit, king mackerel, and grouper.

Sarasota Bay is a broad, shallow body of water separating Sarasota from Longboat Key and the gulf. With its grassy flats and mangrove-lined eastern shore, Sarasota Bay offers ideal habitat for snook, redfish, and seatrout. The passes at the north and south ends of Longboat Key are good spots for migrating Spanish mackerel in spring.

Tampa Bay is the next major fishery up the coast, and a heavily fished one given the number of anglers in Tampa and St. Petersburg. Despite the crowds, there is good fishing for seatrout, redfish, snook, and snapper along the shorelines of the bay and on the grassflats. Tarpon, cobia, and Spanish mackerel enter the bay in the spring. Grouper, pompano, and Spanish mackerel also hang around the islands at the mouth of Tampa Bay. The most popular offshore species is king mackerel.

Homosassa Bay is a late-spring hotspot for tarpon in excess of 150 pounds. It's the place fly anglers go in hope of landing a world-record fish. Beginning in May, the clear waters of Homosassa's flats attract large schools of tarpon, which often go through the prespawn ritual of daisy-chaining. When daisy-chaining, an angler, perched at the bow of a flats skiff, picks out a fish and delivers the bait, lure, or fly just ahead of the swimming tarpon. The island-studded waters where the Homosassa River flows into Homosassa Bay have excellent angling for redfish during the spring.

The Cedar Keys, a collection of islands where Florida begins to bend to the west, is perhaps best known for its seatrout. Fishing peaks during the fall but is good through the spring. Most anglers fish the grassbeds with live shrimp or shrimp-tipped jigs. Redfish also are abundant amidst the islands. Cobia move through the area in the spring. Seatrout and redfish are the predominant species up the coast at the mouths of the Suwannee and Steinhatchee Rivers, in the heart of the state's Big Bend region.

Panhandle

Florida's Panhandle is the long, narrow stretch at the northwest end of the state, bordered by the Gulf of Mexico. The shimmering blue waters of the gulf offer everything from red snapper to blue marlin; cobia cruise the nearshore waters, and a number of broad, shallow bays provide outstanding inshore angling, most notably for seatrout.

Starting at the easternmost end of the Panhandle, in what's known as the Big Bend region, is Apalachee Bay. In April, seatrout and redfish move out of the rivers and onto the lush grassflats of the bay. Initially, the trout stay close to shore as they prepare to spawn, spreading throughout the bay over the course of the summer. Redfish frequent rock-strewn areas along the shore. Both species hit live shrimp, jigs, and jigs tipped with shrimp.

To the west is Apalachicola Bay, which is perhaps most famous for its oysters. Protected by barrier islands, the bay's scattered grassbeds attract trout, while redfish lurk around oyster bars. Each spring, hordes of Spanish mackerel and pompano gather at the passes linking the bay with the gulf.

The next major body of water is St. Joseph Bay, which is best known for its scallops. Redfish and seatrout are abundant on the bay's expansive grassbeds. Up the coast in Panama City is St. Andrew Bay. Scattered grassbeds there hold trout and redfish, as do the grassbeds in the bays, coves, and lagoons around Pensacola.

April is when cobia move into the area, coming up from the south and migrating to the west along the Panhandle's barrier beaches through July. The standard strategy is to cruise the shallow waters just off the beach in a boat, preferably one with a tower, and look for the dark bodies of the cobia against the sandy bottom. When cobia are spotted, the boat is moved ahead of the fish. Then jigs or live bait (pinfish and eels work well) are cast in front of the cobia, which can exceed 100 pounds. Cobia also hang out by channel markers, buoys, artificial reefs, and wrecks.

About a month after the cobia arrive, king mackerel show up in the surf and feast on schools of baitfish, as do big schools of roving jack crevalle. The kings are caught by trolling feathers and dead bait. Live baiting also works.

In June and July, big schools of tarpon move into the area. Most anglers concentrate on the areas in and around passes, bouncing heavy leadhead jigs on the bottom.

Snapper and grouper are caught on wrecks and artificial reefs anywhere from 1 to 20 miles offshore. Farther out, along the 100-fathom curve, anglers catch blue marlin, white marlin, and sailfish.

Freshwater

Florida has excellent fishing for crappie, bluegills, and other panfish, but the largemouth bass is the undisputed favorite of freshwater anglers. Surveys have documented that nearly 80 percent of anglers prefer to fish for bass, while the remainder prefer crappie and bream.

A relative newcomer to the freshwater scene is the peacock bass, which has become a favorite of many former bass diehards. The feisty, colorful peacock is a South American native that was stocked by the state in urban canals in the Miami area in the mid-1980s. The fish, which cannot tolerate water temperatures below 60°F, have taken eagerly to South Florida.

The Everglades

The Everglades used to stretch from Lake Okeechobee to the southern end of the Florida mainland. Agriculture, roads, and homes have hemmed in the northern portion of the 'Glades, but the fishing remains quite good.

Most angling occurs in the flood-control canals that crisscross the Everglades. Although the canals are home to a variety of panfish—including oscars, a South American native that was accidentally introduced—most boaters target largemouth bass.

The edges of canals and cuts leading to the shallow flats of the Everglades are the favored areas to pursue bass. Anglers slow-troll shiners along the canal banks, which typically are lined with sawgrass, cattails, water hyacinths, lily pads, and hydrilla; work topwater plugs along the edge; or flip plastic worms and crawdads in the vegetation. The majority of the bass are under a pound, but the 'Glades does have a fair number of trophy fish, although not many over 10 pounds.

The Everglades can be accessed from three main roads: U.S. Highway 27, which runs north-south through the 'Glades; Interstate 75, also known as Alligator Alley, which runs east-west through the middle of the Everglades; and U.S. Highway 41, also known as the Tamiami Trail, which runs east-west through the southern part of the Everglades, just north of Everglades National Park. Most of the canals are connected, so it is possible to run from one end of the Everglades to the other.

The canals on both sides of Interstate 75 are popular with bass anglers, who have a choice of boat ramps along the highway. East of U.S. 27 is Sawgrass Recreation Park, which has two popular canals, one that runs north along the highway and one that runs east. West of U.S. 27 and south of Sawgrass is Everglades Holiday Park, a hub for canals that run north, west, and south. Some of the best bass fishing is in the L67A Canal, which runs from Holiday Park to the Tamiami Trail.

Bass fishing is at its best in winter and spring. Late winter is particularly productive, when water levels in the Everglades are at their lowest. When the water gets low on the flats, the fish are forced into the canals, and anglers have a field day. During those times, it's possible to catch a hundred or more fish on just about any lure you choose.

Lake Okeechobee

Lake Okeechobee is the crown jewel of bass waters in a state known for its bass fishing. The Big O comprises more than 450,000 acres, most of it shallow and filled with a variety of vegetation.

Due to expansive habitat and an abundance of baitfish, Okeechobee's bass grow big. Anglers come to the Big O from all over North America with the hope of catching a 10-pounder, the magic number for the species. Many of them hit that jackpot. Others are content to catch and release 30 or more 2- to 4-pound bass a day.

The biggest bass are usually caught during the winter and early spring, when the fish move into the shallows to spawn and countless anglers ply the waters with live shiners. In season, anglers commonly catch 7-pounders, and 10-pounders are a regular occurrence. Summer features lots of 2- to 3-pound bass, but the midday heat makes fishing early in the morning or late in the afternoon best.

In addition to large live shiners, bass anglers most often use plastic worms, crawdads, jerkbaits, weedless spoons, spinnerbaits, lipless crankbaits, and topwater plugs. Flipping worms and crawdads amidst the peppergrass, eelgrass, hydrilla, and bulrushes produces fish year-round and is a standard tactic. Weedless spoons and spinnerbaits are favored in spring and summer, when the bass are in the grass at first light, feeding on shad. Burning a crankbait over a submerged bed of hydrilla is a favorite tactic.

Where to fish is often determined by the wind direction and strength. Some areas of the lake can become unfishable because the water gets too dirty for the fish or too rough for boaters to safely navigate. At times the wind has blown parts of the lake dry, leaving anglers and their boats stranded in the muck. Optimal fishing location depends on water levels as well. When the lake is low, some fishing holes dry up, whereas others are crammed with fish. As the water level rises, new areas open and bass quickly move in. Some of these changes are subtle. A certain stretch of bulrushes might harbor lots of bass at a certain water level. A few days of rain can send those fish elsewhere and leave anglers scratching their heads, wondering why the fish are no longer biting. Likewise, a few windy days can shut down fishing at one location and turn it on at another spot 20 miles away.

From the same name/different species file: *Ling* refers to lingcod and to cobia; *rockfish* refers to the rock cods of the Scorpaenidae family and also to striped bass.

F

Following are descriptions of some traditionally productive bass spots on the Big O.

Pahokee Rocks is a good area in the summer. Anglers favor crankbaits and Carolina-rigged plastic worms.

The rim canal, which encircles most of the lake, was created when a dike was built to prevent flooding. It offers protection from the wind and decent fishing for bluegills and speckled perch. Bass fishing is best around the cuts leading to the main lake.

Pelican Bay can be especially good in the winter. Focus on the back of the bay if the water is clean there but the surrounding water is dirty. Use plastic worms, jerkbaits, and spinnerbaits.

Bay Bottom encompasses the area from Belle Glade to Grassy Island and is one of the best winter spots for bass, as the fish come to the area to spawn. Flip plastic worms and crawfish in the peppergrass and eelgrass. Use spinnerbaits if it's windy.

Buzzard Roost can be good as long as the water is clean. If the wind is strong and out of the north, the area tends to get muddy and this makes fishing difficult.

At Ritta Island, fish the cattails on the inside using live shiners or hard jerkbaits.

East Wall/West Wall are two popular areas that get fished hard. In the fall, fish outside the joint grass and cattail edges with live shiners, or flip plastic crawfish and worms. As the fish move inside to spawn, move with them.

Coot Bay is a good shiner spot in the fall.

The Shoal is the area from Uncle Joe's Cut to almost the North Shore. It features a wall of cattails, bulrushes, and patches of grass. Fish the outside early in the fall, before the water gets muddy. When winter cold fronts sweep in, go inside and fish the clean, protected waters of Moonshine Bay, the Monkey Box, Fisheating Bay, and the North Shore.

Indian Prairie Canal is a good winter spot. Fish both sides of the canal on out to the North Shore. Use plastic jerkbaits or spinnerbaits, or pitch/flip plastic worms.

Cody's Cove to Indian Prairie Canal is a good place to use shiners, plastic jerkbaits, and white or chartreuse spinnerbaits. During winter, flip plastic worms on the inside and outside.

The Kissimmee River, which links Okeechobee to Lake Kissimmee, is best when bass are schooling. Chrome lipless crankbaits are the preferred lure.

Kings Bar is good when using live shiners, plastic jerkbaits, or plastic worms around the hydrilla, cattails, and bulrushes on the outside and just on the inside. Do the same when the fish move inside to spawn.

Little Grassy Island is good when bass move inside to spawn during the winter. Use spinnerbaits, plastic jerkbaits, and plastic worms.

Okeechobee also has a phenomenal crappie fishery, with an estimated 10 million of these tasty panfish, which often exceed 2 pounds. The best fishing is in winter, when crappie, known as speckled perch, bed in shallow, nearshore areas. Live minnows fished on cane poles and crappie jigs fished on light spinning outfits are the top producers. In the spring, bluegills and shellcrackers start spawning in shallow areas and under overhanging tree limbs in the rim canal. Live crickets, live worms, and small spinnerbaits are the top offerings.

Lake Kissimmee

Lake Kissimmee is located in about the dead center of Florida. It contains good numbers of big bass, crappie, bluegills, and shellcrackers. Most of the fishing is done around vegetation, primarily hydrilla, reeds, water hyacinths, and lily pads.

During winter and spring, anglers catch a fair number of bass from 7 to 10 pounds. Live shiners are popular with bass anglers, who slow-troll these baitfish along the edges of grassbeds. Whenever a bass bites, probe the area more thoroughly. Flipping plastic worms and crawdads in the vegetation is also a popular technique. The bass bite begins to slow during the summer but picks up again in mid-October.

Winter is prime time for crappie, which take live minnows best. Spring and early summer are the seasons to catch plenty of bedding bluegills and shellcrackers using live worms.

Ocala National Forest

Some of the biggest bass in the state used to be caught in the small lakes scattered throughout Ocala National Forest. The fishing pressure took its toll, and now big bass are a rarity. In addition, many of the lakes are crystal clear, making it difficult to fool a wary largemouth. Some of the best fishing is with live shiners at Lake Kerr, the largest lake in the forest.

St. Johns River

The St. Johns gets its start in Central Florida and flows northward, dumping into several lakes before winding its way to Jacksonville.

The best bass fishing begins in the lower middle portion of the 250-mile-long river, between Lake Harney and Lake Monroe in Sanford. During late winter and early spring, shad migrate down here to spawn. Most anglers either troll or fly-fish for shad, which run 3 to 5 pounds. When the shad run ends, the focus is on largemouth bass, although the river also offers excellent fishing for bluegills. Most anglers target the creeks that feed into the St. Johns.

The river goes from a relative trickle to the broad, shallow expanse of Lake George, on the eastern side of Ocala National Forest. The lake has largemouth bass, striped bass, bluegills, crappie, and shellcrackers. The bass fishing is best in spring and fall, with live shiners, spinnerbaits, and plastic worms the favorite bait. Lake George has an average depth of 5 feet and little structure, so most of the bass fishing occurs in and around beds of eelgrass along the edges of the lake.

Flowing out of Lake George, the St. Johns begins to broaden and is influenced by tidal flow; this is where the bass fishing really gets good. The stretch between the lake and Palatka is the self-proclaimed "Bass Capital of the World."

Fishing is good in the main river, and in numerous creeks and lakes connected to the river. Boat docks and pilings often hold big bass in the river and in Lake Crescent. Boaters can lock through the Cross Florida Barge Canal to gain access to Rodman Reservoir. (Rodman also has access ramps.) This man-made lake has lots of hydrilla and hyacinths, and plenty of bass tournaments. In spring, anglers fish for spawning bass in the shallow creeks that feed into Rodman. On a good day, it's not unusual to catch 40 to 50 largemouths, and Rodman does produce 10-pounders; live shiners are the top bait. Striped bass run into Rodman in the spring, and there is good fishing for bluegills and shellcrackers from early spring through late summer.

Lake Seminole

Lake Seminole forms part of the border between Florida and Georgia in the Panhandle region. The lake was created in 1947 when a dam was built where the Chattahoochee and Flint Rivers meet. The Florida portion of the lake extends north along the Chattahoochee to Alabama. The Flint portion runs northeast and is entirely in Georgia.

The lake has an average depth of less than 10 feet and features lots of standing timber, more than 250 islands, and loads of sloughs and creeks. Fishing is good for sunshine bass and striped bass. Sunshines, which are hatchery-raised hybrid striped bass, average 5 to 6 pounds. Pure-strain stripers average 10 to 12 pounds. Seminole also has crappie, bluegills, channel catfish, and shellcrackers, but most anglers seek largemouth bass.

Much of the bass fishing centers around vegetation, primarily hydrilla. Flipping plastic worms and crawdads in and around the vegetation yields good fish in winter. Spring is the best season, as the bass move into the shallows and creeks and start bedding. Shiners, spinnerbaits, and plastic worms all work well. In the summer, when the bass start schooling, the topwater fishing is at its best.

FLOTATION DEVICE
See: Personal Flotation Device.

FLOUNDER
A group of bottom fish with compressed bodies, flounder are also known as flatfish *(see)*. Another marked characteristic is that both eyes are on one side of the head.
See: Flounder, Gulf; Flounder, Southern; Flounder, Starry; Flounder, Summer; Flounder, Windowpane; Flounder, Winter.

FLOUNDER, GULF   *Paralichthys albigutta.*
Other names—flounder; Spanish: *lenguado tres ojos.*

The gulf flounder is a member of the Bothidae family of left-eyed flounder and is an excellent table fish. It is one of the smaller fish in a large group of important sport and commercial flounder. Because of its size, the gulf flounder is of minor economic significance, and it is mixed in commercial and sport catches with summer flounder *(see: flounder, summer)* and southern flounder *(see: flounder, southern).*

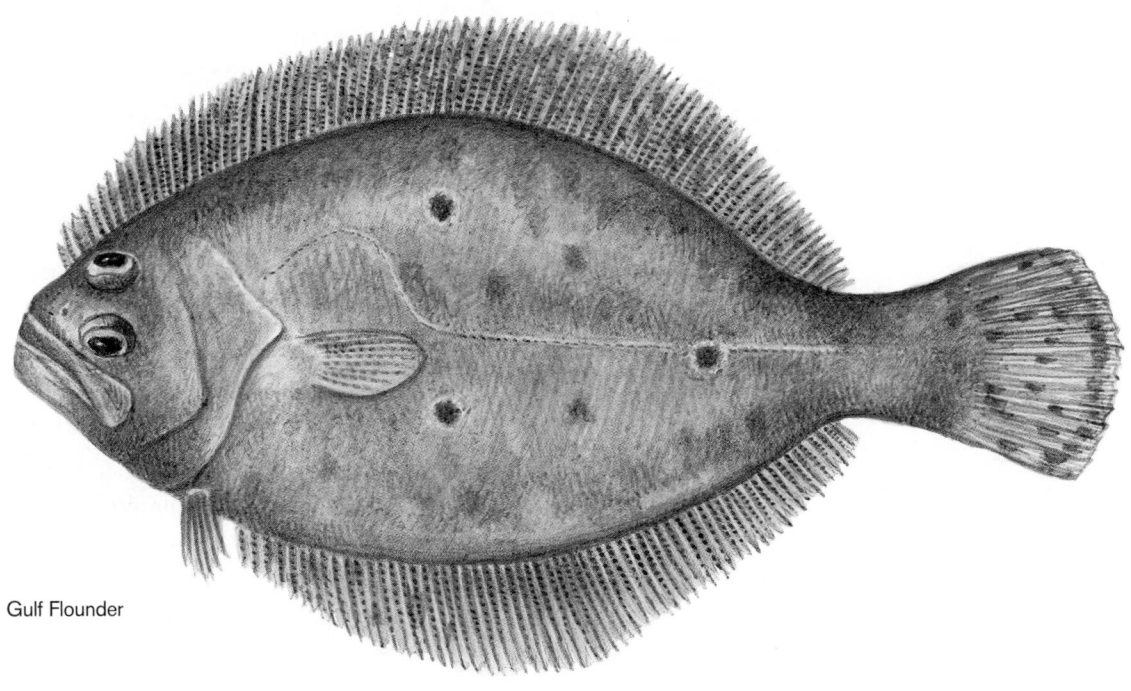
Gulf Flounder

Identification. The gulf flounder has the familiar olive brown background of its relatives, the summer and southern flounder, but it has three characteristic ocellated spots forming a triangle on its eye side. One spot is above the lateral line, one below, and one on the middle, although these spots can become obscure in larger fish. Numerous white spots are scattered over the body and fins (*albigutta* means white-spotted), and the caudal fin is in the shape of a wedge, with the tip in the middle. This species has 53 to 63 anal rays, which is fewer than the 63 to 73 found on the southern flounder. Like other flatfish *(see)*, the gulf flounder can change color dramatically to match the bottom.

Size/Age. The average fish is under 2 pounds and between 6 and 10 inches long, although it is capable of growing to 15 inches. It is believed to live for at least three years. The all-tackle world-record fish is a 5-pounder, caught in Florida.

Distribution. The gulf flounder generally occurs in the same range as the southern flounder; it is common from Cape Lookout, North Carolina, to Corpus Christi, Texas, including southern Florida and the Bahamas.

Habitat. Gulf flounder inhabit sand, coral rubble, and seagrass areas near shore. They often range into tidal reefs and are occasionally found around nearshore rocky reefs. They commonly favor depths of up to 60 feet.

Spawning. Spawning season is in the winter offshore.

Food. The gulf flounder feeds on crustaceans and small fish.

FLOUNDER, SOUTHERN

Paralichthys lethostigma.

Other names—flatfish, flounder, halibut, mud flounder, plie, southern fluke; Spanish: *lenguado de Floride.*

The southern flounder is thought to be the largest Gulf of Mexico flatfish. A member of the Bothidae family of left-eyed flounder, it is a highly desired food fish, and a considerable amount is harvested by trawlers.

Identification. The southern flounder resembles the summer flounder *(see: flounder, summer)* in appearance.

Its coloring is light to dark olive brown, and it is marked with diffused dark blotches and spots, instead of distinct ocelli (spots ringed with distinct lighter areas). These spots often disappear in large fish. The underside is white, the simple fins make an even fringe around the body, and its beady eyes are located extremely close together. It can be distinguished from the summer flounder by having fewer gill rakers and by the presence of distinct spots. It is also similar to the gulf flounder *(see: flounder, gulf),* which has no distinct ocelli.

Size/Age. Mature individuals grow to 36 inches and more than 12 pounds. The average size is 12 to 24 inches and 2 to 3 pounds. The all-tackle record is 20 pounds, 9 ounces. Southern flounder can live up to 20 years in the Gulf of Mexico.

Distribution. The southern flounder can be found from North Carolina to northern Mexico, although it is not present in southern Florida.

Habitat. As an estuarine-dependent bottom fish, the southern flounder commonly inhabits inshore channels, bay mouths, estuaries, and sometimes freshwater. It is tolerant of a wide range of temperatures (50° to 90°F) and is often found in waters where salinities fluctuate from 0 to 20 parts per thousand. No other flounder of the eastern United States is regularly encountered in this type of environment. Anglers regularly catch this fish inshore from bridges and jetties.

Spawning behavior. Southern flounder spawn in offshore waters. In the northern Gulf of Mexico, they move out of bays and estuaries in the fall; this occurs quickly if there is an abrupt cold snap, but it happens more slowly if there is gradual cooling. Spawning occurs afterward, in late fall and early winter. Females typically release several hundred thousand eggs, which hatch and migrate into the estuaries and change from upright swimmers into left-eyed bottom dwellers.

Food and feeding habits. The southern flounder feeds partly by burying itself in the sand and waiting to ambush its prey. Small flounder consume shrimp and other small crustaceans, whereas larger flounder eat blue crabs, shrimp, and fish such as anchovies, mullet, menhaden, Atlantic croaker, and pinfish.

See: Flatfish.

Southern Flounder

FLOUNDER, STARRY   *Platichthys stellatus.*

Other names—rough jacket, great flounder, California flounder, diamond back, emerywheel, emery flounder, grindstone, sandpaper flounder; Japanese: *numagarei.*

The starry flounder is a smaller and less-common member of the Pacific coast Pleuronectidae family of right-eyed flounder. Flounder and other flatfish *(see)* are known for their unique appearance, having both eyes on either the left or right side of the head, although the starry flounder can be either left-eyed or right-eyed.

It is a popular sportfish because of its willingness to bite and its strong fighting qualities. Although the starry flounder has tasty flesh, it is important mainly as a sportfish, having only moderate commercial value. Processing is difficult due to its rough skin, and it must be deep-skinned to remove its unappealing, dark fat layer.

Identification.   The starry flounder belongs to the right-eyed family of flatfish, but, as noted, it can also be left-eyed. Its head is pointed, and it has a small mouth. The anal spine is strong. The caudal fin is square or slightly rounded. Its coloring is olive to dark brown or almost black on the upper side, and creamy white on the blind side. The unpaired fins, its outstanding feature, are white to yellow to orange with black bars. There are patches of rough, shiny, starlike scales scattered over the eyed side of the body, which give rise to its name.

Size.   The average size is 12 to 14 inches, although it can grow to 3 feet and 20 pounds. Females grow faster than males and attain larger sizes.

Distribution.   The starry flounder ranges from central California to Alaska, and south from the Bering Sea to Japan and Korea. This is one of the most numerous fish of central Northern California backwaters, particularly San Francisco Bay.

Habitat.   It is usually found near shore over mud, sand, or gravel bottoms. Often entering brackish or freshwater, the starry flounder is most abundant in shallow water but can be found in depths of at least 900 feet. Juveniles are often intertidal.

Spawning behavior.   Spawning occurs in late winter and early spring in California waters less than 25 fathoms deep.

Food.   Adult starry flounder consume a variety of items, including crabs, clams, shrimp, and sand

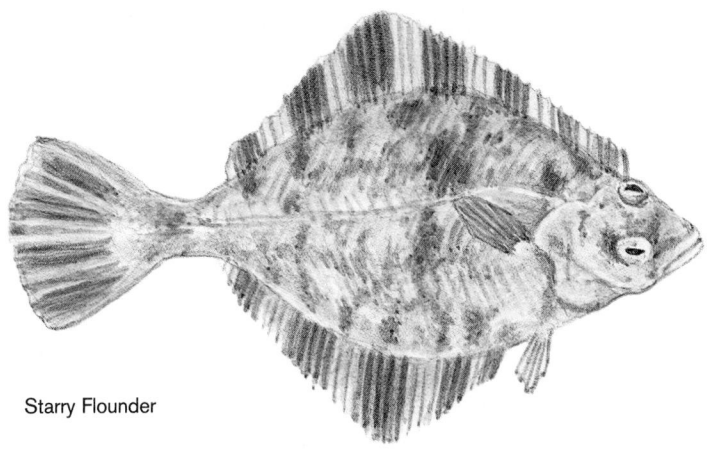

Starry Flounder

dollars. Large individuals also eat some fish, such as sardines, sanddabs, and surfperch.

Angling.   Starry flounder are caught throughout the year in California but are more frequently taken from December through March. They accept a variety of natural baits, including chunks of sardines, clams, shrimp, squid, and worms.

Angling techniques are generally discussed in greater detail under other entries. For more information, *see: Drift Fishing; Inshore Fishing.*

FLOUNDER, SUMMER   *Paralichthys dentatus.*
Other names—fluke, northern fluke, flounder; Dutch: *zomervogel;* French: *cardeau d'été.*

The summer flounder, most commonly called fluke, is a member of the Bothidae family of flatfish *(see),* or left-eyed flounder. Like other flatfish, the summer flounder undergoes a unique maturation from egg to adult flounder in which one eye migrates to the opposite side of the head. It is the most northerly and perhaps abundant of the three

F

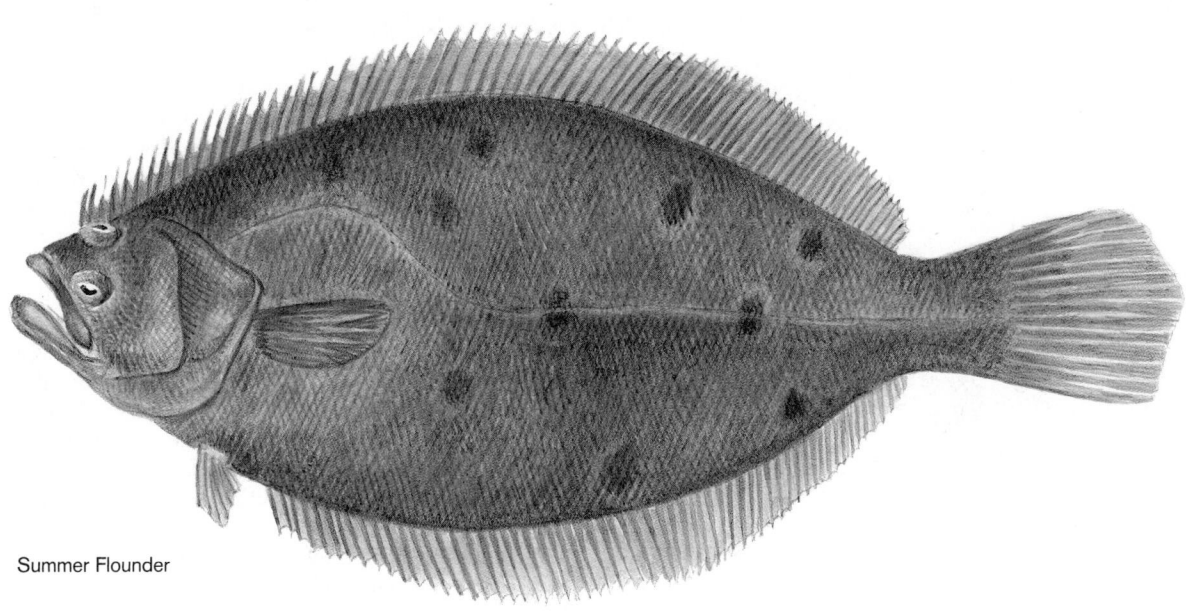

Summer Flounder

bothid species, as well as the largest and most prized flatfish caught in the mid-Atlantic region of the United States.

Fishing for summer flounder off jetties and bridges is a mainstay of Mid-Atlantic coastal sportfishing and a prominent commercial catch, primarily taken by otter trawl. Anglers in the Mid-Atlantic harvest a significant proportion of the total catch, usually about 40 percent, and in some years the recreational take has exceeded the commercial take.

Although not a powerful fighter, this species provides spirited and often dependable action. The meat is firm, white, and delicately flavored, and although some complain about the many bones (as with all flounder) and a dryness of the meat, proper filleting and moisture-retaining cooking methods can eliminate those issues.

Identification. The body is wide and somewhat flattened, rimmed by long dorsal and anal fins. Its mouth is large and well equipped with teeth. The eyes are on the left side of the body, and close together. The teeth are well developed on the right side of the jaw. Its background coloring is usually gray, brown, or olive, but it adjusts to the environment to keep the fish hidden by camouflage. There are also many eyespots that change color. The blind side is white and relatively featureless. The dorsal fin has 85 to 94 rays; the anal fin has 60 to 63 rays. There are only 5 or 6 gill rakers on the upper limb of the first arch and 11 to 21 on the lower limb.

In addition to their different color patterns, the three species of bothids can be distinguished by the number of gill rakers, anal fin rays, and lateral-line scales they possess. Summer flounder have the most eyespots, gulf flounder *(see: flounder, gulf)* have several eyespots, and southern flounder *(see: flounder, southern)* lack conspicuous spots.

Size. The average summer flounder weighs 2 to 5 pounds, the latter being about 23 inches long. It is capable of growing to 35 inches in length but rarely does, and the all-tackle world record is a 22-pound, 7-ounce fish caught at Montauk, New York.

Historical data indicate that female summer flounder may live up to 20 years, but males rarely exceed 7 years of age. Growth rates differ appreciably between the sexes; females attain weights up to 26 pounds.

Distribution. The summer flounder occurs in the western Atlantic from Maine to South Carolina and possibly to northeast Florida, and is most abundant from Cape Cod to North Carolina.

Habitat. A bottom-dwelling fish, the summer flounder prefers sandy or muddy bottoms and is common in the summer months in bays, harbors, estuaries, canals, creeks, and along shorelines, as well as in the vicinity of piers and bridges or near patches of eelgrass or other vegetation. It typically prefers relatively shallow waters and depths of up to 100 feet during warmer months, then moves offshore in winter to deeper, cooler water of 150 to 500 feet.

Life history/Behavior. Sexually maturity is reached at age 3. Spawning takes place during the fall and winter while the fish are moving offshore into deeper water or when they reach their winter location. The eggs, which float near the surface, hatch in three to four days, producing larvae shaped more like conventional fish than flatfish. Water currents carry newly hatched flounder into the estuaries and sounds, where they undergo a transformation in shape and become bottom dwellers.

Food and feeding habits. Adults are largely piscivorous and highly predatory, feeding actively in midwater as well as on the bottom. Extremely fast swimmers, they often chase baitfish at the surface, which is not characteristic of most other flatfish. Fluke also bury themselves quickly, using undulating movements of their fins to throw sand or silt on their backs. The eyes remain uncovered and watch carefully for dinner prospects. Fluke are known to eat what is available, including shrimp, crabs, menhaden, anchovies, silversides, sand launce, killifish, weakfish, hake, and other flounder.

Angling. Although fluke can be caught from shore, fishing is usually best from a boat in 8 feet or more of water during the summer. This is especially true when water temperatures climb above 75°F, because the fish seek the cooler depths.

Commonly used baits are minnows, shrimp, and squid; artificial lures that imitate these items are also effective. A line is generally rigged with two leaders on a vertical spreader so that one hook is fished on or near the bottom, while the second is held about 1 foot off the bottom. If an artificial lure is used in combination with bait, it is attached to the upper leader so it stays off the bottom and can move realistically in the current. A sinker of sufficient size must be used so the line stays on the bottom even when there is a strong tidal flow.

Unless flounder are known to be in a certain area, it is usually best to drift for them, thereby covering a large area. Likely spots to try include places with rough or irregular bottoms, in or near inlets, and around pilings, wrecks, and jetties. Food is abundant

A summer flounder from Barnegat Bay, New Jersey.

F

in these locations. If you are fishing in one spot, it helps to jig the line up and down so the bait does not lie motionless on the bottom, as fluke (and other flatfish) are often attracted by movement.

Other aspects of angling for flounder are discussed in greater detail under other entries. For more information, *see: Drift Fishing; Inshore Fishing.*

FLOUNDER, WINDOWPANE
Scophthalmus aquosus.
Other names—sand flounder.

The windowpane flounder is a small, thin-bodied, left-eyed flounder that is seldom encountered by anglers but is noted for its sweet-tasting flesh. Like other flatfish *(see)*, the windowpane flounder undergoes a unique maturation from egg to adult flounder in which one eye migrates to the opposite side of the head.

The commercial catch of windowpane flounder, primarily via otter trawl, increased in the mid-1980s as a result of an expansion of the fishery offshore, as well as the targeting of this species as an alternative to other depleted flatfish stocks. Like many other flatfish, it is considered overexploited.

Identification.   The windowpane is a roundish flounder with a pale-white or translucent blind side, which gives rise to its name. It has many dark brown spots on the body and fins, and its lateral line is strongly arched to the front.

Size.   It grows to 18 inches and in some areas is common to 16 inches, but many that are encountered by anglers are less than 11 inches and too small to keep for eating.

Distribution.   This species ranges along the northwest Atlantic continental shelf from the Gulf of St. Lawrence to northern Florida.

Habitat.   The windowpane flounder is found from shore out to roughly 150 feet of water, and occasionally deeper.

Spawning.   Sexual maturity occurs between ages 3 and 4. Spawning occurs from late spring through autumn, peaking in July and August on Georges Bank, and in September in southern New England.

FLOUNDER, WINTER
Pseudopleuronectes americanus.
Other names—flounder, lemon sole, sole, black-back, blueback, black flounder, dab, mud dab, flatfish, Georges Bank flounder; French: *plie rouge;* Italian: *sogliola limanda;* Spanish: *mendo limon.*

One of the most common and well-known flounder of shallow Atlantic coastal waters, the winter flounder belongs to the Pleuronectidae family of flatfish *(see)*. It is a right-eyed flatfish, with both eyes on the right side of its body, and gets its name because it retreats to cold, deep water in the summer and reappears in shallower water close to shore in the winter; its relative, the summer flounder *(see: flounder, summer),* does the opposite.

The winter flounder is an important food and commercial species, and a thick, meaty specimen. The meat is firm, white, and delicately flavored, and although some complain about the many bones (as with all flounder), proper filleting methods can eliminate this problem.

Identification.   The body is oval and flat with a tiny mouth. Color varies from reddish brown to dark brown with small black spots. The underside is whitish and occasionally brown, tinged with blue around the edges. The caudal fin is slightly rounded. The winter flounder differs from the similar yellowtail flounder *(see: flounder, yellowtail),* in its straight lateral line, no arch over the pectoral fin, thicker body, and widely spaced eyes.

Size.   Most winter flounder weigh between 1 and $1^1/_2$ pounds and average less than a foot in length, although they are capable of growing to 8 pounds and 2 feet. The all-tackle world record is

F

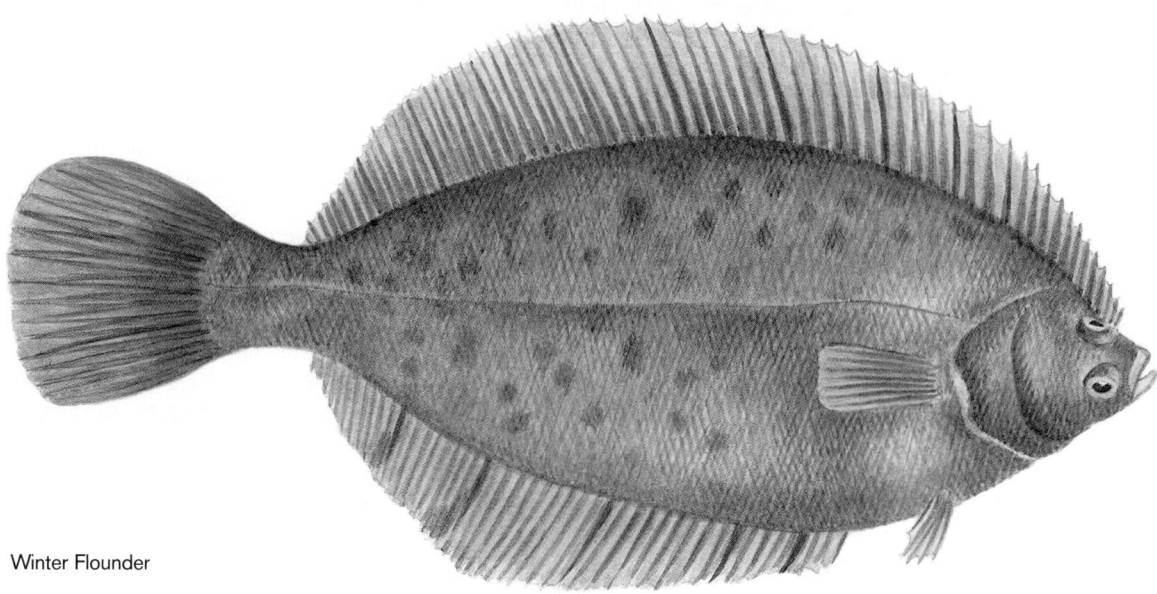

Winter Flounder

A winter flounder from Shark River, New Jersey.

7 pounds. Larger fish are sometimes called "sea flounder" to distinguish them from the smaller bay fish.

Distribution. Winter flounder are mostly inshore fish common in estuaries and the coastal area from Chesapeake Bay north to the Gulf of St. Lawrence. Stragglers occur south to Georgia and north to Labrador.

Habitat. Winter flounder are found inshore in estuaries and coastal ocean areas. In the Mid-Atlantic they stay inshore from January through April. Smaller fish occur in shallower water, although larger fish will enter water only a foot deep. They are range anywhere from well up into the high-tide mark to depths of at least 400 feet. Preferring sand-mud bottoms, they are also found over sand, clay, or fine gravel, and on hard bottom offshore.

Life history/Behavior. Spawning occurs in shallow water over sandy bottoms from January through May. Winter flounder eggs stick together and sink to the bottom, where they hatch in roughly 16 days, depending on water temperature. These fish move from deep water toward shallow water during the fall, and offshore again in the spring.

Food and feeding habits. When on a soft bottom, the winter flounder will lie buried up to its eyes, waiting to attack prey. Because of its small mouth, its diet includes only smaller food like marine worms, small crustaceans, and small, shelled animals like clams and snails.

Angling. Although these fish are caught in midwinter, they are more concentrated in late winter and early spring, and because anglers are more comfortable at that time, fishing activity for this species tends to pick up in March and April. Many anglers chum for winter flounder in order to concentrate them. They will often use a horizontal spreader when fishing two leaders on one line. This lets both baits rest on the bottom where the fish feed. Enough weight should be used to keep the baits on the bottom, and No. 8 or smaller hooks work well for these small-mouthed fish. Winter flounder do not bite particularly hard, and it's necessary to be aware of the light pressure on the line of a nibbling fish. If you are fishing in one spot, it helps to lightly move the line up and down so the bait does not lie motionless on the bottom for a long period, as these fish are often attracted by movement.

Other aspects of angling for flounder are discussed in greater detail under other entries. For more information, *see: Drift Fishing; Inshore Fishing.*

FLOUNDER, WITCH
Glyptocephalus cynoglossus.
Other names—gray sole, craig fluke, witch; Dutch: *witje;* French: *plie cynoglosse;* Icelandic: *langlúra;* Italian: *passera linguadi cane;* Norwegian: *mareflydre;* Spanish: *mendo falsó lenguado.*

The witch flounder, commonly called gray sole, is a moderate-size deep-water right-eyed flounder that is seldom encountered by anglers. It is of some commercial significance, however, and is mainly caught by otter trawl. Formerly, the commercial catch of witch flounder was a byproduct of shrimp trawling, but concerted targeting of this species by long-range fleets as an alternative to other depleted flatfish stocks has resulted in overexploitation. Like other flatfish *(see),* the witch flounder undergoes a unique maturation from egg to adult flounder as one eye migrates to the opposite side of the head.

Identification. The witch flounder is generally uniform brownish on its eyed side, sometimes with obscure darker bars. Its mouth is small and its lateral line straight, and it has large mucous pits on its blind side.

Size. Witch flounder attain lengths up to 31 inches and weights of approximately $4^{1}/_{2}$ pounds, although they are usually less than 25 inches long.

Distribution. The witch flounder ranges in the eastern Atlantic from northern Norway to northern Spain, and in the western Atlantic from the Gulf of St. Lawrence and Grand Banks to Cape Hatteras, North Carolina. It is common throughout the Gulf of Maine and also occurs in deeper areas on and adjacent to Georges Bank and along the shelf edge.

Habitat. Witch flounder appear to be sedentary, preferring moderately deep to deep areas and muddy bottoms. In the western Atlantic few fish are taken shallower than 90 feet by commercial fishermen, and most are caught between 360 and 900 feet. They range much deeper, however.

Spawning. Spawning occurs in late spring and summer.

Food. This deep-water dweller feeds on crustaceans and brittle stars.

FLOUNDER, YELLOWTAIL

Pleuronectes ferrugineus.

Other names—yellowtail, mud dab, rusty dab, sand dab; Finnish: *ruostekampela;* French: *limande à queue jaune.*

The yellowtail flounder is a small, right-eyed flounder that is seldom encountered by anglers. It has been an important component of commercial fishing, mainly caught by otter trawl. The commercial catch of yellowtail flounder has declined drastically in the 1980s and 1990s, and this species is greatly overexploited. Like other flatfish *(see),* it undergoes a unique maturation from egg to adult flounder in which one eye migrates to the opposite side of the head.

Identification. The yellowtail flounder is generally uniformly brownish on its eyed side, with many rusty spots of various sizes. Its mouth is small and lateral line arched toward the front. The blind side has yellow at the edges of the fins and the caudal peduncle.

Size. This species can attain lengths to $18^{1}/_{2}$ inches and weights up to 1 kilogram, but high rates of fishing mortality have greatly reduced the average size and age, leaving fewer larger and older specimens.

Distribution. Yellowtail flounder range from Labrador to Chesapeake Bay. Commercially important concentrations have historically been found on Georges Bank, off Cape Cod, and in southern New England.

Habitat. This fish appears to be relatively sedentary, although seasonal movements have been documented. It is generally caught by commercial trawlers at depths between 120 and 240 feet, over sandy and muddy bottoms.

Spawning. Spawning occurs during spring and summer, peaking in May.

Food. The yellowtail flounder feeds on worms, amphipods, shrimp, crustaceans, and occasionally small fish.

FLUKE

A common name for summer flounder *(see: flounder, summer).*

FLUOROCARBON

Fluorocarbon is the name given to line produced from polyvinylidene fluoride, a nylon alloy that was created in the 1960s and that has seen increasing use in fishing line, particularly in fly and saltwater fishing.

A monofilament line, dry fluorocarbon looks virtually the same to the human eye as dry conventional nylon monofilament, but in water the material has a refractive index—the degree to which light is bent while passing through—that is considerably less than nylon mono and closer to that of water, meaning that it is technically less visible. Decreased visibility in a line should mean that it is less alarming to fish, resulting in more strikes in clear and shallow-water fishing, assuming all other things are equal s(no drag, etc.).

Fluorocarbon also has very high abrasion resistance, does not get weaker through water absorption, and is said to be impervious to ultraviolet light. These characteristics contribute to a very durable line. The lack of water absorption is an important and distinguishing characteristic. Most conventional nylon monofilaments have between 10 and 15 percent water absorption and are weaker in a wet state; fluorocarbon line does not change characteristics, so its breaking strength is the same when wet as when dry.

The combined attributes of abrasion resistance, strength, and decreased visibility offer anglers the advantage to drop down in tippet *(see)* or leader *(see)* size without sacrificing performance. Furthermore, fluorocarbon lines have a super slick finish on them, and as a result they do not pick up little bits of matter on their surface. This means that they produce less friction when going through the rod guides and thus cast better, although the average angler is unlikely to notice much difference, especially if using just a leader length of this material.

Since fluorocarbon is more dense than conventional nylon monofilament, it sinks faster, which can be an advantage or disadvantage depending on the type of fishing being done.

Fluorocarbon is expensive line, largely due to a complicated manufacturing process. And it is also a stiff line, which is why it was first available in short spools and used as tippet material and for shock leaders and not spooled fully onto a fishing reel. Some manufacturers have produced larger spools for filling up an entire reel. Originally available in high strengths, it is now manufactured in a full range of strengths/diameters and to International Game Fish Association (IGFA) record specifications. See: Line.

FLY

(1) A natural aquatic or terrestrial insect, especially one that is consumed by fish.
See: Aquatic Insects; Caddisflies; Dobsonflies; Dragonflies and Damselflies; Mayflies; Midges; Stoneflies; Terrestrial Insects.

(2) In a generic sense, a fly is a type of extremely lightweight lure, also known as an artificial fly (to distinguish it from a natural fly, which is rarely used by anglers), that is cast with a fly line and fly rod. Some flies are more imitative in appearance of natural insects than any other lure. Other flies are highly imitative of baitfish, crustaceans, and various

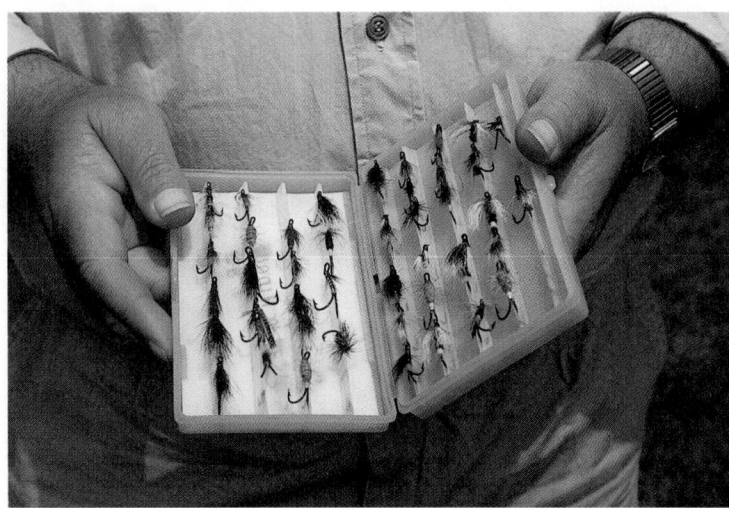

A fly box with assorted Atlantic salmon flies.

lemmings, snakes, and other creatures. Floating flies can be fished in many ways, but overall they are less effective than sinking flies, especially in cool or cold water.

Sinking flies are fished below the surface and are made with materials that absorb water or are more dense than water. They include wet flies, nymphs, and streamers, and also imitate many foods, including natural insects, small fish, crustaceans, worms, eels, leeches, and fish eggs. Sinking flies are likewise fished in many ways but are more productive overall because gamefish feed more often below the surface.

As with any lure used to entice fish, a fly's effectiveness depends on its overall appearance—size, shape, and color—plus its action. Since many flies are created to imitate specific food (especially insects), size and shape are nearly always important. Color is important in some cases and not in others, although it is seldom completely irrelevant and depends on the circumstances and species sought; it is more likely to be important in attractor flies than in imitative flies. Odor, which is an element for some lures, is often not a factor in fly usage, although the materials used for some flies can retain or absorb scents and may be imprinted with scent by the angler to help appeal to certain fish species. Using scent on a fly, however, prohibits any fish caught on it from receiving official world-record certification. Action is largely dependent upon the angler and the design of the fly. Flies do not have any action on their own and must be manipulated to move, although this movement is enhanced in

small, natural, noninsect foods. Still others are more suggestive than imitative, meant as attractors rather than deceivers.

All of the objects considered "flies" by anglers have in common the fact that they are light enough to be presented with flycasting tackle *(see)* and too light to be effectively cast with other types of tackle without the addition of weight (and then not as effectively). Thus, whatever a fly is meant to represent, it is carried to its destination by the act of casting a fly line, which is connected to a leader *(see)*, which is attached to the fly. This is the principle of fly fishing.

For the purpose of adhering to fishing regulations and for record keeping (world records are kept separately for fish caught by fly fishing), the definition of a fly and of fly fishing may be broader than the previous description. For example, some objects used with flycasting tackle are of such weight or design that they cannot be false cast but may actually be lobbed or stripped out with flycasting tackle. This may fit a very liberal definition of a fly, of fly fishing, or of casting, but it does not conform to the conventional and traditional perception of a fly as a lightweight object and of fly fishing as the use of a fly line in the repetitive casting and delivery of a lightweight object.

Types. An extremely wide array of flies is employed in fly fishing for diverse species in all areas of freshwater and saltwater. Flies range from less than $1/8$-inch long up to 10 inches long. Unlike many other lures, flies are entirely handmade, being tied on a single or double hook (seldom the latter) from a variety of natural and synthetic materials. They can generally be categorized as floating or sinking flies, and specifically typed as dry flies, wet flies, nymphs, streamers, and bugs.

Floating flies sit on the surface of the water and are made with materials that are buoyant. They include dry flies and bugs, and imitate a host of foods, including natural insects, frogs, mice or

A fly box with western-U.S. shad flies.

some flies (such as those with feather, hair, or rubber legs).

Patterns. With the exception of bugs, the basic and standard fly has these components: a hook, which includes a point that may or may not be barbed, an eye that may be straight or turned up or down, and a shank that may be straight, curved, keeled, or humped; a head; a body, which is the main section along the shank of the hook and which may have ribs; and a tail. It may also have wings, hackle, a thorax, and sometimes legs.

The particular appearance of a fly—in essence the parts that make up its likeness, the way they are incorporated onto the fly hook, and the colors—not only characterize it by type, but also constitute a pattern, and make a given fly distinguishable from others. There are literally thousands, perhaps tens of thousands, of patterns. This can be confusing and intimidating, and it is impossible for even the most astute fly angler to recognize all of them. The fact that many fly anglers tie flies (comparatively few users of nonfly lures make their own lures) in large part contributes to this proliferation of patterns. A beginning fly angler is best advised to seek counsel at a local fly tackle shop for the recommended fly patterns and sizes for a specific area at a given time.

Fly patterns are named for myriad reasons, most often for their creator, a specific place, and the object they imitate. Dozens of flies are among the most well-known patterns, but there are many specific patterns for various species of fish. The most patterns exist for trout species, because of the long prominence of trout as an angling quarry and the long history of fly fishing for trout; as long ago as 1676, Izaak Walton's *The Compleat Angler* listed 65 fly patterns for trout. There are also a lot of patterns for Atlantic salmon. Patterns for Pacific salmon and steelhead are different than those for Atlantic salmon and trout. Saltwater patterns are entirely different than freshwater patterns.

The myriad of fly patterns is not unlike the existence of many specific nonfly lures for freshwater and saltwater fishing, and specifically for such species as bass, walleye, stripers, etc. Like those products, certain flies have crossover application. Small trout flies are equally effective on panfish, for example, and many saltwater streamers are also effective on northern pike and lake trout.

The huge proliferation of patterns, some of which are barely distinguishable from each other, would seem to suggest that a fly angler, especially one seeking trout in streams, needs hundreds of different patterns to be able to use the right fly that will catch fish at a given time. It is true that many fish, stream trout in particular, can at times be very selective about feeding and about what artificial flies they will take because of its resemblance to their currently preferred food; this makes matching the hatch, whether there is in fact a hatch or merely just a predominance of a certain food item, advantageous if not essential.

However, it is also true that fish take flies that merely suggest food rather than duplicate it, and there are many patterns that are close enough to food duplications to be effective. In truth, even the best flies that imitate specific insects are not clones of those insects. And in any case, the best fly cannot be effective if it is not properly presented and/or retrieved. Therefore, the best course of action is to focus on the type of fly that most closely represents the food that fish are feeding on, and to fish it properly.

Dry Flies

Dry flies are relatively diminutive objects that float on the surface and represent aquatic or terrestrial insects found on the surface of streams, rivers, ponds, and lakes. Most dry flies imitate specific insects, especially mayflies *(see)* and caddisflies *(see)*, which is important, as is their size and profile. They are notable for stiff hackle (water-repellent bird feather wound around the hook) and tail feathers, and also for the use of deer hair, all of which are tied on a lightweight (light wire) hook to float the fly. Many dry flies also have wings, and there are also some that don't have hackle. Depending on the pattern, the materials used, and the way they are tied, dry flies may ride very high on the surface or may rest low in the surface film; they may be bushy and high-profiled, or very sparsely hackled and more diminutive. They are tied on a wide range of hook sizes, with different waters and seasons affecting the appropriate size choice.

Since natural insects float on the water subject to surface current or to movement via a breeze, dry fly imitations must be light enough to do likewise, although they are restrained by attachment to a fine tippet *(see)*, leader, and floating fly line, which may cause drag and may unnaturally move or restrain the fly. Like natural insects, dry flies are generally allowed to drift on the surface subject to whatever natural current or wind influences exist, but to avoid drag the presentation may require in-air or on-water line mending *(see)*.

Less often, some deliberate movement of a dry fly by the angler may be appropriate. This would occur if the natural insect being imitated moved about, such as an adult depositing eggs, which is well imitated by dapping *(see)*. As a means of attracting fish, gliding or skating a dry fly is a technique used for Atlantic salmon and occasionally trout, often with a long-hackled fly referred to as a skater.

In flowing water, dry flies are primarily fished by casting upstream and allowing the flies to float downstream in a natural manner. The line should not be cast directly over the fish, or over the area to be worked with a fly, in order to avoid spooking the fish; the best manner of presentation is to cast up- and across-stream, floating the fly down. Seldom are dry flies fished by casting directly downstream, because this limits the length of the drift owing to

Dry Flies

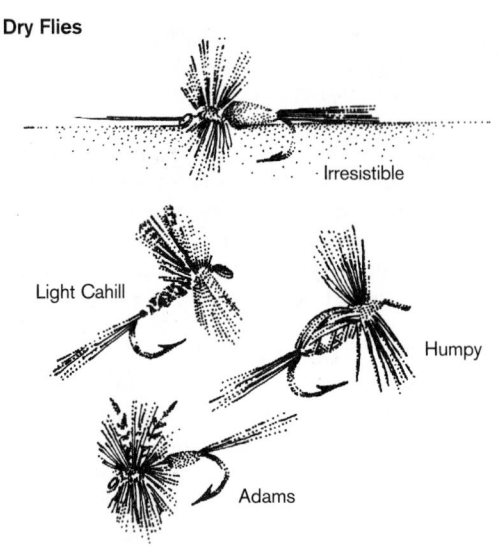

the line that can be dispatched and is almost certain to create drag.

Watch the fly as it floats on the surface so that you know when a fish takes it and so you can react quickly. When a fish rises to a dry fly, it may do so in a violent and splashy manner, which is obvious and exciting, or in a nearly imperceptible dimpling manner, which can be missed if you're not paying attention. In either case, however, do not react with a violent hooksetting motion, which many new fly anglers do; this is likely to pull the fly away from the fish or to break it off if the fish has already hooked itself. Simply react with a moderate flick of the wrist to raise the tip of the rod (keeping the line pinched to the handle with your finger).

Dry flies may become waterlogged after long use and especially after catching fish. When they start losing their buoyancy, some air drying by repetitive false casting, if conditions permit, may temporarily restore floating characteristics, but more likely the fly will need floatant, or dressing, to help it repel water. Silicone and paraffin dressings can be applied to a dry fly to help it float. Some anglers prefer sprays and liquid dips because they keep the hands from getting wet and sticky, but they don't last as long as pastes. If the fly has absorbed a lot of moisture, press it with a cloth to remove the moisture and clean it; then apply dressing to it.

As noted, the patterns and sizes of dry flies vary greatly, and it takes experience to make a selection at any given time and place. A well-rounded dry fly collection should have a representative assortment of fly types. The following patterns are among those that widely work well: Adams, Blue Dun, Brown Bivisible, Dark Cahill, Gray Wulff, Green Drake, Hendrickson, Humpy, Irresistible, Light Cahill, Muddler Minnow (dressed to float), Quill Gordon, some type of hopper, and brown and gray midges.

Wet Flies

Wet flies are very much like dries, although they sink upon entering the water. They primarily represent subsurface forms of aquatic insects that are naturally found in freshwater environs when they are swimming, laying eggs, emerging to head toward the surface, or merely spent and drifting; to a lesser extent, they may also represent a drowned terrestrial insect or small fish.

Wet flies have the following characteristics: the wings are tied to lie backward from the head; the body (often tinsel or chenille) is dense to help sink the fly; there may or may not be a tail; and a lesser amount of hackle at the head, also tied back, is present than on most dry flies. Unlike dries, the hackle on wet flies is soft, being derived from soft and water-absorbing bird feathers.

Parts of a (Wet) Fly

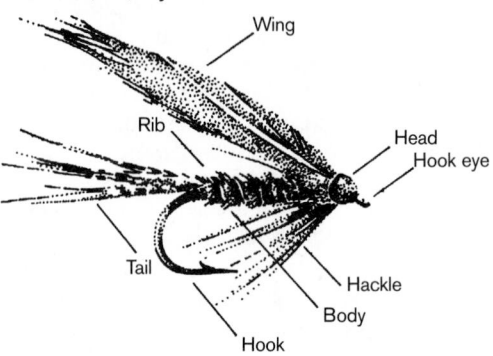

Wet flies are tied on a narrower range of hook sizes (mostly No. 6 to 18) than dry flies, and the hooks are heavier than those for dries to help with sinking. Often a bit of fine lead wire is wrapped on the shank under the body to also help the fly sink, or over the body as ribbing, which has both an appearance and sinking value. Wet flies may be imitative in appearance, or they may be brightly dressed attractors that don't bear close resemblance to natural insects.

Wet flies are unaffected by wind or surface current, but obviously they move with subsurface current; the connecting leader and fly line are affected by current on and below the surface, which may cause drag and unnaturally move or restrain what should be a free-drifting fly. Like natural insects, wet flies are generally allowed to drift in the water subject to whatever natural current exists, but to avoid drag the presentation may require line mending.

In flowing water, wet flies are primarily used by an angler who is above the fish's position, with the angler casting across-stream or across and downstream and allowing the fly to drift down to the (suspected) position of the fish. In this manner the line, leader, and angler are upstream of the fish. They may be retrieved across the flow as well as drifted naturally, and are often employed in tandem, with a second fly as a dropper or with several wet flies (this is usually close to the surface). Depending on the circumstances, especially water depth, a wet fly may be fished with a floating line (fly just under the surface), a sink-tip line (fly at middepths), or a full-sinking line (fly at greater depths).

Wet Flies

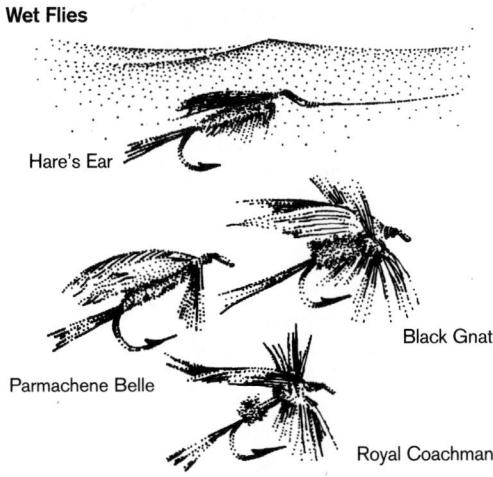

Hare's Ear

Black Gnat

Parmachene Belle

Royal Coachman

In ponds or lakes, a wet fly is generally used with a sink-tip or full-sink line and is fished with a stripping retrieve of the fly line, the speed of which varies according to whatever the fly is supposed to imitate. Wet flies that are attractors are generally fished at a quick pace.

The strike of a fish on a wet fly is typically felt rather than seen. The reaction by the angler should be to quickly pull on the fly line in the line-gathering hand, removing any slack, then pinch the line to the handle with the rod-holding hand, and flick the wrist upward to raise the rod tip.

There are many patterns of wet flies to employ. Sparsely tied and drab-colored wets are often preferred for trout fishing, but gaudy patterns have a good following in fishing for bass, panfish, salmon, steelhead, and brook trout. A wet fly collection should have a representative assortment of fly types. The following are widely known and popular patterns: Black Gnat, Blue Dun, Brown Hackle, Coachman, Dark Cahill, Hare's Ear, Ginger Quill, Gray Hackle, Light Cahill, March Brown, Parmachene Belle, Quill Gordon, and Royal Coachman. Numbers 10 to 16 are most common, with No. 12 being an all-around favorite.

Nymphs

Nymphs are also sinking flies, often more diminutive than wet flies and tied more precisely with wing cases and thorax to represent the larval stage of aquatic insects, including mayfly *(see)*, caddisfly *(see)*, and stonefly *(see)* nymphs. They are also tied to represent such noninsect foods as leeches, scuds, snails, worms, and the like. This covers a lot of food forms; thus, many artificial nymphs are nearly exact imitations of naturals, either the bottom-dwelling larval and pupal stages or the surface-emerging form, and many are more suggestive than imitative.

Natural nymphs, which are the immature stage of aquatic insects, have a long life in the water and are a major, if not the foremost, insect food source for stream-dwelling fish, especially trout. Thus, assorted nymph flies or nymphlike flies are an

essential part of the freshwater angler's repertoire. They are generally dull or drab in color, and many have a thorax, which is material tied to form a hump at the shoulders to represent the undeveloped wings of cased larva.

The body is made from many materials, often fur, and many patterns have soft, sparse, leglike hackles under the head or neck. The materials used help determine whether a nymph sinks or swims (a few are meant to be fished low in the surface film to imitate an emerger) and how quickly it sinks. Various weights are incorporated into nymph patterns to affect sink rate, including wire that is wound onto the shank before the body material is applied, and lead or metal head beads.

Nymph flies run a wide gamut in dressing, from very sparse on the smallest nymphs to bushy and thick-bodied large patterns. They are tied on a wide range of hook sizes, with different waters and seasons affecting the appropriate size choice. Although a common size for nymphs would be in the No. 6 to 10 range, they run to both extremes, and extremely small nymphs (No. 22 and 24) may be used on heavily pressured, shallow small streams. Nymph size is often important in successful fishing, especially on trout streams, and especially when fish are feeding selectively.

All types of fly lines are used to fish nymphs, and choice depends on type of nymph, current flow, depth, and length of drift. Small nymphs, for example, are often fished on a floating line in small shallow waters, using a tiny split shot a short distance ahead of the fly to get it down quickly for what is usually a short drift. As a rule, floating and slow-sinking lines are used in all shallow waters, sink-tip lines in intermediate depths in streams, and full-sinking lines with a fast sink rate in all deep waters.

In moving waters, a nymph is cast upstream or up and across stream with a floating line, with the fly sinking and drifting down with the current for a relatively short drift, or it is cast slightly up and across stream with a sink-tip or full-sink fly line to maintain contact with the nymph either when

Nymphs

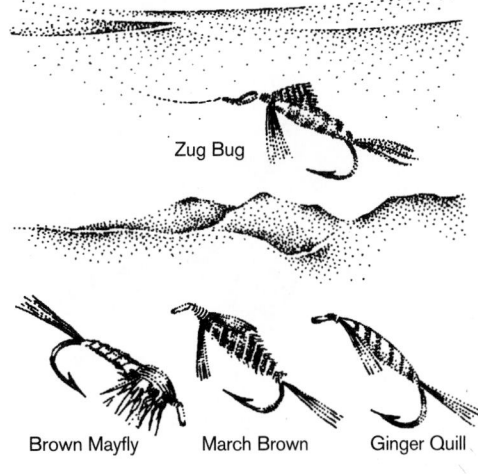

Zug Bug

Brown Mayfly   March Brown   Ginger Quill

F

drifting it downstream or when swimming it. A strike indicator, which may be as simple as a swatch of deer hair, or a colorful adhesive patch, is often used on the leader to help show leader movement when a fly has been taken by a fish in moving water, so the angler can react quickly to a strike.

Often, and especially in small streams, nymph-fishing anglers hold the rod tip high to help maintain a desirable fly drift and keep more of the fly line off the water to minimize drag. In ponds or lakes, a nymph is generally used with a sink-tip or full-sink line, allowed to sink to a desired level, and fished with a generally slow stripping retrieve of the fly line.

As with other fly types, there are many nymph patterns. A nymph collection should have a representative assortment, and the following are widely known and popular patterns: Caddis Nymph, Dark Olive, Ginger Quill, Gray Nymph, Hare's Ear Nymph, Leadwing Coachman, Light Cahill, March Brown, Mayfly Nymph, Montana Nymph, Quill Gordon, Stonefly Nymph, and Zug Bug.

Streamers

As a group, streamers are primarily meant to represent specific or generic baitfish as well as such assorted prey as leeches, worms, eels, etc. They are popular in freshwater, especially in large rivers and in lakes and ponds, and are the foremost type of fly used in saltwater. Although streamers catch trout, they are not a large part of the stream trout angler's repertoire, but they are a factor in stillwater trout fishing. For presentations to large predatory fish, including pike, muskies, lake trout, striped bass, and many saltwater species, especially pelagic species, streamers are the main offering when using flycasting tackle. This somewhat catchall category is sometimes subcategorized as streamers and bucktails.

Bucktails (also known as hairwings) feature hair or other fur, whereas streamers primarily feature feathers. However, other materials, like Mylar, are

Streamer Flies

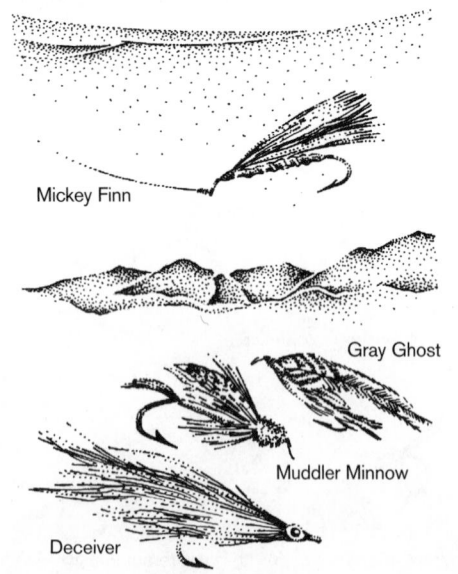

Mickey Finn

Gray Ghost

Muddler Minnow

Deceiver

also used, and some streamers feature a very creative use of both natural and synthetic materials. Obviously streamers incorporate a lot of designs. They are characteristically all tied on long-shanked hooks, however, and are nearly always fished below the surface, although some may be treated with floatant on occasion to fish on the surface and look like struggling surface prey.

Since these flies cover a wide variety of possible forage, many are not exact imitations of specific prey and are dressed rather colorfully as attractors. Many are suggestive in appearance, and a lesser number are strictly imitative. Some are dressed on two hooks in tandem (which are often used for trolling), and many, especially those for big fish and saltwater use, are tied on larger hooks than those used for the most commonly dry flies, wet flies, or nymphs.

Streamers are fished on all line types in a manner that is similar to some aspects of wet fly and nymph fishing; choice is dependent on the type of water and depth to be fished, the circumstances, etc. Sink-tip lines are especially useful for streamers that are fished at moderate depths; full-sink lines are used for deep-water work; and floating lines are used for shallow fishing, where flies are weighted enough to get them beneath the surface a short distance.

These flies are only occasionally fished on a dead, natural drift (and usually when cast directly upstream in a river), and they have to be manipulated with the fly line and/or rod tip, usually by stripping in fly line to swim the fly. The speed of retrieval varies with the behavior of individual species; some require a slow pull-pause movement, whereas for others (often many saltwater fish) the streamer cannot be stripped too fast.

In current, a streamer is normally cast across the current and fished downstream in a combination of drifting and twitching until it reaches the full downstream extension of line, and then it is strip-retrieved back to the angler. It is sideways to the current when moving downstream, which may suggest an imperiled fish or other food; when it darts upstream, it may simulate the action of mobile prey. In open water situations, it is dispatched a full casting distance away or near a breaking fish, allowed to sink to the desired level, and then erratically strip-retrieved.

The size of the streamer and its silhouette are most important, because there are many patterns (and many unnamed creations) available. A collection of representative streamers for various fishing would include the following: Black Ghost, Black-Nosed Dace, Clouser Minnow, Deceiver, Gray Ghost, Mickey Finn, Nine-Three, Silver Doctor, White-and-Red, and Yellow-and-Red, plus assorted colors of Marabous (black, white, yellow), Muddler Minnows (especially brown), and Marabou Muddlers. Woolly Worms, Woolly Buggers, and Zonkers (which are considered streamers by some people but not by others) are great flies that belong in this assortment, and there are many others that are equally effective in specific waters, especially items tied for saltwater use.

Bugs

It is arguable whether the lures known as fly fishing bugs are in fact flies or a separate category of fly fishing lure. They are included here for simplicity in the sense that all items that are cast with flycasting tackle are generically called flies (although many do not imitate insects and are not fished like them). This is just one of many aspects of sportfishing that is rife with confusing and sometimes misleading terminology.

Bugs

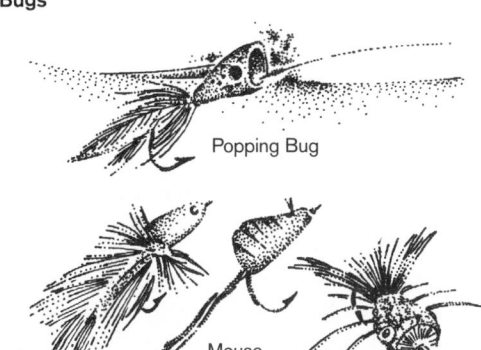

Popping Bug

Mouse

Darting Bug

Hair Bug

In any event, bugs include poppers and so-called bass bugs, and are also known as topwater bugs; they look nothing like other artificial flies or like natural insects. They are made from cork, balsa, cedar, deer hair or buoyant hair from other animals, and some synthetic materials, and are tied on a variety of hook sizes, with larger ones for bigger fish being created on single No. 6 to 2/0 hooks, and smaller ones (for panfish) being tied on appropriately sized hooks.

The range of natural foods that these items imitate includes frogs, rodents, and baitfish that would be found actively swimming or struggling to survive on the surface in freshwater, and primarily struggling or active surface baitfish in saltwater. Bugs are fished on the surface, probably 90 percent of the time with a floating fly line, although a sink-tip line may be employed with some diving and swimming bugs to help pull them briefly under the surface during retrieval.

Poppers are hard- or solid-bodied items made from cork, balsa, or cedar. They usually have some hackle or bucktail at the back of the lure to camouflage the hook or provide extra movement in the water, and they are fished in a popping or chugging manner, being jerked to surge forward and make a commotion that attracts fish through both noise and movement. The way a popper sits in the water, as well as the contoured design of its head or face, governs the action and degree of commotion that it

makes, and there are many styles. Small versions, usually worked slowly, are preferred for panfish; larger ones, fished at various speeds, are intended for largemouth and smallmouth bass, northern pike, striped bass, and other saltwater fish.

Bass bugs have a hair body that is creatively tied and shaped or trimmed into a host of forms, the most familiar ones being mice- and froglike. Some incorporate a loop of monofilament line as a weed-guard, and all are fished slowly. Because they are soft-bodied lures, bass bugs are less likely to be quickly rejected by striking fish.

Other Flies

There are other "flies" used in fly fishing that don't quite fit into categorical peg holes. These include many steelhead and salmon flies, some of which are quasi-streamers; most egg flies, which are simple and bright imitations of fish eggs and are made from yarn; foam-bodied spiders; Mylar-bodied fish imitations; and others. Innovative fly tyers have produced many fish-catching flies that defy categorization.

Fly Tying

From a definitive standpoint, fly tying is the hand manufacture of an artificial fly by winding thread around a hook and attaching assorted materials to the hook with the thread. The attachments are known as dressing, which traditionally meant bird feathers, animal hairs, and metallic tinsel, but

One of the benefits of tying flies is the ability to match food and create flies as necessary when you're out in the field.

Materials and tools used in fly tying.

which today includes a wide range of natural and synthetic materials.

Although all types of flies for all kinds of fly fishing activities are available commercially, many anglers tie their own flies and consider this an important component of their total fly fishing involvement. They derive a lot of pleasure from catching fish on flies that they create, and they view tying as an interesting and challenging hobby that has direct tangible benefits to their angling. They can stockpile flies in the off-season or in other spare time, make creations or variations on standard patterns that are not otherwise readily available, and even tie flies at the fishing site if they need a size or pattern that they do not have. In the long run, fly tying can have an economic benefit; most of the cost of buying commercially tied flies is due to hand labor, so, in terms of materials, homemade flies can cost very little per fly.

Even a beginning fly tyer can produce flies that will catch fish, although, like many other activities, this hobby can be taken to very involved levels and does require knowledge of proper technique. Reaching an advanced level of fly craftsmanship, especially the ability to create specialty flies with some synthetic materials, takes most people years of development. There is good reason for fly tying to be considered an art form, and for the most exquisite flies to be works of art.

Fly tying is one element of sportfishing in which visual and hands-on instruction is immensely valuable, and a beginning fly tyer should receive guidance, if not instruction, from an experienced tyer to get a proper start. Many groups or individuals hold fly tying classes during winter months, and participating in these is probably the best way to get started in this hobby. You will learn to tie patterns that will have local relevance, so that you can successfully use what you create. Getting guidance from experienced tyers will also help you develop an understanding of what materials to use, how to assess the quality of materials, and how to

work with the materials to dress the fly; not the least of your knowledge will be a greater understanding of aquatic and terrestrial insects and other natural fish foods.

There are many books, and some videos, available that teach fly tying, and these are also valuable sources. Fly tying instruction books should have step-by-step illustrations and clear photos that demonstrate every element of the tying process. They should also have good color photos of fly patterns. A good video may be even better for illustrating tying steps and the final look of the fly, although when you're learning to tie by following video instruction, it is annoying to have to keep rewinding a VCR to watch the tying steps (whereas a book is laid out in front of you). Since it takes a lot of photos and space to show the fly tying process for each of the various types of flies, and since that could not be adequately addressed in this book, you should check other information sources for a full and illustrated discourse on the techniques of fly tying.

However, a few general points about fly tying should be noted. It will cost less than a few hundred dollars to get well outfitted with the basic materials for fly tying. From a hardware standpoint, you'll need a vise for firmly holding the fly, hackle pliers for grasping the fine feather ends, sharp needle-point scissors for cutting and trimming, a bobbin to hold the spool of thread, a whip finishing tool for terminating the thread wraps, a single-edge razor blade for cutting and trimming, and a dubbing needle (bodkin) for separating materials and other tasks. Tying thread and head cement will round out the items that will be used time after time. After that, the basic components include the proper style and size of hook and the various components that will be used to dress the fly.

The vise is the most important tool and is more than just a clamp. A good vise should have a wide range of jaw adjustment, because it needs to firmly hold the hook at its bend without deforming it yet still accept a range of hook thicknesses as appropriate for the size of flies being tied; interchangeable vise jaws may be necessary in order to hold both the thinnest and the thickest hooks. There are, incidentally, folding models that are meant for travel and for use along the stream, as well as portable fly tying kits.

A bright lamp, preferably one that swivels to different positions, will be important for use at the fly tying location, and some people will benefit greatly from a magnifying glass on a stand or one that is attached to a band that rests on the head and slips over the eyes.

If you are getting started in fly tying on your own, begin by tying a few streamer patterns, even if it's unlikely that you'll have much need for them. Streamers are easiest to tie, and working on them will help you acquire the fundamentals.

See: Fly Fishing; Flycasting Tackle; Lure.

FLY BOOK

A flexible pouch, also known as a fly wallet, for storing artificial flies, especially streamers, when angling; a fly book is easily stowed in a fishing vest or jacket.

FLY BOX

A light, compact storage device for artificial flies. Fly boxes are made from various plastics and from metal, are rigid, and are sized to fit the pockets of a fishing vest or jacket. Some plastic versions are transparent to allow viewing of their contents. Some are compartmented for loose fly storage, but these allow accidental loss of multiple flies for a variety of reasons; better fly boxes have a means of retaining hooks, such as clips or foam lining, and are also deep and roomy enough to keep the flies from being flattened. Many fly boxes have two-sided interior storage, and they can be opened and laid flat for accessing the top and bottom; such boxes must have some means of retaining flies, or they will be scattered out of the box when it is opened.

Smaller boxes are meant for storing smaller flies, including dries, wets, and nymphs, but some boxes will take larger flies, including streamers, which are also often kept in a fly book or fly wallet *(see)*.

Care should be taken to keep moisture out of fly boxes, because the moisture can lead to rusty hooks. Air drying a used fly on a fleece patch before putting it back into a box is a good idea.

FLYCASTING TACKLE

Flycasting tackle is a special-purpose type of fishing equipment characterized by the use of a heavy and relatively thick line to cast a light, and in many cases nearly weightless, object that is generically referred to as a fly. This tackle is distinct from all other types of tackle, in which a weighty object carries a light and usually thin line (primarily nylon monofilament) when it is cast or when the reel is placed into freespool mode.

This is special-purpose equipment partly because the essential fly line cannot be cast with other tackle. It is also special because most of the objects cast with this equipment in the past, and many of them today—especially in trout fishing—are virtually weightless flies. However, with advancements in rods and lines, some of the "flies" that have evolved in the modern era are extremely large and not-so-weightless objects, in effect greatly expanding the concept of an artificial fly. Thus, it is no longer entirely accurate to say that flycasting strictly involves the casting of weightless objects; huge streamers cast by offshore fly anglers, for example, are far from dainty.

The use of flycasting tackle—which is known as fly fishing—is also distinct in that line does not have to be fully retrieved and spooled onto the fly reel in order to recast the fly. In many situations,

The payoff for matching flycasting gear properly and delivering the right fly is a good bow in the rod.

this feature allows for quick, repetitive presentations. Other forms of tackle don't permit this, or permit it only in special situations, since the object cast must be fully retrieved before it can be recast. Also, because of the light nature of most flies and the terminal tackle used (leader and tippet), presentations with flycasting tackle are usually subtle, and flies can be presented unobtrusively.

Although flycasting tackle has become more popular in recent years and has greatly widened its application, it is much less popular than spincasting tackle *(see)* in freshwater, spinning tackle *(see)* and baitcasting tackle *(see)* in freshwater and saltwater, and conventional tackle in saltwater.

Some dedicated fly anglers are snobbish about the artistry of fly fishing, but on a practical level the advantage of using flycasting tackle is the ability to make quiet presentations and repetitive casts without retrieving the line, as previously noted, and also to use featherweight artificial flies that in many cases are highly representative of natural forage both in appearance and in movement. A dry fly drifted on the surface of a trout stream, for example, can look and move with the current exactly like a natural insect, which is the primary food of trout, more so than a lure can. If the fish are selectively consuming insects, the fly angler has a far better chance of finding (or creating) an imitation to present naturally than the nonfly angler. Thus, in some circumstances, using a fly is the best way to imitate natural forage and fool a fish, and flycasting tackle is necessary to make the proper presentation.

Although it isn't necessarily an advantage, the act of casting a fly line arguably has graceful beauty and symmetry, and many practitioners enjoy and appreciate fly casting as a developed skill. Many fly anglers feel that there is also a measure of special skill in selecting flies (matching the hatch), knowing where to cast, and controlling the line and the presentation, and they feel that these skills make angling with fly tackle stand out from other types of

F

Flycasting Tackle Components

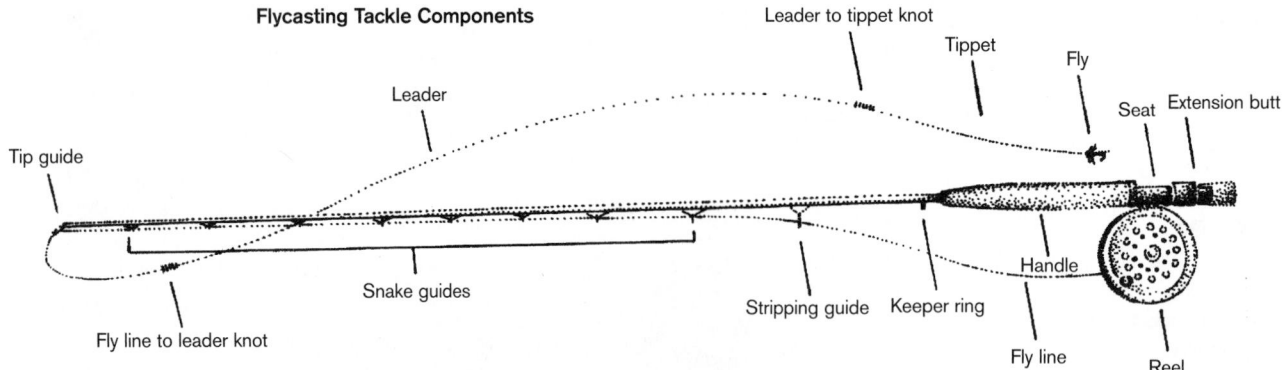

fishing and thus mean that fly fishing is more demanding. However, it is not necessarily more demanding, and this attitude fosters the unfortunate notion that fly fishing is difficult.

Some aspects of fly fishing do have the myth or the appearance—usually wrongly—of being more exacting and requiring exceptional levels of skill. The fact that a number of avid trout fly anglers—who as a group make up the majority of people who fish with flycasting gear—speak about flies and hatches in Latin terminology and with the precision of a single-minded scientist does not help demystify the sport. No matter what tackle anglers use, they all have the same objective of putting their lures or bait in the right place in a manner conducive to getting their quarry to strike, and the skills and complexities in each discipline can be equally challenging. In fly fishing, the methodology is different, but not entirely more complex or more demanding than other forms of fishing.

The art of casting a fly line is, however, a little more taxing to perfect, especially in the learning period, and some would-be fly anglers view this as a disadvantage. No one picks up a flycasting outfit for the first time, makes one or two practice casts, and is instantly fly fishing successfully, as can happen with spinning and spincasting tackle; it requires practice to learn to use fly tackle in even a basic way (no one picks up a baitcasting outfit for the first time either and immediately starts casting like a veteran). Flycasting isn't terribly difficult with the right instruction, but the fact that many schools exist to teach people how to cast with fly rods, whereas hardly any exist to teach other types of casting, is a telling indication. So, too, is the plethora of books, videos, and instructional materials on methods of casting.

Among the real but not insurmountable disadvantages to using flycasting tackle is the fact that it can be more of a problem than using other tackle in windy conditions and in tight quarters, and it has limited casting range for the average user (meaning that you may have to get closer to many fish to reach them with a cast). Fly fishing is also generally an inefficient means of angling deep in open waters, although it can be done.

It is worth noting that little trolling is done with flycasting tackle, and even less fishing with natural bait. Natural baits are mostly too heavy or impractical to cast or use with this equipment, and purists do not consider trolling an acceptable method of fly fishing; trolling is not allowed in flycasting competitions or in recognition of world-record fish caught with fly tackle. This doesn't mean that fly tackle can't or shouldn't be used in such a manner. Some trolling with fly tackle is done for trout and salmon in the spring when these fish are shallow, and also in some other circumstances. Nevertheless, flycasting gear, unlike other forms of tackle, is by tradition and preference almost entirely dedicated to actively casting with some type of fly.

Today, the boundaries between applications for flycasting tackle have blurred because of improvements in reels, rods, lines, and flies. Like other equipment, flycasting tackle has become very specialized (tackle and methods for trout are greatly different than for bass, general saltwater use, tarpon, or billfish), and some of it is much more expensive than other types of fishing equipment. It has become more prominent in saltwater in recent years, especially for pursuing tarpon, bonefish, permit, redfish, striped bass, bluefish, little tunny (false albacore), and sailfish.

There are five main components to flycasting tackle: reel, rod, line, leader, and fly. The last two are discussed in more detail elsewhere, and since the line is unique to this type of equipment and to the method of fishing, it's appropriate to review this component first.

Line

Fly line is critical to the presentation of flies and must be matched to the rod that is used. It is vital to have the right weight of line to bring out the action of the rod, so it's important to understand the fundamental design of fly lines as well as the various classifications and types for different applications. This process is complicated by the wide variety of fly lines now available, so selecting a fly line can be confusing.

Design and construction.   Fly lines were once made of braided horsehair, braided silk, horsehair and silk, enamel-finished silk, and oiled silk. The latter was used into the middle of the twentieth century and required frequent cleaning and dressing, daily drying (being wound onto a line drier), and occasional refinishing. This gave way to nylon fly lines, which were more elastic than silk and not subject to rotting, but cracked easily. After nylon was developed, a succession of technological advances resulted in a revolution in synthetic materials, manufacturing processes, and designs. That lead to the sophisticated products of today, and it expanded fly fishing from what was primarily the use of dry flies and floating lines for trout and salmon in streams and rivers to a much wider activity.

The modern fly line is essentially an amalgamation of a coating and a core. It is a relatively thick product because of these elements, but the coating is necessary to give the line weight and allow it to be cast. Castability is the first and most critical performance characteristic of a fly line.

The core of the fly line is a braided synthetic that determines its tensile strength and stretch and that influences its stiffness. Individual fly lines are designed to be stronger than the heaviest tippet that the product will be used with, so their breaking strength ranges from approximately 20 pounds (lightweight freshwater lines) to over 40 pounds (heavy saltwater lines). The thickness or diameter of a fly line is not correlated to its strength as it is with conventional nylon monofilament line used with other tackle.

The amount of stretch is ideally controlled to achieve the proper medium between having a lot of memory (developing a set from a position in which the line has been placed for a long time), which hinders casting and fishing, and being so soft that the line is difficult to control. Braiding inherently contributes to flexibility and greater castability, which is generally advantageous, but the amount of braiding for the core synthetic may be more or less developed to adhere to the application of the type of line.

For specialty lines used in extreme conditions, the limpness or stiffness of the core can be manipulated to make products conducive to extreme conditions. Since heat can relax line, for example, a line primarily used in heated conditions must have enough stiffness to maintain its castability. On the other hand, since coldness can stiffen a line, a line used in cold conditions must have enough flexibility to maintain its castability. Unfortunately you can't have both properties in the same fly line to satisfy the extremes, and the coating is also a factor in this property.

The coating of fly line is a modern plastic, mainly polyvinyl chloride, and it provides most of the weight needed to load the fly rod for casting and provides some of its flexibility, plus color, shape, and density for specific applications. It also contains ultraviolet inhibitors to make lines last and maintain their color and, in some products, may contain impregnated lubrication to resist rod guide friction. Its construction and properties make it a durable item that can last several years with little maintenance.

Density.   Density determines whether the line floats or sinks, and it is a characteristic determined

Fly Line Types

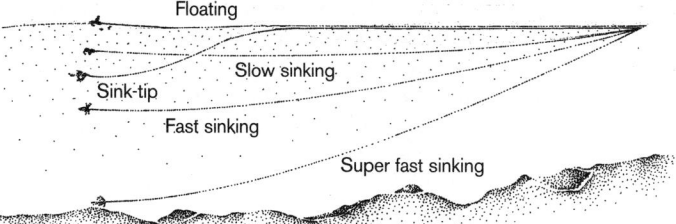

by the material in the coating and its construction. Essentially there are floating, sinking, and floating/sinking lines.

A floating line (designated by the letter *F* in labeling) is for surface or near-surface fishing and is often the first line possessed by a fly angler, particularly a trout angler who uses dry flies and nymphs in shallow water. A floating line is easiest to cast, to pick up off the water, and to fish, which is especially important for someone new to this activity.

A sinking line (signified by *S*) is used only for fishing below the surface. Sinking lines are also known as full-sink lines and are classified according to the speed at which they sink, which is known as sink rate and varies from roughly 1 inch per second (ips) to 10 inches per second; the slowest sinkers were known as intermediate (*I*) lines, a designation no longer used by some manufacturers.

Sinking line use is based upon fishing conditions; a slow-sinking line, for instance, might be used in shallow, gently flowing water, and a fast-sinking line might be necessary to fish near the bottom in a deep, swift-flowing river. Which sinking line to use is based on the depth to be fished and how fast you need to get to and maintain that level. Full-sinking lines can be used for fishing in depths to 30 feet, and they are used for trolling as well as casting.

Floating/sinking (*F/S*) lines possess a floating body and a sinking tip section and are commonly called sink-tip or sinking-tip lines. They are typically used as a second line on a spare fly reel spool to provide the option of easily changing while on the water. The length of the sinking tip varies, usually being from 10 to 30 feet; like full-sinking lines, these lines also vary in sink rate from slow to very fast.

A floating/sinking line allows you to get a fly below the surface but also keep enough of the line on the surface to see it and mend it for a drag-free drift. Sink-tip lines are easier to cast and fish than full-sinking lines, and are especially useful for fishing from 2 to 10 feet below the surface with wet flies, nymphs, streamers, and other subsurface flies. Very fast sink-tip lines keep a fly deeper during a retrieve or drift.

Most sinking lines are dark colored, and most floating lines are light colored. Dark green and white have traditionally been favorite line colors, but floating lines in yellow, orange, lime green, and fluorescent colors are available, mostly as a visibility

F

aid for casting and fishing control, and having no bearing on casting performance and usually no adverse effect on fishing success.

Shape/taper.   Shape, which is also referred to as taper, conforms to the diameter of the fly line throughout its length and determines how energy is transmitted and dissipated during casting. There are basically four shapes: level, double, weight-forward, and shooting.

A level line (signified by the letter *L*) is the same weight and diameter throughout, and essentially has no taper to it. This is the least expensive fly line, but it is more difficult than others to cast and control in the water, and does not afford distance advantages or presentation delicacy. It is adequate for simplified fishing activities, including roll casts and short casts of 20 to 40 feet.

A double taper (*DT*) line has the same taper at both ends and a section of level line in the middle, and it is used primarily in short- to medium-range casting. Although this shape and its large level mid-section is not conducive to casts beyond 50 or 60 feet, it is excellent for roll casting and for making a delicate presentation of a light fly. It has greater life than the following fly line shapes, because the ends can be swapped when the front taper wears out.

A weight-forward (*WF*) line is tapered only at the fishing end. It is designed to fish well at short, medium, and long distances. It is not good for long roll casts but is especially beneficial for standard distance casting since it sports a lighter and smaller-diameter back section that moves with less friction through the rod guides. This also makes it generally beneficial for casting large flies, bugs, and poppers.

A shooting (*ST*) line, which is also known as a shooting head (*SH*), is a 30-foot length of tapered fly line, similar to the head of a weight-forward line. It has a 12-foot tapered end followed by an 18-foot-long level section with a factory-installed loop at the end, which is attached to a long (100-foot) thin-diameter running line. The running line is often 20- to 30-pound nylon monofilament, but it may also be a thin-diameter (.029-inch) plastic-coated shooting line, and the combination results in maximum distance casting and smooth flow through the rod guides. This fly line is used often in big-water fishing and for casting at distances from 70 feet up to about the maximum of 120 (for the best casters); it is difficult to cast and not a line for the novice to start out with.

There are also specialty tapers that are variations of the weight-forward style, usually with different proportions to the overall length of the head or to the sections of the taper. The number of these has grown in recent years, with designs for such specific applications as bonefishing, striped bass fishing, steelhead fishing, and more. Of longer existence has been bass bug and saltwater tapers, which have a specially designed weight-forward portion and short front taper and short belly that facilitates turning over large and wind-resistant flies and popping bugs. Another style is the rocket taper, which has a long front taper that shoots well and allows finer presentations.

A leader (*see*) is always attached to the forward (fishing) end of the fly line. The leader makes the transition from the large and thick-diameter fly line to the fly. It is tapered from a greater strength and diameter at its connection to the fly line to a finer diameter and lighter strength at its connection to the fly, sometimes using a tippet (*see*) to bridge the end of the leader and the fly. The tapered leader is usually about the length of the rod, but this varies with conditions and may be longer or shorter; tapering helps extend the fly to the end of the overall line and to turn the fly over and make a quiet presentation.

Weight and line codes.   Fly lines vary in length according to type of line and are commonly about 85 to 90 feet long; they may vary in overall length from 75 to 100 feet, with the exception of short shooting heads. The portion devoted to the head and the running line varies, but it is the grain weight of the first 30 feet of the line that determines its classification, according to a standard system in which lines are measured in weights from 60 to over 800 grains and translated into line weight or size, which is interrelated with the rods that are designed to properly cast such a class of line.

Line weights range from 1 to 15 in designation, the higher numbers being heavier and more difficult for the average person to cast. Line weights from 3 to 8 cover most freshwater needs, and from 7 to 12 most saltwater needs. The heaviest lines are used for casting huge flies with muscle rods and handling big-game pelagic species, and the lightest lines are used on ultralight rods for minute flies and small-fish angling. Sizes 5 through 8 are most popular nationally, with 6 the most common because of its versatility in freshwater trout fishing.

Fly lines are labeled according to size, function, and taper, all of which must be married to do the job required for the fishing circumstances. To determine the classification and features of a fly line, read the line code of letters and numbers on the outer packaging. A product labeled DT5F, for example, is a double-taper 5-weight floating line. A product labeled WF8S is a weight-forward size 8 sinking line.

Fly Line Tapers

Reel end   Leader end

Level (L)

Weight-forward (WF)

Double Taper (DT)

Bass bug (WF)

Shooting head (SH)

In addition to matching up with the right rod, a particular fly line also matches up with the size and weight of the fly to be used, as well as the conditions (open water and wind being more demanding than sheltered environs). Flies that are very air resistant or that are heavily weighted require greater line sizes, as do windy conditions.

Backing. With the exception of the smallest reels that accommodate the lightest line weights, the nonfishing end of fly line is attached to backing, which is a line that helps fill up the spool and stands in reserve to aid in playing large fish. Without backing it would take more turns of the handle to retrieve line onto the spool, and the line would be stored in small coils, which is harder to stretch out and may inhibit casting by having the line flap against the guides when cast. Backing promotes line storage in large coils, which are more easily straightened for easier use.

Backing also provides a reserve for those instances when a large fish takes a fly and heads to the next county. In most freshwater fishing and some saltwater fishing, the angler seldom gets to the backing on the reel when playing a fish, but when you need it, you'd better have it.

The size of the reel spool in conjunction with the length of the fly line determines how much backing is suitable; in turn, the size of fish that might be encountered and its fighting abilities determine how large a reel and overall capacity (fly line plus backing) is appropriate. Braided Dacron and braided or fused microfilament line, which have very low stretch, are the best products for backing because they wind on easily with less chance of binding than nylon monofilament line; 20-pound strength is standard for use with fly lines up to about the 7-weight class, and 30- or 40-pound strength is used with heavier fly lines. As a rule for the heavier lines, keep in mind the breaking strength of the fly line itself and don't undercut it. Smaller reels require only about 50 yards of lighter backing. The amount of backing necessary on larger reels used for bigger fish is in the 150- to 200-yard range, although greater backing is required for big-game species. Thin-diameter high-tech lines allow for the use of 50- and 60-pound backing line with the diameter of a conventional 20-pound line, and high-tech 30-pound backing with the diameter of conventional 15-pound line means that a much greater amount can also be employed (for more on standard lines, *see: line*).

Reels

Fly reels have long been described as storage devices for fly line that had little or no function in casting or playing fish; this is because they were, until recent decades, mostly used for relatively small fish in freshwater. With the application of fly-casting tackle for very large and strong fish in all environments, reels have evolved into much sturdier products with more functional retrieval and fish-playing characteristics, in addition to being a way to store fly line and backing.

Although some type of reel used for catching fish can be first ascribed to the Chinese around the middle of the twelfth century, the earliest written account of fishing reels appeared in England in 1651 in *The Art of Angling,* a book by Thomas Barker; Izaak Walton even mentioned a "wheel" on a salmon fishing rod in *The Compleat Angler* two years later, and it can be assumed that these developments started an evolution in fishing rods or poles, not the least of which included the creation of guides for the passage of line. By the mid-nineteenth century in Europe, a revolving spool reel called a centrepin was widely used for varied fishing activities, although it had an inert and relatively wide spool and two-handled cranking. This was the forerunner of the fly reel.

Centrepin reels were revolving spool reels, and in appearance they were not unlike the earliest forerunners of baitcasting reels. Still in specialized use today in Europe for coarse fishing with floats *(see),* centrepins are also known as float reels, have a 3- to 4-inch overall diameter, and feature a simple flanged spool on a single axle. They were greatly improved in Nottingham, England, in the mid-nineteenth century by the incorporation of a smooth, free-spinning spool, and the new found sensitivity revolutionized fishing for coarse species.

In the 1870s, several modifications by a number of craftsmen, including Charles Orvis, the founder of that prominent tackle purveyor and creator of the first perforated spool fly reel (1874), made these bulky and heavy reels more suitable for fly fishing

Flycasting reels are basically simple line-storage devices, although some have more advanced drag-control features.

F

and the lighter split cane bamboo casting rods that were being crafted. This included a narrow spool, single-handle cranking, lighter weight, and perforated spools to aid line drying and prevent line rot (the lines of that era required drying after each use). Reels made of aluminum first appeared during the 1870s and became prominent by the end of the century.

It was in the latter decades of that century that fly reels were mounted underneath a fly rod and in-line with it, as well as below the rod grip. The reels of that era are not much different than the simplest fly reels of today, yet these revolving spool products have diversified in many ways, especially in terms of materials, drag, retrieval speed, and features conducive to special and more demanding applications.

One thing that is unchanged, however, and that distinguishes flycasting tackle from many other forms of tackle (except spinning), is that the reel is always situated under the rod and below the handle grip. This placement counterbalances the weight of the rod (which is often relatively long), has a natural and comfortable feel, and reduces arm fatigue from repetitive casting.

Fly reels today are used in freshwater and saltwater, although more commonly in the former primarily by virtue of the greater number of freshwater anglers and the easier use (shorter casting and smaller fish) in those environs. They range from very light small-profile models matched with the lightest line weights in freshwater to large-profile saltwater heavyweights that have a lot of line capacity and drag mechanisms that help pressure the strongest fish. Size is important in terms of capacity to handle large fish, and for matching up with the rod and line being used. Lighter lines used for smaller fish don't need large reels, but heavier lines, which have a larger diameter and which are likely to be used for stronger and bigger fish, obviously require a large reel.

Unlike other reels, a fly reel has no casting or line-dispensing function owing to the different principle involved in flycasting. It holds line, of course, which is pulled out by hand to become available for the actual casting exercise; it retrieves line for storage but not for the act of manipulating a fly; and it provides a variable degree of drag to pressure a strong fish when it pulls line from the reel.

Types

Although fly reels may be referred to as trout reels, salmon reels, saltwater reels, and the like, such type-casting is more a function of a reel's line capacity and features than basic operation. Fly reels are most appropriately identified as being single-action, multiplying action, or automatic, categorizations that are all related to line recovery.

Single-action.   A single-action fly reel is a spool inside a frame with the handle built on the spool. Each turn of the handle causes one turn of the spool, which means that there is a 1:1 ratio in line retrieval. This is also referred to as direct drive. About 90 percent of fly reels in use are of this type, and most of these are fairly lightweight models. When matched to the appropriate line weight for the species sought, single-action reels have plenty of line and backing capacity. A single-action reel has few moving parts and often minimal features, so it is simple and reliable, although models range widely in price due to materials and components.

It is easy to change line quickly on a single-action reel by carrying an extra spool filled with different line. This is most common for freshwater anglers and lets you adapt with one reel to fish throughout the water column. However, in heavier products used for big fish, a second reel might be better than an extra spool; if something goes wrong with the primary reel, having an extra spool won't help.

Single-Action Fly Reel Parts

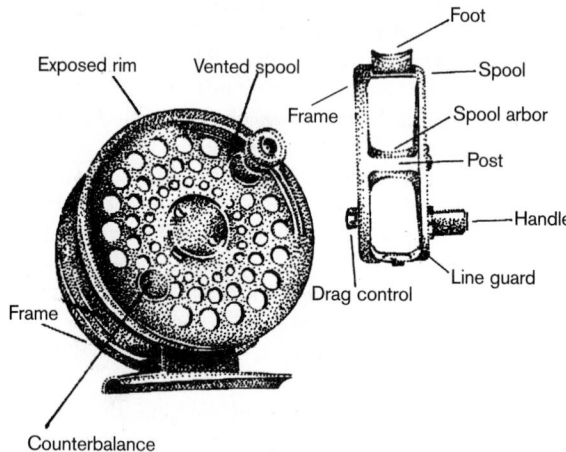

Multiplying action.   A multiplying-action fly reel is similar in design to a single-action reel but sports internal gearing that causes one revolution of the handle to turn the spool more than one time, which is how other categories of reels, such as spinning, spincasting, and baitcasting, operate. Thus, in a multiplying-action fly reel with a 2:1 ratio, the spool revolves two full times for each full revolution of the handle. This gearing makes the multiplying-action fly reel more expensive than an otherwise comparable single-action reel, and it is used in situations where rapid recovery of fairly long lengths of line is important to keep up with a fast-moving fish (it is used by some steelhead, salmon, and big-game saltwater anglers). This type of fly reel has come in and out of popularity over the years and is currently fading because of the greater usage of large-arbor spools on single-action reels.

Automatic.   An automatic fly reel doesn't have manual line retrieval by turning a handle, like single- and multiplying-action reels. It automatically winds line when a trigger is depressed, which releases tension in a prewound spring. That tension is built up when line is stripped off the reel. This is a fairly heavy reel with limited line capacity and without an extra spool option. Such reels are not used in saltwater and are primarily devoted to close-quarters freshwater fishing where quick pickup of loose line is desirable, and for smaller species that will not take a lot of line when fighting. Used mainly for panfish and small trout, they are also a viable fly tackle option for someone who has the use of only one hand or has limited use of both hands.

Features/Components

The key elements of a reel in use include smooth operation, durability, and—in the case of reels used for strong fish—good drag performance. Although most fly reels are fairly simple in construction and have fewer parts than other types of reels, they do have features that play important functional roles and deserve attention when comparing models. The more often that a reel is used, and the more demanding the fishing, the more important these various features become.

Frame. All fly reels have a foot that is attached to the frame or housing and that holds the reel in the rod handle. The frame itself varies in materials, and it includes the rear plate and the pillars or posts that cover the outer rim. The spool rests within this. Most better frames are made from machined or anodized aluminum and also have a line guard or guide that prevents line wear. On better products, the spool-to-frame tolerances are very precise; on poorer ones there may be some gap between these,

which can allow line to slip between the two or increase the chance of getting dirt or sand in the reel (this is more true of older reels than newer ones).

Some frames may be of open or full design, and vented or solid. A full frame provides structural strength for reels made of less expensive materials and requires that line from the spool be directed through the frame before it can be run through the rod guides. Open frames make line changing and rigging easier, and in better reels that are machined from strong materials they do not sacrifice strength. A vented frame (perforated with holes of varying sizes and shapes on the sideplate) is preferred for stylistic as well as practical reasons, and venting exists on spools as well. This originated as a means of helping to dry out older lines, which were subject to rotting; it exists today more for classic appearance but also to aid in rinsing with freshwater, which is important for reels used in marine environments. These holes also reduce weight, which appeals to many anglers who compare relative reel weights, although nearly anyone would be hard-pressed to detect the difference of an ounce or two in loaded reels.

Spool. Fly reel spools in general are deep and narrow, which facilitates line leveling during retrieve, although the angler still needs to guide the line with a finger of the rod-holding hand to prevent center-spool buildup. Newer designs incorporate a large arbor for greater line retrieval per turn of

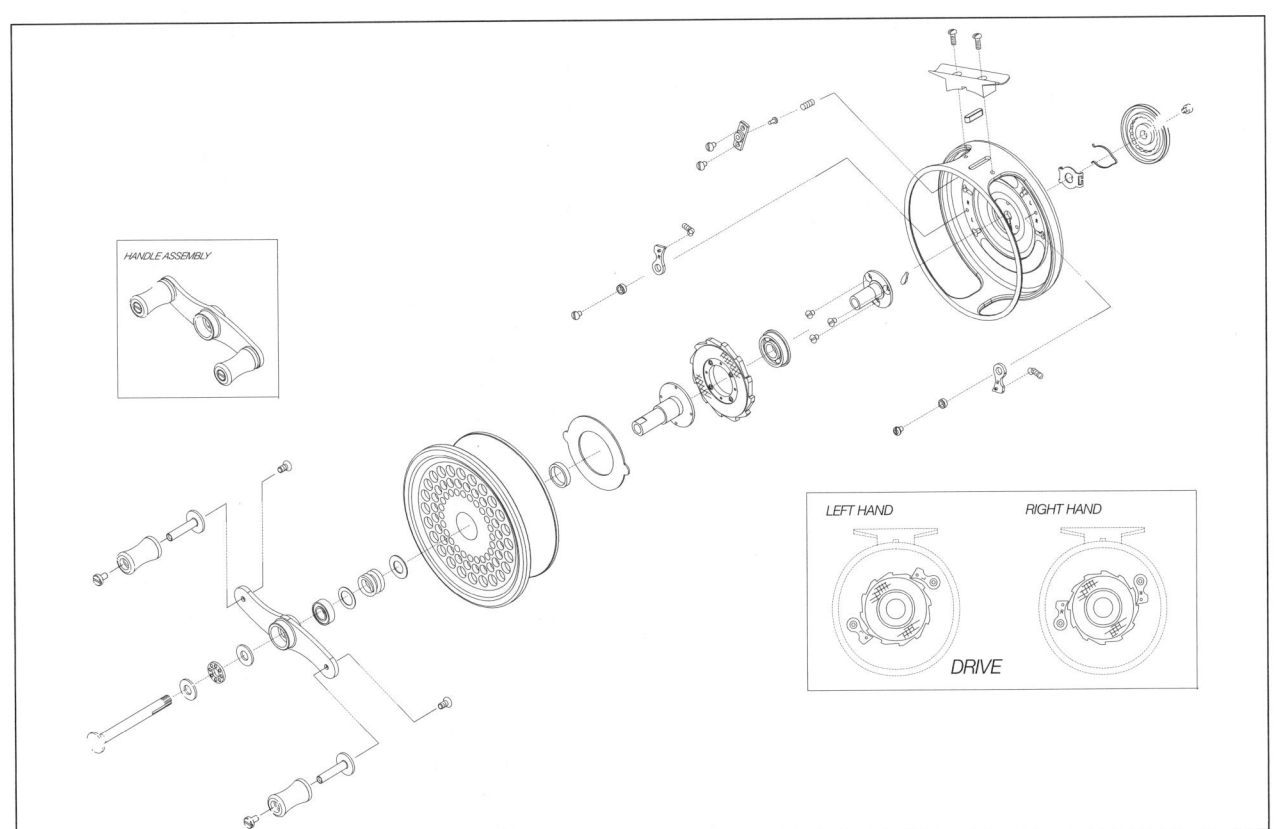

All of the parts of a heavy-duty Penn International saltwater flycasting reel are shown here; this product features a high-tech friction drag, a convertible drive, and an anti-reverse system that prevents the handle from turning backward when a fish strips off line.

the handle without sacrificing capacity. Larger arbor reels are becoming popular and may be the standard of the future on better fly reels. To be of most advantage, they should also be part of a reel with a larger outside diameter than is conventional, in order to maintain necessary capacity. Line recovery is the main benefit here, and large arbor spools recover significantly more line than conventional arbor spools; they also have benefits for outward flowing line (slower speed and fewer turns), drag (shorter duration of application and less tension at greater line lengths), and line memory (less of it).

The handle knob is built on the edge of the spool, and it comes in many lengths and styles, as do knobs for other types of reels, indicating that there is little agreement among anglers about what is best for comfort or performance. Some anglers prefer a handle knob that is fairly short and round to keep loose line coils from wrapping on it when a fish takes and streaks off with line. Others like a large knob that is easy to grab and hold, especially when fighting big fish and when your fingers are wet or cold. A handle should be easy to release (when a fish streaks off), and many anglers prefer not to have a handle with an indentation so that they can let go of it in a heartbeat when they have to. Comfort is especially important in larger reels used for big fish, since a lot of winding is likely to be done; thin and/or short handles are generally not favored for this use, even though they're less likely to catch loose fly line.

Many fly reel spools have an exposed or overlapping rim flange, known as a palming rim, which allows the angler to apply extra, judicious tension on the spool with the fingertips or palm when a fish is taking line (too much pressure will snap the tippet) or, more important, when pumping a large fish during a battle. Some anglers using light tippets will set their drag light and use pressure on the spool rim as their primary control measure.

One-piece machined spools are found on better reels, and top models also have a counterbalanced design and turn easily on ball bearings. Balancing prevents spool wobbling, which occurs on unbalanced reels when a strong fish takes line and makes the spool spin at a furious pace, since the handle is on one side of the spool and there is nothing on the other. (A screw, with the head placed on the inside, can be bolted to the spool opposite the handle to help provide balance in older reels.)

Most spools are also vented with many holes, in some cases of varying sizes, and such reels are sometimes called ventilated spool reels. As noted before with vented frames, this has benefits for cleaning and weight.

Drag. Internally, the activation of a spring-loaded switch on the face of the spool allows the spool to be removed, and this reveals a simple brake or click drag that has one or two pawls engaging a gear. The simplest reels should have a drag that allows for enough adjustment so that when line is

Removing the spool of this heavy-duty Martin fly reel reveals a large surface area of Teflon and stainless steel drag discs.

pulled off the reel quickly it doesn't cause a line overrun and tangling. These pawls cause an audible clicking sound that differs when line is being dispensed or retrieved (some can be used in a silent mode, which is not preferred by guides, who use the sound of the reel to help them determine what the fish is doing).

A lot of fly reels have a compression drag system that utilizes one or more washers (called discs by some) to press against the spool, which is similar to the drag system employed by other types of reels. When an external drag adjustment knob is turned, it puts tension on a friction washer, which applies pressure to the spool to slow it down. There may or may not be a metal drag washer in the system, which presses upon the friction washer, and the material that has long been favored for the friction washer is cork. The drags of some reels employ metal and friction washers via an adjustable caliper-type system that uses friction washers like dual braking pads to apply pressure to the spool. Some reels use O rings in a caliper-like system instead of disclike friction washers. In all cases, the rings or washers that are made of friction material compress with pressure, and in hard use there is a lot of heat built up within the drag system.

As with all other types of reels, the better drags are obviously those that operate smoothly over a wide range of adjustments with good braking systems, and heavier-duty models have various drag washer materials.

Cork is preferred by many fly reel manufacturers as fly reel drag washer material; it is durable, compressible, and light, and has been used for a long time. Cork is a high-service item, however, and can become distorted as well as wear down; when it gets wet, it can be jerky or inconsistent. Anglers who wade have a high tendency to get water in their reels, and wet reels also happen to those who fish from boats, even if only from incidental exposure. An interesting note here is that cork is not used as a friction drag washer material in most other types of reels.

Some top fly reel manufacturers are now using carbon-fiber drag materials, which are prominent in big-game reels. Carbon fiber has a natural slipperiness for smooth operation, but great friction properties. On big-game reels it is installed dry, but on some fly reels it is installed greased. The woven carbon fiber compresses slightly, and that little bit of give contributes to excellent drag range. Just as important, the carbon fiber doesn't change characteristics when it heats up, and doesn't build up friction as it heats up. This is very important during demanding fishing situations and battles with large, long-running, and hard-fighting fish (billfish, tuna, tarpon, etc.), and it is explained in more detail in the entry on big-game tackle *(see)*.

Heat buildup and the ability of a reel (and drag washers) to dissipate heat are important factors, especially for a reel that will be used on strong fish capable of quickly taking a lot of line off a reel. Also a factor is the initial startup of a drag and how easily it can overcome inertia (if it does not, the tippet will break). Many drag washers do not dissipate heat well and/or do not overcome inertia easily, and this is what causes inconsistent drag performance. In saltwater fly fishing, and fly fishing in rivers for salmon and steelhead, this inconsistency of performance is of greatest concern.

How easily the drag can be adjusted and how accessible the adjustment mechanism is, are other important design elements to consider. The adjustment knob, usually a small wheel, should be convenient and easy to grip when your hands are wet or cold. It should turn easily but not so readily that tension can be accidentally changed, and there should be a wide range of adjustment (preferably at least a 360-degree rotation). Too much range, however, such as several full turns of the knob, is just as bad as too little range; some knobs also have click stops to help identify the adjustment positioning.

As with other reel types, you should release drag tension at the end of the fishing day (or trip) in order to enhance the condition of the washer and keep the material from developing a set. This is less important with carbon-fiber drag washers than with other materials. The general principles of using and setting drag are covered in greater detail under that entry *(see: drag)*.

Anti-reverse. Some fly reels have an anti-reverse design, meaning that the spool turns but the handle does not when line is pulled from the reel, depending on the tension placed on the adjustment mechanism. The internal gearing of this adds considerably to their price, but anti-reverse fly reels are favored by some, who would like to avoid the knuckle or fingertip bashing that a furiously spinning spool can inflict when a strong fish streaks away with the fly.

Convertible retrieve. Another feature of some reels is ready convertibility to right- or left-hand retrieve. Fly reels by tradition are commonly set to retrieve right-handed, and many older reels were designed only for this operation (similar to conventional and baitcasting reels). But this seems more suited to left-handed anglers, since they can hold the rod in their dominant hand and retrieve with their subordinate hand. Thus, some right-handed anglers prefer left-hand cranking and right-handed rod holding, and convertibility (with some internal reconfiguring) is important to them,

especially if they'll tangle with large fish that require a lot of pumping and reeling. If the reel is not convertible, they have to hold and fight the fish with their subordinate hand and turn the reel handle with their dominant hand, which also means that the rod is changed from dominant hand when casting to subordinate hand when playing a fish (this is actually what the majority of baitcasting tackle users also do).

Some anglers feel that such convertibility is detrimental for playing really big and tough fish, and they advocate using the dominant hand to turn the reel handle. However, anyone who has used spinning tackle, which is always held in the dominant hand while the reel handle is turned by the subordinate hand, can attest that this is easy to master and preferable. Turning a small handle, such as that of a fly reel, with the subordinate hand is something that anyone can quickly adapt to; working the rod properly to fight a strong fish is much better done with the dominant hand, not only to pump and fight the fish, but also to react to its maneuvers, especially when it is near the boat.

Quality issues. Although many fly reels are suitable for the average range of fishing conditions that anglers encounter, some stand out from others under stress, abuse, frequent use, and most demanding situations. That is when the value of better-quality items becomes apparent. One indication of better quality is a finely machined and finished frame and spool. An anodized finish, or other corrosion-resistant finish, is common to the better reels and any that are to be used in saltwater, and top reels are made of aluminum and stainless steel. Other quality matters include a smooth drag system and easy drag startup, a good range of drag adjustment, and a strong and smooth handle knob. These all add up to durability and top performance for demanding fishing. However, many fly reels are used in routine fishing for generally small or medium-size fish, and they do not require the best drag features or the top materials. As noted previously, most fly reels are used in freshwater, and many times the angler does not get into the backing on the reel.

Rods

Fly rods have developed over the ages in conjunction with other types of tackle and with changes and developments in both reels and lines. For centuries, fishing was accomplished with what was actually a pole *(see)* rather than a rod, and these were mere wooden implements to which braided horsehair line was attached without a reel or line guides. Rod development with an eye toward casting technically had its modern genesis in the midseventeenth century when the first reel or "winch" was used with a pole, and these simple wooden implements were first fitted with guides for the passage of line. Different woods were used for the upper and lower sections, and many different materials were used in rod construction for the following two centuries.

A nine-year-old British Columbia boy hatched rainbow trout in the water tank of a toilet; he put eggs into a container with holes in it, and they got fresh water with every flush.

F

In 1846 Samuel Phillippe, a master gunsmith and violin maker from Easton, Pennsylvania, built the first four-strip split bamboo cane rod and shortly after, the first six-strip rod. These were forerunners in a golden century of fishing rod development in which many famous craftsmen created exquisite bamboo fly rods, and especially the finest functional bamboo fly rods from the 1930s into the 1950s. However, with supplies of the world's best cane from China unavailable in the 1950s at the same time that nylon monofilament line, spinning reels, and fiberglass rods came into prominence, bamboo fly rods were nudged toward antiquity, and they were virtually fully displaced in ensuing decades when manufacturers improved high-quality fiberglass rod production and when high-tech graphite fibers emerged.

Although the old cane rods were long revered by anglers, few would argue that even the finest could match the functionality of the best graphite fly rods of today. Like other types of fishing rods, modern fly rods are vastly superior to what existed in the past, and indeed just two decades ago.

Because fly fishing requires the casting of a special type of line to carry and present a lightweight fly, the rods used have a particular and characteristic role. In situations where the reel is primarily a device for storing and retrieving line, the rod is actually more important than the reel because it is matched to the weight and design of the line and is essential to delivering the fly. The rod stores and transfers energy necessary to cast the heavy fly line; its length, taper, and action are specifically designed for this activity, meaning that other types of rods cannot properly cast a fly line and, conversely, a fly rod and fly line cannot properly cast a heavy lure or weighted bait.

Because they must be matched with a correct fly line weight for best operation, all fly rods today are identified on their shaft by the manufacturer as to the weight of line that they are designed for; some can accommodate two line weights. As with fly lines, weights range from 1 to 15, with 5 through 8 most common. Lengths are normally from 7 to 10 feet, although some shorter models for ultralight fishing exist, as do longer two-handed rods to 17 feet for specialty fishing (mainly big-river salmon casting and including so-called Spey models). Most fly rods are of two-piece configuration, but some long models have more pieces, as do travel models; excellent four-piece travel rods are available from many fly rod manufacturers today and are preferred by experienced traveling fly anglers.

As with spinning tackle, a fly reel mounts under the axis of a fly rod so that the reel sits under the handle instead of on top of it; this is in part because they are both theoretically geared more to casting functions than to fish-fighting functions. This doesn't mean that they do not fight fish well if properly designed, just that casting is generally the greatest attribute of the majority of fly rods (the models designed for big-game fish are designed less for casting and more for subduing fish).

Unlike other tackle, fly rod reel seats are positioned at the very end of the rod below the cork grip. There is a butt cap at the end of the rod just below the reel seat, and this sometimes has or incorporates a fighting or extension butt, which is used for additional leverage and keeps the reel away from the body for easier use when fighting large and strong fish. Unlike many other types of rods, fly rods all have a keeper ring, or wire hook keeper, on the shaft just above the grip, which is used to store the fly hook when the outfit is rigged but not in use.

Most fly rod guides are also different from those of other rods, with the exception of the lowest guide, called the stripping guide, which is a low-friction round ring model. There may be two or three round guides on some fly rods; like the lower guides on other rod types, they gather the outflowing line and funnel it down to run along the rod. The remaining guides of a fly rod are called snake guides; these light wire guides are nearly friction-free and aid the passage of the thick fly line during casting and retrieval.

Most fly rods today are made from graphite or a graphite composite, and few are manufactured of fiberglass. The lighter, more sensitive, and more powerful graphite is far better for picking up line, loading the rod, and propelling it through the air than other materials; and with various grades of graphite available in rods, there are models that can fit all budget ranges.

Unlike fly reels, fly rods have many characteristics similar to those of other rods, and these are more fully detailed elsewhere (*see: rod, fishing*).

Using Flycasting Tackle

Matching and selecting. A balanced system is necessary to cast properly with fly tackle, and matching the rod and line weight is the key element. Casting power comes from the relationship of the fly line to the rod. When fly line is picked up from

Fly anglers learn casting basics at a Colorado ranch before heading to the water.

the water, the rod receives enough weight to flex fully; this is called loading the rod and it sends the fly line backward. With a properly timed cast of a loaded rod, the flexed rod straightens out and then drives the fly line forward. With a mismatched outfit, this process is just about impossible. Therefore, to cast properly you need a balanced system.

Reel-to-Fly Elements

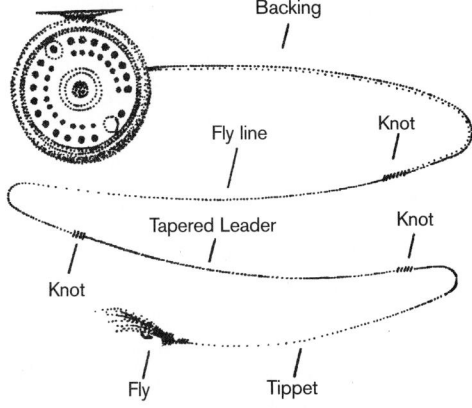

The line, rod, and reel also have to be suited for the type of flies to be cast and the demands of the circumstances or species to be caught. It is often hard for a beginning fly angler to determine what outfit to start with (when you're trying to judge a rod for the first time, you have to cast it to really evaluate the item), and this is where the advice and assistance of knowledgeable personnel at a good fishing tackle shop (especially one that caters to fly anglers and has a lot of fly tackle) can be of great help.

Some general observations can be made, however. First, a weight-forward floating 6- or 7-weight line (WF6F or WF7F) and an 8-foot 6- or 7-weight rod are the standard equipment that most anglers, especially freshwater fly anglers, learn with. A double taper line is marginally better for easier short-distance casting but won't be as useful for fishing purposes. Whether you have a reel with a small amount of backing or one that can handle a lot of backing will depend on the ultimate fishing application.

Line weights are to a large degree related to the size of the fly or flies that will be used. There is a definite progression from the smallest flies for the lightest rods to the biggest and most wind-resistant objects for the heaviest lines. The in-between lines can handle a reasonable range of small to large flies, and that's where the taper of the fly line and the action of the rod also have a considerable influence.

Trout are the main quarry of flycasters, and they are mostly caught on 3- to 8-weight outfits. These outfits are also suitable for panfish, and the reel backing necessary ranges from 50 to 100 yards, the latter being very generous for most activities. The lightest categories are best for small waters, tiny flies, and delicate presentations, and the reels used here need only a minimal amount of backing, if any. The heavier categories are better for bigger

waters, angling in open and windier conditions, using sinking lines in addition to floating lines, and casting longer distances with heavier flies.

Such freshwater species as bass, northern pike, and striped bass are usually caught on 7- to 9-weight outfits. These handle still larger and more wind-resistant flies, but the matching reels do not need a lot of backing, because these species, especially bass and pike, don't usually take great amounts of line. The same weight outfits with more backing are appropriate for big steelhead and salmon in rivers.

In saltwater, for lighter flats species and for inshore and small species, usage runs to 9- and 10-weight outfits with 200 yards of backing. Heavier usage for the likes of tarpon, sharks, and offshore species requires 11- to 15-weight tackle and perhaps 300 yards of backing.

The following list suggests tackle choices for species that are commonly caught by anglers.

Filling and rigging. The fly reel has to be filled appropriately with backing, then fly line and leader, and should be filled so that the business end of the fly line is just below the full spool level. Filling it properly helps reduce coiling and lessens the memory of the fly line on the spool. Technically the process is attaching one end of the backing to the spool of the reel, filling an appropriate amount on the reel, attaching it to the fly line, and then winding the full fly line onto the reel. The sticking point in this is getting the right amount of backing so that the reel is neither underfilled nor overfilled.

Since backing lines vary in diameter, it's hard to do the most logical thing and measure out the manufacturer's suggested backing length and then put it on the reel. You can estimate what seems right, but this often goes awry. The most precise way to fill the reel for the first time is to do it backward, working in an open field or on a large lawn.

Wrap the business end of the fly line around the spool arbor gently so that it gets a bite, and then reel it fully onto the reel, leveling it carefully as you fill it up. Then attach the backing firmly to the exposed end of fly line (use a Uni Knot) and wind the backing on, leveling it until the reel reaches a nearly full level. Cut the backing from the filler spool. Tie the backing to a solid object, and walk off with the reel, allowing the entire line to lie stretched out on the ground. When all the line is off the reel, walk back to where the line is tied and connect the end of the line to the reel arbor. Wind all of the backing and then the fly line onto the reel, leveling it as it fills. Attach a leader to the fly line, and you're ready to rig the rod.

To rig the rod for casting, secure the foot of the reel in the rod's reel seat so that the line guide faces forward; then strip off the leader and a few feet of the fly line. Double the first foot of the fly line, and pass the doubled line through the stripping and snake guides, pulling the leader out once the doubled line is through. Now you're ready to practice casting.

Common Tackle

Fish	First Line	Second Line	Leader
Trout in streams	WF6F	WF6F/S (medium sink)	9-ft, 5x
Trout in lakes	WF6S (medium)	WF6S (fast sink)	9-ft, 4x
Panfish	WF6F	WF6F/S (medium sink)	7.5-ft, 4x
Bass	WF8F (bug)	WF8F/S (medium sink)	7.5-ft, 0x
Northern pike	WF9F (bug)	WF9S (medium sink)	7.5-ft, 0x
Steelhead	WF9F	WF9F/S (fast sink)	9-ft, 0x
Salmon	WF9F	WF9F/S (medium sink)	9-ft, 0x
Bonefish	WF8F (salt)	WF8F/S (slow sink)	9-ft, 10-lb
Snook, redfish	WF8F (salt)	WF8S (medium sink)	9-ft, 10-lb
Stripers, bluefish	WF10F (salt)	WF10S (medium sink)	9-ft, 12-lb
Tarpon	WF12F (salt)	WF12S (medium sink)	9-ft, 16-lb

Straightening leader/line. Both the leader and the fly line may develop a set when they have been left in the spooled position for a while. This can produce coils that may adversely affect how the lines lie in or on the water and how they turn over when cast. The set can be removed from the fly line by stretching it; attach the line to a solid object or have a companion hold it at least a normal casting distance away, pull on the fly line for about half a minute, and then release it. To straighten the leader, have someone hold the end of the fly line taut or attach it to a firm object; work from the butt of the leader toward the tip, holding the lower area of the leader in one hand and stroking the tight section repeatedly with your other hand until it warms to the touch. Repeat this as you work down the leader to the tip. These actions should not be necessary if you've just put the line on the reel or have been using the line and reel regularly.

Holding rod and reel. To cast, hold the rod with a comfortable relaxed grip in which the thumb rests atop the handle and the other fingers curl around it, with the knuckle of the forefinger at about the same level on the handle as the thumb. This is quite similar to how you would hold a screwdriver. Don't wrap your thumb around the handle on top of your index finger, and don't hold the handle in a tight vise grip, both of which cause fatigue. Some casting instructors recommend a grip with the forefinger extended along the top of the rod and the thumb along the side; this can offer good control, but it is not a strong grip for most people, especially with heavier tackle.

If you're retrieving line with the other hand, you can keep holding the rod this way to play a fish, but if you use your casting hand to turn the reel handle, you will have to switch the rod from your casting hand to your other hand to play a fish off the reel.

Holding line for casting/retrieving. Both the casting and noncasting hands play a role in holding the fly line at different times, and line control is an important element of casting, retrieving, and playing a fish.

Small fish in freshwater are often played without using the reel. To do this, as well as to keep the line under control when you have to set the hook, the line should be caught beneath a finger on the rod hand and pulled over the finger and through the guides by the left hand. Fish can be controlled by the pressure from this finger on the line. If the fish starts taking line, lessen finger pressure; when the

The correct grip of a fly rod is with the thumb on top of the handle in line with the reel, and with the other fingers wrapped around the side. The hand should be relaxed for most casting. The left hand grips the line for some casts, especially when hauling and shooting the line.

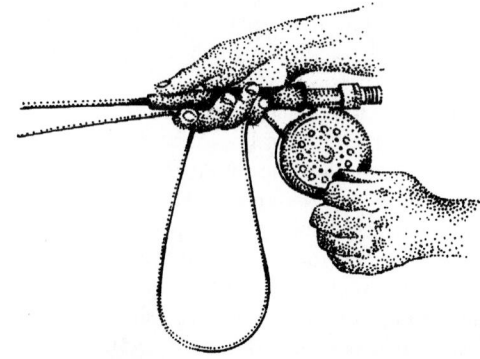

To gather line and lay it evenly on the reel, hold the line as shown, using the pinky to distribute the line from side to side on the spool. This is done whenever you have to spool up loose line, and especially to retrieve loose line quickly to play a just-hooked fish from the reel.

fish comes toward you, strip the line in with your left hand, letting the extra line fall into the water or onto the ground or floor of the boat. Pin the line firmly against the handle when landing the fish and also when setting the hook. Letting the line fall into the water can lead to tangling, however; tangling will be a problem if the fish runs off and takes line from you, and it can interfere with playing or landing the fish.

The line should also be under the same finger control for retrieving a fly, which is done with a stripping motion. When a large fish is hooked, the line stays pinned to the handle by the forefinger so that the hookset can be made; the finger is kept in position, but tension is relaxed to allow the fish to take line if necessary. At this time, any loose line should be quickly reeled onto the spool, so that the fish is played from the reel. Do not leave line lying about when playing a large fish; loose line can wrap

Figure-Eight Line Gathering

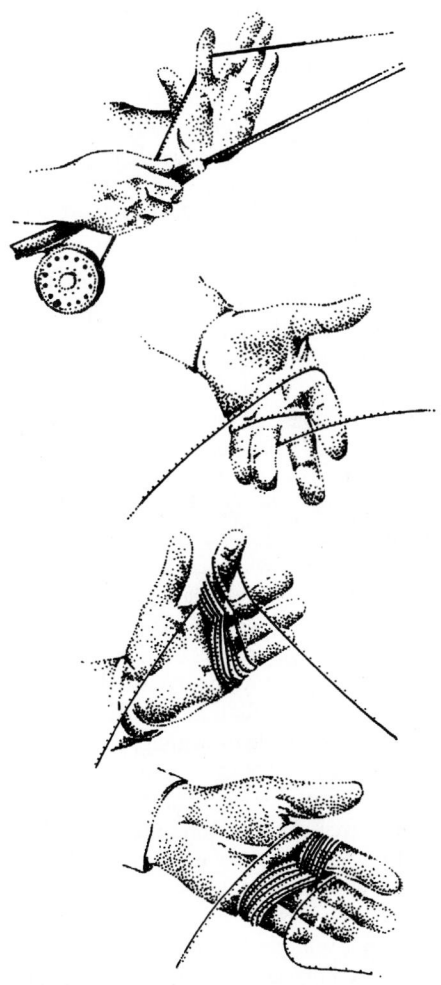

To gather line, drape it under the thumb, over the forefinger, and under the other three fingers; tilt your hand down and drape the line behind the last two fingers and between the second and third fingers to form a figure-eight pattern. Work the line toward your palm by wiggling your fingers, then repeat.

on an object and be snagged when a big fish wants to run, causing the tippet or leader to snap. To gather slack line, keep the forefinger on the line, use your free hand to drape slack nearest to the reel over your pinky, and use the pinky to gather and direct untangled line onto the spool as you turn the handle with your other hand. When fighting a fish off the reel, you still have to use your pinky to level the line on the spool.

Fly line is often held in small loops in the noncasting hand and is freed during false casting to lengthen the amount of line that is cast. Holding it in the hand is more likely to avoid tangling than letting it fall free to the ground or water, but it is not tangle-proof. These loops are gathered on the noncasting hand when line is stripped and retrieved.

To hold moderate amounts of line, try wrapping it in a figure-eight manner over the fingers of your noncasting hand. This is best done when fishing in freshwater for small species of fish, because you don't want line wrapped around your hand when a big fish might strike and suddenly pull on your tied-up fingers. However, this is a very effective way to gather line in small-stream fishing situations, and it allows the line to spiral off the fingers during a cast without tangling and without jamming in the stripping guide.

To use figure-eight line gathering: Drape a section of line under the thumb, over the forefinger, and under the other three fingers; then tilt the hand downward and drape it behind the last two fingers and between the second and third fingers to form a figure-eight pattern. Work the line toward your palm by wiggling your fingers, and then repeat the steps. To release the line, point your fingertips toward the stripping guide on the forward cast and let it spiral off, which will shoot it easily through the guides.

Casting Technique

Casting with fly rod and fly line has the aura of being difficult, but it needn't be. It does require an adroit combination of coordinated wrist and forearm movement, however, but brute strength isn't necessary, nor is a lot of wrist action or quick, whippy rod movements. Flycasting is different from other types of casting because the line is cast instead of the lure and because two hands are used in the process, one for rod control and the other for line control. There are two primary casts: the overhead and the roll, with the former predominating. Hauling is a maneuver used in overhead casting to accelerate the line.

Overhead cast. The overhead cast is the basic cast in fly fishing. It has both forward and backward movements, with a brief pause in between, and starts with picking line up from the water. A good back cast is dependent on picking the line up off the water properly and is important for presenting the fly ahead of you, so all of the elements of this cast are interrelated.

Basic Flycasting

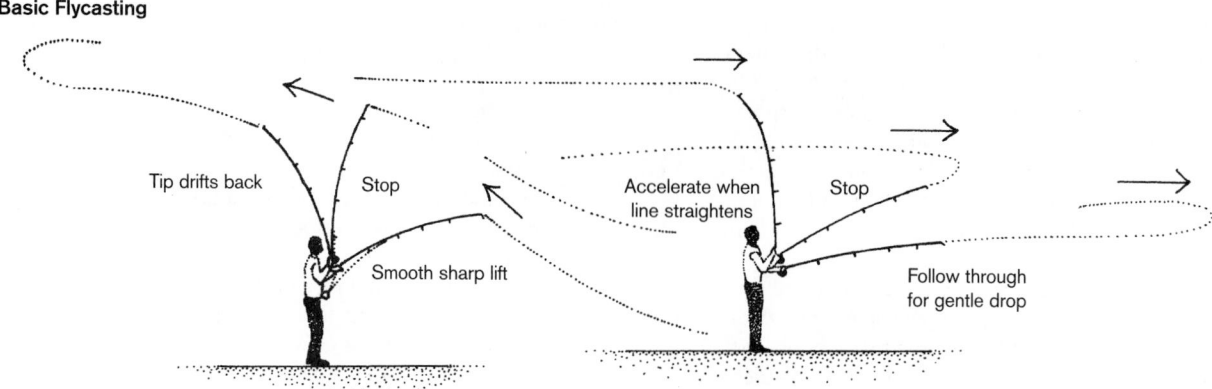

Back cast

Forward cast

This is the basic overhead flycasting process, assuming that you are facing right and casting to the right: Beginning with the fly line and leader fully extended straight out in front of you and the rod in an approximate 3 o'clock position (if viewed from the side with the rod pointed to the right), raise the rod decisively to the 12 o'clock position and flick your wrist sharply, allowing the rod to go no further than an 11 o'clock position. This action brings the fly line and leader off the water and sends it in the air behind you. Pause for an instant to let the line straighten out, and, just as it does, bring the rod forward to the 1 o'clock position. A tight loop should unfurl. As the line straightens and the fly reaches its destination, follow through by lowering the rod tip. The forward casting movement is akin to hammering a nail into the wall, and the right timing is needed to load the rod properly for optimum forward impetus. Realize that the clock positions mentioned are guidelines for casting, but not absolutes, and that the quality of the rod and length of line cast have a bearing on exact positions and variances in timing.

Since this cast starts with the action of raising the rod, which picks up the line in front of you and starts it into the air, it is important to get the initial element right. This is best done with a somewhat slow and deliberate motion rather than a quick, snapping one. Using your left hand to pull down on the fly line, which is known as a single haul, helps.

Unlike casting with other types of tackle, most flycasting is not a series of one-shot casts. It is often necessary to move the fly line and fly through the air in a series of continuous motions to get out the right amount of line to place the fly correctly. This is called false casting, and it means making two, three, or sometimes four backward and forward casting motions without allowing line or fly to touch the water before laying down the line and fly. This is also used to dry surface flies out so that they float better.

The overhead cast is used for all distances, although as the distance to be cast increases, many anglers tend to push at the end of the forward cast, or wait too long for line to unfurl on the back cast. Shooting tapers and weight-forward lines help

achieve distance, as does employing coils of line in one hand for quick release or using the single- or double-haul technique.

Beginning flycasters should practice on a closely cropped lawn with targets and then move to practicing on the water, instead of trying to learn while actually fishing. Beginners, and anglers having casting trouble, should make short-distance casts and watch the line unfurl behind them to get the timing between the end of the backward motion and the beginning of the forward motion right, and to see if they are managing to get tight loops in the unfurling line. If you hear a snapping or cracking sound when casting, the forward cast was started too soon; this rarely happens when you start the back cast because the line is in front of you and you can see it readily. Watch behind you to help develop timing and rhythm.

Getting in-air line loops under control is important to good casting and also for dealing with certain situations. The size or width of the loop is determined by the length of the casting stroke and the movement of the rod tip. If the tip of the rod moves in a wide arc due to a long powerful stroke, the line will have a wide, or deep, loop, and the line will fall on the water with a lot of slack in it. This may be desirable in some situations, such as when you need to have a long natural drift in flowing water. A short stroke produces a tight, or narrow, loop, which has less air resistance and thus is better for distance and accurate fly placement. Generally, a tight loop is preferable for fishing, and it is especially desirable when casting into the wind.

If you are a new caster, it is important to keep your arm movements to a minimum, relying on wrist and forearm action when casting; do not lift your elbow up high or raise your arm so that the rod hand winds up over your head. If your arm moves a lot, casting will suffer. Try to perfect a motion that is more akin to hammering a nail than to tossing a ball.

Hauling. Hauling is a means of accelerating the line to load the rod and is used to help pick the line off the water for the back cast or to shoot out a greater length of it in the forward cast. Doing either one of these alone is a single haul, and doing both

Double Haul Casting

In a double haul, the nonrod hand provides speed both to the pickup and forward momentum of the fly line. On the back cast, use this hand to grip the line (1), then briskly pull the line as you raise the rod (2). The line hand drifts back up toward the reel (3) as it yields some line and as the line straightens on the back cast. On the forward cast, the line hand, now closer to the reel, briefly comes forward with the rod and then briskly pulls the line (4), which speeds up the outflow (5). Release the line from your noncasting hand and allow extra fly line to shoot out the rod guides (6) to gain distance.

in the same casting sequence is known as a double haul. In a double haul cast, the angler uses the non-rod hand to give some speed to both the pickup and the forward momentum of the fly line. It is a technique that takes practice to master because the motions have to be blended properly together.

Assuming that you cast with the right hand and hold fly line in your left, you would accomplish this as follows: Hold the line firmly in your left hand ahead of and close to the reel; at the same instant that you raise the rod to lift line off the water for an overhead cast, pull sharply on the line in your left hand, bringing it down toward your left hip. As the line rises into the air on the back cast, raise your left hand and release some of the line to extend the backward length of the fly line in the air; as the line straightens out behind you, grab the line near the reel with your left hand and, at the same time as your right hand begins to power the rod forward, pull sharply down on the line in your left hand. As the rod comes forward, release the line in your hand to shoot it through the guides and extend the casting distance.

To get greater amounts of line out, which is called shooting the line, you can strip 10 to 12 feet of it off the reel onto the ground (beware of line-catching obstructions) and send it "shooting" through the rod guides by properly hauling it. This is preferable to using a series of tiring false casts to extend the length of line being cast.

Inexperienced flycasters should not attempt hauling until they have mastered a fluid basic over-

head casting motion with tight loops. Start with the single haul, especially for lifting line off the water, and begin with modest amounts of line to master the motion.

Roll cast.   The roll cast is a very practical cast for making fly presentations at a distance of 40 to 50 feet and also as a means of laying out line to pick it up for a standard overhead cast. It is often used as a standard means of manipulating a line and presenting a fly when there is no room behind you to make a back cast for overhead casting. A roll cast has no back casting motion per se, and the line is not lifted off the water into the air as in an overhead cast.

To roll cast: Raise the rod tip up steadily but not too quickly until it is just past a vertical position (generally when the rod gets past your ear) and at a point where there is a curved bow of line extending from the rod tip behind you; then bring the rod sharply forward and downward in a nail-hammering motion. The last action brings the line rolling toward you with leader and fly following, then rolls it over, and lays it all out straightaway. When you bring up the rod to execute this cast, cant it slightly outward; the line coming from the rod tip must be to the outside of the tip, not between the tip and your body.

You can also use the roll cast to straighten out line that is crumpled in front of you, or otherwise lying awkwardly, and lift it smoothly off the water. Make a relaxed roll cast to get the line straight ahead of you, and then immediately lift it off the water to execute an overhead cast.

F

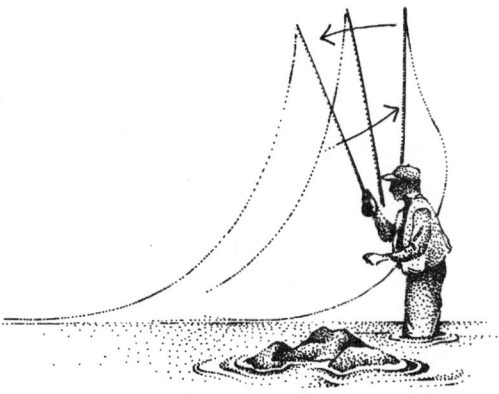

The critical elements of roll casting are smoothly bringing the rod tip up to just past a vertical position, keeping the fly line to the far side of the rod, and punching the rod sharply forward.

Roll casting is easiest with floating and slow-sinking lines and with sink-tip lines that are not too deep. A distance of 20 to 30 feet is easiest to roll cast.

Specialty casts. The fly line, leader, and fly can be manipulated during or after the cast. Manipulation during the cast is called an in-air mend; after the cast, it is an on-water mend. In-air mends include an S cast, curve cast, reach cast, and pile cast *(see: mending)*. The technique of mending fly line is used in flowing water to aid the natural drift of a fly, and it is something not done with other types of fishing line or tackle.

The same motion that is used for overhead fly-casting can be adapted to sidearm casting with a bit of practice, although not many anglers are very accomplished with it. In close quarters and wind, the best way to get a fly to a target is to turn your body directly away from the target, cast in the opposite direction, and use what would ordinarily be the back cast to lay the fly down.

Problems/solutions. Casting problems essentially result from bad habits and poor technique, which underscores the importance of learning fundamentals. Some of the common difficulties experienced by flycasters are briefly noted here, along with ways to deal with them.

A wind knot is an overhand knot that is usually found in the leader and most often results from overacceleration of the rod; a smooth stroke helps eliminate this and also prevents the fly from hitting the rod or hooking the line.

Hitting the water on the back cast is a result of a low back cast, caused by overextending the backward casting stroke, which drives the line down, or is the result of slow line speed; the solution is to cast with a stiff wrist, stop the back cast in a high position, and keep the rod tip from drifting back.

Piling up line, leader, and fly at the end of the cast is caused by a wide loop, which results from an overextended casting arc; shorten the casting stroke, and stop the rod abruptly to get a tighter loop and extended line.

Slapping the water with the fly, leader, and fly line is caused by lowering the rod tip at the end of the forward casting motion; keep a short stroke, and aim the cast higher so that the line and fly settle gently.

Failure to get even a short amount of line out and moving fluidly is often the first problem a beginning caster has and is due to mismatched tackle, letting line slip out during the casting stroke, or waving the rod through a wide instead of narrow arc. Using properly matched tackle and keeping a firm grip on the line will solve this issue. Proper technique requires using only your wrist and forearm to move the rod in a narrow path to create tight loops, which will allow the line to cast smoothly.
See: Baitcasting Tackle; Casting; Knots, Fishing; Line; Reel, Fishing; Rod, Fishing; Spincasting Tackle; Spinning Tackle.

FLY DRESSING
The materials that, when tied on a hook, form the appearance, or pattern, of an artificial fly.
See: Fly.

FLY FISHING
In the broadest sense, fly fishing is angling with fly-casting tackle *(see)*. One of the oldest forms of angling, fly fishing is most commonly associated with casting lightweight objects via a heavy line, which therefore distinguishes it from all other forms of angling in which weighted objects carry lightweight line. There are exceptions to this, because not all lightweight objects are actually cast with fly-casting tackle (they may be trolled or dapped, for example), and some of the objects used are bulky if not weighty (such as saltwater streamers).

To traditionalists, fly fishing strictly connotes the physical act of casting with a fly rod to present conventional flies that imitate natural insects; this

Fly fishing for pike has become popular lately; this angler found a good fish where a tributary emptied into a Saskatchewan lake.

An angler and friend fish for trout at Moose Lake, British Columbia.

narrow view is derived from English sporting traditions for stream trout and salmon. Since the 1960s, however, increased knowledge of fish and fishing techniques, enormously better equipment, and expanded angling interests have led to a much wider view of the scope of fly fishing. Today an extremely wide array of lightweight natural food imitations are employed in fly fishing for diverse species in all areas of freshwater and saltwater.

Avid and overzealous fly anglers often attest that fishing with flycasting tackle is more fun, more productive, or more challenging than fishing with other types of equipment or methods. Such broad testimonials, however, do a disservice to other types of fishing, which, in fact, are far more popular with the majority of anglers and clearly provide high levels of fun, productivity, and challenge. They also ignore the fact that using flycasting tackle is one of many ways to sportfish and that it, like the others, has particular advantages and disadvantages.

While the tackle and technique components of fly fishing are discussed in detail elsewhere, it is helpful to understand the principles and underpinnings of fly fishing, since it differs in a significant way from other forms of fishing and because misconceptions still persist about it to this day.

In general terms, more fly fishing is done in freshwater than in saltwater, although the bounds of saltwater fly fishing have been greatly expanded since the 1980s. Most fly fishing in freshwater is done for trout in streams, but fly fishing for panfish, largemouth and smallmouth bass, northern pike, salmon in streams, and some trout in stillwaters has devotees. Other freshwater species can be caught on flycasting tackle, but many of them, for various reasons, are seldom pursued with this equipment. In saltwater, most fly fishing occurs in inshore environs and tidal rivers and estuaries for striped bass, bonefish, tarpon, bluefish, redfish, seatrout, snook, and mackerel, plus some other species. Pelagic fish, especially sailfish and smaller marlin, are caught with specialized techniques in offshore environs. With all of these fish, except for trout in streams and Atlantic salmon, fly fishing as a method constitutes a minority of fishing effort overall.

Principle.   With the exception of fishing with live or dead natural bait, every type of fishing is an effort to entice fish to strike an object that is meant to represent food. Some of those objects closely resemble food in the way that they swim or are retrieved, some by virtue of their physical appearance, and some by both. Today, plastic, wood, and other materials are fashioned into objects that very closely represent food consumed by various predatory fish; many plastic worms, for example, are nearly indistinguishable from a natural earthworm. Before there were food imitations made from metal, wood, rubber, plastic, or other synthetics, anglers used artificial flies—small hooks dressed with fur and feathers to imitate an aquatic or terrestrial insect. These were used for catching fish, such as trout, that feed on insects. Thus, fly fishing as a method of angling is derived from the creation and use of featherweight artificial flies.

As already noted, an artificial fly today may imitate various types of food, from an insect to a crustacean to baitfish, in appearance as well as in the way it is fished. In some instances, it does this better than other objects that also represent natural food. The fly is carried to its destination by the casting of heavy line that is connected to a leader, which in turn is attached to the fly.

To the uninitiated angler, the mechanics of casting an artificial fly and a large weighty fly line appear difficult. In fact, many aspects of fly fishing can seem complicated if you read one of the many ad-vanced books that are devoted to fly fishing and if you review the thousands of fly patterns and involved esoterica of the activity. In truth, casting an artificial fly is no more, and no less, complicated than other types of fishing, all of which can be taken to extreme levels of involvement by those who desire.

The casting hurdle, however, is a large one to overcome, because if you can't get your offering to the fish, you're completely lost. Despite what many proponents of fly fishing say, it is not simple to learn flycasting, but it is not exceedingly difficult either; flycasting invokes a different principle than casting with spinning, spincasting, or baitcasting tackle, and is a little more involved (which is why fly fishing schools spend a lot of time on casting instruction). Once this is overcome, however, the fact that fly fishing is fun and effective in many situations becomes apparent. For some anglers, it will be the only way that they choose to fish; for others, it will be one of the many ways that they choose to fish. Like all types of fishing, fly fishing can be enjoyed by anyone, with no gender limitations and few physical ones.

Pros and cons.   Besides the casting difference, there are some things that are possible in fly fishing that aren't possible when using other fishing tackle. Precise placement of small flies, for example, is not possible with other tackle choices without the use of casting aids. Likewise, when using flies it's possible to precisely match many food items, especially insects, that some fish eat; this ability can be essential when they are exclusively consuming specific insects. Natural movements and actions of insects are also easily imitated through proper manipulation of the tackle. Furthermore, the ease and quickness of making repeat presentations, especially when using a floating line—since it usually isn't necessary to retrieve all of the line to recast—is often a benefit that is unmatched with other tackle, not to mention that the art of flycasting in itself can be an enjoyable activity. In addition, fly fishing offers a complete package of natural imitation and selectivity, which makes many practitioners more observant in the outdoors.

On the downside, although there are quick, deep-sinking fly lines, fly fishing is often an inefficient method of angling for fish in deep water, especially in large bodies of water and in really turbulent flows. This applies to fish that cruise deep midlevel water as well as those that reside on the bottom. The difficulty is not that you can't get deep enough but that you need time to do so, and also more time to retrieve the line, and these are problems when you're drifting or when there is current.

Also, casting in open environs, such as flats and big rivers, when the wind is blowing hard, is a problem for many anglers, and it hampers their effectiveness; other types of tackle handle this common situation better for the average angler. Likewise, achieving significant distance is difficult with flycasting tackle for all but the most proficient casters, although distance is not a necessity in many angling situations.

See: Dry Fly; Flycasting Tackle; Nymph; Streamer Fly; Wet Fly.

FLYING BRIDGE

A helm station located on top of the salon area of an offshore sportfishing boat *(see)*. These raised helm or steering areas, also known as flybridges, give the captain a clear view of both the cockpit and the water all around the boat. The flying bridge is usually accessed via either a ladder or steps leading up from the cockpit.

FLYINGFISH

Other names—French: *exocet;* Spanish: *volador.*

Flyingfish are members of the Exocoetidae family and are closely related to halfbeaks and balao *(see: halfbeaks and balao)* and needlefish *(see).* They have normal-length jaws, unlike these other species; the fins are soft rayed and spineless; and the lateral line is extremely low, following the outline of the belly. The dorsal and anal fins are set far back on the body. The pectoral fins of flyingfish are greatly expanded, forming winglike structures. The round eggs are generally equipped with tufts of long filaments that help to anchor the eggs in seaweeds.

These fish travel in schools and are abundant in warm seas. They are important food fish for pelagic species, especially billfish, and may be used as rigged trolling bait for marlins, dolphin, and other big-game fish encountered in blue water. On occasion at night, and attracted by light, a flyingfish may leap into a boat, sometimes striking an occupant, which is a startling occurrence and one that may provide a live flyingfish for use as bait.

Frozen packs of flyingfish are found at some marinas and tackle shops, and defrosted specimens are used for offshore fishing in some places, notably

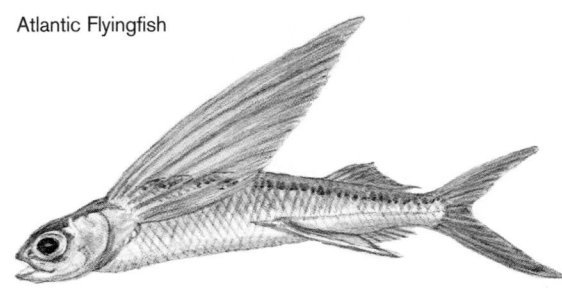
Atlantic Flyingfish

the Florida Keys. The rigged flyingfish is worked away from a slow-moving boat via a kite, and the rod to which the bait is attached is worked by hand to repeatedly lift the flyingfish out of the water as if it were naturally flying.

Flyingfish are readily observed in offshore environs when they suddenly burst through the water's surface and glide for a short distance before re-entering the water. When a flyingfish takes to the air, it comes from below at top speed, which has been clocked at up to 35 mph, and bursts into the air. As soon as it is out of the water—not before—it expands its broad, spineless pectoral fins and, in some species, its pelvic fins. These are held out stiffly, serving only as gliding membranes. They are not vibrated or flapped to help in flying. Last to leave the water is the tail, and the long lower lobe is vibrated rapidly to give additional momentum. As the fish's speed decreases to 20 or 25 mph, it begins to drop back toward the water tail first. As soon as the long lower lobe of the caudal or tail fin enters the water, it is again vibrated rapidly (about 50 times per second), which sometimes gives the fish enough speed to send it airborne again. A succession of these short flights may carry the fish for more than a quarter of a mile.

None of the flights lasts long, usually less than 30 seconds each and often much less for short bursts. Occasionally a flyingfish comes out on the crest of high waves so that its glide starts 15 or more feet above the trough. As a rule, however, flyingfish skim just above the surface of the sea. The young of most flyingfish have long filaments, sometimes longer than the body, trailing from the lower jaw. These are lost as the fish matures.

The reason for flight remains speculative to most observers, although it is presumed to be related to some survival need. Flyingfish feed on small fish and crustaceans, and they spawn in the open ocean around floating weeds and debris.

The largest of all North American flyingfish is the California flyingfish *(Cypselurus californicus)*, which may be 1$\frac{1}{2}$ feet long. It is found only off the coasts of Southern California and Baja California. It is one of several species of flyingfish that are caught commercially for food. They are also used as bait, especially in trolling for big game. It is one of the "four-winged" flyingfish, because the pelvic as well as the pectoral fins are large and winglike.

The common Atlantic flyingfish *(C. heterurus;* also *C. melanurus),* found in warm waters throughout the Atlantic, is two-winged, with a black band extending through the wings. It averages less than 10 inches in length, rarely larger.

Other common species of warm Atlantic and Caribbean waters are the margined flyingfish *(C. cyanopterus),* the bandwing flyingfish *(C. exsiliens),* and the short-winged flyingfish *(Parexocoetus mesogaster),* the latter ranging through all warm seas and noted for shorter wings than found in most species.

The smallwing flyingfish *(Oxyporhamphus micropterus),* which is cosmopolitan in warm seas, also has very short wings, and its glides are never of long duration. Its wings are no longer, in fact, than those of some halfbeaks, and the lower jaw of the young fish is as long as the jaw of halfbeaks.

Another widely distributed genus is *Exocoetus.* About 22 species are found off the Atlantic and Pacific coasts of North America.

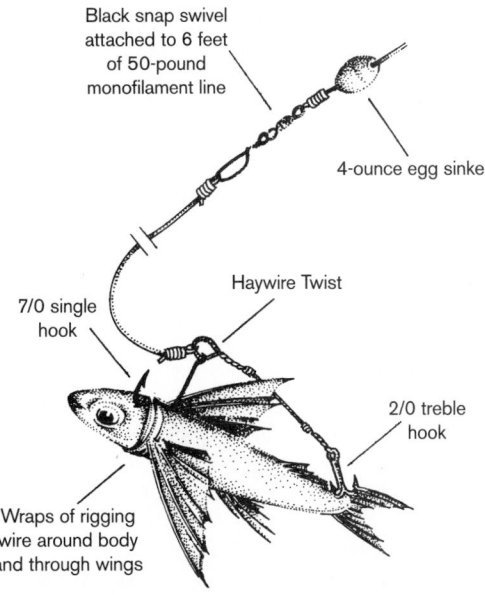
Black snap swivel attached to 6 feet of 50-pound monofilament line
4-ounce egg sinker
7/0 single hook
Haywire Twist
2/0 treble hook
Wraps of rigging wire around body and through wings

A flyingfish rigged as shown is used underneath a fishing kite.

FLYING GAFF
A type of gaff used for large fish.
See: Gaff; Landing Fish.

FLY LEADER
The line connecting fly line and artificial fly, with or without a tippet.
See: Flycasting Tackle; Leader.

FLY LINE
A line of relatively thick diameter with a coating and a core that is essential to casting a fly, because

it is the weight of the line that delivers the fly. There are floating, sinking, and floating/sinking fly lines, and various shapes or tapers.
See: Flycasting Tackle.

FLY REEL
See: Flycasting Tackle.

FLY ROD
See: Flycasting Tackle.

FLYRODDER
A person who fishes with flycasting tackle *(see)*.

FLYRODDING
Fishing with flycasting tackle *(see)*.

FLY TYING
The hand manufacture of an artificial fly by winding thread around a hook and attaching assorted materials to the hook with the thread.
See: Fly.

FLY WALLET
A flexible pouch, also known as a fly book, for storing artificial flies, especially streamers, when angling; a fly wallet is easily stowed in a fishing vest or jacket.

FOLLOWING SEA
Waves coming toward the stern of a boat and going in the direction in which the boat is headed.
See: Waves.

FOOD CHAIN
The progressive, linear passage of food energy from plants to plant-eating animals to carnivorous predators as organisms feed on each other. In a food chain, also called a pyramid, each member uses the member immediately before it on the chain as a food source.

Organisms are not limited to only one source of food but may feed on several sources and on other like members (for example, sharks and tuna both eat herring, but sharks will also eat tuna), so there is an interconnected sequence or cycle of organisms through which nutrients move in an ecosystem, which is called a food web.

Humans are the top predators in the overall food chain. The majority of the fish species pursued by anglers, and especially the most popular ones, are among the top predators in their respective aquatic food chains.

FORAGE FISH
Prey or food species of predatory fish.

FORCEPS
Surgical gripping tool used for removing hooks from small-mouthed fish.

FORK LENGTH
The length of a fish as measured from the tip of the snout to the fork in the tail.
See: Measuring Fish; Regulations.

FORWARD CAST
The forward motion of the rod and line in flycasting.
See: Flycasting Tackle.

FORWARD TAPER LINE
A weight-forward fly line.
See: Flycasting Tackle.

FOUL HOOK
To hook a fish accidentally in some part of its body other than its mouth. Foul hooking is not uncommon when using lures with multiple hooks, when there is an abundance of frenzied fish activity, and when certain aggressive species strike at a lure to stun it rather than initially consume it. Sometimes foul hooking occurs when a fish is properly hooked in the mouth by one set of hooks from a multihooked lure and, in its struggles, also becomes hooked on the outside of the body, usually around the head, by another hook from the same lure; the hook that was in the mouth may or may not remain there, but when it does not, the fish is actually foul-hooked when landed.

The inadvertent foul hooking of a fish is distinguished from snagging *(see)*, which is deliberately hooking a fish in any part of its body. This is illegal in many places, although legal in some for certain species (including paddlefish).

In many places, a fish that is foul-hooked when caught must legally be released. Foul-hooked fish are ineligible for world-record consideration. In waters where illegal snagging (usually of salmon and trout) is likely, there are also regulations regarding the size (hook gap) of a hook that may be used.
See: Regulations; Snagging.

FRANCE
With 58 million inhabitants and a landmass of 551,602 square kilometers, France is the largest country in western Europe, and has one of the widest varieties of landforms and geological features in the region.

Including estuaries and islands, the country has 5,533 kilometers of coastline. This is deeply irrigated by many rivers, and abuts the North Sea, the British Channel, the Atlantic Ocean, and the Mediterranean Sea, offering opportunities for such popular species as tuna, European bass, cod, and pollock, and an assortment of bottom dwellers.

As a result of its terrain and diversity, France has an extraordinary amount of freshwater and thus a great deal of opportunity for diverse species. This includes 123,894 kilometers of salmonid rivers and streams (without tributaries), 65,710 hectares of trout lakes, 100,403 kilometers of cyprinid streams, and 131,353 hectares of coarse-fish lakes and ponds.

Combined with a diversity of climates—from Alpine to continental and oceanic to Mediterranean—France has much to interest anglers.

Freshwater

Although freshwater resources in France, as elsewhere, are either public, which means belonging to the state, or private, which means belonging to landowners, water and fishery management is handled by resident landowners, or by the fishing and water protection associations to which they commit the charge of managing their lots.

The Superior Fishing Council, a national government management agency, is in charge of technical and scientific follow-up as required by the fishing associations. The council is directly related to the Ministry of Environment, whose role is advisory and scientific rather than executive. It collects the piscicultural tax (national yearly sportfishing license) and is in charge of water and fishery policy across the country, which is divided into 22 regions and 96 departments.

French national law assigns the property of the bottom of a waterway to residents, with the water itself being free. No one is allowed to fish on community lots without giving access to one's own lots. Thus, fishing rights belong to the state on navigable public waters, and to the riparian owner (a fishing association or local authority) on private waters. Trout and salmon rights are nearly always privately held, but visitors can obtain permits by checking with the local fishing club or tackle shop. There are closed seasons for some species, as well as regulations pertaining to methods and tackle.

Today people involved in fishing tourism are becoming more aware of the value of wild salmonid streams. In France, many fly fishing circuits, or sections of river, have been established, and these are often also regulated for no-kill (catch-and-release and flies only with barbless hooks). Fly fishing in France has been steadily growing, and practitioners now number about 60,000. Because the large cities are far from the natural and protected fishing sites, anglers often fish on stretches full of trout that are kept exclusively for fly fishing. In France, more than a hundred sites (fly-fishing-only reservoirs or

fisheries) are accessible 12 months a year for a price varying from 100 to 400 French Francs, according to the services offered.

Most French fishing takes place in rivers and streams. Which species a river shelters depends on whether it flows toward the Mediterranean Sea, the Atlantic Ocean, or the English Channel. Shad, sea-run brown trout, European eels, and Atlantic salmon are the most common migrants.

The sea-run brown trout is the most popular freshwater fish in France. In some coastal rivers of Normandy, the biggest specimens can weigh up to 10 kilograms.

Even within species, characteristics vary according which body of water a particular river flows into. The Mediterranean strain of the French sea-run brown, called a zebra trout, has golden tones and many color variations. This fish is covered with small black spots and is the only example in the world of a sea-run brown trout strain with dark vertical stripes on the sides. The sea-run brown found in French rivers that flow to the Atlantic has a much more motley appearance, with large red, blue, or black spots, depending on which rivers it inhabits. Atlantic-strain browns can stay in the sea for a while without being considered a true sea-run brown trout. In that case, they have a silvery coat.

Although it is often overlooked by traveling anglers, coarse fishing is highly developed in France, and native anglers have become so sophisticated in coarse fishing techniques that they have garnered numerous world titles and individual championships. Heavy fishing pressure via club and organized match fishing, and many years of catch-and-release for coarse species, have greatly educated the targeted fish (mostly roach and bream), and made it necessary to use ultrafinesse methods for catching them. Small specialized floats, balanced carefully so that all bites can be detected, are necessary, as are long poles to place and control tackle in areas that are carefully chummed. A method developed near Roubaix on the France-Belgium border, and called *roubaisienne*, which requires the use of take-apart poles from 2 to 12 meters in length for this fishing, is heavily practiced.

Major Rivers

The Rhine system. The Rhine River has a total length of 1,300 kilometers, from its source in Switzerland to its estuary in the Netherlands. It is still an Alpine river in spite of its 190-kilometer-long border with Germany.

The Rhine offers excellent sportfishing opportunities. European grayling are found in some areas, and a few salmon and sea-run brown trout migrate up the Rhine due to the restoration of natural strains (through salmon farms and smolt overflow).

The best sportfishing sites are above Strasbourg, the seat of the European Parliament. The main tributaries of the Rhine are the Moselle, the Meurthe, and the Sarre, which are salmonid streams in their

From the same name/different species file: *Beluga* is used to refer to the white whale and also to the beluga sturgeon; *kingfish* refers to the king mackerel and also to whiting.

F

A pole fisherman angles on the Rhine River.

upper parts. The Haute-Moselle and its tributaries are known for salmonid sportfishing.

The Rhône system.   The Rhône River is 812 kilometers long, from its source in Switzerland to its delta in the Mediterranean Sea. It crosses almost 20 French departments, and all of the main streams from the Alps and the Jura flow into it along its left bank. The tributaries and subtributaries of these streams represent almost 50 percent of the French sportfishing circuits.

The native species in these waters are brown trout, European grayling, and arctic charr in high-mountain lakes. Rainbow trout, brook trout, lake trout, and huchen have also been introduced in many areas.

The best fishing streams are in the upper part of the Rhône after it leaves Lake Geneva. These include its direct tributaries, the Fier, the Arve, the Valserine, the Ain (both the upper and lower stream), the Isere, and the Durance; the sub-tributaries, the Verdon, the Ubaye, the Doubs, and the Loue; and the tributaries and sub-tributaries of the Saône River, which joins the Rhône in Lyon.

Some of the Rhône's numerous backwaters and oxbows are rich in such predatory species as northern pike, zander (also called pike-perch), perch, and especially largemouth bass. The biggest bass reach 3 to 4 kilograms, but there is no management of this species, and all methods of capture are allowed. This practice threatens a fish that is highly popular with anglers.

Almost 30 percent of France's freshwater anglers, especially its fly anglers, live in the regions of Rhône-Alpes, Franche-Comté, and Provence-Alpes-Côte d'Azur. The well-established fly fishing areas are the Franco-Swiss Doubs in Goumois, the Loue around Ornans (Doubs), the lower Ain around Priay (Jura), and the upper Ain around Champagnole (Jura). The hub of this region is the city of Lyon and its surroundings, which house many fly fishing clubs. Anglers from around the world have fished such Franche-Comté streams as the Loue, Doubs, or Dessoubre.

Sportfishing represents a real culture in these regions, and age-old fly-tying traditions remain. The Maison Devaux in Champagnole, for example, on the banks of the Ain River, still makes unique artificial flies of the "forward tying" style created by Aimé Devaux, one of the most famous French anglers. The largest part of the production is now subcontracted to Thailand, but the spirit lingers.

The Garonne system.   The Garonne River has a total length of 647 kilometers, from its source in Spain to its estuary in common with the Dordogne River below Bordeaux. It receives most of the streams flowing down the Pyrenees, the Cevennes, and the Massif Central.

Several of the most beautiful rivers in France—the Tarn, the Ariège, the Lot, and the Dordogne—flow into the right bank of the Garonne, and are notable in their own right. The Tarn is famous for its gorges, which are popular tourist sites; its tributaries, which include the Tarnon, the Jonte, and the Dourbie, provide good trout fishing. The Lot and its tributaries—the Colagne, the Truyère, the Bès, and the Cère—and the Ariège and its tributaries—the Hers and Vicdessos—are worthy trout streams.

Between the towns of Beaulieu and Argentat, the Dordogne is well known for numerous big trout and European grayling. Located downstream from several hydroelectric dams, it is one of the best tailwater fisheries in France. The Dordogne and its tributary the Vézère are part of a plan for reintroducing Atlantic salmon, but this has not been very successful so far. In the lower Dordogne, an important upstream migration of shad occurs in May, and this provides good sportfishing.

The Garonne itself is mainly a coarse fish river, but it offers great fly fishing sport downstream of Agen for mullet, which are locally called "fresh-water bonefish."

The Meuse system.   The Meuse River runs 950 kilometers, from its source in Burgundy to 15 kilometers south of Rotterdam in the Netherlands. In France, it is mainly a whitefish river. The Semoy, which is a good salmonid stream in Belgium, flows into it and can produce Atlantic salmon.

The Loire system.   The Loire is the only one of six major rivers in France that flows entirely within the country. Its total length is 1,012 kilometers, from its source in the Ardeche Mountains to Nantes, where it flows into the Atlantic. Although many salmon used to run up the Loire, numerous dams currently prevent them from migrating upriver.

The main salmonid tributaries of the Loire are the Allier, which was formerly a natural spawning ground for salmon and is now an interesting fly fishing stream for trout and grayling; and the Sioule, Allagnon, Vienne, Gartempe, Thaurion, and Creuse. Most of the Loire's right-bank tributaries, such as the Mayenne, Loir, and Sarthe, cross intensive farming areas and provide anglers with very few fishing opportunities. An exception to this is the Huisne, a tributary of the Sarthe, which is the closest European grayling stream to Paris (150 kilometers distant). Fishing in its downstream sector is possible until around Christmas.

The Seine system. The Seine River is 1,776 kilometers long, from its source in Burgundy to its estuary at Le Havre. This is the most famous river in France because it runs through Paris.

The Haute-Seine is a beautiful trout river in the first 50 kilometers downstream from its source, and is well known for its massive green drake hatch in early June. Nice European grayling exist here as well.

The major sportfishing tributaries upstream from Paris are the Aube and the Haute-Marne, which have trout and grayling. Below Paris the Oise flows into the Seine, and there are several interesting tributaries at its headwaters near the Belgian border.

Chalk streams that originate in Normandy also flow into the Seine and are renowned for their numerous brown trout. In the mid-twentieth century, the Andelle, the Risle, the Avre, and the Epte were famous streams that could be compared to the best chalk streams in southern England. Today the majority of the best circuits on those waters are private and not accessible to the public, but a few possibilities to seduce wild brown trout still exist in the Risle or the Avre.

Normandy is noteworthy, however, for numerous streams in its coastal milk-farming region. The Touques, which joins the Channel in Deauville, is a small stream (a maximum of 30 meters wide), but it has one of the best populations of sea-run brown trout in Europe. Every year more than 1,500 of these fish are caught by anglers, and the total stock is estimated at around 4,000 to 5,000 fish. Most anglers use plugs, but in the fall, fishing is with flies only.

La Touques is undergoing a vast improvement in quality. Sections for fly-fishing-only and for catch-and-release exist along its 100-kilometer length. Nonmigrant brown trout also frequent these waters, as do Atlantic salmon and rainbow trout. North of the Seine estuary and near the Belgian border, other coastal chalk streams like the Bresle, Canche, and Authie support sea-run salmonids.

The Adour system. The Adour is a significant coastal river with a total length of 335 kilometers, from its source in the Hautes Pyrénées to its estuary in the Basque country downstream of Bayonne. The major streams from the Pyrenees flow into the Adour; these streams used to be famous for Atlantic salmon and are now well known for trout fishing.

The Gaves are among the best wild brown trout streams in France. The Gave d'Oloron, Gave de Pau, Gave d'Aspe, and Gave d'Ossau are excellent trout streams; trophy specimens weighing more than 5 kilograms may flourish in the deepest part of the river. Flies and lures work best, although local anglers fish for food by using various natural baits.

Boasting fish averaging 10 kilograms, the Gaves used to be among the best European Atlantic salmon streams. Today, because of commercial and/or illegal net fishing in the river mouth, wild Pyrenees Atlantic salmon populations have decreased dramatically. Nevertheless, a sportfishing tradition once existed on the Gave; the famous Salmon Fishing World Championship took place every year in Navarrenx on the Gave d'Oloron, and a double-handed fly-rod tradition using local fly patterns still exists.

Brittany

Brittany (La Bretagne), the Celtic part of France, is the only region of the country in which good Atlantic salmon populations and reliable fishing for this species still exist. Brittany consists of four departments and benefits from a dense hydrographic network made up of rather short coastal streams, similar to those in Wales and Ireland. Most of them contain migratory Atlantic salmon and sea trout.

There are numerous rivers along Brittany's 1,100 kilometers of coast. The significant ones from east to west on the Channel side include the Trieux (Atlantic salmon and brown trout), the Léguer (Atlantic salmon, sea-run trout, and brown trout), and the Dossen (brown trout). On the Atlantic side the major rivers are the Elorn (the best Atlantic salmon stream in France); the Aulne (at 140 kilometers the longest trout stream in Brittany and also the second best Atlantic salmon stream in France); the Goyen (brown trout, Atlantic salmon, and sea trout); the Odet (flowing through Quimper, the cultural capital of Brittany, and supporting both Atlantic salmon and brown trout); the Laïta and its two tributaries, the Elle and the Isole; and the Blavet and its tributary, the Scorff.

Since the late 1970s these coastal streams have been intensively protected against industrial and agricultural pollution. Although significant water quality problems exist elsewhere in the country, Brittany remains the only part of France with healthy stocks of Atlantic salmon. Ironically, billions of French Francs have been spent for other watersheds like the Loire and the Adour, with few noteworthy results.

The best time for Atlantic salmon fishing is during the fall run from mid-September through the end of October. Atlantic salmon in Brittany are small, with spring salmon having an average weight of 4 to 6 kilograms. Grilse are becoming more numerous each year, with frequent sea lice–fresh fish weighing 1 to 3 kilograms. Fall-run Atlantics weigh from 5 to 7 kilograms and are subject to fly fishing only.

The best months for trout fishing in Brittany are May, June, and September. Drennec Lake, at the headwaters of the Elorn in Parc d'Armorique, offers great sport for rainbow and brown trout. The lake has 110 hectares of pure and clean water surrounded by the picturesque Arree Mountains. Also within that park is Saint-Michel Lake (or Brennilis), which has 550 hectares of pure water in a landscape

F

similar to that of Scotland. Rainbow and brown trout thrive there, and the lake is especially good for northern pike, which enable first-class sportfishing with fly rods and large streamers. With the help of a local guide, one may be able to catch pike up to 10 kilograms.

Although the most common fishing technique combines spinning tackle and worms, Brittany also has an established tradition of wet-fly fishing for brown trout and Atlantic salmon. In the last century in Brittany, peasants fly-fished with long rods made from ash, and flies made from materials found on the birds in their poultry yards and on animals killed by hunting. The traditional wet fly from Brittany is made up of a body in wild boar flock ribbed with copper wire, a collarette in gray-dotted rooster feather, and a wing in peahen feather fiber.

Saltwater

The extensive French ocean coast offers many opportunities for anglers. In France, saltwater fishing is unrestricted, free of charge, and accessible to everyone. The favored methods are surf fishing, lure casting with spinning tackle, and bottom fishing from beaches, piers, and jetties. Trolling from a boat can be very effective for large gamefish species like tuna, and for smaller ones like European bass and mackerel. Anglers also benefit from thousands of hectares of oyster parks, estuaries, beaches, and rocky coasts. Net fishing is free on the coastal fringe for amateur (not commercial) fishermen. Fishing for crustaceans and shellfish is common on the French coasts.

The most common species pursued by anglers is the European bass, a close relative of the American striped bass; pollack; pollock or coalfish; Atlantic mackerel; needlefish; royal sea bream; various mullet (thinlip, thicklip, striped, and golden); spotted bass; Atlantic cod; conger eels; turbot; and burbot.

Despite massive use of its sea resources, France offers excellent fishing opportunities along the coasts of Normandy and Brittany, and also along the Languedoc coast on the Mediterranean, where there is a blue-water fishing tradition for pelagic species, including tuna. Along the northern Brittany coast excellent fishing possibilities for European bass abound, whether one uses spinning or fly casting tackle.

Saltwater gamefish are not managed in France, where the sea is still considered as an endless food resource. Legal capture sizes for some saltwater species have been introduced, but they are extremely low and allow the legal sacrifice of very young fish. To protect fish of high economic value, like European bass, actions on behalf of the breeding and growth areas of juvenile fish have to be taken, especially in the estuaries, but this has not yet occurred. Some coasts are more protected than others and are less in demand by commercial dragnetters.

The first set of stamps to depict fish in color was issued in Mozambique in 1951; it included 24 stamps depicting tropical western Indian Ocean species.

FREEBOARD

The vertical distance from the gunwale on a boat to the waterline.

FREELINE

To remove all resistance from a line and let a live bait—or sometimes a fish that has just taken a live or dead bait—swim freely without the pull of a weight or float or without resistance from the drag on a reel. This is accomplished by putting the reel in freespool (*see*) or by using a drag-bypass feature on some reels (called a baitrunner).

FRENCH POLYNESIA

French Polynesia consists of five main island groups—the Marquesas, Gambier, Austral, and Society Islands, and the Tuamotu Archipelago—spread over a vast portion of the eastern-central South Pacific between Pitcairn Island to the southeast and the Cook Islands to the west. The more than 130 islands here exhibit the complete range of island types possessing a volcanically derived geological origin: towering sharp peaks plummeting steeply into the surrounding sea; older, more weathered islands that have subsided enough to be surrounded by coral-walled lagoons; and low-lying coral atolls, where the central landmass has subsided beneath the sea surface, leaving only a ring of reefs and tiny islets that was once the outer lagoon rim exposed. The land area of these islands totals only 3,543 square kilometers but encompasses 5,030,000 square kilometers of the South Pacific Ocean by virtue of the 200-nautical-mile Exclusive Economic Zone.

The entire area is administered as a French Territory, a process initiated in 1842. The official languages are French and Tahitian, although most formal and business communication is in French. Marquesan and Tuamotun dialects are also spoken, and English is used to some extent, particularly in the tourist-related businesses. The population is approximately 213,000, centered mostly in Tahiti and the Society Islands.

The economy is heavily subsidized by the French. The advantages to visiting anglers are regular air service and at least some degree of tourist accommodation throughout much of the territory. Nevertheless, the number of visitors is a small fraction of the annual number that visit, for example, Hawaii. An even smaller number venture beyond the Society Islands. Thus, sportfishing tourism is nearly completely undeveloped everywhere outside the Societies, and not strongly developed there.

As in other Pacific island areas, however, fishing plays a definite role in the culture and everyday life of the natives. The relative prosperity of the local economy compared to that of some poorer independent Pacific nations results in more modern boats and equipment, all of which are ingeniously applied to traditional fisheries.

F

Small skiffs, propelled by powerful inboard/outboard engines and equipped with bow-steering stations, are used to harpoon mahimahi (dolphin); troll for tuna, wahoo, and other pelagic species; fish outer reef slopes for deep-water snapper and grouper; employ traditional drop-stone fishing near reef and lagoon passes; and troll cane poles armed with pearl oyster shell lures to catch skipjack tuna. Larger "bonito boats," which are fast 35- to 40-foot locally constructed flying-bridge fishing boats usually powered by single turbocharged diesels, are pervasive throughout much of the territory. They speed from school to school of surface-feeding skipjack tuna and troll the same pearl oyster shell lures to commercially cane-pole their catch. On the islands experiencing the highest tourist flow, some of these vessels have been converted to part- and full-time sportfishing.

Ciguatera *(see)* poisoning can be a problem at various locations throughout the territory, and local knowledge should be consulted before consuming any reef-associated fish species.

Marquesas Islands

The Marquesas comprise 10 islands characterized by steep, rugged peaks, jungle valleys, and no significant fringing reefs or lagoons. They form a loose, elongated group oriented over a 300-kilometer northwest to southeast diagonal located 1,400 kilometers northeast of Tahiti. Six are inhabited, and the total population is only 10,000. Tourist accommodations of some kind can be found on each of the inhabited islands, but boat chartering arrangements for sportfishing have to be made with local commercial and subsistence-oriented fishing vessels or tourist dive boats.

The Marquesas are the only French Polynesian island group located squarely in the productive Pacific equatorial upwelling zone. Although the Marquesas are an eastern outlier in terms of inshore fish colonization, with only 350 estimated species, the level of biological production in the surrounding ocean is high. Asian longliners, licensed by the French, continue to record significant catches in this area. Due to the lack of sportfishing data, an indication of available offshore resources has been derived from commercial fishing records. Local anglers are knowledgeable about species targeted closer to shore and near several charted and uncharted seamounts in the area.

Surface-feeding schools of Pacific little tunny, skipjack, and yellowfin tuna (to 40 pounds), often mixed, are pervasive throughout the Marquesas year-round. Larger yellowfin tuna and bigeye tuna are also present. Although seldom targeted, blue marlin are seen and caught year-round. Sailfish are landed on occasion, more often here than in the Society Islands. Large wahoo are particularly abundant from May through September.

Canal Haava, the narrow channel between the islands of Hiva Oa and Tahuata, is a consistent producer of sizable (50- to 60-pound-class) wahoo at this time. Mahimahi in a variety of sizes are inconsistently available through the year. Japanese longline efforts indicate that shortbill spearfish are relatively numerous around the Marquesas. Two tagged blue marlin were recaptured in 1997 near the Marquesas (one tagged off of Kailua-Kona, Hawaii, the other off the tip of Baja, Mexico).

Since Marquesan shorelines frequently fall off abruptly to deeper water, large inshore and pelagic fish are frequently caught in bays and close to shore. Giant trevally, Pacific little tunny, and yellowfin tuna to at least 40 pounds are caught on a regular basis, for example, as they chase bait into the shallows of Taiohae Bay at Nuku Hiva. Motu Iti—a small, rocky pinnacle guarding the eastern mouth of Anaho Bay at Nuku Hiva—consistently holds wahoo close to its outer wall only a few meters from shore. Sharks are numerous, more so in some areas than others.

Inshore trolling, casting, and bottom fishing produce a mixed bag, including bluefin and giant trevally and other jacks, plus queenfish, jobfish, red snapper, emperors, and a variety of small grouper species. Deeper on the outer reef slopes and seamounts, local anglers target red snapper, emperors, deep-water snapper (including queen snapper and similar species, and jobfish), and grouper (white-margined grouper, occasional giant grouper, and others).

In general, most fish populations in the immediate vicinity of the Marquesas remain very lightly exploited due to the small demands of the local population. Offshore longlining operations can be expected to have some influence on sport-catch rates of billfish and other species, but there are no data because virtually no sportfishing is done here, offshore or otherwise. Anglers who journey here can be assured of wetting a line where few have come before them.

Tuamotu Archipelago

The Tuamotu Archipelago is composed entirely of low-lying coral atolls, a complete contrast to the Marquesas 660 kilometers to the north. There are 78 atolls here, only 45 of which are inhabited by a total of 14,000 people. They stretch in a northwest-southeast arc, 600 kilometers wide and 1,200 kilometers long, between the Marquesas and Tahiti. They comprise the world's largest group of coral atolls.

Lying between 1° and 23° south latitude, the Tuamotus are outside the equatorial upwelling zone but more within the main belt of estimated Indo-Pacific fish species colonization. This creates two more sharp differences between the Tuamotu Archipelago and the Marquesas: crystal clear water (the underwater visibility on the outer reefs is routinely unlimited) due to sharply reduced phytoplankton density and lack of runoff from land, and nearly double the number of inshore fish species.

F

Although the details vary from atoll to atoll within the archipelago, most feature sizable enclosed lagoons that communicate to varying degrees with the open sea, often in the form of deep, high-current passes that become focal points for feeding pelagic and inshore fish as they flush tremendous volumes of water out of the lagoon. Large lagoons with ample exchange are often entered by schooling pelagic species normally encountered outside the reef, such as smaller tuna and rainbow runners. They also provide habitat for a large number of inshore species. The outer reef slope is typically steep, plummeting away to great depths, often in the form of sizable sections of near-vertical coral walls patrolled by many larger predator fish. Lack of land, freshwater, and fertile soil has kept human populations historically low, which has helped preserve the pristine natural environment of this island group.

As in the Marquesas, sportfishing here is almost entirely undeveloped, although scattered airstrips and accommodations throughout the archipelago make access possible. Rangiroa, the largest of the group with a 1,020-square-kilometer lagoon, is the most developed, but despite numerous hotels has no dedicated charter fishing boat. Fishing trips on local vessels can be arranged, similar to the routine in the Marquesas.

Offshore fishing can be productive for skipjack and yellowfin tuna, wahoo, and mahimahi. Surface-feeding schools do not appear at quite the frequency seen in the Marquesas, although they are still numerous, particularly in the vicinity of atoll passes on the outgoing tide. Blue marlin are more abundant between November and March but are caught year-round by local anglers in the course of pursuing other species. It is rare to catch a sailfish.

In addition to blue-water species, fishing along the outer reef slope or around the passes of Tuamotun atolls can result in the capture of a wide variety of fish, including various trevally (giant, golden, bluefin, bigeye, and yellow-spotted), dogtooth tuna, barracuda, African pompano, rainbow runners, red snapper and several smaller snapper, and a number of colorful grouper (commonly coral trout, marbled grouper, and peacock grouper). Humphead wrasses that may weigh up to 175 pounds can be baited with crabs or small fish. Deep-water species of snapper and grouper inhabit the greater depths of the reef slope.

Many of these fish are caught inside the lagoon. Spawning aggregations of marbled grouper make periodic mass journeys in and out of lagoon passes on certain moon phases and at specific times of the year in the Tuamotus. Many passes near villages feature numerous fixed fish-trap structures, constructed with wire mesh wings to guide fish transiting the pass into the main section of the trap. These devices capture marbled grouper; giant, bluefin, and other trevally; bonefish; and other species of interest to anglers. These efforts, possibly in combination with subsistence inshore gillnetting activities, may occur in sufficient numbers to depress some potential lagoon and flats sportfisheries in specific locations. Many other atolls are sparsely inhabited or uninhabited, and have been little explored by anglers, despite the existence of bonefish (and appropriate flats for pursuing them), trevally, a small species of tarpon, and other prime light-tackle targets.

High-profile pelagic species, particularly blue marlin and swordfish, are essentially unfished by recreational anglers in the Tuamotus. A growing fleet of local longliners, based in Tahiti, has in recent years become more active in the archipelago, although a significant portion of their effort has been directed toward the capture of a deep-dwelling, ocean sunfishlike species called "salmon of the gods," for which there is a lucrative regional market.

Society Islands

The Society Islands are spread in a loose east-to-west array across 685 kilometers of ocean west of the Tuamotus, between latitudes 15° and 18° south. The five eastern members of the group form the Windward Society Islands, and the nine western entities, the Leeward Society Islands. The main Society Islands are typified by a geological stage intermediate between the Marquesas and the Tuamotus—high, central volcanic islands that have subsided enough to encourage the formation of encircling barrier reefs that create protected lagoons. This constitutes an environment ideal for human inhabitation, with ample rainfall, lush vegetation, mild climate, and numerous protected anchorages. As a result, the Society Islands have been the most heavily populated and developed of the territory, with much of the population centered around the capital of Papeete, Tahiti.

Implications for the recreational angler are a wide choice of accommodations and amenities and the availability of charter fishing boats, and an environment that experiences more fishing pressure than the out-islands, particularly inshore. Several outlying islands within the Societies still offer pristine shallow-water fishing conditions, including five lightly populated coral atolls, but angling visits have to be specially arranged. The traveling angler would be hard pressed to choose a more pleasant, spectacular backdrop.

The Society Islands, like the Tuamotus, lie just south of the equatorial upwelling zone. Lagoon waters are clear near the outer reef but turbid near stream and river mouths and deep bays closer to central island shorelines. Outside the lagoon, blue water is often available immediately adjacent to the reef wall, sometimes tinted green from runoff that forms productive tide lines and plumes as it exits passes on the outgoing tide.

Approximately 633 inshore fish species occur in this island group, lending considerable diversity to potential catches. Many shallow-water species

The lush backdrop scenery for inshore or offshore fishing in Tahiti, as seen here in Papeete, is among the best in the world.

caught by locals for food are in short supply around the main islands due to gillnetting and other subsistence fishing activities. Populations of bonefish, for example, have been depressed below levels necessary for a reasonable angling opportunity; the only easily accessible bonefishing possibilities may be visits by special arrangement to the privately owned atolls of either Tetiaroa or Tupai. Some lagoon action can be had with Pacific little tunny, several species of trevally, queenfish, and scattered reef dwellers like emperors, snapper, and grouper. Deep-water snapper and grouper are fished on the outer reef slopes. Within the Societies, the degree of inshore and reef action is noticeably related to distance from population centers.

Offshore angling prospects are more uniform throughout the group. The Society Islands have a small core of serious anglers, private boats, and charter boats, located mostly in Tahiti, Raiatea, and Bora Bora.

Surface schools of skipjack and yellowfin tuna, usually marked by terns and boobies, are prevalent year-round. Commercial bonito boats tracking these schools commonly encounter blue marlin that chase the small tuna under the boat, frequently signaled by panicky tuna getting hit by the propeller. Black marlin and swordfish are known to pass through the area. Pods of larger mahimahi (over 15 pounds) are fairly common, as are 40- to 60-pound wahoo in the winter months. Several Fish Attracting Devices (FADs) have been deployed in the area. Local sportfishing boats sometimes effectively target bigeye tuna and albacore with natural bait drifted as deep as 900 feet, often near FADs.

Blue marlin are the focus of much of the offshore angling effort in the Society Islands. The season runs from November through March and peaks during the last three months of this period. Significant flurries of blue marlin activity also occur in August, September, and October. Tahitians claim that black marlin also make a consistent annual appearance close to the outer reef slopes in November and December, although they receive little directed effort. Sailfish are a rarity.

Austral and Gambier Islands

The Austral Islands, a widely spaced group of seven isolated isles located just over 600 kilometers south of Tahiti, occupy a lonely 1,170-kilometer northwest-southeast swath of the South Pacific that straddles the Tropic of Capricorn. The Gambier Islands form a tight cluster of 10, protected by a barrier reef on three sides, just above this latitude, 1,100 kilometers to the east below the southernmost extension of the Tuamotu Archipelago. Both groups are isolated, lightly populated, have cooler climates and very little tourism, and are geologically most similar to the Society Islands.

Tubuai and Rurutu in the Australs, and Mangareva in the Gambiers, have air service. Until closure of the French nuclear testing site at nearby Mururoa in 1996, access to the Gambiers was restricted. Thus there are no tourist accommodations. In the Australs, limited facilities exist at Tubuai and Rurutu, and arrangements can be made for other islands, which are accessible only by boat. Rapa, at just below 27° south latitude, is the southernmost outpost of French Polynesia and one of the most isolated Pacific islands, with steep peaks, a narrow fringing reef, and a distinctly cool, misty climate.

Lagoon angling environments exist in the Gambier Islands, and at Tubuai and Raivavae in the Australs. Fringing reefs in various stages of development occur at other islands. Rapa is the most isolated in terms of fish colonization, with only 220 known inshore species. Significant tuna and billfish populations are known for these areas. In particular, striped marlin frequent both the Australs and Gambiers. Sailfish are caught occasionally. Foreign commercial longliners have fished this area intensively in the recent past. Any assisted sportfishing outing requires special arrangements with local Polynesian anglers and could probably be considered, to at least some degree, a pioneering effort.

FREESPOOL

The condition in which line is able to freely unwind from the spool of a fishing reel; the disengagement of gears. When the gears of a reel are disengaged to allow line to come off the spool, the reel is said to be "in freespool." The spool itself may or may not actually turn or rotate. In most spincasting reels and in spinning reels, the spool is stationary; in baitcasting, conventional, and big-game reels, the spool revolves. In most fly reels and in some specialty reels having a direct drive gear, the spool is always free to turn and it is not put into or taken out of freespool.

F

A spinning reel is put into freespool when the bail is lifted; other reels are put into freespool when a line-release button, trigger, lever, or knob is depressed or lifted. All such reels are then ready to be cast, or to otherwise let line flow from the spool.

The term "freespool" is something of a carryover from the use of baitcasting, conventional, and big-game reels. In these types of tackle, the spool does revolve to release line, and freespool really does indicate that the spool is free to rotate in order to easily release line. With spinning and spincasting reels, in freespool the gears are engaged and the bail or pickup pin (respectively) has just been moved out of the way so that line can flow off the spool.

See: Baitcasting Tackle; Big-Game Tackle; Conventional Tackle; Spincasting Tackle; Spinning Tackle.

FREESTONE STREAM
A stream originating from rain runoff and small feeder streams. Freestone streams grow slowly from tiny trickles to broad streams or rivers. Some begin from smaller springs in sandstone bedrock where ridges and mountains have been formed. Freestone streams are more numerous than limestone streams (see) and vary more in chemical and biological makeup. They may have fewer insects than limestone streams, but a greater variety.

FRESH-RUN FISH
A fish that has recently entered a river for upstream migration; also known as a fresh fish. This term primarily applies to salmon and steelhead on their upstream spawning journey. They usually have a silvery sheen, may have sea lice on their bodies, and are very strong.

FRESHWATER
Water with less than 0.5 gram per liter of total dissolved mineral salts.
See: Brackish Water; Saltwater/Seawater.

FRONT
The line along which two air masses of different density and temperature meet, generally identified as either a warm front, cold front, or stationary front.
See: Weather.

FROSTBITE
See: First Aid.

FRY
Young fish, or a group of recently spawned small fish of the same species.

FURUNCULOSIS
See: Diseases and Parasites.

FYKE NET
A net with a long bag and hoops that is set in lakes and streams for catching eels.

F

GABON

Straddling the equator on the western coast of Africa, Gabon is known for its rich mineral and forest resources. In addition, because it faces the Gulf of Guinea in the Atlantic Ocean, it is strategically situated along the migratory route of many pelagic species, especially sailfish, blue marlin, bigeye tuna, and wahoo, as well as sharks—not to mention huge tarpon and other species inshore. Its rivers are virtually unexplored by anglers.

The long shoreline of Gabon is south of Equatorial Guinea and north of the Democratic Republic of the Congo. Much of the country is a flat plain covered by dense equatorial forest; the coastal lowland perimeter encompasses golden beaches and mangrove shores in the vicinity of Libreville, the capital and largest city, and Port Gentil, the easternmost point and estuary for the nation's most prominent watershed, the Ogooué River.

The presence of huge tarpon off Port Gentil was established in the late 1970s and early 1980s, when a number of fish over 200 pounds and up to 250 pounds were captured, some establishing records at the time. Nevertheless, tarpon are lightly fished here, as well as in the other numerous river systems and estuaries along the coast, especially to the south. Many of these waters have undiscovered fishing potential and are believed to hold huge tarpon as well as snapper, jacks, grouper, barracuda, and sharks. The Ogooué River and its numerous serpentine tributaries extend far inland, although its fisheries resources are uncertain.

Offshore, however, Gabon boasts excellent year-round blue marlin angling. During the two dry seasons, when migratory marlin are descending, strikes are more numerous, but the fish tend to be smaller, averaging 350 pounds. A brief dry season occurs from December through mid-January; a longer one runs from June through mid-September. In the wet season, from mid-September through June, blue marlin are in the 500-pound range.

The primary reason for the aggregation of billfish, tuna, and other species off the entire West African coast are the shifts in the frontal zone of the Canary Current and the Equatorial Countercurrent. This is especially significant to the Ekwata Fishing Center, Gabon's principal sportfishing site, situated about a half-hour by boat from the Libreville airport. There is a good five-boat charter fleet at Ekwata, and anglers can troll productive water 50 minutes after leaving the docks. The typical fishing day is a long one, about 11 hours, not because of a long run to fishing grounds, but because the captains are committed to covering as much ground as possible. The weather and sea conditions are usually good in the Gulf of Guinea, but waters can sometimes be rough during the dry seasons.

Arrangements to fish the area can be made through the Big Game Fishing Club of Libreville, and accommodations are available at Ekwata, where there is a comfortable lodge.

GAFF

A sharp hook attached to a pole, stick, or handle used for landing fish. Gaffs come in hand, stick, and flying versions. A hand gaff is short-handled and primarily used for lip-gaffing fish that are to be released unharmed, usually from small boats with low freeboard. A stick gaff features a 2- to 4-inch hook attached to a stick or pole and used for fish up to about 150 pounds; the stick may be aluminum, wood, stainless steel, or fiberglass and from 2 to 6 feet long. A flying gaff features a large hook attached to a pole that is up to 8 feet long and connected to a rope tied to the boat; when the hook enters the fish, it separates from the pole and remains tethered to the rope. The flying gaff is used for large fish of 150 pounds or more.

Gaff hooks are stainless steel and vary from 2 to 16 inches in gap, which is the distance from the point of the hook to the shaft. Gap size should conform to the fish (many offshore saltwater boaters carry several gaffs with different hook sizes and handle lengths). Points may be cone (tapering uniformly to a point) or cutting (sharp edges) style, and a few have a barb; the hook is parallel to the handle for most gaffs, but on some it opens away from the shaft.

Gaffing techniques are discussed in a separate entry (see: landing fish).

GAFFING

See: Landing Fish; Catch-and-Release.

GAG *Mycteroperca microlepis.*
Other names—charcoal belly; French: *badèche baillou;* Portuguese: *badejo-da-areia;* Spanish: *cuna aguají.*

Gags belongs to the branch of the grouper family that is characterized by a long, compressed body and 11 to 14 rays in the anal fin. Gags have white,

Gag

flaky flesh that makes excellent eating, although, like other grouper, they have deeply embedded scales that are virtually impossible to remove.

Identification.   Pale to dark gray or sometimes olive gray, the larger gag is darker than the smaller gag and has blotchy markings on its side and an overall indistinctly marbled appearance. The smaller gag is paler and has many dark brown or charcoal marks along its sides. The pelvic, anal, and caudal fins are blackish with blue or white edges. The gag is distinguished from the black grouper by its deeply notched preopercles, and is distinguished from the otherwise similar scamp by the absence of extended caudal rays.

Size/Age.   The gag weighs less than 3 pounds on average but may reach a weight of 55 pounds (about 51 inches in length). It can live for at least 15 years.

Distribution.   In the western Atlantic, gags are found from North Carolina (sometimes as far north as Massachusetts) to the Yucatán Peninsula, Mexico, although they are rare in Bermuda and absent from the Caribbean and the Bahamas; they are also reported along Brazil. They are the most common grouper on rocky ledges in the eastern Gulf of Mexico.

Habitat.   Young gags inhabit estuaries and sea-grass beds, whereas adults are usually found off-shore around rocky ledges, undercuts, reefs, and occasionally inshore over rocky or grassy bottoms. Adults may be solitary or occur in groups of 5 to 50 individuals.

Spawning behavior.   Gags reach sexual maturity when 27 to 30 inches long or five to six years of age, spawning off the Carolinas in February, and from January through March in the Gulf of Mexico. The female may lay more than a million pelagic eggs.

Food.   Gags feed on such fish as sardines, porgies, snapper, and grunts, as well as crabs, shrimp, and squid; young that are less than 20 centimeters feed mainly on crustaceans found in shallow grassbeds.

Angling.   Like other grouper, gags are primarily caught by fishing at the right depth over irregular bottoms.

See: Grouper; Inshore Fishing.

GALAPAGOS ISLANDS
See: Ecuador.

GALLEY
The kitchen area of a boat.

GAMEFISH
In fishing parlance, gamefish are freshwater and saltwater fish that are sought by recreational anglers and are valued for their fighting virtues and willingness to take a lure, fly, or natural bait. Many species of fish are not encountered by anglers because of habitat, feeding habits, or other reasons, but would put up vigorous resistance if they were and do not make anyone's list of gamefish. Most, though certainly not all, species considered gamefish are predatory and carnivorous, which makes them likely to strike at the offerings of anglers. Species with such highly esteemed traits as ability to jump, strength to make long runs, aggressiveness in taking a lure, and attainment of large size tend to be the most popular gamefish, especially if they are abundant. Edibility is not a factor in whether a fish is considered a gamefish, although many top predatory fish are excellent to eat.

In many places, certain species are designated by law as gamefish, which prevents them from being captured commercially and prohibits their sale by anglers. This is decided by respective governing agencies, however, and varies widely. Legal gamefish status generally confers protective and managerial oversight, and it is reserved for species that are not only popular and intensively sought, but viewed as having more desirable sporting virtues than non-designated species, and also as being more vulnerable. Thus, catfish and most panfish species seldom have gamefish status, whereas bass, walleye, pike, and trout do.

See: Sportfishing.

GAR
Gar are a family (Lepisosteidae) of primitive fish that were once abundant and widely distributed. The few species in existence today are found mainly in eastern North America, ranging as far south as Central America and Cuba. They live in shallow, weedy freshwater, rarely entering brackish water. Like the bowfin, gar have a highly vascularized air bladder that serves as an auxiliary lung, enabling these fish to take in air at the surface and thus survive in water that has become too fouled or too stagnant for most fish to tolerate. Much of the gar's time is spent resting quietly near the bottom or basking at the surface, but they can swim swiftly for short distances to catch their prey.

Gar in general are cigar-shaped, and their tooth-filled snout is broad and flat in some species and slender in others. The single dorsal fin is located far back on the body, directly above the anal fin. The vertebrae resemble those of amphibians, that is, convex in front and concave at the rear, so that they fit together like ball-and-socket joints. In most fish, the vertebrae are concave at both ends. The ganoid (diamond-shaped) scales of the gar fit one against the other like bricks in a wall and are composed of ganoin, an extremely hard compound. Indians used the scales of large gar for arrowheads, and pioneer farmers covered their wooden plowshares with gar hides. The hides have been processed to make luggage and novelties.

The longnose gar *(see: gar, longnose)* is the most widely distributed member of the family, generally ranging from the St. Lawrence River westward through the Great Lakes and southward to Florida and Texas. It occurs most abundantly in the Mississippi River drainage system, usually living in shallow, weedy, quiet waters in the warmer parts of its range but seeming to prefer clearer streams and lakes the farther north it goes.

The shortnose gar *(see: gar, shortnose)* occurs only in weedy, silted streams of the Mississippi River drainage system, and is the smallest of the gar, rarely exceeding $2^1/_2$ feet in length. Sometimes found in the same habitat with the shortnose gar, but ranging farther north and west, is the larger spotted gar *(see: gar, spotted)*. In peninsular Florida, the spotted gar is replaced by the slightly smaller but numerous Florida gar *(see: gar, Florida)*.

The giant of this clan in North America is the alligator gar *(see: gar, alligator),* which lives only in the large tributaries of the Gulf of Mexico. Sometimes, although rarely, it strays far up the Mississippi. Although it was once numerous, and capable of growing to 10 feet long and more than 300 pounds, this species has been greatly reduced; monster-size fish are rare and even 6- to 7-footers are uncommon today.

Gar are voracious feeders that primarily consume forage or rough fish species, especially shad and golden shiners. They are not classified as gamefish in most states where they occur, and although they are strong fighters on rod and reel, they have a very low following among anglers. They are occasionally caught incidentally on lures or on baits by anglers using bottom fishing rigs for catfish; focused angling efforts usually require the use of a wire leader to counter the needlelike teeth of these fish. They are pursued by a limited number of bow-and-arrow hunters.

GAR, ALLIGATOR   *Lepisosteus spatula.*

Other names—garpike; French: *garpique alligator;* Spanish: *gaspar baba.*

The alligator gar is the largest member of the gar family, Lepisosteidae, and one of North America's largest inland fish. It is a primitive species, dating from the Mesozoic era, 65 to 230 million years ago. Fossil remains of gar are often found in limestone quarries throughout the southern United States. The tough, armorlike scales of this species were once used by Indians as arrowheads, and pioneer farmers covered their wooden plowshares with gar hides.

The gar is a resilient fish with an adaptable specialized air bladder that enables it to take in air at the surface, allowing it to survive in the poorest water conditions. Holding a strong resemblance to its namesake, the alligator gar is strong and voracious, and a tough fighter when hooked. It is capable of jumping spectacularly.

The alligator gar has been under siege for most of the twentieth century, eagerly sought and killed. Efforts to eradicate them existed in many of their natural habitats under the ill-advised notion of ridding the waters of gamefish-killing monsters. Many huge fish, including specimens from 100 pounds to more than 300 pounds, were removed by commercial netters, anglers using big-game tackle, and others using steel-tipped arrows while bowfishing. Although their numbers are drastically reduced today, alligator gar are not classified as gamefish by most state fisheries agencies and are not regulated as to size or manner of fishing. There is virtually no concerted sportfishing for this species today.

Alligator gar is edible, but not highly rated. It is used to a slight extent as food; a few are caught commercially and smoked. The alligator gar's green roe is poisonous to humans, animals, and birds, although not to other fish.

Identification.   The alligator gar's body is long and cylindrical, covered with heavy, ganoid (diamond-shaped) scales. The snout is short and broad like an alligator's, and there are two rows of teeth on either side of the upper jaw (other gar have only one). It has a single dorsal fin that is far back on the body above the anal fin and just before the tail. The tail is rounded, and the pectoral, ventral, and anal fins are evenly spaced on the lower half of the body. Its

Alligator Gar

coloring is olive or greenish brown above, and lighter below. The sides are mottled with large black spots.

These and other gar are often mistaken for floating logs. The alligator gar can be distinguished from all other gar by the two rows of teeth in the upper jaw, its broader snout, and its large size when fully grown. The alligator gar most closely resembles members of the pike family in body shape and fin placement, although the tail of these fish is forked, not rounded.

Size.   The alligator gar is the giant of the gar family. It still attains weights in excess of 100 pounds, although such fish are not common; larger fish are occasionally captured in commercial fishing nets. The maximum size of alligator gar is not certain, although the figure evidently exceeds 300 pounds, and the can reach more than 10 feet in length. The all-tackle rod-and-reel record is a 279-pound fish captured in the Rio Grande River in Texas in 1951. There are reports, however of larger fish, including a 356-pound alligator gar that was 8 feet, 5 inches long and taken in Arkansas' Horseshoe Lake in 1931. A 190-pounder caught in a net in Arkansas in 1997 was 7 feet, 11 inches long.

Distribution.   The range of the alligator gar extends from the Mississippi River basin of southwestern Ohio and southern Illinois south to the Gulf of Mexico, and from the Enconfina River of the western Florida Panhandle west to Veracruz, Mexico. It has reportedly been taken from Lake Nicaragua, but this catch could have been confused with a large relative, *L. tristoechius,* taken from Cuban, Central American, and Mexican waters—a fish that rivals the alligator gar in size.

Habitat.   Large lakes, bays, backwaters, bayous, and coastal delta waters along large Southern rivers are the preferred habitat of the alligator gar, although this fish is seldom found in brackish or marine waters. It favors shallow, weedy environs and the sluggish pools and backwaters of large rivers, and can survive in hot and stagnant waters. Alligator gar are often seen floating at the surface. They occasionally come to the surface layer to expel gases and to take air into their swim bladder.

Spawning behavior.   Spawning occurs in spring and early summer in shallow bays and sloughs. The female lays dark green eggs that stick to vegetation and rocks until they hatch in six to eight days. The female is capable of producing as many as 77,000 eggs at once. The young are solitary and float at the surface like sticks.

Food.   Although the alligator gar is infamous for eating almost anything, from dead animals to ducks and popular gamefish, studies have revealed that the vast majority of its diet comprises gizzard shad, threadfin shad, golden shiners, and rough or coarse fish species.

See: Gar.

GAR, FLORIDA   *Lepisosteus platyrhincus.*

The Florida gar is a member of the Lepisosteidae family, an ancient group of predaceous fish once in abundance and widely distributed. Its specialized air bladder enables the gar to take in air at the surface, allowing it to survive in the poorest waters. Although edible, Florida gar are unpopular as food. They are caught by anglers, although not extensively pursued. The roe is highly toxic to humans, animals, and birds.

Identification.   The body of the Florida gar is cigar-shaped, and it has a tooth-filled broad snout. The single dorsal fin is located directly above the anal fin. Its tough scales form a bricklike pattern. Like the spotted gar *(see: gar, spotted),* it has spots on top of the head as well as over the entire body and on all the fins. These spots sometimes run together to form stripes.

The Florida and spotted gar can be distinguished from each other mainly by the distance from the front of the eye to the back of the gill cover. In the Florida gar, it is less than two-thirds the length of the snout; in the spotted gar it is more than two-thirds the length of the snout. The Florida gar can be distinguished from the longnose gar *(see: gar, longnose)*—the only other gar occurring in the Florida's range—by the absence of spots on its head and by the elongated beak of the longnose.

Size.   The average size rarely exceeds 2 feet. The all-tackle record is 21 pounds, 3 ounces.

Distribution.   The Florida gar ranges throughout peninsular Florida and in the Panhandle as far as the Apalachicola River drainage, where there is evidence that it hybridizes with the spotted gar. The Florida gar also occurs throughout part of southern Georgia to the Savannah River drainage.

G

Florida Gar

Longnose Gar

Habitat. The Florida gar is common in medium to large lowland streams and lakes with mud or sand bottoms and an abundance of underwater vegetation. It is also abundant in canals. Gar can be found resting both on the bottom or at the surface. It lives in freshwater but can survive in stagnated water that is intolerable to most other fish.

Spawning behavior. The spawning season is from May through July in backwaters and sloughs. A female can lay up to 6,000 eggs at once. Florida gar often travel in groups of 2 to 10 or more.

Food. Forage and coarse fish make up much of the adult gar's diet, although it also consumes shrimp, insects, crayfish, and scuds.
See: Gar.

GAR, LONGNOSE *Lepisosteus osseus.*
Other names—French: *garpique longnez;* Spanish: *gaspar picudo.*

The longnose gar is the most common and widely distributed member of the gar family, Lepisosteidae, one of the few remaining ancient groups of predaceous fish once in abundance. Its long endurance is due to a specialized air bladder that enables the gar to take in air at the surface, allowing it to survive in the poorest waters.

Although some longnose gar are caught commercially in nets, this fish is of minor sportfishing interest, and some anglers view it as a nuisance, believing that it preys heavily on gamefish. The flesh is edible but not popular, and the roe is poisonous to humans, animals, and small birds, although not other fish.

Identification. The body of the longnose gar is long and slender. It has an extended narrow beak (18 to 20 times as long as it is wide at its narrowest point). The skeleton is part cartilage and part bone. Both upper and lower jaws are lined with strong, sharp teeth. The nostrils are located in a small, bulbous, fleshy growth at the very tip of the beak.

The body is covered with bony, ganoid (diamond-shaped) scales. The dorsal and anal fins are set far back. Its coloring is olive brown or deep green along the back and upper sides, with a silver white belly. There are numerous black spots on the body, although not on the head or jaws. The longnose gar can be distinguished from other gar by its elongated snout.

Size. The average fish is 2 to 3 feet in length, but occasionally reaches 5 feet. The all-tackle record is 50 pounds, 5 ounces.

Distribution. The longnose gar is the most common and widely distributed of all gar. It is primarily found throughout the eastern half of North America, within the Mississippi River system and other drainages. Its range generally encompasses an area from Minnesota and the Great Lakes to Quebec, southward to southern Florida and the Gulf States, and westward to the Rio Grande bordering Texas and Mexico. It may reach as far as Montana in the north and the Pecos River in New Mexico to the south. Large concentrations exist along the Atlantic coast.

Habitat. Longnose gar inhabit warm, quiet water, frequenting shallow weedy areas and the sluggish pools, backwaters, and oxbows of large and medium rivers and lakes. They occasionally enter brackish water and can tolerate murky and stagnated environments.

Life history/Behavior. Groups of adult gar often lie motionless at the surface, strongly resembling floating sticks. In summer, they will roll over and break the surface to gulp air (usually in extremely murky water) and release gases from their air bladder.

Males mature when they are three or four years old; females at six years old. The spawning season is in spring in shallow water. Females can release more than 35,000 eggs, which are fertilized by two or three males. The eggs attach to vegetation and rocks. The young use sucking discs at the front of the snout to attach to submerged objects.

Food and feeding habits. Longnose gar feed on shiners, sunfish, gizzard shad, catfish, and bullhead. They sometimes slowly stalk their prey but are generally known to lie in wait for it to come close.
See: Gar.

GAR, SHORTNOSE *Lepisosteus platostomus.*
The shortnose gar is the smallest member of an ancient family, Lepisosteidae, of predaceous fish. It is the most tolerant of all the gar, as it is capable of withstanding murky and brackish water with the help of its specialized air bladder. The bladder allows the gar to gulp in supplementary air and release gases.

Because large numbers of coarse fish and panfish exist in many waters inhabited by gar, the shortnose gar (as well as other gar) can be useful in controlling these populations. In some areas, however, it is considered a nuisance by anglers and sometimes even a problem because of its abundance.

G

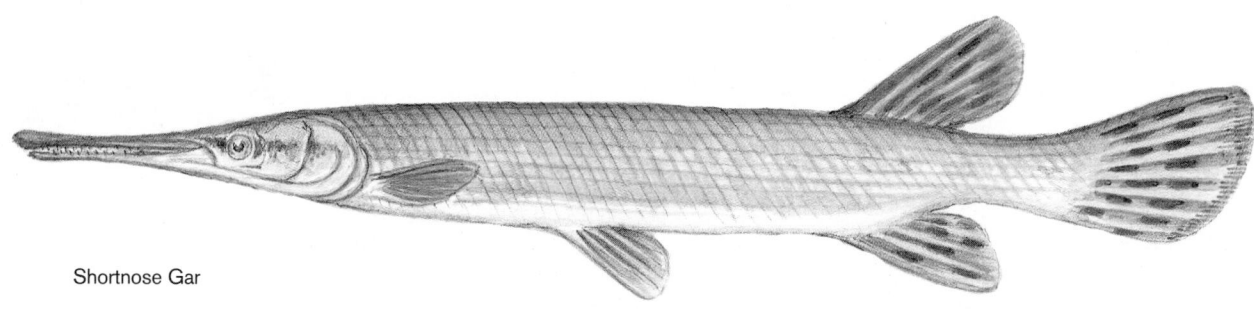

Shortnose Gar

The shortnose gar has good sporting virtues but is not widely pursued. It is often caught incidentally by anglers pursuing other fish. It is not considered a good food fish, and its roe is toxic.

Identification.   The body is long and cylindrical, covered with ganoid (diamond-shaped) scales. There is a single row of teeth in the upper jaw, compared with the alligator gar's *(see: gar, alligator)* two rows. It has a short, broad snout. Unlike its relatives the Florida gar *(see: gar, Florida)* and spotted gar *(see: gar, spotted)*, it has no spots on its head, but it does have spots on its dorsal, anal, and caudal fins.

Size.   The shortnose gar rarely exceeds $2^{1}/_{2}$ feet in length. The all-tackle world record is a 5-pound, 12-ounce fish caught in 1995 in Illinois.

Distribution.   The shortnose gar occurs from the Great Lakes south to the Gulf of Mexico but is essentially limited to the low-gradient portions of the Mississippi River basin. In the United States, it is found from northern Alabama to Oklahoma and down through Louisiana to the Gulf of Mexico. In the north, it has a broad range in the river systems that feed the Mississippi, from southern Ohio to Montana.

Habitat.   This species is common in quiet water, including the pools and backwater areas of creeks and small to large rivers, and in swamps, lakes, and oxbows, often near vegetation. The alligator gar is even more tolerant of muddy water than other gar, and it prefers warm water.

Spawning behavior.   Spawning occurs in the spring in shallow bays and sloughs. The eggs attach to weeds or other objects.

Food.   The diet of the shortnose gar is similar to that of other gar; forage and rough fish comprise the bulk of its food.

See: Gar.

GAR, SPOTTED   *Lepisosteus oculatus.*
Other names—French: *garpique tachetée;* Spanish: *gaspar pintado.*

The spotted gar is a member of an ancient family, Lepisosteidae, of predaceous fish. It is often confused with its close relative, the Florida gar *(see: gar, Florida)*. The spotted gar has good sporting virtues but is not widely pursued, and it is often caught incidental to other fishing activities. It is not considered a good food fish, and its roe is toxic to humans but not to other fish.

Identification.   The body of the spotted gar is long and cylindrical, covered with hard, ganoid (diamond-shaped) scales. It has a single row of teeth in each jaw. The spotted and Florida gar are the only two gar that have spots on the top of the head as well as over the entire body and on the fins. The spots on other gar are limited to the fins and the posterior portion of the body, usually after the pelvic (ventral) fins. The two are generally distinguished by the distance between the front of the eye and the rear edge of the gill cover. If the distance is less than two-thirds the length of the snout, it is a Florida gar; if it is more than two-thirds the length of the snout, it is a spotted gar.

Size.   The spotted gar rarely exceeds 3 feet and averages $2^{1}/_{2}$ feet. The all-tackle world record is a 9-pound, 12-ounce fish caught in Texas in 1994.

Distribution.   The spotted gar ranges from the Great Lakes to the Gulf of Mexico and down through the Mississippi River drainage system. It occurs all along the gulf coast from central Texas to the western portion of the Florida Panhandle. East of the Apalachicola drainage, in the remainder of Florida, the spotted gar is replaced by the Florida gar. Both species occur in the Apalachicola drainage itself, where they are believed to hybridize to some

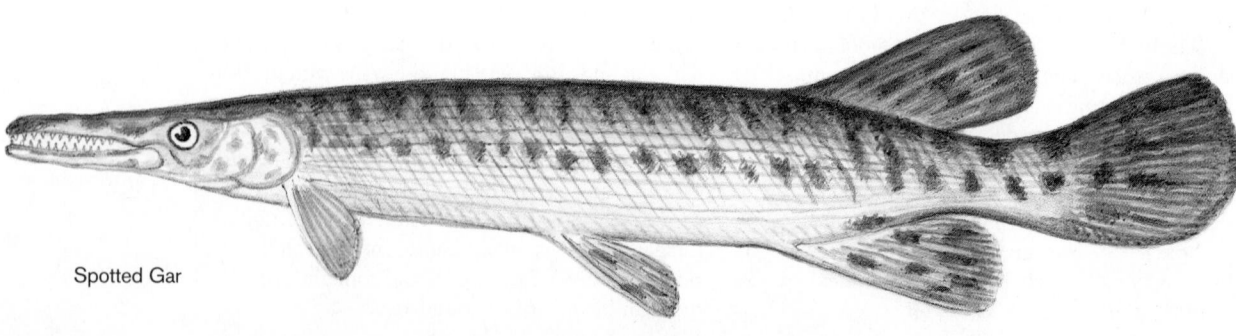

Spotted Gar

extent. In the north of its range, it occurs eastward to the north and south shores of Lake Erie in northern Ohio, Michigan, and Ontario, but it seldom occurs much west of Illinois.

Habitat. The spotted gar is common in the pools and backwaters of creeks and small to large rivers, and in swamps, lakes, and oxbows, often near vegetation. It occasionally enters brackish water and is highly tolerant of warm, stagnant water.

Life history/Behavior. Like other gar, this species is often observed basking on the surface on warm days, resembling a floating log. It occasionally breaks the surface and gulps air from its specialized bladder. Spawning occurs in the spring in grassy sloughs.

See: Gar.

GARFISH
See: Needlefish.

GARRICK *Lichia amia.*
Other names—leerfish; Afrikaans: *leervis;* Arabic: *crhelan, erian, serra;* French: *caranga, liche, liché amie;* Greek: *litsa;* Hebrew: *amit, arian;* Italian: *leccia, lizza;* Polish: *amia;* Serbo-Croat: *bilizma, bjelica, lica;* Spanish: *palometón;* Turkish: *akya baligi, iskender baligi.*

A popular gamefish in the Mediterranean and surrounding areas, the garrick is a large species of the Carangidae family and related to jacks and trevally. It is a fair table fish and has limited commercial food value, marketed mostly fresh.

Identification. A cross between a permit and a mackerel in overall shape, the garrick has an extended body and an unusually curvy lateral line, which arches high over the pectoral fins, dips to or below the pectoral fins, and rises back to the midline as it nears the tail. In many members of the Carangidae family, there is a prominent lobe at the beginning of the long second dorsal and anal fins; however, the garrick has short pectoral fins and no scutes. The first dorsal fin consists of eight very short, almost detached spines. The second dorsal fin has 1 spine and 19 to 21 rays. The anal fin has three spines, two of them separate, preceding the rest of the fin, and 17 to 21 rays. A silvery fish with a leathery, scaleless appearance, it is actually covered with minute embedded scales and is dusky to brown or blue gray, with a white belly. The fin lobes may be black or dusky tipped, and juveniles less than 4 inches long have orangish to brownish black bars on their sides.

Size. The garrick can reach a weight of 71 pounds, which is the South African angling record for the species. The official all-tackle world record is for a 51-pound, 3-ounce fish taken from Italian waters in 1991.

Distribution. In the eastern Atlantic Ocean, garrick occur from the southern Bay of Biscay to

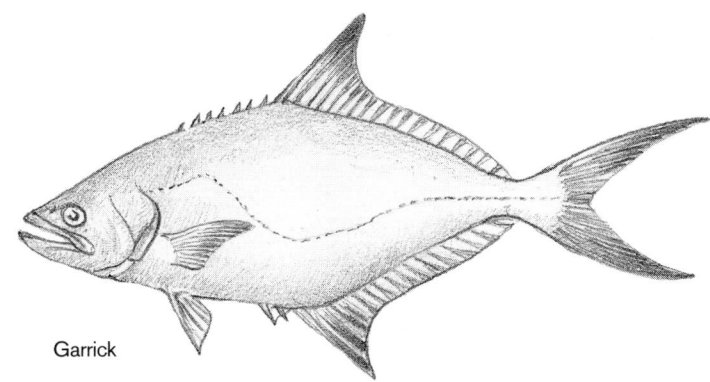

Garrick

South Africa, including the Mediterranean. In the western Indian Ocean they occur from South Africa to Delagoa Bay, Mozambique. The Eastern Cape region of South Africa probably has the best garrick angling in the world.

Habitat. Found in coastal waters, garrick form small schools in estuaries and in the surf zone off beaches and rocky promontories. The garrick is seasonally migratory, some populations moving south to the cape in summer and north to Natal in winter, possibly following the sardine run occurring at those times.

Food. The young eat crustaceans, and adult garrick feed primarily on fish.

Angling. A highly rated sportfish, the garrick is pursued from rocks or from shore, as well as from boats. It takes both live baits, such as mullet and sardines, and lures with zeal. Bluefish (known as elf in South Africa) are one of its favorite foods when aggressively foraging along the coasts, and it is not uncommon to see garrick chasing mullet on the surface.

GEAR RATIO *(and Line Recovery)*
The heart of any reel is the gear set. The moment that the handle is turned, the gears engage and the reel begins to recover line, either for the purpose of retrieving a lure or bait, or for fighting a fish. The demands placed upon the gears vary with the manner of fishing and the species, and performance is influenced by certain mechanical factors and product properties.

Gear Basics
The gear set in a typical fishing reel consists of the drive gear, pinion gear, oscillation gear(s) or levelwind gear(s), and perhaps a transfer gear. Of these, the most important are the drive and pinion gears, which establish the speed or power found in any reel.

The drive gear is usually directly linked to the reel handle in a spinning reel and indirectly through a drag mechanism in a baitcasting reel or a conventional reel. The purpose of the gear is to set the retrieve of the reel. The pinion gear is normally smaller in diameter than the drive gear and connects to the rotor of the spinning reel or to the spool

G

in revolving spool reels. The diametric difference between the drive and pinion gears constitutes the basic numerical ratio of any reel. The number of individual gear teeth machined into each gear is used to calculate the precise ratio.

In almost any simple gear set, one gear material is normally harder than the other. This both directs and controls the action of the two parts throughout their life and actually keeps the gears running smoothly for a longer period. Two hardened gears running together would amplify even the smallest machining imperfection or piece of grit on the gear teeth.

It is common in spinning reels for the pinion gear to be made of brass. This is hard material, and it allows for the more intricate machining required in this smaller part as well as absorbs the greater anticipated wear in this gear with its fewer teeth. The corresponding drive gear is most often made of aluminum in quality reels, and is sometimes made of easily die cast zinc, which tends to be somewhat harder than aluminum. In either case, the gear teeth should be machined as precisely as possible to ensure smooth operation and long life.

Baitcasting and conventional reels typically use brass for the drive gear and bronze for the pinion. Here, too, the hardness differential favors the smaller diameter pinion gear to provide longer life. The gears in these reels are generally smaller than those in spinning reels, and they require a still greater degree of precision and strength. The other gears in any reel will not face anywhere near the stresses and loads encountered by the drive and pinion and therefore do not need to be significantly harder.

Almost all reel gears in better-quality fishing reels are helically milled. This means that each gear tooth is curved, rather than straight, on the gear circumference. Helical milling results in greater strength, thicker cross section, and a high degree of inherent smoothness. The major benefit is that, unlike straight-milled gears where only a single gear tooth is fully engaged at one time, helical gears allow at least partial engagement of several gear teeth at all times, spreading the load and potential wear.

The best way to prolong the life and performance of reel gears is regular maintenance and

This view of helical reel gears helps illustrate the way these objects relate to each other and how numerical ratio is determined by the number of teeth on the respective gears.

lubrication. Heavily used reels should be cleaned and properly relubricated on at least an annual basis. A midseason lubricant check, and possibly a small addition, can also be helpful. Even the best-designed and best-produced gear set can eventually wear out or strip, regardless of regular maintenance or lubrication. Ordinary wear failure results from a weakening of the gear teeth through the removal of material over time. The typical warning of impending failure is that the gears seem to become rougher and "sloppy," with an increase in free play. The final failure results in the gear teeth skipping over one another, particularly in a small area of the handle rotation. Once this occurs, you should replace both the drive and the pinion gears.

Gear Ratio

The basic numerical ratio of the drive and pinion gears in any fishing reel merely establishes the number of revolutions made by the reel spool or rotor per turn of the reel handle. That number is determined by counting the gear teeth on the larger drive gear and dividing that by the tooth count of the smaller pinion gear.

In a gear set consisting of a 60-tooth drive gear and a 12-tooth pinion gear, the ratio would be calculated at 5:1 (read as "five to one"), since the pinion will turn five times for each full rotation of the drive gear. The drive gear is normally linked to the reel handle, and the pinion gear is engaged with the spool or rotor. Thus, in a 5:1 ratio reel, one turn of the handle will cause the spool or rotor to turn five times.

Typical low gear ratios are 3.5:1 or 4:1, and typical high gear ratios are 6:1, although they range both higher and lower. The average or all-around ratio for a spinning reel used in freshwater is 5.2:1. For a baitcasting reel, it is 5.1:1; and for a conventional (inshore trolling) reel, it is 3.8:1. These ratios are often referred to in terms of speed; for example, a high gear ratio reel is frequently called a high-speed reel, but in fact gear ratio does nothing more than designate the mechanical gear action of the reel, which is not the whole story about the true speed of any reel.

Line recovery. To determine the useful speed, the mechanical ratio must also be factored by the size of the reel spool, creating a geometric ratio that establishes how much line is wound onto the spool with each turn of the reel handle. The geometric ratio for every reel is determined by spool diameter, which is a key dimension for any reel and which sets the circumference of the line level on the spool and the amount of line wound onto the spool with each turn of the reel handle. What the geometric ratio really establishes is a more meaningful number than gear ratio: the *line recovery* ability of an individual reel, or the length of line placed back onto the spool per turn of the handle.

For example, a 4.4:1 gear ratio reel with a 2-inch-diameter spool will recover 13.8 inches of line per turn of the handle. A 6.2:1 ratio reel with a

Line Recovery by Spool Diameter/Gear Ratio

Spool (line level)	Numerical gear ratio		
diameter (in inches)	4.4:1	5.1:1	6.2:1
1.25	5.39	6.25	7.60
1.50	7.77	9.01	10.95
1.75	10.58	12.26	14.91
2.00	13.82	16.01	19.47**
2.25	17.49	20.27	24.65*
2.50	21.59**	25.03*	30.42
2.75	26.13	30.28	36.82
3.00	31.09	36.04	43.82
3.25	36.498	42.30	51.42
3.50	42.33	49.06	59.65
3.75	48.59	56.32	68.47
4.00	55.29	64.08	77.90

* A quarter-inch of increased spool diameter makes an average gear ratio reel (5.1:1) faster than a high numerical ratio model (6.2:1).

** A half-inch of increased spool diameter makes a low gear ratio reel (4.4:1) faster than a high numerical ratio model (6.2:1).

1.5-inch-diameter spool will recover less than 11 inches of line per handle turn. Therefore, it is the size of the spool in combination with gear ratio that most affects the recovery of the line. In the aforementioned example, the 6.2:1 reel would be considered a high-speed model based on its numerical gear ratio. But, by comparison, the "slower" 4.4:1 reel will move a lure through the water at a faster speed per turn of the reel handle. Of course, if that 6.2:1 gear ratio reel were equipped with a 2-inch-diameter spool, it would take up almost 19.5 inches of line per handle turn, which is much greater than the 4.4:1 reel.

The point is that you need to know how much line a reel will recover per turn of the handle in order to compare it to another reel; gear ratio alone does not provide enough comparison. Obviously, two reels with identical gear ratios but different spool circumferences will have different recovery rates.

The preceding table shows a line-recovery comparison of spool (line level) diameters by typical numerical gear ratios. These calculations have been simplified by using the maximum line level diameter at all times for the highest resulting linear value, but bear in mind that spools are not normally filled to their maximum possible capacity, and should not be, for practical fishing use. In normal fishing use, the line level will vary as line leaving the spool reduces the working circumference; differences in line thickness can further reduce the line level even when casting identical distances.

The dimensions used in this table are representative of a wide variety of spinning reels marketed for uses from ultralight freshwater through heavy saltwater applications. The same pattern holds for other types of reels, although the range of spool diameters is less broad. A typical baitcasting reel spool will have a diameter between 1.25 and 1.5 inches. Heavier-duty conventional casting and trolling reels can range to spool diameters of over 4 inches.

As shown by the numbers with single asterisks, a quarter-inch of increased spool diameter makes an average gear ratio reel (5.1:1) faster than a high numerical ratio model. An increase of a half-inch in diameter can make a "slow" numerical ratio reel (4.4:1) faster than the one that is generally accepted as high speed, as indicated by those examples with double asterisks.

Thus, selecting a reel for a particular technique, lure type, or species of fish involves not only considering numerical ratio, but also line recovery rate to get the best tackle advantage. But there are still other considerations.

Cranking Power

Although the line recovery rate of any reel affects how much line is wound onto the spool, the numerical ratio of a reel indicates the available cranking power of the gear set. This is similar to the operation of an automotive transmission, where the lower ratio of the first and second gears is much more powerful because these gears transmit greater torque to overcome inertia. Once the vehicle is moving, it is easy to step up in gears through second and third to fourth gear or higher. The low-ratio power gears aren't designed for speed, and the high-ratio speed gears aren't designed for power. Try to move a manual transmission car from dead-still in fourth gear and see what happens.

In a fishing reel, the ability to winch in a sizable fish—or any object with great resistance—is achieved only through a powerful, low-numerical-ratio gear set. "Pumping" a fish during the fight is recommended with any tackle, but it is almost mandatory with high-ratio reels. You have more ability to crank a fish toward you with a power ratio of 3.5:1 or 4.4:1. These ratios in a reel with a respectable spool diameter deliver a compromise of line recovery and gear power that is hard to beat.

Certain applications or situations demand a conscious choice of gear ratios. When using a highly water resistant lure, such as a deep-running crankbait with a large lip, the ideal choice would be

 One of the worst red tide events on record occurred in 1946–47 off Florida and is estimated to have killed 500 million fish.

G

a low-numerical-ratio reel. A 3.8:1 gear set can comfortably deliver the necessary power to drive this bait down and through the water with minimal wear and tear on the angler. A very high-speed reel can bind under the line load created by this lure's water resistance. Trying to fish high-speed lures with a slow 3.8:1 ratio would wear out most casters before lunch time. The effort required to turn the handle fast enough to work a truly high-speed lure would be exhausting.

It is more difficult and fatiguing to reel a slow-ratio gear set fast than to reel a high-ratio gear set slowly. A high-ratio reel can easily be used to retrieve slow-technique lures or bait as long as they do not create a great deal of water resistance. However, some anglers make the mistake of fishing too fast by virtue of using a high-speed reel when they really need to be fishing more slowly. For instance, when a lure or technique calls for a slow presentation or retrieve, anglers sometimes inadvertently retrieve too fast because of their reel; in such a situation, a slow-speed reel would be better if you cannot keep using a fast-speed reel slowly.

Some surf anglers will remember that an ideal choice for use with either high- or low-speed retrieve lures was the original Crack 300 spinning reel, an expensive imported reel that had a spool diameter of 3.75 inches and a power ratio of 3.2:1 and that was a forerunner for that market until production ceased in the 1980s. It provided anglers with a superb combination of line recovery and gear power, and was one of the most respected surf fishing reels ever made. The benefits of such a diameter and power ratio for that activity were such that other manufacturers later developed reels with similar attributes.

The simplest and most powerful reel ratio is 1:1. This is commonly found in almost all flycasting reels, which typically do not have gear sets but are direct drive. They are also typically slow, especially when the level of line is low, such as when a fish has stripped the fly line off the reel and gone down to the much-thinner diameter backing. A few of the more modern designs of saltwater flycasting reels achieve greater line recovery speed by increasing spool diameter. They are employing the geometry factor to achieve a line recovery advantage. The capacity of the reel, however, does not necessarily increase. This is because the central arbor area of the spool is also increased in diameter. This large arbor helps minimize line set, and it reduces the amount of backing required to properly fill the spool. One such 10-weight reel needs 27 percent fewer turns of the handle to retrieve a 90-foot line than a standard design reel. It recovers more line and puts less wear on the angler, and is still a powerful 1:1 reel, but it may not have the total capacity (fly line and backing) that some fishing circumstances warrant.

True big-game fishing reels start out with fairly powerful ratios (3.1:1 to 3.5:1) and large-diameter spools. These reels are expected and designed to deal with big, powerful fish. The large spool diameter allows for sufficient line capacity in a variety of line tests and for acceptable line recovery. Fishing for big game species requires power to control their movements and bring them to the boat as quickly as possible. Large-diameter spools on big-game reels can rapidly recover line when a speedy fish charges the boat or even when clearing lines from the trolling pattern upon hookup. The 3.1:1 ratio is, of course, mechanically powerful. Anglers can quickly wind significant amounts of line onto the spool and have the ability to winch in line against a large fish.

Two-Speed Reels

Sometimes even a powerful 3.1:1 gear ratio isn't enough to control big-game species. Controlling these fish can often require a reel with two separate gear ratios. In the case of the modern two-speed big-game reels, the ratio shifts from the typical 3.1:1 to the still lower and more powerful 1.3:1. The very largest two-speed big-game reels intended for use in fighting giant fish can offer ratios such as 4.0:1 and 1.7:1 or 4.5:1 and 2.0:1. In these cases, the reel delivers both the speed necessary to catch up to a charging gamefish and the power to exert control over its movements.

These reels change gear sets in different ways. Some demand that the angler physically relocate the reel handle to switch gears. Simpler designs require the push of a button to shift in one direction and the turn of a knob or movement of a lever to return to the original ratio. All of these operations have to be fast and easy to permit up and down shifting in the heat of battling a large, powerful fish. And, obviously, the gear sets have to be strong, precise, and durable to withstand the stresses applied.

Attempts at producing multiple-speed spinning reels have not been successful, although a few manufacturers have applied a good deal of time and effort to the project. Two-speed baitcasting reels have been introduced, and these unique tools provided both a higher speed ratio and a true power ratio in a single reel suited for most freshwater and some inshore saltwater applications. Some of these products even offer an automatic shifting design that downshifts as the load on the line increases (as upon hookup). When the load decreases, such as when a fish turns toward the angler, the reel automatically upshifts to permit rapid recovery of line with the higher-ratio gears and to catch up to the movements of the fish. This reel also allows the angler to adjust the amount of force needed to cause the gears to shift up or down. It's a very versatile item and ideal if the amount of tackle available to you is limited.

Retrieval Considerations

Some of the important fishing considerations relative to this subject have already been noted, but it's worth recapping these to emphasize some of the

The first writing devoted to fishing, *The Treatyse of Fysshynge with an Angle,* appeared in *The Boke of St. Alban's* in 1496. Authorship was attributed to Dame Juliana Berners, although some historians dispute this.

advantages and disadvantages of different ratios and line recoveries.

Although recent trends favor high-ratio or so-called high-speed reels, and many people equate speed with fishing value, it is important to recognize that line recovery is the real issue, not speed. Reels with a technically low gear ratio, but a high line-recovery rate, are actually better in situations where large fish are encountered, powerful fish are played, and where hard-pulling lures are cranked. These reels simply have more power, are less likely to bind, are less likely to get stripped gears (assuming the gears are of strong material to start with), and require less effort to land tough fish.

One of the main reasons why high-speed reels are popular in freshwater is because most of the fish caught in freshwater are small on average (bass and walleye, in particular) or do not put up a long tackle-testing struggle. Anglers like the high-speed retrieves because, among other reasons, they feel that they can quickly catch up to fish that run toward them (as many bass do). This is only true when the spool diameter is large enough to permit a lot of line recovery with each turn of the handle, and if the fish is not so large as to be difficult to handle.

People who fish jigs and worms in freshwater are likely to be good candidates for a reel with a high gear ratio, since it lets them pick up a lot of slack with each turn of the handle. But fishing a large spinnerbait and especially a deep-diving plug will be wrist-punishing unless the reel has cranking power for the drive, meaning that a slow-speed reel is preferable there.

For many anglers who cast and retrieve lures, especially those using baitcasting tackle, a reel with 5.1:1 retrieve ratio is a good all-around choice for most fishing, especially if the line recovery is adequate.

See: Baitcasting Tackle; Big-Game Tackle; Conventional Tackle; Flycasting Tackle; Reel, Fishing; Spincasting Tackle; Spinning Tackle.

GEORGIA

Georgia gained what seems like everlasting fame in the freshwater fishing world when George Perry landed a 22-pound, 4-ounce largemouth bass in Lake Montgomery, an oxbow of the Ocmulgee River, in 1932. That fish became the most coveted of all world records and also one of the longest-standing ones.

Catching a fish like that today in Georgia is unlikely, but this in no way overshadows the abundant and high-quality resources existing in the Peach State. In fact, anglers still go to rivers like the Ocmulgee, where fishing is as good or better than ever, especially in the southern half of the state, where lakes are scarce.

Georgia's fishery has changed markedly in many respects. Today anglers can choose from nine huge U.S. Army Corps of Engineers reservoirs, totaling some 500,000 acres, that teem with native large-mouth bass, catfish, and bream, plus such popular additions as pure-strain striped bass, spotted bass, and hybrid stripers. A superb trout management program thrives in north Georgia, taking in some 4,000 miles of mountain streams, as well as the Chattahoochee River down to Atlanta.

Not to be overlooked is Georgia's biggest secret asset: saltwater fishing. The 100-mile-long Georgia coast has the largest saltwater marsh in the eastern United States. This fertile estuary sustains a vast resource of inshore species, especially large populations of seatrout, redfish, and flounder, plus big tarpon.

Freshwater

The largest state east of the Mississippi River, Georgia has a varied landscape that is reflected in its resources and freshwater fishing opportunities. Rolling hills, coastal plains, the Appalachian Mountains, the Okefenokee Swamp, and the rivers that flow to the Atlantic Ocean or the Gulf of Mexico provide divergence. Although it has no large natural lakes, as the result of river impoundments Georgia does have big waters, some of which it shares with neighboring states. Several of these are among the most heavily used recreation sites in North America.

Mountain Waters

Lake Allatoona. Allatoona, a 11,860-acre Corps of Engineers reservoir on the Eltowah River, has a good combination of structure—deep and clear in the main body, and flats around rivers—that gives anglers a variety of fishing.

Striped bass are plentiful here, and have been caught up to 40 pounds. They are a favorite quarry in winter, although some anglers catch stripers in mid-summer in the cool pockets of deeper water. Hybrid striped bass, which are nearly four times as abundant as pure-strain stripers, also provide excitement.

Crappie fishing is good year-round, although most anglers concentrate on the spring. The black bass population is about 80 percent spotted bass, which favor the mountainlike structure, and fishing is considered good. To have consistent success, however, an angler must spend some time learning the lake. Boat traffic can be a problem at Allatoona, which is less than an hour from Atlanta; the lake gets heavy use from boats of all sizes.

Lake Blue Ridge. Walleye, white bass, small-mouth bass, and bluegills are the most sought-after species in Lake Blue Ridge, a 3,290-acre Tennessee Valley Authority (TVA) reservoir in Fannon County. Walleye fishing is best in the spring and fall. The white bass run begins in early February, with a lot of activity centered on Toccoa River shoals at the head of the reservoir. Smallmouth fishing is good except during the annual November to February drawdown, when ramp access is limited. Fishing is also good for yellow perch, channel catfish, and flathead catfish, and the lake has been known for large bluegills (bream), especially around fish attractors in 15 to 20 feet of water.

G

Lake Burton. Lake Burton, a 2,775-acre power company reservoir in the northeast and west of Clayton, is noted for good spotted bass and largemouth bass angling. Trophy-size largemouths are caught in February and March, and fishing for spots peaks in May and November. Burton is also an excellent yellow perch fishery, and although the average perch are not jumbos, a $2^1/_2$-pound state record was caught here. Bream and catfish are also excellent during summer months. Large shellcrackers inhabit the Cherokee Cove area, and good-size channel cats come from Timpson, Wildcat, and Cherokee Coves.

Carters Lake. A popular 3,220-acre Corps of Engineers reservoir, Carters is between Calhoun and Ellijay on the Coosawattee River. With deep, clear water it is known for large spotted bass—many over 6 pounds—and a good population of striped bass, some of which have reached 20 pounds. Walleye, introduced in 1995, are growing into an excellent fishery; catches average 20 inches and 3 pounds, and are expected to do very well here thanks to ample gizzard and threadfin shad forage. Crappie fishing is fair and getting better as the forage fish base grows. The key to success with any species here is power generation. Carters is a pumpback operation, and when generation stops, the fish become inactive.

Lake Chatuge. Spotted bass dominate Lake Chatuge, a 7,050-acre TVA reservoir that straddles the Georgia–North Carolina border. Largemouth bass, which are heavier on average than spots, take a back seat to their cousins, and once-populous smallmouth (home of a 7-pound 2-ounce state record in 1973) continue to dwindle. White bass and walleye populations have been increasing, and hybrid stripers make for exciting catches at times. The state record hybrid, which weighed 25 pounds 8 ounces, was caught here, but most hybrids are in the 2- to 4-pound range. Chatuge also offers a good population of channel catfish.

Lake Hartwell. Georgia and South Carolina share Lake Hartwell, a deep, clear, 56,000-acre reservoir and the northernmost in a chain of Corps of Engineers dams on the Savannah River. Hartwell is distinguished for a number of reasons, perhaps the best being that it receives light fishing pressure when compared with other large Georgia impoundments. Another plus is that it offers the chance to catch spotted bass and largemouths on back-to-back casts, rather than in the usual order of three or more spots to one largemouth.

Although the lake has not been known for large black bass, it does provide a high average catch rate. Crappie fishing is also excellent, and there is always the chance of landing a hybrid or striped bass. White bass are here as well, and the Tugalo River provides notable action in April and May, when the spawning run for this species is underway. Because it is still underutilized, Hartwell provides the chance for a solitary fishing experience in a pristine, rustic setting.

Lake Lanier. Calling the 38,800-acre Lanier a mountain lake might seem improbable, but its qualities—depth and clarity—are those of a mountain lake, and it is in the foothills of north Georgia, even if it is only 45 minutes north of Atlanta. Although recreational boating traffic is heavy, the fishing is still excellent. The most popular species here are spotted bass—very few anglers fish for largemouth anymore—striped bass, and crappie.

Lanier is a championship striper lake. On a good day, catching six isn't unusual, and the average will be 11 to 12 pounds with some in the 25- to 30-pound range. Winter is best for stripers, but there's good fishing in late fall and early spring. The state record spotted bass, which weighed 8 pounds, 5 ounces, was caught at Lanier; and this is not an accident. Fishing for spots is good year-round. The spring white bass spawning run also makes for great action, and crappie fishing is excellent in the winter around major marinas.

Lake Nottely. Largemouth bass, spotted bass, striped bass, and crappie are the most popular species on Lake Nottely, a 4,180-acre TVA lake in Union County, but it also has smallmouth bass, walleye, and large yellow perch. Nottely has a reputation for producing big largemouth bass, which thrive here in greater numbers than do spotted bass. Stripers are plentiful, and many specimens are in the 8- to 15-pound range. Half-pound crappie are numerous. Walleye were stocked in the early 1990s.

Lake Russell. Impounded in 1984, Lake Russell is Georgia's newest Corps of Engineers project. It is a remote, almost pristine, 26,650-acre reservoir and is one of the best crappie lakes in Georgia because of the timber left standing in its depths. An impoundment of the Savannah River on the South Carolina border, Russell is downstream of Lake Hartwell. Largemouth bass average about $1^1/_2$ pounds, but some go to 10 pounds. There is a growing spotted bass population, and increasing numbers of stripers, which are arriving from other lakes in the system. Although walleye aren't stocked, an 11-pound, 6-ounce state record was caught at Russell in 1995, and most catches of this species come from the lower third of the lake.

Lake Weiss. Most of Lake Weiss is in Alabama, but a 2,000-acre portion is in Georgia. Weiss is noted nationwide for its springtime crappie fishing. Groups in convoys from as far away as 1,000 miles make the spring pilgrimage and go home with full creels. Overlooked, however, is the good fishing for largemouth bass, although most are in the $1^1/_2$- to 2-pound range. White bass fishing is excellent during the annual spring spawning run, and striped bass fishing is improving annually on the lower Coosa River.

Trout fishing. Georgia boasts approximately 4,000 miles of trout streams throughout the Chattahoochee National Forest in the north Georgia mountains. The Chattahoochee River, from the mountains down to Atlanta's city limits, is considered one of the top trout streams in the Southeast. Because soils are low in calcium, and trout streams are relatively unproductive in their natural state, most of the fishing is for stocked rainbow, brown, and brook trout. This is primarily an annual put-and-take fishery, but the occasional big brown or rainbow survives the initial stocking and lives two or more years, mainly on the Chattahoochee. More than 100,000 anglers buy trout stamps and enjoy this fishery, which is testimony to its quality and popularity.

On the Chattahoochee, anglers fish with fly rods, waders, and tubes, and cast flies into rushing rapids. They watch their offerings float toward a trout, suspended and waiting in an eddy downstream, in a mountainlike atmosphere—all while traffic roars overhead on an Interstate 285 bridge. Smaller mountain streams yield smaller fish but offer a more gentle ambiance. Many streams are seasonal (March through October), but others, including portions of the Chattahoochee, are open year-round.

Middle Georgia

Clarks Hill. Called Strom Thurmond Lake in neighboring South Carolina, 71,535-acre Clarks Hill is the largest Corps of Engineers reservoir in the Southeast. It might also be the best fishing lake in the state because of its balance of structure and fertility, and because its distance from metropolitan Atlanta enables it to remain relatively uncrowded.

Largemouth bass fishing here rates among the best in the state, and the angling is good year-round, especially at the flats near the confluence of the Savannah and Broad Rivers. Hybrid and striped bass fishing is particularly productive; catches average 3 to 7 pounds. Crappie fishing is excellent and especially good in the spring. Shellcrackers are big, many in the $^1/_2$- to $^3/_4$-pound range, and white perch are numerous and easy to catch. Clarks Hill also is home of the state record blue catfish, a 62-pounder.

Lake Jackson. Relatively small at 4,750 acres, and very old (impounded in 1910), Jackson could still possibly be the best big bass lake in Georgia. From October through February, this power company reservoir in Jasper, Butts, and Newton Counties yields many largemouth in the 5-pound-plus category. It produces big crappie, too, with some slabs reaching 2 pounds (the lake record is $3^1/_2$ pounds). Panfish fanciers will find that Jackson has some of the best and biggest bluegills, shellcrackers, and redbreast sunfish, and a huge population of white catfish.

Lakes Sinclair and Oconee. Some say that 14,750-acre Sinclair, and 19,050-acre Oconee, are among the best crappie fishing lakes in the state. Angling for these species is good year-round on both lakes, but it's best from February through April.

Both are power company impoundments on the Ocmulgee River, but Sinclair is older. Extensive development around Sinclair's shores, and thousands of boat docks, compensate for the deterioration of

West Point is one of Georgia's largest and most popular lakes.

its natural structure. While Oconee retains some natural structure, it is also loaded with boat docks, albeit upscale ones, because this is the hot lake property for metropolitan Atlanta, which is only 60 miles to the west. Largemouth bass fishing on Oconee is good, but mostly for smaller specimens; Sinclair has bigger, though unpublicized, bass. Both lakes have good fishing for hybrid stripers. Anglers also visit Oconee for white bass, and Sinclair for its excellent supply of channel catfish.

West Point. One of the state's most consistent producers of 5- to 7-pound largemouth bass, West Point is a 25,900-acre Corps of Engineers reservoir on the Chattahoochee River, along the Alabama border. The lake's natural fertility and 16-inch minimum size limit for largemouths produce superior fishing for this species year-round. Hybrid stripers have a glowing reputation as well; nearly 40 percent of this species is in the 15- to 20-inch category. Springtime crappie fishing is outstanding, but it runs good year-round. West Point is also the best channel catfish lake in middle Georgia, offering an abundant supply of these fish in the 12- to 14-inch range.

Bartlett's Ferry, Goat Rock, Oliver. These three lakes, forming a small chain, are older power company reservoirs on the Chattahoochee River, downstream of West Point Lake. Bartlett's Ferry, at 5,850 acres, has excellent fishing for largemouth bass and spotted bass; good fishing for white bass, hybrid stripers, and crappie; and good to excellent fishing for catfish. Goat Rock, at 940 acres, has good fishing for largemouth bass, shoal bass, spotted bass, and catfish; excellent fishing for bream; and a growing fishery for hybrid stripers. Oliver, at 2,150 acres and within the city limits of Columbus, is usually too busy with recreational boats during the summer but has good largemouth bass angling in the fall and winter, with some fish up to 10 pounds. Crappie are good in late winter and early spring, and bream are excellent as well.

South Georgia

Lake Walter F. George.   Also known as Lake Eufaula, 45,180-acre Lake George is yet another Corps of Engineers reservoir on the Chattahoochee River. It is one of the best largemouth bass fishing lakes in the Southeast, and definitely the best summertime fishing lake in Georgia, for two reasons: It has great structure, which gives bass shelter, and it has a 16-inch minimum size limit that has produced largemouth averaging 3 to 4 pounds, along with trophies 10 pounds or better. The hottest period is from mid-March through May, but fishing is consistently good year-round. Crappie angling is excellent all year but starts heating up in February and March. The fish average 12 inches and can weigh upward of 2 pounds. The catfish population is dominated by channel catfish, but the population of blue catfish is on the rise. Angling is good for both species. White bass and hybrid stripers are abundant here, and striper fishing, with larger specimens providing excitement, has become more popular in recent years.

Lake Seminole.   Formed at the junction of the Flint and Chattahoochee Rivers, Lake Seminole is a 37,500-acre Corps of Engineers reservoir in the southwest corner of the state on the Florida border. It is like no other lake in Georgia. Topography and wildlife not seen anywhere else—large concentrations of waterfowl, alligators, lily pads, and standing timber—give it a tropical appearance.

Many places claim to be year-round fisheries, but Seminole really is just that. Thousands of northern anglers plan winter fishing vacations to Seminole, where they have great success if they learn the key. Because this lake is covered with aquatic vegetation, anglers have to learn to fish weedbeds by casting worms, spinnerbaits, or topwater lures along the edges of these beds for Seminole's bass. The reward is an average small keeper of 12 to 14 inches, but bass weighing 5 pounds or more exist in the Flint and Chattahoochee arms.

Hybrid bass fishing is also excellent at Seminole. Fish averaging 2 to 3 pounds are caught in open water away from weeds. Crappie fishing is not a main attraction at Seminole, but this fishery is good in the spring and fall. Channel catfish generally provide excellent fishing in the main lake and in the Flint and Chattahoochee arms.

Lake Blackshear.   When the dam broke, the flood of 1994 virtually made a new lake of this 7,000-acre reservoir west of Cordele on the Flint River. It may go through the "new lake" syndrome for a while,

providing south Georgia with hot fishing. This is a shallow, stained body of water with lots of cypress knees, but most of the lake's structure is formed by docks from the many homes on the highly developed western side. Large populations of crappie provide excellent fishing, especially around 12 scattered fish attractors; the best time to fish is February and March. More than 65 percent of the lake's bream are 6 inches long and upward of $^3/_4$ pound. Fishing for these is most productive in May and June. Striped and hybrid bass fishing is good, with special regulations in effect for these species. Fishing is good for smaller channel catfish, especially in deeper water where creek and river channels meet.

Lake Chehaw.   Partly inside the Albany city limits, Lake Chehaw—a 1,400-acre power company impoundment—is fed by the Flint River and creeks. Chehaw is not noted for big largemouth bass, although numbers of 1- to 3-pounders are caught in the backs of creeks in the spring and fall, and in the main lake during the summer. Hybrid bass fishing is also good in summer. Channel catfish averaging 2 pounds are plentiful in coves and on flats in the spring, and along main river and creek channels during the summer. Fishing is fair to good for crappie, bluegills, and redear sunfish (shellcrackers).

The Southeast Coastal Plain

This huge area, nearly half the state, is so flat that it is unsuitable for large impoundments, so anglers fish farm ponds, rivers, and creeks. Fortunately, much of Georgia's 12,000 miles of warmwater streams are in this area, and some of the more notable ones are noted here.

Altamaha River.   The Chattahoochee might be the best known and longest river in Georgia, but the Altamaha is the biggest. It starts at the convergence of the Ocmulgee and Oconee near Lumber City and meanders more than 100 miles down to the Atlantic Ocean. The fishing is so good that the Altamaha hosts many largemouth bass tournaments each year, and catch rates are among the best. Although largemouths can be caught year-round, fishing peaks in the spring and again in late fall. A 44-pound, 12-ounce state record channel catfish and a 58-pound, 7-ounce state record flathead catfish were caught in the Altamaha, and even larger flatheads should be taken in the future. This fishery begins in early spring and continues through the summer. Crappie fishing is good, especially in the oxbow lakes between Georgia Highway 84 and the Seaboard Railroad. The redbreast sunfish have declined, but fishing is still good for bluegills and shellcrackers.

Ocmulgee River.   The large, sluggish Ocmulgee originates at Jackson Lake and flows 251 miles southward to converge with the Oconee River and form the Altamaha River. The fishery north of U.S. 280 differs from the fishery to the south. To the north, sportfish numbers are dominated by shoal bass, redeye bass, and redbreast sunfish in the shoals, and largemouth bass, bluegills, and redear sunfish (shellcrackers) in the slower stretches. Below U.S. 280, largemouth bass are numerous, but pressure is heavy and most are caught soon after they reach the 14-inch minimum size. Redbreast sunfish and shellcracker fishing is good; some shellcrackers weigh as much as 1 pound. The best action is in early spring. As on several other south Georgia rivers, flathead catfish, introduced illegally, are growing in number and have significantly impacted the sunfish population.

The lower Ocmulgee includes Lake Montgomery, home of the long-standing world record largemouth bass. Montgomery is accessible only at high water these days, but fish are still there. Today, however, nothing rivals the size of George Perry's 22-pound, 4-ounce specimen. A few anglers still fish for largemouth bass at this famous sloughlike site, but angling is becoming more difficult as the oxbow slowly fills with silt. Someday Montgomery will be gone but not forgotten; it is part of Horse Creek Wildlife Management Area, where an historical landmark commemorates North America's most famous fish.

Oconee River.   With a stable, abundant, and healthy largemouth bass population, the Oconee could be a hotspot. Although it compares favorably with the Altamaha, the Oconee receives the least bass fishing pressure of any river here. During the summer months, fish in the 12- to 14-inch range are plentiful, and numerous lunker-size largemouth thrive here, too. During the winter and early spring, crappie fishing is very good. Fishing for flathead catfish is very good, but the redbreast sunfish population is down due to predation by catfish. Still, some larger redbreasts are caught, along with bluegills and redear sunfish.

Ogeechee River.   The Ogeechee is a redbreast sunfish hotspot, and nearly a quarter of the redbreast caught range between 6 and 8 inches. The best opportunities come during spring and summer, when the river drops into the 3-foot range on the geological survey gauge at Eden. Fishing is also good in April and May, however, when water temperatures rise and water levels range from 5 to 7 feet. Other panfish include bluegills, redear sunfish, and spotted sunfish (called stump-knockers here). Scattered pockets of black crappie provide good cold weather fishing upstream of Midville.

Satilla River.   The Satilla meanders eastward some 260 miles to the Atlantic Ocean and is considered one of the premier redbreast sunfish rivers in the Southeast. Anglers frequently catch fish 8 inches or longer and weighing a pound or more. Fishing is outstanding in April and May, until the water warms; then anglers turn to largemouth bass, crappie, and several species of catfish. Bass fishing peaks in late winter and early spring, when river levels are too high for panfish.

St. Mary's River.   The river winds eastward from the Okefenokee Swamp to the Atlantic Ocean and is the southernmost point in Georgia. Although it doesn't rival the Satilla for trophy fish, the St. Mary's is one of the better redbreast sunfish rivers in southeast Georgia. The St. Mary's is also known for quality largemouth bass, especially in the lower section around King's Ferry.

Savannah River.   North of Augusta, the Savannah is a series of reservoirs, but southward to the Atlantic Ocean it is an outstanding river angling resource. Largemouth bass average $1^{1}/_{2}$ to 5 pounds, and some people hook into bigger ones. Angling is good in most areas of the river, especially at the mouths of creeks and in oxbows, for redbreast and redear sunfish, bluegills, and channel catfish. The state of striped bass fishing is on hold indefinitely, because altered flow conditions in the lower Savannah caused a drastic decline in stripers. The natural flow has been restored, and biologists are waiting for the stripers to find their habitat again. Both pure-strain and hybrid stripers have populated this water, and the Savannah produced record-class hybrid stripers in the past. The flow rate is largely controlled by upstream water releases, and water levels can fluctuate weekly with hydropower demands. This is especially true in summer and can adversely affect fishing.

Suwannee River.   The 33-mile portion of the Suwannee in Georgia offers an experience that differs from that provided by most other Georgia rivers, owing to the influence of the Okefenokee Swamp. The tea-stained waters of this flowage are excellent habitat for chain pickerel, warmouth, flier (shiners), and bullhead, but largemouth bass, bream, and other catfish aren't numerous because of the water's high acidity.

Saltwater

For years, northern anglers—and most Georgians as well—zipped down Interstate 95 through Georgia as fast as they could on the way to Florida, unknowingly bypassing some great inshore saltwater fishing that now even draws native Floridians. With more than 400,000 acres of rich salt marsh along its nearly 100 miles, and with a series of barrier islands—including Ossabaw, Sapelo, Cumberland (18 miles long and the site of Cumberland Island National Seashore), Jekyll, and Saint Simons—the Georgia coast is a rich but underutilized saltwater fishing resource. Inshore, there's outstanding angling for spotted seatrout and red drum (redfish), whiting, flounder, sheepshead, croaker, and tarpon, as well as opportunities for ladyfish, bluefish, sharks, and jack crevalle. Offshore are king mackerel, snapper, grouper, cobia, sharks, barracuda, and black sea bass.

Inshore fishing is best from mid-May through December for most species. September through December are peak months for spotted seatrout and red drum. Warmer months are better for sheepshead, black drum, and some fairly large tarpon, especially in the Altamaha River.

Tarpon are overlooked here, and although Georgia doesn't provide the type of flats action that

 The largest gulf in the world is the Gulf of Mexico; it covers 596,000 square miles and has 3,100 miles of shoreline.

G

occurs in other places, it does have plentiful fish around islands, creeks, and the many bays and streams feeding the Intracoastal Waterway, as well as within a few miles of the barrier island beaches, including fish from 100 to 150 pounds. Tarpon are available from sometime in June until mid-October; September is an excellent period, as these fish are feasting on migratory bait and on abundant forage flushed from coastal environs by storms.

The tremendous amount of food available in the vicinity of the southern barrier islands, known here as the Golden Isles, also draws other prominent species in the same warmer-month time frame. Red drum, in particular, some of which are in the 40- to 60-pound range, are caught in the holes of channels and creeks, and near sandbars, and may be caught concurrent with sharks or tarpon. Sea trout are caught from the beach, along dropoffs, around structures, and on the edges of grassbeds throughout the region.

The key to inshore fishing here, as elsewhere, is the tide. An outgoing tide pulls bait-rich water from the marshes, and all types of fish search the shallows for food. Fluctuations as high as 9 feet during full and new moons and 5 to 7 feet during the rest of the month can muddy the waters, but they can also be a strong influence on angling. Fishing isn't too good from four days before the full or new moon to four days after, as the water clears.

Tides are an element of catching kingfish, an activity pursued several miles off St. Simons in Brunswick Ship Channel, at Portuguese Slough, and in Doboy Channel at the D Buoy. High tide pushes good-colored water to within 3 miles or so of shore, whereas low tide pushes it several miles farther out.

Offshore from Georgia, the ocean bottom is flat, with little structure other than Gray's Reef. This situation is improving, however, as the state continues to add to its artificial reef program, using tires, cement, and even old Liberty ships. The artificial reefs are identified in various literature.

Gray's Reef, 17.5 nautical miles east of Sapelo Island, is a National Marine Sanctuary encompassing an area of approximately 17 square nautical miles. The reef is 55 to 65 feet deep and hosts a wide variety of species, some seasonally present. Those of sportfishing interest include assorted sharks, jacks, mackerel, bluefish, cobia, barracuda, flounder, sea bass, snapper, grouper, and dolphin. The reef is also a prime spot for divers.

Another hotspot is the Navy Tower, a navigation aid for the King's Bay submarine base near St. Mary's, which attracts huge numbers of fish. A few Georgia anglers will go to the Gulf Stream for pelagic species, but the 98-mile one-way trip discourages many.

GERMANY

Spanning from the Alps to the Baltic and North Seas, and covering more than 137,000 square miles

of landscape that includes mountains, forests, plains, and seacoast, the Federal Republic of Germany is a big country with diverse resources in the heart of Europe. Although it does not attract many visiting anglers, especially Westerners, several million Germans enjoy angling, and the country boasts more than a dozen popularly sought species as well as a wide variety of waters.

Bordering on nine European nations, Germany extends some 800 kilometers from south to north and 400 kilometers from west to east, covering an area similar in size to the state of Montana in the United States. The country is divided into 16 states, each with its own fishing governance and each different according to its particular environment, species, and population of fish.

Although a large country, Germany is highly urbanized; 86 percent of its 82 million inhabitants live in communities of at least 2,000 people. More than 1 million anglers are organized in roughly 10,000 clubs. More than 1.5 million people purchase German state fishing licenses annually, and it is believed that another million people who do not require licenses fish in private waters at home or on holiday in other countries.

Although more than 13 million tourists visit Germany annually, angling tourists number almost none; this may be largely due to the country's licensing structure, which requires that anglers pass a test before being granted a state license. For more on this topic, refer to the section "Legislation" below. The few non-Germans who angle here seldom fish on their own. They use all-inclusive packages offered by hotels and pensions (boarding houses), which usually have creek and brook fishing opportunities, or they employ the services of someone who can provide lake access, boats, and sometimes accommodations.

Very well equipped tackle dealers exist in almost every German city. English is commonly spoken, and it is easy for English-speaking visitors to approach the dealers. These people are the best source of advice on where and how to fish in a certain area for a certain species, as well as for advice on obtaining access to local waters.

Land, Climate, and Resources

The Alps are the southernmost border of the republic, and the Zugspitze (2,962 meters or 9,718 feet) is the highest mountain in Germany. Many creeks and rivers flow out of the Alps. These run in a northerly direction, with very high water in the spring and very low water in the fall. All waters enter the Danube River, which flows eastward into Austria and eventually to the Black Sea, thereby forming a drainage area in Germany with a different ecology than one finds in the rest of the country.

In addition to the creeks and rivers in the south, most notable are the Voralpen lakes. The Bodensee is the biggest of these, encompassing 538 square kilometers and having depths up to 252 meters; it lies partly in Austria and Switzerland as well. Other large lakes are the Chiemsee, the Starnberger See, and the Ammersee. The majority of the southern region is in the state of Bayern (Bavaria); the westernmost part of this region is in the district of Baden-Württemberg.

The character of Germany's midlands is formed by many intermediate-size mountains with an average altitude of 500 meters. Deep, large forests cover the mountains. Numerous brooks and creeks run here; these exit the forests to fill water dams (reservoirs) and form or merge with rivers, which include the Danube, the Rhein, the Elbe, and the Weser, all of which flow into the North Sea; and the Oder, which, along with the smaller Neisse River, forms most of eastern Germany's border with Poland and discharges into the Baltic Sea. The Weser, Elbe, and Oder Rivers flow slowly over the lowlands to the north of the country—a wide, mountainless area with some spots below normal sea level, where water is drained by pumps. High dikes along hundreds of kilometers of coastline protect the land facing the fearful North Sea. Quite the contrary exists along the Baltic Sea coast, where a sandy, sometimes stony littoral is bordered by a steep shoreline that is 60 meters high in places.

Northern Germany is characterized by the wide lowlands of the northwest, where the Weser and Elbe Rivers flow into the North Sea and where very large forests cover wide, infertile sandy heather landscapes that include national parks (in the state of Niedersachsen). The Elbe winds from the Czechoslovakian border in the southeast up to the North Sea. The coast of the North Sea is formed by a large, muddy, and slimy dark substrate called the Wattenmeer (Wadden Sea), which undergoes full tidal drying and flooding. This area is also a national park, and known for its unique bird life.

Offshore from the mainland are many large, sandy, and green islands in a pearl-like string; most are inhabited and popular with summer visitors. Their fine, white sand beaches face open sea and are a surf caster's heaven. The most favored sea angling spot in Germany is the rocky island of Helgoland, situated in the middle of the Deutsche Bucht (German Bay). Sixty kilometers from the closest harbor, Helgoland is a rocky island that is 61 meters high and covers 2 square kilometers.

In northeastern Germany the states of Schleswig-Holstein and Mecklenburg-Vorpommern face the Baltic Sea. This large inland sea has natural connections with the North Sea. The littoral area was formed by glaciers, resulting in a sandy, sometimes stony shoreline. The water is crystal clear, and the salinity is only 2 percent (in the North Sea it is 3.5 percent). In cold winters, ice may keep fishing boats in port during January and February.

Germany's climate is determined by medium temperatures (day/night) in January of minus 4° to plus 3°C, and in July of plus 14° to plus 20°C. Rain falls all year long in short periods, mostly driven by western winds. The midlands and lowlands receive 500 to 700 millimeters of rain per year; the mountain areas are flooded by 1,300 millimeters of rain; and 2,000 millimeters of rain fall in the Alps. High winds or stormy weather usually do not last longer than two to three days, and very stormy conditions are restricted to late winter and late autumn.

Beginning late in the nineteenth century, pollution became a serious problem for many of Germany's creeks, rivers, and streams. Salmon, which were found by the hundreds of thousands in big streams in years past, became extinct. Other fish also succumbed to pollution. It was not until the 1970s that a nationwide campaign resulted in strong legislation, high penalties, and a steady improvement in water quality.

German anglers have done a lot to maintain and increase their revived fisheries resources. Management efforts and stocking activities have reintroduced fingerling fish into the watercourses year-round. Today, many brooks and creeks, as well as rivers, are full of brown trout; the lowland rivers have good stocks of sea trout; and Atlantic salmon restocking programs are progressing, supported by the government, with some angling for this species already available.

For the traveling angler, the most notable fishing regions are Fränkische Schweiz (Bavaria); Voralpenland (Bavaria); Schwarzwald (Baden-Württemberg); Sauerland and Rothaargebirge (Nordrhein-Westfalen); the Harz-Mountain area (Niedersachsen); and the lake district (Mecklenburg-Vorpommern).

Germany has a wide variety of fishing waters. These include deep slow-running streams and rivers; fast-running, well-oxygenated brooks; deep coldwater lakes; shallow, warm brown-water lakes; canals; reservoirs (water dams); and abundant small lakes and ponds. All kinds of European freshwater fish thrive in these waters, with a total of some 70 native species, as well as such introduced species as steelhead, lake trout, grass carp, and numerous subspecies. Largemouth and smallmouth bass have reportedly been introduced in some German waters, perhaps illegally, and are said to be a very rare catch.

The most popular species are *aal* (European eels); *äsche* (grayling); *bachforelle* (brown trout); *barsch* (yellow perch); *brassen* (bream); *döbel* (chub); *hecht* (northern pike); *karpfen* (common carp); *meerforelle* (sea-run brown trout); *regenbogenforelle* (rainbow trout); *schleie* (tench); wels (catfish); and zander (pike-perch).

Since late in the twentieth century, anyone in Germany who owns fishable waters is obliged to replace the catch and to preserve the fish, and restoration of fauna and flora in and alongside the watercourses is practiced. Owners take special interest in the most preferred species, such as brown trout, sea trout, grayling, eels, and carp, and in some waters also rainbow trout and pike.

The first officially weighed tuna (183 pounds) caught on sporting tackle was landed off Catalina Island, California, in 1898; however, a few unweighed tuna had been caught previously.

In general, coarse fishing is good throughout the country; trout fishing is satisfactory in some areas; and perch and pike fishing is good in certain lakes, especially in autumn. In saltwater, angling is good for cod year-round, for tope in September, for herring in March and April, for garfish from May through July, and for mackerel in July and August.

Gamefishing

Brown trout are the most popular freshwater fish in Germany. They are caught in almost all cold, quick-running water that flows from the midland mountains. In bigger waters they grow from 5 to 10 pounds, but the normal size is 2 to 3 pounds, with the national record being 35.64 pounds.

Larger brown trout are rare in small brooks; they generally inhabit larger creeks or small rivers, and lowland waters fed by cold springs, such as those in the district of Lüneburger Heide in the state of Niedersachsen.

The best trout fishing opportunities are in the hands of private owners who typically operate hotels and pensions and sell fishing licenses only to their guests. Some waters are owned by clubs or communities, and they sell licenses, too. Most licenses are subject to strong rules regarding minimum size, bag limits, baits, and methods; fly fishing is the main method. The closed season traditionally falls between October 1 and March 31, but these dates may differ among states.

Waters with brown trout sometimes also hold rainbow trout, but anglers usually find them tougher to pinpoint because they roam widely through an entire watercourse. Rainbows do grow big in Germany; the record fish is a 42-pounder, and the average size is about 10 to 12 pounds. All rainbows are stocked, as they do not spawn naturally in Germany.

The best-known sites for trout fishing, listed from north to south by state, include the following:

Bayern (Bavaria). Brooks and creeks running from the Rhön Mountains to the river Fränkische Saale; waters coming from the Fichtelgebirge and Spessart Forests flowing to the Main River; and chalk streams in the Fränkische Schweiz area. The latter features Puttlach, Wiesent, Ailsbach, Leinleiter, and Trubach Creeks; these are famous chalk waters with very good trout and grayling fishing, and are a preferred destination for anglers from abroad, with many hotels accommodating anglers.

Other sites include the Loisach, Lauterbach, Schwarzach, and Zottbach watercourses in the Fränkische Alb area; these rivers flowing from the Alps: Amper, Glonn, Isar, Isen, Inn, Loisach, Mangfall, Ramsauer Ache, Salzach, Sempt, and Traun; the Allgäu district rivers like the Hopferauer Ache, Iller, Lech, Trauchgauer Ach, Trettach, Upper Donau, Vils, and Wertach; and such Schwäbische Alb rivers as the Breitach, Brenz, and Untere Argen.

Baden-Württemberg. In this wine-cultivating state, the Schwarzwald district (known to many as the Black Forest) is especially notable because of its great number of hotels and pensions with first-class trout waters. These are mostly brooks and creeks, and include such watercourses as the Alb, Elz, Gaubach, Grosse Enz, Gutach, Heimbach, Hundsbach, Kinzig, Langenbach, Lauter, Maisach, Murg, Nagold, Oos, Reichenbach, Rench, Schultach, Schutter, Steinbach, Waldach, Wehra, Wiese, and Wolfach.

Rheinland-Pfalz. Trout rivers include the Ahr, Irsen, Kyll, Nims, Our, Prüm, Rur, and Salmbach.

Nordrhein-Westfalen. The Agger, Bigge, Latropbach, Leune, Ruhr, Sieg, and Sorpe watercourses in the Sauerland region are among the area's notable trout rivers.

Hessen. Trout frequent the upper part of the rivers Diemel, Eder, Efze, and Schwalm.

Niedersachsen. All water dams in the mountain region of the Harz; and the rivers Böhme, Este, Ilmenau, Luhe, Ortze, Oste, and Seeve in the Lüneburger Heide region. The latter rivers are supported by massive plantings of trout fingerlings, particularly sea trout (which grow to 20 pounds or more), and some grayling. Most parts of these rivers are rented to clubs, where licenses are often obtained only through membership.

Schleswig-Holstein. The rivers Stör and Treene are famous for sea trout; these have been maintained by angler stocking, and many thousands of fingerlings are annually planted in the watercourses running into these rivers.

Other Salmonids

The sea trout is not only caught in the aforementioned inland rivers and creeks, but also in all creeks and rivers close to the sea, and in the Baltic Sea itself.

Atlantic salmon restoration has resulted in an ongoing, massive reintroduction in all big streams and rivers, but the results have been generally disappointing. Only one river, the Oste in Niedersachsen, has enough salmon to provide yearly sportfishing.

Huchen growing to 130 pounds still exist but are mainly restricted to the Danube River. Nowadays, big huchen are a rare catch, but some huchen are landed each year in other Bavarian rivers due to reintroduction by anglers. These include the Alz, Iller, Ilz, Isar, Lech, Schwarzer Regen, Tiroler Ache, Wertach, and Wurm Rivers. A tiny stock of natives exists in the river Mitternacher Ohe.

Native stocks of charr inhabit the cold, deep lakes close to the Bavarian Alps, and they are planted into some of the water dams in the Harz area of Niedersachsen. Many subspecies are reared in hatcheries and put into many creeks of the midlands, but they seldom reproduce naturally.

Coarse Fishing

Angling for coarse species is popular alongside the banks of slow-running rivers, streams, and channels, as well as in lakes. It is easy to land a large catch of roach and bream on a given day, and a total take weighing a ton is common when clubs fish in competitions.

British needle manufacturers are said to have started making fish-hooks in the mid-1500s; modern hook manufacturing started with the Mustad Company of Norway in 1832.

G

There is also coarse fishing for such popular species as pike and carp. Large pike are numerous and widespread, but the biggest fish and best overall angling for this species occur in the lakes. German anglers are very fond of lake fishing for pike, and autumn is viewed as the best time.

Carp are second to pike in popularity, and some specimens to 65 pounds have been recorded. Because of their high food value, carp have been introduced to almost all brown-, warm-, shallow-water sites, even the smallest ponds. Although the carp is not an indigenous species, it may spawn successfully in especially warm summers. The great fighting ability of carp has led to the formation of Specimen Hunting Groups by German anglers, and these specialists pursue only big carp.

Eels are found everywhere in Germany, and some are caught up to 25 pounds. They favor slow-moving waters in the lowlands and are even in the smallest trenches. Smoked eels—a highly prized delicacy—are the most expensive freshwater fish product in Germany.

Zander inhabit all brown, warm waters, and some have been recorded to 40 pounds. They are a popular market fish and are common in many lakes and rivers, but they are not easily caught.

The wels catfish is the biggest freshwater fish in Germany; the national record is a 165-pounder. Native stocks inhabit the rivers Naab and Regen in Bavaria, the Oderbruch region alongside the river Oder, and the river Wakenitz in northern Germany. Because wels brought a good price in the market, they were introduced to many lakes in all regions of Germany. It is now possible when fishing for other species, like pike or eels, to have a monster wels take the bait. The fish is said to be rare, but its nocturnal and bottom-hugging habits are the true reason for its alleged rarity.

The best way to catch the aforementioned species is to find a professional fisherman; these locals have access to most of the best lakes and can sell licenses and provide rental boats.

Saltwater

Deep-sea angling. Ocean (referred to as deep-sea) angling in Germany from party boats has increased in popularity since the 1960s. In the Baltic Sea, nearly 50 party boats (called charter boats here) operate from German harbors daily, there are about two dozen of them in the North Sea. Most of the boats are former commercial fishing trawlers, but they now have many amenities on board, including a kitchen, small shops, and toilets. They can accommodate up to 50 anglers and travel from 5 to 20 miles offshore. A growing fleet of smaller boats is available for rent, and these carry four to eight anglers. To operate boats with more than a 5-horsepower motor, one must possess a motorboat driver's license *(Motorbootführerschein)*. Small boats for rent are available only along the Baltic.

Deep-sea angling takes place year-round in the Baltic Sea but is restricted to the spring-to-autumn season in the North Sea due to higher winds and waves. Cod are a predominant species here. The record fish is a 62-pounder, and the best season is in May and June, as well as in autumn. The most popular lure is a *pilker* (pirk, or heavy metal jigging lure) weighing 100 to 150 grams, combined with a soft plastic twist tail. Anglers use 20-pound conventional or spinning tackle in the Baltic; 30-pound gear for wreck fishing is favored in the North Sea.

Mackerel fishing is popular in the North Sea from June through the end of August. Herring are caught at a rate of a hundred per day from jetties in the harbors of the Baltic Sea. Anglers pursue the herring during a short peak period in March and April. Tope are caught around Helgoland Island in the North Sea in early autumn. Some professional fishermen offer their open 30-foot boats *(Börteboot)* for shark fishing a few miles off the island, using 30-pound tackle and mackerel for bait. The record weight for tope around the island is more than 200 pounds.

Surf casting. This sport became much more popular with the reintroduction of sea trout late in the twentieth century. Sea-run brown trout are reared in great numbers in hatcheries managed by anglers.

The entire shoreline of the Baltic is sea trout territory, particularly where gravel, stones, and plants are found. Many eager light tackle anglers wade and cast flies or spoons. The top season is from April through June, and fishing for trout is closed from August through the end of October. The fish average from 3 to 6 pounds but have been taken to 30 pounds.

Traditional surf casting methods are preferred for other species. Surf casters trying to catch cod, flatfish, and the occasional sea trout use rods that are 4 or more meters long, and weights up to 180 grams, to cast from 80 to 150 meters into the surf. Baitfish are available from every tackle dealer along the coast. Best catches are possible in the months of May and June, and again from September through November when the wind is blowing ashore. The Baltic Sea is a preferred surf casting area, second only to the outer islands of the North Sea, whose sandy shores face the open ocean.

Other Issues

Trolling. Trolling is new to German anglers, but it is gaining popularity as Germany's Scandinavian neighbors catch more and more fish annually with this method; trolling with downriggers, in particular, has become more popular. Most well-equipped trolling boats are privately owned, however, and it is uncommon to find such boats for hire. Most trolling is practiced in the Baltic Sea, and in some large lakes for trout.

Put-and-take sites. In the area surrounding big cities there are many ponds and small lakes that provide put-and-take fishing. The quality differs, as do the amenities, but some have facilities, including toilets and shops, and some of these waters offer exceptionally large fish, mainly rainbow trout.

G

Legislation. As mentioned briefly in the opening paragraphs on angling in Germany, each of the 16 German states has its own fishery laws. With the exception of Niedersachsen in the north, all states require a state-issued license (*Jahresfischereischein*) for freshwater and saltwater angling.

Yearly or lifetime licenses exist, and these can be obtained only when the angler has passed an examination (*Sportfischerprüfung*), administered by the German Angling Federation and its district associations. The test is given only in German, and there are no lessons for preparation in the English language; however, if demand grows, this may change. The northernmost state, Schleswig-Holstein, is the only exception; it issues a 40-day license for holiday anglers without requiring an examination.

In addition to possessing a state fishing license, anglers must purchase a site-specific license issued by the owner of the water they wish to fish. Children under 12 do not need a license. Owners of fish waters can be clubs, communities, professional fishermen, or private landowners. Licenses for private waters are issued for a day, a weekend, a week, or a month and sometimes are accompanied by regulations regarding catch limits, size limits, catch-and-release, angling methods, baits, and the like. In Niedersachsen, which has no state license requirements, landowners often require proof that an angler has passed the national examination before they will grant a fishing license for most private waters.

State licenses cover sea angling also, except in the state of Mecklenburg-Vorpommern. A separate license for shore angling is necessary there and is available from tourist information offices.

In Germany it is illegal to fish with live bait, and the laws specify that a fish destined for consumption must be killed immediately and must not be wasted. It is also illegal to use nets to keep fish alive.

Information sources. All-inclusive angling tours for Germany are generally unavailable, and contacting the state or local boards of tourism is necessary to locate hotels, pensions, clubs, and professional fishermen who sell licenses, accommodations, and boats for hire. Contact the Central German Tourist Board to get the address of the official Tourist Board of the German state in question, then contact that state board to locate regional tourist offices.

It's a good idea to read advertisements in one of the big monthly German angling magazines. Fishing club addresses are available from the National German Angling Federation (VDSF) at Siemensstr. 13, D-63071 Offenbach (telephone: 069-8550068; fax: 069-873770), and the German Anglers Association (Deutscher Angler-Verband DAV), at Weissenseer Weg 110, D-10369 Berlin (telephone: 030-97104379; fax: 030-97104389).

GIARDIASIS
See: First Aid.

GIGGING
Taking fish with a handheld prong, harpoonlike device, or spear, any of which may also be known as a gig. These devices are meant to spear or impale fish by means of a pronged or barbed instrument, which is attached to a rigid object such as a pole. Also known in some places as spearing, gigging is primarily a freshwater activity and one that has been practiced traditionally to procure food. The legality today varies in freshwater and is regulated by fisheries agencies. Gigging usually requires a fishing license, is subject to seasons, and may be restricted to certain species. Where legal, gigging is considered a form of recreational fishing; it is not widely employed, however, and is not treated as sportfishing by the general angling community.

Gigging is sometimes confused with jigging and the use of jigs to catch fish by sporting means.
See: Spearing.

GILL
A breathing organ with much-divided thin-walled filaments for extracting oxygen from the water. In a living fish, the gills are bright red feathery organs that are located on bony arches and are prominent when the gill cover (*see*) of the fish is lifted.
See: Anatomy; Gill Rakers.

GILLIE
A fishing guide; also ghillie.

GILLNET
A commercial fishing net in which fish are caught as they swim into the mesh, where they are entangled by the gills. The net is suspended vertically by means of bottom weights and top floats, and the mesh is sized according to the species sought. Gillnets entangle anything larger than the net's mesh size, resulting in tremendous amounts of bycatch (*see*).
See: Commercial Fisherman.

GILL RAKERS
Toothlike extensions, located along the anterior margin of the gill arch, that project over the throat opening and strain water that is passed over the gills. These protect the gill filaments and, in some fishes, are used to sieve out tiny food organisms. The number of gill rakers on the first gill arch is sometimes used as an aid in identifying or separating species that closely resemble one another.
See: Anatomy.

GIMBAL
A pivoting receptacle for fishing rods that may be located on a rod belt (*see*), mounted on the front of a fighting chair (*see*), or located in rod holders. It

contains a receiver with locking mechanism to receive the rod butt, and it pivots when the rod is pumped while fighting a fish. A gimbal is customarily used in saltwater fishing with heavy tackle and large or powerful fish, although it may be used with lighter tackle as well.

GIN POLE
A tall pole with rope and blocks, found in older sportfishing boats and used to hoist large fish out of the water and into the cockpit. No longer prevalent on large sportfishing boats, these have been largely replaced by a transom door/gate *(see)*.
See: Sportfishing Boat.

GLOBAL POSITIONING SYSTEM
An electronic navigation method known by the acronym GPS.
See: GPS; Navigation.

GOLDEYE *Hiodon alosoides.*
Other names—Winnipeg goldeye, western goldeye, shad mooneye, toothed herring, yellow herring; French: *la queche, laquaiche aux yeux d'or.*

A member of the Hiodontidae family of mooneye, the goldeye is one of Canada's most celebrated freshwater fish from an Epicurean viewpoint. When smoke cured, it is sold as Winnipeg goldeye, commands a high price, and is well known among gourmets. The goldeye looks very much like the mooneye *(see)*, but only the goldeye is of commercial interest. Its bony flesh, when fresh, is soft and unpalatable, but it is a delicacy when smoked. In processing, the fish are gutted, lightly brined, dyed orange red, and then smoked over oak fires. It is marketed whole.

Although often called a herring or a shad, it is neither. The goldeye provides good sport for light tackle anglers, but it is not pursued in many parts of its range.

Identification. The goldeye is a small fish whose compressed body is deep in proportion to its length and is covered with large, loose scales. Dark blue to blue green over the back, it is silvery on the sides, tapering to white on the belly. It has a small head and a short, bluntly rounded snout with a small terminal mouth containing many sharp teeth on the jaws and tongue.

The color of its eyes and the position of its anal fin distinguish it from the mooneye. The iris of the large eyes are gold and reflect light. The goldeye's dorsal fin begins opposite or behind its anal fin (the mooneye's begins before the anal fin). The goldeye can be distinguished from the gizzard shad by the absence of a dorsal fin ray projection.

Size/Age. Adults average from 10 ounces to slightly more than a pound in weight, and seldom

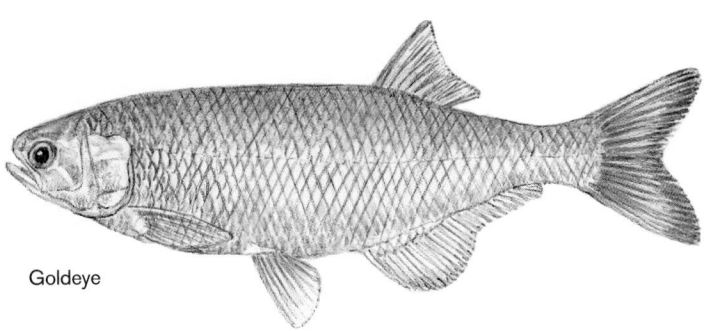

Goldeye

exceed 2 pounds in most waters. They can grow to 5 pounds. The Manitoba record is a 2.3-kilogram fish from the Nelson River. They reportedly can live for 14 years.

Distribution. Endemic to North America, goldeye are found in both Canadian and American waters. They occur from western Ontario to the Mackenzie River at Aklavik in the north, from below the Great Lakes south throughout the Ohio and Mississippi River drainages on the east, and from western Alberta throughout eastern Montana and Wyoming to Oklahoma on the west. Lake Winnipeg in Manitoba has historically been the largest commercial producer of these fish; its stocks were greatly depleted in the 1920s through overfishing, and took decades to recover.

Habitat. Throughout their geographical range, goldeye are most often found in warm, silty sections of large rivers and in the backwaters of shallow lakes connected to them.

Spawning behavior. In the spring, mature goldeye move into pools in rivers, or backwater lakes of rivers, to spawn when the water temperature is between 10° and 13°C.

Food and feeding habits. Goldeye feed on a variety of organisms, from microscopic plankton to insects and fish. They do most of their foraging on or near the surface, and predominantly on insects, although they will eat minnows and small frogs. Small goldeye serve as prey for large predators, including walleye, pike, and salmon.

Angling. Goldeye are caught on flies and on small hook baits, including worms and grasshoppers, suspended below a light float. Light spinning and fly tackle are the favored gear. Most angling for goldeye occurs in central Canadian waters, primarily to produce fish for home smoking. Elsewhere, they are seldom deliberately pursued on rod and reel, but they may be fished live or as cut bait by anglers pursuing other species, notably catfish.

GOLDFISH *Carassius auratus.*
A member of the large Cyprinidae family of freshwater fish, and a relative of carp *(see)*, goldfish are primarily known as aquarium species, but they do exist in the wild.

G

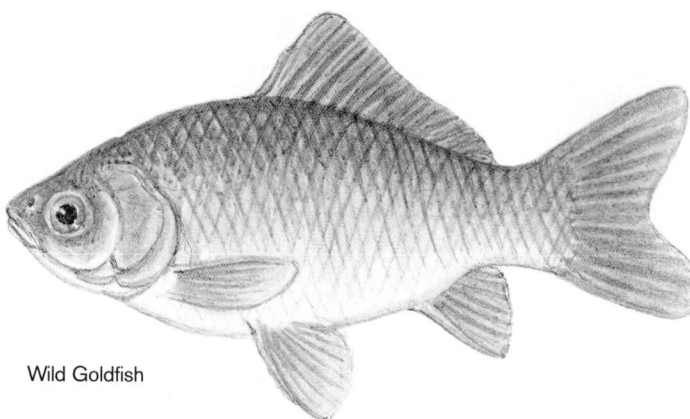

Wild Goldfish

GOOSEFISH   *Lophius americanus.*

Other names—American goosefish, anglerfish, monkfish, lotte, bellyfish, frogfish, sea devil, American angler; French: *baudroie d'Amerique;* Spanish: *rape americano.*

The goosefish has been described as mostly mouth with a tail attached, and reports of goosefish eating prey almost as big as themselves are common. A member of the Lophiidae family of deep-sea anglerfish, the goosefish is an ugly, bottom-dwelling species of temperate waters that attracts prey with a fleshy lure and then sucks it inside its huge mouth. It is not a targeted gamefish, but it is occasionally caught by deep-water bottom anglers. Goosefish and related species have been highly prized in European markets for a long time but have become prominent in North American markets and restaurants only since the mid-1980s, usually under the moniker "monkfish."

Before the mid 1980s, the American goosefish was harvested almost exclusively as a bycatch in groundfish trawl fisheries and the sea scallop dredge fishery, but it became increasingly targeted in response to dwindling supplies of traditional groundfish species and the development of new markets for goosefish parts (tails, whole fish, livers, cheeks, and belly flaps). Meat from the tail of the goosefish is firm, white, and excellent table fare; the liver is a delicacy in France and Japan.

More than two dozen species of anglerfish exist worldwide in tropical and temperature seas, and the American goosefish is the largest among them. Commercial landings of the American goosefish

have so increased that the average fish is smaller and the species is overexploited.

Identification.   The American goosefish is dark brown with a mottling of dark spots and blotches. It has almost armlike pectoral fins located about midway in its greatly flattened body. Small gill openings are just behind them. The head is extremely large for its body size, and the mouth is cavernous, filled with sharp, curved teeth and opening upward. Fleshy flaps of skin margin the head and lower jaw, and smaller flaps of flesh run along the sides of the scaleless body. The first three spines of the dorsal fin are thin and sharp, and they are widely separated from one another. On the tip of the first spine is a flap of flesh that serves as a lure for attracting small fish within grasping range of the mouth. If the prey comes close enough, the goosefish opens its big mouth and sucks its victim inside.

Size/Age.   The growth rate is fairly rapid and similar for both sexes up to about age 4, when they are approximately 19 inches long. After this, females grow a bit more rapidly and seem to live longer, about 12 years, growing to slightly more than 39 inches. Males have not been found older than age 9, with a length of approximately 35 inches, and few grow older than age 6. Their maximum weight is 50 pounds, and the all-tackle world record is a Maine fish that weighed 49 pounds, 12 ounces.

Distribution.   This species ranges from the Grand Banks and northern Gulf of St. Lawrence south to Cape Hatteras, North Carolina. A similar but smaller species, the blackfin goosefish *(L. gastrophysus)* occurs in deeper waters from North Carolina to the Gulf of Mexico and south to Argentina.

Habitat.   Individuals are found from inshore areas to depths exceeding 435 fathoms. Highest concentrations occur between 38 and 55 fathoms, and in deeper water at about 100 fathoms. Seasonal migrations occur, apparently related to spawning and food availability.

Life history/Behavior.   Sexual maturity occurs between ages 3 and 4. Spawning takes place from spring through early autumn, depending on latitude. Females lay a nonadhesive, buoyant mucoid egg raft, or veil, which can be as large as 39 feet long and 5 feet wide. Incubation ranges from 7 to 22 days, after which the larvae spend several months in a pelagic phase before settling to a benthic existence at a size of about 3 inches.

Food.   The carnivorous and rapacious goosefish eats a wide array of fish, some nearly as large as itself, as well as assorted crustaceans and squid. It has been reported to consume diving ducks as well.

GPS

The satellite navigational mode commonly referred to simply as GPS is actually NAVSTAR GPS, which stands for *NAV*igation *S*ystem with *T*ime *A*nd *R*anging *G*lobal *P*ositioning *S*ystem. This system is divided into space and ground control

G

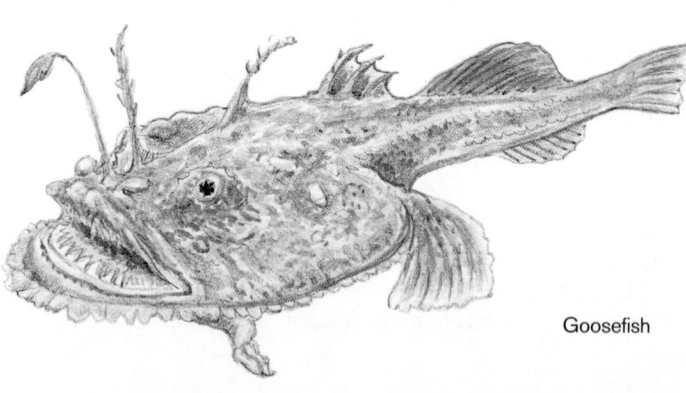

Goosefish

segments. The space segment consists of a constellation of satellites in precise orbits 10,900 nautical miles out in space, arranged so that at least six satellites are always in view from any point on Earth. The ground control segment includes a master control station, a number of monitoring stations, and ground antennas located around the world, which work together to track and communicate with the satellites.

GPS obsolesced the older DECCA and Loran (see) navigational systems, which could be used only by receivers within range of their chains of land-based transmission towers. It also obsolesced the Transit System (sometimes called Sat-Nav) of navigation, which used low-orbit satellites so widely spaced that position fixes were infrequent.

GPS features extremely quick fixes and easy use; you simply turn the receiver on and start navigating. There are no calibrations to make, no chains of towers to select, no operational pitfalls like Loran's baseline extensions to worry about, and, unless you leave the planet, there are no fringe areas. Thanks to the high angle of the satellites and the very high frequency used to carry signals, GPS is immune to weather problems and highly resistant to localized interference, both of which were problems with Loran. It can be used 24 hours a day, in any weather, anywhere where there is an open view of the sky.

In a relatively short period of time, GPS has become a fixture for marine and inland navigation and an increasingly common part of both the sport-fishing-by-boat scene and the backcountry travel scene. The first handheld GPS was introduced in 1988, and early handheld units retailed for about $3,000. A decade later, handheld models were available for $100, and they were far more sophisticated. From a fishing perspective, the major use today is on the water for both navigational and fish-locating purposes. Sportfishing boaters are using fixed-mount and handheld GPS to get to and from selected locations and to determine the exact location of important fishing grounds; in addition, they use GPS as an aid to actual fishing activities, especially when angling in wide-open waters for nomadic schools of fish or pelagic species or when fishing specific bottom structures.

How GPS Works

Principles. Each satellite constantly broadcasts the time and its position. Timing is all-important to accuracy, and the satellites are equipped with atomic clocks reputed to be accurate within one second every 70,000 years.

A GPS receiver calculates its distance from a satellite by measuring the time it takes for the satellite's signal to reach it. The receiver determines its two-dimensional position (latitude and longitude) by measuring its distance from three satellites. It finds its three-dimensional position (latitude, longitude, and altitude) by measuring its distance from a fourth satellite as well. The receiver knows the positions of the satellites overhead and automatically uses those that provide the best geometry for accuracy.

GPS receivers don't have a compass or any other mechanical direction-finding device built into them; they rely entirely on position fixes derived from satellite signals. Normally, they find your position about once every second, and they calculate speed, direction of travel, and distance by comparing where you are one second with where you are the next. You must be moving for GPS to determine your speed and direction of travel; you can't stand still and use the unit as a magnetic compass. It will work at slow trolling speeds, but the faster you travel, the easier and more accurately a receiver can track speed and direction.

Conventional accuracy. The satellites broadcast signals for two levels of service: Standard Positioning Service (SPS) for civilian use and an encrypted Precise Positioning Service for the military. Civilian SPS is accurate enough to get anglers within 25 meters or less of a target destination. However, the United States Department of Defense chooses to degrade SPS accuracy with Selective Availability (SA) interference for military security reasons. The government's accuracy specification for GPS is 100 meters (328 feet) horizontally and 150 meters (492 feet) vertically, 95 percent of the time. In other words, the position shown on a receiver could be up to 100 meters in any direction from your actual position, and your altitude could be plus or minus 150 meters from what is shown on the screen. Most users report seeing latitude/longitude accuracy of 15 to 50 meters on average, but for safety's sake all users need to remember that they could be 100 meters from where GPS says they are at any time.

GPS satellites are arranged in six separate orbital groups to ensure global coverage, and each satellite orbits the earth once every 12 hours. Since the satellites and anglers' boats are in constant motion, the geometry between them is in a state of perpetual change. The best accuracy is possible when a receiver can navigate with three satellites that are low on the horizon and spaced evenly (120 degrees) apart. Less than ideal satellite geometry results in less than ideal accuracy for position fixes, although these errors are negligible compared to SA.

GPS satellites transmit signals in a straight, line-of-sight path. When a receiver can't get a clear view of most of the sky, it may not be able to pick up signals from enough satellites to work properly. A bridge overhead or a high vertical cliff nearby can block necessary satellite signals. A receiver will warn you when it can't receive enough satellites for navigation, and all you should have to do is move clear of these obstructions for the unit to resume navigation.

When installing a GPS antenna on your boat, mount it where things like metal windshield frames, outboard motor power heads, and seated or standing passengers are least likely to block satellite signals. Never mount a GPS antenna in a radar

 Tarpon is one species that rises periodically to the surface to breathe atmospheric air. Young tarpon do this about three times per hour.

G

antenna's transmission path, since the radar emissions can cook some of its delicate internal components.

DGPS accuracy. Accuracy better than 100 meters is required for commercial ships navigating coastal harbors, the Great Lakes, and major rivers, as well as for private and commercial airplane pilots. A system enhancement called Differential GPS (DGPS) was developed to increase accuracy to around 10 meters by countering the effects of SA, and anglers can take advantage of this improved accuracy. DGPS uses land-based receivers installed at surveyed locations. They compare their known location with their satellite-derived position and compute a correction. A DGPS station might, for instance, determine that it is really 100 feet northwest of where the satellites currently say it is and compute a correction. This correction is then broadcast on a special U.S. Coast Guard DGPS radio beacon frequency from a tower located at the same site. Different DGPS station locations use different frequencies, so a DGPS unit always knows which one it's receiving.

In order for a unit to use DGPS, it must contain special built-in circuitry to process the corrections and must be connected to a differential beacon receiver to acquire them. Most units require a separate beacon receiver, but some have them built-in. Units built to use the differential system are advertised as being DGPS-ready or DGPS-capable.

Unfortunately, the maximum broadcast range for a U.S. Coast Guard differential beacon tower is only about 200 miles. Therefore, freshwater anglers more than 200 miles from a saltwater coast, the Great Lakes, or a navigable river are probably out of range of the nearest tower and may not be able to use DGPS; through the phenomenon of skipping, some broadcasts have been received over much greater distances, but this is usually in unobstructed coastal areas rather than inland.

Also on the negative side, DGPS brings land-based towers and their much lower radio transmission frequencies back into the overall equation. Thunderstorms between your boat and the tower can kill reception just as they could with Loran. However, losing the beacon signal just causes a DGPS receiver to revert to normal GPS. You lose the extra accuracy, but you don't lose the ability to navigate as would happen with Loran.

Wide area augmentation accuracy. To overcome the range and tower deficiencies of DGPS, and to get maximum accuracy out of standard GPS for airplane pilots, the Federal Aviation Administration (FAA) is developing the Wide Area Augmentation Service (WAAS). This is a system enhancement signal emanating from very high orbit satellites (covering a wider area than the satellites producing GPS signals); the WAAS signals provide differential information that is collected directly by a GPS receiver, which automatically computes a correction to counter Selective Availability.

This will work in newer GPS products that have a 12-channel receiver, with one channel being preprogrammed by the manufacturer for dedication to WAAS. Older 12-channel products may or may not be retroprogrammed by the manufacturer. There is no need for a differential beacon receiver.

The benefits of WAAS are twofold: First, it works anywhere in North America and all the time because it doesn't rely on land-based towers to relay a differential correction signal; second, accuracy is improved to a range of 3 to 10 meters. Whether Selective Availability is being applied or not, a GPS unit that is WAAS-capable will provide the utmost in accurate position identification.

Types of Receivers

GPS receivers are available as handheld portables, as stand-alone bracket-mounted or in-dash models, and as "black boxes" integrated into sonar and other types of electronics. The actual receiver (sometimes called a GPS engine) has been miniaturized to fit on a small printed circuit board. The same board can be used in nearly any style of unit, which allows a manufacturer's tiniest handheld model to be as fast and accurate as the maker's largest panel-mount unit that incorporates the same board.

A receiver's level of performance depends more on its number of parallel channels and the software used to manage them than just its physical size. Early models had a single channel that could receive the signal from only one satellite at a time. In order to navigate with the three satellites necessary for determining latitude and longitude, it had to lock onto one satellite, get its information, and then unlock and go to the next one. This process was repeated constantly; when signals were lost or blocked, early units sometimes had trouble reacquiring them to start the process over again. The next generation of receivers had multiple channels (usually between 2 and 6) and could keep one channel locked onto each of the satellites it was using for navigation. They took less time to find a position when first switched on, and they were less bothered by temporary signal interruptions. Most newer receivers have 12 channels and deliver performance that, in comparison, is incredible. When first switched on, they find a position in seconds rather than minutes, and they suffer performance interruptions only when the receiver is blocked from the transmitting satellites or the power is disconnected (handheld units may be susceptible to blockage from dense foliage). They have enough channels to lock onto all the satellites in view and can switch instantly back and forth as necessary if signals are blocked.

Handheld portables. These pocket-size receivers have built-in antennas and self-contained power supplies and are the most versatile type of GPS unit. They are a good choice for anglers using canoes, inflatables, rental boats, and other craft without electrical systems, or when temporarily fishing from someone else's boat. They are also perfect for hike-in fishing on remote waters. Although they are a good compromise for anglers who use GPS for a variety of outdoor activities that require portability, they aren't the best choice for a permanent mounting in your boat. It can be more difficult to see their smaller screens and press their smaller keys while bouncing across the water than when using a full-sized, permanently mounted model.

The standard power source for handheld GPS units is AA batteries, and battery consumption varies greatly between models. The more power-hungry versions eat them up as fast as about six batteries every 3 hours, whereas the more conservative units can use as few as four batteries every 24 hours through internal power management systems. Some companies are taking advantage of advancements made in the portable computer industry and offer exotic rechargeable power cells that run units longer than a set of AAs and can be recharged hundreds of times. Manufacturers also usually offer accessory power cords that allow a handheld to run from a cigarette lighter receptacle when used temporarily in a boat, tow vehicle, or even an ice angler's snowmobile. Accessories like remote antennas and mounting brackets are available for many handhelds and make them easier to use in such cases.

Permanent mount units. These receivers are larger than handhelds and have bigger, easier-to-see displays. Most come as two separate assemblies: a head unit that mounts near the helm and contains the display and controls, and a compact antenna that mounts on a gunwale or console. These units are powered by the boat's electrical system. The head is generally designed to be mounted on a gimbaled bracket, but some can also be flush-mounted on a flat panel surface. Beware of flush-mounting any instruments having liquid crystal displays because they have a relatively narrow viewing angle. Once flush mounted, they can't be tilted or turned for better visibility.

The larger screens on permanent units have more room for multiple-window displays and more elaborate graphics than the small screens on handheld models. They can also be clearly read from farther away.

Combination models. GPS receivers are commonly available in combination with sonar units and as plug-in options for chart plotters, radars, and other electronics. Combination units are usually less expensive than separate models and can help ease console crowding on boats where space is at a premium.

Sonar/GPS combinations are probably the most common. Anglers can show either sonar or GPS readings on the whole screen, or they can split the screen to show sonar displays on one side and GPS information on the other. Although this saves space and money, it also has disadvantages. If the sonar breaks, the GPS has to go with it to the service facility because it's in the same case. You may also find yourself in a serious fishing situation that requires precise navigation and maximum sonar detail, wishing that each function could be shown

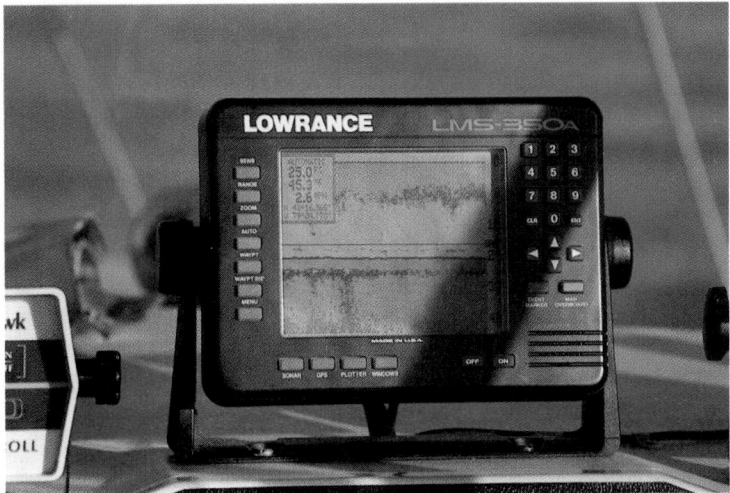

The GPS portion of this combined sonar-and-GPS unit allows an angler to assess speed and location at all times, as well as instantly preserve the location of something observed with the sonar.

full-screen at the same time. Some professional guides, tournament competitors, charter boat captains, and big-water skippers use two sonar/GPS combo units in their quest for maximum redundancy. They use one as a sonar and the other as a GPS, and have an automatic double backup in case of trouble.

There are also combined GPS/communications units that have the ability to send wireless e-mail messages from any outside location. Battery-operated palm-size units can send and receive e-mail messages in wireless form by using orbiting satellites. The number of satellites capable of receiving and transmitting e-mail messages was originally limited but is increasing, so that 24-hour coverage can be provided.

General Use

Anglers can save important locations like favorite fishing spots, launching ramps, marinas, reefs, wrecks, and navigational aids or hazards in the electronic memory of a GPS receiver. Submerged open-water fishing hotspots that are out of sight of land can be almost impossible to find without electronic help. Even familiar launching ramps and marinas can be elusive in fog or darkness.

The locations saved in GPS receivers are called waypoints. Once a location has been saved as a waypoint, an angler can return to it at any time. A waypoint is most commonly saved by pressing a button while the unit is located at the waypoint's position; the position can also be saved by entering its latitude and longitude coordinates through the keypad. These coordinates are important because with the lat/lon coordinates you can find a place that you have never been to; the coordinates can be given to you, or you can take them off a good navigational chart.

It's a good idea to record waypoint information in a logbook as a backup, in case the unit is lost, stolen, or breaks down. You can reenter the waypoints manually after fixing or replacing your unit or acquiring another. Integrating with a personal computer will allow you to store appropriate information as well as plan trips. Some manufacturers have software that allows you to share information with other users and to download, upload, store, and edit navigational data; this can include sorting waypoints, printing route lists and plots, calculating sunrise/sunset times and lunar phases, and determining the bearing and distance between waypoints.

A receiver guides you to a waypoint by providing the compass bearing from your present position to the waypoint's location. When you veer off course, it tells you which way to steer to get back on course, and it constantly provides digital readouts of your speed, direction of travel, remaining distance, and even how long it will take you to get there at the current speed. This information can be displayed in several ways.

Digital box display.   The most basic way to display information is with digital boxes containing numbers and letters. Anglers most comfortable with this type of presentation need only pay attention to three of the boxes. The "Bearing" box shows the compass direction (in degrees) from the present position to the destination waypoint. The "Heading" or "Track" box shows the direction that you are actually traveling as you attempt to steer your boat on the proper course. Forces like wind and current can push a boat sideways as you steer on your bearing and move it in a slightly different direction than your compass reads. The closer the bearing and heading readings are to the same number, the more accurately you are navigating. The third important box is labeled "Distance To Go." You simply steer on the correct compass bearing until the distance-to-go reading counts down to zero.

Some units also have a simple "Direction to Steer" screen that provides navigational information as compass bearing numbers or simply as a directional arrow.

Road/highway display. Some anglers find pictures easier to use than numbers. Some types of displays show a road or highway on the screen with an icon (a graphic symbol) representing your boat traveling down it. You simply steer the boat so that its icon stays in the middle of the road. As you approach your destination waypoint, the waypoint appears as a symbol ahead of you. When your boat icon reaches the waypoint symbol, you're there. The same digital readings found on the first type of display are usually shown somewhere on this screen to let you check your progress.

Track plotter.   This display method is often preferred by anglers used to navigating by the seat of their pants. It shows a bird's-eye view of your boat and the surrounding area. The amount of area shown on the screen is adjustable from a fraction of a mile to hundreds or even thousands of miles. The screen shows an icon representing your boat connected by a dotted line to another symbol representing your destination waypoint. The screen will also show symbols for any other waypoints in the area, and some units can show "event markers" that you can place on the screen at will. They are typically used to mark where fish are caught or hazards are identified. These markers appear whenever you are in the area, but they don't take up any of your valuable waypoint memory.

Anglers maintain the best screen resolution by adjusting the plotter range to show the smallest amount of area large enough to contain both the boat icon and the destination waypoint symbol. As you move, the boat icon leaves a solid line on the screen, marking its track. You simply steer the boat so that the solid track line of the boat icon covers up the dotted line.

Track plotter screens can usually be set for either a north-up or course-up orientation. This means that either the direction "north" or your present direction of travel will always be at the top of the screen. Anglers who like to view maps in the same orientation as they are usually printed (with the direction north at the top) prefer the north-up setting. Those who like to turn the map so that the direction in which they're going is at the top prefer the course-up setting. Either way, when the boat icon covers the destination waypoint symbol, you're there.

Routing.   A routing feature lets you list several waypoints in the order that you wish to visit them and then save the list as a "route" in memory. This is most useful for blazing a safe trail from a launching ramp to a fishing spot, or even from a marina deep within a harbor out through an inlet. Routing lets you overcome problems caused by the fact that GPS navigates in straight-line legs.

When you tell a GPS unit to take you to a waypoint, it plots a straight line from where you are at that moment to where you want to go. It considers that straight line your course, and it guides you along it. If your destination is 2 miles away and there are points of land, islands, or rock bars between you and your destination, GPS will guide you right into them. You can blaze a safe trail by saving a waypoint each time such obstacles force you to make a turn and then listing the waypoints, in order, as a route that leads you around hazards in short, straight-line legs.

When building a safe route, anglers should keep the worst-case accuracy for GPS in mind and strive to stay at least 100 meters from the closest hazard when saving waypoints. If the local geography doesn't offer you that much room on certain legs of a route, be extra careful when traveling them. When running a route, anglers can start at any of the route's waypoints and run the route forward or backward.

Other features and terms.   GPS units employ a number of symbols that all users become familiar with. Icons are used to identify specific positions on the screen and may be used together to delineate a certain area; when placed within a route, they may become waypoints, which are stored in memory as

Tooth loss is a natural and regular occurrence in the well-dentured tigerfish; dozens of teeth were found on the floor of a tank after eight large tigerfish were held in captivity for one month.

G

a specific set of lat/lon coordinates. The number of icons and the type of graphic symbols offered varies.

When you wish to note the occurrence of something on the screen, you may be able to place a mark there; this may be numbered, and a specific symbol may be used for it. An event could simply be a strike while trolling, the location of a net buoy, or something that is unique. The feature that permits this marking may be called an event marker. In a similar vein, some fixed-mount units have a specific function allocated to emergencies, called a man overboard (MOB) feature. When the appropriate button is pressed, the unit instantly records the boat's position and charts a course to that spot. Of obvious use to sailors and boaters in rough seas, it can also be employed when some object has inadvertently fallen out of your boat (like that lucky fishing hat).

Three terms used with regard to obtaining position are acquisition time, cold start, and warm start. Acquisition time is simply the amount of time required for a GPS unit to lock onto the appropriate number of satellites and obtain a position fix. When a GPS unit is started for the first time, and when it has been moved a long distance from where it was last used, the receiver has no idea where to look for satellites and will take a long time, perhaps up to 20 minutes, to find its current position. This is called cold start. Every time that the GPS unit is turned on, the receiver assumes that it is in the same position as it was when previously operating. If it is in, or relatively near, that position, it will rely on the data stored in memory and locate the appropriate satellites fairly quickly. This is called warm start.

When a GPS unit is used in relatively the same area, it should be able to lock onto satellites fast. Speed of acquisition is less of a concern in fixed-mount versions, which are connected to a 12-volt battery and left on all day. It is much more of a concern in handheld units, which are commonly turned on and off periodically. On a warm start, the better handheld units can be fully functional in less than a minute.

Common sense and sonar. Keep in mind that the bearing indicated to reach a desired location is always depicted in a straight-line mode. The receiver does not take into account that an island, another vessel, or any obstruction might be in the path of travel. Thus, following a GPS bearing must be done with the understanding that it is not always possible to follow a straight course and that even when there are no obvious above-water impediments to following a straight course, underwater obstructions such as a shoal, reef, or other object may require altering your heading. As you alter heading, the receiver repositions you and recomputes the direction and time to your destination. Nevertheless, in the same way that using a compass *(see)* is not a substitute for applying common sense, nor is operating a GPS, and it is generally advisable to employ GPS, as well as any other navigational instrument, in conjunction with sonar.

Also keep in mind that these are electronic navigational aids, and they will not be useful if there is an electronic malfunction within the unit or if the power supply is cut off or exhausted. Handheld units that work on battery power are especially susceptible to power depletion, and most have a low-battery warning. Spare batteries will really be appreciated at such a time.

Finally, there are times when a receiver is unable to function properly even though the unit has sufficient power. This is usually when an impenetrable object obstructs the receiver's line of sight to the sky. The biggest problem is with handheld units operated in places where there is a full canopy of cover overhead; handheld units rarely can keep a fix under leafy cover. Most people who fish from a boat and use fixed-mount units do not experience this problem unless they have mounted the receiver in a location that is sometimes obstructed. A person standing in front of a receiver, or an object placed near it, could temporarily block the receiver.

Chart Plotters/Mapping Units

Many anglers find navigating with digital, on-screen maps easier than finding their way with just numbers, virtual highway graphics, or track plotters. Accessories that feature map- or chartlike detail in electronic cartographic form are called chart plotters or mapping units, and the usage of fixed-mount versions in marine environments is referred to as electronic charting. The word "map" is generally used with handheld models, mainly those that are intended for diverse usage, especially inland; the word "chart" is used with fixed-mount units destined for marine applications. Chart plotting and mapping are available on stand-alone devices but may be incorporated into other products, including radar and sonar instruments. Stand-alone versions may be interfaced with these other devices, as well as others, including autopilots.

The highly detailed information for a given area is contained on cartridges that plug into the body of

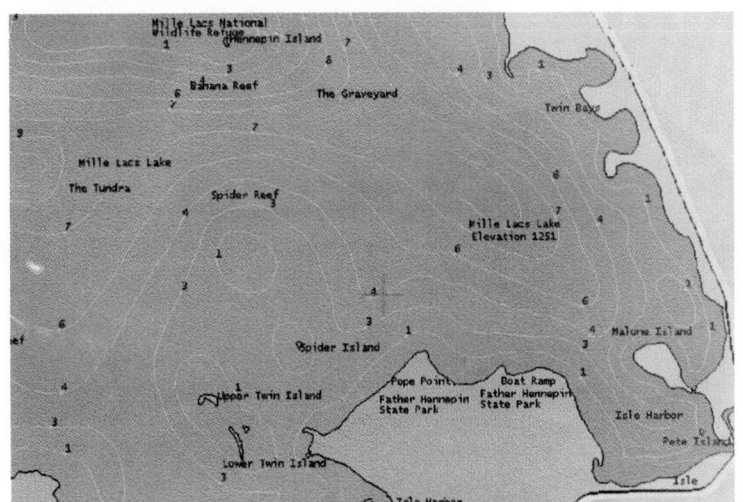

Chartlike details, such as this view of a section of Mille Lacs Lake, Minnesota, are provided in devices that combine charting with GPS navigation.

the unit. The topographic information displayed on-screen looks much like a road map, whereas the hydrographic information displayed looks like a navigational chart and displays detailed information on harbors, marinas, ship channels, and navigational aids. The detailed nautical information is, in fact, derived from navigational charts; thus, these electronic products are only as accurate as the paper government-agency charts from which they are obtained.

The quality of the detailed information in these units will depend on the scale that was used when digitizing the information. The larger the scale, the more detail that will be provided. Some chart plotters show the same information even when the zoom feature is used, which means that the same level of detail is provided on large and close views. Others provide a new set of more detailed information when you zoom in, which means that the more detailed zoom view has come from a different, and larger scale, chart. Naturally, more detailed information requires more memory storage, so it may result in a cartridge that covers a smaller area than one that does not have as much detail. However, this is an important difference between chart plotters. Fewer cartridges to cover a given geographic area may mean that you can view more overall area per cartridge, but you will not necessarily see more specific detail.

Another area of difference between older and newer chart plotters is whether they're "seamless." Older models redrew the chart screen when they jumped from the edge of one chart to the edge of the next; newer versions scroll from one to the other in an uninterrupted fashion.

Like a track plotter, chart plotters show a bird's-eye view of a boat icon and an adjustable amount of the surrounding area, including the locations of waypoints and event markers. Instead of being on a blank screen, however, these objects are shown on a detailed, on-screen chart or map of a lake, river, or coastline that shows a boat's movement in relation to shoreline or coastal features, local towns, highways, etc. This gives boaters the best possible feel for where they are at any given time and where they're going. In all chart plotters, the boat's position is displayed as an icon. In some, the icon moves to the edge of the screen, and then the chart area depicted changes and the icon is returned to the center of the new screen; in others, the icon always remains in the center of the screen and the chart moves beneath it. The former is known as true motion and the latter relative motion.

The most sophisticated contemporary cartridges do more than display depths as lines; they depict the depths in colored shades and even interactively compare the boat's draft with the water depth of the area and sound a warning. Some also depict spot soundings.

Such a high level of detail requires the storage of a lot of memory, so most manufacturers use plug-in cartridges of local areas to do the job. Some cartridges are no larger than a postage stamp. Some GPS manufacturers have developed their own information on their own cartridges, and some have used cartridges from established electronic charting companies; certain GPS units are capable of accepting both. Digital map/chart cartridges vary in the amount of area covered, level of map detail, and price. Some systems require the purchase of several cartridges to cover the entire area of large states or provinces, or large coastal areas, and even people who will use GPS in a relatively small area may need to have two cartridges if the dividing point for coverage happens to be in the area they navigate most frequently. Cartridge-capable GPS units for mapping or charting are available in both handheld and fixed-mount models, and they will become increasingly sophisticated and a greater part of everyday boating electronics.

Fishing with GPS

The navigational value of GPS is obvious. The additional value to anglers is in pinpointing places to fish, schools of fish, or significant underwater structures, and being able to return to them unerringly. In some instances, there is great value to pinpointing the specific part of an area to fish, such as the riprap near a submerged wreck. Trollers, in particular, who spend a lot of time searching for fish on the move (salmon and walleye, for example, in freshwater, or billfish, dolphin, or tuna in saltwater), may get a lot of benefit out of track plotters for returning to schools of fish; it is easy to lose your position when you are trolling at a fast speed or have no nearby visual landmarks. Drift anglers likewise may get a lot of value out of using the plotter and icons to identify places for focusing their efforts rather than covering a lot of unproductive water.

Marking structure. A GPS plotter can be of great use when simultaneously employed in conjunction with sonar to define the edge of any structure, whether that is a canyon in offshore water, a deepwater dropoff in a reservoir, the perimeter of a reef or shoal, or any specific underwater contour. If you have not been to a particular place before, you might want to scout the area first without fishing it; this will help familiarize you with the outline of that structure. The fact that you can visualize on a screen exactly where you have been and where you are heading will make fishing the area much easier.

Generally, the track plotter function of a GPS unit does not provide very precise information when the boat is traveling at slow speeds, as it is when slow-trolling or drifting, because of the effect of Selective Availability. If you are going fast enough to get good plotter detail, then zipping around the edges of the structure that you want to define will create a plot trail that you can reference when you actually fish the area, whether by trolling, drifting, or casting.

When you follow the edge of a structure, place an icon on the screen when there are significant changes; these might be a turn, an intersection with

G

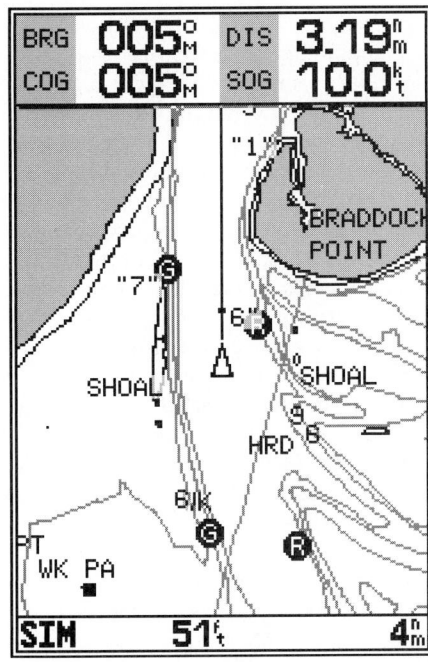 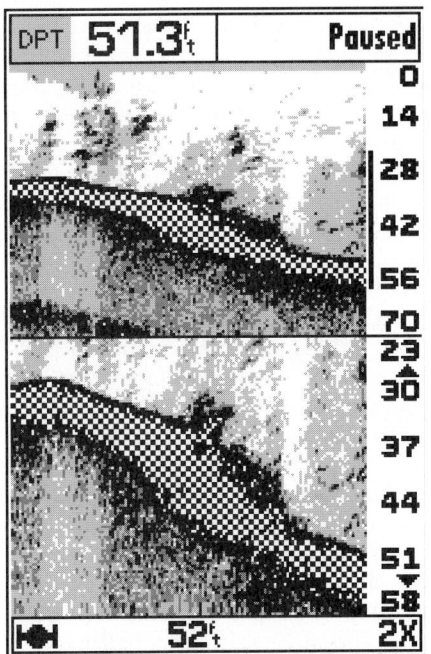

This screen view from a Garmin combined GPS and sonar device provides digital navigational details (left), water depth (right), and chartlike information with a track plotter; the boat is represented by an icon at dead center.

some other structure, or the ends or corners of the structure. When the sonar indicates that you're passing over a significant group of fish or a large individual fish, place an icon there; this might be a place to target your angling effort. When you have completed the scouting of an area, it will be fully defined on the plotter; then you can start to fish the most likely places based upon the depth, species sought, and whatever wind or current might be of influence. To make sense of your information when using icons, allocate specific icons to specific usage; for example, pick one icon to use for corners and prominent edge locations; pick another to use just for schools of fish or for baitfish; pick a third to use for big fish. Learn to manage the information to keep from being confused.

Do you have to use a plotter in this way for fishing? No. But it sure is easier. Without a plotter to provide a visual image of the structure, you can accomplish the same thing by using sonar alone and dropping marker buoys at specific locations; obviously this is an inferior method of defining an area in terms of the time it takes and the numbers of marker buoys (which have to be retrieved). Before sonar, this was done with weighted drop lines and trial-and-error probing.

Trolling.   On the track plotter screen, you can see your course and direction of travel while trolling; when you locate or hook a fish, you can identify that specific locale by pressing the event marker function or by placing an icon on the plotter screen. After trolling onward or after fighting and landing a fish, you can use the plotter screen to show exactly how to get back to the place you identified.

This function is important when you're locating moving schools of baitfish or such wandering species

as striped bass, salmon, and steelhead, or when you are out in the middle of a big body of water and come upon a feeding school of fish. Some anglers regularly use the plotter and event marker functions to help relocate fast and frequently moving schools of fish like striped bass, even when they are in locations (a large river or near a coastal shoreline) where they can clearly see where they are and how to get from one place to another. But if the targeted fish move about quickly because of tide, current, and baitfish activity, you have to stay with them and keep relocating them to stand a good chance of catching them.

In offshore big-game fishing, working the edge of structures or dropoffs can be very important, and many trollers follow a zigzag or S-curve pattern of boat maneuvering while fishing so that they can follow and stay with the contours below as defined on their sonar. If you are doing this, you can place an icon on the screen every time you go over the edge. Later, a series of icons will precisely show the edge so that you can then troll in a straight path from icon to icon. When you hook a fish or if you have a looker come into the baits, mark the spot with a different icon.

When trolling, use different icons to indicate different things; for example, use a fish icon for a school of baitfish and an anchor icon for big, individual fish. Some units have icons that represent schools of fish or large individual fish, so what you use depends on what the machine provides.

If fish are moving and you're retracing your travel, the plotter trail will build up and you may want to erase it; on the other hand, if the fish are stationary, then let the plotter trail build up. It may not be helpful to reduce the plotter screen to the smallest range possible (.10 mile in some units); it's better to get a larger view, perhaps by using the .5-mile range. When trolling, you can set the plotter to update infrequently (say every 30 seconds) instead of using an instant update mode, so the plot trails will last on the screen for a couple of days; if you will be returning to the same places for the same fish, then keeping information available could be very helpful. If you want the plotter trail to last for just the day, then use a 10-second update. For the most detail, use the quickest update frequency possible, although on most units the quickest update will clear out the plotter trail in a few hours.

Some combined sonar/GPS units allow you to construct windows so that half the screen is a sonar view, one-quarter of it is plotter, and the other is a digital depth readout. When not using the plotter, you may want to use full-screen sonar with the following displayed digitally in the upper left corner: depth, speed, surface temperature, and distance traveled.

Drifting and wreck fishing. Drifting across large expanses of water, like a bay or flat, is common for many types of fishing, especially when seeking bottom-feeding fish. The GPS can be used to close in on likely areas for fish or to identify specific places that are producing fish. You thus can maximize your time in productive places and eliminate fishing across unproductive expanses.

Initially, you may have to make a long drift in a particular area. Use the plotter screen to see where you've been and to identify places where fish were caught (by placing an icon there at the time of hookup). Naturally, any drift that is taken without the occasional use of an electric motor for positioning is subject to the direction of wind, current, and tide. These factors may change during a day, and a glance at the track plotter will reveal whether you need to reposition yourself to drift over the proper place because of changing conditions.

Finding wrecks is one of the most important uses for GPS. Keep in mind that simply knowing where a wreck is doesn't mean that you are right on it when the GPS says you have arrived. The waypoint for the wreck may coincide with your position, but the actual underwater wreck is just approximately in this spot. You'll still need to move around to precisely pinpoint it (and in many cases you want to pinpoint the rubble near a wreck). You can then run an east-west or north-south travel pattern to find it with your sonar, using the track plotter to set the trail and sonar to find the object. Do not just drive in circles looking for it.
See: Maps; Navigation; Sonar.

Fishing in Japan dates back at least to 200 a.d., and Japanese interest in angling has continued through the centuries; *Ebisu* is a Japanese god of angling.

GRABBLING
See: Noodling.

GRAND SLAM
Although borrowed from a baseball term—a bases-clearing home run—this expression is used in angling to signify a broad array of feats. A grand slam is commonly associated with tropical water fishing and the capture of billfish or highly prized inshore or flats species, but the expression has been adopted for any combination of species that are highly valued and require a reasonable level of difficulty to catch. Guides, charter boat captains, and tourism promoters have varying spins to put on what constitutes a grand slam, as befits either the most notable or glamorous species in their areas, or the techniques they use.

A grand slam is usually associated with catching these species in a single day of fishing, but this, too, is variable. It may be associated with catching certain species over extended periods of time, since those species are usually not available in a single day (such as catching all billfish species in a year). A grand slam may also refer to accomplishments with certain types of tackle.

In the Atlantic Ocean off North America, for example, catching a blue marlin, white marlin, and sailfish in a single day is a grand slam; adding a swordfish or a spearfish would make it a super grand slam. Varying this in different combinations is possible.

Tarpon, bonefish, and permit are the traditional grand slam of the flats, and in some areas a snook might be added to make this a super grand slam. In backcountry areas, a grand slam might be a redfish, snook, and seatrout, with a tarpon making it a super grand slam.

Obviously a grand slam can be configured any way that makes sense. In the Northwest, a grand slam might be a salmon, halibut, and rockfish, or three major salmon species. In the mid-Atlantic, it might be a red drum, black drum, and cobia. Offshore it might be a variety of different big-game species.

These slams are generally unrecognized by official bodies, although the International Game Fish Association does have four grand slam clubs to honor saltwater catches. These are called Offshore or Inshore Grand and Super Grand Slams, and they recognize accomplishments by a single angler in a single day. They include blue marlin, black marlin, sailfish, swordfish, and spearfish in the offshore categories; catching any three constitutes a grand and any four a super grand. The inshore species include tarpon, bonefish, permit, and snook; catching any three is a grand and all four is a super grand. In both cases, the fish do not have to be landed or weighed (they can be released in the water at boatside, for example) to qualify and receive certificate recognition.

GRAPHITE
A synthetic material, also known as carbon fiber, used as a prominent material in fishing rod construction and in certain components of fishing reels.
See: Baitcasting Tackle; Conventional Tackle; Flycasting Tackle; Graphite Rod; Rod, Fishing; Spinning Tackle.

G

GRAPHITE ROD

A fishing rod that uses graphite material in the construction of the blank. Graphite is the most important material used in rod construction today, and rods made with graphite or a mix of graphite and other materials, primarily fiberglass and secondarily boron, dominate the marketplace.

Graphite came into fishing rod production from aerospace applications at a time when the majority of fishing rods were made of fiberglass. It took a while for manufacturing and design problems to be resolved (with a lot of early breakage and other problems as a result of using fiberglass rod manufacturing technology for graphite, which did not work), but better weights of this material and improved production technologies delivered products that made good on the hallmark characteristics of the graphite: lighter weight, greater strength, and better sensitivity.

The tensile modulus of graphite runs from four to eight times that of fiberglass. Thus, a graphite rod intended for the same type of fishing as one made of fiberglass can have thinner walls and a more slender configuration. The net result in properly designed products is a significant savings in the weight of the finished rod, an improvement in strength, and an improved ability to feel lures or bait working and to detect strikes.

Some confusion has arisen over the modulus (a measure of how effectively a material resists deformation) of graphite available, the generations of graphite that have evolved, and the content of graphite in some fishing rods. However, the most important issue is not so much the material as it is the design of the fishing rod. Even with graphite material, only a well-designed rod can achieve the performance that is necessary for specific angling applications. That performance entails obtaining accuracy, achieving distance, and having maximum sensitivity—all of this with the least amount of effort by the angler. Graphite rods can do this better than any other when properly designed.
See: Rod, Fishing.

GRAPH RECORDER

See: Sonar.

GRASS

See: Aquatic Plants; Seagrass.

ARCTIC GRAYLING   *Thymallus arcticus.*
EUROPEAN GRAYLING   *Thymallus thymallus.*
Other names for the Arctic grayling—American grayling, arctic trout, Back's grayling, bluefish, grayling, sailfin arctic grayling; French: *ombre artique, poisson bleu.*
Other names for the European grayling—grayling; Danish: *stalling;* Dutch: *vlagzalm;* Finnish: *harjus;* French: *ombre commun;* German: *asch;* Italian: *temolo;* Norwegian and Swedish: *harr;* Russian: *kharius.*

Grayling belong to the Salmonidae family and are related to trout and whitefish. They are distinctive-looking fish with a sail-like dorsal fin, and a superb sportfish known primarily in the cool- and coldwater northern regions of North America and Europe. Their firm, white flesh is good table fare, although it is not on a par with that of the wild trout and charr that inhabit similar ranges. Grayling are excellent when smoked, however.

Identification.   With their graceful lines, large fin, and dramatic coloration, grayling are striking fish. Most striking is their large purple to black dorsal fin, which extends backward and fans out into a trailing lobe, speckled with rows of spots. This fin may look bluish when the fish is in the water. Grayish silver overall, grayling usually have shades or highlights of gold and/or lavender, as well as many dark spots that may be shaped like an X or a V on some fish.

Young arctic grayling can be distinguished from similar-looking young whitefish by narrow vertical parr marks (whitefish have round parr marks, if any). When the arctic grayling is taken from the water, a

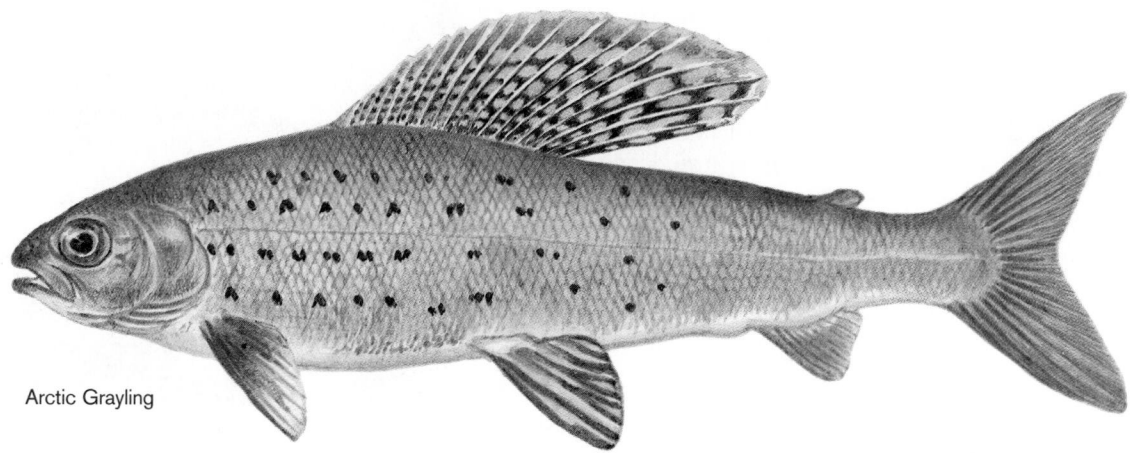

Arctic Grayling

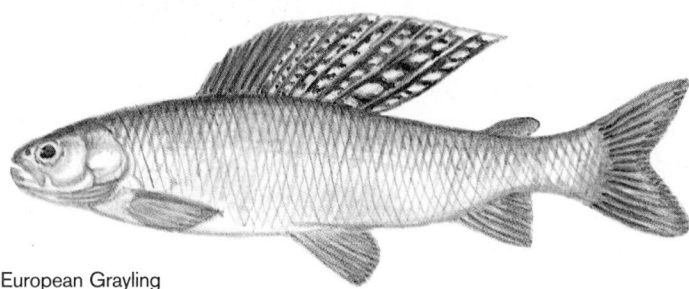

European Grayling

resemblance to the whitefish is especially apparent, as the beautiful colors fade to a dull gray. It has a small, narrow mouth with numerous small teeth in both jaws. The arctic grayling also has a forked caudal fin and relatively large, stiff scales.

Size. A small fish, with maximum lengths to 30 inches, grayling can reach a maximum weight of about 6 pounds. The all-tackle world record for arctic grayling is a 5-pound, 15-ounce fish from the Northwest Territories in Canada, but any arctic grayling exceeding 3 pounds is considered large, and a 4-pounder is a trophy. European grayling tend to run smaller.

Distribution. Arctic grayling are widespread in arctic drainages from Hudson Bay to Alaska and throughout central Alberta and British Colombia, as well as in the upper Missouri River drainage in Montana. Previously known to inhabit some of the rivers feeding Lakes Huron, Michigan, and Superior in northern Michigan, arctic grayling have been considered extinct there since 1936. They have been widely introduced elsewhere, especially in the western United States.

European grayling occur in northern Europe from England and France to the Ural Mountains in northwest Russia.

Habitat. Grayling prefer the clear, cold, well-oxygenated waters of medium to large rivers and lakes. They are most commonly found in rivers, especially in eddies, and the head of runs and pools; in lakes they prefer river mouths and rocky shorelines. They commonly seek refuge among small rocks on the streambed or lake bottom.

Life history/Behavior. Adult grayling spawn from April through June in rocky creeks; fish from lakes enter tributaries to spawn. Instead of making nests, they scatter their eggs over gravel and rely on the action of the water to cover the eggs with a protective coating. The eggs hatch in 13 to 18 days. Grayling are gregarious and flourish in schools of moderate numbers of their own kind. Arctic grayling of northern Canada may be especially abundant in selected areas of rivers.

Food and feeding habits. Young grayling initially feed on zooplankton and become mainly insectivorous as adults, although they also eat small fish, fish eggs, and, less often, lemmings and planktonic crustaceans.

Angling. European grayling are a bit more accessible than their North American counterparts, which primarily inhabit remote and difficult-to-access areas; for this reason, arctic grayling are not known to many North American anglers and are seldom the primary quarry of distant traveling anglers. They do serve as a desirable secondary attraction to anglers primarily seeking lake trout, walleye, northern pike, or charr. Arctic grayling, however, have saved the day for more than one traveling angler who found the main quarry unavailable or uncooperative. Outfitted with a light spinning rod or a fly rod, these anglers could take advantage of the 1- to 2-pound feisty grayling that were available, more likely than not feeding in the evening on the surface.

Most grayling are in the 1- to $1\frac{1}{2}$-pound class, although some waters are noted for fish that are larger in average size than elsewhere. They are routinely found in groups and feed heavily on aquatic insects in all stages of development. Grayling are most commonly observed in flowages while dimpling the water and feeding on surface insects, which in North America are usually mosquitoes; they often do this very daintily, but occasionally feed dramatically by clearing the surface and coming down on the insect.

Primarily caught by fly anglers, grayling provide challenge and thrill. Dry fly fishing with 5- to 7-weight lines is the preferred method. When not rising freely to insects, grayling may be better pursued with a wet fly or nymph. A floating fly line is best most of the time, but a sink-tip line may be necessary. Grayling can be leader shy, and they pursue flies and often strike at the end of a drift, so attention to detail can be important. Fly size ranges from No. 12 through 18, and the favored offering is skimpy and dark. Exact representations aren't usually critical, but using a black or brown pattern is important.

The grayling is an excellent catch on light or ultralight spinning tackle, too, using 2- through 6-pound-test line. Small spinners and spoons are popular, but the best artificial is a small, dark jig. Black or brown marabou or $\frac{1}{16}$- to $\frac{1}{8}$-ounce soft plastic jigs produce especially well in flowing and stillwater.

A tall, spotted dorsal fin is characteristic of grayling.

Although most grayling are caught in the slick water of rivers and streams, and sometimes where it flows quite fast, they are also found in lakes near river inlets, usually along shores studded with small rocks. There, in calm water, they cruise along inhaling surface insects, and are taken on flies, jigs, or spinners.

Grayling have small mouths, so many fish that strike are lost. These are scrappy, feisty fish that jump and fight to the end, but they must be handled gently, as they die quickly when held out of the water or if mishandled. Grayling bleed easily and profusely, and unfortunately squirm and wiggle all the time, making it difficult to unhook them in the water and even harder to grasp them. Barbless hooks are especially useful for grayling fishing, not only for unhooking them easily, but also because these fish are sometimes caught with great abundance in areas where they are active.

GRAYSBY   *Cephalopholis cruentata.*

Other names—Spanish: *enjambre, cherna enjambre, cuna cabrilla.*

A member of the grouper/seabass family, the graysby is a small, secretive reef fish. Graysby are commonly caught on hook and line but their small sides precludes them from being particularly sought after.

Identification.   Varying from pale gray to dark brown, the graysby has many darker orangish, red brown spots on its body, fins, and chin. There are three to five distinctive marks, like pale or dark spots, that run along the base of the dorsal fin. A white line runs between the eyes from the nape to the lower lip. The spots change color, either growing pale or darkening in contrast with the body. The tail of the graysby is more rounded than it is in similar species. There are 9 spines and 14 rays in the soft dorsal fin, compared to 15 to 17 rays in the closely related coney.

Size.   The graysby generally grows to a length of 6 to 10 inches and can reach a maximum of 1 foot.

Distribution.   Graysby range from North Carolina to the northern Gulf of Mexico and south to Brazil. They are common in southern Florida, the Bahamas, and the Caribbean and are also found in Bermuda.

Habitat.   Small ledges and caves in coral beds and reefs are the preferred haunts of graysby, where they blend with the surroundings at depths between 10 and 60 feet.

Food.   Graysby are nocturnal predators, feeding mainly on fish.

GREASED-LINE FISHING

Fishing a wet fly close to the surface and at a uniform swim speed diagonally down and across fast water in a stream. The term was used early in the twentieth century and is derived from the fat that was applied to the line to help float it in the

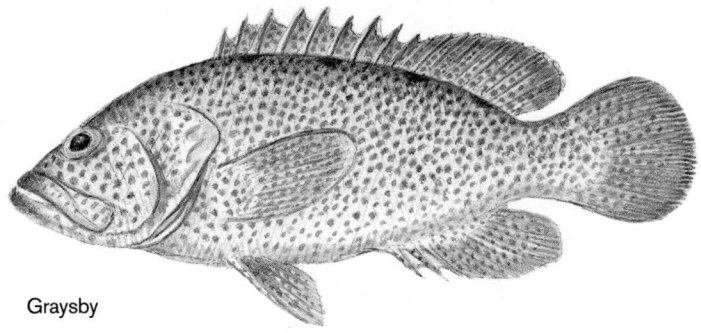

Graysby

pre-silicone era. Mending *(see)* the line is necessary to achieve the right presentation, especially if there are conflicting current speeds, and a high-floating fly line helps achieve this.

GREAT BRITAIN

See: England; Scotland; Wales.

GREEN FISH

A fish brought to the angler so quickly that it is very vigorous, often thrashing about wildly as the angler attempts to land it. Although it is advantageous to unhook and free fish that will not be kept for personal use, landing some fish, because of their nature or size, before they are tired out can be harmful to the fish, and also dangerous to the angler or other person landing it.

See: Catch-and-Release.

GREENLAND

The largest island in the world, Greenland lies northeast of North America and is a self-governing part of Denmark situated between the North Atlantic and Arctic Oceans. Most of this country's nearly 2.2 million square kilometers is north of the Arctic Circle, and 85 percent—the interior plateau—is permanently covered with ice. This plateau is drained by ice fiords, which contribute to the numerous icebergs along its coast. Although reached by air from international locations, Greenland itself has no interior road network and thus requires domestic transport by air and boat. Its population of 55,000, mostly Inuit, has long been dependent on fishing, particularly for shrimp, salmon, charr, halibut, and cod.

In freshwater, sea-run and resident arctic charr are found in lakes, rivers, and streams on both coasts. Inland, because natives net fish, the size of charr increases as distance from settlements increases. Most fish range up to 1.5 kilograms. In remote rivers, 2- to 5-kilogram charr occur. Some of the largest fish inhabit Greenland's glacial rivers, and among these one of the best is the Robinson River. Arctic charr also favor river mouths and coastal waters.

Only one Greenland river, the Kapisigdlit, which runs through the bottom of Nuuk Fiord, has

G

a temperature suited for Atlantic salmon. It features small fish that range from 2 to 4 kilograms. The waters off Greenland, however, are critical grounds for salmon that migrate here from their natal North American and European waters. As late as 1956 the first tagged salmon—a smolt marked in Scotland—was captured in a net off west Greenland; only then was it understood where Atlantic salmon migrated after leaving the rivers of their birth. Both commercial and subsistence netting for salmon in Greenland waters, by Greenlanders as well as non-Greenlanders, partially contributed to the collapse of Atlantic salmon populations. By the late 1990s, fishing quotas (established by international agreement) were the lowest they had ever been. Thus, although there is no sportfishery here for Atlantic salmon, the waters off Greenland are critical to the fishery, not only in terms of population but also for salmon fishing opportunities elsewhere.

Relatively unexplored but good potential for sharks, cod, skate, wolffish, and halibut exists offshore, although these species are not likely to attract visiting anglers. The adventurous and hardy have pursued fish from the ocean ice, the most extreme catch being large specimens of Greenland sharks caught on big-game tackle.

GRILSE
A salmon, usually male, that returns to freshwater rivers after one year at sea. These are small fish, generally weighing from 2 to 4 pounds.
See: Salmon, Atlantic.

GRIP
The part or parts of a fishing rod held by the angler and a major component of the handle. The grip consists of a foregrip, which is not found on some rods (usually light models) but is situated ahead of the reel and used for gripping the rod with the hand that is not turning the reel handle, and the rear grip, which is the section usually held by the angler and which incorporates the reel seat.
See: Rod, Fishing.

GROIN
A man-made structure, usually of concrete or stone, projecting into the water from the shore to protect a sandy beach from erosion. Groins usually exist in a series of parallel structures along a beach and are commonly referred to as jetties *(see)*. They may be constructed of wood and stone, or all stone, and form a perpendicular wall-like extension into the water. They are primarily found in saltwater along the coasts and are intended to prevent erosion by stabilizing the sand in the immediate vicinity. Groins do not usually have navigational aids, but they may be common beach fishing locations.
See: Jetty Fishing; Surf Fishing.

GROUNDBAIT
A chumming preparation made from crushed bread crumbs or stale bread that is soaked, mixed into a paste, and stiffened with bran or cornmeal. These items are made into balls and tossed into the water, clouding and flavoring it. "Groundbait" is a European term and an innovation primarily used in carp fishing.
See: Carp; Chumming.

GROUNDFISH
A species or group of fish that lives most of its life on or near the seabed. The term may be used synonymously with demersal. Groundfish refers to Atlantic cod, haddock, pollock, American plaice, white hake, redfish, and various flounders.

GROUPER
Grouper are members of the Serranidae family of sea bass *(see)*. Most are nonschooling species that generally congregate in the same area. Dozens of species inhabit all warm seas, preferring rocky shores and deep reefs. Grouper in general are good to eat and are a frequent catch of anglers.
See: Coney; Gag; Graysby; Grouper, Black; Grouper, Nassau; Grouper, Red; Grouper, Spotted Coral; Grouper, Warsaw; Grouper, Yellowfin; Hind, Red; Hind, Rock; Jewfish; Wreckfish.

GROUPER, BLACK   *Mycteroperca bonaci.*
Other names—rockfish; Portuguese: *badejo-ferro, badejo-quadrado;* Spanish: *bonaci, cuna bonací, cuna guarei.*

The black grouper is a fairly large and hard-fighting member of the Serranidae family. It is an excellent food fish, although the flesh is occasionally toxic and can cause ciguatera *(see)*.

Identification. Depending on location, the black grouper may be olive, gray, or reddish brown to black. It has black, almost rectangular blotches and brassy spots. It can pale or darken until its markings are hardly noticeable. It has a thin, pale border on its pectoral fins, a wide black edge and a thin white margin on its tail, and sometimes a narrow orangish edge to the pectoral fin; the tips of the tail and the soft dorsal and anal fins are bluish or black. The black grouper has a squared-off tail and a gently rounded gill cover.

Size. Regularly reaching 40 pounds, black grouper can grow to more than 100 pounds; the all-tackle world record is shared by two 114-pound fish, one from Texas and the other from Florida. The average length of the black grouper is $1\frac{1}{2}$ to 3 feet; the maximum is 4 feet.

Distribution. Black grouper occur from Bermuda and Massachusetts to southern Brazil, including the southern Gulf of Mexico, and occur commonly to occasionally in the Florida Keys, the

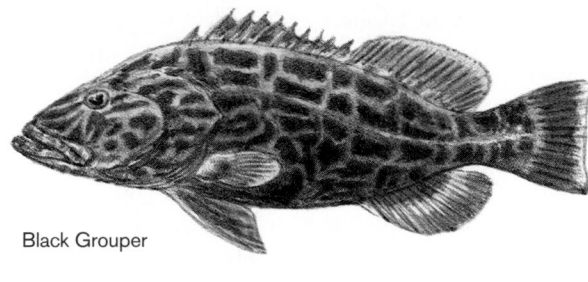
Black Grouper

Bahamas, Cuba, and throughout the Caribbean. Adults are unknown on the northeastern coast of the United States.

Habitat. Black grouper are found away from shore near rocky and coral reefs and dropoff walls in water more than 60 feet deep. Although black grouper typically drift just above the bottom, young fish may inhabit shallow water inshore, and adults occasionally frequent open water far above reefs.

Life history/Behavior. Black grouper spawn between May and August. As in many species of grouper, the young start out predominantly female, transforming into males as they grow larger.

Food and feeding habits. Adult black grouper feed mainly on fish and sometimes squid, and juveniles feed mainly on crustaceans.

Angling. Like other grouper, the black grouper is primarily caught by fishing at the right depth over an irregular bottom.

See: Grouper; Inshore Fishing.

GROUPER, NASSAU *Epinephelus striatus.*

Other names—hamlet; Creole: *negue;* French: *mérou rayé;* Spanish: *cherna criolla, mero gallina.*

The most important commercial grouper in the West Indies and a member of the Serranidae family, the Nassau grouper has been very heavily fished and is continually vulnerable to overfishing, especially during its spawning and migrating seasons.

Identification. Although its color pattern varies, the Nassau grouper usually has a light background with a wide, dark brown stripe running from the tip of the snout through the eye to the start of the dorsal fin, as well as four to five irregular dark bars running vertically along the sides. Two distinctive features are the black dots always present around the eye, and a large black saddle on the caudal peduncle, also always present no matter what color the fish is. The third spine of the dorsal fin is longer than the second, the pelvic fins are shorter than the pectoral fins, and the dorsal fin is notched between the spines. It has the ability to change color, from pale to almost black.

Size. The Nassau grouper is usually 1 to 2 feet in length, reaching a maximum of 4 feet and about 55 pounds, although most catches are under 10 pounds. The all-tackle world record is a 38-pound, 8-ounce Bahamian fish.

Distribution. In the western Atlantic, Nassau grouper are found in Bermuda, Florida, the Bahamas, the Yucatán Peninsula, and throughout the Caribbean to southern Brazil. They are absent from the Gulf of Mexico, except at Campeche Back off the coast of Yucatán, at Tortugas, and off Key West. Once abundant throughout their range, their numbers have been greatly reduced by spearfishing.

Habitat. Found in depths of 20 to 100 feet, although almost always dwelling in less than 90 feet of water, Nassau grouper prefer caves and shallow to midrange coral reefs. Smaller fish are usually closer to shore and common in seagrass beds, whereas adults are usually farther offshore on rocky reefs. Nassau grouper tend to rest on the bottom, blending with their surroundings. They are usually solitary and diurnal but occasionally form schools, as they do when spawning.

Spawning behavior. Spawning around the new moon, Nassau grouper come together in large masses of up to 30,000, making them highly vulnerable to overharvesting.

G

Nassau Grouper

Food.   Nassau grouper feed mainly on fish and crabs and to a lesser degree on other crustaceans and mollusks.

Angling.   Like other grouper, the Nassau grouper is primarily caught by fishing at the right depth over an irregular bottom.

See: **Grouper; Inshore Fishing.**

GROUPER, RED   *Epinephelus morio.*

Other names—grouper; Portuguese: *garoupa de Sao Tomé;* Spanish: *cherna americana, cherna de vivero, mero americano, mero paracamo.*

The red grouper was one of the most abundant grouper in the Caribbean and surrounding waters until spearfishing and general overfishing depleted its numbers. This member of the Serranidae family has firm, white meat and is marketed fresh and frozen, although it is susceptible to toxins.

Identification.   Of varying coloration, the red grouper is usually dark brownish red, especially around the mouth, and may have dark bars and blotches similar to those on the Nassau grouper, as well as a few, small whitish blotches scattered in an irregular pattern. It is distinguished from the Nassau grouper by its lack of a saddle spot and its smooth, straight front dorsal fin. On the Nassau grouper the dorsal fin is notched. It has a blackish tinge to the soft dorsal, anal, and tail fins; pale bluish margins on the rear dorsal, anal, and tail fins; and small black spots around the eye. The lining of the mouth is scarlet to orange. The second spine of the dorsal fin is longer than the others, the pectoral fins are longer than the pelvic fins, and the tail is distinctively squared off. The red grouper pales or darkens in accordance with its surroundings.

Size/Age.   The red grouper is commonly 1 to 2 feet long and weighs up to 15 pounds, although it can reach $3\frac{1}{2}$ feet and 50 pounds. The male red grouper lives longer than the female and has been known to live for 25 years.

Distribution.   In the western Atlantic, red grouper range from North Carolina to southern Brazil, including the Gulf of Mexico, the Caribbean, and Bermuda; some fish stray as far as Massachusetts. They are found only occasionally in Florida and the Bahamas and rarely in the Caribbean, a result of the large reduction in their population.

Habitat.   Red grouper are a bottom-dwelling fish, occurring over rocky and muddy bottoms, at the margins of seagrass beds, and in ledges, crevices, and caverns of rocky limestone reefs; they are uncommon around coral reefs, where they have been replaced for the most part by Nassau grouper. They prefer depths of 6 to 400 feet, although they more commonly hold between 80 and 400 feet. Younger fish (from one to six years old) usually stay closer to shore than do older juveniles and adults. Red grouper are usually solitary, resting on the bottom and blending with their surroundings.

Life history/Behavior.   Like many other grouper, red grouper undergo a sex reversal: The females transform into males, in this case between ages 7 and 14, or when they are 18 to 26 inches long. Although some females can reproduce for the first time as early as age 4, all fish can reproduce by age 7. Spawning takes place from March through July, with a flurry of activity in April and May, in water temperatures ranging from 63° to 77°F and in depths between 80 and 300 feet. The eggs are pelagic and can number 300,000 to 5.7 million, depending on the size of the fish; larvae settle to the bottom after remaining on the surface for 30 to 40 days.

Food and feeding habits.   Red grouper feed on a wide variety of fish, invertebrates, and crustaceans, including squid, crabs, shrimp, lobsters, and octopus. They usually ambush their prey and swallow it whole.

Angling.   Like other grouper, the red is primarily caught by fishing at the right depth over an irregular bottom.

See: **Grouper; Inshore Fishing.**

GROUPER, SPOTTED CORAL

Plectropomus maculatus.

Other names—coral trout (widely used in Australia), coastal trout, island trout, bar-cheeked trout, bluespot trout, common coral trout, coral cod, leopard trout; Arabic: *hamour;* Japanese: *siji-hata;* Malay: *jin hou, kerapu.*

A very beautiful fish and a member of the Serranidae family of grouper, the spotted coral grouper is also a superb table fish that is eagerly sought by anglers and fished for commercially. Large specimens (exceeding 7 to 8 kilograms) are suspected of harboring the toxin ciguatera *(see).* Smaller (4 to 5 kilograms) members appear not to carry this toxin.

Identification.   The spotted coral grouper is strikingly colored and has a remarkable range of coloration. Deep-water specimens are a bright scarlet with round, bright-blue circular spots on the head and body. This coloration can change to pink with blue spots in fish that inhabit shallower waters, or the fish can be grayish, and barred or blotched.

This grouper has a strong, solid, compressed body with a slightly concave caudal fin, a large mouth, large teeth, and a spinous dorsal fin with 8 spines and 11 soft rays. The preoperculum carries three large spines on its lower edge.

Red Grouper

Size. Although known to grow to 21 kilograms, the average fish taken by Australian anglers weighs between 2 and 5 kilograms; an Australian record stands at 11 kilograms.

Distribution. The spotted coral grouper occurs in the western Pacific in Thailand, Singapore, the Philippines, Indonesia, Papua New Guinea, the Arafura Sea, the Solomon Islands, and Australia. Known as coral trout in Australia, this fish and other related grouper inhabit semitropical and tropical waters from central Western Australia to central Queensland.

Habitat. Inhabiting both inshore and offshore reefs, these fish usually prefer shallow water to a depth of 100 meters. Within the reef environment, they dwell in caves and roam from reef to reef to forage.

Life history/Behavior. Spawning takes place during the spring and summer, coinciding with the new moon and a water temperature of 25° to 26°C. The eggs float just below the surface, and when the larvae hatch out they grow rapidly until about three years of age. Individual adults are hermaphroditic, starting off as females and then becoming males.

Food and feeding habits. Adults live mainly on fish such as herring and anchovies; juveniles feed on small fish, crustaceans, and squid. They will take pieces of tuna, mackerel, and mullet, as well as squid and prawns.

Angling. Most angling for spotted coral grouper is a daytime project. Because fish dwell mainly in reef habitat, anglers use heavy tackle. Whether your preference is bait or lure fishing, and spinning or conventional tackle, the minimum line requirements begin at 7 kilograms and range up to 15 kilograms. Rods are built to match. Handlines, which are popular, are even heavier (to 40 kilograms).

Natural bait anglers fishing from anchored boats use 6/0 to 8/0 extra-strong hooks. These are fished just above the bottom and require only the weight sufficient to take the baits down to that level. Jigging the bait will also attract the fish and encourage strikes. The spotted coral grouper is a strong fish that tries to return to the sanctuary of the reef when hooked. The angler must prevent this with a tough

initial response; once the fish has been wrestled to a higher plane in the water column, it can then be played more gently until brought to the boat.

Anglers also use surface poppers, minnow-type lures, leadhead jigs, and spoons, which they either cast or troll. Because lure loss can be high due to the strength of the fish and the coral reefs in which they live, many anglers make their own and find them just as effective as expensive commercially produced lures.

Trollers usually work along the edges of the reefs, offering spoons or saltwater flies. Heavy lines to 40-kilogram strength are necessary so that the hooked fish's instant diving response can be checked, thus avoiding cutoff on the reef.

See: Grouper; Inshore Fishing.

GROUPER, WARSAW   *Epinephelus nigritus.*
Other names—Spanish: *mero de lo alto, mero negro.*

The warsaw grouper is one of the largest members of the Serranidae family of grouper and sea bass, second only to the jewfish *(see)* in size. It has white, flaky meat that is marketed fresh. It is more widespread than the jewfish and caught more frequently.

Identification. The warsaw grouper has a gray brown or dark red brown body, occasionally irregularly spotted with several small, white blotches on the sides and the dorsal fins, although these are indiscernible in death. The young warsaw has a yellow tail and a dark saddle on the caudal peduncle. The warsaw is distinctive as the only grouper with 10 dorsal spines, the second of which is much longer than the third. It also has a squared-off tail. In contrast to the jewfish, the rays of the first dorsal fin on the warsaw grouper are much higher and the head is much larger.

Size/Age. The average weight of the warsaw grouper is roughly 20 pounds or less, although 100-pound fish are not uncommon. It can reach a length of 6½ feet and can weigh up to 580 pounds. The all-tackle world record is a 436-pound, 12-ounce Florida fish. The warsaw grouper grows slowly and can live as long as 25 to 30 years.

G

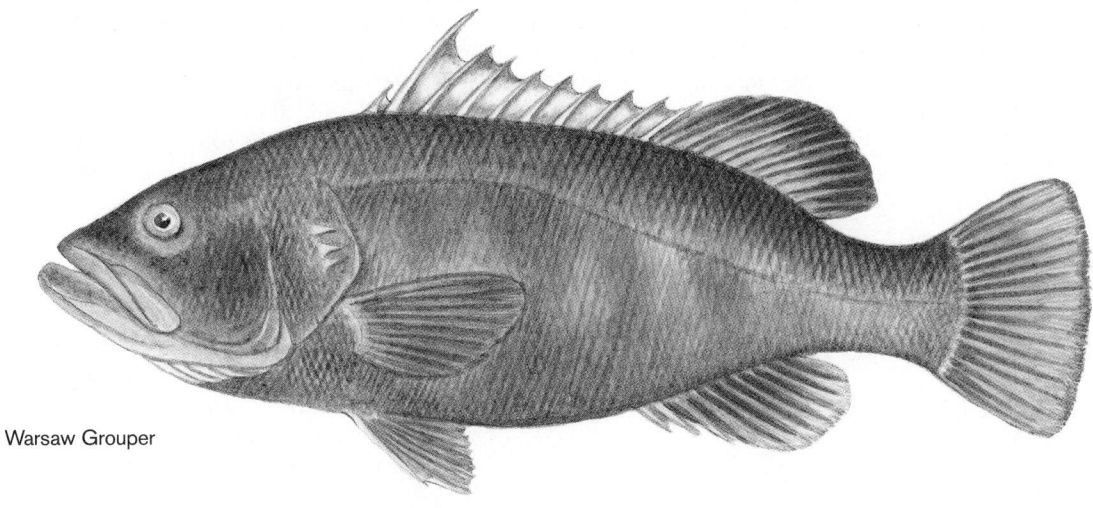

Warsaw Grouper

Distribution. In the western Atlantic, warsaw grouper range from Massachusetts to the Gulf of Mexico, and south to Río de Janeiro in Brazil, although they are rare in Cuba, Haiti, and Trinidad. They are otherwise fairly common along both coasts of Florida.

Habitat. Usually found over rough, rocky bottom, deep rocky ledges, and dropoffs, warsaw grouper prefer depths of 300 to 1,000 feet. Young warsaw grouper are occasionally seen or caught near jetties and shallow-water reefs.

Spawning behavior. The eggs and larvae of the warsaw grouper are thought to be pelagic, although little else is known about spawning and other behavior.

Food and feeding habits. Warsaw grouper feed on crabs, shrimp, lobsters, and fish, swallowing prey whole after ambushing it or after a short chase.

Angling. Heavy tackle is necessary when deep fishing for this species, not only because of the size of the fish but also because they have a habit of taking bait into rocky hideaways and the angler needs to muscle them away. Wire leaders are essential. Preferred baits are whole squid, cut amberjack, or a live red porgy or vermilion snapper. Warsaw grouper usually bite a free-spooled or slack line best. Like other grouper, the warsaw is primarily caught by fishing at the right depth over an irregular bottom.
See: **Grouper; Inshore Fishing.**

GROUPER, YELLOWFIN
Mycteroperca venenosa.
Other names—princess rockfish, red rockfish; Spanish: *arigua, bonaci cardenal, cuna cucaracha, cuna de piedra.*

The scientific name of this member of the Serranidae family means "venomous," a reference to the yellowfin grouper's association with ciguatera poisoning. Despite this, its flesh is good to eat and is usually considered safe for commercial sale.

Identification. The yellowfin grouper has highly variable coloring, usually with a pale background and horizontal rows of darker, rectangular blotches covering the entire fish; the ends of these blotches are rounded, and they can be black, gray, brown, olive green, or red. There are also small dark spots running across the body, which grow smaller toward the belly and usually appear bright red. The outer third of the pectoral fins are bright yellow,

whereas the tail has a thin, dark, irregular edge. An overall reddish cast is present in fish from deep water, and the yellowfin grouper has the ability to change color dramatically, or to pale or darken.

Size. The yellowfin grouper is common to 20 pounds in weight and 3 feet in length; the all-tackle world record is a 40-pound, 12-ounce Texas fish caught in 1995.

Distribution. Found in the western Atlantic, the yellowfin grouper is most common in Bermuda, Florida, and the southern Gulf of Mexico, and ranges to Brazil.

Habitat. Young yellowfin grouper prefer shallow turtlegrass beds, and adults occur on offshore rocky and coral reefs. They also hold over mud bottoms in the northern Gulf of Mexico.

Life history. As with other grouper, the yellowfin undergoes a sex reversal, transforming from female to male in the latter part of life.

Food. Yellowfin grouper feed mostly on coral reef species of fish and squid.

Angling. Like other grouper, the yellowfin is primarily caught by bottom fishing at the right depth over irregular structure, although some anglers land it by surface trolling.
See: **Grouper; Inshore Fishing.**

GRUB
The larva of an insect, especially a beetle, used to tip the hook of a small ice fishing jig or placed on a small-bait hook; also, a term for a small- to medium-size soft body on a jig hook.
See: **Jig; Maggot.**

GRUNION, CALIFORNIA   *Leuresthes tenuis.*
Other names—smelt, little smelt, grunion, lease smelt.

The California grunion is a member of the Atherinidae family of fish known as silversides *(see).* It is an important forage species for predator fish; in season, large numbers of anglers gather on the beaches to fill buckets with grunion undergoing a remarkable spawning ritual in the sand.

Identification. The California grunion has an elongate body and head that are more or less compressed. The mouth is small, and the scales are small, smooth, and firm. Its coloration is bluish green above and silvery below; a bright silvery band tinged with blue and bordered above with violet extends the length of the body.

Size/Age. The maximum known size of grunion is $7^1/_2$ inches; a 7-inch female full of eggs weighed less than 2 ounces. The life span is usually three years, with some individuals surviving four years.

Distribution. The California grunion occurs from Magdalena Bay, Baja California, to San Francisco; however, the principal range is between Point Abreojos, Baja California, and Point

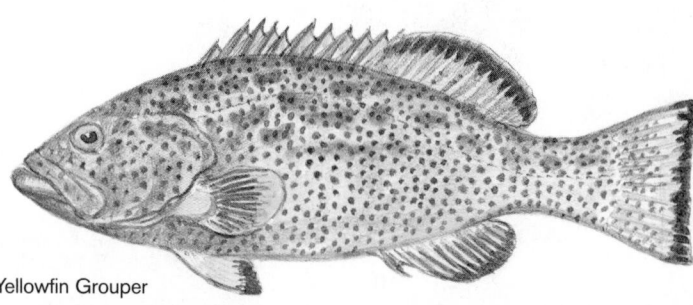
Yellowfin Grouper

G

Conception, California. A similar species, the gulf grunion *(L. sardina)*, is restricted to the Gulf of California.

Habitat. California grunion are nonmigratory and are most often found in schools a short distance from shore in water 15 to 40 feet deep.

Life history/Behavior. The most rapid growth takes place during the first year, at the end of which they are 5 inches long and capable of spawning. The spawning behavior of grunion is one of the more unusual among all marine fish. They are the only California fish known to strand themselves on the beach to deposit their reproductive products in the moist sand.

Females, accompanied by one to eight males, swim onto the beach with an incoming wave, dig themselves into the sand up to their pectoral fins, and lay their eggs. The males wrap themselves around the female and fertilize the eggs. With the next wave, the fish return to the sea. Thus, the spawning process is effected in the short period of time between waves. During spawning activities, grunion may make a faint squeaking noise. Most females spawn from four to eight times a year, producing up to 3,000 eggs every two weeks, and thousands of the fish may be along the beach at a time.

Spawning takes place from early March through September, and then only for three or four nights following the full moon, during the one to four hours immediately after high tide.

Food. The feeding habits of this species are not well known; however, they subsist on small crustaceans and fish eggs.

Angling. California grunion may be taken only by hand. No gear of any kind may be used, and no holes may be dug in the beach. The season is closed in April and May, although these are good months to observe spawning activities.

GRUNT

Several hundred species of grunt exist in warm seas throughout the world. The name "grunt" is derived from the grunting noises these fish make by grinding their pharyngeal teeth, the sounds amplified by the taut swim bladder that serves as a resonator. Their pharyngeal teeth are well developed; the jaw teeth are weak. This dentition distinguishes them from snapper, which they resemble in body form.

Most grunts are deep-bodied fish that range from 6 to 10 inches in length, although a few grow larger. They typically travel in schools. Many grunts have the habit of "kissing" others of their kind, the fish coming face to face, pressing their open mouths together, and then pushing against each other.

Grunts are bottom feeders and are viewed as saltwater panfish. Anglers catch them on light tackle, using shrimp, cut pieces of fish, or other natural baits, or, occasionally, artificials like small jigs and flies. They are typically caught around reefs, where they travel in small or extensive schools, and

White Margate

provide important forage for larger predators. Divers frequently encounter grunts on tropical reefs.

Most of these fish are sensitive to the feel of a line and may also bite lightly, so bait rigs are generally prepared with lead weights that carry the bait or lure to the bottom but permit the line to run freely through the weight. Anglers typically jerk the bait or lure to give it a slight motion, which attracts the fish. Most grunts are good to eat, but they may be ignored by anglers because of their small size; no concerted sportfishing effort is directed at these fish.

Common grunt species encountered by anglers include French grunt *(see: grunt, French)*, white grunt *(see: grunt, white)*, bluestriped grunt *(see: grunt, bluestriped)*, pigfish *(see)*, tomtate *(see)*, and sargo *(see)*.

Other species that may be caught occasionally are various margates. The white margate *(Haemulon album)* is pearl gray, with two or three black bands running the length of its body. The most prominent of these extends from the snout through the eye to the tail. Although most individuals weigh less than a pound, the white margate can grow quite large, and may be found farther offshore than are other grunts. The all-tackle world record for the species is a fish that was caught in Belize in 1996 and weighed 15 pounds, 12 ounces.

One of the most striking of all grunts is the black margate *(Anisotremus surinamensis)*, which averages only about a pound but can grow much larger. A deep-bodied fish with a small mouth and thick lips, it is silvery gray, the fins bordered or edged with black. A broad light band extends obliquely up the body behind the pectoral fins. The inside of the mouth is white.

The closely related Atlantic porkfish *(Anisotremus virginicus)* is a common inshore species that attains a weight of 2 pounds but averages only 4 ounces. It is distinguished by two black bars on the front of the body, one from the top of the head through the eye to the rear angle of the upper jaw and the other from the base of the spiny dorsal to the base of the pectoral fin. Behind this bar, the body is striped horizontally with blue and yellow. Its Pacific cousin is the Panamic porkfish *(Anisotremus taeniatus)*, which ranges from Baja California to Ecuador and is especially common off Cabo San Lucas. It is extremely similar in appearance to the Atlantic porkfish but grows to just 12 inches.

G

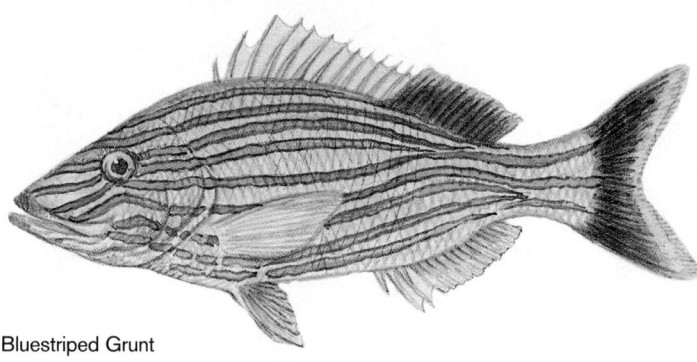

Bluestriped Grunt

GRUNT, BLUESTRIPED   *Haemulon sciurus.*
Other names—Spanish: *ronco catire.*

Frequently used as an aquarium fish when young because of its magnificent coloring, the bluestriped grunt is also considered an excellent table fish and is easily caught on natural baits.

Identification.   The bluestriped grunt is distinguished from all other grunts by its color pattern of continuous blue horizontal stripes over a yellow gold body. The tail and dorsal fins are dark and dusky with a yellow tinge. Other fins are yellow. The inside of its mouth is blood red. It has 12 dorsal spines, 16 to 17 dorsal rays, and 9 anal rays.

Size.   Its average length is up to 1 foot, but it can reach as much as 18 inches in length.

Distribution.   It is common from southern Florida through the Caribbean to the West Indies and southward along the Gulf of Mexico and along the coast of Central and South America to Brazil.

Habitat.   The bluestriped grunt drifts along reefs, especially near the deep edges. It remains relatively close to the shore in shallow water from 12 to 50 feet deep. Juveniles are found in seagrass beds in bays, lagoons, and coastal waters.

Behavior.   A schooling fish, the bluestriped grunt gathers in medium-size groups along reefs during the day. Scaring easily, the grunt will swim away quickly when slightly startled.

Feeding habits.   Adults feed on the bottom at night over open sandy, muddy, or grassy areas, primarily foraging on crustaceans. They also consume bivalves and occasionally small fish.

Angling.   *See: Grunt.*

GRUNT, FRENCH   *Haemulon flavolineatum.*
Other names—Spanish: *ronco amarillo.*

The French grunt is one of the most abundant panfish in southern Florida. These and other grunts often make up the largest biomass on reefs in continental shelf areas. Although it is too small to be of commercial value, the French grunt is an excellent panfish. It is also a common aquarium fish.

Identification.   Its coloring is white to bluish or yellowish with bright-yellow stripes. The stripes set below the lateral line are diagonal. There are yellow spots on the bottom of the head. The fins are yellow, and the inside of the mouth is blood red. It has 14 to 15 dorsal rays, 8 anal rays, and 16 to 17 pectoral rays.

Size.   The average length is 6 to 10 inches, although this fish can reach 12 inches.

Distribution.   The French grunt is abundant in Florida, the Bahamas, and the Caribbean. It also inhabits the waters of South Carolina, Bermuda, and the Gulf of Mexico, and south to Brazil.

Habitat.   Preferring shallower water close to shore, the French grunt inhabits coastlines and deeper coral reefs in depths from 12 to 60 feet. Grunt populations are less prominent around islands lacking large expanses of grassbeds and sand flats.

Behavior.   The French grunt is a schooling fish, drifting in small to large groups that can number in the thousands. The schools travel in shadows during the day. Juveniles hide in grassbeds in bays, lagoons, and coastal waters.

Feeding habits.   French grunts are nocturnal bottom feeders that scavenge sand flats and grassbeds near reefs for crustaceans.

Angling.   The French grunt is easily caught on the lightest of tackle. It takes natural baits, such as pilchards, cut mullet, and dead shrimp.
See: Grunt.

GRUNT, WHITE   *Haemulon plumieri.*
Other names—redmouth; Spanish: *ronco margariteño.*

The white grunt is a wide-ranging and abundant fish. This and other grunts often make up the largest biomass on reefs in continental shelf areas. The white grunt has some commercial value, as it grows to larger sizes than do most other grunts, and it is a tasty panfish that is also commonly used in aquariums.

Identification.   One of the more colorful grunts, this fish has a silver gray body with moderate yellow body striping and numerous blue and yellow stripes on its head. The scales may be tipped with bronze and produce a checkered pattern. The inside of the mouth is red. It has 12 dorsal spines and 15 to 17 dorsal rays, 8 to 9 anal rays, and 17 pectoral rays.

Age/Size.   The average length and weight is 8 to 14 inches and about a pound, although they can reach 25 inches and weigh 8 pounds. White grunts are reported to live up to 13 years.

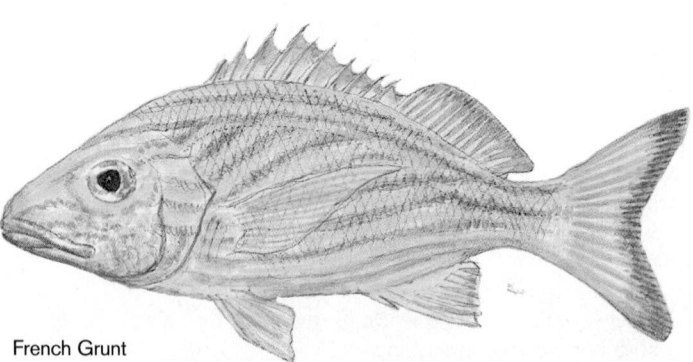

French Grunt

G

Distribution. The white grunt exists in the western Atlantic, from the Chesapeake Bay throughout the Caribbean and Gulf of Mexico south to Brazil. It was reportedly introduced unsuccessfully to Bermuda.

Habitat. White grunts prefer shallower water from nearshore to outer reef areas.

Life history/Behavior. Like other grunts, this species is a schooling fish often found in large groups. Schools travel in shadows during the day and are often located along the edges of reefs and at the base of coral formations. Fish are sexually mature at about 10 inches, and spawning takes place in the southeastern United States in late spring and summer.

Food and feeding habits. White grunts are bottom feeders that root in the sand and bottom matter near reefs. They feed on worms, shrimp, crabs, mollusks, and small fish.

Angling. *See: Grunt.*

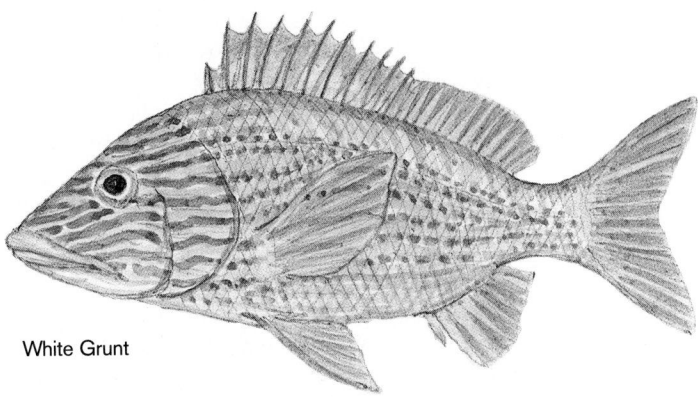
White Grunt

GRUNTER, SOOTY *Hephaestus fuliginosus.*
Other names—black bream, sooty, blubberlips, khaki bream, purple grunter.

A member of the Teraponidae family of grunter and tigerperch, the sooty grunter is a favorite freshwater sportfish among tropical anglers, and, from a recreational fishing viewpoint, is one of the most important of a number of freshwater grunter found in Australia. Despite its poor reputation as a table fish, it is eagerly sought by anglers, who find it a challenge on light tackle. Juveniles are sometimes held in large home aquariums where they will grow rapidly if enough food is available. Dedicated sooty grunter anglers, for study purposes, sometimes keep small specimens in an aquarium environment where their enormous appetite and aggressive nature make them suitable only for the one-species tank. A hardy fish, it is often transported long distances to other streams for stocking purposes. Impoundment stocking is possible, although it will not breed in this situation, nor in aquariums.

Identification. The sooty grunter can be a difficult fish to identify because its members can vary in shape, size, color, and lip size, hence the name "blubberlips." The body is deep and compressed, and color variations appear to be the result of water color. Adults are usually dark brown to blackish purple, but some are a golden color or blotched with patches of brown and gray, or gold on brown, giving the fish a diseased appearance. The single dorsal fin is unnotched, the pectoral fins are gray or gold, and the caudal fin is lightly forked and almost concave. The dorsal fin and height of spine webbing can also differ among specimens.

Size. This species is known to reach a weight of 4 kilograms and a length of 500 millimeters; the average size taken by anglers is about 0.5 kilogram and 250 millimeters. A record specimen of 4.96 kilograms was taken on a lure from Tinaroo Dam in North Queensland.

Distribution. Sooty grunter extend across the tropical north of Australia, from Queensland across the Gulf of Carpentaria to Western Australia. Within these areas they range from tidal freshwater to upstream areas, where natural obstructions such as waterfalls prevent their moving farther. Some have been introduced into streams in central Queensland, and they are known to survive in impoundments. They have also been reported in southern Papua New Guinea.

Habitat. Able to survive within a temperature range of 12° to 34°C, the sooty flourishes in clear or turbid streams, whether flowing or nearly still. It tends to live in and close to streamside cover, under the branches of overhanging trees (especially those that drop berries into the water), and can be found among submerged tree branches and other obstructions, as well as around the mouths of creeks flowing into the main stream.

Life history/Behavior. Sooty grunter breed only in streams during the summer months (December through March) when the water temperature exceeds 25°C and there is a stimulating rise in water levels. This usually takes place in or near areas where current flows. The process usually occurs in the afternoon and takes several hours. More than 100,000 eggs may be produced at one time. Carried by the current, they are nonadhesive and sink to the bottom, where they are lodged in gravel crevices. The eggs hatch out after two days, and the juveniles start to feed after four days. Group spawning appears to occur. They are a hardy and aggressive fish, and anglers have found it easy to transport them above waterfalls into areas they

G

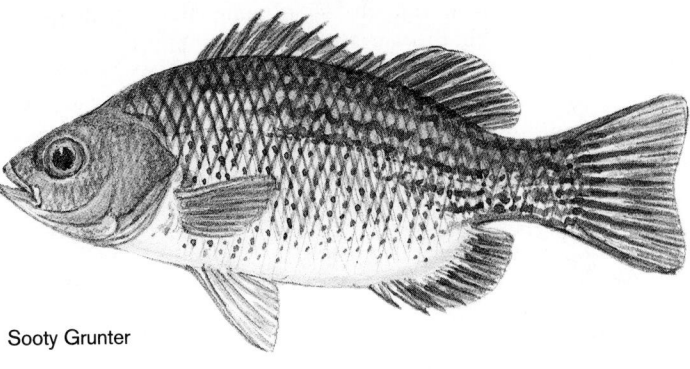
Sooty Grunter

could not otherwise reach. Queensland hatcheries have successfully induced spawning with hormone injections.

Food and feeding habits. This species is omnivorous and will feed on shrimp, frogs, small fish, worms, aquatic and terrestrial insects, plant roots, berries that fall from overhanging trees, and algae growing on the bottom of pools. They have an enormous appetite and will eat almost anything, including bread crust, cheese, and red meat.

Angling. Most anglers pursue these fish from canoes or small aluminum dinghies, or, where possible, from the banks of the stream. When fishing from boats in fast-flowing streams, anglers take turns at fishing and maintaining position. On some streams, the angler wades up the middle while casting to cover on either bank. The most popular technique is casting lures with light spinning or bait-casting tackle. Lures range from diving bass plugs to spinners and surface poppers to soft plastics, and are usually worked slowly at a speed that will just bring out the lure's action. Many of these lures are home-made. This strong, aggressive fish attacks a lure with much the same enthusiasm as does the Australian bass *(see: bass, Australian)*, and is a tenacious fighter.

Lures are cast into waters overhung by the branches of trees like the palm tree; the sooty grunter takes the berries readily when they fall into the water. These trees serve to identify likely sooty grunter territories. Lures are also cast to visible underwater structure, and in the vicinity of the mouths of in-flowing tributaries. So eager are sooty grunter to fill their stomachs that two have been known to be taken on one lure.

The fly angler, using a No. 5 or 6 outfit, will find that the sooty grunter eagerly takes Matuka flies, Muddler Minnows, other streamers, fly-rod poppers, and nymphs and dry flies. Bait fishing is sometimes practiced, but it is not as popular. The sooty grunter is not a good table fish, and most are released upon capture—often as many as 40 to 50 a day.

GUAGUANCHE   *Sphyraena guachancho.*
Other names—guachanche barracuda; Spanish: *picuda guaguanche;* French: *bécune guachanche.*

A member of the barracuda family, the guaguanche is a long, slender, silvery fish often mistaken for a young great barracuda *(see: barracuda, great)*. There is no concerted sportfishing effort for the species, but they are occasionally caught by anglers.

Identification. Silvery olive brown above, the guaguanche has silvery sides with a yellow to golden stripe running along the middle of its body. Like other members of the barracuda family, it has an elongated body and large canine and shearing teeth. Its caudal fin is large, forked, and blackish, and it has widely separated dorsal fins. The pelvic fin begins below a point just in front of the first dorsal fin, which distinguishes it from the similar-looking sennet. On the young guaguanche, there are three broad bars at the rear of the body that are often interrupted in the middle of the side.

Size. The guaguanche can grow to 2 feet, although it more commonly measures 6 to 14 inches.

Distribution. Found occasionally in Florida, the Bahamas, and the Caribbean, guaguanche occur from Massachusetts to the northern Gulf of Mexico and south to Brazil. In the eastern Atlantic, they exist in Senegal, Guinea, Sierra Leone, Côte d'Ivoire, Ghana, Togo, Benin, Nigeria, Cape Verde, Angola, and the Canary Islands.

Habitat. Guaguanche inhabit shallow and generally turbid coastal waters, including sand flats, grassbeds, mud bottoms, bays, and estuaries, although they are rare around reefs. They are a schooling species, forming schools at depths from 3 to 40 feet, and can be found near the surface at night.

Food. Guaguanche feed on fish and shrimp.

GUAM

An unincorporated territory of the United States, Guam is the largest and southernmost of the 15-island Mariana archipelago in the North Pacific Ocean. Roughly 1,500 miles from Japan and the Philippines, and 1,100 miles from New Guinea, this 30-mile-long island was formed millions of years ago when a pair of volcanoes sank beneath the ocean, leaving only their twin peaks above sea level. Nearby is the Mariana Trench, the deepest ocean trench in the world; there, Mount Humuyong Manglo, the highest mountain in the world, rises more than 7 miles from the ocean floor to the highest point on Guam. A majority of the island is surrounded by a coral table reef with deep-water channels. The coastline is characterized by sandy beaches, rocky cliffs, and mangroves.

Sportfishing action heats up in June and July, and peaks in late July or early August, when blue marlin and yellowfin tuna are most abundant. In season, five or six marlin were raised per day on average in the mid-1990s. Skipjack tuna, mahimahi (dolphin), and wahoo are also among the catch. Mahimahi appear in January and peak in late February or March. Wahoo have spring and fall surges but are more closely tied to the full moon. Skipjack tuna are abundant and can be caught all year but peak in summer months.

Boats cruise into 100-fathom water shortly after leaving the harbor at Agaña, the capital city, in search of area banks and seamounts that produce upwellings attractive to baitfish and gamefish. Pelagic species congregate within $1/4$ mile of the shoreline, and the deep water close to shore attracts

Guaguanche

G

fish to the lee of the island. This is convenient when winds prevent travel farther offshore. Most big-game fishing occurs north of Orote Point.

This is not a virgin fishery, and it has been affected by commercial fishing from Asian fleets. Blue marlin are not large on average, ranging from 100 to 200 pounds in summer, which makes this a good light tackle location. A 967-pound fish was reportedly caught in 1991, however, and in 1969 the island produced a former all-tackle world record 1,173-pound blue. The catch rate is fairly high even if fish size generally is not.

Reefs around and near Guam offer a variety of jacks, snapper, and grouper. Some anglers here combine casting on reef flats at remote island groups near Guam with offshore trolling near Guam. Twelve fish aggregating devices are located nearby.

Tourism at Guam is popular, particularly for diving; Guam is renowned for its vivid turquoise lagoons and water clarity (up to 150 feet between December and May), and features undersea observatories and one of the world's few swim-through aquariums. A fleet of well-equipped charter boats specializing in offshore fishing is based in Apra Harbor, a busy recreational and commercial port.

On a par with Nicaragua and Manila at 13° north of the equator, Guam has a tropical humid climate with an average annual temperature of 81° F. The dry season is from January through May, and the rainy season from July through November. Easterly trade winds prevail throughout the year, and typhoons, some of which caused great damage in the 1990s, occur.

GUAPOTE

Guapote (pronounced "wha-poe-tay") are members of the huge, worldwide Cichlidae family of mostly tropical freshwater fish. The *Cichlasoma* genus of guapote is characterized by a moderately deep and compressed body, sometimes with distinctive markings. They are good-fighting but generally small fish and are caught on small surface and diving plugs, usually along the covered banks of rivers and lakes.

The guapote *(C. dovii),* also known as *guapote blanco,* is found in Honduras and Costa Rica; its ultimate length and weight are unknown, but the all-tackle world record is a Costa Rican fish that weighed 12 pounds, 9 ounces. *C. friedrichsthalii,* also known as the yellowjacket cichlid, occurs from Mexico to Guatemala and Belize; the tiger, or jaguar, guapote *(C. managuense)* occurs from Honduras to Costa Rica; and the green guapote *(C. beani),* also known as the Sinaloan cichlid, is found on the Pacific slope of mainland Mexico.

GUATEMALA

The most western and most densely populated of the Central American nations, Guatemala is a rugged country with mountains and rain forest,

A guapote from the Parismina River, Costa Rica.

volcanoes and swamps, a few lakes and various rivers, and coastline on both the Caribbean and the Pacific. The most significant sportfishing opportunity presently is on the Pacific coast, which has experienced some of the world's best sailfishing in the latter 1990s. Tarpon run in the rivers, snook and permit exist on the flats, and the rivers and brackish lakes contain tarpon and snook, but there have been few attempts at organized fishing in all areas of the country through the latter decades. With two-thirds of Guatemala's interior mountainous, and minimum infrastructure to facilitate travel, what little angling occurred was done by intrepid solo adventurers.

Guatemala possesses roughly 250 miles of Pacific coastline, all washed by favorable currents and adjacent to the Middle America Trench. As of the late 1990s, organized sportfishing was concentrated at the small town of Iztapa, about a quarter of the way up the coast from Guatemala's southern border with El Salvador. At least two camps and more than a half-dozen sportfishing boats were operating year-round and enjoying sailfish action supreme.

The confluence of currents here and an abundance of baitfish over deep water (600 to 1,500 feet) have provided sailfishing in all months. Winter offers exceptional action, and calm seas that make it highly conducive to light tackle use. Most of this activity occurs from 15 to 30 miles offshore, but some occurs out to 50 miles. An hour's run by a fast, modern sportfishing boat is standard, but that hour is one of few during which little is happening.

G

The sailfish are so numerous that they are readily coaxed with hookless teasers to the boat wake, and, once excited, pounce on nearly any fly or lure or bait tossed their way. Raising less than 15 to 20 sails (many in the 75-pound class, and some 100 pounds or better) in a single day, per boat, is considered abnormal, and some anglers have more than doubled these figures, which is so outstanding that it is hard to believe. In December of 1997 one boat actually caught and released 166 sailfish in three days—a truly staggering feat. Cold snaps and other weather aberrations can produce poor days, but even the poor days here are akin to good ones in many other locations.

Although the sails are caught year-round, the prime period for greatest action has been from mid-October through May, a season of little or no wind and rain. As if all these sailfish weren't enough, yellowfin tuna are prominent from October through November, dolphin are plentiful, and blue and striped marlin are occasionally caught in winter. At least one grand slam of blue marlin, striped marlin, and sailfish was caught on a three-day charter.

Anglers fly to Guatemala City and then travel by ground transport to Iztapa. The commercial fishery here has been described as casual, and mainly focused on sharks and inshore species; it is illegal to fish commercially for sailfish or to bring a sailfish ashore, and there is no billfish consumption—policies that, if continued, will ensure the health of this fishery.

With everyone's attention focused offshore, little is pursued inshore, although snook have been reported in the Iztapa area. Nearly a dozen small and mostly fast-flowing rivers empty into the ocean along this coast. Roosterfish and jack crevalle have also been reported along this coast.

Over on the short Caribbean coast, no organized sportfishing operation existed in the late 1990s, but speculation about this possibility was intense. This is an area to watch in the future when travel conditions and services improve. The nearby keys and flats, some in the waters of Belize, hold permit and bonefish and should offer similar opportunities in Guatemala; it is possible that these fish are plentiful. Sailfish and white marlin reportedly frequent the offshore environs, but there has been no effort to fish for them.

Tarpon and snook are definitely in the cards here, as seems reasonable, because they are found to the east in Honduras. Respectively called *robalo* and *sabalo*, they should be along the whole coast, especially in the vicinity of the mouths of the two most prominent rivers—the Motagua and the Dulce. The Motagua drains the eastern highlands, and its lower reaches form the eastern border with Honduras. The Dulce is a short, navigable river that flows out of Lake Izabal and into El Golfete Lake before entering Amatique Bay at the town of Livingston. Another coastal river, although smaller than the others, is the Sarstún, which forms a partial boundary with Belize.

Tarpon and snook are reportedly in Lake Izabal, and by extension in Golfete as well as Amatique Bay. In the late 1980s they reportedly entered the Dulce River in large numbers from March through June. Commercial or subsistence fishing efforts here are unknown, and equally uncertain is the availability of a suitable local fishing boat or guide, although it seems possible to find such along the Dulce. That river, and Lakes Izabal and Golfete, cover a wide area (Izabal alone some 300 square miles), and would seem to offer considerable potential.

Tarpon have been reported inland in other Guatemalan lakes that presumably are not brackish environments like Izabal and Golfete. In the early 1980s, Lake Petexbatún in the northern Petén rain forest region had numerous tarpon, including fish well over 100 pounds, mainly in the high-water season of July and August. Snook and peacock bass were supposedly here, but are unverified. This is the heart of ancient Mayan country, with Tikal National Park nearby. Tikal was once a jungle community of 55,000 people in the ninth century.

Guatemala's other interior lakes and rivers have not been known for sportfishing opportunity. Famous Lake Atitlán, about 40 miles west of Guatemala City, reportedly had largemouth bass and crappie. The bass reputedly reached 20 pounds in the 1970s and were the object of extensive spearfishing; their current status is unknown, but stocking has clearly decimated native fish populations and bird life. Atitlán and Amatitlán, south of Guatemala City, also contain mojarra and a variety of small cichlids. At more than 5,000 feet above sea level and with depths exceeding 1,000 feet, Lake Atitlán is a popular attraction known for its mountain beauty and three nearby volcanoes.

Volcanic eruptions elsewhere in Guatemala, as well as earthquakes, have often caused disasters, and hurricanes and tropical storms occasionally strike the coast. The coastal regions are hot and humid, with an annual average temperature of about 82°F. May through October is generally the rainy season.

GUIDE
See: Fishing Guide.

GUIDE BOAT
A generic term that broadly refers to a boat in the 15- to 20-foot class operated by a fishing guide and hired on a daily basis. In earlier times, a guide boat was one that was rowed and was large enough to take one or two passengers in addition to the operator. Today, almost all guide boats are motorized, and they take from one to three passengers aboard, depending on the size of the boat and type of fishing to be done.

A guide boat might be an 18- to 20-foot flats boat (*see*) used for shallow saltwater fishing, a 16- to 20-foot bass boat (*see*) used for freshwater bass fishing,

In the salmon grounds of Nakwato Rapids of Slingsby Channel, British Columbia, the water flow may reach a rate of 16 knots.

G

or a variety of less-shallow draft boats. Those few that are rowed include river-fishing drift boats *(see)* and the occasional skiff, although some guides at lodges in the Campbell River area of British Columbia offer row-trolling for salmon as a means of joining the traditional Tyee Club (membership requires catching a large salmon from a boat that is rowed).

The term "guide boat" may be loosely applied to any boat operated by a fishing guide, although practically the term is meant to be more limited, distinguishing this vessel from a charter boat *(see)*, which is bigger, usually capable of taking more passengers, and built for large waters where seas can become heavy.

Operators of a guide boat may or may not have much formal training or licensing, depending on the locale. In some places, the requirements for guiding are virtually nonexistent and may not even include any permit or license. In other places, more formal training, testing, and certification are required. Any person who takes people for hire onto navigable waterways that are under the jurisdiction of the United States Coast Guard must have a captain's license and pass a rigorous examination. Even if that person operates a boat only on a bay, near-shore flats, or tidal river, and may be called a "fishing guide," the person must still obtain a captain's license.

Generally, you hire a guide as opposed to hiring a guide boat; some guides have more than one boat (especially in saltwater), switching as fishing circumstances warrant. Many guides are booked in advance by reservation and deposit, although in places where guides are numerous it may be possible to hire a guide for a day (through a lodge, hotel, or booking service) without prior reservation. **See: Fishing Guide.**

GUIDE, ROD

The component of a fishing rod that is attached to the exterior of the blank and that aids in dispensing and retrieving line, absorbing stress from the exertion of a strong fish, and keeping the line from contacting the rod blank.

Nearly all fishing rods have guides, the exception being the relatively few line-through-blank rods; this includes a tip-top guide and a variable number of intermediate guides along the length of the blank. Other than the blank itself, guides are the single most significant factor affecting rod performance.

Guides are situated above or below the axis of the rod, depending upon the style and fishing application of the finished rod, and they vary in style, size, number, spacing, placement, and materials of the guide rings (the surface that contacts the fishing line). **See: Rod, Fishing.**

GUINEA-BISSAU

Facing the Atlantic Ocean in northwestern Africa, Guinea-Bissau is sandwiched between Senegal on the north and Guinea on the south. Much of this small country is a low, swampy coastal plain, and it includes about 60 offshore islands, among which is the 18-island Bijagós archipelago. Numerous rivers form wide estuaries here, and a virtually infinite number of small atolls, banks, and sandbars exist along the coast, most surrounded by mangroves and other swampy vegetation.

Due to the presence of four great rivers, the local flora and fauna can count on a great supply of food. Birds, mammals, and fish are particularly abundant in the Bijagós, and after the archipelagos were discovered by French anglers in the early 1980s, the Acaja Fishing Club was established there in 1983.

Situated on large Rubane Island just in front of the Geba River, the club is about 45 miles south of the capital city of Bissau, with a stunning panorama across the clear waters of the Atlantic. Acaja guests can take club boats to the nearby sandbanks and reefs, where they enjoy light tackle trolling and casting with lures and flies around exotic and private sand islands. Inshore and river fishing are also offered.

The major fish of the area are courbine (meagre) and tiger sharks. Up to 150 tiger sharks are taken annually, with an average weight of 400 pounds. Other species regularly caught include bluefish, cobia, barracuda, king mackerel, African pompano, skipjacks, spotted sea bass, garrick, snapper, guitarfish, hammerhead sharks, bull sharks, tope, and various jacks. About 40 percent of these fish are caught by anglers surf-casting from the beach, and the remainder are caught by trolling and light tackle drifting. Bottom fishing and casting are the favored methods for landing red and gray sea bream and grouper. The season is year-round, with a light increase from October through May.

Normally, 400 angling tourists from Europe pass through the Acaja Fishing Club each year, most arriving from Paris via Dakar, Senegal.

GUITARFISH, ATLANTIC

Rhinobatos lentiginosus.

Other names—French: *poisson-guitarre tacheté;* Italian: *pesce violino;* Spanish: *guitarra.*

A cross between a skate and a shark in appearance, the Atlantic guitarfish is a member of the Rajiformes family, along with skate and ray. It is occasionally encountered by anglers but is not a targeted species.

G

Atlantic Guitarfish

Identification. The head and pectoral fins of the Atlantic guitarfish form a triangular disk at the front of the body. The rear of the body is thick and tapered like a shark's, and it has two large dorsal fins and a well-developed caudal fin. The Atlantic guitarfish varies in color from gray to brown, with several pale spots on its body.

Size. This species is normally 1 to 2 feet long and can attain a maximum length of $2^1/_2$ feet. Females are somewhat larger than males.

Distribution. Atlantic guitarfish extend from North Carolina to the Gulf of Mexico, although they are not reported in the Bahamas or the Caribbean and are uncommon in Florida and the Yucatán. The Brazilian guitarfish (*R. horkeli*) and the southern guitarfish (*R. percellens*) are two closely related species that range from the West Indies to Brazil.

Habitat. Inhabiting sandy and weedy bottoms, Atlantic guitarfish are found near small reefs, usually buried in seagrass, sand, or mud at depths of 1 to 45 feet.

Life history. Atlantic guitarfish are ovoviviparous, which means they bear live young, with up to six in a litter. At birth they are 20 centimeters long.

Food. Small mollusks and crustaceans form the diet of the guitarfish.

GULF STREAM

The Gulf Stream is the northern and western swing of the North Atlantic Current and one of the strongest currents *(see)* in the North Atlantic Ocean. It separates the warm, salty Sargasso Sea from the cold, less saline inshore water, moving northerly at between 4 and 5 knots per hour, with a passage that courses off North America through the Florida Straits off Key West, Florida, along the coast to about Cape Hatteras, then away from the coast to the Grand Banks off Newfoundland, after which it joins the North Atlantic Current flowing toward Europe.

The Gulf Stream is normally about 75 miles from Jacksonville, Florida. Anglers who make the long run here and elsewhere fish the edge of the Stream, where different bodies of water meet, especially for pelagic species.

GUNWALE

Pronounced "gunnel" (rhymes with "tunnel"), the gunwale is the upper edge of the side of a boat. Gunwales vary in width, thickness, curvature, and strength. They are often used in fishing for supporting various accessories, especially rod holders, and may be designed to provide underneath storage, especially for unused rods in a horizontal position. Gunwales usually project above any platforms or decks, but in some specialized craft gunwales may be flush with them, especially a foredeck.

See: Boat.

The largemouth bass record of 22 pounds 4 ounces has stood since 1932; however, naturalist William Bartram, exploring Florida's St. Johns River in 1773, reported catching a 30-pound bass on a deer-hair jiggerbob (presumably a bass bug).

GURNARD, FLYING *Dactylopterus volitans.*
Other names—Spanish: *alón, chichara;* French: *poule de mer.*

A member of the Dactylopteridae family, the flying gurnard is a minor commercial species that is occasionally caught incidentally by anglers.

Identification. The flying gurnard may be shades of gray or yellow brown with white spots. It has large, fanlike pectoral fins that extend almost to the tail; these "wings" are used as gliding surfaces for the occasional excursion to the surface. The flying gurnard also has stiff-spined pelvic fins that are directed downward and enable the fish to "walk" along the bottom.

Size. This species ranges from 6 to 14 inches in length; it is usually smaller than 12 inches and can reach a maximum of 18 inches. A 4-pounder caught in Florida is listed as an all-tackle world record.

Distribution. In the eastern Atlantic, the flying gurnard is found from the English Channel south to Angola, including Madeira, the Azores, and the Mediterranean, with the exception of the Black Sea. In the western Atlantic, it is ranges from the Gulf of Mexico north to Massachusetts and south to Argentina.

Habitat. Inhabiting subtropical or tropical seas, the flying gurnard is found in depths of 1 to 35 feet in sandy or seagrass areas, over rocks or coral rubble, and among fringe reefs.

Food and feeding habits. Flying gurnard feed on clams, crabs, and small fish. When foraging, they "walk" along the bottom and turn over rubble with their ventral fins.

GUYANA

Formerly known as British Guiana, this small country in northern South America is bordered by Suriname on the east, Brazil on the south, Venezuela on the west, and the Atlantic Ocean on the north.

The coastline extends for about 270 miles, but coastal fisheries are unreported. The continental shelf is far from shore, and the coastal landmass is low lying, much of it protected by dams and dikes. Several major rivers converge at a substantial bay near Bartica.

Some rivers in the highlands are reported to have lots of peacock bass, payara, pirarucú, catfish, and piranhas, but no infrastructure for sportfishing exists and there are no outfitters in most of the remote, upper watershed rivers.

The Essequibo River and its major tributary, the Rupununi, are sandy-bottomed black-water rivers *(see: Brazil)* that begin in the Guyana Highlands along Guyana's borders with Brazil and Venezuela. Near the Brazilian state of Roraima, the Rupununi meanders through savannas where several large, natural black-water lakes provide excellent peacock bass fishing. The peacocks average 4 to 6 pounds, but some in the 12- to 15-pound class are taken; the action overall can be fast. The river itself produces peacock bass as well as piranhas, catfish, and the occasional pirarucu. A few ranches in the area provide very rustic guest facilities, meals, boats, motors, and native guides, all at reasonable prices.

The Essequibo and tributaries like the Rewa also have peacock bass, catfish, and pirarucu, plus big piranhas and excellent fishing for payara, with 20- to 25-pounders possible. There are also pacu, bicuda, surubim, matrinxa, and other species. One outfitter offers a motorized float trip with primitive tent camping on both these rivers.

Since the Essequibo and Rewa have very few lakes and lagoons, fishing is primarily done in the main rivers, especially below numerous rapids and small falls, through which native guides easily portage boats. The upper tributaries contain only a few small native villages, and the scenery and wildlife viewing can be spectacular.

GYOTAKU

A Japanese art form in which ink prints are made of fish. The process involves the application of ink to one side of a whole fish; an impression is obtained by pressing different types of paper or cloth over the inked body of the fish.

G

HABITABLE ZONES

The various areas that marine organisms occupy in the ocean environment. Life is concentrated in only about 4 percent of the total water area of the world's oceans, primarily because sunlight is needed to permit photosynthesis for plankton, which is the basis of the marine food chain. The greatest abundance of ocean life is found in the open ocean from the lowest tide line to the outer edge of the continental shelf.

HABITAT

In a broad sense, the area or space in which an organism or group of organisms live; an estuary, a pond, a marsh, etc., can be construed as habitat for fish as well as numerous other animals. In a narrow sense, habitat is the specific place occupied by an individual. Anglers often speak of habitat in both senses, but when seeking fish they usually focus on the most definitive aspects of the habitat, especially the specific cover or structure that holds or attracts fish, even if temporarily.

HACKLE

Bird feather of fly-tying quality, which is wound around the hook in constructing an artificial fly.
See: Fly.

HADDOCK   *Melanogrammus aeglefinus.*

Other names—haddie, scrod; French: *eglefin;* Italian: *asinello;* Norwegian: *kolje;* Portuguese: *arinca, bacalhau;* Spanish: *eglefino.*

Closely related to the genus *Gadus,* the haddock is often considered a member of the Gadidae, or codfish, family. Haddock have long been important commercially and are an even more highly valued food fish than Atlantic cod, although stocks of haddock have declined rapidly since the 1960s due to overfishing. Sportfishing for haddock is minor, in part due to current historically low levels of this fish.

Commercial fishing for haddock is principally conducted with otter trawls. Today, the commercial catch of haddock is far below historical levels, and haddock are generally in a collapsed or near-collapsed condition, having been overexploited by commercial fishing. This crisis has occurred in the face of commercial and recreational management of cod fisheries under the New England Fishery Management Council's Multispecies Fishery Management Plan. The 1980s and 1990s experienced record low commercial catches, and haddock abundance and recruitment have been at all-time lows. With spawning stock biomass at unprecedented depressed levels, there is enormous concern for the future of this species.

Identification.   Characteristic of a cod, the haddock has three dorsal fins and two anal fins, and the first dorsal fin is high and pointed. The small chin barbel is sometimes hidden. Its coloring is purplish gray on the back and sides, fading to pinkish reflections and a white belly. There is a black lateral line along the side and a black shoulder blotch commonly called the "Devil's thumb print," or "St. Peter's mark."

The dark lateral line and shoulder blotch can distinguish it from its close relatives in the cod family. The three dorsal fins distinguish the haddock from its relative the silver hake *(see: hake, silver).*

Size/Age.   The average haddock is 1 to 2 feet long and weighs 1 to 5 pounds. The all-tackle record is 11 pounds, 3 ounces, but they have been reported to attain $16^{1}/_{2}$ pounds. Haddock can live for 14 years. The growth rate of haddock has changed substantially over the past 30 to 40 years, possibly in response to changes in abundance. Prior to 1960, when haddock were considerably more abundant than at present, the average length of a four-year-old fish was approximately 19 to 20 inches. Presently, growth is more rapid, with haddock reaching this size at three years. Changes in sexual maturation have also been observed. In recent years, the maturation schedule has shifted downward by about one year; currently, nearly all haddock at age 3, and three-quarters of age 2 female haddock, are mature. Although the presence of early-maturing fish increases spawning stock biomass, it is uncertain if these younger fish are spawning successfully or producing eggs of sufficient quality to contribute strongly to the reproductive success of the population.

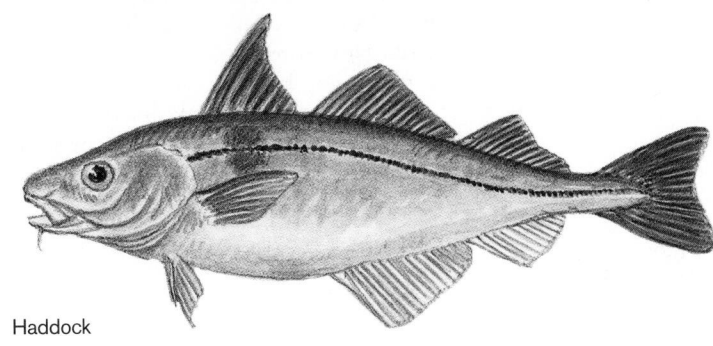

Haddock

Distribution. The haddock is found on both sides of the Atlantic, from the North Sea and Iceland to Newfoundland and Nova Scotia, and southward to southern New Jersey. It occasionally inhabits the deep water to Cape Hatteras. The highest concentrations off the U.S. coast occur on the northern and eastern section of Georges Bank and in the southwestern Gulf of Maine. Two stocks occur in U.S. waters: the Gulf of Maine stock and the Georges Bank stock.

Habitat. Preferring deeper water than do cod, haddock inhabit depths of 25 to 75 fathoms. Although generally a coldwater species, preferring temperatures of 36° to 50°F, they are commonly found in warm water over bottoms of sand, pebbles, or broken shells.

Life history/Behavior. The spawning season is between January and June, and activity peaks during late March and early April, when large congregations form in depths of 20 to 100 fathoms. For several months, the young live at the surface until they settle to the bottom. Individual females can produce up to 3 million eggs, but a 22-inch specimen produces approximately 850,000 eggs. Major spawning concentrations occur on eastern Georges Bank, although some spawning also occurs to the east of Nantucket Shoals and along the Maine coast.

Haddock swim in large schools, and there is some seasonal migration to the north in spring, and south again in the fall. Adult haddock on Georges Bank appear to be relatively sedentary, but seasonal coastal movements occur in the western Gulf of Maine. There are extensive migrations in the Barents Sea and off Iceland.

Food and feeding habits. Primarily consuming crabs, snails, worms, clams, and sea urchins, the haddock seldom feeds actively on fish.

Angling. There is virtually no current sportfishing for haddock, although techniques are similar to those for Atlantic cod (see: cod, Atlantic). **See: Cod and Hake.**

HAGFISH

Hagfish are one of two groups of jawless fish (the other being lampreys), which are the most primitive true vertebrates. They are members of the Petromyzontidae family. Fishlike vertebrates, jawless fish are similar to eels in form, with a cartilaginous or fibrous skeleton that has no bones. They have no paired limbs and no developed jaws or bony teeth. Their extremely slimy skin lacks scales.

The repulsive-looking hag is the most primitive of all living fish, resembling an outsize, slimy worm. The hag is exclusively marine, and only one family, Myxinidae, is known. The hag has the ability to discharge slime from its mucous sacs, which are far out of proportion to its size.

Their habit of feeding primarily on dead or disabled fish makes hagfish doubly unattractive. Commercial fishermen consider them a great nuisance because they penetrate the bodies of hooked or gillnetted fish, eating out first the intestines and then the meat, leaving nothing but skin and bones. The hagfish bores into the cavity of its victim by means of a rasplike tongue. Unlike many lampreys (see), it is not a parasite. Hags' eyes are not visible externally, and they are considered blind. Food is apparently detected by scent, and large numbers of hags are often taken in deep-set eel pots baited with dead fish.

The hag can be differentiated from its close relative, the lamprey, by the following characteristics: The hag has prominent barbels on its snout, no separate dorsal fin, eyes that are not visible externally, a nasal opening at the tip of the snout, and a mouth that is not funnel-shaped or disklike. The largest hags are 2 feet or more in length. They range the cold, deep waters, and at least one specimen was recorded at a depth of 1,335 meters.

HAIR BUG

A deer-hair bug style of artificial fly.
See: Fly.

HAIR RIG

A European bait rig for light-striking fish.
See: Carp.

HAIRTAIL   *Trichiurus savala.*

Other names—hairy, smallhead hairtail, savalani hairtail, spiny hairtail, smallheaded ribbonfish; Malay: *langgai, puchuk, timah.*

Often mistaken for the pike eel *(Muraenesox bagio)* and a related tropical inshore species, the frost fish *(Lepidotus caudatus)*, the hairtail is a rather mysterious fish that is much sought after by anglers along the East Coast of Australia. Although there is no commercial fishery for this species, anglers regard it as very good table fare, provided it is not overcooked.

Identification. The hairtail has an extremely elongated, deeply compressed, scaleless body that is bright silver along its entire length. The single dorsal fin extends the full length of the body, which tapers to a slender threadlike tail. This fine tail readily distinguishes it from the frost fish, whose tail is small but forked, and from the pike eel, whose tail is rounded and much broader. Its pectoral fins are small. The arrow-shaped head has large eyes and an undershot jaw that contains sharp teeth and three or four huge, barbed fangs under the snout.

Size. This fish is known to exceed 2 meters in length and reach a weight of 5 kilograms. An Australian record stands at 4.25 kilograms.

H

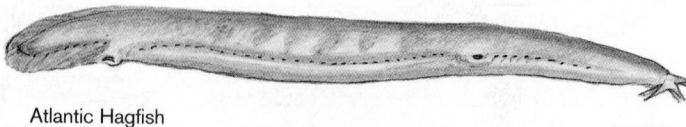

Atlantic Hagfish

Distribution. Hairtail occur in Indo-Pacific waters from India and Sri Lanka to Southeast Asia and north to China and south to New Guinea and Australia. In Australian waters, hairtail are mainly confined to New South Wales waters, particularly the Sydney region. Elsewhere they have been reported from Western Australia, South Australia, and as far north as Townsville in northern Queensland.

Habitat. Hairtail seem to prefer the deep waters of marine inlets and bays, where small yellowtail (scad) and mullet are available.

Life history/Behavior. Little if any serious research has been carried out on the habits of the hairtail. Enigmatic creatures, they are well known for their sudden appearances and disappearances in a waterway. It is not known if they spawn in Australian waters. Small specimens are frequently seen in the fish markets of Asia.

Food and feeding habits. Anglers' experiences show that hairtail feed at any time of the day or night but are most active after dark. They appear to move in schools and will circle a bay as they feed. Hairtail eat small fish such as yellowtail, mullet, pilchards, and garfish, and readily take a bait of king prawn or fish fillet.

Angling. Hairtail fishing is usually carried out from a boat, although occasional captures are made from rocky shores that drop off into deep water. Short boat rods and a reel spooled with at least 5-kilogram (preferably 7-kilogram) line are the norm. Handlines to 10 kilograms are also popular.

When using ganged hooks with garfish or pilchard baits, no wire leader is necessary, but single or double hooks demand the use of wire because of the razor-sharp nature of the hairtail's fangs. A favorite rigging technique is to secure a 15-centimeter wire leader to a curtain ring, the latter offering a secure finger hold when the fish is brought to the surface. Hook sizes vary from 5/0 to 7/0. Small sinkers, riding on the hook eye, are sometimes used when it's necessary to get the bait down quickly to where the hairtail are feeding; when speed is not an issue, the bait is allowed to sink under its own weight.

The last two hours of a rising tide that peaks at around 10 P.M., and for a short time after the peak, are regarded as the best times to fish for hairtail. Boats anchor in a selected area, and chum (usually fish scraps) is fed into the water. Rigged baits are allowed to sink a couple of rod lengths to where the fish are thought to be. Two or more anglers in a boat will vary the depth of their baits. Although some anglers fish during the day, fishing after dark generally produces better results.

Despite its formidable appearance, the hairtail signals its presence by a gentle movement of the line, and the angler's strike is empirical. On many nights, anglers rely on the phosphorescence given off by minute organisms to indicate when the fish has taken the bait; when the fish strikes, the line straightens and disturbs these organisms, causing them to glow.

The fish's strength is considerable, as its length gives it great purchase in the water. When the fish is drawn to the surface, the angler slips a finger into the curtain ring, and the flailing fish is pulled inboard. At this stage, great care is essential in avoiding the impressive teeth of the hairtail.

Lure anglers have found that hairtail respond to metal jigs of various patterns, jigged up and down near the bottom. This method is used during daylight hours.

HAIRWING

A term for a bucktail-style streamer fly, tied with hair or other fur.
See: Fly.

HAKE

See: Cod and Hake; Hake, Pacific; Hake, Silver.

HAKE, PACIFIC   *Merluccius productus.*

Other names—Pacific whiting, whitefish, haddock, butterfish, California hake, popeye, silver hake, ocean whitefish; French: *merlu du Pacifique nord;* Spanish: *merluza del Pacífico norte.*

A member of the Merlucciidae family, the Pacific hake is sometimes classified as a member of the Gadidae family and thus included with codfish. It is the only representative of the hake family in the Pacific. Common in commercial and sport catches because of its abundance, the Pacific hake is not generally sought for its food value, but it is made into fish meal. Because it does not remain fresh very long, once caught, it must be immediately chilled or the flesh becomes soft and undesirable.

Many Pacific hake are caught incidentally by anglers fishing for salmon or bottom fish, and are generally discarded. They are also considered a nuisance because they raid salmon nests for eggs.

Identification. The body of the Pacific hake is elongate, slender, and moderately compressed. The head is elongate and the mouth large with strong, sharp teeth. The thin scales fall off readily. Its coloring is gray to dusky brown, with brassy overtones and black speckles on the back.

The elongated shape, notched second dorsal and anal fin, and coloration separate the Pacific hake from other similar fish in its family.

Pacific Hake

H

Size/Age. The Pacific hake can grow to 3 feet in length. The all-tackle record is 2 pounds, 2 ounces.

Distribution. This fish occurs in the Gulf of California (isolated population) and from Magdalena Bay, Baja California, to Alaska. It has been reported along the Asiatic coast.

Habitat. The Pacific hake prefers a deep, sandy environment, and has been reported in depths exceeding 2,900 feet.

Life history/Behavior. Spawning occurs in the winter or from February through April, beginning at three to four years of age, off Southern California and Baja California, Mexico. After spawning, the adults migrate northward to Oregon, Washington, and Canada and return to their spawning areas in the fall. This species is classified as demersal, but is largely pelagic in oceanic and coastal areas. Adults exist in large schools in waters overlying the continental shelf, except during the spawning season, when they are several hundred miles seaward.

Food. The Pacific hake feeds on a variety of small fish, shrimp, and squid.

Angling. Pacific hake are an occasional, incidental catch and not a targeted species for anglers. They are usually caught on squid, herring, and anchovy baits.

See: Cod and Hake; Hake, Silver.

HAKE, RED *Urophycis chuss.*

Other names—squirrel hake, ling; French: *merluche éureuil;* Spanish: *locha roja.*

Red hake are somewhat of an incidental catch for deep-water anglers and have become less significant to commercial trawlers. Although not considered overexploited, red hake are now caught commercially at much lower levels than previously.

Identification. The body of the red hake is elongate with two dorsal fins—the second one long—and one long anal fin. Its coloration is variable, but the sides are usually reddish and often dark or mottled. The fins are not dark-edged, as they are in some other hake, and the pelvic fin rays are shorter than those of other hake.

Size/Age. The maximum length reached by red hake is approximately 50 centimeters, or about $19^{1}/_{2}$ inches. Their maximum age is reported to be about 12 years, but few fish survive beyond 8 years of age. The all-tackle world record is 7 pounds, 15 ounces, which is their known maximum size; the common size is roughly 2 pounds.

Distribution. Red hake are found from the Gulf of St. Lawrence to North Carolina but are most abundant between Georges Bank and New Jersey. Research from bottom-trawl surveys indicate that red hake have a broad geographic and depth distribution throughout the year, undergoing extensive seasonal migrations. Two stocks have been assumed, divided north and south in the central Georges Bank region.

Habitat. These fish generally occupy deep water over soft or sandy bottoms. Although juvenile fish may frequent shallow water along the coast, adults typically migrate to deeper water, generally between 300 and 400 feet deep, although reports indicate that they exist at depths greater than 1,650 feet.

Life history/Behavior. Red hake winter in the deep waters of the Gulf of Maine and along the outer continental shelf and slope south and southwest of Georges Bank. Spawning occurs from May through November, and significant spawning areas are located on the southwest part of Georges Bank and in Southern New England south of Montauk Point, Long Island.

Food and feeding habits. Red hake feed primarily on crustaceans, but adult red hake also feed extensively on fish.

Angling. There is no significant recreational fishing effort for red hake.

See: Cod and Hake.

HAKE, SILVER *Merluccius bilinearis.*

Other names—Atlantic hake, whiting, frostfish; French: *merlu argenté;* Spanish: *merluza norteamericana.*

A member of the Merlucciidae family, the silver hake is primarily known as whiting. An aggressive fish and a swift swimmer, it is a good species for sportfishing. Whiting are a common fish for party boat anglers, especially in the winter and early spring, and are sometimes an early-season surf catch.

Whiting have been a significant commercial fish, particularly with the demise of groundfish species like cod and haddock. They are primarily caught in otter trawls in the winter and spring. However, the stock abundance of these fish has been low in recent times, there are few older fish, and the pressure on young fish has intensified, resulting in an overexploited fishery. Most of the commercial catch is frozen and sold in packaged form, especially as fish sticks and fish cakes.

Identification. The body of the whiting is long and slender, with a flattened head, a large mouth, and strong, sharp teeth. The second dorsal fin and anal fin are deeply indented, giving the fin a divided appearance. The first fin is short and high. Its coloring is dark gray above, with iridescent purple hues that fade to silvery white on the belly.

The whiting, or silver hake, can be distinguished from the cod *(see),* pollack *(see),* tomcod *(see),* and

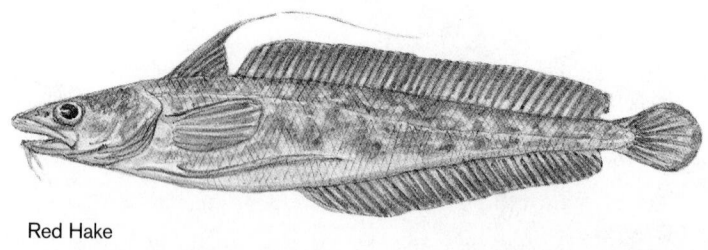

Red Hake

haddock (*see*) by the presence of only two dorsal fins and one anal fin. It also lacks the chin barbel characteristic of cod and haddock.

Size/Age. The whiting can reach 2½ feet in length and a weight of 8 pounds, although the average catch is a fish of less than 14 inches; fish exceeding 4 pounds are rare. Ages up to 15 years have been reported, but few fish older than age 6 have been observed in recent years.

Distribution. Found from the Newfoundland banks southward to the vicinity of South Carolina, the whiting is encountered in large numbers between Cape Sable and New York. Closely related forms are taken in the southern parts of the United States and in the Gulf of Mexico. In U.S. waters, two stocks have been identified based on morphological differences; one extends from the Gulf of Maine to northern Georges Bank, and the second occurs from southern Georges Bank to the mid-Atlantic area. Whiting undertake extensive migrations; in winter, the northern stock travels to the deeper waters of the Gulf of Maine, and the southern stock moves along the outer continental shelf and slope.

Habitat. Whiting primarily inhabit the cool, deep waters of the continental shelf, although they often visit shallower waters in pursuit of prey. Adults stay in deep water offshore, whereas juveniles are generally stay in shallow water closer to shore. They make seasonal onshore-offshore migrations; the range of their location, however, extends from near the surface to 600 feet deep, and they have been reported much deeper. They prefer sand and pebble bottoms, and temperatures between 36° and 52°F. Whiting move toward shallow water in the spring, spawn, and return to the wintering areas in autumn.

Spawning behavior. Spawning occurs in late spring and early summer, when whiting release their buoyant eggs at the surface, allowing them to drift with the current. Future stocks depend on the weather; if the wind blows the eggs away from inshore, very few will survive, having nothing to feed on. More than 50 percent of fish at age 2 (8 to 12 inches), and nearly all fish at age 3 (10 to 14 inches), are sexually mature.

Peak spawning occurs earlier in the southern stock (May and June) than in the northern stock (July and August). Important spawning areas include the coastal region of the Gulf of Maine from Cape Cod to Grand Manan Island, southern and southeastern Georges Bank, and southern New England south of Martha's Vineyard.

Food and feeding habits. Whiting feed aggressively in large groups on herring, silversides, menhaden, young mackerel, and on squid and other invertebrates. They have been known to strand themselves on shoals and in shallow waters during the height of their feeding activity after spawning.

Angling. Because whiting are normally present close to shore in the winter and early spring,

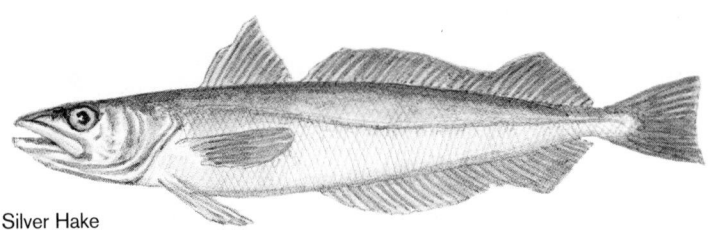

Silver Hake

they are one of few species available to saltwater anglers at that time. The fish are pursued primarily from party boats, but private boaters may catch them as well, and surf anglers can score if the fish are near the beach.
See: Cod and Hake.

HAKE, WHITE   *Merluccius bilinearis.*
See: Cod and Hake.

HALFBEAKS AND BALAO
Other names—French: *demi-bec;* Spanish: *aguja, agujeta, saltador.*

Halfbeaks are closely related to flyingfish (*see*) and needlefish (*see*). These sparkling, silvery fish travel in schools and are abundant in warm seas. They are important food fish for pelagic species, especially billfish, and are used as rigged trolling bait for marlin, dolphin, and other big-game fish encountered in blue water. Although live halfbeaks are seldom available to anglers, frozen packs of halfbeaks (mainly balao or ballyhoo) are sold at most coastal marinas and tackle shops, and individuals are defrosted and rigged for offshore fishing (*see*).

A halfbeak's body is elongated, rounded, and flattened from side to side only in the tail region. The dorsal and anal fins are located far to the rear and directly opposite each other. In halfbeaks, only the lower jaw is long; the upper jaw is of normal length. They stay mainly close to shore, commonly leaping or scooting rapidly across the surface with only their tail in the water. The tail is vibrated rapidly to propel them. Most species lay their eggs in the open sea; a few are ovoviviparous, retaining their eggs in their body until they hatch and then "giving birth" to young.

The wrestling halfbeak (*Dermogenys pusillus*) of southeastern Asia is one of the few halfbeaks kept in aquariums. An ovoviviparous species, the females carry the eggs for about a month, sometimes longer, before giving birth to the young, usually 20 or more. At birth, the fry are less than a half inch long, and they do not have an extended lower jaw. When mature, about 2½ months later, the females are nearly 3 inches long. The males are slightly shorter, and their anal fin is modified as a sexual organ for internal fertilization of the female. These little halfbeaks feed on insects and other live foods, which they capture as they swim along at the surface. Their long lower jaw serves as a scoop of sorts, and the open upper jaw is clamped shut to hold the animals.

H

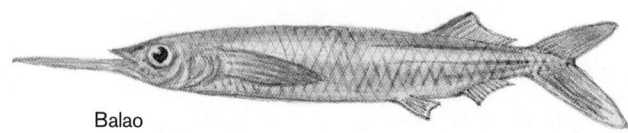

Balao

Male wrestling halfbeaks are pugnacious, circling each other belligerently with their mouths open and their gill covers lifted. Their battles are mainly sparring bluffs, however, and they usually make no physical contact with each other.

The balao (*Hemiramphus balao*) is a halfbeak that inhabits tropical and warm-temperate waters nearly worldwide. In the western Atlantic, it ranges from New York to the Gulf of Mexico and southward to Brazil, including the Caribbean; in the eastern Atlantic, it is found around the Canary Islands and in the Gulf of Guinea from Victoria, Nigeria, to Luanda, Angola. Its pectoral fin is long, the lower jaw and caudal fin have orange red tips, and the sides and belly are silvery. It averages 8 to 10 inches in length and can grow to 16 inches.

The ballyhoo (*Hemiramphus brasiliensis*) is a halfbeak that is common off the Florida coast and in the Caribbean, traveling northward along the eastern coast and occasionally as far north as Massachusetts in summer. It ranges as far south as Brazil, and is also found in the eastern Atlantic, from the Cape Verde Islands and Dakar in Senegal to Angola. Three black stripes extend the full length of the greenish back. The sides and belly are silvery, and the caudal fin is yellowish orange. Ballyhoo average 6 to 10 inches in length, rarely longer. They are netted, often by attracting them to lights at night, and are the most common halfbeak used as bait for pelagic species in North America. The last ray in the ballyhoo's dorsal fin is elongated, much longer than in most halfbeaks. The closely related longfin halfbeak (*H. saltator*) of the Pacific also has a long ray in its dorsal fin. An Indo-Pacific species, *H. far,* is one of the largest, reaching a length of 2 feet. In Japan, the sayori (*H. sajori*), which can attain a length of 16 inches, is commonly harvested for food.

The halfbeak (*Hyporhamphus unifasciatus*), which attains 12 inches in length, lives in the same geographical area of the Atlantic as the ballyhoo but occurs also in the Pacific from Point Conception southward to Peru, including the Galápagos Islands. It has a single grayish stripe down each side of its body and three dark lines down the middle of the back. The tip of the long lower jaw is red, and the body is less deep in profile and more rounded than that of the ballyhoo or balao. The halfbeak is used for bait; it makes good eating itself, although it is seldom caught specifically for this purpose. The

related California halfbeak (*H. rosae*), is smaller, rarely more than 6 inches long. The Indo-Pacific *H. dussumieri* is sometimes 18 inches long.

Included among the Pacific halfbeaks off the coast of North America is the ribbon halfbeak (*Euleptorhamphus viridis*), which grows to as much as 18 inches and has long pectoral fins. The smaller flying halfbeak (*E. velox*), which lives on both sides of the Atlantic and ranges from the Gulf of Mexico to Brazil in the western Atlantic, is so named because of its habit of leaping and skittering over the surface and sometimes gliding for short distances, much as flyingfish do; it can grow to 20 inches in length but seldom enters coastal waters.

HALF-STEPPING
See: Walking the Dog.

HALIBUT, ATLANTIC   *Hippoglossus hippoglossus.*
Other names—common halibut, giant halibut, right-eyed flounder, chicken halibut (under 20 pounds); Dutch: *heilbot;* Finnish: *ruijanpallas;* French: *flétan de l'Atlantique;* Icelandic: *heilagfiski;* Japanese: *ohyô;* Norwegian: *kveite;* Portuguese: *alabote;* Spanish: *flétan del Atlántico, hipogloso;* Swedish: *hälleflundra, helgeflundra.*

The Atlantic halibut is among the largest bony fish in the world and a member of the Pleuronectidae family of right-eyed flounder. Flounder have a unique type of maturation from larvae to adult stage in which one eye migrates to the opposite side of the head.

The Atlantic halibut is a highly prized table fish, with white, tender flesh that has a mild flavor and is often likened to chicken; it has been marketed fresh, dried/salted, smoked, and frozen. It is an excellent fighter, but it is a deep-dwelling fish that is seldom deliberately pursued by anglers. It may be caught incidentally by anglers fishing for other deep ocean dwellers. It has historically been an extremely important market species, but it has been greatly overfished by commercial interests, who primarily catch it by bottom longlining.

Identification.   The body is wide and somewhat flattened, rimmed by long dorsal and anal fins. The lateral line, which has a scale count of about 160, arches strongly above the pectoral fin. The dorsal fin has 98 to 106 rays and the anal fin has 73 to 80 rays. The teeth are equally well equipped in both sides of the jaw. Its coloring is usually pearly white and featureless on the blind side. Some specimens, nicknamed "cherry-bellies," have a reddish tint on the blind side.

Size.   Atlantic halibut weighing between 300 and 700 pounds have been reported, although the all-tackle rod-and-reel record is 255 pounds.

Distribution.   The Atlantic halibut occurs in North Atlantic waters, including the Barents Sea

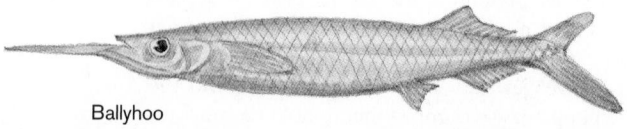

Ballyhoo

H

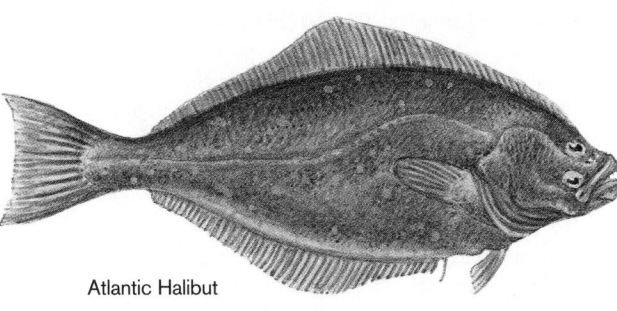
Atlantic Halibut

The California halibut is a large flatfish and a member of the Bothidae family, or left-eyed flounder. It is the largest and most abundant flatfish within its range, although it is greatly smaller than the more northerly Pacific halibut (see: halibut, Pacific). It is an important commercial quarry and sportfish, one that is often deliberately sought by anglers and valued for its excellent firm white flesh.

California halibut were routinely caught to 20 and 30 pounds, often even larger, in California waters in the 1940s, but both numbers and size have dwindled over the decades. However, a minimum length limit (22 inches in California), elimination of gillnetting for this species, improved water quality, and other factors contributed to a resurgence in the population in the mid- to late 1990s.

Identification.   The body of the California halibut is oblong and compressed. The head is small and the mouth large. Although a member of the left-eyed flounder family, about 40 percent of California halibut have their eyes on the right side. The color is dark brown to black on the eyed side and white on the blind side. Rare specimens may be either brown or white on both sides or have partial coloration on both sides. The gill rakers are slender and numerous, totaling about 29 on the first arch. Their numerous teeth, very large mouth, and a high arch in the middle of the "top" side above the pectoral fin make them easily distinguishable from other flatfish.

Size.   The largest California halibut recorded was 5 feet long and weighed 72 pounds. The all-tackle rod-and-reel record weighed 53 pounds, 4 ounces. Females grow larger, live longer, and are more numerous than males. In California, these fish average between 8 and 20 pounds; 20-pounders are considered large, and fish exceeding 30 pounds are trophies.

Distribution.   This species occurs from Magdalena Bay, Baja California, Mexico, to the Quillayute River, British Columbia. A separate population exists in the Gulf of California in Mexico.

Habitat.   Found mostly over sandy bottoms, California halibut appear beyond the surf line and in bays and estuaries. They range from near shore to 600 feet deep but are most commonly caught in 60

and off Iceland and Greenland; it ranges from Labrador to Virginia in the western Atlantic, and from the Barents Sea to southwest Ireland in the eastern Atlantic. This species does not occur in near-freezing polar waters as many people believe; there, it is replaced by the Greenland halibut (*Reinhardtius hippoglossoides*).

Habitat.   A deep-water species, the Atlantic halibut seldom enters water shallower than about 200 feet and is commonly found to 3,000 feet. It inhabits cold (40° to 50°F) water over sand, gravel, or clay bottoms.

Spawning behavior.   Spawning occurs from late winter through early spring in deep water. The eastern Atlantic fish spawn from March through May. Females can release up to 2,000,000 eggs, and the fish move shallower after spawning.

Within a few days of hatching, these and other halibut begin to lean to one side. The eye on the underside migrates upward and across the head so that both eyes are on top of the body. As the eye migrates, the baby fish's skull twists and, in many cases, the mouth does also. In this way, the halibut transforms into a flatfish.

Food and feeding habits.   The Atlantic halibut is a voracious feeder, pursuing its prey in the open water. It forages primarily on fish, including cod and their relatives—ocean perch, herring, skate, mackerel, and other flounder. It also eats crabs, mussels, lobsters, and clams.

Angling.   As noted, there is a minor, concentrated rod-and-reel effort for these fish, owing to their extraordinarily deep-dwelling nature and low population. They are caught in the western Atlantic on banks in 100 to 500 feet of water. Anglers drifting bait rigs or heavy metal jigs on the bottom often catch Atlantic halibut while fishing for such other bottom dwellers as Atlantic cod (see: cod, Atlantic). Although natural baits may differ, techniques are similar to those used in fishing for Pacific halibut (see: halibut, Pacific).

HALIBUT, CALIFORNIA

Paralichthys californicus.

Other names—flatty, flattie, fly swatter (small), barn door (large), alabato, Monterey halibut, chicken halibut, southern halibut, California flounder, bastard halibut, portsider; Spanish: *lenguado de California*.

California Halibut

H

to 120 feet of water. They are not known to make extensive migrations.

Spawning behavior. Males first mature when two or three years old, but females do not mature until age 4 or 5. A 5-year-old fish may be anywhere from 11 to 17 inches long. Spawning takes place in relatively shallow water from April through July, and spawning fish feed actively.

Food and feeding habits. These halibut feed primarily on anchovies and similar small fish, often well off the bottom and during the day, although they also consume squid, crustaceans, and mollusks. At times they are observed jumping clear of the water as they make passes at anchovy schools near the surface.

Angling. California halibut are relatively aggressive fish, and offer variety in terms of technique and location. Although drift fishing with bait on sandy flats is almost synonymous with fishing for this species, trolling with lures and bait, fishing in shallow water, and fishing on deep structure are also productive.

Live anchovies are popular natural bait, and the primary method of fishing these is by drifting along the bottom. Most anglers keep their conventional reel in freespool with a thumb on the line to maintain control, and watch the rod tip, waiting for a sharp tap. When a fish strikes, they yield a little line, then engage the gears and set the hook.

Although this method catches fish of all sizes, it is often less productive for larger halibut, perhaps because many smaller ones are more aggressive. Some anglers have had more success on larger fish not by drifting but by concentrating on gravel and shale bottoms, wrecks, breakwalls, rockpiles, and other structure. They anchor instead of drift, and use a sliding sinker while bottom-fishing with live bait, preferring sardines, queenfish, and squid over anchovies. Leadhead jigs adorned with soft-plastic bodies also work, and both bait and jigs are twitched and moved along the bottom.

When the fish are shallow, trolling with mid- to deep-running minnow-style plugs produces halibut; fly fishing also produces fish at this time. Trolling with wire line is favored when the fish are in deeper water with swift current; plastic squid or hoochies on a multiple-lure bottom rig with a heavy (1- to 3-pound) sinker get down to the fish in the 30- to 100-foot depths.

Fifteen- to 20-pound line is used for most halibut fishing, although wire line trolling is an exception. A stronger leader may be employed to prevent breakoffs caused by the teeth of large specimens. For live bait and shallow plug trolling, a 7-foot rod with a fast tip, and a conventional star drag reel, do fine; line capacity is not a significant issue.

These halibut need to be played with firm, steady pressure, and not with aggressive pumping, which sends them on a getaway run.

HALIBUT, PACIFIC   *Hippoglossus stenolepis.*

Other names—giant halibut, northern halibut, hali (Canada), barn door; Japanese: *ohyô;* Portuguese: *alabote do Pacifico;* Spanish: *fletán del Pacifico.*

The Pacific halibut is the largest flatfish found in Pacific Ocean waters, and one of the world's largest bony fish. It is a member of the family Pleuronectidae, or right-eyed flounder. A strong fighter that grows to impressive size, the Pacific hali-but has long been a favorite among Pacific Northwest anglers. That popularity has soared since the mid-1980s, when halibut populations boomed and large numbers of mostly young fish started to provide excellent fishing from Oregon to Alaska. Pacific halibut populations remain generally healthy, thanks to close monitoring of the sport and commercial longline fisheries, but halibut bycatch *(see)* by commercial trawlers remains a threat.

Table quality. The firm, white flesh of the Pacific halibut is prized by anglers and fish

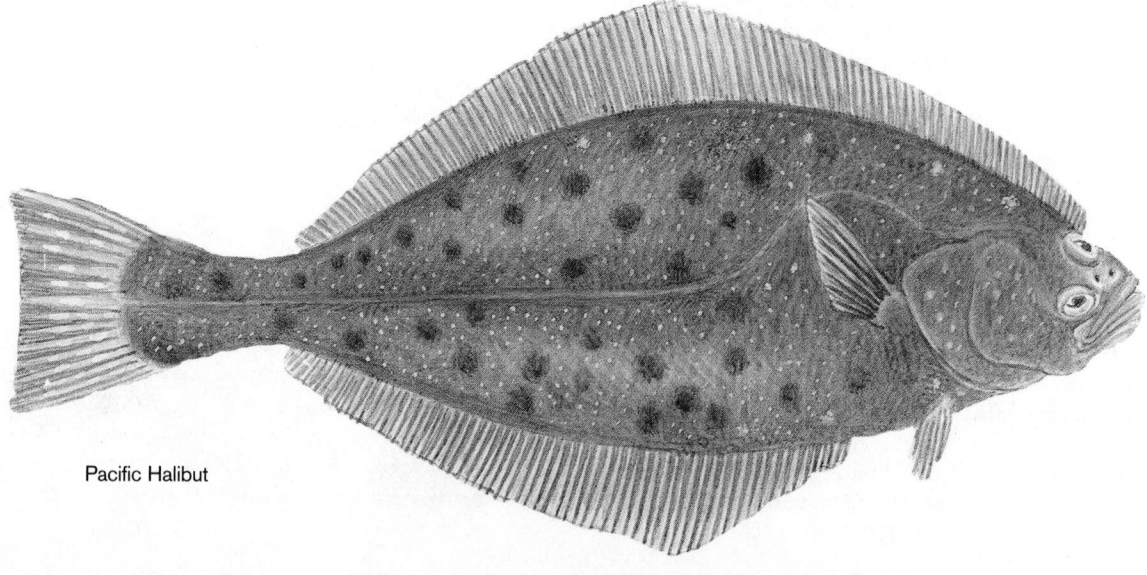

Pacific Halibut

connoisseurs alike. Dryer and with a more delicate flavor than most, the worst thing a gourmet can do is overcook halibut. Otherwise, it provides excellent table fare whether baked, grilled, or poached. For the table, smaller, "chicken" halibut of 50 pounds or less are generally favored over larger fish. Any halibut killed for the table should be bled upon capture to ensure the highest quality and flavor.

Identification.   The halibut usually is dextral; that is, both eyes are on the right side of the head. Its coloration varies from olive to dark brown or black with lighter, irregular blotches. More elongate than other flatfish, the average width of the Pacific halibut's body is about one-third its length. The mouth is large, extending to the lower eye. The small, smooth scales are well buried in the skin, and the lateral line has a pronounced arch above the pectoral fin. The tail is crescent-shaped, longer at the tips than in the middle, which distinguishes it from most other flatfish.

Size.   A typical sport-caught Pacific halibut is a fish of 28 to 50 inches, weighing 10 to perhaps 60 pounds, but the species grows much larger. Rod-and-reel records include several halibut in excess of 400 pounds (the all-tackle record is 459 pounds), and 500-pounders have been caught commercially. Reports of Pacific halibut measuring 9 feet and weighing more than 700 pounds are unverified, but within the realm of possibility. Most Pacific Northwest anglers consider a halibut of 100 pounds or more a trophy. These largest halibut all are females, as males of the species seldom top 90 pounds.

Distribution.   Pacific halibut are found on the continental shelf of the North Pacific Ocean and have been recorded along the North American coast from central California to Nome, Alaska. They are also found along the Asiatic coast from the Sea of Japan to the Bering Sea. They live on or near the bottom and have been taken as deep as 3,600 feet, although most are caught during the summer, when they are at depths of 75 to 750 feet. They generally move back into deeper water in fall and winter.

Life history.   Spawning occurs in the North Pacific Ocean and Bering Sea during winter, with each female distributing 500,000 to 4 million eggs, which are fertilized externally and hatch after roughly 15 days. The eggs and larvae float freely in the ocean current for six months, during which time they are transformed from "normal" fish to flattened creatures with both eyes on one side and become perfectly adapted to life on the ocean bottom. Settling to the bottom in shallow, inshore waters, they continue the counterclockwise migration through the Pacific that is common to the species. Juvenile halibut show a tendency to migrate back toward the place where they were spawned, reaching that destination by adulthood and repeating the life cycle.

Habitat and feeding habits.   Preferring cool water (3° to 8°C), halibut are most commonly found where the bottom is composed of cobble, gravel, and sand, especially near the edges of underwater plateaus and breaklines. Here they wait for tidal currents to wash food within striking range. Halibut are strong swimmers, however, and will leave bottom to feed on pelagic fish such as herring and sand lance. They will also inhabit virtually any kind of habitat if crabs, squid, octopus, cod, pollack, sablefish, or other sources of food are abundant.

Angling.   Its impressive size, relative abundance, and brute strength make the Pacific halibut a popular target of anglers' efforts from the southern Oregon coast to the Bering Sea. Younger, smaller halibut of under 50 pounds constitute most of the sport catch along the Oregon, Washington, and southern British Columbia coasts, and fish in these areas tend to congregate in specific areas where food is abundant. Farther north, off the northern British Columbia coast and Alaska, halibut are more widely dispersed and large fish are more common.

Oregon's top halibut fishing spots are Heceta Bank, Stonewall Bank, and Nelson Island, all within about two hours by boat from Newport. Halibut fisheries also occur out of the Oregon coastal ports of Charleston, Depoe Bay, and Garibaldi. Washington's top halibut producers are Swiftsure Bank and an underwater hump known as Blue Dot, both of which are fished by anglers departing Neah Bay. There are also halibut fisheries out of Ilwaco and Westport, and, on the "inside" waters of the Strait of Juan de Fuca, such places as Sekiu, Twin Rivers, Freshwater Bay, Green Point, Hein Bank, and Middle Bank all support worthwhile halibut fisheries.

Working north up the coast of British Columbia, halibut can be found as far south as Race Rocks and Pedder Bay, near the south end of Vancouver Island. A long bank that runs along the southwest corner of Vancouver Island provides good fishing for anglers out of Bamfield, Ucleulet, and Tofino. Several islands and submerged banks between Telegraph Cove and Port Hardy are good bets around the northeast corner of Vancouver Island. The west side and north end of the Queen Charlotte Islands offer perhaps the best halibut fishing in the entire province but require significant travel from the mainland. Productive fisheries around Dundas Island, Chatham Sound, and Edye Pass make Prince Rupert another popular destination of halibut anglers.

Without question, Alaska offers the best fishing for Pacific halibut. There are rich halibut grounds within easy reach of the Southeast Alaska towns of Ketchikan, Wrangell, Petersburg, Sitka, Juneau, and Yakutat. Farther up the vast Alaskan coast, Kodiak Island and several spots along the east side of Cook Inlet offer both large numbers of halibut and good opportunities for a trophy fish. Best known among these is Homer, the so-called Halibut Capital of the World, and the Deep Creek/Ninilchik area, where

An unusual fly-caught halibut from Seward, Alaska.

halibut anglers launch in the surf to reach the halibut grounds. The Alaska Peninsula also is a halibut angler's dream, and in recent years the peninsula's Unalaska Island has been the focal point of a growing halibut sportfishery. Waters around Unalaska have produced numerous halibut exceeding 300 pounds, including record-class fish of 395, 440, and 459 pounds.

Basic halibut fishing techniques apply wherever the fish are found; the key is to get a bait or lure down to them and keep it there long enough for a fish to find it. Most anglers prefer to fish with bait, and large herring are the most popular choice. Squid, octopus, belly skin off halibut or salmon, and whole cod, greenling, or other small bottom fish also are effective baits. Bait is usually fished on a wire spreader or a sliding-sinker rig, with sinker size ranging from 4 ounces to 4 pounds, depending on depth, current, size of the bait, and line diameter. Bait hooks range from size 5/0 to 12/0, depending on size of the bait and the size of the quarry; some anglers prefer traditional J-style hooks, whereas others like commercial circle hooks. Halibut use their eyes, nose, and lateral line to locate a meal, so anglers often lift the bait well off the bottom to increase visibility and then drop it quickly to create a thumping vibration.

This same "bottom-banging" strategy also works for anglers using artificials. Favorite lures are large, metal slab-type jigs or homemade versions constructed of tubing or small-diameter pipe filled with lead. Both imitate herring and other small fish on which halibut feed. Leadhead jigs also take halibut, especially if adorned with large plastic grub bodies, pork rind, or strips of white belly skin off another halibut.

Rods, reels, and line vary in size depending on fishing conditions. For deep water (more than 200 feet), a 7-foot boat rod with a stiff action, equipped with 4/0 conventional reel, is standard. Such tackle not only helps to level the playing field in the event a monster fish is hooked, but also makes it possible to fish the 2-pound jigs or sinkers required to reach bottom in deep-water halibut spots. For shallow-water fishing, though, some anglers fish much lighter tackle, down to and including bass-action flipping rods or freshwater spinning outfits.

Deep-water halibut anglers use line in the 80- to 130-pound range, whereas light-tackle anglers may prefer line of 15- to 50-pound test. Most serious halibut anglers prefer the low stretch and sensitivity of the modern, high-tech braided lines.

Because of their size and strength, halibut demand respect when they're brought to the boat; many anglers have been injured, or have had equipment destroyed, by fish that weren't controlled quickly or properly. Halibut over about 50 pounds are commonly shot in the head or harpooned rather than simply gaffed or netted, although both activities disqualify fish for International Game Fish Association (IGFA) record consideration. A team effort by everyone on board often is the difference between success and failure when landing a big halibut. Securing a strong line through the jaw and another around the base of the tail will allow a big fish to be controlled without bringing it aboard, a method commonly practiced by small-boat anglers. Once a tough halibut is under control, it should be dispatched with several raps behind the eyes from a heavy club, severing two or three gill arches, or both.

HANDLE

The component of a fishing rod that is usually held by the angler and that incorporates the reel seat and gripping area. Although some rods, primarily those used in big-game fishing, are held by the foregrip while the angler is fighting a fish, most rods, especially those used for casting, are held by the rear grip section, so comfort and ability to control the rod are important elements of the handle.

Handle materials, largely decided by application, primarily include cork and foamed polymers, and are found in varying lengths and styles.
See: Rod, Fishing.

HANDLINE

A line with a weight and a baited hook, which is dispensed and retrieved by hand. In a sense, this is the most basic fishing tackle; it has obvious deficiencies for casting, retrieving line, and playing and landing a strong fish, but a possible advantage in detecting a strike.

Handlines today are primarily used in underdeveloped regions, sometimes with a (baited or unbaited) jig or jigging spoon, and predominately as a means of procuring food rather than providing sport; they may also be used in commercial fishing. Using a handline is the way most people fished throughout history for subsistence purposes.

HANDLING FISH

How fish are handled once they are caught depends on whether they are going to be kept for consumption or whether they will be released.
See: Fish Preparation—Care; Catch-and-Release.

HARBOR

A secure refuge for boats, protected from storms, usually for docking and mooring. Harbors are often associated with inlets *(see)*, jetties *(see)*, piers *(see)*, and tidal marshes *(see)*, and have a variety of features that may be attractive to fish.

HARDWARE

Artificial lures other than flies.
See: Lures.

HARLING

A term for trolling with flies and flycasting tackle for Atlantic salmon in large rivers. Particularly practiced in parts of Europe, especially Scandinavia, harling involves row trolling with a long length of fly line in the water, with the oarsman manipulating the boat in order to maneuver the fly for presentation. This may also be done with bait or lures, and is largely employed in waters that are impossible to cast and wade effectively. Although the length of line is longer in harling, the technique is essentially identical to backtrolling *(see)* in rivers.

HARNESS, BAIT

A device that secures a live or dead bait for trolling. Among these are plastic bridles for whole or headless minnows or small baitfish, and two-hook spinner rigs for nightcrawlers; plastic bridles are used in salmon trolling and the two-hook spinner rigs in walleye trolling. Nightcrawler harnesses are more common to freshwater anglers and are complete rigs that feature a Colorado or Indiana spinner, five or six plastic beads, and two short-shanked snelled bait hooks that are embedded in a whole live nightcrawler.

HARNESS, FIGHTING

Also known as a kidney harness in smaller sizes, this device is worn around the shoulders and upper back, and is connected to a reel; the harness provides back support, arm relief, and reel security. A fighting harness is worn like a vest, may be padded, and is usually made from nylon, canvas, or nylon webbing. Heavy-tackle versions are incorporated into, or used with, a rod belt *(see)* and may be used in conjunction with a fighting chair *(see)* when fishing.

Some harnesses are difficult to get into or do not fit comfortably on the spur of the moment (the decision to wear one may not come until after a fish is hooked and known to be sufficiently large). It is important that the harness fit properly, and offshore regulars usually have their own to avoid the adjustments that must be made to loaned or borrowed harnesses.

Ideally a harness should take pressure off the back, evenly distributing it instead over the hips and thighs. In use, a harness-wearing angler with rod butt in the belt gimbal leans back against the pull of the fish, making the knees, rather than waist or back, the pivot point.

To prevent an angler from possibly being pulled overboard by a fish (if the reel seizes, for example) while the angler is strapped to the heavy tackle, some harnesses are equipped with a quick safety release, and sometimes a safety strap is attached to the harness.
See: Big-Game Fishing; Standup Fishing.

HATCH

The occasion when aquatic insects emerge from the water, shed a skin or case, mate, and deposit eggs on the water. Single species often all hatch into a terrestrial stage in a very short time, and huge numbers may be observed emerging from the stream or as a swirling mass above it.

HATCHERY

A place for the hatching of fish eggs and the growing of fish for stocking or for food. Fish hatcheries may be public or private. Publicly owned hatcheries rear fish for stocking, usually exclusively into public waters, either to create fishing opportunity, sustain existing fisheries populations, and provide prey for predator fish populations, or to restore depleted fisheries. Most publicly operated hatcheries belong to state natural resource and fisheries agencies; some hatcheries are operated by federal agencies. Privately owned hatcheries, some of which are also called fish farms, supply fish to food processors and consumers, to organizations and individuals for stocking in private or public waters (often with a government-issued permit), and on rare occasions to state agencies in times of need to supplement government programs.
See: Fisheries Management.

HATTERAS HEAVER

A heavy-action rod and large reel combination for surf casting.
See: Surf Fishing.

HAWAII

The Hawaiian Islands stretch for 1,523 miles across the north-central Pacific, intercepting the migration routes of marlin, tuna, sharks, and other gamefish that grow to world-record sizes and are highly prized by sport anglers. The archipelago consists of 132 islands, reefs, and shoals, from the southernmost point of the United States (Ka Lae on Hawaii Island) to Kure Atoll, west of Midway Island. Eight main islands (Hawaii, Maui, Oahu, Kauai, Molokai, Lanai, Niihau, and Kahoolawe, from largest to smallest) make up 99 percent of the 6,425 square miles of land area. The six largest provide sportfishing access, and the remaining two have accessible fishing waters.

Hawaiian Island waters are home to more than 700 species of fish, most of which are known throughout the Indo-Pacific. Approximately 30 of these, from billfish to bonefish, are important to sport anglers (fishing is the sixth most popular recreational activity among local residents). Saltwater fishing is paramount because few natural bodies of freshwater exist.

Hawaii was a Polynesian kingdom until 1893, a republic until 1898, and annexed by the U.S. as a territory in 1900. It became the 50th state on May 21, 1959. The earliest settlers arrived at Ka Lae (South Point) in A.D. 124, more than a thousand years before Captain James Cook sailed into Kealekekua Bay in 1778. The 200,000 to 300,000 residents of Cook's time depended greatly on fishing for subsistence and developed many effective fishing techniques that survive today.

Offshore fishing in Hawaii gains most of the world's attention because inshore fishing opportunities are limited. The islands are near the northern limits of coral reef development. Fringing reefs are narrow even on the oldest (westernmost) islands, and nonexistent on the youngest (to the southeast).

Northeast trade winds dominate the weather, generate the dominant wave patterns, and drive surface currents ranging from 0.4 to 0.6 knot. These currents are modified by the shapes of islands, which causes them to create large eddies important to the development of sea life, from baitfish to gamefish. Tides are modest, with less than 3 feet of change everywhere throughout the islands. Two main seasons mark the year. Trade winds (10 to 20 miles per hour) prevail from May through October, which is considered "summer," and winds are more variable (gusting to 30 miles per hour at times, then switching to the south to southwest at others) from November through April, when the weather is a bit cooler and wetter. At sea and on land, August and September are the warmest months, with air temperatures in the 80s to 90s and sea temperatures above 80°F. January and February are the coldest months, with many days in the low 70s, and sea temperatures ranging from 72° to 76°F.

Hawaii's most important offshore species are marlin (blue, black, and striped), tuna (yellowfin, bigeye, skipjack, and albacore), spearfish, sailfish, *mahimahi, kawakawa,* amberjack, and barracuda. Big-game anglers also catch tiger sharks (even tonners), makos (over a half ton), and other types. Deep-sea bottom anglers plumb the depths for red snapper (four or five different species) and grouper. Shore anglers catch jacks (roughly a dozen species, topped off by giant trevally and bluefin trevally), bonefish, barracuda, and ladyfish (the biggest in the world at 24 pounds plus). The giant trevally "slide bait" method of angling, described later, is unique to Hawaii. Assorted panfish are also caught at night.

Hawaii offers limited freshwater angling opportunities. The only native freshwater fish in Hawaii are four gobies and an eleotrid. Streams on the leeward slopes of the major islands are mostly intermittent; on the windward slopes, where there are cliffs and valleys and high annual rainfall, many of the streams are perennial. Throughout the Hawaiian Islands are more than 260 freshwater reservoirs ranging up to 400 acres. Most reservoirs, stream banks, and streambeds in Hawaii are privately owned, however, and require permission from the landowner for access.

Kauai's Waimea River, which runs about 20 miles, is the longest stream. The largest natural lakes are Halalii (1.3 square miles) on Niihau, Kola Reservoir (0.6 square mile) on Kauai, and Salt Lake (0.4 square mile) on Oahu. Various man-made impoundments serving irrigation needs have been stocked with largemouth and smallmouth bass, tucunare (peacock bass), pongee, Chinese and channel catfish, bluegills, oscars, jewel cichlids, and other exotic species. A limited fishery for rainbow trout exists on Kauai. Despite the limited opportunities, more than 5,000 freshwater anglers hold licenses on Oahu alone.

Established Saltwater Fisheries

Billfish. Blue marlin and striped marlin are the main billfish targets. A significant sportfishery also

Thanks to deep water nearby, trolling within sight of the islands is a common part of offshore fishing in Hawaii.

H

exists for Pacific shortbill spearfish. A few black marlin and sailfish are hooked each year but are only an incidental catch.

Most big Hawaii marlin are caught within a few miles of shore. The 100-fathom line curves in as close as 1/4 mile from the beach in places like the Kona coast, and the 1,000-fathom line is only a few more miles away. Substantial island lee eddies help pull bait and big fish back into the protection of the shoreline, creating a boon for anglers.

The biggest fish are usually caught on lures trolled at 8 to 12 knots. That is fitting because Hawaii anglers pioneered lure trolling for billfish back in the 1950s and 1960s, long before the method caught on elsewhere.

Big-game fleets operate out of Kona on the Big Island, Lahaina on Maui, Kewalo Basin in Honolulu, and Lihue on Kauai. A few boats can be chartered in other spots, notably Hilo Harbor on the Big Island.

Blues are caught every week of every month of the year. In a typical year, more are caught in June, July, August, and early September than in other months. In about three of every five years, however, October and early November are just as good as the summer months. Granders can show up at any time. One year, the only grander caught was boated in November. Another, the only two granders caught were landed in July and December. And in still another year, all of the granders were caught in January and February. Hawaii's blues rank high on the all-time list of largest blue marlin caught anywhere in the world and include a 1,805-pounder, the largest on record anywhere.

Summer combines Hawaii's calmest seas, gentlest breezes, and best runs of blue marlin. Warm sea conditions bring huge female marlin (1,000-pounders are caught nearly every summer) to spawn, escorted by eager males. The males are smaller (rarely exceeding 300 pounds) and quicker, getting to bait and lures faster than their more ponderous mates. As a result, the summer marlin catch is dominated by aggressive, quick-hitting, high-jumping billfish of 150 to 200 pounds. Although the males match perfectly with light tackle of 20- to 50-pound class, expect to use heavier gear or lose the chance to boat the occasional big marlin.

Island anglers troll for billfish with locally made plastic high-speed big-game plugs that are run at 8 to 12 knots, or they slow-tow live bait (skipjack tuna) around baitfish schools. For billfish, the burst of skipjack (aku) activity each summer is a major part of Hawaii's attraction. Averaging 3 to 10 pounds, aku are big-game snacks and a reliable supply of energy for the vigorous effort of spawning.

The big challenge for visiting anglers may be finding the charter boat of their choice during the busy summer season. Offshore fishing tournaments crowd the summer calendar, and many of the best-known boats are booked as much as a year in advance.

Striped marlin are a winter-to-spring catch, most abundant from December through June. Blue marlin techniques produce most of the stripers, although trollers switch to smaller lures rigged with smaller hooks when the 50- to 100-pound stripers are swarming in the wake.

Spearfish are the target of dedicated light-tackle anglers, and Hawaii may be the best place to set a world record for this species. Most abundant in January through May, they are caught by trollers who drag hookless teasers to attract the fish. When a spearfish follows a teaser, the angler assesses its size, picks a suitable rod from several ready to cast, and tosses the spearfish a prerigged bait.

Yellowfin tuna. As regular as spring itself, hordes of yellowfin tuna, known as *ahi,* churn into Hawaiian waters at the start of June and remain through September. At times the tuna attack anything in sight, but just as often you can troll through acres of big yellowfins busting around you or breezing by without showing the slightest interest in whatever is trailing behind the boat.

Hawaiian anglers have perfected methods that regularly produce when tuna turn up their noses and clamp their jaws tight. Their successes have produced record catches (Hawaiian waters have rewarded record hunters with dozens of International Game Fish Association [IGFA] yellowfin tuna marks over the years), steady daily catches throughout the summer season, and occasional surprises year-round.

Central Pacific anglers are uniquely situated to learn, develop, and pass on tuna fishing techniques. Their methods combine new ideas fresh from the Orient with traditional ideas from early Polynesian cultures dependent on fishing for survival. Look at a modern arsenal of tuna fishing weapons—birds, jetheads, octopus skirts, bulb squid, shell lures (lures made with pearl-shell inserts), tuna circle hooks, *ika-shibi* gear (using light to attract squid and tuna at night), to name a few—and you'll see ideas that originated somewhere in the Pacific, were introduced and developed in Hawaii, and are now being used successfully around the world.

Central Pacific tuna schools seem to migrate from west to east, which means the first catches are reported from boats berthed at Port Allen, Nawiliwili, and Hanalei Bay on Kauai. The news spreads only slightly faster than the fish. Within two weeks Oahu boats begin bringing *ahi* back to Haleiwa Harbor, Pokai Bay, and Kewalo Basin. Look for them off Maui a few days later, and then almost immediately off the Kona and Hilo coasts of the Big Island.

Some years, sporadic bursts of tuna pop up unexpectedly throughout the islands as early as March. Even so, dependable schools don't usually settle in everywhere until nearly June. Action for *ahi* usually continues throughout the island chain until the end of July, tapers off during August, and disappears by the end of September.

H

Tuna anglers have learned to suffer sporadic lean seasons. Each year's early arrivals generate hopeful predictions for a return to the hot action common in the best years of the past. Hawaii's yellowfins average 100 to 200 pounds, not heavyweight statistics by standards of the eastern Pacific, where only 300-pound fish set records. Local commercial anglers have talked about 300-pound Hawaiian tuna, but the only 300-plus-pounder on record was caught in July 1990, on a catamaran sailing off Lanai. This state-record claimant registered 325 pounds.

At their most aggressive, *áhi* attack in packs. Then, they'll hit every lure in a trolled spread of four or five. Boats in the thick of early action check in with a dozen or more big fish and a crew of exhausted anglers.

Tuna specialists use streamlined jet-style lures skirted with plastic tails. Skirt colors are mixed to match forage. The most popular combinations are "angry squid" (a mix of pink, yellow, and brown) and *"opelu"* (a type of mackerel scad showing silver, green, blue, and yellow). Tuna are sharp-eyed, requiring lures rigged with nylon rather than wire and armed with a single tuna-bend hook to catch the jaw hinge. Such lures are designed for the fast trolling speeds (10 to 12 knots) pioneered on Hawaiian water.

It's not always possible to match the hatch because every year something different happens. One year, it was a filefish hatch that turned *áhi* on and off. Every tuna belly was loaded with the remains of 4- or 5-inch filefish. The following year, action was dominated by huge swarms of little anchovies with schools of bait 2 and 3 miles across and showing 10 to 60 fathoms deep on sonar. Around the anchovies were clouds of skipjack tuna, and below them were large schools of *áhi*.

Some years, live-baiting with skipjacks is the single best way to catch an *áhi*. Other years, the *áhi* won't touch them. You just have to be prepared for anything, then wait and see what weird thing they're doing this year.

Áhi anglers must be ready to change and adapt. When *áhi* aren't showing or are traveling with *mahimahi* schools, boats troll fast with streamlined, skirted lures from 8 to 12 inches long in an assortment of colors. Others tow bait around fish aggregation devices (FADs). They use a downrigger to present a bridled skipjack tuna at depths of 150 to 200 feet, and swim another skipjack at the surface for tuna coming up to feed.

Minnow-style swimming plugs attract smaller yellowfins at the FADs. Chugging a popping plug from a slow-moving boat has taken FAD tuna up to 200 pounds. If tuna show down deep on sonar but not at the surface, stand-up anglers drop a diamond jig down below them and jig it up, alternating each sweep with a drop-and-reel motion.

Spreader rigs and daisy chains are effective in the late afternoon. Spreaders with 16 to 22 small squid in amber or yellow, trolled in clusters of two or three, draw up tuna from considerable depths. *Áhi* gather near inshore bottom features known locally as *áhikoa*. Once located on sonar, they are baited with fillets of mackerel scad dropped down 150 to 250 feet in a modern duplication of Hawaii's traditional "stone drop" method, which early Hawaiians invented to catch *áhi* from dugout canoes. Hawaii's yellowfins spend most of their time in the cooler waters 25 to 50 fathoms down, and gather at the same sites from year to year. Early Hawaiians reached them with a handline carried into the depths by a stone the size of a brick but rounded like a potato. They baited a hook with a fillet of *opelu,* placed it on the stone with a *ti* leaf and some pieces of chum, then wrapped a few turns of leader around the package. With additional wraps, they added more chum, then secured the package with a slipknot. After lowering the baited stone to a predetermined depth marked on the line, they jerked the line to release the knot. The stone fell away to the bottom, the chum dispersed to attract tuna, and the baited hook emerged to flutter in the current. A striking tuna can pull a line across a canoe gunwale so fast, the wood burns and smokes; this is why Hawaiians named this fish *áhi,* or "fire."

Other tuna. Albacore (*tonbo áhi* or *áhi palaha*) may be the most seasonal offshore gamefish in Hawaii. The highly migratory longfins usually begin to show up in late July and are gone by the end of October. During daylight hours, they stay in the cooler waters at great depths (60 fathoms or more), rising to feed at night when they are greeted by drift anglers, who attract them with lights and chum. Most albacore fishing is commercial, but anglers willing to fish overnight can hook record-size longfins. Hawaii's *tonbo* average 40 to 50 pounds and range up to 80 or more pounds.

Skipjack tuna (*aku*) are here year-round but are most abundant from June through August. Schools of 3- to 5-pounders are common and can cover acres. Mostly sought as baitfish for marlin and *áhi,* they are also great sport on light tackle. They hit small jigs, spoons, and plastic worms rigged on very light leaders. Big skipjacks (*otadu*) range up to 35 pounds in Hawaii waters and will sometimes attack the biggest lures in a marlin troller's spread.

Bigeye tuna (*po'onui*) are most often caught when gathered around FADs, flotsam, and jetsam. These "floater" fish range from 1 pound to more than 100 pounds. During the winter months, a few larger bigeyes are caught trolling with lures. Such catches are rare because bigeyes seldom venture up into the warmer surface waters.

Kawakawa, which are closely related to skipjack tuna, are present year-round but are seldom abundant. The Hawaiian name for this tuna species is also the IGFA standard. They average 5 to 15 pounds and grow to 25 in Hawaii waters. Aggressive feeders, they are caught by trolling, jigging, and baiting (whatever you're doing when a *kawakawa* swims by will usually work).

American fishing rods were made of wood through most of the nineteenth century; in the 1860s, Hiram Leonard improved bamboo rod construction by using six, instead of four, strips.

H

Mahimahi. Known in many locales as dolphin or dorado, but as *mahimahi* in Hawaii, these exciting fish are found in island waters year-round but are seasonal in abundance, with annual peaks in April and May and again in October and November. Then, catches can be outstanding, especially off the windward coast of Oahu and in the triangle formed by Maui, Lanai, and Kahoolawe. Fishing is incredible at times, especially when huge schools of fish gather near drifting objects. Catches of 20 to 100 fish totaling up to a ton are not unheard of. Windward coastlines are especially blessed because drifting debris shows up there first. Often, trailered boats are able to reach hot action first because few large craft harbor on the blustery northeast sides of the islands.

Hawaii's biggest *mahimahi* are usually caught on blind strikes by anglers dragging lures for bigger game. The most electrifying technique for hooking *mahimahi* is chugging popping plugs on casting gear. To succeed, the first requirement is finding fish, since blind casting over open water is arm-numbingly tedious. As a result, the normal chugging targets are *mahimahi* gathered around a FAD or flotsam and jetsam. You can also keep a chugging rod rigged and ready for times when you hook a *mahimahi* while blind trolling. The fighting fish often bring in followers, which trail their partner to the transom, excited and ready to pounce on a well-presented surface disturber.

Hawaiian *mahimahi* seem to like a buoyant, level-riding plug with a scooped face cut with very little angle. Although some anglers make their own from wood, the most popular models are produced from surfboard materials. Several local craftsmen have their own versions, but all of these plugs gain their buoyancy from a core of surfboard foam with wire-through rigging for strength and a body envelope molded of plastic casting resin to create shape, action, and casting weight.

Standard practice among FAD anglers is to postpone plugging until after they have hooked a live bait and rigged it for slow trolling from an outrigger. This bait is usually a small skipjack tuna, yellowfin tuna, or *kawakawa*, sewn to a hook with a head bridle. These small tuna gather at FADs by the thousands and attract marlin, *mahimahi*, big yellowfins, and wahoo. *Mahimahi* can't resist the 1-pounders and will even eat the 5-pounders when feeling particularly arrogant.

Live baits are usually tuna or bonito caught right on the scene. The best baits are small slim fish of a pound or less. *Mahimahi* snatch them, turn them headfirst, and swallow them whole, all within a greedy few seconds. Give them a lot of time to get the bait down, as much as 30 seconds or more. The test of strike time is the second run. A *mahimahi* usually grabs the bait in a rush, slows to swallow, then heads back to join its partners. That's the time to hit the brakes and set the hook.

Live baits are usually better than dead baits, but the latter will often do. Rig a dead scad with a stinger hook, drawing a short leader up through the body with a bait needle so the hook is in the hind third. Rigged this way, the scad is trolled very slowly on an outfit with the drag set at strike. The usual dead-bait strike is the sudden appearance of a lit-up *mahimahi* a few feet under the water behind the bait, which then disappears as the reel screams and empty water erases the vivid image.

Although scads are inviting bait, they aren't as durable as ballyhoo. These long, silver halfbeaks are found in Hawaii but can be hard to land. During the early spring, they are caught at night in harbors, where they gather under lights to feed on small organisms drawn to the lights. With ballyhoo, the favored rig is a leader drawn up through the body with the hook positioned behind the vent. Tie the leader to the beak and then sew the hook to the backbone.

Ono. The wahoo *(ono)* catch triples in June, July, and August. Most are caught by patient trollers working jet lures, leadhead jigs, and skirted plastic lures along the near-shore ledges (40- and 50-fathom depths are reachable within $1/4$ mile of the surf line). Here, the wahoo average 20 to 40 pounds, with fish over 60 pounds uncommon. Rig with wire and keep hooks sharp.

Deep sea. Amberjack *(kahala)*, trevally *(ulua, kagami,* and *omilu)*, snapper *(uku, opakapaka, ehu, lehi,* and *ula ula)*, barracuda *(kaku)*, and grouper *(hapu'u pu'u)* inhabit the deep waters around all islands. Amberjack and trevally (some well over 100 pounds) and barracuda (including 50- to 80-pounders) generate great sport for stand-up anglers dropping jigs or whole bait down 70 to 100 fathoms. Snapper (from 2 to 30 pounds) and grouper (usually 5 to 40 pounds, but some monsters exceed 500 pounds) take hooks baited with strips of squid, *aku,* or *opelu* in depths of 40 to 150 fathoms; this is lots of work whether you catch them or not. The best action occurs over bottom structure in the path of moderate to strong currents.

Shore fishing. Shore anglers separate their sport into whipping, dunking, and slide-baiting. Whippers cast jigs, spoons, and surface plugs on light to moderate spinning gear (2- to 20-pound test) to catch bluefin trevally *(omilu)*, giant trevally *(ulua)*, barracuda *(kaku)*, Pacific threadfin *(moi)*, and ladyfish *(awa aua)*. Whipping is best at dawn or dusk, when the fish feed most actively and beach goers are out of the water. Dunkers cast bait (squid, shrimp, and strips of octopus) on hook-and-sinker rigs and wait for bonefish *('o'io)* and trevally. Dunking spots are usually sandy-bottomed bays and channels. Coral-reefed bottoms are avoided because of snags and bait-stealing reef fish.

Slide-baiting is a specialized form of big-game surf casting unique to Hawaii. It makes use of very heavy tackle (stiff 12- to 14-foot rods and trolling reels of 6/0 to 9/0 are common) cast from rock-cliff

shorelines where deep water (100 feet or more) comes within reach of a 60- to 100-yard cast. An unbaited line is cast with a heavy sinker armed with wire hooks to tangle in the bottom. Once the sinker is secured in the coral, a large bait (perhaps a whole octopus, moray eel, or baitfish) on a specialized hook and leader is attached to the line with a slide buckle, which allows it to slide freely down the line until it comes to rest against a stop in the line several feet above the sinker. The quarry, usually a giant trevally, takes the bait and either releases the sinker from the bottom or breaks the sinker line. The best slide-bait fishing for *ulua* is at night along remote coastlines of all islands.

While waiting for the big strike, shore casters fill the time and coolers with some of the prettiest and tastiest panfish ever hooked. The experts use specially designed rods (light, flexible rods up to 14 feet long), but standard spinning gear works, and visiting anglers should feel free to bring their own and get in on the action. The panfish are caught on small hooks baited with luminescent strips or worms, or weighted flies trimmed with luminescent materials. Tackle shops provide advice and a look at gear custom-designed for these unique fishing styles.

Island Details

The Big Island.   The southernmost and largest Hawaiian island bears the name "Hawaii." To avoid confusing the island name with the name of the 50th state, local residents just call this the "Big Island." Roughly the size of Connecticut, it is formed by three large volcanoes, two of which are dormant. The geology is important, because that's what makes it such a great fishing area.

The predominant trade winds blow from the east, driving currents with them. These rivers of water squeeze between the islands and whirl in eddies on the western sides. The lee side of the Big Island is the Kona and Kohala coastlines. The currents in these calm, protected eddies push up against the undersea shelves formed by great masses of volcanic rock. The upwellings churn with baitfish, which are preyed on by marlin, tuna, sharks, *mahimahi*, wahoo, jacks, barracuda, and most other kinds of tropical Pacific gamefish. Kona is served by daily flights from the U.S. mainland (about 2,500 miles away) and by more frequent flights from the largest Hawaii city, Honolulu (about 150 miles away).

Kona is the top choice of veteran and novice big-game anglers from around the world because of its special combination of remarkable conditions. Big fish are caught in calm water near shore. The Kona coast sits in a calm lee; the normal trade winds of 10 to 20 knots are blocked by the looming mass of the volcanoes. The deep blue 100-fathom-depth water needed to attract blue marlin is no more than a $^1/_2$ mile offshore in many places.

At the north end of the Kona coast, the port of Kawaihae is home to a small charter fleet and provides facilities for an active fleet of small boat owners who troll the coastline for *mahimahi* and wahoo. On the east side of the island, Hilo Harbor provides access to the windward coast for recreational and commercial anglers, and Hilo Bay attracts shore casters who dunk for *ulua* and *'o'io*.

Oahu.   Oahu is the most populated island, and its major city, Honolulu, is the seat of state government. Kewalo Basin, near downtown Honolulu, is home to Hawaii's second (to Kona) largest recreational fleet. Boats leaving from Kewalo can head across the Molokai Channel to fish Penguin Bank in the productive Molokai lee, troll the shipping lanes along the south coast, turn east around Diamond Head to fish the windward coast, or head west to the Waia'nae coast. The latter coast, which produced the 1,805-pound all-time record blue marlin, is most easily accessible by boats fishing out of Poka'i Bay. Boats leaving from Poka'i are usually the first to greet the spring *ahi* run.

Freshwater anglers have three good opportunities on Oahu. The best known is Lake Wilson (Wahiawa Reservoir), a hairpin-shaped streambed flooded to create an irrigation impoundment. It holds largemouth and smallmouth bass (over 4 pounds), tucunare, pongee, oscars, tilapia, bluegills, and feral aquarium fish (jewel cichlids and red devils). Fishing quality varies with water level, which fluctuates considerably depending on rainfall and draw-down for irrigation. Wilson sees 20,000 to 30,000 trips per year, and tilapia is a main target.

Feeding activity on Lake Wilson is highest during the first few hours after dawn and the last few hours of evening, when fish are most active on the surface. Tucunare can be so aggressive, they will grab any lure and will gang-attack lures; jerkbaits are particularly effective. At such times, this action stirs up the competitive instincts of bass, who join the melee. By midday, surface waters warm, fish go deeper, and anglers switch to standard bass tactics used in bass waters everywhere. Lures may be the most fun for tucunare, but live bait (mosquitofish, cichlids, and tilapia) are preferred here. Rig a live bait on a bobber, cast it a few feet offshore of the targeted spot, and then let it swim in to danger.

Tucunare spawn from May through June, when they frequent the shallows, guarding their nests. Although they will attack anything nearby while spawning, conservation-minded anglers leave them alone. February is the peak spawning time, and the off-season, for largemouths.

Nu'uanu Reservoir provides limited and restricted fishing for channel cats and convict cichlids. Ho'omaluhia Reservoir (32 acres) in Kane'ohe has channel cats, tilapia, and cobalt/orange cichlids. Both are popular with bank anglers (especially kids with cane poles) because they are easily fished from shore. Baits include bread, chicken liver, squid, tuna belly strips, and worms.

A Canadian study of pike feeding habits determined that pike ate 10 percent of the local duck hatch each year; experiments showed it took 10 days to digest one duckling.

H

Maui. Offshore anglers are served by two Maui ports, Lahaina and Ma'alaea Harbors. Both are in the lee and send boats to fish the triangle between Lanai and Kahoolawe. Maui fleets see exceptional fishing for *mahimahi* and *ono* but do not get as much credit for their marlin catch, which can be outstanding at times (the Lahaina Jackpot Tournament has produced granders on several occasions).

Kauai. The westernmost of the main islands, Kauai sees the first tuna of the spring run. The major fleet operates out of Nawiliwili on the east coast, but others fish out of Port Allen to the south, and Hanalei to the north.

Unique in Hawaii, and to Kauai, is the chance to catch rainbow trout. There is little natural propagation of rainbow trout because streams are not cold enough to support natural reproduction. The single exception is Koaie Stream, and anglers determined enough to fight their way through underbrush to its headwaters are sometimes rewarded by wild rainbows. Rainbows were first stocked on Kauai in the 1920s; the program was intensified in the 1970s and then limited in the 1990s. Eggs are imported from California, hatched at a state facility on Oahu, and transported to Kauai, where they are kept at Pu'u Lua Reservoir. Stocking in streams was discontinued in 1991, and trout stocking is now limited to the reservoir.

Private impoundments on Kauai also hold bass and tucunare, the state records for which (both over 9 pounds) came from Kauai reservoirs. These are not open to the public, but fishing can usually be arranged through private guide services.

Molokai. A rural, agricultural island with few resort accommodations, Molokai is best known for the shore fishing opportunities available to dunkers on its west coast beaches and to skiff anglers on its south coast flats. Whippers cast from skiffs along the outside of the fringing reefs to stir up explosive strikes from *ulua*. Boats operating out of Kaunakakai Harbor have quick and protected access to productive Penguin Banks, an undersea extension of the island pointing to the southwest.

Lanai. Small, rural, and sparsely populated, Lanai has two small-boat harbors. Manele Bay and Kaumalapau offer limited services for anglers trolling the short length of lee coast. When the trade winds ease, Lanai anglers expand their opportunities toward Molokai to the north and Kahoolawe to the southeast.

HAYWIRE TWIST

A method of forming a loop in single-strand wire or Monel wire, the Haywire Twist is primarily used in saltwater fishing to prevent wraps from coming loose under severe pressure.

To form the Haywire Twist, start by making a loop and crossing the strands (1). Hold the loop tightly with one hand or pliers, and with your free

hand press down at point A (the upper strand) with forefinger and up at point B (the lower strand) with thumb; then twist the tag end around the main stem. Check to see that the twist looks as illustrated in step 2, and make four more twists in the same manner. Then wrap (not twist) the tag end of the wire as snugly as possible several times around the main strand (90 degrees to the main stem) to keep the entire rig from unwrapping (3). Bend the end of the tag wire to form a crank (3); holding the loop tightly in one hand, crank the tag wire in a circle in the same direction as the wrap and parallel to the main strand until the wire neatly parts where the last wrap was made. A neat cut is necessary because this wire is likely to be handled, but it is not accomplished by cutting, since cutters cannot cut the wire close enough to avoid a sharp end.

Haywire Twist

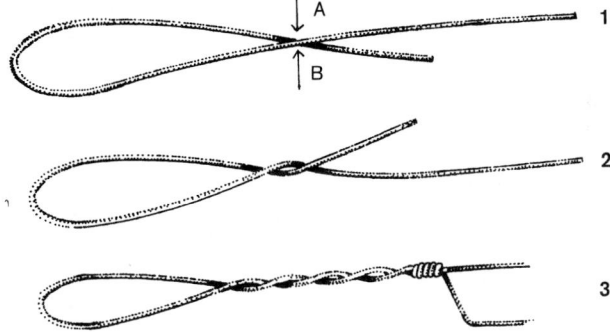

HEAD BOAT

A sportfishing boat that takes anglers out for a per-person fee. Most commonly referred to as a party boat, it is different from a charter boat in that people on a head boat pay individual fees as opposed to one flat fee for renting the boat.

See: Charter Boat; Party Boat.

HEAD SEA

Waves coming toward the bow of a boat and from the direction in which a boat is headed.

See: Waves.

HEADWATERS

The origins of streams and rivers.

See: Basin; Watershed.

HELLGRAMMITE

See: Dobsonflies, Fishflies, and Alderflies.

HELM

The wheel, tiller, stick, or other steering device on a boat.

HEN

A female fish in spawning mode; this term is usually applied to anadromous *(see)* spawners.

HERRING

Herring and their relatives are among the most important of commercial fish worldwide. They are also extremely important as forage fish for a wide variety of predatory fish, sea birds, seals, and other carnivores. In the past, some countries depended entirely on the herring (or related species) fishery for their economic survival. Wars have been waged over the rights to particularly productive herring grounds, which are found in all seas except the very cold waters of the Arctic and the Antarctic.

Large herring are eaten fresh, but many are processed for human consumption by pickling, smoking, or salting. Smaller herring are generally canned and sold as "sardines." They are also used for fish meal, fertilizer, fish oils, and other products. The roe of some herring is a valuable delicacy in certain countries. Many herring species have been depleted through commercial fishing, however.

Most members of the herring family are strictly marine. Some are anadromous and spawn in freshwater, and a few species (those of freshwater origin) never go to sea. Herring typically travel in extensive schools; in the ocean, such schools may extend for miles, which makes harvesting possible in great quantities.

Herring are plankton feeders, screening their food through numerous gill rakers. As such, and because they are generally small, herring are seldom a deliberate quarry of recreational anglers (American and hickory shad are notable exceptions). They are primarily used as bait, either in pieces or whole, by freshwater and saltwater anglers for various game species.

Prominent species with the herring name include Atlantic herring *(see: herring, Atlantic)*, Pacific herring *(see: herring, Pacific)*, blueback herring, and skipjack herring. At least two members of the herring family, alewife *(see)* and blueback herring, are collectively referred to as river herring.

There is minor angling effort for some species, such as blueback and skipjack herring, when they ascend coastal rivers en masse to spawn; this fishery is generally geared more toward procuring food or bait than to pure angling sport. They may, however, be caught on light spoons and small jigs or flies. When massed, they are also taken by snagging (where legal), and also in cast nets. Coastal herring are sometimes also caught, snagged, or taken by a cast net, mainly for use as bait.

See: Menhaden, Atlantic; Sardine, Pacific; Shad, American; Shad, Gizzard; Shad, Hickory; Shad, Threadfin.

HERRING, ATLANTIC   *Clupea harengus.*

Other names—herring; Danish: *Atlantisk sild, sild;* Finnish: *silakka, silli;* French: *hareng de l'Atlantique;* German: *allec, hering;* Norwegian: *sild;* Polish: *sledz;* Spanish: *arenque del Atlántico.*

A member of the Clupeidae family of herring, the Atlantic herring is in the *Guinness Book of World Records* as the world's most numerous fish and is certainly one of the world's most valuable fish. It is used fresh, smoked, salted, and pickled, and is often packed as "sardines," also being shipped frozen as bait and used in the manufacture of oils, fish meal, and fertilizer, and in the pearl-essence industry. Herring are extremely important as forage for predator species; Atlantic herring may be used as bait by anglers but are not a sportfishing target, although they may be caught (or snagged) by coastal anglers who seek to use fresh specimens as live bait.

Atlantic herring inhabit both the eastern and western Atlantic Ocean. Important commercial fisheries for juvenile Atlantic herring (ages 1 to 3) have existed since the last century along the coasts of Maine and New Brunswick. Development of large-scale fisheries for adult herring is comparatively recent, primarily occurring in the western Gulf of Maine, on Georges Bank, and on the Scotian Shelf. Herring stocks have been seriously depleted from commercial overfishing, and some stocks collapsed as long ago as the 1970s; in the late 1990s there were signs of an increase in populations.

A related and similar species in the western Atlantic Ocean is the blueback herring *(Alosa aestivalis)*, which ranges from Nova Scotia to Florida and reaches a maximum length of roughly 13 inches. The skipjack herring *(A. chrysochloris)* occurs in the Gulf of Mexico from Texas to the Florida Panhandle, and ascends the Mississippi River and some of its tributaries, including the Ohio River, and is also found in some impoundments; also

American Shad

Alewife

Atlantic Herring

Threadfin Shad

Members of the herring family have a wide lower jaw that curves, a short upper jaw that reaches only to below the middle of the eye, and a cheek that is longer than it is deep.

H

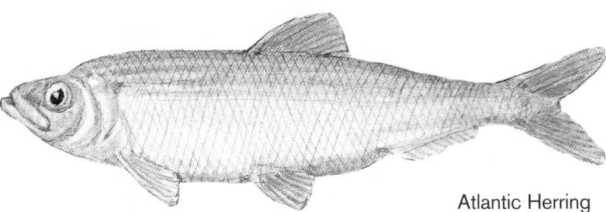

Atlantic Herring

known as skipjack shad and golden shad, it reaches a length of 19 inches.

Identification. The Atlantic herring is silvery with a bluish or greenish blue back and elongated body. The dorsal fin begins at about the middle of body, and there are 39 to 47 weakly developed ventral scutes. At the midline of the belly are scales which form a sharp-edged ridge. Teeth on the roof of the mouth distinguish the Atlantic herring from the similar alewife.

Size. Ordinarily less than a foot long, the Atlantic herring can grow to 18 inches. The all-tackle world record is a 1-pound, 1-ounce fish taken off Long Beach, New York; a 3-pound, 12-ounce record stands for the skipjack herring.

Distribution. Atlantic herring are the most abundant pelagic fish in cool, northern Atlantic waters. In the eastern Atlantic Ocean, they extend from the northern Bay of Biscay north to Iceland and south to Greenland, eastward to Spitsbergen and Novaya Zemlaya, including the Baltic Sea. In the western Atlantic Ocean, they are widely distributed in continental shelf waters from Labrador to Cape Hatteras, and have been separated by biologists into Gulf of Maine and Georges Bank stocks.

Habitat. This species schools in coastal waters and has been recorded in temperatures of 1° to 18°C.

Life history/Behavior. Atlantic herring usually spawn in the fall, although in any particular month of the year there is at least one group of Atlantic herring that moves into shallow coastal waters to spawn. (Blueback and skipjack herring, which are anadromous, spawn in coastal rivers in the spring.)

Spawning in the Gulf of Maine occurs from late August into October, beginning in northern locations and progressing southward. The female lays between 25,000 and 40,000 eggs, which are demersal and typically deposited on rock or gravel substrates, hatching in less than two weeks. Larvae grow by late spring into juvenile brit herring that may form large aggregations in coastal waters during summer.

Almost 5 inches long by the end of their first year, Atlantic herring nearly double their length in two years and reach maturity at age 4 or 5. Schools of herring may contain billions of individuals. In the western Atlantic, herring migrate from feeding grounds along the Maine coast during autumn to the southern New England–Mid-Atlantic region during winter, with larger individuals tending to migrate greater distances.

Food. The Atlantic herring feeds on small planktonic copepods in its first year, graduating to mainly copepods.
See: **Herring.**

HERRING, LAKE
See: **Cisco.**

HERRING, PACIFIC   *Clupea pallasii.*
Other names—herring, north Pacific herring; French: *hareng Pacifique;* Japanese: *nishin;* Spanish: *arenque del Pacífico.*

A member of the Clupeidae family of herring, an important food for many predatory fish, and the principal food of salmon, the Pacific herring also has many uses for human consumption. Sold fresh, dried/salted, smoked, canned, and frozen, the Pacific herring is commercially caught in the eastern Pacific for its roe; it is marketed in Asia as an extremely expensive delicacy called *kazunokokombu,* in which the roe are salted and sold on beds of kelp. Pacific herring may be used as bait by anglers, but are not a sportfishing target, although they may be caught (or snagged) by coastal anglers who seek to use fresh specimens as live bait.

Identification. Similar to the Atlantic herring *(see: herring, Atlantic),* the Pacific herring is silvery with a bluish or greenish blue back and elongated body.

Size. The Pacific herring can grow to 18 inches in length.

Distribution. In the western Pacific Ocean, Pacific herring are found from Anadyr Bay and the eastern coasts of Kamchatka, including possibly the Aleutian Islands, southward to Japan and the west coast of Korea. In the eastern Pacific Ocean, they are found from Kent Peninsula and the Beaufort Sea southward to northern Baja California.

Habitat. Pacific herring inhabit coastal waters, and during the summer of their first year, the young appear in schools on the surface. In the fall, schools disappear as the young move to deep water, in depths of up to 475 meters, to stay there for the next two to three years.

Life history/Behavior. Depending on latitude, mature adults migrate inshore from December through July, entering estuaries to breed. These herring do not show strong north-south migrations, with populations being localized. Like other herring, they school in great numbers.

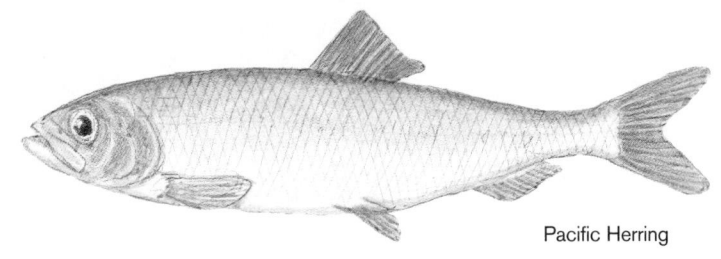

Pacific Herring

Food and feeding habits. Pacific herring larvae feed on planktonic foods, including ostracods, small copepods, small fish larvae, euphausids, and diatoms. Juveniles feed on crustaceans as well as on small fish, marine worms, and larval clams. Adults feed on larger crustaceans and small fish.
See: Herring.

HERRING, RIVER

A term applied collectively to alewives *(Alosa pseudoharengus; see: alewife)*, blueback herring *(Alosa aestivalis)*, and skipjack herring *(Alosa chrysochloris)*.
See: Herring; Herring, Atlantic.

HIGHLINE

A line that is fished far behind a trolling boat.
See: Flatlining; Trolling.

HI-LO RIG

A saltwater term for a two-hook bottom fishing bait rig. Featuring a bank sinker, two three-way swivels, and hooked leaders extending from the swivels, which are 2 to 3 feet apart, a hi-lo rig permits fishing one low bait on the bottom and another higher, as well as allows presentation of two different baits.

HIND, RED　*Epinephelus guttatus.*
Other names—strawberry grouper, speckled hind; French: *mérou couronné;* Spanish: *mero colorado, tofia.*

A grouper of the Serranidae family, the red hind is an important fish in the Caribbean, where large numbers are caught every year. It has excellent white, flaky meat that is usually marketed fresh.

Identification. As with all grouper, the red hind has a stout body and a large mouth. It is very similar to the rock hind *(see: hind, rock)* in appearance, although the red hind is slightly more reddish brown in color with dark red brown spots above and pure red spots below over a whitish background. It differs from the rock hind in having no spots on the tail or dorsal fin, and no dark splotches on the back or tail. The outer edges of the soft dorsal, caudal, and anal fins are blackish

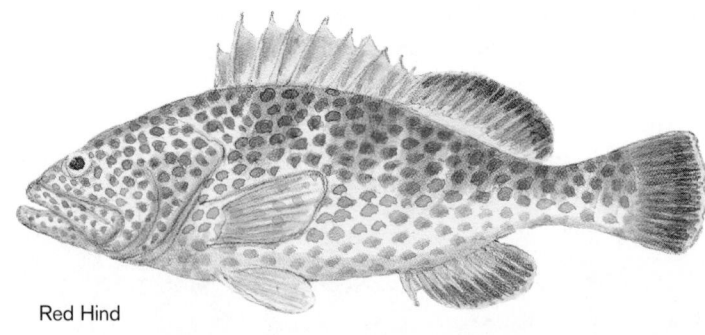

Red Hind

and are sometimes also edged in white. It can pale or darken to blend with surroundings.

Size/Age. The red hind can grow to 2 feet, although it is usually less than 15 inches long; most 12-inch and larger fish are males. Although it can reach 10 pounds, the red hind is rarely larger than 4 pounds in weight; the all-tackle world record is for a 6-pound, 1-ounce fish taken off Florida. The red hind can live for 17 years or longer.

Distribution. In the western Atlantic, red hind occur from North Carolina and Bermuda south to the Bahamas, the southern Gulf of Mexico, and to Brazil. They are common in the Caribbean, occasional in the Bahamas and Florida, and rare north of Florida.

Habitat. Red hind are one of the most common grouper in the West Indies, inhabiting shallow inshore reefs and rocky bottoms at depths of 10 to 160 feet. In Florida and the Bahamas they are usually found in quieter, deeper waters. Red hind are solitary and territorial fish, often found drifting or lying motionless along the bottom, camouflaged by their surroundings.

Spawning behavior. Spawning takes place from March through July in 68° to 82°F waters at depths of 100 to 130 feet. At this time, mature fish of age 3 and older form large clusters over rugged bottoms. They lay pelagic eggs in numbers between 90,000 and more than 3 million. Some fish undergo sexual inversion.

Food and feeding habits. Red hind feed on various bottom animals, such as crabs, crustaceans, fish, and octopus; they hide in holes and crevices and capture prey by ambush or after a short chase.

Angling. As with other grouper, bottom fishing is the best method to catch red hind, using cut fish or squid as bait. Fishing is best inshore over irregular bottom in water 80 to 180 feet deep, and along the shelf break where the depth ranges from 240 to 350 feet. Sturdy boat rods and reels with heavy line are primarily used. Terminal tackle usually consists of a heavy sinker and two 4/0 to 6/0 hooks baited with squid or cut fish rigged on a very heavy monofilament leader.
See: Grouper; Inshore Fishing.

HIND, ROCK　*Epinephelus adscensionis.*
Other names—grouper, jack, rock cod; French: *mérou oualioua;* Portuguese: *garoupa-pintada;* Spanish: *mero cabrilla.*

A grouper in the Serranidae family, the rock hind is found in the same range as the red hind *(see: hind, red)* and is also good table fare. Divers can often distinguish the two species by their behavior alone, as the rock hind is reclusive and shies away from humans.

Identification. The rock hind has an overall tan to olive brown cast, with many large, reddish to dark dots covering the entire body and fins. Similar in appearance to the red hind, it has one to four

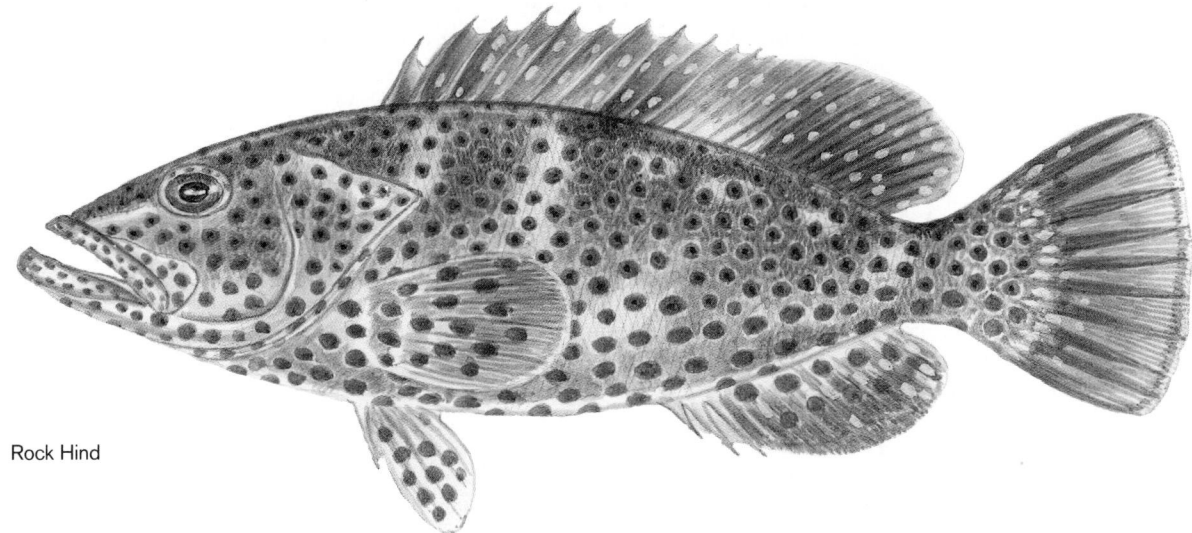

Rock Hind

distinctive pale or dark splotches along its back, appearing below the middle of the dorsal fin, behind the dorsal fin on the caudal peduncle, and below the spinous and soft parts of the dorsal fin. The tail and anal fins have a broad, whitish outer edge but lack the additional blackish margins found on the dorsal, caudal, and anal fins of the red hind. It can pale or darken dramatically.

Size. The rock hind can reach 2 feet in length; the all-tackle world-record fish is a 9-pounder.

Distribution. In the western Atlantic, rock hind occur from Massachusetts to southeastern Brazil, including Bermuda, the Bahamas, the eastern Caribbean, and the northern Gulf of Mexico; they are rare north of Florida. Rock hind are also found in the eastern Atlantic around the Ascension and St. Helena Islands.

Habitat. Solitary fish, rock hind inhabit rocky or rough inshore regions in shallow waters, although they occasionally inhabit deep reefs. They are often found drifting near the bottom.

Food and feeding habits. Ordinarily feeding on crabs and fish, rock hind are said to feed on juvenile triggerfish and young sea turtles at Ascension Island.

Angling. Like other grouper, rock hind are primarily caught by fishing at the right depth over an irregular bottom.

See: Grouper; Inshore Fishing.

HIP BOOTS *(Hippers)*
See: Waders.

HIRE BOAT
A small boat available for rent on a daily, multiday, or weekly basis, operated by the person who rents it, and not accompanied by a fishing guide or boat captain. This is essentially an Australian term for a self-guided rental boat, not to be confused with a guide boat *(see)* or charter boat *(see)*.

HOGSUCKER, NORTHERN
Hypentelium nigricans.
Other names—sucker, hog sucker.

This is a widespread and distinctive-looking member of the sucker family.

Identification. Northern hogsuckers get their name from their piglike appearance, particularly their head. They have a very steep forehead and long, protruding lips, bearing a strong likeness to a pig's snout. Their head also has a concave depression between the eyes, a trait distinctive among suckers. The body is conical, with the head region much thicker than the caudal peduncle. The body is marked with four lateral bars that come together on the fish's back to form saddles. Northern hogsuckers are generally darkly pigmented on the back and lightly pigmented on the belly.

Range. The northern hogsucker is widely distributed across central and eastern North America, occurring in the Great Lakes, Mississippi, Ohio, and some Atlantic drainages.

Habitat. The northern hogsucker inhabits primarily large streams and small rivers. It is usually found in areas with high water quality and clean substrate, free of heavy siltation. It is well suited to a benthic lifestyle, remaining close to the bottom in areas of various depth and flow velocities. Adults may inhabit deep pools and runs, as they are too large to be preyed upon by bass and other predators. The young and subadults live in faster water and in the stream margins.

Food. Like most suckers, the northern hogsucker preys upon many varieties of benthic

Northern Hogsucker

H

organisms, the most common of which are insect larvae, small crustaceans, detritus, and algae. It feeds by disturbing the stream bottom with its large snout and sucking up organisms that it dislodges. It can often be seen with its body angled upward, tail high, nearly perpendicular to the stream bottom as it forages around larger rocks. Its small air bladder and large pectoral fins help support it in the current while feeding.

Size/Age.   The northern hogsucker is a medium-size sucker, reaching up to 12 to 14 inches in length. Sexual maturity is reached between two and three years old, although most fish do not spawn until age 4. The northern hogsucker may live for eight years.

Spawning behavior.   Northern hogsuckers spawn in mid- to late spring as the water begins to warm. They do not make long upstream migrations as many suckers do, but spawn in pool tails, riffles, and stream margins near where they reside. Like most suckers, northern hogsuckers require clean gravel substrate for successful reproduction. They have a reproductive behavior unique among suckers. One female spawns with a group of three or more males that follow her around when she enters the reproductive areas. They will move around each other and move alongside the female, but spawning does not occur until the female begins to quiver.

Angling.   The northern hogsucker is not considered a desired game or commercial fish because of its soft flesh. It is taken by snagging and jigging where legal. It is also not frequently used as bait, although it is likely of value as food for large gamefish.

See: Suckers.

HOLDING
An expression for the position of a fish, usually in a stream or where there is current; this is similar to a lie (see). An example might be, "The shad are holding in the channel at the tail of the pool."

HOLDOVER FISH
Stocked fish, usually trout, that survive through at least one winter in the wild; also known as carryover fish.

HOLE
Angling jargon, primarily used in freshwater fishing, with several related meanings. In the simplest sense, a hole is a place to fish or a place where fish may be congregated and where a person has good success ("My favorite fishing hole is at the first bend of the river"). Generally the term "hole" is used to refer to a deep spot in a river, stream, or creek, which is more widely known as a pool (see). River holes or pools, because of their depth and darkness, and perhaps cooler temperature, are places where

some species of fish are especially likely to be found. In a lake or reservoir, the term "hole" refers to a place that produces a good catch of fish at a given time, or repeatedly over time; such a place might be notable for its depth, structural elements, or other features that cause fish to congregate there.

An angler who is "sitting on a hole" is one who stays in a certain productive spot. A person who has "got a hole" is one who has a somewhat confined location (usually on a big body of water) that may not be known to others and that produces good catches of fish.

HONDURAS
The largely mountainous country of Honduras in Central America is bordered by Nicaragua on the south, Guatemala on the west, and El Salvador on the southeast. A small portion of southeastern Honduras fronts on the Pacific Ocean at the Gulf of Fonseca, but it is not known for sportfishing opportunity. The northern and eastern regions abut the Caribbean, however, and offer more than 400 miles of coastline. Here there are numerous rivers, large estuaries and lagoons, many small islands, and a few offshore islands.

Most of Honduras' rivers flow to the Caribbean, the most prominent being the Ulúa, which drains the western third of the country and empties into the Gulf of Honduras. In these west-central mountains, Lake Yojoa was a hot largemouth bass lake for a brief period in the late 1970s and early 1980s but has fallen off the radar screen in ensuing years. Bass up to 18 pounds were once caught at the clear 13-mile-long, 8-mile-wide Yojoa, mostly by fishing excruciatingly deep, but netting took its toll on the fishery.

In the far east, a great watercourse, the Patuca, originates deep in the eastern highlands and flows through the Mosquito Coast to the sea, just east of Patana National Park; the nearby Coco River does likewise, forming the boundary with Nicaragua. Along the coast and sandwiched between these two systems is a vast network of swampy mangroves collectively known as Laguna de Caratasca, which includes numerous lakes, inflows, and backwater areas that stretch for more than 45 miles. These are difficult to access but are loaded with promise for snook, tarpon, and snapper, and likely other species.

This enormous area is not known to be fished; however, east of the Patuca River mouth by about 30 miles is the entrance to Brus Lagoon, where a lodge set up operations at Cannon Island in the mid-1990s. This location has tremendous fishing for snook and tarpon, including large specimens of both species. Tarpon in the 200-pound class, and snook up to 46 pounds, have been caught here.

The relatively short Sigre River enters the lagoon, and nearby is the Patána River, which flows directly into the sea. Many smaller rivers flow into Brus Lagoon, however, and each is a lush tropical wonder, with dense brush and good fishing at various times. The lagoon mouth is deep and wide and provides excellent angling opportunities. The main river mouth and vicinity have big tarpon, larger apparently than are found farther down in the Caribbean near the mouths of Costa Rican rivers. Snook are caught at the Brus River mouth as well, and along the beach.

This area is still being explored, and its angling opportunities are still evolving. Erratic weather patterns hindered its early development. From September through March snook and tarpon are abundant, as are cubera snapper (including a 78-pound line-class record caught in 1995). September and October, and January through April, are the best times for snook activity. November and December usually bring heavy rains, which greatly swell the area and flush so much muddy water through the lagoon and into the Caribbean that the fishing turns off. Trolling outside the river mouths is the main method for locating tarpon when the water gets muddy.

This area has become an ecological protection zone, and netting is supposedly prohibited in critical areas. If these regulations hold, a good fishery is ensured. Legal and illegal netting activities in areas like this have adversely affected numerous good coastal and inland sportfisheries in Mexico, Central America, and South America.

A number of small keys exist out in the Caribbean, east and north of this coast. These reportedly harbor bonefish and permit, but their distance offshore—roughly 40 to 60 miles from Laguna de Caratasca and much farther from Brus Lagoon—makes them an unknown entity, an area likely to be explored only by long-distance cruisers.

To the west, however, Roatán and Guanaja Islands lie offshore northeast of La Ceiba and are accessible by plane from San Pedro Sula. Guanaja has an established camp that attracts avid reef divers and is known for an abundance of small bonefish and permit on shallow grassy flats. Roatán, a larger island west of Guanaja, has extensive flats, but they are not known to have the bonefish and permit that exist at Guanaja.

HOOK

A recurved piece of metal wire, one end of which tapers to a sharp point, used to impale and capture fish.

Also known as a fishhook, a hook is truly an indispensable piece of sportfishing equipment. Tens of millions of hooks are manufactured daily around the world for use in both sportfishing and commercial fishing, and some manufacturers have tens of thousands of individual hook models. For sportfishing use, hooks are stand-alone equipment used as is with various types of natural or processed bait; they are attached as is or with dressing to an extremely diverse range of hard and soft artificial lures; they are dressed with various materials to become artificial flies; and they are used in molds for the construction of lead and hard-metal lures.

The hook originated long before any other fishing equipment, having been used in some form with spearing instruments in prehistoric time. It is speculated that the oldest fishhooks were made out of wood during the Stone Age, possibly evolving at the same time as gorges. A tree with branches that stick out at acute angles can be the source of a hook strong enough for angling, but the deterioration of wood precludes finding ancient evidence of this.

It is known, however, that gorges were used to capture fish during the Stone Age. These were straight, tapered shafts made of bone, stone, shell, wood, etc., that were placed inside a natural bait to lodge in the stomach or mouth of a fish. Hooks made of bone were used during the latter period of the Stone Age. When used for hooks, bone had a tendency to break, although it withstood hard use, even in saltwater. Historians report that processing bone hooks took patience, but Stone Age people had implements good enough to make extra-fine hooks from this material. Old bone hooks have been unearthed in many places, including Europe, Egypt, and Palestine. The oldest bone hook found in Palestine is reportedly 9,000 years old. Although there was a lot of diversity to the oldest bone hooks, they were not made with barbs, which developed much later.

Hook material evolved over thousands of years from bone to copper to bronze and then iron. The genesis of modern hooks was during the Middle Ages. It is not known exactly when fine hooks for sportfishing were fashioned from steel needles, but the use of steel hooks was noted in print for the first time by Dame Juliana Berners in her 1496 essay *Treatyse of Fysshynge With an Angle;* this essay was included in the second edition of *The Boke of Saint Albans,* the first known manual of sportfishing. Dame Berners recommended using the finest darning needles for small fish, embroidery needles for larger fish, and tailor's or shoemaker's needles for the biggest fish, and she also detailed how to make the steel pliable, fashion a barb, and shape and temper the steel.

Hooks were being manufactured as a business in the seventeenth century, when Izaak Walton recommended buying hooks from London's Charles Kirby, whom he described in *The Compleat Angler* as "the most exact and best Hook-maker this nation affords." Kirby is credited with the advancement of the modern fishhook—through his metal tempering and hardening processes—and the invention of the kirbed offset, which is still in use today.

Hooks were largely made by hand until mechanization took over in the middle of the nineteenth century. For a time, England was the hook-making center of the world (the town of Redditch in particular), and this still accounts for the names that were given to many of the popular patterns that have stayed throughout the years.

Zane Grey had his membership from the Catalina Tuna Club revoked in 1921 when a woman caught a 426-pound broadbill, larger than his own 418-pound catch, and he accused her of having assistance in the catch.

Today hook manufacture is widely dispersed around the globe, and there is an astounding array of hooks in production—many quite similar and many vastly different—and the number of patterns and sizes is impressive and confusing. The array of hooks is due to fishing methods, the differing mouths of fish, and the lures and bait used to attract them.

Characteristics

The majority of fishhooks are made from high carbon steel; a good number are made from stainless steel, and some are made from alloys. The physical parts of a hook include the eye, shank, bend, point, gap, and throat, as depicted in the accompanying illustration. The point may have a barb, and the eye may actually be flattened solid instead of having an eyelike opening. All of these parts have notable features and variations.

In the most basic evaluation of a hook, there are three commonly accepted types described according to the number of points. These are characterized as single, double, or treble hooks; quadruple hooks (four points) have been produced but are not currently in sportfishing use.

Single hooks are the most common hook and the overwhelming favorite for fishing with most types of bait; they are used on all but a tiny percentage of artificial flies and are attached to many types of lures. Double hooks are by far the least common type; they are mainly used in tying artificial flies, but some are employed in baitfishing, and some are fastened to weedless lures. Treble hooks are very popular on a wide range of lures, which are prerigged by lure manufacturers; they are almost never used in fly tying and are only occasionally fished with bait.

Eye.   The eye is the portion of the hook to which the line is attached, and it probably should be called the butt or line connector because it is not always shaped like an eye. The most popular eye style is the ball, which is also known as a ring eye and has a straight-cut end that meets flush with the stem of the eye. A similar but more expensive-to-produce version is the tapered eye, which has a taper-cut end that meets the stem. In both of these,

Hook Eyes

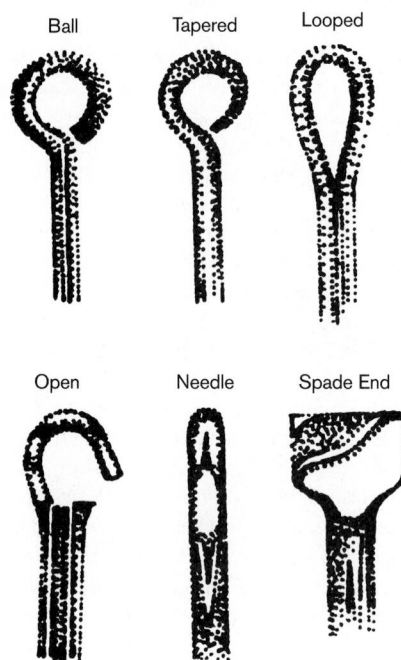

there should be no gap that fishing line can slip through; if a gap exists, the hook is poorly made and you should discard it.

Other eye styles include the oval and needle, which are common on treble hooks, and the looped, which is a traditional style for salmon and steelhead flies. Several versions of open eyes exist; these have a ringlike end. Open eyes are intended for easy changing on lures where hooks are prerigged to lure bodies without split rings; they are subject to loss if the eye isn't fully closed (you need very good pliers) and also to weakening if they are opened and closed a few times.

In addition to being characterized according to shape, an eye can be typecast according to position. Eyes may be straight (in line with the hook), turned up, or turned down; turned-up eyes are preferred on short-shanked heavily dressed flies, and turned-down eyes are preferred by some people for their line of hook penetration. Angled eyes are often snelled to the line when used with bait.

Eyeless hooks are those in which the line is snelled to the shank, since there is no ring or loop to fasten a knot to. The ends of the eyeless hooks are flattened, often to a spadelike form or a knob. These hooks are popular in Europe for coarse and match fishing, especially with very fine-diameter lines and small bait.

Shank.   The shank is that part of the hook between the eye and the bend. Hook patterns have a normal or standard length, but they come several sizes larger and smaller in shank length. A short or long shank designation means that the length of the shank of that item is equal to that of the next smaller or larger regular-shank hook of the same pattern.

Hook Features

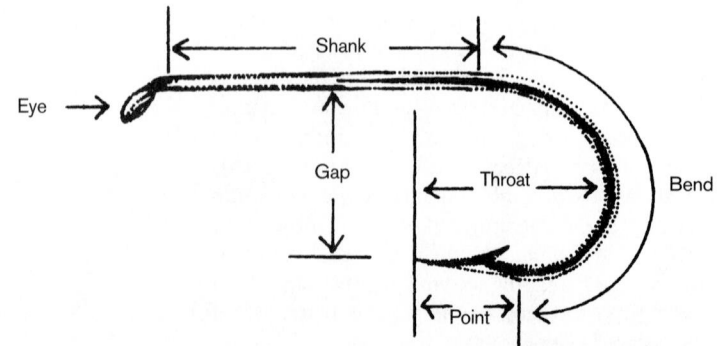

H

Hook Shanks

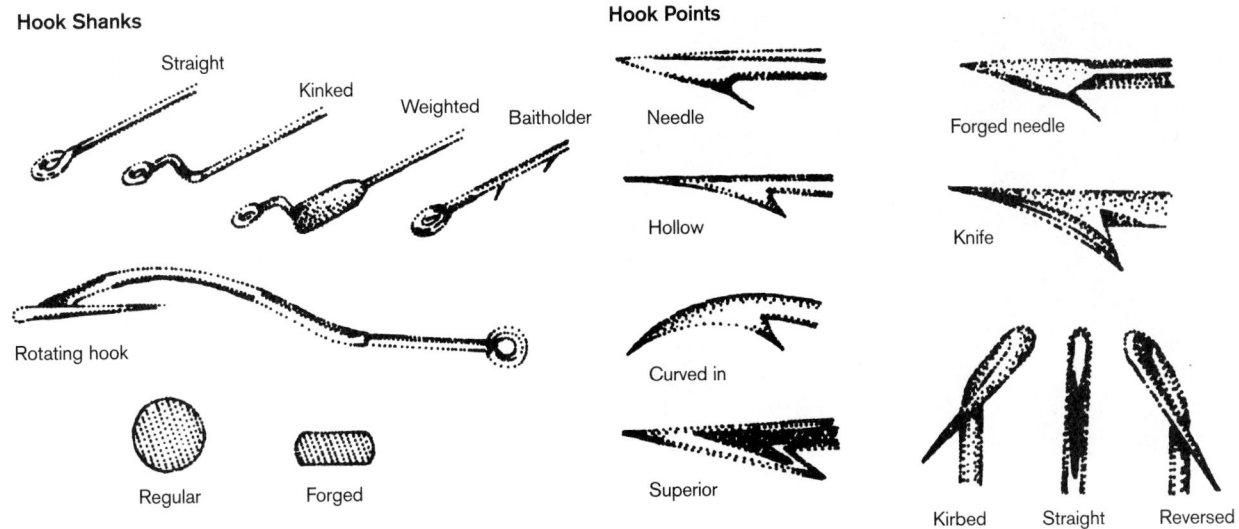

Straight

Kinked

Weighted

Baitholder

Rotating hook

Regular

Forged

Cross Sections

Hook Points

Needle

Forged needle

Hollow

Knife

Curved in

Superior

Kirbed   Straight   Reversed

Variations of more than one step are denoted by the letter *X* or the word "extra." A short-shanked 2X hook, for example, is equal in shank length to a regular-shank hook of the same pattern that is two sizes smaller.

Shanks are straight, bent, curved, humped, and contorted in various ways. Certain styles are favored for their hooking efficiency or for their appearance when dressed with various materials. A keel or humped shank, for example, is popularly used with Texas-rigged soft worms and also for tying some streamer flies. Some shanks have multiple curves for rotating into the fish's mouth, although these may not be as strong as other models. Most shanks are smooth, but some have multiple slices on the upper and lower portions. These are like mini-barbs and are meant for holding bait or soft-bodied lures; hooks with this feature are usually called baitholders. Some shanks also sport a small weight on the shank, either near the bend or just behind the eye; these are mainly used with soft lures that are rigged Texas style without a slip sinker.

Point.   The point is the tapered sharp business end of the hook. It may or may not incorporate a barb, which is the sharp projection behind the point that impedes the hook's backward movement when it has impaled a fish (or clothing, skin, etc.).

Hook points have many configurations. The more common ones in sportfishing hooks are needle or conical, hollow, curved or rolled, knife, and spear or superior. Penetration and holding power are the critical elements of a point. Especially noted for their penetration are the needle point, which is conical in shape, and the knife point, which has triangulated sharp edges. The curved point, which rolls inward toward the shank, has an inward line of pull that helps to keep the hook driving in under sustained pressure.

It is arguable whether long or short points penetrate better, and this is a matter of the sharpness of the hook, the point style, the fish species, and the

hooksetting abilities of the angler, as well as the size of the barb in some cases. If a point is long but slender, it should penetrate as well as one that is short but thicker, although points that are too long are weaker.

As a result of improved manufacturing processes, the sharpness of hooks has progressed significantly in recent years. This is an important advancement because sharpness is the one hook property that anglers readily see the value of. Although most new hooks can still be improved by sharpening *(see: hook sharpening)*, many of the new chemically sharpened hooks are very sharp when fresh. This chemical operation incorporates a series of dips and rinses in extremely potent acids that shave off a tiny layer of the surface of the steel. The result is a perfect shape and superb sharpness.

Hook points primarily lie parallel to the shank when viewed from a straight-on position. However, the point, and sometimes part of the bend, may be offset to one side, in theory for better hooking. If viewed from a straight-on position, a point is called

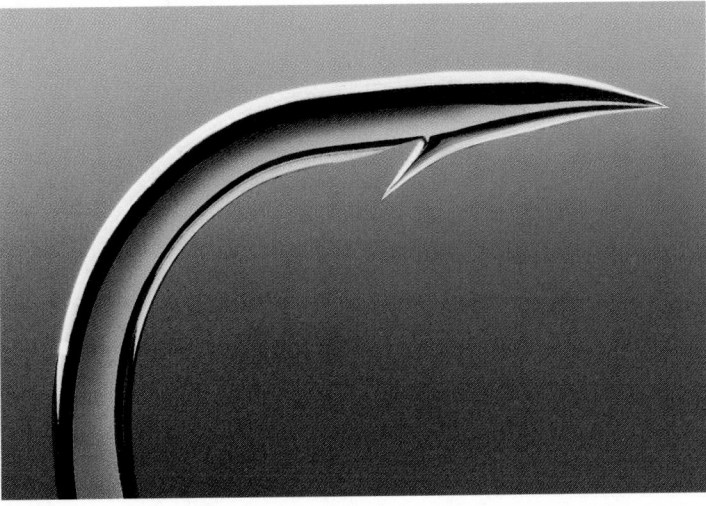

Magnified view of a conical-style hook point.

H

Magnified view of a knife-style hook; note triangulation.

kirbed (after Charles Kirby) when the point is angled to the left of the perpendicular plane; it is called reversed when it is angled to the right. These are more likely to be used in bottom fishing situations with bait than in circumstances where an actively moving hook can drag in the water and cause spinning.

The points of some hooks may also have a wire or nylon guard. Hooks so equipped are called weedless, and the guard extends from the hook eye to the point.

Barb. Barbs exist on the majority of manufactured hooks. Those without them are labeled barbless. Many anglers pinch or file a barb down to make a hook barbless. Some hooks have a slight, smooth bump along the lower point in lieu of a barb. The purpose of the barb is to hold the hook in the fish. A large barb is not necessarily helpful in this regard and may actually make it harder to attain full penetration of the point, not to mention create a large entry hole that can cause the hook to slip out when you don't want it to. Barbless hooks facilitate hook removal and may be mandated in some waters to minimize injury to fish that are released.

Barbs

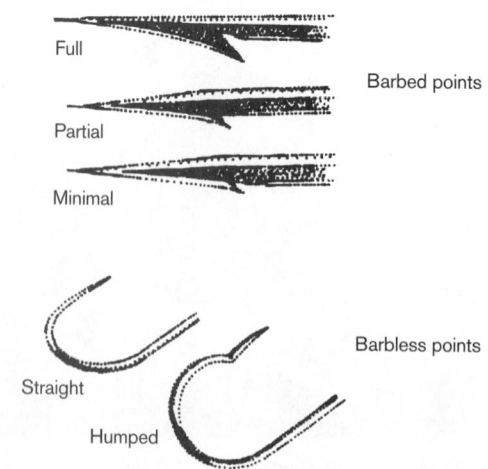

Full

Partial

Minimal

Barbed points

Straight

Humped

Barbless points

The role of a barb in keeping fish on the hook is greatly overrated; many anglers have little or no loss of fish on barbless hooks provided that good fish-playing measures are employed *(see: catch-and-release)*. Nevertheless, it is often hard to find barbless hooks in the range of styles and sizes that you may want.

You can make your own hooks barbless by filing off the barb or by pinching it down. Filing works best with small fine-diameter wire hooks. To pinch the barb down, use a pair of good-quality pliers, place the blunt end over the barb, and squeeze tightly to flatten the barb. Sharpen the point well afterward. Remember to maintain a constant tight line on a fish when using barbless hooks, because the hooks can easily become dislodged if there is even momentary slack in the line.

Bend/pattern. The name by which a style of hook is known is called a pattern, and this is a function of its bend, which is the curved section between the point and the shank. The bend has a lot to do with the strength of the hook. Ideally a hook should resist bending up to a stage where the hook almost would break, preferably bending instead of breaking. Resistance to direct-pull pressure is influenced by hook style and size, is substantially aided by forging, and is related to the bite and gap. The gap is the distance between the tip of the point and the shank. The distance from the peak of the bend to the gap is known as the bite or throat. Most hooks have a deep or relatively deep bite and a fairly wide gap, both of which keep hooked fish more secure than a shallow bite or narrow gap.

Most hooks avoid having a sharp angle to the bend and are formed such that the initial stage of the bend is gradual and the final stage of the bend is pronounced. This design is actually less easily bent than a symmetrically round one.

Popular patterns and attributes include:

Sproat	Straight point; popular with flies and lures.
Kirby	Point offset helps prevent hook from slipping out; good for baitfishing.
O'Shaughnessy	Outward bend to the tip of the point; heavy wire; many applications.
Aberdeen	Light wire, round bend good for use with minnows; will bend before breaking.
Carlisle	Stronger than Aberdeen; used with bait; long shank prevents fish from swallowing the hook.
Siwash	Heavy wire; extra-long point offers good retention; used for big, active fish.
Salmon Egg	Short shank; concealed by small bait.

| **Claw or Beak** | Point is offset and curved inward to aid penetration; used often with bait. |
| **Limerick** | Long shank, wide bend provides extra hooking space. |

There are many more patterns, of course, and many with very specialized applications. Freshwater bass anglers, for example, have such an affinity for fishing with soft lures, especially worms, that there is a whole genre of so-called worm hooks (which should not be confused with fishing with natural worms) having various humps and bends to the shanks, as well as different bends and worm-rigging enhancements. One of the more specialized saltwater hooks is a circle hook, which has become very popular in bait-fishing, especially for tuna, but also other species. The circle hook has a wide bend and long inward point that at first glance makes you wonder how it could ever stick a fish, but not only does it stick the fish, it also doesn't pull out very easily under fishing rod pressure, so a greater number of fish hooked are landed.

Size/gauge/temper. No matter what the pattern, hooks are all designated according to size, which in principle is the width of the gap. This is just a relative designation, however, instead of an absolute one. Gap width may differ between families of hooks, and there is no consistency between manufacturers in sizing, so the matter of size designation is relative to individual manufacturers and specific patterns.

Sizes are specified in whole numbers at the smaller end of the spectrum and as "aught" fractions as they get larger. The smallest hooks, depending on manufacturer, are No. 32, 30, or 28; the largest hooks range from 14/0 up to 19/0.

Hook Sizes

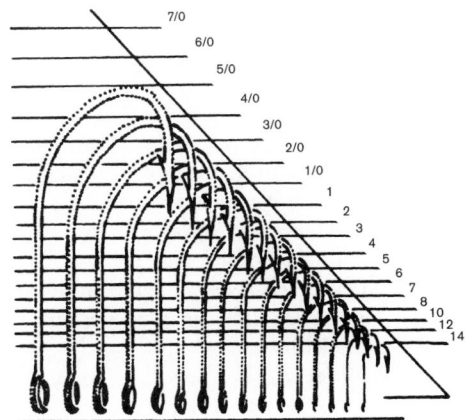

The distance between the point and the inside of the shank, known as the gap, determines hook size. Large hooks (1/0 to 7/0) increase in size as the number increases. Small hooks (1 to 14 and beyond) decrease in size as the number increases, and come in many smaller sizes than are depicted here. This illustration is drawn to actual scale and based on a standard, popular American bait hook, the rolled-point, offset, forged Eagle Claw No. 084.

Hooks

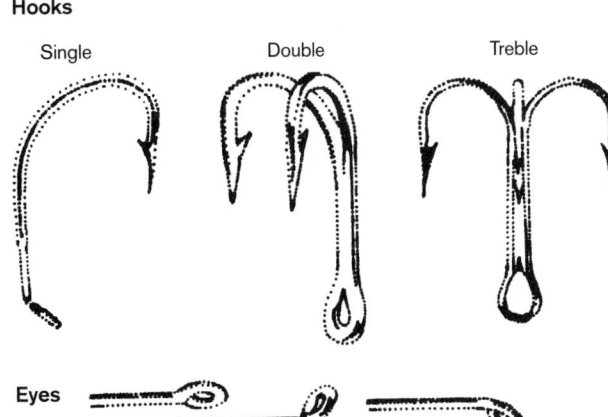

Although not reflected in size designations, the diameter of the wire used to make the hook has a bearing on its performance and its proper use. This diameter is reached in manufacturing by taking steel wire rods and reducing them to the wire gauge that is necessary for a particular pattern. The wire is pulled through a series of ever-narrowing orifices, which reduce the gauge, sometimes by as much as 90 percent.

There are fine, medium, and heavy wire gauges corresponding to relative diameter. Heavy wire is used in making hooks for the strongest applications and for situations where it is beneficial for a hook to sink fast (large wet flies, for example, or big-game baitfishing); fine wire is used in making hooks for light-line fishing, angling with small and delicate bait, and in slow-sinking or floating uses; and medium wire is used for general-purpose hooks.

In the manufacturing process, the drawn wire is machined into shape and then heat-tempered. Tempering is the hardening process that gives the material its strength within that shape. It is a critical operation, because overtempering results in soft hooks that don't adequately resist bending and undertempering results in hard hooks with no flexibility. The ideal is a strong hook that will flex moderately; if the hook has no flex under load, the hook will snap at less of a load. (Incidentally, with the exception of some light-wire hooks, like Aberdeen patterns, when a hook bends out of its original shape and does not spring back, it is permanently deformed and should be discarded.) Some hooks are also given extra strengthening by forging, which is stamping the sides flat. Although this increases resistance to bending on a straight pull, it does not help resist side torque and is often not found on hooks with offset points for this reason, since offset points do not resist side pressure as well as straight points.

Finish/corrosion resistance. In the manufacturing process, different finishes are applied to hooks to provide either cosmetic value (appealing to the angler or, in a few cases, to the fish) or

H

corrosion resistance. Some carbon steel hooks are given color varnishes or lacquers; these are mainly blue, black, bronze, green, and red, but fluorescent and luminescent colors are also applied. Tin, cadmium, nickel, black nickel, gold, and chrome/zinc platings are applied to other carbon steel hooks. Most stainless steel hooks receive no finishing after being polished.

Of the tinted varnishes, bronze is most common and also the most basic one for freshwater use, though it (and the other varnishes) has low corrosion resistance. Gold finishing may involve plating 24 karat gold in better hooks or lacquering lesser-quality products with brass; these are strictly used in freshwater because of low corrosion resistance, and mainly with Aberdeen and salmon egg hooks. Nickel is also a prevalent freshwater finish; it results from electroplating, provides a shiny silver appearance, and has better corrosion resistance than bronze.

An advanced version of nickel plating, called electroless nickel, has an improved corrosion resistance and sharper hooks than standard nickel-plated hooks. A related new multiple-layer finish is nickel Teflon, which is a durable hook with a fast hooksetting property due to the slick Teflon exterior. Black nickel, which is not well known to many anglers, is a newer multiple-layer (zinc oxide over nickel) finish that has a silvery black appearance; it has more corrosion resistance than all of the aforementioned finishes.

Electroplated tin is a standard saltwater finish for carbon steel hooks; this is a step up the corrosion-resistance scale from the aforementioned finishes and is itself exceeded by cadmium-tin plating and chrome-zinc plating, which are finishes that receive different trademark names with different manufacturers. Cadmium is a substance with adverse environmental implications, so manufacturers who use chrome-zinc plating point out the additional safety value of chrome-zinc. These finishes rank with or actually exceed stainless steel in corrosion-resistant properties.

Obviously the ability of hooks to withstand corrosion varies, particularly in saltwater, and is an important aspect of selection. No finish is completely rustproof. As a material, carbon steel is significantly less resistant to corrosion than stainless steel or cadmium-tin and chrome-zinc. Freshwater anglers seldom use the latter three finishes in ordinary fishing activities. In any environment, however, if a hook sits in a wet tray for a long period of time, it will corrode; however, the most important aspect of corrosion applies to hooks purposely left in fish that are to be released (a common occurrence, especially when using bait) or to hooks inadvertently stuck in escaped fish.

Some tests have shown that varnished hooks (bronze, blue, etc.) and nickel or gold hooks, which are most common in freshwater, will break down (defined as being well corroded, brittle, and unusable though not totally decomposed) in two to three weeks of freshwater immersion, compared with 48 to 54 hours in saltwater. Thus, saltwater anglers should not regularly use varnished, plain nickel, and gold hooks unless they release a lot of fish with hooks in them. Stainless steel and cadmium-tin hooks take an indeterminate time to break down in freshwater. In saltwater, stainless steel hooks may take several months to break down, and still longer to decompose entirely. Cadmium-tin takes even longer. Thus, freshwater anglers have virtually no need to use highly corrosion-resistant finishes in freshwater.

The more that a hook is used—meaning that it is sharpened and comes into contact with rocks, sand, and even the teeth of fish—the less resistance it has to corrosion, since the finish becomes partly removed and the underlying carbon steel is exposed.

See Bait; Fly; Hook Sharpening; Lure.

HOOKBAIT

A European term for a bait with a hook in it, used to distinguish this item from a similar or identical unhooked bait that has been distributed for chumming.

See: Carp; Chumming; Float.

HOOK EXTRACTOR

A tool for removing a hook from a fish. This may be needle-nosed pliers, forceps, a long slender pinching device, or other objects that allow a person to avoid teeth and/or reach into the mouth of a fish to remove a hook without injuring the fish or its captor.

See: Catch-and-Release.

HOOK PULLER

A tool used to release fish without having to touch them; a hook puller is primarily used in saltwater by anglers fishing with fairly heavy line or leader. Commercial and homemade models look similar to an old ice block hauling tool, except that the business end is hooked and is used to grab around the bend of a hook when a fish is lifted up with the heavy line or leader.

See: Catch-and-Release.

HOOK REMOVAL
See: First Aid.

HOOKSETTING

Some angling situations and techniques cause a fish to hook itself when it strikes bait or lure; all you have to do is keep tension on the line to keep the

The strongest ebb current on the West Coast: 7 knots at Chatham Strait, Alaska; strongest ebb on the East Coast: 5.2 knots at St. Johns River, Florida.

hook point from slipping free. Most of the time, and nearly always when casting and retrieving hard and soft artificial lures, an angler must react to a strike by setting the hook. This seems rather obvious and easy to accomplish: You just jerk back. Not quite.

Setting the hook on some fish is harder than on others, and there are enough variables—whether the fish is swimming away from or toward you, whether you are sitting or standing, whether you are using a stiff or limber rod, etc.—to make a non-studious appraisal very risky. Indeed, few anglers have an accurate notion of how much force they generate when they set the hook to the best of their ability. Actually, the average angler is quite inefficient when punching home the hook, as tests using instruments that gauge the amount of force applied have demonstrated.

Consider that you may not set the hook as efficiently as desired each and every time, especially when caught unaware by a strike or hampered by a bony-mouthed or strong-jawed fish. Other factors (such as a bow in the line while river fishing or a striking fish that runs toward you) will also impede your efforts. Thus, you can see that it is imperative to do your best to execute the best possible hookset time after time.

Hooksetting starts with proper technique. Its effectiveness has little to do with physical stature or with brute strength. If you doubt this, tie a barrel swivel to the line on any fishing rod and have a friend stand 40 feet away from you, holding the swivel clenched between thumb and forefinger. Raise the rod slowly and apply all the pressure you can to try to pull that swivel out of your friend's hand. If you don't jerk back violently, you can't pull it out.

Effective hooksetting depends on timing and hook point penetration. Pulling back on the rod with steady pressure after you detect a strike is not how you should set the hook, although many anglers mistakenly react to a strike this way.

There are two recognized and effective techniques in hooksetting, one with a no-slack approach and the other with a slight, controlled amount of slack.

With a no-slack hookset, you lean toward the fish, reel up slack until the line is taut, and then punch the hook home. This is accomplished in the blink of an eye, and it is crucial that you reel up slack only until the line is taut but not pulling on the fish. If you tighten the line so much that the fish feels tension, it may quickly expel your offering; this is especially true with bait and with soft-bodied lures. This technique takes timing, which is acquired through experience.

With a controlled slack-line set, the line is not reeled taut to the fish, but nearly so; and the hook is punched home quickly to provide shock penetration. The theory here is that you get better hook point penetration from a snappy shock force than

Proper hooksetting begins with the rod low and pointed toward the fish (top) and concludes with the rod butt held chest high (bottom), where power is delivered and control is maintained.

from a tight-line pull. With the head of a hammer, try to push a nail into a wall, and then use the hammer to strike the nail sharply; you'll see the difference and appreciate how it applies to hooksetting.

Of course, many times a fish strikes without warning; the angler feels tension immediately and reacts by bringing the rod back sharply. Sometimes, that is all it takes, but unfortunately the more typical outcome is that the hook never becomes firmly embedded in the fish. Just reacting and raising back the rod is often not enough, and a second or third hookset may be warranted.

A principal reason why many anglers are ineffective at hooksetting is not their inability to respond quickly and generate rod tip speed, but the way they use their bodies and contort themselves while doing so. Hooksetting is not a whole-body maneuver, but an exercise of wrists and arms. Back and legs have little to do with it. Someone thin and short might deliver more hooksetting force and better hook penetration than a larger, more powerful individual.

Preparing yourself for what is about to happen before it happens is important. Start by keeping your rod tip down during the retrieve (although in some instances this is not the best position for accomplishing a proper retrieve or for detecting a strike). With the tip down, you're in the best position to respond quickly to a strike, even if, as often happens, your attention is elsewhere when the strike actually occurs. If there is little or no slack in the line, you can make a forceful sweep up or back when you set the hook and then be in immediate control of the fish to begin playing it. When working certain lures, however, you need to keep the rod tip up to work the lure properly and to readily detect a strike. When setting the hook, you can compensate for a high rod position by bowing the rod slightly toward the fish while reeling up slack; this action enables you to get a full backward sweep and be in the proper position for the beginning of the fight.

Where possible, you should be reeling and striking all in one motion, keeping the pressure on constantly and not yielding unless the fish is strong enough to pull line off the drag. Good hooksetting technique is never more important than when long distances are involved, and the same is true for fish-playing tactics. Fish a long distance off are harder to control than those up close. Keeping a strong fish away from an obstruction is more difficult when it is 125 feet from you than when it is 40. When fishing from a boat, you may have to maneuver the boat in order to change the angle of pull on a large fish and steer the fish away from obstructions. You have to anticipate and react quickly, however, because often a fish is fairly close to some type of obstruction when it first gets hooked. How you handle the situation from the outset—especially if the fish is a powerful one or if you're using light tackle—can greatly influence the outcome.

Hooksetting should be a quickly accomplished maneuver. When a fish strikes, you should react reflexively, bringing your rod back and up sharply while holding the reel handle and reeling the instant you feel the fish. The position of the rod is important. The butt is jammed into the stomach or midchest area, and the full arc and power of the rod is brought into play, without having hands or arms jerk wildly over your head. In order to countermand line stretch, you must reel hard and fast the moment you set the hook.

Nylon monofilament lines on average have a stretch factor of up to 30 percent when wet, which in part explains why you can deliver more force with a short nylon monofilament line than with a long one (also with a dry line versus a wet one). By comparison, a low-stretch braided Dacron line or a microfilament line, if it had other desirable fish line qualities, would be better for hooksetting over all distances, though you would still generate more force on short lengths. Because of line stretch, an angler is more effective at setting the hook at short and midrange distances than at long distances. If you have a long length of line out, it is harder to counter the effect of stretch when setting the hook. Thus, you can generate more force and be more efficient at setting the hook at short distances than at long distances.

Good hooksetting procedure, however, doesn't end once you have reacted and you feel the fish. Like a golf swing, hooksetting requires follow-through, and that action is sometimes critical. The line must remain tight; bringing the rod tip back behind your head or raising your arms up high often puts some momentary slack into the line when you bring the rod back down in front of yourself. Not having to do this is the advantage of keeping the rod in front of you, and it is also the advantage of reeling continuously until the fish is firmly hooked and offering some resistance. Once you have the fish firmly hooked and everything under control, you can change the angle of pull as conditions warrant; changing the angle usually means applying sideways pressure rather than upward pressure.

The type of rod you use can aid or impede hooksetting efforts. Generally speaking, limber rods decrease your ability to generate hooksetting force and stiff rods increase it. The soft and somewhat spongy response of a limber rod does, however, make it harder to break the line and to cast light lures, so there are functional trade-offs in tackle used. A stiff rod can aid strike detection, but it could lead to breaking light lines if the hook is set particularly hard. Is there a difference in hooksetting effectiveness between types of rods? Not as much as anglers like to think. The difference is really one of rod action.

Light lines can pose hooksetting problems, especially for those who are accustomed to heavier tackle and jaw-breaking hooksets. Again, the problem is usually a rod that is too stiff for the line. Where light line is used, you need a rod with some cushioning effect. With a medium- or light-action rod that is used with light line, and with the appropriate drag setting, it's almost impossible to break the line when setting the hook. You can prove this to yourself when you're hung up on some obstruction while using such tackle; try setting the hook to break the line, and you'll find that it is extremely difficult to do so.

If your line has a belly or bow in it (as it might when river fishing or when a fish takes your offering and runs laterally with it), you may not have time to take out all or most of the slack or to reel up the line for a direct shot, without alerting the fish, when you set the hook. In this situation, you might execute a slack-line snap, being sure to keep the line tight after the hookup. Fly anglers using light tippets and fishing in current don't want to muster much force anyway, so they'll use this method. Most of the time when fly fishing, especially when using light-wire hooks on small flies and thin tippets, you just need to snap the tip up and keep the line taut to set the hook (although the bonier the mouth of the fish, the larger the hook needed, and the heavier the tippet or shock leader, the more you need to "reef" it to the fish).

A line that is impeded by some obstruction presents another problem, since your hooksetting force is directed more at that impediment than at the fish beyond. You can't do much about this situation (which often happens with big fish that take bait and run a short distance) except to realize the problem, fish with heavy line in thick cover, and regularly check your line for damaged spots.

Drag slippage can also impede hooksetting. Some anglers who use baitcasting tackle put a thumb on the reel spool when setting the hook so that they can prevent slippage. However, the better solution is to have the drag *(see)* set precisely for the line strength so you don't have to do this.

One way to deliver better-than-average hooksetting force is to strike with both hands on the rod, one on the handle around the reel and one on the foregrip. Most anglers set the hook with one hand on the rod handle and the other on the reel handle. Usually this is adequate. Certain circumstances, however, may necessitate using two hands to reef the hooks home. Occasionally it is desirable to set the hook two or three times in rapid succession.

What about when trolling? The fish already has the lure when you pull the rod out of its holder. Should you set the hook then? It depends on the situation and the fish. When the quarry is large and hard-mouthed, yes. When using very light line or angling for soft-mouthed fish, no, because you run the risk of pulling out the lure. In either case, you will still have to concentrate on keeping pressure on the fish and on playing it mistake-free.

In big-game fishing and offshore trolling, heavy-duty reels are adjusted with greater drag for setting the hook (called a strike drag) the drag is relaxed to a lighter tension once the fish is on. The heavier drag allows a lot more force to be applied and counters the effect of stretch.

Paying attention to these matters will help you be more efficient at setting the hook. To get the most benefit from this information, however, be sure to sharpen new and used hooks. A super-sharp hook can make all the difference in landing or losing a fish. Most fish are lost because the hook slipped out or was thrown when the fish jumped. A super-sharp hook penetrates easier and increases your chances of landing a fish. The primary advantage of having a sharp hook is to gain penetrating effectiveness. Maximum penetration translates into optimum hooksetting efficiency and better hook retention, which ultimately means more fish hooked and landed.

See: Hook Sharpening; Line.

HOOK SHARPENING

It is certainly true that if anglers paid more attention to the sharpness of their hooks, they would catch more fish. The fact that manufacturers of hook (and knife) sharpeners annually spend more time at consumer shows teaching people why and how to sharpen their hooks than about the products used to sharpen them bears this out. Freshwater anglers in general are less attentive to hook sharpening needs than saltwater anglers, but everyone can benefit

from tending to this detail. Even though modern hooks, especially smaller and finer-diameter wire hooks, are factory sharpened to better levels today than they ever were, hooks quickly lose sharpness through use, especially from impacts.

If you were to look at a standard fish hook under a powerful microscope, you'd see that it has many rough spots. This is especially true of hooks that have been used and have been in a tackle box for a while. Some will also have a bent point (a sure way to lose fish), or have burrs on the barb (which will impair penetration). Sharpening new and previously used hooks smoothes out the rough spots and facilitates getting the point and barb deep enough in the fish to keep it on your line.

You can improve the sharpness of a hook by grinding the point and barb over a sharpening stone or file. The best way to sharpen bigger, hardened thick-bodied hooks, including those of cadmium and stainless steel, and hooks that are forged (flattened around the bend on both sides) is with a file. The file cuts only on the forward stroke, so keep this in mind as you sharpen. Start by sharpening the barb and the inside cutting edges that lead toward the point, as shown in the accompanying illustration; use same angle as the factory-made cutting edge (if there is one). Do both sides; then move the

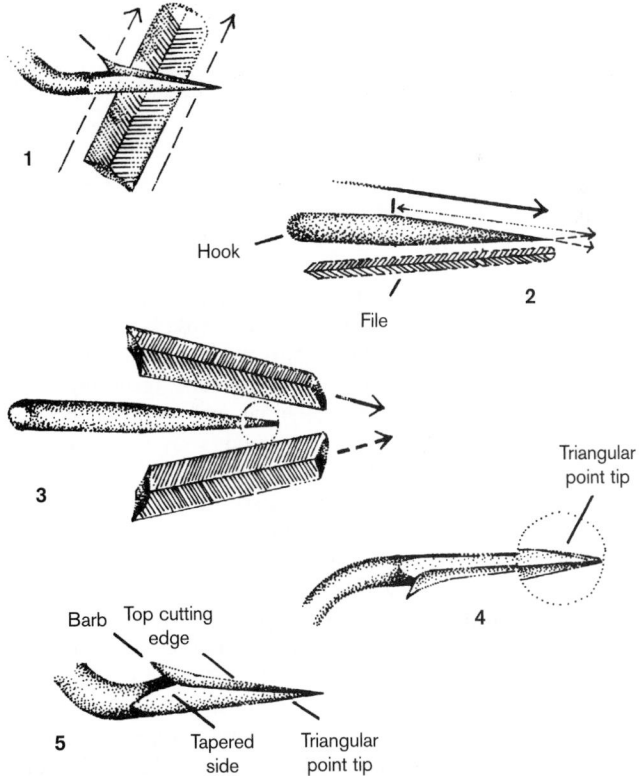

When using a file to sharpen a hook, effect a triangulated cutting area by filing across the inside or top cutting edge, including the barb (1), and by filing along both sides of the hook point (2). With this accomplished, focus on filing the extreme point area (3), creating a mini-triangulated point tip (4). The final result is a well-sharpened barb, top, sides, and point tip (5).

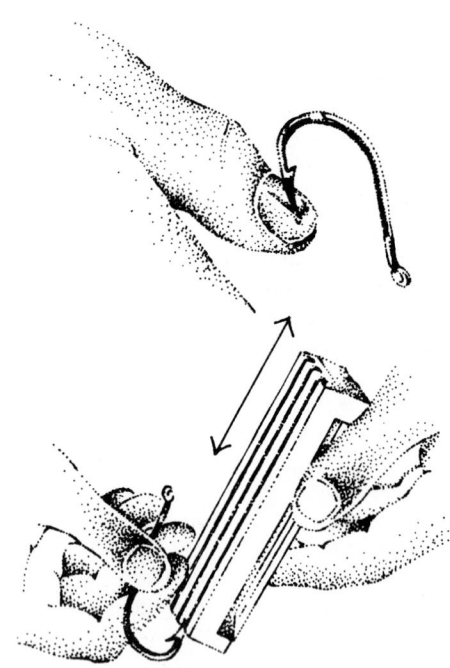

When using a channeled stone, move the hook point back and forth in a channel, changing the angle; then turn the stone crosswise and run it across the barb and sides. The point is sharp enough when it digs into your thumbnail when you drag it across the nail.

file forward and do the same thing to the immediate point area, filing repeatedly toward the point on both sides. It's a good idea to put a mini-cutting edge on the very tip of the point opposite the barb; this little edge really facilitates penetration.

For smaller hooks—the kinds used on most inland waters and nearly all freshwater fish—use a medium-grit honing stone with some type of channel in it. If a file is all you have, use it to the best of your ability. The key to sharpening is not the shape of the sharpening device or its cost, but the fact that it is abrasive and that you use it to put a triangulated shape on the hook. Honing stones (generally in the form of a stick) should be sized to the hook being sharpened, since large models do not adequately reach all parts of a smaller hook.

Sharpening stones can be run forward and backward and should be used in the same manner as a file, first grinding on the inside of the point and then on the left and right sides and the very tip. If you use the channel or groove in a sharpening stone, be sure to rotate the hook so that all parts of the point are affected. Hold the stone and hook firmly to avoid pricking or hooking yourself with the point, and make smooth, deliberate motions.

To test for sharpness: Take a hook, rest the point on your thumbnail, and lightly drag the point across the nail. If the hook is sharp enough, it will catch on the nail; if not sharp enough, it will slide across. Just be careful.

Finally, be wary of oversharpening. If the tapered wedge of the point becomes too short (through excessive sharpening), it may not penetrate as well. If it is ground too thin, it may be susceptible to bending or breaking.
See: Hook.

HOOP STRENGTH
The ability of a hollow tubular structure to resist oval deformation, which leads to the inward collapse of its walls. This is a critical property of fishing rods.
See: Rod, Fishing.

HOTSHOTTING
See: Backtrolling.

HOUNDFISH
See: Needlefish.

HUCHEN   *Hucho hucho.*
Other names—Danube salmon, Danube trout; French: *huchon;* German: *sibirischer huchen;* Hungarian: *dunai galóca;* Polish: *glowacka;* Romanian: *lostrita;* Yugoslavian: *mladica.*

A member of the Salmonidae family, which includes salmon and trout, huchen are closely related to *Hucho hucho taimen,* the taimen *(see).* The huchen is one of evidently four species in the same genus. The huchen and the taimen cannot be separated by conventional scientific analyses but are distinguished by virtue of Asian versus European geographical location and separation.

Other species within the *Hucho* genus include *H. perryi* and *H. ishikawae.* Little is known about both. *H. ishikawae* is found in the upper reaches of the Yalu River in North Korea. *H. perryi* is known as Japanese huchen or stringfish *(itô)* and is a sea-run species that occurs in the Sea of Japan from southern Kuril Island and Primorskii Krai, Russia, to Hokkaido, and in streams on eastern Hokkaido.

Because the huchen is relatively rare, it is not a common food fish, nor is it as highly valued as other salmonids. It is edible and of good quality, however. Huchen populations have diminished rapidly with overexploitation, pollution, and habitat deterioration.

Identification.   Within Europe, the huchen is not confused with any species except the brown trout or the Atlantic salmon, and can be identified by counting the scales along the lateral line. It has by far the smallest scales, numbering 180 to 200, as compared to 110 to 120 in brown trout and 120 to 130 in Atlantic salmon. The huchen is completely covered with minute black speckles, but never has the red spots that may be present on brown trout and Atlantic salmon.

Size.   The huchen grows to at least 114 pounds, making it one of the largest salmonids. The

H

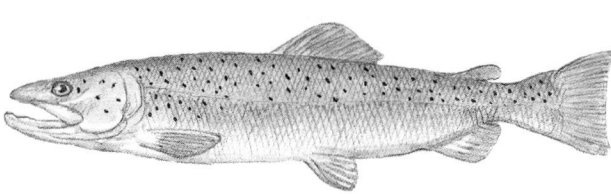

Huchen

all-tackle world record is a 76-pound, 11-ounce Austrian fish.

Distribution. This species is endemic to Europe, where it is restricted to the Danube River and its tributaries, and occasionally to lakes within the Danube basin. It also occurs in the basin of the Prut River and was introduced into other European rivers, including the Thames, in the nineteenth and early twentieth centuries, although unsuccessfully. It stays in river systems and does not migrate to sea.

Habitat. The habitat of huchen is primarily the deeper regions of fast-flowing rivers and streams with oxygen-rich water.

HULL

The structural frame or body of a boat. Hull style is often the most important element of a boat, and for comfort and safety the hull style should depend on the size of the body of water you fish. Generally, there are displacement and planing categories of hulls.
See: Boat.

HUMP

A moderately elevated and generally isolated portion of an otherwise flat lakebed or seabed. Humps vary in size and characteristic, but they do not rise close to the surface as a freshwater reef *(see)* does, nor do they rise as profoundly as an ocean seamount *(see)*. Because they are an irregular feature of the bottom and may be influenced by current and have objects (stumps, rocks, etc.) on them, they can be good places for catching certain species of fish. In saltwater, this would include many different bottom dwellers. In freshwater, it would include striped bass and largemouth bass, provided the water is not too deep. Humps may hold fish at all times or only sporadically. They are fished with deep natural bait, various jigs, plastic worms, and jigging spoons, and by drifting, vertical jigging, and occasionally trolling.

HUMPY

Short for humpbacked, and a term for pink salmon *(see)*.

HUNGARY

Hungary is home to more than 300,000 anglers, and the majority of sportfishing occurs in small bodies of water, primarily canals, lakes, and backwaters connected to rivers. Carp, pike-perch (zander), catfish, pike, bream, eels, and different species of whitefish thrive almost everywhere, but distribution of trout is limited.

Although Hungary has the Danube, its principal river, the landscape is fairly flat and lacks plentiful water reserves. Only 5 percent of Hungary's surface water originates within its borders, and 66 percent of the water used for human consumption originates in the Danube. Pollution, especially from agricultural runoff, has been a problem, as has eutrophication of lakes.

The temperature of the standing water in Hungary is 13° to 15°C at the beginning of April, 18° to 20°C in May, and 20° to 25°C in summer. Temperatures drop back in September and October to 12°C, but this is when really big carp and catfish are caught.

Eastern Region
Bács-Kiskun County. The Main Canal at Kiskunság is the most popular and productive water in the area. About 730 acres in area, it begins at the Ráckeve Danube Branch over the lock of Tass and joins the Danube Valley Main Canal at the border of Akasztó. The water is standing or slow moving, and great amounts of reeds are present. Species include common carp, grass carp, whitefish, tench, pike, pike-perch, and catfish.

Other waters of note include the Canal of Füzvölgy at Kiskunság, the Dead Tisza at Szikra, and Lake Szelidi. The latter is narrow and 5 kilometers long, and has many carp and pike-perch, as well as big catfish.

Jász-Nagykun-Szolnok County. The Dead Tisza of Alcsi Island is a good backwater near Szolnok that has carp, pike, pike-perch, catfish, bream, and whitefish, with potential for record specimens.

Tisza Lake is a large impoundment that spans Szolnok and Heves Counties not far from Budapest. Fishing activities are based in the communities of Porozló, Tiszafüred, Tiszaderzs, and Abádszalók, where accommodations, tackle shops, and guide services available, as well as boats.

The lake impounded the old Tisza riverbed and produced many small bays and coves; it requires some big-water knowledge to fish properly. In winter the water level is particularly low, and in the spring it is very high, covering nearly 25,000 acres when full. Big carp inhabit these waters, as do catfish, pike-perch, pike, bream, tench, and whitefish. Many anglers also pursue fish in the river below the dam.

Csongrád County. Noteworthy waters in Csongrád include the Backwater of Atka, a small but remote and scenic impoundment with a variety of species; the Dead Tisza of Mártély, which is on the road to Mindszent; and the Matyér Lake, located near Szeged. At less than 90 acres, the latter

H

impoundment is small, but it was the site of a world match fishing championship and is known for common carp, grass carp, pike-perch, catfish, and whitefish.

Hajdú-Bihar and Békés Counties. Látókép Lake in Hajdú-Bihar is about 13 kilometers from Debrecen and is known for pike, pike-perch, and carp. The Körös River and its tributaries in Békés County provide a variety of opportunity. The best place on the river is near the dam at Békésszentandrás, where three flows converge; below there are pike-perch, carp, bream, catfish, and whitefish. The backwaters at Kákafog are especially popular. These also contain pike.

Szabolcs-Szatmár-Bereg County. The major fishery in this area is the winding, blind arm of the Szamos River near Tunyogmatolcs, which is similar in species composition to the Tisza River. Camping and accommodation facilities are available practically everywhere here.

Northern Region

Budapest area. Fishing opportunities are somewhat limited near Budapest, although the Danube flows southerly through the city. The Danube itself can provide good angling at times and in certain places, but it is a big water. Pike, pike-perch, whitefish, barbel, and bream are the available species.

A good smaller local site, however, is Stonemine Lake in the Csepel District, at the southern end of the city. Carp, pike, and pike-perch are here, as well as other established area species. Szilas Lake in the 16th District of Budapest at Mátyásföld is also notable for the whole gamut of locally established species.

The Ráckleve Branch of the Danube is a large watercourse that flows behind Csepel Island. It is influenced by two locks here, with water flowing southerly toward Tass. Its depth is 2 to 3 meters at the upper section, and 4 to 5 meters at the lower section. The uppermost portion is in the capital. Grass and reed lines grow alongshore in many places. Common carp, grass carp, whitefish, pike-perch, catfish, pike, and bream are available; and the area is stocked with pike-perch. Some large specimens exist, and record catches are possible.

Below the Tass lock is a small bay that forms before the remaining water from the Ráckleve Branch merges with the Danube. This water is always at the same level as the Danube, and splits into a flowing section noted for pike-perch and bream, and a standing section noted for pike along the banks. Carp, catfish, and whitefish are everywhere between the lock and the mouth of the Danube.

Borsod-Abaúj-Zemplén County. Notable waters here include Rakaca Lake at Szalona, Lake Monok in the village of Monok, the Stonemine Lake of Csorbatelep near Miskolc, and Hámori Lake near Eger. Hámori is a small, beautiful mountain lake

with trout and pike-perch; the others hold pike-perch, pike, and carp.

Heves and Nógrád Counties. Lake Egerszalók in Neves and the Ipoly River in Nógrád are noted for the usual coarse species as well as pike. The Ipoly is Hungary's northern border water, and at 18 to 60 meters wide, it is a pleasant river to fish.

Western Region

Lake Balaton. By surface area, Balaton is the largest lake not only in Hungary, but also in central and western Europe. About 77 kilometers long, it is a shallow lake with an average depth of just 3 meters. The deepest area—more than 12 meters—is near the tip of the Tihany Peninsula.

Pike-perch, pike, common carp, grass carp, wels catfish, asp, eels, and several species of bream are present, with huge specimens of some reported. The lake has produced a 30.5-kilogram carp, a 91.5-kilogram catfish, and a 9.6-kilogram asp. Coarse fishing is very popular from piers and along the shoreline, and especially along weedlines in bays for carp and bream.

Balaton can be reached from Budapest via Route M7, which also passes the southern shore of the lake; Route 17 follows the northern shore. A fishing license can be obtained in nearby tackle shops, at post offices, and at tourist offices.

Gyór-Moson-Sopron County. The best fishing opportunities in the county include the backwater of the Danube River at Moson, in the city of Gyór, and the Zátony Branch of the Danube in the village of Halászi.

Tolna County. The Fadd-Dombori Backwater in the villages of Fadd and Tolna is well known for big catfish and has significant numbers of carp and pike-perch. Lake Szálka, an impoundment situated in a beautiful valley surrounded by forest, is small but very popular for coarse species.

Baranya County. Carp, whitefish, catfish, pike-perch, and pike are the main species at Lake of Pécs, which is known for extremely big carp and catfish. Nearby Orfü and Kovácsszénája Lakes are also worth visiting.

Komárom-Esztergom County. The main angling waters in Komárom-Esztergom County, all of which hold similar species, include Danube Bay at Pilismarót, the cooling power plant lake at Bánhida; and the power plant lake of Oroszlány at Bokod.

Somogy and Vas Counties. In Somogy, Deseda Lake is known for its record fish potential; species include carp, whitefish, catfish, pike-perch, and pike. The Rába River is the main fishing water of Vas County; also notable are the impoundment of Gébart, located near Zalaegerszeg, and Lake Nagykanizsa, in the village of the same name.

Fejér and Veszprém Counties. Lake Velence is the second largest natural lake in Hungary and is located about 40 kilometers from Budapest. Just 2 meters deep, it is a shallow lake,

The largest known sport-caught fish, a 3,427-pound great white shark, was landed in 1988 at Montauk, New York. It was denied record status because the angler chummed with meat from a dead whale.

H

but it covers more than 5,400 acres and is loaded with reeds. Velence is one of the best pike-perch waters in Europe, and here float fishing methods predominate. Anglers can rent boats in many places, and fishing is good from the shore on the southern end of the lake. Also of note in Fejér County are the Cikola Lakes near Adony, and Lake Fehérvárcsurgó near Mór. In Veszprém County, picturesque Inner Lake of Tihany is noted for carp, pike-perch, pike, eels, and whitefish between mid-April and mid-October.

Regulations

Anglers must have a state (national) angling ticket and a regional permit to fish. The latter is specific to the body of water to be fished. With few exceptions, the state angling ticket and the regional permit can be obtained at the same place; county angling associations can provide information. The state angling ticket is valid for the calendar year, and you can apply for any number of regional permits in the year of issue by presenting your state angling ticket. Regional permits, however, are valid only for a specific day or a set period.

Regulations regarding seasons are in effect for some species, as are length restrictions, and these may vary with the authority issuing permissions. There may also be total catch restrictions by weight in some waters. It is necessary to obtain regulations for each site before one begins fishing. For information contact the Hungarian National Angling Association, 1124 Budapest, Korompai út 17.

HYBRID

The offspring of two individuals of different species. The offspring of two individuals belonging to different subspecies of the same species are not hybrids.

Hybridization may occur in the wild or under artificial conditions. Some species that have been known to crossbreed naturally, although not frequently, include lake trout and brook trout (splake), northern pike and muskellunge (tiger muskie), and walleye and sauger (saugeye). Hybrid fish have been cultivated in hatcheries by fisheries managers for stocking purposes; hybrid striped bass (known as whiterock bass, wiper, and sunshine bass), which result from a cross of pure-strain striped bass and white bass, have been extremely popular for stocking and are widely spread in freshwater lakes and reservoirs. Most hybrid fish are sterile (although some, like whiterock bass, are not), so the stocking of these fish is attractive because they can be controlled fairly well; if the initial stocking experiment does not achieve the desired results, the population of hybrids can be extinguished by discontinuing stocking.

See: Bass, Whiterock; Muskellunge; Saugeye; Splake.

HYDROFOIL

A winglike device that attaches to the antiventilation plate on an outboard or stern-drive motor to provide lift when getting on plane. These are available in single- and double-fin versions, which are bolted onto the plate. A hydrofoil is best suited to boats that are underpowered, stern heavy, or with deep-V hulls. Their benefit is getting a boat on plane quickly and increasing visibility; when a boat plows onto plane with the bow thrust up, the driver's visibility may be impaired for a short time. This device also aids fore-and-aft running attitude, somewhat like trim tabs, but cannot control side-to-side attitude. It can improve riding comfort by keeping a boat on plane at lower speeds, but it does not significantly improve top overall speed or fuel economy.

See: Boat.

HYDROGRAPHIC MAP

A map depicting underwater features.

See: Maps.

HYPOLIMNION

The lower and colder layer of water in a lake or pond that is stratified; the layer of water below the thermocline (see).

See: Stratification.

HYPOTHERMIA

See: First Aid.

H

ICE FISHING

Fishing through the ice is a traditional activity in northern locations where the ice is thick enough for people to safely venture onto frozen lakes and ponds. In some places, a winter community develops, and ice houses, also known as shacks, shanties, and bobhouses, dot the surface.

The roots of fishing through the ice extend back to the era before modern reels and line. North American natives speared fish through holes chopped in the ice. They used decoys to attract fish to their holes, or they simply waited for the fish to pass underneath. Lying on top of the holes, wrapped in skins and blankets, kept them warm and blocked out light so they could see into the water.

Spearing is still practiced in some places today, and the use of decoys and spears has some passionate followers. Most decoys are still handmade and designed to behave like a wounded fish. They vary in size, ranging up to 30 inches long for wooden or metal models; the larger decoys are used for sturgeon. However, this is a limited activity and a controversial one.

General Hardware

The only thing that today's ice anglers have in common with those early spear-wielding anglers is the hole in the ice. Making the hole generally requires an auger or spud. Augers can be manual or gas-powered, and they create holes that are 7 to 10 inches in diameter. Larger holes are necessary for landing outsized fish, and the drill bit needs to be sharp. A spud or chisel can also be used to make holes and widen existing holes; these tools are generally used for cutting through in places where the ice isn't very thick, or for testing the thickness of relatively new ice (since a lot of chiseling is needed to get through 2 to 3 feet of ice).

Where the ice is thick, a long-bladed chainsaw can be used to cut large rectangular holes. The large hole allows for plenty of angler movement and for easy landing of any size fish. A chainsaw is also useful for creating a holding pool for the caught fish. The angler cuts a large shallow depression in the ice and pokes a hole through to flood the depression.

A scoop is another necessary item. It is used to clear the hole of ice fragments and may be a wide perforated metal ladle with a long handle or a shallow perforated plastic bucket. A Styrofoam-insulated minnow bucket is also important, especially in very cold and windy weather. The Styrofoam helps keep the bucket water from freezing. A plastic minnow scoop is handy for retrieving bait. Not a necessity but highly valued and important to many ice anglers is a portable sonar unit. A long-handled gaff is useful for large fish, like trout; obviously it is used only on fish that will be kept.

Portable or permanent shelters are used in some locales, although many ice anglers like to be mobile and move from place to place to fish and to search for schools of fish. Permanent shacks, which look like large outhouses, may need to be registered and will require setup and removal, but they provide protection from the elements and are great for serious and regular fishing if they are located in a good spot. Some houses are heated and equipped with various amenities, greatly increasing the comfort level; the most deluxe versions are mini-palaces, with color television, propane cookstove, and beds. Obviously these ice houses are not easy to move, and in most places they must by law be removed from the ice by a certain date (for safety reasons and also to keep debris from falling into the water as the ice weakens).

Mobile anglers need a means of toting their equipment, and some have devised boxes that are dragged on sleds over the ice or are towed behind a snowmobile. (Anglers on foot, incidentally, may need cleated boots for traction on sheer ice.) Likewise, portable tentlike shelters are ferried across the ice. Complete sled-based mobile systems, some with a covered retractable top, are a more deluxe option. The systems are made to be easily pulled so that anglers can keep up with fish that are on the move;

In lakes where the ice gets very thick, chainsaws are used to cut large holes; some anglers use delicate tip-ups for fishing.

When the fishing's good, some frozen lakes draw a lot of activity, although a telephoto lens has exaggerated the clustering in this scene.

these also store tackle and give protection from the wind. Small heaters can be used with them.

Tip-ups.   An essential element of ice fishing, especially with live bait, is a tip-up. This device sports a spool filled with line, to which a baited hook is attached, and sprouts a highly visible flag that stands up when the bait has been struck. Fish are retrieved by handlining. The frame of the tip-up is wooden or plastic, and it sits on top of the ice.

Tip-ups come in many different styles, sizes, and materials, with varied bite-indicating systems. There are basically two types of tip-ups. In wind-assisted tip-ups, the arm moves up and down and jigs the bait with any kind of breeze. The extent of movement can be adjusted. When there's a bite, the spool rotates, which releases a bite-indicating flag. This type of tip-up can freeze up under bad conditions, although retrieving wet line onto the ice can help prevent spool freeze-up.

The more common type of tip-up is a simple line-filled spool placed under the water to prevent freezing up. There is no wind assist or jigging action with this type, and movement of the spool trips a flag to indicate a bite. Both versions are mainly used for larger predators rather than for panfish, and live or dead bait can be fished at any level. Complete outfits ready to fish are found in most tackle stores in areas where there is ice fishing.

Rods/sticks/line.   Short jigging rods and sticks in the 18- to 48-inch range are used for jigging through the ice with assorted jigs and special ice-jigging lures, some tipped with bait. Jigging sticks come in a variety of materials and handle styles and feature 20 to 50 feet of line wrapped around a loop that is in or on the handle.

The angler adjusts the line to the depth selected, lowers the bait into the hole by hand, sets the hook with the stick, plays the fish by hand, and lifts the fish out of the hole with the line. You can use a balsa float (not the old-style round bobber) or spring bobber (a thin strip of flat or round wire attached to the tip) with the stick.

Rod and reel combinations are plentiful. Rod and reel must be matched, and the action of the rod must be soft enough to keep from breaking the line being used. Like sticks, rods should be short, and they usually have few guides, which are large to help minimize ice buildup. Reels are often light spinning or spincasting models.

The line used for ice fishing on rods or sticks varies with the application. A guideline is 2- to 4-pound line for panfish; 4- to 8-pound line for pickerel, walleye, and smaller trout; 10- to 20-pound line for pike and large trout; and 15- to 30-pound line for big flathead catfish. Wire leaders are needed for some species. The golden rule in line choice is to go heavy if the fish are aggressive. You can use heavier line and lighten up the last 10 to 20 feet by using a lighter leader.

Thin-diameter lines are obviously helpful for clear water and for fishing with small baits and tiny jigs. A line that stays limp and doesn't stiffen in the cold is important. Microfilament line is helpful here, since it doesn't change characteristics and is very sensitive. A monofilament leader may be advisable when fishing with heavier microfilament lines, and a softer rod may also be useful for absorbing shock, since this type of line has no stretch. Some anglers like a fluorescent line for its visibility, and it can easily be watched in a dark ice house.

Lures/Bait

Minnows are the favorite live bait of ice anglers, especially when fished on a bait hook below a tip-up. They are most often hooked through the lips, which is the strongest location, and then behind the dorsal fin. They are also popularly fished on a jig hook. Bait anglers who use tip-ups also need an assortment of hooks, split shot weights, floats, and other terminal tackle, as well as small baits like maggots and grubs.

There are loads of jigs and jigging spoons suitable for ice fishing, depending on the target species, as well as some specialty ice fishing lures. Each behaves differently in the water, and the action is also influenced by the addition of bait. Generally, however, any jigging lure should be worked in a subtle manner for panfish and more dramatically for larger predators.

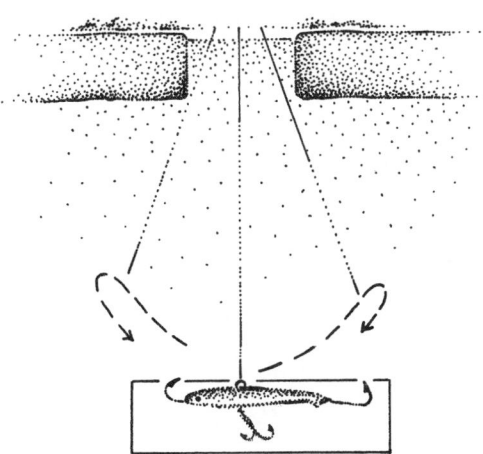

A balanced ice fishing jig has a unique darting, swimming action, moving up and out to the sides as shown by the arrow paths.

Different shapes of small ice jigs are used, as are different types of jigging spoons, most of which weigh from $1/8$ to $1/12$ ounce. Another choice is small leadhead jigs, which are dressed with soft lure bodies or tipped with bait. Balanced jigging lures, which lie horizontally and have a hook at each end as well as under the belly, swim in a unique manner due to a tail fin, and these lures are popular in different sizes for various fish.

Methods

Like open water angling, ice fishing encompasses both passionate devotees and anglers who fish only occasionally. The most serious ice anglers work hard at trying to catch fish and learn new methods; other anglers enjoy just being outside in the winter and aren't concerned with success. Many people, of course, fall in between.

Ice fishing involves a range of approaches for successfully attracting and landing fish. The best ice anglers know they can't make the fish do what they want them to do, so they try to adjust to the fish and avoid being locked into fixed ideas about lures, baits, and locations. If you assume that, in general, fish are aggressive only 10 percent of the time, in a negative mood 60 percent of the time, and in a neutral mood for the remainder of the time, then your best approach is to finesse the situation, being a bit crafty and cautious and assuming that the fish are in a negative mood. This approach will not alarm fish no matter what their disposition is. On the other hand, an aggressive approach, such as jigging a large spoon for perch, will probably scare or turn off most fish. Thus, beginning with a tiny jig baited with a single maggot should bring better results.

When you're starting out, a companion who is an experienced ice angler is a great advantage. Ask questions and try to learn the basics. For catching panfish, you can start very simply with a jigging rod and a thin, small float (see) about $1^1/_2$ inches long and $3/_{16}$ inch wide. The float is held in place on a light line (4-pound test is good) with two silicone tubes (now found in most tackle shops). Use two BB lead split shots (each of which is $1/_{64}$ ounce) to balance your float, placed about $2^1/_2$ inches above a No. 12 or 14 hook (switch to a smaller hook and lighter line if the fish are hard to catch). Carefully place one or two maggots or waxworms on the hook.

This approach will be effective during the first three to five weeks of the ice fishing season when panfish are normally close to the shore in shallow water that is 18 inches to 4 feet deep. Carefully lower your hooked bait in the hole, and watch for any movement of the float up, down, or sideways.

The float can fly down on a strike or move very slowly just an eighth of an inch. This is why a float is best if you are a beginner; you can see the entire range of bites and get accustomed to them. Sometimes it's better to jig without a float, but if you have had success seeing bites, you can easily learn straight jigging and you can imagine how the bites feel (see: jigging).

This approach just described is a good way to get started on ice fishing for bluegills, crappie, or perch. By using a finesse approach, you can readily adapt to those easier times when fish are aggressive.

To be aggressive about catching fish you need to locate them; in ice fishing, using portable sonar and keeping on the move are important elements for locating fish. Make sure your sonar unit can shoot through the ice and can depict both the fish and the weeds where some species may be holding. You can facilitate the effectiveness of the sonar by squirting nontoxic antifreeze on the ice and then placing the

A lake trout like this is a superb catch for any ice angler; this specimen was caught at Lake Simcoe, Ontario.

transducer on the wet spot. Ice has to be fairly clear for this, but thickness is no problem. In heavily marbled ice or snow-saturated ice, make a hole and place the transducer in the hole.

Using sonar allows you to keep moving. When fish appear on the sonar screen, drill a hole and then carefully watch the fish on the screen as you jig. You can often see how the fish respond to your bait or lure (and also to its color) and to the jigging action; you can even watch the fish take the bait. You'll need to jig at various levels for good coverage, just as you would in open-water fishing.

Safety

Never take ice for granted and assume it is safe. Invisible underwater currents, springs, and heat-attracting debris in or on the ice can weaken it dramatically. Some well-frozen lakes develop pressure ridges that you should stay away from. As a rule, always fish with a companion, and test ice thickness before you travel on it.

Right after freeze-up, ice toward the middle of the lake is thinner than that along the shoreline. River ice and lake ice can vary in thickness throughout the winter and in different parts of the river or lake. Do not assume uniform thickness.

The thickness of the ice is not always an accurate measure of its strength. Cracking and sudden temperature drops can severely weaken ice. Heavy snow cover insulates ice, drastically reducing its growth; the snow may cause water to overflow around the edges, thus weakening the ice there.

If you drive on the ice with a vehicle, especially a heavy one, be aware that sudden braking or driving over a bump increases the effective weight of the vehicle and can cause ice failure. Driving fast over thin ice may create an under-ice wave similar to a boat wake; this force can crack the ice ahead of the vehicle under the right conditions. Therefore, it's best to drive carefully and slowly.

As a guideline, the minimum ice thickness for certain loads is as follows: 4 inches for a person walking; 6 inches for a snowmobile; 8 inches for a vehicle weighing 3,500 pounds; and 12 inches for a vehicle weighing 8,000 pounds.

If you're fishing by yourself (which may not be wise) early in the season when the ice is thin, consider hanging ice picks around your neck (two 6-inch nails tied to 15 to 20 inches of nylon cord and covered with a super glue). Cover the points with tissue paper that is taped in place, and hang the whole rig around your neck. If you fall into the water, you'll have something with which you can grab onto the ice and pull yourself out. Carrying extra clothes—even if you leave them in your vehicle on shore—is a good idea, though you'll probably never need them if you're careful.

Always dress properly for ice fishing. The danger of developing hypothermia or frostbite is obvious. Fortunately, excellent clothing and footwear exist to help prevent this.

See: First Aid; Float.

ICELAND

Lying roughly 300 kilometers east of Greenland in the North Atlantic Ocean, Iceland is a mysterious and beautiful island with volcanoes, thermal springs, rolling hills, more than 120 glaciers, and numerous small lakes and swift-flowing rivers. Its northern extremity barely touches the Arctic Circle, and although Iceland has a relatively mild climate, the country features a mixture of nature's extremes, including summer temperatures ranging from 7° to 14°C.

Although Iceland encompasses 103,000 square kilometers and has nearly 6,000 kilometers of coastline, it is sparsely populated with some 260,000 inhabitants. Most have settled along the coastline and in the southwest, and half of these live in the capital city of Reykjavik. The infrastructure is generally good, with plenty of roads and regular domestic flights to most larger towns. Visitors are surprised to find that this lightly populated country has a good road network; with a rented four-wheel-drive vehicle, a lot of waters can be reached. Iceland's Keflavik Airport has excellent connections to several cities in North America and Europe.

Iceland's Atlantic salmon fishery is the main attraction for visitors and is regarded as one of the best in the world, despite the poor state of this species across its range. In Iceland, the standard is crystal clear waters in an unpolluted environment, and salmon fishing has a significant place in the tourism industry. Local newspapers carry daily reports on river conditions and on the number of fish passing by fish counters. The salmon are well looked after in Iceland; coastal netting in the sea has been prohibited since 1932.

Approximately 100 rivers have salmon runs, and from the mid-1970s to the mid-1990s the top 20 had average catches of between 450 and almost 2,000 salmon a year. Over this long period, the best ones were the Laxá i Adaldal, Thverá, Nordurá, and Laxá i Kjos.

In general, Icelandic salmon run 3 to 6 kilograms; a fish over 10 kilograms is unusual. The fishing season is between May 20 and September 20, with variations according to location. Often the fishing takes place in two passes a day, one from 7 A.M. to 1 P.M., and another from 4 P.M. to 10 P.M. On the more expensive rivers it is not unusual for two anglers to share a beat and to fish in shifts. Some of the less well-known rivers may provide good sport at a fair price, along with opportunities to catch charr and sea trout.

The opportunities to pursue freshwater and sea-run trout and charr are equally excellent and more economical. Compared with the Scandinavian countries, only a few districts in northern Norway offer the same quality of fishing for brown trout as does Iceland, and only the rivers in Greenland offer arctic charr fishing of the same caliber. One river, the Laxá i Husavik, offers world-class brown trout fishing from Sog to Myvatn, which is above the falls that prevent salmon from moving upriver. Only fly fishing is permitted on this 30-kilometer stretch of river, and only a certain number of rods per day are allowed.

Anglers catch lots of trout every year in this beautiful river, which flows out of Lake Myrvatn. The upper river courses steadily, with minor falls; then it is forked by islands, and farther downstream it quickens. On the lowest part it flows more gently again. Large streamers and locally productive patterns are favored. The best fishing is from mid-June through July. In August, when the water is low and clear, fishing is more difficult, and nymphs and dry flies are productive. The trout range up to 2 kilograms in the upper river and are a bit larger on average in the lower and more difficult section. Both trout and charr inhabit Lake Myrvatn.

Falls on the Laxá i Husavik prevent salmon from migrating upstream, where there is superb brown trout fishing.

Iceland has much more freshwater fishing to offer, mostly on the northern and northeastern coasts. On the Melrakke flat north of Kopasker, several good coastal lakes with both sea-run and freshwater charr beckon. West of Olafsfjordur near Hraun are more fine coastal lakes and lagoons. The sea-run charr normally enter from mid-July through the end of the season. In Saenautavatn and Anarvatn, between Myvatn and Seidisfjordur, there are fine charr in the 3- to 4-kilogram range.

Nice-size but shy trout hold in the shallow and weedy lakes north and east of Egilstadir. Sea-run charr enter the side rivers of Jokulsás north of Seidisfjordur. The river Svartá and Lakes Isholtvatn and Svartarkotsvatn, 50 kilometers southwest of Myrvatn, are known to harbor large trout.

A particularly good spot is on the south coast near Lake Pórisvatn's adjacent lakes; these are not far from road access. In northwestern Iceland, Anarvatnsheidi is another large lake district. It can be reached with four-wheel-drive vehicles or via horseback, and by snowmobiles in the winter for ice fishing. East of Blónduos in the northwest are several coastal lakes with very good populations of both sea-run and resident charr.

Literally thousands of other small ponds, lakes, and lagoons hold little-known populations of fish. Some waters might produce only smaller fish, others 1- to 2-kilogram fish; and odd lakes have big fish that range from 3 to 6 kilograms. Sea trout enter a number of rivers, especially on the south, east, and west coasts; these fish are normally from 1 to 2 kilograms.

Iceland's economy depends heavily on the rich fish populations in the surrounding sea: fishing and fish processing are the country's most important industries. Cod, sharks, haddock, coalfish, halibut, capelin, crustaceans, and herring are the mainstays, but there is no real charter fishing industry, because anyone with a seaworthy vessel is fishing commercially. Finding a boat to go sportfishing may nevertheless be possible. The Breidafjordur Fiord has a good reputation for halibut between 10 and 25 kilograms, but it also produces some from 80 to 100 kilograms.

ICE OUT

That time when enough ice melts on a lake to make open water fishing possible. Complete ice out may take many days or more than a week on some cold, deep, large, and northerly waters, and the amount of open water will gradually increase over that time.

The legal angling season for some species, especially salmonids, on many northern lakes, usually commences on a certain date, which, in a practical sense, is subject to ice out—the lake is all or partially unfrozen. Fishing for trout and salmon in particular is deemed very good immediately following ice out, because the upper water layers are cold and fish will usually be shallow and more accessible.

ICHTHYOLOGIST

A person who studies fish. This is different from a fishery biologist *(see)*, who studies and manages fisheries, although ichthyologists are frequently referred to as biologists.

IDAHO

Idaho excels in both the variety and quality of its fishing. It has, for example, produced the biggest rainbow trout taken in freshwater by a sporting angler in the United States—a 37-pound Kamloops-strain specimen from Lake Pend Oreille that has survived more than 50 years atop the record books. And an 8-pound, $^1/_2$-ounce smallmouth bass, taken from Dworshak Reservoir near Orofino, would win bragging rights in nearly any state that has this species.

Size isn't the only measure of successful fishing, of course. The Henry's Fork of the Snake River in southeastern Idaho is holy water for trout lovers from around the nation, who come to test their skills against the wariest of trout. The river is as clear as liquid crystal, and its mayfly hatches draw hordes of anglers in early summer. The lucid waters of Silver Creek just south of legendary Sun Valley have been fished by the famous for decades; but the trout aren't impressed by screen credits or anything short of a perfect presentation.

As if year-round resident fish weren't enough, Idaho also boasts sizable runs of steelhead, the mighty rainbow trout that migrate to the Pacific Ocean and back—a journey of at least 1,000 miles from their natal water. If valiant efforts to save chinook salmon succeed, the state may yet reclaim its glory days when the summers marked the return of the kings. In the meantime, Lake Coeur d'Alene holds landlocked chinook nearly as big as their oceangoing cousins.

In addition to its healthy salmonids, Idaho offers respectable largemouth bass fishing, northern pike a few meals shy of 40 pounds, and one of the biggest fish in freshwater—the white sturgeon. The biggest Idaho sturgeon landed with rod and reel and officially recorded was a 394-pound bruiser landed in 1956, when it was still possible to keep a sturgeon landed in Idaho waters. Since then, the Snake River in Hells Canyon has yielded a heavier 12-foot-long sturgeon that was revived and released.

A slogan popular in some quarters proclaims "Idaho is what America was" and reflects the beauty of the state. Indeed, Idaho's lakes and streams are still remarkably pure. Its backcountry remains as rugged and remote as when prospector Elias D. Pierce led the first party that found "color" in the Clearwater River country in 1860.

Idaho possesses 4 million acres of federally designated wilderness, including the massive Frank Church River of No Return Wilderness, which sprawls across 2.4 million acres, or 3,750 square miles, along the Salmon River. Idaho angling may be at its best here. The 78-mile run, from Corn Creek near North Fork at the eastern edge of the wilderness and downstream to Vinegar Creek at its western margin near Riggins, offers scenic solitude normally found only in the wildest parts of the globe. Passage is by brawny welded-aluminum jet boats, or by more quiet craft like kayaks, rubber rafts, or whitewater dories. The exclusive domain of float boats, the Salmon's middle fork offers excellent fishing for west-slope cutthroat.

Trout

In one form or another, Idaho *is* trout fishing. When Ernest Hemingway moved for the last time, it was the allure of Idaho and its trout that caught his eye. At least a part of Hemingway's relocation to Idaho was spurred by the fine trout streams near Ketchum. This included the Wood River and its tributaries, among them Silver Creek, the home of very large and educated trout that demand precision fishing. But also notable is the Snake River to the south, where Billingsley Creek is perhaps less famous but still capable of growing trout as big as those in Silver Creek. To the west is the Boise River and its tributaries, also hallowed waters for trout aficionados. Bear Lake, the turquoise wonder of the state's southeastern corner, produced Idaho's record cutthroat. An ounce shy of 19 pounds, the record held up for nearly three decades.

The focus of trout fishing in America, or at least the West, is the Henry's Fork of the Snake, hard by Yellowstone National Park. The province of flycasters from around the world, the Henry's Fork hits its peak in early summer, when massive mayfly hatches boil off the water. Henry's Lake at the river's headwaters not far upstream produces massive rainbow-cutthroat hybrids and world-class brook trout from its prodigious underwater forest of weedy growth. The Millionaire's Hole in Harriman State Park is a shrine to big trout that demand expertise.

The South Fork of the Snake, the mighty river's other main headwaters tributary, spills over from Wyoming and Jackson Hole. The South Fork is famed for both cutthroats and rainbows. But the biggest trout in the river are browns; specimens weighing in the teens are caught regularly, and monsters in the 20s are rare but possible.

Mountain trout. Reliable fisheries for west-slope cutthroat trout, a fish of the purest mountain streams, attract most of the summertime attention in the upper Clearwater drainage. Kelly Creek, the upper North Fork, and the Lochsa River, which is paralleled by U.S. Highway 12, are recognized nationally as blue-ribbon trout streams. Catch-and-release fishing is the rule for most of these waters because the beautiful cutthroat would be too gullible to survive otherwise.

The neighboring Selway River is also a popular destination in its lower reaches. Its upper waters are tucked away in the Selway Bitterroot Wilderness and accessible only by foot trail or boat. The Upper

Clearwater appears much as it did when the Lewis and Clark expedition faced its most serious challenges here in 1805 and 1806, as it struggled across the Bitterroot and Clearwater Mountains. Today, while camped along Kelly Creek or the Lochsa River, it is possible to hear the song of the wolf and experience a taste of the pioneer days.

More than two-thirds of Idaho remains in federal ownership and much of that, nearly 20 million acres, is overseen by the U.S. Forest Service as national forest land. Here, Idaho's mountainous heart holds some 2,000 lakes tucked into glacial nooks and crannies. Some, like a few in the Sawtooth National Recreation Area near Ketchum, or Seven Devils Lake southwest of Riggins, are relatively accessible by road during the summer months. Others require a major hike to reach, or, better yet, a pack trip with horses to carry the load. The Bighorn Crags west of Salmon and high above the Salmon River's Middle Fork offer a sparkling necklace of high lakes that reward exertion with exceptional fishing and scenes that approach the sublime.

A midsummer adventure to the high country offers mountain lake fishing and a chance to see the heart of Idaho's wilderness from a primitive gravel road. The Magruder Road scratches its way across the Nez Perce and Bitterroot National Forests from east of Elk City, Idaho, to Darby, Montana. The road was pioneered by the Civilian Conservation Corps during the 1930s and has been changed relatively little since. A vehicle with high clearance, preferably with four-wheel drive, is the best bet during late July and August, when conditions are most favorable.

Because the high country reaches elevations of 8,000 feet, even August can bring snow here, and adventurers are advised to take all wilderness precautions. Rain gear, cold-weather clothes, extra food, and means for fire and shelter are all requisites. The Sheep Hill lakes along the corridor provide a spectacular reward to adventuresome anglers up for the task.

Snake River

In Idaho, big waters hold big fish. The Snake River itself reaches more than 1,000 miles from its headwaters to its confluence with the Columbia River, and most of the river's length is in Idaho. With much of its terrain receiving less than 20 inches of precipitation a year, Idaho is like a desert. The state depends heavily on its rivers to irrigate its famous potatoes and other crops that take root in the fertile soils along the wide arc of the Snake River Plain across the south. The reservoirs that catch the Snake's spring runoff so it can be metered out through the long, dry summers or converted into hydroelectricity harbor sizable fish populations.

American Falls Reservoir downstream from the Snake is famed for its trout fishing. Farther downstream, C. J. Strike Reservoir near Mountain Home is noted more for its bass and crappie. At Salmon Falls Creek Reservoir nearby, anglers have a chance to catch walleye, a rare opportunity because proposals to establish them widely were jettisoned by fears they could become serious predators of the state's tiny salmon and steelhead heading to the ocean. Near Boise, waters like Lake Lowell—an irrigation impoundment off the Boise River—provide notable opportunities for panfish and bass.

Brownlee Reservoir, along the Snake to the northwest of the capital, ranks as one of Idaho's most heavily fished impoundments. Smallmouth bass and crappie are the main prizes here, but the lake's rich waters also produce sizable numbers of big flathead and channel catfish. One of the state's largest impoundments, Brownlee is the Idaho Power Company's largest storage reservoir and the keystone of its three Hells Canyon dams. Its water levels fluctuate throughout the year.

After Hells Canyon Dam, the Snake begins its 100-mile whitewater rush out of Idaho. Although what purists would call Hells Canyon now lies under the waters backed up by the dam, popular thinking and official acts say otherwise. The U.S. Forest Service administers the Hells Canyon National Recreation Area along more than 70 miles of the Snake. The river here is a stronghold for the white sturgeon, the largest freshwater fish in North America. Around the turn of the century, a monster estimated at 1,500 pounds was captured from near the mouth of the Weiser River, now at the headwaters of Brownlee Reservoir. But the free-flowing river below the dam complex is the best place left in Idaho to pursue monster sturgeon. In the 1980s, a fishing guide and his crew landed and released a behemoth that stretched the tape at 12 feet long and weighed an estimated 500 to 600 pounds.

In Idaho, sturgeon must be released immediately after they're landed and cannot be removed from the water. Although hearty fish, changes in the rivers caused by dams, and the sturgeon's slow growth rate, make their future tenuous. With strict catch-and-release rules, however, sturgeon are the focus of a sizable community of anglers who both zealously pursue and protect them.

As a result of these regulations, Idaho's two sturgeon records appear unbreakable. The biggest sturgeon officially recorded from Idaho waters was a 675-pounder caught from the Snake with a setline in 1908; the angling record is a 394-pounder caught in 1956. Lewiston, which is downstream along the Snake at its confluence with the Clearwater, is home to a thriving tour boat and guiding industry that includes several outfitters who offer sturgeon fishing.

The Hells Canyon stretch of the Snake, widely known as one of the deepest and most rugged gorges in North America, can also hold large numbers of rainbow trout and crappie, depending on water conditions. When high runoff occurs, rainbows become scarce and are overshadowed by a crappie boom from fish washed out of Brownlee

Tuna can swim 100 miles in a day.

Reservoir upstream. When spring and summer flows are low, the trout prosper. Channel catfish are also present in the canyon, although their numbers have fluctuated widely as well. A more reliable pursuit for anglers is smallmouth bass. Good numbers of bass populate the river, with a few each year approaching 5 pounds. Early spring, when the water temperatures approach 50°F and before the rivers rise and grow murky with runoff, is the most productive time for catching big smallmouths from the lower reaches of the Snake in Idaho waters.

Steelhead and Salmon

The Snake from Hells Canyon Dam downstream, and its largest tributaries—the Salmon and Clearwater Rivers—are also revered by Idaho anglers and others as the home of noteworthy runs of steelhead (sea-run rainbow trout). Classified as summer steelhead because they begin their migration out of the Pacific Ocean about June, the fish begin surging past Lower Granite Dam, 34 miles downstream from Lewiston, as early as August. Located in neighboring southeastern Washington, Lower Granite serves as the last fish-counting station before Idaho waters.

Since the 1970s, a boom in federal hatchery construction to mitigate for lost fish habitat caused by dams has sparked a steelhead renaissance in Idaho waters. The 1980s produced the largest steelhead counts on record, peaking at more than 135,000 fish across Lower Granite, and anglers reaped record harvests of steelhead ranging from 4 to more than 20 pounds.

All this success, of course, demands the tempering of a historical perspective. Idaho's rivers once produced the bulk of the Columbia River's chinook salmon runs. During the 1890s, at least half of the 3 million spring and summer chinook salmon that returned to the mighty Columbia each year migrated upstream to their spawning beds in the Snake and its tributaries. The river's chinook runs now cling tenuously to an uncertain future.

The late 1990s produced seasons with more widespread salmon fishing in Idaho waters than in the prior two decades, a hopeful sign. But salmon numbers have fluctuated widely because of ocean conditions unfriendly to salmon and steelhead and due to the extensive development of hydroelectric dams on the Snake and Columbia. Hatchery production of salmon has proved a hit-or-miss proposition, largely because of the complexities of environmental conditions. The Snake's wild-spawning chinook runs are listed as threatened with extinction under the Endangered Species Act. A massive effort to restore the salmon runs has been underway since the early 1990s, when the fish were first protected by the National Marine Fisheries Service.

In more dire straits than the chinook, Idaho's sockeye salmon are classified as an endangered species. The number of sockeyes making the 900-mile migration home to their last spawning refuge at Redfish Lake near Stanley could be counted on one hand during the 1990s.

Happily for anglers, steelhead have proven themselves tougher than their larger chinook cousins. Although catch-and-release fishing starts in August in Idaho waters, anglers can't take home a fish until September, and the bulk of the run typically doesn't arrive until October. A remarkable aspect of the steelhead's life cycle is that they stop eating once they enter freshwater. They live off the reserves they've built up in their rich ocean pastures until they spawn in the spring. Unlike chinook and other Pacific salmon, steelhead can survive spawning, although the rigors of the process typically claim more than 95 percent of the run.

The Clearwater harbors exceptionally large steelhead. These fish, most of them produced by Dworshak National Fish Hatchery at Ahsahka, average 12 to 14 pounds. Typically each year, several fish topping 20 pounds are landed along the Clearwater or from the nearby Snake. The steelhead that begin their migration in the summer won't spawn until the following spring. That cycle gives anglers nearly six months of fishing most years.

The Clearwater from Ahsahka downstream is a popular winter destination for both Idahoans and Montanans. It remains ice free in all but the coldest weather because of releases from Dworshak Dam across the river's North Fork.

The Salmon River, because of its sizable runs of steelhead, which typically average 6 to 11 pounds apiece, is popular in both fall and spring. Winter along the Salmon, one of the nation's longest undammed streams as well as one of the longest originating and ending in one state, is generally the quiet season. The river becomes icebound in most years sometime in December, and remains so until February.

The lower reaches of the Salmon near White Bird and Riggins offer the best fall fishing. Crowds begin gathering along the upper reaches of the Salmon from Salmon City upstream to Stanley as soon as the ice goes out and the water warms enough to reawaken the fishes' migratory urge to return to their spawning streams.

Idaho's statewide steelhead regulations typically allow anglers to pursue the fish until April, although the anglers' interest typically begins to wane in late March or so. The condition of the fish usually deteriorates quickly as the spring advances and they channel their energy into spawning.

Although the Clearwater River draws much attention for its big steelhead, it offers other notable angling as well. Dworshak Reservoir, which backs up 54 miles of the North Fork, has become the likeliest place to land the next state record smallmouth bass. It boasts two fish that have carried that distinction, including the current record, weighing just over 8 pounds and caught in 1955. Dworshak also has offered a popular kokanee (landlocked sockeye salmon) fishery in past years, although it was in a rebuilding phase in the late 1990s.

The Big Lakes

The Panhandle's Lake Pend Oreille, home of big Kamloops rainbows, is still untainted by development and, at 180 square miles covering 115,000 acres, offers plenty of room to roam. Slightly smaller Lake Coeur d'Alene to the south is richer in nutrients and produces more fish, but it bears some scars, namely elevated levels of heavy metals from a long and storied history of mining in the Coeur d'Alenes to the east. Shallower and more productive are Hauser, Hayden, Spirit, and Twin Lakes. In addition to producing some big largemouth bass, Hauser also produced a 19-pound rainbow that was the state record for more than 50 years. Priest Lake, the least developed and purest of the Panhandle's big lakes, produced a 57-pound, 8-ounce lake trout in 1971.

The big lakes are home to Idaho's largest fish. Record bull trout and a cutthroat-rainbow hybrid have come from Pend Oreille Lake. Although Sandpoint may be the best-known community along the big lake's shoreline, Hope and Bayview serve as fishing centers where charter boats can be found.

IGFA

Acronym for the International Game Fish Association (see).

ILLINOIS

It was not too long ago that serious anglers rarely thought of fishing in Illinois. Farm pond bluegills and silty river catfish were the extent of Illinois' sportfishery. Although a few largemouth bass lived in southern lakes, the fish were small. Northern lakes—especially near densely populated Chicago—were overfished to the point of exhaustion. And the rivers were so putrid and polluted that the fish commonly bore cancerous lesions.

Even southern Lake Michigan was denuded of its bread-and-butter commercial lake trout and herring fishery. By the 1960s, it had become choked with exotic alewives from the St. Lawrence Seaway. Smelly piles of these oily little ocean fish had to be bulldozed from beaches.

If you liked carp and bullhead, Illinois was your place. You went to Wisconsin for walleye, pike, and muskies; to Michigan and Minnesota for smallmouth bass; to Kentucky, Missouri, and farther south for crappie and largemouth bass.

The fishery changed dramatically in the 1980s with the Clean Water Act, which revived the rivers. Today, smallmouth bass richly populate streams in the upper third of Illinois. Walleye and sauger, kick-started by mitigative stocking programs, dominate sportfishing on rivers like the Mississippi, Illinois, and Rock. Catch-and-release ethics nurtured a citizen-driven stocking program on a dozen lakes that now produce steady trophy muskie fishing. Big largemouth—for Illinois (6- to

Size and strength make chinook salmon the premier fish of Lake Michigan.

8-pounders)—thrive throughout the state. And large hybrid stripers, walleye, catfish, and all kinds of bass populate many power plant cooling lakes.

The breakthrough for Illinois arrived with the Jake Wolf Hatchery in 1983, which added a stocking capacity of 60 million fish, spread among 15 to 20 species, to the production of two older, smaller hatcheries. Another hatchery opened at LaSalle Lake, to service cooling ponds and the Illinois River.

Tourism-driven state fisheries management programs were instituted to lure visitors and stop Illinois anglers from flocking out of state. Programs evolved for every type of fishery, augmented by state funds and increased license fees.

The eye-opener was the successful turnaround of Lake Michigan as a salmon and trout fishery, a process that actually began in the 1960s. Illinois joined Michigan, Indiana, and Wisconsin in a bold cooperative stocking program that introduced coho salmon, chinook salmon, steelhead, lake trout, and brown trout, which foraged on the lake's alewives, creating a new shoreline and deep-water sportfishery.

By the late 1960s, derbies and tournaments took place around the lake, broadcasting huge catches of giant fish. A charter boat fishing industry that works all but the coldest winter months blossomed as a result. Marinas proliferated, serving thousands of pleasure boats. Each spring, shoreline anglers and small-craft boaters enjoy a coho run through harbors and along piers and jetties. They typically long-cast spoons and flies for 3- to 7-pound fish that grow larger through the summer.

As these salmon and trout reduced the overabundance of alewives, perch and rainbow smelt proliferated, but those species endured a tailspin in the 1990s. Whether this is cyclical or due to predation or the straining of nutrients by newer, undesirable, exotic species (the zebra mussel, the spiny water flea, the round goby) has not been determined.

One particularly positive result has been the rebirth of smallmouth bass along riprap sea walls and breakwaters from mid-Chicago into Indiana.

Anglers using spinners and crankbaits can have 50-fish days, including the occasional 4-pounder.

Water clarification by mussels, as well as a ban on phosphorus, enables anglers to see fish life as deep as 40 feet on calm days, and Lake Michigan's protected harbors have become virtual aquariums. Deeper sunlight penetration has improved aquatic vegetative cover, causing largemouth bass and panfish—not to mention the occasional northern pike—to enjoy a resurgence in harbors.

These achievements are only part of the Illinois story. Vast improvements have occurred in every region.

Northeast

Fishing pressure can overwhelm the Chicago area. With three-fourths of Illinois' 11 million people living in six Chicago metropolitan counties, local anglers historically traveled far to find productive fishing.

But not anymore. Even the former sewer of the Chicago River and its system of sanitary canals is a viable, reproducing fishery. Anglers have seen a resurgence of bass—smallmouth in the inner harbor of Lake Michigan and largemouth downstream through the industrial belt below the Loop. Following several successful years of European-style carp fishing tournaments in the midst of Chicago's Downtown, anglers now plan other competitions in the revived Chicago River.

Cleaner water and an abundance of wood and rocky bass structure in a thicket of old and rarely used barge slips have contributed to the recovery of Chicago's fishery. Similarly good bass fishing exists in the South Side Calumet River and Lake Calumet and down through industrial CalSag Channel—a canal that joins the historic Chicago Sanitary & Ship Canal in suburban Lemont. Both of these once-dead waterways now host bass and panfish chiefly around massive aeration stations built by the Metropolitan Water Reclamation District.

City anglers' appetites have been whetted by a strong urban fishing program conducted by the Illinois Department of Natural Resources (DNR) and the Chicago Park District in Chicago park lagoons, plus continually improved fisheries management at more than 20 Cook County forest preserve lakes. Walleye as big as 10 pounds have been seen in prolific Tampier Lake on the Southwest Side, and bass up to 5 pounds are pulled from Busse and Maple Lakes, as well as Saganashkee Slough. Rehabilitated Skokie Lagoons has become a major destination for largemouth bass and catfish.

State-managed Wolf Lake on the industrial Illinois-Indiana border has a vastly improved bass program thanks to better aquatic vegetation, as well as a burgeoning smallmouth bass population in its northwest section. Anglers must have licenses from both states to fish the entire lake.

The Des Plaines River—another former sewer coursing from the Wisconsin border through several western suburbs—has seen a spectacular smallmouth bass and pike recovery in its restored northern wetland reaches as well as in the long, rocky stretch below Hoffman Dam in southwest suburban Lyons. The Des Plaines has recovered through its merger with the Sanitary Canal above Joliet and, farther downstream, through its merger with the Kankakee River near Wilmington to form the Illinois.

The Kankakee, Fox, and DuPage Rivers also have become substantial near-urban fisheries, largely due to cleaner water and careful regulations. All three support specific catch-and-release areas for trophy smallmouth bass, demanded by anglers after such regulations were successfully implemented downstate on the Rock River.

Besides smallmouth bass, the Kankakee can yield walleye above 10 pounds in deep holes before the spring spawning run. It also has good fishing for pike and panfish in its upper wetlands and farm runoff ditches.

The Fox sees good walleye action below its numerous dams, as well as smallmouth bass, panfish, and some creditable muskies at creek mouths that drain lakes and reservoirs. In places along the Fox, versatile anglers can work creek mouths for muskies, wade to channel dropoffs for walleye, and then wade toward a nearby riffle for smallmouth bass.

The leafy DuPage was one of Chicago's first suburban streams to develop a recovering smallmouth fishery, now augmented by the state. Protected by several forest preserves, it yields steady catches of respectable bass and catfish.

Major Rivers

More than half of Illinois' borders are rivers—the Mississippi on the west, the Ohio on its southern rim, and the Wabash along southern and central Indiana. The DNR estimates that most of Illinois' fish harvests occur in the substantial backwaters, channels, and dam holes of the Mississippi, which indicates the volume of fishable shoreline along that prolific body of water. The Mississippi's 580 river miles along Illinois have two parts: the pooled reach above St. Louis, with 15 dams creating effective lakes, and the unpooled deeper channel below St. Louis.

These sections are essentially separate rivers with respect to fishing. The pooled stretches offer year-round walleye and sauger fishing. The deep cuts below the dams are productive from fall through early spring; the submerged artificial wing dams, particularly on outer bends, are good in summer. Depending on current speed, anglers use $1/4$- to 1-ounce jigs and minnows on three-way rigs below the dams, and jigs, spinners, and crankbaits cast above or alongside the wing dams.

Channel cats and smallmouth and largemouth bass abound in the upper Mississippi, whereas flathead catfish and a strong, recovering population of blue cats proliferate along with largemouth bass in the lower river. Flatheads and blues frequently top 40 and 50 pounds.

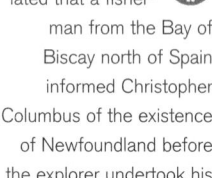

It has been speculated that a fisherman from the Bay of Biscay north of Spain informed Christopher Columbus of the existence of Newfoundland before the explorer undertook his journeys.

Significant tributaries that feed the Mississippi include the smallmouth-rich Apple, Plum, Green, and Rock Rivers—the latter boasting its own substantial walleye population below dams. In fact, the walleye harvest on the Rock quadruples that of the larger Illinois River, which drains half the counties in the state.

Along with walleye, sauger, white bass, and smallmouths in its reaches above Peoria, the Illinois offers good largemouth fishing from Peoria downstream, especially in the labyrinthine backwaters of Bath Chute and Snicarte Slough below Havana. Many duck clubs and managers of waterfowl areas, such as Anderson and Sanganois Lakes, control backwater levels and thereby contribute to the fishery.

Other feeders include the Kaskaskia River, with logjams, root wads, brush piles, undercut banks, oxbow channels, and shoreline riprap that produce substantial numbers of bass and catfish, especially below Fayetteville and above New Athens.

The Ohio River is famed for its maze of backwater creeks in Smithland Pool, 70 miles from the mouth of the Wabash to Smithland Dam below Golconda. Largemouth and Kentucky spotted bass average 12 to 15 inches, with some reaching 21 inches. Crappie and catfish also abound in waters that deeply penetrate the Shawnee National Forest.

The Wabash River is widely known for catfish and largemouth bass, the latter improving measurably in recent years.

The Rock River's trip through northern Illinois dispenses not only substantial walleye below its dams in Oregon, Dixon, Sterling, and Rock Falls, but also a magnificent 9-mile catch-and-release smallmouth area between Oregon and Grand Detour. Large catches of good eating–size channel cats occur in rocky currents. The Rock feeds 96-mile-long Hennepin Canal—a well-stocked panfish and catfish area of many pools between locks (anglers "troll" for fish by walking briskly along the towpath)—and offers deep holes for 30- to 50-pound flatheads between Grand Detour and Dixon.

Other substantial streams include the Mackinaw, Vermilion, Iroquois, Kishwaukee, Pecatonica, and Mazon for smallmouth bass, and the poetically famous Spoon, Embarras, Muddy, LaMoine, and Sangamon for catfish.

Reservoirs and Cooling Lakes

Three main Army Corps of Engineers flood-control reservoirs serve Illinois anglers. Lake Shelbyville, covering 11,100 acres near Mattoon, has developed an excellent largemouth bass and muskie fishery. Many bass are in the 2.2-pound range, and some exceed 5 pounds. Muskies proliferate here, drawing anglers from several states, especially in the weeks before fall turnover. Crappie fishing is another staple.

Carlyle Lake, which spans 24,580 acres east of St. Louis, has largemouth bass up to 6 pounds, and decent crappie, white bass, bluegill, and channel cat numbers, especially in the cover-laden waterfowling areas on its periphery. Rend Lake's 18,900 acres between Mt. Vernon and Benton, has numerous largemouth bass in the $1\frac{1}{2}$- to $4\frac{1}{2}$-pound range, and so many catfish that jug fishermen routinely lay in a winter's supply.

Illinois' array of power plant cooling lakes draws huge numbers of anglers to catfish factories like LaSalle, which also feature smallmouth, hybrid, and striped bass. Decent walleye and bass frequent Heidecke Lake, and Braidwood harbors bass, panfish, and catfish. Powerton's submerged drainage ditches and rocky riprap yield large numbers of 1-pound-plus catfish and flurries of excellent smallmouth in March, April, and early October along rocky ledges and levees in the coolest available water. Newton, Coffeen, and SangChris have good numbers of bass and panfish.

Northern Lakes

The Fox Chain O'Lakes in Lake and McHenry Counties has recovered substantially, although heavy boat traffic remains a pain to anglers on weekends. Muskies proliferate in Lake Marie and other northern reaches, especially on offshore weed beds near channels. Speed trollers have up to eight-fish days in early summer by running shallow-diving shadlike crankbaits no more than 8 to 20 feet from the boat. One lure should be in the prop wash, held down by an 8-ounce weight.

Shabbona Lake was built to field pressure from Chicago, offering trophy muskies, walleye, and bass as well as steady panfish. Four state record muskies have been produced at Shabbona.

Other popular destinations are Pierce Lake near Rockford, and George, Otter, Decatur, Springfield, Spring, Banner Marsh, and Snakeden Hollow Lakes in central and western Illinois. Snakeden Hollow and Mazonia Lakes near Joliet represent an array of bass and panfish challenges, each involving more than 100 flooded strip-mine lakes. Carlton, a tiny lake with numerous shallow bays, routinely yields the highest catch rates of muskies, as well as excellent largemouth bass.

Southern Lakes

Kinkade Lake near Carbondale has achieved premier stature for its large population of 45-plus-inch muskies, as well as excellent numbers of largemouth bass in a wildly beautiful setting. Lake-of-Egypt, and Horseshoe, Crab Orchard, Cedar, and Little Grassy Lakes offer excellent angling for bass and panfish, including occasionally nice crappie. Shawnee National Forest has an abundance of ponds and smaller lakes that yield a variety of action. Also worth checking are numerous county- and city-park lakes with creative management programs.

IMPROVED CLINCH KNOT

A fishing knot for terminal connections.
See: Knots, Fishing.

INBOARD BOAT

A boat powered by an inboard motor.

See: Boat; Sportfishing Boat.

INBOARD/OUTBOARD BOAT

A boat powered by an inboard/outboard motor.

See: Boat; Sportfishing Boat.

INCONNU   *Stenodus leucichthys.*

Other names—sheefish, connie, Eskimo tarpon; Russian: *beloribitsa.*

A member of the Salmonidae family, and a relative of whitefish and cisco, the inconnu is a species with limited northern range. It is poorly known to most anglers, in keeping with the meaning of its French name: unknown. In North America, most anglers know this exotic species as the sheefish. The only predatory member of the whitefish group in North America, it is highly favored by anglers as an exciting and large sportfish, but it is perhaps the least caught of North American and Asian gamefish. Its silvery coloring and tendency to leap high out of the water when hooked have earned it the nickname "Eskimo tarpon." Inconnu also have minor commercial importance, especially when smoked, although it is endangered in some portions of its eastern range.

Identification. The general body shape of inconnu is very similar to that of char or whitefish, but the head is relatively long, pointed, and depressed on the top. Its mouth is large, and the lower jaw clearly projects outward beyond the upper jaw. The maxillary, or upper jaw bone, extends back at least as far as the middle of the eye. Small, fine teeth are found on the anterior part of the lower jaw, and on the tongue, premaxillaries, the head of the maxillaries, the vomer, and the palatines (bones of the roof of the mouth). The tail is distinctly forked. Sheefish have large scales and a dark lateral line, and, like all salmonids, an adipose fin.

Size/Age. Inconnu are said to grow to 60 pounds. The all tackle world record is a 53-pounder from Alaska. Like many arctic and subarctic fish, they are long-lived, which makes large fish vulnerable to exploitation; the largest fish may be between 25 and 35 years old.

Distribution. In North America, inconnu are found in Alaska, from the Kuskokwim River (Bering Sea drainage) north, throughout the Yukon River in Canada, in the Mackenzie River, in Great Bear and Great Slave Lakes in Canada's Northwest

Territories as far as the Anderson River near Cape Bathurst, and in isolated areas of extreme northern British Columbia. The largest North American fish occur in the vicinity of Selawik to Kotzebue, where tributaries enter into Hotham Inlet and Kotzebue Sound. In Asia, inconnu occur westward as far as the White Sea, and an isolated population inhabits the Caspian Sea and its drainage.

Habitat. Although generally viewed as a freshwater species, the inconnu occurs in strictly freshwater lakes and rivers and also in anadromous sea-run forms that winter in brackish deltas, bays, and tidewater areas and ascend coastal tributaries to spawn. It evidently evolved from purely freshwater fish to estuarine-anadromous fish.

Life history/Behavior. Spawning takes place in late summer and early fall, when inconnu ascend freshwater tributaries. Inland inconnu leave lakes and run up tributaries as well. In coastal regions, inconnu migrate from estuaries to river mouths after ice out, then ascend freshwater tributaries; this migration may last a few weeks in short-length rivers, or months in longer ones, such as the Yukon River. After spawning, they do not die, but quickly migrate downstream.

Food and feeding habits. This species feeds mostly on small fish. Salmon smolts, cisco, smelt, and whitefish are among the common forage, and in coastal areas large schools of inconnu will fatten on baitfish prior to their spawning migration, making it possible to spot fish by looking for bird activity.

Angling. Inconnu are aggressive fish, but they can also be spooked by activity. Spoons, spinners, and streamer flies are the common lures, employed mostly in casting. Heavy-bodied spoons are often necessary for casting in windy situations and to get down in the current. Large, weighted flies are likewise usually better for larger fish. Inconnu are caught from boats and by wading anglers, and large coastal fish have the ability to make long runs and take a lot of line. They will leap out of the water when caught and have hard bony mouths that make it necessary to put muscle into the hook-setting motion. Most sport-caught inconnu are released.

INDIA

The Indian subcontinent is a vast country with rich aquatic resources. It offers a variety of fishing opportunities—little known outside its borders—in both its freshwater and brackish water environments.

As the seventh largest country in the world, India stretches 3,200 kilometers from north to south and 2,700 kilometers from east to west. Its territory is one-third the size of the United States but encompasses 25 states, more than 32 million square kilometers of land, more than 50,000 kilometers of rivers and streams, and more than 3,000 kilometers of coastline bordering the Arabian Sea, the Indian Ocean, and the Bay of Bengal.

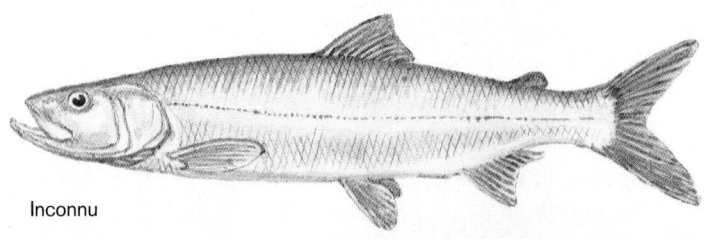

Inconnu

Two major rivers in the north run through the 2,400-kilometer-long Himalayan mountain range, and both are lifelines for the local population. One of these is the Ganga (Ganges), which is 2,512 kilometers long, stretching from its headwaters at Gaumukh in the Himalayas to the Bay of Bengal. It actually has a combined length of 8,047 kilometers when all of its significant tributaries are included. The other is the Brahmaputra, which is 4,023 kilometers long. Important rivers draining peninsular India are the Mahanadi, Godavari, Krishna, and Cauvery, with a total length of 6,437 kilometers. The Western Ghats are drained by the Tapti and Narmada Rivers, and flow all of 3,380 kilometers.

India's population of 950 million is the second largest in the world (after China), and a significant portion of the country's citizens are poor, spending most of their time trying to make ends meet. Three-quarters of the population lives in rural villages. Fishing as a hobby or recreational pursuit is a luxury, and far less than 1 percent of the population partakes in sportfishing. The poor and lower middle-income groups of Indian society fish only for subsistence. Among those who do fish as a hobby, very few appear to practice catch-and-release. Invariably, fish taken by sporting methods end up in the kitchen.

At present, India lures few foreign anglers, primarily because scant outfitting services cater to sportfishing, and detailed information has been lacking; those who visit must be adventurous and adaptable. Access to fishing sites on noteworthy rivers is easy because all major cities and villages are located on their banks, if not within a short distance. For specialized fishing, and especially far northern mountain trout angling, resourceful anglers travel long distances.

Sportfishing for pleasure alone, as practiced in North America and Europe, was virtually unknown in India until the middle of the twentieth century. Prior to that, Indians ranked fishing below hunting for wild animals. For many centuries India was divided into 560 small kingly states ruled by feudal heads and kings who were interested in hunting wild animals. The inclination to hunt wild game permeated to the general population from the nobility, whom they were supposed to help in this pursuit.

Recent American and European influences have spurred interest in recreational angling in India. Because of this trend, sportfishing is likely to grow in economic significance and might provide leverage for tourism.

Various changes and improvements in facilities are necessary, however, to accommodate any growth in recreational angling. There is, for example, an urgent need to build publicly accessible fishing piers in numerous locations. To popularize angling, India must launch an extensive publicity and advertising campaign, and clinics must be organized to teach sportfishing methods to young people as well as adults. These will likely have to be arranged and conducted by the Departments of Fisheries in the Indian states on a regular basis.

Nevertheless, India has opportunities to offer anglers. Sportfisheries exist in the cold waters flowing out of the of the Himalayan, Satpuras, and Aravallis Ranges (respectively in the north, central, and northwestern region) and the hills of southern India; warmwater fishing exists in the great plains, and brackish water fishing can be enjoyed along the extensive coasts of the eastern and western edges of peninsular (south) India. Fishing sites along all the rivers and streams are generally accessible through rail and road connections; however, a certain amount of walking is required to reach some places. Very few people fish from boats; they invariably approach fishing sites by road, and fish from the banks of the rivers or lakes.

There are 31 freshwater fish species in India that are of interest to anglers. Local names of fish differ according to region, but there is, as yet, no listing of standardized local fish names. The species pursued by local anglers are cyprinids (family: Cyprinidae); catfish (families: Siluridae, Bagridae, Pangasiidae, Schilbeidae, Sisoridae); murrel (family: Channidae); and trout (family: Salmonidae). All but trout, which were introduced from Europe around the beginning of the twentieth century, are endemic.

With sportfishing in India gaining strength, in 1982 Raj Tilak and Uma Sharma published their English-language book, *Gamefishes of India and Angling*, as an aid to eager anglers. Tilak and Sharma give an illustrated account of 31 species of freshwater gamefish in India, with keys to their identification, methods of angling, use of lures, and so forth. Through the late 1990s, theirs remains the only book on this topic.

Finding and catching these species is complicated by several factors. The food and feeding habits of some Indian fish are not known to many native or visiting anglers. Also, the complement of gamefish varies regionally, and it is not well known which species inhabit which regions or specific waters, although Indian tourism agencies have been working to make specific details available.

The following information is a general guide to finding and catching fish in Indian waters. Bear in mind that at any given time climatic conditions vary widely in different parts of India. Hence, dry and wet seasons are not necessarily the same from region to region. In the Himalayas, for example, September and October are comparatively dry months with moderate temperatures, allowing access to almost all important fishing sites in the region.

North India

In northern India, the best sportfishing opportunities are available along the base of the Himalayas and the Shiwaliks, and in the plains. The Shiwaliks are low-hill ranges running parallel to the Himalayan mountain region, all along its length on the southern edge.

In the hilly sections of the rivers, the king among Indian sportfish is the mahseer, the largest member of the minnow and carp clan and belonging to the Cyprinidae family. These include the putitor, or yellow-finned, mahseer *(Tor putitora);* the tor, or red-finned, mahseer *(Tor tor);* and the mosal, or copper, mahseer *(Tor mosal).* The putitor mahseer grows to a length of 2.7 meters; the male may reach an astounding 1.9 quintal (190 kilograms, or 418 pounds), and the female can grow to 2.2 quintal (220 kilograms, or 484 pounds). The tor mahseer can reach a length of 1.7 meters and a weight of 100 kilograms (220 pounds). The mosal mahseer does not grow longer than 1 meter.

These fish are omnivorous and accept any kind of natural food, but a paste bait works especially well. Various spoons are also effective. Light to heavy tackle is preferred, depending on the size of the fish targeted. The best fishing is in August and September. Another cyprinid, the chaguni *(Chagunius chagunio),* which does not grow bigger than 450 millimeters (about 17 inches), offers good sport on a small hook.

In Himalayan streams, the schizothoracids, such as the alwan *(Schizothorax richardsonii),* which is a column feeder, and the chhiruh *(Schizothoraicthys esocinus)* and dinnawah *(Schizothoraicthys progastus),* which are bottom feeders, are good sportfishes. These are cyprinids, too, but are found in hilly streams at higher altitudes than are mahseer. They take well on paste baits and are prized table fare. The best time to fish in these regions is September and October.

In the northern Indian plains, a large number of sporty cyprinids and catfish are loved by anglers along such noted rivers as the Ganga and the Yamuna, as well as in many small rivers and streams. Prominent cyprinids here are the katla *(Catla catla),* which attains a recorded size of 1.83 meters; the rohu *(Labeo rohita)* and kalbose *(Labeo calbasu),* which grow to 1 meter; the mirgal *(Cirrhinus mrigala),* which grows to less than 1 meter; and the bola *(Barilius bola),* which grows to 300 millimeters. Most of these are stocked in ponds and reservoirs and form a major part of the fisheries of northern India. They take well on paste and worm baits, and provide a good fight. Among these cyprinids, the rohu is a prized fish and fetches a higher price in the commercial markets than that of all other cyprinids.

Catfish are also loved by Indian anglers. They are carnivorous and destructive to other species, but their size, fighting quality, and tasty boneless flesh make them a favorite quarry. Locals generally catch them using small fish, worms, frogs, and some lures.

The important species of catfish for sport are the aar *(Mystus aor),* growing to 1.8 meters and 68 kilograms; the seenghari *(Mystus seenghala),* growing to 400 millimeters; the boali, or mulley *(Wallago attu),* growing to 1.8 meters and 45 kilograms; the khagga *(Rita rita),* growing to 1.3 meters; the pungas *(Pangasius pangasius),* growing to 1.5 meters and 55 kilograms; the silond *(Silonia silondia),* growing to 2 meters and 45 kilograms; the bachwa vacha *(Eutropiichthys vacha),* growing to 350 millimeters; the garua bachcha, or gaurchcha *(Clupisoma garua),* growing to 1 meter; and the goonch *(Bagarius bagarius),* growing to 2 meters and 135 kilograms (297 pounds).

Also available and pursued here is the murrel *(Channa marulius),* a long-bodied fish characterized as a "snakehead" by some, which grows to 1.2 meters and takes live baits, particularly frogs.

Anglers avoid the rainy season (summer monsoons), which varies according to the region, and extremely cold days.

Peninsular India

In peninsular India, the Mahanadi, Krishna, Godavary, and Cauvery Rivers, as well as other rivers and streams, provide angling for different species. Prominent sportfish include the khudchee *(Tor khudree),* which grows to 450 millimeters and 22.6 kilograms; the mussullah, or high-backed, mahseer *(Tor mussullah),* which grows to 1.5 meters and nearly 90 kilograms; the wulnus, or purree *(Silonia childreni),* which grows to 460 millimeters; and the white carp *(Cirrhinus cirrhosus),* which grows to 450 millimeters. The wulnus takes both live and dead baits employed with a small hook. The white carp strikes like the rohu and can be taken on a small hook with paste or a worm.

With the exception of the rainy season, which starts in June here, anglers pursue fish throughout the year.

East India

The two important sportfishes of the Brahmaputra River and small streams in this region are *Tor progenius,* known as jhungha in Assam and growing to 1 meter, and *Acrossocheilus hexagonolepis,* which attains a length of 0.6 meter and a weight of 9.5 kilograms. This fish is known as bokar in Assam, and as katli among the Nepali-speaking people of Assam and North Bengal.

Trout

In addition to the endemic sportfish of India, two exotic species are well established in hilly sections of northern, eastern, and peninsular India: brown trout and rainbow trout. The browns were introduced in India around the turn of the century; rainbow trout came later. Brown trout are widespread in the wild, whereas rainbows are restricted only to experimental ponds. Trout grow to large sizes in big rivers and lakes—up to 7.5 kilograms in some high-altitude lakes in Himachal Pradesh—and attract foreign tourists. Brown trout are caught here on dry and wet flies and small spoons.

Coastal Regions

India's long coast is flanked by the Arabian Sea on the west, the Indian Ocean on the south, and the

Bay of Bengal on the east. The common marine sportfish targeted by anglers are tuna, marlin, sailfish, mackerel, sea bass, snapper, jacks, croaker, snook, perch, sharks, and tripletail. Some large specimens of these fish have been landed in Indian waters; snook, for example, have been registered as large as 914 millimeters. For brackish water and marine fishes, anglers use heavy tackle and a variety of live and artificial baits. Comparatively, brackish water and marine anglers are much fewer in number in India than those in freshwater.

Fishing in the estuaries and the coastal regions is possible only with the help of boats, of which there are few specifically designated for angling. One can hire boats for any purpose at all seaports in India, but hardly any system for hiring charter boats for fishing exists. There are no fishing guides or charter captains either. Contacting local anglers, or the Department of Fisheries of the coastal state, may lead to information about the availability of boats.

Significant ports along the western coast of India include Kandla (Maharashtra), Bombay (Maharashtra), Nhava Sheva (Maharashtra), Marmagao (Karnataka), New Mangalore (Karnataka), and Kochi (earlier called Cochin in Kerala). On the eastern coast they include Calcutta-Haldia (West Bengal), Paradip (West Bengal), Vishakhapatnam (Andhra Pradesh), Madras (Tamil Nadu), and Tuticorin (Tamil Nadu).

Gamefish Management/Fish Sanctuaries

The fish stocks in various Indian waters have suffered greatly in recent times, both in quality and quantity as a result of harmful direct or indirect human activities. The effect on fisheries resources has been more severe in some places than others.

Radical changes in the occurrence and abundance of fish in certain important river systems is generally related to recent human activities in the area. Technological development, including the construction of dams and hydroelectric power–generation projects, have modified the ecology of rivers by slowing down the flow, increasing the depth, and altering the course. In addition, overfishing, illegal fishing activities, introduction of exotic fast-breeding species, expanded state programs of maximum exploitation of fishery resources, pollution through urban/agricultural/industrial wastes and effluents, and so forth have added to the problem. The construction of vehicular roads, the gradual extension of urban areas, and certain socioeconomic changes appear to have aided the decline. The chain effect of these activities has profoundly influenced fish populations in India, as well as species diversity in the streams and rivers. These influences have led to a pronounced impoverishment or even total disappearance of some important species.

Fisheries agencies of the Indian states are aware of these problems and are attempting to remedy some of them. Good laws to protect fisheries exist in India, but implementation is poor. Although India has not yet achieved total exploitation of its fisheries resources, far-reaching deteriorating effects on fish fauna are strongly manifest. Thus, although angling opportunities are available, they are not as good as they were in the past, nor are they as good as they could be with proper care.

Among the food fish of India, the major carp—such as the katla, rohu, kalbose, and mirgal—form the backbone of fish propagation in northern India, although katla and mirgal have been successfully transplanted into the rivers of peninsular India. Among the major gamefish, the putitor, or yellow-finned, mahseer; the mosal, or copper, mahseer; and the tor, or red-finned, mahseer are distributed by authorities in the waterways of the lesser Himalayas in the north. The khudchee and the mussullah, or high-backed, mahseer are likewise distributed in the rivers in peninsular India.

Hatchery rearing techniques have been perfected for important carp species, and fish are stocked as necessary where natural reproduction is not sustaining fish populations. The natural breeding of important carp and mahseer species has suffered greatly, and as a result the natural production of these fish has substantially declined. Due to a continuing depreciation of fish fauna and reduced natural production, the role of fish sanctuaries has increased as a means of improving the fish stock.

Fish sanctuaries have been in existence in India partly because of the religious beliefs of the people, which require that they protect natural resources, and partly because of legislation introduced by the departments of fisheries or forests in various states. Many such fish sanctuaries exist in India, and they preserve the gene pool of important fish species by providing seed for further propagation of those species. The idea of creating fish sanctuaries is catching on and may become a vital means of maintaining and/or restoring fish stocks.

Angling and Tourism

Tourism ranks sixth among the major industries in India, although it ranks much higher in many other nations. Adequate attention has not been paid to this lucrative trade in India, and much could be done to attract foreign tourists and enhance foreign exchange. The national Department of Tourism is working to provide tourists with incentives to visit various places of interest in the country. Apart from a large number of historic monuments, religious sites, national parks and biosphere reserves, and other rare attractions, India's gamefish and angling sites—if properly managed—could lure many more foreign as well as domestic tourists. Its large carp would interest many Europeans, and the mahseer and trout would entice Europeans and non-Europeans alike. To date, most anglers visiting India are interested in angling for trout.

Among the various efforts undertaken by tourism agencies of the national government and the different states is the circulation of brochures that provide details on India's important gamefish and beautiful angling sites. These have been dispatched to Indian diplomatic missions in other countries. Also available are leaflets describing routes to angling spots, modes of transportation and communication, seasonal weather patterns, campgrounds and lodging, and similar necessities. Tourist information centers provide specifics on current fishing laws and where to obtain fishing licenses.

In addition, some states have constructed fishing lodges and huts at preferred angling sites, making it easier for visiting anglers to enjoy them. Transportation is improving due to better road connections. At some tourist offices, personnel can provide information and plan an itinerary for anglers. Licenses indicate the closed seasons for fishing (mostly the breeding season of important species), but inquire in advance, to spare yourself unnecessary expense and disappointment.

See: Sri Lanka.

INDIANA

Sandwiched between Lake Michigan to the northwest and the Ohio River to the south, and with 21,000 miles of rivers and streams, 452 natural lakes, 580 man-made impoundments, thousands of farm ponds, and gravel pits to its credit, Indiana has water and fishing opportunities that belie its status as the 38th largest state. With this diversity in venues comes a plethora of species, in part the result of naturally occurring features and in part due to the successful introduction of highly desirable gamefish.

For many years, fishing in Indiana meant angling strictly for largemouth and smallmouth bass, bluegills, crappie, and catfish. Today, the largemouth bass is still the most-sought species, the bluegill is still the most caught species, and catfish and crappie are not far behind in popularity. Traditional fisheries for walleye and northern pike, not to mention assorted panfish and such rough fish as carp and sucker, also exist.

The modern Hoosier angler, however, has choices that were not possible in earlier decades, including Skamania steelhead, several species of salmon, purebred striped bass, hybrid stripers, and purebred muskies, thanks to aggressive stocking programs that are not necessarily meant to engender natural reproduction. The Division of Fish and Wildlife (DFW) has also stocked saugeye and tiger muskies, but these programs are being phased out.

Indiana's geographic location, length (300 miles), and weather patterns have a special influence on angling. There are at least three weather zones in Indiana. Like prevailing winds, they run from southwest to northeast, and this often means different weather conditions for the northern, central, and southern regions on a daily basis and over longer periods.

The northern region is the area north of the imaginary line that runs from east to west through the cities of Bluffton, Peru, and Monticello; this is roughly the northern third of the state. The central region is the area from that line south to Indiana Highway 46, an east-west road that runs through Greensburg, Columbus, and Bloomington. The southern region is the area south of that highway.

Anglers in the northern tier counties (the first three or four rows of counties south of the Michigan-Indiana state line) almost always have safe ice for fishing by Christmas. Those in the central part of the state think in terms of safe ice by mid-January or early February, and those of the southern third never know when surface waters will ice up, if at all. Larger waters in southern Indiana seldom have safe ice.

An interesting facet of the influence of geographic location and weather is the difference in growth rates of gamefish, especially largemouth bass, in these regions. In general, it takes longer for bass to attain a certain size in smaller, northerly waters than it does in larger, southerly ones; and there is a difference between growth of bass in natural lakes (smaller) versus impoundments.

Thus, minimum size limits on bass vary greatly from one end of the state to the other and even within the regions. Moreover, they are subject to change. On most standing waters the minimum size limit on bass is 12 or 14 inches. Some standing waters, however, have minimum limits between 15

Skamania-strain steelhead have been a big success for Indiana's Lake Michigan anglers.

and 20 inches. Others have 12- to 15-inch slot limits, and still others have no minimum size limit.

A good thing to remember when seeking hotspots for black bass, bluegills, and other members of the sunfish family is that the DFW occasionally renovates and restocks man-made lakes when imbalances of these species occur and the body of water in question is being lowered for some other reason. Growth rates of all species often are phenomenal a year or so after the renovation, and the good fishing can prevail for several years.

Northern Region

The north is well known for its trout and salmon fishing in Lake Michigan, in the big lake's two tributaries at Michigan City, and in the St. Joseph River. These fisheries are discussed separately later.

Trout and salmon notwithstanding, largemouth bass are by far the most important species to anglers in this region. The effects of the Ice Age are evident in the northern region of Indiana, especially the northeast, which was the southern extremity of glacial activity many thousands of years ago. As a result, the northern-tier counties offer several hundred natural "kettle" lakes that provide especially good angling for bass, several other members of the sunfish family, and numerous other species. However, some very good bass fishing is available in the northwest as well.

Nevertheless, at 3,410 acres, Lake Wawasee is the largest of the state's natural lakes and the undisputed best largemouth lake of the northern region. This Kosciusko County lake is one of those rare Indiana waters that also hosts smallmouth in good numbers. Likewise, the 454-acre West Lakes Chain, a series of four lakes in Noble County, offers very good fishing for both largemouths and smallmouths. Steuben County's 509-acre Hamilton Lake is another top largemouth spot in the region.

Other well-known largemouth bass lakes of more than 300 surface acres include Lake Manitou in Fulton County; Dewart and Syracuse (connected to Wawasee on the north) in Kosciusko County; the Indian Chain in Lagrange County; Koontz, Maxinkuckee, and Lake-of-the-Woods in Marshall County; J. C. Murphey at Willow Slough State Fish and Wildlife Area in Newton County; Worster Lake at Potato Creek State Park in St. Joseph County; and Bass, Crooked, James, and George Lakes in Steuben County.

Robinson Lake covers only 59 acres in Whitley County, but it has big bass in good numbers. It was acquired by the state and is operated as a trophy fishery.

Bluegills, redear sunfish, crappie, and some other sunfish are present in nearly all of the natural lakes of the north, and these species offer both food and exciting action. The smaller kettle lakes are better for the smaller sunfish species than are larger lakes, especially those that do not have shad populations. Biologists say the smaller sunfish species are boosted by a lack of competition for food with shad. However, crappie do well in shad-infested lakes because they feed heavily on this unwanted species. Lakes at Tri-County (Kosciusko County) and Willow Slough (Newton County) State Fish and Wildlife Areas, and Chain O' Lakes State Park, offer very good fishing for these species.

The best smallmouth fishing of this region is in rivers and streams. The St. Joseph River in St. Joseph and Elkhart Counties has been one of Indiana's best smallmouth sites for many years. Bringing salmonids into this river has not changed the smallmouth fishery. Another very good smallmouth site is the Tippecanoe River all the way downstream from Tippecanoe Lake to the town of Buffalo at the upper end of Lake Shafer in White County.

The best lakes for northern pike are Manitou (Fulton County), Chapman and Wawasee (Kosciusko), the Indian Lakes Chain (Lagrange), Fish Lake (LaPorte), West Lake (Noble), and Lakes Hamilton and James (Steuben). The Iroquois River through Jasper County; the Tippecanoe River through Kosciusko, Marshall, and Pulaski Counties; and the Kankakee River in Newton County are also good bets for pike.

Catfish inhabit all the rivers of the northern region. Channel cats are the main species, but there are some flatheads and blues. Thanks to an ongoing stocking program, most northern lakes offer good fishing for channel catfish.

Central Region

Few of the largemouth bass waters of the central part of Indiana compare favorably with those of the north and south. Still, this region offers very good fishing, especially for smallmouth bass.

Among the most notable bass waters are the West Fork of the White River through Hamilton County and the northern part of Marion County (Indianapolis); the headwaters of the East Fork of the White River through Henry, Rush, Shelby, and Johnson Counties east of the capitol city; and such Wabash River tributaries as Sugar, Walnut, and Raccoon Creeks to the west. The headwaters of the Wabash River through Huntington, Wabash, and Miami Counties produce some big bronzebacks.

The West Fork of the White River is as good for smallmouths as any river in the state, and maybe the best, from the 146th Street Bridge south of Noblesville through Lake Indy, a wide, slow-moving stretch on the southwest side of Indianapolis. Below Lake Indy occasional sewage spills lessen the value of this water as a smallmouth fishery, but the river overcomes this handicap by the time it reaches Martinsville. From there downstream to its confluence with the Wabash River at East Mt. Carmel in Illinois, it offers good angling for a wide variety of fish, including largemouth bass, some smallmouth bass, big catfish (channels, flatheads, and blues), and many nongame species.

I

Smallmouths and the other species mentioned inhabit the White upstream from Noblesville, but the fishing is not as good on most stretches upstream from Muncie. It is not as productive from there up to its rise north of Lynn in Randolph County, near the Ohio border. The headwaters of the Big Blue River and Sugar Creek rise east of Indianapolis in Henry and Shelby Counties respectively, and join at the southeastern corner of Johnson County to become Driftwood River as it flows southward to Columbus in Bartholomew County. At a dam on the south side of Columbus the Driftwood becomes the East Fork of the White. The main stem of the White—from the confluence of East and West Forks at the southeast corner of Knox County to the Wabash River—is the best water for large flathead and blue catfish in the state. It is also good for channel cats.

Several other streams of this vast East Fork drainage area also produce good smallmouth fishing. The East Fork of the White is better known for large catfish, however.

The best combined largemouth-smallmouth fisheries in the central part of the state are Freeman and Shafer Lakes and Brookville Reservoir on the Ohio border in Union and Franklin Counties. Smallmouths dominate at Brookville, but the opposite is true at Freeman and Shafer.

Morse Reservoir in Hamilton County, and Geist and Eagle Creek Reservoirs in Marion County, are surprisingly good for largemouth bass. Cataract Lake on the Owen-Putnam County line offers good largemouth fishing, with some bronzebacks.

The best crappie fishing in the central part of the state may be in Mississinewa and Salamonie Reservoirs in Miami and Wabash Counties respectively. All of the reservoirs previously mentioned, however, and Raccoon Reservoir in Parke County, have good crappie populations. Fish of 10 to 12 inches are fairly common, and they get bigger.

The best bluegill and redear fishing is at Summit Lake in Summit Lake State Park in Henry County, and at Glenn Flint Lake northwest of Greencastle in Putnam County. However, all of the farm ponds, gravel pits, and small watershed lakes host bluegill in both good numbers and size. A 6- or 7-inch bluegill or redear sunfish is considered a good catch, but in some waters fish of 8 to 10 inches are fairly common.

All of the reservoirs and rivers have good populations of channel catfish. Flatheads and blues show up less frequently but are present.

Southern Region

Monroe Reservoir not only claims the best largemouth bass fishing Indiana has ever known, but it has maintained that reputation since it was impounded in 1964. This 10,750-acre man-made lake is the largest "inland" body of water in the state, and its bass population is the result of a highly successful stocking that same year.

Monroe is the most likely place to produce a largemouth greater than the existing 14-pound, 12-ounce state record; it still gives up bass that average more than 2 pounds in tournaments. Fish in the 6- to 8-pound range are not uncommon, and a few 9- and 10-pounders are logged there every year.

No less exciting at Monroe is the fishing for crappie, bluegills, and channel catfish. Blue and flathead catfish are also present.

The second best largemouth fishery in this region is Patoka Reservoir, an 8,880-acre multipurpose reservoir in Orange and Crawford Counties. Patoka was a great largemouth fishery for several years after being impounded; then it experienced stunted fish and was subsequently put under slot limit regulations and then a 15-inch minimum size limit. Bass fishing here has been improving.

Patoka also offers particularly good fishing for slab-size bluegills, redear sunfish, and crappie. Excellent fishing for these species is also found at West Boggs Lake in Martin County, and Dogwood Lake at Glendale State Fish and Wildlife Area in Daviess County.

Other top largemouth bass fisheries are the Indiana holdings of the Ohio River. In 1985 the U.S. Supreme Court ruled for Indiana in a suit contending that the navigational dams on the Ohio had raised the river and given Kentucky control of countless acres of Indiana land.

The decision made Indiana a part owner of the Ohio and led to reciprocal agreements between the two states on fishing rights. Now Hoosiers can use their Indiana fishing licenses on all of the Ohio and all of the stream and river embayments on the Indiana side. To fish Kentucky embayments, however, Hoosiers must have a license from that state.

From the southeast corner of Indiana, the pools are Markland, which includes 40 miles of Indiana shoreline; McAlpine, 74 miles; Cannelton, 116 miles; Newburgh, 55 miles; Uniontown, 70 miles; and Smithland, 2 miles. Add to this the waters of the many embayments of Indiana tributaries of the Ohio, and the enormity of this bass fishery becomes apparent. All of the embayments of larger rivers and even smaller creeks and ditches are potential largemouth hangouts.

A few of the larger tributaries of the Ohio are Hogan, Laughery, Grant, and Bryant's Creeks on the Markland Pool; Big Blue River, Little Blue River, and Oil Creek on the Cannelton Pool; and Anderson River and Little Pigeon Creek on the Newburgh Pool. The main stem of the Wabash River flows into the Ohio at the southwestern corner of Indiana, and it offers some angling for bass and other species, especially catfish.

Strip-mined lands and farm ponds in this region offer good bass fishing, but much of this is on private land. These waters are also especially good for bluegills and crappie.

Another outstanding largemouth fishery is Turtle Creek Reservoir, a 1,500-acre man-made hydropower impoundment in Sullivan County. The lake is used for cooling water. It produces good numbers of big bass, and special regulations exist to make it a trophy fishery. Turtle Creek also hosts big crappie and bluegills.

Hardy Lake, a 741-acre reservoir on the Scott-Jefferson County line, is also a good lake for large-mouth bass.

Introduced Fisheries

Trout and salmon. The first, and oldest, salmon fishery on Indiana waters is centered on the state's 234 square miles of Lake Michigan and the big lake's two tributaries between the Indiana-Michigan state line and the Twin Branch Dam east of Mishawaka.

Development of trout and salmon stocking programs date back to 1960, when rehabilitation of Lake Michigan's lake trout fishery was begun by the state of Michigan. This work included the introduction of coho and chinook salmon, brown trout, and steelhead. Although the stocking of lake trout was aimed at bolstering this population, the work with the other species was designed to create put-grow-and-take fisheries and to cut an overabundance of alewives, which were depleting food sources for the alewives themselves and other species.

Indiana has been stocking salmon and trout in Lake Michigan, Trail Creek, and Burns Ditch since the late 1960s, and was the first state to stock the enormously popular Skamania strain of steelhead.

As a result, Indiana's salmonid fishery on its share of Lake Michigan, Trail Creek, and Burns Ditch produces very good angling for coho salmon in the late winter and early spring, for chinook salmon from spring through fall, and for both summer- and winter-run steelhead.

A coho bonus occurs for Hoosiers in the spring, when fish from the stocking of other states congregate on the southernmost shores of Lake Michigan where alewives are spawning. Close-in fishing—even in the harbors and along the shorelines—produces especially good coho action.

The St. Joseph River, which exits Indiana and courses through Michigan on its way to Lake Michigan, is a significant component of the Hoosier State's trout and salmon opportunities, especially since completion of an Interstate Anadromous Fish Project to allow fish passage to its upper reaches. The $15 million project involved natural resources agencies in both Indiana and Michigan and the U.S. Fish and Wildlife Service; it took nearly 15 years to finish. But when the five fish ladders were completed on dams at Berrien Springs, Buchanan, and Niles in Michigan, and at South Bend and Mishawaka in Indiana, trout and salmon could make spawning runs of 65 miles upstream on the St. Joe.

Now Hoosiers can try their luck for salmon in the fall, and for Skamania-strain steelhead from mid-July or August, when this summer-run species starts thinking of spawning, through the fall and winter months. The St. Joe offers good steelhead angling into the late winter and early spring. A fish hatchery was constructed by Indiana at Twin Branch, upriver from Mishawaka.

Muskellunge. The stocking of purebred muskies at Brookville Reservoir in Franklin County in 1974 was the state's first effort at augmenting the few native fish found in tributaries of the Ohio River, and it has been a successful one. Although Brookville has never been a great muskie fishery, it has given up some good fish. More importantly, the work at Brookville did inspire state biologists to stock other waters, and that led to 774-acre Lake Webster in Kosciusko County becoming the centerpiece of the state's muskie fishery. In a national competition in 1997, 80 muskie anglers from around the country caught 27 legal-size fish in three days and encountered 60 others.

Some other good bets for the spreading muskellunge fishery are Ball Lake in Steuben County, Skinner Lake in Noble County, Loon Lake in Whitley, Plover Lake in the Atterbury State Fish and Wildlife Area, and Hardy Lake in Scott County.

Striped bass. Brookville Reservoir in Franklin County, and the Ohio River, have been the only Hoosier waters where purebred striped bass were taken for a number of years, but this species has more recently been introduced at Raccoon Reservoir in Parke County and has been doing well there.

Hybrid striped bass, also known as wipers, also thrive in Indiana. Monroe Reservoir now sports the best hybrid striper action in the state; anglers focus on the big water section just above the dam. Night fishing off the face of the dam is very good in October on full-moon nights and a day or two after a rain.

Some other good bets for hybrids are Lake Freeman, the Tippecanoe River below the Lake Freeman impoundment, and Cataract Lake.

Walleye. Walleye have been stocked in some Indiana waters since the late 1800s, but modern management efforts by the state go back only to 1970. Brookville Reservoir now offers the best walleye fishing in Indiana, but Clear Lake in Steuben County is very good. Monroe and Mississinewa Reservoirs produce sizable walleye in good numbers.

When Mississinewa, Salamonie, Brookville, and Monroe Reservoirs are releasing more than normal amounts of water in the spring, their tailwaters offer very good walleye fishing.

INDIVIDUAL TRANSFERABLE QUOTA

A saltwater commercial fisheries management allotment that grants certain private property rights to commercial fishermen by assigning a fixed share of the total allowable catch *(see)*. An individual transferable quota (ITQ) is a form of management in which entry to an overharvested fishery is limited to help rebuild depleted stocks.

Fossils of ancient fish have been used to shed light on the nature and association of landmasses hundreds of millions of years ago.

I

INDONESIA

Located south and east of mainland Asia and north and west of Australia, the Republic of Indonesia extends 5,100 kilometers from west to east, comprising most of the Malay Archipelago and nearly 13,700 islands. About half of these are inhabited, and in total Indonesia has the fourth largest population in the world.

The major islands of Sumatra and Java, in the western and southern regions, are very densely populated. The primary entry points to this part of the country are the capital city of Jakarta on Java; Medan on Sumatra; and the popular tourist island of Bali. The eastern and northern regions of Indonesia are remote, more inaccessible, and less populated. Major entry points to these regions are Balikpapan on Kalimantan (Borneo), Ujung Pandang and Manado on Sulewasi (Celebes), Ambon in the Moluccas, and Biak on Irian Jaya (the western half of New Guinea).

Indonesia straddles the equator and is surrounded on the north by the South China Sea, the Celebes Sea, and the Pacific Ocean, and on the south and west by the Indian Ocean. It has some 55,000 kilometers of coastline.

Sportfishing is a relatively new activity in Indonesia; consequently, its angling opportunities are little explored. Because of the imbalance between land and sea area, together with the dense population in the west, saltwater fishing is generally more popular than freshwater fishing. There are, however, an increasing number of "managed" freshwater fisheries.

Indonesia has deep blue water where it is bounded to the west and south by the Indian Ocean; there is deep blue water throughout eastern Indonesia. Much of western and southern Indonesia is cultivated, and mangrove swamps have been replaced by cultivated land. Rivers are muddy, and freshwater fishing opportunities are restricted to man-made ponds and lakes. Eastern and northern Indonesia are rugged and forested with clear jungle streams draining into extensive mangrove systems that have hardly seen a rod and line.

The climate throughout Indonesia is tropically humid. Daily temperatures range from the mid-20s to the mid-30s Celsius, and the humidity hovers between 70 and 90 percent. There are two seasons or "monsoons." The southeasterly monsoon, or dry season, runs from April through October. It is hot and humid during this time, but rains are infrequent. Near coastal areas, a constant sea breeze makes the climate balmy. The westerly monsoon, or wet season, runs from November through March. During this season, the weather is often oppressively humid, and there are frequent tropical downpours with associated brief heavy winds.

Throughout Indonesia anglers can find boats for hire. These are usually wooden and slow, or they are local fiberglass designs with outboard motors

This fly-rod-caught narrowbarred mackerel exemplifies the nearshore opportunities available in Indonesia.

(known as longboats), with crews who have no experience at sportfishing. Angling can be a difficult experience on such boats. Sometimes the crew is accustomed to taking anglers. These operations, while safer and faster, are only a little better in terms of their sportfishing experience and equipment. Professional, well-equipped sportfishing charter boats are mainly restricted to areas in and around Jakarta, although new operations are springing up all the time.

All the usual tropical sportfishing species inhabit Indonesia waters, but some areas are better known for certain species than others. Although fishing takes place year-round, it is best just before and just after the rainy season.

Billfish thrive throughout Indonesia; these include black marlin, blue marlin, striped marlin, and sailfish, often in huge numbers. Swordfish are not caught by angling, but they are the most common billfish caught by local handliners! Black marlin are generally small throughout Indonesia; 20- to 25-kilogram fish are common. The current Indonesian record is a 169-kilogram black from Pelabuhan Ratu, and a similar-size fish was caught at Ujung Kulon. Commercially caught black marlin that would push the 450-kilogram mark have been reported from the fish market. Sailfish average 25 to 30 kilograms, but some up to 60 kilograms have been caught.

Several varieties are available, including yellowfin tuna, dogtooth tuna, skipjack tuna, mackerel tuna, frigate mackerel, and occasionally bonito. Yellowfins are big; a 73-kilogram fish was caught at Pelabuhan Ratu and a 71-kilogram tuna at Ujung Kulon. Ambon and Banda have produced bigger ones that remain undocumented and unclaimed, but these locations may hold some specimens over 90 kilograms. Dogtooth tuna run to 36 kilograms.

Wahoo, narrowbarred mackerel *(tenggiri),* and barracuda are common; barracuda are known to reach at least 20 kilograms, whereas the others have been caught to 32 kilograms and may be larger in eastern Indonesia. Giant trevally are huge and plentiful. Several species of sharks are available. Mahimahi (dolphin) are a common catch. Smaller species include rainbow runner, bluefin trevally, bigeye trevally, and a variety of bottom fish.

Western and Southern Islands

Sumatra. Sumatra is bounded to the west by the Indian Ocean and to the east by the shallower waters of the Java Sea and the Malacca Straits. Northern Sumatra juts into the Andaman Sea. Off the west coast is an archipelago chain, of which the largest and most accessible island is Pulau Nias.

Charter operations consisting of longboats exist in some of the more popular tourist destinations. Pulau Nias is one of these, as it is quite famous for excellent surfing. Sumatra has numerous regional airports; the international facility at Medan is the biggest.

Lake Toba in the Barisian Mountains is a popular and prominent tourist destination about 180 kilometers south of Medan. Covering 1,145 square kilometers, Toba is the largest lake in Indonesia; it features steep mountain cliffs, sandy beaches, and large Samosir Island. The freshwater angling potential here and throughout this island is poorly documented, but its numerous ponds and lakes contain the ubiquitous carp and catfish.

Blue water sportfishing is confined to the west and north of Sumatra, where there is deep water close inshore. Black marlin and sailfish have been recorded in many parts, and yellowfin tuna, dogtooth tuna, wahoo, narrowbarred mackerel, giant trevally, mahimahi, and barracuda, together with a host of smaller species, can all be expected. Fishing is best in October, November, April, and May, before and after the rainy season.

Eastern Sumatra has much shallower water and extensive mangroves and tidal inlets. Mangrove jacks, queenfish, barramundi, threadfin salmon, and various species of trevally are present in these waterways, but they are heavily fished, trapped, and netted, as Sumatra is heavily populated. Because the banks are largely inaccessible, casting lures from small boats is the only way to gain access to much of this fishing.

Java. Java is the population center of Indonesia and consequently the most accessible and most explored of the islands. Facilities here are good, and there is a thriving sportfishing community. Jakarta has good tackle shops, and most equipment is readily available.

Freshwater fishing opportunities are limited to managed ponds and lakes where carp and catfish are stocked, although Java does have several rivers.

Saltwater fishing, however, has a strong following. The local marinas have their share of modern yachts, but not many are rigged for sportfishing and none are available for charter. Limited sportfishing centers exist here, but some of these do have sportfishing fly-bridge cruisers—with twin diesel engines, full electronics, and good tackle—for charter. Elsewhere, the common and cheap outboard-powered longboat is the standard for Indonesian charter operations.

Carita, on the west coast of Java, is probably the best equipped of these centers, and charter operations here fish the waters around the remote and beautiful Ujung Kulon Peninsula. Carita is an easy two-hour drive from Jakarta and is consequently very popular with visitors and residents alike.

Ujung Kulon is situated on the southwestern tip of Java. To the south lie the waters of the Indian Ocean, to the northwest is Sumatra, and between Ujung Kulon and Sumatra lie the waters of the Sunda Strait. This is a major seaway leading north to Jakarta and Singapore, and it is here one finds the famous Krakatau volcano. Ujung Kulon Peninsula, a national park and world heritage site, is one of the last strongholds of the Javan rhino.

Ujung Kulon offers an almost endless variety of terrain and angling opportunity. The waters are virtually untapped and have tremendous light tackle potential. The Indian Ocean is very deep close to shore, with steep underwater dropoffs down to the Java Trench. These are some of the deepest and least explored waters in the world. The coastline varies from steep cliffs and rocky headlands with deep water very close in, to sandy beaches with big rolling surf, coral reef fringes, sheltered bays and flats, and mangrove swamps.

Many tropical sportfishing species inhabit Ujung Kulon. Techniques for catching these fish are wide ranging and include trolling with artificials, dead baits, and live baits; trolling with downriggers; kite fishing; casting poppers; jigging; drift fishing with live and dead baits; and bottom fishing. The best time to fish is just before and just after the rainy season, but angling remains good throughout the year—there isn't an off-season per se.

On the south coast, Pelabuhan Ratu, another prime Indonesian sportfishing location, is also a reasonably short drive from Jakarta. Pelabuhan

Fishing the rugged coast of Ujung Kulon.

Ratu is still serviced primarily by longboat operations, and you generally have to bring your own tackle. Boats launch from the beach, as the area lacks a good marina.

The same species are available here as in Ujung Kulon, but Pelabuhan Ratu carries a reputation for yellowfin tuna, which are both large and plentiful. Traditionally, these are caught after the rainy season in April and May, but they are available throughout the year. Like Ujung Kulon, Pelabuhan Ratu doesn't really have an off-season.

Bali. Bali is the main tourist center in Indonesia, and one of its main attractions is diving. Surprisingly, sportfishing is not well advanced, and few truly professional sportfishing operations exist. Charter boats are few as well. Commercial longline operations catch black, blue, and striped marlin from well offshore. Yellowfin tuna are also plentiful, again with the best time being before and after the rains in April, May, October, and November. The high and rocky coastline of southern Bali is home to some outsize giant trevally, which are caught by trolling or by casting big popper-style lures up to the rocks.

Lombok, Komodo, Flores, Sumba, and Sumbawa. The southern islands of Lombok, Komodo, Flores, Sumba, and Sumbawa are little known and little fished, but all have magnificent diving and varying standard accommodations. Sportfishing of any sort is not well documented, although those who have arranged for local boats and taken all their own gear with them say the fishery is excellent. Deep water lies close inshore, and some of these islands also have extensive bays, estuaries, and mangrove systems. The freshwater potential is unknown.

Eastern and Northern Islands

Timor. Timor is accessible through the city of Kupang, but it's a long and arduous flight. Although facilities are limited, guest houses and other accommodations are available. Timor even has limited "transient" charter operations in Kupang, but travelers are advised to expect nothing and carry everything they need. The fishing has been documented as excellent by pioneering Indonesian anglers, and marlin are reportedly common. Boats equipped to catch them, however, are generally nonexistent.

Kalimantan. Kalimantan is yet another little-known, little-fished Indonesian site. Access to the island is through Balikpapan on the east coast. Kalimantan boasts Indonesia's largest rivers, which include the Mahakam, Martapura, and Barito, which originate in the mountains and course through extensive swampy lowlands along the coast. The eastern coastline is dominated by the Mahakam Delta, a huge tidal deltaic complex northeast of Balikpapan. The freshwater and estuary fishing potential is undocumented, but rumor has it that numerous sailfish frequent the waters offshore of the delta mouth.

Farther north, deep blue water predominates, and the fishing consists of marlin, sailfish, wahoo, dogtooth tuna, yellowfin tuna, narrowbarred mackerel, barracuda, sharks, and giant trevally. Access to these waters is difficult due to the lack of suitable boats for charter.

The rest of Kalimantan is unexplored by anglers; however Brunei, which is north of Kalimantan and surrounded by the Malaysian portion of the island, is rapidly establishing a reputation as a superb light tackle fishery for small black marlin. Anglers are just beginning to explore the potential of the South China Sea and the Natuna Sea. Early reports are that the fishing looks good.

Sulewasi (Celebes). Sulewasi can be reached via Ujung Pandang in the south and Manado in the north. Ujung Pandang is relatively commercial, so transfer flights are available to many places in Eastern Indonesia, as are flights to the international airports at Jakarta and Bali.

Manado is tourist oriented and offers excellent facilities catering mainly to divers who come for the superb wall-diving and famed 150-foot underwater visibility. Manado also has a thriving tuna industry based around the yellowfin tuna, which is commercially harvested from a large number of simple fish aggregation devices (FADs) installed by the fishermen themselves. Sportfishing is unexplored.

Ambon. Ambon is famous for its big yellowfin tuna. Deep water is close wherever you fish, and dropoffs and canyons are within a stone's throw of shore. Commercial operations are numerous, and the locals traditionally handline for tuna.

Sportfishing is largely confined to trolling large floating and diving minnow-style plugs for yellowfin tuna, but also available are dogtooth tuna, giant trevally, narrowbarred mackerel, and wahoo. Big black marlin and blue marlin must surely be available, but only a few charter operations exist, and these are restricted to longboats with outboard motors for strictly inshore work.

Although anglers fishing takes place year-round, the catch is likely to be best in October, November, April, and May—before and after the rainy season.

Banda. A small cluster of volcanic islands jutting out from very deep water in the Banda Sea, the Banda Islands are reached by a short flight from Ambon. The waters around Banda hold monster-size yellowfin tuna, which are caught by visiting anglers trolling mainly with big minnow plugs. Other fish are also available, and there must be huge marlin following the bait schools.

The water is extremely deep close to shore, and the wall diving is justifiably world famous. Resorts are of varying standards, and boats are few and cater mainly to divers. There are no sportfishing charter operations in the Banda Islands. The tuna fishing is best from October through December, when large numbers are present. They are normally accompanied by vast schools of spinner dolphin—a dead giveaway for the tuna. The locals fish for them with

Fishing tackle manufacturer Zebco used to be known as the Zero Hour Bait Company when it made electric time bombs for drilling oil wells.

live baits and handlines. For deep-feeding fish, they use an ingenious system of wrapping a rock in a banana leaf hooked onto the bait. When the bait has reached the desired depth, a sharp jerk on the line releases the leaf and suspends a free-lined bait.

Irian Jaya.   Irian Jaya is the Indonesian half of New Guinea and adjoins Papua New Guinea. It faces the Pacific Ocean on its northern side, with deep water and precipitous dropoffs very close to shore; the southern side faces the Arafura Sea and is shallower water, with bays, estuaries, and extensive mangrove swamps. Inland are jungle highlands with clear fast-flowing streams. Some 30 rivers course through Irian Jaya from the central mountains, including the 400-kilometer-long Baliem, which flows to the Arafura and along which live various native tribes.

This area is largely unexplored by anglers, but the superb salt- and freshwater fishing known to exist in Papua New Guinea is hardly likely to stop at the border. Although the potential of Irian Jaya is therefore enormous, the area is inaccessible and has no infrastructure. No guided services or charter boats operate here and, of course, with the exception of Jakarta, there are no tackle shops.

Species to expect in the west of Irian Jaya include blue and black marlin, sailfish, yellowfin tuna, bigeye tuna, dogtooth tuna, skipjack tuna, wahoo, narrowbarred mackerel, giant trevally, barracuda, mahimahi, and various sharks. To the east in the bays and estuaries are narrowbarred mackerel, cobia, giant trevally, golden trevally, queenfish, barracuda, and various inshore sharks. In the mangroves, species include barramundi and mangrove jacks, together with possibly Niugini bass. In the unknown waters of the rivers, Niugini bass and spot-tail bass are likely residents.

INFLATABLE BOAT

A modest amount of fishing, usually in remote locations, is done from inflatable boats, which are lightweight collapsible craft with inflatable pontoonlike sides and bow, powered by a small-horsepower outboard motor. Inflatable boats are usually in the 10- or 12-foot range and are quiet, seaworthy, and durable. They are lacking in stability for most anglers; standing and casting in an inflatable boat without a deck or floor is akin to standing on a waterbed. This can be improved if the boat is outfitted with a full-frame marine-grade plywood floor or deck, but this increases the weight and thwarts portability. Inflatable boats have a shallow draft, but a flat bottom makes them pound in rough water and all gear inside is subjected to open storage. Some inflatable boats have been equipped by manufacturers with rod racks, a bow electric motor bracket, and other accessories, and creative anglers have outfitted them even more elaborately. Though rugged, they are not highly favored by avid anglers.
See: Boat.

INLET

A tributary mouth to a lake or the sea, primarily the latter; an entry point to the sea from a bay, harbor, or estuary. An inlet is primarily the area that connects a safe harbor to a large bay or the open ocean. It often has one or more jetties *(see)* at the mouth; may have been dredged to allow passage of large ocean-going vessels; and has many characteristics of harbors *(see)*, estuaries *(see)*, and marshes *(see)* or wetlands *(see)*.

Inlets are strongly influenced by current, primarily tides in saltwater, and usually receive the outflow of marshes. Bars, channels, cuts between channels or creeks, deep holes, and jetties are prime fishing locations, especially jetties, which have a significant amount of usually channelized flow when the tide is moving. Breakwalls, bridges, piers, docks, and power plant discharge areas are all man-made structures that may provide good fishing as well.
See: Jetty Fishing.

IN-LINE SPINNER
See: Spinner.

INSECT REPELLENT
See: First Aid.

INSECTS
Insects are among the most numerous of all animals and have very diverse forms and habitat. As a food source for trout species, aquatic and terrestrial insects are considered paramount, although they are also a very important food source for the adults and the juveniles, in particular, of many other freshwater species.
See: Aquatic Insects; Terrestrial Insects.

INSHORE

The waters from the shallower part of the continental shelf toward shore. In saltwater fishing parlance, inshore is a loose and variable term referring to that portion of the water from which land is visible or is nearly visible, usually on the shoreward side of major currents or shelves, and populated by nonpelagic species. This term is seldom used by freshwater lake anglers.
See: Inshore Fishing; Nearshore.

INSHORE BOAT
See: Sportfishing Boat.

INSHORE FISHING
Fishing Coastal Estuaries, Rivers, Bays, and Nearshore Ocean Waters
The term "inshore" is a generic one used by anglers to refer to coastal marine areas. Although the spot

where inshore ends and offshore *(see)* begins is not strictly defined, in general inshore fishing refers to angling from a boat for resident and migratory species in estuaries, rivers, bays, and nearshore ocean waters, whereas offshore fishing refers to blue-water fishing for pelagic species.

Inshore environs may be fished from a variety of craft: cartop boats and canoes, outboard-powered rental rowboats and skiffs, a wide array of medium-size runabouts, center console and walk-around cuddy cabin boats, and even cruisers and large sportfishing boats. Anglers also have the option of inshore fishing from party boats *(see),* which sail daily to pursue a wide variety of species.

Inshore waters are popular for many reasons. Chief among these is the limited travel time required to reach the fishing grounds, which makes short outings feasible and facilitates a swift return to port for any reason, particularly stormy weather.

Of course, another reason is that inshore waters hold a variety of popular gamefish and bottom feeders. Coastal estuaries, generally identified as the area where the tide line meets the river current, are the spawning grounds and, in turn, the nursery areas for many species. Estuarine environs provide a delicate balance of water conditions favored by many marine species, and they are also suitable for a few freshwater species that are comfortable living in water of nominal salinity.

Some anglers travel great distances in pursuit of their favorite gamefish and bottom feeders while overlooking fine inshore fishing close to home. Inshore waters often hold an abundance and variety of species to satisfy the most discriminating angler with a fine catch.

Tackle.   Inshore fishing is suitable to a variety of angling methods. Even though drift and bottom fishing with bait may be the most popular methods overall, inshore anglers have opportunities to cast and jig for various species, troll for some species, and, in certain cases, stalk and sight-fish for their quarry. This wide variety opens up the game for many different types of equipment and approaches.

Generally, however, inshore fishing is well suited to light tackle. The waters are protected and usually not very deep, and inshore species for the most part are relatively small, although heavyweight specimens of such species as striped bass, bluefish, snook, tarpon, redfish, salmon, and halibut can test the angler's tackle and skill.

For maximum enjoyment, the choice of tackle should be appropriate to the species sought, so that the angler isn't handicapped by tackle that is too light or too heavy. Those fishing out of private boats have more latitude in gear selection and more opportunities to use lighter equipment than those fishing out of party boats, where maneuverability is less and where more people of differing skill levels have to be accommodated.

Conventional tackle is popular with many inshore anglers; a light- or medium-weight casting or popping rod, $5^1/_2$ to 6 feet long and coupled with a levelwind reel loaded with 150 yards of 10- to 15-pound-test line, is ideal for this type of fishing in most locations. It's well suited to casting artificials, drifting natural baits, chumming, and bottom fishing.

Spinning tackle has some following, although less than conventional tackle, and is more likely to be used for shallow water situations, for casting activities, and for smaller species. Lighter outfits, as opposed to the heavy ones employed in surf fishing *(see),* are best for most applications. Rods that are $5^1/_2$ to $6^1/_2$ feet long, capable of handling lures or rigs ranging from a half ounce through $1^1/_2$ ounces, are ideal for most inshore fishing, coupled with a reel that holds at least 150 yards of 8- to 15-pound-test line. For some inshore fishing, like casting light jigs and small plugs or soft plastics, you can use a lighter weight outfit, like a $6^1/_2$- to 7-foot rod and a reel that holds 6- to 10-pound line.

In saltwater inshore fishing, it's usually better to use a line that is on the heavier side rather than one on the lighter side to reduce the attrition rate of lures and terminal rigs, which often become snagged while drifting or casting. Within reason, line diameter (which often correlates to strength) is not a major factor in most inshore fishing, except in shallow, clear water situations where a lighter, thinner line is less likely to spook the fish and call attention to the lures or bait.

Though less common than either conventional or spinning gear, flycasting tackle is effective on the inshore scene for some species and in certain environs (it is good, for example, for shallow water striped bass but not for deep bottom feeders). Eight-, 9-, and 10-weight outfits are used depending on the species (lighter for bonefish and redfish, for example, and heavier for striped bass and tarpon). The reel needs ample backing for those fish that are likely to make serious runs, and a variety of fly patterns, mainly large streamers, are used in bays, rivers, and the open ocean.

Primary Species and Tactics

The following briefly reviews the primary inshore species and the most popular methods of fishing for them along the Atlantic, Gulf, and Pacific coasts of North America. Not all fishing tactics and opportunities can be mentioned here; nevertheless, the traveling angler far from familiar waters will often find conditions very close to those in home environs and will be able to use favorite tackle to enjoy good sport as well as some fine-eating fish.

Northeastern flounder.   The rock-studded coastline of Maine offers hundreds of rivers and bays that empty into the Atlantic. Many have mud, sand, or pebble bottom where winter flounder take up residence. By anchoring on mud flats or along channel edges and chumming with a mixture of ground clams or crushed mussels sent to the bottom in a chum pot, these tasty flatfish are quickly attracted within range.

Small No. 8 or 9 Chestertown or Wide Gap hooks baited with sandworms or bloodworms readily bring strikes from flounder, and sometimes harbor pollock or small codfish are caught on the same rigs, although most are immature fish that should be immediately released.

Much the same scene is repeated along the Massachusetts, Connecticut, Long Island, and New Jersey coasts. The difference is, instead of a rock-studded coastline, many barrier islands, with broad bays separating them from the mainland, provide an abundance of winter flounder for fine action each spring and again in the fall.

Atlantic mackerel. The Atlantic mackerel summers in the inshore waters of Maine, often traveling in schools that number in the tens of thousands. While mostly found in the close-to-shore ocean waters, they'll often invade large coastal bays as they search for food. These provide fine light tackle sport and will strike tiny diamond jigs, bucktails, or tube teasers. Flies worked with a sinking line will often draw strikes until the angler's arm is weary.

These same mackerel, averaging three-quarters of a pound to 3 pounds, usually winter off the Virginia Capes and provide boat anglers with fine action as they move north to the Maritime Provinces for the summer and then return again in early winter. They're fun to catch and especially well suited to newcomers and youngsters; when you get into a school, the action is often fast and furious, and a great deal of skill isn't required.

East Coast stripers and bluefish. It would be difficult to determine whether striped bass or bluefish are the most popular inshore gamefish along the Middle and North Atlantic coasts. Both species frequent the same inshore waters and are regularly targeted by anglers casting or trolling artificials, chumming, bottom fishing, drifting, and jigging.

Most of the stripers and blues that migrate north to New England have achieved respectable size.

Inshore waters that provide good fishing opportunity include estuary environs such as this marsh area in Chesapeake Bay, Virginia.

Many smaller fish are encountered along their midrange of Long Island and south to New Jersey and through the Chesapeake Bay area. Many of the youngsters of both clans spend their first few seasons in the bays, rivers, and creeks near where they were hatched. The inshore nursery grounds have an abundance of grass shrimp, spearing, sand launce, and other forage to satisfy their ravenous appetites.

Some of the fish are small but provide fine catch-and-release sport for anglers armed with light outfits. Both species are readily caught on plugs, plastic-tailed and bucktail-dressed leadheads, metal jigs, and streamer flies.

Inshore party boat fishing for both stripers and blues is popular throughout their range, because it enables anglers to catch trophy fish with minimal cost. The most popular technique for catching bass and blues is using a diamond or slab-sided chromed jig, with a plastic or feather teaser 18 to 24 inches ahead of it. The schools are often mixed, with stripers on or near the bottom and bluefish closer to the surface.

Party boats use their sonar to locate the schools and then drift over them. Jigging is accomplished by lowering the rig to the bottom and retrieving to the surface. As a rule, a slow retrieve concentrated near the bottom gets strikes from the stripers and a fast, jigging retrieve gets action from the blues near the surface.

Tautog, sea bass, and porgies. Bottom feeders like tautog, black sea bass, and porgies are plentiful in inshore waters along the Middle Atlantic. They're found around most broken, irregular bottom, particularly rock ledges and artificial fishing reefs, and frequent these areas because of abundant food and sanctuary from predatory species.

The most popular technique for catching all three of these bottom dwellers is to use a high-low rig, employing a pair of hooks snelled to 12- to 18-inch leader. Virginia, Sproat, Claw, or Beak style hooks are most popular. Use a No. 8 or 10 hook for porgies, which often average from less than a pound to over 2 pounds, and a No. 4 or 6 hook for the generally larger sea bass. With tautog it's a matter of where you're fishing; in open ocean waters where they range in weight from 3 to 6 pounds or more, Nos. 2, 1, and even 1/0 hooks are preferred.

Small pieces of conch, clam, squid, or seaworm are preferred baits for porgies and sea bass, while tautog prefer green crabs and fiddler crabs, although they'll take the aforementioned baits as well.

This is relaxing fishing; simply find some structure, such as artificial reefs or rockpiles or mussel beds in bays and the open ocean, and anchor your boat so it is positioned directly above the structure. All three species stick very close to the structure; if you're positioned even just a few feet away from the structure over sand bottom, you're apt to not catch a thing.

Once anchored, bait up, using sufficient sinker weight on your rig to hold bottom, lowering the rig

I

to the bottom and waiting for strikes. All three have notorious reputations as bait stealers, so be alert and lift back smartly with your rod tip at the first tug on the bait.

Weakfish and seatrout. The weakfish is a darling of inshore anglers when plentiful because it grows to over 10 pounds, provides a variety of angling opportunities, and is excellent table fare. Caught from New England through the Chesapeake Bay area, the species is also found in numbers through the Carolinas. From Virginia south, the spotted weakfish, locally called trout or seatrout, becomes more prevalent and is found throughout the inshore waters of Georgia and Florida, and up the Gulf Coast of Florida and across through Texas. The only major difference in appearance is the large black spots that are prominent on the backs of the spotted weaks.

The techniques, habitat, and feeding patterns of these species are very similar, and in some places you may catch both in a day's outing. Both are creatures of habit and tend to be lazy when seeking a meal. As a result, they're easily attracted to a chum line of their favorite food, which includes the tiny grass shrimp so plentiful in coastal bays and rivers, as well as the larger shrimp that are targeted as table fare.

The technique of chumming *(see)* for weakfish and seatrout doesn't vary much along the many miles of Atlantic and Gulf Coasts that weakfish and seatrout frequent. They spend much of their time in the shallow reaches of bays and rivers, moving

A small weakfish comes aboard within sight of a New Jersey beach.

across eelgrass and weedbeds where forage is abundant. Often the water on the shallow flats ranges from 3 to 6 feet deep.

Armed with 3 or 4 quarts of live grass shrimp or their larger culinary counterparts, you can easily seek out promising water and double anchor—to keep your boat steady and prevent it from swinging in the wind—and begin chumming.

Dribble only a few shrimp over the side at a time, allowing them to be carried away with the tide over the weedbeds. For larger shrimp, cut them into dime-size pieces and sparingly distribute them to establish a chum line that attracts the weakfish, but don't provide so much food that they hang well back to feed. You want to get them moving toward the source of the food.

Once the chum line is established, it's time to bait up. Tie a No. 1 or 2 Claw or Beak style hook with a bait-holder shank directly to the end of your nylon monofilament line. Bait up with three or four tiny grass shrimp, or use a small piece of a larger shrimp. Ease the baited hook into the water, and permit the current to carry it along, much the same as the current is carrying your chum. Once the bait has drifted off 40 to 60 feet, even more at times, simply reel in and repeat the procedure. Often the strikes will come from as close as a rod's length from the boat on out to the end of your drift. The key is keeping the bait moving naturally with the chum line.

If you're chumming in very shallow water and the weed growth is heavy, the baited hook may sink to the bottom and not drift properly, especially if there's little current. At such times an effective strategy is to add a float to the line so that your bait is suspended just above the level of the weeds. A small split shot or rubber-core sinker may be added to the line between the float and the hook, thus ensuring that it drifts along perpendicularly to the bottom.

Although plastic floats are popular, veteran weakfish anglers have found that a cork or plastic float with a scooped-out head, which emits a popping or gurgling sound as it is pulled through the water, attracts the attention of the fish more readily than an ordinary plastic or cork float.

You can also catch weakfish by working a tiny, quarter-ounce bucktail jig or soft-tailed jig through the chum line. Small swimming plugs work, too.

Drifting across open bottom often brings strikes on an ebbing tide when the weakfish vacate the shallows. At such times a high-low bottom rig with a pair of hooks snelled to a 12- to 18- inch leader works fine. Use a bank or dipsey style sinker of sufficient weight to effortlessly glide along the bottom. Shrimp, strips of squid, spearing, and live killies are effective baits.

Both species of weakfish often migrate as seasons change, and they do so by vacating the protected waters of estuaries, bays, and rivers and moving into the open reaches of the Atlantic Ocean and the Gulf. They travel in huge schools, often moving close to the bottom and feeding on baitfish. On these occasions they offer exciting opportunities to catch them on diamond jigs and teasers, bucktails, or natural baits drifted along the bottom.

Trolling with small plugs, bucktail jigs, or spoons takes many of both species, as the small-boat angler can cover a lot of water. Once a school is located, the troller can continue trolling the area or shut down the motor and drift and jig over the fish.

Southern flatfish. Although weakfish are the darlings of many anglers along a really long stretch of coastline, the summer flounder and its cousin the southern flounder are two of the most popular species sought in much the same range.

Both summer and southern flounder spend a lot of time in the shallow environs of bays and estuaries, and they inhabit open reaches of the Atlantic and Gulf, generally close to shore. However, they often frequent humps or high bottom locations several miles from shore, especially when forage species are plentiful at these sites.

Unlike sea bass, porgies, and tautog, which stick close to structure, summer and southern flounder move about while searching for a meal and are aggressive bottom feeders. They typically forage over sandy bottom, where their backs take on the color of the bottom over which they're traveling. This chameleon-like characteristic is very pronounced, with light sandy color when frequenting light bottom, with mottled or spotted brown and beige tones when over gravel or pebbly bottom, and with dark chocolate brown when feeding over mud bottom.

When resting, flounder usually lie on the bottom and use their fins to partially cover themselves with sand or mud. If a cold snap develops, which is not to their liking, they will lie on the bottom for days without moving about or feeding. At such times the mud will actually stick to their undersides; if you catch one shortly after it emerges from the mud, it will still carry a light covering of the mud on its otherwise snow white bottom.

As flounder rest on the bottom, their eyes extend upward, always alert for an unsuspecting baitfish, shrimp, or crab that happens by. They're extremely fast and will engulf the prey in an instant. As a result of this trait, successful flounder anglers find drifting to be the most successful fishing technique. Although chumming does produce strikes from flounder, as does fishing at anchor, you'll catch more flatfish if you leave the boat unanchored and cover known flounder grounds while drifting at the mercy of the current or wind.

Light tackle is ideal when seeking flounder inshore; however, in more open waters, where you may fish in 25- to 50-foot depths, somewhat heavier gear is appropriate.

The most popular flatfish rig is a simple setup with a small three-way swivel. Tie one end of the swivel directly to your line. To another end tie a 30- to 36-inch leader of 20-pound test, and then snell a No. 1/0 through 3/0 Carlisle, Beak, Claw, or Wide Gap hook to that. To the remaining end of the swivel, tie a 6- to 8-inch piece of monofilament line with a loop in the end of it; slip a dipsey or bank style sinker of sufficient weight to hold the bottom onto the loop.

The summer flounder, popularly called fluke through much of its range, feeds on a wide variety of forage species, including sand eels, spearing, crabs, shrimp, squid, and the young of almost every species in residence. All of these may be used as hook baits. Perhaps the most popular bait is the saltwater killie, or mummichog; it is quickly taken by the hungry flatfish when it is fished live and hooked through the lips and drifted along the bottom.

Redfish. Channel bass, often called redfish, are a formidable target of anglers fishing inshore waters from the Virginia Capes south through Florida and across the Gulf Coast. Often called the southern counterpart to the striped bass, they frequent much the same waters and have very similar habits.

Perhaps the most exciting method of catching redfish is to sight-cast to them as they travel in schools just beyond the surf line off the Atlantic coast during spring. This is also done in Gulf waters and in the backcountry, where schools of a hundred or more redfish may be encountered.

A hammered stainless-steel jig is one of the most popular lures for enticing strikes when the fish are on the move. Schools present themselves in different ways. In open ocean waters, they often appear as a huge dark shadow or dark area while they cruise along, whereas in the shallows of bays and estuaries, their movement often disturbs the surface as the tightly packed schools mill about.

The key is positioning your boat upcurrent from the school and permitting wind or current to move you within casting range. Don't approach too closely while motoring in because you may spook the school. Once positioned, place your cast so it goes beyond and ahead of the fish; then work the lure back toward the school. Properly presented, the spoon draws quick strikes. Bucktail jigs and their plastic-tailed counterparts, swimming plugs, and small spoons all prove effective in this exciting inshore sport.

Not to be overlooked are opportunities to catch redfish on live shrimp, spot, pinfish, or grunts, or to troll for them using spoons. Much fishing for reds is done by seeking and casting to small groups or individuals in the shallows of bays, where they are feeding. These fish are often caught by stalking and making presentations to individual fish, especially with soft-tailed jigs. When the wind is blowing and the water is too deep to spot fish, blind casting can be effective with the same lures, with shallow-running plugs, and with shrimp bait.

Bonefish, tarpon, and permit. Bonefish, tarpon, and permit are among the most prized fish of inshore environs. Although they are usually associated with flats fishing (see) and sight-casting activities, they may also be caught in the bays and in the

I

deeper holes of near-shore waters by using methods suited to fishing for nonvisible fish. All three of these species are caught by a variety of techniques, including live baitfishing at anchor, drift fishing, and in some cases deep jigging.

Unquestionably the most challenging, exciting, and popular technique is to pole across the shallow flats and sight-cast to the fish as they move through water barely deep enough to cover their backs. All flats travelers are spooky, and care must be exercised to avoid approaching too closely. This entails poling until a fish is sighted and then positioning yourself and waiting until the fish moves within range. In some cases, mainly for bonefish on the shallowest flats, you can wade into position and cast to a fish slowly feeding across a flat.

Bonefish are fairly plentiful and, though generally traveling alone, they do sometimes gather in small pods and even schools. Many anglers employ a single live shrimp on a 1/0 Beak style hook and cast just ahead of the cruising fish. Tiny jigs also bring strikes, and fly fishing has become more popular. Permit are sometimes encountered on the flats, and they present a formidable challenge because of their wariness, greater size, and fast speed. Permit are also caught on shrimp; they can be taken on flies, although fly fishing for permit is more difficult than it is for bonefish. The most common offering is a small, live crab.

Tarpon are a particularly good fly fishing species when they cruise the flats; they, too, may take shrimp and crab baits. In the channels between flats and islands, they are popularly caught on live mullet or pinfish. Fishing for big tarpon in such renowned areas as Key West and Boca Grande Pass in Florida, and the many passes emptying into the Gulf of Mexico all the way to Texas, is usually a baitfishing proposition. Live crabs, pinfish, grunts, mullet, squirrel fish, and other small species are drifted through the area frequented by the tarpon, which move with the tides searching for a meal. Frequently, large pods of feeding tarpon are encountered on the surface and may be caught by casting a live bait to the cruising fish.

Grouper and snapper.   Many species of grouper and snapper are popular with inshore anglers from the Carolinas to Texas. They're found on nearly every patch of rock bottom, on myriad coral reefs, and around every shipwreck and ledge where food is abundant.

Inshore small boat anglers fishing these various structures employ a variety of techniques for snapper and grouper. Anchoring and chumming adjacent to and above the structure is very effective for yellowtail snapper and porgies. Fishing live baits in the depths is also productive, particularly with big black grouper, red grouper, mutton snapper, and red snapper. Bottom fishing with a high-low rig produces all bottom dwellers.

An especially enjoyable method of catching all of these species is to drift and deep-jig the reef with bucktail jigs or plastic-bodied leadheads. When there is deep water and swift current or strong wind, you may need to use jigs weighing from 1 to 4 ounces in order to reach the bottom; then keep the jig perpendicular to the bottom as you retrieve.

Schools of grouper and snapper are located by cruising the reef areas and employing sonar. Once fish are located, simply position the boat so that the current or wind will carry you over the fish and away from the reef. In this way, as fish are hooked you'll be drifting to deeper water or away from obstructions.

All grouper and snapper are fast. Make no mistake about it. As a result, an effective method of working your jig is to let it settle to the bottom, then quickly lift your rod tip so that the jig darts toward the surface, and continue reeling and jigging until it reaches the surface. If a strike isn't received, drop it back down and continue jigging and retrieving.

This strategy requires tackle rated at 20 pounds or heavier. Fish that weigh 15 to 50 pounds or more will often break free with little effort if you're using light line. Fish a firm drag; as soon as a fish is hooked, lift back smartly and work hard to get the fish up and away from the bottom. Once a grouper turns back to the coral, it can rip line from your reel and instantly cut you off.

Bonus inshore catches are possible when you're deep-jigging the reefs. This includes species like jack crevalle, king mackerel, wahoo, Spanish and cero mackerel, dolphin, barracuda, and little tunny.

Cobia.   Cobia are still another great inshore gamefish that provide sterling action. Found in nominal quantities along the Atlantic coast from the Carolinas south, they really come into their own along the Gulf Coast, where they're apt to be found cruising around channel markers, buoys, docks, and anchored boats.

Although cobia are found out in the open Gulf where they cruise among the anchored shrimp boats culling their catch, the greatest numbers are inshore residents and found in most every bay and pass. One of the two most popular methods of catching them is anchoring in a pass and using a sliding-egg sinker rig on the bottom with a live pinfish or grunt as bait. The second, more exciting, approach is to cruise the passes, visiting buoys, channel markers, and dock areas; once a cobia is spotted, cast to it. Bucktail jigs and swimming plugs all bring strikes, but a live baitfish hooked just beneath the dorsal fin and cast within range of a hungry cobia will quickly bring an exciting surface strike. Many cobia top the 30-pound mark along the Gulf Coast, so here you need heavier gear than what is customarily used for inshore fishing, with 20-pound-class spinning or casting tackle preferred.

Pacific kelp fishing.   The Southern California coast has a great variety of gamefish and bottom feeders that are a challenge to catch and a welcome addition to the dinner table. Some of the most enjoyable inshore action is had while fishing waters adjoining the kelp beds. The kelp can best be described as a giant tree growing up from the bottom, its big, thick willowy branches adorned with huge leaves. Unlike green seaweed of the Atlantic coast, which is carried along by the current, the Pacific coast kelp, which is a brown seaweed, grows in huge beds and is stationary for the most part. The limbs of the kelp are often as thick as a man's arm, and the leaves are several feet long by a foot or more in width. This mass of kelp provides sanctuary for anchovies, sardines, and a host of small fish and the fry of others, all of which often satisfy the appetites of bigger game.

Chumming is a popular method of fishing the kelp beds. After leaving dockside, boats stop at a bait barge located in most coastal harbors and take aboard a supply of several scoops of anchovies, sardines, or mackerel to be employed both as chum and hook baits. Private and charter boats generally anchor just off from the kelp beds, positioning the boat so that anglers are sufficiently close to cast their baits near to the kelp, or to permit the current to carry the lively baits along the edge of the kelp.

Because tiny anchovies and other small baitfish are the favored bait, anglers prefer a rod with a delicate tip action, one that can softly cast a bait weighing a fraction of an ounce a fair distance from the boat. Correspondingly light lines are used, often only 12- to 15-pound test, with either a conventional or a spinning reel.

The most popular technique is to swim a tiny anchovy bait, hooked lightly through the gill collar or lips with a small No. 1 or 2 fine wire hook, tied directly to the monofilament line. As the bait swims along, often swiftly heading for the sanctuary of the kelp, other anchovies are tossed out sparingly to attract but not feed the fish.

The key is to have the reel in freespool or the bail open and let the bait keep moving. It struggles to get into the kelp, thus attracting the fish that are cruising along the perimeter searching for a meal.

There is no mistaking a strike; in fact, you know it's coming. As a big fish approaches, the tiny baitfish senses the predator and furiously tries to avoid capture. When you feel the bait get excited, you know that in an instant you'll receive a runoff as the bigger fish inhales the helpless anchovy. Here it's important to keep your rod tip in a lowered position, with the tip pointed in the direction the line is moving. In the instant that the line moves off quickly, engage your gear or close the bail, and lift back smartly to set the hook. With the fine wire hook, which is necessary because of the delicate baits, you just set the hook once, as repeated strikes may rip the hook free or spring it open.

You must maintain sufficient pressure on the fish so that it can't reach the kelp. If it does, the line often becomes fouled and you won't be able to work the fish back to the boat. Usually the combination of the line becoming fouled and the fish pulling on it strongly will break the line.

In this kind of fishing, you never know which species will take your bait, because there is variety galore cruising along the kelp searching for a meal. Pacific barracuda and Pacific bonito are two of the most popular, although somewhat smaller, of the targeted species. Pacific yellowtail and white seabass also call this habitat home and are among the prized catches. Kelp bass readily inhale a lively anchovy fished tight to the kelp.

Bottom fishing along the kelp also brings results. Although chumming usually entices strikes from fish that move through the midrange and surface layers, you can often score down on the bottom, too. When the other species mentioned aren't cooperating, many anglers add a weight to their lines, sending the bait right down to the bottom for sand bass, California corbina, or Pacific halibut.

Silver and king salmon. Inshore anglers have opportunities for silver salmon and king salmon off Northern California, where the time-proven technique of using cannonball sinkers to get anchovy baits down to the fish proves most popular. Most of the party boats use cast-iron breakaway cannonballs, often weighing up to 3 pounds. However, many small boats employ downriggers to send their attractors and anchovy- or herring-baited hooks down to the level of the salmon.

This angling takes place in open waters not far from shore, and finding fish is of tantamount importance. At times, slow trolling for the big salmon is fast and furious. Frequently, though, you have to put in the time, searching with sonar for schools of baitfish and, once they're located, systematically slow-trolling the area until the bigger signals, indicating salmon, show up on the screen. When the season gets underway, the fish are usually concentrated, with the professional party and charter boats communicating daily and zeroing in on the fish, and smaller boaters working the same areas.

Rockfish and lingcod. The many species of rockfish that inhabit the cold Pacific waters from the Golden Gate north to Oregon and Washington are among the tastiest fish these waters have to offer, and are regularly sought by inshore bottom anglers. While they are caught well offshore in deep habitats, sufficient numbers are found inshore wherever the bottom is broken and with irregular rocks. Drifting chunk baits using a basic high-low rig with sufficient weight to hold bottom results in fast action when you locate a piece of choice underwater terrain. Small boat anglers will often drop a marker buoy once a productive area is located, and they will repeatedly drift over it. Another option, of course, is anchoring right above the productive spot.

Many consider lingcod to be the Pacific's finest eating species, and they are a favored target of small boat and party boat anglers in Oregon and Washington waters. Although lingcod are the favorite here, literally dozens of species of rockfish are also caught as a bonus, and live baits are favored for these. In fact, anglers who catch a small fish on the lingcod grounds will often bait up with it or will use live anchovies or sardines, with live baits usually providing best results.

Slack tides usually afford the best opportunity to hook lingcod, because it's easiest then to work a bait or lure straight down to the rocky, snaggy bottoms where this big predator is found; too much current or wind results in a flat line angle and constant hookups on the rocky bottom.

Metal slab jigs that imitate smaller fish work well, as do big leadhead jigs with soft plastic bodies or pork rind strips. Many bait anglers use herring, and live baits work much better than dead ones. The ultimate lingcod bait, though, is a live greenling, about 10 inches long, fished with a large, single hook through both lips to pin its mouth shut. Live bait anglers must use a sinker large enough to take the offering down but must exercise care in keeping it just off bottom, or the bait will dodge into a hole and become snagged before a lingcod finds it.

Lingcod also have a habit of diving for a rocky crevice when hooked, so anglers should try to turn them toward the surface and reel them as far off the bottom as possible after setting the hook. For this reason, many anglers use rather stout tackle for lingcod, including stiff boat rods; large, conventional reels; and low-stretch braided line of 40- to 80-pound test. A tough monofilament leader of 50-pound test or larger also helps avoid abrasions and breakoffs.

West Coast stripers.   The waters of the San Francisco Bay delta are home to striped bass of all sizes. The original stock came from New Jersey over a century ago and prospered; then the population was depleted, but it has rebounded to a point where Bay anglers now enjoy superb sport. Enjoyable striper fishing here occurs with light casting or spinning tackle, using plugs and bucktails along the many miles of marsh that border undeveloped areas of the bay. Increasing in popularity is fly fishing from small boats for predominately school stripers in the 2- to 10-pound class.

The world-renowned San Francisco Bay Bridge offers exciting striped bass action. The bridge's supporting tower in the water causes currents to swirl about it, often trapping baitfish and in turn attracting striped bass. The bridge is productive for small boat anglers, since the fish take up a feeding station there and become targets for casting bucktail jigs and deep-running plugs. Position your boat on the downcurrent side of the tower, and cast up into the swirling maelstrom of back eddies that are formed as the tide rushes along. Also try fishing the upcurrent area, where moving water is separated by the tower, resulting in a dead spot of minimal current where the stripers take up station to wait for food to be swept their way.

Northwest salmon and halibut.   Oregon and Washington anglers who fish the inshore grounds have a choice of seeking silver salmon or king salmon on the inshore grounds, or they can send their rigs down to the bottom for Pacific halibut.

Inshore trolling at the river mouths is very popular for catching all salmon species. This is very seasonal sport, with the runs of each species taking place at different times. Deep, fast water at river mouths and turbulent currents result in anglers having to employ conventional outfits rated for 20- to 30-pound line. Trolling whole herring baits has for years been a proven method of scoring with these great gamefish. Depending on tidal flow and water depth, the baits are run into the depths with the aid of heavy trolling sinkers or via downriggers. Using sonar both to locate fish and to ascertain the proper depth to troll is essential.

Its impressive size, relative abundance, and brute strength make the Pacific halibut, which is the largest member of the flatfish clan, a popular quarry from the southern Oregon coast northward. Younger, smaller halibut under 50 pounds comprise most of the sport catch along the Oregon, Washington, and southern British Columbia coasts, and fish in these areas tend to congregate in specific areas where food is abundant, especially near islands and over banks and humps. The large fish are farther north off northern British Columbia and especially Alaska.

The key to fishing halibut successfully is to get a bait or lure down to them and keep it there long enough for a fish to find it. Most anglers prefer to fish with bait, especially large herring. Squid, octopus, and belly skin off halibut or salmon, as well as whole cod, greenling, or other small bottom fish, also are effective baits. Bait is usually fished on a wire spreader or a sliding-sinker rig, with sinker size ranging from 4 ounces to 4 pounds, depending on depth, current, size of the bait, and line diameter. Bait hooks range from size 5/0 to 12/0, depending on size of the bait and size of the quarry; some anglers prefer traditional J style hooks, and others like commercial circle hooks. Halibut use their eyes, nose, and lateral line to locate a meal, so anglers often lift the bait well off the bottom to increase visibility and then drop it quickly to create a thumping vibration.

Heavy tackle is generally preferred for halibut fishing because of the weight of the objects fished, the depth, and the size of the fish possible. A 7-foot boat rod with a stiff action, equipped with 4/0 conventional reel, is standard. For shallow-water fishing, though, some anglers fish much lighter tackle, and deep monster chasers may go heavier. Light-tackle halibut anglers use line in the 15- to 50-pound-test range, but deep-water anglers go heavier.

See: *Individual states and provinces; individual species; Drift Fishing; Jigging.*

INTERMEDIATE LINE
A slow-sinking fly line.
See: Flycasting Tackle.

INTERNATIONAL GAME FISH ASSOCIATION

Known by the acronym IGFA, this nonprofit membership association was founded in 1939 primarily to establish ethical angling regulations and to serve as a central processing center for saltwater world record catch data. Today, it verifies and designates all freshwater and saltwater world record fish catches; creates and maintains the ethical standards and rules used in most fishing tournaments and for world record consideration; serves as an information source for the media, governments, scientists, and the general public; maintains an historical museum documenting the sport of fishing; has the world's largest, and most current, collection of angling literature; and is a leader in fisheries conservation issues.

The IGFA has more than 300 international representatives around the world. In 1999, it opened a stunning Hall of Fame and Fishing Museum complex and headquarters in Dania, Florida (near Ft. Lauderdale Airport), which houses its staff, historical collections, library, and other information; the center is open to the public and is especially notable for its interactive displays. Its E. K. Harry Library of Fishes, open to the public, has 13,000 books on angling, fish, and related subjects; thousands of past and current outdoor and fishing periodicals, films, and videos; the largest collection of historical fishing photographs in the world; and an array of historical artifacts. It publishes its own newsletter and an annual book, *World Record Game Fishes,* which, among other things, lists all current world records in every category and for every species for which records are maintained.

See: **Records.**

INTERTIDAL ZONE

The shallow area along shore and in an estuary between high- and low-water marks that is exposed at low tide and covered at high tide; also known as the littoral zone.

I/O

Acronym for Inboard/Outboard Motor and a boat powered with such motor.

See: **Boat; Sportfishing Boat.**

IOWA

When it comes to angling, this mostly agricultural state is sometimes overshadowed by its Minnesota and Wisconsin neighbors. Yet Iowa has some good fishing that is often overlooked. The fertile soils that grow Iowa's bountiful crops of corn and soybeans also help produce lunker walleye, chunky smallmouths, slab-sided panfish, scrappy trout, and some of the biggest muskies on the continent, not to mention the staple species:

Replicas of world record fish float in the air in the hall between galleries at the IGFA Hall of Fame and Fishing Museum.

channel catfish, largemouth bass, bluegills, and crappie. Improved farming practices and environmental programs—such as the federal Conservation Reserve Program that began in the 1980s—have reduced soil erosion, improved water quality, and boosted fishing.

Close-to-home angling opportunities, with lakes, rivers, and ponds within easy reach of nearly every resident, also make fishing a popular family recreation activity throughout Iowa. One in three Iowans fishes. But they're not elitists; they like action, and they like to eat what they catch.

Thus, channel catfish—prized for both action and table fare—are the most sought-after quarry in Iowa's rivers and lakes. Bass fishing is also extremely popular in Iowa, and the feisty largemouth bass ranks a close second in angler preference. Yet, as in many other states, Iowans take home more bluegills and crappie than any other species, proving their appreciation for a delectable skillet of panfish fillets, even if they don't land a wall hanger.

Natural Lakes

The glaciers that shaped Iowa's prime farmland also scooped out more than 30 natural lakes, totaling 33,000 acres, in northwest Iowa. Residents boast that these waters offer some of the state's best fishing. One of these is 5,700-acre Spirit Lake, the largest natural lake in the state. Spirit owns the Iowa muskie record of more than 45 pounds. Muskie anglers regularly catch and release 50-inch fish around Spirit's weedbeds.

In nearby West Okoboji, biologists confirm bass anglers' beliefs that this deep, clear lake is one of the best in the country for smallmouths. Probing the rock piles with live baits in the fall, smallmouth specialists take plenty of fish over 5 pounds, and most of the bass are released.

Spirit, West Okoboji, and East Okoboji Lakes produce a ton of walleye, too. Some walleye fanciers wade the shoreline on spring and fall nights, casting

I

crankbaits. Others troll with live baits or diving lures along weedlines in the summer. Ice anglers sometimes hit the jackpot with jigging spoons or minnows.

Clear, Storm, Black Hawk, and Lost Island Lakes, all of which are natural lakes in the northwest quadrant of Iowa, share walleye honors. In winter, aerators installed by the Department of Natural Resources (DNR) replenish oxygen in the shallow waters, reducing fish losses and boosting productivity. The aerators have expanded fishing success in lakes that formerly could not sustain gamefish through Iowa's snowy, cold winters.

Even with all the limelight on bass, walleye, and muskies, many vacationers visit Iowa's natural lakes primarily to catch lots of perch, bluegills, crappie, and bullhead. These species may be less sophisticated, but they subsidize many bait shops and resorts. Spring spawning may be the best time for both bullhead and bluegills, but summer anglers also catch big bluegills in the cool shade of boat docks. Try perch in the fall, or through the ice.

Border Rivers

Mississippi River.   If you want an argument, just try to persuade a Mississippi River rat that there's any place better to fish. The "Father of Waters" flows 300 fishable miles along the state's eastern border. It's a 190,000-acre maze of backwaters, chutes, islands, running sloughs, and channels. The scenic, wooded bluffs and array of wildlife add aesthetic appeal to a Mississippi River fishing trip.

Although the Mississippi's locks and dams, built in the 1930s, cater to heavy barge traffic, the pools above the dams, and the tailwaters below them—combined with wing dams and rock levees—provide diverse fishing habitat.

Bass, bluegill, and crappie anglers seek the lily pads and submerged vegetation of lakelike shallows. Stump-field remnants—reminders of the forests that once covered the river valley—often hold bass. Some of the biggest panfish come in early winter, when bluegill and crappie anglers swarm to honey holes in the deeper backwaters.

Eddies and current breaks around submerged wing dams can be action-packed in the summer. For variety, a wing dam is the place to be. An angler can fish with a nightcrawler, leech, jig, or crankbait, and may catch walleye, smallmouth bass, white bass, catfish, bluegills, and freshwater drum.

In the spring and fall, walleye and sauger school in swift water near dams, or around gravel bars. Eager anglers may be elbow to elbow on rock riprap or commercial fishing barges. Boats get in line to troll or drift downstream from the churning tailwaters. Heavy rigs—either large jigs or sinkers on a three-way swivel—are a must.

Tournament anglers have discovered the Mississippi, and the river hosts dozens of walleye and bass contests throughout the season. Veteran river anglers usually have the inside track, as it can take a lifetime to learn the subtleties of the ever-changing currents, sandbars, and channels.

Missouri River.   Iowa may be "The Land Between Two Rivers," but the Missouri River, which forms most of Iowa's western border, is a mere ghost of the once wild and productive stream that pioneers knew. Channelization destroyed countless pools, cutbanks, sandbars, and oxbows, along with many of the fish. Its waters now are squeezed into a rock canal, rushing past wing dikes—but the resilient Missouri still holds good numbers of big flathead and channel catfish, along with occasional sauger. Anglers who can overcome the limited access and swift current can expect to be rewarded well for their trouble.

Big Sioux River.   Iowa's "other" border river, the Big Sioux, winds 130 miles from the Minnesota line to its confluence with the Missouri north of Sioux City. Wooded bends, gravel bars, and occasional rocks make it one of the state's better catfish waters, with a scattering of walleye and smallmouths. For seclusion, try canoeing and fishing the narrow upper stretches.

Interior Rivers

The 19,000 miles of fishable tributaries to the big border rivers bring catfish, walleye, or smallmouth bass within minutes of most Iowans. In the rolling farm country of southwest Iowa, the channel catfish is king. In northeast Iowa's wooded limestone bluffs, smallmouths dominate. Walleye fishing is surprisingly good in many streams wherever there are rocky reaches.

The Des Moines River, which first ambles through Minnesota before cutting 400 miles across the heart of Iowa, typifies river fishing opportunities. Channel catfish love its snags, pools, and gravel bars. Walleye may show up almost anywhere, especially near a couple of big Army Corps of Engineers flood-control impoundments—Red Rock and Saylorville—in Central Iowa.

Veteran anglers always knew where to find pockets of smallmouths in Iowa rivers, but now the secret is out. Length limits on fish caught in all rivers, coupled with catch-and-release mandates on several, have led to a smallmouth boom in most streams with suitable rocky habitat. The best waters are in the northeastern half of Iowa. Favorites include the Upper Iowa, Yellow, Turkey, Maquoketa, Cedar, Winnebago, Middle Raccoon, Iowa, and Boone Rivers. Canoeists can catch some smallmouths, but specialists prefer to wade, casting spinners, leadhead jigs, or crankbaits. Crawdads and minnows can be deadly.

Channel catfish also may grab a bass lure, but serious cat anglers choose live baits or commercial "stink" baits. Savvy cat seekers select their baits by the food that's available. Fishing starts in the spring with sour (rotten) shad or carp for bait. When hot-weather doldrums hit, odoriferous prepared baits are used to get the fish's attention. In late summer, they may feed on grasshoppers, turning to frogs and then minnows in the fall feeding frenzy. Drop the bait where the current can carry it to cats lying in wait under snags or cut banks. But don't pass up pools, riffles, or rocks. A jonboat with a small motor will take a river catfish angler anywhere, but bank or wading anglers catch their share, too.

Biologists fondly call Iowa's prairie streams "catfish factories." Indeed, channel catfish are everywhere, with the possible exception of the coolest, rockiest upper reaches of some creeks. Favorite channel cat rivers include the Boone, Cedar, Chariton, Des Moines, English, Grand, Iowa, Little Sioux, Middle, Nishnabotna, Raccoon, Skunk, and Wapsipinicon.

And don't forget walleye. Anglers who think only of big lakes or the Mississippi River are missing a walleye bonanza in Iowa. Thanks partly to an aggressive state stocking program, many interior rivers hold 10-plus-pound lunkers. Fishing action focuses on low-head dams in the spring, but the walleye don't vanish the rest of the year. Seek them out around rocks and snags in the cleanest, coolest water. The Cedar, Des Moines, Iowa, Raccoon, and Wapsipinicon Rivers rank among the best walleye sites.

Reservoirs

Conservationists still debate the merits of flood-control reservoirs on major rivers, but water regulation issues notwithstanding, four such reservoirs in Iowa offer a variety of fishing opportunities.

Lake Rathbun, an 11,000-acre pool on the Chariton River near Centerville, leads the pack. Rathbun has earned a national reputation as a crappie lake, and regular competitions are held here. The impoundment also produces enough lunker walleye to supply the state's high-tech fish hatchery there, and to draw trophy anglers from all over the region.

Biologists rate Rathbun's catfishing as exceptional. Anglers catch channel cats of all sizes, from pan-size to lunkers pushing 20 pounds. The fastest action typically comes as the shallows begin to warm just after ice out, and the fish devour winter-killed shad and other baitfish. Anglers hold their noses, bait up with evil-smelling cut fish, and hang onto their bucking rods.

White bass add spice to Rathbun's fishing, too. Anglers who find late-summer schools may catch dozens by casting lures or drifting with minnows.

Lake Red Rock, on the Des Moines River downstream from Des Moines, never has drawn as many anglers or produced as many fish as Rathbun. Its fishing goes in spurts, affected primarily by wide fluctuations in water levels, but diehards often find good channel catfish, white bass, or crappie fishing in Red Rock. The tailwaters of the dam also attract hardy winter and early-spring anglers to try for northern pike and walleye.

Saylorville Lake, upstream from Des Moines, is Red Rock's younger and prettier sister. The 5,400-acre reservoir can be crowded with recreationists, but protected shorelines harbor good crappie and channel catfishing, along with largemouth bass and walleye. Hybrid striped bass, called "wiper" here, also provide wild action for fish that may reach 20 pounds.

Coralville Reservoir, built on the Iowa River near Iowa City in the 1950s, may be getting old, but don't count it out for top-notch channel catfishing. The lake grows lots of big flathead catfish, with 10- to 30-pounders common. Coralville also has good numbers of walleye, crappie, and saugeye.

Artificial Lakes

More than 200 artificial lakes, ranging from a few acres to nearly 1,000 acres, put flat-water fishing close to most Iowans. To many anglers, easy access—perhaps near a campground or playground in a county or state park or recreation area—may be more important than a full stringer or livewell. Consider it a bonus that these convenient lakes provide some of Iowa's best largemouth bass, channel catfish, bluegill, and crappie fishing. A few are stocked with walleye or saugeye, too.

The fishing season starts on the ice, when anglers score heavily on bluegills and crappie. The most successful anglers use the lightest tackle, and keep moving until they find the schools.

Come spring, people start catfishing when the ice goes out and the fish feast on winter-killed baitfish. For some of the best results, anglers zero in on lakes where fingerling channel cats are raised in cages on commercial feed before they're allowed to swim free.

Schools of spawning crappie take tiny jigs or minnows around brushpiles or other structure in early May. The bluegill bonanza follows, when the fish move onto their shallow-water, panlike spawning beds.

Bass anglers may cast rocky shorelines, flooded timber, and weedlines all year. As winter approaches, anglers may find the least competition, and the best chance for a lunker largemouth. Nine-hundred-acre Big Creek Lake near Des Moines, one of the state's biggest artificial lakes, has consistently good fishing; but size is only part of the story. Dozens of smaller impoundments fill a real need for close-to-home fishing.

Some favorite artificial lakes in southwest Iowa include Anita, Little River, Twelve Mile, and Green Valley. In southeast Iowa, try Pleasant Creek, Macbride, Sugema, and Geode.

Trout Streams

Tucked away in nine northeastern Iowa counties, 266 miles of spring-fed trout streams provide a sharp contrast to the rest of the state's farm-country rivers and warmwater lakes. But regular stocking of most, along with restrictive regulations on some, have transformed these streams into surprisingly good trout waters. The region's nickname

Flyingfish leap out of the water at an estimated speed of 40 mph, then expand their broad spineless pectoral fins to glide above the surface of the sea.

I

"Little Switzerland" fits the scene of a fly angler working a clear, rocky pool beside a wooded limestone bluff.

Native brook trout survive in a few sites where they're carefully protected by no-kill rules. Rainbows and browns offer decent put-and-take fishing in many streams. Catchable-size trout are stocked by the DNR in dozens of streams; three-quarters of these are rainbow trout, and the remainder are browns and a few brookies. Not all of these are caught immediately, and some holdovers grow large in secluded pools. Hundreds of brood fish are released in these waters annually as well. A small number of streams are managed as special trout fisheries and are subject to special regulations regarding methods, size, and release requirements. In addition there are 28 streams managed as put-and-grow fisheries where fingerling trout—primarily browns—are stocked.

Farm Ponds

Iowa has 90,000 private ponds, and although public access is restricted, farmers often allow fishing. Most of these ponds average about an acre, although some are substantially larger. With landowner permission, a pond angler may have the best chance of catching a real trophy largemouth bass or bluegill. Most people fish from shore, but a small boat helps when working the edges of aquatic vegetation, where the big fish may lurk.

IRELAND

The westernmost island in the British Isles, the enchanted land of Ireland is recognized as a top angling destination in Europe. Atlantic salmon are the favorite attraction for anglers from across the Atlantic, followed by brown trout and sea trout; however, the country is also known for its excellent numbers and size of coarse species, which attract many European visitors, and also for northern pike. Irish anglers are especially fond of salmon and trout fishing, and they also enjoy saltwater angling for a host of species ranging from shark to cod and bass to pollack.

Situated in the North Atlantic Ocean, Ireland is approximately 500 kilometers long and 300 kilometers wide, with a very high ratio of water to land (1 part water to 35 parts land). There are virtually thousands of lakes and 14,000 kilometers of fish-bearing rivers, plus lengthy canal systems.

The main rivers are the Erne and Shannon, which are actually chains of lakes (loughs) connected by sections of river. The Erne and Shannon respectively drain the northern and central portions of the Midlands; the Shannon is longer and enters the Atlantic via a lengthy estuary.

The Irish climate favors most anglers; prevailing warm, moist winds from the Atlantic produce a temperate climate with moderate summers, mild winters, and adequate rainfall throughout the year. With the warm waters of the North Atlantic Drift lapping the south and west coasts, the climate is milder than Ireland's geographical location would indicate.

With salmon and trout the mainstays, few Irish anglers fish for pike and coarse species, which here mean anything other than species of salmon and trout. Thus, excellent populations of pike, bream, tench, roach, rudd, and eels are largely left to the visiting angler, as is the sea angling, particularly along the south and west coasts.

Established Fisheries Boards operate a continuing research and development program for all fresh and marine waters. Lakes, rivers, and coastal stretches are surveyed and mapped, and fisheries are managed and stocked as appropriate, with banks and access routes to the freshwater's edge developed for direct and easy access.

Most Irish angling opportunities are recognized and organized; well-developed angling centers exist and cater to angling tourists. Hundreds of rivers, streams, and loughs are serviced by hotels, lodges, and gillies (guides). Salmon and trout fisheries are usually the property of an individual, club, organization, or the state, and permission (including a permit) is generally required except in the case of some state lakes, such as the great western loughs and those of Killarney. Some waters, however, are seldom fished.

Gamefishing

The quality of Ireland's gamefishing (trout and salmon) is very good, with many opportunities to angle for wild salmon and trout in natural, undisturbed habitat. The main species here are Atlantic salmon, sea trout, and nonmigratory brown trout, but there are some rainbow trout as well.

Trout. Brown trout are available in almost every stretch of freshwater in Ireland. The average size and coloration vary; limestone rivers and lakes produce the larger fish, which can range from all silver to gold with numerous black and red spots.

Resident anglers tend to concentrate on the loughs for their brown trout fishing, although they never completely ignore the rivers. The great western lakes of Corrib, Mask, Carra, and Conn have long been the main brown trout attractions because of their natural wild fish populations. Developed lakes like Owel and Sheelin in the Midlands are also important. Lough trout tend to average 1 to 2 pounds and are primarily caught by standard fly fishing means or by dapping natural insects on the surface, using a long (14 feet or more) pole and fine monofilament line.

Loughs Corrib, Mask, and Leane have a population of very large browns called "Ferox" trout, which can reach 20 pounds or more; fish in excess of 10 pounds are quite common. They are normally taken by trolling.

In Ireland's thousands of mountain lakes and streams, an exploring angler is likely to catch a number of free-rising and beautifully speckled brown trout that have seldom been covered by a fly. The fish in these less fertile sites may be small, but they provide terrific sport.

In areas with a shortage of readily available trout fishing, the local Fisheries Boards operate regulated fisheries. These are maintained at a very high standard by regular stocking with brown or rainbow trout (rainbows exist only in managed fisheries); opening and closing dates vary, but all are open during the summer.

The Irish records for brown trout are 26 pounds, 2 ounces for a lake fish and 20 pounds for a river fish; trophy, or specimen, fish are those that exceed 10 pounds in lakes and 5 pounds in rivers. Spinning tackle and lures or baits are employed successfully in many locations. Permits are required on very few Irish trout fisheries, but the visitor should inquire. Brown trout fisheries open between mid-February and March 1; most close on September 30, but a few close between mid-September and mid-October.

Salmon and sea trout. Most Irish rivers get a run of salmon. Some may produce only a few salmon to the rod each year, whereas on others many thousands are caught. Most of the better fisheries are privately or club owned and permit costs vary depending on their exclusivity and productivity. No permits are required for the "free" fisheries of Loughs Corrib, Mask, Conn, Leane, and Currane. Gillies and boatmen are available on the more organized fisheries.

Some rivers get an early run of "spring" salmon (from 5 to 10 kilograms) and open to fishing on January 1. "Springers," as they are known, are available in many salmon rivers, although they are not as numerous as grilse; this fishing lasts through April but can extend into May. June sees the beginning of the prolific grilse run. These fish usually weigh less than 3.5 kilograms, and the run extends from June through September. The Irish record for salmon is 57 pounds, and a specimen catch is a 20-pounder.

Visitors should check to make sure that the season is open for any particular salmon water. A small number of salmon and sea trout fisheries open on January 1 each year; others open on various dates up to March 1. Most salmon fisheries close on September 30, although a few close between the end of August and the middle of October.

Some of the country's better known salmon waters are the Rivers Liffey, Drowes, Erriff, Moy, Ballinahinch, Corrib, and Owenea. The Drowes, in northwestern Ireland, is just 6 miles long and drains salmon-holding Lough Melvin. It and the Liffey gather several hundred anglers apiece for January 1 opening-day competition, and the Drowes produces about 1,000 salmon per season, with peak results for large fish in March and for grilse in August and September. The first mile of the Drowes is channeled and flanked by fishing platforms, with lies easy to cast to; the remainder courses through fields and woods.

Many more fish are produced by the Moy, which has become one of Europe's top salmon fisheries since commercial netting and trapping operations were bought out by the Irish government. Fishing rods and angling tourists have replaced the nets and traps, and some of the better pools (Ridge and Cathedral) produce a couple thousand salmon apiece each season.

Some salmon fisheries permit only fly fishing, whereas others allow various methods. Many of the smaller rivers, particularly in western Ireland, require a fresh flood to induce the fish to take freely. When in condition, these spate rivers offer tremendous sport, and six or seven fish to a rod is not uncommon. Although catch-and-release angling for salmon (and trout) is gaining in Ireland, angling for both here is predominantly a catch-and-keep fishery, except for private waters with restrictions that exceed those of the state. This ethic is increasing, however, and with a greater effort at environmental protection and fisheries restoration efforts, there could be a good future, for salmon fisheries in particular.

For salmon fly angling, double-handed 13- to 15-foot rods for a 10- or 11-weight fly line are employed locally, although single-handed 10- to 12-foot rods for 8- or 9-weight lines are used for summer grilse fishing. Bring various densities of line to cope with circumstances. Chest waders are essential for much of the spring and some summer angling.

The main run of sea trout is from June through August, but it can last into September. These fish seem to favor the shorter river systems. Both species can be fished in the rivers or on loughs from boats. Many sea trout fisheries close on September 30, but some close between the end of August and mid-October—like the salmon fishery. A 16-pound, 6-ounce fish holds the Irish record, and a trophy is considered one of 6 pounds or more.

Salmon anglers work the River Mourne in Northern Ireland.

Coarse and Pike Fishing

Although there is some fishing for pike by Irish anglers, to a large extent both pike and coarse fishing are very much the domain of the tourist angler. There are thousands of rivers and lakes, and miles of clean canals, packed with well-conditioned bream, rudd, roach, tench, hybrids species, and pike, and these all offer good fishing in tranquil and idyllic rural surroundings. Ireland is known for its superior coarse fishing opportunities throughout Europe, and it attracts dedicated coarse anglers.

The Tourism Board, together with national and local groups, develops coarse fisheries for visiting anglers, and in many places they have provided access points, including footbridges and platforms, to facilitate shore fishing. Charts of developed sites are available locally and from the Fisheries Boards.

Coarse angling is largely focused around fishing centers in towns and villages where experienced providers specialize in servicing angling tourists. There may be many lakes and rivers within reach of a center, and local information is always available. Baits for coarse angling are widely available from tackle shops and bait suppliers in the majority of angling centers, but prior notice is always advisable. Visiting anglers are advised to order in advance.

There is no closed season for coarse angling in Ireland, but there are best periods for the various species. Bream and rudd feed mostly from mid-April through October. Roach are at their best during the colder winter months but are available for much of the year. Tench fishing is best in May and June. Unlike salmon and trout, Irish anglers return all coarse fish alive.

Pike fishing is good throughout the year, but it is at its best during the cooler fall months. Specimen pike (30 pounds in lakes and 20 pounds in rivers) can be taken at any time; Irish pike records are a lake fish of 42 pounds and a river fish of 38 pounds, 2 ounces.

Sea Fishing

Beach, estuary, nearshore, and deep-sea angling opportunities exist along the 3,000 miles of Irish coastline. This includes steep and shingle beaches in the lightly indented east; quiet backwaters and estuaries as well as snug harbors in the south; and massive cliff faces, roaring storm beaches, and hundreds of small islands on the west and northwest.

The most commonly encountered species along the Irish coasts are sharks, tope, ray, skate, monkfish, pollack, coalfish, cod, ling, conger, and various dogfish, flatfish, and gurnard. Angling launches (small party boats up to 45 feet long) are located at harbors all around the coast and generally accommodate up to 10 anglers, with gear on board for rent. Some specialize in fishing over submerged wrecks for large ling, conger, and pollack. Along the east coast and in sheltered bays and estuaries of the south and west, fishing from small dory-type boats is increasing in popularity, and excellent catches are being recorded.

The piers, beaches, and rocky ledges of Ireland's shoreline produce an incredible range of fish. Most of the species already mentioned (including sharks) are also available. Tope, ray, cod, bass, flounder, turbot, conger, wrasses, coalfish, pollack, and dogfish make up the bulk of the catch. Much of this fishing requires little experience, and maps guiding visitors to local hotspots are available from the Central Fisheries Board.

Especially favored fish include mackerel, which are common and sometimes numerous on all coasts; European bass, which primarily inhabit estuaries and beaches south of Galway on the west and south of Dublin on the east, although their numbers have decreased substantially in recent times; pollack, which are taken from both boat and shore on all coasts; and cod, which are also caught off all coasts and are most common in May and June from boats, and in December and January from shore.

Regulations

Fisheries in Ireland are managed by the Central Fisheries Board (in Dublin) and seven regional Fisheries Boards. These were established to protect, develop, and promote all forms of sportfishing; they are not profit-making, and their income is devoted to fisheries management and conservation. For sea angling, the boards update and issue maps and guides of shore, small-boat, and deep-sea angling opportunities. They have developed hundreds of coarse angling lakes, especially catchments at Shannon and Erne, and prepared many watercourses for angling. They manage 150,000 acres of lakes and more than 1,000 miles of rivers and streams for trout fishing. They also manage and control many quality salmon waters, including the Erriff in Connemara, the Galway Weir Fishery, the Lower Lee in Cork, the Owenea in Donegal, and the Glenamoy Bunowen and Carrowinskey in May. Details on these activities are available directly from the boards.

A state (national) angling license is required to fish for salmon and sea trout on private and public waters. This license is available from the Fisheries Boards and from larger tackle shops and angling outfitters. A permit is also required from the owner or manager of a private fishery, and regulations at such a location may differ from those established by the state. Few regulations exist for pike, coarse, and inland trout fisheries, although this is changing under the establishment of local fisheries cooperatives, which may issue permits for regional fishing.

The Central Fisheries Board has provided a general guide to sportfishing in Ireland, and the Irish Tourist Board has general information as well.

ISRAEL

A small country of just 21,596 square kilometers, with a short rainy season, chronic water shortage, and a few rivers that are largely dried up, Israel

I

would not seem to offer much in the way of sport-fishing opportunity. Indeed, although there are reports of some freshwater angling in this narrow 420-kilometer-long country, and although Israel has 195 kilometers of western and largely unin-dented coastline bordering the Mediterranean Sea, it is the narrow tip of southern Israel bordering the Red Sea that is known to provide opportunities for pelagic species, in a location with generally calm waters protected by the Sinai Mountains.

The port of Eilat affords access to the Gulf of Aqaba, a narrow arm of the Red Sea bordered mostly by Saudi Arabia and Egypt, with a small northern portion bordered by Jordan and a compar-atively tiny section bordered by Israel. Eilat is a bustling site, with luxury hotels, a fishing center, and a marina that houses a number of charter boats.

This portion of the Red Sea is known for crystal clear waters and has attracted divers for decades. Offshore game species include sailfish, swordfish, yellowfin tuna, bonito, dolphin, barracuda, amber-jack, mako sharks, and blue sharks.

The area close to Eilat in the northern part of the Gulf of Aqaba offers some fishing, but considerable pleasure-boat activity, much of it stemming from adjoining Jordan, is intrusive. Ras Borka, 40 miles south of Eilat, is a popular site. The Straits of Tiran are also notable; this passage to the deep waters of the Red Sea is more than 150 kilometers from Eilat, and beyond it lie numerous islands and the tip of the Sinai Peninsula at Egypt's Sharm el-Sheik. In the past, overnight and multiday trips have been made to this region, where the fishing is reportedly out-standing. Nevertheless, security concerns are ever-present in this region and may restrict boat travel.

ITALY

One of the most geographically varied countries on the European continent, Italy comprises territory that ranges from the rolling, fertile plains of the Piemonte and Tuscany hills to the southern Calabrian bushes, and from the wide-open crop-lands of the Central Emilia to the peaks of the Alps and the Dolomite Mountains in the north. And although all of Italy's diverse regions amply address most cultural interests, outdoor travelers can easily look to Italy's sportfishery alone for a satisfying visit.

Surrounded on most of its borders by the Mediterranean Sea, Italy offers excellent saltwater sportfishing, especially for tuna, billfish, and numerous inshore and bottom species. In addition to possessing two of the Mediterranean's most pro-lific seas, the Adriatic and the Thyrrenian, the country contains literally hundreds of rivers, lakes, natural and artificial drains, dams, gravel pits, streams, marshes, and river mouths. Excellent road and rail systems, an abundance of top-rated accom-modations, and appealing amenities allow anglers to pursue their passion in comfort. Furthermore, many world-renowned sites, such as Venice, Florence, Rome, Milan, and Naples, are only a few miles from the best fishing hotspots, whether the focus is giant bluefin tuna or trout.

Although Italy's climate has considerable regional variations, temperatures remain uniformly pleasant throughout the year. The best time for saltwater fishing is March through November, and for fresh-water fishing from mid-February through December.

Freshwater

Sportfishing practices in Italy are varied, as befits the country's geographic, ethnic, sociological, and even political diversity. Such dissimilar locales as Sicily and Piemonte, Calabria and Veneto, Puglie and Sardinia, and their wide range of water types, provide a little something for everyone.

Freshwater stocks in Italy include about 80 species, although only a handful are avidly pursued by anglers. Their presence and distribution has been shaped by many factors, predominantly climate.

The most important angling species in the northern and central regions are rainbow trout, lake trout, brown trout, grayling, whitefish, barbel, cat-fish, pike, perch, tench, carp, chub, dace, bream, and roach. In the southern regions anglers primarily target rainbow and brown trout, carp, chub, dace, bream, and roach. The following species, imported and introduced into Italy essentially at the end of the nineteenth century, came from the United States, Canada, and Russia: largemouth bass, smallmouth bass, lake trout, zander, sunfish, catfish, wels, brook trout, and rainbow trout.

Recreational fishing in Italy has been practiced since at least the beginning of the eighteenth cen-tury, when rods, lines, and live baits were used for barbel, perch, tench, grayling, brown trout, carp, chub, dace, bream, and roach. Since the 1980s, increased use of spinning and fly tackle has revolu-tionized fishing in both freshwater and saltwater, but especially the former.

The majority of Italian anglers fish with floats, primarily seeking coarse species belonging to the cyprinid family. The most common freshwater technique is ledgering *(see),* also known as *pesca all'inglese* and *roubaisienne,* because it was imported respectively from the United Kingdom and France.

Coarse fishing is highly specialized here, as else-where in Europe, and competitive fishing has a strong following. Italy is the most passionate and intense match fishing nation in the world (England is not far behind), and Italian match anglers are eager to learn new methods to increase their suc-cess. They have excelled in international champi-onship match fishing events and won numerous world titles.

Italy's climate and geography influence the main coarse fishing techniques, making them different from those in western Europe. All beginners and professionals use telescopic rods, and the preferred quarry is *arborella* (bleak), a species similar to the emerald shiner *(see)* and very abundant across the

Forty-five American states have officially designated state fish; top recipients: brook trout (8), cutthroat trout (7); only 3 states have freshwater and saltwater designees.

country. Italians have mastered the art of catching these small fish at high speed in a three-hour competition (most of the top match anglers can catch 1,500 of these quick silver fish in this time span).

A unique method of coarse fishing, called *bolognese,* developed on the Po River around Bologna. It incorporates a telescopic rod with a reel and allows the angler to fish with a fixed float at depths up to 28 feet. Anglers can cast these rigs 50 yards and present their baits perfectly, even in fast flows.

Italians are developing an interest in casting with lures for appropriate species in private lakes and gravel pits. This interest is met to some extent by the development of put-and-take lakes in all regions of the country. In these waters, which are mostly small, the endemic species have often been eliminated by rotenone poisoning, and restocking has included rainbow trout, carp, and largemouth bass, with the trout and bass being of interest to those casting lures.

Interest in angling for cyprinids (carp and chub, among others), generically referred to as carp fishing, is on the rise. Among members of fishing clubs, carp and related species are often the objects of specimen hunting—the focused pursuit of large or trophy fish; this type of angling has become more popular, and cyprinids are also the principal target of fishing competitions in open waters.

Most freshwater anglers in Italy use baits and apply various technical methods locally referred to as *bolognese, inglese, canna fissa, roubaisienne,* and *al tocco,* either with spinning or fly tackle. Anglers are organized by the Italian Sport Fishing Association (FIPSAS), which has more than 350,000 members.

Italy is divided into many fishing districts that have adopted different regulations and seasons. A national license is required. Detailed information on regulations, as well as maps, brochures, and guides, can be obtained by contacting the local FIPSAS office.

Species

For Italians, the most important family of fish is the cyprinids, due not only to the relatively large number of species they represent (approximately 25), but also to their traditional significance in Europe. More than two-thirds of anglers here are pole fishermen (bank anglers using poles from 7 to 18 meters long) who catch roach, bream, chub, tench, and common carp.

In most of the larger streams that flow through the plains, cyprinids are the species best equipped to resist pollution, even benefiting from some of its environmental effects. These species have increased rather significantly since the 1960s; at the same time, however, their natural predators (perch, zander, and pike) have suffered declines.

Salmonids are the second most important family of fish. Brown trout, which are native to Italy, and the introduced rainbow trout and lake trout (actually a charr), are the mainstays, the latter especially in the northern regions. Brown trout average $2^1/_2$ pounds in the northern and central regions and $1^1/_2$ pounds

elsewhere. European grayling are still rather strongly represented in the northern regions of Piemonte, Veneto, Lombardia, Friuli-Venezia Giulia, and Trentino-Alto Adige. Brook trout are found in the north as well, and can be caught in the streams, lakes, and ponds of Veneto, Lombardia, Piemonte, Liguria, and Trentino-Alto Adige.

Most of these species are pursued by dedicated specialists, especially fly anglers.

Perch, zander, and pike are of interest to Italian anglers. Zander have spread throughout northern and central Italy by migrating among waterways and also through direct importation. Zander represent the second major carnivorous species (wels being first), and where it has prospered it has done so at the expense of northern pike. Pike are prized in Italy, as they are throughout Europe, and large pike are in the dreams of every Italian freshwater angler, although the average size is close to 8 pounds. Pike are fairly numerous in major rivers and lakes in the northern and central regions, and less prominent in the south due to the scarcity of large rivers and lakes.

Other species with constituencies include eels, which are popular throughout the country but especially in the Veneto region (Comacchio Valleys); the Twaite shad, which attracts spinning tackle users in the river mouths of the central regions; and the wels catfish, locally known as *siluro,* which can exceed 500 pounds and has become common in the Po, Italy's greatest river.

Largemouth bass have been introduced throughout northern and central Italy and are prominent in ponds as well as impoundments. Fishing for them became more popular in the 1990s. The fish average 3 pounds and are normally caught on light spinning tackle. Smallmouths have also been introduced into similar waters and in private ponds. Some can be caught in Chiusi Lake in Tuscany, near Florence. A complete list of waters with bass can be obtained from any regional FIPSAS agency. Various sea bass and mullet inhabit the country's numerous river mouths and are popular among anglers who also fish in freshwater.

Northern Region

In the mountainous far north, numerous rivers and streams flow down from the Alps and the Dolomite Mountains into long, narrow, and lush river valleys that resemble linear oases and form beautiful lakes. Due to their isolation, most of these spectacular rivers receive low resident pressure, so the quality of fishing is generally very good.

Within easy driving distance from the cities of Milan, Turin, Verona, Udine, and Venice are a numerous sportfishing spots and many reservoirs locally known as *laghetti a pagamento.* The best of them is Naviglio Langosco, which lies in the Lombardia region.

Rivers and streams in northern Italy offer good fishing to both lure and fly anglers, especially for trout and grayling. Small streams fish well with dry

flies, whereas larger rivers are productive with nymphs. The best time to fish these waters for trout and grayling is between March and September. Fishing for carp and chub is very good year-round, but summertime is the peak season.

Northern Italy is also famous for its good lake fishing. The most well-known lakes are the Garda, the Maggiore, Como, d'Iseo, Mezzola, and Varese. In these lakes, the major angling interests are brown trout, lake trout, perch, whitefish, and some cyprinids; various methods are permitted, including trolling (locally called *traina a tirlindana*) and casting with lures.

In the central portion of this region, the huge water systems of the Po basin (the 405-mile-long Po is Italy's longest river, navigable for 300 miles, and has numerous tributaries) have contributed much to Italy's reputation as a top European angling spot. In fact, this area is one of the most prolific for chub and wels anywhere in Europe. Chub are generally caught with specific pole techniques that require chumming with a natural chum mix. Bottom fishing from a boat or from a riverbank is the most successful method of catching the huge wels, which are abundant in the Po watershed. Fish over 150 pounds are regularly caught, especially during spring and summer.

The most important rivers for sportfishing in northern Italy are the Po, Ticino, Adige, Tagliamento, Brenta, Sarca, Sesia, Tanaro, Mincio, Adda, Piave, Reno, Dora Baltea, Dora Riparia, Panaro, Taro, Trebbia, and Bormida.

A terrific brown trout from one of northern Italy's rivers.

Central Region

The Apennine Mountains are intrinsic to all sections of the central region, especially Emilia-Romagna, Tuscany, Lazio, Marche, Umbria, and Abruzzi. As in the northernmost portion of Italy, numerous rivers and streams flow down from the mountains into long, narrow, and lush river valleys that resemble linear oases and form beautiful lakes and many productive estuaries. Tuscany (Arno River) and Emilia-Romagna are the sources of Italy's long-established sportfishing and hunting traditions, and all important national sportfishing magazines have their headquarters in Florence, the capital of Tuscany.

Sportfishing here is conducted using traditional techniques. Various trout, pike, chub, and other cyprinids are the locally favored species. The most important rivers include the Tevere, Sieve, Tronto, Secchia, Arno, Ombrone, Marecchia, Metauro, Esino, Chienti, and Nera.

Central Italy is also famous for its good lake fishing. The best-known lakes are the Trasimeno, Bolsena, Corbara, Chiusi, Massaciuccoli, Montepulciano, Bracciano, Occhito, Lesina, Piediluco, and Vico. In these lakes, the major interests for anglers are brown trout, perch, pike, and some cyprinids; various methods are permitted, including trolling, fly fishing, and casting with lures.

Southern Region

Southern Italy has numerous rivers and streams with stocked trout and coarse species. On the two major islands, Sicily and Sardinia, freshwater is restricted to a few rivers and lakes due to the warm climate. Several streams and ponds in the interior of these areas are accessible by a series of both paved and woods roads, and offer good fishing for chub and brown trout.

The most important rivers and streams for sportfishing in southern Italy are the Sangro, Liri, Biferno, Volturno, Sele, Calore, Ofanto, Bradano, Fortore, Carapelle, Basento, Agri, Crati, Neto, Simeto, Belice, Platani, and Salso. Most of these rivers are beautiful and, due to their isolation, receive low resident angling pressure, so the quality of the fishing is generally very good

Brown trout, perch, pike, chub, barbel, and other cyprinids are the main species.

Pole fishing with natural baits (worms or insects), and casting artificials with spinning and fly tackle, are prevalent techniques here.

Saltwater

Italy is comprised of three geographically separate and distinct saltwater sportfishing areas: the Adriatic coast, the Thyrrenian coast, and the territory around the Big Islands. The latter includes Sicily and Sardinia; two smaller and isolated deep south-oriented islands, Lampedusa and Pantelleria; and numerous small archipelagos. Each area boasts distinct but varied saltwater sportfishing opportunities.

Adriatic Sea

The Adriatic Sea can be compared to the Sea of Cortez in Baja California, Mexico, as it is enclosed between the Italian peninsula and the former country of Yugoslavia. This 430-mile-long basin consists of two main fishing territories: the North Adriatic, from Venice to Porto San Giorgio, which has a long, narrow, sandy-gold shoreline; and the Central Adriatic, from Porto San Giorgio to Santa Maria di Leuca, which has a rocky shoreline with some short white-sand beaches.

The major angling interest in the Adriatic is the giant bluefin tuna, although considerable enthusiasm is devoted to blue and thresher sharks, albacore, mackerel, and sea bass.

The bluefin tuna was likely the first big-game species encountered by fishermen in this region. They were subsistence fishermen, however, and far removed from the sophisticated population inhabiting Italy today. History suggests that the earliest meetings between tuna and man occurred in the Mediterranean Sea. The northern bluefin began its trek toward exploitation well before the birth of Christ. More than 4,000 years ago, the Phoenicians used the first rudimentary net traps in the Mediterranean to catch this species. The design of nets to catch these formidable fish has been handed down through the centuries, and today two remaining descendants of the practice, called *tonnare,* are still in operation out of Sicily—living legends and the last keepers of an old way of life on the sea.

It was not until the 1970s, however, that the first giant bluefin tuna was caught with rod and reel by trolling a dead mackerel just off the mouth of the Po River in the Adriatic Sea. This discovery became a catalyst for many inshore anglers, who decided to outfit their boats for tuna. The true impetus behind Italy's bluefin sportfishery, however, was importation from the United States and France of drift-and-chum fishing tactics.

Schools of tuna of all sizes were spotted practically all along the peninsula in every region of the country. By the 1980s and early 1990s, hundreds of giants had been caught under International Gamefish Association (IGFA) rules and Italian law. (Italy allows only one bluefin tuna boated per day per boat, except during sanctioned tournaments.) The anglers observed that each size of bluefin— small (up to 70 pounds), medium (70 to 200 pounds), and giant (up to 900 pounds)—did not intermingle and engaged in different seasonal movements. It was eventually learned that small bluefin frequent the southern Adriatic, Ionian, and Ligurian Seas; medium-size bluefin run all along the Thyrrenian, Ligurian, and central Adriatic Seas; and giant bluefin prefer the Sardinian and Sicilian water, and the northern and central Adriatic Sea.

In late spring, after having spawned in the cool waters of the Ionian and Aegean Seas, hungry bluefin scatter in two main directions to pursue huge schools of bait. One moves toward the Adriatic Sea, the other passes through the Sicilian and Sardinian Channels to enter the Thyrrenian and Sardinian Seas.

In this erratic period, the bluefin that have gone the Adriatic way will follow the warm northward surface current that passes close to the Yugoslavian coast, arriving at their final destination in the northern Adriatic in early summer. Some schools of tuna are turned westward in the central Adriatic by a frontal eddy formed around Gargano's Promontory, so the first giants arrive in the southern Adriatic in late spring.

The majority of giant bluefin remain in the shallow waters of the northern Adriatic until early fall, when they return to the eastern Mediterranean, following the hot southward surface current that passes close to the Italian peninsula. They return to the central Adriatic in late autumn.

In essence, the giant bluefin tuna season in the northern Adriatic runs from June through November; July, August, and September are the peak months. In the central Adriatic, giants run from April through December; May, August, September, and October are the peak months. The medium and small bluefin frequent the deeper waters off the central and southern Adriatic year-round. Fishing opportunities for medium tuna peak in spring and winter, and for small tuna in autumn.

At the beginning of the fishing season in the northern Adriatic Sea, giants feed more than 30 miles offshore from Chioggia, Albarella, Porto Garibaldi, Porto Barricata, Rimini, and Pesaro. All of the northern Adriatic Sea is characterized by shallow depths (maximum of 90 feet) and by an extremely variable demarcation line between the inshore and offshore waters. For these reasons the local sportfishing boats, which are small but fast, mount their fighting chair on the bow, so the skipper can chase the big tuna during their long, shallow runs.

The central Adriatic has a longer fishing season, and giants are landed from modern marinas at Pesaro, Porto San Giorgio, Numana, San Benedetto del Tronto, Pescara, and Termoli. It is possible at these sites to charter well-equipped sportfishing boats with experienced skippers and mates who have countless giants to their credit.

Incidental catches while drifting for bluefin tuna include thresher sharks, blue sharks, and swordfish. During the off-season for bluefins, however, anglers can count on a lot of sharks, particularly blues (February through May) and threshers (year-round), together with green mackerel sharks (November through May), and sea bass (year-round). These fish are regularly caught on light drifting tackle.

Thyrrenian and Ligurian Seas

In the early 1980s, the good news concerning the bluefin tuna boom in the Adriatic encouraged anglers in western Italy to give it a try. The bottom

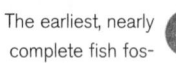

The earliest, nearly complete fish fossils were discovered in sandstone near Alice Springs in central Australia in the mid-1960s and have been dated at 470 million years old.

structure of the Thyrrenian and Ligurian Seas differs greatly from that of the Adriatic. These have deeper waters, and current patterns are particularly influenced by the winds. The western fleets must operate in harder conditions than their Adriatic counterparts, so they tend to mount the fighting chair on the stern and back down while fighting big bluefins.

The tuna fishing operations in the Thyrrenian Sea start in May and June, when the giants invade northwestern Sicily and southwestern Sardinia, passing through the Sicilian and Sardinian Channels. The so-called Sicilian giants move northward in early July, reaching the central Thyrrenian area in August and September, and the northern Thyrrenian and the Ligurian Seas in September and October. The Sardinian schools move northward toward France in July and August, joining the Sicilian groups in September and October. In the southern Ionian Sea, the giants run plentiful in July and August.

The average weight for giants in the Thyrrenian Sea is around 250 pounds, about 180 pounds less than the Adriatic standard. Small and medium bluefins can be caught here in late spring and autumn all along the coasts, about 25 miles offshore.

Through the 1990s, Thyrrenian anglers documented many zones where giant and medium bluefins were most frequently caught by drifting. They vary somewhat from year to year, and each bluefin tuna port has its own prime areas. Many of the best tuna zones are along the 60-fathom curve, between 10 and 40 miles off the coast.

Big concentrations of giants are reported in late spring off Palermo and the Egadi and Eolie Islands in Sicily, and off Portoscuso in Sardinia; summer hotspots are the along the west coast of Sardinia, the Pontine Islands, San Felice Circeo, Anzio, and Civitavecchia. In late summer, prime hotspots include Livorno, Marina di Cecina, Piombino, and Siracusa.

As a result of the country's productive angling, the Italian coasts are dotted with giant bluefin ports that offer good marina facilities and excellent accommodations. Among the most notable are Pesaro in the Adriatic Sea, and Livorno, Palermo, and Siracusa in the Thyrrenian Sea. These latter three ports have excellent restaurants, hotels, marinas, and the best skippers and boats in Italy. During the height of the tuna fishing season, it may be hard to find space, so it is a good idea to make reservations well in advance for accommodations, charter boats, and flights.

In the same months, anglers can troll or drift with live baits and light tackle in inshore waters and catch other gamefish, including amberjack, snapper, grouper, bluefish, and garrick.

Fishing in the estuaries of central Italy is very popular, and species pursued include chub, garrick, sea bass, snapper, jacks, drum, bream, mullet, flatfish, and rays.

In virtually all the estuaries, once the water level drops, big gutters appear along the muddy banks. Casting shallow-running or surface lures or live mullet into the head of the gutter is a locally proven method for catching these species. The best prospects for shore angling are from the end of May until September.

The Big Islands

The territory of the Big Islands includes Sicily and Sardinia, the smaller and southerly Lampedusa and Pantelleria Islands, and such small archipelagos as the Egadi, Eolie, Pontine, Tremiti, and Tuscany Islands. Each island boasts various sportfishing opportunities whether one is angling from shore or boat.

Surf casting and rockfishing all along the wide beaches and rocky shorelines of western Sardinia and northern Sicily provide the best possibilities for barracuda, jacks, sharks, snapper, drum, grouper, rays, and sea bass. These species are also available in the estuaries, as are garrick, which are plentiful in the murky waters.

The species regularly caught around the islands by surf casting and rockfishing include bluefish, bonito, sea bass in great quantities, garrick, snapper, bream, croaker, amberjack, and various other jacks.

Many red and gray sea bream and grouper are caught by bottom fishing and light tackle casting; amberjack, garrick, tuna, sea bass, and snapper can be caught by light-tackle trolling in inshore waters. The season is year-round, with increased activity from September through November.

Fantastic action for spearfish and broadbill swordfish is available around all these islands; some big spearfish cruise these waters. Local anglers show a lot of interest in these species, and in giant bluefin tuna in the same areas and the same seasons.

Most bluefins landed by anglers succumb to drifting dead sardines. In certain areas, such as Siracusa and Marina di Ragusa in Sicily, some anglers pursue bluefins by trolling small feather jigs in October and November, catching up to five fish per day in the 15- to 70-pound range.

Others use the same tease-and-bait methods for spearfish that are applied elsewhere for sailfish, resulting in record-size specimens. The biggest Mediterranean spearfish run in the Straits of Messina from August through November, when fish in excess of 100 pounds are common.

The 60-fathom curve, and the numerous banks off all these islands, produce a good number of broadbill swordfish. Local charter boats assure good swordfish action from April through December, with May through July the peak months. These efforts sometimes produce up to four strikes per night, although the fish rarely exceed 100 pounds.

In Italian waters, swordfish are taken in one of two ways: the classic sight fishing, which consists of seeking, spotting, and presenting a dead and/or live natural bait to the finning fish in daylight conditions; and night fishing by drifting a dead or live squid over canyons, banks, and submerged sea mountains. The latter is the more modern and successful method, and it is most popular with Italian anglers because it can be applied year-round with practically the same chance of success (daylight swordfishing is effective only during their spawning season around the islands from March through May), and because there are fewer swords finning due to severe commercial overfishing. Each method, however, requires skill, preparation, hard work, vigilance, and concentration.

Fishing for broadbills, especially at night, requires increased sophistication in boats, tackle, and crews. This results in additional costs to those chartering a boat to seek this species.

IVORY COAST

Côte d'Ivoire, or the Ivory Coast, is situated about 5° to 10° above the equator on the western coast of Africa. Its southern boundary and coastal region face the Atlantic Ocean and the Gulf of Guinea; to the east lies Ghana, which has the greatest commercial fishing fleet in all of Africa. The Ivory Coast is a leading country of the African continent, serving as both an international crossroads for commerce and a vacation favorite, and it is widely known for its hospitality.

Much of the Ivory Coast is a flat, forest-covered plain; it has golden beaches and a number of mangrove lagoons to the east in the regions of Abidjan and Assinie, and to the extreme east in the regions of Tabou and Grand Bereby. The several rivers here are navigable for short distances and are subject to low water during the dry season. The climate along the southern region is tropical—hot and humid. The wet season, which brings periods of heavy rain, runs from May through October.

The Ivory Coast boasts some of the best blue marlin fishing in the eastern Atlantic, especially during the two peak seasons of November/December (descending migration) and March/April (ascending migration). It is one of the few spots where one can rely on two distinct annual blue marlin migrations, but—depending on a combination of such factors such as wind, current, and water temperature changes—both migrations could be year-round events.

The main reason for the aggregation of billfish, tuna, wahoo, and other species off the entire coast of West Africa is the shifting frontal zone of the Canary Current and the Equatorial Countercurrent, which particularly affects the Ivory Coast ports of Abidjan and San Pedro.

Known as the "Pearl of Lagoons," the city of Abidjan hosts one of the oldest sportfishing centers in Africa, the Marlin Club. Sportfishing and accommodation arrangements are handled by the Mobaya Club (18 BP 347, Abidjan, Côte d'Ivoire; phone: 225-326532; fax: 225-331064), which hosts a good five-boat offshore charter service.

Oversize blue marlin, yellowfin tuna, and wahoo are caught just 45 minutes from the docks of the Mobaya Club Marina. Fifteen miles offshore is a large underwater valley called "The Boulevard," an area between two oil-drilling platforms. The Boulevard is an east-west-oriented rectangle, 30 miles long and 3 miles wide, with a depth that varies from 360 to 760 feet. Inside its perimeter are two fishing zones named "Jacqueville" and "Belier," where blue marlin hunt down tuna and wahoo.

Since 1988, another port on the Ivory Coast, San Pedro, has gained notoriety for large blue marlin. Two hundred miles west of Abidjan, it is the main city of the Ivory Coast's southwest region, and its nearby waters have gained international attention. Despite its reputation, however, San Pedro remains relatively undiscovered, and only a few professional charter boats are available at Club Nautique, where the local sportfishing boats are moored.

The blue marlin fishing zone in front of San Pedro is an ample one. The continental shelf is just 10 miles from port, parallel to the African perimeter. The bottom gradually drops from 180 to 420 feet, then plunges thousands of feet in a span of only 4 miles. All along this passage, constant trade winds and powerful currents create numerous upwellings and provide good concentrations of baitfish.

The typical fishing day here is long—about 11 hours—because the captains are committed to covering as much ground as possible during the day. The boats usually leave the dock at 8 A.M. and, after a 30-minute run, begin trolling in 240 feet of water, where blue marlin frequently chase baitfish into inshore waters. According to local anglers, marlin change direction in midmorning, turning toward the dropoff to find cooler water. The boats troll the dropoff until 3 P.M., then resume inshore trolling for several hours. The weekend captains sometimes work an enormous seamount, 35 miles from the coast, which rises from 3,000 to 900 feet.

The weather and sea conditions are usually good in the Gulf of Guinea, which partly explains the small- and medium-size charter boats found there. Arrangements for anglers fishing out of Club Nautique are handled at the four-star Balmer Hotel, 2 miles from San Pedro and a 10-minute car ride from the airport and marina.

The Ivory Coast also has untapped inshore and estuary fishing potential due to the presence of four large rivers that are navigable for short distances and have related estuaries. These are the Cavally and Sassandra Rivers near San Pedro, and the Bandama and the Comoé Rivers near Abidjan. All hold huge tarpon, snapper, jacks, grouper, barracuda, and sharks. Arrangements to fish these areas can be made through the Mobaya Club and the Hotel Balmer.

  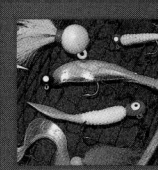

J

JACK

(1) A young, sexually mature male salmon that returns to freshwater rivers during the spawning run.

(2) Jacks are among the most important sport and commercial fish and are distributed worldwide in the temperate and tropical waters of the Atlantic, Indian, and Pacific Oceans. They are among 140 species that constitute the Carangidae family of jacks and pompano, which include such prominent sportfish as amberjack *(see: amberjack, greater; amberjack, lesser),* yellowtail *(see),* and permit *(see),* as well as many others. Jacks are almost exclusively saltwater fish, although some species occur rarely in brackish water. They are strong, fast swimmers and virtually all fight like a bulldog when caught on rod and reel, regardless of their size. Some jacks, but not all, are good table fare, although a few species have been associated with ciguatera poisoning.

These fish are distinguished by a widely forked caudal fin and a slender caudal peduncle. The body is generally compressed, although the shape (and color) varies considerably, from very deep to fusiform. Some jacks resemble mackerel *(see)* and are equally swift, but they lack the distinguishing rows of finlets. Many have extremely small scales, but at the end of the lateral line these are enlarged to form a keel. There are usually two spines in front of the anal fin.

Although young jacks travel in schools, adults of most species are usually solitary or travel in small groups. Some are generally caught in water of moderate depth, some are caught in relatively deep waters, and some are pursued on shallow flats and reefs.

See: Jack, Almaco; Jack, Bar; Jack, Crevalle and Pacific; Jack, Horse-eye; Jack, Yellow; Lookdown; Moonfish; Palometa; Pilotfish; Pompano; Pompano, African; Pompano, Florida; Roosterfish; Runner, Blue; Runner, Rainbow; Trevally.

JACK, ALMACO *Seriola rivoliana.*

Other names—amberjack, greater amberjack, longfin yellowtail; Afrikaans: *langvin-geelstert;* Arabic: *gazala;* French: *seriole limon;* Hawaiian: *kahala;* Japanese: *songoro, hirenaga-kanpachi;* Malay/Indonesian: *chermin, aji-aji;* Portuguese: *arabaiana, xaréu limao;* Samoan: *tavai, tafala, palu-kata;* Spanish: *pez limon, palometa, medregal, huayaipe, fortuno, cavallas.*

A deep-bodied amberjack and a member of the Carangidae family, the almaco jack is an excellent and widely distributed sportfish. It is a fine food fish, although it sometimes has tapeworms in the caudal peduncle area, which can be cut away so that the meat can be eaten safely, and it has been associated with ciguatera poisoning in the Caribbean, especially during spawning season.

Identification. The body and fins can be a uniform dark brown, a dark bluish green, or a metallic bronze or gray, with the lower sides and the belly a lighter shade, sometimes with a lavender or brassy cast. A diagonal black band usually extends from the lip through the eye to the upper back at the beginning of the dorsal fin; young fish sometimes display five or six bars. The front lobes of the dorsal and anal fins are high and elongated and have deeply sickle-shaped outer edges. There are seven spines in the first dorsal fin. The almaco jack is similar in appearance to the greater amberjack *(see: amberjack, greater)* but has a deeper, more flattened body than the greater amberjack and a more pointed head; the greater amberjack

A jack crevalle from the Caribbean waters of Costa Rica.

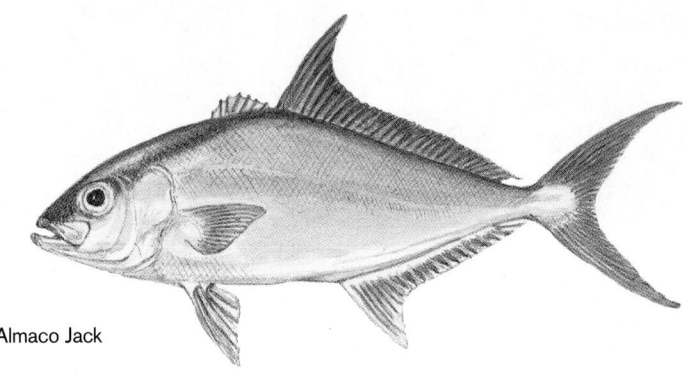

Almaco Jack

oceanic species. Almacos are usually caught around buoys, wrecks, or natural reefs, usually incidental to general offshore trolling for various species, or fishing for assorted reef dwellers, rather than as a deliberate target. Trolling with deep-running plugs or bottom fishing with cut baits are both effective.
See: Inshore Fishing; Jack; Offshore Fishing.

JACK, BAR   *Caranx ruber.*

Other names—runner, skipjack; Spanish: *cojinua carbonera, cojinua negra, negrito.*

A member of the Carangidae family, the bar jack is small and more like a saltwater panfish, but it is a scrappy species and a good food fish.

Identification.   The bar jack is silvery with a dark bluish stripe on the back that runs from the beginning of the soft dorsal fin and onto the lower tail fin. Sometimes there is also a pale-blue stripe immediately beneath the black stripe that extends forward onto the snout. The bar jack bears a resemblance to the blue runner *(see: runner, blue)* but has fewer and less prominent large scales along the caudal peduncle than the blue runner does. The bar jack has 26 to 30 soft rays in the dorsal fin and 31 to 35 gill rakers on the lower limb of the first arch. When feeding near bottom, it can darken almost to black.

Size.   Usually 8 to 14 inches in length, the bar jack reaches a maximum of 2 feet.

Distribution.   In the western Atlantic, bar jacks are found from New Jersey and Bermuda to the northern Gulf of Mexico and southern Brazil, as well as throughout the Caribbean.

Habitat.   Bar jacks are common in clear, shallow, open waters at depths of up to 60 feet, often over coral reefs. Usually traveling in spawning schools, they sometimes mix with goatfish and stingray, although they are occasionally solitary.

Food and feeding habits.   Opportunistic feeders, bar jacks feed mainly on pelagic and benthic fish, some shrimp, and other invertebrates.

Angling.   Bar jacks are usually caught on light spinning outfits and a small jig or small baited hook.

JACK, CREVALLE   *Caranx hippos.*
JACK, PACIFIC CREVALLE   *Caranx caninus.*

Other names for the crevalle jack—common jack, crevally, toro, trevally, horse crevalle; Spanish: *cavallo, chumbo, cocinero, jurel común.*

Other names for the pacific crevalle jack—toro, crevally, cavalla, jiguagua; Spanish: *aurel, burel, canche jurel, chumbo, cocinero, jurel toro, jurelito, sargentillo.*

These two members of the Carangidae family are almost identical in appearance and were formerly thought to be Atlantic and Pacific versions of *Caranx hippos.* Differences documented by scientists have led to the classification of the Pacific crevalle jack in recent years as a validly separate species from

has a more elongated body, a lighter band, and a shorter front dorsal fin.

Size/Age.   A large species, the almaco jack is known to grow to 3 feet in the Atlantic, although it is commonly between 1 and 2 feet long and weighs less than 20 pounds. In the Pacific, it grows to almost 5 feet and 130 pounds but usually weighs 50 to 60 pounds. In the Atlantic, the all-tackle world record is a 78-pound fish taken off Bermuda in 1990, whereas the Pacific all-tackle world record is a 132-pound fish taken off Baja California in 1964.

Distribution.   Found around the world, almaco jacks occur in the Indo-West Pacific from eastern Africa to the Mariana and Wake Islands, as well as north to the Ryuku Islands and south to New Caledonia; they are absent from the Red Sea and French Polynesia. In the eastern Pacific, they occur from Southern California to Peru, including the Gulf of California and the Galápagos Islands. In the western Atlantic, almaco jacks range from Cape Cod to northern Argentina, and they are present in the eastern Atlantic, although distribution is not well established.

Habitat.   A warmwater species, almaco jacks prefer deep, open water and inhabit the outer slopes of reefs, but they rarely swim over reefs or near shore. Young fish are often associated with floating objects and sargassum. Almaco jacks often travel alone and occasionally in schools at depths of 50 to 180 feet.

Spawning.   Almaco jacks spawn offshore from spring through fall.

Food.   An offshore predator, the almaco jack feeds mainly on fish but also on invertebrates.

Angling.   Like other jacks and especially amberjack, the almaco is a tenacious fighter, but it is caught less frequently than its amberjack cousins, probably because it is a generally deeper and more

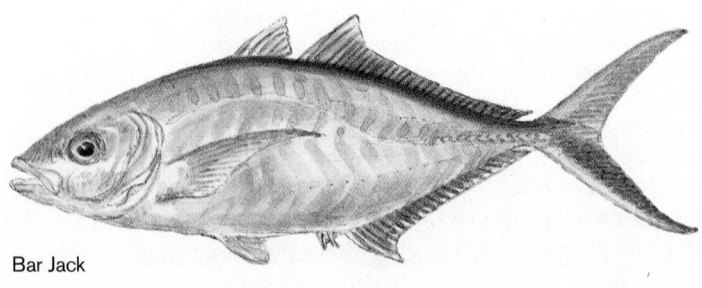

Bar Jack

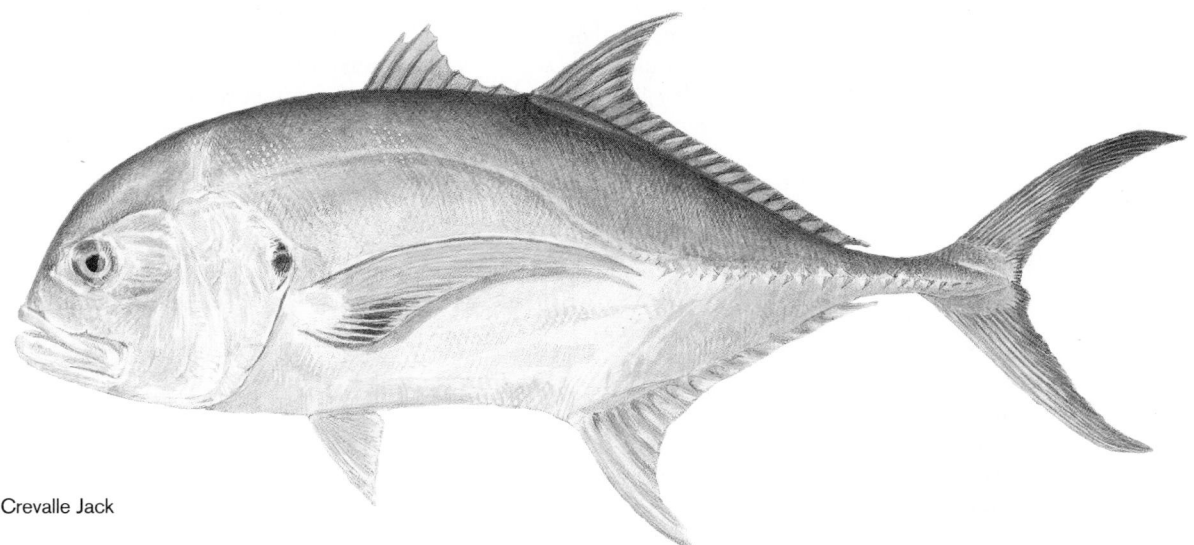

Crevalle Jack

the crevalle jack. These jacks are popular sportfish and are among the toughest of all inshore fish, although they are not highly valued as table fare. In addition, jacks in general have been associated with ciguatera poisoning. The Pacific crevalle jack is marketed fresh, frozen, smoked and salted/dried and may be utilized as fish meal and for its oil.

Identification. Both the crevalle jack and the Pacific crevalle jack are bluish green to greenish gold on the back and silvery or yellowish on the belly. They are compressed, and the deep body has a high rounded profile as well as a large mouth. The tail and anal fin may be yellowish, and the ends of the dorsal and upper tail are occasionally black. There is a prominent black spot on the gill cover and another black spot at the base of each pectoral fin. Young fish usually have about five broad, black bands on the body and one on the head. The soft dorsal and anal fins are almost identical in size, and there are 18 to 21 soft rays in the dorsal fin and 16 to 19 gill rakers on the lower limb of the first arch. The two species are distinguished externally from each other only by the presence of a larger maximum number of scutes, up to 42 on the Pacific crevalle jack, as opposed to 26 to 35 on the crevalle jack. The crevalle jack bears a resemblance to the Florida pompano but has a larger mouth. It can be distinguished from the similar horse-eye jack (*see: jack, horse-eye*) by a small patch of scales on the otherwise bare chest, whereas the chest of the horse-eye jack is completely covered with scales.

Size. Averaging 3 to 5 pounds in weight and 1 to 2^1/$_2$ feet in length, the crevalle jack can regularly weigh as much as 10 pounds; the Pacific crevalle jack is usually smaller. The all-tackle world record for the crevalle jack is a 57-pound, 5-ounce fish taken off Angola, and the record Pacific crevalle jack is a 29-pound, 8-ounce fish taken off Costa Rica.

Distribution. In the western Atlantic, crevalle jacks occur from Nova Scotia south throughout the northern Gulf of Mexico to Uruguay, including the Greater Antilles. In the eastern Pacific, Pacific crevalle jacks occur from San Diego, California, to Peru, including the Galápagos Islands.

Habitat. Both species can tolerate a wide range of salinities and often inhabit coastal areas of brackish water and may ascend rivers, frequenting shore reefs, harbors, and protected bays. Small fish are occasionally found over sandy and muddy bottoms of very shallow waters, as in estuaries and rivers. They are common in depths of up to 130 feet and often move into cooler, deeper water during the summer.

Life history/Behavior. Spawning occurs offshore from March through September. Young fish occur in moderate to large fast-moving schools, and crevalle jacks occasionally school with horse-eye jacks, although larger fish are often solitary.

Food and feeding habits. Voracious predators, they feed on shrimp, other invertebrates, and smaller fish. Crevalle jacks will often corner a school of baitfish at the surface and feed in a commotion that can be seen for great distances, or they will chase their prey onto beaches and against seawalls. Fish of both species often grunt or croak when they are caught.

Angling. Like other jacks, the crevalle and Pacific crevalle are tenacious fighters and excellent candidates for light-tackle fishing. The crevalle jack is most often caught by anglers casting and trolling for other species, commonly using artificial as well as natural baits. This superb light-tackle species can be taken by spinning, fly fishing, trolling, or surf casting, and with such live baits as mullet or pinfish. Anglers should retrieve lures and flies at a fast pace without pausing or stopping, as jacks tend to lose interest in anything that doesn't act normally.
See: Inshore Fishing; Jack.

JACKFISH

A term, often derogatory, used for northern pike and sometimes for chain pickerel, especially common in parts of Canada.

J

JACK, HORSE-EYE   *Caranx latus.*

Other names—big-eye jack, goggle-eye, horse-eye trevally; French: *carange moyole;* Portuguese: *guara-juba;* Spanish: *jurel, jurel ojo gordo, ojón, xurel.*

Like other jack species, the horse-eye is a member of the Carangidae family and a strong-fighting fish suitable for light-tackle angling. Unlike some jacks, it is not highly esteemed as a food fish, although the quality of horse-eye jack meat can be improved by cutting off the tail and bleeding the fish directly after it is caught. This and other jacks have been implicated in cases of ciguatera poisoning.

Identification.   The horse-eye jack is silvery, with yellow tail fins and usually dark edges on the dorsal and upper tail fin. There is often a small black spot at the upper end of the gill cover, and it usually has blackish scutes. The body is compressed, and the entire chest is scaly. There are 20 to 22 soft rays in the dorsal fin and 14 to 18 gill rakers on the lower limb of the first arch. The horse-eye jack is similar in shape to the crevalle jack, although it has a less steep forehead and is either lacking the dark blotch at the base of the pectoral fins of the crevalle jack, or the blotch is more poorly defined. It can also be distinguished by its scales, which the crevalle jack lacks except for a small patch.

Size.   This species is commonly found up to 30 inches and 10 pounds. The all-tackle world record is 24 pounds, 8 ounces.

Distribution.   In the western Atlantic, horse-eye jacks occur from New Jersey and Bermuda throughout the northern Gulf of Mexico to Río de Janeiro in Brazil. In the eastern Atlantic, they occur off the northwest coast of Africa, throughout the Ascension Islands, and scarcely in the Gulf of Guinea.

Habitat.   Horse-eye jacks are most common around islands and offshore, although they can tolerate brackish waters and may ascend rivers. Adults prefer open water and may be found over reefs, whereas young are usually found along sandy shores and over muddy bottoms. Schooling in small to large groups at depths of up to 60 feet, horse-eye jacks may mix with crevalle jacks.

Food and feeding habits.   Horse-eye jacks feed on fish, shrimp, crabs, and other invertebrates.

Angling.   This is a good light-tackle gamefish that can be taken with live baits such as mullet, pinfish, and other small fish, as well as with plugs, jigs, spoons, flies, and other small artificial lures. They are often encountered in fast-moving schools. Lures should be retrieved at a fast pace without slowing or stopping.

See: Inshore Fishing; Jack.

JACK PLATE

A device that raises an outboard motor up on the transom and also moves it away from the transom, increasing speed and fuel economy. Also known as a transom jack, it provides some of the benefits of a bolt-on transom bracket without its greater weight, higher cost, and sometimes engine-immersing problems.

Jack plates are popular on many high-performance boats, particularly bass boats, because they increase speed. Raising the engine 3 to 6 inches lifts that much more of the lower unit out of the water, reducing critical drag and thereby allowing an increase in speed. The higher you can raise the engine, the greater the increase. But you cannot raise the engine unless it is also moved back from the transom far enough to allow water running out from under the bottom to rise sufficiently to keep the required amount of the propeller in the water and ensure that adequate water gets to the motor's cooling system.

Besides increasing speed and fuel economy (some V6 outboards get as much as a 20 percent increase in speed and fuel economy), jack plates also permit shallower water operation at planing speed, shaving several inches off what could be obtained

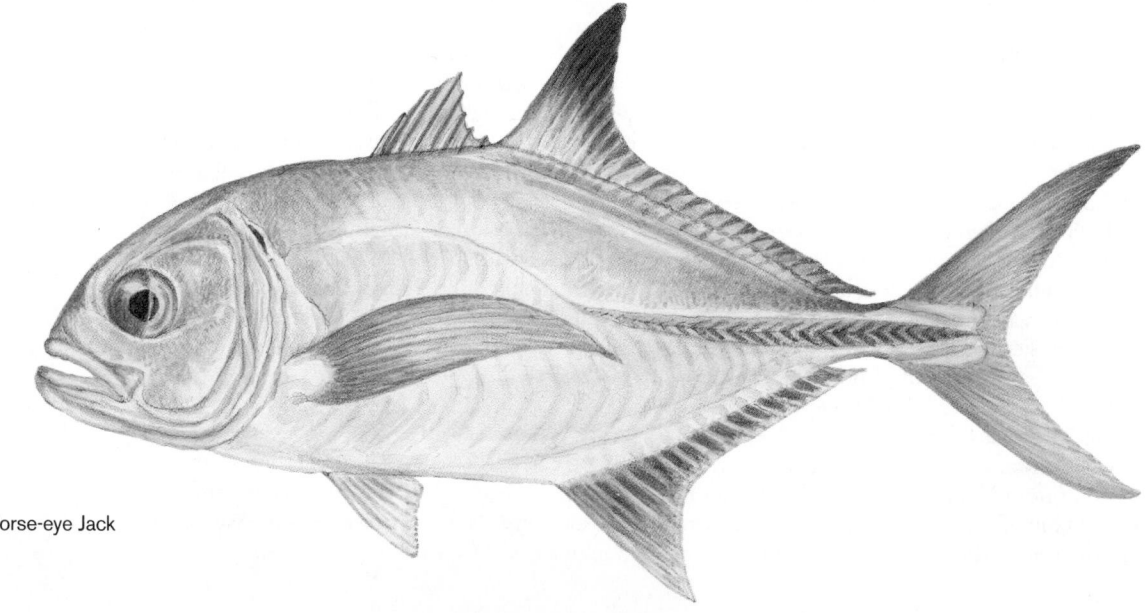

Horse-eye Jack

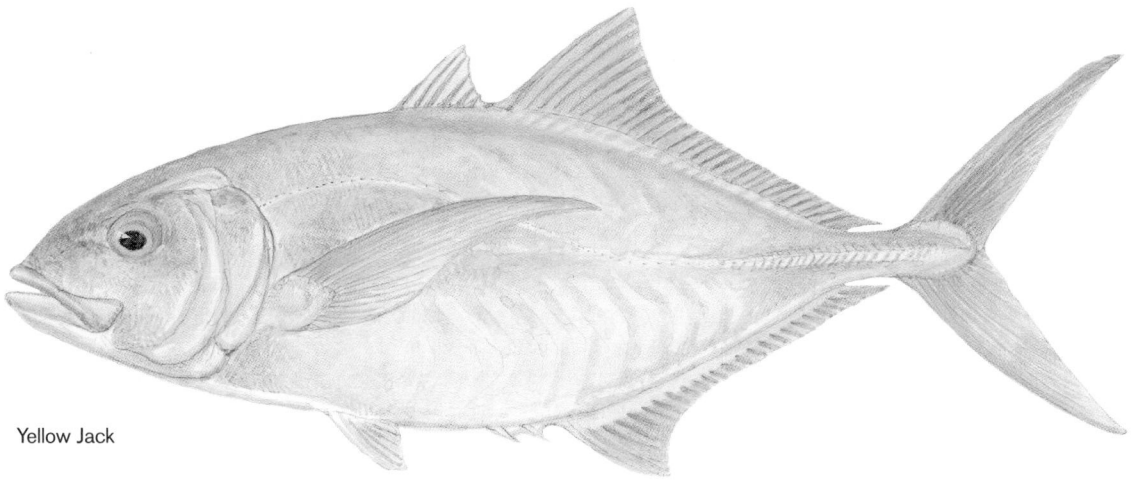

Yellow Jack

with a plate. These extra inches can make a big difference to some anglers, especially those on unfamiliar water who might otherwise nick their propeller or lower unit at an unexpected time.

Jack plates are available in manual and hydraulic electric versions. Adjusting the jack plate's height for optimum performance merely requires trying different elevations.

See: Boat.

JACKSMELT   *Atherinopsis californiensis.*
Other names—silverside, horse smelt, blue smelt, California smelt.

The jacksmelt is a member of the Atherinidae family of fish known as silversides *(see)* and not a true smelt *(see)*. It is an important forage species for predator fish, is a major component of the Pacific smelt commercial catch, and is one of the most common fish taken by pier anglers.

Identification.   The body of the jacksmelt is elongate and somewhat compressed. The head is oblong and compressed, and the eyes and mouth are small. The color is greenish blue above and silver below. A metallic stripe bordered with blue extends the length of the body.

Size/Age.   Jacksmelt can attain a maximum size of $17^1/_2$ inches and a little more than a pound. When 13 to 15 inches long, they are 8 or 9 years old, and they may live at least 11 years.

Distribution.   This species occurs from Santa Maria Bay, Baja California, to Yaquina, Oregon.

Habitat.   Jacksmelt are found in bays and ocean waters throughout the year. They are schooling fish that prefer shallow water less than 100 feet deep and are most common in 5- to 50-foot depths.

Spawning behavior.   The spawning season extends from October through March, and jacksmelt spawn first when two years old and about 6 inches long. Large masses of eggs, about the size of small BBs, are attached to shallow-water seaweeds by means of long filaments.

Food.   Jacksmelt feed on small crustaceans.

Angling.   These fish are often caught from piers but may also be taken in the surf. Sometimes a number of coiled-up worms are found in the flesh. These are intermediate stages of spine-headed worms, the adults of which are harmful to sharks, pelicans, and other fish predators. The worms are harmless to humans when the fish is thoroughly cooked.

JACK, YELLOW   *Caranx bartholomaei.*
Other names—French: *carangue grasse;* Spanish: *cojinua amarilla, cibi amarillo.*

This small and spunky member of the Carangidae family is an occasional catch by anglers. Its flesh is considered fair to good eating.

Identification.   Silvery with a yellow cast, the yellow jack has a bluish back and strongly yellow sides, which grow even more strikingly yellow after the fish dies. The fins are also yellowish, as is the tail. It lacks the black spot near the gill cover that the similar horse-eye jack has, and has a less steep head. There are 25 to 28 soft rays in the dorsal fin, and 18 to 21 gill rakers on the lower limb of the first arch. Young fish are more brassy in color and have many pale spots.

Size.   Averaging less than 2 pounds in weight and 1 to 2 feet in length, the yellow jack can reach a maximum of 3 feet and as much as 17 pounds. The all-tackle world record weighs 19 pounds, 7 ounces.

Distribution.   In the western Atlantic, the yellow jack is found from Massachusetts to the Gulf of Mexico, including Bermuda, and south throughout the Caribbean and the West Indies to Maceio in Brazil. In the eastern-central Atlantic, they are also found off the northwest coast of Africa.

Habitat.   Common on offshore reefs, yellow jacks are usually solitary or travel in small groups in depths of up to 130 feet. Young typically roam inshore in mangrove-lined lagoons, often in association with jellyfish and floating sargassum.

Angling.   Anglers usually catch yellow jacks incidentally, often while trolling.

See: Inshore Fishing; Jack; Offshore Fishing.

J

JAMAICA

At 144 miles long, Jamaica is the third largest island in the Caribbean and about the size of Connecticut. It lies 90 miles south of Cuba's eastern shores and is situated on the southern boundary of the deep Cayman Trench. A lack of shallow flats limits inshore fishing opportunities, but the quick drop-off to deep water provides fertile grounds for marlin, which are influenced by the flow of the Caribbean Current through the Windward Passage between Haiti and Cuba and through the Cayman Trench.

Proponents of Jamaican big-game angling proudly point out that you can fish suitable water for the highly coveted Atlantic blue marlin when you're just a few minutes from the dock, especially if the dock is at San Antonio or Ocho Rios on the north coast.

And it's true. The water drops to 100 fathoms very close to shore, and the marlin in these waters are abundant. Local boats, accustomed to raising a good number of fish per outing, rarely travel more than a few miles offshore. Anglers pursue their quarry from the near-shore drop-off to the 3,000-foot contour; this is a run of just $1/2$ mile to 3 miles from the island, depending on departure point.

The blue marlin in Jamaica are not particularly large as a rule. The normal range is between 100 and 350 pounds. An occasional larger fish is caught (the island record is a 590-pounder), and there is speculation that the bigger blues in these waters are holding well offshore, 30 miles or so, around banks that are hardly touched by anglers embarking from Jamaica.

Nevertheless, this is a great place to be in the fall. In a fall tournament in the late 1980s, 105 marlin were caught in four days, setting a local record. A double-header and a triple-header occurred during the event, and this is not a run-of-the-mill experience with blue marlin.

Blue marlin are reportedly here year-round, although the better fishing is from August through October. This is the breeding season and a period of peak abundance, when smaller males from 100 to 150 pounds are prominent. This doesn't quite overlap with the presence of white marlin in winter; although a few are caught prior to winter, they are most likely to be landed in February and March. In June, the larger female blues (300 to 350 pounds) are present, and they remain through the fall. They are, however, overshadowed by the more abundant smaller marlin, which provide good light-tackle opportunities.

Dolphin, king mackerel, yellowfin tuna, and wahoo round out other year-round possibilities, but dolphin are most abundant from March through May, and wahoo and tuna peak both in spring and fall. Sailfish, skipjack tuna, rainbow runners, and sharks also frequent these waters.

The important fishing ports are Port Antonio, Ocho Rios, and Montego Bay on the north shore, Kingston on the south shore, and Negril on the west end. Well-equipped charter boats with experienced crews are available, and beautiful Port Antonio—situated on the northeastern coast and relatively sheltered from southeast trade winds—is a prominent hub.

Inshore anglers have some opportunities as well, although these have not been widely explored or developed. Such reef species as barracuda, amberjack, yellowtail snapper, and various grouper are available. The coastal rivers hold tarpon and snook.

The Rio Grande, west of Port Antonio, has fair-size snook and tarpon. The Black River, in the southwest, is reported to have produced snook up to 20 pounds and tarpon to 100 in the past.

JAPAN

A small island nation in the western Pacific, Japan is surrounded by saltwater and blessed with freshwater in nearly every valley of its mountainous main islands. It borders the Sea of Okhotsk on the north, the Pacific Ocean on the east and south, the East China Sea on the southwest, and the Korea Strait and Sea of Japan on the west. With its more than 1,000 islands, Japan boasts nearly 30,000 kilometers of coastline.

Japan's waters are influenced by the warm Black Current *(Kuroshio)*, which moves northward from Taiwan, by the Black Current's offshoot, the Tsushima Current, and by the cold Okhotsk Current, which moves southward along the Kamchatka Peninsula. These opposing currents meet near the northern part of the largest Japanese island of Honshu (known as the mainland), making this region one of the world's most fertile saltwater fishing grounds. These are also among the influences that give this small country a diverse climate. The southernmost islands of Okinawa, and the Ogasawara chain, have a subtropical climate; the northern island of Hokkaido has a subarctic climate.

Because of these environmental conditions, Japan is blessed with abundant varieties of fish, and fish have been a food staple for the Japanese since long before recorded history. Both commercial and recreational fishing have a lengthy tradition as important components of Japanese society.

Japanese anglers pursue approximately 30 species of freshwater fish. The most prominent of these are several species each of carp, salmon, and trout, as well as landlocked charr. All of these are native and found throughout Japan except in the southern islands. Prominent introduced species include rainbow trout, brown trout, largemouth bass, and bluegills. Since 1992, however, the introduction of largemouth bass and bluegills has been banned by law to protect native species.

In recent times, Japan's freshwater fisheries have suffered from pollution, the absence of possession limits, unfamiliarity with the practice of voluntarily releasing fish, and an increasing angler population. These conditions have contributed to the depletion

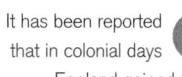
It has been reported that in colonial days England gained more wealth through fish products from the Americas than Spain obtained in gold.

of most native fish populations, and freshwater fishing sites and fish populations are primarily maintained through cultivation efforts and stocking.

Ocean fishing, however, is a different story. The popularity of shore and boat fishing in Japan is among the highest per capita anywhere in the world. Shore fishing is most popular, and almost every harbor and its surrounding area becomes a fishing spot. Fishing from rocky shores is usually practiced only by veteran anglers, and these areas have become top angling locations throughout Japan. Nevertheless, shore fishing has been steadily declining in recent decades due to overharvesting, especially by commercial interests.

Although anglers can pursue more than 80 saltwater species, they completely ignore sharks and fish that are not suitable for eating, even though these species may provide good sport on rod and reel. Furthermore, in Japan, sportfishing is limited to protect commercial fishermen; local regulations throughout most of the country, for example, ban trolling.

Popular small near-shore species of fish include Japanese horse mackerel (ma-aji), Japanese whiting (shirogisu), Japanese common sole (karei), rockfish (kasago), and brown rockfish (mebaru). All weigh less than 1 kilogram on average, but this doesn't detract from their popularity, as most Japanese boat and shore anglers tend to fish for the purpose of catching fresh fish to eat.

Other popular fish include black sea bream (kurodai), greenfish (mejina), Japanese parrot bass (ishidai), spotted parrot bass (ishigakidai), and moara grouper (kue). Except for the moara grouper, which can grow to more than 50 kilograms, the average size of these fish is 0.5 to 5 kilograms.

There are 37,000 boats for hire throughout Japan. These and private boats all strictly bottom-fish with fresh natural baits; fishing with lures and trolling are not practiced, as they are in North America and Europe. Hired boats may include charter boats as in North America, but most are party boats for which individuals pay a per person fee for eight hours of fishing.

In Japan, freshwater sportfishing is not controlled by the government but is managed by local city organizations or local angling cooperatives. Therefore, to obtain a sportfishing certificate or license, or to pay an entry fee to a fishing area, you must deal directly with the local manager of the area.

Hokkaido

Trout. With its generally cold climate, the northernmost island of Hokkaido is well suited to salmon and trout. The predominant species caught with lures and flies here include mountain trout or cherry trout, known as *yamame* (the freshwater-dwelling form of masu salmon); landlocked or whitespotted charr *(Salvelinus leucomaenis),* known as *ezo-iwana;* Japanese huchen, or *itoh;* Dolly Varden, or *oshorokoma;* and rainbow trout, or *niji-masu.*

The Japanese huchen is the largest of the salmonids in Japan and should not be confused with taimen. The range of the Japanese huchen is only Hokkaido and Saghalien; it can reach a length of 1.5 meters and weight of 20 kilograms. These large fish, however, have declined in number as a result of overfishing and development, which has destroyed their natural river habitats. Large Japanese huchen are rarely caught these days; the average catch is less than 80 centimeters (31 inches) long.

Lake Akanko in eastern Hokkaido is the most popular spot for trout fishing. From May through September, landlocked charr, Japanese huchen, rainbow trout, and brown trout can be caught on lures and flies. Dry-fly fishing is possible beginning in June. These fish are wild and put up a spectacular fight. The lakes have an abundance of pond smelt *(wakasagi),* a favorite food of trout. Streamer flies, which imitate the smelt, are thus used to land big trout here. Boat operators line the shores of the lake to take anglers out, and many people fish around the shores while wading.

Salmon. The most common species of salmon in Hokkaido is the chum salmon *(shirozake).* The average fish weighs 2 to 4 kilograms, and the largest is in the range of 8 kilograms. Until just a few years ago, salmon sportfishing in rivers, as well as within 500 meters of river mouths, was prohibited, although commercial fishermen could fish in these places because salmon were viewed as a vital source of food for the Japanese nation. Since 1995, however, when abundance brought down the price of salmon, some rivers were opened to anglers on a trial basis.

Currently, salmon sportfishing is permitted in three rivers: the Churui and Charo Rivers in eastern Hokkaido, and the Motoura River in Hidaka. Anglers commonly fish with spoons and streamer flies.

Saltwater. Charter boats and party boats exist for chum salmon fishing near Nemuro and Funkawan Bay from the end of August to the end of November. By the river mouth on the eastern side of Hokkaido, and in the Okhotsk Sea, anglers can catch pink salmon *(karafutomasu)* migrating upriver to spawn. The best time is August and September; mooching with cut baits, and fishing with metal jigs and spoons, are common tactics.

There is fishing for charr around the shores of Otaru and Shimamaki in Hokkaido from December through May, and this obviously requires appropriate warm clothing. Lure anglers cast spoons or metal jigs. Fly anglers use minnow or shrimp patterns on slow-sinking 8- to 12-weight fly lines. The fish average about 1 kilogram but can be caught to 3 kilograms.

Around Matsumae at the southernmost tip of Hokkaido, bluefin tuna *(kuromaguro)* weighing between 5 and 20 kilograms are caught on lures from July through November. Specimens in excess of 50 kilograms are possible. Here anglers use minnow-imitating lures on 8- to 9-foot spinning rods equipped with 30- to 50-pound line.

J

Anadromous masu salmon *(umimasu)* are found around the south shores of Hokkaido; a particularly good place is along the shores of Tomakomai. The best time is December through April. The average size is 1 to 3 kilograms, but there are occasionally larger specimens, some exceeding 5 kilograms. This area also produces chinook salmon *(masunosuke)* in the 10-kilogram class.

Other ocean fish around Hokkaido that are caught from a boat or from shore are flounder *(karei)*, greenling *(ainame)*, and ribbed greenling *(hokke)*, which are all relatively small fish.

Farther offshore there are Pacific cod *(madara)* in the 7- to 10-kilogram class; these are pursued from charter and party boats, which are available at most harbors.

Honshu, Shikoku, and Kyushu

Trout.   The long and narrow mainland island of Honshu features a mountain range that runs from north to south. Because the island is less than 300 kilometers wide at its widest point, no part of it (nor any other part of Japan, incidentally) is more than 150 kilometers from the sea. The rivers that run off mountains with a height of about 3,000 meters all have a steep incline and therefore run fast. The upper watersheds contain native landlocked charr and mountain trout (freshwater masu salmon).

Throughout all regions of Japan, there are also rainbow trout, which first came from North America. Rainbow trout do not fare as well as mountain trout and landlocked charr in the upper fast-flowing water, however, so they are mostly stocked in fish farms or fishing ponds. The season for all three species is generally from March through September. They may be caught only in fishing ponds after September.

The trout in these rivers, especially those dwelling upstream, are extremely small, averaging 20 to 25 centimeters in length. Due to large numbers of anglers, and no catch-and-release ethic, all of the stocked fish are caught, leaving no holdovers of larger fish for the following year.

Anadromous masu, or cherry, salmon migrate into the larger rivers that flow to the Japan Sea. Although they are few in number, they are targets for lure and fly casting. Their average size is 1 to 4 kilograms, and the occasional 5-kilogram-class fish is a prized catch. The Yoneshiro River in Akita Prefecture, the Aka River in Yamagata Prefecture, and the Kuzuryu River in Fukui Prefecture are known for these fish.

Lakes known for trout include Lake Ashino-ko in Hakone, Lake Kawaguchi-ko at the foot of Mt. Fuji, and Lake Chuzenji-ko at Nikko. Lake Chuzenji-ko is famous as the birthplace of trout fishing in Japan, and even today you can catch brown trout, rainbow trout, lake trout, and landlocked masu salmon in its waters.

Large rainbow trout are stocked in Lake Ashino-ko, and some exceed 70 centimeters and 5 kilograms in size. In Lake Kawaguchi-ko, emphasis has been placed on stocking rainbow trout, and the numbers have been increased in recent years. There are rental boats and lodging facilities around all of these lakes. Perhaps because of their proximity to Tokyo, these lakes host a large number of anglers every weekend.

Bass.   In 1925, largemouth bass were imported from the state of Oregon in the United States and first released in Lake Ashino-ko in Hakone. They have since been spread to other lakes.

Since about 1970, fishing with lures has increased in popularity in Japan, and largemouth bass were released in lakes throughout Honshu, Shikoku, and Kyushu, and fishing for this species has increased in popularity. Popular lakes for bass are Biwa-ko (northeast of Kyoto and the largest lake in Japan, covering about 672 square kilometers), Kasumiga-ura (northeast of Tokyo), Kita-ura, and Hachirogata, all on Honshu. As noted, however, further stocking of largemouth bass has been prohibited by law to protect native species, although fishing for bass is allowed.

These lakes all have northern-strain largemouth bass, but Ikehara Reservoir in Nara Prefecture has Florida largemouths. Although the numbers caught there are small, specimens in excess of 4 kilograms are taken around the month of June. The lake record, caught in 1998, is 6.86 kilograms.

Sweetfish.   Fishing for sweetfish *(ayu)* is a tradition that is unique to Japan. Throughout most rivers in Honshu, Shikoku, and Kyushu, as well as some rivers in Hokkaido, sweetfish fishing continues from the beginning of summer to the end of autumn every year.

There are two common fishing methods. One is Dobuzuri style. This is a type of wet-fly fishing in which two or three wet flies are rigged dropper style on a line attached to an 8- to 10-meter-long pole. Reels are not used. The other is Tomozuri style, in which live sweetfish are used as decoys to attract other fish. The quarry is lured close by and then snagged with a 9-meter-long telescopic pole that has a line just a bit longer than the rod. Reels are not used. A live sweetfish is placed on the line via a metal ring attached to its nose. A treble snag hook is attached to a leader 5 to 6 centimeters in front of the decoy. The average sweetfish is 18 to 25 centimeters long, and any specimen exceeding 30 centimeters is considered large.

Other freshwater fishing.   Other freshwater fishing in Japan is centered on members of the carp *(koi-zoku)* family. Since olden times the common carp *(koi)* and the Crucian carp *(funa)* have been representative catches, and both exist throughout Japan. Other cyprinids are pursued as well. Fishing for carp in Japan usually involves a telescopic rod without a reel for small specimens, and a 5-meter spinning rod with reel and 16- to 20-pound line for individuals that weigh more than 10 kilograms.

Since the Edo period of the eighteenth century, the Japanese have fished for a particular small fish that is normally less than 5 centimeters (2 inches) in size. Known as *tanago,* these fish, even when big, are no larger than 10 centimeters long. They are found mainly in the Kanto area of east-central Honshu in small rivers and ponds, especially during cold winter months. The specialized fishing equipment used is traditional, handmade, and expensive. The rod is 1.2 to 1.5 meters long and comprises six to eight pieces that are each about 25 centimeters long. The rod is used with a small float made from peacock feather and a specially designed small hook that is approximately 4 millimeters long. The best bait is the innards of moth cocoons, but kneaded egg yolk is also used.

Tanago fishing is rare and unique because the fish are so tiny. But the focus required to catch these small fish is the game.

General saltwater.   For the most part, saltwater sportfishing in Japan developed from commercial fishing. The majority of present charter boat captains are former commercial fishermen or people who still work in the commercial fishing industry. The species of fish sought are almost always those that are preferred as food. The species pursued for sportfishing vary according to location, but red sea bream *(madai),* flounder *(hirame),* yellowtail *(buri),* and sea arrow *(surumeika)* are popular throughout Japan.

Red sea bream and flounder are the prize catches. The former are common from 0.5 to 8 kilograms, but specimens from 8 to 10 kilograms are also possible. Traditional methods of catching sea bream are governed by location, but most people jig with prawn as baits. Red sea bream fishing is particularly popular throughout Honshu, Shikoku, and Kyushu.

Angling for flounder occurs throughout Japan except in subtropical areas. Although the largest of these can reach 15 kilograms, the average weight is 1 to 3 kilograms, and a specimen exceeding 5 kilograms is considered big. Live sardines are used as baits in bottom fishing efforts. The fishing season is from October through April. Flounder are also caught on plugs and metal jigs.

The common seabass *(suzuki)* is a popular catch for ocean lure anglers throughout Japan except in the southern islands and Hokkaido (the south shore of Hokkaido is the northerly limit for these species). Angling for these fish is prevalent from the shore, as well as in bays and river mouths; it is most prevalent in Tokyo and Osaka Bays. The median length is 30 to 50 centimeters, but occasionally specimens can reach 80 centimeters in length and 4 kilograms in weight; some grow as large as 1 meter long. Most fishing is done with a metal jig and a minnow-shaped plug. Charter and party boats specializing in common seabass fishing are available from almost any harbor. Spring and fall the prime seasons to pursue these fish.

Similar to the common seabass is the blackfin seabass *(hirasuzuki),* which live around the rocks near shore. This fish is popular among lure anglers

and is usually caught by experienced enthusiasts. Its size is similar to that of the common seabass, and the season lasts throughout the year, although this fish is scarce in midsummer.

Billfish.   Various billfish *(kajiki)* occur on the Pacific side of Honshu from February through October in areas washed by the Black Current. This includes striped marlin *(makajiki)* from 20 to 80 kilograms, Pacific blue marlin *(kurokajiki)* from 60 to 250 kilograms, black marlin *(shirokajiki)* from 80 to 250 kilograms, and sailfish *(bashokajiki),* which average 20 to 35 kilograms. Occasionally, shortnose spearfish *(fuulaikajiki)* from 15 to 30 kilograms are also caught.

Billfishing centers around the islands offshore of the Izu Peninsula, southwest of Tokyo. Charter boats for billfishing depart from Katsuura in Sotoboh, Shimoda in Izu, Miyake-jima in Izu-shichitoh, Nishiki in Kiihantoh, and Kushimoto. The Japanese-style boats usually have an outrigger but no fighting chairs or rod holders. The season begins in June, but July is best for blue marlin and black marlin. Angling success is sporadic, however, as commercial fishing pressure is heavy in this area.

Amami-ohshima and Okinawa

This subtropical area of Japan is part of the Ryukyu Islands and is popular as an ocean resort destination. It has convenient access as well as lodging and is a great place for gamefishing. English is seldom spoken, other than in the hotels, however, so non-Japanese-speaking visitors must be accompanied by an interpreter.

At Amami-ohshima, anglers catch giant trevally *(ronin-aji),* dogtooth tuna *(isomaguro),* and amberjack *(kanpachi)* weighing from 10 to 50 kilograms, plus yellowfin tuna *(kihada),* by casting or jigging. Because the winter months are affected by seasonal winds, the best time to fish for these species is from mid-May through November.

Charter boats for casting and trolling leave from the following islands: Amami-ohshima, Okinawa Hontoh, Kume-jima, Miyako-jima, Ishigaki-jima, Kohama-jima, Iriomote-jima, and Yonaguni-jima.

Casters here use a 7- to 9-foot-long spinning rod with a 2- to 4-ounce popping plug and 20- to 50-pound line. Jiggers use a 6- to 7-foot-long spinning or baitcasting rod with 20- to 80-pound-test line; a 4- to 12-ounce metal jig is fished at depths of between 30 and 200 meters.

Blue marlin are the primary marlin species. Commercial fishermen catch them to 400 kilograms here, but the largest caught by angling usually weigh around 200 kilograms. The average fish is in the 80- to 150-kilogram range. Sailfish are also abundant and are caught from 20 to 40 kilograms on average. Black marlin and striped marlin are small in number.

Among the tuna family, yellowfins in the 20- to 60-kilogram class are possible, but the average fish weighs less than 20 kilograms. The main methods

The largest-growing strain of brown trout once existed in Russia's Kura River, where anadromous sea trout averaged 33 pounds in the 1916 commercial catch.

of tuna fishing are jigging with a metal jig and fishing with baits. Fly fishing has been successfully tried, but only by a few anglers.

Dolphin *(shiira)* are also caught throughout this area, starting in May. The largest weigh from 28 to 30 kilograms, and the average fish weighs between 7 and 10 kilograms. In addition, reef fishing, which in Japan is unique to subtropical areas, is also popular.

Ogasawara (Bonin) Islands

The subtropical Ogasawara chain of islands, also known as the Bonin Islands, are located in the Pacific Ocean roughly 1,000 kilometers south of Tokyo, and north of the Mariana Islands.

This mid-ocean chain is roughly divided into three sections, the northerly Muko-jima islands, the Chichijima islands, and the southerly Hahajima islands. Access is limited to a weekly ferry from Tokyo; there is no air service. This limited access has helped keep these islands well preserved. The presence of steep cliffs all around the islands, as well as fast currents, has also prevented development, as has occurred at Okinawa. Rocky shore fishing, however, is more abundant here than in Okinawa and is especially good at Hahajima. Ferries run between the various islands.

From the rocky shores, anglers catch grouper *(hata)* up to 30 kilograms, two-spot red snapper *(barafuedi)* from 10 to 20 kilograms, amberjack and giant trevally from 10 to 50 kilograms, and dogtooth tuna and yellowfin tuna from 10 to 30 kilograms.

The best season for shore fishing is June through August. Fishing lasts until November, but in late summer and fall typhoons may result in ferry cancellations, requiring two-week ferry schedules. The tackle used for shore fishing is an 11- to 14-foot rod with 15- to 130-pound line and conventional reels. Frozen mackerel scad *(muroaji)* are used for dead baits, and small fish that can be caught around the rocks are used as live baits. Casting with lures and flies is also possible from rocks, but because the fish are large and powerful, heavy tackle is necessary.

Boat anglers can catch all of the aforementioned species and in larger sizes than do shore-bound anglers. They also catch wahoo *(kamasu-sawara)* that exceed 30 kilograms, and amberjack exceeding 50 kilograms, by casting or jigging.

Some areas in the open seas of the Ogasawara Islands remain undeveloped, and Japanese records are being set in these waters. Charter boats leave from Chichijima and Hahajima. Tackle for jigging and casting from boats is the same as that used in Amami-ohshima and Okinawa. Billfish are abundant in this area, but none of the local charter operations specialize in fishing for them or have the appropriate equipment.

JAÚ

A large South American catfish.
See: Catfish.

JERKBAIT

A specially balanced plug or soft worm without a built-in swimming action, fished fairly shallow beneath the surface in a twitching motion. This term once applied only to certain large wooden plugs used in muskie fishing, but today includes many hard- and soft-bodied lures that manifest these characteristics. Strictly used in casting, jerkbaits are mainly freshwater lures and are often grouped within other lure categories, especially plugs and soft worms.

Plugs. Jerk plugs are floating/diving lures that do not have surface fishing merit and do not dive and swim like normal plugs on a steady retrieve. Most are lipless, and the majority are wooden and are usually fished just under the surface. They are very buoyant and are retrieved in a series of pull-pause jerking motions, which makes them dart and roll in short bursts. Large models in 6- to 10-inch sizes are used in muskie fishing; some have rounded broom-handle-like bodies, others are flattened and rectangularly shaped, and some are homemade. One of the most popular muskie standbys has a small metal lip and metal tail, strictly for balance.

Other jerk plugs are in the 3- to 6-inch range and meant for bass, northern pike, and walleye. Some of these are called jerk plugs or jerkbaits mostly because of the manner in which they are best retrieved, which is in a ripping, jerking motion rather than in a straight swim, but they are otherwise similar to shallow-running minnow-shaped plugs. Some also have a suspending characteristic, which is beneficial when they are used around cover.

Worms. Soft worms that are fished in a similar manner to these hard plugs are also called jerkbaits, or jerk worms. The great majority are used in freshwater for largemouth bass, but some are suitable for saltwater casting in estuaries and shallow flats for striped bass, redfish, and seatrout.

Soft worms that suspend or sink slowly under the surface and that are deliberately erratic upon

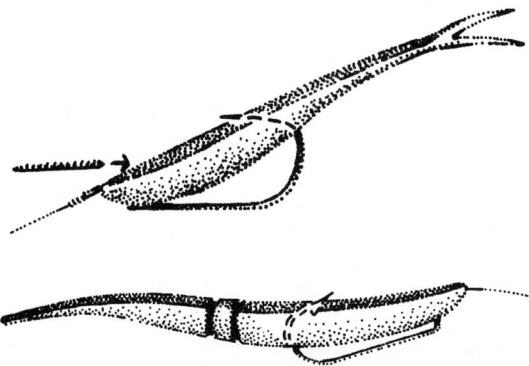

Shown are two common types of soft jerkbaits. Note that in rigging, the point of the hook is pushed through the soft lure, then retracted to just under the surface. Some models are weighted for balance or depth, often with a slender lead weight (top).

retrieval have been part of the freshwater bass angler's repertoire since the mid-1980s. Many of these lures are vaguely wormlike in appearance but could imitate eels, small baitfish, or other creatures in a general way.

These lures are not as supple as conventional soft worms, and they are usually fished suspended or just under the surface in a pull-pause, slow-jerking type of retrieve. This is different from the way most other soft lures are worked. Most soft worms, for example, are known for their slithering, shimmering, undulating type of action, worked primarily on or close to the bottom.

Unlike jerk plugs, jerk worms have a lackluster appearance, and it takes a little use to get accustomed to their rolling, disoriented-fish-like action. Actually, these soft plastics do look a lot like a wounded darting fish when jerked or when paused, because they descend slowly like a dying fish. Like conventional plastic worms, they are rigged with a single hook embedded inside, which makes them reasonably snag-resistant and very capable of being fished amidst heavy cover, especially vegetation. Lily pads, with their frequent openings on the surface and ample clearance below it, are very good locales for these lures.

Soft jerkbaits or jerk worms are usually rigged without a conventional sinker. They may be fished unweighted for shallow use or may be fished with a thin-diameter 1-inch-length lead stick or nail segment inserted into the head for deeper use, longer casts, and less erratic action. The hook should be deployed in a semi-Texas rig manner, with the point slightly protruding through the wider top (or back) of the bait for better hookups. Hook point placement, and style of hook shank, varies with different baits.

Some jerk worms dart well from side to side, and others have more of a slightly canted darting-rolling action. You should experiment a bit with hook size and placement to achieve the desired effect, and you should also be attentive to proper rerigging after a fish has been caught.

When fishing either of these types of jerkbait, you typically have to keep your rod tip down and pointed at the water. You can work them quite well on a raised rod (angled at a 10 to 11 o'clock position) but only when the lure is a long distance away. A low rod angle also aids hooksetting.

See: Plug; Soft Worm.

JET BOAT

A boat propelled by a jet-drive motor and used for navigating in extremely shallow areas, primarily rivers. Jet boats, which are also referred to as jet sleds, are popular with river anglers who travel considerable distances and who at times need to run in mere inches of water. Jet boats are especially popular in the Pacific Northwest and in Alaska but are also used in other areas.

The advantage of a jet boat is obvious to the angler who must traverse shallow rivers and has limited time to fish. It's easy to fish along very shallow rivers via drift boats, canoes, and inflatables, but only in one direction: downstream. It's difficult to cover much distance upstream, even in a canoe, if there is any significant current to beat against. Float trips are a fine way to see and fish a river, if you have the time. But, if you have only a few hours to do your angling, or have a lot of upstream distance to cover rapidly, then jets are the way to go.

A good jet rig is fast. It will even quickly ascend rapids and long stretches of white water if the boat is properly designed and the engine has sufficient horsepower. Some top-end jet boats can cover 50 miles of river, much of it upstream, in little more than an hour.

Jet boats are overwhelmingly aluminum models with flat-bottom hulls, but newer versions include fiberglass models and versions with tunnel hulls. Inflatables also can be used, although they are not as efficient as well-designed aluminum hulls, probably mostly due to air entrainment under the hull that mixes with water in the jet's intake.

Jet-drive motors are not efficient unless they can keep the boat, when fully loaded, easily on plane. A hull that is on plane draws much less water than one that is plowing through the water at displacement speeds. Since the jet unit does not project significantly below the bottom of the boat, it will work just fine as long as there is barely enough water for the boat to plane through.

The lowest point of a jet-drive motor, either outboard or inboard, is the intake; when properly installed, the intake projects only an inch or so lower than the bottom of the boat. When the rig is on plane, the rear nozzle directs a high-velocity stream of water backward through the air, much like a fire hose. Only the skimming intake grill touches the water.

Driving a jet boat is different from driving a conventional boat. When designed for skinny river work, the hull has no significant keel. The jet unit itself has no "rudder" in the water (the skeg and lower unit of a conventional outboard lower unit or stern serve as a rudder) and thus can steer by thrust only. It's more like an airboat, which means a certain amount of planning ahead is required when underway. When making a quick turn, it's sometimes necessary to reduce power a little, momentarily, to prevent sliding. It's also necessary to start each turn a little early, since the boat will slide into turns.

See: Jet Drive.

JET DRIVE

A jet-drive motor is one in which the lower unit features a propeller-less water-intake propulsion system, rather than having a traditional propeller immersed in the water below the boat hull. The intake is covered by a screen and is flush to the hull;

Tests have shown that a fish weighing 20 pounds upon capture will lose 1 pound 4 ounces through dehydration after being left in the open air for 12 hours.

J

an impeller pulls great volumes of water in and expels it out a rear discharge, resulting in forward momentum. To maneuver in reverse, which is not done well in a jet boat, a clam-shaped deflector cups over the discharge area.

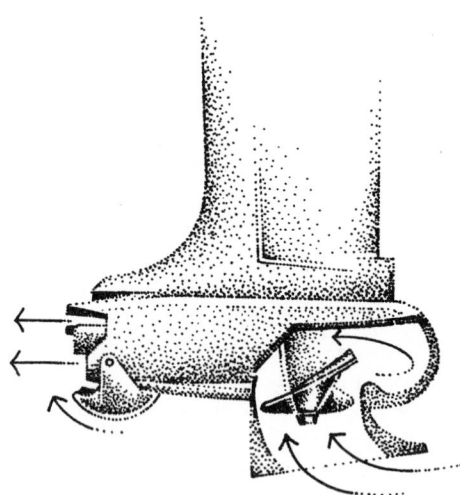

In a jet drive, water is drawn into a pump by an impeller, then forced out at high velocity to provide forward momentum. A gate closes over the outflow area to provide neutral and reverse modes.

Boats equipped with a jet drive are usually called jet boats (including the small and popular vessels called "personal watercraft"), and fishing boats with jet engines in the Pacific Northwest are called jet sleds. Jet-drive motors accelerate quickly, turn sharply, and feature shallow draft when used on appropriate boats. Anglers typically use jet drives on flat-bottomed boats, enabling them to run in just a few inches of water, which is especially useful when navigating many rivers. They also use them on tunnel-hulled boats, which puts the transom in the so-called tunnel and at the transom line for an unimpeded pickup of water and the ability to run in whatever little water the skimming transom can handle.

Jet-drive motors come in basically inboard and outboard versions. The inboard version is rigged more like a stern drive than a regular inboard, with the jet nozzle protruding from the transom where the outdrive unit would be for an inboard/outboard (I/O). The outboard version is either manufactured in whole or fashioned from conventional outboards via a conversion unit; in the latter case, a jet housing is bolted onto the bottom of an outboard exhaust housing, right where the lower unit was before it was removed to make room for the jet pump. It's possible to buy conversion units for almost all of the popular makes of outboards, from 18 to 235 horsepower (hp), and to find manufactured units in a similarly wide range of power.

In the higher ranges, a jet-drive boat can move very fast. When matched with the right hull, it may be actually somewhat faster than a similar size prop-driven inboard with the same horsepower.

With a jet drive, a flat-bottomed boat can run in the skinniest water, and a semi-V can run in just a few inches. Jet-drive motors use more fuel than conventional engines, cut horsepower by up to a third, and have very "loose" steering. They are noisier than a propeller-equipped motor and require some getting used to for steering, especially in rough water and windy situations. They are not suitable for areas with heavy vegetation, which is sucked into the impeller and clogs it. But shallow-water operation is a great advantage in some places. Plus a jet drive is good for fighting strong fish because there is no propeller in the water to cut the line, and a jet drive is safer than a propeller when there are people in the water.

The bottom of the propeller-less jet drive aligns with the bottom of the hull.

Jet-drive motors do not have a neutral gear, and when operating they are always in forward or reverse movement, primarily the former. When the key is turned on a jet drive, even with the throttle in neutral position and with the boat at rest on a boat trailer or tied to a dock, the motor is pulling in water and pushing the boat forward. This can be a disadvantage in docking and at some launch ramps. To depart, especially when the motor is cold, it may be wise to turn the boat around, facing the open water for boarding. This is also a drawback when trying to control a boat slowly, where you might otherwise put the motor in and out of forward, neutral, and reverse. That type of manipulation is not as effective with a jet drive, perhaps making it less desirable for some anglers.
See: Jet Boat.

JETTY

A man-made structure, usually of concrete or stone, projecting into the water from the shore to protect a sandy beach from erosion, funnel current from an inlet, or protect a harbor or pier. Jetties may be constructed of wood and stone, or all stone, and form a perpendicular wall-like extension from a rocky or sandy shore into the water. They are primarily found in saltwater along the coasts.

Technically, a jetty is a structure that extends from inlets and harbor mouths. Its purpose is to protect those places by impeding wave and current action and to keep the entrance to them open for boat traffic; it is also meant to stabilize the beach or shoreline and help prevent erosion. Inlet and harbor jetties support various navigational aids.

Structures extending from a beachfront are technically called groins (see) but are commonly referred to as jetties. Groins are intended to impede the action of waves and current and to prevent erosion by stabilizing the sand in the immediate vicinity; they do not usually have navigational aids.

Jetties also exist on large bodies of freshwater, such as the Great Lakes, where they are primarily intended to aid boat passage and protect harbor entrances; freshwater jetties are often called piers (see), especially if they are topped with a surface that allows easy pedestrian access.

A jetty is slightly different from a breakwater (see) in that a jetty is usually narrower, shorter, and in some cases higher; it serves the same purpose, however. Some breakwaters are detached from shore, not accessible by foot, and may not be perpendicular to the beach or shoreline. Jetties always protrude above the water except under extreme water conditions, and they are a favored place for angling for diverse species.

See: Jetty Fishing; Surf Fishing.

JETTY FISHING
Fishing Coastal Jetties, Groins, Rockpiles, and Breakwaters

For the shore-bound coastal angler, the area close to the beach holds diverse fishing opportunities. These are available along the expansive shoreline, which requires fishing along the shore directly in the surf or fishing around and near various accessible structures. Some of the popular structures that exist are piers, bridges, docks, and bulkheads (see: pier fishing). The most commonly fished structures are the assorted formations of rock, concrete, wood, and rubble that protrude into the water. Such formations include groins (see), inlet jetties, rockpiles that may or may not have been deliberately placed, and accessible harbor breakwaters (see). Though slightly different, these are all commonly referred to by anglers and the general public as jetties (see), and they provide a wealth of angling possibilities.

Fishing these jetties often develops into a lifelong challenge. It is a challenge that depends solely on the angler and the skills and experience that are developed. It can be enjoyed at nominal cost and can provide a wide range of species and angling experiences, as well as some of the sea's most challenging fishing. Jetty fishing is actually among the most physical types of angling you can experience, especially if you move about, visit several jetties, and work along the length of each of them.

Striped bass, shown here, and many other species are found among the rocks of jetties or in the turbulent water nearby.

Jetty fishing is unlike other types of saltwater angling in that there is no comfortable platform like a boat, or secure location like a beach, to fish from. Angling from jetties requires dexterity to move about the moss- and mussel-covered rocks, sometimes in the darkness of night; an ability to present a lure or bait properly to gamefish that are often tough adversaries; and the temerity to land fish from a promontory that is often cascaded with crashing waves and flying spray. Jetty fishing aficionados, known as "jetty jockeys," are a breed of anglers who find excitement, challenge, and reward in an activity that tests their skills every second they are on the rocks.

The testing is worth the discomfort endured and the energy expended, however, not only because of the exciting situation, but because of the great

An angler fishes from the head of the jetty at Barnegat, New Jersey.

variety of species that are caught from rockpiles and jetties on all coasts. Mid-Atlantic and New England jetty anglers, for example, find such bottom feeders as both summer and winter flounder, tautog, sea bass, pollock, and cod around these locations, as well as striped bass, bluefish, weakfish, and the occasional little tuna.

In the Southeastern United States and along the Gulf Coast, flounder, grouper, croaker, sheepshead, and a variety of snapper are caught among the rockpiles and coral outcroppings, as well as more prized species like redfish, bluefish, tarpon, snook, barracuda, and spotted weakfish (trout). Along the Pacific Coast, surf perch, rockfish, Pacific halibut, and sand bass, as well as Pacific barracuda, yellowtail, and Pacific bonito, succumb to those who cast from the many rocky outcroppings.

Other species also are encountered, some less often than others. Jetty anglers who cast from coral breakwaters in the Bahamas, for example, are known to regularly catch bonefish while working a bait on the bottom, and big cobia are occasionally landed from breakwaters in Alabama's Mobile Bay.

The variables of how, where, and when you fish these locations all affect your success, no matter what the geographic location or the species likely to be encountered.

Tackle.   The types of tackle used on jetties vary widely, from heavy-duty surf outfits with levelwind reels, all the way down to light spinning gear and fly rods. Some of the lighter outfits are used by occasional jetty anglers, and they may have success under favorable conditions for smaller species. Generally you need to match the tackle to the water conditions, the lures or bait that need to be fished, and the size of the species. Although room exists for a wide range of equipment under optimum conditions and in certain situations, keep in mind that when the water gets rough, the conditions get difficult, and the species get large, your equipment must be up to the demands.

Rods and reels.   Spinning tackle is by far the most popular gear for jetty fishing, but some anglers use conventional or baitcasting equipment and there are opportunities for flycasters as well.

Two types of outfits are necessary for most jetty fishing. A near-universal choice for small fish is a 6- to 7-foot rod with a fairly stiff action, coupled with a reel capable of holding 200 yards of 10- or 12-pound-test line. This will handle the smaller bottom-feeding species that are found within reasonable casting range.

To deal with gamefish species in the 5- to 20-plus-pound category (like tarpon, snook, redfish, striped bass, bluefish, cobia, and yellowtail), larger lures and baits and heavier gear are in order. Here, you need a 7- to 8-foot rod with a stiff action, capable of casting a 3- or 4-ounce sinker, bucktail jig, metal squid, or large and heavy plug. This rod should be coupled with a medium-heavy spinning reel that can hold 200 to 250 yards of 12- to

17-pound line on conventional or levelwind reels with similar capacity. Veteran jetty anglers feel that if a fish cleans you out of line when you are using such an outfit, it deserves to get away.

Admittedly, fly fishing from jetties is difficult, but it is manageable when using a stripping basket (see). A 10-weight outfit with a sink-tip shooting head line is a good choice; the reel should have between 150 and 200 yards of backing for the time when a bruiser takes a streamer and heads for the horizon.

Bottom bait rig.   Use a basic bottom-fishing bait rig for fishing natural bait around jetties. This is constructed via a three-way swivel, with a sinker on a 3- or 4-inch-long loop of monofilament line attached to one eye of the swivel, and a snelled hook on a 3-foot length of line attached to the other eye. The line to the hook should be 20- or 30-pound test. Use a pyramid sinker for holding qualities if the surf near the jetty is rough, and a bank or dipsey sinker if it is light. Weight varies from 2 to 4 ounces.

You can tie in a dropper loop about a foot from the swivel and place a second hook there. It may be useful to place a Styrofoam float, a half inch in diameter and between 1 and 2 inches long, on the leader where it meets the hook. This strategy suspends the hook and bait off the bottom, within range of cruising fish yet away from pesky crabs on the bottom. When targeting summer flounder, weakfish, striped bass, redfish, rock bass, and species that average a couple of pounds or more, use a 2/0 or 3/0 Beak, Claw, or Wide Gap hook, particularly with seaworms, shrimp, squid, killies, or other small baits. When fishing with large, 2- to 4-inch-long chunks of menhaden, mullet, mackerel, or other fish, or whole squid or clams, use 4/0 through 6/0 hooks.

Work such a rig on the bottom in the waters surrounding the structure you're fishing. Assuming you're fishing from a rockpile that extends several hundred feet seaward, make your initial casts from along the side of the jetty just outside the surf line. Often the churning surf exposes sand fleas, crabs, shrimp, sand eels, and other forage, and the fish move in to feed. Patience is important, but if your bait rests on the bottom in prime water and doesn't receive a strike in 10 to 15 minutes, move farther out on the jetty and make another cast into new water. Keep repeating this procedure until you receive strikes; this way you're covering the entire bottom surrounding the structure.

It's usually not essential to cast great distances while fishing from a jetty or rockpile, since the natural forage is often in close. A good practice is to make a cast of nominal distance, perhaps 100 to 150 feet, and periodically reel in the bait several feet, thus bracketing the entire area.

Freelined live bait.   Live baits are often used when targeting some bigger gamefish. These should be freelined without a sinker so that the bait can swim out and away from the jetty. For this, tie a tiny barrel swivel to the end of the line and then a 3- or 4-foot leader of 20- to 30-pound test. The leader is heavier than the main line because fish often ingest part of the leader when taking the bait, and this helps prevent leader breakage. This basic terminal rig will work for the majority of species found around coastal jetties. The key is tailoring the size of the hook and bait to the species being sought.

Beak and Claw style hooks are favored for live bait; some anglers employ the O'Shaughnessy or Chestertown style, and circle hooks are becoming more popular. If targeting 1-pound winter flounder and using bloodworms as bait, you should try a No. 8 or 9 Chestertown hook with a 2-inch-long piece of sandworm bait, since the flatfish have very small, rubbery mouths. If line-shy Pacific bonito are the quarry, try a No. 4 or 5 Beak-style hook and anchovy.

Anglers who fish live crabs for tarpon often use 5/0 through 7/0 hook sizes; these are honed needle sharp, with the hook placed through the crab's hard shell so that the crab can swim about freely, and with the pincer claws clipped off to prevent getting nipped while handling. Anglers targeting striped bass employ menhaden, mackerel, and herring; they lightly hook the bait just beneath the dorsal fin, cast it out, and permit it to swim away from the jetty. Live eels are fished in a similar manner, except that they are usually hooked through the lips or eyes. Live mullet are also used to tempt strikes from tarpon, snook, and redfish. Some anglers add a sliding float to their line, positioning it so that their bait works from 3 to 5 feet beneath the surface, with the float signaling precisely where the bait is.

Properly hooked, a live baitfish will swim about for a half hour or more, quickly becoming excited as a large gamefish zeroes in on it. Live baits such as these are transported to jetties in 5-gallon buckets, placing just a couple of baits in the bucket so that all of the oxygen in the water isn't quickly consumed. This is just about the only practical way to bring live bait onto jetties and departs from the rule that buckets should not be carried onto rockpiles. When the bait is no longer useful, save it and use it in chunks or strips later, after you've used up all your live ammunition.

Lures. The most popular lures at the disposal of the jetty fraternity include metal squids, plugs, and bucktail or soft-bodied jigs. Within these three lure categories are dozens of combinations.

Metal squids include the time-proven molded-block tin squids, hammered stainless steel jigs, chrome- and gold-plated jigs, and assorted variations of the diamond jig. Some of these are fished plain and others by adding a plastic tail or tube to the hook, or feathers, bucktail skirt, or pork rind strip. The lures are available in sizes ranging from $1/4$ ounce to 3 or 4 ounces. The key is matching lure size and color to the baitfish in residence.

Dozens of plugs also have merit around jetties. Perhaps the most popular one is the swimming minnow version with a side-to-side swimming action. Shallow, intermediate, and deep-diving models come in one-piece or jointed versions and in various sizes and every color imaginable. Matching size is important here also. Other possibilities include an assortment of popping, darting, and skipping surface plugs. All are fun to use, and each requires a different technique when retrieved to maximize its action and draw strikes. These work best when there is a lot of activity around the jetties and competition for food.

A bucktail or plastic-bodied jig may be the best all-around lure for jetty fishing. Various sizes, colors, and soft body styles are possible. With the soft tails, you simply select the size and look that seems best and slip the tail onto the hook. The soft bodies are made to exactly replicate many baitfish, include such important jetty forage as sand eels, herring, and mullet.

Jetty anglers regularly employ some of these lures in combination; they'll use a plug or metal squid as the primary lure at the end of the line and put a hooked soft-tail bait 24 to 30 inches ahead of that as a teaser. This combination is deployed by tying a small barrel swivel to the end of your line, followed by a 30- to 36-inch leader for attaching the main lure. The teaser, which can also be a streamer fly or even just a strip of pork rind on a hook, is then tied off the barrel swivel on a 6-inch dropper line. Sometimes the teaser gets strikes, and sometimes the primary lure. It's not unusual to hook a double, with a fish on each lure; this often happens when a lot of bluefish, seatrout, and striped bass are around.

Live eels are used effectively for striped bass, weakfish, cobia, and other species found around rockpiles, although many anglers employ dead rigged eels with great results. These common eels, ranging in length from 6 to 18 inches, are killed in salt brine. They are then rigged on metal squids designed expressly for this purpose. The metal squid's hook is placed in the head of the eel, and a second hook is run through the eel with a rigging needle so that it comes out near the eel's vent. Rigged in this manner, the eel is a combination lure and bait. It is cast and retrieved much the same as a plug or metal squid and is very effective.

Anglers generally keep six to a dozen eels rigged and stored in Kosher or sea salt brine in 1-gallon plastic jars. These jars, used for mayonnaise, are easily obtained at most delicatessens. Rigged and stored in this manner, the eels are tough and keep for months at a time.

It's easy to make the mistake of carrying a massive lure selection with you and constantly changing. The better tactic is to select two or three lures of each basic type and build confidence in using them, matching the lure to the specific situation. When the surf adjacent to the jetty is running high and the wind is onshore, for example, it's appropriate to break out a heavy metal squid to reach into

Perhaps the oldest ancestor of today's plugs was the Phantom Minnow, an English lure made around 1800 consisting of a metal head, metal fins, three treble hooks, and a silk body.

J

the stiff wind, whereas on a calm, windless night a small swimming plug worked in close to the rocks may be just right.

Footwear. Safety underfoot is unquestionably the most important consideration for accessory equipment when jetty fishing. You'll be walking on a variety of surfaces, from solid rock to concrete and wood, all of which may be wet, covered with slippery marine growth, or sheathed in mussels. Peculiar configurations are the norm, and you must sometimes have the dexterity of a mountain goat to negotiate angles and crevices to reach a spot that is flat enough to cast from and that also provides a decent chance at landing your quarry. Be careful as you move about the rockpiles, and make safety a primary concern.

Wearing ordinary footwear while fishing from jetties, such as sneakers or shoes, or even rubber-soled boots or waders, is sheer folly, and only practical when the jetty is high and dry—which is usually when the fishing is poor. This type of footwear does not give you traction when you're negotiating peculiar angles, nor does it hold securely on slippery, slimy marine growth.

A variety of jetty footwear is available, with the term "jetty creepers" most often used to describe soles designed to secure your footing. Ordinary golf soles, such as those found on golf shoes, which have replaceable aluminum cleats, are ideal, although they do not last long. The golf shoes can be worn as is, especially when fishing from jetties where you're situated well above the water and don't have to wear boots or waders to gain access. You can also wear golf rubbers, which, if large enough, can be slipped over regular boots or waders.

Another option is to have a shoemaker carefully remove the rubber sole from a pair of boots or waders and then cement golf soles to the bottom. This method is used extensively by veteran jetty anglers. Over time, the aluminum golf cleats wear down from the abrasion of the rocks, but they are easily replaced using a wrench made expressly for that purpose. Always lubricate the threads of the cleats when inserting them; this prevents them from becoming corroded and makes replacement easier.

Manufactured strap-on creepers are also used by jetty jockeys, but they are less desirable, because the straps tend to bind and the creepers may be tough to put on and uncomfortable to wear. The creepers have spikes on the soles for gripping; they can be slipped over canvas boat shoes in warm climates or over wader boots but must be sized accordingly. There are also jetty creepers made to slip on over boots and footwear. Some anglers even use felt-soled boots and chainlike slipovers on their boots. None of these options are as effective, safe, or comfortable as the golf soles.

Depending on where you fish and the type of structure you'll be fishing from, select basic footwear as light as you can go. Golf shoes are ideal, followed by knee boots if you'll be sloshing through ankle-deep water, followed by hip boots and waders, the latter as a last resort. You will need boots or waders on jetties or breakwaters where the surf has eroded the beaches, requiring that you wade through water to gain access.

Other gear. A storm suit is still another piece of indispensable gear. In most jetty fishing situations, waves crash against the rocks, producing wind-blown spray. In cold weather, a breeze can be chilling. The suit provides warmth, dryness, and comfort, especially during cold weather.

Mobility is essential while jetty fishing, so carrying a tackle box or bucket is usually not an option. Newcomers who carry a tackle box often suffer the consequences of placing it on a rock: slipping into a crevice and losing its contents, or being showered with a crashing wave. A shoulder bag is the only way to go. Carry a minimum of essential gear and use plastic sealable pouches to keep gear in the bag readily accessible and dry. Many good shoulder bags are available, some compartmented with plastic tubing and sleeves for inserting plugs, metal squids, and bucktails. Store the bag in a well-ventilated spot after each jetty fishing excursion; if you place a wet shoulder bag in a damp place and come back a week later, your lures will be a rusty mess.

If you elect to fish from jetties at night (which is often when the angling is superior as the fish move in close to feed), you'll need a headlamp. This can easily be strapped loosely around your collar, so that the light hangs under your chin. The headlamp

Wet moss and slippery rocks on jetties make walking hazardous; most regulars use cleated soles to improve traction.

Jetty fishing offers the opportunity to fish at various levels and with various techniques, depending on water conditions and likely species.

makes changing lures, moving around the rocks, or putting your beam on a fish about to be landed relatively easy. Forget penlights and regular flashlights because you need hands-free lighting and mobility.

Veteran jetty jockeys who target large gamefish of a size that can't be lifted with their outfit generally employ a long-handled gaff to land their catch. The gaff handle is usually the same length as the rod you're using, with a 2-inch gaff hook. The long handle enables you to reach the fish without getting too close to the water, an important consideration when heavy surf is working across the rocks. Make sure that you can legally gaff a gamefish that is under an established minimum size restriction. Even when there are no prohibitions on gaffing but still a minimum size limit, only employ a gaff if you're absolutely certain the fish is well beyond the minimum size restriction, and you intend to keep it.

If you'll be keeping fish, you should have a 6-foot length of plastic-covered clothesline with you. This makes an excellent stringer, especially for small and medium-size fish.

General Jetty Tactics

Tidal influence.   Tides play an important role when fishing from jetties. High tide may bring 8 or 10 feet of water where only a sand flat existed at low tide. At some jetties, the rockpile isn't even accessible at high tide, and you can get onto the rocks only after the tide has ebbed for a couple of hours. Experience is the best teacher. Visit the spots you plan to fish; if you're new to an area, visit the local tackle shops and ask their advice about tides. Keep in mind there are no set rules, for many of the species move about with the tides, taking up station

to feed for just a short while and then moving on. The key is learning which jetty locations produce results at a given tide stage and planning your strategy accordingly. It's not unusual for a jetty jockey to visit several jetties in the course of a tide, capitalizing on the movements of the fish.

Because erosion and the ravages of the ocean often displace rocks and tumble them about away from the jetty, you will at times foul your rigging on them. It's a good idea to pre-visit the jetties you plan to fish when the tide is low; then you can make a visual observation of spots to avoid later when the water is higher and more favorable for fishing. Often the fronts of jetties are in disarray; at high tide the jetty appears straight and intact, whereas on the ebb tide you'll notice that the front of the jetty actually has boulders tumbled about. Scouting your locations at a time when you can learn about their characteristics is very useful.

Cover it all.   No two jetties are alike, and it takes a while to master the techniques of fishing each. Keep in mind that fish are attracted to a jetty because forage species often seek the protection of the rocks; thus, crabs, lobsters, sand fleas, and shrimp are readily available. Since you have no way of knowing precisely where the fish will be feeding, it is very important that you thoroughly cover with your lures all the water surrounding the jetty.

This is best accomplished by making your first cast shortly after you walk out onto the jetty, placing your lure just outside the curl of the breakers working in toward the beach. Often the churning action of the waves there exposes sand fleas, crabs, and shrimp, and fish will move into the heavy water to feed. After several casts, move out onto the jetty

J

and bracket your casts, making a cast in toward the beach, so that the retrieve almost parallels the jetty. Next place a cast at a 45-degree angle from where you're standing, then straight in front of you, out 45 degrees, and finally almost paralleling the jetty. Then move out and repeat the procedure.

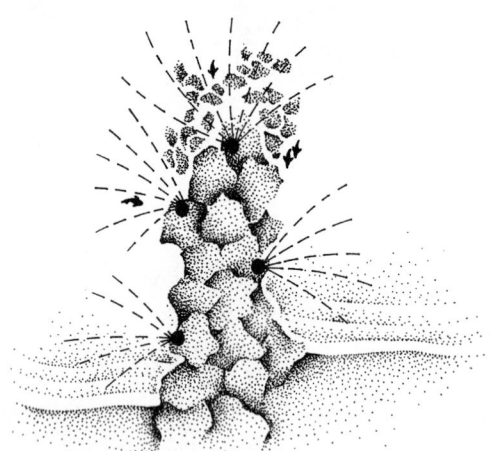

From each casting location on a jetty, an angler should bracket the area with casts to properly cover all water where fish may be feeding.

As you approach the end of the jetty, you'll often find that the seas are crashing onto the rocks and that it's difficult to cast over the submerged rocks and to work your lure. But this is a spot where the fish often feed, so you should work it carefully. Among the tumbled rocks of the jetty front there could be feeding striped bass, redfish, and snook.

Complete the circuit, and work the remaining side of the jetty to the beach. Over time you'll find that each jetty will produce strikes at different spots. Sometimes it's the location of submerged rocks and the way currents swirl around them that results in fish taking up station to feed. With experience, you'll accumulate a wealth of information about each jetty, and instead of working the entire rock-pile, you'll be able to concentrate your efforts in the spots, and with the lures, that regularly produce strikes.

Fish in the rocks. Although casting away from the jetty works for most species, there are exceptions, for example, tautog (blackfish), sea bass, grunts, snapper, and sheepshead. These species often crowd the rocks, even swimming into crevices as they search for crabs and shrimp or rip mussels from the rocks. To catch them, you've got to present your baits in close, with the rig resting among the rocks. These fish will never find the bait if it's 10 or 15 feet from the jetty.

It's easy to snag your rig in the rocks, so when targeting these species simply tie a loop into the end of your line, onto which you slip a $1/2$- or 1-ounce dipsey or bank sinker. Tie in a dropper loop a foot or so above the sinker, and put a 10- to 12-inch leader with a No. 1 or 2 Claw or Beak style hook on it. This is a small, compact rig that is less apt to get

snagged than a multihook rig with a swivel.

Bait the hook with small pieces of seaworm, shrimp, squid, clam, mussel, snail, or cut mullet, and cast out just far enough that the bait rests on either the rocks or the sand immediately adjacent to the rocks where these species are searching for a meal. Most species that feed among the jetty rocks are quick to take a bait, so be alert and strike the fish immediately; delaying often results in a lost bait or a hooked fish that dives into a rocky crevice and cuts your line or leader.

Casting/landing tips. Try to make each cast count. If a fish is feeding in a pocket adjacent to a jetty, it will often strike on your first cast, since it is actively searching for a meal; as your lure comes into range, it's onto the lure in a flash.

Make sure that you work every lure to the very edge of the rocks before lifting it from the water. People often reel fast as their lure approaches the rocks to avoid getting fouled. This is a big mistake, because the greatest number of strikes will come in close. Sometimes the fish are feeding in close; more often they are attracted to and follow the lure and realize that it appears to be seeking the sanctuary of the rocks, so they make a last-second strike lunge to prevent it from getting away. Huge stripers, tarpon, and snook often startle anglers as they crash a lure within a rod's length, an exciting experience that gets the adrenaline moving.

When fishing for smaller fish, you can usually reel them within range of where you're standing and work them in close with the assistance of a wave, or you can simply lift them onto the rockpile. With bigger specimens, once the fish is hooked, permit it to move well away from the jetty, where it can't get the line caught on the rocks and mussels. Let the fish have its head, take drag, and tire itself out. As the fish tires, work it in close and position yourself so that you can get it within range of your gaff or, if someone is with you, within range of their position. Avoid spots where tumbled rocks or pilings or other debris are in front of you; this limits your control, especially when you have a big fish doing its best to get away.

Inlet jetty tactics. Technically, a jetty is a structure that extends from inlets (*see*) and harbor mouths, although the word "jetty" is also commonly used to refer to coastal structures that extend from a beach where there is no inlet (these are actually groins). The purpose of an inlet jetty is to impede wave and current action and thus to protect those places and keep the entrance to them open for boat traffic. It is also meant to stabilize the beach or shore-line to help prevent erosion and to prevent shifting sands from causing the inlets to shoal.

The inlet entrance usually has a pair of parallel jetties or rockpiles on each side of it. These jetties may provide excellent fishing. However, the conditions at inlet jetties vary considerably from other coastal jetties. For one thing, the area between inlet jetties may be a couple of hundred feet wide and over a quarter-mile long. Where most coastal jetties have currents working up and down the beach adjacent to them, in the inlets the tidal flow, moving into bays and rivers or emptying into the ocean, presents a different set of conditions, requiring different tactics.

Tidal influence.   The tidal flow in and out of inlets ranges from just a few feet to 10 feet or more. As this water moves, strong currents develop, often carrying huge quantities of bait with it. This typically occurs on the ebbing tide, when forage species found in bays and rivers are carried along with the tide, as well as quantities of crabs, shrimp, and other food. Gamefish and bottom feeders often take up station in the inlets, usually along the bottom, in areas where they can place themselves out of the heaviest current and wait for a meal to be swept their way.

This presents a different, yet challenging, set of circumstances for the angler casting from inlet rock-piles. The techniques of casting and retrieving, whether with natural baits or lures, are different because of the current. Often the currents are so swift that any lure or the heaviest sinker and bottom rig is just swept along.

Bait presentation.   The jetty angler who uses natural baits with a bottom rig must constantly cast out a rig, permit the current to carry it along, and then retrieve and cast again. Bottom fishing is usually best within an hour or so of either high or low tide; current moves with less velocity just before the slack, and the fish that have taken up station in the quiet water behind or ahead of rocks, ledges, or depressions in the bottom may begin to move about in search of a meal.

Lure presentation.   Many of the lightweight lures that are customarily fished from coastal jetties, especially surface and intermediate-depth plugs and metal squids, don't work as effectively in the swift and often deep water adjacent to inlet jetties. The depth of many inlets ranges from 20 to 25 feet or more, and fish holding at the bottom, where they try to avoid fighting heavy currents, rise only infrequently to the surface for a lure. In fact, they may not even realize it's there, because it's so far above them.

The single best lure in inlets is a leadhead jig, with either a bucktail or a soft plastic body, or a combination of both, perhaps also with a strip of pork rind. These lures get to the bottom quickly in even the heaviest current and can then be worked along the bottom as the current carries them along.

When you start lure fishing at an inlet jetty, you should position yourself low to the water on the rocks and cast out and across the current, beginning with a short cast of perhaps 25 to 40 feet. As the lure enters the water, permit it to settle on a slack line. As soon as the jig touches bottom, the line will pull taut, and you should close the bail or engage the gears. Let the lure be lifted off the bottom and carried by the current; it will often lift off

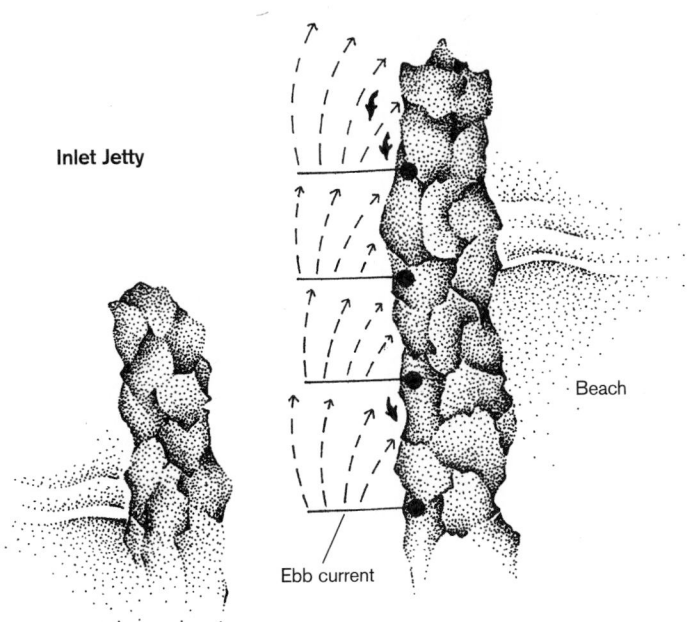

Inlet Jetty

Beach

Ebb current

This scenario depicts an inlet jetty with an ebb current heading seaward. Jetty anglers here should work toward the end of the jetty; at each location begin with short casts and extend outward; then move 20 or 30 feet out and repeat.

the bottom again, move some more, and then bounce. As it moves along, it is being carried in toward the rocks; and as it nears the end of the swing, the current will sweep it off the bottom. This is where the strikes most often occur. Frequently the strike feels as though you've snagged bottom, as a tarpon, snook, redfish, striped bass, bluefish, or weakfish moves up and engulfs the jig as it lifts off the bottom.

Lengthen each succeeding cast by 15 or 20 feet; this action enables the bucktail jig to bounce and sweep across a progressively longer stretch of bottom. Continue extending the distance of your casts as far as you can. If you receive no strikes, move out along the jetty rocks 20 or 30 feet and repeat the same procedure. In this way you'll cover all of the bottom. What often happens is that you'll receive the first strike and then you'll get multiple strikes on successive casts, as your jig works into an area where a pod of fish are schooled up, waiting for a meal to be carried to them.

Getting the feel of a bucktail jig bouncing bottom correctly is best accomplished by getting low to the water and keeping your rod tip pointed downward. Play it safe and don't get too close if a sea is running in the inlet. As the tide begins to slack, especially on the ebb—which is when the bulk of the forage is in the inlet—you'll find the jig moving more slowly. You can enhance its action by working your rod tip, causing the jig to dart ahead, then falter, and be again carried by the tide. At the end of the sweep, you can work the jig back to you, alternately lifting your rod tip, hesitating, then sweeping it upward, reeling, and repeating until you've completed the retrieve.

J

As the tide slackens in the inlet, you can often get strikes on metal squids, rigged eels, and plugs, but most often the intermediate or deep-running models will bring more strikes than surface lures.

An occasional exception to this deep-fishing/ deep lure scenario occurs when the tide is swiftly ebbing and rips are formed to the seaward end of the inlet jetties. Tarpon, jack crevalle, snook, redfish, striped bass, weakfish, and bluefish may take up station in these rips and feed on the baitfish that become trapped in the whirlpool-like eddies. Often this activity is accompanied by sea gulls and other sea birds picking baitfish from the water. This is when a big surface swimming plug cast out into the rips and just held in the current, where it swims as the current pushes against it, may bring exciting surface strikes.
See: Surf Fishing; Tide.

JEWFISH   *Epinephelus itajara.*
Other names—spotted jewfish, southern jewfish, junefish, Florida jewfish, esonue grouper; Fon (spoken in Benin): *tokokogbo;* French: *mérou géant;* Portuguese: *garoupa, mero;* Spanish: *cherna, cherne, mero, guasa, meroguasa.*

The largest of the grouper and a member of the Serranidae family, the jewfish is an important gamefish and an excellent food fish. Marketed fresh and salted, the meat is of excellent quality, finely grained, white, and with a strong flavor. The jewfish has been overfished, mainly through spearfishing and particularly in Florida, where it is completely protected from harvest. Larger fish exhibit a great deal of curiosity, leaving their caves to investigate and interfere with diving operations, sometimes even trying to eat divers.

Identification.   The jewfish is yellowish brown to olive green or brown. Dark brown blotches and blackish spots mottle the entire body, including the head and fins; these markings are variable and more prominent on the young. Irregular dark bands run vertically along the sides of the jewfish, although these are usually obscure. The body becomes darker with age as the blotches and spots increase and become less noticeable in contrast to the body. The first dorsal fin is shorter than, and not separated from, the second dorsal fin. The jewfish is differentiated from the giant sea bass by its dorsal fin soft rays, of which it has 15 to 16; the giant sea bass has only 10. Distinctive features of the jewfish also include a very small eye, a rounded tail fin, and large rounded pectoral fins. Jewfish smaller than $1^1/_2$ feet long bear a strong resemblance to spotted cabrilla but can be distinguished by the number of dorsal spines, of which the jewfish has 11 and the spotted cabrilla 10.

Size/Age.   Jewfish can reach 8 feet in length and 700 pounds in weight. Although the average fish weighs roughly 20 pounds, weights of 100 pounds are not unusual, nor are 4- to 6-foot lengths. The all-tackle world record for jewfish is a 680-pounder taken in Florida in 1961. They have been known to live for 30 to 50 years.

Distribution.   In the western Atlantic, jewfish occur from Florida to southern Brazil, including the Gulf of Mexico and the Caribbean, although they are rare in Florida, the Bahamas, and the Caribbean. In the eastern Atlantic, they occur from Senegal to Congo, though they are rare in the Canary Islands. In the eastern Pacific, jewfish occur from the central Gulf of California to Peru.

Habitat.   Jewfish inhabit inshore waters, and juveniles are common in mangrove areas and estuaries, especially around oyster bars. Both juveniles and adults frequent bays and harbors. Usually found in shallow water at depths between 10 and 100 feet, jewfish prefer rocky bottoms, reefs, ledges, dock and bridge pilings, and wrecks, where they can find refuge in caves and holes. Extremely territorial, jewfish seem to have limited home ranges, where they stay for years at a time.

Life history/Behavior.   There is some indication that the jewfish starts out as a female and undergoes a sex change later in life, as occurs in certain grouper. Spawning takes place over summer months.

Food and feeding habits.   A sluggish but opportunistic feeder, jewfish feed chiefly on crustaceans, especially spiny lobsters, as well as turtles, fish, and stingray.

Angling.   Despite its poor fighting ability (mostly strong pulling through massive weight), the jewfish's great size and weight, and its habit of swimming into a hole or between rocks when hooked, make it difficult to land. It can be taken on live or dead baits fished on the bottom from boats, bridges, or shore. Slow trolling also works on occasion. Baits include crabs, spiny lobsters, mullet, grunts, mackerel, conch, clams, fish heads, and cut baits. Extremely heavy tackle is necessary, given the jewfish's large size.
See: Grouper; Inshore Fishing.

JIG
An artificial lure with a metal head molded to a single hook. The hook shank is never fished plain and may be dressed with fur, feathers, rubber, soft plastic, pork rind, or other synthetic materials, and occasionally with live or dead natural bait. In some cases these materials are permanent; in

Jewfish

J

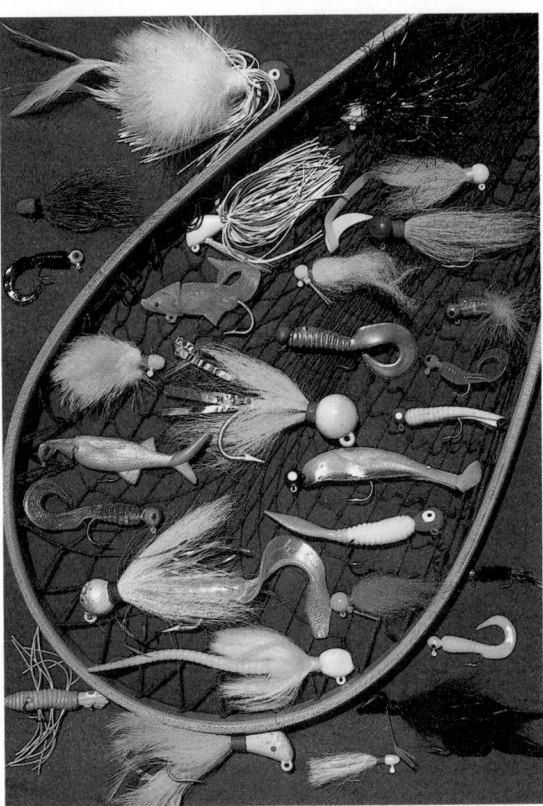

Jigs come in a variety of weights, bodies, and colors.

Although jigs are a preeminent North American type of lure, they do not enjoy quite the international freshwater use that spinners (see) or spoons (see) do. In fact, in some places, terminology and language differences have confused the act of fishing a jig, called jigging, with the act of deliberately snagging (see) or foul-hooking a fish. Deliberately snagging a gamefish is generally illegal and is always unsporting; in fact, the design of a true jig makes snagging difficult to do, and even accidental snagging is an unusual occurrence. Furthermore, true jigs have only a single hook, which is easier to remove from a fish that will be released than the treble hooks found on lures.

Most true jigs have hair, synthetic, or soft-plastic bodies, and smaller sizes see a lot of crossover use, especially in freshwater fishing; if an angler has a decent selection of these lures, some can be pressed into duty at any time for a particular fish or angling circumstance. Many of the same $1/8$-ounce marabou or soft-plastic curl-tail jigs that catch smallmouth bass, for example, can also be employed to catch walleye, bluegill, yellow perch, trout, and white bass, and they can contribute to the unintended catch of such fish as pike or pickerel. The same jigs that will catch big striped bass in freshwater or saltwater will also catch large, deep-dwelling lake trout in freshwater as well as bottom-dwelling groupers in saltwater. Perhaps the preferred colors will differ, but they don't always. When you consider the crossover value, plus the fact that jigs are inexpensive enough that you don't fret over losing one (which happens fairly often, especially when using light tackle), it seems that carrying along a few jigs ought to be as routine as filling your fishing reel with line.

Components. Head design, body dressing, and hook style are the major components of all jigs.

Head design, or shape, influences not only the weight but also the sink rate, action, and ability to avoid getting snagged. There are many shapes of jig heads, as well as variations of standard shapes. The most common shape is the ball head, which sinks fast and has near-universal use. Another popular and fast-sinking style is the bullet head, which is good in current and resists snagging somewhat better than a ball head. The football head is a compact, heavy head that is good with big bodies, sinks fast, and holds

others they're removable and easily replaceable. The shape of the head varies widely (primarily variations of oval, ball, bullet, pancake, and angled designs) as does the color of the head and body. Various metals may be used for the head, although lead is by far the most common and its use is partly why many people refer to this type of lure as a leadhead. Head size primarily determines weight, which is normally between $1/8$ ounce and 2 ounces but can be several ounces more and can be found down to $1/64$ ounce.

A jig is one type of lure that cuts across species, since some type or size of jig has near-universal appeal to the widest possible range of gamefish. Its other virtues include the fact that a jig is aerodynamic and casts very well, it sinks quickly so it gets down in the water column fairly fast, and it can be effective in cold and warm water alike. As with any lure, however, its successful use depends largely upon skillful manipulation by the angler.

Jig Head Styles

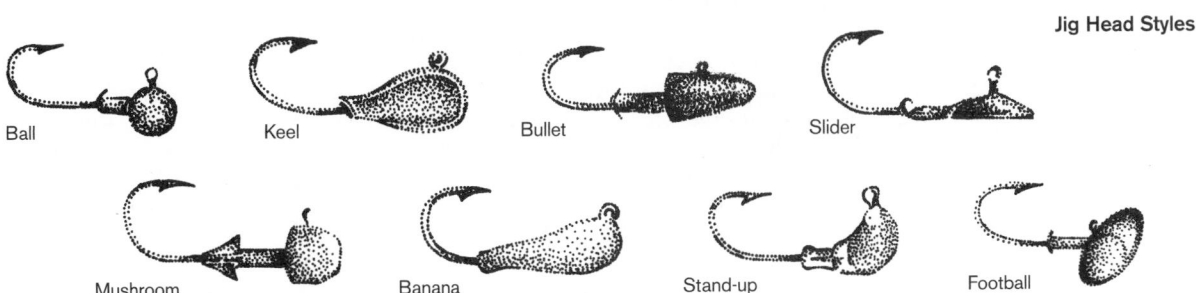

Ball   Keel   Bullet   Slider

Mushroom   Banana   Stand-up   Football

J

bottom well. A keel head is somewhat flattened on the sides and rounded on the bottom; it sinks fast and is especially suited for heavy current. A mushroom head is somewhat of a cross between the bullet and the ball, with a flat inside head that allows a plastic body to fit flush to the head; it usually has a body-holding barb. Other fairly common designs include the slider, a flat slow-sinking head; the pancake, a flat-sided design with little drag and wide action; the banana, a vertical-fishing head with a forward-most line tie (hook eye) and forward weighting; and the stand-up, also a weight-forward design and one that is fairly snag-free.

Just as there are many types of jig heads, so are there many body dressings. Hair jigs, primarily sporting bucktail, are old favorites, durable and active in the water. Some also feature marabou feathers, which have good action but lack durability. Soft bodies, primarily of plastic, but also a mix of plastic and natural organisms, are very popular; these slow the sink rate and have both excellent feel and action, and the appearances of some imitate natural foods. Soft bodies feature curl-tail, grub, fishtail, and paddletail configurations, and though they have good action they lack durability. Various pork rind or soft-plastic products adorn the jigs used by black bass anglers for casting and flipping. Jigs tipped with natural or dead bait, including earthworms, minnows, leeches, chunks of fish flesh, or other items have merit for many freshwater fish, and jigs in saltwater are routinely fished with sandworms or chunks or strips of fish or squid.

The style of hook on a jig also varies. Lighter, smaller jigs have fine-wire hooks that penetrate easily; the lighter models are easily straightened (and freed from snags) when heavy pressure is applied. Thicker hooks, some forged, are used with heavier jig heads in more demanding situations.

In addition to these basic components, some jigs incorporate a very small spinner blade on them. The spinner blade is usually attached to a small stub under the lead head or is affixed to the bend in the hook. The flash and the movement of the blade help attract fish, making this a versatile jig that can be fished conventionally or fished on a slow but steady retrieve and a stop-and-go manner. Some anglers refer to these as spinner-jigs, and they are overlooked by most jig users. Small versions are good for yellow perch, white bass, crappie, and small bass.

Small jigs are also used in conjunction with a spinner blade that is attached to an overhead wire arm. Technically this turns the lure into a spinner-bait *(see)*, although the arm is removable and the lure can be used as a jig or as a spinnerbait on a quicker retrieve if circumstances warrant.

As a category, jigs have the simplest appearance of all artificial lures, but they are a bit of an anomaly in that, at rest, they don't closely resemble fish,

insects, or other aquatic forage. Also, for a lure type that catches such a wide range of species, a jig is not a cast-and-crank product. For an item with such productive potential, many anglers do not use jigs because they find working these lures hard to master. At the heart of such anomalies is the key to catching fish with jigs: Success is directly proportional to your ability to impart action to the lure, effect a proper style of retrieval, and detect strikes. These issues are detailed in the entry on jigging *(see)*.

Although jigs may be broken down by size for categorizing as panfish jigs, bass and walleye jigs, saltwater jigs, etc., the basic categories are simple: jig and pork/eel combinations, which are popularly used in freshwater bass fishing; and jigs with hair, synthetic, or soft-plastic bodies, which are available in all sizes and used widely in both freshwater and saltwater. These types are fished differently and have distinct characteristics and applications, however.

True jigs as described here are sometimes confused with, and categorically lumped with, jigging spoons, which are fished in a vertical manner *(see: spoon)*. There is also a trolling lure known as a feathered jig or simply feathers, which has no true jigging application *(see: trolling lures, saltwater)*. In order to distinguish true jigs from other types of lures that can be jigged, many anglers call these lures leadheads, although lead is not the only material used in the construction of the head.

Jig and Pork

Pork rind has been used for years as a jig garnish, starting with strips and continuing with shaped chunks. These combinations have proven versatile and especially effective in freshwater fishing for largemouth and smallmouth bass. Pork strips are made of pork rind that has been stripped of fat. Chunks have a layer of fat on them, giving them bulk and weight in addition to different action.

A jig with a strip of cured pork rind on its hook is an old-time bait, known as a jig and eel. A jig with a chunk of pork on its hook became popular in the 1980s, and is variously called jig and chunk, jig and pig, jig and frog, etc. Pork baits and similar soft plastics to be used with jigs are available from several manufacturers and in a wide variety of forms.

Whereas the jig and pork combination of yesteryear was principally thought of as a cold-weather, semideep bait, today it's a hallmark of versatility, being fished for bass almost anywhere. With a weedguard, it penetrates the most imposing tangles. Without, it is very effective in open-water sanctums. Fish it deep, shallow, or in between.

The most successful application of this jig is probably in the bushes, brush, and submerged treetops. In the springtime, the shallow bushes along

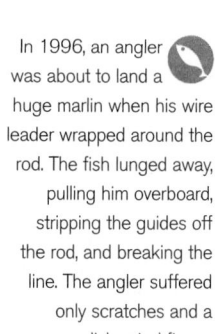

In 1996, an angler was about to land a huge marlin when his wire leader wrapped around the rod. The fish lunged away, pulling him overboard, stripping the guides off the rod, and breaking the line. The angler suffered only scratches and a dislocated finger.

banks often hold bass. The fish are deep in the middle of these bushes, which may be located in 5 to 10 feet of water. Few anglers toss a lure into the heart of these tangles, and a plastic worm, cast from a good distance away, often scours only the periphery of the bush and may not be effective unless bass come out after it. By getting close to these objects, an angler can flip or pitch a jig right into this brush, work it through and out of the entanglement, and snake a hooked bass out with less difficulty than would otherwise be possible. The same is true for logjams and the roots of stumps or trees and other thick hard-to-fish spots. This is why the technique of flipping (see) is so effective, and why these lures are part of that bass fishing method.

Rocky banks can be another strong jig and pork locale, particularly if they have a very steep dropoff and possess a lot of craggy, ledgelike rock formations. Bass will usually seek refuge in the crags and under the ledges but are often not susceptible to lures like diving plugs or falling-away plastic worms. On rocky banks jigs can be flipped or cast. In both cases, present the jig close to the edge of the rock and allow it to fall vertically as close to the bank as you can. Crawl it off each ledge, over each rock, swimming it along as unobtrusively as possible, and working it under the boat or as deep as your cast will permit. Always work the lure slowly, keeping light tension on the line, and be prepared to set the hook the instant a strike is detected.

Yet another prime application for these jigs is a situation in which bass are holding tightly in very dense cover, such as milfoil, hyacinths, floating mats of hydrilla and debris, grassy shoals, or bridge pilings and boat docks. Some of these objects can be very difficult to fish with conventional casting techniques, but by getting close and by quietly (and accurately) flipping a jig around them, you can achieve some highly effective results. In thickly matted clusters of vegetation, drop the jig in any hole that is visible, and jig it up and down repeatedly therein. In some cases you may even have to make your own holes.

The weight of jig and pork that you use depends primarily on the depth of the water, but also upon wind and current conditions. For deep-bank work, a $^1/_4$-ounce lure on light line might do the trick, but more likely you'll need a $^5/_{16}$-ounce jig and may even have to go up to $^1/_2$ ounce. For flipping the bushes and such, size may vary from $^3/_{16}$ ounce to as much as $^3/_4$ ounce. The color is usually dark, with black, brown, or purple being best. It's good to also have some jigs with a weed-guard (the forked style seems best). For pork chunks, a pork rind that weighs $^1/_4$ ounce and measures 1 inch by $2^1/_2$ inches is favored, in black, brown, or multiple colors. The chunk, incidentally, can be trimmed with a knife to make it fall faster.

To care for the pork baits after use, keep them in the container of brine that they came in. After you're finished with a pork chunk, put it back in the manufacturer's jar or some other wet container. While fishing, keep the pork wet; otherwise, it will dry and shrivel up and become useless. One way to keep it wet when it's not being used is to toss the jig and pork into a boat livewell.

To attach pork to a lure, locate the slit at the head of the bait and insert the hook point through it. To remove the pork, turn it sideways at a right angle to the hook point, grab the hook with one hand and the pork with the other, and carefully exert pressure to pull the pork down while pulling the barb out.

These are, obviously, big baits. Even a $^1/_4$-ounce jig with a twin-tailed strip trailer or frog chunk weighs closer to $^1/_2$ ounce. Specifically what they represent is speculative, though crayfish and salamanders seem plausible. Unquestionably, these unobtrusive baits ring the chow bell in both cold and warm water for largemouth and smallmouth bass, and they constitute one of the better big-bass baits in use today.

Soft Plastic and Hair Jigs

Conventional jigs come in various head styles, featuring bucktail or synthetic hair bodies, or soft-plastic bodies. Jigs with a bucktail dressing are commonly called bucktails or bucktail jigs, and are popular in large sizes, especially in saltwater, because they have good bulking characteristics and display movement well. Soft-plastic bodies are more abundant and can be attached to the hook of a jig for use as is or in combination with a hair or synthetic body. They come in many styles. Some are in the form of hellgrammite, crayfish, or shad imitations; others are spider-legged or shaped like a tube or grub. Many are simply long and curly, somewhat like a worm, snake, eel, leech, and so on.

Grubs and tubes are probably the top soft-plastic body forms for jigs used in freshwater

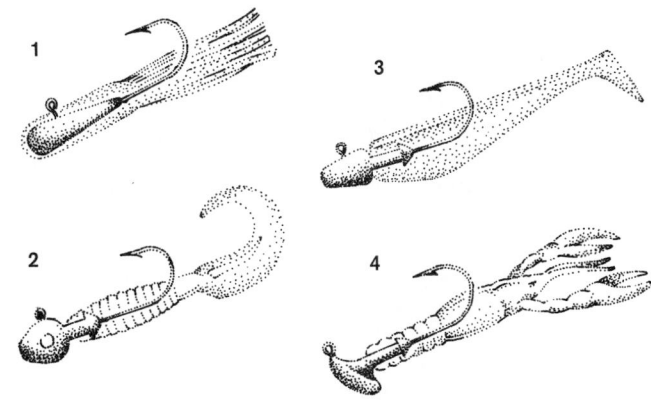

Different soft bodies are rigged on appropriate styles of jig head as shown. Common arrangements from top to bottom include: tube jig (1), grub jig (2), shad-body jig (3), and crayfish (4).

J

fishing; in saltwater these and longer eel-like bodies are equally popular. Grub bodies are solid and either flat-tailed or curl-tailed; they are threaded onto the hook from the head and have a tight, well-defined action if rigged properly. Tube jigs are hollow with many squidlike legs in lieu of a tail; a tube jig head is worked through the body from back to front with only the line-tie hook exposed; the jig has an erratic action when fished on a drop-and-fall.

The weight of the jig itself is the most important aspect in fishing it, and this may vary from $1/8$ to $1/2$ ounce for freshwater bass fishing, from $1/16$ to $3/16$ ounce for panfishing, and from $1/2$ to 3 ounces for saltwater fishing, although this is just a broad characterization. Choice should be dependent upon the depth of the water, its clarity, the wind conditions, the strength of the line used, and the type of jig. This may sound involved, but it really isn't.

Use the lightest jig that you can under the circumstances. You don't want a jig to sink too fast, which would appear unnatural, yet you need the appropriate size to attain necessary depth. When fishing in a lake with current or when fishing in flowing water like a stream or river, you'll need to use a heavier jig than you would if the current were not present. Another influential factor is wind. The harder the wind blows, the more difficult it is for the unanchored angler to hold bottom with a light jig.

Jigging depth is also influenced by the size of your line; the heavier the line, the greater its diameter and the more drag it has in the water, which obviously reinforces the fact that light jigs fall more slowly than heavier ones. Then, too, the clearer and shallower the water, the more you should be using light jigs for less obtrusive presentations. These considerations all add up to interpreting the effects of the elements and selecting the best size of lure according to the conditions.

Light hair jigs, grubs, and tube jigs are usually better fished with spinning tackle than baitcasting gear. They cast better with spinning tackle, where the bail remains open and the lure falls relatively straight once it hits the water. With baitcasting gear, you usually have to pay out line by hand after the cast to get the jig to fall straight. With heavier jigs, of course, this is not a factor.

Flat-tailed grubs should be placed on the shank of the jig in such a way that their tails ride flat, or horizontal, to achieve a good side-to-side falling action. When rigging curl tails, use the side seam as a guideline, and rig it so that the curl tail rides up vertically in the same direction as the hook. The length of these flat-tailed or curl-tailed soft plastics varies from $1^1/2$ to 3 inches. There are many successful colors for soft-plastic bodies; gray (or smoke), green, black, purple, white, and chartreuse are traditional, but pumpkinseed, Junebug, and assorted combinations with embedded metal flecks are very popular. For hair bodies, the best colors are black, brown, yellow, and white.

To work hair-bodied and grub jigs, you must first let them settle to the bottom wherever you've cast. When fishing a moderately sloping shoreline or point, you should slowly pull the lure a little bit off the bottom, let it settle down while keeping in contact with the lure, take up the slack, and repeat this. When working a ledge or a sharply sloping shoreline, slowly pull the lure over the structure until it begins to fall, let it settle, and then repeat. Don't hop the jig up quickly here, because it will fall out and away from the bottom, most likely missing a good deal of the important terrain.

A good technique with grubs is to make them jump quickly off the bottom rather than make short hops. You can also swim a grub on the edges of cover by reeling it slowly across the bottom and giving it occasional darting movements by manipulating your rod tip. The majority of strikes while jigging with these lures will come as the lure falls back down, so be alert for a strike then, and keep both a good feel and an eye on your line to detect this. Tube jigs are better if fished more in a hopping motion than a crawling one. Hop a tube jig off the bottom and let it flutter back. These lures spiral downward rather than dive, and they're often used on lighter jig heads (like $1/16$ ounce) than other lures, as well as on light or ultralight spinning gear, which has led some to refer to their use as "finesse" fishing.

These lures can also be fished in a vertical manner, and this is common in all sizes depending on the circumstances. Crappie, for example, can be caught on light jigs fished vertically over cover such as a brushpile; bottom-dwelling saltwater species can be caught on heavy jigs worked just over a reef or wreck. Vertical jigging is discussed further in the entry on jigging.
See: Lure.

JIG AND EEL
See: Jig.

JIG AND PORK
See: Jig.

JIGGERPOLING

Jiggerpoling is an old-time method of making a quiet, sneaky presentation of a lure close to cover, primarily used in fishing for largemouth bass. Jiggerpoling is done with a minnow-shaped floating plug or a hooked piece of fish belly or pork strip attached to the tip of a long cane pole via a short length of line. The angler sits in the bow of a boat (often a pirogue or small jonboat), prowls shallow cover, and rapidly jiggers or dapples the lure in and around grassy banks and stumps. The angler usually fishes directly in front of the boat, which is paddled or poled by someone in the stern. This is

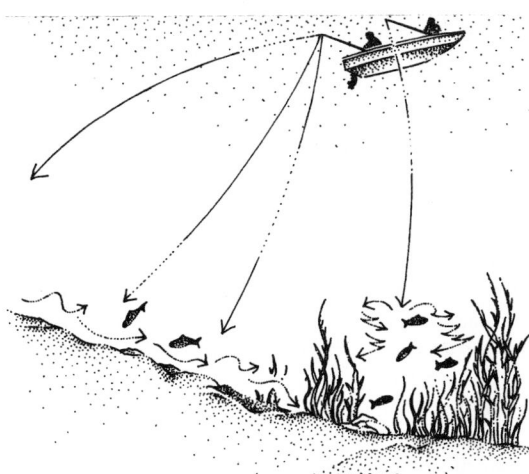

Depending on circumstances, anglers can fish by casting toward shore and jigging a lure back along bottom, or by vertically fishing a jig or jigging spoon on or just slightly above bottom or objects.

effective where the water is murky and where bass are likely to be close to cover, especially along the bank.

JIGGING

One thing that a jig is not is a throw-it-out-and-reel-it-back-in kind of lure, one that can catch fish in spite of the abilities of the person using it. An angler has to put some work into making a jig catch fish and into being able to detect strikes. There is a knack to jigging. Good jig users have a feel for what is happening to their lure and they have a razor-sharp ability to detect and respond to strikes.

The key to jigging success is establishing contact with your lure, getting and keeping it where the fish are, and using the right rod to feel a strike. The greatest concerns are often how deep you need to fish a particular jig and how effective you are at doing that. Jigs excel at being on or close to the bottom, which is where the majority of jig-caught fish are found. They also are productive for covering the area between the bottom and upper levels via vertical presentations.

Covering bottom. When fishing on or close to the bottom, many anglers do not have success because they fail to reach and keep their jigs on the bottom. The simplest way to get a jig to reach the bottom is to open the bail of your spinning reel or depress the freespool mechanism on a baitcasting, spincasting, or conventional reel; let the lure fall freely until the line goes slack on the surface of the water and no more comes off the spool. If the water is calm and the boat still, you can readily detect when you're on the bottom. If it is somewhat windy or if current is present, you have to watch the departing line carefully to detect the telltale slack and to differentiate between line that is leaving the

spool because the lure has not reached bottom and line that is being pulled off by a drifting lure or boat. If you're fishing from a boat, a depthfinder can help you determine when your lure has reached the bottom because you will have some idea of the local depth.

The lighter (and thinner) the line and the heavier the lure, the easier it is to reach the bottom. The stronger the line, the greater its diameter will be and the more resistance it will offer in the water. A quarter-ounce jig will fall more quickly on 8-pound line than it will on 14-pound line, for example. The advantage here (the magnitude of which depends on fishing conditions) is that you will more easily get your lure to the bottom and keep it on the bottom with 8-pound line than with 14-pound line.

A typical scenario for jigging the bottom is to let the jig fall freely until the line goes slack. Reel up slack and lift the jig off the bottom. Once you're on the bottom, you need to maintain contact with it. Assuming that you have cast your jig some distance away, have let it settle to the bottom, and are now retrieving it toward yourself, you should keep it working in short hops along the bottom as long as the terrain and length of paid-out line enable you to do so. If you are in a boat and drifting, the jig will eventually start sweeping upward and away from you and the bottom as you drift, unless it is very heavy; so you need to pay out more line occasionally until the angle of your line has changed

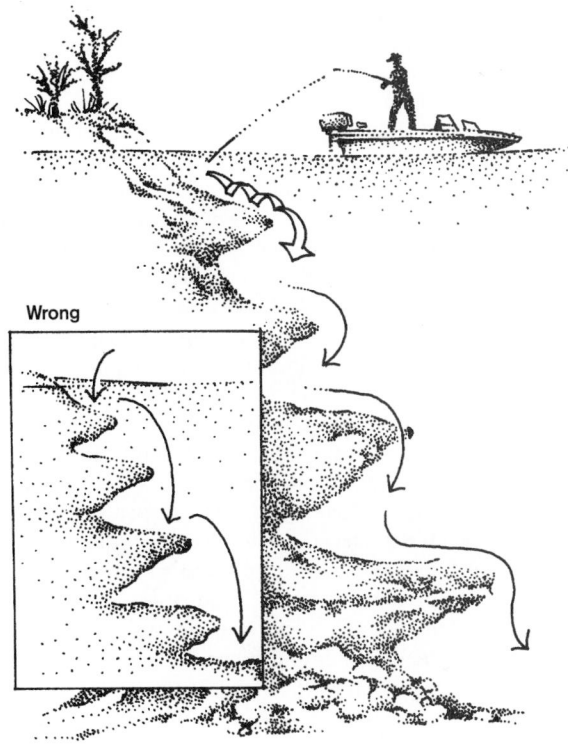

When jigging along a steep shoreline, such as this ledge, retrieve the jig in short, slow hops to crawl the jig along and let it flutter to the next ledge below. Long sweeps of the rod bring the jig out and away (inset), missing some of the best cover.

significantly and then reel in and drop the jig back down again.

Choosing the right weight lure to use is critical to most types of jigging. The ideal is to have a lure that gets to the bottom and stays there under normal conditions but that is not too large to intimidate the fish. Most anglers who fail to reach bottom don't use the right retrieval technique or don't compensate for wind or current; in addition, they may use too light a jig for getting down to the bottom under the conditions that they face.

Sometimes you need to swim a jig by pumping it slowly and reeling, never actually letting it hop along the bottom. Other times you may need to slowly drag it. When fishing a moderately sloping shoreline or point, for example, you should slowly pull the lure a little bit off the bottom, let it settle down while keeping in contact with it, take up the slack, and repeat this. When working a ledge or a sharply sloping shoreline, slowly pull the lure over the structure until it begins to fall, let it settle, and then repeat. Don't hop the jig up quickly here, because it will fall out and away from the bottom and likely miss a good deal of the important terrain. With some jigs, such as grubs, a good technique is to make them jump quickly off the bottom rather than make short hops. You can also swim a jig on the edges of cover by reeling it slowly across the bottom and giving it occasional darting movements by manipulating your rod tip. The majority of strikes while jigging come as the bait falls back down, so be alert for a strike then and concentrate on the feel of your line to detect it.

Jigs also have value in rivers and where there is current. In a fair amount of current, you should cast upstream or up-and-across-stream, engage the line-pickup system as soon as the lure splashes down, reel up slack, and try to keep the line taut by letting the jig drift or by reeling in slack to achieve a natural drift. You virtually fish a jig in quick water the same way a fly angler works a nymph, keeping slack out and rod tip up and feeling the lure as it bounces along. In deep, swift current, you actually need to swim the jig a bit by pumping the rod tip.

Vertical jigging.   Jigging vertically, of course, is useful, especially when fishing through the ice in freshwater, when angling on the bottom in deep water, and when angling for suspended fish in open water. Here, both leadhead jigs and metal or lead spoons are used and you needn't maintain bottom contact, though you might start at the bottom and jig your way upward. Sometimes you'll need to get to a particular depth and regularly jig at that spot.

If you know what depth to fish, you can let the desired length of line out and commence jigging, never reeling in any line and paying out line only if you begin to drift. Here's one way to know how much line you're letting out: Reel the jig up to the rod tip, stick the rod tip on the surface, let go of the

jig, and raise your rod tip to eye level; then stop the fall of the jig. If eye level is 6 feet above the surface, your jig will now be 6 feet deep. Lower the rod tip to the surface and do this again. Now you've let out 12 feet of line. Continue until the desired length is out. With a levelwind reel having a freely revolving line guide, you can measure the amount of line that is let out with each side-to-side movement of the line guide; multiply this amount by the number of times the guide travels back and forth. If you use a reel that doesn't have such a guide, you can strip line off the spool in 1-foot (or 18-inch) increments until the desired length is out. Another method is to count down the lure's descent. A falling rate of 1 foot per second is standard and may be accurate for medium-weight jigs, but you should check the lure's rate of fall in a controlled situation first to ensure accuracy.

For some vertical jigging, you may need to let your lure fall to the bottom and then jig it up toward the surface a foot or two at a time. Bring the lure off the bottom, and reel in the slack; then jig it there three or four times before retrieving another few feet of line and jigging the lure again. Repeat this until the lure is near the surface. The only problem here is that you don't usually know exactly how deep a fish is when you do catch one, and you can't just strip out the appropriate length of line and be at the proper level.

Detecting strikes/hooksetting.   Discerning a strike when jigging can be difficult because so many fish don't slam a jig when they take it. Certainly some do, and there's no question then that a fish has struck, but in most light-jig usage where small fish are sought, something just a little "different" happens that signals a strike. That difference is often barely perceptible. The job of detection is made even less obvious by the fact that most strikes come when a jig is falling, which is often when the line has a slight amount of slack. If you fail to detect the strike quickly enough, the fish may reject the lure or you may be too late to set the hook properly.

In a sense, it's good to tight-line a jig backward as the jig falls, but don't use so much tension that the jig falls unnaturally and stiffly. You need to slightly lower your rod tip as the jig falls; when you feel something take the jig, set the hook quickly, keeping the rod tip high and reeling rapidly at the same time. A lot of jig-struck fish are lost because the angler, in reacting to a strike, raises the rod high but never gets the hook to penetrate the mouth of the fish. So the hook pulls out after a moment, or the fish jumps and throws the hook easily. A forceful hookset that eliminates slack, coupled with constant pressure and rapid reeling, is the way to avoid losing fish on a jig.

Having the right rod is also a big factor, especially in freshwater where jigs are usually fairly light. Light jigs are rarely fished well on stiff, heavy rods, and vice versa; wimpy super-flexible rods don't make good jigging rods, nor do the pool-cue versions. This is where that elusive quality of sensitivity comes into play. A well-tapered rod with a fast tip is preferable, and it's good to keep the tip angled upward. In some types of jigging, a low-stretch line is helpful. Great depths, very heavy jigs or jigging spoons, and fishing for large bottom fish that can quickly get into cover and break off are instances where lines with little or no stretch may be beneficial.

Two conditions that make strike detection more difficult when jigging are fishing jigs under windy conditions and fishing them in and around weeds. These conditions also make it more difficult to maintain jig depth and control. Many anglers tip their jig hooks with bait; for fishing around vegetation, the best bait is a leech. The leeches work better for weed fishing than nightcrawlers because worms get torn up too easily through constant contact with weeds and the constant contact makes it hard to detect a strike, especially if the wind is up.

Developing a keen feel, especially in weeds, takes patience and practice. Realizing that the "tick" you feel is a fish (often a walleye or perch) sucking in your offering, takes some adjustment, although detection is usually easier with larger fish because they take in more water when they inhale a lure and thus the effect you feel is more pronounced. You will lose a number of fish, including a few good-sized ones, that you have momentarily hooked because you don't realize quickly enough that you have a strike instead of contact with a weed. Most of the time you feel the strike as you pull on the jig. Detecting that strike is made easier by using light jigs and light (6- or 8-pound) line on a spinning outfit.

If you must fish a jig in weeds when there is wind, try using a bobber with the jig in the weeds to counter the detection problem. An alternative is to use a split shot and jig, which will keep the lure down but is very hard to feel.

See: Jig.

JIGGING SPOON

See: Spoon.

JONBOAT

The term "jonboat" is used to refer to nearly any rectangularly shaped boat that has a flat bottom, a square bow and stern, and low straight sides. Also referred to as a flat-bottom boat, and frequently called a rowboat, this is one of the most common and oldest types of fishing craft.

Jonboats are frequently used with low-horsepower outboard motors or electric motors, as well as with oars, poles, and paddles. Because of their low draft, they are especially useful in shallow-water fishing, particularly small lakes, ponds, and rivers. In rivers, when shallow sections are

Perfect for small waters and calm conditions, the jonboat is widely used in North America.

encountered, jonboat users simply tilt up a motor if they are using one, get onto the gravel bar, and walk the boat down to deeper water to continue on. Jonboats are primarily used in freshwater but are not meant for big bodies of water or places that might experience heavy wave and wind conditions.

These simple-design boats feature a fair amount of interior room, and they are quite stable if properly loaded, although the shorter and narrower versions can be tipsy. They are light and easily maneuvered and are preferred over canoes by many anglers because of their ruggedness, roominess, and standup fishing stability. Anglers can easily stand up and fish in jonboats, including those 14 feet or longer, as well as some 12-footers; they can also readily transport a jonboat to the water, which is an asset in many places where access is unimproved. Many anglers use 12- to 14-foot jonboats, which can be toted atop a car or on a trailer. Long and narrow jonboats are used in stream and river float fishing, especially in the Ozarks; they sport small outboards placed on a high-backed transom for shallow-water running.

Most jonboats today are made of aluminum, although older models were wooden, which made them heavier and in more need of maintenance; some jonboatlike vessels are made from various plastics. The flat-bottom jonboat hull has been used on boats with more complex interiors, in effect, putting consoles, decks or raised platforms, livewells, and similar options on them, and making them into a form of bass boat or at least a more advanced jonboat.

Many anglers have customized basic jonboats, especially in 14- and 16-foot lengths, with fishing and boating accessories including fore and aft decks, bow-mount electric motors, rod holders, fixed-mount sonar, and other items. Many of these customized boats are used on slightly bigger waters but still require avoidance of rough conditions because of their low freeboard. They also produce a tooth-rattling, rump-aching ride if they have to be taken through rough water. In smaller, less souped-up jonboats, savvy anglers carpet the bottom to deaden sounds, or make a flooring of wooden slats or plywood supported by wooden slats or aluminum braces.

See: Boat.

JUG HOOK

A single hook and line attached to a floating jug rather than to a hand-operated mechanical reel. The hook is usually baited, and it may or may not be attended. A jug hook, also simply called jug or a jugline, is prohibited in some places; where legal, its use and location may be regulated. A jug hook may also be called a setline (see), or set hook (see). Although using a jug hook may be considered fishing, and such usage may be covered under established regulations, a jug hook is not a sportfishing instrument, and jug fishing is not sportfishing.

JUMP BAIT

A term for small, easy-to-cast metal lures that are used in quick-casting to schools of surface-feeding white bass, largemouth bass, and striped bass.

See: Spoon.

JUMP FISHING

Spotting, chasing, and fishing for schooling fish that are feeding on the surface; this term is generally used in freshwater for striped bass.

See: Schooling.

JURUPOCA

A South American catfish.

See: Catfish.

KAHAWAI (Australian Salmon)

Other names—Australian salmon, sea trout (New Zealand), bay trout, salmon trout, black-backed salmon, cockie salmon, sambo, colonial salmon.

This is one of the finest light-tackle gamefish in the world but one known to relatively few people and the subject of confusion. *Kahawai* is a Maori word for fish of the Arripidae family that are found in the inshore waters of New Zealand and Australia. Confusion exists over whether there are two or three species in this family, and the proper terminology; kahawai are also widely known, especially in Australia, as Australian salmon, although they are not a true salmon.

The Arripidae family is believed to consist of two kahawai and possibly one smaller relative, the Australian ruff (*Arripis georgianus;* also known as tommy rough, sea herring roughy, and Australian herring), which occurs off the southern coast of Australia.

The two kahawai consist of the eastern *(Arripis trutta)* and western *(A. esper)* species. Confusion over identity arises between the two species because adults of the eastern species are chiefly plankton feeders, whereas the western species feed mainly on small pilchards, anchovies, garfish, and squid. To compound the problem, in Australia the eastern species rarely moves across to the West Coast, whereas the western species is well known in East Coast waters as far north as Eden on the South Coast of New South Wales. Because eastern Australian salmon are predominately plankton feeders, individuals caught by surf and rock anglers using pilchards, garfish, or lures are most likely to be the western Australian salmon.

Identification. Both species have a moderately rounded elongate body and are difficult to differentiate. The dorsal fin has nine spines and 15 to 19 rays, and the anal fin is much shorter. The caudal fin is forked, and pectoral fins are bright yellow. The back and upper sides are olive green to steel blue with small dark spots, the color changing to pale yellow green to silvery white below. The western species has 25 to 31 gill rakers, and the eastern species 33 to 40. It is doubtful that anglers can distinguish between the two species without counting the gill rakers, which only the rarest angler will bother to do.

Size. Kahawai are known to reach 10.5 kilograms and a length of 80 centimeters. A land-based capture of the all-tackle world record, weighing 8.74 kilograms, was made in Australia in 1994, but the average specimen weighs from 3 to 4 kilograms.

Distribution. The eastern species of kahawai are generally confined to New Zealand, and in Australia to the waters of Bass Strait and along the East Coast of Australia as far north as Brisbane, Queensland, and across to Norfolk Island, Lord Howe Island, and New Zealand. Rarely do they find their way across to Western Australian waters. The western species ranges from Kalbarri in Western Australia, around the bottom of Australia to Tasmania, and as far north as Eden on the south coast of New South Wales. Strays may find their way northward, but they are rarely taken much farther north than Sydney.

Habitat. These fish inhabit estuaries, bays, inlets, and the open sea, especially over reefs and around rocky headlands, and in gutters along surf beaches. They tend to remain well out from the beach, necessitating casts in excess of 50 meters by surf anglers. Juveniles often inhabit the upper reaches of estuaries, where water salinity is low.

Life history/Behavior. The western species spawns from February through June in waters off the southwest corner of Western Australia. Juveniles migrate across the Great Australian Bight to South Australia, Victoria, southern New South Wales, and Tasmania, progressively appearing in bays and inlets from July through October as they travel eastward. Some (western populations) mature in their third or fourth year, and others (eastern populations) in four to six years. Maturing fish eventually return to the Western Australian spawning grounds to complete the cycle.

The eastern species spawns between November and February off the southeast coast of Australia. Juveniles migrate to Tasmanian and Victorian waters, with some dispersing northward along the New South Wales coast. They mature in their fourth year. In Victorian and Tasmanian waters, schools of both western and eastern species are known to mix.

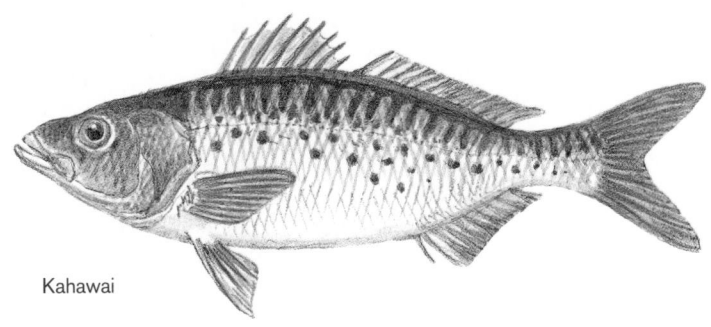

Kahawai

Food and feeding habits. Juveniles of both species feed on small fish, crustaceans, squid, and worms. On reaching maturity, the eastern species feeds mainly on zooplankton such as krill and other small crustaceans, and the western species feeds chiefly on pilchards, anchovies, garfish, and squid. Both are known to eat beach worms, which are often used as baits by surf anglers.

Angling. The kahawai challenges surf, rock, and boat anglers, and is considered by most people to be the finest light-tackle sportfish found in Australian and New Zealand waters. It is superior to the tailor (bluefish) in its fighting qualities.

Surf anglers, using 3- to 4-meter surf rods and spinning, conventional, or side-cast reels spooled with 5- to 7-kilogram monofilament line, resort to high-speed spinning or baitfishing. Favored baits are whole pilchards and garfish, and strip bait, rigged on four or five linked 4/0 hooks. Because these fish rarely venture closer than 50 meters from shore, sinkers up to 113 grams are used to ensure that the necessary casting distance is achieved. Since kahawai tend to be timid, hesitant takers—and will often drop a bait if they feel a weight attached to it—the sinker is rigged so that the line runs freely through it. This also serves to prevent the fish, during a head-shaking run, from using the weight of the sinker to dislodge the hook.

Rock-based anglers use tackle similar to that of the surf angler, but favor high-speed spinning reels. Where bait is used, it is suspended under a float cast to gutters and reefs, or it is cast unweighted and retrieved. Lures are usually metal minnow- or pencil-shaped hexagonals with treble hooks. For productive fishing, both surf and rock anglers must be experienced in the identification of the channels, gutters, and reefs the salmon frequent.

Boat anglers find trolling especially effective, and use pilchards and garfish rigged on linked (ganged) hooks, trolled slowly 15 to 20 meters behind the boat. Lures, including feathered jigs, metal lures, plastic minnow-type lures, and interior-weighted plastic squid (pink is good) are also used. Wire is seldom employed. Fly anglers use large streamers dressed with white, orange, blue, or red feathers (or a combination of these), which they cast from a boat to schooling salmon. Lure casters do likewise, using spoons, jigs, and plugs.

The kahawai is a spectacular fighting fish that head-shakes and tail-walks along the surface when hooked. Fish should not be pressured unduly, as hooks are easily torn from their soft mouth.

Although kahawai can be taken from most southern waters in Australia year-round, the best times to fish for them in southeastern Australia are during the autumn/winter months (March through August). In Western Australia, anglers prefer late summer and early autumn (February through May).

KANSAS

Although Kansas has only one natural lake, the state is a remarkably fine place to fish. Angling opportunities in its 83,000 square miles are provided largely by public impoundments, specifically 24 reservoirs, 46 state fishing lakes, and hundreds of city and county lakes, but also by thousands of privately owned watershed ponds where largemouth bass and panfish reign supreme.

Kansas has an ample array of species; some of the more popular and currently prominent ones are introduced species. Native fish include Kentucky (spotted) bass, channel catfish, flathead catfish, blue catfish, bullhead, several species of panfish, gar, paddlefish, drum, carp, and buffalo. Since the reservoir system was started in the 1950s, introduced species have included striped bass, wipers (hybrid striped bass), smallmouth bass, largemouth bass, white bass, walleye, sauger, saugeye, crappie, rainbow trout, and northern pike.

The most sought-after species statewide is crappie. White crappie are most abundant, primarily because of this fish's ability to do well in environments that vary from the clearer waters of the western and central reservoirs to the murkier impoundments of eastern Kansas.

For folks who enjoy river and stream fishing, Kansas also has hundreds of small and large tributaries to its three primary public river systems. The Arkansas River, the longest in Kansas, enters from Colorado and then travels east and southeast to Oklahoma, eventually joining the Mississippi in Arkansas. The Kansas River system, which begins as a public waterway at the confluence of the Smoky Hill and Republican Rivers near Fort Riley at Junction City, travels east, connecting with the Missouri River at Kansas City, Kansas. The Missouri, which is the largest and most powerful of the state's major rivers, cuts a jagged edge off the northeast corner of Kansas; those who fish from the middle of the river west need a Kansas fishing license; others require a Missouri license.

The Kansas and Missouri Rivers offer a plethora of gamefish species, largely because of the diverse fisheries in reservoirs along their lengths. The primary and most sought-after river species are flathead and channel catfish, but walleye, saugeye, white crappie, wipers, largemouth and smallmouth bass, and the usual mix of bottom feeders and gar also inhabit these waters.

In Kansas, only 1 percent of the state is available to the public for recreation of any form. Ninety-seven percent of the land is privately owned, and the remaining 2 percent consists of roads and right-of-ways. Although the Kansas, Arkansas, and Missouri Rivers are public waters, the land anglers must cross to fish them is often privately owned. Virtually all of the tributaries to the major rivers, save for the state- or federal-owned wildlife areas above and below reservoirs, are accessible to the public "by permission only."

There are, however, numerous public access points along the important rivers, and more continue to be developed. The Kansas Department of Wildlife and Parks produces a guide to Kansas fishing that lists all of the public access points as well as the exact locations of all public fishing areas, reservoirs, state fishing lakes, and city and county lakes.

The state fishing lakes in Kansas are intensely managed and consistently produce more angling success than other fisheries in the state. Each lake is managed individually by district fisheries biologists and each is subject to site-specific regulations that are posted at each lake.

Northwest/Central Region

This region, which incorporates the High Plains and the Smoky Hills, includes 8 reservoirs, 7 state fishing lakes, 10 community lakes, and 8 river access points. It is also the finest region in Kansas for largemouth bass, smallmouth bass, white crappie, black crappie, wipers, and walleye.

Norton Reservoir is a small, relatively clear impoundment with a high density of largemouth bass. Also known as Sebelius Reservoir, it is one of the state's finest saugeye, wiper, and black bass fisheries. Partially submerged tree lines and old roadbeds on the south edge of the lake provide ample fish cover. A deep sand pit at the upper end, on the south side, is a popular hangout for wipers, particularly in May.

Kirwin Reservoir is part of Kirwin National Wildlife Refuge near Phillipsburg. Because half of the lake is on the refuge, the fish are, in essence, protected from angling pressure. Like Norton, Kirwin is relatively clear and has large amounts of flooded trees and aquatic vegetation to provide nursery habitat for young fish. It is regarded as the finest Kansas lake for lunker white and black crappie, and its largemouth bass population is one of the best.

Webster Reservoir is famous for its walleye and wiper populations, and holds its own with black crappie. The lake has flooded timber at the upper end and plenty of rocky shoreline to hold largemouth bass.

Cedar Bluff Reservoir is one of Kansas' few east-west impoundments and has high limestone bluffs along a portion of its south side, a real bonus when battling the prevailing southwest winds. Almost dry in 1992, it was 50 feet below conservation pool and slowly filling with trees and shrubs when floods in 1993 and 1995 refilled the reservoir. An explosion in largemouth bass, walleye, channel catfish, wiper, and white bass populations followed. Cedar Bluff could well be the best fishing lake in Kansas, and, situated just 13 miles south of Interstate 70, it is a great stop for visitors.

Glen Elder and, to a slightly lesser degree, Lovewell Reservoir are excellent walleye fisheries, particularly during the spawn, when anglers "walk-troll" the face of dams. Fed by the Solomon River,

White bass are among the various panfish that provide good fishing at many Kansas lakes and ponds.

Glen Elder also produces high numbers of channel catfish, flatheads, white bass, and crappie. During high inflow periods, anglers routinely take large catfish at the upper end of the reservoir. In June, surface-feeding white bass become the hot ticket as anglers follow gulls feeding on the abundant gizzard shad under attack by white bass near the surface. In October, many anglers fish directly below cormorant roosting sites, a popular hangout for feeding channel catfish. And when Glen Elder ices over, it provides very good crappie fishing.

Wilson Reservoir, only 8 miles north of Interstate 70, is a blue-water gem. It is the clearest, coolest, and deepest public impoundment in Kansas, and certainly one of its finest striper, walleye, and smallmouth bass lakes. Even though stripers don't reproduce at Wilson, the high salinity provided by the inflow from the Saline River seems to enhance the lake's ability to growing large stripers. Although state records come and go, the three that Wilson seems to virtually own are for stripers, walleye, and smallmouth bass. The lake has productive dropoffs, long points, deep areas below the dam, and especially productive river and creek channels. White bass anglers also do well in June, when the whites are on top.

Kanopolis Reservoir, near Lindsborg in the Smoky Hills, is Kansas' oldest reservoir and remains a consistent producer of white crappie, walleye, white bass, and channel catfish. Anglers do well over roadbeds along the eastern edge and in an area

K

known as the humps, an old borrow pit between two boat ramps on the southern shore.

Northeast Region

The densely populated northeast region contains five reservoirs, including the three largest in the state. It also has 13 state fishing lakes and significantly more community lakes and river access points than any other region in Kansas.

Tucked into the Flint Hills is Milford Reservoir, which, at 16,200 surface acres, is Kansas' largest impoundment. Fed by the Republican River, Milford is best known for consistently producing white crappie. But it also has a growing walleye and white bass population and, through a Wildlife and Parks stocking effort, some surprisingly large smallmouth bass.

Just a stone's throw to the east of Milford is Tuttle Creek Reservoir, the state's second largest at 15,800 surface acres. This long, narrow impoundment is embraced by the Flint Hills and is filled with hefty white crappie, flatheads, and channel catfish. The Rocky Ford area below the dam is a well-known hotspot for catfish anglers.

Located between Topeka and Lawrence is Perry Reservoir, the third largest impoundment in the state at 12,600 acres. It is well established as Kansas's best white crappie fishery. In spring, anglers head up into the Delaware River to take advantage of the crappie and white bass spawn, then they follow both species back into the main lake during the summer and winter months. The most famous fishing hole on Perry is the "Hog Trough," a channel cat–rich series of breaks just off the western shore about midway up the lake. Sometime in the 1980s a group of anglers, some say they were farmers, started chumming the area with spoiled, rank-smelling soybeans. The beans attracted the channel cats, and other anglers soon followed suit. Now, every day, rain or shine, scores of boats anchor up over the popular spot. To find it, just follow your nose. And it doesn't hurt to bring a 5-gallon bucket of nasty-smelling soybeans. Stinky cheese baits are the preferred hook bait.

Clinton Reservoir, just under the gaze of the University of Kansas at Lawrence, is another fine crappie lake, and its white bass and channel cat aren't bad either. The stickups at the upper end, where the Wakarusa River enters, offer good opportunities for anglers to jig crappie at just about any time of year.

Hillsdale, the newest reservoir in Kansas, is still a 6,000-surface-acre work-in-progress located south of Olathe. However, it has already established itself as a promising largemouth and crappie fishery.

Southwest Region

Without a doubt the most arid region of Kansas, the southwest has no reservoirs but does hold 11 state fishing lakes, more than a dozen community lakes, and two access points to the Ninnescah River.

But that doesn't mean you won't find good fishing as well as a few geological surprises.

Clark State Fishing Lake may hold only 337 surface acres, but all of them are in an area known as Fatty Evans Canyon, located at the upper end of the Gypsum Hills Region. Unseen until you reach the rim of the canyon, Clark not only offers a good angling experience, it does so in a beautiful setting. Good numbers of largemouth bass, walleye, and channel catfish thrive here.

Another scenic surprise is Scott State Fishing Lake, a 115-acre gem fed by four large springs and tucked into Ladder Creek Canyon, a few miles north of Scott City. The lake has largemouth bass and particularly nice bluegills and redear sunfish. Due to 56°F spring water, Scott also holds rainbow trout.

Encompassing only 80 acres, Meade State Fishing Lake is just a wet spot in the road, but it does offer good largemouth bass angling, especially along the cattails at the northwest end. The lake is near one of the four state fish hatcheries, but it's the only state hatchery that produces largemouth bass.

South-Central Region

South-central Kansas is the focal point for many anglers who fish the Arkansas River drainage. Located in the region are 4 reservoirs, 5 state fishing lakes, 15 community lakes, and several excellent river access points along the Arkansas, Chikaskia, Cottonwood, Little Arkansas, Neosho, and Walnut Rivers, as well as Grouse Creek.

Cheney and El Dorado Reservoirs are on either side of Wichita, Cheney being 20 miles to the west and El Dorado 30 miles to the east.

Cheney is well known for its walleye and striper populations, and for its white bass run each spring as the fish move into the North Fork of the Ninnescah to spawn. It is also a fine white crappie fishery and has been a consistent producer of lunker channel and flathead catfish. Like virtually all Kansas lakes, Cheney is relatively flat-bottomed; most anglers achieve success by jigging over old roadbeds, borrow pits, and submerged tree lines.

With 8,000 surface acres, El Dorado is 1,500 acres smaller than Cheney, but it has thousands of stickups left by the Army Corps of Engineers when the lake was impounded in the early 1980s. Once a powerhouse for largemouth bass, El Dorado has struggled as a bass fishery in recent years because of its lack of nursery habitat. This is primarily due to loss of shoreline vegetation from wind and water erosion. A program to reestablish aquatic vegetation has begun, and biologists are hopeful that the bass population will rebound once the habitat spreads along the shoreline. What El Dorado does have, however, is an ample supply of big walleye, a fish that seems to have found its niche in the windswept environment. The lake also has good white crappie and white bass populations, and the smallmouth bass have found homes in the riprap and borrow

The oldest complete-fish fossils were discovered in central Bolivia in the mid-1980s and have been dated at 450 million years old; the fish possessed armor and rounded head plates.

pits along the dam, as well as in other areas with rocky shorelines.

Marion Reservoir, about 50 miles north of Wichita, is a south-central Kansas hotspot for walleye, white crappie, white bass, wipers, and largemouth bass. And the catfishing is superb. Consistently ranked in the top five Kansas lakes for three to four species of gamefish, Marion is one of many Kansas reservoirs to reap fish population-explosion benefits from 1993 floods.

At the northeast corner of the south-central region is Council Grove Reservoir, a 3,500-acre impoundment on the north edge of Council Grove, the last pit stop on the Santa Fe Trail. Council Grove, fed by the Neosho River, is another white crappie mecca, and, along with Norton, is one of the two best saugeye lakes in Kansas. The main lake is a popular spot for boat anglers, but the spillway and seep stream are heavily fished by bank anglers, who pull in 40- to 60-pound flatheads as well as lunker saugeye. The saugeye get into the seep stream after spilling out of the reservoir.

An excellent river access area is at Grouse Creek, below Silverdale and some 6 miles east of Arkansas City. Located in the KAW Wildlife Area, Grouse Creek is one of the many fine Flint Hills streams that have Kentucky bass, green sunfish, bluegills, channel catfish, and flathead catfish. It also holds good numbers of long-nose gar, which provide entertainment for fly anglers who catch this species while fishing from float tubes. Of the three access points to Grouse Creek, only one has a boat ramp; it is roughly 50 yards above the spot where the creek flows into the Arkansas River.

Southeast Region

The southeastern portion of Kansas is an ecologically diverse area made up of hardwoods, streams, rivers, hills, and farmland. It holds seven reservoirs, and at least two towns on the Neosho River proclaim to be the Catfish Capital of Kansas.

Pomona and Melvern Reservoirs sit at the top of the region. Pomona is best known for producing the 90-pound state-record flathead, a feat that should stand for several years. Like so many reservoirs, Pomona has good numbers of white crappie and white bass. Melvern is the only Kansas impoundment with a viable sauger population. Sauger were introduced by the state in the 1980s to provide eggs and milt that would be combined with similar ingredients from walleye. The resulting saugeye hybrid are hatched and raised in a state hatchery adjacent to Milford Lake. Melvern is also a good walleye, white crappie, and largemouth bass fishery.

Down the road is John Redmond Reservoir, best known for its white bass. Crappie fishing in the Neosho River above the reservoir is rated as very good by the anglers who jig the "jam," an enormous clot of deadfall trees and limbs that span the river for up to a half mile.

Within eyesight of Redmond is Wolf Creek Reservoir, a 5,000-acre cooling lake for the Wolf Creek Nuclear Generating Plant. Closed to the public until 1995, this gem-quality lake has an incredible 70-30 predator-prey mix, the result of front-loading the lake with an enormous predator population of largemouth and smallmouth bass, walleye, wipers, stripers, white bass, and panfish, to keep the gizzard shad population in check. Wolf Creek is the finest smallmouth fishery in Kansas, and although these fish aren't huge, they are plentiful. Tight regulations ensure that Wolf Creek will be a premier lake for many years.

La Cygnes Lake is situated along Kansas' eastern edge. It doesn't officially count as a reservoir, but it certainly fits nicely into that category. Created as a cooling lake for a coal-fired electric generating plant, La Cygnes is the only Kansas lake with an established population of Florida-strain largemouth bass. It holds virtually every other species of fish found in Kansas, but it is the prospect of 9- and 10-pound largemouths that draws bass anglers here. Wipers are another favored species at La Cygnes.

The southern tier of the region has four reservoirs: Toronto, Elk City, Fall River, and Big Hill. In this part of the state it's not hard to find a flathead angler, especially at Toronto, a 2,800-acre lake that many flathead aficionados believe will yield the next state record. Fed by the slow-moving Verdegris River, it could be harboring a fish in excess of 90 pounds. Elk City, at 4,450 acres, is another fine fishing hole for anglers with a preference for white bass and white crappie. During the spawn it's not hard to run into a lunker largemouth or Kentucky bass if you follow the whites up into the Elk River.

Fall River, with 2,550 acres, offers the same mix as Elk City, but it has more angling access to the river above and below the reservoir. The areas above the reservoir are well known to crappie and white bass anglers. Big Hill has a sizable population of largemouth bass, as well as a 21-inch length limit; that limit makes the chance of a bass reaching 5 to 8 pounds better here than in other Kansas lakes. Clotted with stickups and deadfalls, the upper end of Big Hill has more than enough cover to provide ambush points for big bass.

KAWAKAWA *Euthynnus affinis.*

Other names—wavyback skipjack, eastern little tuna, mackerel, tuna, Pacific little tunny, false albacore, dwarf bonito; Cantonese: *to chung;* Hindi: *suraly;* Japanese: *hiragatsuo, obosogatsuo, soda, suma;* Malay: *ayu, bakulan, kayu;* Tagalog (Philippines): *katsarita, manko, pidlayan;* Turkish: *yazili.*

A member of the Scombridae family of mackerel, the kawakawa was classified as *Euthynnus alletteratus affinis* when it was thought to be a subspecies of the Atlantic little tunny *(Euthynnus alletteratus).* It is now considered a separate species. This good gamefish is a prominent commercial

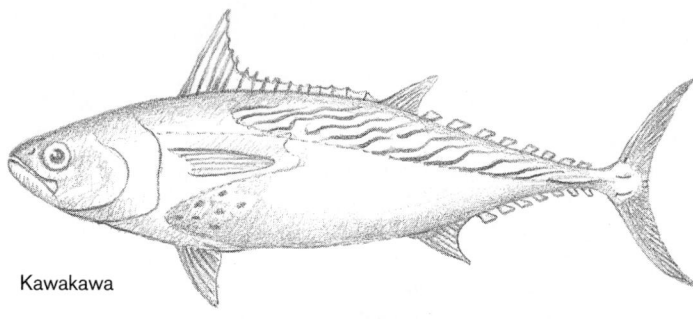

Kawakawa

species in the Philippines, Malaysia, and India. Its flesh is dark red, and in some places it is highly valued as food. In Hawaii it is often prepared as sashimi.

Identification.   The first dorsal fin of the kawakawa has 14 to 16 spines, and the second dorsal fin has 12 to 13 rays. The anal fin has 12 to 14 rays. There are no scales on the body, except on the corselet and lateral line. There are 29 to 34 gill rakers on the first arch, compared to 53 to 63 in the skipjack tuna *(Katsuwonnus pelamis)* and 32 to 41 in the black skipjack *(E. lineatus).* On the back, beginning near the midpoint of the dorsal fin, are a number of oblique, wavy lines over a turquoise background. These squiggly lines run from the lateral line back toward the dorsal fins. Some live specimens may display dark, prominent longitudinal stripes on the venter. These stripes tend to disappear quickly once the fish is removed from the water, leaving only a number of dark spots showing between the pectoral fins and the ventral fins.

Size.   Kawakawa are reported to attain a maximum length of 40 inches and a weight of 30 pounds. The all-tackle world record is a 29-pound specimen.

Distribution.   This species is widespread in tropical and temperate waters of the Indo-Pacific, from the Red Sea and South Africa east to Indonesia and Australia, and from Japan and the Philippines throughout Oceania to the Hawaiian Islands. It is accidental in the eastern Pacific, where it is replaced by the closely related black skipjack *(see: skipjack, black).*

Habitat.   This pelagic and migratory species stays fairly close to land. It may be found near reefs and in estuaries, as well as in open waters, and sometimes forms multispecies schools by size with other scombrids consisting of between 100 and several thousand individuals.

Food and feeding habits.   More than half of the food ingested by the kawakawa consists of crustaceans, although squid and pelagic fish also form a large part of its diet. It is a highly opportunistic feeder.

Angling.   Fishing methods include trolling lures or whole or cut baits, live-bait fishing, and casting. Some effective baits include squid, herring, sauries, mullet, anchovies, mackerel, halfbeaks, and yellowtail.

See: Mackerel.

KAYAK

The term "kayak" usually conjures up an image of someone ensconced in a small, tipsy, canoelike craft negotiating the whitewater of a roiling river. This is not exactly a fishing scene, and a kayak is not the type of craft that often comes to mind for fishing. Yet, anglers are using kayaks to a limited extent, and although kayaks are not about to clog the angling waterways, they do appeal to some people for certain common fishing activities (as canoes do) and, in a few cases, for some extreme activities.

The craft primarily used in saltwater fishing are sea kayaks, made of polyethylene and with raised seats that have a center of gravity near water level. These are very stable and not excessively prone to capsizing (or rollover). In freshwater, kayaks used by anglers include touring models, which are used by adventurers on long-distance forays but not really set up for a lot of fishing, and general-purpose kayaks. The latter are models used for calm rivers (not whitewater) and small lakes and ponds. They range roughly from 12 to 15 feet in length.

Like canoes, kayaks draft hardly any water, so they have obvious benefits for shallow-water fishing and quiet movement; they are eminently portable and less expensive than many boats with trailers, motors, and other accessories. However, most models are not suitable for rough water fishing, require a bit of exertion (not everyone is up to this exercise), can be difficult to get through coastal inlet waves, are short on storage (including fish storage), and have some safety concerns that are not posed by other boats. Moreover, it is not possible to stand up in many kayaks (although it is possible in catamaran-hulled versions, and some agile anglers do stand up in shallow, warm waters, such as tidal flats), and the low level of position changes fishing perspective for people who are used to higher vantage points, although this may be compensated by a quiet, stealthy approach for getting close to fish.

Some anglers are using kayaks to fish shallow waters and get to places that are otherwise hard to access.

Some anglers using kayaks in coastal waters paddle many miles to fish (a few even going offshore to blue water), and others go short distances, but in all cases anglers must pay attention to tides, current, wind, and wave direction when planning the day's activities. Most fishing-related kayaking is done in warm tropical waters, but those who fish in cold water and in cold weather require enclosable cockpits and need to wear wetsuits. Models with scupper holes to drain water are preferred, as are those with waterproof hatches.

A variety of specialized kayak fishing accessories are available, including rod holders and padded high-backed seats. Sea anchors, a folding anchor, dry bags, appropriate PFD, and some standard safety items are among the other items used, as well as portable sonar. Creative anglers have found ways to troll as well as to fish live bait from kayaks, in addition to casting and jigging, and have been expanding the applications for this craft, particularly in saltwater.
See: Boat.

KEDGE

A type of anchor, seldom used on recreational boats, with opposing flukes and used on rocky bottoms.
See: Anchor.

KEEL

The backbone of a boat, the main structural element; also, the lateral fore-to-aft area at the bottom of the hull that provides stability.
See: Boat.

KEEL HOOK

A hook with a raised shank, or keel.
See: Fly; Hook.

KEEPER

A term for a fish that meets legal length limits.
See: Regulations.

KEEPER RING

A small, usually folding, ring ahead of a rod handle; the keeper ring holds a hook that is attached to the fishing line.

KELP

Large varieties of brown algae, or brown seaweeds. Kelp grows in large structures called macrocysts, which may be up to 200 feet long, or grows as elaborately branched mats. Concentrations are known as kelp forests, and they harbor an entire food chain of sea life, which makes them prominent places to locate many species of gamefish.

KELT

A term for sea-run Atlantic salmon that have overwintered in a river and returned to saltwater in the spring. Also called "black" salmon, or spring salmon, these fish are thinner and somewhat darker than fresh bright-silver migrants but lose this darkness as they descend toward the sea. Kelts begin to feed in the spring, the only time when Atlantic salmon do so in freshwater, and can be hungry, aggressive, and thus more eager to take a fly. Some anglers disparage fishing for kelts, in deference to their condition, although there are spring kelt fisheries in some places, and these fish can be good sport.
See: Salmon, Atlantic.

KENTUCKY

"The Happy Hunting Ground," a term Native American Indians used two centuries ago to describe the game-rich landmass that would become the commonwealth of Kentucky, probably took the region's excellent fishing into account as well.

Kentucky is blessed with a wide diversity of fisheries. These range from wild brook trout in the eastern highland region along the Virginia border to world-class crappie and bass fisheries in the lake country of the western lowlands. In between, some 86,000 miles of rivers and streams course the landscape. This is more running water than exists in any other state, and it provides a smorgasbord of flowing-water opportunities for the likes of white bass, smallmouth bass, rock bass, spotted bass, muskellunge, and catfish, plus it offers almost untapped crappie and panfish populations.

Numerous state-owned lakes are scattered throughout the commonwealth, and these provide excellent opportunities to catch bass, crappie, channel catfish, and other species from small boats or by fishing from the banks. A host of large and small impoundments offer outstanding angling as well.

Beginning in the 1940s, when Dale Hollow Reservoir and Kentucky Lake were completed, and extending into the 1970s, when many flood-control reservoirs were constructed across the state, Kentucky anglers underwent a transformation. Having almost exclusively fished streams and rivers, they began to try their luck in the newly formed reservoirs. Some Kentucky anglers now do nothing but fish the lakes, especially the larger ones.

Several small reservoirs provide good fishing in the eastern highland region. Among the better ones are Yatesville, Paintsville, Dewey, Buckhorn, Cave Run, and Carr Fork. In central Kentucky, such famous and larger waters as Lake Cumberland and Dale Hollow receive much of the fishing pressure and publicity. Numerous smaller reservoirs like Barren River, Rough River, Green River, and Nolin contribute a combined 23,000-plus acres of additional angling opportunity.

K

K

The greatest attractions for bass and crappie anglers continue to be huge Kentucky Lake and nearby Lake Barkley. Kentucky Lake, a 184-mile-long reservoir that straddles the Kentucky-Tennessee border at the western end of the state (50,000 acres in Kentucky), grows tackle-rattling largemouth, big smallmouth, and football-shaped Kentucky (spotted) bass. Rod-bending flathead, channel, and blue catfish are so plentiful in Kentucky Lake that it supports a fairly large commercial fishing operation, and the crappie fishing is nearly legendary. Lake Barkley, just across the nearby ridge line, adds 58,000 acres of prime bass and crappie habitat to the already bountiful opportunity of the far western region.

In addition to great bass, crappie, and catfish angling in various waters, Kentucky boasts some of the finest muskie fishing in the South, rockfish (landlocked stripers) up to 60 pounds, and record-size walleye and sauger. It also supports an astonishing number of trout fisheries for a so-called "Southern" state.

Eastern Region

No one really knows if brook trout were ever native to the highlands of eastern Kentucky, but this species has been successfully introduced to some of the region's most remote streams, where they not only survive hot low-water summers, but where they have also been showing strong evidence of natural reproduction. The bulk of the brook trout streams exist in the highlands of the easternmost areas of the state and inside the vast reaches of the Daniel Boone National Forest. Brook trout fishing isn't promoted highly by the state fish and wildlife agency because of the species' delicate habitat, yet more than a dozen streams offer challenges in pursuing these beautifully colored fish, some of which range to 14 inches and more in length. Specific information about this remote fishery is available from the state fish and wildlife agency's regional office at Williamsburg.

There are 19 streams in the hilly to mountainous eastern region of Kentucky that support good numbers of native muskellunge. Heading the list of the top muskie streams are Tygart Creek in Carter and Greenup Counties, the Kinniconick in Lewis County, and the Licking River, which begins in Morgan County and empties into the Ohio River at Covington.

Fish from these streams and others in eastern Kentucky were used to develop one of the finest muskie rearing and stocking programs in America. Minor Clark Fish Hatchery, at Cave Run Lake, annually produces many 10- to 14-inch-long muskie fingerlings for planting in various streams and rivers, and in three lakes. Cave Run Lake, an 8,500-acre standing-timber-infested reservoir in Rowan and Menifee Counties, is not only rated as the finest muskie fishing lake in Dixie, it is also one of the top sites in North America for this species.

Some eastern Kentucky lakes also hold good populations of walleye. Laurel River Lake, a 5,000-acre clear-water mountain gem surrounded by the Daniel Boone National Forest in Laurel County, has large numbers of walleye, some of which have grown to 20 or more pounds. Some believe these giant walleye are remnants of the old river walleye that grew to world-class proportions in the upper Cumberland River system after Lake Cumberland impounded the river in the early 1950s.

From 1955 to 1959, anglers who fished the famed walleye spawning runs in Laurel River and the Big South Fork of the Cumberland during February and March reported catching limits of heavy walleye—10 to 20 pounds and more. Those big walleye virtually disappeared from the rivers by the early 1960s. Whether their gene pool is still in the Laurel Lake population is uncertain, but the fish in that body of water today are still large.

Two lakes in eastern Kentucky—180-acre Greenbo in Greenup County and 700-acre Woods Creek in Laurel County—may contain the biggest largemouth bass in the state. Tiny Greenbo has surrendered two state-record largemouths; the bigger one weighed $13^1/_2$ pounds. Biologists believe that this small clear-water reservoir, which forms the hub of Greenbo Lake State Resort Park, has more trophy-size largemouths per acre than any other body of water in the commonwealth.

Woods Creek Lake, which borders Interstate 75 near London, produced a record largemouth weighing 13 pounds, 10.4 ounces. Poor water clarity makes both lakes difficult to fish during the day. The record fish here, and the two at Greenbo, were caught at night—two on 7-inch plastic worms and one on a spinnerbait.

Rainbow and brown trout are widely spread over this eastern third of Kentucky thanks to a cooperative effort between the state fish and wildlife agency and the U.S. Fish and Wildlife Service. Wolff Creek Federal Fish Hatchery, located below the dam at Lake Cumberland, provides hundreds of thousands of catchable-size rainbow trout, and some brown trout, for stocking throughout Kentucky.

In the hilly and mountainous regions, approximately 30 streams provide good trout fishing for at least six months of the year. This is the result of a mostly put-and-take program. Streams are stocked beginning in April and running through September—provided there is adequate flowage—with a supply of 9- to 12-inch trout each month.

The U.S. Forest Service stocks an additional 15 streams inside the boundaries of the Daniel Boone National Forest beginning in March and extending through June in most instances. In McCreary County, Rock Creek—the state's premier small-stream trout fishery—receives stockings of both rainbow and brown trout through October, with one planting of sub-adult-size fish each fall.

Laurel River Lake is the best lake fishery for trout in the state. This deep, exceptionally clear reservoir provides ideal habitat for rainbow trout, some of which have grown to 8 pounds. Each year, the lake is stocked with about 125,000 catchable-size trout during February. Most of the fish are caught by anglers who troll small spinners and crankbaits just off the shore early in the season. By May, hundreds of night anglers invade Laurel River Lake during weekends, using battery-powered lights attached to the sides of their boats to attract fish close to their offerings of organic baits and vertically jigged artificials.

In addition to these fisheries, eastern Kentucky offers great float fishing opportunities for smallmouth bass, Kentucky bass, and muskies. Tygarts and Kinniconick Creeks are popular for this in the northern end of the region; the remote reaches of Rockcastle River in Rockcastle County is a favorite farther south. Little access development along the streams keeps fishing pressure to a minimum, making a float trip for energetic anglers even more rewarding in the form of more and larger fish.

Central Region

Sprawling Lake Cumberland is a 55,250-acre flood-control and power-generation lake that provides anglers with nearly 1,300 miles of rocky shoreline from Somerset to Jamestown and has long attracted the bulk of fishing attention in the center of Kentucky.

Cumberland has a variety of notable species, with bass being of foremost interest. During its heyday in the 1950s and 1960s, Lake Cumberland was regarded by many bass fishing authorities as one of the best largemouth lakes in the world. That is not the case today, but the big lake still surrenders abundant quality bigmouths, as well as smallmouth bass, to anglers who fish the lake year-round. Rockfish are plentiful in the lower reaches of the lake and offer anglers a good chance to tangle with a powerful swimmer that may weigh in at 50 pounds or more.

Lake Cumberland is the state's best walleye producer. Biologists have reported a huge population of walleye ranging from 20 to 28 inches in the lake. Found throughout the reservoir, walleye are mostly caught incidentally by anglers in pursuit of bass and crappie, although interest in this so-called northern species has been growing among locals.

The Lake Cumberland tailrace, which extends for 55 miles from the base of Wolff Creek Dam at Jamestown south past Burkesville to the Tennessee border, is considered by Kentucky fisheries managers as a blue-ribbon trout producer. Each year, more than 80,000 catchable-size rainbows and 30,000 similar-size brown trout are released into the tailrace below the dam and downstream for about 5 miles. Trout thrive in the cold water released from the bottom of the lake and grow to record-setting sizes. Browns in the 18-pound class have been caught here, as well as rainbows upward of 14 pounds. Trolling, casting, drifting live baits,

and fly fishing are all popular means of taking these wild fish from the underpressured environment.

Dale Hollow Lake straddles the Kentucky and Tennessee border and offers one of the best opportunities in the country to catch a truly large smallmouth bass. An 18-inch minimum size limit and a two-fish-per-day creel limit have contributed significantly to the large number of sizable bronzebacks in the lake.

Dale Hollow also has a good population of walleye, even though few anglers target the species. The 27,000-acre lake is also stocked with rainbow trout and lake trout, which are more numerous in the lower reaches near the dam.

The three river lakes—Barren River (Barren County), Rough River (Grayson County), and Nolin (Edmonson County)—also provide good fishing for largemouth, panfish, and crappie in the central area of the commonwealth. The tailrace below each of these lakes is stocked regularly with several hundred 9- to 12-inch rainbow trout.

Farther north, in Spencer County, 3,300-acre Taylorsville Lake has good numbers of largemouth bass, crappie, and hybrid striped bass. Unfortunately, the relatively small Taylorsville is close to large population centers in Lexington and Louisville, resulting in the heaviest fishing pressure of any lake in the state, much of which comes from organized clubs that hold numerous bass tournaments here. Catch-and-release is practiced almost exclusively among this group, but as one state fisheries biologist noted, every bass in Taylorsville has been caught and released many times.

Less pressured are several streams and rivers that offer excellent populations of smallmouth bass for floating and wading anglers. Foremost among these streams is the South Branch of the Licking River, running between Cynthiana and Falmouth. This wide but shallow limestone-bottomed stream has good numbers of smallmouth bass up to 3 pounds; these are usually taken with both live minnows and artificials, either by casting or fly fishing.

Elkhorn Creek, the state's most historic smallmouth stream (which was once stocked with king salmon), flows into the Kentucky River at Frankfort and offers ideal float fishing conditions on its North Fork. Numerous spots along the river are conducive to wading and fishing with lightweight spinning or fly fishing tackle.

Western Region

Huge Kentucky Lake and Lake Barkley overshadow all other fisheries in the western third of the state. When it comes to largemouth bass, crappie, and catfish, few other lakes in Kentucky can match up in sheer numbers as well in size.

Fisheries biologists believe that Kentucky Lake holds more 4- to 6-pound largemouths per acre than any other lake in the commonwealth. Lake Barkley, no more than a few miles to the east, continuously challenges its sister lake in numbers of

Tarpon have been known to leap as high as 10 feet vertically and 20 feet horizontally, making them one of the most spectacular show-boats an angler could want.

Early-morning fog doesn't stop bass and crappie anglers on Kentucky Lake.

K

Swan Lake, a 300-acre flooded lowland in Ballard County, is the state's only natural lake. It is a part of the large oxbow system that borders the Ohio and Mississippi Rivers in the far western tip of the state. These oxbow lakes are flooded by nearby rivers during winter and spring, bringing in fresh stocks of crappie, spotted bass, and other species. The Kentucky Department of Fish and Wildlife Resources owns many of these lakes and manages the fishery, which includes bluegills, crappie, bass, and catfish.

Ohio River

The Ohio River flows along some 600 miles of Kentucky's northern border and is one of the strongest fisheries in this area of North America. Along this stretch of the Ohio are seven large pools formed by high-lift navigation dams. These pools form lakes as large as 20,000 acres or more, which force the Ohio's waters into every bordering lowland and up the mouths of tributaries, creating numerous backwater areas that offer excellent habitat for largemouth bass and crappie.

The main stem of the river affords countless miles of catfish habitat and good fishing for Kentucky spotted bass during spring and again in autumn. It also has one of the best white bass runs in the world. In recent years, striped bass as well as hybrid stripers have been stocked in the river.

With the exception of bass angling and fishing from the banks near the mouths of tributaries for "anything that bites," most fishing along the Ohio River occurs in the tailraces below the big dams. Here, giant schools of white bass, hybrid stripers, rockfish, and sauger feed on plentiful gizzard shad, emerald shiners, and herring (skipjacks). Action can be fast-paced during late spring and through the early autumn months for white bass and hybrids. In summer, catfish anglers come out in force in the tailraces, using a variety of organic and live baits to catch large numbers of channel and flathead catfish at night.

As the water temperature falls off in autumn, tens of thousands of sauger swim into the tailraces. Blocked in their pre-spawn, upstream migration, the fish mill about the tailrace throughout the winter months, providing late-season anglers with one of the best fisheries for the species in America.

Smithland Pool, near Paducah, is currently one of the top places on the river to take flathead, channel, and blue catfish. Anglers use boats to access and negotiate the turbulent currents beneath the dams, where they slow-bounce organic and live-bait presentations off the bottom. An outboard holds the boat in place against the strong current.

Each of the pools on the Ohio River has excellent access via launching ramps. A reciprocal agreement between states that share the Ohio as a border permits anglers who hold a resident or nonresident angling license to fish both sides of the river.

bass as well as the size of its crappie. Both reservoirs are famous for their world-class crappie fisheries during spring and autumn.

In recent years, Kentucky Lake has developed a trophy smallmouth bass fishery. Smallmouths moved downstream from Pickwick Lake, a stronghold for the species in southern Tennessee (the Tennessee River, which forms Kentucky Lake, flows north to meet the Ohio River near Paducah). Presently, anglers are landing smallmouths in all areas of the lake, but the eastern shore, bordering the Land Between The Lakes recreation area, is most productive.

Lake Barkley, which was formed from the lower reaches of the Cumberland River, is shallower than nearby Kentucky Lake. It has copious bottom structure in the form of submerged stump fields, numerous sunken treetops, and stake beds, created to afford concentrated cover for the lake's large crappie population.

Anglers who test their fishing skills for bass and crappie on Kentucky and Barkley Lakes divert their attention during various seasons to the tailraces. Situated no more than 3 miles apart, both tailraces have large populations of sauger and white bass, as well as striped bass, some of which run up to 25 pounds. Huge flathead catfish, channel cats, and Mississippi blue cats are also plentiful in the tailraces, which are well developed for both bank anglers and boaters.

Anglers traveling to this part of Kentucky typically visit and camp in the 170,000-acre Land Between The Lakes recreation area. This uncommercialized area separating Kentucky and Barkley Lakes has lakeside campgrounds, a nature center, an elk and bison range, and many other recreational facilities.

Lake Malone, a 700-acre lake in Muhlenburg County, has long been a producer of supersize largemouth bass. According to one fisheries biologist, anglers report catching more 10-pound bass from this lake than from any other lake in Kentucky.

KENTUCKY REEL

Term for the original multiplying reel, crafted between 1800 and 1810 in Kentucky by watchmakers George Snyder and Jonathan Meek. This was a multiple-action revolving-spool casting reel, developed at a time when a single-action revolving-spool reel was the only reel available for sportfishing, and anglers exclusively used natural bait or artificial flies. The single-action reel was primarily employed to store and retrieve line, and had no casting function, whereas the revolving-spool multiplier was used for casting—paying out line with the object being cast—and one turn of the crank caused more than one full turn of the spool.

Between 1835 and 1840, Jonathan Meek and his brother started the first commercial manufacture of Kentucky Reels. These and later multipliers would lead to casting with objects other than unweighted flies, and eventually to the development and popularity of artificial lures, including spoons, spinners, and plugs.

See: Antique Fishing Tackle; Baitcasting Tackle; Conventional Tackle; Multiplying Reel.

KENYA

Most often associated with four-legged wildlife, safaris, high mountain peaks, the Masai Mara savanna, Amboselli and its view of Mt. Kilimanjaro, and abundant tourist facilities, Kenya is also one of Africa's best sportfishing destinations. It offers diverse and notable offshore angling opportunities, as well as high-mountain trout fishing. Along the coast these fisheries are more accessible and developed than those in most other countries, especially central and northern Africa, on this continent.

Situated on the eastern coast of Africa and facing the Indian Ocean, Kenya is virtually bisected by the equator. Its coastal region is on the southeast, and to the east lies Somalia, to the north Ethiopia, to the northwest Sudan, to the west Uganda, and to the south Tanzania.

The southwestern border of the country is marked by a small portion of Lake Victoria, the second largest lake in the world.

While much of northeastern Kenya is a flat, bush-covered plain, the remaining geography encompasses pristine beaches, scenic highland and lake regions, the Great Rift Valley, and magnificent Mount Kenya. Although Kenya's varied topography experiences a wide variety of climatic conditions, the coastal temperature remains comfortably warm year-round. Much of Kenya experiences heavy rainfall from mid-April through June and, to a lesser extent, from mid-September through November.

The best time for most outdoor activities (including safaris and fishing) is during the dry season, from November through March. Kenya's saltwater fishing season typically starts as early as August and continues until as late as the end of April. During this time the calm northerly wind, the Kaskazy, provides friendly seas.

One of Africa's top spots for tourists, Kenya is still one of the world's foremost safari destinations. Although its warm climate, exotic animal life, and lush flora and fauna certainly help attract this attention, Kenya's attitude toward its resources may be more responsible for its popularity among nature lovers. Kenyans regard the environment as a primary resource for a wide variety of "clean" incomes, an example ignored by the great majority of African countries. For anglers, this philosophy has resulted in an ocean free of ravaging commercial longlining operations and boasting pristine lagoons and mangrove breaks protected by hundreds of miles of untouched coral reefs.

Saltwater

For all practical purposes, waters within some 30-odd miles of the 300-mile-long Kenya Coast are the main local fishing grounds. This is essentially an area of sea lying above the continental shelf. The seabed here does not plunge to its greatest depths, but it still reaches down in places to about 3,000 feet. The 100-fathom contour, however, roughly marks the landward edge of the coastal current, and, in general terms, is where big-game offshore fishing efforts are focused.

Despite its warm climate and diverse undersea environment, Kenya and other African fisheries formerly had a reputation in international fishing circles for short fishing seasons and limited offshore species, namely sailfish. In the 1960s and 1970s, a primitive infrastructure limited Kenya's billfishing seasons and catches. Captains of small, poorly equipped boats would fish only in the best of seasons, and even then they rarely ventured past the calm "sailfish alley" to search for other species. Of course, at the time there was little reason for them to do so.

Much of this fishing took place out of Malindi, whose prime location near the Sabaki River allows skippers to take advantage of the remarkable color change just a few miles offshore, where river runoff meets the cobalt blue water of the Indian Ocean. This clear area of demarcation has historically been prolific, offering excellent numbers of dolphin, wahoo, kingfish, tuna, snapper, jacks, and sailfish.

In succeeding decades, Kenya's leading charter operators made huge strides in catching up to international standards in boats, tackle, electronics, and fishing techniques, notably so at Malindi and nearby Watamu, and 50 miles south of Mombasa at Shimoni, which borders Tanzania and accesses the promising year-round fishery of the Pemba Channel. As a result, the country's skippers began to explore the far-off rips and banks that had previously been ignored. They found surprisingly productive angling spots and caught not only sailfish, but good numbers of striped, blue, and black marlin, as well as the occasional spearfish.

K

A view of the beach, sportfishing boats, and the Indian Ocean from Watamu.

K

But the biggest surprise for Kenya's skippers was a prolific fishery for swordfish. In 1992, overnight trips to the North Kenya Banks, an undersea chain of mountains 55 miles northeast of Malindi, began producing excellent swordfishing. Another hotspot for broadbills, The Rips, was just 14 to 22 miles from Watamu. Since these discoveries, offshore fishing has diversified along the length of Kenya's coast, although some ports are more focused on gamefishing than others.

Today, Malindi, Watamu, and Mombasa are main ports for offshore excursions. Sophisticated, although limited operations (in terms of the number of boats available) work out of Lamu in the north; out of Kilifi, halfway between Mombasa and Malindi; out of Mtwapa Creek, about 8 miles north of Mombasa; and out of Diani and Funzi Island on the south side of Mombasa.

Off Mombasa are good catches of sailfish, as well as wahoo, barracuda, dorado, tuna, and jacks, and it is not unusual to encounter a marlin. This is also a main site for bottom fishing.

Boats departing from Shimoni commonly fish in the water of the famous Pemba Island Channel. The main fishing areas here extend from Chale Point in the north all the way down to Zanzibar, although it is rare for boats to venture more than 15 to 20 miles south of Shimoni.

The Pemba Channel proper is very deep. The seabed on either side drops abruptly like great escarpments, and these must rival in size the famous Rift Valley hundreds of miles inland. Thus, really deep water is very close to shore and is a main factor in attracting marlin to this area. They may also be attracted by an abundance of food, given the rich pickings along the almost sheer escarpment walls. The many rips here are also significant in this respect.

About 20 miles offshore, Pemba Island is a 15-mile-wide obstruction in the path of migrating billfish. When they reach it, some turn and swim down the channel, whereas others pass the island farther

out to sea. This results not only in a good local population of marlin, but also the diversion of many marlin into the sea. The local Pemba Channel Fishing Club (phone: 254-11-313749; fax: 254-11-316875) has good boats for charter.

Ten miles north of Mombasa lies Mtwapa Creek, a site highly favored by many anglers and offering boats that have helped pioneer big-game fishing locations and techniques in Kenya waters. Kilifi, nearly 40 miles north of Mombasa, lures many private boats, and visitors congregate here to fish from the rapidly expanding Mnarani Club. This is an excellent area for tuna and many other species.

About 70 miles north of Mombasa, Watamu and Malindi have become the most popular ports for big-game fishing off Kenya, in terms of scale of operation and tourist notoriety. Malindi and Watamu fall more or less into the resort category. They are famous for sailfish, striped marlin, blue marlin, black marlin, and swordfish (which, in season, are found and caught in very large numbers). Runs of yellowfins, kingfish, and other species are common as well. Watamu and Malindi host prominent international fishing competitions. At Malindi, the Kingfisher Charter Fleet (phone: 254-123-21168; fax: 254-123-30261) is highly respected, as is Hemingway's Hotel & Sportfishing Resort (phone: 254-122-32624; fax: 254-122-32256) in Watamu.

Freshwater

Trout. There's nothing that takes the breath away like creeping up to a likely trout pool at 9,500 feet in the Aberdare Mountains—especially when keenly aware of nearby populations of buffalo, elephants, lions, and leopards.

The origin of trout fishing in Kenya dates back to the turn of the twentieth century, when Lord Delamare and friends imported the first fish for release into the waters of Mt. Kenya and the Aberdares. Nearly all fish caught today are natives from naturally evolved stock; only a few streams and lakes are planted with hatchery-reared fish. Both rainbow and brown trout thrive, and in some cases inhabit waters fairly close to each other.

Trout fishing in Kenya is restricted to those regions above 5,200 feet altitude. The enthusiastic angler could undertake a trout fishing safari lasting several weeks and still not have fished all the available trout-bearing waters.

The most popular locations for fly anglers are among the slopes of Mt. Kenya, the Aberdare Mountains in the center of Kenya, and in the Mt. Elgan area near the western border. Excellent sites are incongruously tucked away between the tea fields of Kericho, off the track in the Nandi Hills and just a 40-minute drive from Nairobi. Part of the attraction of trout fishing in Kenya lies in the tremendous geographic variety within a practical radius of travel. The real magic, however, is standing knee-deep in a rushing mountain stream, as monkeys peer down from the acacia trees, and giant forest hogs and bushbuck slip down to drink at the water's edge.

Fishing is allowed in Mt. Kenya and Aberdare National Parks, and anywhere outside the smaller Mt. Elgan National Park. An impressive band of Forest Reserve encircles all three mountains, preserving the quality of trout habitat within. A specific trout license is required and can be bought for either 48 hours or a year at the park gates. The only legal offering for trout within Kenya is an artificial fly. Kenyan anglers have designed numerous fly patterns dedicated to meeting the appetites of local trout, two prominent local examples being the Kenya Bug and the Mrs. Simpson. Both are available from local suppliers.

Lakes. Although Kenya has a variety of lakes and a few major rivers, few organized opportunities for other types of freshwater fishing exist. Warmwater species inhabit these, however, and some provide angling for tigerfish and Nile perch, as well as coarse species. Visitors bringing their own equipment may find boats (and drivers) at some sites.

One of these is Lake Turkana. Formerly known as Lake Rudolf, Turkana lies in the Great Rift Valley, where the Ethiopian highlands give way to the northern Kenya desert. It was near the northeastern shore of this lake, in Sibiloi National Park, that anthropologist Dr. Richard Leakey discovered the 26-million-year-old remains of early man.

Turkana is 180 miles long, between 6 and 30 miles wide, and covers 6,400 square kilometers. It contains three main islands. The word *Turkana* means "Jade Sea," so named for the color of its water, which is fed from the highlands by the River Omo, entering the lake on its northern tip. Situated in the middle of the Chalbi Desert, at 1,200 feet above sea level and quite far inland, this site is always very hot, although often a strong wind blows.

Lake Turkana has an abundant population of Nile perch and reputedly harbors monsters that have grown to 300 pounds. Ample tilapia, catfish, barbel, tigerfish, and other species reside here as well. Casting, trolling, and live-bait fishing are popular. The Lake Turkana Angling Club has a lodge on the west side of the lake; Turkana Fishing Safaris (phone: 254-122-312234; fax: 254-122-32266) can arrange a mobile fishing camp with boats for adventure anglers. Be prepared for scorching heat, perennial high winds, and wildlife viewing, which includes crocodiles.

Two other notable lakes are Victoria and Naivasha. Situated at an altitude of 6,200 feet in the highlands 60 miles northwest of Nairobi, Lake Naivasha is the highest lake in Kenya. It has an area of approximately 75 square miles and an average depth of 20 to 30 feet, except around Crescent Island, where the water drops off sharply to depths of up to 45 feet.

Before the 1920s, the only fish native to Lake Naivasha was one species of carp. Theodore Roosevelt unsuccessfully proposed introducing black bass here in 1909. One strain of tilapia was introduced in 1926, another strain was transplanted from Lake Victoria in 1956, and still another was introduced in 1965. Tilapia today are mainly caught in nets by native commercial fishermen, but it is possible to catch them on a rod with a very small spinner.

Fifty-six black bass were imported here in 1928, and these were plentiful by the mid-1930s. With the introduction of crayfish from North America in the 1970s, the supply of food for bass improved immensely, and subsequently there was a boom in largemouth bass fishing. The inner rim of Crescent Island is known for excellent bass, and various techniques work throughout the lake, which has abundant weed growth. Two of the largest bass caught in the lake are displayed at the Lake Naivasha Club, and each weighed approximately 10 pounds; fish up to 13 pounds have been caught in the past.

Access to this fishery is principally through Safariland and the Lake Naivasha Country Club (Lake Hotel), which provides luxurious lakeside accommodations. Camping facilities are located at Fisherman's Camp and Burch's Farm. Good angling can be combined with superb wildlife viewing.

Enormous Lake Victoria is situated 200 miles west of Nairobi and is the second largest freshwater lake in the world (after Lake Superior in Michigan). Lake Victoria borders on the countries of Kenya, Uganda, and Tanzania. Its waters host the voracious Nile perch, which reputedly can grow up to 500 pounds here and has only the giant crocodile as a natural enemy. Other gamefish present are tigerfish and giant catfish, and the lake harbors tilapia and scores of other native species.

Anglers at Lake Victoria favor varied methods, including trolling with a boat, casting with lures or flies from shore or a boat, and bottom fishing with live baits (especially for the biggest fish). Several local fishing clubs organize angling excursions to Victoria from Kisumu; a list can be obtained at the local sportfishing magazine, *The Rainbow Runner,* in Nairobi.

KICK BOAT
A term for self-propelled dual-pontoon float tubes. **See: Float Tubes.**

KICKER
A term for a small outboard motor used for trolling (it saves gasoline and permits slow operation of the boat); also a term for a small auxiliary outboard available for emergency purposes if the main engine fails. **See: Outboard Motor.**

K

KIDNEY HARNESS
See: Harness, Fighting.

KILLIFISH
Also called topminnows and toothed carps, these fish are members of the large Cyprinodontidae family of small fish. They are most abundant in warm climates, but a few species occur in temperate regions. The fins are soft rayed, as in cyprinid minnows, but killifish have scales on their head and have no lateral line. Typical family members have a flattened head, and the mouth opens upward, an adaptation for feeding at the surface. Some species are used as baits, and many tropical species are kept in aquariums.

Killifish travel in schools, generally in the shallows, and are an important link in wetland and estuarine food webs. They are important prey for shorebirds, crabs, and larger fish, and many species are valued for mosquito control, as they feed on the surface and consume whatever insect larvae and small invertebrates are available. Killifish are also among the species most tolerant of high turbidity and low oxygen.

Species
Many killifish live in brackish water as well as freshwater. The best known of these is the mummichog (*Fundulus heteroclitus*), a robust 3- to 5-inch species found along the Atlantic coast from Florida to Labrador. It can tolerate salinities to 35 parts per thousand. The mummichog is noted for its habit of burrowing into the silt on the bottom, sometimes to depths of 6 inches or more in winter.

A rather fat-bodied fish compared to other members of the family, the mummichog varies in color depending on the chemistry of the water from which it is taken. Generally, however, the female is brownish green on the back and sides and light below. The sides are barred with a dark color. Males are brighter and have a much more pronounced contrast between the dark bars and the lighter body color.

Mummichogs are popular bait minnows in some regions, often going by the name of hardheads. They are hardy, remaining alive and vigorous on the hook for a long time. They can also be kept successfully in aquariums, adjusting quickly to freshwater and not demanding a constant high temperature, as do many of the more sensitive tropicals. On the Pacific coast, the California killifish (*F. parvipinnis*) is similar in size and habits to the

mummichog, and occupies the same ecological niche.

The banded killifish (*F. diaphanus*) has many narrow vertical dark bars on its sides. It is a slimmer fish than the mummichog and usually shorter, rarely exceeding 3 inches in length. Also ranging into brackish water (preferring salinities of less than 5 parts per thousand), it occurs from South Carolina northward to the St. Lawrence River and westward through the Mississippi Valley. It is sometimes used for bait, but is not as hardy as the mummichog.

Another well-known species is the gold topminnow (*F. chrysotus*), which inhabits freshwater and brackish estuaries and streams from Florida to South Carolina. Its greenish body is covered with gold or reddish dots that are almost metallic, and the female is duller than the male.

Other common species of *Fundulus* include the banded topminnow (*F. cingulatus*), which has a red belly, red fins, and red dots on its bluish body; the striped killifish (*F. majalis*), a hardy species sometimes as much as 6 inches long, with a metallic-brown body striped with a darker color; the plains topminnow (*F. sciadicus*), a strictly freshwater species found in the Mississippi and its tributaries, primarily in headwaters; and the saltmarsh topminnow (*F. jenkinsi*), a mainly brackish water species of Florida and adjacent states.

Florida has the greatest representation of cyprinodonts in North America. Notable among these is the flagfish (*jordanella floridae*), a short-bodied, almost sunfishlike species attaining a maximum length of 3 inches, and the pygmy killifish (*Leptolucania ommata*), a slender fish that rarely exceeds $1^1/_2$ inches in length.

KILLING FISH
See: Fish Preparation—General Care.

KINGFISH
A term for king mackerel (*see: mackerel, king*), and yellowtail (*see*).

KIRIBATI
The Republic of Kiribati ("ti" is pronounced like the letter *s*) consists of 33 low-elevation coral atolls flung across some 3,800 kilometers of the equatorial South and North Pacific Ocean, organized into three significant island groups: The Gilbert Islands (Tungaru), the Phoenix Islands, and the Line Islands. Kiribati's total land area is only 817 square kilometers, yet the well-spaced geography of tiny landmasses allows 3,550,000 square kilometers of surrounding ocean to fall within the jurisdiction of the country's 200-nautical-mile Exclusive Economic Zone (EEZ). The majority of the mostly

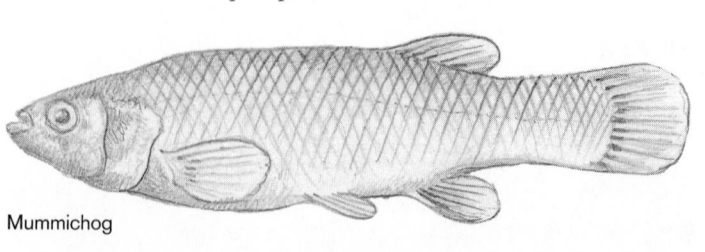

Mummichog

Micronesian population of 80,000 lives in the Gilbert Islands, centered around Tarawa, the capital. Although English is the official language, and enough is understood and spoken by locals for most visitors to effectively communicate, Kiribati is the most widely spoken.

A former British colony, Kiribati gained independence in 1979. It is the poorest nation in the Pacific, with a $32 million gross national product derived from a simple agricultural/fishing economy. With its former phosphate deposits exhausted, the primary exports are copra and fish. Most of the native population lives by subsistence seafood gathering from the reefs and lagoons, fishing, and farming. These are supplemented by part-time cash-generating activities, often copra production. Tourism is only lightly developed.

The country's richest resource is the EEZ. It encircles a vast area of both the equatorial North and South Pacific, on either side of the International Dateline. Ichthyologists estimate that more than 1,000 inshore fish species exist within these bounds. This zone also features particularly prolific offshore tropical fishing grounds. Biological productivity is elevated due to a persistent oceanographic phenomenon called equatorial upwelling, whereby nutrient-rich seawater is drawn from the depths to sunlit surface layers by the spiraling action of opposite-flowing surface currents near the equator. Various Asian and American commercial fishing corporations have been long aware of the area, contributing millions annually to Kiribati for fishing rights.

Sportfishing interests have been slower to gain access to this remote cornucopia of both inshore and offshore angling opportunities due to the overall lack of facilities and promotion. Where facilities do exist, native friendliness, and expertise derived from the strong role fishing plays in local culture—combined with the extremely productive waters—have induced results that are nothing less than spectacular.

Line Islands

The Line Islands extend in a loose, 2,300-kilometer northwest-to-southeast arc from 750 kilometers north of Tahiti to 1,120 kilometers south of Hawaii. Eight of the 10 islands belong to Kiribati, with Jarvis Island and Palmyra Atoll being U.S. possessions. The six members of the group south of the equator are uninhabited.

Christmas Island. The undisputed sportfishing capital of Kiribati is Christmas (Kiritimati) Island, which has the largest landmass of any atoll in the world at 388 square kilometers (nearly half the dry land area of the country). With an estimated population of only 4,000 inhabitants organized into three main villages, nearly the entire 160-kilometer perimeter of the island comprises deserted beaches, fringed by a narrow band of coral-reef flat that seldom falls away to blue water farther than a long surf cast from the shore.

An albatross is undisturbed by a nearby Christmas Island caster.

This long, relatively narrow landmass encloses a large complex of lagoons, some landlocked. Many are connected to the main lagoon, however, which features a nearly 5-kilometer-wide pass to the open ocean on the western side. The lagoon complex is generally shallow and features vast, white and light-colored sand flats, many bordered by beaches, deeper channels, and open bottom sometimes dotted with coral heads and rubble, small islets, and shallow tidal creeks and basins.

The government operates a small hotel at Christmas Island, complete with guide services specializing primarily in outstanding lagoon and reef fishing pursuits. The local private sector now features alternative accommodations and guides, including opportunities to sample the somewhat lightly tested offshore fishing. Most vessels are locally crafted wooden punts and outrigger canoes powered by outboard motors, uniquely suited to the shallow lagoon areas that must be traversed regardless of fishing destination. Anglers can choose between wading or boat fishing, guided or unguided. Vehicles with or without a guide are available for access to lagoon areas via land.

Outstanding flats fishing for bonefish initially put Christmas on the sportfishing map. Visiting anglers drawn by bonefish, however, quickly discovered unparalleled shallow-water opportunities to target bluefin and giant trevally on light tackle, particularly fly fishing, resulting in numerous line-class and fly-rod world-record catches for both species.

The growing number of anglers fishing offshore have experienced consistent action for yellowfin tuna and wahoo. Other species here include mahimahi, rainbow runners, skipjacks and other small tuna, and, less commonly, dogtooth tuna and African pompano. Sailfish and blue marlin have been landed, but very little effort has been expended specifically targeting billfish potential. Hefty giant trevally, and a myriad other species, including various other jacks, queenfish, grouper, snapper, sharks, barracuda, emperors, and sweetlips may all enter the catch along the outer reefs and around coral-head-studded areas of the pass and lagoon.

Inshore and reef species are generally caught year-round. Bonefish (averaging 3 to 6 pounds, with larger fish caught frequently) aggregate monthly at specific locations, apparently to spawn, one to four days after the full moon. The best-known aggregation at Christmas Island is in the vicinity of Paris, located on the point of land due south across the lagoon pass from the main village of London. Fish coming from outer reef areas as they enter the lagoon tend to concentrate here. Most larger fish aggregate in deeper water over gravel-like rubble bottom. Guides position anglers to target these fish as they move along shallower flats en route to other spawning areas. Although this situation can afford stationary anglers a fairly continuous parade of sight-casting opportunities, especially on the middle to top of the incoming tide, actively wading in numerous areas at other times can regularly yield nearly as many bonefish sightings as when fishing near an aggregation. Bonefish are also widespread on the reef flats between outer perimeter beaches and the reef crest, but they are more difficult to land due to abundant sharp coral.

Giant trevally between 30 and 80 pounds are common and are caught in a variety of habitats, including lagoon flats and channels, in the surf near the reef crest, and in deeper water near steep dropoffs to the open ocean around the outside of the atoll. Anglers sight-cast, usually with fly or spinning gear, fish blind in the surf, or troll outer reef margins. Large surface poppers and plugs deployed from the boat, or cast from the beach or while wading, work well, as do a variety of subsurface presentations, most using fast retrieves.

Milkfish, an elopiform species closely related to tarpon and bonefish, are extremely abundant in most lagoon habitats, as well as along the outer reef slopes. These fish feed on benthic algae and sediment and associated invertebrate fauna, and can also be seen in large schools feeding near the surface along windrows and slicks outside the pass. They can be taken on imitation "algae flies," commonly reach 8 or more pounds at Christmas, and are reported to be hard fighters.

Stronger seasonal trends are more evident for some offshore fishing. Wahoo averaging 40 to 65 pounds can be caught all year but are noticeably more abundant during times of cooler sea-surface temperatures (less than 84°F). Yellowfin tuna, particularly school fish under 40 pounds, are available year-round, as are skipjacks and sizable rainbow runners (averaging 6- to 8-pounds). The largest concentrations, as well as bigger individual yellowfins (from 50 to more than 100 pounds), however, occur more frequently during the summer months, from April through November.

This period coincides with the most frequent blue marlin sightings and hookups, often in the vicinity of tuna schools, although at least some seem to be present year-round. The bigger blue marlin (500-pound-class and over) have been encountered in summer. Sailfish are not consistent or abundant; they tend to show up between August and November, and have been seen and caught while showering ballyhoo near the reef shallows. Small packs of larger yellowfin tuna (50 to more than 80 pounds) frequently do the same, most often in the early morning or late afternoon in the sandy shallows just outside the surf between London and the small village of Tabakea to the north. Mahimahi show up occasionally, usually small groups of large fish (more than 20 pounds) during summer.

Most offshore fishing consists of trolling lures on relatively light tackle. Guides also maneuver the boat for casting to bait showers, to mixed surface schools of skipjacks and yellowfin tuna in order to tease or draw direct strikes from the larger individuals, and to selected surf breaks for giant trevally. Lures worked closely along the outer reef slopes, by trolling and deep jigging, catch a large variety of species, including a large, cubera-like red snapper and a colorful Pacific grouper called coral trout, which is bright crimson and covered with electric blue dots. Beware of ciguatera (see) poisoning, and seek local advice before consuming any reef-associated fish at Christmas Island.

Other Line Islands. Other inhabited islands in this group belonging to Kiribati are Fanning (Tabuaeran) and Washington (Teraina), both difficult to access except by irregular government freighters or voyaging sailboats. Fanning Island, 285 kilometers northwest of Christmas, is an 18- by 11-kilometer atoll with a beautiful lagoon harboring a significant population of bonefish, and good flats for pursuing them. Subsistence gillnetting activities in the lagoon for milkfish, mullet, and bonefish by the estimated native population of 2,000, however, are more pervasive here than at more sportfishing, tourism-oriented Christmas Island. Rugged Washington, the next island to the northwest, has no lagoon or not even a tenable vessel anchorage.

Palmyra Atoll, 1,600 kilometers south of Honolulu, is the northernmost Line Island. It is a privately owned, unincorporated territory of the United States, claimed by the Kingdom of Hawaii in 1862 and annexed by the U.S. in 1912, later serving as a naval air station during World War II. The owners maintain a single manager on the island. Palmyra periodically makes the news, when various investors investigate purchasing it for all manner of business schemes, including tourism. The U.S. government has recently enacted a major cleanup of war-era fuel tanks and debris, even reactivating the overgrown airstrip.

In the meantime, the only recreational visitors are maritime, mostly traveling sailors and occasional American commercial fishing boats in transit, who enter the lagoon via the pass blasted out of the reef

Swordfish, which use their bill to slash and maim, are known to rest on the surface and to cruise the ocean's depths; one was photographed by a research submarine at 2,000 feet.

during wartime by the navy. The state of the lagoon and reef-fish populations is nearly pristine. Bonefish feature prominently, with fly-rod catch rates exceeding those reported from various world hotspots. Large giant trevally patrol the edges of the flats, attracted into the shallows along with numerous blacktip reef sharks by the struggles of hooked bonefish. Yellowfin tuna schools are active outside the pass, and wahoo, big giant trevally, and a host of other species are caught by anglers trolling on or near the reef edge. The billfish potential is unknown.

Kingman Reef, an atoll entirely submerged except for a 40-meter sand spit, also belongs to the U.S. and lies 53 kilometers northwest of Palmyra.

Phoenix Islands

The Phoenix Islands lie in a cluster below the equator, just over 1,000 kilometers north of American Samoa and nearly 1,000 kilometers southeast of the Gilbert Islands, slightly more than halfway from the Line Islands to the Gilbert Islands. Kanton Island represents the only realistic sportfishing opportunity within this group of atolls, and it has air service but no tourist facilities.

The lagoon at Kanton is 14 kilometers long, in the shape of an irregular, elongated diamond. Thirteen Gilbertese families totaling 84 people inhabit this government outpost. They are caretakers of vacated facilities, including a substantial wharf left from Kanton's former roles as a stopover for Pan American Airways trans-Pacific seaplanes in the 1930s, a U.S. Air Force base in World War II, and a NASA tracking station in the 1960s. The Kiribati government has studied the possibility of opening a Christmas Island–style sportfishing operation on Kanton.

Like other atolls in Kiribati featuring appropriate lagoon habitat and light fishing pressure, Kanton has a robust population of bonefish and an adequate flats area to support a recreational fishery, but not enough space to support the pressure sustained by Christmas Island's much larger lagoon. Larger inshore species are abundant and similar in composition to those at Christmas Island. Offshore fish activity, most obviously tuna, appears to be at least commensurate with other areas of the tropical Pacific Equatorial Upwelling Zone.

The Gilbert Islands

The Gilbert Islands are the population center and political capital of Kiribati, yet they have relatively few tourist facilities and no business interests specifically serving anglers full-time. Nevertheless, the 16 atolls of this island group, distributed nearly equally above and below the equator in an 800-kilometer-long swath just west of the International Dateline, as well as western outlier Banaba, are in exceptionally productive waters. Fishing plays an intimate role in the fabric of the local culture. Lagoon fish populations in general are depressed in particularly crowded areas, but bonefish do occur in and around the lagoons and reefs, and regular spawning aggregations exist. Migratory pelagics are less affected by local dense human populations and are intensively sought, but mostly on a subsistence basis. Most of the relatively small amount of locally applied modern methods and gear are directed toward commercial fishing.

Some visitors say that the Gilbert Islands remind them of other areas in the tropical Pacific as they were decades ago. Many natives still fish from unpowered, home-built canoes, using traditional techniques such as drop-stone fishing for large yellowfin tuna near the reef edge. With a handline specially knotted to a specific shape and weight of stone, they are able to lower the bait (often a milkfish or bonefish) and drift it at very specific depths. Night fisheries employing coconut-frond torches to attract and net flyingfish still operate. Trolling using an outboard is considered relatively "new," and many trollers use handcrafted lures made of indigenous pearl oyster shells or various materials with fish skin sewn over them. A relatively large proportion of the population is still closely attuned to a vast array of environmental cues and the implications these have for fishing—nuances of wind and current, atmospheric conditions, moon and tide, subtle changes in seasons—and confluences of which can substantially impact the catch.

Where these talents have been focused on sportfishing pursuits, most notably at Christmas Island, the result has been a growing number of sharp, capable young guides. In the absence of a similar arrangement in the Gilbert Islands, hotel and guesthouse operators in, for example, Tarawa and Abemama, regularly arrange for visitors to be taken fishing. A flexible, open-minded angler could likely learn a great deal from a day spent with a skilled Gilbertese angler.

KITE FISHING

Fishing with kites is a tactic employed in saltwater, primarily by offshore anglers fishing for sailfish, but it can be used for many species in both inshore and offshore environs. The main purpose is to work a live bait far from the boat, but kite fishing also offers the clear water advantage of presenting the bait without an obvious fishing line. Although baits fished off kites can be presented at various levels, they are typically fished on or close to the surface and are worked both while trolling or while drifting.

The principle of kite fishing is similar to that of using sideplaners (*see*) or planer boards (*see*) in that the kite carries the fishing line and bait away from the boat at distances that can be varied and, via a release clip, the line is freed from the kite to allow an angler to play a fish unimpeded.

Kites for fishing come in versions suitable for different wind conditions, and they are attached by

 At the Chicago World's Fair in 1893, William Steinway, of piano fame, and Gottfried Daimler introduced a gasoline engine for boats.

K

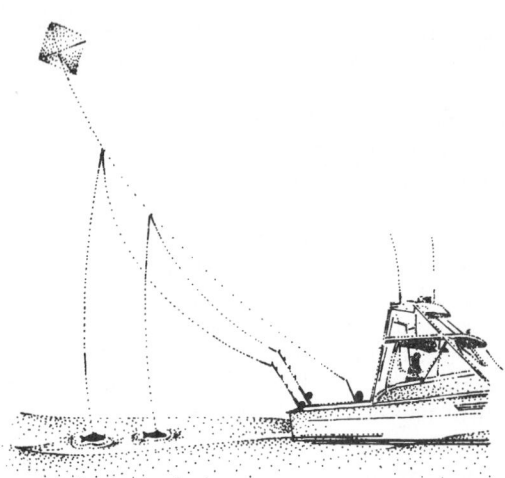

By using a kite, you can get bait an adjustable distance away from the boat and also keep them active on top of the water.

tow line to a retrieval device; this may be an old 6/0 or 9/0 conventional reel and short rod, or a large-wheeled direct-drive manual retriever with a swiveling clip, similar to the devices used for retrieving sideplaners. The tow line is usually Dacron, at least 50-pound strength, which may be subject to fraying but which has the benefit of not stretching. When two kites are fished together, they are kept away from each other by attaching split shot to the kite edges (on opposite sides), and they may be labeled left or right fliers.

In operation the kite is set out a reasonable distance and then the fishing line is attached to it via a release clip on the tow line (running it through a ceramic guide attached to the clip keeps the line in the right position). Multiple baits may be fished via multiple release clips, though few people fish more than two baits from one kite. Baits are fished so that they frantically circle near the surface, which attracts the attention of fish. It's important to keep monitoring the kite lines to make sure that the baits are properly positioned; colorful markers on the line help make the position of the baits visible. If changes in the wind raise or lower the kite, the bait will be affected, and the line has to be adjusted to keep the bait on the surface.

When a fish strikes, the angler grabs the appropriate rod, reels the line until it comes tight to the release clip, and then waits until the striking fish has swallowed the bait and moved enough to pull the line out of the release clip. The angler points the rod at the fish and reels in slack until the line gets tight, setting the hook several times.

Kites are used in drifting when there is ample wind, and in trolling when there is not enough wind, or even when there is wind in conjunction with trolling baits or lures on flatlines and off downriggers. In the latter scenario, kites help round out the offerings and the breadth of water covered.

KNIFE
See: Fish Preparation—Cleaning.

KNOCKER
A device used to free a lure snagged in deep water; also called plug knocker.
See: Unsnagging.

KNOTS, BOATING
Any angler who uses a boat must sometime or other have to tie the boat to a dock or pier, either temporarily or long-term. The security of the boat may depend on how well you tie it up, how quickly you can get it untied if you have to, and whether you take into consideration that the boat's position may be affected by wind, tide, waves, boat wakes, and so forth.

Dedicated boaters, like Boy Scouts, take pride in their knowledge of knots for boating applications. In the boating community, a knowledge of knots is viewed as an indicator of good seamanship.

The majority of anglers are not seamen nor are they rabid boating enthusiasts. They consider the boat a fishing tool, and they know little about knots. This attitude is fine, as long as they make mostly temporary moorings, are attentive to changing conditions, and avoid using an overhand knot (which is extremely difficult to undo after pressure has been applied). The following are commonly used boat knots and ones that all boaters should be familiar with.

Cleating
Almost everyone who uses a boat has had occasion to tie a line to a cleat, usually in a temporary situation, such as at a launch ramp or fuel dock. Each end of a cleat is called a horn. The proper way to tie to a dock cleat is to put the strain on the base of the cleat by bringing the line around both horns at the base and then make no more than two figure-eights around the cleat. Finish it off and bind it by turning the last hitch over on itself so that the tag end is under the cleated line. More turns around the cleat do not hold better and take longer to undo. The line from the boat should come in at an angle.

Cleating

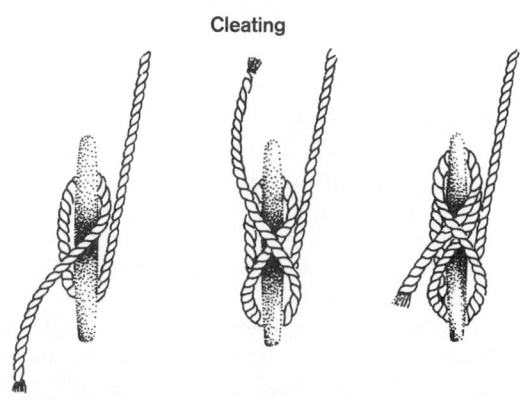

When cleating make sure to tuck the final wrap under (right) and pull tight.

A form of no-knot cleating that is useful for mooring small boats in calm or protected locations (ponds, small lakes, boathouses) is the use of a line-gripping device that lies flush to the dock. These feature an S-configuration through which the line is woven. They hold very well and can be used properly by anyone, but they are best in situations where the boat gunwale is fairly close to the dock so that the line from the boat doesn't come down at a steep angle.

Clove Hitch

A Clove Hitch is commonly used to tie a boat to a piling. Although easy to form, it has a tendency to slip, especially with nylon lines. To avoid slippage, leave plenty of line at the tag end and make one or two half hitches with the tag end around the standing line.

Clove Hitch

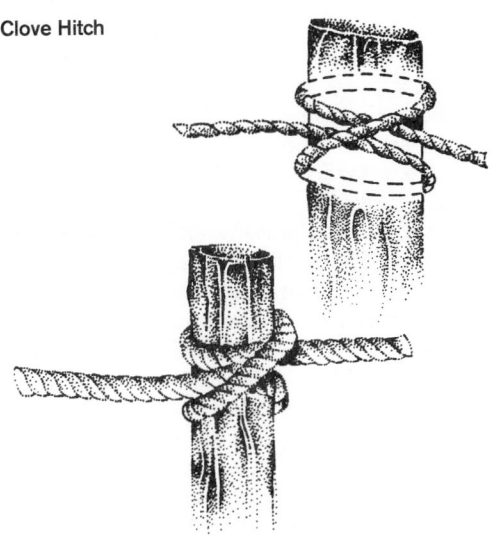

Rolling Hitch

The Rolling Hitch can be used to tie a line to a piling or to tie a bumper to a guardrail without the bumper slipping sideways. The turns should be

Rolling Hitch

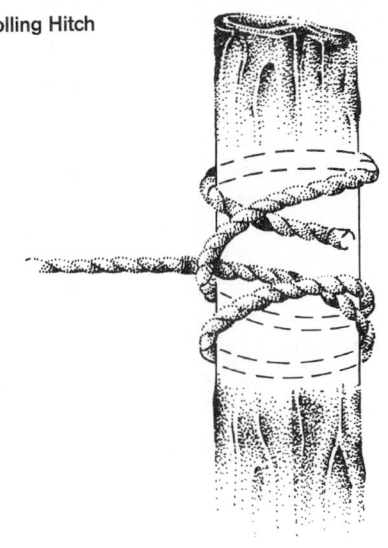

firmed up close and tight, and you should pull on the tag end to help secure it.

Bowline Knot

The Bowline Knot is a customary all-purpose boating knot that doesn't slip or jam when properly tied.

Bowline Knot

Sheet Bend

The Sheet Bend is a good knot for connecting two ropes together, as might be done for towing. It works with lines of different diameter and does not slip.

None of these boat knots retains 100 percent of the breaking strength of the unknotted line or rope, so if your rope is weakened (frayed or cut), be careful. Under maximum-stress conditions, you may get only 60 to 70 percent of the normal breaking strength.

Sheet Bend Knot

KNOTS, FISHING

Just as a strong fishing line is essential in sportfishing, so, too, is a strong knot essential in connecting the fishing line to the object being fished.

Putting a knot in a line changes its breaking strength because the knot is usually the weakest section. Thus, anglers should tie the strongest, most reliable fishing knots they can to achieve the maximum strength possible from their fishing lines. Many people use inferior or poorly tied knots and get away with it because they seldom test their tackle in extreme situations (for example, where ultralight gear is being used or huge fish are being battled).

The ideal knot is one that retains the full breaking strength of the line as if it never had a knot in it. In the ideal scenario, every time that there was breakage, the split occurred at the section of line above the knot. That would be as good as you could possibly hope for. Unfortunately, this scenario seldom happens, partly because anglers use inadequate knots or tie good knots improperly. It is also because there are different knots for different applications, and for some applications no knot yields 100 percent strength.

If you use a knot that regularly achieves only 75 percent of the strength of your line in maximum stress situations, the knot will break before the line. If, however, you tie a knot that achieves 100 percent of the breaking strength of the line, the line will usually break before the knot. Of course, you don't want either one to break, but the important point is that under extreme circumstances your line did as much as it was capable of doing. Perhaps the line was too light for the conditions, the fish was too big, the drag was set too loosely, or the rod was too soft—nevertheless, the line did what it was supposed to do.

However, knot performance varies from one angler to the next. People vary in the way they form their knots, how many wraps they make, how fastidious they are in tying, and so forth. A knot is only as good as the angler tying it. Much can be said regarding the virtue of practice for achieving uniform knot tying, so that once you have mastered a given knot and its use, you can expect it to perform reliably time after time.

Certain lines seem to accommodate particular knots better than others. This may be due to differences in the fiber, material, coating, or molecular structure. Nylon monofilament manufacturers say that knot strength is a characteristic that is built into fishing line and manipulated in the finishing process, so this quality may be stronger in some brands than in others. With nylon, knot failures are usually due to improper tying rather than to the properties of the line itself. With braided and microfilament lines, knot failures are usually due to using the wrong knot.

Here are some pointers for effective knot tying:

1. Learn to tie a knot at home; don't practice on the water. Practice tying it with several different strengths (diameters) so that you can do it uniformly time after time with confidence.

2. Be neat. Keep your wraps and other steps uniform so that when you draw a knot closed, it is neat and precise. Make sure that wraps don't cross over each other.

3. Don't twist a line that is meant to be wrapped. Knots that create a jam do not form as well if the line is twisted, instead of being wrapped over itself.

4. Snug all knots up tightly with even, steady pressure. Knot slippage under pressure can cut the line, so watch the knot for evidence of slippage and redo it if necessary. Don't pop the knot to tighten it. With heavy line, you may need to use pliers to pull on the tag end.

5. Moisten the line as an aid to drawing it up smoothly. If your hands are wet and will wet the line, fine; if not, place the knot and line in your mouth momentarily. Saliva doesn't hurt it. Or dip the entire knot-tying portion of line into the water. Moistening should be done for every knot, especially prior to drawing it.

6. Be careful that you don't nick the knot with clippers or pliers when you cut off the protruding tag end. A nick is a potentially serious and weakening defect. Clip the knot as close as you can; a properly tied knot won't slip. Avoid biting the line with your teeth; this will eventually damage the crown.

7. Check every knot after it is finished by looking at it and by hand-pulling on it in both directions. If a knot breaks repeatedly when you tighten it, check your hook eye or lure connection for rough spots that are cutting the line. If it continues to break, the line may be defective and may need replacement. Try pulling off several feet and retying the knot; often the first few feet of a line are weakened but not the remainder. When you test a knot, you may want to use a glove on your hand or wrap a cloth around your hand before you pull hard on the line.

8. Use plenty of line to complete tying steps without difficulty and to avoid malformed knots. Wetting the line is also helpful. A relaxed line is easier to knot than one that is stiff and coiled or twisted.

9. When using double lines, keep them as parallel as possible and avoid twisting them as the knot is being tied.

10. Test your knots occasionally with a scale to see if they're delivering top performance. You can do this by tying the line to the hook of a reliable spring scale. Have someone wrap the unknotted line around his or her hand several times, using a towel or cloth to keep from getting cut. While your accomplice pulls on the line, you hold and watch the scale, noting the amount of pressure at which the line or the knot breaks. If it is the line that breaks, your knot held.

Using a scale is also a good way to monitor the basic strength of your unknotted line, although this test should be conducted when the lines and knots are wet. Don't be too alarmed if your knot breaks before the line, as long as the breaking point reached is still quite high. A typical top-quality 12-pound-test nylon monofilament line will break in a wet, unknotted condition when roughly 12.8 pounds of pressure are applied. A wet knot delivering 95 percent strength will break when 12.2 pounds of pressure are applied, and one delivering 90 percent will break at 11.5 pounds. If a knot delivers consistent breakage at or near the labeled strength of the line, then you can be satisfied with it until you can find a better knot. Generally, a fishing knot is considered good if it breaks at or above 85 percent of the line's unknotted strength in a wet condition.

If you are experiencing strength or holding problems with an otherwise reputable knot, there are several possible causes. You may be weakening the line by drawing the knot down too roughly or by failing to moisten it first; wetting the line and knot before drawing the knot down smoothly is very important. Another cause may be the type of line; the same knot will not perform as well when tied on some lines as on others. Super thin lines, for example, are more problematic than conventional diameter lines. Try making more wraps or more turns around the hook eye than you might otherwise. When all else fails, try a different knot for the line you're using.

In using a particular knot, you need to consider more than just its maximum breaking strength. Likewise, just because a knot is easy to tie—and some are much easier than others—it is not the best choice in every circumstance. Some knots are very bulky and would not be useful on a small hook or wouldn't easily pass through rod guides when you are casting or—more importantly—when a big fish is pulling the leader or backing off a reel and through a bunch of rod guides at phenomenal speed. By knowing a number of knots, you can adapt to changing circumstances.

Fishing knots are primarily terminal connections and line-to-line connections, but they are also a means of creating double-line leaders. Terminal connections are knots used to tie a line directly to a lure or hook. Line-to-line connections join two lines of similar or dissimilar diameter, including fishing line to a leader or tippet.

Terminal Knots

Improved Clinch Knot. Sometimes referred to incorrectly as a "cinch" knot, the Improved Clinch is probably the most popular terminal connection, especially in freshwater and with nylon monofilament line. It is best used for lines under 20-pound-test. Tied properly, this knot has a strength of 90 to 100 percent; poorly tied, it may yield only 75 to 85 percent, which is insufficient, especially for a light line. It is not a good knot to use on lines with a slick finish or on microfilaments.

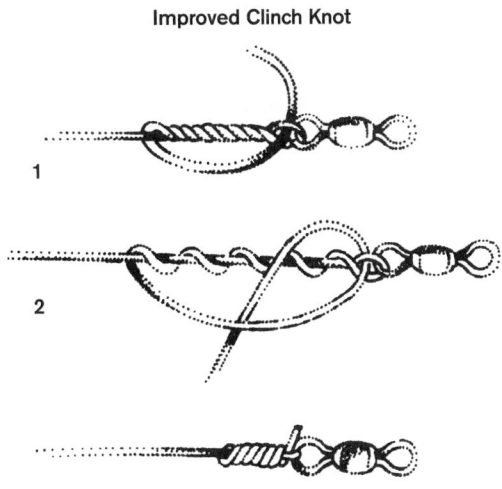

Improved Clinch Knot

To tie the Improved Clinch Knot, pass the line through the eye of the hook and then make five turns around the standing part of the line. Thread the end through the loop ahead of the eye, and bring it back through the newly created large loop. Moisten the knot with saliva, and check that the coils are spiraled properly and not overlapping one another. Pull firmly to tighten. Test the knot with moderate tension, and clip off the loose end.

Depending on the type and diameter of line being used, six spirals may be best for line through 12-pound test and five spirals for 14- to 17-pound test. For 20-pound test and over, make four spirals and use a pair of pliers to pull on the loose end and snug up the knot.

If you experience slippage with this knot, try running the line through the hook eye twice before completing the other steps. This is a Double Loop Improved Clinch Knot. A variation on this is the Double Loop Clinch Knot, sometimes called a Trilene Knot, which also features two turns around the hook eye but the tag end comes back through both turns and then is snipped off.

Palomar Knot. Line manufacturers say this knot is easier to tie than the Improved Clinch and more consistent. Because it is easier to tie, fewer anglers experience difficulty with its use. Tied properly, it yields a strength of 90 to 100 percent and is meant for terminal connections. Some anglers use it mainly for tying leader tippets to flies, since it is a smaller profile knot than the Improved Clinch. It is an especially valuable knot when used with braided and fused microfilament lines, provided that two or three turns are made around the eye.

To tie the Palomar Knot, double about 6 inches of line and pass the loop through the eye of the hook. Tie an overhand knot in the doubled line, and pass the loop over the entire hook. Moisten the knot, pull on both ends, tighten, and clip the tag end.

The only problem encountered with this knot occurs when it is used for large, multihooked plugs, where a longer loop must be created to allow the big lure to pass through it. You should also take care not to twist the doubled sections of line.

Palomar Knot

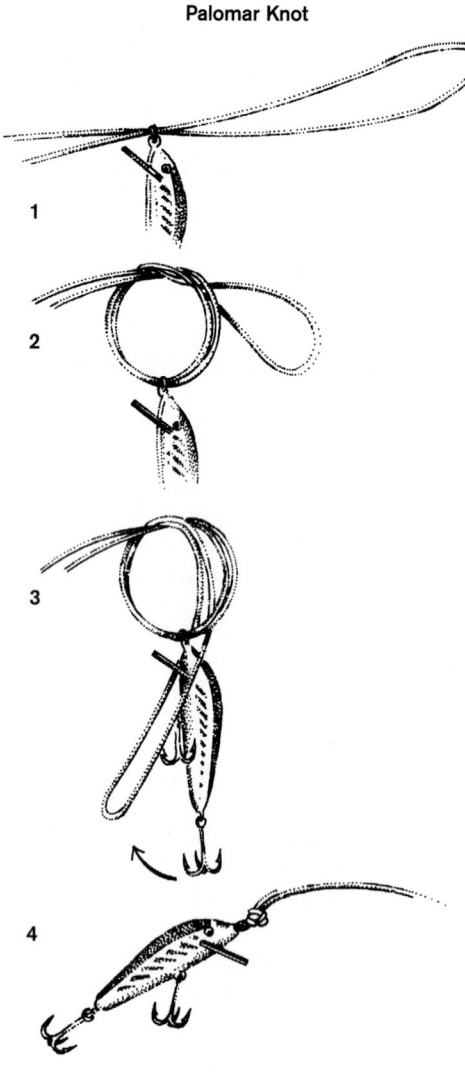

Uni Knot

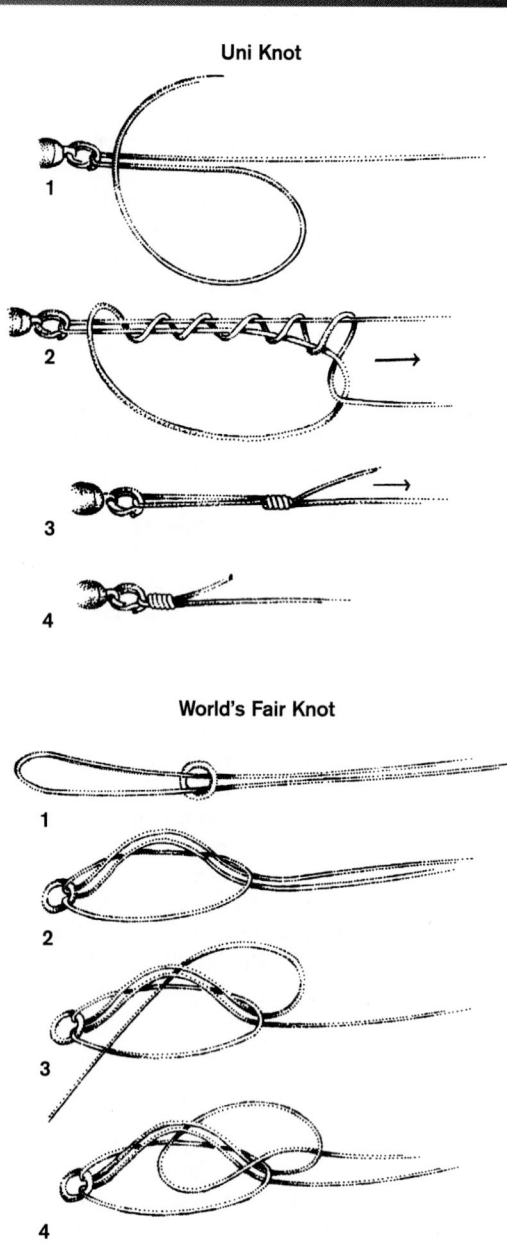

World's Fair Knot

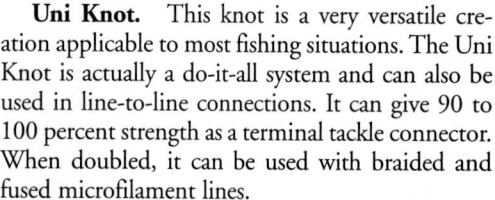

Uni Knot. This knot is a very versatile creation applicable to most fishing situations. The Uni Knot is actually a do-it-all system and can also be used in line-to-line connections. It can give 90 to 100 percent strength as a terminal tackle connector. When doubled, it can be used with braided and fused microfilament lines.

To tie the Uni Knot as a terminal connector, pass at least 6 inches of line through the eye of the hook and make a circle with the tag end. Bring the tag end around the double length and through the circle six times, moistening and then pulling snugly after the last turn.

World's Fair Knot. This knot is not as popular as the previous terminal connections, but it is simple to tie, holds line strength fairly well, and is similar to a common, unnamed knot used in sewing.

To tie the World's Fair Knot, double a 6-inch length of line and pass the loop through the hook eye. Bring the loop back over the standing doubled line, and pull the double line through the loop. Pass the tag end through the double-line loop and then back through the new single-line loop. Moisten, pull snug at both ends, and clip excess.

Nonslip Loop. Loop knots are useful terminal connections when you want to get more action out of a lure and you prefer not to use a snap. These knots are also helpful with some jigs and weighted flies, allowing them to appear more natural on the fall, swim, or drift. Anglers have devised a number of loop knots, and many work fairly well, although some slip under extreme pressure and few hold a high percentage of line strength. Loops can be made with the Uni and

Nonslip Loop Knot

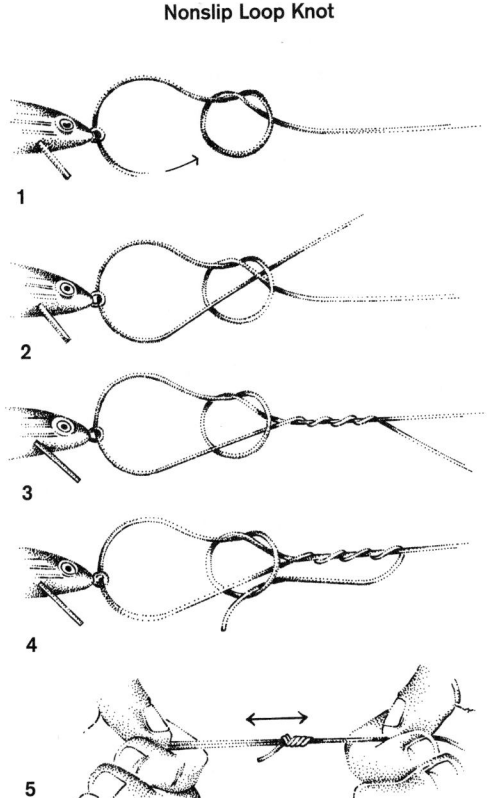

1
2
3
4
5

Offshore Swivel Knot

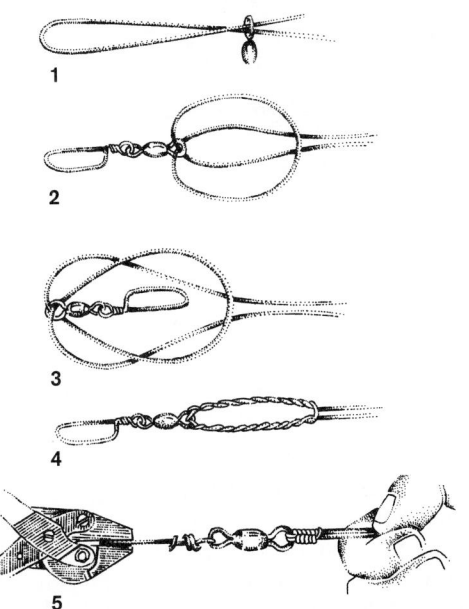

1
2
3
4
5

Improved Clinch Knots by using pliers to grasp the tag end and pull it tightly without pulling firmly on the standing line. However, these knots will slip down under extreme tension and will need to be retied, plus the friction caused by that slipping makes the knot and the line just above it suspect. Therefore, it's better to use a good loop knot that will not slip.

The Nonslip Loop Knot has had several names in the past. Primarily used with nylon monofilament, it is not as difficult to tie as it seems and has very good strength. To tie it, make an overhand knot in the line, leaving about 6 inches at the tag end. Pass the tag end through the hook eye and then back through the overhand knot the same way that it came out. The size of the overhand knot determines the size of the loop; for most situations, keep it small.

Hold the overhand knot softly with one hand, and pull on the tag end of the line to bring the overhand knot down toward the eye. Wrap the tag end around the standing line the proper number of times. (Manufacturers recommend seven wraps for line under 10 pounds, five wraps for 10- to 14-pound line, four wraps for 15- to 40-pound line, three wraps for 50- to 60-pound line, and two wraps for heavier line, but you may need to experiment with this on thin-diameter lines.) Bring the tag end back through the loop of the overhand knot the same way that it exited. Moisten, pull on the tag end to form the final knot, and then pull from both ends to snug up completely.

Offshore Swivel Knot. This knot is a very strong terminal connection for use with a doubled line leader (formed with a Bimini Twist or Spider Hitch), primarily employed in saltwater and by big-game anglers. It is mainly tied on a swivel or a snap but can be tied to a hook or an eyelet, and it will continue to hold if one of the two lines is cut.

To tie the Offshore Swivel Knot, bring the loop end of the doubled line through the eye of the swivel and make one twist in the loop beyond the swivel eye. Bring the end of the loop back against the standing double line, and hold the two together with one hand. With your other hand, slide the swivel to the opposite end of the loop and rotate the swivel through the center of both loops six times. Hold the double line tightly, and release the end of the loop while pulling on the swivel. Grip the swivel with pliers, and pull on both the swivel and the standing double line with even pressure. Push the loops toward the swivel as necessary.

Conventional Snell Knot. Many anglers do not know how to tie a Snell Knot, but it is an important, and very strong, knot when properly formed. A Snell Knot is applied only to hooks with a turned-up or turned-down eye and has the advantage of a direct pull for increased hooksetting efficiency. It is used in fishing with bait and is an especially popular knot with salmon and steelhead anglers, which is why it is sometimes called a Salmon Hook Knot.

To form the Conventional Snell Knot, bring at least 6 inches of the tag end of the line through the hook eye, lay it along the shank, and form a loop. Pinch both sections to the shank with one hand, and with the other hand wrap the looped line tightly and closely without overlays toward

Conventional Snell Knot

1

3

2

4

K

the eye. After making 10 wraps, snug down the knot. Slide the snell toward the eye if it is not going to be used to hold bait and to the midshank if it is to be looped to hold bait (primarily it is used to hold an egg or spawn sack to the shank). Pull the line with equal pressure in opposite directions, and trim the tag end. Unless you have taken pliers to the tag end of the snell and pulled it extremely tight, you can usually move this knot along the shank of a bait hook. If you move it to the middle, hold the shank of the hook in one hand and with the other hand push the standing line in through the eye until a loop forms. The loop can now be tightened around bait, especially a cluster of salmon eggs or a spawn sack, and these can be readily replaced.

Uni Snell.   For many people the Uni Snell is an easier method of snelling a hook and, once mastered, is quicker to tie than the conventional knot.

To tie the Uni Snell, pass 6 inches of line through the hook eye, pinch the line against the shank, and form a circle. Make five to seven turns (fewer for stronger line) through the loop and around the standing line and hook shank. (Locate

Uni Snell Knot

1

2

3

the knot on the midshank if it is to be looped to hold bait or close to the eye if it will not hold bait.) Snug the knot tightly by pulling in both directions, and trim the tag end. See the previous instructions for making a bait-holding loop.

Double Turle Knot.   This knot is a terminal connection that has long been popular with fly anglers. It is easy to tie, has moderate strength, permits a direct pull through a turned-up or turned-down eye, and may help a dry fly sit better on the water.

To tie the Double Turle Knot, pass the tippet end of the leader through the turned-up or turned-down hook eye, going from the eye toward the point. Make a loop, wrap the tag end around twice, and snug up. Open the loop and slip the fly through; then place the loop around the neck of the fly just behind the eye. Pull on the standing line until the knot is tight against the neck.

Double Turle Knot

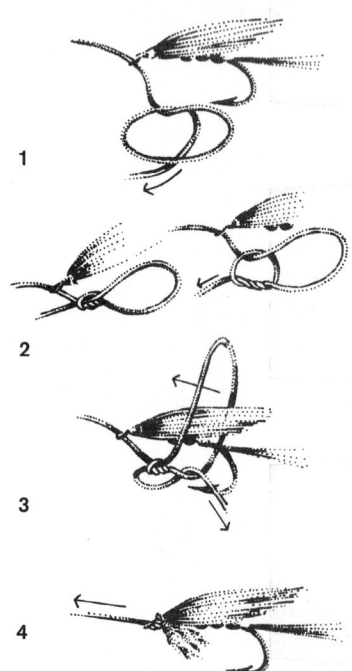

1

2

3

4

Figure Eight Knot.   The Figure Eight Knot is used for connecting a braided wire leader to a hook or lure and is popular for quick-changing lures. It is principally used by saltwater anglers who are fishing deep for toothy species and is not recommended for use with nylon monofilament, braided, or microfilament lines. It is primarily shown here to help illustrate the Improved Figure Eight.

To tie the Figure Eight Knot, pass the tag end of braided wire through the hook eye and bring it back toward the standing end. Pass the tag end under the standing end, up and over it, and through the loop in front of the hook eye. Use pliers to pull on the tag end and tighten the knot. Do not pull on the standing end; this may cause a crimp that could affect lure action.

Figure Eight Knot

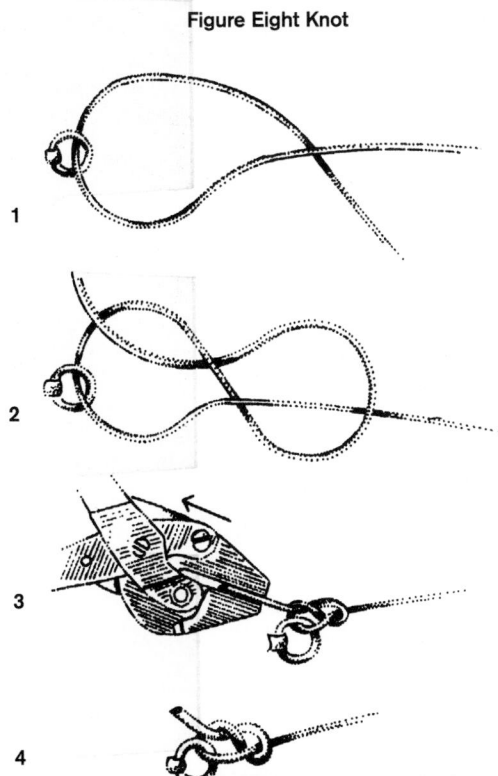

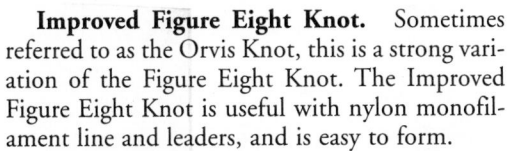

Improved Figure Eight Knot

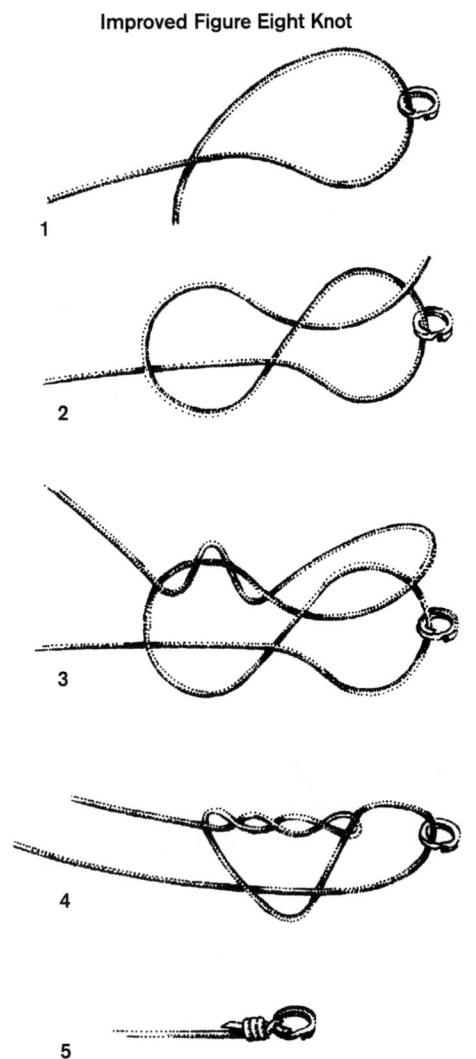

Improved Figure Eight Knot. Sometimes referred to as the Orvis Knot, this is a strong variation of the Figure Eight Knot. The Improved Figure Eight Knot is useful with nylon monofilament line and leaders, and is easy to form.

To tie the Improved Figure Eight Knot, pass the tag end of the line through the hook eye and bring it back toward the standing end. Pass the tag end under the standing end, up and over it, and through the loop in front of the hook eye. Wrap the tag end twice through the loop farthest from the hook eye, and pull on both the hook and standing line to snug the knot.

Haywire Twist. The Haywire Twist is an important means of connecting a single-strand wire leader to a swivel or hook. For tying instructions, *see: Wire Leader.*

Line-to-Line Knots

Line-to-Line Uni. This knot is excellent for joining two lines and is perhaps the easiest line-to-line connection to make. Quicker and easier to tie than the time-honored Blood Knot, the Line-to-Line Uni is equally reliable. It is best for joining lines of similar diameter, especially in strengths up to 20 pounds, but can also work on those of different but not hugely disparate diameter by decreasing the number of wraps on the stronger line. It can also be used to join nylon monofilament and microfilament or braided lines.

To join two light lines of fairly similar diameter, overlap each at least 6 inches. Hold these in the middle of the overlap with your left hand, and

make a circle with the line extended to the right. Bring the tag end around the double length six times, pulling snugly after the last turn. Repeat the process in reverse direction on the other side. Moisten the lines and knots, and pull the two sections away from each other to draw up the knot; then pull the lines firmly and clip both loose ends. Use five wraps for 10- to 17-pound line, four wraps for heavier line.

To tie the Line-to-Line Uni with lines of different diameter, use the appropriate number of wraps for each line. For example, when joining 12-pound to 20-pound, as might be done for a short leader, make five turns in the lighter line and four turns in the heavier line. With heavier lines, you may need to use pliers to pull on the tag ends and snug up. For lines of different material or vastly different diameter, consider doubling the lighter or more slippery line; in other words, when joining 6-pound line to 20-pound line, make a Uni Knot with a double length of 6-pound line, tying it to a single length of 20-pound. You do not need a double-line knot to do this because adding another knot to the equation is not an advantage.

K

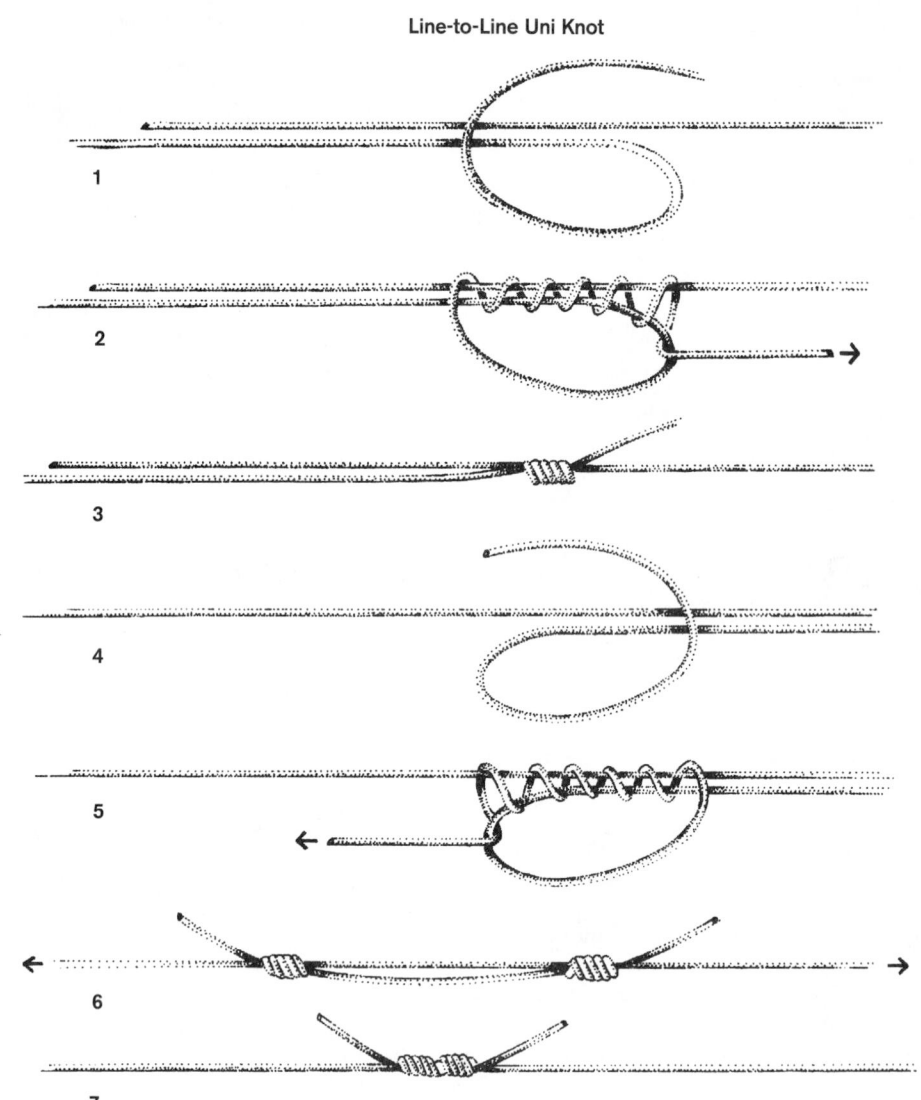

Line-to-Line Uni Knot

1

2

3

4

5

6

7

Simply fold the lighter line back over itself, and make the same wraps with two strands as you would with one.

Albright Knot. Also called an Albright Special, this knot is excellent for joining two lines of unequal diameter but is moderately difficult to tie. It is useful for connecting nylon monofilaments to each other or to microfilament or wire, for making shock leaders, for connecting fly line to braided backing, and for tying a Bimini Twist in the end of the lighter casting line.

To tie the Albright Knot, make a loop in the tag end of the heavier line (or fly line) and hold the loop between the thumb and forefinger of your left hand. Pass 8 to 10 inches of lighter line (or fly-line backing) through the loop from the top, and pinch it tightly against the two loop strands. With your right hand, wrap the lighter line back over itself and the loop strands. Make 10 to 12 tight wraps, starting next to your fingers and working toward the loop end. Pass the tag end of the lighter line through the loop from

the bottom, and exit out the top; both strands of the lighter line should be on the same side of the loop. With the left hand still holding the knot, move the knot gently toward the loop and then pull on both the standing and the tag ends of the light line. Pull tightly on the standing and tag ends of all lines, and trim tag ends.

Surgeon's Knot. This is a good knot for tying a leader with lines of different diameter and is popular with fly anglers for connecting a tippet and leader, especially when using a shock tippet. This is a very simple knot to tie, and people who fish in cold weather love it.

To tie the Surgeon's Knot, bring the tippet and leader lines parallel to each other and overlap about 6 inches. Make a loose overhand knot, bringing the tippet completely through the loop. Bring both lines through the loop a second time, keeping the strands together. Hold both lines at both ends, and pull the knot tight. Trim closely because this knot is slightly bulky and any protrusion could catch in the rod guides.

Albright Knot

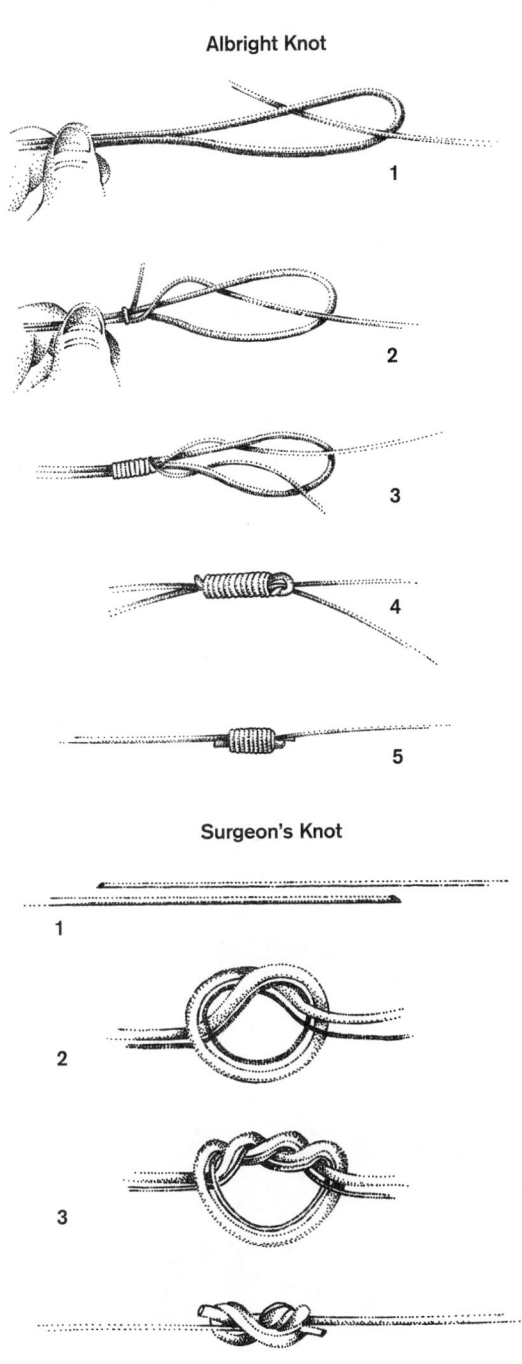

Surgeon's Loop Knot

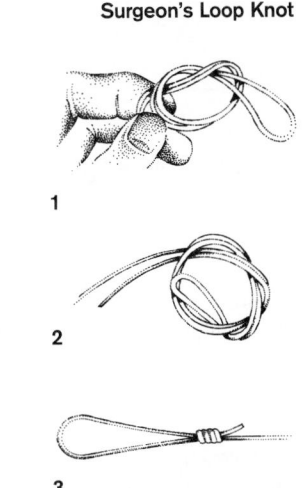

Surgeon's Knot

Surgeon's Loop.   A common and easy-to-tie knot, a Surgeon's Loop is used to put a loop in the end of a line for connecting other lines. It is primarily used in fly fishing for loop-to-loop leaders but is slightly bulky and can snare the rod guides.

To tie the Surgeon's Loop, double the end of a line and make an overhand knot at the point where the line is doubled. Leave the loop open and pass the end of the double line through it a second time. Hold the single standing line and adjust the loop size; then pull on the loop to tighten it, and clip the excess.

Blood Knot.   The Blood Knot is a strong knot if tied properly, and it has long been a popular connection for two nylon monofilament lines, although some anglers prefer the simpler Uni Knot for tying one line to another. However, the Blood Knot has a low profile if properly formed and if the tag ends are trimmed close, and it runs through rod guides nicely. Some anglers consider the Blood Knot an easy knot to tie, but the plethora of tools invented over the years to aid in tying it seems to disprove this statement. It isn't really difficult to tie, and regular users can tie it virtually blindfolded, but some attention to detail is required when it is being learned. The Blood Knot is primarily used by fly anglers for connecting different lengths of line when making their own multipiece tapered leader, and it is best when tied with lines of the same or generally similar diameter. For tying to dissimilar diameters (such as 30-pound line connected to 12-pound line to make a shock leader), double the tag end of the smaller-diameter line and wrap it around the thicker-diameter line by using the same general instructions that follow but making just three wraps in the thicker-diameter line. This variation is called an Improved Blood Knot.

To tie the basic Blood Knot, cross two lines and wrap one five times around the other, bringing the tag end back and between the strands. Pinch this section to keep it from unraveling. Wrap the second line over the first five times in the opposite direction, bringing the tag end of the second line back and into the center loop in the opposite direction of the other tag end. Slowly pull on both of the joined lines to draw the wraps together; then tighten firmly and trim.

A modification of the knot is the Extension Blood Knot, which provides a short length of trailer line for a dropper fly. It is tied in the same manner as an ordinary Blood Knot, except that a longer length of line is used on one section and drawn completely through the middle loop. Leave between 8 and 12 inches of this line extending from

Blood Knot

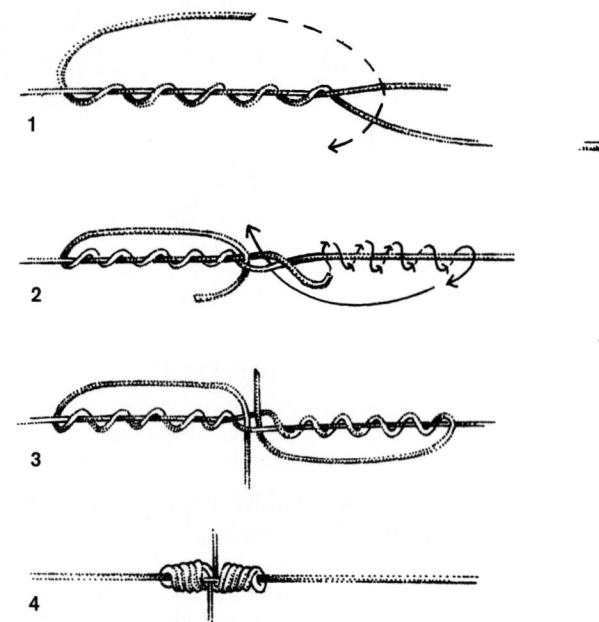

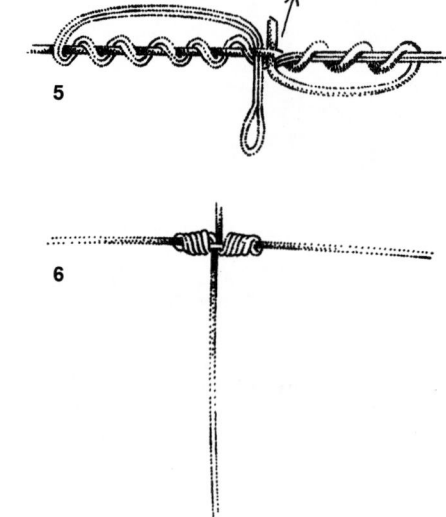

the knot; too little will not be enough to tie a fly to it, and too much will encourage tangling. This extension should be used whenever you plan to fish a dropper fly; it provides the best and strongest connection to the main line (or leader).

Common Nail or Tube Knot. Known primarily as a Nail Knot, but also a Tube Knot, this knot is meant for joining lines of dissimilar diameter. It has long been a preferred method of connecting the butt end of a leader to a fly line, as well as reel backing to a fly line. It is formed with the use of a smooth instrument like a nail, small tube, piece of straw, straightened paper clip, or sewing needle. The Tube or Nail Knot is a nicely compressed knot that moves through rod guides well and does not pull out. Although experienced anglers can tie this knot fairly readily, many people who have infrequent occasion to join lines find it troublesome and time-consuming, usually having to make a couple of attempts until they get it right. The fact that an accessory like a nail or tube is needed (but often unavailable on the water) is also a drawback.

To tie a Tube Knot using a tube (a short piece of rigid plastic from the tube used in a ballpoint pen is great), lay the tube, the butt end of the leader, and the tip end of the fly line alongside each other with the fly line headed left and the leader headed right. Pinch all three in the middle with your left thumb and index finger, and allow 8 to 10 inches of leader overlap. With your right hand, wrap the leader snugly five or six times around the fly line, leader, and tube. Working from right to left, line the wraps up against each other and pinch the entire assemblage in with

Nail/Tube Knot

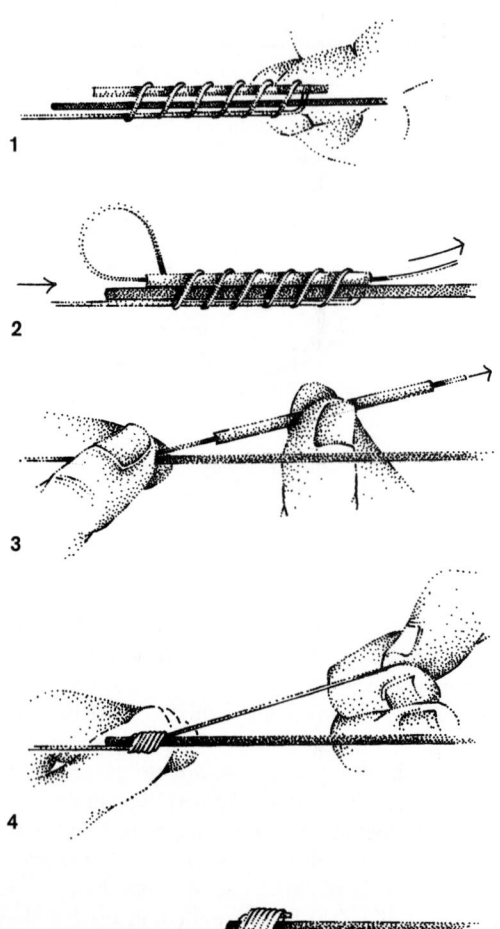

the left fingers. Pass the butt end of the leader through the tube from left to right. Pull both ends of the leader tight and remove the tube. Tighten both ends of the leader again, and simultaneously pull on the leader and fly line tightly before clipping off the ends.

To tie a Nail Knot, place a nail between the two lines and follow the same instructions as for a tube with the following exceptions: Make the wraps less snug, and run the tag end of the leader down alongside the nail. Using a small-diameter tube is actually easier.

Double Nail Knot. The Nail or Tube Knot has a number of variations. One of these is a Double Nail Knot in which two nail knots are tied in opposite directions; it can be used to tie similar-diameter lines together, although the Line-to-Line Uni is far easier to tie and just as useful if you are simply putting more line on a reel. The Double Nail Knot is used with heavy monofilament leaders by some fly anglers because of its lesser bulk; it is used by some big-game anglers for connecting a shock leader to a double line, in part because it can be easily wound through guides and onto a reel.

To tie the Double Nail Knot, overlap both lines with an ample length, form the first knot, remove the nail, and gently draw the knot together without tightening; then form the second knot in the opposite direction, remove the nail, and pull this knot snug. Finally pull both together and tighten firmly.

Double Nail Knot

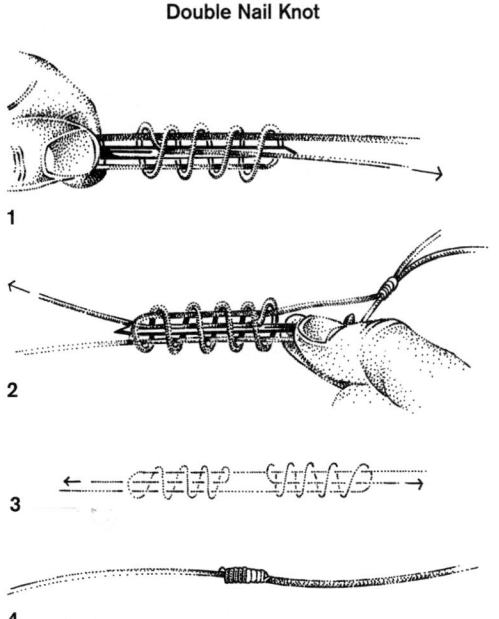

Speed Nail Knot. The Speed Nail Knot, also called an Instant Nail Knot or Fast Nail Knot, is an interesting version of the Common Nail Knot. More like a snell, this knot originated with steelhead anglers who used it for snelling bait hooks. It looks much more difficult to tie than it is and with a bit of practice can be whipped up in mere seconds.

Speed Nail Knot

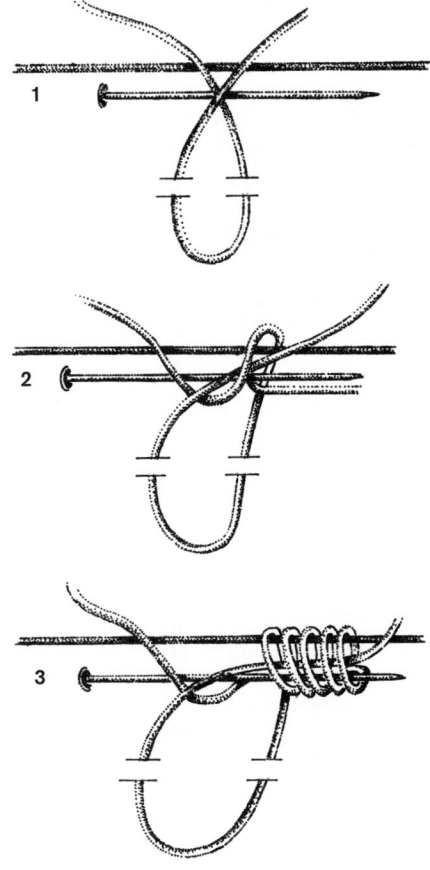

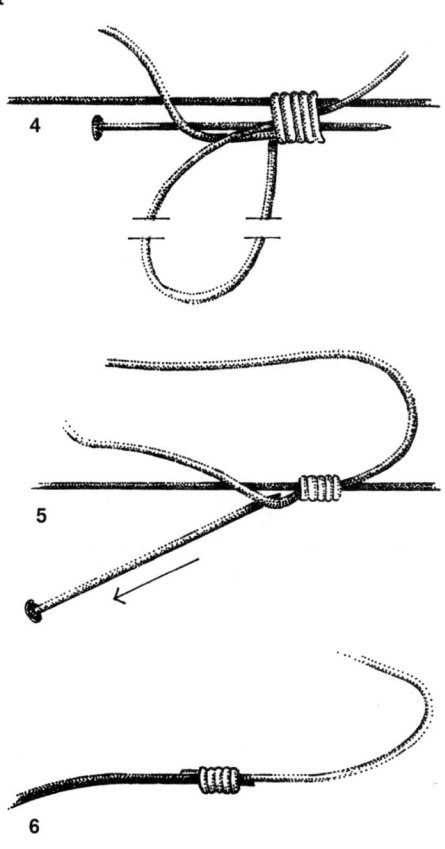

K

To tie the Speed Nail Knot to a fly line, use a nail or something smooth and rigid. Hold the nail parallel to the fly line with the end facing right and extending no farther than the edge of the nail. Take whatever length of leader you want to make, cross the ends, and place the crossed portion against the nail and fly line; pinch all three in your left thumb and first joint of your index finger. Keep the tag end of the leader a short distance from the nail, in effect creating a very large loop that dangles below. Take the upper right side of the loop in your right hand, and wrap only that portion of the loop around the tag end of the leader, the fly line, and nail five or six times, using the tip of your index finger to keep the wraps in place. With the wraps secure in your left hand, let go of the loop with your right hand and grab the tag end of the leader, pulling until the loop dissolves and the knot snugs. Gently slide the nail out, and pull on both ends of the leader to tighten, then on the leader and fly line. Clip the excess.

With practice you can tie this knot in under 20 seconds, and you can do it without the use of a nail. Honest.

Other Line-to-Line Connections

In addition to the knots already described, other knots can be used for line-to-line connections, particularly for big-game wind-on leaders and shock leaders; and for situations where tremendous stress is put on terminal tackle (especially near the boat), where lines of greatly different diameter are coupled for special situations, and where light tackle is employed for big fish. Many of these variations are offshoots of existing knots and hybrid combinations of knots. An example is making a dissimilar-diameter line-to-line connection by using a few wraps of a Uni Knot with heavy leader material and a Blood Knot with lighter material; another example is connecting a fly leader with a Bimini Twist on the class tippet and a Nail Knot on the shock leader. Many of these knots are in some way related to the use of double-line leaders or require doubling lighter line to bulk it up for connecting to a heavier (thicker) line. Experiment with other connections, looking for ease of tying, maintenance of full line strength, and bulkiness of the final knot.

Double Line Knots

A double line in essence is a leader, though one made from the actual fishing line by virtue of a Bimini Twist or Spider Hitch Knot. If properly tied, these knots, especially the Bimini Twist, hold the full 100 percent breaking strength of a line and knot, offer more resistance to abrasion, and offer added breaking protection in the event (which is relatively unlikely) that one of the two strands breaks.

Bimini Twist. The Bimini Twist, once also known as the Twenty Times Around Knot, has such an intimidating reputation that many anglers have avoided learning to tie it. It is a knot primarily associated with saltwater fishing, especially the use of heavy leaders and big-game angling; however, its usefulness extends much further than that, especially for making a double-line leader in light tackle fishing, where a lot of stress might be applied to the last section of the line. This knot is difficult at first to tie, but you can tie it in under a minute once you've got it mastered. If you can walk, chew gum, and think at the same time, you can tie it.

To tie the Bimini Twist, follow these steps, which are keyed to the illustration:

1. Measure a little more than twice the footage you'll want for the double-line leader. (First-time tiers should use shorter lengths.) Bring the end back to the standing line and hold together. Rotate the end of the loop 20 times, putting twists in it.
2. Spread the loop to force the twists together about 10 inches below the tag end. Step both feet through the loop, and bring it up around your knees so that you will be able to place pressure on the column of twists by spreading your knees apart.
3. Grasp the tag ends firmly, and force the twists as tightly together as possible by spreading your knees. Hold the standing line in your left hand, which is just slightly off a vertical position, and keep the line taut. With your right hand, move the other end to a position at a right angle to the twists, keeping it taut as well. Keeping tension on the loop with your knees, gradually ease the tension of the tag end in your right hand so that the tag end line will roll tightly over the column of twists, beginning just below the uppermost twist.
4. Spread your legs apart slowly to maintain pressure on the loop. Steer the tag end into a tight spiral coil as it continues to roll over the twisted line. Keeping a balance of constant tension without slack is critical to this process.
5. When the spiral of the tag end has rolled over the column of twists, continue keeping knee pressure on the loop and move your left hand down to grasp the knot. Place a finger in the crotch of the line where the loop joins to prevent slippage of the last turn; take a half-hitch with the tag end around the nearest leg of the loop, and pull up tight.
6. With a half-hitch holding knot, release knee pressure but keep the loop stretched out. Using the remaining tag end, take a half-hitch around both legs of the loop but do not pull tight.
7. Make three more turns with the tag end around both legs of the loop, winding inside the bend of the line formed by the loose half-hitch and toward the main knot. Pull the tag end slowly, forcing the three loops to gather in a spiral.
8. When the loops are pulled up nearly against the main knot, moisten and tighten to lock in place. Trim the end.

Bimini Twist Knot

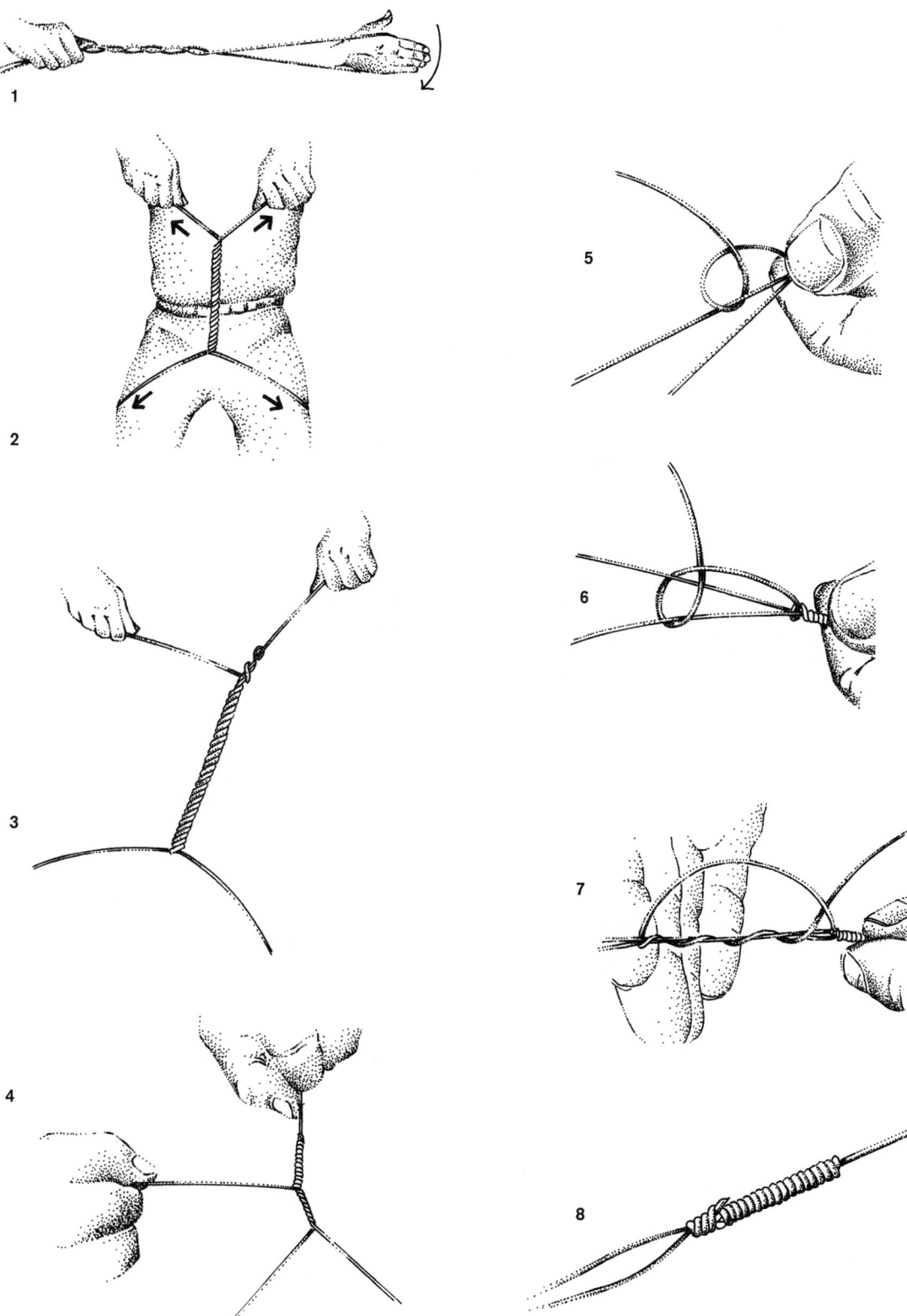

Spider Hitch Knot

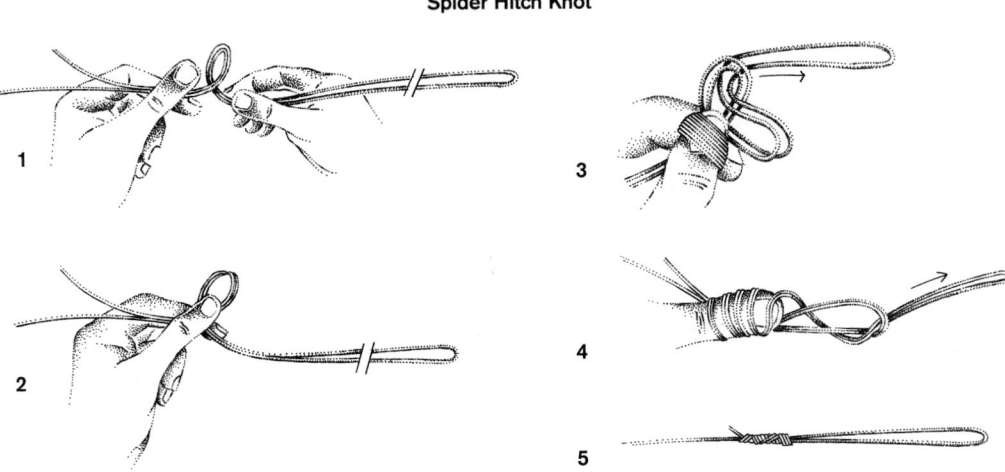

Small, slender fishes with bony spines in front of all their fins existed and disappeared eons ago; some types had bony armor as well.

K

These directions apply to tying double-line leaders of 5 feet or less. For longer double-line sections, two people may be required to hold the line and make initial twists. Or the line could be looped around a firm object, like a cleat, and the twisting done at the tag end. It is also possible to use a Bimini Twist to tie short lengths of double line by placing the loop over one knee that has been tucked underneath your thigh.

Spider Hitch. The Spider Hitch is a very good knot that is an alternative to the Bimini Twist. Although not as well known as the Bimini Twist, it is much easier to tie, especially with cold hands. This knot is very useful in lighter-strength line, particularly as a leader in freshwater fishing.

To tie the Spider Hitch, make a loop of whatever length of line you want to use as a leader, and hold the ends between thumb and index finger at the first joint of the thumb. Make a small loop in the line, tuck it between the fingers, and extend it directly in front of the thumb. Wrap the doubled line around the thumb and small loop five times, working toward the tip of the thumb. Then pass the doubled line through the small loop, making the five wraps unwind off the thumb and using a steady draw. Pull firmly on all ends to snug the knot.

See: Leader.

KOKANEE

The landlocked form of sockeye salmon (see: salmon, sockeye).

KRILL

Small pelagic shrimplike crustaceans with bristled tails. Krill range from about $1/2$ inch to 3 inches long. Most are transparent, and many have light-producing organs. They migrate vertically and are plentiful enough to be a major food source for seabirds, fish, and whales.

KYPE

The curved or hooked lower jaw of male salmonids.

L

LABRADOR
See: Labrador; Newfoundland.

LACTIC ACID
Acid produced in muscle tissues after strenuous exercise. This occurs in fish, sometimes to their detriment, when being landed by anglers.
See: Catch-and-Release.

LACUSTRINE
Having to do with, or living in, a lake.

LADYFISH
Ladyfish are members of the small Elopidae family. They occur worldwide and are related to tarpon *(see)*. They are similar in appearance to tarpon, although far smaller. Ladyfish are excellent light-tackle sportfish commonly found in schools prowling shallow nearshore and brackish waters. They are known for their habit of skipping along the water and jumping energetically when hooked. Ladyfish are pursued commercially in some parts of their range, although a plentitude of bones discourages human consumption; most commercial captures are used as fish meal, and most angler captures are released.

There are at least six species of ladyfish in the genus *Elops,* all of which are similar in average size, behavior, and characteristics. In the western Atlantic, the ladyfish *(E. saurus)* ranges from Cape Cod and Bermuda to the northern Gulf of Mexico and southern Brazil, although it is most common in Florida and the Caribbean. It is also known as tenpounder, as *ubarana* in Portuguese, and as *malacho* in Spanish.

In the eastern Atlantic, two species are found off the African continent and are often confused with each other. These are the West African ladyfish *(E. lacerta),* which occurs from Senegal to Angola and is also known as the Atlantic ladyfish, ninebone, and Guinean ladyfish, and the Senegalese ladyfish *(E. senegalensis),* which occurs from Mauritania to Zaire and is also known as ninebone.

In the eastern Pacific, the Pacific ladyfish *(E. affinis)* occurs from Southern California to Peru, although it is rare in northern Baja California. It is also known as machete, and as *chiro* and *malacho del Pacifico* in Spanish.

The Hawaiian ladyfish *(E. hawaiensis)* occurs throughout the west-central Pacific and is known as *awu'awu* in Hawaiian. In the Indo-West Pacific, the tenpounder or springer *(E. machnata)* occurs from South Africa to the Red Sea and eastward to India and the western Pacific, and is reported from New Caledonia and Taiwan.

Identification.   Ladyfish have an elongated, slender silvery body with a blue green back and small scales. They look very much like a juvenile tarpon, although they can be distinguished from tarpon by the lack of an elongated last ray on the dorsal fin. Their head is small and pointed, the mouth is terminal, and the tail is deeply forked.

Size.   Some species of ladyfish may reach weights from 15 pounds to 24 pounds and a length of 3 feet; such specimens are extremely rare, and in general these fish most commonly weigh 2 to 3 pounds. The all-tackle world records are a 5-pounds, 14-ounce *E. saurus* (from South Carolina), a 12-pound, 9-ounce *E. senegalensis* (from Guinea-Bissau), and a 23-pound, 12-ounce *E. machnata* (from Mozambique).

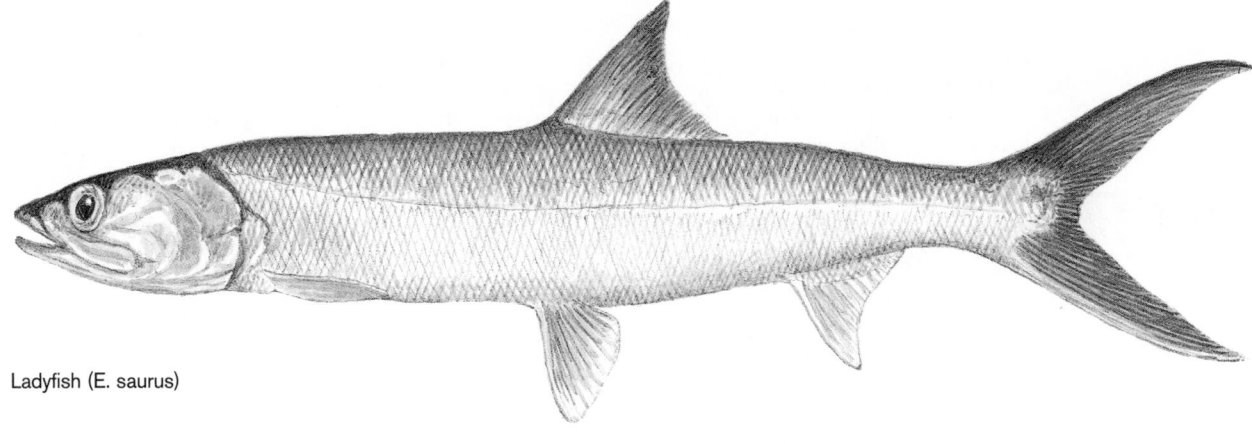

Ladyfish (E. saurus)

Habitat.   Ladyfish are inshore species that prefer bays and estuaries, lagoons, mangrove areas, tidal pools, and canals. They occasionally enter freshwater and are rarely found on coral reefs.

Life history.   These fish form large schools close to shore, although they are known to spawn offshore. Their ribbonlike larvae is very similar to that of bonefish and tarpon.

Food and feeding habits.   Adults feed predominantly on fish and crustaceans. Ladyfish schools are often seen pursuing baits at the surface.

Angling.   Ladyfish take baits, flies, and lures readily and are caught by anglers fishing from boats, piers, bridges, the surf, and on flats. They strike swiftly enough to surprise many anglers, so that the fish often isn't hooked. Nevertheless, multiple opportunities to catch these fish are common when large schools are encountered.

The fight of a ladyfish is disproportionate to its size, as it can make searing bonefish-like runs and also leap repeatedly across the surface. Small spoons, shallow-running plugs, and streamer flies are the best artificial offerings, and a leader is necessary to avoid chafing the line. Ladyfish are not often a deliberate pursuit of anglers owing to their generally small size, and thus do not get the attention that is bestowed upon such prized angling targets as bonefish and tarpon. Most anglers encounter ladyfish incidental to other pursuits.

LAMPREY

Other names for the sea lamprey: lamprey eel, stone sucker, nannie nine eyes (UK); Danish: *havlampret;* Dutch: *zeeprik;* Finnish: *merinahkiainen;* French: *lamproie marine;* Italian: *lamprea di mar;* Norwegian: *havnioye;* Portuguese: *lampreia do mar;* Russian: *morskaja minoja;* Spanish: *lamprea de mar.*

Overview

Lampreys are one of two groups of jawless fish (the other being hagfish), which are the most primitive true vertebrates. They are members of the Petromyzontidae family. Jawless fish are fishlike vertebrates that resemble eels in form, with a cartilaginous or fibrous skeleton that has no bones. They have no paired limbs and no developed jaws or bony teeth. Their extremely slimy skin lacks scales. Fossils of lampreys have been dated back 280 million years.

The jawless, eel-like lampreys are just as ugly as their hagfish *(see)* cousins in form and feeding habits; they differ in other respects, however.

Hagfish are strictly marine, whereas lampreys are either totally freshwater inhabitants or, if they live in the sea, they return to freshwater rivers to spawn.

Lampreys have a large sucking disk for a mouth and a well-developed olfactory system. The mouth is filled with horny, sharp teeth that surround a file-like tongue. A lamprey's body has smooth, scaleless skin, two dorsal fins, no lateral line, no vertebrae, no swim bladder, and no paired fins. Lampreys have no prominent barbels on their snout; their eyes are well developed in the adult and visible externally; there are seven external gill openings on each side; and the nasal opening is on the upper part of the head.

Whereas hagfish scavenge dead or dying fish and secure their nourishment by entering the body cavities of their victims, literally consuming them from inside outward, lampreys are usually parasitic. The lamprey attaches itself to the side of a live fish by using its suctorial mouth; then, by means of its horny teeth, it rasps through the victim's skin and scales and sucks the blood and body juices. The lamprey's mouth glands produce anticoagulating secretions, thereby assisting the flow of blood. After exhausting the blood supply of its weakened or dying host, the lamprey seeks another fish to attack.

There are reportedly 31 species of lampreys worldwide. Not all are parasitic, however. Sixteen are small, inconspicuous, nonparasitic filter feeders in freshwater streams. Of the parasitic species, nine are anadromous, living as adults in the ocean and returning to freshwater to spawn. Most parasitic types attain a length of roughly 12 inches. The marine, or sea, lampreys *(Petromyzon marinus),* are the largest, some capable of reaching a maximum length of 36 inches.

Lampreys spawn in the spring. They ascend streams where the bottom is stony or pebbly and build shallow depressions by moving stones with the aid of their suctorial mouths. Usually, the male and female cooperate in constructing the nest. When ready to spawn, the pair stir up the sand with vigorous body movements as the milt and eggs are deposited at the same time. The eggs stick to particles of sand and sink to the bottom of the nest. The pair then separate and begin another nest directly above the first, thereby loosening more sand and pebbles, which flow down with the current and cover the eggs. The procedure is repeated at short intervals until spawning is completed. The adults die after spawning.

After a period of several days, depending on the species and water temperature, the young appear and drift downstream until they are deposited in a quiet stretch of water where they settle down and burrow into the bottom to spend several years as larvae (called ammocetes). In this stage, they feed on materials strained from the bottom ooze. When they reach a few inches in length (this varies with the species), the ammocetes transform during late summer or fall into adultlike lampreys, complete

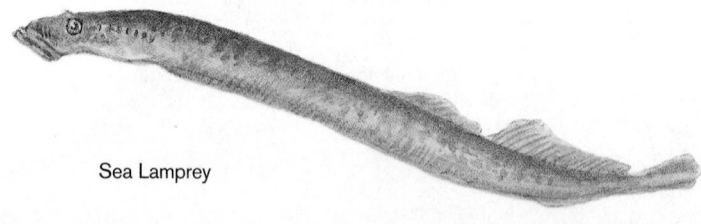

Sea Lamprey

with a sucking disk and circular rows of horny teeth.

The sea lamprey is most notorious as a despoiler of valued sport and commercial fish. It ranges the eastern Atlantic from Iceland and northern Europe (including the North Sea and the Baltic, western Mediterranean, and Adriatic Seas) to northern Africa. It ranges the western Atlantic from southern Greenland, Labrador, and the Gulf of St. Lawrence south to the Gulf of Mexico in Florida. It is land-locked in the Great Lakes, the Finger Lakes, Oneida Lake, and Lake Champlain. It breeds exclusively in freshwater.

Young lampreys, when in saltwater or en route to saltwater, are white underneath and blackish blue, silvery, or lead-colored above. Large specimens approaching maturity are usually mottled brown or dressed in different shades of yellow brown and various hues of green, red, or blue. Sometimes they appear black when the dark patches blend with each other. The ventral surface may be white, gray-ish, or a lighter shade of the ground color of the dorsal surface. Colors intensify during the breeding season.

Mature sea lampreys are from 2 to $2\frac{1}{2}$ feet long. The maximum recorded length is nearly 4 feet, and the maximum weight 5.4 pounds. Reproductive activity is the same as in other lampreys. A single female may contain 236,000 small and spherical eggs.

Little is known of lamprey habits in the sea, except that they are extremely aggressive in their attacks on other fish and are capable of swift travel by body undulations similar to that of an eel. Lampreys do not take the angler's lure or baits but may be accidentally caught in freshwater; they are often seen by trout anglers in shallow water, and are sometimes attached to the bodies of trout or salmon that are caught by anglers. Although lampreys are usually close to land during their stay in the sea, they sometimes stray far offshore to water hundreds of fathoms deep. The sea lamprey is tolerant of a wide range of temperatures and water salinities, ranging from freshwater to that of full oceanic saltiness.

Sea lampreys were considered a delicacy in Europe during the Middle Ages. Also, at one time, large numbers were caught for human consumption in New England, especially in the Connecticut and Merrimack Rivers. Today a few are eaten as table fish, but in general the only value the lamprey has is in its larval form as a bait for anglers.

Commonly, but erroneously, lampreys are known or referred to as "lamprey eels." They are not true eels (see) of the family Anguillidae. For easy differentiation, eels possess jaws and pectoral fins; these are lacking in the lamprey.

Sea Lampreys in the Great Lakes
Several different types of native lampreys (including the silver lamprey, the American brook lamprey,

A lake trout from Lake Michigan bears a scar made by a lamprey.

and the northern brook lamprey) exist in the Great Lakes, but the exotic sea lamprey (Petromyzon marinus) is far larger and more predaceous than native lampreys. None of the Great Lakes lampreys have traditionally had any economic value.

Sea lampreys are native to the Atlantic Ocean and Lake Ontario but not to the upper Great Lakes. Sea lampreys entered the Great Lakes system in the 1800s through man-made locks and shipping canals. Prior to the opening of the Welland Canal in 1829, and prior to its modification in 1919, Niagara Falls served as a natural barrier to keep sea lampreys out of the upper Great Lakes.

Sea lampreys were first observed in Lake Ontario in the 1830s. They did not invade Lake Erie prior to the improvements of the Welland Canal in 1919; sea lampreys were first observed in Lake Erie in 1921. After spreading into Lake Erie, sea lampreys moved rapidly to the other Great Lakes, appearing in Lake St. Clair in 1934, Lake Michigan in 1936, Lake Huron in 1937, and Lake Superior in 1938. By the late 1940s, sea lamprey populations had exploded in all of the upper Great Lakes, causing severe damage to lake trout and other critical fish species.

Sea lampreys attach to fish with their sucking disk and sharp teeth, rasp through scales and skin, and feed on the fish's body fluids, often killing the fish. During its life as a parasite, each sea lamprey can kill 40 or more pounds of fish. Sea lampreys are so destructive that under some conditions, only one out of seven fish attacked by a sea lamprey will survive.

Of the 5,747 streams and tributaries of the Great Lakes, 433 are known to produce sea lampreys. Adult sea lampreys move into gravel areas of tributary streams during spring and early summer. They build nests and lay eggs before dying. After the eggs hatch, small, wormlike larvae are swept downstream from the nest and burrow into sand and silt. The larvae feed on bottom debris and algae carried to them by stream currents.

L

During this stage, which can range from 3 to 17 years, larvae grow to about 6 inches. After the larval life stage, sea lampreys enter their parasitic phase and migrate into the open waters of the Great Lakes. Sea lampreys spend the next 12 to 20 months there (not migrating to saltwater) feeding on fish. The sea lamprey's life cycle, from egg to adult, averages about 6 years, and may last as long as 20 years.

Sea lampreys have had an enormous negative impact on the Great Lakes fishery. Because they did not evolve with naturally occurring Great Lakes fish species, sea lampreys' aggressive, predacious behavior gave them a strong advantage over native fish. Sea lampreys prey on all species of large Great Lakes fish such as lake trout, salmon, rainbow trout (steelhead), whitefish, chub, burbot, walleye, and catfish.

Sea lampreys were a major cause of the collapse of lake trout, whitefish, and chub populations in the Great Lakes during the 1940s and 1950s. These fish were the mainstay of a vibrant and important fishery. Before the sea lamprey's spread, the United States and Canada harvested roughly 15 million pounds of lake trout in the upper Great Lakes each year. By the early 1960s, the catch was only about 300,000 pounds. In Lake Huron, the catch fell from 3.4 million pounds in 1937 to almost nothing in 1947. The catch in Lake Michigan dropped from 5.5 million pounds in 1946 to 402 pounds by 1953. The Lake Superior catch dropped from an average of 4.5 million pounds to 368,000 pounds in 1961. During the time of highest sea lamprey abundance, up to 85 percent of fish somehow not killed by sea lampreys exhibited sea lamprey wounds. The once thriving fisheries were devastated.

In 1958, scientists discovered that TFM (3-trifluoromethyl-4-nitrophenol) was selectively effective in controlling sea lampreys without signi-ficantly impacting other species. Since its discovery, TFM has been used to suppress populations of sea lampreys in the Great Lakes (and also in other areas) by killing their larvae. As a result, sea lamprey populations in the Great Lakes have been reduced by 90 percent from their historic high numbers of the 1940s and 1950s. Decades of exhaustive tests have shown that at the dose needed to kill sea lampreys, TFM is nontoxic or has minimal effects on aquatic plants, fish, and other aquatic organisms, and is nontoxic to humans and other animals.

Despite this success, due to the high cost of TFM and in response to concerns about the use of chemicals, the Great Lakes Fishery Commission and its agents are reducing reliance on the lampricide by 50 percent by the year 2001. The lampricide is being applied more selectively, and alternative control methods, such as traps, barriers, and sterile-male release, are being employed.

See: Exotic Species.

The Jitterbug, a classic American surface lure, was first made by Fred Arbogast in 1937 and named after the popular dance of that era. worth about $500 today.

LANDING FISH

Landing is the act of taking a fish into possession once it has been played close to the angler. In a broader sense, landing also involves the act of setting the hook as well as playing or fighting a fish until it is able to be captured, but these actions are treated separately in this book (see: hooksetting; playing fish).

Landing is accomplished in a number of ways, the most common being hand-holding, netting, or gaffing. The circumstances, species, size of fish, type of terminal tackle used, strength of line or leader, and other considerations affect the decision to use one method or another. An especially important factor is whether the fish will be kept or released (see: catch-and-release).

Many fish are lost at, or close to, the boat because of the actions of the angler or the person attempting to land the fish. Sometimes, even when everything is done right, a fish manages to get free just when it is almost landed; this usually happens when the hook pulls out even though the angler has kept a tight line. However, in most cases, when fish are lost at or near the boat, either just prior to being landed or while in the act of landing, the cause is a mistake or series of mistakes.

Perhaps the greatest mistake made by inexperienced anglers is reeling a fish right up to the tip of the rod when a fish is at boatside—as if they were going to spear it with the tip of the rod. It's better to leave a few feet of line between the rod tip and the fish so that you can direct the fish or lift/swing it onboard. A common mistake made by many people is applying too much pressure on an active fish that is near the boat, as if the game were a tug of war; finesse, not muscle, is the solution. To properly land fish, especially large, strong, and active specimens, the key is to employ common sense, anticipation, and finesse.

Many of the fish caught in freshwater are fairly small, being a pound or two at most in size. Few people have much trouble landing such fish on any type of equipment. Since the majority of all fish caught are small, most freshwater anglers do not often get to experience difficult fish-playing or fish-landing situations, and unfortunately they are ill-prepared to handle them when they do occur. That partially explains why some large freshwater fish are lost after being hooked. Salmon, large trout, steelhead, and large striped bass will fully test the average freshwater angler's playing and landing skills, and anglers who frequently fish for these creatures learn to handle their tackle and use the proper methods to make landing more of a sure thing.

Fish that are caught in saltwater, on average, are larger than those in freshwater, in terms of both length and weight, and many are not as easily landed by hand as a result. Boats for saltwater use typically have a higher freeboard than those used in freshwater, so the distance to a fish in the water next to the boat is different and is more of a factor in how fish are landed. On the other hand, the tackle used in saltwater, especially for bottom fishing and weighted bait, is generally stout, so some fish can be lifted out in saltwater that could not be lifted out in freshwater or with lighter gear.

When a fish is close to the boat, you can take several actions that will greatly improve your chances of landing it, regardless of how it will actually be landed. Often, a fish that is fairly close to you is still energetic. This is a time to cautiously direct the fish. If you're in a boat and the fish streaks toward it (perhaps to swim under it), you could be put at a disadvantage, particularly when using light tackle. You must reel as fast as possible to keep slack out. If the fish gets under the boat, stick the rod tip well into the water to keep the line away from objects and prevent it from being cut.

You should anticipate that a fish will rush the boat and should be prepared to head it around the stern or bow. In some cases a companion can manipulate the boat (especially with an electric motor or with a pushpole) to help swing the stern or bow away from the fish, which is a smart maneuver. If possible, go toward the bow or stern to better follow or control the fish. Whenever possible, fight the fish on the side that it wants to go; don't try to make it come to the side you are on when it wants to go the other way. Also, when there is wind or current, try to get the boat below the fish, so that it is landed on the upstream or upcurrent side. Try to maneuver the fish around the boat at some point in the fight so that this happens. If it is on the wrong side of the boat prior to landing, it may try to dive under the boat and head upcurrent or upriver, and you will be in a terrible position.

The best tactic is usually to move with the fish around the boat according to what the fish is doing. Never hang back in a tug-of-war with a large, strong fish; use finesse rather than muscle.

When the fish swims around the boat, keep the rod tip up (sometimes out, too) and apply pressure to force its head up and to steer it clear of the outboard or electric motor and the propellers. (Sometimes it's best to tilt motors out of the water.) At times it may be necessary to change the angle of pull on a strong and stubborn fish, perhaps to help steer it in a particular direction or away from some obstruction, or to make it fight a little differently. Apply side pressure then, bringing the rod down and holding it parallel to the water, and turning your body partially sideways to the fish. Fight it as you would if the rod were perpendicular to the water.

With very large fish that get near the boat but are still energetic, or with big fish that stay very deep below the boat and can't be budged, the boat may need to be quickly moved a fair distance away so that line peels off the drag. This changes the angle of pull on the fish and usually helps bring it up from the depths. This situation is common in saltwater but does not happen very much in freshwater, except occasionally with big salmon and big striped bass.

In current, a big fish that gets downriver and through rapids where you are unable to follow, may return upriver if you release line from your reel and allow slack line to drift below the fish. The line below the fish acts as a pulling force from downstream (instead of ahead) and may cause the fish to head upstream again.

With some species of jumping fish (Atlantic salmon, for example), and when using fly fishing tackle, you may have to slacken the tension when the fish jumps by bowing the rod toward it so that the jumper cannot use taut line as leverage for pulling free of the hook. Sometimes you can stop a fish from jumping by putting your rod tip in the water and keeping a tight line, which change the angle of pull and may stop a fish from clearing the surface. These and other aspects of fish playing are discussed in more detail in that section (*see: playing fish*).

Eventually the fish is next to you and may be ready for landing. Most fish, especially large ones, will make at least one final effort at freedom, and this will be a crucial moment. Because of the short distance between you and the fish, there will be a lot of stress on your tackle. You must act swiftly when the fish makes its last bolt for freedom. As it surges away, don't pressure it. Let it go. Point the rod at the fish at the critical moment so there is little or (preferably) no rod pressure. A large fish will peel line off the drag, which, if set properly (and if it does not stick), will keep tension on the fish within the tolerance of the line's strength and provide the least amount of pressure possible. As the surge tapers, lift up the rod and work the fish back.

Now it's time to land the fish. But first, a decision has to be made: Are you keeping it or not? If the answer is not, then consider not landing it at all but unhooking it in the water to minimize injury to the fish. You can do this by holding the line with one hand or gripping the fish around the lower jaw with a jaw-gripping tool and using a pair of pliers, a hook gripper, or a hook puller to get the hook out; then let the fish go immediately. In this manner, the fish is never or minimally touched and is least likely to be injured.

However, whenever a fish is on the surface or its head is removed from the water, there is the danger that it will flip, spin, thrash, lunge, or take other action to escape, and this may result in injury to you or the fish or result in a fish that escapes. You have to be very careful when you lift a fish to unhook it, and you should remember that when landing a fish, by whatever means, you should leave the head of the fish in the water to minimize problems (although when you net a fish, it's best to get the head up to the surface). Many fish react instinctively when their heads are lifted and the buoyancy of being supported by water is gone; they'll use their tails to take some type of action. If you keep its

head in the water, a fish may be less inclined to do this; and if you can grab it by the tail, its main source of power is gone and it usually can't take action.

Hand-landing. When you grab or hold a fish with your hands, you may potentially harm yourself or the fish, so do it carefully. If a fish is going to be released, handling should be reduced to a minimum *(see: catch-and-release)* to avoid external damage to the fish or damage to internal organs or to the protective mucus coating (the loss of which increases the possibility of infection). If the fish will be kept, then it doesn't have to be handled as carefully, the major concern then being to avoid personal injury. The sharp fin rays, gill covers, and teeth of some fish, as well as the barbels and pectoral spines on others, can easily cause a cut or stab wound that is likely to be very sore for a while and may become infected.

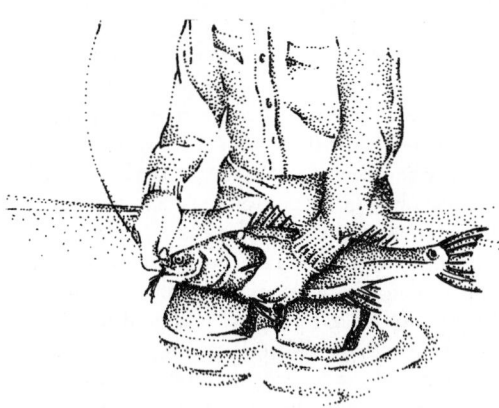

Wading anglers may need to pin a large, strong, or frisky fish to their wet legs, as shown, to land and unhook the fish.

In addition, the landing of fish that are still green, or fresh, or that are very powerful has the potential for causing more serious bodily harm, as well as for damage to equipment. Large saltwater species, for example, if brought into a boat without being subdued properly, can writhe and thrash and do extensive damage. A big fish that flops around in a boat is capable of knocking equipment loose; in a worst-case scenario, it could throw itself against the boat's occupants or get hooked in the tail by loose lures and lash against those in the boat, causing a life-threatening situation. This is extreme, but it has happened. Being careful is mandatory whenever you are handling a fish, especially one that is hooked.

Grasping. There are several locations on a fish that should be avoided if you are going to release them but that make good holding spots if you are keeping them. The foremost location is under the lower edge of the gill; this is a secure, but deadly, place to grasp a fish. A specimen that is tired and on its side may be grabbed under the lower gill cover for landing, and this location usually keeps your hands away from the hooks in a fish's mouth.

Many fish can also be grasped one-handed under the upper gill cover by the back; place the thumb under the upper edge of the gill cover and place the tip of the middle finger under the edge of the opposite gill cover. Another secure but fatal grasping spot for small and medium-size fish is by the upper edge of the eye sockets.

Grabbing by the jaw is a possibility with some fish; the characteristics of their mouths, lack of teeth on the jaws, and size make them quite easy to grasp in this manner. Such species as largemouth bass, panfish, and small stripers can be landed by grasping the lower lip, provided the fish is well tired before the attempt is made.

Simply insert the thumb inside the lower jaw and pinch the jaw against the bent forefinger, which is outside and pressing against the lower jaw. If you'll be landing a lot of fish, you can wear a leather thumb guard to keep from raking your thumb and the skin in the crease between thumb and forefinger. This method of grasping immobilizes the fish and is good for unhooking as well as landing, and has no adverse effect on releasing a fish. It may, however, be hard to accomplish when the mouth opening is covered with one or two treble hooks from the lure.

Larger and stronger fish that lack teeth on the jaws can also be held by the jaw in reverse fashion. For such fish, keep the thumb outside and below the jaw, and put the other four fingers inside the jaw—preferably you are wearing a wet glove when you do this. Gloves, especially versions with a sure-grip surface, aid you in grasping the fish and holding it for unhooking. Wet cotton gloves are best for fish that will be released.

Most fish cannot be held by hand in the mouth, usually because of teeth. One way to hand-land and hand-hold species by the mouth is with a jaw-gripping tool. These clamp over the lower jaw to secure the fish and do not require that you touch

The largemouth bass is one species that can be easily grabbed by the lower lip, but be careful to avoid hooks.

the jaws by hand; these tools don't harm the fish, although many models work best on smaller fish.

Some small fish can be gently lifted with a hand placed under the belly. This may be a good alternative when a fish has been caught on a lure with multiple hooks; however, it is really a technique for small fish. Proper balance cannot be supplied to larger fish this way, a lot of pressure can be placed on internal organs, and a lot can go wrong if the fish squirms and escapes your grasp. Some fish can be calmed by turning them over and holding them upside down. This technique is more useful for a fish that will be unhooked and released than for a fish that will be kept.

A lot of fish, especially small- to medium-size specimens in freshwater, and smaller specimens in saltwater, are hand-grasped behind the mouth and the head in the "neck" or nape area. Holding too tightly here can damage internal organs if the fish is to be released, but bigger fish, with more meat in this area, can be held firmly without problem. Fish with prickly spiny rays may be a problem to land this way; instead, run your hand from head to tail with thumb on top and other fingers on the belly. Depress the dorsal fins with the thumb; now you can safely hold the fish around the middle of the body.

Catfish must be held properly to avoid a puncture from their sharp pectoral fins. The best way to do this is to grab behind, and at the base of, the pectoral fins in order to keep them pointed sideways.

Lifting and swinging. An easy way to boat small fish that are well hooked is simply to lift them aboard with your rod. This method is practical only for small- to medium-size fish caught on sturdy tackle. Bass anglers often bring a fish into the boat by swinging it in because the fish is small and the line and tackle are heavy enough to handle this. Fish under 3 pounds are the usual candidates. Landing is best accomplished by working the fish to the surface and leading it toward the boat; when the head clears the surface near the boat, continue the momentum and lift the fish up, swinging it in. Small fish that are swung into a boat then have to be grabbed by hand, and obviously they may wind up flopping on the floor. Such treatment is not conducive to proper handling and release but is probably all right for fish that are to be kept.

In saltwater, many fish that are taken from party boats, as well as some of the smaller ones caught on other craft, are lifted right out of the water and over the gunwale onto the floor of the boat. Most of these fish are being kept. Lifting and swinging are suitable when fish are well hooked and when a rod and line of appropriate strength are used.

Billing. The long bills of sailfish and small marlin provide a good handle for landing, or at least for holding while the fish is unhooked. That bill is used as a weapon when the fish chases prey, and it can become a weapon used against you if you're not careful enough. To avoid this, try to grab the bill with both hands when it's just below the surface.

On small boats, billfish are usually landed on the starboard side so that the operator can see what is happening, but on larger boats they may be landed on either side or at the stern.

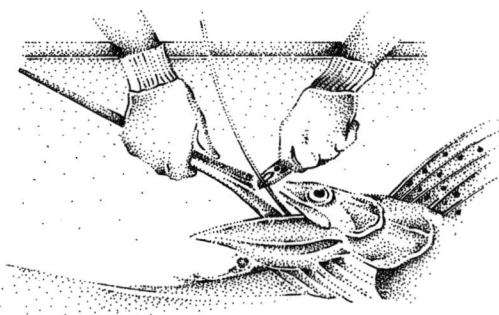

To secure a billfish for unhooking and releasing, grab the bill close to the mouth, using one or two hands, depending on the size of the fish.

In any case, grab the bill with both hands, with your thumbs facing each other but slightly apart. Be prepared to push away from the bill and head if the fish suddenly lunges up and ready to hold on if the fish thrashes moderately.

Tailing. The tails of some fish are rigid enough to permit you to grab them by placing your hand over the caudal peduncle just ahead of the tail fin. You can grab a jack or a tuna this way, and you can grab large salmon and pike by the tail. Smaller fish usually can't be grabbed by the tail, and the tails of many bigger fish are not rigid enough. You can't grab a big largemouth bass securely enough by the tail, nor can you grab most trout (except really large ones) this way. But for some fish, the tail provides a good handle for landing, and it is far enough from teeth or hooks to be an attractive gripping point.

When you do grab a fish by the tail, you can do it either by hand for fish that will be released, or with a tailer for fish that will be kept. A tailer, also called a tail rope or loop, is a nooselike device that slips over the fish and cinches down on the caudal peduncle (the stem just forward of the tail fin). A tailer is best for fish with a stiff rather than flexible caudal peduncle.

If the boat is moving, as is the case when trolling or fishing in open waters for offshore species, a fish can be tailed pretty easily while it is alongside and moving with you. If the boat is drifting or is anchored, or if you are wading and playing a fish to you, then you have to pick the moment to grab the tail. Usually a fish will try to bolt when touched, so you want to get the first try right; otherwise, the fish may sprint off and lengthen the fight, possibly getting free. When the fish is tired and just lying by you, you can grab it easily. If it is still moving a little, bring it around in a circular manner if possible and grab the tail when the fish is headed away from you. When using a tailer, you have to get the noose partway up the body and then quickly draw it tight; after the tail is secured, you have to lift it out of the

L

L

water or you may have a tiger by the tail. Once the fish's tail is raised out of the water, its powerful leveraging agent is gone.

Netting. The three rules of netting should be to avoid netting if you plan to release the fish, *or* if the net is a standard hoop-style, *or* if the fish has been caught on a multihooked lure. Fish that have been hooked with a multihooked lure and then netted may be easily damaged. The hooks inevitably grab the webbing of the net, and the fish thrashes and rips itself while pulling violently against the embedded hooks. If the fish rolls in the net with treble hooks, untangling becomes a real problem; a lot of time is lost before the fish can be unhooked, and the fish's skin, jaws, or eyes may be damaged.

Obviously the decision to release a fish has to be made before the fish is in the net. Cotton mesh nets are softer and don't seem to hurt the fish as much, but hooks are harder to get out, and the cotton nets are not as widely available as nylon or rubber nets.

Fish that are netted usually can be released alive if they have not been handled excessively and have not spent too much time out of water. One way to facilitate the release of netted fish is to keep the net in the water while unhooking the fish. Those who wade, such as stream trout anglers who use flies or single-hook lures, can do this quite easily. Once the hook has been removed, the net can be turned over and the fish gently jiggled out. Obviously, to release the fish alive, you have to be careful how you do this, so that damage is minimized.

How to net. Proper netting technique is as much a matter of knowing what not to do as it is knowing what to do. Under most circumstances, you shouldn't put the net in the water and wait for the fish to come close. Nor should you wave the net overhead where a fish might see it. A net lying in the water or moving above it is foreign and alarming to fish. Moreover, a net in the water cannot be turned or moved swiftly. It's best to keep the net solidly in hand and at the ready, either motionless or out of sight, until a fish is almost within reach.

Don't attempt to net a fish unless it is within reach, and don't try to net it if it is going away from you or appears to be able to go away from you. Ideally, the fish should be heading toward you so that it must continue moving forward, or so that you can move the net in front of it if it turns. As a rule, don't try to net a fish unless its head is on the surface or is just breaking to the surface. A fish that is on the surface has little mobility and cannot be as active as one that has its entire body in the water.

Don't try to net a fish from behind. If a fish is completely exhausted, you may be able to net it from the side, but the most desirable position is from the front. And don't touch the fish with the rim of the net until it is well into the net. Touching fish, particularly if they are still lively, often initiates wild behavior. If the fish acts wild, it could roll on your line and break the line or simply snap the line from the force of its getaway rush. Therefore, resist

The angler has to keep the head of a big, strong fish up and guide it toward the net, and the netter shouldn't stab at or chase the fish.

taking a stab at a fish that may be technically within reach of your extended net but is not in the best position for capture.

Snagging a multihooked lure on the net webbing is a major problem when anglers try to net a fish that is in a poor position or when the fish doesn't come squarely into the middle of the net. Snagging like this is one of the surest ways to lose fish, particularly those that are heavy and cannot be readily hoisted into the boat or scooped up in the now-tangled net.

You can help the netter by making an effort to get the fish's head up so that it is near or on the surface and not deep in the water. When the fish comes up and is being worked toward the net, you should back up in the boat, put more pressure on the fish to gain line, raise the rod high to keep the fish's head up, and tell the netter that the time is right, attempting to lead the fish closer as the netter goes into action. Be prepared for miscues. When a strong fish, and especially a green one, is brought to the net, try to back off a bit on the reel drag, or perhaps open the bail of the reel or put it into freespool, keeping a finger on the line to maintain tension. If the fish flops out, runs through the net (it happens with lousy nets), or charges away, there may be a lot of pressure on your tackle, so anticipate this possibility and let the fish go in the manner noted previously. When it stops, reengage the reel and work the fish back. Don't count the fish as caught until it is solidly in hand.

Netting a fish by yourself is often a tricky chore, made more difficult by the influence of current, wind, and tide. Bringing a fish to net or boat as quickly as possible may not be feasible when you are alone and have a large fish, and often you must play the fish out thoroughly before you can slip the net under it. Try to get the fish to within several feet of the tip of the rod; then raise the rod high over and behind your head while you reach for the fish with net extended in your other hand. Keep the line taut, and don't let your rod hand come down to create slack.

Netting efforts are sometimes more arduous in fast-moving waters because fish are usually below you, and it is hard to get big fish back upcurrent and positioned for proper netting. Another problem is that when you don't gain on fish in current, they rest momentarily and recoup enough strength to prolong the battle or give that last extra kick just when you think you have them. For this reason, those who are netting a big fish for someone else in swift water should usually be a reasonable distance downriver, in a position to land a tired fish as it wallows near the bank, still resisting the angler but unable to swim off with vigor.

If landing the fish isn't feasible—because the net is too small or because you are without a net—you always have the option of landing it by hand or beaching it. In either case, the fish must be thoroughly whipped and under your control before you can do so.

Release cradling.   Perhaps the best method of netting a fish that will be released is to use a type of net called a cradle, or release cradle. This is not a net in the traditional handle-and-dipping sense, but it has similarities and is a benign way of landing and subduing a large or long fish that will be unhooked and released. The most popular release cradles have two long narrow wood boards connected by $1/4$-inch soft-mesh knotless netting that is closed at the ends; the netting droops into the water to envelop the fish. The cradle is laid alongside a boat, and the netting droops into a trough below. The angler leads a captured fish alongside the boat and over the netting, and the net is folded up like a purse to enclose the fish, which remains full-length and in the water. Perhaps most important, the cradle supports the full body of the fish in a horizontal position. Another version, usually homemade and intended for shorter fish, is smaller, with open ends and open-grip handle. In both cases, the fish stays relaxed in the net while the hook is removed and can be released without having to be handled. Moreover, you can rig up the cradle for weighing, keeping the fish in the cradle and providing excellent horizontal support for the fish. A cradle is difficult to use when fishing by yourself; in that case, it is better to avoid a cradle or net altogether and try to unhook the fish while it is in the water.

Gaffing.   Gaffing is a fish-landing option that is primarily used in saltwater and, with one

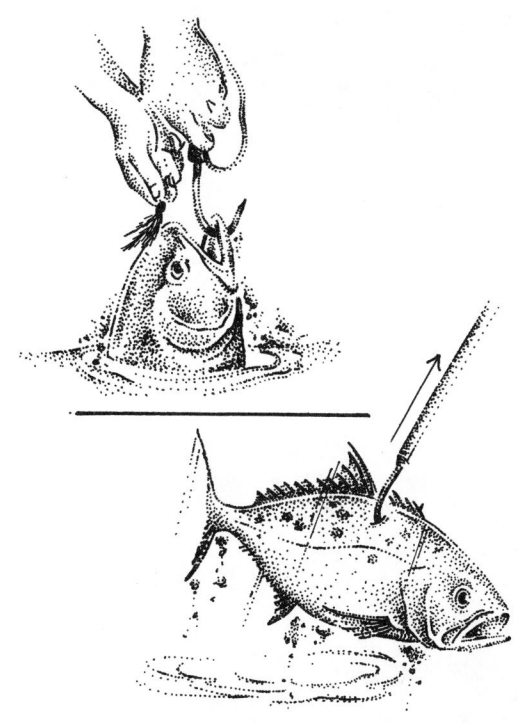

A hand gaff can be used on some fish that will be released, especially those having large mouths (top); the best place to gaff small- and intermediate-size fish that will be kept is in the upper back, as shown (bottom).

exception, is not recommended for fish that are to be released. That exception is when a fish is gaffed in the mouth through the lower jaw.

Like netting, gaffing isn't terribly difficult, although anglers sometimes have trouble executing a proper gaff. In essence, you gaff a fish by getting the point of the gaff in the water beneath the fish and then strike upward sharply. Being too excited or being careless can cause problems. When gaffers flail wildly, they often miss the fish, strike it in a spot that makes control and lifting difficult, or, worse, strike and break the angler's line. Poking the fish with the gaff instead of ramming it home is likely to make the fish act wild, perhaps causing it to surge enough to break free.

The location where you gaff a fish is not critical if you plan to keep the fish, but the gaff is often in the upper back muscle of the midsection of the fish. This may damage some meat, but it is a good secure spot. Gaffing a fish in the belly may cause the fish to react violently and either shake free, pry the gaff out of your hand, or break the gaff. It also contributes to a heavily bleeding fish that makes a mess in the boat or in a fish box.

Gaff the fish with a firm, sure motion and follow through with the upward motion by lifting the fish out of the water if it is small enough to lift; otherwise, a second gaff (or tail rope) or two people hauling will be necessary to get the fish in. To gaff a fish when a boat is moving and the fish is swimming or is being towed alongside the boat, reach across the

L

In these photos, a big dolphin is skillfully gaffed and brought aboard a large sportfishing boat. Note how the mate uses one leg to brace himself as he extends far out, sticks the gaff hook into the fish and instantly grabs it with two hands as the fish starts to thrash, begins to lift up as the fish is under control, and then swiftly lifts the fish over the high gunwale.

back with the hook down and pointed at the side of the fish facing away from you. When the handle is close to the back of the fish, smoothly and sharply drive the point all the way to the bend and keep the gaff coming to you.

The technical procedure is the same when gaffing from a boat that is at anchor or drifting, the difference being that your target is moving and you have to plan the strike well. Try to plant the gaff hook when the fish has just turned and is facing away from the boat rather than when it is headed toward the boat; if you miss, the fish will probably steam away from you rather than go underneath.

Flying gaffs and bridge gaffs are used in big-game and bridge fishing, respectively. The procedure is similar, although a bridge gaff is used more like a snagging tool and is less precise.

Fish to be released can be gaffed in the lower jaw with a hand gaff, preferably by driving the point through the inside of the mouth and out the lower jaw (rather than coming from outside to inside). This is done when the fish is thoroughly played out.

Obviously, the point of the gaff must be razor sharp to do the most effective job. The point should be covered when the gaff is not in use.

What the angler can do. It is worth reaffirming the role of the angler in the fish-landing process, especially during the acts of netting, gaffing, cradling, and tailing.

The angler can do a lot to help the person who is actually landing the fish, or the angler can make those efforts much more difficult. An inexperienced angler can be talked through the process by the person doing the landing. A good mate or captain on a charter boat will tell the angler what to do when the moment of truth draws near. On the other hand, a good angler can play a big fish and still get a successful landing effort out of a totally inexperienced

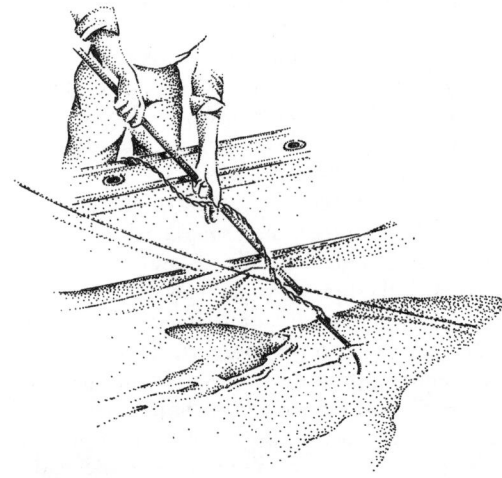

When a flying gaff is used on big-game species, the pole detaches from the hook, and the rope is left attached to the gaff hook in the fish.

lander if the angler tells the person what to do and when to do it.

Generally, however, when the fish is near, the angler can help a lot by keeping up the fish's head so that it is near or on the surface and not deep in the water. When the fish is coming in close, the angler should put more pressure on the fish to gain line by continuing to pump and reel; as the fish is about to be landed, the angler should raise the rod high (keeping it there and not allowing slack), forcing the fish's head to stay up. If a long leader is used, or if there is a lot of hardware on the terminal end (like a dodger and a 6-foot leader to the lure), the angler may need to step back in the boat so that the fish can be reached for landing. If that is not the case, then the angler should remain close to the gunwale in order to see what the fish does and react accordingly.

An angler should be prepared for miscues and ready to lower the rod tip and point the rod at a fish if it streaks away after being touched by a net or gaff or hand. Even if battling the fish of a lifetime, a good angler stays calm and doesn't try to force the results. If the fish is not landed on the first attempt or if something goes wrong in the landing process, the angler stays with the fish and keeps the line away from obstructions. An experienced angler anticipates a problem and prepares to counter it without applying tug-of-war force and thus is often able to bring the fish back for another landing attempt.

Unusual measures. Some situations in saltwater fishing call for more unusual measures for landing fish. Monster-size Pacific halibut and big sharks, for example, can be dangerous fish if they are not killed before being brought into the boat; a knock on the head, which is used to dispatch most fish once they are landed, or hanging from a gin pole, does not do it for these creatures.

Shooting and harpooning are sometimes used by charter boat captains to dispatch a fish before it is actually brought into the boat. A shotgun loaded with bird shot and aimed at the head, and a harpoon whose metal tip is attached to a buoy, are the instruments used for halibut; sometimes, heavy-duty gaff hooks, attached by rope to a cleat, are also used. In the past, large sharks were shot with rifles, shotguns, and pistols, but the wisdom of doing this and concerns for firearms safety have more or less relegated this method to yesteryear status. However, some captains do keep a handgun available for emergencies, including the dispatching of a large shark; others use a 12-gauge bang stick for killing a shark, a device that has to be treated with extreme caution.

LANDING NET

A net with a handle used by anglers to capture hooked fish.

See: Catch-and-Release; Landing Fish; Net.

LANDINGS

The number or poundage of fish unloaded at a dock by commercial fishermen or brought to shore by recreational fishermen. This term refers primarily to saltwater fisheries. Landings are reported at the points at which fish are brought to shore. This term differs from "catch," which is all fish that are caught, including those released or discarded.

See: Fisheries Management.

LANDLOCKED

A term for anadromous *(see)* fish that have adapted to a completely freshwater existence, spending the greater portion of their life in a lake and returning to natal rivers or streams to spawn. Any fish—usually salmon but also striped bass—with such behavior and without access to saltwater is landlocked.

LARVAE

The early life forms of a fish or other animal between the time of hatching and transforming to a juvenile.

LATERAL LINE

A series of sensory cells, usually running the length of both sides of the fish's body, that perform an important function in receiving low-frequency vibrations.

See: Anatomy.

LAUNCH

(1) To put a boat in the water, usually the act of easing a boat off a trailer and into the water at some type of access site.

(2) A place to put a boat into the water, as in boat ramp or boat launch *(see)*.

(3) A multiple-rod-holding device at the back of a seat or backrest, usually found on a center console boat and referred to as a rocket launcher *(see: sportfishing boat)*.

LAUNCHING

Launching primarily refers to the act of getting a boat off a trailer at an access site, but it can also refer to carrying lightweight craft to the water's edge. Many of the same factors that are important when launching a boat are also important when retrieving it (loading it on a trailer).

Fishing boats on trailers are launched at many places, primarily at official and designated access sites called boat ramps or boat launches *(see)*. Launch sites may be improved (paved and maintained) or unimproved. Launching is easier at improved sites with paved ramps, and such sites are

mandated when launching large and heavy craft. Small, lightweight boats on trailers, as well as some midsize boats, can be launched at unimproved sites, although care must be taken to judge the firmness of the ground at the site, the depth of water, and the firmness of the bottom near shore. At unimproved sites, getting a boat out is often harder than getting it in, and much depends on how far the trailer (and tow vehicle) have to be backed into the water, the strength of the towing vehicle in relation to the weight of the boat and trailer, and existing ground conditions.

Whether improved or not, launch sites vary in important ways: steepness or angle of incline, width, depth of water, extension of pavement into the water, docking space, amount of time that a boat may be docked, availability of adjacent parking, fees, and hours of operation.

The best access sites for launching trailered boats are those with moderate inclines and a gradual dropoff to deep water, rather than a steep dropoff or long shallow one. At sites with an immediate steep dropoff, the trailer cannot be backed very far into the water, and this situation places a lot of pressure on the bow when the stern is floating. When the boat is retrieved, the angle is insufficient for it to be winched onto the bow support, especially if the trailer is at a steeper angle than the tow vehicle. For retrieval you need to be able to get the boat onto the trailer far enough that it is centered properly; side bunks or guides if the trailer is so equipped are aids here. An unguided boat floats freely and may not get centered on the trailer when it is winched on. In the worst cases, it may take several attempts to center the boat, a chore made more difficult by wind or current. The assistance of others is welcome when you're trying to position the boat for retrieval.

Access sites with little or no change in the bottom near shore require you to back the trailer and tow vehicle a long way into the water and perhaps push the boat off the trailer if it will not float itself off. The heavier the boat, the more of a problem this is, not to mention that you can wind up with a vehicle whose front and rear tires are in the water and a tailpipe that is submerged. When retrieving a boat in these situations, you usually don't have to put the trailer as far into the water as you do when launching because the motor can be used to push the boat all or part of the way onto the trailer. If you expect to launch in this condition all or most of the time, consider a trailer that cradles the boat lower and thus floats it sooner than one that sits high. Drive-on trailers, incidentally, provide the easiest launching and retrieval at improved sites.

Anglers who keep boats on trailers for portability do not always have an option in picking launch sites, so they have to make do with conditions as they find them. It is tougher to launch at narrow ramps than at wide ones, which accommodate multiple simultaneous launchings. However, the latter are also more crowded, especially at prime days and hours, so if you're new to trailering and launching, practice backing up a trailer beforehand (lay out cardboard boxes at an empty mall parking lot), and try to launch at off-peak hours. Anyone who has watched a busy boat launch knows what a comedy (and tragedy) it can be.

Backing Up

Backing up with a trailer is a problem for many people, and the only way to get good at it is through practice. If you keep your hand on top of the steering wheel, the rear of the trailer heads left when you turn the wheel to the right, so in effect you need to steer in reverse. You may prefer to keep your hand on the bottom of the steering wheel so that when you move your hand to the left, the trailer goes to the left. When you first start, it's a good idea to turn your body sideways and look at the trailer as you turn the wheel and back up. When you get proficient, you won't need to turn around at all but can simply use both side mirrors to watch your progress. Always back up slowly and try to position the trailer as straight as possible in the water.

How to Launch

The first thing to realize about launching is the need for courtesy. Prepare your boat for launching in the parking lot, not while blocking the ramp. Put everything you need into it, and make all installations before you launch, not when you are backed onto the ramp or tied up at the dock or pier.

If you've never been to the launch site before, or if it has changed since your last use, it's wise to inspect the ramp and the area nearby. Look at the length of the pavement into the water, and check to see if there is a drop after the pavement that might be an impediment to trailer wheels. Many boaters have been stuck at ramps when they could not pull trailer wheels over the back lip of a paved ramp, so don't get your wheels in so far as to allow that to happen. Check to see whether the ramp is nonskid or whether conditions have made it slippery (grass and moss can do this). You may need to make sure that the tow vehicle's wheels don't get into the water if that part of the ramp is slippery. Also check or ask about nearby hazards and current, and note the direction of the wind, which may have an effect on launching or retrieving.

Before launching, make sure that the drain plug is in the boat, remove tiedowns, raise the motor or outdrive so it doesn't strike anything, make sure that nothing is sticking out of the boat, disconnect the trailer lights, and, if the ramp is gradual, remove the safety chain on your trailer.

If you are proficient at backing up, try to get the trailer fairly close to the dock or pier. If the ramp slopes properly, you shouldn't have to completely submerge the trailer. The degree to which you put the trailer in the water will depend in part on the trailer design. Roller-type trailers can be backed up so the bottom of the tires are partly in the water and then the boat is pushed off. Drive-on or bunk-style trailers should be backed in until the wheel hubs are almost submerged; this should give some float to the boat and allow it to back off under power without much effort. Back the trailer into the water only until the boat begins to float or can be easily pushed off, or until the trailer tilts.

With the trailer in position, keep the motor of the tow vehicle running. Put an automatic transmission in parking gear and a standard transmission in neutral, and apply the emergency brake. For some vehicles and some ramps, it's not a bad idea to put a chock behind two wheels; cars and trucks have been dunked at ramps. Now disconnect the bow of the boat from the trailer winch cable and push it into the water; a long rope should be tied to the bow or to both the bow and the stern so that a companion can guide the boat to the dock and secure it. If you're alone and cannot push the boat off by yourself or drive it off, tie a long bow rope to the front of your trailer, back far enough into the water to float the boat backward, and then slowly pull forward until the trailer is halfway out of the water. Untie the rope from the trailer, and pull the boat to the dock and secure it.

Depending on the site, boat, and trailer, and the wind, wave, and current conditions, this is the basic launching procedure. Try to avoid getting the trailer hubs in the water unless they are meant for submersion; if you have to submerse the hubs, let them cool down first. Take your time, and launch safely. Don't loiter on the dock or leave your vehicle on the ramp; get it out of the way and leave room at the dock for someone else to come in.

Retrieval

Retrieving your boat at a boat launch is not just the reverse procedure of launching, although many of the same precautions are necessary. It is especially important that you get the boat positioned perfectly on your trailer, and loading a boat on a trailer can be difficult if the trailer is on a bad angle or is not placed into the water at the right depth. Keep in mind that conditions for retrieving your boat may be different than when you launched it; the main differences include tidal fluctuation, presence of wind, presence of wave action from boaters, changes in visibility, and more activity at the launch site. At times when a sudden storm comes up and everyone heads into the launch ramp, there can be near pandemonium, especially if temporary docking space is at a minimum; it's important to watch out for other boaters and to be able to retrieve your boat quickly and get out of the way.

Drive-on trailers are the best for quickness, and if a ramp has a moderate angle, you can usually drive right up onto the trailer to the bow chock (not too fast) if you have the boat centered right at the outset, being careful not to dig the lower unit of the motor into the ramp if the ramp is shallow. You

Anglers load a bass boat onto a drive-on trailer at Lake Sam Rayburn in Texas.

may want to tilt the motor up a bit if you are unsure of the depth. If you can't drive the boat all the way onto the trailer, you may be able to drive it up enough that the boat is firmly on the trailer and then get out and hook up the winch cable to bring it up the remaining distance.

Winch-on trailers provide many chances to get things wrong, usually because the stern of the boat sways to one side (because of wind, current, waves, or bad luck). If you don't get the bow positioned properly along the centerline of the trailer, and centered on the keel rollers, it will not be aligned properly when fully winched up and you'll need to do it all over again, so be sure to get it lined up right. When it is windy, someone on the dock or shore could hold a stern line to help keep the boat centered, with another person pulling the stern in or pushing it out as needed.

Whenever you retrieve your boat, it's a good idea to drain water out of the bilge, livewell, or baitwell so that you don't have to put extra weight on your trailer or crank extra weight out of the water if you're using a winch. Trim the motor or outdrive so it doesn't strike anything. Do not drive away with a boat that is cockeyed on the trailer; back it down into the water and get it positioned properly. Before you pull the boat and trailer off the ramp, fasten the safety chain and make sure the boat is attached to the winch cable. Unload away from the immediate ramp area, fasten tiedowns to the trailer, and reconnect the trailer lights. If you have an outboard motor transom-saver bracket (a device attached to the trailer that supports the weight of the lower unit of the motor), put that on. If not, tilt the motor up, put the motor bracket lock down, and lower the trim, leaving the throttle in forward gear. Secure the electric motor so that it can't bounce. Stow or secure rods, coolers, PFDs, and anything that might blow out of the boat (like containers and cans so you don't become a litterbug). Make sure you turn off all electronics in the boat; turn the engine key to the off position, or you'll have a dead battery. A final

safety check, especially of the hitch connection, safety chains, bow tiedown, rear tiedown, tires, and lights, should be made before you depart. If a brake light or turn signal is out, you may not be able to do anything about it at the launch site, but you should be aware of the problem so that you can take it into account while on the road. Lastly, before you leave, take your vehicle out of four-wheel-drive if you put it in that position for hauling your boat out of the launch site, as many people do.
See: Trailer.

LAWS
See: Regulations.

LCD
Acronym for liquid crystal display.
See: Sonar.

LCR
Acronym for liquid crystal recorder.
See: Sonar.

LEAD
See: Sinker.

LEAD-CORE LINE
See: Weighted Line.

LEADER
A length of nylon monofilament or wire at the end of a fishing line. Also known as a trace, a leader is intended either to have low visibility so that it does not appear to be connected to a lure, hook, or fly or to protect the line from cutting or breaking. No leader material is able to do both of these simultaneously, which would be the ideal. Low-visibility leaders are mainly employed in freshwater fishing, especially for trout and salmon in streams, and in some saltwater situations, like bonefishing.

Leaders are of varying lengths; the terminal end is connected directly to a lure, fly, hook, snap, or swivel, and the butt is connected directly to the fishing line. Sometimes a leader is used from a swivel to a weight, baited hook, diving planer, or bottom rig.

A leader may be lighter or heavier in strength than the main fishing line, depending upon its application, and level or tapered in both diameter and strength. Nylon monofilament leaders are always used in fly fishing because they aid the delivery of a fly and, in most situations, are relatively imperceptible; such leaders are lighter than the fly line, and the terminal end is generally tapered to a fine diameter and a lighter strength.

Most leaders used for other applications have a greater breaking strength than the main fishing line because their primary purpose is to protect against abrasion, cutting, or shock that would cause breakage.

Leaders may be employed in casting, trolling, and baitfishing, and while using all types of tackle. They are more common in saltwater angling than in freshwater, owing to the greater number of nasty fish encountered in the marine environment and some of the different techniques employed; some type of leader, for example, is virtually always used in offshore big-game fishing and shark fishing. Leaders are most likely to be used for fish with sharp teeth, scales, or gill covers; for fish that are very big and powerful; for fish that are hard to land or unhook and release near the boat; and for species that live in places where line-damaging obstructions are frequently encountered.

Tapered Fly Leaders
In fly fishing, using nylon monofilament leaders of varying lengths (up to 9 feet) is a necessity. This is because the fly line is too thick to be attached directly to the fly, and its size would alarm fish if it were attached directly to the fly; the lighter line, when tapered down, is important for turning over and quietly presenting a fly as well as getting it to float or sink naturally. Fly leaders are nearly all tapered from a heavy butt end (which is usually 20- to 30-pound test) through the midsection to a light end, with or without a tippet *(see)*. However, in some situations, a short length of level leader (one length of the same diameter) can be used; this is most common when using sinking lines and leaders under 6 feet long, and when angling for fish that are not highly selective or leader-shy.

In other circumstances, and especially in stream trout fishing and fishing with dry flies, a progressive taper is important to a leader for transmitting the rolling energy from the line throughout the leader. Thus, the butt should have enough stiffness (and usually from two-thirds to three-quarters of the diameter of the fly line) to transfer the rolling energy from the fly line through the rest of the tapered leader to a fine tippet that will allow it to settle lightly and move naturally.

Fly leaders are available in premanufactured knotless tapered versions, or they can be constructed by the angler in knotted compound tapered sections that successively taper down in strength and diameter. The butt is similar in diameter to the fly line, to which it is tied; the midsection continues the taper, and the tip or terminal end tapers still further and is attached to the fly. When using small flies and light leaders, tie a separate light tippet to the end of the leader and then to the fly in order to minimize its visibility; the tippet also helps to turn the leader and fly over with a well-executed cast, and it helps the fly act naturally with less line drag. When using large flies, such as bugs or

L

poppers for bass fishing or big streamers for saltwater species, use a short but heavier tippet, known as a shock tippet *(see)*.

Lengths and strengths of fly leader vary with fish and conditions. Although traditionalists tie knotted compound tapered leaders, most anglers, especially in freshwater, use knotless tapered leaders, since the former take time to construct properly; require an assortment of lines for making the full leader; and can be troublesome when the knots catch on guides, surface debris, grass, or other objects. However, being able to tie your own knotted leader can be helpful when delicate circumstances require a fine leader; in any event, the tip of a knotless leader usually has to be replaced eventually with a newly knotted section of tippet.

Fly leader lengths typically range from $7^1/_2$ feet to 10 feet, but also run to either extreme down to 4 feet and up to 16. As a generality, longer leaders (over 7 feet) are used with floating lines, and shorter leaders with sinking lines. Shorter lengths of nylon monofilament leader are preferable with sinking lines because this material is only slightly more dense than water and thus sinks slowly. Fluorocarbon material, however, is more dense and sinks faster, allowing for longer leader lengths when sinking fly lines are used.

The length of leader varies with fishing conditions and species. Most stream trout anglers use a leader that is about 9 feet long, and many use a longer leader for wary and selective fish if a proper back cast can be made. The problem with long

Depicted here is a fly tippet and wire bite guard used to avoid breakoffs by fish with sharp teeth or rough mouths. The end of the guard that attaches to the fly has a reformable Haywire Twist that gets covered by a plastic tube (inset).

leaders in tight quarters is that the angler often cannot get enough fly line in the air (because of brush and trees) to carry the long leader, or to roll cast enough fly line to unfurl a long leader. This has led to a general belief in using a leader that is about the overall length of the fishing rod, but this is just a convenient guideline, since some anglers are very successful with longer leaders and some with shorter ones. In fact, shorter leaders are preferred by many people who are very capable casters, since they can put the fly where they want it without getting the fly line near or over the fish. Shorter fly leaders are also favored in situations where fish are less wary or generally aggressive.

Fly leaders are typically much stronger for saltwater fishing applications than for freshwater, and they start with heavier butts that commonly taper to 12- or 16-pound-test tippets, although they can be much lighter. Many are constructed with loops in both ends to facilitate quick changing of the leader or of the shock tippet (also commonly used for bigger species). Some shock tippets also employ a short length of braided or single-strand wire ahead of the fly; this is helpful for sharp-toothed fish like barracuda and bluefish.

Many fly anglers, especially those after tarpon, keep a set of shock leaders prepared and ready to fish when the need arises to interchange leaders. They use heavy monofilament, which also takes some work to straighten, so prestraightened line is tied to a fly and kept in traction for use as a spare if needed.

Level Monofilament Leaders

In non-fly-fishing applications, level leaders may be used with any type of tackle and with a variety of techniques. A level leader has one unknotted section of line of the same strength and diameter throughout; this is distinguished from a tapered leader, which is used with flycasting tackle to help present a fly. When casting with other types of equipment, there is no benefit to a tapered leader for presentation, since the weight of the object being cast carries the line.

Whether a leader is necessary or desirable at all depends on the situation and the species. Most freshwater bait and lure anglers seldom use a leader; they tie their nylon monofilament fishing line (the overwhelming favorite) directly to the lure, hook, snap, swivel, or rig because the fish they catch and the circumstances do not endanger the terminal end of the fishing line, or they periodically cut off a small piece of the line as necessary and retie it. Consistent fishing in areas where the terminal fishing line is likely to be abraded might call for a heavy nylon monofilament leader, provided that doing so doesn't alert the fish; the clearer the water, the more you have to be sensitive to the visibility of the end of the line (because of diameter and possibly color). In freshwater, species that often require a leader are pike, muskies, and payara; however, most anglers use a short wire leader for these toothy species rather than a nylon monofilament leader.

In saltwater, a nylon monofilament leader is used for many species but not on others. Line can be tied directly to a hook or to a lure when fishing for striped bass, for example. Most anglers using light spinning tackle for bonefish can tie the fishing line directly to a shrimp hook or to a jig. However, a heavy monofilament leader is desirable for some species because of their sharp teeth or gill covers, or because the act of landing them puts a lot of stress on the terminal end of the line (which is often grabbed in landing fish, whether they are kept or released). Tarpon are a species that require a heavy mono leader; this is called a shock leader, similar to the shock tippet used in fly fishing, but it is simply a nylon monofilament leader, from 60 to 100 pounds in strength, that is tied to a lighter, usually 20-pound, main line. Heavy mono shock leaders may be useful for some toothy species, but a wire leader (also called a bite leader) is preferred in many other instances. As in freshwater, a nylon monofilament leader used in saltwater is almost always heavier than the main line and meant to provide extra strength and/or abrasion resistance.

The length of a nylon monofilament leader is usually short for freshwater fishing and for general casting purposes. As a rule when casting in freshwater, it should be a little less than the length of the rod, or just enough so that the knot connecting the leader and main fishing line doesn't reach the reel when the lure or bait is reeled to the top of the rod. This shorter length is meant to keep the knot off the reel and lessen the chance of it hanging up and impeding casting or freespooling, which it is more likely to do on the smaller baitcasting and spinning reels used in freshwater. However, where big reels and light fishing line are used, a longer leader, which can be wound onto the reel, may be employed; this puts all of the close-to-the-boat pressure on the leader, with the main line wound onto the reel.

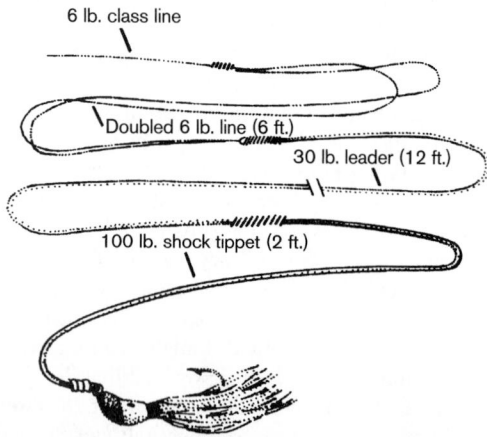

6 lb. class line

Doubled 6 lb. line (6 ft.)

30 lb. leader (12 ft.)

100 lb. shock tippet (2 ft.)

Using double line and line-to-line knots, you can create a heavy shock tippet for a light line. This example depicts lengths that conform to record-keeping rules.

To qualify for a freshwater world record, a leader may not be longer than 6 feet; if a double line is used, the combined length of leader and double line may not exceed 10 feet. For practical purposes, most freshwater fishing doesn't require a leader that is even 6 feet long, and many anglers use a leader that is no more than 4 feet long.

To qualify for a saltwater world record, a leader may not be longer than 15 feet on line classes up to 20 pounds, and the combined length of a leader and double line may be no more than 20 feet. The leader may be no longer than 30 feet on line classes over 20 pounds, and the combined length of the leader and double line may not exceed 40 feet. The greater lengths are geared more to tuna and billfish and to use with conventional tackle *(see)* or big-game tackle *(see)*.

Keep in mind that you need only a short leader to provide protection from teeth, scales, gill covers, and the like. Also, you can combine a short heavy leader with a section of double line, if necessary. Light-tackle anglers in both freshwater and saltwater can use a combination approach to very effectively fish light line with a heavy leader. The most extreme example of this, and primarily for saltwater, is to make a double length of the light main fishing line, connect it to a heavy leader, and then connect this to a short shock tippet. In some cases, the shock tippet is unnecessary. To qualify for a world record, make sure that the respective lengths of each section and the overall length conform to requirements.

In both environments, there are no restrictions regarding the strength of the leader or the material used, and this fact allows wire to be used as leader material under the same stipulations. The strength of the leader, however, should generally be only enough to provide the toughness or protection needed. For leader strength, stronger isn't always better; greater strength often also means greater diameter, which can mean greater visibility, which may translate into fewer strikes.

Nylon monofilament leaders are tied to the double line by using a number of knots *(see: knots, fishing),* with a line-to-line Uni Knot being especially useful. Two important points to consider are making a connection that retains the full breaking strength of the line—this is essential where great pressure, big fish, and light line are involved—and tying a neat knot that flows readily through the rod guides (and in some cases onto the reel spool).

Some reasons for using a nylon monofilament leader are not as obvious as the main issues of resistance to abrasion and cutting. For example, when the fish are very selective and spooky, it might be useful to fish with a leader that is lighter than the main fishing line, or to use one that is less visible (perhaps fluorocarbon). When using a Dacron or microfilament line *(see: line)* for its low stretch and high sensitivity, tying in a nylon monofilament leader may be best because it is less visible and aids in repeated retying. Likewise, using lead-core line calls for a nylon monofilament leader to overcome the visibility of the main line.

Catching large fish on light and ultralight lines is definitely aided by having at least a heavier leader (or a double line or both). And any time there is a lot of stress on the terminal end of the line (especially when landing fish), a leader or a double length of line should be a consideration.

When fish have repeatedly cut off your line or leader, or when the likelihood is high that they will, consider using a wire leader. However, the action of wire leaders is not as good as more supple nylon monofilament, no matter what the strength or diameter, and they are subject to some problems—kinking and curling—that most nylon monofilament doesn't have.

Wire Leaders

The purpose of a wire leader is to prevent the terminal line from being cut. It is generally used in circumstances where nylon monofilament is apt to fail, such as when the teeth, bill, or other portions of a fish will slice or abrade the line. There are essentially preformed and self-made wire leaders, all are level in diameter, and they come in bright or dark brown versions, with the latter preferred by most anglers (the brighter wire is more noticeable and subject to being struck by fish).

Premanufactured wire leaders from 6 to 36 inches in length are mainly used in freshwater lure casting and trolling, primarily for toothy species like northern pike, muskellunge, and payara, occasionally for lake trout, and also for peacock bass and striped bass in rough-and-tumble environs. They are also used in saltwater for some casting and inshore trolling activities, but not for heavy-duty big-game or offshore work, or when fishing bait.

The most common of these leaders are nylon-coated multistrand stainless steel leaders, which have a barrel swivel at the butt end, to which the fishing line is tied, and a snap swivel at the terminal end for connection to the lure. Some versions, however, are uncoated single-strand stainless steel and the newest and most durable ones are titanium coated. They're available in various strengths, primarily from 20 to 75 pounds, and should be used in a strength that at least meets, and preferably exceeds, the breaking strength of the main line. For casting purposes, a short wire leader is preferred, and this can be combined with a nylon monofilament leader or a section of double line. As with all wire, these leaders are subject to kinking and coiling, and you should discard them when they reach this condition because they will impair lure action and may be weakened. Titanium-coated leaders, however, resist kinking and coiling and have a much longer life.

You can make this type of leader with coated multistrand wire, wire sleeves, snaps, and snap swivels, using good crimping pliers. You can also make a less-complicated wire leader with uncoated

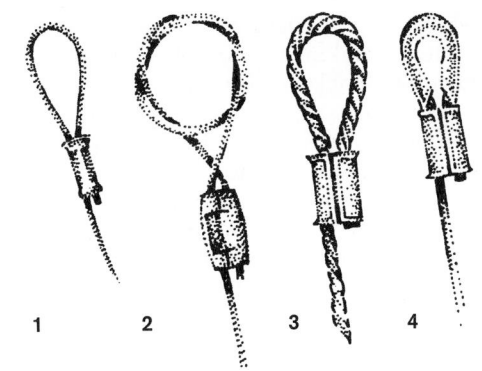

Shown are crimps of nylon monofilament: coated wire (1) cable (2) and wire with stainless steel thimble (3).

single-strand wire by connecting it directly to the lure or fly with a Haywire Twist *(see)* and then forming another Haywire at the other end, which is tied to the main line with an Albright Special knot. Twist-making and wire-straightening tools are available to assist with this, but the drawback is that this permanent wire-to-lure connection precludes quick changing of the lure or fly.

Still another option is a multistrand (braided) stainless steel wire that is flexible enough to be knotted. This has use for both fly and nonfly anglers. Likewise, short preformed light wire leaders with a preformed line tie are available from fly tackle suppliers; known as bite guards, they are available in 4- and 8-inch lengths, with one bent open end that the angler attaches to the eye of a fly by using a clever prefabricated retwistable Haywire Twist that is covered with a plastic tube. The other end is preformed into a closed loop. You can prerig these to be available for instant use as needed.

In saltwater, a heavy-duty system is used to prerig a class tippet to this wire leader, with a bunch of these stored and ready for instant use, as shown in the illustration on page 885. Using a class tippet, tie a 6-inch Bimini Twist in the butt end and then a Double Surgeon's Loop, which will loop onto the monofilament leader (connected to the fly line); tie a 3-inch Bimini onto the tag end of the tippet, then connect that to a black interlocking snap equal in strength to the weakest part of the whole system. The closed loop of the bite guard is attached to the snap.

For offshore trolling and big-game activities, it's necessary to use a longer leader made from single- or multistrand wire, which may or may not be coated with nylon. Coils of such wire are available from under 20-pound strength up to at least 250-pound strength in some varieties, and over 300 pounds in others, and in ample lengths for making numerous leaders.

Single-strand wire, also known as piano wire, is made of stainless steel and is comparatively cheap. It is nearly bulletproof when it comes to resisting cutting by a fish, but it is highly prone to kinking. This causes both minor and severe bends, the latter

L

of which change the molecular structure of the wire and greatly weaken it. Thus, while single-strand wire with a minor kink can be straightened and reliably used, wire with a major kink should be discarded, and a new leader should be used.

Multistrand wire, referred to as cable, is more supple and does not kink as readily, but it has a thicker diameter, creates more drag, and is subject to weakening when thin individual strands are nicked or cut, even though the other strands may be unaffected. It needs to be run over a stainless steel thimble when it is bent or looped to prevent kinking. Cable is more often used in short lengths and for casting, and is often available with a nylon coating, which can be a nuisance because the coating is subject to shredding and fraying by fish teeth, requiring frequent replacement of the cable.

Although premade offshore leaders of different lengths and strengths are available, most expert offshore and big-game anglers prefer to make their own. The length depends on the application, but for offshore trolling and shark fishing, wire leaders are commonly from 12 to 18 feet long but up to 28 feet long in accordance with International Game Fish Association (IGFA) record specifications. Such lengths are necessary where long fish are caught; keep in mind that a big billfish, tuna, or shark, when it swims away, is capable of thrashing its tail repeatedly against the line, which is a major reason why the wire needs to be long enough to withstand this abrasion instead of the fishing line. However, a long wire leader means that the angler can reel the fish only so far to the boat and that crew mates must "wire" the fish by grasping the wire to get the fish close enough to land—preferably the fish will be tagged and released (by cutting the line if the fish has just a bait hook in its mouth, or by unhooking and retrieving a trolling lure). Skilled mates usually do a great job of wiring a fish, but it's dangerous and problematic for a variety of reasons.

Shorter lengths are more common for most applications, with inshore and bottom fishing lengths being from a few feet long up to 10 feet. It is obviously desirable in some situations to use lighter-strength wire, which has a smaller diameter, to enhance bait or lure presentation and minimize detection, and the wire choice should be in accordance with the strength of the main fishing line.

The actual rigging of a single-strand wire leader in its simplest form requires making a Haywire Twist in the butt end that will be attached to a heavy-duty snap swivel at the end of the fishing line (which is most likely doubled); the other end is then run through the eye of a bait hook or through the connection for a prerigged natural bait or lure, and another Haywire is made. The rigged leader is neatly coiled and stored for use as necessary.

Many rigs for trolling, bottom fishing, or baitfishing require other uses of wire (and also heavy monofilament line) that involve crimping with a heavy-duty hand crimper, using single- or double-oval sleeves (which are squeezed and are better than round sleeves, which are crushed), and using nylon or stainless steel thimbles for holding a loop. Crimps should squeeze the line instead of crushing it, and in some cases two crimps are employed instead of one, but that is usually because an inferior crimping tool or sleeve is used.
See: Knots, Fishing; Line.

LEADHEAD
A jig with a lead head.
See: Jig.

LEAN
To "lean" on a fish is to bring as much pressure as the tackle and drag setting can withstand in order to land it.
See: Landing Fish.

LEDGERING
A North American spelling variation of legering *(see).*
See: Carp.

LEE
Being sheltered from the wind, as in the lee side of an island, which is the side that is protected from the wind and where many anglers find themselves fishing on rough days.

LEFT BANK
The left side of a river as viewed when facing downriver.

LEGERING
A European term for bottom fishing with bait rigs without floats, also known as ledgering. This is primarily a shore-based technique in which baits are cast a fair distance from the angler and allowed to rest on or near the bottom, generally using the lightest amount of weight or sinker possible to avoid alarming the fish yet allowing proper presentation and positioning. Rod rests and bite indicators may be used. When the angler does not leave the rod in a rest but holds it, with the reel bail open and the line between the fingers, it is called touch legering.
See: Carp.

LENOK   *Brachymystax lenok.*
A member of the Salmonidae family, the lenok is a nonanadromous troutlike species endemic to northern Asia that has some commercial value and is caught by a few adventurous anglers in remote areas.

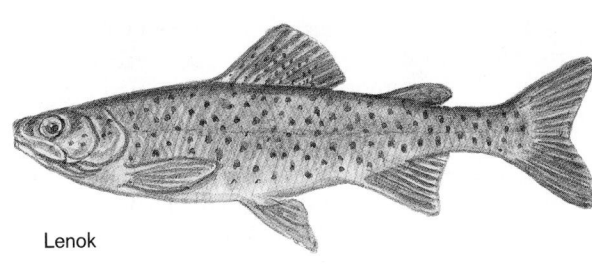

Lenok

There is believed to be just one species of this genus, found in river basins ranging from the River Ob in Siberia eastward and south to the Amur River drainage, as well as in the mountainous sections of the Yellow, Lo, and Han River drainages of China. Two forms of lenok—sharp- and blunt-snouted—have been reported from the Amur basin, however, and may be different species.

Lenok evidently do not grow large; they are reported to attain 16 pounds, and the all-tackle world record is 5 pounds, 6 ounces. They feed mainly on invertebrates, and strike lures and flies readily, including large lemming imitations fished on the surface.

LESSER ANTILLES

The Lesser Antilles are part of the West Indies archipelago and extend from Puerto Rico to the northeastern coast of South America. They include the Virgin Islands (see), Windward Islands, Leeward Islands, Netherlands Antilles, Barbados, and Trinidad and Tobago, and form a demarcation of sorts between the Caribbean Sea and the Atlantic Ocean. Some parts of the Lesser Antilles are independent nations (Barbados, and Trinidad and Tobago); others are dependencies, territories, or possessions of Great Britain, France, the Netherlands, the United States, or Venezuela.

The Leeward Islands are at the northern end of the Lesser Antilles and include Antigua, Guadeloupe, Montserrat, and Saint Kitts and Nevis. The Windward Islands are at the southern end of the Lesser Antilles and include Dominica, Grenada, Martinique, Saint Lucia, and Saint Vincent. The Netherlands Antilles include Curaçao, Bonaire, and Aruba, which are northwest of Caracas, Venezuela, as well as Saba, Saint Eustatius, and the southern half of Saint Martin (Maarten), which are southeast of Puerto Rico. Numerous islets near these main islands are also part of the Lesser Antilles.

Most of the noncoral islands in the Lesser Antilles are volcanic vestiges of submerged mountains. Deep ocean trenches are fairly close offshore and parallel to many of the islands, making some of them conducive to offshore sportfishing for pelagic gamefish. Many feature coral reefs that attract various inshore and bottom fish, and some have shallow flats conducive to sight casting or baitfishing for nearshore gamefish such as bonefish, snook, permit, and tarpon.

Many of the islands have few facilities that cater to angling, and sportfishing as a tourist attraction is lightly developed or undeveloped; boats and knowledgeable guides/captains are limited or scarce. Some have a small number of established guide and charter boat services and are slightly more developed seasonally, usually the result of individual entrepreneurial efforts. Sportfishing at a few islands has developed only lately and is still maturing. Typically, the emphasis is on big game because the deep blue water that exists on both the Atlantic and Caribbean sides of these islands (closer to some than to others), and the currents that flow past them, bring migratory species like blue marlin, Atlantic sailfish, and yellowfin tuna in particular. Islands without charter boats or inshore guide services do not necessarily lack local species or seasonal angling opportunities.

Well-equipped marinas catering to transient boaters exist at many of the islands in the Lesser Antilles, and it may be possible to find a charter service at such facilities. Resorts at the more popular islands may be able to make recommendations, but this information—particularly regarding availability and seasonal fishing opportunities—should be explored well in advance. In the Lesser Antilles, the independent nations are most likely to have some level of organized and experienced sportfishing effort.

Barbados, one of the two independent nations and also the easternmost island in the Antilles, is an island with top-flight sportfishing boats. Wahoo and dolphin are the most prevalent species caught from boats departing this 166-square-mile island, although anglers do land some blue marlin, white marlin, and sailfish.

The blue marlin are generally small, but large fish are present. One angler landed a 910-pound blue in April of 1996, and a 970-pounder was reportedly taken around the same time on a handline by a native bait fisherman. December through April or May is the blue-water season. The island is primarily surrounded by coral reefs, but inshore fisheries are limited. Local shore casters land occasional jack species and the odd permit, usually at night.

Roughly 130 miles southwest of Barbados, Grenada has the same offshore species fairly close to the island, although interest in them is low. Grenada waters harbor snook and tarpon along the east coast, however, where there are several freshwater streams.

Westward in the Netherlands Antilles, a lack of reefs and shallows minimizes inshore fishing potential, but a surfeit of yellowfin tuna, wahoo, dolphin, sailfish, white marlin, and blue marlin makes up for this. Blues are the primary target of the sportfishing fleet; nearly a dozen charter boats make them the primary quarry. They practice catch-and-release only. An 803-pounder is the biggest sport-caught blue marlin reported from Curaçao.

Similarly, eastward and at the southernmost end of the Lesser Antilles off the coast of Venezuela, the independent nation of Trinidad and Tobago offers excellent sportfishing that has garnered attention only since the mid- to late 1990s. Just a few modern sportfishing boats regularly ply its waters, which have a veritable potpourri of species, from tarpon to tuna and barracuda to blue marlin.

Tobago, the smaller of these two islands, is about 20 miles northeast of Trinidad and farther out in the deep blue water of the Atlantic. This makes it an especially attractive spot for blue marlin and yellowfin tuna, as well as dolphin and wahoo. Baitfish are plentiful here, especially in late winter and early spring. Dolphin are abundant from winter through spring, and the average fish weighs between 10 and 15 pounds, but specimens over 50 pounds have been caught. Winter through spring also yields yellowfin tuna, some weighing more than 100 pounds, 10- to 20-pound blackfin tuna, and lots of wahoo. In addition, king mackerel, cero mackerel, mutton snapper, cubera snapper, African pompano, and big barracuda inhabit the waters closer to shore.

Blue marlin are sporadic Tobago catches, although this may reflect marginal effort; huge blues have reportedly been encountered and lost here, and the potential for blue marlin is allegedly strong. Tobago is situated such that the Guiana Current, which flows northwesterly along the top of South America, pushes directly into and around this island, making it a natural for the presence of bait and pelagic species.

Blue marlin and yellowfin tuna are not in the mix at Trinidad, but sailfish and numerous other species are present. Loads of wahoo, sailfish, blackfin tuna, and dolphin frequent these waters. The wahoo often stay close to the northern rocky and steep shoreline, and the others stay a few miles offshore. Sailfishing is good from December through April; wahoo, dolphin, and tuna are good to excellent from October through May.

Relatively large as Caribbean islands go, hilly Trinidad has numerous small islets, mostly along its northern and northwestern coasts (where swift current provides superb wahoo action), and is fortuitously situated 11 miles north of the Orinoco Delta across Boca de la Serpiente. South America's second largest river, the Orinoco produces one of the world's most impressive deltas, a mangrove jungle some 160 miles across. It floods prodigiously every year as a result of interior rains from May through November, and it has a significant influence on this coastal region.

The main influx of the muddy Orinoco is a good distance from Trinidad; borne by currents, however, it turns the water around the island murky. Perhaps pushed out of the delta by increased flows, tarpon appear near the island in increasing numbers sometime in April. Although they are reportedly here year-round, they are most abundant from June through September and are predominantly caught in the passes that separate the islets. So far, tarpon are weighing in at up to 100 pounds, but larger fish are likely. They are also likely to be present in other areas of the island that are seldom fished. King mackerel are available when the tarpon are abundant. Other prevalent species include Spanish mackerel, cubera snapper, pompano, and various grouper and jacks.

Both Trinidad and Tobago have a small number of well-equipped and experienced sportfishing charter boats. Tourism is an important industry, and facilities and services are abundant.

All of the Lesser Antilles islands lie within the Tropical Zone and are influenced by trade winds. There is a dry season from roughly November through May, and a wet season from roughly June through October, although this may vary in certain years due to diverse influences. Like all islands in the Caribbean, the Lesser Antilles are susceptible to hurricanes, some of which do great damage, between July and October.

LEVEL LINE
A taperless fly line with the same weight and diameter throughout.
See: Flycasting Tackle.

LEVELWIND
A mechanism on some conventional reels and most baitcasting reels that automatically disperses line evenly across the spool when line is retrieved.
See: Baitcasting Tackle; Conventional Tackle.

LEVER DRAG REEL
A type of reel used in big-game fishing, and also known as a big-game reel, in which the drag adjustment mechanism is separate from the reel handle and doesn't turn with the handle as the star wheel drag control on a conventional reel does.
See: Big-Game Tackle.

LICE
A common external parasite on marine fish.
See: Diseases and Parasites.

LICENSE
See: Regulations.

LIE
The station or home habitat used for rest or feeding by a fish, primarily salmonids, in a river or stream. Such a location provides feeding opportunity and often shelter. Fish in stillwater adopt specific

The first jawless fishes appeared between 510 and 438 million years ago; the first fishes with jaws appeared between 438 and 410 million years ago.

locations for the same reasons, but these are rarely referred to as lies.

LIFE JACKET

A common term for a Class III personal flotation device *(see)* that is worn by an individual. It usually resembles a vest, and is sometimes called a life vest, but may be jacket style.

LIFE PRESERVER

A common term for a personal flotation device *(see)*, usually referring to a article that is worn by an individual, but also sometimes to a buoyant cushion, ring buoy, or horseshoe buoy that is thrown to someone in the water, who holds onto it until help arrives.

LIFT BITE

The upward lift of a properly balanced float *(see)* indicating that a fish has taken the hookbait.

LIFTING

A manner of taking fish by rod and reel in which the fish is hooked in the mouth without having struck the lure or bait. Lifting is viewed by some (including law enforcement officials) as a manner of snagging *(see)*, except that fish are hooked inside of the mouth, although they did not actively strike the offering. The lure, fly, or bait (generally bait) is repeatedly floated near a resting fish in such a way that it passes across the open mouth of the fish; when the offering is inside the mouth area, the rod tip is raised to set the hook point into the inner mouth of the fish, thus giving the appearance of hooking a fish fairly.

This activity is practiced by unscrupulous anglers on Great Lakes tributaries, primarily for steelhead and salmon, and in close situations where holding fish can be observed and presentations can be deliberately and repeatedly made. It is often difficult to detect a person who is doing this, although repeatedly lifting the rod tip up at the end of a bait's drift may be a giveaway. Inexperienced anglers have unknowingly watched crafty lifters repeatedly catch fish using this method when others were unable to hook a fish. It is a difficult activity to police, and unfair and unethical to practice.
See: Ethics and Etiquette.

LIGHTHOUSE

A prominent aid to navigation supporting a light that is visible for a long distance and that marks a prominent point of the mainland, a harbor entrance, an offshore hazard, or islands and shoals. Technically known as primary seacoast and navigational lights, lighthouses may also issue a fog signal or radar beacon.

LIGHT METER

A portable electronic device used by a relatively small number of freshwater anglers to measure the light intensity of prospective fishing water at various levels as a guide to using the most visible color of lure for the species they seek.

Manufacturers of light meters for anglers maintain that, as a rule of thumb, the depth at which the available light drops to 50 percent is a good point at which to start fishing. Smaller, more natural-colored lures may work best under brighter conditions, whereas larger lures in more reflective colors may work better where light penetration is less. A light meter is primarily of use in situations where vision is the primary sense that fish rely upon for locating prey.

A greater discussion of light, lure color, and fish behavior is contained under the subheading of color in the lure entry.
See: Lure.

LIGHT STICK

A chemiluminescent stick that glows in the dark or in low light conditions and is used in conjunction with bait or some lures to draw attention to them. Light sticks are most often used with deep nighttime angling for swordfish *(see)*.

LIGHT-TACKLE FISHING

Anglers often talk about using light tackle, which is a vague term that means different things to different people. There is no established standard for what constitutes light tackle, since the species, size of average catch, angling circumstances, and other factors all vary on a case by case basis in both freshwater and saltwater. Furthermore, some tackle that would be considered heavy in freshwater is considered light in certain saltwater situations. For example, 4- to 8-pound line on spinning tackle is light for largemouth bass and northern pike, but 12-pound test on baitcasting tackle used for the same species is not. Yet, 12-pound baitcasting tackle is light for muskellunge, and lighter spinning gear is inappropriate for that species. The same 12-pound baitcasting tackle would be light for casting to saltwater stripers and ultralight if used on tarpon.

Although most people directly associate light tackle with the breaking strength of the line, this is not an absolute criterion. Generally, the use of any gear that calls upon above-average efforts to hook, play, and land a fish is light. If even greater effort or more extreme skill is needed to do these things, it is ultralight.

Thus, the hallmarks of using lighter than average fishing equipment are a good bow in the rod, a lot of stress on the line, a good scrap by small fish and a real battle for larger ones, and the need to take extra steps to keep a moderate-size fish from getting free. They also include taking more than a few

Using a long rod with light line, an angler can cast great distances but faces the challenge of delicately working a fish; this scene is in the Beaufort Sea at Victoria Island, Nunavut Territory.

in demanding circumstances, and playing large fish require the most from your line *(see: line)*. Light line must be checked periodically for nicks and abrasions, and replaced more often if severely stressed. Only the best knots, tied consistently perfect, will do for light tackle, since more is demanded of these critical connections.

Hooksetting *(see)* can be more difficult with light line if you're timid, but you must be able to set the hook with authority no matter what tackle you use, and this requires confidence in the condition of your line and the ability of your knots. Hooksetting is enhanced by having the sharpest hooks. Maintaining ultrasharp hooks *(see: hook sharpening)* also helps minimize losing fish.

Another aid to successful fishing with light tackle is using a doubled length of line or a heavier leader, both to ensure greater strength in the knot and to help minimize the effects of abrasion. Some fish writhe a lot in the water near the boat and can easily wrap themselves up in the first few feet of line. They can snap it under the right circumstances, or at least abrade it. The doubled line or heavier leader makes dealing with strong fish on light tackle easier at the boat, which is where a lot of good fish are lost. Depending on the species and the circumstances, you may want to double the last 3 to 5 feet of light line used on casting tackle with a Bimini Twist or Spider Hitch knot *(see: knots, fishing)*, keeping it just short enough that the knot doesn't reach the spool of the reel. You should have no trouble casting these knots through the rod guides if you make them correctly, especially with smaller lines.

When angling for big fish with light line on a spinning outfit, it can be worthwhile to first make a 3- to 4-foot section of doubled line and then add a 2- to 3-foot heavier leader to it using a Uni Knot. Tying good knots is obviously very important here, but this setup really helps avoid abrasion and overcome near-the-boat stress. For some toothy species, add a short wire leader to the heavier monofilament leader or to the doubled line.

Another key component of light-line fishing is using drag *(see)* properly. You should have a reel with a smooth-operating drag, one that doesn't stick when initially needed and doesn't jerk or hesitate during use. Setting the drag properly is critical when tangling with strong fish on light tackle because the drag will be used often. Do not set the drag too loose, which impedes hooksetting (the drag slips) and puts too little pressure on a fish; and don't set it too tight, which might cause the line to snap under the extreme pressure of a surging fish. Knowing your limits, based on the line strength, the effectiveness of your knots, and the type of tackle that you're using, will determine how you play a fish caught on light tackle.

Playing and landing fish.   Under ideal conditions of little boat traffic or few anglers nearby, you can play a strong fish in open water without too

seconds to land even a small fish and using skills and finesse more often than brawn.

Since ultralight fishing is just an extension of using light tackle, and in some cases may be nearly the same thing, it will be considered the same for purposes of reviewing the basic aspects of light-tackle fishing.

Advantages.   In addition to the obvious elements of fun and challenge, there are practical advantages to using light gear, especially line that is lighter in strength than might ordinarily be employed. One of these advantages is producing more strikes. In many circumstances—including when fish are spooky, heavily pressured, or generally turned off—using a fine-diameter line and a lighter lure will induce more strikes, and the lighter tackle is especially beneficial when angling in very clear water. Also, a light line can make a strike easier to detect and make your cast go farther.

Casting distance is an overrated aspect of angling *(see: casting)* because there are downsides to making long casts (it is more difficult to set the hook when a fish strikes a long distance away). However, when you must fish in a stiff wind, a lighter and finer-diameter line offers less wind resistance.

Necessary components.   No matter how you define light tackle or what you fish for, the elements of using it are the same. Rods used for light tackle fishing tend to be a bit limber in order to provide more of a cushion for the lightness of the line. They can be short for small fish like stream trout or panfish, but a longer rod is a distinct advantage for landing big fish. Long rods (7 to 9 feet is the norm but 10- to 14-footers are used by some anglers) give you more leverage to pressure a fish, putting less strain on your arms and wrists, and they're very helpful when a hooked fish is near the boat and you need to steer around obstacles.

An important aspect of light tackle use is having fresh line in top condition. Using light line, fishing much difficulty because the line has nothing to snag on. The deck can be cleared and the boat maneuvered to your advantage. If the drag is set properly, the fish can take plenty of line and do its stuff. But if there are obstructions beneath the surface, or if you hook a big fish unexpectedly in a place having plenty of snags, then you have to be very aggressive and take the fight to the fish as quickly and as well as you can.

Fish captured on any tackle are easier to release if they are landed as quickly as possible. Since a quick landing is a little more difficult with light tackle, an extra effort must be made to play the fish correctly; if the landing takes too long, the fish may be so thoroughly exhausted that it cannot recover when (if) it is released.

By pumping and reeling and keeping pressure on the fish at all times, you tire it out. When you rest on a big fish, it rests and the battle is prolonged. So you must work the fish constantly (see: playing fish).

If you use good equipment, including a quality line with a knot that retains full strength and a rod with backbone, you can pressure a fish very well with light tackle. Depending on whether you're in a boat in open water or on a river bank, you'll probably be unable to land a really big fish by playing tug-of-war. You'll have to pump and reel whenever possible to gain on the fish, but you'll almost certainly have to change your position to work the fish more effectively. You may have to walk the bank or wade downstream after a big river fish because you won't have the muscle to coerce it back upstream. You may have to get below the fish or at least get into a section of river that has less current. On a lake, you may need to move the boat in order to change the angle of pull on the fish.

With light tackle it's important to pressure a fish from the very beginning and to periodically change the angle of tension from vertical to horizontal (left and right), which directs the fish away from obstructions and keeps it disoriented. When the fish swims off, let the drag do the work; otherwise, try to gain line at every chance. If the drag is a bit too loose and the line slips when you pump, use some extra tension (place your thumb on a bait-casting spool, palm on a spinning-reel spool, and fingertips on the inside of a fly-reel spool).

Disadvantages. Using light tackle does have a few disadvantages. It's possible that you might lose a few more fish with light tackle than you would ordinarily. If you can lose a good fish and not be upset about it, if you can lose a good fish and still enjoy the moment, if you can lose a good fish and feel good for the fish—then you have the right attitude for using light (and especially ultralight) gear. You'll definitely lose more lures and hooks with light tackle than with heavier gear; light line is frayed and weakened more easily, mistakes are magnified, and hangups on the bottom are harder to free. Also, since you generally can't use large, heavy lures, casting and hooksetting may pose problems.

These are minor issues, however. Light tackle under the right circumstances is very appropriate for freshwater and saltwater, and more people should gear up for fish of average size than for extreme size. However, some circumstances are inappropriate for light tackle, so be practical. Largemouth bass, for example, are caught in some areas where you can't work an appropriate lure if your tackle is too light; it would not be good sportsmanship to hook a large bass in a field of lily pads by using a wimpy rod and super-fine line, only to have the fish break off with a hook in its mouth and probably trailing a stream of nylon line. Ditto for when you're steelhead fishing in a deep swift pool and have to use many ounces of lead to get a bait or lure down; there you need a heavy rod to muscle fish away from snags, other anglers, anchor lines, and the like.

You can catch big fish on light tackle, as well as more fish of average size, if you know what you're doing. The seriousness and the effect of making mistakes when using ultralight gear is greatly magnified. The margin of error is slim, and there's no gimme even if you use perfect knots, have good reel drag, and skillfully battle fish. Therefore, it takes a more complete angler, with well-rounded skills, to be consistently effective.

LIMBLINE
A line that is anchored at one point, often to the limb or trunk of a dead or overhanging tree, and that is not connected to a hand-operated mechanical reel.
See: Setline.

LIMESTONE STREAM
A stream that flows through a bedrock of limestone or through land laced with varying degrees of limestone deposits. Also known as chalk streams because of their whitish, chalk-colored complexion, limestone streams are extremely rich in aquatic insects and plant life and are a favorite of trout anglers, although they are much fewer in number than freestone streams (see). Their pristine, clear waters produce trout that some anglers consider to be larger, wilier, and often more brightly colored than trout living in most freestone streams.

Whereas freestone streams flowing off mountains or hillsides are fed from a single watershed, limestone streams may collect water from several watersheds through a far-ranging network of underground channels. The limestone aquifers in which the water gathers can carry a large quantity of water over some distance through underground solution channels. These channels usually are no more than 1 or 2 feet in diameter. Several of these channels may come together where they cut through the ground surface to spew cold waters to the outside. These springs are often quite large, with flows of 2,000 to more than 15,000 gallons of water per minute.

Limestone streams generally are meadow streams emanating from calcium-rich rock on the valley floor. Often, these valleys are bounded by sandstone ridges. As sinkholes develop and solution channels and caverns form, limestone is dissolved into the water. The water is gin-clear, but boiling it in a tea kettle will prove that there's a great deal of dissolved limestone present, since the water leaves a residue behind.

Limestone streams have an advantageous ability to neutralize acid precipitation. This natural buffering effect is due to high levels of calcium carbonate, which provides naturally high levels of alkalinity (in many cases from 7.5 to 8.0 year-round). With high alkalinity, these streams are extremely fertile. They hold abundant populations of such aquatic insects as mayflies and midges, and large populations of crustaceans like scuds and sowbugs.

Limestone streams can be shallow or deep, sometimes deceptively deep because of their clarity, and can have a thick growth of aquatic vegetation, which may include waterweed and watercress. They are often bordered by high grasses, rich bogs, and overhanging willow trees.

Most limestone streams support a much heavier food base than freestone streams. The even temperature of these spring-fed waters allows aquatic life to feed and grow throughout most of the year.

LIMIT

A restriction on the size or number of fish that can be taken, caught, or killed. Limit refers to regulations that have been established, usually with reference to recreational fishermen but in some cases also to commercial fishermen. Regulations pertaining to numbers of fish are called bag, creel, daily, and possession limits; regulations pertaining to size are called minimum length, total length, or slot limits.

See: Bag Limit; Creel Limit; Possession Limit; Minimum Length Limit; Slot Limit; Fisheries Management; Regulations.

LINE

Line is the element of fishing tackle that delivers a lure or bait from a rod to the water. In its simplest form, a piece of thread tied to the tip of a willow branch and used to dangle a worm-baited hook in the water constitutes a fishing line. Indeed, horsehair, cotton, and silk are among the materials that were once used as fishing line. Today, fishing line is synonymous with synthetic and technologically engineered products possessing attributes conducive to the various types of angling and manufactured to provide specific performance features, whether cast, trolled, or merely dangled.

Often overlooked and usually unappreciated, especially by freshwater anglers, line is a necessary and important component of fishing. It plays

Fishing line is an angler's most critical connection, and it sometimes undergoes a lot of stress.

arguably *the* prominent role in the three most important aspects of catching fish: presentation, hooking, and landing. When all facets of fishing technique and fishing tackle use are taken into consideration, line becomes the single most important equipment item. To get the most out of your equipment, and to be more successful on the water, every angler should understand the types of line available, the properties of fishing line, and fundamental aspects of line use.

History of Modern Line

Today's angler is incredibly spoiled when it comes to fishing line. Ask contemporary anglers what kind of line was used a century ago and they will be hard-pressed to answer. This is a credit to the role that modern lines—especially nylon monofilament—have come to occupy in sportfishing.

Most fishing line in the early 1900s was made of linen, silk, and even cotton. As natural fibers, those lines required a lot of attention and tender loving care from the angler. Most lines then, for example, had to be rinsed and unspooled periodically to dry off and to deter line rot. And the lines of that time had nowhere near the performance properties of today's lines, much less the early monofilaments.

Although braided Dacron lines came into prominence for casting and trolling purposes, and were a step up from other products, especially in terms of maintenance, they, too, were problematic. However, the real change in line usage that led to today's products occurred in the period from 1934 to 1958. It started with the discovery of synthetic superpolymers, which is credited to the brilliant DuPont research chemist Dr. Wallace H. Carothers, who perfected their development in the mid-1930s. The turning point that came to benefit virtually all anglers happened in 1935 in a chemist's laboratory about 100 yards from Brandywine Creek in Wilmington, Delaware, when researchers succeeded in spinning a synthetic fiber with a high melt point.

In October of 1938, DuPont announced the discovery of a "group of new synthetic superpolymers" from which textile fibers could be spun with a strength-elasticity factor surpassing that of cotton, silk, wool, or rayon. DuPont called this group nylon, a play on the suggested name "no run," with respect to its value as a replacement for silk in the manufacture of stockings. In 1939, DuPont began the first commercial production of nylon monofilament fishing line; that same year, nylon stockings were introduced at the New York and San Francisco World's Fairs. Although both were significant developments, the value of fishing line was not as apparent as that of hosiery; 64 million pairs of all-nylon hose were sold in the first 12 months of production until halted by the advent of World War II.

For nearly 20 years, nylon monofilament fishing line would grow in popularity but not supplant the older fishing lines, particularly braided Dacron. By comparison with today's nylon monofilament, the early nylon line was primitive. Nevertheless, for its time, the early nylon line was durable, resisted abrasion, and didn't break readily; unfortunately, it also was thick and lacked uniformity.

The emergence of spinning reels and later spincasting reels (see: spincasting tackle; spinning tackle) caused line to undergo changes, since the nylon monofilament then was too limp to come off these reels properly. The era of modern lines began when a high-quality product called Stren was introduced in 1958 by DuPont, becoming the first line to be marketed with the DuPont name (previously, DuPont had made the line for others). This product had properties that allowed it to be used with different types of reels for varied fishing activities, and it became known as a premium line. In the vernacular of the modern age, it would be called a "super line."

The development of a thin and uniform-quality line with balanced properties was certainly an evolutionary milestone that made nylon monofilament the dominant (and at times nearly universally used) fishing line. And the uniformly embraced nylon monofilament became a catalyst for other tackle development and for a boom in sportfishing popularity because it helped make the various acts of fishing much easier.

Types

Line is made from different materials in varying strengths, diameters, and colors. It is manufactured in strengths ranging from 1 pound to 200 pounds, with 6- through 20-pound strengths being most popular. Some heavier strengths are made, but these are used only in special applications. Line is supplied on spools of varying but continuous lengths, from 100 yards up to many thousands of yards. The largest spools, with 6,000 yards of line or more, are called service spools and are used by retailers for filling many reels, by fishing clubs, and by some record-seeking anglers who change line often. Bulk spools range in size from 600 to 2,000 yards and may be useful to anglers who fish often. Most anglers use 250-yard spools.

Although there are many hybrid products, line is essentially characterized as being monofilament, braided, or having a core. Nylon monofilament accounts for more than two-thirds of all fishing lines sold, the remainder being essentially braided microfilament, fused microfilament, braided Dacron line, weighted line, wire line, and fly line.

Weighted, wire, and fly lines are distinctly different in principal usage than most other lines. Weighted and wire lines are trolled rather than cast. Fly line is cast but is used to carry nearly weightless objects; other lines that are cast are carried by the weight of the object being cast. These three types of line are discussed elsewhere (see: flycasting tackle; weighted line; wire line).

Monofilament. "Monofilament" is a word that means a single strand of line, but in sportfishing the name has become synonymous with nylon line. Nylon monofilament, also referred to as mono, was first introduced as leader material in 1939, and it became popular as fishing line in the 1950s. It became extraordinarily popular with the introduction and refinement of top-quality spinning and spincasting tackle.

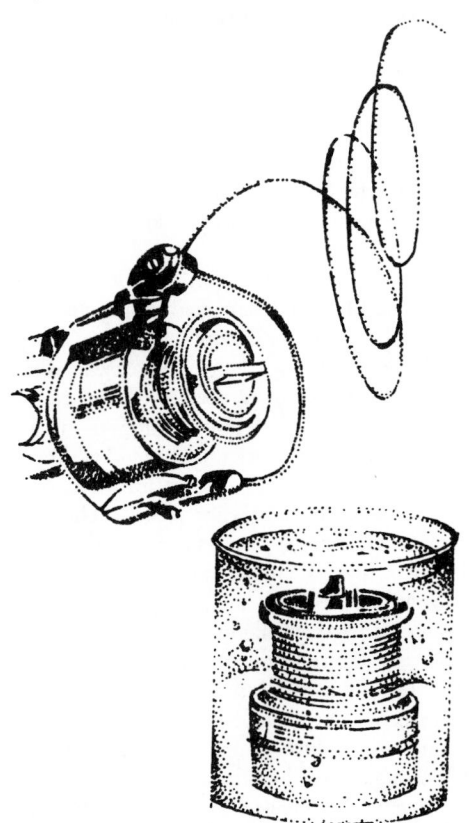

One way to remove coils from nylon monofilament line is to take the spool off the reel and soak it for a while (an hour for line that hasn't been used in a long time); the line absorbs water, relaxes, and becomes limp.

Nylon monofilament line, as the name suggests, is a single-component product. It is formed through an extrusion process in which molten plastic is formed into a strand through a die. Nylon monofilament lines are polymeric by-products of crude oil processing. Nylon alloys, a mixture of various types of nylon, are also used to form fishing line; fluorocarbon *(see)* is such a product. Although various brands of nylon monofilament line possess the same derivatives, the way they are processed and extruded and the way their molecules are compounded determine the different characteristics of the line and its properties. Additionally, premium-grade lines receive more quality-control attention, more additives, and more attention in the finishing processes than non-premium line. As a result, they cost more.

Braided. Braided lines consist of intertwined strands of material, technically making them a multifilament product. Today that material is Dacron, gel-spun polyethylene fiber, or aramid fiber.

Braided line was once synonymous with Dacron, and before the discovery of nylon it was a primary line for fishing. However, nylon monofilament proved to be so superior to braided Dacron (which possessed poor knot strength, low abrasion resistance, and little stretch) that Dacron nearly disappeared in fishing, and today it has an infinitesimally small niche in the marketplace. It remains in use primarily as a backing material on fly reels; for a very few anglers, it is used as a big-game trolling product or a baitcasting reel product.

In the early 1990s, braided lines made from high-tech fibers became available. Because these lines featured great strength with small diameter, and because the fiber and no-stretch characteristics enhanced sensitivity, they became known as "super lines" or "microfilaments." Also called performance lines, microfilaments are braided from gel-spun polyethylene fiber (different grades or generations of Spectra, Dyneema, or Tekmillon) or from aramid fiber (Kevlar). The synthetic fiber itself, which is 10 times stronger than steel, has been used in industrial, aerospace, and military applications, and is incredibly strong yet very thin. Individual strands of fiber are married through an intricate, time-consuming, and costly braiding process. The result is an ultrathin, super-strong, and very sensitive line.

Fused. Braided microfilaments were popular for a while but yielded to a superior product made by fusing, rather than braiding, the same fibers. In this process, multiple microfilaments of gel-spun polyethylene fibers are fused together to produce what appears to be a single-strand line that is also ultrathin, super strong, and very sensitive, yet highly castable. Fused microfilament is a relatively new category of high-performance fishing line that has the same characteristics as its braided predecessor but a more affordable price (fusing is cheaper than braiding). It has garnered a section of the fishing line market, mostly for specific applications rather than all-around use.

Properties

The ultimate test of a fishing line is how it performs when used in all aspects of angling. That performance is based upon the properties that are engineered into the line. Until recently it was believed that a good line was one that had a proper balance of characteristics, primarily being strong, relatively thin, and durable. To a large degree, that is still true, although technological advancements have allowed manufacturers to manipulate properties to improve certain performance features. This has resulted in a wider variety of products than ever, some confusion among consumers, and also much better fishing line.

The most significant advancement in fishing line technology has been the evolution of thinner-diameter products. Anglers have always wanted a line that was strong and thin. Thin-diameter lines enable lures to work better and are less visible to fish. Thin-diameter lines have changed the complexion of line discussions; previously anglers spoke of line in terms of the rated strength, knowing that lines of similar strength also had similar diameter. But with the emergence of lines of conventional strength but unconventional diameter, the game has changed and anglers often unwittingly find themselves comparing apples to oranges.

Most anglers do not take the time to learn about the properties of line; if they did, they would purchase line more wisely and evaluate it more closely when using it. The properties include the following:

Breaking strength. The most prominent feature of any line is its strength, that is, how much pressure must be applied to the unknotted line before the molecules part and the line breaks. Unfortunately, this is an area with a great deal of disparity between products, and one that is poorly understood by many anglers.

All spools of line are labeled to indicate their breaking strength. Some are labeled with the customary United States designation in pounds, some with metric designation in kilograms, some with both. Those that are labeled with both are often not quite accurate; an 8-pound designation may be followed by a small-print designation of 4 kilograms, which actually equals 8.8 pounds.

There are two breaking strength categories: "test" and "class."

Class lines are predominantly used by saltwater big-game tournament anglers, by anglers specifically interested in establishing line-class world records (world records are kept for all species based on strength of line used as well as in all-tackle designations; *see: records),* and by fastidious anglers who want to know exactly what their line strength is. Class lines are guaranteed to break *at or under* the labeled metric strength in a wet condition, in order to conform to the metric world-record specifications of the International Game Fish Association (IGFA), which is the repository for world-record fish. Lines that conform to this guarantee are labeled on the packaging as "class" or "IGFA class." Class line is more expensive than test line and is primarily differentiated from test line in the wet breaking strength feature; its other properties should be similar to those of test lines.

The reason for fishing with a class line is partly to ensure that a fish that might be a record would meet the criteria. If line is tested and found to be slightly stronger than it should be for the parameters of a specific category, then it would be disqualified or bumped into a higher strength category for consideration. Line is tested by the IGFA in a wet condition because line is wet when it is fished and because the wet breaking strength of some lines—most notably nylon monofilament—is weaker than the dry breaking strength. There may be as much as a 20 percent difference in strength among some lines, and a negligible percentage in others. Another reason for fishing with class line is the certainty of knowing the basic strength of your line; the actual breaking strength of similarly labeled test lines varies greatly.

Any line that is not labeled as class line is, by default, test line. Perhaps 95 percent of all line sold is categorized as test, even if the word "test" is not used on the label. Despite the labeled strength, there is no guarantee as to the amount of force required to break the line in either a wet or a dry condition. The labeled strength may not reflect the actual force required to break the line in a wet condition. Since there are no guarantees with test line, they may break at, under, or over the labeled strength. An overwhelming number break above the labeled strength, some just a little above, some very far above.

To illustrate the breaking strength difference, anglers fishing with a class 12-pound line are fishing with a product that will break at slightly less than 12 pounds in a wet state, whereas those fishing with a good-quality test 12-pound line are using a product that will probably break at somewhere between 13 and 14 pounds in a wet state. This difference between labeled and actual breaking strength may not sound like much, but there are situations when it is considerably different. In an extreme example, a poor-quality test 12-pound line may break at 15 or 16 pounds in a wet state, making it a deliberately mislabeled product.

Since there is a great deal of difference in the actual breaking strength of various test lines, and since people only know what the label tells them, many anglers fish with line that is much stronger than what they think it is. And many are mislead into believing that some lines are stronger than others because they physically feel that way. It is meaningless to take a piece of nylon monofilament, wrap it around your hand, tug on it, and proclaim it has great strength. This is dry strength, which is irrelevant.

To determine the actual fishing strength of a line, you have to soak it in water for a while and then test it. Since few anglers have the machinery to

All kinds of line are tested for world-record fish certification by the International Game Fish Association; here, a sophisticated machine tests a line sample and records results on a computer.

calibrate exact breaking strengths, they are usually in the dark as to the actual strength of a line, although some independent analyses (with widely varying results) have been published.

The difference between labeled breaking strength and actual breaking strength exists in braided and fused products as well. Microfilaments technically do not absorb water and do not change in strength from dry to wet. However, tests indicate that their breaking strength varies a good deal from what is labeled (usually being lower) and that they may not break at the same strength consistently. Fluorocarbon line is one in which there is no discernible weakening in a wet state, although there may be some inconsistency in actual versus labeled breaking strength.

To many anglers, who do not push their tackle to the limits and who do not catch large fish or do not angle under difficult circumstances, the amount of difference between labeled strength and actual strength and between wet strength and dry strength is largely nit-picking. However, for anglers who need top performance and who fish to exacting specifications, an understanding of actual breaking strength is vitally important.

Diameter. It used to be that the breaking strength of a line was directly related to its diameter. The greater the breaking strength, the larger the diameter. However, in recent years nylon monofilament line manufacturers have found a way to produce ultrathin lines that have the same performance characteristics as conventional mono but that are markedly thinner. The newer microfilaments are exceptional in regard to thin diameter; a line with 24-pound breaking strength may have a diameter equivalent to a conventional 10- or 12-pound-strength line. Therefore, the diameter of a line is no longer necessarily a corollary to its breaking strength.

This creates some confusion between anglers discussing the merits or demerits of certain products or

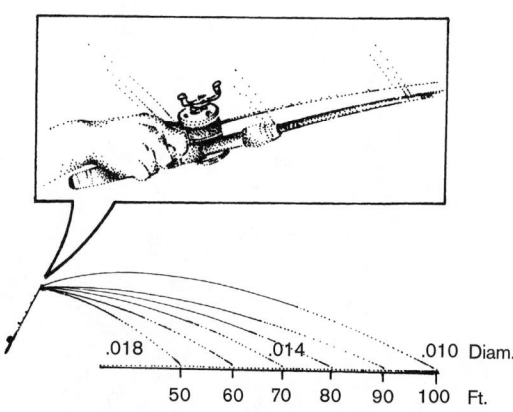

There is a clear relationship between casting distance and line diameter when using the same weight lure.

strengths of line, as well as confusion in anglers doing comparison shopping. There is some concern among anglers that thin-diameter lines are more susceptible to abrasion, since it once was true that thicker-diameter lines were better at resisting abrasion. In some conventional lines, and in poorer-quality lines, that is still true; however, many thin-diameter lines also have a high-degree of abrasion resistance as well.

Line diameter has some bearing on the amount of line that will fit on a spool—and therefore on the amount of line that is available for fighting strong fish. This is of special concern to light-tackle anglers who need plenty of line on a reel. It also impacts the size of knots, especially line-to-line knots, and may affect how well they sit on a reel spool or flow through a reel or rod guides. It is also a factor in achieving distance when casting and in getting lures to work effectively; thinner line has less drag and can be cast farther, and it allows lures to dive or sink deeper or faster. In some cases, it even enhances the action of lures. Because thin-diameter lines are less visible to fish, they are also conducive to getting more strikes, especially in clear water.

Perhaps one day anglers will have to become better attuned to thinking in terms of diameter in order to make valid comparisons between line. Only fly anglers, basically because of their use of fine leaders (see) and tippets (see), have some understanding of numerically based line diameter, some going to the extent of using a micrometer to measure diameter. To really compare products, you have to know what the diameter is as well as what the actual breaking strength is. Some manufacturers are providing diameter information on their nylon monofilaments but not on braided or fused microfilaments. Solid, round, single-strand nylon monofilament provides a uniform diameter and is easy to evaluate, but other products do not provide consistent or necessarily accurate diameter measurements.

Abrasion Resistance. Abrasion resistance is one of the most difficult qualities of line to measure because no laboratory test has yet been devised that accurately reflects the abrasive contact that line is subjected to during fishing conditions. Some lines are more abrasion resistant than others due to greater diameter, the composition of the line, or a coating that is applied to it. Determining the differences among brands is subjective, although some lines do seem to be considerably more resistant to abrasion than others. However, you can make this judgment only through use.

Fishing line manufacturers have often showcased the alleged abrasion-resistant property of their line by mechanically scraping it and competitive lines, all in a dry state, repeatedly over sandpaper. This is irrelevant and unrelated to actual fishing situations, where a wet line is making contact with rocks, fish teeth and gill covers, barnacles, propellers, and all sorts of objects.

Some lines, particularly premium nylon monofilaments and fluorocarbon, have excellent abrasion resistance. Some are just barely adequate. Lack of abrasion resistance was braided Dacron's biggest drawback when it was a commonly used line, and microfilaments, though better than braided Dacron, do not seem to be remarkably good in this area either. Manufacturers claim that fused microfilament lines have better abrasion resistance than nylon monofilament lines, but this has not been proven on the water. Their claim has to do with the fact that because of the high number of filaments used in the manufacturing process, there can be some abrasion without sacrificing the integrity of the line. The experience of some anglers, however, is that the abrasion resistance of microfilament lines is actually poorer than that of good-quality nylon monofilament lines.

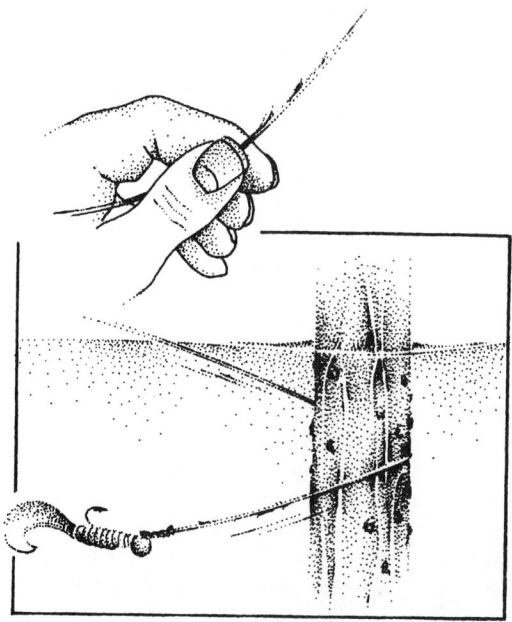

It's a very good idea to periodically run your fingers over the terminal end of fishing line to check for nicks and abrasions because some circumstances are more likely than others to cause abrasion.

Many anglers have to contend with abrasion. Sometimes you have to cut off nicked line every half hour or so while fishing because the conditions are so tough on line. The thinner the diameter of line, the more damaging abrasion can be. Contact with rocks, trees, stumps, vegetation, and fish can wear heavily on line, so selecting one with satisfactory abrasion resistance is important, but not so easy. Keep in mind that no castable line completely withstands abrasion, but some withstand it better than others. The key is to find a line that resists abrasion adequately while still having other properties important for fishing performance.

Stretch. Most lines stretch. The issue is how much they stretch and how this impacts your fishing. Stretch, which is also referred to as elasticity and elongation, is both good and bad. It allows for mistakes in fighting a fish, inadequate drag setting, or countering sudden close-to-the-angler surges by strong fish; yet it hampers the inattentive angler who forgets to keep all of the slack out of the line when setting the hook or who is inexperienced at detecting strikes, especially at long distances.

The average percent of stretch in nylon monofilaments was once around 30 percent in a wet state but now has been reduced in better products to a range of 10 to 25 percent. Nylon monofilament line has slightly more stretch in a wet state than in a dry one. Lines that have high stretch are great for casting, but they are terrible for hooksetting and playing fish because they have the elasticity of a rubber band. The cushioning effect that has been provided by lines with controlled stretch has been important to many anglers, and they are accustomed to it.

On the other hand, having low stretch should increase an angler's ability to detect strikes, aid hooksetting, provide more control in playing a fish, increase the sensitivity of the line so that the angler can feel what a lure or bait is doing, and theoretically help catch more fish. These have been the most important attributes of microfilaments, which have virtually no stretch (or up to 4 percent).

A simple way to detect the difference as it relates to a typical angling situation is to take a 40-foot length of wet microfilament and a similar length of wet nylon monofilament, and connect one end to a firm object and the other to identical fishing rods. Set the hook on each. The lack of stretch and the greater hooksetting ability of the fiber line will be immediately apparent.

A similar way to test this, using the same length of wet line, is to measure the lengths of these lines when you apply an equal amount of pulling tension on them. For instance, if you take a 40-foot length of wet microfilament, connect it to a good scale, and pull on it until only 1 pound of pressure is exerted, you'll see that it doesn't stretch. Take a wet 40-foot length of a good-quality nylon monofilament, do the same thing, and it will stretch a long way.

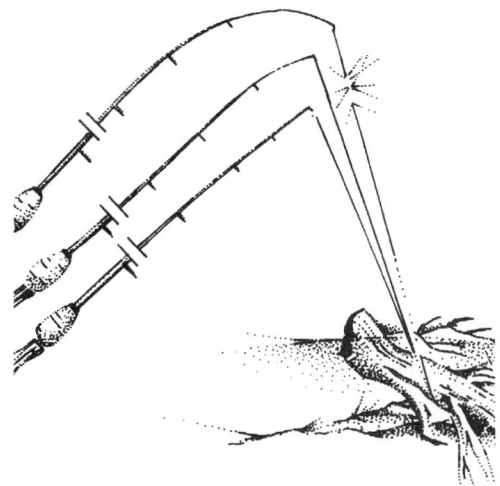

When a line is stretched too far, it reaches a breaking point or is damaged beyond usefulness, which can compromise its strength when you later fight a strong fish.

Stretch is a feature that directly relates to sensitivity. You may have seen film of fish sucking in a lure and then spitting it out, without the angler knowing that he or she had a strike. This illustrates the difference that stretch and sensitivity make. The less stretch, the more sensitivity; the more sensitivity, the better you should detect fish.

Although you would think that it would be best to fish with a line that had virtually no stretch, such as the different microfilaments, many anglers have tremendous difficulty with these products precisely because they have no stretch and are unforgiving. Anglers set the hook too hard or pull too intensely on a hooked fish and yank the hook out of the fish. Because of low stretch, anglers have to use these products differently than nylon monofilament, and they need to make adjustments (such as decreasing the reel drag and using a more limber rod).

It is worth noting that line-pulling tests and demonstrations notwithstanding, a fair amount of stretch in a line may not be as significant a factor in your fishing as it would seem, depending upon the circumstances. For example, a line that has 15 percent wet stretch may not impair your ability to detect a strike or set the hook if it is used at fairly short angling distances and the fish are not especially large or tough. If you go by the numbers, a 40-foot section of line with 15 percent stretch should elongate another 6 feet. But this simply does not happen at the moment you set the hook, say when using a 10-pound line on a jig while fishing the bottom for a 3-pound walleye. Stretch doesn't enter the equation until an appropriate amount of force is applied to the line. If the fish is extremely large, it may, after the hookset and while you are fighting it, stretch the line up to that 15 percent margin, but not before you set the hook. If you fish at closer distances, as you would, for example, when dabbling a minnow for crappies 15 feet below your boat, there is no concern. If you are fishing in places

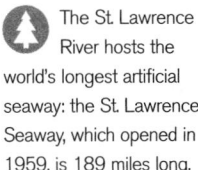

The St. Lawrence River hosts the world's longest artificial seaway: the St. Lawrence Seaway, which opened in 1959, is 189 miles long.

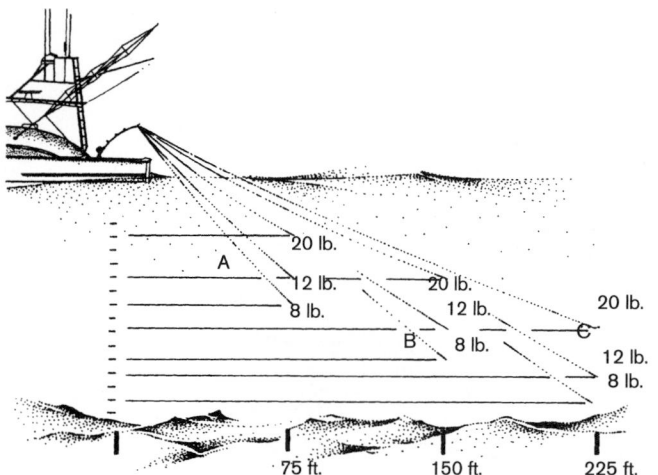

This representation of trolling a deep-diving plug with different strengths (also diameters) and lengths of lines depicts the differences that exist. Longer lines (C) take lures deeper than shorter lines (A and B), and lighter/thinner lines (8 lb.) get lures deeper than heavier/thicker lines.

where a strong fish could peel off a lot of line and cut you off on some obstruction, then you do need to think about stretch very seriously; when a bottom-caught fish applies a lot of pressure to the line, it will cause that line to stretch, and that stretch may allow a fish (like an amberjack or grouper, for example) to get to an object that will cut the line. This happens often to anglers.

At longer distances, there is also reason to be concerned about stretch, which, compounded with the action of the rod, absorbs some amount of energy and does make both strike detection and hooksetting more difficult. For example, if you have 120 feet of line out, which might be common when trolling, and even if you're using a line that stretches only 10 percent, mathematically you might receive 12 feet of undesirable stretch when pressure is applied. Even if the amount is much less than 12 feet, say just 5 feet, that's still a lot to overcome.

The final point on this subject that you should know about is ultimate elongation. Ultimate elongation is the amount of stretch that a line will take before breaking. This does not apply to microfilaments, where ultimate elongation and breaking point are virtually the same. Good-quality nylon monofilament lines have an ability to return to their normal state after severe pressure and stretching and to maintain basic strength. Stretch is not a permanent condition under average fishing conditions. However, lines that have seen the severest stress warrant close examination. It is difficult to determine when a line has been stretched to the maximum—the point where it cannot recover and is no longer serviceable—other than checking whether it holds knots well and can be broken in your hands. If in doubt about the continued serviceability of your line, replace it.

Flexibility. Fishing line has to perform a lot of functions, and in order to fulfill each function it must have the right blend of limpness and stiffness. Somewhere between a limp piece of cooked spaghetti and a rigid piece of uncooked spaghetti is the proper amount of flexibility that will allow an angler to cast a line, spool it, detect strikes, and absorb sudden impacts.

A limp, or very flexible, line is advantageous for achieving casting distance, in part because the line comes off the reel spool easily in smaller coils and straightens out quickly. It can be managed on a reel, especially a spinning reel, more easily than a stiff line, but it lacks some of the sensitivity of the latter. Stiff lines tend to spring off the spool of spinning reels in large coils, which flap against the rod guides, decrease distance, and increase the likelihood of developing a tangle. Stiff lines can affect the appearance or workings of lures, especially light objects such as flies (when used as tippet material), and some types of bait.

The flexibility of a line is hard to judge by observation, although in some instances you can feel that a line is very stiff or very limp. Braided lines are limper than nylon monofilaments, which vary a great deal in flexibility. The molecular structure of nylon is such that nylon monofilament line forms a memory when placed in a certain position (such as being spooled) for an extended period of time. Nylon lines with less memory are considered limp and are more castable than stiff lines, a factor that is important in light-line angling. Nylon lines with a lot of memory are considered stiff, which contributes to spooling and twist problems and makes casting more difficult.

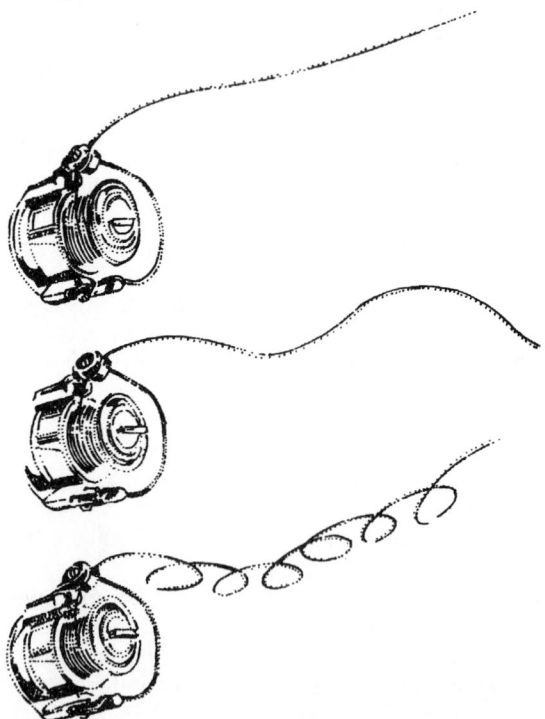

The flexibility of a line depends on its manufactured characteristics, as well as the condition in which it has been stored for a long time. The worst scenario is a very wiry, stiff line that is tightly coiled (bottom). The limpest lines (top) have virtually no memory and come off a reel with almost no coiling.

Castability is affected not only by limpness but also by water absorption in lines that absorb water; wet lines usually cast better than dry lines. It is also affected by line diameter. The greater the diameter, the harder it is to cast. With nylon monofilament, the stiffer the line, the less stretch it has but the more difficult it is to cast. Thus, there is a dramatic trade-off between castability and stretch in nylon monofilament. It's a good idea to wet nylon monofilament line (place the spool in the water) before you start using it on a given day, to help the molecules to relax.

Braided and fused microfilaments are different in this respect. They have low stretch, good limpness, and high castability, wet or dry.

Knot strength. Generally, once you tie a knot in a fishing line, it becomes weaker. Furthermore, knots tied in nylon monofilament that are tested in a wet condition (as they would be when fished) are weaker than when in a dry condition. Nylon monofilament line manufacturers claim that their technological processes produce molecular formations that result in specific knot-strength abilities for their line. Since the same knots are tied with various levels of expertise by different individuals, this is hard to verify when comparing knots tied by one angler with those tied by another. Nonetheless, if you are tying knots carefully and uniformly, and they're not holding, it could be because the knot strength of the line is deficient.

It could also be that the knot you are using isn't well suited to the type of line. The same knots that are used for nylon monofilaments are not as good with braided lines and fused microfilaments, although they may just need some minor adaptation. Braided lines tend to cut themselves when knotted improperly and tend to break at the knot when only moderate pressure is applied, so the proper knot is essential. Braided and fused microfilament lines tend to be slick and don't hold many of the conventional knots used with nylon monofilament, and thus may require different knots. In general, however, microfilament lines lose some of their strength even when tied with a proper knot. That percentage could be as high as 25 percent, a factor that you must take into consideration when evaluating the actual breaking strength of the product being fished.

Uniformity. It is reasonable to expect that what you get at one end of a line spool you should get at every point along that spool to the end. With premium lines you generally do. Sometimes, however, the manufacturing processes may alter the diameter of the line in certain spots or may in some way alter the characteristics in unidentified areas. You may find a spot that is thicker than the rest of the line. Here, the molecules have not been well oriented, and this part of the line will be weaker than the rest. Conversely, a thin spot will be stronger. With the premium lines on the market today, you

should encounter none of this. With bargain-basement specials—those lines selling for a few dollars for a 2,000-yard spool—you get what you pay for: junk.

Visibility. The visibility of a fishing line has no effect on its basic performance and generally has nothing to do with the other properties. Line visibility, or color, is one perceptible property of fishing line, yet it is also a highly subjective feature. Fishing line is available in many colors and shades as well as in fluorescent versions. How the line looks above the water is less of a factor than how it looks on or in the water where it is used. Since only the fish know for sure what they think about that, we're left to speculation and trial-and-error fishing. Because so many variables affect angling success, it is usually difficult to blame line color or visibility alone for a lack of fishing success.

It is known, of course, that some colors are more visible in the water than others. Anglers who fish in shallow clear water have more reason to be concerned about the visibility of line than those who fish in murky water. The background can have something to do with the visibility as well, and most anglers would like their fishing line to be invisible in the water, and highly visible above the water.

High-visibility line, particularly fluorescent line, is of great value to anglers whose eyesight isn't as keen as it used to be. It is also useful to anglers who bottom bounce, troll, fish with jigs or plastic worms, and otherwise have reason to watch their lines for an indication of a strike. Sometimes, high visibility to the angler outweighs high visibility beneath the surface because the angler fishes more effectively by virtue of being able to see the line better. Fluorescent line, which was first introduced by DuPont, was highly successful for them but denigrated by their competitors until the patent ran out; then the competitors eagerly introduced fluorescent lines.

Today there are dark lines and light lines, dull lines and shiny lines, and an assortment of colors picked by enterprising marketers. The so-called clear color remains the distinct favorite of most anglers, with a light-green color perhaps running a distant second in popularity. Fluorescent lines, incidentally, lose some of their brightness after long use because of ultraviolet exposure. And some microfilaments lose their color as well, in part because the color has been added after manufacture and does not hold well.

Anglers should recognize that some lines may absorb light and be more visible, and thus alarming, to some fish under some circumstances. Some lines may alarm fish by casting a greater shadow on the water or by exhibiting flash due to a shiny surface. The trouble is that most anglers use their tackle to angle for different fish in varying circumstances, clear water one moment, cloudy water the next. And those situations are always changing.

Sometimes the diameter of the line is more important than the color. And sometimes having the right lure and retrieving it properly is more important than line color.

Durability. There are many significant properties of fishing line, and their function and importance are interwoven. Some manufacturers emphasize the durability of fishing line as being the most important property; durability is actually a function of all the properties. Although the definition of durability varies, it is agreed that a fishing line should be durable enough to withstand a reasonable amount of hard fishing. However, some of the most durable lines are not the best-performing lines because they are weak in certain properties. For example, a line that is especially resistant to abrasion, perhaps because of its thickness or a coating, may not be as castable because it is stiff. Generally, anglers need a line with a balance of properties, including the ability to hold up to obvious environmental influences as well as specific angling needs.

Line Use

Modern fishing line is so superior to the line available just a few decades ago that anglers are easily lulled into thinking that their line needs no attention. This lack of attention to line, especially in freshwater, also stems from the fact that the average angler seldom catches fish large enough to really test even the poorest line or the angler's own abilities. This is a mistake. Proper care, use, and attention to line pays dividends over and over again in ordinary day-to-day fishing situations.

Controlling line twist.   Probably the greatest problem that most anglers experience in relation to line is twisting. Many anglers incorrectly blame their line for twisting problems. If your line twists and you think it's because the line is no good, take a brand-new consumer spool of that line, lay out the amount you want, and wait for it to twist. You'll be waiting forever. The point is that you have to do something to make line twist; it doesn't twist by itself. Line twist can occur as a result of various factors, including improper spooling, improperly playing a fish, having too loose a drag, using certain lures without a swivel, fishing in swift current, and using a lure that isn't running properly.

If the problem is a faulty lure, you'll need to adjust the lure so that it runs without spinning or else try using a split-ring, snap, or snap swivel, all of which aid in preventing spinning and twisting. Certain lures, such as most spinners used in flowing water, require the use of a snap swivel to prevent twisting. Almost all lures that revolve or turn over, including most spinners and spoons, will put twist in your line and should be used with a snap swivel, preferably a ball-bearing one.

If your drag is too loose, it will slip while you are fighting a fish and reeling in. This results in line twist. Similarly, if you crank a fish by forcefully reeling it in with spinning gear, instead of pumping,

When line on a reel is twisted, you can straighten it out by trolling it behind a boat, without any objects attached to the line. Rewind the line under tension.

retrieving line, etc., you will put a bad twist in the line, since every turn of the rotor puts a full twist in the line.

When you retrieve a lure, you can tell whether your line is twisted by watching how the lure dangles from the tip of your rod. If it begins to rotate, the line is twisted. Another indication is the development of coils in the line when you give it slack. Often an angler will be retrieving a lure, let it momentarily rest, and not notice that a coil develops near the reel. The angler continues retrieving, only to pile up line on the reel arbor on top of the loose coil. During a subsequent cast, the angler is likely to get a bird's nest, the severity of which will depend on how twisted the line has become.

Twisted line is not difficult to cure when you're in a boat or near running water. Line will untwist itself if you let a long length of it out behind your boat, with nothing attached to the end of it (no snap, swivel, split-shot, hook, lure, etc.), and drag it along for a few minutes. The faster your boat travels, the quicker the line unravels. Reel the line back in, and you're ready to attach terminal gear and fish. You can achieve the same effect on moderate- to fast-flowing water by letting the unweighted line float downstream and then holding it in the current for several minutes. This has the same effect as dragging it behind the boat.

Line twist can be impossible to cure if the problem is not recognized until the line is a mass of twists and curls. When line twist is this serious, cut off the problem section and start anew, being careful to correct the cause of the twist before fishing again.

Filling a reel.   Many problems associated with line actually begin at the first step of line use: putting new line on a reel spool. How you put line

Spool Filling

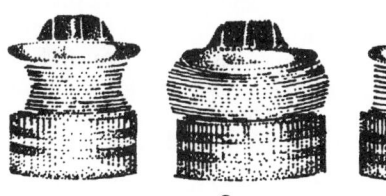

Under   Over   Proper

on and how much of it you put on are keys to minimizing twist and enhancing casting.

The best performance of a line and reel is achieved when the reel has been spooled properly. This means filling it almost to the edge, within $1/8$ to $3/16$ inch. If you overfill a spinning reel, line will fall off loosely when slack is given, causing a snarl to develop; several loops of line will pile up and jam in the spool or in a rod guide. Also, line can become pinched in the side flanges of the spool of an over-filled baitcasting or levelwind reel.

A properly filled reel allows you to achieve good distance in your casts, particularly with light lures. An underfilled reel hampers your casting range, since more coils of line (causing more friction) must come off the spool. After a period of time, through cutting frayed line, tying knots, and experiencing breakoffs, the level of line on the reel will become too low. In addition to hampering casting in some fishing situations, too little line might cost you a big fish if you hook one that takes all the remaining line off the reel. Additionally, drag pressure increases as line on the reel arbor decreases, creating a sometimes difficult situation for the angler when fighting a strong, surging fish.

You can put twist in the line by improperly spooling it, which happens often to inexperienced anglers. Unlike microfilaments, nylon monofilament has a memory factor, and it returns to its "memoried" state after being used. Line thus develops a set in the position in which it has been placed for a long time, such as the plastic spool on which it is wound for packaging.

On a consumer spool, not only has the line taken a set, but it actually is slightly coiled already, which is an inherent part of the manufacturer's spooling process. The manufacturer has huge bulk spools of line from which the smaller retail spools are filled. Line that comes off the extreme periphery of a full bulk spool has less coiling than the line that comes off the core of the bulk spool.

You and a friend could conceivably possess the same brand of line in the same strength, and one would be noticeably more coiled than the other. The reason is probably that they came from different locations on the bulk spool, or that they were produced at different times (when one batch of line was more coiled than the other). In any event, the longer that line stays on the retail spool, the more its coils conform to the diameter of the spool. Coiling is less pronounced in top-grade lines and

lines that come off large-diameter bulk or service spools.

On baitcasting reels, which are aptly called level-wind reels, line is fairly free of the twisting problems caused by spooling. This is because the line is wound straight onto the reel arbor in a direct, level, overlapping manner. The spooling suggestions that follow can also be applied to baitcasting reels.

Open-faced spinning reels and spincasting (closed face) reels pose many problems in line spooling for beginning anglers. The reason is that these systems actually put a slight twist in the line as it rotates off the bail arm and onto the arbor. If the line is of poor quality or if it already has a fair degree of manufacturer-instilled coiling and the angler improperly spools it onto a spinning reel, the result can be twisting, curling, coiling line—endless trouble unless it is run out behind the boat and rewound.

The first secret to successful spooling is watching how the line comes off both sides of the manufacturer's spool. Take line off the side with the least apparent coiling. Then apply moderate pressure on the line before it reaches the reel.

Follow this technique for proper spooling: Place the supply spool on the floor or any flat surface. The line should balloon or spiral off the spool as you pull it up. After you've threaded line through your rod guides and attached it to your reel, hold the rod tip 3 to 4 feet above the supply spool. Make 15 to 20 turns on the reel handle and stop. Now check for line twist by reducing tension on the line.

Lower the rod tip so that it is a foot from the supply spool, and check to see whether the slack line twists or coils. If it does, turn the supply spool upside down. This will eliminate most of the twist as you wind the rest of the line onto the reel. If the other side has more of a coiled or twisted nature to it, go back to the first side and take line off while it is face up. The trick here is to take line from the side that has the least amount of coiling. In effect, this method counter-spools the line on your spinning reel and cancels the curling tendencies that would otherwise exist.

Although manufacturers have recommended placing a pencil or other object inside a spool to let it run freely while you put on line, this is not as good a method as the one previously described. Although the pencil method may suffice for direct spooling of levelwind reels, it seems to compound the spooling problem on spinning and spincasting reels.

Keeping moderate tension on the line with one hand as you reel with the other is important when filling a reel. Do this by holding the line between your thumb and forefinger with your free hand. A loosely wound reel results from not applying spooling tension and causes loops of line to develop on the reel spool. Excessive tension, however, may bind up the line and allow more line to be spooled than necessary—a fact that you will discover later after

Idaho's Snake River sockeye traverse up to 897 miles to and from the Pacific, making them the sockeye migration champs in the lower 48 of the United States.

L

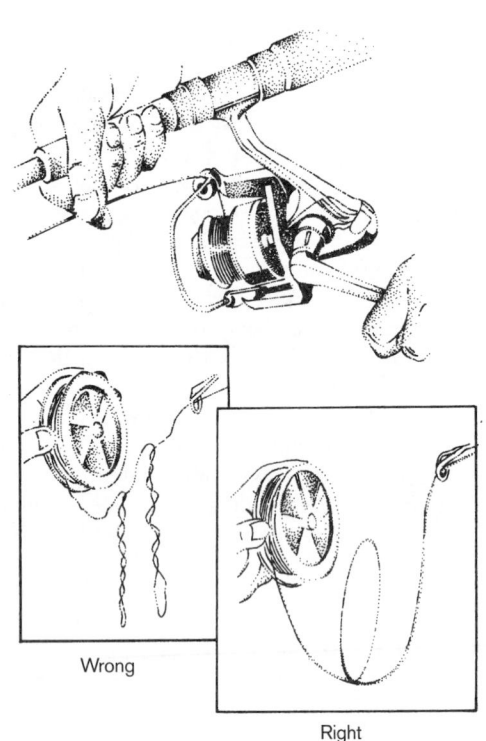

Wrong

Right

Always put line on a reel while applying a moderate amount of tension (top), and be sure to take line off a filler spool from the side that produces the least coiling.

the used line starts to bunch up as you begin to spool it naturally by reeling. So you have to find the right medium.

For some strengths and types of line and some types of fishing tackle, it is important to spool line very tightly onto the reel. Large conventional reels *(see: conventional tackle)* and big-game reels *(see: big-game tackle),* for example, require that line be wound tightly on them so that the pressure of fishing or of fighting a large fish does not cause wraps of line to become buried into a loosely packed spool. A similar issue holds for using braided or fused microfilament lines; when spooled onto the reel, these types of line need more tension than a comparable nylon monofilament.

Removing coils.   Nylon monofilament develops coils because the line has memory and takes a set that conforms to the spool of the reel. This tendency can be troublesome, especially on spinning reels. To remove these coils, relax the line by soaking it in lukewarm water. Dipping it momentarily in water before use may help a bit as well.

Another way to ease coiling is to put a lot of tension on the line. You can apply tension in a controlled way by tying the line to a fixed object, backing off a reasonable distance, raising the rod as if you were playing a fish, and then applying moderate tension to it about 10 times. Don't strain the rod too hard or you risk breaking it, and don't apply so much tension that you break or severely stretch the line.

Changing line.   In a sense, new fishing line is like a new automobile. When you purchase a new

car and drive it off the dealer's lot, it becomes a "used" or old car. When you put new line on your reel and fish with it, it's used. A new automobile that is driven frequently but is garaged and taken on only the best roads is likely to stay in top condition longer than one that is used daily, constantly exposed to the elements, and subject to every type of road condition. Line is very much the same. The age of the line is much less important than how much and under what conditions it has been used.

The primary reasons for changing line are that it is too low on the spool, it's very old, or it has had such extensive, stressful use that a cautionary replacement seems warranted.

When line becomes too low, it hampers casting and reduces effective drag settings, and it needs to be refilled. Many reels have large line capacities, so even when a reel has too little line left on it for good casting, usually it still has half of its capacity left. If the line has not been on the reel very long, it is still worth using. You should consider taking off this leftover line by tying the end to a tree or a post in an open area (or on the water) and backing away so that the line does not bunch up or become tangled. Take off the line, put on a suitable amount of stronger line for backing, and then take the end of the monofilament that you hitched to the post and tie this to the backing. When your spool is full, you have the fresh, unused back section of old line for fishing.

If you have a large-capacity reel but will need only a third or half of it for fishing, and you will not need it for other kinds of fishing, attach a backing to the spool before putting on new line. The backing should be of equal or greater strength than the main line.

If you wish to replace the full capacity of line on a reel, simply strip it all off and discard it in the garbage or in a recycling bin at a tackle shop. You can do this fairly quickly by giving it the old clothesline palm-to-elbow wrap. Another method is to use an electric drill. Affix an old consumer spool or some large-capacity object in the drill bit head, set the reel on freespool or reduce the drag setting to the least amount of tension (this is also a way to break in a drag), and run the drill until the line is off. A third method is to use a battery-operated line stripper.

Old nylon monofilament line needs to be replaced completely, as does line that has been used often in punishing fishing conditions. Some anglers have had nylon monofilament line on their reels for years—so long that they have no idea how old the line may be.

How long line may be used before being replaced is a question with no set answer. This depends on how much fishing you do, the strength of the line, how large and hard-fighting the fish are that you regularly catch, how much care or abuse your tackle receives, and the original quality of the line. An angler who fishes only a few times a year would be well advised to change line at least once a year, preferably before the start of each season. A slightly more frequent angler should change it at least twice a year. And anglers who fish regularly should change their line every few weeks. If your line is exposed to the elements for long periods of time (such as sitting in a sunlit boat or lying on a dock), you may need to change it more frequently than if it had been put away. Line should not be exposed to sunlight or to heat for days or weeks on end.

The type of fishing circumstance can also serve as a guide. Fishing in unobstructed water puts less demand on a line than does fishing around rocks, logs, timber, docks, and the like. Light line, because of its thin diameter, requires more frequent changing than heavy line. Microfilaments may need to be changed much less frequently than conventional line because they are more resistant to light and extremely durable.

Inspecting line.   You can't tell much about the thickness of line by feeling it, since variations are generally in thousandths of an inch. You could use a micrometer to measure the diameter, but very few anglers have reason to own or regularly use this costly piece of equipment.

You can detect abrasion by feel, and this is quite important. A nick, cut, or fray in nylon monofilament can weaken it, sometimes by as much as 50 percent or more. A 10-pound-test line, which would ordinarily need 10 or more pounds of pressure to break it, may need only 5 or 7 or 8 pounds if it is abraded. Microfilaments are said to be weakened less by cuts and frays, but it's not worth taking a chance. The only way to assure 100 percent strength is to cut off abraded sections.

Line breakage as a result of undetected abrasion leads many anglers to question the quality of their line, when in fact the anglers are to blame for not checking the line. Therefore, periodically running your fingers over the first few feet (more if necessary) of line to detect nicks or frayed areas is a good idea. When you do find such spots, cut off the damaged section of line. If, for some reason, you find it hard to detect abrasion by feeling the line, try running it through your lips.

Abrasion usually results from underwater contact with objects and fish, though it can happen after a portion of your line contacts tree limbs or stumps when a lure hangs up. Occasionally, however, imperfections in your rod or reel cause abrasion. A nick or burr on a rod guide, reel pickup arm or levelwind guide, or spool edge can be the culprit. If line abrasion occurs regularly throughout the line or when you're fishing in unobstructed water, you should check the tackle and correct the problem.

Another sign of old line, and possibly well-worn line, is the visibly faded look, which may be the result of age or extensive exposure to sun. With nylon monofilament, this is a result of the fluorescence evaporating from exposure to ultraviolet light. Sometimes anglers find that the line on their reel suddenly seems to have lost its strength. The

reason usually remains a mystery. Old nylon line does, however, become stiff as the result of the seepage of its plasticizing agent (monomer, which is the white chalky buildup that you sometimes get when spooling line on a reel) and thus is brittle and weaker. This condition is evidenced in lighter lines by failure to hold knots well or by the easy breaking of unknotted sections. In some cases, this old line is still serviceable once it is soaked in water, but it's best to consider fading as an indication of wear and to plan on replacing the line.

Care of line.   A lot remains to be learned about the effect of outside elements and substances on microfilaments, so caution is still advisable. Nylon monofilament, however, has a longer track record and is definitely not ageless. Its effective life depends on how it is treated and to what it is subjected. Long exposure to sunlight can affect nylon, so don't store it, either on a consumer spool or a fishing reel, in a position where sunlight falls on it daily. The ultraviolet elements of the sun's rays are very strong, and to diminish their effect, premium lines feature an ultraviolet retardation element, which prolongs the effective life of the line. The fluorescent characteristic of some line is especially vulnerable to ultraviolet light and will fade in time. The best storage for line is in a cool, dry environment, away from extremes in temperatures, water saturation, and sunlight. A garage, closet, or basement might provide suitable storage. Examples of how not to treat line include leaving a spool on the dashboard of your automobile or a reel by a window where sunlight regularly reaches it.

Many anglers lose track of the strength of line on a particular reel or can't recall when they put it on. Sometimes they are mistaken about which brand they are using. This can all be solved by marking the reel. Some line manufacturers supply gummed labels with each spool of their product, so that an angler can jot pertinent information on the label and affix it to the reel.

You should also be careful about what substances come into contact with your line. Some can alter the characteristics of line in unsuspected ways. WD-40, for instance, which is commonly used on reels to inhibit rust, may leach out some of the plasticizers of nylon monofilament, resulting in stiffer line. If the line was in contact with water soon after contact with WD-40, there would be no effect. More effect would be incurred if the reel full of line was sprayed with this substance (and some got on the line) after fishing and then was stored.

Suntan oils can pose a problem, too. Their active ingredients can plasticize nylon monofilament and increase elongation, and the lines become excessively stretchy. Gas and motor oil can also be detrimental to line if there is contact for an extended period of time. In extreme cases of contact (or soaking) with gasoline, a 50 percent reduction in line strength can occur. Motor oil is not as potent as gasoline.

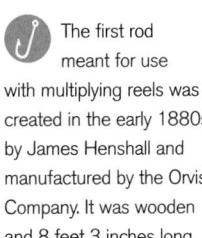 The first rod meant for use with multiplying reels was created in the early 1880s by James Henshall and manufactured by the Orvis Company. It was wooden and 8 feet 3 inches long.

 L

The most harmful substance to line, even for short contact, is battery acid. This sulfuric acid attacks nylon line properties almost immediately and advances oxidization. Light lines in particular are very vulnerable.

Perhaps more serious is the possibility that these substances may imprint an odor on the line that is not noticeable to humans but is detectable by fish. What effect this may have on fish behavior is unclear. It surely cannot be positive.

It is not far-fetched to imagine that you might spray yourself liberally with bug repellent and then touch your line while tying a knot; or that coils of line might fall on an uncovered battery when you laid down your rod; or that gasoline or oil might be inadvertently spilled on your reel. Just take care to keep such substances off your line for extended periods.

Line disposal. Although it does not have a direct relationship to line care, line disposal is an important element of use. Fishing line can have a long residual life and can be harmful to wildlife if discarded outdoors. No type of line should be discarded anywhere but in the garbage or in recycling bins at retail stores.
See: Baitcasting Tackle; Knots, Fishing; Leader; Spincasting Tackle; Spinning Tackle; Tippet.

LINE-CLASS WORLD RECORD
The largest individual of a given species of sportfish that is caught on a specific breaking strength of line, and within parameters established by the International Game Fish Association *(see)*, the certifying organization.
See: Records.

LINE DRESSING
The coating or treatment that is used to help float and/or clean a fly line.
See: Flycasting Tackle.

LINE GUIDE
See: Guide, Rod; Rod, Fishing.

LINEN LINE
Fishing line made from linen, primarily popular with saltwater anglers and replaced by Dacron and nylon monofilament in the mid-twentieth century. Linen line was braided or twisted and had to be removed periodically from reel spools and dried to avoid rotting.
See: Line.

LINEWINDER
An electrically powered device for putting line on, and taking it off, a fishing reel spool; it is usually found in fishing tackle shops.

LINGCOD   *Ophiodon elongatus.*
Other names—cultus cod, blue cod, buffalo cod, green cod, ling; Finnish: *vihersimppu;* French: *terpuga;* Japanese: *ainame;* Portuguese: *lorcha;* Swedish: *grönfisk.*

The lingcod, a Pacific marine species, belongs to the family Hexagrammidae. Its name is misleading because it is not a true cod. A local term for lingcod is "cultus cod"; the word "cultus" is an Indian term meaning "false."

Table quality. The lingcod is an important and highly prized commercial and sportfish, and many consider it one of the finest table fish in the West. Its white, firm flesh is often deep-fried as the main ingredient in fish and chips, but it may also be smoked, baked, grilled, or poached with excellent results. The flesh of the lingcod may be greenish blue, depending on diet.

Identification. The lingcod has a large mouth, large pectoral fins, a smooth body, and a long, continuous dorsal fin divided by a notch into spiny and soft parts. Adults have large heads and jaws, and long, pointed teeth. Juveniles have slender bodies. Its coloring is usually brown or gray with blotches outlined in orange or blue but is closely associated with habitat.

Size. Lingcod may grow to 50 inches or longer. Males are smaller than females, usually reaching no longer than 3 feet in length or 20 pounds in weight. Basically mature by eight years, the male will weigh about 10 pounds and the female about 15. Commercial catches for lingcod sometimes include fish of 50 to 60 pounds. The all-tackle record is 69 pounds.

Distribution. The lingcod occurs in North American waters from Southern California to Alaska but is most abundant in the colder waters of the north.

Habitat. Lingcod inhabit colder waters in intertidal zone reefs and kelp beds that have strong tidal currents. They prefer depths from 2 to more than 70 fathoms over rock bottom.

Life history/Behavior. The spawning season is in winter, from December through February, when the eggs are released in large pinkish white masses into crevices in rocks. Egg masses can contain more than a half million eggs and are frequently found in the intertidal zone. The male protects the eggs, which hatch in one to two months. The young stay at the surface for three to four months before dropping to the bottom.

Food and feeding habits. Adults feed on herring, flounder, cod, hake, greenling, rockfish, squid, crustaceans, and small lingcod. Juveniles consume small crustaceans and fish.

Angling. The aggressive lingcod is as rough and rugged as the jagged, rocky bottom structure it inhabits. When the mood strikes it, the ling may viciously attack any potential meal unfortunate enough to come within striking range, including other lingcod nearly the size of the attacker. Most

Lingcod

West Coast bottomfish anglers have stories about lingcod that grabbed hooked fish and hung on, often long enough to be gaffed or netted at the surface. Just as often, though, lingcod will lose interest in feeding, and these apparent fasts may last hours or even days.

Slack tides usually afford the best opportunity to hook lingcod because that's when it's easiest to work a bait or lure straight down to the rocky, snaggy bottoms where this big predator is found; too much current or wind results in a flat line angle and constant hookups on the rocky bottom.

Metal slab jigs that imitate smaller fish work well for lings, as do big leadheads with large, plastic grub bodies or pork-rind strips. Many bait anglers use herring, and live baits work much better than dead ones. The ultimate lingcod bait is a live greenling, about 10 inches long, fished with a large, single hook through both lips to pin its mouth shut. Live-bait anglers must use a sinker large enough to take the offering down but have to exercise care in keeping it just off bottom, or the bait will dodge into a hole and become snagged before a lingcod finds it.

Lingcod also have a habit of diving for a rocky crevice when hooked, so anglers should try to turn them toward the surface and reel them as far off the bottom as possible after setting the hook. Snubbing that first dash toward the rocks is often the difference between landing and losing a big ling. For this reason, many anglers use rather stout tackle for lingcod, including stiff boat rods, large conventional reels, and low-stretch braided line of 40- to 80-pound test. A tough monofilament leader of 50-pound test or larger also helps avoid abrasions and breakoffs.

The largest lingcod are females, and serious West Coast anglers have, in recent years, gotten into the habit of releasing these bigger fish in favor of the smaller males. Keeping smaller lingcod not only provides somewhat better table fare, it also allows the important mature females to continue spawning and providing lings for the future. Slot limits in some areas require anglers to release both smaller lingcod and the big females.

LINING

Spooking a fish when false casting a fly line over it or landing the fly line on the water over or near the fish.

LIQUID CRYSTAL DISPLAY

A sonar device, also known by the acronym LCD.
See: Sonar.

LIQUID CRYSTAL RECORDER

A sonar device, also known by the acronym LCR.
See: Sonar.

LITTLE TUNNY

See: Tuna; Tunny, Little.

LITTORAL

Living in or related to nearshore waters; the intertidal zone of the marine environment that is exposed at low tide and covered at high tide.

LIVE BAIT

Whole live fish or other natural organisms used to catch predatory fish in both freshwater and saltwater.
See: Natural Bait.

LIVEWELL

A containment device for keeping fish or bait alive; also called a baitwell when used exclusively for holding bait. Livewells may be compartments integral to the interior construction of a boat or may be external containers that are situated within a boat or outside of it on the water's surface. External versions often take the form of insulated coolers or large round plastic wells and should not be confused with bait buckets (see) or small bait containers (see) that have no means of aeration. It is also possible to fashion a livewell out of a food and beverage cooler, if you have a pump to use for aeration and a battery to power it. Livewells feature a pump that aerates the water, either recirculating it or introducing fresh raw water. This oxygenation of the water and the maintenance of appropriate (usually cool) water temperature are key elements to keeping fish and bait alive.

The primary element in effective livewell containment of either sportfish or bait is a quick,

Livewells, such as the one that this largemouth bass is being lowered into, must be big enough and well aerated to properly care for fish.

holding in this environment, as well as the subsequent handling and weighing that fish undergo prior to release. Sportfish kept in a livewell not only have been hooked, played, landed, and handled, but have also suffered long- or short-term captivity in a restricted place, have been bounced around during travel, have been confined with other fish, and then have been released at a later time in a foreign place. Some hardy fish will make it, and some won't. This treatment is not doing the fish any good other than keeping it alive. To retain fish in a livewell that you want to keep for consumption is fine; to retain them to show off at the end of the day and then make a heroic release is false sport and is quite likely to be harmful to the fish.

Largemouth and smallmouth bass and walleye are primary targets for livewell containment, largely because of the popularity of tournaments and the necessity to keep fish alive for weighing and then later release. However, freshwater anglers also use livewells to contain these fish for nontournament purposes and also to contain various panfish species, as well as pike, pickerel, and white bass. Few saltwater anglers keep their catch in livewells because they either release it right away or kill it and put it in a fish box (see); many saltwater species are too large for proper containment in a livewell or would require a livewell so large as to be impractical.

Many fish, and large fish in particular, are not suited for holding in most standard built-in boat livewells, although this varies with the species, the temperature of the water, the size of the well, and the abilities of the pump. In freshwater, small striped bass, trout, and salmon may be kept alive under the best of conditions, but usually larger members of these species are not suitable for containment outside of very large tanks. The size of the livewell is often a factor in keeping fish; the larger the livewell, the better the chance of releasing healthy fish.

Keeping sportfish alive for later release requires frequent if not constant aeration; otherwise, a "livewell" will become a "deathwell." Many freshwater boats, especially bass boats and general-purpose craft, have aerator timers that automatically activate the pump and shut it off at variable intervals. This saves battery power, especially if the main engine battery is also used for powering electrical accessories, including the livewell pump and bilge pump. However, if the water is very warm, it may be necessary to override the timer for frequent manual use, or leave the pump on continuously. Lacking a timer, you have to leave the livewell pump on constantly or manually turn it on and off repeatedly.

Most sportfish survive best in cold or at least cool water. They are hardest to keep alive in a well when the outside temperature and the surface temperature of the water are warm. It is possible to cool livewell water by adding small blocks of ice; however, you cannot take fish from warm water and put them into much cooler water; they must get

preferably continuous, turnover of water. The problems that develop with livewell containment are due to numerous factors, especially warm water, a pump that does not turn over enough volume, poor positioning of the water pickup, pumps that fail or that lose their prime, inferior drainage, lack of top-to-bottom turnover, crowding of bait, and rectangular wells.

Sportfish containment. Livewells are primarily used to hold bait for saltwater anglers and to hold both bait and sportfish for freshwater anglers. The only reasons to keep captured sportfish alive for any period of time are to keep them fresh until you get them home to be cleaned or to keep them alive until they are released at the end of the day in a tournament. The only good way to keep fish alive and reasonably fit is to use some type of aerated livewell. Fish kept on stringers and dragged around for a long time are seldom suitable for release, even though they may still be alive. However, if a fish is to be released alive, then it should be released alive immediately after being captured and unhooked; putting it in a livewell is seldom better for the fish than returning it immediately to its own environment. Nearly all fisheries agencies advise against confining fish that are intended for release.

Many built-in boat livewells are good for keeping a few sportfish alive, but most are not designed to hold many fish or to hold large specimens. There is some question about the effect of daylong acclimated to it. Furthermore, if the ice has come from a source that has been treated with chlorine, the content of chlorine in the water may be sufficient to kill the fish or to require the addition of a dechlorinating powder to the livewell water. It may be helpful, incidentally, to add uniodized (rock) salt to livewells to help reduce stress in fish.

Chemicals are available for livewell use that somewhat tranquilize sportfish and keep them from banging around in the well, lower their requirements for oxygen, and provide some antifungal protection. These measures all require that the livewell system contains a means of recirculating existing water, rather than strictly adding outside (raw) water and discharging used water, which will cause a loss of temperature as well as chemical additives. There is concern, however, about the effect of using chemicals on confined fish that are to be released back into the water, where they might be recaught and consumed by others.

Since boats sometimes move a great deal during a day of fishing, a livewell that will hold sportfish should be capable of operating both when the boat is at rest (taking in fresh outside water) and when it is running from one place to another (recirculating and aerating the existing water). A recirculating system accomplishes this. It is also preferable to have an aerator spray nozzle that delivers water in a sharp showerlike stream, rather than in a faucetlike stream because the former provides better aeration. However, overhead aeration may only aerate the surface and not adequately aerate the lower portion of a livewell, especially if the well is deep, so there are trade-offs. Incidentally, when the boat is moving any distance in rough water, fish should be held in a rear livewell to minimize pounding, if there are forward and aft livewells from which to choose.

Many freshwater boats, especially bass boats, have two small livewells; others have a single large one with a divider. The large ones are preferable, especially if you can remove or retain the divider to give the fish more freedom. Many also have cutoff valves that prevent water from entering or exiting. Leave this valve shut most of the time to keep water out of the livewells because a full livewell contributes a lot more weight in the boat (water weighs roughly 8 pounds to the gallon). When you catch a fish to be kept, open the valve to allow fresh water into the livewells. If the boat does not have a recirculating system and you have a fish in the livewell, you should shut the valves (or plug the drain), since the livewell water will flow out and the fish will be dry if you have to travel any distance. If you have to fill a boat livewell quickly, open the valve or plug, put the engine in reverse, and drive backward. This forces water to come in, filling the livewells.

Make sure that your livewell lines are clean and free of debris for best aeration performance. Be careful about using sportfish livewells for storage of small baitfish unless you have the proper size screens on the outlets. If not, small baitfish will get into drain lines and clog up the aerator. Don't try to keep small baitfish and larger gamefish in the same livewell at the same time. It's a good idea to clean the livewell(s) once in a while because a coating of dirt and scum gathers if you use it enough. You can wash out the drain lines with pressurized water from a garden hose. Be careful about transporting water in a livewell (or bilge) from one place to another, since this can be a means of spreading undesirable and perhaps harmful exotic aquatic life.

The keys to keeping sportfish alive and healthy are cool temperatures, adequate space, and plenty of aeration. Most built-in livewells by manufacturers do not have the water-volume capacity or the pumping ability to treat many fish, so you have to recognize the problems associated with livewell containment; you may need to modify the existing setup with a more powerful pump, or with larger intake and discharge lines to move plenty of fresh water through. Generally, it is best to have a flow-through system that constantly brings in outside (raw) water and constantly flushes the livewell.

Bait containment.   Live bait is most effective when it is energetic and frisky. Some gamefish will not take live bait that is lethargic, especially if other anglers are in the area and there is a choice of food available. Fresh, lively bait is important, and keeping it this way depends on the bait, the size and shape of the well, the amount of aeration, and the water temperature. Some baitfish are very difficult to keep alive. Those that are purchased at bait shops for sums exceeding several dollars apiece represent a considerable investment that has to be protected with the right kind of livewell and good aeration.

The type of livewell and the size are dictated by the bait. Most livewells are circular or oval shaped because many baitfish, especially any member of the herring family, will gather motionless in corners and die. They need to keep moving, and in round

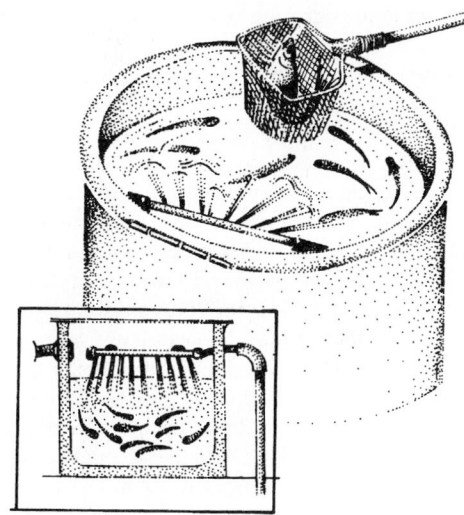

When keeping bait alive, proper aeration is important; some baitfish survive only in oval or round wells, as depicted here.

or oval wells you can create a stream of current that forces the bait to keep swimming. Ideally there should not be any devices sticking into the well because they are likely to become hideouts and death traps. Obviously wells have to be watertight and hold a sufficient volume of water. The larger the size of the individual bait to be stored, the greater the diameter of the well; ditto for numbers and volume.

The most desirable livewell systems are those that pump raw water from outside and deliver it to the well, usually spraying it into the well from above to help aerate it, constantly flushing the old water and removing debris and body waste and maintaining the temperature, which should conform to the surface of the outside water. Some systems merely recirculate existing water, which retains debris and waste matter and usually raises the temperature; this is true for some portable systems, including ice chest livewells, and with these it may be a good idea to occasionally scoop out some of the water with a bucket and replace it with fresh water. However, if the livewell empties its water while the boat is running from one place to another, you should have a shutoff valve or drain plug to stop water from draining out and to allow the pump to recirculate and oxygenate the water while you are underway; after you've reached the destination, you can switch back to outside water intake. In large-volume systems without outside raw water circulation, high-quality filters should be used to draw out bacteria and waste.

In order to process this water efficiently, you need an adequate pump. You can make do with a pump that is also used for other purposes (like washdown), but it's best to have a pump devoted solely to the livewell; have a backup available because if the pump breaks down, there go your bait and maybe your fishing. In a pinch, you may be able to switch over a washdown pump or a bilge pump, or to use one of these or a backup to handle excess bait that aren't making it in an overtaxed main well (a large plastic pail or a cooler can be turned into temporary bait housing if necessary).

If the pump is rated at 300 gallons per hour (gph), it will theoretically turn over a 30-gallon well 10 times per hour, assuming that the drainpipe is of sufficient diameter to accommodate an even exchange. Some gravity-flow drains are too small and become clogged easily and cannot handle the influx of water; this situation leads to overflowing in the well and insufficient aeration when the inflow line is submerged. Overflowing will cause water to spill into the sump or possibly onto the deck or into storage compartments; the bilge pump will then need to be used. Drain lines should be two to three times the diameter of the inflow line but in most cases are not; to achieve this you may have to make some modifications.

Many freshwater anglers use pumps in the 300- to 600-gph range, but greater-capacity models are available and are usually necessary for serious bait maintenance. Some saltwater bait users employ a 2,000-gph pump for larger fish. By talking with other anglers, you can figure out the turnover rate you need for the most demanding bait that you'll use, and make a choice accordingly. For small baitfish and small numbers of bait, pumps with a lower rating are adequate. A 500-gph pump is adequate for holding shrimp and small pinfish, for example, in a 20-gallon-capacity well. If your fishing takes you to extremes in the bait-use spectrum, you might be wise to employ a dual-pump system where either a higher- or a lower-capacity model is used as necessary. No matter what capacity pump you use, if the water gets murky, then your system needs some adjustment. It may be necessary to use a higher-volume pump. Check the baitfish for signs of stress, like loss of scales or color.

Make sure you remove the lower layer of water in the well from time to time if it appears stagnant or does not seem to get mixed with the rest of the water on its own. Stirring the water occasionally may help if you have a large flow-through volume and no standpipe to keep the well water at the proper height. A bottom drain in the tank will help, but you need to have an adjustable riser or standpipe, or else you have to periodically remove the standpipe to flush out bottom water from a bottom drain (and that may cause some problems with the bait). At the very least, remove bottom water when you're finished fishing, and flush all water out of the well at the end of the day. Be aware that flushing bottom debris, especially scales, can lead to clogging the system. Switching between normal and short standpipes allows you to flush out most of the water without trouble, if the short standpipe is covered with a screen. A short pipe is also useful for those times when you want only a small amount of water in the well and want to get at bait easily. An alternative is an adjustable pipe. To fashion it, drill some small holes at the base of the standpipe, and then cover the pipe with tight-fitting PVC tubing that has an inside diameter closely matching the outside diameter of the standpipe. When you need to flush bottom well water, raise the outside tube to expose the holes and lower it back when you're done. Make sure that the outer tube fits snugly so that water doesn't flow out when you don't want it to.
See: **Bait; Boat.**

LIVIES
A term for small live fish used as bait in saltwater.

LOBWORM
A term for nightcrawler *(see)*.

LODGE
See: **Fishing Lodge.**

LOG

A nautical term for a record of the events that occur while boating, usually detailing course, speed, and other details of navigation or the voyage; it is also applied to a record of fishing activities, usually detailing location, success, weather, and other matters.

LONGLINE

A commercial fishing line of considerable length, bearing numerous baited hooks and usually set and drifted horizontally in the ocean. This line is supported in the water column by floats, and baited hooks are suspended from it. Sections of line may be attached to one another, depending on the size of the fishing boat and number of crew, and the total length of connected sections may extend for miles.

Longlines are used in snapper, grouper, cod, haddock, ling, swordfish, and bluefin tuna fisheries, among others, but may catch nontarget species as well as other animals. They are set for varying periods, up to several hours, on the sea floor or, in the case of tuna, in surface waters before being retrieved. Commercial fishing with a longline is a controversial practice that has contributed to overfishing of some primary species and has had a detrimental influence on others.

See: **Commercial Fishery.**

LONG-RANGE BOAT

A party boat *(see)* that makes excursions lasting from several days to two weeks to distant fishing grounds.

LOOKDOWN   *Selene vomer.*

Other names—Portuguese: *galo de penacho, peixegalo;* Spanish: *caracaballo, joro bado, papelillo, pez luna.*

A member of the Carangidae family of jacks, the lookdown is so called because of its habit of hovering over the bottom in a partly forward-tilted position, which makes it seem to "look down." The flesh of the lookdown has an excellent flavor and is commercially marketed fresh.

Identification. Bright silver and iridescent, the lookdown has a deep and extremely compressed body that may have goldish, greenish, bluish, or purplish highlights. One of its most striking features is the unusually high forehead, as well as the low placement of the mouth on the face and the high placement of the eyes. The first rays of the second dorsal fin and the anal fin are long and streamerlike; in the dorsal fin, they may extend to the tail, whereas in the anal fin they do not extend as far. The lookdown may also have three or four pale bars across the lower body. On young fish, there are two very long, threadlike filaments that extend from the dorsal fin.

Size. Ordinarily 6 to 10 inches long and weighing less than a pound, the lookdown may

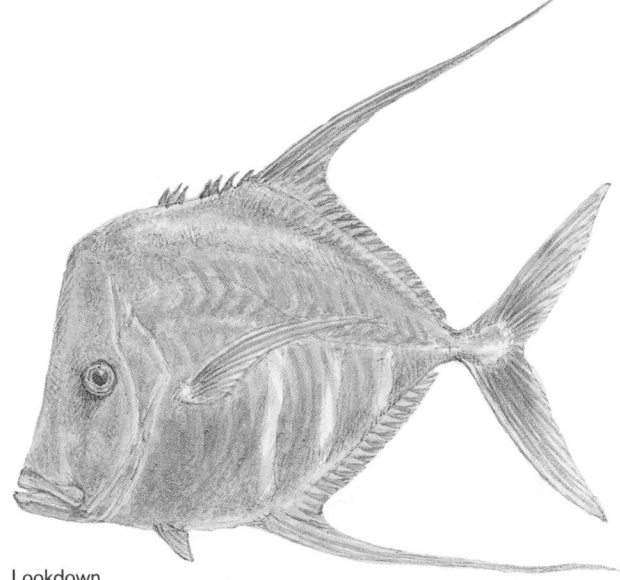
Lookdown

reach 1 foot in length and weigh 3 pounds. The all-tackle world record is a Brazilian fish that weighed 4 pounds, 10 ounces.

Distribution. Endemic to the western Atlantic, lookdown are found from Maine and possibly Nova Scotia in Canada to Uruguay, as well as in Bermuda and the Gulf of Mexico.

Habitat. Lookdown favor shallow coastal waters at depths of 2 to 30 feet, generally over hard or sandy bottoms around pilings and bridges and often in murky water. Occasionally occurring in small schools, lookdown hover over the bottom. Small fish may be found in estuaries.

Food. Lookdown feed on small crabs, shrimp, fish, and worms.

Angling.   See: *Inshore Fishing; Jacks.*

LOOP KNOT

Usually a type of terminal connection in which the line is attached to the hook or lure with a free-swinging loop rather than a snug attachment. There are various types of loop knots.

See: **Knots, Fishing.**

LORAN

An acronym for LOng RAnge Navigation, Loran is a land-based electronic navigation system that was widely employed in coastal areas of North America in the latter part of the twentieth century. Its use and popularity faded in the late 1990s because of the prominence of the far-reaching and satellite-based Global Position System *(see: GPS);* Loran will eventually be obsolete in North America when government-supported transmitting stations are decomissioned.

The current generation of Loran is known as Loran-C. It operates via a network of shore-based transmitting stations covering the coastal areas of

A Loran unit (white) on this boat's console provides navigational information.

Loran-C receivers determine position based on time differences, or time delays; these are commonly called TDs or numbers. They display location information in a set of TDs and in corresponding latitude and longitude coordinates, which correspond to lines connecting TDs of the same value that are overprinted on marine navigational charts. Loran-C receivers are capable of providing such important navigational information as course heading, elapsed time and distance traveled, course necessary to navigate to specific locations (which are called waypoints), time to reach those waypoints at present course, and estimated arrival time; and they can store waypoints in permanent memory to recall for return navigation. Many Loran-C units can also be interfaced with other electronic devices, especially autopilot; the ability to use autopilot can mean significant fuel savings for boaters traveling long distances.

Although Loran-C is useful to anglers for pure navigational purposes, it is more useful for its ability to guide a boat back to a fishing hotspot (reef, wreck, etc.) at any time of the day or night, and with accuracy that under the best conditions—where reception is good and the crossing angles for the TD signals are close to 90 degrees—can be as close as 50 feet. As long as it is being used in an area where reception is reliable and the signals are of good quality, Loran offers great benefits. However, it does experience occasional interference due to severe electrical weather disturbances, and it may be down temporarily when a transmitter goes off-line for maintenance. A distant line of thunderstorms, even out of sight far over the horizon, can sometimes knock out the signals from a critical Loran station.

The advantages offered by GPS navigation are significant: GPS is unaffected by weather and atmospheric conditions, is transmitted via a series of orbiting satellites, can determine position and provide navigational information anywhere (land or water, inland or coastal) in any country, and is capable of greater accuracy.

Nevertheless, Loran is an excellent navigation system. However, any navigation system, like any electronic device, is subject to failure; with Loran this could be because of signal loss or receiver malfunction, so it is best to be prepared with a good chart and reliable magnetic compass, or to be able to revert to dead reckoning basics.
See: GPS; Maps; Navigation.

North America and the Great Lakes, but not extending to other inland areas; it's even somewhat marginal in the northwestern part of the Bahamas and does not reach down through the rest of the islands. Active Loran-C systems are in use in other countries, however, and primarily employed for shipping purposes. In fact, while Loran-C use has been decreasing in North America because of increased GPS use, it is becoming more widely used in other countries where more transmission stations are being constructed. There are European, Far-Eastern, Russian, and Mediterranean Loran-C networks.

Loran-C is the modern form of Loran and followed the original version, which was known as Loran-A. In a basic sense, Loran is a sophisticated radio receiver that obtains signals from two transmission sources, known as stations, that are situated on the ground along a coast. Loran measures the time differences between these signals to obtain a Line of Position (LOP) for each signal, which, when intersected, provides a "fix" to ascertain position. Loran-A required time-consuming plotting with a navigational chart and was subject to a lot of operator error. Loran-C eliminated the need for charting and provided quick electronic depiction of current position.

In operation, land-based stations transmit signals that are obtained by Loran receivers installed on boats. When everything is working right, the best Loran-C receiver can update its position every second, but most do not update that frequently.

LOUISIANA

Louisiana has the resources to back up its claim that it is a "Sportsman's Paradise." Its maze of waterways, for example, offers anglers the rare opportunity to tangle with red drum and trophy largemouth bass on the same day. Within easy reach is the Gulf of Mexico and a chance to battle record blue marlin, white marlin, wahoo, yellowfin tuna, and king mackerel. A full range of warmwater species exists inland, including striped bass, crappie, and big catfish; in saltwater the mix is even broader, including not only pelagic species but also tarpon, seatrout, flounder, amberjack, barracuda, pompano, cobia, and many more. Among the Gulf of Mexico states, Louisiana has the most liberal catch-limit regulations for freshwater and saltwater species.

Abundant water resources are the reason for Louisiana's rare blend of quality and quantity. The state has an estimated 200,000 miles of fishable coastal banks and shorelines, and 41 percent of the coastal wetlands in the United States. This vast, warm shallow-water habitat stretches from Louisiana's eastern boundary with Mississippi to its western boundary with Texas. The National Marine Fisheries Service estimates this eco-system makes up as much as 80 percent of the finfish in the Gulf of Mexico dependent on Louisiana waters at some time in their life cycle.

The state's importance in fish production closely relates to its status as the terminus of the Mississippi River, which, over thousands of years, has carved four distinct paths to the Gulf of Mexico. The present route takes the Mississippi through New Orleans, where it winds 120 miles south and east, then courses through five passes, and finally empties into the Gulf of Mexico. This terminus, where freshwater mixes with saltwater, creates an "edge" effect, a nutrient-rich, brackish water ecosystem that makes Louisiana a vital nursery for finfish and shellfish.

The Mississippi is in effect Louisiana's marsh builder. The rich silt deposits from America's heartland attract freshwater and saltwater species to the same area, making it possible to catch largemouth bass, red drum, and spotted seatrout on the same fishing trip.

The geological effects of the Mississippi River's flow put Louisiana closer to the continental shelf than any gulf state and explain the proximity of blue-water species. Depths of 400 feet are within 12 miles of South Pass, the southernmost of the five passes in the Mississippi River Delta; 1,000-foot depths are within an hour's ride from this pass.

In its never-ending quest to find a shorter route to the Gulf of Mexico, the Mississippi River has graced Louisiana with 14 fishable oxbow lakes. The scouring effect of millions of gallons of sediment-laden water cut these sharp bends off from the river's main flow. Six of the state's rivers still receive water from the Mississippi during spring floods, which also restock the oxbow lakes.

The Mississippi's quest for a shorter passageway to the gulf has also produced in Louisiana the largest overflow swamp in the U.S. When the Mississippi River began to cut through to the smaller Red and Atchafalaya Rivers early in the nineteenth century, U.S. Army officer Amos Stoddard noted that the Atchafalaya River provided a shorter route to the gulf. He concluded that the Mississippi would likely change its course within 100 years. When Captain Henry Shreve searched for a shorter route along the Mississippi River to New Orleans, a canal was dug that cut off a section of the Mississippi at Turnbull's Bend. This canal routed the Mississippi River back into the Red River's channel, which flowed directly into the Atchafalaya. A logjam in the Mississippi then reduced the Red's flow, thereby averting the immediate threat of Mississippi waters running directly into the Atchafalaya.

Over the following century plus, the U.S. Army Corps of Engineers produced further documentation that the Mississippi River was indeed meandering toward the Atchafalaya. In 1959, at a cost of $47 million, the Corps of Engineers constructed the Old River Control Structure. When completed in 1962, the massive project allowed 30 percent of the Mississippi River's flow into the Atchafalaya River and maintained 70 percent of the Mississippi's flow along its present course. The project also sent the river's flow down the Atchafalaya. The structure was upgraded in the early 1990s to further alleviate the hydrological pressure of the Mississippi River's migration toward the Atchafalaya.

Responsible for flood control, the Corps of Engineers earlier in the twentieth century constructed or refurbished levees along the Mississippi River's course through Louisiana and also leveed the 60-mile-long Atchafalaya. The latter project created the expansive Atchafalaya River Floodway, a maze of bayous and lakes that comprises a 5- to 25-mile-wide swamp. The area between the levees holds the Atchafalaya River's flood waters, a vast ecosystem that is one of Louisiana's most productive and visited recreational fishing areas, and a vital commercial fishing location as well. The flow down the Atchafalaya has created one of few expanding river deltas in North America.

This new land is much needed. Levee and jetty projects, along with massive canal digging for oil production and navigation since the 1930s, have put Louisiana's marshlands in a precarious predicament. Hydrologists estimate that Louisiana is losing an acre of land per day, or between 35 and 50 square miles per year.

Several marsh-enhancing projects have been designed. One is operating in the Caernarvon area south of New Orleans along the Mississippi River, and restoration of this brackish water marsh has been documented. Another project is designed to restore the marshlands in the Barataria area southwest of New Orleans, an area made famous as the home of buccaneer Jean Lafitte. Other projects are pointed toward restoration of dozens of barrier islands, a fish-rich string of sandy outcroppings that not only attract anglers but also give the state needed protection from hurricanes.

These natural areas have inherent problems, not the least of which is access. Because the coast is

marshland, all roads must be built over water. Although coastal land routes have been improved since 1980, access is mostly over two-lane roads. Because high, dry ground is at a premium along the coast, boat launches and angler accommodations are limited. These factors have stifled the expansion of Louisiana's recreational fishing populace and pose problems that nonresident anglers find difficult to overcome.

Nevertheless, Louisiana's vast natural saltwater, brackish water, and freshwater areas, as well as its 12 inland reservoirs, offer variety to suit the taste of any angler. As many as 1 million anglers annually take advantage of these opportunities.

Freshwater

As previously detailed, bountiful bayous, swamps, rivers, oxbow lakes, large and small reservoirs, and brackish water marshes give Louisiana's freshwater anglers a wealth of choices. There are no closed seasons here, so these opportunities can be enjoyed year-round.

Extensive environmental cleanup efforts have induced the return of sea-run striped bass to Louisiana's important rivers: the Mississippi, the lower Atchafalaya, the Pearl, and the Mermentau. In addition, state-run hatchery programs have introduced striped bass, hybrid striped bass, and Florida-strain largemouth bass to various waters. Florida largemouth fingerlings placed in oxbows, reservoirs, and city lakes brought trophy bass fishing to a state more well known for its quantity of freshwater fish than their size.

To the nonresident angler, the striking difference between Louisiana's freshwater and that elsewhere in the U.S. is that with the exception of large reservoirs, Louisiana waters are cloudy, murky, or muddy. This makes lure selection a problem for anglers accustomed to fishing clearer environs. As a result, gold- and copper-colored blades are commonly used on spinnerbaits and buzzbaits, and brightly colored crankbaits, and soft lizards or worms are the rule rather than the exception. Gold-sided crankbaits and jerkbaits are popular with bass anglers here because of the water color.

Atchafalaya Basin

Because the 60-mile-long expanse of swamps, bayous, man-made canals, and small lakes is connected at its source to the Mississippi and Red Rivers, the Atchafalaya River Basin is subject to springtime flooding; it is an angler's paradise only after the annual floods recede. During the late winter and early spring, commercial crawfishing holds sway and produces 35 to 100 million pounds annually.

When flows settle down and banks reappear— usually in late May or June—this basin truly is a fishing paradise. Catches of 60 to 100 bass a day are common in the first eight weeks after the floods. Crappie (called sacalait), bream (meaning bluegills,

green sunfish, pumpkinseeds, and redear sunfish— the latter called chinquapin), and catfish are highly sought then as well. These species take a variety of artificial lures and live baits, notably small baitfish, crickets, and nightcrawlers. Anglers also land less desirable species like freshwater drum (called gaspergoo), buffalo, and bowfin (called choupique).

Crawfish are an important food source for all predator species, especially bass. As a result, crawfish-colored jigs with pork or soft-plastic trailers, crankbaits, and spinnerbaits, along with soft-plastic lizards, are preferred offerings for bass. During the postflood period, the prime bass areas are runouts, which drain swamps that provide post-spawn bass and other species with a ready food source, mostly crawfish.

After the water levels stabilize, usually in August or September, the next four to five months are when bass and other species search out deep-water canals and bayous. Except for the Atchafalaya River, the basin is shallow throughout its expanse, and summertime water temperatures can reach the upper 80s. This places a premium on early morning and late afternoon, the most active feeding periods.

The basin's fish stocks were severely depleted by Hurricane Andrew in 1992, when fisheries biologists estimated 175 million fish were killed; but extensive restocking efforts along with significant annual river flooding has replenished stocks of gamefish and other species.

In 1998, the state and the Corps of Engineers joined forces in a 15-year, $335-million-dollar program to enhance access to, and implement water-quality projects, in the Atchafalaya Basin.

Mississippi River and Oxbow Lakes

Because the Mississippi River has continually changed its course over the years, Louisiana is littered with oxbow lakes. The largest accessible and fishable oxbows are Yucatan, Bruin, St. John, Concordia, Deer Park, and Old River. During spring floods, to a greater or a lesser degree, the Mississippi River still flows into St. John, Deer Park, and Old River Lakes. These oxbows, so named because they resemble the "bows" that pioneer farmers used on oxen, can vary from 8 to 14 miles long and from 100 to 300 yards wide.

Lake Concordia, near the communities of Vidalia and Ferriday, is one of Louisiana's "trophy lakes" and has been extensively stocked with Florida-strain bass. Catches of 9- to 12-pound bass are a weekly occurrence from January through April.

Although most oxbows were once lined with fishable cypress, tupelo, and willow trees, development of waterside homes and camps has cut into these tree stands, and most of the structures in the oxbows are now piers and brushpiles planted by anglers. These are suitable holding locations for bass, crappie, and bluegills. The best bass fishing is from late winter through early summer, when top-water lures, jerkbaits, soft lizards, and jigs are top producers. Worms and crankbaits take over in early summer, and crankbaits and Carolina-rigged worms work best from midsummer into fall.

Crappie catches are best in the fall and early winter. Shiners and 2-inch-long black-and-chartreuse, orange-and-brown, and blue-and-white tube baits on a $^1/_{16}$-ounce jig consistently take large numbers of fish daily. Crickets and worms work for bream throughout the spring and summer.

Natural Lakes

Most of the productive natural lakes outside the Atchafalaya Basin are in Louisiana's south-central and southeastern areas. The notable exception is cypress-lined Lake Bistineau in the northwest near Shreveport.

The southeast lakes—Verret, Grassy, Palourde, DeCade, Penchant, and Des Allemands—are productive year-round for bass, crappie, and bream. Because crawfish flourish in these environs, jigs and other crawfishlike lures are especially good for bass. Crappie and bream also thrive on smaller crawfish.

These lakes are popular with fly anglers, who use popping bugs to catch bass and bluegills. Lined with cypress and tupelo, these lakes offer excellent topwater and artificial frog action, although spinnerbaits and soft-plastic lizards and worms hold sway most of the year. In spring, when crawfish are most numerous, black-and-blue and brown-and-orange jigs are most often fished near runouts and around stands of cypress. On hot summer days, working soft-plastic frogs over patches of floating duckweed is a solid technique.

The brackish water chain of Maurepas, Pontchartrain, Borgne, and St. Catherine provide launching pads for bass in nearby rivers, bayous, and grassy marsh ponds. Bass action here is subject to tidal movement, water levels, and wind direction. Spinnerbaits with chartreuse-and-white skirts, small spinnerbaits, and soft jerkbaits, lizards, and worms are the most productive lures.

The Lake Larto-Saline Lake complex in east-central Louisiana is the most productive crappie lake in the state. Crappie weighing over 3 pounds are common here, with March through May and September through December considered prime.

Reservoirs

The king of the hill in Louisiana is 186,000-square-mile Toledo Bend, which straddles the border with Texas. Smaller lakes like Caney Creek, Grand Bayou, Cleco, Indian Creek, and Chicot have been stocked with Florida-strain bass and hold the promise of trophy specimens.

Caney Creek, a smallish 5,000-acre impoundment near Jonesboro in north-central Louisiana, had produced 19 of the top 20 recorded largest bass in the state as of 1998. A state-record 15.97-pound largemouth came from these waters.

These reservoirs are the deepest-water fishing holes in Louisiana; bass, crappie, and bluegills react here as they do in most other lakes throughout the South. The bass tend to hold along points, creekbeds, and humps during late spring, summer, and early fall before moving up to pre-spawn staging areas along the upper reaches of creekbeds in late winter. Because Louisiana is a warm-weather state, even during winter, bass tend to spawn earlier here than elsewhere. They have been known to start preparing spawning areas as early as mid-January.

These lakes also hold large schools of white bass, striped bass, and hybrid striped bass. Crappie and bluegill numbers are highest in Toledo Bend and Indian Creek. These fish move to the old riverbeds in 60- to 80-foot depths in early summer and stay there through the fall and early winter.

Bass respond best to deep-running crankbaits and worms in late spring, summer, and early fall, after which spinnerbaits and buzzbaits take over. Jigs are best in winter and early spring, when jerkbaits and lizards begin to attract bass strikes.

Freshwater Marshes

Other than the Atchafalaya River Basin, Louisiana's bass-rich marshes can be the most confounding and confusing fishing areas for a newcomer. The vast marshes stretch from state line to state line, from the mouth of the Pearl River on the east to the mouth of the Mississippi River, and west nearly 250 miles to the Sabine River. The maze of waterways and mix of freshwater, brackish water, and saltwater provides the state with a nursery ground for countless finfish, shrimp, oysters, and crabs, all of which are food sources for predatory fish. The dividing line is usually the Intracoastal Canal, which spans the entire state.

These inland marshes are dotted with lakes, small bays, and freshwater or brackish water ponds, and are crisscrossed with bayous and canals. They have become a prime target for an increasing number of bass anglers. Increasingly powerful and reliable outboards have opened this area to small-boat owners since the early 1980s. Freshwater diversion projects have helped stabilize several areas, notably the Caernarvon and Delacroix Marshes on the east side of the Mississippi River south and east of New Orleans, and increased largemouth bass numbers such that these are preferred big-bass sites. Small numbers of crappie and bream inhabit these waters, and blue and channel catfish thrive even in areas considered to be brackish.

Because of the wide range of food, bass react to various offerings, including jigs in the winter and early spring, and lizards, worms, and spinnerbaits during late spring, summer, and fall. Crankbaits work best as bass congregate on points in the fall and early winter, when they move from the cooler water in the bayous and rivers into the canals. Topwater lures and soft jerkbaits work best in areas with extensive grassbeds, which occur most often in ponds and shallow canals.

The largest specimen of whale shark, a rare plankton-feeder found in warm oceans, was 41$^1/_2$ feet long and 23 feet around, and weighed more than 16 tons. It was captured near Pakistan in 1949.

L

Coastline and Saltwater

Of the five Gulf of Mexico states, Louisiana boasts the most productive nursery ground, thanks to the Mississippi River. It may in fact be the most productive in all of North America. Deposits of nutrient-rich soils and the Louisiana coast's proximity to the Gulf of Mexico create a fertile area that supports entire life cycles for as many as 300 species of finfish, shrimp, oysters, and crabs.

Among the marshes and throughout the state's 3-mile territorial limit out into the gulf are food and sportfish like spotted seatrout (speckled trout), red drum (redfish), southern flounder, Spanish and king mackerel, black drum, sheepshead, white trout, Atlantic croaker, spot, gray (mangrove) snapper, tarpon, and gafftopsail catfish, all of which use the maze of brackish- and saltwater marshes to spawn and/or raise young.

The two most highly prized and sought-after species are speckled trout and redfish. These, along with flounder, black drum, and sheepshead, move into shallow marshes during the fall and winter, making them available to small-boat anglers. During these months, smaller speckled trout and redfish follow shrimp into marshes, and also find minnows and small crabs to feed on; most of them later move out into the bays and lakes near the gulf to spawn with larger sea-run members of their species. Trout larger than 3 pounds seldom frequent inland waters, yet redfish up to 15 pounds are taken on light tackle in the same areas.

Soft-plastic minnow imitations in a wide array of colors, gold spoons, shad-colored crankbaits, and live minnows and shrimp are the best offerings for "inside" fish. Add a great variety of topwater lures to that list, and your tackle box is complete for fishing coastal bays, lakes, and barrier islands. Sheepshead prefer fresh shrimp. Most anglers also use corks for artificial and live baits, and employ a jerking method called "popping" to trigger strikes.

The best areas to find trout, redfish, and flounder are around rock jetties; in runouts, where shallow ponds empty into deeper canals and bayous; and over oyster beds in bayous, lakes, and bays. Beds of oysters tend to attract schools of baitfish. Tidal movement, either rising or falling, triggers feeding.

Most tackle stores are well stocked with the local maps and information needed to navigate the extensive series of canals and bayous.

Mississippi River Area

Breton Sound and its barrier island hold large numbers of trout, redfish, and Spanish mackerel during late spring, summer, and early fall. Oil platforms serve as artificial reefs for trout and redfish, while passes tend to hold redfish and white trout.

Barrier islands, notably Breton Island and the Chandeleur Island chain, are destinations for anglers looking for the largest trout and redfish. These are accessible only by boat. Wade fishing is the norm at these islands, which also attract particularly large shallow-water sharks swimming in the western gulf. Topwater lures are useful to anglers wading the islands, and fly anglers use topwater poppers along with shrimp imitations to take trout up to 8 pounds and redfish up to 40 pounds. The rock jetties at South and Southwest Passes hold large redfish and trout.

During fall and winter, smaller trout and redfish move into the marshes, even up into the Mississippi River, and provide opportunities to catch these saltwater fish along with largemouth bass, white bass, and striped bass. Shad-colored diving crankbaits and chrome-finished lipless crankbaits are the two most widely used lures. It's possible to catch a largemouth with one cast, a redfish with the next, and a striper with the next in the Mississippi River as far north as the Fort Jackson area, between New Orleans and Venice, which is the southernmost terminus of road travel along the river.

Other treasured spots are the Wagon Wheel, a series of oil-field location canals dug in a spoked-wheel pattern west of Venice; California Bay; Yellow Cotton Bay; Spanish Pass; Fast-Water Canal; and East Bay. The Pointe à la Hache canals, and small lakes and canals near Buras and Port Sulphur, also offer fall, winter, and early-spring trout and redfish action.

To the east, the Delacroix area has first-rate fall/winter bass, trout, and redfish angling. The starting point for most trips is the intersection of the Oak River and the Twin Pipeline Canals, about a 30-minute boat ride from the nearest launches at Delacroix and Pointe à la Hache.

Grand Isle-Fourchon-Cocodrie

Bayou Lafourche, which was a bed of the Mississippi River thousands of years ago, teams up with Barataria Bay and marshes and bays in Terrebonne Parish, to form an expanse of marshes, bayous, lakes, bays, and barrier islands highly favored among Louisiana anglers.

In Grand Isle, Elmer's Island, Fourchon Beach, and Belle Pass provide the only seaside fishing area with roads near the beaches. Local anglers use these three locations extensively to wade for trout, redfish, and Spanish mackerel.

To the east, Grand Terre Island and Four Bayous and Grand Bayou Passes are havens for summertime tarpon and redfish anglers. These areas are reached only by boat.

To the west of Fourchon, notable fishing areas include rock-studded East Timbalier Island and a chain of sandy barrier islands that once made up Last Island, or Isle Dernieres as found on some maps. The latter islands are reached only by boat.

Wade fishing for trout and redfish, and nighttime "gigging" for flounder are favorite pastimes at all islands except East Timbalier, which is ringed by underwater rocks to prevent erosion. Huge boulders here draw anglers for the largest speckled trout in this area of coastal Louisiana. The favorite tactic is to pitch a live 4- to 8-inch-long menhaden (called pogey) into the rocks. No weight or cork is used, and the baitfish is allowed to swim free around the boulders. This method also works on redfish and trout at the rock jetties at Belle Pass.

Redfish action concentrates near the passes from Four Bayous on the east end of this area, to Barataria and Caminada Passes on the east and west ends of Grand Isle, over to Little Pass and Whiskey Pass near Last Isle. Here, anglers use cracked or whole crabs on a 30-pound or heavier leader, with a 1-ounce or larger sinker 30 to 40 inches above the hook, to take "bull" reds, which can run up to 60 pounds (the state record is 61 pounds). They cast the rig into the pass and allow it to sit for 10 to 20 minutes. Because so many smaller fish inhabit these waters, the hook must be rebaited several times an hour.

Speckled trout and white trout are scattered throughout the area, even into Barataria, Timbalier, and Terrebonne Bays and Pelto and Barre Lakes. Numerous oil platforms and oil/gas pumping stations hold the fish, as do the barrier islands. Larger trout and redfish also stake out territory at the close-in oil platforms in the Gulf of Mexico. These fish prefer live baits to artificials. Boat launches are available at Grand Isle, Fourchon, Cocodrie, Dulac, and Theriot.

During fall and winter, speckled trout and redfish migrate into marshes as far north as the cities of Golden Meadow and Chauvin, which are 40 miles by road from the coast. Spots to check out during this time are Lake Laurier just north of Grand Isle; Bully Camp Sulphur Mine Lake and Catfish Lake west of Golden Meadow; Wonder Lake and Boudreaux and Robinson Lakes near Chauvin; Terrebonne, Petit Caillou, and Sale Bayous; Madison Bay near Cocodrie; and the extensive series of canals off the Houma Navigational Canal near Dulac.

Calcasieu Lake

Called Big Lake by locals, this area stretches southward 40 miles from south of Lake Charles to the Gulf of Mexico and offers the best chance to tie into a big speckled trout. Because of its much deeper and cooler water, the adjacent Calcasieu Navigational Canal holds trout and redfish during summer months. Trout up to 10 pounds are common in late spring and early summer, and 6- to 8-pounders show up in catches well into the fall.

Like marshes to the east, this area also holds the promise of first-rate late-fall and winter catches of smaller trout and redfish. Although smaller fish will attack gold spoons, jigs sporting soft-plastic minnow imitations, and topwater baits, anglers mostly cast live shrimp and minnows to oyster beds, small islands, runouts, and rock jetties.

Offshore

For variety of species and proximity to ports, Louisiana is without peer among the five Gulf of Mexico states with respect to offshore fishing.

A redfish is landed at Calcasieu Lake in western Louisiana.

Two factors influence the state's offshore catches: the Mississippi River and the oil platforms constructed off the state's coast after World War II. The river provides nutrients that concentrate baitfish, the first building block of the food chain, and the numerous oil platforms serve as artificial reefs to attract species like snapper, amberjack, grouper, cobia, tripletail, king mackerel, barracuda, Atlantic croaker, triggerfish, rainbow runners, and little tunny. They also attract tarpon, blackfin and yellowfin tuna, and, on occasion at the deeper oil rigs, sailfish, blue and white marlin, mako sharks, jewfish, and large pelagic sharks.

Tarpon is a prized species. From the mouth of the Mississippi River west to the Ship Shoal area south of Cocodrie, large schools of silver kings feed on a wide variety of baitfish. Striped mullet and menhaden are their favorite foods, and huge schools of these species show up in offshore waters during the summer and early fall.

Tarpon fleets from Houma, New Orleans, Golden Meadow, and Baton Rouge go after their quarry with trolled spoons and have taken to casting locally made jigs into schools of rolling tarpon. Since 1990, the hot tarpon spots are near West Delta block 58, the Grand Bayou Pass area, and the Midnight Lumps near the Mississippi River's South Pass. The state-record tarpon is a 230-pound specimen.

The waters south of the Mississippi River hold the best promise of tangling with marlin, yellowfin tuna, mako sharks, sailfish, and an occasional giant bluefin tuna. It is in this area that the river lies nearest to North America's continental shelf and its

1,000-plus-foot depths. Bottom areas east and west of the river tend to flatten out and thus do not have the depths needed to attract these blue-water species.

Anglers can reach blue water by traveling as few as 12 miles south of South Pass, or as many as 80 miles south of the popular launching/docking spot on Grand Isle, which is approximately 40 miles west of the river. Its proximity to this prolific area explains why Venice, on the Mississippi River, has become the busiest blue-water port in Louisiana. Lake Charles also has its share of blue-water anglers, who travel 100 miles south to the Flower Gardens, the only living coral reef in the western Gulf of Mexico that is located in U.S. waters. Once in blue water, and usually around rips, big-game anglers begin by trolling offshore lures in various colors.

Even though the allure of an offshore blue-water adventure is high on most anglers' lists, trips to the oil platforms in West Delta, Grand Isle, South Timbalier, Ship Shoal, and Eugene Island fill charter bookings and most hours of recreational fishing. The abundance of baitfish is evident around the rigs, and most anglers use stout rods and 4/0 conventional reels filled with 50- to 80-pound line to take a variety of species in depths from 60 to 250 feet. Live, fresh, and freshly frozen baitfish are used, either on drift lines or heavily weighted drop lines.

Patterning selected species is often the most difficult task, and anglers drop baited hooks to several different levels, usually at 10-foot intervals and starting at depths of 40-feet, to find species like snapper, grouper, and amberjack. The drift lines are usually reserved for cobia and king mackerel.

The flows of the Mississippi and Atchafalaya Rivers usually suspend a murky layer of freshwater over the gulf. This doesn't stop experienced anglers, who know that under this layer is clean greenish or blue saltwater. They also know, however, that under these conditions live baits or brightly colored jigs must be used to attract strikes. Otherwise, when offshore waters clear—usually by late summer—fresh and freshly frozen bait can be used with equal success.

Louisiana has also enhanced its offshore fishing through its Rigs-to-Reefs Program, a plan that sinks retired oil platforms on the bottom of the gulf to provide additional artificial reefs, which attract many of the same species that converge on standing platforms.

LOWHEAD DAM

A concrete structure in rivers that is designed to maintain a minimum water level above the dam. Because a lowhead dam obstructs fish movement in the river and there is turbulent, highly oxygenated water just downstream of the dam, fish such as shad, walleye, and smallmouth bass may congregate there. However, a lowhead dam is a deceivingly dangerous structure that can claim lives.

The typical dropoff at a lowhead dam is deceptively small, yet the power of the water going over

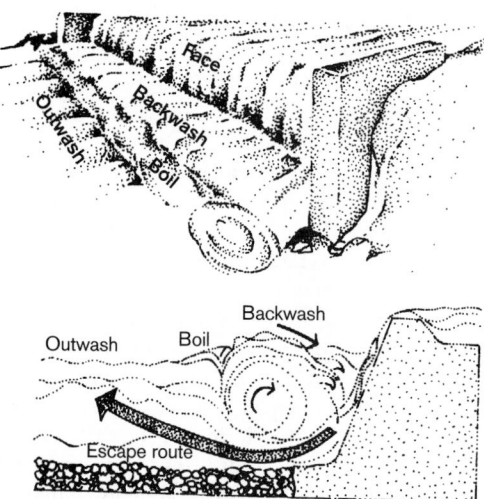

The powerful backwash below a lowhead dam is dangerous; it can pull a person back to the face of the dam, trapping the victim beneath the falling water.

the dam is great. Boaters heading downstream, especially those in nonmotorized craft like canoes or jonboats, can be tempted to shoot over the dam but risk capsizing when they do so. Boaters approaching a lowhead dam from below are tempted to get too close when placing or retrieving an anchor, for example, and they risk instability that causes capsizing as well.

The real danger lies in the powerful backwash that exists behind these dams; its hydraulic effect pulls a person back to the face of the dam, trapping them beneath the falling water without chance of rescue. Wearing a personal flotation device is of no help. It is necessary to stay well away from the upstream and downstream sides of a lowhead dam. **See: Boat; Safety.**

LUDERICK   *Girella tricuspidata.*

Other names—blackfish, black bream, darkie, bronzie.

It has been said that any angler who can master the art of luderick fishing has the necessary skills to catch any fish that swims. Certainly, angling for "loo-drik" has captured the hearts of most Australian saltwater anglers, and the affection shown this species, by old and young alike, is akin to the devotion demonstrated by their freshwater counterparts who angle after the legendary trout. For its mass, the luderick is one of the most determined fighters in the sea, and ranks as high as some of the top gamefish for its extraordinary stamina and fighting strength.

Although luderick anglers are convinced that its edible qualities are improved if it is bled as soon as possible after capture, there is a significant commercial fishery for the species along the East Coast of Australia.

Identification.   The luderick's body, which is moderately elongate and moderately compressed, is generally dark brown on top to silvery gray below. Depending on the habitat, this coloration can change to silvery gray on top to silvery white on the belly, or pale olive brown above with a beautiful bronze sheen extending to the belly. There can be 8 to 12 narrow, vertical, dark bars across the back and sides. The mouth is small, with flattened tricuspid teeth. There is a single, unnotched dorsal fin, and the caudal fin is large and emarginate or concave. Fins are a uniform grayish green.

Size. The largest size recorded stands at 5.2 kilograms, but the average size taken by anglers is around 500 grams to 1 kilogram. An Australian angling record is listed at 2.43 kilograms.

Distribution. Luderick range from South Australia, along the Victorian coastline, and up the East Coast as far north as Hervey Bay in southern Queensland. They are also found on the northern, eastern, and western coasts of Tasmania.

Habitat. Luderick live in estuaries, bays, and inlets, and along rocky coastal shores. They prefer areas where seagrass is prolific but can be found around algae-covered bridge and jetty pylons, rock walls, and submerged reefs. They live close to weed-covered rocks and feed along the edges where the wash dislodges small weed growths.

Life history/behavior. The luderick is a very fecund fish, capable of spawning up to 400,000 eggs. Spawning is a lengthy process and occurs during the months of July through March, the timing depending on location. Eggs are released in the surf and in the estuary mouths, and the larvae find their way into the seagrass beds from where they move well up into the estuaries and coastal lakes. They are schooling fish that hide in the weed-beds, where they are fairly safe from predatory fish.

Food and feeding habits. Luderick are essentially herbivorous, although they are sometimes taken on a prawn. Estuary luderick feed chiefly on green, filamentous algae, and those fish living along rocky shores feed on a lettucelike plant (colloquially called lettuce or cabbage) that grows prolifically on the ocean rocks as far up as the high-tide mark. They will also feed on small crustaceans, marine worms, and the flesh of the cunjevoi, a tunicate that lives on the rocks at about low tide level.

Angling. The tackle of the estuary luderick angler consists of a light, flexible 2.5- to 3-meter rod and a reel spooled with 2- or 3-kilogram-strength line. The line is usually greased so that it floats on the surface, ensuring that there is no slack to interfere with the angler's strike when the float disappears. Accurate timing of the strike is an empirical skill. Hooks are small (No. 10 or 12), suspended beneath a quill or pencil float with near-neutral buoyancy (weighted by sheet lead or split shot to achieve this state), and baited with a twist of green weed. Sometimes small pieces of fresh green prawns are used when the angler runs out of weed. Lures are not used for luderick fishing, nor are flies.

Rock-based anglers use a stouter rod to 3.5 meters, and a larger, sturdier reel. Hooks are No. 8 or 10, suspended beneath a heavier float and usually baited with sea lettuce. Lines are heavier, to 5 kilograms, and may or may not be greased. Although conditions are more boisterous than those experienced in estuary situations, accurate timing of the strike is still required.

Tides and currents are carefully considered, with flood and ebb tides affecting the feeding patterns of the fish. Chumming is considered essential, and a chum of finely chopped weed mixed with sand for estuary fishing, or torn sea lettuce leaves scraped into the wash by the rock plates on the boots of the rock angler, is the ideal. Some anglers mix other ingredients with their chum in order to attract other species to a bottom bait while they concentrate on the luderick.

When hooked, luderick refuse to give up, and patience is essential at all times until the fish is safely in the net. They frequently dive for the bottom, and have been observed rubbing their cheeks along rocks in an attempt to dislodge the hook. The action of the sensitive rod will cushion most of these runs, but the angler must be on guard, especially when the fish reaches the surface, to counter a sudden surge in which the fish dives back to the bottom.

LUMPFISH *Cyclopterus lumpus.*

Other names—lump, lumpsucker, nipisa, kiark-varrey; Italian: *ciclottero;* Spanish: *cicloptero.*

One of the largest members of the Cyclopteridae family of lumpfish and snailfish, the unusual-looking lumpfish is not a quarry of anglers, but it is known as a food fish in Europe and is reportedly valued for its eggs as an inexpensive substitute for caviar.

Identification. The lumpfish is a stout-bodied, almost round fish with a humped upper profile. It has a warty appearance due to a ridge of prominent tubercles running along the middle of the back, as well as three other rows of tubercles on the side, the uppermost of which extends from the tip of the snout to the base of the tail. Another distinctive feature is the way the pelvic fins are fused to form a round suction disk, which enables the lumpfish to attach itself to rocks. Of variable coloration, it is usually olive green or bluish gray with a yellowish belly; this grows red on males during breeding. The pectoral fins are broad and fanlike, and lower rays start at the throat region. The first dorsal fin is apparent only in the young.

Size. The lumpfish can grow to 2 feet and 21 pounds, although it is usually smaller.

Distribution. In the western Atlantic, lumpfish occur from Hudson Bay to James Bay and from Labrador to New Jersey; they are rarely found from the Chesapeake Bay south or in Bermuda. In the eastern Atlantic, lumpfish occur from the Barents Sea to Iceland and Greenland and south to Spain.

Black shale in Ohio and Pennsylvania has produced many complete fossil sharks that have been dated to the Devonian Period, 410 to 355 million years ago.

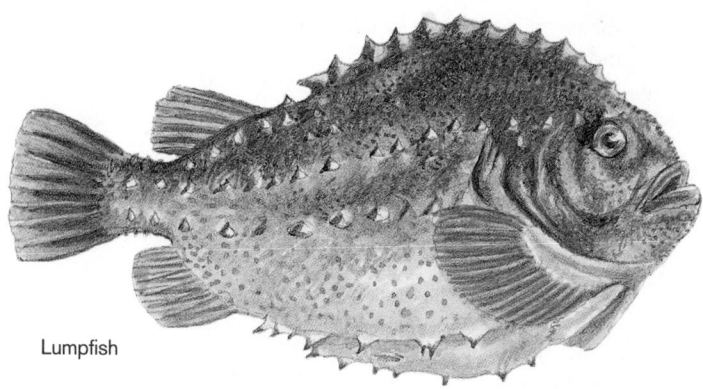

Lumpfish

Habitat. Lumpfish generally inhabit rocky bottoms of cold waters but may also occur among floating seaweed.

Life history/Behavior. Female lumpfish may lay 20,000 eggs or more, which sink to the bottom and stick. They are guarded by the male until they hatch. Lumpfish are solitary rather than schooling fish.

Food. The lumpfish feeds on small crustaceans and small fish.

LUNATE

Used to describe a caudal fin that is shaped like a crescent moon.

LUNKER

A big fish of any of the larger species.
See: Trophy Fish.

LURE

The generic definition of the word "lure" as a noun is "a thing used to entice," and as a verb is "to attract, tempt, or entice." Thus, in the broadest sense related to sportfishing, a lure might be construed as any natural or artificial object with a hook that is used to catch a fish. However, this all-encompassing definition is accepted and referenced only by nonanglers and language purists. Anglers have a narrower view of what constitutes a lure, and it excludes any live or dead natural organism. Thus, an earthworm, a minnow, and an insect aren't lures, even though they're used to tempt or attract fish.

The distinction between broad types of objects used to catch fish has long been clearly delineated between natural organisms, called natural bait *(see)*, and objects that are not natural but imitate natural foods consumed by fish. The latter became known as "artificial lures," but since the mid-twentieth century the word "artificial" has been decreasing in common usage.

Today most anglers classify objects used to catch fish as being either natural bait or lures. Thus, a simple twenty-first century definition of a lure is any nonnatural object with a hook that is used to catch fish. These nonnatural objects are made from a variety of materials, primarily wood, metal, lead, and hard and soft plastic, but also including feathers, fur, yarn, and combinations of materials.

History

The history of lures as described in print dates back to artificial flies, which were used at least in the late fifteenth century, if not earlier. The first published description of artificial flies appeared in the second edition of Dame Juliana Berners' *Boke of Saint Albans,* printed in 1496. Included in the book was her essay *Treatyse of Fysshynge with an Angle,* in which she mentioned a dozen flies. Nearly 200 years later, Izaak Walton's famous book *The Compleat Angler* listed 65 artificial fly patterns for trout. Little progress had occurred in the interim, and lightweight fly patterns for angling with reel-less rods continued to be the only known fishing lures until the nineteenth century, when modern fishing reels evolved and gradually created a means for dispensing, retrieving, and storing line; after this period, fishing horizons began to expand.

Lures made of metal appeared in the nineteenth century, perhaps starting in England around 1800 with the Phantom Minnow, which had a metal head, metal fins, three treble hooks, and a silk body. Julio T. Buel, an American, is credited with inventing the metal fishing spoon; he reportedly had fished with his own invention since 1821 and began the commercial manufacture of spoons in 1848. The first patent for a wooden lure was granted to Americans David Huard and Charles Dunbar in 1874, yet James Heddon of Michigan is credited with creating and manufacturing the first wooden fishing lure in the early 1900s.

The types, categories, and variations of artificial lures mushroomed exponentially every decade thereafter, greatly fueled by the development of plastic molding technology after World War II, fiberglass fishing rods, nylon monofilament fishing line, and the development of both spinning and spincasting reels.

General Information

Lures catch fish because of their appearance and the manner in which they are deployed, which are interrelated factors. Even though some lures don't specifically imitate or suggest food through their physical appearance, they imitate or suggest food in the way that they're used. Thus, in one sense or another, all lures represent some form of food, either mimicking it closely, as is true of artificial flies or minnow-style plugs, or suggesting it broadly, as is true of jigs, spinners, and spoons.

Even though lures represent food, they are not only or always struck by fish that are feeding. Fish strike lures for many reasons. Hunger is a prime motivation. Instinctive reflex, aggravation, competition, and protection are others. Fish refuse to strike lures at times for many reasons, too. Predatory fish, which are of major sportfishing interest, spend

L

varied portions of their time feeding; some species, especially many in saltwater, are necessarily eating machines and constantly forage, whereas others, especially many in freshwater, feed less frequently and are often more selective.

Certainly the range of food consumed by fish is extremely wide, varying with different environments, different species, and different seasons. Thus, some fish are more susceptible to lures, and certain types of lures and fishing techniques, than others, and there is great variety in the types of lures that have evolved and that are appropriate at a given time. A visit to a well-supplied tackle store, with a mind-boggling array of lures, will verify this.

To put the situation into perspective, consider a midsize lure manufacturer. When specific models are taken into account, then multiplied by the various sizes and assorted colors in which the models are produced, the number of different lures that the manufacturer makes may swell to a staggering 1,500 plus. And there are dozens of large and medium-size lure manufacturers, plus many more smaller ones, making fishing lures out of plastic, wood, and metal, not to mention all of the commercial and home tyers of artificial flies.

Either as the cause or the effect of this situation is the fact that anglers have a deep fascination with the objects that they use to dupe fish, and as a group anglers are obsessed with finding, creating, or trying new lures in the never-diminishing hope of increasing success. This not only fuels the array of individual products, but leads to extensive regional preferences in types and colors of lures used for various fish species.

Almost invariably the first question someone asks a successful angler is, "What type of lure did you use?" and this fact underscores the interest that anglers take in items that have caught, or will catch, fish. Some avid anglers possess so many lures that they could open up their own tackle emporium.

Function/design.   No lure, no matter how appealing it is to the human eye, will catch fish of itself. How the angler uses it—in other words, where it is fished and how skillfully it is retrieved—are key factors in its success, although some lures are inherently better than others owing to their design, swimming action, and appearance.

There are two elements to being consistently effective with lures. The first is knowing the quarry: knowing something about the behavior of the food it most often consumes and then matching lure selection to the habits of that fish and the prevailing conditions. The second is being completely familiar with the characteristics of each lure you use: being able to make each work to its maximum designed ability. The more you know about your lures and the fish you seek, and the better you understand the conditions in which you seek them, the better prepared you'll be to make a knowledgeable lure selection.

Categories.   Many lures overlap in application and technique, but others are suitable only to

All lures are somehow meant to imitate natural food; here, a 5-inch-long alewife is contrasted with wooden (top) and plastic minnow-imitating plugs.

particular conditions and require specialized usage. All lures are designed to perform a specific function, however, and thus can be reviewed in a general manner according to type or category. The category is, in part, a function of the materials that are used to create the lures. Flies, for example, are extremely lightweight lures primarily made of feather and fur that is wrapped around a hook. By comparison, spinners and spoons are comparatively heavy sinking lures that are made of metal. Plugs are wooden or molded hard-plastic lures with a lot of buoyancy and built-in swimming action. A detailed review of each category is contained under their respective entries.

See: Antique Fishing Tackle; Buzzbait; Crankbait; Fly; Jerkbait; Jig; Jigging Spoon; Plastic Worm; Plug; Soft Lure; Spinner; Spinnerbait; Spoon; Stickbait; Surface Lure; Surgical Tube Lure; Tailspinner; and Trolling Lures, Saltwater.

Lure Color

How we see color, how we think fish see it, and how this relates to the way we make lure color selections is an intriguing aspect of fishing. Successful anglers are routinely quizzed about what type and color of lure they used, and no other topic fascinates anglers more.

Size, action, vibration, and color complement each other and are all critical to a lure's success. But perhaps the most common modification to lures has nothing to do with their working action. It has to do with changing the lure's color.

You cannot discuss color without discussing light. Color is the result of reflecting (or absorbing) light of different wavelengths: The shortest wavelength visible to humans produces violet, and the longest produces red. Shorter (ultraviolet) and longer (infrared) wavelengths are invisible to the human eye—it is not clear whether fish can see them. Furthermore, colors are perceived differently above water than in the water, and their visibility is

A potpourri of plugs and spoons adorns an angler's Styrofoam "tackle box."

L

greater if they fluoresce. (Fluorescent objects absorb short wavelengths of light, particularly ultraviolet, and re-emit longer, visible wavelengths of light at a higher energy level.)

Although we know a great deal about how humans are affected by light and how we perceive colors, we can't say unequivocally that what we know applies equally to fish. Therefore, anglers form theories and opinions based on experience and information provided by limited research.

It was once thought that fish were color blind and that they perceived colors as gradients of gray. Over the last century, that opinion has changed, however. More than 60 years ago, researchers reported that some fish could definitely perceive colors. Then it was thought that some species of fish could see color and some couldn't. Now it is conceded that most fish see color; only cave fish and extremely deep-dwelling ocean fish do not. Over the past 50 years, various researchers have reported that the vision of some species of fish is tinted yellow, red, blue, or orange. Some had postulated that the most important sense of a fish is its hearing, especially in turbid water; others believe that fish may see far better than we think, even in turbid water.

Anglers have been influenced greatly by scientific studies and by their own attempts to analyze natural conditions. But many anglers still behave as if fish perceived colors exactly as we do; that is why it's said that some lures are designed to catch anglers, not fish. Some anglers completely disregard the color perception of fish in making lure color selections; some work strictly on the basis of natural forage imitation—if baitfish aren't chartreuse, why use a lure that color? And others are ambivalent, vacillating between what looks good to them and what other anglers seem to be successful with.

Despite the fact that we know more about our quarry and its sensory abilities than ever before, there still are some perplexing, fascinating, and unresolved questions. Perhaps the greatest puzzler is this: Why do fish strike a lure that bears no

physical resemblance to any natural food item? It happens all the time, of course. Some effective lures act unlike any known forage, some have a form unlike natural food, and some are colored unlike anything we know or see. Yet at times they are more productive than another lure that in every way seems more representative of real prey. The answer must be that, for some reason, these lures suggest food to that fish. What drew the fish's attention in the first place still begs for an answer.

Another mystery: How important is it to use a lure that we assume is most visible to the fish? At issue here is whether fish are acting principally on the basis of visual stimuli, whether vision is secondary to the fish's other senses, or whether it's important under some conditions but not others. Researchers think they have some clues to the answers to these questions and some insight into how fish perceive color and what makes them respond to our offerings. But we may never really know about these matters—and perhaps we never should, because angling will cease to be a sport when the puzzles have been solved.

Nonetheless, some fish appear to be sight-feeders almost exclusively, and a confirmed way to appeal to them is to use lures that have very high visibility under given water and light conditions at particular depths.

An overlooked and underexplored mystery is where the most prominent color should be located on a lure, especially a plug. Most predator and prey fish are dark on the top and light on the bottom. Did nature make them light on the bottom to be less conspicuous from below? Are they dark on the top so that they will blend in with the environment when viewed from above? Many anglers maintain that gamefish strike their prey (and lures) predominantly from below. If they are coming from below, should your aim be to imitate nature and have a light color at the bottom of your lure? If so, what difference does it make what the top color is? On the other hand, should your aim be to contrast nature and thus have the most visible color on the bottom of the lure? This coloring system, known as countershading, has been tried (with modest success) by manufacturers from time to time.

When someone reports that fish are taking a chrome plug with green ladderback tape on the top, you have to think about this. Fish seldom go down to chase a lure, so how could the ladderback tape atop the plug be influencing the catch? If the ladderback extends onto the sides of the lure, it may offer a bit of visual appeal to a fish. For this reason, when you add prism, luminescent, or ladderback tape to plugs, avoid the top of the lure and place it on the sides or bottom.

Should lure color be based on light intensity? Dark days/dark lures, light days/light lures has been an angling dictum for decades, though it is occasionally admitted that fish sometimes break the rules. There is good reason to use light-colored lures on dark days and dark-colored lures on light days. That might mean, for example, trolling a black spoon for salmon when it is very sunny, for example, especially in the early part of the season and when the fish are shallow. The dark color contrasts well with the brightness from above. However, many good anglers disagree with this.

There are a few facts about light and color in aquatic environments that you should know if you are going to make color work for you. The principal factors to assess are the depth to be fished, the clarity of the water, and the intensity of the light.

Research and conventional thought tell us that as light passes through water its intensity is reduced. This applies vertically as well as horizontally and is further influenced by the clarity of the water. As light intensity is reduced, red and violet are the first to lose their distinctive hue, followed by brown; ultimately these appear black. Blue and green retain their hue much longer, though they fade and don't appear the same shade. Fluorescent counterparts remain visible at greater depths and distances, with fluorescent chartreuse being especially visible. No less an authority than the United States Navy, after testing the visibility of colors at various depths in saltwater, concluded in a report that "fluorescent colors have been shown to be much more effective than regular paints of the same color under almost all conditions of underwater viewing." The Navy also found that background contrast—dark water, sandy or vegetative bottom, and so forth— significantly affected visibility of all colors and that different times of the day produced different results. Fluorescent orange, for example, was most visible early in the morning, but less so later, whereas fluorescent green exhibited the reverse pattern (fluorescent chartreuse was not tested); the Navy report concluded that this effect had more to do with contrast against background colors than with differences in brightness.

These tests relate only to human vision and perception, however. The color preferences of bass vary widely according to a researcher who studied the reactions of largemouth bass to color. He used a light meter to record light transmittance values under clear, stained, and muddy water conditions at specific times of the day and under clear and overcast sky conditions. One of his findings was that the most visible color doesn't necessarily contrast with the background, but the way light disperses in the water is very important. If you have plankton or debris or sediment, these can have different effects on the scattering of light, either reflecting or refracting it, and this seems to modify things so that the consistency of background contrast is not always critical.

Surprisingly, his research showed that fish in muddy water can perceive color at greater distances— up to 4 feet—than had previously been thought. Their range of vision was a maximum of 10 to 12 feet in stained water and up to 40 feet in the clearest water. Anglers who almost always fish under clear water conditions can attest to the ability of fish like salmon and trout to see lures from a great distance, which may account for the fish-catching productivity of brightly flashing, highly reflective silver and chrome spoons and plugs. It is common to catch fish that have not been spotted below the boat on sonar equipment; when attracted to the lure, the fish are far enough away that they are outside the cone angle of the transducer.

Another of his findings was that each color of the spectrum is either camouflaged or highly visible at some time during the day; in other words, colors fade in and out depending on the conditions of the environment. This makes sense if you consider the biological interaction between a predator and prey fish such as shad, minnows, or sunfish, for example. If those forage organisms were highly visible all the time to predators, their population would be limited. But they're not always visible. They're camouflaged a large part of the time. Only sometimes are their particular color patterns highly visible.

Another finding was that certain colors used in combination seemed to be especially attractive. Many anglers can attest to this, whether using different colors of prism tape on spoons or using combined paint colors on their plugs. It is no accident

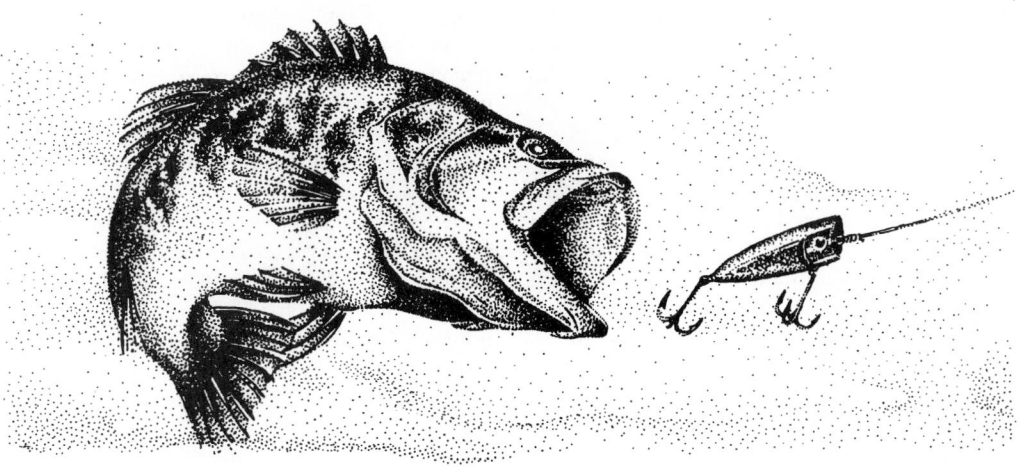

that the hands-down favorite spoon color pattern for northern Canada fishing, for example, is the so-called Five of Diamonds, which is five red diamond shapes on a yellow background. Decades ago before the world of lures and colors exploded, red and red-and-white lures were vitally important to anglers. Surely anglers then thought that those colors were especially visible to fish.

Today not only do we have a greater range of available colors, we even have lures that emit light when there is little or no natural light available. These are phosphorescent and chemiluminescent products, intended for use under low-light conditions. Early morning, evening, night, and dark cloudy days lend themselves to the use of light-emitting lures or colors, as does fishing in very deep water. Anglers have used chemiluminescent light sticks inside plugs to catch lake trout and salmon at night, in early morning, and in deep-water downrigger fishing. Although this strategy has been moderately productive, phosphorescent lures, which have to be exposed to a light source, seem preferable because they are more subtle; however, they are less convenient because they need repeated exposure to light.

Phosphorescent lures have been available for a long time. Phosphorescent paint is used on the exterior of these lures (although you can add phosphorescent tape to conventionally painted lures). You hold phosphorescent lures close to a light source, such as a lantern or spotlight, to "charge" them up. The charge lasts for roughly 20 minutes, after which you have to recharge the lure. This system is good for those who are casting and can recharge lures periodically between casts, but it isn't as convenient for trollers who have to bring lines in to retrieve lures for recharging.

The matter of lure color and color visibility is an especially interesting subject for trollers because they are usually passing by fish fairly quickly and often don't have a chance to make repetitive presentations. The fish are in all likelihood striking out of hunger and reflexive instinct, as opposed to being aggravated or coaxed, and the fish's abilities to hear and see prospective prey seem to be particularly important aspects of foraging. If you adhere to the theory that fish won't strike trolled lures that they can't see, then you must play the color game fastidiously. Trout and salmon trollers, for instance, fish with some of the strangest lure colors and color combinations imaginable, and thus perhaps play to the fish's sense of vision more than many other trollers, although big-game anglers using offshore trolling lures are not far behind in this department.

You can alter lure colors, especially on spoons, if you keep a supply of colored prism tape with you. This tape is sold in sparkle and reflective versions, in sheet form or precut into various patterns, including lightning bolt, ladderback, angled strips, and more. You can completely cover an old color with a new one, or add a strip of color to a lure to enhance it. Before putting on the tape, it's best to keep a lure in the sun or in your pocket for a while to warm it up (in cold weather or when fishing cold water) so that the tape will adhere better.

You should consider visibility as an important aspect of all lure fishing and should realize that on occasion it can be the paramount factor causing a fish to be attracted to your lure, but that it is usually is not the sole factor. A combination of factors, including the action of the lure, its speed, its color, the manner in which it is fished, and the place in which it is fished, all contribute to success.

LURE MAKING

Nearly every generic type of commercially manufactured lure on the market got its start as someone's experimental creation. Since the first angler tried to pull fish out of the water, people have been making tools to catch fish. Nowhere has there been more devotion to making such tools than in the arena of lures. Many of the most successful lure manufacturing companies in the world started with a homemade or handmade creation that was crafted for the purpose of catching fish and that eventually turned into a business. Even today you can buy lures that were made in someone's garage workshop and are sold to tackle stores on a limited or regional basis.

Tinkering with lures has fascinated anglers for generations. Some of this tinkering leads to no more than making modifications (see: lure modifying/repairing), but some leads to actually making lures, not with the intention of starting a commercial enterprise (although it can happen), but with the intention of expanding an interest in angling into a hobby where lures or rigs are made for personal use. Many fly anglers create their own flies and poppers (see: flycasting tackle) and get a lot of pleasure out of this craft, and they enjoy the satisfaction of taking fish on artificials that they have created. From a creative standpoint, making lures is akin to tying flies but obviously much different in terms of process and materials.

Although few people have access to some of the more sophisticated raw-material components of certain lures (imported woods, hi-tech plastics, sophisticated molding materials, machinery, etc.), it is possible to acquire suitable materials and components that will allow you to make or assemble lures that catch fish. Obviously, some lures are easier to make than others, and what you make will likely reflect the kinds of fishing you do and the species you pursue. A river steelhead and salmon angler is going to need spoons and spinners, for example, whereas a reservoir crappie angler is going to need a lot of small jigs. If you fish in places (where it is common to lose a lot of tackle (like brushpiles and other cover, or swift-flowing rivers and streams) then making your own lures not only has a hobby element but a practical one in that you're likely to lower your average cost for terminal tackle items.

Practicalities. The following information will help you get started in lure making. Don't be put off by the list of tools or supplies; a good way to economize is for fishing buddies or members of a club to get together on acquiring some of the materials as well as the bulk supplies. Obviously you should always be careful when working with tools; here, you should be especially careful when you are heating and pouring plastics or metals. These substances not only can cause a bad burn but also can produce undesirable fumes. Using the appropriate protective devices (a breathing mask, glove, eyewear, smock, etc.) is a good idea; proper ventilation is also necessary. Be attentive to issues concerning the use and disposal of lead, since you're likely to work with lead for jig heads, sinkers, and spinnerbaits. If lead is prohibited for terminal tackle use, you may not be able to acquire material for melting and pouring, and whatever old lead that you possess may have to be disposed of properly.

Make sure that you use quality components and those of appropriate size, length, strength, etc. The components must be able to stand up to the anticipated use and to the pressure that will be brought on the terminal tackle. Big, strong fish can decimate components; even good-quality components will split or break if they are too weak for the line strength or the drag tension. Some lures will come apart after being victim to only a few fish because the wire or the hook hangers or other components were not heavy enough. Obviously the quality of paint and the finish that you give will be important, especially for wooden lures, which can soak up water and become unbalanced. The proper paint and finish will help guard against this.

If you'll be making a lot of lures, remember to keep a junkyard of old lures and parts. The components from discarded lures (lips, hook hangers, screws, etc.) can be useful when making or modifying lures. You might get some useful parts from old and cheap throwaways at grab bag bins and flea markets.

Finally, remember that the success of many, if not most, lures, whether they are commercially made or homemade, is dependent upon their action in the water. When you make your own lures, you have to constantly check to see that they work right in the water; if they don't have the correct action, chances are they will not be fish catchers. So keep tinkering with each lure until it does work like it's supposed to.

Tools
Tools for making lures vary widely with the type of lure. In many cases only a few tools are required. Do not buy tools until you have a need for them. Some general suggestions are as follows.

Pliers. Standard pliers can be used to bend wire, hold lure parts, and perform general-purpose tasks.

Round-nose pliers. These are used for making the round eyes on various rigs and lures.

Split-ring pliers. These slim-jawed, long-nose pliers have a tooth on one end of the jaw for easy opening of split rings, and are ideal for changing

free-swinging hooks on lures.

Molds. Aluminum or metal molds for molding jig heads, certain spoons, and sinkers are readily available from several companies. Most are hinged, two-piece styles for use with molten lead. There are also plastic molds for making plug and fly rod popper bodies; they use a special two-part plastic mix that works quickly and easily. Both two-part and open-face molds are available for melting PVC plastic and molding soft plastic lures.

Wire formers. Several types of wire-forming tools are available for making different bends in wire as required with various rigs, spinners, spinnerbaits, and buzzbaits. Instructions are supplied with these easy-to-use tools.

Wire cutters. Wire cutters are necessary to cut wire and finish wire-formed lures. Side-clipping wire cutters that can make a flush cut are best; because they have no bevel along the outside edge of the cutting blades, they can cut very closely to eliminate a protruding tag end.

Snips. Various types of snips can be used to cut sheet metal if you're making spinner blades and spoon blanks from scratch. The best of these are so-called aviation snips, which have compound leverage and are designed for cutting through thicker-gauge metals than what can be cut with standard sheet metal snips.

Carpentry tools. For making plugs from wood blanks, consider tools such as back saws, coping saws, drills, drill bits, carving knives, rules, rasps, files, sandpaper, and emery boards. Some of these, such as files, rasps, and emery boards, are also a must when making certain lures, for example, when the metal on spoons must be smoothed or the seam edges on jig heads sanded.

Brushes. Small plastic-handled disposable brushes are a must for painting and also for coating with clear protective finishes.

Scale netting. This is necessary for putting a scale-pattern finish on lures; it's available from hobby sources and from fabric shops (where it is known as tulle).

Supplies
Lure-making supplies are available from specialty mail-order merchandisers and also from some tackle shops. Some of the items you may need include the following:

Spinner blades. These come in several different shapes, many sizes, and many metallic and painted finishes. They are primarily used in making spinners and spinnerbaits, and sometimes they are attachments on other lures.

Buzzbait blades. Buzzbait blades are like large, wide propeller blades and are designed to be used singly or in tandem (counter-rotating) on the buzzbait shaft. Many finishes, styles, and several sizes are available.

Spinner bodies, beads, and other parts. Beads of different size are used for the bodies of some spinners and are available in many colors of plastic and in solid brass and nickel-plated brass. Odd-shaped bodies are also available in plastic, brass, and nickel-plated metal. Other necessary parts include clevises to hold the blade and allow rotation on the shaft, and colored plastic sleeves to fit over hooks.

Spoon blanks. Spoon blanks are available in many sizes, finishes, and shapes for easy spoon assembly. To complete the lure, you need only add hooks with split rings by using split-ring pliers or add a split ring at the head of the lure for line fastening. Blanks for lipless thin-metal baits, also called blade baits, are sometimes available without hooks, similarly to spoons.

Wire forms. Wire forms for spinners come in straight shafts, with an eye wrapped on one end and with a loop fastener for hanging hooks on the finished lure. Wire forms for jigging spoons and lead tailspinners are made to be molded into the lead lures, leaving an exposed hook hanger(s) and line tie. Those for spinnerbaits and buzzbaits are made in the required shapes and designed to be slipped onto a hook and molded into the head of the lure.

Spinnerbait, buzzbait blanks. These blanks come painted or unpainted; the former requires painting the head, and both require adding blades and skirt to complete.

Plug blanks. Different styles of plug blanks are available, both painted and unpainted. Most have molded-in hook hangers and require only hooks, attached with split rings, to complete. Some wood blanks require hook hangers and lure screw eyes to add hooks and line ties and to hold propellers.

Jig heads. Molded, unpainted jig heads are used as they are and rigged with grubs or worms, but they can also be painted and wrapped with skirt material to make hair jigs.

Hooks. Hundreds of styles, sizes, and finishes of hooks are available for all types of lure making. The most common are treble hooks for crankbaits, large single hooks for spinnerbaits and buzzbaits, and bent-shank jig hooks for molding jigs.

Propellers, lips, hook hangers, plug fittings. Hook hangers, propellers, screw-in lips, and other plug fittings make it easy to complete hard baits.

Various Colorado (left) and Indiana (right) blades are used for making spoons, spinners, and assorted bait rigs.

Skirt material. Plastic and rubber spinnerbait and buzzbait skirt material can be obtained in bulk or in completed form ready for use, often from good tackle shops. Other material for dressing jigs and hooks includes hackle, marabou, natural fur, synthetics, and stranded flash materials in any combination or color; these are available from tackle shops, mail-order houses (especially fly tying suppliers), and craft shops.

Thread. Thread is needed for wrapping tails and skirts on jigs and hooks. Use the 2/0 size for small lures, A for medium lures, and D for large lures.

Liquid soft plastic. Milky-looking liquid plastic is used to make new soft plastic lures and is available from some tackle shops and mail-order houses.

Liquid plastic additives. Hardener, softener, color, and scent may be mixed in the liquid soft plastic to effect the feel, look, or smell of the finished lure.

Plastic for foam-bodied lures. Two-part foam plastic is available to make polyurethane bodies for plugs and popping bugs.

Spinners

Spinners are among the easiest of lures to make, since they require no special skills and no painting. The necessary parts include spinner wire, clevises, blades, bodies or beads, and hooks. Usually the spinner wire is 0.030 in diameter and available straight, with a wrapped eye or with a hooked loop eye. The wrapped eye is often best for standard spinners, since it eliminates having to make a line-tie eye. Use wire several inches longer than the intended spinner to give yourself some working room. Clevises come in folded or stamped styles, with stamped best for spinners. Get the right size to allow shaft clearance with the blades chosen. Shaped bodies in metallic and painted finishes or metallic or plastic beads make up the bodies of spinners. Bodies and beads can be mixed in a lure. Treble hooks are standard on most spinners, but you can use doubles or singles also. Choose the right size, based on experience or comparison with commercially made spinners.

Begin making the spinner by slipping a clevis into the hole on a blade and then sliding the wire shaft through the clevis. Make sure that the concave side of the blade faces the shaft. Then slide on a small metal bead to serve as a bearing for the rotating clevis. Add a body or series of beads as desired. Most bodies are sized to end at the lower end of the blade.

At this point, use pliers to make a right angle bend in the wire, leaving clearance for the wire wrap and also clearance for the turning clevis. The right angle is to position the eye in the center of the wire. Usually a clearance of about $1/4$- to $3/8$-inch is about right. Use round-nose pliers to complete a wrap; then slide on a treble hook. At this point, the eye will be complete, with the excess wire at right angles to the main spinner shaft. Hold the spinner eye and hook with pliers; then wrap the excess wire two turns around the spinner shaft. Use flush-cutting wire cutters to remove the excess wire. Many variations, sizes, and colors of spinners can be made using this basic, simple technique.

Spinnerbaits

Spinnerbaits are almost as easy to make as spinners, although they can be more time-consuming if you mold your own bodies by using wire forms and hooks. You can also purchase the parts needed, which include the body/wire form, skirts, spinner blades, clevises, beads, split rings, and swivels. With a wire/painted body form, begin cutting the upper shaft to the length you desire for attaching the blades. Then use round-nose pliers to form an incomplete eye in the end of the wire. Separately, use split-ring pliers to connect a spinner blade and small swivel to a split ring. Slip the other eye of the swivel onto the partially completed eye on the end of the shaft, and close the eye with pliers.

Skirts are held in place by friction, fitting over the collar of the molded lead body. Slide the skirt over the collar to complete the lure. If the lure is unpainted, paint the body before adding the skirt (see: *lure modifying/repairing*). To make your own bodies, follow the instructions that come for making jigs.

It is also easy to make in-line spinnerbaits (where the blades are on the main shaft). For this, the instructions are the same as for a spinnerbait with an overhead arm, but prior to making the eye in the wire, slide on a clevis holding a blade (concave to the rear) and a few small beads to separate this forward blade from the blade added to the end of the wire. Then complete as with the other lure.

Buzzbaits

Buzzbaits are similar to spinnerbaits except that they're designed to be used on the surface, the blades are different, and the body shape is often slightly flattened. To make buzzbaits, you'll need the wire/body form, skirts, buzz-style blades, and pop rivet-type bearings.

Assembly is easy. First slide a single buzz blade onto the upper straight shaft. Then add a small bearing sleeve, and use pliers to make a sharp right-angle bend in the wire close to the end. Add a skirt by sliding it onto the collar on the rear of the body. That's all there is to it. Variations can include two blades, which should be counter-rotating (they are sold and described that way), with a bearing bead or two between them for separation (you don't want the blades to hit and lock) and easy spinning, and a choice of plastic or metal blades. Plastic is harder to find, but if you've saved the plastic blades from older commercially manufactured models, you can adapt them.

If the lure is unpainted, you have to paint the body before adding the skirt (see: *lure modifying/ repairing*). To make your own bodies, follow the instructions for making jigs.

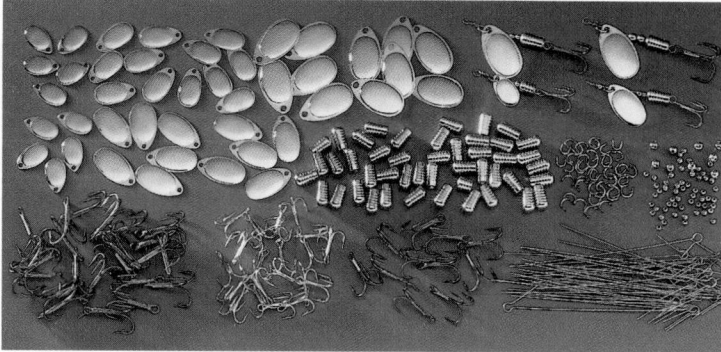

These are the components for making spinners.

Spoons

Spoons can be simply assembled from the basic components, or you can go the extra distance and make them from scratch.

To assemble spoons with free-swinging hooks, you'll have to obtain appropriate blanks, which are the spoon bodies without any parts or hooks. Many sizes, styles, and finishes (metallic and painted) are available. You also need split rings and hooks. Treble hooks are traditional on most spoons, but you can use singles or doubles as the circumstances may warrant; lightweight trolling spoons are popular in single-hook versions, and some places actually require the use of single hooks on lures. To assemble, use split rings and split ring pliers to connect the hole in the rear of the blank to the hook eye. Then use the same technique to add a split ring as a line tie to the forward hole in the blank. The same process, incidentally, is used for lipless thin-metal baits, or blade baits.

To make lightweight spoons from scratch, you can buy sheet metal from hobby shops and use heavy snips to cut out shapes that you wish to try. To shape the blade, hammer it on a scrap of wood until satisfied with the shape and appearance. Then use a drill or drill press to make a small hole ($1/16$ inch to $1/8$ inch) through each end.

You can make fixed-hook spoons (like weedless spoons) by drilling an additional hole in the center of the blank and then turning up (toward the concave side) the tail end of the blank with the hole.

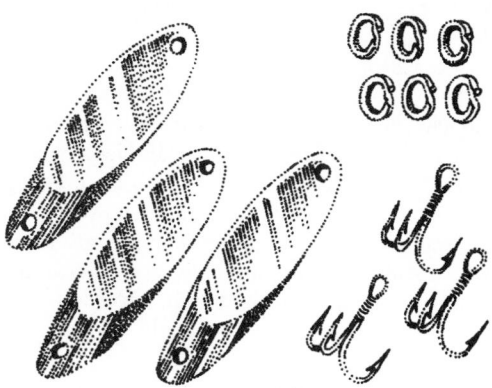

Casting spoons can be assembled from readily available bodies, hooks, and split rings.

Thread a hook through the hole in this bend, and put a bolt or pop rivet through the hook eye to the hole in the center of the blade. Because of the size of hook eyes, this is usually possible only in large spoons. Small fixed-hook spoons can be made by soldering the hook to the concave side of the blade, although some finishes and metals are difficult to solder.

Other variations are to drill small holes on each side of the tailing edge of the spoon and use small split rings to attach tiny willowleaf spinner blades for added flash.

Jigs

Jigs are essentially a leadheaded hook that has various head shapes and that is dressed with some material (perhaps a body of hair, feathers, soft plastic, or a combination of these). The term "jig" technically refers to the entire lure in its dressed form, whereas leadhead refers to the lure without body dressing, and bucktail refers to a lure with a hair body. However, these terms are often used interchangeably, especially leadhead and jig *(see: jig)*.

Making completed or dressed jigs can be simple if you use premolded leadheads; these can be obtained in unpainted or painted versions in virtually any style or size. Making any type of jig can be more involved if you do the actual leadhead molding.

Molding leadheads.   To mold jig heads onto hooks, you need the proper molds (which are the forms into which you pour the molten lead), the right size and style of jig hooks (which are often specific for each mold), any additional required attachments, a pouring ladle, a source of lead heat, heavy gloves, and a sturdy work area. Safety is essential for working with lead. Make sure that the work area is sturdy and large enough and that there is proper ventilation to protect from lead fumes. Do not eat or smoke during this activity (lead can be transferred to your body this way), and make sure that pets, young children, or other distractions aren't present.

Use a strong pot or ladle to melt the lead, and use an old stainless steel teaspoon to strain off any dross or slag floating on the surface. Begin by pouring lead into the mold *without a hook in the mold cavity.* The purpose of this is to heat the mold so that you get complete jig heads. These initial moldings, usually deformed as a result of contacting the cold mold, can be remelted. Once the mold is hot enough (all cavities fill completely), add the jig hook to the mold, close the mold, and rapidly pour the lead into each sprue hole. Allow it to cool for a few minutes; then open the mold to remove the hot leadheads. Continue the process to make up a batch of leadheads. Later use wire cutters to remove the sprue particles from the leadheads. Once the leadheads have cooled, they are ready for painting and/or dressing.

An ideal way to make leadheads is to try to pour a season's supply of leadheads at one sitting, with the aid of a partner and several molds. One person can be responsible for pouring the molds; the other for emptying the poured molds and refilling them with hooks.

Dressing.   You can tie a hair, feather, or synthetic tail to an unpainted head and then paint the head and the thread wrap at the same time, or you can tie onto a painted leadhead and wrap it with an appropriate color wrap, sealing that for protection with a clear finish. For painting details, *see: Lure Modifying/Repairing.*

To tie a skirt of hair, feathers, or synthetics onto a leadhead, you need a vise or locking pliers to hold the hook, skirt material, and tying thread. Skirt material can be bucktail, calftail, saddle hackles, or material known as Ultra Hair, Super Hair, FisHair, etc. Tying thread can be size 2/0 for small jigs, size A for medium jigs, and size D for very large jigs.

To tie a skirt onto a leadhead, the hook has to be held securely, point up. Fly tying vises are ideal, although you can use a small hobby vise or hold the hook in locking pliers that in turn are clamped into a bench vise. With the hook horizontal, use fly tying techniques to tie down the thread and skirt materials. For this, begin by wrapping the thread around the collar or hook shank, wrapping over previous wraps to secure the thread. Then lay bundles of fur, synthetics, or feathers onto the collar and wrap over with thread. This can be done in one bundle or by wrapping several bundles in place to get different colors/materials or a thicker tail. Clip any excess material in front of the thread wrappings. Continue to wrap to make a neat, tight collar of thread, and tie off using a whip finish, such as that used on a rope end to prevent unraveling. Seal and protect the wrap by dipping the head and thread wrap into paint (if not previously painted) or coat with a clear epoxy, fly tying head cement, or clear fingernail polish *(see: fly tying).*

Some leadheads are fished with soft tails, most of which are made of plastic. To put these on a jig, simply slip the soft body (lizard, worm, shad, grub, crayfish, etc.) onto the hook. Most anglers wait until they're on the water to decide which soft body, or at least which color, to put on the jig. And many anglers add a soft body to a jig that has already been dressed with a hair or synthetic tail.

Sinkers

Sinkers can be molded using the same techniques as used for making jig heads. Molds are available for making all sizes and types of sinkers. The same safety and procedural considerations must be followed as for jig heads. You can even make sinkers with special features, such as egg sinkers, worm weights (slip sinkers), and split shot, by using core rods and inserts supplied with the molds. Sinkers do not require hooks, but some require swivels (bass casting), wire forms (walking sinkers), or wire eyes (pyramid, dollar, others). Insert these into the mold before pouring, using the same procedure as the one used for hooks when making jig heads.

Some sinkers such as worm weights are painted; most are not.

Soft Plastic Bodies

Soft plastic bodies can be made through a molding technique similar to that for molding sinkers and jig heads. For this you need the liquid plastic, plastic color, plastic scent (if desired), a melting pan, and one- or two-piece soft plastic molds. Allow plenty of work space and good ventilation.

To mold soft plastic bodies by using an open-face, or one-piece, mold, first melt the liquid plastic on the stove, setting heat very low to prevent burning. Next add color and scent according to the manufacturer's directions. Continue melting and stirring to mix the color and scent. Once the mixture is molten, carefully pour the liquid plastic into each cavity of the open-face mold, filling but not overfilling. Place the mold horizontally in a shallow pan of water to cool. After the lures are cured, remove them from the mold but keep them in cool water for additional curing. Since this process takes a few minutes, it is best to work with a partner and with several molds on a rotation basis.

With two-part molds, secure the mold according to the manufacturer's instructions. Fill the mold reservoir with liquid plastic; then use the mold plunger to inject the liquid plastic into the mold cavities. Allow it to cool in water before opening; repeat.

Plastic Plugs, Bugs

If you don't want to mold your own bodies, you can obtain premolded and prepainted bodies for topwater plugs and crankbaits; these have built-in hook hangers and only require assembly with hooks, using split rings and split-ring pliers.

Some plastic lure bodies are available in unpainted halves, which require gluing and painting. The halves are glued together with cyanoacrylate glues (so-called super glues) or with ketones such as nail polish remover. Often these are not painted externally and are clear so that you can insert Mylar sheeting or prism material for simulated scales or paint the inside prior to gluing.

Molding plastic bodies. There are molds for making good plastic-bodied fly-rod bugs, topwater plugs, and diving crankbaits. They are two-part molds that are easily secured and unlocked, and they're designed to take wire form hook hangers. To mold these lures, you need polyethylene molds, two-part polyurethane plastic, mixing rods, and mixing cups. Most of the fly-rod bug molds make from four to eight lures. The plug molds make one or two at a time, so it helps to have several molds and work on a rotation basis.

Begin by using the supplied jig form to bend the lure wire into the line tie/hook hanger shape. Spray the mold cavities with mold release or nonflavored no-stick cooking spray. Place the completed wire form into the mold and close it, using the locking pins to secure it. Pour out equal amounts of the two-part plastic on separate surfaces, and put them into a common mixing cup. Mix rapidly because you have only 35 seconds until the mix starts to foam and to form the lure. Pour rapidly into the sprue holes in each mold. Do *not* completely fill the mold cavity, since the foam expands to 20 times the original volume. (The amount in the mold cavity can be easily seen through the translucent sides of the plastic mold.)

Set the mold aside for about a half hour; then unlock the mold and carefully separate the two sections to remove the completed lure. Set the completed lure aside for 24 hours to completely cure. Finish by painting (*see: lure modifying/repairing*) and adding split rings and hooks.

You can also add color to the plastic (one-part only, then mix) to make solid-colored lures. Popping bugs are not made with the wire form but by using kinked-shank popper hooks.

Wooden bodies. Shaped wooden bodies can be purchased and require only painting and assembly, using lure-size screw eyes and other fittings. Most premade bodies are of topwater design, such as simple cigar shapes or torpedo shapes, to which one or more propellers can be added. These are best painted before assembly.

Assembly will require small screw eyes for the hook hangers and line tie, along with hooks, any propellers desired, etc. Split rings generally are not used, since the hooks can be attached directly to the screw eye. Even though these bodies are made from relatively soft woods, use a small-diameter pilot drill to make a hole in the wood to take the screw eyes. It also helps to brush the screw eye with bar soap for lubrication when inserting it. Screw eyes come in both open and closed styles, with the closed type used for the line tie and the open type used for hooks. Insert the screw eye almost completely into the pilot hole, add the hook, close the screw eye, and then make the last few turns to completely insert the screw eye. When adding propellers, allow some play and clearance for the propeller to turn.

Wood-bodied lures can also be made by using a wood lathe or by carving with appropriate tools. When using a lathe, use all pertinent safety practices associated with the lathe, including wearing safety goggles, removing ties and loose clothing, rolling up sleeves, and removing jewelry. Since only straight bodies can be made, most lathe-produced bodies are for various topwater lures. It is possible to attach a metal or plastic lip to some straight wooden bodies and make them into shallow or medium divers.

If you intend to make a lot of bodies on a lathe, first make one, paint and assemble it, and then use it to be sure that the shape, size, and action are what you wish. If so, make a cardboard template of that shape for producing more on the lathe.

Carving is necessary to make good diving plugs. This begins with a blank or block of wood. The best

Some species of lungfish, especially those of the African genera *Protopterus*, are able to breathe air and burrow in a dormant state away from the water until seasonal rains come.

L

woods generally available are poplar, basswood, and cedar, which can be cut from planks obtained at craft wood shops. The ideal sizes for most freshwater plugs are about $1\frac{1}{2}$ inches square by 4 to 6 inches long; blanks for saltwater are usually about 2 inches square by 6 to 8 inches long.

Before carving, decide on the shape of the plug and make a life-size template to use in drawing the shape onto the plug blank. Draw center lines down each side of the plug blank. Then use your template to trace the shape of the plug. Realize that you will usually need two templates, one for the top/bottom view or shape of the plug and the other for the side or profile of the plug.

After drawing the lines, begin by removing wood outside of the lines. There are two ways to do this. One is to mount the blank in a vise and use a coping saw to cut out the outlines to reduce the amount of carving necessary. To do this, use the scrap cut-out material as a "frame" to hold the blank. This allows cutting on all four sides. The other way to do this is to use a carving knife to cut out the shape, working on one side at a time. Do not carve randomly on the plug, since the working template lines will be removed early, leaving you with no guides as to shape or size. Carving along first one side, then the opposite, then retracing the lines on the cut sides for final cutting, makes the carving easier and the results more accurate.

After the plug has been carved or sawn into a rough rectangular shape, use a carving knife to round off the sides. Once it is roughly shaped, use a wood rasp to further round the body, followed by successively finer grades of sandpaper. Finish with the finest-grade sandpaper available; then drill pilot holes for the line tie and hook hanger screw eyes. Paint as described elsewhere and finish assembling.

Lure and Bait Rigs

You can make an endless variety of bait and lure rigs by using assorted terminal tackle attachments, single-strand wire, braided wire, and nylon monofilament line. In making any rigs, be sure to use components that are equal or appropriate in size and strength. There is no point in using 200-pound-test wire with a tiny snap, or a huge snap with light 18-pound-test wire.

Learn the best possible connections for each type of component. For single-strand wire, it is possible to make a tight wrap around a hook, snap, or swivel by using a wire former. Another possibility for single-strand wire is the Haywire Twist *(see)*. For braided wire, use leader sleeves, properly crimped in place with crimping pliers. Finely braided multistrand wire allows you to tie standard knots.

Do not use more components than necessary. For example, to put a hook on a wire trace, don't use snaps, swivels, or split rings; connect the hook directly to the wire. To make the hook interchangeable, add a snap. To make it interchangeable and swiveling, use a snap swivel at the end of the wire.

Bait or lure rigs such as this free-sliding-sinker rig (left) and drop rig (right) are quickly made from components.

Most rigs can be figured out easily by comparing them to commercially manufactured versions or by planning the parts necessary and the method of connecting them. Many types of rigs are possible once you have the components and the simple skills required to make the necessary connections. Some typical rigs and rigging follow.

Single- and two-hook bottom rigs. These are easily made in nylon monofilament by tying one or two in-line dropper loops for the snelled hook attachment, tying a loop at the top for the

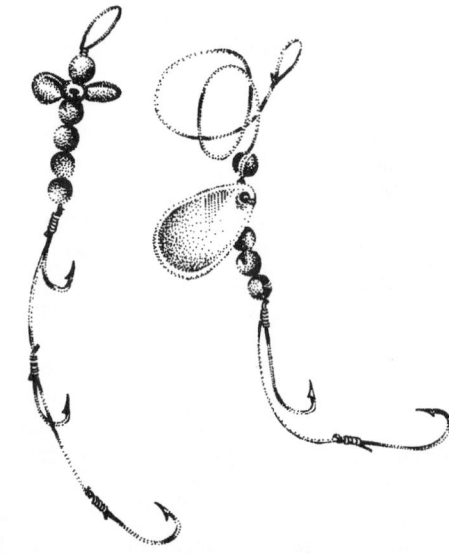

Snelled-hook freshwater bait rigs such as these are easily assembled from spinner blades, plastic beads, and leader material.

line tie and adding a large snap at the bottom for sinker attachment.

If using braided wire, make the same arrangement, using leader sleeves to make the extensions to hold snelled hooks and the line tie and sinker snap attachments. Single-strand wire can be used by making tight or Haywire Twists for the various attachments.

Skirted trolling rigs. Nylon monofilament, braided wire, or single-strand wire can be used for skirted trolling rigs, which are also called hoochies. To provide weight and to keep the vinyl skirt from sliding down the rig, attach a lead sinker to a wire form, with an eye at each end of the wire, the rear eye fastened to a short bead chain leader ending with a single hook.

Slip the vinyl skirt over the end of the wire so that it snugs down on the egg sinker. The bead chain leader and rig must be long enough for the bend of the hook to meet the tail of the vinyl skirt. Another solution is to connect the hook to the wire or mono, thread tri-beads (available at craft shops) onto the line, and then add an egg sinker and the vinyl trolling skirt. Finish with a split ring or loop for attaching to the line.

Fishfinder rig. These surf rigs (which are also good for baitfishing for carp and catfish) are basically a sliding sleeve over the line, with a sinker attached to the sleeve. They can be easily made using nothing more than a large snap swivel and no sleeve, or using a large swivel through holes drilled in the side of a thin PVC sleeve (available at hobby shops), with the split ring holding a large snap-swivel rig.

See: Lure; Lure Modifying/Reparing; Lure Tuning.

A simple skirted trolling rig, sometimes called a hoochy, can be made from a vinyl or plastic squid body attached to a heavy leader.

LURE MODIFYING/REPAIRING

Anglers who use lures eventually accumulate a large collection that represents a sizable investment. Maintaining that investment requires only common sense and a few minutes of care periodically. Many lures that survive repeated fishing efforts are still serviceable with a little bit of care, and others can be made more useful or effective through various modifications. Most lure modifying or repairing is easily done on nonfishing days or during the off-season or, most often, slack times while fishing.

Of course, many lure-modifying activities take place on the water, usually in response to existing circumstances or as a way to stimulate a response by targeted species that are proving evasive. Making existing lures more attractive to fish is the ultimate purpose of all lure-modifying activities, and the ability to modify some lures on the spot to suit fishing conditions is an advantage that shouldn't be overlooked.

Whenever you modify a lure, you're always trying to figure out how to make it look or work better, and you are inevitably pondering the bigger question of what makes any lure work. Whatever answer you get is bound to make you a better angler.

Naturally, many lures are certifiable fish catchers right out of the box and often need no modification to be productive. Some lures that are otherwise effective can be made even better by making certain changes. Others can benefit from alterations because they simply don't work right or because the circumstances dictate an alteration. Fortunately, lures of all types can be repaired, modified, or otherwise refurbished. Some repairs and modifications are specific to certain lures; others are common to all lures. A table of general suggestions for repairs and modifications is contained later in this section, while specific activities follow.

To help with any modifying and repairing efforts, it's a good idea to hold onto lure parts that can be used for modifying and repairing other lures in the future. Don't discard the hooks unless they're corroded or deformed. Retain the split rings, screws, old lips, etc. And when you have lures that don't work as is, hang onto the bodies if there's a chance you could dress up another lure with them or could resurrect them with some alterations.

Refinishing

Most lure refinishing is elective; anglers choose to take an existing lure and do something to give it a different look. That might be painting or polishing, or sprucing up the lure with a marker, tape, or glitter.

Deciding when to refinish a lure is subjective. Some anglers refinish a lure because the circumstances require a new look. Some anglers simply do a cosmetic touch-up on a lure that has seen heavy use. Obviously the painted finish on lures can become chipped, scratched, cracked, and damaged. This will vary with the lure, since some finishes adhere very well to certain lures but not to others.

Paint chips off leadhead jigs, for example, relatively easily. Minor scratches and paint loss are not likely to be a problem in effectiveness, particularly for larger lures with more color on their bodies. However, some metal-bodied lures lose their appeal if they are tarnished, and they may need to be refinished to regain their luster.

Liquid painting. Liquid paints are used for most lure painting. The first step in this activity is proper preparation of the area to be finished. If possible, first remove all the hooks. This is easy on some lures, especially those with free-swinging hooks, and makes it safer to handle them. It is impossible with certain lures, like buzzbaits, spinnerbaits, some spinners, and fixed-hook spoons, but many of these have large hooks that are less dangerous than the small trebles of other lures.

Wash the lure in a warm soapy bath and scrub with an old toothbrush. Once clean and dry, examine the lure finish. If the paint is peeling and flaking, try to remove as much as possible with your thumbnail or a razor blade. Once this is done, or if it is not possible, roughen the finish with fine sandpaper or steel wool to provide some grip to the remaining finish so that the new coat stays on.

If some parts of the old finish are intact and others flake off, it might be difficult to repaint the lure without ending up with an uneven or mottled-looking surface. A possible solution is to paint the bare areas with white paint, let them cure, and roughen as described. Several coats might be necessary to build up the bare area to the level of the remaining paint.

When painting metal surfaces, such as spoons or spinner blades, scrub them with steel wool to slightly roughen the surface. If the surface is corroded, scrub it with steel wool and a powder abrasive cleanser and then clean and dry thoroughly. Paint it after masking any hooks, line ties, weedguards, or similar attachments.

Types of paints vary widely. One basic rule is to stick with sealers, undercoats, paints, and clear overcoats from the same manufacturer to avoid any possible chemical reaction between different paint formulations. The best paints are those that have a glossy finish. Types of paints can include enamel, lacquer, acrylic, epoxy, and powder. Of these, epoxies are the most durable, but they are often not available in small containers for hobby use. They are also two-part products that require mixing (just like the glues), but they may not be as shiny as other paints. Enamel, lacquer, acrylic, and similar paints are available in small containers from hobby and art supply stores and through tackle shops and mail-order companies. All of these are easily applied. Acrylics are especially good since they are bright, durable, and allow a water cleanup.

If you are painting new lures or lures in which all the paint has flaked off, you'll need to use a sealer or base coat first. This is particularly true with wooden plugs, which are porous, but it is important as a base for any lure. Sealers, labeled as such, are available for any of the aforementioned paints. In place of a sealer, or as a base coat over existing old paint, use white, since it will allow the brightness of overlying paints to come through. This is particularly important for fluorescent paints.

Application methods for sealers, base coats, and finish coats include dipping, brushing, and spraying.

Dipping. Dipping is ideal for those lures that are easy to handle, can be dipped into a paint container without affecting the rest of the lure, and can be hung up to dry. For example, dipping would be difficult with spinnerbaits or buzzbaits because you can't dip them without painting either the wire form or the hook. Lures that are good for dipping include topwater plugs, various swimming and diving plugs (with the hooks removed), jigs, and spoons. Dipping does require a container into which the entire lure (or the part to be painted) can be dipped. Hobby shops sell small $1/4$-ounce paint containers that many lure makers like to use for painting lures, but the containers are too small to use for dipping anything but tiny jigs.

Thin paints, or paints thinned deliberately, are best for dipping because they are not as likely to cause runs and sags. You can dip one lure at a time or a whole rack of identically hung lures. To dip a rack of lures, you will need a trough or long pan to hold paint. Whether dipping a rack or one lure at a time, withdraw the lure(s) from the paint slowly so that excess paint can run off and drip back into the container. Hang the lures on a rack, and periodically blot the bottom with a paper towel or cotton-tipped stick to prevent an accumulation at this point.

Dipping is effective when you want an even application of paint in one or two colors. It is possible to make two-tone painted lures, such as a red head/white body topwater plug, by first dipping the body completely in white paint, letting it cure, then partially dipping it into red paint, letting it again cure, and finishing with a complete dip into a clear finish coat.

You can also dye some lures by dipping them, or parts of them, into a dye solution. Dyes are available in small jars and in various colors. Small lures can be dipped into them, but most often dyes are used with soft-bodied lures, particularly for coloring the tails of worms, grubs, and fish bodies.

Brushing. Brushing is best for spinnerbaits, buzzbaits, blades and bodies on spinners, and similar lures where dipping isn't possible. It also works for adding additional colors, such as contrasting bars, to a lure. Brushing will not yield professional results, but the fish usually don't care. Some paints have built-in brushes or felt tips in the caps, although disposable brushes are also ideal for this. When brushing, fill the brush with paint and then brush over the prepared unpainted area. Avoid repeated brush strokes over the same area, particularly with fast-drying paints such as some acrylics. Hang up the lure to dry.

On-the-water paint brushing can be accomplished by applying colored nail polish to a lure. You can easily add an eye, dots, diamonds, stripes, or bars, and the polish dries quickly. Clear nail polish makes a good finishing coat for other painting.

Spraying. Spraying will create beautiful results in terms of color shading, patterns, scale finishes, and similar effects, but on the small area of lures it does waste paint. Canned aerosol enamels and lacquers are typically used for spraying, although other paints can be used with professional-style airbrush equipment. Airbrush equipment is relatively expensive and requires extensive cleanup after painting.

Careful spraying, whether with canned paints or airbrush equipment, requires quick passes of the sprayer to paint the surface without leaving a heavy buildup of paint that will run. Spraying is best for those lures that do not have any attachments or parts that should remain unpainted. Plug bodies are ideal for this. Jigs, spinnerbait bodies, and buzzbait bodies all should have the wire or hooks masked (use masking tape) to protect from the spray paint.

Easy professional-looking results can be obtained by spray painting a base coat of white and then coating the belly of a crankbait yellow, the side silver, and the back black. The result is a professional-looking lure, with the paint colors gradually feathering from one to the other.

Variations require more time but are possible. One is to spray a base coat of paint on the sides, wrap the side with scale netting (available in fabric shops as tulle), and spray a second color to give a scale effect. Templates are easy ways to make individual patterns. To get a smooth finish, don't allow the template to touch the lure. Possibilities include spraying through a coarse comb for a vertical-bar perchlike finish and making templates that will allow you to spray spots, gill plate shapes, stripes, and similar patterns.

To avoid painting anything other than the lure, spray outside on a calm day or spray into a painting box made from a large cardboard carton, open on one side only and lined with cotton batting, sponges, or strips of cloth to catch excess paint.

Keep in mind that, in a pinch, you can spray paint a lure with fast-drying paint and use it within minutes to catch fish. Anglers have literally used an aerosol can of paint (especially fluorescent yellows and ranges) to quick-color a lure that is the right size, shape, and action for the fishing but not the right color. Being careful not to get the paint on your clothing or equipment, you can grip the lip with a pair of needle-nosed pliers, hold the can nozzle the right distance from the lure, and make a fast pass over both sides (remove the hooks first to keep paint off them). Give it a few minutes to air dry, add an eye with a marking pen if desired, put the hooks back on, and you're set. This may not look very professional, but it often doesn't have to. If you like what you've got, then later put a clear finish coat over it to preserve it.

Whether you use one or all of these painting methods, there is no end to the possibilities that you can create. Making a lure that is very lifelike or unique may have the benefit of giving the user more confidence; it also may help because it is unlike the commonly used lures or colors often presented by other anglers. Be careful about getting carried away, however. Remember that forage fish all have a light belly, dark back, and red gills, and are not completely dark or light. The color of the water and the habits of the target species will greatly determine the alterations you make. Lures that will be worked fairly quickly, for example, generally need mostly the proper shading rather than a lot of detail. These might need only a stripe along the side instead of more intricate patterning, including a representation of eyes and gills. However, a lure that is worked more slowly, especially in clear water where the fish's vision is accentuated, may benefit from the extra detailing.

Powder painting. Powder paints allow you to put durable hard finishes on lures easily and quickly using a completely different painting process. Because the lure must be heated in a flame, powder painting is possible only with metal lures, such as spinnerbaits, buzzbaits, spinner blades and bodies, jigs, weedless spoons, jigging spoons, and blade baits.

In all cases, the lure must be heated and then dipped into the powder paint. This is a powder, not liquid, and was originally designed for commercial electrostatic painting of appliances, machinery, and other objects where paint is deposited by electric charge and then baked on.

In appearance, the paint is almost like a talcum powder, but it comes in colors so that various colors or color combinations are possible. The advantages are that the paint is relatively cheap, there is no waste or shelf life or storage problems, and it "dries" instantly. And as with liquid paints, you can mix colors. Yellow and blue can be mixed to make green, white and red to make pink, red and blue to make purple, etc. Powder paint is readily available from some tackle shops and many mail-order companies.

Heat sources can include a cigarette lighter, alcohol lamp, propane torch, or electric heat gun (like the kind used to strip paint). The painting steps are simple. Hold the lure with pliers in a heat source for a few seconds until hot. Then rapidly dip the lure into the powder paint, completely cover it with paint, and remove it from the powder. Done properly, the chalky-looking powder paint will turn glossy and smooth, looking like the best possible paint job. As soon as the lure cools, it is ready to fish or to finish if other assembly or additions are required.

The right amount of heat is the key to powder paint, and experimentation is a must. Controlling the heat is particularly important with leadhead lures, since too much heat will melt the head, ruining the lure. Try for a few seconds first and check the results. If the paint does not adhere completely,

Frog-imitating lures have been around a long time; in 1910 Shakespeare sold the Rhodes Mechanical Swimming Frog, with rubber body and flexible kick-back legs.

L

L

reheat and try again. This is possible at least several times. If the paint covers completely, but looks powderlike rather than glossy, wave the lure through the heat to melt the powder and remove it from the flame while it glosses over. To do this, you must have a "clean" flame; this procedure will not work with a cigarette lighter because carbon will build up on the lure.

Don't overheat the lure. Overheating causes the paint to build up too much or to bubble. If the paint fills the line tie (hook eye) of the lure, as often happens with jigs, use a heated wire to clean out the paint. Once the paint is cool, you can also drill out the paint with a small drill bit or hobby rotary tool.

It is also possible to make several colors, such as a jig head first dipped in yellow and followed by a partial dipping in red, to make a yellow body/red head lure. Glitter can be added to the lure after the first coat and then protected with a clear coat. The clear coat looks powdery white, but after melting, it cures to a clear finish.

For even more durability, bake the finished lures in a standard kitchen oven. Hang the lures on a wire rack, make sure that they do not touch, and bake for 10 to 15 minutes at 250° to 300°F. Hang blades for spinners, buzzbaits, spinnerbaits, and metal lure parts on S-shaped hangers made from paper clips.

Powder paints are obviously best on a new lure that doesn't have old paint on it, but these paints can be used to repaint an older lure if excess paint is removed and if the flame is not so hot that the heat burns the old paint. For best results with an old lure, remove the old paint completely by using tools or paint remover and then repaint.

Polishing.   The metal surfaces of spoons, spinner blades, and the like can become tarnished or corroded, but you can restore the original finish with polishing. For badly corroded lures, first polish with steel wool and then with abrasive cleanser. Metal polishes such as silver polish and brass polish also work well. If the surface is still discolored, consider painting with metallic-finish paints.

Glitter coating.   A simple way to spruce up a worn-out looking lure is to coat it with glitter. In the past, only coarse-style glitter was available, but today's lure refinishing kits use microglitter, which is far more attractive. Glitter is also available from craft stores.

There are two ways to use glitter. One is to coat the lure with a clear finish coat and, while it is wet, shake on glitter. You can use several different colors of glitter, such as silver on the belly of a crankbait, red on the sides, and black on the back. Once the initial coat cures, add a second clear coat to protect the glitter finish.

A second method is to mix glitter into a liquid clear coat of thin epoxy finish or urethane; use a disposable brush to paint the lure body with this mix. You can, of course, put glitter only on certain parts of a lure—sides, vertical bars, or horizontal stripes—using either of these two methods.

Taping.   Adhesive tape also provides refinishing possibilities for lures. Tapes is best used on flat or almost flat lures such as spoons and spinner blades; however, with proper trimming and application, it can be placed on almost any lure.

Tape is available in sheets for customizing, in various small precut patterns and shapes, and in rolls. There is a wide range of plain, glitter, metallic, and prism colors. Tape can be used for the entire side of a lure body, for strips shaped like a bar, or for smaller designs that are simply meant to add a dash of pizzazz.

The key to the most efficient use of tape is to first cut it into the proper shape and then apply it to a dry, warm lure. If you are applying tape outside in cold weather, tuck the tape and the lure in your pocket or under your armpit for a few minutes to warm them up; you'll get better adhesion this way. When you're using tape at home, you can cut with scissors; onboard a boat, you may have to make due with utility scissors on an all-purpose tool or even a sharp knife. Keep in mind that the rounded shape of plugs makes them difficult to refinish with tape; smaller angled strips are best here, and the edges will probably peel up in time. To keep the tape from peeling off on any lure, consider covering it with a clear finish coat.

Marking.   Permanent felt-tip markers are also handy for refinishing or modifying lures. Various designs and patterns can be marked on any lure. The result will not be glossy like paint, but this is a quick easy way to change lures. There are wide- and thin-point markers, and the style depends on the lure and detailing necessary.

A red or black broad-tip marker may be all that you need to make some fish-catching adjustments to plugs, including eyes, gills, stripes, and bars. However, a light color can be used to make a plug belly more pronounced. Most people use markers to detail hard lures, but markers can also be used on soft plastics. Here, a finer point is usually better. With soft plastics, you can use a marker to work on the body, tail, claws, or legs. A little bit of orange or chartreuse, for example, on the extremities of some soft plastics can be very effective.

Additions

One of the most important ways to alter the appearance of lures is to add something to them. The addition might be a hook, rattle, skirts, or eyes. Naturally the appropriate addition depends on the type of lure and the target fish. Lures used for bass and pike are probably the most appropriate for additions.

Eyes.   Eyes that wear or come off lures, or lures that don't have eyes, can be improved with the addition of eyes or by changing to larger, more visible eyes. General theory suggests that eyes are an important triggering signal to fish when they are attacking prey and that large visible eyes on lures, particularly those simulating baitfish, are important.

You can add eyes to lures in a number of ways, but the most common is simply by painting. Eyes can be painted on any lure. This is easily done by making small eye-painting tools from nails or pins having different-size heads. Stick a short length of dowel into the end of the pin or nail to make a handle. Touch the head of the tool to the surface of the paint; do not submerge it. Then touch the tool to the lure where you want the eye. Two- and three-tone eyes are possible by using tools with three different head sizes, allowing each coat to dry before applying the next. Typically colors are light for the outer ring and dark or contrasting for the pupil. You can also paint eyes on lures by using a marking pen or a brush.

Another option is to use ready-made eyes that can be applied onto lures. Craft stores are good sources, and you can buy stemmed plastic eyes there. Select an appropriate size, and apply the eyes by removing the stem with side-cutting wire cutters and gluing the eyes in place with epoxy or a "super" glue. Don't cut off the stem, however, if you plan to apply the eye by drilling a hole in the lure for the stem.

Perhaps an easier method is to use adhesive tape eyes, which are made in various sizes and colors and are very easy to apply. For a different look, you can glue on doll's eyes, which have movable pupils, most of which are black although some are colored. The various eye types are available from tackle shops, mail-order companies, and craft stores.

Skirts.   Skirts of rubber, silicone, LumaFlex, and similar synthetic materials are easily added or replaced on spinnerbaits, buzzbaits, and jigs by taking off the old one and slipping on a replacement. Many of the skirted lures have a collar, with a small bump at the tail end to keep the skirt from sliding off. If the fit is tight, lubricate it with saliva. If you wish the skirt to be permanent and it has a tendency to slip, add a little CA glue once the skirt is in place.

Tying new or replacement hair skirts is similar to, but simpler than, tying flies. To do this for new lures or when repairing old lures, begin by holding the lure or lure part in a vise or in vise-grip pliers held in a bench vise. Dressings are easily tied on hooks for spinners and other lures, jig heads, spinnerbaits, and buzzbaits. Use size 2/0 thread for small hooks and heads, size A for medium-size lures, and size D for large heads and dressings.

Begin by wrapping the thread around the jig collar or hook shank and then wrapping over the thread to secure it in place. Make a half dozen more wraps, and clip the excess thread. Now tie down a bunch of tail material. Tail or dressing material can include hackle, marabou, bucktail, calftail, synthetics, stranded flash material, or a mix of these in any color combination. Place each bunch on in turn, wrap tightly, and clip excess material in front of the wrap. Once all the material is wrapped in place and clipped, continue wrapping; tie off with a whip finish. This is the same as the finish used to

whip the end of a rope and consists of wraps around the standing thread and the dressed area that are finally pulled tight after a half dozen wraps. Do two of these, clip the thread, and then protect with a coating of paint, clear nail polish, fly tying head cement, or epoxy rod finish. When using the thick epoxy, rotate until the epoxy cures to prevent sags and drips.

Trailer/stinger hooks.   Trailer hooks, also known as stingers, are often added to spinnerbaits and buzzbaits, and sometimes to spoons and spinners. Special trailer/stinger hooks are made for this and are usually labeled as spinnerbait hooks because of their prevalent use on these lures. Ideally, they must have an eye that is large enough to slip over the existing hook.

There are several ways to hold the trailer hook in position on the main hook, the primary one being to place a small piece of soft vinyl or rubber tubing over the eye of the stinger hook and then to run the point of the main hook through the tube-cover trailer hook eye. The tubing keeps the stinger hook in proper alignment on the bend of the main hook. Often such tubing is included in packs of stinger hooks, but it can be obtained from medical supply stores or from pet stores that sell aquarium supplies (small-diameter filter tubing) and cut to length. An alternative is to use a button of discarded soft plastic worm in place of the tubing. Slip the button over the eye of the stinger hook; then slip this onto the end of the main hook, as with the tubing.

Another option is to attach a soft grub or worm as a trailer and attractor in the style of a Texas rig. Bury the eye of the hook into the head of the worm, and slip the trailer/stinger combination onto the main hook. The Texas rig also keeps the stinger hook weedless.

Soft bodies added to main lure hooks are common trailers and are often an important element of a given lure's fish-catching effectiveness. Single and

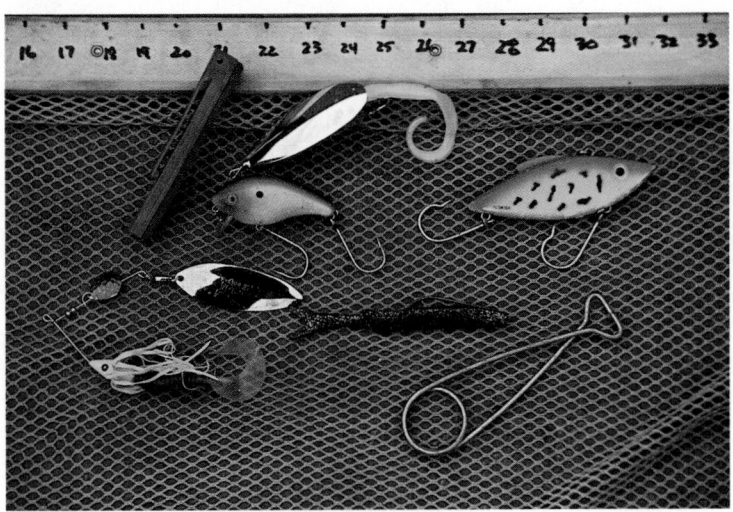

Changing hooks and blades and adding trailers are among the simplest lure modifications.

twin curl-tail trailers, for example, are staple additions to spinnerbaits, and many anglers will not fish these lures without such a trailer. Choose one that is proportionate to the size and weight of the main lure. Snipping off a portion of the forward section of the soft body may keep it the right length and distance for the lure.

These bodies, as well as chunk or strip pork trailers and split-tail eels, provide more action to the lure and also more bulk, which translates into weight for casting distance and into buoyancy for a slower rate of fall. Using soft trailers provides the option of either matching the lure color or offering a complementary or contrasting one.

Trailer blades.   Many lures can benefit from placing a spinning blade as a caboose. Actually it may look more like a fast-moving tail. A rapidly spinning blade certainly offers flash and sometimes a visible attack marker for predators. Various sizes and styles of blades can be used to enhance some lures. Small Indiana or Colorado blades, for example, are good on smaller lures, including little jigs and spoons. Larger models are effective behind a trolling lure, especially the metal-headed lures preferred for high-speed offshore use. As with other applications, willowleaf styles tend to work best for fast use, and rounder styles for slower fishing.

No matter what type you employ, it's necessary to make a good connection via a ball bearing swivel. The spinner blade does no good if it doesn't spin easily. You need a ball bearing with a ring large enough to fit over the barb of the hook and onto the bend; you can put a small piece of tubing (as mentioned with trailer hooks) over the swivel ring before putting it on the hook, which will keep the blade in place and away from other parts of the lure.

On some spoons, particularly weedless models, you can add a spoon on an in-line wire form with or without beads, and attach this to the front of the lure. The spinner revolves while the spoon wobbles, and the spinner produces extra action even when the lure retrieve is stopped and the lure sinks. The combined product has some flash as well as the traditional wobble, and it may be more productive than the unaltered version.

Rattles.   Rattles can be added to virtually all lures. Plain cylindrical "worm" rattles are available in different sizes and are made of glass, plastic, and aluminum. Some are available with extra sleeves and eyes for attaching to line and lures.

Affixing the rattle to the lure is the main trick. Using a rattle with a soft lure is easy, since the rattle can be inserted into the body of the lure. It is possible to glue rattles into holes drilled in the bodies of plugs or crosswise on the lips of plugs. It is also possible to use a dab of silicone sealant for this purpose, as well as electrical tape.

A rattle can be attached to the hooks of most lures, but it must be small in comparison to the hook in order to avoid impeding the gap, the hooking ability, or the action. You can also fix a rattle to topwater plugs, crankbaits, lipless plugs, and jigging spoons, and to upper and lower spinnerbait arms, buzzbait arms, weedless spoon weedguards, spinner bodies, jig hooks (under the skirts), and the wire rigging of skirted trolling lures. However you choose to attach the rattle, make sure you test the lure before fishing it to see that the action is proper. Making an addition can affect the swimming action of some lures; generally, the larger the lip on a plug, the less affect it will have.

Light sticks.   Small chemiluminescent light sticks—the glow-in-the-dark tubes that are often used around Halloween—can be used to add a glowing presence to some lures. Like rattles, they can be attached to various lures, including the body of some spinners, the blades of some spoons, and inside certain hard and soft lures. A few lures are made with holders to grab these sticks, but most need some form of temporary attachment that doesn't hinder the lure action. Unlike a rattle, the light stick has to be bent and shaken to activate the chemicals inside, which produce a bright light for a full day or longer; the stick has to be replaced when it has lost its glow.

Plastic-bodied plugs can be modified to incorporate a small ($1^1/_2$ inches or less) light stick, producing an effect that few commercially made lures can offer. These sticks fit snugly inside many plugs without affecting the action. To install a light stick, drill a hole that is the same diameter as the light stick and then insert the activated stick into the body.

This modification can be made to many plastic plugs, especially diving plugs, crankbaits, and minnow imitators. You may have to sacrifice a lure or two when you first experiment because you need to determine the best place and angle to drill the hole. Generally the best spot is on top at the rear, a location that has no adverse effect on the action or diving depth of most lures, in part because it doesn't promote water resistance.

If you hold the plug up to a very bright light, you can usually see the interior configuration—plastic-bodied plugs are essentially hollow—and approximate the best place to drill. The hole should be made at an angle so that the top of the light stick will just barely protrude. Although not absolutely necessary, putting the plug in a block vise to secure it may help you drill a more precise hole. Use a drill bit that conforms to the size of the light stick; the stick should fit snugly into the lure. With the hole made, don't push the light stick completely into the cavity of the lure; it is very difficult to extricate. If it does go in too far, enlarge the hole and impale the head of the stick with a sharp, strong needle to pull it out.

When you're ready to use one of these modified lures, activate the light stick and insert it into the plug. If the fit is tight, water might not seep into the cavity. If water does get in, it will make the lure heavier and the action of the lure may be affected; simply shake out the water. You can also seal the opening with silicone sealant. Dab the silicone around the top of the stick, give it a few minutes to harden, and you're set. When you want to replace the stick, peel off the sealant and pull out the stick. If the light stick is stuck in the hole, jab the point of a hook into the stick and pry it out.

Try translucent or light-colored plugs for this modification. Dark lures won't allow much of the light stick's glow to come through, and transparent lures may provide too much of a glow. You may want to scrape the paint off a dark plug; some have an undercoat of bone or light gray color, which gives a nice glowing effect. A possibility is to get a transparent plug and then apply a paint finish that will react well to the neon-green light of the stick.

Most light sticks, incidentally, are neon- or chartreuse-green in color, but they may be available in other colors, including red. These small light sticks can also be placed inside some soft-bodied lures like jerkbaits, adding a different dimension to them for night fishing.

Weights. Anglers have long been adding weight to lures for various purposes. Plugs, in particular, have been subject to such modifications, either to increase their overall heft for distance achievement or more likely to affect their balance or buoyancy. Soft plastic lures are also modified with weight to make them sink faster or to swim in a certain way when retrieved.

Plugs. With plugs, the main objective today in adding weight is to affect their buoyancy by making them sink, usually slowly, or suspend once they've been retrieved to a given level. The idea is to keep them in the strike zone longer and prevent them from immediately bobbing up toward the surface. Most floating/diving plugs float at rest, dive when retrieved, and then fairly quickly bob back toward the surface when the retrieve is halted; neutral-buoyancy lures, however, remain at their diving depth or rise or sink very slowly, behavior that imitates the way that baitfish stay at a particular level when they stop moving.

Anglers have put lead wire and split shot on their hooks to try to achieve neutral buoyancy, and this method does occasionally work. However, there is a tendency for any object on the bare hooks of plugs to adversely affect the action of that lure, so this is not a good solution for most plugs.

When fewer suspending lures were available from manufacturers, anglers strategically inserted small weights into wooden floating/diving plugs to achieve neutral buoyancy. This is still possible, but it is a somewhat delicate operation that requires getting things just right to achieve desired results without impairing lure action. Most people prefer to buy plugs that suspend or to use pliable adhesive weights.

You can turn ordinary small wooden crankbaits and small- to medium-size wooden minnow-imitating

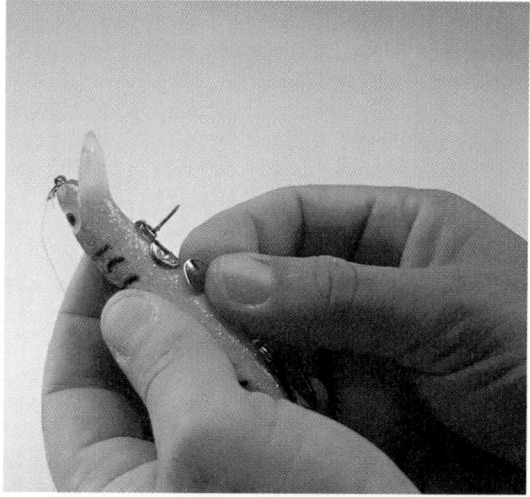

Judiciously adding adhesive pieces of lead to floating lures can make them rise slowly or suspend.

plugs into neutral-buoyancy lures. Take some BBs or similar-size split shot and a short length of thin, but relatively stiff, wire. Put the lure on its side and, using a drill bit the size of the shot, drill a hole in the lure's midline between one-third and one-half the way down from the head, approximately in the location of the balance point of the lure. Place several shot side by side in the hole, pinch them with pliers so they don't stick out the side, and test for buoyancy. You may need to drill another hole and insert more shot. The object is to get the lure to barely rise (or to not rise at all) when submerged. When you're close to achieving this, punch the wire crossways through the lure. Test for buoyancy again, and punch another piece of wire through if necessary. Snip the wire so that it is just shorter than the width of the plug, and use a pick to push the wire inside the lure. Let the lure dry overnight; then give it several coats of lacquer. You might want to put a little quick-drying epoxy in the hole before inserting the shot.

Adding interior weight is useful only for wooden lures, and only for some types and styles. It cannot be done on all wooden lures. However, virtually any plug that is used under the surface, whether a shallow runner or deep diver, plastic or wood, can be modified with the application of exterior adhesive weight. This kind of weight doesn't ruin the lure and requires just a little bit of experimenting.

These adhesive weights, which are known as SuspenDots or SuspenStrips, are placed on dry floating/diving plugs little by little and tested in the water until the proper effect is achieved. They can be removed at any time if the angler no longer wishes the lure to sink or suspend.

The process starts by adding either strips or dots to the lure. The best placement locations, especially for large-bodied plugs like crankbaits, is either beneath the bill or on the forward section of the belly near the front hook hanger. You have to

make sure that the location is the pivot point of the lure, so that the action isn't affected. The adhesive dots and strips (one strip equals two and a half dots in weight) are exact increments of weight, so once you have established the proper number and placement of these on a given lure, you can be reasonably sure that the weight will be the same for identical lures. And you can add parts of these by cutting them.

You can also alter the suspending angle of a given lure according to adhesive placement. To make it suspend more vertically (which might be desirable in timber cover), focus the weight on the front of the plug; to make it suspend horizontally, place it farther along the belly. You can also add weight to the tail section of a lure for the purpose of making it cast better. Some plugs, when cast with light line or in windy conditions, tend to tumble because they're light in the tail, which can cause the line to catch on the hooks. Putting some weight on the tail can make such a lure easier to cast and less troublesome.

Soft lures. The major addition or modification to soft lures is either coloring (by dipping) or adding rattles. However, large soft lures like heavy-body worms and jerkbaits may be modified by putting some weight into them. This is most appropriate for jerkbaits, some of which are packaged with stick- or nail-like lead weights that can be split into different lengths and inserted into the soft lure.

A good tactic is to weight these soft lures in the forward part of the tail section (the forward part of the rear half). The weight changes the retrieval motion so that a quick snap rather than a short sweep is used to work them. But it also lets the lure drop backward when slack is given, rather than float in the same spot or settle down, an action that can trigger otherwise reluctant fish to strike.

The weights shouldn't be placed too far back in the tail, or the movement of the lure will be adversely affected; keep the weights at least $1^1/_2$ inches from the end of the tail. From two to four weights can be added for 6- to 8-inch jerkbaits, usually being placed just aft of the middle. The number will vary with the type of soft lure; those with more dense tails can accommodate extra weight. For deep water, use more; for shallow water, use less. For jerkbaits with a thick belly section, insert the stick weight from the belly straight up and one-half to two-thirds of the way toward the back. For jerkbaits with a thin belly section, insert the stick weight from the back straight down and halfway toward the belly. Snip the ends off so there is no protrusion from the soft plastic.

You can also modify soft jerkbaits by putting a short piece of flexible wire into the head and bending it so that, when retrieved, the lure keeps working to one side rather than darting to and fro, or regularly swims upward or downward when jerked.

Weedguards. The hooks of some lures can be made mostly or partially snag- and weed-free by making various modifications. Spinnerbaits, for example, may benefit from spanning a rubber band from the line tie eye to the hook barb. It is also possible to make the blade weedless by removing it, straightening the wire, adding 1 inch of the end of a clutch-type ballpoint pen (to serve as a shield over the swivel), and then reassembling the blade to the wire.

Most weedless adaptations to lures exist with these enhancements made as part of the original manufacturing, usually using wire or stiff nylon brushlike guards ahead of hook points and fabricated into the lure construction. Heavy jigs and casting spoons are the primary examples. Making existing nonweedless lures snag-free usually requires some workshop tinkering, using stainless steel wire, wrapping thread, and glue. It's difficult to work with multihooked lures and treble hooks, so single hooks lend themselves best to this modifying. The right wire size is important because the final weedguard needs to be strong enough to resist objects yet not impede hooksetting. In essence, this is accomplished by extending the wire from the hook eye to the hook point, aligning a short foot of the wire on the forward bottom of the hook shank, wrapping this tightly with thread, and applying glue to the finished wrap. For more information, *see: Weedguard.*

Lips/bills. Most plug lips are made of plastic and are molded or epoxied into the head of the plug so that they can't be removed. Perhaps you have some old lures sitting around that aren't being used; the parts might be useful on another type of lure, especially older models with metal screw-on lips. If you can locate any of these lips, or are able to purchase metal lips from component suppliers, you can make serviceable lures that have no lips, or repair lures that have lost lips.

For example, you may be able to take a surface stickbait that has a nice body but unimpressive action and make a good shallow-water wobbling plug out of it for bass fishing. For starters, you may need to remove the rear hair-covered treble hook and replace it with an undressed treble. Then, to make it swim, unscrew the small, curved metal lip from an old lure, center it on the stickbait under the head, and screw it on. The combination of a line tie at the nose and a new small lip causes the lure to wobble wide and dive only a few inches below the surface. Use it to fish just over the top of barely submerged vegetation.

Since the line-tie is not connected to the lip, you don't need to worry about the strength of the lip-holding screws. This is an especially important point, since there can be a lot of tension on the line-tie connection. Adding a metal lip or bill to a plug is generally best when the line-tie location is on the head of the lure.

Changes

Replacing hooks. Free-swinging hooks on lures are easily replaced when the originals become rusted or damaged or when you need to switch sizes, styles, or finishes.

Most hooks are easily replaced using split rings, which are commonly employed to attach the hooks to many lures, especially plugs and spoons. The easiest way to replace these hooks is with split-ring pliers, available in several styles and sizes, but always with a tooth at the end of one long jaw to open the split ring. The easiest one-step method of replacement is to open the split-ring with the pliers and then start the old hook onto the split-ring. Once there is enough room, add the eye of the replacement hook. Use the split-ring pliers to grip the ring as you work both hook eyes around the circumference of the ring. The advantage of this method is that you're removing the old ring and adding the new one in the same step, saving time and stress on the ring. If your efforts open the gap on the ring, it may no longer be serviceable for the strength of line you're using, so be attentive to the condition of the split ring; it can become a weak link between the rod and a fish.

If you're replacing treble hooks, note that, in addition to various sizes, styles, and finishes, they come in regular and short-shank lengths. Short-shank lengths can be used to adjust for the additional separation from the lure body caused by the addition of the split ring. Make sure that you choose the right type of treble for lure repairs and modifications.

You can also modify the way a plug works by using a different size of treble hook. Switching manufacturer-supplied treble hooks with slightly larger sizes is a common change. Putting large hooks on a floating minnow plug, for example, will change its buoyancy and may make it into a very slow sinker, or at least cause it to rise upward more slowly when twitched in a stop-and-go fashion beneath the surface. Putting a larger hook on the rear of some surface lures (chuggers and poppers, for example) may make the tail sit lower in the water, raising the head and producing sharper noises and creating more splash. And a larger treble on the front of some diving plugs may help them to run deeper.

Notice that the word "may" has been used with each of these examples. Many plugs, especially smaller ones, are very finely balanced by the manufacturer; putting just slightly larger, and thus heavier, hooks on them can alter the action. You have to test the lure in the water after each change to make sure that it will still have the right inherent action.

Some types of hooks, most notably the popular Siwash or salmon style hook, can be found in open-eye versions as well as closed eye. The open-eye type can be slipped over a split ring (or wire eye), and the eye can be closed by pressing with heavy-duty pliers. This avoids having to thread the hook through a split ring. If you're using double hooks, their parallel shanks make it easy to slide the hooks into place on a hook hanger.

Replacing hooks, especially using single hooks in place of trebles, is an overlooked facet of lure modification that has bearing not only on lure action and fishing success, but also on safety, conservation, and catch-and-release issues. For more information about this aspect of lure modifying, as well as on modifying and changing hooks in general, *see: Hook*.

Segmenting wooden plugs. Anglers constantly talk about the importance of lure action in catching fish; and to the human eye, the belly-dancing action of a jointed plug is about as good as it gets. The trouble is that jointed plugs are expensive for commercial lure manufacturers to make; it's almost like producing two lures. Jointed plugs are vastly outnumbered on retail store racks by unjointed or one-piece models. Fortunately, anglers who are handy with tools and have a home workshop can make single- or double-jointed modifications to otherwise good-running, commercially made one-piece wooden plugs.

One-piece wooden lures can be segmented by carefully cutting through the body with a fine-toothed hacksaw. Cut back all sides on an angle to allow for a wide wobble between segments, put a sufficiently long-stemmed wire loop into both segments, and use slow-curing two-part epoxy to anchor the wire. Unfortunately, you'll have to sacrifice a lure or two in order to get the hang of this. Make sure that the epoxy will hold at least 30 pounds of pulling strength, more if you're likely to use heavier line. You have to segment the lures in the right areas to achieve optimum swimming action; only experimentation will teach this. Give the exposed raw wood several coats of black (or matching) epoxy paint, and cover it with clear lacquer to seal the wood.

This segmenting is particularly worthwhile with small and large diving plugs as well as with minnow-imitating lures. Large-lipped plugs that create a lot of pulling resistance are especially forgiving when it comes to segmenting and usually allow a lot of leeway. The smaller the lip, the more critical it is to segment properly and the easier it is to go awry, especially if you need to retrieve or troll the lure quickly.

People handy with basic tools can make enticing, unique fish catchers by segmenting one-piece wooden lures.

Table of Common Modifications and Repairs

Lure Type	Modifications	Repairs
Plugs	Repaint Refinish with tape or marker Add eyes Add rattles Add split rings Add larger or different propellers Remove propeller(s) Shave, scrape, or trim plastic bills Sand popper lips	Replace hooks Repaint or refinish Reglue or refasten bills Replace damaged propellers
Casting/Trolling Spoons	Paint or add tape Add spinner blade to hook Add rattles Put tail on free-swinging hook Add plastic trailer to hook	Repaint or refinish Add line-tie split ring
Spinners	Repaint Add glitter or tape to blades Tie hair skirt to the hook Add rattles Cup blade with pliers to change speed	Reform wire or clevis Replace hooks Refinish blades As a final repair, cut the main wire shafts to assemble new spinners
Spinnerbaits	Repaint body and/or blades Add plastic trailer and/or stinger hook Add rattles Add crimp-on weight to hook shank for deep fishing Change blade(s) Change skirt; trim length to avoid short strikes Make hook/blade weedless Strengthen open line-tie by bending it into a loop	Repaint body or blades Replace blades Replace skirt
Buzzbaits	Repaint body or paint blades Replace skirt Add plastic trailer and/or stinger hook Add rattles	Repaint body Replace skirt Replace damaged blades
Jigs	Repaint body Add or improve eyes Replace skirt Add grub or worm trailer Glue a grub or shad body onto a bare hook leadhead Add stinger hook Add rattles	Repaint body Replace skirts
Weedless Spoons	Paint or add tape Add weight via rubber core sinker on lower arm or main hook Make weedless with soft plastic body on hook point Add plastic trailer to hook Add spinner blade to tail Add spinner on shaft to head Add rattles	Bend weedguard back into position Repaint or refinish
Jigging Spoons	Add spinner blade to tail Put tail on free-swinging hook Repaint or refinish Add rattles	Replace hook Repaint or refinish Add line-tie split ring
Lipless Crankbaits	Paint or refinish Replace blades Add rattles Add small rear spinner blade	Replace hooks Repaint
Soft Lures	Add rattles Add interior weight/light stick Dip into colored dye Rig tail hook on worm Rig with hooks, propeller, and beads	Trim excess parts, long arms, pincers Remelt and remold

Adapting cut plugs. Cut-plug style trolling lures for salmon and steelhead fishing are different than a lot of other lures and pose a special problem for light-line users when the plug body separates from the rigging and rides up light line. Anglers using noodle rods or other light tackle with 2- through 6-pound test have a lot of strain on the line when a good fish is on, and the sliding of the cut plug up the line can nick the line and cause it to break. To avoid this, put a small tube in the middle of these lures, one that fits snugly so it won't separate from the plug. Some anglers use a piece of air-conditioner tubing wrapped in masking tape; others use a glass insert and ream the hole in the head of the plug to a size that will accommodate the insert.

When using jointed-style cut plugs, try putting a split ring between the joints to give the lure a wilder wobble. However, if you do this, be sure that the split ring is strong enough to take heavy strain.

Remelting soft plastics. Rather than discarding old soft plastic lures, you can save and remelt them to make new lures *(see: lure making).* In addition to getting more mileage out of these, remelting has the advantage of helping to keep these long-lasting plastics out of the environment.

Save old soft plastics and sort them by color. If a lure has several colors in it, cut and separate the parts by color. About once a year, melt down each color separately in an old cooking pan, using a very low heat to prevent burning (to avoid breathing in fumes, consider wearing a nose and mouth mask). The molten soft plastic can then be used to fill soft plastic lure cavities to make new lures, or poured into containers (like old plastic ice cube trays) to make "ingots" of colored soft plastic that can be melted down later for making new lures.

See: Buzzbait; Jig; Lure; Lure Making; Plug; Spinner; Spinnerbait; Spoon.

LURE RETRIEVER

A device used to free a lure snagged in deep water.
See: Unsnagging.

LURE STORAGE

There are a host of versatile ways to store terminal tackle. Traditional portable storage systems evolved from wooden to metal to rigid plastic boxlike containers with pivoting, compartmented trays. They are known as tackle boxes, and plastic models are still available today. However, the realm of items in which to hold tackle has vastly expanded to a potpourri of storage systems, many suited to specialized applications, and with an accent on individual traylike plastic utility boxes of varying size stored within soft-sided carriers or satchels.

Plastic boxes are by far the most popular today because they are easy to care for and come in a great range of designs. However, a few metal boxes, particularly small, pocket-size aluminum models used

to store flies, can still be found, and even some wooden ones. Leather, suede, nylon, and cloth tackle satchels or wallets are also in use, as well as flexible, foldable tackle systems made of dense sailcloth with compartments covered by vinyl. For all but a relatively few anglers (those with big offshore boats and plenty of space), the one common denominator in tackle storage is portability. Most tackle boxes also have in common something that wasn't available with older boxes: movable compartment dividers that allow you to fashion the number and size of storage compartments to suit your needs.

Tackle boxes. The traditional style of tackle box comes in trunk, hip roof, and drawer configurations. A trunk box has one or more trays that pivot up and back together to reveal a large open well at the bottom of the box. These were once the standard but are now rare, partly because the support brackets lacked durability. Hip roof boxes are similar, though they have two sets of trays that open out to face each other; they are also less common today, though more prevalent than the trunk box. The drawer box is the most popular style among larger boxes and has trays that slide out rather than pivot on a bracket; this type usually has more compartments for storage than trunk or hip roof designs and may allow for bulk storage in bottom or top wells.

The type of box to use largely depends on the amount and size of objects that you need to store. Typically most anglers outgrow small or intermediate boxes and purchase more boxes or larger ones as they accumulate tackle and/or their fishing interests expand. Many people who do a lot of angling and/or who fish for various species keep several boxes or storage systems, often organized by lure types or tackle-by-species.

Double-sided plastic tackle boxes with see-through lids were very popular in the late 1980s and early 1990s, and still have devotees. Some have an over/under tray arrangement in which one or two latches (preferably two) open to reveal a lower storage well; only the upper tray has a see-through

This display represents some of the box, tray, and satchel possibilities for lure storage.

lid. Other versions are accessed from the top and bottom via separate latches. These boxes have see-through lids on both sides, which have a tendency to become scratched and cracked or broken more so than the over/under model. Both styles have movable compartments, hold a surprising amount of gear, and can be readily stowed or stacked on top of one another. Some boxes are geared toward specific types of storage needs, such as big lures, and possess features (a rack to hold spinnerbaits, for example) that accommodate this. Compartments are usually wormproof, which means that soft lures will not disintegrate in them; older plastic boxes caused the components of soft-plastic lures to break down, and the lures became unusable blobs.

When you're considering the purchase of a rigid tackle box such as these, check to see whether the box is watertight and has channeling to prevent water from entering the interior, and whether the latches are strong and allow snug closure. Some boxes are designed to prevent accidental spillage (even tipping) in case the latch is left open and the box picked up. Look for a good-quality hinge-pin arrangement in the back rather than one that is part of the molded box; the hinge-pin will last longer. A good handle is critical, too. Large handles aid in carrying and exchanging, but if they stick out too much from the box, they may get in the way. A recessed handle is desirable where boxes will be stacked or objects placed on top of them.

Utility boxes and soft carriers. The biggest change in tackle storage over the past decade has been a trend toward use of opaque-see-through utility boxes of various sizes, stored in soft-sided carriers. These lightweight utility boxes are handleless one-level polypropylene trays, usually with movable compartments, with varying exterior and depth dimensions. Anglers may purchase a good quantity of these, store items by category or application needs, and mix and match boxes in the carriers as their situations require.

Soft carriers, called bags and satchels by some, exist in all types of configurations to accommodate these boxes. The better models are made of waterproof ripstop nylon, and some have a waterproof bottom; others are water resistant. They have zippered access, with front or top tray loading, and most have a shoulder strap as well as top handle. The amount of terminal gear and the number of lures that can be stored in some models is very impressive, especially those with side compartments for small trays and pouches or holders for tools and spools and other miscellaneous items.

Other storage. Not all storage is as formal as a large tackle box or satchel-utility box system. Wading anglers who are mobile need something that can be worn instead of toted. A fishing vest is a multipocketed and compartmented tackle storage system that is worn over shirt or jacket and predominantly used by flycasters and river and stream anglers. Full-length versions are standard, but shorter models are used by deep-water waders and float-tube anglers. Both have many pockets, some designed especially to hold specific items (reel spool or sunglasses), and are intended for the storage of many small items; they even include a pouch in the back for small fish. Alternatives to vests are rigid chest boxes, soft chest packs, and soft fanny packs, which may not hold as much but are the utmost in light portability.

See: Vest, Fishing.

LURE TUNING
See: Tuning Lures.

LUXEMBOURG
This small country in western Europe is bounded by France, Belgium, and Germany. At 2,586 square kilometers it is smaller than the state of Rhode Island, and is largely a plateau comprising the upper basins of the Sauer (Sûre) and Alzette Rivers. Although tourism is important to the country, Luxembourg attracts relatively few visiting anglers, and its modest fisheries resources are highly regulated and similar to those in larger adjoining countries with more numerous and extensive watercourses.

Brown trout, grayling, pike, and various coarse species inhabit most of the rivers of Luxembourg, as well as its small ponds and reservoirs. Large pike reportedly exist in reservoirs along the upper Sauer, as do trout and charr.

Ponds in many villages and towns are accessible to anglers who purchase a permit, and a state license provides fishing access to the public water along the middle Sauer between the mouth of the Alzette River at Ettelbruck and the mouth of the Our at Wallendorf, Germany. Regulations vary with respect to seasons, methods, and equipment for both public and private waters.

MACHACA *Brycon guatemalensis.*

The machaca is a member of the Brycon genus of the Characidae family, which has some 800 species, most occurring in Central and South America.

The machaca inhabits lakes and streams in southern Mexico, Honduras, Nicaragua, Costa Rica, and Panama, and possibly in other Central American countries. It is mainly herbivorous as an adult but is caught on small plugs and jigs by anglers. Like most characins, it is equipped with an adipose fin, and it is silvery overall and has a small mouth. The common catch is 1-pounder, but this fish often reaches several pounds in weight. The all-tackle world record is a 9½-pound Costa Rican fish. In general body shape and appearance, it is similar to a fellow Brycon, the matrincha *(see)* of Brazil. More than one species may be called by this name.

MACKEREL

Mackerel are members of the Scombridae family, which includes tuna *(see)* and numbers some 50 species in 15 genera.

Mackerel and tuna are both mainly schooling fish of the open sea. They provide sport virtually wherever they are found, and they contribute significantly to commercial fisheries, because they are good to eat. And all are good fighters as well; larger mackerel can rip line from a reel with tremendous speed, and some even take to the air on occasion.

Like tuna, mackerel are especially streamlined. The body is literally a spindle, with a pointed head and a much-tapered tail. The large caudal fin is lunate (crescent-shaped). Mackerel are much smaller than tuna overall, but they are just as speedy, displaying swift attacking speeds. Some of these fish have slots into which their spinous dorsal fins fit; this adaptation further reduces friction and enhances their speed. The spiny and soft-rayed dorsal fins are separate, and the soft-rayed dorsal fin is matched in size and shape by the anal fin directly beneath it. Following each fin is a series of finlets, the number varying with the species. In all species, the scales are extremely small or lacking. Most tuna and mackerel are ocean blue or greenish on the back, grading to a silvery shade on the sides and the belly. Some notable exceptions do occur, however.

Angling techniques for mackerel vary to some extent with locations and species. Trolling rigged baits and lures, and fishing baits from a drifting or anchored boat, are predominant methods. Casting plays a minor role, and then typically when chumming attracts the fish close to a boat. Surf and shore fishing are seldom productive, except for a few smaller coastal species.

See: Kawakawa; Mackerel, Atlantic; Mackerel, Cero; Mackerel, Chub; Mackerel, Frigate; Mackerel, King; Mackerel, Narrowbarred; Mackerel, Pacific Jack; Mackerel, Pacific Sierra; Mackerel, Spanish; Offshore Fishing; Wahoo.

MACKEREL, ATLANTIC *Scomber scombrus.*

Other names—mackerel, common mackerel, Boston mackerel; Arabic: *scomber;* Danish: *almindelige, makrel;* Dutch: *gewone makrel;* French: *maquereau;* German: *makrele;* Italian: *lacerta, macarello;* Japanese: *hirasaba, marusaba;* Norwegian: *makrell;* Portuguese: *cavalla;* Spanish: *caballa;* Swedish: *makrill;* Turkish: *uskumru.*

Like other members of the Scombridae family, the Atlantic mackerel is a fast-swimming, schooling,

A string of Atlantic mackerel, caught on a multihook rig, from Long Island Sound, New York.

Atlantic Mackerel

pelagic species that garners both significant recreational and commercial interest. It is known as a feast-or-famine fish; sometimes it is almost completely absent, and at other times it is plentiful in swarming schools. A delicious fish with an abundance of protein, vitamins, and minerals, it has a pleasing oil content. The flesh is firm-textured with a distinctive, savory flavor. Mackerel are available in markets whole or filleted, usually fresh but sometimes frozen, and smoked or salted.

Identification. Atlantic mackerel have smooth, tapering heads, streamlined bodies, and brilliant coloration. An iridescent greenish blue covers most of the upper body, turning to blue black on the head and silvery white on the belly. These brilliant colors fade somewhat after capture but still distinguish these fish. The skin is satiny and has small, smooth scales. The tail is forked. Another distinguishing characteristic is the series of 23 to 33 wavy, dark bands on the upper part of the body, extending to a moderately prominent lateral line. There are two fins on the back, one spiny and one soft, followed by a number of small finlets. There are also finlets present on the under surface of the body near the tail.

Size/Age. The average length for adult Atlantic mackerel is 14 to 18 inches, and the average weight is $1^1/_4$ to $2^1/_2$ pounds. The maximum observed size in recent years has been about $18^1/_2$ inches and weighing about 3 pounds. The all-tackle world record is a 2-pound, 10-ounce fish caught in Norway. The maximum age is roughly 20 years.

Distribution. Occurring in the North Atlantic Ocean, the Atlantic mackerel ranges from Labrador to Cape Hatteras, North Carolina, in the eastern region; and from the Baltic Sea to the Mediterranean and Black Seas in the western Atlantic.

Habitat. The Atlantic mackerel is pelagic, preferring cool, well-oxygenated open-ocean waters.

Life history/Behavior. Atlantic mackerel native to the western Atlantic coast comprise two populations rather than one vast, homogeneous stock as once supposed. The southern population appears offshore in early April, advancing toward Virginia, Maryland, and New Jersey to later spawn off the coast of New Jersey and Long Island. In late May, the northern group enters southern New England waters for a short period and mingles with the southern stock. The northern population soon moves north again to spawn off the coast of Nova Scotia and in the Gulf of St. Lawrence in June and July. These spring movements are probably triggered by water temperatures, and they generally provide the most angling opportunity and result in the greatest harvest.

As autumn approaches, fish that summer along the Maine coast begin to migrate southward toward Cape Cod and, after October, disappear off Block Island. The northern population returns through the Gulf of Maine in November or early December and vanishes off Cape Cod. Both groups winter between Sable Island off the coast of Nova Scotia and Cape Cod in waters generally warmer than 7°C. This annual disappearance, sometimes overnight, has puzzled people for years, and over the years it has given rise to many far-fetched stories.

Atlantic mackerel are moderately prolific, but many factors affect survival of the young. The eggs are released wherever the fish happen to be, leaving adverse winds to push eggs or small fry into areas where their chances of survival are slight. This behavior, combined with predation of large as well as young mackerel, results in a curious pattern of either superabundance or scarcity.

Food. The diet of Atlantic mackerel consists of fish eggs and a variety of small fish and fry.

Angling. Finding mackerel is the necessary element in catching them. Anglers typically locate the fish on sonar equipment or by observing slicks on the surface; when this fails, private boats follow charter and party boats (which do a brisk business in mackerel fishing when this species is available), and otherwise look for clusters of boat activity. Most fishing occurs in near-shore environs or in large bays.

A good deal of mackerel fishing is done with a rig that consists of several small tube lures attached at 1-foot intervals to a main leader and weighted with a heavy (3- or 4-ounce) diamond jig. Because mackerel are midwater fish, it's important to present the bait at the right level. Most anglers find this level by dropping their rig to the bottom, then slowly working it back up in increments, pausing and jigging as they do this. Once they catch fish, they return their rig to the same level. When the fish are not too deep, jigs and flies are also effective, and sometimes chum is used to attract and hold the fish near the boat.

See: Inshore Fishing; Mackerel.

MACKEREL, CERO   *Scomberomorus regalis.*

Other names—cero, spotted cero, king mackerel, black-spotted Spanish mackerel; French: *thazard franc;* Portuguese: *cavala-branca;* Spanish: *carite, cavalla, pintada, sierra.*

A popular gamefish in tropical waters and a member of the Scombridae family, the cero mackerel is a pelagic species that also has commercial interest. It is considered excellent table fare and is marketed fresh, smoked, and frozen. Offshore anglers may use the cero mackerel as rigged bait for larger predatory species.

Identification.   The cero mackerel is iridescent bluish green above and silvery below, with rows of short, yellow brown spots above; there are also yellow orange streaks and a dark stripe below, which runs the length of the body from the pectoral fin to the base of the tail. The front of the first dorsal fin is bluish black and has 17 to 18 spines and 15 to 18 gill rakers on the first arch. The pectoral fins are covered with small scales. The cero mackerel differs from the king mackerel *(see: mackerel, king)* and Spanish mackerel *(see: mackerel, Spanish)* in the pattern of its spots, which are rather elongated and arranged in lines instead of being scattered; the cero mackerel also has a lateral line that curves evenly down to the base of the tail, which further distinguishes it.

Size.   The all-tackle world record cero mackerel weighed 17 pounds, 2 ounces. This species usually weighs less than 5 pounds.

Distribution.   Found in tropical and subtropical waters in the western Atlantic, cero mackerel range from Massachusetts to Brazil; they are common to abundant throughout the Florida Keys, the Bahamas, the Antilles, and Cuba.

Habitat.   A nearshore and offshore resident, the cero mackerel prefers clear waters around coral reefs and wrecks, and is usually solitary or travels in small groups.

Spawning.   These fish spawn offshore in midsummer.

Food.   Cero mackerel feed mainly on small schooling fish, such as sardines, anchovies, pilchards, herring, and silversides, as well as squid and shrimp.

Angling.   As with most mackerel fishing, fast trolling while looking for baitfish is a good way to find ceros. Trollers can catch them on small feathers and baits, but the best sport is on light tackle and in casting small silver spoons and white jigs. They also hit surface swimming plugs, chuggers, and shallow-running plugs. Ceros have sharp teeth, so a wire leader is essential.

See: Mackerel.

MACKEREL, CHUB   *Scomber japonicus.*

Other names—common mackerel, tinker mackerel, Japanese mackerel, Pacific mackerel, Spanish mackerel, scomber, smaach; Afrikaans: *makriel;* Arabic: *baljeh;* French: *hareng du Pacifique, maquereau blanc, maquereau espagnol;* Greek: *koliós;* Hawaiian: *opelu palahu, saba;* Italian: *cavallo, lanzardo, scombro macchiato;* Japanese: *honsaba, masaba;* Portuguese: *cavala, cavalinha, sarda comun;* Spanish: *caballa, cachorreta, macarela, salmonete, verle;* Turkish: *kolyoz;* Vietnamese: *cá thu Nhât-bán.*

This small member of the Scombridae family is commercially cultured in Japan and used in Chinese medicine. In addition, it is a good food fish and is marketed in many different ways.

Identification.   The chub mackerel has a bluish or greenish back with roughly 30 irregular black bars that dissolve into a series of dusky spots near the lateral line. The pectoral fin has a black spot, and there are usually five finlets behind the dorsal and anal fins. The first and second dorsal fins have a large space between them, and the entire body is scaled. The chub mackerel is similar to the

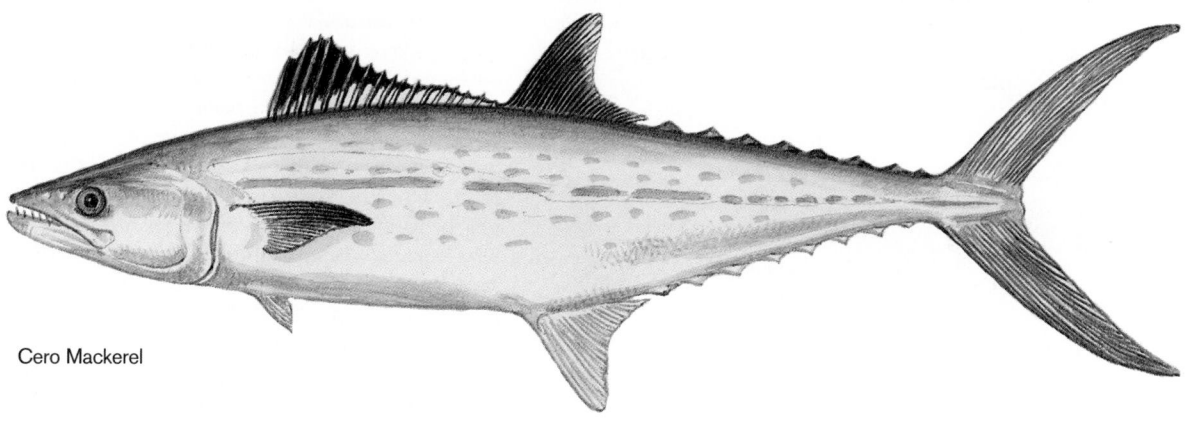

Cero Mackerel

frigate mackerel (see: mackerel, frigate), which also has 30 irregular bars on its back, except that it has scales all over its body; the frigate has scales only in corselets around the pectoral fins.

Size/Age.   The chub mackerel usually grows to 20 inches and 2.2 pounds, although it has been reported to 2 feet and 6 pounds. The all-tackle world record is a 4-pound, 12-ounce fish taken off Mexico in 1986. They can live for 9 to 10 years.

Distribution.   Found in the Atlantic, Indian, and Pacific Oceans, chub mackerel occur in warm and temperate transition waters and adjacent seas. In the eastern Pacific, they occur from Alaska to Cabo San Lucas and are most abundant between Monterey, California, and southern Baja California. In the western Atlantic, they extend from the Gulf of St. Lawrence to the Florida Keys and Cuba, and also from Venezuela to southern Brazil. Chub mackerel are apparently absent from Indonesia and Australia.

Habitat.   Chub mackerel inhabit inshore and offshore waters at the surface, schooling by size in the company of other species of fish, including small bluefin tuna. Huge schools sweep along the eastern Pacific coast in the summer and fall. In the western Pacific, chub mackerel are said to move into deeper areas of Asian waters to remain inactive during the winter season.

Spawning behavior.   A female chub mackerel may produce 1 million pelagic eggs.

Food.   Chub mackerel feed on copepods and other crustaceans, as well as on small pelagic fish and squid.

Angling.   Like other mackerel, chub mackerel are preyed upon by tuna, marlin, sharks, and other fish. Anglers use them as cut- or whole-rigged bait for these species. They are not a significant target of sportfishing, but some anglers pursue them on a variety of baits, flies, and small lures.
See: Mackerel.

MACKEREL, FRIGATE   *Auxis thazard.*

Other names—bullet mackerel, frigate tuna, leadenall, mackerel tuna; Arabic: *deraiga, sadah;* French/Danish: *auxide;* Italian: *tombarello;* Japanese: *hira sóda, soda-gatsuo;* Malay/Indonesian: *aya, baculan, kayau, selasih;* Portuguese: *judeu;* Spanish: *barrileto negro, melva;* Swedish/Norwegian: *auxid;* Turkish: *gobene, tombile.*

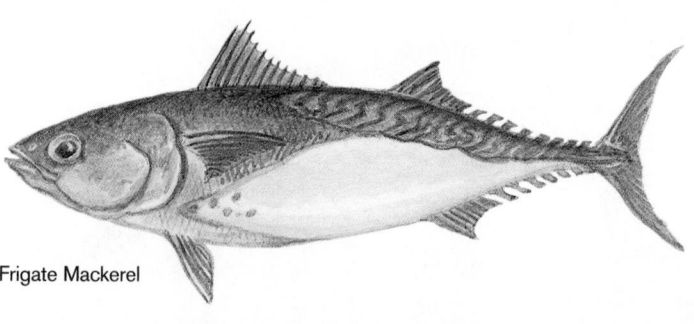
Frigate Mackerel

Frigate mackerel are an abundant member of the Scombridae family and hold an important place in the food web, especially as a forage fish for other species. They are commercially significant and marketed fresh, frozen, dried/salted, smoked, and canned.

Identification.   The color of the frigate mackerel is dark greenish blue above and silvery white below. It has 15 or more narrow, oblique, dark wavy markings on the unscaled back portion of its body. There are eight dorsal finlets and seven anal finlets. It resembles the tuna family more than the mackerel with its more lunate than forked tail; as with all mackerel, however, its first and second dorsal fins are separated by a wide space.

Size.   The average frigate mackerel weighs less than 2 pounds and is less than 20 inches long. The all-tackle world record is a 3-pound, 1-ounce fish taken off Australia.

Distribution.   Frigate mackerel are cosmopolitan in warm waters, although there are few documented occurrences in the Atlantic Ocean. They are subject to periods of abundance and scarcity in particular areas.

Habitat.   A schooling species, frigate mackerel inhabit both coastal and oceanic waters.

Food.   Frigate mackerel feed on small fish, squid, planktonic crustaceans, and larvae.

Angling.   There is little angling interest in this species, although it may be used as bait for other species.
See: Mackerel.

MACKEREL, KING   *Scomberomorus cavalla.*

Other names—kingfish, giant mackerel; French: *maquereau;* Portuguese: *cavala;* Spanish: *carite, carite lucio, carite sierra, rey, serrucho, sierra.*

The largest mackerel in the western Atlantic, the king mackerel is a prized gamefish and an important commercial species, with millions of pounds of fish landed annually. A member of the Scombridae family, the king mackerel has firm meat, most of which is sold fresh or processed into steaks. Smaller quantities are canned, salted, smoked, and frozen. It may be ciguatoxic (see: ciguatera) in certain areas, however.

Identification.   The streamlined body of the king mackerel is a dark gray above, growing silver on the sides and below, and there are no markings on the body, although the back may have an iridescent blue to olive tint. Most of the fins are pale or dusky, except the first dorsal fin, which is uniformly blue; the front part of this fin is never black, which distinguishes it from the Spanish mackerel (see: mackerel, Spanish) and the cero mackerel (see: mackerel, cero). Other distinguishing features include the sharp drop of the lateral line under the second dorsal fin, as well as a relatively small number (14 to 16) of spines in the first dorsal fin and a lower gill rake count, which is 6 to 11 on the first

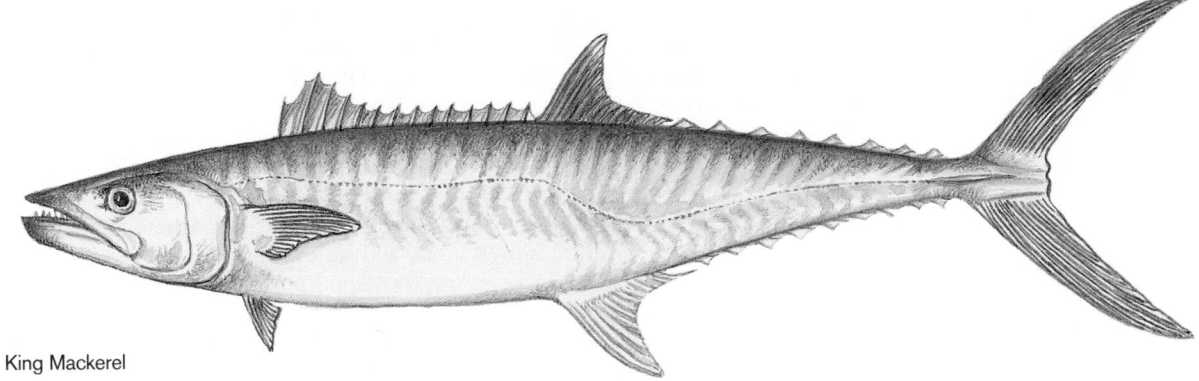

King Mackerel

arch. Young king mackerel may be mistaken for Spanish mackerel because of the small, round, dark to gold spots on the sides, but these fade and disappear with age.

Size/Age. Averaging less than 10 pounds in weight, the king mackerel is usually 2 to 4 feet long and weighs up to 20 pounds. It reaches a maximum length of $5\frac{1}{2}$ feet and a weight of 100 pounds. Females grow larger than males. The all-tackle world record is a 90-pound fish taken off Florida in 1976. This species is believed to reach 14 years old, but those older than 7 years are rare.

Distribution. In the western Atlantic, king mackerel range from Massachusetts to Río de Janeiro, Brazil, including the Caribbean and the Gulf of Mexico, although they are only truly abundant off southern Florida. Two separate populations are suspected, one in the Gulf of Mexico and one in the Atlantic. In the eastern central Atlantic, they have been found around St. Paul's Rocks.

Habitat. King mackerel are primarily an open-water, migratory species, preferring warm waters that seldom fall below 68°F. They often occur around wrecks, buoys, coral reefs, ocean piers, inlets, and other areas where food is abundant. They tend to avoid highly turbid waters, and larvae are often found in warm, highly saline surface waters. A schooling species, king mackerel migrate extensively and annually along the western Atlantic coast in schools of various sizes, although the largest individuals usually remain solitary.

Life history/Behavior. Male king mackerel become sexually mature between their second and third years, and female fish between their third and fourth years. They spawn from April through November, and activity peaks in late summer and early fall. A large female may spawn 1 to $2\frac{1}{2}$ million eggs.

Food. King mackerel feed mainly on fish, as well as on a smaller quantity of shrimp and squid.

Angling. As with other mackerel, the primary chore in catching kingfish is finding them, and anglers can invest long hours looking for these fish. A lot of trolling is done in an effort to locate them, although once located, these aggressive fish can be readily caught in smaller sizes; the biggest fish are more difficult to come by.

Fishing methods include trolling or drifting either deep or on the surface using strip baits, lures, or small whole baits, as well as casting lures and live baits. Balao, mullet, jacks, herring, pinfish, menhaden (pogies), blue runners, ladyfish, croaker, and Spanish mackerel are among the baits used; the largest baits are preferred for bigger mackerel. Spoons, feathers, jigs, and plugs prove effective under various conditions, as do such combinations as feathers and strip baits and skirted strip baits. Chumming works well to attract and hold these fish; at anchor, this method can provide opportunities for fly tackle. Some anglers use extensive amounts of freshly ground chum while trolling.

Many anglers land larger fish by trolling with multiple (two or three) bait rigs, rigs of mullet on feathers, spoons, or live fish slowly in the boat's wake. Another effective big kingfish offering is a

A weakfish from the northern New Jersey shore.

large plain spoon pulled deep with a planer. Downriggers are used in conjunction with live baits, and live fish may also be run near the surface on kites. Deeper fishing produces large individuals when there are plenty of mackerel, as the large ones are below the crowd.

The best months for fishing off North Carolina and Virginia are May and October, whereas winter and early spring are best off South Florida. Many kingfish are caught off inlets and passes, as these areas are important for producing baits, which follow the rising tide in and the falling tide out. Inshore areas with breaks in the bottom depth or with contours are good spots for slow trolling, especially if they hold abundant bait.

Kingfish make a long and powerful run, rest, and then repeat the performance. Now and then a fish will leap from the water. To avoid overpowering the fish and pulling the hook out of its mouth, a rod with a soft tip is helpful.

See: Inshore Fishing; Mackerel; Trolling.

MACKEREL, NARROWBARRED
Scomberomorus commerson.

Other names—barred mackerel, doggie, commerson's mackerel, giant mackerel, kingfish, king seer, seer, serra, snook, barracuta; Afrikaans: *katonkel, koning-makriel;* Arabic: *chanaad, kanaad, khabbat;* Bengali: *champa, matia;* Cantonese: *kau yue;* Fijian: *walu;* French: *coros prêtre, tanzard;* Indian languages: *chumbum, konam, mah-wu-leachi, yellari;* Japanese: *yokoshima;* Malay/Indonesian: *iyot, luding, tenggirri;* Philippine languages: *tangigi, maladyong;* Spanish: *carite estriado;* Swahili: *nguru, ngurumtwane;* Thai: *insi, thu insi.*

The narrowbarred mackerel, a member of the Scombridae family, is an important commercial species throughout its range and also a prominent gamefish. Its flesh is of excellent quality, marketed in various ways, and it is also used as whole bait, strip bait, or chum. Individuals caught off the east coast of Queensland, Australia, have been associated with toxic poisoning *(see: ciguatera).*

Identification. The narrowbarred mackerel is so called because it has many irregular, vertical wavy bars on its sides, which increase as the fish grows. The first dorsal fin has 16 to 17 moderate or low spines, the second has 16 to 19 rays followed by 8 to 10 finlets, and the anal fin has 17 to 20 rays, also followed by 8 to 10 finlets. The lateral line dips below the second dorsal fin. The body is more compressed than that of the similar wahoo *(see),* and

there are three to six gill rakers on the first arch, whereas the wahoo has none.

Size. The all-tackle world record is a 99-pound fish taken off South Africa in 1982.

Distribution. Inhabiting tropical and warm temperate waters of the Indian and Pacific Oceans, narrowbarred mackerel occur from the Red Sea and South Africa to southeastern Asia, north to China and Japan, and south to southeastern Australia. Some populations have immigrated to the eastern Mediterranean Sea through the Suez Canal. In the Atlantic Ocean they are reported from St. Helena.

Habitat. A pelagic and migratory species, narrowbarred mackerel are found in shallow waters, over dropoffs and gently sloping reefs as well as in lagoons. They migrate extensively, but it is thought that permanent resident populations exist in certain areas. They form small schools, although larger fish usually travel alone.

Food. Narrowbarred mackerel feed mainly on small pelagic schooling fish like anchovies and sardines, as well as on flyingfish, squid, and shrimp.

Angling. Although not known to many Western anglers, the narrowbarred mackerel is a highly rated gamefish that sounds often, runs hard and fast, and occasionally leaps. Fishing methods include surface or deep-trolling with squid, mullet, sauries, flyingfish, garfish, and strip baits, as well as with artificial trolling lures. Live-bait fishing near reefs with these and other natural baits is also productive. The best fishing is at dawn or dusk and at high or low slack tide.

See: Mackerel; Offshore Fishing.

MACKEREL, PACIFIC JACK   *Trachurus symmetricus.*

Other names—horse mackerel, jack mackerel, jackfish, mackereljack, scad; Spanish: *charrito, chicharro.*

Not a true mackerel but a member of the Carangidae family of jacks, the Pacific jack mackerel is marketed fresh, smoked, canned, and frozen.

Identification. The body of the Pacific jack mackerel is somewhat compressed and elongate, with a tail that is as broad as it is deep. It is metallic blue to olive green on the back, shading to silver on the belly. Its last dorsal and anal soft rays are attached to the body, or rarely separated from the fins, and the sides are covered with enlarged scales. The Pacific jack mackerel bears a resemblance to the Mexican scad, but the enlarged scales distinguish it, as do the last, attached rays of the dorsal and anal fins. On the Mexican scad, the rays are isolated finlets.

Size/Age. The Pacific jack mackerel can weigh 4 to 5 pounds and live 20 to 30 years.

Distribution. In the eastern Pacific, Pacific jack mackerel range from southeastern Alaska to southern Baja California, extending into the Gulf

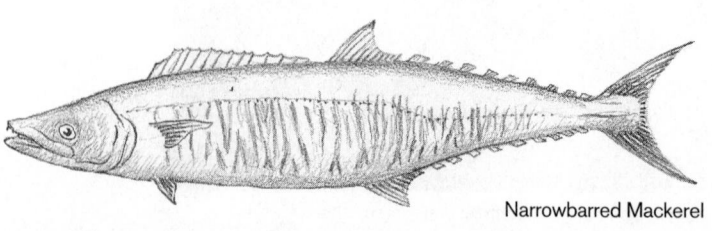

Narrowbarred Mackerel

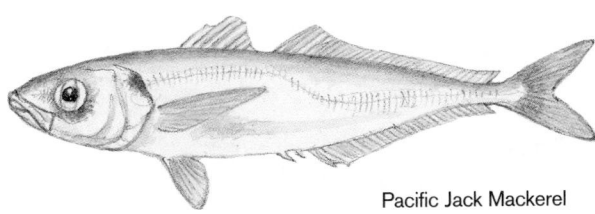

Pacific Jack Mackerel

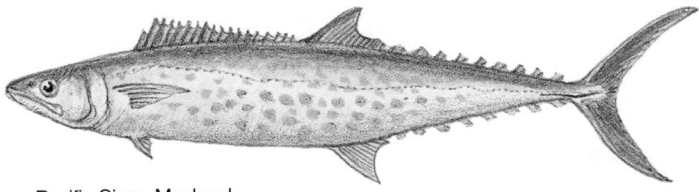

Pacific Sierra Mackerel

of California, Mexico. They are also reported from Acapulco, Mexico, and the Galápagos Islands.

Habitat. Pacific jack mackerel are often found offshore in large schools; adults are found up to 500 miles from the coast and in depths of up to 150 feet. Young fish school near kelp and under piers, whereas larger fish often move offshore or northward.

Spawning behavior. Sexual maturity comes early for Pacific jack mackerel. Half of females are ready to spawn at age 2, and all fish spawn by age 3. Spawning takes place from March through June over a considerable area, from 80 to more than 240 miles offshore.

Food and feeding habits. Pacific jack mackerel feed on small crustaceans and fish larvae, as well as on anchovies, lanternfish, and juvenile squid.

Angling. Younger jack mackerel do not feed extensively on anchovies, do not readily bite on a baited hook or lure, and thus are a much less common addition to the catch of anglers, although they are a common commercial catch. They can be jigged, however, on small feathered hooks and frequently are used as baits for larger gamefish.

See: Jacks.

MACKEREL, PACIFIC SIERRA

Scomberomorus sierra.

Other names—Pacific sierra; Spanish: *macarela, serrucho, sierra, verle.*

The Pacific sierra mackerel is an abundant fish in the Pacific along the coasts of Mexico and Central America. A member of the Scombridae family of mackerel and not to be confused with the Atlantic sierra *(Scomberomorus brasiliensis),* which occurs only in the Atlantic, the Pacific sierra mackerel is an eastern Pacific fish that is excellent to eat. It is marketed fresh and frozen. It resembles the Spanish mackerel in appearance, and the all-tackle world record is an Ecuadorian fish of 18 pounds caught in 1990.

Pacific sierra mackerel extend from La Jolla in Southern California south to the Galápagos Islands and to Paita, Peru. They have recently been reported from Antofagasta, Chile. A schooling species, Pacific sierra mackerel are found in surface coastal waters and over the bottom of the continental shelf. Thought to spawn close to the coast, they feed on small fish, especially anchovies.

See: Mackerel.

MACKEREL, SPANISH *Scomberomorus maculatus.*

Other names—Atlantic Spanish mackerel; Portuguese: *sororoca;* Spanish: *carite, pintada, sierra, sierra pintada.*

The Spanish mackerel is a popular gamefish and a good food fish of the Scombridae family. It is also of significant commercial interest, and whole fish are frequently used as bait for big-game fishing.

Identification. The slender, elongated body of the Spanish mackerel is silvery with a bluish or olive green back. There are 16 to 18 spines in the first dorsal fin, 15 to 18 soft rays in the second dorsal fin—with 8 to 9 finlets behind it, and 13 to 15 gill rakers on the first arch. The lateral line curves evenly downward to the base of the tail. The Spanish mackerel resembles both the cero mackerel *(see: mackerel, cero)* and the king mackerel *(see: mackerel, king),* but it has bronze or yellow spots without stripes; the cero mackerel has both spots and stripes of bronze or yellow, whereas the king mackerel has neither. The Spanish mackerel lacks scales on the pectoral fins, which further distinguishes it from both the cero and the king mackerel, which have scales on them. Also, the front part of the first dorsal fin on the Spanish mackerel is black, whereas it is more blue on the king mackerel, and the second dorsal fin and pectoral fins may be edged in black.

Size/Age. The Spanish mackerel grows to 37 inches and 11 pounds, averaging $1\frac{1}{2}$ to 3 feet and 2 to 3 pounds. The all-tackle word record is a 13-pounder taken off North Carolina in 1987. Fish older than five years are rare, although some have been known to reach eight years.

Distribution. In the western Atlantic, there are two separate populations of Spanish mackerel: one in the Gulf of Mexico and the other along the main western Atlantic coast. The former extends from the Gulf of Mexico throughout Florida waters to the Yucatán, and the latter extends from Miami to the Chesapeake Bay and occasionally to Cape Cod. They are absent from the Bahamas and the Antilles, except around Cuba and Haiti, but are abundant around Florida.

Habitat. Occurring inshore, near shore, and offshore, Spanish mackerel prefer open water but are sometimes found over deep grassbeds and reefs, as well as shallow-water estuaries. They form large, fast-moving schools that migrate great distances along the shore, staying in waters with temperatures above 68°F; these schools occur off North Carolina in April, off the Chesapeake Bay in May, and off New York in June, returning south in winter.

M

Spanish Mackerel

Spawning behavior. Spanish mackerel spawn offshore from April through September. Females release between a half million and $1\frac{1}{2}$ million eggs, and the larvae grow fast to reach lengths of 12 to 15 inches after the first year. They are able to reproduce by the second year.

Food and feeding habits. Spanish mackerel feed primarily on small fish, as well as on squid and shrimp; they often force their prey into crowded clumps and practically push the fish out of the water as they feed.

Angling. Casting, live-bait fishing, jigging, and drift fishing are all employed to catch this abundant fish, and a variety of lures—including metal squids, spoons, diamond jigs, and feather lures—are all effective. Bucktail jigs are particularly

good, especially when retrieved rapidly with an occasional jerk of the rod tip to impart a darting motion. When fish are plentiful, small jigs may be rigged in multiples behind a single line. Minnows and live shrimp are the best natural baits. Light, 6- to 10-pound, spinning tackle provides excellent sport.

After the fish have been located and several hooked, boats make tight circles to stay with the school. Because Spanish mackerel migrate close to land, they are caught from small craft inshore, as well as from larger boats, and by anglers on piers, bridges, and jetties.

See: Inshore Fishing; Mackerel.

MACKINAW
A term for lake trout *(see)*.

MADAGASCAR
Located in the Indian Ocean and separated from Mozambique on the western African continent by the Mozambique Channel, Madagascar was once part of the Gondwana continent, which connected Africa and Asia. After these landmasses separated, Madagascar stood as the fourth largest island in the world, and it is situated in one of the most productive fishing spots in the world.

Known for its unique and superb fauna and flora, Madagascar's landscape has the diversity of high mountains, dry plains, and tropical forests. Its shoreline is dotted with coral reefs, separated only by passages that become long underwater canyons, and by small islands around which fishing is particularly productive. Most of the prominent Indo-Pacific gamefish species thrive here, including black marlin, blue marlin, sailfish, dolphin, wahoo, kingfish, African pompano, amberjack, sharks, grouper, tuna, snapper, jacks, and more. An abundance of sailfish and the lack of fishing effort make this a top site for Pacific sails, as well as a developing fishery for big black marlin.

Madagascar's fishery focuses on three productive centers on Nosy-Be, a small island ideally situated between the northwest coast of Madagascar

A Spanish mackerel from the Arafura Sea near the Cobourg Peninsula, Australia.

M

and the Mozambique Channel and a one-hour flight from the capital city of Antananarivo. The centers include the Italian-owned Marlin Club, the French-owned Sakatia Club, and the locally owned Centre de Pêche Sportive de Madagascar (CPSM). The latter is the oldest center and has not only a small fleet of well-equipped sportfishing boats, but also a boat maintenance and tackle repair facility. It features a fixed beach camp that enables anglers to overnight in remote areas closer to the fishing grounds. Their eight-tent, 16-person beach camp, Terres Rouges, is situated on the northern side of Nosy-Be and can be reached only by boat. The beach camp was built by CPSM because quality accommodations were lacking on Nosy-Be (tourism in Madagascar commenced only in the early 1990s); the facilities now existing on the island, in the main Nosy-Be town of Hellville, are a one-hour boat ride from the major fishing grounds, but they are only a 15-minute run from the beach camp.

The grounds around Nosy-Be are not only diversified but also unexploited. Fishing is good year-round and peaks during the dry season, from April through October. From January through March, occasional rains are common, but the fishing remains good, especially for marlin. More black marlin than blue marlin are landed here. Blacks are most abundant from April through August but are also caught from September through January. As of 1998, the biggest black taken was a 750-pounder, but in 1997 a fish estimated at 900 pounds was hooked and lost. Some striped marlin have reportedly been caught as well.

The sailfish season usually begins around the first week in June and continues through September, but fish are occasionally caught in mid-March. In early October, the Varatraza, a local wind from the east, pushes out the bait for about three weeks, and the sailfish depart. At the end of October the bait returns, along with fewer sailfish, which stay until January. At the height of the season, many sails are raised, and in the best of times in the late 1990s, boats experienced 20 strikes in a half day of fishing.

Although some good boats are available in Madagascar, sportfishing is just developing. It is likely, however, that this could be a hotspot in the future.

MADTOM

The madtom is a member of the catfish *(see)* family, Ictaluridae, often referred to as bullhead catfish. Although the larger members of the catfish family have gained notoriety as sportfish, commercial fish, or food fish, the secretive and diminutive madtom escapes public attention.

These are little-known fish with interesting lifestyles. Madtoms are important links in the food webs of many streams, making it possible for large predators such as bass, wading birds, and water snakes to benefit from the stream's vast energy, represented by larval insect production. They are also a unique natural resource to North America's small streams and are endemic to the continent north of Mexico. The 40 species belonging to the family Ictaluridae occur naturally in the United States and Canada, and 27 are madtoms.

Like other members of the Ictaluridae family, madtoms possess stinging venom in their dorsal and pectoral spines. The venom originates from cells of the skin sheath over the pectoral fin. The toxicity of the venom varies but approximates that of a bee sting, although every person reacts differently to being stung.

Identification. Madtoms are recognized by their unique adipose fin. Non-madtom catfish have a fleshy fin protruding from their back just ahead of the caudal fin. The adipose fin of a madtom is continuous with the caudal fin.

Madtoms belong to the genus *Noturus,* which is divided into three subgenera, *Noturus, Schilbeodes,* and *Rabida,* each with its own distinct appearance. The *Schilbeodes* are dull colored, generally brown or yellow brown. The *Rabidas* have colorful markings with many bands and saddlelike pigmentation. There is only one species in the subgenus *Noturus,* the stonecat *(Noturus flavus).* The stonecat *(see)* possesses the plain appearance of the *Schilbeodes;* however, no other madtoms match this species in size. Stonecats exceed 7 inches as adults and may reach 12 inches in some locations.

There are several tricks to identifying madtoms. Identifying the river where a madtom was collected is the first step to identification. Because most madtom species are limited in distribution (often within one or two states or even one river), many species can be quickly excluded, depending on location. If the madtom possesses body markings, these can be used to determine its species, as the pigmented patterns of each species are distinct.

Other traits used to identify madtoms include their toothpatch, lips, and pectoral spine. On the roof of a madtom's mouth is a toothpatch used for crushing prey. On the stonecat, there are lateral extensions on the ends of the toothpatch. Some, such as slender and freckled madtoms, have differences in their lips. The slender madtom has lips that meet equally, whereas the top lip of the freckled madtom protrudes beyond the bottom lip.

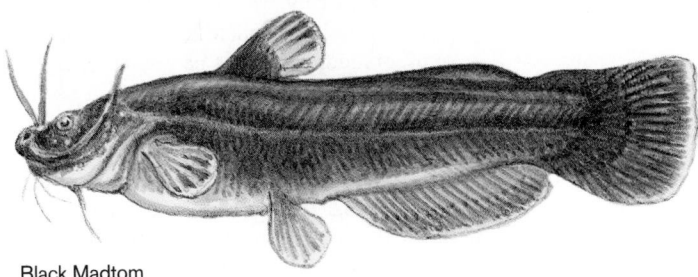

Black Madtom

Another differentiating trait is the pectoral spine. Many madtoms possess spines that are unique in their structure, some possessing many saw-like teeth and some having none. The tadpole madtom has a smooth, straight pectoral spine, whereas the northern madtom has a sharply curved spine with sawlike teeth on both the front and back sides.

Size. Fish size is often correlated with the life history and reproductive strategies a species possesses. Larger fish are often immune to predation as adults; this is not generally so for madtoms, which have a small adult body size. Nevertheless, madtoms avoid predators by virtue of their nocturnal lifestyle, hard spines that artificially inflate their body size when erected, cryptic coloration, and use of cover.

Even so, their chance of survival from year to year may be low. Fish size is often correlated with maximum age, and madtoms are no exception. Larger madtoms live longer. Body size is often an indication of energy stores available for egg production, and therefore will be indicative of the number of eggs each female will produce per spawning season. Because madtoms spawn few eggs relative to other fish, they must invest heavily in each egg to ensure its survival.

To give their young an advantage, madtom females lay large eggs, which provides more energy for embryo growth, allowing young madtoms to hatch at a much larger size and decreasing their chances of being eaten. Madtoms also provide parental care, maintaining a stable and optimum growing environment and protecting the eggs and small, young madtoms from predators.

Madtoms exhibit a range of lifestyles related to body size. At one extreme the stonecat may reach $12\frac{1}{2}$ inches in length, produce 200 to 500 eggs per female, spawn perhaps three or four times in its life, and live six or seven years. At the other end of the spectrum, the least madtom barely reaches $2\frac{1}{2}$ inches, produces about 30 eggs, lives maybe two years with luck, and spawns probably once in its lifetime.

Habitat. Most anglers are probably unfamiliar with madtoms because they tend to be nocturnal, hiding under rocks, logs, and undercut banks during the day. Also, their body markings and color patterns (or lack of, depending on their preferred habitat) help camouflage them from the peering eyes of birds, water snakes, and anglers. Most madtoms prefer the cool, clear water of smaller streams, but some species are adapted to living in lakes, large streams, or muddy rivers. Where aquatic vegetation and beaver dams exist, madtoms take full advantage of their numerous niches.

Most madtoms have strong habitat preferences, and thus use unique habitats. The stonecat primarily inhabits small to large rivers with rubble or boulders and lakes with gravel bars. In contrast, the black madtom prefers vegetation over gravel or sand in the clear moving water of springs, creeks, and small rivers. The margined madtom prefers rocky riffles with fast moving water in small and medium-size rivers. Different species are even known to prefer rocks of specific sizes for cover. Because madtoms are choosy about their homes, they often have problems dealing with the degradation of their preferred habitats.

Food. Madtoms are crepuscular feeders, which means they feed mostly at dusk and dawn. As insectivores, they primarily feed on a diet of midge larvae, mayfly larvae, caddisfly larvae, and crayfish. Most madtoms are not as picky about their food as their housing and will eagerly devour any available prey. Madtoms generally consume smaller amounts of stonefly, beetle, black fly, dragonfly, alder fly, and fish fly larvae. An occasional small fish (such as lamprey larvae), spider, or zooplankton has also been found in their stomachs. When placed together, large adult madtoms have consumed small juvenile madtoms of the same species.

Reproduction. Madtoms start spawning about mid-April and finish spawning in mid-July. Like most fish, the commencement of spawning and the length of the spawning season depend heavily on water temperature. Madtoms usually begin spawning after the water temperature has reached 64°F, and stop spawning after water temperature exceeds 81°F. During the spawning season, adults are sexually dimorphic, which means males look different from females.

Madtoms construct nests to rear their young and provide post-spawning protection. A nest consists of an area with a pebble or gravel substrate that has been cleared of silt and debris.

Most madtoms prefer to nest under rocks; however, the speckled madtom and others have been known to nest in discarded beverage cans or bottles.

Although madtoms are small fish, they have relatively fewer and larger eggs compared to species that do not exhibit parental care. Madtom eggs may be up to 0.2 inches in diameter; they are adhesive and stick to the substrate and each other. Generally, a short time after laying the eggs, the female leaves the nest and parental duties to the male. Eggs hatch in eight to ten days, depending on water temperature. After approximately 21 days of parental care, the male parent will leave the young madtoms on their own.

Threats. More than two-thirds of all madtom species have been listed as threatened or endangered by various agencies in different states. The main threat to madtoms is the degradation or destruction of stream habitats. Madtoms are particularly vulnerable because their naturally small distributions may not provide sufficient refuge for undisturbed areas useful for recolonizing impacted areas. Activities that increase stream temperature and erosion rates are especially significant, as many madtoms depend on cool water for spawning and silt-free nests for juvenile survival. Protecting madtoms, therefore, means protecting small and medium sized rivers.

Madtoms have gained recognition as bait for bass fishing and as an aquarium fish. Because of the problems associated with naturally small and disjunct populations, and because many threatened or endangered madtoms are protected through state and federal laws, anglers and aquarists should exercise caution in the collection of madtoms. Check with local fisheries biologists to make sure that collecting madtoms is legal and that madtom populations in local streams can support such activities.

Another problem with using madtoms as bait is introduction of non-native fish into streams *(see: exotic species)*. Many anglers return unused live baits to the stream before surrendering for the day. However, this may inadvertently introduce non-native fish into new rivers, possibly leading to the elimination of a different madtom species or another fish altogether.

See: Catfish; Madtom, Brown; Stonecat.

MADTOM, BROWN   *Noturus phaeus.*

The brown madtom is a widely distributed and relatively common member of the madtoms *(see)*. This diminutive catfish may be used in bait fishing for bass, and is prominent in moderate to fast flowing water.

Identification. Brown madtoms are dull colored. The upper body possesses a chocolate brown or yellowish-brown tint. The ventral side is pale. Juvenile brown madtoms, especially those collected in complex leaf debris or vegetation, may be black. These fish will adjust the intensity of their body color to simulate shades of their surroundings. The upper lip of the brown madtom protrudes beyond that of the lower lip, and the rear of the pectoral spine has six saw-like teeth.

Size/Age. Male and female brown madtoms grow at the same rate but males reach a larger overall length because they live longer. The largest individual collected to date was a male that measured 6 inches in total length. Females live at least three years while males may live four or five years. The total length of three-year-old fish ranges from 3.9 to 5.1 inches.

Distribution. The brown madtom has a fairly wide distribution covering the following areas: Mississippi River tributaries in Kentucky, Tennessee, Mississippi, and Alabama; Tennessee River tributaries in Tennessee and Alabama; the Gulf Slope in the Sabine River drainage of Louisiana; and Bayou Teche drainage in Louisiana. It has also been reported in the Ouachita River drainage in Arkansas, probably introduced with other baitfish. In areas where brown madtoms are collected, they are usually abundant.

Habitat. This species is usually abundant in springs and small streams where areas of vegetation exist, in accumulations of debris, and underneath

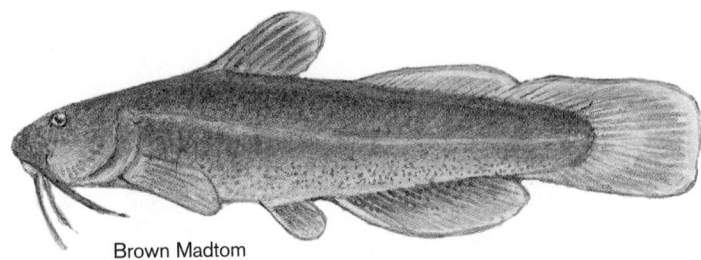

Brown Madtom

undercut banks. Madtoms in one stream in northern Mississippi preferred undercut banks to all other types of cover. Brown madtoms can be found in moderate to fast flowing water over small gravel or coarse sand.

Food. Brown madtoms exhibit crepuscular feeding, with peak feeding activity following sunset and just before sunrise. The diet, similar to other madtoms, is primarily composed of midge larvae, caddisfly larvae, and crayfish.

Reproduction. Spawning, as determined in northern Mississippi research, took place from May through July.

See: Catfish; Madtom.

MAGGOT

Soft-bodied insect larva, especially of the housefly, bluebottle fly (or blowfly), and greenbottle fly. Fly larvae, also known as waxworms, are natural baits used when fishing for coarse fish *(see)* and in ice fishing *(see)*. Maggots are commonly fished in their natural white color but may be available in a darker dyed form; they are hooked through the blunt end or through the midsection. Pupated maggots, known as casters, are also used for coarse species and are fished with the hook buried inside.

MAGNUSON ACT

See: Fishery Conservation and Management Act.

MAHIMAHI

See: Dolphin, Common.

MAHSEER

Mahseer are a fish of mystery and are little known to the angling and scientific community in the Western world. References to this species, even in comprehensive natural-history books on fish, are either lacking or merely mention the mahseer as an Asiatic cyprinid that attains huge sizes. Mahseer are well known in their endemic range, however, and collectively are the largest and most important species for sportfishing within that range, particularly in India *(see)*.

Species

The name mahseer itself is evidently derived from the Sanscrit word *mahasaul,* which is derived from

M

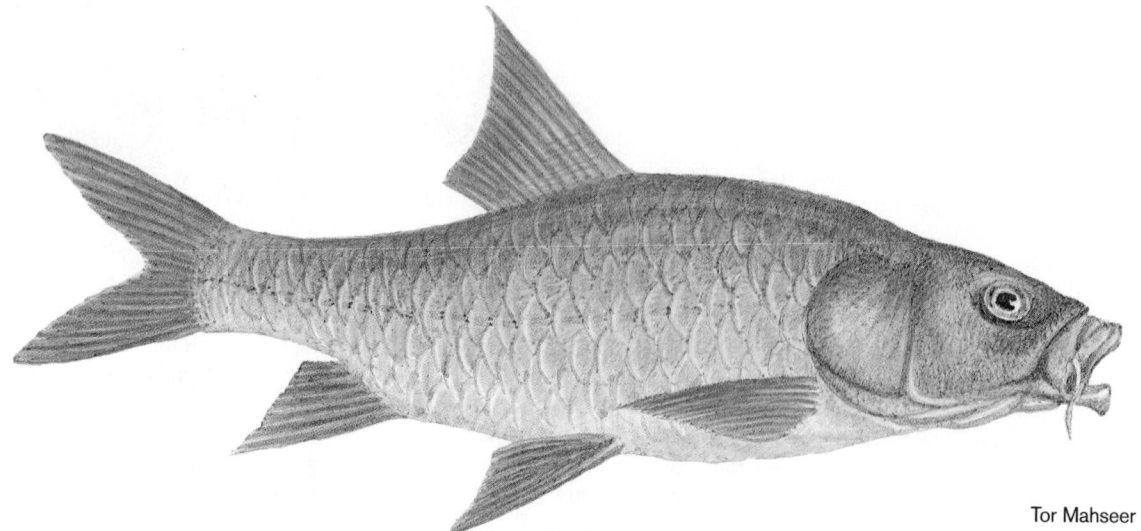

Tor Mahseer

mahasalkalin, meaning "a fish with large scales." Mahseer belong to the huge Cyprinidae family of minnows, which includes carp and their many relatives. For many years, mahseer were classified by taxonomists under the genus *Barbus,* and thus called large-scaled barbels, a nickname that has stuck even though these fish have been reclassified.

The exact number of mahseer that exist is still a bit vague, but at least six species are described under the genus *Tor.* Several of these are the largest of the cyprinid clan. They include the following species.

The putitor mahseer *(Tor putitora).* Also known as the yellow-finned mahseer, common Himalayan mahseer, golden mahseer, and Himalayan salmon, this is the leviathan of the clan. In India it has been reported to attain a length of 2.7 meters. The males reach a weight of 190 kilograms or 418 pounds, and females achieve 220 kilograms or 484 pounds. Modern catches do not reflect fish even approaching this size, however, and contemporary records in some literature indicate a maximum of 132 pounds. It has a high food value and occurs in southern Asia in Afghanistan, Pakistan, India, Nepal, Bangladesh, Bhutan, and the Himalayas.

The tor mahseer *(Tor tor).* Also known as the red-finned mahseer, the golden mahseer, the thick-lipped mahseer, in Bengali as *mohashol,* in Burmese as *nga-dauk,* and in Nepali as *sahar sor,* the tor mahseer can grow to a length of 1.7 meters and a weight of 100 kilograms or 220 pounds. Contemporary records indicate a maximum size of 167 pounds, and a 95-pounder caught in 1984 from India's Cauvery River is registered as the all-tackle world record. It occurs in Pakistan, India, Bangladesh, Nepal, and Bhutan. This is the species most commonly referred to simply as "mahseer."

The mosal mahseer *(Tor mosal).* Also known as the copper mahseer, the mosal mahseer can grow to 1 meter in length. It is found in Himalaya and Burma.

The khudchee *(Tor khudree).* Also known as black mahseer and yellow mahseer, khudchee are found in India and Sri Lanka and grow to 450 millimeters and 22.6 kilograms.

The mussullah *(Tor mussullah).* Also known as the high-backed mahseer, the mussullah grows to 1.5 meters and nearly 90 kilograms.

The jungha *(Tor progenius).* Also known as the jungha of Assamese, this species is found in India and grows to 150 centimeters and nearly 90 kilograms.

Another species that is lumped in with mahseers because of its large scales is the bokar *(Acrossocheilus hexagonolepis).* Also known as the katli, bokar of Assamese, and katli of Nepalese, this species may grow to 11 kilograms and occurs in India, Bangladesh, Nepal, Burma, the Malay Peninsula, Thailand, and China.

Traits and Angling

In general terms, the characteristics of species in the genus *Tor* are an elongate and moderately compressed body with a small head and prominent snout, a strongly curved inferior or subinferior mouth, a protractile upper jaw, lips that are thick and continuous at the corners of the mouth, two pairs of barbels, large scales (on giant specimens, as large as the palm of a hand), a full lateral line, and pharyngeal teeth for crushing food.

Although mahseer are described as omnivorous bottom feeders, most species primarily consume aquatic plant matter, algae, insects, and mollusks. Some, and presumably large individuals, are also piscivorous.

Mahseer primarily inhabit rivers but also occupy the still waters of lakes and canals. The backwaters of rivers, the junctions of rivers, the mouths of tributaries, eddies, and the heads and tails of pools are their favorite habitats. Some species travel up tributaries to spawn, whereas others migrate up a main river; this activity occurs at the onset of the rainy season, and the fish return downriver after the rainy season. In the hilly sections of Indian rivers, the best fishing time is August and September. The rainy season is usually a poor time; turbid water, late spring, early fall, and the lowland sections of rivers all improve the chances of taking large fish.

Large mahseer are powerful fish that can make determined runs in big rivers. They are not flashy fighters, but, similar to their carp brethren, they are powerful and strong. Larger fish have extremely powerful jaws and can do crushing damage to a person's fingers. These fish take many kinds of natural food, but paste baits are especially preferred. Various spoons are also effective. Light to heavy tackle is used, depending on the size of fish targeted.

See: India.

MAINE

Most people associate angling in Maine with images of landlocked salmon or wild brook trout in remote ponds and lakes surrounded by spruce-covered shorelines. Although those attributes remain applicable, the Pine Tree State's abundant waters offer a great deal more, both in freshwater and marine environs.

On the inland front, brown trout, smallmouth and largemouth bass, togue (lake trout), pickerel, and panfish attract residents and nonresidents alike to Maine's 2,500 lakes and ponds and 37,000 miles of rivers, as well as to its untold miles of streams and brooks. The largest state in New England, Maine offers varied terrain and angling opportunities, meeting a wide range of tastes. Indeed, some Maine bass waters would make a Floridian feel at home, and a few brown trout streams resemble pastoral Hampshire chalk streams. Between these extremes are rushing, tumbling rivers, immense lakes, mountain ponds, true limestone streams, and much more.

On the maritime front, Maine's 3,500 miles of rocky coastline—offering innumerable bays, coves, tidal rivers, a sprinkling of beaches, and thousands of rugged islands and ledges—combines with an ecologically diverse sea floor to provide an ideal environment for several dozen gamefish and food fish species. The cold, clear water of coastal Maine is among the cleanest in the United States. Maine's saltwater sportfishery is lightly exploited when compared with that in more populated states to the south. Still, angler participation has increased in recent times, and the value of the recreational fishery has grown considerably. The populations of cod, pollock, haddock, hake, and other bottom dwellers—long the saltwater species for which Maine has been known—are dwindling, however, and are in a troubled state. Angling for these species has been supplemented and in some cases overshadowed by the pursuit of bluefin tuna, various species of sharks, as well as striped bass, bluefish, and mackerel.

Freshwater

Although Maine's once-fabulous northwoods brook trout fishery has declined in response to the growing network of logging roads, brown trout fishing in the southern half of the state is steadily improving, with some browns weighing over 10 pounds. Two- to 4-pounders raise few eyebrows, and 12- to 14-inch fish are routine. Southern and central Maine have brown trout fishing galore in places, some of it world-class, thanks to landlocked salmon, smallmouth and largemouth bass, and striped bass. These gamefish take the pressure off nonindigenous browns.

Mainers love the landlocked salmon, which accounts for its designation as the Pine Tree State's official fish. A smaller landlocked version of the lordly Atlantic salmon, these fish fight with fast runs and high acrobatic leaps that endear them to anglers. Residents and nonresidents prize these landlocks above all and turn—among coldwater species—to brown trout as a distant second choice.

Most of Maine's smallmouth and largemouth bass live in the southern half of the state, near population centers, and offer world-class angling. Until recently, many residents considered these species "trash" fish and concentrated their efforts on salmonids or sea-run striped bass. Their attitude has changed, and more residents are turning from salmonids to black bass or stripers. Anglers routinely catch 16-inch black bass in Maine, and they have a chance to take 4-pound smallmouths and 5-pound largemouths on any cast.

One highly appealing feature of Maine's bass fishery is the profusion of small ponds in pristine settings with little shoreline development. Smallmouths over 7 pounds and largemouths over 10 pounds are possible, particularly in smaller ponds avoided by folks with big, fast boats that require elaborate launching ramps. Bass waters with cartop boat launches are seldom fished, and strict regulations keep the bass population strong in larger waters, despite increasing pressure.

Togue have few followers in Maine, so double-digit specimens can hit a lure on any outing. A 10- to 15-pound togue would make any angler happy, but 20-plus-pound togue are also occasionally caught. And the chance, however remote, exists to take a 30-pounder. Because some Maine waters have too many togue, fisheries biologists have instituted liberal bag limits. This practice allows landlocked salmon and baitfish, especially smelt, to proliferate. Even in waters originally populated by native togue (spread across the state) and brook trout, salmon are far more popular, which has inspired management programs to favor landlocks.

Pickerel and panfish such as white and yellow perch, sunfish, black crappie, and horned pout (bullhead) produce fast fishing for youngsters and anglers who want to eat their catch without hurting the more valuable salmonid and bass resources. Although white perch are actively pursued (their white, flaky meat is prized table fare), pickerel and panfish are generally underutilized in Maine; prolific fishing pressure has put a minimal dent in the populations of these species.

M

M

Maine was once a popular destination for Atlantic salmon anglers, but many formerly prominent Atlantic salmon rivers have dwindled to runs so small, they are not worth fishing. Indeed, this species is experiencing hard times in the Pine Tree State, and restoration efforts are far from bearing fruit.

Southern Maine. In general, Maine waters are sterile. In southern Maine, however, lakes, ponds, rivers, streams, and brooks are richer in nutrients, so fish grow faster. Southern Maine waters therefore produce quality brown trout, landlocked salmon, and largemouth and smallmouth bass. Each year, anglers land 10-plus-pound browns, and on rare occasions 20-pound browns, in this region. Four-pound smallmouths and 5-pound largemouths excite plenty of anglers every season, and some take larger fish. A 7-pound smallmouth or 8- to 10-pound largemouth is possible.

Lakes and ponds produce fast action for brown trout and landlocked salmon shortly after ice out, normally in mid-April. Surface fishing peaks in May and begins to peter out in June; only trollers working the depths with downriggers or lead-core lines linger. Knowledgeable trollers find action all summer. In September, waters cool, and browns and landlocks come to the surface again. Hundreds of Maine waters offer October and November fishing to open-water anglers, but the fall season is strictly catch-and-release for salmonids and bass.

Top spots for giant browns are Square Lake and Mousam Lake, both in the towns of Shapleigh and Acton. These waters produce 10-plus-pound browns most years. Square occasionally yields a 20-plus-pound brown, making this a rare but possible accomplishment.

A classic river for browns is the Saco, particularly around Steep Falls. The Little Ossipee from Newfield to Ossipee Falls, and Pleasant River in Windham, are designated for catch-and-release and host brown trout and brook trout aplenty. Most are pansize, but the opportunity for bigger trout exists.

Sebago, Maine's second largest lake and the deepest in New England (maximum depth 316 feet), holds a smorgasbord of fish, but landlocked salmon, togue, and smallmouths attract the most attention. Sebago is nationally famous for its salmon; the scientific name for landlocks, *Salmo salar sebago,* is derived from this lake. Salmon prowl near the surface of Sebago from ice out in mid-April to early June before descending to deeper water. In September, cool weather brings salmon to the surface again. Today, 4-pound landlocks are a typical trophy salmon from this famous lake, a far cry from a documented 22-pound, 8-ounce landlock caught in 1907. Togue have come on strong in Sebago since a controversial stocking program introduced them in the 1970s. Tributaries to Sebago, such as the Crooked and Songo Rivers, have runs of landlocked salmon in May and again in September, offering top fly fishing action.

Coves around this huge water offer anglers the best smallmouth action in southern Maine, and 3- to 5-pound specimens keep Sebago bass anglers returning. The shallows produce panfish action for white perch and black crappie.

North of Sebago, and in the same drainage, is a cluster of large ponds and lakes that have bass galore. Raymond Pond in New Gloucester routinely yields 3- to 5-pound smallmouths and largemouths each season. Beautiful Crescent Lake in Raymond holds 3- to 5-pound smallmouths and largemouths; 6- to 8-pound largemouths are rare but available. Thomas Pond in Casco has similar fishing and the added attraction of pickerel in the 4- to 5-pound range. Few Maine anglers bother with this toothy predator, so it is an underutilized resource. Moose Pond in Denmark has produced largemouths in excess of 11 pounds; this is a rare catch, of course, but the lake clearly offers big bass. Thompson Lake offers giant smallmouths—at least one documented smallie weighed 8 pounds.

In truth, it would be difficult to find a pond or lake in southern Maine that doesn't have one species of bass, or both. Another plus for this region is myriad streams with brook trout, some holding native fish.

Central Maine. Central Maine has been a great success story for fisheries biologists, beginning with the brown trout fisheries in the Kennebec River between Skowhegan and Augusta. Biologists for the Maine Department of Inland Fisheries and Wildlife tout this large river as one of the best brown trout waters in the Northeast. Fish up to 20 inches are routine; in recent years, at least one documented brown of 30 inches fell to an angler using a dry fly, which is remarkable. Rainbows up to 20 inches make this section of the river even more interesting. June, early July, and September are top months, but people catch fish year-round.

Farther east, the St. George River flows from St. George Lake in Liberty to the ocean in Thomaston. On the way, this small freestone river slides through woodlands, pastoral farm country, and small villages with church steeples. In shallow riffle sections, browns average 8 to 10 inches, but the St. George flows through several ponds before reaching the Atlantic. Near the inlets and outlets, browns run from 10 to 18 inches, but the occasional larger fish does exist. May and early June are prime months to hit the river sections near the ponds.

Damariscotta Lake in Jefferson routinely produces 4-pound browns, and this water improves each year, thanks to intensive management. China Lake in Vassalboro grows browns up to 4 pounds, and larger specimens in years when baitfish thrive.

The ponds along the St. George River have black bass, but a 3- to 4-pound smallmouth would be a trophy here, and a 5-pound largemouth would cause a stir. Central Maine does have world-class bass waters, though. Top bets are Cobbosseecontee Lake just west of Augusta; Androscoggin Lake in

Leeds; Webber and Threemile Ponds in Vassalboro; and China, Windsor, and North Ponds in the Belgrade Lakes. These waters hold plenty of 3- to 4-pound smallmouths and 4- to 5-pound largemouths. Fish grow bigger here, though; 6- to 8-pound largemouths are always possible, and smallmouths of 6 pounds and larger live in these waters. This area also has small remote and semiremote bass ponds that provide solitude and perhaps the trophy of a lifetime. As in southern Maine, few ponds and lakes in central Maine lack bass.

Farther northeast, just above Bangor, the Penobscot River between Milford and Lincoln has arguably the best river smallmouth fishing in the world. Here the river flows over a gravel bottom, and water depths are generally up to 4 feet. Fish average 13 inches, and 3-pounders are common. Anglers do take the occasional $5^1/_2$-pound smallmouth. Islands dot this river in Greenbush and Argyle, the top spot on the river for this species.

Long Pond in the Belgrade Lakes is one of Maine's three top trophy landlocked salmon waters. Four-pounders won't impress many Long Pond regulars because this water gives up 6- and 7-pound salmon every year, and larger specimens are possible. St. George Lake in Liberty routinely produces salmon up to 4 pounds. Ice out in central Maine occurs in mid-April, and salmonids stay near the surface into June. After spending the summer in the depths, they surface in September.

Long Pond also has a good northern pike population, the result of illegal stocking in the 1980s, as pike are not indigenous to Maine. This species has flourished here and attracts crowds. Sabattus Pond in Greene has pike, too, also illegally stocked. Mainers love this new, exotic species.

Waldo County, in the eastern section of central Maine, offers excellent fishing for brook trout. Nearly every brook holds native brook trout, and the ones flowing into the ocean have sea-run brook trout, colloquially called "salters." The time to fish for salters is in April, when spring waters run high, drawing trout from their estuarine environment. Small brooks hold 8- to 10-inch specimens, but rivers like the Passagassawakeag in Belfast have a May run of fish in the 1- to 2-pound range. In general, large waters have later runs.

Down East. Washington County, which contains West Quoddy Head—a small peninsula that is the easternmost point of land in the U.S.—has landlocked salmon and smallmouth bass fishing that attract anglers from around the world. Smallmouths run smaller here than in southern and central Maine, but most of the bass lakes and ponds have little development, and many have no shore dwellings, just forests. The more remote waters lie in pristine country where anglers might not see another person all day.

Although anglers won't take trophy salmon here as readily as in other parts of Maine, trophy specimens do swim in these waters. West Grand and East Grand Lakes are two of Maine's best salmon lakes. These are huge waters with enough coves and peninsulas for anglers to find seclusion. West Grand lies north of the village of Grand Lake Stream, and East Grand is on the Canadian border. Ice out is in late April or early May, and landlocks cruise near the surface until June, when summer heat drives them deeper. They come back to the surface in September. Both lakes also hold bass and togue.

Grand Lake Stream is one of Maine's premier landlocked salmon streams, and fly anglers congregate there in May, early June, September, and early October. This is also one of the few opening-day hotspots in Maine. When fishing season begins on April 1, ice and snow still cover the state, but salmon that have spent the winter in the pool below the dam provide April Fool's Day action.

Top bass waters in Washington County include Third Machias Lake in the Machias lakes chain just west of Grand Lake Stream village. Fifteen-inch smallmouths are average, and 4-pounders are possible. Meddybemps Lake near Calais, and Big Lake west of Princeton, have similar-size smallmouths and attract bass anglers from across the nation. Junior Lake just northwest of West Grand Lake has smallmouths that average 15 inches, but 6-pounders are possible.

The St. Croix River has smallmouths galore that average 13 to 15 inches, but a 4-pounder doesn't surprise St. Croix regulars. This river has fast-water sections that look like salmonid habitat, but parts of the St. Croix look as "bassy" as any water in the country.

Washington County has myriad brooks, and most of them have brook trout. Because the many dozens of lakes and ponds attract the majority of anglers, many brooks are underfished. This is a wonderful place to catch native brookies in secluded woodland settings. Also, brooks and small streams running into the ocean offer sea-run brook trout in early April.

Most Down East bass waters also boast excellent pickerel fishing, with 4-pound catches somewhat common. Many bass waters support white perch, and this area provides Maine's best angling for this species.

Rangeley Lakes. This region attracted wealthy New York City anglers in the mid-1850s, and they caught giant brook trout for 50 years, some weighing as much as 12 pounds. Eight-pounders were possible on any outing. Anglers decided to stock landlocked salmon in the Rangeley Lakes in 1873, and this species flourished. One documented specimen in 1905 weighed $18^1/_2$ pounds. Landlocked salmon, land development, and fishing pressure, however, helped end the era of giant brookies. Today a 4-pound brook trout is a trophy. Larger specimens are possible but rare.

Nevertheless, Rangeley Lake now ranks as one of the three top spots in Maine to catch trophy landlocked salmon. Indeed, the chance always exists to

The Guinness Book of Records lists the largest freshwater fish as the rare pla buk or pa beuk, found only in the Mekong River and tributaries. The largest was 9 feet $10^1/_4$ inches long and weighed $533^1/_2$ pounds.

M

Many of Maine's waters, including Fish River Lake shown here, have notable salmon and trout fisheries.

catch an 8-pounder. Four-pound landlocks surprise no one, and 2-pounders are average. Nearby Mooselookmeguntic and Cupsuptic Lakes, just west of Rangeley Lake, have smaller salmon, and a 3-pound fish would be a good catch. The action in general is better in these two lakes, however, than it is in Rangeley.

Ice out occurs late in this northern, mountainous region, often in mid-May. Trout and salmon stay near the surface through May and most of June, so surface trolling lasts longer than in southern Maine. Fish drop deeper in summer and return to the surface in fall.

Trout and salmon swim upstream here in June and September, when rain brings fresh water rushing down the Kennebago River, the Cupsuptic River, or smaller streams running into the Rangeley Lakes. These are excellent targets for fly anglers. September runs attract anglers from across the nation to cast flies at brook trout weighing 4 pounds and more, and at salmon that weigh from 4 to 8 pounds.

Moosehead Lake region.   Moosehead Lake is Maine's largest lake, spreading over 74,890 acres and extending more than 34 miles in length. With the exception of two small villages (Greenville and Rockwood) on the south end, shoreline development is nonexistent, so the setting is classic northern Maine.

This lake has landlocked salmon, brook trout, and togue, and most anglers troll for these species. Brook trout run up to 4 pounds and occasionally larger, but a 16- to 18-inch brookie is a good fish. Salmon have never run large in Moosehead Lake, and 14- to 16-inch fish are average. Moosehead is a togue lake, although landlocks were introduced about a century ago. The togue average 18 to 20 inches, but 20-pounders are possible on rare occasions.

Ice out on Moosehead occurs in early to mid-May, and high water from the spring melt draws salmon, brookies, and even togue up or down the rivers in this region, including the Moose River, the sprawling East Outlet of the Kennebec River, and the tiny Roach River. These rivers also have September runs of salmon and brookies, and fly anglers hit these waters hard due to abundant fish and a spectacular remote setting. Catching togue in rivers is highly unusual in the U.S.

When anglers head to the Moosehead Lake region, they often think of Moosehead Lake itself; yet, the region stretching from Jackman to the west and over toward Millinocket to the east has an incredible 236,000 acres of water and 4,200 miles of rivers, streams, and brooks—most all of it salmonid habitat.

East of Moosehead lies a cluster of ponds, many of them regulated for fly fishing only. Roads go to a number of these ponds, but some are remote. There are seven Roach ponds that run into Moosehead and attract salmonid anglers, and the Nahmakanta region, a state-owned tract of wilderness, has many more blue-ribbon trout ponds and streams. West toward Jackman is more of the same, with dozens of trout ponds, many remote. Anglers are hard pressed to find waters in this area without brook trout. Togue lakes are also numerous.

Baxter region.   The endless ponds in Baxter, northwest of Millinocket, and the remote and semi-remote ponds on paper company lands north of there, hold brook trout; in many instances, special regulations exist to protect the fishery. Baxter State Park waters are heavily regulated and routinely produce native brookies in the 12- to 14-inch range and larger. Nesowadnehunk Lake just west of Baxter, and Munsungan and Millinocket Lakes north of Baxter, are three of the best spots in Maine for stillwater brook trout in a remote setting. They routinely produce 2-plus-pound brookies.

The rugged West Branch of the Penobscot River, below Ripogenus Dam just south of Baxter State Park, has a national reputation as a landlocked salmon river and is the best spot in Maine for river landlocks. Four-pound fish are common. The lower section of Nesowadnehunk Stream also has salmon, many of them running up from the West Branch. A private road parallels the Penobscot River, but lower Nesowadnehunk Stream is remote, offering only a foot trail.

Waters in this region peak in late May and June and again in September. The high elevation and northern latitude help keep waters cool all summer. In addition, northern Maine receives as much as 60 more days of rain than does southern Maine. In short, summer fishing can be spectacular.

Much of Maine's north country belongs to large corporations that allow access for a minimal fee. This is truly a sportsman's paradise, and one of the nation's best examples of big business accommodating the public's recreational needs.

Aroostook County.   Much of Maine caters to tourists, but a large section of Aroostook County is

M

an agricultural area, worked mostly by potato farmers, with few sporting camps and motels. This should not discourage anglers, though, because the region offers brook trout, landlocked salmon, and brown trout in different settings, ranging from remote boreal forests to pastoral farmlands and, surprisingly, true limestone waters.

Three major limestone waters—Prestile Stream, Meduxnekeag River, and parts of the Aroostook River—lie in eastern Aroostook, right in the middle of potato country. They flow through a limestone belt and hold fat trout that feed voraciously on myriad caddis- and mayflies. This is limestone fishing at its best, with little pressure.

Prestile Stream and the Aroostook River harbor brook trout and the occasional Atlantic salmon, although the latter is rare. Meduxnekeag has browns and brookies. These main rivers can produce small trout in the 8- to 10-inch range all day, discouraging folks who are after bigger fish. When dusk comes, though, a 2- to 3-pound brook trout is possible, and the Meduxnekeag has 20-inch browns and larger. Best of all, every brook running into these primary rivers has trout. Often, even the smallest of brooks has trout that are 12 inches or larger, even during summer.

Southwest of Fort Kent near the Canadian border is a state-owned township colloquially called the Red River, or Deboullie Lake, region. This tract of public land has several blue-ribbon brook trout ponds that lie in remote woods. Trout average 10 to 12 inches, but Black Pond holds 4-pound brookies. Island, Denny, and Galilee Ponds have the typical Maine brookies running from 8 to 12 inches, but the occasional 16-inch fish livens a day. Deboullie has landlocked salmon, brook trout, and the rare blueback trout, which is a landlocked arctic charr. June brings heavy hatches on these waters.

In northeastern Aroostook, the Fish River chain of lakes and the thoroughfares between them offer anglers excellent opportunities for trophy landlocked salmon and brook trout. Late May, June, and September promise the best fishing, but in the north country, abundant summer rains keep fish active throughout the season. Eagle, Square, Cross, Mud, and Long Lakes are huge waters, and the latter is one of the three best spots in Maine for trophy landlocks. Fly anglers hit the thoroughfares between these waters each June and September and catch salmon that average 2 pounds; 4- to 5-pound specimens don't raise an eyebrow. Brookies around 16-inches are common, but 4-pound trophies are possible.

Saltwater

Historically, most recreational fishing in Maine has been conducted on party and charter boats targeting cod, pollock, haddock, hake, and other bottom dwellers. Several thousand pounds of fish was not an uncommon day's bounty for a boatload of 20 anglers from the 1950s through the 1970s. As groundfish stocks in the Gulf of Maine plummeted in the 1980s due to commercial overfishing, the number of larger deep-sea passenger boats declined proportionately, but a few continue to operate, and catches can still be good. Many charter boats began to pursue bluefish during this period, a species that had resumed its annual summer migrations north into Maine waters in 1973 following a 51-year hiatus. Today, most offshore charter boats, and a large and growing fleet of private sportfishing and commercial craft, focus their efforts on giant bluefin tuna. Fishing for blue, mako, and porbeagle sharks has become increasingly popular, but most of the catch is tagged and released.

Inshore recreational saltwater fishing in Maine has centered around the plentiful Atlantic mackerel for nearly a century. Mackerel thrive all along the state's coastline from late spring through fall, and thousands of residents and summer visitors enjoy light-tackle sport with these accommodating little gamesters. Striped bass fishing, both as an activity and as an industry, has burgeoned since the early 1990s, when seasonal bluefish populations began to recede. Anglers quickly turned their attention to bass, which became plentiful enough to attract thousands of new sportfishing participants and to fuel many new coastal guide services, charter boats, outfitters, and tackle shops. In the late 1990s, some 75 percent of Maine's nearly 300,000 residents and visiting saltwater anglers primarily targeted striped bass.

The Downeast coast.   The upper half of the state's rugged shoreline, from Penobscot Bay to the Canadian border, is referred to as the Downeast coast, as old-time sailing ships from Boston often ran downwind on an easterly course to get there. Despite a tremendous area of seemingly prime habitat for a number of game and food species, sportfishing pressure is extremely light here due to a short summer season, fewer striped bass and bluefish than in the southern waters of the state, and a corresponding dearth of party and charter boats.

Groundfish, including cod, pollock, cusk, and haddock, are available all along this section of Maine's coast, in water depths from 60 to well over 300 feet. Experienced anglers seek out the rocky humps and ledges that rise from the sea floor and around which these bottom feeders congregate. They send down 8- to 24-ounce chrome-plated diamond or Norwegian-style jigs attached to sturdy 30- to 50-pound-class outfits. Natural baits such as sea clams, squid, and mackerel chunks also work well, especially for haddock and cusk, but may attract dogfish—small sharks regarded as pests. Party boats specializing in bottom fishing can be found in Eastport, Jonesport, Bar Harbor, and Rockland. These normally provide half- or full-day trips.

Atlantic mackerel are available from mid-June through September in bays and harbors virtually everywhere Downeast, ranging from "tinkers" of 6

M

to 10 inches up to "clubs" approaching 2 pounds. They are taken on small pieces of bait, tiny diamond jigs, or trolled multihook feather or tube rigs, and it's not uncommon to catch several dozen in an hour when the fish are schooling. Fly fishing for mackerel is popular in many areas, and any small streamer dressed with a bit of Mylar for added flash will produce.

Anglers pursue striped bass in the tidewaters of numerous rivers along the Downeast coast, notably the Penobscot, although a good amount of local knowledge as to specific areas and stage of the tide is necessary for consistent success. Bluefish migrated north annually to this region of the coast during the 1980s but were scarce in the 1990s, as stocks have diminished; populations of menhaden, a prime forage species for blues, have likewise decreased.

The Midcoast. The stretch of shoreline from Penobscot Bay south to Casco Bay, referred to as the Midcoast, offers very good fishing. The Camden-Rockland area has launch ramps for private boaters seeking mackerel and groundfish, and Thomaston, at the navigable head of the St. George River, provides access to both Penobscot and Muscongus Bays. Island-studded Muscongus Bay, as well as the Medomak River that empties into it, see comparatively little sportfishing pressure, although mackerel, groundfish, and striped bass are available during the summer months. Johns Bay, on the eastern side of Pemaquid Point, holds plenty of mackerel and can host fair numbers of bluefish in the 6- to 15-pound range in summer, along with stripers in the Johns River.

The Damariscotta River, just west of Johns Bay and separated by Rutherford Island, is comprised of channels, estuaries, and mud flats and is navigable as far upriver as the town of Damariscotta on Route 1, where there is a public launch facility. Although not as heavily fished as rivers to the south, the Damariscotta provides fine striped bass action, including 50-plus-pounders, for small-boat anglers. The river is dotted with thousands of lobster trap buoys, however, which can make fishing difficult in some sections.

Boothbay Harbor, just around the corner from the mouth of the Damariscotta, is the northernmost destination for serious saltwater sportfishing on the East Coast. A bustling summer resort as well as an important lobstering port, the Boothbay region is home to a number of guide, charter, and party boats, along with a half-dozen marinas that accommodate private boats. The most popular offshore area is a plateau-like expanse of bottom 200 to 350 feet deep. Called The Kettle, it is situated 10 miles south of Seguin Island. Jigging produces good numbers of cod, pollock, cusk, hake, and other groundfish; trolling or chumming can produce giant bluefin tuna between 200 and 1,000 pounds from mid-June through September. Anglers also land blue, mako, and porbeagle sharks on The

Kettle and in adjacent deeper waters. Inshore fishing for mackerel, striped bass, and bluefish is productive in most of the Boothbay area's bays and around the islands.

The Sheepscot River, the western boundary of the Boothbay region, is one of Maine's coldest waterways year-round, yet it never freezes over. Bluefish are taken on trolled plugs at the river's wide mouth, known as Sheepscot Bay, and striped bass are caught all the way up to the town of Wiscasset on Route 1 and several miles beyond. The beach at Reid State Park on the western shore of the mouth offers good striped bass fishing for surf casters, especially in late summer and early fall.

The Kennebec River. Once polluted by industrial discharge many miles upriver, the Kennebec once again hosts populations of Atlantic salmon, striped bass, sturgeon, and shad thanks to stringent environmental laws. Home to a world-class, small-boat sportfishery for stripers that has expanded steadily since 1990, the Kennebec annually yields thousands of bass each summer from the river's mouth all the way to the Edwards Dam in Augusta some 35 miles upriver, as do the waterways connecting the Kennebec to the Sheepscot River. These include the Sasanoa River with its Upper Hell Gate, Hockomock Bay, the Cross River, and Lower Hell Gate. Live baits, plugs, jigs, and flies all produce stripers in the Kennebec system, and much of the best fishing occurs during the outgoing tide. Launch ramps are available at Bath, Phippsburg, and Hallowell (on the Kennebec), and at Wiscasset (on the Sheepscot). A number of licensed striper guides operate out of these towns as well as Boothbay Harbor and ports in Casco Bay.

Popham Beach, on the western shore of the mouth of the Kennebec, is a popular and easily accessed surf fishing spot for stripers and blues. The coastline around the corner and stretching southwest to Small Point, which is mostly sand beach dotted with rocky islands and ledges, is good striper territory and can be worked from shore or boat. Seguin Island, 2 miles offshore, is surrounded by deeper waters that produce bass and bluefish on trolled swimming plugs.

Casco Bay. Casco Bay is the watery backyard of Portland, Maine's largest city. Bounded by Cape Small to the east and Cape Elizabeth to the west, the bay is 18 miles wide at the mouth and extends nearly the same distance inland. Studded with islands and shoals, Casco Bay waters and the rivers that empty into it—notably the New Meadows, Harraseeket, Royal, and Presumpscot—provide good fishing for striped bass, bluefish, mackerel, and groundfish during the warm-weather months. Blues are landed almost anywhere, especially on swimming plugs trolled around the ledges in the outer bay, which include Temple and Lumbo Ledges, Halfway Rock, Bulwark Shoal, and Alden Rock, yet they will often chase baits up onto the shallow mud flats along the northwest side of the

Cod was the first species established as a state fish. There has been a life-size wooden carving of the "sacred cod" hanging in the Massachusetts state house since 1784.

M

bay from Portland to Brunswick. Each of these rivers holds striped bass from June through September, as do many of the islands and ledges. Cod and pollock prefer the underwater humps from 50 to 150 feet deep in the outer portions of the bay, and anglers take them on jigs or baits. Numerous marinas and launch ramps exist along the bay's perimeter, and the area boasts more than a dozen guide, charter, and party boats that target groundfish, stripers, and blues. Sharks and bluefin tuna are available in South Harpswell and the greater Portland area.

The Southwest coast. The southwest coast, stretching from Casco Bay to Kittery, offers excellent fishing.

The Spurwink River, which marks the southerly border of Cape Elizabeth just below Portland, provides good action for striped bass in the summer and is a favorite among flycasters. Adjacent Higgens Beach is one of Maine's top surf fishing spots and yields some of the largest striped bass taken in the state each year. Crescent-shaped Saco Bay, home of famous Old Orchard Beach, is bounded on the south by Biddeford Pool and the mouth of the Saco River, an excellent striped bass river that can hold bluefish as well. Public launch ramps and access to the shore are available in the Camp Ellis area.

The 5-mile stretch of coast from Biddeford Pool down to Cape Porpoise offers good inshore fishing for stripers, blues, and mackerel. Kennebunkport, a mile up the Kennebunk River, is home to several deep-sea party boats. Perkins Cove at the town of Ogunquit, some 10 miles down the coast from Kennebunkport, hosts a small fleet of party, commercial, and pleasure boats. York Harbor, 7 miles farther downcoast, provides good access to Boon Island and its adjacent ledges 6 miles offshore, where action for bluefish, bottom fish, and bluefin tuna is good.

All of the ports along the southwest coast are jumping-off spots for Jeffreys Ledge, which ranges from 20 to 30 miles offshore and stretches southwest from Kennebunkport to Newburyport in Massachusetts. Jeffreys is the most popular and heavily fished offshore ground off the southwest coast and consistently yields good catches of cod, pollock, haddock, bluefin tuna, and sharks. Other bottom-fishing and tuna grounds farther east in the Gulf of Maine, including Platts Bank and Cashes Ledge, are accessed from these ports as well.

The Piscataqua River, the natural border between Maine and New Hampshire, provides fine striped bass fishing from May through October; live baits (mackerel, menhaden, pollock, and eels) are especially productive on larger fish. Bluefish roam the Portsmouth Harbor area at the river's mouth and the outer shoreline, and bass, blues, groundfish, and tuna are taken around the Isles of Shoals, a cluster of rocky islands 7 miles offshore. Anglers who land stripers on the Piscataqua should be aware that size and possession limits for striped bass in Maine and New Hampshire may differ. Fish landed from the Maine riverbank fall under Maine regulations, and vice versa.

MAINTENANCE

See: Tackle—Care, Maintenance and Repair.

MALAŴI

By African standards, the 45,700-square-mile landlocked country of Malaŵi in the southeastern corner of central Africa is small, but an impressive 30 percent is covered by water, primarily by Lake Nyasa. Formerly known as Lake Malaŵi, Nyasa is the third largest lake on the African continent, and the twelfth largest freshwater lake in the world.

Malaŵi does not offer the abundant game and wildlife viewing opportunities available in some African countries, and fewer international tourists visit Malaŵi. Yet, with lush green hills, spectacular mountain ranges, lofty plateaus, and abundant bird life, as well as Lake Nyasa, Malaŵi has varied attractions, and many Africans are attracted in particular to the sandy shores of Nyasa. Nevertheless, fishing opportunities for the traveling angler, especially the international visitor, are modest.

This is unfortunate and ironic, because crystal clear Lake Nyasa, which is 567 kilometers long and up to 80 kilometers wide, has more endemic species of fish than any other lake in the world. Accounts of the number of species vary from 200 to 500, and some biologists suggest that even these numbers are conservative.

Although Lake Nyasa is touted in tourism literature as an angler's paradise because of its multitude of fish species, the greatest portion of these are small aquarium fish and members of the Cichlidae family, including many varieties of mbuna rockfish and assorted tilapia. The tilapia, and other coarse fish—including vundu (African catfish growing to 30 kilograms), tsungwa (growing to 2 kilograms), and mpasa, or lake salmon (a member of the carp family growing to 3 kilograms)—although valued as table fare, are not compelling gamefish, nor are they especially attractive to international anglers. Mpasa are strong fighters, however, and are caught in some of the 14 rivers that feed the lake, most notably Bua, Luweya, Lufira, and North Rukuru. Tigerfish are also reputed to be in the lake, which has hosted light-tackle fishing tournaments.

Many thousands of people living around Lake Nyasa rely on it for commercial or subsistence fishing, and, although angling opportunities are minimal, visitors can enjoy snorkeling, whereby they can observe great schools of small, colorful cichlids. Boats are available for hire at lakeside hotels, but good information on where to fish is lacking. Because of its size and great depths, Nyasa can get very rough in windy weather.

M

There are other possibilities in Malaŵi, however, including river tigerfishing and rainbow trout angling, both in or near the Shire Highlands south of Lake Nyasa. The highlands include Mount Mulanje, central Africa's highest peak at 9,849 feet.

Tigerfish are concentrated in the lower Shire River, which exits Lake Nyasa and eventually merges with the Zambezi River in Mozambique. The lower Shire plunges through chasms, and tigerfish up to 7 kilograms favor the rapids and eddies below Kapichira Falls. Access from Chikwawa can be rugged in the wet season, necessitating a 4-wheel-drive vehicle. The lower Shire is wide here, and a boat is generally necessary. The dry season (May through November) brings optimal fishing conditions.

Not far to the east and northeast, mountain streams and lakes are stocked with rainbow trout. Anglers can fish rivers on the lower slopes of the Mulanje Mountains, or on the Chambe and Lichenya Plateaus. In the Zomba Plateau, rainbows thrive in many streams, as well as in Lake Mulunguzi. Streams and lakes in Nyika National Park also contain trout. Licenses from either the park or forestry offices are required, only fly fishing is permitted, and the period from September through April is recommended.

Numerous reservoirs of various size exist here, and reportedly some on the tea estates in Mulanje and Thyolo have been stocked with largemouth bass. The rainy season is from November through March, and it can be humid between December and February, although evenings are cool in the colder altitudes.

MANGROVES

A tropical to semitropical treelike plant (genus *Rhizophora*) found in tidal conditions in salt marshes, muddy swamps, lagoons, and estuaries. Mangrove forests are found in eastern North America (Florida and the Caribbean), eastern South America, West Africa, Southeast Asia, and Australia.

Able to extract freshwater from their saline environment, mangroves grow with their roots in the water to heights of 30 to 40 feet, and have edible fruit. Three different mangroves—red, black, and white—are most commonly known, and all occur in Florida.

Red mangrove trees suggest big green millipedes walking on the water, their prop roots desperately grasping the bottom. Their long, arrowlike seed pods hang vertically, with the seed at the bottom. Black mangrove trees have pencillike roots and usually occupy slightly higher elevations upland from the red mangrove. White mangroves occupy the highest elevations farther upland than either the red or black mangroves.

Mangrove systems help purify the water in estuaries by filtering runoff; they provide breeding and nesting areas for many marine animals and birds, prevent shoreline erosion, and buffer inland areas from storm winds and tides. Mangrove thickets offer so much protection from the elements that boaters facing a hurricane emergency may take their boats far up mangrove creeks for shelter.

The waters beneath mangroves are used as nurseries by many important fish species. As the leaves die and decay, they become food for the community of animals living on the bottom. Snook, jacks, snapper, sheepshead, grouper, small jewfish, and barracuda hide and forage through the tangles of roots. Tarpon prowl the channels just outside the mangroves. Juvenile tripletail are seen lying on their sides, floating alongside and resembling mangrove leaves. Occasionally, mangroves growing in slightly brackish water harbor largemouth bass.

Anglers in shallow-draft boats drift along mangrove shorelines, tossing surface plugs and flies as near the roots as possible, to draw fish out from concealment, and then work hard to keep hooked fish from getting back into the roots.

MANITOBA

In a country with wall-to-wall fishing opportunities, Manitoba stands second to no Canadian province. It offers diverse species and notable locations that run the gamut from metropolitan catfish to tundra trout. The tourism literature calls this province an angling paradise, a lofty description not without merit.

One of Canada's heartland provinces, Manitoba is sandwiched between Ontario and Saskatchewan on its east and west, and Minnesota/North Dakota and Nunavut Territory on its south and north. Within its boundaries is a landmass of 251,000 square miles, slightly smaller than Texas. Despite its central North American location, Manitoba is a maritime province: Its northern boundary straddles Hudson Bay and Nunavut Territory at the 60th parallel. There, Churchill is Canada's only arctic seaport, with 63 frost-free days, ocean-sailing vessels, and saltwater fishing for arctic charr.

Fifteen percent, or 39,000 square miles, of Manitoba's landmass is water. It boasts 100,000 freshwater lakes and 75 species of fish. With these abundant resources, it is no wonder that many anglers, residents and nonresidents alike, visit its waters, many with hopes of catching a trophy fish.

Through the Manitoba Master Angler program, a province-supported initiative to recognize notable catches, trophy fish have been recorded since 1960. Today some 10,000 trophy fish among 28 species are registered annually, the most popular being northern pike, lake trout, walleye, channel catfish, brook trout, whitefish, and smallmouth bass. Other species in the province, and with varying constituencies, are arctic charr, arctic grayling, black crappie, brown trout, bullhead, burbot, carp, freshwater drum (silver bass), goldeye, kokanee,

largemouth bass, mooneye, muskellunge, perch, rainbow trout, rock bass, sauger, splake, sturgeon, tullibee, and white bass.

Manitoba is a world leader in progressive fish management, with aggressive catch-and-release programs and legislated mandatory use of barbless hooks. In fact, barbless hooks are mandatory throughout the province, for all species of fish. More than 75 percent of the trophy fish caught and recorded in the Master Angler program are released to fight again. A tape measure and camera are standard equipment.

Manitoba consists of three distinct geologic regions. Mesozoic shale covers the southwest portion; Paleozoic limestone extends through the north-central portion; and Precambrian granite extends outward in a northwesterly direction to the Hudson Bay Coast and beyond the provincial boundaries.

The Mesozoic region is typified by small shallow lakes in the agricultural belt. Through control of water levels in rivers, these lakes have become great producers of northern pike, walleye, and stocked trout.

The Paleozoic region contains large, relatively shallow lakes that are excellent producers of walleye, sauger, whitefish, and white bass. Lake Winnipeg, the seventh largest freshwater lake in North America and covering an area of 9,398 square miles, is an excellent example of this type of lake. Two other very large lakes of Paleozoic limestone are Lake Winnipegosis, which covers 2,086 square miles, and Lake Manitoba, which has a surface area of 1,817 square miles.

In general terms, the best angling waters are in the Precambrian shield country to the north and northeast, which is typified by fertile deep lakes and countless rivers. Gods Lake, Island Lake, and Big Sand Lake are good examples of this type of Precambrian granite.

Provincial Parks

Whiteshell Provincial Park. With an area of 672,334 acres, Whiteshell is Manitoba's largest park. The northern boundary is the Winnipeg River; the eastern boundary is the Manitoba/Ontario border; and the Trans-Canada Highway traverses the park to the south. The park is characterized by numerous lakes, rivers, and rugged Precambrian shield terrain, with a forest of spruce and fir, intermixed with aspen, poplar, and poorly drained tamarack or black spruce fens and bogs. Fishing is superb here, and in most Whiteshell waters, targeted species include northern pike, walleye, lake trout, whitefish, smallmouth bass, lake sturgeon, goldeye, mooneye, and sauger.

The Winnipeg River to the north, which became very prominent in the 1700s when it was an important fur trade route, is one of the great fishing rivers of Manitoba. Rising in Lake of the Woods and sweeping in a giant arc across the northern limit of Whiteshell Provincial Park, the river starts at Eaglenest Lake at the Ontario border, which is noted for large northern pike, trophy walleye, and scrappy smallmouth bass. At Seven Sisters, the river broadens to form a series of lakes: Natalie, Sylvia, Margaret, Eleanor, Dorothy, Nutimik, and Lac du Bonnet. It then drops through a series of cataracts and bays to join Lake Winnipeg. There are seven fishing lodges and five provincial campgrounds on this series of lakes, and fishing is consistent for northern pike, walleye, smallmouth bass, and sturgeon. The area is a paradise for wildlife, and it offers a variety of hiking trails, canoe routes, and archaeological sites.

Anglers fish primarily from boats, which are available from numerous camps. Walleye thrive in rapids and fast-moving waters. Northern pike prefer quiet bays, weedbeds, and waters near rapids. Smallmouth linger around deep, rocky ledges, and sturgeon feed on the bottom near large rapids or falls. Pike run from 5 to 10 pounds, but occasional 15- to 20-pounders exist. Walleye run from 2 to 7 pounds, and smallmouth average 2 pounds. Sturgeon vary from 10 to 80 pounds; Manitoba's record is 126 pounds. Anglers practice all methods of fishing, but spoons, spinners, and jigs are the most popular offerings. Sturgeon are taken on dead baits or minnows. Goldeye are landed with wet and dry flies.

The rest of Whiteshell Park stretches along Highway 307, which runs north to south and connects a large quantity of lakes with many facilities. Although family cottages dominate most of the lakes, good fishing is available throughout the season. This is ideal country for a family vacation, and the more adventurous angler can take a canoe trip to many backwoods areas, including the Mantario Wilderness. Mantario was set aside for hiking, canoeing, and fishing, and no motorized craft are allowed. The fishing is excellent, especially for northern pike, walleye, and smallmouth bass.

Nopiming Provincial Park. A little farther north of Whiteshell Provincial Park is Nopiming Provincial Park, a new wilderness area. *Nopiming,* an Anishinabe word meaning "entrance to the wilderness," is set in the Precambrian shield country east of Lake Winnipeg and is accessible only via an isolated gravel road from Provincial Trunk Highways 304 and 314. Rock and water are the prominent features of the park.

Because of its relative isolation, Nopiming Provincial Park has excellent fishing. Walleye, northern pike, lake trout, and smallmouth bass abound in the many lakes and rivers in the area. Only three lodges exist in the park, but campgrounds are available throughout. The main campgrounds are at Tulabi Falls, Black Lake, Beresford Lake, and Quesnel Lake. Backcountry camping is also allowed, and the area offers exceptional road-accessible canoeing. Notable canoe routes are Seagrim Lake, Rabbit River, Bird River, and Manigotagan. Excellent walleye thrive in Black,

The largest entirely artificial reservoir in the United States is Lake Mead, an impoundment of the Colorado River in Nevada.

M

Quesnel, Manigotagan, Gem, and Bird Lakes. Northern pike exist throughout Nopiming, and noteworthy smallmouth bass are caught in Shoe and Tooth Lakes.

Atikaki Provincial Park. The vast area north of Nopiming Provincial Park, between Lake Winnipeg and the Ontario border, is accessible only by air. This region offers excellent sportfishing, and lodges are scattered throughout the park. The northern portion is known as Atikaki Provincial Wilderness Park. *Atikaki* means "county of the caribou," and roughly 350 woodland caribou range in or near this park, which was designated as a wilderness zone in 1985.

The boreal forest and Precambrian shield make this park a true and typical Manitoba wilderness for canoeing and trophy angling. Notable lakes are Aikens, Sasaginnigak, Dogskin, Amphibian, Family, and Moar. All are excellent for northern pike and walleye, with Aikens also having lake trout. Lodges, as well as outpost camps, are available at some of the smaller lakes.

The Interlake District
A large area ranging from farmland in the south to coniferous forest in the north lies between Lake Winnipeg and Lakes Manitoba and Winnipegosis. The northernmost two-thirds of this area is sparsely settled and has few roads, making it a natural home for wildlife. The region supports many worthwhile angling spots, and although these places are widely scattered, all can be reached via Highway 6, which runs north out of Winnipeg and parallels the eastern shore of Lake Manitoba.

The Narrows of Lake Manitoba, 130 miles north of Winnipeg via Highways 6 and 68, is renowned for large walleye, jumbo perch, silver bass (drum), and common carp. Forty miles north of Ashern, Lake St. Martin and the Fairford River offer good northern pike and walleye action. A new road, Provincial Trunk Highway 513, which runs off Highway 6, has opened a new area at Dauphin River on Lake Winnipeg, where the walleye action is superb. Northern pike to 15 pounds are also common.

At Grand Rapids, 250 miles north of Winnipeg on Highway 6, is a large hydroelectric generating station connecting Cedar Lake to Lake Winnipeg. Cedar Lake is a large body of water renowned for huge northern pike. Fish exceeding 25 pounds are common, and some in the 30-pound class have been taken. Cedar Lake is part of the Saskatchewan River, which flows from the Alberta Rockies and empties into Hudson Bay, and also has excellent walleye and whitefish angling. The 14.2-pound Manitoba record whitefish came from this system. Some of the best local walleye and northern pike fishing is in the vicinity of Waterhen.

Gods Lake/Gods River Area
Gods Lake/Gods River. The Gods Lake/Gods River country of northeastern Manitoba has long been famed for trophy lake trout, brook trout, and northern pike. Located 365 miles north of Winnipeg and serviced by four lodges with all-weather landing strips, Gods Lake itself is 65 miles long and 20 miles wide, and provides superb fishing. Lake trout average 6 to 12 pounds, with many exceeding 20 pounds; northern pike average 6 to 16 pounds, with some in the 30-pound class; and brook trout average 3 to 5 pounds, with many in the 7- to 9-pound class. Walleye and whitefish are also present.

Single barbless hooks are mandatory for brook trout fishing in the Gods and Island Rivers, and only one brookie over 18 inches can be kept. Spoons and large spinners are popular for lake trout and northern pike, and small spinners and flies for brook trout. Jigs can be especially effective on all species at certain times in the summer, and fly fishing is most effective in July, when insects are hatching. Even large whitefish can be taken when fishing for brook trout on the river.

Gods River water is very clear and fast, with many shallows and rapids, and navigation here is recommended only for skilled canoeists. The brook trout in these waters are brilliantly colored, large, and naturally strong because of the fast-moving water. They are famous throughout the continent and live up to their hard-fighting reputation. These are native, wild fish who deposit their eggs in early September on gravel beds in slack waters behind islands and along boulders in the main river itself. Early in the following summer, the fry inhabit warmer quiet waters along the banks and enjoy a plentiful supply of aquatic insects. The young fish triple in size during the brief midsummer and adapt to hiding and feeding among rocks in deeper and faster water. Trophy brookies over 20 inches or 4 pounds are about 6 years old, and their diet includes minnows as well as insects. These brook trout do not retire into Gods Lake itself, but live in the big river year-round.

Other waters. Several other great fisheries have been developed near Gods Lake, most notably Knee, Molson, Edmund, Bolton, Gunisao, Utik, and Silsby Lakes. All are serviced by lodges and have better-than-average northern pike fishing.

Knee Lake lies 400 miles north of Winnipeg and is 45 miles long, with a width of up to 5 miles. The lake comprises numerous islands, bays, and reefs, which create ideal structure, and therefore, some of the finest fishing habitat in North America. Utik, Bolton, Silsby, Gunisao, and Edmund are smaller but produce excellent trophy northern pike, along with fast action for walleye and whitefish.

Trophy northern pike are the predominant species in these waters. They average 8 to 18 pounds, and many are in the 20- to 30-pound category. Anglers can expect good fishing throughout late June, July, and August. The timing of ice out can affect the catch in the early season, but northern pike are always available in shallow bays or near the spawning beds in rivers.

Gunisao Lake is noted for trophy walleye and is probably the best trophy walleye lake in Manitoba. It is 16 miles long and has approximately 75 islands that provide extraordinary walleye habitat, as well as sheltered fishing in all weather.

The Far North

Because the Precambrian shield runs in a north-westerly direction up to and including the 60th parallel, the far north has developed into a unique and marvelous fishery. This area of sand eskers and tree-less tundra creates a vacation destination with the freshest, cleanest air and trophy fishing that Manitobans say is second to none. Sites with fully developed lodges, complete with all-weather landing strips, are Nueltin, Nejanilini, North Knife, and Big Sand Lakes, and the North Seal River chain.

Nueltin Lake. Nueltin Lake is 800 miles north of Winnipeg, straddling both the 60th parallel and the borders of Manitoba and Nunavut Territory. Shaped like an hourglass, the lake is 125 miles long and up to 35 miles wide. The southern third lies in Manitoba and is heavily tree-lined with stunted spruce and tamarack. The northern part of Nueltin is only 380 miles from the Arctic Circle and is situated in nearly treeless, flat, and lichen-covered tundra where caribou are occasionally seen.

Nueltin is as remote as one can get in Manitoba, with wild, unspoiled beauty, countless islands and bays, many incoming rivers, and plenty of sandy beaches where you might see the tracks of a moose, wolf, fox, or bear if not the animal itself. Granite outcroppings are the only breaks in the barren land.

The lake is cold and deep, and therefore supports huge lake trout and trophy northern pike. There are no walleye this far north, but the added attraction is grayling up to 4 pounds, which can be caught in the frigid, fast-flowing streams and rivers that feed into Nueltin, especially around Nueltin Narrows. Lake trout in the 30- to 50-pound class live in Nueltin, as do northern pike in the 15- to 30-pound range. There is one main lodge on this enormous body of water, but it is open only 10 weeks each year, starting with ice out in mid- to late June, and there are outpost camps at Windy River and Nueltin Narrows as well as access to other area waters.

Nueltin has benefited from an enlightened lodge-instituted trophy-only policy that was begun in 1977 and subsequently changed to a catch-and-release-only policy (with the exception of a shore lunch fish). As a result, Nueltin lays claim to being the first catch-and-release lake in North America and, along with requiring the use of only single barbless hooks, the first to ensure that it will have preserved long-lived trophy fish for generations to come. As a result, 20-pound pike and 40-pound lakers go back into the water, as do 5- and 15-pounders, and a steady increase has occurred in the

Nueltin Lake has some of Canada's best lake trout fishing; this is a 35-pounder.

number of trophy specimens caught and released at Nueltin.

The Manitoba Master Angler program is testimony to the lake's great pike and lake trout fishing, even though two-thirds of Nueltin lies in Nunavut Territory, and trophy fish caught in those waters aren't registered in this government program. In effect, Nueltin would dominate the stat sheet far more than it usually does were this not so.

Lots of fish, even pike and lakers of enormous size, are an honest-to-goodness possibility for any angler, even those who are moderately skilled. The biggest laker taken to date weighed 56 pounds, and bigger ones have been lost.

Nueltin lends itself to various angling techniques. For big lake trout, trolling is undoubtedly the best tactic, especially in the main part of the lake. Early in the season, however, when the ice is still receding, the bays and river inlets with open water offer the best chances for huge fish, with possibilities for light-tackle angling as well as casting and jigging. Spoons and large jigs are the best lures, and DeBartok Rapids and Sealhole Lake are two prime locales.

For pike, the period from mid-June (when the camps open) through early July offers the most action, with plenty of fish in shallow water that are eager to strike surface lures, spinnerbaits, and weedless spoons cast into the shore in the backs of countless bays. Good pike and lake trout fishing are available throughout the season.

Nearby and accessed from Nueltin's camp by floatplane is Kasmere Lake, which has similar species to Nueltin and which has only been fished by the occasional fly-in day angler. Minimal fishing effort, however, has already tabbed the lake as a hotspot for big pike. A new lodge was built on Kasmere in 1999.

Big Sand Lake. Big Sand Lake is 525 miles north of Winnipeg and 200 miles west of Hudson Bay. It is the headwaters of the South Seal River, and supports fishing for trophy northern pike plus lake trout, walleye, and arctic grayling. There is one lodge on the lake, which opened in 1988, and outpost camps exist on Leclair, Wood, Wolf, Otter, and Jordan Lakes. The serenity of the location coupled with incredible trophy fishing opportunities is enough to excite even the most experienced angler.

Big Sand Lake is 50 miles long and has produced northern pike in excess of 35 pounds. It is not uncommon to catch 100 or more pike per day, and good opportunities abound for fish up to 20 pounds. Cabbage weeds flourish in bays and along points and deep shorelines, creating great habitat for these sulking predators.

Walleye are plentiful at Big Sand as well, and can be caught in abundance even close to the lodge near the outlet of Katimew Lake, one of many tributaries to Big Sand. The lake is not known for huge walleye, but there are many in the 3- and 4-pound class, readily caught on crankbaits and jigs.

The lodge practices a strict no-kill (except small fish for shore lunch), barbless-hook-only angling policy. Once commercially fished by the Indians, Big Sand Lake has been off limits to commercial ventures for some time, and only sportfishing is practiced today. Good-size grayling (3-pounders) inhabit the South Seal River, which is a pleasant two-hour boat ride from the lodge.

North Seal River.   The North Seal River system is another fish factory, one that has been newly developed for anglers. It comprises a series of lakes on the North Seal River chain and includes Chatwin, Minuhik, Egenolf, Blackfish, Nicklin, Steven's, Maria, and Burnie Lakes. Located 700 miles north of Winnipeg, the North Seal River watershed has opened a new remote fishery dominated by the Robertson Esker, a stunning geographical formation of sand dune and rock some 300 miles long.

Formed by a subglacial riverbank, Robertson Esker gives shape and character to the region. Rising above the land, then falling below the water, the esker has become an area where rivers become lakes and lakes revert to rivers. Sandbars, rocky shoals, and fast-flowing rivers add up to excellent fishing for northern pike, lake trout, grayling, and walleye. A main lodge, several mini lodges, and outpost camps service the system.

The Northwest

The so-called northwest portion of Manitoba is actually the central region north of the 53rd parallel. All but a small portion of this section of the province is in the Precambrian shield country. It is a very popular destination for visiting anglers and has many facilities. Although this renowned area is several hundred miles north of the international boundary, paved highways make this easily accessible in all weather.

The Pas, Flin Flon, Thompson, and Lynn Lake are significant centers and have daily air and bus service. Clearwater, Cormorant, and Athapapuskow

Lakes are probably the most famous, with Rocky, Reed, Kississing, and Cranberry Lakes following close behind.

Clearwater Lake is astonishing for its crystal clear waters with visibility to a depth of 40 feet. The lake itself is 15 miles long and 15 miles wide, and ranges from 80 to 100 feet in depth. Because of this depth, ice out is always late at Clearwater—usually not until the first week of June. Lake trout, northern pike, and whitefish are frequently taken by trolling or vertical jigging with heavy spoons. The average lake trout is 3 to 5 pounds, but many trophies of 15 to 25 pounds have been landed. Northern pike are available from 10 to 20 pounds, and whitefish run 3 to 5 pounds. Cormorant Lake is just a little farther to the northeast and is accessible by gravel road. This is an excellent walleye and northern pike fishery, with many bays and islands for protection.

The balance of the lakes in this area are all accessible by road, and all provide excellent northern pike and walleye fishing. There are lodges at each of the lakes and many campgrounds in the area, making this an excellent family vacation destination. Lake Athapapuskow held the world's lake trout record of 63 pounds for almost 30 years. Even today, at least one or two trophy fish in the 35- to 40-pound range are caught in Athapapuskow every year.

The Southwest

Manitoba's southwest also offers some fishing opportunity, although most of the lakes are relatively small and shallow. Stocking programs, especially in the Duck, Porcupine, and Turtle Mountains, have given these areas new life. Such exotic species as kokanee salmon, splake, brook trout, brown trout, and rainbow trout are among the fish stocked here. Muskies have been successfully stocked in Line Lake in the Duck Mountains, and northern pike and walleye inhabit most of these waters.

The southwest contains two of Manitoba's largest southern rivers: the Red, which originates in the United States, and the Assiniboine, which runs east and north from Saskatchewan. Both are excellent producers of some 12 to 15 fish species, particularly giant channel catfish, trophy carp, and walleye, along with bullhead, freshwater drum, sauger, northern pike, white bass, sturgeon, perch, tullibee, goldeye, mooneye, black crappie, and rock bass.

Several man-made structures, including Lockport Dam, the Portage Diversion, and Shellmouth Dam, have created reservoirs and lakes that have become meccas for bank and boat anglers. Although only a few lodges exist along the rivers, ample facilities are nearby.

Red River.   The Red River is unquestionably one of the best bets in North America for large walleye, producing an awe-inspiring number of specimens weighing 10 pounds or more. These fish are migrants from Lake Winnipeg.

Generally dirty and roily, especially in spring and early summer, the Red River flows northward in farm country from the Dakotas through southern Manitoba and into Lake Winnipeg. The hotbed of big-fish activity is in Manitoba, in the Selkirk area just north of the city of Winnipeg and below the Lockport Dam. Big walleye, however, can be caught anywhere in the river. They fall for a variety of presentations, with slow trolling one of the more reliable techniques for newcomers to this waterway.

October, when a tremendous run of big walleye migrates out of Lake Winnipeg, is the best time to fish. The run starts in mid-September, when the water cools and the north winds blow. Incidentally, the Winnipeg River, which is about 60 miles from Lockport, is another good producer of walleye. It does not seem to hold as many large fish, but its walleye are more aesthetically appealing, sporting an emerald green coloration in the fall. Winnipeg River fish are locally called greenbacks.

Actually, all walleye here are called "pickerel," and most local anglers fish with so-called pickerel rigs, which sport a long-shanked bait hook for a nightcrawler and a small spinner blade. Drifting and stillfishing with live bait or jigs tipped with bait is also popular. Some anglers, mostly visitors from the U.S., troll with plugs, and this method merits attention as well.

The Red River is also known as one of the premier spots in North America for giant catfish. In Manitoba, the Red dominates the Master Angler citation list, and rates among the best places to pursue 20-pound or better specimens. The huge cats are almost exclusively taken on baits, predominantly chicken liver or gizzard shad chunks, fished along the bottom. Several other rivers in this area also offer good catfishing.

MANTA

See: Rays and Skates.

MAPS

The word "map" is frequently used by anglers to convey several different products. Technically, a map details land features, and a chart details water features. Topographic maps depict land features in great detail but do not provide subsurface details about water. They may help some freshwater anglers locate places worthy of fishing (ponds or river backwaters, for example) but are of no value from a hydrographic standpoint. Navigational charts, on the other hand, and underwater contour maps depicting hydrographic information, provide little information about land areas but significant detail regarding depth, obstructions, and navigational aids. When used in conjunction with a compass or a GPS, they help you maintain course, especially in fog, low-light conditions, or at night.

Every angler who fishes a large or unfamiliar body of water should have a good map or chart of that place and use it in conjunction with sonar. The best and most detailed of these are navigational charts, which exist for virtually all bodies of water that are deemed by federal agencies as navigable. This includes coastal waters and large inland waterways but does not include many bodies of freshwater. Maps that are not navigational charts but that do show underwater detail usually contain a notice that they are not to be used for navigational purposes; nevertheless, depending on the degree of detail, they can be of general navigational value and an important source of information to anglers.

Maps and charts that show underwater contours and hydrographic features can help you navigate without getting lost or possibly running into obstructions, and can help you find areas that may provide good fishing. Maps that are studied at home, prior to on-the-water fishing, often allow anglers to devise a plan and avoid haphazard fishing, which is especially useful when time is limited.

Navigational charts (and topographic maps) are produced by American and Canadian federal agencies and are available at some sporting goods stores, marinas, and major-city map stores. Dealers usually stock local area charts and maps and can order others for you. To order maps yourself, obtain a map index from the appropriate government agency. United States topographical maps are produced by the U.S. Geological Survey; navigational charts of U.S. waters are distributed by the National Oceanic and Atmospheric Administration, Distribution Division; Canadian topographic maps are distributed by Natural Resources Canada, Ottawa; navigational charts of Canadian waters are produced by the Canadian Department of Fisheries and Oceans, Hydrographic Section, Ottawa.

Order maps long before you expect to depart on a trip. Remember that the larger the scale, the more detail is provided. Other maps of big waters may be

M

A compressed map of a large reservoir depicts submerged river and creek channels as well as access sites and relative depths.

available from jurisdictional agencies such as the Corps of Engineers or the Tennessee Valley Authority (TVA), although their maps are rarely detailed enough to give you more than general information.

Maps supplied by private firms are often geared to anglers' interests and provide a good deal of underwater contour information. Their size and scale will determine how helpful they are as boating and fishing aids. Many useful maps can be found at tackle shops, sporting goods stores, and marinas near popular waterways. In addition, state freshwater fisheries agencies often have contour maps (ranging from large-scale to reduced size on an 8 $\frac{1}{2}$-by-11-inch sheet of paper), particularly for smaller lakes and ponds, and you should check with these agencies for such availability.

Not all of the information on underwater contour maps or navigational charts is totally accurate or complete, and anglers must use good judgment when using them, but these products are substantial aids to anglers who know the habits of their quarry and its habitat and can identify areas that are likely to be productive. This is particularly so where big lakes are concerned and where it would take an inordinate amount of time to explore. Moreover, once you've had success at finding fish, you may refer to a map to locate other areas that may be similar.

The features of an underwater contour map or navigational chart are evident once you've read the symbols index. Navigational charts especially should be studied, because many aids to navigation are identified.

It's a good idea to store maps in a large, clear, sealable plastic pouch or to treat them with a waterproofing material to help them last in marine environments. Color coding the different contour levels or marking certain areas with indelible markers is also worthwhile.
See: Navigation.

MARGATE, WHITE
See: Grunts.

MARGIN
The edge of a body of water, especially stillwaters such as ponds or lakes. This is a European term, coincident with margin fishing, which refers to short-range, or close-in fishing efforts.

MARGIN FISHING
A term for fishing the edges of ponds and lakes for carp (see) by using long rods and dappling the surface with a bait when cruising or basking fish are attracted there.

MARIANA ISLANDS
See: Portugal.

MARICULTURE
The raising of marine fish or shellfish under some controls, usually for the purpose of commercial sale. Ponds, pens, tanks, or other containers may be used. Feed is commonly used. This term is often used synonymously with, and secondarily to, aquaculture, which is a more generic term that encompasses cultivation of fish in freshwater environs as well as in saltwater. Fish farming (as well as oyster farming, shrimp farming, etc.) is another term used to describe mariculture operations; and a marine hatchery may be a form of mariculture, although hatcheries operated by government agencies usually release fish before commercial harvest size is reached, and usually raise them for the purpose of supplementing sportfishing stocks. Private hatcheries may raise fish to be sold for private stocking efforts or for commercial sale to food processors, fish markets, and restaurants.
See: Aquaculture; Hatchery.

MARINA
An establishment along the water where boats are kept and where varying services and supplies are available. Marinas usually have mooring docks in the water and provide dry storage on trailers or on ground supports or inside closed buildings; they may offer boat and engine repairs and servicing. They may sell or rent boats as well as supply drive-up fuel and fresh water. Some marinas have a store where various provisions, including ice, navigational charts, and sometimes bait and fishing and boating equipment, are available.

Marinas are usually occupied by recreational boats and provide seasonal, long-term, and/or temporary dockage. They often have a boat launch, and some have a heavy-duty facility for hauling large vessels out of the water.

MARINE
Pertaining to the sea and saltwater environs from the open oceans to the high-water mark and into estuaries; also used to refer to seawater or saltwater.

MARINE RADIO
A general term for radiotelephones used in boats, primarily applied to VHF radios.
See: Communications.

MARKER BUOY
Not to be confused with channel- or shoal-marking buoys (see) anchored as strategic aids to navigation, marker buoys are small portable floats, usually attached to a heavy weight, used by casting and trolling anglers to temporarily mark the location of such underwater hydrographic features as channels, dropoffs, shoals, points, and bars in mid-depth waters.

Most marker buoys are nothing more than plastic floats, usually brightly colored for easy spotting, attached to heavy weights by strong line. They are tossed in the water at a specific site, the weighted line drops to the bottom of the water, and the float marks the spot. The float is retrieved later along with the line and weight wrapped around the float. Flat markers are better than round, barbell versions because the former are more resistant to the effects of current, wind, and waves. Round markers can be blown quite a distance from the site they are supposed to identify, which does not happen with the square, flat marker buoys.

Marker buoys are frequently used in conjunction with sonar equipment. Most big-lake and saltwater anglers, and most deep-water trollers, don't use marker buoys because they roam so widely in search of fish, because the buoys aren't functional in really deep water, or because placement of the buoys could interfere with fishing. However, marker buoys can be effectively used by boaters on small- to medium-size bodies of water who are looking to define specific and relatively shallow underwater structures or contours for casting, vertical jigging, or trolling; and by those who may be trolling to locate schools of fish that they will stop and cast to.

MARLIN, BLACK *Makaira indica.*

Other names—Pacific black marlin, giant black marlin, silver marlin (Hawaii), white marlin (Japan); Arabic: *kheil al bahar;* Indonesian: *layaran, mersuji, suji;* Japanese: *kurokawa, shirokajiki;* Portuguese: *espadim negro;* Spanish: *aguja negra, marlín negro.*

The astonishing power of the black marlin, combined with its immense size—it rivals the blue marlin *(see: marlin, blue)*—make it one of the most sought-after fish in the sea. A member of the Istiophoridae family of billfish, the black marlin is renowned for its inspiring fighting qualities and its spectacular jumps as it struggles to escape. It challenges anglers from all parts of the globe.

The meat of the black marlin is firm and white and brings a high price on the commercial market.

It is prized in Japan, where it is eaten as sashimi, but banned in Australia's State of New South Wales because of the threat posed by high mercury and selenium levels.

Identification. The black marlin is the only marlin, regardless of size, whose pectoral fins are rigid and cannot be folded flat up against the body without breaking the joints. The pectoral fins also have an airfoil shape, whereas those of other marlin are flat. The ventral fins are extremely short, almost never exceeding 12 inches in length. The first dorsal fin is retractable and fits into a groove along the back; it is proportionately the lowest of any billfish, usually less than 50 percent of the body depth. The leading edge of the second dorsal fin sits slightly in front of the second anal fin. The lateral line, which is rarely visible in adults, is a straight double row of pores.

Its body is laterally compressed, rather than rounded—much more so than in the similar-size blue marlin, and the upper jaw is elongated in the form of a spear. Dorsally, the body is a dark slate blue, but this coloring changes suddenly to a silvery white below the lateral line. Light-blue body stripes are usually visible on live marlin, especially when the fish is excited; these fade after death. Slight variations in color cause some specimens to have a silvery haze over the body. In Hawaii this has led to the name "silver marlin" (once thought to be a separate species). The name "white marlin," applied in Japan, refers to the color of the meat rather than the external color of the fish, and should not be confused with the white marlin *(see: marlin, white)* species.

Size. The black marlin has been known to reach a length of 15 feet; the long-standing all-tackle world record was caught off Cabo Blanco, Peru, in 1953 and weighed 1,560 pounds. The Australian national record is a fish of 1,439 pounds, taken off Cairns in 1973. Australia consistently produces the largest specimens today, particularly specimens exceeding 1,000 pounds. Although exceptions exist, giant black marlin are larger than giant blue marlin taken on rod and reel. This may be because large black marlin are more accessible and more

Black Marlin

often occur within the range of sportfishing vessels. Japanese longline fishermen contend that giant blue marlin taken far out at sea beyond the range of sportfishing boats are larger than giant blacks. Marlin exceeding 300 pounds are almost always females; a 500-pound male is a rarity.

Distribution/Habitat. This species appears to be confined to the tropical and subtropical waters of the Indian and Pacific Oceans. In tropical areas, distribution is scattered but continuous in open waters, and denser in coastal areas and near islands. Occurrence is rare in temperate waters. A few stray black marlin travel around the Cape of Good Hope into the Atlantic, moving up the southwest coast of Africa until they reach the Ivory Coast. Some have been known to cross the ocean from there, traveling in a southwesterly direction as far as Río de Janeiro, Brazil, or in a northwesterly direction as far as the Atlantic coasts of the Lesser Antilles. Such excursions, however, are exceptional and very rare. Little is known of the migrations of this pelagic species, but they do not appear to be extensive except in unusual cases.

In Australia, black marlin extend from the east coast of Tasmania in the south to Cape York in the north, and from the west coast of the Gulf of Carpentaria to Albany in southern Western Australia. They are rarely seen along the South Coast of Australia. The principal recreational fisheries are off North Queensland and New South Wales. They prefer the warm ocean currents along the edges of the Great Barrier Reef, but also migrate into the cooler waters off the coast of New South Wales.

Life history/Behavior. The black marlin is an oceanic, highly migratory, pelagic fish that is generally found no deeper than 75 meters. The fecundity of the black marlin is high, with estimates running to more than 220 million eggs for large females. In Australian waters, spawning takes place in the northwest region of the Coral Sea between October and December, and in the Timor Sea until March. No research has yet determined if the eggs are released at once, or in batches throughout the season. The larvae have been identified in the northwest Coral Sea off northwestern Australia, and off Lizard Island in North Queensland. Some adult fish and juveniles, on both the eastern and western coasts of Australia, migrate southward in summer. The large fish tend to stay close to the edge of the continental shelf, which, along the Great Barrier Reef, can be within a few hundred meters of the outer edge. In New South Wales waters, smaller specimens are taken within 100 meters of the rocky coastline.

Food. Large black marlin feed primarily on scad mackerel, frigate mackerel, trevally, squid, tuna, and mackerel tuna. Smaller fish are known to feed on herring, kahawai, pilchards, squid, scad and frigate mackerel, and others.

Angling. In Great Barrier Reef waters, the most productive fishing is from October through December, which coincides with the black marlin's spawning time. This is when the big females are present.

Most big black marlin are taken by anglers trolling dead or live whole fish, but methods of trolling with lures—using both soft- and hardhead lures, and live-bait fishing—are increasing in popularity as techniques and lure designs improve. All methods require careful consideration of many varied factors, including water temperature (15° to 30°C), time of day, weather conditions, moon phases, location of bait schools, and empirical knowledge.

When trolling natural dead or live baits, anglers in the Great Barrier Reef fishery of North Queensland use gamefishing tackle from 6 kilograms to 60 kilograms and baits up to and often in excess of 10 kilograms in mass, and work in waters to 30 fathoms. Hook size and type (straight, not offset), wire type and strength, knots, doubles, leaders, and swivels must be immaculate in their presentation.

Where big baits are used in the heavy line classes, only two rigs are normally deployed, clipped to outriggers. In light-line classes, more rigs can be fished. Baits are rigged so that they skip and swim naturally without spinning. The most popular trolled bait in Great Barrier Reef waters is the scad mackerel (known familiarly as "scad"), perhaps because of its ready availability and the documented successes with it. Other baits are tuna and bonito.

Trolling with lures is highly successful, and in many instances it is favored over baits because of its

A black marlin is about to be released near Isla Coiba, Panama.

M

effectiveness and the no-mess ease and speed with which the lures can be used. Trolling speeds, lure shape and color (both head and skirt), lure size, distance behind the boat, whether fished from outriggers or not, line-weight-to-lure ratio, and number of lures out are but some of the vital considerations upon which success hinges.

In the lighter line classes (6 to 15 kilograms), both small, natural live baits, and strip baits taken from larger mackerel and tuna, are used successfully. Teasers are towed to attract the marlin to these baits and are brought inboard when the marlin has sighted the baits. Drift fishing with live baits is sometimes practiced, but more often than not sharks find the baits before the marlin do.

Much importance is placed on the competence of the boat's skipper, whose skills in controlling and positioning the boat for maximum assistance to the angler are critical to a successful outcome.

Australian anglers have an opportunity to fish in a unique manner for black marlin; that is, they can fish from land. On March 6, 1979, a rock angler using 10-kilogram line landed a 64-kilogram black marlin along the south coast of New South Wales. This was the first recorded land-based marlin capture in Australian waters. In 1986, a record black marlin weighing 110 kilograms was taken on 10-kilogram line from the rocks in the same general area.

The favorite bait for the land-based angler is the frigate mackerel, which is abundant in these waters. Bridle rigging, as for boat fishing, is the proven method of bait presentation. Basic tackle is a medium- to fast-taper 2.5-meter rod with roller guides, and a finely tuned big-game reel with sufficient line capacity (using 10- to 24-kilogram line) to cope with the stripping runs of the marlin.

Assisted by current and offshore winds, which take them away from the rocks, baits are supported by balloons or polystyrene foam attached to leaders that break away from the main line when the fish strikes. Land-based anglers usually fish in pairs for safety reasons and for gaffing purposes; gaffing from a rock platform can be a dangerous and difficult operation requiring the assistance of another party. Long-handled gaffs to 6 meters, or sliding gaffs attached to heavy cord and designed to slide down the line, are favorites.

See: **Big-Game Fishing; Billfish; Offshore Fishing.**

MARLIN, BLUE

Makaira nigricans and Makaira mazara.

Other names—Atlantic blue marlin, Pacific blue marlin, Cuban black marlin; French: *espadon, makaire bleu;* Japanese: *makajiki, nishikuro;* Portuguese: *agulhao preto;* Spanish: *abanco, aguja azul, castero, marlín azul.*

A premier member of the Istiophoridae family of billfish, the blue marlin is one of the foremost big-game species worldwide. Some taxonomists

A blue marlin is revived off Chub Cay in the Bahamas.

believe that the blue marlin that occurs in the Atlantic and Indo-Pacific Oceans are closely related but separate species. They identify *M. nigricans* as an Atlantic-only species and *M. mazara* as the species occurring in the Pacific and Indian Oceans. Others treat the two populations as subspecies, *M. nigricans nigricans* and *M. nigricans mazata.*

The blue marlin has exceptional size and strength, and is a powerful, aggressive fighter. It runs hard and long, sounds deep, and leaps high into the air in a seemingly inexhaustible display of strength. Because of these characteristics, and because it is more widespread than other marlin, the blue marlin is arguably the most popular and sought-after by anglers. Intensively pursued commercially in many parts of its range, it is overexploited. The flesh is pale and firm and makes excellent table fare, especially when smoked. In the Orient it is often served as sashimi or in fish sausages. Blue marlin are seldom eaten in North America, and the vast majority caught by anglers are released after capture, and many of those released are tagged.

Identification. The pectoral fins of blue marlin are never rigid, even after death, and can be folded completely flat against the sides. The dorsal fin is high and pointed (rather than rounded) anteriorly, and its greatest height is less than its greatest body depth. The anal fin is relatively large and also pointed. Juveniles might not share all of these characteristics, but the peculiar lateral line system is usually visible in small specimens. In adults it is rarely

M

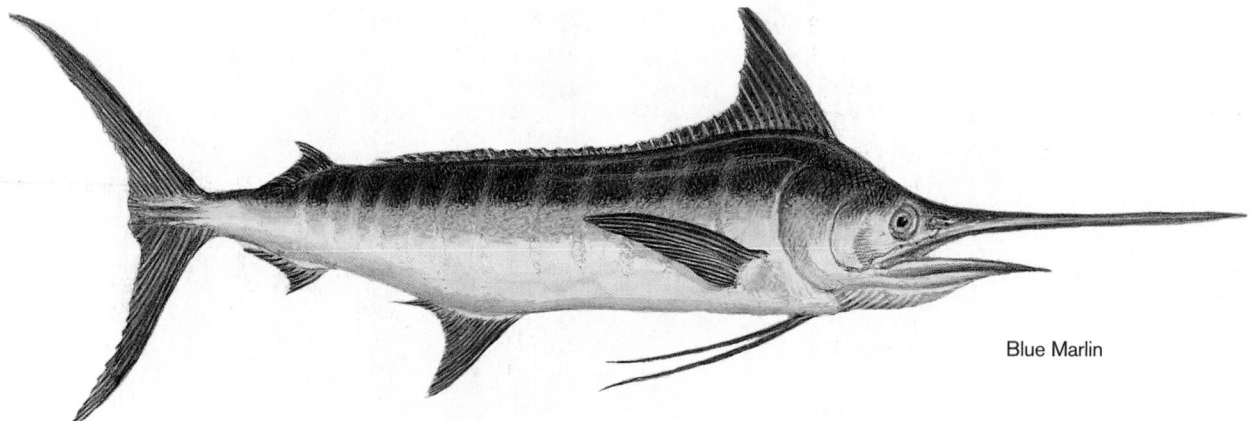

Blue Marlin

visible unless the scales or skin are removed. The lateral line of a Pacific blue marlin is a series of large loops, like a chain, along the flanks. The lateral line of all Atlantic blue marlin is a reticulated network that is more complex than the simple loops of Pacific specimens. The vent is just in front of the anal fin, as it is in all billfish except the spearfish, and the upper jaw is elongated in the form of a spear.

The back is cobalt blue and the flanks and belly are silvery white. There may be light-blue or lavender vertical stripes on the sides, but these usually fade away soon after death, and they are never as obvious as those of the striped marlin *(see: marlin, striped)*. There are no spots on the fins. Small blue marlin are similar to white marlin *(see: marlin, white)*, but the blue has a more pointed dorsal fin at the anterior end, more pointed tip on the pectoral and anal fins, and lacks dorsal fin spots.

Size/Age.   The blue marlin is the largest marlin existing in the Atlantic Ocean. Elsewhere, it is capable of growing to sizes that equal or exceed those of the black marlin *(see: marlin, black)*. Japanese longline reports indicate that the blue marlin is the largest-growing member of the Istiophoridae family. It apparently grows larger on average in the Pacific Ocean, where decades ago one commercially caught specimen reportedly weighed 2,200 pounds, and an angler-caught specimen (which did not qualify for world-record status) weighed 1,800 pounds. The all-tackle world record for Atlantic blues is a 1,402-pounder caught in 1992 at Vitoria, Brazil; the all-tackle world record for Pacific blues is a 1,376-pounder caught in 1982 at Kona, Hawaii. The giants are all females, as male blue marlin rarely exceed 300 pounds. Most blue marlin encountered by anglers range between 150 and 400 pounds. Blue marlin are believed to live for more than 15 years, although fish exceeding 10 years of age are uncommon.

Distribution/Habitat.   This pelagic, migratory species occurs in tropical and warm temperate oceanic waters. In the Atlantic Ocean, it is found from 45° north to 35° south latitude, and in the Pacific Ocean from 48° north to 48° south latitude. It is less abundant in the eastern portions of both oceans. In the Indian Ocean, it occurs around Ceylon, Mauritius, and off the East Coast of Africa. In the northern Gulf of Mexico, its movements seem to be associated with the so-called Loop Current, an extension of the Caribbean Current. Seasonal concentrations occur in the southwest Atlantic (5° to 30° south latitude) from January through April, in the northwest Atlantic (10° to 35° north latitude) from June through October, in the western and central North Pacific (2° to 24° north latitude) from May through October, in the equatorial Pacific (10° north to 10° south latitude) in April and November, and in the Indian Ocean (0° to 13° south latitude) from April through October.

Life history/Behavior.   The life history of the blue marlin is poorly known. The full extent of its oceanic wanderings, as well as its open-sea spawning activities, are unknown. These fish are found in the warm blue water of offshore environs, usually over considerable depths and where there are underwater structures (for example, canyons, dropoffs, ridges, seamounts) and currents that attract copious supplies of baitfish. They are usually solitary.

Food and feeding behavior.   Blue marlin feed on squid and pelagic fish, including assorted tuna and mackerel, as well as dolphin. They feed on almost anything they can catch, in fact, and they feed according to availability rather than selectivity. Because they require large quantities of food, they are scarce when and where prey is limited.

Angling.   Fishing methods for blue marlin include trolling large whole baits such as bonito, dolphin, mullet, mackerel, bonefish, ballyhoo, flyingfish, and squid, as well as various types of artificial lures and sometimes strip baits.
See: Big-Game Fishing; Billfish; Offshore Fishing.

MARLIN, STRIPED   *Tetrapturus audax.*
Other names—striper, marlin, Pacific marlin, Pacific striped marlin, barred marlin, spikefish, spearfish, New Zealand marlin, red marlin (Japan); Arabic: *kheil al bahar;* French: *empéreur;* Hawaiian: *a'u, nairagi;* Japanese: *makajiki;* Portuguese: *espadim raiado;* Spanish: *agujón, marlín, marlin rayado, pez aguja.*

Widely distributed in the Pacific Ocean, the striped marlin is the most prevalent marlin in the

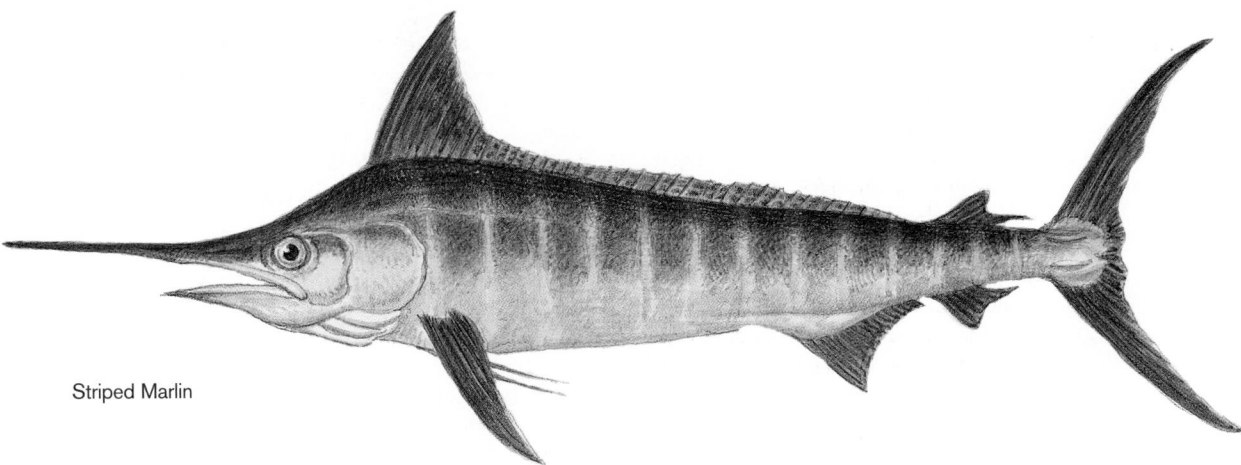

Striped Marlin

Istiophoridae family of billfish, the most common Indo-Pacific billfish species, and a prized catch of anglers. It is well known for its fighting ability and has the reputation of spending more time in the air than in the water when hooked; lacking the overall size and weight of the blue marlin *(see: marlin, blue)* or the black marlin *(see: marlin, black),* it is more acrobatically inclined. In addition to making long runs and tail-walking, it will "greyhound" across the surface, performing up to a dozen or more long, graceful leaps. It is caught fairly close to shore in appropriate waters.

The striped marlin has red meat and is the object of extensive commercial fishing efforts, primarily by longlining. Many people throughout its Indo-Pacific range hold its flesh in high esteem, and it is rated best among billfish for sashimi and sushi preparations. Heavy fishing pressure has resulted in reduced stocks, however, as is true of all billfish.

Identification.   The body of the striped marlin is elongate and compressed, and its upper jaw is extended in the form of a spear. The color is dark or steely blue above and becomes bluish silver and white below a clearly visible and straight lateral line. Numerous iridescent blue spots grace the fins, and pale-blue or lavender vertical stripes appear on the sides. These may or may not be prominent, but they are normally more prominent than those of other marlin. The stripes persist after death, which is not always true with other marlin. The most distinguishing characteristic is a high, pointed first dorsal fin, which normally equals or exceeds the greatest body depth. Even in the largest specimens, this fin is at least equal to 90 percent of the body depth. Like the dorsal fin, the anal and pectoral fins are pointed. They are also flat and movable and can easily be folded flush against the sides, even after death.

Striped marlin have scales, fins on the belly, and a rounded spear, which set them apart from swordfish, which have no scales or ventral fins and a flat bill; from sailfish, which have an extremely high dorsal fin; and from spearfish, which do neither the long spear on the upper jaw nor the body weight of the larger marlin.

Size.   The largest striped marlin on record is a 494-pound fish caught in New Zealand in 1986; in the United States the largest known is a 339-pound California fish. They are common from under 100 pounds to roughly 200 pounds.

Distribution/Habitat.   Found in tropical and warm temperate waters of the Indian and Pacific Oceans, the striped marlin is pelagic and seasonally migratory, moving toward the equator during the cold season and away again during the warm season. It has been occasionally found on the Atlantic side of the Cape of Good Hope. Striped marlin are especially abundant in the southern Pacific Ocean, where New Zealand produces most of the largest specimens.

In the eastern Pacific, the striped marlin ranges as far north as Oregon but is most common south of Point Conception, California. It usually appears off California in July and remains until late October. The best California fishing locality is in a belt of water that extends from the east end of Santa Catalina Island offshore to San Clemente Island and southward in the direction of the Los Coronados Islands. The waters around the Baja Peninsula, Mexico, are especially known for striped marlin, which are particularly abundant off Cabo San Lucas.

A striped marlin caught off Malindi, Kenya.

Life history/Behavior. The life history of this species is poorly known. Striped marlin are found in the warm blue water of offshore environs, usually above the thermocline. They are mostly solitary but may form schools by size during the spawning season. They are usually present where there is plenty of forage.

Food and feeding habits. The striped marlin is highly predatory, feeding extensively on pilchards, anchovies, mackerel, sauries, flyingfish, squid, and whatever is abundant. The spear of the marlin is sometimes used for defense and as an aid in capturing food. Wooden boats frequently have been rammed by billfish, and in one instance the spear penetrated $18^1/_2$ inches of hardwood, $14^1/_2$ inches of which was oak. When it uses its bill in capturing food, the striped marlin sometimes stuns its prey by slashing sideways with the spear rather than impaling its victim, as some believe.

Angling. Fishing methods for striped marlin include trolling whole fish, strip baits, or lures, and fishing with live baits. Most striped marlin are taken by trolling 8- to 12-inch skirted offshore lures. Blind strikes are the rule, but a fish spotted on the surface can occasionally be tempted to strike if lures are trolled past it, or if live baits are cast to it.

Spotting, stalking, and casting or trolling to surface-located stripers is an exciting possibility, as the fish are often visible in favorable conditions. Surface stripers may be "tailers," which are free-swimming fish with their sickle-like tails exposed; "sleepers," which are inactive fish with their dorsal and tail fins sometimes exposed; "jumpers," which are simply unhooked free-jumping fish; and "feeders," which are fish actively feeding along the surface. Different methods may be employed depending on the disposition of the fish. Lob-casting live baits to surface fish works well but requires considerable effort. Once a striped marlin is located, the angler should cast a bait in front of and beyond the marlin, and then reel the bait back toward the fish. Strikes usually result from properly presented live baits, of which Pacific mackerel is the favorite.

These fish are often fickle, and areas where they congregate may change each year. Savvy anglers concentrate on temperature breaks and converging currents in areas with plentiful baitfish and clean blue water.

See: Big-Game Fishing; Billfish; Offshore Fishing.

MARLIN, WHITE *Tetrapturus albidus.*

Other names—spikefish, Atlantic white marlin; French: *espadon;* Italian: *marlin bianco;* Japanese: *nishimaka; nishimakajiki;* Portuguese: *agulhão branco, espadim branco;* Spanish: *aguja blanca, aguja de costa, blanca, cabezona, marlin blanco, picudo blanco.*

The smallest of the four marlin in the Istiophoridae family of billfish, the white marlin is a top-rated light-tackle gamefish and an active leaper. It is the most frequently encountered marlin along the East Coast of the United States, where it is almost exclusively released (often tagged) after capture. There is an active commercial fishery for the white marlin in many parts of its range, however; the flesh is of good quality and is especially tasty when smoked.

Identification. The body of the white marlin is elongate and compressed, and its upper jaw extends in the form of a spear. In overall appearance, the white marlin is generally lighter in color and tends to show more green than do other marlin, although it may at times appear to be almost chocolate brown along the back; the flanks are silvery and taper to a white underbelly. Several light-blue or lavender vertical bars may show on the flanks, especially when the fish is feeding or leaping. Some specimens have a scattering of black or purple spots on the first dorsal and anal fins.

Its most characteristic feature is the rounded, rather than pointed, tips of the pectoral fins, first dorsal fin, and first anal fin. Some specimens apparently vary from the norm in that the dorsal and pectoral fins may be more pointed; the anal fin is more consistently rounded than the other fins. The first dorsal fin resembles that of the striped marlin in that it is usually as high or higher than the greatest body depth. It differs from that of the striped marlin (*see: marlin, striped*), or any other marlin, in that both margins are convex. The flat, movable pectoral fins can easily be folded flush against the sides of the body. The lateral line is visible and curved above the pectoral fin but is otherwise straight.

Size. The largest rod-and-reel-caught white marlin is the all-tackle 181-pound, 12-ounce world record, taken off Brazil in 1979. Fish to 8 feet in length are common throughout their range, although white marlin can attain a length of 10 feet. The largest specimens are caught in Brazilian waters. Off North America, the white marlin is prominent in offshore waters off Maryland, North Carolina, and Florida.

Distribution. The white marlin occurs throughout the Atlantic Ocean from latitudes 45° north to 45° south in the west, including the Gulf of Mexico and the Caribbean Sea, and from 45° north to 35° south in the east. A few eastern strays have been recorded in the western Mediterranean and off France.

Life history/Behavior. Although this pelagic and migratory species usually favors deep-blue tropical and warm temperate (exceeding 27°C) waters, it frequently comes in close to shore where waters aren't much deeper than 8 fathoms. It is normally found above the thermocline, and its occurrence varies seasonally. It is present in higher latitudes in both the Northern and Southern Hemispheres during the respective warm seasons. It is usually solitary but sometimes travels in small groups, the

White Marlin

latter tendency reflecting feeding opportunities. Spawning occurs in the spring, with both sexes reaching maturity at around 51 inches in length. Females are capable of producing many millions of pelagic eggs.

Food and feeding behavior. White marlin feed on assorted pelagic fish and squid, concentrating on whatever is most abundant at a given time and place; this especially includes sardines and herring. It may use its bill in capturing food, stunning its prey by slashing it sideways and then turning to consume it. It also captures prey without using the bill as a weapon. The actual feeding habits of individual fish are not well known, but on a few occasions white marlin have been observed balled up in a small group herding baitfish for feeding purposes. This trait is believed to show cooperative hunting instincts, which also exist at times in other pelagic species.

Angling. White marlin can be caught by trolling with small whole or strip baits as well as with small spoons, feathers, or any of a variety of other artificial lures. Live-bait fishing with squid, ballyhoo, mullet, bonefish, mackerel, anchovies, herring, and other fish is also effective in specific situations. A good deal of successful northwestern Atlantic fishing employs whole rigged small- and medium-size ballyhoo. These are usually fished undressed (without an accompanying colored skirt) and trolled offshore in 100 to 1,000 fathoms over specific underwater contours and where there are surface temperature changes and color breaks, both of which tend to concentrate baitfish. Aficionados use outrigger lines and flatlines, as well as teasers, and fast speeds—around 6 knots. Tackle is often in the 20- and 30-pound conventional range, and anglers may keep spinning or levelwind outfits handy with a rigged bait for fish spotted within casting distance of the boat (often when the boat is idle or just getting started). Trolled baits taken by whites are dropped back on a 3- to 10-count, to give the fish a chance to get the bait in their mouth before the angler sets the hook.

Due to their size and activity, white marlin make good candidates for fly rodders, provided the fish are numerous and can be teased into casting range. Anglers fishing for whites often encounter other pelagic species, inviting a chance at larger blue marlin (*see: marlin, blue*). For blues, it's best to have a larger bait or lure, on a heavier outfit, ready to employ in the trolling spread.

See: Big-Game Fishing; Billfish; Offshore Fishing.

MARSH

A freshwater marsh is wet or periodically flooded treeless land, usually characterized by grasses, cattails, or other freshwater-tolerant plants. Although some scientists might make a narrow definition differentiating a marsh from a wetland (*see*), they are virtually the same.

A salt marsh is flat land with grasses and possibly shrubs subject to overflow by saltwater during high tide. Salt marshes are generally quiet areas and vary in size, although some bays may contain thousands of acres. An important component of estuaries (*see*), salt marshes receive food organisms and detritus with the incoming tide, and send detritus and waste materials into the estuary with the outgoing tide. They help filter impurities and nutrients from the

A white marlin, hooked off Bimini in the Bahamas, makes an effort to throw the hook by coming to the surface.

M

water and also hold shorelines in place. Mussels, crabs, snails, killifish, and many other small and medium-size fish use the salt marsh and are preyed upon by larger fish, some of which also spawn here; the young of many species grow up in tidal marshes, making them vitally important nurseries.

In a salt marsh, sportfish are caught on sandbars or in the deeper water behind sandbars, on the downstream side of points, around mussel beds, at undercut banks and along banks with steep dropoffs at high tide, in deep channels at low tide, in holes and troughs, on sand flats at high tide, and along the edge of a flat. The inlet, especially if it narrows, is a good spot, as are funneling points, like channels underneath bridges and between land points. See: Inshore Fishing.

MARSHALL ISLANDS
See: Micronesia.

MARYLAND
With trout streams in the west, bass in the restored Potomac River, a restored striped bass population in Chesapeake Bay, and marlin in the Baltimore Canyon, Maryland holds many and divergent fishing possibilities. This befits a state with the Allegheny Mountains and Piedmont Plateau among its topography, and half its landmass consisting of coastal plain.

The fact that Maryland ranks 42nd in size among the United States may be reflected in its freshwater fishing opportunities, as there are no large natural lakes, and the Potomac and Susquehanna Rivers are of prime importance, but it is certainly not reflected in its saltwater opportunities, especially the inshore and tidal interface areas, which are influenced by the expansive reaches of the Chesapeake Bay. Most of the eastern half of the state drains toward the Chesapeake Bay; the bay is largely responsible for the 3,190 miles of tidal shoreline that exists in Maryland, although Maryland's Atlantic coast is formed by a narrow barrier that establishes three bays.

Naturally, the primary angling quarry in the Free State is striped bass, locally called rockfish. However, speckled trout, bluefish, weakfish, flounder, red drum, black drum, white perch, and other species draw near-shore interest; white marlin, blue marlin, tuna, sharks, dolphin, and wahoo are the major offshore interests. These are complemented in freshwater by smallmouth and largemouth bass, crappie, bluegills, northern pike, walleye, brook trout, brown trout, and rainbow trout. Few anglers are able to take advantage of all this bounty, but there's certainly plenty to choose from.

Freshwater
Conowingo Reservoir/Susquehanna River. The 4,000-acre Conowingo Reservoir in Hartford

County is the largest impoundment in Maryland. It backs up the Susquehanna River behind Conowingo Dam on U.S. Route 1. Boat ramps are available, and outboard motors are permitted. Some areas of the reservoir have a rocky bottom that can eat up a prop or lower unit, so caution is advised.

Striped bass and hybrids are available and give the unsuspecting angler plenty to handle. The hybrids run smaller than their purebred cousins, as is normal, but what they give up in size, they more than make up for in spirit.

Striped bass are more common in the tailrace below Conowingo Dam, which is the continuation of the Susquehanna River and shortly flows into the Chesapeake Bay. Anglers land them from the catwalk and from the shoreline, or by wading in the river. Boaters using special prop guards work the rocky waters just below the tailrace, and cast or troll small swimming plugs.

Smallmouth bass exist in good numbers farther down the Susquehanna near Port Deposit, along the rocky shoreline. Largemouth bass are taken less than a mile farther down the river.

The entire area from Havre de Grace and Perryville to the Patapsco River flowing out of Baltimore holds plenty of white perch, striped bass, catfish, and largemouth bass. These fish will move up and down the bay and river as saltwater intrusion moves in and out. Saltwater reaches its highest level in late summer, especially during periods of drought. At this time, bass and other freshwater species may be concentrated in the headwaters.

Tidewater bass fishing is also found along the eastern and western shores of the bay. The Chester River from Millington to Kings Town is very good bass water. Runs of white and yellow perch in the spring attract legions of anglers to the Millington area, where a small shad dart tipped with a minnow is the favored bait.

The Wicomico River in Salisbury is a good spot for tidal largemouth fishing. The remains of old docks and sunken boats are the most likely hiding places for these fish. Crankbaits and plastic worms or lizards are popular offerings.

Potomac River. The Potomac River forms most of the western boundary of Maryland, and its tributaries drain most of the western half of the state. Restored to better health after years of abuse and neglect, the Potomac provides important recreational opportunity today, especially for bass anglers, and some of this is available right at the doorstep of the nation's capital.

On its western shore the restored Potomac River provides excellent fishing for bass in sight of America's most famous monuments. Largemouth bass are numerous from the capital down to the Route 301 bridge. The dense vegetation growing in the feeder creeks and over the flats near the Woodrow Wilson Bridge hold tremendous numbers of largemouth bass. The vertical walls that line the shorelines in Washington, and the numerous docks along the Virginia side of the river, are equally good locations for largemouth. Crankbaits work well around the docks and vertical walls; spinnerbaits and plastic worms draw strikes in the thick weeds. Striped bass mingle with largemouths but are governed by strict seasons and bag limits.

Smallmouth bass, which were introduced to the Potomac watershed in the mid-1800s, are primarily abundant from the capital north. Fishing from float boats or canoes and by wading the shallows produce good catches. Crankbaits or plastic lures that imitate small minnows or crawfish work very well, madtoms are the favored live baits, and streamers are most effective for flycasters.

Good areas to float and fish for smallmouths exist around Knoxville, Harper's Ferry, Sandy Hook, and Brunswick. It's possible to use boats up to 16 feet long with small motors, although you must be careful around rocks; a propeller guard, used by many river veterans, is advisable.

There are many access sites for the Potomac River. Boat ramps at Edwards Ferry and the C & O Canal Aqueduct near Dickerson in Montgomery County provide access to the upper Potomac. A boat ramp on the Anacosta River at Bladensburg Road can be used by shallow-draft boats. A better access site for fishing in D.C. is found on the Virginia side near National Airport. Areas south of D.C. are accessed from ramps at Tantallon on Piscataway Creek, Marshall Hall Road in Piscataway National Park, Sweden Point in Smallwood State Park, and Friendship Landing Road on Nanjemoy Creek.

Deep Creek Lake.   Located near McHenry in Garret County in the far western part of the state, Deep Creek Lake provides a wide range of warm- and coldwater fishing opportunities. Largemouth and smallmouth bass are available, the former more common in shallow, weedy areas or around boat docks or piers, and the latter more common on rocky bottoms, steep dropoffs, and points. Other prime warmwater species include pickerel and northern pike. Brown trout, brook trout, and rainbow trout also call Deep Creek Lake home, providing what biologists call two-story fisheries.

Deep Creek Lake has access via a boat ramp, cartop boat launch site, and a fishing pier; various facilities are available at Deep Creek Lake State Park on the east side of the lake.

Prettyboy and Loch Raven Reservoirs. Prettyboy and Loch Raven Reservoirs provide a total of 3,900 acres of fishable water close to the major urban complex of Baltimore/Washington, D.C. Loch Raven is located off Route 146, whereas Pretty Boy is farther north at the junction of Routes 25 and 111. Both sites offer largemouth and smallmouth bass, crappie, sunfish, perch, and carp. Loch Raven additionally offers pickerel and northern pike.

Both reservoirs supply the Baltimore area with drinking water, so regulations require that only elec-

tric motors be used. Due to the size of these lakes, it can take a good deal of electric power to cover all the fishing areas. Boat ramps and cartop launching are available at both lakes, and Loch Raven has boat rentals.

Bass anglers flock to Prettyboy and Loch Raven, but other available species draw legions of fans. The crappie run in the spring sees boat anglers working underwater brush piles, with a fair number of people lining the roadway bridge. Large carp inhabit Loch Raven as well, and they may readily feed on the surface in summer, when locusts emerge from their shells and fall into the water. This provides some surface action for anglers; the better the locust crop, the better the sight fishing.

Other sites.   Garrett County has excellent trout fishing sites, with the Youghiogheny River offering more than 29 miles of fishable water. Brook, brown, and rainbow trout are available upstream of the Route 42 bridge at Friendsville. Special management areas are located along the river, where regulations stipulate fly fishing or catch-and-release only. This is a long stretch of water with plenty of room for everyone, but anglers must respect the rights of property owners who have granted public access.

Eastward in Allegany County, Rocky Gap Lake in a state park of the same name is a 250-acre impoundment with largemouth and smallmouth bass, walleye, crappie, channel catfish, brown trout, and rainbow trout. The rainbows are governed by special fishing regulations. Boaters must use electric motors, but launch sites are available for trailers or cartop craft. Boat rentals and a fishing pier are available, and the adjoining state park, which is 5 miles east of Cumberland, offers various facilities.

The Beaver Creek Watershed near Hagerstown covers 8 miles of trout streams holding brown and rainbow trout. The watershed is accessible upstream of Route 68, which is south of Hagerstown. Here, too, the rainbow trout fishery is governed by special regulations.

Greenbrier Lake, in Greenbrier State Park on Route 40 near Interstate 70, has largemouth bass, crappie, and bluegills. It also harbors rainbow trout, but the availability is seasonal and governed by special regulations. Boats can be powered by electric motors only; launch sites for cartop and trailered boats, and rental boats, are available.

Saltwater

Chesapeake Bay.   This large inlet of the Atlantic Ocean is aptly referred to as Maryland's greatest natural treasure. The bay in its entirety is America's largest estuary, and its 46 principal rivers and streams drain 64,000 square miles in six states. About 1,725 square miles and 123 linear miles of the bay are in Maryland, and its exceptional number of tidal shorelines and tributaries make it one of the most important nursery grounds in North America for various aquatic resources.

Nova Scotia biologists report that about 1 in 10 young Atlantic salmon survive to become smolts, which migrate to sea; in many rivers fewer than 1 in 25 survivors will return to spawn.

Among those resources is a plethora of saltwater fish that are accessible from many sites. The population of each species may vary from year to year, but the quality of the angling is uniformly good.

Saltwater fish may venture as far up the bay as the mouth of the Elk River or the Susquehanna Flats when late-summer droughts enable saltwater intrusion to reach this area. This is not a consistent condition, and the Chesapeake Bay Bridge is normally the northern boundary for most saltwater species—except striped bass, which, being anadromous, inhabit the bay year-round, all the way to the base of the Conowingo Dam.

The town of Rock Hall is named for striped bass, which are locally known as rockfish, and a few charter boats operate from this location to pursue these admired fish. Most upper-bay stripers are taken on trolled bucktails, tube lures, or spoons. When the fishing is good, anglers find schools of breaking fish on the surface; then light tackle and small jigs can provide plenty of activity.

Rock Hall Harbor and the Chesapeake Bay are accessible from two area boat ramps and from two fishing piers, one on Sharp Street and one at the junction of Bayside Avenue and Walnut Street in Rock Hall.

Various notable angling locations are farther down the Eastern Shore in or near Kent Island, which is surrounded on the north by the Chester River and on the south by Eastern Bay. Kent Narrows separates Kent Island from the mainland and offers boat ramps, marinas, and a small charter boat operation. A pier at Matapeake State Park is open for fishing and produces good numbers of white perch and striped bass.

The mouth of the Chester River on the back side of Love Point can produce striped bass, croaker, white perch, spot, and small blues. The water depth falls off from a few feet to 25 to 30 feet, and action centers along this dropoff.

A very steep edge runs along the bay side of Kent Island down to Bloody Point. The bottom drops from several feet to 117 feet at the deepest part along this edge. Trolling for stripers is good here in the spring and fall, with bluefish prevalent in the summer. Anglers who work the bottom find croaker, spot, trout, and flounder, catchable on squid, cut baits, and jigs.

Directly across the Bay from Kent Island is Annapolis. Anglers here find access at Sandy Point State Park and head to the pilings of the Chesapeake Bay Bridge for striped bass. Casting bucktails or live eels is the favored technique. Trolling with bucktails, tube lures, or spoons, and drifting with live eels are proven methods for stripers at Dolly's Lump, Hackett Point Bar, or Tolly Bar. Spot, croaker, weakfish (also called gray trout, or trout, locally), white perch, and flounder are taken by bottom anglers using squid, bloodworms, or cut menhaden.

The South River and West River possess numerous marinas and boatyards, and the heavy boat traffic does not improve fishing. The area between Thomas Point and Curtis Point, however, where both rivers empty into the bay, holds fair numbers of striped bass, bluefish, croaker, spot, and trout.

Chesapeake Beach is a small town on the western side of the bay with access to particularly productive areas. The big fleet of charter boats that operates from Chesapeake Beach fishes for a variety of species from spring into the fall. Striped bass and bluefish are the primary targets and are usually taken by anglers trolling with bucktails, spoons, and tube lures. Chesapeake Beach charter captains have a system for trolling six or eight wire lines from a narrow deadrise boat that instills envy in those who cannot run more than three lines without getting at least two tangled.

The boats out of Chesapeake Beach run as far north as Holland Point Bar or the Old Gas Buoy, and as far south as the Gooses and Calvert Cliffs. There is a sharp drop at Calvert Cliffs, where the bottom falls from 5 to 50 feet along an edge that runs south to Cove Point. Stripers and blues stack up along this structure, especially in the spring and fall.

During the summer, small blues, weakfish, flounder, and croaker become more numerous, and the fishing shifts to bottom bouncing with squid, bloodworms, and cut fresh fish. During warm weather the boats may run to the Eastern Shore, where this type of fishing is more productive.

The Choptank River is east and south of Chesapeake Beach, and boasts good fishing all the way up to Cambridge. An old bridge over the river here has been turned into a fishing pier, and it can be especially productive for striped bass and white perch. The channel edge running from Cambridge to Tilghman Island is a good area to fish for stripers, blues, and weakfish. At times, any of these fish will chase baits on the surface; then, small bucktails and spoons are very effective.

Tilghman Island has been a fishing hotspot for many years. Boats pass out to the bay through Knapps Narrows in search of striped bass, bluefish, weakfish, flounder, and black drum. The drum are caught near Popular Island on peeler crab in late spring and early summer. These fish weigh 40 to 80 pounds and give upper-bay anglers a chance to tangle with a real saltwater monster.

Trolling with bucktails, spoons, or tube lures is the most common method for catching blues, striped bass, and weakfish. Bottom-fished peeler crab is the primary method for taking flounder, weakfish, and croaker.

The Little Choptank River holds striped bass in shallow, sheltered water. Casting bucktails or bottom fishing with peeler crabs will catch stripers along with some weakfish, flounder, and small blues. Boat ramps are located on Ragged Point Road and Taylors Island Road; these respectively access Brooks Creek and Slaughter Creek, which empty into the Little Choptank.

The Honga River, Fishing Bay, and Tangier Sound meet at Hooper Strait and funnel gamefish and baitfish into this area. The edge of the deep channel running down the Honga River is a good location for weakfish and striped bass. Bottom fishing with peeler crabs is the most popular technique here, but a bucktail tipped with a peeler crab will often catch weakfish or stripers.

Fishing Bay is a wide yet shallow body of water with excellent summertime fishing for weakfish and small blues. The ever-popular peeler crab is the preferred bait for weakfish, too; spoons and bucktails attract bluefish. Anchoring in Hooper Straight and soaking peeler crabs on the bottom will produce a mixed bag of weakfish, spot, croaker, flounder, and bluefish. Trolling around Hooper Light with spoons and bucktails is good for bluefish and striped bass.

Charter boats and a boat ramp are located at the marina at the junction of Routes 336 and 335; there are several other ramps in the area. Crisfield is the last town on the Maryland side of the Eastern Shore with access to the bay, and it has a large charter fleet and many facilities.

Boats leaving Crisfield head into Tangier Sound for weakfish, blues, croaker, spot, and striped bass. To the south, the same species, and speckled trout and red drum, inhabit the waters along Pocomoke Sound. In summer, boats anchor along the edge of the channel in Tangier Sound where the bottom drops almost straight down from a few feet to more than 100 feet. Weakfish move up this wall in the evening to feed on soft crabs hiding in the shallows. Anglers intercept them by soaking peeler crabs on or close to the edge. They use the same technique throughout Tangier and Pocomoke Sounds.

Point Lookout marks the entrance to the Potomac River and access to fishing hotspots in the middle sector of Chesapeake Bay. Solomon's Island on the Patuxent River just north of Point Lookout has a charter boat fleet, launch ramps, and many amenities. The deep harbor promises good fishing for weakfish, striped bass, croaker, and spot. The shoals between Drum Point and Hog Point are good trolling areas for stripers and blues.

Charter boats running out of Smith Creek near Ridge, and from the St. Mary's River, carry patrons past Point Lookout into the bay. A boat ramp and fishing pier in Point Lookout State Park offer access to the good fishing.

Chumming is the most widely used method for catching weakfish, bluefish, and striped bass. Boats anchor on the Middle Grounds, where they grind up fresh or frozen menhaden to create an oily chum. Even small private boats carry a portable grinder to make fresh chum. Once the fish are in the slick, small pieces of menhaden are dropped into the current. The action can be fast and exciting.

Big-game species are prime attractions for Maryland's offshore fleet, which often ventures out to the canyons.

Atlantic Ocean. Maryland's coastline along the Atlantic Ocean is only 31 miles long, but it packs a wallop that is disproportionate to its size.

From the coastline, the Atlantic is accessible only through the inlet at Ocean City. Just over 100 miles from Washington, D.C., and 120 miles from Norfolk, Virginia, this is a popular site for vacationers as well as anglers. At one time Ocean City billed itself as the white marlin capital of the world, and it still sees some impressive numbers of these elusive billfish. Today almost all billfish, including white marlin, are released, as anglers realize these fish are too valuable to catch only once.

The big boats that sail out of Ocean City in pursuit of marlin, tuna, dolphin, and wahoo must run 50 to 70 miles east to the region where the warm blue water of the Gulf Stream meets the edge of the continental shelf. Baltimore Canyon, Poor Man's Canyon, and Norfolk Canyon traditionally produce the best action. Most fishing occurs over the 50-fathom curve, and more often than not out at the 100-fathom curve. Some captains pull rigged ballyhoo, mackerel, or squid, while others use trolling lures.

The best concentration of white marlin hereabouts is usually from mid-August through mid-September, although whites show up as early as the beginning of June. The major tournaments are scheduled in early September, to coincide with peak fishing, when the marlin are migrating southward. The fish have averaged in the 55- to 70-pound range in the past. These numbers won't break any records, but if the fish are pursued with light tackle, they provide the best of sport.

Closer to the beach, tuna, big bluefish, and sharks inhabit the shoals. Jack's Spot is one of the better locations. Chumming and chunking produce most of the tuna and sharks, whereas trolling spoons is a primary technique for big blues. Ocean City once had the 30-pound line-class record for bluefin tuna, and yellowfins are often found in the

M

30- to 90-pound class. Some monster bigeye have come into Ocean City, including a number of past or present world records, the best of which is the all-tackle and 50-pound line-class Atlantic bigeye, which weighed a mammoth 375$\frac{1}{2}$ pounds.

Behind Ocean City, the shallow waters of Isle of Wight and Assawoman Bays hold good numbers of flounder, weakfish, and croaker. Jetty anglers take small blues, striped bass, and weakfish out of the inlet, and boaters cast to the submerged south jetty.

Surf casters work the entire coast from Ocean City to the Virginia line. Most of Assateague Island National Seashore is open to four-wheel-drive vehicles that have the proper equipment and permits. Surf fishing is best in the spring and fall, when the fish bite and the bugs don't. King whiting, croaker, blues, red drum, weakfish, and striped bass are caught on an assortment of lures and baits.

MASSACHUSETTS

The Commonwealth of Massachusetts may rank only 44th in size among U.S. states, but one wouldn't know that from an overview of its fishing opportunities. Striped bass, tuna, cod, Atlantic salmon, brook trout, and yellow perch are among the fish that have long been associated with the Bay State, and although each has had its peaks and valleys, sportfishing for these and myriad other species reaches into every sector of this heavily populated state.

From its prominent Atlantic islands to its seaboard lowlands, Massachusetts' 192 miles of coastline and 1,519 miles of tidal shoreline reflect the prominence of the sea and its fisheries past and present. Indeed, a codfish still hangs in the statehouse here. In the upland hills and valleys, trout and salmon—equally traditional New England staples—present a diversity of opportunity that in many cases is found shoulder-to-shoulder with bass and such imports as northern pike and muskies.

Rivers and streams, brooks and ponds, reservoirs and lakes, tidal waters and estuaries, coastlines and bays, inshore and offshore—it's all here.

Freshwater

Rivers. A number of the Bay State's rivers, and some of the brackish ponds and estuaries, are not only loaded with warmwater and coldwater fish species, but lunkers from the salt as well.

This fresh and salt double dipping includes striped bass up to 50 pounds, some of which have been taken 100 miles inland.

The Connecticut River, which travels from northern New England across Massachusetts, and the Merrimack River, which meets the Atlantic at Newburyport, are the primary rivers for anadromous species. They not only provide stripers in the spring but also American shad and blueback herring, as well as Atlantic salmon.

Salmon, of course, began to disappear after the construction of dams and the advent of industrial pollution in the 1800s. Before then, it was said that one could "walk across the Connecticut and Chicopee Rivers on the backs of the salmon." Those days will never be seen again here, but some remnant of this abundance may occur if federal and state Atlantic salmon restoration efforts prevail.

With respect to numbers of returning fish, these efforts have produced moderate results at best. The bright light, however, has been the discovery of spawning salmon in the Connecticut and its feeder streams. These fish must be released, but at some future date perhaps fish could be kept if there is a major breakthrough in numbers of returning fish.

Now that rivers are cleaner, and fish lifts and ladders have been constructed, it is encouraging to observe the fish migrating farther north. Salmon and shad, in fact, have once again made their way upstream through Connecticut and Massachusetts and into Vermont.

American shad are abundant not only in the Connecticut and Merrimack but also in the North and Palmer Rivers. They are also being established in the Charles and Taunton River Basins. Labeled "the poor man's salmon" in this state, shad are caught on darts and other small colorful lures, as well as on flies during their spring migration.

Among the Bay State's rivers, the Connecticut stands out for its diversity, offering the aforementioned species as well as such standbys as bass, trout, pickerel, pike, catfish, carp, and crappie, and some walleye. Giant sturgeon are present but rarely landed, and an occasional alligator gar is encountered in the backwaters or oxbows.

Crossover fishing isn't limited to the large rivers. Both migratory striped bass and resident largemouth bass are taken side by side in freshwater on the Bass River in Yarmouth, more than a mile upstream at the first bridge.

Two rivers that draw serious anglers and beginners alike are the Deerfield and Swift. These wind through the mountains of the Berkshires and the rolling hills of the Connecticut Valley, the Swift being fed by Quabbin Reservoir. The fishing is excellent because of continuous trout stocking, and the scenery is equally commendable.

Similarly, the Westfield River and its branches are heavily stocked with trout, and sections of this waterway also wind through mountains, providing valley fishing where a solitary experience can be enjoyed. The Millers, Green, Chickley, and Cold are streams in the Western and Valley Districts that also offer heavy trout fishing in a wildlife-rich area, and on many stretches there is solitude for the day. A great number of feeder brooks offer an excellent combination of well-stocked rainbow and brown trout, as well as a few native brookies.

Elsewhere, the Nashua, Shawsheen, Concord, and Ipswich Rivers offer trout, bass, pickerel, pike, and plenty of panfish. Even the once-polluted Housatonic in the Berkshires, and the Charles of Boston fame (the longest river wholly within

Massachusetts, incidentally), have cleaned up their act and offer angling opportunities.

Coldwater lake fisheries. Atlantic salmon captured in the Connecticut and Merrimack Rivers and used as brood stock in the anadromous salmon restoration program are replaced each spring with new returning spawners, because it was discovered that the larger holdover brood stock did not provide as many eggs as the smaller fish of each new spring. Thus, one of the best-received fish-stocking programs in the state was started, and now holdover specimens are released into a number of ponds each spring and fall. Brood salmon between 5 and 25 pounds have been released in various ponds statewide. Many of these locations also have trout, and anglers fishing for 1-pound rainbows can find themselves battling a salmon up to 35 pounds, as the stocked fighters grow quickly.

Massachusetts' biggest body of fresh water, Quabbin Reservoir has a diverse fishery.

Landlocked Atlantics are taken both in open water and under the ice in much the same manner as trout, mainly by stillfishing with live baits or a variety of cast or trolled lures, flies, and streamers. Favored artificial offerings for casters and trollers often have the blue, green, and silver coloration of herring. Ice anglers must drill large holes, as the big salmon rarely fit through the standard ice hole. They mostly take large live shiners on tip-ups or on a jigged perch eye or rainbow smelt.

In the Northeastern District, the main lakes that receive brood stock each year are Forest Lake in Methuen, Baddacook Pond in Groton, Lake Saltonstall in Haverhill, Pleasant Pond in Wenham/Hamilton, Lake Cochituate's middle and north ponds in Framingham/Natick/Wayland, Hopkinton Reservoir in Ashland/Hopkington, and Lake Pearl in Wrentham.

In the Southeastern District, they include Little and Long Ponds in Plymouth, and Cliff and Peters Ponds in Brewster. In the Central District, they include Wallum Lake in Douglas, Whalom Lake in Lunenburg/Leominster, Comet Pond in Hubbardston, Lake Quinsigamond in Worcester, and Webster Lake in Webster.

In the Connecticut River Valley District, these include Lake Mattawa in Orange, Five Mile Pond in Springfield, and Congamond Lakes in Southwick. In the Western District, they include Laurel Lake in Lee, Onota Lake in Pittsfield, Otis Reservoir in Otis, and Goose Pond in Lee/Tyringham.

In addition to these Atlantic salmon brood stock plantings, landlocked salmon are also stocked in Quabbin Reservoir. Sockeye (kokanee) salmon have been stocked in Onota Lake in Pittsfield and Laurel Lake in Lee, where little or no reproduction was noted and only rare catches are recorded.

The state plants rainbow, brown, and brook trout in all the major coldwater lakes and ponds. More than a half-million pounds go out each year, with the greatest number in the spring and a moderate amount in the fall. More than 50 percent of the fish are a foot or longer when planted, and 25 percent are 18 inches or larger. Hundreds of 2-foot-long trout are surprise plants throughout the state. Many trout are also stocked by sporting clubs.

Very few waters have native trout populations, so lake stocking is primarily a put-and-take activity, not one that supplements native fish. Whereas most of the state gets heavy trout angling pressure, many of the trout ponds on Cape Cod are underfished, and as a result their inhabitants can grow to truly lunker size. Brackish waters such as Mashpee/Wakeby Ponds in Mashpee and Sandwich offer up large fish.

Sea-run brown trout, known as salters, were introduced into Cape Cod streams—the Mashpee, Quashnet, Coonamessett, and Childs—to supplement the small but holding native brook trout salties. They provide a challenge to fly and ultralight-gear anglers.

Tiger trout are a favorite of Bay State anglers and are also stocked in all the major coldwater lakes and ponds. These showy hybrids put up a strong fight, but when not actively feeding they can be finicky and require great patience from an angler. They take bright streamers and flies and small lures.

Rainbow smelt, which are an eating favorite of both humans and predators, are common in southeast coastal streams, while landlocked populations exist in Quabbin Reservoir, Onota Lake in Pittsfield, Lake Quinsigamond in Shrewsbury, Littleville Reservoir in Huntington, Higgins Pond in Brewster, and Long Pond in Plymouth.

Warmwater lake fisheries. Most of Massachusetts' trout ponds and lakes are two-story fisheries, supporting warmwater species in addition to trout and/or salmon. The primary warmwater fish are crappie, smallmouth bass, largemouth bass, chain pickerel, yellow perch, white perch, suckers, pumpkinseed, bluegills, white catfish, channel catfish, and horned pout (bullhead). There are two special stocking programs for several of the more predacious fish not normally found in this state, and these have met with well-publicized success.

M

One is for the tiger muskie, the nonreproducing cross between a muskie and a northern pike. These fast-growing eating machines can hit the 30-pound class in relatively few years. First stocked to reduce the number of runt-size panfish, they soon became one of the state's top freshwater quarries due to size and fighting ability. Many tiger muskies are released by successful anglers until they reach top-end trophy size.

The important muskie waters in Massachusetts include A1 Site and Chauncy Pond in Westboro, Cheshire Reservoir in Cheshire, the Chicopee River in Ludlow, Cochituate Lake in Framingham, Cook Pond in Fall River, Desmond Pond in Rutland, Hamblin Pond in Barnstable, Hampton Ponds in Westfield, Indian Lake in Worcester, Mascopic Lake in Tyngsborough, Maseapoag Lake in Sharon, McCleod Pond in Colrain, Monoponsett Pond in Halifax, Nippenicket Pond in Bridgewater, Norton Reservoir in Norton, Otis Reservoir in Otis, Pontoosuc Lake in Pittsfield, Quannapowitt Lake in Wakefield, Red Bridge Impoundment in Ludlow, Rohunta Lake in New Salem, Sabbatoa Lake in Taunton, Spy Pond in Arlington, and Webster Lake in Webster.

Northern pike were introduced into Massachusetts waters and are stocked in all the tiger muskie locations mentioned, as well as other waters. These have also proven popular with open-water and ice anglers, and some dandy catches have been made through the ice.

Waters that possess pike but not tiger muskies include Attitash Lake in Amesbury, Lake Buel in Monterey, Buffumville Reservoir in Charlton, the Charles River in Natick, Cheshire Reservoir in Cheshire, the Concord River in Concord, Dark Brook Reservoir in Auburn, East Brimfield Reservoir in Sturbridge, Forge Pond in Granby, Hamilton Reservoir in Holland, Lashaway Lake in East Brookfield, Leverett Pond in Leverett, Manchaug Lake in Sutton, Massapoag Pond in Lunenburg, North Spectacle Pond in New Salem, Onota Lake in Pittsfield, Quaboag Pond in Brookfield, Silver Lake in Wilmington. Snipatuit Pond in Rochester, South Watuppa Pond in Fall River, Wequaquet Lake in Barnstable, Whitehall Reservoir in Hopkinton, and Winnecunnet Pond in Norton.

Walleye were stocked in the state until 1960, and only small populations persist in the Connecticut River in Northfield and Turners Falls, where reproduction is fair to good. There are a few walleye in Lake Chauncy in Westboro, Quabbin Reservoir, and the Assawompsett Pond system. Incidentally, Assawompsett, which is a 2,400-acre "pond" in Lakeville, has some historical significance. Here, a white man was murdered by Indians while fishing in the 1670s, and this precipitated King Philip's War.

Bass waters. In Massachusetts, the size of the pond does not dictate the size of the bass; both smallmouth and largemouth lunkers inhabit big waters, like the Connecticut River and Quabbin Reservoir, and small no-name farm ponds alike.

Among the better-known bass waters are Ashland Reservoir in Ashland, Ashumet in Mashpee and Falmount, Auburn Lake in Auburn, Barehill in Harvard, Big Alum in Sturbridge, Billington Sea in Plymouth, Buffumville Reservoir in Charlton, Canton Reservoir in Canton, Chebacco Lake in Hamilton, Chequaquet in Barnstable, Congamond in Southwick, Cook in Fall River, Cranberry Meadow in Spencer/Charlton, Dark Brook Reservoir in Auburn, Dayville in Huntington, Dudley in Wayland, Dunham in Carver, and East Brimfield Reservoir in Brimfield.

Also, East Waushaccum in Sterling, Flint in Tyngsboro, Fort Meadow Reservoir in Hudson/Marlboro, Fresh in Plymouth, Glen Echo in Charlton, Goose in Tyringham, Great East in Acton, Great Herring in Plymouth, Hamilton Reservoir in Holland, Indian in Worcester, Jamaica in Boston, John's in Mashpee, Knop's in Groton, Lackey Dam in Uxbridge/Sutton, Attitash in Amesbury/Merrimack, Lake Boone in Hudson/Stow, Lake Chauncy in Westboro, Lake Cochituate in Natick/Framingham, Lake Mirimichi in Plainville/Foxboro, Lake Monomonac in Winchendon, and Littleville in Huntington.

Also, OxBow in Easthampton, Pearl in Wrentham, Lake Quinsigamond in Worcester, Lake Sabbatia in Taunton, Long in Brewster, Long in Lakeville, Manchaug in Sutton/Douglas, Mascuppic in Tyngsboro/Dracut, Mashpee/Wakeby in Mashpee, Massapoag in Sharon, Monponsett in Halifax, North in Hopkinton, Norton Reservoir in Norton, Onota in Pittsfield, Putnamville Reservoir in Danvers, Quaboag in Brookfield, and Sampson's in Carver.

Also, Santuit in Cotuit, Shirley Reservoir in Lunenburg, Singletary in Sutton/Milbury, South Watuppa in Fall River, Stockbridge Bowl in Stockbridge, Tispaquin in Middleborough, Upper Mystic in Winchester, Webster in Webster, Whitehall Reservoir in Hopkinton, Whittins in Whittinsville, Wickaboag in Brookfield, Winthrop in Holliston, Long in Lakeville, and Lower Mystic in Arlington.

Reservoirs. Quabbin Reservoir, located in the Connecticut River Valley District, is the state's main water supply and, at 28 miles long and 25,000 acres, its largest and best-known lake. The better part of five towns were covered by damming feeder rivers, and the area offers the closest thing to wilderness fishing in the state. Quabbin attracts anglers from several New England states for bass, trout, pickerel, and panfish, but to have success there with any regularity, one must study lake maps and talk with locally experienced anglers and bait shop owners.

This closely controlled reservoir opens to the public in April and closes in October, the exact dates often depending on weather and water

M

The first baitcasting reels were made by Kentucky watchmakers in the early nineteenth century; the first multiplying reel was reportedly produced in 1810.

conditions. There are several access gates for boaters and shore anglers.

Quabbin has a population of self-sustaining lake trout, some of which reach the 20-plus-pound class. These are a major draw, especially in early spring, and are caught in waters accessed from Gate 8 near Pelham (off Route 202), and from Gate 31 in New Salem (off Route 122). Both areas offer boat launch facilities as well as boat and motor rentals. Numerous walk-in gates along Routes 202, 122, and 32A provide shore fishing opportunities.

Lake trout are caught at Quabbin on trolled or stillfished live or dead shiners, and large trolling rigs with a variety of lures. After ice out they are often near the surface and can be caught from shore or boat. As the weather warms, veterans here switch to free-swimming live baits, weighted with a barrel sinker and fished on the bottom.

Landlocked salmon in the 2- to 5-pound class are also plentiful in the Gate 8 portion of Quabbin. They are primarily caught on wobbling spoons and streamer flies.

Gate 43 in Hardwick is the third main gate and also offers boat launching and rentals. This site accesses one of the sections of Quabbin that is well known for bass (another is the area near Gate 31), although these fish are plentiful throughout the reservoir and respond to the entire line of presentations. Discovering an old streambed or a submerged stone wall can lead to excellent bass action.

Largemouths to 6 pounds and smallmouths to 4 pounds are regular catches. Many Quabbin bass anglers practice catch-and-release even though the population is self-sustaining and healthy. Anglers seeking good-eating fish can tie into a healthy population of white perch in the vicinity of Gate 8.

Although Quabbin is the major reservoir draw, smaller Wachusett Reservoir in the Central Wildlife District offers a self-sustaining lake trout population and has produced many state-record fish in the past. The highlight is superior smallmouth bass fishing.

About an hour west of Boston, Wachusett is an old reservoir, impounded in 1908. It is 8¹/₂ miles long and has 37 miles of shoreline. It receives water from the Quinnapoxet and Stillwater Rivers, as well as via an aqueduct from Quabbin. Wachusett has produced state-record brown and rainbow trout and white perch in the past, has an abundant rainbow smelt population, and is especially favored for bass and trout in the spring. Controlled access is provided by means of gates, and the lake is open from ice out in April through November. Only shore fishing is permitted, however, so the bulk of trout activity takes place in April and May, when the water is cold and the fish are most accessible.

Saltwater

New Hampshire border to Cape Ann. Extending from the New Hampshire border to the Merrimack River, Salisbury Beach offers surf fishing for large striped bass beginning in June, with nighttime, dawn, and dusk trips producing best in summer. Bluefish are also caught here, close to shore from July through September, although numbers are down from years past. Boat anglers score during the day by trolling or chunking deep around dropoffs, ledges, and other structure just offshore. From April on, Atlantic mackerel gather near the surface over ledges, wrecks, and lumps. Cod and pollock are available in near-shore waters from late fall through April, then move to offshore structure during the warmer months.

Moving south, the Merrimack River offers a wealth of fishing options. American shad begin migrating upstream to their spawning grounds in late April/early May. They readily hit small shiny spoons and flies, and can weigh up to 9 pounds. Although not a dependable catch, hickory shad can spice up river action throughout the season. Another spring option is Atlantic mackerel. The larger specimens weigh up to 5 pounds and are caught near the mouth of the river beginning in April. Tinker mackerel will often stay in the area through the summer, providing a ready source of bait for bluefish and striped bass anglers. Look for schools dimpling the surface over prominent bottom structure.

Stripers of all sizes can be caught virtually anywhere inside the river, from the Joppa Flats to the bridges and jetties and along the grassy banks. Nighttime fishing is especially productive in summer, when big bass move into the shallows to feed close to shore. Deep-drifting bait at the river mouth account for lots of big stripers and the occasional bluefish, even during midday hours. Strong currents at the mouth of the Merrimack demand extreme caution for both shore and boat anglers.

Boaters launching from the river have ready access to the Isles of Shoals (actually in New Hampshire waters) to the northeast. The deep, rocky shoreline of these scenic islands holds lots of big stripers due to an abundance of baby pollock, mackerel, and other baitfish. Jumbo bluefish also cruise the chilly waters in summer, and can be taken on trolled swimming plugs and chunk baits fished near the rocks.

Plum Island, which begins at the Merrimack's south jetty, is a classic barrier island that has long been famous among surf casters seeking stripers and blues, plus the occasional cod or pollock, along the ocean shore. Nowadays, early-season beach access is limited because of efforts to protect the endangered piping plover, but good fishing still exists. Boat anglers do well during the day by trolling jigs, plugs, and spreader bars on wire line in deeper water, or by drifting baits at night over sandbars. The southern tip of the island, known as Sandy Point, is a particularly productive spot due to strong currents that sweep bait in and out of Plum Island Sound.

M

M

The Parker River and the labyrinth of tidal creeks that meander through the expansive salt marshes behind Plum Island hold white perch and striped bass, including some surprisingly big specimens. Schoolie bass provide fast action all along the grass banks for fly and light-tackle anglers, especially at night, dusk, and dawn.

Just south of the Parker, the Ipswich River offers plenty of calm, sheltered water and a meandering estuary with good striper fishing all along its length. The rocks just outside the mouth of the river produce good striper fishing for wading anglers. To the east is Castle Hill, where stripers are taken right along the shore. Castle Neck (Crane's Beach) offers good striper and bluefish action early and late in the season for shore anglers, before the summer crowds and boat traffic all but eliminate any chance of daytime fishing. The bass and bluefish grounds in 20 to 30 feet of water off Castle Neck produce well for trollers during summer. Boaters often score big fish at night by drifting baits near the bottom.

The Essex River begins at the eastern end of Castle Neck. Flounder are caught here over shallow, mud-bottomed areas in spring and fall. Beautiful Essex Bay comprises a broad expanse of protected tidal creeks, sand flats, and deep holes, making it a perfect spot for anglers in small boats, canoes, and even kayaks. Look for stripers cruising the flats on a rising tide. Work the marsh banks at night, and the deeper pockets and channels during the day.

At Cape Ann, the coast begins to take on a distinctly New England appearance, with rocky headlands plunging into cold Atlantic swells. Striped bass are found all along this rocky coast; the key is to present baits, lures, and flies in the foaming water along the base of the rocks, where bait is tumbled in the wash. Fishing the bottom with fish chunks and live eels is another productive method, especially for those seeking big bass. Bottom anglers can also score with cunner, small cod, and pollock by fishing baits over rocky zones. Flounder can be taken over a mud bottom. A mile or so off Halibut Point, the Dry Salvages serve as a rocky oasis that holds cod, pollock, cunner, mackerel, striped bass, and blues. The same applies to Thacher and Milk Islands.

During summer and fall, bluefin tuna occasionally move in close to Cape Ann, in some years just a few miles from shore. Cape Ann also offers a short run to the productive bluefin grounds of Jeffreys Ledge. Traditional hotspots on Jeffreys include The Cove, New Scantum, and The Fingers. The ledges also offer decent bottom fishing for pollock, cod, and haddock.

The offshore waters hold good numbers of sharks, including blues, makos, threshers, porbeagles, and browns. Shark anglers seek their quarry by setting up long chum slicks over prominent underwater structure and around offshore temperature breaks.

Cape Ann to Boston Harbor. The rugged, scenic shoreline from Cape Ann to Boston, also known as the North Shore, is an inshore angler's paradise, especially for those seeking striped bass. Myriad protected coves offer shelter for small boats, and the clear, cold water keeps gamefish active during the hot summer months. Mackerel appear along the North Shore in April, taking up station around such inshore structures as jetties, ledges, and wrecks. Flounder, tomcod, and small pollock are available to anglers working baits along a muddy bottom. Deeper ledges, wrecks, and hard-bottom areas hold bigger cod, pollock, and cunner. These fish move closer to shore from late fall through spring, whereas in summer they're commonly found in depths ranging from 60 to 180 feet.

The near-shore waters of Gloucester and Rockport host excellent striped bass fishing, and numerous spots provide shore anglers with action. Farther along the coast, the coves, islands, and promontories around Marblehead and Manchester-by-the-Sea provide a spectacular backdrop to any striper trip. Flies, plugs, spoons, soft plastics, and bait all produce. Bluefish cruise here, too, but not in the numbers of years past.

The granite ledges and numerous islands (such as Cat, Bakers, Eagle, and Great Misery) from Magnolia to Nahant provide a sanctuary for all kinds of prey species, from eels and silversides to crabs and lobsters, all of which serve as food for big striped bass. The key is to focus on any sort of rocky structure, but note that marinas and docks serve as prime striper hangouts. Small boats are ideal for this type of fishing, as a lee shore is almost always available. The Danvers River in Beverly also holds a large population of stripers throughout the summer that shouldn't be overlooked by small-boat and shore anglers.

Boston area. Boston Harbor is rapidly shaking its reputation as one of the country's most polluted and fishless waters. The rugged, scenic islands (such as Spectacle, Lovell, Long, Georges, the Brewsters, Gallops, and Peddocks) that lie scattered about the mouth of the harbor offer the same type of great fishing opportunities as the North Shore. Better still, the Harbor Islands have received national park status, and there are plans to make them more accessible to visitors.

Mackerel are crowd pleasers in the early spring, whereas groundfish such as tautog, tomcod, cunner, and small pollock can be taken by bottom anglers among the numerous wrecks and rocky zones. Beginning in late May/early June, hordes of school-size stripers make their appearance, and are often seen busting on the surface around the harbor islands, especially at dawn on a dropping tide. Bigger bass are available from June through October. Chunking with baits; drifting live eels; trolling spreader bars, tubes and plugs on wire line; and retrieving big flies on fast-sink lines all produce keepers. These techniques also produce action with slammer blues throughout summer and early fall.

Keeper bass can even be caught in downtown Boston! Each season, big fish are taken off Logan

Airport, the New England Aquarium, and in front of the Charles River locks during the spring herring run.

Just south of Boston are Quincy, Hingham, and Dorchester Bays, once known as the country's most productive winter flounder grounds, but now depleted by overfishing. Flounder are still caught here, however, particularly in the spring, and indications are that these waters might again host a healthy population of flatfish.

The Neponset River, which feeds into Dorchester Bay, features a classic New England estuary often overlooked by anglers because of its proximity to Boston. Nevertheless, it serves as sanctuary and nursery to many types of baitfish and crustaceans, which in turn attract striped bass. Anglers enjoy prime light-tackle and fly fishing all along the river's grassy banks. White perch and winter flounder are other Neponset residents.

Offshore offerings. Rising from the middle of Massachusetts Bay some 30 miles due east of Boston, Stellwagen Bank is readily accessed by anglers from both the North and South Shores. This popular piece of bottom structure, which rises from roughly 180 feet to a peak of 90 feet, acts as a giant fish factory, attracting an enormous range of gamefish. The bank's plankton- and nutrient-rich waters produce huge shoals of sand eels, butterfish, and whiting, which sustain a resident population of cod, pollock, flounder, hake, and other bottom fish. Mackerel are thick in the upper levels of the water column. Although it's considered an "offshore bank" by many anglers, Stellwagen also attracts huge striped bass and bluefish, which can sometimes be seen feeding on the surface. And even if the fishing's slow, there are plenty of whales to keep things interesting.

Starting in July, big-game anglers keep an eye out for the arrival of bluefin tuna on the bank. Stellwagen also draws its share of sharks, among them blues, makos, and threshers. Sharkers who want to stay clear of all the activity on the bank seek out temperature breaks farther offshore. The basic method is to set out a long chum slick, which draws the fish to the hooked baits, or within casting range.

Boston to Cape Cod Canal. The towns of Quincy, Hull, and Hingham offer quick access to the many inshore ledges and islands in and around Boston Harbor, which hold big bass and bluefish beginning in June. Atlantic mackerel arrive in April and provide light-tackle action around jetties, wrecks, and underwater structure. Winter flounder are available to bottom fishermen drifting sandworms in protected harbors and coves in early spring and fall. Farther south, off Cohasset, Stellwagen Ledges in 60 feet of water may serve up small cod, tautog, and pollock from late fall to early spring, with striped bass and bluefish taking up residence for the summer. Also in summer, large cod and pollock are targeted over deeper wrecks out in Massachusetts Bay.

The South Shore is a prime area for those who like to fish bait chunks and live eels for big stripers and blues, especially at night. Fly anglers enjoy good success by working large "slab-type" flies around rocky areas washed by swells.

Scituate's three cliffs have long been known to produce great striper action for both surf and boat anglers. The North River, which flows into the Atlantic between Scituate and Marshfield, is another important waterway for sportfishing. Shad arrive in May, followed shortly by hordes of schoolie stripers. White perch are also available, providing early-season sport for light-tackle anglers who fish small jigs, flies, and pieces of worm. Bigger bass hit the river in June and often cruise along the grassy banks at night. Mackerel can be jigged outside the jetties in April and May. The mouth of the North River is always a good spot to fish chunks and eels for big bass and blues, but anglers should use caution in this heavy-current spot, especially at night.

Duxbury Bay, Plymouth Harbor, and Kingston Bay are prime bass territory, including areas of shallow, sandy flats where stripers can be sight-fished with fly tackle and light spinning gear. Winter flounder are available inshore in spring and fall but move to deeper water in summer.

Summer bottom anglers out of this area pursue cod, pollock, flounder, and big tautog around the deep wrecks in Massachusetts Bay, which serve as oases on an otherwise featureless bottom. These wrecks often hold chopper bluefish in summer. Expect these bottom fish to move into shallower areas as the waters cool in late fall.

Some 15 miles out from the Duxbury/Green Harbor area, Stellwagen Bank serves up everything from cod and pollock to striped bass and bluefish to sharks and giant bluefin tuna during the course of the season. Serious sharkers go beyond the bank and establish chum slicks near temperature breaks. Their targets are blues, makos, and threshers.

From Plymouth to Sagamore, the coast is mostly beach, save for scattered rocky outcroppings. Mackerel schools move through in April and May, with some good-size fish swimming within reach of small boaters. Striped bass are caught from shore all along this stretch of coast, with sandbars, deep holes, and rocks producing action, especially at night. Daytime trollers score by using wire line to present tubes, jigs, and umbrella rigs along contour lines. Come fall, schools of bluefish and bass often mix together on the surface, chasing baitfish on their way south; diving birds may point the way to some great topwater action.

Cape Cod: Sandwich to Provincetown. The east end of the Cape Cod Canal serves up small cod and pollock action in early spring and late fall, as well as through the winter for those willing to tough it out. Mackerel gang up around the jetties and near-shore structure in April, and the first striped bass are close behind. The jetties and the power plant outflow (just inside the canal) are

 According to *The Guinness Book of Records*, the largest piranha in captivity weighed 3 pounds 6 ounces and died of self-inflicted electrocution; it chewed through the heating cable in its tank.

M

Surf anglers fish for striped bass and bluefish off Cape Cod.

good spots to cast for stripers and bluefish throughout the season.

The Cape Cod Canal itself is a fantastic and famous fishing spot, especially among striped bass fanciers. While boat fishing is not permitted in the canal, shore anglers line the riprap banks, casting jigs and plugs to the stripers and blues that often chase baitfish to the surface during slack water. Chunks of mackerel and live eels fished on the bottom also take their share of fish. Best fishing takes place at night and dawn, when boat traffic is minimal.

Moving onto the Cape, Scorton Creek in Sandwich is a great striper spot, and even holds schoolies throughout the winter. Fish are landed well back into the creek and all along its grassy banks, making it a great spot for shore anglers, as well as those in small boats and canoes. Scorton also boasts a population of sea-run trout, which are available during winter. Sandwich Harbor offers good wade fishing for stripers and blues, especially at night, but anglers should use caution when working along the bars, which are subject to strong currents.

Barnstable Harbor offers more protected striper fishing for fly and light-tackle anglers, from the east end of Sandy Neck well back into the marshes. Look for schools busting under diving birds, especially in June and September/October. The harbor also yields good catches of flounder, both black-backs and fluke. Look for the latter around sandy areas washed by strong currents.

Sandy, gently sloping flats run the length of the inner arm of the Cape, offering great sight fishing for stripers and even bluefish from June through September. Casting to big stripers is possible as they cruise through water just a few feet deep. Bluefish arrive in June and are taken through September. Wire-line trollers tow umbrella rigs along the deeper contours for bass and blues with good success. Cod and an assortment of other bottom fish, along with big bluefish, are available over the deep wrecks in Cape Cod Bay. Billingsgate Shoal off Wellfleet is a famous fishing spot, producing everything from fluke to stripers to bluefish because of the fast currents that sweep baitfish over the raised bottom. The channel leading into Wellfleet Harbor is another good place to fish for the same species.

The shallows from Barnstable to Provincetown are thick with sand eels through the summer, which attract fluke, bluefish, and stripers. Good spots to fish include the mouth of inlets and any pockets, rocks, or near changes in bottom composition. Casting lures and flies along the edge of grassy or weedy patches often draws strikes from bass hiding in the darker zone.

Cape Cod: Provincetown to Falmouth. Provincetown Harbor produces world-class fluke fishing, especially in September, with bluefish and stripers mixing into the catch. Turning the corner and heading down Cape Cod's Outer Beaches, you'll find Race Point, long a mecca for surf anglers on the trail of trophy bass. Boat anglers do well by drifting bait or trolling spreader bars and parachute jigs near the bottom on wire line and downriggers. During the day, deep holes, troughs, and rocky areas are prime places to drift eels or troll with deep-diving plugs and umbrella rigs.

The coastline from Race Point to Nauset Inlet, once a bastion of beach-buggy subculture until access was severely restricted, still produces many huge striped bass and bluefish from June through October for those willing to hike the strand. At night, stripers often move into the surf zone to feed just a few feet from shore.

Hardy anglers can take cod and pollock on bottom baits from late fall through early spring, before these fish move to deeper zones for the summer. Nauset Inlet off Chatham is well known for huge stripers, yet it can be a dangerous place for both boaters and surf casters because of the fierce currents that flow in and out of Pleasant Bay. The bay itself harbors lots of big bass, which often hold in pockets on the grassy bottom and cruise the shallows after dark.

Jutting into the ocean south of Chatham is Monomoy Island, another famous landmark that's surrounded by great fishing. Bearses and Pollock Rips lie off the island's east end and southern tip, respectively. Both shoals are swept by strong currents, making them great places to catch stripers and blues. Experts drift eels and live pogies (menhaden), or use wire line to fish jigs and spreader bars down deep.

This is also the northernmost range of the so-called summer migrants—bonito, false albacore, and Spanish mackerel—which arrive in late summer and depart in early October. The miles of shallow sand flats along Monomoy's western shore offer phenomenal sight-casting opportunities for anglers seeking striped bass and bluefish from June to September.

Good striper and bluefish action are enjoyed all along the Cape's south side, from Chatham to

Falmouth. The Bass River in Hyannis is one of the first spots on the coast to produce schoolie stripers, with bigger bass available from June through October. Hyannis Harbor sees big bluefish in June, and again in late August and September. Blues are also encountered on the sand flats close to shore off Cotuit and Osterville in June. As the waters warm, the big blues move out to the rips like those at Succonesset and Horseshoe Shoals, although small "snarbor" blues may provide fast action in the shallows through the summer.

This stretch of coast is prime territory for bonito, false albacore, and Spanish mackerel from late July through September. Pods of these fish typically cruise the beaches or gang up around the mouths of saltwater ponds and bays, such as Green Pond, Great Pond, Eel Pond, Waquoit Bay, Osterville, and Popponessett Bay. These spots also hold stripers and bluefish, although summer action is generally best at dawn and dusk. Anglers profit from great schoolie action inside the ponds and harbors throughout the season, even during midday. Fly and light-tackle anglers can score by simply working streamers, jigs, and spoons around the numerous dock pilings.

The waters between the Cape and "The Islands" (Martha's Vineyard and Nantucket) are rife with shoals and rips that hold blues, bass, bonito, false albacore, and fluke throughout the season. These spots are especially productive during the hot summer months, when inshore areas quiet down during the day. Most of the aforementioned species are occasionally caught on or near the surface, especially at dawn and dusk, but most of the time you'll need to get baits and lures down deep to score.

Woods Hole in Falmouth offers prime access to great fishing along the scenic Elizabeth Islands chain and Vineyard Sound. Woods Hole's rocky rips can be a great spot to fish for stripers, especially at first light, although the swift currents and summer boat traffic demand constant vigilance on the part of the helmsman. In August, the rocky ledge extending from Nonamesset Island into Vineyard Sound is a perennial hotspot for bonito and false albacore. Small-boat anglers enjoy good action with stripers by throwing plugs and flies all along the shores of the Elizabeths. Early morning and late evening yield the best results, but be sure to keep an eye out for rocks. June is a good time to cast and retrieve live eels in the shallows for stripers, especially around Cuttyhunk Island. Famous Sow and Pigs Reef off the tip of Cuttyhunk is filled with scary boulders, but many anglers think the payoff with big bass is worth the risk.

The powerful currents that sweep through each of the cuts, or "holes," between the islands tumble all kinds of baitfish, making them vulnerable to bluefish, bass, bonito, and albacore. While schoolies and occasionally keeper bass will chase baits on the surface, usually around slack tide, the biggest fish normally hug the bottom. Wire-line trollers do well with parachute jigs, tubes, and plugs through the holes, while bait dunkers often chunk at anchor or drift with eels and pogies. Fluke fishing is quite good around the mouths of the holes, while rocky outcroppings and wrecks on the Buzzards Bay side of the Elizabeths hold good numbers of tautog, big scup, and the occasional black seabass for bottom anglers.

While fishing along the Elizabeths, keep an eye out for birds working over busting fish in Vineyard Sound and Buzzards Bay. Bluefish, bonito, or false albacore are often below them.

Martha's Vineyard and Nantucket. For many anglers, Martha's Vineyard and Nantucket represent the promised land of inshore fishing, boasting hotspots too numerous to list. The Vineyard is famous for its shore and surf fishing for striped bass, bluefish, bonito, and false albacore. The numerous saltwater ponds (for example, Tashmoo, Menemsha, Lagoon, Tisbury Great Pond) around the island provide shelter for numerous prey species and offer protected fishing for both shore and small-boat anglers. On outgoing tides, predators from bass to bonito line up at the inlets to intercept baitfish being flushed out of the ponds. On the island's west shore, Tashmoo Pond hosts scads of schoolie stripers in June, and outgoing tides produce well, especially at night. Bluefish often lurk outside the jetties, too.

Moving south, anglers score with big stripers by working plugs, flies, and jigs around boulders in Lambert's Cove and off Cedar Tree Neck and the Brick Yard. Menemsha Pond hosts a big run of herring in May, producing some of the season's first action with really large bass. Farther down, between Menemsha and Gay Head, Lobsterville Beach and Dogfish Bar provide wade-fishing access for anglers after blues, bass, bonito, and albacore. The rocks in front of the famous Gay Head cliffs and Squibnocket make these spots prime territory for big stripers.

The island's exposed, wave-pounded south shore produces huge fish each season for surf casters, who patrol the beach in four-wheel-drive vehicles looking for diving birds over breaking fish. Night fishing can be especially good here, with stripers and blues feeding close to the beach. Big brown sharks move in along the south shore during summer, and some adventurous anglers have even taken them from the shore. The big rip that forms off Wasque Point on the very southeast tip of the island serves as a magnet for everything from bass to bonito, making it a crowded spot in summer.

Along the east coast, Cape Pogue, Chappaquiddick Point, Edgartown Light, Big Bridge, Little Bridge, East Chop, and West Chop are all productive shore spots. It's worth noting that the Vineyard also offers some decent sight casting for stripers and blues on the sand flats, such as those off Cape Pogue, Edgartown (Middle Flats), Dogfish Bar, and inside Tashmoo Pond.

Bonito and false albacore fever grips the island from late July to mid-October. Some perennial hotspots for these fast and frequently finicky fish are Vineyard Haven, the entrance to Cape Pogue Bay (The Gut), Lobsterville Beach, Menemsha Pond, Tashmoo Pond, Hedge Fence Shoal, Edgartown Light, and Wasque Point. Expect Spanish mackerel and bluefish to join in the fray at times.

For boat anglers, the numerous shoals surrounding the Vineyard are particular attractions. Lucas Shoal and Middle Ground in Vineyard Sound produce outstanding catches of summer flounder (fluke), stripers, blues, and, in summer and early fall, bonito and albacore. Three nautical miles northeast of Vineyard Haven, Hedge Fence is another excellent spot for all the above species, as is L'Hommedieu Shoal, another 2 miles beyond Hedge Fence.

Bait and wire-line anglers on the trail of trophy bass often visit areas like Devil's Bridge off Gay Head, Squibnocket Point, Wasque Shoal, and the Hooter Buoy at the end of Muskeget Channel. Big bluefish are caught in these spots, too.

Like Martha's Vineyard, Nantucket is surrounded by phenomenal fishing. Surf anglers cruise the sandy beaches from June through October, looking for blitzes and haunting hotspots such as Great Point, Sankaty Head, Smith Point, the harbor jetties, and Eel Point. The rip-filled waters off Nantucket hold big bluefish throughout the summer, when mainland hotspots fizzle. The waters off Tuckernuck Island and the nearby shoals (for example, Old Man, Great Point, Pochik, Rose, and Crown) give up numerous keeper bass and chopper blues, especially for anglers who jig deep with wire line. Flycasters and surface pluggers can score big blues here all season.

Nantucket is a fantastic spot to chase bonito and false albacore in late summer and early fall. Smith Point, Eel Point, and Nantucket Harbor are good spots to try, as well as the rips. And on calm, sunny days, anglers stalk striped bass and bluefish on the shallow sand flats of Madaket Harbor and Tuckernuck Bank, as if sight fishing for bonefish on tropical flats.

Bait-rich Nantucket Shoals to the east also holds big striped bass down deep, as well as cod and pollock. Deep wrecks in this area provide oases for some of the biggest cod and pollock still found in New England.

Southeast of the islands, offshore species like yellowfin tuna and white marlin may show up on traditional grounds like The Fingers, The Star, The Dump corners, and The Claw in July, August, and September, although there are no guarantees. The key is to look for the arrival of warm Gulf Stream water curling in from the canyons. Some trollers locate the action by trolling along the 20-fathom edge until they find a concentration of baitfish or a temperature break. Those willing to make the long run to the edge of the continental shelf can troll or chunk for blue and white marlin; bigeye, yellowfin, and albacore tuna; wahoo; and big mako sharks.

Buzzards Bay. The entrance to Buzzards Bay has numerous ledges and wrecks that offer great bottom fishing, especially in early spring and mid- to late fall. Spots like Mishaum Ledge, Coxens Ledge, Hen and Chickens, and Negro Ledge all hold big tautog, seabass, scup, and winter flounder. From May through November, these ledges are magnets for stripers and bluefish. Trollers using wire line and tube-and-worm combos score big by working along the rips that form over these rocky rises.

Along the eastern shore of Buzzards Bay, numerous points, coves, creeks, and harbors hold schoolie bass throughout the season. The best action occurs in June and October, when bass often chase baits on the surface. Look for schools of blues feeding in shallow zones from Memorial Day through early July, providing fast surface action. Summer fluke fishing is good along sloping shorelines in 10 to 40 feet, and muddy zones hold winter flounder in May and November.

The strong currents flowing back and forth between Cape Cod Bay and Buzzards Bay make the western end of the Cape Cod Canal a great spot to fish throughout the season. Schoolie bass usually chase baitfish on the Mashnee Flats or in front of the Massachusetts Maritime Academy, and bigger fish lurk in the depths around Hog Island, Wings Neck, and the "Old Canal" channel. The Mashnee Flats, Onset Harbor, and the tip of the Stony Point Dike give up lots of fluke during the warm months, and scup and tautog are caught near riprap "islands" and rocky patches. From mid-August through September, bonito and false albacore arrive in the upper bay. Good spots to look for them include the entrance to Onset Harbor, Scraggy Neck, Toby's Island, the Maritime Academy, and near the tip of the Stony Point Dike.

The Wareham and Weweantic Rivers at the head of Buzzards Bay hold white perch and loads of small bass in season, with the occasional lunker to keep things interesting. Herring enter the rivers in May, making this one of the best times to score a keeper. Bluefish arrive in this area near Memorial Day and provide prime plugging action through June as they gorge on squid. The big fish depart by July, but small (1 to 5 pounds) "snarbor" blues may linger through the summer. In August and fall, menhaden (pogy) schools sometimes become trapped in coves and harbors along the western shore of the bay, providing fast-paced action with "gorilla" bluefish. Bird Island's rocky shallows and the boulders off Butler Point are prime spots to cast for bass and blues throughout the season, especially at dawn and dusk. During summer, when hot weather chases striped bass to deeper water, drifting eels and trolling tubes around Nyes Ledge, Cleveland Ledge, Great Ledge, and Wilkes Ledge often produces big fish. Shallower rocky spots like Bird Island Ledge, Dry Ledge, Sippican Neck, and the Bow Bells hold

In June 1903, the New York City firm Abercrombie & Fitch, calling itself "The World's Headquarters for Fishing Tackle," advertised its first catalog; it contained 160 pages and cost 3 cents.

M

tautog, flounder, and scup in the early spring and fall, and are good places to fish the bottom for bass in June, particularly at night.

The rocky shallows along Aucoot Cove and Converse Point off Marion are great areas to toss a plug or fly for stripers. Bluefish move into the waters around Ram Island in June. Apponagansett Bay in South Dartmouth often sees late-season bluefish blitzes. Barney's Joy Point, Gooseberry Neck, and Mishaum Point feature lots of rocks that attract big bass throughout the season, although careful boat handling is necessary. Try working big, slow-swimming surface plugs and huge streamer flies around these shores for big bass at first light. Live eels and pogies should produce similar results. Sandy, sloping beaches like Horseneck and Demerest Loyd provide good fluke fishing in spring and fall. For sight fishing, try poling, drifting, or wading the sand flats on an incoming tide; you're bound to see stripers and even blues looking for a meal, especially in June.

The Westport River near the Rhode Island border offers miles of protected water for stalking stripers in small boats and from shore. At dawn, watch for schoolies busting baitfish along the edges of the marsh grass; bigger fish cruise the same shallows at night, looking for eels and crabs. The mouth of the Westport is a great place for shore anglers to fish plugs and baits at night. Bonito and false albacore often chase baits outside the river mouth from August through mid-October.

Westport is a great jumping-off spot for boaters, since it offers easy access to the Elizabeths, Martha's Vineyard, Buzzards Bay, and eastern Rhode Island.

Saltwater Species Overview

Winter flounder (blackbacks)   Found year-round in all state waters. Inhabits shallow, mud-bottomed bays, harbors, and estuaries during May and in mid- to late fall.

Summer flounder (fluke)   Most common around Cape Cod, the Islands, and in Buzzards Bay. Prefers sand or mud bottoms with good current flow. Peak season runs from May through October. Available in shallow water (10 to 30 feet) early and late in season, but may seek deeper areas (40 to 60 feet) in midsummer.

Tautog (blackfish)   Available year-round. Most common from Cape Cod south, particularly in Buzzards Bay. Inhabits rocky bottom, ledges, and wrecks. Peak fishing from April through June and from October through December, when present in fairly shallow water. Seeks deeper zones in summer.

Black seabass   Most common in waters south of Cape Cod, including Buzzards Bay. Inhabits wrecks, reefs, and ledges. Found in deeper water (30-plus feet) through summer. Frequently found on same grounds as cod, pollock, tautog, and other bottom dwellers.

Atlantic mackerel   Available in cold Atlantic waters beginning in April. Most common from Cape Cod Bay north in summer. Large schools gather near surface around near-shore structure (wrecks, jetties, ledges) and over offshore banks.

Cod and pollock   Available year-round in all waters except Buzzards Bay. Small fish move into near-shore areas (20 to 60 feet) from late fall through early spring. Usually inhabit wrecks, rocky bottom, shoals, and deep banks. Larger fish found on deeper (60-plus feet) wrecks and banks.

Scup (porgy)   Available year-round in inshore waters. Most numerous south of Cape Cod. Inhabits rocky areas, docks, piers, and wrecks.

White perch   Available year-round in salt marshes, estuaries, and tidal creeks.

Striped bass   Enters inshore waters south of Cape Cod in April and departs in late November. Enters waters north of Cape Cod in May and departs in October. Inhabits shallow flats, rocky coastlines, estuaries, tidal creeks, shoals, ledges, wrecks, channels, and high surf.

Bluefish   Available in waters south of Cape Cod from early June into late October. Available north of Cape Cod from late June through October. Inhabits flats, surf, shoals, wrecks, ledges, offshore banks, and channels. Big fish most numerous inshore early and late in season. Moves to deeper, colder water in summer.

Bonito   Available in waters south of Cape Cod from late July to mid-October. Found along beaches, shoals, and inlets.

Little tunny (false albacore)   Available in waters south of Cape Cod from mid-August through mid-October. Found along beaches, shoals, and inlets.

Spanish mackerel   Available in inshore waters south of Cape Cod from late July through October. Found along beaches, shoals, and inlets.

Bluefin tuna   Available from July through November. Schools gather over deep banks, ledges, and shoals, although also encountered in open water.

Yellowfin tuna   Found in offshore waters (120-plus feet) south of Nantucket and Martha's Vineyard. Availability dependent upon influx of warm Gulf Stream water. May first show in July.

Sharks (blue, mako, thresher, brown, porbeagle)   Available in offshore waters from July through October. Found over deep banks and around temperature breaks.

White marlin   Found in offshore waters (120-plus feet) south of Nantucket and Martha's Vineyard. Availability dependent upon influx of Gulf Stream water. May arrive in July and depart in September.

MATCHING THE HATCH

An expression for the selection and use of artificial flies that exactly, or as closely as possible, mimic the look, size, and behavior of naturally occurring aquatic insects. The origin of this expression is in fly

M

fishing, and principally used when angling with dry flies for trout; however, the principle of imitating the existing prominent natural forage for any species at any point in time is common to all methods of angling and may be generically referred to as matching the "hatch."

See: Hatch.

MATE

A person who assists the captain on a charter boat *(see)* or party boat *(see)*. The chores of a mate are usually broad, from netting or gaffing fish to tying up fishing rigs, preparing bait, filleting fish, cleaning up the boat and equipment, and much more. The mate usually performs all the chores necessary for fishing, with the exception of running the boat (and sometimes may assist with this as well). Generally, it is the captain's job to pilot the boat, locate fish, and constantly keep the boat in position to maximize angling effort.

Some large charter boats have two mates, and party boats always have at least one mate, sometimes two or more; on party boats they may also be called deckhands. Small boats that are operated by a fishing guide *(see)*, and some charter boats (usually those in freshwater that are in the 20- to 25-foot range), do not have a mate; in these instances the guide or captain does all of the necessary chores. When trolling is involved, passengers must assist in holding the steering wheel (maintaining the boat's course), which sometimes works out well and sometimes does not. The absence of a mate under certain conditions may lead a small-boat skipper to keep unproductive lures in the water or stay in one place unnecessarily long instead of making the effort to change lures or places.

Often the quality of the fishing experience is directly related to the ability of a mate to do important chores, and sometimes to the speed with which they are done. Demeanor and effort are important as well. Good mates make a big difference in some outings and should be rewarded with an appropriate gratuity for the services rendered.

In some places and situations, one of the qualifying requirements for obtaining a captain's license is demonstrating experience on a fishing boat for hire, and having been a mate for a certain length of time fulfills this.

MATRINCHA

Other name—Portuguese: *matrinxã*.

The matrincha is a member of the Brycon genus of the Characidae family. There are reported to be some 800 species of Brycons, most in Central and South America. "Matrincha" is the English-language name for a Brazilian fish known as *matrinxã* and is identified in some literature as *Brycon hilarii*. Brazilians say that it is closely related to a similar species known as *jatuarana*. Both are

A matrincha from the Cururu River, Brazil.

characins. They are superb gamefish on light tackle and provide delicious table fare. Few anglers are familiar with either fish, although more have encountered the matrincha.

Identification.   The matrincha has a stout, rounded body with a small head, a high dorsal fin that is centered on the body, an adipose fin, and a broad, squared tail. Its coloring is silvery to bronze and dark across the back; the pelvic and caudal fins are dark.

Size.   The maximum attainable size of the matrincha is uncertain, although Brazilian literature indicates that it may reach 31 inches and 11 pounds. The world record is 7 pounds 5 ounces, and 3- to 4-pounders are common. The *jatuarana* is said to be darker and reaches a maximum weight of 17 pounds.

Distribution.   In Brazil, the matrincha reportedly occurs in some sections of the states of Amazonas, Acre, Pará, and Rondônia. The São Benedito River in southern Pará, and its tributaries, have been good fisheries for this species, but the full range both in Brazil and elsewhere is uncertain.

Habitat/Behavior.   A schooling species, the matrincha is found in small groups in clear rivers during the dry season. It reportedly occurs in large schools prior to the flood season, when spawning takes place in the whitewater of large rivers. During the high-water season, they scatter into the flood lands.

Food.   The matrincha is believed to be omnivorous, consuming fruit, seeds, plant matter, and small fish as season and water stages dictate.

Angling. Most anglers encounter this species in low clear water, where the fish cluster in small groups and are fairly skittish. They are caught below rapids and in the head of runs or pools but are easily spooked or moved off after being fished for a while. They are also caught from under trees and logs along riverbanks.

Although large lures—such as those meant for peacock bass—may occasionally catch a matrincha, smaller offerings, such as spinners, spoons, and jigs, are better. Matrincha are good targets for light-tackle fishing with spinning and fly gear, and their broad profile allows them great purchase in rivers. This results in a strong fight not unlike that experienced with American shad, including impressive aerial displays. Spinning tackle with 6- to 10-pound fine-diameter line is the best equipment.

MAURITANIA

The Republic of Mauritania is a large country within the Sahara Desert in northwestern Africa whose coastline bisects the Tropic of Cancer and fronts the eastern Atlantic Ocean. Although numerous gamefish exist along Mauritania's coast, there is limited sportfishing.

The Sport Fishing Club of Nouadhibou was created by the promotional office of the airline company Air Afrique in 1973. Anglers began to test the Baie de l'Etoile (Star Bay), and a newly constructed Fishing Centre was inaugurated in 1977. By 1998, about 350 angling tourists from throughout Europe annually passed through the Air Afrique Nouadhibou Fishing Centre. An international fishing competition at this site brings together more than a hundred anglers from 10 nations each year.

The courbine, or meagre (in the drum family), is the premier fish in Mauritania. The Fishing Centre reports that between 300 and 350 of these fish, with a mean weight of 40 kilograms, are taken annually. The record is a 63-kilogram specimen. At the centre, anglers catch 30 to 35 tons of fish of various species annually, 60 percent by surf casting from the beach; they catch the remainder by trolling and drifting.

Surf casting produces other species with regularity, including bluefish, skipjacks, spotted seabass in great quantities, garrick, snapper, guitarfish, hammerhead sharks, tope, and various jacks. Anglers land many red and gray sea bream and grouper by bottom fishing and with light-tackle casting. The season is year-round, with a light increase in October, November, and December.

The Mauritanian government, in cooperation with Air Afrique, has reserved a portion of sea that is 25 kilometers long and 5 kilometers wide in the Bay of Levrier, which contains Star Bay. The purpose is to reserve a site exclusively for sportfishing and to prohibit commercial fishing.

MAURITIUS

The 720-square-mile island of Mauritius is just north of the Tropic of Capricorn at 20 degrees south latitude, and about 535 miles east of Madagascar in the Indian Ocean. This locale places it in the migratory crossroads of many pelagic fish species and brings them close to the island itself. The big blue marlin is the foremost angling attraction.

In the Western world, many people are better acquainted with the dodo bird than with Mauritius. That large, goofy-looking, nonflying bird with the hooked bill was one of many fascinating creatures and remarkable flora that Dutch explorers found on Mauritius when they arrived at the end of the sixteenth century. Mauritius was then uninhabited, which no doubt caused Mark Twain to comment that God had modeled heaven after this island.

Mauritius is densely populated today and has become a booming tourist destination. Although known to the jet set and among the European and South African big-game fishing community, the independent sovereign British Commonwealth nation of Mauritius is little known to North American anglers, and is often described as a "new discovery." It is only "new" because it is so far away to so many. Tourism has become an important industry, however, and a half million visitors journey to Mauritius annually, many of them to enjoy beautiful beaches, to dive on extensive coral reefs, and to surf.

The 206-mile-long coastline of Mauritius is almost entirely surrounded by coral reef, and within a mile of shore the ocean drops to more than 2,000 feet. The Indian South Equatorial Current washes around these islands, and with current pushing bait and gamefish upward at these and associated volcanic islands and seamounts, opportunities to catch fish exist year-round.

As mentioned, marlin are the premier gamefish in Mauritius. Outstanding action can be had for either blue or black marlin, although the former clearly shine here because they are especially large.

More than two dozen Pacific blue marlin granders—fish weighing more than a thousand pounds—have reportedly been caught in Mauritius waters since people took note of such things. A 1,100-pound blue caught off Le Morne in February 1966 remained an all-tackle world record until 1982. And in November 1984, a 1,430-pound blue marlin was taken here on 130-pound tackle; unfortunately, it did not qualify as a world record because it struck two lines at the same time. Nonrecord granders were caught in the 1990s, and a 950-pound blue caught off Le Morne in December 1994 established a women's line-class world record.

In 1989, a fish just under the 1,376-pound world record (Hawaiian) was taken. Naturally, anglers land many smaller blue marlin in Mauritius, with an average weight of roughly 350 pounds. The availability of so many big blues, however, has fueled speculation that the next all-tackle world

M

record, and possibly the first rod-and-reel blue marlin over 1,500 pounds, may come from Mauritius.

As for black marlin, they run large on average, although no fish caught here has yet contended with the granders of other locales. Nevertheless, fish up to 700 pounds have been landed, and black marlin here consistently average in the 300- to 500-pound range, providing plenty of excitement. A catch of a 300-pound blue and a 300-pound black on the same day is theoretically possible (though unlikely), and gives great fodder to the imagination.

The prime time for marlin is from October through March—the spring and summer seasons in Mauritius, and the peak of the tourist trade. Good catches of both blues and blacks occur throughout the year, however, and some striped marlin enter the catch at times. Offshore trollers fish from large, well-equipped sportfishing vessels and use live baits, mainly bonito and skipjack tuna, but also lures.

A particularly pleasant aspect of Mauritian big-game trolling is that it can be done within minutes of shore. A nine-hour fishing day involves little running and a lot of angling—one covers a great deal of potentially productive water in the course of a day.

Most of the Mauritius sportfishing fleet is harbored near the southwestern or northwestern sections of the island, respectively, at Black River and the Le Morne Peninsula; some originate out of Grand Baie on the east coast. Many marlin are caught off the southwestern area of the island, offshore but in sight of the Le Morne Peninsula, where the dropoff from reef to great depths is sharp and an upwelling draws schools of baitfish to the surface. The fishing is concentrated from the dropoff to about 7 miles offshore.

Closer inshore, one might encounter such other billfish as striped marlin and sailfish. Neither of these are considered abundant in Mauritius waters, but specimens to 240 and 80 pounds, respectively, have been recorded, and these two fish are taken from time to time each year.

Several species of tuna are abundant in this area of the Indian Ocean. Yellowfin tuna are found all year long, and the most and biggest fish, up to 240 pounds, are caught in March and April.

Skipjack tuna are especially prevalent all season. Mauritius holds the all-tackle world record, which is shared by two 41-pound fish, and has established numerous other line-class and fly-rod skipjack world records. An abundance of skipjack makes for light-tackle and fly-rod opportunities that are seldom explored here.

Dogtooth tuna, which inhabit tropical reef waters, are plentiful as well. Mauritius holds the 50- and 80-pound line-class world records for this species; a 224- and a 230-pounder, respectively, were caught off Le Morne.

Wahoo, small dorado (dolphin), barracuda, and a variety of sharks, plus such reef fish as grouper, are other gamefish possibilities. The Mauritian record for wahoo is 125 pounds, but these fish are usually landed at one-third that size. The best action is from September through January. Anglers land dorado year-round.

Sharks are fairly abundant, although they don't pose the big-game fighting problems—mutilated billfish—that occur in other marlin hotspots. Mako sharks grow quite large, and a world-record 1,115-pounder caught by a boat from Black River in November 1988 is the largest mako taken on sporting tackle. Hammerhead, tiger, and blue sharks are available too, and a 400-pound blue from Mauritius holds an International Gamefish Association (IGFA) line-class world record.

Mauritius is roughly comparable in size to Maui in the Hawaiian Islands. It is ringed by a coral reef, and inshore the waters are calm, gorgeous, and conducive to all manner of water sports, with warm lagoons, soft powder-sand beaches, and tropical greenery. The interior landscape includes thick forests, waterfalls, gorges, mountains, and lush vegetation; there are several small lakes and streams originating in the highlands, but freshwater fisheries are undetermined.

The climate of Mauritius is tropical and generally humid. In the summer months, from November through March, the coastal temperature varies from 73° to 90° F. The rainy season occurs from January through March, and cyclones may occur between November and February.

MAXIMUM SUSTAINABLE YIELD

The largest average catch that can be taken continuously from a stock under average environmental conditions. Maximum sustainable yield is different from optimum yield, which is the recreational and/or commercial harvest level for a species that achieves the greatest overall benefits, including economic, social, and biological considerations. See: Fisheries Management.

MAYFLIES

Mayflies are members of the scientific order Ephemeroptera, a term derived from *ephemera*, meaning short-lived, and *ptera*, meaning wing. They are the best-known aquatic insects *(see)* and include approximately 700 species, all of which have aquatic larvae and a relatively short-lived terrestrial adult stage. Their life cycle consists of egg, nymph, and adult stages, with most of this being in the nymph, or immature, form.

The larval development period depends on species and local climate but can last from two weeks to two years. Because of the large numbers of different species and varying life cycle times, mayfly larvae can be observed in a healthy stream at any time of year. They can be found in a variety of habitats, including exposed rock surfaces in fast current or buried in soft bottoms. Generally, they are confined to streams with high levels of dissolved oxygen and good water quality.

Nymphs range from barely visible in size up to 1¹/₂ inches, feed on algae or plant debris, and are timid creatures until the eve of their emergence. They may be flat-bottom clingers, soft-bodied burrowers, torpedo-shaped swimmers, or cylindrically shaped crawlers.

When mature, the nymph loses its timidity and becomes active. It may make several trips to the surface and back to the bottom. Some swim to the surface and immediately pop out of their nymphal skin, or case, and fly away. Some struggle to get free of the case. Some fall to the surface several times before they are able to fly away. In streams, trout have a limited opportunity to feed on the adult, but they take advantage of it, and this makes a great opportunity for the dry fly angler. Most fishing opportunity is in the nymphal stage.

The first adult stage of the winged insect is called a dun, or subimago. When the dun molts, or sheds its skin, it is sexually mature and is called a spinner, or imago. It mates in the air, and females then fly down to the water's surface to lay their eggs. Both males and females die shortly afterward. Some females repeatedly dip their abdomen into the water while sustaining flight. Others land on the water, drift with the current, and lay their eggs at rest. Some species actually submerge to lay their eggs. Young nymphs soon emerge from the eggs.

Single species often all hatch into a terrestrial stage in a very short period of time, and huge numbers may be observed emerging from the stream or as a swirling mass above it. This occasion is widely referred to as a hatch.

Mayfly larvae are mostly distinguished by these characteristics: platelike, filamentous or feathery gills along the abdomen; three (sometimes two) long hairlike tails on the abdomen (the tails may appear webbed), which extend from the body at the same level; three pairs of segmented legs (six legs in total) on the middle section of the body; a usually flattened body; and one claw at the end of each leg. Adult mayflies have large, upright wings that are sail-shaped.

Mayfly larvae may be distinguished from stonefly larvae by the presence of platelike or feathery gill

Mayfly

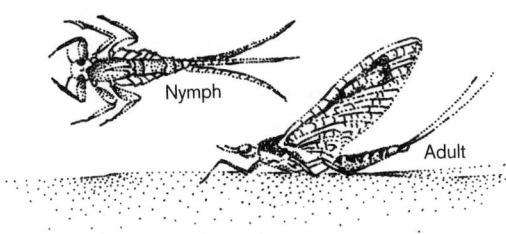

Nymph

Adult

Mayfly Life Cycle

tufts along the sides of the abdomen. In addition, mayfly larvae usually have three hairlike tails and very short antennae (usually shorter than the head length).

Damselfly larvae can also be similar to mayfly larvae, except damselfly larvae have no gills on the sides of their abdomen and they have three broad oar-shaped tails (these are the damselfly larvae's gills) that extend from the back end of the damselfly in a tripod formation. Mayfly larvae have tails that extend from the back end of the abdomen all in the same plane with (parallel to) the ground.

MEAGRE *Argyrosomus regius.*
Other names—croaker, salmon bass, shadefish; French: *maigre commun;* Italian: *bocca d'oro;* Spanish: *corvina.*

The meagre is a large member of the Sciaenidae family (drum and croaker) common to the eastern Atlantic. An important food fish, it is prominent in commercial trawl fisheries and is also a target of anglers.

It occurs in the eastern Atlantic, from Norway to Gibraltar and south to the Congo, including the Mediterranean and the Black Sea, and migrated into the Red Sea via the Suez Canal. It generally inhabits inshore and shelf waters, close to bottom, but is also found at mid- and surface levels when foraging on schools of baitfish.

The meagre is commonly found to 60 inches in length, but it is reported to attain a maximum of 78 inches in length and a weight of 284 pounds. The all-tackle rod-and-reel record is a 105-pound, 13-ounce specimen caught in 1986 in Mauritania.

Meagre spawn inshore during spring and summer. Young fish may enter estuaries and coastal lagoons; adults and juveniles migrate along coastlines and from inshore to offshore environs in response to changes in water temperature.

M

MEALWORM

The larva of a meal beetle, also called a mousie, used to tip the hook of a small ice fishing jig or placed on a small bait hook.

See: Jig; Maggot.

MEASURING FISH

Fish are measured in various ways and for a variety of reasons. The simplest kind of measurement and the most common reason for measuring involve fish that the angler wants to keep; such fish need to be measured for length to comply with existing laws pertaining to that species. Many species of fish, especially those in freshwater, cannot be kept by anglers unless they meet certain length requirements. How to measure fish in accordance with applicable laws, and the reasoning behind this, is detailed in other entries *(see: fisheries management; regulations)*.

Another common reason for measuring involves large fish that will be kept by an angler who desires to know the weight. This information may be simply for personal gratification, for submission in a contest, or for the sake of claiming a record. Although measuring can also include taking length and girth measurements (which are required for world-record certification), it especially involves the weighing of a fish. Many types of spring and digital scales are available and can be carried with anglers. The accuracy of these varies widely, not to mention that they are often used when a boat is unsteady and moving with wind or waves—a condition that tends to allow the fish to surge on the scale. Some spring scales, however, especially the brass tube Chatillon models, are so accurate that they can be calibrated well enough to pass official weight-inspection tests and may actually be certified for use in record keeping. For record establishment, it is absolutely necessary to have a fish weighed on a scale that has been recently certified for accuracy. Most weighings of fish are performed on scales at stores (grocery, meat, and produce scales), at fishing lodges or camps, at marinas, and at fishing clubs. For conscientious anglers who catch fish that are large but not record class, even ordinary pocket or tackle box scales should be checked periodically against known weights so that their degree of accuracy can be determined.

Estimating Weight

Weighing on the water can be harmful to big fish, because they may be out of the water for a long time and held in a position that doesn't support their internal organs well (being hung by the mouth); thus, for really large fish that are to be released, weighing may be harmful or may not be practical. Weighing fish that will be released is specifically not recommended by some fisheries agencies and, as a practical matter, it is good to minimize handling of a fish for all purposes, weighing included *(see: catch-and-release)*.

Large fish that are released and not weighed, however, are often subject to speculation—even outlandish guessing—regarding the actual live weight. For many years, anglers and fisheries biologists have been working on ways for people to reasonably determine weight based upon length and/or on length and girth measurements. No single table or formula applies to all species, owing to the vast differences in body shapes that exist. And no method has been totally perfect time after time, but there are ways to come close enough to knowing the live-released weight for most fish.

In all cases you need to know the length. To make measurements, use a soft tailor's tape measure or a piece of marked cord or thin-diameter rope that will not shrink and is marked at regular intervals. In a pinch, you can measure small fish by spreading your fingers and using the distance from pinky to thumb. Another emergency measure is to use your fishing rod, aligning the butt with the tip of the fish's jaw. Still another is to cut nylon line off the reel and cut it to the exact length (and girth) of the fish.

Tables.   The best way to get a quick, on-the-spot idea of the fish's weight without having to do multiplication and division (what if you have no pen?), and when you have forgotten to stick a calculator in your tackle box, is to refer to a table. In some of the finest lakes in northern Canada, where lake trout must be released unharmed and people catch huge specimens, all boats are equipped with a waterproof length-girth-weight table, affixed to the seat or gunwale, that can be instantly referenced as soon as a tape measure (also supplied) is wrapped around and along the trout.

An increasing number of freshwater fisheries agencies are publishing weight estimation tables for the most popular and common species in their jurisdiction; these are correlated to total length only (no girth) and are based upon the average weight for fish of that length in that jurisdiction. One of the best of these tables, offered by Pennsylvania, is a waterproof, pocket-size booklet covering 16 freshwater fish, which also has instructions for photographing and releasing the catch. Tables for use in saltwater with billfish are appearing, although these are specific to regions rather than being worldwide.

Formulas.   Formulas have long been developed in freshwater and saltwater for using length and girth to estimate the weight of a fish, and these have been evolving since the days (at least the 1940s) when a formula for fish with a cylindrical body shape was applied to all fish, although this didn't take into account especially elongate or round species.

The following formulas, published by the Minnesota Department of Natural Resources, take body shape into account:

Walleye *Length³ ÷ 3,500 (length × length ×*
         length ÷ 3,500)
Pike   *Length³ ÷ 2,700*
Sunfish *Length³ ÷ 1,200*
Bass   *Length² × Girth ÷ 1,200*
Trout   *Length × Girth² ÷ 800*

The formula for pike is not accurate when applied to large, heavy muskies (it makes them far too large), although some people use *Length × Girth² ÷ 800* for these fish (which is also above the actual weight by a small amount). Very heavy specimens of any species are often tough to fit into these formulas because their bellies tend to become distended, and fish of equal lengths can have much different thickness (just as every human being that is 68 inches tall doesn't weigh the same, even though there are average weight charts).

Formulas and tables are based on averages using standard-size fish up to large-size fish, but seldom extraordinary sizes of fish (because there are so few extraordinary fish). So these formulas are guidelines, not absolutes. The difference between an estimated 39-pound fish and an estimated 42-pound fish is really minor in the overall scheme of things unless a record is involved, which likely means killing the fish anyway; and the main purpose is releasing the fish unharmed.

Likewise, in saltwater, determining the weight of virtually all released billfish species is mostly an estimate. The same is now true for tarpon, since almost no tarpon are actually killed and weighed and many people fishing for them have no real experience in weighing tarpon of any size, let alone of all sizes. Eyeball estimates are usually well off the mark, generally being higher than the fish actually weighs (as determined by actual weights when tagged fish are recovered and actual weights are compared with estimated weights).

The old formula of *Length × Girth² ÷ 800* is still used by some people for billfish and other saltwater species, but this is as much off the mark as it is close; some people divide by 900 for species that are very long and thin-bodied, like wahoo, king mackerel, and barracuda. Some private parties and some research groups or fisheries agencies have developed a formula or created preliminary tables that convert length to weight, but these have been calculated for fish in specific oceans and regions of oceans (you can't compare Pacific sailfish to Atlantic sailfish, for example, since the former are much larger on average than the latter).

With catch-and-release fishing being more prominent, it's likely that existing tables and formulas will be refined and that ways to estimate weights for other species will be developed. Spreading your hands apart doesn't suffice any longer.

See: Records; Tagging.

MENDING

Mending is an important and basic line-manipulating skill used by fly anglers to effect a proper presentation and/or drift of a fly without drag. Drag is the influence of current on a fly that inhibits it from drifting in a free manner as if it were a natural insect. A drag-free drift is highly desirable and often necessary for all, or as much as possible, of the presentation, and certainly for the period when the fly is in the likely zone where a fish lies. In some situations a drag-free drift is possible for only a few seconds before the current grabs the line and pulls the fly downstream too fast.

To avoid or minimize drag on the fly, an angler must maneuver the line in such a manner that the fly floats unhindered with the current. It is usually the effect of converging current, or of currents that operate at different speeds, that causes the fly line to flow either faster or slower than the fly and pull on it, either dragging it across the surface if it's a dry fly, or up- or across-current if it's a nymph.

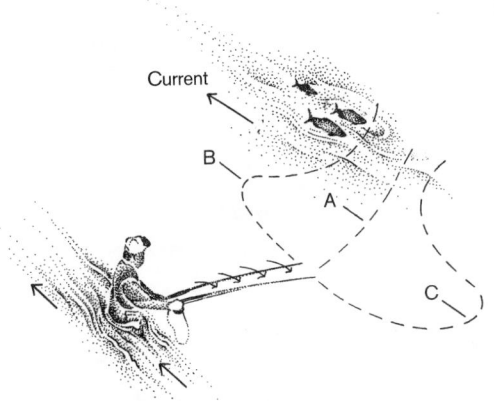

When a fly line is laid across current (A), a strong mid-stream flow will catch the belly (B) and place unnatural drag on the fly. This can be countered by mending line that is already on the water. After making the initial cast (A), use your rod to pick up the belly of the line and drop it upstream (C), which permits a drag-free float of the fly that lasts long enough for it to drift naturally to the fish.

There are various methods of mending the fly line to prevent or postpone the current from dragging the fly. This mending is accomplished by throwing additional slack into the line; most often slack is thrown into the belly of the line when the line is already on the surface, but it may also be accomplished in other ways and in a variety of situations, some of which are briefly described here.

On-water mends. A standard mend on a cast made quartering upstream is performed the moment the fly and line are on the water; the angler lifts the rod quickly and flips the belly and forward part of the line upstream. This is best done with some slack line hanging between the reel and the stripping guide on the rod. If the cast is long, the forward part of the line may be mended several times to lengthen the drift. This tactic can also be employed to lift the line a few inches above the surface to get it over an object, like a rock, in the current. The objective is not to move the fly from the path of its normal drift, but to extend the length of a natural drift.

A series of roll casts or tip rolls of the slack line is also another way of mending a small amount of line, and is especially useful when you're already well into a drift and need to extend it but cannot with an upstream mend, which would in itself pull on the floating fly. Stripping some slack off the reel and feeding it out will also give the drift a little more mileage.

A variation on this technique would be throwing a mend downstream when you're casting across slow-moving water and placing your fly in swifter current. Flipping the line downstream allows the fly to float naturally and faster and then meet up with the pace of the line.

In-air mends. Mending can also be accomplished by manipulating the fly line and leader in the air at the end of the forward cast but before the line contacts the water. This is done in several ways that throw slack into the line, resulting in the term "slack line casts."

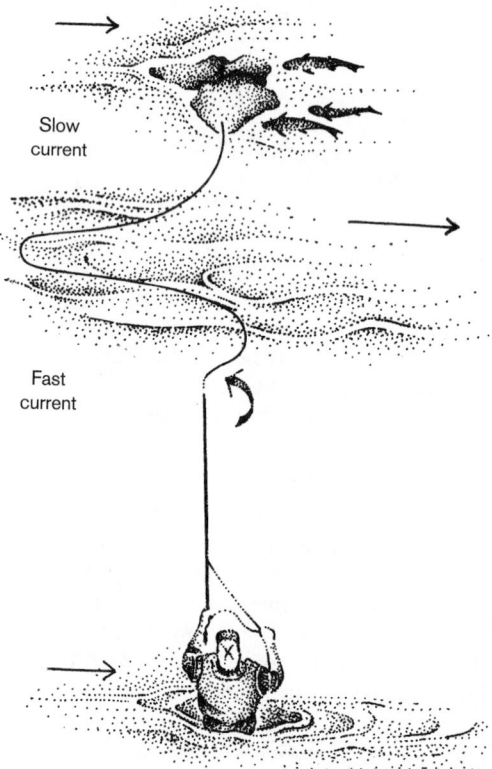

Slow current

Fast current

When making a presentation across a fast, narrow flow of water, you can avoid instantaneous drag on a fly by making an upstream curve cast. Here, as the forward cast nears completion, the angler throws an upstream in-air curve in the line, which deposits most of the belly into the fast current, allowing the fly to float for a short distance drag-free in the slower current.

One way to do this is to drop the rod tip from a vertical position to one side and then return it to the vertical position while the forward cast is in progress and before it lands. In essence, this action forms a curve in the line and is thus called a curve cast; it can be accomplished upstream or downstream.

Another version, sometimes called a reach cast, is done by reaching upstream with the rod while the line is in the air and then laying the line on the water. In a similar fashion, slightly overpowering the cast and stopping the line so that the fly stops in midair and bounces a bit backward, then letting the line fall to the surface, creates a series of curves in the line on the water. This is called an S-cast, or S-curve. In all of these maneuvers, further mending can be accomplished without creating drag by sending slack out in a tip roll, which is an abbreviated roll cast. A version of this for short drifts in quick water, or pocket water (*see*), is called a pile cast. It is accomplished by casting high above the target spot, stopping the cast abruptly, and dumping the line on the water. This action piles up the line closer to the fly and allows a short drag-free float.

MENHADEN, ATLANTIC   *Brevoortia tyrannus.*
Other names—pogy, bunker, bughead, bugfish, fatback, menhaden, mossbunker; Danish, Finnish, Norwegian, Polish, Swedish: *menhaden;* French: *menhaden tyran;* Spanish: *lacha tirana.*

A member of the herring family, the Atlantic menhaden is a hugely important commercial species; greater numbers of this fish are taken each year by commercial fishermen than of any other fish in the United States. Although it is marketed fresh, salted, canned, or smoked, the Atlantic menhaden is mainly used for the production of oil, fertilizer, and fish meal. Excessive fishing of the species has caused population declines.

Identification.   The Atlantic menhaden has a deep and compressed body, a big bony head, and a large mouth with a lower jaw that fits into a notch in the upper jaw. It also has adipose eyelids, which make it appear sleepy. It has a dark blue back, silvery sides with an occasional reddish or brassy tint, pale-yellow fins edged in black, a dark patch on the shoulder, and two or three scattered rows of smaller spots.

Size.   The Atlantic menhaden can reach a length of $1^{1}/_{2}$ feet.

Distribution.   This species occurs in the western Atlantic Ocean from Nova Scotia to the Indian River in southern Florida. In the northern regions, it is primarily known as bunker.

Habitat.   Atlantic menhaden inhabit inland tidal areas of brackish water and coastal saltwater. They migrate in and out of bays and inlets, and are found inshore in summer. Some populations move into deeper water in winter.

Life history/Behavior.   Atlantic menhaden form large and very compact schools consisting of

Atlantic Menhaden

both young and adult fish; this makes them vulnerable to commercial fishermen, some of whom use spotter planes to locate the schools and direct commercial vessels to the fish, which are then encircled.

Menhaden have distinct seasonal migrations—northward in April and May, and southward in early fall. Spawning occurs year-round, although not in the same locations at the same time. For example, because high water temperatures are detrimental to breeding, the peak spawning season off the southern coast of the U.S. is October through March. Egg estimates run in the tens of thousands to hundreds of thousands. They are free floating and hatch at sea. Once hatched, the offspring are carried into estuaries and bays, which serve as sheltered nursery areas in which young Atlantic menhaden spend their first year. The fish mature between their first and third years.

Food and feeding habits. Using long filaments on their gills, Atlantic menhaden filter zooplankton and other small plants and animals out of the water.

Angling. Although there is no angling for menhaden, they are widely used as baits for such species as mackerel, Atlantic bonito, bluefish, striped bass, and sea trout, as well as other species. When menhaden schools are located, specimens may be snagged for use as live baits, or taken with a cast net, the latter being productive at night when the fish are attracted to lights; chunks are commonly used for hook baits and for chumming.

Like all herring, live menhaden are difficult to keep alive. The water has to be kept cool and well aerated, and a circular well is a must. Live fish can be hooked through the lips or the back behind the dorsal fin, and they are drifted or slowly trolled, usually without weights. Because whole live menhaden are large, anglers must give gamefish time to swallow the fish before setting the hook.

MESOTROPHIC
Moderate nutrient levels. A mesotrophic lake is one that is intermediate between oligotrophic *(see)* and eutrophic *(see)* lakes, with moderate levels of nutrients and capable of supporting both coldwater and warmwater fisheries in different portions. Lake aging goes through a process from oligotrophic to mesotrophic to eutrophic.

METAL LURE
In a strict sense, a metal lure is any artificial lure that is all or mostly made of metal. Today this is primarily spoons, spinners, and jigs. Lures are usually categorized by their type or function, rather than the material that they are made from, since there is so much overlap in the use of materials. Thus, it is uncommon today to refer to a lure as a metal lure. However, in an antiquated sense, a metal lure is an old and collectible item that was made of metal or that had mainly metal components, created in the early days of artificial lure making. Perhaps the oldest ancestor of today's plugs, for example, is the Phantom Minnow, an English lure with metal head, metal fins, three treble hooks, and a silk body, first crafted around 1800; this lure existed at a time before metal spoons or spinners and before wooden plugs.
See: Antique Fishing Tackle.

MEXICO
Mexico has been a great draw for anglers, especially those from the United States, for many years and continues to provide surprises, with new hotspots being discovered periodically in inland bass fishing, offshore billfishing, and flats fishing. A large country, Mexico is blessed with an exceptional amount of coastline on the Pacific, the Gulf of Mexico, and the Caribbean, but it lacks significant water reserves inland.

Much of Mexico's saltwater fishery is explored through established sportfishing operations, and because some areas of both coasts have minimal access, they have not been thoroughly investigated for angling potential. Opportunities for self-guided exploration exist for the adventurous angler, although this is most reasonable for those fluent in Spanish. The farther one gets from the more popular tourist sites, the less likely it is that the locals will speak English. The language difference is one factor that probably keeps most northern-based anglers from fishing on their own in Mexico, particularly in the most southerly areas of the mainland. In addition, certain areas of the country present security concerns for self-guided travelers.

Nevertheless, hot bass fishing lakes; striped marlin off Cabo San Lucas; Pacific sailfish off the western mainland; Atlantic sailfish at Cancún and Cozumel; and tarpon, permit, and bonefish along many areas of the Yucatán coast present world-class opportunities.

Freshwater
Mexico does not have the abundant inland angling opportunity or diversity that characterizes most U.S. states and all Canadian provinces. Its freshwater fishing pales in comparison to its saltwater opportunities, and yet many people equate Mexico with fantastic largemouth bass angling.

To understand freshwater fishing in Mexico, it helps to know a few things about the country as a

M

whole. Mexico is a large nation with varied terrain and climates. Although about half of Mexico is a dry plains plateau, and a continuation of the plains of the southwestern U.S., it has high peaks, canyons, mountain ranges, valleys, and coastal plains. It has relatively few sizable rivers and almost no large natural lakes. Most of the rivers aren't navigable, and many are in the valleys and canyons of mountain regions. The longest river is the Rio Grande, or Rio Bravo del Norte, which runs along the Mexican–U.S. border. It has been identified as one of the most polluted waterways in North America.

Although Mexico is generally arid and warm, its climate varies with altitude and has some bearing on Mexico's fisheries, particularly in the winter in those locations subject to high-mountain (that is, coldwater) runoff. Some areas have very low average annual rainfall and are subject to drought, which may continue for years, whereas others are subject to peaks and troughs in temperature and precipitation.

The largest lakes are artificial, having been formed by dams that were primarily constructed by federal engineers for irrigation, hydroelectric power generation, or both. There are perhaps 50 of these waters in various parts of the country; many of them are in the northwestern region in the foothills of the Sierre Madre Occidentals. Some were constructed as long ago as the 1930s, although the majority were formed in the last four decades. Some were constructed as recently as the mid-1990s, and undoubtedly others are likely to be created in the future, although the rate of large, new-water creation slowed to a near halt in the late 1990s. These lakes are usually full of brush and trees; some are literally flooded forests, and catching large, strong fish from them can be a challenge.

Sportfishing in freshwater is not a tradition for Mexicans. Most resident fishing efforts in this country have long been directed at subsistence or commercial activities, using handlines or nets. Few Mexicans have had the means to obtain modern angling or boating equipment, and even today only a small percentage of residents fish for sport in freshwater.

As mentioned, there is considerable interest in freshwater fishing in Mexico among nonresident anglers, mainly from the U.S.; approximately half of these come from Texas, Oklahoma, and Louisiana, and their interest focuses almost entirely on black bass, *negra lobina.*

Rainbow trout are said to be indigenous to Mexico, presumably in the higher and cooler western mountain region, from the northern part of the state of Durango toward the southern part of the state of Sonora, and a species of golden trout was identified in a small area there. Still, there is no identifiable fishery for trout.

Catfish are present in many Mexican lakes, and some species are likely indigenous. Although federal authorities have stocked channel cats in some waters, neither angling nor commercial fishing for this species has caught on. Lake Comedero has many catfish, as does Lake Oviachic.

Most of the predominant fish in Mexican lakes are the result of planned or unplanned introductions. Mojarra and largemouth bass were among the first species introduced, dating back to at least the 1930s. Mojarra, common to Central America, were replaced in the early 1980s by tilapia, which were introduced by the federal government. The high-protein tilapia have no sport value, but the planting has been very successful, providing a thriving commercial fishery. They have also become a food source for bass, but this is an unintentional benefit of their introduction. Tilapia are plentiful in many lakes; on hot days in some waters, it is possible to see thousands of these fish milling about near the surface, feeding on minute organisms. Tilapia are prolific, and in some Mexican lakes they spawn three times in a season. Nevertheless, they have been overfished by netters in certain lakes, and, although not eliminated, reduced to small sizes.

Crappie are present in Lake Novillo in the state of Sonora. Bluegills are present here, too, as well as in other waters. Both species are believed to have been introduced by Americans with homes on the lake, as a means of providing food fish for introduced largemouth bass. Some lakes have gar and some carp, but many lack rough fish species entirely. Most have threadfin shad and gizzard shad, although in northern waters the threadfin shad are subject to die-off during extreme cold weather.

There are no known peacock bass in Mexican waters, although rumors suggest that they were placed in Lake Baccarac in the mid-1980s; none are known to have been caught. Peacock bass purportedly would not attain large sizes in Mexico and would succumb to extreme cold swings, although the southernmost region of the country, in and around the state of Chiapas, might be conducive to this species.

In some lakes in the southernmost regions of Mexico the fisheries are unknown, unpublicized, and undeveloped. These areas have long been politically unsettled; operators interested in exploring the region and possibly setting up fishing camps have been dissuaded for safety and security reasons. This is true in some other areas as well.

Mexico does have some natural lakes, called *lagunas,* but few hold largemouth bass or have notable fisheries for this species. Bass anglers have focused their attention over the years on impoundments (known as *presas,* or reservoirs), primarily on newer ones as they first became accessible, and, in a few instances, on older ones. Larger impoundments and lakes with bass include, but are not limited to, Lakes Angostura, Novillo, Macuzari, and Oviachic in Sonora; Dominguez, Hidalgo, Baccarac, Mateos, Ocaroni, El Salto, Comedero, and Huites in Sinaloa; Aguamilpa in Nayarit; Palmito and Tortuga in Durango; Chapala in Jalisco; Pátzcuaro in Michoacán; Malpaso and Angostura in Chiapas;

Miguel Alemán in Oaxaca; several small lakes near the city of Tampico; Guerrero, Española, and Azúcar in Tamaulipas; Cochillo in Nuevo León; Don Martín in Coahuila; Boquilla and Granacia in Chihuahua; and Falcon and Amistad on the Texas border.

The federal government constructed most of the larger man-made lakes, but some are cooperative ventures with power companies. The construction of western reservoirs in the foothills of the Sierra Madre has been extremely successful. These lakes were intended to provide water for irrigating fertile lands among the coastal plains and valleys along the Sea of Cortez and to help grow food products to feed Mexicans. These goals were achieved and resulted in the exportation of food to other countries, especially the U.S. These efforts have produced hard-currency benefits.

Largemouth bass have been stocked throughout Mexico at least since the 1930s, and they have been transplanted and introduced widely. How the bass got into some Mexican waters is open to speculation. Americans were evidently involved, often deliberately introducing bass both with and without the blessing or knowledge of Mexican authorities.

Northern-strain largemouths were the only known bass in Mexican waters until the late 1970s. At that time, the results of stocking pure Florida-strain largemouths in American waters that did not previously have this species, especially in California and Texas, were becoming evident; Mexico seemed like another suitable location for these fish.

Around 1977, fishing camp operators arranged for the state of Florida to donate 30,000 pure-strain Florida bass fingerlings to the Mexican state of Tamaulipas. These were placed in rearing ponds there, grown to 8 or 9 inches, and then introduced into Lake Guerrero. Until those fish matured, huge largemouth bass were not known in Mexico.

Since then other lakes, in the states of Sinaloa and Sonora, have been stocked with Florida bass, many with the assistance of Mexican officials. Naturally, some of the fish that have been moved from one place to another are second- or third-generation Florida bass, and in some cases have crossed with northern-strain largemouth. Baccarac, Comedero, El Salto, Huites, and Oviachic are some of the impoundments that hold these fish, in addition to Guerrero.

Anglers have caught very big largemouth bass (from pure Florida stockings), including a confirmed 17-pounder from Guerrero. Rumors suggest that bigger fish have been caught, including some 18-pounders from Guerrero and a 19-pounder from Baccarac, but these reports are clouded with suspicion of netting. Two 18-pounders were reportedly caught by commercial fishermen in Comedero in 1997, and it is likely that bass of this size or larger have been caught by netters in Mexico. Because some Florida bass have grown to more than 10

pounds in just $3^{1}/_{2}$ years, some people speculate that newly created western Mexico lakes, which have ample forage and which are not netted, have the potential to grow a bass exceeding the long-standing 22-pound, 4-ounce world record.

Veterans of the Mexican bass fishing scene have watched a succession of boom-and-bust lakes develop. The boom is usually due to the typical pattern that envelops new lakes with good forage and bass populations—quick-growing bass that are aggressive and uneducated. Their feistiness is due in part to a fat torso. This results in high numbers of fish caught per boat or angler on a daily basis. The mantra of camp owners and operators in Mexico has historically involved numbers; 100 bass (or more) a day is the calling card for legions of anglers who could not experience such fishing on their home waters in their wildest dreams.

The bust has followed within a few years (sometimes as few as two or three), when either the average size or the number of fish has dropped. These changes are often blamed on local netting, which has certainly contributed to the problem (as has spearfishing). Even lakes officially designated as sportfishing-only lakes have lost that status in just a few years, and netting or poaching crept into the picture.

Netting, both illegal and legal, is practiced sooner or later on virtually all Mexican lakes. Tilapia are primarily pursued, but other species are sought after too, including the abundant largemouth bass, even though Mexico's congress passed a law in 1994 that protects these fish and prohibits them from being the target of commercial fishing. The law has not been well enforced, however. In a country with many poor people, and where it is difficult to convey to local residents and to public officials the value of fishing-oriented tourism, netting is virtually inevitable.

Netting is not the only problem. For various reasons, many of the once awesome and highly touted hotspots become mediocre or average fisheries, or fisheries with ample bass but few medium or large specimens, or fisheries that have ample but hard-to-catch bass. As new lakes age, they mature, creating an ecologically based retreat from their former productivity. Furthermore, many Mexican impoundments, especially mountain lakes, are subject to extreme fluctuations, which adversely impact a maturing population of bass. The bass may go deeper, and the population may become oriented to the security of deep water, which makes them more difficult to locate and catch.

Two of the biggest problems with Mexican lakes are drought and fluctuating water levels. Lowland impoundments are prone to drought and may be very low for many years. Some went dry and had to be restocked when they were refilled.

The water level in mountain lakes can vary dramatically. In late 1997, for example, Lake Huites, then touted as one of the greatest bass lakes in

If there are fish in the depths of Russia's Lake Baikal, it will take a lot of line to reach them; Baikal is 5,371 feet deep and has seven times the volume of Lake Superior.

M

North America, was dropped at a rate of $2\frac{1}{2}$ to 3 feet a day for weeks in anticipation of predicted precipitation from El Niño. The lake was down about 120 feet from full pool and still falling when, just after Christmas, a freak heavy snow fell in the upriver mountains, quickly melted, and caused the reservoir to rise 47 feet over $2\frac{1}{2}$ days. Neither of these circumstances was beneficial to the fishery, even though the lake was new and chock-full of largemouths.

Unstable water levels, which are generally unusual in closely maintained American waters and which cause havoc with bass, are a normal occurrence on most Mexican lakes. In irrigation lakes, the water level normally drops; unless the water falls too fast, there is no need for concern. Rising water, however, can cause bass to withdraw for long periods; it may take three to four weeks—preferably with the water high and stable—before they become active again.

Ironically, although many people think of Mexican bass lakes as conducive to shallow fishing and surface action, this is often not the case, except in new lakes that are full, or when a lake has experienced stable conditions for a long period. In mountain lakes, bass have a tendency to stay deep, perhaps due to the often falling water, and, of course, they become harder to catch when they stay deep.

The age of Mexican bass lakes varies, and some of the older lakes, including Guerrero, Baccarac, Oviachic, Palmito, and Novillo, have windows of opportunity, primarily around spawning time, during which some anglers will catch enough fish to be happy. When conditions on these lakes are ideal, the angling will be good. Unfortunately, it may not be good every year at the same time, or it may be good for just a short period, or it may be downright poor for several years and then revive.

Before and during the spawn are the preferred times for largemouth bass fishing in Mexico. Spawning season varies with altitude and location. Bass in mountain lakes normally spawn between mid-March and early April; those in the flatland lakes spawn in January. Some lakes that are just $1\frac{1}{2}$ hours apart have spawning seasons that are months apart. October and November can be good months as well, and sometimes provide the best fishing, although this may vary from year to year due to other conditions.

The lack of summertime anglers is one element that skews the fishing results in Mexico. In fact, January through March is preferred by many visiting anglers because of poor weather and fishing conditions at home, because it is usually warm in Mexico at this time, and because the fish are usually shallower and more accessible. Many camps are closed between May and September.

The catch-and-release ethic has produced a dramatic change in Mexico's bass fishery, one that came about only in the early to mid-1980s.

Previously, visiting anglers commonly kept excessive numbers of bass of all sizes, especially in the lakes that could be reached by car. Guerrero, one of the most accessible lakes, was particularly vulnerable, and thousands of pounds of largemouth bass were hauled away from Guerrero in freezers in the back of pickup trucks by people who thought there was no end to this resource and for whom no limits had been established (and some of these anglers complain today about Mexicans netting fish!). This lake, and other drive-in lakes in northern Mexico, were seriously hurt by such actions. Voluntary and involuntary limits, a changing ethic, and the realization of the damage incurred on some lakes eventually resulted in changed attitudes and practices. For many mountain lakes, where access is difficult, their isolated location made them secure from excessive sportfishing, although not from legal or illegal netting. There, the greater problem may be that eventually the fish will become smarter after being caught.

It is hard to be definitive about the prospects for Mexico's bass lakes, as they are continually changing. New lakes offer many more fish than some anglers could get at home, bass that are much easier to catch, and a better climate. So January through March will probably always be peak periods for most anglers. When people have to work hard to catch only 15 or 20 bass a day, however, the yield does not warrant the expense. In fact, when bass fishing productivity drops below a standard of about 40 quality fish per boat per day, and the chances of landing an 8- to 10-pound bass diminish, the better camp operators look for greener pastures, even though this type of action would be a terrific day on almost any bass lake elsewhere in North America.

A person visiting Mexico on a self-guided vacation, with plenty of time to spare and bringing a boat to fish from (likely a cartop boat), can probably find acceptable bass fishing in many lakes that do not have established fishing camps. The very mention of netting in a lake is enough to keep foreign visitors away, but that may not necessarily imply that the fishing is awful (although it probably means that large specimens are unlikely). Even if the lakes are netted, there's a good chance they will have plenty of smaller bass (2 to 5 pounds) that are unsophisticated and very susceptible to angling, as virtually no one will have been tossing lures at them. Moreover, at least one lake that is netted for tilapia—El Salto—was producing large bass as recently as 1999, in part because the lone camp operator there instituted a successful clothes-for-bass program designed to encourage netters to release bass.

Keep in mind that bass exist in many Mexican waters that are not among the more well known or currently popular sites. A traveler with time and a boat can cheaply sample many waters that don't draw tourists or are not prominent on road maps.

Lake Guerrero. Lake Vicente Guerrero is in the state of Tamaulipas, about 175 miles south of Brownsville, Texas, and about 20 miles from Victoria. It covers about 100,000 acres when completely full, is loaded with brush and timber, and has many flats, islands, and creekbeds.

Lake Guerrero's history is typical of many Mexican bass lakes. It was formed in 1971 and was not supposed to be fishable for several years, but five incoming rivers filled the new reservoir quickly, flooding farmlands, ranches, roads, and the village of Padilla. Half-submerged at full pool, Padilla's church was a dramatic and frequently used photographic backdrop for anglers posing with their catch.

Throughout the 1970s, Guerrero provided what some considered the greatest bass fishing in the world. If you could make even a feeble cast, with virtually any lure you could catch a bass. The early game was to fish for many small bass and lots of 4- to 7-pounders. In the clear shallows, anglers could see a fish coming to strike a lure from 8 or 10 yards away. At times, three to five bass, each weighing perhaps 5 pounds, would follow a hooked brethren to the boat. It was, in essence, the ultimate bass fishing experience, one that would be repeated on many other newly created reservoirs in the decades that followed.

These experiences were nearly the ultimate in freshwater fishing excess. For at least a decade, with the exception of a ban on live bait, this was a no-holds-barred catch-and-keep fishery. The larger bass disappeared first, although hordes of small fish remained. Then the population of small bass dwindled, the anglers dwindled, and the camps closed. A prolonged drought drew Guerrero down drastically. Some camps, once at water's edge, were left a mile or more from the shrunken lake, and Guerrero was declared finished. Nearly a decade later, big bass began to show up, thanks to the planting of Florida-strain fish. The lake experienced a rebirth, and the anglers returned.

The big bass were not the 7-pounders of years past, but fish weighing more than 10 pounds. Fifteen- and 17-pound specimens, and reputedly some larger, were caught in the early 1990s. Guerrero was a gold mine once again, this time for lunkers. But this fishery also peaked, perhaps because the original pure-strain fish passed on, but the lake still produces 10-pound fish today.

One reason for Guerrero's resurgence in the mid- to latter 1990s was a prolonged drought in Tamaulipas, which kept the lake 25 feet below normal and roughly half full for about a decade. These conditions produced a stability that is unusual for Mexican impoundments. Experienced anglers have had good success in Guerrero in recent times, some fishing methodically in deep water; those with lesser skills have experienced varied results. Being present when the fish are active, which is often hit-or-miss, can provide a lot of action. February and

A 10-pound largemouth is landed at Lake Guerrero, long known for its bass fishing.

March, when the fish usually spawn, are favorite times for many Guerrero veterans. Some of the best big bass fishing has occurred in midsummer at night, although large fish are caught in all seasons.

Due to a shifting clientele, the availability of replica taxidermy mounts, new government harvesting restrictions, and a generally improved conservation ethic, there is a much better attitude toward releasing big bass. These days, 3- and 4-pound fish are plentiful, and some monsters do inhabit these waters. How Guerrero's bass fishery will develop in the future, however, is anybody's guess.

Lake Huites. Lake Huites stands in sharp contrast to Lake Guerrero for many reasons. It was not impounded until 1994; it was first stocked with pure-strain Florida largemouth bass; it is a mountain lake situated in the remote Sinaloan foothills; and for anglers it was a catch-and-release fishery when it first opened to fishing in 1997. Like Guerrero and other Mexican lakes, however, especially highland impoundments, it is subject to extreme fluctuations, and netting started soon after the first spinnerbaits hit the water.

All 240 people from the village of Techobampo, as well as those from two other villages, were relocated in 1994 when a dam on the Río Fuerte was completed and a new impoundment—built for irrigation and hydroelectric power—started to fill. That dam also backed up the Chinipas River, a serpentine watercourse that flows into Huites from rugged peaks near renowned Copper Canyon. Barranca del Cobre, Mexico's larger and deeper version of the Grand Canyon, is a nearby scenic wonder with a maximum depth of more than 6,000 feet.

Southwest of canyon country, on the outskirts of the Sierra Madre Occidentals, Lake Huites is 22 miles long and covers 30,000 acres when full. It is so remote that most of the first guides employed at fishing camps there had never seen a boat or outboard motor before, and the nearby villages got

Lake Huites in the western mountains is one of Mexico's newest bass fisheries.

electricity only once the dam was built. The drive from Los Mochis, 18 miles of which follows a winding, rutted, neck-wrenching burro trail, takes more than three hours.

It is extremely still in the narrow sections of the lake, especially on the Chinipas. Boats travel through chasms so steep that the sun doesn't penetrate until midmorning. Overhead, huge boulders hang on precipices hundreds of feet up, and every osprey that flies by has a fish in its talons. Below, the tips of 40-foot-tall trees barely reach the water's surface, and the bass might pull your fishing rod into the water if you don't hold onto it.

Adventurous American anglers, showing the tenacity of burros themselves, flocked to Huites for stupendous largemouth bass fishing action. Florida-strain largemouths, planted in 1994, grew quickly, producing football-shaped bass with small heads and a large girth, and a hot chili pepper disposition.

Landing these dynamos is not guaranteed and is always a challenge. Flooded *au natural,* Huites is loaded with trees and brush, and the bass linger along the shorelines amidst this protective cover. When the fish strike a lure, they dive for the nearest wood, often a multilimbed cactus, and either break the line or achieve freedom when an exasperated angler is unable to extract them.

There were so many bass in the early days at Lake Huites, losing half the fish that struck your line was not a problem. In fact, the bass often congregated in spots, usually off points near deep water.

These areas produced so much action, anglers didn't have to search all over this expansive water to find them, a rarity in most U.S. bass lakes. When unusual cold spells hit Huites, or when extreme changes in water level occur, however, the fishing can be off for a while.

The effects of tilapia (and possibly bass) netting and of angling pressure, as well as the ultimate size potential of Huites' bass, remain to be seen. The peak for this fishery, at least in terms of giant bass, could be yet to come.

Other lakes. Although Huites has been the latest darling of the avid visiting bass angler, other lakes in the northwest still have a following. All of them have never-ending brush and tree cover, remote locations, waters that are quiet and virtually empty when compared with lakes in the U.S., and they are surrounded by beautiful mountain scenery. They are characteristically long and relatively narrow, with steep shorelines that are often protected from wind. Many are usually clear, at least by most standards, and are replete with rocky points, coves, and many bassy nooks. When the water level changes, these lakes present a whole new look.

Lake Comedero, also known as Lake José Lopez Portillo, is a 30,000-acre impoundment that was stocked with northern-strain largemouths in 1985. Located about 45 miles southeast of Culiacan, this was a tremendous fishery in the early 1990s, and still has a following. In recent times it has not produced massive catches, but it does have big fish potential. Sportfishermen have caught bass to 15 pounds here, and in 1997 local commercial fishermen allegedly caught two 18-pounders.

Lake El Salto was another hot lake shortly after it opened in 1990. This 24,000-acre timber-studded lake was stocked with 200,000 Florida-strain bass in 1985 when it was filling. About 1 1/2 hours from Mazatlan in the Sinaloan mountains, El Salto quickly forged a reputation for 8- to 10-pound bass and plentiful small fish but no midsize specimens. Soon, the large fish appeared to be gone, leaving only small bass. El Salto had a large number of netters, and after just a few years it was written off by anglers.

However, in 1998, a deluxe lodge was built by a prominent outfitter, and visiting anglers once again started catching a lot of bass in the 10-pound class, with some up to 14 pounds. In December 1998, El Salto produced a lake-record 14-pound, 3-ounce bass, and a newly implemented conservation program to discourage netting of bass makes some think the lake could be ripe for a 20-pounder. In 1994, a 16-pound, 3-ounce bass was found dead in El Salto; it had choked to death with a tilapia wedged in its throat. As of the spring of 1999, El Salto's reputation as a big-bass lake had been reclaimed.

Lake Baccarac near Los Mochis opened to fishing in 1984. A 35,000-acre impoundment on the Sinaloa River, and also known as Lake Bacubirito, it has produced some huge Florida-strain large-mouths, including a reputed 19-pounder around 1994, and was drawing anglers throughout the late 1990s.

Lake Oviachic, better known as Lake Obregon, is both an old lake and a new lake. This 30,000-acre impoundment on the Yaqui River was originally impounded in the 1950s. The lake went dry in the early 1980s, was refilled and restocked with northern-strain largemouth bass in 1990, and took on a new life. Although it hasn't produced trophy-caliber bass, the 27-mile-long lake is known for an abundance of action. Muddy water from upstream releases (out of Lake Novillo), however, can turn the fish off.

Lake Novillo, a 25-mile-long impoundment below the convergence of the Moctezuma and Yaqui Rivers, has drawn people since the early 1970s, but it has not been a prime spot for visiting anglers in recent times.

All of these lakes are subject to changes, some of which happen almost overnight. Due to their remoteness, it is difficult to maintain current information on their status. Some turn on briefly when rainfall or clearing water occurs. Some turn off quickly due to other factors. As mentioned in the introductory section, when the fish are not actively hitting in the shallows of these mountain lakes, they must be pursued deep.

Many claims are made about the quality of the fishing in Mexican waters; it takes some legwork to procure reliable information from those who have fished them recently, or from local operators and their representatives. Almost without exception, each of the lakes mentioned has at one time been called the greatest bass fishing lake in Mexico. Be advised that superlatives are thrown about easily here.

Large spinnerbaits and large plastic worms are the standard fare for Mexican bass, incidentally. It may be necessary to use $1/2$-ounce sinkers with the worms. Big jigs, jigging spoons, and surface plugs get some play, too. Anglers should be prepared to shuttle from their accommodations to the lake, especially in the mountainous west and when the water levels are low. You may have to take a camp van or bus to reach the water.

Saltwater

Baja. Situated immediately south of the California border, the Mexican states of Baja California Norte and Baja California Sur constitute a great expanse of angling territory. This large area offers remarkably limited opportunities for freshwater anglers; a few trout in the mountains near Ensenada are one exception. Understandably, most of Mexico's angling action occurs in saltwater.

Unlike other parts of Mexico, Baja California is separated from the mainland by a large gulf called the Sea of Cortez. With this inland sea to the east, and the Pacific Ocean to the west, the 760-mile-long Baja Peninsula is virtually surrounded by water, and the Baja presents tremendous fishing opportunities along both coasts. Boaters experience the best action, but excellent shore fishing opportunities exist on the Pacific side as well.

The more-developed towns have fishing fleets and cater to traveling anglers, especially those interested in blue-water species. Mexico offers significant opportunity to the adventurous angler with plenty of leisure hours; learning where to fish for the most rewarding and desirable species takes time, much of it spent traveling unpaved roads. If this potential appeals to you, learn Spanish, rent a van, load it with fishing tackle, get a map of the Baja, and start fishing when the road meets the water.

To cover in detail every fishing nook and cranny of this close to 2,000-mile coastline would require volumes. So, the following is only a review and offers a summary of the major species available, and the places and seasons to pursue them. We'll begin in the north, on the Pacific side of the Baja, and work south to Cabo San Lucas, then north along the Sea of Cortez to the fishing village of San Felipe. Many of the fish landed around the Baja are nomadic, and the water conditions may vary little from place to place. As a result, the species and techniques noted bear repeating.

Tijuana to San Quintín. Along the Pacific Ocean near the California border from Tijuana to Ensenada, surf anglers can expect to catch barred perch, corbina, and various croaker by using natural bait, small jigs, and soft-bodied grubs. Farther from shore, on local reefs, are rockfish and lingcod, as well as kelp bass, barracuda, and bonito.

Offshore, pelagic blue-water species include albacore, striped marlin, bluefin tuna, yellowfin tuna, and yellowtail. The best action for these larger open-water fish occurs during summer and fall, and at other times in years when the warm water lingers.

Many of the same gamefish inhabit the waters farther south, but here they are generally more abundant. There is less pressure on these species, as access is difficult for surf anglers and only larger fishing boats are able to cruise the longer distances required to ply these waters.

San Quintín to Guerrero Negro. From San Quintín south to Guerrero Negro, the offshore fishing is excellent, offering good numbers of bluefin, yellowfin, and bigeye tuna. These species are caught during summer and fall. Dorado and yellowtail are common too. Because of the distance from good ports, few private sport boats ply these waters. Anglers fishing from long-range boats that depart from San Diego dominate this fishery.

For shore-based anglers who want to work the surf zones of this region, the only access to beaches is via unpaved dirt roads, mandating the use of a four-wheel-drive vehicle. But anglers who brave the tough road conditions will find hard-fighting

M

gamefish, among them white seabass and corvina, and excellent surf fishing for barred perch and corbina.

Anglers who travel out to the beaches must be completely self-sufficient, bringing all the necessary camping items, food, water, fuel, and fresh or frozen bait. Artificial lures such as metal jigs and soft-bodied jigs work well for many species, but bait is necessary to catch big white seabass consistently. Squid is especially favored because it is tough, relatively inexpensive, stays on the hook, keeps well on ice, and attracts all of the aforementioned species.

Guerrero Negro to Magdalena Bay (Mag Bay). Not far offshore in the waters off Guerrero Negro are numerous pinnacles and reefs, plus a few islands, that provide food and cover for hungry gamefish. Here, anglers fishing from long-range boats can expect some tuna, as well as dorado, yellowtail, white seabass, and black seabass. Close to shore in nearby estuaries are cabrilla, grouper, and some snook. In the surf line, croaker, corbina, corvina, and white seabass will take baits and lures.

Farther south at Mag Bay are several offshore banks that attract schools of gamefish. Some of the more well known ones are Uncle Sam, Thetis, and Potato Banks, and they provide excellent tuna and wahoo action. In the fall, at times, large numbers of striped marlin and big sailfish can be seen pounding schools of bait, providing excellent nonstop action.

Inside Mag Bay is a huge network of channels lined with mangroves. The best access here is by small boat. One can launch at the small town of San Carlos and head out to these channels, which hold a large variety of fish. Snook, cabrilla, grouper, corvina, halibut, Sierra mackerel, and pargo will eagerly grab lures and baits.

Magdalena Bay (Mag Bay) to Cabo San Lucas. Offshore anglers who head south of Mag Bay will still catch marlin, dorado, and yellowfin tuna, but not always in the same quantities as when fishing over the productive banks. Shore-bound anglers will find it tough to access the surf, because only a few unpaved roads head out to the Pacific Coast. Those who make it to the beaches will find the standard fare: croaker, corbina, corvina, surfperch, cabrilla near rocks, and white seabass.

North of Cabo San Lucas, offshore anglers will pass over the Goldengate Banks, which produces good action for marlin, dorado, yellowfin tuna, black seabass, grouper, and pargo. South of here by 20 miles or so, anglers will pass over the Jaime Banks just before reaching Cabo. Here, striped marlin fishing in winter and early spring can be fabulous.

The southernmost tip of the Baja, known as Cabo San Lucas, is world famous for billfish. Large numbers of striped marlin invade the waters near Cabo from about the first of the year into early spring. At that time, nearby Jaime and Goldengate Banks host large numbers of striped marlin in the 90- to 150-pound range.

Here, marlin feed on extensive schools of mackerel that forage near the banks. Striped marlin are receptive to trolled marlin lures and are especially fond of live bait. Live mackerel are the most common baitfish, but small green jacks, locally called *caballito,* are key menu items. Large yellowfin tuna, some exceeding 200 pounds, also cruise these banks at this time of year. A handful of anglers out of Cabo target big tuna and are rewarded with good numbers of 200- to 275-pound yellowfins.

As the season progresses into summer, fishing for the larger blue and black marlin improves, and peaks in the fall, when major tournaments, such as the renowned Bisbee and Gold Cup, are held. The larger marlin are hooked on trolled jigs and large live baits such as skipjack, small dorado, and football-size yellowfin tuna. Although marlin are the main target in this area, wahoo, dorado, roosterfish, and school yellowfin fishing are especially good inshore.

Northeast of Cabo San Lucas, toward the Sea of Cortez, is the town of San José del Cabo. This former small fishing town has grown rapidly, with new hotels and golf courses springing up along the landscape. The fishing is particularly good here, and anglers work the nearby Gordo Banks for all the important billfish, and also enjoying some good reef fishing for grouper and pargo. The spring and summer months see good numbers of wahoo grabbing trolled lures and baits on the Gordo Banks. Large cruisers from Cabo San Lucas will fish this area, as will numerous 20- to 25-foot local center-console *pangas.*

East Cape to La Paz. The area known as the East Cape covers roughly the waters northeast of Cabo San Lucas, from Punta Frailles to the southern end of Cerralvo Island near La Paz. This is a popular area for anglers because of consistently great fishing. Several fishing resorts thrive here, offering well-equipped fishing fleets comprised of both cruisers and *pangas.*

This region is a great producer of striped, blue, and black marlin during the spring and summer. But other blue-water residents such as swordfish, yellowfin tuna, dorado, wahoo, and sailfish will be among the catches.

Closer to shore, roosterfish, jack crevalle, and ladyfish inhabit the waters along the beaches and the edges of rock formations. At nearby reefs, leopard grouper, pargo, triggerfish, African pompano, and a few amberjack are available.

La Paz to Loreto. The waters near La Paz provide ample fishing opportunities. During the winter and early spring, large schools of yellowtail frequent the offshore reefs and islands. Large grouper and large pargo are also available here. In the offshore waters near La Paz, striped, blue, and black marlin provide action during the summer months.

As one travels farther north, to Loreto, yellowtail become a primary offshore target, along with dorado, school tuna, and sailfish. Anglers land an occasional marlin as well.

Loreto to Bahía de los ángeles. Like most areas in the Sea of Cortez, the waters from Loreto to Bahía de los ángeles provide anglers with ample opportunities to stretch their lines. The region is interspersed with numerous rock reefs and small islands. Yellowtail abound during the late winter and spring, when they grab jigs and live baits. Grouper and cabrilla inhabit the reefs along with several species of pargo.

Offshore, yellowfin tuna appear in summer, as do schools of hungry dorado. Billfish will show up as well, and the occasional striped marlin and sailfish are taken. Loreto is a favored destination not only because the fishing is excellent, but also because the town is conveniently located near a large airport, allowing anglers quick access from all of the western states.

From Loreto north toward Bahía de los ángeles and the islands in the Cortez Midriff, action focuses on the current rip lines boiling near small islands and reefs. This is great habitat for schools of baitfish, because currents around the islands concentrate plankton, which baitfish—like sardines—love. Among the baitfish are such hungry predators as bonito, Sierra mackerel, grouper, cabrilla, and hordes of yellowtail. Anglers can produce excellent action using live baits and by casting jigs to yellowtail ranging from 10 to 30 pounds.

Bahía de los ángeles to San Felipe. North of Bahía de los ángeles, the schools of yellowtail begin to thin out and anglers target cabrilla, Sierra mackerel, grouper, and other near-shore species. At the northern end of the Sea of Cortez is the small town of San Felipe, a popular site for anglers from Arizona and California, especially in winter, when temperatures here are warm and balmy.

This particular region differs from the rest of the Baja because of tremendous tidal influences. Between high and low water the tide drops 20-plus feet. Anglers here normally do not pursue the bluewater glamour fish but are content with many types of croaker, including corbina, yellowfin croaker, shortfin corvina, white seabass, and orangemouth corvina. One type of croaker once common to this area is now close to extinction. Called the *totuava,* this fish reportedly reached up to 200 pounds, but due to overfishing and changes in habitat it is now a rare, protected catch that must be released.

Farther offshore, anglers can expect good numbers of Sierra mackerel. These slim silver torpedoes range from 2 to 5 pounds and take a variety of metal jigs and small tuna feathers. A short wire leader is required when fishing for Sierra because they have a well-developed set of sharp teeth that will sever both monofilament line and careless fingers. Along with the Sierras are small bonito and skipjack.

Pacific mainland coast. The western mainland shore of Mexico is most renowned for its beaches, cruise ship landings, and such popular sun-and-fun spots as Acapulco, Mazatlán, and Puerto Vallarta. There is much more, however, including excellent angling and many miles of lightly fished or unfished waters, from the northern reaches in the Sea of Cortez south to the open waters of the Pacific. Although the fisheries along some sections of this coast have been influenced by commercial fishing activities (longlining affecting billfish and tuna, and netting affecting inshore species), some areas have rebounded due to new regulations, and the fisheries in other areas have varied due to the changing effects of warm currents, El Niño in particular.

The entire western mainland coastline has a diversity of pelagic, bottom, and inshore species, including such popular quarry as Pacific sailfish, striped marlin, Pacific blue marlin, black marlin, dolphin, yellowfin tuna, roosterfish, cubera snapper, and corvina among many others, pursued from big charter boats, little skiffs, long wooden *pangas,* or surf and shore. Moreover, the adventurous can have much of the best angling with little, if any, competition.

Sails here are caught within a few miles of shore. Blue marlin are caught a few miles farther out and typically weigh in the 150- to 300-pound range, although larger fish, including a line-class world record, have been caught. Billfish are present year-round, but the best chance of scoring is during the winter months.

Dolphin (dorado) are perhaps the foremost quarry, being swift, able jumpers and great table fare. They are especially abundant from summer through fall in the northern reaches of the Cortez, although they generally move southward as the season progresses. In the fall, smaller school fish wander into shallower water and provide light-tackle opportunities. These dolphin range from a few pounds to 40 or 50 pounds. The larger ones are usually caught in the heat of summer, and live mackerel, if available, are the preferred local bait, although trolling is done as well.

Many line-class world records for the popular roosterfish have been set in the Sea of Cortez. Cubera snapper and assorted bottom fish, including massive grouper and seabass, are abundant all along the coast in rocky locales. Overshadowed by the more glamorous species, but still possessing qualities that endear it to anglers in the know, is the corvina. These weakfish-like creatures are perfect for small-boat and inshore anglers who prefer to work the bays, estuaries, and surf-line rips. They are caught in several subspecies, and although they can grow larger, corvina range from 3 to 15 pounds.

The favored, accessible locales for sportfishing along the western mainland are—from the north—Kino Bay, Guaymas, Topolobampo, Mazatlán, Puerto Vallarta, Ixtapa/Zihuatanejo, and Acapulco. Some of these, especially Mazatlán and Acapulco, are popular tourist sites with large sportfishing charter fleets and tend to attract vacationers who want to spend a day fishing offshore for dolphin or

M

Bombay Duck is a term for a marine lizardfish abundant in the Ganges Delta and the Arabian Sea. Also called bummalo, this ordinarily small fish is split, boned, sun-dried, and used as a condiment.

sailfish (pez vela). Consequently, these areas do not typically attract serious anglers. In fact, the best angling destinations, albeit without the best boats and facilities, are the smaller towns farther south along the coast that don't attract large numbers of tourists and where, in some cases, visiting anglers can launch from a beach in a panga. Puerto Escondido and Huatulco, for example, are more than an hour south of Acapulco and offer excellent fishing for adventurous travelers. These areas were lightly explored until the 1990s.

The Pacific mainland coastline of Mexico is extensive, and a good map will reveal its many inlets, points, bays, and estuaries. Some of the estuaries wander inland, miles from the sea, and many are mangrove-lined, offering opportunities for snook, corvina, snapper, and jacks, especially in the winter. These sites promise light-tackle action for the inshore angler no matter what the weather or water conditions offshore. Snook and snapper prefer the edges of these areas, and anglers usually land them by casting to cover. Jacks and corvina linger around the mouths of inlets and estuaries and prefer cast spoons and jigs.

The northern section of this coast is within the confines of the Sea of Cortez and offers quarry similar to that found along the Baja Peninsula. Kino Bay is close to various islands that attract diverse species; Tiburon is especially notable. Topolobampo, near Los Mochis, lies both north and south of a bay- and inlet-studded coast, with an abundance of explorable inshore water.

Guaymas, which is easily reached by highway from Nogales, Arizona, was a billfish hotspot in the mid-twentieth century, suffered from commercial fishing, then enjoyed a renaissance in the early 1990s, when sailfish, all three species of marlin, plus yellowfin tuna, wahoo, and dolphin were caught offshore from San Carlos Bay. Greater numbers of billfish and tuna congregate here when warmer currents are present, and summer through fall has been the best period. Good reef fishing can be had within a few miles of the bay; grouper, red snapper, triggerfish, cabrilla, and yellowtail are among the species anglers pursue. Surf fishing for pompano, corvina, and mackerel was once very popular but has waned and is showing no signs of a revival.

Just below the Tropic of Cancer and at the southern end of the Cortez, Mazatlán has scores of well-equipped charter boats, and although some light-tackle inshore fishing is possible, the focus is primarily offshore. Mazatlán is known for producing sailfish year-round, but the prime period for these fish, called pez vela, is from June through September. This is also a good period for large dolphin. Two line-class world records were established in this port in the past; one specimen weighed a phenomenal 83 pounds, 6 ounces. Blue marlin and black marlin are landed from May through December, and striped marlin are present from December through May. Swordfish, tuna, roosterfish, and red snapper are among the other species caught here.

Farther south and nicely situated in the Bay of Banderas, close to deep water, Puerto Vallarta has many of the species found in Mazatlán. Sailfish are prevalent from May through December, tuna from September through March, wahoo from September through December, and marlin from August through December. Although not known for snook, in 1997 Puerto Vallarta's surf produced a snook that could have been a new world record had it been weighed on a certified scale; the fish hit 63 pounds on a truck scale.

The adjacent villages of Ixtapa and Zihuatanejo, which lie north of Acapulco, receive minimal sportfishing attention because they are small and out-of-the-way. Nevertheless, the area is a growing resort destination and offers good sailfish action. As of the late 1990s, sailfish could still be pursued at reasonable prices. A roosterfish line-class world record was established here, and the local bounty also includes yellowfin tuna, blue marlin, black marlin, dolphin, jack crevalle, skipjacks, and Sierra mackerel. December through April is the primary period for offshore fishing, but billfishing can be spotty. With no shelf nearby to concentrate fish, trolling efforts are geared to hooking up with migrants, which may be plentiful or hard to locate. Even in poor times, some sailfish are raised and/or caught. Inshore fishing has been lightly explored here.

The same is true of the coast from south of Acapulco to the border with Guatemala. A close look at a map reveals substantial shoreline but a lack of reasonable access. Yet various small villages dot the area, so there is clearly much to be explored.

Huatulco, for example, is a small village east of Puerto Angel and west of Salina Cruz in the state of Oaxaca. It was unheard of until a resort facility sprang up there in the late 1980s. Although the community has grown into a small tourist destination, it is still unlikely to be found on most maps. Situated on the edge of the Gulf of Tehuantepec, and not far from the Middle America Trench, with associated dropoffs and several seamounts, Huatulco is nicely positioned to receive a warm northerly flowing current, and this brings with it a bounty of baitfish as well as lots of sailfish, plus marlin, yellowfin tuna, and dolphin.

Although the inshore opportunities are unexplored, the sailfishing is so good that poorly equipped anglers, even first-timers, have explored a few miles offshore in pangas and hooked up with a number of Pacific sails. When the area was first fished in 1990, pangas were the only game in town. Later, at least one modern sportfishing operation with a well-equipped boat established itself. This area could become one of Mexico's top billfishing destinations.

The nine bays around Huatulco are noted for numerous beautiful, soft sandy beaches. Anglers

M

have landed sailfish at the outskirts of the bays and within 2 miles of the beach. Although the fish are present year-round, the best season is from late spring through summer; some days in this period see 20 or more sails raised, and the size is fairly large on average, many in the 125-pound range. Blue and black marlin are both caught here, predominantly in winter and early spring. A 750-pound black was reportedly caught in August of 1996, and blue marlin have been landed to about 500 pounds.

With all of these sailfish, light-tackle opportunities are excellent. It will be necessary to bring your own equipment, especially fly or light-tackle gear, if you expect to hire a local *panga* (which can be done economically). They may have heavy tackle and a limited amount of terminal gear; tackle is not available locally.

Gulf of Mexico.   The eastern coast of Mexico fronting the gulf contains many of the species found throughout the coastal areas of the gulf from Florida through Louisiana and Texas, but these waters have been seriously affected by commercial fishing, much of the region is populated and of moderate interest to tourists, and it is lightly visited by traveling anglers. Better and more accessible fisheries exist both to the north, in Texas waters, and to the south along the Caribbean at the Yucatán Peninsula in Mexico and in Central American countries.

Tarpon, snook, redfish, seatrout, jewfish, mackerel, barracuda, snapper, jack crevalle, and grouper are among the species that inhabit the coastal areas from Matamoras and Laguna Madre south to the Bay of Campeche; the more popular species like snook, tarpon, and redfish are endemic to numerous bays and estuaries, especially those with moderate-size rivers. The Pánuco River at Tampico was once a hot tarpon spot, particularly in April; Laguna de Tamiahua, south of Tampico, was a top seatrout spot; and farther south the area around Tuxpan was noted for tarpon, snook, and many other species. Offshore reefs in this region, from just north of Tampico to just south of Tuxpan, are noted for a variety of species, and tarpon and snook are known to inhabit the rest of the coast, at Alvarado, for example, and the eastern region of the state of Tabasco.

To the west, in the eastern state of Campeche, Laguna de Terminos was a top North American tarpon site from the mid-1950s to the mid-1970s. Little has been heard from this area in recent times, but all sizes of tarpon thrived here, including fish reportedly to 190 pounds. Winter produced difficult fishing for tarpon, but the late spring and summer months, from June through August, brought the best tarpon action, although the heat makes this the least comfortable season.

Located between Ciudad del Carmen and Isla de Aguada, the lagoon spans 60 miles and is fed by five rivers, of which the Candelaria is the most significant. An extensive network of jungle creeks, man-grove swamps, and flats exist here, with one major pass to the shallow Campeche Bank on the coast. Snook were a prominent catch in the past, and other species in the lagoon complex or along the coastal shore included jack crevalle and permit in summer, as well as seatrout, barracuda, ladyfish, kingfish, grouper, jewfish, and more.

Yucatán Peninsula.   The Yucatán Peninsula is one of the foremost archaeological regions of the world and the home of numerous Mayan ruins. Estimates suggest that several hundred years ago up to 4,000 Mayan canoes on trading missions navigated regional waters at any one time—such was the thriving, ancient Mayan culture. Today, the watercraft of this area are more modern, their numbers far less, and their activities quite different.

Geographically, the low, flat Yucatán Peninsula is to the country of Mexico what the point is to a fishhook. And, even considering the excellent fishing at Mexico's westernmost region around the Baja Peninsula, the Yucatán can arguably be called the country's leading edge for anglers. Jutting into the sea, and bounded by the Gulf of Mexico to the north and the Caribbean to the east, the Yucatán is so fortuitously situated that it is blessed with some of the finest inshore and offshore angling in the world.

Most of the Yucatán's fishery centers along the coast of Quintana Roo, a state that comprises the eastern region of the peninsula. At the northeastern corner, Isla Holbox offers good fishing for tarpon and has recently become more accessible through the addition of new facilities catering to anglers. Small tarpon are available year-round, but late spring and summer are reportedly the best times for tarpon in the 70- to 100-pound range, and larger tarpon are present. Snook inhabit these waters, as do bonefish, jack crevalle, and some permit.

Better known are the highly touted fisheries nearby to the southeast at Isla Mujeres, Cancún, and Cozumel, and farther south at Boca Paila and Ascension Bay. There is year-round fishing on all of the Yucatán flats, but the favored time to visit is from late fall through spring, which coincides with the popular tourist season, although a cool spell then could diminish flats success. The summer and fall are good times here as well, and less visited.

Cancún/Isla Mujeres.   The offshore fishing at the tip of the Yucatán Peninsula—which doesn't in fact take place very far offshore—centers around the islands of Cancún and Isla Mujeres. They lie adjacent to the Yucatán Channel, which separates Cuba and Mexico and is dominated by strong northward-flowing currents that funnel baitfish and pelagic species along the tip of the Yucatán Coast.

As a result, the sailfish population is extraordinary—as good as anywhere in the Atlantic. It is so good, in fact, that the best days witness multiple hookups, with glowing reports of not just two, but even three and four of these high-dorsal-finned creatures at a time. White and blue marlin add to this already incredible fishery, and the whites are so

M

plentiful at times that they, too, can be a source of multiple strikes or hookups.

Anglers land the white and blue marlin around the 100-fathom curve off Cancún and Isla Mujeres, which is just a few miles offshore. Whites are typically taken a bit shallower, however, and sailfish shallower still. Most of the fishing occurs directly offshore or to the northeast or southeast. Arrowsmith Bank, less than 20 miles to the southeast of Isla Mujeres, is another hotspot, although good fishing close to the island often dissuades anglers from making the run.

There is no real shelf or quick dropoff around Isla Mujeres and Cancún, but an upwelling of sorts exists out in the 100-fathom water, where currents sweep by. This area is productive for dolphin and marlin, and attractive to baitfish.

It is the presence of prodigious schools of baitfish, especially in the spring and early summer, that makes the waters off the northern tip of the Yucatán such an attractive area for billfish, especially sailfish. It is routine to find sailfish balling bait, so trolling methods commonly involve looking for such activity and fishing with bait. Dorado, bonito, and other fish find the bait schools, too, and sometimes make it harder to focus on just the sailfish, but facing too many eager and hard-fighting creatures is one problem most anglers can cope with.

Lots of activity makes this a hot place to try fly fishing, although when the sailfish are ganging up on bait, a fly may not turn their heads. Unquestionably, the light-tackle fishing, using spinning rods and 8- to 20-pound line (these sailfish average 40 to 50 pounds) is great. The best period for billfish and dorado is in the spring. Other species you might catch while trolling for sailfish and white marlin include wahoo, kingfish, and blackfin tuna; grouper, cubera snapper, mutton snapper, and jack crevalle are hard-fighting inhabitants of local reefs and inshore environs.

The big news inshore are the glamour species: bonefish, and plenty of them, plus tarpon, snook,

and permit. None of these fish run to giant sizes here, but they are so readily available that experienced anglers say catching one is almost a sure thing.

Some of this action occurs less than an hour's drive from Cancún. This resort city, which was just a small village of a few hundred people in the mid-1970s, was carved out of the mangrove coast by the government and made into a Mexican Riviera. An image of what the fishing used to be like on the Cancún flats is close by, however, especially at Isla Blanca lagoon, 20 miles to the north. There are extensive flats here, as well as numerous coves, bays, mangrove islands, and other fishable locales up the coast, most of them lightly explored and generally reached via a 7-mile-long dirt road. A boat trip requiring some 20 minutes to the area around Cabo Catoché follows.

Bonefish, mostly in small groups, and permit are plentiful on the flats. Snook and tarpon (in the 20- to 30-pound class, and a few larger) are in good supply around the mangrove islands, shores, and inlets. All of these species are sought after by boaters (wading is hard on the flats, most of which are very soft), stalking and sighting fish to cast to—the most exciting of all inshore angling pursuits. A grand slam of all four of these highly coveted species is quite possible on spinning gear, and remotely possible on a fly (you'd have to get the permit first, always the most difficult chore). Tarpon and snook fishing here is good all season, but it's best from May through August, a time that is also good for other species.

Cozumel. Long before the Spanish conquest, Cozumel was a pilgrimage site for Mayan worshipers of Ixchel, the fertility and moon goddess. There is perhaps irony in this; today, many anglers make a different sort of pilgrimage to this well-known Caribbean island because its waters are so fertile, and they often do so around the time of full moon. Atlantic sailfish—the premier quarry and found more abundantly here than in most other locales worldwide—begin their migration off this island around the time of full moon in March. The sailfish actually show up in numbers (some can be caught all year long) in February and really get cooking in March, peaking from then into June.

Cozumel is 33 miles long and 9 miles wide and situated off the east-central coast of the Yucatán Peninsula. The accessibility of Cozumel, which is a prime fun-and-sun tourist destination that is easily reached from the United States, has attracted large numbers of anglers in private boats, as well as tourists, looking for a one-day venture in hopes of catching their first sailfish. Cozumel is *the* place to do that, and also *the* place to catch sails on a fly rod as well as on light spinning tackle and on casting tackle. Cozumel is also an excellent place for a realistic chance at a multiple hookup, a grand billfish slam (white and blue marlin plus sailfish in a single day), or a super grand slam (the other three billfish plus swordfish).

A hooked sailfish leaps in front of a boat near Cozumel.

Cozumel's offshore fishery has held up well for years, sometimes raising double-digit numbers of fish. In the best of times on a *slow* day off Cozumel, you might catch three or four sailfish (this would be a good day almost anywhere else). Dolphin, kingfish, bonito, and blackfin tuna are also in the offshore mixed bag, sometimes in good numbers and sizes (dolphin especially), although they are usually an incidental catch in billfishing.

Trolling at Cozumel predominantly takes place in the 12 miles of deep water that separates the island and the mainland; in fact, this is where most offshore trolling occurs, often close to the Yucatán near Playa del Carmen in 10 to 60 fathoms of water. Sailfish apparently migrate northward with the strong current, coming from the open waters of the Caribbean and working their way up the coast past Cozumel, passing the head of the peninsula at Isla Mujeres and Cancún, and then moving into the Gulf of Mexico.

The Caribbean is deep here, with well over 100 fathoms of water between mainland and island. There is a sharp drop from 10 to 60 or so fathoms near the mainland, and this is the zone that is heavily worked. Up the coast, the bottom rises to a bank and is not nearly as deep close to shore.

Baitfish are abundant along this area, especially off several coves south of Playa del Carmen, and sailfish, migrating through in groups, are obviously drawn to them. Boats trolling and zigzagging north-south along the mainland edge frequently encounter pods of these billfish and experience multiple hookups. After such an encounter the savvy skipper may run north a fair distance and then troll southward with the hope of engaging other fish from that pod.

Anglers also encounter white marlin in along the mainland shoals and edges, sometimes catching them in the same locales as they do sailfish. Blue marlin, however, are more likely to be caught farther offshore and over deeper water, typically in the channel, which has some irregular bottom structure.

Less attention is devoted to reef and flats fishing in Cozumel, and the area has not been publicized for this. Although bonefish are abundant along the Yucatán flats on the mainland, they are not as abundant at Cozumel because the island has little shallow water. The island does harbor some bonefish and permit, however, and although this may not be a world-class fishery, it is good enough to provide a very pleasant day, especially if you don't favor big-water fishing, or a heavy blow comes up that keeps big boats off the water, or you just want to take a spinning or fly rod in tow and poke around. These bonefish and permit are in and near a small lagoon at the south end of the island, and in one at the north end. The fish aren't big in either locale, but the setting is pristine and peaceful.

The reefs around Cozumel are another matter entirely. Rated among the world's finest for diving, they are the island's main draw after angling. Palancar Reef, which surrounds Cozumel, is one of the world's largest coral reefs. and its edges yield big grouper, red snapper, and other bottom fish, as well as the occasional dolphin and kingfish.

Southern flats and bays. World-famous shallow-water light-tackle flats fishing exists along southeastern Quintana Roo. The shoreline drops off sharply just south of Cancún and doesn't offer flats fishing, but south of Tulum— the most visited of all Mayan archaeological sites—are tarpon, bonefish, permit, snook, and assorted other species. This is the region in and around the Sian Ka'an Biosphere Reserve, a 1.3-million-acre region with tangled mangrove swamps, vast tropical forests, and isolated swampy beaches. Netting is prohibited in the preserve, and the number of local inhabitants is minimal, leaving the fish undisturbed and plentiful. Boca Paila, Ascension Bay, and Espiritu Santo Bay are the main fishing areas, and facilities are available at each location.

As with the flats to the north at Isla Holbox, the fish are not generally large, although some huge permit have been caught here, including 40- to 50-pounders on fly tackle. Catching the grand slam species (tarpon, bonefish, and permit) or super grand slam (plus snook) in a day is a realistic goal, especially at Ascension and Espiritu Santo Bays. Indeed, this may be the foremost place in the world to achieve these accomplishments.

Bonefish and permit are the stars here, both often traveling in large schools on the flats. Tarpon mostly inhabit the mangrove backwaters, and range from small specimens up to 70 and 80 pounds. The snook run to 20 or 25 pounds but are generally less numerous than the other species. Big barracuda, plus sharks and jacks, also frequent these waters. Although some flats can be waded, most are soft and muddy, making poling and casting from boats the standard angling method.

Boca Paila is roughly two hours by auto from Cancún and was originally fished in the early 1970s by anglers taking a long boat ride from Cozumel and camping on the beach. Protected from prevailing winds and boasting many easily reached flats, Boca Paila has the mother lode of small bonefish and has long been renowned for its plentiful permit. Tarpon, snook, and barracuda, as well as various reef species, are also targeted here.

Much the same can be said for vast Ascension Bay as well, 25 miles south of Boca Paila and with a cornucopia of mangrove islands, channels, flats, and creeks. Other fish encountered here include jack crevalle, cubera snapper, and large barracuda. Large permit cruise the flats at Ascension Bay, as do big schools of bonefish ranging from 1 to 5 pounds. There are tarpon in the mangrove areas and also in some landlocked lagoons accessible via a rugged dirt road.

Espiritu Santo Bay is roughly 15 miles south of Ascension Bay and less known and visited. Loads of

M

flats and mangrove lagoons exist in this large area, too, and a barrier reef parallels the shoreline and crosses in front of the mouth of the bay. Huge permit and ample schools of bonefish inhabit the flats, and small tarpon favor areas near mangrove shores, between the reef and shoreline, and the lagoons.

MICHIGAN

Michigan is a state of outdoor fanatics. And with a combined 2 million resident and nonresident fishing licenses sold annually, angling ranks as a big facet in the state's immense tourism and recreational matrix.

Two factors account for the wild popularity of fishing here. First, with more big-water coastline than Florida and Oregon combined, plus 11,000 inland lakes and 3,000 rivers, Michigan has as much and as varied sportfishing as any other state, and far more than most. The St. Clair River alone has 90 species of fish, more than a dozen of them sought by anglers. Gull Lake near Kalamazoo has 52 species and is probably the only place in the world where you'll hear locals complain about "nuisance" Atlantic salmon that prey on the fish anglers really want to catch, bluegills!

The second factor is that Michigan has something many states lack but which is just as important to anglers as fish: widespread access to virtually all of those waters through some 9 million acres of publicly owned land.

Michigan's fisheries are primarily coolwater and coldwater, and the state has three distinct climatic and geographic zones.

The Upper Peninsula (UP) is a continuation of Ontario's Laurentian shield country, where a thin layer of soil over rocky outcroppings grows trees and not much else. Winter comes early, stays late, and brings arctic conditions. Fishing here usually means brook trout on the inland streams, smallmouth bass and pike in the smaller lakes, and salmon in the Great Lakes.

The northern Lower Peninsula, a gigantic sand and gravel pile left behind by the glaciers and that also doesn't grow much but trees, gets almost as cold as the Upper Peninsula, especially the central highlands. But winter starts a couple of weeks later, spring comes a couple of weeks earlier, and a network of fast-flowing rivers provides much of the best trout water in the state. This zone also offers magnificent smallmouth bass and northern pike fishing, both inland and in the Great Lakes; plenty of walleye, sunfish, perch, and smelt in inland lakes; and anadromous brown trout, steelhead, and Pacific salmon (mostly chinooks) in Lakes Michigan and Huron. The northern waters of the latter two lakes also provide especially fine carp fishing, in waters so clear that fly- and spinning-tackle fans stalk 20- to 30-pound carp like oversize bonefish and can often see their quarry coming at 200 yards.

From Saginaw Bay south, the climate is much milder. Snow and below-zero temperatures occur each year, but they're generally confined to midwinter, and by March anglers are out in boats while enthusiasts in the northern parts of the state are still ice fishing. There are few trout streams here but lots of bigger, warmer rivers with excellent concentrations of smallmouth and largemouth bass and pike. The area is dotted with lakes teeming with crappie, sunfish, perch, and bass.

The state has shoreline on four of the five Great Lakes: Superior, Michigan, Huron, and Erie. The principal gamefish in all the big lakes is the chinook salmon, which was imported from the Pacific in 1968, a couple of years after the state's Department of Natural Resources (DNR) first stocked the Platte River on Lake Michigan with coho salmon. Chinooks grew large and plentiful for a couple of decades, and a state record of 46 pounds, 1 ounce was set.

An outbreak of bacterial kidney disease in the early 1990s drastically reduced the chinook populations in Lakes Michigan and Huron, especially the former. Better disease control in the hatcheries and increased care in selecting eggs from returning fish at weirs have brought the salmon back to excellent levels, and with increased emphasis on stocking lake trout, brown trout, and steelhead, it's common for anglers to boat five-fish limits comprised of three or four species in a morning.

Cohos also inhabit all four lakes, but these smaller and more acrobatic fish are most common in Lake Michigan. They don't hang around Michigan waters much, however, and make a big annual circle of the lake, spending the summers largely off Indiana, Illinois, and Wisconsin. Thus, chinooks are the primary salmon stocked today.

Steelhead are another immensely popular fish with trolling anglers, and whereas there is some evidence that the first rainbows stocked in Michigan rivers 100 years ago included sea-run subspecies that reached the Great Lakes, all of the rainbows there today are anadromous, although most come from stock that hasn't been in saltwater for generations.

Before the salmon, there were lake trout—both the fat and the lean species. The lean was far preferred, and it was virtually wiped out by the 1940s due to overfishing, pollution, and the arrival of parasitic lamprey eels. The fat trout, which lives deeper, didn't come as close to extirpation, but their numbers were also decimated.

Today, lakers are making a comeback in most of the Great Lakes, with the exception of northern Lake Huron. The U.S. Fish and Wildlife Service determined that lake trout once again reached a self-sustaining level in much of Lake Superior in 1997, and stocking has produced good populations in Lake Michigan. Ironically, the lake trout that provided eggs for the restocking were mostly descendants of Lake Michigan fish that had been planted in a lake in Wyoming before World War II. Evidence of the well-being of these fish is seen in the Michigan record laker, a 61$\frac{1}{2}$-pound fish caught in 1997 in Lake Superior. It is reportedly the largest lake trout ever caught in the U.S.

Trolling, with crankbaits in spring and spoons throughout the summer, is the principal method of catching Great Lakes salmonids in Michigan. The introduction of the downrigger vastly increased the catch of salmon and lakers in summer, when the fish run deep. Previous to that invention, anglers usually fished wire line, which required far more laborious cranking to wind 200 to 300 feet back onto the reel. Another major breakthrough was the sideplaner board, which dramatically increased the catch of walleye and steelhead by covering more water and positioning the lures away from the boat.

Pacific salmon are one of the primary tourist attractions and economic mainstays of many small towns on the Great Lakes, supporting hundreds of charter boats and tackle shops. Yet many people believe that the DNR has bestowed the salmon fishery with an importance far out of proportion to its economic value and its overall place in the Michigan fishing picture. They argue that far more people spend far more time fishing inland lakes and streams that get short shrift from the DNR, which spends the bulk of its fish hatchery dollars on Great Lakes salmonids.

In the fall, the salmon run up dozens of streams and provide wonderful sport for pier anglers and wading anglers miles from the big water. The primary limiting factors are hydroelectric dams on most rivers, but a new licensing agreement between the federal government, the state, and the hydroelectric companies has regulated water flows through the dams and should improve salmon spawning conditions downstream.

In fact, although trout anglers have generally fought for removal of these dams where possible, in a few instances they objected to the dams' removal because they feared that allowing salmon and steelhead to run up a stream like the Au Sable would decrease populations of resident brown trout.

Steelhead make their runs mostly in the winter and spring, although the number of summer-run fish is increasing. Steelies often use the same lies as salmon, but smart anglers know that when the salmon are in the streams, fishing a spawn sack below the salmon redds can prompt a smashing strike from a holdover rainbow.

Expecting Michigan walleye anglers to get excited about angling elsewhere is like carrying coal to Newcastle. If you were to name the five great walleye grounds in the world, Michigan accesses three of them: Saginaw Bay on Lake Huron, Little Bay de Noc on Lake Michigan, and Lake Erie. Many inland lakes also abound with walleye, and plants by walleye clubs in places like Whitefish Bay on Lake Superior are expected to spawn new world-class fisheries within a few years.

Michigan's numerous Great Lakes tributaries are noted for salmon, trout, and steelhead fishing.

The involvement of these clubs in running ponds under the aegis of the DNR has been of immeasurable value in improving and preserving the state's walleye populations. Showing enlightened self-interest, the clubs use volunteer labor to produce fish more cost effectively than a state or commercial hatchery can, and the benefits accrue directly to club members.

Inland, Michigan has thousands of miles of trout streams, ranging from mile-wide major rivers like the St. Marys to creeks you can step across but that can still hold big browns. The grayling that filled rivers in the northern Lower Peninsula before the turn of the century are just a memory, but imported brown, rainbow, and brook trout replaced them everywhere.

A small population of grayling still live in Neff Lake 10 miles west of the town of Grayling, the last survivors of a failed attempt to reintroduce Montana grayling in the 1980s.

Grayling is the city where Michigan's angling industry began, with Chief David Shopenagon, a revered Indian guide, teaching the craft to white disciples like Rube Babbit before the turn of the century. There were virtually no trout streams in the Lower Peninsula before about 1880. These were the days of the grayling, and the old chief and his fellow guides led sports from across the U.S. and Europe on expeditions that yielded hundreds of fish a day (and sometimes sent thousands of salted fish in barrels to Chicago, New York, and Detroit).

M

The wretched excess started the grayling's decline, but the nails were pounded into the coffin by the lumbering industry, which literally hacked down every tree in northern Michigan that was worth cutting. When the loggers were finished, in many areas stump fields that stretched from horizon to horizon were all that was left. Chemicals and sawdust from lumbering operations were poured willy-nilly into the streams, the loss of the forest canopy raised their temperatures, and by the 1920s this fish was extinct.

But anglers abhor a vacuum as much as nature, and it wasn't long before they began dumping trout into streams that were virtually empty of a top-rank predator. Browns were introduced to the Pere Marquette in 1883 (one of the first plantings in the U.S.), rainbows shortly thereafter in several rivers, and brook trout from the Upper Peninsula were spread to every creek and rivulet that flowed near a railroad line.

The brook trout has been adopted as the official state fish, and its range has spread from its original Upper Peninsula habitat to the southernmost regions of the state. But many people think that a better choice would have been the scrappy smallmouth bass, which was not only native everywhere in the state but today commonly reaches the 4-pound mark.

Michiganders like to boast that their state has more registered boats—about 900,000—than any other, something to be expected in a state populated by fishing fanatics. While bigger boats are required for the rougher water of the Great Lakes, inland-lakes fishing tends to be more of a tin-boat activity. Small aluminum boats in the 10- to 14-foot range, rigged with small outboards, are ideal for launching on many lakes and rivers where the ramps are dirt or grass and the path to them is a narrow forest two-track.

Although these offer some good fishing, the larger specimens of most species are found in the big Great Lakes waters and their bays. As a result, Michigan has some impressive rod-and-reel game-fish records. These include an 11-pound, 15-ounce largemouth bass; a 9-pound, 4-ounce smallmouth bass; a 17-pound, 3-ounce walleye; a 47-pound, 12-ounce muskellunge; a 39-pound northern pike; a 32-pound, 10-ounce Atlantic salmon; a 9-pound, 8-ounce brook trout; and a 26-pound, 8-ounce rainbow trout.

Commercial fishing for game species was virtually ended by the state in the 1970s, but a federal judge ruled that native Americans could still carry on commercial fisheries for salmon, lake trout, and whitefish. This ruling has led to an ongoing conflict between anglers and Indian commercial fishermen, with the former accusing the latter of overharvesting the resource, and the latter accusing the former of attempting to wriggle out of legal obligations. The conflict is greatest in places like Grand Traverse Bay and northern Lake Huron, where the nets of tribal anglers tend to be concentrated in the same small areas where anglers fish.

The present agreement between the state and Indian tribes runs out in the year 2000, and many observers think that the recognition of several new tribes by the federal government in the 1990s, all of which have claimed fishing rights, will make the problem even more difficult to resolve.

Upper West Coast

A couple of fly anglers once made a bet on who could get the most chinook salmon hookups in one day on the Pere Marquette River. Some of the takes were only headshakes that lasted seconds, but the winner recorded 126 strikes over 10 hours, and landed and released 23 salmon that ranged from 8 to 25 pounds. The "loser" had 94 strikes and landed 21 fish.

No one ever planted chinooks in the "P-M," as Michigan anglers refer to this big stream that runs 150 miles from its headwaters to Ludington on Lake Michigan, about halfway up the western shore of the Lower Peninsula. But some of the fish planted in nearby streams in the 1960s and 1970s strayed there and created the finest self-sustaining run in the state, averaging about 40,000 fish each fall.

Anglers from other states are often amazed to learn that Michigan has better Pacific salmon fishing, both in streams and in the Great Lakes, than most of the Pacific regions where these fish originated. The runs in rivers like the St. Joseph, Grand, Big and Little Manistee, Pere Marquette, Platte, and Betsie usually begin in late August, peak in late September, and trickle off through October, but genetic drift appears to be creating summer runs.

In the rivers, anglers catch salmon and steelhead on a variety of flies (including Woolly Buggers, nymphs, and egg flies), spoons, and spawn. The steelhead runs continue off and on throughout the winter, usually peaking in March and April, just before the inland trout season opens.

What has really kicked up the success rate of Michigan anglers is a locally developed technique called light-line nymphing. The angler uses a fly rod and reel, but instead of traditional fly line, the reel is spooled with the synthetic running line normally used as backing.

The leader is about 10 feet long, and the 18-inch tippet (normally 6 to 10 pounds) is tied to a three-way swivel, with a point fly on the end of the tippet and a second fly on a dropper from the swivel. Weight in the form of split shot in a slinky (a thin fabric tube filled with three to eight shot) is clamped onto another dropper off a barrel swivel about a foot above the top fly.

By adjusting the amount of shot for the water depth and current flow, anglers can flop the flies into the water, and the "tick, tick, tick" of the shot bouncing along the bottom ensures them that the flies will pass by the fish just at eye level.

M

Anglers run light-line rigs through deep holes where they know large numbers of fish concentrate. Although the fish are almost always hooked in the mouth, some critics say this is merely a form of legalized snagging for fish, which constantly open and close their mouths while holding over the bottom.

Offshore in the Great Lakes, as mentioned earlier, the salmon have rebounded from the decimation caused by bacterial kidney disease a decade ago. Today they are the most abundant species in the daily mixed bag landed by charter boats. The catch also commonly includes steelhead, lake trout, and brown trout up to 10 pounds.

The primary forage fish is the alewife, which apparently reached the Great Lakes from the Atlantic with the construction of the first shipping canals in the nineteenth century, and by the 1950s these fish constituted the primary biomass of the four lower lakes. But the decimation of lake trout populations by pollution, lamprey eels, and overfishing enabled alewife populations to explode, and many people can remember days in the 1960s and 1970s when summer algae blooms consumed so much dissolved oxygen in the water that the alewives died off in the millions and washed up on the beaches, leaving stinking windrows of rotting fish 2 feet high.

Salmon were introduced to Lake Michigan by the Michigan DNR in 1966, primarily to control the alewife population. In the early 1970s, coho numbers exploded in response to a virtually unlimited food supply, and the wait to launch boats at ramps was sometimes measured in hours during the wildest days. By the early 1990s, the Pacific salmon had proven so successful that biologists said alewives were on the verge of becoming an endangered species in Lake Michigan.

Coho and chinook numbers stayed very high through about 1990, until the outbreak of bacterial kidney disease knocked the salmon back and caused another, smaller, alewife boom. For a few years, boat operators reported seeing occasional rafts of dead alewives floating on the surface, skinny fish that apparently couldn't handle the twin stresses of spawning and starvation. But a salmon comeback and increased numbers of other salmonids by 1995 apparently resulted in at least a temporary balance of power that satisfied both the alewives and the predators.

Steelhead fishing is outstanding on Lake Michigan. These anadromous rainbows support an important summer charter boat fishery that usually requires skippers to run 15 to 20 miles offshore. The steelhead boats fish the scum line, a region where upwelling currents and prevailing winds concentrate enormous numbers of ants, bees, butterflies, caddisflies, houseflies, and other terrestrial insects that are carried offshore by the return flow of upper-level winds that fill in the low pressure created over the lake by the daily breezes.

Large boats venture onto Lake Michigan from many ports.

This rich food source in turn concentrates steelhead from all parts of the lake, and biologists estimate that more than a million of the big rainbows spend the summer in this one patch in the middle of northern Lake Michigan.

Incredibly, anglers routinely catch 10- to 15-pound steelhead 20 miles from shore that have nothing in their stomachs but bugs, whereas steelhead taken inshore have stomachs filled with smelt, alewives, and other forage fish. This is an eye-popping lesson in the biomass of insects carried offshore by the lake-breeze weather machine.

The coastline of the northwestern Lower Peninsula has fine smallmouth bass populations wherever rocky bays exist. Both arms of Grand Traverse Bay are excellent, and the annual return of the smallies to spawn on the shallow rock reefs at Waugoshance Point off Wilderness State Park on the Lower Peninsula's extreme northwestern tip draws thousands of anglers who come just to catch and release the fish before the season officially opens (often as many as 80 fish a day, ranging from 12 to 19 inches).

Southern Lake Michigan ports like Grand Haven and St. Joseph once were renowned for party boats that returned to shore with perch that were so big, they looked like small walleye. But something has happened to the perch population, which has fallen off by as much as 80 percent. While biologists are investigating the problem as a Great Lakes–wide phenomenon, it is most evident in Lake Michigan, and scientists suspect it is largely the result of competition for food with a host of exotic invaders at all levels of the perch's life cycle.

Upper East Coast

Salmon and steelhead fishing continue to be good to excellent in Lake Huron, but sea lamprey levels were so high by 1998 that the Michigan DNR said they were killing virtually every lake trout before it became old enough to reproduce.

M

The problem results from a fantastic explosion of lampreys from the St. Marys River and some biological similarities between the two species. Both sea lampreys and lake trout like water temperatures below 45°F, and both concentrate off the shoreline on reefs in the fall and winter—the trout to spawn on the deep reefs and the lampreys to prepare for their spawning run up nearby rivers. Having lampreys and lake trout in close proximity in high densities results in extremely high predation of the latter by the former.

Biologists hoped that new lamprey control programs scheduled through 2005 would alleviate the problem, but some Michigan DNR biologists insist that it is a waste of time and money to stock lake trout in northern Lake Huron until it has been proven that the controls will work.

In addition to salmon, the primary species sought along the Lake Huron shoreline of the Upper Peninsula is perch, and even here there were problems. Perch numbers were declining, as they had been for five years throughout most of the Great Lakes, and local anglers believe that an exploding cormorant population was largely responsible. Although cormorant numbers have increased remarkably over the past 15 years, their daily feeding requirements show that they cannot account for such a drastic reduction in perch.

A bit farther south, along the Lake Huron shore of the northern Lower Peninsula, the fishing for chinook salmon and steelhead is usually very good. But many anglers say that an even better fishery is the big, lake-run brown trout population planted off Alpena and other ports in the area. As fat as a football and often twice as long, these fish are powerful fighters, albeit not as spectacular leapers as their close cousin, the Atlantic salmon, and they are also wonderful table fare.

Because of the emphasis on salmon, anglers here tend to overlook the exceptionally good walleye fishing, which consists mainly in trolling crankbaits in early spring, and spoons through the summer.

From the mouth of the Au Sable River at Oscoda, anglers can fish for salmon, steelhead, and walleye by trolling out through the pier heads or casting from the rocks and jetties. The lower reaches of the Au Sable, below a dam that blocks upstream passage of fish, is a popular place for steelhead anglers pulling plugs from downstream-drifting boats.

The Singing Bridge area near Oscoda was once the scene of fantastic smelt runs, but this species, too, has declined dramatically throughout the Great Lakes since the late 1980s. Introduced to the Great Lakes less than 100 years ago, smelt ran up every creek and river on spring nights just after ice out, often in such numbers that people could reach into the water and pull out silvery fish by the handful.

Smelt are among the tastiest of fish, either headed, gutted, and deep-fried or simply tossed whole into the hot fat, which some gourmands claim is the only way to prepare them. A night of smelt

dipping was once a Michigan spring ritual from the balmy shores of Lake Erie to the icy beaches of Lake Superior. A father could take his small children to a creek that ran onto a beach, turn them loose with a long-handled dipnet, and head home within a couple of hours, transporting 10 gallons of smelt in the trunk and sleeping kids in the back seat.

But those runs have largely failed to materialize in recent years in most of the Great Lakes. Today's smelting often means catching two or three fish at a time rather than two or three dozen, and biologists say it may reflect the Great Lakes' vastly increased numbers of smelt-gobbling big predators, from salmonids to walleye.

Lower West Coast

Here, too, salmon—cohos in the spring and chinooks through the summer—are the dominant species for offshore anglers. The original Great Lakes salmon plants were far to the north in Platte Bay, but the DNR stocked descendants of those fish in the St. Joseph River, the major stream in southeast Michigan, through the 1970s, and continued to stock chinooks into the 1990s.

The most productive fishing isn't from a boat but from the river pier heads. Anglers casting spoons and spawn start the year with steelhead and big brown trout just after ice out; walleye, flathead catfish, and channel catfish are the summer quarry; and salmon are the ticket in the fall. Smallmouth and largemouth bass are usually caught at any time.

The offshore waters at this southern end of Lake Michigan warm much earlier than do the northern waters (which in some years never crack the 40s, even in midsummer). The cohos move south along the Michigan shoreline and provide angling activity through early June, after which they continue their annual migration through Indiana, Illinois, and Wisconsin waters, where they spend most of the summer before heading straight across the lake to the mouth of the Platte in fall.

But the chinook are found offshore all year, and although the key to catching them is always to find the cool water they like, in southern Michigan they often tend to be more concentrated simply because there's less cold water to inhabit.

Whereas Michigan coho salmon primarily provide fishing for anglers in other states, the huge numbers of Skamania steelhead planted by Indiana have been a boon for southwestern Michigan anglers. The silver rockets are an offshore fishery all summer, and rivers like the St. Joseph now get both spring, summer, and fall runs of steelhead originally planted by both states. The fish that run in late winter and early spring usually weigh roughly 5 pounds, but summer-run steelhead are regularly caught into the midteens.

The most overlooked fishery here is probably the big brown trout inhabiting the waters just offshore (the state record, incidentally, is 34 pounds, 6 ounces). They can be taken within a long cast of

The Guinness Book of Records lists the sailfish as the fastest fish based on speed trials in which one sailfish peeled off 300 feet of line in 3 seconds, equal to 68 mph.

M

shore in April, and even in the heat of summer are usually found along reefs and bottom structure in 60 to 90 feet of water, less than a mile offshore along most of this shoreline.

The area is speckled with hundreds of inland lakes that have good public access and are stocked by the DNR. One of the most interesting is Gull Lake, where some anglers complain because the state has stocked it with landlocked salmon. These anglers would prefer to catch panfish, and they say that when they catch landlocks, the salmon usually have sunfish in their stomachs.

But many other lakes are stocked with sunfish, and some have excellent populations of hybrid sunnies that run to 10 inches and will put a healthy bend in a light fly or spinning rod. This is also Michigan's best largemouth country, with a climate that sees spring arrive a month before it does in the northern regions, fall last a month later, and winter temperatures moderated by the prevailing westerly winds off the relatively warm waters of huge Lake Michigan (although most of the four Lower Great Lakes usually freeze in a normal winter, parts of Lake Michigan often remain open).

Lower East Coast

An angler's heaven, Saginaw Bay holds prodigious numbers of big walleye, perch, and bass in its inner reaches, and chinook salmon, steelhead, and lake trout where its green, turbid waters meet the clear seas of open Lake Huron. On a fall day, a person can hunt ducks in the morning, fish in the afternoon, and hunt with a bow or gun for deer in the evening until sunset.

But Saginaw Bay can also be rough, and each fall usually brings a tragedy or two, when small-boat owners disregard the warning signs and are overwhelmed by big seas and icy water as the wind starts to howl.

The south shore of the bay is laced with myriad canals and creeks that provide bank fishing opportunities as well as havens for boaters when the weather turns stormy. The canals are the best areas to pursue perch and panfish, and in spring they hold impressive numbers of carp that are the subject of a controversial weekend bowfishing tournament. The critics object to what they call a senseless slaughter of fish; many of the archers post scores that are measured in the tons of carp killed.

If small-lake anglers want to get a grasp of the size of Lake Huron, they need only realize that Saginaw Bay, some 60 miles long and 30 miles wide, is larger than most other lakes in the U.S. except the five Great Lakes. And yet Saginaw is not the biggest of Lake Huron's bays. That honor goes to Georgian Bay on the Canadian side.

Saginaw Bay is known nationally for its fabulous walleye fishery. During the spring spawning run in April and May, anglers routinely cull 7-pounders, and 40 or more pounds of walleye are often boated in just a couple of hours. Walleye fishing continues through the winter, and ice anglers on snow machines can rival summertime anglers in productivity on a sunny winter weekend.

South of Saginaw Bay, the shoreline has a paucity of streams and offers few places of refuge for boaters. The section from the mouth of the bay south to Port Huron at the head of the St. Clair River sees mostly salmon trolling, with a few steelhead, walleye, and brown trout mixed in.

The Upper Peninsula

"Nine months of winter and three months of poor sledding" is how locals often describe the climate of this 350-mile-long witch's finger, bordered on the north by the world's largest freshwater lake, Superior, and on the south by enormous Lakes Michigan and Huron.

This is the area many Michiganders think of when they talk about "Up North," the place they go to get away from it all. Yoopers, the residents of the UP, refer to Lower Peninsula denizens as "trolls," because they live below the Mackinac Bridge that connects the two landmasses.

The hills and second-growth forests of the UP make up a third of Michigan's 57,000 square miles, but they are home to only about 300,000 of the state's 9$^1/_2$ million residents. And that's why fishing is still so good in the thousands of lakes and beaver ponds and hundreds of creeks and rivers that fill every low spot. After the logging companies cut down the virgin forests at the end of the last century, and usually abandoned the land afterward to avoid paying taxes on it, the resulting economic bust cleared out much of the population.

Although mining and logging continued as the major industries, there were few enough people that the landscape was able to recover from the worst excesses. Today, about 2 million acres of the UP are owned by the state or federal government and another 2 million acres are in Conservation Forest Reserve, which gives the lumber and mining companies a tax break if they keep the lands open for public recreation.

Lake Superior offers excellent chinook salmon trolling from ice-out until freeze-up. Charter boats are available at various ports, including Munising, Marquette, and Ontonagon. Covering more than 31,000 square miles and stretching 350 miles in length, Superior is larger than some states. It is also home to America's least-visited national park, Isle Royale, located near the western end of the lake, some 40 miles off the nearest Michigan shoreline and accessible by ferry from Houghton and Copper Harbor on the Keweenaw Peninsula, or via a 30-minute airplane ride from those ports.

Some 44 miles long and 8 miles wide, Isle Royale boasts several large lakes of its own that have excellent brook trout and pike fishing. The island's shorelines are the site of runs of coaster brookies, inland equivalents of the anadromous salter brook trout that run to the ocean off New England.

M

Little Bay de Noc provides some of North America's top walleye fishing.

Another unusual angling opportunity in the UP is lake trout fishing at Stannard Rock, 40 miles off Marquette. A seamount rises from depths of 600 feet to within 60 feet of the surface, and anglers who make the long and often rough trip out are rewarded by lakers up to 40 pounds that hang out along the upper slopes and take cast spoons.

Each fall, coho and chinook salmon run in the Rock, Sand, Carp, and numerous other Upper Peninsula rivers, and both summer- and winter-run steelhead strains are found all along Superior's shoreline, although spring offers by far the best angling. Although this is the biggest water on the Great Lakes, it is also the coldest and the least rich; salmon and steelhead here tend to run slightly smaller than those caught in Lakes Michigan and Huron.

Salmon is the glamour species along the UP's southern shore on Lake Michigan as well. Nearly all of these are chinooks that average about 12 pounds, but Little Bay de Noc, near the town of Escanaba, shares with Lake Erie and Saginaw Bay a fabled reputation for walleye, both in number and in size.

Needless to say, these waters also harbor excellent smallmouth fishing just about anywhere an angler can find submerged rocks, and when the smallies come to spawn on the inshore reefs in spring, it's common for wading fly and spin anglers to take 50 a day on artificials. Although the majority are under the 14-inch legal limit, enough 18- to 20-inchers hit to bring many anglers back year after year.

From the Brule River on the Wisconsin border on the west to the St. Marys River on the Ontario border to the east, the UP is the land that John Voelker made famous in books written under the pen name Robert Traver. A former Marquette County prosecutor and state supreme court justice who owned a fishing cabin at Frenchman's Bend, Voelker especially loved the native brook trout thronging hundreds of UP streams, which ranged from yard-wide rivulets to springtime brawlers with Class V rapids.

Brook trout are still the primary stream species here, and many UP anglers know of a creek where they can take 15- to 19-inch "specks." Many of the streams are fishable with fly tackle, although others are so brushy that they are more suitable for the worm-dunking techniques described in "The Big Two-Hearted River" by UP brook trout aficionado Ernest Hemingway.

Hemingway often fished here as a young man when his family owned a summer home on Walloon Lake in the northern Lower Peninsula. And proving that he was as savvy an angler as he was a writer, if you follow the route that Hemingway has young Nick Adams take in "The Big Two-Hearted River," you'll arrive not at that stream but at the Fox near the old logging town of Seney.

The mouths of many streams on the Lake Superior watershed offer excellent spring fishing for steelhead, and fall sees chinook salmon run in the same waters. While fly fishing is effective using Woolly Buggers, Black Stonefly Nymphs, and local patterns, most anglers prefer to cast spoons.

This region is famous for phenomenal smallmouth bass fishing too. Craig Lakes State Park and Lake Michigamme are well known, but anglers who explore the back roads and forest two-tracks with a canoe or a small rowboat atop their vehicle will find access to literally hundreds of fish-rich lakes and ponds that may not appear on most maps.

Tremendous angling is available to anyone who visits Porcupine Mountains Wilderness State Park on the Lake Superior shore in the western Upper Peninsula. This 100-square-mile roadless area was slated to become a national park, until World War II claimed all of the federal budget, and the state bought it. Its myriad lakes, rivers, and creeks abound with pike, smallmouth bass, and brook trout, and often all three.

The Porkies, as the locals call this mountain region, offer backpacking anglers walk-in sites where they are unlikely to see another angler for two or three days at a time, but the wilderness cabins scattered throughout the hiking-trail system are always booked months in advance.

At the opposite end of Lake Superior is the St. Marys River. To fish the famed rapids here, take a fly or spinning rod in one hand, a heaping measure of courage in the other, and wade very, very carefully through the labyrinth of rocks and whitewater below the locks.

The area's incredible rainbow trout fishing was praised in print already in the 1930s; if anything, the angling is even better today. Not only are there wonderful steelhead runs (with the fish averaging 8 to 10 pounds), the river also hosts runs of chinook, coho, and pink salmon, and anglers fishing the rapids sometimes catch all four salmonid species in one afternoon, along with a walleye or whitefish or two for good measure.

Below the mile-long stretch of rapids, the river broadens and slows and offers superb angling for

M

walleye, smallmouth bass, and muskellunge, the latter largely ignored by the locals. Another interesting fishery is the Atlantic salmon run created by a stocking program that Lake Superior State University runs at the big hydroelectric plant.

Raised in old penstocks, the Atlantics return each summer to their release site, and can be seen holding in the fast currents of the crystal clear water a few feet from the generating plant. Like all Atlantics, they show a maddening disregard for everything that boat and bank anglers throw at them, but every now and then someone hooks and lands one of the silver devils up to 20 pounds. Biologists have recovered tags from St. Marys' Atlantics that were caught in Lakes Huron and Michigan, some 250 to 300 miles away.

In northern Lakes Michigan and Huron, anglers have discovered a wonderful new sport in sight fishing for 20- to 30-pound carp. They employ the same fly fishing and spinning techniques as for bonefish, redfish, and tarpon on saltwater flats. The water on these shallow Great Lakes flats is so clear, anglers can spot cruising carp against the bottom at 200 to 400 yards. Enthusiasts must wade or fish from poled boats for this extremely spooky quarry.

Although this type of fishing exists virtually anywhere in the Great Lakes that has a bottom covered with fist-size rocks (which shelter the insect larvae and crayfish the carp feed on and yet don't get roiled by wave action), the best sites are mostly on the Upper Peninsula shorelines of Lakes Michigan and Huron. Among the hottest of the hotspots are the Garden Peninsula and associated islands, several bays just west of the gigantic Mackinac Bridge, and the stony flats around Les Chennaux Islands at the eastern end of the UP.

The favored tackle is an 8-weight fly rod or a 7-foot spinning rod that casts a 6- to 8-pound line. The fish are extremely shy and sensitive to any line slapping on the water, a lure cast too close, or even the reflected flash of a rod.

The lures are similar to those used in stream fishing for smallmouth bass: small rubber-tailed jigs for spin anglers, and No. 6–8 dark Woolly Buggers, Stonefly Nymphs, and crayfish patterns for flyrodders. This is a summer fishery, and the carp usually come out of deep water onto the flats by about 9 A.M. as the sun warms the shallows. They cruise and feed actively for a few hours and then spend the afternoon lazing by the dozens in a protected bay before returning to the deep water in the evening.

Anglers who have worked out their patterns either pole a boat along a shoreline or stake out a point of channel on a stony flat, where the fish move through on routes that are as predictable as a train.

It's common for anglers to catch and release 10 to 20 of these powerful fighters a day. The average is about 15 pounds, and it's interesting that most anglers will catch a dozen fish weighing more than 20 pounds for every one under 10 pounds.

Another exciting and gustatorially rewarding form of fly fishing that may be unique to northern Michigan is the midsummer whitefish binge on mayflies. Commercial netters or ice anglers usually pursue these Great Lakes whitefish. But when they dimple the surface like brook trout during the brown drake and hexagenia hatches on the Great Lakes in July, they're suckers for almost any spent-wing dry fly in sizes 4 to 6.

These whitefish average about 5 pounds, but they run to 10 pounds, and when a big whitefish decides to use its slab-sided body against a 6-weight fly rod and a 5-pound tippet, the angler is in for a long fight. But a trip for a day of whitefish angling during the hatches is well worth it, because many people consider the whitefish the best-tasting species in freshwater, and summer whitefish binges are also common on many inland lakes in the UP.

Anglers can get the same opportunity with the Menominee, the smaller round whitefish that's sometimes called a lake herring. Running to about 2 pounds, they also will feed on hatching mayflies, but not with the predictable annual regularity of the bigger lake whitefish.

In the mid-1990s, anglers trolling the St. Marys landed what appeared to be three world-record pink salmon in a week. These fish didn't just break the existing record of 8 pounds; at 11 and 12 pounds, they demolished it. Taxonomic evaluation established that the fish were not purebred pinks but a hybrid between a pink and a chinook, and locals soon adopted the term "pinook" to describe them.

Pinks got into the Great Lakes supposedly by accident in the 1950s. Canadian scientists wanted to introduce them, but the American states involved in the Great Lakes stocking project did not. Fisheries technicians supposedly dumped a few thousand fry into Lake Superior, theorizing that they would never survive spawn.

Forty years later the little humpbacks are not only thriving, they now run in the St. Marys every year rather than in alternating years, the pattern they follow in most places. This frequency is attributed to genetic drift, and now that anglers have reported catching stray pinks in many Lower Peninsula streams that have salmon runs, the fish are expected to eventually establish themselves there.

Famed for its gamefish production, the St. Marys also harbors the scourge of the Great Lakes, the sea lamprey. More of these parasitic eels are spawned in the St. Marys than in all other Great Lakes tributaries combined.

In the 1990s, lampreys rebounded to the pandemic levels at which they virtually wiped out lake trout in the Great Lakes in the 1950s and 1960s. Ironically these anadromous eels are even more susceptible to pollution than brook trout, and by cleaning up rivers, humans have given the eels more and better places to spawn. The eels have reached such high levels in northern Lake Huron that they

M

kill virtually every lake trout before it reaches maturity. And with a shortage of lake trout to feed on, the eels began preying in greater numbers on salmon and whitefish.

This problem has been compounded by the size and huge flow of the brawling St. Marys rapids, which made conventional chemical and mechanical lamprey treatment techniques ineffectual. But biologists believe that they will gain control of the eels through a program that uses a new chemical that is toxic to eels but not to other creatures, and sterile male eels that are released into the river to mate with females who subsequently produce sterile lamprey eggs.

Urban Area Fisheries

Detroit. Most muskie lakes don't give up one 48-inch fish in a year, but at least six Lake St. Clair anglers caught and released muskies between 48 and 52 inches in one day in the summer of 1997. Incredibly, they weren't fishing for muskies; they were drifting worm harnesses on 6- to 10-pound line for walleye. And if that's not startling enough, summer isn't the best time to catch big muskies here. The experts say that if you want a really big fish, troll traditional foot-long muskie lures in October when the monsters are trying to put on fat for the winter.

Angling-club records show that not only are Lake St. Clair's muskies bigger today than at any time on record, there are a lot more of them. It's common for muskie tournament boats to catch and release 15 to 20 fish a day, and all within view of the skyscrapers of America's fifth largest city.

Muskie fishing is almost a religion for some anglers on these waters, where trolling shallow lures within yards of the boat was perfected. The $4^1/2$ million residents of Greater Detroit live on the edge of what is probably the finest urban fishery in the world, and certainly in the U.S. Lake St. Clair, which lies about 2 miles east of Detroit, is a shallow bowl about 40 miles across, an aneurysm between the St. Clair and Detroit Rivers, which carry water from Lake Huron 60 miles north of the city to Lake Erie 30 miles to the south.

Anglers who fish here should buy both Michigan and Ontario licenses. The best walleye fishing is usually on the Canadian side of these waters, and the best angling for other species crosses the unmarked international boundary line as weather and bait movement dictate.

The spring walleye run is remarkable. About 3 million walleye spawn in the Thames River on the Ontario side of Lake St. Clair. Most of these fish come up the Detroit River from Lake Erie, and self-described Detroit River rats think they've been cheated if a March or April outing doesn't provide a bunch of 6-pounders in a couple of hours, with an excellent shot at an 8- to 10-pound wall hanger. And even after the spawning run ends, anglers can count on catching 2- to 7-pounders most of the rest

of the year. Jigging early in the year and drifting crawlers or trolling crankbaits later in the spring are the usual methods.

Walleye and muskies draw so much attention that most locals virtually ignore other fisheries that approach world-class status. When a national bass tournament was held on this system in the mid-1990s, the top 10 anglers had 20 smallmouth bass apiece that averaged $2^1/2$ to 3 pounds. One angler practicing for that tournament caught and released about 60 smallmouths in one afternoon, fish that averaged more than 3 pounds.

Lake St. Clair has some largemouths, but more are found in Detroit River backwaters that have the structure and habitat bucketmouths prefer. An excellent smallmouth fishery exists in the Detroit River in the heart of downtown. A favorite spot is around the pilings in front of the 800-foot glass tower of the Renaissance Center.

Like most major cities, Detroit has hidden its riverfront behind concrete cliffs of office towers, commercial buildings, and moldering warehouses. But the city has built a new fishing pier, there is access to the river behind many of the commercial sites, and local anglers are beginning to take advantage of the city's excellent bank fishing for walleye, smallmouths, white bass, and carp.

Steadily clearing waters throughout the St. Clair River–Lake St. Claire–Detroit River system (thanks to zebra mussels) have resulted in steadily increasing populations of smallmouths and other sight feeders. There are even excellent numbers of northern pike, an extremely unusual occurrence in waters that have big muskie populations. Pike and muskies have a relationship similar to that between wolves and coyotes; in this case, the northerns hold the upper hand. Pike eggs hatch roughly three weeks before the muskie eggs; when the muskie eggs do hatch, they are just the right size to provide a meal for the pike fry, so it's rare to find fishable numbers of both rapacious species in the same lake.

Lake St. Clair also maintained good perch populations in a period when these little cousins of the walleye were on the decline in the rest of the Great Lakes system, and offers plenty of bluegills, white bass, catfish, and carp.

A local secret brings specialist anglers each spring to the St. Clair River a few miles upstream from Lake St. Clair. Fishing mostly after dark and before dawn, they drift 4-inch minnows and round gobies for Great Lakes sturgeon that occasionally exceed 50 pounds. While most sturgeon species elsewhere are in serious decline, the Great Lakes fish are holding their own, especially in Lake St. Clair, although it has been years since any have lived long enough to match the 200- to 300-pound specimens caught at the turn of the twentieth century. The fish are plentiful enough that anglers are catching and releasing several a night, and they are allowed to keep one fish over 50 inches per season.

An overlooked resource is the Huron River, best known for the riffles that hold smallmouth bass and rock bass. But it also has stretches with brown and rainbow trout, and lakes with excellent populations of catfish, panfish, and northern pike.

This stream flows through Ann Arbor, home of the University of Michigan, where canoe liveries offer excellent access to the fishery. In spring and fall, anglers concentrate at the Flat Rock Dam near the river mouth to catch steelhead in March and April, and chinook salmon in September, but the DNR and anglers' groups are raising money for a series of salmon ladders that will enable the anadromous species access to upstream stretches.

Saginaw/Bay City/Midland. These three cities share more than the Statistical Metropolitan Sales Area. In addition, they are on the Tittibawassee–Saginaw River drainage, which offers hundreds of thousands of urban residents angling that matches some wilderness opportunities. This is especially true in spring, when walleye mass in the rivers to prepare for spring spawning.

The Tittibawassee also features a huge spring sucker run that attracts thousands of worm dunkers, and both it and the Saginaw are home to large numbers of big channel cats, crappie, and largemouth bass.

Just outside these cities lie the Shiwassee Game Refuges, a 15,000-acre complex of marshes, sloughs, and creeks where five significant rivers come within a few hundred yards of each other. This is a wonderful small-boat fishery; it is shallow and includes hundreds of miles of protected waterways that hold excellent numbers of largemouth bass, pike, panfish, and carp.

Grand Rapids and Lansing. One of the best steelhead holds in America doesn't have a location. It has an address.

The Grand River in downtown Grand Rapids, Michigan's second biggest city, has spring and summer runs of big rainbows. Commuting motorists idling in traffic can glance down from a bridge or high-rise building and see an angler playing a leaping trout. Visiting anglers have no trouble locating fish. They just look for the gaggles of local anglers working the broken water in front of the art museum or upstream from the Sixth Street Bridge.

And Grand Rapids anglers can drive just 20 minutes and find themselves wading an excellent trout stream, the Rogue River, which runs just north of town and supports a fine fishery despite the intense angling pressure.

Other quality fisheries near Grand Rapids are the Thornapple and Flat Rivers, which hold enormous numbers of smallmouth and largemouth bass. Anglers access both streams by wading or from a canoe, and both cater to those who fish with light spinning tackle or fly rods.

The Grand River is Michigan's longest, and improvements in water quality and fish ladders have resulted in salmon runs through the center of the state capital, Lansing, 68 miles upstream from Grand Rapids, and in tributaries on the Michigan State University campus. A new riverwalk in downtown Lansing, just a long cast from the state Capitol building, is popular with lunchtime anglers, many of them in suits and ties, and a local tackle shop has started an enormously popular rough fish tournament that sees anglers vie for the biggest carp, sucker, and bullhead, just like their counterparts in England.

The Grand also has excellent populations of smallmouth bass in riffle sections, and largemouth in the backwaters along its entire length, but the Portland State Game area a few miles downstream from Lansing has wadeable water that is among the best for both. And it's a great place to catch channel catfish up to 10 pounds, which often smack plugs being cast for smallies.

The owner of a Lansing fly shop has developed a new sport that is gaining in popularity and respect. He sight fishes with 2- and 3-weight rods and No. 20 to 28 nymphs for the various sucker species in the Grand. It's a highly specialized form of angling, and it takes time to develop the knack of hooking the fish, with skilled anglers often outfishing the more ham-handed 20-to-1.

Lake Erie

At the time of The Toledo War, when Michigan and Ohio almost came to blows, most people figured Michigan lost because Ohio kept control of most of western Lake Erie, whereas Michigan had to settle for the then howling wilderness of the Upper Peninsula as compensation. But 150 years after the state militias laid down their arms, hordes of Ohio anglers make the cash registers of UP tackle shops jingle, and Michigan still has access to Lake Erie and what is unquestionably the finest walleye fishery in the world.

Michigan's share of the shallowest, warmest, and second smallest Great Lake is a 50-mile stretch of shoreline between Monroe and the Ohio border in the extreme southeast corner of the state. That's more than enough, because only 20 miles to the south is Ohio's Maumee River, which each spring sees an annual walleye spawning run that averages an incredible 10 million fish. Any angler who wants the experience of catching a batch of smaller fish within two hours and then spending the rest of the morning culling 8-pounders needs to visit these waters in spring, just after the run.

The sonar screens in the western basin of the lake are black with post-spawn walleye for miles off the shorelines, and although these fish are usually in a neutral mood, their numbers are so fantastic that 10 minutes of trolling puts a crankbait in front of so many fish, a strike is almost guaranteed.

Michigan anglers launch from ports like Luna Pier and Monroe, but those who fish here regularly also carry a license for Ohio, which lets them work the waters around the Bass Islands and Put-in-Bay, and Ontario, giving them access to Pelee Island and the Canadian shore.

And although the walleye is king (or queen, in the case of the 8- to 12-pound spring giants), western Lake Erie, which has a deeper basin than its eastern counterpart, also has excellent populations of 10- to 15-pound steelhead, coho salmon of similar size, and chinooks that average 12 pounds and run to 20.

Smallmouth and largemouth bass and northern pike offer excellent fishing along the Lake Erie shoreline and offshore shallow reefs. Most anglers prefer to cast jigs or crankbaits. Yellow perch continue to hold their own here despite a general decline in the rest of the Great Lakes.

Despite its size, Erie is the shallowest of the Great Lakes, averaging 40 feet and having a maximum depth of 210 feet. It is also the warmest, routinely exceeding 70°F in midsummer. One of the great ironies is that most of the walleye in its waters today were restocked from outside sources after overfishing and pollution destroyed the original stocks by the 1960s. In fact, the walleye subspecies found here, called the blue pike by local anglers, is now thought to be extinct.

Inland Northern Lower Peninsula

On warm, muggy nights in late June, when bats and whippoorwills swoop above the silky currents of trout streams and fly anglers in most parts of the country are climbing out of the water, tens of thousands of anglers set out for the rivers in northern Michigan. They usually try to reach their selected spot while they can still see well enough to wade safely, and then wait patiently and hopefully for something that many of them think about all year: the hex hatch. The night-hatching *Hexagenia limbata* is the nation's biggest mayfly, and it can appear in such incredible numbers that huge cannibal brown trout that normally wouldn't even dream of feeding on a surface fly lose all sense of caution and go on a nightly mayfly binge.

The Au Sable and Manistee Rivers in north-central Michigan have the best-known hex hatches (the flies usually start the hatch downstream and work up toward the headwaters over a two-week period). But hexes, often referred to by locals as the Michigan caddis, can be found virtually everywhere in the state, even on Lake St. Clair near Detroit, where the locals curse the "Canadian soldiers" that can gather under street lights in such numbers that cars skid on the greasy patches created by their crushed bodies.

Hexes are maddeningly unpredictable, but as a rule the hatch usually starts after midnight and can consist either of a smattering of flies lasting 10 minutes or a blizzard hatch that goes on for two hours. The spinners can return to the water anytime from dark to dawn, and anglers often observe two peaks of activity during the night, switching from hatcher to spinner imitation as needed.

The fish can be just as schizophrenic as the insects. Sometimes a fantastic hatch or spinner fall will fill the air and water with hexes, yet not a fish rises. Experts say this usually occurs in the first few days of the hatch, when the fish haven't yet keyed on the big flies, and near the end of it, when they are so stuffed with food that they don't need to eat.

Hex anglers usually fish No. 8 to 12 imitations, although the bodies of the flies are only about $1^1/_2$ inches long at a maximum. The usual routine is to locate undercut banks and bends that have good habitat for big trout, listen for the "gloop" sound of a feeder, and then stare into the darkness until eyes accustomed to the gloom can spot the rising fish.

Sometimes anglers come back to work the same monster night after night, and these two weeks probably see more trout over 20 inches taken from these waters than the rest of the season combined, largely because of the hex hatch but probably also because so many anglers are out fishing at night. The biggest confirmed fish taken on a dry fly during the hatch is a 10-pound 8-ounce brown landed near Grayling.

The forests of northern Michigan have largely grown back, albeit different forests than the horizon-wide stands of enormous white pines that once covered the landscape. The Au Sable, one of the most storied trout streams east of the Rockies, fell on hard times again in the 1980s and 1990s. With sewage, phosphates, and other pollutants removed, underwater plant growth declined dramatically, and many anglers say that a lack of plants to feed insects and hide fish is the reason that the population of trout over 8 inches has declined, although baby fish are still plentiful.

The state plans two long-term experiments to fix the problem. One involves increasing the amount of "large woody debris," (such as fallen trees). The other involves grinding up oak and maple leaves and dumping them into the river in an effort to enrich and improve the chemistry of the river bottom. Some scientists believe that decades of mismanaged timbering operations resulted in the gradual impoverishment of the river's ability to sustain large amounts of insect life.

That's not to say that this fishery is poor. A declining Au Sable is still a better trout stream than many that are still in their prime. The spring Hendrickson hatch, which usually coincides with the opening of trout season, still produces excellent dry fly fishing for 12- to 18-inch brown trout. Many anglers prefer to fish the Manistee, which flows west to Lake Michigan, even though its headwaters lie within 10 miles of those of the Au Sable, which flows east to Lake Huron.

One of the most popular ways to fish both streams is from an Au Sable riverboat, which is somewhat of a cross between a canoe and a bateau. Between 18 and 23 feet long, and 3 to 4 feet wide, this boat was designed to separate two fly anglers, with the anglers at the front and the guide at the rear. Instead of a paddle, the guide usually steers the boat with an ash pushpole. The boat's speed downriver is controlled by dragging chains and by increasing the amount of chain let out as the current gets stronger.

Another hatch that causes fish to go wild is the gray drake hatch on the Pere Marquette, usually in mid-June. This river gets regular stockings of brown trout (many anglers have fought against similar stockings on the Au Sable). When the gray drakes get going, it's common for flycasters to take 10 or more 12- to 16-inch browns in an evening, and most anglers say that by the time the fish reach that size it's impossible to tell stocked trout from those born in the stream.

Relicensing the hydroelectric dams resulted in agreements between the states, federal government, and utility companies that have provided better-regulated water flows. As a result, a marvelous brown trout fishery has developed in the Manistee below Tippy Dam, where anglers routinely catch stream-resident browns that run from 3 to 8 pounds. Most of these fish are taken on spawn or plugs, but fly anglers take a few on streamers.

The northern Lower Peninsula abounds with smaller streams that hold excellent populations of brook and brown trout, nearly all of them dependent on natural reproduction. Most of these streams have healthy populations of aquatic insects that start popping out with the little black stonefly hatches in April, just in time for the traditional last-Saturday trout opener, and continue through a sequence of caddisflies, stoneflies, and mayflies that almost always sees the season close before the hatches end. Indeed, on streams with extended seasons, Indian summer can bring excellent dry fly fishing on Blue-Winged Olives, tiny Tricorythodes, and white mayfly patterns well into October.

The area also has hundreds of lakefront resorts, ranging from mom-and-pop cabins to world-renowned lodges, which offer excellent fishing for walleye, smallmouth bass, and panfish. Among the best lakes in this region are Leelenau, Mullet, Burt, Cadillac, Mitchell, Walloon, Fletcher Floodwaters, Houghton, and Higgins.

Ice Fishing
In many Michigan lakes more fish are taken through the ice in winter than from open water the rest of the year. Even southern Michigan is far enough north that anglers can count on six weeks to two months of ice fishing, and one of the best spots is Lake St. Clair's Anchor Bay near Detroit. A hotspot for spearing pike, it's best known for marvelous winter perch and panfish production.

Houghton Lake, in the north-central part of the Lower Peninsula, hosts the annual Tip-Up Town Festival every winter, an event that has outgrown its ice fishing roots to become a snowmobile festival that sees as many as 8,000 machines a day zipping across the ice. The quarry here is perch and northerns, but driving 10 miles farther to Higgins Lake produces excellent opportunities to fish for lake trout, rainbows, and smelt, the latter usually being taken deep on small minnows. If you've never caught a 10-inch smelt on a light rod from 60 feet of water, you're in for a real surprise.

This far north and inland, ice fishing usually starts in December and ends in March (in the UP it can last until May). Walleye, perch, and sunfish are the primary rod-and-reel targets. Pike anglers mostly use tip-ups and spears.

Another spearing target through the ice is the sturgeon, in Black Lake. Because they are allowed only one sturgeon 50 inches or larger per season, many anglers save their efforts for winter, when they can spend hours staring through a green hole in the ice, waiting for the few seconds when the big, dark shape attacks the spearing decoy.

Trout and salmon are caught year-round on inland lakes not designated as trout lakes, and ice fishing probably accounts for the primary harvest of splake, which often is found in less than 3 feet of water once the ice is on.

The Exotics Problem
The captain of a research vessel was standing on the bridge wing of his ship in Saginaw Bay when he saw something beneath the hull near the stern. Alarmed, he ran back, leaned over the side and realized that he was looking at the bottom of the rudder 15 feet below, a new experience in waters that used to be so murky one couldn't see more than a yard beneath the surface.

The reason Saginaw Bay and the rest of the Great Lakes are clearing so rapidly (approaching almost tropical clarity in some areas) is the zebra mussel, a dime-size, filter-feeding bivalve from the Baltic that reached the lakes in the ballast tanks of oceangoing ships about 20 years ago. Without natural enemies, the zebra mussel population exploded, reproducing at a rate that researchers say is 1,000 times greater than in their home waters.

The mussels quickly caused problems by coating and clogging city and industrial water-intake pipes and other underwater structures, but, for anglers, the short-term results of the infestation have been largely positive. What the long-term results will be, no one knows. While the clear waters over tropical reefs appear to teem with life, scientists and anglers know that the richest freshwater fishing grounds are usually in murky waters, living soups that can sustain much larger biomasses.

Some biologists believe that because the mussels feed by filtering tiny organisms from the water, they will compete directly with juvenile gamefish and forage fish for food, or indirectly by removing that food from the water column by excreting it as waste in a form that is unusable by the small fish or the even tinier creatures that the small fish eat.

Minnesota has more boats per capita than any other state in the United States and claims more shoreline than California, Florida, and Hawaii combined.

In the eastern basin of Lake Erie, water clarity had reached a point by 1998 that biologists were worried it could no longer sustain the massive forage base needed to feed the huge numbers of salmon, steelhead, and walleye. Given the rate at which the mussels were spreading, they were concerned that the trend would eventually be repeated even in the vastly greater volumes of Lakes Huron and Michigan.

But for the present, the clearing waters in most places have improved weed growth and populations of sight feeders like smallmouth bass, pike, and muskellunge. The clearer water resulted in a decline in the walleye population in Lake St. Clair near Detroit, but anglers learned to change fishing methods, and many walleye still inhabit the deep, dim channels of the nearby St. Clair and Detroit Rivers.

Another major concern is the continued arrival of exotic species to the Great Lakes in the ballast of seagoing ships. The European ruffe, a perch relative of no angling value but with an enormous appetite for gamefish eggs, showed up in Duluth Harbor at the extreme western end of Lake Superior in the early 1990s. Within five years it was the predominant species in the harbor, but at first it spread only slowly along the northern shoreline of the lake, a few miles a year. Then scientists discovered ruffe in the harbor at Alpena, Michigan, on Lake Huron, about 500 miles to the southeast. It became evident that Duluth ruffe had been transported to Alpena in the ballast of the freighters that carry cement between the two ports.

More than 100 exotic plants and animals have been documented in the Great Lakes over the past 100 years, and most of them arrived in the past three decades. Some of them, like the spiny water flea, have so far been little more than a nuisance to anglers; but others, like the zebra mussel, are considered an economic threat to water intakes and other underwater structures, and the ruffe and round goby could be major threats to sportfish.

Michigan, with a share of four of the Great Lakes, is at the center of the effort to solve the exotics problem, but most scientists believe that these species will continue to arrive until the federal government devises an enforceable solution affecting ships entering the lakes from other countries. Ironically, exotic species here also include the salmon and steelhead that have become the glamour attractions of Great Lakes sportfishing.

MICROFILAMENT (Line)

See: Line.

MICRONESIA

Micronesia is a substantial grouping of islands in the North Pacific Ocean, east of the Philippines (see) and north of the island of New Guinea, and stretching from just north of the equator to about the 20th parallel. In Greek, *Micronesia* means tiny islands, and indeed this region contains some 2,000 islands (mostly coral atolls and islets) that are spread out among the Northern Mariana Islands, the Marshall Islands, Guam (see), Kiribati (see), the Caroline Islands, and Nauru. The largest island is Guam, and it is followed in size by Babelthuap in the Republic of Palau, which is part of the Carolines; both are volcanic in origin.

The Northern Marianas are a U.S. commonwealth and include approximately 16 coral and volcanic islands, the major ones being Saipan, Tinian, and Rota. The Caroline Islands are much larger in overall size, consisting of many hundreds of islands, islets, and atolls, with the principal subdivisions being the states of Chuuk (formerly Truk), Pohnpei (formerly Ponape), Kosrae, and Yap, all of which are in the independent Federated States of Micronesia, and the Republic of Palau, which is a U.S. Trust Territory. The independent Marshall Islands consist of 34 atolls and coral reefs that are divided into the Ratak and Ralik Chains; Kwajalein is the largest atoll, and Bikini the most renowned.

Hardly anyone can tell you where Micronesia is, let alone which islands it comprises or what the angling situation is. Sportfishing is still virtually unknown in this part of the world, and although the true potential here has yet to be determined, it appears to be vast. Many parts of Micronesia are essentially untapped and virgin by modern standards, although they still bear the scars of World War II and subsequent nuclear testing actions. This is especially true of the Marshall Islands, which were subjected to devastating nuclear bomb and megabomb testing and ensuing radioactive fallout.

Bikini Atoll in the Marshalls consists of 36 islets that surround a lagoon that is 21 miles long and 11 miles wide. Atomic tests were begun here in 1946. A megabomb that was detonated in 1954 produced radioactive fallout on the ocean and islands for great distances around Bikini. Although concerns regarding radioactive contamination of the soils and plants on islands in the region existed into the late 1990s, resettlement of Marshallese to some islands has occurred, and attempts at surface restoration of the atolls are underway. The long-term effect on marine life has been much more favorable, and dive camps have been established at some, including Bikini.

Divers are more likely than anglers to have visited Micronesia's coral reefs, and they have reported tremendous marine life, including in and near the Marshall Islands. A 1997 *National Geographic* expedition to Rongelap Atoll, which is about 100 miles east of Bikini and was the recipient of 1954 fallout due to westerly winds, found no visible scars from nuclear radiation to the atoll's coral reef and aquatic life, and described it as "an Eden for fish."

The Caroline Islands have been explored by a few anglers, especially around Chuuk and Pohnpei. Lagoons, reefs, dropoffs, channels, and varied interesting terrain exist here, much of which has never seen sportfishing activity. Likewise, Bikini Atoll, where flats, coral reefs, and nearby deep blue water produced a potpourri of species, was visited only in the late 1990s.

Given the location of the Micronesian atolls in the Pacific, it seems billfish might be plentiful here. Marlin haven't been aggressively targeted by the few anglers who have plied these waters; encounters have been largely accidental, in part because there are few proper boats available and in part because only so much ground can be covered by a few vessels in a limited period of time in such a vast area. When a big-game sportfishing boat was brought to the Caroline Islands in the late 1980s as part of a touring mother-ship operation, however, anglers on board caught more than a dozen billfish in several weeks, including both sailfish and blue marlin. The biggest of the latter nearly hit 500 pounds. Reportedly, these were the first sport-caught billfish in Micronesia. Blue marlin have also been landed more recently off Bikini Atoll and are accompanied by virtually all the pelagic species found throughout the central Pacific, including dolphin, wahoo, and assorted tunas, some in terrific numbers.

The coral reefs, atoll channels, and lagoons abound with sportfish, a full listing of which is still to be completed. Angling reports from these virgin waters have been replete with unabated action; clearly, a bountiful light-tackle fishing paradise exists. Large barracuda, yellowfin tuna, dogtooth tuna, bigeye tuna, bluefin trevally, wahoo, mahimahi (dolphin), kawakawa, rainbow runners, and the usual assortment of grouper, snapper, and sharks are caught close to the atolls.

Flats in the region also contain bonefish, as well as several species of trevally, various snapper, and an assortment of other species. The coral atolls are hard and wadeable, and they are plentiful not only throughout the Marshall Islands, but also in all of Micronesia. As more and better flats become known and accessible, this region will offer among the best flats fishing in the world.

With so few boats and so few anglers currently exploiting these waters, the better locales throughout the vast area of Micronesia have yet to be fully identified.

MIDGES

Midges belong to the scientific order Diptera, a term that is derived from *di,* meaning two, and *ptera,* meaning wing, owing to the presence of just two wings. These aquatic insects are much smaller than many other aquatic insects and are often overlooked, but they are extremely abundant and important food sources for fish in shallow areas of streams, lakes, and most vegetated areas. Two-winged insects represent a broad group of organisms, including deerflies, mosquitoes, blackflies,

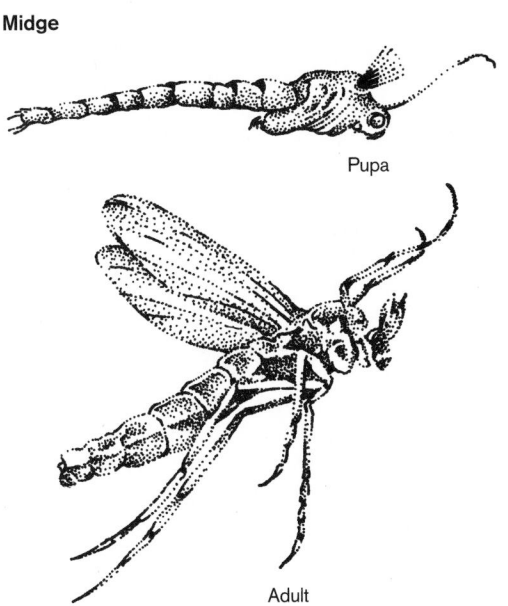

Midge

Pupa

Adult

no-see-ums, and tiny insects that are commonly called gnats in North America or buzzers in Great Britain, but the major food is represented by midges (all midges belong to the genus *Chironomus* and are called chironomids) and secondarily by the larger craneflies. The larvae of these insects are most important as trout food.

The life cycle of these insects is similar to caddisflies *(see)* and consists of egg, larva, pupa, and adult stages, with most of this being in the wormlike or grublike larva stage. Midge larvae, which are only $\frac{1}{8}$ to $\frac{1}{2}$ inch long, burrow into bottom muck or cling to bottom debris, and are widely consumed by trout. After several months, the larva turns into an actively moving pupa, the preadult form that it maintains for several weeks until it matures and swims to the surface. Just under the surface, it hatches into a winged adult, a process that takes enough time to attract the attention of fish, which consume the metamorphosing pupae and emerging adults in large numbers. This activity presents excellent fishing opportunity to fly anglers, who must correctly represent the appropriate stage and size and color of insect species, as well as fish their imitation naturally just beneath the surface. Adults look like mosquitoes, and after emerging they sit on the water surface, where they are preyed upon. When they leave the surface, they often appear in such swarms that they are a nuisance, although they do not bite.

Craneflies are two-winged insects that are less common than midges, but as adults are larger and sometimes very prevalent along stream banks, where they dance over and along the water, becoming a target for trout. Their larvae is also longer than midge larvae, ranging up to 3 inches long and looking very wormlike (they may be called water worms), but their pupae are terrestrial.

See: Aquatic Insects.

M

MIDWATER

In or near the middle layer of water. This term is generally used by biologists to describe the habitat of fish that are not surface or bottom (benthic or demersal, respectively) dwellers.

MIDWAY ATOLL

The coral atoll of Midway consists of Eastern and Sand Islands, situated near the geographic center of the Pacific Ocean and about 1,300 miles northwest of Honolulu, Hawaii. A strategic air and naval base during World War II, Midway was closed to the public and utilized by the United States Armed Forces until September 1993. It is now under the jurisdiction of the U.S. Fish and Wildlife Service, and Midway Atoll National Wildlife Refuge is the first remote island refuge open to the general public in the Pacific.

The Fish and Wildlife Service entered into a public-private partnership to provide refuge operations and support, as well as opportunities for public education and enjoyment. Sportfishing, as well as diving and eco-touring activities, have been conducted at Midway since the late 1990s to benefit overall operations. Anglers practice catch-and-release, except for record fish and consumption.

Essentially a virgin fishery, although similar to that of Hawaii for most pelagic species, the waters around Midway are productive and provide diverse opportunities. Species that were caught in the earliest explorations of the waters around Midway include blue marlin, black marlin, striped marlin, sailfish, bluefin tuna, yellowfin tuna, mahimahi (dolphin), wahoo, giant trevally, bluefin trevally, kawakawa, amberjack, rainbow runners, and grouper. A handful of giant trevally line-class records have been set here, and this species is especially prevalent; 50- to 60-pounders are common and some reach 100 pounds.

A 600-foot dropoff exists just a few miles from the reef, and this is where most big-game fishing has so far occurred. Although 400-pounders have been common, specimens to 850 pounds have been recorded, and expectations for larger fish are realistic.

This area is likely one that will receive much more attention in the future. Several well-equipped sportfishing boats operate here, with experienced crews and opportunities for both inshore and offshore fishing. Accommodations are comfortable, and there's wildlife viewing to be enjoyed as well.

MIGRATION

A regular journey made by a particular species of fish, on an annual or lifetime basis, usually associated with propagation patterns but also associated with the seasonal availability of food. Most migrations are mass movements and involve travel over a particular route, usually at the same time annually. Migration is not to be confused with the relocation of fish because of pollution, sedimentation, storms, or the temporary relocation of food sources. Anglers, for example, often refer to fish as making migrations from deep water to shallow water to feed, an action that is really a localized movement. The periodic movement of fish in a water body is not necessarily a migration, although the movement of a fish species to and from breeding grounds (such as walleye in spring moving from a spawning river back to the main lake) is a migration.

Migrations occur in various species and in both freshwater and saltwater. All freshwater fish that move from lake or river environs to a tributary in order to spawn will migrate to and from the spawning grounds at or around the same time each year. All anadromous (see) and catadromous (see) fish undertake spawning migrations, the former from saltwater to freshwater and the latter from freshwater to saltwater, also around the same time annually. Pelagic (see) ocean species migrate from winter to summer grounds, both for spawning and for food procurement, also around the same time annually. Migrations occur in north-south, south-north, offshore-inshore, and inshore-offshore patterns, and in combinations of these (some sea organisms migrate up and down in the water column). Some fish migrations cover great distances, even thousands of miles, and some are extremely short, perhaps just a short distance up a river.

Water temperature is an important factor in the migration of many gamefish. Although they may appear in a certain area at about the same time each year, their arrival, and in some cases departure, does not occur until specific water temperatures are established or no longer exist. This is usually what makes the migratory arrival of a given species earlier or later than usual, as well as the departure.

Homing instincts are not fully understood, but it is known that the chemical difference in specific tributaries is what allows anadromous species such as salmon to return to their river of birth as adults to propagate. They receive the chemical imprint of their birth water as smolts prior to migrating out to sea.

The migratory habits of many freshwater and saltwater species are important to anglers, even if they are not fully understood, because these habits dictate the appearance and availability of the species. It is when many species of fish are undertaking their spawning migrations, like American shad and the various salmon, that they are most accessible. Likewise, when many pelagic species are following schools of pelagic baitfish, such as herring, their location can be better defined, and thus they become more accessible. When factors that change the presence or abundance of baitfish (like a temperature change) occur, the predators will follow, meaning that anglers should be trying to find the food and should be fishing in places where the primary food sources are most abundant.

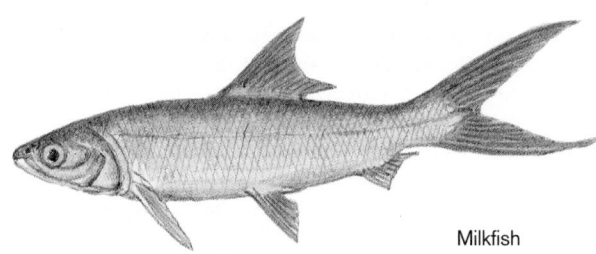

Milkfish

MILKFISH *Chanos chanos.*

Other names—salmon herring; Afrikaans: *melkvis;* Fijian: *yawa;* French: *chano, thon;* Hawaiian: *awa;* Japanese: *sabahii;* Philippine languages: *bangos, banglis, bangolis, bangris, banglot;* Tahitian: *tamano;* Thai: *pla nuanchan;* Vietnamese: *cá máng.*

A herring-like fish, the milkfish is very important in the Indo-Pacific, where it is used widely for food. The fry are collected from rivers and used for stocking ponds, where they are raised to juvenile status and eventually marketed fresh, smoked, canned, and frozen.

Identification. Looking somewhat like a large mullet or a tarpon, the milkfish has a streamlined and compressed body, large eyes, and silvery metallic coloring. It also has a small, toothless mouth, a single spineless dorsal fin, and a large forked tail fin.

Size/Age. The milkfish can reach 5 feet in length and a weight of 50 pounds, and live for 15 years. The all-tackle world record is a 24-pound, 8-ounce Hawaiian fish.

Distribution. In the Indo-Pacific, milkfish occur from Japan south to Australia, west to the Red Sea and South Africa, and east to Hawaii and the Marquesas Islands; in the eastern Pacific, they occur from San Pedro, California, to the Galápagos Islands.

Habitat. Adults travel in schools along continental shelves and around islands where there are well-developed reefs and where temperatures exceed 20°C. Milkfish flourish in water as hot as 32°C.

Life history/Behavior. Milkfish spawn in shallow, brackish water, and a single fish may produce 9 million eggs. These float on the surface until they hatch, and the new larvae enter inshore waters two to three weeks after hatching. Older larvae settle in coastal wetlands during the juvenile stage, occasionally entering freshwater lakes, and older juveniles and young adults return to the sea to mature sexually.

Food and feeding habits. Milkfish larvae feed on zooplankton, whereas juveniles and adults eat bacteria, soft algae, small benthic invertebrates, and sometimes pelagic fish eggs and larvae.

Angling. Not readily caught on rod and reel, milkfish are usually an incidental catch for anglers.

MINIMUM LENGTH LIMIT

A restriction pertaining to the minimum size of fish that may be kept; the restriction prohibits anglers from keeping fish that are less than the specified length. A minimum length limit is the shortest length of a fish, and it is determined by measuring the fish with a ruler. There are several methods of measuring fish, and the appropriate method is often specified in applicable fishing regulations brochures.

A minimum length limit is a legal game regulation established by the fisheries agency with jurisdiction over the location being fished, and enforced by fish and wildlife conservation officers.

See: Measuring Fish; Slot Limit; Fisheries Management; Regulations.

MINNESOTA

Sportfishing is more than recreational pursuit in the Land of 10,000 Lakes; it is a way of life. About 1.4 million fishing licenses are sold in Minnesota every year, and about one in four residents own a fishing license. Every year on the second weekend in May, an estimated 1 million people participate in the general fishing opener, a day regarded more as a celebration of spring than the beginning of the fishing season. Sportfishing tourism is among the top five industries in the state.

With its bounty of water and its northern forests, Minnesota has come to epitomize the northwoods fishing experience. The phrase "going up North"—a standard in Minnesota vernacular—means piling into the family car for a weekend at the cabin, usually to fish for walleye, northern pike, bass, or panfish. Perhaps the most enduring postcard image of Minnesota is that of a canoe floating serenely on a remote northern lake, its occupant holding a fishing rod.

But Minnesota offers much more than northwoods lakes. The Minneapolis–St. Paul metropolitan area boasts one of the nation's largest and most diversified urban fisheries. Twin Cities lakes are populated with trophy muskies (in excess of 30 pounds), feisty walleye of all sizes, unlimited numbers of panfish, and largemouth bass up to 7 pounds. Lake Minnetonka, which is within sight of downtown Minneapolis, became the darling of competitive bass angling in the mid-1990s, in part because it yielded catches of bass with an exceptional average weight of 4 pounds.

Lake Superior, the world's largest body of freshwater, abuts the far northeastern edge of Minnesota; this deep and cold lake is home to chinook and coho salmon, two species of rainbow trout (steelhead and Kamloops), and a burgeoning lake trout population.

Minnesota also contains the headwaters of the Mississippi River. As the river winds south from Itasca State Park, it develops into a world-class fishery for smallmouth bass and walleye, even in the urbanized stretches within Minneapolis and St. Paul. The renewed fishery there is due to dramatic improvements in water quality.

The St. Croix River, a federally designated wild and scenic river, supports thriving numbers of smallmouth bass, walleye, crappie, and muskies. Several other major river systems—notably the Minnesota, St. Louis, and Rainy Rivers—are established walleye fisheries.

For trout lovers, the southeast corner of the state offers hundreds of miles of streams full of browns, brookies, and rainbows. Inland streams along Lake Superior's North Shore hold native populations of brook trout, while dozens of northern inland lakes supply anglers with brook, rainbow, and lake trout. Minnesota enjoys a large and growing population of fly fishing enthusiasts, despite the state's obsession with walleye, the official state fish.

For true trophy seekers, Minnesota has some of North America's finest muskie waters; indeed, two fish exceeding 50 pounds in 1996 came close to bumping off the 54-pound state record. Large northern pike are also found in select trophy waters.

In the winter, anglers turn their attention to ice fishing, which is a story unto itself. Some lakes support entire communities of heated fish houses. Minnesota is also the birthplace of the modern portable ice fishing shelters that have revolutionized the way many anglers spend their winters.

More than 1 million acres of roadless forests and nonmotorized lakes are at the disposal of backcountry anglers in the Boundary Waters Canoe Area Wilderness. Most canoeists regard a Boundary Waters trip incomplete without a sizzling meal of fried walleye.

Unheralded but equally important are the dozens of lesser rivers, hundreds of smaller prairie lakes, and thousands of farm ponds—there are actually 15,292 lakes and nearly 15,000 miles of rivers and stream in the state—that provide opportunities for all manner of warmwater species.

Species Overview

The fisheries in many of Minnesota's lakes, particularly those in the central and northern regions, are so diversified that it is possible to catch all of their prime species in the same day. The following information applies to nearly all of these lakes.

Walleye.   Spring and early summer are best suited to fishing for walleye throughout Minnesota. These fish are typically oriented to shallow-water structures such as sand and gravel bars, rocky points, dropoffs, and shallow bays. The universal lure for walleye at this time of year is a jig and minnow, the latter being a shiner or a fathead. Jig sizes vary depending on how deep they are fished, but generally a $1/8$- or $1/4$-ounce size is sufficient. The minnow is impaled through the head, cast, and slowly bounced across the bottom. Walleye always attack the jig-minnow combination during its falling motion.

Leeches and nightcrawlers become the baits of choice as summer progresses. Anglers favor using them under a slip float, usually over or near shallow structures such as rockpiles and reefs. They can also be trolled slowly using a variety of live-bait rigs, or

threaded on a jig and cast. Crankbaits and stickbaits also come into play later in the summer; they are typically trolled in shallow water (3 to 15 feet) for more aggressive fish. In the fall, walleye return to the shallows, where anglers land them on all manner of live-bait rigs. Throughout Minnesota, walleye fishing is done using light- to medium-weight spinning equipment rigged with 6- or 8-pound-test monofilament.

Some of the more popular walleye lakes in north-central Minnesota are Gull, Pelican, Mille Lacs, Leech, Winnibigoshish, Osakis, the Whitefish Chain, Ottertail, Cass, Cut Foot Sioux, and Fish near Duluth.

Northern pike.   Aggressive and plentiful, northern pike are often considered a nuisance by walleye anglers. However, they are a popular species when walleye are not biting. Most pike weigh between 2 and 8 pounds, but trophy lakes can yield specimens larger than 20 pounds. Pike are caught most of the year, even in the warmest summer months. They are often taken incidentally on jig-minnow combinations, but anglers serious about catching large pike use large crankbaits, spoons, or large sucker minnows suspended under a float or a bobber.

Most lakes in the central and northern region harbor northern pike, but truly large pike are found in Mille Lacs, Leech, and Winnibigoshish. To grow large, pike need a prey base of tullibee or cisco, a rough fish found generally in larger lakes. This is not to say some smaller lakes don't produce the occasional lunker.

Largemouth bass.   Bass inhabit most shallow, weed-filled lakes. Starting early in the summer, spinnerbaits are popular lures. So are jigs tipped with plastic grubs and pork rind. The universal plastic worm is a particularly popular lure in Minnesota, with many variations in colors and sinker sizes. Crankbaits are effective in the summer, as bright sun drives bass deeper. Some of the more notable Minnesota bass lakes are Le Homme Dieu, Gull, the Chisago Chain, and numerous waters in the Detroit Lakes area.

Smallmouth bass.   Smallmouth are more plentiful in the lakes of northeastern Minnesota, but one of the most important smallmouth fisheries cuts through the heart of the state. The Mississippi River boasts smallmouths in good numbers and sizes up to 23 inches in length. The best stretches of the river lie between Brainerd and Elk River, sections of which have special regulations to promote trophy fishing.

Most anglers float the Mississippi River in small boats or canoes. Minnow-imitating lures are popular baits, as are jigs tipped with minnows. The river has become a popular destination for fly anglers, who have success with poppers and wet flies.

Crappie.   Crappie are plentiful in central and northern Minnesota, but most anglers keep their top spots a blood secret. The best crappie lakes are

A one-third-inch-long clam, collected at 12,350 feet in the ocean, was estimated by scientists to be over a century old.

those that are lightly fished; otherwise, word of good crappie fishing spreads quickly and the tasty panfish fall prey to overfishing. The best crappie fishing occurs in late April and early May, when the fish congregate in shallow, dark bays to feed on insects and small minnows. The most common fishing technique is to employ a small minnow fished under a slip bobber. A tiny jig lends color and extra weight.

Central and Northern Lakes Region

Minnesota's central and northern lakes region represents the core of the state's walleye, northern pike, panfish, and bass fisheries. The region could be roughly defined as that north-south area between St. Cloud and Bemidji and extending from Detroit Lakes east to Duluth. Sportfishing permeates the economy of this region; every town, no matter how small, has at least one bait shop.

North-central Minnesota is dominated by several large lakes: Mille Lacs (132,000 acres), Leech (111,000 acres), and Winnibigoshish (58,000 acres). These shallow, hard-bottomed lakes are ideal walleye factories. Within this area lie hundreds of other lakes ranging between 500 and 20,000 acres. This is the heart of Minnesota's vacation country; resorts, lodges, and summer cabins dot the shorelines here.

Lakes in this region share many similarities. Most are multispecies lakes, although walleye are the primary target. A few are stocked with walleye, but most have naturally sustaining populations. Bass and panfish are the second-most sought-after species, followed by northern pike and yellow perch.

Lake Mille Lacs. This is Minnesota's most treasured walleye lake and one of the finest such fisheries in the nation. Bowl-shaped, shallow—few spots exceed 30 feet; and measuring a grand 132,000 acres, Mille Lacs is ideally suited for producing walleye. Consequently, scarcely a foot of this lake's shoreline isn't occupied by a resort, lodge, private cabin, or launch service. In the winter, hundreds of ice fishing houses, ranging from shanties to palatial cabins with televisions and hot tubs, crowd onto the lake, creating small ice fishing villages complete with plowed roads. Nearly a half-million pounds of walleye (none are stocked) are pulled from Mille Lacs in an average season.

In recent years the lake has earned a deserved reputation for trophy muskies, northern pike, and smallmouth bass. The lake's emerging muskie population has specimens pushing 40 pounds; pike can range from small "hammer handles" to 20-pounders; and smallmouth as big as 7 pounds have been caught. When nothing else is biting, jumbo perch can fill an angler's stringer in the summer and winter. Many people believe that Minnesota's next state-record muskellunge will come from Mille Lacs. It is not uncommon for anglers to see 20 or more of these fish in a day and, if they are lucky,

land one or two. Most cast heavy jerkbaits, surface lures, or bucktails.

Despite these riches, the walleye is king on Mille Lacs, and for many Minnesotans the pursuit of these fish borders on obsession. A typical "keeper" walleye ranges between 1 and 4 pounds, but fish in excess of 8 pounds are not uncommon, with a few 11- to 12-pounders taken each year. In the late 1990s, courts allocated portions of the Mille Lacs walleye fishery to Chippewa tribes, which has resulted in different sportfishing regulations almost on a yearly basis.

Despite its rather plain appearance, Mille Lacs can be a challenging lake. The bottom is composed of a variety of substrates—sand and mud "flats" and rocks—and walleye linger in these areas depending on the season and time of day. Jigs tipped with minnows or leeches are a primary bait for walleye, fished either over shallow rocks and sand, or over the lake's famous mud flats. Live-bait rigs are equally successful, as are crankbaits trolled over the rocks. The bulk of the walleye are caught in May and June; in the summer, the fish head for deep water.

Because the lake is huge, a good-size boat (16 feet or larger) and a map are recommended. Heavy winds can produce big waves and make the lake unfishable. Fishing launches are popular, and scores of guides call Mille Lacs home.

Leech Lake. Like Mille Lacs, Leech Lake near the town of Walker is a fine walleye fishery, in terms of numbers of fish and their size. Walleye fishing is best in the early summer and again in the fall, but savvy anglers are able to find them in deeper waters all summer long.

This huge, many-armed lake, however, is perhaps most famous for its muskie fishing. In the 1950s, during a period of warm, stagnant summer weather, the lake's muskies went on a "rampage." Anglers caught so many that they filled wheelbarrows. Black-and-white photos from the era show anglers standing next to racks bulging with dozens of large muskies.

The lake's reputation continues. In 1996, an Iowa angler caught a muskie weighing 52 pounds, the state's largest in several decades. Fish in excess of 40 inches are not uncommon. Muskies bite all summer, but the prime angling occurs in September and October, when the fish aggressively chase bait. Popular lures are bucktails, jerkbaits, and topwater plugs.

Northern Border Lakes

Lake of the Woods. This huge lake straddling Canada claims the title "Walleye Capital of the World," a moniker shared by a half-dozen other major walleye fisheries in the nation, including Minnesota's own Lake Mille Lacs. Suffice to say that Lake of the Woods is a formidable walleye lake. Because it is 55 miles wide at its greatest point and covers 65,000 miles of shoreline, it appears on most national maps and occupies that distinctive knob of

M

northern Minnesota that protrudes into Ontario. It is home to a substantial resort and lodge community accessible through the towns of Baudette and Warroad. Another geographical aberration called the Northwest Angle—accessible only through Canada or across the lake—supports numerous fishing resorts.

Lake of the Woods offers walleye and sauger in both good numbers and size. The end of commercial fishing gave the fishery a much-needed boost. Photos on resort walls tell the story: smiling groups of anglers posing with catches ranging from 1-pounders to 12-pounders. The prime periods are late May and June, and the early fall, when walleye stay shallow and succumb to a variety of live-bait rigs and jigs. Otherwise, downriggers and crankbaits have emerged as a prime summer technique for deep-dwelling walleye. Locating prime underwater structure, such as reefs and sandbars, is key to catching Lake of the Woods walleye.

Ice fishing is another big attraction at Lake of the Woods. Resorts employ specially designed tracked vans, hovercraft, and amphibious vehicles to travel far out on the lake, where ice houses provide heated fishing environments. An estimated 84,000 anglers visit Lake of the Woods to ice fish every winter. Air service is also available for winter and summer anglers wanting access to resorts on distant Oak Island.

Large muskies inhabit Lake of the Woods, although dedicated muskie chasers will fish both Minnesota and Ontario waters. Lake of the Woods arguably offers an angler's best chance to land a 50-plus-inch muskie in the United States. Muskies are caught from mid-June through the fall, but August may be the best month; the fish can be active and shallow then, and may strike surface lures. Some trolling is done here, but most muskie anglers favor casting, as shallow water, rocky reefs, and submerged weed growth are bountiful.

Big pike are also plentiful; many are caught through the ice early in the winter. Largemouth bass exist in some areas of Lake of the Woods, but the lake is a haven for smallmouths, which, though not huge, offer abundant and relatively shallow action all season. With 14,000 islands in this gigantic and confusing body of water, anglers will find numerous rocky nooks to work.

Other large border lakes. Island-studded Rainy Lake lies on the Minnesota-Ontario border near International Falls. It is an enormous lake with a resurgent walleye population. It is also a first-class smallmouth bass and crappie lake. Portions lie within Voyageurs National Park, which is one of the nation's few water-based national parks. Special permits aren't needed to fish in the park, and backcountry camping opportunities are numerous and scenic. With many reefs and shallow rocks, Rainy Lake is a tricky lake to navigate, but the scenery and sportfishing are well worth the visit. A lake map is recommended. Houseboats are a popular means of

seeing and fishing the lake; several local companies rent them.

Lake Kabetogama is the next water east of Rainy Lake. It, too, lies within Voyageurs National Park and is a reputable walleye fishery. Smallmouth bass are fewer here. Like Rainy, it hosts a thriving resort industry. The next lake, Namakan, is another fine walleye fishery.

Boundary Waters Canoe Area Wilderness

The 1-million-plus-acre Boundary Waters Canoe Area Wilderness is a gem in America's wilderness system. Located in northeastern Minnesota along the Canadian border, this sprawling network of pristine lakes and rivers is completely roadless and open to nonmotorized boats only, although a handful of border lakes allow outboards of 25 horsepower or less. Tens of thousands of canoeists flock to the Boundary Waters every season, making it the most heavily used wilderness in the nation.

Boundary Waters offers superb backcountry fishing for walleye, northern pike, smallmouth bass, lake trout, and stream trout, but novices should do their homework before planning a trip. Fishing success varies greatly from lake to lake and season to season. Most veteran anglers plan circuitous canoe routes that include stops at prime fishing lakes, which enables them to fish a variety of lakes while enjoying new scenery. Otherwise, a common strategy is to set up a base camp on a prime fishing lake and take day trips from there.

Either way, this takes planning and research, so it is advisable to hire a guide for a first trip. With literally hundreds of lakes and routes to choose from, novices can easily waste time on unproductive waters.

Two time periods offer the best fishing: late May through June, and September through October. In the spring and earlier summer, walleye and bass still roam the shallows, typically in such areas as rocky points, bays, river inlets and outlets, and shallow reefs. Lake trout and stream trout also inhabit the shallows. Once summer arrives, most species head for deeper reefs and rocky structures where they can still be caught, but only by those who know where these specific structures lie. Likewise in the fall, walleye, bass, and lake trout move back into shallow areas. For fishing and scenery, fall is a particularly spectacular season in which to visit the Boundary Waters.

Because most Boundary Waters fishing is done from canoes, camping and fishing gear must be lightweight to ensure feasible portages. A well-conceived fishing outfit should include a medium-weight spinning rod and reel; a minimum selection of crankbaits, spoons, and spinners; and terminal tackle for live-bait rigs. Minnows, nightcrawlers, and leeches are the natural baits of choice.

Several large lakes are famous Boundary Waters fisheries. They include Basswood, which is the home of the state-record northern pike, and Saganaga, Seagull, Gunflint, and the Minnesota portions of Crooked and Lac La Croix Lakes. Saganaga, which has depths to 240 feet, is the deepest Minnesota Lake. Walleye and smallmouth bass are the target species, but northern pike are also found in most Boundary Waters lakes. Lake trout inhabit only the deeper lakes, and stream trout are available in state-designated trout lakes.

The Boundary Waters are accessible through major entry points in Ely, Grand Marais, and the Gunflint Trail. Special permits and fees are required to enter the wilderness; reservations must be made well in advance. Numerous outfitters, guides, and well-stocked tackle shops are available at major entry points. A number of popular guidebooks serve as valuable tools for planning a fishing trip.

Prairie Lakes and Rivers

As one heads south from northern Minnesota, the state slowly transitions from northern spruce and pine forests to central hardwoods and then to farmland and prairies. A steady dose of farmland greets the traveler south of Interstate 94. This region maintains a remarkable number of thriving fisheries.

Big Stone Lake, located in extreme western Minnesota, rates as one of the state's best walleye fisheries. It is actually a dammed portion of the Minnesota River that straddles the South Dakota border. As a border lake, Big Stone opens earlier than other lakes and offers superb walleye

fishing. Just up the road, Traverse Lake is considered another good walleye lake.

Farther downstream is Lac qui Parle Lake, one of the state's least-known walleye meccas. Nearby Artichoke Lake is another sleeper walleye site.

Several counties west of Lac qui Parle is Kandiyohi County, which is home to three fine walleye lakes: Green, Diamond, and Big Kandiyohi. Farther south, the lakes surrounding Mankato are renowned for their bass fishing. Lake Tetonka, located farther west near the town of Waterville, is home of the state-record largemouth bass.

Lake Superior

The recovery of Lake Superior's lake trout fishery is one of the great ecological success stories of this century. Attacked by invading sea lampreys, lake trout were nearly wiped out of the lake in the 1950s. But by the 1960s, federal and state biologists had devised ways to control lampreys and, buoyed by stocking programs, lake trout began a slow recovery in Lake Superior waters of Minnesota, Wisconsin, and Michigan.

While the lake trout recovery was underway, fisheries managers in Minnesota and the other states tried experimental stockings of Pacific salmon, subspecies of rainbow trout, and even Atlantic salmon. For the most part, these fish thrived; through the 1980s, Lake Superior became a menagerie of big gamefish, sating the appetites of anglers seeking large salmonids and giving rise to a huge charter boat industry.

That success story was tempered significantly in the 1990s, at least in Minnesota waters of Lake Superior. Runs of chinook salmon and steelhead declined significantly, and the state's Atlantic salmon stocking program was discontinued. Coho stocking also ceased. Meanwhile, lake trout became more abundant than ever.

Along the Minnesota portion of Lake Superior, anglers still catch salmon, but in fewer numbers. Steelhead anglers still ply the waters of the Knife,

M

Minnesota's renowned Boundary Waters offers winter fishing via dogsled team access and summer fishing via canoe-portage access.

French, and other rivers, but the fishery is catch-and-release only for wild stocks. (The nonnative Kamloops strain of rainbows are still relatively plentiful and can be kept.) Lake trout now make up the bulk of the catch, including specimens up to 20 pounds and even a rare 30-pounder.

Minnesota's portion of Lake Superior's shoreline is stunning in its beauty, and it is relatively undeveloped. The North Shore starts in Duluth and ends at Canada's border. The lake is clear, cold, and dangerous to those who don't know its moods. A large boat (20 feet or more) is recommended, although locals often use deep-V inland boats as small as 16 feet. A small fleet of charter boats still operates out of the Duluth harbor.

Downriggers are a popular tool for pursuing salmon and trout in Lake Superior. Anglers employ a variety of plugs and spoons, which can be moved with downriggers through varying depths and according to water temperatures. Anglers often search shallow reefs and use heavy jigs for lake trout. Shore casting is also popular, using spoons and plugs. Steelheaders ply the rivers in the spring with spawn sacks and flies.

Lake Superior's inland streams and lakes. Tumbling out of the rugged North Shore ridges are numerous streams and creeks that harbor native brook trout. These streams are remote and overgrown with brush; they offer a challenge to anglers willing to explore the backcountry. Most of the trout are small—a 15-incher is a trophy—but these streams are beautiful and relatively untouched by the angling hordes.

Likewise, numerous inland lakes in Lake and Cook Counties offer fishing for rainbows, larger brook trout, lake trout, and splake. The Gunflint Trail, which heads northwest from Grand Marais, provides primary access to many of these backcountry lakes. Trout are typically caught all season long, but the prime periods are spring and fall.

Southeast Bluff Country

The landscape of southeastern Minnesota departs dramatically from the rest of the state. As the prairies approach the Mississippi River, they rise to form rolling, oak-studded hills, scenic valleys, and limestone bluffs. From theses highlands bubble hundreds of miles of creeks and streams that eventually empty into the Mississippi River. Southeastern Minnesota—a region that includes Fillmore, Houston, Winona, Olmsted, and Wabasha Counties—has a strong resemblance to New England, with small farming communities, narrow winding roads, and big red barns. It's a beautiful part of the Midwest.

It is also trout country. Brook, rainbow, and brown trout make their home in streams and rivers, some of which are stocked by the Department of Natural Resources (DNR). Most, though, support wild browns or brookies. When the trout season opens in mid-April, anglers pursue trout that range from 6 inches to several pounds. Occasionally, browns in excess of 5 pounds are caught in deeper pools.

The streams are too numerous to name, but most belong to two major watersheds: the Whitewater and the Root River systems. Some streams are small enough to jump across; others, such as the main stem of the Root River, can handle canoes and small, flat-bottomed boats. The DNR publishes a comprehensive map of designated southeast trout streams, which are accessible through easements and at road and bridge crossings. Finding a place to fish isn't difficult, but intrepid anglers must take the time to seek permission from private landowners to access pools away from the crowds.

Bait anglers can get by with a simple nightcrawler, hook, and split shot. Others rely on a variety of small in-line spinners and small crankbaits, whereas fly anglers typically employ Elk-Hair caddis, Bead-Head Pheasant Tails, Blue-Winged Olives, Tricos, and other small mayfly imitations. Fly hatches can sometimes be quite heavy through the late spring and summer, offering fly anglers terrific opportunities to fool trout with their own creations. In recent years, fly fishing in the southeast region has become popular; local tackle shops, even in small towns, often stock good selections of popular patterns.

Smallmouth bass are an overlooked species in the southeast. Fly anglers with surface poppers can have terrific action throughout the summer; otherwise, small crankbaits and surface plugs work with spinning gear. Bass up to 19 and 20 inches are available.

The Twin Cities

The state-record tiger muskie came from Lake Calhoun, just a mile from downtown Minneapolis. Portions of the Mississippi River in St. Paul provide such a wealth of walleye that regulations require catch-and-release only. Lake Minnetonka regularly yields bass over 5 pounds, and a recent state-record crappie came from Coon Lake in the northern suburbs. These are a few examples of the superb fishing opportunities found in and around the Twin Cities.

The Twin Cities muskie population is a result of an intense state stocking effort. Prime lakes include Calhoun, Harriet, Independence, Owasso, Bald Eagle, Cedar, and Rebecca. The best fishing typically occurs from midsummer through fall. Casting heavy lures is the main technique, but trolling is also effective.

Pool 2 of the Mississippi River, which is below the Ford Dam in St. Paul, is one of the most popular open-water winter fisheries in the state. Catches of 50 or more walleye in a day are not uncommon. Sauger are also plentiful. Most anglers use jigs and minnows; crankbaits are more effective for trolling the river's rocky shores in the summer. Walleye up to 10 pounds are caught regularly.

Many people regard Lake Minnetonka as one of the best largemouth fisheries in the nation, not because it holds extremely large fish (7 pounds is about the maximum because of the short growing season) but because it produces large numbers of fish in the 2- to 5-pound range. Jigs adorned with plastic bodies and tails, soft-plastic worms, and crankbaits are among the more popular baits. Ironically, the invasion of a fast-growing exotic weed, Eurasian milfoil, is credited with bolstering the lake's bass population. Lake Minnetonka is also a good walleye and muskie lake.

Other popular Twin Cities bass lakes are Lake Waconia, Demontreville and Olson Lakes, Big Marine, and Forest Lake.

Quality panfish opportunities are plentiful in the Twin Cities, too. Coon Lake is famous for its crappie, as is Minnetonka. White Bear Lake holds good crappie and sunfish populations, as do Lake Phalen, Lake Harriet, and Prior Lake. Popular walleye lakes are White Bear, Prior, Calhoun, Harriet, Phalen, Forest, and Bald Eagle.

Mississippi River, Southern Reaches

Once it leaves the Twin Cities, the Mississippi River winds its way south along the Wisconsin-Minnesota border through scenic river towns such as Hastings, Red Wing, Lake City, Wabasha (the setting for the popular movie "Grumpy Old Men"), and Winona. Walleye and sauger are plentiful throughout the system. Spring and summer fishing in the stretch from Hastings to Red Wing is superb. Anglers focus their efforts around wing dams—sub-surface structures that jut into the river. Red Wing is another well-known walleye and sauger fishery virtually year-round. Anglers congregate near the dam on warm days in the winter; catches of 50 to 100 fish daily are not uncommon. Jigs and minnows, live-bait rigs, and crankbaits are preferred offerings.

The river widens and forms Lake Pepin near Lake City. Pepin is another reputed walleye fishery, and white bass are also popular here. Anglers track schools of white bass by following feeding gulls. Both predators key on migrating schools of baitfish. Backwaters of the river provide fast northern pike action in the spring.

MINNOW

More than 2,000 species constitute the minnow, or Cyprinidae, family of freshwater fish, making it perhaps the largest family of fish. "Minnow," "shiner," and "dace" are three names commonly associated with members of this family, which also includes carp *(see)* and chub *(see)*.

Minnows occur in Africa, Asia, Europe, and North America. Although this family attains its greatest diversity in Asia, it is the largest family of freshwater fish in North America, where more than 300 different species occur. The greatest diversity in North America exists in the southeastern United States, but minnows are widely distributed

Minnows are used extensively as bait by anglers; keeping them lively in a proper well or container is especially important.

throughout North America—from Alaska to southern Mexico—and often represent a large proportion of species within regional fish faunas.

Well-known genera of native North American minnows include *Campostoma* (stonerollers), *Cyprinella* (satinfin shiners), *Gila* (Gila chub), *Luxilus* (highscale shiners), *Lythrurus* (smallscale shiners), *Nocomis* (chub), *Notropis* (true shiners), *Phoxinus* (redbelly dace), *Pimephales* (bluntnose minnows), *Ptychocheilus* (squawfish), and *Rhinichthys* (dace).

Identification. Minnows are characterized by a single dorsal fin, abdominally located pelvic fins, soft fin rays, cycloid scales, and a set of bones connecting the inner ear to the swim bladder. This last attribute is known as the Weberian apparatus and enhances the ability of minnows to detect sound.

Minnows do not have teeth in their mouths but instead grind food with pharyngeal teeth located in their throat. Males of many minnow species have keratinized bumps known as tubercles on their head, body, and fins. Tubercles may facilitate body contact during spawning, or they may be used in aggressive interactions between males. The large tubercles of chub and stonerollers have earned these species the nickname "hornyheads" among many anglers.

Even for ichthyologists, exact minnow species can be especially difficult to identify. Some useful characteristics include breeding coloration, location of tubercles on nuptial males, pharyngeal tooth

M

counts, mouth shape, anal fin ray counts, various scale counts, and the presence or absence of barbels. Knowledge of species distribution aids in identification, especially when two similar-looking species have nonoverlapping ranges.

The best approach to minnow identification is to obtain a regional guide to fish containing both dichotomous keys and illustrations. Many excellent guides are available and can usually be obtained from university libraries, natural-history museums, and specialty bookstores.

Habitat.   The ecological habitats of minnows are as diverse as the family itself. Minnows occur in creeks, streams, rivers, swamps, ponds, lakes, and impoundments. The majority of minnow species, however, occur in flowing waters and do not fare well in impoundments.

Food and feeding habits.   Most species feed on aquatic insects, crustaceans, and detritus, but a few are specialized for feeding on algae or plankton. Larger species, such as chub in the genus *Semotilus,* or squawfish, prey on other fish.

Size/Age.   The body size and life span of minnows vary widely. Adults of most minnow species are less than 100 millimeters long and live for two to five years. One of the smallest species is the blackmouth shiner *(Notropis melanostomus),* which may not exceed 37 millimeters in length. At the opposite end of the spectrum is North America's largest native minnow, the Colorado squawfish *(Ptychocheilus lucius),* which has been recorded to reach a total length of 1.8 meters and a weight of 45 kilograms. Minnows in this genus may live for more than 10 years.

Life history.   Minnows exhibit a variety of life history attributes. The breeding season can be as short as one month, or last throughout the year. Many species reproduce between March and August, probably because warmer water temperatures are more conducive to the production of gametes and survival of larvae. Accordingly, the length of the breeding season is generally longer for species occurring in lower latitudes.

The number of eggs produced (or fecundity) by female minnows varies both within and among minnow species. In general, larger females can produce more eggs. The flagfin shiner *(Pteronotropis signipinnis),* for example, matures at lengths under 30 millimeters and releases an average of 32 eggs per clutch. In contrast, the giant Colorado squawfish *(Ptychocheilus lucius)* may produce around 20,000 eggs. Total fecundity is often underestimated because many minnows produce multiple clutches of eggs within a single spawning season. Aquarium-held bannerfin shiners *(Cyprinella leedsi),* for example, may release up to 228 eggs every 3 to 10 days. Multiple clutch production may ensure that individuals from at least one clutch survive, especially in stream environments where rapid changes in physical conditions can impact the survival of larval or juvenile fish.

Mature egg sizes in minnows range from about 0.6 millimeter to 2 millimeters in diameter. Species exhibiting territorial behavior or occurring in fast-water habitats generally produce the largest eggs. For example, the central stoneroller *(Campostoma anomalum)* is a territorial species that produces 2-millimeter eggs. In contrast, the cherryfin shiner *(Lythrurus roseipinnis),* a species characteristic of slow-flowing Gulf of Mexico coastal-plain streams, produces eggs that average 0.77 millimeter in diameter.

Spawning behavior.   The reproductive behavior of North American minnows is fascinating and complex. Substantial variation in reproductive behavior exists within the family, but species can be grouped into a few general categories.

Broadcasting species scatter their eggs over plants, gravel, or the nests of other species and then abandon them. Broadcasters can spawn as pairs in which males clasp individual females, or as large groups in which it is less clear which males fertilize which eggs. The broadcasting strategy is used by the majority of species for which spawning behavior is known.

Crevice spawning occurs in many species of satinfin shiners and in the California roach *(Hesperoleucus symmetricus).* Males guard territories around the crevices associated with rocks and logs. Males and females swim next to each other alongside the crevice, and the female deposits eggs into it. Males may deposit sperm during solo runs along the crevice or while swimming with the female. Although no post-spawning parental care occurs in these species, fertilized eggs situated within the crevice are well protected from predation.

Pit, pit-ridge, and mound building all involve manipulation of the substrate by territorial males for the construction of spawning nests. Eggs laid within these types of nests may suffer lower mortality rates because of the presence of territorial males (which may deter egg predation), partial or full concealment within the substrate, and better aeration as a result of the hydraulic properties of the nest. The widely distributed striped shiner *(Luxilus chrysocephalus; see: shiner, striped)* is a pit spawner.

Eight species within the highscale shiners, as well as stonerollers, dig circular spawning pits in gravel with their snouts and mouths. More than one male may attempt to fertilize a female that swims over the pit.

Pit-ridge nests are constructed by chub in the genus *Semotilus.* Gravel is piled at the upstream portion of the nest upon completion of the initial pit. After spawning, males cover the eggs with gravel and dig another pit downstream of the just-formed ridge. The ridge can approach 2 meters in length as the male continues to bury the eggs from each spawning act. The pit-ridge nest of the fallfish *(Semotilus corporalis)* is the largest nest known among fish.

Mound building occurs in eight species of chub and cutlips minnows *(Nocomis* and *Exoglossum* species). As with pit-ridge nesters, the eggs are covered by the male after fertilization.

The ornate shiner *(Codoma ornata)*, the pugnose minnow *(Opsopoeodus emiliae)*, and the bluntnose minnow are egg clusterers. Eggs are laid in a single layer on the underside of a flat object. In addition to guarding the cavity, male bluntnose minnows increase survivorship of the eggs by removing fungused eggs with their mouths and fanning the egg mass. Male bluntnose minnows also rub the eggs with their nape, which may spread protective mucous layers over them.

Nest-associating minnows include roughly 25 species that spawn over the nests of other minnows, and about 10 species that spawn on sunfish nests. Most nest associates are categorized as broadcasters, but some species of highscale shiners and stonerollers can build pits or spawn over the nests of other species.

Value. Minnows are extremely important ecologically. They transfer energy throughout aquatic ecosystems by converting their detrital, algal, and microorganismal diets into fish flesh that can be eaten by larger fish. They are also an important food source for birds and other wildlife. Minnows serve as hosts to freshwater mussel larvae *(glochidia)*, which attach to fish gills in order to disperse and complete early development. Many mussel species require a particular fish host, so the decline of certain minnow species may result in the decline and possibly the extinction of certain freshwater mussels.

Nest-building minnows are sometimes referred to as "keystone species" because their presence has a strong effect on many other species in aquatic communities. These nests not only provide spawning habitat for many other minnows, but the large number of eggs deposited in them may also be consumed by other species of fish and stream invertebrates.

Minnows are sought after and eaten by many anglers. In addition, they are used as bait and constitute a large proportion of the natural forage base upon which freshwater gamefish depend. Examples of species that are commonly fished for and eaten include chub of the genera *Nocomis* and *Semotilus,* the peamouth *(Mylocheilus caurinus)*, the Sacramento blackfish *(Orthodon microlepidotus)*, stonerollers, squawfish, and carp. Many of these species are taken with flies or artificial lures, and put up a good fight when caught with light or ultralight tackle.

Almost all minnow species are suitable for use as bait. Species such as the golden shiner *(Notemigonus crysoluecas)* and the fathead minnow *(Pimephales promelas)* are widely sold as bait because they are easy to culture in large quantities. Anglers can easily collect other species from streams by using a small seine net, but they should be familiar with state regulations before doing so.

Because of their abundance and broad range of body sizes, minnows are important forage items for many game species. Given their wide distribution throughout North America, the introduction of nonnative forage fish is usually unnecessary and potentially harmful to native fish.

Beyond their value to anglers, minnows contribute much to humanity. Many naturalists enjoy observing minnows in nature and keeping them in aquariums. Minnows that are sensitive to pollution can be monitored by aquatic biologists and used as indicators of stream health. The diverse lifestyle of minnows makes them ideal subjects for both education and research in biology, ecology, and evolution. Finally, the diversity of minnows makes them a significant component of aquatic biodiversity.

Conservation. Many species of North American minnows are endangered, threatened, of special concern, or thought to be declining by aquatic biologists. As of the early 1990s, 10 species were thought to be extinct and nearly 70 were listed as needing some form of legal protection. One group of minnows, the blackline shiners, is especially sensitive to habitat change and thus highly imperiled. Imperiled species in this group include the pugnose shiner *(Notropis anogenus)*, the blackchin shiner *(Notropis heterodon)*, and the bridle shiner *(Notropis bifrenatus)*.

Other groups of minnows characterized by a high degree of imperilment include the satinfin shiners *(Cyprinella* species*)*, minnows in the genus *Dionda,* and chub in the genus *Gila.* Examples of imperiled minnows from these genera are the turquoise shiner *(Cyprinella monacha)*, the Devils river minnow *(Dionda diaboli)*, and the Borax Lake chub *(Gila boraxobius)*.

Imperiled minnows occur all over North America, but a high proportion of declining species occurs in the southwestern U.S. and northern Mexico. Causes of decline include chemical pollution, sedimentation, channelization, changes in flow regime, impoundments, introduced species, and general degradation of aquatic habitats.

A large threat to minnows and other fish is competition for food and other resources from introduced species. Introduced minnows can also transmit diseases to native fish and other aquatic life. Minnows are easily introduced outside their native range when they are transferred long distances in anglers' bait buckets. In addition, many bait shops sell nonindigenous minnows. To solve this problem, anglers could collect their own baits from the water they plan to fish and discard the unused baits in the same location. Alternatively, anglers can demand that local bait dealers stock only native minnows, and fisheries managers can monitor bait suppliers. Enforcement of water-quality regulations and the protection and restoration of aquatic habitats is also important.

See: Minnow, Fathead; Shiners; Shiner, Common; Shiner, Emerald; Shiner, Golden; Squawfish, Northern; Stoneroller, Central.

The production of baitcasting or levelwind reels began in 1810 when watchmaker George Snyder, President of the Bourbon County Anglers Association, built the first Kentucky reel.

M

MINNOW, FATHEAD   *Pimephales promelas.*
Other names—minnow; French: *tête de boule.*

The fathead minnow is a small, hardy, and widely cultivated member of the Cyprinidae family of minnows that is commonly used as bait, and it is an important forage species for gamefish. It is also commonly used in toxicity studies.

Identification.   The fathead minnow has a stubby, deep, compressed body with a short head that is flat on top. The snout is blunt. The mouth is small and slanted and possesses pharyngeal teeth. The body is generally dull in color, being dark olive or gray above and fading to muted yellow to white below. The scales become larger toward the tail and smaller toward the head, and the lateral line curves downward and is incomplete. There is a dark spot at the middle of the anterior dorsal rays, the caudal rays have dark outlines, and the leading edge of the pectoral fins is black. There is also a stout half-ray at the front of the dorsal fin. There are no barbels, but breeding males develop tubercles on the snout and become darker.

Size/Age.   Fathead minnows average $1^1/_2$ to 3 inches long, and grow to only 4 inches. Most die in their third year.

Distribution.   This species ranges widely (in part through introductions) across North America, from Quebec to the Northwest Territories and south to Alabama, Texas, and New Mexico, as well as in Mexico. It is most common in the Great Plains and scarce in mountainous regions.

Habitat.   Fathead minnows prefer ponds and pools or slow-moving water in streams, creeks, and small rivers. They can tolerate muddy water and are occasionally found in roadside ditches.

Spawning behavior.   Fathead minnows have an extended spawning period, from late spring into summer. It commences when the water temperature exceeds 60°F. They are nest spawners, often creating nest sites under floating or suspended objects or beneath logs or stones, generally in 1 to 3 feet of water. Males create the nests, herd the females into them, and guard the nest until the eggs hatch; several females may deposit eggs in one nest site, and the adhesive eggs hatch in six to nine days.

Food.   The diet of fathead minnows is mostly algae, as well as bottom detritus, zooplankton, and insect larvae.

Angling.   The fathead is a hardy minnow and widely used as a bait by anglers. It is raised commercially and sold not only to bait shops but also for stocking in ponds as forage for gamefish. Because of their small size, fathead minnows are consumed as forage by many species.
See: Minnows.

MINNOW PLUG
A floating/diving plug that is minnow-shaped and mostly fished on or just beneath the surface.
See: Plug; Surface Lure.

MINNOW TRAP
See: Trap.

MISSISSIPPI
Mississippi anglers do not lack for places to fish. The Magnolia State offers not only large reservoirs, but also a number of large and small river oxbows on the Mississippi and Yalobusha Rivers, several impoundments on the Tennessee-Tombigbee Waterway, 21 publicly managed smaller lakes, and literally hundreds of miles of float fishing opportunities on several large creeks.

All told, some 175 different freshwater fish species have been identified in the state's waters. The most popular for anglers by far are largemouth bass, black crappie, white crappie, channel catfish, flathead catfish, blue catfish, bluegills, and redear sunfish. Other well-known species are also present, however, including smallmouth bass, pure-strain and hybrid striped bass, and sauger.

The southern portion of the state offers the added bonus of brackish water conditions where anglers may catch several common saltwater species, including redfish, flounder, and speckled trout. Farther offshore, easily reached barrier islands provide excellent small-boat and wading opportunities for additional species like Spanish and king mackerel, cobia, red snapper, and an occasional tarpon. Yet farther offshore, charter skippers search for billfish and dolphin.

Because of the state's generally warm climate, fishing is popular year-round. In the larger reservoirs, anglers use a variety of artificial lures for bass, but prefer live baits, primarily minnows and earthworms, to take crappie and sunfish.

Large Reservoirs
The best known of Mississippi's large reservoirs is Ross Barnett, a 30,000-acre impoundment of the Pearl River near the capital city of Jackson. The lake features a distinct mixture of open water, shallow grassbeds and flooded stumps, and winding river channel. Depending on the time of year and the type of water being fished, bass anglers often do well with spinnerbaits, topwater and shallow-running spoons, and plastic worms rigged weedless but weightless that are worked through stumps and over vegetation.

Fathead Minnow

M

The spring months traditionally rank as the best time for crappie on Ross Barnett, and anglers use both live minnows as well as $^1/_8$- and even $^1/_{16}$-ounce hair jigs, sometimes tipped with a minnow, around stumps and timber along the Pearl River channel south of State Highway 43.

Other major impoundments wholly within Mississippi include Lakes Arkabutla, Sardis, Enid, and Grenada. All are old and basically shallow flood-control lakes, but at times each produces fine fishing action for several species, particularly bass, crappie, and catfish. The four lakes are located along a north-south line near Interstate Highway 55 between Memphis, Tennessee, and Grenada, Mississippi, and draw many anglers from western Tennessee.

Arkabutla is the northernmost of these four lakes; because it muddies quickly after a rain, it is best known for its blue and flathead catfish populations. Likewise, crappie fishing can be excellent at Arkabutla, particularly farther up the lake's two main tributaries, the Coldwater River and Hurricane Creek. Live minnows fished under floats work best for crappie here, whereas cat anglers prefer homemade baits concocted from a variety of foods like beef or chicken livers.

Crappie are also the primary attraction at Sardis Lake, but bass anglers do well in spring and fall, when the fish tend to move shallow on gravel banks and points. Major tributary creeks that have gained reputations for both species include Clear, Toby Tubby, Hurricane, Greasy, and Big Spring, all of which feature a variety of cover and structure.

Enid Reservoir, approximately 20 miles south of Sardis, is, like Sardis, an excellent crappie lake. In 1957 Enid produced the current 5-pound, 3-ounce world-record white crappie; heavier-than-usual crappies, generally referred to locally as "slabs," are caught each spring. The primary technique is working small hair jigs in 3 to 4 feet of water around brush and stumps, but plastic jigs and live minnows are also popular. When the fish are deeper than 5 or 6 feet, anglers here often use longer fly rods rigged with small spinning reels and light monofilament line, as the longer rods offer more precise depth control of lures or baits. Another technique is to cast a minnow or jig with a bobber and begin reeling it back. Periodically the retrieve is stopped to allow the bait or lure to sink slowly, and this is when strikes often occur.

At maximum pool, which is 64,000 acres, Grenada Lake is the state's largest reservoir. Autumn brings crappie anglers to the lake by the scores, but throughout the rest of the year anglers stay busy with largemouth bass, white bass, and channel catfish. A popular summer fishing technique is slow-trolling with live minnows, a tactic that often catches bass in addition to crappie.

In the northeast corner of the state, the Tennessee River makes a brief swing through Mississippi on its way from Alabama into Tennessee. This part of the river is impounded as Pickwick Lake, and, as in the Alabama portion of the lake, it produces excellent smallmouth fishing. Two significant tributaries, Yellow and Indian Creeks, flow into the lake from Mississippi, and both are well-known hotspots.

Mississippi's best smallmouth—a 7-pound, 15-ounce specimen—came from Yellow Creek. Spinnerbaits slow-rolled near deeper brush and over rocky points do well on smallmouth much of the year, but many anglers here have learned to drift small plastic grubs in the current on 6- or 8-pound line. In fall, large topwater plugs also produce well. In winter, walleye and sauger are also present, both of which are usually caught on $^1/_2$-ounce and heavier jigs crawled slowly along the bottom over rocky banks.

Near Meridian, Okatibbee Lake is a smaller impoundment but one that provides top action for bluegills, particularly in Twitley Branch and Gin Creeks. Special fish attractors have been constructed in various parts of this 3,800-acre lake, and these provide good places to try for crappie.

Tennessee-Tombigbee Waterway Lakes

The U.S. Army Corps of Engineers created a number of lakes along its 234-mile-long Tenn-Tom Waterway project between Pickwick Lake and the Gulf of Mexico, including several in Mississippi. Among these are Aberdeen, Columbus, and Aliceville, the last of which is shared with Alabama. Although the Tenn-Tom Waterway itself is essentially a 300-foot-wide barge canal, the lakes themselves provide extensive backwater areas for fishing.

In most Southern backwater areas, vegetation is common because the water is generally shallow. Stumps and standing timber are also present, especially at Columbus Lake, which, while making small-boat navigation occasionally difficult, provides excellent habitat for fish. Bass over 10 pounds have been taken from several of these Tenn-Tom lakes, usually in spring on spinnerbaits, buzzbaits, and shallow-running minnow-imitation plugs.

Mississippi River Oxbows

Anglers can choose from literally dozens of small to fairly large oxbow lakes of the Mississippi River, formed when the silt-laden river changed course and isolated a curve. Sometimes the oxbows are completely separated from the river; at other times they are open at one or both ends, and size can vary from less than 100 to several thousand acres. Most oxbows usually include an abundance of standing timber like willows and/or cypress trees, and they tend to have distinct deep-water channels as well as shallow-water flats.

Among the largest and best known Mississippi River oxbows are Tunica Cut-Off in northern Mississippi near the city of Tunica, DeSoto Lake

M

near Clarksdale, and Lake Ferguson near Greenville. All three offer 2,500 or more acres of bass, crappie, and catfish action. Sunfish, particularly bluegills, are also present in most oxbow lakes and provide hours of entertainment for anglers armed with a simple cane pole and a bucket of small minnows.

Largemouth bass as well as striped bass are targeted by many anglers here. The stripers are taken with large topwater lures, jerkbaits, and heavy plastic grubs, whereas largemouth anglers often flip $^1/_2$-ounce jigs or soft-plastic lures around the cypress trees.

Game and Fish Commission Lakes

Over the past several decades, the Mississippi Department of Wildlife, Fisheries, and Parks has constructed 21 small public fishing lakes totaling 5,111 acres throughout the state. Ranging in size from 12 to 1,200 acres, these mini-impoundments are designed to provide fishing opportunities in areas where previously there were none. They are heavily stocked annually with largemouth bass, catfish, and sunfish to provide optimum enjoyment, and at least one of the lakes, Waller, has produced bass over 11 pounds. Neshoba County Lake is well known for its crappie population.

The lakes are open daily on a fee basis, and small aluminum boats may be rented on site. All boat operation is restricted to trolling speed only. Concession stands selling licenses, tackle, and limited picnic supplies are also available on each lake.

Float Fishing Streams

Mississippi offers a number of excellent streams for quiet float fishing, including Black Creek, a portion of which has been protected as a National Wild and Scenic Stream. Highway bridge crossings offer excellent put-in/take-out points for lengthy trips; one popular Black Creek float begins at U.S. Highway 98 east of Hattiesburg and continues to U.S. Highway 11, a distance of about 12 miles. Other Black Creek float trips are available in the Desoto National Forest south of Hattiesburg.

Another popular waterway for canoe and jonboat anglers is the Bogue Chitto River south of Brookhaven. Many different trip options are available on this stream, which actually leaves Mississippi and flows through lower Louisiana all the way to the Gulf of Mexico. The Pearl, Leaf, and Chickasawhay Rivers also offer scenic floats through the southern portion of the state.

On all of these waterways, anglers find both largemouth and spotted bass, crappie, warmouth, a variety of sunfish, and channel catfish. Most use lighter spinning tackle with down-size lures like spinnerbaits, crankbaits, and topwater plugs to fill a stringer. In some areas fly fishing is popular but can be difficult because of low, overhanging branches. Overnight camps are frequently set up on river sandbars, and here anglers bait bottom rigs with doughballs or homemade "stinkbaits" for catfish.

Gulf Coast

Because several important rivers, including the Pearl, Pascagoula, and Biloxi, flow into the gulf along the 90-mile-long Mississippi coast, anglers have the chance to fish brackish water, where largemouth bass and channel bass may hit on successive casts. The Biloxi and Pascagoula areas, especially, offer dozens of miles of winding rivers, secluded bays, and small bayous for this type of fishing.

Inshore saltwater opportunities in St. Louis Bay near Pass Christian as well as Biloxi Bay offer protected fishing for flounder and other shallow species. Offshore the coastline is also somewhat protected by a string of small, separate islands—Grand, Cat, Ship, Horn, and Petit Bois—which together form the federally controlled Gulf Islands National Seashore. These islands offer good surf, wading, and small-boat angling for speckled trout, flounder, bluefish, and redfish. Still farther offshore the Chandeleur Islands are nationally famous for redfish and trout action; anglers can charter boats or planes in Gulfport to take them to the islands for trips lasting one to several days.

Biloxi, Gulfport, Ocean Springs, and Pascagoula all support charter fleets that regularly comb gulf waters for mackerel, snapper, dolphin, grouper, tripletail, and other species. Many skippers have created private artificial reefs just offshore for red snapper. Bottom fishing and trolling are popular around the area's many old oil platforms and artificial reefs. In the blue water 50 to 100 miles out, sailfish and blue marlin are taken during the summer months by many of these charter boats.

MISSOURI

The angler looking at a map of Missouri might suppose that two mighty rivers, the Missouri and the Mississippi, provide a lot of fishing. They don't. Both suffered such severe navigation development that the immense fishery they once represented is today a fragment of its former self. Nevertheless, Missouri offers abundant angling for a landlocked state, and this potential is fairly diverse, thanks to 13 large reservoirs, thousands of smaller reservoirs, and many rivers and streams.

The quality of the state's gamefishing is largely due to an excellent conservation agency. The Missouri Conservation Department, which for several decades has been the best-funded and best state conservation agency in the nation, has used scientific research to develop and maintain healthy fish populations in most of the state's waterways.

The largemouth bass ranks first with both resident and nonresident anglers in the Show-Me State, and it is followed closely in popularity by crappie. Next, in descending order, come catfish, sunfish, white bass, smallmouth bass, walleye, sauger, and, surprisingly, trout. Missouri even has muskellunge, which are stocked in two of the state's reservoirs, and includes among its fish populations in certain waters striped bass, hybrid stripers, paddlefish, freshwater drum, and carp.

Most people coming to Missouri to fish do so in one or more of the larger reservoirs. Many also come to fish and float the streams of the Ozarks. A smaller number pursue trout, primarily rainbows and, in a few places, browns, stocked in water kept cold by either spring discharges or deep-reservoir discharges, usually referred to as tailwaters.

Major Reservoirs

Missouri's important reservoirs are primarily in the southern half of the state. These vary in size but generally support a great deal of recreational activity. They are subject to some water-level fluctuation, as they are also used for generating power and controlling floods. They're listed here in order of total acreage, which is not necessarily an indication of fishing prominence, which can vary.

Lake of the Ozarks. This sprawling, twisting mid-Missouri reservoir is about 35 miles southwest of Jefferson City, nearly midway between Kansas City and St. Louis, and is at the heart of Missouri's biggest and most developed vacation area. Lake of the Ozarks is a 59,520-acre reservoir originally built for power generation but now little-used for that purpose. Much of its acreage is subject to intense use from all manner of boaters, and the lake is ringed with houses and boat docks. Those docks, in fact, provide the primary cover for bass and therefore the main fishing action for largemouths.

Lake of the Ozarks is deep, clear, and beautiful, particularly in the lower end, which is more like a typical highland impoundment. The lake becomes progressively more stained as you head to the upper sections, especially in the Osage and Niangua arms. It has an excellent number of largemouth bass, and has been known for many of these in the 3- to 5-pound range. It also has good numbers of white bass, crappie, and catfish, as well as paddlefish (a state-record paddlefish—134 pounds, 12 ounces—was snagged in the Niangua arm in 1998). Many of the biggest bass are caught in late winter, prior to the spawn, and April and May are especially good for quantity.

Truman Lake. Located in west-central Missouri and west of Lake of the Ozarks, Truman Lake, also known as Harry S Truman Reservoir, is a 55,600-acre U.S. Army Corps of Engineers flood-control and recreation reservoir on the Osage, Grand, and Pomme de Terre Rivers. With 958 miles of shoreline, it has countless coves, sloughs, and embayments along the main lake as well as in the many creek and river feeders.

Truman is unlike many other Missouri reservoirs in that it does not contain great depths or clarity. The water is predominantly muddy or stained, and the average depth at normal times is just 15 feet. It contains good populations of largemouth bass, white bass, crappie, bluegills, and catfish, as well as burgeoning walleye and striper numbers. The

The flooded timber of Truman Lake provides challenging cover to fish for bass.

tailwater below Truman Dam, which forms the upper reaches of the Osage Arm of Lake of the Ozarks, is an excellent place to fish when water flow is heavy.

Bull Shoals Reservoir. Straddling the Arkansas-Missouri line in the deepest part of the Ozarks, Bull Shoals is a 45,440-acre Corps of Engineers flood-control and recreation reservoir on the White River. It has 740 miles of shoreline, most of it rocky bluffs and ledges. Like other mountain waters, it is extremely clear and deep, and sometimes difficult to fish, yet it is annually considered one of the best lakes in Missouri. Bull Shoals is favored over its neighboring reservoir, Table Rock, by many anglers because it doesn't get as crowded with other boaters, due to fewer amenities and houses on the lake and a more remote location.

Bull Shoals is known for excellent largemouth bass, smallmouth bass, and spotted bass fishing, as well as renowned tributary runs of white bass in the spring. Crappie, bluegills, catfish, and walleye, as well as some rainbow trout in the lower end, round out most of the fishing, and there's good striped bass angling as well. The cold water in the White River below Bull Shoals Dam provides some of the country's best trout fishing.

Table Rock Reservoir. Located in far southwestern Missouri near Branson, this is a popular lake for varied recreation, yet one that annually supports excellent bass fishing. A highland reservoir with deep structure and rocky shoreline, Table

M

Rock is 70 miles long and covers 43,100 acres at conservation pool. Viewed on a map, Table Rock is serpentine, with countless nooks, crannies, and bends that befit its location in the up-and-down Ozark hills.

Though it was impounded in the 1950s, Table Rock continues to produce good fishing for largemouth bass, spotted bass, smallmouth bass, white bass, and crappie, and also holds catfish and paddlefish. A lot of deep fishing is done here, and angling can be good throughout the year. Winter fishing for spotted bass and largemouths is good, and larger specimens tend to be caught from February through April.

Lake Stockton.   About 51 road miles northeast of Springfield in the Ozarks of southwestern Missouri, Lake Stockton is a 25,000-acre Corps of Engineers flood-control, power, and recreation reservoir on the Sac River that was fully impounded in 1971. It contains good populations of largemouth bass, walleye, and crappie, and is considered by many an overlooked body of water. Smallmouth bass, white bass, bluegills, and catfish are also present. Smallmouths aren't abundant, but they have been of good size; the lake produced a state-record 7.2-pound smallmouth in 1994.

Ultraclear water often makes this lake hard to fish. That water clarity makes it a favorite with divers, however. It is also popular with sailors, who take advantage of its preponderance for wind. Being somewhat like a prairie lake, Stockton does not benefit from the protection of hills, as other Missouri impoundments do, so it is prone to wind at all times, especially early in the year.

Norfork Lake.   Straddling the Arkansas-Missouri border, Norfolk is a 22,000-acre Corps of Engineers flood-control and recreation reservoir on the North Fork River. Only a small segment of the lake actually extends into Missouri.

Norfolk contains good populations of largemouth, smallmouth, spotted and white bass, crappie, bluegills, and catfish, as well as a good population of striped bass, which are maintained through annual stocking by Arkansas. It is an extremely clear, deep reservoir that is sometimes tough to fish. Cold water from Norfork Dam provides some of the country's best angling for large brown trout in the lower North Fork River in Arkansas.

Mark Twain Lake.   Located in northeastern Missouri between Perry and Monroe City and about 30 miles southeast of Hannibal, this is an 18,600-acre flood-control and recreation reservoir on the Salt River. Pretty, and with many protected coves, Mark Twain Lake was created in 1984, making it one of the newer reservoirs in this state. The lake contains good populations of black bass, white bass, crappie, bluegills, and channel catfish, but also has flathead catfish and walleye.

Smithville Lake.   Located about 20 miles north of Kansas City in northwestern Missouri, Smithville Lake is an 8,040-acre Corps of Engineers

reservoir impounded in 1980 for flood control and recreation. Despite intense fishing pressure, the lake has produced good fishing, in part owing to an abundance of weeds and flooded timber, and in part to 175 miles of shoreline fishing opportunity. Largemouth bass are the mainstays here, but the lake also has crappie, bluegills, and catfish. March through May are good times to beat the crowds and garner largemouths.

Pomme de Terre Reservoir.   A 7,820-acre Corps of Engineers flood-control and recreation reservoir on the Pomme de Terre River, this lake is situated in western Missouri south of Truman Lake and northeast of Lake Stockton, and about 60 miles from Springfield. It has good populations of largemouth bass, white bass, crappie, bluegills, and catfish, and Missouri's best population of muskellunge. Despite being small, Pomme de Terre has been ranked among Missouri's best bass fishing waters, and it has had less angling pressure than this state's better-known and larger reservoirs. Fall and winter are top bass periods.

Wappapello Reservoir.   This southeastern-Missouri impoundment is 15 miles north of Poplar Bluff, with major access on the southern part of the lake around the town of Wappapello. A Corps of Engineers flood-control impoundment, Wappapello has 7,200 acres at normal summer level, and is narrow, shallow, pretty, and relatively easy to fish. It usually provides good crappie fishing all winter, and is one of the state's best early-spring fishing spots.

Thomas Hill Reservoir.   A 4,500-acre reservoir built to provide cooling water for a coal-fired power plant, Thomas Hill is roughly 30 miles northwest of Moberly. It has a good population of catfish of all sizes, some largemouth bass, and a good population of white crappie. The best fishing usually occurs in the winter, especially around the hotwater outlet in Brush Creek Cove.

Long Branch Lake.   Although it often doesn't get the credit, Long Branch is one of the best big-bass waters in Missouri. Situated near Macon in Mark Twain's area of northeast Missouri, Long Branch is a 2,400-acre Corps of Engineers flood-control lake that is not heavily fished. It has a good population of channel catfish of all sizes, a good population of largemouth bass, including fish larger than 6 pounds, plus many small crappie and carp. It is frequently muddy because of siltation in the watershed.

Lake Taneycomo.   Near Branson in far southwestern Missouri, Taneycomo is a 1,730-acre hydroelectric and recreation reservoir on the White River, sandwiched between Table Rock and Bull Shoals Reservoirs. Cold water from Table Rock Dam makes this small lake hospitable for rainbow and brown trout, which are stocked frequently by state fisheries personnel. Narrow, protected, and more river than lake in its upper half, Taneycomo provides some of the best trout fishing in mid-America.

Clearwater Reservoir. Situated in southeastern Missouri about 150 miles south of St. Louis, Clearwater is the smallest of Missouri's major reservoirs and sometimes difficult to fish because of superclear water. A 1,650-acre Corps of Engineers flood-control and recreation reservoir on the Black River, it contains good populations of largemouth bass, spotted bass, white bass, crappie, bluegills, and catfish.

Smaller Reservoirs

In one count made several decades ago, Missouri was found to have some 200,000 ponds and small lakes. The biggest and best of these for public fishing are impoundments either owned or managed by such government agencies as the Missouri Department of Conservation (MDC), the U.S. Forest Service, and the Division of Natural Resources (the state park agency), or by individual counties and municipalities.

The MDC manages or shares management of nearly three dozen of these reservoirs, which range in size from less than 100 up to 300 acres. Fishing in these impoundments varies from pretty good to excellent, primarily with warmwater species. These reservoirs exist all over the state, and information about them is available from the MDC.

Streams

The streams of the northern half of Missouri are prairie-like in character. Access can be difficult, but access sites have been developed on many. Catfish are the primary species caught from these streams.

The primary stream fishing interest in Missouri exists in the Ozarks, a river-carved uplift covering much of this state south of the Missouri River and extending into Arkansas. Ozark Mountain streams, which draw many out-of-state anglers, are gentle, clear, and crooked, which makes for perfect canoeing water. The rocky bluff banks provide habitat for smallmouth bass, which are highly prized among Missouri anglers, although the primary species is the goggle-eye (rock bass).

Most Ozark streams are not floatable, being too small to be passable most of the year. These "wading streams" represent a good many areas to fish, but it isn't easy to find them or get access because almost all of them flow through private land. Fishing on them can be tough because of the small size and clarity of the water. But so pretty and pleasant is a float on these streams that catching a fish, even a small one, is a bonus.

A brief description of the most important float streams in the Ozarks follows. Access to these is easy because they are all served by liveries, which provide both canoes and transportation to and from the river. All an angler has to do is show up.

Meramec River. About 100 miles of this fine stream is considered canoe water. The best floats and most of the liveries are in the upper third of the Meramec, from Missouri Rt. 8 near St. James to

Meramec State Park near Sullivan. Many stretches as far down as St. Louis County are optimal for fishing and floating.

Huzzah and Courtois Creeks. Pretty little tributaries of the Meramec, the Huzzah and Courtois offer excellent floating when they have enough water. The most dependable floats are the lower 12 miles of the Huzzah and lower 18 miles of the Courtois. Some of the liveries on the Meramec offer floats on these creeks.

Bourbeuse River. The Bourbeuse is a gentle, crooked little stream with some attractive stretches. Not all sections are served by canoe liveries.

Big River. A long tributary of the Meramec, the Big River features sporty riffles spaced between long, slow holes. Fishing is surprisingly good. Not all stretches are served by liveries.

Black River. This beautiful Black River is extremely popular with St. Louis-area floaters. The best floating is in the 13 miles below Lesterville. On the three forks above Lesterville, canoeing is fun only when water flow is sufficient. Below Clearwater Lake the Black is somewhat slower and better known for its fishing.

Current River. The Current is the most famous of Missouri's float streams. About 135 miles of this stream, which with the Jacks Fork forms the Ozark National Scenic Riverway, is considered float water. From Montauk for the first few miles downstream the flow is sometimes not adequate for canoeing. Below Doniphan the river broadens and slows. Canoe liveries rent canoes only within their districts.

Jacks Fork River. The beautiful Jacks Fork River, which is part of the Ozark National Scenic Riverway, offers the best floating in Missouri when it has enough water. Only the 13 miles below Alley Spring are floatable all summer. The stretch above Alley, when floatable, is not for beginners.

Big Niangua River. The Big Nianqua is within an easy drive of Lake of the Ozarks. About 44 miles, from Williams Ford to Mill Creek, is considered canoe water. The most popular floats are those above and below Bennett Spring State Park, near Lebanon.

Gasconade River. Known more as a fishing stream than a canoeing stream, the Gasconade nevertheless has many stretches rewarding to the canoeist. Over most of its 300 miles, though, the Gasconade spaces its sporty stretches between long, slow holes. The best canoe water is the 150-mile section between Competition, near Lynchburg, to the Paydown access, near Vienna. Some stretches are not served by canoe liveries.

Big Piney River. A long, gentle tributary of the Gasconade, the Big Piney is scenic in its upper and middle stretches and is worth floating and fishing all the way through Fort Leonard Wood to the Gasconade above Jerome.

North Fork River. Clear, cold, and beautiful, the North Fork has few long holes and many

According to *The Guinness Book of Records*, the ocean sunfish (*Mola mola*) produces up to 300 million eggs at a single spawning.

M

sporty stretches with spectacular scenery. Flowing through rugged, remote segments of the deep Ozarks, it eventually joins Bryant Creek and becomes Norfork Lake just north of the Arkansas border. About 29 miles, from Twin Bridges to Tecumseh, is prime canoe water in all but the driest summers.

Bryant Creek. A tributary of the North Fork, Bryant Creek is smaller, more crooked, and less popular, but almost as beautiful. Only about 17 miles, from Hodgson Mill to the North Fork, is considered year-round float water.

Eleven Point River. Eleven Point, a national scenic river administered by the U.S. Forest Service, flows through some of the most rugged and remote country in the Ozarks. For several miles it forms the western border of the famed Irish Wilderness. The best floats are from Greer Spring to Riverton. Inflow from Greer nearly doubles the size of the river. The stretches above Greer are floatable only during wet weather.

Other Waters

The Missouri River provides relatively little fishing in Missouri and is not a pleasant place to be, thanks to channelization done for navigation between 1950 and 1980. The river is a flop for navigation because it is so swift and narrow. Its fishing is primarily for catfish with some crappie, bass, and carp fishing in the small remaining backwaters.

The Mississippi in Missouri, too, is channelized and provides limited sportfishing. Above St. Louis, the pools behind navigation dams provide some slack water and some angling opportunity. The most notable fishery in the Mississippi is for sauger in the raceways below the dams at Winfield, Clarksville, and Saverton. The fishing is good only in winter, when the freeze-up in northern states clears the river and limits its flow.

Trout fishing in Missouri is essentially found in three venues. One is Lake Taneycomo, previously described. Another is the four trout parks: Maramec Spring, Bennett Spring, Montauk Spring, and Roaring River. These public parks provide put-and-take fishing for rainbows stocked daily in major spring branches. The third trout fishing possibility is the dozen or so small spring branches both public and private; four have small populations of self-sustaining rainbows, and the rest are stocked.

MODULUS

A measure of how effectively a material resists deformation. Modulus can also be considered a measure of how quickly a material recovers after being flexed. This term is used in conjunction with tensile, which means to place a material under a tension load, and is often used by fishing rod manufacturers in describing rod blank properties. A high-tensile-modulus material, for example, is one that has a stiff structure and a high stiffness-to-weight ratio.

This is an overused and often misunderstood word in fishing rod manufacture. Modulus alone is not an indicator of the quality of a rod, since many other factors, including the amount and quality of the resin, the taper design, and the wall thickness of the blank, affect action and performance.

See: Rod, Fishing.

MOJARRA

Mojarra are members of the Gerridae family of tropical and subtropical saltwater fish. Roughly 40 species are in this family, some of which also occur in brackish water and a few rarely in freshwater. They are small and silvery and have a protractile mouth. The upper jaw of the mojarra fits into a defined slot when the mouth is not extended, or "pursed." When feeding, the mouth is protruded and directed downward. The dorsal and anal fins have a sheath of scales along the base, and the gill membranes are not united to the isthmus. The first, or spiny, dorsal fin is high in front, sloping into the second, or soft-rayed, dorsal. The tail is deeply forked.

Most mojarra are less than 10 inches long. They are important for predator species and are used as baits by some anglers. Some species are observed in schools on sandy, shallow flats.

The spotfin mojarra *(Eucinostomus argenteus)* is abundant in the western Atlantic off the coast from New Jersey to Brazil. It occurs in the eastern Pacific along the coast from Southern California to Peru. The yellowfin mojarra *(Gerres cinereus)* is common in Florida and the Caribbean.

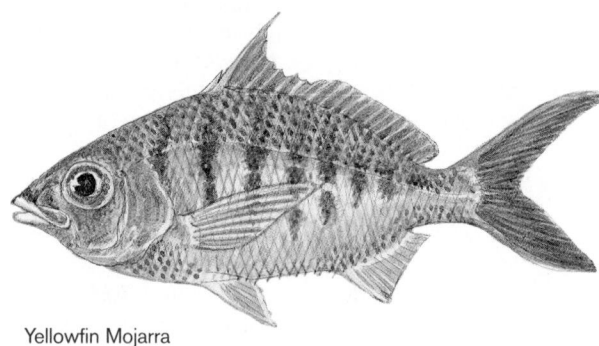

Yellowfin Mojarra

MOLD

A preshaped form into which molten lead or plastic is poured for making sinkers, weights, and soft-plastic lure bodies by hobbyists; molds for hobby use may be purchased from large tackle retailers or mail-order suppliers. Molds are used in the commercial manufacture of many fishing and boating products, including lures, terminal tackle, fishing reels, boat hulls, and many other items.

MOLLUSK

A group of freshwater and saltwater animals with no skeleton and usually one or two hard shells made of calcium carbonate. This group includes the oyster, clam, mussel, snail, conch, scallop, squid, and octopus. Mollusks may be used as bait when angling, but they are not targeted by anglers or deliberately sought with sporting equipment.

MONGOLIA

Sandwiched between Siberian Russia and northern China, Mongolia is a large country about the size of western Europe. It has a small population of 2.4 million that is 40 percent nomadic. It encloses the Gobi Desert and is distinguished geographically by Inner Mongolia, which is the area between the Gobi Desert and the Great Wall of China on the south, and Outer Mongolia.

Tourism is not well developed; it opened to Westerners only in 1990. Nevertheless, opportunities for adventurous anglers exist in unusual places for various species, including grayling, pike, whitefish, lenok, several species of sturgeon, and, especially, taimen, the world's largest salmonid. Dry fly fishing is said to be excellent in the northern regions of Mongolia, where ultraclear water offers superb sight fishing conditions. Taimen there range from 27 to 66 inches in length; they can be caught in the 30- to 40-pound range and may weigh from 60 to 100 pounds. Lenok, which are a brown trout look-alike, range from 2 to 8 pounds.

Mongols are generally hunters, not anglers, and fish is not part of their diet, so there is little to no subsistence, commercial, or recreational angling for fish by natives. When they do fish for taimen, Mongols use heavy trotlines that are baited with meat, or they use lures made of marmot or sheep skin and that look like rodents.

Mongolia's geographic location causes its rivers and streams to be located in or course through the Arctic, Pacific, and Central Asian drainage basins.

The Arctic Basin contains about one-fourth of Mongolia's landmass and is comprised of the Selenge River and its tributaries, which flow northerly and across the Russian border into Lake Baikal; the Shishkhed River west of Lake Hovsgol; and the Bulban River in Khovd Province. There are 25 species here, including sturgeon, burbot, northern pike, lenok, perch, and whitefish.

The Pacific Basin, which is in the northeastern region and contains about 11 percent of the country's landmass, includes the Onon, Uldz, Kherlen, and Khalkhin Gol Rivers. These flow easterly and merge with Russia's Amur River. The area harbors 41 species, including sturgeon, grayling, taimen, carp, and whitefish, and possibly pike, Dolly Varden, and charr.

There is no ocean drainage for the remaining 64 percent of Mongolia's territory, which blends into the vast closed Central Asia drainage basin. In the northwest, this area includes saline Uvs Lake, which is Mongolia's largest lake by surface area, as well as Khar Us, Khar, and Khyargas Lakes. In the central region, it includes the Gobi Altai Mountains and the Valley of the Lakes between the Khangai Mountains. Only five species have been identified here, among them grayling.

There are reportedly more than 4,000 lakes in Mongolia, most of them freshwater. Thirty percent of the lakes are found in the mountainous regions. Lake Hovsgol is the 14th largest lake in the world, the deepest lake in Central Asia, and the largest in Mongolia by water volume. There are nearly 100 tributaries to Hovsgol, but just one outflow, the Egiin River, which runs southeast to the Selenge River. Siberian grayling and lenok are the major sportfishing attractions among nine species of fish in this lake, which is said to be one of the purest large bodies of freshwater in the world.

Mongolian lakes experience a large swing in climatic conditions. They become warm in the summer, peaking in July and August; the temperature drops markedly in September and gradually until mid-November. Lakes are thickly frozen from late November until late May or early June.

There are some 1,200 rivers and streams in Mongolia with a total length of 70,000 kilometers. The rivers generally start to warm up in late April and rise in temperature until July. In August they gradually decrease until November when they freeze. All of the rivers freeze, and stay frozen for between 140 and 180 days. Late summer is reportedly a prime time for taimen sight fishing, as this is when the rivers are at their lowest and clearest stage, although the best chances for catching large individuals at this time may be at night; smaller fish are reportedly plentiful during the day in some locations in August.

Opportunities to fish in this wild and rugged country are provided by several adventure travel agencies.
See: China.

MONKFISH

A common name for the goosefish (see).

MONOFILAMENT (LINE)

See: Line.

MONTANA

Montana's fisheries are vast and varied, as befits a state that ranks fourth among the 50 United States in land area, encompasses 1,490 square miles of inland water, and contains a plethora of rivers, some of which progress eventually to the Gulf of Mexico and the Pacific Ocean. These are among the most heralded trout flows in North America. Though piscatorially associated with various trout, the Treasure

M

State also has warmwater fishing opportunities, and provides anglers with great choice in fishing experiences due to a large land area, a low population density, and a broad diversity of water types.

These waters include 26 sizable rivers and their attendant tributaries, at least 10 mountain ranges and wilderness areas offering breathtaking alpine angling opportunities in streams and ponds; 30 large lakes and reservoirs; and nearly a hundred smaller lakes.

As a headwaters state, Montana features pristine waters that are born in mountain snowmelt and grow from unnamed trickles and streams to celebrated rivers and lakes. The headwaters of both the Missouri and Columbia Rivers, for example, begin high in the mountains, and there are many others along the Continental Divide, which runs through Montana from Canada and Glacier National Park in the north to Idaho, Wyoming, and Yellowstone National Park in the south.

As is true in other places, fishing in Montana may be approached by type of water, targeted species, or location. In general, warmwater fisheries are east of a north-south line running from the Canadian border to just west of Billings, and coldwater fisheries are west of that. Both fisheries exist in some bodies of water, however, and the various geographic regions of Montana are delightfully distinct, offering different fishing experiences.

No matter where or when an angler fishes in Montana, the time of year and weather conditions play a major role in determining success. For example, many Montana rivers experience huge runoffs in late spring to midsummer, which can affect how to fish a particular river. Factors like snowmelt in the spring, or irrigation on some rivers in the summer, could suggest that another time of year or a different site be selected.

Tourism is among the leading industries in the state, so visitors can expect to be treated cordially in Montana, and tackle shop owners are more than happy to offer sound advice on local conditions.

Species

The cutthroat trout is Montana's state fish, and although it is native to the state, it is gone from much of its original territory. The Westslope cutthroat is native west of the Continental Divide and in some of the drainages located east of the divide, where it is referred to as the upper Missouri cutthroat. Yellowstone cutthroat are native to the Yellowstone River drainage. The cutthroat also goes by the names blackspotted, red-belly, native, and flat cutthroat. It inhabits cool, clear mountain streams and lakes. The cutthroat is similar to a rainbow trout but has a red slash on its lower jaw. There are crosses between the different cutthroat species and between cutthroats and rainbows, all of which are difficult to identify. Cutthroat trout in Montana are roughly 10 inches long but may grow to 18 inches.

Rainbow trout are found throughout Montana but are native to the Kootenai River drainage in the northwest. Montana rainbows typically average 12 inches but may reach 24. Brown trout are an introduced species most common in the lower reaches of fairly large streams and also found in reservoirs or lakes that have suitable tributaries for spawning. Browns here are often 13 inches long but seldom longer than 24 inches.

Brook trout were also introduced to the state and inhabit small spring-fed streams and ponds. Widespread in clear, cold streams and lakes, and frequently found in high-mountain beaver ponds, they are often 9 inches in length but seldom more than 16 inches.

The golden trout, also introduced, exists in fewer than a dozen high-mountain lakes in southern and southwestern Montana, whereas numerous lakes have golden-rainbow hybrids or golden-cutthroat hybrids. The golden trout does well in the harsh conditions of high-mountain lakes and streams as well as in clear, cold lakes at lower elevations. Golden trout routinely are 10 inches but seldom bigger than 18 inches.

The bull trout is native to Montana and was called the Dolly Varden until 1978, when the primarily inland form of the fish was designated as a separate species—the bull trout. The fish does best in large, coldwater streams but also inhabits smaller streams and lakes that have a tributary to ascend to spawn. Bull trout routinely are 16 inches long and may get as big as 36 inches. Their numbers are dwindling in Montana.

The lake trout is native in Elk, Twin, St. Mary, and Waterton Lakes and is also known as mackinaw. Inhabiting deep, cold lakes and reservoirs, this species averages 22 inches but may grow to 40 inches.

The kokanee is a landlocked sockeye salmon that was introduced to the state. It inhabits cold, clear lakes and reservoirs and ascends streams to spawn. Kokanee are found in the far northwestern region, at three or four sites in central Montana, and in Fort Peck Reservoir in northeastern Montana. The typical size is 11 inches, but the fish may reach 18 inches.

Native mountain whitefish are found throughout the western third of the state and in the streams of the mountainous portions of southern Montana. It is common in medium-size and large, clear, cold rivers and some lakes and reservoirs. Whitefish are common at 12 inches and may reach 20 inches.

The arctic grayling, also known as the Montana grayling, is rare in the lower 48 states, but they are found in certain areas of Montana. Historically, the fish is a stream species but now mostly inhabits mountain lakes where it has been planted. The upper reaches of the Big Hole River in southwestern Montana, as well as a few mountain streams in northwestern Montana, can yield grayling. Grayling normally are 10 inches long but may reach 18 inches.

Northern pike are native to the St. Mary River drainage but are also found extensively throughout eastern, north-central, and northeastern Montana. They are prevalent in some far northwestern waters. The fish is common at 20 inches but may grow to 45 inches.

The shovelnose sturgeon is a large-river and reservoir fish that can tolerate turbid water. Native to Montana and also known as hackleback, this fish has a snout shaped like a shovel. It is similar to the pallid sturgeon. The shovelnose commonly is 32 inches long in Montana but can reach 41 inches.

Paddlefish are native to Montana and thrive year-round in Fort Peck Reservoir and in the tailwater below Fort Peck Dam. In the spring, these fish spawn upriver in the lower reaches of both the Missouri and Yellowstone Rivers. They commonly grow to 60 inches, but some 72-inch specimens have been caught.

Channel catfish are native and are found in many reaches of the Missouri and Yellowstone River systems. A 17-inch channel cat is common, but they seldom exceed 30 inches. Black bullhead were introduced and are found in creeks, rivers, and farm ponds of eastern Montana, as well as in a few lower areas of far northwestern Montana.

Burbot, also known as ling, are native to Montana and are a popular species. Found in large rivers and cold, deep lakes and reservoirs, burbot are commonly caught at 20 inches long, and they sometimes attain 30 inches.

All of the various sunfish and perch in the state were introduced. Largemouth bass inhabit the eastern third of the state and a small portion of northwestern Montana, which is at lower elevation. Smallmouths favor isolated stretches of the Bighorn, Musselshell, Yellowstone, Milk, and Tongue Rivers, and Fort Peck, Homestead, South Sandstone, and Tongue River Reservoirs. Both species are regularly 11 inches long but can grow to 18 inches.

Pumpkinseed may be found in some of the same waters as smallmouth bass; bluegills are in only about a dozen or fewer areas in eastern Montana; green sunfish are present in some far southeastern waters; rock bass are in the Tongue River; crappie are in the Bighorn, Stillwater, and Yellowstone Rivers, Fort Peck Reservoir, Lake Elwell, and portions of the Missouri River above Fort Peck Reservoir.

Yellow perch, which are a favorite panfish with Montana's ice anglers, are available throughout the eastern third of the state, a large portion of northwestern Montana's lower-elevation waters, and the Missouri River and its tributaries. Eight-inch perch are most common, and they occasionally reach 15 inches.

Walleye are found in the Bighorn, Marias, Milk, Missouri, Stillwater, and Yellowstone Rivers, in Lake Elwell, and in Fort Peck and Canyon Ferry Reservoirs. Sixteen-inch walleye are common, and

A brown trout comes to the net of a Montana fly angler.

occasionally 30-inchers are taken. Canyon Ferry has produced some 19- and 20-pound walleye.

Sauger, also called sand pike, are prevalent in all of the walleye waters and in the Tongue River in southeastern Montana. They range from 13 inches all the way up to an occasional 24-incher.

Northwest Region
Flathead Lake/Flathead River. Flathead Lake is the largest natural freshwater lake west of the Mississippi River and a particularly scenic Montana destination. Its surface encompasses more than 125,000 acres, and its shoreline covers 185 miles. Fishing is a prime draw, but the highly accessible lake is also heavily used by sailors, powerboaters, cruise boat enthusiasts, and the like, which makes for a lot of summertime activity.

Nevertheless, Flathead is known for trout, salmon, perch, and whitefish angling. Lake trout to more than 40 pounds have been recorded, as have bull trout of 26 pounds. The deeper waters between Melita and Wild Horse Islands, in Skidoo Bay north of Finley Point, and in the vicinity of Angel Point south of Lakeside on the west shore, are prime laker territory.

Kokanee salmon are found in Flathead also, especially in Big Arm and Elmo Bays; off the islands in the Narrows at the north end of Polson Bay; and in Skidoo, Blue, Yellow, and Woods Bays. At least a dozen public access points beckon around the lake.

The Flathead River is part of a system unique to Montana. The North, Middle, and South Forks converge to form the Flathead River, which eventually flows into Flathead Lake. Fishing any of the forks is more of a sightseeing trip than a fishing expedition. The forks run out from the wilderness and are spectacular rivers, but they are low on nutrients and support marginal populations of fish. Most of the fish live in Flathead Lake and run up the river to spawn. All three rivers are spotty at best for cutthroat and bull trout.

M

The Kootenai River. The Kootenai is rainbow trout water, and what's left of the river in Montana—Libby Dam flooded the upper half—produces some lunkers. Anglers occasionally land cutthroats, which probably were washed over the dam, and bull trout. A population of white sturgeon frequents the river, but their numbers are scarce and their fate is uncertain.

Anglers using baits, lures, and flies can all do well on the Kootenai. Fly anglers might be advised to try the waters between Libby and Kootenai Falls, known locally as "the Rocks." The river from Libby Dam to Libby and from below Kootenai Falls to the old Troy Bridge has some fine holes and would be good territory for bait and lure users.

Lake Koocanusa. Lake Koocanusa, created by damming the Kootenai River above its confluence with the Fisher River above the town of Libby, is entirely surrounded by national forest land, but access is challenging because the surrounding terrain is steep and boat launch sites are scarce. The reservoir is subject to large water-level fluctuations because of the dam. At 95 miles long, the reservoir is huge but narrow. Kokanee salmon, cutthroat trout, rainbow trout, and bull trout are present, as are whitefish and burbot.

Lake Mary Ronan. A 1,500-acre lake, Mary Ronan is west of Flathead Lake and northwest of the town of Dayton, and sustains a rainbow trout population. The lake is closed to angling during the spring spawning season but opens in May. Public access is good on the east side of the lake.

McGregor Lake. This scenic 1,500-acre lake is roughly 30 miles west of Kalispell on U.S. 2 and offers good fishing for lake trout. It is planted with rainbow, and there are decent numbers of brook trout and yellow perch. The lake is a popular ice fishing destination.

Swan Lake. Just off State Highway 83 near the town of Swan Lake, at the north end of Swan Valley, this 2,500-acre lake is roughly 10 miles long and a mile or so wide. It offers excellent fishing for rainbow, cutthroat, and bull trout, as well as kokanee salmon, perch, northern pike, and sunfish. Swan Lake once had a sizable bass population, but these fish have dwindled. Both the inlet and the outlet of the lake are typically productive.

Whitefish Lake. Whitefish Lake is just northwest of the town of Whitefish and offers cutthroats, bull trout, lake trout, and whitefish. The lake also has a good population of northern pike.

The Yaak River. The Yaak is located in arguably the most remote corner of Montana. A tributary to the Kootenai, it produces nice rainbows and cutthroats. The river above Yaak Falls is fairly gentle and accessible by road, whereas the area below the falls is mostly canyon and tough to get to.

Eastern Region

Bighorn River. The Bighorn River, which flows from Yellowtail Dam to the Yellowstone River near Custer, is one of the best big-trout fisheries in Montana and gives up some mighty browns and rainbows. For much of the year, water temperatures in this tailwater fishery are moderate, and the water is rich in nutrients from the area's limestone streams. The Bighorn is clear, and sunlight helps moss and weeds grow on the bottom. It all adds up to good habitat and great growth rates. Browns in the river operate on a boom and bust cycle, depending on the most recent drought, which in a severe year can de-water the river, raise water temperatures, and cause brown trout mortality. Rainbows, once planted in the river, have become a stable population and no longer need to be planted.

The Bighorn is a large river but in a few spots anglers can wade across. It flows through Crow Indian Reservation, and anglers should be aware that tribal lands are off-limits to anglers. Be attentive to stream access laws and stay within the high-water mark on the stream. Because of access limitation, the best way to fish the Bighorn is from a boat.

Dry flies and nymphs work well on this river, depending on conditions, and streamers can be deadly. Those who use spinning gear take many fish, but this method can be tricky when moss and weeds are heavy, typically from late spring to early autumn.

Bighorn Lake. Bighorn is a 70-mile-long reservoir situated in a red-walled canyon and was created by damming the Bighorn River. The lake is home to brown and rainbow trout, crappie, largemouth bass, sauger, walleye, yellow perch, burbot, and channel catfish. It is surrounded by the Bighorn Canyon National Recreation Area south of Billings at the Montana-Wyoming border. State Highway 313 leads to the lake, but only two public access sites exist on the Montana end of the lake, and one of those is reached by road from Wyoming.

Fort Peck Reservoir. Fort Peck is one of the nation's best walleye fisheries, but it has not experienced the angling pressure seen at other lakes and reservoirs in the upper Midwest. It is home to some 40 species of fish, including channel catfish, crappie, lake trout, northern pike, sauger, smallmouth bass, yellow perch, and an occasional rainbow trout.

Formed by Fort Peck Dam on the Missouri River, the reservoir covers roughly 250,000 acres and stretches more than 130 miles through the Missouri Breaks, a rugged and unforgiving landscape. This is gumbo country, and those who drive into the area must either be ready to leave in the face of threatening weather, or be prepared to stay until the clay dries out after a rain.

Access to the reservoir is through a handful of boat launches and campgrounds around the huge reservoir. Naturally, a body of water this large is best fished by boat.

Nelson Reservoir. The 4,500-acre Nelson Reservoir is 15 miles northeast of the town of Malta, close to U.S. 2. Northern pike, walleye, and yellow perch offer great fishing from April through

Though only a fraction of its rivers are well known, Eastern Canada has over 400 salmon rivers, the greatest such resource in the world.

about November. The fishing slows down in mid-summer, but late spring and early autumn are productive.

South-Central Region

The Yellowstone River.   This is hallowed fishing ground. Born in Wyoming's high country, the Yellowstone flows through Yellowstone National Park before entering Montana. The upper reaches of the river are nurtured by the pristine waters of the park and a nearby wilderness area. The river is particularly special because its 670 miles of unimpeded flowage makes it the longest free-flowing river in the continental U.S.

Along its route from Yellowstone National Park to Billings, the river holds native cutthroat, rainbow, and brown trout. Momentous occasions on the river include the caddisfly hatch in late spring, the salmonfly hatch in late June or early July, and exceptional hopper fishing in late summer.

The upper Yellowstone runs through Montana's Paradise Valley where, for a fee, anglers tired of the big river can test their skills on the educated trout of the area's crystal clear and famous "spring creeks."

Tributaries to the Yellowstone are the Boulder, Shields, and Stillwater Rivers. Angling on the upper Yellowstone can be challenging. Cutthroats dominate the upper reaches of the river, and there is deep water through Yankee Jim Canyon. Below the canyon the river widens, and a few islands appear. Bank fishermen can do well here, and brown trout are the dominant species.

The river, which has been heading north thus far, turns east several miles below Livingston at what is known as the "big bend." Below Livingston, the water is classic fly water. The river uses several channels from year to year. From Springdale to Columbus, the "middle Yellowstone" is underfished but remains excellent trout water.

Perhaps on the Yellowstone as much as any other river in Montana, knowing where to fish is crucial. It takes several trips to the river to become familiar with it.

At Columbus, the river begins to change to a warmwater fishery, and the change continues until below Billings. The trout give over almost completely to such warmwater species as catfish, sauger, paddlefish, and walleye. There are smallmouth bass in the river, too, along with burbot and northern pike. Channel catfish are most prevalent from Huntley downstream, and smallmouths are most common from Forsyth downstream.

Southwest Region

The Beaverhead River.   The Beaverhead River meanders for some 45 to 50 miles as the crow flies, from where it begins south of Dillon at the Clark Canyon Reservoir to Twin Bridges, where it joins the Big Hole. Good habitat makes this an excellent fishery for big rainbow and brown trout, but the river is among the toughest in Montana to fish.

Access is one problem. Because of the thick streamside willows that hang over the steep banks, the river is tough on the wading angler. Those who fish from boats do better, but the river is swift and tricky, and tensions with landowners run high.

The upper stretch of the Beaverhead, from Clark Canyon Dam to Barretts Diversion, winds through a narrow, rocky valley. The lower river courses through a wide valley. Unlike some of Montana's other classic trout streams—which have riffles, pools, and runs—the Beaverhead is a slick river that belies its swift nature.

The upper portion of the river is a favorite for outfitters and guides, but the lower portion of the Beaverhead is much less heavily fished. Fishing suffers below Dillon, where the river loses it clarity. Irrigation draws off some of the water in summer, and the habitat in general declines.

Most of the fishing on the Beaverhead is with heavy, weighted flies, although dry flies can be productive. Bait users do well in the high turbid waters of spring runoff, and lure users have success in summer and fall.

The Big Hole River.   One of Montana's blue-ribbon trout streams, the Big Hole River is classic water. It flows for 150 miles through one of the state's most picturesque high-mountain valleys and joins the Beaverhead River at Twin Bridges.

Rainbows and browns inhabit the lower river, but the brown trout don't get much above where Fishtrap Creek joins in. State fisheries biologists have found a number of 5-pound browns above the village of Divide, and a 20-pounder was taken during electroshocking just below Divide. Big Hole's potential seems clear.

Cutthroat trout, brook trout, and limited numbers of grayling populate the higher reaches of the Big Hole. The grayling has a tough time holding its own against some of the other introduced species, and is primarily located in high-mountain tributaries and the river itself, from Wisdom to Jackson. Grayling are a catch-and-release species.

Cutthroat, too, did not compete well and are now only a small portion of the Big Hole's fishery. But the brookies do well and are relatively easy to catch in the river's upper reaches and tributaries.

Like the Beaverhead, the Big Hole is hit hard by irrigation, and in extremely dry years is practically de-watered. In some years the river has been closed to fishing.

One of the hottest times on the Big Hole is the spring salmonfly hatch that runs up the river for about three weeks in June. That is perhaps the busiest time on this great river, but there is good fishing before that hatch, too.

Fishing is best by boat during spring runoff and the salmonfly hatch, but later in the year, after July, a wading angler can fish the river well. Fly anglers are in the majority on the Big Hole. Lure anglers will not do as well there as on other Montana rivers.

M

Clark Canyon Reservoir. Clark Canyon Reservoir, which is about 20 miles south of Dillon near Interstate 15, gives up big trout. There is ready access to the water and camping, and boat launches are available. The reservoir covers roughly 6,500 acres and was formed by damming the Beaverhead River. It is primarily home to rainbows, but these waters also contain brown trout and burbot. The reservoir offers good fishing year-round and is particularly popular with ice anglers from southwestern Montana.

The Gallatin River. The Gallatin River is born in the northwest corner of Yellowstone National Park, then grows up along a 100-mile race to where it joins the Madison and the Jefferson Rivers to create the Missouri River near Three Forks. Along the way, the river provides a variety of water from the easily accessible but small-stream-like Upper Gallatin to the not-so-accessible and slower-moving lower river. In between is Gallatin Canyon, which is classic riffle-pool trout water. For most of the way from the park boundary to the mouth of the canyon, the river is followed by a highway, offering numerous public access points.

There are no dams on the Gallatin, and spring's high water means great fishing for anglers using bait. High water comes in mid- to late May and subsides near the end of June.

Cutthroats are prevalent in the upper reaches of the stream, and brown trout are more common in the lower, slower water. In between are brookies near the mouths of feeder streams, and rainbows throughout the main stream. The East Fork of the Gallatin meanders through private land just west of the town of Bozeman and offers primarily good brown trout fishing. Access can be difficult, however.

Spinners, bait, dry flies, and nymphs all work on the Gallatin, another Montana river with a reliable salmonfly hatch beginning early in June.

Georgetown Lake. This 6,000-acre high-mountain lake about 20 miles west of Anaconda is as heavily fished year-round as any lake in the state. Georgetown Lake is shallow, but the grassy bottom provides great habitat for kokanee salmon and rainbow trout. The lake is easily accessible, as State Highway 1 follows it for much of its northern shoreline. This is an extremely popular destination for ice anglers from Butte, Anaconda, and Missoula.

Jefferson River. The Jefferson is unlike the other two rivers—the Gallatin and the Madison—that come together to form the Missouri River. Gentle and deep, Jefferson River flows a little more slowly. Born when the Big Hole and the Beaverhead come together just north of Twin Bridges, it is made up of long slow stretches interrupted by short riffles. This makes for superb brown trout water, and there are occasional rainbows. The slow water also makes for an abundance of undesirable species like carp, chub, and suckers, however, and also for plenty of whitefish.

The Jefferson is a tough place to be a trout during long, hot summers because of heavy de-watering due to irrigation. But autumn on the Jefferson, as on most other southwest Montana streams, can be a magical time.

The Madison. The Madison is probably the most heavily fished river of the trio that come together at Three Forks to make up the Missouri River, and with good reason: It is classic dry-fly water; the river has comparatively high numbers of fish; and it is all situated in spectacular scenery.

The Madison originates in Yellowstone National Park where the Firehole and the Gibbon Rivers meet, then flows about 100 miles to where it joins the Gallatin and the Jefferson. There are two sections. The upper river, from Quake Lake to Ennis Lake, is one long riffle. Where the stream flows through Beartrap Canyon, the lower river contains some of the wildest water in Montana. Below the canyon, the river widens and slows for the rest of its 30-mile trip to the Three Forks area.

The upper Madison is catch-and-release only, and fishing is restricted to artificial flies. A few stretches are closed to fishing altogether. Access to this part of the river is good because it is followed closely by roads.

Madison Meadows is the section from the Highway 289 crossing to the confluence with the Gallatin and the Jefferson. This stretch is about 20 miles long and is bordered mostly by private land. Fishing here is marginal during warm months but good during the winter.

The Ruby River. The Ruby River is a tributary of the Beaverhead and hard to access in its lower reaches. Expect to encounter some fee fishing, although several access sites have been achieved through a coalition of landowners, state officials, and anglers. The river flows into the Beaverhead above Twin Bridges. Fishing is good above Ruby Reservoir for foot-long rainbows, but, again, access is tricky. The river originates on national forest land, where the access is better and the stream is good for neophyte anglers.

Western Region
The Blackfoot. The Blackfoot River gained notoriety with the release of Hollywood's version of the novel *A River Runs Through It*. But the Blackfoot River today is not the same as it was in the past. Logging has contributed siltation to the river, and a sizable body of gold ore located above the town of Lincoln keeps the threat of mining hanging over the headwaters.

Still, the Blackfoot runs for roughly 100 miles from its beginnings on the western slope of the Rocky Mountains to the lumber mill town of Bonner, where it joins the Clark Fork River. The river offers deep-forest stream banks and open-meadow stretches. There are campsites and frequent access points along the river, which has largely escaped subdivision to date.

Portheus, a fish that resembled the modern tarpon in appearance, lived in the times of the dinosaurs and grew to be 14 feet long.

Cutthroats are prevalent in the river above Lincoln, but this stretch of water has small numbers of fish and the habitat is poor. Below Lincoln the fishery improves rapidly, as more tributaries pour into the river. The free-flowing Blackfoot is ripped with logjams, and the water is home to some fine brown trout, plus brookies, rainbows, cutthroats, and a few bull trout. Rainbows dominate the river from where the North Fork enters.

Floating the Blackfoot can be tough, especially above Johnsrud Park, but from there on the river settles down and is manageable.

The Bitterroot River. The Bitterroot River is born high in western Montana and runs north following the Bitterroot Range to its confluence with the Clark Fork River in the town of Missoula. The valley was among the first to be settled in Montana, and settlement continued well into the late twentieth century with the subdivision of many Bitterroot Valley farms and ranches. Logging, too, contributes to the decline of the fishery, but in spite of closed access and siltation, the Bitterroot River still is one of Montana's better trout streams.

The Bitterroot mostly gives up rainbows and brown trout, but brookies, cutthroats, and bull trout are present, too. The river holds a surprise or two: northern pike, thanks to illegal plants, and largemouth bass inhabit some of the slower backwater stretches.

Flies, nymphs, lures, and bait all work well on the river, which, depending on the time of the year and condition of the water, is noted for its clarity. Spring runoff is dramatic and, until that ends, the water will be cloudy. Irrigation also hits the river hard, and when that happens, most anglers head upstream.

The river offers dynamite dry fly fishing before the spring thaw raises water volume and turbidity. Runoff is generally in late May and June.

The Clark Fork River. The Clark Fork River is still making a comeback from the sad heydays of mining in the Butte area and smelting in the Anaconda area. But the river, which flows on to exit the state at Huron, where it is a mighty river indeed, provides a wide variety of water.

Silver Bow Creek and Warm Springs come together below a mining company's settling ponds just upstream from the burg of Warm Springs to form the Clark Fork. From there to Garrison Junction the river is home to mostly brown trout. Among the hottest water on the upper Clark Fork is that section from Gold Creek to Drummond. Trout numbers are poor until Rock Creek dumps in, and then the numbers are good to Milltown Dam. The Blackfoot River joins the Clark Fork here, but from this point until below the town of Missoula, the fishing is usually poor.

When the Bitterroot and the Clark Fork come together, the fishing changes. Browns give way to rainbows. There is outstanding fishing on the Clark Fork from Missoula to Superior, if you can find it.

The fish seem to congregate in particular areas, and the water in between is lackluster. This is a river that demands to be known before it gives up its good fish.

Rock Creek. Rock Creek is a tributary of the Clark Fork River, but the similarities are few. One of Montana's blue-ribbon trout streams, Rock Creek is roughly 50 miles long and has a road running beside it. The stream is classic trout water, with riffles, runs, and pools; it supports rainbow trout, brown trout, cutthroats, brook trout, and bull trout.

Like the Big Hole, Rock Creek experiences a tremendous salmonfly hatch beginning in early June.

Some of the land is private, but access points exist along most of the stream, including a number of U.S. Forest Service campgrounds along the upper and middle reaches. Rock Creek receives some of the heaviest pressure of any stream in Montana.

North-Central Region

Lake Elwell. Lake Elwell is a 17,000-acre reservoir created by Tiber Dam on the Marias River and located southwest of Chester in Liberty County. The lake is relatively deep at about 150 feet and offers a truly good walleye fishery. It also yields an occasional burbot and rainbow trout, and regularly produces perch and pike.

Fresno Reservoir. Created by a dam on the Milk River, Fresno Reservoir is about 10 miles west of Havre and is easily reached from U.S. Highway 2 by county road. The reservoir encompasses about 6,000 acres and is used for irrigation, so the water level can fluctuate. The lake provides northern pike, perch, and walleye fishing. There have been plantings of trout and bass, but few anglers report taking these species.

Lake Frances. Just southwest of the town of Valier, Lake Frances is a 5,500-acre lake on the Dry Fork of the Marias. The lake is home to burbot, perch, pike, rainbow trout, and walleye, and it provides good ice fishing. Trout are becoming less common here.

The Missouri River. The Missouri River wears many faces in its long, long run from Three Forks to Fort Union, where it is joined by the Yellowstone just after it leaves the state of Montana.

For the trout angler, the truly fine water is a 90-mile stretch from below Holter Dam to just above the town of Cascade. This section is rated a blue-ribbon trout stream because of its big browns and rainbows. But with greatness comes fame, so this stretch of river is heavily fished. Outfitters who once would have touted the Bighorn as Montana's best river, now bring their clients to the Missouri. The river can be a busy place.

Trout fishing declines at about the town of Cascade, where the river runs deeper and slower. Where the Smith River dumps into the Missouri, trout numbers fall off substantially. This area of the river does offer some walleye fishing, however.

M

Downstream, the complexion of the Missouri changes even more, and although trout are present, most anglers go after walleye, sauger, perch, catfish, or burbot.

The Smith River. The Smith River was the first river in Montana to be regulated for use by floaters and campers. The floatable portion of this little river is only about 60 miles long, yet it receives some of the highest use of any stream in the state. A permit system is in place, and roughly 80 percent of these permits are going to local or nonguided anglers; 20 percent is set aside for guided floaters.

The river is a quality fishery for rainbows in its upper reaches, and brown trout in the middle to lower stretches. But angling pressure, like floating pressure, is heavy on this river.

Stream Access

According to state law, the public may access waters within Montana for recreational use within the "ordinary high-water mark." The high-water mark is the line where water is present for "sufficient periods to cause physical characteristics that distinguish the area below the line from the area above it," such as soil and vegetation. The ordinary high-water mark does not encompass flood plains. This applies to stream-related recreational use such as fishing, swimming, boating, and hunting, and it is important for all anglers to understand.

In Montana there are two classes of streams: Class I and Class II. Class I streams are those that have been declared navigable or that support commercial use and include most of the state's largest rivers. Class II streams are not navigable but support stream-related recreation.

Anglers do not need permission from landowners for use of water between the ordinary high-water mark and the stream. But anglers should get permission from the landowner to cross private land.

You may camp within the bed and banks of Class I streams if it is necessary for recreational use and occurs out of sight or more than 500 yards from a dwelling. Camping closer requires landowner permission. You may not camp on Class II waters.

Anglers and boaters may portage around barriers above the ordinary high-water mark but only in the least intrusive manner. Barriers are defined as artificial obstructions in or over water that totally or effectively obstruct recreational use. Montana's stream-access law does not speak to portages around natural barriers.

MOOCHING

The most common technique for catching salmon in Pacific Northwest coastal waters is "mooching." Mooching involves the use of bait and is practiced in a way that includes a bit of drifting and subtle trolling. There are a number of ways to mooch; the differences revolve around the size of bait used, the

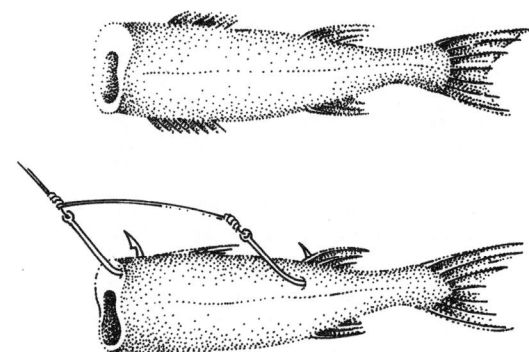

Plug-cut herring, shown here, mooch well if the proper cutting angle is achieved on the bait, and the hooks are correctly placed.

speed of the boat, and the strength of the tackle. A lot of mooching is done in areas where there is current—in rivers as well as in coastal areas where tides and eddies are prominent.

For mooching, anglers use herring, sometimes live, sometimes freshly killed and fished whole or cut, and sometimes fished as thawed/treated/cut bait. Cut bait is preferred in most areas, but the angle of the cut is important because it influences the speed of the roll as the bait is drifted or trolled. An angled cut is made behind the gills by the pectoral fin; the innards are pulled or routed out. Snelled salmon hooks in two- or three-hook rigs are used. Positioning the hooks is important and varies according to the number of hooks used, size of the bait, and the speed of the roll desired. In any case, the lead hook is impaled through the head, inserted inside the cavity behind several ribs and hooked out through the top of the bait.

Tackle consists of a long rod, generally $10\frac{1}{2}$ feet, and a reel capable of holding several hundred yards of line. In some locales, notably British Columbia, anglers are partial to so-called "mooching reels," which are 1:1 direct-drive devices akin to large fly reels. Levelwind reels and fly reels are also used. The latter are used with lighter line, shorter rods, and smaller bait when smaller fish, especially coho salmon, are abundant.

Fairly heavy sinkers, from 2 to 6 ounces, are used; these are keel-shaped and fished several feet above the bait. A barrel swivel is used a few feet ahead of the sinker, and the length of the leader from swivel to bait is roughly equal to the length of the rod.

Boat control is very important in this type of fishing, whether drifting or trolling under power. Tides, wind, and swells dictate positioning, but the object is to achieve a proper roll of the bait, as well as to keep it in the most advantageous locations. When trolling, or "motor mooching," the boat operator frequently (in some cases constantly) puts the tiller-steered motor in and out of gear, and sometimes may go backward a short distance to maneuver.

Although some strikes are vicious and result in instant hookups, many are soft—the fish may bump the bait—and the angler has to pay out line quickly to give the fish time to get the bait well into its mouth without feeling resistance. Most fish are hooked just inside the mouth and can be released without harm if that is desired.

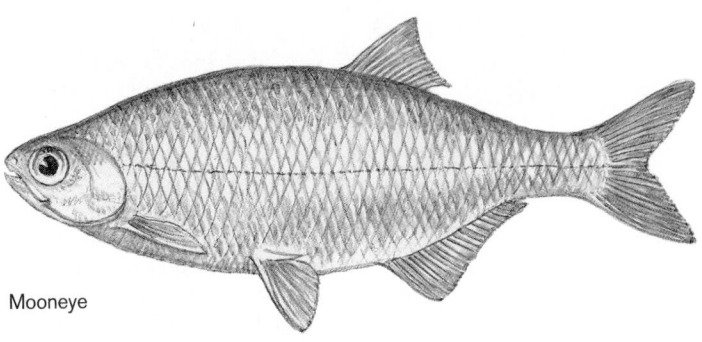

Mooneye

MOONEYE *Hiodon tergisus.*

A member of the *Hiodontidae* family, the mooneye is a close relative and very similar in appearance to the better known goldeye *(see)*. It is most important as forage for assorted predator species. Its flesh is soft and bony and of no human food value, and it is not a target of anglers, although it may occasionally be an incidental catch and can be consumed after smoking. Though often called a herring or shad, it is neither.

Identification. The mooneye is a small fish whose compressed body is deep in proportion to its length and is covered with large, loose scales. Dark blue to blue green over the back, it is silvery on the sides and tapers to white on the belly. It has a small head and a short, bluntly rounded snout with a small terminal mouth containing many sharp teeth on the jaws and tongue.

The color of its eyes and the position of its anal fin distinguish it from the goldeye. The iris of the large eyes of the mooneye are silver colored (unlike the gold-colored iris of the goldeye). The mooneye's dorsal fin begins before the anal fin (the goldeye's begins opposite or behind its anal fin). The mooneye can be distinguished from the gizzard shad by not having a dorsal fin ray projection.

Size/Age. Mooneye are slightly larger on average than goldeye and are often found to be 2 pounds in weight, although their maximum attainable size is uncertain. They may live at least 10 years.

Distribution. Endemic to North America, mooneye occur in the St. Lawrence–Great Lakes region (except Lake Superior), the Mississippi River drainage, and the Hudson Bay basin from Quebec to Alberta, and southward to the Gulf of Mexico. Mooneye are also present in Gulf Slope drainages from Mobile Bay, Alabama, to Lake Pontchartrain, Louisiana.

Habitat. Mooneye inhabit deep, warm, silty sections of medium and large rivers, the backwaters of shallow lakes connected to them, and impoundments.

Spawning behavior. Mooneye spawn in the spring, moving up tributary rivers or streams.

Food. This species feeds on plankton, insects, and small fish. Small mooneye are preyed upon by large predators, including walleye, pike, catfish, and salmon.

Angling. Though seldom the target of angling effort, mooneye can be caught on flies and on natural bait that are impaled on small hooks and suspended below a light float. Light spinning and fly tackle is used. Mooneye may be fished live or as cut bait for other species, notably catfish.

MOONFISH, ATLANTIC *Selene setapinnis.*
MOONFISH, PACIFIC *Selene peruviana.*

Other names for Atlantic moonfish—French: *lune;* Portuguese: *corcovado, galo verdadeiro, peixe-galo;* Spanish: *corcobado, jorobado, lamparosa.*

Other names for Pacific moonfish—horsefish, Peruvian moonfish, pug-nosed shiner, blunt-nosed shiner; Spanish: *caraja, jorobado, pez luna.*

Small members of the Carangidae family of jacks and not well known to anglers, moonfish are a good food fish and are commercially marketed fresh and salted/dried.

Identification. Similar to the lookdown *(see)*, Atlantic and Pacific moonfish are shiny, silvery, and platelike, but their bodies are more elongated. They have the similar steep head profile, but it is more concave than in the lookdown. Another difference is that the front rays of their dorsal and anal fins are not elongated. The young Atlantic moonfish has an elongated black spot on its midside, and the Pacific moonfish has a black spot at the upper edge of the operculum.

Size. Moonfish may reach 10 to 12 inches in length.

Distribution. The Atlantic moonfish occurs in the western Atlantic from Nova Scotia to Mar de Plata, Argentina, including the Caribbean Sea and the Gulf of Mexico. The Pacific moonfish occurs in the eastern Pacific from Redondo Beach in Southern California and throughout the lower Gulf of California to Peru, but is usually rare north of Baja California, Mexico.

Habitat. Bottom-dwelling species, moonfish usually form schools and inhabit inshore waters of up to 50 to 60 meters in depth. Young Atlantic moonfish are found over muddy bottom in bays and river mouths, whereas young Pacific moonfish may be found near the surface.

Food. Moonfish feed on small fish and crustaceans.

Angling. *See: Inshore Fishing; Jacks.*

MOON PHASE
See: Solunar Tables; Tides.

MOORING

A place where a boat is kept at anchor. A boat is said to be moored when securely anchored or when tied to a dock, pier, or other structure.

MOROCCO

For most people Morocco means heat, bazaars, and Casablanca, but for many European anglers this country on the northwest corner of the Sahara Desert is an idyllic backdrop to diverse and breathtaking fishing.

Situated on the northwestern tip of Africa, Morocco is separated from the rest of the continent by the towering Atlas Mountains and the Sahara. Its coastline faces the Atlantic Ocean on the east, and the Mediterranean Sea on the north. Morocco's climate, geography, and history are all more closely related to the Mediterranean than to the rest of Africa, and visitors are often struck by the odd sensation of having not quite reached Africa. In the north on the Mediterranean coast, fine beaches, lush highland valleys, and evocative old cities like Marrakech, Fez, and Meknes reinforce this impression. This Mediterranean character melts away as one moves south and east, into and over the starkly beautiful ranges of the Atlas Mountains.

The climate in Morocco is reliably dry, although a small amount of rain does fall between November and March. Temperatures vary considerably by season and locale. Whereas the southern and southeastern desert regions can reach extremely high temperatures during the hot summer months, the higher altitudes of the mountains are cool during summer evenings and freezing in winter.

Due to these extremes of climate, Morocco offers many hotspots both for saltwater and freshwater fishing. In fact, it is possible to fish for white marlin on deep-blue ocean waters, and the following day catch largemouth bass on a placid mountain lake.

Although angling locations are plentiful, sportfishing facilities are scarce. In 1999, there were only two local professional sportfishing operators for both saltwater and freshwater: Sochatour (71 Avenue des FAR, Casablanca 01, Morocco; phone: 212-2-314694 or 212-2-314719; fax: 212-2-314699), and Louis Champeaux (phone: 212-2-206401). There is a European sportfishing operator in Great Britain, The Best of Morocco, Ltd. (Seend Park, Seend, Wiltshire SN12 6NZ; phone: 0380-828533). It is necessary to bring your own fishing equipment.

Saltwater

The Moroccan coastline offers wide sandy beaches as well as a number of interesting rocky shorelines. The diversity of fishing in this fascinating country is great, particularly around Dahkla and Agadir (for surf casting) in the deep south, and around Casablanca (for deep-sea fishing) in the northwest.

Near Morocco's southern border, Dahkla is washed by the cool Canary Current and offers some truly breathtaking scenery and sea fishing. From high above fossil-rich cliffs the view is absolutely beautiful: mile upon mile of white-gold sand and a seabed that drops away beyond the third or fourth breaker into deep water. It is a completely unspoiled and virtually unfished haven.

The best prospects for angling are from the end of May until September, when stingrays, shovelnose rays (guitarfish), jacks, snapper, bluefish, garrick, grouper, sharks, bream, and a variety of different species of bass are plentiful.

One particular fish, the courbine (or meagre; in the drum family) moves close inshore in good numbers during June and July. Fish between 30 and 80 pounds are commonly caught at this time of year. The best baits for this giant fish are squid, cuttlefish, and octopus (known locally as *calamar, choco,* and *poulpe*). All are available at the local market in Dahkla.

Facing the Atlantic Ocean at about the same latitude as Bermuda, the thriving seaport metropolis of Casablanca sits in the northwest corner of Africa, a temperate, agriculturally rich region that bulges toward nearby Spain just across the Straits of Gibraltar. Though Casablanca's fame was made in the movies, the white marlin grounds near this city have won it a different kind of recognition. Since 1987, the clear blue waters off Mohammedia, a suburb 12 miles north of Casablanca, have gained international fame through the consistent exploration and world-record-setting catches of skilled French and American skippers and anglers.

White marlin are found from 8 to 35 miles off Mohammedia Marina's docks, depending on the shifts in the warm currents that converge off this coast. Anglers troll rigged needlefish or mackerel where the surface temperature rises abruptly from about 70° to 77°F, as this is where schools of white marlin and sometimes swordfish are found chasing skipjack tuna. The best season for white marlin runs from August through mid-November. In the same months it is also possible to troll or drift with live baits in inshore waters for amberjack, snapper, grouper, bluefish, garrick, and tuna.

Freshwater

In the southeast, Morocco's mountain ranges yield to the desolate expanse of the Sahara. The rivers that flow down this side of the Atlas support long, narrow, and lush river valleys that resemble linear oases and are dammed to form beautiful lakes.

Within easy driving distance of Morocco's ancient city of Marrakech are three large reservoirs, each one with good to excellent sportfisheries. Twenty miles south of Marrakech is the Lalla Takerkoust Dam, which hosts a prolific stock of carp. Forty miles north of the city is El Massina Dam, home to a big population of largemouth bass. Twenty miles east of Marrakech is Ait Aabel, which boasts the best fishing of the three. Fed by the Tessaout River, Ait Aabel is huge, wild, and secluded, and has been stocked with largemouth bass, which are abundant. They are especially found among the massive boulders at the base of the dam, where shore anglers have an opportunity to catch them.

Going afloat (boats are hired through the two local operators) enables the angler to explore the steep-sided gorges of the rivers that help fill Ait Abel during the winter rains. The changes in depth along the course of this flooded canyon are tremendous and keep the sonar on the fishing boats bobbing up and down like a yo-yo. The greatest concentrations of bass are around sunken trees, bushes, rocky outcrops, and ledges.

MOSQUITOFISH   *Gambusia affinis affinis.*

The mosquitofish is a member of the large Poeciliidae family of livebearers, which is closely related to killifish *(see)* or cyprinodonts, differing from them mainly in bringing forth their young alive rather than laying eggs.

Also known as the North American topminnow or the western mosquitofish, this species is famous as the number-one scourge of mosquito larvae. Although there are other larvae-eating species of fish, the mosquitofish tolerates salinity and pollution levels that would kill most other species, and it produces up to 1,500 young in its lifetime.

Native to the southeastern United States, the mosquitofish has been introduced to suitable warm waters around the world since 1905, when it was experimentally introduced to Hawaii and virtually eliminated mosquitoes. It has been transplanted to the southwestern U.S., the Caribbean, Central America, Europe, and the Middle East, and coldwater strains have gone to Canada, Russia, and the northern U.S., among other areas. All of this has made *Gambusia affinis affinis* the widest-ranging freshwater fish on earth (other species of mosquitofish have not been as successfully introduced).

Female mosquitofish are about 2 inches long, and the males are only half as large. As with other species of livebearers, the anal fin of the male is modified to form an intermittent organ for introducing sperm into the female. A mature female may produce three or four broods during one season, sometimes giving birth to 200 or more young at a time. When she is carrying young, the female becomes obviously plumper and develops a large black area on each side just in front of the anal fin. This fish is easily raised in aquariums and is not sensitive to temperature variations, but it does not adjust well to living with other fish.

Although it has been highly effective at controlling malarial mosquitoes, the mosquitofish is not a panacea. Mosquitofish larvae cannot survive without water (as mosquito larvae can), they do not control mosquitoes in places with abundant surface

Mosquitofish

vegetation to hide mosquito larvae, they may consume the young of forage and game species, and they can have adverse effects on indigenous fish species.

MOTOR, ELECTRIC

An electric motor is one of the most important and useful items that any boating angler can have. An electric motor, called a "trolling" motor by most of the angling fraternity, allows you to maneuver and position your boat in the proper angle for casting and to make the type of presentation that is required for the fishing circumstances, all as quietly and carefully as possible. An electric motor could most appropriately be called a maneuvering motor or a positioning motor because its main purpose is keeping anglers who cast from a boat in position to make more and better presentations, and thus fish effectively.

Electric motors essentially take the place of oars and sculling paddles, but they are quieter and interfere less with fishing activities. They can be used in trolling but are primarily used for positioning while casting. Electric motors are predominantly used by freshwater anglers, especially bass and walleye anglers; saltwater usage has been less widespread, in part because of difficulties in keeping electronic equipment that is exposed to corrosive elements in working order. However, this is changing. Manufacturers have vastly improved the corrosion resistance of motors meant for saltwater use. Previously, many motors used in saltwater were beefed-up versions of freshwater motors, but now they are specifically designed for the harsh salt environment, having stainless steel and corrosion-resistant parts, tighter seals, improved torque, remote-control operation, and more power.

All electric motors are battery powered. Some run off a single 12-volt battery; others require 24 or 36 volts. Still others have the capability of running off either one or two 12-volt batteries. Not all electric motors are alike. Some are more powerful; some more battery efficient. The amount of energy (designated as amperes, or amps) consumed by electric motors varies, and this figure, when known, will tell you how many hours of continuous use you can get out of a battery at varied speeds. Modern electric motors are much more efficient at consuming and conserving battery power than in the past. However, it is a fact that the heavier the boat and boat load, the more power, or thrust, is needed.

M

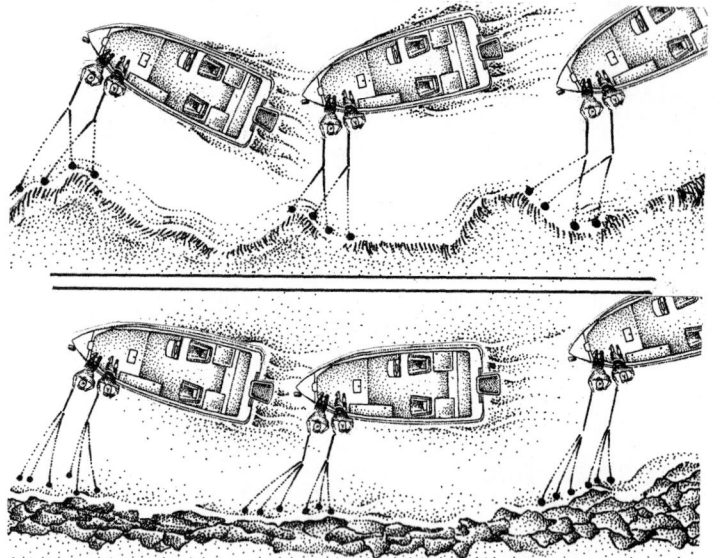

Electric motors are primarily used for getting and maintaining position for good casting presentations. Paralleling a ragged shoreline (top) and steep bluff (bottom) as depicted here allows two bass anglers to cover the area well, sometimes overlapping casts.

M

As a rule, to position a boat effectively in wind and/or current, you will need at least a pound of thrust for every 100 pounds of gross boat weight (including yourself and companions). Thus, if the gross weight is 2,000 pounds, you'll need an electric capable of delivering at least 20 pounds of thrust at full power. If the wind and current conditions tend to be particularly bad in your area, you might even need 50 percent more thrust, or a 30-pound thrust electric in this example.

An important factor to consider is how much fishing is done in areas of substantial current or wind; both of these drain the reserves of a battery quicker than calm-condition operation. Saltwater operation, in general, is more demanding than freshwater, partly because a lot of power is needed to combat currents and wind, and partly because saltwater casters may have to do a bit of moving to keep up with quickly moving and widely roaming fish. Boat weights, wind and current demands, and angler interest have consistently pushed electric motor manufacturers into offering more powerful products, and if batteries ever improve to provide more power over extended periods, there will be a new race for greater thrust.

On most fiberglass and on many aluminum boats in freshwater, the electric motor is mounted permanently on the bow, with the bracket support installed on the bow port to put a little weight on that side and counterbalance the console and driver weight on the starboard side. On small boats such as rowboats and jonboats, electric motors can be mounted on the front or back. Boats move with greater ease when pulled rather than pushed, so many anglers prefer bow mounting; plus, with bow mounting, they can see where they're headed and

know when to avoid objects. Bow mounting is preferred for casting to cover and working along specific edges, but a single motor (you can't put two on the bow) may not have the power needed in open water conditions.

Saltwater anglers, particularly those who use flats boats, are most likely to employ one or two long-shafted transom-mount motors, which are operated either manually or by remote control. They prefer transom mounting because it is close to the stern poling platform and does not require lowering into the water, making motion and noise that might spook fish. Two transom motors provide the gusto to follow quickly moving fish, which cannot be done by poling; however, maneuverability, especially in wind is tougher with transom operation.

Some anglers, especially guides and tournament anglers, put bow and transom-mount motors on their boats, using either or both when conditions warrant. However, numbers and power aren't always in the best interests of the angler, because no electric motor is completely quiet. Some anglers firmly believe that certain fish, under certain conditions, are attuned to electric motors and are turned off or alarmed by the sounds that they make. This is especially true in clear water and on exposed flats, and in the shallows.

Small boats usually require only a single 12-volt electric motor, though you can employ more than one motor at a time. Some anglers who fish in places where gas outboards are prohibited rig up two or three electrics in unison, and some manufacturers have units specifically for this application. Small-boat electrics feature a turnscrew-clamp transom mount, which makes them adjustable and removable. With some, you can leave the bracket installed and remove the rest of the motor. Some of these models can also fit on the front of a small boat, but it pays to first check out your boat and then see whether the motor you like will fit the design of your bow.

Permanent-mount electrics are used on conventional bass boats and large craft and can be operated manually or remotely, depending upon the unit. Most remote units are operated via a foot-control pedal on the bow deck; some have merely a long electric cord, and some are totally remote controlled, operated by a wireless touch pad or by voice command. The latter types eliminate the hindrance of wires and cable, and have become increasingly popular in both freshwater and saltwater. Completely remote units operate by radio frequency control and by air pressure (pneumatic) control. Some of the remote models can be operated from 200 feet away from the boat, meaning that in gentle flats conditions, anglers can get out of the boat and walk along the flats, keeping a low profile, while the boat stays an unobtrusive distance away, ready to be called closer when needed.

For years, many anglers shunned cable-controlled bow-mount electric motors because they were prone to cable or foot-lever pad breakage. These items have improved, but they aren't foolproof, and when a cable breaks or the foot control malfunctions, you're out of commission. Moreover, some people struggle with the actual movement of the foot control because it isn't smooth, isn't situated well on their boat, or, as is the case with some long-cable remote motors, is hard to operate and unresponsive. You can run the foot control when standing or seated.

Manual models do not have a foot control pedal or cable running to the motor and are steered by turning a fixed handle or a handle extension device. They are mostly operated by hand but may be maneuvered with your foot or knee, although you have to be properly balanced to do this. Manual bow-mount motors are relatively easy to steer, but they are poor in rough water, in sharp turns, or in reverse because you have to physically turn the motor around, which can mean reaching out over the boat. They're usually operated from a standing position, are less prone to breakage, and are best for agile people.

One important feature to look for in an electric motor is a breakaway bracket; this device allows the shaft of the motor to slip back should the motor collide with an immovable object. This feature will save you from having bent shafts and damaged lower units, and will prevent extraordinary stress on the mounting bracket when objects are struck head on. Another important consideration is the length of the shaft. Big boats and boats that will be used in rough water conditions require a long-shaft motor so that the prop will grab properly and, in the case of manual models, so that the control handle is at an accessible height (although there are accessory devices that attach to the upper shaft and extend upward to make manual control easier.

Another important feature is a good armature and easy-release/take-up system for getting into and out of the water with minimum effort. Different motors vary greatly in this regard. There are also automatic devices for raising and lowering bow-mounted electric motors.

Batteries and Chargers

With an electric motor you'll also need one or more batteries, plus a means of recharging the battery. An electric motor does not automatically recharge the power source, and in the course of a full day's fishing, you may drain the energy of a battery considerably. With pulse modulation, good electric motors today don't drain a battery as much as they did in the past, and depending on the fishing circumstances, you may be able to get two or three days out of a battery without recharging it. But you'll still need a battery charger.

The best products for powering electric motors are deep-cycle batteries. Deep-cycle batteries are often called marine batteries, but not all "marine batteries" are deep-cycled, so you should check to

be sure that the batteries you obtain for electric motor use are deep-cycle products. These are constructed with special plates that allow them to be regularly drawn down and recharged; standard batteries are not meant to do this and do not have nearly the life of deep-cycle batteries when used for electric motor operation.

Deep-cycle batteries for electric motors are rated by size or amp-hours as well as by voltage. Make sure you get the right voltage for your motor's needs. Amp hours are the amount of amperage that a battery can consistently produce over a 20-hour period. A size 24 battery yields typically 60 to 70 amp hours, and a size 27 might yield 70 to 85. Batteries may also have a marine cranking amp rating, which is the amps it produces for 30 seconds at 32°F, and reserve capacity, which is the number of minutes during which a battery will produce 25 amps. For maximum performance, get the highest-amperage batteries you can, plus a high-amp-capacity battery charger with multiple features. For starting the outboard motor, you don't need a deep-cycle battery. A conventional automotive battery will do, but opt for a non-deep-cycle marine battery. However, if you want to reduce weight in your boat, then you can use one battery for all electrical needs, and it should be capable of being repeatedly drawn down and recharged.

Remember that the batteries are the lifeline to your boat's operation. Clean the terminals and connections regularly for good contact. Signs of a weak battery include low electric motor propulsion, weak sonar signals, low temperature gauge readings, low tachometer and speedometer readings, and weak fuel gauge indications.

Batteries on a full charge last longer, so keep your charge level high at all times, even through the winter. It is best to recharge a deep-cycle battery as soon as possible after it has been drawn down. Staying in a weakened condition can damage the plates and promote a shorter life. If you are charging directly to a battery, you can use the clamp-type terminal connectors, being sure to place the positive and negative wires properly and keeping the battery compartment ventilated. If your boat is wired for automatic charging, you need an adaptor that is attached to your charger's lead wires and that merely needs to be plugged into the boat receptacle with the system switched into the charging mode. There are also onboard automatic battery chargers that can be wired into the system; these will charge the batteries by themselves, shut off when charged, and monitor the battery status to recharge as necessary.

Checking open-cell batteries used to be done by monitoring the acid levels in the cells and filling them with distilled water. Their charging state was checked with a hydrometer. That system has been rivaled by popular maintenance-free sealed liquid acid and gel batteries. The technology and performance of the sealed liquid acid battery is much the

In 1999, an empty two-piece cardboard box for a lure called the "Michigan Life-Like Minnow," which was manufactured in February 1908 by A. Arntz of Muskegon, Michigan, sold at auction for $2,600.

M

same as its open-cell predecessor, but the sealed gel battery theoretically allows less liquid dissipation.

You cannot check the amount of electrical energy left in a sealed battery with a floating hydrometer. You must resort to more sophisticated means in the form of electronics, which allows you to monitor the amount of remaining charge via a dash-mounted gauge. This type of electronic hydrometer works by accurately measuring the battery's voltage, and translating that number into percent of charge remaining. Some instruments will display total amp hours withdrawn from the battery at any time, as well as the precise battery voltage, and even the rate at which the current is being withdrawn.

The total lifetime of your battery depends greatly upon the charger you use. Some batteries are more sensitive to excessive charging voltage than others, and if you have an onboard-charging system but an unregulated output alternator, you can damage a battery, especially a gel version. Overcharging increases the internal temperature of the battery, which accelerates destruction of its positive plates and results in reduced storage capacity and battery life.

The ideal AC charger for a maintenance-free battery is not the old standard type that reverts to a trickle when full charge is reached, because constant current can cause damage. A charger should be capable of automatically not exceeding safe voltage levels for either gel or liquid acid batteries, and should shut off when the charging cycle is complete.

If you must charge two or even three batteries at the same time with a single charger, you're going to need at least a 20-amp heavy-duty model. You can safely charge two or even three in parallel, provided they are all equally discharged. Otherwise, connecting them in parallel will result in the battery(ies) with the higher charge trying to recharge the battery(ies) that is lower, and enough heat could be generated in the connecting wires to start a fire. Obviously, if you use those batteries connected in parallel at all times, then they will always all have exactly the same state of charge.

One way of keeping batteries alive for long periods and keeping them capable of accepting full charges is to use pulse technology maintenance products. These somewhat help prevent sulfation of the battery plates. When crystallized sulfate molecules build up on the lead plates, they prevent full recharging, which leads to more sulfate buildup and eventually to a dead battery. Pulse technology is a system that discharges a pulsating DC current into the battery, removing sulfates from the plates and, if used continuously, preventing them from returning. Some models are connected to solar panels that permit full-time pulsation and that are capable of maintaining batteries at all times, even when they are not being used (in a boat, recreational vehicle, etc.). Products with pulse technology have been used by the military for various applications, and in recent years these products have spread to recreational and consumer automotive applications. Extending battery life for several years is possible with such systems and has obvious economic benefit; helping to reduce the disposal of (toxic) batteries also has environmental benefits.

It is important to note that in typical lead-acid batteries, the failure to routinely monitor and replace battery-consumed water results in irreversible plate damage. In sealed maintenance-free batteries, the user has no opportunity to monitor water level to minimize plate damage and maximize battery life. Newer low-maintenance batteries exist that have an oil-water mixture that serves to retain water and minimize its loss, yet also allows for the addition of more water to maintain proper fluid levels and to keep the plates covered.

Batteries are the lifeblood of the electric motor. Frequent use of an electric motor battery means that the battery constantly goes through the process of being charged (often overcharged), then drained at varying levels of discharge, and often neglected before or during charging again; and all of this happens over a wide range of time and temperatures. Obviously batteries have to take a lot. Although battery technology has improved, it has not kept pace with angling needs. Batteries are also the main thing that is holding up the further development of electric motors for fishing. Smaller batteries with increased life and with much greater power are needed for the demands that anglers put on their motors.

Some of the more sophisticated electric motors, such as this bow-mounted unit on a bass boat, provide remote cableless operation.

Maneuvering Tactics

Speed and position are the key elements to fishing effectively and to properly running a boat with an electric motor. It takes a little practice to learn how to pilot a particular boat with a particular motor, especially to learn how to control it along and around places that you cast to. The strength of the motor, the weight of the occupied boat, and the conditions encountered determine how best to run the motor. Eventually, dealing with constant on/off operation and directional maneuvering becomes second nature.

In one sense, maneuvering a boat with an electric motor is similar to driving a car around town, where you alter speed frequently and manipulate the steering wheel constantly. However, it is also unlike driving a car because you have no brakes to slow down and no pavement or lane markers to easily follow, and you are more susceptible to being blown off course.

Maneuvering a boat with a bow-mounted motor, which pulls the boat bow-first, is a bit different from maneuvering with a transom-mount motor, which pushes it bow-first. The latter is harder to use in the wind, because the bow gets shoved by the wind and the boat quickly slips off course, requiring constant correction.

In small, light boats with a transom electric you would do well to fish stern-first to better control positioning. You can turn the motor around and run it with handle facing away from you, or you can rotate the head so that the handle faces the bow but the motor pulls away from the stern.

Under calm or near-calm conditions, maneuvering a boat is relatively easy. You'll get plenty of casts in, and you can keep the boat positioned properly for long periods of time. When underway, the main issue is selecting the proper speed to allow you and companions ample opportunity to make presentations in desired places.

The stronger the wind, the harder this becomes. Often it is not beneficial to manipulate your boat with the wind. Even with the motor set on the slowest possible speed, you're likely to blow past desirable fishing locations quickly. Fishing fast is seldom productive, except perhaps when chasing schooling surface-feeding fish. When white bass or stripers are on top and moving, for example, you need to quietly stay with them and rapidly get lures amongst them.

When casting to specific places, such as weedbeds, points, mangrove edges, rocky shorelines, etc., you generally need to make an accurate cast and a measured retrieve, sometimes more than once, which cannot be done properly in a poorly controlled boat. Running the boat into the wind at a speed that keeps you in the right place for the right casts is necessary. It is now possible to run a well-charged battery hard all day without killing it, so there is no battery-power-saving excuse for not bucking the wind.

Sometimes the wind comes crosswise at your boat, and this is especially difficult to counter when you're casting to a particular shoreline or weed edge. Head into and across the wind, and keep up speed to maintain position. In this situation, and some others, it may be advantageous for a companion to move to the front of the boat to fish. Doing so minimizes concern for where the back of the boat is positioned, and both anglers will have equal opportunity to make good presentations.

Running the boat properly and fishing effectively at the same time is not very difficult except in the wind or when navigating through heavy vegetation or timber. At all times you have to anticipate where the boat is headed and simultaneously observe what is coming up to cast to. You have to be on top of the boat position at all times, not wait, for example, until you've drifted close to cover to adjust position. Getting close to cover, incidentally, is all right when the water is murky, but not when it's clear. And, of course, this may still depend on the species. Using an electric motor on high power in shallow water is likely to spook most species of fish, even if the water is murky.

Another consideration in boat positioning is the depth below your boat, as well as the depth where you're casting and retrieving. It is often desirable to keep your boat positioned in a certain depth of water. Let's say, for example, that you're fishing crankbaits along a moderately sloping shoreline and that there's a sharp break to deeper water at 10 or 12 feet, which is where most bass are being caught at the time. That break may be 70 feet from shore, which is where you might situate the boat if you were casting close to the bank. By studying your sonar as you fish, you see that if the boat is in 25 feet of water, you can cast your lure into the shallows where it is 4 or 5 feet deep and retrieve the plug through the 12-foot range and then on out to the boat in an effective manner. So you slowly keep following that 25-foot contour, and if you notice a change in contours—such as a hump or extended point—you immediately maneuver the boat accordingly so that you keep your casts and lures in the proper places. This is fishing effectively.

MOTOR, TROLLING

A common term for electric motors, which are used rarely for trolling but mostly for maneuvering boat position while fishing, especially when casting. See: Motor, Electric.

MOUSIE

See: Mealworm.

MOZAMBIQUE

Mozambique is a large and lengthy country in southeastern Africa with 2,470 kilometers of coastline on the Mozambique Channel of the Indian Ocean. It has had a checkered saltwater sportfishery in the latter decades of the twentieth century, owing to civil strife and a poorly developed infrastructure—a situation common to many developing African nations. Freshwater sportfishing is virtually unknown, and the entire coast, stretching from the southern border with South Africa to the northern border with Tanzania, possesses some of the least-explored coastal fishing in the world. Saltwater gamefishing was outstanding in the past, although lightly pursued with both primitive equipment and primitive vessels. It has the potential to be a great attraction in the future.

Saltwater

Inhaca Island, Paradise Island, Bazaruto, Pomene, Xai Xai, and Tofo are all names that stir distant memories for some anglers and fuel a desire to return and fish the magnificent coast of Mozambique. Those memories, however, date back to before 1970.

Early in the 1970s, a fierce war put an end not only to Portuguese colonialism (the country became independent in 1975), but also to public fishing along this unspoiled stretch of African coast. Twenty years of civil war followed, and for most of that time Mozambique was closed to all but a very limited number of foreign diplomats who managed to fish the waters adjacent to the capital city of Maputo, at the extreme southern tip of the country.

In more recent times, a few intrepid anglers have visited the smattering of islands that exist off this coast. These islands are separated from the mainland by 20 miles of tidal flats, a fact that deterred rebel forces from approaching the islands and protected the small band of loyalist soldiers guarding their sovereignty. Reports filtered out about fantastic fishing, with some indication that the years of inactivity had resulted in regeneration of this coast. Some anglers believe that all that is needed now is boats, fuel, and accommodations to draw anglers in droves, possibly creating one of the world's foremost big-game centers.

Before the early 1970s, Santa Carolina, or Paradise Island, as it was commonly known, was southern Africa's answer to Cairns of Australia, Kona of Hawaii, and Cabo Blanco of Peru—all famed for their big marlin. Situated in the huge bay within the Bazaruto archipelago, it was a prime port for anglers to take advantage of pelagic fisheries opportunities brought about by the close southerly flow of the warm Aghulas Current coursing through the Mozambique Channel between the mainland and Madagascar.

Big black marlin, many over 1,000 pounds, were then boated from craft barely suitable for big-game fishing. Single-diesel-engined tubs with jury-rigged fighting chairs and makeshift outriggers were on the brink of giving way to modern sportfishing boats when the civil war commenced. At that time, other billfish included Pacific blue marlin, striped marlin, Pacific sailfish, and swordfish. Black marlin were the main quarry, with special emphasis placed on late in the season, when larger catches were registered, especially at Bazaruto (south of Beira).

Today, a band of ardent anglers and scuba divers, mainly from South Africa, journey to the lower Mozambique coast to make use of the rustic lodges and campsites built there, and they use high-speed 18- to 23-foot craft powered by dual outboards.

An abundance of king mackerel, wahoo, barracuda, dorado, bonito, and small tuna can be caught, but it is angling for sailfish and marlin that will spearhead the future redevelopment of the angling infrastructure of the area. With a current lack of big boats, a chicken-and-egg situation exists; the full potential of the Bazaruto archipelago, as well as the rest of the lengthy coast, will be realized only when fully equipped offshore charter craft make their appearance.

Some fishing efforts have indicated that a viable sailfish resource still exists here, but the full extent of this is unknown. Concerns exist about conserving fisheries resources here, because the region has a prevailing lack of protein and food, and local fishing crews, such as they are, need financial persuasion to release captured species, particularly large specimens like billfish.

Beach anglers have opened up new horizons along the white sandy shores of the islands. Prior to the war, a limited number of anglers fished from a few of the rocky promontories that stretch out into the ocean at the extremities of numerous bays and coves. Often they caught an abundance of gamefish, the main one being giant trevally.

At present, shore-based anglers—fishing from sand spits and channel edges—seek ocean predators as they await the vast array of food being swept out of the bay off the seemingly endless sandbanks and through the gaps between islands. Using lures, freshly netted sardines, or live bait, anglers question the need to take a craft to sea to access the diversity and quantity of fish. An ample supply of fish has even made fly fishing—a technique that is altogether new in this part of the world—more promising. It is possible that bonefish on the shallow flats will be targeted eventually, opening up a new vista of opportunities for light-tackle angling. Decades ago, huge bonefish, including specimens from 18 to 23 pounds, were reportedly landed around coastal Mozambique, although the status of this fishery is uncharted today.

With peace, government stability, and a vastly improved road system, the Mozambique coast is becoming a popular spot for South African anglers. The mystique of primitive Africa combined with excellent fishing either from shore or in modern high-powered craft (though small) makes this a unique experience, and the day may come when exploration of the entire coast and offshore waters unveils terrific treasures.

M

The heaviest giant squid ever recorded weighed $2\frac{1}{5}$ tons and had one tentacle that measured 35 feet long.

Freshwater

As primitive as the coastal fishery is, the inland fishery is even more so. Mozambique has numerous rivers and lakes, and the status of their fisheries is relatively unknown today. Forty percent of the country is comprised of coastal lowlands, but westward in the interior the land rises to low hills and plateaus, with mountainous regions in the west and north. It is purely speculative to suggest that the higher reaches may contain trout; however, some regions border highlands that do possess rainbow trout, especially in Malaŵi (see).

The rivers are likely to contain some of the same species found in neighboring countries, possibly including tigerfish. It is reasonable to expect that these can be found in the Zambezi River, as the Zambezi is a hotbed for tigerfishing upriver in Zimbabwe. There, after exiting Lake Kariba, it flows into extreme western Mozambique, where it forms a large lake behind Cabora Bassa Dam, which on a map appears to be slightly smaller than the 180-mile-long Kariba. The Zambezi flows southeasterly from here to the Indian Ocean, widening considerably in its lower sections. The lake and the river in Mozambique almost certainly possess tigerfish, vundu, and tilapia, as well as other species, although the size of the fish and extent of the population are completely speculative.

Other significant rivers with unknown fisheries resources include the Ruvuma, which forms most of the northern border with Tanzania, and the Limpopo, which is in the far south and flows from South Africa into Mozambique and through a large delta before reaching the sea near Xai Xai. Numerous other rivers and tributaries flow from the highlands.

In addition to Cabora Bassa, Lake Nyasa forms part of the Malaŵi border, as do Lakes Chilwa and Chiota, although the fisheries of the latter are unknown. A short stretch of the Shire River, which in Malaŵi is known to have tigerfish, flows in Mozambique before entering the Zambezi River.

MUDDING

The behavior of bottom-feeding fish in shallow water, especially the bonefish, which creates a mud trail as it roots while feeding, often with head down and the upper lobe of its tail out of the water.

MUDLINE

The edge created in a large body of water by the influx of turbid current, usually a river. The mudline is obvious at the river mouth and for a variable distance (depending on the volume of incoming water and big water current) along the shore near the river mouth. The clearer edge of the mudline is attractive to some species of gamefish.

MULLET

Mullet are members of the Mugilidae family, a group of roughly 70 species that range worldwide in shallow, warm seas. A few species live in freshwater and some are reared in ponds. All are good food fish, especially in smoked form, although smaller ones may be too bony to eat. Mullet roe is considered a delicacy. Mullet are important food fish for many predator species, and anglers use them alive or dead, in chunks or strips, as baits.

Identification. The striped mullet (*Mugil cephalus*) is bluish gray or green along the back, shading to silver on the sides and white below. Also known as the black mullet, or fatback, it has indistinct horizontal black bars, or stripes, on its sides; the fins are lightly scaled at the base and unscaled above; the nose is blunt and the mouth small; and the second dorsal fin originates behind that of the anal fin. It is similar to the smaller fantail mullet (*M. gyrans*) and the white mullet (*M. curema*), both of which have a black blotch at the base of their pectoral fin, which is lacking in the striped mullet.

Fantail mullet have an olive green back with a bluish tint, shading to silvery on the sides and white below. Its anal and pelvic fins are yellowish; there's a dark blotch at the base of the pectoral fin; the mouth has an inverted V-shape; and the second dorsal fin originates behind that of the anal fin.

The white mullet, also known as silver mullet, is bluish gray on the back, fading to silvery on the sides and white below. It lacks stripes; small scales extend onto its soft dorsal and anal fins; there's a dark blotch at the base of the pectoral fin; and the second dorsal fin originates behind that of the anal fin.

Size. The striped mullet may reach a length of 3 feet and weigh as much as 12 pounds, although the largest specimens have come from aquariums. Roe specimens in the wild are common to 3 pounds, but most striped mullet weigh closer to a pound. The fantail mullet is small and usually weighs less than a pound. The white mullet is similar in size to the fantail.

Distribution. The striped mullet is cosmopolitan in all warm seas worldwide and is the only member of the mullet family found off the Pacific coast of the U.S. The fantail mullet occurs in the western Atlantic in Bermuda, and from Florida and the northern Gulf of Mexico to Brazil. The white mullet is found in the western Atlantic in Bermuda and from Massachusetts south to Brazil, including

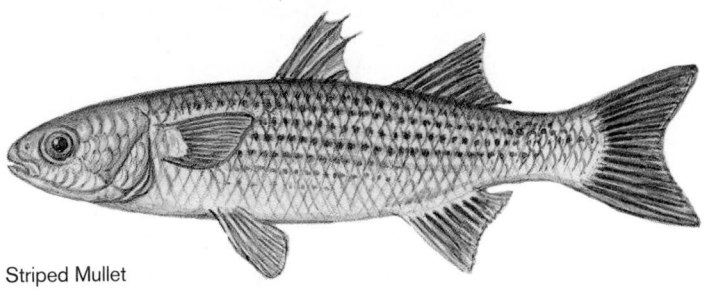
Striped Mullet

M

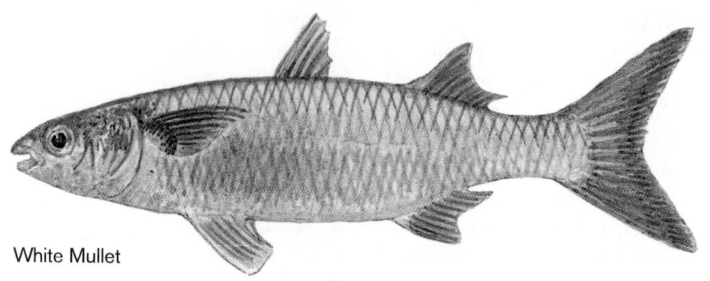

White Mullet

the Gulf of Mexico; in the eastern Atlantic from Gambia to the Congo; and in the eastern Pacific from the Gulf of California, Mexico, to Iquique, Chile.

The Brazilian mullet *(M. brasiliensis)* is prevalent in the southern Caribbean southward along the South American coast. Common species off the coasts of Europe and Africa and in the Mediterranean are the thick-lipped mullet *(M. chelo),* the thin-lipped gray mullet *(M. capito),* and the golden mullet *(M. auratus).* Some common species in Indo-Pacific waters include the 3-foot-long blue-tail mullet *(Valamugil buchanani),* which is found in Indonesia, Micronesia, Melanesia, the Mariana Islands, and southern Japan; and the 2-foot-long fringelip mullet *(Crenimugil crenilabis),* which occurs in the Red Sea, along the East Coast of Africa, and from southern Japan to Lord Howe Island, Australia. A freshwater mullet *(Myxus petardi),* called pinkeye, occurs in Australian coastal streams and migrates downriver to spawn in estuaries.

Life history/Behavior. Mullet are schooling fish found inshore in coastal environs. Many, but not all, species have the unusual habit of leaping from the water as they race along in schools. Some have stiff bodies when they jump, and fall back into the water with a loud splat, which usually draws the attention of people nearby; most newcomers to mangrove coasts think these leaping fish are a sporting species or are being pursued by gamefish, although this is often not the case.

Theories as to why mullet jump abound: to escape predators, remove parasites, coordinate spawning migrations, aid respiration, and so forth. Some research has supported the respiration theory. Research on striped mullet showed that the fish uses the upper portion of the pharynx for aerial respiration, obtaining air by jumping or holding its head above the water. The research showed that the jumping frequency of this species seemed to be inversely related to dissolved oxygen concentration. The less oxygen, the more often the fish jumped. Biologists say that the upper pharyngeal cavity of the striped mullet can hold about 2 percent of the fish's body volume, and could supply oxygen for at least five minutes. This would enable the fish to feed in waters with a low oxygen concentration. If this fish can obtain air by sticking its head above the surface, however, why does it jump?

Adult striped mullet migrate offshore in large schools to spawn; juveniles migrate inshore at about 1 inch in size, moving far up tidal creeks. Fantail mullet spawn in near-shore or inshore waters during spring and summer, and juveniles occur offshore. White mullet spawn offshore, and the young migrate into estuaries and along beaches.

Food and feeding habits. These mullet feed on algae, detritus, and other tiny marine forms; they pick up mud from the bottom and strain plant and animal material from it through their sievelike gill rakers and pharyngeal teeth. Indigestible materials are spit out. In most species, the stomach is gizzardlike for grinding food.

Angling. Mullets do not ordinarily take hooked baits or lures, but anglers may pursue them for use as bait by snagging them with small treble hooks (cast into schools). They are commonly captured by cast net. Occasionally they are caught on flies or doughballs or even wads of algae; when hooked, they fight gamely.

MULLOWAY *Argyrosomus hololepidotus.*
Other names—southern meagre, jewfish, silver jewfish, river kingfish, butterfish, soapy, kob (South Africa); French: *maigre du sud, maigre africain;* Italian: *bocca d'oro.*

The mulloway, because of its size and the availability of the waters it inhabits, is a much-sought-after prize among both shore-based and boat anglers, especially in Australia. A rather slow-moving fish that exhibits an initial burst of great power when hooked, it is considered a straightforward fighter with few, if any, nasty habits. Small mulloway, known as soapies, are short on reputation as table fish, hence the name, but adults are excellent fare, and the species is commercially valuable.

Identification. The mulloway has a body coloring that varies from bluish gray to bronze green on top. It is silvery below. Fish taken at night, however, can be a silvery color all over. A row of prominent pearly spots extends along the lateral line. There may also be a large black blotch at the base of the upper margin of the pectoral fin, although this is sometimes missing. The caudal fin is rounded, and the long dorsal fin—consisting of a spined section and a rayed section—extends from just above the pectoral fin to the "wrist" or caudal peduncle. The teeth are short and sharp within a large mouth, the inside of which is bright orange.

Size. This fish is known to grow to more then 70 kilograms and a length of 2 meters in some parts of its range. In Australian waters, the largest mulloway recorded by rod and reel weighed 43.7 kilograms. This species can live for at least 30 years, with 6-year-olds weighing about 8 kilograms. Juveniles, or soapies, weigh up to 2 kilograms and are around 50 centimeters long. Most mulloway taken by anglers in Australia weigh less than 10 kilograms.

Distribution. This species occurs along the western and eastern coasts of Africa to Australia, including Oman and the east coast of India. It ranges around the southern half of Australia from North West Cape in Western Australia, across the southern portion, and up the East Coast to as far north as Bundaberg in Queensland.

Habitat. Small mulloway tend to remain in estuaries, where they are found in schools. As they grow, they spread out into bays and inshore waters, frequenting coastal reefs, ocean beaches, and rocky shores. In flood conditions, they congregate around river mouths to feed on thousands of small fish that are washed into the sea.

Life history/Behavior. Fecundity is unknown, and larvae have not been identified, but juveniles as small as 5 centimeters have been found in rivers along Australia's East Coast. They grow rapidly, increasing in length by about 2 centimeters per month. Spawning probably takes place in summer. As they mature, mulloway are inclined to become solitary, moving along the coast from river to river, along coastal beaches, and up into the estuaries when searching for small fish.

Food and feeding habits. Mulloway feed on various fish species, including mullet, garfish, bream, luderick, leatherjackets, common mackerel, pilchards, and yellowtail (scad). They also eat sand crabs, prawns, and worms. They are especially fond of giant beach worms *(Australonuphis)*, which they may identify by smell. These worms grow to more than 2 meters in length and are found along the Australian coast.

Angling. In Australia, every recreational angler aspires to catch a big mulloway (30 kilograms or more), but the majority must be content with smaller specimens to roughly 10 kilograms. The most popular method is to fish the ocean beaches, points, and river entrances using surf fishing tackle, and a minimum of 200 meters of line testing 15 kilograms or more. Boat and estuary anglers prefer shorter, stout boat rods, and some estuary anglers use heavy handlines. Offshore anglers will target reefs and wrecks surrounded by a sandy bottom. Hook sizes vary from 5/0 to 10/0.

Baitfishing is the first choice except where mulloway are feeding on small fish washed into the sea at flooding river entrances, which makes large surface lures and poppers effective. Surf anglers normally use strip baits of mullet, bluefish, bonito, or tuna flesh, or dead whole baits of pilchards and garfish rigged on ganged 5/0 hooks. While waiting for the sun to set before fishing for mulloway, surf anglers fish for bluefish to be used as bait; fresh fillets of bluefish are certain to attract mulloway moving along a surf beach. Where they can be caught, the giant beach worms are likely to take priority over other baits.

Mulloway travel well up into estuaries and are often taken 10 kilometers from the ocean. Within estuaries, anglers land small individuals at all hours of the day. The large, old specimens are almost invariably taken at night, usually during the two hours on either side of the change in the tide. Estuary mulloway respond well to fresh prawns, bloodworms, small squid, and small live mullet and yellowtail, in addition to the other baits mentioned.

Fishing in estuaries with soft-plastic lures and minnow plugs has increased in popularity during daylight hours, and is sometimes effective when fishing under bridge lights that have attracted small baitfish. Occasionally, a small mulloway is tempted by a trolled metal spoon meant for bluefish.

The initial run of a hooked mulloway can be long and powerful, often stripping 100 meters of line from the reel. Skilled anglers make no attempt to stop the fish during this run. Instead, the strike is registered when the run stops and the fish swallows the bait, as evidenced by recognizable head shaking. The subsequent fight becomes a test of stamina, drag control, and patience on the part of the angler.

Fly fishing for mulloway is rarely practiced, although a fly presented to schooling mulloway can be just as effective as any surface lure.

MULTIFILAMENT *(Line)*

See: Line.

MULTIHOOK RIG

Using multiple hooks on bottom fishing rigs is a standard process, and it is usually accomplished with two, and occasionally three, hooks separated vertically off the main fishing line. However, in gathering baitfish for sportfishing purposes in saltwater, the term "multihook rig" has come to mean a string (half a dozen or so) of small fine-wire hooks on a single rig. These have variously been known as quill rigs, fish catchers, lucky joes, and other terms; most are handmade and tedious to tie. In recent years, a small variety of such rigs have been commercially manufactured, by far the most common and popular of which is the Sabiki rig, a Japanese creation used to catch pilchards, herring, goggle-eyes, cigar minnows, mackerel, and an assortment of baitfish.

These rigs are employed in situations where it is impractical to use a cast net *(see)* to gather bait (usually because of depth or current), and they feature six hooks on small leaders that branch off a main line. Each hook on the rig is dressed with a small trimmed piece of iridescent dried material (often fish skin or shrimp), and many also have a small luminescent paint bead head, which can be charged under light to glow. The branch line is lighter than the main line, and the components of the rig may vary depending on the application.

These rigs are fished with or without chum, and in water that varies from 10 to 15 feet deep to many hundreds, provided that schools of baitfish have

M

Multihook (Sabiki) Rig

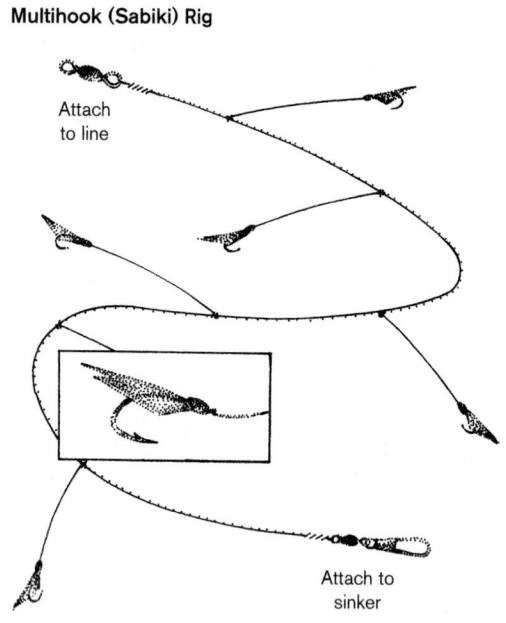

Attach
to line

Attach to
sinker

been located. In some cases, the baitfish are attracted by chumming; in others, large schools are pinpointed with sonar before the rig is lowered. Heavy sinkers, attached to a swivel at the bottom of the rig, are used to get the rigs down and help keep the bait from getting tangled in the rig when retrieved. The rig is jigged in short motions, and when a fish grabs hold, it is held still for a few seconds to allow the wriggling caught fish to attract its brethren. Multiple catches are common.

Fish should be removed from the bottom hooks first, working up the rig and being careful not to get impaled on the super sharp points. A small hook extractor will help in unhooking. To store the rigs, use a rectangular piece of cardboard with notches cut in the middle of each end; wrap the main line over the notches and clip each branch hook off to the side of the board.

MULTIPLYING REEL

A revolving spool reel with multiplying action as opposed to single action, that is, a reel whose spool revolves more than one time for every turn of the handle. Single-action reels are those that have essentially a 1:1 retrieve ratio, where one turn of the crank causes one turn of the spool; multiplying reels have a greater than 1:1 gear ratio, where one turn of the crank causes more than one full turn of the spool.

The term "multiplying reel" or "multiplier" began at the turn of the nineteenth century and is generally associated with American craftsmen who fashioned the famous Kentucky Reel, which was the forerunner both of today's baitcasting reels and of other revolving spool reels in which the spool turns at a greater than 1:1 ratio. Before that time, the only reels available were single-action revolving spool versions, primarily employed for storing and

retrieving line. Throughout the nineteenth century and well into the twentieth century, the term "multiplying reel" was in common use; today, it is used only when referring to antique tackle.
See: Antique Fishing Tackle; Baitcasting Tackle; Conventional Tackle; Flycasting Tackle; Kentucky Reel; Single-Action Reel.

MUMMICHOG
See: Killifish.

MUSKELLUNGE   *Esox masquinongy.*
Other names—maskinonge, muskallonge, mascalonge, muskie, musky, 'lunge, silver muskellunge, Great Lakes muskellunge, Ohio muskellunge, Allegheny River muskellunge, spotted muskellunge, barred muskellunge, great muskellunge, great pike, blue pike, etc. Occasionally, it is referred to as a "jack" in some areas.

The muskellunge is the largest member of the Esocidae family of pike. Its name is derived from the native Indian word *maskinonge,* which has had numerous interpretations. Among them are deformed pike *(mashk kinonge);* ugly fish *(mas kinonge);* and large pike *(mas kenosha).* Unlike its blood relative, the northern pike *(see: pike, northern),* which has circumpolar distribution, the muskellunge is strictly a North American species, native to central and eastern North America. Although it is bodily pikelike and does occur in some of the same waters, it is vastly different in behavior and abundance (or lack thereof). It is one of the world's foremost gamefish by virtue of its size, strength, and predatory habits, and also by virtue of its contrary nature. The muskellunge is one of the most difficult freshwater sportfish of North America to willfully catch, and its habits and feeding behavior are as, or more, difficult to understand than those of any other freshwater species, including the most highly touted and lowly populated Atlantic salmon. Although a devoted coterie of anglers fervently pursues muskellunge, these enthusiasts are a fraction of the total angling populace, most of the rest of whom do not have the opportunity to catch this species or prefer more dependable or more abundant species.

Although the range of the muskellunge has expanded through stocking efforts, this fish is abundant only in portions of its range. It has not been pursued commercially for many decades, but the number of large individuals has declined since the 1960s as a result of many environmental factors, especially habitat destruction and alteration that has affected spawning and predator-prey relationships, as well as the capture and killing by anglers of many of the largest individuals. The voluntary release of muskies has increased since the mid-1980s, and today muskie fishing is mostly a catch-and-release endeavor, especially among devotees of this fish.

Muskellunge

The flesh of a muskellunge is white and flaky and of excellent quality, but many anglers have never tasted it and have no need to because there are equally good table fish available among more abundant species like walleye and northern pike, one or both of which are usually found in the same environs as the muskie.

Identification. Like other species belonging to the *Esox* genus, the muskellunge has an arrowlike body that is long and sleek. A single soft-rayed dorsal fin is located very far back near the tail. The pelvic fins are located relatively far back on the belly, about halfway between the pectoral fins and the tail, instead of directly under the pectoral fins. The mouth is large, with the maxillae reaching back at least to the middle of the eyes, and it is broad like a duck's bill, but full of teeth.

The coloration and markings on muskellunge are highly variable but usually consist of dark markings on a brownish or green background. There are numerous dark, vertical bars that may appear as vermiculations or spots, and sometimes the body has no markings. The northern pike, by comparison, has light-colored, oblong or kidney-shaped spots against a darker body, and the chain pickerel *(see: pickerel, chain)* has a unique chainlike pattern on the sides, although the spaces between the "links" of the chain may be seen as large oblong spots, depending on one's point of view. The grass and redfin pickerel look much more like the muskie in their markings, but they grow only to roughly 15 inches in length.

The muskie can also be distinguished from other *Esox* species by both cheeks and the gill cover, which are usually scaled only on the top half. In the pickerel, the cheeks and gill cover are fully scaled; in the pike, the cheeks are fully scaled, but the gill cover is usually scaled only on the top half. Another distinction occurs in the number of pores under the lower jaw. In the muskie there are 6 to 9 pores along each side (rarely 5 or 10 on one side only). In the northern pike there are 5 along each side (rarely 3, 4, or 6 on one side only). In the pickerel, there are 4 along each side (occasionally 3 or 5 on one side only).

The variable markings and colorations of muskellunge have lead to identity confusion over the years, and at one time it was believed that there were at least four species or varieties of muskellunge, but these patterns occurred throughout the range of the muskellunge, and subspecies are no longer recognized. An exception is the tiger muskellunge *(see: muskellunge, tiger)*, a sterile hybrid resulting from the breeding of true muskellunge and northern pike parents.

Size/Age. Muskellunge are among the largest North American fish dwelling entirely in freshwater. Although reports suggest the existence of fish from 80 to 100 pounds that were netted, speared, or otherwise encountered (including scales from an angler-lost St. Lawrence River fish that a biologist verified as being from a muskie that he estimated at 100 pounds), there is no hard verification of any muskie weighing more than 70 pounds. Even some of the known 60-pounders are subject to doubt. The former all-tackle world record and current New York State record muskellunge is a 69-pound, 15-ounce fish that was caught in 1957 in the St. Lawrence River. This fish has been disputed, however, and a slightly smaller and previously caught 69-pounder from Wisconsin has replaced it. Thus, 70 pounds stands as the maximum known size for muskellunge. Most muskellunge encountered by anglers weigh between 7 and 15 pounds and are less than 40 inches long; specimens exceeding 20 pounds are not uncommon, but it is extremely hard to come by one weighing more than 30 pounds. Very few in excess of 40 pounds were caught throughout the 1990s, and most released fish are not weighed; their size is measured by estimated or actual length in inches. They have been known to live between 25 and 30 years, and many fish live for 15 years, although the average life span is closer to 8 years.

Distribution. The muskellunge is endemic to eastern North America. It is native to the Great Lakes, Hudson Bay, and Mississippi River basins from southern Quebec to the Red River of the North in Manitoba, and extends south in the Appalachians to Georgia and west to Iowa. It has been introduced (including the hybrid version) widely to Atlantic coast drainages as far as southern Virginia, and elsewhere in the southern and western United States, although its representation in many of these areas is minor.

M

Muskellunge/Barred Variation

Dark markings, light background

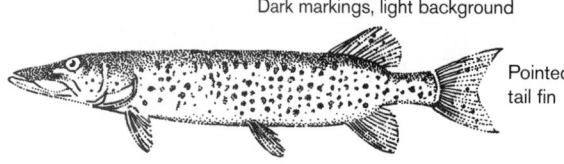

Pointed tail fin

Muskellunge/Spotted Variation

Dark markings, light background

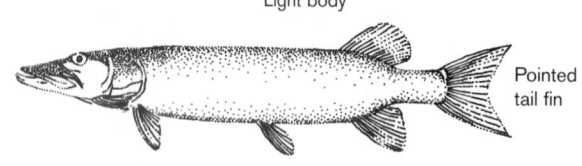

Pointed tail fin

Muskellunge/Clear Variation

Light body

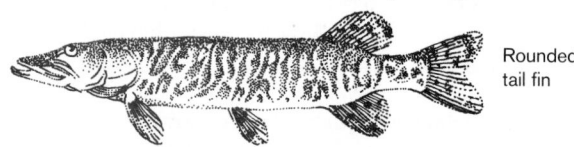

Pointed tail fin

Tiger (Hybrid) Muskellunge

Dark markings, light background

Rounded tail fin

Subtle distinctions differentiate the four variations in muskellunge coloration and marking.

M

Habitat. Muskellunge live in medium to large rivers and in lakes of all sizes, although their preferred habitat is cool waters with large and small basins or both deep and shallow areas. They are found in waters no more than 75 acres in size, as well as in enormous waters like Lake of the Woods, Ontario; Lake St. Clair, Michigan; or the St. Lawrence River.

They rarely venture far from cover and favor shallow, heavily vegetated waters less than 40 feet deep, but they sometimes inhabit deep water that lacks vegetation but offers ample prey.

Life history/Behavior. Muskies spawn in the spring in 1 to 3 feet of water, in shallow bays covered with vegetation. This occurs just after ice out, and when the water temperatures are between 49° and 59°F. They are broadcast spawners and disperse the fertilized eggs randomly. The eggs sink to the bottom but are not as adhesive as northern pike eggs. Their spawning season usually occurs after the northern pike's in areas where the two species co-exist. On rare occasions, a hybrid tiger muskie *(see: muskie, tiger)* results, but this situation also causes small northern pike to mature before small muskies do, making predation on the muskies more likely.

Muskie eggs usually hatch in 8 to 14 days, and within 10 weeks the young may be 4 to 6 inches

long. Females grow larger than males at all ages, and both reach sexual maturity in three to five years.

Food and feeding habits. The muskie is a solitary fish that tends to stay in the same area, lurking opportunistically in thick weedbeds and waiting for prey. It is seldom a wandering, roaming fish, although it may migrate from deep to shallow environs to feed. Its diet is varied, with a preference for larger, rather than smaller, fish, as the muskie is well adapted to capturing and swallowing fish of considerable size. Yellow perch, suckers, golden shiners, and walleye are among its favorite foods, but it also consumes smallmouth bass and many other fish, as well as the infrequent animal (duck, muskrat, and the like).

Angling. Muskellunge are generally harder to catch than any other freshwater species. They are unpredictable, even for those who constantly seek them. Sometimes, and in some waters, they are not as difficult to catch as the oft-quoted "fish of a thousand casts" or "fish of 100 hours" clichés suggest. This is especially true of smaller individuals, and an extremely small number of people catch these fish with some degree of consistency. Generally, however, muskie fishing requires hard work, many hours on the water, and a great deal of patience—and there are no guarantees. Muskie fishing is the one form of freshwater angling (Altantic salmon angling runs a close second) in which merely glimpsing the quarry is a feat. A "follow"—when a muskie is visually observed as it trails a lure to the boat—is as meaningful as tossing a horseshoe close to the peg.

Muskies generally lurk in or near places where they can lie relatively concealed to ambush forage fish, so anglers must seek places that provide feeding opportunities. Muskies are large fish that have big mouths that strike big lures, perhaps because they are prone to eating big fish. A 15-inch walleye isn't imposing to a 40-inch muskie; muskies position themselves in strategic locations that attract prey large enough to make an ambush attack worthwhile. The nature of the cover, the depth of water around the cover and nearby, and the presence of current determine which places are better than others. Following are prime locations to concentrate on.

Submerged vegetation. Muskies are attracted to the edges of vegetation, particularly to the breakline where weeds end and deep water begins, and to corners, pockets, or other irregular contour features of weedbeds. In the fall they move away from dead and decaying vegetation, and anglers should look for them in whatever green and healthy weeds exist.

Points of land. Whether they extend from the shore or from islands, points are natural impediments to fish movement and serve as attractants to prey and predator alike. Concentrate on points with a long underwater slope adjacent to deep water, especially if they break sharply from 10 feet off to 20 or 25 feet, or those that have some form of heavy vegetation around their perimeter, or those with rockpiles on the underwater breaklines.

Shoals, bars, submerged islands.   With or without a hard bottom or vegetation, these structures attract baitfish and gamefish, making them reliable feeding areas.

Confluences.   Near and just below a warmwater discharge, feeder creek, or other tributary is a prime place to seek muskies. In the fall, for example, the immediate area near a warmwater discharge is affected and may be attractive to forage fish and muskies. Where a tributary meets a major flow is a promising locale as well, especially in summer, when the tributary may be dumping cooler and more oxygenated water into the main flow.

Current.   A point or shoal that is washed by a strong current is a promising place to find muskies. A locale where strong current can bring baitfish washing by, or which retards the movement of weak, crippled, or wounded fish, is also a top spot. Back eddies, slicks, and current edges are worth a look, too.

Although muskies may inhabit deep water, most fish are taken in less than 30 feet of water; depths of 15 to 30 feet are the norm. In many places, they hold in much shallower water. Most casting anglers catch muskies in depths between 5 and 15 feet; trollers usually catch them in depths ranging from 8 to 30 feet.

Casting and trolling both have devotees, partially by law (trolling for muskies is not legal in a few places) but mostly by traditional preference. Trolled lures are fished on fairly short lines, as there is seldom much reason to put out more than 75 feet of line. Muskies are not spooked by boat noise, and some trollers catch them right in the prop wash, within 10 to 25 feet of the boat and just a few feet below the surface.

The primary advantage of trolling for these fish is the ability to cover a lot of territory on large bodies of water, although heavy vegetation on some waters hinders trolling efforts. Also, trollers don't see fish that might follow their lures, but casters often do. Muskies will pursue a cast-and-retrieved bait right to the boat, occasionally striking at boatside but more often vanishing. This activity shows an angler where a fish is located; good muskie casters remember all of the places where they have caught and seen fish on their favorite waters, and they continue to visit those places regularly. The choice of whether to cast or troll should be based on your own interests and abilities as well as the habitat and angling situation.

Muskie lures don't have the diversity of lures intended for other fish. And although no sure-fire lure exists, there are some contenders. Large jigs, jerkbaits, a few surface plugs, bucktail spinners, and assorted diving plugs are the common lures; bucktails are the runaway favorites for casting, followed by jerkbaits. Some anglers land muskies on large jigs or surface plugs, but it's best to focus

A muskie, tagged in the dorsal fin, is about to be released at Lake of the Woods, Minnesota.

on bucktails and diving plugs until you've become proficient.

Bucktail spinners (weighted in-line spinners heavily dressed with bucktail hair over one or two treble hooks) are mainly used in shallow- to mid-depth casting, over the top of submerged cover and along the edges of shallow submerged cover. They are seldom used for trolling. They are manufactured in a host of color combinations, but black is the hands-down top muskie producer. If you're new to casting for muskies, start with a black bucktail around cabbage beds.

Among diving plugs, shallow-running minnow-style baits account for many catches. Anglers use them around the edges of weedy habitat and sometimes retrieve them over the top of deeply submerged vegetation.

Deeper-diving plugs are both cast and trolled. A good tactic with a deep-diving plug is to reel it down until it hits vegetation, then stop the retrieve (which allows the lure to float upward), then reel it in a few feet until you hit vegetation, then stop, and so forth. This action is similar to that of a jerkbait except that the lure is far more enticing when retrieved. Deep-diving plugs are better than other lures for casting around reefs and points and quick-current edges that don't tend to accumulate vegetation. Shallow, medium, and deep divers all have trolling applications. Five- to 8-inch-long plugs are customary for this, preferably in single- or double-jointed versions, but also in unjointed models. Popular muskie plug colors include black, black-and-white, chartreuse, silver-and-black, and yellow, plus perch, walleye, bass, and muskie patterns, but there is no clear favorite.

No matter what lure you tie on, the way you use your boat and equipment to cope with the conditions can be a factor in your success. Drift along the side of, rather than through, prime habitat. This permits many casts around an area without alarming any fish. An electric motor is just as

M

beneficial to a muskie caster as it is to a bass angler, primarily for precise boat control and positioning. Sonar can be a substantial aid, too, for achieving proper boat positioning over areas likely to hold muskies.

Most muskie anglers use heavy tackle. Twenty-five to 40-pound line and a stiff rod is standard, but some anglers are successful with 12- to 20-pound line and a 6-foot fast-action baitcasting rod. Muskies fight well but not laboriously, although they can provide spectacular jumping action. They are noted for being hard to drive a hook into, and for escaping from anglers who thought they had a well-hooked fish. Repetitive hook setting and sharp hooks, as well as low-stretch lines, can be advantageous. The muskie's formidable dentures make a steel leader and sharp hooks advisable.
See: Pike.

MUSKELLUNGE, TIGER *Esox masquinongy x Esox lucius.*

Other names—tiger muskie, norlunge, nor'lunge, hybrid muskellunge.

A member of the Esocidae family, the tiger muskellunge is a distinctively marked hybrid fish produced when true muskellunge *(E. masquinongy)* and northern pike *(Esox lucius)* interbreed. This occurs when the male of either species fertilizes the eggs of the female of the opposite species. This is not a common occurrence in the wild but has happened naturally in waters where both parent species occur, making it an unusual and prized catch.

The tiger muskie was believed to be a separate species until scientists succeeded in crossing a northern pike with a muskellunge, thereby discovering the tiger muskie's true origin. Deliberate crossbreeding of these species in hatcheries by fisheries managers is now much more common than natural hybridization, and tiger muskies have been stocked in many waters where neither parent occurs naturally. Fish culturists prefer to cross a male northern pike with a female muskellunge because the eggs of the muskie are less adhesive and don't clump as badly in the hatching process.

Populations of introduced tiger muskies are naturally self-limiting because this hybrid is sterile and cannot reproduce itself. Its numbers can therefore be controlled over time. It also grows quickly and is aggressive, making it an excellent catch for anglers.

The tiger muskie has a distinctive look and should not be confused with the true muskellunge, which has been called a tiger muskie in some areas. In most respects, notably in size and appearance, the hybrid is very much like the true muskellunge, and anglers hold the naturally occurring hybrid in higher esteem than the true muskie because of its rarity, its beautiful markings, and its game nature. The true muskie may have either bars or spots on the sides or no markings at all, but it is rarely as strikingly beautiful as the tiger muskie, which has dark, wavering tigerlike stripes or bars, many of them broken, that are set against a lighter background.

As is true with many hybrid fish, the body of the tiger muskie is slightly deeper than that of either comparable-length parent. The cheeks and jaws are usually spotted, with 10 to 16 pores existing on the underside of the jaws. The tips of the tail are more rounded than in the true muskie, and the fins have distinct spots. In very large specimens, the fins, especially the tail fin, appears to be much larger than for a comparable true muskie.

Naturally occurring tiger muskie in excess of 30 pounds are extremely rare, and most have come from Wisconsin lakes. A 51-pound, 3-ounce fish, caught in 1919 at Lac Vieux Desert on the Wisconsin/Michigan border, is the all-tackle world-record tiger muskie. For a time, it was thought to be a true muskellunge and thus held the world record for that species.

Methods of fishing for tiger muskies are no different than those for true muskies. Naturally occurring tiger muskies are caught incidentally by anglers fishing for true muskellunge or other fish species. Introduced muskies are caught both as targeted and incidental catches. Most are released alive, particularly those of natural origin.
See: Muskellunge.

Tiger Muskellunge

NAIL KNOT

A fishing knot for line-to-line connections.
See: Knots, Fishing.

NAMIBIA

This southwestern African nation, bounded by Angola to the north, South Africa to the south, and primarily Botswana to the east, is something of a study in contrasts. Its entire coastal region is low lying and marked by the 60- to 100-mile-wide Namib Desert, which faces the South Atlantic Ocean. Here, these waters are cooled by the northerly flowing Benguela Current. Farther inland, Namibia's terrain is mountainous, and the important permanently flowing rivers are primarily at its extremities, forming boundaries. Relatively few traveling anglers visit Namibia. Those who do are mostly from South Africa and focus their attention along its nearly deserted, vast coastline. One gets the feeling that no one has been here before.

Coastal Fishing

For the first-time visitor, the endless expanses of beaches fringing the Namib Desert are eye-opening, and a party of anglers seldom will encounter others throughout an entire day's fishing. These areas are a great distance from anywhere—it is roughly 2,000 miles from Pretoria, South Africa, to Terrace Bay—and along the coast itself, local ingenuity has devised a road built from salt. It does not break up easily and manages to ward off the ravages of the desert climate to provide a smooth, tarlike surface that is dangerous only when moistened by sea mist.

Along the coast the cold Atlantic provides a belt of cool air that seldom exceeds 18°C. Anything above this is regarded as hot. In winter months, however, a dreaded wind comes off the desert, turning the length of the coast into a furnace, with temperatures reaching 40°C. The wind starts at dawn and lasts until 2 P.M., almost to the minute. Mornings are thus spent in protected environs. No one dares travel against this wind, as it is a veritable sandblaster that quickly peels paint off vehicles and scars windscreens.

Although coastal fishing throughout the year is good, December through April is the prime period, and the most sought-after species include kob, steenbras, blacktail, and galjoen for lighter-tackle anglers, and bronze whaler, gulley, and cow sharks for heavy-tackle artists. Caught by the thousands every year is the saltwater silver catfish. Normally frowned upon by visiting anglers, this species is eagerly sought by local anglers, who regard smoked catfish as a delicacy.

Three significant fishing regions define this coast. The first is called Long Beach and stretches from Walvis Bay at midcoast to Swakopmund some 19 miles north. Local anglers just about always make good catches there. The second is some 40 miles north of Swakopmund at Henties Bay, which owes its existence to visiting anglers, who either rent a cottage or stay in the hotel there.

The third is the so-called Public Recreational Area, which is the region from Henties Bay north to Mile 108 (various locations are marked according to their distance from Swakopmund). Each year it attains the status of a "holy fishing pilgrimage" for thousands of anglers. Here, people are at liberty to do more or less what they like, and this must be the last true wilderness left in southern Africa. Only the salt road to Terrace Bay cuts across the Public Recreational Area, and 4×4 vehicles are necessary when traveling off it. There are no telephones, no lights, no doctors: in short, nothing. Self-sufficient camping, some of it at various caravan parks, is the norm.

Beyond Mile 108 lies Skeleton Coast National Park. A ranger's post is established at the Ukab River, and only those with a firm booking at Terrace Bay (or Tora Bay during December) are allowed in. Terrace Bay's fishing lodge, about 250 miles north, was converted from an old mining enterprise and accommodates only 48 guests.

All along the coast, the most popular species is the galjoen, mainly caught on red baits, which wash ashore during high tides. The surf line is filled with sea bamboo and seaweed, and anglers land galjoen by casting into this. Some years the galjoen are found in more open water.

Blacktail is popular and is also caught with red baits. Bronze whaler sharks are targeted in the summer with traditional sardine baits. Gully sharks are pests that break up the light galjoen tackle. Galjoen of 10 to 12 pounds are taken during mid- to late winter. They are the fattest fish here and, when barbecued over an open fire, are delicious.

The usual route anglers take in Namibia begins with a week at Terrace Bay, catching galjoen and blacktail. Then, they move down the coast in search of kob and steenbras. Baits for the latter two are white mussels dug from the beaches, sardines, chokka, and red baits. When kob and steenbras are running, it's difficult to stop angling.

After fishing the Public Recreational Area, many anglers spend a few days at Henties Bay or Swakopmund, whereas others visit a famous spot south of Walvis Bay—the vast lagoon area of Sunwich Harbour.

Recreational boat fishing was unknown in Namibia until a few enterprising individuals began to operate a ski boat out of Henties Bay. Their catches, however, are not greater than that of the beach anglers. Boat fishing is more popular from the harbors at Swakopmund and Lüderitz. The lagoon at Lüderitz is famous for its cow sharks (weighing 150 pounds and more).

When anglers have had their fill of these favored species, they turn their attention to sharks, particularly during the summer months. Heavy tackle notwithstanding, some anglers have enjoyed tremendous battles with big bronze whalers that frequent the inshore line.

Inland Fishing

Few traveling anglers think of fishing in Namibia's freshwater impoundments, even though coarse fishing for bream, catfish, and yellowfish is quite good. The most notable freshwater opportunity is in the Caprivi Strip, a panhandled piece of land northeast of Namibia and possibly one of the best wildlife areas in southwestern Africa. There are three main rivers in the Caprivi Strip: the Zambezi, on the border with Zambia; the Kwando; and the Okavango, which originates in Angola and forms a border with that country, then enters Botswana to reach the world-renowned Okavango Swamp. All three rivers have the best angling for tigerfish and bream that Namibia can offer.

The Zambezi River tigerfish has lured many an angler to the Caprivi. Living as they do in fast-flowing water, these fish are fit and very strong. The speed at which they leave their lairs, which are in the eddies and the lee of channel walls in the vast sandbanks, to hit trolled spoons, launches them into the air like missiles. Thereafter, provided the hook stays embedded in the tiger's armor-plated jaw, a long and spectacular fight ensues.

Another favorite lair of the Zambezi tiger is slightly downstream of a herd of wallowing hippos, where small bream—the tigerfish's main food source—are attracted by the stirred-up detritus of the riverbed.

Fishing the hippo herds can be an exciting way to catch tigerfish; it's necessary to get a boat close enough to the herd to find the fish, yet be nimble enough to maneuver away quickly should an irate bull take exception to your presence.

The meandering Zambezi allows anglers to travel for many miles downstream from Katima Mulilo, fishing the quieter deep-water eddies or the fast-flowing sections over sandbanks, at the same time enjoying the river's beauty and harshness. Excellent light-tackle bream fishing is possible where the river slows down in deep channels, and between reed-lined banks. To end a perfect day on the river, a toast to the setting sun over one of Africa's mightiest rivers is a haunting, unforgettable experience.

NATIONAL FISHING LURE COLLECTORS CLUB
An organization of fishing tackle collectors.
See: Antique Fishing Tackle.

NATIONAL MARINE FISHERIES SERVICE
Founded in 1871 as the United States Commission of Fish and Fisheries, the National Marine Fisheries Service (NMFS) is the federal agency charged with managing and sustaining most living marine resources and their habitats in U.S. waters. These resources include many species of fish, lobster, shrimp, crabs, clams, whales, dolphins, seals, and sea turtles, as well as the environment where these animals live, feed, and breed.

The agency is part of the National Oceanic and Atmospheric Administration (NOAA) within the U.S. Department of Commerce, where it was placed in 1970 after previously being known as the Bureau of Commercial Fisheries, a part of the U.S. Fish and Wildlife Service. Its jurisdiction is federal waters, which start 3 miles from shore and extend 200 miles into the ocean, although seaward boundaries of Texas, Puerto Rico, and the Gulf Coast of Florida extend 9 miles from shore.

The mission of NMFS is to build sustainable fisheries, recover protected species, and sustain healthy coasts. It has the responsibility of protecting endangered and threatened marine species and their habitat, and conducts cooperative marine research with other federal agencies, state fisheries agencies, universities, and other organizations. It also measures the economic effects of fishing practices and fishery regulations, enforces federal fisheries laws, and plays a role in managing fish and marine mammals that swim between waters of the United States and other countries.

NMFS has the obligation to work with eight Regional Fishery Management Councils (see: fisheries management council), created by the Magnuson Fishery Conservation and Management Act (see: Magnuson Act) and responsible for managing marine fish stocks. This brings together many parties, but recreational anglers largely feel it is heavily biased toward commercial fishing interests.

Other responsibilities of NMFS are derived from such federal laws as the Endangered Species Act, which protects species that are threatened or endangered; the Marine Mammal Protection Act, which regulates interactions with marine mammals; the Lacey Act, which prohibits fish or wildlife transactions and activities that violate state, federal, native American tribal, or foreign laws; the Fish and Wildlife Coordination Act, which authorizes NMFS to collect fisheries data and to advise other agencies on environmental decisions that affect

Fish that live in Arctic and Antarctic waters produce their own antifreeze.

N

living marine resources; and the Federal Power Act, which allows NMFS to minimize effects of dam operations on anadromous fish, such as prescribing fish passageways that bypass dams.

NMFS is not involved with the management of strictly freshwater fish, which falls under the jurisdiction of respective state fish and wildlife agencies and the Fish and Wildlife Service *(see),* which is part of the Department of the Interior.

NATIVE

A species of fish that is endemic to a region, watershed, or specific body of water. A native species is distinguished from an introduced or exotic species *(see),* which occurs outside its endemic range and has been placed there by unnatural means (usually deliberate but sometimes accidental planting by humans). The term "native" is particularly applied in North America to endemic trout, especially brook trout.

NATURAL BAIT

Live or dead organisms that occur in nature and which are used to attract and catch fish. The term natural bait is used to differentiate such items from artificial baits, which are technically lures *(see);* from processed baits *(see),* which are food items (corn, cheese, bread, etc.); and from chum *(see).*

Natural bait is used popularly in both freshwater and saltwater around the world, and includes a wide array of items. These include, but are not limited to, alewives, anchovies, ballyhoo, bunker (mossbunker or menhaden), butterfish, chubs, clams, corn, crabs, crayfish, crickets, eel, eggs, frogs, grubs, grasshoppers, hellgrammites, herring, killifish, leeches, mackerel, maggots, minnows, mullet, mussels, pilchards, pinfish, porgy, salamanders (waterdog), sand eels, sardines, sculpin, seaworms, shad, shiners, shrimp, silversides, smelt, spearing, squid, suckers, sunfish, waxworms, whiting, and assorted earthworms. Brief categorical reviews follow.

Freshwater Natural Bait

Prominent freshwater natural bait includes the following.

Earthworms/nightcrawlers.   These are used in whole or in parts, on one or more bait hooks, and are tipped onto jig hooks, crawled behind spinner harnesses, and weighted and fished under a float. They are especially used in fishing for such panfish as bluegills and perch, as well as walleye, bullheads, stream trout, and river steelhead, primarily with No. 6 or 8 hooks. Nightcrawlers are generally preferred, but small and lively angleworms are also used, though primarily for panfishing.

Crayfish.   Also known as crawfish or crawdads, and fished in both hard-shell and soft-shell versions (the latter preferred but not always available), crayfish are hooked through the tail with

Freshwater Live Baits

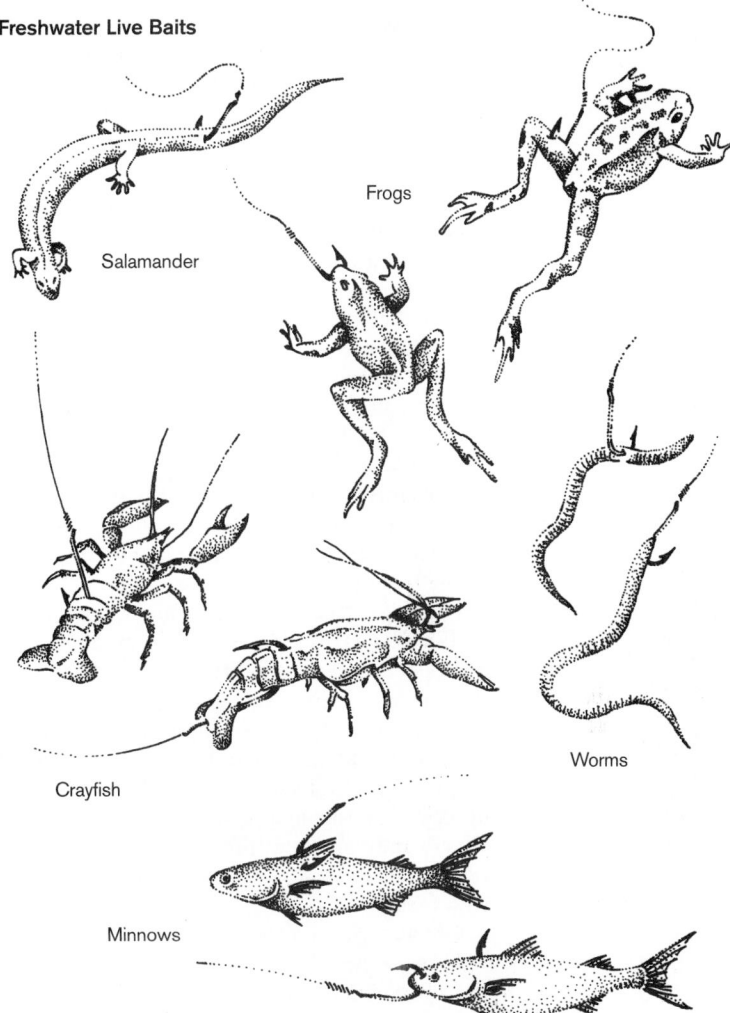

Salamander

Frogs

Crayfish

Worms

Minnows

a long-shanked hook. They are primarily used for smallmouth bass fishing. Tails and pieces of the tail are used for other fish, however, most notably for steelhead drift fishing.

Minnows/shiners.   There are numerous species and sizes of these baitfish (including fathead minnow, dace, Arkansas shiner, golden shiner, and chub) used primarily as live bait for a host of large and small fish. Smaller bait may also be hooked through the lips to adorn the hook of a jig or jig-spinner combination. Small minnows are used for crappies, ice fishing, bass, walleye, and trout. Very large shiners are popularly used in Florida for big largemouth bass, and large baitfish (including suckers) are fished for such species as pike, muskellunge, and lake trout.

Leeches.   These are used whole primarily for walleyes and smallmouth bass. They are rigged similarly to worms, and when cast or trolled are hooked through the sucker with a No. 6 or 8 hook.

Waterdogs.   Also known as mud puppies, these salamanders are not available everywhere but are used for a variety of gamefish, including striped bass.

Crickets, grasshoppers, and hellgrammites. These delectables are used for many small fish. Hellgrammites attract stream trout and smallmouth

N

bass; grasshoppers and crickets are good for various panfish species as well as crappie and stream trout. Hellgrammites should be hooked under the collar with a No. 6 or 8 hook, and the others through the body with a long-shanked light-wire hook.

Frogs. Live frogs are quite popular in some Canadian and northern U.S. locales and rather ignored most everywhere else. The prime quarry is bass, followed by pike. They can be hooked through the lips or thigh.

Salmon eggs. Salmon eggs are popularly used for drift fishing for trout and salmon. Rainbow trout and steelhead, in particular, are major quarries. These are fished singly with small salmon egg hooks, or as a group in an unwrapped cluster or in a nylon mesh spawn bag (called a spawn sack). Imitation eggs and egg sacks are quite popular as well. The natural eggs are cured and preserved for fishing applications.

Herring. Included here are such fragile baitfish species as alewives, which are also called sawbellies and found in northern climes where they are popularly used alive for trout in lakes; shad (primarily gizzard but also the threadfin variety), which are found in southern U.S. climes and fished live or as dead or cut bait; and herring, which are coastal, river-run fish used alive or dead for stripers and various catfishes on the East Coast and for salmon (via lift-and-drop mooching) on the West Coast.

Chum. Most of the chumming *(see)* done in freshwater is not with natural baits, although there are opportunities for this if you can procure enough bait economically to be able to chum. An angler who cast-nets for shad, for example, might be able to procure enough bait to dispense live shad as chum for largemouth bass or stripers. Saving old bait and using it to lightly chum in chunks is a possibility when fishing for catfish and stripers in big reservoirs and rivers.

Others. Some miscellaneous baits include caddis larvae for stream trout; mayflies for trout, crappies, etc.; bluegills for striped bass (where legal); grass shrimp for panfish; perch eyes for tipping on a jig when ice fishing for yellow perch; cisco, whitefish, and other large species fished alive for northern pike; and chunks or strips of fish meat, for tipping on a jig, especially for lake trout, or behind a spoon for pickerel or pike, or in some instances, dead-bait bottom fishing for assorted species (pike, lake trout, catfish, sturgeon).

Saltwater Natural Bait

Prominent saltwater natural bait includes the following.

Marine worms. Worms such as sandworms, clamworms, and bloodworms are used whole or in parts, on one or more hooks, or behind a spinner rig for stillfishing, trolling, or drifting for a variety of small inshore fish, as well as blackfish, flounder, and others.

Eels. Eels are a hardy bait, primarily used in inshore drift fishing and casting. They are fished on jigs as well as lip-hooked on a bottom rig, and are a top live bait for striped bass.

Shrimp/crabs/crayfish. Live shrimp are a highly popular bait for a wide variety of coastal fish. They can be hooked through the top of the head for free swimming, or threaded on a bait hook or jig head. Live blue crabs are also used for many species of fish; smaller versions take tarpon and permit, while larger ones are fished deep for snapper, grouper, redfish, and others. They are hooked through the tip of the shell, often with claws removed. Fiddler crabs, which are abundant in many tidal areas, are used for snappers, groupers, sheepshead, and other fish. Saltwater crayfish, which are quite large, are used in southern marine waters for cubera snapper and large groupers.

Assorted live fish. You name the fish, and if it is the right size, it can probably be used as live bait for some saltwater predator. Depending on locale and availability, of course, such species as pinfish, blue runner, anchovy, menhaden, grunts, sardines, pilchards, mackerel, and herring are favored. These fish are hooked through the lips or back, sometimes with a double-hook setup, or through the eyes (soft-fleshed fish).

Offshore baits. An assortment of natural baits is used in offshore trolling situations for billfish, tuna, dolphin, wahoo, king mackerel, and so forth. Squid, ballyhoo (balao), mullet, mackerel, and bonito are the main baits, usually fished whole, but sometimes in strips. Many of these baits are purchased frozen, then thawed in water and rigged with wire and thread on stainless steel hooks and wire leaders *(see: bait rig)*.

Chum. A good deal of chumming *(see)* is done in saltwater, especially for tuna, shark, and reef species. It is done inshore as well as offshore

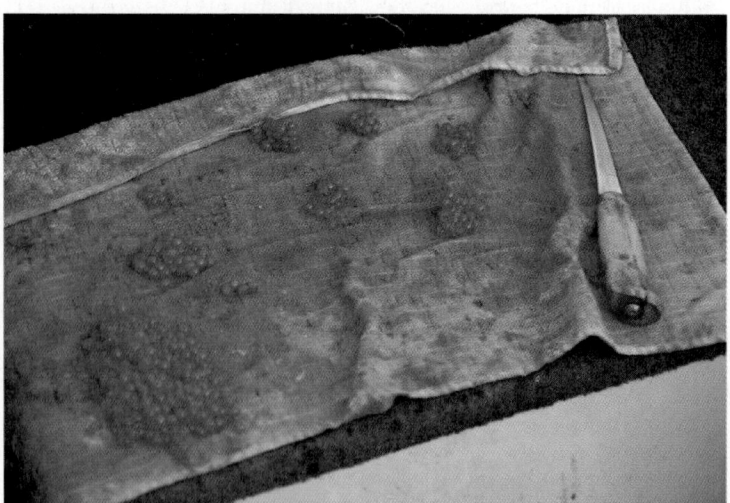

A skein of preserved salmon eggs is cut into chunks for direct use on a hook or as part of an egg sack.

Saltwater Live Baits

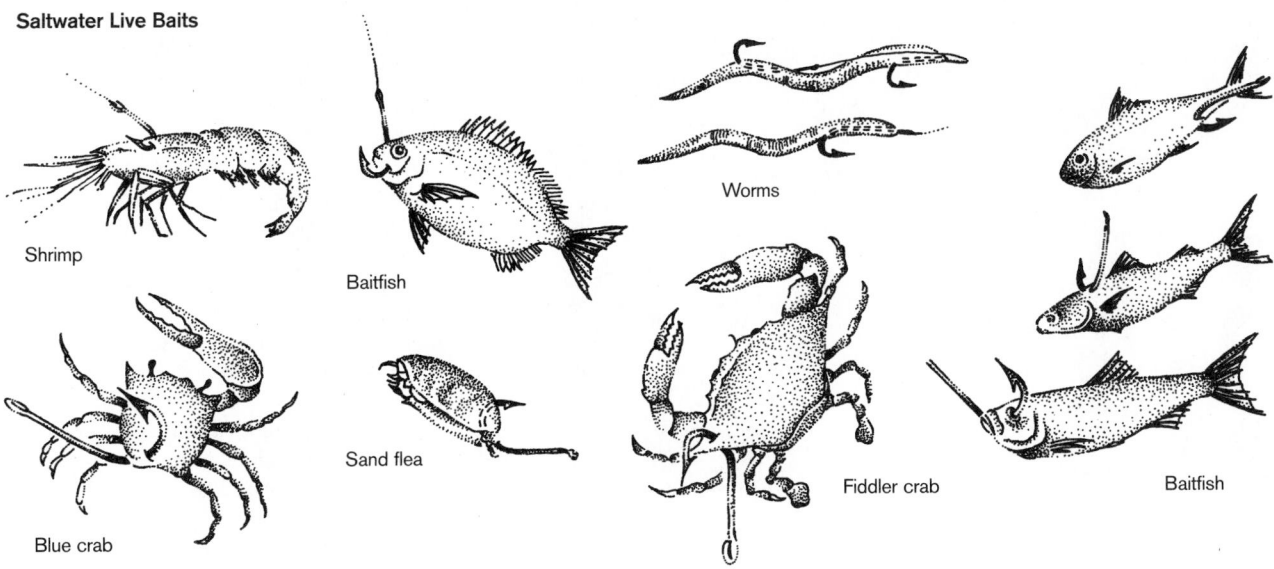

Shrimp

Baitfish

Worms

Blue crab

Sand flea

Fiddler crab

Baitfish

by small private boat anglers as well as party and charter boat anglers. The same species that are used as live bait, as well as smaller fish that are ground up (like menhaden), are used as chum, and also as cut or strip bait that is placed amidst the chum.

Others. Other morsels used for various saltwater fish include sand fleas, which are used by surf and pier anglers for pompano; cut plug baits, used for mooching (trolling with cut herring for Pacific Northwest salmon) or bottom fishing; octopus chunks for drift fishing or stillfishing; and dead baits, including clams, mussels, snails, fish chunks/strips/heads, used for drifting or stillfishing.

A dead bait rig that is very effective for bottom fishing for tarpon can be made by tying a 10/0 hook to one end of a 6-foot 120-pound-test monofilament leader and a barrel swivel at the other end. Behead a mullet and attach a bait needle with an open eye to swivel. Then pull the leader through the bait and out the tail until the hook is placed as shown in the following illustration.

Dead Bait Rig

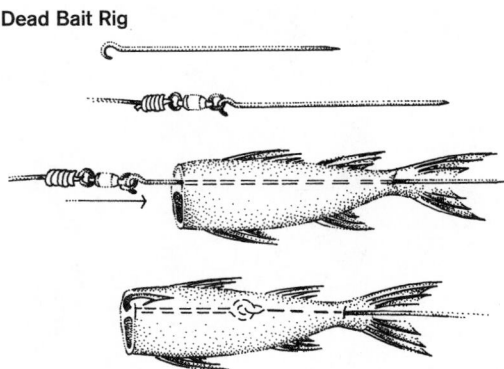

General Tips

Most live baits are hooked through the head or lips (tail for crayfish) for casting and free-lining, but

through the midsection for stillfishing with or without a float.

Bait has to be presented properly to be effective. This includes the physical appearance as well as the movement, or in some cases, lack of movement. Natural bait is generally fished in a more passive manner than lures, because the target fish have time to watch it, smell, it, and perhaps touch it before striking. If it moves in a swift or unnatural manner, it may cause alarm, although a natural bait that appears to be struggling, as many do when hooked, can in itself be attractive to a predator because it appears more vulnerable and easier to capture. There are some exceptions to this slow-fishing mantra, however, such as when live bait is trolled below the surface or when rigged dead bait is pulled over the surface for pelagic species, although these tactics are still designed to represent natural prey actions. Another exception is when a live natural bait is hooked on a jig and fished more actively than it would be if fished alone.

Where live bait is used, liveliness is vital. Many fish aren't interested in inactive or dead bait, so it's important to keep your bait as fresh and vigorous as possible. Change live bait whenever the current offering seems to be losing its vitality, and make sure that it acts naturally. A crayfish that rolls instead of crawls, for example, or a minnow that doesn't swim energetically, lessens the chance of success.

The water that bait is kept in ideally should be oxygenated or changed periodically to keep it healthy for the fish. Pay close attention to the freshness of the water, as well as the temperature, to ensure that bait remains in good condition. Some bait, such as alewives and herring, can only be kept in circular or oval baitwells or livewells *(see)*; they bunch into the corners of other wells and die, so the method of retaining them is important.

It is helpful to hold your line when live-lining bait. When fishing with a float or bobber, it's easy to tell if a fish is mouthing your live offering. But

N

Different fish require different rigging; a butterfish (top) is hooked through its belly, while a ling is hooked through its head.

that isn't the case when letting bait run freely. Then, it is often difficult to know if a fish has picked up your offering or if your bait is hung on brush, rock, or grass. Keep a light hold on the line to detect gentle strikes, and when in doubt, pull ever so softly on the line. If it moves off vigorously, you've got a fish.

Unless a fish has savagely attacked your bait offering and run off with it, it may be necessary to wait before setting the hook. For some fish, it does not pay to be in a rush to set the hook when live-bait angling. Certain fish need time to consume their quarry because they grab the bait crosswise in their mouth and swim a short distance away before swallowing the fish. By waiting a short time, and by not putting tension on the line during this period, you stand a better chance of hooking such fish.

This is not always the best move for all fish, however, and it can lead to deep hooking of some specimens that you must or want to release unharmed. Considering the type and size of bait used, the kind of hook, and the tendencies of the targeted fish, striking fairly quickly after the take may be better to minimize deep hooking. When you do have a deeply hooked fish, be especially careful about handling and unhooking it. There's a good chance that a fish released with a hook in it will survive if it is not bleeding. More about this issue is discussed in the entry on catch-and-release *(see)*.

NAVIGATION

From a boating perspective, navigation is the act of steering a boat, plotting a course, and/or determining boat position. Every angler who uses a boat is a navigator, most to a very minor degree, some to a major degree. The extent to which anglers are familiar with navigation is largely influenced by the waters on which they boat and the type of vessel employed. The principles of navigation should be

familiar to anyone venturing on big waters—whether ocean, lake, or river—or likely to boat in the dark or fog or in inclement weather, or likely to travel in any locale featuring official aids to navigation such as buoys.

No matter where an angler boats or what craft is used, the safety of the operator, the occupants, the boat, and others is a primary concern. Moving a boat necessarily entails avoiding hazards and obstructions that may be visible or out of sight; negotiating current, wakes, and waves; piloting under changing and sometimes severe weather conditions; encountering other boats; and maneuvering in and around docks, harbors, canals, and other areas. Piloting any type of boat is a serious responsibility, and the operator should be able to navigate safely under all circumstances.

In addition to being able to properly steer and maneuver a boat, anglers should be familiar with various tools used in navigating. These include a compass *(see)*, electronic navigation devices such as Loran *(see)* and GPS *(see)*, navigational charts and maps *(see)*, and sonar *(see)*.

Sonar is not actually a navigational tool, but it is probably more widely used during the act of navigating by fishing boat operators than any other instrument. This is because many angler-boaters (the majority in freshwater) rely heavily on sonar for bottom-depth information while fishing and while moving from one place to another. Although bottom depth has only minor value in determining position, it has obvious value in helping to avoid running aground. Likewise, radar has some value in determining position, and more value in avoiding running aground or preventing collision, but only the largest sportfishing boats are equipped with it. It used to be that only midsize and larger fishing boats used electronic navigational devices, especially Loran, but that has completely changed. Today, many freshwater and saltwater boats in the

One of the most embarrassing navigational errors is running aground; hopefully this happens on a sandbar, as here, where no damage is done.

16- to 21-foot range are equipped with such devices, primarily GPS, although handheld GPS units make navigation via that instrument easy for any anglers in any vessel. Navigational charts or maps are used by many anglers not just for their value in showing the proper routes to take on a given body of water, but also for locating suitable fish habitat.

Navigation can be made more difficult by adverse weather, so it is advisable for anglers to keep an eye on weather conditions and be alert to changes that may signal a storm.

Anglers and boaters have become increasingly reliant on electronic devices to give them information relevant to fishing, boating, navigation, and the weather. But if the electronic devices on a boat fail, which they sometimes do, and there is no quick way to determine depth, course, position, or speed, an angler who can't make adjustments could be in a very serious situation. There have long been ways to determine this information without electronics, including dead reckoning *(see)*, and anglers are advised to become acquainted with these through boating and piloting literature.

With or without electronic devices, angler-boaters need to use common sense and good judgment whenever they are boating, especially in difficult circumstances or on unfamiliar waters. Unfamiliar waters, especially those likely to have unmarked obstructions (rock reefs, sandbars, trees, etc.), require special attention. On large and unfamiliar bodies of water, consider using various launch sites to minimize distance traveled. Studying a good map, preferably a navigational chart, is important, and it's a good idea to ask local boaters, marina operators, and tackle shop personnel about hazards to avoid. Whenever you enter a new part of that body of water, do so carefully, operate your boat slowly, watch your sonar, and observe the water and shoreline closely. In tidal waters, be attentive to water level changes, and don't take risks.

NAVIGATIONAL CHART

A chart depicting hydrographic information and significant detail regarding depth, obstructions, and navigational aids.

See: Maps; Navigation.

NEAP TIDE

See: Tides.

NEARSHORE

The shallow portion of inshore saltwaters adjacent to the shoreline. In fishing parlance, inshore is a more common term than nearshore, and they are generally interchangeable, although nearshore is more specific.

See: Inshore; Inshore Fishing; Onshore.

NEBRASKA

Because Nebraska is a prairie state, few fishing opportunities exist that are not the result of man-made reservoirs. Notable exceptions are the hundreds of small, shallow, natural lakes that dot the Sandhills in the north-central region.

Nebraska anglers long have been accustomed to traveling in order to pursue their favorite species. Four-fifths of the population lives in the eastern third of the state, and there are no major reservoirs in that region. The Missouri River, which marks the state's eastern boundary, is that area's most important body of water. But the river is channelized below Gavins Point Dam at Yankton, South Dakota, and is not much more than a water chute for barge traffic from Sioux City, Iowa, to where it empties into the Mississippi River near St. Louis.

The majority of big reservoirs are in the southwest, including Lake McConaughy, the state's largest impoundment. Big Mac, as it is known, covers roughly 35,000 surface acres and is nearly 20 miles long.

Nebraska boasts several distinct geological features, including the Sandhills, and fishing opportunities vary accordingly. All of the state's coldwater trout streams are in the northwest and north-central regions, which include the Panhandle's canyon-laced Pine Ridge County. The midsection is flat and accommodates the Platte River, which each spring and fall lures millions of waterfowl in a spectacular migration through a narrow Central Flyway opening roughly from Grand Island west to North Platte.

Most of the state's reservoirs are showing signs of aging as siltation and shoreline degradation suffocate the habitat. But in 1997, the Nebraska legislature took a unique and important step in the rehabilitation process by requiring anglers to purchase an annual $5 aquatic habitat stamp along with a fishing license. Money generated by the sale of the stamp can be used only to enhance and restore aquatic habitat in Nebraska's reservoirs, lakes, and streams. Nebraska's commitment to the future was assured when it became the first state to require such a stamp.

The importance of habitat to Nebraska's fisheries was brought sharply into focus during a five-year (1988 to 1992) drought that left moisture-starved reservoirs at or near all-time low-water levels. Harlan County Reservoir, the state's third-largest reservoir, was so depleted that most biologists didn't expect it ever to fill again. But it did fill, miraculously almost overnight, and most of the other reservoirs were in flood pool as well by the spring of 1993.

All the vegetation and trees that grew along the shorelines during the low-water years were then covered by water. The nutrient-rich mix provided food, spawning habitat, and cover, and many species pulled off fantastic hatches. The good old days returned, and the size of walleye caught in

N

McConaughy in the latter 1990s rivaled that of Lake Erie's western basin and Lake Huron's Saginaw Bay. Proof of this is evidenced by the results of a two-person team, two-day walleye tournament held on Big Mac in 1997, when the winning team posted 20 fish that weighed a phenomenal 5.72 pounds on average.

Nebraska is the crossroads of the United States—where east meets west, and where north meets south. As a result, a rich biological diversity exists within its borders. Hunters have long taken pride in Nebraska's reputation as the mixed-bag capital of the nation. It's the same for anglers, who somewhere in the state can catch everything from chinook salmon to paddlefish, trout to flathead catfish, bluegills to walleye, and hybrid stripers to muskies.

Channel catfish, because they are available in nearly all Nebraska waters, likely are the most popular fish. Walleye are a close second.

Northeast

This region relies on agriculture, and its rolling hills make the land highly readable. It contains several small reservoirs—most of which cover fewer than 250 acres—and Lewis and Clark Lake, a Missouri River impoundment above Gavins Point Dam that is the state's second-largest reservoir and shared with South Dakota.

Upper Missouri River. A 45-mile-long unchannelized portion of the Missouri River is tucked away between Fort Randall and Gavins Point Dams. This scenic area is particularly productive. The upper Missouri is wider here than anywhere below Gavins Point Dam. It contains quite a few sandy islands and many oxbows, and the depth usually averages between 5 and 10 feet.

This is the state's top smallmouth bass spot, but largemouth bass also linger far back in the oxbows. Northern pike, walleye, sauger, crappie, and bluegills, along with flathead and channel catfish, are available, too. Because they must fight the current, the walleye here are more trim than their bulkier reservoir brethren.

Lewis and Clark Lake. Lewis and Clark produced a 101-pound blue catfish in 1990. The Nebraska jug fisherman who caught it missed a chance at the state record (100 pounds, 8 ounces from the Missouri River near Wynot in 1970) when he cleaned the fish after weighing it on an uncertified scale. The 30,000-acre reservoir is slightly smaller than Lake McConaughy and is the last impoundment on the Missouri River. Most anglers seek its walleye and sauger.

Gavins Point Dam tailwaters. The tailwaters of Gavens Point Dam on the Missouri is the only area in the state where paddlefish are allowed to be snagged. The paddlefish season annually runs the full month of October, and only those who have special permits are allowed to pursue the filter-feeding fish. At times, especially during the spring and fall, paddlefish crowd into the area below the dam in such numbers that anglers jigging for walleye or sauger routinely snag them. The state-record paddlefish weighed 91 pounds, 8 ounces and was landed in 1978. Although anglers prefer to catch walleye and sauger, they catch all species of fish, including rainbow trout and smallmouth bass, below the dam. The smallies and trout come from South Dakota reservoirs upstream.

Willow Creek Lake. Located 2 miles south of Pierce, Willow Creek Lake is a 700-acre impoundment. It is the largest in the northeast region with the exception of Lewis and Clark. Although it contains walleye, largemouth bass, northern pike, and tiger muskies, its worth as a panfish lake surfaces during the winter months, when ice anglers drill for bluegills and crappie.

Fremont State Lakes. The thirst for fishable water by eastern Nebraskans is evidenced by the popularity of the Fremont State chain—20 sandpit lakes that cover 280 acres in all. These small lakes draw about 800,000 visitors a year, making them the second most popular destination for water recreation in the state. Largemouth bass, panfish, and channel catfish are targets of anglers who crowd onto these small bodies of water.

Southeast

Several small flood-control reservoirs have been built near Omaha and Lincoln. Branched Oak and Pawnee are among a series of Salt Valley reservoirs that were constructed near Lincoln during the 1960s and 1970s. All these metropolitan reservoirs receive extremely heavy fishing pressure, but Branched Oak (1,800 acres) and Pawnee (740 acres) are in a league of their own in terms of drawing power. They rank first and third, respectively, among the state's reservoirs in the number of visitors each year.

Branched Oak. Branched Oak used to be one of the state's premier walleye fisheries, but an infestation of white perch has whittled down the walleye population. Little if any natural recruitment is occurring, and stockings of fingerlings have failed because the young walleye are either eaten by the white perch or are unable to compete with them for food. Crappie are beginning to rebound, and the lake is loaded with channel and flathead catfish. Biologists, however, say that the only way to make this a viable fishery once again is to apply rotenone, eradicate all the fish, and start over. Those in power are reluctant to do this because the water level would have to be drawn down before the rotenone could be applied. Emptying the state's most popular lake among pleasure boaters might be too much of a political hot potato, and these issues could prevent biologists from restoring this once excellent fishery.

Burchard Lake. The Salt Valley reservoirs had life expectancies of 100 years when they were built. Burchard, only 7 miles from the Kansas border, is not a Salt Valley impoundment. But it sets a standard for clean water and good watershed that biologists want to duplicate in all other eastern Nebraska reservoirs. The clean water enables weeds to grow. This in turn creates excellent habitat, which provides for good populations of bluegills and largemouth bass, along with some crappie. This 150-acre lake will become a model for all rehabilitation projects using money generated by the sales of aquatic habitat stamps.

Missouri River. Wing dams and river bends offer about the only habitat along the channelized portion of the river. Flathead and channel catfish are available for the few river rats who know how and where to catch them. But change is in the wind. There is a movement to restore more natural conditions—opening up some oxbows and reconnecting them to the river, giving it more of a natural meander. As the natural conditions are reestablished, fishing for additional species will improve, and more people will look to the river as a fishing destination. It's unlikely that federal funds will ever become available to construct a large reservoir in eastern Nebraska. But the river already is there, and its restoration one day will provide a vibrant fishing opportunity for the water-starved residents of eastern Nebraska.

South-Central

Interstate 80 lakes. Motorists traveling on Interstate 80 between Grand Island and Sutherland can observe what have become important fisheries to Nebraskans. A series of 41 borrow pits located along I-80 were created in the 1960s when dirt was taken from those pits to build the interstate highway. Because of the high water table along the Platte River, the pits quickly filled, and the state initiated stocking programs.

Most are small pits—only three are larger than 30 acres—and few have good access for boats. The majority of anglers either fish from shore or use small boats, canoes, or tubes. Those who do manage to launch larger boats do so for the comfort, not the added horsepower, as only electric motors are allowed. Although some receive fairly extensive fishing pressure, as a whole the lakes are overlooked by hard-core anglers, who drive right by them en route to much larger reservoirs.

The small lakes primarily offer largemouth bass, bluegills, and channel catfish. Some have rock bass, a few have yellow perch or northern pike, and a couple contain walleye. Smallmouth bass initially were stocked in many of the lakes, but largemouth bass eventually found their way into the lakes, where they were better able to compete for food. The smallmouths have slowly gone by the wayside.

Harlan County Reservoir. Traditionally, the state's third-largest reservoir (13,500 acres) has been an excellent walleye fishery. But a gradual decline in the fishery is in progress, and the walleye catch in the late 1990s was very poor. The recruitment has been very weak the last several years. The species of choice now seems to be white bass. The crappie population has increased dramatically in the aftermath of high water levels, and the number of channel catfish has improved. Biologists are hoping to make this an excellent fishery for hybrid striped bass, which are known as wipers here.

Sherman Reservoir. A 2,600-acre impoundment, Sherman is the state's most consistent crappie fishery. It has numerous coves and consistent water levels each year. About two-thirds of the crappie anglers fish from boats, but the many coves allow bank anglers easy access to the fish, too, especially during the May spawning period. A 10-inch minimum length limit for crappie went into effect in 1998. Walleye also attract attention, and there's an 18-inch minimum size limit. White bass success varies from good to excellent.

Johnson Reservoir. Walleye and white bass help make Johnson, a 2,800-acre lake, a strong magnet for anglers. Crappie are also beginning to draw attention, and the lake had a good number of crappie more than 10 inches long in the late 1990s. Numbers of channel catfish are low, compared to those in other reservoirs.

Elwood Reservoir. Elwood is one of three state reservoirs that utilize alewife as a food source, and this 1,200-acre impoundment is considered among the best walleye producers in the state. The lake level, however, is subject to extreme changes in water elevation because of irrigation demands. This fluctuation causes a loss of shoreline vegetation and apparently hampers panfish recruitment. Reproduction of channel catfish also is restricted, but there are good numbers of big channels.

Southwest

Nebraska's big reservoirs are in this region, and all are established walleye and white bass fisheries. But there are bonus fish, too, such as the state-record 64-pound, 15-ounce striped bass caught from Sutherland Reservoir in 1993. Biologists believe the huge striper initially was stocked in McConaughy and made its way down the canal system to Sutherland. That canal also produced the state-record 14-pound, 2-ounce rainbow trout in 1975. Other Platte Valley reservoirs—Maloney and Jeffrey—along with Medicine Creek and Enders, all produce good numbers of 15- to 18-inch walleye. Medicine Creek also can be exceptional for white bass and crappie.

McConaughy Reservoir. Nebraska's largest reservoir was a world-class walleye fishery in the latter 1990s, when it experienced the best years for walleye in its history. Five-fish limits of between 8- and 10-pounders were not uncommon in 1997, which prompted the Nebraska Game and Parks Commission to lower the state's walleye limit to four and to allow anglers to keep only one walleye a day longer than 25 inches. The state-record walleye of 16 pounds, 2 ounces was caught in 1971,

The method of angling with a fly developed earlier and faster than any other type of artificial lure fishing—perhaps because early anglers were concerned mostly with trout in rivers and streams.

long before alewives became the primary prey fish. Alewives produce big walleye, and the state's top three walleye fisheries—Big Mac, Merritt, and Elwood—are the only alewife-based reservoirs.

There is a trade-off, though. The alewife population at McConaughy has exploded, and walleye eggs or small fry are being eaten by them at such a pace that there is little if any natural recruitment occurring. Stocking of fingerling walleye appears to be the only way to beat the alewife. Biologists also plan to stock chinook salmon and brown trout in an attempt to reduce alewife numbers.

Lake Ogallala.   Although Lake Ogallala covers only 590 acres, this small reservoir, which lies beneath Big Mac's Kingsley Dam, is the state's most important trout fishery. Biologists are managing this as a trophy lake for rainbow trout, brown trout, and chinook salmon.

Red Willow Reservoir.   A 1,630-acre lake, Red Willow might be the state's best all-around fishery, barely edging Merritt and Elwood for that honor. It has become the premier wiper lake, but an angler never really knows what might gulp a lure. A guide and his client once stayed in one spot long enough to catch five Master Angler (the state's large-catch recognition program) species—channel catfish, largemouth bass, walleye, wipers, and northern pike. It yields lots of white bass, and the crappie population is building up once again.

Swanson Reservoir.   Wipers in Swanson Reservoir are beginning to put on bulk and could one day rival those in Red Willow if anglers release this sterile hybrid cross between a white bass and a striped bass. This 5,000-acre lake has mostly a flat bottom and is essentially void of structure, yet it still manages to produce good classes of walleye, white bass, and crappie. This might be the state's best lake for flathead catfish.

Panhandle

Most of the state's coldwater trout streams are in this region, but a vigorous stocking program is necessary due to the decline of Lake McConaughy as a rainbow trout fishery. A breed of rainbow trout known as the McConaughy strain flourished in Big Mac until the late 1970s. Most trout anglers blame the decline of rainbows on the stocking of stripers. The stripers are about gone now, and the Nebraska Game and Parks Commission has ordered that no further striper stockings can take place in the state. Biologists, however, still can't revive the rainbow trout population, even though federal fish hatcheries have maintained the McConaughy strain. It's believed alewives are outcompeting the rainbows for the small food that once was available.

The McConaughy strain is unusual. These rainbows have an inclination to migrate out of the lake and to travel far up the coldwater streams to spawn. In the glory days of McConaughy as a trout fishery, most of the fish migrated from the west end of the lake up the North Platte River. When they ran into a tributary they liked, they left the river and headed up the creek to spawn.

Many of the streams run through the Pine Ridge, which stretches from north of Rushville to the Wyoming border, a distance of more than 80 miles, and varies in altitude from 3,100 feet to just over a mile high. Pine forests stretch as far as the eye can see, and the cool, gravel-bottomed streams are stocked with brook, brown, and rainbow trout. Public access is available on many of the streams, such as Soldier, Squaw, Chadron, Nine-Mile, Pumpkin, and Otter Creeks. But they and other streams meander mostly on private ground, and obtaining permission to fish is a necessity. A few reservoirs also are available, along with some Sandhill lakes. A sandpit near Scottsbluff in 1997 yielded the state-record northern pike, a 30-pound, 1-ounce specimen.

Box Butte Reservoir.   Box Butte is a 1,600-acre lake that is subject to severe irrigation drawdown each summer, yet it still produces decent panfishing for yellow perch, crappie, and bluegills. It has a good population of northern pike, and some walleye and largemouth bass also inhabit the lake.

Lake Minatare.   Lake Minatare is the largest impoundment, at 2,300 acres, in the Panhandle region. It is closed during the fall/winter waterfowl migration because it harbors so many waterfowl during that period. The good news for western Nebraska anglers is that it's beginning to rebound as a walleye fishery. Also available are smallmouth bass, channel catfish, wipers, white bass, and perch.

North-Central

The Sandhills, one of the geological wonders of the world, cover one-fourth of Nebraska. A satellite picture of the Sandhills taken from 500 miles up shows that the hills lie in a diagonal pattern, running northeast to southwest. All are steep on the southeast side because they are wind-blown dunes; it appears the predominant wind was out of the northwest when the Sandhills were formed. This was once a largely bare sand system, but a growth of grass that anchored the dunes was likely triggered by increased rainfall and perhaps decreased temperature.

This is range country, and the native grasses are grazed by cattle. Large ranching operations and a few small villages dot the Sandhills. The region has a high water table, and hundreds of shallow lakes are interspersed among the stabilized sand dunes, some of which rise to a height of 400 feet.

Sandhill lakes.   The Sandhill lakes are shallow and average between 6 and 10 feet in depth. Many are so saline that they can't support fish, but those that have freshwater are very productive. Most have abundant aquatic vegetation—unless they have a high population of carp—and they become weed-choked and difficult to fish during the summer. The best time to fish is in the spring and winter. Some, such as Pelican Lake in the Valentine

Atlantic Needlefish

National Wildlife Refuge, offer world-class ice fishing opportunities for bluegills that run 2 pounds and larger. Northern pike, largemouth bass, and perch also are sought by many Sandhill lakes anglers.

Merritt Reservoir. A 2,900-acre lake, Merritt is a premier Nebraska fishery for a variety of species. It is the state's top water for channel catfish and muskellunge. The state record for both species was set here, and each weighed 41 pounds, 8 ounces. The channel was caught in 1985 and the muskie in 1992. The lake is best known for its walleye, even though there is little if any natural recruitment. Stockings preserve its status as a walleye fishery. Good populations of bluegills, crappie, and perch make it the state's best panfish lake.

Calamus Reservoir. Nebraska's newest reservoir is showing signs of finally becoming a viable fishery after 18 years of Dead Sea status. It was among the nation's best lakes for northern pike during its early years. Panfish and largemouth bass are other shallow-water species that flourished when it was first flooded. But when the flooded habitat decayed, the shallow-water species crashed. Now, some open-water species have finally begun to emerge. Walleye fishing was excellent in the latter 1990s, and a huge population of small fish has been building. Wipers and white bass are improving, too. The reservoir finally is able to sustain fish populations that biologists thought it could when it was built. The future looks bright for this 5,200-acre lake.

NEEDLEFISH

There are 32 species in the Belonidae family of needlefish, many of which are also known as longtoms or sea gar. Most live in tropical seas, a few inhabit cooler waters of temperate regions, and some stray occasionally into freshwater. They are often observed by coastal anglers, and some are caught frequently.

The most distinguishing feature of these fish is their elongated upper and lower jaws, which have numerous needlelike teeth. The upper jaw is shorter than the lower jaw; however, in two species the lower jaw is shorter. They have slender elongate bodies that are silver on the flanks and bluish or dark green along the back, and also feature small scales and a wide mouth. In most species, both the bones and the flesh are greenish, but they make good eating. Some species are pursued commercially, with Europeans and Scandinavians exhibiting the most interest in this species as a food fish.

Garfish

Needlefish commonly skip across the surface when hooked on rod and reel, when alarmed, and when attracted to lights. They leap from the water and hurtle through the air like an arrow. Since they have a habit of leaping toward lights at night, they present a serious hazard to night anglers and people on low well-lit boats. People who have been struck or impaled have been badly injured, and in rare cases killed. Beneath the surface, these fish swim very rapidly. Plugs, streamer flies, spoons, jigs, and live baits will all catch needlefish. Light tackle ensures a good fight.

Species

One of the most widely dispersed species is the houndfish *(Tylosurus crocodilus crocodilus)*, which is found nearly worldwide in tropical and warm temperate waters. It is common in the western Atlantic, ranging from New Jersey southward through the Caribbean to Brazil. In the eastern Atlantic it ranges from Cameroon to South Africa; in the Indian Ocean it occurs in South Africa; in the western Pacific it ranges from Japan to Australia. In the eastern Pacific it is replaced by *T. c. foditor*, the Mexican houndfish.

The houndfish averages 2 feet or less in length but occasionally attains a length of 4 to 5 feet. It is also known as hound needlefish, crocodile needlefish, and crocodile longtom, and the all-tackle world record is 6 pounds, 11 ounces (the record for Mexican houndfish is 21 pounds, 12 ounces). Compared to other, generally smaller members of the family, houndfish have a relatively short, stout beak. They are found singly or in small groups, readily strike artificial lures, and are exciting to take on rod and reel.

The Atlantic needlefish *(Strongylura marina)* is a smaller species that inhabits coastal areas and mangrove-lined lagoons and also enters freshwater. It occurs in the western Atlantic and ranges from the Gulf of Maine to Brazil. It is absent from the Bahamas and Antilles. It grows to 31 inches and can weigh slightly more than 3 pounds.

Similar in size is the garfish *(Belone belone belone)*, which occurs in the eastern Atlantic from Norway and south Iceland to the British Isles, including the Baltic Sea, with related species (or subspecies) present from France to the Canary Islands, including the Mediterranean. The garfish has considerable commercial interest and is known as *hornfisk* in Denmark, *orphie* in France, *agugila* in Italy, *horngjel* in Norway, *agulha* in Portugal, *aguja* in Spain, *hongädda* in Sweden, and *zargana* in Turkey.

NEOPRENE

A prominent wader *(see)* material that provides warmth in cold water.

NEST

A visible bed, often circular, made by egg-laying fish on the bottom of a body of water for spawning. Eggs are laid in the nest, and sometimes they are guarded by one or more of the parents.

NET

A mesh bag mounted on a wooden or metal frame with one or more handles. Used for capturing individual hooked fish, this device is also known as a landing net to distinguish it from a seine or commercial fishing net. Landing nets are an important and regularly used accessory for freshwater anglers, from stream trout waders to big water boaters. They are less frequently used by saltwater anglers, mostly for smaller fish in bays and shallows.

Nets should be suited to the kind of angling being done and the fish anticipated. Stream nets for trout have a short handle and small hoop diameter (12 to 14 inches) for use with small fish while boat nets have longer handles (perhaps collapsible) and larger hoops. The further one has to reach (from boat or pier), the longer the handle needed; however, the heavier the fish you may catch, the sturdier the handle necessary (usually reinforced). Pier and bridge anglers use a large, handleless net that is lowered and raised on a rope. A few nets incorporate a scale into the handle in order to weigh a fish that has been netted.

With all nets, the larger the fish, the bigger the hoop and the deeper the bag necessary. Although it seems foolish to net small fish with big nets, it's worse to be caught with a net that can't fit the fish. For small-boat fishing, a net that is at least 4 feet long from net rim to handle butt, with a wide rim and a deep net bag, is a popular choice. For very big fish in big water and boats with high freeboard, a 6-foot handle is better. Most nets feature aluminum handles and frames. Mesh bags are rubber, polyethylene, nylon, or cotton, although cotton tends to rot. All nets should be rinsed after use to increase their longevity.

Mesh bags with wooden side handles, called cradles, have been used by fisheries technicians and some anglers to support fish without handling, but they are cumbersome and difficult for a lone angler to use. With help from a companion, however, they're very good for landing long fish that are to be released, and make a good net for long toothy species like pike and muskie.

See: Cast Net; Catch-and-Release; Landing Fish.

NETHERLANDS

Upon landing at Schiphol Airport near Amsterdam, few people realize that they are at that moment not only near some good fishing areas, but also several meters below sea level, a situation that also exists throughout much of the western and northern provinces of the Netherlands. Should the sea level rise considerably in the next century, as has been forecast by some scientists, and if not enough is done to avert these problems, many people in the Netherlands will have serious problems. Still, light-hearted Dutch anglers say that angling from the bedroom window has certain charms.

Also known as Holland, the Netherlands covers just 41,526 square kilometers and is bordered on the west and north by the North Sea, on the east by Germany, and on the south by Belgium. With a population of more than 15 million, it is one of the most densely populated countries in the world. Most of its residents live in the relatively small delta area of rivers like the Maas, Rijn, and Schelde.

Those rivers and deltas transport water to the sea near the port of Rotterdam and between the islands of the southwestern province of Zeeland. The Rijn once held one of the world's largest stocks of Atlantic salmon, a unique run of fish almost completely extinct since World War II. These fish started to reappear a few years ago, however, due to the improvement of fish habitat, stocking programs, and the construction of fish ladders. Holland is, and probably always has been, a passageway for fish like Atlantic salmon and sea trout, and even the water in small creeks in the east and south holds too much sand for these fish to deposit their eggs with any chance of success. The total number of mature salmon going upriver was very small in the late 1990s, offering only a slight chance to hook one, but there may be a viable fishery for salmon someday if the numbers improve.

Other species, of course—including pike, pike-perch (zander), and trout, which are tops among freshwater gamefish—draw the attention of resident and visiting anglers. Interest in eels, perch, carp, bream, and roach is high as well. In saltwater, mackerel, cod, whiting, and assorted flatfish are the main species.

Freshwater

Freshwater fish in Holland inhabit a network of canals, lakes, and rivers. Significant Dutch rivers include the Rhine, which flows from Germany, and its tributaries; the Maas, which is an extension of the Meuse from Belgium; and the Schelde, which also enters from Belgium. Many small lakes grace the northern and western regions. The world-renowned Dutch delta redevelopment and reclamation program has created numerous freshwater lakes, the largest of which is the IJsselmeer in the central part of the country; this is the former Zuiderzee, which was created after being diked by the Afsluitdijk.

Club and organized match fishing are major activities throughout the country. As in the rest of western Europe, roach and bronze bream are the most common and favorite species. Pole fishing for these fish is how most anglers begin, and if they master this method up to championship level, they will eventually use take-apart poles up to 12 meters in length.

Coarse species in canals and rivers that are continually fished for matches are very difficult to catch, and this has become a challenge that Dutch anglers thrive on. They must continually improve their delicate floats, rigs, and chum recipes to outwit the fish and other anglers. They have done this successfully enough for the country to have won a pair of world titles and individual championships. Incidentally, the challenge of catching big carp (more than 25 pounds), which started in England, has caught on lately in Holland.

Rivers. The first part of the river Maas, the Grensmaas, is shallow and runs with considerable speed. It is ideal habitat for coarse species like barbel, carp, and chub, which are sought with match rod, feeder rod, pole, and fly tackle. This area also contains sea-run trout.

In general, match rods are between 3.3 and 4.5 meters long and are used with spinning reels to fish floats at considerable distances from shore. Feeder rods are equipped with delicate tips to telegraph the light take of a fish. The "feeders" are wire or plastic cages, weighted with lead, that are filled with groundbait before being cast to the spot to be fished. A short, light length of nylon monofilament line with a hook is connected somewhat above the feeder. Dutch anglers use poles in lengths from 5 to more than 14 meters. To improve control over a drifting float, the line is often considerably shorter than the rod, and the pole is taken apart when a fish is landed and/or new bait is put on the hook. The natural and processed baits used most often when fishing these types of tackle include maggots, casters, worms, bloodworms, bread, hemp, and corn.

Numerous gravel pits have been created along the rivers, and these range from just a few acres to thousands of acres. These are often much deeper than the rivers to which they are connected—down to 20 meters in some cases—and are frequented by anglers for coarse species and zander.

Fishing with jigs equipped with shad bodies and other soft plastics straight below a boat or float tube—a method called *vertical fishing* in Holland—can produce zander up to 100 centimeters in length and 20 pounds in weight, although smaller zander around 50 centimeters are the norm. Perch and pike are a much appreciated bycatch of this method. In winter these gravel pits host match anglers who fish for roach with wagglers at depths of between 5 and 15 meters.

Where canals enter the rivers, and on a larger scale upstream from where the river IJssel flows into the IJsselmeer, there is an annual "spring run" in April and May of great numbers of roach and bream (and to some extent ide), which move upriver to

spawn. Exceptional catches are possible during this period on pole, feeder rod, and match rod.

Fly anglers along the river IJssel have developed a style of nymph fishing suited to these conditions. A 4- to 5-meter-long leader, heavy nymphs with fluorescent materials incorporated into the body, and a clearly visible strike indicator are the main tools of the trade. Good-size roach and bream take a well-bent fly rod to pull them from the main flow of the river.

Another fish regularly inhabiting Dutch rivers is the bleak, a small silvery fish found and pursued in the top layers of the water. They take small dry flies well, but their speed in taking these, as well as their small mouths, makes them hard to hook.

The asp is a fish that has entered Holland's waters in recent years, originating in Germany and evidently washing downstream during high water periods. Ten years ago this fish was unheard of in Dutch rivers but is now an exciting prospect for anglers using flycasting and spinning tackle.

River anglers also have an opportunity to pursue zander. During the long summer evenings, many fly anglers cast fast-sinking lines and 10-centimeter-long streamers for zander. The take on a streamer can be hardly noticeable, just a little increased resistance, so anglers set the hook when they feel this, and a good-size zander could be heading for deeper water in the next instant.

In the saltwater or brackish water of harbors close to where main rivers enter the sea, anglers have challenging sport catching mullet. It's impressive to see these torpedo-shaped fish 'sunbathing' in

An angler fishes for coarse species in a Dutch canal.

summer months, and some can be 80 to 100 centimeters long. Catching them is not too easy, as they mainly feed on weeds, but anglers who use bread or small parts of herring do catch mullet.

Lakes.   The shallow waters of Holland's *polders,* or sections of land reclaimed from the sea and protected by dikes, provide diverse fishing opportunity. The oldest polders are found in the provinces of Utrecht, Zuid-Holland, Noord-Holland, Friesland, and Overijssel. Many of these waters badly need to be restored to their former depth, whereas others suffer from the inflow of manure and pesticides. A good polder water is gin clear (even though it appears otherwise because of the dark bottom) and filled with numerous aquatic plants.

The polder canals and lakes are hunting grounds for anglers who cast unweighted spinners, little wobblers, and spoons for pike and perch. Ultralight-tackle enthusiasts cast maggots or bread in search of rudd. Fly anglers catch rudd as well as roach and perch on dry flies and nymphs, and northern pike on streamer flies. Carp anglers have success in polder waters by sneaking along and dropping a bait in likely looking places, or by baiting certain areas and fishing over this chum until their electronic strike indicators go off.

Another member of the cyprinid family, the tench is an inhabitant of waters that are crowded with plants. Some anglers will first clear a few square meters of aquatic plants, drop some groundbait (with worms added) there, and await the arrival of the tench.

Until mid-1998 it was legal to fish for pike, perch, and zander with live baits, but new legislation stopped this popular and successful technique. In discolored waters, dead fish used as baits can be as successful as live baits; anglers use roach, herring, sprat, or mackerel to attract pike in particular.

Zander and big pike inhabit the larger lakes scattered throughout Holland, and these include the Vinkeveense, Nieuwkoopse Plassen, and the Friese Meren. Trolling lures and baits is a popular method for pike, whereas vertical fishing with jigs or using small dead baits is popular for zander. Drifting along the shoreline while casting jerkbaits, minnow plugs, and spoons is also popular.

Wherever there is access along the shoreline of these lakes, anglers pursue perch and zander using assorted methods with baits and jigs. Anglers fishing from belly boats cast either flies or pieces of bread toward the reeds and other vegetation along the shore. The float tube has firmly established itself in Holland as an excellent device for fishing waters that are otherwise difficult to access. Still, rowboats are available for rent on all the established waters.

Wels have been inhabitants of a small number of waters in Holland for a considerable time, and in recent years they have spread to other sites as well, like those connected with the river Maas. Most wels are hooked and lost by anglers fishing for zander or pike, but in late 1997 a wels of more than

45 kilograms was caught in the Biesbosch. Wels are a protected species in the Netherlands and must be returned to the water immediately.

The trout fisheries Eemhof, Kempervennen, Berenkuil, and Baggelhuizen are four examples of popular daily-fee privately operated fisheries. These are rather large natural or man-made lakes where fly anglers have room to enjoy their sport and where newcomers can get casting and fishing instruction if needed. A fee for the day or several hours is charged, and the waters are stocked primarily with rainbow trout, and sometimes brown trout; these may be released if handled with great care, or they may be kept for an additional fee. They are similar to commercial fishing preserves in the United States. Other, usually smaller, trout fisheries are managed as strictly put-and-take waters, and may be fished with various tackle and methods. The rainbow trout caught here are plate-size, but some waters are stocked with larger specimens.

For sea-run trout, the Veerse Meer and Oostvoornse Meer, especially the latter, have in recent years gained international recognition as two of the best sea trout fisheries of Europe. The Oostvoornse Meer is situated just below Rotterdam; the Veerse Meer lies farther south, near Veere in the province of Zeeland.

Both lakes are brackish, and their great supply of baitfish, saltwater scuds, and shrimp means plenty of food for trout. In the Oostvoornse Meer, trout have been known to grow up to 2.5 centimeters per month. The largest trout to come out of these lakes are well over 20 pounds.

In the Oostvoornse Meer, all trout have to be returned to the water, no motorboats are allowed, and one can only fish with a fly or an artificial lure. Fly anglers must use at least a 2X tippet to cope with the fish that can be expected here. The shallow water between shore and the many dams in the Oostvoornse Meer are prime feeding grounds for these trout, and easier for most anglers to fish. Beyond the dams, the water gains depth rapidly.

Saltwater

The coastline of the North Sea in the Netherlands consists mainly of dunes, but in the southwest there are gaps formed by river mouths, which forged an expansive delta of islands and waterways. In the north, the dunes were broken through by the sea, creating the West Frisian Islands; behind these is a tidal sea called the Waddenzee, which is popular for anglers seeking flatfish. Some areas of this beautiful seascape produce mackerel, garfish, bass, and sea trout.

Surf casting for flounder, whiting, cod, and bass is a common activity along the coast, using weights from 80 to 200 grams and baited hooks that are cast with long rods great distances from the shoreline. A wind blowing toward shore is usually preferred; summer is the best time for bass, whereas cod move in closer to land in the colder months.

N

Piers and dams like those near IJmuiden, Hoek, Scheveningen, Haringvliet, and Zierikzee are popular fishing sites, too. Garfish are caught here close to the surface. Bass are hooked here but are often lost among the rocks by shore-based anglers. Casting toward shore from a drifting or anchored boat results in more bass landed. These are caught by various means, but fly tackle, using heavy sinking lines to fish down to 8 meters, has earned a place for this species in recent years as well.

Hundreds of small boats also set out to sea regularly from a number of harbors when the conditions and weather are right. Fishing over shipwrecks in late autumn, winter, and early spring often produces large cod, up to 40 pounds on some occasions. In summer, the same boats are on the hunt for bass. Party boats are also available from many ports along the coast, and some fish all year. Mackerel are the main pursuit from June through September, and cod during winter. Whiting and flatfish are also caught.

Licenses and Regulations

Licenses and regulations are a complex matter in Holland. Two types of licenses are needed for most Dutch waters, although none is needed for sportfishing in saltwater. *Sportvisakte,* the national license, is a yearly one available from post offices, tackle shops, and some fishing clubs. This license gives anglers the right to fish with a maximum of two rods, one of which has to be devoted to predator species (i.e., equipped with an artificial lure or streamer).

The second license is one that allows an angler to fish a particular waterway. Depending on the specific watercourse, one has to be a club member, have a weekly ticket or daily tickets, or be covered by the *Grote Vergunning* (large license), which covers a lot of water across Holland. The *Grote Vergunning* is offered by the national federation of anglers (NVVS, in Holland); most fishing clubs in Holland belong to this organization and only their members can receive the license. It cannot be bought in a shop (although one can purchase a membership to some fishing clubs in a large number of fishing tackle stores). The Oostvoornse Meer and Veerse Meer are just two examples of waters covered by the *Grote Vergunning.*

A number of public waters exist in Holland for which the *Sportvisakte* is the only license needed if you do not fish for pike, perch, or zander. A membership for one year in a fishing club varies in cost depending on the number of members and the number of waters to which they have fishing rights. Some have no more than twenty-five members; the biggest ones have thousands of members.

In the Netherlands, closed seasons are enforced for certain species of fish, and some regulations cover bait types, as well as special considerations for certain waters. Minimum size limits apply to most species, with the exception of carp, garfish, and twaite shad *(Alosa fallax),* although many Dutch anglers practice catch-and-release in freshwater. Nearly all fishing clubs have their own regulations in addition. These may pertain to an extended closed season for pike, prohibition of treble hooks, or the prohibition of night fishing. Ask about these issues when you buy a license or decide to become a member of a club.

NET KEEPER

A device that tethers a landing net to the body of a wading angler so that it is out of the way when fishing yet easily accessible. Net keepers are fastened to a retractable chain or string, or to a quick-release clip.

NETTING

See: Landing Fish; Catch-and-Release.

NEVADA

Nevada's fishing opportunities are surprisingly abundant and widely varied, particularly since the state receives less precipitation than any other state in the United States.

In its northwestern corner, Nevada has an abundant lake trout population in forested Lake Tahoe; at the opposite end of the state, it has the Colorado River, which winds across the Mohave Desert, forming canyonlike Lakes Mead and Mohave and boasting famous largemouth bass and striped bass fisheries. In between are numerous natural lakes and man-made reservoirs—mostly used as storage for flood control or irrigation—that also provide terrific fisheries for stocked and wild trout.

Nevada has approximately 535 fishable streams with nearly 3,000 miles of habitat, mostly in the northern two-thirds of the state, that are underutilized; most anglers head for the larger rivers and more developed lakes and reservoirs. Yet these flowages possess reproducing populations of brown trout, brook trout, Lahontan cutthroat trout, redband trout, bull trout, mountain whitefish, and other species.

Northern Region

Wildhorse, Wilson Sink, and South Fork Reservoirs. Wildhorse, Wilson Sink, and South Fork are all in the northeastern corner of Nevada and are "put-grow-and-take" trout fisheries. They are primarily stocked with rainbow trout, but also with browns and rainbow-cutthroat hybrids. They have secondary opportunities for such warmwater species as smallmouth and largemouth bass, yellow perch, crappie, and channel catfish. Additionally, South Fork has wild brown trout and native Lahontan cutthroat trout.

Wildhorse is a 2,830-acre irrigation storage reservoir on the East Fork of the Owyhee River. It's about 60 miles north of Elko, with good year-round access via Route 225. Located off Route 226, nearby Wilson Sink Reservoir is small at 800 surface acres. Access at Wilson is less dependable in the winter when the dirt road thaws enough to become mud. South Fork Reservoir, which covers 1,650 surface acres and is 3 miles long, is 20 miles southwest of Elko off Route 228 on the South Fork of the Humboldt River. Access is good year-round.

All three reservoirs are stocked with 8- to 10-inch trout, mostly rainbows, in the spring and fall, which quickly grow to 13 to 17 inches if they're not caught first. Fishing off the bottom from shore with worms and prepared baits is popular during spring and fall, as is casting spinners and spoons. Boaters troll with small spoons and spinners. Float-tube anglers like fishing the "no wake" zone in the willows at the south end of South Fork for bass and trout. The rock dam face and rocky points, especially those jutting out on either side of the dam, are good places to fish for smallmouth bass in April, May, September, and October.

Ice fishing for trout is popular at these reservoirs during the winter, from late December through much of February. Yellow perch are a welcome winter bonus at Wildhorse. Smallmouth bass, crappie, and catfish also inhabit Wildhorse, and Wilson has largemouth bass. Spring and early summer are the best times for these species.

Fishing beneath the dams at both Wildhorse and South Fork can be good when high flows have washed fish into the rivers.

Ruby Mountains and East Humboldt's lakes and streams. The Ruby Mountains and East Humboldt Mountains are among the most scenic and glacier-carved in Nevada. Twenty high-mountain lakes and dozens of streams provide angling opportunities to backpackers searching for wild brook trout and native Lahontan cutthroat trout. The only stream stocked with rainbow trout is Lamoille Creek in Lamoille Canyon, which receives more fishing pressure than any other stream in Elko County. Much access to other fishable streams in the ranges is blocked by private property, although the upper reaches of many streams are accessed downslope from the Ruby Crest Trail.

Ruby Lake National Wildlife Refuge. Located 65 miles southeast of Elko, the 37,632-acre Ruby Lake National Wildlife Refuge consists of marshes, open ponds, and islands bordered by wet meadows and grass- and sagebrush-covered uplands.

Fishing for abundant, but usually small, largemouth bass is popular throughout the marsh area. The Collection Ditch flowing on the west side of the North and East Sump units is a favorite among fly anglers because it can be fished only with artificials. Anglers can catch rainbows and 5- to 10-pound brown trout here.

Rye Patch Reservoir. Located 22 miles north of Lovelock and 50 miles southeast of Winnemucca, Rye Patch Reservoir is an impoundment on the Humboldt River. Built for irrigation storage and flood control, it provides good habitat to walleye, spotted bass, white crappie, hybrid stripers, yellow perch, channel catfish, black crappie, bluegills, and green sunfish.

The Pitt-Taylor Arm at the upper end of the 22-mile-long reservoir has many islands with rocky shorelines that hold walleye and crappie, as well as brushy areas that hold spotted bass. Angling for walleye up to 12 pounds begins late in March and extends through mid-May, then picks up again in September. Anglers use deep-diving plugs and yellow or white crappie jigs on the windswept shorelines in 8 feet of water over structure. Fishing for walleye below the dam is good when that structure is spilling water.

A deep-spawning fish, spotted bass are caught in typical largemouth bass habitat. The spotted bass on average here are small but can run up to 5 pounds. Catfish up to 27 pounds have been caught at Rye Patch and are mainly landed on stinkbaits fished in areas where fresh water flows. Hybrid striped bass, locally called wipers, are caught up to 8 pounds and provide excitement in open water from June through September.

Smaller waters. Excellent stream fishing opportunities exist throughout many of the mountain ranges in northern Nevada. The East and West Forks of the Jarbidge, Bruneau, and Mary's Rivers in northeastern Nevada offer excellent opportunities to catch native wild trout. Bull trout in the 6- to 10-inch range inhabit the East Fork of the Jarbidge River or the upper stretches of the West Fork. The East Fork is rather remote, offering little access but excellent fishing. Due to aggressive conservation measures, fishing is excellent on the Bruneau River, primarily for redband trout. The Mary's River and its tributaries are under extensive management to restore Lahontan cutthroat trout. The upper stretches of the Mary's River offer the best fishing.

Notable small reservoirs and lakes include: Squaw Creek, Chimney, Knott Creek, Onion Valley, Big Springs, Dry Creek, Crittenden, and Dorsey Reservoirs, as well as Blue Lakes and Angel Lake.

Central Region

Pyramid and Walker Lakes. Pyramid and Walker Lakes are two premier Lahontan cutthroat trout lakes. They are dependent on good flows of high-quality water to sustain fish populations; otherwise, they would become too alkaline. Both are also at the end of closed basins; the Truckee River flows into Pyramid, and the East Fork and West Fork of the Walker River join to flow into Walker Lake. Because flows from the Truckee River have been committed to Pyramid Lake to protect the endangered cui-ui, a native sucker that also inhabits the large desert lake, Pyramid's fishery seems to hold up better than Walker Lake's, which receives less dependable flows from the Walker.

Just 30 miles northeast of Reno on the reservation of the Pyramid Lake Paiute Tribe, Pyramid

Lake is 26 miles long, up to 11 miles wide, and 350 feet deep in spots. It is open to trout fishing from fall through spring. The best times to catch trophy Lahontan cutthroat are November through April; flycasting big woolly-looking flies or fishing deep from boats with spoons are common tactics at this artificials-only site. Boaters should be cautious of quick-changing weather conditions that can make this lake treacherous.

The entire west shore of Pyramid Lake between Warrior Point on the north and Popcorn on the south is good for shore fishing and trolling. Trolling is popular on the eastern shoreline between Hell's Kitchen and Anderson Bay. The western shoreline of Walker Lake produces cutthroats in the 1- to 4-pound range. Sportsman's Beach and the Cliffs are particularly popular with shore anglers.

Spawning Sacramento perch (not a perch but a sunfish) at Pyramid can be caught by jigging off the rocky shorelines during May or June.

Lake Tahoe.   Lake trout, known here as mackinaw, filled the niche in Lake Tahoe left by the demise of Lahontan cutthroat trout, a species that once migrated into the lake on their spawning runs up the Truckee River from Pyramid Lake.

Although most of Lake Tahoe lies in California, plenty of action still exists along the northern and eastern shores for those fishing on the Nevada side. Lake trout here are found in 100- to 400-foot depths, and successful deep fishing for them requires heavy, specialized equipment. Boaters here troll with downriggers or lead-core line, whereas others jig with heavy spoons.

Fishing year-around is good, although dedicated Tahoe anglers prefer the colder months of November through March. Mackinaw in the 5- to 15-pound range are common, and fish in the 20-pound class are available.

From Sand Harbor to Cave Rock, anglers can also fish shallow near the surface with lighter gear for native rainbows (reared in Marlette Lake for return to Lake Tahoe) and browns, and can occasionally pick up a lake trout. Shore fishing at Cave Rock for brown trout and stocked rainbows is also popular.

Truckee, Carson, and Walker Rivers. Western Nevada's largest rivers are the Truckee, East Carson, Carson, and East and West Forks of the Walker. These are only small streams by some standards, but they all offer good fishing for stocked and wild rainbow trout, as well as a diversity of other wild, and some native, species.

The Truckee River, which flows out of Lake Tahoe, down through the mountains, through the middle of Reno, then east and north to Pyramid Lake, is a premier trout stream of the West. The section from the California line down to the Interstate 80 bridge (upstream from Crystal Peak Park) is designated for artificial lures only and is managed as a wild trout area. This section offers a little bit of every kind of water a fly angler could want.

Anglers can catch stocked rainbow, cutthroat, and brown trout throughout the trophy section and down through the cities of Reno and Sparks and beyond. Brown trout populations increase in those areas where the river is warmer because they tolerate changes in water temperature better. Mountain whitefish are caught upstream from Reno. When water flows are high, the fishing can be excellent east of town downstream to Wadsworth.

The Carson River and the East Fork of the Carson offer good fishing for 12- to 15-inch stocked brown, rainbow, and cutthroat trout near Carson City on the Carson River, and above Dresslerville on the East Carson.

The West Walker flows out of Topaz Lake as the Topaz Canal and offers good fishing in Wilson Canyon for 12- to 15-inch stocked rainbows, browns, and cutthroats in the late fall and winter, when irrigation seasons are over and water flows are reduced.

The first 15 miles of the East Walker in Nevada offers excellent fishing for wild browns and rainbows up to 3 pounds. The catch-and-release area once known as the Rosaschi Ranch, and now managed by the Forest Service, is 2 miles from the California border and extends 7 miles. This catch-and-release area has become crowded because of attention to its special designation; however, the adjoining stretches offer fishing that's just as good.

Lahontan Reservoir.   With 10,000 surface acres, 17 miles of length, and nearly 100 miles of shoreline, Lahontan Reservoir is one of the state's top warmwater fisheries. Approximately 20 miles from Fallon, this impoundment has white bass, hybrid stripers, walleye, channel catfish, white catfish, bullhead, yellow perch, largemouth bass, spotted bass, and the occasional rainbow trout.

White bass and 3- to 4-pound wipers concentrate on the confluences of water inflows such as the Truckee Canal and the Carson River at the end of March, and can be caught from shore on a jig or minnow. Popular areas are the No. 9 and 11 beaches. Fish become more widely distributed as the season progresses.

Walleye range up to 14 pounds and are caught where sandy and rocky bottoms combine with emergent vegetation. The end of May signals the beginning of walleye season.

Topaz Lake.   Fishing the January 1 opener at Topaz Lake is a good way to celebrate the new year for many anglers. This popular reservoir offers good boat and shore fishing for stocked rainbows. Boaters troll the rocky eastern shoreline to the mouth and then back up the center of the lake.

Smaller reservoirs.   Central Nevada has numerous other small lakes and reservoirs that offer anglers good opportunities to catch stocked rainbows and some warmwater species, particularly bass. Trout fisheries include Illipah Reservoir, Cave Lake, Groves Lake, and Eagle Valley Reservoir. Trout and bass can both be found at Echo Canyon

 It has been reported that the first tagging of fish in the United States occurred in 1873, when an angler tagged Atlantic salmon in the Penobscot River in Maine.

N

Reservoir and the reservoirs at Kirch Wildlife Management Area—Adams-McGill, Cold Springs, and Haymeadow. The ponds at Mason Valley Wildlife Management Area offer bass and panfish.

Southern Region

Lake Mead.   Located on the southern border of Nevada and Arizona on the Colorado River, Lake Mead was formed when Hoover (now Boulder) Dam was completed in 1935. When full, the water rises to a maximum depth of 590 feet, creating an impoundment that is 110 miles long with 550 miles of shoreline and 162,000 surface acres.

Soon after the dam's completion, the lake was stocked with largemouth bass, black crappie, bluegills, green sunfish, and threadfin shad for forage. To enhance the fishery, biologists tried stocking different species, including striped bass in 1969, although it was not expected that stripers would reproduce in the Colorado system. Reproduction was documented, however, in 1973. Now, the striped bass is the premier gamefish in the reservoir.

The best areas to fish for all species in Lake Mead are in Las Vegas Bay, Calville Bay, and the upper Overton; feeder streams and washes at these sites add nutrients to the lake and enhance the production of forage fish.

Anglers jig cut bait, like frozen anchovies, or troll shad-imitation lures to catch stripers that average 2 pounds. Fish in the 20- to 30-pound range are possible, more commonly in the fall and usually on shad imitations. Beginning in July and continuing through much of the rest of the year, anglers can take striped bass using a variety of topwater lures, often by fishing early and scouting for surface activity.

Largemouth bass are popular at Lake Mead, too. Bass from 4 to 8 pounds are available in addition to smaller specimens. Las Vegas Bay produces good-size bass because of the available nutrients and forage fish.

The Overton Arm is a top spot to fish for black crappie, some of which range up to 3 pounds. Channel catfish up to 8 to 10 pounds are taken on cut anchovies or stinkbaits. Anglers have landed tilapia and smallmouth bass in Lake Mead, although there is no fishery for either, and the lake has a big population of carp.

Lake Mohave and the Colorado River. When Davis Dam, above Laughlin on the Nevada side of the river, was completed in 1951, it formed narrow 67-mile-long Lake Mohave.

The upper 15 miles of the reservoir, where trout are stocked regularly, provides the best fishing for striped bass, which were first found in Mohave in 1980 after being washed over Boulder Dam in high-water years. While most of the stripers in Mohave are less than 14 inches, some weigh up to 60 pounds or more. The best time to pursue them is at night or on slightly breezy days from September through November, on cut anchovies, squid, or large shad-imitating lures.

Striped bass in the Colorado River beneath Davis Dam range from 10 inches to 20 to 30 pounds. Late spring and early summer are good times to fish the river for stripers that have moved up from Arizona's Lake Havasu to spawn.

Anglers can catch stocked trout in the Willow Beach area or below Davis Dam, where there's good access for shore fishing.

Largemouth bass up to 9 pounds inhabit most Mohave coves that have weedbeds, except the cold upper 15 miles, in the spring. When water levels decline in the fall and weedbeds are uncovered is another good time.

Channel catfish up to 15 or 20 pounds are caught throughout the summer on cut bait or stinkbait fished on the bottom. Bluegills are caught throughout the lake below the upper 15 miles.

NEW BRUNSWICK

The largest of the three Maritime Provinces of eastern Canada, New Brunswick is best known for its Atlantic salmon fishing. The province contains several rivers that are among the more renowned and important Atlantic salmon fisheries in North America. In recent years, however, nonresident anglers are also traveling in increasing numbers to this coastal province for smallmouth bass fishing, as New Brunswick has excellent fishing for this species in rivers and lakes.

New Brunswick's inland fishery resource includes 46 freshwater, anadromous, and catadromous fish species. Approximately 90 percent of sportfishing efforts are directed at brook trout, Atlantic salmon, smallmouth bass, landlocked salmon, white perch, yellow perch, and chain pickerel. Only 5 percent of angling effort is directed at coastal species. This is spread among striped bass, American shad, mackerel, cod, flounder, and pollock, and these species are greatly underutilized.

Early summer mornings find Lake Mead's stripers active.

N

New Brunswick attracts many American anglers because of its proximity to the eastern United States; these anglers are primarily interested in salmon and bass. It attracts other Canadian visitors because of its Atlantic salmon. The catch and effort overall for Atlantic salmon have increased in recent years, despite a decline in the total Canadian salmon abundance and catch since 1970. The Miramichi watershed supports 60 to 70 percent of the provincial angler effort for Atlantic salmon. Angling restrictions have been placed on many New Brunswick salmon rivers with insufficient juvenile and adult populations.

Brook trout are the most popular species among resident anglers and are widely available in the province. Effort and catch per day for this species, however, have decreased in recent years, primarily due to overfishing, habitat degradation, and introduction of competitive fish species.

Smallmouth bass angling continues to increase in popularity in southwestern New Brunswick waters. The overall catch of these fish doubled between 1990 and 1995. According to creel surveys, more than 95 percent of bass are released. Other warmwater fish—particularly white perch, yellow perch and chain pickerel—are significantly less popular than the aforementioned species. Ice fishing, which is legal from January 1 through March 31, is permissible in selected waters for all species; this method is not especially popular, although ice fishing in frozen estuaries for smelt has a good following.

Catch and effort for coastal species such as flounder, mackerel, and pollock have remained relatively constant for several decades. Recreational fisheries for striped bass have declined, and highly restrictive harvest limits have been imposed.

Nonresidents are required by law to be accompanied by a licensed guide when angling in New Brunswick's designated Atlantic salmon waters. A licensed guide is not required when angling in other waters for landlocked salmon, brook trout, or smallmouth bass; however, there is no substitute for local knowledge, and the services of a licensed guide are recommended for visitors, at least in the short term.

Atlantic Salmon

Atlantic salmon are locally considered the "king" of sportfish, a reputation derived from their strong fight and acrobatics when hooked. They are the fish most sought after by nonresident anglers.

New Brunswick rivers currently produce 80 percent of the Maritime Provinces' overall Atlantic salmon fishery. In the past, when the commercial fishery was operating, Canada harvested about 17 percent of the world's Atlantic salmon, of which 25 percent were fish originating in New Brunswick.

Atlantic salmon inhabit nearly every stream with unrestricted access to the sea. Adult salmon are known to frequent 100 streams and rivers, and approximately 50 of these support an angling

Anglers fish the Miramichi River for Atlantic salmon.

fishery. The best known salmon waters in New Brunswick are the Miramichi, Restigouche, Saint John, and Tobique Rivers. The Main Southwest Miramichi, which is extremely popular, is a lovely, long, winding, generally shallow river with many bars and pools, and it is an easy river to wade under most circumstances. It is wide by the standards of most trout anglers, and its regular visitors are known for long casting, although that is not an absolute necessity.

New Brunswick offers 2,528 kilometers of fishable salmon waters, of which 850 kilometers provide unrestricted public access. Approximately 45 percent of the salmon water is adjacent to private or freehold property, and landowner permission is required to angle there. The province leases about 7 percent, or 182 kilometers, of good salmon water to clubs and corporate interests. Another 205 kilometers of Crown Reserve water is available exclusively to residents fortunate enough to have their applications drawn from a lottery-type process.

On the Miramichi system, access to private waters is readily available through several lodges catering to visiting anglers. Guests at these operations enjoy exclusive angling on the waters controlled by the host lodge. The Restigouche system is accessible only to anglers invited as guests of the controlling club or corporate interests. The Saint John and Tobique Rivers are public domain and readily accessible.

Angling for Atlantic salmon in New Brunswick was first recognized as sport in the 1850s, but took on a modern popularity only after World War II. Since the 1920s, Atlantic salmon abundance has declined substantially. Although Atlantic salmon returns from the ocean have been declining, most juvenile populations in New Brunswick's rivers appear reasonably healthy. Anglers remain optimistic that improvements in salmon returns to the rivers and to the recreational fishery will occur.

Fly fishing is the only legal method of angling for Atlantic salmon in this province. Atlantic

N

salmon angling has historically been that of catch-and-retain, yet hook-and-release regulations for all large salmon greater than 63 centimeters (25 inches) in total length were implemented in New Brunswick in 1984. The province has a season-total bag limit of eight grilse (fish less than 63 centimeters in total length). Nonresident anglers require a guide when angling for salmon. Angler catches have averaged 41,645 grilse (42 percent released) and 14,800 multi-sea-winter fish (100 percent mandatory release) during the period 1987 to 1995. This is for combined kelt and bright fish.

Nonresidents continue to go to New Brunswick to angle for salmon regardless of the requirements for guides or the lower catches in the past few years. Angler and nonangler alike recognize the importance of the fishery to the economy of the province, especially to the smaller communities along the rivers. More than 100 businesses provide outfitting services to salmon anglers.

Atlantic salmon season opens annually on April 15; this includes the time frame referred to as kelt fishing, as there is no longer a distinct kelt season. Actual angling opportunity begins when the rivers are ice-free.

New Brunswick has two distinct Atlantic salmon fisheries, the kelt, or "spring," fishery and the summer, or "bright," fishery.

The kelt fishery is primarily focused on the Miramichi system and runs from opening day until late May. This fishery focuses on Atlantic salmon that are descending the river, having spent the winter under the ice. Local terminology describes these as "black" salmon; however, this is clearly a misnomer, as fish regain their bright ocean camouflage immediately upon starting their descent. This is the only time when Atlantic salmon actively feed while in freshwater and are therefore eager to take a fly. Angling for kelts is almost entirely done from a boat, in high, coldwater conditions. The most common tackle is 8- or 9-weight full-sink or sink-tip lines, 9- to 10-foot rods, and large, brightly colored streamer flies.

The bright fishery is focused on the timing of runs, and the timing varies from river to river. The earliest fish show up in the Restigouche system in early June, in the Saint John in mid-June, and in the Miramichi in early July. Peak timing on all systems is the first three weeks of July. The Miramichi system receives a second important run in mid-September, and enjoys excellent angling from then until the season closure in mid-October; the availability of these fish is subject to annual variation, depending on water levels, rainfall, and temperatures.

Most angling on the Restigouche is from long motorized canoes, whereas on the other rivers it is by wading. In all cases, the most common tackle is 8- or 9-weight floating lines, 9- to 14-foot leaders (8- to 12-pound tippets), reels that hold 150 yards of 25-pound backing, 9- or 10-foot rods, and both wet and dry flies in sizes 2 to 10.

The importance of Atlantic salmon angling to New Brunswick is reflected in the province's decision to proclaim an Atlantic salmon fly as an official symbol in 1993. The symbolic salmon fly was designated as the "Picture Province" and designed by Warren Duncan. It comprised the following: a tag of gold symbolizing the value of Atlantic salmon to New Brunswick; a butt of green floss honoring the fiddlehead; a tail of red goose fibers to match Canada's flag, indicating New Brunswick's ties with the nation; a body of cranberry, as cranberry is one of New Brunswick's official colors; a rib of medium oval gold tinsel; a hackle of lemon yellow, which is the background color of New Brunswick's flag; and a wing of hair from the black bear, which roams widely in the province.

Landlocked Salmon

Landlocked salmon are managed in approximately 40 lakes and two rivers, all located in the Saint John, Musquash, Magaguadavic, and St. Croix watersheds in New Brunswick. Landlocked and sea-run salmon have similar life cycles, except adult landlocked salmon substitute freshwater lakes for the ocean. The importance of landlocked salmon to the recreational fishery has increased substantially over the past decade with the implementation of an effective stocking program that produces native strains of fish. Restrictive daily catches and minimum length limits have also improved the quality of the fishery.

Lakes that support landlocked salmon have basically clean, cool, well-oxygenated water. Other physical and biological requirements include adequate forage species and access to suitable spawning/nursery grounds. Sixteen lakes, notably East Grand, Chamcook, Magaguadavic, Digdeguash, Oromocto, Loch Alva, Crystal, and Sisson, currently provide the majority of the landlocked salmon fisheries in New Brunswick. River fisheries occur in the St. Croix and Magaguadavic Rivers.

The present landlocked salmon distribution is heavily weighted toward the southwestern portion of the province. The remaining populations are randomly scattered throughout northwestern and southeastern New Brunswick. In total, New Brunswick's landlocked salmon lakes cover less than 150,000 acres, with the southwest having more than three-quarters of the provincial total.

The best landlocked salmon fishing occurs in the four- to five-week period following ice out and again in September. Trolling with tandem streamer flies or minnow-imitating plugs is the most popular and productive technique.

The demand on landlocked salmon continues to increase, although effort is light in comparison with many other jurisdictions in eastern Canada and the U.S. Fishing pressure has especially increased on the prime landlocked salmon waters. Landlocked salmon angling, to many anglers, offers a suitable alternative to brook trout and sea-run Atlantic salmon fishing, and with ample opportunity to harvest fish for the table as well.

Brook Trout

As the most abundant coldwater gamefish in New Brunswick, the brook trout has always been, and still is, the most sought-after species by resident anglers. Brook trout are found virtually everywhere in the province, with the exception of acid peat moss lakes in the eastern region. This includes many coastal rivers and streams. Most bodies of water, with the exception of a few in the north-central region of the province, are now accessible to the brook trout angler.

New Brunswick contains approximately 40,000 kilometers of streams that are suitable habitat for brook trout, and more than 2,000 lakes that contain this species. The most productive brook trout lakes are small, less than 80 hectares. The biggest concentration of lakes under 80 hectares is in the northern and western portions of the province, while the largest lakes are in the southern portion. The absence of predatory species such as chain pickerel and smallmouth bass in northern and western drainages benefits brook trout production.

The average size of brook trout in the province is 5 centimeters by the end of the first growing season, 10 to 13 centimeters after the second, and 20 to 25 centimeters after the third. Brook trout older than five years are rare, with two- and three-year-olds constituting the bulk of the catch. Brook trout in certain lakes have reached 2 to 3 kilograms.

Some New Brunswick brook trout migrate to saltwater or brackish water, where they put on extra growth and become known locally as "sea trout." Virtually all coastal rivers and streams once had sea-run fish; however, sea-run populations of brook trout have been declining due to increased predation by seals and overexploitation by anglers. The Miramichi River system offers excellent opportunity for angling. Stems of note include Cains River, North Branch Main Southwest Miramichi River, Beadle Brook, Dungarvon River, and the Northwest Miramichi River. The Tabusintac River is another excellent river for sea-run brook trout.

Migratory behavior is variable from river to river, but in all cases, growth in the estuary and marine environment is rapid. Returning fish may weigh as much as 3 kilograms, although the average is considerably less.

New Brunswick waters still provide good-quality brook trout fishing, although the number of larger fish available has decreased. In some waters, recreational angling has contributed to reduced stocks. In recent years, however, effort for this species has been reduced overall, partly as a result of a shift in angler preference to smallmouth bass angling and of the introduction of competitive fish species.

Most of New Brunswick's trout lakes have natural or wild fish. The lakes with the best wild specimens tend to occur in waters that are distant from major population centers, and many are in geologically elevated areas.

Generally the best fishing is from mid-May through late June. After this time, brook trout congregate in coldwater spring holes; at this time, intimate local knowledge is required for success. The most popular method of fishing for brook trout is with live worms and a small spinner. Fly anglers use standard streamer patterns in the early season and match the hatch as the season wears on.

The stocking of 120 lakes with up to 190,000 brook trout per year has resulted in the creation of additional angling opportunities for fish of 20-centimeters and larger. Hatchery releases, however, account for a minute portion of the total brook trout catch.

Smallmouth Bass

Although smallmouth bass are not native to the province, increased interest and enthusiasm have been demonstrated by anglers, and this species now ranks second in popularity with nonresidents. Smallmouth bass were introduced into New Brunswick about 1870, and have become established throughout southwestern New Brunswick in the Saint John, Magaguadavic, and St. Croix drainages.

Self-sustaining populations of smallmouths are known to inhabit 40 lakes, which range from shallow mesotrophic ponds to deep, clear oligotrophic lakes having both warmwater and coldwater fisheries. The provincial government has taken a cautious approach in establishing smallmouth bass populations outside its present range. The geographical range of the smallmouth bass has been extended in recent years through the good intentions but illegal actions of individual anglers. Bass are opportunistic, competitive, and hardy, and in some instances are responsible for the decline of brook trout populations.

The most obvious of New Brunswick's smallmouth bass waters is the massive (60-mile-long) lake just north of the capital city of Fredericton, locally called the Mactaquac Headpond. This is an impoundment of the St. John River and it has plentiful, and large, smallmouths. Most of the other rock- and boulder-laden smallmouth lakes in southwestern New Brunswick are easy to find and cool enough to provide good angling throughout the summer. Among the more notable ones are Harvey, Oromocto, East Grand, Little Magaguadavic, and George. These are places where you can fish with a guide or on your own (if the latter, be extremely careful, as some are tricky to navigate), and they hold enough bass to provide reasonable success even when angling conditions aren't prime.

Some good river fishing is possible as well. One of the most notable waters is the Meduxnekeag River from Jackson Falls to Woodstock (which also has nice brown trout). A wide range of tackle

N

choices makes fishing suitable to anglers of all interests, but fly and spinning gear are favored, especially early in the season.

Natives of New Brunswick have only recently recognized the social and economic benefits of smallmouth bass, as bass fishing increased dramatically in the 1980s and 1990s. Catches increased approximately eightfold. One unique aspect of this fishery is the ability of bass to be successfully hooked and released. This provides an opportunity to increase angling effort without greatly affecting total mortality.

The spawning period in New Brunswick is from mid-May to mid-June but varies slightly from year to year and area to area depending on water temperature and spring freshet. The best angling also occurs from mid-May to mid-June and picks up again from late August through the season closure in mid-October. Although smallmouth bass weighing more than 5 pounds have been caught in New Brunswick, most bass average $1\frac{1}{2}$ to 2 pounds.

Other Species

Brown trout/lake trout. New Brunswick has a limited brown trout population. These fish occur in the Loch Lomond Lakes, Meduxnekeag River, and the lower Digdeguash River system, and are most popular with a handful of anglers from those areas. The average size is 1 pound, with specimens in the 3- to 5-pound range not uncommon.

Lake trout inhabit 12 lakes in the province. The most notable of these are Long and Serpentine Lakes in the north, and Chamcook Lake in the south. To most provincial anglers, fishing for lakers is strictly an ice-out fishery, enjoyed by trolling with assorted lures and tandem streamers. The average size is 2 to 5 pounds, with an occasional fish over 10 pounds.

American shad. Shad are a virtually overlooked fishery in New Brunswick. They are most abundant in the Saint John and Miramichi Rivers, and angling effort is concentrated predominantly in the latter. In the vast lower reaches of the Saint John River, concentrations of shad are difficult to locate and are not normally a targeted species. Because the Miramichi is a designated Atlantic salmon river, fishing for shad there is with flies only. The best fishing is during the first three weeks of June. Suggested tackle is an 8- or 9-weight outfit, with sinking-tip lines, 4- to 8-foot leaders, and unweighted white or yellow flies.

White perch. The white perch is known to inhabit 28 lakes in New Brunswick, all but one in the southwestern region. This species is also found in the St. Croix, Bocabec, Gaspereau, Miramichi, and Saint John Rivers. Lakes known to have good angling populations include North, McAdam, Bolton, and Second Eel.

New Brunswick anglers catch a fair number of these good table fish annually. The largest recorded fish taken from freshwater weighed 4.75 pounds and was 19 inches long— several times larger than the average catch. Most white perch are caught in freshwater, but some are taken from waters in the upper estuaries. Saltwater populations along the New Brunswick coastline are scattered and of small size.

The best white perch angling occurs just after ice out and again in mid-September, primarily with spinning gear and angle worms or small plastic jigs and grubs.

Yellow perch. Yellow perch exist throughout the province and are treated as coarse fish by most anglers in New Brunswick, although some angle for them as table fare. Endemic to many waters in New Brunswick, yellow perch are found in all counties except Albert and are particularly abundant in the southwestern region. The species is documented in 82 lakes and several streams, and has been found in the Miramichi River estuary. The highest catches occur in the Saint John watershed followed by the St. Croix and Miramichi drainages.

Yellow perch reach 38 centimeters in length in the Canaan River, but in most waters they average 17 to 23 centimeters. They are caught quite shallow here in the summer. There are no creel limits or minimum length limits for the yellow perch, which does not have sportfish status. Angling for yellow perch in inland waters is restricted to those seasons that are open for sportfish.

Saltwater and Estuarial Fisheries

The New Brunswick coastline is irregular, possessing deep bays, inlets, and estuaries. It is distinguished by its border with the 160-mile long Bay of Fundy, which is narrow in the headwaters region and produces remarkable 30- to 50-foot variations between high and low tides. Lower estuarial and coastal species in New Brunswick include smelt, striped bass, American shad, mackerel, cod, flounder, pollock, and dogfish sharks. Guide or charter boat services are minimal at best. Visitors are best advised to consult with locals at the wharves in the numerous fishing communities along the coast.

The majority of angling effort occurs in Passamaquoddy Bay, Bay of Chaleur to the northeast, and Northumberland Strait, which separates New Brunswick from Prince Edward Island. Striped bass, cod, and mackerel are angled in northern coastal or estuarial waters, whereas cod, flounder, and pollock are caught primarily in Bay of Fundy waters to the south. Striped bass are taken primarily in Tabusintac, Richibucto, Kouchibouguac, Nepisiguit, and Miramichi estuaries, and to a lesser extent the lower Saint John River.

New Brunswick has two distinct populations of striped bass. One is that of the most northern strain of this species in the southern Gulf of St. Lawrence. These fish primarily spawn in the Miramichi estuary and migrate locally in the southern Gulf of St. Lawrence. They average 2 to 3 pounds; 20-pounders are considered trophy size.

Overexploitation by both commercial and sport-fishing interests has contributed to declining numbers. The commercial fishery, including the sale of bycatch, has been stopped. Angling for these fish is restricted to catch-and-release only. Most angling effort occurs in the Miramichi, Tabusintac, and Nepisiguit estuaries.

The other striped bass population is a migratory one that spawns in rivers of the Bay of Fundy. It is part of the same population that migrates through American coastal waters south to Florida; New Brunswick waters are the extreme northern edge of its range. The average size of these stripers is 6 to 8 pounds, but some are in the 30- to 40-pound class. Anglers are permitted to retain one fish (check the size limit) per day, with a minimum size restriction. The decline in population is attributable to man-made structures, such as the Mactaquac Dam on the Saint John River and a municipal causeway across the Petticodiac River in the Moncton/Riverview area, which prohibit these fish from reaching their spawning grounds. Most angling effort is concentrated in the estuaries of the Saint John, St. Croix, and Magaguadavic Rivers.

The potential for saltwater angling expansion along the province's extensive coastline is huge, as hundreds of thousands of angler days could be supported without overexploitation of prolific species, especially mackerel, flounder, dogfish, and pollock.

NEWFOUNDLAND AND LABRADOR

Canada's easternmost province comprises two geographically separate and distinct areas: Newfoundland, a large island of more than 42,000 square miles situated off Canada's east coast, and Labrador, a much larger landmass of nearly 115,000 square miles lying to the northeast of Quebec. Each boasts a wide variety of freshwater, as well as limited saltwater, sportfishing opportunities.

In Newfoundland, the major interests are rainbow trout, brown trout, brook trout (locally called Eastern brook trout), anadromous (sea-run) brown and rainbow (steelhead) trout, sea-run brook trout, arctic charr, and Atlantic salmon. In Labrador they are Atlantic salmon, brook trout, ouananiche (land-locked Atlantic salmon), sea-run brook trout, northern pike, whitefish, burbot, arctic charr, lake trout, landlocked charr, and splake.

Salmon are of special interest in this province. About 60 percent of North America's Atlantic salmon rivers exist here. More than 180 waterways have been identified as rivers with significant migrations of salmon. Several smaller flowages sustain small annual salmon runs. The major streams are called "scheduled" rivers and are restricted to fly fishing during the short summer season between early June and early September. Two rivers—the Humber and Gander—have later runs and also offer an extended period of catch-and-release angling lasting through the end of September.

In freshwater, the majority of river angling is restricted to fly fishing and casting techniques; in most large lakes and ponds, various methods are permitted, including trolling or angling with lures and baits.

Saltwater angling is generally confined to stream estuaries, where sea-run brown, rainbow, or brook trout prepare to migrate upstream. Local anglers occasionally pursue mackerel by lure and spinning rod, and a fledgling shark fishery with heavier tackle is gaining popularity among tour boat owners.

The giant bluefin tuna fishery that once existed in eastern Newfoundland disappeared with declines in such food fish as capelin and herring. Collapse of northern cod stocks due to overharvesting has virtually eliminated the commercial cod fishery. "Cod jigging," a traditional method of snagging codfish with a strong waxed-cord line and heavily weighted hook, has been a mainstay of the resident food fishery for centuries, but even this practice is under strict control and annual review. The need to rebuild stocks has put any permanent recreational saltwater fishery for groundfish, especially cod and halibut, on the back burner for the immediate future.

One Russian Beluga sturgeon was weighed in at 3,359 pounds.

Newfoundland

A large, sparsely populated island, Newfoundland is about equal in size to the combined states of Maine and New Hampshire and has a surprising 8,498 miles of rugged coastline. About one-third of the island's population of 500,000 resides in the capital city of St. John's and surrounding communities on the east coast's Avalon Peninsula.

Although Newfoundland has a modern highway system, it is accessible to nonresidents only by air or sea. Four airports serve the island portion of Newfoundland: Deer Lake and Stephenville on the west coast, Gander near mid-island, and St. John's on the east coast. Major carriers fly into these, and smaller regional airlines service outlying areas. Large, oceangoing ferries transport vehicles and passengers from North Sydney, Nova Scotia, to Port aux Basques, Newfoundland, on a year-round basis, a 90-mile jaunt that lasts about 6 hours. During summer months an alternate service lands on the southeast coast at Argentia, site of a former U.S. naval base. This crossing takes about 16 hours and is available twice weekly. Anglers wishing to spend some time in Newfoundland with their own vehicles have these choices; in both instances, reservations are recommended.

The Trans-Canada Highway runs across Newfoundland for 540 miles, from Port aux Basques to St. John's, with paved secondary roads opening access to coastal communities. Modern lodging, restaurants, and other facilities across the island provide a variety of services and amenities for the traveling angler, the majority of whom are interested in salmon.

Thanks largely to a moratorium on commercial salmon nets and a buyout of most commercial

N

salmon licenses imposed by the Canadian government in 1991, Atlantic salmon stocks have made a strong recovery. This political decision was hailed by many anglers as one of the most significant conservation actions of the twentieth century. The vast majority of commercial fishermen relinquished their salmon licenses, and wild Atlantic salmon are now free to enter streams directly from their ocean feeding grounds without encountering gillnet obstructions.

All rivers on the island are considered "public" water. Although all of the scheduled salmon rivers are open to nonresident anglers, they must employ local guides or outfitters. Many government-inspected and -licensed outfitters and guiding services offer packages in various locations across the island. Facilities range from rustic to resort class.

For those seeking privacy and an undisturbed wilderness setting, some outfitters provide access to remote rivers inland or along the island's south coast, where there are no (or very few) roads. Tourists are able to fish within a half mile (800 meters) of a provincial highway for trout only, without hiring a guide, which offers family recreational opportunities.

Salmon populations in most rivers are dominated by grilse—salmon that have been at sea only one year before returning to spawn. These fish generally measure under 26 inches and weigh 6 pounds or less. With escapement of large salmon from commercial nets and an increase of repeat-spawning grilse, the relative mix of larger salmon to grilse has increased significantly.

In addition to salmon, the island of Newfoundland contains some of the world's most productive, and interesting, trout waters. Sea-run brook trout, brown trout, and rainbow trout enter many of the island's rivers at various times of the spring and summer. Visitors to St. John's might consider bringing along a fly rod, as some of the best brown trout angling can be found on several streams weaving through the city.

Most small ponds or lakes contain populations of small, wild resident Eastern brook trout, called "mud trout" by residents. In the more remote areas of the island that have limited access, 2- or 3-pound brook trout can be caught on occasion.

Near L'Anse aux Meadows, a UNESCO World Heritage site where Vikings landed and settled in North America long before Columbus, lies Pistolet Bay and its rivers. Here, wild arctic charr can be attracted by skilled fly anglers.

Arctic charr that escaped an aquaculture-rearing project inhabit Grand Lake on the west coast. At 87 miles long, Grand is the island's largest lake. Another product of aquaculture escapement, the rainbow trout, is found in the Bay d'Espoir area of the south coast, where large specimens may be taken below the hydrogenerating plant.

Western region. The west coast of Newfoundland has some of the finest salmon rivers in the province. Typical rivers are spate streams—crystal clear and icy cold—which peak during the spring breakup and become more logy as summer progresses. They are fed from the Long Range Mountain highlands, a plateau that rises majestically some 2,000 feet from the coast and extends from Port aux Basques to the tip of the Great Northern Peninsula. The Trans-Canada Highway and other roads in the provincial network pass over many of these rivers, providing ready access to nearby salmon pools.

Angling pioneer Lee Wulff made many of these rivers well known in his writing and films. They include the Grand Codroy, Serpentine, Harry's, River of Ponds, Portland Creek, Lomond, and the mighty Humber. Other rivers of interest include Crabbes, Robinsons, Southwest Brook, Bottom Brook, Sop's Arm, Main River, Fishell's, St. Genevieve, Castors, Big East, and Torrent, although these are just a few. Numerous opportunities to pursue Atlantic salmon exist on this coast.

The dominant waterway is the Humber River, which begins high in the mountains behind Gros Morne National Park and, after flowing nearly 90 miles, exits into the Bay of Islands near the modern city of Corner Brook. The Lower Humber is known for its genetic strain of large salmon that can tip the scales at more than 50 pounds, and each season experienced veterans are able to subdue and release salmon in this weight class.

One mecca for resident salmon anglers on the Upper Humber River is Sir Richard Squires Park. This site is accessible by road and lies to the northeast of Deer Lake via the community of Cormack. The river here is wide and shallow, and dominated by Big Falls, a natural barrier that temporarily slows fish migration. Peak runs usually occur here in early July and last for three to four weeks.

Popular salmon flies are the Blue Charm, Thunder & Lightning, Orange Puppy, Green Highlander, and many more that are variations of classic British patterns. The original complicated feather wings are generally replaced with a thatch of black moose hair, which is plentiful on the island. Productive locally tied flies are readily available at area stores.

As noted, Pistolet Bay at the top of the Northern Peninsula has small runs of arctic charr, while Eastern brook trout may be found in numerous lakes and ponds throughout the west coast. Sea-run brook trout can be caught later in the summer at most estuaries. The Cloud River is a popular sea trout river on the northeast side of the peninsula. The Cloud also contains Atlantic salmon and is accessible primarily by boat from the community of Roddickton.

Grand Lake, and interconnecting Sandy and Birchy Lakes, contain landlocked salmon, known here as ouananiche, as well as trophy-size brook trout and aquaculture-raised charr escapees. Spring season, just after ice-out, is the best time to pursue these species, usually with spinning tackle or live bait.

Access to Grand Lake is in the community of Howley, which is about 20 road miles east of Deer Lake.

Several ponds in the interior of the Great Northern Peninsula are accessible by a series of woods roads and offer casual fishing for brook trout. Many of the larger or more remote watersheds such as Bluey, Adies Lake, Star Lake, Cat Arm Reservoir, Ten Mile Lake, and Southwest Pond once held trout in the 5-pound class, and a few such specimens are still taken from time to time, although the relative size declined as woods-road construction provided ease of access.

Gros Morne National Park near Bonne Bay manages its own salmon rivers and resources, and requires a special park fishing license for angling. These are available at park offices.

South coast. Most salmon rivers of the south coast are isolated and difficult to access, and these conditions have preserved excellent angling for Atlantic salmon. Rivers such as the Garia, LaPoile, and Grey are accessible only via a boat trip on saltwater from small communities, or by helicopter.

A partially paved road system leads from the Trans-Canada Highway through a rugged landscape to Burgeo, once a prosperous south coast fishing community, and the site of Grandy's Brook. The road also provides access to interior lakes and ponds that provide recreational angling for trout and landlocked salmon. It is a popular jumping off point for canoeists.

Due to their isolation, most south coast rivers receive low resident pressure, and the quality of angling is excellent, although a high percentage of salmon here are grilse. Outfitters provide nonresident access to these remote areas.

The Conne River, in addition to salmon angling, sustains a limited food fishery for the Conne River Indian Band, Newfoundland's only status band with a reserve located in Baie d'Espoir. A major attraction here is the river below the Baie d'Espoir hydroelectric facility, where escaped pen-raised rainbow trout are plentiful and can be taken readily by lure or fly throughout a long season.

Interior region. In central Newfoundland, the Exploits and Gander Rivers, and their tributaries, dominate the much flatter landscape. Both rivers were monitored for several years by counting fences and showed significant increases in salmon populations following the moratorium. By the late 1990s, the runs on each had increased from an average of 5,000 to 7,000 fish in previous years to more than 25,000. The Exploits watershed, including connecting lakes and ponds, is the island's longest at more than 200 miles.

The lower portion of the Exploits is readily accessible and is most popular with resident anglers, as it flows near the communities of Bishops Falls and Grand Falls–Windsor. At peak times, hundreds of anglers can be observed from the Exploits bridge near Bishops Falls as they fish local pools by wading or from boats.

A project completed in the late 1990s at the Exploits River near Grand Falls-Windsor is a migration bypass route and Salmon Interpretation Centre. Spearheaded by the Environment Resources Management Association volunteer group, the complex provides a glass-walled viewing area for visitors to watch salmon on their way upstream. The fish ladder provides an unobstructed path for salmon to reach spawning areas farther upriver.

A hidden gem of the Exploits is Great Rattling Brook, a small, intimate tributary that contains a high percentage of large salmon. Accessible by a gravel woods road and short hike, or with the aid of a local outfitter, the stream contains numerous small pools and excellent dry-fly water.

Farther east, the main stem of the Gander River is roughly 32 miles long as it exits from Gander Lake near the community of Appleton and enters saltwater at George's Point in Gander Bay. The river is shallow and contains four ponds, or "steadies" as they are known locally, connected by intimidating rapids and narrows. There are numerous pools on this river, and the ratio of salmon to grilse is good. The Northwest Gander is a major tributary that wanders through a remote wilderness area as it nears headwaters.

Much of the main river is accessible only by boat, and a unique river craft has been developed over decades to navigate the shallow and often narrow access points. The Gander River boat is a 25-foot-long freighter canoe built from locally cut and seasoned spruce planks and juniper ribbing. A typical craft is powered by a 20-horsepower outboard. Intimate knowledge of the river is a must, and local guides have passed this information down from generation to generation.

The Gander River Management Association secured approval from the provincial government to initiate a pilot project in a specific watershed management scheme. Begun in 1997, it was the first for the province and included a special Gander River license to fish these waters. The permits are available at local stores and through any of several outfitters.

In a similar pilot project, regeneration of the Indian Bay watershed near Gander began in the early 1990s and was designed to rebuild populations of the trophy brook trout that were once plentiful in this series of interconnected ponds and streams. Positive achievements have resulted, and large trout stocks there have been rebuilding.

Other salmon rivers of interest in the central region include the Indian River located near Springdale, the Gambo River to the east of Gander, and the Terra Nova River, a popular cottage area where a successful rebuilding of salmon stocks was achieved in a project led by the local rural development association.

Eastern region. The eastern region as described here excludes the Avalon Peninsula but does include several salmon rivers located on the Burin Peninsula and watersheds. These are within the Bay du Nord Provincial Wilderness Reserve.

The existence of rods for fishing dates back to 2000 B.C. in Egypt, but the use of rods for more than just an extension of the line didn't come about until the advent of flycasting in the eighteenth century.

N

The most significant waterway here is Long Harbour River, with lesser streams including Bay d'Loup, Piper's Hole, North Harbour, and Northwest. Many rivers are accessible by road or a short hike.

Terra Nova National Park lies between Glovertown and Port Blandford, and, as in the case with Gros Morne, a special park license is required to fish on salmon rivers within park boundaries.

There are many secondary streams on the Bonavista and Burin Peninsulas that have small runs of Atlantic salmon and sea-run trout. One such stream near Clarenville, the Shoal Harbour River, is unique due to a resource mix that includes sea-run and resident brook trout, brown trout, rainbow trout, Atlantic salmon, and the remnants of an experimental Pacific pink salmon introduction from the 1960s.

Rivers in this area generally have earlier migrations of salmon than west coast or central rivers and are populated primarily by grilse. Most interior areas offer angling for brook trout and landlocked salmon. A handful of outfitters provide access to the few salmon rivers lying within boundaries of the Bay du Nord Wilderness Reserve.

Avalon Peninsula. The Avalon Peninsula, which is as far east as you can go in North America, contains the highest density of human population and the widest diversity of salmonid species on the island. Rainbow, brook, and brown trout, as well as Atlantic salmon, can all be caught on rivers of the Avalon.

Visitors to St. John's are often surprised to learn that excellent brown trout angling is available on streams that flow through the city center and border on busy thoroughfares or meander through residential areas. The Waterford River, Quidi Vidi, and Long Pond are among the best bets for quick, casual fly fishing.

Indigenous species are highlighted in a glass-walled fluvarium at the Freshwater Resource Centre, where visitors may see fish in their natural habitat. This site on Long Pond is a stone's throw from Confederation Building, the seat of government; across the pond are the grounds of Memorial University. Brown trout are plentiful in Long Pond and connecting streams.

Large anadromous brown trout of more than 20 pounds have been caught within a half-hour drive of the capital at other parts of the Avalon Peninsula. Sites include Renews River estuary, Cape Royal, Bay Bulls, Manuels River, Kelligrews River, and Topsail Beach, to name but a few.

Rainbow trout inhabit several rivers and ponds between St. John's and Portugal Cove, including Three Island Pond, Ocean Pond, Great Cove, and Gallow's Cove Pond.

The Avalon's top salmon river is the Salmonier. Other salmon streams include the Renous, Biscay Bay, Northwest Trepassey, Branch, and Little Salmonier. The Rocky River and Colinet River,

virtually destroyed by commercial overfishing, have slowly recovered thanks to projects by local conservation organizations.

Small brook trout are found in most ponds of the Avalon Peninsula, especially within boundaries of the Avalon Wilderness Reserve, where access is limited. Other productive ponds are located near the Witless Bay line and St. Mary's Bay.

Many Avalon-area salmon anglers, however, prefer a trip to less-populated regions of the province, where abundance and choices of rivers may be greater and crowding less a problem.

Labrador

For a genuine wilderness experience and quality of angling equal to the world's top exotic locales, Labrador still ranks among the best. There are few remaining pristine wilderness areas in eastern North America that contain such a diversity of resources as Labrador, and there is plenty of elbow room. This huge landmass contains a population of only 35,000 people; this distribution is akin to spreading the population of Bangor, Maine, over an area as large as all of the New England states. To say it is underpopulated is a gross understatement.

This enormous region is dotted with hundreds of pristine lakes and raging rivers, expansive forests of fir and spruce, and some of eastern North America's highest mountains. Labrador has a diversity of landscapes, ranging from breathtaking fiords rising from the sea to giant icebergs floating south on the Labrador current, resembling a fleet of white sailing ships on the horizon.

Several species inhabit the waters of Labrador, including northern pike, lake trout, splake, landlocked salmon, brook trout, landlocked charr, and whitefish in the south and west; Atlantic salmon in coastal rivers; and sea-run arctic charr in the northern areas.

Dozens of government-inspected and -licensed outfitters provide access to nonresident anglers, who are required by provincial regulation to hire outfitter services above 52° north latitude. This includes most of Labrador. Facilities vary from simple and efficient to opulent and luxurious, and a range of creature comforts is offered. Most of the fishing camps are fly-in operations, and pressure on their resources is minimal.

The majority of outfitters impose catch-and-release restrictions; retention of one or two trophy fish enables them to preserve the quality of the fishery. Fly fishing for trout and salmon is particularly popular, but casting with spinning gear and some trolling are also practiced. Atlantic salmon are enticed to any of the normal hair-wing patterns and to large Bomber dry flies constructed of spun and clipped deer hair and a bright orange palmered hackle. The Bomber and smaller Orange Bug are also good for taking large trout.

Fishing with large flies for big brook trout (and to some extent northern pike), especially surface

Excellent brook trout fishing exists in streams like this in Labrador.

products such as hair mice, is a Labrador phenomenon that has to be seen to be believed. One reason why large surface flies work so well, sometimes drifted freely and sometimes skittered or riffled across the surface, is that brook trout here include lemmings in their diet. It is not unusual to capture a trout with a belly containing one or more of these creatures. Although mouse imitations work on these fish, such large flies as the Bomber, Muddler Minnow, and Woolly Worm are also effective.

In addition to lemmings, Labrador is known for its large hexagenia hatches, although other natural insect foods include stoneflies, mayflies, caddis, and sedges. Good trout flies here include stimulators and enticers, Stoneflies, Irresistibles, Muddlers, Wulffs, and most of the insect simulations. Charr are normally taken on lures and spinning tackle but provide an excellent challenge for fly fishing. Small, dark nymphs or brightly colored streamers are good choices for charr. Lake trout and pike are caught on a wide range of offerings, as are landlocked salmon.

Roads are few in Labrador, and travel to the vast interior has been limited to float-equipped aircraft or helicopters. This isolation has helped in part to preserve Labrador's fabulous angling resources and pristine wilderness. The Trans-Labrador Highway has opened road access to towns such as Happy Valley-Goose Bay, but is normally under construction or repair due to extreme weather conditions, and motorists should exercise caution. A road is planned along the east coast to connect the

communities of Red Bay and Cartwright. Once a link is completed between Cartwright and Happy Valley-Goose Bay, road access to much of Labrador will be a reality.

One railway operates within the province and connects Sept-Iles, Quebec, with Shefferville, Quebec, in the north and has a spur line running to Wabush-Labrador City. Passengers and vehicles are carried on this, but its primary role is to transport iron ore pellets from mine to market.

There is scheduled air service from mainland points to airports at Happy Valley-Goose Bay, Churchill Falls, and Wabush-Labrador City. Smaller airlines connect with most coastal communities and to points within the province. Most visitors arrive by air to these sites, then connect with their outfitter for further travel, especially by floatplane.

Western region. In western Labrador, the iron ore mining towns of Wabush-Labrador City are step-off points to access interior lakes and streams via float-equipped aircraft. Most watersheds here are affected by the enormous Smallwood Reservoir and its series of electronically operated dams, which control water flow through giant turbines at the distant Churchill Falls.

The Ashuanipi River system connects two large watersheds, Menihek Lake to the North and Ashuanipi Lake to the south. Lac Joseph and Atikonak Lake are two enormous watersheds that lie to the southeast of Labrador City-Wabush; lakes to the north and east include Shaw, Dyke, Crossroads,

N

Ashtray, Albert, Woods, Lobstick, Gabbro, and Andre. Fly-in outfitting camps are located on many of these waterways. These lakes and numerous others are affected by energy needs at Churchill Falls, one of the world's largest hydroelectric-generating facilities, and they are all a part of the massive Smallwood Reservoir system.

The fish species of this region include northern pike, lake trout, splake, brook trout, whitefish, burbot, and ouananiche (landlocked salmon). The 22-pound, 11-ounce world-record landlocked salmon was caught on Smallwood Reservoir at Lobstick Dam in 1983, and several more have come close to breaking that record.

Lake trout to 40 pounds, and northern pike in the 20- to 30-pound range, have been caught in the reservoir, although lakers in this region are usually in the 8- to 15-pound class and pike are in the 5- to 12-pound range. Really big specimens are rare; however, in some places you can catch lakers one right after the other, and in other places plenty of pike, although there's not much in the way of traditional weedbed fishing. Whitefish and trophy-size brook trout favor the rapids below the various dam structures, where water is normally cold and highly oxygenated. These have high concentrations of whitefish, a plentiful food base that attracts the other, larger species. Indeed, whitefish are plentiful enough to be caught on spinners and plugs as one fishes for other species.

Accessed only by floatplane, and primarily from Wabush-Labrador City, this region sees few visitors each year, and then only from late June through early September. The better fishing for landlocked salmon occurs in June and again in late August and September. Smaller fish are available all summer long in the rivers, especially in the pools and quick water between lakes. They are typically caught on spinners, spoons, and flies.

Although this is not the heart of Labrador's brook trout fishery, this species is plentiful in certain places in the region and can be had up to 7 pounds. Some sections of this area rival the better-known brook trout waters in the central part of Labrador, and 4- and 5-pounders are regularly caught. The Ashuanipi and McKenzie Rivers produce many trout in the 3- to 5-pound class, which is outstanding by any standards, as well as the occasional larger fish. Murray River and the outflow of Crossroads Lake are also very good, and undoubtedly many locales produce great results at certain times, especially if the water is not too low. These fish can be caught all season long and on various lures.

The preferred method of angling in this region is with spinning or baitcasting tackle and lures or baits, although fly fishing is productive for brook trout and whitefish. Ouananiche often take large streamers, lake trout prefer large lures trolled deep, and pike strike a variety of offerings, but there is room for all types of fishing, depending on the location and time of year.

Burbot, a freshwater cousin of the cod, are found in cold lakes, usually at extreme depths, and are receptive to baits, although there is little interest in these fish among visiting anglers. Splake, a cross between lake and brook trout, inhabit some western Labrador watersheds and will strike a lure or large fly under varying conditions.

Central region.   East of Smallwood Reservoir, the central region features Happy Valley-Goose Bay as the primary hub for visiting anglers. This region is known to generations of fly anglers for its superb resource of large brook trout (in the 4- to 8-pound class). To the southwest of Goose Bay is an area with several lakes containing trophy-size brookies, including the famed Minipi Lake, Little Minipi, Anne Marie, and Minonipi watersheds. Landlocked charr are also taken in this system, generally in early autumn as water cools and spawning time approaches.

Several outfitters provide access to the southeast interior, which contains a portion of the Eagle River headwaters, including Igloo Lake, Park Lake, Osprey Lake, Eagle Lake, and Crook's Lake. Awesome Lake and English River lie farther east at the edge of the Mealy Mountain range. These watersheds, with the exception of Awesome Lake, also contain northern pike in addition to a trophy brook trout resource. Giant brook trout have been caught in the English River, which flows out of Awesome Lake, and at several of the inlets that leave the mountains and flow over waterfalls to enter the lake. Awesome Lake is ringed on the west by mountains, including two reaching to 3,500 and 3,800 feet, making for an inspiring angling backdrop. Snow remains on the slopes throughout the season.

Peripheral lakes that offer outfitter camps and contain a mix of brook trout, lake trout, and northern pike include Night, Shapio, Border, and Double Mer.

No roads exist in this wilderness region, so access to these remote outfitter camps is provided via floatplane or helicopter. The combination of distance and difficulty of access has helped preserve these unique brook trout resources and a high quality of angling.

South coast region.   Road access is available to the Straits area in the far southeastern corner of coastal Labrador, where two well-known salmon rivers—the Pinware and the Forteau—are easily accessible from the island of Newfoundland via a 90-minute ferry ride from St. Barbe, Newfoundland, to Blanc Sablon, Quebec. Scheduled airline services carry passengers and freight to nearby Blanc Sablon airport.

These two rivers receive significant resident pressure, but there is an outfitter camp on the Forteau, and several outfitters provide service on the Pinware. Facilities are comfortable, and local guides have firsthand knowledge of these important streams.

Road access disappears at Red Bay, a few miles farther north along the south coast. A road system to connect Red Bay to Cartwright, a major settlement at the mouth of the Eagle River, is planned.

This isolated coast contains four rivers with runs of Atlantic salmon, and small communities lie at the base of each. These include Port Hope Simpson at the Alexis River, Mary's Harbour at the St. Lewis River, Charlottetown at the Gilbert River, and Norman Bay at the Hawke River. A fishing camp sits at the base of the Gilbert River, and farther north are lodges at the more remote Sandhill River.

The renowned Eagle River is the favored salmon stream on this part of the coast. It empties into Sandwich Bay near Cartwright, and there are outfitter lodges and private camps in operation on the Lower Eagle. Nearby rivers with good salmon runs but limited access include North, White Bear, and Paradise Rivers. Sea-run brook trout of significant sizes are taken from all these rivers during early summer.

Labrador has experienced a reduced commercial fishery for salmon, but a strict quota has been in effect in this area—designated by the federal Department of Fisheries & Oceans as Salmon Fishing Area (SFA) 2—and farther north, above Lake Melville, in SFA 1.

North coast region. The coastal area and interior region above Lake Melville, identified as the north coast, is isolated except for scheduled air service and a shipping route in summer. A mix of Atlantic salmon, arctic charr, and sea-run brook trout are taken at outfitter lodges located at Michael's River, Big River, Adlatok River, Voisey's Bay, and Flower's River. Northern pike and lake trout are found in lakes at the lower extremes of this vast area.

The facilities vary from basic to semiluxurious, and fishing is excellent during the peak, from mid-July through late August. This region is dotted with numerous lakes and rivers, some of which hold a mix of fish species. Access is extremely limited, however, and the terrain is generally unfriendly to the unprepared. As in much of Labrador, outfitter lodges are a necessity.

Above the northernmost community of Nain are several rivers offering excellent arctic charr angling. Outfitter camps operate in this area at Tasiuyak Lake and Umiakovik Lake during the short summer season. Even farther north, near the site of a former U.S. radar installation, is a charr and caribou camp at Saglek Bay.

NEW HAMPSHIRE

Between the Canadian border in the north and the Atlantic Ocean in the south, New Hampshire has diverse fishing opportunities, probably more than the average angler can sample in a lifetime of trying. More than 4,000 miles of trout and Atlantic salmon streams and in excess of 200 coldwater lakes and ponds in New Hampshire hold brook, brown, rainbow, and lake trout as well as landlocked salmon.

The warmwater fishery consists primarily of roughly 1,200 bodies of water located chiefly in the south. Although the coastline is relatively short, an abundance of striped bass draws anglers from far inland to the marine fishery.

The coldwater resource is the focus of the majority of management efforts and programs. Bass anglers, however, are increasing in number, and as they voice their expectations the warmwater fishery is receiving more attention from state agencies. Trout and salmon management still relies on hatchery and stocking programs, but the objective of providing anglers with a quality experience supersedes any put-and-take philosophy.

Major Rivers

In the northern half of the state, the Connecticut, Pemigewasset, Androscoggin, and Saco River basins are the major watersheds and provide classic mountain-stream trout fishing.

Connecticut River. The Connecticut River rises just below the Canadian border in Pittsburg and flows south into Massachusetts, forming the New Hampshire and Vermont border along the way. From its headwaters down to Lancaster, the Connecticut offers anglers some of the best public waters in the East. Brookies and rainbows averaging 10 to 12 inches are the mainstay, but there's always the chance of hooking a huge brown. Every season, local youngsters fishing the town pool haul in brown trout weighing in the double digits.

In the special regulation sections of the river between Second Connecticut Lake and Lake Francis, landlocked salmon are a spring and fall wild card. Fly anglers new to this portion of the river should bring caddis and stonefly patterns in black, brown, tan, and olive.

From Pittsburg to just north of Lancaster, the water is a mixture of rapids, riffles, pockets, long glides, and occasional deep pools formed by bends in the river where it flows through flat farmland. This stretch gets fished hard, but it is productive all season long. To avoid crowds, move downstream, below Colebrook, where the pressure is considerably lighter and the fishing often is even better.

Below Lancaster, the stream widens, deepens, and gets much bigger. This section is good trout water, but there is much more of it. Noteworthy is the brown trout tailwater fishery below Moore Dam in the Littleton area. Downstream of Lebanon to Massachusetts, the river changes into big, slower-flowing water that provides excellent fishing for bass, and the occasional northern pike in the setback sloughs. The lower half of the Connecticut is generally boating water.

Five Connecticut River tributaries merit specific recognition: the Ammonoosuc River at Woodsville, the Mascoma at Lebanon, the Sugar at West Claremont, the Cold at Actworth, and the Ashuelot at Hinsdale. Each is a good trout fishery in its own accord.

N

Pemigewasset and Merrimack Rivers. The second most significant north-to-south watershed in New Hampshire is comprised of two rivers. The Pemigewasset rises in the northern reaches of the White Mountains and joins the Merrimack River at Franklin. The Merrimack flows southward from Franklin into Massachusetts.

Gin clear and gravel-bottomed, the Pemi looks like a trout angler's dream stream, and often it lives up to those expectations. Route 3 runs beside the Pemi for much of its length, and stream access is easy. Fly anglers especially favor the Pemi because its technical fishing aspects test them thoroughly over the course of the season.

At Franklin, the Pemi and the Winnepesaukee Rivers merge to form the Merrimack River. The upper Merrimack sustains a trout and salmon cold-water fishery through much of the summer, and the stretch from Concord to the Massachusetts border has outstanding smallmouth bass fishing.

Particularly noteworthy are the Atlantic salmon brood stock fishery and access opportunities along the Merrimack and lower Pemigewasset Rivers. In conjunction with an Atlantic salmon restoration program, surplus adult fish weighing up to 15 pounds and more are released into these rivers, providing a first-class salmon fishery rivaling that found in famous streams. For a fishing license and a salmon permit, anglers can experience sport that would cost big bucks elsewhere.

Portions of the Merrimack and Pemigewasset Rivers and their tributaries to the first upstream bridge are subject to special regulations, some of which require fly fishing only, or the use of artificial lures only, with one hook point.

Androscoggin River. Located in east-central Coos County between Errol, New Hampshire, and Gorham, Maine, the Androscoggin River is New Hampshire's version of a "western" trout stream. This is big water that holds plenty of big fish all year long. Two-pound brookies, 5-pound rainbows, and log-length browns can come at any time and virtually anywhere. The occasional landlocked salmon hooked in swift water makes things even more interesting. Most anglers find the river productive throughout the season, even in the dog days of summer. Fly anglers mark their calendar for the third week in June, when the alderfly hatch triggers a trophy-trout feeding frenzy.

Saco River. In the Mount Washington valley, a network of feeder streams joins the Saco River. From the Conway area and downstream about 20 miles into Maine, the Saco is a first-class trout stream. This section of the river lies amidst many tourist attractions, so it gets heavy pressure from visiting anglers seeking the big browns and rainbows that give the river its reputation. Savvy local anglers tend to give more play to Saco feeder streams, such as the Ellis and the Swift.

North Country Lakes and Ponds

Lakes and ponds in the northern half of the state generally tend to be coldwater fisheries, whereas those in the southern half typically are either warmwater or two-tier fisheries.

In Pittsburg, near the Canadian border, Lake Francis and First, Second, and Third Connecticut Lakes fall into the big-water category, best fished from a seaworthy boat. Brook, rainbow, and brown trout share the waters with landlocked salmon and lake trout. Whether the fishing is trolling for salmon and lakers during the day, or casting a fly to visible trout cruising the surface film and sipping evening-hatch caddisflies, these lakes offer good, consistent fishing from ice out in May through October.

Among the best northern trout ponds are the following: Boundry Pond (covering 18 acres and also called Mountain Pond) in Pittsburg, Lower Trio Pond (68 acres) in Odell, Little and Big Greenough Pond (303 acres) in Wentworth Location, Nathan Pond (26 acres) in Dixville, Little and Big Diamond Pond (230 acres) in Stewartstown, Connor Pond (86 acres) in Ossipee, and Big Dan Hole Pond (408 acres) in Tuftonboro.

Lakes Region

The Lakes Region in the midsection of the state gets its name from several famous fishing lakes. Chief among these is Lake Winnipesaukee, New Hampshire's angling crown jewel and largest body of water. It has 44,586 surface acres, hundreds of islands, underwater structure that drops off to depths exceeding 100 feet, and grassy or sandy shallow bays. Winnipesaukee gets its well-deserved angling reputation from lake trout and landlocked salmon; but among bass anglers, the big lake is also acclaimed for superb smallmouth bass action.

From ice out in late April to roughly Memorial Day, anglers take landlocked salmon on the surface by trolling lures and flies that imitate smelt, the lake's primary forage fish. As the water warms and gives up its oxygen, salmon retreat to the colder water in the 20- to 40-foot depths. Salmon prefer temperatures in the mid-50s; during July and August this means they'll be in the 40- to 70-foot depths in this big lake. Many salmon anglers think that a brisk trolling speed is best for salmon; however, maintaining a slower speed—as close to 1.8 miles per hour (mph) as possible—is consistently most productive for Winnipesaukee salmon.

In spring, just after ice out, lake trout may be taken in the shallows on light-tackle rigs, such as live smelt fished under a bobber. In summer, lake trout seek their preferred 50°F water temperature in the 40- to 100-foot depths. This means slow, deep trolling. A rule of thumb for summertime Winnipesaukee lakers is to troll the 55-foot contour at less than 2 mph. Trolling lures work well, but the old standby here of trolling sewn-on bait, such as jack smelt, is tough to beat.

From spring through fall, Winnipesaukee's smallmouth bass fishery is as good as any other in the Northeast. Bass boats are now as numerous there as other types of craft, especially when there's

Squam Lake is noted for its smallmouth bass as well as lake trout and salmon.

a fishing tournament in progress. The old-time technique of using crayfish or hellgrammites for baits is still a good bet here for anglers who want to tie into a 5-plus-pound smallmouth bass.

In late September and October, smallmouth bass in Winnipesaukee and other waters in the Lakes Region return to the shallows and indulge in a feeding binge. The fishing can be truly terrific during this time.

In winter, ice anglers take over the lakes, and colonies of ice fishing shacks—locally called "bob-houses"—dot the prime areas. The main species of interest to ice anglers are lake trout, rainbow trout, pickerel, bass, yellow perch, and white perch. Salmon are protected during the ice fishing season.

The large-lakes rainbow trout program is a key component of Lakes Region fisheries management. To mitigate fishing pressure on lake trout and provide a high-quality alternative, the state stocks rainbow trout. Rainbows in Winnipesaukee can exceed 5 pounds. No fail-safe tactic has yet been developed, however, for targeting and catching these fish locally. In most instances, large lake rainbows are caught by chance, not by design.

Year-round, Lake Winnipesaukee incurs heavy fishing pressure, but the fisheries are closely monitored and aggressively managed because they are among the state's most valuable recreational and economic resources.

Much of what pertains to Winnipesaukee is generally true for the other Lakes Region waters.

Squam and Winnisquam Lakes offer smaller versions of Lake Winnipesaukee's fisheries. Newfound and Sunapee Lakes no longer merit their former reputations for lake trout and salmon, but the state Fish and Game Department is trying to restore them to their former glory.

Squam Lake, which at 6,764 acres is the second-largest lake in New Hampshire, deserves special note because it is one of the unsung jewels of New England. This predominantly deep body of water has numerous islands and rocky shoals. The water is pure and crystal clear, and you can watch a lure drift off to the bottom in depths twice your body length and then some.

Located near Holderness in the foothills of New Hampshire's White Mountains, Squam is a premier New England smallmouth bass fishery. It also offers fine landlocked salmon angling, harboring larger landlocks on average than its much bigger nearby sister lake, Winnipesaukee. Lake trout thrive here, too, although these favor deep water and are tough to come by most of the year. The lake has been noted for large white perch in the past.

The finest time for smallmouth fishing is in the spring, from early June through the fourth of July. Once the weather sets in and the surface layers warm up, bass retreat to the areas around deep, rocky shoals. Some great fishing can be had at Squam in midsummer, if you locate these spots and work them carefully, using jigs, live crayfish, and perhaps surface plugs in the evening.

For landlocked salmon, the months of April and May, when the fish are closer to the surface and near shore in pursuit of spawning smelt, are the best times to fish. There is little nonfishing boat traffic at that time, and the salmon are plentiful. Most anglers fish traditionally, trolling streamer flies on a fly line or lead-core line. Later, the fish move deeper and are harder to locate.

Warmwater Fisheries

Although there are roughly 1,200 bodies of warm water in the Granite State, only a third of them are managed to any extent by the New Hampshire Fish and Game Department. Most of these waters are located south of the White Mountains. In New Hampshire, ponds and lakes are categorized according to the fish species inhabiting the waters, and the warmwater/coldwater distinction is fuzzy in instances where waters that contain bass are stocked with trout to provide a seasonal put-and-take trout fishery.

It is common here for a given body of water to hold and sustain both trout and bass, a situation known as a two-tier fishery. For example, 707-acre Spofford Lake, located in Chesterfield, not only has trout and bass, but it also produced a state-record northern pike that weighed 21 pounds, 4.6 ounces.

Where waters tend to be on the warm side, brook trout don't fare well; rainbows and browns adapt moderately well among the largemouth and smallmouth bass that may be there. Massabesic Lake in Auburn is a 2,512-acre site that does an acceptable job of supporting both trout and bass. Depending on tackle and technique, anglers here can take rainbow trout, brown trout, largemouth and smallmouth bass, white perch, and bluegills.

New Hampshire does possess pure, classic largemouth bass waters, mostly in the southern end of the state. About 10 miles southwest of Concord, in the Weare and Hopkington area, is a loosely connected network of water between Hopkington and Everett Lakes. When fish biologists studied these waters, they found big bass and plenty of them in the midst of extensive reaches of flooded standing timber. This ideal bass habitat produces big fish and good fishing. Anglers have landed largemouths up to 8 pounds in these waters, and fish in the 4- to 5-pound class are definitely possible.

Largemouth bass may not readily come to mind when one thinks of New Hampshire, but the bass fishery is extensive enough to keep a plethora of bass clubs and bass anglers happy.

Saltwater

New Hampshire's coastline is short, about 15 miles as the crow flies, but its marine resources are varied and the saltwater fishing grounds are well known. Offshore structures like the Isles of Shoals have been drawing anglers since the Vikings found and harvested an abundance of cod, haddock, pollock, and flounder. These groundfish species have declined in number, as is true all along the Atlantic coast, but striped bass and bluefish provide an exciting recreational fishery. From May through October, the Great Bay estuarine waters provide one of the best inshore striped bass fisheries of the Northeast. For pure sport and fast action, anglers use light tackle or fly gear and focus on schoolie stripers. Effective methods for taking big fish include freespooling live mackerel, eels, and pogies; drifting chunk bait in the rips; and trolling a tube and worm combination.

Charter and party boats operate out of Rye and Hampton Harbors. Some focus on offshore groundfish species, whereas others work the inshore waters for mackerel, stripers, and bluefish.

NEW JERSEY

Perhaps overlooked by nonresident anglers because of its dense population, industrialized character, proximity to Manhattan, and relatively small size, New Jersey nevertheless has surprisingly diverse angling, as well as wildly enthusiastic anglers. From Greenwood Lake's bass fishing to the Pine Barrens' pickerel and the Delaware River's shad, and from Sandy Hook's stripers to Cape May's drum, not too many important East Coast species escape the hook.

New Jersey has no large lakes, only one major river, and only 130 miles of Atlantic coastline. But this coastline is studded with beaches, inlets, and marinas far beyond what many locations with much longer coastlines can offer, providing access to perennially popular flounder, weakfish, striped bass, and bluefish inshore, and even marlin, tuna, and dolphin offshore. These opportunities have resulted in exceptional catches, which include the largest striped bass ever caught, the second largest known bluefish ever caught, and numerous line-class records for weakfish, flounder, and black drum, as well as bigeye tuna. Inland, numerous small to medium lakes and streams provide opportunities that range from four species of trout to pure-strain muskellunge, landlocked hybrid stripers, walleye, and plenty of largemouth and smallmouth bass, plus what is arguably the best fishery for American shad in North America in the Delaware River.

Freshwater

One of the most covert angling stories in the northeastern United States is the existence and indeed expansion of freshwater fishing opportunities within the confines of the Garden State. Known as the most densely populated state in America, and a heavily industrialized one at that, New Jersey does not bring to mind outstanding freshwater fishing to outsiders. It has no nationally renowned freshwater opportunities, with the possible exception of the Delaware River, and no large bodies of water; yet it offers a diversity—in fact more than is found in a lot of states—it seldom receives credit for.

This diversity exists throughout New Jersey's three distinct inland geographic regions. Indeed, myriad freshwater venues—including lakes, ponds, rivers, impoundments, and a latticework of streams and creeks, all of which support good populations of gamefish and panfish—await the angler. From wild brook trout to pure-strain muskellunge, anglers can find it all in New Jersey.

Northern region. *Greenwood Lake.* Passaic County's 1,920-acre Greenwood Lake shares a border with New York and is recognized as a supreme largemouth bass fishery within the tri-state (including Pennsylvania) area. Smallmouth bass, pure-strain muskies, walleye, and chain pickerel are among the players at Greenwood, and healthy populations of robust yellow perch, sunfish, channel catfish, and bullheads thrive here, too.

The lake is heavily weeded and its complexion fairly turbid. Largemouths get big here, and 7-pounders are not uncommon. Fishing for both largemouth and smallmouth bass begins in mid-April and intensifies into the summer months. Smallmouth average about 2 pounds here, and 4-pounders are caught annually. During the late May to early June spawning period, they are encountered in close to dockside cover; later, they frequent Greenwood's rockier flats and dropoffs.

The muskie is the ultimate prize of Greenwood, one eagerly sought by dedicated fans all season long. Early spring and late autumn are the optimum times to pursue these fish.

Greenwood draws many New York anglers because of its early bass fishing opportunities (the season is still closed in April and May in most New York waters), and because it is one of the larger publicly accessible lakes in the tri-state area. Many tournaments are scheduled here, and the lake is a beehive of activity in summer months. In winter, Greenwood offers excellent ice fishing.

Monksville Reservoir. Also in Passaic County, 505-acre Monksville Reservoir is situated just below Greenwood Lake and provides superb fishing for largemouth and smallmouth bass, walleye, pure-strain muskies, tiger muskies, trout, and panfish. This impoundment boasts a plethora of sunken islands, humps, dropoffs, and flats, as well as stands of drowned timber. It sports a mean depth of nearly 43 feet and a maximum depth of 90 feet, and it is restricted to electric motors.

Stocked trout receive most of the attention in early spring, but come May, walleye usurp the limelight. The bulk of the walleye activity occurs in the south-central and southern sections of the reservoir. Walleye average 3 pounds or thereabouts, but fish up to and exceeding 6 pounds are present.

Both largemouth and smallmouth bass are common throughout Monksville and are caught from April through November. Muskies prowl submerged weedbeds, sunken timber, and breaklines. October to ice-up (usually by mid-January) is the most opportune time to encounter Monksville muskellunge, and the fish also strike baits under the ice.

Lake Hopatcong. New Jersey's largest lake, Hopatcong spans 2,658 acres and is situated in portions of Morris and Sussex Counties.

Undoubtedly the most heavily utilized freshwater resource in the Garden State, Lake Hopatcong offers outstanding fishing. Largemouth and smallmouth bass, chain pickerel, channel catfish, walleye, crappie, yellow perch, rock bass, and sunfish are all present, as are stocked populations of trout (some of which hold over through the winter to attain larger size), hybrid stripers, and both pure-strain and tiger muskies (experimentally). The hybrid striper is the star attraction of Hopatcong, followed in popularity by the largemouth bass, channel catfish, and walleye.

Hybrid striper fishing here is dynamic, with specimens caught in excess of 10 pounds. Stripers begin hitting in earnest in early May and continue into October. The largest fish of the year are taken at night during the latter part of summer. Top areas include Nolan's Point, the River Styx cove, Henderson Bay, Woodport, and the Brady Bridge area.

Largemouths that frequent the many docks and boathouses are particularly susceptible to a flipped or pitched jig, and also assault spinnerbaits and plastic worms. Plenty of submerged weedbeds throughout Hopatcong also hold largemouths, and the lake yields 3- to 5-pound specimens regularly. Fish to 7 pounds are taken every year.

Channel cats are the stunning overachievers on Hopatcong, attaining weights of 20 pounds or more. They are caught throughout the lake from May into October.

Although taken from Hopatcong since the early 1980s, walleye are now just beginning to establish a foothold. Anglers can find walleye to about 5 pounds, and expectations are high for the future of this fishery.

Chain pickerel are also notable on Hopatcong, as they thrive in its weedy environs. Chainsides wax fat on the rich shiner and alewife (also called a sawbelly here) forage base, and larger specimens can exceed 5 pounds.

Hopatcong is New Jersey's most popular ice fishing lake, and crappie, pickerel, yellow perch, and bluegills are the top winter targets.

Round Valley Reservoir. The standard by which all other Jersey waters are judged, 2,350-acre Round Valley Reservoir in Hunterdon County is the Garden State's finest stillwater salmonid fishery. Boasting depths to 160 feet, "The Valley," as it is known to regulars, offers outstanding fishing for brown, rainbow, and lake trout.

This impoundment, which has a 9.9-horsepower outboard motor restriction, is heavily stocked by the Division of Fish, Game and Wildlife, and also receives thousands of rainbows and browns annually

 Federal excise taxes on fishing tackle and some marine products are collected by manufacturers and used for fish restoration and access improvement projects.

N

from a local association. Trout are taken on a year-round basis, although there is a closed season on lakers that extends from mid-September to the beginning of January, to protect spawning fish.

Round Valley is managed as a trophy trout fishery with minimum size restrictions and very conservative daily limits. The regulations are succeeding; lakers to 24 pounds, browns to 21 pounds, and rainbows to 8 pounds have been pulled from its depths.

Drifting with alewives is the most popular technique, and many people anchor and swim an alewife below a slip bobber. Trolling plugs and spoons also pay handsome dividends. Both the North and South Tower areas are productive, and during the summer months boaters score well after dark. Shoreline anglers have a crack at trout during April and May and again from October through December.

Round Valley also offers excellent largemouth and smallmouth bass fishing along the shorelines and coves, and anglers have a good chance at largemouths over 5 pounds and bronzebacks over 3 pounds.

Spruce Run Reservoir. Located within a 10-minute drive from neighboring Round Valley, Spruce Run Reservoir is a 1,290-acre hotbed for largemouth bass, hybrid stripers, and northern pike. This impoundment, which has a 9.9-horse-power outboard motor restriction, is not as deep as Round Valley, so it has a different angling character.

Spruce Run largemouths hang close to the plentiful submerged weedbeds, creek channels, sunken islands, humps, and dropoffs. The cove to the left of the launch ramp in the state park is a good bet for early-season bass, as is the entire stretch of shoreline extending from the camping area to Black Brook Cove. Hepler's Cove and Black Brook Cove are prime locations for northern pike. This is especially true when using live shiners during April and May and again during October-December.

Hybrids exploded onto the Spruce Run scene and provide thrilling action on drifted alewives and trolled minnow plugs, particularly during May and early June and again during September into October.

Spruce Run is stocked with trout during the spring, although the holdover potential of the habitat is at an absolute minimum. This fishery is, for all intents and purposes, an annual put-and-take proposition. Salmonids are caught into June.

White catfish are also abundant here, as are heavyweight carp. When the lake freezes, northern pike, yellow perch, and crappie spark interest.

Merrill Creek Reservoir. Considered by many to be the state's premier smallmouth bass venue, 600-acre Merrill Creek Reservoir in Warren County also provides good opportunities for rainbow, brown, and lake trout, as well as largemouth bass, yellow perch, and sunfish.

This 210-foot-deep impoundment, which has an electric-motor-only restriction, possesses a variety of structure, including submerged timber, boulder fields, rockpiles, dropoffs, humps, creek channels, and weeds, and is ideally suited to trophy bronze-backs. On an angler-per-hour basis, Merrill Creek provides the best in both sizes and numbers. Smallmouths are found along the entire expanse of the reservoir's shoreline out to depths of 40 feet, but the immediate area surrounding the handicapped access is a place to focus special attention.

Drifting from a boat with alewives and shiners accounts for the majority of salmonid catches, although shore anglers score during April, May, and June.

Big Swartswood Lake. Big Swartswood Lake in Sussex County has been one of the Garden State's most consistent producers of big largemouths for decades. Just 494 acres in size, and 42 feet deep, and with an electric-motor-only restriction, Swartswood has ample and expansive weedbeds, rockpiles, and rocky points to attract largemouths, which are active from mid-April into November. This fishery continues to be first-rate, and largemouths up to 10 pounds have been caught here. Many fish are in the 2- to 4-pound range.

Pickerel, yellow perch, rock bass, and crappie are sure bets year-round and have earned Swartswood a reputation as a first-class ice fishing venue.

Stocked trout contribute to frantic action from April through May on Big Swartswood, and salmonid numbers are augmented by releases from a local club. The holdover potential of the lake is marginal, but every year big browns are wrestled from the depths.

Delaware River. Known outside the region primarily for its run of migratory American shad from April through May, the East's largest free-flowing river also provides exemplary angling for walleye, pure-strain muskies, tiger muskies, smallmouth and largemouth bass, channel catfish, striped bass, carp, a variety of panfish, and, in the state's northernmost stretch from Columbia to Montague, the occasional brown trout.

Top areas on the upper New Jersey portion of the Delaware include Montague, Worthington, Poxono Island, Walpack Bend, and Kittatinny Beach (all in the Delaware Water Gap National Recreation Area), and Columbia, Belvidere, Phillipsburg, Carpentersville, Riegelsville, Bulls Island, Kingwood, and Frenchtown.

On the central stretch of the Delaware, favored areas are Byram, Stockton, Lambertville, Washington's Crossing, and Trenton. Trenton Wharf draws anglers during the spring herring run.

Lower-river hotspots include Bordentown, Florence, Burlington, National Park, Greenwich, Pennsville, Penns Beach, and Salem Cove. Of special interest in the lower Delaware is the Commodore Barry Bridge locale, a prime striped bass spawning ground. Thirty- to 40-pound stripers are caught here each spring.

N

Tributaries on the lower river provide exceptional angling for striped bass (which spawn in some of them), largemouth bass, and channel catfish. These include Salem Creek, Cohansey River, Oldmans Creek, Rancocas River, Raccoon Creek, Salem River, Big Timber Creek, Crosswicks Creek, and Mantua Creek.

Raritan River. New Jersey's second major river system, the Raritan offers fine fishing for smallmouth bass, channel catfish, largemouth bass, rock bass, white catfish, carp, and sunfish from its genesis at the North Branch/South Branch confluence at Old York Road in Somerset County downriver to New Brunswick in Middlesex County.

Trout are stocked at Dukes Island Park (in Somerset County), and downriver from this location anglers have a fair chance of encountering walleye, muskies, and northern pike. White perch are prolific throughout the lower reaches of the Raritan, especially near New Brunswick. The Johnson Park beat, also in New Brunswick, is one of the Garden State's best-kept largemouth bass secrets.

Millstone River. The 20-mile south-to-north Millstone River, from Princeton (Mercer County) to Manville (Somerset County) is a vastly underrated and ignored venue for largemouth bass, northern pike, channel catfish, chain pickerel, rock bass, sunfish, and carp. Smallmouth bass linger in the lower reaches of the Millstone, particularly where it merges with the Raritan at Manville.

Top spots are in Somerset County at Blackwells Mills in Belle Mead, in the hamlet of Millstone, and at Wilhousky Street in Manville.

Delaware & Raritan Canal. The narrow D&R Canal hosts stocked trout, channel catfish, largemouth bass, crappie, yellow perch, white perch, striped bass, carp, and sunfish. Muskies, walleye, and northern pike, although rare, also frequent the turbid precincts.

Weedbeds, logs, sunken brush, undercut banks, and overhangs typify the D&R Canal habitat. Depths range to 10 feet. Flowing slowly through the counties of Mercer, Hunterdon, Somerset, and Middlesex, the canal provides ample shoreline access via the D&R Canal State Park system and is an ideal venue for the canoe and cartop boat angler.

The D&R Feeder Canal in Hunterdon and Mercer Counties is also heavily stocked with trout and offers good opportunities for largemouth bass, channel catfish, bullhead, sunfish, and crappie.

Other sites. Other northern New Jersey waters worthy of effort are Little Swartswood Lake and Wawayanda Lake in Sussex County, Sheppards Lake in Passaic County, Lake Musconetcong and Budd Lake in Morris County, and White Lake and Mountain Lake in Warren County.

The Newark Watershed reservoirs in Passaic and Sussex Counties offer excellent fishing for a variety of species. Largemouth and smallmouth bass, rainbow trout, and brown trout are notable at

Canistear, Oak Ridge, and Clinton; muskies are present in Echo Lake; and they all have pickerel, yellow perch, crappie, and sunfish. These four reservoirs are under the auspices of the city of Newark, however, and access is controlled with a seasonal permit.

The northern region of New Jersey is laced with premium-quality trout streams, brooks, and small rivers. The best include the Big Flat Brook, Wanaque, Ramapo, Rockaway, Paulinskill, Black, Pequest, Musconetcong, Spruce Run Creek, Pequannock, South Branch of the Raritan, and North Branch of the Raritan.

Not to be overlooked are the state's 33 Wild Trout Waters, most of which are in the northern region, where native trout reign and only artificial lures can be used. Many of these are in Sussex, Warren, Morris, Passaic, and Hunterdon Counties; Flanders Brook, India Brook, Parker Brook, Rocky Run, Van Campens Brook, Willhoughby Brook, and Little York Brook really shine.

Central region. *Manasquan Reservoir.* At 740 acres, Monmouth County's Manasquan Reservoir offers a wide range of angling opportunities. Largemouth and smallmouth bass, and stocked trout, are the primary attractions, although numerous crappie and sunfish draw marked interest. During April and May, the put-and-take fishery for brookies and rainbows draws legions of anglers to the impoundment.

The smallmouth bass population at 'Squan has been very good, typically offering fish up to 3 pounds, but this trend may decline as the habitat falls victim to natural progression. Then, it will be better suited to largemouths, which are active from late April through November. Fish over 4 pounds are possible.

This impoundment, which has an electric-motor-only restriction, has been stocked with hybrid striped bass, channel catfish, and tiger muskies. These fisheries are expected to be more prominent in the near future.

Lake Assunpink. Considered the finest largemouth bass venue in central New Jersey, 225-acre Lake Assunpink in Monmouth County is a consistent fish producer, which explains its popularity among statewide bass clubs.

A shallow electric-motor-only impoundment with an average depth of just 5 feet, Assunpink is loaded with road beds, weeds, and brush. It has plenty of bass up to 3 pounds, and some in the 5-pound class. March through June, and September through November, are the most productive periods. Channel catfish also contend for fishing attention on Assunpink, and many anglers frequent this impoundment for a chance at 12-plus-pound specimens.

Two notable small lakes include nearby Stone Tavern Lake and Rising Sun. Both are within a few minutes' drive and offer good largemouth bass, crappie, and catfish angling.

A great deal of freshwater fishing in the Garden State occurs in small waters, such as this south Jersey pond.

Farrington Lake. Farrington Lake in Middlesex County is rated as one of the Garden State's finest pickerel waters and as a fine largemouth bass site. Chainsides attain very respectable sizes in the 290-acre Farrington, with 30-inch fish present. Thick-bodied largemouths exist throughout the long and narrow length of this electric-motor-only impoundment, hugging the shoreline brush, blowdowns, and weedbeds.

The lake also has panfish, stocked trout, and northern pike. The pike—many of which exceed 15 pounds—hug the weeds like bass and can be found close to the banks or on outside vegetation.

Other sites. Other worthwhile waters in central New Jersey include Carasaijo, Prospertown, and Shenandoah Lakes in Ocean County; Deal Lake in Monmouth County; and Lake Mercer in Mercer County.

Central New Jersey's better trout streams include the Manasquan River and Mingamahone Brook in Monmouth County, plus Toms River and the North Branch of the Metedeconk in Ocean County.

Southern region. *Union Lake.* A particularly productive largemouth bass water, Cumberland County's 898-acre Union Lake has a bountiful forage base of herring, gizzard shad, and shiners; natural structure like weeds, sunken trees, and brush; man-made tire structures; and rockpiles. All of these elements contribute to the lake's optimum largemouth conditions. The average largemouth

tips the scales around the 2-pound mark, but 3- to 5-pounders are regularly caught. Smallmouth bass, although rare, show up just enough to provide an occasional surprise.

Union's burgeoning herring population is attributed to the newly constructed fish ladder on the Maurice (pronounced "Morris") River, which permits upstream passage for these fish and provides ample forage so the bass can gain size rapidly. The ladder has also impacted the lake's striper population.

Union's landlocked striper population, once one of New Jersey's shining fisheries, has waned to insignificance, even though the odd 10-pounder might be caught here. However, increasing numbers of 5- to 8-inch estuary-run striped bass from the Maurice River have been using the ladder and entering this impoundment. Because the fish will be entrapped here, there's hope that they will prosper, eat heartily, and grow to tackle-bending proportions in future years.

This lake, incidentally, has a 9.9-horsepower outboard restriction.

Maurice River. The approximately 13-mile stretch of the Maurice (pronounced "Morris") River flowing from the Union Lake dam just above the city of Millville (Cumberland County) southward to Delaware Bay is an amazingly productive stretch of river.

It is one of the hottest striped bass venues in the Garden State, with linesiders up to and exceeding 15 pounds caught here during the spring, summer, and autumn. Swarms of smaller fish inhabit this branch- and brush-infested flowage.

This is prime largemouth habitat as well, with bass up to 5 pounds feasting on herring, shiners, and elvers. Trophy-size channel catfish and white catfish, and jumbo yellow bullhead are here, as are pickerel, white perch, carp, sunfish, crappie, and yellow perch.

Parvin Lake. Ninety-five-acre Parvin Lake in Salem County is newly managed and regulated as a trophy bass fishery, and is expected to be a prime small water for big bass in the future.

With an average depth of just over $3\frac{1}{2}$ feet, the slightly stained Parvin is jammed with bass-holding structure, including weeds, stumps, brush, and sunken timber. There's an abundant forage base on this electric-motor-only lake, primarily consisting of shiners and elvers. The average bass is near 2 pounds, but 5-pounders are not uncommon.

Lake Lenape. Atlantic County's 350-acre Lake Lenape on the Egg Harbor River offers excellent opportunities for largemouth bass, yellow perch, crappie, and chain pickerel. Because of its unlimited outboard access (although park registration is required), Lenape is a popular tournament site for southern New Jersey and southeastern Pennsylvania bass clubs.

The lake has weedbeds, sunken timber, sand flats, and stump fields, and its water is stained

N

brown to black owing to the cedar and pitch pine topography bordering the headwaters. It yields largemouths up to 4 pounds and pickerel up to 24 inches, with an occasional larger specimen.

Malaga Lake. Malaga Lake in Gloucester County packs a lot into just 105 acres of electric-motor-only fishing. Heavy concentrations of lily pads, grassbeds, and other weeds, as well as channel edges, stumps, and brush, make this an optimal site for largemouth bass. The lake produces specimens over 4 pounds each year, especially in spring and fall.

Malaga has a good supply of chain pickerel, which are found throughout the lake and caught year-round. March through June, and September through December, produce the better pickerel.

Other sites. Other noteworthy southern New Jersey waters include Menantico Sand Wash Pond in Cumberland County, Maskells Mill Pond in Salem County, Hammonton and Maple Lakes in Atlantic County, Mirror Lake in Burlington County, Iona Lake in Gloucester County, East Creek and Dennisville Lakes in Cape May County, and Oak Pond in Camden County.

Saltwater

New Jersey has one of the largest saltwater recreational fisheries in the United States due to its long shoreline and the fact that all of its large population is within a two-hour drive of the briny. The northeastern end of the state has the greatest proportion of that population and shares the lower Hudson River with New York. Just below such cities as Newark, Jersey City, and Elizabeth is Raritan Bay, which separates New York's Staten Island and the bay shoreline that stretches to the east.

The 120-mile-long coast starts at the tip of Sandy Hook and is treated as three different areas. The northern portion between Sandy Hook and Barnegat Inlet is referred to as "The Shore," and attracts both vast numbers of anglers and summer visitors, primarily from northern New Jersey. The central coast, from Barnegat Inlet to Atlantic City, is oriented toward Pennsylvania and western New Jersey anglers; the southern coast, from Ocean City to Cape May, is geared toward servicing Pennsylvanians as well as a great many Canadians who summer at Wildwood and Cape May. Although the extremes of the northern and southern areas are separated by only 40 miles, these regions might as well be two different states—the interchange of fishing information is so limited and the techniques and even some species are so disparate.

Delaware Bay separates New Jersey from Delaware, and in its upper reaches is vastly different from other parts of the state. The lower end of the Delaware River is shared between New Jersey and Delaware, but an oddity of law from colonial days gives the First State control of the waters up to the shores of the Garden State. New Jersey does have equal rights to the rest of the river, however, where it borders with Pennsylvania and New York. Saltwater fisheries in New Jersey are controlled by the state Division of Fish, Game and Wildlife, which falls within the Department of Environmental Protection.

Many of the marine species taken off New Jersey migrate up the coast in the spring and are generally encountered a week or two earlier within range of Cape May. For instance, mackerel fishing may start there during March as Cape May boats run south off Delaware to locate the first schools. That season generally lasts three to four weeks as schools gradually move north and out of range. The movement tends to speed up along the central coast before those spawning fish sometimes pause for two to four weeks in the New York-New Jersey Bight. In mid-April, northern boats usually begin to seek mackerel, and that fishery can run into May, depending on water temperatures and the proximity of bluefish schools. In general, mackerel move east when water temperatures climb above 50°F, although the presence of even a few bluefish may be an even more important factor.

Bluefish move in from offshore as well as up along the coast from the south. Cape May boats see some on the heels of the mackerel and usually start night chumming trips by the end of April; northern anglers often catch blues moving into warmer inshore waters around the same time, although party and charter boats rarely try to schedule trips before the second week in May. Throughout May and June there's a steady inshore movement of blues, which can be seen finning along the warm surface at first, before gradually moving deeper as the thermocline drops lower.

Sharks also tend to work up the coast and come in from warmer offshore waters. Cape May usually has a good fishery by the first week in June, and northern areas experience similar action a week later. School bluefin tuna move into both areas two to three weeks after the sharks arrive.

The reverse occurs in the fall, as northern areas get the migratory runs first. For instance, migratory striped bass from Chesapeake Bay feed in northern areas before passing by South Jersey from mid- or late-November into December. Cape May often has good bass fishing by October, however, as Delaware River fish start returning through the rips.

Hudson River. Heavily populated areas in northeastern New Jersey have nearby fishing opportunities in the lower and salty portions of the now much cleaner Hudson River. Even though river waters rarely display much clarity, the quality of those waters is far better now than it was for many decades when both industrial and municipal dumping polluted the river. Most of the species that live in the Hudson have shown signs of being pollution-resistant, but they also tend to taste of the river and, in the cases of species with higher oil contents, may contain levels of pollutants that require health warnings. This is especially the case with eels, but PCBs dumped years ago by General Electric accumulated in the tissues of striped bass to such an extent that commercial fishing for that species was prohibited during the 1970s. Ironically, these events ultimately benefited the species, which has since enjoyed many outstanding spawning years and provided a decent fishery in the Metropolitan area—even when the Chesapeake stocks hit rock bottom in the early 1980s.

The abundant Hudson River striped bass population continues to spread out along the coast each spring after providing a good pre-spawning fishery, which occurs a bit farther upriver in New York. Jersey anglers join their counterparts from across the river in catching stripers there from spring through fall. Shore anglers score in March and April from such areas as the Englewood Boat Basin in Bergen County, near the George Washington Bridge, where they cast sea worms for mostly short stripers as well as tomcod and white catfish.

Boaters do best in the lower reaches of the river from May on. Some of the best areas are around the Statue of Liberty and Ellis Island. Anglers can catch bass close to the islands by casting plugs, poppers, and bucktail jigs, but most of the larger stripers fall to bunker chunks fished from anchored boats. The current is very strong and often requires heavy sinkers, but bass in the teens and 20s are abundant. Bluefish also become common in the harbor area of the river by June.

Ironically, although boaters can be observed by literally millions of people in Manhattan and Brooklyn on the New York side, and from the solid line of waterfront communities across the river, anglers can often fish in virtual isolation except for river traffic—and the fishing may be better than anything found outside the river. The Staten Island end of the Verrazano Bridge is a good spot for stripers at times, although with only one support on each side it doesn't provide the fish-holding structure typical of most bridges.

A relative lack of marinas and launching facilities is the biggest problem in accessing the river, although the Liberty State Park development outside Jersey City has made it much easier for anglers seeking marina space and a launching ramp close to some of the river's best fishing. Stripers are caught from the park shores at times, and also from any pier that is accessible along the river. The state is investing some money into providing that access. The Hudson River Fisherman's Association in Cresskill keeps close track of changes in shore access and is the best source of information.

Raritan and Sandy Hook Bays.   This may be the most underrated bay system in the country. Although surrounded by densely populated areas with vigorous industry, and subject to water flow from the polluted Kill Van Kull, Raritan Bay has been cleaned up considerably over the years. This bay was once famous for its oysters, but pollution

shut down all shellfishing except for relay to clean waters for later harvest or for processing in depuration plants. Although rarely clear, the bay waters are extremely fertile, and bountiful harvests of baitfish and grass shrimp attract droves of such predators as summer flounder (fluke), winter flounder, bluefish, striped bass, and weakfish.

Except for pound nets and the purse seining of menhaden (bunkers), netting isn't allowed in the bay. Even that is prohibited on the New York side of the bay, and efforts are underway, aided by spotter planes, to end the decimation of that most important forage fish each spring and summer by mostly out-of-state bait purse seiners. Unfortunately, a great deal of illegal dragging has been conducted at night by "pirate" trawlers primarily operating out of Belford, although that activity recently has been reduced as law enforcement agencies implemented night scoping technology to nab the well-organized bandits.

A unique fixture on the Jersey side is the Naval Ammunition Pier at Earle, which extends far out in the bay. Fishing is off-limits for boaters inside the buoy line around the pier, but navy personnel enjoy great sport off the pier, especially for striped bass at night. A large party and charter boat fleet sails out of the modern port at Atlantic Highlands, which is near the mouth of Shrewsbury River and also features a large launching ramp. Nearby Leonardo State Marina has a party boat and some charters but caters mostly to private boats and features a good ramp with ample parking. Other party and charter boats sail from Highlands, Keyport, Morgan, and Perth Amboy.

The season starts in March as winter flounder become active; that fishery continues into early May, and the peak usually occurs during April. Although the flounder population along the coast was extremely depressed during the 1990s, Raritan Bay produced excellent angling every spring. Many fish ranged into the 2- to 3-pound class and shorts were few. The clam beds off Staten Island often attract weekend fleets in the hundreds, although many productive flounder grounds are spread throughout Raritan and Sandy Hook Bays. The latter comes alive in April as fish drop out of the Shrewsbury and Navesink Rivers.

The Shrewsbury and Navesink are also noted for their flounder fishing. The Shrewsbury may produce as early as February if the winter is warm and the season is open. March is a sure thing, although the fishery comes and goes with weather conditions. Early flounder turn on when the weather is sunny and mild, leading to warmer and clearer waters. Avoid fishing after rain or snow, which will turn the waters cold and dirty—driving flounder back into the mud. Larger female flounder move out first to spawn and leave the river, so the best fishing usually starts in March and may be over before mid-April, after which small male flounder take over. Most of the early effort occurs between

A great white shark in Australia was hooked and landed twice in the same day by the same angler—even gaffed in the mouth and photographed—but it escaped both times. Its estimated weight was 3,000 pounds.

the Sea Bright and Highlands Bridges, whereas the mouth of the Shrewsbury is best in April. The Navesink flows into the Shrewsbury just above the Highlands Bridge and provides excellent flounder catches a bit later than the other river, with small boats doing best during April in shallow waters around the Rumson Bridge.

The last shot at flounder usually occurs from late April into May in the ocean off the Cedars on Sandy Hook, where big flounder may be mixed in with ling (red hake). A Raritan Bay fall run usually develops in November and December, although relatively few anglers seek flounder. More glamorous fish such as striped bass are still available.

Striped bass also start biting in March, when many are hooked on sandworms cast from bay shorelines stretching from South Amboy to Atlantic Highlands. Almost all of these stripers are shorts (sublegal size) caught in waters that are only a few feet deep and warm up faster than deeper waters. As a general rule, this fishing is best from the middle of the flood into the beginning of the ebb both day and night. Flounder anglers catch short stripers from boats starting around late March, but striper enthusiasts rarely make a concentrated effort before April and May, when they begin to drift worms at the usual bay hotspots such as Sandy Hook Rip, Flynn's Knoll, and Romer Shoal, as well as the Highlands and Sea Bright Bridges in the Shrewsbury. Again, the vast majority of these early bass are shorts.

Chunking with cut bunker is a deadly method from June to August in many areas of the bay that have mussel bottoms. Flynn's Knoll and Ambrose Channel draw the largest fleets. Live eels drifted in Sandy Hook and Ambrose Channels and in Flynn's Knoll are the top producers in September and October, unless purse seiners leave enough bunkers in the bay to create an attraction for big bass. If schools of bunkers are available in October and November, there should be good action drifting live bunkers or trolling bunker spoons on wire line. Trolling often produces some bass within the bay into early December.

Bluefish arrive during early May and are usually abundant by midmonth. In some years these are 2- to 3-pounders, although on occasion there may be schools of 10-pounders that not only enter the bay but also go right up into the rivers. Shore casters usually get good shots at blues for a week or two before the fishery becomes primarily a boater's game, and then trolling and jigging are favored. Schools of mostly 1- to- 4-pound choppers remain in the bay throughout the summer, and many larger ones are also caught by those chunking for stripers. The fall fishery is primarily outside the bay, however.

Fluking also starts in May, and is normally worthwhile after midmonth. These fish are the predominant bay fishery from June through August. Pursuing fluke throughout the bays is a large party boat fleet at Atlantic Highlands, which is joined by others from such ports as Highlands, Leonardo, Keyport, Morgan, and Perth Amboy. Charter and private boats partake in this fishery as well, and thousands of boats may be involved on weekends. Some fluke tournaments draw well over 200 entries. At times, the best fishing is in the western end of the bay, but sometimes it's preferable to fish closer to the ocean or down the beach at Sandy Hook. Fluking continues through September, when the departing fish tend to pile up in Ambrose Channel, and it often remains viable well into October.

Weakfish arrive early, but very few are caught on hook and line until July. Earlier attempts occur upriver in the Shrewsbury, but volume weakfishing is mainly a bay proposition. Large concentrations of these fish are usually found in Raritan and Chapel Hill Channels. After years of depressed weakfishing, the species bounced back in the mid-1990s and has been improving steadily with ever-larger specimens and relatively few shorts. The best fishing usually occurs in August and September, although schools may remain available into October if there aren't too many early cold northwesters. Whereas jigs work when weaks are feeding actively, the Raritan weakfishery is almost exclusively pursued with sandworms drifted a few feet above bottom on a three-way swivel rig. Although night fishing is effective for weakfish in many areas, those found in the bay almost always stop biting at dark.

Anglers sometimes encounter the full range of bottom fish in the bay. Blackfish (tautog) are caught by fish potters as they come in to spawn during the spring, but anglers take relatively few then. Fall provides the best shot for blacks around rocks supporting navigation aids and on a few shallow wrecks. Some mostly small sea bass are mixed in with the late-summer weakfish, but porgies (scup) are rare except in tiny sizes. Raritan Bay hosted massive runs of large porgies into the middle of the century, before pirate netters from Belford wiped them out.

Northern Shore.   Boats that are berthed within Raritan Bay often fish the ocean, but most activity along the Northern Shore comes out of Shark River and Manasquan Inlets, two of the busiest inlets along the East Coast. The large municipal boat basin at Belmar includes a busy party and large-group charter fleet. Boats fishing out of Manasquan Inlet are berthed at Manasquan, Brielle, Point Pleasant Beach, and Point Pleasant. Brielle Yacht Club and Hoffman's Marina on that northern side berth one of the world's largest private offshore sportfishing fleets. Some run from the opposite shore at Southside Marina and upriver at Clark's Landing in Point Pleasant. Still others come out of northern Barnegat Bay via the Point Pleasant Canal.

The only volume of inshore rocky, mussel-covered bottom along the New Jersey coast is located north of Shark River Inlet, primarily from Deal to the famed Shrewsbury Rocks. Not only are those areas noted for bottom fish such as blackfish and sea bass, which prefer a rough seabed, but also for striped bass, bluefish, and large fluke. When door-mat fluke were much more common, before intensive trawling sharply reduced the population and prevented most fluke from surviving much beyond their third year, these rugged bottoms attracted many anglers seeking the fluke of their dreams, and they were willing to break off many rigs in the process. Some party boats specialized in that fishing, although most fluke boats today generally opt for smoother bottoms most of the time.

In addition to the rough bottoms, there are many lumps just a few miles offshore all along this coast. The most famous of those is the Klondike, a large area of lumps covered with mussels, which held huge quantities of sea bass and porgies well into the 1900s. That area between the Shark River and Manasquan Inlets was a major attraction when Manasquan Inlet was stabilized in the early 1930s. Unfortunately, extensive dragging has so smoothed the bottom that the Klondike is no longer productive of sea bass and porgies. The lumps do hold sand eels, however, which in turn attract fluke, bluefish, bonito, little tunny, and even stripers at times. Augie's Lump, the Ammo Grounds, and Eagle's Lump are smaller hills close to the Klondike that are particularly noted for bonito chumming during late summer. Manasquan Ridge, about 6 miles from that inlet, offers similar fishing, as does a string of others running to the south, such as Southeast Lump, Tolten Lump, and J. B.'s Lump. Tolten, 17 miles southeast and near the wreck of the same name, is often bathed by blue water late in the summer, which attracts great numbers of little tunny and bonito and an occasional dolphin.

The most prominent structure off the Northern Shore is the Mud Hole, a deep trench that appears to be a geological extension of the Hudson River out to the edge of the continental shelf. Depths range to more than 250 feet in parts of the trench, from the BA Buoy at the northern end to Monster Ledge, which is about 22 miles east of Manasquan Inlet. Beyond that, the Mud Hole acquires different names in the deeper spots farther off. These include Glory Hole (about 35 to 45 miles), which is noted for sharking, and Chicken Canyon (50 miles), which often attracts both bluefin and yellowfin tuna and sharks.

The inshore bluefin tuna fishery focuses on the Mud Hole, especially at Monster Ledge and even closer to shore around the Oil Wreck and the Arundo. This is primarily a late-summer to early-fall fishery. It was depressed during the mid-1990s, but in the past it often produced outstanding action with school, medium, and giant tuna. A small mesh dragger fishery that just about eliminated whiting (silver hake) and greatly reduced the ling (red hake) population is probably to blame for the lack of larger bluefins, because those fish provided the forage that drew the bluefins to the area. Sharking is also popular in the Mud Hole, and little tunny, bonito, skipjack tuna, and chicken dolphin are frequently caught there in late summer by both trollers and chunkers.

Just inside the Mud Hole to the north are some of the most famous fishing grounds worked by northern New Jersey and western Long Island boats. The Mud Buoy, also called the Mud Dump, was the most consistent area for chumming bluefish in August and September during the 1990s, but dumping of dredged muds from New York Harbor was stopped in 1997. The lack of this activity may discourage the bluefish, as happened when the dumping of acids in the stained Acid Waters was stopped three decades earlier.

Just offshore of that huge mound of mud is 17 Fathoms, a rough-bottom area named for its average depth. Bluefish feed there on numerous small bottom fish, and there is very good blackfishing in December and January, as inshore areas get too cold for the tautog. The Farms is a similar area, located nearby just inside the Mud Hole, which is noted for bluefish from May through November. Another rocky area farther inshore and just offshore of Shrewsbury Rocks is the Rattlesnake. This 55- to 60-foot rough bottom produces large quantities of blackfish. Farther north off Sandy Hook is the Scotland Grounds; the wrecks and rough bottom there provide good ling and blackfish catches in spring and fall, and it is the closest such spot for bottom anglers coming out of Raritan Bay.

Due to its proximity to one of the busiest harbors in the world, the Northern Shore has more than its share of wrecks from both collisions and sinkings during two world wars. Those hundreds of wrecks are scattered from just beyond the surf line out to near the canyons. While the inshore pieces harbor blackfish, sea bass, porgies, and ling in season, deeper wrecks often hold cod and pollock even during the summer, although those species were overfished and have been in short supply during the 1990s. Bluefish also commonly gather around wrecks and may even be found over those in 200 to 300 feet in December. The major offshore wreck fishery in recent years has been for jumbo sea bass, in depths over 200 feet and 60 to 80 miles from Brielle. They are caught from late fall through early spring and often run 3 to 5 pounds, although some specimens occasionally range up to 8 pounds.

Among the best-known and hardest fished offshore wrecks during the summer and early fall are the Bacardi and Texas Tower. Both are on the 30-fathom curve, about 65 miles out. They attract a June run of medium and giant bluefin tuna that may be replaced by yellowfins in the summer. In 1989, there were tuna to be caught at the Bacardi every day from June into the fall, and weekend fleets often exceeded 200 boats. These arrived from ports as far apart as Montauk and Barnegat, but that phenomenon has never been repeated. Large school bluefin used to be caught regularly at the Bacardi in October, whereas cod and pollock resided on the bottom, although few have been caught in recent years.

Winter codfishing is conducted mainly on wrecks 30 to 40 miles offshore in depths of 100 to 140 feet or so. The *Virginia* and the many wrecks in the Red Square, plus others to the southeast once produced lots of large cod, although that fishery dropped off to a pick of smaller cod and just a few cows during the 1990s.

Canyon fishing has become a favored attraction for anglers all along the New Jersey coast, and large fleets out of Belmar, Brielle, Manasquan, and Point Pleasant fish 80 to 90 miles off in Hudson Canyon from late June into October for yellowfin, bigeye, and albacore tuna; dolphin; blue and white marlin; and an occasional wahoo. Trolling dominates during early summer, when overnight chunking produces state-record mako and blue sharks but not many tuna. This tends to change around mid-August, when the night bite for yellowfins turns on. A few swordfish are also caught in that fashion, especially around Labor Day. Northern Shore boats also commonly fish a bit farther southeast in the much smaller Toms, Lindenkohl, and Spencer Canyons, but they sometimes have to make longer runs farther south to Wilmington Canyon when cool water moves into northern canyons early in the fall.

Surf fishing is a very important sport along the Northern Shore, especially since the revival of striped bass and weakfish during the late 1990s. Sandy Hook attracts great numbers of anglers to its parking lots, but the best fishing is often at the tip, which requires a walk of more than a mile. On the bay side of Sandy Hook, anglers cast into the mouth of the Shrewsbury River or Spermacetti Cove for weakfish, school stripers, and winter flounder at times. Numerous jetties above Shark River Inlet provide good sport for anglers using cleats to avoid slipping on the rocks. In addition to stripers and bluefish, many fluke and blackfish are caught from the jetties.

Some of the jetties between the Shark River and Manasquan Inlets were filled in by sand during beach replenishment projects, but the area remains very productive for surf casters. The jetties at the Shark River Inlet are short and provide limited fishing, but both Manasquan Inlet jetties are longer and provide extremely popular platforms for anglers seeking stripers, blues, weaks, blacks, and fluke.

The stretch of beaches from there to Barnegat Inlet is almost entirely sand and offers only a few very short jetties in Bay Head and Lavallette. These beaches provide classic surf conditions with fairly deep water nearby and lots of bars, cuts, and sloughs. The "structure" constantly changes, but good-looking water is always available. The roaring northwesters of fall are at the angler's back, and the dunes are high enough in most areas to block the wind somewhat. The surf is sometimes so calm under those circumstances that anglers ply the waters in sneakers in November. After a few days of northwest wind, so much water is pushed offshore that surf casters can wade to the outer bars at low tide.

Beach buggies are permitted after the bathing season from the Brick Township beaches south, although drivers must obtain a permit from each municipality they will pass through. Anglers without buggies can get along fine, however, because end-of-the-street parking is readily available in many spots after Labor Day; it's just a few yards from the parking areas to the surf. Island Beach State Park provides the best access for buggy operators, thousands of whom purchase seasonal permits. Many others pay by the day. An annual Governor's Surf Fishing Tournament is held there in October.

All of the usual species are caught from these sand beaches. The emphasis is on baitfishing during the spring and summer for stripers. Sea worms are the usual choice at first, but from May into December surf clams are the standard, as they are much cheaper and seem to attract larger bass. These clams became particularly popular during the 1990s. The fishery tends to be best right after a hard easterly blow, which tosses clams up on the beach. As the clams die, those not consumed by sea gulls are washed into the surf, where stripers wait for a treat they otherwise can't partake of. As a result, long casts are rarely necessary, and kids often do best with clams because they can't cast far beyond the wash. Mullet have traditionally been prime baits for bluefish, and that's especially the case in September, when the first cold snaps send those small forage fish down the beach in large schools.

Casting lures for bass, blues, and weaks attracts large crowds of anglers in the fall. Popular lures are swimming plugs that are smaller (usually $5/8$ to 1 ounce) than those used to the east, as surf casters here generally opt for light 7- to 8-foot rods and 10- to 14-pound lines with small spinning reels. Jigs

Anglers are attracted to jetties and beaches all along the Jersey coast.

from $1/4$ to $5/8$ ounce tipped with soft plastics are very popular for school stripers and weakfish, whereas metal is particularly effective when long casts are required and when bluefish may also be present.

Most surf anglers here fish a teaser a few feet ahead of the lure when bluefish aren't a problem, as the weightless fly or soft plastic often produces more stripers and weaks than the lure. Popping plugs work at times for stripers and blues but aren't a standard. Dawn and dusk are traditionally prime periods for casting, but some of the best catches are made at night. As the season progresses, hot action on lures is possible at any time during the day. Bluefish blitzes are difficult to predict; they appear suddenly to blast baitfish, especially bunkers, and quickly move on.

For jetty jockeys fearless enough to risk their limbs, the north jetty at Barnegat Inlet may be the best spot on the coast for stripers during a northeaster. Fly anglers have done very well casting into the inlet for little tunny (locally called false albacore) during late summer. Anglers land many fluke and small blues in the inlet from the jetty, and there's good weakfishing on jigs cast from bulkheads inside the inlet.

Shore fishing is comparatively limited here. The Long Branch Fishing Pier, the only long public fishing pier along the Northern Shore, burnt down and wasn't replaced. Not only was that a fine summer fishing spot for fluke, but it was also famed for whiting fishing at night during early winter. Anglers often caught bags of whiting there at virtually no expense, but both the pier and the whiting were gone by the 1990s. A short fishing pier still exists at Seaside Heights, as do private piers at Ocean Grove and Belmar. Quite a few docks and sedge banks offer free fishing possibilities on Raritan Bay, and there is a fishing pier at Keansburg.

The Shark River is small, but it offers very good spring and fall winter flounder fishing from both designated piers in Belmar Marina and from rental skiffs, as well as seasonal opportunities for stripers, fluke, kingfish, and blowfish. The Manasquan River also provides only a few miles of tidal waters, although it's heavily fished by small-boat owners for flounder, fluke, weakfish, and school stripers. The walls within the inlet on both sides draw hundreds of anglers. They catch lots of fluke, sea robins, and hickory shad but also get a good shot at bluefish when these species first flood in for a week or so in early May.

The Manasquan River connects with Barnegat Bay through the Point Pleasant Canal, which constitutes the start of the Intracoastal Waterway. The canal is an excellent shore fishing area. Anglers mostly bottom-fish for flounder, blackfish, sea bass, and porgies during the day, but striper and weakfish pros roam the banks at night. Due to roaring currents, the best fishing is usually around slack water. The rough bottom claims lots of sinkers and jigs,

and nets are required to get larger fish over the fence that runs along both sides of the canal.

The northern half of Barnegat Bay is ideal for small boats, as this is all shallow water that provides excellent opportunities for flounder, fluke, weakfish and blue claw crabs. The small Metedeconk River, just beyond the canal, is a good spot for weakfish. The somewhat larger Toms River farther south attracts a spring run of white perch, although the wintering stripers that used to reside there were cleaned out by netters long ago. Holes near the Mantoloking Bridge provide an early-spring haven for flounder and are very good for fluke and weakfish later on.

Good-size stripers are caught off sedge banks near Barnegat Inlet during the spring on live herring, and live eels fished at night from summer into fall produce some 30- to 50-pounders in the same areas. A large run of small bluefish usually invades the bay in May and June, producing fine sport over endless shallow eelgrass bottoms. Enthusiasts favor small popping plugs cast on light tackle. The great runs of school stripers that hit bucktail jigs and flies during April and May in the 1960s haven't returned. It was this fishery that sparked establishment of the Salt Water Fly Rodders from Cap Colvin's Tackle Shop in Seaside Park. The ancient practice of chumming with grass shrimp for weakfish in Barnegat Bay has returned, however, because the eelgrass that harbors those tiny baitfish has recovered from a blight that afflicted the entire Northeast Atlantic coast.

Central shore. Barnegat Inlet is much wider than its counterparts to the north, and much more dangerous as well. Shifting sands have been a problem since Henry Hudson first spotted it from sea and gave it a Dutch name—one that roughly translates to Breakers Inlet. A recent project to stabilize the inlet with a new, longer south jetty was only partially successful, but it did provide a great, flat-topped fishing platform. A substantial fleet of private, charter, and party boats is located just around the southern corner of the inlet and within yards of the famous red lighthouse, Barnegat Light. Known as Old Barney, it sits at the northern end of Long Beach Island. Many other boats run a few miles across the bay to the inlet from such ports as Waretown and Forked (pronounced fork-ed) River, which is the site of a state marina. Beach Haven is the major port toward the southern end of the island, but those boaters access the ocean via Little Egg Harbor Inlet.

Stripers and blues of all sizes are commonly caught in Barnegat Inlet, and the north jetty is a favorite for casters who work the broken-down seaward section before it rises up again at the light on the tip. Anglers also troll and jig for plentiful stripers and blues from October into December off Island Beach State Park and at the clam beds just northeast of the inlet and a couple of miles south on Harvey Cedars Lump. Fluking is very good both within and just outside of the inlet. Some of the best sea bass and blackfish wrecks along the coast are located within a short run from Barnegat Inlet. Blackfish specialists regularly catch tautog in the 10- to 15-pound class from those wrecks, especially in April.

Fishing within southern Barnegat Bay is similar to that in the northern section, although Double Creek Channel and Myer's Hole at Barnegat Light provide the deepest holes within the shallow bay and are often the best spots for winter flounder and weakfish. The Forked River Power Plant on the mainland side pushes hot water into the bay and attracts an early run of flounder as well as wintering school stripers.

Offshore fishing centers around Barnegat Ridge, about 16 miles east. The ridge area actually consists of the North, Middle, and South Ridges, which are famed for bluefish but also attract school bluefin tuna, little tunny, bonito, and even dolphin at times during late summer. Barnegat boats also fish lumps to the north, including Ole's Lump, which is a favorite for trolling and chunking school tuna as well as skipjacks and little tunny.

Most northern boats sail toward Barnegat during June to get the first shots at mako sharks along the 20-fathom line near the Resor Wreck, and in such depressions as the Dusky Hole and The Fingers. The sharking area referred to as The Star is at the northern end of The Fingers, where the compass star is located on the nautical chart. Unfortunately, those traditional sharking grounds have been producing mostly blue sharks rather than makos and browns (sandbars) because longlining pressures impacted the latter two species. Therefore, sharkers more frequently run even farther offshore, such as to the Triple Wrecks area, which is about 60 miles to sea but still gives up a few large makos. The Barnegat fleet is closer to Toms, Lindenkohl, and Spencer Canyons but also runs up to the Hudson or south to the Wilmington when necessary.

The Beach Haven charter fleet was much larger earlier in the twentieth century and attracted anglers from all over the East for school bluefin tuna trolling. That fishery has gone downhill over the years, and the Beach Haven fleet now fishes primarily for bluefish, fluke, and sea bass inshore plus canyon tuna and billfish. Little Egg Harbor Inlet produces large stripers on live eels during the fall, and the inshore waters of Great Bay are especially good for fluke and weakfish.

The Mullica River flows into Great Bay and is noted for excellent white perch fishing through the ice during very cold winters. Some stripers also overwinter in the Mullica. Graveling Point, where the river meets the bay, is usually where the first stripers of the season are caught by anglers casting sandworms from the sedge banks in March.

Long Beach Island is also noted for its surf casting, although the light-tackle lure fishing that dominates north of Barnegat Inlet in the fall isn't as common at Long Beach. Baitfishing is standard. Bunkers are most popular for both stripers and blues in the fall, when the chamber of commerce conducts its annual six-week Surf Fishing Tournament for those two species. It usually takes a striper of 40 to 50 pounds or more, and bluefish close to 20 pounds, to win the grand prize for each species, and almost invariably they and the vast majority of other entries are hooked on cut bunker. Clams and worms work here just as they do to the north, but anglers land few really big stripers on those baits.

The entire nature of the coast changes below Beach Haven Inlet, as the shoreline becomes a series of small sandy barrier islands separated by shoals. Brigantine Inlet, at the north end of Absecon Island, is also known as Wreck Inlet and is used only by small boats. At the south end of the island is Absecon Inlet; this wide, stable inlet carries much charter and private boat traffic from Atlantic City, which is on its south side. Fluke and weakfish are the featured species within Absecon Bay; outside fishing includes bluefish at such nearby spots as Atlantic City Ridge, and wreck fishing for sea bass and blackfish. Sharking is popular at the 28 Mile Wreck, which also provides good inshore trolling for school bluefins and dolphin. Canyon anglers from here south tend to run to the Wilmington and Baltimore rather than to the northeast canyons.

Surf casting south of Long Beach Island isn't as good as that to the north due to a more gradual deepening from shore. While stripers and blues aren't as frequently encountered, there is often good baitfishing for kingfish and weakfish. The mouths of inlets are also productive, and it should be noted that the all-tackle world-record $78\frac{1}{2}$-pound striped bass was plugged from an Atlantic City jetty on the stormy night of September 21, 1982.

South Jersey. Great Egg Harbor Inlet is used by boats sailing out of Margate to the north and Ocean City on the south side. No large party and charter boat fleet exists in this area; however, the very lack of pressure on wrecks has made it possible for some party boats to consistently take the largest blackfish in the state. Many trophy blackfish of 10 pounds or more, some to 18 pounds, have been landed. An all-tackle world-record 25-pounder was taken in January 1998.

Boats in this area find good sharking 20 to 30 miles offshore and frequently encounter large quantities of Spanish mackerel while trolling inshore for bluefish both on grounds toward Atlantic City and farther south to such areas as the Stone Beds. They also share areas closer to the inlets directly below them (Corson, Townsend, and Hereford), such as Sea Isle Lump, Sea Isle Shoal, and Avalon Shoal. The many creeks and channels inside barrier islands provide good action with fluke and weakfish. Striped bass and blackfish are caught at bridges near the ocean.

From Wildwood to Cape May, anglers can experience excellent variety thanks to the mouth of

Rods with shorter sections developed not only out of carrying convenience but also because they could be concealed or camouflaged as walking sticks at a time when angling was considered dishonorable.

N

Tournament anglers returning from canyon fishing attract a crowd in Cape May.

Delaware Bay. Boats here have the unique opportunity to sail through protected waters in either direction to reach the ocean or bay. The navy cut a canal through Cape May that boats can follow from the harbor into Delaware Bay. The ocean is a shorter run through wide Cold Spring Inlet, which is more often simply referred to as Cape May Inlet. Only North Wildwood boats normally run out of Hereford Inlet, which has shoals that limit it to small boats.

Not only is the bay itself cleaner these days, but the legendary oxygen block in the Delaware River near Philadelphia also has been eliminated. This much cleaner river has once again become a major striped bass spawning area. Delaware Bay is an established spawning area for several species, including the weakfish. Although that species is very cyclical, it may well be that the incredible slaughter of them by trawlers, gillnetters, and pound nets, as well as recreational anglers, during periods of abundance is the reason for their sudden disappearance.

The last great cycle, which started in the early 1970s and ran into the mid-1980s, produced tremendous catches of ever-larger weaks during the May to June spawning run. Ultimately, 8- to 10-pounders became routine, and it took weaks in the midteens to win contests. These beautiful fish were coming back again in the late 1990s, but this time the fall and winter slaughter by trawlers in federal waters was prohibited by the Atlantic States Marine Fisheries Commission Management Plan and cooperation from the National Marine Fisheries Service.

Anglers catch most smaller bay weakfish by casting small jigs tipped with shedder crab or on that bait directly. The larger fish taken during the previous cycle, however, were easily attracted to jigs tipped with long plastic worms and other such artificials. Hotspots near the mouth of the bay include Brandywine Shoal in midbay (marked by Brandywine Light), Round Shoal, Sixty Foot Slough,

Brown Shoal, and the adjacent deep-water anchorage for large vessels coming into the bay on the Delaware side.

Delaware Bay also represents the practical northern range of several species. Black drum follow behind the weakfish each spring, and June is the prime month of the spawning run. Those fish can run up to more than 100 pounds and were almost wiped out for years after tuna purse seiners began to make huge sets on the drum. Bottom fishing at night with clams on the bottom is the usual method for attracting drum. Croaker and spot are frequent summer catches in the bay. Cape May Harbor also produces the northernmost spotted seatrout fishing, as a few anglers wade from the marsh banks in the fall to cast lures for the southern version of the weakfish. There is some fishing throughout the marsh areas for small stripers, as well as for flounder, in the fall.

Shore fishing along the Atlantic here is marginal, as the bay and plentiful nearby structure make this more of a boater's fishery, but jetty and surf anglers connect at times, especially in fall, with striped bass, and occasionally bluefish, from Wildwood to Cape May Point. Accessible jetties with end-of-street parking are available in Wildwood, Cape May, and Cape May Point, but the prime jetties at Cape May Inlet are inaccessible, as they're surrounded by Coast Guard property.

Bluefishing was generally better off the Northern Shore during the 1990s, especially during the summer, than it was in South Jersey, which was spotty at best most of the time. However, a state record 27-pound, 1-ounce blue (which may be the second largest ever weighed) was caught in October 1997 on a Cape May party boat that was chumming at night on Five Fathom Bank.

Because any winter flounder found this far south are usually small and not particularly abundant, fluke are referred to simply as flounder. That fishery is an important one for the Wildwood-Cape May fleet, who get into them as early as April and often continue well into the fall.

The mouth of the bay is protected by dozens of underwater sandbars that create rips. These have become one of the finest places to fish for striped bass in the fall. From October into November and sometimes December there is usually good action in at least some of those rips for anglers drifting live eels. Hundreds of boats pursue the stripers on weekends, but the abundance of rips often makes it possible to get away from the crowd. Strong northwest winds muddy waters at the mouth of the bay, but easterly winds are good if not too strong, as the technique involves drifting through the rough water at the edge of the rip. The bass wait here for prey to be drawn to them. In addition to the private and charter fleets, several party boats also participate in this fishery. A smaller spring run occurs in the rips, but jigs tipped with baits are usually more effective than eels at that time.

N

The largest stripers caught around Cape May during recent falls haven't come from the rips, where volume is greatest, but from shallow waters near shore where bunker chunking draws big bass to those baits. South Jersey anglers also get into hot diamond jigging for migrating stripers and blues from late November into December, although that sport is primarily pursued on Five Fathom Bank. During the 1990s, it was illegal to retain any size striper from these waters, which are roughly 9 miles offshore and well into federal territory.

Offshore fishing is extremely important to the Cape May fleet, and South Jersey Marina is one of the largest of its kind on the coast. The marina sponsors several offshore tournaments, starting with a shark contest in early June. The king of all East Coast tournaments, however, is held out of The Canyon Club Resort Marina. The Mid-Atlantic $500,000 is actually misnamed, because the official calcuttas bring the pot—in a contest that draws more than 130 boats in mid-August—to well over a million dollars. The target species are blue and white marlin plus yellowfin and bigeye tuna, which are mostly caught in local canyons such as the Wilmington, Poorman's, and Baltimore.

South Jersey boats have a considerable advantage over their northern counterparts in that runs of only 60 miles or so are required to reach the closest spots, although tournament anglers regularly blow past the 100-fathom line to fish 500- to 1,000-fathom areas 100 miles and more from Cape May. The offshore fleet gets into especially good chunking for 50- to 150-pounders during June and July on hills off Delmarva. Yellowfins mix into the same grounds, 40 miles or so from Cape May, during the summer.

Weakfish, fluke, and small blues are featured farther up the bay off the Maurice (pronounced "Morris") River and Fortescue, where a large charter fleet concentrates on these species. Popular areas include Miah Maull Shoal and Egg Island Point. Striped bass have become a more prominent quarry since the art of bunker chunking was introduced to the area, and 60-pound bass have been hooked at the bug light off the Maurice River. Local anglers fish stripers primarily in October and November, although schoolies are present in the Maurice River much of the year. Good bay fishing for private boaters continues up the bay to at least the Cohansy River. Stripers can be caught even during the winter by shore casters around the Rt. 95 Bridge from New Jersey to Delaware. The best Delaware River striper fishing, however, occurs farther upriver.

The Division of Fish, Game and Wildlife has been acquiring parts of the extensive wetlands along Delaware Bay. In cooperation with the federal government and private groups, they plan to eventually have 60 percent under their protection in order to ensure protection for the many juvenile species such as weakfish and fluke that are dependent on those marshes.

NEW MEXICO

Although some perceive New Mexico as a desert state, anglers who frequent the area know better. From its high alpine lakes in wilderness areas to its small streams and rivers that feed large reservoirs, there is ample water to provide varied fishing opportunities. Whether you're a fly fishing purist, a dedicated bass angler, or just enjoy a day on the water or relaxing on the bank, there's plenty of action on the state's 6,000 miles of permanent streams and rivers and 170 lakes and reservoirs—all with good fish populations that are mostly accessible to the public.

The "Land of Enchantment" has seven major watersheds. Among them, they offer almost any kind of fishing. This state is blessed with diverse habitats, ranging from arctic-alpine to mountain forests, prairies, and deserts. These areas are home to various cold- and warmwater species. Of the former, there are rainbow, brown, brook, cutthroat, and lake trout, as well as kokanee salmon; of the latter, largemouth, smallmouth, striped, white, and spotted bass thrive throughout the state, as do good populations of walleye, northern pike, crappie, bluegills, and three species of catfish.

A wealth of public land is another of New Mexico's blessings, giving anglers easy access to recreation statewide. The state's five national forests and 2 million acres of public land are managed by the National Forest Service, the Bureau of Land Management, and other federal agencies. State parks and wildlife areas abound. In addition, many Indian tribes have good fishing waters for which no state license is needed, although tribal permits are required. Excellent fishing opportunities also abound on private land, but permission is required and some landowners charge access fees.

The state Game and Fish Department has regulations and projects aimed at improving fishing for everyone; this is a challenge in a state where drought and demands for irrigation constantly impact the fisheries resource. The state stocks 6.7 million trout each year for a growing number of anglers. Some areas are designated as "special trout waters" and have regulations that promote quality fishing by restricting baits and bag limits. The rules and fees are subject to change, so anglers are advised to check first.

Northwest

Navajo Lake. A 15,000-acre irrigation reservoir, Navajo Lake holds good populations of warm- and coldwater fish. In the spring, there's excellent fishing for large crappie, which are predominantly caught by jigging plastic grubs and spoons around submerged vegetation. Trolling for kokanee salmon is productive throughout the season. In the fall, these fish school to spawn at the spillway and in Francis Canyon. Roe sacks are prime baits for trout in these areas. Navajo also supports smallmouth bass up to 5 pounds, northern pike that approach

20 pounds, and brown trout, some weighing in at more than 10 pounds. Try slow-trolling in the winter months for the big browns.

San Juan River. One of the finest tailwater trout fisheries in the nation was created below Navajo Dam when it was completed in 1962. On this section of the San Juan River, anglers can consistently catch trout from 15 to 19 inches and larger. The well-nourished fish, mostly rainbows, grow 6 inches a year and weigh an average of 3 to 5 pounds. Eight-pounders are not uncommon. Twenty miles of excellent fishing can now be found in what was formerly a muddy catfish river. The cool, clear water flowing from the reservoir's 300-foot depths makes ideal habitat that grows trophy rainbow and brown trout and even a few cutthroats. To enhance and protect this valuable fishery, the state has established special rules. The first quarter-mile below the dam is a catch-and-release section; all fish must be immediately returned to the water. The next 3½-mile section is restricted to the use of artificial flies and lures with barbless hooks, and has a bag limit of one trout that must be 20 inches or longer. The river downstream from the "quality" sections does not have special regulations, yet it maintains fine fishing albeit with fewer trout.

The San Juan River flow varies according to yearly snowpack and reservoir storage, but usually runs at 600 to 800 cubic feet per second (cfs) in the winter and summer, and as high at 5,000 cfs in the spring. The current is swift and deep, with intermittent pools, riffles, and flats, some of them 30 to 40 yards wide. Chest waders are recommended, but the big water can be hazardous. There is good fishing in numerous side channels where the wading is easier. Best results come from a modified nymphing technique in which the fly is sunk until it floats just off the bottom. Put a single split shot about 18 inches above the fly and cast upstream, letting it drift back down in a natural manner. Long casts are not necessary.

San Juan trout don't strike like most fish. Instead, they lie on the bottom, rise to take the fly, and slowly float back down with no perceptible hit. A small colored marker, serving as a strike indicator, is placed where the leader and line meet. This is an effective way to determine strikes. Watch the indicator and when it stops or twitches, however slightly, set the hook. This, along with the weighted fly, should guarantee success.

A No. 10 black Woolly Worm and a local fly called the San Juan Worm, along with several locally tied patterns that resemble trout eggs, are good most anytime. Generally, the darker patterns work best, but in one area called the "orange hole," anything seems to work as long as it is orange. Due to stabilized water flows, insect hatches also provide excellent dry-fly fishing using small No. 18 to 20 Renegade and Iron Blue Dun patterns.

The reputation of this river brings anglers from all over the country and beyond. A problem with this is an overabundance of people, particularly on the weekends. Guides who use boats are available and are very successful, and hiring a guide is probably the best option for a first-time angler.

Navajo Indian Reservation/Morgan Lake. At 12,000-acre Morgan Lake, a power plant takes water for cooling purposes, and this keeps the temperature around 60°F in the winter. Thus, Morgan is good for catching 3- to 4-pound largemouth bass from November through March, using slow retrieves with deep-diving crankbaits, jigging spoons, and small plastic worms.

Jicarilla Apache Reservation/Stone Lake. Stone Lake is one of the better trout waters in the state for large rainbows, but it does suffer from occasional winter kills. It is best fished from boats or float tubes because of an abundance of weeds. Anglers are limited to using flies and lures here. Other reservation lakes are La Jara, Mundo, Horse, and Dulce. Some winter ice fishing is available.

Rio Chama. This watershed has three major impoundments. Heron Lake's 8,000 acres is home to the only viable population of lake trout (mackinaw) in the state, with a record 25-pounder in the books. Troll deep via a downrigger or lead-core line, using a heavy jig or some type of swimming lure. Heron also holds good numbers of kokanee salmon, which are best caught by trolling in summer and which gang up to spawn in the late fall. Rainbow trout also show up in creels from this location, where boats are limited to no-wake speeds. Just downstream is El Vado Lake, another reservoir that is best fished from a boat. A state-record 20-pound, 4-ounce brown trout was taken from the river just below the dam. Farther downstream is Abiquiu Reservoir, where there are good populations of trout, crappie, channel catfish, and smallmouth bass. The Chama is fed by numerous smaller tributaries, the most notable being the Rio Brazos, which is mostly on private land.

Jemez Mountain streams. The watersheds of the Jemez Mountains are host to many small trout-filled streams, some of them limited to flies and lures only. Most rainbow and brown trout are in the 8- to 12-inch range, but 20-inch lunkers are not uncommon. Every spring, anglers look forward to the stonefly hatch in the Guadalupe, San Antonio, and East Fork Rivers.

Rio Grande River. The Rio Grande River flows north to south, nearly bisecting the state. As it enters New Mexico it runs through a deep gorge, part of which is designated as a federal Wild and Scenic River. Those who walk into this section are rewarded with large rainbow and brown trout, along with northern pike that have migrated downstream from Colorado. The Red River upstream from its confluence with the Rio Grande is particularly inviting in the fall, when brown trout migrate upstream to spawn. Coldwater species predominate in the Rio Grande's northern section and tributaries, where Hopewell Lake is recognized for its

Some species of fish can make their own light, and only fish can produce electricity from their bodies.

brook trout. Cochiti Lake, a U.S. Army Corps of Engineers impoundment, offers coldwater and warmwater species. The lake has some trout and good numbers of crappie, white bass, and channel catfish. The spillway provides good fishing for trout, primarily with baits. Severe drawdowns do have an adverse effect, and the upper end has been silting in. Boats are recommended, but be advised that this is a no-wake lake.

Pueblo Indian waters. The Jemez, Santa Clara, Sandia, Nambe, Zuni, Acoma, and Isleta Pueblos all have lakes, and some have streams that are stocked and open to the public. Permits are required.

Bluewater Lake. At 2,000 acres, Bluewater Lake always produces nice rainbows for those fishing from the bank or through the ice, as well as for lure trollers and bait anglers. Try casting flies in early morning and late evening as well; a spinning rig with a fly and bubble is sometimes a good combination. Water levels in the lake fluctuate significantly.

Northeast

Wilderness trout. In a triangle of the Santa Fe and Carson National Forests bordered by the towns of Santa Fe, Taos, and Las Vegas, are 20 small lakes and 150 miles of streams that can be reached only by foot or on horseback. All have excellent fishing for rainbow and cutthroat trout, but don't expect any lunkers, as the fish grow slowly in the high mountains with their short summer seasons. The 167,000-acre Pecos Wilderness in the Sangre de Cristo Mountains contains the headwaters of the Pecos River, the state's second-largest watershed. Popular secluded lakes include Spirit, Pecos Baldy, Katherine, and Stewart. An ultralight spinning rod and an assortment of small lures, hooks, bubbles, and flies are all that is needed. In the summertime, catch grasshoppers for live bait; this is a killer combination in the high country.

Red River. Small headwater lakes for the Red River include Middle Fork, Goose, Heart, and Lost, all with cutthroat and rainbow trout. Cabresto Lake and stream has brook trout. The main river is stocked with rainbows, and the lower portion below the Red River hatchery is great for brown trout in the fall.

Eagle Nest. Located in the 8,500-foot Moreno Valley, this 3,000-acre Eagle Nest is one of the state's best public trout waters. It provides year-round fishing for all who want a truly quality angling experience. This lake produces 200 pounds of trout per acre. Although 14- to 16-inch rainbows are common, a true trophy is always a possibility. Kokanee salmon are stocked regularly. A former private lake, it is under a long-term lease that provides public access for bank anglers. Boaters do best by trolling. Fishing is most successful in the early morning and late evening, especially casting flies to rising fish. This is also a popular spot for ice anglers.

Cimarron River. A 21-mile stretch of heavily fished water below Eagle Nest Lake, the Cimarron River is stocked throughout the summer, but fishing is mediocre at best. In the fall, this river does a flip-flop, providing exceptional brown trout action, especially for lunkers that become aggressive before spawning. Some portions of the river flow through private land, although most of it is open to the public.

Pecos River. The Pecos is a major river beginning in the Pecos Wilderness and flowing south into Texas. Trout are caught in the upper reaches, and warmwater species in the lower sections. Santa Rosa Lake, a 1,500-acre reservoir, has bass, walleye, crappie, and catfish.

Ute Lake. Located in the broad grasslands, Ute is a large reservoir (8,200 acres) and one of the best warmwater lakes in New Mexico because it is not subject to irrigation drawdowns. Smallmouth bass do well here, and the state record of just over $6\frac{1}{2}$ pounds was caught in Ute. White bass, large walleye, largemouth bass, and crappie are also available.

Conchas Lake. A 25-mile impoundment on the Canadian River, Conchas is the top walleye lake in New Mexico. A rocky bottom cut by submerged cliffs makes ideal habitat for this species. Boats equipped with sonar help locate these spots. Conchas is also known for large crappie, which provide best action during April and May.

Southeast

Pecos River. Fishing along the river is good for channel and flathead catfish in isolated holes. Anglers park and walk a 2- to 3-mile stretch using chicken livers, cut baits, and grasshoppers. Much of the river is marginal due to erratic and low water flows. On-stream reservoirs provide good angling for warmwater fish. In addition to Santa Rosa, 4,500-acre Lake Sumner has the usual warmwater species, including white bass. Try fishing here during July and August when the pressure drops off. Use buzzbaits along rocky bluffs and mini-coves. When the water rises after summer showers, fish shallow at the upper end. Brantley Reservoir (3,400 acres) is the last major impoundment with similar species and angling techniques to those at Sumner. Carlsbad Municipal Lake provides urban angling opportunities for trout in the wintertime, as well as warmwater species year-round.

Sacramento and White Mountain streams. These areas have assorted small streams and lakes, plus Ruidoso, Carrizo, and Eagle Rivers. Alto and Grindstone Lakes in the south-central mountains are stocked with rainbows. A natural population of brook trout thrives in Bonito Lake and in the streams. The best fishing is at dawn and dusk.

Mescalero Apache Reservation. A large reservoir at the edge of Ruidoso, plus two other smaller lakes nearby, provide good trout fishing; permits are required.

Southwest

Elephant Butte Lake. This is New Mexico's largest and finest warmwater fishing spot. Its 40-mile length and 40,000 surface acres will satisfy any angler, and it has produced striped bass up to 54 pounds, largemouth bass to 9 pounds, flathead catfish up to 78 pounds, and above-average numbers and sizes of all the other warmwater species. Unsurpassed largemouth opportunities make it home to national bass tournaments. It is one of the first lakes in which spring bass fishing picks up due to its southerly location and shallow, south-facing, protected brushy areas. Better fishing early in the year is in the area above the "narrows" at the upper end of the lake. White bass get active at the same time and in the same area.

Caballo Lake. Located just below Elephant Butte, Caballo is the last reservoir on the Rio Grande River before it leaves the state. It harbors the same fish species, but not the reputation of its neighbor, possibly because of its smaller size and severe drawdowns during irrigation season. It is a good fishery and seldom crowded, best known for its white bass fishing in the summer.

Gila National Forest. The permanent waters offered by Gila National Forest support good populations of smaller trout, but the areas separating them can be very dry. And some of these waters head into the wilderness area, where access is restricted. Others host populations of the Gila trout, an endangered species, and are closed to fishing. Rainbow and brown trout, with a few brookies at higher elevations, are the primary local species. Lakes include Lake Roberts, a 71-acre site with rainbow trout and catfish; Wall Lake, a 10-acre puddle with rainbows; 100-acre Snow Lake, which also has rainbow trout; and 22-acre Bear Canyon, which has rainbow trout, bluegills, catfish, and crappie.

Bill Evans Lake. This 62-acre off-stream reservoir consistently produces big largemouth bass, including a 15-pound, 13-ounce state record. Bluegills, crappie, and catfish are present, and trout are stocked in the winter.

Rio Grande River. The Rio Grande is primarily a warmwater fishery. The only exception is the section between Elephant Butte and Caballo Reservoirs, which runs through the town of Truth or Consequences. There, cool water from the depths of Elephant Butte is home to large rainbow trout, some of which approach 6 pounds. Food is plentiful here. The section is channelized, and access is limited to a few public stretches of bank. Best success here is had by drift fishing with flies or baits from flat-bottomed boats, but launch points are limited.

Gila River. The Gila is a large river flowing from the Gila National Forest into Arizona. Warmwater species include catfish and smallmouth bass. It is stocked with rainbow trout upstream in the national forest.

Best Waters

Although natural circumstances have unpredictable affects on fisheries resources or on anglers' success rates, some waters stand out in New Mexico for particular species. These include the following.

Rainbow trout: San Juan River below Navajo Reservoir, Rio Chama above and below El Vado Lake, Pecos River, Rio de Los Pinos, and the Jemez watershed

Brown trout: Navajo Reservoir, Wild Rivers section of the Rio Grande, San Juan River below Navajo Reservoir, Rio Chama, Cimarron River below Eagle Nest Lake, Mora-Pecos River system, and the Jemez watershed

Brook trout: Hopewell and Cabresto Lakes, and Bonito and Carrizo Creeks

Lake trout: Heron Lake

Kokanee salmon: Heron, El Vado, Navajo, and Eagle Nest Lakes

Largemouth bass: Elephant Butte, Ute, and Conchas Lakes

Smallmouth bass: Ute, Conchas, Elephant Butte, and Abiquiu Lakes

White bass: Elephant Butte, Caballo, Cochiti, and Brantley Lakes

Walleye: Ute, Conchas, Caballo, Santa Rosa, and Sumner Lakes

Catfish: All of the larger waters in the state

Crappie: Conchas, Abiquiu, Ute, Cochiti, Elephant Butte, and Caballo Lakes

Bluegills: Elephant Butte, Sumner, Santa Rosa, Ute, and Conchas Lakes

Green sunfish: Canadian, Pecos, Rio Grande, Gila, and Black Rivers

Yellow perch: Lower Charette, Springer, and Stubblefield Lakes

NEW YORK

To many non–New Yorkers, and even to many people who live in or near New York City, it's a surprise to learn that the Empire State has among the most diverse and abundant fishing resources in North America.

North of Manhattan's skyscrapers and pavement are some 70,000 miles of rivers and streams, 7,500 lakes and ponds, 324 reservoirs, and two Great Lakes that offer angling for most of North America's important freshwater species. To the east, the marine waters of the Atlantic abut more than 1,500 miles of coastline and offer bay, inshore, and offshore opportunities for a broad spectrum of large and small gamefish. The number of species pursued in New York—from yellow perch to yellowfin tuna and brook trout to blue marlin—rivals that found in Fulton Fish Market, the Big Apple's fabled fishmonger's paradise. Accordingly, New York annually ranks in the top 10 in both number of licensed anglers and number of registered boats, despite its large and mostly urban population.

This state discharges water from all of the Great Lakes, the Adirondack Mountains, the Catskill Mountains, and the Delaware Basin, and contains a plethora of warmwater and coldwater environments for the likes of such popular and widely dispersed fish as trout (which once thrived in the waters around Manhattan), bass, salmon, pike, and walleye. The estuary of the Hudson River, a major Atlantic tributary, is the second most important nursery for striped bass on the East Coast. And Montauk, at the eastern end of Long Island, maintains its long and well-deserved reputation as a world-renowned saltwater angling port.

In saltwater, the most prominent inshore and bay species include striped bass, bluefish, flounder, fluke, weakfish, mackerel, black sea bass, blackfish, and porgies. Offshore, various shark species are regularly sought, as are bluefin, yellowfin, and bigeye tuna; albacore; bonito; dolphin; striped marlin; and blue marlin. Among warmwater species in freshwater, largemouth and smallmouth bass are extremely popular. Other prominent fish include northern pike, walleye, chain pickerel, muskellunge, yellow perch, crappie, rock bass, bullhead, and assorted sunfish. Eels, fallfish, suckers, and carp have some following, and migratory American shad are a favored springtime catch. Brown and brook trout top the popularity charts among coldwater species, but the state offers prominent fisheries for rainbow trout, lake trout, and steelhead, as well as chinook, coho, kokanee, and landlocked Atlantic salmon.

New York has the distinction of being the birthplace of fly fishing and fly tying in North America, owing to the efforts of Theodore Gordon, who, around the turn of the twentieth century, applied then exclusively British tactics to trout in the Neversink River and created the first dry-fly patterns appropriate for New World waters. By contrast, New York also has the distinction of producing some of the largest muskellunge ever recorded, among them numerous world records caught by trolling in the St. Lawrence River. It also produced the second-largest striped bass ever taken on rod and reel—a 76-pound former world record from Shagwong Reef off Montauk Point. And it produced one of the most heralded and disputed fish ever landed—a 3,427-pound great white shark taken from a boat captained by a man who the shark-hunting character Quint was patterned after in the book and movie *Jaws*.

From east to west and north to south, from salmon to shark and stream to surf, from farm pond to Finger Lake and rowboat to party boat, New York unquestionably has something to offer any angler.

Hudson Valley

The densely populated and largely suburban southeastern Hudson Valley has surprisingly more fishing opportunities on both sides of the scenic Hudson River than might be expected. These include numerous small rivers and streams, a plethora of ponds and small lakes, and a few publicly accessible motorboat lakes. Warmwater species are the main target in the smaller and shallower waters, but trout—primarily stocked—exist in numerous places.

On the east side of the Hudson River are 15 small to midsize reservoirs that are part of the Croton River watershed and that partly supply New York City with water. These strictly regulated reservoirs are off-limits to everyone except anglers on foot or fishing from rowboats. A prohibition against motors keeps many anglers from venturing onto them, but these bodies of water, as well as their inlet and outlet streams, are home to several trout species as well as bass, and comprise some of the most significant yet underutilized publicly accessible waters in the area. West Branch, Croton, Kensico, and Cross River Reservoirs are among the larger and more notable options, and quality stream fishing for trout can be had on Amawalk Outlet as well as on the East Branch of the Croton River.

Hudson River.   From the Tappan Zee Bridge spanning Haverstraw Bay, the widest section of river, to the dam at Troy, the tidal Hudson River offers surprisingly good and diverse fishing. Oft-maligned, oft-abused, but ever-potent, the remarkable Hudson has enjoyed a water-quality comeback and a resurgence in top-rate angling. It is ranked as a top Northeast fishery for largemouth and smallmouth bass, and an awesome spring hotspot for stripers. This reputation perseveres despite marginal shore fishing opportunities and insufficient access for transient boaters.

Fisheries biologists say that between 1 and 2 million stripers migrate into the Hudson each year to spawn. In the process, they traverse 154 miles from Manhattan to Troy, although the greater portion stays in the Hudson Highlands. These fish generally begin moving into and up the river in mid-March. By mid-April they reach Newburgh, and by late April they arrive in the area from Kingston to Catskill and beyond.

Spawning takes place when the water has warmed to the mid- to upper 50s, usually around mid- to late May. By mid-June, the main body of stripers has moved downstream and disperses in New York Harbor and along the coast, a few traveling as far as Cape Cod. Some fish, mostly small schoolies, remain in the river throughout the summer.

With the East Coast striper population having rebounded from historic lows, the number and size of fish in the Hudson amazes anglers. Those trolling with downriggers have run into schools so thick that their weights have bounced over the backs of fish and their sonar screens have turned black. In recent times, stripers up to 53 pounds have been caught, but they reportedly can run to 60 pounds and maybe more. Many anglers catch fish in the 20- to 30-pound range.

On September 2, 1927, O. C. Grinnell caught the first swordfish ever taken on rod and reel off the North Atlantic coast; Grinnell had been trying to catch a swordfish since the middle of June that year.

N

The prominent spring striper fishing areas in the lower Hudson include Croton Point, Storm King Mountain, Denning Point, Esopus Meadows, and the vicinity of Rondout, Esopus, and Catskill Creeks. Very few anglers cast for these deep spring fish; most drift, anchor, or troll. The tide changes are important, and most activity occurs on a moving tide. In colder weather, more fish are caught on bloodworms, but some are taken on pieces of herring. When the water warms, trolling with large plugs is somewhat effective, usually at depths of between 20 and 25 feet. The largest stripers regularly fall to baits, primarily from early May to early June. Live herring, chunks of herring, and live eels are the mainstays. More people use eels because they are readily available, whereas herring have to be caught and kept lively or fresh. The herring run, which coincides with the striper presence, is also strong, and stripers feed heavily on them.

Overshadowed by the abundance and popularity of stripers in the Hudson are another spring migrant, American shad. Hudson River shad were historically plentiful and among the largest specimens on the East Coast, making them primarily a commercial quarry. Their numbers have fluctuated in recent times, and sportfishing effort for them is marginal even when the population is high.

Shad are bottom-hugging fish that stay in main channels, and the sheer expansiveness of the Hudson daunts would-be shad pursuers. Some anglers have success with flies and darts that are fished behind boats anchored in midriver on the downstream edge of shoals, flats, and islands. The time just before and during low slack tide is good, especially near dawn and dusk; the peak of the run is from late April until early June.

Throughout the year, anglers interested in largemouth and smallmouth bass have plenty to enjoy on the Hudson. All of the major creeks, and portions of the main river from just south of the U.S. Military Reservation at West Point to north of Coxsackie, produce bass. The better creeks get most of the attention, especially from anglers launching smaller boats.

Tidal influences on the Hudson create a unique bass fishery within New York. Cover, current, and tide are interrelated here, and sometimes so is salt content. The Hudson is slightly brackish or completely freshwater somewhere around Cornwall Bay, although the exact location may vary with runoff. Bass do move and become active with tidal changes, as significant water-level fluctuation can occur between tides. Bass fishing is usually best when the water is at peak movement—either rising or falling. A falling tide is prime.

The average size of Hudson bass is fairly good, with 2-pounders common. This is in spite of heavy fishing pressure and is largely due to the release of virtually all bass. Largemouths here have been caught to 7 pounds and smallmouths to 5 pounds, and they are very scrappy fish. Shoals, sandbars,

islands, and rockpiles are main river spots. In creeks, the focus is on assorted structure.

The Hudson River offers other species, although none are as highly touted as the aforementioned ones. Crappie and trout are common in many of the creeks, and carp—some large—are plentiful in the main river, as are white catfish and white perch. Sturgeon have historically been present, but there is no sportfishery for them. Bluefish range into the saline parts of the lower river and provide excitement when available.

Catskill Region

West of the Hudson Valley and just a two-hour drive from New York City, the Catskills are renowned for trout fishing, yet the angling is as diverse here as in the rest of the Empire State. In fact, largemouth bass, pickerel, and panfish are virtually as popular as trout. The region is blessed with numerous small lakes and ponds that support these species, particularly in the outlying areas of the Catskill Forest Preserve. Many of these waters are private and provide good angling, yet they seldom attract publicity. Nevertheless, the highlighted focal points for anglers are the New York City reservoirs, the major trout rivers, and the Delaware River. Each system offers something different but is connected to—and to some degree dependent on—the others.

New York City reservoirs. The Catskill watershed and Delaware River Basin are rooted in the rivulets and creeks of the Catskill Mountains, whose waters were dammed long ago to provide water for New York City. The outlet flow of these reservoirs provides cold water for exceptional downstream trout fishing, whereas the reservoirs themselves—Pepacton, Cannonsville, Neversink, Rondout, Schoharie, and Ashokan—are the Rip Van Winkles of New York angling.

These deep but moderate-size (1,145 to 8,300 acres) and undeveloped mountain reservoirs provide the bulk of Gotham's water (the rest coming from Croton watershed reservoirs), yet they are relatively unknown in angling circles. This is due in part to onerous restrictions placed upon their use—no motors, rowboats of a specific size kept at designated sites, mandatory inspections and steam-cleaning, no fishing near the dams, etc.—and rigorous enforcement. Yet in the mid-1990s, nearly 3,000 boating permits were granted for Pepacton, the most popular of the reservoirs.

At all of these waters many boats are chained to trees, and their owners—parking along the roadways—tote oars, cushions, rods, and fishing paraphernalia down steep banks, pull the boats to the shoreline, and row for a chance at brown trout that average between 5 and 8 pounds. Some are in the 10- to 15-pound range. These clear waters, most of which are full of alewives, have also produced 20-pound browns (a 22-pounder caught in the mid-1990s is believed to be the largest). They also contain smallmouth bass and other species. Landlocked salmon, for example, swim in Neversink Reservoir, which drowned some of Theodore Gordon's historic angling grounds; lake trout thrive in Rondout; and Ashokan possesses rainbow trout and walleye.

Some trolling for trout is done in the Catskill reservoirs by anglers using spoons and cowbell attractors on weighted or lead-core line. A fair amount of early-season casting occurs from shore; ice-out varies from late March to mid-April, and open patches of water, usually by creeks, provide some light-tackle near-surface angling. The majority of big trout, however, are taken by anglers who drift or slow-troll with live alewives (locally called sawbellies) fished deep at various levels.

Trout rivers.   Possibly no other trout river in North America is known as widely within the continent, and outside it, as New York's Beaverkill. And no other river has been as widely written about or so detailed in contemporary trout and fly fishing literature.

Situated in the southwestern section of the Catskills, the Beaverkill is, in general terms, a relatively modest body of water, flowing some 45 miles to its confluence with the East Branch of the Delaware River. The upper half is almost entirely privately owned. From Roscoe, which is billed as "Trout Town USA," the Beaverkill is joined by the (mostly publicly accessible) Willowemoc Creek at famous Junction Pool. Here, it becomes a larger river with a generous amount of classic water, and the remaining 20-mile length is open to public fishing. This includes a good bit of renowned no-kill water, which produces excellent catch-and-release fishing with artificial lures only all season long, but especially when major hatches occur. The two stretches of water with these special regulations provide the best angling, but these oft-released fish are no dummies.

Brown trout are the primary catch, although anglers take an occasional rainbow. Dry flies are preferred by most anglers, especially because the many well-known pools of the Beaverkill are hallowed dry-fly waters. There's barely a time when the favored pools are bereft of anglers. Many travel from faraway locales to give the Beaverkill a fling.

The Beaverkill receives perhaps disproportionate glory, as numerous Catskill trout rivers and streams are noteworthy in their own right. These cold, clean mountain waters include Esopus Creek, the East and West Branches of the Delaware River, Willowemoc Creek, Schoharie Creek, Catskill Creek, Callicoon Creek, the Neversink River, Rondout Creek, East and West Kill Creeks, and Batavia Kill. Numerous brooks exist as well, and more than 1,500 miles of trout flowage grace the Catskills.

Brown trout, the bulwark of these waters, were imported to the region eons ago. Today, they are found in "native" and stocked forms, primarily in lower and midreaches. The truly native brook trout is widely dispersed as well, especially in headwater streams and spring-fed tributaries. Rainbow trout are the least common species but are scattered about; they occur mainly in larger flowages, especially the stems of the Delaware River, and inhabit some unexpected small waters.

Although Catskill trout fishing starts on the traditional April 1 opening day, better conditions occur after the cold runoff ebbs, the water warms, and the hatches are more pronounced. May and June are terrific months. Insect hatches vary, but a partial and general guide is as follows: quill gordons and hendricksons from mid-April through mid-May; March browns from mid-May through early June; sulfur duns from late May through early July; green drakes from early to mid-June; light cahills and yellow drakes from mid-June through mid-August.

The summer often produces low water conditions, although spring seepages and forested banks help keep small streams cool. Trout anglers focus their attention on Beaverkill River, Willowemoc Creek, and Esopus Creek, as well as the upper Delaware River and its branches. These locations witness many visitors on weekends and summer evenings.

Delaware River.   The Delaware River in New York is a multifaceted recreational playground. It is one of the finest wild trout rivers in the Northeastern United States, a prime fishery for American shad, a terrific smallmouth bass river, one of the most popular canoeing and rafting flowages in the East, and part of the National Wild and Scenic Rivers System administered by the National Park Service. Although the degree of superlatives attached to these attributes might be debatable, there is no question that this river, especially the upper reaches, which split the New York and Pennsylvania boundary in the Catskill Mountains and its foothills, is a top angling draw.

The main stem of the river—from Hancock, New York, down to Delaware Bay—has much to

A fly hatch is in progress as anglers fish the upper reaches of the Delaware River.

N

recommend it, but 75 miles of the upper reach, which was designated as a National Wild and Scenic River in 1978, is most notable aesthetically and piscatorially, as are the tributaries, which include the East and West Branches of the Delaware, and the Lackawaxen (Pennsylvania), Mongaup, and Neversink Rivers.

Perhaps no species is more abundant in the Delaware or more energetically pursued than the American shad, albeit for a short period of time. The bulk of the fishing activity takes place from late April through mid-June, when the shad migrate all the way upriver and into the upper tributaries to spawn. These fish are frequently caught in 4- to 6-pound sizes, occasionally in great numbers, and they are pursued by both boaters and wading anglers. Enthusiasts focus their attention around Port Jervis, Sparrowbush, Barryville, Lackawaxen, and Narrowsburg. The pools and holes below riffles are the primary spots, and the best action occurs early and late in the day. Most anglers use shad darts, but fly fishing for shad has increased in popularity and is very effective.

Although trout inhabit the main stem of the Delaware, the prime trout water lies in the 27-mile main section from Hancock to Callicoon, and in the two upper stems, which are essentially tailwater fisheries. The stretch of the East Branch of the Delaware between Pepacton Dam in Downsville and Hancock runs for 32 miles, and 18 miles of the West Branch runs from the Cannonsville Dam in Deposit to Hancock. The West Branch is the most intensely fished section, followed by the East Branch. The former has the most consistently cold water and a less diverse fish population.

These waters have abundant brown and rainbow trout. Browns predominate in the East and West Branches; rainbows are abundant in the East Branch from the village of East Branch to the confluence with the main river at Hancock, and southward on the main river. These are primarily wild fish, particularly the rainbows, and anglers have a good chance of landing some in the 16- to 20-inch range—exceptional figures anywhere in the Northeast. Fly fishing is the preferred method, although other artificials and baits are used where regulations permit. Various mayfly hatches are strong from late May on, stonefly hatches occur from June into August, and caddisflies are common in June and July.

The quality of these fisheries, as in all tailwaters where trout are found, depends on continuous releases of water from New York City's reservoirs that is ample in volume and appropriate in temperature. Drought conditions can force a water district to cut back or alter releases, producing thermal stress and potentially seriously impacting coldwater species. Maintaining release levels necessary to the fisheries has been a constant problem here. It is even more problematic in the Neversink River, which enters the Delaware below Port Jervis.

Smallmouth bass are found throughout this river, but good fishing exists in the upper river south of Callicoon, where the water temperatures are more favorable. The smallmouths are not large, although they once were when author Zane Grey cut his angling teeth here. That was before the construction of tributary reservoirs in both New York and Pennsylvania, and prior to a dependence on cool-water discharges to maintain water flow. Few smallmouths over 14 inches long are caught, but plenty of small fish are caught on light spinners, flies, jigs, and small plugs. The bigger fish haunt the deeper pools.

Walleye inhabit the river, too, although they are not intensely pursued. Some large walleye, 8 to 10 pounds, are taken annually. Most angling—largely by locals—occurs in spring and fall.

Access for waders and boaters is limited on the Delaware, and anglers cannot cross private property without permission. Several publicly accessible spots are located on each side of the upper river. Fishing during the day in the summer, especially weekends, is hampered from Callicoon to Port Jervis by heavy canoe and raft traffic.

Central Region

Ample opportunities for all types of angling are at hand in the section of New York that reaches from the capital district westward through the Finger Lakes and that lies between the Catskill and Adirondack Mountains. Bass, walleye, and trout are the mainstays here, and there are numerous large bodies of water to ply.

Finger Lakes.   Eleven lakes dot New York's wine country region, just south of the east-west arm of the New York State Thruway connecting Rochester and Syracuse. Some are fairly small, all are relatively narrow, and most have notable fisheries.

The two largest of these lakes, Cayuga and Seneca, are 40 and 36 miles long and have maximum depths of 435 and 632, respectively. The next three largest lakes—Keuka, Canandaigua, and Skaneateles—have water ranging from 187 to 350 feet deep, so you know these are serious trout waters. Some have the potential for monsters. Lakers, browns, and rainbows are prevalent in these locations. Landlocked Atlantic salmon exist in these waters, too, most notably Cayuga. Keuka is often overlooked but once held state records for brown trout and rainbow trout.

Cayuga Lake, which has all of these salmonids, is much like a ravine, with steep sides in many places, no reefs or shoals, and a few bars off points. Here, as is typical of the Finger Lakes, the shallows provide good springtime trout and salmon trolling in the south. As the water warms, angling effort moves northward and deeper. The lake also has a good warmwater fishery—especially in the northern end—for largemouth and smallmouth bass, yellow perch, and crappie.

N

Seneca Lake, immediately to the west of Cayuga, is similarly long but nearly 3 miles across at its widest point. Seneca is known for plenty of smallmouth bass, large lake trout, large pike, and abundant yellow perch. It has rainbows and browns as well, and fishing for all trout species is hot in the springtime in the warming shallows, especially when smelt and alewives congregate. Seneca has produced northern pike to 20 pounds and is one of the better pike waters in the state. Good fishing exists all along the lake and especially at the northern end near Geneva.

A major tributary of Seneca, Catherine Creek is a famous spawning rainbow trout stream in March and April. Other Finger Lakes tributaries, including Cayuga Inlet, Grout Brook, Keuka Inlet, and Naples Creek, offer spring-run rainbow fisheries. Eggs or egg sacks, worms, and nymphs on light lines or tippets are the primary offerings.

There's fine smallmouth bass fishing in Keuka, Otisco, Owasco, and Canandaigua Lakes. Tiger muskies are present in Otisco, as are walleye. Perch are abundant in most and large in a few. Dipnetting for smelt, which occurs from late March through April, is popular on many Finger Lakes tributaries.

Oneida Lake. Located on the northeastern fringe of Syracuse, Oneida Lake has long been New York's best walleye water. Although Lake Ontario eclipses it in size, the numbers at Oneida make this *the* place. More than 200,000 walleye are caught annually in poor years; in better years, the numbers are several times that. Fish weighing more than 5 pounds are an occasional catch, but 15- to 18-inch walleye are typical. Roughly 100 million walleye fry are stocked in the lake each year, produced by the lake's adults at a nearby state hatchery. Although walleye are the primary target on Oneida, smallmouth bass and yellow perch are also important. Lesser fisheries exist for crappie, carp, catfish, bullhead, largemouth bass, and various panfish.

Oneida is a large but uniformly shallow lake. It is 21 miles long and has a maximum width of $5^1/_2$ miles, resulting in nearly 52,000 acres of water. The maximum depth is 55 feet, but more than half the lake is less than 30 feet deep. Wide open and with few bays and many bars, reefs, and shoals, the lake can be rough under windy conditions.

Walleye are popular in open water from May into fall, and again in winter through the ice, particularly in the eastern half of the lake. Intense walleye fishing coincides with the opening of walleye season in early May, and continues for several weeks thereafter because the post-spawn fish are shallow and near the shorelines, especially in the vicinity of tributary bays. For most of the summer the fish are in 15 to 35 feet, primarily on the bottom, and are caught by drifting.

Especially popular on Oneida, yellow perch have suffered cyclical swings over the years but are normally abundant. Prime fishing occurs in late summer and early fall and later through the ice. Smallmouth

fishing on Oneida is good to excellent, with lots of fish and many of good size. Crayfish are abundant, too, and readily stirred up through wave action. The shallowness of Oneida keeps bass accessible throughout the season.

Other waters. A number of rivers in the central region offer varied fishing, particularly for bass and walleye; these include the Chemung, Chenango, and Susquehanna. Of greatest note, perhaps, is the Mohawk River, a section of the Erie Canal running west to east from Utica to the Hudson River near Troy.

Most of the fishing in the Mohawk takes place in the section from St. Johnsville east. The 9-mile-long portion known as Crescent Lake, between Locks 6 and 7 from Schenectady to Albany, is a premier spot boasting varied species, including some striped bass that pass through from the Hudson.

Smallmouth bass and walleye are the favored attractions in the Mohawk River, which provides ample cover, dropoffs, bridge abutments, islands, vegetation, and other structure. Tiger muskies, many of which are caught coincidentally, as well as many yellow perch and crappie also inhabit this turbid waterway.

Just north of the Mohawk at Gloversville, and just inside the southern boundary of Adirondack Park, is Great Sacandaga Lake, New York's bona fide big pike king. Sacandaga yielded a 46-pound state-record northern in 1940, a fish that stood as the all-tackle world record until dethroned in 1986 by a European pike. A spawned-out 39-pounder was caught in this 29-mile-long lake, also known as Sacandaga Reservoir, in the spring of 1982, and other monsters have been landed over the years, but 20-pounders are a more realistic catch, especially early in the season when suckers are moving in and out of feeder streams.

Western Region
Lake Erie. The whole of Lake Erie appropriately owns the appellation "Walleye Capital of the World," but much of its fame is attributed to the western basin and the majority of its waters in Ohio. The deeper eastern basin between New York and the province of Ontario, and leading to the Niagara River, however, is no slouch, either in number or size of both walleye and smallmouth bass. It is a mixed-bag fishery, as it also holds most of the salmonid opportunities for Erie's lake and tributary anglers. Steelhead and rainbow trout have adapted especially well; in New York, they have been emphasized in salmonid stocking programs. At Dunkirk, a warmwater discharge in the harbor provides open-water fishing for various species in the winter. Charter captains in eastern Lake Erie can provide anglers with an offshore trolling outing that combines lake trout, steelhead, salmon, and walleye.

Walleye are the main interest, however. Due to clear water, walleye on Erie have become sight feeders and often roam near the surface or at suspended depths in vast schools pursuing alewives, perch, shad, and whitefish. The clear water, which looks almost offshore-ocean-blue from high above, has made walleye—a notoriously light-shy fish—wary of bright colors, noise, boats overhead, and any offering presented close to a moving powerboat. As a result, longline fishing is popular now, especially trolling with sideplaners and in-line planer boards. Big fish—8- and 10-pounders—have been common for many years, and some of those in the know deliberately stay away from schools of fish that weigh under 5 pounds; they're simply not large enough to bother with.

It seems that wherever there are rocks on Lake Erie, there's also smallmouth bass. New York shores produce numerous bass, including 3- to 5-pounders, and the potential for 6- to 8-pounders exists; indeed, this area yielded the state-record 8-pound, 4-ounce smallmouth. Jigs, vertical jigging spoons, vibrating lures, and live baits account for most catches. Soft-shelled crabs are a favorite natural, if you can get them. Some of the best bass angling is within sight of downtown Buffalo; Seneca Shoals and Donnelly's Wall are two top spots.

The changes in the lake and fishery are due in large part to zebra mussels, which filter and clarify the water by removing microscopic plants with unbelievable proficiency. Their long-term impact is uncertain, however. Anglers should remember that Lake Erie is a large body of water, one that can get rough in a hurry. When the water is cold and the wind is severe, Erie can be inhospitable.

Niagara River. To most of the world, the word Niagara conjures up visions of thundering falls, tumultuous spray, and a honeymoon haven. But anglers have had a love affair with the Niagara River because it offers excellent and varied angling that is widely famous among the Great Lakes and its tributaries.

Most notable is perhaps the best run of large salmon in the Great Lakes each fall in the Niagara

Gorge at Devil's Hole. No boats pass above this spot; it possesses some of the most treacherous whitewater in the East. From the falls to Lewiston, the lower Niagara River is a steep, forbidding gorge. But it yields spectacular fishing to the diligent and careful angler. Drifting with preserved salmon egg clusters is most productive, but flatline trolling with deep-diving plugs is a hot second, especially early in the day. Shore casters fish eggs, plugs, and spoons.

From mid-October through April, steelhead are present in good number in the swift water of the lower Niagara, but the best action is in February and March. Drifting with eggs is the main technique, but other methods are possible, including fly fishing. The river gets a virtually neglected run of lake trout in May, and angling for this species is surprisingly good. At other times, walleye, smallmouth bass, and perch fill the bill. Smallmouth are especially plentiful here, as are walleye that top 10 pounds. These are not caught in the turbulent flow but from Lewiston to the mouth of the river at Lake Ontario. The boat-able section of the lower river is 8 miles long, extending from Devil's Hole to the Niagara Bar.

The upper Niagara River—the section above the falls and extending to Lake Erie—is noted for bass, walleye, perch, pike, and muskies throughout the summer and fall. This outflow water is clear and tricky, and has one of the most unheralded muskie populations in the country, including 40-pound specimens. This is a tricky clear-water trolling fishery, however. Numerous launch sites, piers, and docks exist. If you don't venture north of Grand Island, it's unlikely that you'll be swept over the falls (although great fishing might exist in the pool below the thunder, no one has tried).

Chautaqua Lake. Chautaqua Lake was once long recognized as a formidable muskie fishery and a producer of large fish. The muskies are still there, but they've gone through some hard times. Sizes have dropped, and 20-pounders are less common. The walleye and bass populations have prospered, and although Chautaqua may not bask in the walleye and bass glory of nearby Lake Erie, it has much to offer for these species, and for crappie as well.

The walleye are plentiful; smaller fish are generally heavy in the thick weeds, and larger fish frequent the deeper waters of the north basin. Largemouth bass are found throughout Chautaqua, but smallmouths—some in the 4- to 6-pound range—shine. Crappie, known here as calicos, are a favorite quarry, especially in the south basin.

Lake Ontario

In a state with abundant resources, no fishery has stood out with more distinction in recent decades than Lake Ontario. This lake draws anglers from all over the Northeast for salmon, trout, bass, and walleye fishing that is among the best in the Great Lakes. Although it has shone since the early 1970s, it is also a lake in transition—one that perplexes

Early morning anglers find salmon success in the turbulent flow of the Niagara River.

N

anglers and fisheries managers and doesn't live up to expectations every year. Variable wind and weather patterns, as well as changing water conditions, contribute significantly to these problems. This should come as no surprise, however, on the 19th largest lake in the world, one that is 193 miles long and 53 miles wide and has an average depth of 283 feet. This voluminous water has an abundance of riches for the savvy angler, in both the lake proper and in its tributaries.

Chinook salmon, lake trout, steelhead, brown trout, walleye, and smallmouth bass have all provided premier fishing opportunities on Lake Ontario. Largemouth bass, northern pike, muskellunge, coho salmon, Atlantic salmon, and yellow perch have also figured significantly. But the main attraction is chinook (king) salmon.

For some time, Lake Ontario has had the best angling and the largest chinooks in all of the Great Lakes. The Oswego and Salmon Rivers in the eastern basin—which are small, narrow, shallow, and generally slow—are magnets for salmon and anglers alike. There has long been shoulder-to-shoulder fishing in these tributaries in September, when dark and soon-to-die chinook and coho migrate upstream. But the western end of Lake Ontario, where the bottom drops off more steeply close to shore and where the incomparable Niagara River enters, has been the best big-water place to consistently catch these nomadic fish from April through September. It is the only section of the lake that has dependable angling for schools of king salmon in the spring and early summer, when the fish are brightest and strongest, primarily because the forceful incoming current piles up baitfish. Most of the big spring kings are caught in the Niagara area.

The western basin can stake a claim for producing the biggest lakers as well. In early 1994, a modern-day Lake Ontario lake trout record was established near the mouth of the Niagara River by a 39-pounder; in November, anglers can jig and release up to 40 fish per day. Although the western end of the lake produces big lake trout and plenty of them, the extreme eastern end of the lake is generally considered the prime laker habitat. Near Henderson Harbor, the rocky reefs and islands make lakers a bread-and-butter fish.

Lake trout are a native Lake Ontario species that were once decimated by lamprey eels and commercial overfishing. The last sport-caught native-strain laker was taken in the 1930s, and the last commercially caught laker by 1950. Restocking efforts began in Lake Ontario in 1973 and have been sustained with federal help. Management regulations have been aimed at making them self-perpetuating, a process that has had modest results. Some anglers feel it is detrimental to more popular nonnative species. Nevertheless, lakers are a reliable catch and a fallback option on tough days throughout most of the lake. Still, their deep-dwelling nature and mediocre fight when taken from deep water lessen their sporting value.

The acrobatic and aggressive steelhead, however, are highly prized. These fish are especially sought by winter and early spring anglers in the tributaries. Steelhead are most reliably found in the established rivers, especially the Salmon, Niagara, Black, and Oswego, throughout the winter. Fresh runs occur at various times and peak when these fish spawn in April. Some early-season near-shore fishing for steelhead exists, and limited offshore fishing is available if and when there is a thermal bar.

Brown trout are the spring mainstays for most of the lake, especially from Rochester to Pulaski. At this time, they're inshore and shallow and make up the majority of the early season catch. In local contests, it usually takes a 15-pound fish to place in the top 10, and a 20-pounder to win; the lake and state record is 30 pounds. Most people troll via flatlines with plugs, graduating to spoons and downriggers as the water warms and fish disperse. But in the early going, pier- and shore-based casters score well, too. Brown trout are widely dispersed along Lake Ontario, but the mideastern section from Mexico Bay to Fairhaven seems to annually outproduce the others for big fish.

These coldwater species, plus coho and Atlantic salmon, are the subject of most interest across the lake. Atlantics have been stocked in greater numbers, especially in the eastern basin and in the Black River. Atlantic salmon were once native to Lake Ontario, the only Great Lake that had these fish. Efforts continue to reestablish this species.

On the warmwater front, walleye and smallmouth bass populations are exceptionally good and, with some localized exceptions, underexploited. Both species are not as widely dispersed as trout and salmon, but along the lake's 712 miles of shoreline there are many places to find them. The far eastern end of the lake, especially from Cape Vincent at the head of the St. Lawrence River to Henderson Harbor, is known for outstanding smallmouth bass fishing, and possesses great numbers of these fish. Bass habitat here is excellent, with plenty of rocky shoals, islands, points, and weed-edged rocks. Walleye are abundant in the same places; the average fish were once so large that 8- to 10-pounders seemed common, although the big fish were heavily exploited. Many good-size fish still exist in this section of the lake, however, and the overall population is relatively lightly tapped.

Good smallmouth action is reliable in the Sodus-to-Oswego sector of the lake, and a nearly unpublicized spring walleye fishery (including fish to 10 pounds) exists at Oswego. Across the lake in Canada's Bay of Quinte is an extraordinary population of walleye that is targeted in spring, fall, and winter; these fish reportedly contribute to walleye numbers across the far eastern end of the lake, as well as in the St. Lawrence River.

N

Lake Ontario's great fisheries resources have depended heavily on a healthy and prolific population of baitfish, principally alewives and smelt (the record 39-pound laker had 99 smelt and alewives in its stomach). Concerns about these populations will always exist, but Ontario has escaped some of the baitfish-related problems affecting other Great Lakes; many anglers annually see massive numbers of baitfish on their sonar.

Huge baitfish numbers have led to terrific growth rates and a lot of fat fish. Good fishing for many, and large, trout and salmon spoiled many anglers. When the fishing got harder due to adverse weather and increasingly clearer water—thanks to zebra mussels—some thought the lake had gone downhill. Heavy stocking levels and plentiful baitfish, however, essentially means that there are plenty of fish. In this huge and deep lake, finding them is usually the main problem.

St. Lawrence River

It is no secret that the St. Lawrence River is one of the great North American fishing locales. Steeped in history, tradition, and fishing renown, the St. Lawrence has been in the sportfishing limelight ever since there was a limelight. Its natural resources were of tremendous value as long ago as 1535, when French explorer Jacques Cartier discovered it while looking for the Northwest Passage to the Orient.

But it is the 52-mile-long section of the St. Lawrence called the Thousand Islands—known to the Mohawk Indians as the "Garden of the Great Spirit"—that has produced not only a famous salad dressing, but also places it among the continent's foremost bass and muskellunge fishing.

The St. Lawrence is not a typical river featuring pools, eddies, and riffles. It is akin to a mammoth lake, holding a half million surface acres of water. Also known as the St. Lawrence Seaway, the river flows northeasterly from Lake Ontario for 700 miles and serves as a shipping channel for colossal freighters carrying assorted cargoes from Great Lakes ports. It is 200 feet deep in spots, several miles wide at most points, and possesses more than 1,600 islands—the largest of which is 21 miles long—in the Thousand Islands sector.

The St. Lawrence River in New York is bounded on the north by Ontario, Canada, and reaches from Wolfe Island and Cape Vincent at the outflow of Lake Ontario 97 miles to Massena and a boundary with Quebec. That area encompasses 300,000 acres of water, most of which harbors something worth fishing for. Prominent departure points for anglers in this region are at Cape Vincent, Clayton, Alexandria Bay, Ogdensburg, and Massena in New York, and Kingston and Gananoque in Ontario.

The prime angling interests in this great body of water are smallmouth bass, largemouth bass, walleye, northern pike, and muskellunge, although there are ample perch, rock bass, bullhead, carp,

and other species, as well as salmonid stragglers from Lake Ontario. The St. Lawrence is a fabled muskie water, and has been renowned for its large muskellunge. The now-dethroned (and disputed) all-tackle world-record muskie (69 pounds, 15 ounces) was caught somewhere in the Thousand Islands stretch in 1957, and several line-class-record 60-pounders were caught in that area during the heyday of the 1950s. No other single locale in North America has been as closely identified with mighty muskellunge as the St. Lawrence.

The huge fish have not been caught here in decades, however, and angling interest has shifted to more abundant and more cooperative species, especially to large salmon in nearby Lake Ontario. Still, dedicated trollers can land 30- to 40-pound muskies here. Much emphasis is still placed on tra- ditional locales, such as Hinckley Shoal off Carleton Island and Forty Acre Shoals off Gananoque. This is almost exclusively a trolling fishery, partaken of from September through early November.

Many more people ply the St. Lawrence for bass. Area chambers of commerce have long billed the local waters as the "Smallmouth Bass Capital of the World," and although some would dispute this claim, there's no arguing that the river has a tremendous population of smallmouths. This is thanks in part to a notable quantity of rocky bars, shoals, bluffs, and island heads near deep water with plenty of current. Largemouths, too, are abundant, in the main river along deep grassbeds and weedlines as well as back in the weedy and lily-pad-filled bays and creeks. The places to find both species are numerous.

Jigs and live baits have historically been the foremost presentations on the St. Lawrence for bass, but the entire gamut of bass tactics and tackle are applicable. Good fishing can be had almost all season long from the opening in mid-June until early November. The last half of June and early July are especially popular. The main section of the St. Lawrence stays cold until summertime. Although the severity of the winter, the timing of ice breakup, and spring weather are factors in river water temperature, the early season usually arrives while the water is cold enough to keep the bass in the shallows; some may still be spawning on shoals and island bars in late June.

Northern pike, although not particularly large here, are abundant and a good spring and winter quarry. They are commonly caught by bass anglers who aren't trying to catch them, and they are a major ice fishing attraction in bays. Walleye were once abundant, then nonexistent, and have now reestablished a substantial population, primarily near Cape Vincent and at the eastern end of Lake Ontario. The 1990s saw a bonanza of walleye over 10 pounds in the confluence with Lake Ontario, making this one of the least-known big walleye fisheries in the country, but the opportunity was overexploited. Walleye are still plentiful, however, and they have become an important fishery once again throughout this section of the river.

No matter what species one pursues, the St. Lawrence is not a place for timid boaters. There are many dangerous places and some swift water, and the river has a propensity for getting riled up by westerly winds, especially in late summer and fall. Traveling from the launch site to various fishing spots one can cover a lot of water; a suitable craft and some boating savvy are required.

Adirondack Region

The northernmost area of New York—bounded by Vermont, Quebec, and the St. Lawrence River—the Adirondack region is an enormous area replete with fishing opportunity and largely devoid of people. Within its borders is Adirondack Park. At more than 6 million acres, it is the largest state park in the contiguous United States and offers 1,300 miles of rivers, many small to medium-size lakes, big waters like Lake George and Lake Champlain, and a surfeit of remote ponds. Although this is considered trout country, it has a great diversity of species, especially some terrific bass fishing, and there is no lack of places to fish afoot or by any type of watercraft.

Trout waters. The region's trout waters flow in every direction from the high peaks of the Adirondacks and have been described as the best trout rivers east of Montana. Adirondack rivers and streams are synonymous with fishing for brook trout, which are still native in many of these waters, and abundant in small flowages, especially feeder streams. Brown trout are very common, however, and rainbows are present as well. Some of the tributaries hold landlocked salmon, and some of the lakes have kokanee salmon, so there's diversity no matter where you turn.

The Ausable River is considered the preeminent Adirondack trout river. Situated in the northeast, it originates in the high peaks and flows northward to Lake Champlain and has two stems. The West Branch of the Ausable is widely favored and has been heavily touted over the years. It is a 30-mile-long, rugged river that flows through the gorges of Wilmington Notch and directly under the chairlift at Whiteface Mountain. This is a cold, steep, and shady river with exceptional aquatic insect forage and copious cover. Upper sections have deep water with undercut banks and some pools; lower reaches have interspersed pocket water and pools below islands. The Ausable is noted for large brown trout, including fish in the 15- to 20-inch range, as well as some in the 7- and 8-pound category, and has a short stretch of specially regulated water offering year-round angling. The East Branch, which originates in the Keene Valley, is a fine trout stream in its own right, although it doesn't possess the size or numbers of fish of its sister flowage.

North of the Ausable, the Saranac River runs for 65 miles from Saranac Lake to Plattsburgh and affords diverse conditions and varied angling for warmwater as well as coldwater species. The river forks at Clayburg, creating a short South Branch that is popular for trout for 5 miles up to Union Falls. Also of special interest for trout—including brookies, browns, and rainbows—is the North Branch. Both are cold, quiet, and in many places thickly wooded. The main stem has several hydroelectric impoundments; fishing below the dams or in the tailwaters is good for brown trout, smallmouth bass, and walleye.

South of the Ausable and on the eastern fringe of the Adirondacks is the Bouquet River, New York's finest landlocked Atlantic salmon river excepting the Lake Ontario tributaries. This is a tributary of Lake Champlain, in fact, and runs for about 40 miles from the headwaters to the big lake. The 12-mile-long lower stretch, from the dam at Wadhams, concentrates salmon, which run from late April through May and from mid-September through October. Salmon up to 10 pounds have been common, and in the lower reaches the action can be mixed with lake trout, bass, and walleye.

Flowing westerly from the Adirondacks eventually to the St. Lawrence River at Ogdensburg is the underrated and often ignored Oswegatchie River. This 102-mile-long flowage is varied in its characteristics. The steep and quick 35-mile-long section above Newton Falls is difficult to access and marked by dams and whitewater rapids. Trout are the main quarry here, and although they may not be as abundant or large as in other Adirondack rivers, they could be found in no lovelier setting nor with more wildlife viewing opportunity. The lower section is generally wider and slower moving, with more diverse angling opportunities, including smallmouth bass, walleye, pike, and panfish.

These are among the more obvious and larger rivers in the Adirondacks, but there are many others, not to mention tributary waters, that also deserve consideration. These include the short but famed section of the Battenkill River in the extreme southeastern corner of this region; the headwater section of the Hudson River, especially above North River and in the Boreas and Cedar tributaries; the North Branch of the Chazy River; Chateaugay River; West Canada Creek; the St. Regis River; Raquette River; and Schroon River. Of the 1,200-plus miles of rivers just within the confines of Adirondack Park, 155 are classified as wild and 511 as scenic, attributes that add immensely to any angler's fishing experience.

It should be noted that in addition to rivers and streams, hundreds of lakes and ponds abound throughout the Adirondacks, offering good fishing, especially for trout. The Adirondack region in particular is noted for its many brook trout waters, the majority of which are ponds of varying sizes. Some of these exist along roadsides, but most are remote, accessed by foot or portage, and located by reviewing topographic maps.

 The highest large lake in the world is Titicaca in the Peruvian Andes. It is 12,500 feet above sea level and 900 feet at its deepest point.

N

Lake Champlain.   Tourism boosters call 110-mile-long Lake Champlain the "Sixth Great Lake," and they have a point. Twelve miles wide and boasting 585 miles of shoreline and more than 300,000 surface acres, Champlain is a formidable body of water. What to catch here is mostly a matter of what you want and where you are. The bass and walleye fishing is exceptional but rivaled in popularity by lake trout and landlocked salmon. Steelhead, pike, yellow perch, pickerel, and muskies are also prominent, and there are numerous other species as well.

In the New York portion (Champlain borders Vermont), smallmouth bass are the principal quarry along bays, islands, and points. The northern end produces fish up to 5 pounds, and it is not an overstatement to say that you can hardly fail to catch a smallmouth here. Largemouth bass are also present, although less prominent, as they mainly frequent the bays and weeds; they are more evident in the southern section of the lake, where the water is more stained in color due to heavy traffic.

Lake trout and landlocked Atlantic salmon are found in various places around Champlain, but the midlake section, which has depths to 400 feet, garners the most attention. Smelt are the favorite forage of these fish, and deep-water angling is the norm for most of the open-water season, although near-shore and near-tributary fishing coincide with the spring and fall salmon runs. Lakers and salmon from 3 to 8 pounds are frequent catches.

Walleye, perch, and pike are popular with anglers along the lake and are especially sought through the ice. Smelt are another prominent winter catch. Ice fishing for them peaks through mid-February.

Lake George.   Considerably smaller than its northern neighbor, Lake George is nonetheless a big body of water. Its 44 square miles of picturesque and fairly narrow water provide good fishing for lake trout, landlocked salmon, smallmouth bass, largemouth bass, and northern pike, as well as various panfish, smelt, and other species.

Angling for lakers and salmon commences with ice out, which occurs around mid-April in the south and later in the north, when the fish are shallow and the smelt are spawning, especially around tributaries. Deep fishing is the game from June on; the lake has a maximum depth of 201 feet, and lakers are usually way down in the summer. Fall provides good opportunity for shallower fish, especially salmon early and late in the day.

Smallmouth bass are found all over Lake George. Hundreds of rocky coves, points, and islands invite smallmouth angling, but anglers land some in very deep water during midsummer. September and October provide splendid opportunity amidst colorful vistas. Largemouths, too, are ample, primarily in bays. This fishery is good from the beginning of the season through fall.

Long Island (Saltwater)

Long Island is shaped like a huge fish whose head and mouth touch Manhattan at the west and whose tail, which is divided into huge flukes called North and South Forks, juts eastward 130 miles into the Atlantic Ocean. The size and location of this landform are unique. It encompasses the Hudson River estuary on the west; is well placed on the continental shelf, which parallels the south side of the island; and within its perimeter are many large, shallow bays that serve as nurseries for numerous species. These physical features have produced one of the greatest marine habitats in the world and contribute to exceptional saltwater angling that is enjoyed by more than 800,000 anglers annually.

Trapped between this island and the continent is Long Island Sound. Extending more than 150 miles, it varies in width to 19 miles near its middle and less than 8 miles at Orient Point on the east. Extending off Long Island's North Fork is a series of islands that end on Wicopisset Passage, which is shared with Rhode Island. The South Fork points into the open Atlantic as Montauk Point, touted as the saltwater fishing capital of the world. The ocean side of Long Island is relatively straight, a great stretch of barrier beaches. Trapped behind this are numerous shallow bays that open into the Atlantic through six inlets. Here, the variety of fishing environments is almost limitless, ranging from back bays and tidal creeks to sounds and the open ocean. Long Island offers anglers 130 miles of ocean surf on the south side and twice that on the North Shore. In between, there's a plethora of docks, bulkheads, floats, bridges, and jetties from which to angle.

Fish variety is particularly abundant, offering a diversity of migratory species, some of which move short distances inshore and offshore while others trek thousands of miles. Because of this, what you catch is determined by when (and sometimes where) you're fishing. During cold months, cod, ling, whiting, and flounder are prime species. From April through November, prominent inshore species include striped bass, bluefish, weakfish, winter flounder, fluke, blackfish, black sea bass, mackerel, and porgies. Offshore, anglers fish for sharks, bluefin, yellowfin, and bigeye tuna, albacore, bonito, and hordes of dolphin, as well as striped and blue marlin.

The size of fish populations is determined by various factors, including commercial and recreational fishing pressure, natural variations due to climatic occurrences—especially during spawning and nursery periods—and natural cyclic fluctuations occurring within every species. Enlightened state and federal fisheries managers have been attacking overfishing, which has been a problem in New York waters, as it has been along the entire Northeast coast. Today, every species has one or more restrictions as to season, minimum size lengths, and creel limits, all designed to provide enough breeding stock to ensure species survival. Remarkable gains have been made in this direction in relatively few years, but a continuing need for vigilance and proper stewardship is required.

While saltwater fish feed all the time, they do not always feed with the same frenzy and this affects an angler's ability to catch fish. In the waters surrounding Long Island, the best fishing months to catch most species are May, June, September, and October. This doesn't mean that fish cannot be caught at other times. They can, but it takes more skill on the part of the angler to do so.

North Shore (Long Island Sound). *Western Long Island Sound.* Long Island Sound narrows in the west, and anglers from Oyster Bay to City Island and east along Westchester County's shore fish virtually in each others backyards. Little Neck, Manhasset, and Hempstead Bays are spring hotspots for striped bass, flounder, bluefish, and fluke when waters warm. Shoals surrounding City Island, Stepping Stones Reef, and Execution Rocks are well known for flounder and porgy catches. Numerous smaller bays and harbors along the north side of the sound, from Mamaroneck to Rye, harbor the area's biggest bluefish in August and September, as well as numerous striped bass and blackfish.

Lloyd Neck/Cold Spring Harbor/Centre Island. This section offers excellent striped bass fishing. Anglers commonly pursue these fish at night by trolling long, unweighted lines baited with gobs of sandworms. They favor small boats with nearly silent engines and waters from 3 to 10 feet deep, and work along all the beaches of these bays and harbors. The boulder-strewn shores are ideal bass waters. Mixed with bass at night are weakfish and bluefish. In spring and late fall, these beaches produce good blackfish catches. Most fishing in Cold Spring Harbor centers around the northern half. The shallower southern sections produce flounder in April and May, and in August house hordes of snapper bluefish.

Eatons Neck. For numbers, variety, and quality of fish, the shoal north of Eatons Neck Point, known as Eatons Neck Triangle, is exceptional. It is a large extension of shallow water pushing northward into the Sound. The area is filled with sand eels and spearing. Access is easy because of numerous boat ramps in the area. Schools of small bass are abundant here in spring. Eatons Neck also produces weakfish, and big blues are taken for granted. Fluke to 12 pounds have been caught here. The so-called Triangle is derived from three buoys marking the shoal: Can 13 north of Eatons Neck Point, the OB Buoy a mile northwest of Can 13, and Buoy 11B. Waters to the west and north drop from 30 to 100 feet. On the eastern side, the bottom slopes gradually from 22 to 80 feet. Most weakfish and bluefish are taken inside these buoys, whereas striped bass are caught between Can 13 and the lighthouse.

Smithtown Bay/Crane Neck. Smithtown Bay, between Eatons Neck Point and Crane Neck Point, offers 15 miles of good fishing waters. East of Crane Neck is boulder-strewn Oldfield Point, an area with the same characteristics as Crane Neck that is ideal for blackfish. At night, these areas are taken over by striped bass. Three streams flow into Smithtown Bay with varying degrees of salt-, fresh-, and brackish water. Stony Brook Harbor's flow is primarily saline. It offers bass fishing in the channel. Near the SH Buoy, catches of bluefish in August are common. At times, weakfish mix with blues, which are the main summer fishery. A favorite place for striped bass and weakfish is the mouth of the Nissequogue River, a substantial stream that flows into Smithtown Bay. Flounder show here first in the river and are outside by June. Bluefish concentrate off the river's mouth. Short Beach and Sunken Meadow Beach flank the river's mouth and at night offer surf anglers a chance at bass and weakfish.

Mt. Misery Shoal. This is a uniformly flat piece of bottom that extends northeasterly for about a mile under 15 to 25 feet of water off Mt. Misery Point, just east of the entrance to Port Jefferson Harbor. Its outer edge is marked by Buoy C11. In late May and June, it attracts weakfish. At night, surf casters on the beach take weakfish and striped bass. Bluefish are a certainty off the shoal, where anglers head when weakfishing slows. Fluke move into this area during the summer. Closer to the beach, catches are mixed with blackfish. Porgies are on the flat; in late September, jumbo porgies school here. When boat concentrations are dense, the best fishing method is to drift and jig. With light traffic, trolling umbrella rigs produces a potpourri of species.

Mattituck Inlet. One of the most lightly fished areas in all of the marine waters of New York is the north side of Long Island's North Fork, from Mattituck Inlet east 12 miles to Rocky Point. Difficult access is the reason; the few existing ramps in the area are marginal. Striped bass are the prime species, fished off the beaches or along the shore at night, or by drifting or trolling. Daytime anglers usually drift to catch weakfish, fluke, and flounder. The best porgy area is east of Mattituck, from The Firing Range to Duck Point. A shoal north of Horton Point concentrates fluke. Bluefish are along the shore to mid–Long Island Sound. Find feeding birds and fish under them.

East End. *Orient Point.* Long Island's south side offers excellent early season flounder from Long Beach Point to Orient. In late spring, fluke replace flounder, moving into these waters from June through September. They concentrate from Trumans Beach to Orient Shoal. Blackfish dominate catches on the rocks. Plum Gut, between Orient Point and Plum Island, offers great striped bass and bluefish angling. Blackfishing is superb all along the north side of Plum Island. Just north of Plum, in 50 feet of water, the tide rips over a submerged shoal,

Astacopis gouldi is a crayfish found in the streams of Tasmania, Australia, that has grown to a length of 2 feet and weight of 9 pounds.

Pigeon Rip, one of the area's best bluefish grounds in August. This is deep-water fishing, and jigging is the only way to get to the blues. The wide expanse of shallow, rocky bottom between the eastern tip of Plum Island and Great Gull Island is the domain of striped bass.

The Race, Fishers Island. The waters between Little Gull and Fishers Island are no place for small boats. In its depths, throughout summer, are the area's biggest bluefish. Twenty-pounders are not uncommon. Fishing here requires big boats, heavy tackle, and strong-armed anglers. In topography, Fishers Island is more akin to New England than New York. It is rocky and irregular, and ideal for blackfish. During spring and fall migrations of striped bass, drifting eels parallel to the rocky shores on the island's south side has produced great catches.

Gardiners Island. Located between Long Island's North and South Forks, Gardiners Island offers big-bay fishing on its east side, while the more protected west side offers harborlike conditions. The Ruins mark the northern tip of a shoal, both sides of which produce excellent striped bass catches at night with trolled plugs. During the day, these flats produce fluke and flounder. Eastern Point Plains and Tobaccolot Bay, on the east side, are prime snowshoe flounder grounds. Fish to 3 pounds are taken just off the beaches in 25 to 30 feet of water. On the west side, in Bostwick Bay, southwest to Crow Shoals and then southeast to Cherry Harbor, the island offers bluefish anglers excellent inshore fishing in July and August.

Peconic Bays. "The Peconics" include Flanders, Great Peconic, Little Peconic, Hog Neck, and Noyack Bays and Shelter Island Sound, and offer great fishing for porgies and weakfish. Traditional hotspots, which include the hole south of Buoy 16, the cut just west of Buoy 18, the rip south of Buoy 22, and the rip at South Robins Island Race from Buoys 23 to 30, produce most weakfish catches. Porgies prefer deeper waters in the middle of Little Peconic, Great Peconic, and Noyack Bays. There is excellent flounder fishing here in April from Buoy 2, on the western end of Great Peconic Bay, westward through Flanders Bay.

South Shore. *Montauk Point.* In any language, *Montauk* means fishing. This easternmost extension of Long Island juts deeply into the Atlantic and is the focal point for both inshore and offshore activities. There are three fishing locales at Montauk: the north and south shores and off "The Point." It is on the beaches surrounding Montauk that an army of surf casters comes in spring and fall to catch striped bass. The fish migrate close to south-side beaches and The Point when going north or south. Weakfish are also found in the surf and placate striped bass anglers between bass bites. Here, too, bluefish are regular fare.

Inshore fishing at Montauk is world renowned. Water around The Point is moderately deep, between 30 and 50 feet within a mile of shore. Fish

A striped bass is landed near Montauk Point.

are attracted by a great rip formed as the tide from Long Island Sound escapes seaward and boils over a long underwater reef that connects Montauk Point with Block Island, 12 miles away. This confusion of water is known as Pollock Rip. East of The Point is mainly a striped bass fishery, in an area known as The Elbow. However, bluefish often fill the charter boat boxes here. During some years, good catches of weakfish as well as blues are possible in August and September.

Offshore fishing at Montauk rivals the best in the world. From this famous port, angler's boats fan out east and south for such ocean leviathans as giant tuna, mako sharks, blue and white marlin, and swordfish, plus a host of small tuna on the edge of the continental shelf. On the bottom, anglers fish primarily for cod and pollock. The closest offshore areas south of Montauk are the Cartwright Grounds in 90 or 110 feet of water, the CIA grounds just to the east, and Mud Hole East, which is southeast of Block Island. Farther offshore, the well-known blue-water fishing areas include The Fingers, Butterfish Hole, Fish Tales, and others.

Shinnecock Bay. Shinnecock Bay is 8 miles long and 3 miles wide, but it is really two bays constricted in the middle by Ponquogue Point. The eastern part, with the inlet on its southern end and the canal on its northern end, produces the most fish. Three-quarters of its waters are 6 feet deep or less. The main tidal flow is through the western edge of this part of the bay, from Ponquogue Point north along the shore to the canal's entrance. The main navigation channel is located here and is the focal point of the fishery.

The inlet produces good fluking, and at night striped bass are taken on live baits. The rowboat fleet concentrates in the channel just off, and north, of the Coast Guard station, searching for flounder and fluke. An area in the eastern part of the bay known as The Basket yields good flounder catches in April and May. Early fishing for flounder, fluke, and weakfish can be exceptionally good in Shinnecock Canal. The bays here are fine places to start the fishing season because they are better protected from the elements; even more important, the canal concentrates fish.

Moriches Bay. Moriches is a unique body of water but comparatively shallow for a Long Island Bay. It is 12 miles long and less than 3 miles wide, and more than half the bay is less than 3 feet deep. Fishing is restricted to the east-west channel and a large widening west of Moriches Inlet, from Masury Point east to Tuthill Point. The bay is known for excellent fluking and almost year-round flounder catches. This fishery is best from Buoys 15 to 19 in Narrow Bay Reach, around Buoys 27 and 29, and east to 41. Fluke hotspots are around the inlet, or deeper inside, from New Cut to Buoy 29, and the flats from Buoy 36 to the inlet and between Buoys 39 to 41. Waters just inside the inlet have produced large striped bass, usually only at night by anglers drifting live eels or bunkers. Blackfishing can be quite good along the rock jetties. Bluefish are almost always at the 2B Buoy 2 miles outside.

Great South Bay. Long Island's largest enclosed bay, Great South measures roughly 32 miles from east to west and 5 miles at its widest. It is the deepest of South Shore bays, ranging from 7 to 10 feet with some 15-foot spots in dredged channels. A series of channels were cut through it to allow for boat traffic. Most fishing takes place in these channels and where they meet.

On the western edge of Great South Bay is Babylon Cut. There's good fishing for striped bass and weakfish at the cut's southern edge where it meets the State Boat Channel. West Channel, from Buoy 6 on the north to the RB obstruction buoy to the south is one of two prime weakfishing areas in Great South Bay. The other is the main east-west channel on the south side of the bay. Two weakfish hotspots are located off East and West Fire Islands and off Ocean Beach. North Channel is hardly a channel, but a wide area of deep water, 8 to 12 feet between the Fire Island Flats and Nicoll Point in Heckscher State Park. It is the main east-west channel on the northern side of the bay and is well marked with buoys. Heckscher Flats is a wide, level-bottomed part of the bay, south and mostly east of Nicoll Point, and is the outflow of Nicoll Bay and the Connetquot River. The flounder season starts here in Great South Bay in the spring.

Fire Island Inlet. Fire Island Inlet is a complicated piece of turbulent water with traffic and current. If you don't fish from the beaches, you need a stable boat. The area around the remnants of the Sore Thumb is a striped bass hotspot; a barge was sunk there in 1980, and its lee produces good flounder and fluke catches. There's good striper fishing in this area when bass are migrating. Some of Great South Bay's better flounder and fluke fishing takes place in the Oak Beach hole. Another channel, hard against Great South Beach (Fire Island), carries most of the ebb and flow of the tide.

The deepest part of this channel runs against the beach, and the cut from the bridge to the inlet is a prime striped bass area. Fish at night while drifting live eels in an area just south of Buoy C13; this spot can really produce bass, especially off the remains of an old construction dock.

Jones Inlet. Waters inside Jones Inlet receive the most intense saltwater fishing pressure off all of Long Island. The area north of the inlet is cluttered with low-lying thatch islands that developed a natural drainage system of guzzles, drains, and creeks to handle the tidal flow. This watershed system has been enhanced and developed by dredging and sand mining to facilitate traffic between the inlet and towns along the south side of Long Island.

The back bays themselves are generally shallow, containing little or no water at low tide. Reynolds Channel is the main east-west waterway just inside Jones Inlet and also the main route taken by migrating fish. Long Creek is the main north-south waterway in the western part of this area, draining a collection of canals and bays. Good, early-season flounder fishing occurs in Baldwin Bay. Several well-known "crossroads" fishing areas have developed, such as where Long Creek and Scow Creek meet and cross Sea Dog Creek. Good flounder and fluke catches are made here. A second major north-south channel is Swift Creek. It produces fluke, flounder, snapper, and weakfish. Swift Creek drains waters as far north as Merrick Bay and yields flounder and some weakfish catches in the summer.

A series of creeks and canals drain into East Bay from Merrick to Wantagh and flow into either Broad Creek Channel, Haunts Creek, or Great Channel. Meadowbrook and Wantagh State Parkways cross over these and other passageways. Some of the South Shore's best blackfishing occurs under their bridges. At night, sharp anglers anchor and dole clam bellies into the current to chum striped bass.

East Rockaway Inlet/Reynolds and Broad Channels. Nine-mile-long Reynolds Channel runs from East Rockaway Inlet to Jones Inlet. Between these points are scores of good fishing areas. Anglers after bluefish and striped bass concentrate between Buoy 5 on the north side of East Rockaway Inlet and a shoal that builds seaward off the Boardwalk in Edgemere. Chummers take bass at night around the base of Atlantic Beach Bridge; worm anglers take flounder and blackfish during the day. A good flounder, and sometimes fluke, spot is the 26-foot hole at the entrance to Banister Creek.

Halfway down the length of Reynolds Channel, Broad Channel from the north drains a series of guzzles and bays. The best fishing is off Duck Point on South Green Sedge, and where Woodsburgh Channel meets Broad Channel at the OB Buoy. South of the buoy is a 20-foot hole that has produced fluke and flounder, and at night some big weakfish and an occasional large striped bass. To the north, in the southern end of Hewlett Bay, flounder are taken in May and June.

N

New York Harbor, East River, and Hudson River. *Lower New York Harbor/Staten Island.* Efforts to clean up the Hudson River have paid off in fishing dividends as well as clean water. Fishing for striped bass has increased remarkably off piers in the East River; along the waterfront of Queens and Brooklyn; around Ellis, Liberty, and Governors Islands in Upper Bay; around Hoffman and Swineburne Islands in Lower Bay; and on Romer Shoal. Many of these areas are accessed from boats leaving Sheepshead Bay as well as New Jersey. Flounder catches on Romer Shoal, and fluke catches—especially in the cut between Buoys 4S and 5 on the south end of the shoal—have also increased. Bluefish have again returned to the wide expanse of Rockaway Inlet. In fall, stripers up to 40 pounds have been caught by anglers pulling dead bunker baits off the beach into deeper water.

East River. In the late nineteenth century, when someone wanted to fish for striped bass on the East Coast they usually chose one of two places: Cuttyhunk Island in Massachusetts or the East River between Manhattan and Queens. The East River hotspot was, and is still today, Hell Gate, between Wards Island and Astoria. Most fishing now takes place from piers or bulkheads, but anglers are finding it worthwhile to run their boats from distant ramps to the area.

Hudson River. Marine fishes move up and down the Hudson River with the tides; some regular and some unusual species have migrated far upriver, but most go only as far as the George Washington Bridge, which straddles New York and New Jersey in the lower river. When rainfall is lacking, however, the brackish Hudson becomes more saline, and bluefish are taken as far upriver as the Tappan Zee Bridge. The Hudson is an important coastal spawning river for striped bass in the spring, and huge numbers of stripers migrate upriver from March through early June. Many are caught upriver in brackish or freshwater sections. Most leave the river after spawning, but a few hold over, so that some degree of striped bass fishing is always possible in the Hudson. Shad, however, are only a spring visitor, mainly caught farther north near shoals and flats.

Offshore grounds. Fishing the waters among, around, and behind the New York islands is good because they lie over a relatively shallow continental shelf that is from 60 to 80 miles wide. Its outer edge drops off into abysmal depths on the Atlantic's floor. Over this shallow shelf flows the Gulf Stream, a river of warm water that starts in the Caribbean and flows north, then east, to Europe. It carries numerous species of migrating fish.

The shelf is gouged by several canyons, cut by rivers formed from melting glacial ice that 20,000 years ago stood high above Manhattan. These canyons offer great fishing, but comparatively few anglers have the boats to make it to the shelf's edge. Instead, most concentrate their shelf fishing inside the New York Bight, a triangular area from about Cape May on New Jersey's coast to Montauk Point. Inside the bight are dozens of recognized, identifiable offshore fishing grounds that offer a wide variety of species: tuna, albacore, dolphin, bluefish, sharks, and marlins, and, on the bottom, schools of hake, tilefish, cod, pollock, and black sea bass.

Many of the first-accessed fishing areas are close to Rockaway Inlet and Long Beach, and they include such well-fished spots as Iberia Wreck, Black Warrior Wreck, Big Wreck, Nor'west Bass Grounds, Nor'east and Sou'east Grounds, Middle Grounds, The Oil Spot, The Cedars, Flynn's Knoll, Southwest Pit, England Banks, The Elbow, Tin Can Grounds, Subway Rocks, and Scallop Ridge. A bit farther offshore are the Angler Banks, Lightship Ridge, Steel Wreck, COD Wreck, 17 Fathoms, The Farms, and Three Sisters Grounds. Probably the area's most famous fishing ground is the Mud Hole. It is part of the drowned Hudson Canyon and begins south of the BA Buoy. It is not a well-defined hole but the beginning of a trough, 170 feet deep, with banks under 70 to 90 feet of water.

Long Island (Freshwater)

The quality of Long Island's freshwater fishing opportunities suggests that anglers should be standing in line to get their turn. Because of the great variety and quantity of saltwater here, however, the island's freshwater fishery is overlooked and unexploited, except by a small cadre of anglers.

Long Island is a huge terminal moraine, and on its predominantly sandy back are some 40 lakes, ponds, and reservoirs and more than 100 spring creeks, sometimes erroneously called rivers. Because of Long Island's sandy nature, runoff watersheds cannot develop. Instead, all the surface waters are spring fed. About half of the shallower, warmer ponds offer largemouth bass (and pickerel and panfish), whereas the other half offer brook, brown, and rainbow trout.

Thousands of springs and weeps create four predominant streams—the Connetquot, Nissequogue, Carmans, and Peconic Rivers. At 10 miles, the Peconic is the longest, but because it was dammed from colonial times to produce mill power and cranberries, it is too warm for trout but excellent for bass and chain pickerel. The others are idyllic trout streams. The Connetquot, in fact, was the site of one of America's first trout hatcheries and is today a world-class trout stream.

A sea-run fishery has prospered on the Nissequogue and Connetquot Rivers. Early each spring, steelhead to 20 pounds are taken on both rivers, and fall sees brown trout of almost the same proportions. All three streams have developed sea-run brook trout fisheries, and fishing is open throughout the year in their tidal sections.

With all these resources lying so close to the more than 17 million people living in New York's metropolitan area, one would expect the fishery to suffer. To the contrary, fishing in the two state parks—Nissequogue and Connetquot—is conducted with fly fishing and barbless-hook mandates under the English-style beat system. For a modest fee, an angler reserves a beat with its limits marked on the river and gains access to one of three exclusive daily sessions.

NEW ZEALAND

New Zealand is a small nation at the lower end of the South Pacific Ocean, about 3,000 kilometers to the east of Australia. A long, narrow country, it consists of two major islands (the North and South Islands), as well as numerous offshore isles. Several of the latter, including Stewart and Great Barrier Islands, are in excess of 80 kilometers long. As the run of the 2,000-kilometer-long group is roughly north-south, it straddles a wide range of climatic regions, ranging from sub-tropical to sub-temperate.

New Zealand was first occupied by Polynesian voyagers, the Maori, around 1,000 years ago, with European colonization on a large scale over the last 200 years. This nation of $3^1/_2$ million people is today about 25 percent Maori and 70 percent European (Pakeha in the Maori tongue), with English the common language. Approximately 2 million people live in the top half of the North Island, 700,000 in the lower half of the North Island, and only 800,000 in the more sparsely populated South Island.

The geography of New Zealand ensures that no site is more than 170 kilometers from the sea, and nearly all the cities are clustered about large sheltered ports. Away from the coastal plains, rugged mountain ranges trap moist oceanic winds and precipitate rainfall that feeds a multitude of lakes and rivers.

Isolated from other countries by the wide sweep of the Pacific Ocean, with a light population and relatively little heavy industry, New Zealand has few pollution problems compared to other Western Nations. A total ban on nuclear weapons and power plants is enshrined in law in this conservation-minded nation.

It is little wonder, then, that fishing ranks as New Zealand's most popular participatory sport. A survey showed that a staggering one-third of the population tries their hand at some form of fishing each year, with one-seventh of the population classified as regular anglers, and saltwater participation outnumbering freshwater by about five to one.

Freshwater

Isolated from any continental landmass for millions of years, New Zealand developed its own unique native species. Free from predation, this included many flightless birds, including the kiwi, New Zealand's national symbol and the derivation of the nickname "Kiwis" for its residents. Likewise, the many rivers and lakes were populated mostly with small native fish of the galaxid family and several species of freshwater eel.

European settlers brought with them many species of plants, animals, and fish from their home countries. Some of the fish most successful at adapting to their new homes were European brown trout, which were introduced in 1867, and rainbow trout brought from North America in 1883. Both of these species are widespread throughout the waters of much of New Zealand, which can justifiably claim to have the finest wild trout fishery on the planet.

Another successful American import was the chinook salmon, often called "quinnat" salmon in New Zealand. Runs of these great fish were established in many of the rivers on the east coast of the South Island. Also established were restricted populations of sockeye salmon, mackinaw (lake trout), Atlantic salmon (landlocked populations), and brook trout (brook char). Of these three, only the brook trout is available to anglers in any quantity. The prime fishery for brook trout is Lake Emily in the Canterbury region of the South Island, although they are established in a number of other waters.

New Zealand freshwater fishing is split up into a number of regions, each overseen by a Fish and Game council elected by the fishing license holders. A freshwater fishing license bought in any individual region is valid for both trout and salmon over nearly the whole country. The single exception is the Taupo region in the center of the North Island. This is run by the Department of Conservation, and a separate license is required to fish here.

Trout fishing regulations vary widely throughout the country, and even from water to water. Any Fish and Game license will have a précis of the rules for that region printed on it, but, while the license is valid in other regions, it will not have those local regulations. Visiting anglers who are not using the services of a local guide are advised to seek advice

A trout angler lays out a cast on a crystal clear South Island stream.

N

from the region's Fish and Game office, or a local tackle store, before fishing.

Trout

Most, but not all, of New Zealand's lakes, streams, and rivers contain trout, usually a mix of browns and rainbows. Space considerations do not permit a review of New Zealand's expansive trout fisheries in great detail, but a number of locally published fishing guide books are available, many of them dealing with just one of the main islands, such is the volume of material.

After trout were first introduced into the virgin, food-filled waters of New Zealand, initial growth rates were incredible, with rainbows averaging over 4.5 kilograms and browns close to 9 kilograms. With the introduced trout today striking more of a balance with their environment, average weights have settled to more like 1.5 to 1.8 kilograms. This is still impressive by world standards, and fish over the old magic "double figure" mark of 10 pounds (4.5 kilograms) are still regularly caught.

New Zealand is primarily a fly-fishing-for-trout country. Most fishing laws here were established before spinning tackle was invented or gained popularity, so most of the angling is divided into fly fishing only areas or trolling areas, and, in the latter, non-fly fishing tackle and methods are allowed.

Lakes and tributaries. In a large number of pristine clear water lakes, fish are easily taken by trolling, even by anglers who have never fished before. For the price of a boat and guide, fish are pretty much guaranteed. This is no idle boast; some Lake Taupo accommodation houses offer a free room if their guide cannot hook the guest into a fish.

The most popular fishing lakes include the Rotorua Lakes and Lake Taupo in the North Island, and the Nelson Lakes, Lake Brunner, Lake Hawea, Lake Wanaka, and Lake Wakatipu in the South, in addition to a great many other worthwhile fisheries.

The lake systems of Rotorua and Taupo are in the central region of the North Island, and these two watersheds have been largely responsible for making New Zealand's trout fishing highly respected in international circles. This area has the most prolific rainbow trout fisheries in New Zealand; there are browns here, too, but they're generally outnumbered by rainbows.

The rainbows are of primarily steelhead stock and, though confined to the lakes, are prevented from going to sea by dams. They live in the lakes all summer (December to March), but leave the lakes to run up the streams and spawn. The best fly fishing in streams that flow into the lakes is in April and May, when the big fish move out of the lakes; good fishing also is had in November and December, when the trout return to the lakes. In the summer, most lake fishing is done from boats by longline trolling with lures or flies. However, fly fishing opportunities do exist at the stream mouths, where trout gather for food and also colder water. Streamer flies that imitate smelt are fished on sinking lines when the fish are deep, and on floating lines when the fish are shallow and chasing bait.

There are a number of lakes within a 32-kilometer radius of Rotorua, the most popular being Rotorua, Okataina, and Tarawera. October to June provides good trolling, with May and June offering stream mouth fishing opportunities for fly casters.

Covering 616 square kilometers and stretching for 40 kilometers, Lake Taupo is a huge lake and a recreation and resort showpiece. It is a giant craterlike lake, filled with blue water and reaching a maximum depth of 155 meters. Scores of streams feed into it from all sides, with the major source being the Tongariro River, a major fishery which enters at the southern extremity through a five-fingered delta, and which is filled with spawning rainbows in the winter months. Strong runs of rainbow trout move into the Tongariro (and other tributaries) during June to August and can provide exceptional cold weather fly fishing.

Rainbow trout are the mainstays in the lake, and though the fish may be deep enough in the summer to require weighted lines (lead core) to get down, a lot of trolling is simply done by flatlining a lure or fly (the latter is called harling here). Lake fishing via trolling is essentially effective year-round on this lake, with the western bays being especially favored. Large boats are used to take multiple excursions to areas accessible only by boat, with overnighting done on the boats.

In some locations, trollers can fish within touching distance of rocky cliffs, yet still be over deep water and in rainbow territory. In the summer, the trout tend to be close inshore feeding on smelt, which primarily shoal along shallow sandy beaches, especially where a river or stream enters. Fly fishing at stream mouths is good in November–December and May–June, and often before dawn or after dark on summer days at these stream mouths.

A rainbow trout comes aboard a Lake Taupo charter boat.

Rivers. New Zealand has dozens of rivers that flow to the sea, some directly from the mountains, others from lakes to the sea. These have populations of resident trout, and an annual migration of sea-run brown and rainbow trout (steelhead). On the North Island, the upper reaches of these provide good dry fly and nymph fishing. On the South Island, South Westland has a fine fishery for silvery spawning sea-run browns in late summer and again in the spring when they follow whitebait into the river.

These provide good fishing, but the major river emphasis is on rivers that are connected to lake systems, and on the high mountain flowages. For the more experienced fly angler, gin-clear mountain rivers and streams on both islands offer the challenge of spotting, stalking, and hooking trophy trout. These fish may range from 2 to 6 kilograms, and are well educated. A cautious approach and flawless presentation is needed to take the large fish regularly. The unspoiled high country waters where they are found are usually flanked by mountainous virgin rain forest or native tussock grasslands.

Most of these high country fisheries are in the mountains of the central North Island, or the alpine region of the South Island. Access is not easy, and may involve backpacking or the use of four-wheel-drive vehicles, inflatable rafts, jet boats, or helicopters.

Lowland rivers of a more pastoral character tend to hold good numbers of smaller, but still substantial, fish which may range in size from 1 to 2.5 kilograms. Access to many waters is free, and, where they run through private land, a friendly approach to the landowner will see access granted in many cases.

Generally, stream and river trouting in New Zealand is a case of quality not quantity, with very few fish on the best waters being caught under 1 kilogram. For good anglers, the average size is more likely to be 2 kilograms or better for rainbows and slightly higher for browns.

The streams are very clear, and it's often necessary to locate and see fish, then stalk them and make pinpoint presentations, often using fine tippets and long (in some cases 12- to 18-foot) leaders. Long casts are seldom necessary, but accuracy often is. Nymphs are used extensively on many waters, dry flies on others, and wet or streamer flies are very popular in rivers that flow into lakes.

Seasons. Although some rivers (including many lakes) are open to fishing year-round, the best time to fish for trout in New Zealand is from November to April, which in this hemisphere is the spring-summer-autumn period. Most waters are open to fishing and the best climatic and river conditions may be expected in this period. The exception to this is the winter rainbow run on the Tongariro River, as previously noted.

In November and December (spring and early summer) the rivers and stream of both islands usually fish well. January and February (midsummer) are considered by some to be the best time for dry fly fishing on the South Island, and a good time for the small streams at Rotorua and Taupo. March and April (late summer) usually still have settled weather, and provide good dry fly and nymph fishing. May and June (autumn) primarily offers stream mouth and big-lake tributary fishing.

Quinnat Salmon

Although there are some small populations of Atlantic and sockeye salmon in New Zealand, it is the chinook, or quinnat, salmon that is the successful species in New Zealand. Introduced from stock captured in the Sacramento River in California around 1900, the kiwi chinook represent the only self-sustaining sea-run salmon fishery established in the Southern Hemisphere.

The bulk of the New Zealand salmon fisheries center on the East Coast rivers of the South Island. The most prolific are the Waimakariri, the Rakaia, the Rangitata, and the Waitaki Rivers. Lesser fisheries are found on the Waiau, Hurunui, Ashburton, Opihi, Orari, and Clutha Rivers.

In addition, there are some salmon runs in rivers on the West Coast of the South Island, with the Hall and Paringa being the most consistent. Both of these drain small lakes only a few kilometers from their mouths, and it is in these lakes that most salmon are caught, mostly by deep trolling from boats.

Other places that chinook salmon may be caught are Otago Harbour, where a stocking program has salmon returning to the harbor each year. Here, fishing a herring under a float or trolling lures from a boat are the common practices. The waters around large salmon ocean-ranching operations in the Marlborough Sounds and Stewart Island also produce salmon, escapees from the cages.

The rivers on the East Coast of the South Island are braided freestone rivers. Fishing is carried out from anchored boats out off the mouth, by shore-based anglers thickly clustered around the river mouths, and in pools upstream as the salmon move up to spawn. Some upriver anglers and those that work off the river mouths use jet boats, a Kiwi invention developed for shallow water work in this region, to access their fish. Fat-wheeled farm bikes or all-terrain vehicles are also a popular means of getting around for shore-based anglers.

The salmon runs start around late November, which is the beginning of the New Zealand summer, and finish around the end of April, as autumn starts to close in.

Fed by snow melt, actively changing their beds much of the time, and carrying glacial-ground rock flour, the salmon rivers are seldom clear running. Local wisdom has it that the best fishing is when the rivers are starting to clear after a flood, or "fresh," has encouraged a run of salmon into the river. Water visibility of about 30 centimeters (approximately 12 inches) is counted as fishable.

N

Most salmon fishing in New Zealand is done with spinning tackle. In the surf around the river mouths, hex wobblers (a locally made, heavy casting spoon) are the lure of choice, while lighter types of locally made spoons called zed spinners are favorites to use on fish that have entered the river.

Kiwi chinook average 7 to 9 kilograms, with 14 kilograms counted as a trophy and rare specimens of 18 kilograms taken. Salmon fishing is permitted on the same license as is used for trout. The daily bag limit is two fish kept per person, and fishing must stop if the second fish is taken. Any fish foul-hooked must be returned.

Fishing around the mouths of the salmon rivers can be high density when the salmon are prime, as many anglers favor catching fish when they are in the peak of condition. These mirror-scaled beauties fight the best and are prime eating at this time. Anglers preferring a bit more solitude fish further up the river, seeking out fish where they hold in pools, resting after running rapids, or waiting for a rise in river levels to help with their upstream run.

Saltwater

The long island chain of New Zealand is oriented roughly north-south and consequently bridges a wide range of water temperatures and habitats mainly falling into the temperate category.

Although New Zealand does not boast the wide variety of fish species found in tropical waters, the combination of cooler, nutrient-rich waters and a large continental shelf area has resulted in strong populations of a wide range of popular sport and table fish.

New Zealand has long been a gamefishing Mecca. Early Maori colonists considered the capture of the powerful mako shark as a feat equal to killing an enemy in battle. Early European settlers brought a sporting heritage with them, and although early fishing efforts were aimed at filling the cooking pot, they soon discovered the challenges of catching the large yellowtail, or kingfish as it is known in New Zealand. Kingfish grow in excess of 50 kilograms in these waters and were a considerable challenge on the primitive tackle of the day.

Angling for this species led to the 1910 founding of the Bay of Islands Kingfish Club, which eventually became the Bay of Islands Swordfish Club and was one of the world's first gamefish clubs. Kingfish anglers constantly had their tackle broken up by large striped fish with bills, and one of these was finally caught in 1915, a striped marlin of 223 pounds.

Interest then swung to the greatest gamefish of New Zealand waters: striped, black, and blue marlin, and the high-jumping mako shark. The visits of Zane Grey in the late 1920s and early 1930s, and the publication of his book *Tales of the Angler's Eldorado: New Zealand,* put New Zealand game-fishing on the international map.

During the mid 1980s, however, New Zealand's saltwater angling reputation was at risk, as foreign longline fleets plundered New Zealand waters and recreational catch rates plummeted. After considerable pressure by recreational anglers, in 1987, a ban on foreign longline boats and local longline boats taking or selling marlin was secured. The result was a return to the "good old days," with plentiful fish and catch rates exceeding the golden era just after World War II.

Gamefishing for many of the larger species is seasonal in New Zealand, as water temperatures only reach the comfort zone for many species during the summer and autumn (December to May). The positive side of this is the biological fact that the largest members of a population group live on the fringes, in this case because their larger thermal mass copes better with lower water temperatures, and they have the ability to swim further and faster than smaller specimens. Consequently, very large specimens of many species are encountered.

Striped marlin are still the premier catch off New Zealand's coast, and this is arguably the best fishery in the world for that species, having established many world records. Other billfish are also of varying importance here, and various tunas and sharks, especially makos, are major attractions, with record-setting fish possible. Kingfish are still a major sport-caught fish in New Zealand, and the offshore pinnacles here support the world's best fishery for this species. The widely scattered but little-known (outside of New Zealand) kahawai present outstanding inshore light-fishing opportunities. During high summer, mahimahi (dolphin) are occasional visitors to New Zealand waters, and there are incidental catches for some lure-trolling anglers from February through April. A handful of wahoo captures have been made in recent years, and it may be that, due to oceanic warming, these fish are starting to penetrate New Zealand waters.

Striped Marlin

Striped marlin are the mainstay of New Zealand saltwater gamefishing and it is fair to say that the combination of numbers and size would make this the world's premier fishery for the species. The average size of Kiwi striped marlin is about 90 kilograms (200 pounds) and a fish of over 500 pounds was caught in 1995, although disqualified from the record books on a technicality.

A review of IGFA records reveals that New Zealand "owns" nearly all the world striped marlin records, including a 224.10 kilograms (494 pounds) specimen, and a fair percentage of these caught in recent seasons. This is a live fishery, not one living on past glories. In 1997, a charter boat broke all New Zealand records by catching 156 marlin for the summer season. This included a fifteen-fish day, a magnificent effort considering the high average size of these fish.

The first striped marlin of the New Zealand season are usually caught in the month of December, and January through April represents the bulk of the fishing on the mainland. Fish move as far south as the bottom of the North Island in a good year, although the top half of this Island sees most of the action.

Most of the gamefishing charter fleets are based on sheltered East Coast ports in the top half of the North Island, although fishing charters are available in most areas of the country. Houhora, Whangaroa, Mangonui, The Bay of Islands, Tutukaka, Whitianga, Tauranga, and Whakatane are the main charter boat centers.

About 30 kilometers north of the top of the North Island lie the Three Kings Islands. These islands and the associated King and Middlesex Banks support an incredible variety of bottom and pelagic fish, and provide a prime feeding area for a wide range of predatory species. But first and foremost, over the months of March to the end of June, the area has an incredible striped marlin fishery, with "pack attacks" of six or more marlin a regular occurrence.

Recent changes in charter boat regulations have made it easier for boats to fish this area, but there is not a great deal of shelter at either of the anchorages at these islands. These remote pieces of rock are wildlife sanctuaries and landing is prohibited. There are no facilities, so anglers live aboard the charter or private boats. This is a usual thing in many parts of New Zealand, and most boats are set up for this sort of trip.

The Three Kings mostly seems to start producing billfish around mid-February, but they hold large numbers at the end of the season, as fish withdraw from the cooling mainland waters.

Other Billfish

Shortbill spearfish, blue marlin, black marlin, and broadbill swordfish are also found in New Zealand. Spearfish are mostly an incidental catch when fishing for other species, but during some seasons, over 400 of these enigmatic little billfish are caught, mostly in the 20 to 30 kilogram range.

Blue marlin are caught in New Zealand water during the hottest months, usually February and March. Although they are not as common as striped marlin, most blues are between 200 and 300 kilograms. The largest landed weighed 461 kilograms, the only "grander" caught in New Zealand. Most of these fish are captured north of East Cape. Boats targeting blue marlin tend to troll large lures over offshore deep water structures such as canyons.

Black marlin are also caught in much lesser numbers than stripies, but are mostly good-size fish in excess of 150 kilograms. The national record for this species stands at 444 kilograms. Few of these fish venture south of East Cape, and are mainly caught by fishing live or dead baits around inshore reefs and other structures.

Swordfish have been occasional captures in New Zealand waters for many years, but these were mostly incidental, caught by anglers fishing for marlin. The techniques used in the past were not particularly effective on broadbill, so numbers caught were not great, although bycatch from commercial fishermen targeting tuna or deep water grouper (hapuku in New Zealand) indicated a healthy population.

Night fishing with light sticks was first tried by recreational anglers in 1989, and captures have been regular since then. High numbers are not caught (around ten to twelve per season), but this reflects a low effort from anglers rather than a lack of fish. Although commercial longliners are permitted to take broadbill as a bycatch, as of the late 1990s it appears that the fishery is not under stress, and large adults are regular captures. A swordfish of 291.9 kilograms caught on 24-kilogram line in 1998 is an example.

Broadbill are present throughout the country, right through the year, as shown by longline catches, strandings, and sightings. However, nearly all recreational captures have been made off the East Coast of the North Island between East Cape and North Cape, although this represents a concentration of fishing effort in these regions, rather than any pattern of fish distribution.

There have been several sailfish strandings and reported sightings, and although New Zealand waters are a long way south of their usual range, an eventual capture is likely.

Tuna

New Zealand waters are host to eight species of these most migratory fish. Yellowfin are the most common of the large tuna here. They appear in New Zealand waters around December as the water temperatures rise, and leave again around late April. During this period they range south to Taranaki on the West Coast and Hawkes Bay on the East Coast, although occasional stragglers make their way a little further south than this. The average size of sportfishing captures is 20 to 40 kilograms. Fish are caught each year in excess of 70 kilograms, but these are considered to be trophy fish.

The Bay of Plenty, especially the region based near the town of Whakatane, is considered to be New Zealand's tuna capital. Yellowfin in this area are taken by trolling lures, casting jigs, chunking, and live baiting. This last method is most effective when the yellowfin are marauding schools of anchovies and pilchards in the February-March period.

Bigeye tuna are regularly taken by longliners in New Zealand waters, but only occasionally by anglers, usually on trolled lures over offshore canyons early in the morning. Those fish that are caught are often in excess of 100 kilograms, but there may be only half-a-dozen taken on rod and reel each year. The best areas seem to be the eastern

In May 1914, Evinrude and Sears Roebuck both ran advertisements for their "rowboat engines." The Evinrude Magneto cost $80; the Sears Motorgo $49.95.

N

Bay of Plenty, the Gisborne coast, and the North Cape region. Fish are mostly caught in the summer months, although this may be a reflection of fishing effort rather than bigeye concentrations.

Both the southern and northern bluefin tuna are found in New Zealand waters. The bulk of these fish are southern bluefin, with rare northern giants in excess of 300 kilograms occasionally caught by commercial longliners. Southern bluefin were commercially fished to near-extinction in the 1970s and '80s, but a catch limitation agreement between New Zealand, Australia, and Japan has seen a modest increase in the numbers of these fish, despite the depredations of other Asian fleets and a degree of illegal fishing by Japanese boats in the Tasman Sea.

Bluefin migrate into New Zealand waters from Australia, arriving at Fiordland on the southwest corner of the South Island around March. From here, the fish travel up both coasts, mostly sticking to the edge of the continental shelf. The best chance for anglers to intercept these fish is off Fiordland, a rugged, isolated, magnificent, but often storm-beaten region of New Zealand largely protected by national park status. Only a handful of charter boats ply this region, but bluefin can be caught here on trolled lures from March to June. The largest in recent times was a 110-kilogram fish taken in 1997. Fish average between 25 and 50 kilograms.

Skipjack tuna are summer fish in New Zealand, arriving in December and lingering through May. Their distribution is similar to yellowfin tuna. They are popular as a light-tackle sportfish, and much sought after as a cut bait for a wide range of bottom species. The average fish is 3 to 4 kilograms, and the local all-tackle record is 10.26 kilograms. Trolling small lures is the usual method of capture, but casting with spinning gear is successful, as is the use of small live baits and fly fishing when these fish are feeding on a "meatball" of anchovies or pilchards.

Albacore are a common tuna of New Zealand waters and can be captured at any time of year. Most fish are caught over the summer months (partly a reflection of fishing effort), but of note is a midwinter run of large fish in the Bay of Plenty. A popular light tackle sportfish, albacore can be caught the length of the country on both coasts, and are often an incidental catch of anglers seeking larger species. Size is variable, with larger specimens tending to be caught in deeper water. The average fish is 5 to 6 kilograms; 10-kilogram fish are common, and local records are mostly in the 20- to 25-kilogram range. Mostly taken on trolled lures, they are also susceptible to chunking, jigging, small live baits, and fly fishing.

Two less common species are the slender and butterfly tunas. The slender tuna is an elongated fish ranging from 5 to 12 kilograms. Not a good table fish, they are left alone by commercial netters. They do fight well on light tackle, and limited sportfishing is carried out for them off the East

Coast of the South Island in April, May, and June, as they move north from Dunedin to Kaikoura. These fish are targeted by casting to surface schools, as trolling results in constantly losing tackle to the razor-toothed New Zealand barracouta (snake mackerel). Slender tuna also put in erratic appearances in the Bay of Plenty in spring months (September–November) where they are sometimes caught on lures set for albacore.

Game Sharks

Sharks listed as "gamefish" by the IGFA and found in New Zealand waters include mako, blue, thresher, white, porbeagle, tiger, hammerhead, and tope.

The most commonly caught game sharks are probably makos, which are usually encountered in the summer months throughout the country in every size from "just-born" to "scary monster" class. A number of specimens over 1,000 pounds have been caught, and very large individuals are encountered each year. They are not heavily pursued by anglers in the northern half of the North Island, but are still commonly caught on lures and baits intended for marlin. They are a popular gamefish with anglers in more southern regions, however.

Blue sharks are also common in New Zealand waters in all sizes from freshly pupped to world record class fish. They, too, are not actively pursued by northern anglers, except for those specializing in light tackle or saltwater fly fishing, but are more popular in the colder waters of the south.

Threshers and hammerheads are less common than the two previously mentioned species, but still regularly encountered. The system that has produced many of the largest fish in years gone by—deep drifting with dead baits—is seldom practiced now, as surface trolling is more popular. But on occasions when it is tried, it can still be effective, as proven by a 312-kilogram thresher caught off Tauranga in 1997. The five heaviest threshers in the IGFA record book, each in excess of 300 kilograms, have all come from northern New Zealand waters.

With recovering seal populations, white sharks seem to be increasing in numbers in New Zealand waters. In recent years there have been several attacks on abalone divers by these creatures. Whites are still far from common, and are seldom actively pursued by New Zealand anglers. The isolated Chatham Islands, or the Manukau Harbour adjacent to Auckland (the country's largest city), are two areas where these sharks are encountered.

Tiger sharks sometimes spread into New Zealand waters from the tropics, but are not often caught. Like whites, they should not be considered a target species by visiting anglers.

The porbeagles is a relative of the mako shark and is sometimes caught by anglers fishing deep water for grouper and bass (wreckfish). In recent years southern sportfishing clubs have given this species some attention, and 'beagles of up to 100 kilograms have been captured.

The smallest world-record fish is a 1-pound grass pickerel, caught in June 1991 in Indiana. One pound is the minimum weight allowed for record classifications.

N

Tope are medium-size bottom-dwelling sharks, often called school shark in New Zealand. They are common and regularly captured by anglers targeting other bottom species. Although seldom pursued by anglers, they are strong fighters, and New Zealand claims most of the world records on this species, the result of intensive effort by a small group of anglers fishing Northland's Parengarenga Harbour.

In addition to these species, a large inshore shark is the brown New Zealand whaler, called narrow-tooth shark by the IGFA. Regarded as a game shark in New Zealand, these fish are common in northern inshore waters during summer, When water temperatures are high, they move into large harbors and estuaries to give birth. They are bottom feeders and relatively harmless to man, but the largest inshore fish likely to be encountered by small boat anglers. They have been captured in excess of 300 kilograms, but average between 100 and 200 kilograms. They occasionally jump when hooked, but are not heavily fished.

Inshore

Although lacking the wide range of sportfish present in tropical waters, New Zealand makes up for this with good populations of what fish are available. Although commercial overfishing has greatly reduced the numbers of many species, angling is still good by world standards.

Kahawai. Kahawai are feisty little fish and one of the most common species caught by coastal and shore-based anglers. The Maori name by which they are known means literally "strong-in-the-water," and these fish freely strike a wide range of lures and baits, fight powerfully, and often jump. If they populated the oceans in the rest of the world, they would probably be one of the foremost light tackle fish in the annals of sportfishing.

In New Zealand, their range is nationwide, and they are found in many coastal areas, frequently penetrating into estuaries and the tidal reaches of large rivers. Schools of surface feeding kahawai are still regularly encountered, and these fish are ideal for light tackle, surf, and fly fishing. They are a reasonable table fish with a strong flavor, and are improved in this area by bleeding soon after capture.

Yellowtail. Southern Yellowtail (called kingfish here) are the kingpins of the inshore fishery. In New Zealand, these fish grow to unprecedented sizes. A glance at the IGFA record book confirms the almost total dominance of the New Zealand branch of the family, including a two-way tie of 52-kilogram fish. Most common in the North Island, yellowtail straggle halfway down the coasts of the South Island in a warm summer. In the northern half of the North Island these fish are available pretty much year-round, although they head out to spawn in deep water around January.

Commercial interests are allowed to take yellowtail only as a bycatch, and recreational anglers are limited to three fish per day with a minimum size of 65 centimeters. In one of the top yellowtail areas around White Island, a voluntary code restricts anglers to one kingfish kept per day each.

These restrictions seemed to have worked well in preserving yellowtail numbers. Top areas for kingfish include the Three Kings Islands, White Island, and the Ranfurly Bank, although fishing for these powerful fish is good in most areas. The average size is around 12 to 15 kilograms, with fish over 24 kilograms not uncommon. A handful of fish in excess of 40 kilograms are caught each year.

Popular fishing methods include drifting with both live and dead baits, chunking, jigging, casting with surface lures ("popper" fishing), casting rigged dead baits, and fly fishing. Some of the largest fish are taken fishing from rocky shores (called "land-based gamefishing" or LBG in New Zealand), as well as from boats of all sizes. New Zealand can confidently claim to have the world's best yellowtail fishery.

Snapper and trevally. In terms of the numbers of anglers that pursue them, snapper are probably the most popular fish in New Zealand. Listed as a gamefish by the IGFA with the locally unheard-of tag "squirefish" attached, these fish are not true snapper, but members of the sea bream family. Excellent table fish, they are handsome, still reasonably common despite heavy commercial and recreational fishing pressure, and a fairly strong fighting fish.

Peak populations are found on both coasts in the northern half of the North Island, but they are reasonably prevalent through to the Marlborough Sounds-Nelson region at the top of the South Island. Available year-round in the north of their range, they are mostly only available in the warmer summer months in the south.

The quality of New Zealand snapper fishing can again be seen by the dominance of the record books, and these are all catches made fairly recently. Average size varies a lot, but any fish over 4.5 kilograms is considered a substantial one, over 9 kilograms is a trophy, and occasional captures of over 13.5 kilograms are made.

Snapper are often caught from rock and sand shores; by small boats fishing unweighted baits in estuaries, harbors and shallow coastal areas; and over deeper reefs. Snappers are usually caught on baits, with strip baits of skipjack tuna or whole pilchards (sardines) popular. Bottom jigging with metal lures is also successful, and snapper can also be caught on flies.

The white or silver trevally is New Zealand's sole representative of this widespread family. Their distribution is similar to that of the snapper. These hard-fighting fish are often found in surface feeding schools around offshore islands, rocks, and reefs in the Bay of Plenty and northern regions of the country. They also feed over deeper reefs and hard on the

N

bottom. Average fish are 2 to 3 kilograms in weight, while 5-kilogram specimens are considered large. Occasional fish exceeding 10 kilograms are captured.

These fish, particularly when surface feeding, are excellent targets for light tackle casters and fly anglers. They are a good table species, although not highly rated by some local anglers.

Bottom fish. Hapuku (grouper) and the closely related bass (wreckfish), in addition to the unrelated bluenose (rudderfish), are keenly sought by both recreational anglers and commercial fishermen using bottom baits in deep water between 100 and 400 feet. The first two species average around 15 to 25 kilograms, but are sometimes taken in excess of 46 kilos. Bluenose are more commonly 10 to 15 kilograms, with large specimens exceeding 25. These excellent table species are found nationwide over moderate to deep coastal reefs and are very popular table species. Previously, fishing for these species was regarded as a food-harvesting exercise; however, the advent of low-stretch braided lines has added a sporting aspect to their capture.

Other popular small- to medium-size species sought for both sport and the table are tarakihi and red gurnard (nationwide); warehou and blue moki (central); and blue cod, red cod, and trumpeter (most prevalent in the south). Several species of flounder and mullet are also common, but are mostly taken by net, and also, in the case of flounder, by spearing in shallow water at night.

NICARAGUA

From a natural resources standpoint, Nicaragua seems to be a paradise. Like its southerly neighbor, Costa Rica, Nicaragua is bounded by the Caribbean on the east and the Pacific Ocean on the west; despite some deforestation, it has the largest rain forest reserves in Central America as well as its two largest lakes, Nicaragua and Managua. Rivers form large sections of its northern and southern borders and are numerous along the eastern lowlands. And, it is the least densely populated country in this part of the world.

Nicaragua was rarely fished through the latter part of the twentieth century due to civil unrest. From a general tourism as well as recreational fishing standpoint, Nicaragua fell off the radar screen. As a result, its fisheries resources have been barely explored with modern equipment and methods; based upon what has been known to exist in the past, plus minor sorties along the southwest coast from Costa Rica, some people are looking at this country's sportfishing opportunities in "new frontier" terms. With changes in the late 1990s occurring in Nicaragua that seem likely to encourage more tourism, sportfishing opportunities may open up, and the country's tarpon, snook, bonefish, permit, marlin, and sailfish resources will be better evaluated. Given the nature of the fisheries in Costa

Rica, however, and what is known from the past, there is reason to be optimistic about future angling on both coasts.

It is known that the San Juan River, which forms part of Nicaragua's southern border with Costa Rica, as well as its nearby tributaries and the delta mouth they form, have exceptional numbers of snook and tarpon, as well as machaca, guapote, and mojarra. This area has lately been accessed via a mothership (a 65-foot houseboat towing fishing skiffs), and with permanent facilities planned, it is expected to provide near-virgin fishing in the rivers, lagoons, and near-coast areas.

Anglers will be able to explore hidden lakes and lagoons that don't even appear on maps, including San Juanillo, Silico, La Barca, Ebro Lagoon, Misterioso Lagoon, Fish Creek, the upper waters of Indian River, and Rio Caño Negro (also known as Black Creek). There reportedly is a tarpon nursery in the estuary of Spanish Creek that abounds with 10- to 40-pound tarpon.

These waters have been lightly fished, and there's opportunity to fish the inland lakes for snook, guapote, mojarra, machaca, and other species; in brackish lagoons for the occasional tarpon, as well as snook and snapper; or outside the river mouth for tarpon and occasionally for such species such as jacks, tripletail, barracuda, dorado, snapper, and wahoo when the blue water species move in during certain times of the year.

The vicinity of the river mouth is the most consistent place to find large snook, which run from 15 to 20 pounds. Snook are available all year, but peak from April through June and August through October. Fat snook, which are a smaller species and average 5 pounds, are abundant in the rivers and lakes from November through March. Fall is a good time for the tarpon, too, although they're also available all season. Fifty- to 100-pounders are in the surf, where leadhead jigs do the job. The beaches and surf can be walked, and when conditions are right, a boat can get through the *boca,* or river mouth, to prowl the deeper environs on the oceanside. Reputedly, there are offshore flats that have bonefish and permit.

While this is strictly the activity in the far southwestern corner of Nicaragua, there is reason to believe that the remainder of Nicaragua's Caribbean coast has more, possibly a lot more, of the same. The trouble is that there are few villages along the entire coast (only 5 percent of the country's population is in this area) and extremely poor access. But there's an impressive amount of lagoons, deltas, and small islands here, plus coral reefs scattered offshore. Inland, numerous rivers originate in the highlands and flow through tropical rain forest and the entire lowland area known as the Mosquito Coast.

Fishing up and down this coast from Bluefields to Puerto Cabezas is reputedly excellent, and intrepid adventurers may be able to hire out boats at those two ports from local fishermen. Bluefields is a more popular site, and in the late 1990s, there were regular flights there from the capital, Managua, and continuing on to the Corn Islands. An easterly road from Managua stops far short of Bluefields.

There are two Corn Islands, Big and Little, about 30 miles offshore. Little Corn has a large shallow reef and may provide bonefish and permit; kingfish and dolphin are caught nearby.

Up the coast, northeast and offshore of Puerto Cabezas, is a group of small islands known as Miskito Keys. Flats here contain bonefish and permit; snappers and other species are found in lagoons; and wahoo, mackerel, and barracuda are among species caught in the area. This location has only been lightly fished, and other opportunities are possible.

On the Pacific side, there is some sportfishing out of the southern port city of San Juan del Sur. Sailfish are the main attraction and said to be present all year, with best results from June through October. Blue marlin are caught from November through February. Tuna, bonito, Spanish mackerel, and other species are also found, and more about the Pacific Coast's entire fishery may be learned as tourism develops.

Inland, the freshwater opportunities primarily consist of the aforementioned guapote, machaca, and mojarra species in the middle and upper reaches of rivers. There have been unconfirmed reports of trout in the highlands north of Jinotega. Rivers in the mountainous outback may have gamefish, although the effects of timber harvesting and subsistence fishing are uncertain.

Nicaragua's major rivers run into the Caribbean, with the Rio Grande and its tributaries being the most extensive system. The San Juan River begins in Lake Nicaragua and flows some 110 miles to the salt. Lake Nicaragua is an enormous lake, nearly 100 miles long and containing over 350 islands. With two volcanoes and a national park containing archaeological sites, Lake Nicaragua is a tourist draw and reputed to have plenty of guapote, which are fine light-tackle fish, but unlikely to contend with tarpon and snook along the coast for the attention of traveling anglers. However, it was known to contain a unique species of freshwater shark *(Carcharhinus luecas),* referred to as a bull shark.

NIGHTCRAWLER

The most common earthworm *(see),* usually from 6 to 8 inches long, and a highly popular and effective freshwater bait.

See: Natural Bait.

NIGHT FISHING

In terms of the overall number of people who fish, fishing at night is not nearly as popular as fishing during the day. This is mainly because people are more comfortable fishing during daylight hours than at night. There are many places, and many species of fish, that could provide good night fishing experiences if anglers were more willing to try it. In some cases, less competition from other anglers, chances for larger fish, and sometimes opportunities for a better overall catch are clear incentives to be angling at night.

Some species of fish are very active at night and have physical adaptations that make them more prone than others to night activity. The glossy white, large eyes of walleye, for example, are actually due to a special reflective layer in the retina of the eye known as *tapetum lucidum,* and this same layer is also found in the eyes of cats, raccoons, and deer. It gathers light that enters the eye, making the eye extremely sensitive to bright daylight intensities but well adapted to nocturnal vision.

Species that have an especially well-tuned sense of smell, like catfish and sharks, are more nocturnal than others. And some species that are very reliant on their hearing abilities will use this sense, especially their lateral line, to detect food opportunities even when vision is limited. It is a well-known fact that many fish, especially in midsummer when daylight is greatest, are more active in the low-light hours of dawn and dusk. This may be partly due to the fact that there is less human activity on the water at that time, and the same can be said about fish activity at night. Places such as trout streams that tend to have a lot of human activity in the day may be more productive at night because the fish have found night feeding more advantageous, whether or not they are physiologically attuned to this.

Among the fish that are known to be nocturnally active and that are typically fished for at night are largemouth bass, striped bass, catfish, trout, coho and chinook salmon, and swordfish. Ironically, a good amount of angling is carried out at night under the lights of bridges, roadways, and docks, because the light draws insects, baitfish, and larger predators; a host of species, in both freshwater and saltwater, may be attracted.

The methods used for after-dark fishing vary widely, from casting surface lures in the pitch black for largemouth bass to using glowing lures for deep salmon trolling, and from fishing live eels off a wave-whipped jetty for striped bass to sitting in a lantern-equipped boat while fishing deep bait for catfish or trout. One thing that can be said with certainty about fishing for all species of fish in the inky blackness of night is that you just don't fish like you would in daylight.

Naturally, anglers are accustomed to seeing what they're doing and watching the line or the lure, and this is seldom possible at night, although black lights make it possible to watch fluorescent lines very well. Therefore, intuition and a feel for the line become more important at night than in the daylight. Obviously, your vision is better on nights

Modern-day salmon fishing in the Great Lakes started in the early 1960s with Michigan stockings, but coho salmon were planted (unsuccessfully) in the Great Lakes as early as 1873.

N

Early evening is a prime time for bass fishing, especially in the summer.

with moonlight than on dark or overcast nights (some people also feel that fishing is better before or around the full-moon phase, although this is arguable). Keeping the use of lights to a minimum is a good idea for some types of fishing (like largemouth bass), though it is unnecessary for others. A small headlamp is a dandy accessory for night fishing, since it frees both hands and issues only a small amount of light.

Acclimating yourself to night fishing and to seeing in the blackness takes some adjustment, so you're smart to keep a couple of rods handy with different lures or baits on them in order to minimize the need to use a light and retie. If you're casting with a baitcasting outfit and get a bad backlash, you can put that rod aside and employ a different one. If you're prone to backlashes with baitcasting tackle, consider using spinning gear at night, especially if circumstances don't require accurate lure placement close to cover.

Be attentive to safety when you're fishing in the dark. Landing and unhooking fish caught on lures with multiple hooks is more of a problem in the darkness. Be careful about losing your balance while standing up in a boat at night; in daylight you often brace for a collision with objects, but in the dark you rarely see the objects and are jolted off balance when the boat bumps something. You could wind up in the water, or fall against something inside the boat. Don't leave a lot of things underfoot in a boat, especially hooked lures. When in a boat, keep a high-powered

flashlight handy so you can warn an approaching motorboat about your presence. And when you're under power, have bow and stern lights on.

When fishing in pure darkness, you can do several things to enhance your success. Familiarize yourself with the place that you're fishing. It's best to slow down and work an area well rather than hustle all over. And, in many freshwater situations, it helps to concentrate on quiet and stealth. Noise from operating the motor constantly, moving things around in the boat, chucking an anchor overboard, plunking the electric motor into position, etc., can transmit bad vibes to fish, at least for a while. Being silent and stealthy is an attribute at night. When speaking, use a muted tone so that you don't alarm the fish. Smacking the oars against an aluminum boat is bad news. Similarly, when wade fishing, you need to move slowly and walk carefully, since falling and splashing about are seldom conducive to good fishing.

In a boat, you should approach an area silently from afar as opposed to running up on it with motor on. Drifting quietly and working methodically all around a boat is effective in some situations. Ease the anchor into the water if that helps keep you in place or from moving too far too fast.

Finally, have great respect for the water and the forces of nature, especially at night. If you get into some trouble, chances are that there will be few people around to help.
See: Safety.

NIGHT VISION EQUIPMENT

Electronic night scopes and binoculars multiply available light up to about 50,000 times and can almost turn night into day. This equipment can make night anglers safer and more efficient and is being increasingly used by anglers and boaters who spend considerable time on the water after dark. Night vision equipment makes locating buoys, reading channel markers, and spotting other public or personal navigation markers much easier. Hazards, such as floating debris, shoals, poorly marked jetties, partially submerged standing timber, and boats either anchored or running without lights, are made less dangerous. Both binocular and monocular models are available.

Equipment generations. Night vision units are referred to as generation zero, 1, 2, or 3, depending upon their level of technology. Generation zero units represent the oldest technology and require an infrared light source to work. Generation 1 models include improvements that allow them to operate with ambient starlight. Generation 2 models offer better performance with less visual distortion and are usually lighter and more compact. Generation 3 models offer even more performance and can use a broader spectrum of light; their most important internal component, the intensifier tube, should last longer than those in earlier models.

Light enters a night vision unit's objective lens and then is amplified and passed on to the user's eye. Generation 1 units are the most common among imports and offer light amplification from about 2,000 to 30,000 times, depending upon internal enhancements. Generation 2 models boost light about 30,000 times, and generation 3 models multiply light about 50,000 times.

The actual image improvement that your eye sees when switching from one generation to the next depends upon the ambient light on the scene. A major manufacturer did a comparison test to determine how far away a 6-foot-tall man could be seen through generation 2 and 3 models under different light conditions. There was only a 16 percent difference under bright moonlight (.1 lux), but under a dark, overcast sky (.0001 lux), generation 3 performed 50 percent better than generation 2. Generally, the darker the night the more difference a unit's generation and amplification factor makes.

Stepping up to the next higher generation of equipment can mean more than just extra light amplification and a higher cost. Generation 2 and 3 units may have less visual distortion, better resolution, and a wider field of view than generation 1 models. Again, the differences are more apparent under darker conditions. Depending upon conditions, a good night vision unit can provide a view comparable to what the eye sees in normal daylight.

How it works. Light is amplified inside a generation 3 night scope by passing through three components. Each is about the diameter of a quarter, and they are lined up and sandwiched together inside a vacuum tube. The disc closest to the objective lens is called a photocathode. The middle disc is called a microchannel plate and the disc closest to the eyepiece is a phosphor screen.

Light is made up of tiny particles called photons. A photon enters the objective lens and hits the surface of the photocathode. This component is a glass plate with a surface coating of Gallium Arsenide, which converts the photon into an electron. The photon-turned-electron then travels to the microchannel plate to be amplified. This component looks like a wire mesh with more than a million holes passing through it. The holes, called channels, are tilted at a 5-degree angle, and millions of electrons cling to the channels' sides. As the traveling electron enters the closest tube, it can't pass straight through because of the tube's 5-degree tilt. Instead, it ricochets down the sides of the tube, knocking loose more electrons, which join it. The more electrons that join the original one, the higher the tube's amplification factor. The electrons exit the channel and strike the phosphor screen causing it to glow.

Each of the millions of photons entering the front of a scope follow a parallel path through the tube to the phosphor screen. A photon entering at the upper-left edge of the objective lens strikes the upper-left edge of the phosphor screen. Because the particles maintain their orientation as they travel through the tube, the glowing image that meets your eye is an accurate representation of the scene in front of the scope.

Accessories. Accessories include infrared illuminators, head mounts that let you wear a binocular unit like goggles when you need both hands free, lenses that magnify image size, and even adaptors for connecting camcorders or still cameras. Illuminators add light under extremely dark conditions and can help to replace light lost when using a magnifying lens—less light going in means less coming out to your eye. A head mount is helpful when fishing or maneuvering around an unlighted dock or when snaking between hull-threatening obstacles.

Not for high-speed use. Manufacturers warn that boats should be operated at slow speeds while wearing this equipment; it isn't intended for high-speed operation. Military users train for long periods of time before attempting to operate vehicles or vessels at speed, or to fly, using night vision equipment. Although most units have built-in safeguards to keep sudden flares of light from damaging their intensifier tubes, the user can be momentarily blinded by them, perhaps long enough to lose control of his boat.

NIUE

They call Niue "The Rock of Polynesia," and it is just that—the world's largest raised coral atoll,

N

thrust upward by some titanic submarine upheaval. Protruding from abyssal depths, its 260-square-kilometer landmass is fortressed from relentless Pacific swells by rugged hundred-foot-tall limestone cliffs in which the forms of ancient coral heads are still evident.

There are no lagoons or long sandy beaches. Rather, the island is girdled by a narrow, flat, wave-cut coral platform, which drops off rapidly into deep water. The cliffs are broken by intimate coves, canoe landings, and chasms where splits in the bluff open out into ravine-like saltwater swimming pools filled with colorful fish. In some ways Niue is the reverse of a normal island. Instead of the reefs extending out from the shore, many of them extend inland.

Situated in the South Pacific Ocean, Niue (pronounced new-ay) is 2,100 kilometers northeast of New Zealand and 460 kilometers east of Tonga. It has been a New Zealand protectorate, but is now an independent nation in free association with New Zealand, and still dependent on its larger brother in many ways.

The island is around 17 kilometers long by 10 kilometers wide. Because of a lack of job prospects 10,000 Niueans now live in New Zealand and Australia, leaving only 2,000 people on the island. To try boosting tourism there has been much investment in infrastructure, and there's a wide range of good quality accommodation and other amenities.

Niueans are of Polynesian background and amongst the friendliest, peaceful, and honest people that could be encountered anywhere. Crime is virtually unheard of on this island. Many locals have been educated in New Zealand, have worked there, or have relatives there. It is rare to encounter anyone who does not speak English well.

The main town is Alofi, situated near the airport, which is serviced from New Zealand and Tonga. With no sheltered harbor on Niue, it is important that all boats can be pulled out of the water for safe storage in rough weather. This is done with a large crane mounted on Sir Robert's Wharf in downtown Alofi. A 6-meter craft is about the top of the range that can be handled, and most boats are between 3 and 6 meters. A boat ramp and smaller crane facility is available at nearby Avatele.

Launching and retrieving by crane all adds to the experience of fishing out of Niue but does make access to the fishery completely weather-dependent. A series of deep water moorings for visiting boats are available off Alofi, but with little shelter, visiting boats are often forced to cut and run if the weather turns bad.

Charter services, existing only since 1997, are filled by three fishing operators and one dive operator. Safety is of paramount importance, and all charter boats are regularly inspected for safety equipment and required to have a second engine. A VHF radio system is maintained, but the excellent cellular phone system is often used instead. Boats are equipped with basic tackle, but serious anglers might be wise to supplement this with their own equipment.

Seafood is an important part of the Niuean diet, with many people fishing for their own tables, and there's a strong domestic market in pelagic species, particularly tuna and wahoo. There is not much catch-and-release here, although charter operators will usually release billfish at an angler's request. This should be discussed before fishing starts. The rule is that any fish caught belong to the boat, and are usually sold on the local market. This is reflected in reasonable charter rates. Charter operators will usually offer the angler a share of the catch for their own consumption.

For charter trips, early morning starts (5:30) are the norm. This catches the dawn bite and allows a reasonable stretch of fishing before the wind starts to come up around midday. Anglers are back in time for lunch on shore, with the afternoon free to relax and take advantage of the many other activities available.

Local fishermen fish for food from small aluminum boats or one-man outrigger canoes, using heavy monofilament handlines. They are surprisingly sophisticated fishermen in their own way, and familiar with the fine points of chumming, live baiting, chunking, and careful rigging of baits like flying fish.

Baitfish are captured at night by pursuing them with boats equipped with lights and long-handled nets. This nighttime fish netting is an interesting experience in itself, and at least one local operator specializes in taking out guests on these trips.

With basic tackle and small canoes, local fishermen regularly catch wahoo (which many locals claim to be able to smell while they are still in the water) and tuna. Sailfish and larger marlin are also occasionally captured after epic battles. Canoe fishermen often use their legs to brake or slow their handlines and you can tell the most intrepid ones by their line scars!

With a narrow littoral zone, the amount of fish life that can be supported is not great, so the conservation-minded local fishermen tend to pursue pelagic rather than bottom species if possible. During the winter months this is usually wahoo, supplemented with more tuna and some mahimahi in the summer.

Wahoo is the fish of choice. It is the fish that everybody in Niue wants to eat, and so it is also the one everybody wants to catch. Trolling with big bullet-headed lures, or rigged whole flying fish, are popular techniques.

There are strict limitations on the taking of crayfish (lobster) and shellfish. Full protection is accorded to live coral, turtle, moray eel, rays, giant wrasse, and the timid but plentiful Niuean banded sea snake. In this aspect, Niue is well ahead of many Pacific islands.

New Brunswick does not have an officially designated fish, but it does have an official Atlantic salmon fly, "The Picture Province."

N

Along with attempts to stimulate the tourism industry has come the influence of visiting anglers, mostly New Zealanders. In 1997 the Niue Sportfishing Club, now affiliated with the IGFA, was formed and it has established a local record chart. Rod and reel fishing is becoming more common than it used to be, compared with the practical, results-oriented method of heavy handlines. Visiting anglers are encouraged to join the local club, which can be contacted through the Niue Tourism Office in Alofi. Fishing is strictly prohibited on Sundays, and this restriction is taken very seriously.

There are two main fishing seasons. The October through February summer period sees a predominance of skipjack tuna, yellowfin tuna, and mahimahi (dolphin), with blue marlin in attendance. It is likely that black and striped marlin are also present in these waters, but as the offshore sportfishery is new, this is yet to be confirmed. Inshore, trevally (giant, bluefin, bigeye and goldspot) hunt the reefs during this period.

During the May through September winter months, wahoo are more common, and sailfish are encountered along with some marlin. Inshore, the trevally seem to depart and the reefs are left to the barracuda and red bass (called *fagamea* locally, pronounced fonga-me-a). The red bass is an aggressive tropical snapper, a smaller relative of the cubera snapper.

In deeper waters off the shoulders of the island there are dogtooth tuna, amberjack, various snappers, black trevally, groupers, sharks (including whalers and tigers), and the usual rash of unidentified fish that can't be stopped. Deep-water fishing with baits fished off low-stretch braided lines can produce some very interesting fishing.

Because of the steep dropoff from the island, much fishing at Niue is done within a few hundred meters of shore. A series of fish aggregation devices (FAD) are only about 400 to 500 meters from the lee coast and are a main focus of fishing effort, as are several underwater ridges extending out off the island. FADs are sometimes set on the latter and provide excellent fishing, but they are not well protected from bad weather and are more prone to loss than those inshore.

Shore casting off the reef at low tide with both lures and baits is good sport, and is at its best in the summer months when trevally are present. Be aware that there are danger spots around the island where unexpected waves can sweep in and endanger shore anglers. The quaint Niuean expression for this disaster is "to lose your hat." Fishing prohibitions also apply to some areas. Seek local advice before going fishing.

NMFS

Acronym for National Marine Fisheries Service *(see)*.

NO KILL

A term applied to a body of water, usually a section of river or stream, that is subject to complete catch-and-release *(see)* fishing regulations. In other words, all fish caught must be released alive and unharmed by anglers. No-kill waters are also often subject to regulations regarding method of fishing or equipment, such as fly fishing only, mandatory use of single or barbless hooks, artificial lures only, etc.
See: Regulations.

NOODLE ROD

A long, limber fishing rod primarily used for light-line river fishing, especially for steelhead, but also employed in open-water trolling. Noodle rods are primarily custom-made, usually about 12 to 14 feet long, manufactured for use with 2- through 8-pound line, and feature a long handle and many guides. The guides are placed so as to curve around the blank, starting near the butt on top of the rod and ending at the tip under the rod; the purpose of this arrangement is to keep the line from contacting the shaft of the rod when it is bent. Being long and limber, these rods get a great bend in them when a stout fish is on, and playing fish requires some adjustment from the normal mode.

When fighting a fish with a noodle rod, the butt should be pointed at the fish; the rod will bend completely over in a large semicircle-like manner. When wading in a river, this can be done with the rod held upright. From a higher vantage point, however, including a boat, it may be necessary with large and strong-fighting fish to play it sideways, with the entire rod held horizontal to the water rather than vertical, although the butt is still pointed at the fish.

NORTH CAROLINA

Although many states claim to have diverse sportfishing opportunities, North Carolina is one of the few that really do. Tourism interests call the Tar Heel State a "Variety Vacationland," and anglers with eclectic tastes can find that holds true in saltwater, where inshore or offshore this is one of the best places to fish on the Atlantic Seaboard, as well as in freshwater, where mountain stream fishing is complemented by swampland wading.

Inland, the opportunities range from coldwater trout fishing in over a thousand miles of mountain streams to largemouth bass fishing that is virtually within a stone's throw of the fabled surf fishing at Cape Hatteras. Deep mountain lakes are contrasted by shallow, vegetation-filled marsh lakes. Swift-flowing streams and large impoundments are augmented by slow-moving rivers amid swampy floodplains. Popular freshwater sportfish include brown, rainbow, and brook trout; largemouth, spotted, and smallmouth bass; striped bass and their hybrid cousins; crappies, bluegills, and assorted panfish; walleyes; muskellunge; and spawning-run shad in coastal rivers.

In the marine environment there's tidewater fishing, surf fishing, inshore fishing, and offshore fishing, each with highly notable components, whether that be big bluefin tuna in the winter off Hatteras, red drum in the surf on the barrier beaches, or striped bass in the rivers.

About 175 miles of barrier beaches known as the Outer Banks encircle the great Currituck, Albemarle, Pamlico, and Core Sounds, where a variety of popular species also include bluefish, spotted seatrout, cobia, flounder, and croaker, plus the occasional tarpon. Oregon, Hatteras, and Ocracoke Inlets are gateways to marlin, tuna, dolphin, king mackerel, albacore, and many other species.

The North Carolina Wildlife Resources Commission maintains many excellent launch ramps across the state where there are no fees to launch a boat, and there are many privately maintained ramps throughout the state that provide access for a launching fee.

Freshwater

Mountain streams and lakes. North Carolina is home to the largest mountains east of the Mississippi River, and this produces a surprisingly good trout fishery. In fact, some 2,100 miles of high, coldwater streams are recognized as Designated Public Mountain Trout Waters and closely managed by the state's Wildlife Resources Commission for brook, rainbow, and brown trout fishing. The state tries to manage its coldwater streams as mostly wild trout waters, but those with marginal habitat that are incapable of supporting a wild trout fishery receive supplemental stockings of hatchery reared fish.

The federal government manages streams inside the Great Smoky Mountains; many are intensively managed as native trout waters with emphasis on the eastern brook trout, which is the only truly native salmonid found in North Carolina. Some of the streams within the national park are accessible only by crossing Fontana Lake with a boat and hiking into some of the most pristine trout country in the United States. Hazel, Forney, and Eagle Creeks are but a few of the notable trout streams that empty into Fontana, and lack of easy access makes these and other streams lightly fished.

Another outstanding trout fishery exists within the Cherokee Indian Reservation in Jackson County. The reservation's fishery consists almost entirely of stocked fish, but what the fish lack in being truly wild they make up for in sheer numbers and size.

The headwaters of the Nantahala River are high along the border of North Carolina and Georgia and constitute what is probably North Carolina's coldest trout stream. The Nantahala has some of the finest trout of all three species in the state. Small

feeder streams, including Big Indian and Kimsey Creeks, hold good populations of small but colorful brookies at their origins. Campgrounds and other facilities are available in the Nantahala National Forest. The lower Nantahala River is heavily used for whitewater rafting, but offers fine fishing for those who get out before the major rafting action takes place.

Some of the best trout streams are small flows that many anglers overlook simply because of their size. They're seldom fished and can hold outstanding populations of surprisingly large, albeit spooky, fish. Stealth plus the ability to make short, accurate casts are important for success.

In contrast, some of North Carolina's larger mountain trout streams are tailwater fisheries. Tailwater rivers such as the Tuckaseigee and Green hold some very large trout. Public access may be a problem at some, however, so anglers need to check into this issue.

Many tourists visit North Carolina's mountains every year and there are numerous pay-to-fish ponds in these areas. For the non-purist, these ponds represent a fine way to collect fresh trout to be cooked at the campfire or cabin.

Trout aren't the only species in the mountain rivers, incidentally. The French Broad River near Black Mountain and the New River are highly regarded for their muskie populations. Local guides have done remarkably well for these fine sportfish.

The mountains also hold some of North Carolina's finest lakes, which are unusual in that they hold coldwater, coolwater, and warmwater fish species. Most notable are Fontana, Hiwassee, Calderwood, Nantahala, Cheoah, Santeetlah, and Chatuge.

Several species of trout are usually present in these, and all contain a good population of smallmouth bass, spotted bass, walleye, and muskie. Panfish, especially bluegill and crappie, are fairly abundant.

Fontana Lake has rainbow, brook, and brown trout, and a remnant population of steelhead, which were introduced there years ago and may migrate up into the feeder streams to spawn in the winter. The winter fishing on these streams is scarcely used and can be quite good; conversely, fishing in the deeper waters of the lakes has produced some very large trout during the warmer months. In spite of its high elevation and relatively cool water, Fontana has produced some very sizable largemouth bass. For years the state record largemouth bass came from this deep lake.

Piedmont region. The larger lakes of North Carolina are east of the mountains in the Piedmont region and have excellent populations of crappie, largemouth bass, catfish, landlocked striped bass, and all varieties of panfish, especially shellcrackers and bluegills. Hybrid striped bass are popular newcomers in these lakes, and are locally called Bodie bass.

Lake Norman near Charlotte is noted for striped bass and largemouth bass fishing. There are numerous campgrounds and marinas located on this lake, and access is easy.

Kerr Lake along the North Carolina-Virginia border is a noted largemouth bass fishery and holds a strong population of striped bass that were trapped in this impoundment when the Roanoke River was dammed. Spring fishing for spawning stripers on the Dan River, a tributary to Kerr, is very popular. Other lakes along this river system, such as Gaston and Roanoke Rapids, also contain large numbers of gamefish.

High Rock Lake near Lexington is acclaimed as one of the state's best largemouth bass lakes, and some prominent fishing tournaments have been held here. It is the second lake in the Yadkin River chain.

Badin Lake was formed when the Yadkin River was dammed near Albemarle. It is bordered on one side by the Uwharrie National Forest, which has excellent campsites and outdoor facilities. Below Badin Lake is the Pee Dee River and Lake Tillery, both of which offer fine warmwater fishing.

The major rivers of the Piedmont—the Haw, Yadkin, Catawba, and Roanoke—offer good float fishing for panfish, catfish, and rock bass. There are numerous impoundments along the rivers that have excellent populations of largemouth and hybrid bass. Some also have a good population of white bass.

Many smaller lakes in North Carolina are owned by the various municipalities or counties. They are usually reservoirs for drinking water. Most allow fishing but are restricted to electric motors only.

These smaller lakes are managed intensively for recreational angling and usually have rental boats available at the site for a nominal fee. Contact the local city or county recreation departments for details on fishing these lakes.

Many small privately owned ponds and lakes are located throughout the state. With proper permission these lakes usually offer fine fishing.

Coastal plain. North Carolina's coastal plain contains some of the most interesting angling that the state has to offer, including saltwater fish in brackish or freshwater environments.

The aforementioned Roanoke River, which is dammed along its upper parts, has a spawning run of striped bass, locally called rockfish, that is one of the strongest and finest on the East Coast. Each spring stripers swarm into the lower river, migrating upstream to the dam at Roanoke Rapids Lake where they spawn.

Thanks to the conservation efforts of many individuals and organizations, stripers are now protected during spawning time, when anglers can catch them but must release virtually all. Single, barbless hooks are required on all waters of the Roanoke River from the Highway 258 bridge at Scotland Neck to the

first dam on the river at Roanoke Rapids. Fly anglers flock to the Roanoke Rapids/Weldon area during the spawning run. Some stripers remain in the river on a year-round basis but the truly spectacular fishery is in the early spring.

There are many tributary streams along the lower Roanoke River that have excellent fishing for largemouth bass, crappie, white and yellow perch, and assorted panfish. These streams are bordered by some of the more spectacular scenery in eastern North Carolina, as vast tracts of bottomland hardwoods are still intact there. These tributaries of the Roanoke River wind in and out of huge swamps and it's entirely possible to get lost if you're not very familiar with the waters, making it necessary to have good charts and maps.

Both hickory and American (white) shad also spawn in the Roanoke River, and light tackle anglers have a lot of sport with these gamefish here. Other notable shad rivers include the Cape Fear and the Pamlico/Tar.

The most notable American shad fishery in the state is found below the locks on the Cape Fear River near Fayetteville. This is strictly a springtime fishery when the shad make their spawning run, but angling is quite good for that period of time. Bank fishing is possible but most people prefer to fish from boats, as there is swift current below locks.

In eastern North Carolina, and just across Pamlico Sound from Cape Hatteras, is Lake Mattamuskeet. This is an unusual lake which many people consider to have the finest largemouth bass fishing in the state.

At some 50,000, acres Lake Mattamuskeet is the largest natural lake in the state. It is unique in that it is oblong in shape and extremely shallow. Many other natural lakes in the coastal plain are similar in shape and depth resulting in the theory that the lakes were formed by a meteorite shower at some point in the past. Other lakes such as Phelps, Waccamaw, White, and Pungo are smaller.

Most of this lake is part of the vast Pocosin Lakes National Wildlife Refuge and falls under special rules because of this. The lake is primarily a waterfowl refuge and is closed to fishing for several months of the year.

During the summer months, however, Lake Mattamuskeet is open to boats and fishing and is a light tackle bass angler's dream lake. The best way to fish it is by wading. Anglers use shallow-draft boats to reach their destination on the lake, then anchor the boat and wade in water that's seldom more that waist deep.

While spinning and baitcasting tackle are the most widely used equipment on Lake Mattamuskeet, flycasting tackle is especially useful here, since much of the time the only water clear for fishing is the small pocket of open water between mats of aquatic vegetation. With a fly rod the angler can work small openings and not have to retrieve the entire lure and line through the vegetation.

A European eel held in a Swedish aquarium lived to be 88 years old; it was born in the Sargasso Sea and captured in a river as a 3-year-old elver.

N

Aquatic vegetation is thick due in part to the enrichment of thousands of tons of waterfowl manure that were deposited in the lake during the winter months. Because of this, weedless or top-water lures are most effective.

Because of its shallow, vegetation-rich nature, Lake Mattamuskeet does not get pressure from the large, high-powered bass boat crowd. Many believe that the majority of fish in the lake have never seen a lure before, which is practically unheard of in this age of high fishing pressure. Other fish found in Lake Mattamuskeet, incidentally, are striped bass, flounder, panfish, and crappie.

Lake Phelps, which is near Mattamuskeet, is quite different in nature. Phelps is deeper, not as rich in vegetation, and much clearer. Most of this lake is best fished by boat but the shallower edges are wonderful for wade fishing. Frequently, large-mouth bass can be sighted in the shallows and stalked and sight-fished much the same as bonefish are on saltwater flats. A large state park with camp-grounds and full facilities adjoins one side of Lake Phelps, and public boat ramps are available.

One of the most picturesque fishing lakes in North Carolina is found in Merchant's Millpond State Park near Gatesville. This is a large millpond full of standing, live timber. Gasoline motors are not allowed on this lake, canoes are available for rental, and camp sites exist. Largemouth bass, assorted panfish, and catfish are abundant.

Lake Waccamaw, located in the southern coastal plain, is also a popular largemouth bass lake. It is deeper than many of the other lakes that dot the eastern part of the state, and, since it is easier to maneuver bass boats here than in many of the more shallow bodies of water, it receives more fishing pressure.

Coastal plain rivers such as the Alligator, Chowan, Pungo, Pasquotank, Tar (which becomes the Pamlico River at Washington, NC), Neuse, Trent, New, Cape Fear, Northeast Cape Fear, and Waccamaw are widely known as fine largemouth bass rivers. They also produce good catches of red-breast sunfish, various catfish, and the primitive bowfin or blackfish. Many of these rivers also pro-duce striped bass seasonally.

There are many brackish water coastal streams where an angler may catch both saltwater and fresh-water fish on the same lures or bait in the same water. Largemouth bass populations are good in these mildly saline rivers, but also present are red drum, bluefish, speckled trout, striped bass, white and yellow perch, and flounder. Any of these might be caught on the same fishing trip to these coastal rivers.

Don't discount the possibility of catching the larger saltwater fishes in these coastal streams. Even trophy tarpon or large red drum (redfish) are found well into the "fresh" waters of some of these rivers.

Many coastal streams are classified as "commer-cial" waters below a certain, arbitrary, point, and no fishing license is necessary there, although a pro-posed universal fishing license might change that. Be sure to check local fishing regulations.

Perhaps the most widely recognized bass fishing in the coastal plain is found in Currituck Sound in the northeastern part of the state. Like Lake Mattamuskeet, this is an extremely shallow body of water that is filled with aquatic vegetation during the warmer months. Like other shallow bodies of water that have large amounts of weeds, lures must be worked through brush and submerged vegeta-tion in order to be effective, and shallow draft boats are the best transportation.

The most unusual freshwater fishing in North Carolina is found in several small ponds located a few hundred yards behind Cape Point at Hatteras. Surf anglers can literally go a small distance behind the famed point and fish for largemouth bass and bluegills.

Saltwater

Atlantic Inlets.   Saltwater fishing in North Carolina is divided by Diamond Shoals. This 12-mile-long sandbar marks the meeting place of the cold Labrador Current from the north and the warm Gulf Stream from the south. The merger of these produces excellent fishing, but also treacher-ous conditions that cause it to be referred to as the "Graveyard of the Atlantic." The shoals that extend seaward from Capes Hatteras, Lookout, and Fear, are littered with broken, rusted skeletons of ships wrecked by storms or sunk by enemy torpedoes, and they also possess artificial reefs.

Waters to the north of Diamond Shoals tend to be colder and harbor fish more common to the north Atlantic, while waters to the south are warmer and hold fish more common to the south Atlantic. Fish such as yellowfin tuna, dolphin, blue marlin, and white marlin are found along the edge of the Gulf Stream on both sides of Diamond Shoals.

Proximity to the Gulf Stream means that the off-shore waters harbor lots of white marlin and record-size blue marlin. In fact, the waters off North Carolina can lay claim to having the best potential in the coastal U.S. for catching a grander, if not an all-tackle record.

Oregon Inlet has been the port of record for sev-eral Atlantic blue marlin granders. Others have been registered at Hatteras and Morehead City. A 1,142-pounder taken in August of 1989 at the 80-fathom mark northeast of Cape Lookout is a former all-tackle world record holder, and a 1,128-pounder caught in June of 1975 held the 80-pound line class world record until replaced in 1993 with a fish from the Azores.

While there is opportunity for large blue marlin out of any of the major coastal ports, the area to the northeast of Oregon Inlet has been especially pro-ductive in modern times. In the late 1980s, there were four blue marlin caught in a three-day span off Oregon Inlet that each weighed over 800 pounds.

The marlin season off North Carolina generally begins earlier than it does further north, thanks to the warm Gulf Stream influence, and this brings northern boats down for the June and July action. Hatteras often produces well in the beginning of the summer, and then the attention in August and September shifts more to the Oregon Inlet waters.

As for white marlin, the offshore waters have plenty in season. It has been called the best white marlin fishery in North America, and in a productive year the action can border on the unbelievable at times. Locals still talk about the phenomenal catch and release of 108 white marlin made in a single day in 1983 by one sportfishing boat, and that during a tournament.

Certainly that was a blitz, but in a good day a boat here might see upwards of 15 fish. Pods of white marlin are a frequent sighting, especially when they're chasing bait in the fall. These fish aren't large, with 45 to 60 pounds being average size. There are no record-makers here, but they provide good light-tackle action, as well as opportunities for casting a fly or using spinning tackle. The problem, however, with white marlin fishing here is that it occurs offshore where the big blue marlin roam as well, meaning that there are many times when the bigger blues hit a small bait meant for whites and a great tackle mismatch can occur.

Of course, coastal North Carolina is also noted for other species, particularly channel bass and bluefish. Most of the biggest, and record-setting, bluefish caught in North America have come from coastal North Carolina, including the 50-pound line-class and all-tackle record of 31 pounds 12 ounces. That particular trophy was garnered in 1972, when bluefish reappeared here in great numbers. They had been missing for several decades prior to that.

Virtually all of the monster fish have been taken between November and January in their respective years, which is fitting. The bluefish blitzkrieg in the fall on the Outer Banks is renowned, and as long as the bluefish population—thought by some to be cyclical—remains at a high level, the fall action will be excellent.

Nevertheless, small blues are available here all season long. Bluefish provide surf casters and inshore boaters with a good level of action in the fall, so good, in fact, that using light tackle, including a fly rod, is feasible. However, the bigger blues do not always migrate into the surf for the shore fishermen, nor do they necessarily stay long when they come in, so sometimes there will be light action off the beach while a good mass of fish is offshore.

Outer Banks blues average about 12 pounds in the spring prior to their northward migration, and 15 in the fall. They winter off the various capes and generally provide the best fishing in the months of May and November. The Nag's Head–Oregon Inlet area is one of the better locales, as is Cape Hatteras.

A cobia is boated off the North Carolina coast.

When the blues aren't the quarry, big red drum (also called channel bass) can fill the void. As with bluefish, North Carolina waters have produced a lot of record fish, at one point filling 15 of a possible 20 categories, including the all-tackle and 50 pound line-class record with a 94-pound 2-ounce monster. The hottest fishing is in November, with action all along the banks, but great activity in the surf at Cape Hatteras.

Oregon Inlet is the first opening to the sea south of the North Carolina/Virginia boundary. There are large charter fleets on Manteo Island, plus an excellent launch ramp and varied accommodations. The charter fleet here works the offshore waters on a year-round schedule. Yellowfin tuna are taken all year, with best fishing in the spring and fall. White marlin provide great action during the summer, with the occasional big blue marlin moving into the trolling spread for added excitement.

About 30 miles from Oregon Inlet, the Point is the center of all fishing activity. A very steep drop from 28 to 224 fathoms and another from 200 to 600 fathoms a few miles to the east draw bait and gamefish. The fleet may work north and south of the Point but this is the place where they are likely to begin the day.

Trolling with ballyhoo, mackerel, mullet, and squid is about the only technique used by the Oregon Inlet offshore fleet. A few lures find their way into the spread and chunking has found a few followers, but trolling some type of dead bait is the standard operating procedure.

Not every boat out of Oregon Inlet runs offshore. King mackerel and amberjack are caught over inshore wrecks and around the Navy Towers on live bait, plugs, and spoons. Spanish mackerel, big bluefish, and striped bass are taken on trolled plugs, spoons, and bucktails just beyond the surf line and over the shoals at the mouth of the inlet. Mackerel and amberjack are common in the summer, with the best bluefish and striper action in the spring and fall.

N

The next outlet to the sea is in the shadow of Diamond Shoals at Hatteras Inlet. Several marinas in the town of Hatteras Village offer charter boats, slips, and a launch ramp.

Hatteras is the nearest point—about 12 miles—to the Gulf Stream north of mid-Florida. Working along the edge of the Gulf Stream out of Hatteras Inlet produces yellowfin, blackfin, and bluefin tuna, as well as marlin, dolphin, and wahoo. The appearance of giant bluefin tuna during the winter has drawn anglers from all over the world and been the subject of a lot of publicity. Fish approaching 1,000 pounds are taken on dead bunker tossed out a few feet behind the boat. When the fishing is hot, and it often is, catches of 25 or more giants per boat per day are recorded. Due to federal regulations, most of these fish are released and many tagged; tagging data from released and recaptured tuna have been valuable to marine biologists.

In the fall, a run of big king mackerel develops over inshore wrecks and shoals. Slow-trolled live menhaden account for most of these big fish. Under favorable conditions the king mackerel run will carry into the winter, adding to the great fishing for giant bluefin.

The inshore grounds out of Hatteras Inlet produce Spanish mackerel, bluefish, red drum, and amberjack. Bottom fishing shows the influence of warmer southern waters, as grouper and snapper replace sea bass and tautog.

It's a long way from Hatteras Inlet to Beaufort Inlet, which is the next major outlet heading down the Tar Heel coast. Barden Inlet behind Cape Lookout Lighthouse serves Harkers Island, but Beaufort Inlet carries the larger charter, private, and head boat fleet out of Morehead City and Atlantic Beach.

King mackerel are major players of the inshore fishery here. Trolling with live menhaden or with dead cigar minnows and ribbonfish has been raised to an art form along this stretch of the North Carolina coast. Small treble hooks and light wire leaders are hidden in the bait in an effort to fool the keen eyes of the mackerel. The big mackerel are played with a light drag to prevent pulling the small hooks out.

Offshore action centers on the Big Rock, an upwelling close to the 100-fathom drop that produces tuna, dolphin, wahoo, and marlin. Big blue marlin show up in late spring to get the offshore season off to a fast start. Several head boats fish the waters near the Gulf Stream for grouper, snapper, triggerfish, amberjack, and African pompano. The boats run all year and most schedule 18- or 24-hour trips at least once a month.

Masonboro Inlet serves the charter and private boat fleet running out of Wrightsville Beach. New Topsail Inlet to the north serves a smaller fleet at Topsail Beach. Both inlets are serviced by several launch ramps and marinas.

King mackerel provide most of the inshore fishing excitement, with yellowfin tuna the major focus on the offshore grounds. Live bait is used for the kings, and trolled rigged ballyhoo for the yellowfins. Bottom fishing for grouper, snapper, triggerfish, and other deep water species is done from both head boats and charter boats. Natural rocks and artificial reefs attract bottom fish and king mackerel.

The Cape Fear River empties into the ocean at Bald Head Island creating shoals that attract numerous species. Anglers troll or drift live baits along the edge of the shoals or at the color change where the turbid water from the river meets the cleaner water of the ocean. This is a good area to find big king mackerel and cobia. There's a marina on the south side of the Cape Fear River at Southport, and a boat ramp on the Intercoastal Waterway at Dutchman Creek.

There are several more inlets between the Cape Fear River and the South Carolina line at Little River Inlet. Lochwoods Folly, Shallotte, Tubbs, and Mad Inlets provide passage to the ocean, but all are a bit dangerous due to shifting sandbars that can change the channel overnight. Boat ramps and marinas are located behind the barrier islands on the Intercoastal Waterway.

The Sounds.   The famous Outer Banks of North Carolina is a sandy strip 175 miles long that runs from the Virginia line south to Cape Lookout and then curves back to the mainland. This open-beach barrier reef encompasses 2,000 square miles of sounds or shallow bays that hold great fishing potential, and which offer a potpourri of freshwater, saltwater, and brackish water angling. This is the ideal situation for light-tackle anglers. Even though the bigger sounds can get rough, they have an abundance of sheltered water that can be fished from a small boat or by wading.

In North Carolina, enormous volumes of freshwater daily enter the upper sounds. This water piles up and, depending on volume, creates a lot of brackish water that supports some freshwater species, especially largemouth bass. Currituck Sound, an upper sound that begins at the Virginia line, was once one of the greatest bass factories and shallow-water fisheries in the nation, but the salinity of Currituck has increased greatly since the mid 1980s due to lower freshwater inflows. Bass cannot tolerate it when the salinity becomes too high, and such species as speckled trout, flounder, croaker, and white perch become more prevalent. A good deal of the fishing for these species takes place in the Currituck before it meets up with Albemarle Sound at the Wright Memorial Bridge in Kitty Hawk. This is a very shallow body of water that will not accommodate large boats. Most of the fishing is done from prams or skiffs, or from shore. Albemarle Sound is deeper and larger than Currituck with a greater variety of fish. Striped bass are a primary catch here and found throughout the year, but strict regulations keep the season short and the bag limit low.

Croatan Sound and Roanoke Sound surround Roanoke Island before emptying into Pamlico Sound. Speckled trout are taken from the shallow edges of both waterways on live bait, jigs, and plugs. Striped bass are common at the Mann's Harbor Bridge over Croatan Sound, where plugs, jigs, and bucktails take fish all year. Weakfish, flounder, blues, croaker, and spot keep bottom bouncers happy.

Pamlico Sound is a huge inland sea stretching from Roanoke Island in the north to Cedar Island in the south. It is wide but shallow, seldom reaching over 20 feet in depth. Weedbeds are common along the shoreline, and speckled trout find this a suitable home. The water is 3 to 5 feet deep and usually clear, requiring a careful approach to avoid spooking fish. Live shrimp or mullet will fool even the biggest fish, but many anglers prefer to use jigs, plugs, and flies.

In recent years more anglers have taken up wading in Pamlico Sound, using spinning, baitcasting, and flycasting tackle. Speckled trout are the primary target, but bluefish, channel bass, flounder, croaker, and spot are also caught. It takes experience or an experienced guide to consistently find productive weedbeds or deep holes in the sound, but the action can be fast and exciting with lures or bait.

Tarpon range as far north as Hatteras, and the best action for them in North Carolina is in Pamlico Sound during the summer. They can be difficult to find, however. Most are caught on dead or live bait fished on the bottom in sloughs and holes known to be tarpon hangouts. Local guides have the best idea of where the tarpon hotspots are. Tarpon in the 100-pound class are usually taken each year.

Core Sound runs behind Core Banks from Cedar Island to Cape Lookout, and Bogue Sound begins at Cape Lookout and runs behind the Bogue Banks to Bogue Inlet at Swansboro. Core Sound doesn't see the fishing pressure that Bogue Sound gets because Cape Lookout National Seashore has protected the barrier islands of Core Banks. This is a very shallow sound, but trout, flounder, blues, croaker, and spot are caught in the deeper holes and sloughs.

Bogue Sound lies between the well-developed Bogue Banks barrier island and the equally populated mainland. Morehead City and Atlantic Beach anchor the east end with Cape Carteret and Swansboro at the western end. In spite of the heavy boat traffic, good fishing is found throughout the sound. Speckled trout take refuge in the shadow of bridges crossing the sound. Gray trout are caught in the turning basin at Morehead City, with croaker, spot, and flounder taken in the channels.

From Bogue Inlet south, the narrow Intercoastal Waterway separates the mainland from the barrier islands. Speckled trout, flounder, croaker, and spot

are caught here but boat traffic is always a problem. There are boat ramps located on both sides of the sounds and along the Intercoastal Waterway. Few charter boats work these shallow waters but guides with skiffs are found in most waterside communities.

The Surf. North Carolina offers the surf caster more fishing opportunities than most are able to use. Most of the North Carolina beach between Virginia and South Carolina is open to surf fishing, and a good deal of that is accessible by beach buggies. The fishing is so good that even a beach with poor structure can produce good action.

Corolla provides the northernmost access point for beach buggies. Anglers can drive north from here to the Virginia line where access is denied at False Cape State Park. The beach is natural, with no bulkheads or other manmade structures, and fishing can be good for drum, bluefish, speckled trout, and croaker. The beach south of Corolla is developed and vehicular access is restricted.

Development really becomes a problem from Duck to Nags Head. Walk-on fishing is possible but beach buggies are restricted to fall and spring. Special permits to drive on the beach are required in each town, but the fall run of big blues and striped bass can be worth the cost and trouble of obtaining a permit.

Oregon Inlet has a variety of surf fishing possibilities. The beach north of the inlet has good structure with deep holes and sloughs where drum, trout, bluefish, and mullet are caught. At the mouth of the inlet, an old trawler went aground and its bones attract big blues and striped bass in the fall.

Pea Island from Oregon Inlet to Rodanthe is closed to vehicles due to beach erosion. Walk-on access is allowed but parking alongside Route 12 can be a problem. This is a great stretch of beach for big blues in the fall, especially around an old boiler left over from one of the many shipwrecks along this dangerous coastline.

Beach buggies can be used from Rodanthe all the way to Buxton, and from the Hatteras Lighthouse south to Hatteras Inlet. A small section of beach behind the motels in Buxton is set aside for walk-on fishing. Those who stay in one of the motels and walk to the beach often do as well if not better than their motorized brethren.

The Point at Cape Hatteras is the greatest surf fishing location in the world. The Labrador current hits it on the north side and the Gulf Stream hits it on the south, resulting in a mix of bait and gamefish found nowhere else.

Big red drum drop by in the spring and fall, and are often joined by big blues and stripers. Most are caught on chunks of cut bait fished on rods designed to handle big fish in rough water. Known as Hatteras Heavers, the rods have pool cue-size tips and enough backbone to tip over large boulders. Matched to a big conventional reel filled with 30-pound line, the combination can throw 8 ounces of lead and a big hunk of bait into a gale.

N

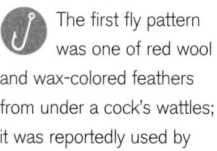

The first fly pattern was one of red wool and wax-colored feathers from under a cock's wattles; it was reportedly used by the Macedonians in the third century A.D.

Ocracoke Island across Hatteras Inlet has a wide beach that is open to vehicles. This is a quiet outpost that can only be reached by ferry, and the fishing is as good as found anywhere along the coast.

Portsmouth Island was once a busy seaport but is now part of the Cape Lookout National Seashore. It, too, may only be reached by ferry. Known for a good run of red drum in the spring and fall, the island still attracts a hardy band of surf casters.

Cape Lookout National Seashore also protects all of the Core Banks. Surf fishing is allowed here but access is difficult. Small boats can travel across Core Sound to the barrier island, where anglers can walk over the sand to the surf. This is too much work for most people, but those who make the effort are pleased with the quality fishing experience.

A private ferry from Harker's Island will carry anglers and their vehicles over to the beach above Cape Lookout Lighthouse. Primitive camping is allowed, so anglers may enjoy an extended stay.

Bogue Banks is highly developed but most of the beach remains open to vehicles. Speckled trout, bluefish, flounder, and croaker are the most common species here, with an occasional puppy drum and Spanish mackerel caught from the beach.

Bear Island at Bogue Inlet can only be reached by boat, but red drum are taken here on a regular basis in the spring and fall. Fresh cut bait is the best choice, but the heavy tackle required at Cape Hatteras is not needed here.

The federal government controls the beach from Bogue Inlet to New River and they do not let surf anglers on the property. The rest of the coast from New River to the South Carolina line is open to fishing. Vehicle use may be restricted in some locations by local ordinances, but the walk to the surf is usually short.

Big fish are rare here but spot, croaker, flounder, speckled trout, weakfish, and Spanish mackerel provide good action. The best fishing for trout and flounder is in the fall and winter when they stage in the deeper sloughs and around inlets.

Piers. North Carolina has an abundance of fishing piers extending into the ocean, some reaching more than 1,000 feet out. They begin in Kitty Hawk and continue down to Sunset Beach. Pier fishing is a great way for the whole family to enjoy the sport at a reasonable cost. Most piers have some type of entertainment center, a restaurant or snack bar, and a tackle shop. The cost is less than a movie and you get to take your catch home.

A few serious pier jockeys will spend hours fishing live baits in hopes of hooking a big king mackerel, tarpon, cobia, or bluefish. This takes patience, skill, and a serious investment in tackle. It is easier and more productive to soak a bait on the bottom and catch a mixed bag of blues, trout, sea mullet, croaker, spot, and anything else that happens to swim by. Blues and Spanish mackerel often stage feeding frenzies at the end of the pier early in the

morning or late in the afternoon. Lures cast into this melee will bring instant strikes and exciting action.

In the spring and fall, big red drum and striped bass are caught from piers north of Cape Hatteras. Chunks of cut bait fished on the bottom at night collect most of these trophies.

NORTH DAKOTA

In North Dakota, the water meets the prairie and fishing season never actually closes. North Dakota is open to angling activity throughout the spring, summer, winter, and fall seasons, each of which offers a unique freshwater experience for a variety of gamefish, including northern pike, walleye, sauger, saugeye, chinook salmon, rainbow trout, brown trout, muskellunge, smallmouth bass, largemouth bass, and a wide variety of panfish. The most popular year-round species is the walleye, closely followed by a relative and favorite winter quarry, yellow perch.

The diversity of species in North Dakota is largely a result of stocking programs by the state game and fish department and a combination of natural reproduction in some waters. To add to existing fisheries, chinook salmon were introduced to the Missouri River system. A growing population of these fish represents one of the most successful inland populations of disease-free salmonids in the country. Though void of blue-ribbon trout streams, North Dakota's lakes and farm ponds are becoming popular inland trout fisheries also, a direct result of stocking programs and the catch and release ethic of anglers.

However, most angling effort in the state centers on warmwater and coolwater species, and the three large bodies of water that comprise the state's most popular fisheries are the Missouri River System, which includes two reservoirs (Lake Sakakawea and Lake Oahe), Devils Lake, and the Red River of the North.

The Missouri River System

A main character in the prairie landscape, the Missouri River runs from the North Dakota border in the northwest through the central part of the state and along the capital city of Bismarck. From its headwaters at the confluence of the Yellowstone River, the Missouri is broken into four sections: the upper Missouri River, Lake Sakakawea, the Missouri River Tailrace, and Lake Oahe. Anglers know these sections of water for their excellent populations of walleye, northern pike, chinook salmon, and world class sauger and saugeye fishing.

There are more than 60 recreational access points along the Missouri River system, making it a favorite destination for both the casual and trophy angler. For the heavily favored walleyes, pre-spawn early spring angling, and late fall angling, typically produce trophy fish from 8 to 13 pounds. Average

Though black marlin have been intensively pursued in recent decades, no one has bested the world-record 1,560-pounder caught at Cabo Blanco, Peru, in August 1953.

weights depend on the life cycle of the river section and can vary from 2 to 5 pounds.

The Upper Missouri. Originating from Montana, the Missouri River enters North Dakota's northwest border near Williston. Here, the confluence of the Missouri and Yellowstone Rivers form the upper section of a 180-mile-long reservoir called Lake Sakakawea. This area holds the largest remnant population of naturally reproducing paddlefish in the United States. Both fish and angler congregate in this area each spring. The largest paddlefish landed on rod and reel was a 120-pound specimen caught in 1993, and the oldest fish on record was 45 years old.

Lake Sakakawea. The Garrison Dam that contains giant Lake Sakakawea was built for hydroelectric power and flood control and completed in 1953. It is the third largest rolled-earth dam in the world. The United States Army Corps of Engineers manages the lake project. As a result, Sakakawea, named after a legendary American-Indian woman who helped guide the early 1800s explorers Lewis and Clark up the Missouri, is largely void of private development and is unpopulated along its shoreline.

Lake Sakakawea's fishing opportunities heat up at ice out, which usually occurs in early to late April. Twenty-pound northern pike can be found cruising the shallow bays at this time. Shore anglers fishing with floats and quick-strike rigs tipped with dead bait often produce lunkers. Noted hotspots for pike, which incidentally is the official state fish, include Parshall and Steinke Bays. Jigging and live bait rigging in 12 to 20 feet of water produces many nice catches.

Walleyes are usually found in the upper third of the reservoir in late April and early May as they haunt the traditional spawning grounds of White Earth Bay and the Van Hook Arm. Meanwhile, rainbow and brown trout offer anglers on the lower end of the reservoir plenty of rod-bending opportunity near the Garrison Dam and the Riverdale Bluffs.

By midsummer, fishing action heats up throughout the reservoir. The lake's midsection holds many traditional hotspots for walleye, including Nishu and Beulah Bays, as well as points and bays near Indian Hills. Crankbaits and spinner rigs pulled in 8 to 25 feet of water are top producers.

The Missouri River Tailrace. The Missouri River begins again immediately below the Garrison Dam and stretches downstream for 70 miles until it reaches the headwaters of Lake Oahe.

Fishing action on the river begins below Garrison Dam at the Missouri River Tailrace, where Lake Sakakawea's water is generated into hydroelectric power. The fast current and generators create a constant buffet of churned-up baitfish, which provides a smorgasbord to both fish and angler. The Tailrace chute produces catfish, chinook salmon, rainbow trout, sauger, walleye, and burbot, plus a variety of non-gamefish species. This area is a favorite year-round open water fishery.

From the Tailrace, the Missouri River winds downstream through heavily wooded timber bottoms and sparsely populated areas to the riverside city of Washburn and the metropolitan areas of Bismarck-Mandan. The fast current changes the river's flow constantly, challenging even the best anglers' navigational ability. The walleye fishery within this section is good, but primarily a resident secret. The stretch from the dam to around Stanton has good-size rainbows, and with riffles and holes is a rather surprising trout river.

Lake Oahe. Lake Oahe's headwaters begin in south-central North Dakota, below the capital city of Bismarck. Identifying where the Missouri River ends and where Lake Oahe begins is often disputed. The Fort Rice boat landing, a fishing hotspot, marks the headwaters of Lake Oahe, which, at full pool, contains 90,000 acres of water in North Dakota, although vastly more in neighboring South Dakota.

Famous for spring and fall runs of northern pike and walleye, North Dakota's section of Lake Oahe has gained notoriety for its wintertime production of lunker pike, and it gets heavy angling pressure during peak periods.

Devils Lake

As North Dakota's largest natural prairie lake, and one of the United States' only closed basin lakes, Devils Lake is unique by nature's design. With no direct tributary inlet or outlet, the emerald waters of this lake are difficult to predict. Since the mid-1990s, this prairie lake has been on the rise, surpassing a 500-year high-water mark and offering more than 35 square miles of new fishable water.

The prairie waters of Devils Lake originally consisted of 70,000 acres of spring-fed waters and runoff. The lake's maximum depth is 35 feet, with an average depth of 15 to 18 feet. The basin structure is edged with rocky points, sand, weedbeds, and hardwood timber. Since the lake is a prairie basin in a valleylike floor, the water spreads out instead of climbing to higher elevations.

Devils Lake is a top producer throughout the seasons, with a special emphasis on the winter fishery. Local promoters use snow removal equipment to keep and provide good access onto the lake's traditional winter fishing areas, which wind miles around the lake. Winter anglers move a lot here, looking for jumbo yellow perch, some 2 pounds or better. Wax worms tipped on small jigs are the main offering for these fish. Walleyes are also a winter favorite here.

Spring and summer activity heats up an abundant population of white bass, the so-called piranha of the prairie. These feisty schooling fish turn on in numbers at Devils Lake. Shore anglers do exceptionally well for white bass along bridge abutments and roadbeds in the spring. The vicinity of the

N

Highway 19 bridge and Graham's Island State Park are both white bass hotspots.

Suspended walleyes are caught in the summer on Devils Lake by those using big-water trolling tactics. A growing population of walleye has proven that Devils Lake is a "sleeper" for this species.

The Red River of the North

The great Red River of the North is unique for its northbound flow toward Manitoba, Canada. Serving as a natural border between North Dakota and Minnesota, and aptly named for the color of its runoff from nutrient-rich soil found in surrounding agricultural lands, the Red River is known as one of the most volatile rivers in the country, and is prone to both drought and floods.

The mighty Red's claim to fishing fame is the annual production of lunker channel catfish, some weighing 20 pounds or more. The northern portion of the Red is considered one of the premier catfish spots in the nation, producing up to 30-pound specimens. The Drayton Dam area north of Grand Forks has been a traditional catfish hotspot for years, but the entire river system offers good opportunities.

From its headwaters in Wahpeton, where a tribute to the catfish was built as a tourist attraction, through the cities of Fargo and Grand Forks, anglers find plentiful access to good-old-fashioned riverbank fishing. Heavy-duty rods and reels are employed here for the behemoths, with dead baits and stink baits being the preferred bottom offerings. Night fishing is very common here. Although catfish reigns as king on the Red, the river also supports sauger and walleye fishing.

Other Waters

Because of the notoriety of the larger bodies of water, anglers often overlook North Dakota's smaller lakes. There are 53 counties in North Dakota that host more than 170 fishable waters that are listed by the game and fish department as publicly accessible. Notable major lakes include Audubon, Ashtabula, Darling, Pipestem, Sweet Briar, and Nelson.

A sister to Lake Sakakawea, Lake Audubon has summer and winter popularity for walleye, northern pike, and yellow perch. Located in central North Dakota, next to Lake Sakakawea, it is the headwaters of a chain of irrigation lakes known as the McClusky Canal System, where the state's highest density of largemouth bass and muskellunge are found.

Nelson Lake, in the west-central region of the state, is unusual here because it receives the warm-water discharge from a nearby power plant. Good populations of panfish exist in Nelson, with bluegills a favorite, and some believe that this lake has the potential for a new state record largemouth bass.

The state record walleye, which weighed in at 15 pounds 12 ounces, was taken on Wood Lake in 1959. Though Wood is a small natural lake, that older catch nevertheless underscores the fact that some good fishing, and indeed big fish, can be had in the smaller and lesser known waters of North Dakota. Furthermore, some small lakes have limited success rates as summer fisheries but become extremely popular as through-the-ice winter fisheries.

NORTHWEST TERRITORIES

The newly reconfigured Northwest Territories is the vast western Arctic region of Canada's far north. The eastern Arctic region, now known as Nunavut Territory *(see)*, was separated from the former configuration of the Northwest Territories (NWT) in 1999, leaving a huge region that encompasses 1.5 million square kilometers of land—equal in size to Alaska and comprising 15 percent of the entire country of Canada. It includes two of the largest lakes in the world, Great Bear and Great Slave, one of the most formidable rivers in North America, the Mackenzie, and is populated by more caribou than people.

Arguably the best lake trout fishing region in the world, but indisputably home to the biggest lakers on the planet, the NWT has some of the finest and least pressured fishing waters anywhere, with Arctic char, northern pike, and grayling being premier attractions besides lake trout, and with opportunities for less-noticed species like walleye, Dolly Varden, bull trout, whitefish, and inconnu.

Nearly all fishing in the NWT is done on wild rivers and lonely lakes. The big waters dominate the angling scene but are contrasted by diminutive spring creeks in the Mackenzie Mountains and secluded small Canadian Shield lakes. East of the Mackenzie drainage, waters flow to the polar sea via barren land rivers. The Anderson, Horton, and Hornaday Rivers drain the tundra north of Great Bear Lake. Further east, the famous Coppermine, Thelon, Dubawnt, and Kazan Rivers all rise along the treeline before flowing into Nunavut.

Often referred to as the western Arctic, the Northwest Territories extends north from its boundary on the 60th parallel with the Canadian provinces of British Columbia, Alberta, and Saskatchewan to the islands of the western Arctic archipelago. To the west, the mainland portion of the NWT bounds the Yukon Territory along the continental divide. The new eastern boundary with Nunavut skirts the barren lands east of the tree line.

Settlements of three land claims in the northern part of the territory have created a vast amount of private land. Generally, casual passage along waterways is provided in the claims, but fishing parties traveling on their own need to determine if they will be crossing land where they need permission. Optional stamps are now required to validate NWT fishing licenses for the Inuvialuit claim area and within the Great Bear Lake special management zone. Land claims in the southern part of the

NWT are not finalized, but may have an impact on sportfishing for the adventure traveler. The angler who visits a lodge will be largely unaware of the changes that have occurred, as nothing will have altered the vast, wild, open spaces of the north.

Most visitors to the NWT arrive by commercial air carrier, and many lodge visitors arrive via chartered flights that go direct to the lodge from the south, often from Winnipeg or Edmonton. Highway access from the south (through Alberta) exists on the Mackenzie Highway system, which reaches the communities south of Great Slave Lake, the capital city of Yellowknife on the north shore of Great Slave Lake, and the small Dene community of Wrigley midway down the Mackenzie River. Inuvik in the Mackenzie River Delta is serviced by the Dempster Highway through the Yukon Territory. The roads lead to jumping off points, but fishing along the highways in the NWT is not good by Arctic standards. The famous waters of the NWT are only accessible by air and long boat trips.

Typically, the Arctic angling season is compressed into the short period of open water from Late May to mid-September. The lakes are ice covered for the remainder of the time, although this varies from north to south, with some being open only briefly (or in cold years not at all) and others (usually smaller and more southerly ones) being open for up to 120 days in warm years. Even when open, most NWT waters are cool or cold, meaning that fish are seldom very deep in the lakes. While this means that fish are more accessible to anglers than they would be in warmer climes, it also means that midsummer days here can be inhospitable. The air temperature ranges from the 70s to 30s, occasionally on the same day, so visitors must be appropriately attired. Wading anglers are advised to wear neoprene chest waders, and since there is much use of float planes, it is necessary to pack judiciously.

Fishing has traditionally been limited to the open-water season; however, recently outfitters from Fort Resolution, Yellowknife, and Inuvik have begun to offer ice fishing packages. These winter expeditions are often coupled with snowmobile treks to isolated waters, like the Anderson River, which are hard to reach in the summer. In late March, when longer periods of daylight return to the north and the hard bite of winter is past, it is a wonderful time to travel and fish.

As anyone who has flown over this region can attest, the NWT is chock full of lakes of all sizes, as well as rivers, many of which drain from one lake to another and another. Not every body of water contains sportfish, although most do. Not every one has huge specimens, and some have lots of fish that are generally small. There is a lot of area in the NWT that is lightly if at all touched by anglers, since most sportfishing is clustered at lakes that can be serviced by outfitters and where there are established camps.

Although adventure travelers can have extraordinary experiences by undertaking wilderness canoe-camping excursions, due to the ruggedness of the land and wildness of many waterways, this activity is only advisable for experienced adventurers. While it is possible to enjoy bountiful fishing on these expeditions, the largest fish, especially lake trout, are usually found in the biggest bodies of water and seldom caught by those who run the rivers and have to cover a lot of territory from put-in to take-out locations.

Just as there is a great breadth of waters in the NWT, so, too, is there diversity in fishing methods and tackle. Trolling, though a staple for lake trout fishing in the lakes, is by no means the only method of fishing. Casting and jigging in lakes, and casting in rivers, are very productive, and the range of tackle choices for different methods runs the gamut from ultralight spinning gear for river grayling to heavy-action rods with large levelwind reels for trolling 2-ounce spoons. Light- to medium-weight fly fishing outfits, light to medium spinning outfits, and light to medium-heavy baitcasting tackle all have a place as well, depending on the location, the size of fish likely, and the means necessary for achieving success. This may seem wide open, but it underscores the fact that the abundant resources of the NWT truly provide a diversity of angling opportunities.

Species

The NWT is the "land of charr," the foremost native species of the Arctic. In this region, that includes lake trout (which, despite their name, are actually a species of charr), arctic charr, Dolly Varden, and bull trout. Populations of these distinctive native charr have spread across the territory since the last Ice Age. The wild charr of the NWT are an extraordinary treasure when contrasted with the diminished ranges of wild salmon and trout in North America.

That these extraordinary fish are generally little known has both protected them by keeping them out of sight and out of mind, and has left them exposed because they lack strong champions. The consequence is that, other than lake trout, which grow largest of these fish, northern charr have historically been undervalued to all but the native peoples. Most visiting anglers pursue lake trout in the NWT, and occasionally take a side trip to a famous arctic charr river in Nunavut. A journey to fish for all of the northern charr found in the NWT, would take an angler from the high country of the Mackenzie Mountains to lakes on the edge of the barrens and along the Arctic coast.

Lake trout. The long-lived and large-growing lake trout is king of NWT charr. Great Bear and Great Slave Lakes have produced a string of angling records for this species dating back to 1938, when pioneering outfitter Warren Plumber first fished Taltheilie Narrows on Great Slave Lake. He opened the first fishing lodge on that lake in 1950, and ever since, lake trout have been the staple of 60-odd lodges and guiding services in the NWT.

The New York City Common Council passed a law on May 28, 1734, to regulate the method of taking brook trout in Fresh Pond to "angling, with angle-rod, hook and line only." No nets allowed.

N

A big laker is netted from the deep water of Christie Bay at Great Slave Lake.

Great Bear and Great Slave are likely the two most prominent waters for lake trout fishing, although these monstrous lakes are only fished by a few thousand people in total annually. But they have produced a disproportionate number of North America's giant lakers, including numerous all-tackle and line-class world records. Leviathans from 60 to 72 pounds have been registered, some of these in the 1990s, and bigger fish have been hooked, especially in Great Bear.

Big waters notwithstanding, spectacular lake trout fishing is found in many smaller lakes, like Coville, Providence, and Mackay, and they have also been known to yield some monster lakers; a 54-pound lake trout, for instance, was caught at Point Lake on the Coppermine River.

As a general rule, small lakes produce smaller fish, and most bodies of water that contain lake trout can offer ample numbers of fish daily. Lake trout are also caught in flowing water here, and scores of large and small rivers have terrific light-tackle angling opportunities for these fish.

One great river angling adventure for lake trout is during the so-called "river run" at Lac la Martre, which offers great action on light spinning and fly tackle. This occurs in late August when the fish start their spawning run. Five- to 12-pounders are common and bigger ones are regularly taken. An unusual situation occurs near the coast in the Eskimo Lakes, which is part of a native settlement area in the northwestern part of the territory. Lake

trout there haunt the area where the lakes join Liverpool Bay on the Beaufort Sea, and this is likely as close as lake trout in North America come to having a "sea run."

Lake trout records, as well as the majority of large specimens (over 20 pounds) are usually taken by trolling. Flatline trolling is the norm, primarily in shallow water. As the value of the native stocks of lake trout has become better understood, outfitters have discouraged the use of downriggers and weighted lines, which were never very prominent in a lot of places here, as a means of getting very deep, since there is so much action to be had from shallower stocks of fish.

Many outfitters now encourage their clients to replace treble hooks with single barbless ones to facilitate the easy release and minimal handling of the fish. Single, barbless hooks, though not mandated, are much more prevalent, and may be a policy at better lodges and camps. Likewise, catch-and-release has become much more prevalent; the excessive removal of many trophy lake trout from NWT waters in past decades was felt for many years with reduced numbers of big fish. The longevity of these fish and their slow growth have mandated that a new conservation ethic be practiced, and this has been evolving throughout the NWT among anglers.

Ice out on the lakes in the NWT generally occurs between mid-May and early July depending on the water and location. This late breakup and brief summer help maintain very cold water temperatures throughout the open-water season. Cool waters encourage lake trout to stay shallower for most of the fishing season. This allows anglers to use lighter tackle for much of the season.

Immediately after the ice goes out, it's common to catch lake trout at creek and river mouths on the lakes, and some of the fastest fishing can be had then. If there are baitfish available at the sites, large lakers may be present. The fish are more scattered when the ice is fully gone. Late season fishing can produce some heavyweights and is an overlooked time, partly because of the possibility of poor weather (wind, cold, and occasionally snow). Lake trout spawn in late "summer" here, primarily on shallow reefs.

Arctic charr/Dolly Varden/bull trout. The NWT lies at the western boundary of the eastern subspecies of arctic charr that are so famous in the Nunavut Territory. These venerable fish are only found on the Horton and Hornaday Rivers in the northeast corner of the mainland, and on Banks Island and western Victoria Island (*see: Nunavut Territory*) in the archipelago. West of the Tuktoyatuk Peninsula in northwesternmost NWT, there is a change in subspecies. The landlocked arctic charr found in lakes along the north slope of the Yukon and Alaska is related to Siberian strains.

There is a small population of landlocked eastern arctic charr in the Keith Arm of Great Bear Lake, and anglers occasionally pick up one of these when fishing for lake trout near the Great Bear River. According to lodge owners, they are not found anywhere else on the lake.

The charr in rivers west of the Mackenzie River is the northern subspecies of Dolly Varden. Their range extends west from the Mackenzie River in the NWT to the Alaskan Peninsula in southwestern Alaska. (Lakes west of the Mackenzie in the Yukon Territory have the landlocked form of arctic charr.) Anglers can differentiate the northern Dolly Varden from the arctic charr based on its red spots, which are generally smaller than the eyes of the fish and have a blue halo around them. The spots on anadromous eastern arctic charr are splotchier, typically larger than the eye of the fish, and lack the bluish halo. However, to confuse things somewhat, landlocked lake-dwelling arctic charr tend to have small, pupil-size red or white spots. There are anomalies and variations as well.

Anglers familiar with arctic charr will notice that the Dolly Varden has a more compressed, or flatter, profile and a less rounded tail fin. The tail in Dolly Varden is large and is not forked, as it is in char. These differences reflect the Dolly Varden's adaptation to flowing water, and the arctic charr's preference for flat water. Arctic charr generally spawn and overwinter in lakes. Dolly Varden spawn in moving water, and overwinter in deep runs and river spring holes.

Anadromous northern Dolly Varden run into four rivers along the west side of the Mackenzie River Delta and the north slope of the Yukon Territory. These are the Rat, Big Fish, Babbage, and Firth Rivers, and they also have nonmigratory populations of smaller grilselike male fish. The highly aggressive nonmigratory males sneak in behind the redds of bigger, mating sea-run fish and may fertilize up to half of the eggs. The Big Fish and Babbage Rivers have landlocked populations above their barrier falls.

The headwater lakes and rivers of the Mackenzie Mountains are home to Dolly Varden and their cousin the bull trout, which are difficult for most people to tell apart. Locals lump them together as "river trout." They are vigorous feeders and enjoyed by both lure and fly casters. The North Nahanni, Redstone, Keele, Carcajou, Godlin, and Mountain Rivers all have fine populations.

Dall sheep hunters taking a rest from the saddle have found some fine fish under the overhanging banks of the Godlin River. Further south, a healthy run of Dolly Varden hit the Drum Lake outlet around Labor Day. The Dolly are on the go at the same time that lake trout move into the Cabin Creek tributary of Drum Lake. Between the two charr runs and frisky Arctic grayling, Drum Lake is worth the trip.

Landlocked arctic charr, Dolly Varden, and bull trout feed readily and can be voracious. While small charr concentrate on insects, bigger specimens feed on fish and opportunistically on mice, baby ducks, and even small muskrats. The number of large carnivorous charr in a lake is very small compared to the total population. In small Arctic lakes, it is easy for anglers to remove the few really big cannibals from the food chain. Maintaining large fish in the population of lakes is one of the reasons many guides and outfitters now advocate catch-and-release.

Anadromous arctic charr and Dolly Varden go to sea for 2 or 3 months a year to feed on a diet of invertebrates, capelin, cisco, herring, and sculpin. After they return to freshwater to spawn, they hang out under the ice for the next 10 months. They will continue to feed throughout the winter but the edge is off their appetite.

The feeding habits of arctic charr, Dolly Varden and bull trout make them ideal for spinning tackle users. Anglers use light- to medium-weight spinning rods with 6- to 10-pound lines. A variety of small to medium spoons, especially with orange and pink inserts and in the hallowed five of diamonds pattern, are a must. Silver-bladed spinners are also effective. Generally, fly anglers use sinking lines and streamers. Successful fly patterns include the red-and-yellow Seaducer, Mickey Finn, and large sculpin imitations.

Northern pike. Though northern pike aren't the first fish that nonresident anglers associate with the Northwest Territories, their popularity has been steadily increasing. These shallow and near-surface fish are widely distributed throughout the drainage

N

systems of the mainland from the southern boundary of the NWT to saltwater in the Mackenzie River Delta, with big lakes usually producing the better specimens.

Northern pike here generally average from 18 to 30 inches in length. The slow growth of a northern pike in Arctic drainages with little fishing pressure makes it possible to frequently break 30 inches. A 10-pound, 32-inch Great Bear Lake northern pike is a fifteen-year-old fish. Forty-inch fish from near Trout Rock in the north arm of Great Slave Lake average around 20 pounds.

It is reasonable to expect that in a week of fishing at a hot pike spot, an angler will take some fish that verge on 20 pounds. One reliable pike location is Beaver Lake on the upper Mackenzie River; it produces pike up to 27 pounds on a fairly regular basis, and a few every season break 30 pounds.

The unexpected happens frequently enough that anglers take considerably larger northern pike. Rare fish are found that exceed 50 inches. The largest known pike from Great Slave Lake is a reputed 60³/₄-inch fish taken through the ice near Trout Rock; the fish was not weighed or officially recorded.

Action for northern pike commences with ice out in the spring. Pike are abundant in the shallows and often pounce on lures or flies. On the big waters, large pike stay in shallow water most of the summer. When the water warms in the shallower lakes, pike go deep.

Grayling. The Arctic grayling is the signature species of the NWT. A resident of clean and cold water, this colorful fish is found across the region. The average mature grayling is a 1¹/₂- to 2-pound fish. Three-pounders are 12 years old and have reached the average life expectancy for this species in far northern waters. Fish over 3 pounds are trophies.

Great Slave and Great Bear Lakes and their tributaries have some of the best Arctic grayling fishing in the world. Great Bear's tributaries have produced most of the line class and world records, including

some over 5 pounds, and have superb grayling fishing. The tributaries to Great Bear River, which flows to the Mackenzie, are also excellent. Northeast of the lake, Colville Lake provides access to grayling for anglers who really want to get away.

The outlet of Great Slave in the Mackenzie River is an especially productive grayling habitat. The fishery there took a hit in 1989 when high water temperatures nurtured a deadly gill infection. Since that time, a combination of undisturbed habitat and restrictive angling regulations have helped grayling bounce back.

In the same region, the well-known Brabant and Kakisa River runs are recovering. Some years, the Kakisa is the only river on the east side of the mountains from the Arkansas River to the Mackenzie River that is clear and full of fish in late May and early June.

On the East Arm of Great Slave Lake, the mouth of the Lockhart River, Taltheilie Narrows, and the Stark River are famous for grayling. Both the lower Lockhart and Stark Rivers have rapids that stay open throughout the winter. Open rapids that force oxygenated water under the ice are characteristic of the best grayling haunts.

Arctic grayling are generally caught on flies or light spinners, the latter in gold or silver in sizes from 0 to 2. On the surface, they rise for a range of caddisflies, mayflies, stoneflies, and terrestrials, including grasshoppers. A good selection of dry fly patterns in sizes 12 to 18 is advisable, although in many places almost any small dark offering will do. Grayling often respond better to a fly in the meniscus than one floating on the surface, so soft-hackle flies can be effective. When grayling are not rising, they are normally on the bottom nymphing. A broad selection of nymphs in sizes 2 to 16 is then necessary.

Walleye. Walleye are among the three most popularly sought fish in the NWT. Consistent walleye fishing is found in parts of the Talston River system, Great Slave Lake, the Hay River, the upper Mackenzie River, and small lakes northeast of Yellowknife. The spring fishing at Trout Lake in the southwest corner of the NWT is locally famous.

The most productive time to fish for walleye in the NWT has been in the late May and early June spawning period when the fish are congregated. In the summer, with coldwater temperatures, walleyes can often be found shallower than in more southerly climates. For example, walleye are taken in 4 or 5 feet of water in the Hay River in early July, and in 8 to 10 feet of water in midsummer on the upper Mackenzie River. As a result, they offer an opportunity not only to successfully use plugs and jigs, but also flies. Fly anglers work a full sinking line, a short tippet, and a weighted yellow or tan minnow imitation along the bottom. A soft plastic worm on a sinking fly line is also deadly.

On the upper Mackenzie River, walleye average 2 to 4 pounds, with a few each year reaching about

Major flows, like the Stark River here, course throughout the Northwest Territories.

6 or 7 pounds. Nine to 10 pounds is the top end of the walleye weight scale in the NWT.

Whitefish. Lake whitefish are available in most lakes and many rivers in the NWT. Broad whitefish are found along the western Arctic Coast and up the Mackenzie River to the Camsell Bend below Fort Simpson. Few lodges advertise them and relatively few visiting anglers deliberately pursue whitefish, but these are a commendable fish, and an increasing number of Arctic fly anglers claim them as their favorite. Whitefish are one of the best table fish in the north. Fried whitefish makes a great shore lunch, and smoked whitefish (some lodges have smokehouses) is a real treat.

Like grayling, whitefish are almost never caught on the hardware and tackle used for pike and trout, and angling for them is more specialized, requiring light or ultralight spinning and fly gear. They can be taken on light jigs, and to a lesser degree small spinners, but are best caught on flies, including soft-hackle and emerger patterns, and they are a delightful fish to catch.

Whitefish are sometimes seen dimpling the surface in the evening, and can be available to anglers then. Rising whitefish on a midsummer's eve are not actually rising to flies on the surface; they are nymphing for caddis and mayflies swimming up to hatch. The slight downturn of the whitefish's small mouth does not allow it to easily snip dry flies from the surface. If you watch their rises carefully, you'll see that it is the back of the fish which breaks the surface as it positions itself to come down on the rising insect. Ideally, an emerger should be fished several inches under the surface for whitefish. Small spinners fished in the top of the water column will often take them, too. When whitefish aren't feeding on the surface, they're often munching on scuds further down; count your offering down to locate the depth where they are feeding.

Other species. The waters of the Mackenzie River drainage and the Anderson River are home to the elusive inconnu, a species that few people are acquainted with. Known as sheefish in Alaska and the Yukon, they are commonly called "conni" in the NWT. Averaging 18 to 30 inches long, this member of the whitefish clan is a strong fighter that deserves more attention.

Good early spring inconnu fishing is found near the community of Fort Resolution, in the Slave River Delta. Many are also caught to the west in the Hay River in May or early June. Anglers fish shallow bays with bright spoons as the ice goes out. Later in the summer and in early fall, strong runs are found in the Big Buffalo and Talston Rivers, below the Slave River Rapids at Fort Smith, and in the small creeks of the Mackenzie River Delta. A local guide is needed to successfully fish for inconnu. They average from 9 to 20 pounds, but some specimens weighing up to 70 pounds have been reported by commercial fishermen.

The ugliest, but perhaps best-tasting, fish in the NWT is the burbot. A freshwater cod, and also known as ling cod and eelpout, it is found in most of the lakes and larger rivers of the Northwest Territories. They are commonly caught to 24 inches in length, and some up to 30 inches and 8 or 9 pounds have been reported.

Burbot, which live in deep water and prey on smaller fish, are rarely caught by anglers fishing for the more prominent species. Local guides from Aklavik take people out to jig for burbot in the Mackenzie Delta byways, and some still use traditional jigs made of sheep, muskox, or caribou antler. It's common for an angler jigging for burbot near Aklavik to pick up an inconnu. The Dene and Inuit prize the burbot's liver, incidentally, which is a good source of vitamin B. The fillets of a burbot make delicious fish and chips.

On the outer northwest edge of the Northwest Territories, the Mackenzie River has the only run of dog or chum salmon east of the continental divide. Chum salmon are the least predictable of the NWT's gamefish, but are taken annually in gill nets by Dene harvesters on the Mackenzie River, Liard River, and below the Slave River Rapids. On rare occasions, one is picked up in Great Bear Lake near the Great Bear River, where they are referred to as "the strangers."

Fresh chum salmon enter the Mackenzie River from the Beaufort Sea in July. There are unconfirmed reports that fish have been taken by anglers in some of the small rivers that flow into the Mackenzie Delta. Local guides in Aklavik or Inuvik might know where to find this elusive fish, and it is conceivable that salmon might be encountered on a trip for sea-run Dolly Varden.

Locations

Fishing destinations in the NWT can be broken down into six angling regions: south of Great Slave Lake, the western barren lands, Great Slave Lake and the upper Mackenzie River, Great Bear Lake, the Mackenzie Mountains, and the Mackenzie River Delta.

There are numerous fly-in lodges on Canadian Shield lakes east of Fort Smith. These operations specialize in northern pike, lake trout, walleye, and whitefish, with plentiful and large lake trout and pike the foremost attractions. Some of the better sites are along or close to the Saskatchewan *(see)* border, and include Selwyn, Snowbird, Scott, Kasba, and Wignes Lakes.

The western barren lands contain the headwaters of the Kazan, Dubawnt, Thelon, Lockhart, and Coppermine Rivers. Notable lakes include Mackay Lake on the Lockhart River, and Providence and Point Lakes on the Coppermine River. Treeline lodges here offer lake trout, northern pike, whitefish, and trophy grayling.

Great Slave Lake. The 11th largest lake in the world, Great Slave is 298 miles long and in some places over 2,000 feet deep. Containing over 11,000 square miles of water, it can hardly be missed on almost any map, and its fishing has to be viewed by four areas: the East Arm, the North Arm, the Slave River region, and the Mackenzie River outlet.

This lake has long been renowned for its lake trout. The laker fishing was especially prime in the mid-1960s, when 20- to 25-pounders were caught (and kept, unfortunately) regularly. Then it slumped in terms of producing large fish, and is still rebounding, helped by conservation practices. Now, rare is the large fish that gets kept at the fishing lodges here.

The prospect of catching giant lake trout, however, remains the lake's prime lure. A 74-pounder is reputed to have been netted at Great Slave some years ago, and anglers have caught them to $58^1/_2$ pounds. This mammoth body of water does contain some monsters. It also contains plenty of trout that have never seen a lure, and you don't have to be a veteran angler to catch fish. Trolling near shore around points, reefs, and islands has long been the predominant tactic for lakers here. The water is always cold, and most trout are caught only 10 to 20 feet deep.

The East Arm is blessed with islands and peninsulas, which make it geologically distinct from the wide-open remainder of the lake. It has been made famous by Talteilei Narrows and the Stark and Lockhart Rivers, which are known for big lake trout, grayling, pike, and whitefish. Some lodges feature side trips to inland lakes for walleye.

Talteilei Narrows acts as a river or channel between McLeod and Christie Bays. Wind-driven currents on the big bays push the water back and forth through the narrows creating wonderful eddies and backwaters, and the Talteilei area continues to produce spectacular trophies. If the East Arm of Great Slave Lake is gold medal water, Talteilei is in a class by itself.

Remarkably good angling takes place at the shallow, cold, and swift Stark River, using light spinning or fly gear for grayling up to 3 pounds, small pike, and the occasional whitefish. At the best of times it is a virtual bonanza, and there is good reason to understand why some have called the Stark the greatest grayling river in the world. The possibility of catching 3- to 4-pound grayling is very good.

The North Arm is a maze of granite reefs that shelter some of the best northern pike fishing in the NWT. Not only do the low islands and submerged structures provide great habitat, but they protect the spectacular pike waters around Trout Rock from casual boaters. Visitors to the North Arm are only a few air minutes from jet service to southern Canada at the Yellowknife airport.

Fort Resolution is the jump-off point for fishing the Slave River Delta and the lower Taltson River. Local outfitters take clients out for northern pike,

inconnu, walleye, and whitefish. Road access allows Mackenzie Highway travelers to drive in and meet their guides.

Perhaps the best-kept angling secret in the NWT is the outlet of Great Slave Lake into the Mackenzie River. The waters around Brabant and Lobstick Islands have superb grayling, pike, whitefish, and walleye angling. The Mackenzie Highway spur to the community of Hay River on the south shore of Great Slave Lake is a short bush flight from the lodge at Brabant Island.

Great Bear Lake.   There is no locale that is known more widely for lake trout than this one, and considering its stature as the eighth largest freshwater lake in the world, Great Bear Lake perhaps might be more appropriately called the Great Bear Sea, or, better yet, Great Trout Sea.

Great Bear is actually the fourth largest lake in North America, ranking behind Lakes Superior, Huron, and Michigan in size. When you consider that it has an infinitesimally small percentage of the boat traffic and fishing pressure of those other large North American lakes, and that it is so remote as to straddle the Arctic Circle, you can comprehend the allure it has as a distant fishing locale, especially for lake trout aficionados.

Great Bear has been known as the world's best fishery for record-size lake trout and Arctic grayling since it was first sportfished in the early 1960s. For over 20 years it held the all-tackle laker record with a 65-pounder, which it bested with a $66^1/_2$-pounder in 1991 and then a 72-pound 4-ounce fish in August of 1995. The current IGFA all-tackle world record for Arctic grayling, 5 pounds 15 ounces, was also established here, and more than a score of line-class world records have been certified from Great Bear or its tributaries.

Each year, fewer than 600 anglers have the opportunity to experience the waters of Great Bear. The lake remains frozen until the early part of July, and fall winds and freezing temperatures put an end to angling at the beginning of September. The closest road to Great Bear is over 100 miles to the south, so the only way in is by plane.

A prominent aspect of Great Bear's legendary fishing is the relative shallowness of its lake trout fishing throughout five major arms. With 12,000 square miles of surface area, depths of up to 1,400 feet, and only three months of ice out, the waters of Great Bear never warm to the same extent as smaller lakes in the area. The middle of the lake will not go above 35°F all summer. Due to the frigid waters, lake trout move to shallow bays and reefs to find the baitfish in warmer waters. Lake trout are caught all summer in depths of 4 to 35 feet. They are never caught in the 60- to 100-foot range synonymous with lake trout fishing in smaller bodies of water.

Lake trout at Great Bear average 6 to 15 pounds. Every year more than a thousand in the 20-pound range will be caught, with many reaching 30 to 50

N

pounds, and some in the 50- to 70-pound range. Experts believe that the lake trout in Great Bear grow at a rate of just $1/4$- to $1/2$- a pound per year. That dates some trout between 100 and 150 years old. Current lodge policies ensure the survival of these fish. No lake trout over 28 inches (10 pounds) is allowed to be harvested.

The tried-and-true method of lake trout fishing here, trolling with the biggest spoons and plugs, is the technique that works day after day, week after week, and season after season.

Great Bear anglers also get in some mighty fine arctic charr fishing on the Tree and Coppermine Rivers, via fly-outs from main lodges. These rivers have been known to produce really big charr, from 15 to 22 pounds, plus the all-tackle world record, a 32-pound 9-ounce fish taken in 1981.

Mackenzie Mountains and Delta. The Mackenzie Mountains, with feisty Dolly Varden, bull trout, grayling, lake trout, and whitefish, is the most underrated and poorly known angling destination in the NWT. Difficult access makes the mountains a dream destination for adventurous anglers who have advanced wilderness canoeing and expedition skills.

A trip to the Mackenzie River Delta or the Eskimo Lakes offers lake trout, Dolly Varden, northern pike, grayling, whitefish, inconnu, and burbot. Whether you arrive by road or air, it's a good idea to utilize a local guide, and it may be necessary to obtain a separate sportfishing license (in addition to the NWT license) from the Inuvialuit and/or Gwich'in Settlement Regions as well. The lands within these regions are privately owned by natives, and a permit to cross private lands may also be required and obtained in local villages.

To the east of the Delta are the Horton and Hornaday Rivers, which have arctic charr but no sportfishing facilities or outpost camps. The small community of Paulatuk, located near the mouth of the Hornaday, is a possible source of local guides, but there's no organized angling service.

Arrangements for local charr guides can also be made in the community of Holman Island on Victoria Island to fish the Kuuk and/or Quunnguq Rivers on the western end of Victoria Island. The western portion of Victoria and other westerly islands in the Arctic Ocean are within the NWT, but most anglers access it via Nunavit through Cambridge Bay and an established charr and lake trout camp on Merkley Lake.

NORWAY

With magnificent waterfalls, tens of thousands of lakes and tarns (mountain lakes and ponds), deep fjords, spectacular mountains, large forests, rich wildlife, and a long beautiful coast, Norway is a dream destination of world-traveled anglers. To most visitors, sportfishing in Norway is synonymous with big powerful rivers and equally big and powerful Atlantic salmon. However, few visitors realize that this country also has a wealth of trout and sea fishing opportunities.

Situated in the heart of Scandinavia northwest of Denmark and west of Sweden, Norway runs from the 58th parallel in the south to the 71st parallel north of the Arctic Circle. It covers an area of 301,585 square kilometers, a third of which is more than 300 meters above sea level. Norway has a 2,542-kilometer border in the east with Sweden, Finland, and Russia, and its coastline is 21,347 kilometers long (including bays and fjords), which, in proportion to the country's area, is longer than that of any major country in the world. That coastline faces the North Sea in the south, the Norwegian Sea (Atlantic Ocean) in the west, and the Barents Sea in the north, all of which is dotted with over 85,000 islands. And the whole country only has a population of 4.5 million people!

Amongst all these bounties, Norway has over 700 registered salmon and sea trout rivers. It is believed that 16,000 years ago Norwegian waters were populated only with such salmonids as sea charr, salmon, and brown trout, but after the last Ice Age, such white-fleshed species as pike, perch, grayling, and carp slowly made their way here from the Baltic in the east, and spread into Norwegian water systems.

With so many natural resources, fishing and hunting in Norway have long provided—and still do for many families—not only recreation but a substantial supplement to the larder. Angling for salmon in particular has a long rich history that goes back to the beginnings of European gamefishing, and was dominated and cultivated by the English fly fishing gentry. Wealthy Englishmen at the turn of the twentieth century, in their constant pursuit for bigger and better sport, leased large stretches of all the best Norwegian rivers from local landowners and farmers. These fishermen built fine and extravagant fishing lodges, most of which still exist today, to accommodate their guests and staff. They remained close by the river the whole summer in order to pursue their Victorian dream of landing not only the biggest but also the greatest volume of salmon.

Trout Fishing

The most common and probably the most popular gamefish in Norway is the native brown trout, which is found here in thousands of small forest lakes, tarns, rivers, and streams. Many of the remote mountain lakes and especially the tarns are surrounded by floating mats of living boggy peat, which drift around according to the wind direction. For the first-time angler these are a little unnerving, as traveling over this is similar to walking on a giant grass-covered waterbed, which moves underfoot with every step. They are generally safe enough, although due caution should be taken. These floating mats can also have small holes or pockets of

N

water, which should not be forgotten when fishing, and should be approached carefully. In hot weather conditions, as exists in late summer, the trout use these large insulating mats to keep cool and shaded from the brightness of the midday sun, and these holes are used as feeding windows.

The average weight of a wild trout in Norway varies from place to place, but fish of 0.5 to 1 kilogram are common. Hip waders or rubber boots are adequate for most lake fishing but chest waders are a must in rivers. For trout fly fishing a 9-foot No. 5 or 6 rod with a floating line is a normal outfit, and will cover most conditions.

The main insect staples for trout are mayflies, midges, caddisflies, damselflies, and dragonflies. The only terrestrials of any importance are ants and craneflies. The most productive fly patterns are deer-hair caddis imitations, but muddler minnows and large nymphs also work well. Spinners and small spoons designed for trout fishing constantly produce good fish. Trolling with large spoons and wobblers (minnow plugs) on big lakes can produce very large brown trout up to and over 15 kilograms, but smaller fish are normal, with individuals between 5 and 10 kilograms possible. Lake fishing for trout is sometimes done with a set of five or six hookless attractor spoons or blades that are all attached to a leader ahead of a worm-baited hook. This is trolled deep and slow, normally from the back of a rowboat.

Southern Region

Southern Norway has quite large areas of wilderness that are dominated mostly by coniferous spruce and pine forests, with birch also present in smaller numbers. Fish populations and fishing in the south were devastated in the 1960s by acid rain from Great Britain and eastern Europe, but in recent decades the cultivation of waters through a restocking and liming policy has re-introduced indigenous fish into all but a few waters. Although brown trout is the most common species, pike, perch, and charr are very widespread. Brook trout can also be found in some areas instead of brown trout; due to their greater tolerance of acidic water, brown trout were formerly stocked in lakes that had a low pH.

Norway's largest lake, Mjøsa, which covers 368 square kilometers, is in the southeast, as is its longest river, the 598-kilometer-long Glåma (Glomma), which, with its tributaries, drains about one-eighth of the country's area. Both are rich in fishing possibilities. Mjøsa is 60 miles long and 10 miles wile at its greatest point. On the banks of Mjøsa lies the town of Gjøvik, home and museum of the Mustad fish hook company. The lake is famous for it's trolling for huge trout and pike, and has produced many double-digit specimens of both, some over 15 kilograms.

Glomma has a reputation as Norway's best and most diverse sportfishing river with over 25 fish species, and just about every type of river condition from almost still to fast rapids. Although coarse fishing is very new in Norway, most of it is done here, along with grayling fishing.

East of Glomma is the Femundsmarka National Park. Dominated by the effects of the Ice Age, this is a typical glaciated landscape, with boulder fields, spruce forests, and bare mountain. Also found here is an abundance of some of Norway's best trout lakes and streams, which make it a Mecca for fly and spin anglers alike. The rich natural pH level in the lakes here makes them high in insect life, which includes the largest mayflies. The trout here are also very special, dressed in a butter-yellow color and with large thumb-size spots of red and black along the sides. These are some of the best and most beautiful brown trout that exist.

Norway has 18 national parks, the southernmost and largest being Hadangarvidda, which encompasses 3,422 square kilometers and lies to the west of the capital, Oslo, and is northern Europe's largest high mountain plateau. Famous for large herds of wild reindeer, mountains, and glaciers, Hadangervidda National Park provides wild brown trout sport in spectacular surroundings.

There are also landlocked charr in many lakes in southern Norway, but these are not really of interest to the visiting angler, as they spend the warmer months of the year in the deepest colder water, only coming shallower and being caught when the water is covered with a thick layer of winter ice.

Winter ice fishing is very popular in southern Norway, not only for charr, but also for trout, pike, perch, and sea fish such as cod. The tackle for this sport consists of a small rod that is 30 to 40 centimeters long, special "anti freeze" monofilament line, and small weighted and baited hooks and spoons that are jigged through a hole in the ice.

Trout, pike, and perch fishing locations are readily accessible in southern Norway. There are normally local fishing clubs and organizations that sell licenses, but many private farms and landowners also supplement their income by selling day tickets on private lakes, but this can be a little hit-and-miss regarding quality. Pike and perch can also give excellent sport, after spawning is over in the spring. Fishing with plugs, spoons, wobblers, and even flies can be very effective.

Salmon and sea trout.   Common belief has it that all of Norway's finest salmon rivers are situated in the north. However, as with the rest of the country, the southern region has many salmon and sea trout rivers. Fishing on most is reasonably priced and well organized. Rivers such as Mandalselva, Otra, and Drammenselva, have had good runs in the late 1990s. Perhaps the foremost attraction in this region is the Numedalslågen River, which, with stable yearly catches of about 20 metric tons, is rated as one of Norway's top five most productive salmon rivers every year.

With its source in Haddangervidda National Park, the Numedalslågen runs 325 kilometers downstream to Larvik, where it enters the sea into the Oslofjord. Like many other large rivers in Norway, this is regulated for power production but still has a fairly stable water flow. The upper stretches that have no salmon can also provide good fishing for brown trout, pike, and ide throughout the summer.

There are two "best" times for salmon fishing here. The first is in mid-June. There are fewer fish in this first run but they are big, with an average weight of around 7.5 kilograms. The second major run of fish occurs about late August or early September. These are smaller (3 kilogram average) but are normally in great numbers.

The archipelago coastline of the southern region is excellent for sea trout fishing with both fly and spinning tackle from shore. During winter and spring, sea trout often swim within a few meters of land, occurring in or near sandy beaches with weed growth, boulders, and small rocky bays that have patches of kelp. Areas with lots of small peninsulas and bays are also ideal fishing sites.

The best time for sea trout is normally at high tide. But in southern Norway there is no real "high tide" because tidal fluctuations only differ from 50 centimeters to 1 meter most of the year. The sea trout come in with higher water to hunt in the shallows for ragworms, prawns, baitfish, and sand eels, all of which come out of their hiding places to feed on what the tide brings in. The optimum opportunity is presented when high water occurs in the evening just after dark, or in the morning just before daylight. If you're lucky enough to be in the right place with a warm southerly wind (which experienced Norwegian sea trout anglers call "happy hour") the sport can be tremendous. Saltwater sea trout here normally weigh up to 1 kilogram, but fish of 10 kilograms have been taken on a single-handed fly rod or lightweight spinning tackle.

With it's lengthy coastline and greatly varying sea depths, southern Norway is an el dorado for the sea fishing angler. The small village of Langesund in Telemark has gained an international reputation with deep sea anglers, breaking many European and world records for such species as ling, tusk, and mackerel. Although you can enjoy traditional sea fishing here, the bay of Langesund offers deep sea fishing for some species weighing over 150 kilograms, such as halibut and Greenland shark. Fishing at a depth of 300 to 400 meters is not uncommon here. This is an extremely physically tough and demanding sport and only for the experienced angler.

Sea fishing in general is very well organized and reasonably priced, with many charter boats of varying size, accommodation, and tackle available for hire in most coastal towns throughout Norway. The best seasons vary from species to species, but fishing in general is available year-round. A medium-weight spinning rod is suitable when fishing from

A Norwegian salmon angler lays out a long cast.

land, but deep bottom fishing requires specialized tackle, such as a minimum 50-pound-class boat rod with roller eyes fitted with a heavy conventional reel that has enormous line capacity, and a line of at least 50-pound strength. Leader material should be 2-millimeter monofilament, and Swedish pilks (heavy jigging spoons) or lead weights of 1 kilogram are the norm.

Middle and Northern Norway

The middle and northern regions of Norway are well known for their big salmon rivers, and the latter has what is arguably the best salmon rivers in the world.

Along the west coast are such famous rivers as Gaula, Orkla, Stordalselva, and Namsen, the latter of which alone produced 21.1 metric tons of salmon and sea trout as recently as 1997.

Although there has been a clear downfall in recorded catches of salmon in Norwegian rivers over the last few years, in 1997 the Tana and Altaelva together still produced a fantastic 62.3 metric tons of salmon and sea trout, and both yielded fish over 20 kilograms, but these are special rivers and fishing on them is sometimes difficult to arrange. Fishing on Altaelva in the month of June is for local residents only, and in July and August licenses are obtained by a lottery method. All applicants who apply in January have their names placed in a box and the first to be drawn get to fish. There are some special beats available but these command a very high price. But there are other rivers. The Neiden, Repparfjordelva, Vefsen, and Lakselv all have delivered steady numbers of fish in the late 1990s.

These are all big rivers with named pools and beats, but it's still advisable to book a gillie *(kleppe)*, as this will definitely increase the chance of success. Powerful rivers and fish mean big, powerful, two-handed rods and deep wading; a recent trend with Norwegians is to fish with a single-handed trout rod, although many look upon this as madness. The

N

most popular methods for salmon fishing here are with fly, worm, and spoon.

All of these rivers have world-famous fly patterns named after them, but most successful fly anglers use their own simple-dressed hairwing patterns, normally tied on a double hook.

Sea fishing on the coast in this region also has a reputation for giant cod, and the angling record stands at over 40 kilograms. Excellent sea fishing in spectacular scenery can be had at the Lofoten archipelago. This is a group of 80 islands off the coast of Nordland that are dominated by high snow-clad mountains that rise steeply out of the sea. The best season here for big fish is from January to April.

Arctic Region

For most would-be visitors, Arctic Norway conjures up visions of constant snow and ice, though nothing could be further from the truth. Northern Norway is also the "land of the midnight sun," and can often produce Mediterranean-like summers. The explanation for this is simple: when the sun doesn't go down, it's bound to get warm. Thus, it's possible to fish around the clock.

Finnmark is Norway's largest, least populated, northernmost county, and borders Finland and Russia. Øvre Anarjåkka National Park is a remote and wild part of Finnmarksvidda and adjoins Lemmenjoki National Park in Finland. Together they form a large area of undisturbed wilderness that is characterized by an ancient rolling landscape with birch forests, extensive bogs, and numerous lakes. This region contains some of the largest glaciers in Europe. Here, there is first-rate fishing for charr, grayling, and trout. All are common in sizes up to 2 kilograms. East of Finnmarksvidda, the waters are heavily populated with perch and pike, and guides are necessary to help one find the trout and charr spots. There are several tour operators and fishing camps here that have helicopter fly-in service for those who don't have the time or interest to walk and find their own way around. This is highly recommended for the first-time visitor.

This region is also a popular destination during the late winter months, when there is a combination of sun, snow, and ice fishing for big charr and pike.

Regulations and Seasons

Rod-and-reel fishing in the sea from land or a boat can be done year-round without charge, but some special rules apply to salmon, sea trout, and sea charr.

To fish in freshwater, anglers need to purchase a state (national) license, which is available from any post office, has weekly and yearly terms, and can be for an individual or family. Anglers under the age of 16 don't need a state license except for water systems where there are salmon, sea trout, and sea charr. Licenses for private waters are issued by their owners or by clubs.

Salmon fishing in general is from May 15 through September 30. Trout fishing, other inland fishing, and sea fishing can be done year-round. Local regulations vary from county to county. There is no "catch limit" in Norway, except on rivers with salmon, sea trout, and sea charr, or where stated in the local regulations. Live bait fishing is not allowed. The use of float tubes is forbidden in most fishing club waters. Rules and regulations will also vary with different fishing clubs, so there may be a minimum size limit, boat restrictions, maximum hook size, etc., that is imposed by them; fishing should not commence until one has purchased the appropriate area license, and checked the local fishing seasons and regulations.

Norway also has a "right of access law." Access to woods, fields, mountains, rivers, lakes, etc., regardless of who owns them, is an ancient right in Norway. When using a boat or canoe, you can go where you like in the sea, rivers, and lakes. With the exception of some canals and locks, this is totally free of charge. But you are not allowed to fish unless you have gained the owner's permission or purchased the appropriate local license.

NOVA SCOTIA

While salmon and trout are both synonymous with angling in Nova Scotia, the province should be known for its diversity in both species and angling opportunities.

The mainland portion of this Maritime province is connected to New Brunswick via an isthmus; to the north, separated by the Strait of Canso, is the island of Cape Breton. Between these two, Nova Scotia has a total area of 55,491 square kilometers (21,425 square miles) and is shaped somewhat like an old boot sticking out into the Atlantic Ocean. This boot runs nearly north and south, with the southern tip located below the 49th parallel, meaning that some parts of the United States are north of some parts of Nova Scotia.

If unraveled, the shoreline would stretch 7,500 kilometers (4,625 miles) across North America. Since the province is bordered on the east by the Atlantic Ocean and on the west by the Bay of Fundy and the Gulf of the St. Lawrence, it offers abundant opportunities for saltwater sportfishing, which is lightly utilized, although saltwater species were of great historical importance to colonists, and the province harbors a large commercial fishing fleet.

Inland, Nova Scotia has 6,674 lakes that are over a hectare (2.4 acres) in size, and over 1,200 watersheds fed by 5,000 rivers and streams, offering a profusion of diverse freshwater angling opportunities.

No place in Nova Scotia is any farther than 60 kilometers (37 miles) from saltwater, so the rivers are fed by moderate watersheds and tend to be small and intimate. With a population of approximately one million people, finding open water for fishing is rarely a problem.

Freshwater

With the exception of American shad, Nova Scotia does not offer a world-class fishery for any single species, but it is an exceptional area for species diversity, and it has a plethora of angling opportunities. Different species, in distinctive types of terrain, makes for interesting fishing in Nova Scotia. The pastoral rivers of the Annapolis Valley, the rolling hills of Cape Breton, the tumbling streams along the South Shore, and the wilderness lakes, are all only a few hours apart, making Nova Scotia a unique destination for the versatile angler.

Most angling regulations in the province are similar to those elsewhere; however, when angling for Atlantic salmon, only fly fishing is permitted, and that with only single or double hooks. Additionally, some streams are posted for fly fishing only, regardless of the species present or sought by the angler. Although it is not mandated, catch-and-release for smallmouth bass is the rule of thumb for anglers. This is particularly true during the spawning season in May and early June.

Freshwater management can be divided into six geographic areas, and the species fall in different climatic, terrain, and water-quality regions. Although Nova Scotia is known for Atlantic salmon and trout, few people have taken advantage of the abundance of such warmwater species as smallmouth bass, chain pickerel, white perch, and yellow perch. It is also home to lightly fished but magnificent spring runs of American shad in numerous rivers. Introduced brown and rainbow trout have also found an appropriate niche in many parts of the province.

Cape Breton

The four counties in Cape Breton offer some of the most magnificent and unique salmon rivers in Nova Scotia, as well as some fine trout fishing.

The Margaree River in Inverness County is a beautiful river that has the distinct characteristic of a spring, summer, and fall run of salmon. The fall run is the most popular, not only because water levels are at their highest, but because of the high percentage of large multi-sea winter fish. The Middle River has a good fall run of salmon, while the Cheticamp River offers a spring-summer run. As an added bonus, all these rivers are surrounded by spectacular scenery.

The Baddeck River in Victoria County is a fall river with a large run of salmon, and the North River features an excellent run of spring-summer Atlantics.

In Richmond County, the Grand River is fished mainly along the lower stretches during the spring-summer run of salmon. There are also minor tributaries that, if timed right, will offer smaller runs of Atlantic salmon.

An Atlantic salmon angler casts on the Margaree River.

Speckled trout (brook trout) inhabit hundreds of small streams throughout Cape Breton. Their size is modest, but their abundance can make up for this in action. The Cape Breton National Park has a number of streams in a wilderness setting that provide excellent trout fishing. The Baddeck, Middle, Margaree, and River Inhabitants all offer a sea run of speckled trout in June. If timed right, the fishing can be excellent.

Lake Ainslie in Inverness County is one of the largest lakes in the province and has a unique speckled trout population, which moves into Trout River in late summer. It is restricted to fly fishing only, and at times the bottom is literally covered by large schools of trout.

Rainbow trout have become established in Bras' d'Or Lake, with the western side of the lake a preferred fishing area. But, the best angling is when these trout move up the Baddeck, Skye, and Middle Rivers to spawn.

White perch are found in a large number of lakes in Nova Scotia. Generally, they are not a target species but are simply an incidental catch when angling for other fish. The spring spawning run, which is on the south side of Lake Ainslie, is very impressive.

Northern Mainland

The northern end of the mainland adjoins Cape Breton and covers the counties of Antigonish, Guysborough, and Pictou.

River John in Pictou County features a favorable run of sea-run brown trout each spring. There are also smaller rivers here with respectable runs, but much depends on water levels.

The St. Mary's River has a spring-summer run of Atlantic salmon. Excellent dry-fly fishing can be found in the many pools on this river, but changes in water levels and water temperature make fishing difficult as summer advances.

The best area for speckled trout is on the eastern shore of Guysborough County; the area around the

N

Liscomb Game Sanctuary is probably the most productive, and the most popular.

The rivers in Guysborough also have sea-run trout in late spring and early summer. Some of the most popular rivers are the Musquodoboit, Sheet Harbour, and Ecum Secum. The headwaters of these rivers are remote and can produce a good wilderness fishing experience. Sea-run brown trout are also found in the estuary of the Salmon River and are angled mainly in the tidal pools.

Southcentral Region

This is a large area encompassing the county of Lunenburg and the Regional Municipality of Halifax (RMH). There are a number of Atlantic salmon rivers in this zone and they all have spring-summer runs. The main rivers are the Medway and La Have in Lunenburg County, and the Moser in RMH. All have large pools that are excellent for dry-fly fishing. Although crowded during the mid-June peak run, both the number of available pools, and the practice of anglers rotating through the pools, provides everyone with an equal opportunity. The exception to this are the boat pools, with a few on the La Have, and for the majority of the Medway. The runs of Atlantic salmon vary from year to year and are very water-dependent. As the season advances, temperatures rise and water levels decline, and fishing becomes much more difficult.

Halifax is the capital city of Nova Scotia, and the regional municipality of Halifax also includes the city of Dartmouth. This metropolitan region has innumerable lakes containing smallmouth bass. Dartmouth is known as the City of Lakes for good reason. The majority of these lakes, all of varying size, are classified as urban fisheries. Of the 20 or more lakes in this area, the two largest, Porter's and Grand, are the most popular and the most productive.

Along with smallmouth bass, Grand Lake also features a sizable population of landlocked salmon and striped bass. The big lake is subject to sudden changes in wave and wind action, so boaters should exercise caution. The salmon and striped bass are usually fished by trolling with downriggers, while smallmouths are pursued by casting to limited structure and using deep tactics.

Southern Region

This area covers the southern tip of Nova Scotia and the counties of Yarmouth, Digby, Shelburne, and Queens. The latter two have particularly felt the effects of acid rain, and subsequent damage to habitat has reduced the number of salmonids in many rivers. Trout and salmon can still be caught, however.

There is a spring-summer run of Atlantic salmon on both the Medway and Tusket Rivers. Brook trout can be found in a number of streams, but their numbers are reduced through competition with smallmouth bass and chain pickerel.

Smallmouths are becoming the most popular species in this region, with a 20-inch specimen always a possibility. While Nova Scotian smallmouths typically inhabit lakes, the Mersey is the one river in the province where these bass can be found. Good bass fishing can be had in Killams, Ogden, and Parr Lakes (Yarmouth County); Spectacle, Lac d'en Bas, and Salmon River Lakes (Digby County); and Ten Mile Lake (Queens County).

It is believed that chain pickerel were first established in Digby County in 1924. From this introduction, the species has spread throughout the area. The most popular pickerel sites include June, Spectacle, Henriette, and Amero's Lakes (Digby County); and Utley, Annis, and Long Lakes and Western Duck Pond (Yarmouth County).

As smallmouth bass and chain pickerel expand their range, the opportunities to fish for both these species continues to grow.

Northcentral Region

This area comprises Annapolis, Kings, and Hants Counties, all presenting great angling opportunities. The topography of the northcentral region encompasses everything from rolling agricultural land to wilderness retreats, with fast running brooks, slower rivers, and very productive lakes. All this flows to the floor of the Annapolis Valley, which is bounded on each side by the North and South Mountains.

The valley floor has three main rivers, the Annapolis, Gaspereau, and Cornwallis. All three ultimately flow into the Bay of Fundy, so the waters are tidal in their lower reaches. The Cornwallis is a unique limestone river, which accounts for its alkaline water. The upper part meanders slowly through a tranquil pastoral setting, and although the lower parts have limited shore access, the tall grass and low gradient make this a beautiful float trip. The river has a large population of both resident and sea-run trout. The sea-run fish arrive from mid-May through mid-June, with a later run in September. Although both rivers share the same headwater, the Annapolis flows in a westerly direction while the Cornwallis flows eastward.

The paramount feature of the Annapolis River is the major run of American shad late in May. The run is mainly fished at the confluence of the Annapolis and Nictaux Rivers in the town of Middleton. Angling is primarily from the bank, but there is excellent flycasting opportunity. Neither river is very large, and once a school is located, it is quite possible to hook and land over 20 shad. Some tributaries can provide interesting brook trout fishing, but the numbers and size of the fish are not great.

The Bay of Fundy has the highest tides in the world (commonly 20 to 40 feet), which accounts for the largest tidal generating station in North America at the estuary of the Annapolis. This creates a headpond with a good population of striped bass, which travel upriver to spawn and provide freshwater angling.

Also within this region is the smaller Gaspereau Valley. The Gaspereau River is a hydroelectric generating system with its headwaters as a series of lakes. George, Gaspereau, Aylesford, Little River, and Black River Lakes all provide some of the best smallmouth bass fishing in the province, both in sheer numbers and size. These impoundments have great structure for bass and rarely experience anything more than low to medium fishing pressure. The lakes also feed the lower river, which has spring-run salmon in May, June, and July, with the main pool located below the White Rock power plant. Another lake in the valley, Lumsden, is heavily stocked with trout. White perch are said to be abundant in all of these lakes.

Isthmus

This area connecting mainland Nova Scotia to New Brunswick is comprised of Cumberland and Colchester Counties.

Cumberland borders the neighboring province with Northumberland Strait to the north and the Bay of Fundy to the south. It has few lakes of any size but many small streams and rivers. The rivers feeding Northumberland Strait have good runs of sea-run brown trout in the spring, with the best being at River Phillip and Wallace River. A number of smaller rivers have good runs, but this is very dependent on water levels that are heavily influenced by short length of flow and a limited watershed.

There are also good runs of Atlantic salmon in Cumberland County, with the best time being October when the water levels should be higher. While there were some salmon rivers on the Minas Basin side, the runs there have disappeared despite ongoing restoration efforts.

Colchester County has several good rivers, with the main river system being the Shubenacadie. This is fed by a series of lakes and rivers, with the Stewiacke being the principal tributary. The Stewiacke once had one of the largest runs of Atlantic salmon in the province, but this has also disappeared in recent years, although there is hope for return of these fish. In the meantime, spring runs of American shad, and resident brown trout throughout the season, are the major fisheries. The Waugh River also produces good angling for sea-run brown trout in the spring.

Saltwater

With so much coastline, one would expect Nova Scotia to be a saltwater fishing Mecca. It is, to a degree. But, it is largely underutilized by recreational anglers. As more people are introduced to this marine activity, mainly promoted through saltwater sportfishing tournaments around the province, interest is slowly increasing.

Historically, big game fishing here centered around giant bluefin tuna, but now blue-water fishing includes mako and blue shark. Inshore fishing features striped bass, mackerel, bluefish, cod, flounder, halibut, and haddock.

Nova Scotia was historically *the* place to be for catching giant bluefin tuna. A major fishery years ago made the province a favorite haunt of Ernest Hemingway and top big-game anglers. But bluefin tuna numbers worldwide have declined, and the number of fish that can be caught is federally regulated.

Nevertheless, the bluefin tuna is one of the most sought-after fish in Nova Scotian waters, Tuna boats depart from Halifax and along the eastern shore up to the Canso Causeway. The fishing peaks in the last week of August through October in the area of Port Hood and Mabou on Cape Breton Island. The size can be impressive; a 1,000-pounder is not uncommon, and in 1979, the all-tackle world record specimen, a 1,496-pounder, was caught out of Aulds Cove.

There are charters available through the commercial sector, principally out of Aulds Cove at the Canso Causeway. In Nova Scotia, tuna must be fished on rod and reel on a registered commercial fishing vessel to which a bluefin tuna license is attached.

Shark fishing is growing in popularity here each year, with the blue shark being the main species. Blues weighing from 200 to 300 pounds and being from 10 to 12 feet long are not uncommon, with the average running approximately 100 pounds. Larger mako and porbeagle sharks are occasionally taken. Recreational shark fishing is on a catch-and-release basis except for tournaments, where the catch is weighed and sold with all proceeds going to a provincial charity. Shark are fished here by chumming to a floating bait. The best season is in August and September, with a number of charter boats operating out of the Halifax area.

Fishing for groundfish (cod, haddock, pollock, and others) is widely available via charter boats around the coast. The best time is from July through September.

In August, people fishing from wharves, shore, and small boats set their sights on mackerel, a migratory species that runs in the millions along the coastline of Nova Scotia. The hotspot for mackerel is either Mahone Bay or St. Margaret's Bay along the south shore.

Bluefish hit Nova Scotia in August as well, but the runs are unpredictable and of short duration. Basically, this fish is only found on the southwestern end of Nova Scotia, through the numerous islands in and around the mouth of the Tusket River. When you do catch the run, its an unforgettable experience, as these voracious predators attack baitfish (mainly mackerel) with such ferocity that slicks of fish oil calm the waters and overpower the salty scent of the sea.

Perhaps the most primitive of the commonly known fish is the sturgeon, which dates back 350 million years and whose flesh was considered a delicacy even in Roman times.

N

There was a time when large striped bass (up to 70 pounds) sought out the estuaries of many rivers around the province, but overfishing adversely impacted the population. More recently, a resurgence of this fish has re-invigorated its popularity. The sizes have been smaller than they were years ago as it takes a number of years for the fish to reach maturity, but that may change. Because of the reduced populations, this fish is highly controlled and regulations should be carefully checked before you go fishing. The May spawning run in the Annapolis River can produce good results, but the best time is during July and August. The Tusket, Annis, Bear, and Annapolis Rivers in the southern part of the province are best for stripers, although Porter's Lake near Halifax also produces good runs. In fact, any river on the mainland can produce a reasonable run. There are no runs, however, on Cape Breton.

NUMBERS

The latitude and longitude coordinates for a given position. Someone who is navigating by the numbers has called up specific lat/lon coordinates from the memory of an electronic navigational device such as GPS or Loran to determine the direction to steer a boat in order to arrive at a specific destination.

See: GPS; Loran; Navigation.

NUNAVUT TERRITORY

Officially existing only since April 1, 1999, Nunavit Territory is the vast eastern Arctic region of Canada's far north that was separated from the former configuration of the Northwest Territories *(see)*. Nunavut means "our land" in the native language, and was formed for Canada's Inuit (Eskimo) people after a plebiscite in 1992. The country's newest territory, Nunavut is an enormous region that encompasses 1.9 million square kilometers of land—about one-fifth of the entire country of Canada. It includes the geographic and magnetic North Poles as well as the geographic center of Canada (30 kilometers northeast of Baker Lake), and is populated by less than 25,000 people. The Inuit have direct ownership of 350,000 square kilometers of this new territory, and now own some of the best fishing waters in the world.

Despite the change in land ownership, the right of innocent passage along waterways is guaranteed to non-beneficiaries in the Inuit land claim settlement. For those who angle the Arctic by canoeing its many splendid rivers, there will be little or no change. The shift in land ownership may see some lodges change hands, and it may see the names of some of its lakes, rivers, and towns change. Gradually, there is likely to be improved access to many previously uncelebrated and lightly visited angling "hotspots," such as Chantrey Inlet on the far northern mainland, as the Inuit selectively develop sportfishing in one of the last great wildernesses on earth.

It's not as if this region hasn't seen any anglers. Some of Canada's most famous and heralded angling waters are within this region, and they have been fished to varying degrees for decades. But due to remoteness, expense, and short seasons, and given the number and size of its waters, the region has hosted comparatively few anglers, and there are many lakes and rivers that rarely see a sport angler. In essence, the adventurous people who have ventured into Canada's remote eastern Arctic have had the arctic charr, lake trout, northern pike, and Arctic grayling virtually to themselves.

Visiting the far north to angle is an experience that goes beyond the act of catching frisky fish. This is a land of stark contrasts that ranges from the edge of the trees on the western barren lands to the towering barren cliffs of north Baffin Island's fjords. The Nunavut Territory is huge, stretching from it's southern boundary with the Province of Manitoba to the North Pole and from the tundra of the barren lands to the icebergs in Davis Strait off Greenland. It is equal in landmass to the entire country of Mexico, larger than Alaska, and could fit the entire states of Texas, California, Michigan, and Minnesota combined within its borders. And the amazing thing, as anyone who has flown over it in a plane can attest, is that there is water everywhere.

Typically, the Arctic angling season is compressed into the short period of open water from late June to mid-September. The lakes in Nunavut are ice covered from 240 days a year near the tree line, to 300-plus days a year in the northern islands of the Arctic archipelago. Recently, Inuit outfitters on Baffin Island have stretched the old open-water fishing season by offering adventurous anglers the opportunity to travel by dog team and jig for arctic charr and tomcod through cracks in the sea ice. Traveling by sled on a bright Arctic spring day to a distant bay, where you will jig with traditional Inuit caribou bone lures, provides a new and unique dimension to ice fishing.

Species

Arctic charr.   The arctic charr is the storied fish of Nunavut. Anglers who know them well consider arctic charr a fish worth the same passionate pursuit which many accord steelhead and Atlantic salmon. They are spirited fighters on both spinning and fly tackle, capable of solid drag-burning runs when at their peak and newly arrived back in their home rivers from the salt.

Feeding in the ocean on small silvery herring and capelin, arctic charr are particularly good sportfish. They can be very aggressive and frequently fall victim to bright silver spinners and wobbling spoons. Although arctic charr can be taken on dry flies, fly anglers are generally more successful with bright steelhead patterns and large weighted sculpins fished near the bottom.

The eastern arctic charr found in Nunavut is broadly considered one of two distinct subspecies of arctic charr found in North America (the other being western arctic charr). It is a fish that challenges taxonomists and geneticists, who have split and re-lumped the various subspecies and relatives over the years as they have sought to understand the relationship between the broadly dispersed circumpolar populations. Anglers who have fished widely in Nunavut know that there are even some visible differences between populations within the eastern Arctic stock.

The connection between arctic charr and Dolly Varden is strong, since they are closely related. The Tree River arctic charr live on the western boundary of the eastern arctic charr. They are well east of the known range of Dolly Varden. Despite this, they exhibit some characteristics reminiscent of the northern Dolly Varden, found west of the Mackenzie River in the Northwest Territories.

Tree River charr have small reddish spots with blue halos around them that are typically smaller than the eye of the fish; their bodies exhibit a compressed or flattened profile. Arctic charr generally have splotchy spots that are larger than the eye of the fish, they lack the blue halos, and they have a rounder body profile. If you compare a Tree River arctic charr with one from Victoria Island a few miles north across Coronation Gulf, the differences are visible, even though the scientific certainty of the lineage of the Tree River fish is undecided. Taxonomic subtleties aside, the Tree River contains one of the Arctic's great charr stocks, and it is where the biggest fish run.

Arctic charr in Nunavut occur in anadromous, nonanadromous, and lacustrine or landlocked forms. Anadromous males and females go to sea yearly to feed after spending five to eight nursery years in freshwater. They return to freshwater lakes in the autumn to spawn. The nonanadromous arctic charr are smaller males that stay in freshwater rivers that have access to the sea. Landlocked arctic charr are found in many isolated interior lakes that no longer have free passage to the sea. They are generally smaller than the sea-run form, but they are still an impressive gamefish on light tackle. Historical accounts by early missionaries from the Bathurst Inlet region refer to lakes fished by the Inuit with large populations of landlocked arctic charr.

Today, the arctic charr is found in many isolated interior lakes, and most of the coastal rivers and streams that rise from lakes that can support spawning. The majority of charr are caught in rivers; however, the larger specimens are primarily caught in the lower stretches closer to the salt. Arctic charr rivers flow into the Arctic Ocean, Hudson Bay, and the Atlantic coastlines of Nunavut. The well-known charr of Lake Hazen on northern Ellesmere Island are, at 82 degrees north, among the most northerly known populations. Lake Hazen has two distinctive stocks of arctic charr, incidentally; one is larger and has longer fin rays than the other; these charr, sometimes referred to as landlocked, do have access to the sea but apparently do not go to sea. Technically, the most northerly known populations are found in lakes near Alert and on the northern end of Greenland (about 84 to 85 degrees north).

Charr do not run huge distances inland like Pacific salmon, and it is usually small specimens that are in the lakes. The charr that are caught early in the season are very bright fish, looking in coloration like a steelhead or fresh-run salmon, but they develop remarkable colors, and the later-season fish can possess beautiful shades of red and orange, plus spots. Non-spawning fish, especially the sea-run forms, tend to be silver. Many lacustrine populations have individuals which haven't sexually matured and which retain a pale color even at non-spawning times.

The most lasting image of the arctic charr is that of a spawning fish's brilliant orange belly set against a dark-green back, highlighted with orange spots and white-edged fins. However, non-spawning fish range from the dull-silver coloration of landlocked specimens to the blue silver flash of the returning sea-run specimen. Arctic charr average 15 to 18 inches in length in Nunavut; specimens longer than 30 inches are rare but possible in some runs. Sea-run fish average 2 to 10 pounds.

The largest known arctic charr taken by anglers have come from the Tree River. The Tree River stock and related runs from the Coppermine and others rivers that flow along the Northwest Passage have consistently produced big fish. This is where the great pictures of huge, brightly colored charr draped across anglers' arms comes from. The IGFA all-tackle world record for arctic charr is a 32-pound 9-ounce Tree River fish caught in 1981.

Practically speaking, to trophy-seeking anglers a large charr is one that is over 15 pounds, and Nunavut has several locations known to produce such fish, in addition to the Tree and Coppermine Rivers. Chantrey Inlet is one, although it has a very small window of opportunity at the time of ice out. More reliable are various rivers on Victoria Island (shared with the Northwest Territories), which have produced 18- to 24-pound arctic charr and assorted line-class world records over the years. Although there are plenty of charr in the various rivers of Baffin Island, these waters have not been known for large specimens, and fish over 15 pounds have not been common there.

Size aside, most of the Inuit maintain that the best-tasting arctic charr comes from around Pelly Bay on the central Arctic coast's Boothia Peninsula, although any visiting angler who has eaten freshly caught charr, especially small and midsize specimens, has enjoyed a gastronomic delight.

Lake trout. Lake trout, of course, which are actually in the charr family, are perhaps Nunavut's

N

Creation of the first glass fishing rod is credited to Dr. Glen Havens, who experimented with fiberglass and resins starting in the mid-1930s.

greatest claim to the angler's affection. Lakers are found in the greatest numbers in the rivers and lakes of the barren lands on the Arctic mainland. These rivers flow north to the Arctic Coast's Coronation Gulf and Queen Maud Gulf, and east into the west side of Hudson Bay.

Lake trout are also found on the southern half of Victoria Island on the western end of Nunavut. On many rivers, lake trout inhabit and dominate the upper reaches, while arctic charr inhabit the lower and share it with smaller-size lakers. Unlike their cousins, lake trout are generally intolerant of the saltwater in coastal estuaries.

The extremely cold water of the lakes and rivers of the barren lands allow lake trout to remain at shallower depths in the lakes and to thrive in the oxygen-rich water of brawling rivers. This characteristic of Nunavut lake trout allows the angler to pursue them with varied tackle, including lighter spinning gear and fly tackle. On those rare occasions when big caddis hatch in early July, it is not uncommon to pick up 6- or 7-pound fish on a bushy Goddard caddis.

In lakes, the abundance of trout at shallow depths, including the availability of good-size fish, makes it generally unnecessary to use the deep trolling tactics and equipment that are common for catching lakers in the southern parts of their range, especially after ice out and in late summer. Almost no lodges provide downriggers, for example, and it is rarely necessary to get down more than 35 or 40 feet in most Nunavut lakes, even in the middle of the (short) summer. Not all of the fish are caught by trolling, although the majority are; jigging and casting are possible, especially at inlets and along shorelines. The cold water also contributes to distinctively marked and hard-fighting fish.

There are few places outside of Nunavut where it is common to catch lake trout in rivers. The largest lakers are not likely to be in swift-flowing water; however, they are very likely to be in the vicinity of a tributary, especially where it enters a big lake, since this will also attract a lot of forage fish, including suckers, whitefish, and small trout. However, smaller fish, in the 5- to 10-pound range, are often caught in the rivers of this region, and they are a terrific prize for the light-tackle angler.

The largest lake trout of the Nunavut Territory are generally found in the biggest lakes. Although there are some huge lakers on Victoria Island, mainly in Merkley Lake, the northernmost waters don't seem to produce the monster fish, probably because of the short open-water seasons. The big lakes of the more southerly region of the territory, from Baker Lake south to the Manitoba border, most reliably produce huge trout. Nueltin Lake, which is a 125-mile-long body of boundary water, two-thirds or more of which is in Nunavut, is the most renowned lake trout water in the territory. Huge in this region means over 30 pounds, as there are great populations of small trout in nearly all of the places that

hold this species, and most lakes can produce fish in the 15- to 20-pound range. Some lakes, however, have been subject to netting by native people, and these are less likely to have a good supply of large lake trout.

Northern pike. Northern pike are distributed across the barren lands from the tree line to Hudson Bay and north to the southern edge of the Arctic coastal plain. The upper Thelon, Dubant, Kazan, and Thlewiaza Rivers have good pike fishing. Nueltin Lake is the most renowned pike water in the region and has produced numerous 50-inch fish.

The popularity of barren-land pike fishing has increased over the years, either as an adjunct to people seeking lake trout, or as a sole quarry unto itself. Shallow-water casting, which appeals to many anglers, dovetails nicely with northern pike in Nunavut waters, as these fish are accessible and aggressive throughout the limited season. A greater interest in fly fishing for these fish has been evident, and flies sometimes succeed at moving fish when other offerings do not. Nevertheless, as is true elsewhere in Canada, the great majority of Nunavut's pike are caught on spoons, and there is virtually no trolling done for this species. The greatest action for shallow fish is usually had early in the season, especially in the backs of bays, which lose their ice early and warm up.

Grayling. The Arctic grayling is a favorite fish of the far north for light-tackle devotees. Like charr, it's a species that is primarily found in the remote north, with a similar range to that of northern pike. Though caught in some lakes, it is mainly found in rivers here. Light spinning and fly tackle is more than adequate for these fish, which typically run about $1^{1}/_{2}$ pounds but may be much larger. A 3-pounder is a fairly large grayling, but fish of this size are caught in various Nunavut locations, and are common in a few. Record-size grayling have been caught in various locales here, including the Kazan River.

This frisky and flashy blue fish lives off insects and very small fish fry. Its keen interest in flies makes it a natural for the fly caster. However, the grayling is a fragile fish—one that never stops squirming when caught—making it susceptible to harm through handling and requiring careful release.

Some of the largest grayling can be found in lakes, but they are generally overlooked in stillwaters here. It is possible in some places to spot cruising fish in the shallows nearshore, taking insects off the surface, and to cast to them. This is often an evening affair, and most lake anglers are resting then, having spent all day casting or trolling for the pike and lake trout in these waters. Evenings in summer, however, seem to never end in Nunavut, as this is the fabled Land of the Midnight Sun, and it presents delightful opportunities.

Grayling are rarely the sole, or even primary, quest for far-north anglers. They are usually caught

Piled rocks are a traditional Inuit marker for an important fishing site; this one overlooks Bloody Falls on the Coppermine River.

as an adjunct, or side excursion. A suitable light rod must be brought for these fish, however, as the small-mouthed grayling almost never succumb to the larger offerings made for lake trout and pike. Focusing exclusively on grayling requires having a guide or outfitter who is well acquainted with the white water on the rivers, and the small streams that feed the lakes.

Whitefish.   Lake whitefish are found in the lakes and rivers of the barren lands and in the littoral zone along the Arctic Coast and Hudson Bay. No lodges advertise them and relatively few anglers seek them out, but when the opportunity presents itself the lake whitefish is a prize worth pursuing.

Like grayling, whitefish are almost never caught on the hardware and tackle used for pike and trout, and angling for them is more specialized, requiring light or ultralight spinning and fly gear. They can be taken on light jigs, and to a lesser degree small spinners, but they are best caught on flies, including soft hackle and emerger patterns, and they are a delightful fish to catch.

Whitefish are sometimes seen dimpling the surface in the evening, and can be available to anglers then. Rising whitefish on a midsummer's eve are not actually rising to flies on the surface; they are nymphing for caddis and mayflies swimming up to hatch. The slight downturn of the whitefish's small mouth does not allow it to easily snip dry flies from the surface. If you watch their rises carefully, it is the back of the fish which breaks the surface as it positions itself to come down on the rising insect.

Whitefish is one of the best table fish in the north. Fried whitefish makes a great shore lunch, and smoked whitefish (some lodges have smokehouses) is a real treat.

Locations

There are several ways to approach a fishing trip to Nunavut, but each depends on the type of experience and the species the angler is interested in. It is important to remember that Nunavut is still a remote (and often harsh) land that has no roads, limited scheduled air service, and a tourist industry that is still evolving and developing. The options for the angler include well-established lodges (which are not as numerous as one might think in this vast region), community-based guiding services, guided canoe trips, and self-managed canoe expeditions. Self-managed canoe expeditions are only for accomplished wilderness travelers and often do not provide the type of angling, or amount of fishing time, that dedicated anglers want, although they can provide access to rarely visited locations. For anglers going to Nunavut with a limited amount of time and a desire to get in a lot of fishing, visiting

N

an established lodge is the best option, and it is the one most frequently taken.

The most varied angling opportunities are available at the lodges on the barren lands. There are well-established facilities at Nueltin Lake, Kasba Lake, and Ferguson Lake/Yathkyed Lake, which can provide excellent lake trout, Arctic grayling, and northern pike fishing. There are also community-based guides in the Inuit community of Baker Lake on the barren lands, and some outfitters provide tent camping expeditions to locations that are not serviced by established lodges. There is also good arctic charr fishing along the north shore of Baker Lake and along the lower Thelon River.

There are established arctic charr lodges on the Tree River along the central Arctic Coast, and at Merkley Lake on Victoria Island, with an outpost on Hadley Bay. The latter is in close proximity to the most northerly lake trout in North America. More adventurous anglers will find community-based angling services for arctic charr available in Kugluktuk on the Coppermine River, at Rankin Inlet on the west coast of Hudson Bay, at Coral Harbour on South Hampton Island in northern Hudson Bay, at Iqaluit on Frobisher Bay on southern Baffin Island, at Pangnirtung on Cumberland Sound in the central section of Baffin Island, at Pond Inlet on north Baffin Island, and near Resolute Bay on Cornwallis Island along Barrow Strait in the High Arctic. Bloody Falls on the lower Coppermine River has fine charr fishing in late August or early September. Close proximity to the community of Kugluktuk means that Bloody Falls is not a wilderness experience, but it can be very good fishing.

Fishing gear is almost never available at Nunavut locations, or extremely expensive, so anglers must bring a good supply of whatever they will need. Since most access is by float plane in this country, it is necessary to pack gear compactly so that it will fit with others in a small aircraft. It is often said that summer lasts one day, or one week, in this country, and while that is an exaggeration, a beautiful, warm 75°F day can be followed by a dark cloudy day with blustery winds, which, when blowing across cold water, can make it seem like fishing in the winter. Therefore, good rain gear, boat boots, sweaters, and wind breakers are imperative *(see: travel)*.

Nueltin Lake

Although most of this huge lake is located in Nunavut, it is generally viewed as a Manitoba lake. Greater details about this lake are noted in that entry *(see: Manitoba)*. There is one lodge on the lake, located at the southern end in Manitoba, although there are several outpost camps for this lodge, two of them situated in Nunavut. This outflow of Nueltin, which is above the tree line and flows to western Hudson Bay, is one of the more interesting and least visited sites of the far north, primarily hosting lake trout and, further along,

grayling. Sealhole Lake at the outflow of Nueltin has prodigious water flow and terrific lake trout fishing, and it is probably visited by only a handful of people each season.

Ferguson Lake and Vicinity

By far north standards, Ferguson Lake is a small body of water south of the community of Baker Lake and west of Rankin Inlet in south-central Nunavut. However, in addition to good July and August fishing on its own waters, Ferguson provides access to excellent angling in the nearby waters of 35-mile-long Yathkyed and 125-mile-long Kaminuriak Lakes. Although there are some grayling in this area, this area is almost entirely a lake trout experience.

There is one base camp lodge in this area, on Ferguson; a few outpost facilities in the region, including several at Kaminuriak and one at the north end of Yathkyed (where the Kazan River enters); and some daytrip fly-in access to other areas. Undisturbed by commercial fishing, domestic netters, and few other anglers, these huge lakes have become places for multi-faceted lake trout fishing, where trollers and casters each enjoy success.

Light-tackle angling is especially feasible in these waters, since the trout are usually shallow, ice out normally doesn't occur until about July 4, and there are many feeder rivers and outlet tributaries that stack the fish up. Smaller lake trout are available in the various rivers, some of which provide adventurous hike-to whitewater fishing, and bigger specimens are available in the lakes and at tributaries where heavy flows exit, creating back eddies that are magnets for lake trout.

Ferguson Lake, being relatively shallow, and the other lakes here, are conducive to thin-water fishing through the entire open-water season, and most of the fish that are caught here are taken in under 12 feet of water. Catching a 20-pounder is a distinct possibility in these waters, and fish to 30 are likely. There are big lakers here, too, and specimens up to 50 pounds and more were caught in the 1990s.

Some of the largest far-north herds of caribou traverse the tundra in this region, and anglers are quite likely to see varied numbers of these in this area, as well as, perhaps, musk ox.

Chantrey Inlet

Located in the Arctic tundra on the mainland Nunavut Territory, Chantrey Inlet is the place where the mighty Back River courses through Franklin Lake. It attracts a prodigious run of big charr (10 to 20 pounds) in early July as the ice leaves, and it hosts scores of lake trout, including specimens that have reputedly topped the 60-pound mark, the rest of the season till mid-August. Most of the trout are in the 10- to 20-pound range, but there's a good chance of getting one from 30 to 40 pounds here. Grayling, too, exist along the shoreline in less tumultuous water and in two nearby small lakes.

Swift water and back eddies provide challenging moments for shore or boat anglers hooked to charr or lakers, with most anglers using heavy spoons to troll or jigs for casting and drifting. This is not the place to try light tackle, fly fishing, or gear of questionable endurance. Deep, rapid water, a boulder strewn bottom, and extremely hard-fighting fish combine to provide some of the most demanding freshwater fishing and boating.

This remarkable place has had varied accessibility over the years. In the past, some operators have brought groups of anglers in for a few weeks, but the stability of these operations has varied. The problem with Chantrey is that everything is dependent on ice out, which varies from year to year. The big charr run through so fast that even in the best case, the hottest charr angling, and the big fish, lasts less than two weeks at the mouth of the mighty Back. No established operation was being run here as of the late 1990s; however, this is an area—including the upriver lakes—that bears watching.

Victoria Island

The moment that you step off the commercial airliner at Cambridge Bay you realize that Victoria Island is a special place. Across from the airport is a Distant Early Warning (DEW) radar site. In the bay is the wreck of the Maud, the round-hulled vessel used by Norwegian explorer Roald Amundsen to make the first east-west crossing of the Canadian Arctic at the turn of this century. A few yards from that is the site of the first church here, a Roman Catholic building made of double stone walls, with caribou hides for insulation. Perhaps a visit will coincide with the biggest event of the season, the arrival of the supply barge that is laden with goods ordered a year earlier, and whose passage is cleared by icebreakers. In Cambridge Bay, drying charr and animal skins hang outside houses. Dog sleds lie next to ATVs and snowmobiles.

Above the mainland Northwest Territories, 270 miles north of the Arctic Circle, in the lower reaches of the Arctic Ocean, Victoria Island is a long way from anywhere. It's a particularly long way to go to stand waist-deep in a river that never gets warmer than 40 degrees, under a gray, sometimes drizzly or snowy sky, and cast for a fish that may not be there. Much of the time there is only the whistling of wind for company, or an occasional caribou a half mile away on the horizon. Other than caribou, musk oxen, and rocks, there is nothing here that rises more than a few inches off the ground. The nearest tree is 400 miles to the south, across a spongy, moss-covered, nearly level plain that hides an always frozen substrata.

But in this apparently desolate spot are treasures that only several dozen anglers are able to enjoy each summer. In some of Victoria Island's rivers, which flow north to the Viscount Melville Sound

Cold Victoria Island rivers produce colorful spawning-run charr.

and south to the Coronation and Queen Maud Gulfs, not far from the permanent polar icecap, the lucky ones will intercept the elusive, brilliantly colored arctic charr on the way to its spawning grounds. This is one of the premier spots in North America for a chance at catching trophy charr.

Although most visitors fish the western and northern rivers for this species, arctic charr run along the south coast of Victoria Island near the community of Cambridge Bay in early July. Locals search for them by driving along the coast on ATVs watching for flocks of seabirds and seals swarming after capelin. The charr will be found feeding in the middle of the scrum. Casting bright spoons, spinners, and wet flies from shore often brings explosive action. Surf casting for charr is good fun.

Certainly arctic charr are found all across the North American Arctic. The largest charr appear to come regularly from Victoria Island and the Tree River on the mainland Northwest Territories. Geographically, these places are not that far apart, yet their charr are distinctly different. Tree River charr in their spawning colors have a dark back and are not fully swathed in red or orange. They have a humped back, too, and often a more pronounced kype. Many taxidermists, more familiar with these trophies, have painted this pattern on Victoria Island trophies.

The biggest charr caught at Victoria Island was a line-class world record 24-pounder taken in 1982. Several other line class world records have been established here as well. Summer charr here typically run from 12 to 20 pounds, a weight well above that found in most other regions.

Charr spawn approximately every three years, and it is the spawning fish that change color and are largest and most prized. Silver charr, those descending lakes and rivers and running out to the ocean for the summer, are smaller and bright, though a lot of fun to catch. Fishing is done for silver charr in

N

July and holdover (spawning) charr in August. The season, which is just six weeks long, begins in mid-July and runs through August, by which time the weather is already starting to get worrisome.

In addition to having tremendous charr fishing, Victoria Island has some exceptional lake trout angling. Lakers up to 44 pounds have been caught in relatively shallow 15-mile-long Merkley Lake. The larger lakers are usually taken right after ice out during the first two or three weeks of fishing. Casting and fly fishing opportunities are best then for both trout and silver charr. Throughout the season, small lake trout can be taken on ultralight spinning tackle and fly rod in shallow water by sight casting to feeding/cruising pods.

Victoria Island has various fishing locales that have seldom, if ever, seen a lure in years. This is partly due to the fact that some waters here open up only every few years, usually after a mild winter.

NUN BUOY

A cylindrical buoy, tapered at the top and usually red, used as an aid to navigation.
See: Buoys.

NURSERY

The part of a fish's or animal's habitat where the young grow up.

NYLON LINE

See: Line

NYMPH

The immature form of some aquatic insects in freshwater; also an artificial fly that imitates or suggests the natural insect.
See: Fly.

N

OCEANIA

The combined island areas of the western, central, and southern portions of the tropical Pacific Ocean. The area is subdivided into Micronesia, Melanesia, and Polynesia.

OCEANIC

Pertaining to or living in the open ocean.

OCEANOGRAPHER

A person who studies the environment of the oceans, including currents, wind, tides, sea-air interactions, geology of the sea floor, and the living organisms.

OFFSHORE

Although this term practically signifies the direction away from land, in fishing parlance it generally means that portion of the water from which land is not visible, and to most saltwater anglers it pertains to deep-water areas, on the edge of ocean currents or shelves, where big-game species, particularly billfish and tuna, are pursued.
See: Inshore; Offshore Fishing; Sportfishing Boat.

OFFSHORE BOAT

See: Sportfishing Boat.

OFFSHORE FISHING

The term "offshore" is largely a generic one used by saltwater anglers to refer to deep-water areas on the edges of ocean currents or to shelves commonly called blue water. Although there's no strict definition as to where offshore begins and inshore *(see)* ends, in general offshore applies to the pursuit of big-game species, particularly billfish and tuna, and inshore refers to angling for resident and migratory species in estuaries, rivers, bays, and near-shore ocean waters.

Because of the expanse of water and the nature of the pelagic species there, offshore environs are primarily fished by trolling and by chumming while the boat is drifting or at anchor. Trollers use both lures and rigged natural baits, but some live bait fishing occurs. Although offshore fishing is done at great distances from some mainland coasts, it can be done fairly close to other coasts if hydrographic contours and currents provide appropriate conditions suitable to the presence of big-game species. Thus, offshore fishing may be enjoyed by anglers fishing from private sportfishing boats of various sizes, from charter boats, and, less commonly, from long-range party boats.

Generally, offshore fishing is done with medium- to heavy-duty conventional tackle or big-game tackle *(see)*, even though some of these species, or smaller specimens, may be caught with other equipment where circumstances permit.

The various elements of offshore fishing—from setting and using drag to lures and baits and tactics for specific species—are covered in more detail in separate entries.
See: Bait Rigs; Billfish; Billfish on Fly Tackle; Conventional Tackle; Kite Fishing; Sharks; Sportfishing Boat; Stand Up Fishing; Trolling; Trolling Lures, Saltwater; Tuna.

OFFSHORE LURES

See: Offshore Fishing; Trolling Lures, Saltwater.

OHIO

With an army of anglers and a meager sprinkling of small reservoirs, Ohio certainly depends on a large share of Lake Erie to satisfy its residents. The most fertile and productive of all the Great Lakes, Erie and its sprawling waters and plentiful fish schools can easily accommodate a crowd.

Lake Erie's shallow Western Basin is a world premier freshwater spawning ground, a bonanza that has earned it its reputation as the "Walleye Capital of the World." The walleye fishing is great, and the often ignored smallmouth bass fishing is even better. The wide range of gamefish inhabiting Lake Erie will test any angler's interests and abilities.

Although anglers flock to northern Ohio to feast on Lake Erie's bounty, if they ignore the Buckeye State's inland lakes and the Ohio River, they're missing out on a smorgasbord of treats. Ohio's collection of small reservoirs features fine angling for panfish, catfish, bass, and walleye, as well as surprisingly good muskies. The darling of the modern fisheries programs is the saugeye, a walleye-sauger hybrid generously stocked in many of the state's reservoirs.

Most visiting anglers fail to realize that although Lake Erie and the Ohio River have a long history of pleasing recreational anglers, natural inland lakes are few and far between. The largest natural lake in Ohio is little Chippewa, a 300-acre private patch of water about 40 miles southwest of Cleveland. The 31 inland lakes that boast 1,000 acres of water or more are all reservoirs. Most have been created over the past 50 years, and some are considerably younger.

Lake Erie

Western Basin. Ohio shares western Lake Erie with Michigan and Ontario, but Buckeye anglers have the largest slice of the big lake and the best of the fish-attracting reefs. Since the removal of Ohio's commercial gillnet fishery, bought out by the Ohio Division of Wildlife on behalf of anglers many years ago, the walleye angling on Lake Erie has flourished. There have been changes, however.

A parade of exotic species of fish and organisms have found their way to the Great Lakes over the years, most from European waters. The pace accelerated in the 1980s, with clouds of spiny water fleas and even Chinese mitten crabs making an appearance. The most notable critters hitchhiking in the bellies of ocean freighters have been the zebra mussel, a small mollusk; and the round goby and ruffe, two small but aggressive and prolific species of fish. The zebra mussel has significantly impacted the fishery, and although their initial appearance prompted a forecast of doom and gloom, the effects haven't all been bad.

Billions of the filter-feeding mollusks now live in Lake Erie, covering every available piece of rock and rubble, and the once dingy Western Basin has become a place of clear water. That clarity has liberated the walleye, allowing them to do what they do best, which is to use their large, opaque eyes to feed primarily after the sun goes down. This is, of course, a frustrating change in behavior for daytime anglers.

At the same time, the clear waters have broadened the spawning grounds for fish, allowing light to penetrate and letting some species, especially smallmouth bass, find success in deeper waters. As a result, hordes of smallmouth bass have been a delight for anglers.

Western Lake Erie is at its very best in the spring. The average depth of the Western Basin, from the Bass Islands to the Michigan shoreline, is just 30 feet, a reason why walleye swim here from all over Lake Erie and beyond to spawn each March and April.

If the winter is chilly enough to provide safe ice along the mainland and around the Bass Islands, ice anglers often get the first taste of walleye. When Lake Erie warms in spring, and walleye swarm over and around the limestone reefs to spawn, the fishing season begins in earnest. Although roughly 70 percent of the walleye spawn on Lake Erie's reefs, the remainder that head up the Maumee, Portage, and Sandusky Rivers give wading anglers a spring walleye fling in late March and early April, followed by some hot white bass fishing.

In May, western Lake Erie's smallmouth bass move to the shallows as post-spawn walleye head for open water. Many walleye will roam the big lake, some even heading up the Detroit River to Lake St. Clair and beyond. Large schools of walleye will remain, however, and June through August are excellent months for western Lake Erie anglers.

During the spawning season, walleye anglers rely on jigs and jigging spoons tipped with minnows. When the spawn is winding down, anglers begin casting traditional weight-forward spinners tipped with nightcrawlers, and pull out diving plugs to troll for trophy fish. The clear waters of Lake Erie and the scattered schools of walleye now make trolling the most consistent technique, whereas drifting was favored in the days before the zebra mussel.

The smallmouth bass fishing is especially impressive along the western Lake Erie shoreline and around the western lake islands, and it's also very consistent. The bass are vulnerable during their April and May spawning seasons, which can extend into June in deeper, cooler Canadian waters. When the spawn is over, though, smallmouths simply move to deeper waters and begin to feed on crayfish and emerald shiner minnows.

Almost all of Ohio's bass tournament trails have set their records on Lake Erie because of the plentiful smallmouth bass and the faithful fishing. At times, the arsenal of bass baits, from jerkbaits and deep-diving plugs to spinners, will catch big bass. From spring through fall, the Lake Erie favorites are tube jigs, jig-grub combinations, live crayfish, and sparkling live emerald shiner minnows.

Anglers looking for smallmouth bass can narrow their focus to two critical ingredients. Successful anglers must find the depths the bass prefer, which can vary from day to day and throughout the day, and the rockpiles that are magnets for this species.

Western Lake Erie yellow perch are popular, but they are generally slightly smaller than their deepwater cousins in central Lake Erie. They make up for that by being more plentiful and easier to find.

Put-in-Bay on South Bass Island is a major departure point for Lake Erie walleye and smallmouth bass fishing.

Yellow perch prefer deep-water dropoffs along the mainland and around the islands. Local anglers keep tabs on their whereabouts, hoping to learn where they can find a supply of perch fillets for dinner.

Central Basin. The spring and fall yellow perch fishing attracts legions of boat anglers to Lake Erie, and for good reason. The large schools of perch can provide nonstop action, and they're not hard to catch. Using weighted crappie rigs or wire spreaders with long-shanked hooks tipped with lively shiner minnows, anglers can easily find success.

Yellow perch populations have fluctuated over the years, but the bar sided fish are still the second most popular for Lake Erie anglers. When the perch gather in near-shore schools in spring and fall, it's easy to spot the small flotillas of perch boats that have pinned down the largest concentrations of the flavorful fish, a staple of northern Ohio fish fries. These flotillas will be stationed off ports like Lorain, Cleveland, Fairport Harbor, Conneaut, and Ashtabula.

Although some walleye spawn in Central Basin rivers and streams, most spend the spring spawning season on western Lake Erie reefs and up western Ohio rivers. When the spawning season has ended, they head for the deeper, cooler waters of central Lake Erie; there, large schools of walleye thrill anglers from Huron to Conneaut.

Deep-water schools of walleye often suspend along the thermocline in summer, heading to the surface to feed on schools of shiner minnows after dark. Although the schools are often surprisingly large, trolling techniques designed to catch scattered walleye work best. Planer boards, diving planers, and a range of one-line weighting systems are used to take lures to the walleye. Veteran walleye anglers know that techniques must take into account that walleye are exceptionally shy of the sight and sound of fishing boats.

Crankbaits and spoons dominate the choice of trolling lures, although spinner rigs tipped with nightcrawlers and even heavy weight-forward spinners and nightcrawlers will catch many walleye. A good sonar unit is a must, and electronics that measure trolling speed and water temperature can help to fine-tune lure presentation.

As a bonus, walleye anglers can also catch Lake Erie's steelhead. Not as plentiful as the walleye, these trout are often caught on walleye lures, and at the same depths as walleye.

The secret of the Central Basin is its superb smallmouth bass fishery. Generally neglected by anglers more eager for perch or walleye, the near-shore bass fishing can range from good to spectacular, and trophy bass are always a possibility. Lake Erie's Central Basin has a featureless sand, sediment, and clay bottom, offering bass little deep-water structure. Bass flock to the harbor areas, where breakwalls provide bass habitat. Artificial reefs in the Lorain and Cleveland areas are gold mines for bass anglers, as are even the smallest rock humps.

As in the Western Basin, bass are generally easiest to find around structure, but temperature and water clarity dictate the preferred depth. When schools of minnows are suspended, the bass will rise to the occasion.

Northeastern Streams

Steelhead are the glamour fish of Lake Erie tributaries ranging from the Rocky River in Cleveland to Conneaut Creek near the Pennsylvania border. The young trout are stocked each year in the Rocky, Grand, and Chagrin Rivers, and in Conneaut Creek, and head to Lake Erie to feed and grow much larger than stream rainbow trout. In early winter, they head back to the streams where they were stocked, and can be caught there by wading anglers through April.

Both fly and bait anglers target the big trout, which favor the deeper pools and will run many miles up the rivers in a mostly futile effort to spawn. Fly anglers cast with 7- and 8-weight fly rods, and the choice of flies ranges from traditional egg patterns to small nymph imitations, Woolly Buggers, and sucker spawn. The top bait choices are spawn bags, jig-maggot combinations, and minnows worked near the bottom of the deep pools under a float, as well as nightcrawlers weighted to bounce along the rocky stream bottom.

High water conditions after rain and snowmelt lure trout into the rivers. Prime fishing conditions arrive when the water levels decline and the stream flow is lightly stained but not clear.

Ohio River

The Ohio River can be the Buckeye State's most frustrating of bass fishing holes, but it's a grand, old river for channel and flathead catfish and for walleye, sauger, and saugeye, as well as white bass, striped bass, and hybrid stripers. Anglers can also expect to find carp, crappie, bluegills, and smallmouth bass, with a few spotted bass and even muskies tossed in to the fisheries mix of the muddy river.

The distribution of Ohio River fish is curtailed by 19 dams designed to accommodate barge traffic, not populations of fish. The dams have slowed the flow of the Ohio River, creating a series of smaller "pools," much like lakes, and each is a bit different.

The best Ohio River fishing is in the dam tailraces, where gamefish are attracted by large numbers of baitfish in the highly oxygenated water. That's where many of the walleye, sauger, and saugeye are caught, as well as the big hybrid bass, white bass, and stripers.

Anglers commonly cast jigs tipped with plastic tails or minnows, or jigging spoons or blade baits, to the tailrace current. The catch is often surprising; instead of a walleye, a rough and rugged striped bass may test their tackle.

The best largemouth bass fishing occurs in the backwaters of the Ohio River; the creek channels provide suitable spawning habitat, and the snags, stumps, and weedbeds offer the cover fancied by largemouth bass. Bass fishing in the main river usually begins to warm up in May and June, and can be good throughout the summer if main-channel weedbeds are abundant.

Smallmouth bass prefer to hang around the rock and rubble in the river current. The smallmouth and spotted bass are especially abundant in areas downstream of tailwater areas, and around the heads and tails of the many main-channel islands. Warmwater discharges are bass magnets during the cold weather. Once plentiful in the Ohio River, spotted bass ("Kentuckies") have lost a territorial battle to the hybrid stripers, as well as the smallmouth and largemouth bass.

Reservoirs

Dozens of bass clubs are sprinkled around Ohio, and bass tournaments are held on many of the reservoirs each weekend from spring through fall, although sometimes one wonders why there's such a big effort. The bass fishery on inland lakes isn't much to brag about, as trophy fish are difficult to find.

Not surprisingly, the best bass lakes are those with motor restrictions and those closed to high-powered bass boats. Clendening, Piedmont, Leesville, and Pymatuning all have 10-horsepower motor limits and boast the best bass fishing in Ohio. Bass anglers have discovered that small lures work best in Ohio; tiny 3- and 4-inch plastic worms and small jigs are the mainstays. Summer pleasure boaters crowd the lakes, and bass anglers—while dodging aggravating personal watercraft—have learned to move away from wave- and wake-washed shorelines to probe the deeper waters with crankbaits and Carolina rigged worms.

Ohio has surprisingly good muskie fishing, and trophy muskies are caught each year at Piedmont, Leesville, Clear Fork, Alum Creek, West Branch, and Milton, and at sprawling Pymatuning Lake when it's at its peak. Trolling a big lure is the best way to hook a trophy muskie.

Just as the walleye is king on Lake Erie, so is it on many inland lakes. The best inland walleye waters are Pymatuning, Mosquito, and C. J. Brown Reservoir. Most anglers resort to jig-minnow rigs early in the year, and either drift spinner-crawler combos or minnow-style plugs once summer arrives.

The walleye certainly isn't Ohio's fish of the future, at least not on the state's inland waters. Ohio fisheries experts have turned to the saugeye, a walleye-sauger hybrid, to provide the best fishing. Saugeye will thrive better in dingier, warmer water than will walleye. They'll hit the same lures as walleye and are more likely to bite during the waning days of summer, when walleye prefer deeper waters and are hardest to catch.

Saugeye have become a welcome addition on Ohio fishing waters, from the Ohio River to such inland reservoirs as Alum Creek, Atwood, Beach City, Burr Oak, Caesar Creek, Charles Mill, Clendening, Deer Creek, Dillon, Hoover, Indian Lake, O'Shaughnessy, Paint Creek, Piedmont, Tappan, and Turkeyfoot. Whereas hybrid fish such as saugeye won't spawn, walleye have experienced little spawning success on Ohio's inland lakes.

Central region. Alum Creek Lake is busy with summertime boaters, but this 3,387-acre impoundment has good largemouth bass, crappie, and bluegill fishing. Muskies are making a splash, and saugeye stockings have been a success. Some saugeye are caught in the tailwaters during the cold weather months.

Buckeye Lake is a 3,300-acre lake whose shoreline is crowded with homes and whose waters can be filled with summer skiers. Big hybrid stripers and channel catfish are plentiful. Anglers also catch largemouth bass, bluegills, crappie, and saugeye, and a few focus on the plentiful carp.

Deer Creek Lake spotlights white bass, saugeye, and channel catfish among its 1,277 acres. Its tailwater fishing for saugeye is famous for producing state-record fish.

Delaware Lake covers 1,330 acres and is managed for big crappie. It is also a favorite of weekend recreational boaters from nearby Columbus, and has good fishing for largemouth bass and saugeye.

Hoover Reservoir's 10-horsepower motor limit helps trim the crowds. Fish production at this 3,843-acre Columbus-area lake is hampered by fluctuating water levels. Anglers focus on largemouth bass, crappie, white bass, and saugeye.

Indian Lake, covering 5,800 acres and built in 1852, is large, shallow, and weedy. Largemouth bass are a traditional favorite, and saugeye and channel catfish are plentiful.

Southwestern region. At 2,210-acre C. J. Brown Reservoir, walleye are the top fish. The main lake is at its best in spring, and the tailwaters lure anglers in winter. Channel catfish and crappie are good bets in spring and summer.

Caesar Creek Lake's largemouth bass fishery attracts large numbers of fair weather boaters, and shallow water anglers find fulfillment by dunking small baits for bluegills. Schools of late-summer white bass are an annual attraction at this 2,830-acre lake, and saugeye are fairly plentiful.

Grand Lake St. Marys draws crappie anglers from afar. This sprawling 13,500-acre reservoir is shallow, and channel catfish are easy to find throughout the summer. Ohio's oldest reservoir, built in 1845, it also offers bullhead, yellow perch, and some largemouth bass.

Paint Creek and Rocky Fork Lakes are a stone's throw from one another. Respectively 1,190 and 2,080 acres, they have slightly different complexions. Paint Creek is noted for its saugeye, largemouth bass, crappie, and channel and flathead catfish. Rocky Fork features muskie and channel catfish, with a taste of walleye, largemouth bass, and crappie.

Northwest region. Charles Mill Lake draws springtime anglers for its crappie and saugeye. This shallow, marshy 1,359-acre lake also provides channel and flathead catfish in the summer.

Clear Fork Lake is an excellent muskie reservoir and provides muskie eggs for Ohio stocking programs. The 1,000-acre lake also has good largemouth bass and crappie fishing.

Pleasant Hill Lake's spring crappie and summer saugeye fishing are high points; the tailwaters are a saugeye hotspot winter. Weekend boaters fill the 850-acre lake, which also has good crappie, largemouth and smallmouth bass, and channel catfish populations.

Northeast region. Atwood Lake's saugeye have slowly become the fish of choice. This 1,540-acre lake was once known only for its sailboat races. The good largemouth bass fishing is usually overlooked, and spring anglers can score on crappie.

Berlin Lake's smallmouth bass, crappie, and white bass have long been favorites, making spring a prime time to visit its 3,590 acres. Walleye are caught in good numbers, as are a few muskies.

Clendening Lake is a rural 1,800-acre lake with little shoreline development and numerous largemouth bass. Rated Ohio's best little lake for bass, perhaps due to its 10-horsepower motor limit, Clendening also has good fishing for saugeye.

A stone's throw from Cleveland, LaDue Lake covers 1,500 acres and allows only electric motors. This restriction makes it tougher to cruise the ample shorelines for the big bass that live here. Big channel catfish, some walleye, and little perch are also caught.

Leesville Lake's muskies thrive along its long and narrow 1,000 acres, and catch rates are high. With a 10-horsepower motor limit, the lake is conducive to trolling the extensive weedbeds. The bass fishing is also top-notch, and crappie are a spring treat.

After Milton Lake's dam was renovated, the 1,685-acre lake became known once again for its trophy muskies. This time around, crappie and largemouth bass numbers have improved, and walleye are also present.

Lake Mogadore has fast-growing redear sunfish among its 1,000 acres, where only electric motors can be used. The best fishing is actually for bullhead, but some nice largemouth bass are caught each summer.

Mosquito Lake walleye anglers can get bit by the Mosquito walleye bug, with huge stockings of walleye fry helping to maintain bountiful schools of fish in the face of heavy fishing pressure. Largemouth bass and crappie are also favored, and some northern pike are caught each year.

Pymatuning Lake is Ohio's largest inland lake, if you count Pennsylvania's share of this 14,650-acre border reservoir. With outstanding walleye fishing and lots of crappie, smallmouth bass, and largemouth bass, Pymatuning is protected by a 10-horsepower motor limit. It was once Ohio's best lake for trophy muskies.

Tappan Lake's 2,350-acres experience light fishing pressure, although excellent numbers of channel catfish and good fishing for saugeye and largemouth bass are available.

West Branch Lake's muskie fishing has peaks and valleys, but when it peaks, the muskie catches are spectacular. A few large striped bass are caught here every summer along the dam, and some largemouth bass inhabit the bays and coves and linger along main-lake weedbeds.

Southeastern region. Dillon Lake is a rural 1,330-acre lake that has surprising numbers of channel catfish, largemouth bass, and saugeye.

Piedmont Lake is a clear, 2,270-acre lake with a 10-horsepower motor limit. It has some of Ohio's biggest muskies and owns the state mark for that species. Walleye schools are thinning, whereas saugeye are on the upswing. The good largemouth and smallmouth bass fishing is one of the lake's big secrets. In summer, plenty of channel catfish are caught after the sun goes down.

Salt Fork Lake was known for largemouth and smallmouth bass, but the spotlight has turned to muskies. Walleye and channel catfish are available in good to outstanding numbers.

Seneca Lake has been a mainstay for channel catfish and largemouth bass, and anglers often hook a few walleye on this 3,550-acre lake. Striped bass are a rare treat.

Small Lakes

For big largemouth bass, Knox Lake's 495 acres and 12 miles of shoreline in central Ohio can't be beat, thanks to length limits and a 10-horsepower motor limit. Just north of Lancaster, Rush Lake also features largemouth bass and 10-horsepower motors.

In northeastern Ohio, Highlandtown Lake is managed for trophy bluegills and allows only electric motors. The Portage Lakes around Akron get lots of pressure, with Nimisila Lake's largemouth bass fishing a bonus. Punderson Lake, east of Cleveland, is stocked with trout and plenty of bluegills. Spencer Lake, south of Lorain, has 78 acres of bluegills, bass, and catfish.

Southwestern Ohio's East Fork Lake has 2,160 acres of water and numerous hybrid bass, crappie, channel catfish, and largemouth and spotted bass.

Jackson Lake in southeastern Ohio is a narrow, winding largemouth bass haven, where anglers with electric motors can hook a trophy fish. Nearby Jackson City Reservoir also has lots of largemouth bass, some redear sunfish, and stockings of trout and saugeye. Southeastern Ohio channel catfish waters include small Lake Logan, smaller Monroe Lake, and Lake Rupert, which is also a 325-acre sleeper for bass, bluegills, walleye, and saugeye. Tycoon Lake allows only electric motors and has plenty of bass and catfish.

Kiser Lake, north of Dayton, prohibits all motors on its 396 acres, but anglers catch many bluegills there. The top bluegill fishing hole in Ohio is the Lake La Su An Wildlife Area in northwestern Ohio, near Toledo; permits are needed to fish this series of lakes and ponds, where bluegills grow to surprising size.

 One out of five Americans age 16 and older fish and/or hunt in the United States and create a total nationwide economic impact of $106.1 billion.

OKLAHOMA

To those unfamiliar with the Sooner State, Oklahoma is often stereotyped as a dry, desolate landscape of oil wells and flat grassland. The real Oklahoma, though, offers anglers more surface acres of freshwater to fish in than every state in the nation—except its southerly neighbor, Texas—and more miles of shoreline than the Gulf of Mexico and Atlantic coast combined.

Almost 5,000 lakes and a quarter-million farm ponds beckon anglers in this state. All together, Oklahoma offers more than a million acres of fishable water in lakes and ponds. Largemouth bass, reservoir-strain smallmouth bass, and spotted bass all inhabit Oklahoma's many lakes, as do walleye, saugeye, striped bass, hybrid striped bass, channel catfish, blue catfish, flathead catfish, black crappie, white crappie, white bass, and a variety of sunfish species.

Stream fishing opportunities also abound; some 25,000 miles of streams and rivers cross Oklahoma's diverse landscape. Although stream and river fishing are available throughout the state, the eastern half of Oklahoma contains the most popular clearwater streams. These cool flows offer excellent smallmouth bass angling, and two even provide year-round fishing for brown and rainbow trout.

Lake Texoma

Undoubtedly Oklahoma's most productive fishery, Lake Texoma sprawls along the Oklahoma-Texas border, creating an 88,000-acre angling paradise, one that boasts some 300 fishing guides. Nationally recognized as a top inland striped bass location, Texoma's clear waters have supported a self-sustaining striper population that has numbered in the millions for more than 20 years.

Although the lake was built in the early 1940s, it remains particularly productive and fertile, primarily due to naturally occurring salt deposits that flow from the western reaches of the Red River into the lake. The salt binds with clay particles, thereby taking the clay out of suspension and leaving the lake's water clear.

Striped bass get top billing at Lake Texoma. The hottest striper fishing takes place during fall and winter, when large schools of fish actively chase shad. Locating stripers at this time of year is fairly easy; just look for large schools of sea gulls diving into the water. The birds feast on injured shad driven to the surface by voraciously feeding stripers.

Once the fish have been located, catching them usually isn't hard. Slab spoons—1- to 3-ounce chunks of lead with a hook attached—are lowered into the depths and pulled in an upward motion. Crankbaits and soft-bodied paddle-tailed jigs are also effective.

The most reliable fishing occurs during the summer months, when stripers are taken in most parts of the lake using a vast array of tactics. Trolling is a common technique, and flatline trolling with crankbaits and plugs regularly takes large numbers

A striped bass is landed on Lake Texoma.

of fish holding in 10 to 30 feet of water. Downriggers are used to catch stripers that suspend in deep water off points and creek channels.

Summer also offers the most exciting topwater action of the year, when stripers often break the surface, particularly on calm days. Popping plugs are local favorites, but anything that splashes on the surface is apt to draw a bone-jarring strike.

Live shad are particularly effective baits, regardless of season. Many anglers use a cast net to catch shad for baits, but it can be difficult to locate shad at times. Special holding tanks are required to keep these baitfish lively.

Texoma stripers typically run between 12 and 22 inches, although fish up to 15 pounds are not uncommon. Trophy fishing opportunities are available in the Red River, immediately below the dam. During periods of heavy water releases, stripers up to 40 pounds move up below the dam to feed on stunned baitfish that have gone through the dam's turbines. Free-lining live baits is an effective tactic, but many large fish are caught on jigs and topwater plugs.

While Texoma's great striper fishing draws the most attention from anglers, excellent smallmouth bass fishing is also available. The lake produced three straight state-record smallmouths, and fish in the 5- to 7-pound class are not out of the question.

February through March are prime months for catching big smallmouths, although good action also can be had from late spring through early summer. Smallmouths congregate on the lake's many rocky points, and the top fishing locations offer deep water close to shore.

Jigs tipped with either soft-bodied crayfish or pork chunks are excellent smallmouth producers. Spinnerbaits and crankbaits are also good bait choices. Because of the lake's relatively clear water, light line (4- to 8-pound test) is recommended.

Catfish anglers also call Texoma one of the state's best. Blue and channel catfish are numerous here, and anglers employ diverse tactics to land them. Drifting with live or cut shad, a method favored by striper anglers, is dynamite for catching both channels and blues. Drift anglers usually concentrate on flats—the mid-depth areas between the shoreline and deeper creek channels. Platter Flats, Willafa Wood, and Willow Springs are favorite areas to drift for catfish.

For those who prefer a more relaxed style of fishing, Texoma offers excellent jug fishing and trotlining. A state-record 116-pound blue catfish was taken at Texoma by a jug angler, and trotliners usually report heavy catches for both channel and blue catfish. Cut or whole shad are standard bait choices for channels, whereas anglers concentrating on blue catfish favor live shad or live sunfish.

Texoma is also known for good crappie and largemouth bass fishing. Crappie enter shallow water to spawn in late March and early April. Anglers who dabble small jigs or soak live minnows in and around shoreline cover do well then. Largemouth anglers do well fishing in and around flooded cover in spring. Spinnerbaits, jigs, and plastic worms are productive lures.

Lake Eufaula

Often called Oklahoma's gentle giant, Lake Eufaula covers more than 105,000 acres of the state's east-central landscape. A relatively shallow, murky water lake, Eufaula offers a little of everything in the way of fishing opportunities.

Known throughout the state for its excellent springtime crappie fishing, Eufaula each year produces hundreds of catches of slab-size crappie weighing between 2 and 3 pounds each. Crappie action usually heats up first on the southern portion of the lake, and the fishing peaks in April. As the lake warms, fishing in the northern half of the lake improves, usually a few weeks after it turns on in the southern half.

Wading and fishing from float tubes or belly boats are two of the most common tactics at Eufaula. Although much of the lake's standing timber has disappeared, enough woody cover remains to provide constant targets for spring crappie anglers. Cane pole fishing with either live minnows or crappie jigs is a local tradition, one that's hard to beat. Regardless what equipment is used, anglers who concentrate on timber in 2 to 5 feet of water consistently report the best catches.

Eufaula is also a top catfishing destination. Trotline users and jug anglers do well from spring through fall, and drifting is a popular technique during the winter months. Those using trotlines usually concentrate on coves, whereas jug users usually target flats in 10 to 20 feet of water and main-lake points. Whole or cut shad are popular bait choices for both trotlines and juglines.

Drift fishing with live or cut shad is particularly productive during the dead of winter. Deeper water in the main body of the lake yields the best wintertime catches. Old creek channels and flats near creek channels are top midlake areas.

Another popular catfishing technique involves probing nooks and crannies along riprap during the early-summer spawning period. Catfish are cavity nesters that make spawning nests in rocks in shallow water. Big cats are extremely territorial, so dropping a bait in front of them is sure to draw a voracious strike. Shrimp, shad, live sunfish, and nightcrawlers are standard baits for catching spawning catfish.

In summer, Eufaula produces good white bass action. Large schools of sand bass, or sandies as they are called locally, can be seen surfacing from July through September. The fish are actually chasing shad, and any lure thrown in the middle of the slashing, splashing melee will usually result in an immediate strike. In-line spinners, slab spoons, topwater plugs, and crankbaits are all productive for catching sand bass from surfacing schools. Once the fish retreat to deeper water, surface activity decreases, and then trolling with crankbaits becomes productive.

The lake is also home to a rapidly developing smallmouth bass fishery. First stocked in the early 1990s, smallmouth bass took hold in the lake's rocky, clear-water areas, and natural spawning has been documented. Porum Landing and the Number Nine area are the best spots for smallmouth fishing, and plastic crayfish, jig-and-pork combos, and crankbaits are favored offerings.

Eufaula also has good largemouth bass fishing, and the lake holds some walleye. Largemouth bass anglers often concentrate on woody cover and flooded bushes, particularly in the spring and early summer. Main-lake points and dropoffs are good areas for largemouth later in the year. Walleye hold in some of the same places as smallmouth bass. Live worms and minnows fished on jigs are good walleye fare, as is an assortment of crankbaits.

Northeast

Grand Lake O' the Cherokees. One of Oklahoma's crown jewels, Grand Lake offers 46,500 acres of diverse fishing opportunities. More than 10,000 square miles of Ozark Mountain foothills drains into Grand Lake, and the Neosho and Spring Rivers provide significant inflows at the lake's north end. Largemouth bass, spotted bass, crappie, and white bass are abundant at Grand Lake, which is known not only for producing large numbers of fish, but also for yielding many trophy bass and crappie each year.

Spring (April through June) finds both bass and crappie in shallower water. Bass anglers do well fishing with spinnerbaits, jigs, and topwater lures at this time. Flooded willow bushes, grass, and timber are top springtime bass-holding locations, and these areas also attract spawning crappie.

The lake is widely known for excellent nighttime bass fishing during the heat of summer. July and August are top months for night fishing. Plastic worms, spinnerbaits, and surface lures are top local

O

offerings. Boat docks, which are plentiful on the big lake, provide excellent structure during the summer.

Live minnows and small jigs are tops for spring-time crappie fishing. Specimens up to 3 pounds are reported each spring, but fish in the 10- to 14-inch range are most common. Winter angling for crappie is also popular at Grand Lake, where heated fishing docks draw many anglers from December through February.

The Neosho River above Grand Lake is home to a nationally famous paddlefish run each April. Fish up to 140 pounds have been taken during the spawning season. Grand Lake also contains good populations of catfish, walleye, and white bass.

Sooner Lake. This unique lake is home to a power-generating station that keeps the lake's waters relatively warm year-round. During winter, warmwater discharges concentrate baitfish, and large numbers of largemouth bass and hybrid striped bass enter the discharge canal to feed heavily. Trophy hybrids in the 12- to 15-pound range are a real possibility at Sooner Lake, especially during December and January.

Live minnows, topwater plugs, and large jigs catch both largemouth bass and hybrid striped bass here. In addition to fishing the discharge area, local experts ply deep-water areas near the dam, and underwater islands in the main lake.

Sooner also produces good action for crappie, white bass, and catfish, although these species are not as popular as largemouths and hybrid stripers.

Lake Tenkiller. A deep, clear-water impoundment, Lake Tenkiller offers fishing for all three types of black bass species: largemouth, smallmouth, and spotted bass. Largemouth and spotted bass are far more common than smallmouth bass, and night-time fishing is often necessary during the summer months due to the lake's extremely clear water. Boat docks, deep-water points, and rocky structure are key black bass locations.

Although not widely known, Tenkiller offers good sunfishing, particularly for bluegills. May and June are top months for catching spawning panfish, with live worms, crickets, and small jigs among the top bait choices. White bass are also abundant at Tenkiller. Trolling small crankbaits and casting small spinners to surfacing schools are two popular techniques.

Below the lake's dam, the lower Illinois River offers year-round rainbow and trophy brown trout fishing. Almost eight miles of trout stream are found below Tenkiller, and wintertime and early spring are most productive for trout anglers. Artificial and prepared trout baits like salmon eggs are popular with anglers, as are small spinners and spoons. Light line (2- through 6-pound test) is recommended for these finicky fish.

The section of the lower Illinois that contains trout, and the 2 miles of river below the trout area, is widely regarded as the state's number one trophy striped bass resource. Anglers have landed stripers nearing the 50-pound mark, and numerous 20- and 30-pounders are taken from this coldwater fishery each year.

Summer is the best time to pursue these tackle-busting monsters. The cold water of the lower Illinois River is a refuge for big stripers, drawing fish from the Arkansas River and Robert S. Kerr Lake. Both live bait fishing and casting artificials are productive, but drifting, trolling, or anchoring and then fishing with live shad or trout is by far the best technique. Standard bass tackle can be used, but strong line in the 15- to 25-pound class is a must.

Northwest

Canton Lake. One of Oklahoma's premier fishing destinations, Canton is a walleye mecca, both in total numbers of fish caught and numbers of trophy fish (6 to 10 pounds) taken. Spring and summer find Canton's walleye most cooperative; April through June are excellent months, and anglers employ a variety of fishing methods.

Trolling is a popular technique for covering large expanses of water to locate active fish. Mid-diving crankbaits are good lure choices. Drifting with bottom rigs, weight-forward spinners, and live bait also yields good results. Weedy bays provide good cover and forage for walleye, but fish also congregate on midlake underwater islands and creek channels.

Although walleye are Canton's claim to fame, the lake also hosts incredibly hard-fighting hybrid striped bass. Anglers can catch hybrids by using the same techniques as those employed to catch walleye, and hybrids are even found in many of the same locations as walleye. In addition, hybrid striped bass tend to school around the many small islands along the lake's northwestern shore. Drifting and trolling live sunfish, crayfish, or large minnows are good tactics for catching big hybrids in the 5- to 15-pound range.

White bass and crappie are frequently taken incidentally when anglers troll crankbaits or drift live minnows. Both species are quite common at Canton, but angling pressure is focused on walleye and hybrid striped bass.

Lake Carl Etling. Located in Black Mesa State Park in Cimarron County in the Oklahoma panhandle, Lake Carl Etling offers incredible angling diversity in its 160 acres. Walleye, hybrid striped bass, and white bass are key species of interest. Rainbow trout fishing is available in the winter months (November through April).

Both bank and boat fishing opportunities are available, and excellent primitive camping facilities are located within the state park. Live minnows and worms are good choices for trout, walleye, and hybrid striped bass. Crankbaits and stickbaits are effective for walleye and hybrids, and they will also produce white bass.

Great Salt Plains Lake. Characterized as a shallow, windswept lake, Great Salt Plains offers good fishing for saugeye and channel catfish.

It has been calculated that a stream trout can swim up to 102 inches per second, but you shouldn't try to fish a lure or fly at anything approaching that speed.

Saugeye anglers mainly rely on shallow-running crankbaits and jigs tipped with minnows or nightcrawlers. The spillway, located below the dam, is a great spot for these tasty fish.

Top catfishing techniques include jug fishing and trotlining. Whole, cut, or fresh shad are top baits for these activities. For those who prefer drifting, dragging nightcrawlers or stinkbait on the bottom is a popular technique.

In addition to catfish and saugeye, the lake also offers fishing for hybrid striped bass and white bass. Jigs, crankbaits, and spinners are recommended for catching these species.

Southwest

Altus Lugert Reservoir. At 6,200 acres, Altus Lugert is one of southwest Oklahoma's bigger lakes. Walleye, hybrid striped bass, white bass, and largemouth bass are all abundant at Altus Lugert.

Anglers regularly have excellent success fishing the east side of the lake when the wind has been blowing from the west, and their results speak loudly. State-record hybrid striped bass and walleye both were taken by anglers fishing from the bank at Altus Lugert.

Midlake humps and underwater islands are key locations for those fishing from boats. Trolling is an excellent method for locating these structures. Once identified, vertical jigging and live bait fishing can be employed to fish these areas.

Summer action for white bass and hybrid striped bass is good, whereas walleye bite best from fall through spring. The top seasons for catfish are spring and fall. Jug fishing and trotlining opportunities are good, but catfish are also taken from the bank with live baits or stinkbaits.

The North Fork of the Red River, located below the dam, offers rainbow trout fishing during the winter months (November through March). Prepared baits, small jigs, and in-line spinners are standard trout fare.

Ft. Cobb Reservoir. Known as an excellent lake for bowfishing, Ft. Cobb also offers good opportunities for white bass, largemouth bass, walleye, catfish, and hybrid striped bass. Running primarily north and south, Ft. Cobb offers white bass, walleye, and hybrid anglers a wide variety of potential hotspots from late April through June. Trolling around points is a popular approach to catching fish, as is casting or drifting live baits around the large island on the lake's west side.

A common method for catching various species at Ft. Cobb is to cast from the dam, located on the lake's south end. After successive days with a north wind, baitfish will be pushed toward the dam, with hungry white bass, walleye, and hybrid striped bass following closely along behind. Soft-bodied fish-imitating jigs are extremely effective, but heavier jigs are usually necessary for long casts out from the dam.

Catfish anglers find that a variety of tactics work at Ft. Cobb, including bank fishing, trotlining, and jug fishing. For largemouth bass, May and June are good months, and plastic worms, topwater lures, and spinnerbaits usually produce good results.

Southeast

Konawa Lake. Known for its high fertility and productivity, Konawa is a premier trophy largemouth bass lake that is affected by a power plant. Due to warmwater discharges, December, January, and February are the best months to fish here. Plastic worms and lizards, crankbaits, jigs, and live minnows are effective baits on Konawa.

Hybrid striped bass and white bass also thrive in good numbers on this lake. Trolling and casting crankbaits or spoons are effective approaches to catching these species. Riprap along the dam, the discharge canal, and main-lake submerged roadbeds are prime fishing locations.

McGee Creek Reservoir. Situated in the scenic mountains of southeast Oklahoma, McGee Creek is an excellent bass lake, although naturally high levels of mercury have caused consumption advisories to be placed on larger bass. Bigger fish are generally taken in March and April, but summer produces the fastest action from surfacing schools of bass in the 1- to 3-pound class.

McGee Creek also contains good populations of spotted bass, and smallmouths have been introduced. The lake offers good channel catfishing, and crappie cause excitement during the spring spawning season (April and May).

Murray Lake. A deeper, clear-water lake, Murray is an exceptional smallmouth bass fishery. It contains good populations of largemouth bass as well, offering fish weighing up to $13\frac{1}{2}$ pounds. April through June is prime for black bass action. Rocky shorelines and submerged timber attract bass during spring. Soft-plastic baits, spinnerbaits, and jigs are standard bass catchers.

Murray offers good catfishing, too. Because of its clear water, drifting live bait is a good way to catch channel cats at Murray; live minnows, cut baits, and nightcrawlers work well for this.

White bass and crappie are in abundance at Murray, although bass and catfish are the primary angling targets.

Oklahoma City—Metro Area

Thunderbird. A murky water lake close to the Oklahoma City metropolitan area, Thunderbird happens to be one of the most productive reservoirs in Oklahoma. It hosts an outstanding saugeye fishery, with good numbers of large saugeye (3 to 6 pounds) taken each year. Live minnows, jigs tipped with minnows or nightcrawlers, and crankbaits are good saugeye medicine.

Winter is the best time to fish for this species, and fall and early spring also offer good angling. Main-lake points, sunken brush rows, and dropoffs are ideal places to prospect for saugeye.

Excellent channel and flathead catfish are another mainstay at Thunderbird. The lake favors trotlines and juglines, but many catfish are caught each year by bank anglers.

Crappie populations are high, with late April through early June being most conducive to catching large numbers of shallow-water crappie. Flooded brush, sunken brushpiles, and shallow coves usually contain spawning crappie during these times. Small tube jigs and live minnows are local favorites for these panfish.

Rivers

Arkansas River. From Kaw Lake to Webbers Falls Reservoir, the Arkansas River offers multiple angling opportunities ranging from striped bass fishing to limblining for catfish. The river is subject to varying flows depending on rainfall and lake releases. Anglers achieve the best success by searching for deeper pools filled with submerged rocks and timber.

Live minnows will take a variety of species, including flathead catfish, striped bass, white bass, and largemouth bass. Live worms and cut shad are good choices for channel catfish.

Because access to the river is mostly over private land, anglers must gain permission to fish from the banks. Boat anglers can travel the river by putting in at boat ramps scattered along the river.

Lower Mountain Fork River. Towering pines and submerged bald cypress trees mix along the lower Mountain Fork River to form spectacular scenery. Running from Broken Bow Lake to the Little River, the lower Mountain Fork is most noted for year-round rainbow and brown trout fishing.

Opportunities exist for both fast action and trophy specimens. Catfish and largemouth bass inhabit some stretches of the river, and white bass are available during the spring spawning season.

OLIGOTROPHIC

Low nutrient levels; an absence of nutrients. An oligotrophic lake is one that is young and deep-sided, with clear waters and a rocky or sandy bottom. It is usually located in areas where the surrounding substrate is rocky and where soils are limited and generally infertile. Both planktonic and rooted plant growth are sparse; thermal stratification is usually pronounced in the summer, and there is abundant oxygen at deeper levels. Oligotrophic lakes support such coldwater fisheries as trout, salmon, charr, and cisco.

See: **Eutrophic; Mesotrophic.**

ONSHORE

Waters abutting a coastline. This word is also used synonymously with ashore, meaning physically on the land adjacent to water, but is even more specific than nearshore (*see*). It is not the opposite of offshore (*see*) in common angling usage.

ONTARIO

Few localities in the world can match Ontario, Canada's second largest province, in diversity and quality of freshwater fisheries. About one-sixth of Ontario's 413,000 square miles is water, including 34,000 square miles alone in its share of four of the Great Lakes. In a typical year, Ontario caters to roughly 2.5 million anglers of all ages, including residents and nonresidents, and its angling opportunities are unlimited.

Ontario has 250,000 lakes and countless waterways spread over distances of 1,050 miles from east to west, and 1,075 miles from south to north—an area almost the size of Texas and California combined. Fishing destinations vary in size from 350-mile-long Lake Superior, which demands the sturdiest of boats; to peaceful cottage lakes that can be fished by canoe; to powerful rivers such as the Niagara, St. Lawrence, and Ottawa, which challenge even the most experienced anglers; to small trout streams that can be crossed in chest waders.

Ontario's fishing country is as varied as the many species found within its boundaries. Southern areas bordering the Great Lakes are characterized by extensive agricultural lands and urban development. The heavily forested, rocky terrain of the Canadian Shield spans the middle of the province, an area that has become prime cottage country and a scenic fishing haven. To the north, the flat bogs, small spruce, aspen, poplar, birch, and balsam fir trees, and complex river systems of the Hudson Bay Lowlands beckon anglers seeking true wilderness adventure.

Of the 158 species of fish found in the province, about two dozen are of special interest to anglers. Walleye (known as pickerel here), yellow perch, lake trout, brook trout, steelhead, rainbow trout, brown trout, smallmouth bass, northern pike, muskellunge, largemouth bass, coho salmon, and chinook salmon are the predominant fish, although trout, pike, perch, and walleye probably draw the most attention province-wide.

Southwest Ontario

Lake Erie. Lake Erie, once proclaimed a virtually dead fishery because of pollution, has made a remarkable comeback. Although it is the shallowest of the Great Lakes with an average depth of 62 feet, Lake Erie supports a variety of both warm- and coldwater species.

In a typical year, data from the Ministry of Natural Resources (MNR) show that more than a half million sportfish are caught in Ontario's 4,783 square miles of the lake (the equivalent of 48 percent of the lake's total area). Walleye, smallmouth bass, yellow perch, and freshwater drum make up 70 percent of the catch. Unlike anglers from bordering states, Ontario anglers share the fisheries resource with commercial interests, which account for an additional 20 to 40 million pounds of various species, nearly half of which are rainbow smelt.

The prime sportfishing target is walleye, which average 5 to 7 pounds, but 9- to 12-pounders are not uncommon. In western Lake Erie—from Holiday Beach, near the mouth of the Detroit River, eastward to Leamington—in May and early June, walleye are taken by anglers trolling, drift fishing, or casting weight-forward spinners armed with a minnow or worm. As summer progresses, the fish move toward the deeper middle and eastern sections of the lake.

Pelee Island, 14 miles off Kingsville, is an early season walleye favorite. It is also a prime spot for smallmouth bass, some up to 4 pounds, which hang out over rock, rubble, and gravel bottoms. The best smallmouth opportunities are in late June, September, and October; in midsummer they often suspend in deeper waters. Anglers in large boats can make the run across the open lake to the island; those with smaller craft cross on the ferry.

Walleye and yellow perch are favorite catches from piers and near shore in the central and western parts of Lake Erie in May and June. As the water warms in July and August, anglers may have to venture out 10 miles or more to 100-foot depths to find walleye that suspend while feeding on baitfish; departure points for this trip include Port Burwell, Port Dover, Port Maintland, and Port Colbourne.

Zebra mussels have made the pursuit of walleye throughout Lake Erie somewhat more difficult by dramatically increasing the water clarity. Anglers have been forced to travel farther and farther offshore as the walleye move deeper to find their preferred light levels. The long-term impact of these exotic bivalves on fish populations and on fish size is uncertain.

Steelhead, Pacific salmon, and lake trout are also popular in Lake Erie. In the spring, steelhead ascend the creeks and small streams that notch the clay bluffs so predominant along Ontario's Lake Erie shoreline, but receive less attention from anglers than they do in Lake Ontario or Lake Huron because of the primary interest in walleye and yellow perch. The most significant runs are in the eastern portion of the lake on Big Otter Creek at Port Burwell, Big Creek at Long Point, and Young Creek near Simcoe. In the summer, these fish roam the deeper portions of the lake and return to nearshore waters in the fall for pre-spawn staging.

Angling for salmon and trout in July and August calls for locating fish and trolling minnow-imitating plugs and spoons via downriggers, sideplaners, and flatlines. From late August into the fall, salmon move closer to shore off the mouths of the numerous larger creeks found along the central and western portions of the lake from Erie to the Niagara River.

The inner bay at Long Point, bordered by the Big Creek and Turkey Point marshes, provides the best inshore fishery along the lake. The shallow, weedy waters are a haven for walleye, smallmouth bass, largemouth bass, northern pike, sheepshead, and a variety of panfish (yellow perch, crappie, and catfish). Within sight to the east is the Nanticoke Generating Station, which attracts the largest spring run of white bass along Erie's north shore.

The fast currents at the mouth of the Niagara River at Fort Erie hold ample feed for a mixed bag of sportfish and keep the water ice free so keen anglers can fish most of the year. Depending on the season, catches from shore or from small boats in the vicinity of the Peace Bridge can include walleye, smallmouth bass, yellow perch, rainbow trout, brown trout, chinook salmon, and coho salmon.

Grand River. The Grand River at Port Maintland is the only significant river on Lake Erie's north coast. The 175-mile-long Grand flows through southern Ontario's heartland of farms, cities, marshes, Carolinian forest, deep valleys, and cliffs. It is the first nonwilderness river to be designated as a Canadian Heritage River and has an excellent fishery to match.

Walleye, rainbow trout, and white bass run as far as 20 miles upstream to the Caledonia Dam during spring spawning. Largemouth and smallmouth bass, northern pike, and panfish are also found throughout the river below Kitchener. There are 15 miles of classic brown trout water on the Grand's upper reaches between Inverhaugh and Belwood Lake. Browns here, which average 15 to 22 inches but can reach 30 inches, are a delight for fly anglers, and special regulations have been adopted to promote catch-and-release.

Lake St. Clair. Ontario possesses two-thirds of heart-shaped Lake St. Clair, which measures 35 miles by 26 miles and has an average depth of 11 feet. It remains a productive and important recreational fishery despite significant ecological changes over recent decades. These were caused by such things as chemical pollution, population explosions of white perch and gobies, and the appearance of zebra mussels.

The clearer water caused by the filtering action of the zebras has resulted in expansive areas of new weed growth that have befuddled walleye anglers using traditional methods. But sight feeders, such as smallmouth bass, yellow perch, and muskellunge, seem to have benefited from the improved visibility.

In May, anglers intercept post-spawn walleye moving away from the Thames and Ruscom Rivers along the southern shore. As the water warms, anglers have to adapt to fishing in the weeds or go 3 or 4 miles offshore to find clear bottoms for trolling crankbaits or drifting live baits.

Mitchell's Bay is a top panfish and smallmouth bass area, with plentiful largemouth bass in and around the 63 square miles of the Walpole Island marshes. A special license is available from the native community to fish the island's maze of channels and backwaters.

Lake St. Clair has a strong muskellunge population, which benefits from abundant forage found in the vast shallows and from a relatively long growing

Placoderms, which were primitive jawed fishes existing 420–355 million years ago, were generally torpedo shaped with bony plates that formed head and trunk shields.

season. Trolling spoons and large plugs in 12 to 15 feet of water from late September to November is the best tactic for boating fish that average 15 to 20 pounds but could reach 30 pounds. Muskies inhabit the southern shore from the Thames River westward to Belle Island at the mouth of the Detroit River, and range to the northeast in Mitchell's Bay and St. Luke's Bay.

The seasonal walleye patterns in the nearby Detroit and St. Clair Rivers are somewhat similar. This includes a spring run of migrating mature fish returning to Lake Erie or Lake Huron after spawning in the Thames River, and a resident summer population of smaller fish. Clear water and heavy boat traffic call for trolling near bottom with minnow-imitating plugs at night.

Steelhead, brown trout, and chinook and coho salmon are also in the St. Clair River in the spring, from the warmwater discharge at the Port Lambton Power Plant north to Sarnia.

Lower Lake Huron. In spring and early summer, steelhead and chinook salmon are the predominant fish along the sandy shores of lower Lake Huron, from Sarnia north to Southampton. Steelhead have been in Lake Huron since 1904, having been introduced by the U.S. Fish Commission in Lake Superior in 1895. Annual stocking supplements natural reproduction in such rivers as the Maitland, Bayfield, Lucknow, Sauble, and Saugeen. Chinook, first planted in Lake Huron by Michigan in the late 1960s and later by the

An angler fishes the shoreline of a Georgian Bay fjord for smallmouth bass.

MNR and volunteer fishing clubs, have been the catalyst for popular salmon derbies along lower Lake Huron and southern Georgian Bay.

The Saugeen River at Southampton is one of Ontario's best-known steelhead waters. Here, anglers can wade and drift spawn bags in the fast water below the Denny's Dam lamprey control barrier, or troll from small boats downstream for 3 miles to Lake Huron. Steelhead enter the river in April and May and again in October and November. In summer, walleye, channel catfish, and stray Skamania-strain steelies from Michigan plantings attract anglers who don't have the boats or equipment to pursue salmon and trout in the deep offshore waters. In the fall, chinook and brown trout add variety to river fishing.

Above Denny's Dam, rainbow and chinook move upstream as far as 30 miles to Paisley and Walkerton in the spring and fall, respectively. The Upper Saugeen, as it twists and bends through farmland, also holds resident smallmouth bass, northern pike, and muskellunge.

Bruce Peninsula and Southern Georgian Bay. Virtually all of the agricultural watersheds along the southern shore of Georgian Bay support migratory steelhead populations. Heavy stocking has created opportunities for chinook, brown trout, lake trout, and splake offshore.

The city of Owen Sound is a focal point for fishing the nearby Georgian Bay waters of Owen Sound, Colpoys Bay to the north, and the numerous nearby rivers that flow into Georgian Bay to the east. These include such legendary steelhead waters as the Pottawatomi and Sydenham Rivers at Owen Sound, the Bighead River at Meaford (with 80 miles of fishing), the Beaver at Thornbury, and the Nottawasaga at Wasaga Beach.

The Nottawasaga—along with such tributaries as the Pine, Boyle, and Mad—is the largest river system flowing into Georgian Bay and has more than 400 miles of pools and riffles open to steelhead. A 29-pound, 2-ounce Ontario record steelhead was caught off its mouth. Although best known for rainbow and walleye, the Nottawasaga also harbors browns, chinook, northern pike, smallmouth and largemouth bass, and a variety of coarse fish.

Although whitefish are often thought of as a commercial species, Colpoys Bay near Wiarton has produced some whoppers for recreational anglers over the years. In 1996, the Ontario record of 14 pounds, 12 ounces was caught in the bay through the ice.

South-Central Ontario

Niagara River. The mighty 27-mile-long Niagara River is best known as the site of the famous Niagara Falls and as a place for honeymooners and daredevils, but with all of Lake Erie's water—with the exception of what flows through the Welland Canal, exiting here and entering Lake Ontario—there is much to attract a smorgasbord of species.

The Upper Niagara River from Fort Erie to Grand Island has smallmouth bass and walleye throughout the summer, and the channels in and around the smaller islands offer good trolling opportunities for muskellunge. The muskellunge fishery is unheralded but highly commendable. This is a clear-water trolling fishery that produces 25- to 40-pound fish for dedicated anglers.

Steelhead and brown trout, and the occasional salmon, move into the upper river from Lake Erie in the fall. Ontario's long-standing and somewhat controversial 22-pound, 4-ounce record walleye came from the Fort Erie end of the Niagara River in 1943.

The Lower Niagara River (that section below Niagara Falls) is not for the faint-hearted or ill-prepared. It can be dangerous water, with daily fluctuations in levels caused by upstream power-generating stations. Fishing by boat is possible from Niagara-on-the-Lake up about 8 miles to the Devil's Hole pool near Queenston, although the upper reaches are turbulent and demand sturdy craft and capable boat handling.

Anglers on foot have access to the swirling water in the river's pools from the Niagara River Parkway. Above Queenston, this means a long hike down steep man-made trails carved into the rugged Niagara Gorge.

In winter and throughout spring, steelhead move into the Lower Niagara from Lake Ontario and are found as far upstream as the Niagara Whirlpool. Anglers land lake trout at the mouth of the river in early spring. In summer, yellow perch, silver bass, walleye, and smallmouth bass are the predominant catches for both boat and shore anglers from Niagara-on-the-Lake to the vicinity of Queenston. Walleye are plentiful here, including some in the 6- to 8-pound class, as are smallmouth bass. From August through October, chinook salmon are the main attraction, but coho, lake trout, and browns are available as well.

Western and central Lake Ontario. The recreational and economic spinoffs of massive plantings of salmon and trout have benefited the heavily populated northern side of 193-mile-long Lake Ontario more than any of the province's other waters on the Great Lakes. Although stocking levels have fluctuated, especially through the 1990s, and the species mix has varied, salmon and trout continue to be important and prominent in this region. Introduced species of chinook salmon, coho salmon, and steelhead are especially popular; and the native lake trout are not only popular, they are also being revitalized. Biologists have planted Atlantic salmon, once native to Lake Ontario, in an effort to reestablish this species with a self-sustaining population, but they are so far largely incidental to the other fish. Nevertheless, specimens to 24 pounds have been recorded.

The earliest salmonid angling action occurs in the western end of Lake Ontario in late April and May from the mouth of the Niagara River west to St. Catharines and Burlington primarily from downrigger- and sideplaner-equipped boats out of such places as Niagara-on-the-Lake, Port Weller, Port Dalhousie, and Grimsby. Coho, chinook, steelhead, brown trout, and lake trout are likely catches.

As the water warms, salmon move deeper, swinging eastward and south into New York waters. Later in the summer they migrate back to the central and eastern portions of the north shore, where trollers intercept them at such places as Bowmanville, Brighton, and Wellington.

From September into November, chinook and coho school off the mouths of most Lake Ontario rivers, especially in the western end, where they are within reach of small-craft trollers and casters on piers and breakwalls. Ontario's 45-pound, 6-ounce record chinook was caught from the Credit River at Oakville in 1980, and the 26-pound, 10-ounce coho record came from nearby Lake Ontario off Bronte in 1987. Lake Ontario also produced the provincial brown trout record in 1994, a 34-pound colossus. Huge browns, some in the 15- to 20-pound class, are a possibility for shallow trollers in the spring, and for deep anglers in the summer. Cohos are normally caught in the 4- to 8-pound range, whereas chinook run the gamut, with most heavyweights taken in late summer and fall.

In 1994, a 39-pound lake trout was caught off the mouth of the Niagara River. Lakers are abundant here but are not as popular in this part of the lake as salmon and steelhead. In contrast, lake trout are the bread-and-butter fish for anglers at the Kingston end of Lake Ontario, especially around Main Duck Island, because migrating salmon are outside the reach of all but the largest boats.

In summer, shallow-cruising steelhead are often caught in offshore Lake Ontario waters as a bonus for salmon anglers, but the spring and fall fisheries off the mouths of rivers and streams are more popular.

The Credit River is the best steelhead water west of Toronto, with lesser runs in Bronte Creek and the Humber River. The best-known steelhead hotspot to the east is the Ganaraska River at Port Hope. Other area creeks noted for substantial spring and fall steelhead are Duffins, Sopers, Wilmot, and Shelter Valley.

Lake Simcoe. An hour's drive north of Toronto, Lake Simcoe is the fourth largest inland lake in the province and one of Ontario's most important year-round recreational fisheries, providing a million hours of angling throughout an average year. A surprisingly rich and diverse fishery has been maintained in this 287-square-mile lake, despite heavy development and angling pressures.

Simcoe made its reputation from lake trout and whitefish, but native strains have seriously declined since the 1970s; populations are now maintained by heavy annual stockings. Typical lake trout range from 3 to 6 pounds, but fish up to 20 pounds are always a possibility. Whitefish in the 10-pound category are now rare, but hatchery-raised specimens average a respectable 2 to 4 pounds. Smelt appeared

in Lake Simcoe in 1962 and are thought to be an additional detriment to both trout and whitefish.

Lake Simcoe's present water quality favors yellow perch, smallmouth bass, and other warm- or coolwater species. Anglers target perch, especially in April and May, at the Atherley Narrows between Lakes Simcoe and Couchiching, at Cook's Bay, and from public wharves and private docks around the lake. Perch up to 2 pounds have come from Simcoe; this is large by Ontario standards, but the average is under 10 inches. Black crappie appeared in significant numbers in Lake Simcoe and adjacent Lake Couchiching in the mid-1990s.

During the summer months, smallmouth bass move to the shoals, reefs, and weedbeds along the eastern side at Brechin, Beaverton, and Big Bay Points, and around such islands as Thorah, Georgina, and Snake.

Lake Simcoe has walleye over 10 pounds, but the fish are difficult to locate in summer. The best opportunities are in mid-May, when post-spawn fish drop back into the lake from the mouth of the Talbot River, a major spawning area, and head out to Thorah and Georgian Islands. Other opportunities exist in the south end in Cook's Bay off the Holland and Jersey Rivers. The shallow waters of Cook's Bay, however, primarily favor largemouth bass, northern pike, muskies, and panfish.

Lake Simcoe has been dubbed the "Ice Fishing Capital of the World." It supports more than 4,000 registered huts—both commercial rentals and privately owned structures—and hosts 6,000 to 10,000 anglers on a good February weekend. Yellow perch are the most common catch, followed by lake trout, whitefish, and herring. Popular jumping-off spots for winter fishing include Georgina, Big Bay Point, Jackson's Point, and Beaverton.

Trent-Severn System and the Kawarthas. The Trent-Severn Waterway, which winds for 230 miles through the heart of central southern Ontario, linking Lake Ontario to Lake Huron's Georgian Bay, is one of Ontario's busiest recreational playgrounds for boaters and anglers alike. Its 15 major natural and man-made lakes, connected by an intricate network of canals and locks, provide excellent shallow-water habitat for walleye, bass, muskies, yellow perch, rock bass, bluegills, crappie, and bullhead.

Anglers land walleye around many of the dams and locks throughout the system in the spring and fall, and in the interconnecting rivers and lakes in the summer. Pigeon is considered the best lake for walleye, followed by Rice, Clear, Stony, Lovesick, Buckhorn, Chemung, Sturgeon, and Balsam Lakes. A typical walleye weighs 2 pounds, but trophies up to 10 pounds are not unheard of.

Largemouth and smallmouth bass range throughout the system in varying abundance. Buckhorn is a top lake for both varieties, Pigeon and Stony are noted for largemouths, and 10-mile-long Balsam hosts smallmouths.

The Kawartha lakes in the Trent-Severn system provide the best opportunity in Ontario to catch that first muskellunge. This situation is unique in that muskies aren't in competition with northern pike as they are elsewhere in the province. Among the better muskie lakes are Rice, Stony, Buckhorn, Chemung, Pigeon, and Balsam. The fish are mainly 6- to 10-pounders but are relatively abundant; the occasional lunker is in the 20- to 30-pound range. Nearby Lake Scugog, connected to the Trent-Severn through the Scugog River, also offers good muskie fishing in early June and from mid-September until the end of October. With an average depth of only 5 feet, the lake's massive weedbeds are a haven for largemouth and smallmouth bass, and myriad panfish, including black crappie and pumpkinseeds.

Haliburton/Muskoka. North in the Haliburton Highlands, muskellunge are found only in Elephant Lake northwest of Bancroft. Adjoining Baptiste Lake also has muskies but achieved some notoriety when a 37-pound lake trout was landed in 1980. Both lakes have populations of walleye, smallmouth bass, and largemouth bass.

To the west, in the heavily cottaged Muskoka country, smallmouth bass have been the predominant sportfish for generations in Lake of Bays, Lake Muskoka, Lake Joseph, Lake Rosseau, and Skeleton and Three Mile Lakes.

From Bancroft to Dover, numerous small lakes deep enough for trout are stocked with lakers, brook trout, rainbow trout, and splake. Among these waters, the ones with road access are most sought after. Liberal regulations are in place for rainbow trout and splake lakes, to ease the fishing pressure on lakes with native populations of lake trout and brook trout (called speckled trout here).

For a small daily fee, anglers have a choice of 21 lakes in the privately owned Haliburton Forest and Wildlife Reserve, 15 miles north of the town of Haliburton. The 78-square-mile forest has easily accessible lakes varying in size from 12 to 450 acres, and these have lake trout, rainbows, splake, speckled trout, and smallmouth bass, which are maintained by regular stocking.

Algonquin Park. Algonquin Park, which boasts 325 lakes and rivers within its 2,900 square miles, has a reputation for both quality fishing and wilderness canoeing. It's still possible to catch a 5-pound speckled trout within 150 miles of downtown Toronto if you're prepared to work at it.

The 55-mile-long corridor along Highway 60, which cuts across the southern end of the park, provides road access to Lake Opeongo, the largest lake in Algonquin and the major jumping-off point for the backwaters. No motors are allowed in the interior lakes, and special regulations are in effect to protect native speckled and lake trout.

Specks, or brookies, are the most widespread species in Algonquin, occurring in 230 lakes and typically weighing from 1 to 4 pounds. Coveted wild brookies are found in lakes requiring one or more portages; hatchery trout predominate in the eight smaller lakes along the highway. The best fishing is in May, and three-quarters of the season's harvest from the park is taken then.

Eleven park lakes are noted for lake trout, notably Smoke, Canoe, Cache, and Opeongo along the Highway 60 corridor. The average lakers weigh 2 to 4 pounds, but a 20-pounder can always come along in remote interior waters. Splake have been introduced in 10 area lakes.

Smallmouth bass inhabit 15 of the park's lakes, many along Highway 60 and within easy reach of campgrounds. Popular smallmouth lakes are Opeongo, Canoe, Cache, and Smoke. Late June and early fall are best.

Eastern Ontario

Bay of Quinte and Eastern Lake Ontario. After a hefty pollution cleanup, curtailment of commercial fishing, and a string of ideal spawning years, Bay of Quinte and its adjoining Long Reach and Hay Bay have become one of North America's top sites for walleye over 10 pounds and have plenty of them. The larger fish, which can reach 18 pounds, move into the bay from Lake Ontario in the late fall, positioning for spawning in the Napanee, Salmon, Moira, and Trent Rivers in April. Walleye that remain in the bay over the summer average 1 to 4 pounds.

The MNR has counted close to 4,000 boats along the 50 miles of bay waters from Trenton to Picton at the opening of the walleye season in early May. Many anglers find success bouncing bottom with a jig-and-minnow from an anchored or drifting boat. Trolling with a crankbait that resembles an alewife, the primary food for Quinte walleye, has also been effective. In 1997, the MNR estimated that anglers caught 80,063 walleye during the open-water season and an additional 22,631 through the ice. The average weight, including released fish, was more than 2 pounds.

In the quest for walleye, other Quinte gamefish are often overlooked. Smallmouth bass averaging $1\frac{1}{2}$ pounds inhabit the channel edges near Belleville, largemouth bass are in the back bays between Rossmore and North Port, and northern pike haunt Muscote Bay and the mouths of the Trent and Salmon Rivers. Hay Bay has produced numerous muskellunge over 20 pounds in past years. Both yellow and white perch, along with other panfish, are also common in Quinte waters.

In waters offshore from the bay are lake trout and salmon. The eastern end of the big lake is noted for smallmouth bass and walleye. Offshore, the Main Duck Islands are a long run but produce good fishing for various species. Muskies are caught at the far eastern end, off the head of Wolfe Island at the entrance to the St. Lawrence River, and closer to Kingston.

St. Lawrence River. The scenic Thousand Islands is without a doubt the most famous fishing region along the Ontario portion of the vast St. Lawrence River and the stretch least affected by the massive seaway construction of the 1950s.

It's a structure angler's dream, with countless points, rocky shorelines, shoals, sharp dropoffs, and brisk current all concentrated in a 30-mile stretch from Wolfe Island, at the mouth of the river, eastward past Gananoque to Brockville. A traditional fishing technique here, and one still employed successfully by charter captains, is stillfishing with a shiner minnow on the bottom from an anchored boat around Howe, Tar, and Grenadier Islands, and around hundreds of smaller islands and reefs. More mobile and well-equipped anglers, however, cast around the countless reefs, bays, islands, weedbeds, and docks for fish, particularly largemouth and smallmouth bass.

Northern pike, yellow perch, and bullhead are popular catches in May and June. Smallmouth bass are numerous and are found throughout the islands in summer; they are caught shallow early in the season, as the water is still cool, then move to deeper haunts. Largemouths are not as abundant as their smallmouth cousins but are still available in ample quantities, especially in creeks, bays, and shallow, weedy environs. Roaming walleye are intercepted at the west end of Howe Island and around the Ivy Lea Bridge. Muskellunge are most active in September and October.

This section of the St. Lawrence was once internationally known for huge muskies, especially 50- and 60-pound fish, and produced the disputed world-record 69-pound, 15-ounce muskie in 1957. Although believed to have been caught downriver near Ogdensburg, New York, the record fish was also claimed by Gananoque, Ontario; it was purged from the world-record books in the mid-1990s, although it is still honored by New York.

In recent decades, trophy muskies have become scarce in the river, and especially at renowned Forty Acre Shoals, a patch of river bordered by Howe, Wolfe, and Grindstone Islands and historically the most famous fishing reef in the Thousand Islands. Overharvesting and ecological changes appear to have been at fault. Although the glory days are gone, fall trolling around the islands can still produce muskies in the 15- to 17-pound range, and 25-pounders are caught every season. Occasionally, someone lands a 40-pounder or better. Northerns up to 20 pounds are also attracted to baits intended for muskies, especially in the Bateau Channel along Howe Island. Ice fishing for pike is especially popular in the bays.

Carp are available throughout Ontario waters, but nowhere are they more abundant than in Lake St. Lawrence between Morrisburg and Cornwall. Conventional sportfishing pressure is minimal for these fish; a small number of anglers have focused on these species and experience good and virtually uncontested angling. There is significant interest in bowfishing for these lumbering giants during June,

The Henshall Van Antwerp Black Bass Reel, patented in 1887, was a forerunner of the baitcasting reels used through the first half of the twentieth century.

when they come into the marshes to spawn. Area derbies take place then, and a fish weighing between 40 and 45 pounds is generally needed to win.

Lake St. Francis, as the St. Lawrence River east of Cornwall is known, is a productive section of the Ontario portion of the St. Lawrence River because of its large weedy areas interspersed with numerous channels and holes. The walleye and perch runs in May at the mouth of the Raisin River at South Lancaster attract anglers from across eastern Ontario and from as far as Montreal. The yellow perch, known here as "Lancaster perch," are a local favorite because they feed heavily on small river snails, which gives the flesh an exceptional flavor.

In summer, anglers pursue walleye, which average 4 pounds, with spinners and nightcrawlers in the cooler currents of the shipping lanes while dodging oceangoing freighters. The lake has an abundant population of northern pike up to 15 pounds, smallmouth bass up to 4 pounds, and muskellunge in the 15- to 25-pound class, all of which are largely ignored except by a small core of serious anglers.

Rideau Lakes and Canal.   The Rideau Canal and its 120 miles of lakes, rivers, and cuts has been renowned for fishing since colonial times. The system, opened in 1832 for possible military use, runs from Kingston on Lake Ontario north to Ottawa, Canada's capital city.

At the shallower southern end, the Cataraqui River and Cranberry, Whitefish, Opinicon, and Newboro Lakes are prime habitat for largemouth bass that can reach 7 pounds, which is roughly the largest found in Ontario. Splake have been stocked in deeper Indian Lake with mixed success.

Big Rideau Lake, the jewel of the Rideaus with depths exceeding 200 feet, is a popular trolling water for lake trout in the 2- to 10-pound class. The islands near Portland hold good populations of small- and largemouth bass and panfish.

In the north, the Rideau River from Burritts Rapids near Kemptville to downtown Ottawa holds good numbers of muskellunge in the 10- to 20-pound range, walleye that can exceed 10 pounds, and smallmouth and largemouth bass to 5 pounds for anglers who have the skills and patience to fish heavy weeds. Black crappie are a popular target in April and May along the creek mouths and numerous canal locks.

Most of the other Rideau lakes have a variety of bass, pike, walleye, bluegills, crappie, and other panfish. Loughborough, Bob's Lake, Crosby, Christie, Otty, and Wolfe Lake (which produced a 9-pound, 4-ounce smallmouth in the 1980s) are known as consistent producers.

Ottawa River and Ottawa Valley.   Shared with Quebec over much of its 350-mile length, the Ottawa River is eastern Ontario's second major river after the St. Lawrence. Power-generating stations have created numerous vast reservoir systems that harbor a variety of warmwater gamefish.

The 50 miles of the lower river from Ottawa downstream to Hawkesbury is the most productive section. Walleye in the 2- to 3-pound range are actively sought by anglers throughout the seasons, but the largest fish, some over 10 pounds, are taken through the ice in late December and January. Smallmouth and largemouth bass, northern pike, and a variety of panfish are abundant.

Interest in the muskellunge fishery has grown in recent years, and fish up to 50 inches are being caught in the fall by dedicated and knowledgeable muskie enthusiasts. A 62-inch muskie was caught and released in 1997 in the Ottawa-Hull area.

Upstream, the shallower bays of Lac Deschenes, from Ottawa to the dam at Fitzroy Harbour, are noted for walleye, smallmouth bass, northern pike, and the occasional muskie. The Lac des Chats portion at Arnprior holds walleye, smallmouth bass, and muskies in the 35-pound class. The upper reaches past Pembroke, Deep River, Mattawa, and New Liskeard on to Lake Timiskaming are vast waters primarily holding walleye, northern pike, and smallmouth bass. It's worthwhile for visiting anglers to contact outfitters located along the river for guidance about the best fishing areas.

The foremost draw here is walleye. Most of these fish are in the 2- to 3-pound range, and some are in the 8-pound class. Pike are plentiful, as are smallmouths, some of which weigh up to 4 pounds; there are no muskies up here, but there's an overlooked supply of largemouth bass in backwater locales.

Smallmouth and largemouth bass are found in nearly all of the cottage lakes within a few hours' drive of Ottawa, such as Mississippi, Bennett, Christie, Clayton, Dalhousie, and White. But north and west of Ottawa, throughout the Pembroke and Bancroft regions, trout fishing is a tradition, and bass are generally underexploited. Healthy bass populations also inhabit such lakes as Constance, Golden, Round, Dore, and Muskrat.

Madawaska River.   The Madawaska River, which flows southeast from Algonquin Park to the Ottawa River, is another significant fishing water in eastern Ontario. Power dams have created a series of reservoir lakes that include Centennial, Black Donald, Calabogie, and Lake Madawaska.

In these flooded waters, jigging for walleye in depths up to 60 feet may be necessary for success. Smallmouth bass exist throughout the river, and largemouth frequent the weedy bays of Lake Calabogie. There is a chance of catching a muskellunge just about anywhere, but most angling effort is concentrated on Lake Madawaska at Arnprior.

Eastern Ontario trout waters.   Eastern Ontario lake trout have declined in recent decades, but they remain an important recreational catch in 46 Canadian Shield lakes, of which 29 have some natural reproduction. A higher fertility compared with lakes farther north helps maintain natural populations, which are augmented with stocking programs, despite easy road access and high angling interest.

The father of modern taxonomy—the biological ordering system—was Swedish naturalist Carl von Linné, known as Linnaeus; many fish were first identified and named by him in 1758.

Popular trout lakes south of Highway 7 are the Big Rideau, Charleston, Devil, Big Salmon, and Sharbot. North of the highway they include Lucky, Mair, Mazinaw, Palmerston, Mosque, and Weslemkoon Lakes.

In the mid-1980s, large stocking programs of splake were begun on a put-grow-take basis in 26 lakes that were no longer suitable for lake trout. The splake have done well in some of these waters; the better ones include Little Salmon and Little Clear in Frontenac Provincial Park, and in Indian, Draper, and Upper Rock Lakes.

The Near North

Lake Nipissing. Covering 350 square miles and extending 40 miles in length and 15 miles in width, huge Nipissing is a lake of contrast and marks the transition into northern Ontario. The east end is shallow and possesses the sand, mud, and rock shoals suited to walleye and yellow perch, whereas the west end is a melange of rocky islands and bays, reefs, and sheltered waters best known for northern pike and muskellunge.

Nipissing is a very productive lake by northern Ontario standards, but not by southern standards. Fishing, especially for walleye, gradually slid downhill in recent times but has shown signs of bouncing back in the late 1990s, thanks to restocking programs and tighter angling regulations.

In May and early June, walleye are found close to shore off the sandy bottoms at North Bay, and the mouths of the Sturgeon, Veuve, Wasi, and South Rivers. The Manitou Islands in the center of the east end of the lake are a year-round favorite location. Fish in the 1- to 2-pound range are abundant, and prospects of hooking into an old-timer up to 12 pounds still exist.

The lake has good populations of smallmouth bass, which are often ignored. The best areas are Callender Bay and the south shore, the islands near the mouth of the French River, and the West Arm.

Catching a 40-pound muskellunge from Lake Nipissing is still possible, but its reputation, along with that of nearby Nosbonsing and Restoule Lakes, of the 1950s and 1960s for numbers of big muskies has diminished from too much fishing pressure. The best opportunities today are in South Bay, West Bay, and Cache Bay. Ling, sheepshead, and sturgeon are also well established in the lake. White bass run the Sturgeon River on the north shore in May.

There is as much fishing on Nipissing in winter as there is during the summer. An average of 1,700 ice shacks pop up in January, and walleye are the prime target, followed by yellow perch, northern pike, whitefish, and herring. In 1996, MNR surveys indicated that 165,118 walleye, pike, and perch were caught during the open-water periods, and 213,639 were hauled in by ice anglers.

French River. Mention the French River and people immediately think of fishing amidst glacier-scoured bedrock of pink and gray granite. This scenic and historic river is a 68-mile-long series of island-dotted lakes connected by rapids and falls between Lake Nipissing and the isolated eastern shoreline of Georgian Bay.

Most fishing effort is devoted to walleye that migrate from Georgian Bay in search of alewives in the maze of channels and outlets of the French River delta, which include the Bad and Pickerel Rivers. May until August are the best times for trolling deep-diving plugs or stillfishing with live baits in the fast waters. In July, night fishing is best for walleye that could weigh 10 pounds, but they are usually half that. As fall progresses, the walleye move farther upriver.

Northerns up to 15 pounds and smallmouth bass up to 4 pounds permeate the French River system. October is the best time for trolling for trophy muskellunge, especially in Hartley Bay. Many muskies fall in the 25- to 40-pound class, but a 59-pound, 7-ounce leviathan was boated here in 1989.

Ahmic and Cecebe Lakes. Two of the lakes in the Magnetawan River chain, Ahmic and adjoining Cecebe, are among the largest lakes in the Parry Sound District and are prolific walleye, northern pike, and smallmouth bass waters. In summer, night trolling with minnow plugs, and stillfishing in the evening with a leech suspended under a float, are locally proven ways to catch elusive Ahmic Lake walleye, which average 4 pounds and gorge themselves on smelt.

Moon River. The Moon River, flowing into Georgian Bay farther south, has remained a top-notch fishing location but with an emphasis on quality rather than quantity. The river gained fame for huge walleye in the 8- to 14-pound range, with the occasional eye-popper hitting near the 20-pound mark. The size of walleye now is more modest, in the 5-pound class. Popular places in the basin for walleye that move in for the winter are Woods Bay, Captain Allan Straits, and Moon River Bay.

Abundant populations of smallmouths and largemouths are there but are often overlooked in the quest for walleye. Pike up to 25 pounds thrive throughout the river. Muskies are present, too, including some monsters; the Moon River produced a Canadian-record 65-pound, 58-inch muskellunge in Blackstone Harbour in 1988.

Manitoulin Island and the North Channel. Rural Manitoulin Island, the largest freshwater island in the world at 100 miles long and up to 60 miles wide, dominates the northern shore of Georgian Bay and is a focal point for Ontario anglers.

Smallmouth bass, northern pike, and yellow perch are abundant in most of the island's 19 inland lakes and surrounding waters. Small walleye, 2 pounds or under, are found in Mindemoya and Windfall Lakes. The May run of jumbo perch at Lake Wolsey draws a lot of attention. Sixteen-mile-long Lake Manitou, the largest of the island's lakes, has a lake trout population that is critically

important to the province, not only for sportfishing, but also as a source of trout eggs for a nearby government hatchery. The lakers have been known to reach 30 pounds, but the average catch weighs closer to 5 pounds.

Some island creeks have resident speckled trout, but better known is the migrant steelhead fishery in the spring and fall near the mouths of the small rivers. The most prominent of these are along the south shore and include Blue Jay Creek and the Manitou River on Michael's Bay, and the Mindemoya River at Providence Bay.

Manitoulin's 250 miles of rocky shoreline, with its sheltered bays and nearby island waters, also host Pacific salmon, steelhead, brown trout, and lake trout, which have been stocked by the millions over the years or wandered in from the massive plantings in Lake Huron waters by Michigan. Salmon fishing is centered at Meldrum Bay, followed by Providence Bay and Gore Bay, from mid-July through October.

Manitoulin Island was the site of a greatly influential fisheries research program aimed at restoring Georgian Bay's lake trout fishery, which collapsed in the 1950s due to lamprey eels and overfishing. The program involved planting millions of first-generation splake in the 1970s, followed by millions of the second generation of these hybrids in the 1980s. Although these fish filled a gap in the spring fishery, they failed to reproduce or to live long; the MNR then switched to annual plantings of pure-strain lake trout in the 1990s.

In the shadows of the nearby La Cloche Mountains, McGregor Bay has one of the few remaining populations of native Georgian Bay lake trout. Northern pike, muskellunge, and smallmouth bass are also found throughout the rocky islands and small bays.

To the west, northern pike, smallmouth bass, and yellow perch are the most common species throughout the North Channel waters, which extend 100 miles from Little Current to Thessalon. In May and June, opportunities for walleye exist at the mouth of the Spanish River.

In the fall, stray chinook show up at the mouths of such rivers as the Thessalon, Mississagi, and St. Mary's, but pink salmon—accidentally released into Lake Superior in 1956—are a curiosity. The pinks, which typically weigh 2 pounds but have been known to exceed 10 pounds, show up every odd year when they can be caught from shore by anglers using flies, spinners, and other small lures.

Ontario's North
Lake Temagami region. Walleye populate the lakes north of Lake Nipissing, but their size diminishes with the shorter growing season. The Marten River system and nearby smaller lakes are noted for eating-size "pickerel" under 2 pounds; anything over 5 pounds is trophy class. Walleye up to 7 pounds inhabit Lake Temagami and its four sprawling arms, but this 78-square-mile site is better

known for lake trout and whitefish in both the open-water and ice fishing seasons.

Highway 17 to Highway 11 Belt. Walleye, northern pike, and smallmouth bass are common in hundreds of lakes in the huge belt of rock and forest terrain between Highways 17 and 11 from Sudbury to Lake Superior—Obabika, Gowganda, Wanapitei, Onaping, Biscotasi, Missinakwa, Mattagami, Panache, Chiblow, Wakomata, Horwood, Missinaibi, Dog, and Remi, to name a few.

This rough, lightly populated region is also the heart of Ontario's trout country. Of the 2,000 Ontario inland lakes holding lake trout, the districts of Sudbury and Algoma have a significant share. Northwest of Espanola, former logging roads provide access to numerous trout lakes. Mozhabong, Sindaminda, Savage, and Whiskey are among the better-known waters. The greatest concentration of trout lakes, however, is in the Elliot Lake–Blind River area, where Rawhide, Kirkpatrick, Semiwhite, Flack, Matinenda, and Bark Lakes are among the most consistent producers of large lakers.

As a bonus, countless difficult-to-reach and not-easy-to-find smaller lakes in the Sault Ste. Marie–Chapleau area have healthy native populations of speckled trout. It's said that woods-wise locals may take the locations of the best brookie waters—where a 6-pound speck is still a possibility—with them to the grave.

Lake Superior. The rocky cliffs, deep crystal water, rushing rivers, and limited access along Lake Superior, which is the largest of the Great Lakes, make the northern shore one of Ontario's most awesome fishing destinations. Lake trout, steelhead, coho salmon, chinook salmon, and pink salmon are the primary coldwater attractions. In the shallower bays and rivers, northern pike, yellow perch, and remnant walleye are the dominant warmwater species.

Pacific salmon have given a boost to a declining lake trout fishery, especially in the east end of the lake. Summer and fall trolling are popular in Goulais Bay, Batchawana Bay, Montreal River, and Michipicoten Bay. This latter bay, located at Wawa, is the best spot on Superior for spring and fall chinook, boasting salmon to 30 pounds. In the west, salmon and lake trout linger offshore around the lake reefs at Marathon, Terrace Bay, Rossport, and Thunder Bay.

Lake Superior's north shore is the preserve of Ontario's finest classic steelhead waters, although getting there can be a challenge. Steelhead runs can be short because the rivers are quickly blocked by falls. Among the dozens of unpolluted rivers that can be fished from Highway 17 (the Trans-Canada Highway), the better-known ones are the Batchawana, Montreal, Michipicoten, Steel, and Nipigon. In Pukaskwa National Park, steelhead run the Dore, University, and Pukaskwa Rivers, but there is no road access. Anglers must boat in from Lake Superior.

North in the Lake Superior drainage are hundreds of coldwater lakes, rivers, and streams scattered throughout an exceptionally rugged terrain with few good roads. These waters are low in productivity but suited for brook and lake trout and provide a wilderness trout experience for those willing to make the effort.

Lake Nipigon/Nipigon River. The speckled trout is king in the huge undeveloped waters of Lake Nipigon, which, at 1,740 square miles, is the largest lake entirely within Ontario's borders.

The best time for a trophy, which can weigh up to 7 pounds, is from ice out in late April through early June. Proven techniques include trolling a spinner-and-worm rig around the lake's profusion of rocky points and islands. Lake trout are found throughout the lake, and walleye and northern pike inhabit the mouths of such rivers as the Ombabika, Gull, and Poshkokogan.

The 20-mile-long Nipigon River spilling into Lake Superior is one of the most famous speckled trout rivers in the world, still reveling in the past glory of a 14$\frac{1}{2}$-pound world record caught in 1916. Although such a catch is unlikely today, specks of half this size are still possible from the fast current around various dams and narrows, especially in May and September.

Jesse Lake, a widening of the river about halfway between Lake Nipigon and Lake Superior, has walleye, northern pike, yellow perch, and whitefish for midsummer action.

Northwest

Northwest Ontario, the region west and north of Thunder Bay, has more fishing camps than any other part of the province, with countless Canadian Shield lakes and rivers flowing either easterly to Lake Superior or northerly to Hudson Bay.

Quetico region. The 1,750 square miles of Quetico Provincial Park, south of Atikokan and north of the Ontario-Minnesota border with a labyrinth of interconnected waters, is a popular destination for canoeists and anglers seeking the solitude and beauty of the wilderness. Smallmouth bass, northern pike, walleye, lake trout, and whitefish range throughout the park. Beaverhouse, Quetico, Sturgeon, and Lac la Croix are among the better lakes.

To the west, 30-mile-long Rainy Lake, with Fort Francis at its center, has good to excellent populations of walleye, smallmouth bass, and northern pike, especially in Ash, Alexander, and Seine Bays in the north arm. A 51-pound, 8-ounce muskie came from nearby Pipestone Lake in 1975.

Dryden District. To the north, the Dryden District contains among Ontario's most famous muskellunge waters: Lac Seul, Eagle Lake, Wabigoon, and Big Vermilion Lake. Here, dreams of a 50-pound muskie could come true. In particular, 60-mile-long Eagle Lake claims more trophies than any other water in Ontario, yielding fish in the 30- to 40-pound class every year. Special catch-and-release regulations are in place on some lakes, to protect a world-class fishery.

Lake trout, walleye, and northern pike are abundant in many Dryden District lakes. Stocked decades ago, smallmouth bass are found in lakes accessible by road, but not in remote waters.

This is the home of the floatplane, and anglers have a choice of hundreds of waters to fly into for unpressured walleye, northern pike, and lake trout. Planes depart from such locations as Sioux Lookout, Red Lake, and Pickle Lake.

Lake of the Woods. Ontario shares the 1,485-square-mile area of Lake of the Woods with Minnesota and Manitoba. The Ontario waters are sheltered by most of the 14,000 rocky islands found in the lake. Those islands contribute to an estimated 3,800 miles of shoreline, which gives anglers plenty to focus on. The lake has a reputation for its variety of sportfish—especially pike, lakers, and muskies—to match its vast size.

Walleye are the primary target of both resident and nonresident anglers out of such places as Rainy River, Nestor Falls, Sioux Narrows, and Kenora. Anglers will find walleye throughout the lake, although they're less common in deep Clearwater and Whitefish Bays. Walleye here are typically in the 1- to 3-pound range, and older fish weigh near 10 pounds; although good and above the average size for Canadian Shield waters, these fish are not in a league with the lunkers found in Lake Erie or the Bay of Quinte.

Smallmouth bass of 2 to 3 pounds are abundant, especially in the waters around Nestor Falls and Sioux Narrows, but they are often overlooked by anglers in their pursuit of walleye. Largemouth bass, which are less abundant, are found in the back bays and weedbeds in these areas.

Northern pike exist throughout the lake and are often called "jackfish" in this part of the province. Pike are typical in the 5- to 8-pound range but can reach 25 pounds. As big as they are, it seems unlikely that Lake of the Woods northerns will break the long-standing Ontario record of 42 pounds, 2 ounces, caught from nearby Delaney Lake in 1946.

Lake trout are a particularly important species in Lake of the Woods and can reach 30 to 35 pounds. Prominent areas for them are Whitefish Bay at Sioux Narrows, and Clearwater and Echo Bays near Kenora.

Lake of the Woods is among Ontario's top producers of large muskellunge, and numerous fish in the 55- to 58-pound class have been taken over the years. Today, however, there's a greater likelihood of encountering a fish in the 30-pound range, and enough of these are hooked every year to make this one of the most likely places in North America to have a good chance at such a fish. Mid-August to early October is the peak time in proven spots such as the Nestor Falls-Sabaskong Bay area and Labyrinth Bay.

Lake Superior, which covers 31,800 square miles, has the largest surface area of any lake in the world.

Among other species in the lake, yellow perch is the most common. Black crappie are targeted in Sabaskong Bay in the spring and through the ice. Other established species include sauger, bullhead, cisco, lake whitefish, and sturgeon.

To the north of Lake of the Woods, the sprawling Winnipeg and English River systems have good populations of walleye, northern pike, smallmouth bass, muskellunge, lake trout, and whitefish. The Winnipeg River near Minaki has a reputation for muskies in the 10- to 30-pound category, and legendary past catches have exceeded 50 pounds.

Far North (James/Hudson Bay Watersheds)

Rivers. The pristine and remote large river systems that drain north into James Bay and Hudson Bay, accessible mainly by air, are the answer for the true angling adventurer. This area of northern Ontario, its gateway to the Arctic, is rich in North American and Canadian history. Here, near the southern shore of James Bay at Moosonee, the Hudson Bay Company originated, amassing a fortune and helping to forge a country through the trapping and trading of beavers. This is where the Moose River and such tributaries as the Missinaibi, Kwataboahegan, Kapuskasing, Mattagami, Onakwahegan, and Abitibi Rivers now beckon wilderness adventurers and explorers. These are rough, rugged rivers, however, and fishing on them is seldom the main focus of visitors.

Moosonee is the only locale in this region that is accessible by ground, via train from Cochrane. This train, the Little Bear, provides dropoff and pickup service to those making multiweek canoe expeditions. A village of 3,500, Moosonee sits along the mile-wide Moose River in a large deltalike area that experiences 6- to 7-foot tides and is still a 20-minute boat ride from James Bay. Fishing opportunities are limited, mostly for small pike and walleye and an occasional whitefish. Three- to 6-pound charr come into the bay from mid- to late May, and again in September. This is not an angling hotspot,

but it is one worth taking a day to see when headed into or coming from the interior.

The interior portions of rivers such as the Ogoki, Attawapiskat, and Albany, however, are less accessible and have more angling attraction. They are virtually untapped waters for northern pike up to 15 pounds and walleye to 7 pounds, with the occasional larger specimen. Speckled trout averaging 2 to 3 pounds are found at the mouths of tributaries of many of these rivers in early summer and move farther up the tributaries into the cooler water of deep holes and whitewater rapids as the main rivers warm. The brookies return as the temperature falls in late August and September.

Farther north, resident speckled trout in the lower reaches of the Sutton, Winisk, and Severn Rivers are augmented by sea-run trout that spend most of their time in saltwater and enter freshwater in preparation for fall spawning. These far-north brookies, although respectable in size, seldom reach the weights of those found in Northern Quebec and Labrador. The Sutton River has the province's most northerly established lake trout population.

Outfitters from jumping-off points such as Nakina, Jellicoe, and Armstrong provide fly-in services for anglers to outpost camps and dropoffs for canoeing/fishing expeditions to these remote watersheds.

Kesagami Lake. One of the finest and most unique pike and walleye lakes in northern Ontario, Kesagami is a little-known gem in the northeast corner of the province, about 60 miles south of James Bay and accessed via floatplane from Cochrane or Moosonee. An isolated water without road access, Kesagami Lake makes up most of Kesagami Provincial Park in a flat and poorly drained region of peat bog and muskeg. It's an unusually shallow lake, with an average depth of 7 feet and a maximum depth of 29 feet, and offers 180 miles of shoreline, many bays, and seven islands.

Being shallow, Kesagami warms early, contributing to a growth rate well above normal for the region. This, combined with a baitfish population of cisco, suckers, and whitefish, produces prodigious walleye and many unusually plump northern pike. Many Kesagami pike weigh 15 pounds or more, and some are in the 25- to 35-pound range. The only lodge here has instituted conservation policies, including catch-and-release for pike, and the use of only barbless hooks and fish cradles for landing pike.

An evening walleye fishing scene at Kesagami Lake.

OPALEYE   *Girella nigricans.*

Other names—green perch, black perch, blue-eyed perch, bluefish, Jack Benny, button-back; Japanese: *mejina*; Spanish: *chopa verde.*

A member of the nibblers in the Kyphosidae family of sea chub *(see: chub, sea)*, the opaleye is a tough species to catch but a determined fighter on rod and reel.

Identification. The body of the opaleye is oval and compressed, the snout is thick and has an evenly rounded profile, and the mouth is small. Its coloring is dark olive green, and most individuals have one or two white spots on each side of the back under the middle of the dorsal fin. Bright-blue eyes and a heavy perchlike body distinguish it from related species.

Size. They are reported to attain a maximum weight of $25\frac{1}{2}$ inches and weight of $13\frac{1}{2}$ pounds.

Distribution. Opaleye occur from San Francisco, California, to Cabo San Lucas, Baja California.

Habitat. This species inhabits rocky shorelines and kelp beds. Concentrations of adults are found off California in 65 or so feet of water.

Life history/Behavior. Opaleye form dense schools in shallow water when spawning, which occurs from April through June. Eggs and larvae are free floating and may be found miles from shore. Juveniles form schools of up to two dozen individuals. At about 1 inch in length, they enter tide pools, gradually moving deeper as they grow. Opaleye mature and spawn when they are roughly 8 or 9 inches long and between two and three years old.

Food and feeding habits. Opaleye primarily eat marine algae with or without encrustations of organisms. Other food sources include feather boa kelp, giant kelp, sea lettuce, coralline algae, small tube-dwelling worms, and red crabs.

Angling. Although extremely difficult to catch due to their largely vegetarian diet and nibbling nature, opaleye are strong battlers. They are not the subject of intensive angling effort but may take mussels, sand crabs, and cut baits. Some anglers use hooked plant matter.

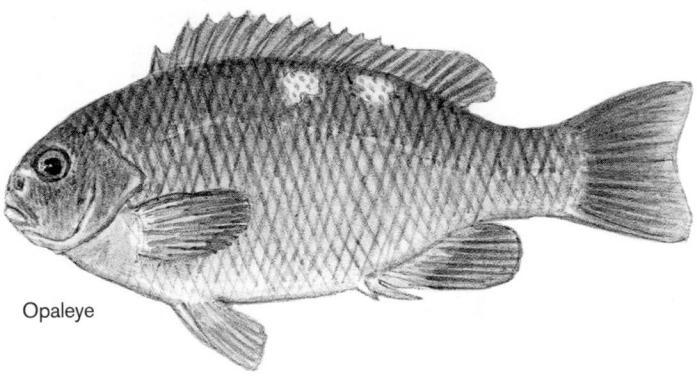
Opaleye

OPEN-FACE REEL
A spinning reel.
See: Spinning Tackle.

OPEN WATER
(1) A term used to distinguish a lake or pond that is not frozen from a frozen one. In locations where lakes are subject to freezing in the winter, the "open-water season" begins when the lake is free of ice.

(2) A loosely used reference by freshwater anglers to indicate that area of a large body of water, usually a reservoir or lake, that is away from the shore, with no visible structure or cover. "Open water" is used by some anglers to differentiate between fishing along or close to the shoreline, and fishing the broader expanse (as in "We caught them out in open water"). In a sense, it is analogous to the primarily saltwater term "offshore" (see).

OPERCULUM
The largest and uppermost bone that forms the gill cover of a fish.
See: Anatomy.

OPTIMUM YIELD
The recreational and/or commercial harvest level for a species that achieves the greatest overall benefits, including economic, social, and biological considerations. Optimum yield is different from maximum sustainable yield, which considers only the biology of the species.
See: Fisheries Management.

OREGON
Oregon spent much of the waning part of the twentieth century trying to beat back the warm ocean conditions of El Niño and save several of its salmon and steelhead populations. Unfortunately, headlines surrounding these matters overshadowed the presence of Oregon's truly diverse sportfisheries, most of which are alive and well.

Fishing for fall chinook salmon on the Oregon coast, for example, is the better than it is in either of the neighboring states, and the chinook in some Oregon estuaries are, fish for fish, larger than those in most Alaskan rivers.

The nation's largest sturgeon fishery, a million fish strong, lies within a few minute's to an hour's drive from Portland. Sturgeon coming and going from the lower Columbia River reenter river estuaries from Washington to northern California.

Some anglers believe that the next world-record walleye will be caught in the Columbia River, where these fish were introduced in the 1940s. State records in the river's border states of Oregon and Washington are nearing 20 pounds, and 12- to 16-pounders are no longer rare. Big walleye are so numerous that many salmon managers consider walleye unwelcome predators on baby salmon and steelhead and would just as soon see them all caught.

And although the salmon are imperiled in the Columbia, more shad (several million) enter this river every spring than most East Coast rivers,

where the species originated. So many shad make it to spawning grounds 200 miles upriver that biologists worry about shad plugging fish ladders designed for salmon.

Additionally, two Oregon rivers routinely produce catches of more than a hundred smallmouth bass a day; 3-pounders there are hardly worth noting. And Oregon's fine trout fishing remains intact, if changing.

Offshore fishing for bottom fish and rockfish is excellent and improving as federal regulators tighten controls on commercial fishermen. And you don't even need a license for the state's most popular fishery, Dungeness crabs.

Saltwater

Oregon has more than 350 miles of coastline to take the brunt of Pacific storms, and U.S. Highway 101, which runs within a few feet to a few miles of the beach for its entire length, offers a path to the West Coast's most accessible and diverse saltwater fishing.

Coastal bays. A diversity of sportfishing opportunity is the hallmark of Oregon's bays, and many also have excellent crabbing.

Columbia. The end of Lewis and Clark's journey is now a long jetty with good fishing from large rocks for most species of rockfish, sturgeon, and salmon (in season). Large Columbia Bay has long reaches that can get choppy with afternoon winds, yet there's excellent crabbing here—the largest Dungeness crabs, sometimes 8 or 9 inches across, on the coast. The estuary up to freshwater (about 20 miles) usually has good sturgeon fishing. There's a nasty bar here that should always be crossed on an incoming tide; watch for shipping traffic and don't anchor in the channel.

Nehalem. Pleasant, scenic little Nehalem Bay is popular for crabbing and has good chinook salmon fishing on the bar during incoming tides from July through September. The south jetty is accessible, but fishing is not as good as at Tillamook, a short distance south. A bonus for sightseers occurs when elk herds on the Nehalem Spit come to the water's edge; playful calves often chase harbor seals into the water.

Tillamook. Extremely diverse, Tillamook Bay is fed by five tributaries and has good winter crabbing if it hasn't rained enough to force the crabs out into the ocean. Sturgeon anglers welcome the rain because the same freshwater that pushes crabs out draws sturgeon inside when there are no pesky crabs to rob the bait. Jetty fishing is good for greenling and sea bass, and some crabbing occurs off the jetty instead of from boats. There's a long public fishing pier, and bay tidal flats are good for clamming. Tillamook's biggest draw is large fall chinook salmon; a few 50- to 60-pounders are caught each year from September through Thanksgiving. The bar is tricky and narrow, and shouldn't be crossed during a strong ebbing tide.

Netarts. When freshwater runoff stops crabbing on Tillamook Bay, locals head just a few miles east of Tillamook to Netarts, a bay without tributaries and thus always salty enough for crabbing. It also offers an unusual shore fishery for surfperch from a highway shoulder that hugs the bay's northeast shoreline. Boat launches are available, but no jetties or channel. This is not an ocean-access bay.

Nestucca. Limited crabbing occurs in Nestucca Bay, but the bay entrance is several miles from boat ramps and there's no ocean access. Two tributaries provide good fishing for spring chinook from May through June, and fall chinook from August through November. Fall chinook fishing is best from the bank, with spinners, or slip-stop bobbers over clusters of salmon eggs. Pacific City, on the ocean side of the upper bay, is home to Oregon's famous beach dory fleet. Dories launch directly into the surf at all times of the year to gain access to bottom fish, halibut, salmon, and albacore.

Depoe Bay. Tiny Depoe Bay has a good public launch and is home to an active charter-fishing and whale-watching fleet. Offshore reefs harbor lingcod, sea bass, cabezon, red snapper, and other species. The ocean floor drops sharply, allowing easier access to deep-water fishing. The bay erupts abruptly from a hole in the rocky coastline, over which U.S. 101 passes on a bridge. There is no jetty, but the bay is so small it has no runoff problems. Turn two corners and you're immediately into sea swells that are easily read before launching.

Siletz. Although there's little boat access or angling opportunity at Siletz, it is a pleasant and scenic bay with a good run of fall chinook into the estuary and an unusual beach fishery for salmon and steelhead crossing the bar in a narrow channel. It's best to fish toward the top of an incoming tide.

Yaquina. A premier Oregon coastal estuary, Yaquina has a generally forgiving bar and plenty of crabbing, perch fishing, jetty angling, and seasonal salmon fishing. A marina and public launch are on the south shoreline, between the Oregon State University Hatfield Marine Science Center and the Oregon Aquarium, and there's also a public crabbing and fishing pier. Crabbers should use caution with their bait because the bay houses Oregon's most aggressive, trap smashing sea lion population. Locals avoid trouble by baiting crabs with mink carcasses, chicken and turkey wings, and watermelon rinds. Killer whales sometimes enter the bay specifically to hunt and eat seals and sea lions. Bay flats east of the Marine Center offer good clamming plus sand shrimp for use as baitfish on the jetty, for perch fishing in the bay, or steelhead fishing in several nearby rivers. Surfperch give live birth to young fish in the bay from late March through early May. This is also the coast's only reliable jigging fishery for herring, which spawn from February through early May. Some winter and spring sturgeon fishing exists upriver to Toledo.

Alsea. A good crabbing bay, Alsea has a solid fall chinook run in September and October. Do not cross the bar.

Siuslaw. One of Oregon's longest estuaries, Siuslaw has good fall chinook fishing in September and October. Crabbing is seasonally fair in the lower bay from November until May. As in all bays, crabs molt and get soft during the summer. Unlike blue crabs of the East Coast, soft-shelled Dungeness crabs are not good to eat. Jetty fishing can be good, but access is a hike. Be cautious about crossing the bar.

Winchester. The outlet of the Umpqua River, Winchester is a good winter and spring sturgeon fishery and has Oregon's best striped bass fishing. Stripers live in a tributary, the lower Smith River, and the long, wide Umpqua estuary. Sturgeon are found from Winchester upriver past Reedsport to deep holes just below Scottsburg. Crabbing is good, and the bar can be treacherous.

Coos. The Coos is a large, relatively calm bay that also serves as southern Oregon's seaport. Crabbing is almost always good out of Charleston, at the bay's entrance, and charters offer access to bottom fish and tuna in season. Surfperch and sturgeon use the bay, and striped bass are found in three large sloughs. Jetty fishing is good for lingcod, but getting to the jetty is a bit tricky, requiring a drive across sandy tidal reaches. North and south shorelines outside the entrance offer a unique surf fishery for stripers. The bar here is more forgiving than others and can be good for chinook salmon fishing on incoming tides in the fall.

Coquille. Coquille Bay is a small scenic bay that has good crabbing and seasonal jigging for smelt. The entrance is narrow. Use caution when crossing the bar.

Port Orford. Although there is no bay or river at Port Orford, it instead has a protected harbor and a unique system of lowering boats into the harbor with a lift. This provides almost instant access to numerous offshore reefs and bottom fish.

Rogue. The Rogue is a small bay with an outlet to the ocean that is relatively safe because there is little or no tidal runoff. Crabbing is available but limited, and some smelt jigging occurs in the spring. The bay's primary attraction is Oregon's longest trolling season for chinook salmon, which extends from March through October.

Chetco/Brookings. Even smaller than Rogue Bay, Chetco/Brookings has good, instant ocean access to offshore reefs for bottom fishing and a productive late season for chinook salmon in October.

Coastal salmon and steelhead. Coho salmon seasons have been limited since the late 1970s. Chinook salmon, however, are available offshore most months of the year, and the fishing season runs from April through October. Most anglers troll deep off harbor entrances from August through October.

The best fishing occurs in estuaries in the late summer and fall, when trollers pull cut-plug herring across the bottom in or near bay entrances, and spinners in the midbay zones, or cast bobbers and baits (egg roe or sand shrimp) in tidewater sloughs.

Most rivers have runs of both native or hatchery steelhead or a combination. Wild steelhead must be released unharmed in most rivers, but hatchery steelhead with clipped adipose fins may be kept. There is little fishing for steelhead in estuaries.

Crabbing and clamming. Dungeness crabs are prevalent in most coastal bays and offer plenty of excitement. The best baits are salmon parts or bits of bottom fish, but many shad anglers freeze their catches for use in crabbing.

Don't pass up clamming and mussel gathering. Like crabbing, a license is not required, but there are daily limits. The best beach for digging razor clams is at Seaside and Gearhart, in about the first 20 miles south of the Columbia River entrance. Look for low tides and a calm ocean, as pounding surf tends to drive clams deep into the sand.

Jetties. Jetties always require caution, often being awash in large waves. Huge rocks require tennis shoes or rubber boots. The rewards for jetty fishing are perch, greenling (a small member of the lingcod family with brilliant blue-green flesh), and other bottom fish.

Sand shrimp, clam necks, and herring pieces are good baits. Don't cast too far from the rocks, as fish often bite within a few feet of rocks showing at the surface. The best time for jetty fishing is the last two hours of an incoming tide through the first 30 minutes of the ebb.

Albacore. Albacore tuna have rebounded since the high seas driftnet fleet was forced off the Pacific Ocean. From July through September, schools of albacore work north off the Pacific Northwest coast to Vancouver Island. They usually pass within striking range, no more than 100 miles for overnight charter boats, of Oregon ports. In the late 1990s, the same warm ocean currents that wreaked havoc on coldwater-loving salmon drew tuna to within 10 to 15 miles of some ports, and even the small private boat fleet reaped the rewards within sight of coastal mountains.

Tuna are slashing, diving fighters that don't give up and fight far harder, pound for pound, than any other coastal Oregon fish. Oregonians aren't equipped for live bait fishing like California boats, opting instead for pulling feathered and rubber-skirted jigs at high trolling speeds.

Freshwater

Coastal region. Oregon stocks rainbow and cutthroat trout into most of the lakes in the strip of land between the ocean and the Coast Mountain Range. Trout fishing in streams is a catch-and-release effort, to protect sea-run cutthroat trout and juvenile steelhead.

Many lakes also contain good populations of largemouth bass, and Tenmile Lakes between Coos Bay and Reedsport is such a good bass fishery that

A big female largemouth bass can lay up to 30,000 eggs in a nest, but she never stays to watch over them; males guard the eggs and fan the nest to keep silt away.

it supports year-round angling and several tournaments in the spring and summer.

Columbia River. For more than 200 miles from its mouth upriver, the Columbia is both the boundary between Oregon and Washington and a jointly managed fishery that provides the most and largest fish in both states. To prevent confusion, angling regulations along the Columbia are the same in both Oregon and Washington, despite different rules in other parts of both states. The following is a condensed review of angling opportunities starting from the mouth upriver.

Buoy 10. This channel marker near the entrance of the Columbia River has become synonymous with Oregon's best-known coho salmon fishery. Actually, both chinook and coho are caught in the lower river from Buoy 10 upriver to Tongue Point, east of Astoria.

Astoria to Bonneville Dam. The lower Columbia's estimated 1 million white sturgeon come and go at will from their birthplace in this stretch of river to numerous other coastal bays. Sturgeon fishing is good most of the year out of Astoria but concentrates from Longview to Portland in February and March, as sturgeon follow the smelt run to the mouth of Washington's Cowlitz River. After March, they move upriver to below Bonneville, where large fish spawn in the heavy spring runoff current below the dam. Anglers catch and release 7- to 10-footers, and some specimens are even larger. When the shad are in, whole shad make good sturgeon bait; at other times, sand shrimp, smelt, and herring are popular.

Shad enter the Columbia in May, when fish move well into Washington's reaches of the upper Columbia and through Portland up to Willamette Falls near Oregon City. Shad strike small bright spinners and shad darts, both trailed from the sterns of anchored boats or fished from shore.

Bonneville Dam upriver. Four major hydroelectric dams are barriers to salmon and steelhead runs, but they also provide rich reservoir pools for smallmouth bass, walleye, channel catfish, and other species. Smallmouths love the rocky shorelines and are plentiful. The best fishing is from The Dalles to Umatilla, and plugs and jigs are especially preferred.

Large walleye are caught well below Bonneville Dam, even in and around Portland, but the best fishing is below John Day Dam from April through September and from Arlington to McNary Dam at Umatilla year-round.

Willamette River/northwest region. Portland is Oregon's largest city and also has one of the state's largest spring chinook salmon runs; the fish pass between skyscrapers from March through June. The Willamette River here sometimes has a thousand or more boats during the run's peak, and businessmen often fish during lunch hour.

The lower Willamette from the falls at Oregon City to where it enters the Columbia also holds good numbers of sturgeon, small- and largemouth bass, crappie, walleye, and yellow perch. On state-owned lands of Sauvie Island, within half an hour's drive of most of Portland, crappie, bullhead catfish, and carp attract year-round attention. Upriver from the falls, the Willamette and its sloughs are good for large- and smallmouth bass.

The Clackamas River, which drains the southwest flank of Mount Hood and enters the Willamette at Oregon City, gets spring chinook and summer and winter steelhead. So does the Sandy River, which drains the northwest flank of Mount Hood and enters the Columbia directly at Troutdale, east of Portland.

Tributaries with salmon and steelhead runs are the Molalla, South and North Santiam, and McKenzie Rivers. The Santiam, McKenzie, and upper Willamette systems are dammed, and reservoirs here teem with stocked trout, kokanee salmon, and landlocked chinook salmon.

Trout fishing in valley streams is limited by rules requiring the release of wild fish to help protect juvenile steelhead, which closely resemble small trout. Ponds and borrow pits (where gravel has been extracted for construction and the depressions filled with water) in Albany, Canby, Willamina, Junction City, Salem, and Eugene are routinely stocked with trout in late winter and spring, before they become too warm.

Southwest region. The Umpqua River originates in the Cascades and flows through Roseburg. From Roseburg to Scottsburg, above tidewater, this is a trophy smallmouth bass fishery. Daily catches in some stretches exceed a hundred fish a day. A strong run of shad inhabit the lower river, and there are good spring chinook and winter and summer steelhead runs. The summer steelhead run into the fly fishing–only waters of the North Umpqua is legendary.

The Rogue River is consistently Oregon's best steelhead and salmon producer, offering long stretches of scenic water and plentiful fish almost year-round. Portions of the river are accessible by boat only, and this has spawned an entire industry devoted to building the famous Rogue River drift boat. The river is also large enough to accommodate jet powered boats, but rapids inhibit powerboat navigation in places. The Rogue also harbors an unusual run of "half-pounder" steelhead. These are young fish that go to sea and return the same fall as 12- to 16-inchers, then return to the sea again to come back the following year as adult steelhead. Half-pounders travel all the way upriver to Medford.

Lakes and reservoirs throughout southwest Oregon are routinely stocked. Applegate and Selmac Reservoirs hold some of the state's biggest largemouth bass.

Central region. The Deschutes River is often called the queen of trout rivers because of its rich population of native redside trout that stuff

Drift boat anglers prepare to float an Oregon river for steelhead.

themselves on the rich aquatic insect life of this desert tributary. By far the best time of year on the Deschutes is May and June for the salmonfly hatch, but October and its huge caddis hatch is terrific, as is the March brown hatch. The Deschutes, which empties into the Columbia 100 miles east of Portland, also shortstops much of the Inland Empire's run of summer steelhead. Steelhead get to the mouth of the Deschutes and choose its cool, mountain-fed water instead of continuing on through the reservoir-warmed Columbia. This makes the lower 25 or so miles of the Deschutes a steelhead haven. Baits are not allowed and aren't necessary.

Upriver from impassable Pelton Dam, the Deschutes creates Lake Billy Chinook, which offers a good population of bull trout that feed on the lake's abundant kokanee. Kokanee are so numerous in Billy Chinook that the state allows anglers to keep 25 fish per day.

South of Bend, the Deschutes is born in subterranean rivers that erupt from lava cliffs and create several natural and man-made lakes in the famous 120-mile-long Century Loop, a collection of trout waters with trophy lake trout, rainbows, kokanee salmon, brown trout, and brook trout.

Located southeast of Bend, natural East and Paulina Lakes in Newberry Crater have huge brook trout and kokanee big enough to sometimes look much like their seagoing sockeye salmon brethren.

Odell and Crescent Lakes southwest of Bend are premier kokanee and lake trout waters, and they offer good services at several resorts. Both lakes are often snowbound and ice covered well into April and May.

Diamond Lake is at the headwaters of the North Umpqua River and in the shadow of Crater Lake National Park. Diamond was once only a fish-barren puddle of snowmelt runoff inaccessible to trout because of impassable falls. Voracious Klamath basin rainbow trout are stocked annually and grow to huge proportions.

The Klamath system flowing to the sea through Northern California is born in legendary streams like the Williamson and Sprague Rivers north of Klamath Falls. Klamath Lake itself has several cold-water spring inlets where native rainbow trout seek protection from warm summer temperatures.

Central Oregon also has several private ponds where anglers can pay a fee to fish for various stocked trout and warmwater species. These are more than mere fish ponds but can be extremely expensive.

Northeast region. The John Day River enters the Columbia a short distance east of the Deschutes but is neither a product of glaciers nor cool mountain streams. Instead, it flows through desert country and warms quickly as sunlight bakes its canyon walls. This makes it the second of Oregon's premier smallmouth bass streams. Fish aren't quite as large as those in the lower Umpqua but are nearly as big and just as numerous. The water is best run in kayaks, canoes, and rafts in spring. Water levels get very low in the summer. It also has good runs of spring chinook and steelhead, which get through the lower sections well before the water warms.

Grande Ronde, Imnaha, and Wallowa Rivers are heavily stocked with summer steelhead. Some of these fish fail to head for the ocean and remain in freshwater, which makes the rivers excellent summer trout fisheries in a pristine, nearly alpine setting beneath the flanks of the Wallowa Mountain range and Eagle Cap Wilderness.

The Snake River forms the border between Idaho and Oregon, and dams along its length create an ideal habitat for more smallmouth bass and the state's best channel catfish populations. Brownlee Reservoir and its Powder River Arm create a crappie fishery so good that fish grow up to 12 inches long and are frequently taken illegally for the black market in Portland.

Numerous alpine and high desert lakes are good trout fisheries; Phillips and Thief Valley Reservoirs near Baker City are the best.

Southeast region. Oregon's largest fishing region is almost totally owned by the federal government and is thus public land. The Bureaus of Land Management and Reclamation provide fish habitat and offer numerous ponds, small reservoirs, and large impoundments. The state stocks these with fingerling trout every spring. The alkaline-base waters are insect rich, and trout grow up to an inch a month. By the following spring, the holdover fish are large and hungry.

Owyhee Reservoir is a 54-mile-long impoundment on the Owyhee River that was built to irrigate desert farms along the Snake River. It holds healthy crappie and largemouth bass populations, a few trout, and even some sturgeon. The river flowing into the reservoir is tough to reach but rewards the hardy with a good smallmouth bass and channel catfish experience.

Mann Lake, southeast of Burns, is a small, windswept natural lake at the base of Steens Mountain, an escarpment several thousand feet high. Only fly fishing is allowed for Lahontan cutthroat trout, and this is one of only a few Lahontan fisheries north of Pyramid Lake in Nevada.

Oregon protects many of its desert redband trout streams by closing them, but it stocks some of the same fish in lakes. The state has stocked hybrid striped bass in Ana and Thompson Valley Reservoirs to control scrap fish populations, and these battlers are best fished in early spring.

Crayfish. Nearly all of Oregon's freshwater holds populations of crayfish. The meat in the tails of these crustaceans is delicious, although some anglers prefer to use them as baitfish.

"Crawdads," as they are called here, are usually caught in mesh traps, baited with a variety of fish and animal parts to lure them inside. Chicken wings, fish heads and carcasses, and tuna liver catfood tins are favorites. Some Oregon lakes, like Timothy and Lake Billy Chinook among others,

are so rich in crawdads that they support commercial fisheries for the Portland restaurant market.

Crawdads are prepared just like crabs; pop them into water heated to a roiling boil and leave them there for 12 to 15 minutes. The tail breaks off from the body, and you can pull or work out the flesh as you would with a miniature lobster.

OUTBOARD BOAT
A boat powered by a transom-mounted outboard motor.
See: Bass Boat; Boat; Flats Boat; Jonboat; Sportfishing Boat; Walleye Boat.

OUTRIGGER
Indispensable tools for offshore trolling, outriggers consist of long poles mounted on the top or sides of offshore sportfishing boats. Once made of bamboo, outriggers are now almost exclusively aluminum.

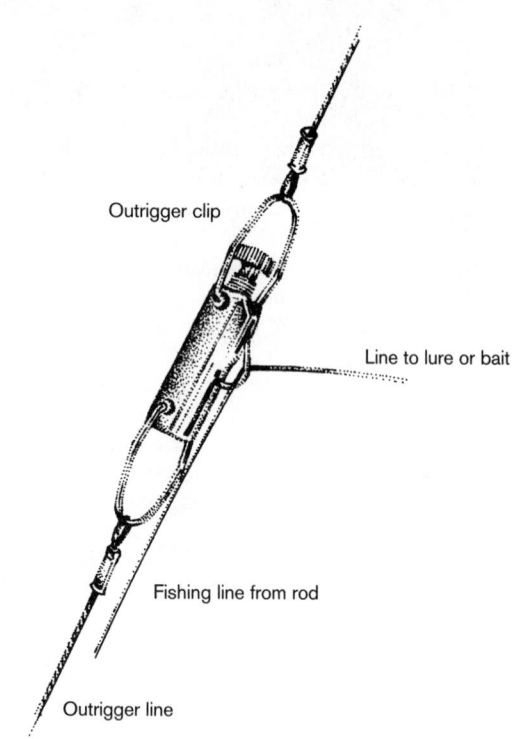

Outrigger clip

Line to lure or bait

Fishing line from rod

Outrigger line

Outriggers are designed so that they can be raised or lowered. They are kept in the raised position when running and not trolling. They are fished in the lowered position, with some type of cord running in a loop to the outrigger's tip. This lanyard contains a release clip, to which the fishing line is attached. The clip is then run up the outrigger pole so that the fishing line leaves the rod tip, goes up to where the release clip is situated on the outrigger line, and then back to the bait behind the boat.

Outriggers are used for several purposes, depending on the kind of fishing being done, and the bait or lures being trolled. The most common

use is when trolling either bait or offshore lures for pelagic species. Here, using an outrigger causes the bait or lure to be pulled from an elevated point, making it skip across the surface (on a fairly short line), thereby imitating the action of many important bait species.

In big-game fishing, and also when used in freshwater trolling (on large lakes and primarily for trout and salmon species), outriggers allow for a greater horizontal spread of lures or bait, permitting increased spacing of these objects and sometimes less likelihood of tangling trolled lines. Increased spacing is often a benefit in freshwater angling to reach fish that are outside of the boat's path of travel, although there are also other means of doing this *(see: sideplaner)*.

When fishing bait in big-game trolling, using an outrigger creates an automatic dropback when a fish strikes the bait, and the line releases from the clip and comes tight. This gives the fish a moment to mouth the bait and results in a better hookup.

Outriggers vary in length according to the size of boat. A 40- to 45-foot boat might have 33-foot outriggers; a 28-foot cabin boat might have 24-foot outriggers. Smaller versions are mounted on the gunwales or T-Tops *(see)* of shorter cabin and center console boats, with the latter seldom having outriggers over 15 feet in length due to the stress they exert on the top itself. The longer outriggers used on large boats employ spreaders to eliminate flex and stiffen the poles. Extra strong models are advisable for towing heavy objects when trolling, and when setting the release clip tension heavy, because a hard strike can put a lot of stress on the outrigger. Trolling with large baits and lures puts a lot of drag tension on the outriggers, as does getting whipped about in rough water.
See: Sportfishing Boat.

OVERFISHING
Harvesting fish at a rate that does not generate a desirable, sustainable, or "safe" population or stock level. This term is especially applied to saltwater, where many fish stocks have been depressed owing to overfishing, primarily, but not entirely, as a result of national and foreign commercial efforts. It is ordinarily used with respect to the harvesting of fish and the landings *(see)* reported, although it can be generally applied to fishing effort, with or without harvest; excessive fishing effort in freshwater, which may not reduce populations but which may result in more difficult angling and a lower success rate, is a form of overfishing, and is usually referenced as fishing pressure *(see)*.
See: Fisheries Management.

OVERHEAD CAST
A basic cast when using all forms of tackle.
See: Casting; Flycasting Tackle.

OVERRUN
A backlash *(see)* in a revolving spool reel, caused when the spool turns faster than the line is carried off that spool, resulting in a snarl of line that must be untangled to continue fishing.

OXBOW
A small lake or channel to the side of a river, formed when the main river meanders and cuts through a point of land and then rejoins itself downstream, creating an island that separates the two sections of water. Generally, the upstream opening of oxbows becomes silted and the meandering side channel is abandoned except in high water periods, thus creating a small lake in the abandoned channel. Oxbows may harbor some species of fish that do not acclimate to the large or swift flow of the river.
See: Backwater.

OXYGEN
The presence or absence of oxygen in various levels of a water body determines where such organisms as fish and zooplankton, which require oxygen, are found. Some waters—especially lakes, ponds, and still backwaters of rivers, or some sections of estuaries—are especially prone to oxygen depletion.

In most water bodies, oxygen concentration is chiefly caused by the infusion of molecular oxygen at the surface and by photosynthesis. In the ocean, there is usually sufficient oxygen throughout all but the most extreme depths, although coastal waters and estuaries may receive such an amount of nutrients and inactive organic matter (including the dumping of waste materials) that areas with slow circulation may be subject to excessive oxygen demand and possibly oxygen depletion. This situation has been known to cause fishkills *(see)*.

The same can happen in freshwater, but lakes and ponds have a different situation, since they are more often prone to poor water circulation, especially in the heat of summer, and they have clear thermal stratification *(see)*.

In the spring, when water in a lake is well mixed, oxygen is usually present at all depths and organisms may be distributed throughout the lake. In the summer, under layering conditions, little or no oxygen is produced in the lowest layer, or hypolimnion *(see)*. As oxygen is consumed through decomposition, levels may become too low for fish and zooplankton, which then must occupy the upper waters. If these low levels are prolonged and the upper waters become very warm, species that require cooler temperatures may die or be forced to move to places that have both suitable temperatures and sufficient oxygen (a tributary spring, for example). With the onset of cooler temperatures and wind activity in the fall, the lake layers break down and the turnover *(see)* replenishes oxygen to the bottom waters.

Formation of ice in winter severs the atmospheric supply of oxygen to the lake. If sunlight can penetrate through the snow and ice, algae and weeds will continue to produce oxygen. If the snow cover is too great, this process will be inhibited. Since respiration and decomposition continue, the amount of oxygen consumed may exceed the amount produced. This is quite common in lakes that have large amounts of weeds, leaves, and other organic debris available for decomposition in the sediment. If oxygen levels fall too low, fish and other aquatic life may die.

Monitoring oxygen would seem to be a strategy that anglers would employ under the theory that an area with insufficient oxygen will not contain sportfish. Although oxygen monitoring devices (meters) have been developed for testing this aspect of water, they have not been popular because the most popular sportfish species seldom inhabit the more stagnant waters that are likely to have low oxygen levels. Nevertheless, factors that cause oxygen depletion should be of concern to anglers, at least from the standpoint of environmental awareness.

OXYGEN METER

A portable electronic device used by a relatively small number of anglers, primarily freshwater bass anglers, to measure the oxygen content of prospective fishing water. If the oxygen level is unsuitable to the fish they seek to catch, they reason that those fish are unlikely to be in that location, and they move elsewhere.

Fish, like people, must have oxygen to survive. Most of the oxygen in our fishing waters comes from photosynthetic algae, bacteria, and plankton.

A lesser amount comes from rooted plants and the interaction of wind and waves. The oxygen level in water is often directly connected to the amount of available light and water pH. Photosynthesis, for instance, has a localized effect on both pH and available oxygen. Whether due to rooted plants in shallower water or from plankton in open water, photosynthesis tends to raise pH as it removes carbon dioxide and generates oxygen. When dead plants decay, however, an almost opposite situation occurs: The process of decay removes oxygen from the water, generates carbon dioxide, and lowers the local pH.

Most research with regard to the effect of oxygen levels on fish has been done with freshwater bass. Oxygen dissolved in water is measured in parts per million (ppm), and 8 to 9 ppm is considered ideal for bass. In research, investigators report that bass were seldom found where oxygen levels dropped below 5 ppm.

An oxycline, or a layer of water containing enough oxygen to support fish, may form in freshwater lakes although the water stratified beneath it may not contain a survivable amount. Naturally, this varies with species because some can survive in less oxygenated water than others, and it varies by time of year. In some lakes and reservoirs that have trout, the oxygen content at the depth that contains their preferred temperature may be inadequate in the midst of the summer; this may cause the fish to die, or send them to cool shallow tributaries with springs, where both temperature and oxygen needs can be met.

The use of an oxygen meter may be helpful in determining where to fish for selected species in stillwater environments, but it has not been demonstrated to be a necessity for anglers.

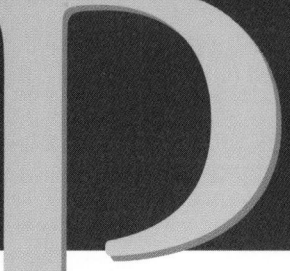

PACK ROD

A multi-piece fishing rod whose sections (usually three or more) are of small enough length to be packed inside a protective tube and carried within or outside of various luggage, especially a daypack or backpack used by hikers and campers. Pack rods are usually either of fly or spinning configuration (a few are convertible) and may also be called travel rods *(see)*.

See: Rod, Fishing.

PADDLEFISH   *Polyodon spathula.*

Other names—spoonbill, spoonbill catfish, spoonbill cat, American paddlefish, Mississippi paddlefish, shovel-billed cat, duck-billed cat, spadefish, shovelfish.

Members of the primitive Polyodontidae family of bony fish, paddlefish are distant relatives of sturgeon *(see)*, whose closest living relatives are gar *(see)* and bowfin *(see)*. They are large, slow-maturing, and long-lived freshwater fish of large inland rivers. They have a distinctive appearance and a prehistoric lineage that dates back hundreds of millions of years. They are not related to catfish.

There are only two known species of paddlefish. The American species *(P. spathula)*, which is profiled here, is commonly referred to simply as paddlefish, lives only in the United States in the Mississippi River system, and is a threatened species, although it is pursued in some areas by both commercial fishermen and recreational anglers. The other species is the Chinese paddlefish *(Psephurus gladius)*, which is native to the Lower Yangtze River in China; also known as the Chinese swordfish, it is believed to be near extinction due to dams and overfishing, and, according to one report, attained a maximum weight exceeding 1,000 pounds.

Paddlefish have been steadily declining in numbers due to overexploitation in the late nineteenth and early twentieth centuries, habitat degradation (e.g., construction of dams, locks, and other migratory obstructions), and pollution. The life history of this species, and its slow-maturing and intermittent spawning, have contributed to its vulnerability to these activities. Paddlefish are protected in some states, and restricted fisheries exist in others. Populations of North American paddlefish that can sustain fishing pressure exist in only a few localities, and poaching is a continued threat. Poaching occurs for the purpose of securing eggs, which are substituted for sturgeon eggs and valuable when made into caviar.

Paddlefish became commercially important for their flesh in the late 1800s and early 1900s after the collapse of sturgeon fisheries. Some states established regulations in the early 1900s in hopes of protecting paddlefish from similar overexploitation.

The roe carried in large, gravid female paddlefish was not recognized as valuable until the 1970s, when diplomatic relations between Iraq, Iran, and the U.S. deteriorated and a ban was enacted to stop all imports from Iraq and Iran into the U.S. This fueled a demand for caviar, with an associated price increase for roe to $26 to $33 per kilogram by 1979 (which more than doubled 10 years later). Although caviar has traditionally been made from sturgeon, the caviar made from paddlefish is said to be equal in quality to that of sturgeon.

The paddlefish caviar market was strong in 1980, when 340 kilograms of roe were taken from Tennessee and Cumberland River impoundments, the major source of paddlefish in the U.S. By the mid-1980s the Tennessee River populations had been overexploited, and commercial fishermen turned to less exploited stocks. They went to other areas, such as Louisiana, where emergency closures were necessary to study the population dynamics before the species collapsed. There is still a demand for paddlefish caviar because sturgeon, especially in Asia, continue to be imperiled. In addition some recreational fisheries for the species still exist, although they represent a fraction of the interest experienced in the late nineteenth and early twentieth centuries.

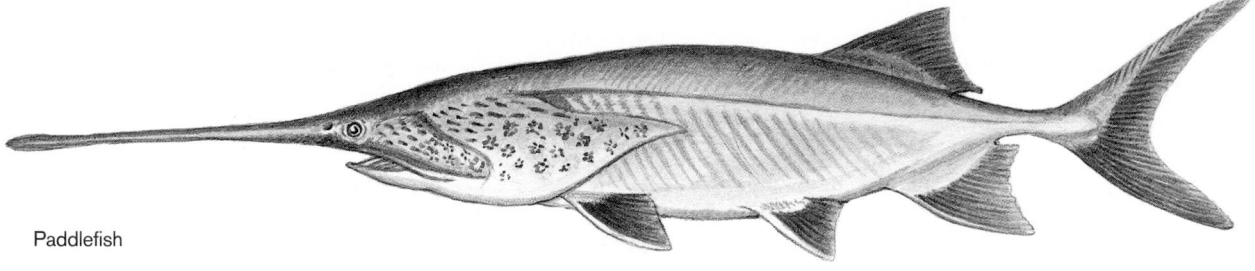

Paddlefish

Identification. The paddlefish is almost sharklike in appearance, and if its long paddle extension were cut off, it would look even more like a shark. Unlike sharks or other fish, paddlefish have a unique, long, paddle- or spoonlike snout. The function of the snout has not been completely determined, although it is highly enervated. Paddlefish are suspected of using their snout to locate prey, perhaps to stir sediments on the bottom. There are two small barbels on the snout, and the underside is dotted with sensory pits.

Paddlefish also have a greatly elongated operculum flap, an extremely large basketlike mouth, long gill rakers, and a deeply forked tail with a high dorsal fin that resembles a shark fin. Adult paddlefish are toothless, but juveniles have teeth on their jaws. The color is slate gray to purplish above. They have an almost white belly, and the skin is smooth, like that of a catfish, with the only scales being on the caudal peduncle.

Size/Age. Paddlefish may live to be 25 to 30 years old. They often grow to 100 pounds, although the average fish is much smaller. Literature from the past contains reports of paddlefish that grew to more than 200 pounds. World records are not kept for this species by the International Game Fish Association (IGFA) because they are not hooked in the mouth, but snagged. Nevertheless, state records show that Montana produced a 142-pound, 8-ounce fish in 1973 in the Missouri River; Missouri produced a 134-pound, 12-ounce fish in Lake of the Ozarks in 1998 and a 130-pounder in 1992; North Dakota produced a 120-pounder in the Missouri River in 1993; and Oklahoma produced a 112-pounder in the Grand River in 1992. The 130-pound fish from the state of Missouri was determined to be 20 years old. The 134-pounder from Missouri was more than 20 years old, 76 inches in overall length, 52 inches from eye to tail fork, and 44 inches in girth.

Distribution. The American paddlefish ranges throughout the Mississippi River drainage, from the Missouri River in Montana southward. Some populations are self-sustaining, whereas others are maintained with stocking. American paddlefish have been sent to Russia (50,000 paddlefish eggs were shipped from Missouri in the mid-1970s) in an attempt to establish the species there and augment caviar production, which has suffered due to dwindling sturgeon populations.

Habitat. Paddlefish prefer low-gradient rivers, pools, backwaters, and oxbows; they also exist in flood-plain reservoirs as a result of dam building. When not spawning, they are pelagic and are found in open water.

Life history/Behavior. Adults migrate upstream to gravel bars in the spring, spawning in high currents with temperatures between 50°F and 60°F. They are commonly found in tailwaters below dams, which impede their upstream migration. In rivers where they are able to travel unimpeded, sturgeon may migrate significant distances; in 1996, Iowa biologists tracked a radio-equipped 32-pound female paddlefish more than 100 miles from its suspected spawning site in the Cedar River, through the Iowa River and into the Mississippi River.

Spawning occurs in midstream, and the adhesive eggs attach to the gravel on the bottom. When hatched, the fry are moved downstream by swift currents into deep pools with lower water velocities. Where oxbows occur, they may serve as alternate spawning sites and important nursery areas for young paddlefish, whose early growth is rapid. Males mature at 7 years of age and females at 9 to 10 years, sometimes longer. Females are very fecund, with 10,000 eggs per kilogram, but they are intermittent spawners, breeding approximately every 2 years. Several males spawn with each female. Growth and fecundity of paddlefish vary with latitude; higher growth and lower fecundity occur in the more southerly portions of its range; the inverse is true for more northerly populations.

Food and feeding habits. Paddlefish eat zooplankton, microscopic plants and animals that live in open water. They swim through the water with their large mouth open and strain out the zooplankton with numerous (hundreds) gill rakers. Contrary to popular belief, they are not bottom feeders and move about in shallow water or near the surface of slow-moving currents with favorable foraging conditions.

Angling. Because they eat only plankton, conventional angling methods using lures, flies, and baits are not applicable for paddlefish. For this reason, and also because they are usually encountered only in spring when spawning, these fish are taken by snagging *(see)*, a practice that cannot be considered sportfishing or angling, and one that disqualifies any fish from world-record consideration.

Snagging seasons exist in some states, and casting or trolling with snag hooks takes place in tailwater pools, where paddlefish are most likely to be found. Snagging fisheries exist for paddlefish in Montana, North Dakota, South Dakota, Missouri, Arkansas, Oklahoma, and Iowa, primarily in the Mississippi, Arkansas, and Missouri Rivers, but also in some inland waters. This species is still part of legal commercial fisheries in some states and may be part of indigenous fisheries, which often entails netting.

Due to the generally low numbers and feeding habits of paddlefish, it is extremely rare for anglers to legitimately catch one, or even to inadvertently snag one while fishing legitimately for other species. Anglers should check regulations regarding fishing for, or catching, paddlefish. Although they are fairly hardy, to help preserve their existence, paddlefish should be handled carefully and returned to the water quickly.

See: Sturgeon.

P

PAKISTAN

As with other southwest Asian and also Middle East countries, little has been reported in the Western world about sportfishing opportunity in Pakistan, and it is not a hotbed of international angling travel. Situated in the northernmost part of the Arabian Sea in the western Indian Ocean, Pakistan's coast is the recipient of warm ocean currents moving up from East Africa and also up along the coast of western India. In addition, the main port and largest city of Kar chi is in close proximity to the deep Indus Canyon and its neighboring shelf.

As a result, a wide variety of pelagic species remains close to Pakistan's shores throughout the year, among them Pacific sailfish, striped marlin, yellowfin tuna, bigeye tuna, wahoo, bonito, and dolphin. Other available fish include various sharks, barred mackerel, cobia, barracuda, amberjack, giant trevally, queenfish, rainbow runners, and barramundi, as well as an assortment of grouper, snapper, and coral reef species.

The Arabian Sea is rough in summer, making September through late April the locally preferred angling period. Cape Montze, Churna Island, and Kaio Island are the favored nearshore fishing spots; offshore trolling occurs in the shelf waters beyond Churna Island. Some boats available for charter may be found in Kar chi.

PALATINE TEETH

Teeth located on the palatine bones inside the upper jaw bone, usually behind the vomerine tooth patch.
See: Anatomy.

PALM

To apply variable pressure with the palm of the hand or, more often, with several fingers, to the revolving or turning spool of a reel when fighting a fish that is taking line. This technique is used with smaller reels, primarily fly, spinning, and baitcasting versions, and may be practiced with concurrent tension on the reel from its own drag *(see)* mechanism. If a fish surges, the hand or palm can be immediately removed from the reel, lessening drag tension and returning it to the tension previously set. Palming a reel spool is often done when the preset drag tension setting on the reel is insufficient to help tire or control the fish, or when a large fish is close to being landed.
See: Playing Fish.

PALMING RIM

The overlapping rim flange on the spool of a fly reel, manually used as an auxiliary spool brake.
See: Flycasting Tackle.

PALOMAR KNOT

A fishing knot for terminal connections.
See: Knots, Fishing.

PALOMETA   *Trachinotus goodei.*

Other names—gafftopsail pompano, joefish, longfin pompano, sand mackerel; French: *carangue quatre;* Portuguese: *galhudo;* Spanish: *palometa, pampano.*

This small species is a member of the Carangidae family of jacks and pompano.

Identification. A bright silvery fish with a deep body, the palometa may be grayish green and blue above and yellowish on the breast. It has dark, elongated dorsal and anal fins that are bordered in a bluish shade, and a black-edged tail. It also has four narrow bars that vary from black to white and are located high on the sides. Traces of a fifth bar appear near the tail.

It is similar to the Florida pompano *(see: pompano, Florida),* but the front lobes of the dorsal and anal fins are blackish and very elongate (the tips reach back to the middle of the caudal fin).

Size. The palometa rarely reaches 1 pound in weight and is usually 7 to 14 inches long; 18 inches is its maximum length. The all-tackle world record is a 1-pound, 3-ounce Bahamian fish.

Distribution. In the western Atlantic, palometa extend from Massachusetts to Argentina as well as throughout the Caribbean Sea, the Gulf of Mexico, and Bermuda. They are common in the eastern and southern Caribbean, occasional in the Bahamas and Florida, and uncommon to rare in the northwest Caribbean.

Habitat. Inhabiting waters up to 35 feet deep, palometa generally form large schools in clear-water areas of the surf zone, along sandy beaches and bays, occasionally around reefs, and in rocky areas.

Spawning behavior. This species is thought to spawn offshore in spring, summer, and fall.

Food. Palometa feed on crustaceans, marine worms, mollusks, and small fish.

Angling. The palometa readily strikes small artificial lures but is seldom a deliberate quarry of anglers owing to its small size.
See: Inshore Fishing; Jacks.

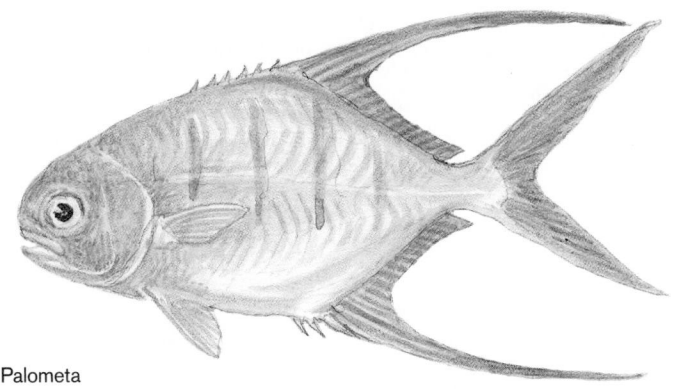

Palometa

PAN DRESSING

A method of cleaning small fish that may not be suitable for filleting or that are to be cooked whole. See: **Fish Preparation—Cleaning/Dressing.**

PANAMA

One legend concerning the derivation of the word *Panama* says that when Cuna Indians were asked where to find gold by Spanish soldiers hundreds of years ago, they responded in their language with the words *panna mai,* which means "far away." Panama is neither far from nor near to most of the North American anglers who are likely to visit it. Linking Central and South America and hosting the famous east-west canal passage, however, it is well situated to receive anglers, and well positioned to host popular gamefish, which are found in abundance both near and far from its Pacific shores.

Ironically, the second explanation for the derivation of this country's name is that it came from an Indian word meaning "land of many fish." Among the various species common to Panama are black, striped, and blue marlin; sailfish; wahoo; dolphin; yellowfin tuna; sharks; roosterfish; cubera snapper; skipjacks; jack crevalle; bigeye and bluefin trevally; mullet and Colorado snapper; houndfish; rainbow runners; snook; tarpon; and corvina. You know the quantity and variety of fish must be substantial when you see just how many specimens caught in Panamanian waters currently fill, or previously filled, the International Game Fish Association (IGFA) record book, especially in the fly-rod categories.

These include wahoo fly-rod records for dolphin, roosterfish, Pacific sailfish, and wahoo, and line-class world records for swordfish (now rare), Pacific sailfish, black marlin, and dolphin. Most of these and others are light-line/light-tackle catches of considerable accomplishment, further underscoring the evidence of great abundance. Many attempts and many lost opportunities must typically occur before an angler connects with a record-setting fish on fly or light tackle.

The freshwater angler, incidentally, will also find angling opportunities in Panama and can catch peacock bass in Gatún Lake, an impoundment along the Río Chagresito, which flows into the Panama Canal. Although not known for large peacocks, these waters offer them in abundance.

Caribbean

Panama is washed by the Caribbean Sea to the north and the Pacific Ocean to the south. The Caribbean winter is often windy and rough, whereas winter on the Pacific is the dry season and features generally sunny, warm, and calm days. Saltwater sportfishing was virtually undeveloped along Panama's Caribbean coast until the late 1990s. It is best fished from May through December. Isla Grande, 35 miles east of Colon (the beginning of the canal), features excellent wahoo trolling, plus yellowfin and blackfin tuna and a shot at sailfish or blue marlin. Bottom fishing and jigging for grouper and cubera snapper are also productive. The San Blas Islands to the east are the home of the Cuna Indians and remain very primitive. The offshore opportunities are complemented by inshore angling for tarpon and snook. The latter are also found around some mainland rivers draining into the Caribbean, but many have been ruined by agricultural pesticides.

Tarpon and snook live in the Panama Canal, too. Tarpon by nature are strictly an Atlantic species, and it was long assumed that the colder water on the Pacific side kept them from adopting a new home. During the 1990s, however, tarpon were caught in many areas along the Pacific coast.

Pacific

For most of the latter part of the twentieth century, the Pacific side of Panama has provided the most notable angling. Many anglers equate Panamanian fishing with live baiting for large black marlin over Hannibal Bank, a seamount off the nation's southwest Pacific coast. Others think of both billfishing and light-tackle angling near Piñas Bay on Panama's southernmost Pacific coast on the South American mainland near the border with Colombia. To still others it means fabulous light-tackle action for inshore species off that same coast or around the island of Coiba.

The Hannibal Bank area sees large numbers of black marlin, and occasionally Pacific blues, from January through March each year. Pacific sailfish and wahoo pass through in great numbers in the summer months. Pelagic species are attracted to Hannibal Bank, a hump that rises from 1,000 fathoms to merely 20 fathoms, and when the proper mix of currents washes by here, the marlin fishing is excellent. This bank is also fished for bottom fish and other nonbillfish species.

At Piñas, the big blacks run from December through March and are soon followed by sailfish throughout the summer. Light-tackle inshore fishing is excellent year-round at Piñas. Inshore anglers generally seek roosterfish and cubera snapper on plugs, baits, or jigs close to beaches or rocky outcrops near shore. Various jacks, plus grouper and offshore targets such as rainbow runners, yellowfin tuna, and dorado, also keep the light-tackle angler busy at Piñas Bay and around Coiba Island. Piñas Bay has long been serviced by the only camp in the area, Tropic Star Lodge, noted for first-class accommodations and food. Anglers are flown in to a nearby airstrip and then driven partway before boarding small boats to complete the trip to the camp.

The 100,000-acre island of Coiba, at the edge of the Gulf of Chiriqui, has long been a prison camp. Club Pacifico de Panama was established there in the early 1970s but stopped operating after 1987 and is now the National Park Headquarters, as

Panama's government encourages ecological tourism even while maintaining the prison. It is possible to run to Hannibal Bank from Coiba, but an abundance of all varieties of fish inshore makes this unnecessary. Access to Coiba is provided by the mother ship *Coiba Express*. Anglers are flown into the prison landing strip on Coiba and transferred to the mother ship by the smaller fishing boats.

Some billfishing and a full range of inshore fishing are also available in the Contadora Islands between Panama City and Piñas. Those islands are mostly a tourist destination, however.

The excitement of black marlin fishing in Panama is heightened by a popular and effective technique: catching and rigging live skipjacks for bait, then power-drifting them behind the boat. The hapless baits (small yellowfins are also used but rarely available) are first to sense the predators approaching, signaling their panic by swimming frantically to the side of the fishing boat in an attempt to flee. When this happens, the angler experiences a great sense of anticipation, an adrenaline rush exceeded only by the fight that follows. The 2- to 3-pound skipjacks are trolled alive and rigged with a hook in front of their snout via a loop of line sewn through their eye sockets, a method that takes practiced anglers just a few seconds, keeping the baitfish alive and frisky.

Although Hannibal Bank is known for black marlin, billfishing enthusiasts have focused more attention in recent times on the Piñas Bay area, and this trend is responsible for many of the aforementioned records. Piñas is situated close to deep water and the influence of currents that lure clusters of baitfish.

At Piñas, a great deal of the billfish trolling occurs out in the Gulf of Panama, about 10 miles from the mainland at Zane Grey Reef, named after the pioneering author/angler but evidently not because of local exploits. Seamounts there feature dropoffs from 130 to 600 feet, and these are the main attractions for marlin. In fact, many species favor this area, sometimes so many that preventing nontargeted fish, such as dolphin, from nabbing baits becomes difficult.

Although billfish are caught off the Panamanian coast year-round, the hot marlin action generally runs from December through April. Blue marlin, which are the least prominent of the three marlin species found here, show up first in December in a normal year, followed closely by blacks. Blues are more prominent to the east than they are near Coiba, and blacks are the mainstay of the fishery in both locales. Both fish average in the 300-pound range, although fish in excess of 500 pounds are taken, as are some blacks in the 700-pound category. The biggest black marlin taken from Piñas waters weighed nearly 900 pounds.

Striped marlin become available in March at Piñas but are rare around Coiba; they are a less-frequent catch than black marlin at any time.

Piñas Bay is a focal point for excellent light-tackle and big-game fishing.

March also brings the heaviest concentration of sailfish; although sails are present throughout the year, April and May are prime times. On the most extraordinary days, boats have reported landing between 15 and 30 sailfish, but an average good day takes in roughly 20 billfish. Sailfish are also present all year off Coiba, but never in such large quantities. The best sailfishing there is during the May to December rainy season, which features mostly late-afternoon and nighttime rain, except during September and October, when it can be persistent.

The billfishing slows from late September through early December. That, however, is also when the wahoo fishing is at its peak, and reports indicate that several dozen of these fish have been caught in a single day, although this is not the norm. Wahoo are noted as rainy-season fish and can be trolled in great quantities at times during that period. Most range from 15 to 30 pounds, with some larger specimens mixed in. Throughout the rest of the season, they are an occasional catch.

With an abundance of fish, opportunities are plentiful to use light big-game tackle for marlin, spinning tackle for sailfish, and fly tackle for sails, striped marlin, and small blacks. These waters are one of the foremost locations for light-tackle (and big-game fly) angling precisely because so many fish are raised. The boats favored here are predominantly small because the water is often calm, and the ability to fight and land such attractive species from smaller craft does enhance the fishery. The boats used at Coiba are generally diesel-powered 23- to 28-foot open boats that operate from the mother ship. At Piñas, 31-foot Bertrams have been used since the early days. When fishing is at its peak, anglers in Panamanian waters actually switch to lighter tackle to increase the challenge. Surely that speaks reams about the angling.

Trolling and billfishing are not the only pursuits here. As mentioned, many opportunities are present inshore for casting and jigging for hard-hitting, strong-pulling creatures. This is especially true off

Coiba Island, where casting popping plugs, plug trolling, jigging, and making deep drops with live or dead baits can yield cubera snapper, jack crevalle, bigeye trevally, bluefin trevally, mullet snapper, and roosterfish, plus assorted other species. It is not uncommon to ring up a catch of 20 fish species over several days.

The bottom drops off significantly around Coiba, so anglers needn't go far to reach productive territory. And, with plenty of baitfish schools around, anglers are virtually guaranteed opportunities to cast to various species marauding baits during a normal day.

Tarpon and snook are also present in Panama's Pacific waters. Tarpon have migrated to new grounds in the Pacific via the Panama Canal, and they have been caught at Coiba. Some rivers near Panama City seem to be developing regular runs of tarpon. Among them is the Bayano, about 35 miles to the west. Fish of 100 pounds are common here, and there are reports of commercially netted specimens weighing between 200 and 250 pounds. The activity is seasonal, concentrating in January and February. Snook are also present in that river, primarily from December through May, and have been caught to 47 pounds.

PANFISH

This term is used widely by anglers and fisheries managers to collectively describe a variety of small fish of several species. There is no individual species called a panfish. The term is used almost universally in freshwater, seldom in saltwater; although common to anglers, it may be unfamiliar or even confusing to nonanglers.

The term "panfish" often refers to fish that, when fried whole, can fit into a pan, but it is also often understood to mean species that are not technically classified as gamefish *(see)* and that are usually abundant and as valued for their tasty flesh as for the enjoyment of catching them.

Yellow perch are a popular panfish for ice fishing.

As explained elsewhere, the classification of species as gamefish, and the public view of their sporting value or virtue, are variable issues. Therefore, in some quarters, panfish are viewed as gamefish, whereas in others they are not. "Gamefish" or not, small species that are susceptible to angling are valued highly for the recreation they afford, and for the delicious table fare they become.

Although panfish are commonly linked by these factors, the species that fit under this umbrella are not all linked biologically. Many "panfish" are members of the sunfish *(see)* family, the perch family, the bass *(see: black bass)* family, the catfish *(see)* family, and the sucker *(see suckers)* family. These include, but are not limited to, such sunfish as the green, longear, orange spotted, spotted, and redear varieties; plus bluegill, Sacramento perch, rock bass, warmouth bass, black crappie, white crappie, yellow bass, white bass, yellow perch, and white perch. In some areas, people include suckers, bullhead, pickerel, and even carp in this category. The primary, and most widely distributed, panfish are discussed separately here.

Whether panfish fit into a pan or are classified as gamefish is immaterial to most people who fish for them. Although black bass, trout, and walleye garner higher accolades for sport, and thus greater media attention, it is an indisputable fact that more time is devoted to angling for the collective group of panfish than for any other freshwater species. They are not only a strong component of spring and summer open-water fishing, but in many places they are also the prime quarry for ice anglers.

Furthermore, panfish are especially significant for peaking children's interest in angling, and for providing family fishing opportunities.

The fun in catching panfish is a significant factor in their popularity, as most are very scrappy when hooked on light tackle. Sunfish, rock bass, perch, crappie, and other panfish dart and dive, run and turn, and offer a fine short-term fight on light fishing equipment, even if they are only 6 or 7 inches long and a half pound in size. Compared on an ounce-for-ounce basis, panfish are among the most determined and vigorous fish caught by anglers.

As mentioned, the popularity of panfish—crappie, perch, white bass, and bullhead in particular—rests equally in their appeal as table fare. They are among the most favored freshwater food fish, in part because of their size, and they are delicious when prepared in a variety of ways. A feast of fresh panfish is one of the finest—and usually simplest—meals that a fish lover can have.

Feasts, in fact, are usually possible because panfish are relatively abundant in most places where they are found. Fisheries managers generally encourage harvesting panfish and apply a fairly liberal creel limit *(see)* to facilitate this. Although panfish provide a good forage base for larger gamefish, they can quickly overpopulate a lake or pond. Most panfish are generally prolific spawners, and harvesting them is helpful in keeping fish populations in balance. When populations get out of balance, a body of water can be populated by stunted sunfish, crappie, or other species, and removing significant numbers is necessary to help with this problem. Fortunately, delectable flesh makes this a task that many anglers are willing to take on.

There would be a lot more eating and catching, however, if more anglers would take more time to learn about panfish and to pursue them more carefully. The following information is condensed, somewhat generalized, and focused on the bluegill, crappie, yellow bass, white bass, and white perch, although much of what is contained here applies to species with more limited or similar ranges. Yellow perch *(see: perch, yellow)*, bullhead *(see)*, and pickerel *(see: pickerel, chain)* are covered under their respective headings.

Most people think panfish are caught strictly on live baits, and much of the time this is true. At times, however, lures or flies will take more panfish than will live baits. So don't become a one-bait or one-tactic panfish angler. The more versatile your approach, the more panfish you'll get on your line.

Panfishing isn't difficult, but it can be frustrating, and catching the larger specimens with some consistency often involves more than being on the right body of water. If you are a beginner, consider seeking out an experienced angler for the species you're after; offer to furnish the lunch and soft drinks in appreciation for the coaching. Lacking that, hire a good guide for a day; guides who take clients panfishing are hard to find in many northern states but are more common in Southern waters, especially on big lakes and impoundments.

Bluegill

Bluegills are a schooling fish; where you find one, there are others nearby. They are aggressive and will eat most anything you offer them when hungry, but they can be mighty picky on occasion. So it pays to take along both live baits and artificial lures when you're specifically seeking these fish. When bluegills are on a feeding spree you can often see them churning the water, voraciously attacking a larvae hatch, mosquitoes, or the eggs of nesting bass or crappie.

Where to fish.   The cliché that "fish are where you find them" is old but so true with bluegills. And, except for springtime, when bluegills are bedding against shallow-water shores, you just have to shop around from one cover type to another until you meet up with a school.

Spring is when the fishing is easiest. Be out early in the day, when the water usually is calmest. Move quietly around the shoreline and look for two things: gravel, rock, or sandy bottom areas; and shallow water off points or around weeds and lily pads. All of these are typical spawning spots.

As you move, keep your eyes ahead to watch for the sudden darting movement of bluegills spooked by other fish, fish-eating birds, or your approach. Have a cold drink, wait until things quiet down, then quietly approach and fish the spot.

After spring gives way to summer, finding bluegills can be tougher because they hie to deeper hangouts. Now is the time to pay attention to cover, including logs, bushes, and brush, and to places like grassy flats, channels, lily-pad clusters, and away-from-shore humps.

When midsummer weeds become denser, try this old trick: Take along a sickle and run your boat into the weed mass. Usually the weeds are no more than a foot deep. Cut a bushel-basket-size hole on each side of the boat, then leave for about an hour. While you're gone, the minute zooplankton and algae you have shaken loose may have attracted nearby bluegills. When you return, approach quietly and fish your handmade hotspots.

During fall and early winter, food is scarcer, forcing bluegills to roam in search of food supplies. Keeping this in mind, anglers should investigate both shallow and deep dropoff areas, remaining alert for any school movement. Try a bait at different depths until the float nods its head to signal not only a strike, but also the location of a school of fish.

Once you locate seasonal hangouts, you're set for the year. Keep notes on these spots, and be aware of feeding times. You'll discover that habit patterns are dependable from one year to the next. However, these times and places will differ from one lake to another. Much of this is due to variances in cover types, lake temperatures, and hangouts in deep and shallow lakes.

Tactics.   A cricket comes as near to being infallible for bluegills as any live bait. Never take along just a few dozen. Feeding crickets to bluegills is like feeding popcorn to a hungry youngster. It disappears in a hurry, so be sure to bring plenty. Many old-timers never venture out without a couple hundred. Keep the crickets cool and feed them oatmeal between trips, and they won't go to waste.

A commercial cricket box makes them easy to grab in a hurry. You can make a cricket container out of a large oats box. Near the top edge, cut a quarter-size hole and staple it over with a half-dollar-size flexible rubber cover. When you want a cricket, just raise the flap, shake out a cricket, and the flap will automatically close the hole.

Use a No. 8 long-shanked Aberdeen hook with crickets; this is easy to grasp and remove when the fish is deeply hooked. Impale the cricket through the tougher shoulder area and let it wiggle loosely on the bend. Bluegills will swipe a bunch without getting hooked, but the catch is worth it.

One way to reduce fish pilferage and increase your catching average is to learn to read a sensitive float *(see)* or bobber. Use one shaped like a slim pencil, and paint the very tip bright red. Watch this for the slightest movement. If it tilts to the left, it means a bluegill has sucked in the cricket from the

P

right side. If it rises the slightest bit, a bluegill has slurped the cricket from above. Set the hook at any of these indications and you'll not only catch more but also bigger bluegill.

The best artificial lure is a green, sponge-rubber spider with white legs on a No. 10 hook. This can be used on a fly rod, below a float on a casting rig, or dunked at the end of a line on a cane or graphite pole.

As it absorbs water and sinks naturally, the rubber legs make a minute movement that seems to trigger a bluegill's feeding instincts. Cast near cover, let it sink very slowly, and if the line stops sinking, set the hook—a bluegill has inhaled the spider. At times, a tiny bit of red worm on the hook barb adds a touch of magic.

When using the spider with a spinning or spin-casting outfit, try attaching a small spinner to it. If it is too light to cast, add a couple of split shot in front of the spinner to give needed weight. Keep the retrieve very slow; the blade should barely turn over. If you get followers but no takers, try adding a dab of marshmallow on the hook.

Bluegill are caught on other items, of course. Pieces of worms and small grubs impaled on small hooks and fished under a float are commonly used when crickets aren't available. You need to use a small hook and fully thread the bait onto it to keep the bluegill (and other sunfish) from nibbling it away. Small spinners sometimes catch bluegill, although seldom in quantity to compare with natural baits. Small flies (wet flies, nymphs, and dry flies on No. 12 and 14 hooks) and tiny cork-bodied popping bugs catch shallow-water bluegill, especially during the nesting season, and getting these fish to take on the surface is great fun.

Crappie

There actually are two species of crappie, the black and white varieties *(see: crappie, black; crappie, white),* but there's so little difference between the two that they can be treated as one when it comes to finding and catching them.

Also a sunfish family member, the crappie is considered by many to be the most desirable for table fare because of its tender, succulent flesh. Commonly called specks, crappie in the South are considered better tasting than those up North; however, northern waters are likely to hold yellow perch, which are as good to the palate as any crappie.

Where to fish.   When you set out on a strange lake in search of crappie, think brush, brush, or the nearest thing resembling brush. The reason is simple. Crappie are mostly minnow eaters, and minnows hide around any kind of brush, or weeds, to avoid being eaten. So crappie go where minnows hide. Other hideouts are fallen trees, bushes, old piers, flooded weeds, or shoals covered with coontail or sphagnum moss, plus wrecked boats, docks, building blocks or brushpiles *(see)* that have been planted to attract minnows, and undercut banks.

Big yellow perch, sunfish, and crappie add up to a memorable day of panfishing.

When these don't pay off, try drifting with the wind or slow-trolling across a lake, plying a minnow at different depths until you cross paths with a school of roving crappie.

Tactics.   Get a long cane pole, or a telescoping graphite one for handiness, and attach an equal length of No. 6 nylon monofilament line. A popular crappie hook is a No. 2 Model Perfect or Carlisle fine wire. Either will make a small hole in a minnow's carcass and have a bend wide enough not to injure a minnow as you insert the hook.

For drift fishing, hook the minnow in the lips and be careful not to go deep enough to enter the brain area. For dunking the minnow into brush, hook it through the dorsal fin base, being careful not to penetrate the spine.

Keep moving from brush to brush, easing in close so you can dunk the minnow right against the cover—the closer the better. Be sure to keep minnows lively to catch the bigger crappie, called "slabs." An aerated minnow bucket helps. Drifting is also a standard tactic because crappie roam around in schools, and it sometimes takes a roaming angler to find them.

When you catch your first crappie, remember this: Let it splash around a bit on the surface, then toss in a live minnow right beside it. Crappie are like chickens; each chicken wants a piece of what the eating chicken has. So it is with avid crappie. The minnow helps keep other crappie looking for food.

As a last resort, when crappies seem to be in Nowheresville, try this old cracker trick. Anchor your boat near a patch of weeds, brush, or lily pads. Spend about a minute slapping the surface with the tip of your crappie pole. Wait five minutes, then repeat.

Other anglers will think you're a bit daffy until you begin hauling in crappie. This commotion sounds like a school of feeding crappie. Again, like chickens, a roving school will come to the sound believing minnows are there for the gorging.

Although crappie are caught from time to time on various lures (occasionally on a surface lure or a diving plug), the one artificial that pays off regularly is a small leadhead jig with a soft-plastic body resembling a minnow. The trick is to fish this so s-l-o-w-l-y you yawn. Jigs weighing from $1/64$ to $1/16$ ounce are often better than heavier ones, and obviously this technique requires light line. It also reveals how crazy crappie can be— they want minnows lively but prefer artificial lures as near dead as possible.

White Bass

The white bass is the largest and most sporting of all the panfish. In fact, some are so big that one specimen can more than fill a skillet. Few fish in freshwater hit harder, pound for pound, or fight longer, than an energetic white bass. Maybe that's because it's a member of the saltwater striped bass family. Many a fishless day has been saved by a school of white bass showing up when all other species are void. At many impoundments today, an abundant population of white bass is a saving grace when other popular species fall off.

Where to fish. Much of the time you needn't worry about where to fish for white bass. They tell you either by sight or sound. You'll see anglers cruising around open water, or in backwater bays, standing up, looking in all directions. They're scouting for white bass.

The silvery bodies of these fish can be seen flashing at a distance; you'll spot them much sooner than you hear them. Other times, you'll be fishing for other species and suddenly hear a terrific commotion as a school of white bass erupts nearby and slashes into shad minnows just under the surface.

When you see, or hear, a feeding school, approach as quietly as possible, using the wind to drift you toward them if possible. Once within casting distance, cast your lure ahead of, not into, the moving school. If you spook them, they dive deeply and appear elsewhere, usually out of casting range. Stay with a school until it sounds from sight, then scout for another.

At times, such as in early spring, finding white bass can be extremely difficult. Just remember that these fish are a gravel spawner, so look for long shorelines showing white stones, rocks, or riprap.

Catching tactics. White bass are easier to catch on artificial lures than on live baits for one salient reason: They spook easily, and an angler must normally get closer to use live baits than artificials. A good caster can power an artificial lure a long distance and catch a number of white bass before the school gets jittery.

Among live baits, of course, the threadfin shad is tops because it's the favorite food of white bass. Most seasoned anglers use a baitcasting, spinning, or spincasting outfit with just enough sinker to cast the minnow. Two split shots placed about 2 inches apart above the minnow will tangle less than one sinker. No float is used because this would impede the cast. A free-running minnow looks more natural to a white bass and rarely has time to move before a white bass nabs it.

Artificial lures must meet certain requirements to be effective. They must be compact, close to the size and look of shad, and cast well into a breeze. The most popular is a weighted tailspinner, with a lead body, a treble hook on the belly, and a spinner on the tail. Also effective is a minnow-type surface lure that will dart and sashay when twitched, and a shiny slab spoon with a treble hook.

Each of these lures will cast well into a wind, and will enable long casts that don't alarm the school. Stay parallel with a working school and cast ahead of it to avoid spooking the leaders. To take bigger bass, try this trick: Cast over and beyond the working school, then let the lure sink for a 10-count before retrieving. This lets it get down below the school where the bigger, smarter white bass cruise along to slurp up the wounded shad drifting down from the slaughter going on above.

In early spring, when white bass are scarce, look for gravelly or rocky shores. Put on the tailspinner, cast into shallows, and let the lure sink until slack line tells you it is on bottom. Lower your rod tip, reel in slack line, and, with a sharp upward sweep of the rod tip, jump the lure off bottom. Keep it coming, fast, until something almost jerks the rod from your hands. At this moment, you will know how hard a white bass can sock a lure!

Remember these spots and return next year about the same time. White bass cruise here following urges for the spawning season. Even though they may not be hungry, the super-fast lure causes impulse strikes.

Yellow Bass

Yellow bass are somewhat similar to white bass in behavior; although smaller on average, they'll amaze you with the impact of their strikes and vigorous fight. Yellow bass are more bottom dwelling than are white bass and rarely give away their presence. When they do, they are typically feeding on a bottom hatch, especially during the early, warm days of summer.

Here's a sign to watch for. As you fish, keep examining surface waters close to you and look for large patches of tiny bubbles. These are caused by a school of yellow bass grubbing on the bottom. Ease

P

a small spoon vertically down from the tip of your rod until it touches bottom. Jig it in a small circle. The action will be fast and superb.

White Perch

No relation to the yellow perch, this fish is a member of the true bass family, white and yellow. Why they hung the name "perch" on it is anyone's guess, but the misnomer is here to stay. Like many panfish, however, the white perch is a schooling species and a fine sportfish; it is similar in many respects to the white bass, which it somewhat resembles.

Where to fish. Look for tributary streams and long points in moving water, which are favored hangouts of roaming schools of white perch. They also inhabit sandy and gravelly bottom estuaries and shallow bays. Finding them is a matter of moving about, and being alert to school movements.

White perch are creatures of habit. If you find them in an area one day, return there the next day. They usually run the same daily courses, as long as the food supply continues.

Catching tactics. The majority of white perch are caught on live bait, including crabs, minnows, and worms. But canny anglers take an appreciable number on artificial lures that require less fuss.

Some anglers use the first-caught white perch for bait, cutting it in small pieces and impaling these on light leadhead jigs. Fly anglers use tiny nymphs and larvae flies inched slowly over bottom on a sinking line and leader. Miniature crankbaits, spinners, and spoons are good.

Spring is the best time for the biggest catches. In any season, it is important to keep artificial lures as weedless as possible for fishing right on bottom in varied cover.

Simple Care and Cooking

The following brief advice will help you get the most out of a fresh batch of panfish. A comprehensive review of caring for fish, cleaning, and cookery issues is contained elsewhere *(see: fish preparation—care; fish preparation—cleaning/dressing).*

Proper keeping. The sooner you eat panfish after catching them, the better the flavor. Here is a condensed review of ways to keep them as fresh as possible.

If the water is cold, panfish can be kept on a stringer. In hot weather, keep them in a big plastic bag laid on ice. Because these fish are small, laying them directly on ice can turn their flesh soft, which will deteriorate the flavor.

If your catch is big enough for freezing a batch of fillets, you need to avoid freezer burn, which turns flesh white and robs it of both juices and natural flavor. The best thing is to freeze the fillets in water for long-term storage. For short-term freezing, place the fillets flat on a sheet of plastic wrap, fold the four flaps over, and squeeze out all possible air. Enfold this packet in a sheet of aluminum foil

or freezer wrap. Lay the packets side by side, not atop each other, and freeze as fast as possible.

Tasty cooking. What constitutes a "fine kettle of fish" to some is a mess to others, but it's hard to go wrong with the small fillets or whole bodies of panfish unless you overcook them.

To deep-fry, wipe off excess moisture, dip small whole panfish or fillets in buttermilk, dredge in flour seasoned to your taste, and deep-fry until they are done as crispy as you like them. Drain on folded paper toweling and cover with foil to hold the heat until the entire batch is ready.

To broil, place whole panfish on a broiling pan, baste with Italian salad dressing, broil five minutes on one side, turn, baste, and broil three more minutes. The oil in the dressing melts and drains into the pan. The seasoning remains, and the result is surprisingly tasty.

To bake, try this simple and delightful Swedish recipe. Place each serving in foil; add a quarter stick of butter, a squeeze of lemon juice, a shake of salt and pepper, and a few small potatoes and carrots, then garnish with a sprig of fresh dill. Fold the foil lengthwise and pucker up the ends. Broil in an oven or over charcoal for about 30 minutes, or until done to suit.

See: Sunfish; and individual species.

PAPUA NEW GUINEA

This nation in the southwestern Pacific consists of the eastern half of New Guinea, the second largest island in the world, and an assemblage of more than 600 islands of varying sizes. With its mainland separated from Australia's Cape York Peninsula by just 150 kilometers across the Torres Strait linking the Arafura and Coral Seas, and bordering the Irian Jaya territory of Indonesia, Papua New Guinea is diverse in cultures, wildlife, natural resources, and fisheries.

Volcanic islands, coral atolls, low-lying mangrove swamps, plunging valleys, fog-shrouded mountains, dense rain forests, numerous jungle rivers, and tropical seas characterize this country, which contains lightly explored fisheries along the coasts and in the lush interior. That interior, although marked by many rivers and some lakes, is not known so much for its variety of fish but for two of the meanest and hardest-battling species—Niugini bass and spottail bass—caught in freshwater. The abundant low-lying swampy regions along the coast are known for equally compelling species, including barramundi, saratoga, and threadfin salmon; offshore, the reefs and blue water contain marlin, sailfish, various tuna, mahimahi, trevally, and a host of gamefish.

Regarded as one of the last sportfishing frontiers, Papua New Guinea has had little infrastructure for freshwater and saltwater angling, and relatively few angling-oriented operations have been established here, mainly due to the remoteness of opportunities

Fish have been in existence for approximately 470 million years, making them the oldest vertebrates.

(in freshwater) and to the difficulty in attracting people from afar for saltwater fishing (when there are other more well-developed and easily accessed locations, like Australia's Great Barrier Reef). Some mobile operations have existed for coastal and interior fishing expeditions, however, and a few island or coastal camps do provide inshore and offshore fishing.

Just south of the equator, Papua New Guinea has a tropically humid climate. Daily temperatures range from the mid-20s to the mid-30s Celsius, and the humidity is between 70 and 90 percent. There are two seasons, or "monsoons." The southeasterly monsoon, or dry season, runs from April through October. It is hot and humid during this time, but rains are infrequent (although rain in the interior at this time can still bring several inches). Near coastal areas, a constant sea breeze makes the climate very balmy. The westerly monsoon, or wet season, runs from late November through March. This period tends to be oppressively humid, bringing frequent tropical downpours and associated brief heavy winds. From late September into November, oppressive days leading up to the rainy season can be good for fishing, but April through June is also prime. Although many saltwater species are caught year-round, fishing is generally best just before and just after the rainy season.

Saltwater

Papua New Guinea is bordered by the Bismarck Sea on the north, the Solomon Sea on the east, and the Coral Sea and Gulf of Papua on the south. The northerly coast faces deep water with steep dropoffs close to shore and is especially productive for a range of pelagic and reef species. The southern coast, particularly in the western sector, is shallower and deeply indented with bays, estuaries, and extensive mangrove swamps along the low-lying coast.

The major center for inshore and brackish-water species is at Daru in the Western Province. The entire southwestern coastline from the Irian Jaya border east to the city of Kerema is lowland swamp and sparsely populated, most prominently containing the expansive Fly River Delta north of Daru. Navigable in its lower reaches, the Fly is one of the country's major rivers and drains much of the western interior. Barramundi are the principal catch here, followed by saratoga and threadfin salmon.

Farther east, some sportfishing along the southeastern coast originates out of the capital city of Port Moresby, and on the eastern coast near Huon Peninsula out of Lae in Morobe Province.

Off the northwest coast of Papua New Guinea, anglers have experienced extraordinary light-tackle fishing for a host of offshore species, without going far offshore. Blue marlin, black marlin, Pacific sailfish, yellowfin tuna, dogtooth tuna, bigeye tuna, kingfish, wahoo, giant trevally, barracuda, mahimahi, and various sharks are among the area's plentiful species, caught close to the mainland as well as at several islands nearby, including Karkar and Bagabag, respectively about 18 and 43 kilometers from the mainland.

Marlin and sailfish are available here year-round. The best season for blue marlin is from September through November, for sailfish from December through March, and for black marlin from April through June. Blue and black marlin between 200 and 500 pounds have been caught, although larger fish have reportedly been lost. During periods of greatest abundance, sailfish hunt in packs and run to good sizes. Reefs offer fishing for dogtooth tuna, Spanish mackerel, giant trevally, sailfish, and other species. Dogtooth tuna are especially plentiful, large, and powerful.

Freshwater

The inland region of Papua New Guinea features tropical rain forest, jungle vegetation, and grassland, as well as rugged mountains running through the center of the mainland. Jungle highlands have clear, fast-flowing streams coursing from either slope to larger flows and the sea. In some areas, especially along the southern coast, the rivers wind through plains and swamps infested with mosquitoes (malaria is a concern).

The jungle rivers are known for Niugini bass and spottail bass, freshwater relatives of cubera snapper with deep muscular bodies; these fish grow large and are truly ferocious. They are seldom caught in great numbers, owing to their demeanor and to their proclivity for thick cover, which demands accurate casting. They number among the most demanding river fish to catch. They have a well-honed knack for striking a lure as they turn and swiftly head back to cover; so strong are they that a high percentage are never landed.

Niugini bass (locally called black bass or Papuan black bass) and spot-tail bass are commonly caught from 15 to 20 pounds; 30- to 40-pounders are considered large. Some have reportedly been caught to 60 pounds, and Australian anglers with experience in angling for this species use stout 6-foot rods, wide-spool baitcasting reels, and 40-pound line, and that often doesn't do the job. Large, heavy diving plugs and surface plugs are used to entice the fish from bank-side log and tree cover. Known for busting up tackle, demolishing lures, and making blistering initial runs, these fish do not have great stamina for long fights, but the first-moment encounter is usually so explosive that, in snag-infested jungle rivers, they win their freedom in a short but furious tussle.

Barramundi are caught in some of the rivers as well, and the lower tidal reaches provide action for a variety of species. Numerous rivers have Niugini bass and spot-tail bass fishing potential, although opportunities to fish these are scarce and have not been continuously reliable. The Kikori River of the Southern Highlands has been fished by a mothership houseboat operation with fishing skiffs in tow;

P

it empties into a large deltaic region of Bevan Sound at Saumao Peninsula but is flanked by such large systems as the Purari, Turama, and Guavi Rivers, not to mention the many tributaries to all of these—all with angling potential. On the northwest coast, the Sepik River flows more than 1,200 kilometers, beginning high in the central mountains near the Irian Jaya border. It is navigable for almost its entire length, and floods numerous lakes, including the vast, shallow expanse of Chambri Lake, although the fisheries here are unknown.

Niugini bass and spot-tail bass also thrive in the rain forest rivers of New Britain, Papua New Guinea's largest offshore island. Dogtooth tuna, trevally, and other species are found near shore around this and other easterly islands and reefs.

Sections of interior Papua New Guinea's pristine wilderness have been compromised in recent years through timber harvesting, including clearcutting along rivers, and the watersheds have been impacted. The effect on rivers and their fisheries, as well as on the deltas and possibly beyond, is already being felt, according to some accounts.

PARAGUAY

Nestled in the middle of South America and surrounded by Brazil, Argentina, and Bolivia, the country of Paraguay is true to the meaning of its name—"land of rivers." These rivers contain a host of warmwater fish species—some 250 in fact—not unlike those of the Amazonian region of Brazil. An exception is the greater prominence in Paraguay of dorado, a species of great sportfishing interest. The dorado is the one species with which this country is most identified by anglers.

All rivers and watersheds in Paraguay belongs to the Plata (Plate) Basin, which is formed by the Paraná River—the most important river in the basin and one of the world's largest rivers—and the Paraguay River. Both originate in Brazil, where the Paraguay is formed from various tributaries in

southwestern Brazil's Pantanal, a large swamp or a huge marsh that is the only river here not affected by dams.

The Paraguay River divides the country into diverse regions: the Gran Chaco alluvial plain in the west, and Paraguay Proper, which is the southerly portion of the Paraná Plateau. The latter has elevations up to 2,000 feet and gives rise to numerous tributaries of the Paraguay River on its west and the Paraná River on its east.

The mighty and beautiful Paraná forms part of the border with Brazil until it is joined by the Iguaçu River downstream of famous Iguaçu Falls, and then forms the border with Argentina until it is joined by the Paraguay River near Corrientes and leaves the country. The character and fisheries of the Paraná River have been affected by several huge hydroelectric constructions, including one of the world's largest, the Itapúa Dam, and the Yacyreta Dam. Unfortunately, fish ladders were not constructed to allow upstream passage of migratory fish, including dorado, to their spawning grounds, and because fish congregate in the spillway below the long dams, poaching has been common and resulted in adverse impacts.

The Uruguay River, incidentally, is the third of these important flows that are part of the Plata Basin, although it is not in Paraguay. It, too, has been seriously affected by dams. The Uruguay River borders Brazil and Argentina, then Argentina and Uruguay, before emptying into the Plata estuary at the Atlantic Ocean near the mouth of the Paraná River.

The Paraná is the most significant river for sportfishing, although the dams have changed habitats and gamefish behavior. Nevertheless, there is still good fishing along its length, and the best season is spring. In this hemisphere, spring occurs from September through early December.

Along the southern Paraguay River, there is notable fishing in its tributary, the Tebicuary River, which flows westerly and is easily reached by road 100 miles south of the capital city of Asunción. Sportfishing here is particularly attractive, especially for dorado, although the river is affected by rains; angling success is therefore dependent on the river level. The Tebicuary is best in spring, summer, and fall; the winter months of May and June provide slow action due to colder water temperatures.

Other important tributaries that also flow into the Paraguay River are the Manduvira—located 35 miles north of Asunción—the Negro, the Ypane, the Aquidaban, and the Apa. The Apa is Paraguay's northernmost tributary and forms the border with Brazil. All are excellent rivers when water conditions are good. These tributaries and the upper Paraguay River are fishable year-round but are best in spring.

There are several species of the golden fish, dorado, in Paraguay, but the most important of them is *Salminus maxillosus (see: dorado);* the hard-fighting

Successful dorado anglers pose with their trophy along the banks of the Paraná River.

glamour species, it runs strong, jumps in the air like a tarpon, and fights to the last moment. This fish may reach 40 pounds in Paraguayan waters (though larger fish were known in the past), is the object of considerable local attention, and is highly sought by international anglers.

Sportfishing for these aggressive predators is approached in many ways. Trolling with lures is the most common activity; anglers frequently drift from a boat with live baits, depending on water clarity and the type of river. Casting from a drifting boat or from the shoreline is possible at some times and places, and is great sport with light tackle.

In northern Paraguay, some pristine jungle rivers like the Apa provide exciting light tackle and flycasting for dorado in the dry season from September through November, when fish are moving upstream and can uniquely be caught in the rapids. The occurrence of rains, however, floods the rivers and ends low clear-water sport.

Some of the better dorado fishing occurs along the Paraná's southernmost border with Argentina, on the Paraná above its merger with the Paraguay River to south of Posadas, and across into Argentina *(see)* in a large swampy backwater region known as Esteros del Ibera, where consistently clean water provides good action, including casting with lures and flies.

The equipment normally used for dorado is 16- to 25-pound line on appropriate spinning and bait-casting tackle. Steel leaders are mandatory, and lures and terminal gear must be of premium quality, as the power of the dorado's jaws can destroy equipment. Eight- and 9-weight flycasting tackle with large streamers are also used, and line types vary with the circumstances.

Other prominent sportfishing targets in Paraguay are the spotted catfish, *Pseudoplatistoma coruscans,* and striped catfish *Pseudoplatistoma fasciatum,* locally and regionally called *surubi.* The striped catfish appears in both the Plata and Amazon Basins, whereas the spotted catfish occurs only in the Plata. These species can be caught with artificial baits and even by fly fishing. The spotted catfish easily reaches 120 pounds and is a good fighter that does not jump, but makes strong, sometimes tackle-busting runs, looking for stumps or rocks to snag the line. It is found in large rivers and tributaries, feeds mainly on other live fish, and prefers strong currents.

Both species are night feeders, roaming shallow banks and sandbars, but both are easily spooked. Anglers approach them quietly from shore or anchored boats, and they are usually caught on a single-hooked live bait attached to a sliding sinker. During the day they linger in deep channels or in deep eddies, near the mouths of tributaries to a large river. Trolling for catfish with deep-diving lures in the channels is a common practice in the Paraná River, as is drifting with live baits.

Surubi are highly prized for their flesh in South America, and considered top gourmet fare. They are widely offered in restaurants as a special menu item. Dorado are also good tasting, and are preferred when grilled.

Another important gamefish is the pacu, *Colossoma mitrei,* a mainly herbivorous fish that is not considered a predator. It is, however, great to hook on light tackle and provides a powerful, deep fight. Pacu occur in all rivers and lagoons in the Plata Basin and reach 30 pounds or more. Pacu are pursued with natural baits from shore or from a drifting boat. Hooks are baited with fruits, snails, freshwater crabs, parts of fish, or processed corn baits.

Sportfishing season in Paraguay is generally good almost year-round; however, the peak angling season for most species is from September through early December. Some waters still do not receive much fishing pressure, although others are subjected to excessive fishing, including killing fish, and also to poaching problems.

PARASITES
See: Diseases and Parasites.

PARR
Small, young anadromous fish, particularly salmon and trout, living in freshwater prior to migrating out to sea. During this life stage, parr develop large vertical or oval rounded spots (sometimes called bars) on the sides. Called parr marks, these help camouflage the fish and also identify it; they will gradually disappear as the fish becomes silvery, regardless of whether the fish goes to sea (some do not). In the silvery phase, the fish is known as a smolt *(see).* Migration to sea occurs between 2 and 8 years.
See: Salmon, Atlantic.

PARTY BOAT
The term party boat encompasses a variety of sportfishing vessels that are known by various local names, including drift boats, long range boats, head boats, and day boats. A party boat is usually a large vessel that accommodates individual anglers, mostly on a nonreserved basis and with daily fares applied per head, generally paid upon boarding. This is different from a charter boat *(see),* which charges a boat rate and is generally reserved by a small group of people in advance. Party boats offer an economical way for people of any skill level to spend a day fishing on a large body of water, sometimes for a diversity of species.

Party boats range in size from vessels carrying as few as a half dozen anglers to huge vessels a hundred feet or more in length, complete with bunks, galleys, and accommodations for trips of a week or more. They are primarily a saltwater angling possibility, found in most every coastal port on the

P

Atlantic, Pacific, and Gulf Coasts, and depending on the season, offering angling for a range of fish species. In freshwater, midsize party boats are found on a few large bodies of water, such as Lakes Michigan and Erie, and their species options are much narrower. Party boats are usually easy to find in major ports, and in popular sportfishing areas there are often many options as to what you can fish for, the time of day that party boats sail, and the duration of the trip.

In the United States, the Coast Guard licenses the captains of these vessels, and the owners must adhere to strict regulations designed to ensure the safety of passengers. Each vessel must undergo a meticulous inspection to be certified as safe, ensuring that the fishing public's best interests are foremost. Captains of these vessels (as well as captains of charter boats) must pass a comprehensive written exam before receiving their license to carry passengers for hire.

Party boat anglers catch everything from giant bluefin tuna and marlin to bottom feeders weighing but a pound, with most fish being small- to medium-sized inshore specimens. They catch fish by trolling, drifting, chumming, bottom fishing, jigging, and occasionally casting, and employ a wide variety of tactics within these disciplines. Mastering all of this aboard the fun-filled party boats that head daily to the fishing grounds is an exciting challenge.

Benefits of Party Boats
Good for beginners. Party boat fishing is a great way to get started in sportfishing. Newcomers are usually welcomed aboard by veteran anglers, who are quick to share techniques and to help in any way they can. The captain and mates also go to great pains with the beginner, realizing that they may gain a regular customer as a result. Among the regular customers aboard party boats, this type of fishing becomes almost an addiction, with anglers often sailing on a specific day each week the year-round, taking advantage of the changing seasons and changing species and types of fishing.

Camaraderie and diversity. Many people feel that fishing aboard a party boat is among the most enjoyable of angling experiences. The camaraderie of those who board these vessels, in addition to the actual fishing, adds to the excitement of the trip.

On a party boat a group of people is brought together with the common interest of going fishing and catching fish. They are young and old, male and female, from all ethnic and religious backgrounds. Most have never met before, but during the course of the trip relationships develop, fishing stories are exchanged, and a bond develops. Some people enjoy this fishing so much that people have been married on party boats, and it's not unusual for just-married couples to spend part of their honeymoon onboard, enjoying the fresh air, sunshine, good fishing, and, importantly, the affordability.

The duration of the fishing day aboard a party boat varies, depending on the location, time of year, and species availability. The normal day trip usually leaves dockside at seven or eight in the morning and returns at three or four in the afternoon. There are, however, half-day, three-quarter day, and twilight-fishing party boats. In many areas a second shift takes over the craft on its return for the night schedule. There may be half-, three-quarter, and all-night trips.

Along sections of some coasts, there are trips of several days' duration. Examples include weeklong excursions off Mexico's Baja Peninsula, two- and three-day trips to the Dry Tortugas off Florida, deep-water wreck fishing off Massachusetts' Nantucket Island for two days or more, and multi-day trips to the underwater canyons along the edge of the Continental Shelf off New York and New Jersey. Depending upon the boat, some include a bunk as part of the regular fare, while on others a bunk is optional for a limited fee.

Wide variety of species. Anglers may elect to board a particular party boat to seek a certain species of fish via a specific method of fishing. Almost all party boats have signs prominently displayed at the docks identifying the species that will be sought and the method of fishing.

Bottom fishing is the hallmark of party boat angling. This may be with the boat either anchored over wrecks, reefs, or irregular broken bottom, or while drifting over smooth bottom. Some boats specialize in chumming, and this may be done at anchor or while drifting. Trolling is often done, too, but this limits the number of anglers who can stream their lines from the stern. Trolling is often used to locate schools of fish, after which chum is used to hold the school close to the boat and attract the fish to hooked baits. Jigging is still another popular party boat activity, also done either at anchor or while drifting.

There are many variations to the above. In the Great Lakes, downriggers may be used while

Open to the public, party boats depart daily during the season from major ports.

P

trolling, and an angler is assigned a specific station. On the Pacific Coast, when deep-water trolling with breakaway sinkers to get baits deep, anglers often rotate positions with their tackle, to ensure that each has a chance of his baits working in a productive area as the grounds are covered.

Because sea conditions change frequently and the habits of fish change just as quickly, the party boat captain and his mates or deckhands quickly adapt. So, although you may anticipate bottom fishing all day, if the skipper locates a school of surface-feeding fish, he may ask anglers to switch techniques to take advantage of the developing opportunity.

General Issues

Selection.   Whether you're a veteran or a newcomer to party boat fishing, it's wise to do some homework before boarding a boat. As a first step, you might watch the local fishing reports in coastal newspapers. Fishing reporters talk with captains regularly and usually relay reliable fishing information, from which you can make a determination as to the length of the trip, species sought, and costs.

Perhaps the best approach, especially if you're new to this fishing or visiting an area for the first time, is to go to the docks and visit as the boats come in after a trip. Find out what time they usually return so you can be available when they first arrive. Talk with the people who are disembarking. Ask how the fishing and weather was, and whether or not they were satisfied with the attention of their captain and crew, and their diligence on the fishing grounds. Toward this end you have good and bad in every profession. You want to board a boat where the captain and mates work together as a team and will move from spot to spot until they score. If a disembarking passenger tells you the captain anchored on a reef and spent the day in one spot, asleep in the pilothouse, while the mate handled the decks, you may be best served looking elsewhere.

It's fair to say that you'll find party boats that are dirty, but you'll find charter boats and guide boats that are dirty, too. Appearance may or may not be an indication of whether they are worth fishing on, but conscientious captains try to keep their boats reasonably clean and in good shape. When you're at the docks taking stock of things before paying to fish on a party boat, don't hesitate to ask the captain if you can board, and then discreetly inspect the boat. In this way you'll know what's in store for you before you sail. Look at the restrooms. They should be as clean as your bathroom at home. If the toilets are grimy it's generally a reflection on the crew. Likewise in the galley. If it's a greasy grill or dirty microwave that doesn't appear to have been cleaned in ages, perhaps you should move on to another boat.

Tackle is another consideration. Look at the tackle in the event you'll be renting an outfit. Is it what you'll enjoy using? If the reel only has half a spool of line, or a guide is missing on a rod, or the metal parts of the reel are corroded, it shows lack of concern on the part of the crew, and using this kind of gear will diminish your enjoyment. Find a boat that's right for you before you enlist, by walking the docks, talking to people, and just plain observing.

Costs.   It's difficult to identify the exact cost to be encountered aboard a party boat. The general rule is, the closer to shore that you fish, and the shorter the duration, the lower the cost. Many of the half-day boats that bottom fish close to port charge $30, or $35 if chum is used, when targeting bluefish and bonito. The three-quarter day boats are around $40, while all-day fishing fares are usually $45 to $50 for close-in runs. For night trips, the same applies, depending on duration and distance to the grounds.

As you move into specialized fishing, such as twenty-four hour trips to far offshore wrecks and reefs, and trips to the Bahamas and Dry Tortugas, fares move into the $100 to $125 range. For two-day trips, such as those targeting tuna and other pelagic species in the Northeast canyons, the fares move up to $225 per angler. In some cases bunks are included, but it's best to check this out before boarding. Ask about tackle rental too, as the charge is often $20 for the heavier gear required for big game.

On really long range trips, such as those bound for Mexican water from San Diego, Newport Beach, and other California ports, it's all a matter of the boat and its accommodations, whether or not meals and bunks are included, and the length of the stay. Figure in the range of $100 to $150 per day. While this may seem costly, it's really quite economical when you consider that the same trip on a charter boat would cost several times that per person daily. Considering the camaraderie of those aboard, the excellent sport for truly great gamefish, and the prospects of bringing home great table fare, these long range trips are certainly worthy of consideration.

Regulations and Limits.   Each state has jurisdiction over fishing in its coastal waters, while the Federal government presides over offshore ocean fishing. It's wise to check with the party boat captain to determine whether or not you need a state license (issued by the state of the port from which you sail). In some jurisdictions you do not need a separate license while onboard a party boat, as the boat is licensed. However, some jurisdictions require an individual license, and these may be obtained for varying time periods, usually at a tackle shop in the area of the docks.

There are state and, in some cases, federal regulations (see: regulations) in effect in most jurisdictions with respect to specific seasons in which fish may be caught, minimum and sometimes maximum size that may be kept, and the quantity, or daily bag limit. Some jurisdictions have possession limits, too. It is generally prudent to be guided by

P

the instructions of the captain or mate in this regard. They are usually very knowledgeable, and the mates carefully measure regulated fish, ensuring that undersize specimens, or those in excess of the limit, are carefully returned to the water. However, you are ultimately responsible for your own fish and for knowing current regulations, so it's wise to obtain a booklet of regulations (usually available at bait and tackle shops) and keep it with you.

Because of numerous regulations governing size and bag limits, many fish caught on party boats must be released. Fish are carefully measured so as to comply and then promptly released. It's important that fish be handled carefully and released quickly to ensure survival. Many captains and mates take this very seriously because they realize the future of the sport rests with the released fish surviving. However, aboard some boats the opposite is true, particularly with part-time mates, who are employed during the summer months at the peak of the party boat tourist season. They sometimes do not realize that the fish will not survive careless handling and ripping hooks from their mouths or gills. Anglers and mates should be encouraged to release fish carefully and properly (see: catch-and-release; handling fish).

As with any other type of fishing, when you do keep fish on party boats, you should keep only what you can use, even when there are very liberal (or no) bag limits. Before size and bag limits were established for many coastal species, there was often a horrible practice by some irresponsible anglers who killed everything they caught, failed to properly care for the catch, and later dumped much of the fish in the trash. Thanks to regulations, this practice has for the most part disappeared from the coastal scene, but not all fish are covered by regulations. There are still instances where excessive killing continues, especially in fishing for Atlantic mackerel, scup, sea bass, croakers, spot, and other species. This excessiveness and greed is unnecessary, and certainly does not mark the participant as a sportsman. All species, big or small, popular or unpopular, are resources that should be treasured; releasing fish you can't or won't use ensures a viable fishery in the future.

Equipment and Fishing

Renting.   Of particular interest to the beginning party boat angler is the fact that you're not required to supply anything. Rental rods and reels are available with a nominal fee in addition to the regular fare. The rental outfit is equipped with the basic rig to be used that day, including a bottom rig, drift rig, or artificial lure for jigging or trolling. If you should lose the rig, you may purchase another from a mate, whose job it is to assist you in any way possible. They are always circulating around the rail, rigging tackle, baiting hooks, gaffing or netting fish, or otherwise being helpful.

In the Florida Keys, party boats generally charge a fixed fare, and if you lose a hook or bottom rig

while fishing the reef, the mate simply replaces it as a part of the basic fare. The additional nominal amount that the fare is increased as a result of not charging for hooks, lines, or sinkers is a welcome convenience to passengers and results in less work for the mates.

Using your own.   Anglers who regularly fish on party boats have their own tackle and bring it with them, usually needing to be supplied only with bait. After you have made a few excursions on party boats and seen what veteran anglers have and what the boats provide, you'll probably want to outfit yourself and bring your own equipment.

Much can be learned from veteran party boat anglers, as they have this type of fishing down to a science. Because time on the fishing grounds is often limited, the veteran is extremely well organized with his tackle, so not a moment is wasted. Many of the pros develop a personal party boat checklist to ensure that they have everything with them necessary for a successful day. This includes:

❏ Proper clothing, including rain gear and hat
❏ Ice chest with ice for fish, and a compartment for food and beverages
❏ Plastic bags in which to place cleaned fish on ice
❏ Deck shoes or slip-on boots to keep dry
❏ Pills for seasickness, headache, or pain relief
❏ Polarized sunglasses
❏ Folding toothbrush and toothpaste
❏ Sunscreen of 25 SPF or higher
❏ Sleeping bag for overnighters

These items ensure that you'll have an enjoyable trip, regardless of duration. Little things like a toothbrush to freshen your mouth after a night in a bunk, or an antacid tablet for indigestion, or especially sunscreen to prevent a burn, often make the difference in a trip's enjoyment. Regulars carry all of this gear with them and at least one completely rigged rod and reel. Since there is plenty of room on the bigger party boats, they also bring a spare outfit as insurance, and a tackle box loaded with essentials.

A party boat tackle box should be roomy, plastic, and waterproof, with all items easily accessible. It should contain:

❏ Sharp filleting knife
❏ Serrated knife for steaking, cutting bone
❏ Diamond knife sharpener
❏ Stainless steel dehooker
❏ Vise-grip cutting pliers in sheath
❏ Eight-inch broomstick for wrapping line around to pull free from bottom snags
❏ Sinkers for the type of fishing expected
❏ Terminal rigs for the type of fishing expected
❏ Jigs, spoons, feathers, and other lures and rigged leaders

French spinners were introduced to America after World War II by Mepps, which was known as the manufacturer of precision equipment for sportfishing.

Getting started. Having boarded with this array of equipment and tackle, most veterans discuss with the mates the exact method to be used on arrival at the fishing grounds, and the techniques that have proven most effective. They rig accordingly as the boat travels to the fishing grounds and wear their cutting pliers and bait knife in a sheath on their belt. Time on the fishing grounds is limited, so it's smart to be totally prepared.

Many party boat anglers wear a carpenter's tool apron in which they place a couple of extra sinkers and complete terminal rigs so they can quickly retie and get back in the water should they lose a rig. This saves time from rummaging through a tackle box, or having to make up a rig or purchase one from a busy mate.

Included in the tool apron is the 8-inch piece of broomstick; this is a godsend when it's necessary to break off a snagged bottom rig. It prevents breaking costly tackle as you try to break off, but, more importantly, it keeps the line from cutting your hands.

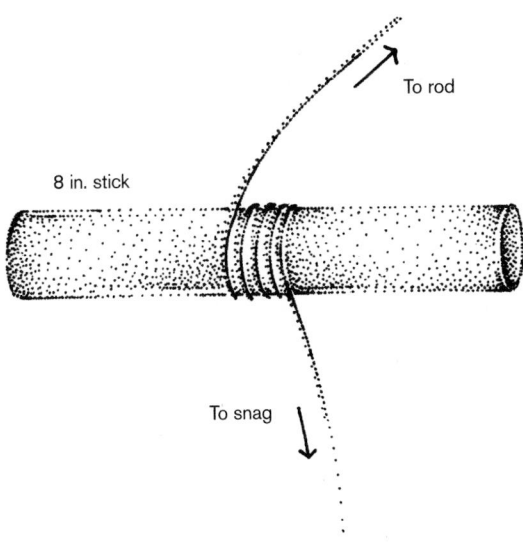

To free a bottom-snagged rig when fishing on a party boat, wrap the line several times around an 8-inch piece of broomstick, hold it with both hands, and pull to free the rig or break it off. This is especially useful when fishing with strong and low-stretch lines.

Once the fishing grounds are reached, the captain either announces over the boat's loudspeaker that fishing will begin, or signals this by sounding the horn. At each fishing location along the rail, the mates will have placed a container of bait; if live bait is used, it is readily available at the circulating tanks. After you are baited up and fishing, it's a good practice to be aware of the actions of other anglers. Watch the first people to score, and don't hesitate to mimic their technique.

Rail position. Although initially it may sound unimportant, rail position in certain types of party boat fishing can often put you at a decided advantage.

In many types of reef and wreck fishing, the boat is anchored over sand bottom and the current holds the boat in position either close to or over the choice bottom. In this kind of situation, the people who occupy the stern have the choice spots; as the fish are chummed, the first baited hooks they respond to are those of anglers positioned at the stern.

As a rule of thumb, it's difficult to beat the stern position for any kind of party boat fishing, and it's not unusual to see party boat regulars arrive extra early, even hours before boarding time, so they can place their outfit in a choice stern location.

When drift fishing, the captain usually positions the boat so the lines of anglers on one side will stream away from the boat, and the lines of those on the other side will drift under the boat. Every half hour or so the skipper will make a move over new bottom, and alternate the position of the boat, so the anglers whose lines drifted under the boat will stream away from it and vice versa for the other side. It is usually best to have your lines drift away from, rather than under, the boat.

The best position on boats that drift is the bow, where only two or three anglers can fish. In this way they can take advantage of their lines streaming away on either drift, and it enables them to cast out and away from the bow, which results in more bottom being covered.

When party boats are crowded, each angler has a spot at the rail, usually marked by a painted stripe on the rail, or where there is a piece of cord tied, to which you can attach your outfit. Some boats have rod holders at each position.

When the boat isn't crowded, it's much more comfortable and you can move about more readily. At such times, it's often wise to move away from where the anglers tend to cluster near the stern, and to situate yourself alone, which often results in more strikes and less chance of a tangle.

Bring two outfits. As anglers become proficient on party boats, some expand their horizon from the species normally targeted to seek bigger game. As a case in point, many boats chum for yellowtail snapper throughout their southern range. These average 2 to 4 pounds and are pursued with small hooks and light tackle. Frequenting the same grounds as yellowtails are big grouper and snapper, some weighing 50 pounds or more, which are targeted by anglers who bring heavy tackle and use big baits to catch these Goliaths of the deep. Many anglers bring a pair of outfits aboard, one heavy and one light; they first make a catch of the smaller gamesters and then switch over to target the heavyweights, making for a fun-filled and well-rounded day.

Along the mid-Atlantic Coast, the catch of species such as summer flounder is limited with respect to size and bag limits, and once anglers have filled their limit, they'll often switch over to diamond jigging or squidding for species such as bluefish, striped bass, Atlantic bonito, and Spanish

P

mackerel, which often frequent the same grounds and result in a bonus catch.

Pacific Coast anglers fishing off kelp beds often experience mixed-bag action, with Pacific bonito, white sea bass, and kelp bass being the target of baits drifted near the surface, while bottom rigs down on the sand bring strikes from Pacific halibut, rockfish, and other bottom feeders. The key on all three coasts is to be prepared, and to quickly respond as situations develop.

Patience with big fish.   In some types of party boat fishing, such as when working the Pacific kelp beds, chumming around shrimp boats in the Gulf, or seeking bluefish when chumming in the Atlantic, the fish that are hooked are so large and strong that you just can't stand at the rail and bring the fish directly to you. At such times, it's necessary to follow the fish up and down the rail. Most party boat anglers are extremely courteous and when they hear the time-honored call, "fish on, coming through," they'll clear the rail, and raise or lower their line to permit you to follow your fish. With a big fish, the mate frequently accompanies the angler making certain no tangles occur en route.

As a big fish is brought alongside, it's especially important to be alert to any last-minute runs. The mates are at the ready with a long-handled net or gaff (sometimes two gaffs are necessary, as with large yellowfin tuna) and as soon as the fish is within range, they either net or gaff it. At this time, it's critical that the angler just reel the fish close enough for the mates to handle. Sometimes, in the excitement, anglers try to lift the fish, and with a big fish thrashing at boatside, this can often result in a line break. Stay calm, reel the fish within range, and let the mates show their skill. It's much easier for a fish to be gaffed or netted when it is a foot or so beneath the surface, and not thrashing on the surface or with its head lifted from the water. As the fish is brought aboard, place your reel in freespool or open the bail on a spinning reel, so the mate can move away from the rail and other anglers can move freely as he unhooks your fish.

The road to success.   It's worth noting that party boat regulars often become extremely proficient, and their skills are on a par with the best of guides, mates, and charter skippers. This doesn't just happen. It's a result of dedication, learning fundamentals, and honing techniques to perfection. It's not at all unusual to see veteran anglers aboard party boats consistently catching more and bigger fish than other anglers. This should never be construed as luck, although occasionally it may be, but more as an understanding of the species

sought, its feeding habits, the weather conditions, speed of drift, current, water clarity, and a host of other factors.

It's often the little things that count. On a summer morning with a lazy drift, all of the anglers onboard may be catching summer flounders while using a 4-ounce sinker to hold bottom. As afternoon winds develop velocity, the boat's speed of drift accelerates, and at times it may take a full 16 ounces of sinker weight to keep a rig on the bottom. Those anglers who respond by changing weights continue to score, while those who maintain their 4-ounce sinkers actually have their baits drifting at midlevel, well above the bottom-feeding fish.

Always having a fresh bait on your hook, keeping the hooks sharp, using lightweight or fluorocarbon leaders less visible to fish, tying the correct knots, and, above all, being alert, are just a few of the many small things that collectively make a big difference in success.

Other Matters

Fish care.   When bottom fishing or drift fishing, where the species sought are small in size, it's customary for anglers to reel their catch to boatside, lower their rod tip, and gently swing the fish aboard. The mate will quickly unhook your fish, rebait, and place your fish on ice or in your bag. On some boats, the mate places the catch on a stringer and then puts the fish on ice in a community box. On long-range boats or party boats whose excursions last several days, when the target is big species such as tuna, wahoo, and dolphin, the fish are often identified by a tail tag, then placed either on ice or refrigerated until you return to dockside.

In some areas, particularly in Florida and along the Gulf Coast, where the weather is often hot and fish can easily spoil, the mates place fish in a community box filled with crushed ice. Each fish is scored with a specific marking that is assigned to each angler onboard. As an example, the first angler to catch a fish is assigned "one cut on the bottom," which means the mate makes a single knife cut on the bottom of the fish near the head. The next angler to score is assigned "two cuts on the bottom." After four cuts are assigned, the next spot is the top of the head, with one to four cuts assigned. Next, the top of the tail is cut, then the bottom, and a single X on the left side of the head, then the right, then a double X, and so on.

The system works extremely well. The angler doesn't have to handle the fish, as it is unhooked, marked, and placed on ice immediately by the mate, who is often assisted by the captain when the fishing is hectic. Upon returning to dockside, the anglers disembark and form a semicircle with their opened ice chests. The mate removes each fish from the community box, calls out "top tail," and places the fish in the ice chest belonging to the angler assigned the top tail cut. "Two cuts on the bottom," "bottom tail," "double X on the left," and

the chant goes on. In just a few minutes, hundreds of fish from the community box can be distributed. The fish are in excellent condition with this system.

Immediately after distributing the fish to the people who caught them, the mate goes to the cleaning table, where he will fillet and package your fish if you wish. For his efforts, he is rewarded with a tip based on the size and number of fish cleaned.

In tourist areas, many mates have Styrofoam coolers available and will clean your fish, pack them in double plastic bags, and then bury them in bagged ice in the cooler, sealing it with duct tape so that the fish may easily be transported home by air or car. Double-bagging fillets keeps them from becoming soaked with water, and double-bagging ice prevents water from leaking as it melts. Packed in this way, the fish easily keep for several days, arriving home in prime condition.

In many tourist locales, restaurants encourage you to bring your catch in, and they'll use their local recipes to prepare it, which is a great way to conclude a pleasant day's fishing on a party boat.

Selling fish.   As a general rule, the fish you catch aboard a party boat are yours to keep. However, some mates on party boats will agree to clean your catch for you at no charge, providing you share some of the catch with them. They subsequently sell the fish they accumulate this way, which supplements their regular income.

Some boats permit experienced anglers to sail at a reduced fare or, in some cases, no fare at all, providing the angler agrees that the fish he catches become the property of the boat, which sells them at market. This is most likely to be an option when the action is exceptional and the fish price high. Often, just one or two fish are worth more on the commercial market than the boat's fare; this is especially so in the case of bigeye tuna, yellowfin tuna, and albacore. This works to the advantage of both boat and angler when the fishing is good, and good anglers are onboard. But if fishing is poor, the angler financially benefits while the captain suffers.

In those few places in freshwater where party boats operate, this is not an option, since freshwater sportfish are also designated as gamefish and cannot be sold. In saltwater, this is often different; sportfish may not be designated as gamefish in certain places, and may legally be sold, although there's an ethical question (*see: ethics*) as to whether it is right for an angler to sell fish and whether the selling of sport-caught fish in fact makes an angler a commercial fisherman.

Certainly party boat patrons may give their catch to the mate, captain, or other customers if they don't want them (although there is another ethical question: If you couldn't use the fish, why not release them when they were caught?). But certain saltwater fish have a lot of market value, and in some places they may be sold with or without a special permit or commercial license. Because it is normal for customers to assume that whatever they

The iridescent appearance of a fish is created by a waste product called *guanin*, which appears in the form of colorless crystals that are deposited in the outer layer of the skin and reflect light.

P

Rail positions are often important on party boats; the stern, which produced a bluefish for this angler, is one of the preferred locations.

catch is theirs, they should be advised up front if that is not the case; if the option to sell fish exists, they should consider whether this is a practice they wish to engage in.

Big fish pools.　Almost all party boats have a pool, to which anglers contribute a nominal amount, ranging from a couple of dollars to ten or more. The pool money ultimately goes to the angler catching the largest fish of the day. Rules identify which species of fish are eligible for the pool money, and it's great fun if momentum swings from one angler to the other as the size of the biggest fish increases throughout the day. Often the pool money is divided into two or three places, especially if the boat is crowded. It's not unusual to be rewarded with several hundred dollars for the biggest fish of the day, a double-barreled bonus considering that you've got a big one for the dinner table.

There are, however, those rare occasions when not a single fish is caught during the trip. Then the pool money is awarded via a drawing, so even on the poorest fishing day some lucky angler disembarks with a bonus. It's customary that the pool winners share a portion of the pool with the mate(s). These deckhands work hard, and it's their deft gaffing or netting that brings the winning catch aboard, so they deserve the consideration.

Gratuities.　The crew members aboard many party boats are paid on a per diem basis. Their wages are fair, and they depend in part on gratuities from passengers for services rendered. Use the same tipping judgment you might render when at a restaurant, with a 10 to 15 percent tip in order for good service.

If, however, you board a boat in the morning and the mate is sitting there reading a newspaper instead of helping you with your gear, and throughout the day he's not helpful in removing the hook from a deeply hooked fish, or isn't interested in cleaning your catch, then it's certainly appropriate not to tip. Be leery of the mate who is more interested in catching fish for the market, instead of being concerned with your welfare.

If, on the other hand, he greets you with a smile, gets you set at a spot, keeps your bait container filled, is immediately at hand to net or gaff your fish, and gets them into the cooler or on ice, and back at dockside does a professional job of cleaning your catch, then certainly some extra consideration is in order.

No GPS.　With increased fishing pressure on all coasts, party boat skippers must continually work hard to find fish for their patrons. Often this means finding spots not fished by others. Historically, party boat captains have taken pride in their own "spots." During periods of slow fishing, many party boat owners sail far from shore with their sonar probing the depths as they look for new places that could provide good fishing. Frequently, these spots, such as wrecks, reefs, rocks, and ridges, are reported from commercial men who get their nets fouled in bottom obstructions. Party boat skippers reward finders of such locations with sizable cash payments because it expands their fishing opportunities and results in more enjoyment for their anglers.

The captains are very secretive about some of their spots, as they are indeed investments.

On the inshore grounds, private boaters could easily follow the party boats and record the Loran or GPS locations. With the passage of time, party boats have had to go great distances offshore, as is the case off New England, the New Jersey and North Carolina Coasts, the Florida Keys, and Gulf Coast ports, in order to find spots never before fished. When they find a wreck, ridge, or reef they're often able to provide exciting fishing for their patrons for a short period of time. But because of sophisticated electronics and the fact that private boaters have fast, long-range boats, the spots aren't "secret" for long. This is a sad dilemma for the party boat owners whose livelihood depends upon providing a relaxing trip and good fishing on a daily basis. The world has gotten smaller as a result of electronics, and this has certainly had a negative impact on the exclusivity that party boat captains and their patrons have enjoyed for years with respect to their spots.

In recent years, there has even been piracy of some spots from aboard party boats. Individuals have brought electronic equipment, especially handheld navigation devices like GPS units *(see)* and recorded the locations when they were on the fishing grounds, much to the consternation of the captains. As a result, some captains will not permit portable GPS units, or similar electronic position monitoring gear, to be carried aboard by passengers.

The following is language from a notice to patrons that one may find upon boarding a coastal party boat:

"Party and open boat fishing is one of the few businesses where you still find a spirit of friendly competition. The captains on these boats compete to find the most productive fishing grounds. This is a long-time tradition, and part of what makes fishing fun. Finding these spots is also time-consuming and a lot of hard work. New technology is wonderful, but greedy unscrupulous people can always find a way to use it for ill purposes. In this case it is being used to steal the location of fishing grounds. This information is then sold. Everyone should understand that it is policy aboard this boat to not tolerate this form of stealing, nor will the boat's owners participate in this scheme by purchasing information stolen from other boats and their captains. Be aware that a diligent effort will be made to prevent GPS and other devices from being brought aboard. If such devices are found after departure, they will be confiscated by the captain and destroyed."

While no captain lays claim to any spot, as the oceans are available to anyone, they feel very strongly when people try to take advantage of them. This is particularly true of captains who use their off-season time or slow days to run many miles seaward as they methodically monitor their electronics to search for bottom conformations and wrecks that may hold a bonanza catch.

See: **Bottom Fishing; Charter Boat; Chumming; Fishing Regulations; Inshore Fishing.**

PATTERN

The particular appearance of an artificial fly, comprised of the parts that make up its likeness, the way they are incorporated onto the fly hook, and the colors.

See: **Fly.**

PAVÓN

The Spanish word for peacock bass *(see: bass, peacock).*

PAYARA   *Hydrolycus scomberoides.*

Other names—dogfish, saber-toothed dogfish; Portuguese: *cachorra, peixe-cachorra, pirandirá;* Spanish: *payara, chambra.*

The payara is an excellent South American gamefish and a fearsome-looking characin that is noted for its saberlike teeth. A member of the Cinodontidae family and a relative of tigerfish and piranha, it is only known to a small number of anglers, and little has been reported about it in the scientific literature. The total number of species in this family is unknown, and there are three genera.

Identification. The payara is distinctive because of its unusual head and mouth. It has two long canine teeth on the tip of its upturned lower jaw, which slip into a sheath inside the tip of the upper jaw when the mouth is fully closed. These slightly backward-curved saberlike teeth can be between 2 and 3 inches long in a 20-pound fish. On some large individuals, these two long lower jaw teeth may be broken. The snout of the upper jaw is also equipped with two shorter forward-curved canine teeth, and the rest of the mouth has shorter but sharp-pointed teeth, more of which are on the lower jaw.

The body of the payara is compressed and elongate. The dorsal fin is high, originates at midbody, and is squared off. There is an adipose fin just ahead of the caudal peduncle, and the tail is squared in some specimens and rounded in others. Both tail and adipose fins darken on their posterior, and may have a small whitish fringe. The body coloring is a steely gray with blue gray to olive tones, darker on the back and lighter on the belly. The lateral line runs the length of the body and is slightly decurved toward the head.

Size. The maximum size that *H. scomberoides* can attain is uncertain. It was reported as 33 pounds until a 39-pound, 4-ounce all-tackle world-record specimen was caught at Uraima Falls, Venezuela, in 1996. It can evidently attain 4 feet in length.

Distribution. *H. scomberoides* occurs in the Orinoco and Amazon River basins. A species that is believed to be smaller (up to 20 inches) is reported to exist in southern Brazil in the upper watershed of the River Plate. This fish is called biara *(Raphiodon vulpinus)* and is also known as *cachorra* in Portuguese, and *chafolete* and *machete* in Spanish.

A payara from the São Francisco River, Brazil.

P

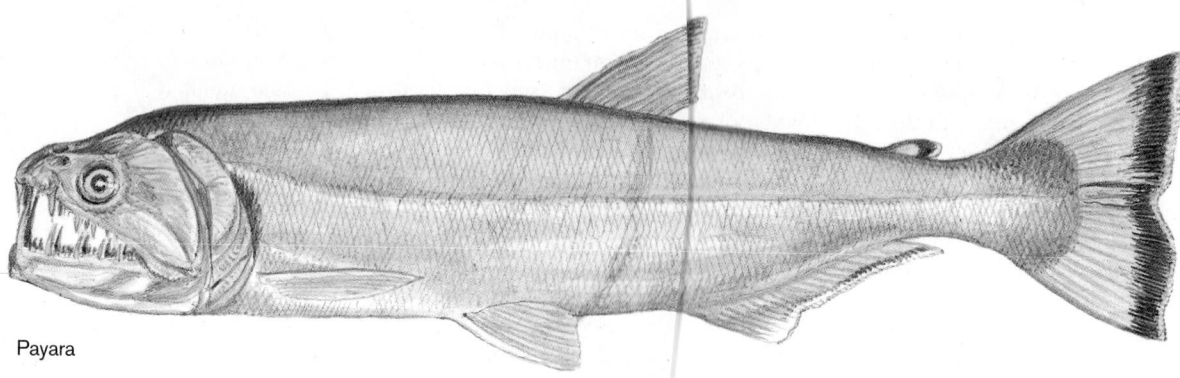

Payara

Habitat. Payara are primarily a river fish and prefer swift-flowing areas. They also exist in flooded backwaters and in the shallows and depths of lagoons and impoundments. They are said to be a schooling species, but it is unclear whether they are actually schooling fish or happen to be concentrated at certain locations.

Food. The complete diet of payara is unreported, but their dentition and aggressive nature make them clearly a formidable predator of other fish.

Angling. Payara strike hard and usually leap out of the water upon being hooked. Although good fighters, they tire fairly easily (at least in comparison to species like dorado). They are not difficult to land, although in slower flows big payara can be challenging if they turn their considerable broadside mass against the current, and in thickly timbered waters they may be initially hard to coax away from obstructions.

A variety of plugs are effective on payara, particularly noisy, flashy lures. Shallow-running crankbaits, lipless crankbaits, and large minnow-shaped swimming plugs are productive; big spoons and jigs may also be effective. In lakes and flooded backwaters, payara are usually caught incidentally by anglers pursuing peacock bass. In some rivers—especially the clearer, swifter flows of tributaries and headwaters—they can be deliberately targeted, particularly in the pools and eddies below falls and in the head of pools below a rapids.

In rivers, payara often prefer the swiftest water and areas near the largest boulders. In reservoirs, they are a less predictable catch and are sometimes landed by deep jigging. A specimen exceeding 20 pounds will make several runs and spectacular jumps. Their sharp teeth frequently puncture plastic and wooden lures. A strong steel leader and snap swivel are necessary, and lures must be durable and the hooks and attachments extra-strong. Heavy-action rods, with baitcasting reels capable of holding 100 yards of 17- to 30-pound-test line, are commonly used in locations where bigger fish may be present.

Payara caught in swift waters may be difficult to revive and release, especially if taken on light tackle. As the distribution of these fish is somewhat limited, especially the large specimens, it is important for anglers to handle and release them carefully. The flesh of payara is edible but not notable; they are regularly consumed by local peoples.

Venezuela and Brazil are known for payara, although mainly in certain types of waters. The upper tributaries of the Orinoco and Amazon Rivers, with blue- and black-water characteristics *(see: Brazil; Venezuela),* are best. Venezuela's interior waters produce among the biggest payara; Brazil has payara in certain waters from the upper to lower regions of the country; and Colombia has good payara waters.

PECTORAL FIN

The fin usually found on each side of the body directly behind the gill opening.
See: Fish.

PELAGIC FISH

Free-swimming fish that inhabit the open sea and are independent of the seabed or water bottom.

PELVIC FIN

The pair of adjoining fins ventrally located beneath the belly and in front of the anus; also called ventral fins.
See: Fish.

PENCIL FLOAT

Also known as a pencil bobber, this is a term for a long and slender-profile float *(see),* usually one made of plastic.

PENDULUM CAST

A long-distance cast used by surf anglers.
See: Casting; Surf Fishing.

PENNSYLVANIA

Called the Keystone State because it was the link binding the original 13 northern and southern states, Pennsylvania is also a "keystone state" for sportfishing, serving as a link between northern and

P

southern fisheries, and between the Atlantic Ocean and the Great Lakes. Although Pennsylvania has no saltwater fishing to speak of—other than for tidal-river species—fishing opportunities are diverse and surprisingly good here; Pennsylvania annually ranks among the leading states in fishing license sales, and this is reflected in angler enthusiasm.

Except for narrow strips along the southeastern and northwestern corners of the state, the terrain is hilly to mountainous. Trout streams, larger creeks, or rivers flow through most valleys. Several small lakes and ponds dot the glaciated northeast and northwest corners. There are four substantial man-made reservoirs—Pymatuning, Allegheny, Raystown, and Wallenpaupack—and numerous smaller reservoirs and lakes. Important watersheds are the Ohio/Allegheny Rivers, the Susquehanna River, and the Delaware River.

The favorite gamefish in Pennsylvania are brook trout, brown trout, rainbow trout, smallmouth bass, largemouth bass, walleye, muskellunge, northern pike, chain pickerel, and channel catfish. American shad and striped bass migrate into the Delaware River, and steelhead are plentiful in Lake Erie and several tributaries.

The most popular or widespread panfish are white crappie, black crappie, yellow perch, bluegills, pumpkinseeds, rock bass, and brown, yellow, and black bullhead. Additionally, white bass, white catfish, white perch, warmouth, green sunfish, and redbreast sunfish are common in some waters.

Carp are prevalent throughout the state, as are several sucker species. Freshwater drum are abundant in Lake Erie. Through stocking, lake trout are common at Lake Erie and a few inland lakes. Flathead catfish are especially common in the Allegheny River. Sauger and spotted bass are available in the lower Allegheny and Monongahela Rivers and in the Ohio River. Some chinook salmon are still stocked in Lake Erie, which also has a small population of pink salmon.

Trout Streams/Small Lakes

Trout have traditionally been the most popular fish among Pennsylvania anglers. The state stocks trout in nearly 5,000 miles of streams and has more than 400 miles of Class A Wild Trout Water. Roughly 10,000 miles of streams and rivers provide suitable trout habitat, and there's good trout fishing in every part of the state. Many streams, or sections of streams, are subject to special regulations that restrict fishing methods and/or the harvest.

The Pennsylvania Fish and Boat Commission stocks brook, brown, and rainbow trout in streams. Brookies are the only native species, but browns and rainbows have established self-sustaining populations in several flows.

Trout anglers can go wild in the Allegheny Highlands, a rugged, hilly, forested, sparsely populated region covering most of north-central Pennsylvania. The Allegheny National Forest and several enormous state forests provide public access to hundreds of miles of fine trout streams. Many small flows are populated by wild brook trout and are rarely visited by anglers, as numerous stocked streams experience most of the pressure. Famous area creeks include the Kettle, Pine, Tionesta, Kinzua, and First Fork of the Sinnemahoning.

There may be snow on the ground when trout season opens in mid-April. Fly fishing is best during the great hatches of May and June. During summer, stream flows are normally very low, making fishing difficult; then, early morning is best for those who are extremely cautious and use fine tippets.

Pine Creek forms in Tioga County and eastern McKean County, then turns southward at Ansonia through the Pine Creek Gorge. The first 17 miles through the "Grand Canyon of Pennsylvania" to Blackwell are accessible only by foot, bicycle, or water. A float trip through the canyon is one of the finest trout fishing adventures in the East. Camping is permitted along the creek.

Kettle Creek is the next major drainage west of Pine Creek, flowing southward from Oleona to the West Branch of the Susquehanna River at Westport. Its deep, narrow valley is about as far off the beaten path as you can get in a car. Most businesses survive here only because of trout anglers. Cross Fork, an important tributary, is a favorite of fly anglers.

Tionesta Creek flows through the Allegheny National Forest from Barnes, where its east, west, and south branches join, to the Allegheny River at the village of Tionesta. It can be canoed from Barnes to Tionesta Reservoir during April and May. The better fishing is in the main branches. As with most Allegheny Highlands creeks, wild brook trout are abundant in many tributaries.

Pennsylvania limestone streams are part of America's fishing heritage and are frequently cited in classic angling literature. These streams are characterized by a stable pH of 7.5 to 8.0, low gradient, large numbers of aquatic plants, and abundant aquatic insects, particularly mayflies, midges, and freshwater shrimp. These streams tend to emerge from springs at nearly full flow, preferring stable flow and virtually constant temperature year-around. Trout grow quickly in this environment.

The limestone streams are located generally in the south-central and southeastern portions of the state, in the Appalachian Mountains and Piedmont. Penns Creek in Union County is considered by many people as the finest trout stream in the state. Access is much better here than along most limestone streams, and much of it is floatable during April and May.

Limestone creeks include Ottown Run (Bedford County); Moselem Run, Peters Creek, Spring Creek, Willow Creek, and Wyomissing Creek (Berks County); Boiling Spring Run (Blair County); Cooks Creek (Bucks County); Buffalo Run, Cedar Run, Elk Creek, Lick Run, Little

Deep-dwelling halibut are prolific fish; a female halibut weighing 150 pounds is capable of producing as many as 2 million eggs.

P

Fishing Creek, Logan Branch, Penns Creek, Pine Creek, Sinking Creek, Slab Cabin Run, and Spring Creek (Centre County); Little Valley Creek and Valley Creek (Chester County); Bald Eagle Creek, Cedar Run, and Fishing Creek (Clinton County); and Big Spring Creek, Cedar Run, Green Spring Creek, Hogestown Run, Letort Spring Run, and Trindle Spring Run (Cumberland County).

Also Buck Run and Falling Spring Branch (Franklin County); Spring Run (Fulton County); Donegal Creek, Eshleman Run, Indian Run, Londonland Run, and Swarr Run (Lancaster County); East Branch Mill Creek and Mill Creek (Lebanon County); Catasaqua Creek, Cedar Creek, Coplay Creek, Little Lehigh Creek, South Branch Saucon Creek, Spring Creek, and Trout Creek (Lehigh County); Antes Creek, the source of which is the largest limestone spring in Pennsylvania (Lycoming County); and Allegheny Creek, Bushkill Creek, East Branch Monocacy Creek, Jacoby Creek, Monocacy Creek, Nancy Run, Saucon Creek, and Shoeneck Creek (Northampton County).

Roughly 100 small lakes covering more than 5,000 surface acres are heavily stocked with trout. Stocking is spread out through the year to provide recreation in every season. Because these lakes are stocked by formula, one is about as good as another, although fishing pressure varies. Lists of stocked lakes are widely published, and any tackle shop should be able to assist. Many of these lakes are in state parks, and many have special boating regulations, predominately permitting only electric motors.

A shad comes into the boat on the Delaware River.

Ice fishing is particularly popular at some lakes stocked with trout. Those along the northern tier typically freeze over by Christmas. Lakes along the southern border do not have any safe ice during many winters.

Most lakes are stocked with brook, brown, and rainbow trout. Marginal fisheries do exist, however, at a few inland lakes that have been stocked with lake trout. The best opportunities may be at East Branch Lake in Elk County, and Raystown Lake in Huntingdon County.

Delaware River

The Delaware River is Pennsylvania's link to the Atlantic Ocean. Forming the eastern border with New York and New Jersey, it enters the state in Wayne County, flowing southward about 200 miles past Philadelphia and into Delaware Bay. Tides reach upriver as far as the Route 1 bridge at Trenton Falls.

The Pennsylvania portion of this river contains a diverse and high-quality fishery. Many American shad and some striped bass migrate in from Delaware Bay; trout fishing is superb in the headwaters; and in between there's smallmouth bass, largemouth bass, walleye, muskellunge, white and channel catfish, and a variety of panfish.

The Delaware is a popular floating river, but it has several treacherous rapids. Among the worst are Skinners Falls, 5 miles above Narrowsburg in Wayne County; another about 2 miles above the Zane Gray House access site in Pike County; Sambo Riff just below the mouth of Flat Brook in Monroe County; Foul Riff just above the PP&L access site in Northampton County; and wing dams in Bucks County. In the tidal portion, boaters must beware of the wakes of seagoing vessels and tidal rips.

The upper Delaware from Hancock, New York, down to the Delaware Water Gap adjoining New Jersey is a designated National Wild and Scenic River. Scenery is spectacular, with hills rising 800 feet above the river. This is all Class I water, a series of short riffles and long pools, perfect for relaxed float fishing. Float fishing for brown and rainbow trout is popular along Wayne County from Hancock to Callicoon, New York, a distance of about 31 miles. Excellent insect hatches occur from late May through September.

The Delaware has especially fine shad fishing. Shad move into Pennsylvania water during early to mid-April. They'll reach the Delaware Water Gap by late April, and Wayne County by mid- to late May. Action continues through June in the upper river. Shad darts are the traditional lures, but small spoons, sometimes fished behind downriggers in the deeper midriver sections, are also effective. Fly fishing has gained popularity in the upper reaches. The best fishing is generally in the main channel.

Striped bass migrate up the Delaware into Bucks, Philadelphia, and Delaware Counties from

May through July, and a few stragglers go much farther upriver. In the lower section, look for them where tidal currents are heaviest. Bloodworms are the top natural baits, but these fish are also caught on white jigs and silver or white crankbaits.

Largemouth bass inhabit tidal water near tributary mouths and in weedy coves. Smallmouth bass are more abundant from Trenton Falls upriver to Damascus in Wayne County. Anglers also encounter walleye and muskellunge through this stretch, although very few muskies are caught above Delaware Water Gap. The deep Narrowsburg Pool is a favorite spot among walleye anglers, especially during spring and fall.

Larger tributaries generally have fair to good warmwater fisheries in the lower areas, and coldwater fisheries toward the headwaters. The Schuylkill River, which meets the Delaware at Philadelphia, has both smallmouth and largemouth bass, channel catfish, walleye, and muskies. The Lehigh River, entering at Easton, has good smallmouth bass fishing and some largemouth bass, muskellunge, channel catfish, and panfish. The Lackawaxen River in Pike County is fine trout water. Big browns migrate from the Delaware into the Lackawaxen seeking cooler water during summer. The area near the Delaware is a favored shad spot in May.

Susquehanna River

The Susquehanna River is a nationally renowned smallmouth bass fishery. Walleye, muskies, catfish, and panfish are also fairly abundant in some areas. Before dams were built and water quality declined, large numbers of American shad, eels, herring, and other anadromous fish migrated into the river from the Chesapeake Bay. The restoration of shad runs was one main reason for the establishment of the Pennsylvania Fish Commission (now the Fish and Boat Commission) in 1866. The same act that established the commission directed dam owners to provide fish passage facilities, but it was not until the last three decades of the twentieth century before any real progress was made in this regard.

The Susquehanna River forms in the northeast corner of Pennsylvania, flowing northward into New York. It re-enters Pennsylvania in Bradford County, near Sayre, flowing southward. Its largest tributary, the West Branch, enters at Northumberland, where an inflatable dam creates Lake Augusta. The Juniata River joins at Clarks Ferry. At Harrisburg, the Susquehanna is a mile wide. Its watershed is the second largest in the eastern United States and includes more than half of Pennsylvania. Four hydroelectric dams between Harrisburg and Maryland create large lakes.

Except for the dams, the Susquehanna is all floatable. Typical low-water conditions in summer, however, make floating difficult in many areas, particularly above Laceyville and from Halifax to Harrisburg. Below Harrisburg, a low-head dam and three larger dams make long floats burdensome. The more rugged rapids of the river are in this area.

The Susquehanna is ideal smallmouth habitat all through Pennsylvania; it is rocky and, except above the hydroelectric dams, shallow. Through Bradford and Wyoming Counties, the bottom is a mix of gravel and rubble. Smallmouth anglers here often drift hellgrammites in the current. This is a delightful stretch for float fishing. Pools are short but can also produce walleye and muskies.

Farther downstream, the Susquehanna flows through the Appalachian Mountains. The river offers long pools, lengthy stretches where it flows swiftly over exposed bedrock, and numerous islands. Smallmouth fishing is spectacular. For a change of pace, channel catfish are also quite abundant.

Lake Clark, Lake Aldred, and the Conowingo Pool, created by three large hydroelectric dams, offer excellent fishing for smallmouth bass and channel catfish, along with some walleye, muskellunge, crappie, and yellow perch. Largemouth bass are common in the Conowingo Pool. Striped bass have been stocked as well. All three lakes are deep enough for powerboats. There are many rocks just beneath the surface, however, primarily toward the heads of the lakes.

The West Branch Susquehanna River drains most of the Allegheny Highlands, a sparsely populated forest. Despite its beautiful scenery and clear water, the West Branch is virtually without fish until it reaches Lock Haven, primarily due to acidic coal mine runoff, and does not become a good fishery until the Williamsport area. From that point, fishing for smallmouths, walleye, muskies, and panfish gets progressively better.

The Juniata River is smallmouth bass heaven. Along its headwaters, smallmouths are incredibly abundant, if somewhat on the small side. Farther downstream, larger smallmouths become more common, as do walleye and muskellunge. Stonecats (madtoms) are the favorite live baits here, and natural-colored jigs work during summer when the water is low and clear.

Walleye and muskellunge are fairly plentiful in the Juniata, although not nearly as widespread as smallmouths. Look for muskies in the calmer pools, especially in the lower half of the river. Walleye fishing is usually best during winter in the deeper pools up to Huntingdon. Rock bass, locally called redeyes, are the most popular panfish.

The Little Juniata River and the Frankstown Branch, which meet to form the Juniata River, are both loaded with smallmouth bass and trout. The smallmouths tend to be quite small. The trout, mostly browns, tend to be larger, however.

Ohio/Allegheny Rivers

West of the Appalachian Mountain divide, most waters flow into the Ohio/Allegheny River system. The Ohio River begins at Pittsburgh, where the

Allegheny and Monongahela Rivers meet. These are all large rivers at this point, made navigable to heavy barges by a system of navigation dams and locks that provide a water transportation link to the Mississippi River. Upriver, the Allegheny and Monongahela flow over rocky beds in a series of riffles and pools. Fair to excellent fishing is available throughout most of this watershed.

The Allegheny River seeps from the ground on a farm near Coudersport, in Potter County. Within a few miles it becomes a fine trout stream and gains volume quickly. Only a few miles below Coudersport, pools are deep enough to hold a few muskellunge.

By Port Allegheny, the river has become a warmwater fishery that can be floated, although only with light boats or canoes. The valley is broad, and the river is surrounded by either farms, swamps, or dense bottomland forest. Floating is the only practical way to reach most of this stretch, although it gets very shallow during summer, when it is often necessary to get out of the boat to pull. Much of the water between Port Allegheny and the New York border experiences minimal fishing pressure. Smallmouth bass are scattered throughout most of this area. Walleye and channel catfish lurk in the deeper water, and muskies lay by abundant wood cover.

After making a swing through New York, the Allegheny re-enters Pennsylvania as the Allegheny Reservoir, which is created by the Kinzua Dam. The middle Allegheny, from the Kinzua Dam 107 miles downstream to the head of the navigation pools near Emlenton, provides exceptionally fine multispecies fishing. Most of this stretch, except for the areas around Warren and from Oil City to Franklin, has been designated the Allegheny National Wild and Scenic River. Shore access is good, especially from the dam to Tionesta, where the river either borders or is surrounded by the Allegheny National Forest.

Suitable for canoes and light boats, the middle Allegheny is perfect float fishing water. Riffles are mild, although shallow, during normal summer flow. Seven islands between Irvine and Tionesta, 30 miles by river, have been designated the Allegheny Wilderness Islands. Primitive camping is allowed on these and on several other islands.

From the Kinzua Dam to the mouth of Conewango Creek at Warren, and to a lesser extent for another 15 miles or so downstream, is among the best big trout water in the state. The typical trout is 15 to 18 inches long, and a few in the 6- to 8-pound class are taken. Small spoons or shallow-running minnow-shaped plugs provide action in the riffles around the many islands, but the biggest browns fall to large minnow lures in the pools. The best fly fishing is during May and June, preferably when outflow from the dam is no more than 1,200 cubic feet per second.

Muskie fishing is good throughout the middle Allegheny, and particularly from the dam to Oil City. Look for muskies in the calmer pools. The best fishing occurs in October, November, and June.

The middle Allegheny might be the best trophy walleye fishery in the East. The trophy standard is 10 pounds, but a few weighing more than 15 pounds have been caught. Favorite areas during fall and winter are the Kinzua Dam tailwaters and the dredged pools at Warren, Starbrick, and Tionesta. During summer, look for walleye in deeper troughs, more than 4 feet deep, in the riffles. Live minnows are the best winter baits. Use either nightcrawlers or minnows in summer.

The rock-bottomed Allegheny is perfect smallmouth bass habitat. Fishing for smallmouths is only fair for the first few miles below the Kinzua Dam, but it improves considerably below the mouth of Conewango Creek, peaking between Irvine and Kennerdell. Soft-shelled crayfish are the best summer baits, but you'll have to catch your own. The best fishing occurs during June and October, and most of the larger smallmouths are caught then.

Less known but enthusiastically sought by a few anglers are channel and flathead catfish. Channel cats to 20 pounds, and some larger, are found in most of the deeper pools throughout the river. Flatheads are not abundant above Tidioute. Commonly weighing 6 to 10 pounds, and with a few more than 40 pounds, they primarily inhabit pools that are at least 15 feet deep and filled with boulders. Above Tidioute few pools are deep enough.

Several of the larger tributaries also provide good fisheries. Conewango Creek has fine smallmouth bass and pike fishing, and a few walleye in the deeper pools. Brokenstraw Creek, which meets the river at Irvine, has some smallmouths and walleye in its lower half, good stocked trout fishing in its midportion, and pike where it drains swamps near the headwaters along the New York border. French Creek, which flows into the river at Franklin, has spotty but good fishing for smallmouth bass, walleye, and muskellunge.

The Clarion River, which meets the Allegheny between Emlenton and Parker, has fair smallmouth bass fishing and excellent scenery. A 36-mile float fishing trip from Ridgeway to Clarington is a relaxing experience. In Armstrong County, the lower portions of Red Bank, Mahoning, Cowanshannock, Crooked, and Buffalo Creeks offer good smallmouth bass action, along with walleye, pike, and muskies.

The Monongahela River flows northward into Pennsylvania from West Virginia. Fishing is fair for smallmouth bass, walleye, muskies, and channel catfish. Its major tributary, the Youghiogheny River, drains the highest land in Pennsylvania. Best known for whitewater rafting, it has fair to good smallmouth bass, and trout fishing from the Youghiogheny Dam to Connellsville.

Fishing is surprisingly good even within the urban and heavily industrialized region along the navigable portions of the lower Allegheny and Monongahela Rivers, and the Ohio River. The biggest challenge lies in evaluating the surface; almost everything looks the same from above. Good places to fish are around the many bridge piers, which can hold walleye, sauger, smallmouth bass, spotted bass, white bass, and crappie.

Below the navigation dams is another likely place to find bass, walleye, sauger, hybrid stripers, channel catfish, and flathead catfish. Look for walleye near the mouths of tributaries, especially during fall, winter, and spring.

Lake Erie

Though only a small portion of Lake Erie lies within Pennsylvania, Erie is still the biggest fishing hole in the state, covering 640,000 surface acres and 42 miles of shoreline. Here is excellent fishing for walleye, smallmouth bass, lake trout, and steelhead. Several of the 14 permanent tributaries are visited annually by steelhead. The only natural bay, Presque Isle, and its connecting lagoons, hold good numbers of both largemouth and smallmouth bass, northern pike, muskellunge, and panfish.

Erie was declared dead in the national news media during the 1960s, although it never was; water quality has improved considerably since, as has the fishery. Unfortunately, some species were lost. Most notable was the blue pike, a close relative of the walleye, which was a mainstay of both sport and commercial fisheries. It is now presumed extinct. Gone also are the native lake trout, although strong efforts are being made through stocking to re-establish a self-sustaining population.

Exotic species have also had an enormous impact on the native fish, sea lampreys being most notorious. This species may have done more to wipe out the native lake trout than anything else. Other exotic intruders include alewives, white perch, zebra mussels, and spiny water fleas. Pacific salmon were heavily stocked in Lake Erie and flourished for a while, but they are now only a minor part of the Erie's sportfishery.

Lake Erie is a notoriously treacherous body of water, one that requires big-water boats. Anglers unfamiliar with it need to be cautious. The popular access areas in Pennsylvania are at Walnut Creek, the City of Erie, Presque Isle State Park, and Safe Harbor Marina near Northeast.

Smallmouth bass fishing is exceptional at Lake Erie. Five-pound smallmouths are common, and 6-pounders are caught frequently enough. Skilled anglers expect their daily catches to number in the dozens. The best smallmouth action is during May and June, before and following the spawn, when these fish are in relatively shallow water.

Water clarity, wave action, and sunlight play significant roles in determining where the smallmouths are. As a general rule, the larger bass will be

Lake Erie provides Pennsylvania's most significant big-water fishing.

beyond the depth where bottom disappears (on calm, sunny days when the water is clear, you can see bottom in under 35 feet). Smallmouths congregate near irregular, rocky structure and over rocky rubble; dropoffs and humps are best located with sonar, and vertical jigging is effective when there's a concentration of smallmouths.

This is the only place in Pennsylvania where guiding is big business. The guiding or charter boat business was first built on salmon, but now walleye are the primary goal, and guided anglers, as well as many good private boaters, have no trouble catching 6- to 8-pound walleye. During July and August, anglers troll using various methods for walleye that are suspended over deep water (90 to 130 feet).

There are two distinct types of walleye behavior in Lake Erie. One group spawns in the western basin, in Ohio, then migrates throughout the lake in summer and provides deep-water suspended fishing. Another group spawns in Pennsylvania and inhabits nearshore water generally less than 75 feet deep. These walleye tend to hug bottom. Although not as widely known as the deep-water fishery, anglers land them by trolling, drifting, or jigging at night in water as shallow as 15 feet. Probably the best shore-fishing pattern for these walleye occurs as they feed on young steelhead entering the lake from tributary creeks during spring.

Steelhead management was intensified, and salmon management reduced, after it was determined that the return rate (from the lake to tributaries) was

P

much better for steelhead. An aggressive stocking program has built an excellent steelhead fishery, although in the lake steelhead are caught incidentally. The best steelhead fishing, however, occurs when they migrate into tributaries from late September through the following May, and the best action is usually when creek flow is rising.

The significant Lake Erie tributaries in Pennsylvania are, from east to west: Twentymile Creek, Sixteenmile Creek, Twelvemile Creek, Walnut Creek, and Elk Creek. Because most of the Lake Erie shore is privately owned, fishing access is limited. The Fish and Boat Commission maintains access along Elk and Walnut Creeks.

Although it is adjacent to the third largest city in the state (Erie), Presque Isle Bay and connecting lagoons in Presque Isle State Park offer good fishing for smallmouth bass, largemouth bass, northern pike, muskies, panfish, and steelhead. Ice fishing is very popular.

Inland Lakes/Reservoirs

Aside from Lake Erie, Pennsylvania's natural lakes are small. The largest is 928-acre Conneaut Lake, in Crawford County. It has good numbers of muskellunge, smallmouth bass, largemouth bass, northern pike, crappie, sunfish, and some large white bass. Boating pressure is heavy during summer, and anglers prefer October or November.

Conneaut is one of several glacial lakes in the northwest corner of the state. Others are Edinboro, LeBoeuf, Canadohta, and Sugar Lakes. All have native muskie populations, as well as bass and panfish.

Pymatuning Reservoir straddles the Ohio border in Crawford County. Covering 13,920 acres, it is a relatively shallow lake with a maximum depth of 35 feet. Best known for its walleye and muskies, it also provides good fishing for smallmouth and largemouth bass, crappie, and channel catfish. A favorite walleye fishing pattern occurs during spring, when they move onto shallow bars and shoals at night. During summer, walleye anglers troll or drift in the central and lower parts of the lake, concentrating their efforts close to humps and dropoffs.

Few waters can match Allegheny Reservoir for producing trophy fish. Located in northeastern Warren County and reaching across the New York border, the reservoir has 99 miles of shoreline and roughly 12,000 surface acres. Maximum depth near the dam is about 135 feet. Shoreline access is limited because there are no roads along most of the lake. Allegheny Reservoir has given up walleye over 17 pounds, pike over 33 pounds, and several muskies over 40 pounds. Smallmouth bass are abundant. Although not a major part of the angling catch, brown trout are highly prized. The prevalent panfish are yellow perch, white bass, rock bass, and crappie. The white bass fishery is overlooked by most anglers, but fish over 15 inches

long are common. Some of the largest walleye, pike, and brown trout are taken through the ice. During summer, local anglers favor fallen trees and artificial structures. Vertical jigging with spoons around major points is an effective method for walleye.

A number of notable but smaller man-made lakes are in the northwest corner of the state. These include Tionesta Lake in Forest County, which has excellent smallmouth bass and muskie fishing; Woodcock Creek Lake and Tamarack Lake in Crawford County, which have an abundance of bass, muskies, and panfish; 1,860-acre Lake Wilhelm in Mercer County, which offers good crappie fishing along with walleye, largemouth bass, and pike; and 3,560-acre Shenango Lake in Mercer County, which has a good supply of largemouth bass, smallmouth bass, walleye, muskellunge, pike, catfish, and crappie.

Lake Arthur, a 3,225-acre impoundment in Butler County, is the premier lake in the west-central part of the state. Although fishing pressure is particularly heavy, wise management practices have led to a quality fishery—the best trophy largemouth lake in the state. Many largemouths over 5 pounds have been caught through the ice. Fishing is also good at Arthur for muskies, crappie, hybrid stripers, channel catfish, walleye, and pike.

In the southwestern region, Glendale Lake—a 1,600-acre impoundment in Cambria County—is among the state's better pike waters. It also has fine largemouth bass, along with muskellunge, channel catfish, chain pickerel, crappie, and other panfish. This is one of the few Pennsylvania waters where anglers stand a reasonable chance of catching a bowfin.

In Armstrong County, smallmouth bass, muskies, walleye, pike, and crappie are abundant at Mahoning Creek Lake; Crooked Creek Lake provides good largemouth bass fishing. In Somerset County, smallmouth bass and walleye are the main attractions at Youghiogheny River Reservoir, which is shared with Maryland; Lake Somerset has fair to good pike fishing, and High Point Lake, which is near the top of the highest mountain in Pennsylvania, is a sleeper for walleye.

Anglers usually think trout when they look at the north-central region. A few small man-made lakes provide good warmwater fishing, however. Cowanesque Lake in Tioga County is one of the best, providing smallmouth and largemouth bass, muskies, walleye, channel catfish, and crappie. Others include Hammond Lake, which offers bass, pike, muskies, walleye, and channel catfish; and Hills Creek Lake, which occasionally yields exceptionally big muskellunge and largemouth bass.

In Centre County, Blanchard Lake has plenty of largemouth bass, smallmouth bass, and crappie. Black Moshannon Lake is a good largemouth bass fishery. Kettle Creek Lake, a deep but small impoundment in Clinton County, supports a fair

About 1860, Robert Barnwell Roosevelt, uncle of Theodore Roosevelt, complained that "streams in New York [City] that were formerly alive with trout are now totally deserted . . . ."

P

smallmouth bass fishery in addition to stocked trout. In Elk County, 1,240-acre East Branch Lake had produced a few exceptionally large muskellunge and brown trout to go along with fair smallmouth bass, yellow perch, and lake trout. In Cameron County, George B. Stevenson Lake has a little-known fishery for largemouth bass and crappie to accompany stocked trout.

Raystown Lake steals the show among south-central Pennsylvania lakes. Winding 30 miles in a serpentine manner through the Appalachian Mountains, it has a surface area of 8,300 acres and, except for a few areas that have been developed for recreation, is surrounded by forested mountains. Fishing pressure is heavy, yet with the help of stocking it sustains a lively sportfishery.

Stripers bring hordes of anglers to Raystown Lake. These fish have been taken to 50 pounds here, including state-record specimens, but the big brawlers are elusive. Visiting anglers might consider hiring a guide. Largemouth and smallmouth bass, lake trout, muskies, and crappie are plentiful. Some very large brown trout are caught occasionally. Because of its rich forage base, this lake has the potential to grow extremely large trout. Walleye have been stocked, but so far anglers have been able to make good catches only during spring when walleye are in shallow water.

Lake Marburg, a 1,295-acre York County impoundment, has the best pike fishing in the area, along with smallmouth bass, walleye, channel catfish, muskies, and better-than-average yellow perch, bluegills, and crappie. In Blair County, much smaller Canoe Lake is best known for largemouth bass and panfish, but some anglers also find large walleye.

Lake Wallenpaupack, with a surface area of 5,700 acres, is the largest body of water in the northeastern corner of the state. Although heavy pleasure boat traffic makes fishing difficult during the tourist season, a rich forage base sustains a quality fishery. Get on the water before sunrise during summer and cast surface lures along rocky banks. The better fishing is generally during May, October, and November, when most boats belong to anglers. Smallmouth bass fishing is very good at Wallenpaupack, and the lake also offers largemouth bass, muskies, walleye, and stripers.

Numerous small natural lakes and reservoirs dot the northeast, especially in the Pocono Mountains region. Some are private. Most have a mix of bass, chain pickerel, panfish, and trout. The state's best native pickerel fishing is found here. Pike and muskellunge, although they have been stocked into some northeast lakes, are not natives.

Among the better lakes in the Poconos are Lake Idlewild, Sterns Lake, Stillwater Reservoir, and Tuscarora Lake in Susquehanna County; Prompton Dam in Wayne County; Shohola Falls Dam in Pike County; and Lackawanna and Newton Lakes in Lackawanna County.

South of the Poconos in Carbon County, walleye and muskellunge highlight a fishery that includes largemouth bass, smallmouth bass, channel catfish, and panfish at Beltzville Lake. Mauch Chunk Lake has fine largemouth bass fishing along with smallmouth bass, walleye, channel catfish, muskies, and panfish.

Largemouth bass action is good at Harveys Lake in Luzerne County, at Lake Chillisquaque in Montour County, and at Stevens Lake in Wyoming County.

Several small reservoirs support quality fishing in the heavily populated southeast. Most have a good mix of fish, including largemouth bass, walleye, channel catfish, and panfish. Largemouth bass and muskies provide the best fishing at Blue Marsh Lake in Berks County and at Chester-Octoraro Lake in Lancaster County. Crappie fishing is better than average at Ontelaunee Reservoir in Berks County. Largemouth bass and walleye are mainstays at Lake Galena. In Delaware County, largemouth and smallmouth bass are the primary sportfish at Springton Reservoir, and Marsh Creek Lake in Chester County has good crappie fishing.

PERCH

The Percidae family of freshwater fish consists of hundreds of species, some of which are unarguably among the best-tasting species available and among the most important sportfish in North America and Europe. By far the largest number of species in this family are much too small to be eaten by humans, although they are important and presumably tasty forage for a host of larger predators. Among the smaller species are some 160 species of darters, which represent 20 percent of all fish in the United States.

All members of the perch family share basic features, however. The body is typically long and slender, and the two dorsal fins are distinctly separate. The anal fin has one or two spines, and the pelvic fins are located far forward, near the throat. The gill covers end in sharp, spinelike points. The scales are heavy and toothed along their exposed margins.

See: Darters; Perch, European; Perch, Yellow; Sauger; Saugeye; Walleye; Zander.

PERCH, EUROPEAN   *Perca fluviatilis.*

Other names—perch, English perch, English river perch, Eurasian perch, redfin (Australia), redfin perch, reddie; Dutch: *baars;* Finnish: *ahven;* French: *perche europeénne, perche fluviatile;* German: *barsch, berse, flubbarsch;* Hungarian: *süger;* Italian, Portuguese, and Spanish: *perca;* Norwegian: *abbor;* Russian: *okun;* Swedish: *abborre;* Turkish: *tatlisu levregi.*

A member of the Percidae family, the European perch is popular with many anglers for its table fare and light-tackle virtues, and it is a common target

P

European Perch

of anglers throughout Europe. In places where it was introduced, especially those where trout exist, it is viewed less favorably, as it competes with trout for food and feeds on small trout. In some areas, anglers are asked not to return caught fish to the water.

Identification. A deep-bodied fish with a large mouth, the European perch is olive on the back, which grades to green on the sides and merges into white on the belly. The two dorsal fins are distinctly separated, the first being spinous with a black spot or blotch at the rear. There are five to six vertical bars across the back and sides, and these are more prominent among younger fish. The pelvic fins, anal fin, and the lower margin of the caudal fin are bright orange or red, hence the name.

Size. Although this species has been reported to grow to 500 millimeters in length and 10 kilograms in weight, most specimens are far smaller; 6.5 kilograms is reported to be the maximum for Eurasian specimens.

Distribution. European perch are native throughout Europe (except in Spain, Italy, and Greece) and to Siberia's Kolyma River. They have been widely introduced elsewhere, including Australia (Tasmania) in 1862, where they are now found in many streams and impoundments across the bottom half of the continent.

Habitat. This fish prefers slow-moving or stillwaters, and favors those areas where weed growth and underwater structures offer shelter and food. In streams they prefer slow-flowing pools and backwaters. In large farm dams and impoundments, they choose to roam in schools.

Life history/Behavior. This species is capable of breeding in both streams and dams, and females can produce more than 100,000 eggs, each about 2 millimeters in diameter. Spawning takes place in late winter and spring (August through October) at night in quiet waters away from strong current flow and among aquatic plants or underwater structures. The egg mass can be up to 3 meters long, and the eggs hatch out in seven to eight days. Growth in impoundments can be rapid, and overpopulation often results. High fecundity leads to a lot of small fish and few large ones, so overfishing is never a problem. Regular fishing and harvesting reduces numbers and the demand on food stocks, and the quantities of larger fish increase as a result.

Food. The carnivorous perch feeds on other fish, crayfish, mollusks, shrimp, worms, and insect larvae.

Angling. Fishing methods in general are similar to those for the North American yellow perch *(see: perch, yellow)*. Bait anglers use a variety of natural baits, including pieces from fillets of fish (especially saltwater mullet). Lure anglers choose among plugs, spinners, or soft plastics, either casting or trolling. Fly anglers use streamer patterns worked deep. European perch in lakes and impoundments tend to school more readily than in streams, and jigging for them is often popular among boat anglers, as well as for those fishing through the ice.

PERCH, GOLDEN   *Macquaria ambigua.*
Other names—yellowbelly, callop, Murray perch, white perch, Murray bream, tarki.

A member of the Percichthyidae family of temperate bass and native to Australia, the golden perch is one of that country's most important inland fish. At one time, it supported a commercial fishery in the Murray-Darling system in the West of New South Wales. The impact of farming, irrigation schemes, drought, and pollution has reduced numbers considerably, but increased culture and stocking of small and large impoundments has secured their future. A placid fish that can be handled quite easily, it is, nonetheless, a fine sportfish and provides excellent table fare.

Identification. The golden perch is a deep-bodied, laterally compressed fish that has a conspicuous shape, especially in the adult: a concave forehead profile, a tapered snout, a protruding lower jaw, and a humped back that accentuates the small head and is more prominent in large females. A small eye sits above and behind the corner of the mouth. Although there is some variation in color due to water clarity, the back coloration can vary from dark brown to olive green, shading to yellow and white on the lower sides and belly. The soft dorsal and rounded caudal fins are muddy black, and the other fins are yellowish.

Size. This species is known to grow to 23 kilograms and a length of 760 millimeters; the Australian angling record stands at 9.52 kilograms. Captures of specimens up to 5 kilograms are not uncommon and are usually taken by anglers in large impoundments.

Distribution. The golden perch appears naturally in the rivers and tributaries of the Murray-Darling system in central and southern Queensland, western New South Wales, Victoria, and South Australia, and in some coastal streams in northern New South Wales. They have also been introduced to many large impoundments in these states, as well as in northern Queensland and the Northern Territory.

P

Habitat.   Most of the waterways in which golden perch live are slow moving, turbid, and warm. They are also found in clear-water environments to a lesser degree, as well as in backwaters and billabongs that form after floods. They swim at all depths, and generally live among weedbeds; in and around underwater structures such as submerged trees, logs, and rocks; and under overhanging banks.

Life history/Behavior.   Golden perch migrate upstream to spawn at night during spring and summer. This movement, which can exceed 1,000 kilometers, ensures that the eggs and larvae are not washed downstream into the sea. The spawning urge appears to be triggered by a rise in water level, runoff from flooding, water temperature, and water chemical content. Their fecundity is high; a female can produce more than 500,000 eggs. The floating eggs are nonadhesive and are carried away by the current. Hatching occurs within 24 to 30 hours at a water temperature between 20° and 31°C, and the fish mature within 20 to 25 days. Growth rates in water impoundments where food is plentiful and little effort is required for swimming (as opposed to stream effort) are usually high.

Food and feeding habits.   The carnivorous golden perch feeds chiefly on yabbies, shrimp, small fish, mollusks, and aquatic insect life. They also take worms and moth larvae.

Angling.   Trolling, lure casting, and baitfishing are all favored for golden perch. Light to medium weight spinning and baitcasting outfits with lines to 7 kilograms are favored, and 15-kilogram handlines are used where underwater obstructions are a hazard. Plug casting from a streambank or from a canoe, particularly in the clearer headwaters of a stream, is frequently successful.

Slow trolling with deep-diving plugs while also casting plugs or spinners to likely spots is another successful technique. If fishing is slow, some boat anglers circle a pool at high speed to disturb the bottom conditions, a tactic that can uncover mollusks and crustaceans and other aquatic life. This ruse will often evince interest from golden perch and, if live baits are suspended under a float, it will cause the fish to home in on their prey. A deep-diving, rattling lure cast into the roiled water is also productive.

Anglers should exercise care when handling golden perch. The spines on both dorsal and anal fins can puncture a wayward hand, and the wound can become inflamed if not treated. The gill covers also have a sharp cutting edge that must be avoided, and it is preferable either to grasp the fish by the lower jaw in much the same manner as that used to grasp a bass, or swim it into a net.

The golden perch is a highly regarded table fish with white, firm flesh. Unfortunately, however, it sometimes carries a muddy flavor if the perch has been taken from muddy water.

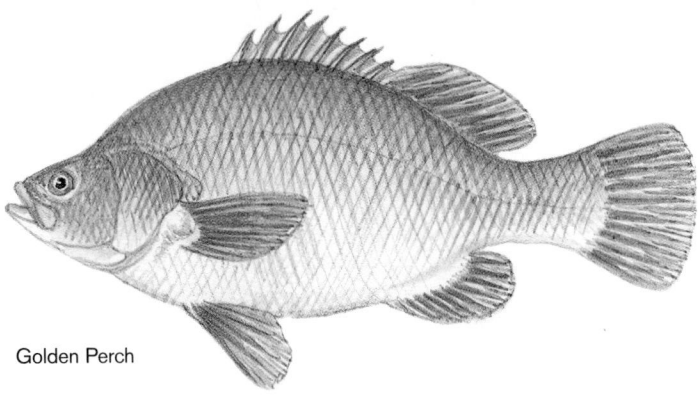

Golden Perch

PERCH, JUNGLE   *Kuhlia rupestris.*
Other names—rock flagtail; Japanese: *okuchi-yugoi;* Tagalog (Philippines): *damagan.*

A member of the Kuhliidae family of aholeholes, the jungle perch was once a celebrated freshwater sportfish in Australia. Its numbers have declined, however, and today in Australia it is viewed as a species to be released upon capture. It is a fine food fish.

Identification.   A strong, sturdy species, the jungle perch has a compressed body that is colored brown over the back and becomes paler on the sides, fading to silver or white on the belly. Its large mouth extends back to below a large eye. The majority of its scales have a central black spot, and the tail is emarginate with rounded lobes. The dorsal fin is deeply notched and almost forms two separate fins. A white bar on the upper lobe, and a cream bar on the lower lobe, serve also as identifying characteristics.

Size.   This species grows to 500 millimeters and 3 kilograms, but such specimens are rare. Most Australian anglers are lucky to catch one larger than 1 kilogram.

Distribution.   Jungle perch have been recorded from Fiji, Papua New Guinea, and from Durban, South Africa, north to the Red Sea and most islands of the Indian Ocean. In Australia they range from Fraser Island in southern Queensland to the eastern streams of Cape York.

Habitat.   Jungle perch live in the crystal clear waters of rock pools in rain forest streams. They are

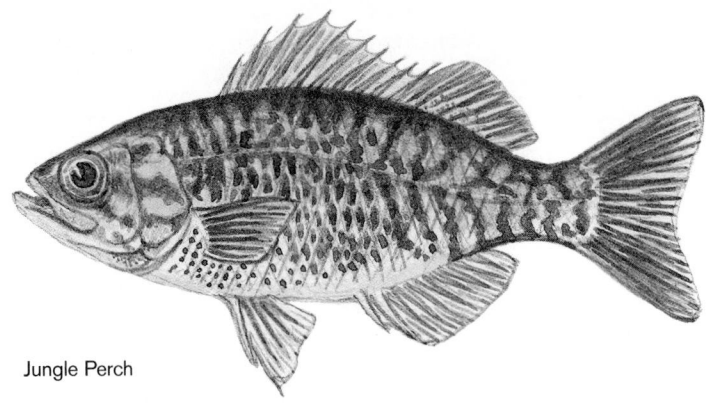

Jungle Perch

P

capable of surviving in brackish water and are thought to move downstream to brackish waters to spawn.

Food and feeding habits. The jungle perch is primarily carnivorous and lives on crustaceans, insects, and small frogs and fish.

Angling. Considered a challenge by anglers using plugs and lures, the jungle perch is a clean, strong fighter that responds well to casting with baitcasting and spinning tackle. Lines to 4 kilogram-strength, and rods up to 2 meters long, are the norm; shallow- to mid-diving plugs, surface poppers, and small plastic jigs are favored. The fish will take an artificial fly, but the difficult terrain and the overhanging nature of streamside vegetation make this technique less popular. Although it will readily attack a lure, it can be easily spooked if the angler carelessly approaches the crystal clear rock pools of its home stream. It can be found in greater numbers in streams accessible only to the dedicated and adventurous angler.

PERCH, NILE   *Lates niloticus.*

Other names—giant perch, Niger perch; Arabic: *Am'kal, Am'kaltyâya;* Swahili: *mkombozi, sangala.*

A member of the Centropomidae family and a relative of snook and barramundi, the Nile perch is one of the world's largest freshwater fish and one of the most highly valued food and angling species of the African continent. It was cultivated by Egyptians in fish ponds at least 4,000 years ago (along with tilapia) and has been widely introduced to other areas, sometimes with disastrous results for native species.

Identification. The Nile perch looks very much like a large version of the barramundi *(see).* Juveniles are mottled brown and silver. By age 1, they measure 8 inches in length and are completely silver. Adults are generally brown to greenish brown above and silvery below. The top of the head is strongly depressed, and the tail is rounded (convex). The first dorsal fin consists of seven or eight strong spines, and the second dorsal fin, which immediately follows the first without a complete break, has one or two spines and 12 to 13 soft, branched rays. Large Nile perch have deep, distended bellies, and pack a lot of girth.

Size. In some parts of their range, Nile perch up to 6½ feet long and weighing 176 pounds have been caught and recorded by native fishermen and were once common. Much larger ones, up to 500 pounds, are said to have been taken in nets but have gone unrecorded. An all-tackle world record was a 191½-pound fish landed in Lake Victoria, Kenya, in 1991. A 213-pounder was caught on rod and reel in Lake Nasser, Egypt, in 1997.

Distribution. The Nile perch is endemic to the African continent and exists naturally or via introduction in various river systems and lakes in Egypt, Ethiopia, Uganda, Kenya, Zambia, and Zaire. It is present in the Blue and White Niles, and the Niger, Benue, Chad, Senegal, Volta, and Zaire Rivers, and in Lakes Rudolph, Albert, Tanganyika, Turkana, Victoria, Kyoga, Nasser, Fayoum, and Menzaleh. Good Nile perch fishing is well known below the Aswan Dam and at the junction of the Blue and White Niles. Nile perch were introduced to Lakes Kyoga and Victoria in the 1950s and 1960s, and were extremely successful, to the detriment of native cichlids and other smaller fish.

In many if not most of these sites, Nile perch are valued more for commercial and subsistence fishing (their white meat is tasty, especially in smaller fish) than for angling, and various pressures have made the largest specimens less common.

Life history. Nile perch grow about 9 or 10 inches a year during their first two or three years,

P

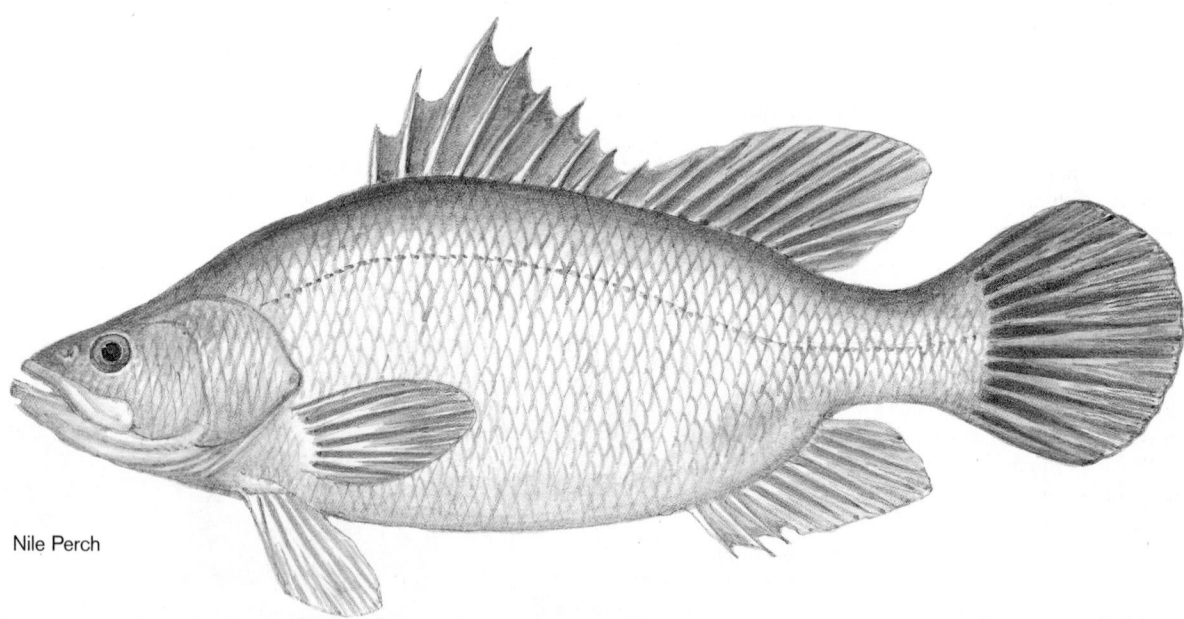

Nile Perch

then growth slows. They reach maturity at a length of about 20 to 24 inches, the females being larger at maturity.

Food.   Nile perch are voracious predators, as well they have to be to reach their enormous sizes. Any abundant small fish are targeted, and tilapia are believed to be a primary food source, although they will eat other perch.

Angling.   Fishing for Nile perch is done primarily by drifting or stillfishing with live baits, and trolling with large plugs or spoons. Some casting may occur, especially in smaller portions of rivers where the fish are likely to be in pools or eddies. Casters may use plugs, spoons, and large streamer flies. Baits may include any common fish up to a pound, such as tigerfish but especially tilapia. In lakes, anglers concentrate on rocky bays and inlets.

Nile perch are good fighters in small and medium sizes, and sheer brutes in the heavyweight class. They make several sustained runs and may take considerable line if large enough. Anglers fishing with large natural baits and lures for giant specimens often use extremely heavy tackle. River perch are much more challenging to land than those in lakes, especially by anglers who must fish from shore, do not have the assistance of boats to chase after running fish, and have to accommodate swift currents and eddies. Behemoths can take hundreds of yards of line from a reel. Heavy concentrations of water hyacinths increase the level of difficulty of catching large fish in some rivers and lakes.

See: Kenya; Uganda.

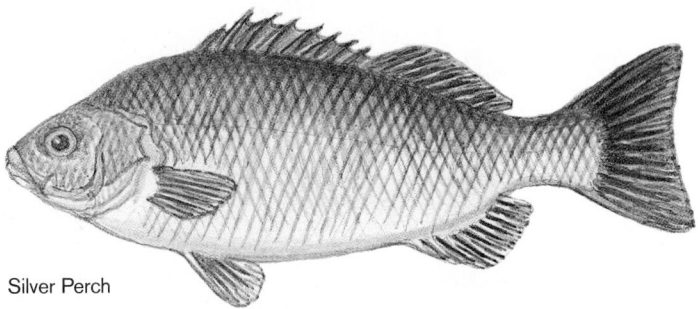
Silver Perch

Size/Age.   The average fish is less than 12 inches long and weighs $1/2$ pound or less; it never weighs more than a pound. The silver perch can live up to six years.

Distribution.   Silver perch occur from New York southward along the Atlantic coast and also in the Gulf of Mexico.

Habitat.   The silver perch is an inshore fish, most common in bays, seagrass beds, tidal creeks, small rivers, and quiet lagoons near estuaries. It is sometimes found in brackish marshes and also occasionally in freshwater.

Life history/Behavior.   The silver perch migrates offshore in winter and returns inshore to breed in spring. Spawning occurs inshore between May and September in shallow, saline areas. Silver perch reach maturity by their second or third year, when 6 inches long.

Food.   Adults consume crustaceans, worms, and small fish.

Angling.   The silver perch is easily caught on shrimp and cut baits.

PERCH, SILVER   *Bairdiella chrysoura.*
Other names—sand perch.

The silver perch is a member of the Sciaenidae family (drum and croaker). It is one of the most common and abundant Atlantic drum, harvested by commercial netters but seldom prominent in the angler's catch. This small panfishlike species is good to eat, but it is more likely to be used by anglers as live bait for larger predators.

The closely related bairdiella, or gulf croaker *(Bairdiella icistius),* is one of a number of marine species introduced successfully to the Salton Sea from the Gulf of California. It grows to 12 inches there and is an important forage fish.

Identification.   The body of the silver perch is high and compressed. As with others in the drum family, its dorsal fins are separated by a deep notch. There are five to six pores on the chin and no barbels. Its mouth is terminal and has finely serrated teeth. Its coloring is silvery, with yellowish fins and a whitish belly. It commonly has no spots.

The silver perch can be distinguished from the unrelated white perch *(see: perch, white)* by the dark stripes that line the sides. It can also be distinguished from the sand seatrout *(see: seatrout, sand)* by its lack of prominent canine teeth, and by its chin pores.

PERCH, WHITE   *Morone americana*
Other names—silver bass, silver perch, sea perch, bass, narrow-mouthed bass, bass perch, gray perch, bluenose perch, humpy; French: *bar blanc d'Amerique.*

White perch are something of a mystery to many anglers. They are abundant in some places, rare in others, similar enough to other species to be misidentified, and underappreciated as table fare. Many anglers catch white perch incidentally while pursuing other species, except in places where they are numerous. In all, there is not much of a constituency for the white perch, but it is a robust fish that provides excellent sport on light tackle.

In some places, white perch are disdained because they compete with favored gamefish for food. In other places, a lack of harvesting—either by anglers or other species of fish—can lead to large populations of stunted, small white perch. Nevertheless, where there is a population with larger than average size, white perch could rival crappie as a desirable quarry.

There is a limited commercial fishery for them in coastal areas, especially in the Chesapeake Bay and in the Great Lakes. Many restaurants that offer "lake perch" are serving white perch in lieu of the

P

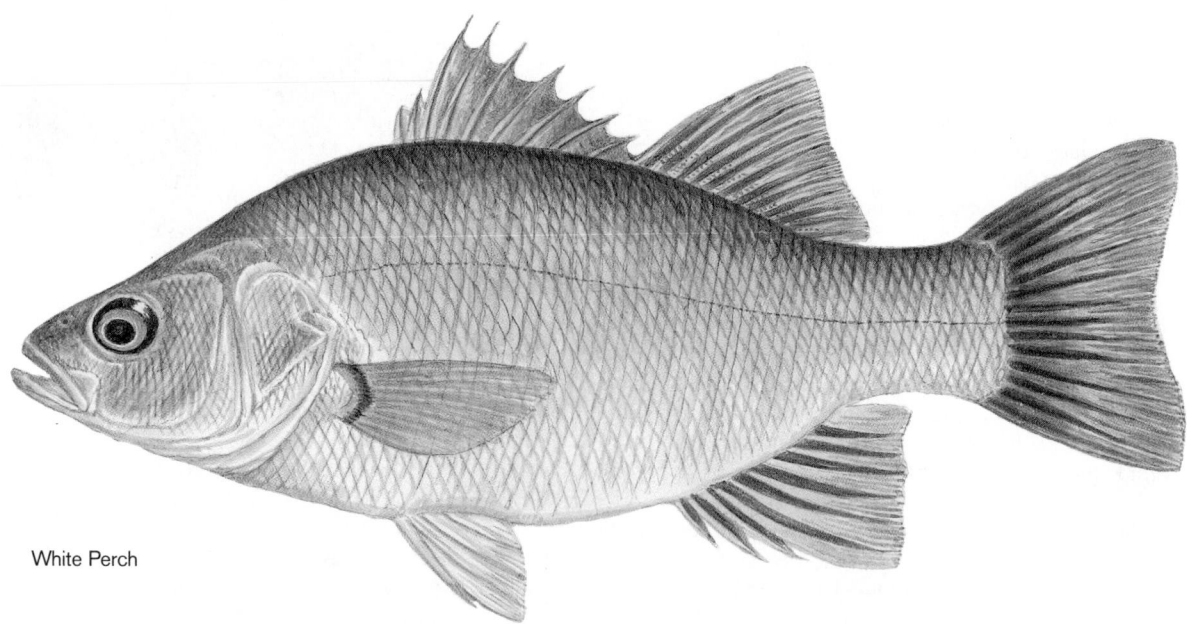

White Perch

more traditional yellow perch. This usually happens when the latter are less available. White perch taken from coolwater lakes have a firm, white flaky flesh and are of excellent eating quality.

Identification.   The white perch is not a true perch but a member of the temperate bass family and a relative of white bass and striped bass. It is similar in shape to the striped bass, but it has a deeper, less-rounded body and lacks the horizontal lines found on striped bass. Although shorter, stockier, and smaller in weight than a striper, it is very similar in appearance to a white bass *(see: bass, white),* except that it has no stripes. A more appropriate name for this species would probably be silver bass, and it is called by that name in some areas.

The white perch has a deep, thin body that slopes up steeply from the eye to the beginning of the dorsal fin and which is deepest under the first dorsal fin. On large, older specimens, it can be nearly hump-backed at that spot. Its colors can be olive, gray green, silvery gray, dark brown, or black on the back, becoming a lighter silvery green on the sides and silvery white on the belly. The pelvic and anal fins (both on the belly) are sometimes rosy colored. Like all members of the temperate bass family, it has two dorsal fins on the back, and the pelvic fins sit forward on the body below the pectoral fins. The first dorsal fin has nine spines, but the second one is soft rayed. There are three spines at the front of the anal fin, and a single spine precedes the second dorsal fin and each pelvic fin. The white perch has no teeth on its tongue, its scales are relatively large, and the lateral line is complete.

Size/Age.   White perch are generally small and slow-growing after attaining juvenile size. The average white perch caught by anglers weighs under a pound and is probably close to three-quarters of a pound and 9 inches in length. These figures can obviously vary among regions and populations.

In some places, the average white perch is just 6 inches long.

These fish have a normal life span of between 5 and 7 years, but some specimens may live for 14 to 17 years. They are said to be able to grow to 19 inches and 6 pounds, but these dimensions are extremely rare; the largest white perch in angling records is a 4-pound, 12-ounce Maine fish that was caught in 1949.

Distribution.   White perch are found along the Atlantic coast from the southern Gulf of St. Lawrence to South Carolina and inland along the upper St. Lawrence River to the lower Great Lakes. They are present in all three Maritime Provinces, common in Lake Ontario, and especially abundant in the Hudson River and Chesapeake Bay areas. The white perch is far more coastal in occurrence than is the white bass, and most of the overlap in their distributions occurs in the area of the Great Lakes and upper St. Lawrence River.

Habitat.   Like its striped bass cousin, the adaptable white perch is at home in saltwater, brackish water, and freshwater. In marine waters, they are primarily found in brackish water, estuaries, and coastal rivers and streams, and some of the latter have sea-run populations. Some white perch remain resident in brackish bays and estuaries, whereas others roam widely in search of food.

White perch inhabit scattered freshwater lakes and ponds throughout their range, but in varied abundance. A prolific fish, they have overpopulated some ponds and small lakes and have been deemed a nuisance, especially when crowding out black bass, trout, and other species. For marine purposes, white perch are considered demersal (bottom dwelling), and in general they do tend to stay deep in their home waters, on or close to the bottom.

Life history/Behavior.   White perch are spring spawners, usually accomplishing this act

P

when water temperatures are between 14°C to 24°C, and in shallow water over many kinds of bottom. Males and females each spawn several times in random fashion, and females may produce from 15,000 to more than 200,000 eggs. The tiny eggs become sticky after fertilization and attach to vegetation and bottom materials. The length of time for hatching depends on the water temperature. When the water is cooler, hatching takes longer (four days at 15°C versus about 30 hours at 20°C). Newly hatched white perch are 2.3 millimeters long and feed on plankton. For unknown reasons, white perch in some bodies of freshwater are extremely successful at reproduction, whereas in others they are virtually unsuccessful.

These fish are a schooling species that group even while young, and continue to stay in loose open-water schools through adulthood. They do not orient to cover and structure, and tend to be deeper than yellow perch, with whom they occupy the same lakes and ponds in parts of their range.

Food and feeding habits. White perch in lakes are known to feed both during the day and night but are generally more active in low light and nocturnally. Freshwater and saltwater populations move to surface (or inshore) waters at night, retreating to deeper water during the day.

Perch eat mostly aquatic insect larvae when they are small. As they grow, they eat many kinds of small fish, such as smelt, yellow perch, killifish, and other white perch, as well as the young of other species, particularly those that spawn after them. They also reportedly consume crabs, shrimp, and small alewives and herring.

Angling. In those freshwaters where white bass are not numerous, white perch are usually caught at random and accidentally, although it is possible to catch more than one if not many in the same location. Where white perch are abundant, creel limits are generous, and fish are caught with rapidity at times. In saltwater and in brackish environs, an angler who locates a white perch has typically come upon a school and may catch a few dozen fish.

Despite the sometimes relative abundance and schooling nature of white perch, the biggest problem many anglers face is finding these fish, or finding them when they are active. Tides, current, and water movement may affect their activity in estuaries, but in lakes and ponds the stimulant may more likely be low morning light or nightfall. In some places it is possible to find schools of white perch behaving a lot like white bass and chasing small baitfish to the surface. If the water's surface is fairly calm, you may observe this behavior, and if you carefully and quietly approach the school, you can experience steady casting action. More often than not, however, you have to search for schools of fish that are not visible to the eye, using sonar in open water, casting in estuary creeks and current-funneling pools, and otherwise prospecting.

Some anglers troll in freshwater, primarily with small spinners and spinner-bait combinations, but casting with jigs, small jigging spoons, diving plugs, and minnow-shaped plugs is more common, as is drift fishing or slow-trolling with worms or minnows under a float. Small spoons and jigs equipped with grub tails or small eel-like plastic tails are effective in the shallow backwaters of estuaries. Getting any of these offerings near the bottom is usually important, except when surface schools are present. Whatever you use, when you catch a white perch, stop and work the area thoroughly for more fish.

And don't overlook ice fishing with small jigs and baits either. There is some constituency for this in freshwater, and especially in coastal rivers that have enough ice for safe travel. It may be necessary to move to keep up with active schools.

Although small on average, and not prone to acrobatic maneuvers, white perch are extremely robust fighters, and a highly enjoyable catch on light spinning or flycasting tackle.

PERCH, YELLOW *Perca flavescens.*

Other names—ringed perch, striped perch, coon perch, jack perch, lake perch, American perch; French: *perchaude.*

The most widely distributed member of the Percidae family, the yellow perch is one of the best loved and most pursued of all freshwater fish, particularly in northerly states and provinces in North America. This is due to its availability over a wide range, the general ease with which it is caught, and its delicious taste. Yellow perch do not attain large sizes and are not known for superior fighting characteristics, so they receive much less press than some freshwater species, including such equally popular panfish as crappie and bluegill. Nevertheless, the yellow perch is a favorite in large and small lakes alike, and it has some commercial importance, particularly in the Great Lakes. This role is limited by the small size of the fish and by its varying abundance. It is particularly popular for ice fishing; typically generous bag limits allow anglers to provide a family's worth of meals on a given outing.

Identification. Unlike the white perch, which is actually a temperate bass, the yellow perch is a true perch. Although it resembles true bass in many ways, it is more closely related to fellow Percidae family members, the walleye and sauger. Its most striking characteristic is a colorful golden yellow body, tinged with orangy fins.

Yellow perch are colored a green to yellow gold and have six to eight dark, broad vertical bars that extend from the back to below the lateral line, a whitish belly, and orange lower fins during breeding season. Their bodies are oblong and appear humpbacked; this is the result of the deepest part of the body beginning at the first dorsal fin, then tapering slightly to the beginning of the second dorsal fin. This trait is somewhat similar in white perch

P

Yellow Perch

(see: perch, white), to which the yellow perch is un-related, although both fish may inhabit the same waters.

Yellow perch are distinguished from trout and salmon by their lack of an adipose fin, which is ordinarily located between the dorsal and tail fins, and from sunfish by their separate dorsal fins (connected in sunfish) and two or fewer anal fin spines (sunfish have three or more). They are distinguished from walleye and sauger by their lack of canine teeth and by a generally deeper body form.

Size/Age. The average yellow perch caught by anglers weighs between $^1/_4$ to $^3/_4$ pound and measures 6 to 10 inches in length. In lakes with stunted populations, the fish are on the lower end of this range, and a 10-inch fish is usually considered fairly large. Some lakes produce perch in the 1-pound and larger class, although fish greater than $1^1/_2$ pounds are infrequent. The all-tackle world-record yellow perch, taken in 1865, weighed 4 pounds, 3 ounces and is the oldest freshwater sport-fish record in the books. Yellow perch can grow to 16 inches in length and can live up to 12 years. In general, northern populations grow more slowly but live longer, and females grow faster than males.

Distribution. Yellow perch are widespread in the northern United States and Canada. They range east from Nova Scotia to the Santee River drainage in South Carolina and west throughout the Great Lakes states to the edge of British Columbia and into Washington. A small number extend north through Great Slave Lake almost to Great Bear Lake in Canada's Northwest Territories. Although they appear in nearly every state due to stocking, they are sparsely distributed in the South, most of the West, and parts of the Midwest; they are also sparse in British Columbia and northern Canada. Although the yellow perch is a freshwater fish, Nova Scotia fisheries personnel report that it is occasionally found in brackish water along the Atlantic coast.

Habitat. Yellow perch are found in a wide variety of warm and cool habitats over a vast range of territory, although they are primarily lake fish. They are occasionally found in ponds and rivers. These fish are most abundant in clear, weedy lakes that have a muck, sand, or gravel bottom. Smaller lakes and ponds usually produce smaller fish, although in very fertile lakes with moderate angling pressure, yellow perch can grow large. They inhabit open areas of most lakes and prefer temperatures between the mid-60s and the low 70s.

Life history/Behavior. Yellow perch usually spawn in early spring when the water temperature is between 45°F and 50°F. Eggs are spawned in the shallow areas of lakes or up in tributary streams in gelatinous ribbons by an adult female and are fertilized by as many as a dozen males in weedy areas several feet deep. The ribbons, which may be up to 7 feet long and several inches wide, attach to vegetation until one-quarter to one-half of the 10,000 to 48,000 eggs hatch into fry in 10 days to three weeks after spawning. Without protection from parents, slow-swimming and slow-growing yellow perch travel in schools and are avidly preyed upon, especially by walleye, during the first year of life. Their odds of survival are perhaps 1 in 5,000 in the first year, yet yellow perch manage to produce in abundance in favorable habitat.

Yellow perch travel in schools composed fish that are similar in size and age, and there is some evidence of the sexes dividing into separate schools. In large lakes, adults move in schools farther offshore than the young. They move between deeper and shallow water in response to changing food supplies, seasons, and temperatures.

Because of their predaceous nature and swift breeding, overpopulation is a problem in many lakes where yellow perch have been introduced; the fish may become stunted, and other species may be adversely impacted as a result. The introduction, through natural or artificial means, of yellow perch

P

into ponds containing trout usually results in a collapse of the trout population, and this may be true for other species of fish that were dominant before yellow perch entered.

Food and feeding habits. Young yellow perch feed on zooplankton until they have grown to several inches in length and then feed on larger zooplankton, insects, young crayfish, snails, aquatic insects, fish eggs, and small fish, including the young of their own species. Yellow perch are commonly believed to feed in shallows at dawn and dusk, remaining inactive at night, but the conditions under which they feed and under which they can be caught vary widely with their environment and the skill of the angler.

Angling. Yellow perch are very popular for food and sport. They are not strong fighters, but in cold water and on light spinning or spincasting gear they engage the angler in a feisty battle. Their inclination to avoid turbid and muddy environs and to reside in clean and cool habitat no doubt accounts for their firm white flesh, which has a flavor equal to that of its cousin, the highly touted walleye.

Anglers land yellow perch in open water throughout the season, and these fish are especially popular among ice anglers. They are also caught during their spring spawning runs, in which they ascend tributaries and seek warm shoreline areas in bays and back eddies. Primarily, yellow perch like cool water and will school deep wherever surface temperatures are warm, although they will move shallower to feed.

Yellow perch are a schooling fish, so when you catch one, there will be more in the vicinity. It pays to scour an area thoroughly. The best locations are often the weedbeds in shallow lakes, where it is advisable to fish on or close to the bottom. Fishing deep, vertically with jigs or baits, is also important in larger bodies of water.

Yellow perch are caught on a variety of baits and lures, with live worms, live minnows, small minnow-imitating plugs, jigs, spoons, and spinners being among the best attractors. Small jigs with hair or curl-tail grub bodies are productive. The range of acceptable colors varies but includes white, yellow, shad-imitation, and gray or silver, especially if imbedded with flakes. Baits are very effective, but these fish are adept at nibbling and stealing baits. Floats and bobbers are frequently employed with live baits; nightcrawler rigs, sporting a No. 2 hook and a No. 2 spinner, are also effective. Chumming has its devotees as well, including those who use mealworms and more fragrant ground concoctions.

Light spinning or spincasting outfits, equipped with 2- through 8-pound-test line, are more than adequate for perch. Fly fishing, although less popular, is also effective, particularly when yellow perch are in shallow water in the spring.

Seldom are yellow perch caught on larger lures that are meant for other gamefish, and rarely do they come to the surface or travel far in pursuit of a

Float-fished bait lured this yellow perch from a New York pond.

lure. It is usually important to work slowly and deep, with smaller lures.

In the winter through the ice, minnows, worms, waxworm larvae, small jigging spoons, and small jigs are the top producers.

PERIGEE

The point in the moon's orbit closest to the earth, producing a greater tidal range.
See: Tides.

PERMIT   *Trachinotus falcatus.*
Other names—French: *carangue plume;* Portuguese: *sernambiguara;* Spanish: *palometa, pampano, pampano erizero, pámpano palometa.*

An important gamefish and a particularly prized member of the Carangidae family of jacks and pompano, the permit is a tough fighter and a handful on light tackle. This is especially true for sight casting on shallow flats. The permit is also an excellent food fish, although it is much less important commercially than the Florida pompano. The greatest concentrations of permit are off southern Florida, and this is also where the biggest fish are taken.

Identification. In overall appearance, the permit is a brilliantly silver fish with dark fins and a dark or iridescent blue to greenish or grayish back. The belly is often yellowish, and sometimes the pelvic fins and the front lobe of the anal fin have an

Permit

orange tint. Many individuals have a dark, circular black area on the side behind the base of the pectoral fin, and some have a dusky midbody blotch. The body is laterally compressed, and the fish has a high back profile; young fish appear roundish, adults more oblong. Small permit have teeth on the tongue. The permit has 16 to 19 soft anal rays, and the second dorsal fin has one spine and 17 to 21 soft rays, compared with 22 to 27 in the similar Florida pompano. It is further distinguished by its deeper body and a generally larger body size. Also, the second and third ribs in the permit are prominent in fish weighing more than 10 pounds, and these ribs can be felt through the sides of the fish to help in differentiating it from the Florida pompano.

Size. Permit commonly weigh up to 25 pounds and are 1 to 3 feet long, but they can exceed 50 pounds and reach 45 inches in length. The all-tackle world record is a 53-pound, 4-ounce Florida fish caught in 1994.

Distribution. This species occurs in the western Atlantic, ranging from Massachusetts to southeastern Brazil, including the Bahamas and much of the West Indies. They are most common in Florida, the Bahamas, and the Caribbean and are rarely encountered in the northern part of their range.

Habitat. Permit inhabit shallow, warm waters in depths of up to 100 feet, and young fish prefer clearer and shallower waters than do adults. Able to adapt to a wide range of salinity, they occur in channels or holes over sandy flats and around reefs, and sometimes over mud bottoms. They are primarily a schooling fish when younger, traveling in schools of 10 or more, although they are occasionally seen in great numbers, and they tend to become solitary

with age. They are sometimes attracted to areas where the bottom is stirred up.

Food and feeding habits. Over sandy bottoms, permit feed mainly on mollusks, and over reefs they feed mostly on crustaceans such as crabs, shrimp, and sea urchins. Like bonefish, they feed by rooting in the sand on shallow flats.

Angling. An elusive, coveted, and heralded saltwater fish, permit are renowned for being difficult to approach, difficult to entice to strike, difficult to set a hook in, and difficult to land. As a warmwater fish pursued mostly in South Florida, the Florida Keys, and the Bahamas, permit are unavailable to most North American anglers, and these conditions only enhance their mystique.

Although some anglers favor bait fishing or jigging in intermediate depths over reefs, wrecks, and the like, the vastly preferred practice is to sight-fish for permit while stalking the same shallow flats inhabited by bonefish and casting a jig, fly, or live crab or shrimp. Permit venture onto sandy flats on a rising tide to scour the bottom for food and are often seen cruising or tailing while feeding on the bottom. They feed much like bonefish do, rooting in the sand for shrimp or crabs. As mentioned, these fish travel in schools, which are occasionally large, but the big fish are usually solitary.

On the flats they are skittish creatures, and anglers stalk them carefully in a boat or by wading. Although it is often critical to make a precise presentation, this is made easier and less critical when a school is encountered, as the competitive instinct may prevail. Nonetheless, it should be noted that relatively few fish are hooked, and fewer still landed, in comparison to the number of fish seen, so the importance of stalking and presentation should not

P

be underestimated. Furthermore, the nature of their feeding behavior—rooting down on the bottom—reduces their field of vision, making it important to position the offering where the fish can see it, and then to move it just enough to interest them.

Most permit are caught on live crabs; some respond to live shrimp. Medium-size blue crabs about 2 inches across are best, and many anglers clip the claws off before impaling them on a 2/0 or 3/0 hook. Small jigs produce a fair number of fish. Weighted flies are a more challenging offering, and therefore less effective, but a select few patterns produce consistently. Overcoming the difficulty of maneuvering into an optimal casting position while countering the effects of wind and other factors, and simultaneously making an accurate presentation with an enticing crab-imitating fly, are among the top challenges and achievements in sportfishing.

No matter what the offering, the hook must be sharp, and it is advisable to set the hook forcefully several or more times to effect penetration, as a permit's mouth is extremely leathery. Similarly, if slack develops during the fight, the hook will likely drop out; it is essential to keep a constant tight line.

To provoke a strike, it is important to work the bait or lure into position, but not by casting right on top of the fish, or by casting beyond the fish, letting the offering sink, and then retrieving it across the bottom (where it may snag). The angler should cast the offering a few feet in front of the fish, keeping the rod tip high and working the bait, lure, or fly on the surface toward the permit, then letting it swim or fall down to the fish. A moving object presented in this way is likely to get the fish's attention.

When the hook is set, permit bolt off like a streak of lightning, zooming over the flats on a long, sustained run toward deep water. They might try to cut the line on an obstacle or try to dislodge the hook, so the angler must keep the rod high and use a reel with ample line capacity and an excellent drag. Permit have superior stamina and will fight for a long time (a 40-minute or longer fight for a 20-pound fish is likely). They are often caught on light- to medium-action 7-foot spinning rods and 8-pound line. Fly rodders use a 9- or 10-weight fly rod and floating sink-tip line.

Although the fishing method is similar to that for bonefish, most permit are caught in slightly deeper water—2 to 4 feet; bonefish prefer only a few inches or so. Sighting permit, and knowing when and where to find them, are key elements of the game.

A rising tide, as noted, brings permit onto shallow flats, but they also congregate around channel edges, where a falling tide will wash food off the flats. Early mornings on warm days are good for bringing these fish into the shallows. If the water is calm, however, the fish are so spooky that maneuvering within casting range is nearly impossible. A breeze improves the odds greatly.

A large permit landed near Marathon, Florida.

Although spring is a highly desirable time for permit angling in South Florida, these fish are on the flats from spring through fall there. Only when the water temperature turns cooler (mid-70s or less) do they head for deeper water and the reefs.
See: Jacks.

PERSONAL FLOTATION DEVICE

Commonly referred to as a PFD, this is a lifesaving device that is meant to float a person in the water and to hold their head above water so they can breathe. In an emergency, it could be the most important item that you have.

PFDs are primarily used by people in boats, but they may also be worn by anglers who wade in swift water, by anglers who fish out of float tubes and kick boats, and by young and old people when they are on a dock, pier, or other location where it is possible that they might fall into the water. In the latter instances, it may be prudent, although not mandatory, that a PFD be either worn or available. However, Federal and state laws require that every vessel have a U.S. Coast Guard–approved personal flotation device of correct size for each person onboard. It is not required that they be worn in some places, but it is required that they be available. Regulations vary between states, provinces, and countries, and may depend on what agency has jurisdiction over a particular body of water; in some locations, children under a certain age, as well non-swimmers, must wear a PFD.

P

PFD Types

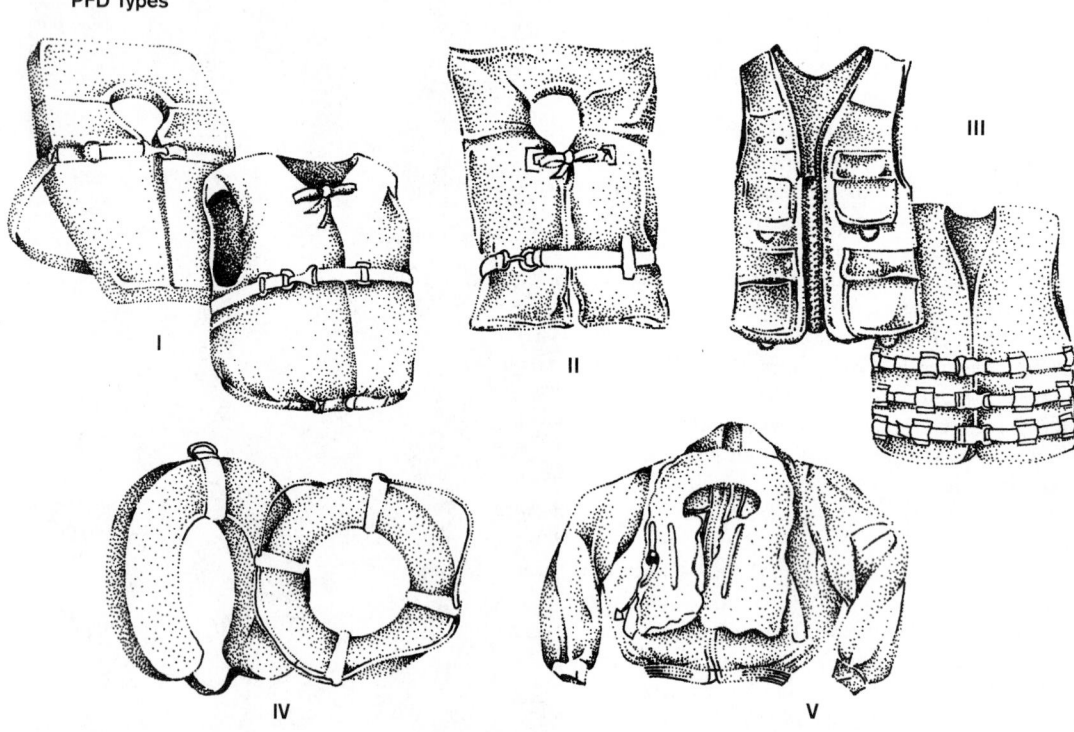

I

II

III

IV

V

Most anglers do not wear a PFD in their boat, or wear it only in adverse conditions or when operating a boat at high speed. Look at most of the photos that appear in this book, as well as current outdoor periodicals, and you'll see few anglers, especially adults, wearing a PFD. People who are good swimmers, who are in stable boats, who fish in shallow water, who fish in warm water, and those out on fair weather days in moderate or calm water conditions usually are in no danger. However, accidents happen; even a good swimmer can slip and fall out of a boat, knocking himself unconscious on the gunwale. Novice anglers and novice boaters typically underestimate the consequence of changing wind and wave conditions or current, and fail to realize that they can be very vulnerable, especially in a small boat, even on a day that looks harmless or in a location with warm or placid water.

Few people expect to end up in the water when they go fishing from a boat. But it happens, and not just in the extreme case of a boat sinking or capsizing. Small boats and canoes do get swamped, and people do fall out of boats. It is one of the leading causes of boating-related fatalities. Falling into the water without a PFD increases the chance of drowning, especially if the water is cold and/or a person is injured. In cold weather and when boating on cold water, it is smart to wear a PFD all the time because the degree of danger is heightened due to quick onset of hypothermia.

Of course, it does little good to have a PFD in the boat, but not on or at least available when you need it. People who suddenly find themselves in the water may not be able to locate their PFD, or may

be too panicked or numb from cold water and shock to put it on even if they do find it. In most fatal boating accidents, PFDs are onboard but not worn; 80 percent of boating-related drowning victims were not wearing PFDs.

Types.   There are five categories of PFDs:

Type I   Also known as an offshore life jacket, this is designed to turn most unconscious wearers to a vertical or slightly backward position. Adult sizes provide a minimum of 22 pounds of buoyancy and child sizes a minimum of 11 pounds. This is the best PFD to keep a person afloat in large and rough waters where rescue may be slow in coming; it is commonly found aboard commercial craft, and is regarded as the easiest to put on in a sudden emergency. There are bib and jacket versions, the latter generally favored for warmth and comfort.

Type II   Also known as a nearshore buoyant vest, this is designed to turn some unconscious wearers to a vertical or slightly backward position, but does not do so as effectively as a Type I. Adult sizes provide a minimum of 15.5 pounds of buoyancy and child sizes a minimum of 11 pounds. This PFD is more like a bib design than a vest, and is intended for calm inland water where there is a chance

Type III	Also known as a flotation aid, this is generally considered the most comfortable PFD, available in many different styles for different activities; vest styles are frequently referred to as a life vest or life preserver and coat styles as a life jacket. They will not turn an unconscious person face up, but are designed to make it easy for a conscious wearer to place themselves in a face-up position. They have the same minimum buoyancy as Type II devices and are intended for calm and moderate nearshore waters where there is a chance of a quick rescue. Some of these devices provide warmth for a bit of hypothermia protection, and some are available also as fishing vests. Some versions have collars that help keep a wearer's head up. Type III PFDs are a favorite of many freshwater anglers, but few people actually find them comfortable enough for all-day use.
Type IV	Also known as a throwable device, this is not intended to be worn in a boat, but to be tossed to someone in the water. Buoyant boat cushions, ring buoys, and horseshoe buoys are the main devices, that are grasped by the person in need of help and should be kept at hand for sudden use. They are intended for calm inland water, especially where there is heavy boat traffic, for a quick rescue.
Type V	Also known as a special use device, this is any PFD approved for restricted use, including wet suits, so-called survival or anti-exposure suits, boardsailing vests, and whitewater vests. Most Type V PFDs must be worn to be acceptable to law-enforcement authorities, and they must be used for the type of activity for which they are approved as a flotation device. In other words, if you are alone in a boat and your sole PFD is a Type V device that is stowed in storage, it will not meet legal requirements.

of a fast rescue. It is a commonly used PFD, although not one that is preferred by anglers and rarely worn continuously by anglers.

Some inflatable vests and jackets had been listed as Type V garments, but newer (and Coast Guard approved) versions have been reclassified as Type III. The label of Type V garments indicates the approved use and limitations. Coverall-style Type V PFDs, such as survival and anti-exposure suits, offer excellent hypothermia protection in cold water, and also provide wind and cold air temperature protection for fishing in extreme conditions.

Practicalities. All PFDs that are approved by the U.S. Coast Guard bear labeling certification and type designation. In order for these devices to be useful, they must be worn or closely available, they must be in serviceable condition, and they must fit the wearer. Such fitting is based upon the weight of an individual, keeping in mind that sometimes anglers wear bulky clothes. They must also provide enough buoyancy. Not all flotation is the same in PFDs. A PFD with $15^1/_2$ pounds of flotation will not keep the head of many people out of the water; one manufacturer claims that at least one in every four persons will float under the water surface when wearing a PFD with this amount of flotation. Not all PFDs of the same classification (Type III, for example) have the same amount of buoyancy; some may have $15^1/_2$ pounds, some 22 pounds.

The amount of buoyancy that you need depends on such factors as height, weight, and body fat, since body weight on the water is not the same as on land, evidenced by the fact that heavy or husky persons do not necessarily need more flotation support than lighter individuals. Nevertheless, the greater the amount of buoyancy, the more its influence on flotation for a given person.

Another factor that affects the usefulness of any PFD is its condition (see the following information on maintenance), and it is possible that a PFD, despite its labeling, might no longer be capable of providing flotation support. You should check your PFD occasionally in a controlled setting to see how it performs and to verify that it is still serviceable.

Still another factor that one should consider in a PFD is the amount of hypothermia protection it provides. Type I PFDs have virtually no protection against hypothermia while Type V anti-exposure suits have the most you can get. In between, there are varying levels of protection. Body heat is primarily lost from the head, the sides, and the groin. PFDs that trap cold water and mix it with the ambient heat of the body provide more protection than others. Although many people think of hypothermia in regard to cold weather and cold water, serious body temperature cooling can develop if you are exposed for a sufficient time in water that is 70 degrees Fahrenheit, a temperature that is much different when you are in the water than when you are exposed to it in the air.

The main reason why people do not wear PFDs is that they aren't comfortable enough, especially when worn over a moderate amount of clothing. So you should make sure that your own PFD fits you properly, with or without heavy clothes. To get some confidence in it, you should try it out in the water (a pool is a good place). Make sure that it

Australia's Great Barrier Reef, which stretches 1,260 miles and holds the world's finest black marlin fishing, comprises thousands of small reefs.

P

doesn't ride up on your body, which makes swimming difficult. Remember that you could be in the water some time, so you want enough buoyancy to keep your head out of the water. Also remember that you might need to swim a considerable distance to safety, so your PFD should accommodate that.

In recent years, the U.S. Coast Guard has approved some manually inflated PFDs as Type III life vests (and was evaluating automatic-inflating PFDs as Type II vests. Inflatable PFDs will probably become more popular in years to come because they are mainly suspender-like devices that are very comfortable to wear even over bulky clothing, and they do not inhibit arm movement for casting or normal fishing activities. Some inflatable PFDs (using a CO_2 cartridge) inflate upon impact, while others have to be activated by the wearer or can also be blown up orally; automatic-inflating PFDs are best for people who do not swim, since they might be prone to panic and unable to activate a manual model if suddenly thrust into the water. Approved inflatable PFDs (manufactured after 1996 and bearing a Coast Guard–approval certification on their label) will be of special interest to freshwater anglers who use small boats, to those who use canoes and inflatable boats and float tubes, and also to those who wade in cold rivers. Inflatable PFDs are the kind of item that is meant to be worn all the time, so they are available when needed and activated by a replaceable CO_2 cartridge (get a rearming pack so you have a spare cartridge on hand).

Anglers who travel to distant or exotic locations often find that only boat cushions are provided as PFDs (which may be acceptable there but is certainly not safe), or that the PFDs available are inadequate because of their poor condition or improper size. If your fishing activity will take you into potentially dangerous situations (long hauls over rough cold water), you should find replacements or plan accordingly. This is a situation where carrying an inflatable PFD makes a lot of sense; it is light, takes up little space, and provides top security (but it will have almost no anti-hypothermia protection).

Maintenance. PFDs are usually used more often as seat cushions, boat fenders, and kneeling pads than they are worn, and this compression and fabric tension can adversely affect their primary function. If the fabric is torn or if it is faded and worn, consider replacement. If the fabric tears when you pull on it, get rid of the PFD. A Kapok-material PFD will lose its buoyancy due to splitting or compression, so check this carefully as it may actually sink.

Whether they have been used or not, it's a good idea to check the serviceability of your PFDs every summer in shallow warm water or in a pool. They should float the wearer for an extended period and should not restrict breathing. After you've tested them, dry them in a well-ventilated area and make sure that no mildew or rotting develops. Clean PFDs with a mild soap and warm water, and replace any worn or broken parts, like buckles or straps. Store PFDs in a dry well-ventilated place away from heat, moisture, and frequent sunlight. Keep them away from oil, grease, and gas, which could deteriorate some PFDs and cause them to lose buoyancy. For inflatable PFDs, make sure to replace a used CO_2 cartridge, and keep a spare cartridge or rearming packet on hand for each device. You should also inspect the inflatable material periodically.

Know the law. As mentioned, Federal and state laws require that every vessel have a U.S. Coast Guard–approved PFD of correct size and in good serviceable condition for each person onboard. Boats less than 16 feet in length, and canoes and kayaks of any length, must have one approved Type I, II, III, or V device for each person, and boats over 16 feet must have one approved Type I, II, III, or V device for each person plus one throwable Type IV device. Type I, II, and III devices must be readily accessible; a Type IV device must be immediately available or on hand; and Type V devices must be worn to qualify. These are minimum requirements.

Check local regulations for requirements regarding who is legally required to continuously wear a PFD, or under what circumstances (some competitive events require that a PFD be worn whenever the main engine is operated). Remember that a PFD could be the best insurance you'll ever have, and a lifesaver.

See: Boat; First Aid.

PERSONAL WATERCRAFT

An ambiguous term that through aggressive marketing has primarily come to mean small one- or two-person jet-drive vessels. Since the late 1980s, personal watercraft have been the fastest growing segment of the boating market, and the vessels responsible for a high percentage of boating-related accidents, usually due to reckless operation. Personal watercraft are seldom used for fishing, although a few operators have employed them on occasion for this purpose. They are more likely to be a source of annoyance for anglers, even more so than water-skiers and accompanying tow boats, due to their noise, the fast speeds at which they are operated, the shallow waters that they can navigate, and the tendency of some careless operators to interfere with others on the water. As a result of problems with the operation of personal watercraft, their use has been banned in some places (such as sections of the Florida Keys) where they threaten habitat. The term personal watercraft is sometimes also applied to float tubes (see).

PERU

The third largest country in South America, with 2,700 kilometers of Pacific coastline, as well as

Only 1 percent of the freshwater on Earth is contained in surface reservoirs, lakes, and streams; of that, 20 percent is located in the Great Lakes of North America.

mountain rivers, jungle waters, some of the highest peaks in the world, and the continent's largest lake, Peru is something of an enigma to anglers. It has been of minor sportfishing interest for traveling anglers since at least the early 1980s.

Saltwater

Although most general accounts of the natural resources of Peru indicate that its coast is rich in fish life, these statements mostly reference commercial catches of anchovies, smelt, pilchards, mackerel, and flatfish; they usually don't indicate that Peru's marine resources have been hard hit by national and international commercial fishing operations.

Peru's greatest piscatorial claim to fame was northern coast big-game fisheries that diminished long ago. Cabo Blanco was a hotspot for huge black marlin, and it drew many top anglers, personalities, and skippers to the sardine-rich waters nearby, where the (Peru) Humboldt Current helped make it the first place in the world where anglers had a good chance of encountering "granders," or marlin weighing more than 1,000 pounds. In August of 1953, Alfred Glassell caught the still-standing all-tackle 1,560-pound world-record black marlin, and in April of the following year Mrs. Charles Hughes caught a women's 130-pound world-record 1,525-pound black. These are two of the Babe Ruth–like records of sportfishing. Even in its heyday, however, Peru did not produce large numbers of black marlin; striped marlin were more common, as were swordfish. Yellowfin and bigeye tuna rounded out the big-game menu.

During the best times, however, fish were caught within sight of land, and sometimes within sight of the historical Cabo Blanco Fishing Club, which ceased operations in 1965. Whether due to current changes, overfishing of baitfish, or other factors, the glory days are ancient history, and big-game species have since been evidently far from shore in an area with few or no appropriate vessels capable of distant voyages.

Peru's coast was also home to other species, including snook, corvina, and various flatfish. Surf fishing was once popular and productive in accessible sites. Numerous tributaries entering the Pacific from the coastal plains would seem to still invite fishing opportunity, but current information about these, or about sportfishing operators, is lacking.

Freshwater

The Peruvian freshwater fishing scene—its current fisheries status, operators, and accessibility—is likewise largely unknown, with the exception of some rain forest opportunities in the northeastern region.

In the southeastern Andes, Lake Titicaca was once not only reputed to be the world's highest trout lake, but, between 1940 and 1960, also one of the world's best producers of trophy rainbow trout. Titicaca had yielded a 34-pound specimen and was a source of numerous fish weighing between 12 and 20 pounds. Situated in the Andes at around 12,500 feet, and the largest freshwater lake in South America, Titicaca is 110 miles long and has an average width of 35 miles; its gamefisheries were heavily exploited, and nothing has been heard of its angling significance in decades. The region remains noted for its ancient civilization and is a tourist draw. Titicaca drains into Lake Poopó in Bolivia via the Desaguadero River, and it has several northerly tributaries that once held trout.

Perhaps because it is a large and generally undeveloped and unpopulated area, the eastern and northeastern tropical forest region of Peru (the *montaña*) bordering Brazil and Colombia has the most viable currently known sportfishing opportunity in this country. In the northeast, the fishery is accessed from the city of Iquitos. It is in this large region that Peru's tributaries of the Amazon River originate, abound, and gain size and character, and where peacock bass and other warmwater species predominate. The many rivers and fishing opportunities here are described in the Amazon review under Brazil *(see)*.

PFD
Acronym for Personal Flotation Device *(see)*.

PFIESTERIA
A harmful algal bloom, resulting from a toxic single-celled dinoflaggellate, *Pfiesteria piscicida*. The Latin name means "fish killer," and it has been dubbed "cell from hell" by some, since it has been responsible for huge fish kills and also illness among humans.

This algal bloom has attracted great media attention in the 1990s, particularly in Chesapeake Bay and in North Carolina, because of the fish kills that it caused. Between 1992 and 1995 in North Carolina, it reportedly killed billions of fish in estuaries.

What stimulates these organisms to bloom and become toxic is unknown. However, when it happens, the toxins eat into the skin of fish, and ugly lesions the size of a quarter are common. The fish die when their bodies become wracked with the infection.

See: Algae Bloom; Dinoflaggellate.

pH
A measure of the acidity or alkalinity of water on a logarithmic scale from 1 to 14. A pH of 7.0 is neutral; the lower the reading below 7.0 the more acidic the water, and the higher the reading above 7.0 the more alkaline the water. Normal rainfall is slightly acidic, with a pH ranging from 5.6 to 5.7.

The majority of freshwater fish require pH levels from 6.0 to 8.5. Changes to either end of the spectrum can have adverse impacts on fish, as well as other organisms, with some more susceptible than others. Brook and brown trout numbers are severely reduced at a pH value of 6.5, and rainbow trout eggs have a much reduced hatching rate. Smallmouth and largemouth bass are unable to survive at a pH value of 5.5. Most species are absent at levels below 5.0, and even if they are able to survive, their food sources may not be able to do so. Some waters have become so acidified that no life can survive.

PHARYNGEAL

Bones in the throat of certain fish that are used like teeth to crush food. These bones are hard and strong and will crush such objects as clams, mussels, and snails. Carp (see) have pharyngeal teeth, which play an important role in their forage habits.

PHILIPPINES

The Philippine Islands are not a prime destination for globe-trotting anglers, and very little is heard in most quarters about sportfishing opportunities, facilities, or services there. The waters of the western Pacific in and around the Philippines, however, have produced at least five line-class saltwater world records, and big Pacific sailfish and great barracuda are known to frequent its tropical waters. Numerous yellowfin tuna, dolphin, wahoo, and assorted jacks are here as well. To the surprise of many anglers, largemouth bass have been introduced in the country's freshwater resources.

Any country that covers roughly 115,830 square miles is bound to offer some angling opportunities. Sandwiched by Taiwan to the north and Indonesia to the south, and bordered by the South China Sea on the west, the Celebes Sea on the south, and the Philippine Sea on the east, the Philippines comprises more than 7,100 islands, only 460 of which are more than 1 square mile in area. The largest of these is Luzon in the northern Philippines, bounded by the Babuyan Channel on the north. Along Luzon's irregular western coastline is the well-known harbor of Manila Bay.

The northeastern region of Luzon is locally known as sailfish country, and in the months of May and June it hosts national and international billfish competitions. Sailfish are the main quarry here, but this species is found in many areas throughout the islands. A 93.75-kilogram 30-pound line-class record Pacific sailfish was caught far to the south of Luzon at the Tubbataha Reefs in the Sulu Sea in May 1990.

Dolphin, wahoo, and yellowfin tuna are among the offshore catch as well. Philippine anglers are fond of drift fishing for yellowfins at night. Tuna in the 60- to 90-kilogram range are commonly caught, and anglers use 30- and 50-pound outfits, which occasionally also bring in a swordfish.

Two spots in particular are favored for this fishing. One is off the island of Palawan, where sportfishing is based out of the city of Puerto Princesta. The ecologically compelling Palawan is reached via a 1-hour plane trip or a 20-hour ride on a modern air-conditioned ferry. The other is off Surigao on the northern part of Mindanao, the second largest of the islands. There, fishing is often done from local outrigger boats called bancas. Powered by reconditioned diesel truck engines or 16-horsepower inboard engines, the bancas are an adventurous way of pursuing tuna, as well as sailfish and marlin, although they are cramped.

The bancas are used for nearshore lighter tackle angling, too, and various species are enjoyed along the irregular shorelines throughout the islands. Barracuda are prominent in the Philippines, and some are huge; Scarborough Shoals produced a line-class world-record 38.5-kilogram specimen in March of 1991. Jacks from 1 to 10 kilograms provide the majority of inshore interest, however. They are especially prominent and popular near the resort area of Matabongay, a three-hour drive from Manila, where locals hire out their bancas for anglers who cast with live shrimp.

Inland, the bigger islands are mountainous, some with navigable rivers. On Luzon the larger rivers include the Cagayan, Chico, Abra, Pampanga, and Bicol. The longest river of the Philippines, the Cagayan flows northerly for about 354 kilometers. The Río Grande de Mindanao (also called the Pulangi in its upper reaches) and the Agusan are the principal rivers of Mindanao. On Luzon, south of Manila, Caliraya Lake hosts largemouth bass that were brought to this island as bass fry evidently from the U.S. The two largest lakes on Luzon are Laguna de Bay and Taal, but it is unknown if they contain bass.

The Philippines possesses some modern sportfishing vessels, but most angling for the visiting tourist is rather adventurous and unorganized. The Philippines are within the Tropics and experience a lot of rain. In most of the region the rainy season lasts from May through November—the summer monsoon. Typhoons sometimes occur from June through October.

pH METER

A portable electronic device used by a relatively small number of anglers, primarily freshwater bass anglers, to measure the acidity or alkalinity of prospective fishing water to determine its pH level. If the pH level is unsuitable to the fish they seek to catch, they reason that those fish are unlikely to be in that location, and they move elsewhere.

The common pH scale ranges from 0.0 (highly acid) to 14.0 (highly alkaline). A reading of 7.0 is considered neutral, having equal parts of acidity and alkalinity. Most of the research done to determine the effect of water pH on fish has involved largemouth bass. In freshwater, some biologists feel that pH is critical because it affects the ability of fish to use oxygen, to feed in a wide range of temperatures, to reproduce, combat disease, handle stress, and even to survive pollution. Fish can survive in a pH range of from 4 to 10, but researchers say they are least stressed and hypothetically most catchable in a range between 7 and 9.

Manufacturers of pH meters advise looking for a surface pH between 7.5 and 8.5. If all of the water seems to be below 7, find the highest pH you can. If all of the water seems to be above 9, fish where you find the lowest pH. The level of pH usually drops as you go deeper, so check below the surface for a pH cline; this is where there is a pH change of two tenths or more per foot of depth. If there is a pH cline, they advise that the most catchable fish will probably be at or above it. A pH cline is generally tied to water clarity. If the water is clear, the pH cline will probably be deeper. If the water is murky, it will be shallower. Its depth can change from one part of a lake to another.

The use of a pH meter may be helpful in determining where, or where not, to fish for selected species in some environments, but it has not been demonstrated to be a necessity for anglers.

PHYTOPLANKTON
Microscopic suspended algae *(see)* in the surface waters of seas and lakes where there is enough light for photosynthesis to occur.

PICKEREL, CHAIN   *Esox niger.*
Other names—jack, pike, eastern pickerel, eastern chain pickerel, lake pickerel, reticulated pickerel, federation pickerel, mud pickerel, green pike, grass pike, black chain pike, duck-billed pike, river pike, picquerelle, water wolf.

This member of the Esocidae family of pike is a lean, sporting, evil-eyed bandit, yet it is virtually neglected by most nonwinter anglers, rarely specifically pursued by open-water anglers, and often downgraded by those who catch it unintentionally while seeking more popular fish. Respectable battlers on appropriate tackle, these aggressive, available fish also offer a good chance of angling success.

Long, slimy, toothy, camouflaged in green brown and bearing chainlike markings, the chain pickerel has cold-blooded eyes and is a smaller but equally fearsome-looking version of its northern pike and muskellunge cousins. It has an unusual arrangement of bones, but the flesh is generally white, flaky, and sweet. At some times and from some places, however, the flavor is not as good. This deficit may be remedied by removing the skin before cooking. Many chain pickerel are caught through the ice.

This fish is sometimes confused with the walleye, particularly in southern Canada where walleye are called "pickerel," but the walleye is a member of the perch family and is unlike the true chain pickerel in all respects save one: It too has many teeth. Chain pickerel are abundant where pike and muskies are not found or are not particularly abundant.

Identification.   With its long, slender body, the chain pickerel is very similar in appearance to the northern pike *(see: pike, northern)* and the muskellunge *(see),* especially when young. It gets its name from its markings, which appear in a reticulated, or chainlike, pattern of black lines that cover the golden to yellowish or greenish sides. The small, light-colored oval spots on the sides of the northern pike resemble the very large, light oval areas on the chain pickerel but may be distinguished by the dark background behind the pattern on the northern pike; also, the northern pike's spots never appear large in relation to the background, whereas in the chain pickerel the lighter areas are more prevalent. The chain pickerel has fully scaled cheeks and gill covers. These further distinguish it from the northern pike, which usually has no scales on the bottom half of the gill cover, and from the muskellunge, which usually has no scales on the bottom half of either the gill cover or the cheek. It has only one dorsal fin, which is located very far back on the body near the caudal peduncle. There is a dark vertical bar under the eye, and the snout is shaped like a duck's bill. The lower jaw has a row of four sensory pores on each side, and the mouth is full of needle-like teeth.

Size/Age.   The chain pickerel can exceed 30 inches in length and 9 pounds in weight, although the average fish is under 2 feet long and weighs less than 2 pounds. In some waters it may be even smaller. The all-tackle world record is a 9-pound, 6-ounce fish caught in Georgia in 1961. The maximum age is roughly 10, although the average is around 4. Females grow larger and live longer than males.

Chain Pickerel

P

Two big chain pickerel caught on a large minnow plug.

Distribution.   This species extends along the Atlantic slope of North America from Nova Scotia to southern Florida, as well as along the Gulf Coast west to the Sabine Lake drainage in Louisiana and from the Mississippi River basin north to southwestern Kentucky and southeastern Missouri. Chain pickerel have been introduced to Lakes Ontario and Erie drainages and elsewhere. Their primary abundance is from the mid-Atlantic states north and in Florida and Georgia.

Habitat.   Chain pickerel inhabit the shallow, vegetated waters of lakes, swamps, streams, ponds, bogs, tidal and nontidal rivers, and backwaters, and the quiet pools of creeks and small to medium rivers, as well as the bays and coves of larger lakes and reservoirs. Solitary fish, they prefer water temperatures between 75°F and 80°F and are occasionally found in low-salinity estuaries, although they can tolerate a wide range of salinity. They move into deeper water during the winter and continue to feed actively.

The environs preferred by chain pickerel are somewhat similar to those of largemouth bass, particularly in regard to vegetation and abundant cover. Their primary hangouts are among lily pads and various types of weeds, and they sometimes hold near such objects as stumps, docks, and fallen trees. Invariably, the waters with the best chain pickerel populations are those with abundant vegetation, much of which is found near shore.

Life history/Behavior.   This fish reaches sexual maturity when three to four years old, perhaps earlier in more southerly climates. They spawn in the swampy or marshy backwater areas of lakes and rivers, from late winter to early spring (March through May) just after ice out in 46°F to 51°F water. Parents do not build nests or guard the eggs, and the 5,000 to 50,000 eggs are dropped in long glutinous strands over the bottom, where they stick to vegetation and brush. The eggs hatch in 7 to 10 days or in a couple of weeks, and the young fish stay among the weeds and close to shore throughout their first summer.

Food and feeding habits.   Capable of eating fish almost as long as they are, chain pickerel feed primarily on other fish, as well as the occasional insect, crayfish, frog, or mouse. Small minnows and fry are among their favorite prey, but they are fond of midsize fish like yellow perch and other pickerel in the 4- to 6-inch range. They will often eat larger fish, and it is not uncommon to catch a large chain pickerel that is still trying to digest another pickerel half its own length. Mainly sight feeders, they lie motionless in patches of vegetation, waiting to snatch small fish, but they can sometimes be lured from a distance to prey that appears vulnerable.

Angling.   Not many other sportfish will follow a lure right to the boat with impunity as chain pickerel will, and it is common for them to strike viciously just as a lure is about to be lifted from the water. They often make a V-shaped wake in shallow water when dashing out from cover to intercept a lure, and they may hit a lure three, four, or five times in a row while chasing it.

Chain pickerel are primarily attracted to movement and flash. Nearly any lure with a spinning blade or sparkling appearance will catch at least one chain pickerel in its lifetime. Standard spinners and small spoons are traditionally effective lures, but they are prone to hanging up in thick cover. Spinnerbaits, weedless in-line spinners, and weedless spoons are a better option. Worms and jigs are also taken by chain pickerel, but the result is often a line severed by the fish's teeth. Fly fishing is also worthwhile for pickerel, with streamers being especially ravished. Tandem-bladed spinnerbaits with a white or chartreuse skirt are probably the single most popular pickerel lure, fished with a trailer hook and equipped with silver, copper, chartreuse, white, or yellow blades. A variety of colors works in other lures, but silver and shad are among the favorites.

Live baits may be the top chain pickerel catchers for most anglers, certainly in the winter. Minnows or shiners up to 6 inches long are popular. Chain pickerel often strike their prey to stun or cripple it so they can reattack and consume it headfirst. Therefore they usually take a bait sideways in their mouth and run off with it a bit, maneuver it around, then swallow it headfirst.

In typical chain pickerel water, the best fishing occurs in spring. Chain pickerel spawn in shallow bays and marshy areas after ice out in the north, and in the mid- to late winter in the south. Warmer water temperature and the development of cover are usually two indicators of progressing activity. Chain pickerel feed all year and can be caught in modest numbers in the cold water of early spring. When the water temperature exceeds 50°F, they become more active; 55° to 70°F temperatures offer excellent conditions. At this time, weed growth is developing, providing more cover in which the

P

chain pickerel can lie motionless in anticipation of the inevitable baitfish ambush. When vegetation becomes thick in late spring or early summer, there is usually more forage available, which lessens fishing productivity. From this time through midfall, it is important to fish heavy cover effectively. In the coldwater conditions of early spring and fall, fish slowly for chain pickerel, as you would for bass. Shallow-running crankbaits and minnow-imitation plugs are best.

Many anglers unfortunately pursue and land chain pickerel on tackle that is too heavy to allow these fish to make a good showing. The best gear for chain pickerel is a spinning outfit with 4- or 6-pound line, as the average chain pickerel weighs no more than $1^1/_2$ pounds. On light tackle or a fly rod, chain pickerel will run, jump, and cavort in a pleasing manner. Only large chain pickerel put up a really good fight on medium to heavy tackle. Where cover is extremely thick, and where largemouth bass are also being pursued, you'll have to temper this go-light advice with practicality.
See: Pike.

PICKEREL, GRASS AND REDFIN

Grass pickerel   *Esox americanus vermiculatus.*

Redfin Pickerel   *Esox americanus americanus.*

Other names—banded pickerel, little pickerel, mud pickerel.

The grass pickerel and the redfin pickerel are two nearly identical subspecies of *Esox americanus,* differing only slightly in range. Because they occur only in small populations and are of small size, they have little importance as sportfish, although they are significant predators in many waters of more prominent small sportfish. Although the white, sweet flesh of these members of the Esocidae family is bony, it has an excellent flavor.

Identification.   Slender and cylindrical, grass and redfin pickerel look much like the chain pickerel *(see: pickerel, chain),* with the same fully scaled cheeks and gill covers. They are dark olive to brown or black above, amber to brassy white below, with 20 or more dark green to brown wavy bars along the sides. On the grass pickerel, there are pale areas between the bars that are wider than the bars. The grass pickerel is lighter in color than the redfin pickerel and has a pronounced pale midlateral stripe. The grass pickerel also has yellow green to dusky lower fins and a long narrow snout (although shorter than the chain pickerel's) with a concave profile, whereas the redfin pickerel appropriately has red lower and caudal fins as well as a shorter, broader snout with a convex profile. Both have large mouths with sharp canine teeth and several sensory pores on the lower jaw. A dark vertical bar extends down from the eye, which is more vertical in the grass pickerel than in the redfin. An easy way

Grass Pickerel

to distinguish the redfin from the grass pickerel is to examine the scales on the sides of the redfin, of which there are more notched or heart-shaped ones, specifically six in the area between the pelvic fins. There are up to three on the grass pickerel. Also, the redfin has more than seven of these scales between the dorsal and anal fins, whereas the grass pickerel has four or fewer.

Size/Age.   Both species seldom exceed 10 inches in length (the redfin pickerel can reach 14 inches) and three-quarters of a pound in weight; the redfin pickerel generally grows faster and slightly longer than the grass pickerel. The all-tackle world record for the grass pickerel is a 1-pound Indiana fish; for the redfin pickerel, the record is a 1-pound, 15-ounce New York fish. They can live up to eight years, although they usually live five years or less. Females live longer and grow larger than males.

Distribution.   In North America, grass pickerel range from the Great Lakes basin north to southern Ontario in Canada, and to Michigan, Wisconsin, and Nebraska; they also occur in the Mississippi River and gulf slope drainages west of Pascagoula River in Mississippi to the Brazos River in Texas. Redfin pickerel are found in Atlantic slope drainages, from the St. Lawrence River drainage in Quebec to southern Georgia; they also occur in gulf slope drainages from the Pascagoula River in Mississippi to Florida. Populations for both species are generally small on a local level.

Habitat.   Grass and redfin pickerel inhabit quiet or small lakes and swamps, bays and backwaters, and sluggish pools of streams. Both prefer heavy vegetation in clear waters, but the grass pickerel favors waters with neutral to basic acidity, and the redfin inhabits comparatively acidic waters.

Life history/Behavior.   Reaching sexual maturity when they are roughly 2 years old and at least 5 inches long, grass and redfin pickerel spawn in late fall, early winter, or spring; grass pickerel require water temperatures between 36° and 54°F, and redfin favor waters approaching 50°F. Spawning takes place in heavily vegetated, shallow areas, and the backs of the fish appear at the surface as they scatter eggs in small batches over the vegetation.

Redfin Pickerel

P

Grass pickerel may produce twice as many eggs as do redfin pickerel. They do not build nests. The grass pickerel's eggs hatch in 11 to 15 days, the redfin pickerel's in 12 to 14 days, without the protection of the parents.

Food and feeding habits. Grass and redfin pickerel are largely piscivorous, feeding mainly on other fish such as minnows, although they occasionally eat aquatic insects, small crayfish, and frogs. They will remain virtually motionless among the vegetation for hours at a time, waiting to dart out and seize a potential meal.

See: Pike.

PIER

A structure raised on piles that extends perpendicular from shore out into a body of water. Most often found in coastal areas, piers are usually made of wood but may be made of masonry or metal. Many piers are important fishing locations for land-based anglers.

See: Pier Fishing.

PIER FISHING
Fishing Coastal Piers, Bridges, Docks, and Bulkheads

Fishing from the shore varies from freshwater to saltwater and from one species to the next in either environment. Most land-based freshwater anglers fish from open shore or bank, or from a small dock although in huge bodies of water, such as the Great Lakes and its connected rivers, they may fish from larger docks that are used to accommodate yachts and ships, or from long piers that are usually part of a wharf or harbor jetty.

In coastal areas, these include fishing from the beach (see: surf fishing); from a jetty, groin, rockpile, or breakwater (see: jetty fishing); and fishing from or around a pier, bridge, dock, or bulkhead. Structures

Piers that are washed by current or have other features that either attract or hold fish provide the best angling.

such as piers, bridges, docks, and bulkheads exist in tidal rivers, harbors, inlets, waterways, and marinas; and, in some cases, they are also found in open bays or along otherwise unobstructed oceanfront. The diversity and the productivity of the fishing opportunity offered by these structures will vary with location, and are influenced by many factors, including water depth, water salinity, tides, current, season, size and location of the structure, amount of cover present, and, of course, species of fish.

Most of the following information is directed at coastal structures. However, it is also applicable to fishing such structures in tidal estuaries and rivers, in brackish water, and in some entirely freshwater environs (primarily large lakes, rivers, and canals that provide navigation for large vessels), even though the species differ and even though tides may not be an influence, or a minimal one.

Before general points about what to use and how to work these structures can be given, it is necessary to explain what they are, especially because different terms are often used to describe the same things. "Dock," "wharf," and "pier" are examples of such words.

Technically a pier is a structure, usually wood but sometimes masonry or metal, that is raised on piles and extends in a perpendicular manner from shore out into a body of water. It is usually meant for pedestrian access but may be large enough to accommodate vehicles. Some piers are not accessible to boats and do not provide a landing place, usually because of location. For example, a pier that extends from a beach would be exposed to the elements, and a boat fastened to such a pier might be subject to the full force of wave and current action, a situation that would often make the loading or unloading of passengers unsafe and subject the boat to damage during docking.

Many of the coastal piers that are used strictly for fishing are too far above the water, even at high tide, to be a suitable boat landing; these are seldom confused with docks or wharves, and they are often quite long. Some fishing piers extend hundreds of yards into the ocean or an inlet; South Carolina's Paradise Pier, for example, reaches 1,120 feet into Fripp Inlet.

In a more-protected environment, however, a pier is typically used for docking and landing, often for temporary (short-term) dockage or for loading and unloading passengers and gear.

Although a pier might serve purposes similar to a jetty (see) or breakwall it is neither. A pier may be referred to as a wharf, although a wharf is a structure that is parallel to the shore and used for the docking, loading, and unloading of large vessels.

Both piers and wharves are commonly called docks by many people, and the word "dock" is often used to refer to any site where a boat of any size might be berthed, as well as to the entire area where wharves and piers are located ("I'm going down to the docks"). Technically a dock is an enclosed or nearly enclosed water area that is relatively small and is used for mooring a boat. However, in today's usage, the small wooden structure alongside a waterfront home is known as a dock, as is the large area alongside a pier or wharf. The former, however, will almost always be close above the water surface, regardless of tide, whereas the latter will usually be high above the water and at a level that will fluctuate with tidal changes.

Although the upper structure of a pier or a dock will offer shade, it is the support pilings that are especially important (this applies to the old free-standing pilings of dilapidated docks as well). The pilings break the force of the current and attract small fish that feed on the organisms encrusted on the pilings.

A bulkhead is simply an embankment or retaining wall along the waterfront. Also known as a sea-wall, it might be metal or masonry but is often wood, positioned parallel to the water. It is used to buffer boats, but its chief purpose is to keep the water from eroding the shore behind. The water is usually moderately deep alongside a bulkhead, although the depth obviously varies with tidal extremes.

Bridges don't need explanation, although they do vary from small road bridges over streams, rivers, marsh creeks, and canals, to long expanses over open water, usually bays. Bridges have varying numbers of piles or pilings, and sometimes bulkheads. Bridges that expand over large water bodies are fished from boats; smaller bridges, and the ends of larger bridges, can be fished from land. Such smaller bridges that are fished from land are the focus of review here.

At first glance, fishing at or around these structures may not seem challenging, but there is exciting angling to be had for a wide variety of species, which may be sought with diverse tackle, using both natural baits and lures. Methods, in fact, can become a matter of choice.

The species available at these structures range from large to tiny, from major gamefish to major table fish. Huge tarpon are regularly taken from bridges in the Florida Keys; snook and redfish are also common southern bridge catches. In South Carolina, which is known for its fishing piers, anglers may catch such larger game as cobia and king mackerel, and possibly sharks. Anglers casting from New Jersey piers often encounter big striped bass, bluefish, and weakfish, all of which strike a variety of lures and natural baits. In San Diego, it might be fast-moving Pacific bonito and barracuda, and in the Northwest it might be king salmon.

Although the gamefish in these structures are the attraction for many anglers, bottom feeders are the bread and butter quarry. In New York, miles of structures located along the north shore of Long Island attract both summer and winter flounder, plus tautog. In Maine, dock anglers tussle with harbor pollock and small cod. Structure anglers in the DelMarVa Peninsula can often catch spot, croakers, and seatrout until their arms are weary. The broad expanse of Pacific offers many species of surf perch, rockfish, sand bass, and halibut that are within reach of bridge, bulkhead, and pier casters. (Whiting and ling once provided pier and bridge casters with a great winter fishery along the mid-Atlantic Coast, but foreign factory trawlers decimated these species. If these fish ever return to plentiful numbers, they might provide pier and bridge casters with the great sport and fine eating enjoyed in an earlier era.) All of these species are excellent table fare and provide some of the finest and freshest seafood available for the dinner table.

Perhaps the most leisurely type of fishing available to coastal anglers is fishing from the piers, bridges, docks, and bulkheads that are readily accessible and are located almost everywhere along the seacoast. In certain places, some of the best publicly accessible non-boat angling is at these structures and may be nearly unknown to casual or unobservant anglers. Small bridges, road causeways, and old docks or piers or bulkheads, for example, are less obvious than piers but can provide some good results, often to anglers who fish at night on the right tide, especially in estuaries and canals. These structures can be enjoyed at nominal cost compared with other types of fishing; in fact, although there is usually a fee to access piers built expressly for fishing, for the most part there is no cost associated with using structures and enjoying the relaxed atmosphere and camaraderie associated with this type of fishing.

Fishing these structures can develop into a lifelong activity for some anglers. This kind of fishing is rather easy to master and is especially suited to those who are prone to seasickness when boating. Because it is not very physically demanding (especially in the case of piers and large docks), it is accessible and enjoyable for those with physical limitations. Not to be overlooked either, especially when bottom-feeding species are available, is that these structures provide an excellent opportunity for family fishing and offer an inexpensive means of introducing children to angling.

Tackle

Conventional, baitcasting, and spinning tackle may all be effectively employed when fishing from most piers, bridges, docks, and bulkheads. Choice is generally a matter of personal preference or suitability to the species, water conditions, and necessary means of fishing. There is no perfect all-around outfit, since you need heavier gear for big fish like tarpon, redfish, striped bass, and bluefish than for bottom feeders like flatfish, seatrout, sand perch, and rockfish.

All of the species sought around these structures are mostly attracted to them because they provide foraging opportunity. Forage species take up residence in and around these structures, and predators

P

A variety of species are caught from piers, both by fishing with bait and by casting lures.

move in and out of them when tides and current make that forage more abundant or more vulnerable. As a result, the predominant activity is fishing with bait rigs; casting, though frequently practiced, is often less of a consideration than it is when fishing from jetties or the surf.

Rods and reels. For heavier gamefish, a rod measuring $6\frac{1}{2}$ to 8 feet long is ideal. Because you'll often use big baits and heavy lures for tarpon, stripers, bluefish, and redfish, a rod with a stiff action is preferable, since it handles baits and lures with ease and has the muscle to pressure a big fish. Graphite and graphite composite rods are preferred. Reels are usually conventional models for heavier fishing, and baitcasting or spinning versions for lighter duty, such as casting small plugs and jigs.

Since snags or other obstructions are seldom found around these structures (with the exception of barnacle-encrusted pilings), you can usually get by with lighter lines than in many types of coastal fishing. A reel holding 150 to 200 yards of 12- to 15-pound-test line is usually more than adequate. However, big tarpon and striped bass have been known to spool a reel, especially when hooked from a bridge where the current is swift and the angler is unable to follow the fish. Obviously, such situations dictate stout tackle.

For the bottom fishing enthusiast, a spinning outfit with a 6-foot rod, or a baitcasting outfit that includes a $5\frac{1}{2}$- to 6-foot rod with a long handle for two-handed casting, is fine for fishing from piers, docks, and bulkheads. Because the bottom feeders usually range from half a pound to 5 or so pounds, there's no need to use big reels. Indeed, the reels used by many people for this type of fishing are too heavy and cumbersome. A spinning or baitcasting reel capable of holding 100 yards of 8- to 12-pound-test monofilament line is more than adequate.

Bottom bait rig. When fishing from most piers, bridges, and other structures, anglers are elevated from the water by levels that will vary from just a few feet to 50 feet or more. Although occasionally the line may be cast out, most often the fishing line will be nearly perpendicular to the bottom. This differs from surf and jetty fishing, where the line and rig lay parallel with the bottom once they've been cast out.

Dozens of different bottom rigs can be used for fishing from these structures, and naturally there are regional favorites. However, a few time-proven favorites always bring good results no matter where they are used.

The fish-finder bottom rig is a popular rig that may be used to present a natural bait to anything from a half-pound spot to a 100-pound tarpon. It's built around an egg-shaped sinker that has a hole through the middle. Slip a sinker of sufficient weight to hold bottom—usually $\frac{1}{2}$ ounce to 4 ounces or more—onto your line. Next tie in a tiny barrel swivel, which will prevent the sinker from slipping off the line yet permit it to slide on the line ahead of the swivel. To the barrel swivel, tie a 12- to 36-inch-long piece of monofilament or fluorocarbon leader material, of a size balanced to the hook and bait you're using. When pursuing winter flounder, spot, or croakers, use a No. 6 Claw or Beak style hook and 12 inches of 8-pound-test leader. If the target is channel bass or snook, use a 5/0 or 7/0 Claw or Beak style hook and 36 inches of 30-pound-test leader material.

When this rig is adorned with bait and lowered from a structure, it rests on the bottom, and a feeding gamefish is able to pick up the bait and move off with it without feeling the weight of the sinker. This gives the fish an opportunity to get the bait well into its mouth before you set the hook, and the result is more hooked fish. Several variations of this rig are commercially available; some have a plastic sleeve that you slip onto the line, with a sinker snap attached to the sleeve, whereas others have a metal ring through which the line is slipped, with a sinker snap attached to the ring. All three methods are very effective.

Another popular bottom rig is the single hook version, which is built around a three-way swivel. Tie the three-way swivel directly to the end of your line. Attach a snelled hook to one eye of the swivel; the hook should be appropriately sized for the targeted species and should be snelled to a length of leader. Finally, to the remaining eye of the swivel, either tie-in your sinker or use a small duo-lock snap to attach it. Bait the hook and lower the rig into the water.

A high-low rig is a third type of bottom rig favored by many who fish from these structures. With the line perpendicular to the bottom, the high-low rig enables you to fish one bait directly on the bottom and a second (or high hook) bait 24 to 30 inches off the bottom. Many tackle shops have ready-made high-low rigs available, but with a little effort you can tie up your own right on the fishing grounds.

P

To make this rig, begin by using a Double Surgeon's Knot to tie a loop in the end of your line and attach the sinker to this loop. Tie in a dropper loop just a few inches up from the loop; when the loop is completed, it should extend approximately 10 to 12 inches from the standing part of the line, meaning in effect that you've used 20 to 24 inches of line in preparing the dropper loop. Next slip a Claw or Beak style hook (with a turned-down eye) onto the loop, looping the hook through the loop twice. If you loop it only once, it will slip and slide free, but putting it through twice will firm it up tight and, in effect, will result in a double leader leading to the hook. Repeat the same procedure where you want to place your high hook, which should be anywhere from 12 to 36 inches up from the low hook.

These three rigs will work effectively in most situations where you want to present a bait to a bottom-feeding fish. They work effectively either when cast away from the structure or when just dropped to the bottom from it.

Lures. Most of the same lures employed in the surf and on jetties may be used effectively from bridges, piers, docks, and bulkheads. However, an important difference is that at the latter structures you usually fish from a greater height above the water. Although you may be fairly close to the water when fishing from bulkheads and docks, you're likely to be fully 30 feet or higher off the water when casting lures from bridges and piers. As a result, the techniques used from the surf or jetty simply don't apply when fishing from these structures. In fact, these structures present new challenges and really exciting fishing once you master the variables.

The most popular items in the arsenal of lure casters are plugs, bucktail or plastic-tailed leadheaded jigs, and metal squids and jigs. Lures ranging in weight from $1/2$ ounce to $1 1/2$ ounces, which are sufficiently heavy to be easily cast from these structures, are among the most popular. Since they are relatively light, they don't require heavy tackle to make a good cast and presentation.

Other gear. Unlike other kinds of fishing, pier fishing doesn't require a lot of gear beyond the basics. You will need a tackle box/satchel and bait container; for nighttime bridge casters, a miner's headlamp, worn loosely around the neck, may come in handy.

Many of the species caught from these structures are of a size that can readily be reeled in with little difficulty. But if you have the good fortune of hooking a big striper, bluefish, or tarpon, landing it can present a problem. Sometimes you can walk it to shore and beach it with little difficulty, or bring it close enough for a companion with a long-handled net to capture. Other times, bridge tender facilities, light poles, bulkhead features, and other obstructions make this impossible.

To help in the landing of heavy fish, many public piers have landing nets fabricated from a heavy round metal rod to which is attached a net bag and a length of $1/8$-inch cord. The net is lowered into the water, and the fish maneuvered above it; an assisting angler lifts the net, capturing the fish, and then lifts net and fish to the top of the structure. Large treble hooks, with lead molded around their shanks (elsewhere known as snag hooks), can be lowered to the water with nylon cord and used as a gaff to snatch the fish when it is brought within range, although the use of this method has decreased in recent years because of various size limit restrictions in coastal states (to avoid misjudging the fish and gaffing an undersized fish).

Anglers fishing for snook and tarpon, which are often released, regularly crimp the barbs of the hooks on their lures. Once a fish is brought within what would be landing range, they give it slack line; usually the fish then either jumps or rolls, ridding itself of the hook and gaining its freedom. Thus, the angler is not obliged to handle a fish that would have been released anyway.

General Tactics

Casting bait away from structure. In some instances it is good to cast a bait rig away from the structure. For certain species, a cast and retrieve approach is best; this is especially true when seeking summer flounder and weakfish, since they like to work shell beds that are located in the vicinity of structures. To cast effectively away from structure, cast as far as you can from the structure, let the rig settle to the bottom, and then lift your rod tip. This causes the rig to slide along the bottom, hesitate, and then slide forward again when retrieved. The fish spots the bait, which is usually a live minnow, sees it move and falter, and is often on it in a flash.

With some species, a motionless bait placed away from a structure gets the most strikes. This is particularly true with spot, croaker, rockfish, surf perch, and other species that move about searching for seaworms, shrimp, clams, and other forage on the bottom. Keep in mind that the stage of the tide may have a bearing on whether you should fish away from a structure or close to it. When the current is strong, some fish, flounder in particular, are more likely to be away from the structure; when it is very slow or nonexistent, they may be under the structure or within a few feet.

Fishing bait close to structure. Some species, such as tautog and sheepshead, often feed extremely close to the pilings that support piers, bridges, and bulkheads. They search for crabs, shrimp, and other forage that cling to these structures, and they'll also use their teeth to rip mussels from the piles. To score, you've got to present your bait just inches from the pilings or concrete. It's not unusual to see veteran pier and bridge anglers moving from piling to piling, carefully lowering their high-low rig and permitting it to rest motionless for a few minutes; if no hits are received, they move to the next piling and then the next until they receive a strike. Both sheepshead and tautog are extremely fast, and you've got to strike immediately or else they'll strip your bait from the hook.

Fishing live bait.   Fishing from piers, bridges, docks, and bulkheads proves extremely effective when using a wide variety of live baits, which can easily be presented in a natural manner to many species of gamefish. There are many ways of fishing a live bait, though unquestionably the simplest technique is to tie a hook directly to the end of the line, bait it, and lower the bait into the water. As simple as this rig is to make and use, it is among the most effective of live bait rigs.

Wherever striped bass are found, anglers use this setup with excellent results. They employ a size 1/0 or 2/0 Claw or Beak bait-holder hook and place a single large sandworm on the hook by inserting the hook into the sandworm's mouth, exiting about an inch down on the worm. This enables the angler to lower the worm into the water and drift it out with whatever current moves about the structure, where it swims enticingly and draws strikes.

This same rig is also effective for striped bass and weakfish when used with live eels, which are hooked through the lips and fished in the same manner. Live spot account for many big weakfish when used in this manner, and both grunts and pinfish are very effective baits when live-lined for snook and redfish; these baits are hooked either through the lips or eyes, or just forward of the dorsal fin, which permits them to swim about freely.

Because many live baits are small and will invariably stay close to the structure you're fishing from, you might add a float to the line anywhere from a foot to several feet above the hook. Favored floats are those that can be easily snapped anywhere on the line to hold the bait at the desired depth. The float rig is particularly effective for weakfish.

Many bridge and pier anglers chum *(see)* for weakfish and seatrout by using tiny grass shrimp, which they sparingly dribble into the water, to be carried by the current and attract the fish to the baited hook. A favored float of those seeking weakfish and seatrout is one with a scooped-out head; when you pull on the fishing line, it causes the float to pop and gurgle, often arousing the attention of the fish, which then sees the bait suspended just beneath it.

Buoy rig for live bait.   Live baits such as herring, mackerel, mullet, menhaden, and pinfish will often stay very close to the structure you're fishing from, seeking what little sanctuary it offers. Because big baits are difficult to cast and are easily ripped from the hook when the angler casts with force, many pier and bulkhead anglers employ a unique buoy rig approach to get the bait far from the structure from which they're fishing.

To prepare this rig, tie a 2- to 4-ounce pyramid sinker directly to the end of the line. Next tie a 36-inch-long piece of 20- or 30-pound-test leader material to a barrel swivel with a coastlock snap on it. Tie

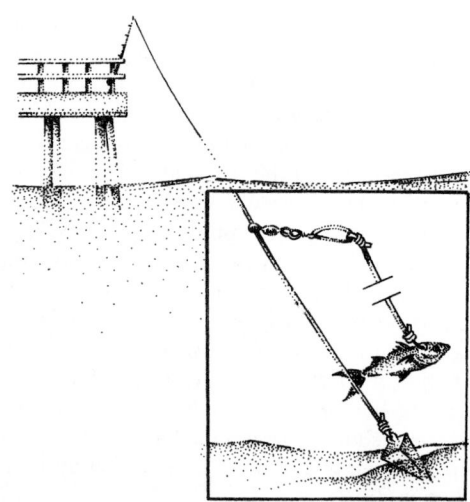

Shown here is a live bait rig fished at a good distance from a pier. Setup begins by casting a pyramid sinker without bait and lodging it securely in the mud or sand; then, live bait, which has been attached to a leader and snap swivel (inset), is placed on the fishing line. The bait slides down into the water and achieves a free-swimming position. This method allows the angler to make a distant presentation of live bait without having to actually cast the bait.

a Claw or Beak style live bait hook, or a treble hook, to the end of the leader material.

Cast the pyramid sinker to the general area where you want your bait to be. Once the sinker is firmly secured into the sand or mud bottom, slip the coastlock snap over the line and close it so that it can slide on the line. A live baitfish, usually impaled through the back, is then placed on the hook and is permitted to slide down the line and into the water. Once the bait enters the water, it can swim only from its entry point down to the sinker; often it will move back and forth, perhaps excitedly fluttering on the surface and attracting striped bass, bluefish, snook, tarpon, redfish, king mackerel, barracuda, and other large gamefish. If sharp-toothed species, such as king mackerel, barracuda, and bluefish, are in an area, it's often wise to use a 6-inch-long piece of No. 8 or 9 stainless steel leader material between the hook and the monofilament leader, employing a tiny barrel swivel to join the two.

This method of fishing a live bait from piers and bulkheads often brings exciting strikes because the baitfish moves to the surface when being stalked by the quarry. Once the bait is taken, the hook is usually set as the fish mouths it, so you quickly reel up the sinker until it comes taut with the coastlock snap and then you lift back to ensure that the hook is set.

Chumming.   Used in concert with the techniques just discussed, chumming *(see)* often enhances your fishing opportunities from these structures by attracting fish within range of your natural baits. Many operators of commercial fishing piers regularly chum from their structures. Ground menhaden is often used to attract baitfish and keep them in the vicinity of the pier, which in turn attracts a variety of species.

The time-proven technique of using a weighted chum pot, filled with ground menhaden, herring, mackerel, mussels, clams, or crabs, is regularly used to bring fish within range. Almost all bottom feeders will move toward the source of chum when it is carried along by the current.

Chumming with live grass shrimp readily attracts weakfish and seatrout to dock areas. Pacific bonito and rock bass will respond to small pieces of fish dispersed from structures. The same is true for bluefish, striped bass, snappers, and groupers. When an easily obtained meal is available, most bottom feeders and gamefish will take advantage of it, much to the advantage of the angler who employs any of the wide variety of chums.

Casting from Bridges and Piers

Both bridges and piers position you high off the water. Currents moving through beneath these structures are most often caused by tidal flow but are affected by wind as well. As these currents reach the pilings, towers, or other structure that support the pier, they cause what are popularly called "dead spots" just before the structure, or behind it as the current passes swiftly through. At both dead spots, the current separates and fish can take up station in quiet water, waiting for food to be swept along. Freshwater anglers have long known that trout often take up station ahead of, or behind, a large rock in a stream, as do smallmouth bass where a deadfall breaks the current in a river. A similar situation occurs at coastal bridges and piers. Knowing this, the bridge and pier caster can target placement so that lures can be worked to these areas, much like a baitfish being swept along by the current.

Many gamefish, especially weakfish, striped bass, tarpon, and snook, take up a feeding station in the quiet water facing the current. If the structure permits, position yourself so that you can make your

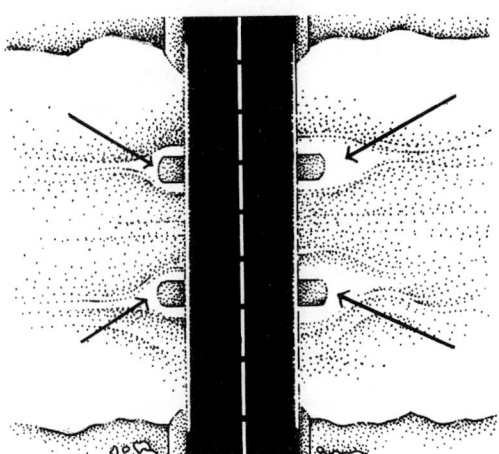

Bridge pilings deflect current, and the dead area (arrows) in front of upstream pilings and below downstream pilings may hold fish.

cast to position the lure 20 or 30 feet up from where you expect the fish to be feeding. This enables you to work the lure and to swim it with the current to within range of the fish. Often this requires a faster rate of retrieve than you would employ elsewhere, since the current is pushing the lure. You've got to speed up the retrieve to give the plug a swimming action or to make the jig appear to be darting downcurrent and faltering as it moves along.

If you don't receive strikes casting directly upcurrent, move to the left or right of where you think the fish are holding. Cast up and across at a 45-degree angle, with the lure dropping in a spot past where the fish may be feeding. Work it across and downcurrent, within view of the fish. Sometimes you can work a swimming plug or leadheaded bucktail or plastic-tailed jig so that it comes within the sight line of the feeding fish, which will often dart out to engulf it, right within view from your vantage on the bridge or pier.

Situations such as described often occur during the swiftest of tides with boiling currents that the fish prefer to avoid. Often, as the tide or current moderates, the fish will expand their range, moving up and down along the structure looking for a meal, and you should adjust accordingly. Don't hesitate to move about. Most veterans look for spots devoid of anglers, so that they can work their lures through new territory, often receiving strikes on their first presentation.

By crossing to the other side of the bridge— watch out for bridge traffic—you experience an entirely different set of circumstances. The current is running beneath the structure, often forming rips and eddies, with the same dead spots of minimal current where the fish like to hold and feed when the current is heavy. In this situation, you can often cast out a swimming plug and "swim" it in the current. If the current is sufficiently swift, only a very slow retrieve, or a twitching of the rod tip, is necessary to keep the plug working. Many anglers just walk the plug, moving it back and forth along the bridge or pier rail, permitting the lure to move in and out of the spots holding fish, much as a struggling baitfish would do in order to stem the current.

Leadhead jigs work effectively in this situation, too. The lighter jigs will work near the surface, and the current will do tricks with them, permitting them to settle, be shifted to the side, and then swept toward the surface as they ease into the fast current. In this kind of situation, the addition of a strip of pork rind or a soft tail does wonders to enhance the action in the current. Twitch your rod tip, and move it back and forth, ensuring that the lure resembles a struggling baitfish.

Don't hesitate to switch to a heavy jig that will get down in the current. The old adage that "if there's a fish feeding on the surface, there's a dozen down on the bottom" holds true with fishing these structures. A heavy jig, perhaps in the $1\frac{1}{2}$-ounce range, can be worked deep while fishing either upcurrent or downcurrent. The key is using the

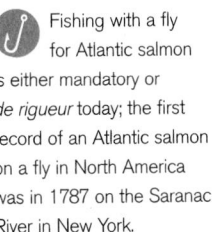

Fishing with a fly for Atlantic salmon is either mandatory or *de rigueur* today; the first record of an Atlantic salmon on a fly in North America was in 1787 on the Saranac River in New York.

P

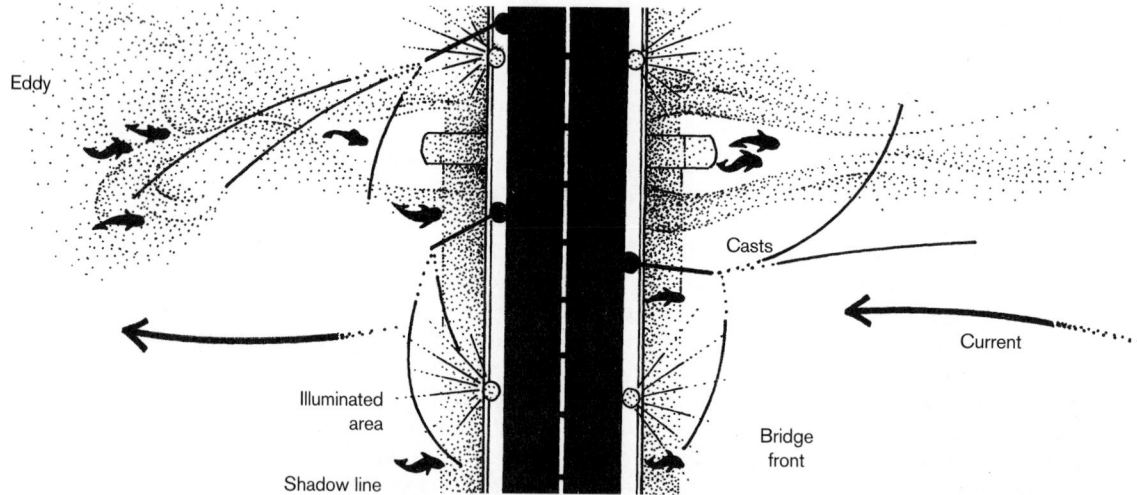

Depicted is a typical major bridge with walkways and with lights that illuminate the water beyond a shadow line at night. Feeding fish will locate in the shadow line on the bridge front and outside of the shadow line on the back (downstream side) of the bridge, as well as in dead water ahead of and below bridge pilings and where the water eddies. Anglers fishing from the bridge should position themselves to make casts to these areas.

current to your advantage and always maintaining control of the jig's movement. A heavy jig bouncing on the bottom is often observed as it's swept along; and just as the current, or the angler, works it off the bottom, it's taken by a hungry snook, striper, weakfish, or tarpon.

Fish it all. On all piers and bridges, it's important to thoroughly fish all the water surrounding the structure. Anglers tend to bunch up at the end of a pier or the middle of a bridge. Veteran anglers avoid the crowds and work the perimeter. This is especially true where a pier extends out from the beach. Often there are eelgrass beds, marsh grass, or reeds extending out from the beach that hold baitfish, and the fish know this and move in close. An ocean pier —along the surf line where the tumbling waves harbor baitfish or expose crabs, shrimp, and seaworms—is another spot often devoid of anglers, yet one certainly warranting several casts.

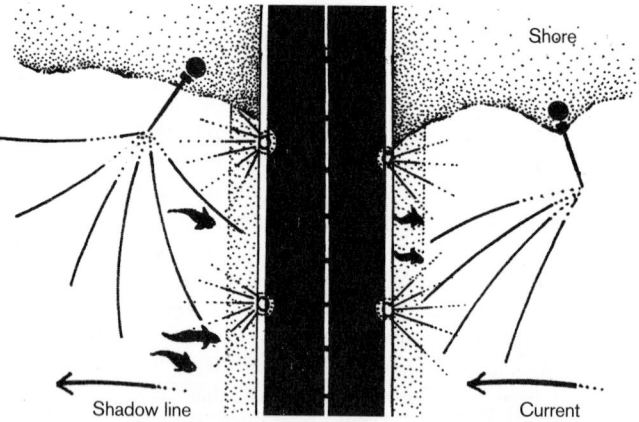

Anglers fishing from shore at night should cast out and across the current to properly scour the area around a bridge. It is especially important to work the shadow lines above and below the bridge. Note the positions of fish near the bridge relative to overhead lights.

Work shadow lines. Although daytime sport is enjoyable, there is excitement on the night tides because many coastal species are more active nocturnal feeders and the success ratio is often far superior at night. A unique situation develops after dark on many structures. Illumination from bridge or pier lights, and even a bright moon, develops a shadow line, with the water close to the structure in total darkness and the water beyond the shadow line brightly illuminated.

With the water flowing toward the bridge or pier, which is popularly called the "front of the bridge," gamefish often take up station facing into the current in the darkness, with their noses tight to the shadow line. On the opposite side, or the "back of the bridge," the opposite occurs, with the fish in the brightly lit area, but still with their noses tight to the shadow line, facing into the current or darkness. It's not unusual to see 100-pound tarpon lined up side by side in the shadow line of the bridges in the Keys or to see striped bass doing the same in the waters of many bridges.

Use the same techniques described earlier: Either cast up into the current and retrieve your lure within the vision window of the fish, or cast at an angle and work the lure across and toward the shadow line where the fish are holding. The key with either plugs or leadhead jigs is to fish the lure parallel with the surface, whether working it near the surface or in the depths. Strikes often come as deep-running lures lift off the bottom at the conclusion of a retrieve.

Cast under bridge. If you observe fish holding on the backside of the bridge, waiting for forage such as crabs, shrimp, and small fish to be carried under the bridge toward them, you have to work extra hard to properly present a lure. Often the shadow line is tight to the bridge, and if you permit a lure to work in the rips and eddies, it is many yards behind the line of vision of the feeding fish. At such times, by pointing your rod tip downward and properly timing your cast by rocking the rod and flipping the lure up into the current beneath the bridge, you can then quickly take up the slack as the lure is swept along by the current and to the shadow line and waiting fish. At first this may seem awkward to do, but once you master the motion you'll find it rewards you with many strikes.

Work the corners. Not to be overlooked are the corners where the structure meets land. Often you can fish from rock riprap that is adjacent to the bridge foundation. Sometimes this is a beach or shore, and sometimes it is a bulkhead. Frequently the bridge is located at a narrow point of a bay or river, so there is an open expanse of water funneling through beneath the bridge structure. This can cause back eddies, tidal rip lines, and currents of varying speed, which, when combined, sometimes cause miniature whirlpools that trap forage species and attract gamefish.

By positioning yourself in the corner, using a bracket approach to present your lures, and using the tidal flow to your advantage, you can cover a lot of water and catch some beautiful fish. Corner spots often provide exciting tarpon, redfish, and snook angling in southern waters, and striped bass, bluefish, weakfish, and summer flounder in northern waters. All of these bunch up in corners where food is swept their way on a moving tide.

Casting from Docks and Bulkheads

Somewhat different techniques are brought into play when you're positioned fairly low to the water while fishing from docks and bulkheads. Both structures provide good fishing because they offer sanctuary for forage. Shrimp tend to cling to bulkheads and dock pilings, and hungry fish regularly cruise along these structures. Crabs often cling to the pilings, too, or can be observed at night in the area swimming beneath the dock lights. When there is a seaworm hatch, it's not unusual to observe literally millions of inch-long squirmers swimming just beneath the surface. At such times the water often boils as practically every species in residence gorges on the tiny, yet plentiful, food. Where there is abundant food around docks and bulkheads, there will be predators to catch.

Natural drift. Under natural drift conditions, a single sandworm or bloodworm, impaled on a hook and drifted along with the current, quickly brings strikes. A plastic worm may also bring strikes. The key is presentation, with the most successful approach being to drift these items with the current as unimpeded as possible. Veteran bulkhead casters often "walk the worm," permitting the current to carry it along just inches from the bulkhead.

Work tight to bulkhead. Plastic-tailed leadhead jigs also produce excellent results when worked tight to the bulkhead; often snook, redfish,

striped bass, bluefish, seatrout, tarpon, ladyfish, snapper, and other species feed just inches from where you may be standing. Tight to the bulkhead means just that, casting out and permitting the current to carry your jig as you walk along the bulkhead or dock, working your rod tip so that the jig darts ahead into the current, then falters and is swept along again, much like a struggling shrimp or tiny baitfish. Work the jig just 6 to 12 inches from the bulkhead or pilings, and you'll be surprised by exciting strikes. Do not overlook the corners of these structures either.

Know the tides. Depending on location, many dock and bulkhead areas come alive at or near slack tide. With swift currents, many gamefish take up station anywhere they can get out of the quick flow, which may be in the middle of a bay or river. As the current slows, they move about, searching for food; they know that the dock and bulkhead areas often have an abundance of forage.

To capitalize on this situation, try to time your visits to key locations an hour before to an hour after either the flood or the ebb tide. By timing your movements, you can often cover three or four spots in different areas, capitalizing on the slow-moving water in each location. As you gain experience, you'll no longer be surprised to see a spot having a 4-knot current and no fish life whatsoever suddenly erupt in a maelstrom of surface-crashing, feeding gamefish. Then, as the current begins to boil, the bonanza shuts off as quickly as it began.

This phenomenon proves that gamefish typically move several miles per day. Anglers often observe huge schools of fish before, during, and after the slack tide. As the current begins to boil, their sonars go blank, indicating that the fish promptly vacated that area rather than fight the energy-sapping current. This happens at docks and bulkheads, too.

Dead spots and shadow lines. Some of the techniques employed by bridge casters have application for fishing from docks. As current flows to the pilings or supports of the dock, there is a dead spot in the current, as is the case on the downcurrent side of the dock. Work these spots diligently with swimming plugs and leadhead jigs.

The same can be said for a shadow line from the dock lights. The difference is that you're usually close to the water. Keep your rod tip low so that the plug or jig works parallel with the surface, and work the lure right up close to the pilings.
See: Tides.

PIGFISH *Orthopristis chrysoptera.*
Other names—Spanish: *corocoro burro.*

Anglers catch this species in large numbers on hook and line and also in nets in warm temperate waters. It is used mainly as a bait for larger predators.

Identification. Pigfish have long anal fins, matching the soft dorsal fin in shape and in size. The head is sloped and pointed, the snout almost

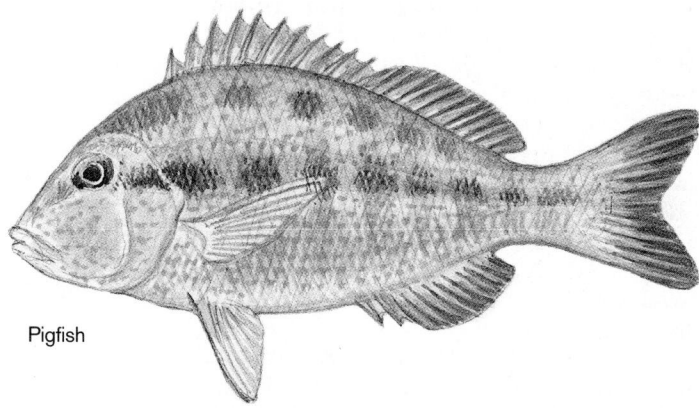

Pigfish

piglike, and the lips thin. A background color of bluish gray is marked with brassy spots in indistinct lines that are horizontal below the lateral line but extend obliquely upward and backward above the lateral line. These oblique markings are also found on the cheeks. The fins are yellow bronze with dusky margins.

Age/Size. The maximum length and weight is 18 inches and 2 pounds, but pigfish are commonly 7 to 9 inches long and weigh no more than a half pound. Pigfish normally live for three years.

Distribution. The pigfish exists in the western Atlantic, from Massachusetts and Bermuda to the Gulf of Mexico. They are most abundant from the Chesapeake Bay south and do not inhabit tropical waters.

Habitat. Pigfish are found in coastal waters over sand and mud bottoms.

Life history/Behavior. These schooling fish are mostly nocturnal. Spawning occurs inshore in spring and early summer, prior to when the fish move into estuaries.

Food. Pigfish are bottom feeders that forage on crustaceans, worms, and small fish.

Angling. A common catch in late summer and fall, pigfish are taken by bottom anglers offering various natural baits.

See: Grunt.

PIKE

The Esocidae family of fish, categorically known as pike, numbers some of the most popular, aggressive, and important sportfish of cold and cool waters in the Northern Hemisphere. Six species constitute one genera in this circumpolar group, and they are categorized as pike, pickerel, and muskellunge. The three pickerel and one muskellunge occur naturally only in North America. The pike include two species, *Esox lucius* (northern pike) and *E. reicherti* (Amur pike); the latter is found only in Eurasia, and the former is widely distributed in North America and Eurasia.

All species have slim, elongated bodies with dorsal and anal fins located far to the rear, just in front of the forked caudal fin. The front of the head is flattened, and the long, depressed jaws and snout, when viewed from overhead, appear shaped like a duck's bill. The overall bodily appearance is very much arrowlike. The rays in the fins are soft, the large mouth contains numerous sharp canine teeth, and the coloration is usually greenish or brassy. Pike are distantly related to salmonids, although they lack an adipose fin and do not look or behave like salmonids.

Pike, pickerel, and the muskellunge are solitary, aggressive predators. They do not build nests. In spring, the female scatters or broadcasts her eggs in shallow water where the males fertilize them. The young are given no parental attention, and the species, where they overlap, readily prey upon and compete with each other. Where their ranges overlap, some species hybridize, making the identification of certain individuals extremely difficult. This is compounded by variations in color due to water characteristics and habitat, and some fish having extremely distinctive body markings. Some northern pike have a genetic color variance that results in a markedly silver or bluish appearance, causing them to be called silver pike (*see: pike, silver*).

Pickerel are the smallest of the group, and only the chain pickerel is capable of growing to more than 5 pounds and no more than 8 pounds. The muskellunge is the largest, once capable of attaining at least 70 pounds if not more. The northern pike routinely exceeds 20 pounds in some waters and is capable of growing to more than twice that weight. The latter two are among the most prized freshwater sportfish.

See: **Muskellunge; Pickerel, Chain; Pickerel, Grass and Redfin; Pike, Northern.**

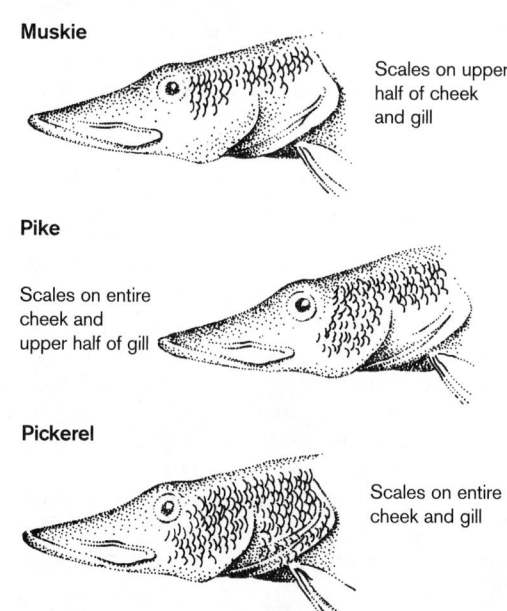

Muskie

Scales on upper half of cheek and gill

Pike

Scales on entire cheek and upper half of gill

Pickerel

Scales on entire cheek and gill

The scale pattern on cheeks and gills helps differentiate the pike species.

P

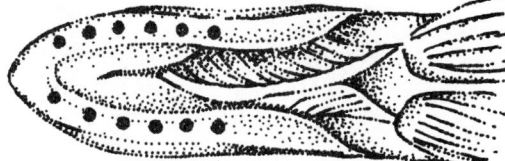

Muskellunge

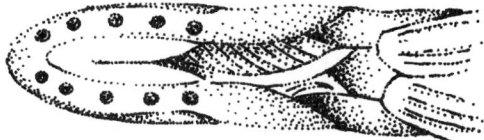

Northern Pike

There are six or more pores on each side under the jaw of muskellunge, and five or fewer pores on the northern pike.

PIKE, BLUE

(1) *Stizostedion vitreum glaucum.*

Not a pike, but a subspecies of the walleye *(see)* and a member of the Percidae family, the blue pike is believed extinct. It was a deep-water species endemic to Lake Erie and of great commercial significance in the 1920s, possibly more so than the native lake trout. The blue pike was distinguished from the larger walleye (walleye were called walleyed pike or yellow pike at one time) by virtue of its larger glassy eyes, lack of yellow pigmentation, and narrower distance between the eyes. This bluish or blue gray walleye was said to be present in Lake Erie into the early 1970s, and may have occurred in limited numbers in Lake Ontario, Lake Huron, and some other connected Great Lakes waters, although this has never been confirmed. Commercial overfishing, interbreeding with walleye, and the introduction and spread of lamprey eels are among the factors that may have led to the demise of this species.

(2) A term for the so-called silver pike *(see: pike, silver).*

PIKE, NORTHERN   *Esox lucius.*

Other names—pike, northern, jack, jackfish, snake, great northern pike, great northern pickerel, American pike, common pike, Great Lakes pike; Danish: *gedde;* Dutch: *snoek;* Finnish: *hauki;* French: *brochet;* German: *hecht;* Hungarian: *csuka;* Italian: *luccio;* Norwegian: *gjedde;* Portuguese: *lcio;* Russian: *shtschuka;* Spanish: *lucio;* Swedish: *gäddo.*

Malevolent-looking and spear shaped, the northern pike might well have been named "water wolf." Often likened to the notoriously vicious barracuda of saltwater, it is the namesake member of the Esocidae family of pike. Although disparaged by a few people who catch it while seeking other species of fish, the pike is a worthy angling quarry, one that grows fairly large, fights well, and accommodates anglers frequently enough to be of substantial interest in the areas where it is found.

The majority of northern pike are released by anglers, but a minor amount of commercial fishing for them exists in North America and also in Eurasia. This species is not usually thought of as a good food fish, but it is actually excellent, especially those specimens that come from cool, clean waters. Although bony, the flesh is sweet, white, and flaky, and cooking preparations are best with the skin removed to avoid flavors that may accompany its mucus-coated skin.

Identification. The northern pike has an elongated body and head. The snout is broad and flat, shaped somewhat like a duck bill. The jaws, roof of the mouth, tongue, and gill rakers are armed with numerous sharp teeth that are constantly being replaced. A single soft-rayed dorsal fin is located far back on the body.

Male and female pike are similar in appearance, and both are variable in color. A fish from a clear stream or lake will usually be light green, whereas one from a dark slough or river will be considerably darker. The underparts are whitish or yellowish. The markings on the sides form irregular rows of yellow or gold spots. Pike with a silvery or blue color variation are occasionally encountered and are known as silver pike *(see: pike, silver).*

The northern pike can be distinguished from its relatives by three main features. Most noticeably, the greenish or yellowish sides of these fish are covered with lighter-colored kidney-shaped horizontal spots or streaks, whereas all other species have markings (spots, bars, stripes, or reticulations) that are darker than the background color. Its markings are most likely to be confused with those of the chain pickerel *(see: pickerel, chain).* The second distinction is the scale pattern on the gill cover and cheek. In the northern pike the cheek is fully scaled, but the bottom half of the gill cover is scaleless. In the larger muskellunge, both the bottom half of the gill cover and the bottom half of the cheek are scaleless. In the smaller pickerel, the gill cover and the cheek are both fully scaled. The third distinctive feature is the number of pores under each side of the lower jaw; there are usually 5 in the northern pike (rarely 3, 4, or 6 on one side), 6 to 9 in the muskellunge (rarely 5 or 10 on one side), and 4 in smaller pickerel (occasionally 3 or 5 on one side only).

Size/Age. Pike are normally 16 to 30 inches long and weigh between 2 and 7 pounds. Females live longer and attain greater size than males. Pike up to 20 pounds are common in some Canadian and Alaskan rivers, lakes, and sloughs, and fish weighing up to 30 pounds and measuring 4 feet in length are possible. Fish exceeding 25 pounds are quite rare, and the North American record is a 46-pound, 2-ounce New York fish caught in 1940. Larger northern pike have been recorded from various European countries, and the all-tackle world record is a 55-pound, 1-ounce German fish captured in 1986. The average life span of northern

Northern Pike

pike is 7 to 10 years, but in slow-growing populations they may live up to 26 years.

Distribution. The northern pike occurs around the world in northern or arctic waters, extending from northwestern Europe across northern Asia to northern North America. It is densely distributed throughout Alaska with the exception of the offshore islands, and widespread throughout Canada and the arctic islands above Hudson Bay, being conspicuously absent from the coastal plains (most of British Columbia and the Canadian Atlantic coast east of the St. Lawrence River). In the United States, it is found south of Maine in New Hampshire, Vermont, and Massachusetts (except along the coast), and in all the Great Lakes states (although it is largely absent from lower Michigan and Indiana), as well as west of the Great Lakes in Minnesota, Wisconsin, Iowa, Illinois, Missouri, Nebraska, and Montana. It is restricted primarily to the extreme eastern portions of North and South Dakota. It has been widely introduced outside this native range, even into southern and western states.

In Europe and Asia, this fish is primarily known as pike, not northern pike, and is accompanied in northeastern Asia by the Amur pike *(E. reicherti),* which is native to the Amur River system. Also known as the blackspotted pike, this fish can grow to more than 3 feet in length and weigh up to 35 pounds; it is of some commercial interest, and has been introduced to a few waters in the U.S.

Habitat. Although classified by biologists as a coolwater species, the northern pike exists in diverse habitats, somewhat like largemouth bass but without a tolerance for extreme warm conditions. It is especially known to inhabit the weedy parts of rivers, ponds, and lakes, but it may be found in deeper, open environs in waters without vegetation, or when the temperature gets too high in warm shallower areas. Warm shallow ponds and cold deep lakes both support pike, but large individuals have a preference for water that is in the mid-50°F range. Smaller fish are more likely to be in warm shallow water.

Life history/Behavior. Northern pike spawn in spring, moving into the heavily vegetated areas of lakes and rivers either just after ice out or in some cases prior to ice out. In many places they spawn in wetlands or marshes that will have little or no water later in the season. They are broadcast spawners, and the scattered eggs that fall to the bottom are adhesive. They usually hatch in 12 to 14 days, but do so

later in much colder waters. In waters that also contain muskellunge *(see),* the two species may crossbreed naturally; this occurs rarely and is more likely to be achieved deliberately in a hatchery, but it has occurred naturally, as muskies spawn in the same or similar environs, although usually after pike.

Young pike grow rapidly and in much of their range are capable of attaining 6 inches by the end of their first summer. Females mature at age 3 or 4, and males at age 2 or 3, although they may do so later in more northerly waters.

Food and feeding habits. Pike are voracious and opportunistic predators from the time they are mere inches long. They are solitary, lurking near weeds or other cover to ambush prey. Their diet is composed almost entirely of fish, but it may occasionally include shorebirds, small ducks, muskrats, mice, frogs, and the like. Other pike—as well as whitefish, walleye, yellow perch, and suckers—are common food items in waters where these species are abundant. The northern pike is highly specialized for feeding individually on large food items, and it may attack and eat forage that is one-third its own length; in pike waters, it is common to find scarred fish that were grabbed by but escaped the large toothy maw of a pike. Pike feed most actively during the day and are heavily sight-oriented. They are less affected by cold fronts than are other gamefish.

Angling. Born in weedy waters, pike spend much of their life in similar habitat, holding motionless in the vegetation, camouflaged to strike suddenly at passersby. Key locations in lakes include weedy bays, river inlets where weeds are plentiful, shoreline points with beds of cabbage weeds on their open-water sides, reefs with coontail weeds, marshy shorelines, lily pads, and reedy pockets along sandy and rocky shorelines. Many other areas may hold pike, but some form of vegetative structure obviously hosts a significant portion of the pike population. Some pike, especially large ones, inhabit open waters where they forage on schools of baitfish, so it is not necessarily the case that every pike in a given environment will be in the weeds.

Pike remain fairly shallow in the early part of the year, and some (mostly smaller ones) stay in shallow water throughout the season. Bigger pike, however, usually gravitate to deeper, heavy-cover haunts as the water warms. During early summer, they move to cabbage weeds (also called pike weeds), for example, in water that exceeds 6 to 7 feet and drops off to 15 feet or so. Look to the outer edge of these weeds for trophy fish, and especially in pockets or indentations.

In rivers, pike are a lazy fish and usually try to establish an easy ambush position. Look for them where small rivers and streams merge with the main flow, in the small eddy beneath a beaver hut, downstream from islands, in shallow backwaters, under docks, on shorelines just below riprap or wing dams, on the inside of large eddies, and where brush and slow water meet.

Even relatively small pike may attack a big lure, so the big lure/big fish theory doesn't necessarily hold with these game creatures. Smaller pike are often more eager and more vulnerable to angling, and they out-hustle larger fish to a lure of any size. This is especially true where pike are very abundant. Using fairly large lures is nonetheless advantageous, not only because they discourage some smaller fish from attacking, but also because they represent more of a meal to a larger pike than would a diminutive lure, which makes them more worthy of pursuit.

Pike lures include the traditional red-and-white spoon, plus a fluorescent orange-bladed spinnerbait or bucktail spinner; an orange-and-yellow-backed minnow-imitation plug; a yellow, Five-O-Diamonds pattern spoon; a black bucktail with a single fluorescent spinner; and various shallow- and deep-diving plugs in gaudy and metallic colors. Good pike lures often tend to be brightly colored and to work with a broad, wide-wobbling action. Lethargic fish may be more inclined to hit large hair- or rubber-bodied jigs, as well as soft-plastic jerkbaits and weightless plastic worms.

Pike are attracted not only to a lure's size and shape, but also to its swimming action, flash and visibility, and noise. They are one of the more curious freshwater fish, and getting their attention is often a key to catching them. That would seem true of most fish, but many other freshwater species are keenly aware of the presence of certain lures in their domain yet remain otherwise disinterested.

Lure types and the techniques used to present them vary greatly for northern pike, although many would-be pike catchers stick to the simplicity of casting spoons in and around weeds. Although casting weedless spoons directly into a mass of shoreline vegetation and retrieving outward can have merit, it is a fairly standard tactic that suffers in heavily fished waters.

All types of plugs can be useful in catching pike—surface plugs, shallow-running plugs, and medium to deep divers—but shallow runners are especially popular, as are long and slender plugs that imitate small fish. Most anglers think only of shallow-running minnow-style plugs for pike; these are useful, of course, and are perennial pike catchers, but anglers should broaden their arsenal. Many of the larger minnow-shaped plugs used for striper and muskie trolling, for example, are effective pike catchers, both in casting and trolling applications.

A northern pike from Scott Lake, Saskatchewan.

An overlooked hot pike plug is a super-shallow-running (1 foot deep and less) bulbous crankbait that rattles noisily. This plug not only calls pike up out of deep weeds in the summer, but it can also be worked in back-bay shallows in the spring. In lieu of this particular lure, you could try a surface plug, such as a walking-type stickbait or a propellered plug (perhaps even a popper), to get a pike's attention and bring it up for a strike. Another option is a medium- or deep-diving crankbait that possesses rattles; these are worked stop-go fashion over and through the weeds. Still another option is a nonrattling deep-diving plug; this type should first be worked around the edges of the vegetation to entice the pike to move out of the weeds, and then worked through the weeds in a slow, twitching style.

The diving minnow is ideal for parallel casting to banks and weedlines, and also for shallow pull-pause retrieves; it's helpful to use the same lure—which has good flash and looks like a small fish—for deep edges as well as for relatively shallow work. Barbless hooks, incidentally, are the only way to go when using multihook lures, especially plugs, for pike. Some plugs can be switched to single barbless hooks, which diminishes the chances of inflicting damage (on you and the fish) and facilitates unhooking.

A spinnerbait is another effective northern pike lure, fished through weedbeds, around timber, up against stumps, in and about brush, and across rocky points. Their weedless nature is especially beneficial, and they work especially well in the spring, when pike stage in extremely shallow water during spawning and post-spawning periods.

Jigs work well for these fish, although when used without a wire leader, many jigs are lost to a pike's razor-sharp teeth. Good pike jigs include plastic eel-like versions, or those formed of natural hair, in bright colors. Some anglers slow-troll these along the deep edge of weedbeds, slowly lifting and lowering the rod tip. Casting along the edges is also productive.

Fly fishing for pike has gained a following in recent times, simply because these fish are aggressive and are often available in shallow water, which makes presentation less difficult. In the northern parts of their range, where pike stay shallow in cool water well into the season, pike can be stalked and sight-fished. This method allows flycasters fishing from boats to make presentations akin to those used on tropical saltwater flats.

Fishing with live or dead baits is a small overall component of the pike angling scene, although in some areas a dead bait stillfished on the bottom in spring takes the larger pike.

Baitcasting, spincasting, and spinning gear are all suitable for pike fishing, although baitcasting is most preferable for large lures or baits or when the opportunity exists to catch large fish. The generally stiffer baitcasting rod has an advantage over other types of tackle in hook setting, which is not always accomplished well in the big toothy maws of a pike. Line capacity is not a big factor in pike fishing. Rods should be $5\frac{1}{2}$ to 7 feet long, with a stiff butt and midsection, and a rather fast tip. Most pike anglers prefer heavy line; 12- to 17-pound test is favored, but many opt for 6- to 10-pound-test line where the cover is not thick.

Steel leaders are used by many pike anglers, but avoided by others. A large pike may take a lure deep or get some of the line in its mouth, and certainly many lure-hooked pike get free when they cut leader-less line. Yet many fish are caught without the use of leaders, although this is sometimes pure luck. Small, 6-inch, 20-pound-test leaders do not hamper casting but afford some protection.

Pike aren't hard to subdue. They do a lot of thrashing and short-distance darting, and some don't really fight until they eyeball the boat or angler. Reel drag is significant when playing larger fish, but only briefly. The heavy weeds these fish prefer can cause a problem with light lines; big pike tend to make long, steady runs through thick vegetation. A leader can be beneficial in these instances.

The greatest difficulty in landing pike is facilitating a smooth release that doesn't injure the fish or the fish handler. Netting pike is inadvisable, as they often thrash wildly when captured, and multihook plugs can be dangerous and harmful. Unhooking and releasing fish in the water, by the boat, is the best tactic. Leading them into fish cradles is also useful.

See: Pike.

PIKE, SILVER

Taxonomically there is no species of fish, or subspecies of northern pike *(see: pike, northern)*, that is identified by the name "silver pike." This term is occasionally used to describe pikelike fish that have a silvery or blue gray coloration but otherwise look like northern pike. Most scientists classify this fish as a color variation of the northern pike, the result of genetic mutation. This determination has not been scientifically proven. Some North Americans refer to it as "silver muskellunge," although it is a pike; many call it a blue pike, and some call it a deep-water pike.

Smaller than the northern pike (it has been reported up to 20 pounds) and distinctly uncommon, the silver pike has occurred across most of the range inhabited by northern pike in North America and Eurasia. Its body coloration is light and predominantly silver, although it may be bluish; it is darker on top and lighter on the belly, and has no spots. Silver pike that have mated with "true" northern pike have produced offspring with black mottled markings on a silver base, similar to crappie and leading to the term "black pike."

See: Pike.

PIKE-PERCH

Also written as pikeperch and pike perch, "pike-perch" is a European term for zander *(see)*.

PILCHARD

(1) An angling term for various small members of the Clupeidae family of herring *(see)* that inhabit the western Atlantic. These include three members of the *Harengula* genus: false pilchard *(H. clupeola)*; redear sardine *(H. humeralis)*; and scaled sardine *(H. jaguana)*. It may also include the Atlantic thread herring *(Opisthonema oglinum)*.

A silver pike from Wollaston Lake, Saskatchewan.

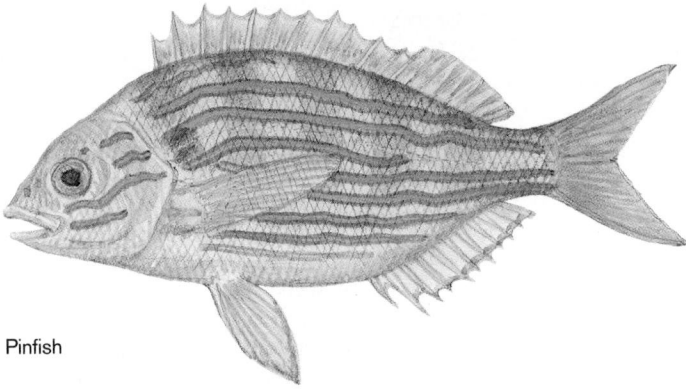

Pinfish

These species occur from Florida and the Gulf of Mexico southward to Brazil, and some range farther north. They are commonly 5 to 7 inches in length and are caught on small multihook bait rigs and with cast nets for use as inshore and offshore live baits. Pilchards may also be known as white baits in parts of Florida.

(2) A term for Pacific sardines *(see: sardine, Pacific)*.

PILE CAST

An in-air technique for presenting a fly or mending a fly line.
See: **Mending.**

PILOTFISH   *Naucrates ductor.*

Pilotfish are a unique and circumtropical species widely found in the Atlantic, Pacific, and Indian Oceans. They are renowned for accompanying large sharks on their oceanic wanderings, as well as whales, ray, schools of various other fish, and ships. A pilotfish is said to have followed a sailing ship for 80 days.

This species has no angling value but is often observed by offshore anglers. It feeds on scraps of the host's leftovers, as well as on parasites, small fish, and invertebrates. Minor commercial interest exists for this species, which is of the jack family and looks somewhat like an amberjack.

Pilotfish have five to seven dark vertical bars on their elongated body, and a low spinous first dorsal fin with four spines. They can grow to a maximum of 27 inches.

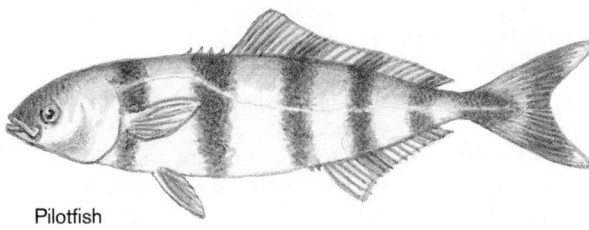

Pilotfish

PINFISH

Other names—bream, saltwater bream, sailor's choice, Canadian bream; Spanish: *sargo salema.*

This abundant, small member of the Sparidae family is important as forage for predatory species of fish and is widely used by anglers as bait. There was once a fairly good commercial fishery for pinfish, but it is now a minor one; the flesh is oily and has a strong flavor.

Identification. Pinfish have a compressed panfishlike body with a head that is high through the area just in front of the dorsal fin. It has a small mouth and incisor-like teeth with deeply notched edges. Its coloration is silvery overall, with yellow and blue horizontal stripes. A round black spot at the upper rear margin of each gill cover is distinctive. The name of the species comes from the

needle-sharp spines on the first dorsal fin. All fins are yellowish.

A similar small porgy, the spottail pinfish *(Diplodus holbrooki)* averages less than 10 inches in length, but occasional larger individuals do exist. It is identified by the large black band across the base of the caudal peduncle and by the black margin on the gill covers. Otherwise, the body is silvery, with only faint black bars. The spottail pinfish is common over rocky bottoms and around docks and piers. In the Caribbean it is replaced by the almost identical silver porgy *(D. argenteus).*

Size. Pinfish are capable of growing to 15 inches, but they rarely reach 10 inches in length and are common at about 7 inches. They live at least seven years, and probably longer.

Distribution. The pinfish occurs in the western Atlantic, from Massachusetts to the northern Gulf of Mexico, including Bermuda, to the Yucatán Peninsula in Mexico. The spottail pinfish is found in the Gulf of Mexico and in Florida.

Habitat/Spawning behavior. Pinfish are coastal and inshore species that travel in schools, sometimes in great numbers, over vegetated and sometimes rocky bottoms and around docks and pilings; they also frequent mangrove areas and may enter brackish water or freshwater. Pinfish move out of coastal waters in winter, and spawning occurs in winter in offshore waters.

Food and feeding habits. Pinfish consume crustaceans, mollusks, worms, and occasionally small fish associated with grassy habitat. They nibble at most foods, a habit that makes them a nuisance for anglers fishing baits for other bottom-dwelling species.

Angling. To catch pinfish, anglers use small pieces of bait on small hooks and bottom rigs around docks and piers, and in shallow nearshore water. They are captured with cast nets for live (and cut) bait use and for chumming.
See: **Inshore Fishing.**

PINTADO

A shovelnose catfish of South America, also known as spotted sorubim.
See: **Catfish.**

P

PIRAÍBA

The largest South American catfish and one of the largest freshwater fish in the world.
See: Catfish.

PIRANHA

Piranhas (pronounced pee-ron-yahs) are the best known and most storied members of the Characidae family, most of which are minnowlike but possess teeth and an adipose fin. There are reportedly some 800 characins, and piranhas make up a large group that are related to such gamefish species as payara, dorado, and tigerfish.

Also known as *caribe* in Spanish, piranhas and some closely related species belong to the subfamily Serrasalminae, which has two different groupings. One includes seven genera and some 60 species that are primarily plant-eating fish. The tambaqui *(Colossoma macropomum)* of the Amazon is the most prominent member of this group; it is an important food fish, eats fruit, grows to 66 pounds, and is occasionally caught incidentally by anglers.

The other group has six genera and includes silver dollar fish, which belong to the genus *Metynnis* and are well known to aquarium hobbyists. It also includes four genera of piranhas—*Pygopristis, Pygocentrus, Pristobrycon,* and *Serrasalmus*—which include approximately 50 species. Some of these piranhas have yet to be described by scientists, and a good deal remains unknown about many of them, especially the extent of their range.

It is known that piranhas, like most characins, are schooling species. Most are fairly small, under 10 inches in maximum size. They are also good sportfish on appropriate tackle, and their firm, white meat is excellent table fare.

The fearsome flesh-eating image of piranhas is exaggerated on the whole, as many piranhas are herbivorous and eat seeds, although many also eat other fish. Many species of piranhas are termed harmless to humans; however, some species can be extremely dangerous. The questions, of course, are which ones are harmless, are they always harmless, are the dangerous ones always dangerous, and what gets them excited?

Red Piranha

A black piranha from the Trombetas River, Brazil.

Native South Americans are known to swim in waters that contain dangerous piranhas; in some Brazilians waters, it is not unknown for an angler to catch a large black piranha, a dangerous species, from a particular section of water, only to have the native guide slip over the side of the boat a short while later to retrieve a snagged lure.

The presence of blood is generally thought to be a stimulant to a feeding frenzy of flesh-eating piranhas. However, there is ample evidence to indicate that schools of these fish are triggered into attacking behavior by the frenzied and panicked activity of victims, and many if not all piranhas have a highly developed auditory ability. Many gamefish hooked by anglers, particularly peacock bass, are literally attacked by piranhas while they are in the midst of a wild struggle against a fishing rod. They may suffer minor or major mutilation in the process, perhaps being consumed from the tail to belly in such a manner that the angler lands little more than a still-breathing head. This action is not unlike the frenzied behavior of sharks. It is true that people and animals have been killed by piranhas, and that some animals have been reduced to a carcass within a few minutes.

Piranhas can be such effective eating machines because they have numerous upper and lower teeth that are short, triangular, and sharp. The teeth interlock and the jaws are extremely powerful, allowing these fish to chew continuously and to remove flesh in clean bites. There is some belief that the larger the school of piranhas, the greater the propensity for an attack.

Piranhas are confined to the Orinoco, Amazon, Paraguay, and São Francisco River basins of South America, but few species apparently occur across this entire range. They are primarily river species but can adapt to stillwaters, and are commonly found in rivers, lakes, and lagoons in most watersheds within their range.

Species of note. Piranhas are deep-bodied and generally slender fish. Although they vary in size, color, and pattern, all have an adipose fin and a broad tail, and most have a rather blunt snout with a slightly upturned lower jaw. Many piranhas are hard for nonscientists to distinguish from each other. Species of prominence are given below.

Red-bellied piranha *(Pygocentrus nattereri)*. This species is also known as red piranha and red pirai; and in Portuguese as *piranha caju* and *piranha-quexicuda;* and in Spanish as *paña, paraña, caribe boca de la locha, palometa,* and *palometa de rio.* Perhaps the most wide-ranging of these fish, the red-bellied piranha occurs from Venezuela to Argentina's Paraná River system, as well as in the tributaries of the Amazon River in Peru. It is classified as dangerous; shows hierarchies in schools; feeds on insects, worms, and fish; and is reported to be active mainly at dusk and dawn. This species is relatively small; a 3-pound, 7-ounce specimen holds the world angling record.

White piranha *(Serrasalmus rhombeus)*. The white piranha occurs in the Orinoco and Amazon basins; in Brazil it is known as *piranha-preta,* and it may also be called redeye piranha and yellow piranha. A potentially dangerous fish, it is a small species that grows to a maximum of 13 inches.

Black piranha *(Pygocentrus piraya)*. This species is also known as blacktail piranha and São Francisco piranha, and in Portuguese as *chupita.* It is endemic to and widely spread in Brazil, including the São Francisco River basin, and may occur elsewhere. The dangerous black piranha is the largest of all piranhas and is also a commercial species. It is reported to grow to 13 pounds; the all-tackle world record is a 6-pound, 15-ounce Venezuelan fish, and 2- to 4-pounders are common in some waters.

The black spot piranha *(Pygocentrus caribe)*. A small and harmless species from Venezuela, this fish is also called blackspot piranha and, in Spanish, *caribe pinche.* It is listed among record species, with a 1-pound, 4-ounce fish being the largest caught.

The pirambeba *(Serrasalmus humeralis)*. This is a Brazilian piranha that established a breeding population in Dade County, Florida. It is believed to be the only escaped piranha species to have accomplished this, and it was eradicated in 1981.

Angling. Piranhas are great sport on light tackle. Large specimens are especially good fighters. Most piranhas are caught incidentally by anglers fishing for other species, primarily peacock bass, and are seldom the deliberate target of angling.

White Piranha

Because of this, they are usually caught on heavy tackle that mitigates their fight. Anglers can take advantage of the schooling behavior of piranhas, however, by having on hand lighter tackle and smaller lures. Small spoons, jigs, and lipless crankbaits are very effective for these species. A steel leader is advisable.

PIRARARA

A South American catfish.
See: **Catfish.**

PIRARUÇU

See: **Arapaima.**

PISCIVOROUS

Fish eating. Most predatory fish, and most of those considered sportfish, are piscivorous.

PISTOL GRIP

A type of handle, especially common on short baitcasting rods.
See: **Baitcasting Tackle.**

PITCHING

Pitching is a technique for casting under obstructions by using a low-trajectory approach to the targeted area. It is a cast that does not develop a lot of rod tip speed and isn't used for great distances, yet one that provides accuracy and soft presentations for lures dispatched to hard-to-reach places.

Pitching is often confused with flipping *(see),* perhaps because of its use by bass anglers and because it primarily involves baitcasting reels and long rods. Although both techniques have similar purposes and achieve similar results, they accomplish them differently, and in pitching, unlike flipping, the reel is used to cast.

Pitching works best where there is heavy cover and where the clarity of water prevents you from getting close enough to make a short flip cast

P

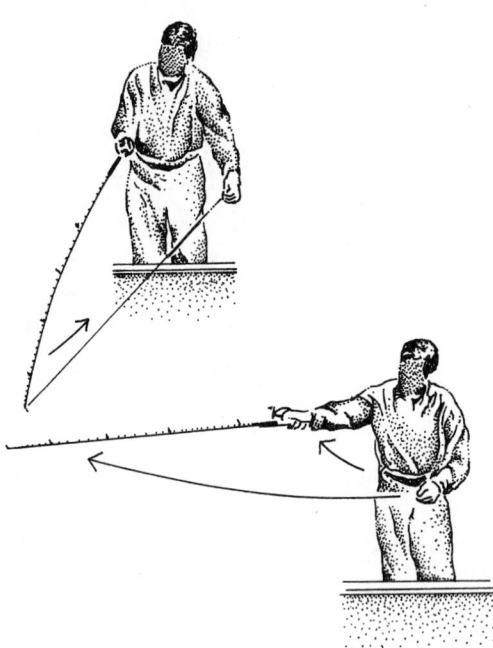

A two-handed pitch cast is made by holding the lure (be wary of hooks) in your left hand and pulling on the line to bring your rod tip down so that it has a slight bend (top). Bring the rod up as you let go of the weight, and take your thumb off the reel spool (bottom) to send the lure toward its target on a low trajectory.

without spooking fish. In many places where pitching is used, there are overhanging obstructions, especially tree cover. In such situations, a conventional overhead cast will cause the lure to get hung up. Pitching lets you keep the lure down close to the surface all the way from your position (usually in a boat) to the target. If you make a pitching cast properly, you can get your bait under most kinds of overhanging cover.

Rods that are best for pitching are often $6\frac{1}{2}$ feet long, shorter than a standard flipping rod, and are designed for lines ranging from 8 to 17 pounds. This is a versatile tool that can be used for many other activities. It should be matched with a good-quality baitcasting reel, preferably one with a flipping feature for versatility, since you might get a strike as soon as your lure enters the water, in which case it's good to have a reel that engages the moment you release pressure on the freespool device.

The pitch cast is made with either a two-handed, low-trajectory cast or with a one-handed pendulum motion. Both work well but serve slightly different purposes. Practice is the key to learning either one.

To execute the pendulum cast with a practice casting weight, let out line so that the weight hangs down to just above your reel. Put the reel into freespool, and keep your thumb on the spool. Raise the rod tip to swing the lure forward, and then permit it to swing back toward your body. Swing it forward again, and release thumb pressure on the reel's spool as the lure comes forward. If your timing is

right, the lure will fly out in low, level flight to its intended target. When practicing on land, the weight should stay down close to the ground so that in actual fishing the lure stays down close to the surface of the water. The key to making this cast properly is getting enough movement in the practice weight to pull line off the spool as you release thumb pressure.

Be sure to use a $\frac{5}{8}$-ounce weight in practice sessions. This weight may be heavier than the lure you'll use for fishing, but the beginning objective is to learn how to execute the cast and polish your timing, and such a weight makes it much easier to do this.

An educated thumb and a low spool-tension setting on the reel are critical to successful pitching. You won't be able to develop the power in pitching that you get with a conventional cast. Unless you've got your reel set so that the spool operates fast and easy, you might as well forget about pitching. Having the tension set lightly means you have to control things with your thumb. The only way to do that is through practice.

The pendulum method for pitching is best when using fairly heavy lures and where most of the targets are close in. Most pitching is done with a jig and pork frog or perhaps a jig and grub combination. The pendulum method works best with a leadhead jig weighing $\frac{3}{8}$ ounce and up.

Like the pendulum cast, the two-handed pitch technique permits you to keep a lure down so that it can be made under an overhanging obstruction. The main advantage is greater distance without sacrificing accuracy or soft presentation.

To make a two-handed pitch cast, put the reel into freespool and let out enough line that the practice weight drops down even with your reel. Hold the practice weight in your left hand, and pull on the line to bring your rod tip down until it has a slight bend. Bring the rod up as you let go of the weight, and take your thumb off the reel spool at the same time. If you do it right, the lure will speed away to its target with a low trajectory.

Make sure you don't overload the rod on the two-handed pitch. If you pull the tip of your rod down hard to get more distance, the reel will start with a quick jerk that even an experienced thumb can't control; you don't have to pull hard on the line to bring the rod tip down. It is essential that your pitching rod have a fast enough tip to send the lure to its target with just one smooth movement. Practice lifting your rod arm at the exact instant you release the casting weight. This is the key to good pitching. If your timing is just right, the practice weight or lure will shoot out easily and give you adequate distance.

Some may question the wisdom of holding a lure with a sharp hook in the left hand to execute this two-handed pitch cast. It's not a problem if you handle the lure carefully. Practically all of the lures used for pitching while bass fishing have some kind

P

of weedguard or have the hook buried inside them. With reasonable care you can hold them without hooking yourself. Of course, when practicing, you'll be using a dummy plug that doesn't have hooks.

Timing and coordination are critical in mastering both of these pitching casts. Practice is the way to develop your timing and coordination. Don't be frustrated if you fail to get things together in the first 10 minutes of practice, since few do. But stick with it, and you'll become a better angler.

Make certain that you become adept at keeping the lure down close to the surface of the water. This is accomplished by having the proper timing when you release the lure with your left hand. If you release the lure too late, it will go right up. If this happens, learn to let go of it sooner. If you're right-handed, hold the lure in your left hand and bring it back so that your hand is alongside and slightly to the rear of your left leg. Try releasing the lure (or practice weight) when your hand is about even with your left leg. If you do it right, this should bring the lure down where you want it.

See: Casting.

PITHING
A method of killing fish.
See: Fish Preparation—Care.

PLAICE, AMERICAN   *Hippoglossoides platessoides.*
Other names—dab, long rough dab, plaice, Canadian plaice; Dutch: *lange schar;* French: *balaide de l'Atlantique;* Icelandic: *skrápflura;* Norwegian: *gapeflyndre;* Spanish: *platija americana;* Swedish: *glipskädda, ler flundra.*

The American plaice is a large-mouthed, right-eyed member of the Pleuronectidae family of flatfish *(see)* that is currently an insignificant catch by anglers, but has been an important component of commercial fishing, mainly caught by otter trawl. The commercial catch of American plaice has seriously declined over recent decades, and this species is greatly overexploited. Like other flatfish, it undergoes a unique maturation from egg to adult in which the one eye migrates to the opposite side of the head.

Identification.   The mouth of the American plaice is large and reaches below the rear edge of the eye. The lateral line is nearly straight, but the front part is slightly higher. The color on the eyed side is uniformly reddish to grayish brown, the edge of the dorsal and anal fins is whitish, and the blind side is white. It has a rounded rather than a forked tail, which helps distinguish it from the immature Atlantic halibut.

Size.   The American plaice can grow to 32 inches and 14 pounds. Growth is rather slow; three-year-old fish are normally between 9 and 11 inches long and weigh less than one-third of a pound. After age 4, females grow faster than males.

Distribution.   This species occurs along the northwest Atlantic continental shelf, from southern Labrador and western Greenland to Rhode Island, in relatively deep waters. It is now less abundant off Georges Bank, and greater commercial landings occur in the Gulf of Maine. In the eastern Atlantic, it occurs off eastern Greenland and from the English Channel to the coast of Murmansk.

Habitat.   American plaice are commonly found between 300 and 600 feet over a soft bottom.

Spawning behavior.   Sexual maturity begins between ages 2 and 3, but most individuals do not reach maturity until age 4. Spawning occurs in spring, generally from March through May.

Food.   Invertebrates and small fish make up the plaice's diet.

See: Drift Fishing; Inshore Fishing; Plaice, European.

PLAICE, EUROPEAN   *Pleuronectes platessa.*
Other names—plaice, fluke, hen fish; Dutch: *schol;* French: *carrelet, plie, plie d'Europe;* Icelandic: *scholle;* Italian: *passera, solla;* Norwegian: *gull-flyndre, rödspette;* Spanish: *solla europa;* Swedish: *rödspätta, schol.*

The European plaice is a right-eyed member of the Pleuronectidae family of flatfish *(see),* which has long been prominent in commercial and recreational fishing in the eastern Atlantic but has seriously declined over recent decades. Mainly caught by commercial trawlers, it has been an important market fish, and the most important flatfish in Europe. Like other flatfish, it undergoes a unique maturation from egg to adult in which one eye migrates to the opposite side of the head.

Identification.   The lateral line is nearly straight, curving only near the pectoral fin. The color on the eyed side is uniformly reddish to grayish brown, with red spots on the body, and on the dorsal, anal, and caudal fins. The edge of the dorsal and anal fins is whitish, and the blind side is white. It is distinguished from the similar-appearing and larger-growing American plaice by its red spotting.

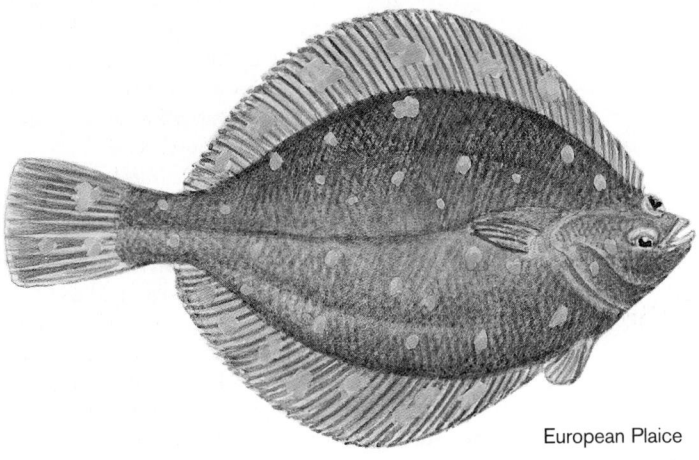

European Plaice

Size. The European plaice can grow to 30 inches and 10 pounds, although fish weighing 15 pounds have been reported.

Distribution. This species occurs in the northeast Atlantic, from Greenland and Norway south to Morocco; in Spain and France in the Mediterranean; and in the White Sea.

Habitat. European plaice range from tidal shallows out to depths of 650 feet over mixed bottoms. They move into shallower water in summer and into deeper water in winter. Small plaice are occasionally observed along beaches; older individuals seek deeper environs. Their preferred water temperature is between 2° and 15°C.

Food. Their primary diet is mollusks, but plaice also consume worms.

Spawning behavior. Sexual maturity occurs between ages 2 and 3, but most individuals do not reach maturity until age 4. Spawning occurs in offshore environs from February through May.

Angling.   *See: Drift Fishing; Inshore Fishing.*

PLANER BOARDS

Planer boards are devices that aid flatlining substantially and increase the versatility of trolling presentations. Planer boards can be used for all kinds of fish but are primarily used in freshwater for trout and salmon. Planer boards increase presentation capabilities by allowing lures to pass near fish that may be spooked by your boat or that are in areas where you can't, or don't want to, take your boat.

There are two versions of planer boards, sideplaners and in-line planers. A sideplaner is a plastic or wooden surface swimming board that evolved on the Great Lakes for trout and salmon trolling and works something like a downrigger on the surface. A nonfishing line or cable tethers the board to the boat and allows it to run at varied distances off to the side (there are port and starboard models that sport two or three runners). One or more fishing lines, using almost any type of tackle, attaches to the planer or tow line via release *(see)* clips; you fight a fish unencumbered when it strikes your lure and the release frees the fishing line.

There are commercially made sideplaner boards and retrieval devices, but many people make their own. Most sideplaners are about 30 inches long with double runners, but some homemade models are longer, up to 4 feet in length for some charter boat captains who deal with rough water.

An in-line planer is smaller but similar to a sideplaner. As the name suggests, an in-line planer attaches directly to your fishing line; a lure is set out the desired distance; then the fishing line is run through a snap at the rear of the board and also into a release clip at the towing point. The in-line planer is set out at whatever distance off the side of the boat you desire. When a fish strikes, the line pulls out of the release and the board slides down the line. The board can be rigged to stop ahead of the hooked fish by using a barrel swivel, bead, and leader. It can also be rigged to fall completely away from the fishing line, but then it will have to be retrieved from the water; few anglers use it this way. Because of the heavy towing strains, a stout rod and fairly strong line are necessary for in-line planer fishing.

Several types of in-line planers are commercially made. In-line planers should have a large snap at the back—on some the snap is positioned on the side at the rear, which may cause the planer to run awry. Many anglers change the connecting release on their in-line planers and wrap (or tape) their favorite release into place. If a release fails to let the line go when a fish strikes, you'll have to reel the planer up to your rod tip and then unfasten it, which is not a good move when you're trying to keep pressure on a fish. If it doesn't release, you can tell that a fish is on because the board will fail to pull out to the side, and the tow will be more toward the stern.

How far you set out the boards depends on how close to shore you want to be, how far apart you want to spread your lures, how much room you have to fish, and how much boat traffic there is; 80 to 100 feet out is standard when boat traffic is moderate. They can be run out as much as 200 feet if you have a high anchor point in your boat for the tow line. Some anglers use a 6- to 8-foot pole. In-line boards are run 30 to 100 feet out.

You can run a lure behind a planer board any length that seems feasible. Because lures are trolled well to the side of the boat behind a relatively unobtrusive planer, they often don't have to be run as far back as when a flatline alone is used. You still need a lot of line on your reel, though, because the fishing line extends first to the release clip on the planer board, then to the lure.

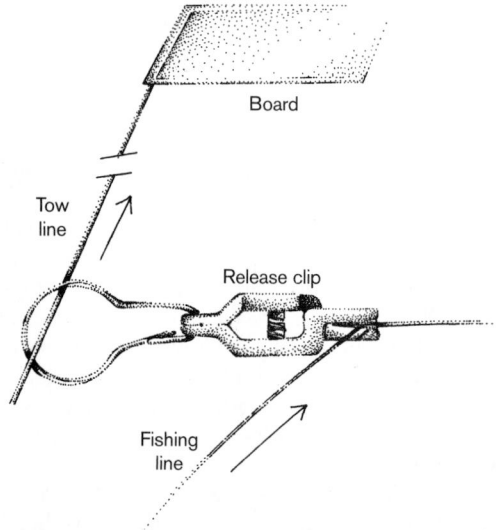

A release clip, which is attached to both the tow line and fishing line, is critical to using a planer board; fishing line can be placed deeper within the clip to increase tension.

Lines fished off boards don't have to be run shallow, and they needn't be fished with only shallow running plugs or spoons. You can use whatever lures are appropriate for the conditions; moreover, by adjusting the tension of the line release, you can troll a hard pulling, deep diving plug or a line with weights on it. The keys to success are knowing how deep those lures run at the length of line you have them set behind the planer board tow line, and having the tension on the release set properly. The tension must be tight enough to withstand the force of the lure or the weight being trolled, but not so tight that it is hard to pull out on a strike or free from the boat.

There are a number of releases suitable for sideplaner-board trolling, and they work much the same as downrigger releases, except that their position on the tow line is not fixed—it is determined by the length of fishing line let off the reel. Many anglers use spring tension, rubber-pad releases with large clips that fasten to the tow line easily and run down it smoothly.

One of the advantages of sideplaner-board fishing is that if you have multiple lines on one side of the boat and the outermost release pops, you can slide the inner lines out, then put the released line back out as the inside line. This is all accomplished without having to pull in fishing lines or the board. If you want to replace one lure without bringing the board and other lures in, you can pick up your fishing rod, reel up the stack, pop the fishing line out of the release, reel in the lure to be changed, reposition the other lines and releases on the tow rope, and set the new lure out in the inside position.

There are a few drawbacks to using sideplaners, though. They require a little more equipment and cash outlay than flatlining (though some trollers make their own sideplaners); it takes some practice to get used to them and to drive the boat properly; it can be tough to work everything if you're alone; and sometimes they pose logistical problems in heavy traffic. Planer-board fishing is most efficient with two or three people, all of whom are capable of setting lines and maneuvering the boat effectively as a team.

Retrievers.   You must have a method of tethering sideplaners to your boat and retrieving them. Several companies make sideplaner retrievers with one or two reels mounted on a pole, and some people fashion their own, spooling it with 150- to 200-pound-test line and attaching it to a pole with a swiveling pulley at the top. Most sideplaner tow line is made of braided, low-stretch, highly visible green Dacron.

Ideally, the sideplaner retriever should be mounted as far forward in the boat as possible to get a high line angle to the board and to keep the boards relatively abreast, instead of behind, the boat. On small boats, mount the poles as close to the bow as you can. On large boats, such as those with cuddy cabins that don't allow you to get up to

Trolling tools include a planer-board retriever, large planer boards, and small in-line planers.

the bow quickly, it's best to mount sideplaner retrievers on the gunwales amidships, or flush to the cabin wall. Some big-boat trollers mount a retrieval pole on the bow, despite the difficulty of getting to it. They have plenty of releases, so they seldom have to pull in the boards, and they use a loose tether (wrap a line around a cleat, connect a snap to the line, and snap it onto the tow line) to reach the tow line to clip a new release and line onto it.

Fishing with planer boards.   Sideplaners exert a lot of pull. They act much like a rudder, especially on small, lightweight boats—the pull of the board turns the boat toward the board. When using one double-runner board in a small boat, you'll constantly fight the steering to compensate for the drag. If you want to fish off only one board (when you're alone or want to get lures close to only one side, near shore, for example), it may be necessary to put a board out on the other side of the boat, without a fishing line, in order to offset the drag of the board being fished. With big boats, the effect of using one sideplaner isn't much of a problem. Some planers, incidentally, are available as triple-runner models; that is, three boards spaced about 10 or 12 inches apart but bolted together as one unit. Triple runners exert much more pull and are principally for use in rough water.

There will be times when you won't want to run either sideplaners or in-line planer boards because of the water conditions. In extremely rough water with high waves, boards do a lot of bouncing, which can knock the line out of the release if the tension isn't set tight enough, or they can flip over, which could cause a big problem by tangling lines and sending the board off in the opposite direction. In rough water, the releases also may foul by flopping over behind the tow line; when that happens, you can't pop the line out of the release properly, especially if light line is being used.

Under windy conditions, boards don't run as far off to the side of the boat as you might like; sideplaner releases may be hard to run down the tow line. When this happens, jiggle the fishing line or the tow line to bounce the release along, or turn the boat so that the angle of pull of the trailing line forces the release down to the proper spot. Strong wind also causes boat maneuvering problems when a good-sized fish is hooked.

If you catch a fish while heading downwind, you can, if you like, leave the motor in neutral and play the fish in. When heading upwind, however, you cannot stop the boat because of the possibility of tangling lines, tow ropes, and the like if the boat drifts backward. If the fish is really big or fights particularly well, or if you're using very light line, you should play it while a companion retrieves the other lines and the boards and maneuvers the boat for landing. If it's a small fish, you may be able to keep the boat headed into the wind, with the other tackle out, moving slowly with several stop-and-go actions executed by a partner. If you're alone, you must manage as best you can. Because they are attached to the fishing line, in-line planers don't pose this problem.

When using either type of board, a host of fishing combinations is possible. In nearshore areas, you can run two or three strategically spaced lines

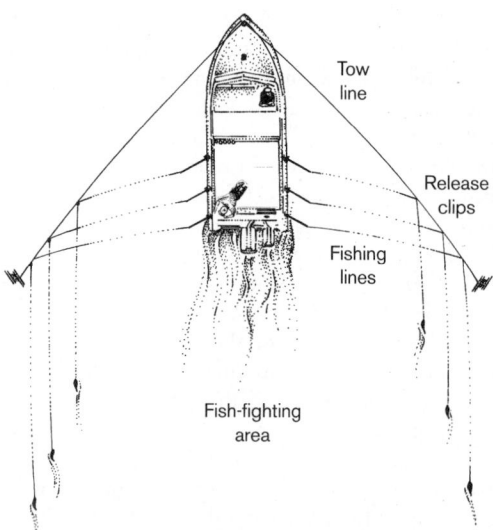

You may not fish this many lines, but this is how they would be arranged with sideplaners. Note that the setback distance is staggered on both sides. When a fish takes any lure, it is played in the middle ground behind the boat, and the other lines are moved outward along the tow line.

off the shoreward sideplaner. On the open water side of the boat, you have the option of running a surface or diving lure on a long flatline, running a lure deep via a downrigger, or running one or more lures off another sideplaner. Moreover, the range of water that can be covered is vastly increased. If you run two sideplaners, each 60 feet off the sides of the boat, and have two anglers in the boat, you could run four lines over a 40-yard span of water. If the bottom drops off sharply near shore, as it does in many inland lakes, you could work water a few feet deep on the nearshore side of the boat and over 40-foot depths on the opposite side, presenting lures to fish that would not ordinarily see them—and they won't be frightened by the passage of your boat.

When you're using sideplaners and fishing several shallow lines, you can experiment with their distance from the boat and with the distance the lures are set behind the tow line. Sometimes, when running two or three similar lures off one sideplaner, you may run them at approximately the same distance behind the tow rope to imitate a small school of baitfish. Be careful not to put short lines on the outside. If a fish strikes a short outside line, there's a chance it would cross over one or more of the longer inside lines after the hookup. Take this into account when setting lines out, and try to arrange them so that a fish caught on the outside line will drop back, clear of the inside lines, and can be played up the unfished center alley. Perhaps it's coincidence, but a high percentage of fish fall to the outside line.

Trolling strategies and boat maneuvering techniques when using boards are similar to those used for flatlining. When you turn, however, the outside board increases its speed and the inside one slows (or stalls). But because the fishing lines are well separated, there is less chance of tangling when you turn, particularly if all the lines are nearly the same distance behind the boat, or if the inside lines are not as far back as the outside lines. Be careful though not to turn so sharply that the inside board stops dead in the water and the lures attached to it don't move; if you're in shallow water and using a sinking plug or a spoon, the motionless lure can settle to the bottom and hang up. The release on the tow line can also get tangled when the board picks up speed. Furthermore, many fish strike a lure on a turn. If your lure is floating upward or fluttering down and a fish strikes it, there will be no tension on either the fishing line or tow rope line; the release cannot be snapped or the hook set, and you could potentially lose a fish. If you must make a sharp turn, make sure you keep the inside board moving slightly, which keeps tension on the line.

Boat maneuvering in heavy traffic when boards are being fished is a little more complicated than usual. That's why many big-boat trollers run flatlines off outriggers, and small-boaters shorten the distance they run their boards away from the boat. If your sideplaner hasn't yet collided with someone

Not all fish swim horizontally. A catfish indigenous to the Nile and other African rivers swims in the vertical posture. Many mid-water deep-sea fish swim or rest vertically.

else's sideplaner, you've missed one of trolling's most embarrassing, aggravating, and mayhem-causing experiences. If a collision seems imminent, the worst thing you can do is turn the boat away because that causes the outside planer to speed up and arc outward, making a collision all the more probable. You might turn inward, but then you'll have to sit still until the other boat passes. The best tactic is to reel the board in toward your boat as quickly as you can.

Those who find sideplaner boards too much trouble simply run flatlines. But when it is necessary to get your lures away from the boat, when you want to cover a wide spread of water with each passage of your boat, or when you troll some hard-to-reach places, boards will put your trolling lures over a lot of fish that you couldn't reach otherwise.
See: Flatlining.

PLANER, DIVING

A diving planer is a trolling accessory that attaches to fishing line a few feet ahead of a lure and dives deeply. No weights are used with this device; the design of the planer and the forward motion of the boat make it dive. When a fish strikes, the back-pulling tension trips a release that causes the diver to flatten and offer minimal water resistance as the fish is played. Diving planers are an alternative to using downriggers, wire or lead-core lines, or weighted lines to troll deep.

There are two versions: nondirectional, which only run straight down, and directional, which can be run straight down as well as down and off to the left or the right of a straight path. Directional divers are more versatile and more popular.

Diving planers offer several benefits in addition to taking lures deep. Their size, color, and swimming motion make them attractive to trout and salmon. They offer an action that can't be attained by lures set behind downriggers: Because the lures are set a short distance behind the boat, they are less responsive than divers to boat movement (turns and wave effects, for example).

Because directional divers can take lures down and to the side of a boat, many anglers use them in conjunction with downrigger-set lines. Some fish in the path of the boat are spooked by downrigger weights and move down or away from them. Directional diving planers direct lures off to the side of other presentations. They help to cover more deep territory and, as a result, offer further presentation opportunities to shores, piers, and the like.

To determine the depth that a diver will run, consult the chart supplied by the manufacturer. Because divers run deep, you cannot estimate the amount of line let out; you must use the pull or pass method of line length determination *(see: flatlining)*. You have to let out a certain length of line to get to a specific depth. This varies with different diving planers and with the diameter of line being used.

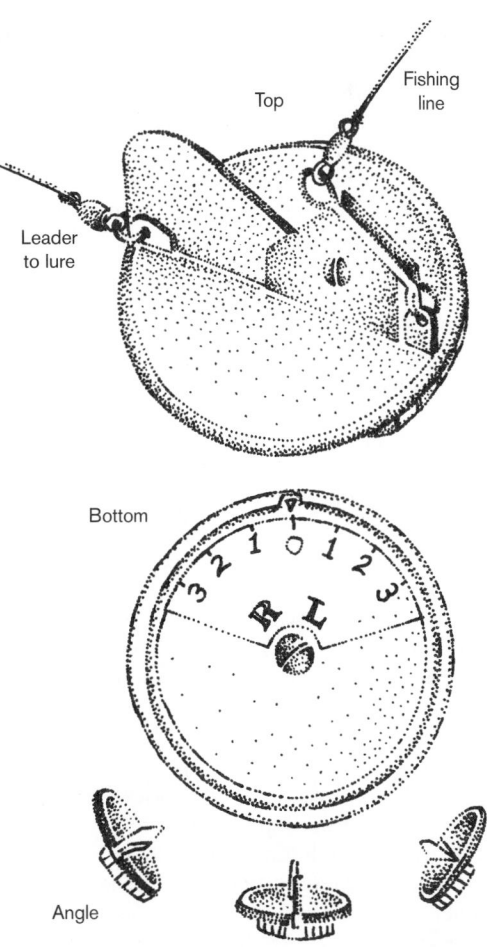

This representation of a directional diving planer shows how the line is attached to the device via a release pin, and how the keel on the bottom can be moved from right to left to affect swimming angle; the greater the adjustment, the more the planer swims to either side.

Many diving planers have an adjustable tension screw release, and you need to set this just right for the strength of line you're using and the depth you'll fish. Diving planers pull awfully hard. If you want to retrieve one and the release won't trip (or, worse, if a small fish is on and the release won't trip), it's hard work bringing it in. There are a few planers that can be reset without retrieving the planer, although you still need to watch line length in order to get it to the desired depth.

A variety of lures can be fished successfully behind a diving planer. Spoons and cut plugs are especially favored because these devices are used primarily for trout and salmon trolling. Minnow plugs of various sizes also get the nod, as do dodger-fly or dodger-squid combinations. Diving plugs aren't usually worked unless they are very shallow-runners and can withstand sometimes erratic planer action. It's best to use a short setback because of the difficulty of netting a fish that is 5 or so feet behind a diving planer; 3 to 5 feet is a common setback length. Leader strength should be as strong or stronger than the main fishing line, preferably 17 to

20 pounds if big fish are likely to be encountered, and perhaps 25 to 30 if a dodger is trolled.

The main fishing line should be strong, at least 14 pounds; most anglers use 20. High-tech braided lines can be very effective, but beware of pulling the hooks out of fish since these lines have no stretch and many strikes with diving planers are very sharp. Also, a 20-pound braided line with the same diameter as 8-pound monofilament slices through the water so easily you have to completely reevaluate diving depth attainment.

Long, stout rods are necessary for diving planer use. On big boats, beefy 9- to 10-footers are used, and on smaller ones, beefy 7- or 8-footers are worked. Because diving planers pull so hard, a good rod holder is necessary, preferably an adjustable one that can take a lot of handle torque and that is easy to get the rod out of. It's better to place diving planer rods on the gunwale, several feet ahead of the transom, and at a low angle.

One drawback to diving planer use is occasional uncertainty about the depth the planer (hence your lure) is running. Therefore, it's important to judge accurately how much line you've let out, especially if you catch fish and want to reset the rig at the same level.

Another criticism is that planers inhibit the fight of some fish. But the extent to which this is true depends on the fish. Large fish pull very hard, and some, including cohos and steelhead, jump. When fighting a fish, you'll know that the planer, even though it has tripped, is there; the fight is not quite as satisfactory as on an unencumbered line. A way to get around this is to use a diving planer like a downrigger—that is, attach a release clip to the diving planer, attach a handline or separate rod to the diving planer, and attach the fishing rod and line to the release clip. (Just about no one does this, but it is a way to fight a fish on a free line.)

In any event, diving planers can account for an extra fish or two during the course of a day's trolling when used as an adjunct to downrigger fishing. They merit consideration to round out your trolling repertoire, or for use in places where other systems are unavailable.
See: Trolling.

PLANER, IN-LINE
See: Planer Boards.

PLANING HULL
One of two broad categories of boat hulls that are noted for speed and quick steering response; speed is largely a function of engine power, but is enhanced by planing hulls because most of the hull, usually in some form of V shape, is raised out of the water while running.
See: Boat.

PLANKTON
Passively floating or weakly swimming organisms in a body of water. Planktonic organisms may drift and float freely, range widely in size, and include the larval stages of many fishes. Some are invisible without magnification and others are visible to the unaided eye.

PLASTIC WORM
A highly popular soft plastic lure that primarily imitates a worm, but may also imitate a snake, leech, or salamander.
See: Soft Worm.

PLATFORM
A raised section on a small boat used for increasing visibility when shallow-water fishing. A transom platform is most common, and some boats are equipped with smaller bow casting platforms; a few shallow-water guide boats possess a tall midship console platform that is more like a mini tower.

Transom platforms are a signature characteristic of flats boats, and are used for poling as well as sighting and/or fishing in inshore waters. They are raised several feet high, enough to cover an outboard motor when fully tilted, are usually 36 to 48 inches wide and 20 to 30 inches deep, and are bolted to the deck and transom. This platform is also useful for sitting and casting, and can be used in conjunction with a remote-controlled transom-mount electric motor. Some flats boats feature a bow casting platform that elevates the angler a shorter distance than the transom platform, and which can also double as a seat while playing a fish. It may be bolted to the deck or removable, like a wide stool.
See: Flats Boat; Tower.

PLAYING FISH
Once a fish has been attracted to your lure, bait, or fly, and before you can either release it or toss it on ice, you have to hook it, play it, and land it. For many species of gamefish, these activities are significant enough to warrant thorough separate discussions (see: hooksetting; landing fish).

When it comes to playing a fish, which is also commonly referred to as fighting it, the degree of work that is involved obviously varies from a second or two for the smallest species jerked out of shallow water, to many hours of muscle-aching, perspiration-inducing, and tackle-straining exertion for offshore leviathans. There is not much out of the ordinary involved in the playing of small or less powerful species, but those that strain fishing equipment—and that includes small but very strong fish caught on light tackle—require more than just holding the rod and winding the reel handle to catch.

P

This is an elementary part of angling, one taken for granted by many anglers in part because they rarely (especially in freshwater) experience difficult fish-playing situations and are unfortunately ill-prepared to handle them when such situations do occur. That partially explains why many large fish are lost after being hooked. Guides and charter boat mates and captains constantly have to teach their clients how to deal with large and strong fish.

There are certain techniques for manipulating the rod that help land fish without adversely affecting the tackle (such as causing twist in the line). These techniques help you to apply maximum pressure to a fish throughout the entire period of playing, keep the fish away from obstacles that might cut the line or tear out the hook, and land the fish as quickly as possible.

Why would you want to apply maximum pressure constantly and land a fish quickly? For a number of very important reasons other than the obvious one of simply wanting to catch the fish. First, there is no glory in having a hooked fish cut or break the line on obstacles and then be left swimming freely with a hook or hooks in its mouth. For some species of fish and in some circumstances, it is critical immediately after hooking them, or later during the fight, to use pressure and angle position to keep the fish away from any objects—reef, piling, vegetation, the bottom of the boat, etc.

In addition, a prolonged period of fish playing may result in losing the fish because the hook has worn a large hole in its mouth and then pulled out. Furthermore, in some saltwater environs, long battles attract large predators, primarily sharks, that will attack and kill a hooked fish. This may happen even during shorter fights, but it is more likely the longer the fight plays out.

Also, and sometimes most important, prolonged fish playing can exhaust a fish to the point that it cannot recover its strength and be released alive and well, whether you are releasing it by law or by choice. Lactic acid buildup *(see: catch-and-release)* can be fatal to fish, and this is increased during a long fight.

It should be noted that in some instances landing fish as quickly as possible is not advantageous to releasing the fish. This occurs for some very deep and generally bottom-dwelling fish in both freshwater and saltwater, which need a slower playing time so that they depressurize.

Methods. Fish-playing activities generally take place in a short period of time, and the action is often fast. Your reactions must be swift and instinctive, and your tackle, particularly line and reel drag, must be capable and of good quality. Many fish are

1

2

3

4

In this sequence of a guide and angler landing a 9-pound bass in a Mexican lake, note how the angler strains to direct the active fish toward the netter and into the outstretched net; he keeps a tight line even as the fish nearly escapes while the guide is trying to get both hands on the handle.

P

lost as a result of the way in which the angler plays the fish, usually by allowing the fish to do things that it could be prevented from doing. Within the capabilities of your tackle, take the fight to the fish; don't sit back and be casual. Confidence in playing fish well and hard is derived from experience and also from knowing what your tackle can do.

Line breakage is often the reason for losing large fish, and much of this boils down to inferior-quality line, line that is damaged, or bad knots (see: line). Another reason for losing fish is an improper reel drag setting. When the drag is set too tightly, line won't freely come off the spool under the surges of a strong fish (see: drag). Granted, the drag is meant to put pressure on a fish that is streaming off, making it exert itself rather than swimming without impedance; but when the drag is too tight, it's a problem because tension increases as the diameter of the spool decreases and as the amount of line in the water increases.

Playing a fish begins with hooking it well and staying with its antics from the moment that the hooks gets stuck in its mouth. The position of the rod is very important. Right from the start, the rod butt should be jammed into the stomach or mid-chest area, and the full arc and power of the rod should be utilized. You cannot play and land a fish well if your rod is held up over your head or extended out and away from your body. These are not power, or control, positions. You do have to keep the tip up, however, throughout a normal fight and constantly maintain pressure on the fish. Slack line must always be avoided.

In a boat, you generally don't need to move once a fish is on the hook; but if the fish is a very large one, you will need to move to one corner of the stern so that the captain has a clear view of the line and the action in case it's necessary to move the boat quickly. If you are wading in a lake or river and hook a good fish, you should immediately and carefully step backward until you're in ankle-deep water or on the bank, where you can move quickly up or down a river if necessary. Do not be afraid to move, but do it carefully, not in a panic. Keep an eye on obstacles in the river so that you can work the fish in advance away from any obstruction (like a fallen tree along the bank), or be prepared to move swiftly to get your line safely beyond the obstacle.

"Pumping" is a technique that is used for playing all but the smallest fish, and it is critical when fighting a large or strong fish and/or when using light line. It is employed whenever a fish is deep and often when the fish is straight away and shallow but not budging or swimming to one side or the other. To pump, keep the rod butt in the stomach, lower the rod tip and reel in line simultaneously, and then pressure the fish as you bring the rod back up. Once the rod is up, lower it and reel. Continue doing this. Some fish and some tackle require constant short pumping motions, often called short stroking; this is more common when using stand-up tackle (see)

for tuna and billfish. To best really tough bruisers, the pumping must continue unabated because on some fish, like tuna, if you stop to rest, the fish does too, and it can regain strength and prolong the battle when it rests.

Often when a fish is fairly close to you, it is still energetic. Continue to keep the rod tip high or fully taut when held to the side. This is a time to be directing the fish. If you're in a boat and the fish streaks toward it (perhaps to swim under it), you could be put at a disadvantage, particularly when using light tackle. You must reel as fast as possible to keep out slack. If the fish gets under the boat, stick the rod tip well into the water to keep the line away from objects.

You should anticipate that a fish will rush the boat and should be prepared to head it around the stern or bow (easier done in an uncluttered boat). Sometimes a companion can manipulate the boat to help swing the stern or bow away from a fish; this is a smart maneuver that can aid the playing of a large fish. If possible, go toward the bow or stern to better follow or control the fish. Walk around the whole boat if you have to (several times if necessary). Don't hang back in a tug-of-war with a large, strong fish; use finesse rather than muscle.

When a fish swims around your boat, keep the rod up (sometimes out, too) and apply pressure to force its head up and to steer it clear of the outboard or electric motor and the propellers. (Sometimes it's best to tilt motors out of the water.)

At times you need to change the angle of pull on a strong and stubborn fish, perhaps to help steer it in a particular direction or make it fight a little differently. For example, when a strong fish continues

To deal with stubborn fish, change the angle of pull. When a fish is running straight away, change the rod from an overhead to a side position (1) and continue with this method until the fish changes attitude (2). To dissuade it from streaking to the side, switch rod position and apply pressure from the opposite direction (3).

P

to bulldog straight away from you, slow it down and change its direction by applying side pressure. Bring the rod down and hold it parallel to the water while turning your body partially or entirely sideways to the fish. Fight the fish as you would if the rod were perpendicular to the water. Instead of the rod tip being high and bent, it is sideways and bent. You can pump fish while in this position. Switch sides as necessary when the fish moves far enough in any direction.

With very large fish that get near the boat but are still energetic, or with big fish that stay very deep below the boat and can't be budged, you may have to quickly move the boat a fair distance away, letting line peel off the drag. This changes the angle of pull on the fish and usually helps bring it up from the depths. This situation does not happen very much in freshwater but is more likely in saltwater.

Using a boat to play a very big fish is a standard practice in large bodies of water. Under some circumstances, it may be questionable from an ethical standpoint, though not from a practical one. Chasing a fish is sometimes necessary to prevent the reel from being de-spooled, or to avoid obstacles (lobster or crab pots, buoys, anchor lines, etc.), or to help a struggling and inexperienced angler. Many big fish in offshore waters are caught as much by the boat-handling and boat-maneuvering actions of the captain than by the angler. In some cases this includes backing down in reverse toward the fish,

Keeping the rod too high is not an effective way to control a strong fish when it is very close to the boat. To keep it clear of the boat and motors, reel down, dip the tip of the rod in the water if necessary, and steer the line clear of objects.

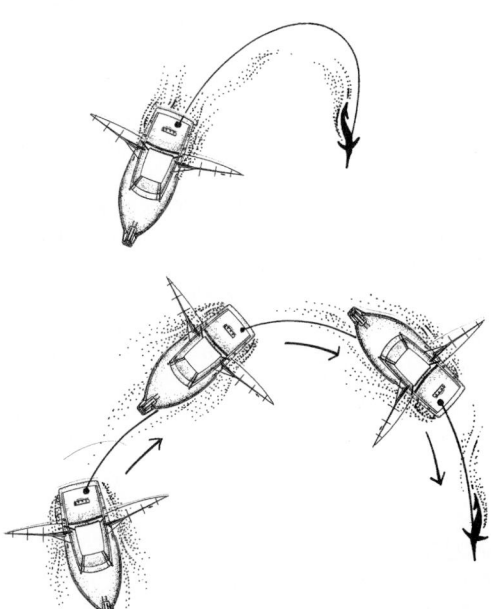

In this exaggerated view of a big-game fishing scene, hundreds of yards of line separate the angler and a turning fish, forming a belly in the line (top) that causes a great amount of drag tension, which in turn can lead to line breakage. When this belly forms, the boat needs to move in the direction of the line (bottom), not directly toward the fish, to remove the belly; this action also lets the angler quickly regain line on the reel and puts the line in a straight position with the fish.

and in others it involves circling to redirect the angle of tension or head a fish away from a certain direction.

In current, a big fish that gets downriver and through rapids where an angler is unable to follow, may return upriver if the angler releases line from the reel and allows slack line to drift below the fish. The line below the fish acts as a pulling force from downstream (instead of ahead) and may cause the fish to head upstream again. If this strategy does not work, your chances of pulling the fish to you are slim, and you'll have to figure out a way to get below it or break it off. On the other hand, if you get below a fish before it gets to the end of a pool and into the rapids, and pull from the downstream angle, it is likely to want to head away from you and upriver, which is a better scenario.

With some species of jumping fish (Atlantic salmon and tarpon, for example), and when using flycasting tackle, you need to slacken the tension when the fish jumps by bowing the rod toward it so that the jumper cannot use taut line as leverage for pulling free of the hook. Sometimes you can stop a fish from jumping by putting your rod tip in the water and keeping a tight line, which changes the angle of pull and may stop a fish from clearing the surface.

A momentary slack line also may prevent a fish from jumping, although slack is an invitation for the hook to fall out. The only good reason to prevent a fish from jumping—and jumping is one of the thrills that anglers live for—is that you know the fish is poorly hooked and you fear that a jump will cause the fish to throw the hook. Otherwise, you should enjoy the jumps, because leaping out of the water takes considerable energy and helps tire the fish.

P

Final moments. Eventually the fish is next to you and may be ready for landing. If it still has a last burst of energy, however, this will be a crucial moment. Because of the short distance between you and the fish, there will be a lot of stress on your tackle. You must act swiftly when the fish makes its last bolt for freedom.

As it surges away, don't pressure it. This is no time for a standoff. Let it go. Point the rod at the fish at the critical moment so that there is no rod pressure, just pressure from the drag on the reel. A large fish will peel line off the drag, which if set properly (and not sticking), will keep tension on the fish within the tolerance of the line's strength and provide the least amount of pressure possible. As the surge tapers, lift up the rod and work the fish.

If a companion is landing the fish for you—by netting, gaffing, hand-landing, etc.—guide the fish toward that person, and try to get its head or snout out of the water, or partially so. If you and the lander work as a team and are proactive, your chances of a successful landing are much better than if you stand like a statue and wait for your companion to snare the fish.

Do not reel the fish right up to the rod tip; stop reeling at the point where the line is equal to the length of your rod, or slightly less in the case of a long rod (offshore fishing may differ, since you need only get the wire leader to the rod tip or within reaching distance of a crew member). In some instances, it is better to walk backward (on shore or in a boat) to bring the fish within landing range rather than to reel down and heft up more; however, in some large boats, this takes you away from the action, keeping you from seeing where the fish and the terminal end of the line are and preventing you from reacting appropriately if necessary. Even when the fish is initially captured, anticipate a landing miscue (it slips out of hand, falls out of the net, etc.); be prepared for the fish to bolt away by making sure that no line has been wrapped around your rod tip and that you're in position to give it line or to point the rod at it the instant it flees. This sudden dash happens from time to time with big strong fish and can spell disaster, since the fish is making a furious last sprint for freedom. To prepare for such an emergency, with baitcasting or conventional tackle, put the reel in freespool but keep your thumb on the spool; with spinning tackle, open the reel bail but keep your index finger on the spool; and with a lever drag reel, move the preset drag lever back from the running or full drag position to a lesser drag position, and keep your thumb on the spool. If the fish gets free, exert just enough contact on the spool with your thumb or finger to prevent an overrun when the fish stops; as soon as the fish stops or slows sufficiently, re-engage the drag or gears. Don't set the hook; just keep steady pressure on the fish and pump it back to the boat, whereupon it is often much more docile.

More information about the actual landing of fish is contained in that entry (see: landing fish). **See: Hooksetting.**

The deepest lake in the world is Lake Baikal in Siberia at 5,371 feet. The deepest in the United States is Crater Lake in Oregon at 1,932 feet.

PLIERS

Pliers are nearly indispensable tools for a host of applications in fishing and boating. A wide variety of pliers is used for such common and important purposes as cutting fishing line, heavy leaders, and wire; unhooking fish; pulling on knots; pinching lead weights or sinkers; crimping connector sleeves; and tightening bolts.

For the most part, the tool needs of freshwater anglers are different from those of saltwater anglers; the former predominantly use light nylon monofilament lines, and the latter are likely to cut heavier material, crimp hard objects, and grasp and unhook large and thick hooks. Freshwater anglers generally are well served with standard needle nose pliers, for example, which are very popular for unhooking fish and used in conjunction with nail clippers for cutting line and trimming fishing knots. Pliers with side cutters are also useful, and multipurpose utility pliers—those with knife blades, screwdriver blades, awl, and so on—are also favored by many people for general use, although they are generally not as well suited for heavy-duty uses, especially in saltwater applications, as specialty pliers.

From a fishing perspective, the major concerns with pliers are durability, ability to stay sharp, performance at cutting fishing line and wire, and ability to crimp objects such as sleeves and sinkers. Pliers with side-cutting blades are generally preferred for wire and most monofilaments except the lighter strengths; models with spring-loaded jaws, which keep them open when at rest, are favored by many users. Some pliers have replaceable cutting blades so that the worn-out cutting surface on an otherwise serviceable tool can be replaced. Anglers who regularly make up wire or nylon monofilament leaders and fishing rigs must have a top-quality pair of crimping pliers to do the proper job because crimping the retaining sleeves, not simply crushing them, is essential.

Most pliers come with sheaths that are worn on a belt so they are immediately handy; sheaths should keep pliers snug but be open for fast access. Taking care of pliers by cleaning them, rinsing with freshwater, and coating with a corrosion-inhibiting lubricant, is important to proper performance. **See: Leader.**

PLUG

A plug is a relatively buoyant wooden or molded hard plastic lure with built-in swimming action, although due to diverse materials with different properties and a plethora of lure designs, there are many plugs that do not exactly fit this umbrella-like description. Most plugs float, but some sink and others combine floating and sinking characteristics. Most imitate or suggest some type of fish, although they may also imitate or suggest many other types of aquatic food. Though the vast majority are constructed from wood or hard plastic, many are

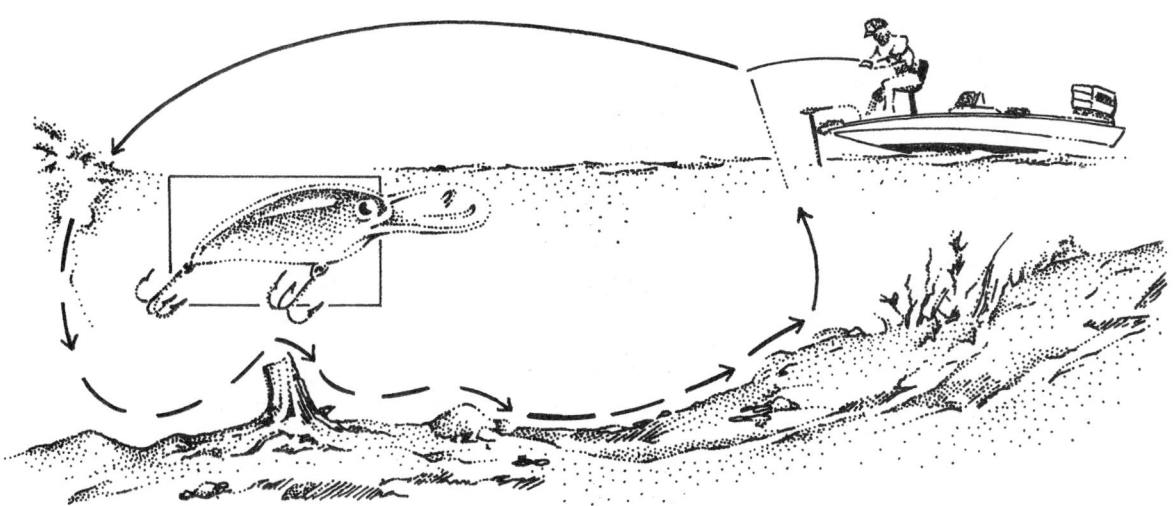

Although most plugs, especially diving versions, are fished along the shoreline, it can be worthwhile to cast deeper running versions (inset) away from shore. A bottom-scouring stop-and-go retrieve is often best.

boat, the lure may not be reaching all of the bottom that it should and therefore not getting to the depth of water where the fish are holding. Try casting parallel instead of perpendicular to the shore and make sure that your plug is working the right depths.

Bottom scratching is critical in most fishing situations when casting with plugs. Try to keep your plug rooting along the bottom, over objects, and along impediments. This is no problem with the right floating/diving crankbait. For sinkers, let it settle to the bottom (or count it down to a particular level) and make your retrieve at a rate slow enough to keep the plug on or as close to the bottom as possible.

Many floating/diving plugs are exceedingly buoyant, a feature that adds a different dimension to their retrieval than to other lures. If you stop the retrieve, such plugs bob toward the surface like a cork. You can take advantage of this feature. A pull/pause action is easily accomplished by retrieving in the standard fashion and stopping momentarily, then repeating the procedure. In its most exaggerated form, this can be extended to stopping the retrieve long enough for the lure to float to the surface, and then resuming the retrieve. When fishing for bass, try making the lure hesitate by objects that might hold gamefish. This technique can be used repeatedly throughout the entire retrieve and might be the tactic to stir up otherwise unexcited fish.

The buoyancy of plugs varies from one product to another. Obviously, sinking models sink and floaters rise. How fast they rise or fall depends on their density in relation to the density of the water. Some plugs that rise quickly are not as beneficial to anglers as those that rise more slowly. At times, fish strike a plug only when a retrieve that produces a steady swimming action is interrupted momentarily, which lifts the lure up slightly.

A few plugs (usually smaller sizes) have little buoyancy or are neutral in buoyancy. These lures remain stationary in the water when stopped. Suspension has a lot of validity in fishing plugs, especially smaller crankbaits, which essentially represent small baitfish. Baitfish rarely rise or sink to a significant extent in their natural environment. When they stop, they stay at the same level, using their fins as stabilizers and relying on their internal organs to maintain their level. Making a lure stop and suspend at its running level has the most usefulness when fishing over some type of cover. A good example would be when working a crankbait over a submerged grassbed, which likely holds bass buried in the holes in the vegetation. These bass might hit a crankbait swimming briskly by. They probably won't be induced to strike a lure that is stopped but floats quickly back up to the surface. But a lure that is stopped and that hovers over the grass could be the most attractive offering of all. The same can be true when fishing over treetops or dropoffs. You can make plugs suspend or rise slowly by adding adhesive lead strips or dots to them.

Certain places are particularly well worked with plugs. In freshwater this includes rock walls and roadways, underwater islands, and other irregular features that the lures can reach. Sunken or exposed bridge abutments are worth working and so is flooded timber; in all cases fish to, from, over, and around these objects, and don't be concerned about bumping the lures against them.

The best way to fish a particular object with a plug is to cast beyond it so that when you retrieve, the lure will be able to get down to its running depth before it reaches the object. This is only possible, of course, when there is enough area behind the object to permit this. When casting to a long fallen log, for instance, cast beyond the target but position yourself to be able to retrieve your plug down the length of the log as closely as possible.

It is possible to work plugs around heavy cover, a tactic that can be successful if you can keep from getting hung up or enmeshed in weeds. Six or more

P

wiggling, vibrating, exposed hook points do not make much of a weedless bait; however, for fallen trees, heavy weed growth, thick lily pads, etc., a specifically weedless lure can be used with more effect and less chance of being alarming. Occasionally a plug that gets hung up can be freed by giving slack to the line, allowing the lure to float free. Plugs will work well for the shore-based angler, too, if nearshore weed growth is not too great.

One critically important aspect of plug fishing that is overlooked by many anglers, particularly beginners, is the diving ability of the lure. If bass, for example, are holding at 12 feet on a rocky bank and you're using a plug that you think dives that deep but in reality only reaches 8 feet, you can cast till your arms fall off and be unsuccessful. You must know how deep any diving plug runs to be effective with it. Diving abilities depend on the lure, the size of your line, and the speed of retrieve. Use the information supplied by the manufacturer with its product as a guideline, but don't rely on it. Find out for yourself how deep your lures run.

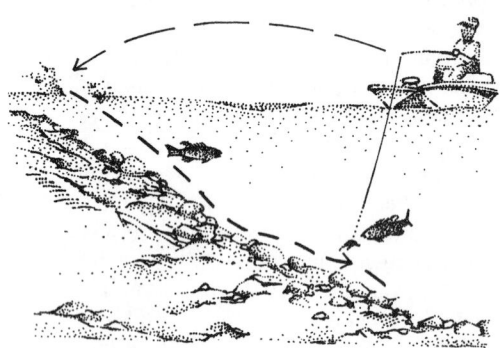

To fish a crankbait deep, you have to use the right plug, make a fairly long cast, keep your rod tip down, and reel at a moderate, steady pace.

When retrieving, it is not necessary to crank the handles as fast as possible to achieve maximum depth. In fact, some lures lose depth when worked too fast. Crank the lure fast for a moment to get the plug down, then effect a moderate pace of retrieve; this keeps the lure as deep as it will go depending on your line. High-diameter lines offer more resistance and inhibit lure diving. The thinner the line, the deeper a diving plug will go. If you are flinging long casts, this makes a difference. If you are trolling, with relatively long lines out, this is especially significant. Also, remember that current, if it is present, affects diving ability. Lures retrieved with the current, or sideways to it, do not run as deep as those worked into it.

Determining the diving depth of a plug can be simple if you fish it over known bottom terrain or around objects of a known depth. For example, find a flat that is 7 feet deep. Try a medium- or deep-diving plug; if it touches bottom you know it will go that deep. Move out a little deeper until you lose contact with the bottom to determine running depth at its maximum. If you're not hitting bottom, go shallower until you make contact.

There are, incidentally, lipless plugs that are not used as divers so much as swimming plugs. Many of these sink; some float. They are primarily used in bass fishing (sometimes for northern pike and redfish) and are excellent for catching schooling fish, for casting over submerged vegetation, and even for deep running using a count-down method to get sinking models near the bottom. In cooler water, these are often fished in a stop-and-go manner, retrieving a few feet and then pausing momentarily before retrieving again.

When fishing any kind of plug, it is usually a benefit to keep the rod tip down. This not only assists in hook setting and reacting to a strike but also allows the lure to run deeper. If the rod tip is close to the water, you'll gain an extra foot or two of depth over someone in the same boat with the same lure whose rod is angled toward the sky. Those extra few feet could make the difference in getting down where the fish are holding, which is especially relevant in dingy water. To attain the most depth possible when casting, you can kneel or sit down in the boat and lean over and stick the rod tip into the water. The longer your rod is and the farther you stick the tip into the water, the deeper the lure will go. It makes no sense to do this, however, if you can achieve the same thing by using a similar plug that dives deeper. On the other hand, you may find a situation where one particular size and color of plug is working and you have just one of these; then you may need to do whatever you can to get the lure down to the proper level.

Another key pointer for successful plug usage is how to present your lure and position your boat when working the shoreline or a weedline. The best way to cast to such areas is by working parallel, rather than perpendicular, to it. When two anglers are in the boat, it is a good tactic for both of them to fish from the front (as when casting from a bass boat), with each one's cast overlapping the other as the boat is maneuvered close and parallel to the area.

The vibration and noise of some plugs is another aspect worth considering. The best plugs have an enticing side-to-side action that does more than look good. It produces vibrations that are detectable to fish and that may signal not only the presence of potential forage, but a wounded, erratically swimming prey. Fish like bass strike some plugs they cannot see, such as in murky water or at night, because they've been able to detect them due to the water they displaced and the vibrations produced. The better the lure, the better its action and vibration qualities.

Some plugs also possess rattle chambers within their bodies. These lures feature one or more BB-like spheres, which are free to move back and forth in the chamber, creating a rattling sound. These can be especially effective near a riprap bank or rocky cliff shore.

P

Of course, the food eaten by predatory fish doesn't rattle; however, fish do produce vibrations, and some prey, such as crayfish, may very well produce audible noise as they crawl over rocks. Most important is that the rattle can draw the attention of a fish and make the lure more detectable under low light and turbid water conditions. Sometimes rattling plugs are more effective than nonrattlers, but many times there's no difference. However, it pays to realize what the advantages of rattling plugs are and when they can be useful.

The last major element of good plug usage is color. The color choice of a plug should relate to that of the major forage where you're fishing as well as to the color of the water and its visibility. Although many colors are available, the bestsellers for most manufacturers year in and year out are the silver, shad, and crayfish versions. These best resemble the predominant natural forage of most fish, especially bass. A full palette of lure colors is available, however, and there are good reasons for using some of the ones that do not conform to the norm. Chartreuse and neon red plugs, for example, are top colors for trout and salmon in some waters, purple has worked well as a plug color for many walleye anglers, and so forth. The issue of color in lures is addressed in more detail elsewhere (see: lure). It pays to have a varied selection of plugs in your tackle box, not only in terms of color, but also body shapes and diving abilities, so you can handle whatever conditions you may encounter.

A troller displays an assortment of plugs for catching walleye and lake trout.

Two remaining aspects of crankbaits should be mentioned in this section. The first is that crankbaits must run true to be effective. They must run straight on the retrieve, not lie on their side or run off at an angle. Some lures do this fresh out of the box, and some don't. There are ways to "tune" your crankbaits and ways to make them run true. The fine-tuning of these and other lures is reviewed separately (see: tuning lures). The second is the issue of when and how to replace treble hooks with single hooks, which sometimes has distinct fishing advantages.

Replacing Treble Hooks with Singles

Spoons are commonly used with single hooks, especially lightweight trolling versions. In the Great Lakes, many anglers replace the manufacturer supplied treble hook on a trolling spoon with a single hook, with no apparent loss in catch rate, in order to make the lure work better. Spinners can accommodate a single hook quite well, and all spinnerbaits, which are favored for bass and pike, are single-hooked. So are virtually all flies and nearly all jigs.

But these lures have different actions and are used in different ways than plugs. So, do anglers use treble hooks on plugs or other lures on the theory that more hooks equal more chances to catch a fish, or because treble hooks make lures work better by providing stability, affecting buoyancy, and enhancing swimming action? Both. Most anglers take out-of-the-box plug action for granted. The fact that plugs can accommodate two, three, or more treble hooks means to most anglers that they have extra chances to stick a fish, and a lot of them want, or feel they need, every chance they can get.

Yet there is good reason to use single instead of treble hooks on plugs with some species and in certain situations. Many plugs swim nearly or just as well with single hooks as they do with ordinary trebles. A few actually have enhanced swimming action and even enhanced hooking effectiveness. Some do not swim properly when modified—usually those that are more delicately balanced by design and which have poor tolerance for alteration. In general, diving plugs and swimming plugs that pull hard and show a lot of action are especially good lures for single-hook modification, and these are lure types that are especially prone to causing damage to fish.

Getting the right action, however, is largely determined by which size and style of single hook you use. You can replace manufacturer supplied trebles with out-of-the-box singles, but some lures (especially saltwater plugs) don't swim well enough that way, so you can cut two points off the existing treble (making a "cut-down single"). Cutting two hooks away from each treble at a point slightly past the middle of the bend, and therefore a tad closer to the shank, leaves enough of the treble's dynamic configuration to keep the plug swimming convincingly. The small part of each hook bend remaining perhaps acts as a micro "keel."

P

However, hook-cutting also slightly reduces the overall weight of the lure, which is sometimes critical and which affects action. So, while cutting two hooks off each manufacturer supplied treble is a quick way to produce a single-hooked plug in the field, using a treble two sizes larger than the original, with two hooks similarly removed, may be better. This obviously requires advance preparation, but it eliminates the weight loss problem, and the larger gap of the remaining hook misses less strikes.

The alternative to using cut-down singles is a conventional single hook that is many sizes larger to get good action and also hooking efficiency. As a replacement, the Siwash, or so-called salmon hook, is an excellent choice. Siwash hooks have a short strong round bend with a long point. Most manufacturers make them with an open eye, so putting them on the split ring of a plug is easy, provided you have a pair of sturdy pliers to crimp the eye closed.

On a smaller lure in which two trebles are replaced by two singles, it may be necessary to place the hooks so they face in opposite directions to get the best action; for some lures, the direction makes no difference. But that raises the question: Do you replace all the trebles with singles?

Even without any other hook modification, some anglers remove the center treble hook from some plugs that come with three sets. When doing this, if the two remaining trebles are also replaced with hooks two sizes larger, the action of the lure is essentially unaffected. The hookup rate is higher, and hook tangling is far less of a problem.

Taking that one step further, you could remove all three trebles and replace the front and back sets with cut-down singles that are three sizes larger than the original trebles, or with the appropriate single hooks. You might be able to get good action and hooking effectiveness out of a plug with just one cut-down single (at the tail), but if not, try two cut-down singles, one at the tail and the other at the forward part of the lure.

Reducing a plug's multiple treble armament all the way down to one hook, a cut-down single or an out-of-the-box single, isn't always cut-and-dried. One clever way to do this is to remove both treble hooks from a deep diving plug and attach a single large short-shanked Siwash hook to the front hook eye via a split ring, with a small barrel swivel located between the split ring and the eye of the single hook. This creates a lure that, for some types of fishing, is more active than the original and even more effective.

This replacement approach seems to work best with shorter plugs, since the single on floater/divers and swimming plugs must usually be attached to the forward hook hanger. If the plug body extends much farther back than the bend of the single belly hook, the odds of missing strikes increase with that distance. One way to reduce that threat is to attach the single to the tail of the plug, and on the forward hanger use a treble three sizes larger than the original with all three hooks cut off at their bends.

Another advantage for using single-hooked plugs is that it increases their snagless and weedless abilities. Floating grass is always a great frustration when it comes to using surface plugs. For example, summertime fishing on the shallow flats for redfish is a great time for using a slowly slurping surface plug, but only if it's not loaded with vegetation. Getting the fish's attention is almost a guaranteed thing if you can keep the hooks from fouling on the overabundant turtle grass.

Going to one or two single hooks, either cut-down singles or out-of-the-box versions as appropriate for the specific plug, may solve the weed problem by using light wire or heavy monofilament line to make weedguards for them. As long as the attachment point for the line is placed so it doesn't create a sideways V to catch grass (right on the end of the "nose" is ideal), a plug with weedless single hooks swims and crawls through a hayfield without catching anything except fish.

Fishing surface, shallow-running, and diving plugs around and among brush and flooded timber is also very effective, but when it is important to cast accurately, and when the dirty water impedes your ability to see obstructions, treble-hooked plugs hang up frequently, and are difficult to reach by boat to unsnag. By using single hooks, with or without a guard, and by fishing with a deft touch to stop a lure when it strikes a limb and let it float up, you can effectively fish a plug in thick stuff.

This prompts the question: just as a single-hooked plug hooks less grass and brush, might it also hook less fish? Often the answer is no, although admittedly this is a subjective issue that is hard to quantify. Some hard-mouthed fish, such as tarpon and snook, are especially difficult to hook with plugs sporting single hooks. Some fiercely aggressive fish, like northern pike, are no problem at all.

Generally, as long as you can get the right action out of a plug with single hooks, you can catch fish well. As well as the same plug with treble hooks? Overall, probably not, but close enough. Obviously, you will not be able to catch fish that swipe at a lure and get foul-hooked by one out of six or nine hook points. On the other hand, you can fish single-hooked plugs in places that others with treble-hooked plugs can't, and you can release fish without injury to them and with far less chance of problems to yourself. Who is to say what those benefits are worth?

Not everyone wants to use single-hooked plugs. Tournament anglers, including many bass and walleye devotees, probably don't want to do so except in isolated instances, especially if they fish in open, unobstructed waters, and/or seldom use a net. Comparatively few other people fish for money, but that doesn't mean they aren't serious about *catching*. Nevertheless, anglers who've had very little problem with releasing fish that are caught on treble-hooked lures and are not hurt or bleeding, are likely reluctant to take a chance on losing fish, especially a trophy. Also, many people have gotten along well by unhooking treble-hooked fish with pliers and don't feel compelled to use single hooks, even for personal safety reasons.

Because replacing the treble hooks on plugs with single hooks is not a common tactic yet and because you may need a specific type of hook, you'll probably have to do some searching to find the type and size of single hook or treble (to cut down) that you'll need. If you have a lot of lures, especially older ones that aren't in use, you may find suitable replacements among your supplies. Some well-stocked tackle shops may have the hooks that you need, especially in areas where trout and salmon are caught (for the Siwash hooks), and you should check mail-order tackle suppliers as well.

See: Antique Fishing Tackle; Catch-and-Release; Lure; Surface Lure.

PLUG CASTING

A term for casting and fishing with baitcasting tackle (see), derived from its early-day use, which was primarily with plugs (see).

PLUMBING

Determining the depth, usually with a plummet (see), of the water when using a float (see).

PLUMMET

A small weight clipped onto the fishing fine and lowered to the bottom to determine depth when fishing bait on a float (see).

POCKET WATER

A boulder-strewn or large rock-studded section of river or stream composed of fast and slow current, in which the commotion downstream of one rock meets another rock and so on, creating small pools or eddies downstream of the rocks. The creases or edges of the currents along these places hold trout.
See: Finding Fish.

POD

A small, tight group of fish swimming together.
See: School.

POINT

A place where the land juts out in the water away from the shore and where the bottom terrain that is underwater continues to taper down and off. Some points are very obvious, some are subtle; some taper gradually and extend (almost like a bar) a long distance into the water body, although others end abruptly and drop off quickly.

Points are important features in lakes and reservoirs, in large tidal and nontidal rivers, and in saltwater along the shorelines of bays and along the coast. They are much more numerous in freshwater, especially in lakes and reservoirs, where bass, walleye, pike, muskellunge, and trout in the spring are reliably caught on or near points.

For certain species of fish, points are natural obstacles for travel and good places to eat. Baitfish congregate at points, a fact that means consistent and reliable feeding opportunity for other fish. In many places they are washed by current, which also presents feeding opportunities.

Not all points are the same. There are main points, secondary points in back bays, points with long gradual tapers, points with sudden dropoffs, points with little cover, points with plenty of cover, brushy points, rocky points, woody points, grassy points, sand-and-clay points, and long underwater points not obvious to the eye when scanning the shoreline.

No one place has every type of point, but at various times some are more attractive than others. In freshwater, points with some cover, for example, are usually better than those without cover. Yet some points that yield good fish have scant cover; many reservoir points, for example, are nearly bare unless someone has planted brushpiles. Proximity to cover or to deep water are factors that make some points stand out.

Fishing a point properly means knowing which parts to work, and how. Using sonar (see) is an important element of fishing a point from a boat because you need to define the underwater contour of the point and the depth variations so you can identify them properly. You also need to locate any submerged objects, such as stumps, boulders, stone walls, and the like, which are not obvious and which may be on or slightly off the point, since these can be particularly important objects on which to concentrate effort. Using sonar also helps to locate baitfish that may be present on a point, as well as predatory species themselves. If you can locate the latter with sonar, then you can spend more productive time on a point. This knowledge is especially important when you're fishing large, unfamiliar bodies of water; eliminating some points and narrowing the search on others can help you to establish patterns that work elsewhere.

Casting lures around points is a common technique that is useful for many fish, especially bass, but trolling is also highly effective, as is drifting. Trolling is a good way to get lures down to fish off points, especially when there is substantial wind or current to affect cast-and-retrieve presentations. It's one of the best ways to fish the edges of points, especially those that drop off sharply. When casting around points, essentially you can cast and retrieve across points, cast to the shallows and retrieve toward deep water, or cast from shallow water and retrieve your lure from deeper to shallower water.

 Julio T. Buel is credited with inventing the fishing spoon; he began the commercial manufacture of spoons in 1848, but had fished with his own invention since 1821.

The last approach is the least practiced but worth remembering when times are tough and especially when using deep-diving plugs and surface lures.
See: Finding Fish.

POISON
See: Ciguatera; Diseases and Parasites; Pfiesteria.

POLE
(1) A misnomer usually applied to a fishing rod.

(2) A fishing implement unaccompanied by a reel or by rod components, and used for making quiet presentations, primarily of bait, to specific places, some of which are not readily accessible by casting. A pole is not used for casting and there is no running line; bait is swung or dropped gently into place and a fixed length of line is attached to the tip of the pole.

Most poles in North America are made of bamboo, and referred to as "cane poles," although they may be made of synthetic material (fiberglass and graphite) and also telescopic. North American poles are commonly 10 to 15 feet in length, mainly fished from shore or bank for panfish species, but often employed from a boat. In Europe and Asia, poles may be two to three times this length (some expensive specialty poles are 60 feet long), and almost exclusively used from the bank, primarily in coarse fishing; they are made of graphite and are light in weight despite their great length.

Hooked fish are retrieved by being jerked or lifted out of the water with shorter poles and heavy line, and are led to a landing net with long poles and light line.
See: Cane Pole; Coarse Fishing; Float; Rod, Fishing.

POLING
A method of propelling a boat silently in shallow water, common to angling on saltwater flats and some rivers.
See: Flats Boat; Flats Fishing; Pushpole.

POLLACK
A European member of the cod family, similar to pollock (see).

POLLOCK   *Pollachius virens.*
Other names—coalfish, Boston bluefish, green cod, blisterback, saithe, coley.

A member of the Gadidae family, the pollock is the most active of the various codfish and has been popular with anglers. It is an important commercial species, taken primarily by trawls and gillnets, and generally marketed fresh or as frozen fillets, although it is not as popular a market fish as its cousin the Atlantic cod *(see: cod, Atlantic)*. It is not

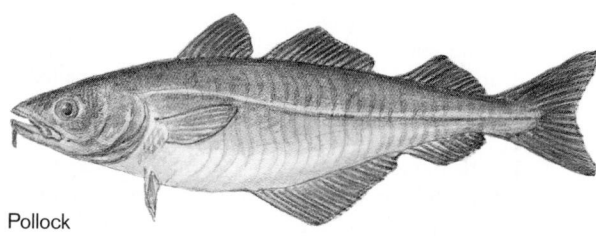

Pollock

to be confused with another cod family member, the Alaska, or walleye, pollock *(Theragra calcogramma)*, which is not an angler target but an important commercial species, particularly in the Bering, Okhotsk, and Japan Seas. A similar species sought by anglers is the European pollack *(Pollachius pollachius)*.

Identification.   Pollock are olive green to greenish brown on top and yellowish gray on the sides and belly, with silvery overtones. They can be distinguished from other members of the cod family, such as the Atlantic cod, haddock *(see)*, and the tomcod *(see)*, by three features: The lower jaw of the pollock projects beyond the upper jaw, the tail is forked, and the lateral line is quite straight, not arching above the pectoral fins. Young pollock have codlike barbels on the chin, but these are small and usually disappear with age. The European pollack is distinguished from the pollock by its lateral line, which is decurved over the pectoral fins.

Size/Age.   Pollock can grow to $3\frac{1}{2}$ feet, although most adults are much smaller. The average fish weighs between 4 and 15 pounds. The all-tackle record is 50 pounds. A slow-growing fish, the pollock reaches about 30 inches at age 9. They have been reported to live as long as 31 years, but few pollock live longer than 12 years.

Distribution.   These fish inhabit waters on both sides of the Atlantic, from Greenland and Labrador to Virginia on the west side, and on the east, from Iceland to northern Spain, including the Bay of Biscay, the English Channel, and the western Baltic and North Seas.

Habitat.   Generally a deep or midwater fish, the pollock prefers rocky bottoms in waters shallower than those the cod or haddock prefer. They occur in depths of up to 100 fathoms, although they are found as shallow as 4 fathoms.

Life history/Behavior.   The spawning season for pollock is in late autumn and early winter. Their eggs are free-floating and drift on the surface, and for the first three months, larvae are present on or near the surface. Juveniles travel in large, tightly packed schools near the surface.

Food.   Pollock feed in large schools on small herring, small cod and their relatives, and on sand eels and various tiny crustaceans.

Angling.   A sporting fish, pollock make powerful runs and occasionally leap and shake, providing a good fight. Angling for this coldwater species occurs year-round, but activity peaks in late fall through early spring.

Most pollock fishing occurs in conjunction with cod fishing, typically on wrecks; those far offshore tend to produce better fishing and larger specimens. Ledges, rockpiles, and other structures also produce pollock, however, and these fish are not necessarily caught close to the bottom. Many are caught well off the bottom in the lower third or near the middle of the water column, making it worthwhile to fish baits or jigs through these areas, dropping them down and fishing up through the water column while drifting.

When baits like sand eels, squid, or herring are present, pollock are susceptible to jigging. Generally, successful jigs, baits, and rigs are similar to those used in cod fishing (see: cod, Atlantic).

Skimmer clams are the primary natural baits, and diamond jigs the main lure. Jigs can also be fished with a soft-plastic lure or a small bucktail rigger on a dropper line about 18 inches above the bottom lure.

POLYETHYLENE (Line)

See: Line

POMPANO

Related to the jacks, pompano are a small group of tropical species that are members of the Carangidae family. They include such outstanding food fish as the Florida pompano and such highly coveted gamefish as the permit.

See: Jacks; Palometa; Pompano, African; Pompano, Florida.

POMPANO, AFRICAN   Alectis ciliaris.

Other names—Cuban jack, Atlantic threadfin, pennantfish, threadfin mirrorfish, trevally; Afrikaans: *draadvin-spie lvis;* Arabic: *bambo, tailar;* French: *aile ronde, carangue, cordonnier;* Hawaiian: *papio, ulua;* Malay/Indonesian: *cermin, ebek, rambai landeh;* Portuguese: *xaréu africano;* Spanish: *caballa, chicuaca, elechudo, jurel de pluma, paja blanco, palometa, pampano, sol, zapatero.*

The African pompano is the largest and most widespread member of the Carangidae family of jacks and pompano, surrounded by a great deal of confusion because until recently adults and young were classified as entirely different species. A strong fighter and an excellent light-tackle gamefish, it is a superb food fish and is marketed fresh or salted/dried.

Identification.   The most striking characteristic of the African pompano is the four to six elongated, threadlike filaments that extend from the front part of the second dorsal and anal fins. These filaments tend to disappear or erode as the fish grows, although in young fish the first two of these may initially be four times as long as the fish. The body shape of the African pompano changes as it grows; starting out short and deep, it becomes more elongated by the time the fish is 14 inches long, and the forehead becomes steeper and blunter. In both young and adult fish, the body is strongly compressed, and the rear half of the body is triangular. The lateral line arches smoothly but steeply above the pectoral fins and has 24 to 38 relatively weak scutes in the straight portion and 120 to 140 scales. Shiny and silvery on the whole, larger fish may be light bluish green on the back; on all fish there may be dark blotches on the operculum on the top part of the caudal peduncle, as well as on the front part of the second dorsal and anal fins. Young African pompano have five to six ventral bars.

Size.   This species is known to attain a length of 42 inches and a weight of 50 pounds, but it can grow to 60 pounds; the all-tackle world record is a 50-pound, 8-ounce Florida fish. Twenty- to 30-pounders are common in South Florida.

Distribution.   Found worldwide in tropical seas, African pompano occur in the western Atlantic, from Massachusetts and Bermuda to Santos, Brazil, as well as throughout the Caribbean Sea and the Gulf of Mexico. In the eastern Atlantic, they occur from Senegal to the Congo, with some populations existing off the coast of South Africa. In the eastern Pacific, they range from Mexico to Peru. In the western Indian Ocean, they range from the Red Sea to Sri Lanka and south to South Africa. They are also reported around Fiji and Tuvalu.

Habitat.   Inhabiting waters up to 300 feet deep, young fish prefer open seas and linger near the surface, whereas adults most often prefer to be near the bottom over rocky reefs and around wrecks. African pompano may form small, somewhat polarized schools, although they are usually solitary in the adult stage.

Food.   African pompano feed on sedentary or slow-moving crustaceans, small crabs, and occasionally on small fish.

Angling.   An excellent gamefish, African pompano are greatly appreciated for their hard fight, stamina, and beauty. Although they look and fight much like a permit, the similarities are superficial, as these fish are not observed on shallow flats like permit and are mainly caught over wrecks and reefs, and in many places incidentally by anglers trolling or baitfishing for grouper, snapper, kingfish, and sailfish. Wreck and reef fishing for these species became more prominent in South Florida in the 1990s, as anglers identified locations that had good populations of baitfish to attract this species. Since then, targeted efforts for African pompano have borne good results. Fish are caught deep on jigs and on baits, and when attracted to the surface by chumming, they are caught on cast hooked baits, or plugs or flies.

In addition to wrecks and reefs, these fish are attracted to humps, rockpiles, ledges, and irregular bottom structures that might hold baits.

P

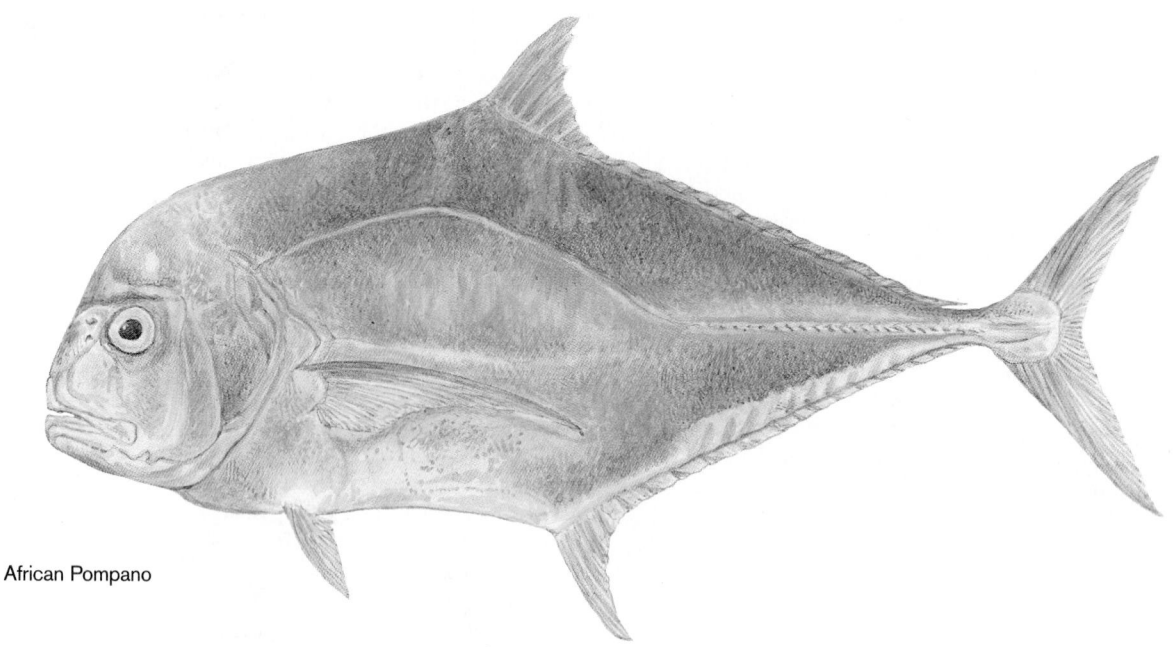

African Pompano

Large bucktails (1 to 3 ounces are standard), are used to jig deep, and white is the preferred color. Subtle strikes usually follow when the jig falls during the jigging motion, but making a wide-sweeping jigging motion with a tight line is also productive. Specialists drift over the targeted areas, jigging above structure to attract the fish away from the confines of that structure, making it easier to play the fish once hooked. Slow trolling with deep-fished live baits may also be productive.

Prodigious amounts of live baits are used as chum to attract African pompano to the surface. Anglers offer live pilchards, menhaden, or herring, and often there's action for various other species before African pompano come around. When they do, however, they are caught on live hooked baits, or cast popping plugs, shallow swimming plugs, and streamer flies or fly-rod poppers.

Shallow-caught fish make a strong first run, followed by successive runs and boat circling. Spinning and casting tackle suitable for 8- to 20-pound lines are favored, and the drag must be in good shape and the rod capable of putting pressure on a fish to keep it in check.
See: Inshore Fishing; Jacks.

POMPANO, FLORIDA   *Trachinotus carolinus.*
Other names—Portuguese: *pampo, pampo-verdadeiro;* Spanish: *palometa, pampano, pampano-amarillo.*

A member of the Carangidae family of jacks and pompanos, the Florida pompano is an excellent gamefish for its size and is an exciting catch on light tackle. It is also considered a gourmet food fish because of its delicately flavored and finely textured meat. It is netted commercially and bred in ponds, and it is among the highest-priced marine food fish per pound in the United States.

Identification.   Mostly silvery when alive, the Florida pompano is one of the few fish that is more striking in color after death. It then has greenish gray or dark blue shading on the back, and a golden cast to the belly and fins. Deep- or dark-water fish tend to also have gold on the throat, pelvic, and anal fins; young fish tend to have a yellowish belly, anal fin, and tail. The Florida pompano has a deep, flattened body; a short, blunt snout with a small mouth; and a deeply forked tail. Unlike most jacks, it has no scutes on the caudal peduncle. The first and spinous dorsal fin is very low and usually hard to see, whereas the second dorsal fin has one spine and 22 to 27 soft dorsal rays. The anal fin, which begins slightly farther back on the body than the second dorsal fin, has three spines and 20 to 23 soft anal rays. The Florida pompano is similar to the permit *(see),* although the permit is deeper-bodied and tends to be a much larger fish, growing to 40 pounds.

Size/Age.   The Florida pompano rarely grows larger than 6 pounds and 25 inches long, and usually weighs less than 3 pounds. The all-tackle world record is an 8-pound, 1-ounce fish taken in Florida in 1984. The Florida pompano has an estimated life span of three to four years.

Distribution.   Occurring in the western Atlantic, the Florida pompano range from Massachusetts to Brazil and throughout the Gulf of Mexico, although they are absent from clear waters around the Bahamas and similar islands. They are most prominent from the Chesapeake Bay to Florida and west to Texas, and are abundant in the warm waters of Florida and the Caribbean.

Habitat.   Inhabiting inshore and nearshore waters, adult Florida pompano occur along sandy beaches, including oyster bars, grassbeds, inlets,

P

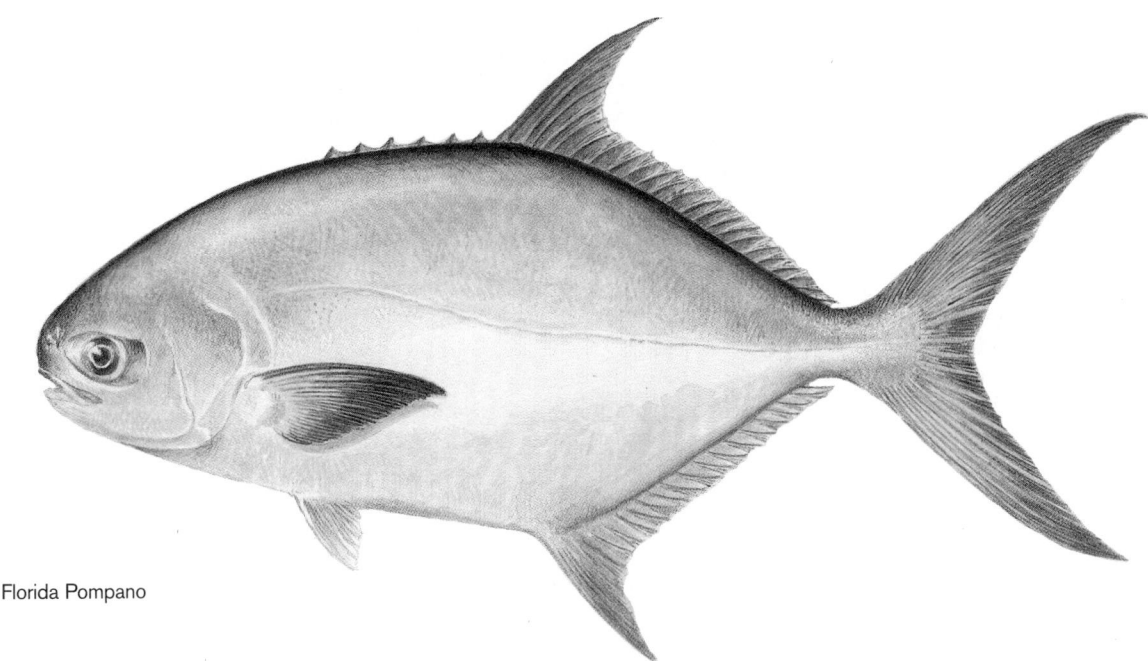

Florida Pompano

and often in the turbid water of brackish bays and estuaries. They usually prefer shallow water but may occur in water as deep as 130 feet. Young fish inhabit sandy, muddy, or open beaches. Florida pompano generally form small to large schools that travel close to the shore and migrate northward and southward along the Atlantic coast, staying in waters with temperatures between 82° and 89°F; local activity is determined by the tide and by temperature.

Life history/Behavior.   Reaching sexual maturity at the end of their first year, Florida pompano spawn offshore between March and September, with a peak of activity from April through June. Females are capable of laying hundreds of thousands of pelagic eggs, and larvae grow rapidly, attaining a length of about 8 inches by the end of the first year.

Food.   Florida pompano feed on mollusks, crustaceans, and other invertebrates and small fish.

Angling.   Anglers pursue Florida pompano while fishing from bridges, jetties, piers, the surf, and small boats. Fishing on the bottom with natural baits is a successful method, but some anglers cast and troll small artificial lures. Because these fish are sensitive to cold water, late summer and early fall are the best times to catch Florida pompano in their northern range; they are available in Florida waters from late spring through fall in normal years, and year-round during mild winters. Runs have been sporadic and rarely sustained in the past, but numbers and availability have improved with changes in commercial netting.

Terminal tackle favored by bait users consists of two or three No. 1 or 1/0 hooks tied on short dropper loops one above the other. Sand fleas, shrimp, clams, and small crabs are good baits. The best fishing conditions are early morning or late afternoon, on an incoming high tide with light to moderate

surf and clear water. The baits should be allowed to rest on the bottom for a few minutes and then retrieved very slowly. Florida pompano hit the bait hard and fast, usually hooking themselves.

Anglers who fish bays, passes, and grassflats from boats are more likely to use small jigs on light spinning tackle. The time-honored pompano jig—a round leadhead equipped with a short bucktail body—is still extremely popular with casters, but also effective are jigs with different head shapes and soft-plastic bodies. Occasionally they may be tipped with pieces of shrimp or with sand fleas, although this tactic is mostly unnecessary unless the fish are skittish or not aggressive. Sizes range from $1/4$ ounce to 1 ounce depending on depth and current.

Jigs can be fished vertically over reefs and on the edges of deep-water flats. Sandbars, passes, clam beds, and other inshore structures, including grassflats, are also targeted, often while the boat drifts and the angler casts ahead, constantly twitching the jig to give it action. Deeper fishing requires a slower movement. Before and after a flood tide are often better times.

In some places, small jigs on light line can be blind-cast by anglers wade fishing in water that is too deep to see fish; the jig should be worked very slowly. Small pink or white soft-plastic grubs on a $1/8$-ounce leadhead will do, and may also catch small snapper and bonefish.

Like all jacks, these fish have a bulldoglike disposition and make repeated strong runs, rendering them a fine light-tackle species.
See: Inshore Fishing; Jack; Surf Fishing.

PONTOON BOAT

Essentially a platform on dual pontoons, these vessels used to be known only as general fair-weather cruise-and-party craft, but have been adapted for various fishing applications, primarily in freshwater. General use includes casting for largemouth bass, white bass, and stripers, or stillfishing for the same species plus crappie, catfish, and walleye. They are also used for trolling when outfitted with the right accessory equipment.

Pontoon boats range in length from 18 to 30 feet, and use long-shaft outboard motors as their primary propulsion. For fishing, they are also outfitted with an electric motor on a front deck (center position), an electric motor attached to the main outboard so it can be directed via the steering wheel, or a small-horsepower auxiliary outboard motor next to the main motor and also connected for steering purposes.

Most pontoons sport a canopy, which can impede casting unless it can be fully retracted. High railings can also be an impediment to landing fish, and models with low railings all-around are preferable for fishing. Manufacturers of pontoon boats have taken these and other matters into consideration in fishing packages that are offered with some of their pontoon boats; in deluxe versions, that includes being fully rigged with sonar, rod holders, livewell, and the like.

Pontoon boats are best suited to calm waters. Controlling them in the wind is difficult due to their boxlike structure, and they roll atop the waves. They can be trailered but keeping them in a boat dock or marina slip is preferable.
See: Boat.

POOL

(1) A section of any flowing waterway, usually deeper than other portions and without turbulence.

Because of its depth, and sometimes breadth, the water in a pool flows more slowly than in the shallower runs and riffles, and it is where many species of gamefish are found resting or feeding. Pools vary greatly, affected by the size of the

An angler plays a fish in a long pool on this Nova Scotian river.

waterway and the amount of current (which depends on season, rainfall, etc.). They have varying depth, width, and length. A pool may be the size of a bathtub or a bedroom in a creek; it may be 100 yards long in a medium-sized river; and it may be several miles long in a large river that has been dredged and channeled.

In large pools the depth may vary along the pool's length. In deep pools, the bottom of the pool may be darker and/or cooler than the upper portions. A typical pool becomes shallower at the tail end because sediments carried in the current sink and build up, although this condition may be altered and moved through ice gouging. The tail of a pool may move gradually into a run *(see)* and then into a shallow riffle *(see)*. At the head of a pool, the bottom often drops abruptly from a riffle, creating a clear change from one type of water to another.

These and other factors make a pool likely to hold desirable gamefish species (including trout, walleye, smallmouth bass, steelhead, salmon, and catfish), either for security, comfort, feeding, or all of these reasons. Depending on depth, current, species, and other factors, fish may locate at the head of the pool, at the tail of the pool, or in between; fish at or close to the head of the pool are likely to be active feeders, although this is a generality. The amount of current, the presence and location of cover in the pool (boulders, deadfall trees, etc.), the type and availability of forage, and the characteristics of individual species are factors that have a bearing on when and where fish will be located in a pool, and whether it is advantageous to fish on the surface, at midlevels, or along the bottom.

Objects that offer cover enhance the likelihood of fish presence, especially if they are in deep water; and the more cover that a pool has, especially at the head and upper third of the pool, the better it will probably be. These objects may deflect current, cause eddies, create defined current edges, provide current-free holding water, and bring food to fish, so they are important. And the best cover, or the cover most strategically located, is likely to have the biggest fish.

(2) The capacity of an impoundment.

A reservoir containing the maximum amount of water that it was designed to hold is said to be at "full pool." This level is measured at the height above sea level; thus, if full pool is 290 feet, and the surface of the reservoir is currently gauged at 283 feet above sea level, then it is said to be 7 feet below full pool. This is a common gauge of water levels in impoundments; water levels are often published in local newspapers. Sudden changes may be indicative of fishing conditions; swiftly dropping pool levels due to drawdowns for energy or irrigation needs, for example, may cause fish to locate deeper.

POPPER

(1) A hard- or solid-bodied artificial fly, also called a bug or popping bug.
See: Fly.

(2) A wooden or plastic surface plug with a concave, scooped-out mouth, also known as a popping plug.
See: Surface Lure.

POPPING PLUG

See: Surface Lure.

POPPING ROD

A term for casting rods used with revolving spool reels in saltwater. If used in freshwater, these would be called baitcasting rods or even muskie rods, but in saltwater the application is with heavy lures, usually from ⅝-ounce up to 2 ounces. These rods range from light saltwater versions (which is equivalent to medium-heavy freshwater), perhaps used for fishing with topwater plugs, to heavier rods used in deep jigging, even though casting is not involved in the latter.

Popping rods have medium- to short-length handles, depending on application, with the latter preferred by many inshore and shallow water casters. They are matched with revolving-spool reels, often with levelwind baitcasting versions, and frequently with models having wide spools and large capacity.
See: Rod, Fishing.

POPULATION

Fish of the same species inhabiting a specified area. This term is used more often with respect to freshwater species and is slightly different from a "stock" of fish, a term that is used more commonly with respect to saltwater species and in regard to a grouping of fish usually based on genetic relationship, geographic distribution, and movement patterns.
See: Fisheries Management.

PORGIES

The Sparidae family of porgies comprise roughly 112 species, and as a group they have worldwide distribution in the tropical and temperate waters of the Atlantic, Pacific, and Indian Oceans, although a few range into cooler waters.

Porgies are similar to grunts (see), but their body is even more flattened from side to side, or compressed, and high through the area just in front of the dorsal fin. As in some grunts, the eyes are located high on the head and just behind the posterior margin of the mouth. The second, or soft, dorsal fin and the anal fin are both large and are about the same shape.

Porgies are medium-size to small. Some live close to shore, others in offshore waters. They are prevalent around reefs, but some are found only over sandy bottoms; others inhabit rocky bottoms. Most species can change their colors from solid to blotched or barred and from dark to light, effecting a better camouflage. They are omnivorous and typically travel in schools. Included in the group are a number of species that are harvested for food. Many also provide good, generally light-tackle, sport for anglers. They are relatively easy to catch and, for their size, put up a strong fight.

In the United States, porgies, like grunts, are predominantly an Atlantic species off the coast. The scup (see) averages less than 10 inches in length but is one of the most prominent members of this family. It is valued by both anglers and commercial fishermen along the northeastern and mid-Atlantic U.S. coast. The jolthead porgy (see: porgy, jolthead) is one of a large group of porgies found in warm waters of the Caribbean and off southern Florida, occasionally drifting with the Gulf Stream as far north as Bermuda. Distinctively shaped, it is the largest member of its genus.

Other porgy relatives that are common in their respective regions and encountered by anglers include the most popular sheepshead (see), sea bream (see: bream, sea), and pinfish (see), as well as the squirefish (see: snapper) of Australia, the dentex (see) of Europe, and the black porgy (Acanthopagrus schlegeli) of Japan.

Angling. These slightly humpbacked fish are bottom dwellers and are caught on or within a foot or two of bottom. Most porgies are landed in relatively shallow water, often 10 to 30 feet deep. Larger fish are typically taken deeper, however, and some species are located in deep offshore water.

In bays or inlets, look for porgies over a sandy or hard bottom. They also inhabit shellfish beds and the edges of reefs. Most anglers fish a two-, and sometimes three-, hook bait rig, using sandworms, bloodworms, squid, clams, and grass shrimp as bait.

Porgies are notorious bait stealers; fishing a small piece of bait, usually just enough to cover the hook, is sufficient to curtail nibbling and bait loss. Chumming is sometimes helpful for increasing the catch.

As mentioned, porgies put up a good fight for their size and are respectable battlers on light tackle. When light sinkers are used, a light to medium spinning outfit, with 8- or 10-pound line provides good sport. When heavy weights are needed because of tide, current, or depth, a boat or bay rod may be required.

Porgies are sometimes quite plentiful and can be caught in good numbers. Other times the reverse is true. In northern environs they usually become available in spring, and fishing lasts through summer. Many porgies are caught by anglers fishing the bottom for some other species.
See: Inshore Fishing.

P

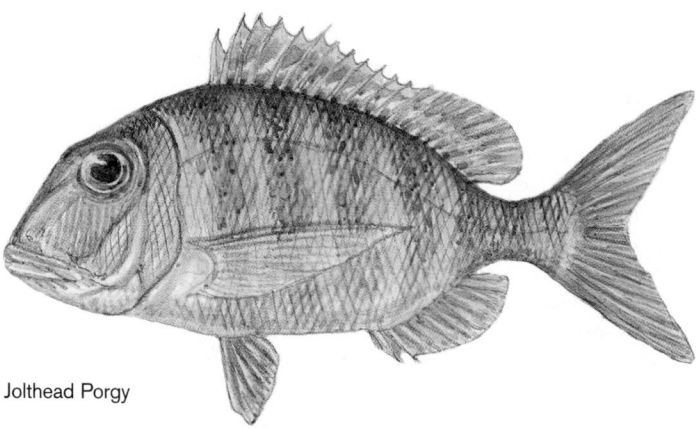

Jolthead Porgy

PORGY, JOLTHEAD   *Calamus bajonado.*
Other names—porgy; Spanish: *pluma bajonado.*

A member of the Sparidae family, which includes about 112 species, the jolthead is an excellent food fish with some commercial value, and a species that bottom-probing anglers often encounter along the eastern United States; it has been associated with ciguatera *(see),* however. The common name presumably comes from the fish's habit of using its head to bump or jolt clams or other mollusks loose from their attachments.

Identification.   The high, rounded forehead gives the body a distinctive profile, typical of the genus. It eyes are large and are located high on the head. Yellowish brown, with an almost metallic luster, it may be blotched with dusky splotches or nearly solid in color, depending on the bottom over which it is swimming. Some individuals are grayish. Over each eye is a blue streak, and sometimes there are faint blue lengthwise stripes on the body. The caudal fin is lunate (crescent-shaped).

Size.   Among the largest of the porgies, this species is typically 20 inches long, but it can attain a length of 26 inches and a weight of 23 pounds. The all-tackle world record is a 23-pound, 4-ounce specimen.

Distribution.   The jolthead porgy occurs in the western Atlantic, from Rhode Island to the northern Gulf of Mexico, including Bermuda, and south to Brazil. It is most abundant in the West Indies.

Habitat.   The jolthead occurs in coastal environs over vegetated sand bottoms and more frequently on coral bottoms between 6 and 45 meters deep. Large adults are usually solitary.

Food and feeding behavior.   The diet of jolthead porgies is sea urchins, crabs, and mollusks. Small schools are often seen feeding near shore.

Angling.   Joltheads are not a prime angling target, but anglers fishing for various bottom and reef dwellers sometimes catch them incidentally. They are primarily caught on baits.
See: Inshore Fishing; Porgies.

PORK RIND
A strip or chunk of pork attached to a weedless spoon or jig.
See: Jig; Spoon.

PORT
(1) The left side of a boat facing the bow.

(2) A harbor, especially one with dockage, maintenance, and launching facilities.

PORTUGAL
Spanning 91,905 square kilometers, including the Azores and Madeira, Portugal is roughly the size of Indiana in the United States and twice that of Switzerland. The westernmost country in continental Europe, it is bounded by Spain on the north and east and by the Atlantic Ocean on the south and west. Its capital city, Lisbon, has been the gateway to the Atlantic for navigators and explorers for centuries.

Portugal's primary stake to sportfishing fame, especially for visiting anglers, is not on the mainland but out in the Atlantic at Madeira and the Azores. It does offer sportfishing for local anglers along the coast and in the interior, however.

The Mainland
In freshwater, trout are the primary game species in the cooler reaches of the hundreds of miles of rivers that exist in Portugal (and are also present on Madeira). Barbel and carp are also prominent in nearly all rivers and streams. The major rivers in the mountainous northern region include the Minho, Mouro, Castro Laboreiro, and Douro; in the central region, they include the Mondego, Zezere, Alva Nabao, and Avelar.

Perch are here as well, especially in the southern part of the country; shad run up the coastal rivers from early February into July; and largemouth bass are also present. The introduced bass, known as *achigã,* have flourished, and are present in a number of waters, including Maranhão Reservoir, Vale de Gaio Reservoir, the Sado River, and the Beja and Algarve Dams, which are impoundments in the southeast on the Guadiana River.

Along the 625 miles of coast, Portuguese anglers fish for the likes of tuna, blue shark, tope, conger and moray eels, grouper, pollock, European bass, plaice, mackerel, garfish, bream, ray, and other species. The northern region generally favors colder-water species, with the area between Moledo in the far north and Oporto having the most opportunities. A number of rivers empty into the Atlantic here. Fishing ports include Esposende, Ofir, Póvoa de Varzim, Vilado Conde, Espinho, Figueira da Foz, and Nazaré.

South of this region, from Peniche on through the Algarve region, the coast becomes rockier and

P

broken by scattered sand beaches, and the ports offer more temperate-water fishing with big-game possibilities. Fewer rivers enter here. Fishing ports include Peniche (for the Berlenga Islands), Ericeira, Sesimbra, Sines Sagres, Lagos, Paraia da Rocha, Albufeira, Faro, and Monte Gordo.

Madeira Islands

Lying 1,000 kilometers southwest of Lisbon and 800 kilometers from the African coast, Madeira is a volcanic archipelago of four islands with a temperate year-round climate and great positioning in the North Atlantic Ocean for intercepting pelagic big-game species, especially huge blue marlin. The archipelago consists of two inhabited islands, Madeira and Porto Santo, and two uninhabited groups, the Desertas and the Selvagens, which are respectively 11 and 156 nautical miles south of Madeira.

Until the late 1980s, the Madeiras were known more for their wine production, tropical beauty, and place in early trading history than for their fisheries, even though big marlin had been taken from nearby waters. Throughout that decade, most available boats and equipment were geared toward casual tourists and inshore fishing that focused on barracuda, sharks, bonito, mackerel, and some tuna. Even today, only a handful of modern top-rate sportfishing operators exist, and facilities for visiting boaters are extremely limited. The chances of reaching the marlin grounds are not good unless one makes arrangements very far in advance.

The operators who do exist are busy during the marlin season (July through September) because the blues here have been fairly mind boggling. Some top marlin experts call this the best marlin fishery in the world. As long ago as 1980, a near-grander was caught here on rod and reel, and sporadic reports throughout the 1980s filtered out about blues weighing between 550 and 800 pounds. In the late 1980s, a 1,200-pound Atlantic blue was caught by a French angler, and bigger fish were reportedly registered by commercial fishermen, including a 1,320-pounder in 1986 and a 1,540-pounder in 1985.

Throughout the 1990s, with intensified and expert angling efforts targeting blue marlin, the catches have skyrocketed. Two developments have become apparent: a very large average size (500 pounds according to some, even higher according to others), and many fish close to or exceeding the 1,000-pound mark. Where many billfish sites talk about the potential for granders, or the two or three that have been caught over the years, this area produces many such fish in a season, and, in at least one reported instance, produced two blues exceeding 1,000 pounds in a single day. Most of the marlin are released, and most of the few that are kept are those that died during the fight. Of the released fish, some were estimated at weights between 1,100 and 1,200 pounds. Just as remarkably, these monster blue marlin are almost all caught on trolled

A large bigeye tuna is boated off Madeira.

lures, the seas are calm during the billfish season, and the run to the fishing grounds is just 10 miles from the islands.

Fishing is centered out of Funchal on the island of Madeira and commences for blue marlin sometime in late June or early July, tapering at the end of September and early October. In addition to blue marlin, these waters have an abundance of bigeye tuna (some of which are large, including two current world records), plus large bluefin tuna, mako sharks, blue sharks, and hammerhead sharks. Some swordfish have also been caught, as have a fair number of spearfish. The Madeiras hold world records for spearfish, including the a 90-pound, 13-ounce fish that is the 50-pound-line-class and all-tackle record holder. The tuna fishing is reportedly best from January through April, and shark action is good from September through November.

Formed from volcanic action, the Madeiras have extremely deep water near their clifflike shores (the world's second highest cliff is here by Cabo Girao). It can be argued that the sportfishing potential here is as limitless as the depths, and the balmy climate is one that everyone finds endearing.

Azore Islands

The Azores are a group of volcanic islands due west of Portugal in the North Atlantic. Separated from Europe by almost a thousand miles, and from North America by 1,600 miles, they are volcanic mountains, rising from great ocean depths along the Mid-Atlantic Ridge. Fittingly, their shorelines are craggy and steep, but within a few miles of shore the ocean depths plunge to more than 2,000 feet.

The Azores, which are spread over more than 350 miles, are divided into three groups: the eastern group consists of São Miguel and Santa Maria; the central group consists of Faial, Pico, São Jorge, Terceira, and Graciosa; and the northwestern group includes Flores and Corvo. Sportfishing occurs out of Faial, Terceira, and São Miguel, but the bulk of the effort originates on Faial, where there is a fishing center at Horta, the island's capital. A handful of charter boats operate here, plying four significant offshore banks that lie between 10 and 45 nautical miles from port. Fishing conditions are usually good throughout the summer but are rough in winter and spring. A second fishing center is situated in Ponta Delgada, the capital of São Miguel, and big-game fishing occurs at three offshore banks situated between 12 and 25 nautical miles from port.

Much effort has been concentrated on Condora Bank off Faial. Because the bank is located along the Mid-Atlantic Ridge, the water drops off steeply fairly close to shore, and into the abyss a few miles away. When a big marlin or tuna wants to go deep here, you need more than muscle; you need a reel with loads of line capacity.

There are only a few more boats fishing these waters than in the Madeiras. Another impediment is the often heavy seas created by blustery days that make big-game trolling unfeasible. Nevertheless, the Azores have come into their own as outstanding marlin grounds. Expanded fishing efforts here since the mid-1980s have proven that there are many blue and white marlin to be caught. The blues are very big, and the whites average 80 pounds. The average weight of the Atlantic blues caught in the Azores far exceeds the average in most other—and much better known—areas. These fish weigh in at 500 pounds or better, as in the Madeiras. And the stories of granders and much bigger fish being seen and lost are not mere stories.

In the mid-1980s, the first reports of these fish were mind boggling. Commercial fishermen were said to be spotting groups of marlin. One account had it that Azorean harpooners had snared a 1,144-pound blue marlin and a 1,188-pounder. Anglers related losing monster blues, one estimated at 1,500 pounds.

In August of 1988, an angler came just shy of catching the first grander in the Azores, taking a 980-pound blue on 130-pound line and establishing a European line-class record. A published report then noted that in 10 days of angling, 15 blues with an average weight of 600 pounds were caught, including an astounding double of 650 and 500 pounds. Then, that September, a 1,146-pound blue was caught to establish a new world record on 50-pound line. Since then, more boats have joined the action, and the records have tumbled, with six line-class world records being currently taken from the Azores, the largest a 1,189-pounder captured in

1993. Scores of 1,000-pound fish have been caught, many of which were released, and one boat accomplished the extraordinary feat of catching three such fish in a single day.

One reason why the marlin are here is because the volcanic and high-rising Azores benefit climatologically from a branch of the Gulf Stream, the North Atlantic Current, which protects against extreme warmth or cold on the islands and provides plenty of forage opportunity. When the nutrient-rich water is warm enough, in the 75°F range, marlin abound. The period from May through December produces blue marlin, but July through September is best.

Other billfish that show up in these waters include white marlin, swordfish, and long-billed spearfish. Spearfish are still a bit of a mystery creature, as few have been caught worldwide, yet quite a few have been boated in the Azores. White marlin appear frequently, arriving generally before the blue marlin, but are available from May into October. At times, they are more likely to be caught by anglers trolling for tuna than by blue marlin enthusiasts, as the whites prefer more diminutive offerings that move at a slower speed. Nevertheless, offshore prospecting with lures or baits that will attract either whites or blues is the best option. Broadbill fishing is still lightly explored, although swordfish weighing up to 350 pounds have been caught here.

The Azores can offer sensational fishing for tuna. The primary target is the yellowfin, and it is not uncommon to run across these fish by the acre. Many very big yellowfins, in the 200- to 300-pound class, are caught here, particularly between July and October. Bluefin tuna are also found in the Azores, although not in the same abundance as yellowfins. Some giants have been caught, including a 974-pound 80-pound-line-class women's world record in October of 1996. But bigeye tuna are here in great quantity and in large sizes, beginning in April, and there is excellent action for these fish into June, especially off of Ponta Delgada. This is when yellowfin action picks up. Yellowfin and bluefin action heats up again in September and October, although these fish are overshadowed by the billfish at that time.

In addition to all of this, big mako sharks also frequent Azorean waters. Some 500-pounders have been trolled up unexpectedly, providing great excitement to anglers pursuing other species. Blue sharks, threshers, and several others are here as well, and such species as dolphin, skipjack tuna, and bonito are also in the mix. Inshore fishing can produce barracuda, amberjack, grouper, bluefish (several world records have been established in the Azores), and a slew of bottom species. Certainly these aren't the target of expeditions to the Azores, but by bringing some extra gear along, on a blustery day you can get into a leeward shore and still keep the lines wet and stretched.

Fish do not chew their food; they would suffocate if they tried to chew, which would interfere with the passage of water over the gills, necessary for obtaining oxygen.

P

POSSESSION LIMIT

A restriction on the total number of fish of a species or group of species that may be legally possessed by one person. In the field, the possession limit is usually the same as the daily bag or creel limit, which means that an angler may not take in a single day more than a daily creel limit. In some places, it is legal to have in possession a number exceeding a daily creel limit, for example, when the catch is stored at home in a freezer. Usually a possession limit is twice the daily creel limit, although in certain places it is more liberal than that. However, in other places the possession limit and daily creel limit at all times are the same no matter where the fish are stored.

A possession limit is a legal game regulation established by the fisheries agency with jurisdiction over the location being fished, and enforced by fish and wildlife conservation officers. Possession limits vary widely, and anglers who will be keeping fish must know the regulations that apply to both daily creel and possession limits wherever they are fishing. **See: Creel Limit; Fisheries Management; Regulations.**

POTAMADROMOUS

Fish that migrate within rivers or streams to spawn. **See: Anadromous.**

POUT, HORNED

A regional name (primarily in New England) for black or brown bullhead *(see: bullhead, black; bullhead, brown).*

POWER

The amount of pressure that it takes to flex a fishing rod. **See: Rod, Fishing.**

PRACTICE PLUG

A hookless, cylindrical, plastic- or rubber-coated weight used for practice casting with spinning, spincasting, and baitcasting tackle. **See: Casting.**

PREDATOR

A species that feeds on other species. Most of the fish species that are pursued by anglers are predators at or near the top of the food chain.

PRESENTATION

The act of delivering a bait, lure, or fly to a fish is an intrinsic element of every type of angling, whether casting, trolling, stillfishing, drift fishing, or jigging. Even though the term "presentation" is the one most often used with respect to casting, and especially fly fishing (as in upstream presentation, or upstream fishing), presentation is all about how objects are delivered and manipulated. Although many astute anglers are fastidious about presentation, many more are haphazard about it, even though they pay a lot of attention to lure or fly selection, to specific places to fish, and to the act of locating fish.

Good presentation begins with such obvious skills as accurate casting, using a bit of stealth, minimizing noise, and not coming right up on, over, or through areas to be fished. Stream trout anglers are among the craftiest of all people in approaching their quarry. This craftiness is largely due to the fact that stream trout, which are often found in clear and relatively shallow water, are respected for their wariness. So, anglers approach them carefully in very particular ways and try to offer flies or lures as naturally and unobtrusively as possible. Other species, especially inhabitants of stillwaters and of turbid or more cover-laden environments, do not typically enjoy the "crafty" reputation, and anglers tend to be less refined about the deliverance of their offerings, which may be a mistake.

Good presentations are aided by getting within proper casting range to make accurate casts and timely retrievals. For example, as a rule, the farther you are from specific objects that may shelter fish, the harder it is to make a really precise presentation with certain lures. If you can get close without spooking the fish, you can make a greater number of presentations in a given time period than if you were farther away, and you can be more thorough. On the other hand, if you cannot get close enough without spooking the fish, then you have to be able not only to make long, accurate casts, but to position yourself to make each one count.

In many cases, the first cast to a prospective fish lie is the most important one, so getting yourself in the best possible position is especially important. However, repetitive casting to the same spot sometimes proves more effective, but a lot of anglers who cast from boats are in too much of a hurry to do this. Making repeated presentations to cover, for example, is not something that many bass anglers, who tend to run-and-gun from one likely piece of cover to the next, do often enough. Sometimes it pays to be more like steelhead, salmon, or trout anglers, who routinely make many presentations through the same river lie before connecting with a fish. And they make exactly the same presentation drift after drift after drift, knowing that their offering has to be made at just the right depth, speed, and place time after time.

Varying the angle of presentation, however, is a good move for mobile anglers, and this is where boat manipulation skills come into play, or where wading anglers need to be patient and maneuver themselves into the proper place. When bass anglers fish cover, for example, such as fallen trees and vegetation, they have to fish it in ways that will make

P

their lures reach the fish and will let the lures swim or be retrieved as naturally and convincingly as possible. This is why electric motors are such valuable devices. Most cover should be approached from the edges first, working deeper into it with successive casts.

The nuances of making good presentations also have to do with positioning a boat properly to drift in current or with the wind, maneuvering a boat when trolling (since this is what actually puts the lure or bait in a place for the fish to get it), and using retrieval methods for various lures. These and more aspects of presentation are discussed in many places in this book, especially under the respective lure entries.

See: Casting; Retrieving; Trolling.

PREY
A species that is fed upon by other species.

PRIEST
A short club for quickly and humanely killing a fish that is to be kept for consumption.

See: Fish Preparation—Care.

PRINCE EDWARD ISLAND
The smallest province in Canada, Prince Edward Island (PEI) is in the Gulf of St. Lawrence on Canada's east coast, separated from New Brunswick and Nova Scotia by the Northumberland Strait. Just 175 miles long and between 4 and 40 miles wide, PEI is connected to the mainland by a 10-mile-long bridge and summer ferry service. This island is the most densely settled province in Canada, with 135,000 residents, most of whom depend on renewable resources for their livelihoods.

PEI has 1,100 miles of coastline, deeply indented with many estuaries and bays. Other than barrier-beach ponds, which are found at the mouths of many streams, there are few natural lakes. There are, however, more than 800 artificial ponds, many originally constructed as mill ponds. The streams themselves are short and spring-fed; most originating from springs that discharge 7°C water in summer and winter. As a result, streams on PEI are less reliant on surface runoff and maintain good flows, even in summer.

PEI hosts a limited number of sportfish, but the numbers are deceptive. Recreational fishing here, both in freshwater and saltwater, is very good. This fact is largely unknown outside the province, excluding the island's storied tuna fishery.

Freshwater
PEI is one of the few places in North America where the brook trout, also called the speckled trout, is still king. The large input of mineral-rich groundwater and nutrient-rich runoff from agricultural land, combined with short streams and large estuaries, have created ideal conditions for brook trout. These fish inhabit virtually every stream on the Island. Sea-run trout, the fish most sought after by anglers, range up to 6 pounds.

The trout season runs from April 15 to September 15, with a generous daily limit of 10 fish. The Trout River in western PEI now has an experimental Trout Management Zone, with a shorter season, reduced creel limit, and a barbless-hook requirement.

Until mid-June, anglers most often use bait or lures to take sea trout, particularly in estuaries or ponds. The timing of runs varies from river to river, but many waters have a run of sea trout beginning in mid-June and lasting until mid-July. From the middle of June until early August, small dry flies are preferred, with large flies used in estuaries or after dark. The streams on PEI are small, and rods from 6 to 8 feet are preferred by fly anglers.

Many people enjoy fishing for trout in ponds, using baits or flies. Some ponds, however, can become overly enriched and weedy in the summer, making fishing difficult. Some ponds become too warm in summer, and angling at this time is generally less successful.

Rainbow trout are an introduced species on PEI, and only a half-dozen streams exist where they can regularly be taken. The season for rainbows is the same as for brook trout. In the winter, however, there is a put-and-take rainbow trout fishery in a few small lakes.

Atlantic salmon were once common in many PEI streams; however, overfishing and habitat degradation have reduced the number of salmon throughout the province. With habitat enhancement and stocking of salmon smolts raised in semi-natural rearing ponds, there are now five principal streams where Atlantic salmon can be angled. These are the Morell, Valleyfield, West, Naufrage, and Trout Rivers. Most of the salmon angled on PEI are taken in the Morell River, located on the northeastern side of the Island. This is the only river on PEI that is a scheduled river, and its main branch can be fished only by fly after June 1.

Although the salmon run is primarily composed of grilse, some salmon in excess of 20 pounds have been encountered. Because more than 90 percent of grilse caught on the island originate from semi-natural rearing ponds, catch-and-release is less important on PEI than in other regions where returning fish are needed to meet spawning requirements. The season extends from June 1 through late November, but the best fishing for salmon occurs from mid-June through late July. On the Morell River, many anglers enjoy trolling flies for salmon in Leards Pond, a large former mill pond. Most angling for salmon is done by wading the main river, however.

Other species found in freshwater include white perch, rainbow smelt, and eels. Perch are taken from July until September, but only in a few locations with relatively warm water temperatures. This fish was formerly restricted to warm areas, such as barrier-beach ponds, but in recent years has expanded its range to include a few artificial impoundments in some rivers.

Rainbow smelt are caught through the ice with spears in winter, although they are also fished from many wharves in late summer and autumn. Hundreds of "smelt shacks" cover the ice in estuaries and bays across PEI. Although eels have traditionally been speared through the ice in ponds and estuaries in winter, or caught by "flambeau-ers" using lights in spring, the drop in eel numbers has virtually decimated any recreational opportunities associated with this species.

Saltwater

Saltwater angling on PEI continues to be the most underutilized component of its recreational fishery. The island's many estuaries and bays, and offshore areas, offer recreational anglers excellent opportunities for a variety of saltwater species. No saltwater recreational license was required as of 1999, but a change in this policy is anticipated.

Deep-sea fishing along PEI provides good family fishing opportunities, and is a great way to enjoy beautiful coastline vistas. Mackerel, cod, and dogfish are the species most commonly caught, and numerous deep-sea charters are available throughout the island from midsummer through early autumn. Visitors can obtain a brochure about saltwater sportfishing from the provincial tourism agency.

Mackerel can be exceedingly abundant and are superb fighters if taken on a fly or even a spinning rod. There is no limit on the number that can be caught, and when runs are on, anglers can fish from wharves or near causeways, where flatfish are also taken. The commercial fishery for cod has been curtailed, but a viable recreational fishery still exists off the coast of PEI. This fishery also occurs from midsummer through early autumn, but, as is not the case with mackerel, there is a daily limit. Dogfish, a small shark, is another species of interest to the recreational angler. In autumn, dogfish can be so abundant that some commercial fishermen consider them a nuisance.

For those interested in larger fish, three species of sharks are commonly caught off the coast of PEI: blue, mako, and porbeagle. Although sharks are abundant, catch-and-release is recommended because of their low reproductive rate. Fishing for these sharks generally occurs in autumn. Chum is used to attract sharks to the vicinity of the boat. Most of the blue and mako sharks top out at about 100 pounds, but the porbeagle can run two to three times this weight. Sharks of this size are excellent fighters and provide plenty of excitement.

North Lake, in eastern PEI, boasts of being the "Tuna Capital of the World," with a historical catch

A bluefin tuna is brought to the dock at North Lake.

of many bluefin tuna in excess of 1,000 pounds. The tuna boom at North Lake took place from the 1970s through the mid-1980s but was followed by nearly 10 years with few reported tuna landings. Bluefin tuna numbers worldwide have declined, and the number of fish that can be caught is now federally regulated. The late 1990s have witnessed a return of the tuna and a subsequent resurgence in tuna charters off North Lake.

Four existing world-record giant bluefin tuna have been caught in PEI waters or by PEI anglers. Three of them weighed more than 1,000 pounds and include the all-tackle 1,496-pound world record, landed at Auld's Cove, Nova Scotia, by a PEI angler in 1979. This is the largest bluefin ever captured on rod and reel.

With PEI at the northerly migratory range of bluefin tuna, fish appearing here are, on average, at or near peak sizes. Since the mid-1990s, numerous giants in the 800- to 1,000-pound class have been caught annually off PEI. In 1997, for example, roughly 150 giants were landed in the southern gulf district (there are three districts here), and their average weight was 974 pounds; many of these were not landed by recreational anglers, however. Approximately another 330 tuna were landed in the other districts; their weights averaged between 500 and 600 pounds.

This fishery takes place from August through October, and in recent years the largest tuna have shown up in August and September. The fishery is closed when a total weight quota is reached, as all of

P

the giants are killed upon capture and sold and shipped away, primarily to Japan. The arrangement with charter boat captains here is that tuna belong to the boat, even when caught by a client who has paid for the charter (though charter fees may be waived when a tuna is caught). These boats are otherwise used in commercial deep-sea and lobster fishing but are outfitted for the pursuit of tuna in season. Tuna must be sportfished on rod and reel on a registered commercial fishing vessel to which a bluefin tuna license is attached. The established tuna ports are North Lake and Tignish.

PROCESSED BAIT

Foodstuffs that are used to attract and catch fish even though they do not occur naturally in aquatic environments. The term processed bait is used to differentiate such items from natural baits *(see)*. Examples of processed baits include bread, dough, cheese, sweet corn, cubed meat, seeds, vegetables, and protein boilies *(see)*. Most of these are used in angling for coarse fish *(see)*, although some take a few predatory species, including trout and catfish.
See: Bait; Chumming; Float.

PROPBAIT

A surface lure with a propeller.
See: Surface Lure.

PROPELLER GUARD

A propeller guard is an outboard motor accessory for small-boat anglers who fish shallow rivers or venture into uncertain waters. Made of heavy metal and encircling the propeller, it is primarily used on 7.5- through 15-hp motors and protects the propeller and part of the lower skeg. In appropriate situations, the motor is operated in the tilted shallow-water-drive position so it will kick up when it hits an object. Some anglers have devised homemade guards, including pitchforks hose-clamped around the lower unit, but many of these devices impede high-speed operation. An alternative to propeller guards is a jet drive *(see)* outboard motor.

PUERTO RICO

Known to some as the "Land of Enchantment," Puerto Rico is an island with a strong and certainly beckoning offshore fishing reputation. The charm for anglers is a year-round fishery for blue marlin, one mostly pursued by trolling. Neither the blue marlin nor other big-game species are sought far offshore, especially along the north coast. Puerto Rico's fortuitous positioning in the eastern end of the Greater Antilles, with the Atlantic Ocean on the north and Caribbean Sea on the south, makes this possible.

Although it is a self-governing commonwealth in association with the United States, Puerto Rico is in fact closer to South America (480 miles) than to North America (1,063 miles). It lies roughly 80 miles east of the Dominican Republic, separated by the Mona Passage, and 37 miles west of the Virgin Islands, separated by the Virgin Passage.

A generally mountainous island (Cerro la Punta is the highest peak, at 4,390 feet) spanning 3,515 square miles, Puerto Rico has several small islands around its 311-mile-long coast. Desecheo is just 10 miles from Puerto Rico to the west, the popular tourist site Isla Mona ("Monkey Island") is 41 miles to the west, and Caja de Muertos ("Dead Man Chest") is the most prominent of several small islands a few miles from the southern coastal town of Ponce.

There are no significant islands to the north, but to the east lies the 51-square-mile Vieques, which is mostly a U.S. military installation and internationally known as a target and training area for the U.S. Navy. The eastern region of Puerto Rico has abundant rock formations, cays, and islands. Of principal interest is Culebra ("Serpent Island"), 17 miles to the east, which has guest houses, small hotels, restaurants, skin-diving operations, and good sportfishing. Crystal clear waters, breathtaking beaches, and coral formations are abundant, and many seabirds use the area for nesting.

Offshore

Obviously, Puerto Rico has numerous blue marlin in its waters. As well it should. Neighboring St. Thomas is generally viewed as the blue marlin jewel in the Atlantic/Caribbean, especially for big fish, and Puerto Rico is surely a close second. In fact, these two destinations are among the top locales anywhere to fish for big Atlantic blue marlin.

They do, of course, share much the same waters and are in the same migratory path for marlin. They might be spawning, or at least nursery, areas for young fish as well, as a great many small blues are seen in these waters. Puerto Rico has yet to produce a rod-and-reel grander, unlike St. Thomas, which gets more notoriety as a result. But the big fish are sure to be in Puerto Rican waters, and many visiting anglers each year try to be the first to set the grand standard.

Local boat skippers see marlin in the monster category every season, and two fish have been caught that were close to the 1,000-pound mark. One of those is the present Puerto Rican record, a 984-pounder taken in 1985; another giant blue weighed in at 980 pounds. Marlin in the 500- to 800-pound class come to the boat every season.

The trade winds can produce rough seas, incidentally, although this seldom stops the big sportfishing boats from venturing forth. Easterly or northeasterly winds, usually between 10 and 20 knots, are the rule,. Hurricane winds, of course, are another matter, and Puerto Rico was wracked hard in September 1989 by Hugo.

North coast. The currents, trade winds, deep water, and upwellings offshore from Puerto Rico all interact to create a favorable situation for pelagic species and baitfish, and especially for marlin. The Puerto Rico Trench runs parallel to the north shore of this 110-mile-long island, creating depths well beyond the reach of the most advanced sportfishing sonar. In fact, the deepest water in the Atlantic—28,374 feet—is in the western end of this abyss, approximately 75 miles from the main island.

Puerto Rico is washed by currents flowing from the Atlantic into the Caribbean and thence becoming the Yucatán Current headed into the Gulf of Mexico. The flow washes around the island to the west in the Mona Passage. It is believed that billfish migrate past the north coast and funnel by the west coast into the Venezuelan Basin. Blue marlin, white marlin, sailfish, yellowfin tuna, wahoo, and dolphin are abundant along the north coast.

Of the billfish, the blue marlin is most numerous. Blues are caught year-round, usually only 2 to 5 miles off the coast. Relatively small blues are captured between February and June. In June they begin to appear in numbers, and from July through October the fishing is unusually bountiful. The blues that remain from June until the middle of August are larger than those caught in September and October. Blues usually vary between 225 and 450 pounds in summer; however, 713- and 895-pounders were boarded in a single summer day, and a 980-pounder was caught off the north shore. The summer fishery here may be good because the blues are then the main catch rather than one of many species to be caught. At other times of the year, the catch is peppered with all the typical offshore nomads that one sees elsewhere in blue water.

A number of charter boats operate out of San Juan, the capital city, and weekend fishing is popular among local anglers. Despite relatively small fishing effort, approximately 500 blues are caught annually off San Juan alone, and twice that number are taken off the rest of the northern shores.

Such prolific results are reflected in the records of the prestigious Club Nautico de San Juan Billfish Tournament, which holds the unofficial world record for most blue marlin—190—caught in a single four-day tournament in August 1988.

More than 15 blue marlin tournaments are held annually around the island; these are sanctioned by the local sportfishing ruling body, Asociacion de Pesca Deportiva de Puerto Rico, and the country has been honored with conservation awards for its development of sportfishing regulations and conservation ethics. Nine of these tournaments are held along the northern shore.

White marlin are caught every month, year-round, but are more plentiful in April, May, and June. Whites usually range from 45 to 65 pounds, but some over 90 pounds have been caught. Sailfish occur along the north coast in October and are most abundant in November and until the middle of December.

May through July is the best period for yellowfin tuna. Anglers sometimes encounter large tuna schools during early summer months. The usual size of yellowfins is from 60 to 150 pounds, and some approach 200 pounds.

Dorado (dolphin) numbers are abundant off the north coast, especially in summer. Yet the best months for dorado fishing here are from early December through the beginning of March. The average weight is from 10 to 15 pounds, but fish of 30 to 50 pounds are not uncommon.

Wahoo fishing is especially good close to shore off San Juan in January. These fish are also abundant in late December, and available in good numbers during the rest of the year.

There is fair reef fishing off the north coast as well. This is much better in the northwestern sector than it is near San Juan.

East coast.   Offshore fishing is excellent on the east coast closer to the southwestern region of the island. Here, a few miles off Humacao, is Grappler Bank, whose edges drop from 30 to 500 fathoms a mile from the bank; and Little Bank, whose edges drop from 45 to 400 fathoms. Grappler is the larger bank, and wahoo are most abundant on its eastern side. Little Bank produces tuna, dolphin, and skipjack tuna, as well as wahoo.

Although blue marlin over 700 pounds have been caught here, these banks are known as a wahoo paradise. Thirty- to 50-pound wahoo are the norm, even though several over 80 pounds are caught yearly and a few over 100 pounds have been reported from Grappler. The prime time for these fish is October and November.

There was once an abundance of sailfish near Culebra, but the large balls of sardines that attracted them to this area disappeared in the mid-1990s. A resurgence of sailfish occurred in the late 1990s, but not great numbers as before.

The reefs on this coast, in the Fajardo, Vieques, Culebra, and Humacao perimeter, provide the best reef fishing of the island. Fishing in these waters is also productive for wahoo, tuna, and other small migratory species. A full-service marina exists at Humacao.

South coast.   Billfish, tuna, wahoo, and dorado are plentiful along the south coast from Guanica to Cabo Rojo. Blue marlin are caught most consistently south of Guanica and La Parguera, and often the largest blues of the year come from here.

The billfish found along the south coast are also migratory but seem to come and go with the currents more than those in the north. Billfishing here begins in March and is consistently good until May; April and May are the best months.

A large run of dorado lingers here during the tropical winter months, when the water temperature is cooler and the winds stronger. These fish average 30 to 50 pounds, and several 60- to 80-pounders are caught yearly from the 100-fathom mark close to shore and up to 15 miles offshore.

The first fishing and hunting club in the New World was Pennsylvania's Schuylkill Fishing Company, founded in 1732 along the banks of the Schuylkill River in present-day Philadelphia.

P

Reef fishing is particularly good at La Parguera, where snapper, grouper, and mackerel are the main species. Private marinas exist at Ponce and La Parguera.

West coast. This area could be called a big-game angler's dream. Here the Mona Channel has depths to 3,600 feet and contains a line of ridges and canyons. Multiple blue marlin hookups and more than 10 strikes daily are common in peak periods. World-record dorado and wahoo have also come from this area.

There are two blue marlin runs off Mayaguez. One is in the summer and may have its origin in the run off San Juan. The larger run is in August, September, and October and may consist of fish migrating through the Mona Channel on their way to Central and South America. The larger run produces many fish from 75 to 200 pounds and provides great light-tackle fishing opportunity.

The run to the 100-fathom curve is about 15 miles from Mayaguez. The most productive blue marlin areas along the west are the Pichincho, Guineo, and Esponjas Banks, and the waters near Desecheo and Mona Islands. Marlin here average 150 pounds, and a 984-pounder is the largest yet caught. Pichincho has a series of peaks and a rapid dropoff. A sharp dropoff a mile from Mona Island's east end is excellent for blue marlin. Desecheo is prime for blues and sailfish along its abrupt dropoff from 600 to 2,400 feet.

Charter boat services are much more limited in this region than they are at San Juan.

Baits, lures, tackle. Trollers place great emphasis on watching for bait, feeding fish, and other signs that might indicate the presence of marlin. Both natural baits and lures are part of their arsenal.

Blue marlin here display a varied diet. Tuna, dorado, mackerel, and needlefish are among their fare. White marlin eat a great quantity of squid, as well as blue runners, surgeonfish, and little tuna. Sailfish feed on essentially the same forage as white marlin, plus flyingfish, which are the chief food of dorado.

The most popular angling baitfish in Puerto Rican waters is the ballyhoo, which is naturally abundant locally and used to catch all species of big-game fish. Mullet may be used for billfishing, as are ballyhoo, small barracudas, and bonito. Small dorado, tuna, and tarpon are also successfully employed. As in most big-game areas, the baits used do not necessarily reflect the actual diet of the fish sought.

High-speed trolling with large offshore lures is favored by some anglers over slower trolling with natural baits, in part to cover lots of ground while searching. These are effective, as are smaller lures used by light-tackle enthusiasts.

Generally, big-game tackle here consists of 30- and 80-pound International Game Fish Association (IGFA-class) outfits. Some tournaments mandate a maximum of 30-pound tackle. Many anglers choose even lighter tackle for dorado or billfish. Fly fishing has increased, as good numbers of fish make this method a more feasible proposition.

Inshore

With all the attention placed on marlin in the past, little has been detailed about Puerto Rico's inshore fishing opportunities. However, snook, tarpon, bonefish, barracuda, ladyfish, snapper, and assorted other species exist here, principally along the shore where there are flats and bays. In recent times, a little more attention has been paid to these resources, and even some skiff guides exist for inshore, mangrove, lagoon, and tidal river fishing

San Juan Bay is known to have large schools of tarpon, and the mangrove-lined creeks and lagoons that branch off from the bay are also prime for tarpon and occasionally snook and jacks. October through December brings schooling action from small tarpon; larger fish roam here from January through March, when 50- to 100-pounders are available. Fish to 150 pounds have been caught here, however. Some anglers concentrate on the mouth of San Juan Bay, where big tarpon swim along the edge of the ship channel. The Loiza River, and several lagoons, enter on the east side of the bay. The mouth of the Loiza is favored for tarpon and jacks after heavy rains muddy the water and draw in schools of fish to forage on bait; however, the river flows significantly only when heavy rains cause the upstream reservoir to overflow. The mouth of the Espiritu Santo River nearby is similar.

Flats and reefs on the south and east coast are generally lightly fished. On the east, Culebra Island, which is a national wildlife refuge, features good bonefishing, especially inside the bay of Ensenada Honda on the island's southwest tip. Numerous cays along the south mainland coast reportedly contain bonefish. The mangrove flats near La Parguera once harbored snook and bonefish but have suffered from netting.

PUMPING

The act of systematically raising the rod tip, then quickly lowering it while simultaneously reeling in line, in order to tire a fish and bring it to the boat. This is a key component of fighting a large or strong fish.

See: Landing Fish; Playing Fish.

PUNCTURING

A technique, usually used by fisheries professionals and occasionally by anglers, for relieving the pressure built up in the air bladders of fish that have been retrieved too rapidly from deep water and that are to be released. Puncturing is also known as venting and fizzing, and it is performed on species that do not have a pneumatic duct connected to the air bladder and that cannot expel air; these fish, when

P

retrieved quickly from deep water, cannot naturally adjust their air pressure and cannot make rapid vertical movements. Puncturing entails the insertion of a sharp object, usually a long needle, through the body wall of the fish to let the pent-up air escape through the puncture hole.

See: Catch-and-Release.

PUPA

A resting stage in the life cycle of some insects; the larval insect is enclosed in a protective case where it changes into the adult form.

See: Insects.

PURSE SEINE

A commercial fishing net that is used to encircle a school of fish (sometimes located by spotter planes); the net hangs curtainlike and is pulled tight much the same way as a string closes a purse.

See: Commercial Fisherman; Seine.

PUSHPOLE

A pole made of wood, aluminum, fiberglass, or graphite that is used to propel a boat quietly, or to temporarily stake (anchor) it in shallow water. Probably as old as the boat and possibly older than the paddle, a pushpole of some form has been intrinsic to boat use and, even with the sophistication of modern gas and electric motors, it is today still an important element of fishing, most popularly used in the shallows of marine estuaries, bays, flats, canals, and inshore environs.

Almost any open boat under 20 feet long can be propelled by a single pushpole. Though many people associate fishing use of a pushpole with saltwater flats angling, any small boat can be poled in a situation where the water is shallow and it is desirable to quietly move along. Pushpoles are used to propel a canoe upstream against a current, glide a skiff across a bonefish flat, or muscle a bass boat through heavy weeds.

The advantage offered by a pushpole is accomplishing movement with less noise than the quietest electric motor, with no batteries to become depleted or moving parts to wear out. The disadvantage is that a person who poles cannot fish while in the act of poling; if it is necessary to continuously pole, the poler does not fish while a companion does. Pushpoles may come in handy, incidentally, for retrieving lures that get snagged on objects. Some freshwater models are equipped with a head that sports a spike for such a purpose (or pulling down a tree branch to reach a stuck lure or fly).

Features. Pushpoles are between 12 and 22 feet long, depending on the size of boat and the usual depth of water fished, with most saltwater models 18 to 20 feet. The depth of water to be poled is the best guide for how long a pole should be, but many people base length equivalent to the overall size of the boat, so the pole, when fastened along the gunwale, doesn't extend much beyond the bow and/or transom.

Pushpoles were once solely fashioned from round lumber stock, then made out of hollow fiberglass tubing similar to that used for pole vaulting in track and field athletics, as well as from aluminum. Today the basic length of a pushpoles is made primarily from fiberglass; some are made from graphite, some from a composite of graphite and fiberglass, some from wood, and a few from aluminum. Though light, aluminum tends to be noisy, is prone to eventual rusting in saltwater, and can be cold to the touch; it is less popular and primarily restricted to small-boat use in freshwater. Wooden pushpoles are still used in some places, especially in northern river canoeing; they work for light applications, but don't last long in heavy-duty use, especially when asked to propel a relatively large boat in wind and/or current. Wooden poles have always been subject to sudden breakage, and while any pole can break, when you depend on a pushpole a lot, having it break can be as traumatic as losing your engine far from shore. Therefore, the majority of use has shifted to synthetic poles, primarily for durability and, in the case of graphite or composites, also for lightness. In saltwater, commercially made poles are virtually all made from synthetic materials and cost hundreds of dollars.

The diameter of a pushpole is generally from $1^1/_4$ to $1^1/_2$ inches, with the smaller diameter being better for smaller hands. A large-handed person

A guide uses a pushpole to quietly stalk the flats.

generally needs a thicker pole to avoid hand fatigue and cramping. The main section of the pole may be one piece or multiple pieces (some are three-piece units). Aluminum models may have two sections that telescope. You can make a wooden one from $1\frac{1}{4}$- to $1\frac{3}{8}$-inch round lumber yard stock, and attach a couple of 6-inch pieces of round stock side by side to one end of the pole for a foot.

Length and material has a bearing on weight, which can range from under 4 pounds to nearly 8 pounds in synthetics, and lighter in aluminum versions (which are smallest). Graphite pushpoles are most expensive, but they tend to be lighter, which is important because even the lightest poles feel heavy by the end of a day of poling. Graphite is also more slippery than other material, and some users wear light leather gloves for a better grip. Among synthetic poles, light colors, usually a cream or off-white, are less prevalent than dark colors, mainly black. Although dark colors get hot in the sun, they are believed to spook fish less than light poles. Wooden poles are usually unpainted; aluminum poles may be painted with a dull finish that does not produce glare.

Graphite poles are usually stiffer than other synthetic poles, and this endears them to many flats guides. Stiff poles are powerful but not very flexible, which means that beginning polers find them hard to use because they seem unresponsive. The real problem is that experienced polers know how to plan and anticipate every move in advance, while less experienced or beginning polers are more reactionary, and thus rely on the flex of a pole a good deal while maneuvering. Veteran guides prefer the stiffest and lightest poles for those times when they need to pole fast; a stiff pole enables quicker movement.

The ends of a pushpole may be round and blunt, tapered to a point, or fitted with a triangular or forked foot. Usually one end has a point and the other a foot or fork, so the pole can be reversed depending on the bottom material. The pointed end is used for burying in a soft bottom—to hold the boat in position for a while or to stake out—and for poling over hard bottom. It features a silent and relatively splashless entry and exit from the water. The larger foot end is used for poling over soft bottom or mud. Feet shapes include a Y, triangle, or hybrid of the other two. A triangular-shaped foot is popular for grabbing bottom and not sinking too far into a soupy bottom, and it can also be used for paddling, since it has more surface area. Both ends may be made from different material than the basic body of the pole, and can be replaced or changed, although aluminum ends are likely to be noisy in rock or hard-bottomed areas.

Pushpoles are usually mounted along the gunwale of a flats boat, and secured with J-shaped brackets. Three brackets are required to hold long synthetic poles in place, two facing inward at the ends and one facing outward in the center. These should be situated so as to put a bend in the pushpole while it is in the brackets, which supplies the friction to keep it in place. Telescoping aluminum poles can be stored in a rod locker. Wooden one-piece poles are usually just laid down in the boat.

Poling. Poling is not difficult and is entirely a function of practice. A South Florida flats guide can pole a 16- to 18-foot skiff all day for many miles without fatigue using finesse rather than brute power. So can the weekend angler who is in reasonable shape and learns the proper technique. Proper poling is seldom a matter of muscles and brute strength, although someone who has been poling for a long time is much more proficient than someone who has just started.

The important thing to remember is that travel in a straight line requires a balance of the effects of wind and/or current. To go straight ahead in calm water, just push the pole straight astern. If the water is calm and there is little or no wind, the bow of the boat moves in exactly the opposite direction from the thrust of the pushpole. If that thrust is essentially parallel to the keel and straight astern, the boat moves straight ahead regardless of whether the poler is in the center or to one side. Usually, however, there's wind and/or current, and this must be countered by "crabbing" the boat against those forces in a slightly right or left turning attitude, similar to but not quite as emphatic as necessary for turning. To pole continuously in a straight line

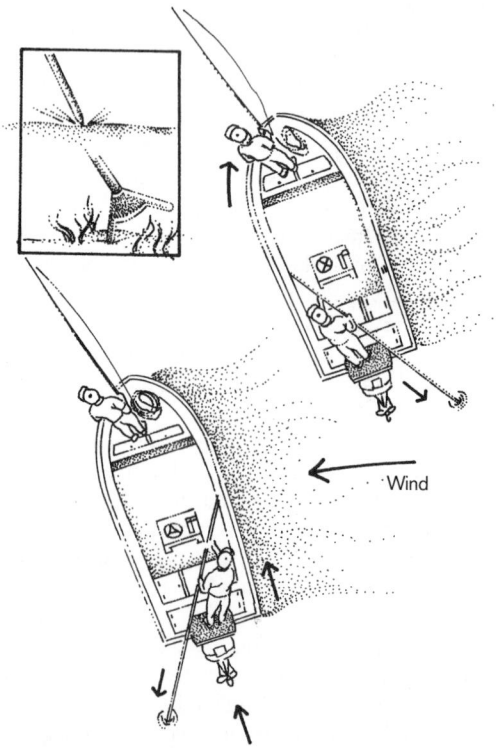

To turn the bow toward the wind, push off from the upwind side (right); to quarter with the wind instead of turning broadside to it, push off from the downwind side (left). Use a pointed end on a hard bottom and a forked end on a soft bottom (inset, top).

P

downwind, you do not need to keep switching from side to side. Angle the tip of the pole to one side or the other of the centerline to correct direction. Use short pushes when first learning and gradually you'll be able to use longer ones, walking your hands over each other down the pole as you push.

To turn left, stick the pole against the bottom off the left (port) corner of the stern and push. To turn right, the pole must be off the right (starboard) corner. The greater the pole's angle to one side or the other of the boat's centerline, the quicker the turn. Often it is necessary to push out the stern of the boat to give the bow angler a better angle at the fish; this is a modified turn which is executed by jamming the pointed end of the pole into the bottom a few feet from the stern and repositions the bow. It is especially useful so that the angler and poler are not aligned, which might be problematic for a fly caster.

If you're facing downwind and need to move quartering the wind, turn the boat to a 45-degree angle by pushing off at the stern on the upwind side, then keep the boat headed straight by pushing off on the downwind side.

Use the forked end for a soft bottom and the pointed end for a hard or in-between bottom. To prevent a pole from getting stuck in soft bottoms, twist it when completing the push to break the suction. Keep the angle of the pole high in hard bottoms to prevent it from slipping.

Staking out. Many anglers use a pushpole to keep the boat stationary if the water is reasonably shallow and the bottom soft enough. This is usually a temporary form of anchoring, and it is often done in such a way that if a strong fish is hooked, the pole can be untied and retrieved quickly to start moving as necessary. Some even carry a second shorter "stake-out" pole so that the boat can be immobilized at both ends. The long pole is usually thrust into the bottom at an angle of 30 degrees or less (from the horizontal and as low as possible to reduce the stress of bending), to also reduce the likelihood of interfering with casting, before being bent over even a little farther and tied to the boat. A strong pole will hold a boat in a surprising amount of wind and current, but if it is poorly made, or stressed too much via a sharp bend, that's the time when it will most likely fail. Before you buy a ready-made pole or blank, make sure the manufacturer stands behind its product under reasonable circumstances.

See: **Flats Boat.**

PUT-AND-TAKE FISHERY

The placing of hatchery-raised fish in waters where they can be caught by anglers. This term applies primarily to freshwater and refers to the stocking of fish in areas where there is little expectation of creating a naturally sustaining population of fish. Thus, the objective is stocking fish to provide recreation and food, not to enhance native populations of fish. This objective may apply to privately operated pay-to-fish preserves or farms or to public waters stocked by government agencies.

See: **Hatchery; Stocking.**

The Guinness Book of Records lists the longest earthworm as a South African one that reached 22 feet long when naturally extended.

P

QUARTERING SEA
Waves coming toward the quarter, or side.
See: Waves.

QUEBEC
Covering 523,859 square miles, Quebec is by far the largest of Canada's 10 provinces. Offering more than 1 million lakes and countless thousands of miles of rivers, it stands to reason that Quebec is also an angler's dream. More than that, the province offers a wide spectrum of angling experiences and species that would be difficult to match anywhere in North America.

A great many popular freshwater gamefish—northern pike, walleye, muskies, black bass, yellow perch, sunfish, brook trout, rainbow trout, brown trout, lake trout, arctic charr, landlocked salmon, and Atlantic salmon—abound within Quebec's borders. The potential surroundings are nearly as varied as the fish, allowing anglers to choose from a range of backdrops, including Montreal skyscrapers and distant wilderness settings in which hearing a floatplane would be a big event. Great fishing is accessible by vehicle, but if adventure is the goal, some of Quebec's waters are accessible only by air or pack trip. This province offers hidden headwater lakes, brawling rivers, and windswept tundra barrens, not to mention thousands of cottage lakes and some of Canada's largest and most sprawling impoundments.

Naturally, not every waterway teems with all species of gamefish, and certain areas are better for some species than others. For instance, muskie fishing is best along the St. Lawrence and Ottawa Rivers, whereas anglers will find the best arctic charr fishing in the rivers flowing into Ungava Bay 900 miles and more to the north. By the same token, excellent northern smallmouth bass fishing is available in the Gatineau region near the Ontario border; 600 miles to the east, the angler would be hard pressed to find a black bass of any kind. This is, instead, superb Atlantic salmon country. It's all a matter of knowing where in this vast province to go, and which locations provide the better opportunities. The waters mentioned below are only representative of the areas discussed.

St. Lawrence River Lowlands
From the last foothill of the Laurentian Range south to the U.S. border, southern Quebec offers the most diverse fishery within the province. By virtue of its population density, Quebec also has the most heavily used fishery. Transecting the region is the St. Lawrence River on its way from the Great Lakes to the Gulf of St. Lawrence. It offers variety of gamefish, high numbers, and trophy potential, especially in bodies of water like Lakes St. Francis, St. Louis, and St. Pierre, which are actually basins within the river's course, as well as Lake of Two Mountains at the confluence of the Ottawa and St. Lawrence Rivers.

Together, these four basins, as well as the Ottawa River upstream from the Carillon Dam, offer among the best trophy muskellunge fishing in North America. Fish of less than 30 pounds hardly get a second look from the region's dedicated muskie fishing fraternity, not when fish exceeding 50 pounds are being caught and released annually.

This level of success, however, is rarely enjoyed by casual anglers, as it requires specialized equipment and techniques. Although the muskie season opens in mid- to late June, few muskie anglers fish seriously here before mid-August. One reason is that muskies need most of the summer to regain the weight and strength lost over the winter and ensuing spawning period. The second is that late-season muskies are generally more aggressive; as summer yields to autumn, anglers record improved success. When weather permits, some diehards fish well into December, and specimens in the 50-pound class have been taken amid blizzards. Most muskies, in all sizes, are taken by anglers fast-trolling big plugs over shoals and ledges in 15 to 25 feet of water.

Northern Quebec offers many wilderness fishing experiences, among them brook trout fishing on the Broadback River, shown here.

Q

In an effort to control and even suppress introduced yellow perch, smallmouth bass, and rock bass numbers, Quebec fisheries biologists released muskie fingerlings in many lakes of the Lower Laurentians during the 1960s and 1970s. In the presence of abundant prey, the muskies quickly established self-sustaining populations and provide surprisingly good angling in bodies of water like Lakes Tremblant and Maskinongé, as well as in countless other smaller lakes throughout this cottage country. Casting a big jerkbait is the most productive method, and, although most of the fish are in the 5- to 15-pound class, their numbers more than compensate for their size.

The basins of the St. Lawrence River also consistently produce big walleye, thanks to the abundance of baitfish in the murky, nutrient-rich waters. Walleye weighing up to 4 pounds are common, and anglers targeting big walleye catch fish of 8 to 12 pounds throughout the summer. Most conventional techniques like bottom bouncing, jigging, and trolling produce results when varied according to water and weather conditions. The common denominator, however, is that the majority of bigger fish are caught in areas of some current around the islands and along the edges of the shipping channel on Lake St. Francis and Lake St. Louis. On Lake of Two Mountains, it's important to work the edges of the shoals that follow the current of the Ottawa River.

The easternmost of the St. Lawrence River basins, Lake St. Pierre has not traditionally produced many big walleye, but it does regularly yield sauger worth bragging about. These oddly marked kin of walleye occur in most waters linked to the St. Lawrence, but St. Pierre is known as a consistent sauger producer, offering a reasonable chance at a fish in the 3- to 4-pound class.

Black bass thrive throughout southern Quebec as well as in many of the cottage country lakes of the Lower Laurentian. Smallmouths are the dominant variety, and, although most are small—a 4-pounder is classified as trophy size—they are every bit as feisty as their reputation dictates. The St. Lawrence River, the Ottawa River, and Lakes St. Francis, St. Louis, and Two Mountains are all good bets throughout the summer. So are the Chateauguay River from the U.S. border to Lake St. Louis, and, east of that, the Richelieu River, Chambly Basin, and Missisquoi Bay—an arm of Lake Champlain that extends into Quebec. Lakes Memphremagog, Massawippi, and Brome, as well as many smaller bodies of water in the eastern townships along the U.S. border, also have excellent populations of smallmouths.

In the Lower Laurentians, Bark Lake near Barkmere, Tremblant near St. Jovite, Achigan near St. Hippolyte, and Ouareau near St. Donat, along with many other lakes, offer good smallmouth fishing.

Good largemouth bass fishing spots are something of a rarity in Quebec and are rarely divulged. There are fishable pockets in the weed-choked bays of Lake St. Francis, among the Peace Islands of Lake St. Louis, and also among the Boucherville Islands of the St. Lawrence River off the east end of Montreal Island. The fish tend to be in the 2- to 4-pound class, and one double that from Quebec waters is definitely worth writing home about.

Northern pike are present in most of the region's waters. A few notable exceptions, among them Memphremagog, lie in the eastern townships. Pressure on these pike is such that most weigh less than 6 pounds, although specimens twice that size are caught on occasion. Anybody looking for trophy pike stands a better chance in the more remote waters of central Quebec. This region does boast a fishable population of chain pickerel, however, especially in Lake Memphremagog, where a 3-pounder is better than average.

Although not native to these waters, rainbow and brown trout were introduced so long ago and so frequently that they have indeed taken hold. Thanks to regular supplemental stocking efforts, the fishing is surprisingly good. One of the prime areas is Lachine Rapids, a fast-water stretch of the St. Lawrence River where it squeezes around the south side of the island of Montreal. Although browns and rainbows of 8 to 14 pounds are caught there every year, a more reasonable expectation is a fish half that size. From February through April, shore fishing is productive along the south side of the rapids, but boat fishing is distinctly more productive because a larger number of pools are accessible. The rapids can be extremely treacherous, however, and anglers are advised to venture out with a reliable craft and someone who knows the water. Casting a variety of lures works well here.

Good fly fishing for rainbows, browns, and even some brook trout exists along the Chaudière, which flows from Lake Mégantic near the Maine-Quebec border north to enter the St. Lawrence River near Quebec City. Although the river is treacherous in high water, many areas are easy to wade. Fish of a pound or less are most abundant, but it isn't unusual to hook a trout of 3 pounds. Coaxing it from the currents is another matter.

Browns and rainbows have been stocked in numerous lakes in the eastern townships, the most popular of which are Memphremagog and Massawippi. Although both harbor bigger fish, a reasonable expectation is trout between 2 and 4 pounds. The most productive time is the two-week period after the late-April opening (or early-May ice out, whichever comes first), when the trout forage close to shore and can be caught by fast-trolling plugs or streamers about 4 feet below the surface close to the shoreline. The technique also produces landlocked salmon in the 2- to 6-pound range on Lake Memphremagog. Lake trout are also present in both lakes, although these fish are much more difficult to catch, especially after they've moved to deeper water. Shallow trolling works early, but by June deep trolling is the game, using lures that resemble rainbow smelt.

Lake trout tend to be more abundant in the lakes of the Laurentian playground, north and west of Montreal. Among them are Lakes Cayamant and Poisson Blanc near Gracefield, Lake Simon near Duhamel, Lake McGregor north of Buckingham, and Lake Tremblant near St. Jovite. Although the latter produces hefty lakers on occasion, it is better known for its big landlocked salmon. Biologists introduced Atlantic salmon fry throughout the 1960s, and with large numbers of rainbow smelt present as well as ideal spawning redds available on the Caché River, the fish quickly took root.

Tremblant has produced salmon topping the 23-pound mark and regularly yields fish of between 8 and 16 pounds. Smelt-imitation lures trolled close to the surface during the first three weeks of the season work well, after which deep fishing comes into play.

Despite the variety of high-profile gamefish found through southern Quebec, the greatest angling effort is expended on various panfish species. Without question, yellow perch are the most widely distributed panfish. This distribution is partly natural and partly due to human carelessness; thus, these fish are abundant all along the St. Lawrence River from the Ontario border east to Quebec City, including Lakes St. Francis, St. Louis, and St. Pierre; along the Ottawa River and Lake of Two Mountains; and in Richelieu River and Missisquoi Bay. Eastern township lakes like Memphremagog, Massawippi, and Brome are good bets all through the summer, and in the winter ice fishing season.

Most of the cottage-country lakes in the Laurentian playground also have large populations of perch, but they tend to be rather small. Lakes St. Francis, Two Mountains, and St. Pierre offer the best fish, in number and size. Dunking a night-crawler in the pockets among the many weedbeds yields the best catches.

Where perch are present, there are apt to be rock bass, pumpkinseeds, and even some bluegills as well. The most prized of the panfish, however, is the black crappie, which is found in large schools on the St. Lawrence and Ottawa Rivers. In May, bull-head fishing is popular along waterways like the Chateauguay River. Most of the fishing occurs at night from shore. You'll find the most productive spots by looking for a collection of lights from lanterns along the shoreline.

In addition to the aforementioned fishing in southern Quebec, runs of shad and a winter tommycod fishery exist here. Atlantic shad first show up in Montreal-area waters toward the middle of May and linger for about three weeks before continuing on their migration to the spawning grounds at the base of Carillon Dam at the head of Lake of Two Mountains. During their all-too-brief stay, they provide good fishing on the Rivière des Mille Iles near Terrebonne, and on the Rivière des Prairies near the hydroelectric facility located between the Pie IX Bridge and the Papineau Bridge. Most anglers wade waist-deep and then cast small, brightly colored shad darts out into the current on light line. This is shoulder-to-shoulder fishing most of the time, but when one of these fish starts to peel line, one quickly forgets the crowd. Most of the shad weigh 3 to 4 pounds, but fish up to 8 pounds have been taken here.

Tommycod are also migrants from saltwater, but they make their spawning runs in the middle of winter after the Christmas holidays. The major spawning ground is at the mouth of the Ste. Anne de la Pérade River, which flows into the St. Lawrence about halfway between Montreal and Quebec City. Traditionally, between Christmas and New Year's, a village of some 1,200 fishing shanties is set up on the ice in preparation for the onslaught of anglers, who arrive by cars, vans, and buses. Some tommycod are caught at the beginning of January, but the prime time is usually between January 12 and 20. Few if any fish are left come the beginning of February.

These fish look like miniature cod and average between 8 and 12 inches in length; a big one runs to 18 or 19 inches. The singularly unsophisticated fishing method consists of dangling a bank of lines off a 2 × 4 into a hole that runs the length of the shanty. A heavy lead weight holds each line to the bottom, and from these lines two short pieces of cord are suspended that each hold a hook baited with a cube of half-frozen liver. By monitoring the vibrations of a matchstick tied into the line at eye level, the angler detects the bites and then simply hauls up the line. Sometimes you have only one fish, sometimes two, and occasionally it's possible to haul in four fish, two clinging to each cube of bait!

The fishing goes on around the clock, but the best action is at night. The fish come in waves and, when the bite is on, hit faster than the lines can be rebaited. Periods of incoming tide seem to be most productive.

Eastern Region
Lower St. Lawrence River: Gaspé Peninsula, North Shore, and Anticosti Island. Almost all of Quebec's more than 100 scheduled Atlantic salmon rivers flow through this region. Among the most popular and perhaps best known are those of the Gaspé Peninsula, an idyllic coastal region of rugged headlands buffeted by brisk onshore breezes from the Gulf of St. Lawrence on one side and rolling lands caressed by the gentle waters of the Baie des Chaleurs on the other. The peninsula alone boasts 26 salmon rivers, among them such fabled waters as the Matapédia, Grand Cascapédia, Bonaventure, York, and St. Jean, as well as lesser-known waters such as the Patapédia, Little Cascapédia, Grande, Dartmouth, and Ste. Anne. Also found on the peninsula is the Matane, where many of today's finest salmon anglers learned to fish for Atlantic salmon, as well as a number of restored rivers. These include the Nouvelle, Pabos, Port Daniel, Cap Chat, and Ouelle.

Perhaps the popularity of these waters lies in a century of unbroken angling tradition, but it more likely rests in their present-day accessibility. With a couple of minor exceptions, Highway 132 crosses the lower reaches of these rivers, making it possible to do a complete loop of the Gaspé.

Starting in the highlands of the peninsula's interior, these streams change abruptly in nature along their short and tumultuous course to the sea. Initially their waters tumble across basalt ledges, then over boulders, and finally around freestone banks before reaching the estuaries. The habitat is well suited for the sea-run Atlantic salmon that spawn in these rivers, and the pools in which they linger on their way to the upriver redds are considered by many salmon anglers as among the most classic in the world.

Two-sea-winter salmon in the 8- to 12-pound class dominate the runs, but three-sea-winter fish of 14 to 18 pounds are a reasonable expectation on the bigger rivers like the Grand Cascapédia, York, and Matapédia. Multiple spawners on their way back to the redds a second or third time are caught every year, and these can weigh well in excess of 30 pounds. Salmon of 35 to 45 pounds stand as the record on just about every river. Some, like the Matapédia and Grand Cascapédia, continue to produce fish of those dimensions even today. One-sea-winter fish, called *grilse* and weighing 3 to 5 pounds, typically enter freshwater after the beginning of July.

Some salmon are rumored to enter the rivers in the spate waters of May before the salmon fishing season opens, but the first major runs show up in the majority of Gaspé rivers between the middle and end of June. Because the dime-bright fresh fish are most aggressive, and the water conditions at their best, prime salmon fishing time is considered to be the last week of June and the first two weeks of July, although the fishing can be good at any time of the summer, especially on a rise of water.

Although Atlantic salmon are king in the Gaspé region, brook trout also inhabit these waters. In fact, many headwater lakes of the salmon rivers provide excellent fishing for handsomely colored brookies, most of them weighing under a pound, although 2- to 4-pound fish are caught in some of the bigger bodies of water.

The sea-run trout fishing on virtually all of this region's rivers is well known to local anglers, but it is almost completely overlooked by visitors who come to pursue salmon. Sea-run trout here are brook trout that leave freshwater to gorge themselves on the abundance of the sea, returning only to spawn in their rivers, much like the salmon with whom they share the pools. When they first enter the streams, the fish are silver-flanked and possess barely discernible halos along their flanks, but after only a few days in the freshwater pools, the flamboyant markings characteristic of brookies begin to emerge.

On average, sea trout weigh a pound or two, but 3- to 4-pounders can be encountered on most rivers of the Gaspé region. On some, like the Bonaventure, York, Ste. Anne, and Patapédia, even larger sea trout are taken every summer. The West Branch of the Little Cascapédia is probably the most productive, having yielded specimens up to 10 pounds. Four- to 6-pounders are regularly seen finning in the pools. They're skittish fish, however, and duping them into taking a fly is often a difficult challenge.

Barely visible across the Gulf of St. Lawrence from the Gaspé Peninsula is the rugged North Shore escarpment. It, too, is an area noted for Atlantic salmon fishing as well as both sea trout and freshwater brookies. In fact, there is salmon fishing from as far west as the provincial capital of Quebec City all the way east to the boundary with Labrador near Blanc Sablon. The westernmost salmon river is the Jacques Cartier, site of a highly successful salmon restoration program throughout the 1980s and early 1990s. Unfortunately, because of the sharp, towering escarpment that rises virtually at the water's edge, most rivers from there east to the mouth of the Saguenay, a distance of some 100 miles, have insurmountable waterfalls within the first mile or so from the sea.

Three modest streams flowing northwest into the Saguenay have surprisingly good Atlantic salmon runs: the St. Jean, the Petite Saguenay, and, thanks to dedicated restoration efforts between the mid-1980s and mid-1990s, the Rivière à Mars. On the opposite shore of the Saguenay is the well-known St. Marguerite, accessible via Tadoussac and Sacré-Coeur. Both snake through gently rolling country, and most of the watercourse runs over gravel and sand banks. If you have any doubt at all about the presence of salmon, investigate the big holding pool in the sanctuary above the fishing sectors. In addition to salmon, this river offers excellent sea trout fishing, especially in September after the salmon season closes.

As one moves eastward along the North Shore, there are a number of worthwhile salmon rivers to choose from. The first of these is another successfully restored stream called the Escoumins, which today offers as reasonable a chance of hooking a good salmon as it did in the 1960s. Next is the Laval, a dark and brooding river due to its tannin-stained waters. Although it produces nearly a hundred salmon per season, a surprising proportion are large fish.

Several minor salmon rivers flow to the coast beyond Baie Comeau. The next notable salmon river is the Godbout—a pleasant freestone river above the gorge, a sandy river below the gorge, and a rough and untamed river in between. As is the case with most streams along this stretch, it sees the first heavy runs after the first week of June but provides good fishing as long as good water conditions prevail. The Trinite also merits a look.

At Port Cartier, there is the aux Rochers River, which is sometimes overlooked, although it shouldn't be. Inland from Port Cartier is the Port Cartier Wildlife Reserve, which offers excellent fishing for lake trout, big brook trout, and northern pike.

The Moisie, a world-famous salmon river, flows into the Gulf of St. Lawrence east of Sept Iles. Statesmen and kings, tycoons and magnates, have cast their flies over its waters in the hope of hooking one of the Moisie's legendary salmon. Fish of 20 and 30 pounds are relatively common, and much bigger ones are hooked every year but are not always landed. This is a big river that flows out of a rugged, unkempt land, so it's necessary to make the right connections to fish it.

Another excellent salmon river is the Rivière St. Jean, some 85 miles farther east. Although the salmon on average do not compare to those of the Moisie in size, they more than compensate in number. The best pools are 10 miles and more upstream from the mouth and largely inaccessible other than by boat. Advance arrangements are essential.

The road ends a short distance beyond the town of Havre St. Pierre, and access to all salmon rivers farther east is by air. Notable among them are the Natashquan, Étamamiou, Mécatina, and St. Augustin, although there are several others as well.

Between the North Shore and the Gaspé Peninsula lies Anticosti Island. Some 130 miles long and 40 miles across at its widest point, this wedge of limestone offers numerous small, quaint salmon streams. Most are small enough to cast across with line to spare, and, except in the Jupiter, the salmon tend to be in the 6- to 8-pound class. The grilse here are smaller. Most of Anticosti's rivers depend on rain and therefore offer inconsistent fishing. The most dependable is the Jupiter, followed by Rivière aux Saumons, Chaloupe, and La Loutre. Others, like the Bell, might not have a drop of water one week and yet have spate conditions and great fishing the next.

Brook trout are the only other fish inhabiting Anticosti Island. All of the rivers that are accessible from the sea have good runs of sea trout. Most have native populations of brookies, as do the few lakes with sufficient water for winter survival. An overlooked opportunity is coastal fishing for big sea-run trout near the mouths of the rivers.

Northeastern Region

The region east of the Saguenay River, west of the Labrador border, and south of the 50th parallel is essentially a remote land of endless black spruce forests and open taiga, punctuated with countless lakes and wild rivers. Moose and woodland caribou still roam without ever crossing a fence, and few people other than loggers, miners, hunters, and anglers ever venture deep into this realm. It is an angler's haven, especially for trout devotees.

Brook trout are the primary species found in virtually all the streams and countless headwater lakes.

The sheer number of large and small waters throughout this region make any attempt at listing them and evaluating their fishing potential a monumental if not impossible task, but many can be described by touching on a few.

As a general rule, most of the lakes tend to be deep and tannin-stained and have sandy shorelines that drop off quickly. Brook trout are abundant in the smaller lakes as well as in the streams that etch their way south around the rounded topography of the Canadian Shield. Most of these rivers flow toward the Gulf of St. Lawrence, but those in the western portion of this region flow into Lake St. Jean and the Saguenay River.

Starting in the eastern portion of the region, the majority of the watersheds produce brook trout; some are also home to Quebec red trout, a landlocked arctic charr. A few also have landlocked Atlantic salmon, and several significant rivers have runs of Atlantic salmon, as discussed in the section on the North Shore of the St. Lawrence River. As a general rule, it is safe to say that, because of the short growing season and the poor food base in the waters flowing down out of the Labrador escarpment, the trout (both brookies and Quebec reds) that spend their lives in freshwater tend to be rather small. Sea-run brook trout, which feed in the gulf and return to freshwater only to spawn, inhabit many of these rivers as well.

Typical of the smaller North Shore watersheds is the Watshishou, located east of Havre St. Pierre. A number of tributaries gather water from the rugged interior of the North Shore highlands, flowing into and through a string of fairly large, deep lakes and finally becoming a full-fledged river dashing to the Gulf of St. Lawrence. The lower portion of this watershed is frequented by Atlantic salmon, whereas the lakes have an abundant supply of brook trout up to 16 inches and Quebec red trout up to 12 inches. Landlocked salmon of 4 pounds and more are caught both in the lakes and in the fast-water streams that connect them. Anglers occasionally catch larger brookies in the 2- to 4-pound class, especially in the lower lakes. These are thought to be sea-runs.

The larger watersheds like the Olomane, Natashquan, Magpie, and (largest of them all) Moisie, reach deep into the backcountry of the North Shore, almost to the border of Labrador. Most are scheduled Atlantic salmon rivers for at least the lower portions, but the tributaries and lakes offer a wider variety of gamefish.

An example is Lake Magpie, which is actually a widening and deepening of the Magpie River entering the Gulf of St. Lawrence roughly halfway between Havre St. Pierre and Sept Iles. About 45 miles long and barely 2 miles wide, it is fed by 27 tributaries and surrounded by magnificent rock faces that resemble coastal fiords. The lake itself is home to five primary gamefish, as well as lake whitefish.

Most species of fish lay many thousands of eggs. Spawning walleye, for example, in extreme cases, have reportedly laid over 600,000 eggs.

Q

As is the case for most North Shore drainage basins, the brook trout tend to be on the small side, but abundant. The average size is 12 to 14 inches; some are caught on the lake itself, but they're most common in the numerous tributary streams. Although landlocked salmon are present as well, they're not abundant, and the fish are mostly under 2 pounds. The long-standing lake record is an 8-pound specimen.

Lake Magpie does have a good population of lake trout, and anglers can reasonably expect fish of 15 to 20 pounds. The lake record is a 26-pound fish. The northern pike fishing is notable, too, offering opportunities for trophy specimens of 25 pounds and more. Anglers report seeing large pike lying like logs on the surface of shallow bays.

Farther to the west along the North Shore, near Port Cartier, Lake Walker has a known lake trout and northern pike fishery, as well as larger brook trout. Brookies to 2 pounds are common, fish in the 2- to 4-pound range are hooked regularly, and larger individuals are taken from time to time, especially near the more remote north end of the lake.

One of the most imposing drainage basins along the North Shore is the Manicouagan River, which enters the gulf near Baie Comeau. Although much of its flow has been fettered by a series of massive hydroelectric dams, it continues to provide reasonably good fishing in the lower reservoirs and surrounding lakes. The prime spot, however, is the immense Manicouagan Reservoir some 60 miles inland. This doughnut-shaped body of water is fed by countless tributary streams, most of which provide excellent fishing for brook trout up to 2 pounds, although trophy specimens up to 8 pounds are occasionally caught in both the lake and the tributary pools.

The Manicouagan watershed has long been known for its excellent landlocked salmon fishing, even prior to the construction of dams. The fish are abundant, but they tend to be small, averaging about 2 pounds on the more remote waters. Fast trolling with silver smelt-imitation spoons in the deep bays is among the most productive methods throughout most of the summer, the exception being the occasional period of intense heat and sun. Lake trout are abundant throughout most of the watershed. These fish weigh between 6 and 8 pounds on average, but substantially bigger trout are present. Northern pike tend to grow large in the Manicouagan region, and trophy fish in the 20- to 30-pound range are liable to take trolled lures in the shallow bays. You'll need to be well equipped and largely self-sufficient for this jaunt.

Two additional reservoirs of significance in this region of eastern Quebec are the Outardes and the Pipmuacan. Both are remote and provide excellent fishing for lake trout. Trophy fish are regularly caught in the latter. Characteristically, the tributary streams and headwater lakes surrounding them offer good brook trout fishing.

In the Sacré Coeur region, a number of inland lakes provide good freshwater brook trout fishing as well as superb Quebec red trout fishing. Quebec reds rarely grow to more than a pound or so in most provincial waters, but this particular area regularly produces reds twice that size, and 4- to 6-pound specimens have been caught in the past. Lake des Sables in the Rivière des Sables watershed is a prime spot. This watershed also produces big brookies, but the same can be said for many of the drainage basins of the Lake St. Jean-Saguenay region of Quebec. Among them is Lake Poulin de Courval and its surrounding headwater lakes in the Rivière des Sables watershed. They consistently produce 3- to 5-pound brook trout, and the action on 12- to 16-inch fish is steady to the point of redundancy.

Lake du Dégelis and surrounding lakes in the Rivière Portneuf watershed also have large brook trout, and several of the lakes also produce 2- to 4-pound Quebec red trout. The Rivière Portneuf itself can be waded once the spring runoff abates. It offers good stream fishing with flies and spinners for brook trout up to 3 pounds.

Lake St. Jean and its surrounding waters are perhaps best known for landlocked salmon fishing, however. The main lake is a large round basin some 15 miles across. Although it produces good fishing for walleye up to 4 pounds, as well as northern pike up to about 15 pounds, its name is synonymous with angling for landlocked salmon, better known in this region as *ouananiche*. That's partly because since the 1880s anglers have been drawn to this body of water from throughout eastern North America and even Europe in search of the lake's feisty salmon.

Lake St. Jean's salmon tend to be small, averaging around 2 pounds, even though 4- to 6-pounders are caught from time to time. What they lack in size, they more than make up for in aggressiveness and spunk. They eagerly hit smelt-imitation lures trolled in the prop wash less than 20 feet behind the boat and, once hooked, typically jump a half-dozen times.

To experience the best fishing, it's important to follow the schools of salmon around the lake, starting in the Chambord area shortly after ice out. As the summer progresses, salmon make their way north along the western shore of the lake, passing Roberval around the middle of July and reaching the mouth of the Ashuapmushuan River toward the middle of August.

Larger landlocked salmon inhabit this region as well, but anglers must travel into the backcountry northwest of Lake St. Jean to find them. Several of the reservoirs on the Péribonka River, a major tributary to the lake, contain landlocks averaging 4 to 6 pounds, with fish pushing double digits from time to time. Farther north, in the headwaters of the Péribonka, Lake Duhamel regularly produces landlocked salmon between 4 and 8 pounds, and fish to 14 pounds have been caught. Access to the

Some primitive fishes from the Jurassic Period have a trout-like appearance and are believed to have been able to live in both marine and freshwater environments.

Lake St. Jean backcountry is largely by vehicle over gravel lumber roads or by floatplane.

Central and Northwestern Regions

For a dedicated angler, the region stretching from Lake St. Jean to the Ontario border and from the foothills of the Laurentians to the 50th parallel is the realization of every dream. It has more bodies of water than one person can hope to fish in a lifetime, with countless lakes, tumbling streams, and big rivers. In concert these waters offer a variety of sportfish, including walleye, pike, lake trout, brook trout, landlocked salmon, and black bass. Best of all, the region has just the right mix of waters that are either road-accessible, reachable on foot, or accessible only by air.

As a general, although not rigid, rule, brook trout are the predominant species in the eastern portion of the region, whereas pike and walleye are most prevalent toward the west. The larger, deeper lakes of the central and western portions are home to lake trout. Landlocked salmon also do well, although they are an introduced species in the region as are, for the most part, smallmouth bass in the southwestern corner. Some of those introductions date so far back that the gamefish have established self-sufficient numbers and are considered native by local anglers.

With a few exceptions, the area contained by Highway 155 from Lake St. Jean to Trois Rivières, down the St. Lawrence River to Tadoussac, and up the Saguenay River to Lake St. Jean is brook trout country. Because much of this area is easily reached from Quebec City, a steady level of fishing pressure is exerted and many bodies of water are stocked on an annual basis. As a result, the bulk of the trout caught are in the 10- to 12-inch class. Nevertheless, on a fair number of lakes 2- to 4-pound brookies are a reasonable expectation. Among them is Lac des Neiges in Laurentides Provincial Wildlife Reserve, a lake once set aside, along with nearby Lac à l'Épaule, as a retreat for politicians and dignitaries. Stream fishing can be particularly good in the upper reaches of rivers like the Bostonnais, the Kiskissink, and the Métabetchuane.

Also in this region is Portneuf Wildlife Reserve; in addition to having quality lake and stream fishing for brook trout, the reserve offers surprising, and surprisingly good, muskie fishing. A number of lakes in the territory were stocked with this species during the 1970s, and the experiment proved more successful than anyone dreamed possible. The muskies aren't huge—20 pounders are the exception rather than the rule—but muskies in the 5- to 10-pound class are present in numbers and ever willing to take a lure or streamer fly.

To the west of Highway 155 and the St. Maurice River, there's a far greater variety of gamefish. Brook trout are still the most common species in the watersheds draining into the southwestern quadrant of Lake St. Jean, as well as the lakes in the southern drainage basins. But in the heart of the region, brook trout are banished to headwater lakes by the abundant walleye and pike in the lower waters. Many of the larger lakes also have lake trout.

Some of the best road-accessible brook trout fishing is available at Mastigouche and St. Maurice Provincial Wildlife Reserves. Most of the lakes in St. Maurice produce small fish in the 10-inch class, although bigger fish are possible for anglers familiar with the area. For instance, Lake Polette averages fish of 15 inches, yet at Lake St. Thomas, a walk-in lake, the average weight is $2^1/_4$ pounds.

In addition to good brook trout fishing in lakes such as Grand Lac des Iles, Lac au Sable, and St. Bernard, Mastigouche Wildlife Reserve also offers good fishing for landlocked salmon in Lac Sorcier. The fish were introduced during the 1960s and have established a self-sustaining population. The majority are in the 3-pound size, and fish double that are rare, but they react well in the early season to a streamer or lure trolled close to the surface.

The lakes situated northwest of Lake St. Jean, however, are more representative of the diverse fisheries of central and western Quebec. Innumerable small headwater lakes teem with pan-size brook trout, and virtually all the larger collector lakes like Nicabau, Charron, and Aigremont offer strictly walleye in the 2- to 4-pound range, and northern pike running to 15 pounds, although larger specimens are present.

In the heart of central Quebec is one of the province's most prolific bodies of water. Created in 1917 by the damming of the St. Maurice River at the La Loutre Rapids, Gouin Reservoir has a massive surface area of more than 500 square miles, most of it highly productive northern pike and walleye habitat. In fact, it is so prolific that a commercial fishery annually harvested more than 3,000 pounds of fish without any apparent impact on the stocks until it was abandoned in 1972.

Accessible by gravel lumber roads or by air, the recreational harvest falls far short of the toll formerly taken by the nets. Although trophy walleye may well swim forgotten here, in the bays, fish in the 3- to 5-pound range are incredibly abundant and provide outstanding action throughout the summer. Northern pike are plentiful in these sheltered bays, where anglers can reasonably hope for fish weighing up to 15 pounds; some larger ones are present. Gouin is accessible by fly-in to established camps, and also by a rugged drive. It is a vast lake, one that is easy to get lost on. Flooded timber, reefs, and mazes of islands make this a place to exercise great caution.

Another excellent destination for walleye and northern pike anglers is the Cabonga-Dozois Reservoir system. Created in the late 1920s by damming the Gens de Terre River at the outlet of Bark Lake and the Outaouais River at La Barrière, this immense reservoir complex is a confusing maze of islands and extended bays. The walleye, lake trout, and northern pike that once teemed in Lakes

A northern pike is landed on Dozois Reservoir in Verendrye Provincial Reserve.

Bark, Rapid, Washkega, Wagoose, and Cabonga adapted well to the vastness of their new environment; and walleye are so plentiful that, given the right conditions and the right spot, it's possible to hook fish on virtually every cast. Most Cabonga walleye weigh between 2 and 4 pounds, but larger ones to 10 pounds are taken every season.

The key to successful walleye fishing on Cabonga-Dozois waters is knowing where the fish are. From the late May opening to the end of the first week of June, look for them at the mouths of incoming rivers. After the middle of June, fish along sandy shoals, in sandy bays, and off rocky points. Most of the big walleye lurk along the edge of the stickups, the vestiges of a drowned forest.

Northern pike are so abundant, they verge on becoming a nuisance at times, but anglers who target these fish can catch many up to 10 pounds—and some specimens in the 15- to 25-pound class—simply by working the shallow bays and the mouths of tributary streams. Lake trout, on the other hand, are less predictable. Fish weighing up to 40 pounds have been caught by anglers working the shoals off Cabonga Dam with gang trolls. Smaller lakers of between 5 and 10 pounds are caught by anglers working jigs and spoons through the fast-water pool at the base of the dam itself during early summer, when water flows are at their peak.

The Cabonga-Dozois Reservoir system can be confusing and, every summer more than one party of anglers wanders into one of the many blind bays,

convinced that they are in the channel back to camp, and eventually runs out of gas around nightfall. Either an experienced guide or a GPS unit is a must, as is a sturdy, deep-hulled boat of 16 feet or more, capable of withstanding sudden summer storms.

Downstream about 50 miles along the Gens de Terre River, which in itself provides excellent fishing for big walleye, is Baskatong Reservoir—an excellent road-accessible fishery for pike and walleye. The fish tend to be somewhat smaller on average than in Cabonga as a result of Baskatong's greater accessibility and heavier fishing pressure. The backcountry behind Baskatong provides a wide range of fishing opportunities for brook trout, lake trout, splake, walleye, and pike. Gravel lumber roads cut into the territory provide dusty access, but many of the best lakes are accessible only by floatplane.

Farther to the west, along the Ontario border, Lake Kipawa is known for pike and walleye, although other opportunities exist as well. Some of the finest smallmouth bass fishing in the north is available locally, especially at Lake Beauchene and adjacent smaller waters, which are south of Kipawa and southeast of Temiscaming. Smallmouths grow to 5 pounds in Beauchene, and the walleye and northern pike are good size, too. The region also has brook trout, some to 4 pounds.

To the southeast, Gatineau River country offers more opportunity for smallmouth bass. Exceptional northern smallmouth fishing brings anglers to Lake

Blue Sea near Gracefield and to Lake McGregor north of Buckingham. On average, these fish weigh less than 2 pounds, but they definitely make up for their small size in pugnaciousness and abundance. This is also lake trout country, and lakes such as McGregor, Poison Blanc, Simon, Sept Frères, and des Iles, are just a few of the better spots.

Northern Region

That part of Quebec north of the 50th parallel is an immense territory covering about 74 percent of the total land area of the province. Typically, it is remote, sparsely inhabited by barely 42,500 humans, and stretches from the boreal forests and muskegs north to the subarctic barrens, where summer is measured in weeks, and frigid winds scour the earth's exposed crust. To count and catalog the lakes and rivers of this vast wilderness would requires a lifetime of devoted service; to fish the more accessible ones would take many lifetimes.

At one time, only a small corner of the far northern region was accessible by vehicle. Now a road runs northwest from Lake St. Jean to Chibougamou, then west-southwest to Lebel sur Quévillon and Senneterre. A spur runs north from Chibougamau to Lakes Waconichi, Albanel, and Mistassini. All three provide excellent fishing for lake trout, brook trout, walleye, and northern pike. As a rule, the walleye are small, but northern pike tend to grow big, with fish in the 10- to 20-pound class a reasonable expectation. Anglers easily land pike by trolling close to the surface, but the sandy flats at the inlet of the Papas, Cheno, and Toqueco Rivers at the north end of Mistassini are ideal for casting big streamer flies.

Lake trout are abundant but small on Waconichi, although anglers equipped with the proper gear can pick up fish in the 15- to 20-pound range. Lake trout tend to be somewhat larger on Albanel, but the best lake for this species is Mistassini, where trout over 35 pounds have been taken. The majority of the lakers, however, are between 5 and 15 pounds.

The brook trout fishing is legendary. Waconichi can provide steady angling for 2-pound brookies to enthusiasts trolling small minnow-imitation plugs or casting streamers. On Albanel, the same techniques can produce fish of 3 pounds, and this lake's major tributary, the Témiscamie River, has a trophy fishery. Brookies up to 4 pounds are fairly common, and fish twice that size are logged on occasion. Mistassini also offers excellent angling for big brookies among the many islands that run like beads up its middle. A variety of techniques works, but every now and then a hatch will bring fish of 2 to 4 pounds to the surface, providing exciting surface fly fishing. The Papas, Cheno, and Toqueco Rivers at the north end offer outstanding late-summer fishing for trophy brook trout.

Although not accessible by road, LakeAssinica and several other bodies of water in the headwaters of the Broadback River are home to the famous Assinica strain of brook trout. The average pocket-water brookie here weighs roughly $2^1/_2$ pounds, but the deeper holes consistently produce 5- to 6-pound specimens. Nine-pounders are taken annually, and the past record for the area is over 10 pounds. Hardware is productive on the lakes, but fly fishing brings the most fish to hand in the river. The best dry fly fishing for big brookies occurs in July and early August. From mid-August to early September, anglers fish the spawning runs for big, full-color brookies. The region is accessible by air from Chibougamau, and it's possible to mount a float-camp expedition in the region.

Until the middle 1980s, the Mistassini region was essentially the northern limit of road-accessible fishing in Quebec. But then a new network of wide and well-graded roads, initially built to haul massive generators to the James Bay hydroelectric project, was opened, and these have provided access not only to the rivers of the James Bay region, but also to the Caniapiscau Reservoir in the heart of this northern land. Excellent fishing for pike and walleye is within easy striking distance from the town of Radisson. In fact, superb pike and walleye are taken by anglers fishing off the top of the dikes built to contain La Grande 2 and La Grande 3, although the aesthetics might be sorely lacking. Continuing eastward along this stretch, the town site of Brisay is the gateway to the vast Caniapiscau Reservoir. Despite the short growing season, this body of water consistently produces northern pike and lake trout in the 10- to 20-pound class, and larger fish are common. Trophy brook trout from 3 to 8 pounds are caught fairly regularly throughout the short summer.

About a decade after the reservoir was created by damming the headwaters of the Caniapiscau River, biologists found that the landlocked salmon grow, on average, two to three times as big here as in surrounding waters. Typically, the Caniapiscau watershed has always produced landlocked salmon in the 3- to 6-pound class, and the speculation is that the reservoir's salmon grow more rapidly on a steady and nourishing diet of abundant whitefish, enabling them to quickly attain 10 pounds and more.

Beyond the reach of roads, northern Quebec offers fishing that dreams are made of. Access is primarily by floatplane out of four major gateways: Radisson in the James Bay region, Labrador City on the Labrador-Quebec border, Schefferville on the Labrador-Quebec border, and Kuujjuaq on the shores of Ungava Bay. The Radisson gateway is mostly used to access the angling opportunities of the James Bay and Hudson Bay drainages. The rivers and lakes lying to the north of Radisson are legendary for trophy brook trout.

Typical of these is the Seal River, which flows down out of the sparse taiga through a chain of relatively small lakes to finally reach the sea at Cape Jones, the northern tip of James Bay before it becomes Hudson Bay. Brookies in the 2-pound

Q

class are the average on both the river and the lakes, whereas fish double that size are a reasonable expectation, especially during the onset of the spawning run in mid-August. In addition, these waters also produce excellent fishing for northern pike in the 6- to 20-pound class.

Brook trout are also abundant in the rivers of the Hudson Bay coast, but arctic charr become increasingly dominant northward. One of the best-known charr fishing areas along this coastline is Richmond Gulf near the village of Umiujaq. Although the fish tend to be in the 3- to 5-pound class, they are abundant and strike readily.

Farther north along the coast is the Tuksukatuk watershed. Three- to 4-pound brookies hold in the shallows of the main river, and lake trout are caught in the same area, even on flies. In the lower portion of the river, fresh-run arctic charr congregate in the shallow runs, where they take streamer flies and silver spoons readily. The rivers around the Inuit settlement of Povugnituk, well up near the northern tip of the peninsula, also produce charr in abundance.

Across the Ungava Peninsula to the east is the village of Kangirsuk at the mouth of the Payne River. Large schools of arctic charr congregate in the saltwater just off the mouth of the river through late June and most of August, providing steady action. Most anglers cast spoons from big, stable freighter canoes, but the fishing can be equally good from shore as well when the schools swing close to land.

Tidal pools inside the river offer tremendous sight fishing for charr. Around the middle of August, charr move upriver on the Payne, and in-river fishing in fast water outshines the river-mouth fishery. In addition, anglers frequently hook into hefty lake trout in the same pools. An angler landed a laker of about 35 pounds while charr fishing in the mid-1970s. The best lake trout fishing, however, is in Payne Lake, where fish of 20 to 40 pounds cruise the shallows for prey through the short barren-land summer, and they pounce on virtually any lure cast to them. The tributary streams are home to small brook trout.

Between the Payne and Leaf Rivers to the south along the Ungava Bay coast there are about a dozen other rivers that drain the heart of the peninsula, all with their own runs of sea trout and arctic charr. The Leaf is a significant river, drawing much of its flow from Lake Minto very close to the Hudson Bay coast. Two- to 3-pound sea-run and freshwater brook trout are found in many of the pools and countless tributary streams along its 200-mile-long course, but the river fishing for charr in blazing spawning colors is the foremost attraction. Schools of charr are caught in Leaf Bay through late July, and the schools start to move up the river in August to provide good fishing throughout the month and in early September. A small run of Atlantic salmon also enters the river in August, but this is largely a hit-or-miss proposition.

Atlantic salmon runs are more predictable on the Koksoak River, which enters the southern basin of Ungava Bay at the gateway community of Kuujjuaq. Two major branches—the Larch (shown as the Rivière aux Mélèzes on most maps) and the Caniapiscau (the same river that was dammed in its headwaters to create the Caniapiscau Reservoir discussed earlier)—meet about 80 miles inland to create this river. Virtually all of the Koksoak's Atlantic salmon runs turn into the Larch River branch, then into the Rivière du Gué, and finally the Delay River. Overwintered salmon provide good fishing in the Delay in July, and fresh-run salmon reach these waters later in August.

The 250-mile-long Caniapiscau River is rumored to have some salmon, but it is better known for its excellent brook trout and landlocked salmon fishing. Anglers also land lake trout on the river itself, although the best fishing is in the many lakes drained by its tributaries. For instance, Lakes Lemoyne, Nachicapau, and Canichico—located just east of the Caniapiscau itself and linked to it by way of a short river—offer fishing for large lake trout as well as landlocked arctic charr and brook trout.

East of the Koksoak, the Whale River (listed as the Rivière à la Baleine on most maps) has a long-standing reputation for its Atlantic salmon fishing. It flows into Ungava Bay about 100 miles east of Kuujjuaq and, in most years, salmon are present in numbers from ice out in June through freeze-up in late September. The early fishery focuses on over-wintered salmon that have not yet spawned, but by mid-July, dime-bright estuarine salmon that mature in the brackish water of the river's mouth make up the bulk of the fish. In August, they're joined by heavy runs of salmon from the Atlantic feeding grounds. As a rule, Whale River salmon average between 8 and 12 pounds, although some runs consist almost entirely of fish in the 14- to 16-pound class. The record is a 24-pound fish taken in 1976.

A short floatplane hop farther east is the Tunulik River, well known for excellent arctic charr in the pools at its mouth. During the first half of the arctic summer, most of the charr are taken just off the coast in the open water of Ungava Bay; but by the end of July, the tidal pool at the base of the first falls provides most of the catches until the end of the season in early September. The Tunulik is known for its big charr; most fish are in the 8-pound class, but trophy charr from 14 to 18 pounds are taken regularly on bright silver spoons cast into the pools. After the middle of August, the charr linger in the upriver pools of the Tunulik, where they share the water with brook trout up to 2 pounds and lake trout averaging about 10 pounds.

The next major river system to the east is the George, considered one of the top Atlantic salmon rivers in the world. Some 400 miles long, the George sees runs of more than 10,000 salmon, and all of them pass through one of the best-known stretches of water in the world: Helen's Falls, a

3-mile-long torrent barely 20 miles from the coast. The fish generally show up in early to mid-August, and the runs keep coming until the end of September. Three-quarters of the fish are salmon in the 6- to 10-pound class; the remainder of the run is evenly split between one-sea-winter fish (grilse) and three-sea-winter fish of 14 to 18 pounds. The biggest salmon recorded on the George is a 28-pounder.

Salmon here take flies well and seem to have a special penchant for black patterns. Helen's Falls, however, is not the salmons' only resting place on their way to upriver spawning grounds. Numerous excellent holding areas reach as far as the de Pas River, some 300 miles inland.

The George also offers excellent fishing for arctic charr and sea-run brook trout, primarily from the mouth to Helen's Falls and in the Ford River, a tributary to the George just downstream from the falls. Farther inland, freshwater brookies and lake trout share the pools, and, close to the headwater, big northern pike lurk in the shallow backwaters.

The George is the last of the four scheduled Atlantic salmon rivers of the Ungava Bay region, and the remaining watersheds emptying into the eastern basin of Ungava Bay are primarily arctic charr rivers, although a sea-run brook trout fishery exists as well. Keglo Bay, Weymouth Inlet, and the Koroc River produce consistently good charr fishing from mid-July on, although open-water fishing on the saltwater of the bay for dime-bright charr is good from the time the ice goes out in late June or early July.

Northern Quebec features trophy brook trout, along with lake trout and big northern pike, in the southeastern corner of the region, along the Labrador border. Accessible through Gagnon or Labrador City gateways are Lakes Chambeaux, Ternay, Justone, Lucault, and Matonipi, to name just a handful from among the hundreds in the region. Brook trout of 2 to 4 pounds are fairly common, and fish twice that size are caught from time to time during the short 10-week season imposed by the elements. Lake trout are also numerous and vary between 5 and 25 pounds. Northern pike inhabit most of the region's watersheds, and, because of the light fishing pressure, anglers can encounter trophy fish of 15 to 30 pounds.

QUEENFISH (CROAKER)   *Seriphus politus.*
Other names—herring, herring croaker, kingfish, shiner, queen croaker; Spanish: *corvina reina.*

The queenfish is a small croaker and a member of the Sciaenidae family (drum and croaker). Essentially a panfish-size bottom scrounger, it is not an esteemed sport or food fish, but it is commonly caught from Pacific coast piers and may be desirable as whole or cut bait for other species.

Identification. The queenfish has an elongated, moderately compressed body. The upper profile is

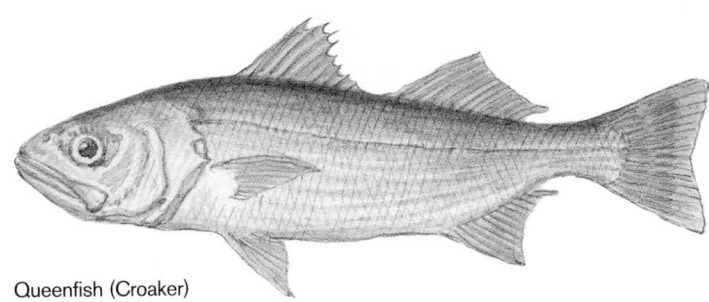

Queenfish (Croaker)

depressed over the eyes, and it has a large mouth. Its coloring is bluish above and becomes silvery below. The fins are yellowish. This species is distinguished from other croaker by its large mouth; by the base of its second dorsal and anal fins, which are roughly equal; and by the wide space between its two dorsal fins. There is no chin barbel on the lower jaw.

Size. The maximum length of the queenfish is 12 inches, but most fish are considerably smaller.

Distribution. The queenfish is found along the Pacific coast, from Yaquina Bay, Oregon, to Uncle Sam Bank in Baja California, Mexico. It is common in Southern California but rare north of Monterey.

Habitat. Queenfish commonly inhabit shallow water over sandy bottoms in summer. They mostly occur in water from 4 to 25 feet deep but have been known to dwell as deep as 180 feet. They often gather in tightly packed schools, sometimes with white croaker (see: croaker, white), in shallow sandy areas near pilings and piers, and they migrate to deeper water at night.

Spawning behavior. Spawning occurs along the coast in summer. The eggs are free floating, and newly hatched juveniles appear in late summer and fall; they gradually move shoreward from depths of 20 to 30 feet into the surf zone.

Food. Queenfish feed on small, free-swimming crustaceans, crabs, and fish.

Angling. This species is often caught as a byproduct of other bottom fishing efforts, using natural baits on small hooks. Live sardines are a common bait.

QUEENFISH (JACKS)
Other names—leathery, queenie, leatherskin, whitefish, skinny-fish, giant dart, talang queenfish, doublespotted queenfish.

Members of the Carangidae family of jacks, pompano, and trevally, the species *Scomberoides lysan* and *S. commersonianus* are together popularly referred to as "queenfish," the former generally as doublespotted queenfish and the latter as talang queenfish. Very fast moving and powerful fighters when hooked, queenfish are noted for their long runs and a dogged struggle that is often punctuated with spectacular and repeated leaps as they try to throw the hook. Most anglers who have hooked up to a queenfish regard the experience as one of their

Q

Talang Queenfish

most exciting, light-tackle challenges. It is also a reasonable table fish if bled immediately on capture, although the flesh of large specimens tends to be a bit dry.

Identification.   Queenfish have a long, laterally compressed, deep, thin body that is covered in a leathery skin with deeply embedded scales. Silvery green with yellowish reflections, it carries a series of blotches that on *S. commersonianus* lie above the lateral line, and on *S. lysan* on either side of the lateral line. Both the second dorsal and anal fins of *S. commersonianus* are sickle shaped, which distinguishes it from *S. lysan*. The soft dorsal fin of *S. lysan* carries a distinct black area not present in *S. commersonianus*. The tail of each species is deeply forked.

Size.   *S. commersonianus* are known to exceed 14 kilograms in weight, and *S. lysan* 7 kilograms. The world record for the former stands at 15.6 kilograms. Most captures fall in the 1- to 5-kilogram range.

Distribution.   Queenfish range across the tropical top third of Australia, from about Gladstone in central Queensland to Carnarvon in Western Australia. Although not a common occurrence, they are sometimes taken from coastal waters near Brisbane, southeast Queensland. Elsewhere, they are broadly found in Indo-Pacific waters, including the Gulf of Thailand, Okinawa, Indonesia, the Philippines, Papua New Guinea, and the East Coast of Africa. *S. lysan* also occurs in Hawaii but is unconfirmed in the Gulf of Thailand.

Habitat.   Mostly taken by boat anglers, the queenfish occurs around the coral cays on Australia's Great Barrier Reef, and close in to rocky headlands, bomboras, bays, river mouths, and wharves. They are also frequently caught by anglers chasing barramundi in mangrove creeks.

Life history/Behavior.   Little research has been carried out on the queenfish, and its spawning behavior is not known. Adults prefer waters with a fast tidal movement, although anglers target the top of the tide and the start of the runout when fishing in mangrove creeks and estuaries.

Food and feeding habits.   The queenfish is well known for its voracious attacks on schools of small food fish. At night, it is not uncommon for schools of queenfish to swim close to well-lit areas and attack a shoal of small baitfish. They may occasionally eat crustaceans.

Angling.   High-speed, heavy-duty baitcasting or spinning outfits with a 7- to 10-kilogram line are the standard for taking queenfish. Queenfish will also take most natural baits, whether live or cut fish. Ganged hooks rigged with pilchards or garfish are also popular, as is the casting and fast retrieval of strip baits. By far the most favored method is casting fast-moving surface poppers, spoons, bucktail jigs, or minnow-type lures to sighted feeding fish. Wire leaders are frequently used, especially by bait anglers, although many use a heavy monofilament leader.

Because of the queenfish's habit of feeding on bait schools close to reefs and rock formations, small-boat anglers should maneuver close to these structures to cast or troll along their fringes. Gaffs are almost invariably used for boating the fish, as only small queenfish will fit into the average net.

Fighting a big queenfish is largely a matter of ensuring that a cool head and a pounding heart work in complete harmony. Aerial displays of shaking head and twisting body are common, and care should be taken not to hurry the playing process. Queenfish tend to remain in open water rather than adopt the tactics of some species (trevally, for example) of finding the sharpest rock edges against which to rub the line. Jumping tactics will quickly tire them.

Fly anglers can approach within casting distance of feeding fish and can be assured of fast responses and tackle-testing runs. Large saltwater flies, rapidly retrieved, are the best bet.

QUINNAT
A term for chinook salmon *(see)* in New Zealand.

QUOTA
A saltwater fisheries management term for the maximum number of fish that can be legally landed in a specified time period. This limit can apply to the total fishery (commercial and recreational catch) or to an individual fisherman's share. Quotas are primarily assigned to commercial fishermen, but in cases where stocks are low and there is a significant shared catch between commercial and recreational fishermen, such as with tuna, quotas apply to both.

RACE

An area of disturbed or confused water caused by the clashing of currents *(see)* and tides *(see)*.

RADIO

See: Communications; Weather.

RADIO DIRECTION FINDER

A radio direction finder (RDF) is an electronic device primarily used for navigation and to determine radio signal bearings. Some big-boat anglers use an RDF to scan for radio chatter from anglers and to identify the location of anglers who report being on a school of fish. If they are not having success at their own position, they may pick up and head to where others are located.

RADIOTELEMETRY

Electronic tracking of fish for purposes of research and fisheries management *(see)*.

RAFT

An inflatable boat. When used on large vessels, including commercial craft, an inflatable boat is called a life raft. Heavy-duty rafts are used in big-river recreation, especially for whitewater boating.

RAISE *(A Fish)*

Raising, a term used in various forms of sportfishing, occurs when a targeted species is attracted to the lure or bait and can be seen on the surface as it pursues lures or bait that are being fished on or close to the surface. Saltwater big-game anglers are said to "raise a fish" when it comes into their trolling spread and either shows interest in a teaser, lure, or bait, or actually attacks it. If they "raised" three fish in a given day, it would mean that on three separate occasions they saw a fish (usually a billfish but also tuna) swimming with or chasing their lures, even though they may not actually have caught any of them.

Stream trout and salmon anglers are said to raise a fish when they can see one move and look at their offering, and muskie anglers are likewise said to raise a fish when they see one pursue or follow their lure on the retrieve, generally near the boat.

This term is often used in referring to fish that are difficult to catch, and to conditions in which an angler is unlikely to catch, or even see, many specimens in a single outing. This is especially true for giant tuna, marlin, Atlantic salmon, and muskellunge.

RAYS AND SKATES

The various families that belong to the order of fish known as Rajiformes are generally referred to as ray and skate, and include such groupings as sawfish, guitarfish, electric ray, stingray, eagle ray, manta ray, and skate. Among the dominant distinguishing features of this order are gill openings wholly on the ventral surface and forward edges of the pectoral fins connected with the sides of the head and situated forward, past the five pairs of gill openings; eyeballs not free from the upper edges of the orbits, as they are in sharks; and no anal fin.

Most Rajiformes are easily recognized by their form. Their bodies are flattened dorso-ventrally, and the pectoral fins extend widely and seem to be part of the body. The tail section is more or less defined from the body, the eyes and spiracles are on the top side, and the mouth and entire lengths of the gill openings are situated on the bottom side. Sawfish, however, are sharklike in general appearance. They are classified among the order Rajiformes on skeletal considerations as well as for the relationship of the pectorals to the gills and because of the absence of upper eyelids. The shape of the majority of guitarfish resembles a cross between sharklike and skatelike forms.

Some members of this order have no dorsal fin, others have one or two. Some possess a distinct caudal (tail) fin, others do not. The spiracles are larger than those of most sharks and are always located on top of the head. The majority have well-developed eyes. In a few species, however, the eyes are degenerate. Without exception, the order Rajiformes has five pairs of gill openings. Some have smooth skins; others are covered with thorny or prickly protrusions; and some have tails armed with dangerous, saw-edged spines. The shape of the teeth varies. Teeth may resemble thorns, knobs, or plates, or be sharply pointed. They may be in bands, transverse rows, or mosaic patterns. None of the members of this group has luminescent organs, but some have electric organs.

In those Rajiformes that lie on the bottom or bury themselves in the sand, the spiracles are important in the process of respiration. Water taken in through these passages courses over the gills and

R

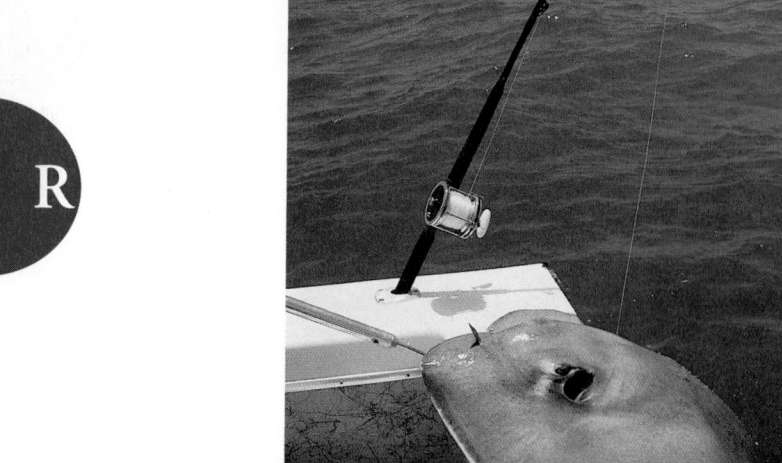

A big ray from Marco Island, Florida.

Development in the skate family is oviparous. The eggs encased in horny capsules are commonly seen washed up on sandy beaches. As far as is known, however, all other members of this order are ovoviviparous; that is, embryos develop inside the oviducts of the female until ready for extrusion. In this type of development, there is no placental attachment between mother and young.

Most Rajiformes live on the bottom or close to it and are comparatively sluggish. Some of them lie buried in the sand or mud most of the time and are poor swimmers. Skate are capable of swift propulsion when necessary, although they usually swim slowly and close to the bottom. Sawfish also spend a good part of the time along the bottom but rise to pursue fish at middepths or higher. Eagle ray are quite active and often swim close to the surface, although they feed on the bottom. In opposition to its close cousins, the mantas seem to have abandoned bottom living and spend most of their lives swimming near the surface or not too far beneath it.

Ray and skate subsist on a variety of animal food, including all available invertebrates that inhabit sandy or muddy bottoms. Eagle ray, as a group, prefer hard-shelled mollusks, while the sawfish occasionally leave their bottom foraging to crash into a school of closely packed fish. Electric ray are strictly fish eaters, sometimes taking surprisingly large prey in comparison to their size. The mantas, including the giants of the group, feed on tiny plankton, small crustaceans, and small fish. Their mode of feeding is similar to that of the huge whale sharks and basking sharks. Food is carried into the mouth by the intake of water and sifted by the so-called prebranchial apparatus, as the water passes over the gills and out through the gill openings.

Commercially, ray and skate are of little value. Small quantities are used from time to time as fertilizer and as baits for traps, although the meat from the wings of some specimens is used, and has been passed as scallops in the past. When caught along North American coasts, the great majority are released. There has historically been a greater demand for skate in northern Europe. Various ray are available in fish markets in many tropical areas, but the quantity used is small. These bottom dwellers can be a great nuisance to anglers because they take baited hooks meant for other fish. Also, they are capable of inflicting a painful wound with their serrated spines when stepped on or handled incautiously.

Rajiformes are widely distributed in latitude and depth in the Atlantic, Pacific, and Indian Oceans, including adjacent seas. They also cover a broad thermal range, from cold polar waters to warm tropical seas. The most numerous group are skate, which primarily inhabit the temperate belts of the two hemispheres. Their cousins are found predominantly in tropical and subtropical waters. Electric ray may be grouped as occupying an intermediate geographical position.

out through the gill openings. Skate, however, may hold their heads slightly above the bottom when resting and take in some water through the mouth. Mantas swim more freely and inhale water mostly or completely through the mouth; they have proportionately smaller spiracles.

The members of the Rajiform clan range in size from only a few inches to giant mantas with a breadth of about 23 feet. The spectacularly armed sawfish reach a length of more than 20 feet.

The mode of locomotion varies within the group. Skate and stingray are propelled forward smoothly along the bottom by undulating the pectoral fins from front to rear. Guitarfish use their tails chiefly in swimming, with an assist from the pectorals. Mantas and eagle ray, with their more pointedly shaped pectoral fins, swim with a flapping motion of the fins or "wings," more or less resembling bird flight. In the process of swift motion, some eagle ray and mantas hurl themselves into the air, often completing a somersault, one of the most spectacular sights of the sea. Sawfish swim chiefly by lateral undulations of the posterior portion of their trunk, aided by the caudal fin and to a lesser degree by the pectorals.

All members of this order effect fertilization internally; the act is facilitated by a pair of claspers developed along the inner edges of the male's pelvic fins, in the same manner as it is in sharks. The inner edges have deep grooves, with the edges more or less overlapping, thereby aiding the transportation of the sperm into the female.

As an order, Rajiformes constitutes a saltwater group, but several species of stingray have colonized in freshwater in the lower portions of South American rivers draining into the Atlantic. They are found far up some rivers, however. Sawfish also frequently inhabit freshwater.

Although these fish are seldom sought by anglers, some are encountered or at least observed by them, especially by people fishing in shallow tropical and subtropical waters, so brief reviews of the families follow.

Pristidae (sawfish). These sharklike ray have a long snout that is formidably armored with sharp teeth along each side. They are bottom dwellers like typical ray but will rise toward the surface to slash through a school of baitfish, turning to pick up any that have been stunned or wounded. Sometimes they succeed in impaling several fish on their toothed snout; these are then scraped off on the bottom and eaten. The long snout is also used to probe into sand or mud to dig up shellfish. If molested, a sawfish turns this food-getting snout into a powerful weapon of defense and can inflict serious injury, but there is no evidence of unprovoked attacks.

Like ray, sawfish have gill slits on the underside of the body on each side just behind the mouth, and the large pectoral fins are joined broadly to the head. The body is long and slim, more like that of a shark. The four species of sawfish are cosmopolitan in distribution in warm to tropical seas, inhabiting shallow waters and straying into brackish water or even freshwater. A sizable population has become landlocked in Lake Nicaragua.

The smalltooth sawfish *(Pristis pectinata)* is commonly 15 feet long and sometimes reaches a length of 20 feet. It can weigh as much as 800 pounds. This species is common throughout warm Atlantic waters, from the Mediterranean southward to Namibia and from North Carolina to Brazil. The largetooth sawfish *(P. perotteti)*, a western Atlantic species, is similar but has larger teeth in proportion to its body. Sawfish that live in Indo-Pacific waters are the giants of the clan.

Rhinobatidae (guitarfish). Guitarfish have a distinct raylike body, with the forward part rounded or heart shaped. The snout is wedge shaped, and the tail sector is not clearly distinguished from the body. The caudal fin is relatively short and thick, but the dorsal and anal fins are well developed. The gills are on the underside of the body, which is typical in ray.

Guitarfish inhabit tropical and subtropical seas around the world and are sometimes found running up into freshwater. There are 43 species in the family. Like typical ray, guitarfish are bottom feeders, eating mainly small crustaceans and mollusks. They are ovoviviparous. Most species are 5 to 6 feet long, although the giant guitarfish *(Rhyncobatos djiddensis)* of the Indo-Pacific region reaches a length of 10 feet.

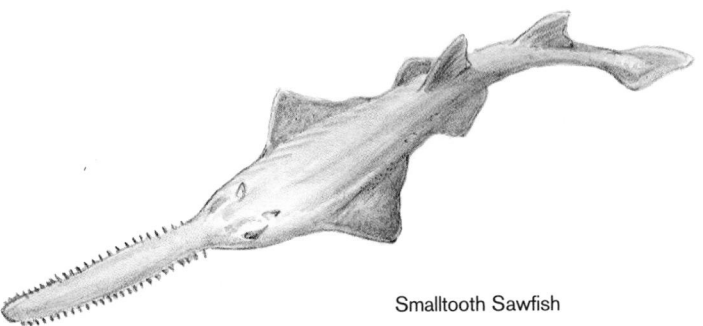

Smalltooth Sawfish

The Atlantic guitarfish *(Rhinobatos lentiginosus; see: guitarfish, Atlantic)* is widely distributed in warm waters and is especially common in the Atlantic. Its average length is 2 feet, but some reach a length of 3 feet; the females are larger than the males. The grayish brown body is covered with small whitish spots. The shovelnose guitarfish *(R. productus)* is a 4-foot species found in the Pacific from the Gulf of California to San Francisco.

Torpedinidae (electric ray). Roughly 14 species of electric ray inhabit seas throughout the world. Some live at great depths, others in shallow inshore waters. Some are as much as 6 feet long and weigh 200 pounds; others are less than a foot long. The eyes are small and functional in most species but are rudimentary or obsolete in a few deep-water forms. None of the electric ray are good swimmers; they spend most of their time partly buried in the sand or mud on the bottom and move only sluggishly. Their bodies are soft and flabby compared to those of skate and other ray, and the skin of most species is soft and marked. Development is ovoviviparous.

All electric ray are able to generate jolting charges of electricity. Any diver, swimmer, or angler who has come close to or tried to handle an electric ray knows the power of their shock. This defense protects these ray from would-be predators and delivers stunning blows to prey that would otherwise be too fleet for these slow-moving fish to capture. Ordinarily, however, these ray eat crustaceans, worms, and similar small animals that can be captured without the need for discharging electricity.

The Atlantic torpedo *(Torpedo nobiliana)*—which ranges in the eastern Atlantic from Scotland to South Africa, including the Mediterranean, and in the western Atlantic from Nova Scotia to North Carolina—is the largest of these ray. It averages roughly 30 pounds in weight, but individuals as much as 6 feet long and weighing 200 pounds have been reported. Despite its name, this fish is anything but speedy or torpedo-like; instead, it is sluggish, and therefore characteristic of the Latin meaning of the word "torpid." A related $1^1/_2$-foot-long species, *T. marmorata*, lives in the Mediterranean and along the eastern Atlantic coast from the United Kingdom to South Africa. The Pacific electric ray *(T. californica)* is similar to the Atlantic species but smaller, and it is found from British Columbia to

R

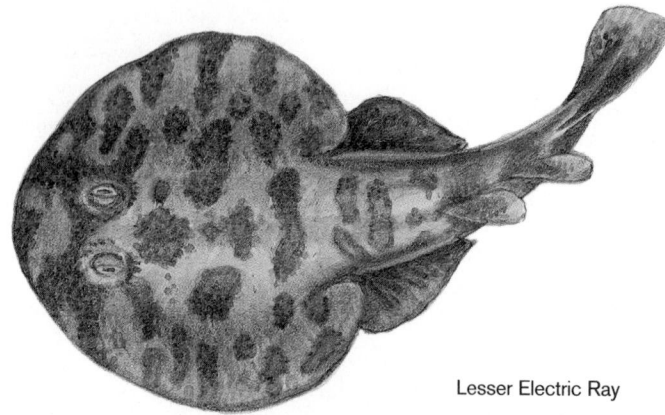

Lesser Electric Ray

Baja California, Mexico. Also small at seldom more than a foot long is the lesser electric ray *(Narcine brasiliensis),* which ranges from North Carolina to the Gulf of Mexico.

Dasyatidae (stingray). Stingray are best known for their long, slim, whiplike tails that are armed with one to several spines near the base. When caught or stepped on, a stingray lashes its tail and invariably manages to impale a spine in its molester. Poison from glands along the grooves on each side of the spine flows into the wound, delivering additional and excruciating pain. The venom should be flushed from the wound as soon as possible, and it is best to see a doctor for treatment and antibiotics. Deaths have resulted from untreated stingray wounds, particularly when they have been inflicted in the trunk area rather than on the limbs.

Stingray generally lie on the bottom, almost completely buried in the sand or soft sediment. Camouflaged also by their grayish brown and often mottled coloration, they are almost impossible to see. Wading anglers walk slowly in a bottom-shuffling manner that usually, but not always, sends a nearby stingray scuttling off.

Fifty species of stingray in six genera are distributed in warm, shallow waters around the world. A few stray into brackish water or even into freshwater. They range in size from species that measure only a foot across their wings to others that have spans as great as 7 feet. In nearly all species, the body disk—including the winglike pectoral fins—is nearly round. Although stingray feed on worms, their main diet is crustaceans and mollusks, which they crush between their flat-topped teeth. A few stingray are active and aggressive enough to catch fish.

One of the most common stingray along the Atlantic coast of North America is the bluntnose stingray *(Dasyatis say),* which measures about 3 feet across its pectorals. It ranges from New Jersey to Argentina and is widespread in the West Indies, sometimes straying into cooler waters during warmer months. The Atlantic stingray *(D. sabina)* measures only slightly more than a foot across its wings, which are very rounded. This uniformly yellowish brown stingray is found in the western Atlantic, from the Chesapeake Bay to southern Florida and the Gulf of Mexico, and has occurred in the Mississippi River. More common than the Atlantic stingray and ranging from New Jersey to Argentina is the southern stingray *(D. americana),* which averages about 3 feet wide. On the underside of its tail, just behind the spine, are finlike folds; above them, the tail is keeled.

The round stingray *(Urolophus halleri)* is common in the eastern Pacific, from Northern California to Panama. It measures about $1^1/_2$ feet across its pectorals. In the Atlantic, from North Carolina to the Caribbean, is the closely related yellow stingray *(U. jamaicensis).* In both species, the rounded disk is mottled with dark on a light brown background. The tail is short and stout, and the venom is extremely potent.

Stingray of one group live so exclusively in freshwater that they are usually placed in a separate

Atlantic Stingray

Southern Stingray

family, Potamotrygonidae, and are referred to as river ray or river stingray. There are 14 species in three genera of this family, and they are found in South America.

Myliobatidae (eagle ray). As a group, these are among the most pelagic of the ray, although not as completely as the mantas. They still seek their food mainly from the bottom, however, probing for shellfish and crustaceans, which they crush with their powerful flat teeth to get at the soft insides. At other times, they swim almost swallowlike through the water. Now and then an eagle ray will burst into the air in a brief, spectacular "flight."

Unlike the typical bottom-dwelling ray, the 22 members of this group have a distinct head region, with the eyes and spiracles located on each side rather than on top. A distinctive fleshy lobe, or crown, caps the front of the head. Most species have one or more poisonous spines at the base of the tail, but the spines are so short and so close to the body that they cannot be used very effectively even in defense. Eagle ray occur in all warm and tropical seas.

The spotted eagle ray (*Aetobatus narinari*) is cosmopolitan in warm seas. One of the giants of its clan, it may measure more than 7 feet across its "wings" and reaches weights of between 400 and 500 pounds. Its tail carries more than one spine, frequently as many as five. Because its snout resembles a duck's bill, this species is known also as the spotted duckbilled ray. Its wings and body are heavily spotted, earning it the name of leopard ray as well.

The bullnose ray (*Myliobatis freminvillii*), which occurs in the western Atlantic from Cape Cod to Brazil and possibly in the Gulf of Mexico and the Caribbean, lacks spots and is considerably smaller, measuring only about 3 feet across. The bat ray (*M. californica*) occurs in the Pacific, from the Gulf of California to Oregon. Like other eagle ray, it has a special fondness for shellfish and becomes a destructive pest where oysters and clams are being harvested commercially.

Mobulidae (mantas). The mantas, also called devil ray, comprise a 10-member family that spans a wide spectrum of size, from ocean giants to species that measure only a few feet across the pectoral fins. Mantas are easily distinguished by two flexible head protrusions, called cephalic fins, that form narrow lobes, one on each side of the head. These appendages are used chiefly to facilitate the entrance of small pelagic food organisms into the wide mouth. The cephalic fins, separated widely and extending forward from the head, resemble "horns," from which the name "devil ray" originates.

Mantas lack a caudal fin. Their skin, aside from tail spines, is naked or covered with small tubercles or prickles. The minute teeth are in both jaws or in only one, in series and forming a band. The Atlantic manta and the Pacific manta have a terminal mouth (at the end of the snout) rather than one that is directed downward as in their close cousins, the

Atlantic Manta

mobulas. Development is ovoviviparous. They range in tropical to warm temperate regions of all oceans.

The giant manta (*Manta birostris*) is circumtropical and the largest species; its wing span can exceed 20 feet, and it can weigh well over 3,000 pounds. The dorsal color of the giant manta is dull, varying from dark olive brown to black. There may be a lighter patch on each shoulder and various blotches and indistinct markings. The superficial areas of coloration may be natural in some and accidental in others because the dark pigmentation is easily rubbed off. The underside of the body is white or creamy white.

The European manta (*Mobula mobular*) belongs to a genus of mantas that have teeth in both jaws and that have the mouth on the underside of the head. Measuring about 4 feet across its wings, the European manta is further distinguished by its possession of a spine, or sometimes two, at the base of the tail, as in other types of ray. This species occurs from Iceland south to Senegal but is most abundant in the Mediterranean region, and strays have occurred off New Jersey and Cuba.

In the western Atlantic, the devil ray, or little devilfish (*M. hypostoma*), occurs from New Jersey to Brazil and is about the same size as the European manta; it has a long tail that lacks a spine. The devil ray is extremely active in its feeding habits, commonly forcing schools of small fish into the shallows as several mantas rush into the milling fish to scoop up a mouthful. This manta also easily and regularly leaps clear of water, whereas the giant Atlantic manta, because of its size, has difficulty in getting completely into the air. The devil ray usually travels in small schools.

Rajidae (skate). In skate, the dorsal and anal fins are greatly reduced in size, and the pelvic fins are deeply notched so that they appear as four fins rather than two. The pectoral fins are large and winglike, joined at the front of the head to form a shelflike snout. The tail is moderately slender. Males have long, prominent claspers used in mating.

Skate produce unusual leathery egg cases called sea purses or sailor's purses. At each of the four corners of the case is a thin projection that helps to anchor the case to objects on the sea bottom. These egg cases are nevertheless commonly washed ashore and are among the curios picked up by beach wanderers.

R

Skate Egg Case

Skate can dart swiftly, when necessary, using their pectoral fins in undulating motions for graceful underwater propulsion. But they are essentially bottom dwellers, usually lying quietly half buried in the sand or mud during the daylight hours and stirring to feed at night, although they also take an angler's bait during daytime. Skate are brown or grayish, commonly mottled, blending well with the bottom. When they rest, they usually fan the sand or soft sediment as they settle so that only their eyes and spiracles are above the surface. By creating suction with their body, they can cling to the bottom so tightly that they are difficult to dislodge. If forced out of hiding, they squirm and twist, frequently managing to impale a victim with their tail spine. A few species can deliver a mild shock; their electric organs are located in the tail and are connected to spinal nerves.

Skate sometimes eat fish, making their catches by darting up quickly from the bottom and then holding the fish down with their body until they can grab their victim with their mouth, which is on their underside. Mostly, however, skate feed on shellfish and crustaceans, which they secure by grubbing them from the bottom. Skate have flat, pavementlike teeth for crushing the shells. In many countries, skate are caught commercially and are prized as food.

Most skate live in rather shallow water and close to shore, but there are some deep-water species. The largest genus is *Raja,* which contains more than a hundred species found in cool to temperate waters throughout the world.

The little skate *(R. erinacea)* is the most common species along the Atlantic coast of North America, ranging from Nova Scotia to North Carolina. Also known as the hedgehog skate, it is about $1\frac{1}{2}$ feet long and weighs only about a pound. It has a row of spines along its back, from just behind the eyes to the end of the tail fin. The big skate *(R. binoculata),* reaches a length of 8 feet. It is found from the Bering Sea and the Aleutians to Baja, California, Mexico. The more abundant California skate *(R. inornata)* averages only about 2 feet in length and has four to five rows of prickly spines on its tail; it occurs from British Columbia to central Baja California. Also notably thorny is the clearnose skate *(R. eglanteria),* which has spines on its back as well as on its tail. This species is common along the middle and northeastern Atlantic coast in summer but retreats to warmer waters off Florida and in the Caribbean in winter. It gets its name from the translucent areas on each side of its snout. The barndoor skate *(R. laevis)* is one of the most aggressive of all skate and grows to a length of about 5 feet. It is common from Newfoundland to Cape Hatteras and is often caught on baited hooks. The barndoor skate's counterpart off the coast of Europe is the common skate *(R. batis),* which is harvested commercially. It ranges from Norway and Iceland to Senegal, including the western Mediterranean.

RDF

See: Radio Direction Finder.

REACH CAST

An in-air technique for presenting a fly or mending a fly line.

See: Mending.

READING WATER

A term for watching water conditions to determine where fish may be located and how to present lures, flies, or bait to them.

See: Finding Fish.

RECORDS

The largest individuals of a particular species of fish taken by anglers, according to the characteristics or type of equipment used, the body of water, the geographic or governmental region, or other method of classification. Most official records are kept by a government or private organization by state, province, or nation, usually for the major species that are pursued by anglers, but in some cases also for species that are uncommonly caught or rare. These records are based on the weight of the fish without regard to the time it took to make the catch or the difficulty involved.

The criteria for establishing state, provincial, and national records vary widely. The equipment permitted in one, for example, may not be

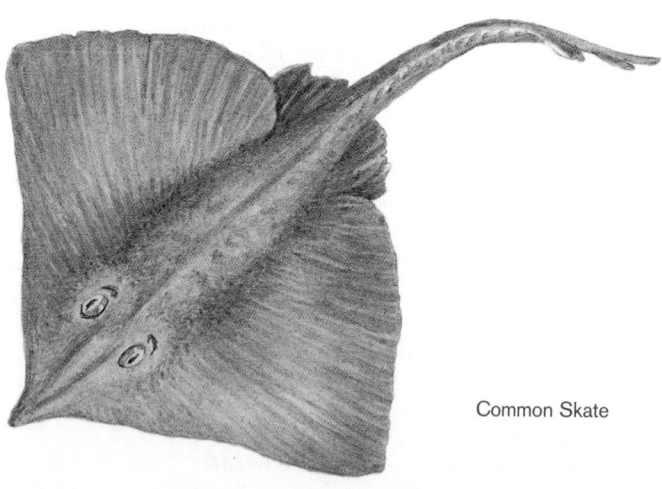

Common Skate

The most celebrated world-record catch is commemorated by the state of Georgia.

permitted in another; likewise, the circumstances surrounding the catch (foul hooking, more than one person handling the rod, etc.) may cause disqualification in some but not in others. Thus, there may a good deal of discrepancy between these types of records.

On a worldwide basis, records for both freshwater and saltwater species—known as world records—are kept by the International Game Fish Association *(see)* in several methods of categorization, and they are based upon defined internationally accepted rules regarding the equipment, methods, and circumstances.

The IGFA keeps these records according to line-class and all-tackle categories for fish caught on all types of fishing tackle except fly tackle; there is a separate category for fish caught on flycasting equipment. The latter is kept according to tippet class, with seven tippet strengths ranging from 1 to 10 kilograms. Line-class records correspond to the specific breaking strength of line, and range from 1 to 60 kilograms, although line-class records do not exist in the heavier strengths for species that do not attain large weights. An all-tackle record is the heaviest individual of a given species of sportfish caught on sporting tackle, using line up to 60-kilogram (130-pound) breaking strength; it may also be a line-class world record.

Certain important requirements must be met when submitting applications for world record recognition. One of the more important is the requirement that the catch be weighed on certified scales, and preferably be witnessed by disinterested parties who will attest to the weight. Another is that a sample be sent of the line used to catch the particular fish being considered for a world record; the line is tested by IGFA to determine its actual breaking strength *(see: line)*, since this may differ from the label strength. A clear photograph of the fish, with the tackle used, is also required to assure proper identification of the species.

Hundreds of world records exist, and scores of new records—usually displacing previous records—are established every year. Just as many are denied record status as are granted; denial is usually because the line is found to be heavier than the category for which the fish was submitted or because the fish was weighed on uncertified scales.

Over the years, much controversy has surrounded some records, especially ones for very popular species or species that people are especially passionate about. As a result, some of the older records, which were established before rigorous criteria and evaluation methods were adopted, have been "retired" or disallowed.

Because of media attention and/or the length of time that existing records have gone unbroken, the all-tackle records for certain species are especially coveted. These include largemouth bass, muskellunge, northern pike, walleye, striped bass, bluefish, tarpon, bonefish, sailfish, blue marlin, and black marlin.

RECREATIONAL FISHERMAN

A person who catches fish and shellfish for personal use, fun, challenge, and leisure. This broad term is primarily applied to noncommercial fishermen in saltwater who do not sell their catch, regardless of the means used to capture the fish or shellfish, provided that such means does not involve high-volume harvesting techniques and equipment. It may also apply to noncommercial fishermen in freshwater who use methods other than rod and reel to capture fish.

Technically, the U.S. Department of Commerce considers fishing to be recreational when "pleasure, amusement, relaxation, and/or home consumption or subsistence are the primary motivations." Marine recreational fishing is defined by the National Marine Fisheries Service as "any fishing in marine waters that does not result in the sale or barter of all or part of the fish harvested."

The term "recreational fisherman" is used by marine fisheries managers as all-inclusive and to delineate commercial fishermen from noncommercial fishermen. However, to the sportfishing community, this term differs from "angler," or "sportfisherman," which are both used to signify people who use sporting equipment (i.e., rod and reel) during the act of fishing and who, in theory, are not pursuing large numbers or volumes of fish species. Thus, a scuba diver who uses a speargun to "catch" fish is not an angler, but would be considered a recreational fisherman. A person who uses a rake to dig clams for personal use would likewise be categorized by marine fisheries managers as a recreational fisherman but not an angler. And a person who uses a trotline *(see)* or setline *(see)* for personal use would also be categorized by freshwater fisheries managers as a recreational fisherman but not an angler.

Furthermore, and also muddying an understanding of this term, is the fact that some saltwater anglers who consider themselves recreational anglers—using rod and reel exclusively and fishing primarily for sporting purposes—also sell a portion of their catch in states where such sales are not prohibited for certain species (dolphin and tuna especially), evidently as a means of offsetting the high cost of traveling to offshore environs to fish for those species. The sale of fish by so-called recreational fishermen is a controversial one among anglers, and causes difficulties when sportfishing interests are pitted against commercial fishing interests.

See: Angler; Angling; Commercial Fisherman; Sportfishing; Sportfisherman.

RECREATIONAL FISHERY

A fisheries management term, primarily used in saltwater fishing, referring to all aspects of the act of fishing or the harvest of fish for noncommercial purposes, under conditions in which the proceeds are released or kept for personal use and are not sold. This term includes fisheries resources, the people who utilize those resources, and businesses providing goods and services.

See: Recreational Fisherman.

REDD

A pit or trough made by female salmon and trout in the gravel bottom of rivers or streams for spawning. Eggs are laid in the redd, which is sometimes also called a nest.

RED TIDE

An area of water, frequently discolored, that is formed by accumulations of large numbers of microscopic plants or animals. These phenomena are not tides; and although some are red, they may be amber, brown, purple, or pink, or not visibly colored. A red tide may be confined to relatively small patches, or it may cover several acres or even many square miles of sea.

Red tides have been documented worldwide for thousands of years in cold temperate to tropical waters. In North America, red tides occur on both sides of the Atlantic, off Florida, and along the Pacific coast into Alaska.

Red tides are caused by dinoflagellates. These and other types of microscopic algae (about $1/1000$ inch long), collectively called phytoplankton, are plentiful (hundreds of thousands per liter of water) and serve as a foundation for the marine food web. Dinoflagellates can produce some of the most powerful poisons in nature. When certain dinoflagellates are present in higher-than-normal concentrations, a "bloom" is created that releases poison, or toxin, into the water. This poison can cause various effects; for example, it may paralyze fish, causing them to stop breathing, after which the result may be large dieoffs. Sometimes, a bloom discolors the surrounding water. Some instances of red tide have been linked to pollution, but many are unrelated.

Most red tides are harmless. However, toxic red tides can kill fish and other marine animals and can contaminate shellfish such as clams and oysters. People can become ill by eating shellfish tainted with red tide toxins. Some toxic red tides cause debilitation through paralytic shellfish poisoning (PSP), a disease that is contracted by eating infected shellfish and that attacks the human nervous system; additionally, toxic particles in sea spray at the shore can cause respiratory discomfort. Although the term "red tide" is widely used to indicate the presence of poisonous shellfish, only a very small percentage of red tides cause shellfish to be unsafe. However, outbreaks of poisonous shellfish may occur when there is no discoloration of the water, or they may be caused by other factors.

REDFISH

A common term for red drum *(see: drum, red)*.

REDWORM

Also known as a red wiggler, this is a type of earthworm *(see)*, normally about 3 to 4 inches long, and a popular freshwater bait.

See: Natural Bait.

REEF

A mass or ridge of rock in a body of freshwater or saltwater. Rock reefs are submerged parts of land rising from the bed of a lake, large river, or the ocean; they are permanent objects (unlike a bar or shoal, which consists of unconsolidated sediment) and can be hazardous to navigation when they rise close enough to the surface. Many reefs that are in the navigational zone of well-traveled waterways are marked with buoys, but they may not be marked in infrequently traveled areas of oceans, rivers, and lakes, or in seldom-visited far northern lakes.

Reefs may be places where various forms of aquatic life find shelter and food, and they are thus attractive to many species of sportfish, such as lake trout, walleye, and smallmouth bass in freshwater and many species of jacks, snapper, and grouper in saltwater. Fishing efforts around them include trolling, jigging, and bottom fishing with bait; in saltwater, a lot of chumming *(see)* is done.

In the oceans, there are also biogenic reefs, which are composed of various living organisms and are called coral reefs *(see)*; these are either fringing reefs (close to mainland shores), barrier reefs (separated from the mainland), or atolls (surrounding volcanic peaks).

See: Inshore Fishing.

REEL, FISHING

Fishing reels are basically line management devices that are affixed to some type of rod. Their primary functions are storing, dispensing, and retrieving fishing line.

The storage function relates to the ability of the reel to contain sufficient line to allow continued fishing in the event of a tangle and breakoff, as well as to provide for sustained runs by large fish. The dispenser function is more complex; it ranges from the ideally friction-free event of long-distance casting to the action of a clutch, which allows line to slip outward under tension (called the drag; *see*). The retrieval function likewise ranges from the high speed recovery necessary to impart lure action to the powerful cranking power required to raise a stubborn fish away from its protective bottom structure.

Fishing reels accomplish these functions by several means. In each case, the design of the reel tends to favor one function over the others, and leads to several basic divisions of fishing reel types.

Types

Fishing reels can be divided into two major categories, depending upon whether the spool revolves or is stationary.

Revolving-spool reels. Conventional, or revolving-spool, fishing reels receive their name because the motion of the line is considered conventional; it is pulled from a spool that revolves the same way that sewing thread is taken from its spool. Such reels are mechanically straightforward; they are characterized by strong cranking power and the ability to handle heavy lines. Although revolving-spool reels hold the majority of distance casting records, they are relatively difficult to cast and require considerable skill and practice to avoid catastrophic errors.

Revolving-spool reels can be categorized as single- or multiplying-action versions. Single-action reels, which include fly fishing and mooching products, are simply spools with handles that revolve on a shaft. The spool is large because each rotation of the handle must retrieve a reasonable amount of line. However, the large spool severely limits casting distance because the energy to start the spool rotating requires unsuitably massive terminal weights. In the case of fly fishing, the reel is simply a line storage device, and the line is pulled by hand from the reel to facilitate the cast.

Single-action reels are mounted below the axis of the rod so that forward winding retrieves the line. Because of the direct drive nature of the handle, the mechanical efficiency can be excellent, and the simplicity of the design offers great reliability. The drag function—applying pressure to make it harder for the spool to permit line to flow outward when pulled by a large fish—may be as simple as using the hand to apply friction to the edge of the spool, or may include the use of adjustable mechanical friction washers.

Multiplying-action reels are commonly referred to as multipliers and today are represented by a group of products that are generally termed "conventional " reels. These have comparatively small spools that are driven by a mechanical gear train. The gear train can be disconnected to free the spool, allowing for excellent long-distance casting in lighter weight products. Spool overrun can occur, however, leading to a vividly descriptive condition of line tangle called a "bird's nest." Avoiding this catastrophe requires considerable skill by the caster.

Because the gear train consists of parallel axes for the shafts, the mechanical forces are simply constrained, frictional losses are minimal, and cranking power is superb. Likewise, the drag system is uncomplicated and extremely effective. In addition, the line is wound directly onto the spool, easing line flexibility requirements and allowing the use of very heavy lines on very small spools. Some models of these reels can be used efficiently with a wide variety of line strengths. Multiplier reels range from freshwater baitcasting reels to big-game reels for offshore fishing applications.

Fixed-spool reels. Spinning reels are called "fixed-spool" reels as well as "stationary-spool" reels because the line is dispensed from the end of a nonrotating spool. The spool axis is parallel to the rod, and the line is pulled over the spool lip when cast. Such a system does not require energy to rotate a spool, and is not subject to overrun; thus, it is extremely simple to cast and relatively tangle free.

Retrieval is accomplished by winding the line around the fixed spool with a rotating arm. Because this motion requires a 90-degree change of direction, there are mechanical losses even with relatively limp lines. Likewise, the drive gears from handle to rotating arm require a 90-degree change of direction, leading to thrust forces and mechanical losses. Fixed-spool reels thus excel in casting, even for users who are relatively unskilled and unpracticed, but are not as efficient in cranking power as revolving-spool reels.

A wide variety of reels, with different features and capabilities, are on the market.

R

Two types of fixed- or stationary-spool reels are widely used and very popular, especially in freshwater fishing. One features a spool that is exposed and always visible to the user, and is commonly called a spinning reel. The other features a covered spool and is commonly called a spincasting reel. The latter has convenient push-button casting operation, and a top-mounted hand position identical to that of the (revolving-spool) baitcasting reel. Individual spinning reels can typically be used efficiently with three, or perhaps four, strengths of line; individual spincasting reels can be used with only two or three strengths of line.

The features and use of each of these types of reels is described in greater detail in their specific section.

Production and Materials

The manufacture of fishing reels requires a fairly large capital investment in dies, designs, tooling, computer design/manufacturing software, and so forth. The finished product is a mass-produced item, each as nearly alike as the other. This is true as well even for limited-production items that are "machined" from barstock, which require an enormous development cost. Fishing reels are not custom-made products that can be created for individual needs and interests, although there is a substantial amount of after-market tinkering that occurs with some, particularly reels that are put to the most demanding big-game fishing uses.

Many of the components and features of reels are discussed in detail in their respective entries, but one factor that has become more variable is the actual materials used. Many manufacturers have stressed the use of metal, or the use of plastic, in their products, but a lot of anglers do not understand why or how this may be relevant. Materials may vary greatly with freshwater and lighter-duty reels, and the subject warrants a brief review here.

Metal.   The metals used to fabricate fishing reels range from simple diecast alloys (aluminum and zinc) through machinable, tough aerospace alloys (hardened high tensile strength aluminum). The choice is typically determined by engineering requirements and costs.

Positive attributes of metal in reels include strength, rigidity, and durability.

For a given-sized part, metals are generally stronger than polymers; this is true even with less expensive alloys. For this reason, the internal gears of reels are almost universally metals, such as brass, stainless steel, aluminum bronze, or other alloys. Similarly, the metal body of a reel is stronger than its polymer counterpart. In the case of high-end reels, the body is often machined from a solid block or billet of metal, resulting in the strongest possible structure, without regard for cost.

Metals are also stiff, or rigid, by nature and are able to maintain precise alignment between gears, even when subject to heavy stresses. Frame distortion under load leads to gear misalignment and loss of cranking power. The losses in cranking power are actually delivered as wear to the gear train, and measurably decrease gear life. Being rigid, metals resist this distortion and power loss.

Durability is achieved through the superior wear properties of metals. Many alloys are not only used for the frame, but may double as load-bearing surfaces.

The negative attributes of metal reel bodies include weight, corrosion, and lack of shock resistance. Aluminum and its alloys comprise the bulk of metal reel components, offering about a threefold decrease in weight compared to steel, stainless steel, or brass alloys. Titanium, although extremely light, is presently too expensive and difficult to machine to be practical.

Metal reels generally require surface treatment to inhibit corrosion, particularly in a saltwater environment. This can be done to certain aluminum alloys by an electrochemical coating process called anodizing, which can be both tough and colorful (nearly any color can be permanently dyed into the coating). Almost all top-end reels with golden or flat-black finishes, for instance, use dyed anodized coatings for protection. Some reels even have anodized coatings on internal parts, such as gears. Other alloys are finished with paints, epoxy, or other bases, and, depending on quality, can give adequate corrosion protection.

Plastics/graphite.   Polymer (sometimes called "graphite") reel bodies are injection-molded from a mixture of plastics and strength fibers. The polymers or plastics include ABS, nylons, and similar materials, and the strength fibers are chopped fiberglass, graphite (hence the name "graphite"), or even silicon carbide whiskers. The injection-molding process is well suited to economical mass production. Plastics should not necessarily be confused with "cheap," as in toys; plastics are structural parts of modern firearms, for example, and can withstand enormous loads.

Positive attributes of plastics and graphite in reels include economy of production, light weight, and corrosion resistance. The cost of production and raw materials is extremely economical for these products. The fabrication process is at lower temperatures than with metals, and the die lifetime generally longer; both result in a lower cost product. Additionally, the weight of such products is about two-thirds that of aluminum alloys, although this number must be modified to include metal parts such as gears, shafts, and screws, which are internal to the reel.

Especially noticeable is the fact that plastics are inherently resistant to corrosion and often do not require any finishing; colored fillers can be added to the polymer before molding. Note also that metallic finishes, often vacuum deposited, can be applied so that the part appears to be made of metal. The durability of the finish is a matter of quality, ranging from those of the toy industry to those in high-wear applications such as the metal-finish knobs on stereo equipment.

Negative attributes of plastics and graphite in reels include distortion and wear. Distortion results because polymers must retain a degree of flexibility to avoid brittleness, particularly at extremely low temperatures. This is because an overly rigid polymer can fracture through propagation of a crack, much like a piece of glass. The purpose of the strength fibers is to limit crack propagation, so the final mixture must be a compromise of properties. (In the case of metals, brittleness is controlled by grain structure, which is a function of the alloy and heat treatment.) Furthermore, the flexibility of polymer parts should not be regarded as entirely negative; reels made of these materials have wonderful shock resistance and will survive hard falls much better than metal reels. The most important factor in producing a viable polymer frame fishing reel is careful structural design; done correctly, the product is excellent.

Polymers have many self-lubricating properties but are fundamentally soft and therefore can wear quickly, especially through the abrasive action of sand, dirt, and grit. Again, careful designs that restrict bearing and other movement have generally succeeded in eliminating this potential problem. In firearms, for instance, steel inserts are molded into the plastic body to provide bearing surfaces.

For both metal- and polymer-bodied reels, many of the potential problems that can be negative attributes may be avoided through minor maintenance. Generally, the potentially bad aspects of a product are exacerbated through neglect, and the reel is perfectly capable of delivering good service and value whether made of metal or plastics.

Bushings and Ball Bearings

The basic task of bushings and ball bearings is to precisely support a rotating shaft with minimum friction. In revolving-spool reels and fixed-spool reels, a rotating shaft supports the handle and gear train, which the angler cranks for retrieve; in revolving-spool reels, the rotating shaft also supports the spool, and in fixed-spool reels, it also supports the rotor.

Bushings. A bushing, sometimes called a sleeve bearing, supports the rotating shaft with a smoothly finished hole and a lubricating film. The bushing material can be the same as that of the reel body itself but is typically a distinctly separate material for better wear and lower friction. The physical contact between bushing and shaft is subject to sliding of one surface over the other, so there's a need for smooth mechanical finishing and lubrication.

For relatively low loads, the body material of diecast reels is a suitable bushing material. The common diecast metal is Zamak, a zinc/aluminum alloy with good machining characteristics. Its coefficient of friction with a steel shaft (a measure of the amount of friction between the metals) is low,

and a lubricating film makes it even lower. The lubricating film is required to keep the surfaces from actually touching, and must not only withstand the pressure of the contact, but retain this property at higher temperatures as well.

Bushing materials which differ from that of the reel body are used for greater loads and include such metals as brass and bronze, as well as fiber-reinforced polymers. These bushings are firmly installed with a press fit, or even adhesives, because inadvertent rotation of the bushing would disastrously wear an oversized hole in the reel body. The bushing materials are selected to optimize mechanical properties, such as abrasion resistance and low friction. The metals are often sintered from granules (much like a graham cracker pie crust), and the resultant porous structure allows either storage or free passage of lubricants, which extends service life for the bushing. Other alloys contain graphite flakes which "self-lubricate" the bushing. Polymer bushings are strengthened with chopped fibers in the matrix. A well-made bushing gives extremely smooth rotation for the operation of a fishing reel.

Ball bearings. The major advantage of ball bearings over bushings is under heavy load conditions. Under low load conditions, the difference between the two systems is virtually indistinguishable, but as the load on the shaft increases, the superior performance of ball bearings becomes increasingly apparent. Ball bearings support their load through a rolling action in contrast to the sliding contact of the bushing. The difference can be compared to moving a rock on wheels versus dragging it along the ground; the heavier the rock, the more apparent the difference between the two methods.

The rolling action of a ball bearing depends on the roundness, precision, and hardness of its components. Lubrication is of secondary importance. High quality ball bearings have extremely close tolerances or imperceptible "play," and the small ball bearings in fishing reels rotate freely when spun. Many ball bearings are sealed with precision fitted covers, front and back, to keep contaminants out and lubricants in. In all, the ball bearing is a complex structure, and the many steps required for its manufacture make it expensive. It, and the related roller bearing, are without doubt the best engineering solution to the support of a rotating shaft under load.

Most production fishing reels are designed with both bushings and ball bearings. Because of the difference in cost of the two types of support, the more expensive models contain a larger number of ball bearings, and have a longer projected service life under harder use conditions. Various cost/performance tradeoffs give excellent value and satisfy the needs of all levels of anglers.

Cantilever supports. Although most rotating shafts are supported on both ends, some designs are cantilevered, or supported at one end only. Small flycasting reels are a typical example. The spool is supported on a shaft, which is cantilevered to the

A 14-pound 8-ounce brook trout caught in the Nipigon River, Ontario, in July 1916 is the second-oldest freshwater world record chronicled.

R

R

sideplate. The handle shaft on some conventional and baitcasting reels is another example.

In these latter cases, the flex allowed by cantilevered designs (also called set plate designs) can seriously affect performance under load because gear teeth engagement becomes compromised, and severe wear can result. The important point is that ball bearings can deliver their full capability only when the total reel design offers rigid support for all of its components. Thus, you cannot simply associate increased ball bearing count with increased quality.

Lubrication.   The primary purpose of a lubricant in a fishing reel is to reduce wear. Greases are generally used in lubricating bushings, gear teeth, and sliding shafts to prevent direct metal-to-metal contact. The essential property of the grease is that its viscosity is sufficient to resist extrusion from the contacting metal surfaces by the pressure generated by heavy loads. This viscosity should be relatively independent of temperature and unaffected by water.

Suitable greases are sold by fishing reel manufacturers; if they are locally unavailable, white or "lithium-based" general-purpose greases serve well. Flake additives, such as graphite, further enhance performance but can be messy unless carefully applied, and will transfer stains to clothing.

Other flake additives include molybdenum disulfide and Teflon. Flaked molybdenum disulfide is designed for high temperature automotive disk brake service; it is messy to apply but an excellent lubricant for gears in some large conventional reels. Flaked Teflon is comparatively expensive and is used for some drag washer lubrication. The same chemical inertness that characterizes the non-stick Teflon coating in cookware also yields non-stick drag performance. It is a singular and unusual property, and leads to extremely smooth starting and stick-free drag performance, particularly in reels designed for light lines. These and other greases, however, should only be applied if the manufacturer recommends it. Some manufacturers have specific grease recommendations, or advise no greasing, so you should follow their instructions.

Light oils are intended for lubrication of ball bearings on the shaft of revolving spool reels, which must rotate freely for long casts. These ball bearings are designed to operate with a rolling action, and the light oil is intended as much for surface protection as lubrication. Grease or heavy oils inadvertently applied to spool bearings seriously degrade their performance. Such ball bearings should be washed in alcohol or acetone (in proper ventilation) and then lubricated with light oil. The oil also serves the secondary purpose of reducing bearing noise. Such oils can be used for lubricating the shaft ends, and for other light-duty uses such as baitcasting reel clutches and yokes.

If you get oil on your hands while fishing, clean your hands well to avoid the possibility of repelling fish with the odor of the lubricant when you touch lures or natural bait. In some cases, this makes no difference in fishing, but in others it can. Wipe off any lubricant on the exterior surface of a reel with an alcohol soaked rag, or use a covering scent.

See: Baitcasting Tackle; Big-Game Tackle; Conventional Tackle; Flycasting Tackle; Rod, Fishing; Spincasting Tackle; Spinning Tackle; Tackle Care, Maintenance.

REEL SEAT
The component of a fishing rod handle or butt that contains the reel.
See: Rod, Fishing.

REGULATIONS
When anglers obtain a fishing license, they should also receive a brochure, booklet, or pamphlet that details the regulations pertaining to fishing in the area covered by that license. This literature is usually a synopsis of regulations that have been adopted by law under the direction of the resource agency responsible for fisheries in that area of jurisdiction. Such regulations exist for all freshwater fishing, since licenses are required throughout North America to fish in freshwater; it is partly true in saltwater, since licenses are required in some places but not in others. Even where licenses are not required, there are still regulations pertaining to limits, seasons, angling methods, and the like, and these are detailed in some type of booklet.

Often the regulations are formidable, extensive, and perhaps confusing. Although some are straightforward and easy to understand, the trend in recent decades, as the management of people and resources has become more complex, is toward more detailed and site- or species-specific regulations. Difficult reading or not, however, these regulations are must reading for anyone who wants to fish. While most anglers realize they must know and abide by dates and limits, there are many other points that require checking. Things you may take for granted as accepted practice in one place may be against the law in another. Since ignorance of the law is no defense, you should know what the regulations are wherever you fish. Be aware that regulations vary considerably from one state or province to the next. It is a fact that some of the legal differences come from special regulations or exceptions for specific waters. It is also a fact that many regulations are difficult to enforce.

While the plethora of regulations may seem excessive and like a lot of governmental intrusion to some people, bear in mind that the reason for most regulations is to give the fish a chance and to set restraints upon people, some of whom would exercise no moderation if left unchecked. In fact, some regulations are based more upon the need (real or perceived) to control the actions of people than upon sound biological principles. It is also important to realize that many regulations have been requested or encouraged by anglers, or supported by their organizations.

No matter how stringent the regulations may be, and no matter how stringent or how difficult the enforcement may be, ethics, morality, and sportsmanship count for the most in the end, and, on this, each angler knows his or her own score.

The following is an overview and explanation of common regulations.

Licenses

Fishing licenses in North America are not federal licenses but are issued by state and provincial government agencies, which set their own fee structure. There is seldom fee reciprocity for nonresidents. The license *(see)* is usually referred to by the public as a fishing license or as a sportfishing license, but it is actually granted to people who use various means of fishing, including some methods not generally considered as sporting. These can include the use of spears, certain types of nets, setlines, trotlines, and other means.

A fishing license is not restricted to specific waters but allows an angler to fish throughout the state or province and for all or most species. The revenues received from these licenses, as well as from the sale of stamps or permits or other fees, are kept by the states or provinces and theoretically used for the management of fisheries resources. Management funds in the United States also come from a federal excise tax that is apportioned to the states *(see: Federal Aid in Sportfish Restoration Act)*.

The regulations specify who qualifies as a resident and who must have a license or who is exempt from a license (some people must have a license, but it is free). They also specify which activities are covered by this license, and they define what is meant by sportfishing for the purpose of this license; in other words, capturing fish with commercial harvesting equipment is not a means of sportfishing and doesn't qualify for a sportfishing license. A license is valid only within the boundaries of the government that issues the license. In border waters, there is sometimes a reciprocal agreement between governments honoring licenses, but in many cases, and especially in international boundary waters, there is no such reciprocity, which means that an angler needs two licenses to freely fish in waters that have divided jurisdiction (and may have to abide by different regulations when in the respective jurisdiction).

A sportfishing license is required in freshwater throughout North America, with some exceptions. Those exceptions may include people over and under a certain age, in the military, with disabilities, and members of native or aboriginal communities. A license is required of both residents and nonresidents, although the fees for the latter are greater.

The situation in saltwater is less straightforward. Some states include saltwater fishing as part of a general statewide license that is applicable to both saltwater and freshwater. Some have a saltwater fishing license that is separate from, and in addition to, a freshwater fishing license. In some places, a freshwater license may be required in tributaries and in nontidal portions of a coastal river, but no license may be necessary in the tidal portions or elsewhere in saltwater. In some saltwater environs, there is a boat license, which is a blanket license granted to the operator or captain of a boat and covering, in effect, all people who fish in that boat. The scenario is diverse, complicated by the fact that saltwater fish hinder state management efforts because they do not acknowledge governmental boundaries.

Seasonal licenses are normally valid for a 12-month period, which may or may not be on a calendar basis; they are nontransferable and nonrefundable and may not be valid until signed. There are no tests or courses required in order to receive a license, but that may change in the future; some countries in Europe have such a requirement. Licenses for nonresidents often can be bought for limited periods (a day, a week, etc.). Regulations usually require that the license be in the angler's possession when fishing and that it be shown to a conservation officer upon request. In a few states, a license must be displayed on the outer clothing above the waist, and in some it must be shown to anyone who asks to see it. In certain places, a license is not required on private waters or on farms. Many states offer lifetime licenses that are expensive when bought but economical over one's life if purchased at an early age. Combined licenses for spouses or family licenses are sometimes available, and the cost of a fishing license is usually less if purchased in conjunction with a hunting license. So-called "conservation" licenses, primarily required in Canadian provinces, have more stringent provisions for keeping fish.

Some localities may levy other governmentally imposed costs in addition to the license fee, such as a stamp. Stamps are usually issued in freshwater fishing and for particular species or to support a particular management program; the revenue derived from the sale of such stamps is used for purposes that are specific to the management of those species, instead of being put into general fisheries management coffers. Also, some places, such as state or federal parks or private preserves, require an additional license or permit for fishing; these are separate from those required by the state or provincial fisheries agencies.

State and provincial licenses, stamps, and permits can usually be obtained at tackle and bait shops, some sporting goods stores, marinas, lodges and camps, town or county clerk's offices, and at the offices of the presiding fisheries agency. They are increasingly becoming available by phone through credit card purchase.

Comparing the cost of a license with the cost of other goods (food, beverage, boat gas, etc.), and considering that a fishing license is valid for a full year and that it permits fishing for many if not all species throughout a state or province, a fishing license is pretty inexpensive. It is one of the original user fees, and for the most part, the management of

i Color is a big element in fishing lures today, and as long ago as 1883, Earnest F. Pflueger was granted a patent for artificial lures coated with luminous paint for fishing at night.

both game and nongame fish is supported by the funds derived from angling licenses, with little if any financial contribution to fisheries management from nonanglers unless a small amount comes from general tax funds.

Problems.   Angling without a license is the most frequent fish and game law violation. Some violations occur innocently, but the majority are made by people who should know better.

In most localities, an angler needs a license to fish on privately owned waters. Many places allow fishing in private waters without a license if you are the owner, a direct relative of the owner, or a tenant of the owner. Often the decision depends on whether the private water is stocked with public fish, has public water flowing in or out of it, is navigable, is an agricultural pond, or is stocked with fish purchased from commercial sources. In many states, regulations for private water differ from those for public water; in some cases, where licenses are not required, there are no regulations on size or bag limit, season, or manner of taking fish. In others, a license is not needed, but general regulations still apply. If a license is required on private water, it is the same license that any member of the public would buy from the appropriate government agency; this is different in some European countries, where licenses (actually permits) are granted by individual property owners.

Children under a certain age (usually 14, 15, or 16) usually don't need a fishing license, but an adult who takes children fishing may. Generally, that adult does not need a license if he or she is just supervising but does need one if he or she assists or is fishing too. The interpretation of supervision depends on the government: You may not need a license as long as you don't handle the rod while the line is in the water, or you may not be able to handle any tackle unless you are licensed. Some states consider baiting a hook to be assisting. You may need a license if you are helping children under a certain age, and a licensed adult may have to accompany a nonresident child.

Seasons

Seasons in which anglers can or cannot fish are established for certain species or for some fish in specific locations. For popular species, a closed season is usually established to protect them when they are spawning. In theory the closed season prevents too many fish from being taken and permits adequate replacement, although fisheries biologists do not agree on this issue; and it may be regarded differently depending on the fish population, the number of anglers, and the habitat. Differences in season dates for the same species exist among agencies; also, a state may have a closed season for a particular species during the spawning period but no closed season for a different species during its spawning period.

Usually those species that are abundant and for which a liberal harvest is encouraged do not have a closed season, and angling may take place on a continuous or year-round basis. A closed season may exist on a year-round basis for those species whose populations are low and in need of complete protection.

When the season opens, angling may legally begin; the start of the season, referred to as opening day, is often a very popular and eagerly anticipated event, subject to a peak of angling activity. In eastern U.S. states, the opening day of trout season, which is in early April, is a much-heralded occasion, although one that is more notable for social enjoyment than for productive angling. In the Midwest, the early May opening of the walleye season brings throngs of people to the water.

Where there are established seasons, they usually begin at 12:01 A.M. on the opening day of the season, and close at midnight on the last day of the season. With some exceptions, there are no restrictions on the hours in which a person can fish during an open season (unlike hunting), meaning that fishing is permitted at all hours of the day during the season. Exceptions usually allow fishing to begin at or just before sunrise and end at or just after sunset; these are usually established to help minimize the illegal taking of spawning fish, particularly Great Lakes salmon and trout.

Problems.   One of the major causes of game law violations is the possession of fish out of season, and it is very obvious that people who possess a fish out of season have broken the law. These people usually do not have a fishing license either. Regulations not only specify that it is illegal to possess fish out of season, but that it is also illegal to fish for a species during a closed season. There are times when people inadvertently catch out-of-season species while angling for in-season species. This is not unlawful if you release them immediately. However, if a body of water is closed to the taking of all species, you cannot legally fish there out of season even if you release all fish. In some northern areas, it is illegal to fish in trout-stocked waters for any species prior to the opening of the trout season, even if the season for other species is otherwise open.

Some people deliberately catch and release certain fish out of season, under the guise of angling for species that are legal; this is a gray area that is problematic for law enforcement, since it is difficult to prove intent in court. However, there is an ethical question to fishing out of season even if you intend to release the fish, and there is the issue of adhering to the spirit of the law. Fishing prior to the beginning of the season is most common among bass anglers, and has led in some places to the establishment of special "early-season" regulations prohibiting the use of bait and permitting very restrictive harvest, or stipulating catch-and-release.

Bag/Creel/Daily Limit

A bag or creel limit regulates the number of fish that can be taken daily and is also called a daily

R

limit. The purpose is to achieve one or more of the following: distribute the total catch among more people over a greater time period; keep populations from being reduced to such a low level that fishing is unacceptable; keep populations at a level that allows them to forage on abundant or stunted populations of other species; provide larger and (to anglers) more acceptable fish; and protect populations, if reproduction is limited, so more fish will reach sexual maturity and thereby spawn at least once.

A creel limit is commonly based on an aggregate number of specimens of one species; thus a daily limit of five walleyes means that no more than five walleyes can be kept by one angler during the period from 12:01 A.M. until midnight. It does not mean that an angler can keep five walleyes in the morning, go home, return in the afternoon, and keep five more. However, an angler could keep two in the morning, go home, come back later, and keep three more.

The creel limit is usually different for each species or grouping of fish. For example, in a recent year in Tennessee, the daily limit was 5 fish for largemouth bass, 5 for walleye, 1 for muskellunge, 2 for striped bass, 20 for rock bass, 30 for crappie, and unrestricted for bluegills and catfish. Top predator fish, which receive more angling pressure, are usually subject to more restrictive daily limits because there are fewer of them in the overall fish population and they can be more readily overharvested. Species that are not the top predators, such as bluegill, crappie, and perch in freshwater, are much more abundant than the top predator fish, and the populations of these species are influenced to a greater degree by environmental conditions. Thus, unless there is a serious problem with the population of those species, daily limits tend to be more generous than they are for predators and usually exist more as a means of preventing some anglers from being game hogs than as a means of population control.

Crappie are among the freshwater species that often have liberal harvest limits.

In a similar vein, some creel limits apply to all fish that are caught, without regard to species, and all species are grouped in an aggregate amount. This is prevalent in Canadian provinces and is likely to become more popular in the future as a way to reduce the total catch of anglers in a single day. In this case, a daily bag limit of seven fish for all species might include seven of one species, or it might stipulate that no more than a certain number could be of a particular specie or species. The primary purpose here is to regulate anglers and minimize total take rather than to control specific populations of fish.

A creel limit may also have a stipulation pertaining to the size of the fish; usually the stipulation would apply to keeping a restricted number of specimens over a certain length (or size). For example, the daily limit for northern pike might be six fish, only one of which could be larger than 75 centimeters (an actual Saskatchewan regulation).

Many anglers who have caught their limit customarily continue fishing but release, or cull *(see: culling),* their later catches. Many provincial and some state regulations specify that it is illegal to continue to catch or fish for a species once the daily limit is in the angler's possession. If an angler has a limit of five bass, for example, and then catches a sixth bass, he or she could technically be in violation of the law when holding (reduced to possession) that sixth bass, even though it is for the purpose of release, unless the regulations specifically permit this. The culling aspect of regulations is very loosely (if at all) enforced in most states, but it is more closely followed in Canada. However, in some jurisdictions, including Canadian provinces, regulations specify that an angler must stop fishing upon reaching his or her limit.

Some people think that anglers should abide by a voluntary limit equal to the existing law, whether they keep or release the fish; in other words, if the daily limit is six northern pike, the angler should stop fishing for pike once he or she has caught six of them, even if all are released. Such a notion might become a regulation, although its enforcement would clearly be difficult. In most places, however, fish that are released are not considered "taken" and do not count against the daily limit.

What many anglers fail to take into account is the fact that even when they practice careful catch-and-release, a certain amount of delayed mortality is unavoidable. This fact means that you still have an impact even if you release every fish that you catch. By taking a percentage of your released fish totals into account as part of your limit, you would voluntarily reduce your impact. For example, assume that 10 percent of all released fish die (which some studies indicate) and that the daily limit for a particular species is 10 fish. On a given day, you catch a total of 20 of this species, keeping 10 and releasing 10. Of the 10 released, 1 fish (10 percent) can be expected to die later; thus, your total impact for the day is a mortality of 11 fish,

R

even though you have kept only 10 and have complied with the law. However, if you had kept less than the daily limit and released the others, your total take, or total impact, for the day, would have complied with the spirit of the law.

Admittedly this issue is really more about ethics *(see)* than fisheries management, but you can see that if an angler has a good day on the water and catches a lot of fish for which there is a low limit, even if he or she releases all or nearly all of those fish, the angler is still having an impact.

Daily limits are also associated with possession limits, which are explained later. In some places, again especially in Canadian provinces, the daily limit and the possession limit are the same. In other words, you may possess no more than one limit for each particular species at any time. This includes all fish that you have in hand, at home, in camp, and in transportation. Thus, if the limit is five walleyes and you have three in your home freezer and one in your boat livewell, then you are allowed to keep only one more walleye.

Length Limit

For some species of fish, there are no size limits, meaning that it is legal to keep a fish of any size. And in some locations, there are no size limits for any species, but simply aggregate daily limits. However, in many locations and for many species, there is a minimum legal size, largely to prevent small fish from being kept and to allow fish to grow to a size where they will have an opportunity to spawn at least once. That size is expressed in terms of length, not weight, and is measured in inches or centimeters. Where a minimum length limit exists, you must immediately release any fish of that species that is under the minimum size, and you may keep, or voluntarily release, a fish that equals or exceeds that minimum length.

It is critical that anglers understand how to measure a fish that they will keep. Measuring is done differently in some places, and it may vary with the species, especially in saltwater where some fish have forked tails. Many regulations brochures define how to determine length and illustrate it graphically. Some are rather vague, simply saying that minimum

length is determined from the tip of the snout to the tip of the tail. Some can be confusing when they also refer to total length.

To measure any fish, you should lay it down, preferably on a clean, wet surface, and take the length measurement in a straight line starting at the snout with the mouth closed. It is helpful to have a ruler with the beginning point blunt and angled up so that the snout of the fish can be pressed against it.

Total length.   Length is commonly obtained, especially in freshwater, by measuring to the end of the compressed tail. Some regulations refer to a pinched tail, others compressed, but the idea is to bring together the upper and lower portion of the tail fin, called the lobes, and measure to the longest point. This is also referred to as total length and is how freshwater fish, and saltwater fish without forked tails, are measured.

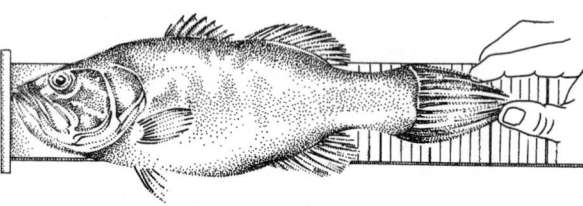

Total length is the distance from the tip of the snout to the end of the tail, as measured with the fish laid flat, the mouth closed, and the tail slightly compressed.

Fork length.   To determine fork length, measure the straight-line distance from the tip of the snout to the center of the tail fin. This method is used for saltwater species with a forked tail; often fish with a rigid forked tail will suffer damage to their tails during transportation from fishing grounds. If they were measured on a total-length basis back at the dock, they may no longer be legal, even though they were legal when initially caught. Measuring these fish by fork length removes that problem and standardizes measurements to make it easier for anglers.

Slot Limit

A slot limit is a special adaptation of a length limit meant to encourage the protection of fish of a certain size. It can be applied in two ways. Generally a slot limit allows harvesting of fish within a defined size range and prohibits the taking of fish smaller or larger than that size. For instance, if bass can be kept only when they are between 15 and 20 inches in size, then fish smaller or larger must be released immediately. Many biologists believe that a slot limit is a better way to limit catches than a minimum length limit, since it not only protects the smallest of the species but also requires release of trophy fish. These trophy fish can then theoretically be caught another day, and their return to the water helps to repopulate the species during spawning season and maintain predator-prey balance.

In less common situations, fish within a specified size range are protected, and fish within that

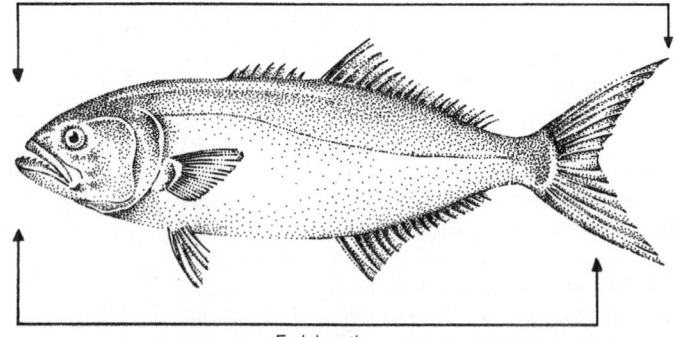

Total length

Fork length

Fish are measured according to total length or fork length.

range must be released. For instance, if lake trout between 22 and 28 inches are protected, specimens of that size must be released, but specimens smaller or larger than that can be either kept or released. Such a slot limit might be used to help protect a size or age group of fish that is underrepresented in the overall population, perhaps because of environmental factors when those fish were born.

Possession Limit

A possession limit is similar to a creel limit, but it specifies the total number of fish that can be in the angler's possession, whether the fish are in hand, in transportation, in camp, at home, on the grill, or in some combination of these. The purpose is to prevent people from repeatedly keeping daily limits and storing them for future use, thus becoming a game hog, and also to help prevent the waste of fish that have been accumulated and stored for long periods.

Possession limits are a confusing issue to anglers, and they vary, particularly between states and provinces. In some places the daily limit and the possession limit are identical. This is more common in Canada than in the United States. Where the daily limit and the possession limit are the same, you may not have more than a daily creel limit in your possession, no matter where the fish are individually stored. In a hypothetical case of a (daily and possession) limit of four lake trout, let's say that an angler goes fishing on Saturday and keeps a daily limit of three lakers. That night the person eats one, cans one, and smokes and freezes the third. The angler is now in possession of two lake trout. On Sunday the angler goes fishing again but now may keep only two lake trout total. The person keeps two and freezes them both, and has reached the possession limit. During the week the angler eats one, which reduces possession to three lake trout. The following Saturday the angler again goes fishing but technically may keep only one lake trout, even though the daily limit is listed as four lake trout.

In many states, a possession limit is equal to a two-day creel limit. Let's use a hypothetical example of a three-fish daily limit for chinook salmon, with a two-day possession limit. An angler catches and keeps the daily chinook limit on Saturday, and cans or freezes it on Saturday night. The person goes fishing again on Sunday and catches and keeps another daily limit, which is stored at home that night. The person now has a legal two-day possession limit of chinook salmon in storage. If the angler goes fishing on Monday and catches and keeps one chinook salmon, he or she is technically in violation of the law, since the angler already has a full possession limit at home. But if the person ate one of the salmon for dinner on Sunday night, then he or she would be in possession of five fish, and on Monday could legally keep one more chinook salmon, but not two or three.

The possession limit may be more liberal than a two-day creel limit. However, in those places where

This notice, posted at a Texas lake, illustrates the slot limit regulation in force.

the possession limit and daily limit are the same, a person can usually transport no more than a two-day creel limit. This regulation allows people who have been fishing at a distant location the opportunity to have in their possession more than one daily limit, but not a limit for every day that they might have been fishing.

Possession is usually defined as any means of home storage, including canned, preserved, smoked, or frozen, as well as the obvious immediate possession of fish in a boat or vehicle, or in temporary storage (at camp or trailer). Therefore, it's important to read the regulations thoroughly to understand what you may and may not do. Obviously, conservation officers or wardens are unlikely to raid your permanent residence to check for the storage of fish, unless you are a repeat violator of wildlife laws. Over the course of a season, many anglers find that they have inadvertently accumulated a few more fish than what the possession limits stipulate. This doesn't necessarily make them game hogs. Furthermore, the issue is complicated by the fact that daily and possession limits differ among jurisdictions and that anglers may visit more than one jurisdiction, and thus keep and possess fish from different places.

As noted, the purpose of possession limits is to prevent excess and to avoid waste. It is one of those areas where conscience and ethics determine a person's adherence to the limits more than formal regulations do.

R

Transportation

Dead fish. As much as resource managers would like you to enjoy the fish that you keep, they have no particular interest in how you store your fish or in what you transport them *(see: fish preparation—care)*. Nevertheless, there are regulations covering the state of the fish being kept while they are transported to your permanent residence, or to the place where they will be stored or consumed, and how they may be transported. This subject is referred to in regulations literature as transportation.

Increasingly, many places require that fish be identifiable when transported. Many states and provinces stipulate that you may not alter the fish in such a manner that the species would be unrecognizable. And many require that a portion of skin (often 1-inch square) be left on all fillets for identification purposes. Where there are length limits on fish, the body of the fish must usually be kept intact, except for removing the entrails and gills, so that a conservation official is able to determine the length. The fish must remain in this manner until reaching the place of consumption or residence. This restriction would preclude beheading and filleting the fish at the place of capture.

The amount of fish that can be transported is either a daily or a possession limit, but one person cannot usually transport (or store) another angler's catch in addition to his or her own, unless the other person's fish are labeled (perhaps including license number) or that person is present. The manner of storing during transportation may be regulated, too, perhaps requiring that transported fish be packaged in such a way that they can be "readily unwrapped, separated, identified, and counted," which is the exact wording of Minnesota's regulations.

Live fish. Transporting live fish is illegal in most places. This regulation prevents the introduction of those fish into other waters, which in itself is usually an illegal act, and also reduces the spread of exotic or nuisance animals or aquatic plants. Many anglers transport their catch from the place of capture to their home by keeping the fish in the boat's livewell; although this practice may keep them fresh, it may also be illegal. Bass, walleye, and panfish are especially subject to such treatment,. In the past, such treatment, where prohibited, was not enforced, but today it is a much more serious issue *(see: exotic species)*.

Methods and Equipment

The methods of fishing that are subject to regulation cover a wide gamut. Some methods are obviously illegal: using explosives and the like, trapping fish by damming the waterway or otherwise preventing their passage, stunning the fish through electric means, or using chemicals that would stun or kill. Fishing with a bow and arrow, or with a spear, as well as using trotlines, setlines, and other non-rod-and-reel methods are usually addressed in the regulations booklets but are not covered here because they are not considered sport in the commonly accepted sense of sportfishing *(see: angling)*.

Most regulations specify what is legally defined as "angling" and detail any limits on the number of hooks that can be used, as well as the number of lines. It is important to review these matters because they may change periodically or may differ by jurisdiction. Throughout Canada, for example, it is illegal to fish with more than one line, except when ice fishing. In most states, it is illegal to fish with more than two lines, except, perhaps, when ice fishing. In a few states, the number of lines is unlimited. There are usually limits to the number of hooks that may be used on a line, and a hook is defined in the regulations. In a few places, it is illegal to use wire line for rod-and-reel fishing or to use a treble hook that is not attached to a lure.

The use of chum is generally legal in freshwater or saltwater, but in many cases the legality is due to omission rather than stipulation by law. There are odd pitfalls here, though; in a few states, using corn as chum for trout is illegal, and some places make using live baitfish illegal. In Canada, nonresidents may not bring in bait. Applying scents to plastic bait or lures is not classified as chumming, but no chum or substance may be toxic, stupefying, or a pollutant. The use of scents or other chemical potions may someday be deemed an unfair advantage to anglers; these practices may then be prohibited.

Foul Hooking

Deliberately foul-hooking fish *(see: foul hook)*, also known as snagging, means hooking a fish anywhere on its body other than inside the mouth and is generally prohibited except for certain nongame species, such as paddlefish, and for some Great Lakes fish, such as salmon, during their spawning runs. However, sometimes anglers unintentionally foul-hook fish, play them, and land them. In the majority of states and provinces, an angler cannot keep fish that were foul-hooked, even if they otherwise conform to regulations, such as size. Those fish must be released immediately. Check to see whether the regulations pertain to where on the fish the foul hook occurs. Some specify that a foul-hooked fish is one that is caught behind the gill covers; this makes sense for some species, such as bass and pike, which often take a lure with two sets of hooks, one of which may lodge on the head outside of the mouth. Bait hooks seldom manage to foul-hook fish outside of the immediate mouth area unintentionally.

Other Common Regulations

Besides the regulations just discussed, there is still a host of others that apply to angling. Make sure that you review the regulations booklets, even when you think you know what the law is because laws change and because many anglers have mistaken notions or interpretations of fishing regulations based on what they have been told by others in the past.

A common area of misinformation concerns bait. Usually, anglers may catch their own bait provided they conform to accepted methods (you can't seine gamefish for use as bait, for example) and provided that they are catching bait that is legal to be caught and/or used for fishing. There are a few important exceptions, and you should check to find out what those are. Also, be advised that in many places it is not legal to release unused bait into the water.

Regulations vary widely as to whether gamefish may be used as bait. In a few states, they may be used dead; in others, only portions of gamefish (viscera, eyes, etc.) may be used. The definition of gamefish is a key factor, For instance, bass may not be used as bait but carp may, or vice versa if the state is trying to control the spread of carp. In states where gamefish species may be used as bait, they may be possessed in size and numbers only in accordance with the fishing regulations for that particular species.

Buying, selling, or trading gamefish is almost universally illegal in freshwater except, obviously, for those who are fish farmers, possess special permits, or have commercial fishing licenses. This is a much murkier issue for marine fish. Generally, species that are classified by state law as gamefish (this has no relationship to whether sportsmen consider them to be gamefish) are considered protected and usually may not be sold by anglers. Fish that are not so classified are unprotected and may legally be sold, although there is a lot of controversy attached to this. Some so-called sport or recreational anglers have been selling some or all of their catch, especially tuna and dolphin (and before that bluefish, striped bass, and maybe other species), for many years, although it would seem that they ought to be required to have a commercial license and be classified as commercial fishermen. That has happened to a limited degree in the case of giant bluefin tuna, where quotas are established and recreational anglers or boat captains must pay a fee and obtain a permit in order to be able to sell that species. The issue of selling saltwater fish has been a hotly contested one and still remains unresolved in many states, especially those on the East Coast *(see: commercial fisherman; recreational fisherman; sportfisherman).*

Usually you must be present when you have a fishing line in the water and you may not leave it unattended, although you can be a specified distance nearby, as in ice fishing. In some places you may not fish by trolling with a motor. In some places you may not deposit fish entrails into the water. In all locations, you may not trespass over private property.

Read the Regulations

If you have read through this entire section, you have probably noticed that the words "usually" and "generally" are employed often. This should be a tip-off that there are many different regulations and many exceptions to standard regulations, and that it

Dolphin are often kept in quantity and in all sizes by anglers.

is important to understand which regulations apply in the state or province where you are fishing, to the body of water that you are fishing, and to the species that you seek or actually catch.

Make sure that you read all the regulations, not just the obvious table of length and bag limits. Also read the fine print. When you do, you may find such interesting and perhaps unknown or overlooked dictums as these, taken from recent regulations booklets:

California	"It is unlawful to cause or permit any deterioration or waste of any fish taken in the waters of this state."
Kentucky	"All sportfish incidentally taken while capturing live bait with seines, dipnets, or cast nets must be released immediately and unharmed into the water."
Minnesota	"No person may have a spear in a dark house or fish house [ice fishing shanty] while angling; nonresidents may not spear from a dark house."
Missouri	"Gamefish not hooked in the mouth, except paddlefish . . . , must be returned to the water unharmed immediately."
Montana	"It is unlawful to waste any part of gamefish suitable for food."
New Hampshire	"Littering is sufficient cause to revoke your [fishing] license."
New York	"No aquatic insect nor any insect that lives in the water during any of its life stages shall be taken from waters inhabited by trout nor the banks thereof at anytime."
Ontario	"It is illegal to harm spawning grounds and nursery, rearing,

R

Pennsylvania	food supply, and migration areas on which fish depend directly or indirectly, in order to carry out their life processes." "It is unlawful to kill any fish and fail to make a reasonable effort to lawfully dispose of it."
Saskatchewan	"It is illegal to take more fish than the limit specifies, including fish eaten for shore lunch."
Wisconsin	"It is illegal to fish for any variety of fish in excess of the daily bag limit."

See: Catch-and-Release; Fisheries Management.

RELEASE

A release is a device that is used both to secure fishing line to some towing mechanism (downrigger cable, planer board tow line, or outrigger) and to free it from that mechanism when a fish strikes or when the angler wishes to change lures. Most releases have adjustable tension settings to allow for changes in pressure exerted by the object being towed. Most of the time, a release is used in trolling, but it can also be used for live or cut-bait fishing.

Releases are critical in many forms of trolling and present a lot of room for experimentation, as well as problems. The release must free the fishing line when a fish strikes or when the angler chooses to detach it in order to retrieve it (otherwise, the line must be brought in to manually free the line).

In downrigger fishing, releases can be attached to the weight, to the downrigger cable at the weight, and to the cable at any location above the weight. In planer board fishing, releases can be attached to the board and to the tow line at any location ahead of the board. When using outriggers, a release (also called a clip) is used on a short length of line attached to the outrigger, and generally placed midway up on the outrigger.

In all releases, the fishing line is clamped into it under variable pressure. Some feature a trigger that can be set to open under greater or lesser tension. Some feature spring-loaded jaws capped with rubber pads; how far into the pads you set the fishing line determines the tension. A release used on a downrigger cable should be small and streamlined to avoid causing drag. A release used on a sideplaner should be able to slide freely down the tow line.

With some releases used in downrigger and planer board trolling, it's a good idea to make several twists in the fishing line and place the loop into the releases. This prevents the line from slipping through without tripping the release. However, on outriggers, when fishing on the surface for big game, it may be best to set untwisted line into the release so the distance that the lure is set back can be quickly changed.

If the line has been placed properly, when a fish strikes, the line immediately pulls free of the release, which remains attached to the tow device. If the line frequently pops free of the release under rough water conditions, increase the adjustable tension. If fish strike and pop the release but seldom get hooked, the tension is too light. However, when the tension is set overly tight, small fish may not be able to free the line from the release.

Anglers can free a line attached to a release by pointing the rod directly at the release, reeling up all slack, and then snapping the rod back. Give the trailing lure a moment to rise, sink, speed up, or slow down before reeling it in, as a following fish might pounce on it when the action changes.

See: Big-Game Fishing; Downrigger; Downrigger Fishing; Flatlining; Planer Boards.

RELEASING FISH

See: Catch-and-Release.

REMORAS

Members of the Echeneidae family, remoras and sharksuckers are slim fish that have a flat sucking disk on the top of their head. They attach themselves usually to sharks or other fish—including marlin, grouper, and ray—but sometimes to the bottoms of boats or other objects. These hitchhikers take an effortless ride with their host, feeding on parasitic copepods found on the host's body and gill chambers.

Developed from the first dorsal fin, the sucking disk consists of a series of ridges and spaces that create a vacuum between the remora and the surface to which it attaches. By sliding backward, the remora can increase the suction, or it can release itself by swimming forward.

On his second voyage into the West Indies, Columbus saw natives using remoras to catch giant sea turtles. When a big turtle was sighted basking at the surface, a remora with a line tied to its tail was let over the side of the boat. Typically it headed immediately for the turtle and fastened itself tightly to the turtle's shell. Then the turtle was carefully drawn back to the boat, the remora refusing to let loose.

The sharksucker *(Echeneis naucrates),* which averages $1\frac{1}{2}$ feet in length but may be as much as 38 inches long and weigh up to 2 pounds, is the largest member of the family. Worldwide in distribution in warm seas, it is gray with a broad, white-edged black band down each side, tapering to the

Sharksucker

tail. It prefers sharks and ray as hosts, and often enters shallow beach and coastal areas; it has been known on rare occasions to attach itself to bathers or divers.

Also cosmopolitan is the remora *(Remora remora)*, which is common to 12 inches long and may attain a length of 34 inches. It is black or dark brown and is also found worldwide. It, too, prefers sharks as hosts. Some other species show distinct host preferences. The whalesucker *(R. australis)*, for example, generally fastens itself to a whale; the spearfish remora *(R. brachyptera)* commonly attaches to billfish such as marlin.

Although often observed by anglers, remoras have no angling merits.

REPAIRS

See: Tackle—Care, Maintenance, Repair.

REPELLENTS

See: First Aid.

REPLICA TAXIDERMY

See: Taxidermy.

REPRODUCTION

A process used in taxidermy *(see)*.

RETRIEVING

An intrinsic element of angling, retrieving is the act of manipulating objects that have been cast or lowered into the water and that need to be worked by hand in order to impart fish-attracting action to them.

The keys to successful retrieval of most lures are depth control, action, and speed, all of which vary in importance depending on the situation and the lure. Achieving the proper depth is perhaps the most important factor, since you can't hope to catch fish without getting your offering to the fish's level. With many lures, the ability to achieve a certain depth is a function of the design of the lure and the way in which it is used. Action is also a function of the design, but only to the extent to which the lure is properly fished; achieving the proper action is a necessity in order for the lure to have maximum attractiveness. Speed is often the most ignored factor in retrieval and is influenced by the diameter of line being used, type of lure, current, and the retrieve ratio of the reel.

Every lure is designed to do a certain function, but that function must be coordinated with the existing fishing conditions and must be achieved through proper lure retrieval. Specific retrieval techniques for lures *(see)* and flies *(see)* are discussed throughout this book.

RHODE ISLAND

Despite being the smallest of the United States, Rhode Island offers respectable and diverse fishing opportunities. And although the interior measures only 40 miles at its widest point, the state is deeply indented in the southeast by Narragansett Bay and has 384 miles of tidal coastline. This geographic characteristic prompted its moniker, the "Ocean State," and helps explain why saltwater fishing is the primary focus of attention among Rhode Island anglers.

Saltwater

Rhode Island has among the best saltwater fishing in the eastern U.S. It possesses a convoluted coastline that ranges from craggy granite outcroppings—both above and below the water—to long, smooth, sandy beaches punctuated by inlets and backed by scores of tidal bays and ponds.

Rhode Island is a surf caster's delight, and its south-facing barrier beaches are a favorite with both striped bass and bass anglers. Striped bass are *the* fish for most Rhode Island anglers, and although no world records have been pulled onto the state's beaches, there have been many close calls. Favorite surf fishing areas for this species include Misquamicut Beach and Weekapaug Breachway (inlet/outlet), Quonochontaug Breachway and State Fishing Area, Charlestown Breachway, the outlet to tidal Ninigret Pond, the beach and outlet to Cards Pond and the Harbor of Refuge, and, in the far eastern corner of the state, the outlet to Quicksand Pond. The rock-strewn waters around West Island, off Sakonnet Point and home of one of the more famous striped bass clubs of the late nineteenth century, also offer great angling, but the public can fish this area only from a boat, as beach access is restricted.

Rhode Island is a boat angler's mecca for stripers as well, with its vast areas of inland marine waters, especially Narragansett and Mount Hope Bays and the Sakonnet River (not a river but a long, attenuated saline bay), to ply. These are protected from the elements by nearly three dozen islands and the mainland. Narragansett possesses most of the islands; at 26 miles long and up to 12 miles wide, it nearly always provides some lee in which to fish.

Rhode Island, called Aquidneck Island by everyone but cartographers, is the largest island in the bay, almost filling it, and is followed by Conanicut and Prudence Islands in size. Bristol, too, is almost an island, separated on its north end by a few yards of dirt between the Warren and Kickemuit Rivers.

For fly rodders and ultralight tackle anglers, some of Rhode Island's most exciting saltwater fishing occurs during the "worm hatch" on Washington County's salt ponds. Beginning on the full moon in May, bloodworms emerge from the mud to mate. They appear around dusk on days when the sun's heat warms the mud; cloudy days generally do not produce large "hatches." About $1\frac{1}{2}$ inches long, the

In 1956, Sir Willoughby Norrie, Governor of South Australia, caught a 2,224-pound great white shark on rod and reel; found inside was the remains of a pet dog buried at sea.

R

pink worms attract schools of striped bass that feed like bluegills just beneath the surface. The stripers generally range from 18 inches long to 18-pounders.

Fly anglers catch most fish on red-and-white or pink-and-yellow bucktail streamers, cast on 6- to 8-weight intermediate fly lines. Spinning tackle enthusiasts fish small, pink, soft plastic baits to match the hatch. It is critical to fish the hatch when it is just beginning around sunset; once the emergence is in full bloom, the fish key in on the real worms and become extremely selective. The most active hatches occur on the north end of Point Judith Pond, as well as on Potter and Ninigret Ponds; worm emergences have been reported in coves on Narragansett Bay as well.

With stripers in relative abundance in recent years, anglers are catching these fish within the city limits of Providence. Some of the best bass angling in early summer occurs in the city in Narragansett Bay's uppermost reaches, along the shores of the Providence, Seekonk, Warren, and Barrington Rivers.

Inshore fishing for stripers is just part of Rhode Island's saltwater story, of course. There is plenty farther out, as Block Island and Rhode Island Sounds are extensions of the Atlantic Ocean that front upon the coast. Tear-shaped Block Island is a dozen miles east of Montauk Point and 8 miles south of Point Judith. The North Rip there is a favorite for pollock, cod, and fluke anglers, especially on the south side. Inside Great Salt Pond, flounder are tops.

Rhode Island boat anglers are torn between two popular and plentiful species: blackfish, alias tautog, and bluefish. Bluefish are subject to cyclical variances, and blackfish populations have been a source of concern in recent years. At times, when blackfish are ashore in the spring to spawn, fishing for them from the beach, bridge, bank, and bulkhead is almost as good as fishing from a boat. Early in the season, however, and again in November and December, the bigger blackfish concentrate in deeper water and are taken by boaters. The largest blackfish landed within this species' range is a 20-pounder from Rhode Island waters.

Bluefish are scattered throughout the state's marine waters from late May through late November. A spot that has always produced bluefish, even during the August doldrums, is the protected water of Greenwich Bay. Elsewhere, the numerous small bays, tidal rivers and creeks, and back-bay marshes provide important nursery grounds for bluefish; in late August and September, when they have their "coming out party," snapper blues provide excellent fishing.

Ranking near, if not on, the top, is another fish that is more often pursued for its food, rather than sporting, value: winter flounder. Because of this species' popularity as a food fish, its numbers have suffered in recent times due to commercial and recreational pressures. Seasons, minimum lengths, and bag limits have been placed on these fish to halt overharvesting.

The return of fluke, alias summer flounder, has caused this species to rival bluefish as the summer's best bet. The fluke are taken on almost all inside waters, but the better fishing occurs along the outside beaches, especially near the breachways from Watch Hill to Point Judith, and along Block Island's Charlestown Beach. Most fish range from 1 to 3 pounds, but anglers have taken specimens weighing more than 12 pounds in recent years.

Weakfish, which locals call by the Indian name *squeteague,* are another possible Rhode Island catch. When squeteague are abundant, Narragansett Bay hotspots include the waters near Halfway Rock and both the east and west sides of Prudence Island, and Greenwich Bay.

The state of Rhode Island is also synonymous with big-game offshore fishing. Nebraska Shoals in Block Island Sound was once *the* place to catch giant bluefin tuna. In recent times this has changed drastically, as the baitfish upon which tuna feed changed their migration patterns. Still, every season a few tuna over 600 pounds are landed from boats leaving Rhode Island ports. The better offshore fishing nowadays is farther out, off Block Island. Here, sharks, yellowfin and bluefin tuna, as well as albacore and white marlin, are the sought-after species.

When all the warmwater marine species have headed south for the winter, cod and pollock replace them. The Cox Ledge fishing grounds, east of Block Island, still produces good catches of these species.

Incidentally, to catch what locals call a "grand slam"—a striped bass, bluefish, bonito, and little tunny in one day—fish streamers or small lures near the center and west walls of the Harbor of Refuge during the last weeks of summer and the first weeks of autumn.

Freshwater

Saltwater anglers greatly outnumber freshwater fishing enthusiasts in the diminutive Ocean State, but Rhode Island offers ample fishing opportunities to catch trout, northern pike, and a variety of warmwater fish in its streams and ponds.

Streams. The flowages in Rhode Island are not long, and they course through uneven topography. As a result, some have falls and rapids, which have been used to power textile mills and other industries. In the late eighteenth century, the first U.S. textile mill driven by water power was built in Rhode Island.

The state's premier trout fishery, the Wood River, rises in West Greenwich near the Connecticut border and flows south to join the Pawcatuck River, which separates Rhode Island and Connecticut. The Rhode Island Division of Fish and Wildlife stocks brown, rainbow, and brook trout throughout the Wood-Pawcatuck system, and small populations of wild brookies—referred to as "natives"—

have managed to survive in the headwaters of such tributaries as the Falls River and the Flat River. Whether stocked or wild, trout in the Wood-Pawcatuck system have access to plenty of natural foods. Among the aquatic insects are caddisflies, small stoneflies, and many mayflies, most notably the giant *Hexagenia limbata,* which emerges on July nights. The river system's baitfish include minnows and suckers as well as Atlantic salmon fry, stocked by the state in an effort to restore the Pawcatuck's salmon run. Occasionally, there are reports of sea-run trout in the lower Pawcatuck.

Flowing from Connecticut into west-central Rhode Island, the Moosup River also receives generous trout stockings from the state. A small free-stone stream with a remnant population of wild brook trout, the Moosup is an especially scenic Rhode Island river.

Several small streams throughout the state hold small populations of brook trout, but none is as rich as the little Queen River. This stream rises in West Greenwich and flows through Exeter into Glen Rock Reservoir in South Kingstown. Almost all of the land through which the river flows is closed to the general fishing public, so the state does not stock it. Access by canoe and kayak is extremely limited. For generations, the Queen's wild population of brook trout has thrived through the stewardship of private landowners.

Once one of the filthiest streams in the U.S., the Blackstone River rises in Massachusetts and flows south to Narragansett Bay in Rhode Island. Redbrick factories—relics of the Industrial Revolution and its accompanying pollution—still line the river's banks. Thanks to the Clean Water Act, the Blackstone's water is pure enough to support a run of anadromous blueback herring and stocked trout in some faster stretches, but the streambed holds several generations of heavy metals and other pollutants from industrial waste. Slower stretches of the Blackstone River hold large bass, pickerel, and carp. Access to the river abounds, as it is part of the federal Blackstone River Valley National Heritage Corridor in Massachusetts and Rhode Island.

Two other restored rivers, the Pawtuxet and the Woonasquatucket, flow through the state's most densely populated metropolitan area before spilling into Narragansett Bay. The state stocks trout on the uppermost reaches of the Pawtuxet, in the village of Hope, and the lower and slower stretches of both streams contain largemouth bass, pickerel, and carp. A survey of the Woonasquatucket also found a few native brook trout. Several stretches of the rivers near shopping malls and city buildings are lined by enough vegetation to provide pleasant canoe paddling and good fishing.

Lakes and ponds.   Many of the state's ponds were built in the nineteenth century to store water for mills and other industries; the generally flat topography of the region prevented dam builders from creating very deep-water storage facilities, and most of the natural ponds in Rhode Island also are shallow. The state stocks trout in dozens of lakes and ponds—listed in the division's annual booklet of freshwater fishing regulations—but only a handful of lakes are deep and well oxygenated enough to sustain trout through the summer. They include Wallum Lake in Burrillville, on the border with Massachusetts, and Beach Pond in Exeter, on the border with Connecticut. Deep Pond, on Narragansett tribal land in Charlestown, is also capable of holding trout throughout the summer, but the state has not stocked it for several years.

The Fish and Wildlife Service also maintains a program to stock northern pike. Introduced to a limited number of Rhode Island waters in 1962, northern pike have spread through natural migration and illegal introduction to several other ponds and the Blackstone River. Anglers have caught pike as large as 35 pounds, but 10- to 12-pounders are more common. Perennial hotspots include Worden Pond, Thirty Acre Pond, and Hundred Acre Pond, all in South Kingstown; the Woonasquatucket Reservoir, also called Stump Pond, in Smithfield; Pascoag Reservoir in Burrillville; Waterman Reservoir in Greenville; and Chapman's Pond in Westerly.

There is little or no stocking of the state's other prominent warmwater and coolwater species: largemouth bass, smallmouth bass, yellow perch, white perch, redfin pickerel, chain pickerel, white catfish, brown bullhead, and several species of panfish, including black crappie, banded sunfish, redbreast sunfish, and bluegills. Large carp, goldfish, and other exotic species also inhabit some of Rhode Island's ponds.

Fishing for smallmouth bass is limited in Rhode Island. Although smallmouths as large as 5 pounds have been caught, most smallmouth ponds hold much smaller fish. The best prospects for smallmouth bass fishing include Indian Lake in South Kingstown and Stafford Pond in Tiverton. Other ponds holding smallmouths include Spring Lake in Burrillville, Tiogue Lake in Coventry, and Watchaug Pond in Charlestown.

Anglers have caught largemouth bass as heavy as 10 pounds in Rhode Island, and each year several specimens in the 5- to 7-pound class are taken. Most lakes and ponds in the state, including all of the reservoirs, support largemouths. Among the most interesting spots, however, are ponds with spawning runs of anadromous alewives, called "buckeyes" or "herring." Alewives spend most of their adult lives in saltwater. Around the first full moon in April, they begin running up small coastal streams to their spawning ponds. The adult alewives and their fry are an enriching food source that nourishes largemouths to become exceptionally healthy and generally large. Among the ponds where bass feed on anadromous alewives are Gorton Pond in Warwick, Brickyard Pond in Barrington, Belleville Pond in North Kingstown, and Carr Pond, also in North

American shad, a spring treasure along coastal rivers, make their first spawning run between ages 4 and 5 years; about 70 percent of the spawning fish will die afterward.

Kingstown, where access is controlled by the curator of the Gilbert Stuart Birthplace.

A population of landlocked alewives and other baitfish, as well as an abundance of perch and sunfish, are prey for largemouth bass on Worden Pond in South Kingstown and the two ponds connected to it by streams: Hundred Acre Pond and Thirty Acre Pond. The state has built a boat launching ramp on Worden Pond, but access to the other two ponds is difficult to obtain.

Most of Rhode Island's reservoirs also offer fine fishing for largemouth bass. These include Flat River Reservoir, also called Johnson's Pond, in Coventry; Pascoag Reservoir, also called Echo Lake, in Burrillville; Upper Slatersville Reservoir in North Smithfield; and Smith and Sayles Reservoirs in Glocester.

Many small ponds in Rhode Island offer a smorgasbord of fishing opportunities for stocked trout, largemouth bass, and panfish; among the most reliable spots—each with boat ramp access—are Carbuncle Pond in Coventry, Breakheart Pond in Exeter, and Silver Spring Lake in North Kingstown.

Rhode Island's largest body of freshwater, the Scituate Reservoir, has been closed to fishing and all other recreational uses for decades, despite its populations of largemouth bass, pickerel, yellow perch, and trout. Built on the north branch of the Pawtuxet River and commissioned as a source of drinking water in 1926, the Scituate and its five tributary reservoirs cover a total surface area of 4,557 acres in the center of the state.

RIFFLE

A hard-bottomed area of a creek, stream, or small river that is shallow and characterized by a choppy disturbed surface. Riffles have a hard bottom that isn't washed away by the action of moving water, so they are not scoured out. Riffles usually exist above a pool (see), where a softer bottom has been gouged out, and may exist between pools, or between a pool

and a run (see), which is a generally uniform section deeper than a riffle and without the disturbed surface, yet lacking the characteristics of a pool.

Riffles may be short in distance, just 20 to 60 feet long, which is common in farm-country flows, or up to several hundred yards or more long, which is common in wide and long rivers in rocky terrain. Because a riffle is shallow, water builds at the head and rushes over it, so the flow quickens. Usually a riffle is shallow enough to produce wavy, rippled surface water, which provides increased oxygen and may also result in surface foam downstream. Most fish don't inhabit riffles or spend much time there because it is unproductive to waste a lot of energy constantly fighting current, especially swift current. Fish may move through riffles, especially those on upstream spawning migrations and post-spawners returning downcurrent, but in neither case are these fish likely to be doing anything more than passing through. Exceptions, of course, exist: If a riffle is comparatively slow and larval aquatic insects are on the bottom, then fish (like trout) may spend some time in the riffle foraging for these invertebrates.

The area above and below riffles, however, is usually more likely than the riffle itself to hold fish, either resident fish or those that are temporarily resting before migrating upstream. Small fish and other aquatic life are often disturbed, disoriented, or overwhelmed when they get into a riffle, and become easy prey at the end of the riffle where it empties into a pool. If there is a boulder or series of large rocks or other protection in a riffle, the object may have a deep pocket behind it that is out of the current and is conducive to capturing food that comes by or is washed into the pocket; in such an instance, gamefish (like trout or smallmouth bass) might reside in that specific location in a riffle.

RIFFLING HITCH

Also known as the Portland Hitch, this is a supplemental knot tied on a wet fly to plane it across the surface of a river. Used primarily in Atlantic salmon fishing, a fly with this hitch leaves a trailing wake and is very effective at attracting recalcitrant salmon. The fly is fished down- and across-stream and retrieved at a speed that causes it to leave a visible V wake; the hitch may be tied so that it sits on the left, right, or underside of the foreshank of the fly to achieve the right effect, depending on which way the fish is being approached.

Foreground anglers fish the top of a riffle on New York's Beaverkill River.

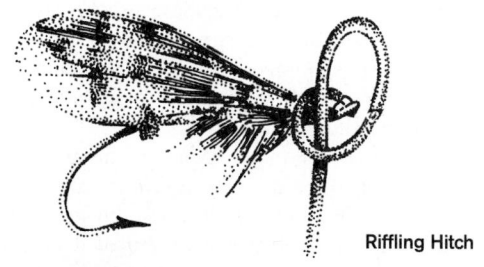

Riffling Hitch

The Riffling Hitch is created by making two half hitches behind the head of a fly that is already tied with a standard knot. When this is done, the tippet extends from the shank of the fly near and behind the head at an angle. Some flies are tied in such a manner as to leave extra room at the head for the hitch.

RIG

An arrangement of terminal tackle *(see);* the ready-to-fish final configuration of a lure and leader; and a ready-to-fish natural bait prepared with hook, weight, line (often wire), and other accessories.

See: Bait; Leader; Lure; Natural Bait; Trolling Lure, Saltwater.

RIGHT BANK

The right side of a river as viewed when facing downriver.

RIP

See: Tidal Rip.

RIPARIAN

Pertaining to the bank of a natural waterway, usually a river, sometimes a lake or tidewater. Riparian rights refer to the legal rights of the owner of property on a river bank.

See: Regulations.

RIPRAP

A collection of loose stones that serves as a foundation for, and to prevent erosion of, an embankment supporting a levee, dam, bridge, road, or similar man-made structure. Banks or shorelines with riprap vary greatly in length, in the size of the stones, and in the depth of the water nearby, although the riprap usually has a good pitch as it extends from above to below the waterline.

Riprap is typically found along the face of a dam, along the banks lining a tailrace, along the banks of a roadway or railroad bed that crosses water, and around the shoreline support foundation for bridges. Some species of fish are attracted to riprap banks at certain times, and the banks are especially likely to harbor largemouth bass, walleye, and catfish in freshwater because the stones provide hiding places for young fish and the food they feed upon, which attracts other species. There is usually a sharp slope to the riprap underwater, providing good depth nearby, and in many places there is also current along the face of the riprap.

RIP TIDE

See: Tidal Rip.

RISE

The visible disturbance of the water's surface by a fish that is feeding, usually on insects that are on or just under the surface. In principle, this visual disturbance, which may be the dainty sipping of a surface insect, the swirl caused by a fish that has taken food from under the surface and turned downward, or the prominent and audible splash of an aggressive strike, can apply to all forms of fish and various feeding activities that produce visible surface disruptions, but it is usually ascribed to salmonids in rivers and lakes, and to the consumption of insects. Other fish are mostly said to "swirl," even though the behavior that causes the visual disturbance may be similar. Different feeding behavior produces different types of rises, called rise forms, and these can be indicative of the food of the fish, and sometimes the size of the fish.

RIVERINE

Of or living in a river or flowing water.

ROACH   *Rutilus rutilus.*

Other names—French: *gardon, vangeron;* German: *plötze, rotauge.*

A prominent coarse fish *(see)* that is widely sought by anglers, the roach is the subject of minor commercial interest. It is a member of the large Cyprinidae family, which includes minnows *(see)* and carp *(see),* and is of similar size and color to its relative, the rudd *(see).*

Identification. The roach has a somewhat cylindrical yet deep body, a moderately forked tail, a terminal mouth, and an erect dorsal fin. The scales are strongly marked, the back is gray to blue green, and the sides are silvery and taper to a white belly. The pelvic and anal fins are reddish orange, and the dorsal and tail fins are dusky. The roach may be confused with rudd *(Scardinius erythrophthalmus);* however, the pectoral fins of the rudd are reddish orange and the body is more golden brown.

Size/Age. Roach are believed to be able to live for 12 years; they grow to a maximum of 4 to 5 pounds, although the common catch is under a pound, and in some waters half of that.

Distribution. Roach are found in Europe, excluding Spain, Italy, and Greece. They have been introduced to Australia.

Habitat. These fish inhabit virtually any water, including rivers, lakes, reservoirs, and canals. The quality of the water is no impediment to their well-being, and they are equally at home in slow-flowing, still, muddy waters.

Life history/Behavior. Spawning takes place in heavy weeds in spring, when roach broadcast numerous adhesive eggs rather than construct a nest; this activity is usually accompanied by an obvious splashing commotion. The fry stay in schools and gather in large congregations, and they

Roach

provide forage for numerous predators. Roach remain a schooling fish as adults, and their schools (called shoals) generally comprise similar-size individuals. Shoals of roach wander and feed in a homing area.

Food and feeding habits. Roach are primarily algae eaters, but they also consume mollusks, crustaceans, worms, and aquatic insects; most of their food is small, although larger fish consume bigger food items. They are similar to bronze bream (*see: bream, bronze*) in feeding habits, although they do not roil the water as much. They occasionally feed at the surface, and often at midlevels, but most feeding taking place on the bottom. Small roach feed at any time, but larger individuals are more active in low light.

Angling. Like other coarse fish, roach are not spectacular fighters, but they are especially popular with many Europeans, especially British anglers, and are one of the mainstays of competitive (match) fishing.

Bottom fishing with assorted baits—particularly maggots, bread, and worms—is the primary technique for roach, and this may involve prebaiting or chumming. Roach are caught at other levels, and in a variety of locations, water clarity, and current, so diverse options must be considered.

Rods from 11 to 13 feet in length, line from 2 to 4 pounds in strength, and No. 14 to 20 bait hooks are the preferred tackle. Hooked baits are fished with or without a float.

ROCKET LAUNCH
A term for the multiple-rod-holding apparatus, often part of a center console helm seat backrest, that is used to store fishing rods in sportfishing boats (*see*).

ROCKET TAPER
A fly line with a long front taper.
See: Flycasting Tackle.

ROCKFISH
(1) A term for striped bass (*see: bass, striped*).

(2) A diverse and important group of marine fish, rockfish are members of the Scorpaenidae family, which includes 310 species generically characterized as scorpionfish. There are roughly 68 species of rockfish in the genus *Sebastes* and two in the genus *Sebastolobus* that are found along the coasts of North America. Nearly all occur in Pacific waters. Both species of *Sebastolobus* and 32 species of *Sebastes* occur in Alaska's coastal waters, and at least 12 species range as far north as the Bering Sea.

Most of these species are important to the commercial fishing industry, which uses otter trawls to catch them, and some are important to anglers. They may also be referred to as rock cod, sea bass, snapper, and ocean perch because of their resemblance to these species or to the quality of their fillets, but the latter species are not related to rockfish. One rockfish in the Atlantic, *S. marinus,* is commonly called ocean perch in commercial markets and may also be labeled redfish or rosefish. Rockfish as a group have white, flaky meat with a delicate flavor, as befits deep-dwelling coldwater species.

Only a few rockfish species are too small to be useful for human consumption. Rockfish species are seldom marketed separately; they are generally all good to eat, but differentiating among the species—many of which are caught in the same locations and are very similar—can be difficult.

Directed fishing efforts for rockfish have resulted in overharvesting of most stocks, and elimination of some. Rockfish are extremely slow to become reproductively mature; this trait, and the tendency of many stocks to remain in one location, makes their populations especially vulnerable to overexploitation.

In addition to these factors, rockfish are deep dwellers with a swim bladder that possesses a special gas-producing and -absorbing gland. This gland changes the volume of gas in the swim bladder, which enables the fish to maintain buoyancy at different depths. This swim bladder is easily damaged when a fish is subjected to sudden changes in water pressure, such as when it is brought to the surface. The gas gland does not have sufficient time to absorb the gas in the swim bladder as the gas expands with a decrease in water pressure. Consequently, as the fish is brought to the surface, the swim bladder expands and becomes too large for the fish's body cavity and explodes out through the mouth. Countless rockfish are wasted when caught incidentally and thrown back into the water.

Most rockfish are landed in deep water by anglers using bottom fishing tactics or midwater drifting. Although commendable as food, rockfish are not known for their great battles, like salmon or tuna, or for their large size, like halibut, although the larger specimens of some species will provide good sport.

Identification. Adult rockfish range in size from 5 to 41 inches, but most species grow to between 20 and 24 inches in length. These fish are characterized by bony plates or spines on the head and body, a large mouth, and pelvic fins attached forward near the pectoral fins. The spines are venomous, and although not extremely toxic they can still cause pain and infection. Some species are brightly colored. Rockfish appear somewhat perchlike or basslike and are often called sea bass.

Life history. Rockfish can generally be separated into those that live in the shallower nearshore waters of the continental shelf and those that live in deeper waters on the edge of the continental shelf. The former comprise species that are always found in rocky bottom areas (called shelf demersal by biologists) and those that spend much of their time up in the water column and off the bottom (shelf pelagic).

All rockfish of the genus *Sebastes* are ovoviviparous, giving birth to live young after internal fertilization.

Rockfish are slow growing and extremely long lived. Black rockfish *(Sebastes melanops),* which are a common pelagic species, become sexually mature at about 10 years of age and have been reported to reach age 40. Yelloweye rockfish *(S. ruberrimus),* which are a shelf demersal rockfish, are a longer-lived species, becoming sexually mature around 15 years of age and living in excess of 100 years. There have been unconfirmed reports of fish at age 114.

Members of some species, such as the yellowtail rockfish *(S. flavidus),* do not wander far and actually have an extremely strong preference for a specific site. If a fish is captured and relocated elsewhere, it will quickly return to its original home site.

Food. Rockfish feed on a variety of food items. Juveniles eat primarily plankton, such as small crustaceans and copepods, as well as fish eggs. Larger rockfish eat such fish as sand lance, herring, and small rockfish, as well as crustaceans.

Common species. The most common species encountered in Alaska include the black *(S. melanops),* copper *(S. caurinus),* dusky *(S. ciliatus),* quillback *(S. maliger),* and yelloweye *(S. ruberrimus).*

Common species in Washington include the black, copper, quillback, and yelloweye.

Common species in Oregon include the black, blue *(S. mystinus),* bocaccio *(S. paucispinis),* China *(S. nebulosis),* copper, Pacific ocean perch *(S. alutus),* and yelloweye.

Common species in California include the black, blue, bocaccio, canary *(S. pinniger),* chilipepper *(S. goodei),* copper, cowcod *(S. levis),* greenspotted *(S. chlorostictus),* olive *(S. serranoides),* starry *(S. constellatus),* vermilion *(S. miniatus),* widow *(S. entomelas),* and yellowtail *(S. flavidus).*

Angling. As their name implies, rockfish are found around rocky bottoms—the craggier the better—and at depths of 200 to 700 or more feet. Ledgelike dropoffs, deep rock valleys, and craggy peaks are especially good, as they contain holes and crevices where these fish can hide. In deep-water bottom fishing, it's necessary to use heavy weights or jigs to get to the bottom. Eight to 16 ounces of lead are used depending on the depths. The favored offerings are heavy metal lures, called "jigbars," diamond jigs, and similar heavy lures, often with a plastic grub or piece of squid attached. These are typically bounced off the rocks, but they can be fished up through the water column, as some species are not tight to the bottom.

In shallow water, usually under 100 feet and to maybe only 10 feet, anglers use lighter lures and multibait rigs, although this is usually where smaller rockfish are found. Herring, shrimp, worms, squid, small live fish, and strips or pieces of fish are used for bait. Some rockfish are caught near the surface and are susceptible to cast lures, even flies, although this usually occurs when the water is not rough or murky. The usual bottom rig is made up of three to six hooks above a sinker that is heavy enough to take the line to the bottom on a fairly straight course.

Because of the extreme depths fished, it takes a lot of weight and a lot of line on tackle; low-stretch lines are helpful. The bait should be sufficiently firm to stay on the hook while being chewed upon; squid are commonly used for this reason.

See: Bocaccio; Rockfish, Black; Rockfish, Copper; Rockfish, Yelloweye.

ROCKFISH, BLACK   *Sebastes melanops.*

Other names—black snapper, black bass, gray rockfish, red snapper, sea bass, black rock cod.

A member of the Scorpaenidae family, the black rockfish is widely distributed in the eastern Pacific. It is an excellent food fish.

Identification. The body of the black rockfish is oval or egg shaped and compressed. The head has a steep upper profile that is almost straight; the mouth is large and the lower jaw projects slightly. The eyes are moderately large. The color is brown to black on the back, paler on the sides, and dirty white below. There are black spots on the dorsal fin. This species is easily confused with the blue rockfish; however, the anal fin of the black rockfish is rounded, whereas the anal fin of the blue rockfish is slanted or straight. The black rockfish has spots on the dorsal fin, and the blue rockfish does not.

Size. This species can attain a length of 25 inches and a weight of 11 pounds. The largest recorded weighed $10^{1}/_{2}$ pounds.

Distribution. Black rockfish occur from Paradise Cove, California, to Amchitka Island, Alaska.

Habitat. This wide-ranging fish can live on the surface or on the bottom to 1,200 feet near

Black Rockfish

rocky reefs or in open water over deep banks or dropoffs. Offshore and deep-water individuals are larger than nearshore specimens.

Life history/Behavior.   Like all members of their family, black rockfish are ovoviviparous, with egg fertilization and development taking place in the body of the mother. When embryonic development is complete, the female releases the eggs; the exposure to seawater activates the embryo, and it escapes from the egg case. The young hatch in spring and form large schools off the bottom in estuaries and tide pools in summer. Adults may be abundant in summer in shallow water near kelp-lined shores, but they occupy deeper water in fall and winter. They may school over rocky reefs from the bottom to the surface and are caught at varied depths, from near the surface to 1,200 feet.

Food.   The diet of the black rockfish includes squid, crabs eggs, and fish. They are occasionally observed feeding on sand lance on the surface. Salmon anglers sometimes catch this fish on trolled herring.

Angling.   *See: Rockfish.*

ROCKFISH, COPPER   *Sebastes caurinus.*

Other names—never die, whitebelly, chucklehead, rock cod, bass.

The copper rockfish is a member of the Scorpaenidae family and is a widely distributed, hardy species. It often appears in aquarium displays.

Identification.   The body of the copper rockfish is moderately deep and compressed. The head is large with a slightly curved upper profile; the mouth is large, and the lower jaw projects slightly. Its coloring is copper brown to orange tinged with pink. The back two-thirds of the sides along the lateral line are light, the belly is white, and there are usually two dark bands radiating backward from each eye.

Size.   This species can attain a length of 22 to 23 inches and a weight of 10 pounds.

Distribution.   The copper rockfish occurs from San Benitos Islands, Baja California, to the Kenai Peninsula, Alaska.

Habitat.   This fish is commonly found in shallow rocky and sandy areas, and is generally caught at depths of less than 180 feet; however, some have been taken as deep as 600 feet.

Life history.   Copper rockfish are ovoviviparous, like all species in the genus *Sebastes.*

Food and feeding habits.   The diet of copper rockfish includes snails, worms, squid, octopus, crabs, shrimp, and fish.

Angling.   *See: Rockfish.*

ROCKFISH, YELLOWEYE

Sebastes ruberrimus.

Other names—red snapper, rasphead rockfish, turkey-red rockfish.

Also a member of the Scorpaenidae family, the yelloweye rockfish is known to many anglers as "red snapper," although it bears only slight resemblance to true snapper. It is one of many red to yellow species in the eastern Pacific, however, and resembles several others, making identification difficult. The large size and excellent flesh of this species make it a favorite among anglers.

Identification.   The yelloweye rockfish is orange red to orange yellow in body coloration; it has bright-yellow irises and black pupils, and a raspy ridge above the eyes. The fins may be black at the margins. Adults usually have a light (perhaps white) band on the lateral line. Juveniles have two light bands, one on the lateral line and one short line below the lateral line. A large rockfish, the yelloweye is a heavy-boned, spiny fish through the head and "shoulders."

Size/Age.   The yelloweye rockfish can attain a length of 36 inches and weigh up to 33 pounds. The all-tackle world record is an Alaskan fish that weighed 33 pounds, 3 ounces.

Distribution.   This species occurs from the Gulf of Alaska to Baja California, Mexico.

Habitat.   Rocky reefs and boulder fields, from 10 to 300 fathoms, are the usual haunts of the yelloweye. They are abundant during summer in shallow water along kelp-lined shores and are found in deeper water at other times.

Life history.   Yelloweye rockfish are ovoviviparous, like all species in the genus *Sebastes.*

Food.   The diet of yelloweye rockfish includes assorted fish, crustaceans, squid, and shrimp.

Angling.   *See: Rockfish.*

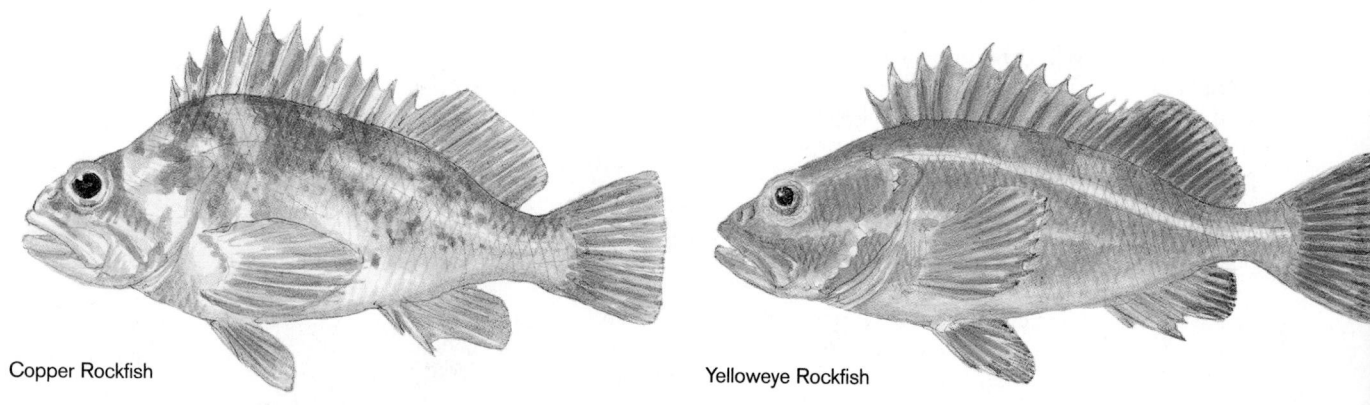

Copper Rockfish   Yelloweye Rockfish

A good rod belt greatly helps anglers fight strong fish.

ROD BELT

A beltlike device with a receptacle for holding the butt of a fishing rod and used for playing large fish while protecting the angler's lower abdomen, kidney, and groin. The primary purpose of a rod belt, which may also be called a fishing belt or a fighting belt, is to relieve the pressure that an unprotected rod butt can exert on the body while fighting a fish, especially one that takes a lengthy time to pursue, either due to its size and strength or the lightness of the tackle. Rod belts are believed to have originated with surf anglers, but are used by surf, pier, and boat anglers alike if the circumstances warrant. A rod belt is commonly used in saltwater, sometimes in conjunction with a fighting harness *(see: harness, fighting)*; it is seldom used in freshwater, but may be employed by some, such as anglers pursuing giant species like sturgeon. A rod belt may be used with any type of tackle, including fly rods with butt extensions, but is most often associated with stand-up fishing *(see)* and the use of conventional and big-game tackle.

There are rod belts to suit light-, medium-, and heavy-tackle fishing. Original belts were made from leather, and some are still in use today, but most modern belts are made from highly durable synthetic materials, and some designs offer fish-playing benefit as well as personal protection. The leather models belted behind the back and in the front featured a wide reinforced area with a molded cup that may or may not have included a gimbal pin. Modern versions of the light tackle variety are essentially the same, and may have an open cup, a gimbaled cup, or an angled cup entry to facilitate rod butt placement. Putting a rod butt into the belt holder usually takes place in the heat of a battle and under a lot of tension, so it needs to be easy to accomplish.

The more experienced the angler and the more strenuous the fight, the more it is likely that an angler will prefer having a gimbal rest, which locks a gimbal-butt rod in position and allows it to pivot easily when the rod is raised and lowered. A rod that does not have a gimbal butt should be used with an open-receptacle belt. This includes most spinning rods, some conventional rods, and nearly all fly rods.

Medium-tackle belts are larger and worn lower on the abdomen, and provide more leverage. They are used with 30- to 50-pound tackle. Most feature a gimbal cup, but some do not; some models have an integrated rod butt receptacle that swivels in all directions. Heavy-tackle belts are still larger and bulky, and meant for positioning the rod butt receptacle across the thighs. These are used with 50- to 130-pound tackle and usually in conjunction with a fighting harness.

When using medium or heavy tackle in boats, it is a good idea to have a safety strap attached to the reel in case the outfit (with or without angler) gets yanked overboard, which has happened.
See: Big-Game Fishing.

ROD BLANK

The shaft of a fishing rod.
See: Blank; Rod, Fishing.

ROD, FISHING

An instrument with a handle, shaft, and reel seat, which connects a reel and line for the purpose of making a controlled presentation of bait, lure, or fly. It is an intrinsic element in all forms of sportfishing, being essential to casting, retrieving, detecting a strike, setting the hook, and playing the fish.

Effective fishing is in part determined by the use of the proper tackle for the situation; choosing the right rod is an important element of this. However, just as there are many different species of fish, diverse habitats, and methods of angling, so, too, are there many categories and types of fishing rods, each suited to a particular application. Some fishing rod manufacturers produce scores, if not hundreds, of different rods, covering a gamut from fly, spinning, baitcasting, spincasting, surf, trolling, boat, big-game, flipping, popping, noodle, and downrigger models, to name just some of the possibilities, not to mention specialized subtypes within many categorizations.

Obviously, a fly angler can't do justice to fly fishing without the right type of rod, but neither can the same type of spinning rod be used adequately in stream trout fishing as in trolling for trout with downriggers. Even when there is cross-application, some compromise must be made. Different species, special applications, and regional preferences have led to a proliferation in rods that anglers who do a variety of fishing will need. Although anglers do stretch the use of some fishing tackle, and although some rods can be used for multiple species and means of fishing, it is generally important to have the right type, length, and style of rod for a particular fishing situation. To make this choice from a potpourri of possibilities it is helpful to understand the functions, materials, features, and components of fishing rods.

Categories/Types

All fishing rods have a handle, shaft, and reel seat. The materials used for each of these features may vary. The shaft is primarily referred to as the blank; this is where the rod guides are attached, and the number and type of these vary widely. A very small number of rods do not have a series of external guides; in these, the line runs through the blank within the hollow interior and exits at the tip. Fishing rods are most commonly of one- or two-piece configuration. Some have three or more pieces; a lesser number, usually for specialty applications, have multiple telescoping sections or a telescoping butt section. Prices range widely, and though many of the specialist and top-quality performance rods are costly, high price is not necessarily indicative

To select a fishing rod, you should have a clear idea of your needs and the general properties of rods.

of the best quality and may not be synonymous with best value. Many good-quality fishing rods are to be found at midprice ranges.

The following text briefly details the most prominent different categories of rods. This information is rather generalized, as there are exceptions and special products in most categories.

Baitcasting. Used with levelwind or baitcasting reels, which sit on top of the rod handle and face the angler, this tackle provides excellent casting accuracy for the skillful user, although achieving top-level proficiency takes practice and experience. Most baitcasting rods are one-piece models, though larger, heavier duty ones may have a telescoping butt and are generally stiffer than spinning rods. Guides are usually small to medium in size, and handles may be straight or with a pistol grip, both having a trigger hold under the handle.

Spincasting. These rods are similar to those used in baitcasting and are fairly uncomplicated. The guides are mounted atop the rod, and guide rings are generally small. Reels mount a little higher on top of the rod's reel seat, and the handles feature either straight or pistol grip design with a trigger hold under the handle. Spincasting rods usually aren't as stiff as baitcasting rods, having generally lighter action for use with light lines and lures. They are made in one- and two-piece models, mostly of fiberglass, and a few are telescopic.

Spinning. Used with open-faced spinning reels that mount underneath the rod, this tackle is very popular for a wide range of fishing situations and is relatively uncomplicated. Guides are big to accommodate the large spirals of line that come off the reel spool when casting. Handles are straight, with fixed or adjustable (ring) reel seats, and both one- and two-piece models are common.

Fly. Unlike other rod types, fly rods use a large diameter, heavy line to cast a very light object. Guides are small, and rod length varies from 5 feet to 12 or 14, although most fly rods used in North America are $7^1/_2$- to 10-footers. Fly rods are rated for casting a specific weight line; a fly reel usually sits at the bottom of the handle, but some rods have extension butts for leverage in fighting big fish.

Surf. These long rods are used for casting great distances from the beach into the surf and come in both spinning and revolving-spool reel versions. Length varies from 7 to 14 feet, though most are in the 10- to 12-foot range with long two-handed handles. They are heavy, in order to cast objects weighing 2 to 4 ounces, and guides are large.

Boat and bay. A lot of different rods fall into this catchall category predominantly devoted to saltwater fishing. These are usually workhorse products with beefy two-handed handles that accommodate conventional reels. They are generally stiff, heavy-action rods, with longer models used in pier fishing and shorter ones in boat work.

Big-game. These rods, meant for subduing the largest creatures of the sea, have the sturdiest construction. Generally short, they feature a roller guide on the tip top or throughout the blank, and sport an extra-heavy-duty handle with a gimbal mount butt for insertion into rod holders. These rods are rated according to the class of line (and reel size) they are suited for.

Other rods.   Travel or pack rods are found in baitcasting, spinning, or fly versions and are three- or four-piece products (some also have telescoping butt sections). Ice fishing rods are usually very short rods with a soft tip for use around holes in the ice, mostly necessary for storing and dispensing line. Flipping rods are long (7 to 8 feet), heavy-action rods with telescoping butts that are used for making short casts in close quarters to heavy cover when largemouth bass fishing. Noodle rods are whippy 12- to 14-foot rods with guides that curve around the rod blank; they are primarily used in stream steelhead and salmon fishing for presentation and fish-fighting advantages, and sometimes in trolling. Downrigger rods are 8- to 9-foot slow-action products that are primarily found in baitcasting versions and take a long, deep bend for use when trolling with downriggers. Some other rods are made for special applications, and many manufacturers make rods designed for particular species of fish or for use with certain lures or baits (crankbait rods, worm fishing bass rods, mooching rods, and popping rods, for example).

Dynamics of the Fishing Rod

It is impossible to construct a single rod providing top performance for all types of sportfishing. This is naturally obvious to the experienced angler, but not to many beginners, who can be observed with grossly mismatched tackle. The mismatch may be in the form of reel to rod, or it may be in the form of a rod and reel combination that is too light or too heavy for a particular species of fish or method of angling. In either case, the result is less enjoyment than would be had with the proper equipment.

Although the tackle industry has taken measures to provide guidelines on balanced outfits, a lot remains to be accomplished in educating anglers about their equipment, especially rods and especially knowledge of basic nomenclature. Furthermore, an understanding of the dynamics of the fishing rod—especially how rods are used and how such use affects rod construction—is fundamental to knowing what type of rod is best for particular fishing needs, and also how to get the most enjoyment from it.

Function

Designating a rod by classifying it as being a certain type is meant to denote the intended application. Many rods today are subcategorized; for example, a baitcasting rod may be typed or labeled as a bass worming rod or a flipping stick, a big-game rod may be typed as a 30-pound-class offshore trolling rod, and so forth. Type is not completely separable from function, which is the specific task the angler wants the rod to perform.

Angling with a rod entails at least four specific functions: casting, detecting a strike or bite, setting the hook, and fighting/landing the fish. Some of these require opposite properties for optimal performance, which obviously complicates rod design.

Casting.   The process of casting consists of a combination of body movements and rod action intended to project terminal tackle. The rod acts as a storage device to deliver smoothly the energy of the angler's arm, wrist, and hand, and it acts as a lever arm to increase tip velocity in the forward casting arc.

A longer rod generally casts farther than a shorter one, subject to the limitations of the individual angler's physical stature. This is because the tip velocity of a rod is directly proportional to length, although this ignores excessive bend, which tends to shorten the physical length of the rod. A higher launch velocity—the speed at which the lure, at the point of release, leaves the arc of the moving rod tip—results in a longer cast. In rods of equal length, a superior stiffness-to-weight ratio of one rod material over another provides a lighter fishing tool and thereby reduces angler fatigue after hours of repetitive use.

Stiffness-to-weight ratio is an engineering term used to quantify the ability of a material to be used effectively in structures. The higher the ratio, the larger the load that can be borne without excessive weight penalty. An aircraft constructed of solid steel, for example, would be very strong, but wouldn't fly. Likewise, a solid steel rod would be strong, but relatively unfishable by modern standards. Because some rod materials provide a distinct advantage in stiffness-to-weight ratio, they can be incorporated into longer rods to cast the same total weight of lure or bait for which a heavier rod, made of material having a less advantageous stiffness-to-weight ratio, might be considered.

Another factor in the process of casting is energy storage. During a strong cast, the human muscles act in an almost explosive manner. The rod must be designed to smooth this impulse and efficiently cast the terminal rig or lure. Failure to do so results in thrown-off rigs, snapped-off lures, inaccurate casts, and backlashes *(see)*.

Energy storage is enhanced by loss-free materials in rod construction and by rod taper. Loss-free materials are generally those with long, uninterrupted fibers with strong, mutual bonding. Ideally, a loss-free material acts like a perfect spring and returns all stored energy. Any loose ends to the working fibers, or gaps in the bonds, cause frictional losses, and the angler's energy goes into "heating" the rod rather than casting the lure. This latter case is much like bending a paper clip back and forth; it does not spring, but instead deforms and noticeably heats up.

In most fishing situations, the ideal taper for casting is very gradual, probably best illustrated by the highly developed field of fly rod design. When flexed, fly rods typically have a gradual bend from

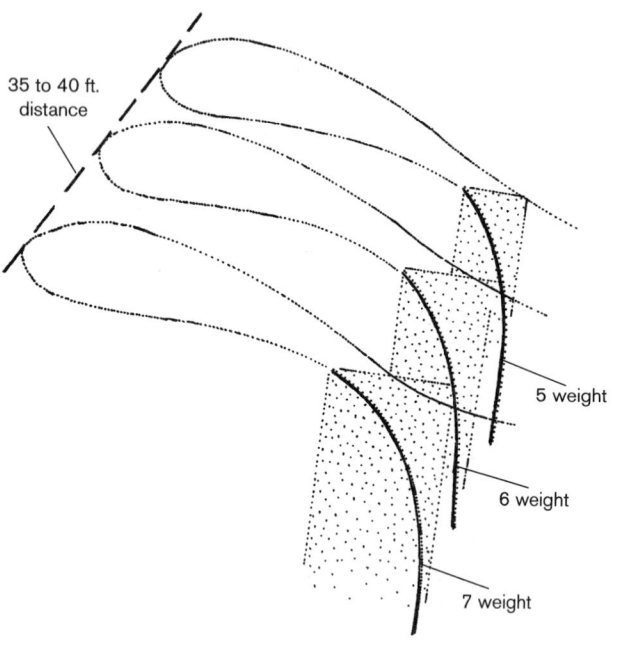

35 to 40 ft. distance

5 weight

6 weight

7 weight

Casting distance and rod action vary with line weight. A 9-foot rod rated for a 6-weight fly line (WF or DT), balances at 35 to 40 feet.

tip to butt, so that all portions of the rod assist in the storage and smooth transfer of energy from the angler to the fly line. The fly angler spends a great deal of time casting, often making delicate presentations, so it is appropriate that the fly rod emphasizes properties that are designed for casting.

Detecting a strike. From the standpoint of rod design, detecting a strike is limited to sensations transmitted by the line through the rod and into the angler's hand. Watching for line movement and noticing telltale ripples on the water are not directly involved with characteristics of the rod.

Here, the requirements for ideal rod design fortunately are aided by the laws of physics, which state that energy transfer occurs equally well in both directions through most structures. When we speak into a device, it is called a microphone; when the device emits a sound, it is called a loudspeaker. An intercom, however, uses a single device in both directions equally well. Likewise, an angler imparts energy to a lure when casting, and receives energy in the form of a vibration during a strike. A rod that casts well also exhibits great sensitivity to strikes. Thus, rods that smoothly transfer energy from angler to line and lure reciprocally transfer energy well from lure and line to angler. This property is quantified in physics as a mathematical statement called the Reciprocity Theorem.

There are some fine points to consider, however, because the strike signal can be so miniscule that fishing rod components such as reel seats and reel materials may affect the angler's ability to detect the strike. The rod, then, is not a separate entity, but rather a part of a complete system. In this regard, purposeful design of rod accouterments and reels affects optimal performance in strike detection.

Setting the hook. This is a rod function that may require a property that is opposed to those of other rod functions. An analogous example of opposing functions is a catalytic converter on an automobile; the component is not advantageous for engine efficiency, but a necessity to help provide for a cleaner environment. Rod design, too, is a balance of tradeoffs.

Ideal rod construction for hook setting requires great stiffness, so that minimal delay occurs between the strike and the angler's reaction to it. Additionally, such stiffness aids in maximizing the amount of line taken up, which in turn compensates for whatever stretch and slack may be inherent to the line being used *(see: line)*. In this circumstance, fast acceleration is desired. Consider the situation of a fish picking up bait and the angler's reaction. In one moment, the hook is motionless; an instant later, it is moving at great speed to become imbedded in the fish's jaw.

The bass angler's worm fishing rod is an excellent example of optimal rod design for hook setting. This type of rod is designed to set the hook hard, fast, and deep. In this type of fishing, failure to "cross a fish's eyes" not only translates into a missed catch, but, in many instances, impacts on verifying whether a detected irregularity in retrieval is the subtle strike of a fish or merely the lure bumping on bottom structure.

Fortunately, the function of setting the hook can be compromised in rod design, in light of special angling techniques and advancements in the design of certain hooks and terminal tackle.

Fighting/landing the fish. This process—bringing the fish to the angler—is also essentially one of energy transfer; this time, that transfer is from the fish to the drag elements in the reel *(see: drag; reel, fishing)*. The construction of the rod is an important factor because it smoothes the pulsing thrusts of the fish's tail and fins, and accommodates changes in the direction and angle of the fish's runs.

In fighting a fish, there are also secondary energy losses in the friction of line bellying through the water, and in fiber bond slippage within the rod structure itself. This latter characteristic is called damping or dampening.

Damping is the process of converting vibrational energy to heat. In an automobile suspension system, for example, the task is accomplished by the shock absorbers. The energy imparted to automobile springs when there is a bump in the road is converted to heat by the shock absorber. Though desirable in some situations, damping is undesirable in others. A pole vaulter, for example, stores energy in the bending (or loading) of the pole in order to be flung over the crossbar. If a shock absorber were placed on the pole, performance would suffer greatly. Likewise, a good casting rod should not be excessively dampened.

When deflected, a properly designed rod returns to equilibrium rather quickly, instead of continuing to vibrate up and down. From a casting point of view, this is an important consideration after the rod has flexed in the forward casting arc.

To some extent, all fishing rods damp; it's a matter of degree. Rod damping helps wear down a fish. Excessive rod damping, however, can cut down casting distance because casting energy is too quickly being dissipated into heat as fiber bond slippage occurs. A well-damped rod is comfortable to use when a fish is on, just as a well-damped automobile is comfortable to ride in, compared with the ride experienced in a stiff-spring pickup truck.

The ideal taper for a rod designed to fight fish is generally abrupt. Abruptly tapered rods are usually called "fast tapers," "magnum actions," or "power rods." They are fashioned through large butt-to-tip diameter-ratio differences.

A good example of this type of rod taper is the classic West Coast albacore or tuna rod. It is characterized by being "tippy," meaning much more flexible at the tip than at the butt. When a fish is hooked, the bend of such a rod may resemble an inverted L shape, with very little deflection near the butt. The location of the bend varies according to the size of the fish and the angler-applied force exerted when pulling on the fish.

For larger fish, the bend of the tippy rod occurs downward toward the grip as well, and the rod can adjust to such a circumstance because of its thicker-walled section near the butt. On the other hand, a small fish causes a bend higher up in the more flexible portion of the rod, at a smaller cross section. A wide range of fish can be accommodated by such a rod. Furthermore, by designing in sufficient butt stiffness, this type of rod will not "bottom out," or tend to exceed its elastic limits, and the angler can exert a great deal of power against the fish. The fishing conditions automatically select that particular portion of the rod cross section best suited to fight the fish.

When such a rod is cast, however, in a like fashion only very particular and limited portions of the rod act elastically to store energy. Therefore, it is a relatively poor casting instrument.

Obviously, ideal rod construction entails a number of compromises. Some of the qualities we seek in rods have similar requirements; others have opposing ones. Thus, there must always be a certain amount of give and take in designing a truly fishable rod. In most instances, the particular degree of compromise is intended to give the best possible performance for the type of rod and its function. In other words, good rod design and construction should emphasize those properties most vital to each particular type of fishing.

As noted, fly rods tend to favor casting, but at the risk of bottoming out, or exceeding the elastic limit on a truly strong fish; the exception is big-game saltwater fly rods that are very effective fighting tools but troublesome to cast unless they are of superior overall design. By contrast, the power rod

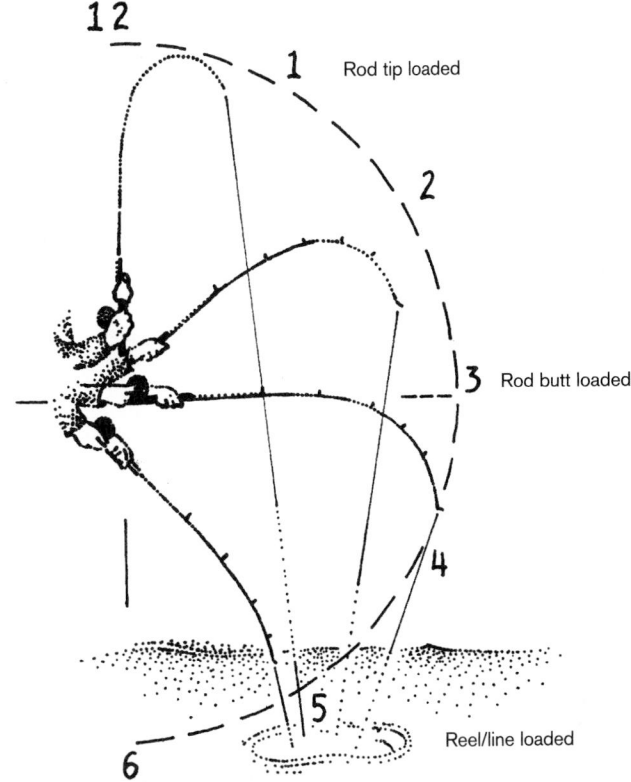

Rod tip loaded
Rod butt loaded
Reel/line loaded

When playing a strong fish directly below your position, power is exerted when the rod is approximately between the 2 and 4 o'clock positions; this is when the rod butt carries the load. When the rod is approximately between the 4 and 6 o'clock positions, the reel and the line carry the load and the rod does little. When the rod is approximately between the 12 o'clock and 2 o'clock positions, the tip carries the load; this can be harmful to the rod and creates a situation in which the angler can do little to influence the fish.

can quickly exhaust a wide range of fish, but at the risk of tearing the hook out of the baitfish or snapping off a lure on the cast.

Power/action. The performance and function of rods are commonly described in terms of power and action, which are somewhat nebulous terms that refer to the design of the rods based upon their construction and materials and incorporating all of the issues that have been noted so far.

In a practical sense, power is defined by the amount of pressure that it takes to flex the rod; the less pressure it takes, the lighter the rod's power. Designations are made according to an individual rod's ability to efficiently handle a certain range of lure weights and line sizes. These designations are ultralight, light, medium light, medium, medium heavy, heavy, and extra heavy.

The related concept of action denotes where a rod flexes along its blank, which is determined by the taper. A fast-taper rod flexes mostly at or near the tip, a moderate-taper rod flexes through the middle of the rod, and a slow-taper rod flexes through the butt. Specific designations include slow, moderate, moderately fast, fast, and extra fast.

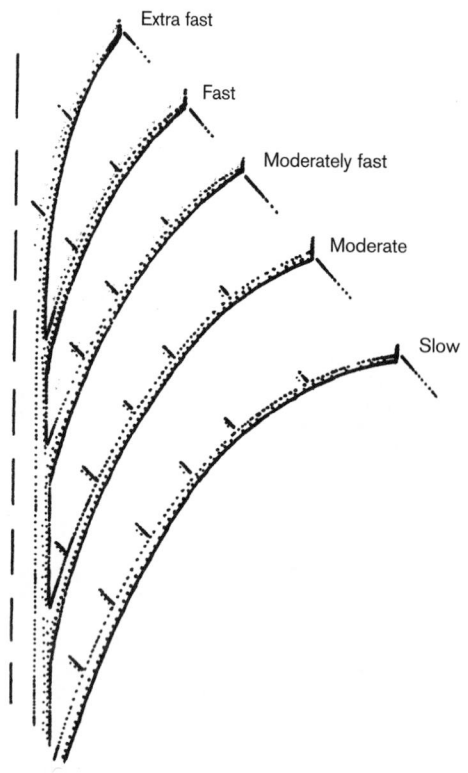

Rod Action

Construction and Materials

Rods are mass produced by major manufacturers, but only insofar as the blanks are fabricated by large-scale methods. The overall properties of the finished product are extremely dependent on what is done to the blank after manufacture. Thus, the number, type, and placement of guides; the wrapping; and the choice and placement of handle material totally affect the end use.

Unlike the situation with reels, rod building can also be a cottage industry, and many small custom rod builders exist, most of them buying blanks from established manufacturers and custom tailoring the final product. This tailoring might be done, for example, to make an offshore casting rod suited to the build of a particular angler, or it might be done to wrap a fly rod blank with spinning rod guides to create a special river fishing rod. In addition, individual anglers purchase blanks and component materials to build rods for themselves or family members, either to suit special needs or to have the satisfaction of catching fish on a personally made rod.

A typical rod is manufactured by first cutting a cloth formed of strength fibers pre-impregnated with a bonding resin This resined cloth is normally referred to as "prepreg" by fishing rod manufacturers. From a chemical standpoint the most commonly used resin systems are phenolic, polyester, or epoxy, the latter two being more commonly employed in modern rods.

The prepreg is cut into the proper shape to provide the appropriate thickness of rod wall along the entire blank. In some rods, for instance, the butt

section may utilize a wider cut of prepreg or even additional layers for a specific taper.

After it is cut into a shape, the prepreg is wound around a form called a mandrel, which is contoured to define the shape and taper of the finished rod blank. By a number of different processes, pressure and heat are applied to cure the wrapped prepreg and mold it over the mandrel. After the cure cycle, the mandrel is removed from the blank and the rod's exterior is subjected to finishing operations.

To some degree, all rod-building materials are composites. Each rod shaft consists of a strength or stress element, typically a fiber, and a bonding element, typically a resin. The stress element stores and transmits energy by elastic deformation, and the bonding element both fixes the location of the stress element and prevents the failure of one fiber from directly propagating to another.

This latter property is the principal reason why single-material rods are impractical. The failure or development of a defect would easily propagate like a crack in a windshield and the entire structure would fail. Therefore, superior construction techniques entail many small fibers to reduce the risk of breakage.

Another reason for using small fibers in rod construction is that it is far easier to manufacture small fibers without defects than it is to manufacture larger ones without defects. This is because fewer atoms are involved.

Bamboo. Bamboo (Tonkin cane) is a natural composite. The stress element consists of tiny fibers that distribute nutrients through the plant, and the bonding element is a material called lignin.

The principal limitations of bamboo are variations in quality and the presence of discontinuities (nodes) within the stalk of the plant. From the manufacturing standpoint, variations in the natural product, even within a single stalk or culm, necessitate an enormous amount of painstaking selection and hand work. It is labor-intensive and very costly to manufacture, which is why the very best split-cane rods are enormously expensive.

The situation with split-cane rods is much like it is in a winery. The correct circumstances and precise production control of the grapes lead to a truly outstanding wine; otherwise, the product is merely grape juice. Though capable of giving fine performance under somewhat limited conditions, bamboo is largely a material for the custom rod builder.

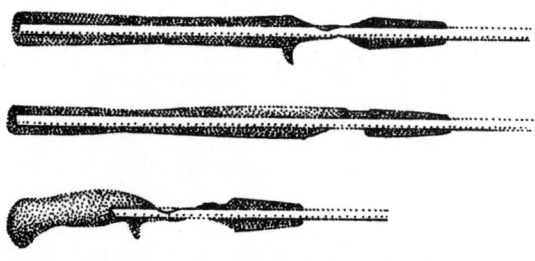

In some rods, the blank runs completely through the handle.

Fiberglass. Fiberglass is manufactured by flowing molten glass through tiny orifices in a melting furnace. The glass strands are pulled through the miniscule holes at high speeds and stretched while partially molten into fine filaments.

The glass filaments are then conditioned, coated, and woven into yarns or cloth fabrics, depending upon their intended application. The diameter and other physical parameters of the glass filaments are continuously monitored to assure a uniform product.

This uniformity was the key to successful early fiberglass fishing rod construction. The manufacturers were not only able to design rods, but were confident that quality would be uniform throughout each production run.

Uniformity also aided in developing mass-production techniques with reduced labor costs, and thereby made it possible to offer excellent fishing rods at attractive prices. Moreover, as fiberglass rod technology matured, the uniformity of the fiberglass materials permitted fine-tuning of manufacturing processes to improve the product.

One example of fine-tuning was the introduction of variations in the chemical composition of the glass melt. Of the types of glass available, E-glass, which is an alkalai borosilicate glass, is widely used because of its high resistance to water damage and its high-tensile-modulus. (Modulus is a measure of how effectively a material resists deformation. Tensile means "to pull" or place under a tension load. A high-tensile modulus material produces a stiff structure and thus aids in achieving a high stiffness-to-weight ratio. There also are other kinds of moduli, for example, compression modulus and shear modulus, which are not all independent but relate to one another.)

A higher-priced, low-alkalai, high-aluminum-and-magnesium kind of product called S-glass *(see)* can be produced with an approximately 30 percent improvement in tensile modulus. S-glass was originally developed for aerospace use but has been largely supplanted in that industry by other materials. It remains in the tackle industry as an intermediate rod material in price and performance between regular fiberglass and graphite.

Graphite. Graphite, or carbon fiber, as it is called in some parts of the world, has become a generic term. As originally developed for the aerospace industry, graphite was intended to maximize the strength-to-weight ratio, and the aim was to achieve the highest possible tensile modulus. Performance, such as in fighter planes, was more important than price. However, the proliferation of graphite products into the fishing tackle industry, beginning from high-end rods but eventually trickling down to mid- and low-priced rods, encouraged the development of a much wider range of graphite fibers, both in cost and in modulus.

The present situation requires that graphite as rod material must be evaluated in very specific terms for comparison purposes; this is hard to do because graphite has become as generic a word in common usage as "wood."

There is a further complication in that rods are frequently required to flex to a much larger angle than would be practical for an aircraft structural member; thus, another engineering quality is the elastic limit. Other complexities include the fact that most rod-building graphite fibers are used in prepreg form and proprietary processes can be used to control the ratio of fiber to resin, greatly affecting the properties of the final product. Also, the prepreg itself may consist of unidirectional, angled, or even woven graphite fibers. As a final confusion, chopped graphite fibers may be used to supplement the strength of polymers, such as used in reel seats and reel bodies.

The bottom line, however, remains delivered performance. All of this confusion aside, the "fishability" of a rod remains the final parameter; the type and configuration of the graphite fibers merely describe the fabrication method.

Graphite is produced by passing a polymer fiber, which is much like an ultra-fine monofilament fishing line, through a heated vacuum oven until only carbon atoms remain in the exiting fiber. The process is called pyrolization and is relatively expensive. The combination of advances in production techniques and substantial increases in the volume of graphite sales has lowered the price of graphite until it has become an attractive fishing rod material.

The tensile modulus of graphite runs from four to eight times that of fiberglass. Thus, a graphite rod intended for the same type of fishing as one made of fiberglass can have thinner walls and be of a more slender configuration. The net result is a significant savings in the weight of the finished rod.

A second property of graphite has both positive and negative aspects. The combination of configuration and bonding properties enhances the alignment of unidirectional graphite fibers in rod construction, so graphite rods can be designed with fibers extending unbroken from tip to butt. This construction style provides smooth energy transfer, which results in excellent casting qualities and more sensitivity than found in a fiberglass rod made from woven cloth. But there is a limitation imposed on the variety of rod tapers that can be designed with unidirectional fibers.

It is evident that the correct combination of graphite with fiberglass can produce rods with both good sensitivity and a wide variety of tapers. This process requires extremely careful design, however, and the graphite should not only be unidirectionally aligned within the rod, but also uniformly distributed around the rod shaft. Such a composite rod offers both performance and value, for it can be offered at a price between fiberglass and high-content graphite.

It is noteworthy that the percentage of graphite in a rod is not the major factor in value or performance, but rather how it is used. There has been

Fish in captivity have been trained in various ways; as long ago as 1914, Washington resident C. W. Lange trained trout to jump through hoops, among other stunts.

R

considerable controversy over "graphite content" alone as a sales point, but such thinking has little foundation in scientific fact.

Boron. Boron is produced by the reduction of gases in contact with a heated filament. In effect, the boron is plated on the filament in the form of a coating, resulting in a fiber of great tensile strength. However, the filament (usually a tungsten alloy) is heavy and contributes substantially to the total weight of the fiber. Overall, boron fibers have a significant advantage over graphite in strength-to-weight ratio, but by themselves are not practical in mass-produced rod construction due to weight.

Because of this, boron fibers are usually employed with graphite to form composite rods and thus are subject to the same rigorous design requirements of unidirectional fiber alignment and uniform distribution around the shaft for top performance. High-boron-content tubular rods usually contain less than 15 percent boron fibers by weight, but, again, content alone does not constitute an accurate assessment of performance.

Future materials. Several interesting materials, both fibers and bonding matrices, are currently being evaluated by aerospace laboratories. However, these are exotic, both in manufacturing technology and price. For these to be worth producing, anglers would have to see a considerable performance advantage to warrant the expenditure, and/or a great reduction in manufacturing cost.

The probable future of rod construction seems to be with improved application of those materials presently used, rather than with the introduction of new materials. Advances in construction techniques, lower production costs, and perhaps sharper pricing should lead to increased sales of high-performance rods suitable to the varied types and functions needed in the sport of angling.

Features and Components

A fishing rod is used in conjunction with some type of reel and line and, therefore, has features and components necessary for various functions. Some are derived from the manufacturing process, such as hoop strength and spine, while others are additions that are basic to every use.

Hoop strength. Whenever a beam is flexed, its outer surfaces are under the greatest stress and provide the maximum restoring forces for returning the beam to its original shape; the central portion of the beam acts mostly to keep these surfaces spaced apart. This stress distribution holds true for any beam shape. It helps to explain the shape of the steel "I" beam used in bridge construction, for example; the outer surfaces carry the load and the central web acts to keep the outer surface apart. Likewise, the construction of snow skis consists of upper and lower strength surfaces, separated by a simple foam or cell filling.

In simplest terms, a hollow tube delivers better stiffness-to-weight ratios than a solid bar (or beam);

Handle, guides, action, and material are all important elements in using a rod to cast, retrieve, and play a fish.

in the latter, the middle of the object increases weight but does not contribute much to the stiffness. The logical conclusion of this is that the "best" fishing rod would be hollow, and of maximal diameter with minimal wall thickness. The ultimate examples of such a product are current production rods for specialty fishing in Asia, which have eight telescoping sections that extend to a total length of 31 feet, with a total weight of 9.2 ounces! These are production rods, and they are enormously expensive.

There are, however, complications with having a hollow rod with maximal diameter and minimal wall thickness. The first is hoop strength, which is a measure of the ability of a hollow tubular structure to resist ovaling deformation leading to inward collapse of its walls. A typical soda straw has low hoop strength and fails under bending loads by collapsing or folding in half. In tubular rod blanks, hoop strength limits the maximum diameter and minimum wall thickness attainable in mass production. There are further complications specific to rod taper, materials, and assembly techniques. Mainly though, hoop strength is enhanced by such methods as winding around the rod blank (which acts like barrel hoops), exterior mesh (which acts like support stockings), and interior fillings (which act to space the walls apart).

Winding around the rod blank can be in the form of unidirectional fiber tape, or as a cross weave in a cloth prepreg. The former can be extremely expensive and technically difficult to apply; the latter often leads to a bumpy, non-uniform rod surface. Both methods are also used to relieve the additional stresses that occur at "built-in" ferrule joints (the place where sections connect) in premium rods. Lower priced rods often enhance this vital hoop strength at ferrules by a thread wrap.

Exterior meshes, particularly those of a high-strength polyamide such as Kevlar, also enhance hoop strength. It is essential that the mesh is strongly bonded to the rod blank for best effect; think of support stockings for the legs, or of the woven mesh in garden hoses. It is further noteworthy that Kevlar and similar fibers act strongly in tension, but are soft in compression, and therefore act not as "springs," but more in the nature of damping elements. Expert fly casters have reported that Kevlar-meshed graphite fly rods cast more akin to expensive hand-built Tonkin cane rods than any other synthesized fiber.

The simplest interior filling is a solid one. Some of the earliest fiberglass fishing rods were of solid construction; they were extremely heavy in weight and slow in action, but they were virtually indestructible. They were also eventually considered unfishable. However, technology has gone full circle, and advances in rod fabrication have wedded the best of both worlds: super slender, high-sensitivity solid tips at the first 12 to 18 inches of the rod, smoothly blended into a responsive and powerful hollow tubular rear section. The bonded joint is undetectable, both visually and in performance.

Even more advanced fabrication technology has led to a tapered, precision-ground graphite core, which is used as the traditional mandrel in rod building but is left inside the finished blank for hoop strength. The rod is light, slender, yet virtually unbreakable under fishing conditions. Unidirectional fibers are exposed at the first 12 to 18 inches of the tip, giving unparalleled sensitivity, strength, and power characteristics; again, this is the best of several worlds.

In each of these latter cases, the advances in rod performance are not so much due to the materials, which are various graphite fibers, but how these materials are assembled into a rod.

Spline. The spline, or spine, is a softer direction or preferred orientation of flexing or bending for a rod blank. In other words, the rod bends more easily along one plane, which is known as the spline. This preferred orientation stems from the fabrication of a rod blank by winding prepreg cloth around a mandrel; the prepreg must have a starting and ending edge, which distresses the absolute uniformity of the blank wall and thereby defines a direction of easier bending.

Manufacturers and rod builders usually locate the spline prior to affixing rod guides to make sure that their placement is not counter to the preferred bending orientation. The spline can be located by several methods; it is typically found by gripping the rod tip, then flexing while rotating about the rod axis and noting the preferred orientation for the easiest bend.

The spline of many rod blanks can be subtle, depending on the manufacturing technology and the type of rod. For instance, rods with a Kevlar support mesh usually exhibit diminished spline characteristics due to enhanced hoop strength.

When a rod has a weakly defined spline, determining precise orientation is less important for affixing guides. An example of this would be a multi-section spinning rod. In part, this is because each section is a separate blank made by a separate process and producing a separate spline, and because the location of the guides below the rod axis becomes the dominant factor defining the bending plane.

However, for rods used with baitcasting, conventional, and big-game reels, and specifically blue water tuna rods, spline orientation can be critical because these rods tend to torque under load in even the best of cases. The guides are located above the rod axis, which is an inherently unstable situation, and incorrect spline can aggravate the tendency to torque, leading to a requirement of extra forces to keep the rod oriented vertically. The angler ends up not only fighting the fish, but also fighting the rod.

In general, however, in spite of a great deal of folklore to the contrary, spline orientation is a secondary effect and relatively unimportant. A statement such as this may agitate some custom rod builders, but spline orientation is controlled at the level of the rod fabricators, and there is little the angler can do to alter the completed rod. Additionally, advances in rod blank fabrication technology in many cases has caused the spline to be less pronounced, and therefore of diminishing concern.

Ferrules. The longest practical one-piece rod is about 5 to 6 feet in length. The reason for this limitation is that one-piece rods longer than that will not fit easily into an automobile, and the possibilities for accidental mechanical damage abound. For instance, having the wind blow a car door shut when a longer rod is carefully being maneuvered into place is disastrous. Rod manufacturers are constantly requested to make warranty replacements of rods with the characteristic creased damage of car doors and, even more common, doors in the home. (The absolute worse place for storage of a rod is behind a door; if it slips into the door jamb, it will join the Legion of Mashed Rods.) It is estimated that such accidental mechanical damage exceeds rods broken in actual fishing conditions by many orders of magnitude.

Therefore, most rods of moderate or more length are produced in several sections. (There are notable exceptions, such as the custom one-piece 11- to 15-foot products used by dedicated surf casters, who regard car-top or bumper roof racks as a

R

necessary part of their sport.) In the distant past, these sections were produced by cutting the rod blank and joining the sections with a separate metal fitting or ferrule; the additional weight and stiffness, however, degraded the action, and most rods today are joined with integral ferrules that are part of the blank itself.

The merit of integral ferrules is obvious: no discontinuity or significant alteration of the rod action. As an example, backpacking rods for the hiker are produced as five or more sections of about a foot each, yet the assembled rod is very fishable and it requires a diligent search to locate the joints. Even better are the high-end three- or four-piece travel products that result in eminently fishable 6- to 9-foot spinning, baitcasting, and flycasting rods.

The integral ferrule is fabricated in inside and outside forms. The inside ferrule is the lightest and simplest to produce in that the lower section is made a bit larger and the tip section slides into it. The joint is ground with a precision taper, and the friction fit is sufficient for a secure grip. Many experienced anglers lubricate this joint (if not already done by the manufacturer) with beeswax, both to increase the grip and to promote smoother assembly. Do not apply the wax excessively or it will trap abrasive dirt particles; always wipe a ferrule before assembly.

Hoop strength at the ferrule is usually increased with a string wrap. The outside ferrule, in turn, is stronger because the thinner tip section is built up at the joint to fit outside the lower section. The tip section is thus as strong as the rear section, which was already strong because of the increasing rod taper toward the butt. The outside ferrule is more expensive to produce because the built-up joint requires the application of separate hoop windings on the rod blank, and each such operation increases costs. When made well, both types of ferrules deliver good service and are very fishable.

Several special products deserve distinct mention. One is telescoping rods in which the ferrules are joined from the inside. Telescoping rods are generally of three or more sections, extending to lengths in excess of 12 feet and popular for poking among bushes for species such as crappie and bream. The guides are usually of a "slip-on" configuration, always on the rod, and are slid into their correct places as the rod is extended. This process is much simpler in practice than the description. In Europe and Asia, where this style of rod is extremely popular, the guides are fitted with a plastic "stringing needle," which not only aligns but also pulls line through the guides before extension so that the rod is ready to tie on terminal tackle as soon as it is extended (you have to try stringing a 15-foot rod in a boat to truly appreciate the convenience of this accessory).

Another example is blue water rods for large fish. These conventional rods use the powerful drags of revolving-spool reels to subdue fish that easily outweigh the angler and are many times heavier than the breaking strength of the line. Because the top-side guides generate torque forces on the rod, the blanks are always of one-piece construction to prevent rotation at a ferrule.

In general, however, the ferrule is an essential part of most practical rod designs, and the convenience it provides for transport and storage far outweighs any effect on rod action.

Guides. Nearly all fishing rods have guides; this includes one tip-top guide, which is obviously at the top or casting end of the rod, and a variable number of intermediate guides, which are along the blank between the top and the handle. Of all accouterments, guides are the single most significant factor affecting rod performance beyond the blank itself. The style, height, number, spacing, and weight are all part of the guide, and therefore important parameters.

Rod guide styles can be termed either "spinning" or "conventional." Although there is some degree of universality, the basic choice that distinguishes these is large-ring bottom-mounted guides for spinning rods (as well as fly rods), and small-ring top-mounted guides for conventional rods, which are used with revolving-spool reels (baitcasting, conventional, and big-game).

Guide style includes the frame material, which includes welded stainless steel, graphite polymer, brazed wire, and others. However, the fundamental guide parameter is whether it has single or double attachment points to the rod blank, which respectively are called single- or double-foot guides.

Because casting is what spinning tackle does best, the appropriate guides for spinning rods should favor the casting function. Thus, a single-foot guide least perturbs the typical light action of a spinning rod, and is the primary choice. The single-foot guide is also suitable for withstanding the forces of the line acting on the guide when subduing a large fish. These forces are directed downward, and the frame of a single-foot guide slung below the rod has sufficient strength to withstand severe tension load on the guide ring.

Double-foot construction is favored for conventional rod guides, especially for models used to subdue strong ocean species. This is because fish fighting is what such tackle does best, and the load of a gamefish on the line applies both a crushing downward force on the guide ring and frame, and a simultaneous tendency to torque or twist the rod. This latter phenomenon occurs because the line is located directly above the rod axis and is fundamentally at unstable equilibrium; when torquing begins, the lever arm for twisting increases and the condition avalanches. Such stresses require the rigid configuration of a double-foot frame (the double attachment points of the frame to the rod act in the manner of a triangle, the extremely sturdy building block of bridge spans). Light-duty baitcasting rods, such as those used for freshwater bass fishing, have

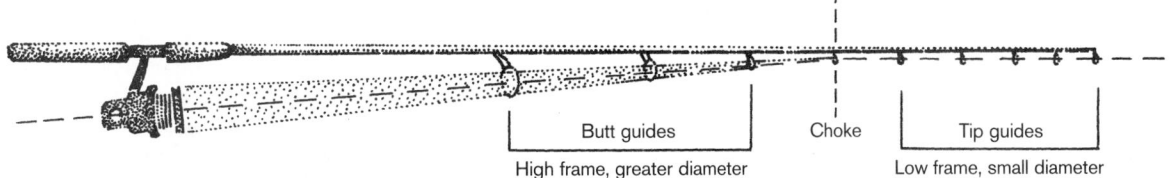

A spinning rod characteristically has the largest guides closest to the butt and the smallest guides closest to the tip. The choke guide is the intersection point where larger spirals of line funnel down when cast.

a mixture of guide styles, usually double-foot guides toward the stiffer rear section and single-foot guides toward the slender tip section, which is often designed to enhance strike detection (as with jigs or plastic worms).

An important function of the guide on all rods is to prevent contact of the line with the rod blank. During a cast, such contact or "line slap" results in shorter casts due to increased friction; when fighting a gamefish, such contact is regarded as an unfavorable and irregular additional force retarding the line.

The height and spacing of guides on the rod are interactive; these parameters are mutually dependent and must be considered simultaneously. In the case of spinning rods, the line leaves the reel in the form of a cone-shaped envelope, defined by the spool diameter at its base and the tiptop at its apex. The theoretically ideal guide ring diameter, height, and spacing precisely lies along the surface of this cone because such a configuration would minimize friction and thereby lead to maximum casting distance. Although there is some disagreement about the location and effects of the lowest or first guide along this cone, most spinning rods are fabricated in a sensible manner and small departures from this ideal cone are not serious.

During retrieval of a large fish, the stress on the line is applied through the guides to the attachment points on the rod. If the number and spacing of the guides is insufficient, the stress is concentrated at these points and the rod will be bent into distinct segments instead of a smooth curve. The final result could be a catastrophic failure.

How many guides are sufficient? The optimum solution requires a compromise because too many guides leads to heavy weight, slow action, and high costs; too few lead to stress concentration and rod failure. A simple test of spinning rod design is to string the rod with monofilament line, and then lift the rod against a load to verify the quality of its design. Note that the common practice of simply wiggling the rod back and forth, or flexing the rod tip against the ceiling, reveals the rod taper but does not generally validate correct guide spacing and number.

In the case of the conventional rod, during a cast the line leaves nearly tangent to the spool so that the guide rings can be relatively small. Because controlling gamefish is what conventional tackle does best,

the guide configuration favors the retrieval function. During the fish fighting process, in the ideal case the guides are required to support the line above the axis of the rod. Compromises are necessary here, too, because increasing guide height reduces the number required but also increases the "lever arm" and therefore the tendency to torque. The optimum height and spacing depends on the rod action but is generally regarded as the minimum number that will not permit the line to cross the axis of the rod during maximum bend.

Although some rod designers abhor even slight contact between line and rod surface, the process of the line crossing below the rod axis certainly exacerbates the always present problem of torque. In essence, pulling the line past the rod axis is an unstable state, and the structure responds by torquing, or twisting over. The test for correct design here is the same as for spinning: thread the rod with line and check for contact under load.

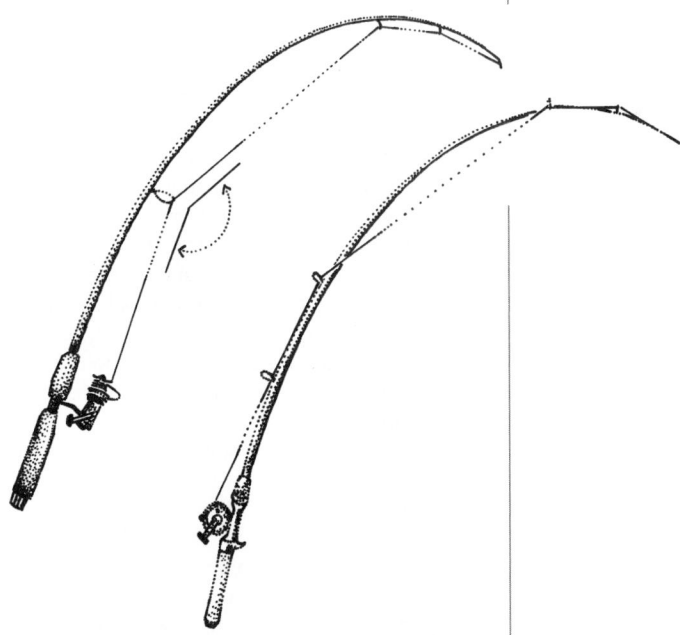

This is a greatly exaggerated depiction of poor guide placement on a spinning rod (top), where guides and line are under the blank, and on a baitcasting rod (bottom), where guides and line are on top of the blank. It helps illustrate the fact that when there is too great an angle (arrows) of line from one guide to the next, there is excessive strain on the rod and loss of power.

R

Guide rings.   In order to effectively confine the line with minimum disturbance, the ideal guide ring should have several properties: low weight, low friction, and high durability. Low weight is particularly important for casting applications where the additional mass of the guide can affect the action of the rod blank.

In the specific case of fly fishing, where superior casting properties for a delicate presentation are of foremost importance, the lightest of all guides, simple helixes of thin wire, are the rule. At the other end of the scale, as in blue water trolling where weight is unimportant because the rod is supported by a gimbal mount and shoulder harness, the norm is massive roller guides to minimize the friction of heavy lines and to maximize fish-fighting power. Other fishing tackle falls between these extremes. Practical guide ring materials include chrome-plated stainless steel or brass, common and technical ceramics, and various carbide and nitride compounds. These are available, depending on their configuration, in a wide range of weights.

Low friction is attained through good surface polishing, but, as usual, contradictory requirements arise from the property of durability. The wear aspect of durability concerns abrasion of the guide ring by the line; this is usually due to the action of microscopic particles of suspended sediment (quartz) carried by the line. Therefore, an ideal guide ring material should be harder than quartz, and this requirement is identical to that of a precious gemstone.

Common guide ring materials include aluminum oxide (alumina, or in its gemstone form, red ruby or blue sapphire), tungsten carbide (Carboloy), silicon carbide (SiC), titanium nitride (TiN), and zirconium nitride (ZrN). While some of these materials can be formed as a ceramic before firing, all require grinding and polishing, the same as any gemstone. This leads to a contradictory requirement: The desirable hardness property in these materials is the very feature that causes that same material to be stubborn to shape and polish. Silicon carbide guide rings, for example, typically require one week of continuous diamond dust polishing to attain a good surface finish. This manufacturing cost is naturally reflected in the finished product.

Another aspect of durability is "shock resistance," or the ability of a guide ring to withstand a sharp blow. Of the foregoing materials, tungsten carbide is reported to be the most brittle, followed by silicon carbide and aluminum oxide. Titanium and zirconium nitrides can occur in the form of solid technical ceramics, or may be applied as vacuum-deposited coatings on various substrates. The latter materials are routinely used as protective coatings on the turbine blades of jet aircraft; they may sound exotic but are extremely practical and durable. Another application of these coatings is on premium drills and cartridge case dies, where their hardness and low friction properties offer

significant benefits. These are definitely guide ring materials for the near future.

The tip-top guide is a type of terminal guide ring, but its service load is substantially more severe due to increased contact and friction where the line has its greatest angular change at the rod tip. As a consequence, many rods are offered at a lower price by mounting a higher quality material such as Carboloy or silicon carbide for the tip-top ring, and using hard chrome or other materials for intermediate guides. In like manner, the stripping guide of a fly rod has the major angular change for the line (the tiptop tends to lie parallel to the line due to the combination of line stiffness and soft rod tip action), thus, its "stripper" guide is usually of higher quality than the remainder, typically the best aluminum oxide or silicon carbide. In general, the rod manufacturer is well aware of the requirements for superior guide service; its choice of materials reflects compromises on cost, quality, and perceived value.

Guide wrapping.   The guide is normally wrapped onto the rod with thread, which both affixes it to the blank and serves in a decorative capacity. The thread can vary in thickness, ranging from approximately the fineness of a hair, to the coarseness of 4-pound-test monofilament, and in materials from costly silk to common spun nylon. Generally, the finer thread wraps are most highly regarded because more turns are required per linear inch, which likewise requires a higher level of craftsmanship.

Under load, the guide acts as a point of stress concentration on the rod blank, so the stiffer double-foot guide is often provided with a cushioning underwrap (called "double wrapping") to better distribute the stresses. In fact, for all types of rods, stress concentration at the guide foot is statistically the most frequent cause of failure under load; most rod breakage from a large fish is located at a site of guide attachment. This situation is further exacerbated by the common practice of grinding the end(s) of the guide foot to knife edges to allow smooth thread wrapping.

The transparent coat of epoxy resin is the final step to protect the wrapping thread and, perhaps more important, to firmly affix the guide in place because any movement could lead to scratches on the rod blank and promote premature failure.

Once the resin has cured, the guide and wrap are now an integral part of the rod blank and affect the action. The wrap acts in the manner of an athletic support bandage, adding to the stiffness of the rod, and the weight and stiffness of the guide also affect the action. The completed rod is typically stiffer and slower in action than the unadorned blank as it was originally fabricated. Thus, proper rod design must plan for the overall effects of adding guides and wrapping.

The guide wrapping is additionally the focus of artistic expression. Its coloration can be somber or brilliant, it may be complementary or contrasting to that of the blank, it may be a single color,

Determining the number of fish that exist today is complicated by the fact that present fish species and subspecies can adapt and change within a few years.

tiger-striped, or multi-banded; all of these are a reflection of the preference of its builder or user, and can be a source of great pride.

The acme of artistic expression is represented by the "diamond wrap" at the base of the rod blank just above the foregrip; this is a beautiful, time-consuming (expensive), and challenging bit of crafts-manship and is the hallmark of the custom-built rod. Intricate patterns are worked into the thread, and are often breathtaking in their execution. Each diamond wrap is unique and an expression of individuality. The diamond wrap is to the custom rod builder what the air brush paint finish is to the custom automobile builder. Though some may be gaudy, there is no doubt as to its vigor as an art form.

Incidentally, some custom rods have the same color combinations for the entire tackle selection of the angler: freshwater ultralight spinning through blue water trolling, all with identical color wraps. These are "matched sets," akin to the custom color striping of target and hunting arrows for the avid archer. They can be as beautiful and pleasurable to use as a set of matched and boxed sterling silver forks, knives, and spoons.

Line-through-blank rods. Because the use of guides and wrapping necessarily affect the action of the rod blank, the concept of threading fishing line through the center of a rod is as old as the first tubular rod. The absolute simplicity of eliminating not only the guides and wrapping, but torque and stress concentration points, was universally alluring. The nodal segments of early bamboo rods were drilled through, and line was inserted down the axis. The practical problems that arose were those of extreme friction, which impeded the ease of casting and the distance achieved, and caused power losses when retrieving lures, bait rigs, and fish. These problems remained with line-through-blank rods until the 1990s, with none commercially available.

The key to solving this dilemma was recent advanced technology, which precisely finished the *interior* as well as the *exterior* of the rod. These advances include internal polymer finishes and complex internal integrated structures. To date, only one manufacturer, Daiwa, has developed this for models of spinning and baitcasting rods, and these cast and retrieve as well as similar rods with external guides; in addition, they offer "perfect" bends without stress concentration, unprecedented light-ness (the rod wall can be made thinner because it does not have to withstand stress concentration due to the guide foot), and torque-free characteristics.

The ability to be torque free is particular to line-through-blank rods; the fish-fighting ability is effective not only to the front, as with external-guide rods, but acts equally well for strong runs to either side. The tiptop and front section of the rod is axially symmetrical and therefore omnidirectional. Whichever direction the fish runs, the rod responds with equal bending forces. An additional benefit to the omnidirectional tiptop is that it is tangle free.

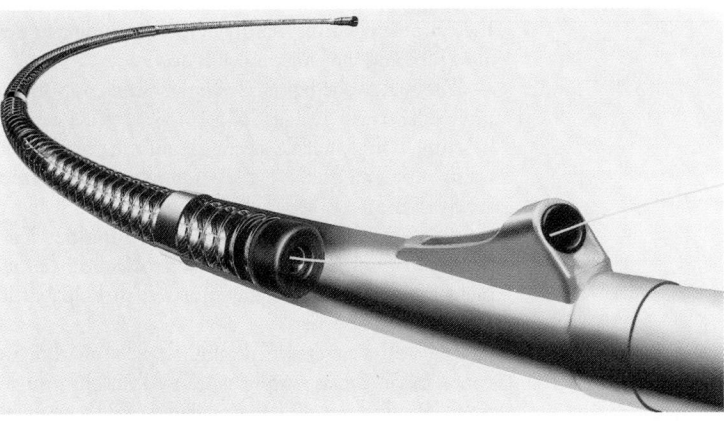

This computer-generated image depicts a Daiwa Interline rod, in which fishing line passes through the graphite blank.

At this point, these line-through-blank products are being used primarily for freshwater fishing applications, but in time, this technology may spread to a wider range of applications.

Grips and handles. Rod grips and handles serve several functions, including comfort and con-trol for the angler and a seat for mechanically mounting the reel.

The traditional grip material is cork because it is thermally insulating (and therefore warm in cold weather), light in weight, sensitive to vibration transmission, and provides a good grip, even when wet. Drawbacks include relatively rapid wear because of softness (cork is easy to shape but also easy to crumble), difficulty to obtain as a uniform material (it is the bark of a tree with all of the implied variations from piece to piece), and being relatively expensive in premium grades (inspection and sorting is labor intensive).

Ground and reconstituted cork, which is the equivalent of particle board, is a compromise mater-ial but is generally regarded as physically unattractive. It is used extensively in the form of rubber-bonded tape, which is spiral-wound directly onto the blank for specialty surf rods because of its light weight and durability.

Man-made handle materials include foamed polymers such as Hypalon, typically found in black but available in colors or even "laminated" configu-rations. These can range from foamed cylinders to molded and shaped offset pistol grips.

The choice of material is largely determined by application: cork for more finesse-like fishing and foamed polymers for rugged applications. The forces that a big-game angler applies to the rod grip would tear many materials right off the blank. On the other hand, a person casting ultralight micro-jigs would likely find the weight of polymer grips oppressive. The former needs Hypalon, the latter premium cork. Both types of grips have shapes which reflect their application; the Hypalon for the big-game angler is often a hand-filling triangular cross section to better control torquing; the premium cork for the ultralight caster is bullet shaped to better encourage

R

the natural pointing tendency of the index finger along the rod axis for pinpoint accuracy.

The reel of the big-game angler needs not only a physically sturdy reel seat of formed stainless steel or machined high-tensile-strength aluminum, but is often supplemented by a separate accessory clamp (part of the reel) secured around the reel seat by stainless steel bolts. Angled tie rods, shoulder harness, and gimbaled butt are accessories that complete the fishing outfit, all intended to help battle the strongest species.

The reel seat of an ultralight spinning rod, in contrast, can be as simple as a few thin aluminum rings, offering not only light weight, but the convenience of positioning the reel anywhere along the handle for best balance. These rings, incidentally, should be secured not by just sliding onto the reel foot, but by rotating them several times to "bite" into the handle.

A more common reel seat is one with a threaded closure, which is regarded as more secure but suffers the drawback of fixed location. Threaded reel seats are offered over a wide range of sizes for various fishing applications. The reel seat materials for these applications are machined aluminum alloys and molded graphite (polymers with strength fibers).

In applications requiring sensitivity, the reel seat is often cut away to allow direct contact of the rod blank and reel seat so that the transmission of the most subtle strike is maximized. The choice of reel seat is determined just as in the case of the handle or grip: it should represent the combination of best comfort and utility that pleases the angler.

Some spinning rods, incidentally, do not possess either a threaded reel seat or adjustable aluminum rings, but have merely unaltered cork handles. These are expressly designed to allow the user to position a spinning reel where it feels most comfortable, using black or colored electrician's tape (preferably 1-inch width) to firmly secure it to the rod. This is preferred by some light jig users, and it is possible for anglers with sliding ring reel seats (which often don't stay put) to remove the rings and use tape to secure the reel to the handle. The main drawback to this is that the reel cannot be easily removed from the handle for storage or changing, and even the tightest manual tape wrapping may not prevent some flex or stretch in the tape at the reel foot when the rod is put under severe stress.

See: Baitcasting Tackle; Big-Game Tackle; Conventional Tackle; Flycasting Tackle; Reel, Fishing; Spincasting Tackle; Spinning Tackle; Tackle Care, Maintenance.

ROD HOLDER

A device that a fishing rod is inserted into when not being used or held by hand. Rod holders come in many forms and are made by many manufacturers. Adjustability, ease of rod removal, sturdiness and stability, and placement options are the key factors in selecting and using these accessories.

Some rod holders are primarily used for stowing rods out of the way when not in use. There are various ways to do this, depending on the design of the boat. Open boats, center consoles, and cuddy cabin craft often sport through-the-gunwale or flush-mounted holders that store rods upright. This isn't practical for many small boats, though, and horizontal mounting is preferable for some. The decks of many small boats are often cluttered with rods, and many anglers leave these to bounce freely when the boat is underway; here, a snap-in floor holder can be used to secure rods.

Holders used to contain rods that are being used—stillfished or trolled—are mounted on or in the gunwale and transom, as well as on a guard-rail, handrail, trolling board, or downrigger. Holders should be adjustable to different positions and angles, although some rod holders mounted on downriggers are not adjustable. They should be able to support a long-handled rod, a rod with a trigger grip, a spinning rod, and a heavy-duty rod with crosshair style gimbal footing. Holders should allow quick removal of the rod; some designs cause anglers to fight with the holder to remove a rod when a fish is on the line and exerting a lot of torque on the handle, which is buried in the holder.

ROD REST

A bank- or shore-planted device that supports a fishing rod being used in bait fishing and not held by hand. Rests may be used to support the entire rod or the tip section, and may hold a single rod or multiple rods.

A rod supported by a rest can be grabbed and lifted upward without having to slide or pop it out of a holder, which makes it useful when fishing with very light lines and floats, but impractical for fishing from a boat.

See: Rod Holder.

ROD STORAGE

Rod storage in a fishing boat takes many forms, but it is a sure bet that in most boats, except for big sportfishermen, there is rarely enough room for safely stowing all the rods you want or may need. Most anglers bring and use several rods in a day of fishing. They usually want them rigged up and accessible, but out of harm's way when not being used. When several people are in a boat, especially one in the 16- to 20-foot range, this can be a tall order. Leaving rods lying around is a poor option for fairly obvious reasons: They tend to get tangled, which makes for frustrating untangling when a rod is needed quickly, and they are subject to being broken or damaged in many ways. Rods should be secure, not bouncing around, in a moving boat, and when fishing, extra rods should not be in locations that impede fishing.

These holders keep casting rods out of the way but ready on a center-console boat.

Bigger boats can use a combination of storage schemes, and open areas pose few problems for rod storage. Holding racks may store rods horizontally under the gunwales, vertically along the sides of a console, and vertically along the aft edge of a tuna tower, not to mention horizontally inside the cabin. Some open fishing boats have lockable horizontal rod storage inside floor compartments on the recessed foredeck, much like the rod-holding compartments of bass and some multi-purpose freshwater fishing boats. But in small open boats, accessible rods, especially fly rods that can't fit into upright holders, must be stored under the gunwale horizontally or along the interior sides.

Horizontal rod racks are feasible on all but the very smallest of boats (it isn't practical to stow a 9-foot fly rod horizontally along the gunwale of a 10-foot cartopper, at least not fully assembled), and you aren't going to be able to carry six rods per side in a really small boat either. But you can get many rods per side in even a 16-foot skiff with the right rack, although you may have to customize one yourself to do it. In fact, many small-boat anglers do customize their boats for rod storage purposes, and this takes on the forms of both horizontal and vertical storage, particularly in vertical systems using PVC pipe.

Properly designed and installed rod holders can contribute substantially to angling efficiency and at the same time considerably lengthen the usable life of your fishing tackle.

See: Boat.

RODE
A nautical term for anchor line.

ROE
The eggs of a female fish; also a term for a female fish with eggs.

ROLL CAST
A common and practical cast used in fly fishing.
See: Flycasting Tackle.

ROLLING HITCH
See: Knots, Boating.

ROOSTERFISH   *Nematistius pectoralis.*
Other names—Spanish: *papagallo, gallo, pez de gallo, reje pluma.*

The roosterfish is a superb light tackle gamefish and a member of the Carangidae family of jacks, so named for the comb of long dorsal fin spines that extend far above the body of the fish. It has been exploited at a local level because of its excellent quality as a food fish and is marketed fresh.

Identification.   A striking, iridescent fish, the roosterfish is characterized by seven long, threadlike dorsal fin spines, which are found even on young fish. This comb stands erect when the roosterfish is excited, as when threatened, but ordinarily the fin remains lowered in a sheath along the back. There are also two dark, curved stripes on the body and a dark spot at the base of the pectoral fin.

Size.   Roosterfish can grow to 4 feet in length and exceed 100 pounds. The all-tackle world record is a 114-pound fish taken off Baja California in 1960.

Distribution.   Endemic to the eastern Pacific, roosterfish occur from San Clemente in Southern California to Peru, including the Galápagos Islands; they are rare north of Baja California, Mexico.

Habitat.   Roosterfish inhabit shallow inshore areas, such as sandy shores along beaches. Young fish are often found in tidal pools.

Angling.   This inshore species inhabits moderate depths of water and fights particularly well. It will jump several times after being hooked, dive deeply, and engage in a slugfest. A good-size roosterfish, roughly 20 pounds, will make a startling first run with its dorsal comb high above the water.

Roosterfish are found in loose groups and are often spotted under working birds. They are caught by boaters who drift and troll, but also by surf anglers and those who cast from boats. Sandy-bottomed locales are good, as are bays and sections of mild surf. Smaller fish are usually closer to shore.

Trolling with strip baits, live baits, plugs, and feathers is popular; casting and live bait drifting, particularly when a group of roosterfish is located, can be particularly effective.

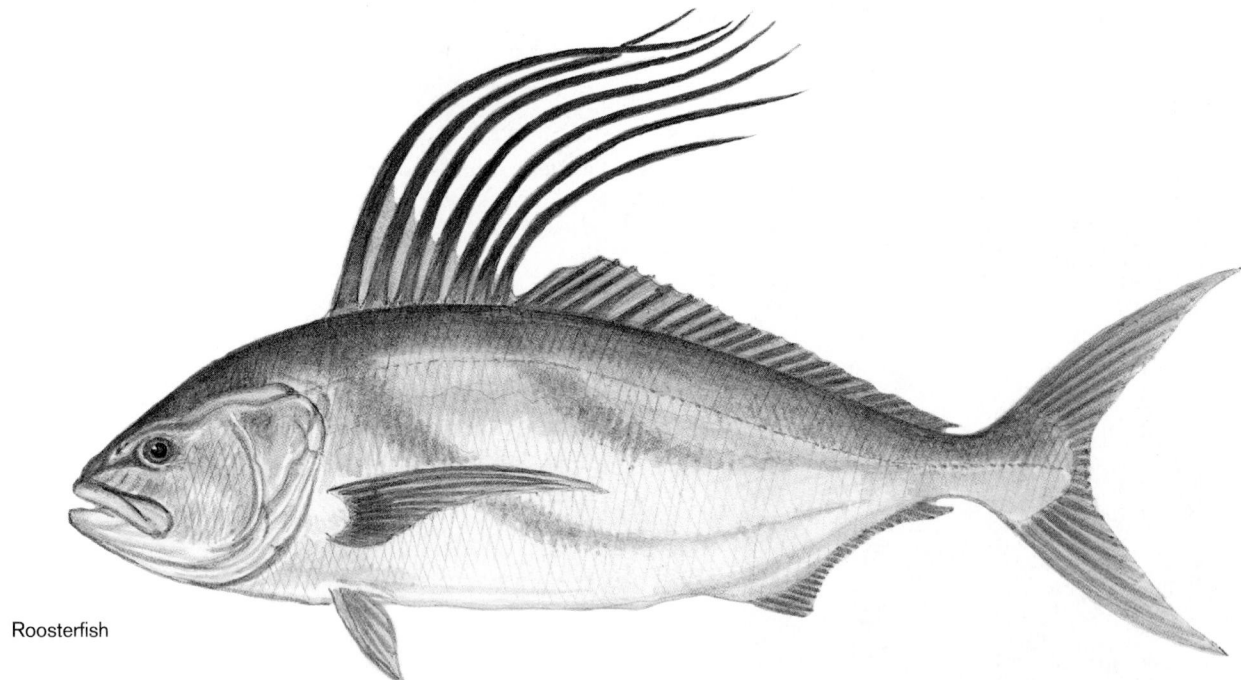

Roosterfish

The tackle for these fish is often quite stout, but medium-action gear with 15- to 20-pound line has merit, and fly rods and light spinning or baitcasting gear are good choices as well.

See: Inshore Fishing; Jacks.

ROTENONE

A chemical used by fisheries biologists to poison all or a section of a lake or pond in order to kill fish. Rotenone is not known to be harmful to humans and is usually applied as a method of last resort for sampling purposes or for complete eradication of existing fish populations in order to restock the water with other species.

ROUGH FISH

A subjective and generally unofficial term for freshwater species that are not considered gamefish.

Exactly which species fall into this lump category is debatable. Species that are designated by law as gamefish do not technically warrant inclusion; however, some species may be officially listed as a gamefish in one state and not in another. Fish that are considered gamefish by general consensus do not fall under this category either; nevertheless, there are many species that a majority of anglers do not deem sporting but that a minority of anglers do.

Clearly no official listing of rough fish species exists, but on the basis of general attitudes and interest this term includes carp, catfish, bullhead, gar, buffalo, drum, suckers, bowfin, burbot, sturgeon, and whitefish *(see each species)*. Catfish, sturgeon, and whitefish probably draw a little more esteem than the others.

"Rough fish" is a term that obviously has negative connotations. This viewpoint has evolved for various reasons. Some fish, like carp, are either nonnative or their feeding and spawning behavior are such that they can be detrimental to other more highly esteemed species in certain environments. Some are less highly esteemed simply because they are more reclusive, less abundant, hard to locate or catch, scrounge for food rather than pillage, are not carnivorous, or look odd or different.

The puritanical and undemocratic attitudes that have evolved toward rough fish species have to some degree continued even in the current enlightened fishing age because highly popular species (salmon, trout, bass, and walleye in particular) have become the focus of almost faddish specialization and marketing, and because popular sportfishing literature has overwhelmingly been oriented to those fish that are perceived to be more glamorous and with greater followings.

What this means, of course, is an unbalanced approach to sportfishing effort as well as harvest, with extreme emphasis on a few top predators or highly valued food fish, and little, or no, interest, in others. That may be human nature, and it may be a cultural phenomenon. Attitudes toward neglected fish may change if the populations of more esteemed fish suffer greatly or if pursuing the less-esteemed species becomes more acceptable for other reasons (marketing, economics, food).

In the meantime, in many places, people who devotedly pursue these so-called rough fish have little competition for the resource. For those who desire to keep a good thing to themselves, this may be a good thing. However, with more interest in rough fish and with greater numbers of people pursuing them, there might be more dissemination of

information and more knowledge, and perhaps opportunities for even better angling.
See: Coarse Fish.

ROW
To propel a boat using oars.
See: Boat; Rowboat.

ROWBOAT
A small craft with a displacement-type hull that is propelled by oars fitted in oar locks. The term is primarily applied to 10- to 14-foot boats, usually with a flat or semi-V bottom. Many jonboats *(see)* are called rowboats, as are many small boats available for rental at camps and marinas.
See: Boat.

RUBBER WORM
A common term for an artificial worm, few of which are made of rubber today.
See: Soft Worm.

RUDD   *Scardinius erythrophthalmus.*
Other names—European rudd; German: *rotfeder;* Italian: *scardola.*

A prominent coarse fish *(see)*, the rudd is widely sought by anglers. It is a member of the large Cyprinidae family, which includes minnows *(see)* and carp *(see)*, and is of similar size and color to its relative, the roach *(see)*.

Identification.   The rudd is somewhat cylindrical yet deep bodied. It has a moderately forked tail and an upturned mouth. The scales are strongly marked, the back is dark brown, and the sides are golden brown tapering to a white belly. The pectoral, pelvic, and anal fins are reddish orange, and the dorsal and tail fins are dusky. The rudd has 8 to 9 dorsal rays, 10 to 11 anal rays, and eyes that are red or have a red spot. The rudd may be confused with the roach; however, the pectoral fins of the roach lack the reddish orange color, and the body is more silvery. It is similar in appearance to the golden shiner *(see: shiner, golden)* but is distinguished from that species by its scaled ventral keel.

Size.   The maximum size for rudd is in the 4- to 5-pound range, although fish of that nature are rare. A 2-pound rudd is typically a large one.

Distribution.   Rudd range from western Europe to the Caspian and Aral Sea basins but are absent from Russia; they have been introduced to the United States.

Habitat.   Pools, canals, lakes, and slow-running rivers with muddy bottoms are the prime locations for rudd. They spend much time in or along the edges of vegetation.

Life history/Behavior.   Spawning takes place in heavy weeds in spring, when rudd broadcast

Rudd

numerous adhesive eggs rather than construct a nest. The fry stay in schools and gather in large congregations, and they provide forage for numerous predators. Rudd remain a schooling fish as adults. Their schools (called shoals) generally comprise similar-size individuals.

Food and feeding habits.   Rudd feed on snails, aquatic insects, and small fish, and spend a lot of time in beds of vegetation. They are largely surface feeders, but they also feed on the bottom and at mid-depths. Many rudd are observed taking food from the surface or from the underside of aquatic plants. These observations indicate where to fish.

Angling.   Like other coarse fish, rudd are not spectacular fighters, but they are popular. Maggots, bread, grubs, and worms are the main baits for rudd, and most fishing occurs in or close to weeds. Fly fishing with nymphs, however, is also an option. Anglers use rods from 11 to 13 feet in length, line from 2 to 4 pounds in strength, and No. 14 to 20 bait hooks. Hooked baits are fished with or without a float.

RUFFE   *Gymnocephalus cernuus.*
Other names—Eurasian ruffe; French: *grémille;* German: *kaulbarsch;* Polish: *jazgarz;* Russian: *yersh obyknovennyi.*

A member of the Percidae family of perch *(see)*, the ruffe has no sporting virtue and only minor commercial value in its native European range. It was largely ignored until it was introduced into North America, evidently through ballast water discharge by transoceanic ships. Since its discovery in 1986 in Lake Superior's St. Louis River, the ruffe has been a considerable threat to the delicate predator-prey balance necessary to maintain flourishing commercial fisheries and sportfisheries in North American waters, especially in the Great Lakes. It has been reported only in Lake Superior waters but is likely to exist, or spread, elsewhere.

The species found and multiplying in Lake Superior has been identified as *Gymnocephalus cernuus.* Other members of the same genus include the striped ruffe, or schraetzer *(G. schraetser);* the Donets ruffe *(G. acerinus);* and the Danube ruffe *(G. baloni).* These are eastern European and western Asian species, native to the Danube River and tributaries to the Black Sea. The native range of *G. cernuus* is from France to the Kolyma River in eastern Siberia, and it has been introduced to England, Scotland, and Scandinavia.

Identification. The ruffe's body shape is very similar to that of the yellow perch, and its body markings are similar to those of the walleye. It has a spiny first dorsal fin connected to a second soft dorsal fin, two deep sharp spines on the anal fin, one sharp spine on the pelvic fins, and sharp spines on the gill cover. The dorsal fins have rows of dark spots, the eyes are large and glassy, and the mouth is small and downturned. There are no scales on its head.

Size/Age. The ruffe seldom exceed 6 inches in length but can attain a length of 10 inches. Most female ruffe live for 7 years but may live up to 11 years. Males generally live 3 to 5 years.

Habitat. In Europe and Asia, the ruffe occurs in freshwater and in brackish waters with 3 to 5 parts per million salinity. It exists in a variety of lake environments, preferring turbid areas and soft bottoms without vegetation. In rivers, it prefers slower-moving water. It is more tolerant of murky and eutrophic conditions than are many other perch.

Life history/Behavior. The ruffe generally matures in two to three years, and spawns between mid-April and July, depending on location, temperature, and habitat. Young ruffe have a faster growth rate than many of their competitors, and adults reproduce prolifically, which allows for quick population expansion. It is a nocturnal fish, spending its days in deeper water and moving shallower to feed at night.

Food. The ruffe's primary diet is small aquatic insects and larvae, although it may consume fish eggs. Although there is much to be determined about this fish, researchers have found that the diets of ruffe and yellow perch do not overlap much; if they did, it was feared that ruffe populations would explode and cause a decline in yellow perch, and possibly other fish species.

Angling. As noted, in North America there is no angling interest in ruffe. Where it has been located, it is illegal to fish with ruffe as bait and to transport the species dead or alive. Efforts to control the spread and impact of ruffe to other areas are urged, including being careful not to unknowingly transport the adults or juveniles in bilge water or water from bait buckets.

See: Exotic Species.

RULES OF THE ROAD
Also known as Navigation Rules, this a general term for regulations established for boats to prevent collision.

See: Boat; Navigation.

RUN
(1) A seasonal migration undertaken by fish, usually as part of their life history; an upstream migration, particularly of anadromous fish. Run is sometimes used by anglers to refer to a temporarily increased abundance of fish without respect to migratory behavior *(see: running)*.

(2) A generally uniform section of a stream, creek, or small to midsize river that is deeper than a riffle *(see)* and without the disturbed surface, yet not as deep and slow-flowing as a pool *(see)*. A run usually has uniform depth throughout most of its length, commencing as the depth of the tail end of a pool tapers upward and ending by shallowing to a riffle. Runs generally exist between upstream pools and downstream riffles.

Runs may also be called flats, and they vary considerably in length, depth, and width, as well as in bottom features. The bottom may have a soft sand or silt character, a mixture of sand and rock, or interspersed sections of both, as well as possess some large rocks or other cover objects. Some species of fish (or some sizes of certain species) are very active in runs, especially when the flow is moderate; others visit these areas to feed but do not take up full-time residence.

(3) The behavior of a fish taking line off a reel under tension and swimming away from the angler. A fish makes a "run" when it swims any distance with a hooked bait, lure, or fly, while the drag of the reel is employed.

RUNABOUT
A general-purpose motor-driven boat, usually seating four to six people, without sleeping quarters, and used for general pleasure boating but seldom appointed with sportfishing accessories.

RUNNER, BLUE *Caranx crysos.*
Other names—hardtail, hard-tailed jack, runner; French: *carangue coubali;* Greek: *kokali;* Italian: *carangidi, carangido mediterraneo;* Portuguese: *carangídeos, xaralete;* Spanish: *atún, cojinua, cojinúa negra, cojinuda.*

Ruffe

The blue runner is a small, spunky member of the Carangidae family that is valued as bait for big-game fishing. It is an excellent food fish and is marketed fresh, frozen, and salted.

Identification.   The body of the blue runner is bluish green to brassy, silvery, or light olive above. There is a black, somewhat elongated spot near the upper end of the gill cover, and there may be faint bluish bars on the body. A characteristic feature is the blackish shading on the tips of the tail fins. The blue runner is easily distinguished from the crevalle jack because it lacks the dark blotch found on the pectoral fins of that fish.

Size.   This species usually weighs less than 1 pound and is typically 1 foot long; the all-tackle world record is an 8-pound, 7-ounce fish taken off Texas.

Distribution.   In the eastern Atlantic, blue runners range from Senegal to Angola, including the western Mediterranean. In the western Atlantic, they occur from Nova Scotia to Brazil, including the Caribbean and the Gulf of Mexico.

Habitat.   Blue runners inhabit offshore waters in large schools. They are occasionally found over reefs, sometimes in pairs or solitary. Young fish frequently linger around sargassum and other floating objects.

Life history.   Sexually mature when they reach 9 to 10 inches in length, blue runners spawn off-shore from January through August.

Food.   Blue runners feed primarily on fish, shrimp, squid, and other invertebrates.

Angling.   The blue runner is not a primary target of anglers, although these fish are caught incidentally by anglers trolling, casting, or fishing with bait. They are caught on small baited hooks drifted in chum lines, and are often kept as live or dead (rigged) bait for larger pelagic species.

See: Jacks; Offshore Fishing.

RUNNER, RAINBOW   *Elagatis bipinnulata.*

Other names—runner, rainbow yellowtail, skip-jack, shoemaker, Hawaiian salmon, prodigal son; Afrikaans: *re nboog-pylvis;* Arabic: *aifa, garaeiba, gazala, mujlabah, sagla;* Creole: *carangue saumon, dauphin vert, sorcier;* Fijian: *drodrolagi;* French: *carangue arc-en-ciel, comère saumon;* Hawaiian: *kamanu;* Japanese: *taumuburi;* Malay/Indonesian: *pisang-pisang;* Portuguese: *arabaiana norte, salmao;* Samoan: *samani;* Spanish: *cola amarilla, corredores, macarela, pez rata, salmon, sardinata;* Tahitian: *roeroe;* Tuvaluan: *tekamai.*

A member of the Carangidae family of jacks, the rainbow runner does not look like other jacks because it is a much slimmer, more streamlined fish. It is also an excellent food fish with firm white flesh, marketed fresh and salted/dried. In Japan the rainbow runner is cooked with a special sauce or eaten raw and is considered a delicacy.

Identification.   The rainbow runner is blue green above and white or silver below with a yellow or pink cast. On both sides there is a broad,

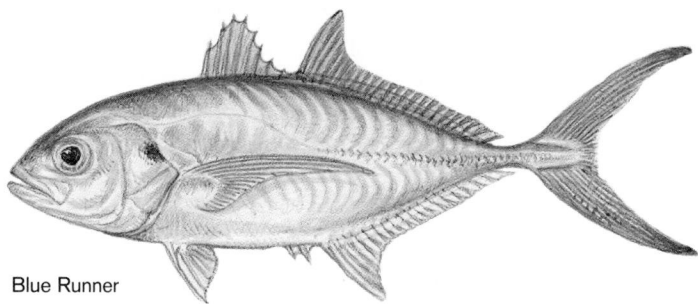
Blue Runner

dark-blue, horizontal stripe from the snout to the base of the tail; a narrow, pale-blue stripe immediately below it that runs through the eye; a pale to brilliant-yellow stripe along below that; and then another narrow, pale-blue stripe. The tail is yellow and the other fins are a greenish or olive yellow. The rainbow runner has a slender body that is more elongated than that of most other jacks. The first dorsal fin has six spines and the second has one spine and 25 to 27 connected soft rays. Behind this is a 2-rayed finlet. The anal fin has a single detached spine with 16 to 18 soft rays followed by a 2-rayed finlet. The rainbow runner is similar to the cobia in shape but can be distinguished by its coloring, as well as the finlets that follow the dorsal and anal fins.

Size.   The rainbow runner is typically 2 to 3 feet long, although it can reach 4 feet and 22 pounds. The all-tackle world record is a 37-pound, 9-ounce Mexican fish.

Distribution.   Found worldwide in marine waters, the rainbow runner occurs in the western Atlantic, from Massachusetts throughout the northern Gulf of Mexico to northeastern Brazil; and in the eastern Atlantic from the Ivory Coast to Angola, including the areas around St. Paul's Rocks and Genoa, Italy, in the Mediterranean. They range throughout the western Indian Ocean. In the eastern Pacific, they occur from the mouth of the Gulf of California, Mexico, to Ecuador, including the Galápagos Islands; in the western Pacific, they are found near Fiji and Tuvalu.

Habitat.   Rainbow runners form either small polarized groups or large schools that usually remain at or near the surface, although they can inhabit depths of up to 120 feet. They occur over reefs and in deep, clear lagoons, preferring areas with a current.

Food.   Rainbow runners feed on invertebrates, small fish, and squid.

Angling.   Rainbow runners are not ordinarily a target of anglers, but they are commonly caught on baits or lures trolled for other species. Fishing

Rainbow Runner

R

methods include trolling with small baits and lures, or live bait fishing. The rainbow runner is sometimes caught on heavy tackle intended for larger fish, but its fighting ability is then reduced. When hooked on light tackle, it is an excellent gamefish and a tough fighter prone to fast surface runs.

See: Jacks; Offshore Fishing.

RUNNING

A term applied to the seasonal appearance of significant numbers of fish, usually in rivers while undergoing their spawning migration, but also moving along the coast. When someone says, "The shad are running," it means that schools of these fish are known to be migrating; similarly, when someone says, "The bluefish are in," it means that numbers of bluefish are now in the area and being caught.

RUNNING DRAG

A position on lever drag (big-game) reels that allows line to slip from the spool freely without backlashing the reel; this position is reached when the drag lever is initially advanced from the freespool position.

See: Big-Game Tackle.

RUNNING LIGHTS

Navigational lights required by law to be used on boats from sunset to sunrise, in order to avoid collision. For most sportfishing boats, running lights must include red and green sidelights on the bow centerline (red to port, green to starboard), and a single white stern light visible over a 135-degree arc. There are different requirements for large vessels, and these lights must be visible when the boat is at rest, as well as when it is underway.

RUNNING LINE

A portion of a fly line behind the head that is lightweight and small in diameter, and aids distance casting by minimizing friction on the line guides.

See: Flycasting Tackle.

RUNOUT

A term for the site where shallow marsh ponds or swamps drain with falling tides or receding flood water into deeper canals and bayous. The area where the departing water drains, the runout, tends to collect certain fish species and supply them with a ready source of food, making it also a favorite target of anglers.

RUSSIA

Since the breakup of the former Soviet Union in late 1991, new countries and self-governing areas have been created and are still evolving. The vast region that was once the Union of Soviet Socialist Republics and the largest country in the world is now the Russian Federation. It still spans Europe and Asia, covering more than one-ninth of the world's land area, a region more than twice the size of China or the United States, and akin to Canada in climate. It encompasses the countries of Russia, Ukraine, Byelorussia, Moldavia, Armenia, Azerbaijan, Georgia, Kazakhstan, Uzbekistan, Kirghizia, Turkmenistan, and Tadzhikistan.

This vast area includes the world's longest continuous coastline, spanning more than 37,650 kilometers, mostly along the Arctic and Pacific Oceans; borders that face the Black and Caspian Seas; an exceptional number of rivers—many of them large, long, and prominent—that course through all regions; and many lakes, including Lake Baikal, the deepest freshwater lake in the world.

These enormous resources portend a significant freshwater sportfishery, the surface of which has been virtually untapped and little explored. The lack of infrastructure for general as well as angling tourism throughout the Russian Federation, the distance and great expense of traveling within the region, language barriers, and the state of the political and economic climate have left many questions about the actual status of the fisheries' resources unanswered. The only fairly well-developed sportfishery to date is for Atlantic salmon, and that for a relative few rivers in the northwesternmost region.

Nevertheless, Russia reportedly harbors more than 450 species of freshwater fish, of which some 20 to 30 are of interest to anglers. Chief among these, of course, is Atlantic salmon; but charr, taimen, lenok, brown trout, various sturgeon, pike, grayling, and Pacific salmon species are among Russia's coveted gamefish, although some have been adversely affected by pollution and other problems.

Although international air travel from eastern and western countries is well established, domestic travel within Russia is sometimes an adventure in itself. Flights operate to nearly every town or settlement but are sometimes problematic. Helicopters are used in many remote places, especially on the salmon rivers, but these are often subject to weather and mechanical delays. In most of Russia, roads provide very limited access to good fishing. Visitors who want to fish on their own, but who don't know the language or don't use a reliable tour operator, have minimal chance of success and would likely need an exceptional amount of time and patience.

European Region

The European, or westernmost, region of Russia is most populated and most accessible. Unfortunately, it is heavily polluted, although the pollution is localized and the region still has vast fishing potential when compared to the rest of Europe. This area contains the one fishery that is somewhat known to the rest of the world, especially to a small coterie of international anglers: the Atlantic salmon of the Kola Peninsula.

Virtually all of Russia's salmon fishing and overall sportfishing is currently concentrated in the Kola Peninsula. Some 65 peninsula rivers presently contain, or once contained, Atlantic salmon. Foreign anglers today visit only a handful of these. Among the rivers noted for their salmon fishing are the Varzuga, Varzina, Ponoi, Umba, Jokanga, Litsa, Rynda, and Kharlovka; the Ponoi has garnered the most notoriety. All provide fly fishing from camps run in cooperation with Western investors and outfitters, most are up to international standards, and all are either very expensive or extremely expensive. Because most of the peninsula is without roads or airports, chartered helicopters are often the only option for accessing many rivers. Visitors are funneled through the city of Murmansk.

Bounded on the west by Finland, the Kola Peninsula is otherwise surrounded by the Barents and White Seas. Salmon rivers in the north of the peninsula enter the Barents Sea and generally are shorter and steeper, with hearty rapids and falls and runs of shorter duration, but they also possess larger fish on average. Those rivers entering the White Sea (an arm of the Barents) are in the southern and central parts of the peninsula; they are longer and gentler in grade, void of significant falls and rapids, and generally have runs of small to medium salmon that last four to five months.

Overall, the Kola's salmon, which are plentiful and typically host an excellent ratio of adults to grilse—better than virtually all other hallowed Atlantic salmon waters—have been more or less accidentally saved by the existence of a large military installation on the peninsula. This institution kept civilians, prying eyes, and coastal netters far at bay, allowing salmon to migrate in and out unfettered, save for local poaching and minor local river mouth netting. The first foreign visitors fished the area in 1989, camps and more exploration soon followed, and today—not without bureaucratic headaches, poaching problems, territorial disputes, and other troubles—enough of a fishery has developed to rate this region as excellent, although some apprehension as to its future still lingers.

At least 14 of the top 20 Kola rivers have, or did have during the 1990s, established fishing camps. A high percentage of Kola salmon are believed to enter just four rivers: the Varzuga, Ponoi, Kola, and Umba; however, the exact number of fish running all of these rivers is not completely known, and modern statistics have been kept for only a decade and are subject to many variables.

The salmon season generally begins in late May or early June (the snow melts in May) and ends in late September or early October, but varies from river to river. Rivers with larger fish but runs of shorter duration end their season in early to mid-August; those with smaller fish or a second run have a longer season. The first part of the season, which

Salmon anglers fish the Varzina River.

experiences the highest water levels, also tends to produce the largest fish. Some rivers yield fish from 20 to 40 pounds during the spring freshet, although the high flow and rougher water conditions of some early season rivers result in many bigger fish breaking off. The early June weather can be cold, damp, and wet.

Among the north-coast rivers, the Varzina is one of the more notable fisheries. This is a swift-flowing canyon river that runs to the Barents Sea from Yenozero Lake; reaching it requires some hiking over rugged ground, but it has produced good-size salmon up to 15 kilograms that are full of stamina and tough to land. East of the Varzina is the Jokanga River. The fifth largest flow on the peninsula, the Jokanga has more than 200 kilometers of watercourse and good fishing for salmon of various sizes. Five of its tributaries—the Suhaja, Lyljok, Puiva, Tichka, Pokkryei, and Pulongi—which respectively range from 97 to 34 kilometers in length, are said to be suitable for salmon fishing as well. East of the Varzina are the Rynda and Kharlovka Rivers, both of which are difficult if not impossible to wade early in the season.

The Ponoi River, which is the Kola's largest, flows roughly from west to east through the east-central region of the peninsula and into the White Sea. It is just above the Arctic Circle, and is primarily fished in the lower 80 or 90 kilometers, as well as in it tributary, the Pornache River. The Ponoi is not only large in length, but also wide in many places. Yet it has a gentle flow that makes it easy to wade and good for anglers of all skill levels. It is restricted to fly fishing only (some rivers allow spinning and fly tackle) and catch-and-release, and has proved a fairly reliable producer. The river has been the subject of cooperative tagging for a research project.

Nearly all anglers ply the river with floating fly lines, and some fish in lower water with skated dry flies. Wade fishing is most popular, but Ponoi anglers also fish some locales from the bank and from a boat.

R

The Ponoi has two distinct runs of salmon: one that enters in June and July and spawns in the fall, and another that enters in mid-August, stays in the river for more than a year, and spawns the following fall. There are evidently far more fall-run fish.

The Kola's fisheries are primarily accessed through established operators who mete out one guide for every one or two clients. Pollution has not been a factor for most Kola rivers, but poaching has caused problems, and the fishing has varied in some rivers over the relatively short period during which anglers have had access. Visitors with an adventurous bent can buy a catch-and-release day license for a modest fee on most rivers, if they can find the right office and, furthermore, get to the rivers. These are not easy tasks, and do-it-yourself expeditions require time, patience, and a command of the Russian language, not to mention an understanding of the culture and local customs. The difficulties are so great that few foreigners, primarily Russian-speaking Europeans, visit fishing sites on the Kola, or elsewhere in the country, on their own. Most visitors require a local host or a reservation with an established fishing camp.

In addition to salmon, sea-run brown trout inhabit several Kola rivers, and arctic charr thrive in some of the northern waters. Pink salmon were introduced in the 1960s, and most rivers today have runs. Some of the upper rivers have excellent fishing for nicely spotted resident brown trout, which average 1.5 kilograms and may reach 4 to 6 kilograms or more. The inland lakes and rivers of the peninsula hold arctic charr, and in the southern areas there are some pike and grayling.

Atlantic salmon are also found east of the Kola Peninsula in other rivers that enter the Barents Sea, ranging all the way to the Ural Mountains. The last of these is the Kara River, which is beyond the island of Novaya Zemlya in the Kara Sea and on the western shores of Bajdarackaja Bay. East of here the arctic waters are too cold for salmon.

Thus, potential salmon waters exist along a coastline extending close to 3,000 kilometers, including the regions of Kola, Karelen, Archangels, and Komi. This broad territory has arguably the world's best current potential for salmon fishing. The area east of the Kola Peninsula is not fished much for Atlantic salmon by anglers, but includes the Pechora River, which is the largest Atlantic salmon river in the world. The Pechora is 1 kilometer wide where it enters the sea, and salmon travel more than 1,500 kilometers up the river, reportedly spawning in more than 62 tributaries. Commercial fishermen have fished it extensively in the past. The Pechora also is the only known river where both Atlantic salmon and taimen live. Other major salmon river systems in the region east of the Kola Peninsula are the Mezen, Archangels, Onega, and Dvina.

The rivers and easterly arctic coastline also harbor inconnu, which normally run to 10 kilograms, although 40-kilogram specimens have been taken.

Elsewhere in the European or western region of Russia, grayling are spread out through the area, as are whitefish and brown trout; the latter species is more prominent in the western areas and absent from the northeastern polar region. The area south of the Kola Peninsula bordering Finland is loaded with lakes and rivers, and many of these contain good brown trout fishing. Fine possibilities for brown trout also exist in the southerly Caucasus region bordering Turkey. In that same region, sea trout inhabit some rivers entering the Caspian Sea. Pike and perch are widespread in western Russia, and zander (pike-perch) are found in the southern regions; a saltwater- or brackish-water-tolerant zander reputedly exists in the northern region of the Black Sea, allegedly spawning in lower rivers and weighing up to 3 kilograms.

The sturgeon is by far Russia's largest sportfish to inhabit freshwater, and also probably its most valuable in light of the caviar resource it represents. In the European region of the Russian Federation, sturgeon are found in the Volga and Ural Rivers, which enter the Caspian Sea, and also in rivers entering the Black Sea. Recent sportfishing for sturgeon in the Ural and Volga Rivers has produced specimens up to 125 kilograms, but the numbers and sizes of the various sturgeon species have declined dramatically. Poaching for eggs and meat is a constant problem, and most Russian sturgeon are considered endangered by Western scientists.

Finally, the Gulf of Finland, which separates westernmost Russia from southern Finland and is a brackish water extension of the Baltic Sea, receives the flow from many rivers and is said to contain salmon year-round. Sportfishing for salmon occurs around islands on the Finnish side of the gulf's boundary, and some large specimens are caught by casters and trollers. Opportunities for salmon and sea trout in Russian waters, along the coasts and in the tributaries—especially in the northeastern region of the Gulf of Finland near the Finnish border—are unknown.

Asian Region

Extending nearly 8,000 kilometers east of the Ural Mountains, the Asian region of Russia is immense, lightly visited, and little fished. Three salmonids—taimen, lenok, and grayling—are found throughout this region.

Several subspecies of grayling reportedly thrive here. Lenok occur in waters that range from brooks to large rivers. This species has red dots on its side like a trout, but white flesh; it normally reaches 2 to 3 kilograms but is said to range up to 6 kilograms.

The taimen is the world's largest salmonid, and Russian scientists have reported that at least one specimen weighing 96 kilograms was once taken by commercial fishermen. Taimen usually weigh 7 to 20 kilograms. They are not found on the Kamchatka Peninsula, or in the far northeastern region, and are best caught on big spoons and floating plugs—

or something that imitates a mouse—and, for larger specimens, fished during the night. Fly fishing is also productive, especially for smaller fish in the clear rivers. The largest taimen are said to inhabit isolated parts of the Jakutskaya district to the east, and southward to the Khabarovsk region (the Uda River here yielded an 80-pounder to a float-camping angler in 1989), and in the region north of Mongolia, where lakes and tributaries drain into the mighty northerly flowing Jenisej River.

A sea-run taimen, called Sakhalin taimen, is reportedly found on Sakhalin Island (north of Japan in the Sea of Okhotsk) and in coastal rivers in the Khabarovsk region down to the North Korean border. Good rivers are the Koppi, Khuttu, and Tumnin. This fish has larger scales and a deeper body than its strictly freshwater relative, and the largest weight reported is 70 kilograms. There is a run in April and May and another in September and October.

Arctic charr—strictly freshwater as well as sea-run versions—range along the Asian region's unused and uninhabited arctic coast. Normally these fish weigh from 1 to 7 kilograms. Their cousin, Dolly Varden, as well as other charr, are found along the northern part of the Pacific coast.

Six species of Pacific salmon inhabit the eastern coastal rivers, though organized sportfishing efforts for them or the viability of various runs for sportfishing are little known. Chum salmon range from the Lena River in the north, which flows into the arctic-region Laptev Sea, all along the coastline to the North Korean border. The smaller pink salmon are almost as widespread as chum salmon, and also appear in the Kuril Islands. Sockeye salmon are found from the Bering Strait to the southern border. Coho salmon inhabit the northern part of the Pacific coast. Chinook salmon are mainly found on Kamchatka Peninsula. Cherry salmon, which are found only on the Asian side of the Pacific Ocean (the others range to North America), are found in the Kurils, on Sakhalin Island, and along the Khabarovsk coast, with a few found on Kamchatka Peninsula.

Rainbow trout and steelhead mainly occur on the western side of the Kamchatka Peninsula. Pike and perch exist throughout Russia's Asian region, except in the extreme Arctic, along the Pacific coast, and in Alpine areas. Whitefish are plentiful as well, evidently in several species, and several species of sturgeon inhabit the Pacific basin.

R

SABIKI RIG

See: Multihook Rig.

SAFETY

Sportfishing is generally not a dangerous activity and seldom results in accidents. However, any activity that takes place on or around water; involves the operation of motorized vessels; causes people to come into contact with sharp objects like hooks, knives, and fish teeth; results in interaction with wild animals; and may be pursued in inclement weather can justly raise some safety concerns. Accidents may be rare, but they do happen.

Wading swift waters; walking on slippery jetties; floating in an inflatable tube; landing large, strong, and toothy fish; fishing on ice; and similar matters all require obvious precautions. Safety matters pertaining to these and other specific activities have been addressed within the respective entries. Although anglers can find themselves in an unsafe situation in many not-so-obvious ways—encountering a grizzly bear while walking the banks of a wilderness stream, for example—the greatest safety issues are related to boating, weather, and exposure to the elements.

Water Safety

The greatest concern for anyone who spends time around water is the possibility of drowning. The four major causes of drowning, in order, are: not wearing a personal flotation device; abuse of alcohol; lack of sufficient swimming skills; and hypothermia (chilling of the body because of exposure to cold). Two-thirds of the people who drown never had any intention of being in the water; this includes most people who fish, since they either wade, fish from the bank or shore, or fish from a boat, but don't intend, or expect, to get into an unsafe situation.

Personal flotation devices *(see)*, also known as PFDs, are reviewed in detail elsewhere. The most important basic points to know are that anyone who cannot swim should be wearing a PFD when on or near the water; that rough weather and water conditions and some tricky boating situations require that a PFD be worn out of prudence; and that a PFD must be worn to be helpful, because it is almost always too difficult to put on once a person is in the water and in trouble.

People who spend time around water not only should develop a healthy respect for it, but should become comfortable with it. Learning to swim, at least to be able to float and tread water, means that if you do take an unexpected plunge in the water, you know enough to somewhat help yourself. Small children, of course, need constant supervision around water.

Alcohol (and drugs) and water are a lethal mixture. More than half of the people who drown annually have consumed alcohol prior to their accident, so it is obvious that no one who is on or in the water should consume alcohol.

Being in cold water is much more of a concern than being in warm water, even if you know how to swim and are wearing a PFD. This can lead to hypothermia, which is reviewed elsewhere *(see: first aid)*.

Boating

Safety issues for boating anglers arise when towing, launching, fueling, and operating a boat, and have been mostly addressed under a separate entry *(see: boat)*. It is especially important not to overload a boat (too much weight or too many people), to make sure that a proper-fitting PFD is available for every passenger, and to have the required safety equipment (warning device, navigational lights, fire extinguisher, etc.) aboard.

Other than reckless boat handling, the chief causes of boating safety concerns for anglers are dams, dangerous currents, navigational hazards, anchoring, and winds or storms. Most of these concerns can be minimized by prudent boat operation

Fishing during a snowstorm and in very cold water, these anglers are smart to have life jackets on, but they'd be safer sitting than standing.

S

and good boat-handling skills, but it's important to learn to recognize situations that can present a problem and to not underestimate them. The force of current *(see)* and the effects of strong converging currents, for example, are commonly not respected enough. The dangers inherent in improper anchoring *(see: anchor)* are significant, especially in heavy winds or strong current, and many boaters run into problems by anchoring poorly or in unsafe places or circumstances.

River tailraces *(see),* for example, can be extremely dangerous because of the velocity and turbulence of discharged water, changing water levels, and unpredictable current patterns. In these places, anglers should not tie their boat to the dam or anchor at it; downstream anchoring should be done with a quick-release device, and the engine should always be kept running in fast water. It's important to be alert for rising water and to keep a safe distance from other boats as well.

In large bodies of water and in big rivers, prudent navigation requires not just evaluating what lies ahead on the open water, but what may lie below. The water isn't like a highway, where everything is visible. Reefs, sandbars, rockpiles, and other objects are commonly present in many water bodies, and not necessarily marked; boaters must be sure of their path of travel, or proceed cautiously otherwise. The sudden striking of objects has unexpectedly and quickly sunk fishing boats, pitching occupants into the water. An otherwise delightful day can become a crisis, an emergency, or a survival situation in an instant.

Fishing and boating at night, which is common in summer for freshwater and saltwater anglers, brings added concerns for navigation and boat handling, and a greater concern for caution. This obviously applies to those who are moving under power, and not as obviously to those who are not; people in a boat that is anchored in a channel need to use lights to indicate their presence to others, or risk unintentionally being in harm's way.

Strong winds are often a natural element that causes a problem for boaters. Sometimes, coping with the wind is not terribly prudent, and the sensible thing to do is head for port. This is especially so if the winds appear to be building; don't wait for the worst conditions to arrive.

The first concern when fishing in heavy wind—especially when the water is cold, the waves are high, the boat is small or tipsy or flat-hulled, or there is a far distance to go—should be safety. You must put on and fasten a proper-fitting PFD that will keep your fully clothed body afloat and your head upright.

When the wind and weather are rough, you have to consider whether you, and the boat you expect to use, are up to fishing. On the personal comfort level, taking a pounding by running through heavy waves is hard on the back and neck, particularly for older anglers. And though the fish may be biting like crazy, that is small comfort to a companion who gets seasick *(see: seasickness).*

But the boat is another story. You have to realistically assess what your boat can handle, going forth only if you're are completely sure and prepared, or turning back when good sense demands it. Of course, going out to fish under severe wind is much different than being on the water and angling when conditions change from calm to frothy. Too many anglers push their luck each year, not noticing shifts in wind speed or direction, or thinking they can run themselves out of trouble. Sometimes they pay for it. Most people are guilty of not looking enough to the horizon for squalls and thunderstorms. That is one reason why on large bodies of water the wise angler has a VHF radio or handheld weather radio to stay informed of weather patterns, changes, and potential problems when in a locale where these devices function.

If the wind has picked up enough to put whitecaps on the water or, worse, a trail of foam, beware. It's already late, especially on large shallow lakes, which are among the most dangerous bodies of water because big waves build up quickly there. So are lakes with many reefs and shoals. Small boaters get caught in troughs, or get pushed up into shallows or shoals or boulders and bang up the outboard's lower unit or the boat hull, maybe even causing capsizing (especially watch out in a canoe). Recognize the dangers that lie ahead and be smart enough to avoid them so that you remain safe.

In addition, you need to be sure that nothing impedes your boat's progress when you're faced with strong winds and their accompanying waves. A crippled boat is very tough to handle properly in the worst conditions. You shouldn't be out there with a motor that isn't working well, for example. And make sure that any ropes—anchor rope or otherwise—aren't laying out where rough-water bouncing could cause them to be swept overboard. If so, the rope will be in the boat's propeller in an instant, probably seizing up the motor, and you'll be in a lot of trouble.

Thunderstorms

Although all types of storms pose danger to anglers, a thunderstorm is the one significant weather event that is most likely to be encountered by people who fish. Lightning is the leading cause of weather-related deaths and a high cause of weather-related injuries. Approximately one in four lightning strikes on humans happens to people involved in recreation; many such strikes are on or near water. Over the last half century in the United States, lightning was responsible for many more deaths than tornadoes and for many more than hurricanes and floods combined.

Whenever the slightest chance of a thunderstorm exists, the first safety precaution is to check the latest weather forecast and keep an eye on the sky. Recognize the signs of an impending storm: towering thunderheads, darkening skies, lightning, and increasing wind. Tune in an NOAA weather radio, the weather band of a VHF radio, or an AM/FM radio if you can, for the latest weather information.

When a thunderstorm threatens, getting inside a home, large building, or all-metal automobile (not a convertible or the bed of a truck) is the best course of action. This is usually not possible for anglers unless they act well in advance of a storm. Many people put themselves in unnecessary danger by waiting too long to take action when a thunderstorm approaches.

Anglers who are wading or who are along the bank or shore need to get out of and away from the water. Anglers in boats should quickly get to a safe place on land whenever possible; if not possible, they may be able to get out of the storm's path by moving, but only if they act well ahead of its arrival. You cannot outrun a thunderstorm that is imminent. If the storm is still very distant, you can try to outrun it. To do so, you need to know what direction the storm is moving in. Thus, running is effective only on large bodies of water and when storms do not cover wide expanses.

If you are caught outside on land, do not stand underneath an isolated tree, a telephone pole, or isolated objects, or near power lines or metal fences. Avoid projecting above the surrounding landscape. In a forest, seek shelter in a low area under a thick growth of small trees. In open areas, go to a low place, such as a ravine or valley. If you're in a group in the open, spread out, keeping people 5 to 10 yards apart. Stay away from metal vehicles and objects, and do not carry or raise any objects. Remove any metal objects from your hair or head, and remove metal-cleated boots.

Lightning may strike up to 10 miles from the center of the storm, so precautions should be taken even though the parent cloud is not directly overhead. If you are caught in the open, far from shelter, and if you feel your hair stand on end, lightning may be about to strike you. Drop to your knees and bend forward, putting your hands on your knees. Do not lie flat on the ground.

If you are stuck in a boat and the same thing happens, or your fishing rod begins to buzz or the line rises out of the water, lightning is about to strike. Immediately crouch down, lean forward, and put your hands on your knees, making sure not to touch anything else in the boat.

The reason behind these positions—and why you don't lie flat—is that when lightning strikes, it seeks the quickest way through the object it strikes. The more things that you touch or have contact with, the more lightning will travel through the body in an effort to seek a way out.

Many lightning strikes occur without the warning of thunder, so precautions are necessary even when there is no thunder. When there is both thunder and lightning, you can tell how many miles the lightning is from your position by counting the seconds between the sound of the thunder and the sight of the lightning, then dividing that by five. Scientists say that if you can hear thunder, then you are in range of being struck.

Thus, to avoid becoming a statistic, anglers should watch the sky for signs of an impending storm, get off the water early and especially if they hear thunder, and pick the proper places for refuge on land.

See: Boat; Navigation; Survival; Waves; Weather.

SAILFISH *Istiophorus platypterus.*
Other names—spindlebeak, bayonetfish; French: *voilier, espadon vela;* Hawaiian: *a'u lepe;* Italian: *pesce vela, pesce ventaglio;* Japanese: *bashôkajiki;* Portuguese: *veleiro, algulhão;* Spanish: *pez vela, aguja voladora, aguja de faralá, aguja de abanico.*

With its characteristic large dorsal fin and superlative aerial ability, the sailfish is arguably the most striking member of the Istiophoridae family of billfish. Although present taxonomy suggests that the Atlantic and Pacific sailfish are the same species, some experts are not yet convinced. It has long been believed that Indo-Pacific specimens of sailfish attain a much greater size than their Atlantic counterparts (and this is reflected in record catches), but a recent study of size data from the Japanese longline fishery provided evidence that eastern

An Atlantic sailfish provides a thrill near American Shoal in the Florida Keys.

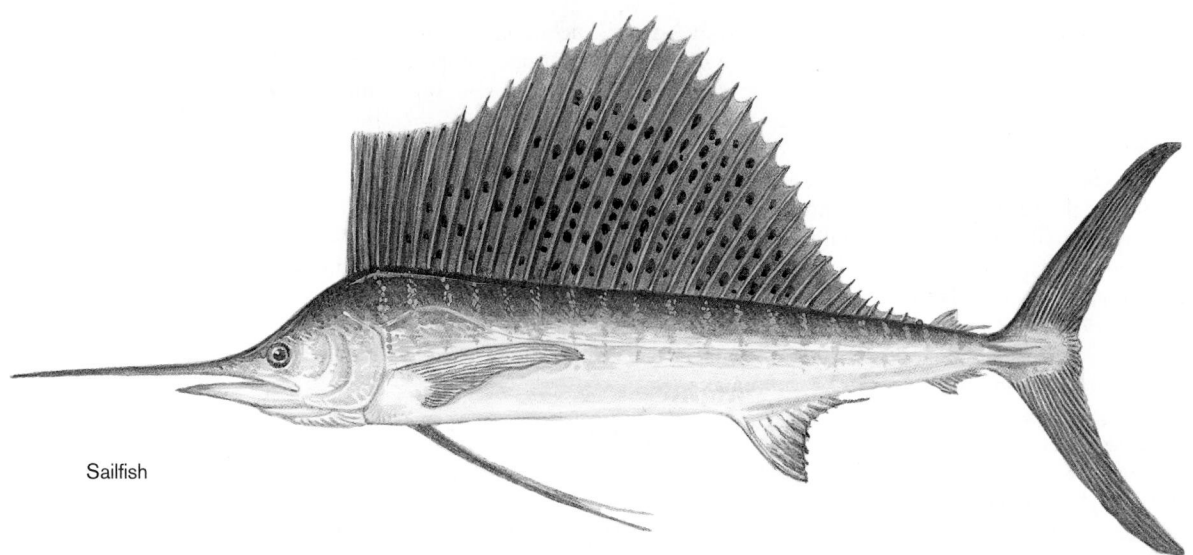

Sailfish

Atlantic specimens (identified by some ichthyologists as *I. albicans*) can attain much larger sizes than previously recorded.

The speedy sailfish is among the most exciting light-tackle big-game fish to catch. Light conventional gear, as well as spinning, baitcasting, and fly outfits, are all suitable for pursuing sailfish. The smaller specimens found in the Atlantic are especially good fun and are relatively easy for even inexperienced anglers to enjoy. Sailfish are rarely kept by western Atlantic anglers (and many are tagged when released) but are commonly kept in other places, especially off Mexico and Central America. They do have commercial significance in many parts of their range and are heavily exploited.

Identification. The sailfish is dark blue on top, brown blue laterally, and silvery white on the belly; the upper jaw is elongated in the form of a spear. This species' outstanding feature is the long, high first dorsal fin, which has 37 to 49 total elements; it is slate or cobalt blue with many black spots. The second dorsal fin is very small, with six to eight rays. The single, prominent lateral line is curved over the pectoral fin and otherwise straight along the median line of the flanks. The bill is longer than that of the spearfish *(see),* usually a little more than twice the length of the elongated lower jaw. The vent is just forward of the first anal fin. The sides often have pale, bluish gray vertical bars or rows or spots.

Although sailfish look like similar-size white marlin *(see: marlin, white)* and blue marlin *(see: marlin, blue),* they are readily distinguished by their large sail-like dorsal fin.

Size/Age. Sportfishing records for sailfish have long been maintained by the International Game Fish Association (IGFA) according to their Atlantic and Indo-Pacific distribution; the all-tackle world record for Atlantic fish is a 141-pounder caught off Angola in 1994; its counterpart in the Pacific is a 221-pounder caught off Ecuador in 1947. Fish from 20 to 50 or 60 pounds are commonly caught off the eastern U.S., and fish from 50 to 100 pounds are common in many places in the Pacific. They can exceed 10 feet in length.

Distribution/Habitat. Sailfish occur worldwide in tropical and temperate waters of the Atlantic, Indian, and Pacific Oceans. They are pelagic and migratory in warm offshore waters, although they may migrate into warm nearshore areas in parts of their range. In the eastern Pacific, sailfish range from Baja California, Mexico, to Peru, and in the western Atlantic from Massachusetts to Brazil. They are most common in warm waters along the edges of the Gulf Stream.

Life history/Behavior. Like other pelagic species that spawn in the open sea, sailfish produce large numbers of eggs, perhaps 4 to 5 million. These are fertilized in the open water, where they float with plankton until hatching. Sailfish grow rapidly and reportedly can attain 4 to 5 feet in length in their first year. They reportedly swim at speeds approaching 68 mph, making them the swiftest short-distance gamefish. Sailfish may form schools or small groups of from 3 to 30 individuals and sometimes travel in loose aggregations spread over a wide area. They appear to feed mostly in midwater along the edges of reefs or current eddies.

Food and feeding habits. Sailfish eat squid, octopus, mackerel, tuna, jacks, herring, ballyhoo, needlefish, flyingfish, mullet, and other small fish. They feed on the surface or at mid-depths.

Angling. Fishing methods for this species are similar to those for other billfish, although lighter tackle is more appropriate. Fishing methods include trolling with strip baits, whole mullet or ballyhoo, plastic offshore trolling lures, and trolling feathers or spoons. Another option is live-bait fishing with or without kites, using jacks, mullet, and other small natural baits. Sailfish are usually caught in depths exceeding 6 fathoms but are occasionally caught in lesser depths and even from ocean piers where currents and baitfish bring this species near shore. Generally, however, they are pursued in clear, blue offshore water and are located on or near the surface.

The spectacular jumping of the sailfish makes it a superb light-tackle quarry, as this leaping and a generally small size prevent it from having long-term stamina. Spinning and baitcasting rods with 12- through 30-pound line are standard, and fly gear is very effective with bait-and-switch *(see)* tactics.

See: Big-Game Fishing; Billfish; Billfish on Fly Tackle; Offshore Fishing.

SALINITY

The total amount of inorganic minerals or salts dissolved in a kilogram of seawater. Rain, snowfall, and the inflow of rivers dilute seawater and lower salinity; evaporation and freezing increase salinity. Other factors that may affect salinity at a given time and place include wind, wave motion, and ocean currents. These elements cause vertical and horizontal mixing.

The average salinity of seawater is 35 parts per thousand (35 pounds of salt per 1,000 pounds of seawater), which is 220 times saltier than fresh lake water. Concentrations as high as 40 parts per thousand have been observed in the Red Sea and the Persian Gulf. Salinities are much less than average in coastal waters, in the polar seas, and near the mouths of large rivers.

The salinity of seawater may affect the availability of species, because some gamefish are much more tolerant of low salinity or variable salinity.

See: Brackish Water.

SALMON, AMAGO *Oncorhynchus rhodurus.*
Other names—Japanese: *amago, biwamasu.*

This small member of the Salmonidae family is one of two species of Pacific salmon *(see: salmon, Pacific)* that occur only in Asia and the western Pacific. It is closely related to masu salmon *(O. masou; see: salmon, masu),* and there are diverging ichthyological opinions about whether the two are the same; they are currently considered separate species. Compounding the matter is the existence of anadromous and freshwater versions of both species. Technically, the word "amago" refers to the anadromous or stream-dwelling version, *O. rhodurus macrostomus;* the nonanadromous and permanently freshwater-dwelling version is *O. rhodurus rhodurus,* which in Japan is known as *biwamasu.* Thus, "amago" refers to the seagoing salmon and "biwamasu" to the freshwater dweller, although the word "amago" is often used interchangeably to refer to both.

Both amago and biwamasu are small, the former being half the size of the latter on average, and

generally less than 10 inches long. Their distribution in Japan is extremely limited, ranging from the Tokyo Bay area southwesterly along the Pacific coast of Honshu Island to the northern tip of Kyushu Island, including Shikoku Island. Most amago salmon remain in rivers for their full life span, but some are anadromous, and most of the latter remain in bays and inlets rather than wandering through the open ocean. Those that migrate to the ocean spend only six months there. Spawning in coastal rivers occurs in spring. Amago were reportedly introduced unsuccessfully in Germany.

SALMON, ATLANTIC *Salmo salar.*
Other names for sea-run fish—grilse, grilt, fiddler, Kennebec salmon; Danish and Norwegian: *laks;* Dutch: *zalm;* Finnish: *lohi;* French: *saumon Atlantique, saumon d'eau douce;* German: *lachs, las, salm;* Italian: *salmo, salmone;* Japanese: *sake masu-rui;* Portuguese: *salmao;* Russian: *losos;* Spanish: *salmón del Atlantico;* Swedish: *lax.*

Names for post-spawn adult fish—black salmon, slink, kelt.

Names for salmon living entirely in freshwater—landlocked salmon, ouananiche, grayling, lake Atlantic salmon, Sebago salmon; French: *ouananiche.*

Atlantic salmon are possibly the most important single species of fish in a historical and an economic sense, having been esteemed since the days of the Romans and being mentioned even in the Magna Carta, not to mention the high price that fishing on a beat of prime Atlantic salmon river fetches. The only salmon in the Salmonidae family that occurs in the Atlantic Ocean and its tributaries, the Atlantic salmon has been coveted for its excellent flesh since recorded history. Likewise, anglers since before Izaak Walton's time have known it for its acrobatics when caught, which gave rise to its name *salar,* derived from the Latin word *salio,* meaning leaper.

Confusion sometimes arises because the Atlantic salmon is classified as a member of the *Salmo* genus, which consists of various trout species, rather than the *Oncorhynchus* genus, which includes all seven Pacific salmon species. Despite the confusion, this system is unlikely to change. The name "salmon" arose in Europe and originally referred to the Atlantic salmon. New World settlers carried the name with them from the Old World and applied it not only to the Atlantic salmon in eastern North America, which was identical to the species in Europe, but also to the similar-bodied fish of western North America.

Although it has been proposed that the name Atlantic salmon be changed to end confusion concerning its taxonomical relationship to trout, this name is deeply rooted in history and has been published in the literature worldwide. The fish is broadly regulated under the name Atlantic salmon

S

Atlantic Salmon

S

as well, and it is reasoned that a name change might cause greater confusion and be an injustice to the species with which the name "salmon" originated.

Ironically, the Atlantic salmon is like some members of the Pacific salmon group in that it has both anadromous and freshwater forms. The former migrate from freshwater streams to the ocean and then return to those streams to spawn, whereas the latter remain in freshwater all their lives. Called landlocked salmon or ouananiche in North America, the freshwater form is the same species as the anadromous Atlantic salmon and shares identical characteristics, except that the freshwater fish is smaller. Landlocked salmon occurred naturally in some large lakes that were cut off from saltwater many thousands of years ago. In modern times, stocking has spread the landlocked form to many other waters. Landlocked Atlantics are also fine gamefish and excellent food fish.

Atlantic salmon have suffered greatly throughout large portions of their range due to dams, other habitat alteration, pollution, and overfishing, especially by commercial interests. Some stocks of sea-run and landlocked Atlantic salmon have become extinct, and many are endangered or threatened. As a consequence of industrial and agricultural development, for example, most of the runs native to New England have been extirpated.

Concern for Atlantic salmon accelerated after the mid-1960s. Until that time, little was known about the life of the Atlantic salmon in the sea. Then, a common feeding ground for Atlantic salmon was discovered off Greenland and exploited by commercial fishermen. Another feeding ground was later located off Norway. The ensuing commercial pressure and the return of these fish to birth rivers they found impassable or unsuited to spawning accelerated the decline.

Atlantics have been reared in hatcheries for decades to provide smolts for river stocking programs, and although this has been of limited success, it has not proven an antidote to greater problems and has also resulted in stocks with different, and often lesser, genetic adaptability to specific rivers. Atlantic salmon are also commercially farmed in large ocean pens. This is a rapidly growing industry in some locations, one that supplies many salmon to market. Some concern does exist, however, regarding escapees and their possible interaction with natural stocks.

As a gamefish, the Atlantic salmon is showy when it leaps out of the water, capable of making strong runs up and down (usually the latter) swift-flowing rivers when hooked, and often a challenge to entice. Landlocked fish are known for long runs and superior fighting ability, and they are widely sought by anglers in lakes and rivers. The reddish orange flesh of both, but especially of the sea-run fish, is excellent to eat and is highly valued when fresh or either hot- or cold-smoked.

Identification.   Compared to the size of its body, a mature Atlantic salmon has a small head. Its body is long and slim, and in adults the caudal or tail fin is nearly square. Individuals that return to spawn prematurely (called grilse) are mostly males and have a slightly forked tail. While in the sea, the Atlantic salmon is dark blue on the top of its head and back; its sides are a shiny silver, and the belly is white. The fins are dark, and there are numerous black marks in the shape of an X or Y on its head and along its body above the lateral line.

When the fish enters freshwater to spawn, it gradually loses its metallic shine and becomes dull brown or yellowish. Many, particularly males, are splotched with red or have large black patches on the body, and may look a lot like the brown trout *(Salmo trutta),* their closest relative. Often brown trout may have circles, or halos, around some of their spots, and the spotting may be heavier than in the Atlantic salmon, extending onto the lower half of the sides and the fins, including the adipose fin. The spots do not normally take the form of Xs or Ys. At spawning time the males are further distinguished by their greatly elongated hooked jaws that meet only at the tips; the fins become thicker, and a heavy coat of slime covers the body. Post-spawn fish appear very dark, leading to the name "black salmon."

In a general sense, the body shape of an Atlantic salmon is similar to that of a trout and is distinguished from salmon and trout of the genus *Oncorhynchus* by coloration, size, and location of occurrence, among other characteristics.

Landlocked Atlantics look the same as their anadromous counterparts, although spawning fish may be darker.

Size/Age. The Atlantic salmon can live for eight years and is the second largest of all salmon. It is capable of attaining weights to 80 pounds, although no such sizes have been recorded in decades. Unofficial historical reports talk of specimens weighing as much as 100 pounds. The largest known sport-caught fish is the all-tackle world record, a specimen weighing 79 pounds, 2 ounces when taken from Norway's Tana River in 1928. Most specimens today weigh 20 pounds or less, and fish exceeding 30 pounds are rare, even in the better waters. Historically, the biggest fish came from Europe. In North America, the largest known Atlantic salmon was a 55-pounder caught in the Grand Cascapedia River, Quebec.

Landlocked Atlantic salmon do not grow to such ultimate sizes, although they are capable of growing to between 30 and 40 pounds. A 22-pound, 11-ounce specimen from Lobstick Lake in Labrador is often cited as the largest sport-caught landlocked salmon, but these fish historically grew to 45 pounds in New York's Lake Ontario, and modern introductions in that lake and in Lake Michigan have produced numerous fish in excess of 30 pounds. A $35\frac{1}{2}$-pound specimen was once taken from Sebago Lake in Maine. Lake Vanern in Sweden, and some Russian lakes, have reportedly grown landlocks to 40 pounds. In most places, the average size is under 10 pounds and closer to 5 pounds.

Distribution. The anadromous Atlantic salmon is native to the North Atlantic Ocean and coastal rivers in North America and Europe. Its endemic range in the western Atlantic was from Long Island Sound and the Housatonic River in Connecticut north to Ungava Bay, Quebec, including the Gulf of St. Lawrence and the Labrador Sea; in the central North Atlantic, its range included southwestern Greenland and most of Iceland; in the eastern Atlantic, it ranged from the Dour River in Portugal north to the Kara River in Russia, including the British Isles, the North and Baltic Seas, the Norwegian Sea, and the Barents and White Seas.

In North America, landlocked Atlantic salmon were endemic to many lakes in eastern Canada and Maine, as well as to Lakes Champlain and Ontario; in Europe they existed in Norway, Sweden, and northwestern Russia.

Although anadromous Atlantic salmon still inhabit much of their original range, some stocks are no longer of the original genetic strain, which was wiped out. They therefore consist of introduced or augmented anadromous fish. Anadromous Atlantic salmon have been extirpated from most of their more southerly range on both sides of the Atlantic, a victim of industrial growth, dams, pollution, and other factors. In North America, numerous self-supporting runs of anadromous Atlantics exist in Canada, especially Quebec, but also in Newfoundland, New Brunswick, and Nova Scotia, although the size of these stocks is severely depleted. Self-supporting runs of Atlantic salmon in the United States are found only in Maine. Restoration efforts have been attempted in various rivers and presently continue in the Connecticut, Pawcatuck, Merrimack, and Penobscot Rivers of New England, which is a far cry from the 28 New England rivers that once contained this species.

Although some original landlocked populations have also been extirpated, landlocked Atlantic salmon have been introduced to many waters where they did not originally exist, and reintroduced to waters where they once existed. Landlocked Atlantics have been widely introduced to the Great Lakes, where the larger specimens exist today, and are widely dispersed in eastern Quebec, Newfoundland, and Labrador.

Habitat. Anadromous Atlantic salmon spend most of their lives in the ocean, ascending coastal rivers to spawn. They are found in freshwater only during their spawning runs, after engaging in extensive and complex migrations throughout their range by relying on their acute sense of homing for navigation. In coastal rivers, they primarily inhabit deep runs and pools, and seldom favor fast water or riffles.

Although some landlocked salmon may exist in rivers all year, the great majority spend most of their lives in the open water of lakes, ascending tributaries to spawn. In rivers, they inhabit deep runs and pools. In lakes they stay in cooler, deeper levels, where baitfish are abundant.

Life history/Behavior. Spawning usually occurs in gravel bottoms at the head of riffles or the tail of a pool, and in the evening or at night. The female looks for places where the water seeps down into clean gravel. The female digs a nest, or redd, 6 to 14 inches deep in the gravel by turning on her side, flipping her tail upward, and pulling the gravel up until a hole is excavated. After the female and male spawn in the redd, the 5- to 7-millimeter eggs are buried with gravel by the female. The whole process is repeated several times until the female has shed all of her eggs. Females produce an average of 700 eggs per pound of body weight. After spawning, the adults, which are then called kelts, usually drop downstream to rest in a pool.

Unlike Pacific salmon *(see: salmon, Pacific)*, the adults do not die after spawning. Exhausted and thin, they often return to sea immediately before winter or remain in the stream until spring. Some will survive to spawn a second time, but few survive to spawn three or more times.

Salmon eggs develop slowly (roughly 110 days) over the winter while water flowing through the nest keeps the eggs clean and oxygenated. In most rivers, the eggs survive well and are protected from freezing or silt. The eggs hatch in the spring, usually April,

S

S

and the young salmon, called alevins, remain buried in the gravel for up to 5 weeks while they absorb their large yolk sac. Many young fish are lost at this stage. Over the winter, silt and sand often move into the nest and can trap the young fish. If they survive this stage, the young salmon that emerge are about 1 inch long in May or June. During this freshwater stage, before they migrate to sea, they are known as parr. Salmon parr are territorial, feed during the day, and live in shallow riffle areas 10 to 26 inches deep that have gravel, rubble, rock, or boulder bottoms.

After roughly three years (but within two to eight years) in freshwater, salmon parr become smolts and prepare for life in saltwater. In the spring, these parr become slimmer and turn silvery. During the spring runoff, as water temperatures rise, smolts form schools and migrate downstream at night. It is during this downstream migration that smolts "learn," or become imprinted with, the characteristics of their particular river, which will play a role in their eventual return.

Atlantic salmon will stay at sea (or in a lake) for one or more years and are known to travel long distances. Many salmon from Canada's Maritime rivers travel as far as the western coast of Greenland, where the waters are rich in food. Grilse, or salmon that spend only one year at sea before returning to freshwater, are smaller, weighing from 3 to 6 pounds; most are males. Salmon that return after two winters usually weigh from 6 to 15 pounds. Salmon that remain in the sea for two years or longer before making their first spawning run become the largest, heaviest individuals. Rivers with runs of fish that spend more than two years in the ocean, therefore, are known for larger salmon. Some Atlantics may make a spawning run only once or twice during their lifetime of roughly eight years; others will spawn three or four times, returning in consecutive years to the same spawning grounds, and these are usually the largest fish of all.

Atlantic salmon that are ready to spawn begin moving upriver from late spring through fall. The exact timing varies according to the particular river and the distance the fish travel upstream, but these spawning runs are surprisingly consistent and occur at the same time each year for each river. Salmon populations are often spoken of as "early run" or "late run," and these are relative, overall designations. In some places, the spawning areas are actually close to the sea, not far above the high-tide level. In other streams, the spawners may travel long distances, as much as 312 miles upstream; they are known for their ability to leap small waterfalls and other obstacles. During this journey, the salmon does not eat. Landlocked salmon living in lakes move up into tributary streams to spawn in a similar manner, although they usually don't do so until late summer.

The early spawners appear in streams in spring and are usually the largest fish. These individuals have the firmest flesh and are most sought after. They are followed soon by the grilse and then by more mature fish, the runs slacking off during the hot summer months but increasing again in early autumn. Early-run fish do not move upstream rapidly; their gonads are not yet well enough developed for the actual spawning act. Sometimes the late arrivals catch up with them, and they reach their destination at the same time. Spawning occurs from October through December.

Large river systems may have several runs, which reflects different races heading to their own tributaries. In a few rivers, especially in northerly regions, some Atlantics enter rivers in late summer, fall, or early winter, a year before they spawn.

Food.   In rivers, salmon parr feed mainly on the immature and adult stages of aquatic insects. In the ocean, salmon grow rapidly, feeding on crustaceans and other fish such as smelt, alewives, herring, capelin, mackerel, and cod. Landlocked salmon in lakes eat pelagic freshwater fish, primarily smelt and alewives. Neither feeds during its upstream spawning migration, which leads to endless curiosity and speculation as to why it strikes a lure or fly during this time.

Angling (for Atlantic and landlocked salmon). Much has been written about salmon fishing and the intricacies thereof, and even a volume such as this cannot do justice to the full scope of fishing techniques and strategies for both the sea-run and freshwater fish in their respective environments, so the following information is intended as an overview.

It is during their limited spawning run that seagoing Atlantics are pursued by anglers in rivers; there is no ocean sportfishing for this species in North America, although Scandinavian anglers practice ocean fishing for this species in the Baltic Sea. The average sea-winter fish weighs less than 15 pounds, and one weighing more than that is considered large in most rivers. Nevertheless, smaller fish fight extraordinarily well, and the possibility of landing older 20- to 30-pound fish exists in some rivers.

Atlantic and landlocked salmon hug the river bottom, resting in pools and deep-water sections. They are not usually caught in the fast-water reaches, although they will frequent the head and tail of pools, and slick-water runs. A common tactic is to start fishing above the head of a pool or run, methodically working down through a stretch, casting down and across and letting the fly swing at the end of each cast. Most fish are caught when the fly makes its swing or hangs momentarily in the current at the end of the swing.

Fly fishing is the angling method by law or tradition in most of North America for seagoing Atlantic salmon. These fish usually hold shallower than other salmon, making sight fishing—casting to a specific fish that has been seen rather than casting blindly for unobserved fish as is usually done when angling for coho or chinook salmon—

a favored method. Some waters have restrictions on weighted hooks or flies to minimize accidental or deliberate foul hooking of fish.

Wet flies in various colorful patterns and sizes are popular for Atlantic salmon fishing, and the larger flies are generally reserved for fast, high rivers. Dry flies work at times, too, which is an anomaly considering the nonfeeding disposition of these fish; the dries used, however, such as Bombers, are large flies typically tied with tightly packed deer hair.

Atlantics may take on the first, fiftieth, or one-hundredth cast, acting out of reflex or annoyance, and they may be put down easily or be relatively undisturbed by the angler's presence and activities. Unlike other salmon in rivers, Atlantics and land-locks are prone to jump high and often, in addition to making long, demanding runs. Long rods and reels with plenty of backing are required. Standard fly tackle consists of an 8- or 9-weight rod equipped with a floating fly line and a reel with 200 yards of 20- or 30-pound-test backing. Leader length should match rod length, or be slightly shorter. A sinking fly line or sink-tip fly line is not used. A 9-foot rod with 9-weight line is a standard outfit in North America. This setup accommodates the bulk of some salmon flies; however, longer rods, including two-handed versions, are popular in many European rivers.

Long casts in the 70- to 100-foot-plus range are the norm on many Atlantic salmon rivers, although they aren't always a necessity. Getting a good drift on the fly, mending it where necessary, and at times even riffling it across the surface gently, are important aspects of presentation. The evening and early-morning hours are good times, and overcast days bode well for daylong fishing, although there is no guarantee on such matters. When pools are fished by a number of anglers, it is customary to take turns; anglers slowly work their way downstream from the head of the pool, with one angler beginning at the top of the pool as the previous angler approaches the end of it.

The principal method of pursuing landlocked salmon in lakes is trolling. Most activity occurs in the spring, after ice out and until these fish move deep. Although some salmon are caught when the ice is breaking up and water temperatures are in the 39° to 42°F range, better action doesn't begin until the water hits the mid 40s. Landlocks are caught from the surface to 20 feet deep at this time and are found near shore over relatively shallow bottom or in open areas over deep water.

As the surface temperature increases, landlocks are more likely to be found near tributaries if they attract large spawning runs of smelt, or inshore where schools of smelt or spawning alewives may be located. Water temperatures then are in the low to mid-50s. This activity takes place in May and throughout June, but by mid- to late June in a normal year the surface water is warming, and

A landlocked Atlantic salmon is released on a river in Labrador.

landlocks will move to deeper water and locate in the thermocline, roughly staying in 52° to 57°F water and roaming as widely as the size of the lake and water temperature zones will allow. They are usually hardest to locate and catch at this time.

The traditional and still widely practiced method of landlocked salmon trolling employs a fly rod and a streamer fly. The rod is between 8 and 9 feet long and equipped with a large-capacity fly reel loaded with 100 yards of backing, a level sinking line, and a long leader. The leader is between 20 and 30 feet in length and usually 6 to 10 pounds in strength. A streamer fly is tied to the end, and sometimes a split shot or two is added to the leader. The rod is often held in the angler's hand and kept parallel to the water, and it is jerked backward frequently to give the fly a darting motion.

Another traditional method is to use a fly rod or conventional rod with a levelwind reel and lead-core line, fishing a spoon or fly at the business end. The favored rods are long, and anglers pulsate them as they do fly rods. Downrigger and sideplaner fishing have increased on the landlocked salmon scene, especially where spoons and plugs are preferred. These are fished in conventional manners.

Lure selection should follow the baitfish patterns in a given lake. Smelt are the foremost, and preferred, landlocked salmon food. Alewives are a major forage in some locales. Elsewhere, cisco, shiners, and yellow perch make up part of their lake diet. Smelt are usually the bread-and-butter prey, and most landlocked salmon lures are meant to imitate smelt. These lures include minnow-imitating plugs in straight and jointed versions from 4 to 6 inches in length, long thin spoons, and single or tandem streamer flies.

The best fishing, especially in spring, is often in the first few hours of the day, but a late-afternoon or evening flurry is common. Midday, particularly under bluebird conditions, is dubious. A relatively fast trolling speed is employed for landlocks, and whereas lines are usually set from 75 to 200 feet behind the boat on flatlines, and from 40 to 80 feet back on deep downriggers, some spring fish are literally caught in the prop wash.

SALMON, AUSTRALIAN

See: Kahawai.

SALMON, CHINOOK   *Oncorhynchus tshawytscha.*

Other names—king salmon, spring salmon, tyee, quinnat, tule, blackmouth, Sacramento River salmon, Columbia River salmon; French: *saumon chinook, saumon royal;* Japanese: *masunosuke.*

The chinook salmon is one of the most important sportfish and commercial fish in the world, especially, and historically, to the Pacific coast of North America, where this and other salmonids have long had great cultural and food significance. It is the largest member of the Salmonidae family, and both the largest and least-abundant member of the Pacific salmon genus *Oncorhynchus.* By nature an anadromous species, it can adapt to an entirely freshwater existence and has done so with such remarkable success in the Great Lakes of North America that it has formed the backbone of an enormous and extremely valuable sportfishery there, becoming one of the greatest fisheries transplant/management/revitalization projects of all time.

Pacific stocks of chinook, as well as other Pacific salmonids, however, have suffered greatly throughout large portions of their range due to dams, other habitat alteration, pollution, and excessive commercial fishing. Some chinook runs in the Pacific Northwest are threatened or endangered.

As a gamefish, the chinook is not flashy; it rarely leaps out of the water, unlike coho salmon *(see: salmon, coho)* and Atlantic salmon *(see: salmon, Atlantic),* but it is bulldog strong and has great staying power. Fresh river migrants are more than a handful for many anglers, and large fish in all environs are not only tenacious but also greatly prized. The sea-run chinook is the only Pacific salmon in which the meat can be regularly either red or white. Although white meat is rare, red meat commands a higher price in any Pacific salmon species. It is sold fresh, fresh-frozen, canned, or smoked, and has an excellent taste in all forms.

Identification.   The body of the chinook salmon is elongate and somewhat compressed. The head is conical. For most of its life, the chinook's color is bluish to dark gray above, becoming silvery on the sides and belly. There are black spots on the back, upper sides, top of the head, and all the fins, including both the top and bottom half of the tail fin. Coloration changes during upstream migration; spawning chinook salmon range from red to copper to olive brown to almost black, depending on location and degree of maturation, and they undergo a radical metamorphosis. Males are more deeply colored than the females and are distinguished by their "ridgeback" condition and by their hooked nose or upper jaw, known as a kype. The young have 6 to 12 long, wide, well-developed parr marks, which are bisected by the lateral line, and no spots on the dorsal fin.

One distinguishing feature of the chinook is its black mouth and gums. The very similar looking coho salmon has a black mouth but white gums, except in the Great Lakes population, in which the gums may be gray or black.

Size.   This species is the largest of all Pacific salmon; individual fish commonly exceed 30 pounds in Alaska and British Columbia and 20

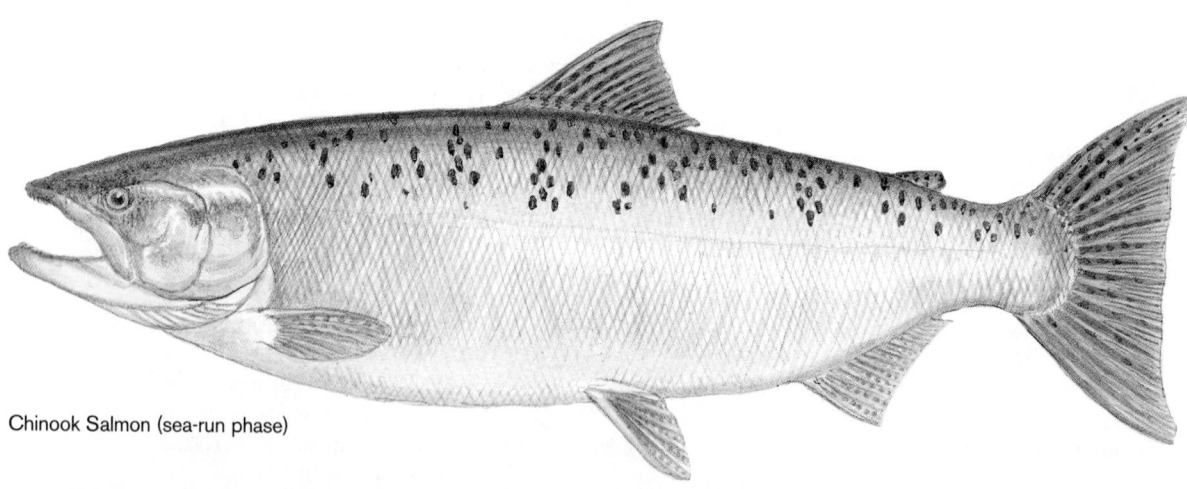

Chinook Salmon (sea-run phase)

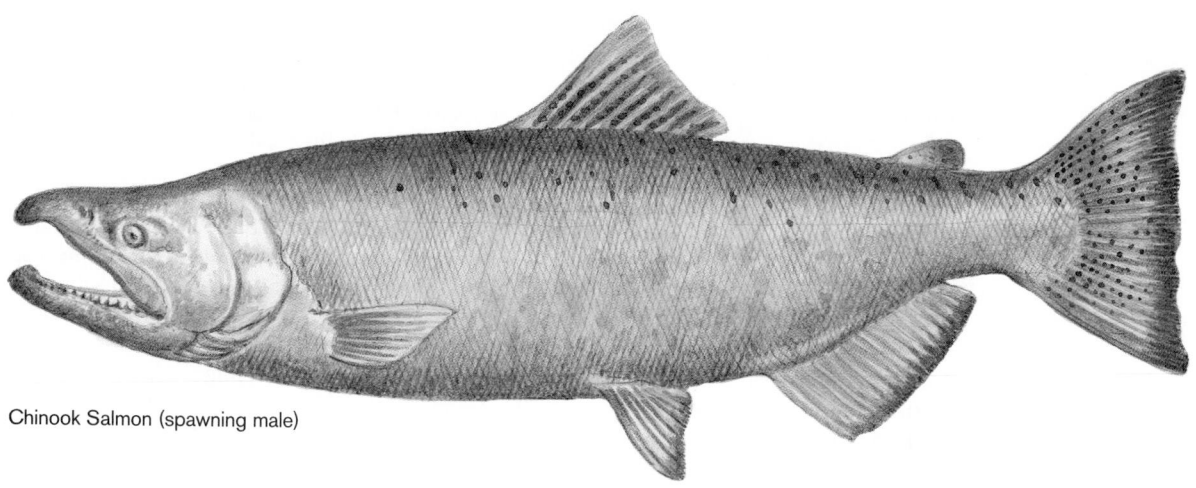

Chinook Salmon (spawning male)

pounds elsewhere. A 126-pound chinook salmon taken in a fish trap near Petersburg, Alaska, in 1949 is the largest known specimen. The all-tackle world sportfishing record is a 97-pound, 4-ounce fish caught in Alaska's Kenai River in 1986. Chinook transplanted to the Great Lakes commonly weigh from 15 to 30 pounds, and the largest specimens recorded weigh under 50 pounds.

Distribution. The chinook salmon is endemic to the Pacific Ocean and to the Bering Sea, the Okhotsk Sea, the Sea of Japan, and most of the rivers that flow into these waters. On the Asian coast, they occur naturally from Hokkaido in northern Japan to the Anadyr River in the former USSR, and generally from San Luis Obispo County in Southern California to the Chukchi Sea area of Alaska; the greatest concentrations are along the British Columbia coast and Alaska. In Alaska, where the chinook is the state fish, it is abundant from the southeastern panhandle to the Yukon River. Major populations return to the Yukon, Kuskokwim, Nushagak, Susitna, Kenai, Copper, Alsek, Taku, and Stikine Rivers. Important runs also occur in many smaller streams. The chinook is rare in the Arctic Ocean. Most sea-run chinook are encountered by anglers along the coasts and in spawning rivers. Scientists estimate that there are in excess of a thousand spawning populations of chinook salmon on the North American coast. An uncertain but much lower number inhabits the Asian Coast.

Since as early as 1872, the chinook salmon has been introduced into other waters around the world, including the Great Lakes and Atlantic and Gulf states in the United States, some areas of Central and South America, Europe, and the South Pacific. These transplanted populations apparently failed due to an inability to maintain self-perpetuating spawning levels, with the exceptions of South Island in New Zealand, and to some degree in the Great Lakes of the U.S. (which experience minimal natural reproduction, although large populations are sustained by intensive

stocking). Anadromous chinook have returned to sea ranching operations in southern Chile as well. Transplanted and strictly freshwater-dwelling chinook are widely distributed throughout the Great Lakes and their tributaries in Canada and the U.S., with greatest concentrations in Lakes Michigan and Ontario; these fish also exist in some large inland lakes in the U.S., and in other countries.

Life history/Behavior. Like all species of Pacific salmon, chinook are anadromous. They hatch in freshwater rivers, spend part of their life in the ocean, and then spawn in freshwater. Those chinook that have been transplanted to strictly freshwater environments (as in the Great Lakes) hatch in tributary rivers and streams, spend part of their life in the open water of the lake, and then return to tributaries to spawn. In both cases, all chinook die after spawning.

Sea-run chinook salmon may become sexually mature from their second through seventh year; as a result, fish in any spawning run may vary greatly in size. For example, a mature three-year-old in Alaska will probably weigh less than 4 pounds, whereas a mature seven-year-old may exceed 50 pounds. Females tend to be older than males at maturity. In many spawning runs, males outnumber females in all but the six- and seven-year age groups. These life spans and maturities may vary with different coastal runs of chinook as well as with freshwater transplants; in the latter case, they usually live no more than four to five years and are much larger at two and three years. Small chinook that mature after spending only one winter in the ocean or lake are commonly referred to as "jacks" and are usually males.

The period of migration into spawning rivers and streams varies greatly. Alaskan streams normally receive a single run of chinook salmon from May through July. Streams throughout the Great Lakes primarily receive chinook from late August into October, but there are some spring runs.

Chinook salmon often make extensive freshwater spawning migrations to reach their home streams on some of the larger coastal river systems. Yukon River spawners bound for the extreme headwaters in Yukon Territory, Canada, will travel more than 2,000 river miles during a 60-day period. In the Great Lakes, however, some migrating salmon are restricted to only a few miles of river (and do not spawn successfully in that stretch).

Chinook salmon do not feed during their freshwater spawning migration, so their condition deteriorates gradually during the spawning run. During that time, they use stored body materials for energy and for the development of reproductive products. Each female deposits from 3,000 to 14,000 eggs (usually in the lower range) in several gravel nests, or redds, which she excavates in relatively deep, moving water. They usually hatch in late winter or early spring, depending on time of spawning and water temperature. The newly hatched fish, called alevins, live in the gravel for several weeks until they gradually absorb the food in the attached yolk sac. These juveniles, called fry, wiggle up through the gravel by early spring. Most juvenile chinook salmon remain in their natal water until the following spring, when they migrate to the ocean in their second year of life. These seaward migrants are called smolts.

Scientific understanding of the distribution of chinook in the ocean is still sketchy. It has been speculated that most North American chinook do not wander more than 1,000 kilometers from their natal river, and that fish from western Alaska streams roam farther than others from North America. Large numbers are found relatively close to their respective shores, and also in distant offshore waters, and their depth preferences vary.

In the Great Lakes, chinook migrate many miles from their natal water, apparently in relation to the abundance of forage and appropriate water temperature. Thus, as surface levels warm, the colder water preferred by both salmon and their forage is found deeper (or shallow but farther offshore, depending on wind and other factors). The fish wander considerable distances, and their location varies regularly.

Food and feeding habits. Juvenile chinook in freshwater feed on plankton, then later eat insects. In the ocean, they eat a variety of organisms, including herring, pilchards, sand lance, squid, and crustaceans. Salmon grow rapidly in the ocean and often double their weight during a single summer season. Likewise, chinook that live entirely in freshwater feed on plankton and insects as juveniles, and pelagic freshwater baitfish in the lakes. Alewives and smelt are the primary food items, and, in fact, chinook and other salmonids were introduced to the Great Lakes and other inland waters especially to help control massive populations of baitfish, which they consume voraciously. Thus, they quickly develop large, stocky bodies.

Angling (for chinook and coho). Because coho and chinook salmon inhabit a variety of environments, anglers practice multiple fishing methods to pursue them. Overall, angling for these fish is far more prevalent in freshwater—either in rivers when the spawning run occurs or in the open water of the Great Lakes—than in saltwater. Identifying habitat, structure, and so forth, as one might do for many other fish, is less critical when targeting Pacific salmon than when enticing nonfeeding river fish to strike through careful presentation, or locating the right depth and temperature of open water in which salmon schools will be located. Essentially, then, open-water and river fishing techniques are the primary angling methods.

The coastal fishery for sea-run salmon in Pacific waters primarily occurs in nearshore, tidewater, and estuary environs. The favored angling methods are trolling with spinners and cut herring, trolling with flies (mostly for coho), mooching (see), some jigging, and some live-bait fishing. The most opportune time to pursue these fish is when they have returned from their sea wandering and are gathering in the vicinity of coastal rivers, waiting for rains to send new water out the rivers and signal the beginning of the "run." Salmon in the midst of their life cycle—not ready to spawn and not migrating to natal waters—are rarely sought far at sea, especially by small-boat anglers. The great travel distances are inconvenient, and because of the deep-wandering nature of salmon, finding them is akin to locating a needle in a haystack. Confronted by these obstacles, coastal anglers wait for sea-run fish to come close to shore during their migration toward coastal rivers.

When pursuing chinook in the ocean, anglers principally troll dead baits or artificial lures. Occasionally, they offer live baits or use metal jigs while stillfishing or drifting. Chinook salmon normally stay well beneath the ocean's surface, making a heavy weight or downrigger necessary to maintain a trolled bait at the desired depth. Chinook favor depths between 40 and 250 or more feet, depending on location, temperature, currents, and other factors. Channels, passes, and straits that funnel current are popular sites, particularly along current seams and where a back eddy exists. In northern areas, steep rocky shores—near the mainland or islands—that are well washed by current and tidal movement are prime spots; here, anglers offer a cut herring, fished very close to the bottom. Fishing in low light, especially at sunset and at dusk, is often more productive than during bright midday light, especially for chinook. Surface trolling with light tackle for coho salmon is possible when the fish are congregated on or near shoals where food is abundant. Streamer flies are the main offering, trolled fairly fast over bull kelp beds so that the fly skips over the water.

Coho and chinook in the Great Lakes are widely pursued throughout the season in open water. They are inshore early in the season and ultimately seek out a water temperature of between 48° and

55°F, which occurs at the thermocline. The thermocline is usually deeper as summer progresses; its depth changes, however, due to shifting winds. Coho tend to remain closer to shore than do chinook, although the depth and location of each species is a highly variable factor. Both gather in schools and traverse great distances as they seek out desirable water conditions and alewives or smelt forage.

Because freshwater salmon migrate extensively and exist at varied levels in open water, particularly below 30 feet and as much as 70 to 120 feet deep in the summer, anglers must typically search and fish deep in open water where there are few, or no, shoals or islands. Thus, freshwater tactics differ considerably from the tactics practiced in coastal fishing for sea-run salmon. Various trolling techniques are the primary focus, and among them downrigger fishing is most popular. Some drift fishing and limited jigging are also done.

Although open-water salmon fishing is essentially a boating proposition, the land-bound angler can score on open-water salmon in the spring and fall, and occasionally in the winter. Spring is the best all-around time for salmon in the Great Lakes. When the fish are in close to shore seeking out the most comfortable water temperature (influenced by wind direction and the introduction of warm tributary waters), they are just as accessible and vulnerable to shore-based anglers as they are to boaters. The only edge boaters have at this time is mobility, as they can cover a large expanse of water. Shore fishing close to the tributaries is generally best, as this is where the warmer water is. At this time, breakwaters, piers, beaches, and other access points become jammed with casters equipped with long rods. As the fish move out, shore fishing becomes markedly less productive. It increases in productivity again in late summer and early fall, when many salmon return to migrate upriver.

Chinook and coho salmon anglers seldom practice live-bait fishing in freshwater, principally due to the wandering nature of the quarry and the prodigious amount of available natural forage, including alewives, smelt, herring, and anchovies. Under these circumstances, a hooked offering often goes unrecognized. In Pacific waters, cut herring is extremely effective and has been used much more in recent years inland. Particularly effective baits, salmon eggs are used for drift fishing in coastal rivers and Great Lakes tributaries; they are usually fished in gobs or egg sacks and are sometimes combined with crayfish meat or tails, frequently with just a pencil or ball lead rig, or with a float.

Tributary fishing is the predominant Great Lakes method of catching chinook and coho salmon in late summer and fall. Fish that have just entered rivers or have been in them only a short while may still exhibit a feeding urge, striking a lure or fly as a conditioned, reflexive act. But the longer they are in the river, the less this is so. The same is

A chinook salmon from the coastal waters of Rivers Inlet, British Columbia.

true in coastal rivers where sea-run fish are migrating, although these fish have a much longer distance to run and their behavioral timing is more spread out. None of these fish actually feed, however, so imitating a natural food source in appearance or action is unnecessary. Getting the attention of a fish that will aggressively swipe at your offering is the whole game.

Often it can be difficult to get river fish to strike any offering, and it is usually vital to make the presentation right in front of the salmon. A precise presentation, therefore, is of foremost importance; the trick is to position the bait or lure on the bottom and directly ahead of the fish.

Long rods, medium-heavy lines, and small offerings are the main outfits for coho and chinook fishing in small to medium streams. Eggs, spinners, spoons, and wobbling plugs all have devotees. Fly fishing is more popular in western waters than in the Great Lakes, primarily because the rivers in the former are bigger and longer than those in the latter, affording a greater expanse of fishing opportunities and somewhat less crowding. Shallower sections, however, provide the best opportunity for anglers using fly tackle and light spinning or baitcasting tackle. Bright flies and fast-sinking fly lines (usually the high-density full-sink versions) get the nod.

Salmon hug the bottom, resting in pools and deep-water sections. They gather in the tail of a run, ahead of swifter water, and in holes and runs along deep-water banks. They are not usually caught in the fast-water reaches. Lures must be cast slightly upstream and quartered, drifting with the current to the end of the swing. Whatever the offering, it must bounce or swim along the bottom, and the right-size sinker is critically important: too little, and the offering never reaches the bottom and is totally ineffective; too much, and it drags in the current, acting unnaturally or hanging up repeatedly.

Much river salmon fishing is done by bank or wading anglers, but in large rivers, angling from boats for coho and chinook is not only practical but also effective. Nonfly anglers usually use wobbling plugs in the river more than they do other hardware, or they use salmon eggs or spawn sacks. Forward trolling is not a popular tactic, not least because of boat and angler traffic. Anchoring or controlled drifting via backtrolling (see) are the primary boat fishing methods. Those who anchor do so in or above selected pools, setting their lines out 50 to 75 feet behind the boat and allowing the plugs to work constantly in current, perhaps bouncing them back slowly and then retrieving to repeat the procedure.

In rivers, tackle ranges from 14- to 30-pound-test line, the latter used in narrow rivers and where heavy weights and big fish are encountered. Levelwind reels are preferred, and long (8- to 9-foot) rods are employed. Fly rods suitable for 9- and 10-weight lines with plenty of reel backing are necessary. In open-water trolling, 8- to 9-foot downrigger rods get the most play; for this method, levelwind reels are most popular, and line strength ranges from 12 to 20 pounds, although lighter line can be used.

See: Salmon, Pacific.

SALMON, CHUM   *Oncorhynchus keta.*

Other names—calico salmon, dog salmon, fall salmon, autumn salmon, chum, keta; French: *saumon keta;* Japanese: *sake, shake.*

The late spawning run of the chum salmon severely affects its popularity as a sportfish. In general, it is caught by anglers fishing for other Pacific salmon. In arctic, northwestern, and interior Alaska, this member of the Salmonidae family is an important year-round source of fresh and dried fish for subsistence and personal use, although elsewhere its flesh is not favored for human consumption. Overall, it is not as popular or as desirable as other Pacific salmon. The frequently used name dog salmon reportedly originates with its prevalent use as dog food among aboriginals.

The flesh is creamy white or pinkish to yellowish and the lowest of all salmon in fat content; it is sold fresh, frozen, dried/salted, smoked, and canned. After entering freshwater, chum salmon are most often prepared as a smoked product. The chum was formerly commercially cultured in Russia and used as dog food in Canada. The development of markets for fresh and frozen chum in Japan and northern Europe has increased the demand for these products.

Identification. In the ocean, the slender, somewhat compressed, chum salmon is metallic greenish blue on the back, silvery on the sides, and has a fine black speckling on the upper sides and back but no distinct black spots. Spawning males turn dark olive or grayish; blood-red coloring and vertical bars of green and purple reach up the sides, giving the fish its "calico" appearance. It develops the typical hooked snout of Pacific salmon, and the tips of the anal and pelvic fins are often white. The breeding male develops distinctly large front teeth, another explanation for the name dog salmon. The color of spawning females is essentially the same as that of males but is less vivid, with a dark horizontal band along the lateral line. Young fish are exceptionally slender and have 6 to 14 narrow, short parr marks along the sides, located mostly above the lateral line.

The chum salmon is difficult to distinguish from the sockeye (see: salmon, sockeye) and the coho salmon (see: salmon, coho), which are of similar size, without examining gills or caudal fin scale patterns; the chum salmon has fewer but larger gill rakers than do other salmon. The sockeye salmon also lacks the white marks on the fins, and the chum salmon is generally larger than the sockeye.

Size/Age. The chum salmon varies in size from 4 to more than 30 pounds, but the average weight is 10 to 15 pounds. Females are usually

A chum salmon from King Salmon, Alaska.

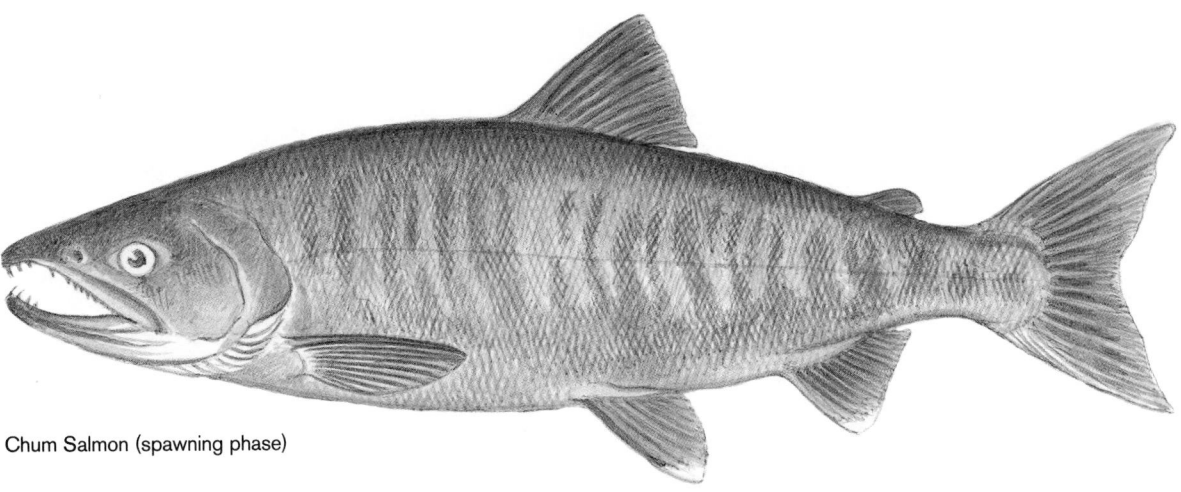

Chum Salmon (spawning phase)

smaller than males. These fish can reach 40 inches in length. The all-tackle world record is a 35-pounder from British Columbia. Chum salmon can live as long as seven years.

Distribution. Chum salmon are the most widely distributed of the Pacific salmon, native to the Pacific and Arctic Oceans, the Bering Sea, the Sea of Japan, and the Okhotsk Sea. They range south to about the Sacramento River in California and to the island of Kyushu in the Sea of Japan. In the north, they range east in the Arctic Ocean to the Mackenzie River in Canada and west to the Lena River in Siberia. In the Mackenzie, they travel all the way to the mouth of the Hay River and to the rapids below Forth Smith on the Slave River, entering both Great Bear and Great Slave Lakes and traveling through the Northwest Territories to the edge of Alberta.

Life history/Behavior. The chum salmon is an anadromous fish; with the exception of a few landlocked populations, chum salmon inhabit both ocean environments and coastal streams. Spawning takes place from ages 2 to 7, most commonly at age 4 and at a weight of 5 to 10 pounds. Like pink salmon *(see: salmon, pink)*, chum salmon are sometimes called "autumn salmon" or "fall salmon" because they are among the last salmon in the season to take their spawning run, entering river mouths after mid-June but reaching spawning grounds as late as November or December. Occasionally there is one run of chum salmon in summer and another in fall in the same river; the summer-spawn fish are smaller and less likely to swim far upstream. In general, they are not strong leapers, swimming upstream only as far as the first significant barrier, although some fish in the Yukon River have been known to travel more than 2,000 miles to spawn in the Yukon Territory. Chum salmon often spawn in the same places as pink salmon, such as small streams and intertidal zones and in small side channels. As many as 4,000, but an average of 2,400 to 3,100, eggs are deposited in nests, or redds, dug by females in gravel riffles. The

female guards the redd for a few days, then both sexes die.

Chum salmon enter streams in an advanced state of sexual maturity and thus do not stay in freshwater as long as chinook, coho, and sockeye salmon, remaining for perhaps two to three weeks. Their fry do not move out to sea as quickly as do pink salmon fry in the spring. They move to salt-water estuaries in schools, remaining close to shore for a few months and waiting until fall to move into the ocean. Chum salmon are known to hybridize naturally with pink salmon.

Food. Juvenile chum salmon in freshwater feed on plankton, then later eat insects. In the ocean, they eat a variety of organisms, including herring, pilchards, sand lance, squid, and crustaceans. Adults cease feeding in freshwater.

Angling. Chum salmon are not a focused target of anglers. They are an incidental catch on occasion, both in coastal nearshore saltwaters and in tributaries.

See: Salmon, Pacific.

SALMON, COHO   *Oncorhynchus kisutch.*

Other names—silver salmon, silversides, hookbill, hooknose, sea trout, blueback; French: *saumon coho;* Japanese: *gin-zake.*

A member of the Salmonidae family, the coho salmon is an extremely adaptable fish that occurs in nearly all of the same waters as does the larger chinook salmon *(see: salmon, chinook),* but it is a more spectacular fighter and the most acrobatic of the Pacific salmon. It is one of North America's most important sport- and commercial fish, especially to the Pacific coast of North America, where this and other salmonids have long had great cultural and food significance.

By nature an anadromous species, the coho can adapt to an entirely freshwater existence and has done so with remarkable success in the Great Lakes of North America. Like the chinook, it has declined through large portions of its endemic range due to

S

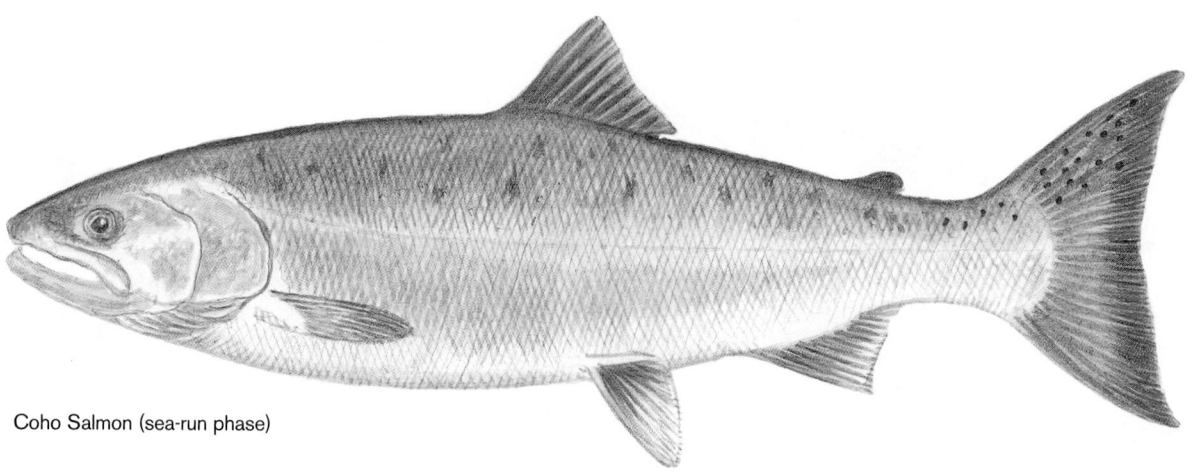

Coho Salmon (sea-run phase)

dams, other habitat alteration, pollution, and excessive commercial fishing. Some runs in the Pacific Northwest are threatened or endangered.

Although they are smaller on average than chinook salmon, and in many places less abundant, coho are popular sportfish wherever they are found. Their Pacific coastal range parallels the chinook's. As with the chinook, coho populations in the Great Lakes are supported almost entirely by hatchery production. Both species are intensively sought by boat anglers in coastal estuaries and bays and in the Great Lakes proper, and by boat, bank, and wading anglers in rivers.

As a gamefish, the coho is a much more suitable light-tackle quarry than the chinook, although it is caught with most of the same tackle and methods. Unlike the chinook, it is a streaky, near-surface, and aerial battler, rather than a deep and dogged fighter, although it, too, has great stamina. The coho's flesh is red and of excellent quality. It is a significant commercial catch for food markets, and is processed fresh, fresh-frozen, canned, or smoked.

Identification.   The body of the coho salmon is elongate and somewhat compressed, and the head is conical. For most of its life (in saltwater or lake as well as newly arrived in a spawning river), this species is a dark metallic blue or blue green above, becoming silvery on the sides and belly. There are small black spots on the back and on the upper lobe of the caudal fin. They can be distinguished from chinook salmon *(see: salmon, chinook)* by their lack of black spots on the lower lobe of the tail, and the white or gray gums at the base of the teeth; chinook have small black spots on both caudal lobes of the tail, and they have black gums.

Spawning adults of both sexes have dark backs and heads, and maroon to reddish sides. The males turn dusky green above and on their head, bright red on their sides, and blackish below. The females turn a pinkish red on their sides. The males develop a prominent doubled-hooked snout, called a kype, with large teeth, which make closing the mouth impossible.

Juvenile coho salmon have 8 to 12 well-developed parr marks evenly distributed above and below the lateral line; the parr marks are narrower than the interspaces. The adipose fin is uniformly pigmented. The anal fin has a long leading edge usually tipped with white, and all fins are frequently tinted with orange.

Size.   Coho do not attain the size of their larger chinook brethren and in most places are caught around the 4- to 8-pound mark. The all-tackle world record is a Great Lakes fish of 33 pounds, 4 ounces, caught in the Salmon River, New York, in 1989. Fish to 31 pounds have been caught in Alaska, where the average catch is 8 to 12 pounds and 24 to 30 inches long. All coho are exciting to catch, as they are strong and acrobatic, but coho exceeding 15 pounds are a real handful for most anglers.

Distribution.   The coho salmon is endemic to the northern Pacific Ocean and the rivers flowing into it, from northern Japan to the Anadyr River, Russia, and from Point Hope, Alaska, on the Chukchi Sea south to Monterey Bay, California. It has been infrequently reported at sea as far south as Baja California, Mexico. Most sea-run chinook are encountered along the coasts and in spawning rivers.

The coho has been transplanted into the Great Lakes and into freshwater lakes in Alaska and along the U.S. Pacific coast, as well as into the states of Maine, Maryland, and Louisiana; the province of Alberta, Canada; and in Argentina and Chile. Natural successful spawning has not noticeably occurred in these transplanted populations, with the possible exception of the Great Lakes in Michigan; the Great Lakes contain substantial populations of coho, which are sustained through extensive stocking.

Life history/Behavior.   Like all species of Pacific salmon, coho are anadromous. They hatch in freshwater rivers, spend part of their life in the ocean, and then spawn in freshwater. Those coho that have been transplanted to strictly freshwater environments (as in the Great Lakes) hatch in

Coho Salmon (spawning male)

tributary rivers and streams, spend part of their life in the open water of the lake, and then return to tributaries to spawn. All coho die after spawning.

Adult male sea-run coho salmon generally enter streams when they are either two or three years old, but adult females do not return to spawn until age 3. All coho salmon, whether male or female, spend their first year in the stream or river in which they hatch.

Generally speaking, the larger the female, the greater the number of eggs produced. Females spawn from 1,500 to 4,500 eggs, but the average production is 2,500 eggs. This number also varies with specific runs.

The timing of runs into tributaries varies as well. Coho salmon in Alaska, for example, enter spawning streams from July through November, usually during periods of high runoff. In California, the runs occur from September through March, and the bulk of spawning occurs from November through January. Streams throughout the Great Lakes primarily receive coho from late August into October. Run timing has evolved to reflect the requirements of specific stocks. In some streams with barrier falls, adults arrive in July when the water is low and the falls are passable. In large rivers, adults must arrive early, as they need several weeks or months to reach headwater spawning grounds. Run timing is also regulated by the water temperature at spawning grounds: Where temperatures are low and eggs develop slowly, spawners have evolved early run timing to compensate; conversely, where temperatures are warm, adults are late spawners.

Coho salmon do not feed during their freshwater spawning migration, so their condition deteriorates gradually during the spawning run as they use stored body materials for energy and for the development of reproductive products. Adults hold in pools until they ripen, then move onto spawning grounds; spawning generally occurs at night. The female digs a nest, or redd, and deposits her eggs, which are fertilized by the male. The eggs develop during the winter and hatch in early spring, and the embryos remain in the gravel utilizing the egg yolk until they emerge. The emergent fry occupy shallow stream margins and, as they grow, establish territories, which they defend from other salmonids. They live in ponds, lakes, and pools in streams and rivers, usually among cover in quiet areas free of current, from which they dart out to seize drifting insects.

During the fall, juvenile coho may travel miles before locating off-channel habitat, where they pass the winter free of floods. Some sea-run fish leave the river in the spring and rear in brackish estuarine ponds, then migrate back into freshwater in the fall. Coho spend one to three winters in streams and may spend up to five winters in lakes before migrating to the sea as smolts. Time at sea varies. Some males (called jacks) mature and return after only 6 months at sea, at a length of roughly 12 inches, whereas most fish stay 18 months before returning as full-size adults.

Little is known of the ocean migrations of coho salmon. Evidently there are more coho salmon in the eastern Pacific and along the coast of North America than in the western Pacific. High-seas tagging shows that maturing southeast Alaska coho move northward throughout the spring and appear to concentrate in the central Gulf of Alaska in June. They later disperse toward shore and migrate along the shoreline until they reach their stream of origin. Although most coho do not seem to migrate extensively, tagged individuals have been recovered up to 1,200 miles from the tagging site.

In the Great Lakes, coho migrate many miles from their natal water as abundance of forage and appropriate water temperature dictate. Thus, as surface levels warm, the colder water preferred by both salmon and their forage is deeper (or shallow but farther offshore, depending on wind and other factors). The fish wander considerable distances, and their location varies regularly.

Food and feeding habits. Juvenile coho in freshwater feed on plankton, then later eat insects. In the ocean, coho salmon grow rapidly, feeding on a variety of organisms, including herring, pilchards, sand lance, squid, and crustaceans. Likewise, coho

A coastal coho salmon from Campbell River, British Columbia.

S

that live entirely in freshwater feed on plankton and insects as juveniles, and on pelagic freshwater baitfish in the lakes. Alewives and smelt are the primary food items, and, in fact, coho and other salmonids were introduced to the Great Lakes and other inland waters especially to help control massive populations of baitfish, which they consume voraciously and thus quickly grow large, stocky bodies. Like all Pacific salmon, the coho does not feed once it enters freshwater on its spawning run.

Angling. Because the coho's habits are similar to those of the chinook salmon, angling methods and locations are similar as well. Coho are at times an incidental catch when chinook are the focus; most likely, however, fishing efforts target either or both species. The timing of availability may be different, especially in coastal rivers and in nearshore coastal waters. In addition, coho salmon are likely to remain shallower in open water than are chinook. Sometimes coho hold on or close to the surface, which is not a likelihood for chinook. Fishing methods are detailed under the entry for chinook salmon.

See: Salmon, Pacific.

SALMONFLIES
See: Stoneflies.

SALMONID
A term for any member of the Salmonidae family; this includes the various trout, salmon, charr, whitefish, and grayling. It is frequently, but erroneously, expressed as salmonoid.

SALMON, LANDLOCKED
A term for strictly freshwater-dwelling salmon, which spend the greater portion of their life in a lake and return to their natal river or stream to spawn. Any species of salmon with such behavior

and without access to saltwater is "landlocked"; this includes freshwater sockeye salmon, which are called kokanee, as well as coho and chinook salmon. In the northeastern United States and Canada, however, the term "landlocked salmon" specifically refers to freshwater-dwelling Atlantic salmon (see: salmon, Atlantic).

SALMON, MASU   Oncorhynchus masou.
Other names—cherry salmon, cherry trout; Japanese: honmasu, sakuramasu, yamame, yamabe.

This member of the Salmonidae family is one of two species of Pacific salmon (see: salmon, Pacific) that occur only in Asia and the western Pacific. It is generally called cherry salmon in English, because the meaning of its most common Japanese name, sakuramasu, is "cherry trout." This appellation alludes to the masu's presence on the spawning grounds at cherry blossom time, which occurs from March through May in Japan.

Although ichthyological opinion varies as to whether this species and amago salmon (O. rhodurus; see: salmon, amago) are the same, these species are currently classified as separate but closely related. Moreover, there are anadromous and freshwater versions of both species. Technically the word "masu" refers to the anadromous fish, O. masou masou, which in Japan is known as sakuramasu; the nonanadromous and permanently freshwater-dwelling version is O. masou ishikawae, which in Japan is known as yamame. Thus, "masu" refers to the seagoing salmon, and "yamame" to the freshwater dweller. The masu is subject to commercial fishing in the ocean and is reared in hatcheries in Japan.

Size. Masu salmon on spawning grounds in Russian rivers may range up to 8.5 kilograms, but the average fish weighs between 2 and 3 kilograms. They are generally smaller in Japanese rivers. On average, yamame are roughly half the size of masu.

Distribution. The masu salmon occurs in more southerly waters than do any of the other Pacific salmon. It is found in the Sea of Japan and the Sea of Okhotsk, and migrates up rivers on all sides of the Japanese islands of Hokkaido and Honshu and on some of Russia's Kuril Islands and Sakhalin Island; along the Asian mainland in rivers from southeastern Korea to Russia's Amur River; as well as in rivers of the western Kamchatka Peninsula. It is not found in the Bering Sea and was unsuccessfully introduced in Canada. The yamame has the same range but is also present on Japan's

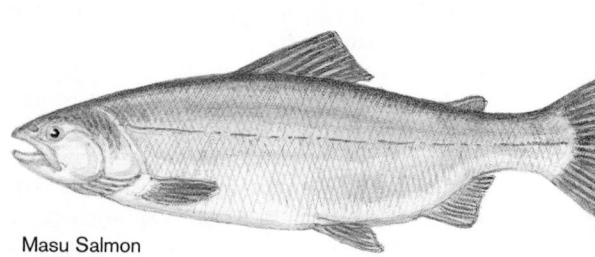

Masu Salmon

Kyushu Island and some southernmost Korean rivers fronting the western Korea Strait, as well as on Taiwan.

Habitat.   Masu live in the Japan and Okhotsk Seas while maturing and migrate up large and small coastal rivers for spawning. Their migration range in the Pacific is extremely limited compared with that of other Pacific salmon. Yamame are present in coastal rivers.

Life history/Behavior.   Spawning takes place from March through early July; the exact time varies among the rivers but begins earlier in the southern part of the spawning range. Masu and yamame salmon have been observed spawning together. Male yamame salmon mature at age 1 and females at age 2—a year earlier than their masu counterparts, some of which do not mature until age 4. Yamame do not migrate downstream in spring after one winter in freshwater, as masu do. Adult masu do not feed while in freshwater, and yamame do not feed when undergoing the reproductive process. Both die after spawning, although in some hatchery rearing experiments, some yamame males have successfully spawned two or more times.

SALMON, PACIFIC

The term "Pacific salmon" describes certain members of the genus *Oncorhynchus* that occur naturally in the North Pacific Ocean and its drainages in Asia and North America. They are members of the Salmonidae family of fish, which includes trout, salmon, charr, whitefish, and grayling, all of which are endemic to the temperate and cool regions of the Northern Hemisphere but have been introduced widely outside their native range, including the Southern Hemisphere.

In the Salmonidae family there are either 11 or 7 "salmon" of Pacific origin, and 1 of Atlantic origin. The latter is *Salmo salar*, simply known as Atlantic salmon *(see: salmon, Atlantic).* In order of general prominence and value to anglers, the 7 most widely recognized Pacific salmon include chinook *(Oncorhynchus tshawytscha),* coho *(O. kisutch),* pink *(O. gorbuscha),* sockeye *(O. nerka),* chum *(O. keta),* masu *(O. masou),* and amago *(O. rhodurusi).* Masu and amago salmon occur naturally only in Asia, and the others occur naturally in both Asia and North America.

Some scientists count 11 species because 4 additional species that were historically called "trout" and were, at least among nonscientists, not considered "salmon" have been classified taxonomically as belonging to the *Oncorhynchus* genus. Not even a taxonomist can explain the reasons for this very well, but these newcomers include two prominent "trout" species that were formerly in the *Salmo* genus—steelhead/rainbow trout *(O. mykiss)* and cutthroat trout *(O. clarki)*—as well as the lesser-known golden trout *(O. aguabonita)* and the

Apache trout *(O. apache).* The placement of these four "trout" in this Pacific salmon genus would seem to make them members of the Pacific salmon family.

Biologically, salmon and their relatives are primitive fish, with fossil remains dating to more than 100 million years ago. Evidence indicates that many of the more advanced or specialized families of modern-day bony fish have ancestral stocks closely resembling these primitive fish.

The most clearly evident primitive feature of the group is the lack of spines in the fins. Most of the soft rays in the fins are branched. The pelvic fins are situated far back on the body—in the "hip" region, where the legs of amphibians articulate with the body *(see: anatomy).* This location contrasts with the placement of the pelvic fins in many other species, including largemouth bass, for example, which are so far forward they are almost directly beneath the pectoral fins. Other indications of their primitive nature are an adipose fin and a primitive air bladder.

Most members of the Salmonidae family are in some way associated with cold, often rushing waters and high oxygen demands. Some, including all of the salmon, are also tied to the sea, spending a good portion of their lives there. All members of the family spawn in freshwater, and most require cold running water. Members of some sea-running species, including most salmon, have become accidentally or deliberately landlocked, living and reproducing successfully entirely in freshwater without ever taking a journey to saltwater.

Pacific salmon spawn in gravel beds in rivers and streams, and sometimes along the lakeshore. Their progeny have a relatively short freshwater existence and migrate out to the sea. When mature, Pacific salmon usually return to the waters of their birth to reproduce, after which all but some amago and some nonanadromous masu males die.

Contrary to earlier beliefs, many salmon from North American rivers roam far at sea in the North Pacific Ocean and the Bering Sea. The oceanic distribution of the salmon is dependent on the species and point of origin. Sockeye and chinook salmon from northwest Alaska, for example, may migrate across the Bering Sea to areas close to Kamchatka, Russia, and south of the Aleutian Islands into the North Pacific Ocean; the sockeye also migrate eastward to the Gulf of Alaska. Salmon such as the pink, chum, and coho from central and Southeast Alaska, British Columbia, and Washington State migrate out into the northeastern Pacific Ocean and the Gulf of Alaska. Some salmon migrate several thousand miles from the time they leave the rivers as juveniles until they return as adults. A chinook salmon tagged in the central Aleutian Islands and recovered a year later in the Salmon River, in Idaho, had traveled roughly 3,500 miles.

The homing instinct of salmon is one of nature's greatest wonders, and something that is still not

Most Pacific salmon, such as this chinook from the Taku River, British Columbia, are caught during their upstream spawning migration.

fully understood by scientists. Some degree of straying from natal waters does occur, but all Pacific salmon species are likely to develop reproductively isolated populations, which are known as stocks, and these stocks are individually vulnerable to highly efficient harvesting and to adverse conditions affecting the waters where they spawn.

Collectively and individually, the Pacific salmon species are of great historical, cultural, food, and sport significance to people of the coastal regions of the North Pacific Rim. The market for chinook, coho, pink, and sockeye salmon, because of their excellent table qualities and high value in canning, has long been strong, and the subsistence catch has been important for centuries. Although a long tradition of recreational fishing for these species exists, only since the 1950s has it gained momentum. Today, it is of great economic value, especially for tourism in Alaska and British Columbia.

Virtually all angling attention focuses on chinook and coho salmon, especially in North America. Today, for example, although five species of Pacific salmon occur along the Pacific coast, more than 99 percent of all salmon caught in the ocean off California are either chinook or coho. Most sportfishing for Pacific salmon occurs in rivers and streams when these species are undergoing their spawning migrations, and a fair amount occurs in saltwater, predominantly in bays, estuaries, and inshore waters near the coast. In these waters, anglers target fish that are migrating to their natal tributaries, or those that are gathered nearby awaiting the run. Sportfishing for this species is almost entirely centered around fish that are preparing to spawn, as this is when they are most accessible. (An exception to this is the chinook and coho salmon that have been introduced into the Great Lakes of North America; these fish live their entire lives in freshwater and are pursued extensively in lakes, where they feed heavily.)

Although some commercial and subsistence fishing for Pacific salmon occurs once they have entered or are in the process of entering spawning rivers, the bulk of the harvest is in nearshore and offshore waters through gillnetting and trawling. The U.S., Canada, Japan, Russia, and North and South Korea are the major harvesters, essentially in that order. Alaskan vessels harvest the highest percentage of the North American catch.

The troubles plaguing Pacific salmon stocks have been well publicized throughout the 1990s and have resulted in harvest treaties between some of the aforementioned countries, harvest quotas, and assorted management plans; these have not stemmed the decline of some Pacific salmon stocks (especially in California, Oregon, Washington, and certain portions of British Columbia), although they are supposed to address overharvesting.

Some salmon stocks are at historically low levels. Catch reductions have been imposed on all recreational anglers and on commercial fishermen. Anglers are a small part of the overfishing problem, however. In British Columbia, where salmon sport-fishing is a big business, anglers account for 4 percent of the total annual salmon harvest.

Excessive commercial fishing is just one of the problems affecting Pacific salmon. Dams, logging, pollution, water use, overfishing, habitat destruction, hatchery impacts, mismanagement, and other human-induced factors are among the factors. No single factor is responsible for the full extent of the decline, and no single action will restore the fish. Because salmon cross so many state and national jurisdictional boundaries, there is insufficient focus and accountability to ensure effective management of the overall system, as well as a lack of coordinated overall fisheries management.

Some observers feel that the entire Pacific salmon fishery could suffer the same fate as the Atlantic striped bass did in the late 1970s: perilously low stocks, curtailment of sport and commercial fishing, a ban on sale. But Pacific salmon differ greatly from Atlantic striped bass, which have rebounded strongly and are a single species dependent on relative few major rivers and estuaries. There are five eastern Pacific species of salmon. They eat different food, return to a wide range of home waters (more than 1,000 for chinook alone), and migrate according to different cycles.

See: Salmon, Amago; Salmon, Chinook; Salmon, Chum; Salmon, Coho; Salmon, Masu; Salmon, Pink; Salmon, Sockeye.

SALMON, PINK *Oncorhynchus gorbuscha.*

Other names—humpback salmon, humpy, fall salmon, pink, humpback; French: *saumon rose;* Japanese: *karafutomasu, sepparimasu.*

An important commercial catch, the pink salmon is the smallest North American member of the Pacific salmon group of the Salmonidae family. In many Alaskan coastal fishing communities, particularly south of Kotzebue Sound, it is considered a "bread and butter" fish because of its commercial significance to fisheries and thus to local economies. It has some sportfishing value in Alaskan rivers, less

so than coho or chinook salmon, but little elsewhere. The flesh is pinkish, rather than red or white, and it is mostly sold canned but also utilized fresh, smoked, and frozen. It is valued for caviar, especially in Japan. The flesh is of most value when the fish is still an open-water inhabitant, as it deteriorates rapidly once the fish enters rivers.

Identification.   The pink salmon is known as the "humpback" or "humpy" because of its distorted, extremely humpbacked appearance, which is caused by the very pronounced, laterally flattened hump that develops on the backs of adult males before spawning. This hump appears between the head and the dorsal fin and develops by the time the male enters the spawning stream, as does a hooked upper jaw, or kype.

At sea, the pink salmon is silvery in color, with a bright metallic blue above; there are many black, elongated, oval spots on the entire tail fin, and large spots on the back and the adipose fin. When the pink salmon moves to spawning streams, the bright appearance of the male changes to pale red or "pink" on the sides, with brown to olive green blotches; females become olive green above with dusky bars or patches, and pale below. Young pink salmon are entirely silvery and lack the parr marks, or dark vertical bars, that the young of other salmon species have. All pink salmon have small, deeply embedded scales.

Size/Age.   The average pink salmon weighs 3 to 6 pounds and is 20 to 25 inches long, although these fish can grow to 15 pounds and 30 inches. The all-tackle world record is a 13-pound, 1-ounce Great Lakes fish taken from Ontario, Canada. It lives for only two years.

Distribution.   Pink salmon are native to Pacific and arctic coastal waters from the Sacramento River in Northern California northeast to the Mackenzie River in the Northwest Territories, Canada, and from the Lena River in Siberia to eastern Korea. They occur throughout the Aleutian Islands, the Bering and Okhotsk Seas, the Sea of Japan, and the island of Hokkaido, Japan, as well in the rivers that flow into these waters.

Pink Salmon (sea-run phase)

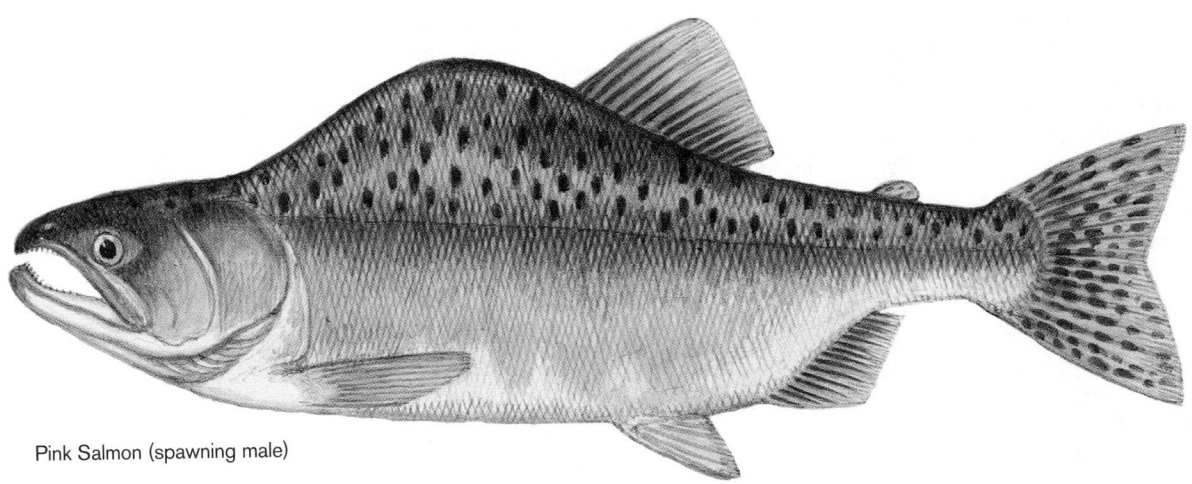

Pink Salmon (spawning male)

Pink salmon have been introduced to Newfoundland and to the western coast of Lake Superior, and currently maintain populations in these locations; there have been sporadic reports of pink salmon in Labrador, Nova Scotia, and Quebec since their introduction into Newfoundland. Introduced accidentally into Lake Superior, pink salmon are now spawning in tributaries of Lake Huron and are possibly the only isolated freshwater population to ever survive.

Habitat. These anadromous fish spend 18 months at sea and then undertake a spawning migration to the river or stream of their birth, although they sometimes use other streams. They tend to migrate as far as 40 miles inland of coastal waters, occasionally moving as far as 70 miles inland.

Life history/Behavior. Pink salmon are often referred to as "autumn salmon" or "fall salmon" because of their late spawning runs; these occur from July through mid-October in Alaska. Females dig a series of nests, or redds, depositing hundreds to thousands of eggs, which hatch from late December through February. Young become free-swimming in the early spring soon after hatching, often returning to sea in the company of young chum and sockeye salmon. Adults die soon after spawning. Pink salmon can hybridize with chum salmon.

Almost all pink salmon mature in two years, which means that odd-year and even-year populations are separate and essentially unrelated. In particular streams and overall areas, the odd- or even-year cycle is dominant, whereas elsewhere odd- and even-year pink salmon are equally abundant. Sometimes cycle dominance will transfer, so that the previously abundant cycle becomes weak, and vice versa.

Food and feeding habits. While in freshwater on spawning runs, sea-run pink salmon may eat insects, although they often do not feed at all. At sea, they feed primarily on plankton, as well as on crustaceans, small fish, and squid. They do not feed during the spawning run.

Angling. In open waters, pink salmon are caught by anglers trolling for other Pacific salmon, although generally smaller lures and flies are necessary to attract this species. They become a deliberate open-water target when either coho *(see: salmon, coho)* or chinook *(see: salmon, chinook)* are unavailable. They may be fairly abundant off river mouths for several weeks prior to spawning. In rivers, they are readily caught on small spinners, small spoons, and flies, and on the spinning and fly tackle used for trout.

See: Salmon, Pacific.

SALMON PLUG
Term for a cutplug *(see)*.

SALMON, SOCKEYE   *Oncorhynchus nerka.*
Other names—sockeye, red salmon, blueback salmon, big redfish; French: *saumon nerka;* Japanese: *beni-zake, himemasu.* The landlocked form is called kokanee salmon, Kennerly's salmon, kokanee, landlocked sockeye, kickininee, little redfish, silver trout; French: *kokani.*

A member of the Salmonidae family, the sockeye is like some other members of the Pacific salmon group in having both anadromous and freshwater forms. The former migrate from freshwater streams to the ocean and then return to those streams to spawn, whereas the latter remain in freshwater all their lives. Called kokanee, the freshwater form was once thought to be the subspecies *O. kennerlyi* but is now accepted as the same species with characteristics identical to that of the anadromous sockeye, although it is a smaller fish. It occurred naturally in some waters in the drainages of the Pacific and has been spread through stocking to many other waters. Kokanee can be fine gamefish and excellent food fish; sockeye salmon are predominantly prized more for their food value than for sport, however, as the upstream migrants are not aggressive at taking baits or lures.

The name of sockeye salmon is a corruption of the coastal Indian word *suk-kegh,* which meant

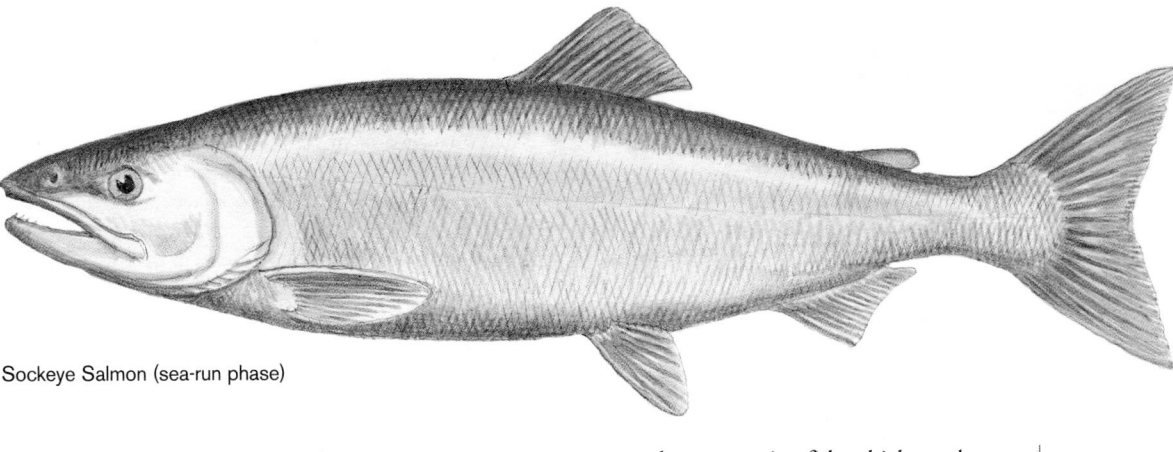

Sockeye Salmon (sea-run phase)

medium salmon. Sockeye leave the ocean to spawn in freshwater, as do other Pacific salmon, but they enter only those rivers having lakes at their headwaters. These fish were so abundant historically, especially in North America, that they left indelible imprints on the culture and geography of states and provinces. Many place names were derived from these salmon, and the spawning red sockeye were both an important food source and an element of religion for native tribes. In some places they remain an important mainstay of many subsistence users. The erection of dams and alteration of habitat, however, as well as commercial overfishing and other factors, have caused an overall decline in sockeye stocks and the loss of some specific runs. Sockeye populations in the Pacific Northwest outside of Alaska are especially troubled.

The flesh of the sockeye is deep red and high in oil content, making it the most commercially valuable of all the Pacific salmon. The meat is especially delicious when smoked, excellent for canning due to the rich orange red color, and also marketed fresh, dried/salted, and frozen. Canned sockeye salmon is marketed primarily in the United Kingdom and the United States; most frozen sockeye salmon is purchased by Japan. Sockeye salmon roe is also valuable, and is salted and marketed to Japan.

Identification. The sockeye is the slimmest and most streamlined of Pacific salmon, particularly immature and pre-spawning fish, which are elongate and somewhat laterally compressed. They are metallic green blue on the back and top of the head, iridescent silver on the sides, and white or silvery on the belly. Some fine black speckling may occur on the back, but large spots are absent. Juveniles in freshwater have the same general coloration as immature sockeye salmon in the ocean but are less iridescent; they also have dark, oval parr marks on their sides. These parr marks are short, less than the diameter of the eye, and rarely extend below the lateral line.

Breeding males develop a humped back and elongated, hooked jaws filled with sharp, enlarged teeth. Both sexes turn brilliant to dark red on the back and sides, pale to olive green on the head and upper jaw, and white on the lower jaw. The totally red body distinguishes the sockeye from the otherwise similar chum salmon, and the lack of large, distinct spots distinguishes it from the remaining three Pacific salmon of North America. The number and shape of gill rakers on the first gill arch further distinguish the sockeye from the chum salmon; sockeye salmon have 28 to 40 long, slender, rough or serrated closely set rakers on the first arch, whereas chum salmon have 19 to 26 short, stout, smooth rakers.

Kokanee are smaller but otherwise identical to sea-run sockeye in coloration; they undergo the same changes as sockeye when spawning.

Sockeye Salmon (spawning male)

Kokanee Salmon

Size.   Adult sockeye usually weigh between 4 and 8 pounds. The all-tackle world record is an Alaskan fish that weighed 15 pounds, 3 ounces. Kokanee are much smaller; in many places they do not grow much over 14 inches or 1 pound, especially where the plankton food resource is low or where many other species compete for it; the all-tackle world record is a British Columbia fish that weighed 9 pounds, 6 ounces.

Distribution.   The sockeye salmon is native to the northern Pacific Ocean and its tributaries from northern Hokkaido, Japan, to the Anadyr River, Russia, and from the Sacramento River, California, to Point Hope, Alaska. Kokanee exist in Japan, Russia, Alaska, at least three western provinces in Canada, seven western U.S. states, and three eastern states.

Habitat.   Sockeye salmon are anadromous, living in the sea and entering freshwater to spawn. They mainly enter rivers and streams that have lakes at their source. Young fish may inhabit lakes for as many as four years before returning to the ocean. Kokanee occur almost exclusively in freshwater lakes, migrating to tributaries in the fall to spawn (or to outlet areas or shoreline gravel in waters without suitable spawning streams).

Life history/Behavior.   Sockeye salmon return to their natal stream to spawn after spending one to four years in the ocean. Mature sockeye salmon that spend only one year in the ocean are called jacks and, almost without exception, are males. They enter freshwater systems from the ocean during the summer months or fall, some having traveled thousands of miles. Most populations show little variation in their arrival time on the spawning grounds from year to year; kokanee spawn from August through February, sockeye from July through December.

Once near their natal system, these fish use olfactory cues to guide them home. Freshwater systems with lakes produce the greatest number of sockeye salmon, as fish run upstream to just below a lake outlet, some spawning in the lake itself or in inlet streams. The female selects the spawning site, digs a nest, or redd, with her tail, and deposits eggs in the downstream portion of the redd. One or more males swims beside her and fertilizes the eggs as they are released. After each spawning act, the female covers the eggs by dislodging gravel at the upstream end of the redd with her tail while males drive off intruders. Depending on size, a female

produces from 2,000 to 4,500 eggs. Like all Pacific salmon, sockeye die within a few weeks after spawning.

Eggs hatch during the winter, and the young alevins remain in the gravel, living off the material stored in their yolk sacs until early spring. At this time they emerge from the gravel as fry and move into rearing areas. In systems with lakes, juveniles usually spend one to three years in freshwater before migrating to the ocean in the spring as smolts weighing only a few ounces. In systems without lakes, however, many juveniles migrate to the ocean soon after emerging from the gravel.

Although most sockeye salmon production results from the spawning of wild populations, some runs have been developed or enhanced through human effort.

Food and feeding habits.   Anadromous salmon rarely feed after entering freshwater, although young fish will feed mainly on plankton and insects. In the ocean, sockeye salmon continue to feed on plankton, plus crustacean larvae, larval and small adult fish, and occasionally on squid. Kokanee feed mainly on plankton but also on insects and bottom organisms.

Angling.   The largely plankton-eating sockeye was often judged difficult to catch in the past, which may in part have been due to anglers using the same approach for the sockeye as for the larger and more aggressive chinook and coho salmon. Sockeye are strong, however, and leap out of the water, and they have become the object of more angling effort. Small hooks baited with eggs or a piece of worm, small flies, and small spoons or spinners will catch them in rivers; because they don't feed on their river spawning run, however, deep presentations that place the offering directly in front of the fish are necessary to provoke a reflexive strike.

The same items work for river kokanee, and in lakes the best approach is deep trolling, using tactics not unlike those for other trout and salmon species, although with offerings that are on the small side. Some fly fishing opportunities exist when the fish are shallow in early-season cold water, and ice fishing is generally productive, using small ice jigs and small natural baits.

Open-water fishing for kokanee is similar to fishing for lake trout or other salmon in open water: the angler must find cool (usually deep) waters and fish them consistently at the correct depth. These tactics require lead-core lines, downriggers, and weighted flatlines with attractors when the fish are deep, and unweighted flatlines and floating fly lines when the fish are shallow after ice out.

Once the surface water has warmed, kokanee move into deeper, cooler (roughly 50°F) water. They cluster in a small deep band or, in lakes with entirely warm water, on or near the bottom where there are springs or in old channels where it is as cool as possible. Very small spoons, spinners, and occasionally plugs are used, often tipped with a piece of natural bait. Small cowbell attractors are especially popular with many deep trollers, and a rubber snubber may be used to help prevent ripping the hook from the kokanee's tender mouth. Sometimes a piece of nightcrawler or other bait is fished without a lure, directly behind the attractor.

See: Salmon, Pacific; Trolling.

SALMON TAILER

A nooselike device that cinches over the caudal peduncle of a salmon for landing.

See: Landing Fish; Tailer.

SALMON, THREADFIN

See: Threadfin, King.

SALTER

A sea-run brook trout (see). This fish is not truly anadromous but may go to saltwater for short periods to feed or for temperature reasons.

SALT FRONT

The upper limit of saline intrusion in a tidal river. Saltwater is more dense than freshwater and pushes upriver as a wedge beneath the freshwater to a certain point, which is then known as the salt front.

SALT MARSH

See: Marsh.

SALTWATER/SEAWATER

Commonly used terms for water with many dissolved salts in or from the ocean, as well as in connected seas, bays, sounds, estuaries, marshes, and the lower portion of tidal rivers.

See: Brackish Water; Freshwater.

SALTWATER TAPER

A specially designed type of weight-forward fly line for casting large flies.

See: Flycasting Tackle.

SAMOA

Previously known as Western Samoa, the independent Pacific state of Samoa consists of nine volcanic islands, four of which are inhabited. It is situated in the heart of the South Pacific Ocean, west of American Samoa and northeast of Tonga.

The population is 170,000, three-quarters of which lives on the island of Upolu, where the capital city of Apia and the international airport are both located. Most of the rest of Samoa's population lives on the largest island in the group, Savai'i.

Upolu and Savai'i constitute most of Samoa's landmass. They are high, rugged, volcanic islands, still covered in many areas by lush rain forest. Both islands are roughly 75 kilometers long. The capital of Apia is clean and progressive by Pacific island standards. Although violent crime is minimal, theft is a problem in urban areas.

Indigenous Samoans are of Polynesian descent and make up more than 90 percent of the population, the bulk of whom maintain a traditional village way of life. For example, the traditional waist-to-knees body tattoo of Samoan men is still popular and is still achieved with bone tools in the old way. An extremely painful ritual, the tattoo is a sign of a warrior who has suffered and shown courage.

Samoa became independent in 1962. The official languages are Samoan and English. Samoans are an affable people, and most of them do speak English. Good-quality hotels, as well as resort, motel, and guest house accommodations, are available. One famous landmark is the former home of Robert Louis Stevenson, who spent his last years in Samoa. Stevenson, who was buried on the summit of Mount Vaea overlooking Apia, still casts a long shadow in Samoa, where he is known as "Tusitala," the teller of tales.

Temperatures average between 25° and 30°C, and December through April is the wet season. Samoa is subject to trade winds from the southeast quarter throughout much of the year. Because Upolu and Savai'i Islands lie in a northwest-southeast direction and have high mountainous interiors, they tend to split the winds like a sharp rock in a stream. Consequently, there is little in the way of a lee shore for anglers fishing in windy conditions.

Sportfishing is still in its infancy in Samoa, and the Western concept of fishing for recreation remains somewhat alien to the locals, who have always considered fishing as a way of putting food on the table. The first tagging and release of a billfish here was recorded in only 1995; the fish, a black marlin, was recaptured 17 days later in American Samoa, 75 nautical miles away.

In 1994, Samoan anglers became affiliated with the International Game Fish Association (IGFA) under the banner of the Tautai-O-Samoa Association. In 1996 they ran their first international gamefishing tournament, which has shown strong growth, drawing boats from American Samoa and New Zealand.

One full-time charter boat works out of Apia, and New Zealand boats occasionally spend their winter off-season (June through September) working here. These boats offer good-quality sportfishing gear. Other, less formal, charters can sometimes be organized with local boatowners; in these instances, anglers are advised to bring their own equipment.

Sea temperatures are usually around 28° to 32°C, and a wide range of tropical sportfish are available throughout the year. Blue marlin are the predominant billfish, gathering here in good numbers. Rod-and-reel captures to 300 kilograms have been recorded, and longliners have brought in fish weighing more than 1,000 pounds.

Black marlin are also present, although the waters seem to be a bit too warm for striped marlin in any numbers. Pacific sailfish are also regular captures, and shortbill spearfish have been taken. Other offshore gamefish include yellowfin tuna averaging around 40 kilograms, and plentiful skipjacks, tuna, wahoo, and dolphin (called *masi-masi* here).

About 5 nautical miles off Apia, the inshore shallow water drops from 60 to 80 meters down to 3,000 meters, and this spot is where gamefishing normally starts, including visits to several fish aggregation buoys installed by the Samoan government. Trolling with lures is the favored technique.

In the mid- to late 1990s, the domestic longline commercial fishing effort increased, based from Apia. This fishery was aimed mainly at tuna for the domestic market and had evidently not made significant inroads into the local fish populations at that time.

Trolling small lures along the reef edge can provide fine sportfishing for species such as rainbow runner, bluefin trevally, barracuda, kawakawa, giant trevally, and dogtooth tuna. Anglers catch many of these species by casting lures, including surface poppers.

Fishing from the shore with both cut baits and small metal or soft-plastic lures produces a wide range of small emperors, snapper, trevally, and grouper. Some lagoon areas reportedly produce bonefish, but this has not been confirmed.

SAMSON FISH *Seriola hippos.*

Other names—sea kingfish, sambo, samsonfish.

Often confused with the yellowtail kingfish and the amberjack to which it is closely related, the samson fish is a power-packed sportfish and a member of the Carangidae (jacks) family. It has a formidable reputation among anglers and is renowned for its astonishing strength and unrelenting efforts to escape when hooked. There is a small commercial fishery for them, especially in Western Australia, where they are caught together with yellowtail kingfish on handlines and drop lines. The flesh tends to be coarse in older specimens but reasonable in smaller fish, especially if the fish is bled immediately when captured.

Identification.   Samson fish have elongate, moderately compressed bodies that are bluish green above, fading to a golden yellow on the sides and white on the belly. There is usually a golden stripe along the midline. Young specimens have three or four brown vertical stripes along the body. The head, by comparison with the slender head of the yellowtail kingfish, is blunt and more rounded,

although this is less pronounced as the fish ages. The first dorsal fin is usually dark blue, and the other fins are greenish gray. The second dorsal fin is elevated in front.

The teeth and tail of the samson fish are distinguishing characteristics. Its teeth are reddish (the kingfish's teeth are white), and the forked tail, which has a keel at the base, is never yellow (the kingfish's is yellow). They are also more trevally-like in appearance, although they lack sickle-shaped pectorals.

Size.   Samson fish are known to grow to 55 kilograms and a length of 1.8 meters. An Australian record stands at 35 kilograms. Specimens exceeding 30 kilograms are rare.

Distribution.   Samson fish are endemic to New Zealand and Australian waters. In Australia, they are distributed along two regions of the southern coastline: from the Brisbane area (Moreton Bay) in southern Queensland to Montague Island off the coast of New South Wales, and from Marion Bay in South Australia around the coast to Shark Bay in Western Australia. The specimens in Western Australian waters are usually bigger than their counterparts from the east.

Habitat.   This species prefers deep water, both inshore and offshore, and is found around reefs, bomboras, and coastal headlands. Their habitat closely parallels that of the yellowtail kingfish; unlike kingfish, however, which tend to school in large numbers, older samson fish travel in pairs. Smaller fish move around in small schools.

Life history/Behavior.   Very little is known about the history and behavior of the samson fish. No details of spawning activity are available.

Food.   Samson fish feed on small fish, squid, and crustaceans.

Angling.   Most samson fish are taken incidentally by anglers pursuing yellowtail kingfish, although Western Australian anglers fishing off Rottnest Island just west of Perth, and the Abrolhos Islands to the north, will target this species with success. Occasionally they are taken by shore-based anglers fishing from rocky headlands along the coast, but mostly they're caught over rocky reefs from anchored or drifting boats.

The tackle of shore-based anglers fishing from rock platforms and cliffs usually consists of a 3.6- to 3.8-meter rod and a sturdy reel spooled with 10- to 15-kilogram line. Both spinning and baitfishing are practiced. Where a rock platform formation allows safe fishing, shorter roller-tipped rods to 2.4 meters and medium game rods are popular. Long-handled gaffs to 6 meters are essential, as are sliding gaffs (fed down a line), when cliff fishing.

Boat anglers prefer light- to medium-weight tackle comprising fully rollered or roller-tipped rods wedded to conventional reels holding at least 400 meters of line. Hook sizes vary from 5/0 to 9/0. Stout handlines to 50 kilograms are also occasionally used. Baits include whole live fish or dead yellowtail

(scad), mullet, and garfish; strips of mullet and bonito; small squid and octopus; and king prawns.

Samson fish will respond to trolled dead fish, or
lures such as plastic squid, metal jigs, spoons, offshore trolling lures, and feathered lures, and they
will show interest in lures dropped to the bottom
and retrieved in a series of upward sweeps.
Chumming with a mix of fish scraps, chopped
squid, pilchards, and tuna oil, all tossed with sand
and bran to help it sink to the bottom quickly, will
attract this fish within angling distance and hold
them in the area.

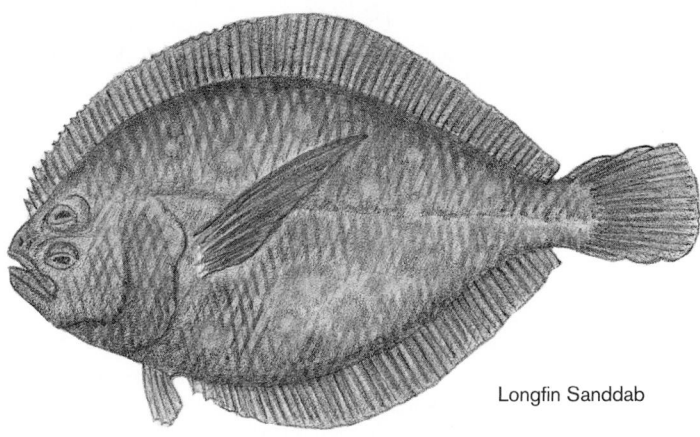
Longfin Sanddab

SANDDAB, LONGFIN   *Citharichthys xanthostigma.*

Other names—sanddab, soft flounder, Catalina
sanddab; Spanish: *lenguado alón.*

A member of the Bothidae family of left-eyed
flatfish *(see),* the longfin sanddab is a small but
common bottom fishing catch by anglers, particularly in Southern California.

Identification. The body of the longfin
sanddab is oblong and compressed. The head is
deep, the eyes are large and located on the left side,
and the mouth is large. The color is uniformly dark
with rust orange or white speckles, and the pectoral
fin is black on the eyed side. The blind side is white.

This species can be distinguished from the
Pacific sanddab *(see: sanddab, Pacific)* by the length
of the pectoral fin on the eyed side, which is always
shorter than the head on the Pacific sanddab and
longer than the head on the longfin. Sanddabs are
always left-eyed and can be distinguished from all
other left-eyed flatfish by having a lateral line that is
nearly straight along its entire length.

Size. These fish are common to 10 inches in
length but are reported to reach a maximum length
of $15^3/_4$ inches.

Distribution. Longfin sanddabs occur in the
eastern Pacific from Costa Rica to Monterey,
California, including the Gulf of California. They
are rare north of Santa Barbara.

Habitat. These flatfish are usually dwell on
sand or mud bottoms from 8 to 660 feet deep.

Spawning behavior. Females are larger than
males and normally mature when three years old
and roughly $7^1/_2$ inches long. They produce numerous eggs, and each fish probably spawns more than
once a season. The peak of the spawning season is
July through September.

Food. The diet of longfin sanddabs is wide
ranging and includes small fish, squid, octopus,
shrimp, crabs, and worms.

Angling. Where these and other sanddabs are
abundant, it is difficult to keep them off the hook.
Anglers use bait on small hooks, often two or more
on one bottom setup. A food-gathering variation
from the typical rig incorporates several dozen small
hooks dangled on an iron ring or hoop. This rig is
lowered on a stout line to a position just off the

bottom and allowed to remain a sufficient period to
fill all the hooks. Normally this does not require as
much time as is needed to rebait the rig after removing the catch. Small pieces of squid or octopus are
best because they are tough and stay on the hook
best, but fish works equally well as a bait.
See: **Drift Fishing; Flatfish; Inshore Fishing.**

SANDDAB, PACIFIC   *Citharichthys sordidus.*
Other names—mottled sanddab, sole, sanddab,
soft flounder, megrim; Spanish: *lenguado.*

A member of the Bothidae family of left-eyed
flatfish *(see),* the Pacific sanddab is an excellent food
fish that has both commercial significance and a
popular sportfishing following. This species is often
listed on the seafood menu of California restaurants, and is viewed by some as a delicacy.

Identification. The body of the Pacific sanddab is oblong and compressed. The head is deep,
and the eyes are large and on the left side. The color
is light brown mottled with yellow and orange on
the eyed side, and white on the blind side.

The Pacific sanddab can be distinguished from
the longfin sanddab *(see: sanddab, longfin)* by the
length of the pectoral fin on the eyed side. It is
always shorter than the head of the Pacific sanddab
and longer than the head of the longfin. Sanddabs
are always left-eyed and can be distinguished from
other left-eyed flatfish by their lateral line, which is
nearly straight for its entire length.

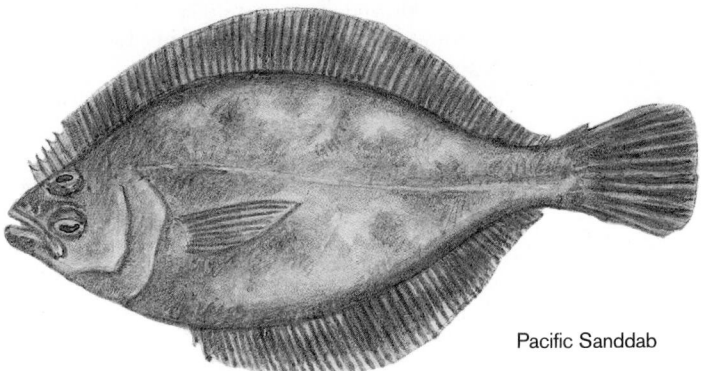
Pacific Sanddab

Size. These fish may reach 16 inches and 2 pounds but are common to just 10 inches in size and under a half-pound.

Distribution. Pacific sanddabs occur in the eastern Pacific from the Sea of Japan, Aleutian Islands, and Bering Sea to Cabo San Lucas, Baja California, Mexico. They are common in shallow coastal water from British Columbia to California.

Habitat. These flatfish are found on sand bottoms in water that ranges from 30 to 1,800 feet deep, but they are most abundant at depths of 120 to 300 feet.

Spawning behavior. Females are larger than males and normally mature at age 3, at roughly 8 inches in length. They produce numerous eggs, and each fish probably spawns more than once in a season. The peak of the spawning season is July through September.

Food. The diet of Pacific sanddabs is wide ranging and includes small fish, squid, octopus, shrimp, crabs, and worms.

Angling. Sportfishing activities are similar to those for the longfin sanddab.

See: **Drift Fishing; Flatfish; Inshore Fishing.**

SAND EEL

Common term for sand lance *(see)*.

SAND LANCE

American Sand Lance   *Ammodytes americanus.*

Northern Sand Lance   *Ammodytes dubius.*

Pacific Sand Lance   *Ammodytes hexapterus.*

Other names—Sand launce, sand eel, launce-fish, sandlance; French: *lançon.*

Resembling small eels, sand lance are burrowing fish that are important as food for many gamefish. They are excellent to eat when prepared in the style of whitebait.

Identification. Sand lance are small, slim, elongated, and round-bodied fish with no teeth, usually no pelvic fins, no fin spines, and a forked tail. Although they have a long soft dorsal fin, they do not have a first dorsal fin. The body has sloping fleshy folds, and there is a distinct fleshy ridge along the lower side; the straight lateral line is close to the base of the dorsal fin.

Fin-ray and vertebral counts distinguish the American sand lance from the northern sand lance; the American sand lance has 51 to 62 dorsal fin rays, 23 to 33 anal fin rays, and 61 to 73 vertebrae, whereas the northern sand lance has 56 to 68 dorsal fin rays, 27 to 35 anal fin rays, and 65 to 78 vertebrae. Sand lance can be distinguished from young eels by their separate rather than continuous dorsal and anal fins, and by the rounded caudal fin of the eel.

Size. Sand lance grow to a length of about 6 inches.

Distribution. Sand lance occur in temperate and colder parts of the Atlantic and Pacific Oceans and in the Indian Ocean. On the western Atlantic coast, sand lance range from north Quebec to North Carolina. Northern sand lance are believed to inhabit deeper waters, whereas American sand lance inhabit inshore areas. Pacific sand lance range from the Sea of Japan to arctic Alaska, the Bering Sea, and to Balboa Island in Southern California. The arctic and Pacific sand lance may be separate species, distinct from Atlantic populations.

Habitat. Schools of American sand lance are often abundant in shallow water along sandy shores and are found in salinities of 26 to 32 percent. For protection, the fish quickly burrow into the sand, snout first, to a depth of about 6 inches. Quantities of sand lance are often dug up in the intertidal zone by people seeking clams.

Angling. There is no angling value to sand lance; they are important as a food for many gamefish, including arctic charr, coho salmon, mackerel, and striped bass, and their appearance and burrowing activity invite angling imitation both with lures and technique.

SAND SPIKE

A rod-holding tube, pointed at one end for insertion into the sand, used by surf anglers to secure a rod.

See: **Surf Fishing.**

SÃO TOMÉ AND PRÍNCIPE

The independent and democratic Republic of São Tomé and Príncipe comprises islands of the same name, as well as several small islets anchored in the Atlantic Ocean in the Gulf of Guinea. São Tomé and Príncipe is 320 kilometers off the west coast of Africa and 230 kilometers from Gabon. It is recognized as an exciting and different location for tourists and offshore fishing enthusiasts.

Part of an archipelago, the islands are volcanic in origin, leaving a jumbled mass of rocky peaks, tropical rain forests, and striking waterfalls. The southern portion of São Tomé Island crosses the equator, yet the weather is unexpectedly sublime.

Sportfishing in São Tomé and Príncipe is limited exclusively to the exclusive Bom-Bom Island Resort on the northern end of Príncipe. One of the most elegant and full-featured resorts in Africa, it caters to diving and ecotours in addition to sportfishing.

American Sand Lance

The waters off Bom-Bom (also known as Bombom) host an enormous range of gamefish, particularly sailfish, blue marlin, kingfish, yellowfin tuna, dorado, snapper, barracuda, and bonito. Many world records have been established locally, especially for Atlantic sailfish. The best fishing times appear to be between July and December; January through March are largely unproductive. Blue marlin are plentiful in August, and sailfish run in packs in October and November.

The resort has a fleet of well-equipped charter boats with English-speaking skippers and mates from South Africa (Portuguese is the official language), and both offshore and inshore fishing are offered. Anglers access São Tomé and Príncipe from Lisbon, via Abidjan (Ivory Coast), and arrive on the island of São Tomé, where they overnight at the Marlin Beach Hotel before flying to Bom-Bom the following morning.

SARATOGA   *Scleropages leichardti.*

Other names—spotted barramundi, 'toga, Dawson River salmon, southern saratoga, spotted bonytongue.

Not to be confused with the barramundi, to which it is unrelated, the saratoga is one of eight species of the family Osteoglossidae, two of which live in Australia. Its counterpart is the gulf saratoga (or northern spotted barramundi; *Scleropages jardinii*). Both species appear, naturally, to be confined to the freshwater streams of the Northern Territory, Gulf of Carpentaria, and Cape York in Australia, and the latter also appears in Indonesia. Spectacular fighters when in open water away from weedbeds and underwater obstructions, they are highly respected by recreational anglers who practice catch-and-release. Being very bony and lacking in flavor, saratoga do not make good table fare.

Identification.   The saratoga is a long-bodied fish with a straight forehead profile, a scaleless head, and a large, upturned mouth with two chin barbels, large body scales, and a small, convex caudal fin. Both the dorsal and anal fins are posteriorly placed and dark brown in color and a bluish tinge along the edge. The lighter-colored pectorals are pointed, and the pelvic fin is small. Body coloration changes from dark brown on the back to silvery below, and there are one or two large orange or red spots on most of the scales. The gulf saratoga, which is of similar body design, has a convex forehead profile, and spotted dorsal, caudal, and anal fins.

Size.   The saratoga grows to a length of 900 millimeters and a weight exceeding 4 kilograms. A record for this species stands at 4.2 kilograms. The gulf saratoga has been recorded to 17.2 kilograms and more than 900 millimeters in length.

Distribution.   The range of the saratoga extends from the Adelaide River in the Northern Territory to the Jardine River in Cape York, and

into southern Queensland, where it has been stocked in some impoundments and river systems.

Habitat.   Although found in numerous freshwater streams, the saratoga prefers stillwater conditions such as those encountered in billabongs *(see)*, backwaters, and lagoons. In these waterways, they prefer areas of lily pads, weedbeds, and overhanging banks and pandanus trees.

Life history/Behavior.   The fecundity of the saratoga is low, up to 200 eggs, and spawning usually occurs during spring (September through November) and at night. The eggs are carried in the female's mouth, and although the larvae leave her mouth from time to time, they return until the egg sac is used up. As the upturned mouth indicates, this fish is a surface feeder, and adult fish patrol close to the surface as they seek out insects and other food. They are known to jump from the water to take dragonflies or other insects.

Food and feeding habits.   The saratoga's diet is a varied one, consisting of insects, small fish, frogs, crayfish, shrimp, lizards, mice, and whatever else they happen upon as they cruise just below the surface.

Angling.   Lure casters will find the saratoga an exciting fish to catch, especially on lines of up to 4- to 5-kilograms breaking strength. Subsurface plugs, surface poppers, spinners, and streamer flies are effective. Sight fishing to surface-feeding saratoga, or tossing lures under overhanging pandanus trees or along the edges of lily pads, are favored methods.

The flycaster who tosses a streamer about a meter in front of a patrolling fish can expect a split-second attack when the fly settles on the water. The resulting fight will be both spectacular and hard, provided the fish can be prevented from gaining sanctuary among subsurface structures or weedbeds.

Natural-bait anglers frequently use floats rather than probing the bottom, where it is unlikely fish will be searching for food. If the bait, which can be pieces of fish, frogs, shrimp, and the like, is suspended about 50 to 60 centimeters under the float, it will lie in the path of any patrolling saratoga. Hook size can be as large as 4/0. A wire or heavy mono leader is not necessary unless the fish is being sought in waters where barramundi are likely to exist.

SARDINE, PACIFIC   *Sardinops caeruleus.*

Other names—pilchard, California pilchard, California sardine, sardina; Spanish: *pilchard California, sardina de California, sardina Monterrey.*

Unlike the young of herring *(see)*, which are often marketed as sardines, the Pacific sardine is a true sardine. Once one of the most important commercial fish along the Pacific coast, the Pacific sardine population has been depleted by pollution and overfishing. The bulk of commercial fish is canned or processed to make fish meal, fertilizer, or oil, but Pacific sardines are not marketed fresh.

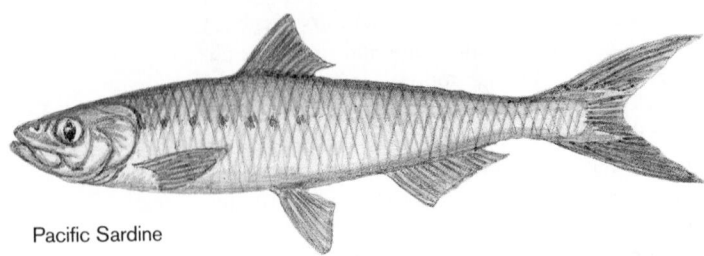

Pacific Sardine

Identification. The Pacific sardine has an elongated body, a compressed head, and a small mouth with no teeth. It is silvery with dark blue on the back, shades of purple and violet along the sides, and black spots along both the sides and the back. It can be distinguished from the typical herring by the absence of a sharp ridge of scales (which is found down the midline of the belly of herring), and by vertical ridges on its gill covers.

Distribution. In the eastern Pacific, Pacific sardines occur from southeastern Alaska to Cabo San Lucas, and throughout the Gulf of California, Mexico.

Life history/Behavior. In summer, Pacific sardines migrate northward from California to British Columbia and return in autumn or winter. They form large schools of various-size fish. Their eggs are pelagic, and unlike the eggs of herring, they float. Individuals generally mature in their second year.

Food. The Pacific sardine feeds mainly by filtering zooplankton and phytoplankton.

SARGO   *Anisotremus davidsonii.*

Other names—China croaker, blue bass, black croaker, grunt, xantic sargo; Spanish: *burro piedrero.*

The sargo is the largest of the Pacific grunts and is commonly caught incidentally by anglers fishing for other species, primarily during the summer.

Identification. The body of the adult sargo is a compressed oval shape, and the back is elevated. The head has a steep, straight upper profile and a small mouth. The sargo's coloring is a metallic silver, with a grayish tinge on the back. It is silvery below, and there is a distinguishing dark vertical bar running across the body from the dorsal fin to the base of the pectoral fin. Occasionally, sargo are entirely bright yellow, orange, or pure white.

Sargo

Young sargo, up to 4 inches, have several dark horizontal stripes. The vertical bar begins to appear when they are 2 to 3 inches long.

Size. These fish can reach a maximum length of 22 inches.

Distribution. Sargo occur in the eastern central Pacific from Magdalena Bay in Baja California, Mexico, to Santa Cruz, California.

Habitat. Sargo are found inshore and in bays over rocky and rock-sand bottoms, often near kelp beds, and around pilings or submerged structures. Although they can dwell in up to 130 feet of water, they are most common in water between 8 and 25 feet deep.

Life history/Behavior. Sargo swim close to the bottom in loose schools. The fish spawn in late spring and early summer. Spawning first occurs when the fish are about 7 inches long and two years old.

Food and feeding habits. Sargo are bottom feeders that primarily forage on small shrimp, crabs, clams, and snails.

Angling. *See: Grunts.*

SASKATCHEWAN

Driving through Saskatchewan on the Trans-Canada Highway, a traveler might form the impression that this province is an arid one dominated by wheat fields and dusty rolling hills with cattle ranches. This major-highway vantage point, however, doesn't reveal that this prairie province is home to more than 94,000 lakes and countless rivers and streams. In fact, fully one-eighth of Saskatchewan's one-quarter million square miles is covered with freshwater, resulting in a rich and varied sportfishery.

Indeed, Saskatchewan has several important river systems that drain large areas and provide significant habitat for many popular sportfish. Prominent native species include lake trout, grayling, walleye, sauger, northern pike, perch, whitefish, burbot, goldeye, and lake sturgeon. Throughout Saskatchewan, however, introduced species have also enriched the opportunities. Brown, rainbow, brook, cutthroat, and tiger trout, as well as splake, have been stocked in ponds, lakes, and streams throughout the province for most of the past 50 years, and a strong trout fishery is the result. One southern lake even offers a successful largemouth bass fishery.

Saskatchewan boasts an exceptional road-accessible fishing, especially in the far northern reaches of the province. Several paved and gravel highways and roads reach remote wilderness fishing lakes that would otherwise require long and expensive flights. And these same roads take the adventurous angler to jumping-off points where floatplanes provide still greater wilderness exploration.

More than 200 outfitters are scattered throughout the central and northernmost areas of the province, providing services that range from rustic to downright luxurious. In addition, outpost camps exist on hundreds of remote lakes where few have wet a line.

Although Saskatchewan's far north offers numerous trophy fisheries, especially for northern pike and lake trout, the southern region also has outstanding opportunities to catch trophy specimens. In the valleys of the North and South Saskatchewan Rivers, walleye (called pickerel here by many anglers) over 10 pounds are caught with remarkable frequency, and northern pike in the 10- to 20-pound range are fairly numerous. Although they are increasingly rare, large lake sturgeon are available, and big carp are a definite possibility. And some of the largest members of all species are caught in winter through the ice.

Southern Region

Trout streams.   Most of the southwest corner of Saskatchewan is characterized by rolling hills, remnants of short grass prairie, and one of the driest climates in western Canada. But tucked into small valleys and the folds of the Cypress Hills are among the best and most unheralded small trout streams in the Canadian west. Cypress Hills is named for a tree that doesn't actually grow in the area; the one that does is the lodgepole pine, and it suggests an alpine region far from the prairies. The hills rise to an altitude of more than 4,000 feet, on a par with Banff in the Rocky Mountains. Brown, brook, and rainbow trout inhabit streams and ponds throughout the area. Some of these streams have been managed since the 1920s, whereas others have been enhanced more recently.

One of the more notable trout waters is Battle Creek, which flows from Alberta through Fort Walsh National Historic Park and the west block of Cypress Hills Interprovincial Park, eventually joining Montana's Milk River. It is accessible by a dry-weather road, Highway 27, southwest of the town of Maple Creek. Some parts of Battle Creek can be reached only on foot. Cool water flows through alternating cobble riffles and deep pools. Parts of the creek are heavily overgrown and are best fished with small fly rods or light spinning tackle. Rainbow trout in the 1- to 2-pound range are common between the Alberta-Saskatchewan border and the southern boundary of Fort Walsh National Historic Park.

Another good site is Boiler Creek, which runs through the center of Cypress Hills Park. Surrounded by lodgepole pine in its upper reaches and open meadows below, the creek holds a series of beaver ponds that have good angling for pan-size brook trout. Anglers can reach it on foot or on a dry-weather vehicle trail. The creek is stocked annually with brookies.

Flourishing populations of brown, brook, and rainbow trout exist in Belanger Creek, which flows out of the Cypress Hills into Frenchman River to the south. Large brown trout are found in the slower waters of the southern reaches of the creek, and large rainbows dominate in the central section. Brook trout are most abundant in the upper reaches, which have lower water temperatures and fast riffles. The creek is accessible by road at several points along Highway 21 south of the town of Maple Creek.

Bear Creek runs down the north slope of the Cypress Hills south of the town of Piapot. Initially stocked in the 1920s with brown trout, it is now managed for brookies, which have been naturally reproducing for years. The population is occasionally supplemented by stocking, but fishing is generally rated from fair to excellent. Some sections of the creek are overgrown, but there are open sections and beaver ponds.

Bone Creek rises near the eastern edge of the Cypress Hills and flows eastward into Swift Current Creek. It has been managed as a brown trout fishery since the 1930s and is known as the area's best trout stream. Browns up to 10 pounds have been taken along its 27-mile length from reaches such as Klintonel, Tompkins, Garden Head, and Carmichael Bridges. Brown trout are still stocked annually to supplement natural reproduction in the creek. Big browns have been caught on dry and wet flies, and on spinning tackle.

Anglers land brown trout in Conglomerate Creek as well, which flows south out of the Cypress Hills to join Frenchman River. Browns are stocked here each year to augment natural reproduction. A number of reaches are readily fished by anglers, as there is plenty of open pasture land along the length of the creek. Access and parking are available at several points just off the Highway 614 grid road north of the town of Eastend. Calf Creek, a tributary to Conglomerate, has brook trout; the upper section runs swiftly over cobbles and farther down is a series of beaver dams that hold fish in good numbers.

Nearby Caton Creek runs south out of the Cypress Hills. Its cold upper reaches are home to pan-size brook trout. Fly fishing opportunities are very limited because of heavy cover along the stream bank, but fishing with light spinning tackle can be excellent, especially in some of the beaver ponds along the creek's length.

Swift Current Creek, an important watershed, flows north and east into the river arm of Lake Diefenbaker. As it passes through Pine Cree Regional Park, 33 miles south of the town of Tompkins, it is accessible to anglers seeking pan-size brook trout.

Running through a steep valley south of the Cypress Hills, Sucker Creek provides excellent fishing for pan-size brookies. South of the town of Maple Creek on Highway 21, Sucker Creek is best fished with light spinning tackle, as dense cover grows along the stream's banks.

Flowing across the southwest corner of Saskatchewan is the Frenchman River, the area's

S

main watershed, which has brook, brown, and rainbow trout, as well as walleye and northern pike. Accessible at many points, the Frenchman can be fished from shore or boat.

South Saskatchewan River. The waters that flow through the South Saskatchewan River rise in the Alberta foothills of the Rockies, then wander across southern prairies and the Badlands to meet with the North Saskatchewan River. The South Saskatchewan is home to trophy walleye, as well as sauger, pike, perch, rainbow trout, burbot, lake sturgeon, whitefish, goldeye, and carp.

In its western reaches toward the border with Alberta, the South Saskatchewan produces small numbers of the increasingly rare and pressured lake sturgeon, which are protected from overfishing by catch-and-release regulations, severe limits, or closed seasons, depending on the location. Both the South and North Saskatchewan Rivers hold lake sturgeon.

At Saskatchewan Landing Provincial Park, a half-hour north of the town of Swift Current, the river begins to widen into a classic impoundment called Lake Diefenbaker.

Lake Diefenbaker. One of the finest big-water fisheries in western Canada, T-shaped Lake Diefenbaker is 84 miles long from the southwest end at the park to the junction with the top of the T at the town of Elbow. From here it is 15 miles in either direction to the two dams. Although it is no more than a few hours' drive north of the border with the United States, and is accessible from all directions by paved highways, Lake Diefenbaker holds northern pike in excess of 20 pounds, walleye into the midteens, jumbo perch, and big rainbow trout. A rainbow trout over 20 pounds was caught by a shore angler in 1997, in the fast water below Gardiner Dam.

Big walleye are the most sought-after species in the lake. They're caught by anglers jigging off hundreds of lake points, trolling the edges of dropoffs and weedbeds with live-bait rigs, or trolling crankbaits for active fish feeding on minnows. Prime times for trophy walleye are spring and fall. In spring, look in shallower bays off the main lake where water temperatures have made the fish more active. In fall, large fish are linger off points, and in riprap near both dams.

Rainbow trout, some of which are escapees from commercial fish-farming operations, have done well in Diefenbaker Lake, and 5- to 10-pounders are not uncommon. They are caught by anglers casting from shore, trolling in boats, and fishing through the ice.

This large lake is underfished, in part because it is big and subject to high prairie winds from time to time. Big winds make for big waves and dangerous conditions for small craft. Close to almost every launch access on the lake, however, are areas that are protected from wind and that hold fish throughout the summer season.

This lake has notable opportunities for shore-bound anglers. When the region was flooded, many small side valleys, called coulees, filled with water. In springtime these sites are havens for large walleye that succumb to anglers casting jigs, crankbaits, or in-line spinners, and to those stillfishing with bait rigs from shore. Each year, large rainbow trout are caught on spinning or fly gear cast from the rocky face of the Qu'Appelle Dam at the southeast end of the reservoir. In fall, good-size rainbows are caught by shore anglers within sight of the Riverhurst Ferry, on the western arm of the lake.

Beyond Gardiner Dam at the northeast corner of Lake Diefenbaker, the South Saskatchewan continues to flow north through farmland and past Saskatoon, ultimately joining the North Saskatchewan River east of Prince Albert. The river produces excellent fishing along its length. Anglers working the banks in Saskatoon have caught walleye over 10 pounds during autumn.

Qu'Appelle River system. The Qu'Appelle River originates at the rock rubble dam at the southeast corner of Lake Diefenbaker. The Qu'Appelle drainage, which influences most of southeastern Saskatchewan, is a series of natural lakes and impoundments linked by the river as it flows eastward to meet the Assiniboine, which flows eastward into Manitoba.

Buffalo Pound, a very shallow impoundment, is the first significant lake to the east of Diefenbaker. It produces good numbers of perch, walleye, and pike in both summer and winter.

Downstream and about 60 miles northeast of the capital city of Regina lie Pasqua, Echo, Mission, and Katepwa Lakes. All four natural lakes hold good populations of walleye, perch, pike, and whitefish, as well as suckers, burbot, and some very large carp weighing in at 30-plus pounds.

Available launch facilities, provincial parks, major paved highways, and nearby services in the town of Ft. Qu'Appelle, make these four lakes amongst the most popular summer fishing holes in southern Saskatchewan. They are very fertile, and produce excellent numbers of pan-size perch, walleye in the 1- to 4-pound range, and pike over 10 pounds. Trophy walleye in excess of 10 pounds are taken from these lakes each year. Among the largest walleye are those taken during late-season ice fishing in March, off the mouths of the channels connecting these lakes.

Still farther east, Round and Crooked Lakes hold good populations of pike, walleye, perch, and whitefish. All of the Qu'Appelle drainage lakes sprout small towns of ice fishing shacks during the winter season.

Souris River drainage. One of the more unusual fishing opportunities in Saskatchewan is Boundary Dam Reservoir, a few miles south of the town of Estevan and virtually on the Saskatchewan–North Dakota border. This lake is home to a successfully reproducing population of introduced largemouth bass that are doing extremely well, protected by a reduced limit. Three- to 4-pounders are not uncommon, and trophies up to 7 pounds have been taken in the weedbeds and along the riprap of this reservoir.

The water from the reservoir is used to cool a coal-fired power-generating plant, and the warm water returning into the lake keeps its average temperatures well above normal year-round. Open-water fishing is possible near the warmwater discharge well after the rest of the province's lakes are frozen solid.

Two of Saskatchewan's newest reservoirs, created by the Rafferty and Alameda Dams on the nearby Souris River, are proving fertile and productive for walleye.

Last Mountain Lake.   Locally known as Long Lake, this narrow body of water runs nearly 70 miles from its southern edge at the Valeport Marsh to the shallow, rocky spawning waters at its northern end.

A one-hour drive from the capital city of Regina, it is accessible at numerous points along its length. Both shorelines host numerous resort communities with excellent launch facilities that are open to the public. Despite its southern location and ease of access, this is a world-class trophy lake for the patient angler.

Large walleye, many over 10 pounds, are caught in this lake every year. In spring, big fish concentrate at opposite ends of the lake near spawning areas. As summer progresses and water temperatures warm, large schools of walleye migrate toward the central portion of the lake, where they can be caught off main lake points, bars, and sunken rockpiles. The biggest fish are usually caught in fall, or just after freeze-up through the ice.

Last Mountain Lake also holds good populations of northern pike; fish over 10 pounds are common in spring and fall. Excellent carp, some over 30 pounds, are taken each year by anglers traveling here from as far away as Great Britain. Good populations of jumbo perch, some well over a pound, are here, too. Larger pike inhabit shallower bays off the main lake in spring and are taken by anglers casting plugs, spoons, and large streamer flies. In fall, large pike will strike spoons or plugs trolled along the outer edge of shoreline weedbeds and dropoffs.

Lake of the Prairies.   Lake of the Prairies is formed by a dam on the Assiniboine River, which rises in eastern Saskatchewan and flows through Manitoba. One-third of the lake lies in Saskatchewan.

It is home to an excellent population of walleye, pike, perch, and large carp. Visiting anglers should note that Manitoba angling rules apply to this body of water regardless of where it is fished.

North Saskatchewan River.   The North Saskatchewan River winds its way across central Saskatchewan, creating a majestic river valley and rich habitat for the production of large fish. Big walleye, pike, perch, suckers, carp, sauger, lake sturgeon, and goldeye are here. In many places the river is shallow, braiding its way through sandbars that shift with water at varying levels and changing currents. It is fishable from shore or from a boat.

Anglers fishing from shore in the city of Prince Albert have caught walleye well over 10 pounds, some on a simple leadhead jig adorned with bright plastic tail. Jigs tipped with frozen or salted minnows (live minnows are not legal for fishing in Saskatchewan) are often used for walleye, and are more effective the farther north in the province one travels.

Saskatchewan River.   Formed from the merger of the North and South Saskatchewan Rivers just east of Prince Albert, the Saskatchewan River flows easterly toward Manitoba through a series of impoundments that produce some of the best walleye fishing in North America.

The first of these is the newest, Codette Lake, formed when Francois-Finlay Dam was built. This relatively new reservoir is a good place to fish for pike and walleye, and many of the latter are in the 3- to 5-pound range. Jigs and live-bait rigs are the tools of choice, but take lots of extras for working the plentiful flooded timber here.

Just downstream of Codette Lake is a section of the Saskatchewan River that runs past the town of Nipawin and into Tobin Lake. This stretch is one of North America's top producers of trophy walleye. The provincial record was broken every year for four consecutive years in the mid-1990s, and the largest lunker weighed in at more than 18 pounds.

Both drifting downcurrent with jigs, and trolling crankbaits along the breakline between shoreline flats and the deep river channel, produce trophy fish, but the primary tactic here is drifting with a long-snelled (10 feet or more) bottom-bouncing bait rig with small hooks and a live leech.

Although the river has been subjected to intense angling pressure, and catches of 4- to 8-pound fish have declined, the patient angler can still find success. Fish over 10 pounds are caught almost daily throughout September and October. Anglers fishing the river will also catch good numbers of sauger, goldeye, suckers, and the occasional lake sturgeon. The river produces best for walleye in spring and fall, and fishing in Tobin Lake is good throughout the warmer summer months. Tobin also produces pike from 15 to well over 20 pounds in the open-water angling season. Tobin is one of the most heavily fished waters in the province, and special regulations have been placed on it to protect the midrange walleye and pike.

Below the E. B. Campbell Dam, which forms Lake Tobin, and downriver to Cumberland Delta and Cumberland Lake, a number of fishing lodges and camps host anglers looking for walleye, large pike, sauger, sturgeon, whitefish, and goldeye in a wilderness setting. Cumberland Lake links the

In 1915, 400 million pounds of salmon were harvested in Alaska, an amount that would then have filled 10,000 freight cars whose total length would have exceeded 100 miles. According to surveys, each year anglers in Minnesota keep about $3^{1}/_{2}$ million walleye totaling 4 million pounds.

Saskatchewan River, which continues eastward into Manitoba, to the Churchill River to the north, through the Sturgeon-Weir River; this was a crucial hub in the historic "Voyageur Highway" canoe route that brought fur traders all the way from Montreal to the Northwest Territories. Much of this part of Saskatchewan is still isolated wilderness, not much changed from the days of the *voyageurs*.

Central Region

Prince Albert National Park. Prince Albert National Park is one of two national parks in Saskatchewan. Within its boundaries are Crean, Waskesiu, and Kingsmere Lakes. Crean and Kingsmere hold lake trout, pike, walleye, and whitefish. Waskesiu has no viable lake trout population. Anglers wishing to fish in national parks should note that separate regulations and licenses apply within these parks.

Hanson Lake Road. Known both as Highway 106 and Hanson Lake Road, this route runs north through Narrow Hills Provincial Park and then east to the Manitoba border, providing access to exceptional fishing. It leads anglers along prime trout waters in the Narrow Hills Park area, including such stocked streams as McDougal Creek, Mossy River, Steep Creek, and White Gull Creek. For anglers willing to drive on gravel roads a little farther off the beaten track, this highway affords access to lakes like Piprell, Little Bear, East Trout, and Big Sandy.

Piprell is a trophy rainbow trout fishery and has produced a 19.2-pound specimen. Other species of trout are stocked in nearby lakes. East Trout and Little Bear Lakes hold lake trout, northern pike, whitefish, and perch. Big Sandy holds walleye, pike, and whitefish.

A short drive to the southwest are the Whiteswan Lakes, which contain good populations of lake trout and pike, and Candle Lake, which is an excellent walleye, pike, and whitefish site in both open-water and ice fishing seasons.

Farther east are larger lakes like Big Sandy, Hanson, Deschambault, Jan, Amisk, and Mirond.

One of the largest lakes in the area, Deschambault has a big, southern sandy basin that is particularly good for pike. The two northern arms of the lake are rocky and better habitat for walleye. Fish creek mouths in spring until the water starts warming up, then move out to the deeper edges of points. Jan holds an excellent population of pan-size walleye.

All of the lakes along the Hanson Lake Road are "drive-to" wilderness lakes serviced by outfitters and lodges set in the rugged scenery of the Canadian Shield. They hold a variety of species, from walleye and perch to northern pike and whitefish, and—in those lakes farther north of the road—lake trout.

Meadow Lake area. The region north of the town of North Battleford in west-central Saskatchewan is dotted with dozens of lakes and a number of parks, and has very little human population. Most of the lakes here, like Chitek, Ministikwan, Makwa, and Delaronde, are home to good populations of perch, northern pike, walleye, and whitefish. Turtle Lake holds large trophy pike and is the home of the "turtle lake monster," a creature occasionally sighted by anglers and boaters and thought to be a very large sturgeon.

Flotten Lake, in the northeast corner of Meadow Lake Provincial Park, is a northern walleye lake with rocky islands, reefs, and points. This lake has such classic walleye structure as rocky shoals and steep dropoffs, and serves up lots of 2- to 6-pound fish. Farther north, Dore and Canoe Lakes are remote wilderness waters that can be driven to on paved and gravel highways. They hold good numbers of walleye, pike, and whitefish.

Limited services are available at nearby First Nations communities, and provincial campgrounds exist in the area. Lac La Plonge, deeper and colder than other area lakes, has lake trout in addition to other typical species.

Lac La Ronge and vicinity. In the center of Saskatchewan amidst hundreds of fishing lakes, Lac La Ronge is a seven-hour drive north from the province's capital city of Regina. This huge northern Canadian Shield lake has two distinct characters: The northern half is dotted with hundreds of islands, and the shoreline is cut with long, fiordlike bays; the southern half is a large open basin, exposed to strong winds that sometimes whip its waters into 9- and 10-foot waves.

Lac La Ronge has literally hundreds of good fishing spots for walleye, northern pike, and lake trout. Although lakers have been severely pressured in recent years and stocks are lower than they once were, recent reductions in both commercial and sportfishing limits have helped to strengthen lake trout numbers. Prime time for walleye and pike is between mid-June and the last week of August. Lake trout are in shallow water in early to mid-June for a short period, and again during spawning in the fall, between mid-September and mid-October, depending on weather and water temperatures. During the warmer days of midsummer, lake trout are deep and are found off midlake reefs or deep-water points, perhaps as far as 100 feet down.

The lake is well serviced by outfitters, guide services, and lodges, especially those based in the town of La Ronge, and on the eastern shoreline in the Hunter's Bay area.

La Ronge is not only a significant fishing lake in its own right, but it is also the hub for hundreds of fishing destinations farther north. In summer, constant floatplane traffic buzzes over the town as anglers head for fly-in destinations lying within an hour or two of their departure point.

For the drive-in angler, however, there are dozens more road-accessible lakes and rivers to the north. Just an hour from the town of La Ronge, on

S

gravel Highway 102, is Saskatchewan's largest northern river, the Churchill. Along the way, anglers will drive past several excellent fisheries. Nemeiben Lake, just north and east of La Ronge, is a high-quality walleye, lake trout, and pike fishery, serviced by resorts and campgrounds.

As the road winds northward, it passes many small pothole lakes holding rainbow and speckled trout, as well as McKay Lake, which is a small lake trout fishery. Anglers who like to canoe and get off the beaten path should seek out lakes like Mekewap, to find rainbow trout that are not heavily fished and will rise to dry flies readily throughout July and August. Getting there is half the fun. From Highway 102, paddle across Lynx Lake and portage across to Duck Lake. Travel up Duck Lake and cross over into Sulphide Lake, then portage into Mekewap.

North of the Churchill River, 102 continues far into the northern bush. It travels past wilderness lakes such as Waddy, Brabant, and McLennan, which are noted pike and lake trout fisheries. It also connects to Highway 905, a gravel road that runs north past Reindeer Lake to Wollaston Lake and remote northern Saskatchewan.

There is no lack of opportunity throughout the area along 102, as well as farther east and west. West of La Ronge, in fact, is Besnard Lake—a large, rocky walleye and pike lake that provides especially good fishing in the peak season between June and August. Reached via Highway 2 north from Prince Albert Park to Highways 165 and 910, this lake has recovered in recent years from depressed walleye numbers and now produces steady action.

Churchill River drainage. In the northwestern section of the central region, the waters of Turnor, Frobisher, and Peter Pond Lakes flow into Churchill Lake and then into the Churchill River, one of Canada's most historic river systems. The Churchill River flows southeast through Lac Isle-à-la-Crosse, runs northward to the village of Patuanak, and then turns eastward and winds across Saskatchewan into northern Manitoba and eventually to Hudson Bay.

This river was at the heart of the old Voyageur Highway. The Saskatchewan portion of the Churchill was the essential link between southern and northern watersheds. Today the Churchill has been nominated as one of Canada's Heritage Rivers, in recognition of its cultural, historical, social, and environmental significance.

In Saskatchewan, the Churchill forms the boundary between the true Canadian Shield country to the north and the forest lands to the south. This is a territory of rocks and clear water, spruce and birch. It is also an area in which opportunities for great fishing abound. The Churchill is a series of lakes connected by short passages of fast water, rapids, or waterfalls. It is home to abundant wildlife and waters containing walleye, northern pike, whitefish, and lake trout. The Churchill River is also a world-class canoeing destination, and few trippers paddle it without adding meals of fresh fish to their packed-in food.

The Churchill drainage is home to literally dozens of fishing camps and lodges, located all along its length. Although it is a true wilderness river, in many areas virtually unchanged since the days of the fur traders, it is accessible by numerous roads.

Highway 155 is a paved two-lane highway that runs to the village of Buffalo Narrows on Churchill Lake at the river's headwaters. Gravel road No. 918 runs north to the village of Patuanak. Gravel road No. 914 runs north to Pinehouse Lake in the middle section of the river. Gravel Highway 102 runs north from La Ronge to Otter Rapids and Otter Lake, a favorite departure point for anglers and canoeists. It is the site of several lodges, the village of Missinipe (which is the Cree name for the Churchill, meaning "big river"), and a floatplane base for north-bound adventurers. Just before it enters Manitoba, the Churchill meets gravel road No. 135 at the village of Sandy Bay, just downstream from the Island Falls Dam. This is the only dam on the Churchill in Saskatchewan. Up to this point, its flow is unimpeded along its entire length.

Some anglers tow their own boats along these roads and launch them on the Churchill, where provincial parks have provided access, or at outfitters, where they may be charged a modest docking fee. The Churchill River is drive-in wilderness fishing at its peak. Lakes all along the Churchill that aren't accessible by road are readily reached by floatplane from La Ronge or Otter Lake.

Northern Region
Smaller lakes. Gravel Highway 905 gives anglers access to some of the northernmost drive-in fishing in Canada. Lakes like Davin, Pardoe, and Wathaman lie adjacent to this route and provide excellent angling for lake trout, northern pike, and walleye. The Geikie River crosses the highway as it flows into the south end of Wollaston Lake, and here, in ice-cold fast water below rapids and falls, anglers find arctic grayling holding behind rocks and in eddies.

The highway travels remote northeastern Saskatchewan all the way past the west side of Wollaston Lake to Points North Landing. From here, floatplanes take anglers into the most remote northern fly-in lakes in northern Saskatchewan (many of these lakes are also accessed directly from points south, such as Regina or Saskatoon or Winnipeg, via wheeled charter planes that land on private airstrips).

Although a few of the big waters in this region can be accessed by driving to their southern extremity, these and other near-north wilderness lakes are mainly or entirely accessed by air. Fly-in-only sites include Cree, Foster, Hatchet, Waterbury, Close, Deception, Paul, Hepburn, and Unknown Lakes.

S

These locations are typically supported by one or more full-service lodges. They hold excellent populations of lake trout, northern pike, and whitefish. Some, like Cree and Hatchet, are well known and have produced trophy pike and lakers for many years. The more southerly lakes, or those with areas of shallower water and sand, may hold walleye as well, although seldom huge specimens. The farther north a lake is situated, the more likely it is to hold arctic grayling. Grayling are typically found where there is moving water; a stream flowing into or out of a lake is a good place to look for them.

From the Churchill River drainage northward, there are scores of small, isolated lakes that have only an outpost camp or are accessed only for day trips. Many lodges established on big lakes will fly anglers in to these places. Some such lakes are virtually virgin waters, seeing at most only a few dozen anglers a year.

Reindeer, Wollaston, and Athabasca Lakes. In the same northern reaches of Saskatchewan are the three largest lakes in the province. Two, Wollaston and Reindeer, are accessible by road, although many anglers prefer to avoid the lengthy wilderness drives and fly in. The third, Athabaska, is accessible only by air.

These lakes are big water. Reindeer, the most southerly of the three and partly stretching into Manitoba, stretches more than 120 miles from end to end. It is littered with thousands of islands and is especially known for an abundant northern pike population, as well as for producing many specimens over 20 pounds. The lake harbors large numbers of medium-size lake trout and loads of walleye. Several full-service fishing lodges accommodate anglers.

Wollaston Lake is farther north than and roughly half the size of Reindeer, yet it has more than 800 square miles of water, making it the third largest lake in the province. All of that water holds good-size lake trout as well as a tremendous population of northern pike and plenty of walleye in shallow,

sandy areas. The walleye are average in size, but the pike here grow big, and Wollaston is known for pike over 20 pounds. Some specimens are in the 25-pound class and range up to as large as 35 pounds. Wollaston is also serviced by a number of lodges, and some of these have plenty of fly-out opportunities. The season on these two northern lakes is from early June to early September.

Of the three great northern fishing lakes, Athabaska is by far the largest. It lies between the 59th and 60th parallels, just south of the Northwest Territories border. It runs 180 miles east to west, extending from Ft. Chippewyan in Alberta to Fond du Lac at its eastern end. One of Canada's largest lakes, Athabasca covers more than 1.3 million acres and is part of the Mackenzie River drainage that flows to the Arctic Ocean.

Athabaska is home to huge lakers and monster pike. Lake trout over 50 pounds have been caught on rod and reel, and a reported 102-pounder was landed here in a commercial net in the 1960s; 20-pound pike are common. The lake also has walleye and arctic grayling. Despite these attributes, Athabaska has light fishing pressure and is serviced by very few outfitters. Remoteness has something to do with that, as do the lake's enormity and open expanses. Athabaska can be a dangerous lake in high winds. The best fishing occurs between mid-June and late August.

The far north.   Still farther north are several wilderness lakes situated virtually or actually on the border with the Northwest Territories. Accessible only by air, these include Ena, Tazin, Scott, and Selwyn Lakes. With minimal fishing pressure, these remote lakes are trophy waters for northern pike and lakers. Catch-and-release policies are the rule. Two lodges operate on Tazin, and one each on the others. Opportunities exist to fly to remote sites for day trips or to more isolated outpost lakes. Grayling thrive at some sites. Although they are typically in the 1 1/2-pound range, specimens weighing more than 3 pounds inhabit some waters.

Lake trout over 20 pounds are probable, and lakers ranging from 30 to 50 pounds are possible; pike are numerous to 15 pounds, and specimens from 20 to 25 pounds or more are caught fairly often. Anglers often catch 5- to 12-pound fish of either species all day long. The period following ice out is favored for shallow action, but good deep-water anglers can score on lakers throughout the summer. The big fish are caught late in the season when they come to spawn on reefs. Because late August and early September can bring rugged weather, these periods are often bypassed; but hard-core trout anglers score very well then. It's a very limited season, of course, generally running from the second week of June through the first week of September.

Scott Lake, which sprawls over the 60th parallel into the Northwest Territories, is somewhat typical of these far-north lakes. Scott is a big, interesting lake, 40 miles long and 40 miles wide at its greatest

Pike anglers navigate the back bays of Scott Lake.

points. Just 100 miles below the arctic tree line, the lake bears some tundra influence in the north, yet in the south it is distinctly reminiscent of southern Ontario, with craggy cliffs, jackpine shorelines, and plenty of birch trees. It has five long arms, an extraordinary number of bays, and all the islands, nooks, crannies, and shoreline you can possibly imagine.

Pike fishing starts with ice out in early June and continues throughout the summer. Many visitors will catch a 20-pounder if they work at it, and some do far better. Pike up to 38 pounds having been landed here. Lake trout are plentiful, too, including trophy specimens in the 20- to 40-pound class. These fish tend to cluster in deep-water areas throughout the summer. Anglers catch many of the biggest lakers from mid-July through August, when the fish are deep and hard to access, favoring more sophisticated angling methods than those used in most far-north camps. For both pike and lake trout, the camp policy is catch-and-release only, with barbless hooks.

Several top-quality fly-out experiences are available from Scott Lake. There is an outpost camp at Premier Lake, a distant water connected to Scott where a 30-pound pike and 40-pound laker have been caught, and there's an outpost camp on Wignes Lake. Outstanding day-trip fishing for grayling is available on the Dubawnt River, and also at Lefty Falls.

Lefty Falls, officially known as Hunt Falls and the tallest waterfall in central Canada, is packed with grayling. This falls is among the province's most impressive natural wonders and a site often used for advertising the wilderness charm of Saskatchewan. It is theoretically accessible by boat: You would have to run 60 miles of the Griese River from Scott and Wignes Lakes, negotiate its rapids, and make a grueling portage around the falls. Otherwise, you fly in by floatplane and trek through thick and mosquito-laden bush to reach the splendorous falls.

A premier Saskatchewan lake trout haven, Ena Lake is a 15-mile-long glacial-carved body of water that straddles the 60th parallel northeast of Tazin Lake. It has never known commercial fishing (a factor that impacts resources in northern lakes) and has been visited by relatively few anglers since a lodge opened there in 1990.

A well-sheltered scenic wilderness lake that sports many bays and islands, Ena is blessed with numerous deep troughs that keep the water cool all season. The best angling for lake trout occurs in June, following ice out, and in September, when the fish are spawning on reefs. Many 25- to 30-pound trout thrive here, and lakers have been caught to 53 pounds. Ena Lake also provides good fishing for northern pike. They, too, are frequently caught in trophy proportions, from 18 to 26 pounds, and all are released alive. Bays and islands provide suitable cover, and in summer, pike are favored over deep lakers. This is a catch-and-release, barbless-hook-only fishery.

SAUGER   *Stizostedion canadense.*

Other names—sand pickerel, sand pike, blue pickerel, pike, gray pike, blue pike, river pike, pike-perch, spotfin pike, jack, jack fish, jack salmon; French: *doré noir.*

A member of the perch family, the sauger is a smaller, slimmer relative of the walleye, which it closely resembles. It is an important commercial species in some places, especially in Canada, and a gamefish that is often overlooked in some parts of its range. Most of the commercial Canadian catch is taken in Manitoba, where fishing with gillnets and pound nets occurs in summer, autumn, and winter. Sauger are marketed almost entirely as fresh and frozen fillets, and much of the catch is exported to the United States. Their flesh is slightly softer, sweeter, and finer in texture than that of the walleye, but this difference is generally indistinguishable to most people, and commercially they are sold as one and the same fish.

Identification.   The sauger's body is slender and almost cylindrical, and the head is long and cone shaped. The back and sides are a dull brown or olive gray flecked with yellow and shading to white over the belly. There are three or four dark saddle-shaped blotches on the back and sides. It is easily distinguished from the smooth-cheeked walleye by the presence of rough scales on its cheeks and two or three rows of distinct black spots on the membranes of its spiny dorsal fin, by the absence of a large blotch on the anterior portion of its spinous dorsal fin, and by the absence of a white tip on its tail. The eyes are large and glossy, and the teeth are large and sharp.

Size/Age.   Sauger are commonly caught at sizes ranging from 10 to 16 inches and up to $1\frac{1}{2}$ pounds. Specimens exceeding 22 inches and 5 pounds are rare. The maximum size is about 9 pounds, and the all-tackle world record is an 8-pound, 12-ounce fish caught in North Dakota in 1971. The life span is 10 to 12 years.

Distribution.   This species has a general distribution in mid-central North America from Quebec to Tennessee and Arkansas, and northwesterly through Montana to about central Alberta. Between Alberta and Quebec it occurs in southern Saskatchewan, Manitoba, and Ontario and throughout the Great Lakes to James Bay. It does not occur east of the Appalachians or much south of Tennessee except in a few drainages where it has been introduced, principally from the Carolinas

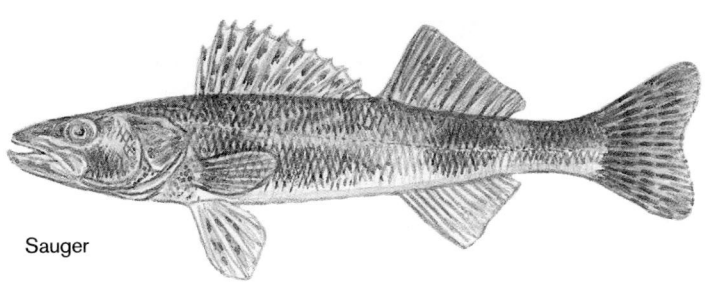

Sauger

around through the lower coastal states to as far south as Texas on the lower Gulf of Mexico.

Habitat.   Habitat preferences of the sauger tend to large, turbid, shallow lakes and large, silty, slow-flowing rivers. It is more tolerant of muddy water and swifter current than are walleye, and it prefers water temperatures between 62° and 72°F. It is often found in tailwaters below dams, and along rocky riprap. Eddies near turbulent water are often staging and feeding areas. Gravel bars and points are prominent holding locations in lakes.

Life history/Behavior.   Male sauger mature at age 2, females at ages 3 or 4. They spawn when the water temperature is between 41° and 46°F. Adults enter backwaters or tributaries or congregate in tailwaters and search for gravel or rock substrate where they can deposit their eggs. In large river systems, the upstream spawning run can cover 100 to 200 miles, although it will be just a short distance from reservoirs into tributaries. In waters where they occur with walleye, they will usually spawn immediately after walleye. Sauger can naturally interbreed with walleye, producing a fish called a saugeye *(see)*. Sauger grow more slowly than do walleye, however, and are primarily a river fish that locate near the bottom on a variety of bottom types. Like walleye, they are a schooling species.

Food and feeding habits.   Sauger feed on such small fish as shad, sunfish, and minnows, as well as on crayfish, leeches, and insects. Most feeding occurs over rocky gravel bottoms or along sparsely weeded sandy bottoms.

Angling.   Sauger can provide year-round fishing, although they are often deliberately targeted only in specific seasons in certain locales (through the ice in the north, or in winter and spring in the south) and are otherwise caught incidentally. Although locations and fishing methods for sauger are similar to those for walleye *(see)*, these fish tend to live deeper and are also more aggressive when located, usually striking solidly. They also are even more bottom-oriented. Scaled-down presentations, including lighter and smaller lures, are more appropriate. Blade baits, tail-spinners, in-line spinners, and jigs tipped with minnows are good artificials, and deep-running small-bodied plugs are also effective when deep-trolled. Live minnows are preferred baits, and bait rigs fished deep are also productive.

SAUGEYE

The saugeye is a hybrid fish resulting from the interbreeding of walleye and sauger. It occurs naturally, although infrequently, where the two species mix together. Most populations are produced in hatcheries and are usually stocked in locations where neither parent species has been able to maintain a population. In some literature, it is identified as *Stizostedion vitreum x S. canadense,* which

Saugeye

refers to a cross between a female walleye and a male sauger. The meat of saugeye is similar to that of its parents, making it excellent table fare.

Identification.   The body of the saugeye is more similar to that of a walleye than to that of a sauger, although the dorsal fin is sometimes spotted (it is on the sauger and is not on the walleye). It also has saddlelike markings on the back and sides, as the sauger does; and the caudal fin has a white border on its lower lobe, as the walleye does. Saugeye also have a dark blotch on the membranes of the spiny dorsal fin. The body may have a yellowish cast.

Size/Age.   This fish grows rapidly and has the potential to reach the intermediate sizes, although not the overall size, that walleye typically attain. The all-tackle world record is a 12-pound, 6-ounce fish from Ohio. Typical saugeye are about 15 inches in length, and normally range from 10 to 24 inches.

Distribution.   The saugeye has been introduced to waters in the United States from western Ohio, Kentucky, and Tennessee to the eastern Dakotas and southward to Oklahoma.

Habitat.   Like their sauger parent, saugeye are more tolerant of muddy or turbid water than are walleye, and seem better suited to impoundments that receive a high rate of water exchange (which increases turbidity). The introduction of saugeye to new waters, however, is still in its early stages.

Spawning behavior.   Unlike some hybrid species, saugeye are not sterile and do have the ability to produce offspring with either parent stock. Spawning occurs in tributaries or in tailwater areas when the temperature is between 40° and 50°F.

Food.   Small fish are the primary food for saugeye. Shad are especially favored in many lakes and rivers.

Angling.   Winter tailwater fishing for saugeye is especially popular in some areas, as these fish are aggressive and one of the few gamefish that are concentrated and active then. Many of the same areas that would be fished for walleye *(see)* are appropriate for saugeye, although saugeye are likely to hold deeper. Midsummer fishing on lakes or impoundments can be tough, as the fish are more scattered, although they are highly structure oriented. Jigs tipped with minnows or worms, live-bait rigs, and medium-size crankbaits (which are trolled) are all good saugeye catchers.

Pacific Saury

SAURIES

Abundant offshore fish, sauries are members of the four-species Scomberesocidae family. They have only moderately elongated jaws that are beaknon, and are easily distinguished from needlefish *(see)* and halfbeaks *(see: halfbeaks and balao)* by the five to seven finlets behind the dorsal and anal fins, as in mackerel. Sauries as a group have small scales, a relatively small mouth opening, small teeth, and no swim bladder. These relatively abundant fish are heavily preyed upon by tuna, marlin, bluefish, and other predators.

The Atlantic saury *(Scomberesox saurus)* travels in schools containing thousands of fish. They are commonly attacked by a variety of predators that sometimes drive the schools into shallow nearshore waters. Often a whole school will rise simultaneously from the sea and skitter across the surface (for this reason commercial fishermen refer to them as "skippers"). They are sometimes caught commercially when abundant, but they are not fished for regularly.

The Atlantic saury occurs in the eastern Atlantic from Iceland and Norway along the British Isles to the Baltic Sea and throughout the Mediterranean, Adriatic, and Aegean Seas to Morocco. In the western Atlantic, they occur from the Gulf of St. Lawrence south to North Carolina and Bermuda. Atlantic saury are also known as, in French: *balaou;* Italian: *costardella;* Norwegian: *makrellejedde;* Portuguese: *agulhao;* Turkish: *zurna.*

The Pacific saury *(Cololabis saira)* is similar and has a significant commercial interest as well. Also known as mackerel pike and skipper (and *sanma* in Japanese), it also occurs in large schools, generally offshore near the surface, and, like the Atlantic saury, feeds on small crustaceans and the eggs and larvae of fish. The Pacific saury occurs from Japan eastward to the Gulf of Alaska and south to Mexico.

Both species may reach a length of about 14 inches but are usually shorter.

SAWFISH

See: Rays and Skates.

SCALE

A scale for weighing fish is one of the most popular accessories that anglers have, although it may be one of the least discussed and least used, since it is generally reserved for weighing fish that are of significant size.

Handheld scales are of the spring variety, and they have exterior incremental markings to show weight or depict weight on a digital readout. They are notoriously variable and, with few exceptions, are best for getting a "ballpark" estimate of the weight of a fish. Some, however, are surprisingly accurate—enough to be used for record purposes. If absolute weight is a concern to the angler for any reason, it's a good idea to verify the ability of a given scale by checking it against a known weight (take it to the grocery store, put a bag of potatoes/apples/grapefruit on their certified scale, then weigh it with your own scale), so you'll know if it's off the mark and by how much. A fish that might be a world record must be weighed on a certified scale, however, and not in a rollicking boat, so you need to observe certain protocol for such special fish.

Fish to be released shouldn't be indiscriminately weighed. Weighing can be harmful, as can taking the fish out of the water for the extra handling and time necessary to weigh it. If you must weigh a fish to be released, it's best to keep the fish in a cradle *(see)* and weigh the whole thing with the fish properly supported horizontally, then weigh the cradle separately and deduct that from the total. An alternative is to get a girth and length measurement and use a formula for estimating weight. This and other aspects of weighing and handling fish are covered in greater detail in other entries.

See: Catch-and-Release; Landing Fish; Measuring Fish; Records.

S-CAST

An in-air technique for presenting a fly or mending a fly line.
See: Mending.

SCENTS

An aromatic substance applied to or made part of artificial lures. These substances may be applied to hard or soft lures in the form of a paste, gel, or similar element, or in the form of a liquid that is sprayed or used as a dip; they are also incorporated into soft lures in the manufacturing process, or in some cases are added to a pouch or other receptacle that is part of a lure or attached to it. Most usage with lures occurs with items that are capable of absorbing and retaining the scent for a period of time. Scents are more popular in freshwater than in saltwater. They are viewed with suspicion by many anglers, yet used religiously by some, particularly catfish and bass anglers in freshwater.

The major question regarding scents is whether they attract fish and/or mask offensive odors, thereby increasing hooking success. This is difficult to prove in actual angling conditions due to the number of variables that influence fish behavior and angling effort.

It is well known that some fish have much more developed smell and taste senses than others. Any

S

fish with barbels or whiskers is an example. However, many predatory fish rely primarily on their vision, some rely heavily on their hearing, and some use both; these fish rely little, if at all, on their sense of taste and smell.

Many scents are generally targeted at all fish, and others are targeted for particular species. Advertising claims notwithstanding, whether any fish are attracted to scents, to what extent they may be attracted, and under what conditions (how close it is to the fish, the effect in current versus stillwater, and other factors) is difficult to prove. In freshwater, catfish are well known to prefer baits that emit odors; scents are used regularly in fishing for these bottom-scrounging creatures. Beyond this, however, the major predators are not known to heavily rely on scent in natural environs. Most scents are aimed at bass, but these fish principally use their vision and lateral line for detecting prey when feeding. In saltwater, a high use of bait, and in some cases chum *(see),* for certain species, plus an abundance of clear water to aid visual feeding, diminishes angler interest in scent products.

Equally uncertain is whether fishing scents mask odors that might be offensive to fish, such as human scent or chemicals (as in sunscreen or insect repellent). This, too, is a claim of scent manufacturers and one that is hard to prove or disprove. Some frequently cited instances of lures that were dipped into gasoline and lubricant and yet fished successfully have been used to refute the merits of this aspect of scents.

It is fairly clear that using scents or scented products is not repelling to fish. Therefore, if it is a confidence booster for anglers and helps them to fish more effectively, it may have some value. But there are many instances in both freshwater and saltwater fishing (using most flies, fishing with surface lures, and casting spinners) where there is little if any merit to these products.

See: Anatomy; Bait; Chumming; Processed Bait.

SCHEDULED WATER

A term used in some Canadian provinces for waters that (usually) contain significant runs of Atlantic salmon and that are subject to regulations restricting angling to the use of flies and fly fishing. Other species may be present besides salmon, but only fly fishing is permitted regardless of the species targeted. Both lakes and rivers may be scheduled, although rivers, and often their tributaries, are the primary scheduled waters and may be scheduled only during that portion of the season when salmon are historically present, leading to open and closed seasons.

SCHISTOSOMIASIS

See: First Aid.

SCHOOL

A closely spaced collection of fish that swim in association with each other. Fish in a school are often of the same species and of similar size, but species may intermingle and vary in size. Some species are noted for their tendency to school, while other species are more solitary.

See: Schooling.

SCHOOLIES

Small fish that run together, often used to refer to saltwater fish that are sub-legal size or less than a foot long, especially bluefish and striped bass.

See: Schooling.

SCHOOLING

(1) The behavioral grouping of fish, usually of the same or related species, which move together as a unit and exhibit a specific geometrical relationship. Similar to herding, schooling may be a natural means of reducing predation and ensuring survival of some individuals. Many species of fish school throughout their lives, and young fish, as well as prey species, are especially likely to school. Fish of different species seldom intermingle, although related species (such as white bass and striped bass, for example) may do so.

Schooling of fish has very little to do with their education. It does have much to do with their ability to survive and reproduce in sufficient numbers. Schools are composed of many fish of the same species moving in more or less harmonious patterns throughout the oceans. A very prevalent behavior, schooling is exhibited by almost 80 percent of all fish species during some phase of their life cycle. Many of the world's commercial fishing industries rely on this behavior pattern to produce their catch, especially for species like cod, tuna, mackerel, and menhaden.

Fish school for a number of reasons. For some, schooling helps reduce water friction. When traveling in schools, fish that swim in fairly precise, staggered patterns create a to-and-fro motion with their tails that produces tiny currents called vortices, which are swirling motions similar to little whirlpools. Each individual, in theory, can use the tiny whirlpool of its neighbor to assist in reducing the water's friction on its own body.

Another advantage is the safety factor against predators. A potential predator hunting for a meal might become confused by the closely spaced school, which can give the impression of one vast and frightening fish. Additionally, schooling fish benefit from the concept of safety in numbers. A predator cannot consume an unlimited quantity of prey; the sheer number of fish in a school allows species to hide behind each other, thus confusing a predator by the alteration of shapes and colors presented as the school swims along. Of course, those on the outside edges of the school are more likely to be eaten than those in the center. Predatory fish also benefit from schooling because it gives them the ability to travel in large numbers in search of food and to corral prey.

Schooling fish respond quickly to changes in the direction and speed of their neighbors, and can do so while still retaining a close swimming pattern. They can move from one configuration to another and then regroup almost as one unit.

When young, most fish species do not exhibit the schooling pattern. As they mature, they begin to swim in pairs and then in larger and larger clusters until they attain the classic parallel pattern. Thus, schooling appears to be a formed behavior pattern genetically imprinted. Researchers believe that as the sense organs of the young fish mature, their schooling behavior strengthens. The first sense used is that of sight, which begins to function immediately after birth to allow for feeding. Fish eyes cannot focus directly forward because they are located on the sides of the head. This placement does, however, permit the eyes to be especially sensitive to lateral movement—a very helpful attribute in schooling. The fish can see what other members of the school are doing in relation to themselves and respond accordingly.

Of special interest in the phenomenon of schooling is the lateral line system on the sides of a fish. This is a series of sensory cells usually running the length of both sides of the fish's body; it performs an important function in receiving low-frequency vibrations. These two lateral lines are highly sensitive to movements and the displacement of water as a fish swims close to its neighbor. They aid in keeping all the fish in a neat, orderly pattern. Some fish do not have lateral lines, nor do they have the sensitive cells; thus, they rely on their eyesight. Research suggests that if fish are blinded and their lateral lines cut, schooling does not take place; but if the lateral lines are left in place on blind fish, they are still able to school. The lateral lines are especially important to fish living in murky waters where sight is not particularly useful.
See: Anatomy.

(2) The phenomenon of gamefish actively feeding upon prey species and vulnerable to angling effort. Some species of gamefish, especially those that are pelagic or roam open water, like tuna and salmon, forage as a school and prey upon schools of baitfish. Some species do not ordinarily school but will do so in a loose sense when there is ample feeding opportunity; largemouth bass, for example, which are a cover-oriented fish, may school in reservoirs when large numbers of shad are available in shallow water. When gamefish are grouped and actively feeding upon large numbers of prey, they are said to be schooling, which refers both to their own association as well as to their (sometimes frenzied) foraging behavior. They may be particularly vulnerable to angling at that time, and the activity may generate a high level of action and angler enthusiasm, although it is usually a phenomenon of short duration.

Angling for Schooling Fish

The phenomenon of schooling is commonly associated with freewheeling activity. However, it does not occur everywhere and with all species. Some of the more popular fish that school in saltwater include dolphin, bluefish, striped bass, and tuna. Tuna are caught by trolling and baitfishing and very rarely by casting; they are such fast movers that they are seldom appropriate for the school-fishing tactics that are characteristic of most other species.

In some places people actually depend on schooling fish behavior for the bulk of their deliberate angling activities. In many freshwater locales in the fall, striped bass, hybrid stripers, and white bass chase and consume pods of baitfish (usually threadfin or gizzard shad) and roam over a wide area as they keep up with the bait and maraud them. Often this phenomenon is best observed in early and late daylight hours. With white bass, it happens on points and along rocky shores as well as in open water, but with stripers it may happen anywhere. The key to finding it is observation.

Striper anglers usually motor to places where schooling fish are frequently observed or were seen the morning or evening before. They shut the outboard motor off, and watch and wait. When a sudden splashing occurs in the distance, and/or a flock of seagulls is seen hovering expectantly and diving to the water, that is a giveaway and also the signal to shift into breakneck gear.

The tactic is to race to the site of the commotion, glide to the outer edge of it, cut the motor,

Striped bass are the quest of these Oklahoma anglers; boats in the background are moving to keep up with the fast-traveling school of fish.

S

and cast into the melee. Sometimes nearly any lure will do; sometimes it must be close in size and shape to the baitfish being pummeled. Two or three anglers may get into fish this way; if the school moves on, you try to move with it, being careful not to put the fish down (which often happens anyway, because of the fish you catch or the intrusion of your boat or that of others) and trying not to lose their direction.

The same thing happens with bluefish in saltwater, except that when bluefish and bait are really thick, the blues are reasonably undisturbed by boats, and fish-catching can be fast and furious for a longer period of time.

Likewise, bird activity in inshore or offshore waters can be an indication of feeding by schools of some species or several species, from mackerel to albacore to dolphin, and here the open waters may be conducive to trolling around the edges of the melee to pick off fish, as well as getting into position to cast lures or pitch out live bait. Many offshore anglers will use the high vantage point of towers to spot dolphin schools near floating weedlines, and will pitch some unhooked live bait to them to start a flurry of feeding, then cast some hooked bait among the fray. It is also possible to use chum to get the fish into casting position with light spinning tackle or a fly rod, since the school will keep feeding toward the boat.

Some species of freshwater fish are known as "schooling" fish because they tend to be found in groups. Walleye, yellow perch, and crappie are popular species that are usually clustered, and it is common knowledge that in nearly any place that you catch one of these fish, there are surely others. Panfish anglers well know that they can locate a school of fish, especially crappie, and catch them by the score with jigs or live bait as long as they are fishing at the proper depth. Crappie will school heavily in deep locales in summer and fall, and stay in one particular area. They require a presentation with some finesse, rather than the slam-bang action that is associated with the frenzied behavior of other species. But at least with these fish, once you have found a concentration, you don't have to work to keep locating them.

More species of freshwater fish may cluster than what people think. And in places with little or no fishing pressure, this is more likely to be observed; the difference being that fish in highly pressured waters are wary and more likely to be spooked by any activity, whereas those in virgin or lightly pressured waters are more tolerant.

Northern pike and chain pickerel are great examples of fish that can be deceptively abundant, although not actually schooled per se. In northern Canadian waters, schools of 2- to 5-pound lake trout cruise shallow rocky shorelines on summer evenings to feed on bugs, and they are caught by stealthy anglers using flies and small jigs on light tackle, who cast to wandering pods of fish. If you're patient, you can sit and wait for these trout to come by; if not, you can intercept them by boat, shutting the motor off before getting to the fish, then casting to their midst as they cruise by. These fish are in no way behaving like surface-busting striped bass would, yet they are cruising en masse and they are aggressive. In these shallow, clear waters, you can actually stalk the school, and several fish will charge your lure.

Walleye, charr, and lake trout may be found in heavy concentrations in those northern locales where there is a large inlet to a lake at various times of the season, and the fish seem to be secure because of the depth and heavy current present. Such a place can provide fast fishing for a while, but it may need to be rested when the action slows, perhaps for 30 to 60 minutes before you return and get into more fish. This seems to be more likely for charr and lakers than for walleye, but it also seems to be because the fish come in to feed and then leave, rather than taking up permanent local residence. In any event, finding these types of situations—where there's an abundance of active schooling fish—can result in terrific action.

Largemouth bass, which are very oriented to cover for hiding and feeding purposes, do gather in loosely defined schools, as previously mentioned, when there is ample open-water bait. The bait are primarily surface or near-surface feeding fish, usually detected by observation. Their appearance may be short-lived and may be fairly obvious to those close enough to be able to observe this behavior. Bass that appear to be schooling generally herd baitfish, primarily shad but sometimes alewives, against some type of underwater structure, like a reef, hump, or weed edge. Keeping up with these fish is often difficult, and they are usually spooked easily by boats that get too close.

This is a liberal definition of schools and schooling behavior, however, since largemouth and smallmouth bass are generally not a schooling type of fish once they have passed the juvenile stage. Many anglers refer to bass schools when discussing an abundance of these fish in one particular location, but this is not a school nor is it true schooling behavior, just a lot of fish of the same species coexisting, usually in an area with plenty of cover and forage opportunity.

SCOOTER

A shallow water low-freeboard style of flats boat (see) used in the Gulf Coast, primarily for anglers seeking redfish and seatrout in calm inshore waters.

SCOPE

The term for rode (anchor line) length in relation to water depth and anchoring point on a boat.
See: Anchor.

SCORPIONFISH, CALIFORNIA

Scorpaena guttata.

Other names—spotted scorpionfish, scorpion, rattlesnake, bullhead, scorpene, sculpin; Spanish: *rascacio californiano.*

The California scorpionfish is an excellent food fish and the most venomous member of the scorpionfish family. It has venom glands that are attached to the dorsal, pelvic, and anal fin spines, and if these spines penetrate the skin, an intense and excruciating pain in the area of the wound occurs almost immediately. If there are multiple punctures, the wound can induce shock, respiratory distress, or abnormal heart action, and sometimes leads to hospitalization of the victim. The California scorpionfish is often called sculpin but is not a member of the sculpin family.

Identification. The California scorpionfish has a stocky and slightly compressed body as well as a large head, mouth, and pectoral fins. Colored red to brown with dark patches and spots on the body and fins, this fish is capable of dramatic color changes to blend with its background. It has large pectoral fins, 12 poisonous dorsal spines, and poisonous anal and ventral fin spines.

Size/Age. The California scorpionfish can grow to 17 inches and live 15 years.

Distribution. In the eastern Pacific, this species occurs from Santa Cruz, California, to Punta Abreojos, Baja California, including a cloistered population in the northern Gulf of California and at Guadalupe Island in Mexico.

Habitat. California scorpionfish usually live in caves, crevices, and rocky areas of bays along the shore, from just below the surface to 600-foot depths. Resting quietly during the day among rocky reefs and kelp beds, they emerge at night and are often seen by night divers in the open near kelp and eelgrass beds. Some are occasionally found over sand or mud bottoms.

Life history/Behavior. California scorpionfish start spawning at age 3 or 4. Spawning activity occurs from April through August, most likely at night. The eggs are implanted in a single layer on the gelatinous walls of hollow, pear-shaped "balloons" of 5 to 10 inches in length; these are released on the bottom and rise to the surface, and the eggs hatch within the next five days.

Food. The California scorpionfish feeds on crabs, squid, octopus, fish, and shrimp.

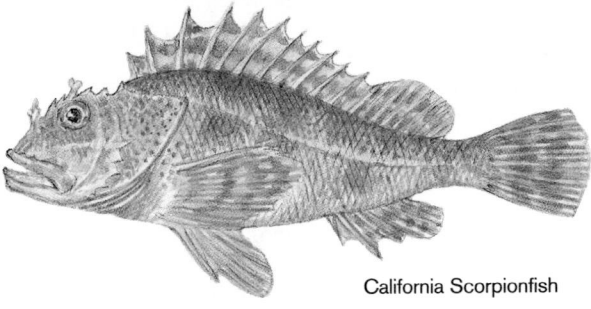

California Scorpionfish

Angling. California scorpionfish readily take a hook that has been baited with a piece of squid or fish and lowered to the bottom in a rocky area they are known to inhabit. Tough baits like squid are useful because they are difficult to steal and save rebaiting time. On occasion, a considerable amount of chumming with ground fish will attract California scorpionfish to the surface. Hooked California scorpionfish are not noted for their fighting qualities.

SCOTLAND

For general information about fishing in Scotland as a country within the United Kingdom, *see: England.*

Gamefishing

Trout. Scotland offers excellent wild brown trout fishing on its abundant rivers, lochs, and tarns, and on the lochs in the Shetland, Hebrides, and Orkney Islands. The season for brown trout varies considerably from river to river, running from spring to autumn, and the visiting angler should check this beforehand if possible. Stocking is carried out in comparatively few of these waters, and catching a 3-pounder is often a considerable feat.

Preferred flies for these small wild brownies include such old favorites as Black Gnat, Black and Peacock Spider, Teal Blue and Silver, Peter Ross, Black Pennell, Zulu, Kate McLaren, Kingfisher Butcher, Alexandra, Whickham's Fancy, Soldier Palmer, and various sedge patterns.

This angling comes at a reasonable price. If you wish to stick strictly to wild browns, you can fish at a low cost; indeed the fees for getting to some of these out-of-the-way places will be far greater than the direct angling costs. Boat hire is often extremely cheap as well, although boaters should beware of being caught out in the big lochs in rough weather, which can blow up suddenly. On waters that support a run of salmon and sea trout, the charge for fishing will be greater than that for angling solely for brown trout.

In addition to browns, Scotland offers some rainbow trout as well. Stocking rainbows in Loch Leven in the early 1990s was a controversial move because of the natural brown trout population. But the rainbows have settled in well and have put on a surprising amount of weight.

The Scottish Tourist Board can direct you to the main inland trout fishing areas, but British angling publications will give you much more detailed help, as the beats on rivers change hands frequently. They may also be able to put you in touch with a local expert.

There is also a thriving and steadily increasing business in commercial, small, stillwater (in a broad sense, anything that is not a river, stream, or tributary) trout fisheries, primarily in the south of Scotland. These waters hold mainly rainbows.

S

Some are open most of the year, closing only in winter. As the climate is colder here, the trout tend to be fitter than in some commercial stillwater trout fisheries in England, but they tend not to be stocked as large at most sites, although some specialize in bigger fish.

Salmon and sea trout.   Scotland is famous for its salmon fishing, and anglers travel from all over the world to partake of the sport and the tradition, but above all to fish in beautiful locations that range from deep majestic lowland rivers to faster runs through magnificent glens, with mountains all around. Scotland offers salmon fishing for anglers from all walks of life, including royalty. Anglers can rent private beats and association waters on a daily or weekly basis. The prices range widely and are dictated by exclusivity and previous years' yields. It is possible, however, to catch good numbers of salmon from the cheapest of beats, given perfect conditions, especially when there is plenty of water to encourage Atlantic salmon to run upriver.

It is illegal to fish for migratory fish (salmon and sea trout) in Scotland on a Sunday; hence, many weekly accommodation/fishing packages run from Sunday to Sunday.

Until the mid-1990s it was common for nearly all sport-caught salmon on Scottish rivers to be kept by anglers, but this has changed somewhat—on a voluntary basis on some rivers and by legislation on others. Many waters now restrict the number of salmon that can be kept. These restrictions vary, and in some cases a strict one-fish limit followed by

River Spey anglers display their salmon catch.

catch-and-release is practiced, to conserve future salmon stocks. Such practices are essential on Scottish rivers, as some have lost their spring salmon runs altogether, and the main run on many rivers is now from June onward. Diminishing stocks of sand eels—a major element of the diet of salmon and sea trout in the sea—and netting in the high seas and estuaries have had an enormous, negative impact on stocks.

As a basic guideline, salmon rivers in the west of Scotland can be classed as spate rivers. They are shorter than those in the east and are heavily reliant for their flow on rainfall coming down from the mountains, which produces quick changes in water levels. Increases in flows quickly bring fish into the river, but the run stops rapidly if levels decrease rapidly. These rivers include the Doon, Nith, Anann, Ayr, Cree, and Bladnoch. On the east side are the more famous rivers, including the Tweed, Spey, Tay, Aberdeenshire Dee, Helmsdale, Beauly, Deveron, Don, and the North and South Esk.

Many of these rivers have runs of both salmon and sea trout. The Spey, for example, has a fine run of sea trout of good average size, but they are rarely sought by anglers obsessed with catching the mighty salmon. Large sea trout (6-plus pounds) are taken on the Spey by salmon anglers using double-handed rods and salmon flies.

The Spey, of course, is arguably Scotland's premier salmon river and—along with the Tweed, Tay, and Dee—among the rivers most noted for large fish and large populations. The Spey courses northerly about 48 miles, from its origins in the Highlands southeast of Loch Ness to the sea. It is a fast flowage with plenty of breadth and wide, shallow runs. Casting a long line across large pools is a trademark of salmon fishing here, but heavily wooded banks have led to so-called Spey rods and casting methods. This gear enables anglers to overcome the intrinsic difficulties of big water and little casting room.

The Scottish Tourist Board relies heavily on visiting salmon anglers, so they will be helpful to those looking for waters to fish.

If you are tempted by the wild salmon fishing in Scotland, you should be armed with the right equipment. On some of the smaller spate rivers, it is possible, and sometimes a benefit, to use a single-handed 10-foot rod suited to an 8- or 9-weight line. If you're fishing a river in spate, or one of the longer and more well-known rivers, however, you'll need a rod of around 15 feet with a 10- or 11-weight fly line. Take various densities of line to cope with circumstances.

Flies vary depending on water conditions, but in general low water is fished with a fly of size 6 down to a size 14, and in high water a size 6 up to a brass Tube or Waddington that is almost 3 inches long. Favorite patterns include variations of Willie Gunn, Stoat's Tail, Hairy Mary, Munro Killer, and the ever-popular Ally's Shrimp. Tie these on single, double, and treble hooks, and on brass tubes and Waddingtons, and you shouldn't go far wrong. Local experts may have a few secrets in their fly box; it might be worthwhile to befriend them.

A pair of chest waders is essential in most cases, and on some of the bigger, more treacherous rivers, a wading staff is advisable.

Coarse Fishing

The only coarse fishing commonly associated with Scotland is for the beautifully marked pike present in many of the country's lochs. Several are renowned for producing pike over 30 pounds, and anglers go there in the hope that they can produce a fish to match the legendary Endrick pike. The Endrick legend surrounds the skull of a pike that was found at the mouth of the River Endrick and Loch Lomond, which experts have calculated could have weighed more than 70 pounds.

The Scottish record specimen of 47 pounds, 11 ounces came from Lomond, which is just outside Alexandria, and many experts believe giants over 50 pounds favor the Endrick (south) bank of the 26-mile-long loch. The River Endrick itself produces excellent coarse fishing, offering large catches of roach and dace; giant bream are taken at night. On the loch itself, there is excellent roach fishing at Balmaha, where you can also hire boats.

Many other lochs are capable of producing pike that weigh 20 or more pounds, including Loch Ken in Dumfries and Galloway County, which is also a superb roach water; the underrated Loch Awe in Strathclyde, which is also home to giant wild brown trout; and Kilbirnie Loch, where it's also easy to find plenty of roach. Excellent bream and carp fishing are available at Castle Loch at Lochmaben in Dumfries and Galloway County. This venue boasts the Scottish bream record and also holds plenty of carp. Lochrutton Loch, which is full of bream and roach, is another venue that offers a large mixed catch in summer.

Of the rivers, the old River Forth at Stirling is good for roach, and the River Clyde from Motherwell down to Glasgow harbors roach, dace, and bream. The River Tay at Perth has built a superb reputation for big roach to over 2 pounds and is known for large catches. Another jewel is the Forth and Clyde Canal. This venue is rarely fished, and "swims" (immediate fishing areas) need to be created, but it offers fantastic tench fishing, and large catches are possible throughout the summer around Kirkintilloch and Cumbernauld.

No national license is required to fish in Scotland, and there is no officially closed coarse fishing season on still waters, rivers, or canals. You might have to respect local bylaws, however, which restrict fishing at certain spawning times. Although some fishing is free—and what isn't is all pretty cheap—you will often have to buy day tickets to fish. These are best purchased in advance and are generally available from local shops, hotels, and farmers. Unlike salmon and sea trout fishing, coarse fishing is permitted on Sundays.

Sea Fishing

Nearly 4,000 miles of coastline surrounds Scotland, and like its neighbor England, Scotland's species vary according to whether one is fishing in the North Sea, in the Atlantic Ocean, or fronting the Irish Sea.

The southeast corner of Scotland around the Solway Firth fronts the Irish sea and holds among the best marine fish populations in the United Kingdom. Available everywhere, dogfish are considered a local pest but have saved many anglers from a blank day. Also expect flounder from the many estuaries, and pollack, wrasses, small conger (known in the UK as "strap" conger), possibly thornback ray, and dabs from most other marks. Boat fishing around Luce Bay can be fantastic, especially for tope in summer. The main ports are Whithorn, Luce Bay, Drummore, and Stranraer.

Up the coast is the Firth of Clyde, where incredible catches of cod to 30-plus pounds were taken from the shore in the 1960s. Now it is but a shadow of its former self, although there are plenty of keen anglers, and flounders tend to be the main quarry.

Farther north anglers will find good fishing around the coast from hundreds of estuaries and sea lochs, although local advice is essential. Just getting to some of these out-of-the-way venues can be difficult. But the scenery is breathtaking. On this rocky coast, wrasses, pollack, and conger are among the targeted fish.

The Isle of Mull is famous for common skate, which run to 150-plus pounds; the main season is in July and August, and advance booking is essential. Look in the sea fishing magazines for advertisements from the few charter boats offering fishing for common skate. All common skate are returned, usually tagged. Oban is another port where boats target common skate. Up to 2.5 kilograms of lead may be required to hold bottom in the fast tides found off this coast, so be prepared for heavy-tackle angling.

The Hebrides offer excellent shore fishing, and visitors may be able to assemble a boat trip in conjunction with local anglers. Well-organized clubs exist on the islands. Halibut are caught occasionally and are perhaps the most prized marine sportfish in the UK. Some haddock are caught hereabout in winter.

Moving to the northeast mainland, Scrabster is a good charter port, and codling (small cod) are the main winter species. Local specialists occasionally land huge catches of porbeagle sharks, primarily in November. Shore fishing all around the northern and eastern coasts tends to be for codling and flounder; wrasses and red codling are prevalent in summer. Again, local knowledge is essential, and visitors should contact the local fishing club.

S

The marine waters of the southern part of Scotland are naturally more heavily fished than those in the north, because they're closer to Glasgow and Edinburgh. The southeast corner of Scotland, from Aberdeen south to Edinburgh, offers very good year-round sport, including excellent winter fishing for flounder in the estuaries and for codling from the rocks. The winter codling sport is superb, although weather conditions can curtail boating activities. Anglers also take haddock in winter. The main charter ports are Peterhead, Stonehaven, Johnshaven, Arbroath, Anstruther, North Berwick, Burnmouth, and Eyemouth. Many small-boat owners, and several clubs, ply the area south of Edinburgh, targeting plaice and codling.

The Orkney and Shetland Islands tend to be ignored by UK sea anglers because of the traveling required, but visitors will find plenty of fish, and some local clubs are willing to help.
See: Wales.

SCROD
Fish market terminology for a small cod or haddock with the head on.
See: Cod, Atlantic; Haddock.

SCUD
Scuds are small freshwater crustaceans of the order Amphipoda that are a favorite food of trout and other fish. They are side swimmers, moving rapidly on their sides, and are usually associated with aquatic vegetation. Unlike most crustaceans, the scud has no upper shell; it breathes by means of gills, a fact that sets it apart from insects.

Scuds have a shrimplike appearance but lack the large hard covering over the head and upper body. The body is white to clear with many segments, and is flattened laterally, being higher than it is wide. Scuds have two pairs of antennae and seven pairs of tiny legs.

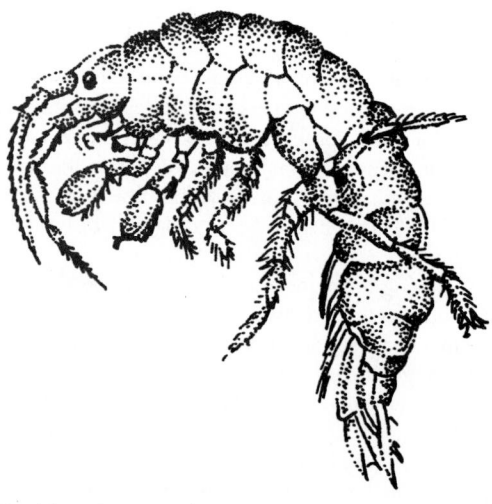

Scud (greatly enlarged)

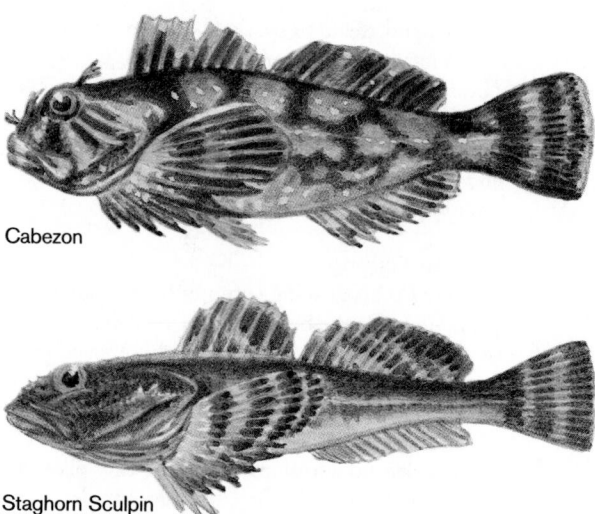

Cabezon

Staghorn Sculpin

SCULPIN
The Cottidae family of sculpin is made up of more than 300 species, most of which are marine but many of which also occur in freshwaters throughout the Northern Hemisphere. They are important as food for larger fish and as predators of the eggs and young of gamefish. Bottom-dwelling fish of cold waters, sculpin live in shelf waters and in rocky tidalpools. A few species of larger sculpin inhabit depths of up to 4,200 feet in saltwater.

Sculpin are characterized by wide bodies that taper to slender, compressed tails. They may be unscaled or have spiny prickles or platelike scales, although the development of these vary within species depending on habitat and are not necessarily useful in identification. All sculpins have a bony support beneath the eye, which connects bones with the front of the gill cover. The dorsal fin is deeply indented between the spiny and soft-rayed portions, and the pectoral fins are large and fannon. The color and pattern vary, although they are mainly mottled with various shades and are protectively camouflaged by their mottled pattern; freshwater sculpin are among the most difficult North American fish to identify because of their indistinct mottling. Freshwater sculpin are tiny, ranging from 2 to 7 inches, whereas saltwater sculpin are slightly larger; most species of sculpin are less than 1 foot long. Sculpin are primarily carnivorous, clinging to the bottom and pouncing on small invertebrates, crustaceans, and mollusks for food.

Of the marine species, the cabezon, or great marbled sculpin (*Scorpaenichthys marmoratus*), is the largest and best known, weighing up to 30 pounds. It is good table fare and is a coveted catch in California waters, taken on cut baits or with jigs. The staghorn sculpin (*Leptocottus armatus*) inhabits the same waters as does the cabezon and is sometimes caught accidentally by anglers and used for bait. The grunt sculpin (*Rhamphocottus richardsonii*) is so called because of the noises it makes when removed from the water. It is featured in aquariums.

Of the freshwater species, the banded sculpin *(Cottus carolinae)* and the mottled sculpin *(C. bairdi)* often inhabit the cold rapids of streams. The prickly sculpin *(C. asper)* is so called because of the many prickles on its body, and it can reach a foot in length. The deep-water sculpin *(Myoxocephalus thompsoni)* of the Great Lakes is threatened.

SCUP   *Stenotomus chrysops.*

Other names—porgy.

A member of the Sparidae family of porgies, which includes about 112 species, the scup is most commonly known as "porgy" and is a common angling catch along the eastern United States. It is a fine food fish that has had significant commercial interest. Primarily caught through trawling, it was overexploited and at low population levels throughout the 1990s.

Identification. Somewhat nondescript, the scup is rather dusky colored, being brownish and almost silvery, with fins that are mottled brown. It has a deep body, about the same depth all the way to the caudal peduncle, where it narrows abruptly. The fins are spiny. The caudal fin is lunate (crescent-shaped). The front teeth are incisor-form, and there are two rows of molars in the upper jaw.

Size/Age. Scup attain a maximum length of about 16 inches. The all-tackle world record is a 4-pound, 9-ounce Massachusetts fish. Ages up to 20 years have been reported.

Distribution. Scup are found in the western Atlantic from Nova Scotia to Florida but are rare south of North Carolina, occurring primarily in the Mid-Atlantic Bight from Cape Cod to Cape Hatteras. An introduction to Bermuda was unsuccessful.

Habitat/Behavior. A schooling species, scup are common in summer in inshore waters from Massachusetts to Virginia; in winter, they frequent offshore waters between Hudson Canyon and Cape Hatteras at depths ranging from 70 to 180 meters. Sexual maturity is essentially complete by age 3, when the fish $8^1/_4$ inches long; spawning occurs during summer months.

Food and feeding habits. The diet of scup consists of crabs, shrimp, worms, sand dollars, snails, and young squid. Although they sometimes eat small fish, scup usually browse and nibble over hard bottoms.

Angling. Sportfishing for scup mostly occurs when these fish are in inshore environs. They are a common catch of anglers on small boats and party boats, especially those fishing with bait on bottom. Because of their schooling tendencies, they can be a nuisance when larger fish are sought, usually causing boaters to change locations. Specific fishing for scup may entail the use of a chum pot to attract them. Two-hook bottom rigs (and occasionally small jigs)

Scup

baited with shrimp, worms, clam pieces, or squid are effective.

See: Inshore Fishing; Porgies.

SEA ANCHOR

A sea anchor is a large megaphone- or parachute-shaped bag that is used in fishing applications to slow down a drifting or trolling boat. Sea anchors, also known as drogues, have long been used by sailboaters and cruisers, can be found in very large sizes, and have varying uses for controlling a boat's action in heavy seas; smaller sea anchors have been adopted by big-water, big-boat trollers who need to reduce speed, either in flat, calm conditions or in a stiff tailwind, and by anglers who are drifting while casting or bottom bouncing but need some way to decrease or neutralize the speed of their drift in order to fish effectively.

The need for using a sea anchor arises when a boat is moving so fast that a lure or bait cannot be presented properly, or spends almost no time in the strike zone. It is also important on windy days when you have to fish a particular place where the fish are very finicky about presentation, or are tightly

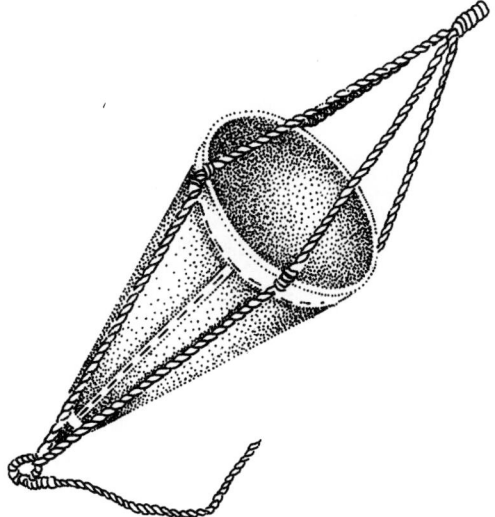

A sea anchor works by catching water in its wide end and funneling it through a narrow end, which slows momentum.

grouped. An alternative to using sea anchors is to set out one or two bottom anchors so that the boat does not move, but often this does not fill the bill for the circumstances.

Sea anchors usually are made of ripstop nylon and open up like a huge funnel or rounded bag when pulled through the water. Their wide-mouth opening can be restricted to lessen drag according to conditions, so that a lesser amount of water passes through the narrow end.

Many anglers attach sea anchors to the gunwales amidship, especially for drifting in open water and in situations where two or three anglers are casting downwind across an area (often a flat). Guides who use flat-bottomed boats and who ordinarily pole may, on windy days, employ a sea anchor amidship on the windward side of the boat, and use their pushpole to help maintain position parallel and within casting distance of a shoreline, weedline, or grassbed. This is commonly used in redfishing on grassy windblown flats.

Similarly, a walleye angler might use a sea anchor in conjunction with an electric motor or small

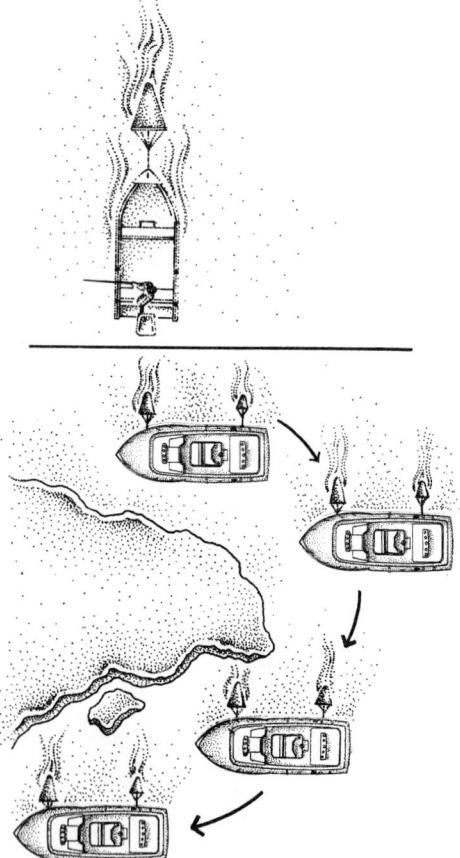

When trolling downwind in open water, you can slow boat movement by heading backward and dragging a sea anchor off the bow (top). For two people to effectively drift and slowly fish around an object, such as a point (bottom), hang two sea anchors off the starboard side of the boat, and use an electric motor to position the boat around the point.

outboard motor to maintain position while drifting along a flat or around a point. The sea anchor slows the boat, and the motor does the maneuvering without the boat being blown around as it might otherwise if just relying on motor power.

Sea anchors are often tied amidship, but may be tied to the bow if conditions warrant. For forward trolling, a sea anchor can be tied to the bow, with just enough rope to reach midship; tie a tail rope to the funnel end so that when you need to retrieve the bag, you can pull on the tail to collapse it. For slow back-trolling *(see)* with the wind you can tie a sea anchor to the bow so that it extends in front of the boat facing the bow, and then, if necessary, supplement control with a transom-mounted electric motor or outboard motor. If you backtroll into a wind, the bow-tied sea anchor helps reduce splashing by keeping the bow angle lower. With boats that are easily pushed around by the bow in a wind (high-riding aluminum boats, for example), a bow-tied sea anchor negates the sideways wind push and makes the bow a pivotal point for very effective boat control.

Sometimes one anchor will slow a boat adequately, but when trolled, it may cause the boat to veer to the side. Port and starboard sea anchors, both fixed to the bow, may be necessary, perhaps decreasing the size of the opening on each to get the proper speed. Some anglers use two sea anchors when drifting, one positioned close to the bow, the other close to the stern. Others keep two sea anchors of different size on hand, a small one for use on nearly calm days and a large one for wind.

Sea anchors need to be tied to sturdy cleats or to bow eye bolts. Sometimes it has to be off the bow eye bolt and not a gunwale cleat for best results. These devices exert a lot of pull, especially in the larger sizes, so they must be tied to the sturdiest points. Be leery of tying them to a handrail or guardrail or around rod holders. And be prepared to bring one in quickly if necessary should some problem arise; a line tied to the tail and to the boat will make it easy to collapse the bag. Lastly, try to position them so as not to interfere with your fishing. **See: Drifting.**

SEA BASS

(1) Members of the Serranidae family of fish, which includes over 400 species of widely varying physiques, habitats, and natures. Many are important gamefish and food fish. They include such diverse and large-growing species as striped bass *(see: bass, striped)*, jewfish *(see)*, giant sea bass *(see: sea bass, giant)*, barramundi *(see)*, and Nile perch *(see: perch, Nile)*, as well as kelp bass *(see: bass, kelp)*, black sea bass *(see: sea bass, black)*, white perch *(see: perch, white)*, and many different grouper *(see)*.

(2) A spelling variation of "seabass," which are actually members of other fish families *(see: seabass, blackfin; seabass, Japanese; seabass, white)*.

SEA BASS, BLACK   *Centropristis striata.*

Other names—blackfish, sea bass, black bass, black will, black seabass, rockbass, common sea bass, humpback (large males), pin bass (small specimens); Spanish: *serrano estriado.*

Black sea bass are members of the Serranidae family and popular sportfish in the western Atlantic along the coast of North America. Their firm, white flesh makes excellent eating, especially if they are iced after capture and properly cared for, as their flesh deteriorates rapidly when warm. Anglers must handle this fish with caution, as the dorsal fin has stiff, sharp spines that can puncture human skin. These stand straight up when the black sea bass is alive, but even when the fish is dead and the spines lie flat on the back, they can be dangerous.

Identification.   The black sea bass has a relatively stout body that is three times as long (excluding the tail) as it is deep. It also has a high back, a flat-topped head, a slightly pointed snout, and a sharp spine near the apex of each gill cover. Both dorsal fins are joined into one continuous dorsal fin, and the tail is rounded; the elongated top ray of the tail that sticks out past the rest of the tail, particularly pronounced in larger specimens, is the most distinguishing feature of this fish. Because of the high back, which creates a noticeable rise just behind their heads, some large male black sea bass are called "humpbacks."

Like many rock-bottom dwellers, the body color of the black sea bass is variable, ranging from black to gray or brownish gray. The dorsal fins are marked by several slanting, white spots arranged into lengthwise lines or a more random pattern; the spots in rows make the dorsal fins appear to be striped a light color. There also appear to be thin stripes on the sides, with wide vertical bands overlapping the stripes on some fish, and a large dark spot on the last dorsal spine. The upper and lower edges of the tail are white, as are the outer edges of the dorsal and anal fins. Smaller fish may lack the white edge on the tail and anal fins.

Males differ from this coloration, having a completely bluish black body, except for some white areas on the head and the edges of fins. Their tail lobes are prolonged, although on smaller fish they may be very short.

Size.   Big sea bass range from 3 to 8 pounds, and the average fish weighs between 1 and 3 pounds; the all-tackle world record is a 9-pound, 8-ounce fish. They can grow to 2 feet long, averaging 6 to 18 inches. They are known to live for 10 years, but in rare cases they may live longer. Females rarely live beyond 8 years of age, whereas males may live up to 15 years.

Distribution.   Found in the western North Atlantic Ocean along the United States, the black sea bass ranges as far north as Maine and south to northern Florida, as well as into the Gulf of Mexico. It is most common between Cape Cod, Massachusetts, and Cape Hatteras, North Carolina. It also occurs in southern Florida during cold winters.

Black sea bass consist of two stocks, one north and the other south of Cape Hatteras, North Carolina. The northern group winters along the 55-fathom depth contour off Virginia and Maryland, then migrates north and west into the major coastal bays.

Habitat.   The black sea bass is a bottom-dwelling species found around wrecks, reefs, piers, jetties, and breakwaters, and over beds of shells,

Black Sea Bass

coral, and rock. Small fish are found in shallow and quiet waters near the shore, such as in bays, whereas most larger fish prefer offshore reefs, in water ranging from roughly 10 feet deep to several hundred feet deep. Black sea bass prefer relatively cool waters, living offshore in winter and moving inshore in spring.

Life history. Black sea bass are hermaphrodites; most begin their lives as females and later become males. Large fish are males, and females reach reproductive ability in their second year. Transformation from female to male generally occurs between ages 2 and 5. Their protracted spawning season extends from February through May in the southern range and from June through October in their northern range. Spawning begins in March off North Carolina and occurs progressively later farther north.

Food and feeding habits. Clams, shrimp, worms, crabs, and small fish constitute the diet of the omnivorous black sea bass, and most anglers offer them some form of bait. Many bass that are caught in deep water and quickly brought to the surface will regurgitate all or part of their stomach contents, which may attract more fish.

Angling. When hooked on light tackle, the black sea bass fights hard all the way to the surface. The action is fast and vigorous, and in spite of its generally small size, this species is very much a gamefish. The best angling is in depths of 6 to 20 fathoms from May through June and from November through December, especially around ledges and rocky heads, although these fish are landed year-round. Some are caught by anglers on docks, piers, or the shore, but most are taken by anglers bottom fishing with baits or by anglers jigging with 2- to 4-ounce metal jigs from anchored or drifting boats. Fishing over wrecks often produces large specimens. Finding the structure that produces the large fish is the real trick, as the better places are usually a well-guarded secret, especially among the party boats. Preferred baits includes fish pieces, shrimp, squid, and assorted crabs, worms, and clams, especially skimmer clams.

Black sea bass have a fairly good-sized mouth and can take a relatively large offering. Where bigger sea bass are likely, a large piece of clam or squid or a small whole fish might be used for bait, although smaller baits are used inshore. It is practical to use a two-hook rig, leaving the lower hook on the bottom and the upper one 2 to 3 feet off the bottom. Sea bass can be nibblers and bait stealers, so it pays to keep an eye on your bait.

Appropriate sinkers vary with the conditions. Bank sinkers are popular, ranging from perhaps 3 ounces in shallower water to 8 ounces in deep water where current is swift. Medium-action boat rods and 15-pound line are the tackle used to catch these spirited fighters. They are predominantly caught in the spring and summer.

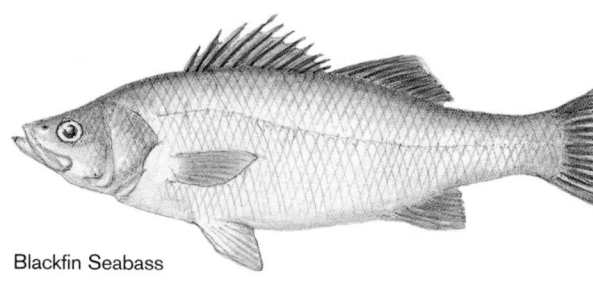

Blackfin Seabass

SEABASS, BLACKFIN   *Lateolabrax latus.*
Other names—Japanese: *hira-suzuki.*

Similar in shape to the striped bass, the blackfin seabass is highly regarded as both a food fish and a gamefish.

Identification. The blackfin seabass has a large mouth, a lower jaw that projects beyond the upper jaw, and a slightly forked tail. It has an elongate, compressed, silvery body, that is deeper, more stocky, and more silvery than that of the Japanese seabass *(see: seabass, Japanese).* Other elements that distinguish the two are the row of scales on the lower jaw of the blackfin seabass; the blackfin seabass also has 12 dorsal fin spines, 15 to 16 soft rays, and 3 anal fin spines with 9 to 10 soft rays; the Japanese seabass has 12 to 15 dorsal fin spines, 12 to 14 soft rays, and 3 anal fin spines with 7 to 9 soft rays. The eyes of the blackfin seabass seem slightly larger than those of the Japanese seabass, possibly due to its deeper body. Unlike the Japanese seabass, the blackfin seabass rarely has any spots.

Size. The blackfin seabass grows to 40 inches and 23 pounds. The all-tackle world record is an 18-pound, 4-ounce fish taken off of Wakayama, Japan, in 1990.

Distribution. This species occurs in the northeastern Pacific Ocean from the Shizuoka and Chiba Prefecture in central Japan to the Nagasaki Prefecture and the East China Sea.

Habitat. Blackfin seabass inhabit shallow rocky areas. They are often caught in the vicinity of shallow rocks and reefs, and large individuals are sometimes caught in the brackish waters of river mouths.

Angling. In the southern waters of Japan, the blackfin seabass is caught more often than its close relative, the Japanese seabass *(L. japonicus).* Anglers land this fish by surf casting with flashy, minnow-shaped artificial lures or metal jigs; by using small live baits; and by fly fishing with streamers.

SEA BASS, GIANT   *Stereolepis gigas.*
Other names—California black sea bass, California jewfish, giant bass, black, black sea bass; French: *bar gigantesque;* Japanese: *kokuchi-ishinagi, ishinagi-zoku;* Spanish: *lubina gigante.*

The giant sea bass, a member of the Serranidae family, is not only a formidable fish in size, it is also renowned for its lengthy life span. Mostly an eastern Pacific gamefish, specimens exceeding 500 pounds have been caught.

Identification. The body of the giant sea bass is elongate and has dorsal spines that fit into a groove on the back. Greenish brown or black, the giant sea bass has black or transparent fins, with the exception of the ventral fins, which appear lighter because of a white membrane between the black spines. There is usually a white patch on the throat and underneath the tail, and the membranes between the rays are also light. Young fish are mottled with prominent dark spots and a few pale-yellow blotches on a mostly brick-red body; these markings are periodically seen on fish up to and exceeding 25 pounds.

The first dorsal fin is separated from the second by a single notch; the first is extremely low and has 11 spines, whereas the second is higher and has 10 soft rays. The presence of more spines on the first dorsal fin than soft rays on the second distinguishes the giant sea bass from similar related species such as the jewfish (*Epinephelus itajara; see: jewfish),* with which it has been confused in the past.

Size/Age. The giant sea bass reaches maturity by the age of 11 or 12 and weighs roughly 50 pounds, although it has been known to weigh more than 600 pounds and measure more than 7 feet in length. The all-tackle world record is 563 pounds, 8 ounces; the most common catch is in the 100- to 200-pound range, and much smaller fish are seldom caught. Large specimens are usually found in water deeper than 100 feet. Some of the largest giant sea bass are believed to be 75 years or older; a 434-pound fish was estimated by ichthyologists at between 72 and 75 years of age. The ovaries of a 320-pound female fish were estimated to contain 60 million eggs.

Distribution. Giant sea bass occur in tropical and subtropical inshore waters of the northeast Pacific off the California and Mexico coasts, specifically from the Gulf of California southward to Humboldt Bay and Guadalupe Island. They have also been found off the Asiatic Pacific coast. In California waters these fish have been in short supply but were rebounding in the 1990s due to a moratorium on keeping them.

Habitat. Inhabiting inshore waters, giant sea bass are bottom-dwelling fish, preferring hard, rocky bottoms around kelp beds. The young occur in depths of about 6 to 15 fathoms, whereas larger specimens usually inhabit depths of 15 to 25 fathoms.

Food and feeding habits. The giant sea bass diet includes crustaceans and a wide variety of fish. Anchovies and croaker are a prominent food source off California, mackerel, sheepshead, whitefish, sand bass, and several types of crabs are also favored. Although these bulky fish appear to be slow and cumbersome, they are reputedly capable of outswimming and catching a bonito in a short chase.

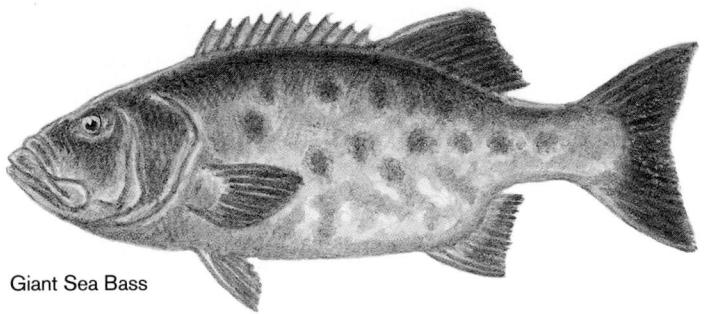

Giant Sea Bass

Angling. Fishing methods include live- or dead-bait fishing from an anchored or drifting boat with cut baits and such large natural baits as mullet and mackerel. Fishing is best in the 10- to 25-fathom range in summer, over rocky bottoms and around kelp beds.

Giant sea bass do not instinctively run for cover when they are caught, and they have no teeth to cut the line, so catching them is primarily a matter of having the tackle to match the fish and being able to outlast the fish. Encountering larger specimens, which often happens while using lighter tackle for calico bass or halibut, requires staying on top of the fish to minimize the chance of the line running into an obstruction, and applying enough constant pumping pressure to pull the fish away from the bottom. Real giant specimens are seldom landed by anglers, and deeply caught species will need to have their swim bladder deflated *(see: releasing fish)* before being returned to the bottom.

SEABASS, JAPANESE *Lateolabrax japonicus.*
Other names—sea perch; Japanese: *suzuki.*

Apparently more wide ranging than its very close "cousin" the blackfin seabass (*see: seabass, blackfin),* the Japanese seabass is a less frequent catch in southern Japan waters but is a highly rated gamefish and valued as table fare, making it also the object of commercial fishermen.

Identification. The Japanese seabass has an elongate and compressed body, resembling the weakfish or spotted seatrout in shape. It has a large mouth, a lower jaw that projects beyond the upper jaw, and a slightly forked tail. Its body is less deep and stocky than that of the blackfin seabass. Other elements that distinguish the two

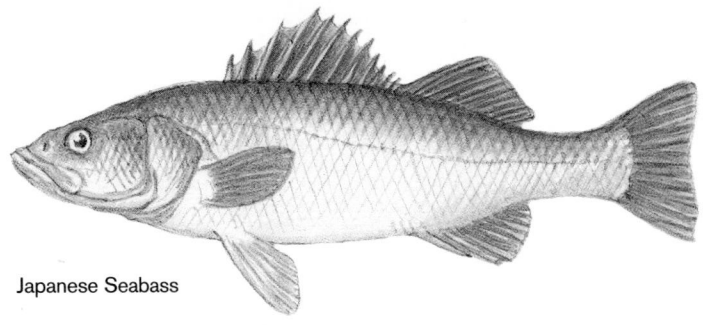

Japanese Seabass

species are the fin spines and rays. The Japanese seabass has 12 to 15 dorsal fin spines, 12 to 14 soft rays, and 3 anal fin spines with 7 to 9 soft rays; the blackfin seabass has 12 dorsal fin spines, 15 to 16 soft rays, and 3 anal fin spines with 9 to 10 soft rays. Young Japanese seabass have small black spots on the back and dorsal fin, which usually disappear as the fish grows, although some adults retain small spots and others may have large spots. The eyes of the Japanese seabass seem slightly higher on its head than those on the blackfin seabass, possibly because its body is not as deep. The Japanese seabass is also darker on its back than the more silvery blackfin seabass.

Size.   The Japanese seabass grows to 40 inches and 23 pounds. The all-tackle world record is a 19-pound, 2-ounce fish taken off of Shizuoka, Japan, in 1988.

Distribution.   This species occurs in the northeastern Pacific Ocean from Japan south to Taiwan and the East and South China Seas.

Habitat.   Japanese seabass inhabit river mouths, shallow inshore bays, surf, moving water of inshore rocky reefs, and deeper waters. The young may ascend rivers in summer.

Spawning behavior.   Japanese seabass spawn from November through January on deep rocky reefs, then move shallow to feed.

Food.   The diet of adult Japanese seabass consists of anchovies, sardines, and other small fish, plus crustaceans and shrimp.

Angling.   Anglers land Japanese seabass by baitfishing with small fish or crustaceans; slow trolling; jigging; and casting with minnow-type plugs, flashy jigs, or spoons at any level from the surface to the bottom. The best fishing is said to be at night and at dawn near the surface. The largest fish are caught in fall and winter.

SEABASS, WHITE   *Atractoscion nobilis* (also *Cynoscion nobilis*).

Other names—Catalina salmon, white corvina, corvina blanca, white weakfish, weakfish, king croaker; French: *acoupa blanc;* Spanish: *corvinata bronzeada.*

A member of the Sciaenidae family, the white seabass belongs to the grouping of weakfish or corvina and is not a true bass or sea bass. The name "weakfish" refers to the tender, easily torn mouth tissue characteristic of these fish, and not their fighting ability. "Seabass" is a misnomer for the *Atractoscion* species, not related to bass.

The white seabass is a fish that has been much sought after commercially and by anglers. Its flesh is white and tender and highly valued, but it spoils quickly without proper care. White seabass stocks have struggled due to overfishing by commercial gillnets, which are now illegal in California for this species. Attempts have been made to assist white seabass stocks through hatchery means and by raising newly hatched fish in enclosed marine grow-out facilities until they are large enough to be released; the results have been encouraging.

Identification.   The body of the white seabass is elongate and somewhat compressed. There is a characteristic raised ridge along the middle of the belly between the vent and the base of the pelvic fins. The head is pointed and slightly flattened. The mouth is large, with a row of small teeth in the roof and a projecting lower jaw. The first dorsal fin has nine spines and the second two spines and 20 soft rays. The anal fin has two spines and 10 soft rays. There are no barbels on the chin. Its coloring is bluish to gray above, with dark speckling, and becomes silver below. Juveniles have several dark vertical bars; with a sleek profile, young fish are often mistaken for sea trout, which can be a problem where size restrictions are in effect.

The white seabass can be distinguished from its Atlantic relatives, the weakfish *(see)* and the spotted seatrout *(see: seatrout, spotted),* by its lack of canine teeth. It is most closely related to the California corbina *(see: corbina, California),* but it is the only California croaker to exceed 20 pounds. It is most easily separated from other croaker by the presence of a ridge running the length of the belly.

Size/Age.   The average weight of a 28-inch fish is $7^1/_2$ pounds. The all-tackle record is 83 pounds, 3 ounces, which was established in 1953 at San Felipe, Mexico. White seabass generally live for five years. In Southern California they are commonly caught in late fall and early winter, and weigh between 5 and 15 pounds. Larger fish, including some up to 60 or more pounds, are landed from midwinter through May. A 30-pounder is a good catch.

Distribution.   White seabass inhabit the eastern Pacific, mainly between San Francisco, California, and Baja California, Mexico, and in the northern Gulf of California. They are found as far north as southern Alaska and as far south as Chile.

Habitat.   Preferring deep, rocky environments, white seabass are usually hold near kelp beds in depths of 12 to 25 fathoms. They are sometimes found in shallow surf or deeper waters. Juveniles inhabit shallow nearshore areas, bays, and estuaries.

Life history.   Spawning occurs in spring and summer. White seabass are schooling fish and are present in California waters all year long. They are especially popular in the spring, and also in the winter when they converge on spawning squid.

White Seabass

Food and feeding habits. White seabass feed on anchovies, pilchards, herring, and other fish, as well as on crustaceans and squid.

Angling. White seabass are fished primarily with live baits in relatively shallow water, but they will also take a fast-trolled spoon, an artificial squid, or a bone jig. Live natural baits appear to be the best offering, but large anchovies and medium-size sardines are also good. At times, large white seabass will strike only large, live Pacific mackerel.

Live and dead squid are the primary natural baits in the winter off Southern California, when the squid are abundant and spawning. Fished on a jig or a baited hook with a sliding egg sinker, the squid is freespooled to the bottom, often being pecked by other fish on the way, then worked a few feet off the bottom by repeated lifting and dropping movements. Tackle with 25- to 30-pound line is used on party boats and where there is a lot of kelp; 10- to 15-pound gear can be used on smaller boats.

SEABREAM

See: Bream, Sea.

SEA GRANT

Sea Grant, formally known as the National Sea Grant College Program, is a network of 29 university-based programs in coastal and Great Lakes States involving more than 300 institutions nationwide in research, education, and transfer of technology regarding coastal, marine, and Great Lakes issues. Through a cost-sharing relationship with universities, Sea Grant plays a vital national role in estuarine research, science-based fisheries management, marine education, coastal engineering, resource policy analysis, pollution remediation, seafood safety, and marine engineering. Focal points of Sea Grant leadership are research expertise in aquaculture and marine biotechnology, and research in areas promising new products, job creation, economic growth, and improved international competitiveness.

The National Sea Grant College Program has succeeded despite little public fanfare or significant taxpayer dollars. Few citizens, and few recreational anglers, have heard of Sea Grant, but the 100 million Americans living within 100 miles of a coastal waterway—the Great Lakes, the Atlantic and Pacific Oceans, and the Gulf of Mexico—have likely benefited from its works and, at the very least, educational programs.

Sea Grant provides critical, objective information leading to the intelligent use, conservation, and management of coastal and marine resources through problem- and issue-oriented basic research. Its scientific research is peer-reviewed with a unique value-added component that also enables Sea Grant to educate and transfer technology to citizens. By addressing its research into areas that will make a difference in large sectors of society, such as coastal communities, Sea Grant is a model for inventive and flexible approaches to problem solving.

The real-world problem-solving applications of Sea Grant research have built bridges between academic scientists and the needs of citizens, and have produced, among many things, improved hurricane-resistance construction designs, new medical products produced from crab shell wastes, desalination of sea water for irrigation and drinking water, oil spill cleanup procedures, and a better understanding of the science of fisheries resources to ensure that they will be available for the future.

The Program

Congress established the National Sea Grant College Program in 1966 to hasten the development, use, and conservation of the nation's marine and Great Lakes resources. The legislation called for a network of Sea Grant colleges that would conduct education, training, and research in all fields of marine study, and directed that grants and contracts would go to "suitable public and private institutions of higher education, institutes, laboratories, and public or private agencies which are engaged in, or concerned with, activities in the various fields related to the development of marine resources."

The Secretary of Commerce has designated 29 Sea Grant college programs in coastal and Great Lakes states and Puerto Rico. These programs are the heart of a nationwide network of over 300 participating institutions and over 3,000 scientists, engineers, educators, students, and outreach specialists. This network has provided a powerful national capability in marine resource research and public outreach.

Some notable examples of Sea Grant achievement include leading the development of hybrid striped bass aquaculture, which has grown from a university demonstration project to a valuable fish-farming industry; developing new strains of salmon that grow three times faster than wild stocks; conducting research on nutrient runoffs from agriculture into bays that has led four states to adopt management practices resulting in improved water quality; improving marine safety and lifesaving practices, from survival training for the fishing industry to major advances in the revival of coldwater drowning victims; and supporting the training of thousands of students in oceanography and marine biology. It also organized the first systematic effort in the United States to discover and develop new drugs from marine organisms; this biotechnology effort resulted in the discovery of more than 1,000 compounds—including at least 50 with significant potential for treating inflammatory diseases like arthritis and asthma—and the awarding of numerous patents.

Although many Sea Grant programs are oriented toward general resource and commercial issues, some are focused on issues of direct concern to consumers and to recreational anglers. The 29 Sea Grant programs have extensive educational materials, especially relating to environmental matters, seafood, and recreation, that are available to the public; and some of their work has been incorporated into various sections of this encyclopedia.

Addressing Resource Issues of Public Concern

Sea Grant plays a unique and important role in advancing the nation's interest in marine resources. Together with the Office of Naval Research (ONR) and the National Science Foundation (NSF), Sea Grant provides the only sustained federal contact and funding source for universities with marine research capabilities. Moreover, Sea Grant provides the major source of research support for marine-related subjects that fall outside biological, physical, and chemical oceanography, and marine geology and geophysics. These include, for example, coastal and ocean engineering, fisheries science, and marine-related social sciences and law. Where NSF and ONR have remained steadfast in their support of basic oceanographic research, Sea Grant has supported scientific research to address marine and coastal resource issues of more immediate public concern. To ensure that programs respond to local as well as national concerns, the law requires that one-third of the program funds come from state or local governments, industry, or other sources. This has provided outstanding leverage to limited federal funds.

Sea Grant is also the only National Oceanic and Atmospheric Administration (NOAA) marine program with sustained, legislatively mandated responsibility for linking NOAA with university researchers and educators. The Marine Advisory Service (MAS) provides a key link between NOAA programs and residents in coastal and Great Lakes states and in Puerto Rico. Many Sea Grant–supported research projects are pursued in collaboration with NOAA specialists associated with the Office of Coastal Resources Management, the Coastal Ocean Program, the National Marine Fisheries Service, and the National Weather Service; and these projects contribute to a wide range of NOAA responsibilities, including fisheries and coastal management, aquaculture development, coastal water quality, habitat protection and restoration, marine sanctuaries and estuarine reserves management, and protection of life and property from natural hazards. Sea Grant is strengthened to the extent that it draws on the extensive technological and scientific resources available in NOAA. These include its forecasting and remote sensing capabilities; sophisticated environmental and resource information databases; and access to NOAA ships, laboratories, and computing capabilities.

Planning for the Future

The strategic planning framework for Sea Grant assumes the persistence of various trends. One of the most important of these is continued population growth along coastal areas; 127 million people are expected to live in coastal areas by 2010, and this population growth will place increased demands on the coastal environment and its resources as well as engender conflicts over use and access. The cumulative effect is to disrupt the natural processes of coastal ecosystems and to threaten the ecological, aesthetic, and economic values that attract people to the coast. Contaminated waters, saltwater intrusions, erosion, habitat and wetlands losses, fishery declines, and shellfish bed closures are indicative of these pressures and are not likely to diminish.

Public support for environmental protection is widespread but is moderated by a belief that it is possible to use natural resources while, at the same time, minimizing environmental destruction and preserving resources for future generations. These attitudes foster expectations for a balanced approach toward resource use and conservation and for expanded public access to coastal resources. At the same time, technological innovations continue to shape events, although the development and use of these technologies, and understanding their social, economic, and political implications, will continue to be a challenge.

Despite general public support, political support for ocean and coastal programs is severely limited by fiscal and political conditions. Prospects are limited for major capital investments and for increased funding of ocean programs, so collaborative approaches become necessary. Although the variety of issues facing Sea Grant far exceeds available resources, Sea Grant's intent is to respond to those conditions likely to persist and to identify areas where it can have greatest impact.

SEAGRASS

An aquatic plant of the marine environment, primarily of the intertidal zone. Seagrasses are a major component of coastal regions and may grow to depths of 20 feet, but they are mostly associated with the shallows of flats and estuaries. Seagrasses provide life for a wide variety of organisms and help to stabilize the substrate. Some prominent sportfish use seagrasses as a nursery, and others frequent seagrasses during certain tidal stages to feed.

Environments that contain seagrass are vulnerable to habitat destruction, which may happen via anchors being dragged through the grass and motorboats run through the shallows. Damaged seagrass does not grow back readily.
See: Aquatic Plants.

SEAMOUNT

A mountain rising 1,000 meters or more from the sea floor with limited extent across the summit. Seamounts are usually fairly isolated but may exist in groups or chains; they are seldom very steep on the sides, being more elliptical in shape. The vicinity of seamounts may provide fishing opportunity, particularly for big-game species; the presence of currents and the upwelling of water in the vicinity of this structure may enhance feeding opportunities and cause predator fish to frequent that area.

SEA ROBIN

Sea robins are mostly tropical and subtropical fish of the Triglidae family, characterized by split pectoral fins that consist of stiff separate rays on the lower half and broad, soft, winglike rays on the upper half. The upper rays are not as large as in the similar-looking flying gurnard *(see: gurnard, flying)* but are used for the same purpose—swimming; the lower rays are used to find food by sifting through debris and turning over rocks. Sea robins also use their pelvic and pectoral fins to "walk" across the bottom as they search for fish, shrimp, squid, clams, and crabs to satisfy their insatiable appetites. They are often brightly colored, are capable of making loud noises by vibrating muscles attached to the air bladder, and inhabit moderately deep waters. At least 19 species occur in the Atlantic and a few in the Pacific off the coasts of the United States and Canada; other species exist off the coasts of Europe, Africa, and in the western Pacific south of Japan. These fish spawn throughout the summer, their eggs float on the surface, and the young grow quickly during the first year.

One of the more well-known fish of this group is the northern sea robin *(Prionotus carolinus),* which occurs from Nova Scotia to northern South America but is uncommon north of Massachusetts. It averages 12 inches in length and may reach a length of

Northern Sea Robin

18 inches. A black, mottled fish with an olive brown or gray background, the northern sea robin has a large head that is covered with bony plates and spines and has a distinct black chin. It is a bottom-dweller, moving close to shore during the summer and to deeper water in winter. Other Atlantic species are the striped sea robin *(P. evolans),* which is distinguished by a few dark bands on its sides, and the leopard sea robin *(P. scitulus),* an almost foot-long species with dark blotches, common in the Gulf of Mexico and the southern Atlantic.

Sea robins are a delicacy in some areas and are occasionally caught by anglers in particular seasons and localities, although they are more often thought of as bait stealers and oddities.

SEA-RUN

Another term for anadromous *(see),* referring to fish that move from the sea to freshwater to spawn.

SEASICKNESS

Seasickness is a form of motion disorder due to sensory confusion. It results from a sensory mismatch in the brain in which the vestibular system of the inner ear sends messages about body position and movement that contradict information relayed by the eyes. Inside the cabin of a rocking boat, for example, the inner ear detects changes in body position as it bobs with the movement of the boat. But since the cabin moves with the passenger, the eyes register a relatively stable scene. The brain is confused by the information it receives, and this causes dizziness, blurred vision, nausea, and other symptoms. It happens to many people and can afflict anyone as a normal consequence of putting the body into unnatural motion.

Seasickness usually does not occur in freshwater except on the largest bodies of water, and then chiefly when waves cause a lot of boat rocking. For this reason, many people who have boating experience in freshwater do not realize that they are susceptible to this disorder until they venture out into the more rollicking surface of the sea (perhaps that is why it is not called "water sickness"). In any case, many people experience seasickness for the first time, more or less as a surprise, when the symptoms start occurring while they are out on a boat in saltwater—and when it is too late to take any drugs to ward off the problem. If you get sick, don't expect the boat to turn around and return to the dock. Deal with it as best you can, because you will get better.

Adapting.   One school of thought in the treatment of seasickness is similar to the adage about treating the common cold: An untreated cold will last about seven days, and a treated cold will go away in about a week.

Over time, most people adapt to the motion that makes them sick. Once the brain determines that the confused sensory signals are the "norm," it shuts down the nausea, cold sweats, drowsiness, and other symptoms. Unfortunately, this does not happen quickly enough for many people. For some, it is possible to ease symptoms naturally, especially if they act fast at the onset of symptoms.

The more you move around, the sooner you become accustomed to the motion of the boat. Be sure you have a broad view of the horizon, and try to anticipate the vessel's motions. Do not lie down, even though it may allow you to feel better temporarily. Don't do anything that requires a close visual focus. It may help to join the captain near the helm, so you can focus attention on the boat's course; this corresponds to the fact that automobile drivers almost never get car sick.

Treatment. Prescription and over-the-counter drugs are the most common treatments for seasickness, but the wide variety available indicates that there is still no ideal solution, and they must be taken in advance of a boat trip. For the most part, these treat symptoms, not causes. On an extended voyage, they can help keep symptoms under control while you adapt to your new surroundings or get your "sea legs."

How a specific drug will affect anyone is unpredictable. What works for one person may not work for another. The only way to know for sure is to try it after consulting with a physician.

If you know that you're prone to seasickness, you might first try a nonprescription drug like Marezine, Dramamine, or Bonine. Marezine may be more desirable because it does not cause drowsiness, but this side effect varies among users of all of these drugs. If nonprescription drugs aren't effective, a doctor can prescribe prescription medication. Transderm-Scop is a prescription drug that works well for many people. It comes in the form of a small patch worn behind the ear, and it dispenses medication into the bloodstream over time.

Most drugs for seasickness must be taken 1 to 2 hours before the boat leaves the dock, so plan ahead. Like all drugs, seasickness preventives can have side effects. If you have a history of drug effects, consult your family doctor and, if possible, try the drug on land before you use it at sea.

Ginger root has recently received some attention as a seasickness preventive. Capsules of powdered ginger root have been reported to curb motion sickness better, in some cases, than over-the-counter anti-nausea drugs. Powdered ginger, available in health food stores, is effective because it works in the digestive tract where the problem is, rather than on the brain as drug remedies do.

The use of acupressure point treatment for seasickness has also become popular recently. This technique can be used after the onset of symptoms, which can be a real advantage over preventive drugs. Fabric wristbands are commercially available that operate by exerting carefully controlled pressure on an acupuncture point on both wrists (called the neikuan point). Some users have had good results, but many people are skeptical. As with almost all seasickness remedies, if it works for you, use it.

Diet. Some people believe that eating can lessen motion sickness symptoms. Your diet before going aboard and during a voyage can play a role. Eating lightly and wisely so that your digestive tract is relaxed is a good idea, because a light or calm stomach is not as easily disturbed as a stuffed one. Enjoy the food you like to eat, in moderation. There really is no scientific evidence that consuming specific foods prevents or causes seasickness. For some people, eating after they have gotten the queasy or dizzy symptoms of sickness, or even watching others eat, can induce nausea. Most importantly, do not consume alcoholic beverages; alcohol affects inner ear function and can make a seasick person feel worse.

Additional measures. Although seasickness is not a life-threatening condition, some of the symptoms (i.e., dizziness, drowsiness, loss of balance) have the potential to cause personal injury onboard a rolling, tossing vessel. If you do become seasick on a boat, tell the captain. You will probably be directed to the area of the vessel with the least motion and away from fumes.

If you feel as if you might vomit, get to the rail or head (toilet) before you do. The rail is a better spot, because the smells that accompany vomiting are reduced by boat movement and wind, and are less likely to cause others to feel nauseated. If you must lie down on a bunk (not recommended unless you have serious symptoms), make sure you leave a bucket or container handy. Most captains treat their seasick passengers with kindness, unless they lose their lunch in the wrong place. Lying down, however, stimulates the inner ear and will probably make you queasy all over again.

If you do vomit, you'll probably feel better afterward. This may be temporary or it may be the onset of recovery. To improve your chances of rebounding, once your stomach has quieted, move around and get your body in tune with the motion of the boat. Try to adapt. There's a good chance that you may still be able to enjoy the outing.

SEASON

(1) Fisheries agencies regulate fishing by recreational and commercial fishermen for certain fish or groups of fish, setting opening and closing dates and thus creating open and closed seasons. Seasons differ by species, locality, type of water, and other considerations.
See: **Regulations.**

(2) In a broader, fishing-parlance sense, season refers to the time when migratory species of fish are present, as in: Shad are in season in the Northeast during May.

SEA TROUT

A term for the anadromous or sea-run brown trout; this is not to be confused with purely saltwater seatrout.

See: Seatrout, Sand; Seatrout, Silver; Seatrout, Spotted; Trout, Brown.

SEATROUT, SAND   *Cynoscion arenarius.*

Other names—white trout, sand weakfish, white weakfish.

A member of the Sciaenidae family (drum and croaker), the sand seatrout is a small and frequently caught fish. Found primarily in the Gulf of Mexico, it supports a minor commercial and sportfishing industry. It is closely related to the weakfish *(see)* of the Atlantic coast.

Identification. Its coloring is pale yellow on the back and silver to white below, without any real defined spots. Young sand seatrout have cloudy backs, sometimes forming crossbands. The inside of the mouth is yellow. There are 10 to 12 soft rays in the anal fin. It does not have any chin barbels and can be distinguished from the silver seatrout *(see: seatrout, silver)* by the presence of 10 anal rays, the silver seatrout having only 8 or 9.

Size. The average fish is 10 to 12 inches in length and rarely weighs more than a pound. The all-tackle record is a 2-pound, 3-ounce fish caught in Texas.

Distribution. The sand seatrout occurs mainly in the Gulf of Mexico from the west coast of Florida through Texas and into Mexico and as far south as the Gulf of Campeche. It also exists on the extreme southeastern Atlantic portion of Florida.

Habitat. The sand seatrout is predominantly an inshore fish found in bays and inlets. The young inhabit shallow bays, particularly in less saline areas. Adult fish move offshore in winter.

Spawning behavior. There is a prolonged spawning season inshore from spring through summer. Fish mature during their first or second year.

Food and feeding habits. The main food source is shrimp and small fish.

Angling. *See: Seatrout, Spotted.*

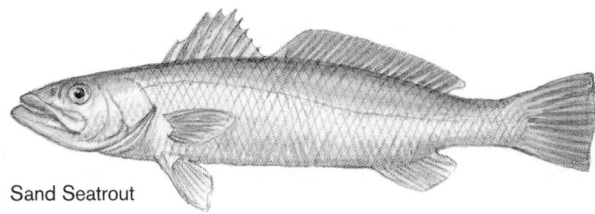

Sand Seatrout

SEATROUT, SILVER   *Cynoscion nothus.*

Other names—silver trout, silver weakfish.

A member of the Sciaenidae family (drum and croaker), the silver seatrout is smaller than other seatrout and generally similar in body shape. It is often misidentified with the spotted seatrout *(see: seatrout, spotted).*

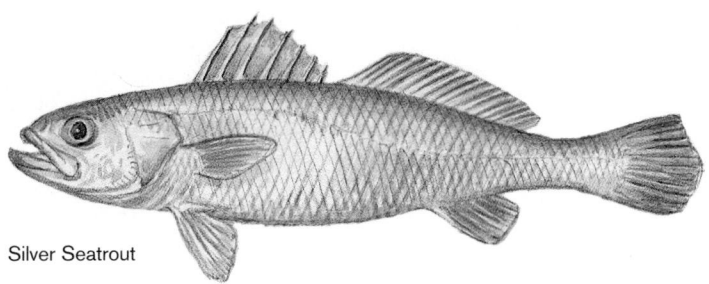

Silver Seatrout

Identification. Its coloring is pale straw or walnut on the back and silver to white below, without any real defined spots, although faint diagonal lines may be present on the upper body. There are 8 to 9 rays in the anal fin, which distinguish it from the sand seatrout *(see: seatrout, sand),* which has 10 rays. Silver seatrout have large eyes and a short snout, no chin barbel, and one to two prominent canine teeth usually present at the tip of the upper jaw. The lower half of the tail is longer than the upper half.

Size. Silver seatrout seldom weigh more than a half pound and are usually less than 10 inches long.

Distribution. The silver seatrout occurs mainly throughout the Gulf of Mexico and is also in the Atlantic from southern Florida to Maryland.

Habitat. Predominantly an offshore fish, the silver seatrout is usually found over sandy and sandy mud bottoms. It migrates in bays in winter months.

Spawning behavior. There is a prolonged spawning season offshore during spring, summer, and fall.

Food and feeding habits. The main food sources are shrimp, small crustaceans, and small fish.

Angling. Owing to their size and the availability of other species, silver seatrout are seldom the deliberate target of anglers but may enter the inshore catch in winter, especially over sandy bottoms near beaches and inlets.

SEATROUT, SPOTTED   *Cynoscion nebulosus.*

Other names—trout, speckled trout, speck, spotted weakfish, spotted squeteague, gator trout, salmon trout, winter trout, black trout; Spanish: *corvinata pintada.*

The spotted seatrout is a member of the Sciaenidae family of drum and croaker. It belongs to the genus *Cynoscion* (weakfish and seatrout), which is named for their tender mouths from which hooks tear easily. Considered a exceptionally valuable commercial fish, and an even more valuable sportfish to anglers, it is intensely pursued throughout its range, especially in the Gulf of Mexico. Most Gulf and Atlantic coast states have experienced a decline in spotted seatrout populations due to overfishing and exploitation, and fishing is strictly controlled; in some areas the cessation of gillnetting is leading to stock recoveries and providing optimism for the future.

S

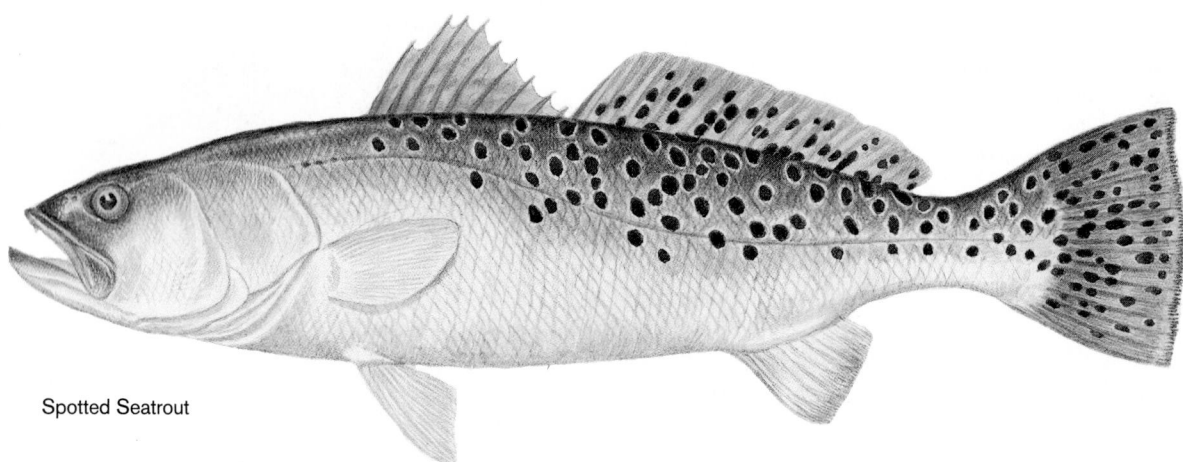

Spotted Seatrout

S

The spotted seatrout is also known as an excellent table fish. Its flesh is fine and delicately flavored, but it spoils quickly and should be cleaned or stored on ice when possible after being caught. It usually appears on the menus of Southern restaurants as "trout" and can be substituted in recipes for seabass or redfish.

Identification. The spotted seatrout has an elongated body with a slightly more regular and even tail fin, with a black margin, than that of sand or silver seatrout *(see: seatrout, sand; seatrout, silver).* Its coloring is dark gray or green on the back, with sky-blue tinges shading to silvery and white below; the dorsal fins are gray green, and many round black spots speckle the back, tail, and dorsal fins. The lower jaw protrudes beyond the upper, which has one or two prominent canine teeth. The first dorsal fin has one spine and 24 to 27 soft rays, and the anal fin has two spines and 10 to 11 soft rays. There are eight or nine short, stubby gill rakers on the lower limb of the first gill arch. There are no barbels, and the interior of the mouth is orange. Very young fish have a broad, dark lateral band. The presence of spots on the fins can distinguish the spotted seatrout from other seatrout.

Size/Age. Mature spotted seatrout commonly range from 12 to 24 inches and average 4 pounds, although they can reach 48 inches and weigh as much as 16 pounds. The all-tackle record is 17 pounds, 7 ounces, caught at Fort Pierce, Florida, in 1995. They can live up to 10 years; three-year-old fish in Alabama are generally 12 to 13 inches long, and four-year-old fish are 14 to 15 inches long. Anglers commonly catch spotted seatrout weighing between 1 and 3 pounds; fish exceeding 7 pounds are considered large, and 10-pounders are definitely trophies.

Distribution. Spotted seatrout occur along Atlantic and Gulf of Mexico coasts. They are most abundant along the coasts of Georgia, Florida, Alabama, Mississippi, eastern Louisiana, and Texas but range as far westward as Tampico, Mexico. In late spring, they can range as far north as Long Island, New York, but are more prominent in the mid-Atlantic in the Carolinas, Virginia, and Maryland.

Habitat. An inshore bottom-dwelling species, the spotted seatrout is inhabits shallow bays, estuaries, bayous, canals, and Gulf Coast beaches. They prefer nearshore sandy and grassy bottoms, and may even frequent salt marshes and tidal pools with high salinity. They also live around oil rigs, usually within 10 miles of shore. Ideal water temperatures are between 58° and 81°F. Cold water is lethal to spotted seatrout, and although some move into slow-moving or still, deep waters in cold weather, the majority remain and may be killed by the low temperatures.

Life history/Behavior. It is believed that water temperature and salinity levels are more important to spawning than a specific location, because newly hatched spotted seatrout will not survive low salinity and low temperature conditions. Optimum spawning conditions for spotted seatrout exist when salinity is 20 to 34 parts per thousand and temperatures reach 70° to 90°F. Spawning occurs at night in coastal bays, sounds, and lagoons, near passes, and around barrier islands from March through November. Females may lay up to 10 million eggs. The eggs hatch within 20 hours and are transported to estuaries by winds and currents.

Spotted seatrout are schooling fish and are not considered migratory, as they rarely move more than 30 miles, although they do move into deeper waters or deep holes to avoid cold temperatures. Juveniles spend two to four years in shallow grassy areas and then tend to move into the nearshore passes and along beaches.

Food and feeding habits. Spotted seatrout are predatory, feeding primarily on shrimp and small fish. When shrimp are scarce, they often consume mullet, menhaden, and silversides. The larger specimens feed more heavily on fish. Juveniles feed on grass shrimp and copepods.

Angling. In Florida and on the Gulf Coast, especially in Louisiana and Texas, spotted seatrout are caught throughout the year, although the most productive time is during summer and early fall for overall numbers of fish, and in mid- to late fall and early spring for big fish.

Lures and live baits are both effective. Live shrimp and minnows are the most common live baits, but cut mullet, soft-shelled crabs, worms, and squid are among other effective natural baits. Popular lures include soft worms, bucktail jigs, grubs and jigs with assorted soft tails, surface and shallow-swimming plugs, spoons, and streamer flies. Light tackle is very appropriate for these fish, and many anglers use light baitcasting or light to medium-light spinning tackle. A lesser number employ flycasting gear.

In the gulf, especially throughout Texas, sight fishing for trout and redfish *(see: drum, red)* is extremely popular. Anglers use shallow-water craft to negotiate the abundant grassflats—many of which are just inches deep—where they visually locate and then cast to the fish with baits, lures, or flies. In other areas, fishing by wading or casting from boats is common, usually for unseen fish that are moving through an area or are located in feeding or resting places, such as grassbeds and shellfish beds or in deep holes or channels, where blind casting or even trolling can be effective.

Spotted seatrout are caught on a variety of offerings because they feed throughout the water column. Anchoring and casting lures or stillfishing with bait, drifting under the occasional control of an electric motor or pushpole and casting, and trolling slowly through holes and channels are all practiced in appropriate places and conditions. Among lures, however, jigs with soft tails—either curly, grub-shaped, or shrimp-shaped—are especially favored, and these are usually worked slowly via casting.

On occasion, these fish will actively feed on or close to the surface, and at such times surface plugs and popping bugs for fly rods will catch them. More productive, however, is fishing below the surface with shallow-swimming plugs that imitate small baitfish like finger mullet, or fishing along the bottom with slow-moving jigs. An extremely popular technique, particularly throughout the Gulf of Mexico, employs a popper and natural shrimp; the angler works the surface popper to attract the attention of a trout to the shrimp.

Bigger seatrout are not typically found with concentrations of smaller ones, and it is necessary to work deeper areas and, in general, to use larger baits and lures for bigger fish. The period before and after spawning is a good time for large spotted seatrout, and this is also when the coldest water is just coming or going. The coldest period of midwinter is generally not productive for spotted seatrout, as the fish are nearly dormant.

Large spotted seatrout are not as widely distributed as smaller ones. In the Gulf of Mexico, the largest trout are taken in spring, and again in winter. In the spring, fish move into shallow beach and

A spotted seatrout from Calcasieu Lake, Louisiana.

bay habitats en masse for their first spawn of the season. For the rest of the summer and early fall, the larger fish tend to stay in cooler Gulf waters and only periodically enter the beach and bay habitats for subsequent spawns. Most of the large fish winter offshore, and a few winter in interior marshes, where they are especially sluggish.

Large trout have different food habits than do smaller ones. Smaller trout eat large amounts of shrimp and other crustaceans. As they become larger, their diet shifts more to fish, the larger the better. Studies in Texas and Mississippi have shown that really big spotted seatrout prefer to feed on mullet. They found that, invariably, a large trout will find the largest mullet it can handle and try to swallow it. Often the mullet is half to two-thirds as large as the trout. Thus, the key to catching large spotted seatrout is to find those places where they are located at the respective season and to use big lures or baits.

SEAWEED

Algae that grows in the sea or on rocks; kelp *(see)* is a form of seaweed. This is distinguished from seagrass *(see)*.

SECCHI DISK

A circular black-and-white disk lowered into the water to determine transparency.
See: Water Clarity.

S

SEINE

(1) A small fine-mesh net used for collecting bait or other aquatic organisms, primarily used by one or two people in streams or shallow waters. A two-person seine usually has a float line (upper) and lead line (bottom) designed to be pulled through the water for the purpose of catching bait, particularly minnows, although a form of seine can be made of fine-mesh net stretched over a frame and used by one person. Such devices are normally used to catch baitfish for personal use, and their size and place of use may be regulated. In some locations, seines may be used, under permit, to collect bait for sale.

(2) A large commercial fishing net designed to hang vertically in the water, with one end held at or near the surface with floats and the other end held at or near the bottom with weights. The sides are drawn together to encircle fish. The net and contents are drawn onto a boat or shore. A purse seine operates on a similar principle, although it is used by two boats and spread out to encircle schools of fish; it is interwoven and can be drawn together for collecting the entire contents. The size of the mesh is supposed to correlate to the target species. Purse seines have been attributed with the bycatch of porpoises, and there have been efforts to develop means of escape for nontarget mammals and fish.

See: Commercial Fisherman.

SENEGAL

Senegal is situated between the equator and the Tropic of Cancer, on the western coast of the African continent. Its coastal region is on the west facing the Atlantic Ocean. Mali lies to the east, Mauritania to the north, and Guinea and the Guinea Bissau to the south. In the middle of the country is Gambia, a small nation encircled by Senegal, which extends inland along the Gambia River and fronts the Atlantic Ocean.

Jutting into the eastern Atlantic, especially at the Cape Verde Peninsula, Senegal has a variety of notable offshore and inshore fishing opportunities, with sailfish being the premier attraction. Senegalese waters host more than 30 gamefish species, most of which are caught year-round by anglers trolling artificial lures or small natural baits just off the rocky peninsula of Cape Verde.

Much of Senegal is a flat, bush-covered plain, whereas the rest of the country encompasses gold beaches and mangrove swamps in the extreme south. The main rivers are the Sénégal, which forms the northern boundary, and the Saloum, Gambia, and Casamance; these are subject to seasonal fluctuations but are navigable in the lower reaches. Senegal experiences a wet season from June through October (wetter in the tropical south and drier in the more arid north), and a dry season from November through May. The best time for offshore fishing is during the rainy season, whereas inshore fishing is possible year-round.

Since the 1960s, this country has had a strong reputation among light-tackle billfish enthusiasts as a top Atlantic sailfish destination. The first sailfish—*espadon voilier* in the local French idiom—captured with rod and reel in the waters off Dakar, the capital city, dates to 1965 and led to the creation of the Gorée Sportfishing Centre in 1966 and the Big Game Fishing Club of Dakar in 1967. Senegalese sportfishermen soon improved their craft, realizing that they had access to a solid fishery for medium-size sailfish. Light-tackle angling became popular by 1970, and in 1973 a 96-pound sailfish caught on 12-pound line established Senegal's first International Game Fish Association (IGFA) line-class world record. In 1978, local anglers developed the Sport Fishing Centre of Dakar, and this group now organizes most Senegal's international tournaments. Further line-class records were established in the late 1980s and helped influence a new trend among local sportfishing operators, who have since standardized the use of light tackle aboard their charter boats.

Centre de Peche Sportive (also known as Air Afrique Sportfishing Centre), which is owned and managed in Dakar by Air Afrique, represents the pride of West Africa's sportfishing operators with its fleet of well-outfitted 28-foot Bertrams. This is where anglers wait to meet their charter boats, just a few minutes from the Savana Hotel. Only a few other serious sportfishing organizations exist in Senegal, including two dozen private boats at Africa Safari in Dakar, and the Club Espadon in nearby Saly.

Sailfish are scattered everywhere along the Senegal coast, but the locals usually target three precise zones where the fish feed most actively. One is between 4 and 25 miles northwest of the northernmost point of the Cape Verde Peninsula; this zone is the area's best bet for blue marlin and swordfish. The second zone is 8 to 25 miles southeast of Cape Manuel, the southernmost point of the peninsula, where sportfishing boats troll for sailfish and roaming blue marlin, zigzagging along the continental shelf. The third one, located 8 to 35 miles southwest of Dakar, is considered a "sailfish alley" because these fish are present almost year-round here.

Senegal's sailfish season starts at the end of May and runs until the end of October, peaking in July, August, and September. The average sailfish weighs around 65 pounds, but beginning at the end of August larger sailfish—up to 90 pounds and more—move into the area.

Yellowfin and bigeye tuna migrate through the area in two distinct movements. From April through July, schoolies averaging 30 pounds run offshore; from October through December, fish up to 200 pounds pass by roughly 30 miles off the coast. Along with the bigger tuna, anglers often have a chance to catch wahoo, sailfish, and, many times, blue marlin. Wahoo are present virtually all year, peaking from May through August, but they usually stay far off the coast, so the catches of this species are not plentiful. Local anglers report occasional encounters with bluefin tuna in December and January, but the bluefin also seem to prefer offshore waters from 30 to 200 miles from the coast.

Another great predator frequenting the waters off Dakar is the elusive broadbill swordfish. Night drifting becomes possible during the quiet nights of June and July, and again in December.

If there's any downside to the area's prolific sailfishing, it is that the large schools of sailfish tend to deter anglers from seriously exploring the blue marlin potential. Even those clients who do put in a few hours of trolling offshore often give in to the temptation to change gears and put out light tackle for sailfish, simply because the tactic produces reliable action.

Blue marlin generally follow two migration routes off the coast of Senegal. In May, June, and July, medium-size blue marlin swim southward down the coast; in October and November, the bigger fish seem to swim back up the coast. During this second northward migration, the marlin feed on yellowfin tuna, a species that prefers clear, blue waters. If the currents do not push blue water into the nearby continental shelf, blue marlin may stay as far as 50 miles off the coast.

Although most of the angling attention, especially from distant travelers, is focused on offshore action, plenty of inshore species thrive in Senegalese waters. Surf casting all along the wide beaches of St. Louis, Mbour, Cambérène, Sangomar, and Cape Skirring give the angler the best possibilities to catch big barracuda, meagre, jacks, sharks, snapper, drum, grouper, rays, and sea bass. These species are also caught in the estuaries of Casamance and Sine Saloum, but tarpon are present, too, especially along the mangroves and in the murky waters of the various rivers (which also host hippos and crocodiles).

The best spots for inshore fishing are located near three lodges: the Hotel Savana au Cap Skirring, the Centre de Peche de la Petite Cote au Mbour, and the Village Hotel Keur Saloum au Toubakouta.

SENNETS

Sennets are members of the Sphyraenidae family of barracuda, although they are smaller and less wide ranging than barracuda. Northern sennet (*Sphyraena borealis*) grow to a maximum of 18 inches; they occur in the western Atlantic from Massachusetts to southern Florida and the Gulf of Mexico. Southern sennet (*S. picudilla*) are similar, occurring in Bermuda, Florida, and the Bahamas south to Uruguay; also known as *picuda china,* they have more commercial relevance than the northern

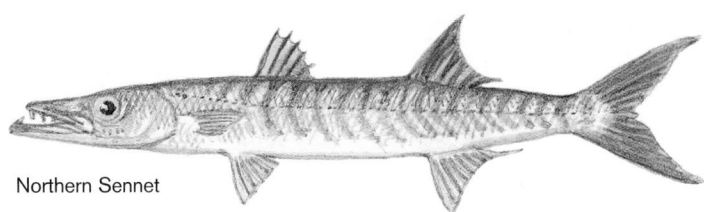

Northern Sennet

sennet and are found near the surface, sometimes in large schools.

These fish are seldom far from the coast, often preferring to be near rocky bottoms. They are good table fare and not known to be poisonous (as barracuda may be). They provide good sport for light-tackle anglers and have been known to take small spoons, plugs, and flies.

SETBACK

The distance that a lure or bait is placed behind the boat, or behind an object such as a sideplaner.
See: Downrigger Fishing; Planer Boards.

SET HOOK

A single hook and line attached to some object rather than to a hand-operated mechanical reel. The hook is usually baited and may or may not be attended. A set hook is prohibited in some places; where legal, its use and location may be regulated. A set hook may also be called a setline *(see)*, jug hook *(see),* or limbline *(see).* This is not a sportfishing instrument.

SETH GREEN RIG

One of the oldest deep-trolling, multi-lure presentation methods, developed by renowned New York fish culturist Seth Green in the late nineteenth century. A few anglers still use this rig, or a variation, principally as an adjunct to other methods of deep trolling, and generally when they're desperate.

The Seth Green rig features five to eight lures, usually spoons or flies, on individual leaders that snap to the main fishing line and stay at a fixed position because they are attached to swivels set 10 to 20 feet apart. A heavy lead weight is used to get the rig down. To fish it, you lower the weight and line into the water until the first barrel swivel is reached, then you take a leader and snap it to the barrel swivel; the line is lowered in the water until you reach the next swivel, and attach another leader. Continue in this fashion until all lures are out.

This setup requires a heavy rod and reel and some adroit manipulation to retrieve—when you reel in, you must stop to remove each of the snapped on leaders. Leader length varies; old-timers used 15- to 30-foot leaders, but if you're fishing deep, you can use shorter ones. This setup has also been called a "thermal rig" and is primarily used in midsummer trout and salmon fishing for covering

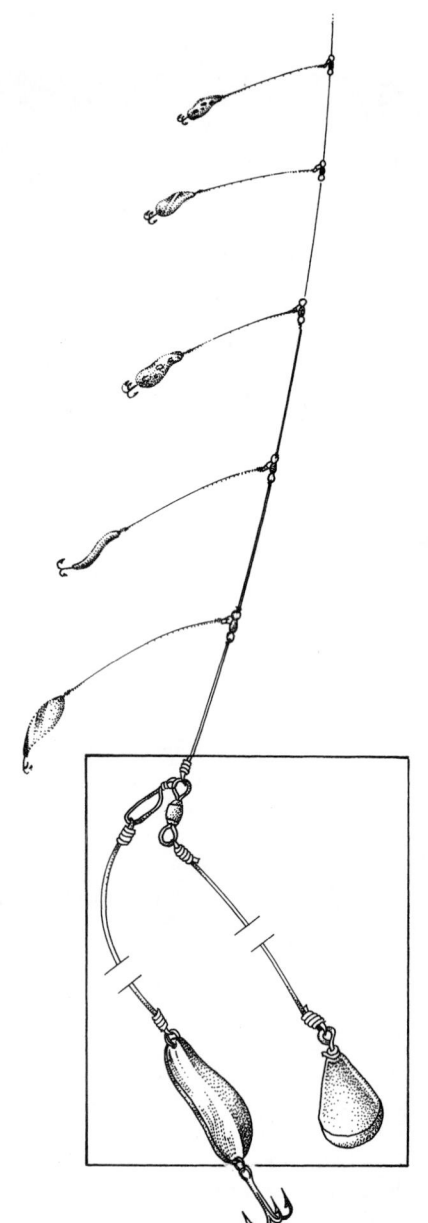

The cumbersome Seth Green Rig features multiple trolling lures attached to barrel swivels that are spaced out along the main line.

a deep column of water. It was adapted from commercial fishing applications. Anglers should check local fishing regulations to be sure that it is legal to use this many lures or hook points on one fishing line.

SETLINE

A line that is anchored at one point and is not connected to a hand-operated mechanical reel. The line is attached to a hook or hooks that are baited to catch fish. A setline may also be called a limbline or logline. Setlines are illegal in some places; where legal, they usually must be tagged or marked with the owner's identifying information. Regulations

also govern the length, number of hooks, spacing of hooks, and other issues. Usually a setline is not under the direct view and control of the person placing the line. From the standpoint of fishing regulations, such a line would be unattended. Although using a setline may be called fishing, and such usage may be covered under established regulations, a setline is not a sportfishing instrument, and setline fishing is not sportfishing.

SETTING THE HOOK
See: Hooksetting.

SEYCHELLES

An archipelago of 115 granite and coral islands northeast of Madagascar in the Indian Ocean, Seychelles is 4° south of the equator and 1,000 nautical miles from the east coast of Africa. Tourism is the economic mainstay of this 472-square-kilometer republic, and in the latter twentieth century the region has been a popular destination for European tourists, including anglers who have discovered outstanding and diverse big-game fishing and an abundance of bonefish.

Seychelles consists of 83 largely uninhabited coral islands, and 32 granite islands in the northerly Mahé group. The predominant islands in this group include Mahé—which is the largest and contains 90 percent of the country's population of 75,000—as well as Praslin, Silhouette, and LaDigue. Two other islands, Denis and Bird, are especially popular with big-game anglers, as they lie close to deep water.

Recreational fishing in the open sea here is a recent sport; its development coincided with the advent of tourism in 1972. Prior to this, the Seychellois fished with hook and line for daily subsistence requirements, and used fish traps inside the reefs. Spearfishing was banned with the arrival of the first tourists in 1972. Commercial fishing has become well developed, however, and is an important economic activity, the primary targets of which are yellowfin and skipjack tuna, as well as swordfish.

The tourism policy of the Seychelles champions sustainability and aims at a limited number of visitors. These restrictions allow for high-standard facilities that maximize economic benefit and minimize environmental degradation. More than 47 percent of the territory is classified as marine or national parks.

Today, most of the upmarket resort hotels on Mahé, Praslin, and La Digue, and on the islands of Desroches, Bird, and Denis, offer big-game fishing to clients. From the latter, the trip to the blue-water dropoff is just a few hundred yards; there, upwellings produce nutrient-rich conditions and excellent fishing. A typical half-day trip sees the regular tag and release of sailfish, dorado, wahoo, bonito, tuna, rainbow runners, and barracuda. Blue and black marlin are also present, and in 1996 three black marlin over 500 pounds were tagged and released. Tuna are abundant and available all year, and Seychelles has established a number of world records for dogtooth and yellowfin tuna. Great potential exists for light-tackle and fly fishing, possibly for record specimens of some species.

Being close to the equator, Seychelles experiences two annual monsoon periods. The southeast monsoon occurs from April through September, is usually associated with dry and windy conditions, and is noted for producing sailfish, marlin, and tuna. The northwest monsoon occurs from October through March, is wet but calmer, and brings a more plentiful supply of both pelagic and demersal fishes.

Desroches Island, which is part of the Amirantes Group of Seychelles islands, has recently become a hotspot for bonefish and is the bonefish capital of this country. This island group spans for 90 miles southwest of Mahé. Exploration in the late 1990s identified areas of great potential in the vicinity of Desroches, and numerous fish in the 10-pound class are reportedly present. Bird Island is also known to have bonefishing opportunity.

Seychelles are prominent grounds for Hawks Bill and Green turtles; both are protected by law, and conservation efforts are achieving encouraging results. With all of its coral reefs, the Seychelles are also popular diving sites. Travel to Seychelles is accomplished via London, Kenya, and South Africa.

S-GLASS

The common term for low-alkali, high-aluminum and -magnesium fiberglass, a very high tensile modulus fiberglass used in fishing rod construction.
See: Rod, Fishing.

SHAD, ALABAMA   *Alosa alabamae.*
Other names—Gulf shad, Ohio shad.

This member of the Clupeidae family of herring *(see)* and shad is an anadromous species virtually ignored by anglers. It does have some commercial significance, however.

Identification.   A silvery fish like its other relatives, the Alabama shad has a large terminal mouth with upper and lower jaws of almost equal length. Its tongue has a single median row of small teeth, there is no lateral line, the posterior of the dorsal fin lacks an elongated slender filament, and there are 18 or fewer anal rays. In general, it is nearly identical to the larger-growing American shad *(see: shad, American)*, but adult fish have 42 to 48 gill rakers on the lower limb of the first gill arch.

Size.   The Alabama shad can grow to just over 20 inches but is usually under 15 inches long.

Distribution.   This species occurs in the northern Gulf of Mexico from the Mississippi Delta and Louisiana eastward to Choctawhatchee River in Florida; it also occurs in rivers from Iowa to Arkansas and across West Virginia.

Habitat/Life history.   The Alabama shad is a schooling species that spends most of its life in the ocean; when mature, it returns from early spring through summer to rivers and streams to spawn, inhabiting open water of medium to large rivers. Young shad descend rivers in autumn.

Food/Angling.   The feeding habits of this species at sea are unknown but are presumably similar to those of hickory and American shad. The Alabama shad is anadromous and only a potential angling target during upriver spawning migrations, during which time it does not feed. This smallish shad is a largely incidental catch and a rare deliberate angling target.
See: Shad, Hickory.

SHAD, AMERICAN   *Alosa sapidissima.*
Other names—poor man's salmon, common shad, Atlantic shad, Connecticut River shad, North River shad, Potomac shad, Susquehanna shad, white shad, Delaware shad, alose; French: *alose savoureuse.*

Frequently referred to simply as "shad," this species is an anadromous member of the Clupeidae family of herring *(see)* and shad and is highly regarded as a gamefish due to its strong fighting and jumping characteristics. American shad spawning runs provide a popular but seasonal sportfishery on both coasts of the United States, although these fish receive scant attention in Canada. The white, flaky flesh of this shad is full of bones but makes good table fare if prepared with patience and care; the scientific name *sapidissima* means "most delicious," an appropriate appellation for a fish that supports a considerable commercial fishery and whose roe is considered a delicacy and commands a premium price.

Other North American shad to which they are closely or distantly related include the smaller hickory shad *(A. mediocris; see: shad, hickory)*, a western Atlantic species whose range overlaps with the American shad; and the Alabama shad *(A. alabamae; see: shad, Alabama)* of the Gulf Coast. Several herringlike species called shad occur in the eastern Atlantic; these include the twaite, Killarney, or Mediterranean shad *(A. fallax);* and the allis shad *(A. alosa).* These smaller species occur in western Europe and the Mediterranean, and also ascend coastal streams in spring to spawn.

The American shad has a history of intensive exploitation for its flesh and roe, and landings in the past century have steadily declined due to this and other factors. Overfishing, dams, and pollution have been the chief causes of severe declines in the abundance of American shad. Some of these factors have been mitigated but others, most recently excessive commercial ocean exploitation, have caused continued concern. Along the eastern U.S.,

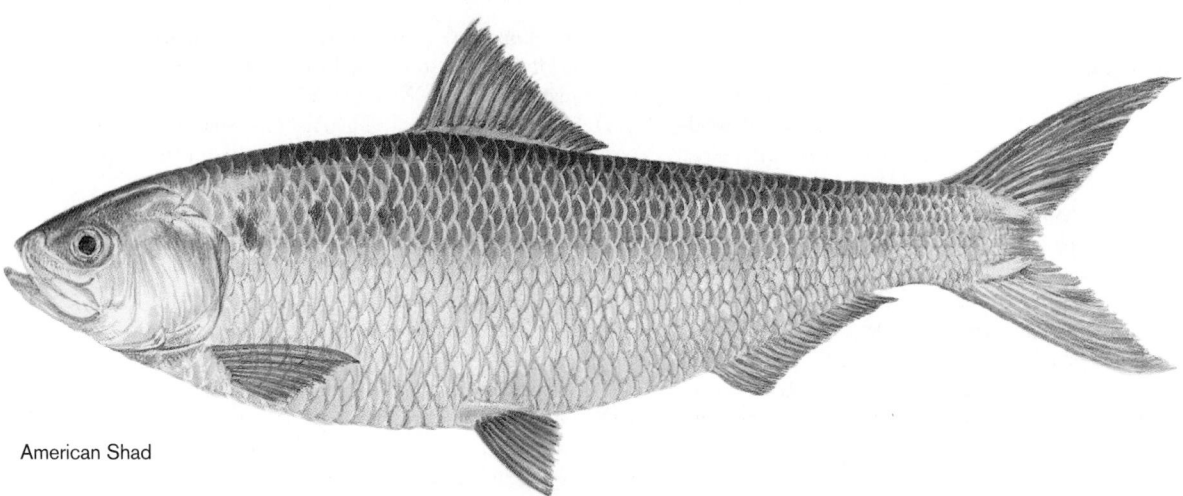

American Shad

a coastwide management plan has been created to assist cooperation and restoration efforts among states, which includes habitat improvement, fish passageways, and stocking programs. Although there has been some improvement in shad populations in some rivers, the number of American shad continues to decline.

Identification.   The laterally compressed, fairly deep body of the American shad is silvery white with some green to dark blue along the back, frequently with a metallic shine. The coloring darkens slightly when the fish enters freshwater to spawn. There is a large black spot directly behind the top of the gill cover, followed by several spots that become smaller and less distinct toward the tail; sometimes there are up to three rows of these dark spots, one under the other. The American shad has large, easily shed scales, as well as modified scales called scutes, which form a distinct ridge or cutting edge along the belly. It has a single dorsal fin in the middle of the back, the tail is deeply forked, and there are soft fin rays and long anal fins. It has weak teeth or no teeth at all.

Bearing a close resemblance to the hickory shad, the American shad is distinguished by the way its lower jaw fits easily into a deep, V-shaped notch under the upper jaw, whereas the lower jaw of the hickory shad protrudes noticeably beyond the upper jaw.

Size/Age.   The normal size of American shad are 2 to 5 pounds, but specimens weighing up to 8 pounds are not uncommon when fish are abundant. They reach a maximum of $2^1/_2$ feet and possibly $13^1/_2$ pounds. The all-tackle world record is an 11-pound, 4-ounce fish taken from Massachusetts waters in 1994. Although American shad can live to age 13, few live past age 7. Females (called roe fish or hens) grow more quickly and generally larger than males (called bucks).

Distribution.   The endemic range of this species is east of the Appalachians along the Atlantic coast of North America from Sand Hill River, Labrador, to the St. John's River, Florida; practically every significant coastal river along the western Atlantic seaboard has supported a distinct spawning population at one time or another. Important sportfisheries currently exist in the Connecticut and Delaware Rivers. The Hudson River has historically had major runs, but sportfishing for shad in this deep, wide river is negligible, although it has in the past been commercially significant. The Susquehanna has been undergoing restoration of its runs. In 1871, American shad were introduced into the Sacramento River in California and today are found up and down the Pacific coast, ranging from Bahia de Todos Santos in upper Baja California, Mexico, to Cook Inlet, Alaska, and the Kamchatka Peninsula. Most sportfishing occurs in the U.S. portion of this range, and a major run occurs in the Columbia River.

Habitat.   American shad spend most of their lives in the ocean, ascending coastal rivers to spawn. They are found in freshwater only during their spawning runs and cannot tolerate cold waters below 41°F. Predominant in more northerly climates, American shad engage in extensive and complex migrations throughout their range, relying on their acute sense of homing for navigation. In coastal rivers, they primarily inhabit deep runs and pools.

Life history/Behavior.   Most fish spawn for the first time when they weigh 3 to 5 pounds. Males reach sexual maturity at age 3 to 4, females at age 4 to 5. Some life history patterns of American shad depend on the river of origin; for instance, in Southern rivers the average spawning age is 4 and fish generally spawn only once, laying 300,000 to 400,000 eggs; however, the average spawning age for more northerly fish is 5, and these fish generally spawn several times in a lifetime, laying a smaller number of eggs per spawning, usually ranging from 125,000 to 250,000.

Shad "runs" are extremely dramatic, as thousands of fish ascend rivers within the space of a few weeks, sometimes traveling long distances up the rivers where they were hatched. When water temperatures range from 41° to 73°F, the fish swim upriver and as far inland as 300 miles. Peak migrations occur when the water temperature is in the 50s. These migrations usually take place in April in southern rivers and through July in northern regions, even beginning as early as mid-November in Florida.

Most spawning activity takes place in deep areas with moderate to strong currents, particularly during the night, when water temperatures are in the mid-60s. A single female is accompanied by several males, swimming close to the surface and splashing and rolling as anywhere from 50,000 to 600,000 eggs are laid. The nonadhesive eggs drift with the current, gradually sinking and then hatching from 3 to 12 days later. Larvae are found in rivers during the summer, feeding on insects and plankton and entering the sea by autumn, where they remain until maturity. Post-spawning adults attempt to return to the sea after spawning; many die immediately after spawning, whereas others have been known to live long enough to spawn as many as seven times.

Food and feeding habits. American shad primarily feed on plankton, swimming with their mouths open and gill covers extended while straining the water; they also eat small crustaceans, insects, fish eggs, algae, and small fish. They cease feeding during upstream spawning migration but resume during their relatively quick downstream post-spawning migration.

Angling. Shad provide drag-screeching runs, broadside-to-the current fight, and frequent aerial maneuvers. They are as spunky a river fish as there is to be found and are especially exciting when caught early in their upstream migration (they are spent after spawning and are therefore less challenging). But they are also of limited availability seasonally. The shad spawning run lasts only six to eight weeks in the spring. These fish often move through a river in stages or waves. They are affected by water conditions and are often not present in the same locales on a day-to-day basis.

Shad are not much for midday activity. Anglers often experience the best shad fishing in the evening, and early morning is considered prime time. The first two or three hours of the day may be the best because shad migrate upriver at night and there is a new wave of migrants in the morning, and perhaps also because of the low level of light. Shad will move during the day, however, particularly in cloudy or rainy weather. They may migrate from pool to pool or even move around in a large, slow-flowing section of water during the day, being visible on or just below the surface as they cruise en masse. Anglers frequently see this activity when the fish are on the spawning grounds and appear to be daisy-chaining, much like tarpon.

Shad typically remain in river channels, preferring deep water to the swift, riffling, shallow sections. The primary place to fish for them is in the pools. The water is slower, calmer, and deeper here than in the rest of the river, and shad primarily rest in such spots before continuing upriver. You may find a large school of fish occupying a particular pool on a given day, or you may find few or none. Sometimes, when success tapers off in a given spot, you merely need to move slightly up, down, or across the river to find action again.

Light spinning tackle is standard for shad. A 6- to 7-foot light-action rod and a spinning reel equipped with 4- to 8-pound line are best. The reel should have a smooth drag, as large shad will take varied amounts of line during the fight. Terminal gear largely consists of shad darts; a dart is a lead-bodied bucktail jig with a tapered form and slanted nose. Darts are the perennially favored shad catcher, although some anglers have success with flies, small spinners, and tiny spoons, the latter being fished less often on a bead-chain-style sinker and more commonly behind a downrigger weight.

It is usually necessary to maneuver these offerings down to the bottom, a task that is influenced by the depth of water, strength of current, weight of lure, and size of line. Shad do not feed during their spawning runs but apparently strike out of reflexive action; thus, they don't seem to go out of their way to chase a lure. The offering has to be placed in front of a fish's nose to be effective. For this reason, it's common to get hung up and to lose many lures in the pursuit of shad.

Shore anglers, waders, and those casting from anchored boats should cast across and upstream, allowing their lure to sink to the bottom, then, with

An American shad is landed on the Annapolis River, Nova Scotia.

the line tight, let the lure swing downstream with the current until it reaches the end of its sweep. Boat anglers either troll into the current or anchor and stillfish their lures by letting them hang in the current. In either case, approximately 75 feet of line is let out behind the boat, using a heavy enough lure (or weighting it with split shot on the line about 18 to 24 inches ahead of the lure) to present the offering just off the bottom.

Darts range in size from tiny to $\frac{1}{2}$ ounce. Heavy versions are used in early spring, when the river is high, swift, and roily; at this time, a lot of weight is needed to keep the lure down. But heavy darts are large and may not attract fish even when they do stay down, so anglers often resort to smaller darts and add split shot; the extra weight keeps the dart down, and the smaller dart is more favorable to the shad. The mostly widely used darts weigh between $\frac{1}{8}$ to $\frac{1}{4}$ ounce.

A red-headed, white-bodied dart (with white or yellow bucktail) is the time-honored favorite color and is effective. But darts come in a host of colors and combinations, and it pays to have a selection of sizes and colors available. Black head/green body, green head/chartreuse body, red head/chartreuse body, and red head/yellow body are among the most successful combinations. It's a good idea to switch colors frequently, however, especially when you know there are fish in the locale you're working but they haven't responded to your initial offering.

Especially effective for trolling are tiny spoons with No. 6 hooks. A good shine is important, and the lure must have perfect balance to run properly, as action is critical. The spoon, which should twirl fast, is fished in a manner similar to that for darts, although it is not necessary to put out as much line; 50 feet or thereabouts will do if the river section is from 8 to 12 feet deep. With spoons, use a swiveling bead-chain sinker ($\frac{1}{4}$ ounce is standard) about 18 inches up the line. With a downrigger, it isn't necessary to use weight, but the downrigger release must be set just right.

Fly fishing for shad is popular on both coasts, especially when the water is not in spate condition. Rods should be suited for an 8-weight line (although you can do with less) and be in the 8- to 9-foot range. Sinking, fast-sinking, and sink-tip fly lines are employed according to river depth and current flow. A short leader is adequate. Flies are mostly short-shanked streamers, sometimes brightly colored and often weighted with bead eyes. Using bead eyes and lead strips on the body is illegal in some places (especially New Brunswick) where weighted flies are prohibited (mainly for salmon fishing, to avoid deliberate snagging of fish). Check regulations carefully. It is usually necessary to get the fly down to the bottom, so an across, swing, and hang presentation is best. Most fish strike as the fly makes its downcurrent turn or when it is stripped back in retrieval. Some fly-caught shad are taken close to the surface, however, usually when milling in slow pools. Then, a short stripping retrieve is employed.

SHAD, GIZZARD   *Dorosoma cepedianum.*

Other names—shad, eastern gizzard, hickory shad, mud shad, nanny shad, skipjack, winter shad.

Although the gizzard shad is important forage for large fish, its rapid growth rate causes it to exceed a consumable size for most predators early on in its life. It is often labeled as a nuisance fish by anglers and biologists, due to large die-offs, which happen because the species is especially susceptible to drastic changes in temperature and low concentrations of oxygen. A member of the Clupeidae family of herring *(see)* and shad, the gizzard shad is used to some extent as fertilizer and livestock feed.

Identification.   The gizzard shad is one of two freshwater members of the herring family that has a distinctively long, slender last ray on its dorsal fin. The body is silver blue on the back and silver white underneath, with either blue-and-green or gold reflections on the head and flanks; occasionally there are six to eight horizontal dark stripes on the back, starting behind a large purple blue or black shoulder spot (which is faint or absent in large adults). The gizzard shad also has dusky fins, a blunt snout, a subterminal mouth, and a deep notch at the center of the upper jaw. It lacks scales on the nape. There are 52 to 70 lateral scales, 10 to 13 dorsal rays, and 25 to 36 anal rays.

Size/Age.   Growing a maximum of $20\frac{1}{2}$ inches and averaging about 10 inches in length, this species commonly reaches more than a pound in weight. Although it is rarely pursued for sport by anglers, the all-tackle world record is a 4-pound, 6-ounce Indiana fish. Most gizzard shad die before they reach age 7, although the species is known to reach 10 years of age.

Distribution.   Found in most parts of the St. Lawrence–Great Lakes, Mississippi, Atlantic, and Gulf drainages, this fish ranges from Quebec to central North Dakota and throughout New Mexico, as well as south to central Florida and Mexico; it has been introduced outside this native range.

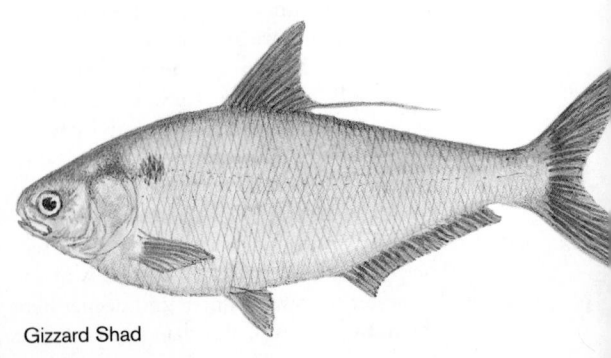

Gizzard Shad

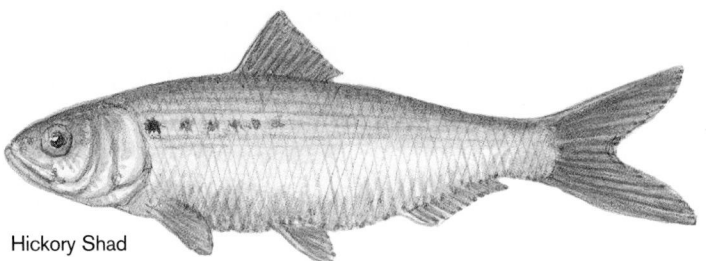
Hickory Shad

Habitat. Gizzard shad mainly occur in the deep open water of medium to large rivers, reservoirs, lakes, and backwaters; adults are also found in brackish or saline water of estuaries or bays, as they prefer calmer open waters.

Life history. Gizzard shad occur in schools and are first able to spawn when two to three years old or 7 to 13 inches long. They breed near the surface in freshwater from March through August, when water temperatures range from 50° to 70°F. The adhesive eggs sink to the bottom, varying in number from about 3,000 to more than 380,000. Gizzard shad prefer warm waters and cannot tolerate extreme cold conditions, which may cause a fishkill of significant numbers. They roam open waters in search of plankton, which occurs at various levels according to the season and conditions.

Food and feeding habits. Gizzard shad are filter feeders that strain microscopic organisms from the water or pick through mud and organic matter on the bottom; in some environments they appear more oriented to bottom feeding.

Angling. There is no concerted angling interest in gizzard shad, although larger specimens are sometimes caught incidentally, or when concentrated in certain areas (for example, the tailrace below a dam). Smaller specimens are caught on ultralight line and small hooks, taken in cast nets, or snagged, for bait purposes.

See: Shad, Threadfin.

SHAD, HICKORY   *Alosa mediocris.*
Other names—shad herring, hickory jack, freshwater taylor, fall herring, bonejack.

A member of the Clupeidae family of herring *(see)* and shad, the hickory shad is of significant recreational interest, being a friskier although smaller cousin of the American shad *(see: shad, American)*. It is also of commercial value, particularly its roe.

Identification. Gray green on the back and fading to silver on the side, the hickory shad has clear fins with the exception of the dusky dorsal and caudal fins, which are occasionally black edged. It has a strongly oblique mouth, a lower jaw that projects noticeably beyond its upper jaw, and a cheek that is longer than or about equal to its depth. There is a blue black spot near the upper edge of the gill cover, followed by a clump of indistinct dusky spots that extend below the dorsal fin. There are also teeth on the lower jaw, and 18 to 23 rakers on the lower limb of the first gill arch.

Size. The hickory shad can reach almost 2 feet in length, and averages 1 to 3 pounds in weight. It can weigh as much as 6 pounds.

Distribution. Found only along the Atlantic coast of North America, the hickory shad ranges from Kenduskeag River, Maine, to the St. John's River, Florida. It is most common in the Southeast and in the Mid-Atlantic regions. This species overlaps with American shad and ascends some of the same rivers when spawning.

Habitat. The hickory shad is a schooling species that spends most of its life in the ocean; when mature, it returns in early spring through summer to rivers and streams to spawn, inhabiting open water of medium to large rivers. Young shad descend rivers in autumn.

Life history/Behavior. Hickory shad mature when they are two years old and about 12 inches long. Adults ascend coastal rivers during the spring. Preferred water temperatures range from 55° to 69°F, but the lower end of that range seems to trigger the spawning urge. Females lay up to 300,000 eggs. Young fish remain in rivers, estuaries, and backwaters, migrating to the sea by fall or early winter.

Food and feeding habits. At sea, hickory shad feed on small fish, as well as on squid, small crabs, other crustaceans, and fish eggs. In an irony that is common to most anadromous species, they are not pursued or caught by anglers in places where they do feed, but are pursued and caught when migrating upriver in natal waters when they do not feed.

Angling. Angling for hickory shad is akin to that for American shad.

SHADOW LINE
The sharp edge between water that is illuminated and that which is not, as created by overhead light. The shadow line is a nighttime phenomenon that exists wherever overhead lights fall on the water; it occurs on bridges, piers, bulkheads, seawalls, all types of docks, and wherever a structure is in or on the edge of the water. Usually the water close to the structure is dark while the water beyond the shadow line is brightly lit. A shadow line may also be created by moonlight in places where there is no artificial light.

Because gamefish often position themselves close to one edge of the shadow line to forage, a shadow line can be an important place to fish. Whether the fish are in the dark water facing the illuminated water, or in the illuminated water facing the dark water, may depend on the circumstances, especially if there is current.

See: Pier Fishing.

S

SHAD, THREADFIN   *Dorosoma petenense.*
Other names—shad, threadfin.

A well-known forage fish and member of the Clupeidae family of herring *(see)* and shad, the threadfin shad rarely grows larger than 5 inches long, remaining small enough to be one of the most important open-water forage species for important freshwater gamefish, especially bass and stripers.

Identification.   The threadfin shad is silvery with a deeply compressed body and is most easily recognized by the elongated, thin last ray on its dorsal fin. It has a small, dark shoulder spot, and its upper jaw does not project past the lower jaw. It is similar in appearance to other herring, including the similar-size but more northerly ranging alewives *(see)* and the larger gizzard shad *(see: shad, gizzard)*, with which it shares overlapping ranges and many of the same waters. It is distinguished from gizzard shad of similar size by its more pointed snout, terminal mouth, black dots on its chin and bottom of the mouth, and yellow fins. It has 40 to 48 lateral scales, 11 to 14 dorsal rays, and 17 to 27 anal rays.

Size.   This species is commonly found at $2^1/_2$ to 4 inches long and can attain a maximum length of 9 inches. Many threadfins do not live longer than 2 years, although they can live as long as 4 or more years.

Distribution.   Threadfin shad occur throughout the Mississippi River basin, from the Ohio River of Kentucky and southern Indiana southwest to Oklahoma and south to Texas and Florida, as well as in other Gulf of Mexico drainages and Atlantic drainages in Florida. They are also present in rivers around in Guatemala and Honduras. They have been introduced as a forage species in Hawaii and the western United States, and to other areas in the mainland U.S.

Habitat.   Occasionally found in the brackish waters of estuaries and bays, threadfin shad are mainly a freshwater fish occurring in large rivers, reservoirs, lakes, and backwaters, where they principally inhabit open-water environs.

Life history/Behavior.   Threadfin shad spawn in the spring and autumn near or over plants or other objects. They are prolific but short-lived and are highly susceptible to winter kill from extreme cold temperatures, which helps keep their numbers in check.

Food and feeding habits.   Threadfins are filter feeders that primarily consume plankton and organic detritus in open water; they occasionally feed on fish larvae and on the organic material found on or over sandy or silty bottoms. In reservoirs and large lakes, these fish are constantly on the move, searching for and feeding on minute plankton, the location and level of which will vary seasonally and according to various factors.

Angling.   There is no angling effort for threadfin shad, although they may be captured with cast nets for use as live baits. Like all herring, they are difficult to keep alive and must be contained in a circular, rather than rectangular, livewell that is highly aerated at the proper temperature.

SHARKING
A popular term for shark fishing.
See: Sharks.

SHARKS
Sharks evolved as predatory fish some 400 million years ago in the Devonian period, long before vertebrates began to walk on land. Ever since, they have been among the most successful predators in the sea. A rich record of fossilized shark teeth, ranging from $1/_8$ inch to more than 6 inches long, indicates that many species of sharks have come and gone over the ages. Fossil records show that at least one species of carnivorous shark, *Carcharodon megalodon*, which lived 4.5 million years ago, reached some 40 feet in length.

Today there are at least 370 species of sharks worldwide, and new ones are still being discovered. They range in size from 6 or 7 inches long (the dwarf dogfish, *Etmopterus perryi*) to the world's largest fish at 40 or more feet long (the whale shark, *Rhincodon typus*). Eighty percent of all sharks are less than 5 feet long when fully grown.

Sharks obviously are a diverse and adaptable group of fish. They inhabit almost every marine ecosystem, and a few species are found in freshwater. Although almost all sharks are carnivorous predators, a few—the whale, basking, and megamouth sharks—filter plankton from the water. Sharks are often thought of as solitary, but some species commonly occur in schools. Many sharks, particularly those found in temperate waters, are migratory, heading toward the equator in the winter to take advantage of food sources available in different locations at various times of the year.

Characteristics
Like all fish, sharks are vertebrates, but ichthyologists place them in a separate class from most fish because the shark's skeleton is made of cartilage instead of bone. Within this class, the Chondrichthyes, are two subclasses. One is the Holocephali, or chimaeras, strange-looking fish

Threadfin Shad

seldom seen outside aquariums or research facilities. The other subclass, the Elasmobranchi, includes sharks, skates, and rays *(see: rays and skates)*.

In addition to their unique skeletal structure, sharks have five to seven gill slits on each side, allowing each gill to vent separately into the surrounding water. Bony fish, in contrast, have one gill opening on each side of their bodies that is covered by a bony plate called the operculum.

Sharks also lack the gas-filled swim bladders of most bony fish. Instead, sharks have evolved a different means of maintaining buoyancy: They have extremely large livers (it constitutes up to 25 percent of their body weight) that contain oils that are lighter than water. These oils, coupled with the cartilaginous skeleton, make sharks almost neutrally buoyant.

Swimming ability.   Not all sharks must swim constantly to force water over their gills for respiration. Some, like the nurse shark, the angel shark, and even some of the larger requiem sharks (the group that includes tiger sharks), can actively pump water over their gills and will occasionally rest motionless on the bottom, particularly in the rare places where the water is supersaturated with oxygen. And many bottom-dwelling sharks pump water over their gills most of the time. Sharks must literally swim or sink, however, because their bodies are slightly denser than water. Like airplanes, they require forward motion to stay afloat. Water is 800 times more dense than air, so swimming takes a lot of energy. Sharks have a number of physical adaptations that make them exceptionally efficient swimmers.

As mentioned, most sharks achieve near-neutral buoyancy through the oil stored in their livers. A shark's skeleton also contributes to its buoyancy and swimming efficiency, as cartilage is less dense and more flexible than bone. (Out of the water, however, the skeleton isn't strong enough to support the shark's body adequately, and the shark will soon die, crushed under its own weight.) The only place heavy bone is found on the shark's body is in its teeth and scales. The scales—called placoid scales— have small bony projections that hook backward. These projections, called dermal denticles, work along with the shark's streamlined shape to facilitate the flow of water over the shark's body, reducing drag and enabling the shark to swim faster.

Not all sharks are fast; some are sluggish and stay close to the bottom. One of the fastest swimmers, however, is the mako shark, which is thought to reach speeds of more than 40 mph for short bursts and is capable of spectacular leaps into the air. The power behind this amazing ability is the tail. The sculling motion of the tail both steers and propels the shark forward. All sharks have heterocercal tails, which means that the spinal column extends into the top lobe of the tail. In most sharks, the top lobe is larger than the bottom lobe, giving the tail an asymmetrical shape. The fastest swimmers have nearly symmetrical tails.

A blue shark cruises through a chum line off Montauk, New York; a hooked bait drifts under the red balloon.

A shark's fins help create lift and stabilize the shark as it turns or dives. Because shark fins are relatively fixed and lack the pliability of fins from bony fish, sharks have more limited maneuverability than many bony fish. Some people have suggested that this is like comparing the capabilities of a fixed-wing jet, which can turn and roll but must be moving forward, to those of a helicopter, which can hover, rise straight up, or even move backward.

Sensory ability.   As a shark swims, it constantly samples the water for odors and sounds. The nostrils of a shark play no role in breathing and are used only for smell. Sharks have been called "swimming noses" because they can detect odors at a few parts per million. Sharks can smell blood at the 1 part-per-million level or less and are drawn to bleeding prey.

Sound also plays a role in locating food. Low-frequency vibrations (40 Hz or less), such as the sounds made by something splashing in the water, attract sharks. A small duct connects the shark's internal ears to the outside. Hearing is further enhanced by the lateral-line system that extends along the head and sides of the body and is sensitive to vibrations, currents, and pressure changes.

Both odor and sound are important for locating possible food sources, but actual feeding is dependent on vision and the detection of electrical fields. The visual system of sharks is well developed and functions well in high and low light. A special structure in the eye called the tapetum lucidum increases

S

their sensitivity in low light. Other animals with good night vision, such as cats, also have a tapetum. It is responsible for eyeshine, seen when light shines on a cat's eyes at night. Sharks also have eyeshine, and it varies from blue green to gold in color.

At close range, the shark's electroreception system comes into play. Receptors located in pores on the shark's snout and lower jaw can detect tiny electrical fields created by the prey's muscular movement. This sensory system may also help the shark navigate relative to the planet's magnetic field.

Feeding and digestion. When a shark has procured its prey, it swallows the food whole or in chunks. Once the shark is satiated, it may not eat again for several weeks. As the food is digested, it passes through the intestine, which has a spiral valve structure unique to sharks. The spiral valve increases the interior surface area of the intestine for more efficient absorption of nutrients.

Sharks are opportunistic feeders and will often eat whatever is available. Even extraordinary indigestible items have been among the flotsam that has turned up in their stomachs. Sharks reportedly have some ability to regurgitate unwanted food items.

Teeth. Shark teeth come in as many shapes and sizes as sharks do; in fact, they are useful in identifying individual species. They can also say something about the shark's diet. Some sharks are specialized predators; their teeth are adapted for efficient capture of their preferred prey.

The upper and lower teeth of a mako shark.

Others eat whatever is available, and their teeth are amply suited for many types of food. The great white uses its triangular, serrated, bladelike teeth for grabbing and biting off chunks of large fish and marine mammals. At the other end of the spectrum, the smooth dogfish uses its flat teeth for crushing the shells of mollusks and crustaceans. Others, like the mako or sand tiger, have narrow, pointed teeth for impaling and holding onto prey small enough to swallow whole.

Shark teeth are simply embedded in the shark's gums, not its jaws; they fall out easily but are also easily replaced. Sharks generally have several rows of teeth, one or more of which may be functional at a time. As the teeth are broken, pulled out, or worn down, they are replaced from the row behind

in conveyer-belt fashion. It is estimated that some species may shed as many as 30,000 teeth in a lifetime. Each replacement tooth is larger than the one it replaces, allowing the shark's teeth to keep up with its growing body. This also allows scientists to estimate the size of a shark based solely on a tooth.

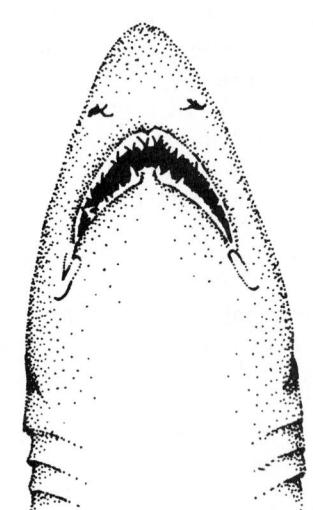

The underside of the head of a sand tiger shark.

The shark's jaw is rather loosely attached to the rest of its skull, which enables it to open its mouth very wide. A shark bite involves several distinct movements, usually taking place in a second or two. First, the shark raises its snout and lowers its bottom jaw. This not only gets the snout out of the way, it exposes the many electrosensory receptors located on the underside of the snout, which help the shark home in on the prey. This is crucial, as many sharks can't see during a strike. These species protect their eyes either with a special eyelid called a nictitating membrane or by rolling their eyes back into their heads. Next, the upper jaw protrudes forward, exposing the teeth, and the lower jaw moves upward and forward toward it. Finally, the shark lowers its head, and the upper jaw returns once more to its normal position.

Skin. Sharks don't have scales like other fish. Instead, they have placoid scales, or denticles. The denticles are tiny, bony projections implanted in the shark's skin. They come in many shapes and sizes but usually completely cover the shark's skin like a coat of armor. Their main functions are protection for the shark and reducing drag as the shark's body slices through the water. The word "denticle" means small tooth, and the teeth in the shark's mouth are actually just modified placoid scales. The teeth and the skin denticles are very similar in structure and not all that different from human teeth. A center pulp of nerve cells and blood vessels is surrounded by dentine, and the tooth has a thin, hard outer layer of enamel.

Denticles give the shark's hide a rough texture like sandpaper. In fact, shark attack victims often receive scrapes from contact with a shark. Shark skin has been dried and used as an abrasive, called shagreen, for sanding wood. This use is now rare because there are cheaper substitutes. Shark hides are used to make a strong leather, however, once the denticles have been chemically removed.

Reproduction. Sharks have a number of reproductive strategies. Some enclose fertilized eggs in tough, leathery egg cases that are released into the water for subsequent development and birth. Some female sharks retain the eggs within their bodies and hatch the young internally, so they are born alive and fully formed. Others have a sophisticated placental arrangement similar to that of mammals.

Regardless of the strategy, sharks devote most of their reproductive energy to producing a few large, well-developed young with a good chance of surviving to maturity. Shark gestation, growth, and sexual development all take a relatively long time. Many sharks take 10 to 20 years to mature sexually, and they produce as few as one pup at a time. Tagged sharks have been recaptured more than 30 years after the initial tagging. A number of species are estimated to live for 40 or 50 years.

Longevity, slow development, and low reproductive rates mean that shark populations depleted from overfishing or other causes require more time to recover.

Issues

Sharks are not only important ecologically, but they also serve humans in many ways other than sportfishing. Because they are poorly understood and the subject of fear among many people, they are also controversial and have been subject to overexploitation in recent decades.

Uses. Worldwide, sharks are a significant source of food for humans. One hundred million sharks (600,000 tons) are consumed annually. In many cultures, they are a preferred fish. In North America, sharks were considered unappetizing until the 1980s, when the demand for shark flesh rose steeply. One reason for shark meat's bad reputation may have been that proper preparation of the meat was not commonly understood. Shark blood contains high amounts of urea, which helps sharks regulate the amount of water in their bodies as they travel to areas of varying salt concentrations. If given the chance, bacteria break urea down into ammonia, which gives the meat an unpleasant odor and flavor. Freshly caught sharks should be bled and iced down immediately after capture to prevent this problem.

Sharks can command premium prices at fish markets around the world. In Hong Kong, people were buying 7 million pounds of shark fins annually in the late 1990s. To meet the demand, some commercial fishing fleets pursued sharks exclusively for their fins, cutting the fins off live sharks and returning them to the ocean to die a lingering death.

Virtually all parts of a shark have commercial value; even the entrails are used to make fish meal. Shark hide is stronger than cow hide and many times more expensive, as demonstrated by the cost of belts, shoes, and wallets made from shark skin. Indigenous people have used shark teeth to tip arrows, harpoons, and other weapons. Today, shark jaws and teeth are sold as curios or jewelry.

One of the most valuable but least-known uses of sharks is in medicine. Various parts of sharks are, and have been, used for research purposes, in antibiotics, as organic supplements to enhance human body parts (especially cartilage), and in cosmetics, as well as for other aims.

Shark attacks. A few places, such as Australia and South Africa, are infamous for shark attacks, but attacks on humans anywhere are extremely rare. Most shark attacks occur in tropical or subtropical waters, the exception being cooler waters inhabited by the great white shark. The great white is greatly feared thanks to media hype, but it is actually the tiger shark that is responsible for most attacks on humans. Many scientists now believe that most attacks by sharks are not related to predation, but rather to territoriality, or provocation.

In the entire United States, two to three dozen attacks occur on average each year. The vast majority occur in California, Florida, and/or Hawaii; fatalities are rare, and higher numbers of attack incidents seem to coincide with storms and greater water disturbance. The fear of shark attack is, for

This is all that's left of an angler's bluefin tuna after being attacked by a shark.

S

the most part, unwarranted. The chances of being killed by a bee sting, lightning, or a poisonous snake are much greater than those of being the victim of a shark attack. Yet, even with shark numbers declining and shark control programs being enacted in some places, lingering concerns about public safety and the possible impacts of shark attacks on tourism have led to debate concerning the desirability and practicality of shark management/ control programs in certain locales.

Conservation. Sharks are remarkably suited to their role as efficient predators and are critical to the natural balance of the oceans. But human beings have been even more efficient predators of sharks, and shark populations are now in trouble throughout the world. There is widespread concern over increased commercial fishing (and also recreational fishing) and the consequences this has for the populations of some shark species in several of the world's oceans.

Unfortunately, there is a general lack of public awareness about shark conservation needs, especially in light of their low productivity. This is compounded by the historically low value of shark products, by a general lack of management efforts in many countries and a lack of international management mechanisms actively addressing the capture of sharks, by difficulties in identifying sharks at the species level, and by the lack of information about their migratory routes, seasonality, and rates of movement between different regions. A general lack of knowledge about critical habitat areas for sharks and sharklike species is also problematic. Insufficient funding for both research and management of sharks and sharklike fish compounds the problem as well.

Sportfishing

History.   With a few exceptions, sportfishing for sharks has a very recent history. Classic books detailing the early days of big-game fishing don't even discuss sharks, except to mention them in a negative context, such as when they attacked hooked tuna or billfish. Prior to the 1960s, only a few areas throughout the world boasted specialists who caught sharks for sport, and in some cases they did so from shore.

Captain William Young from California was one of the early sharking pioneers at the turn of the century, and he popularized adventure with sharks in his writings about killing 100,000 of them from Hawaii to Australia and the Red Sea.

Australia became a hotbed of sharking before the sport became popular in most other areas due to a relative abundance of the great white. Alf Dean was the most famous of the early recreational sharkers, capturing six white sharks weighing more than a ton, including the 2,664-pounder at Ceduna on April 21, 1959, which the International Game Fish Association (IGFA) still recognizes as the all-tackle and 130-pound line-class world record. Dean also holds the 80-pound line-class record with a 2,344-pounder caught in November 1960. Yet those whites were small fry compared to one he lost after a $5^1/_2$-hour battle; that fish was estimated at 30 feet and 4,000 pounds. Fossil shark teeth indicate that even such modern monsters are much smaller than the really great whites that once ruled the oceans.

The once consistent white shark fishery in South Australia and the east coast of that country also produced a 2,240-pounder for Bob Dyer, who holds the 20-, 30-, and 50-pound line-class records with whites of 1,068, 1,053, and 1,876 pounds. Dyer's wife, Dolly, caught a women's record 1,052-pounder, which stood until Janet Forster boated a 1,164-pound white at The Pages in March of 1994. Ms. Dyer still holds every white shark women's record from the 20- to the 80-pound line classes, however, with fish under 1,000 pounds caught from 1954 to 1957 off Cape Moreton, Queensland.

It's unlikely that these records will be broken, at least not soon, as white sharks are becoming ever scarcer and have received protection from exploitation throughout most of the world. Furthermore, those early anglers both chummed and baited with mammals, a practice since banned by the IGFA, although the old records continue to be recognized.

South Africans were also great shark anglers. S. Schoeman, in his classic book *Strike,* cites a 986.98-kilogram shark landed from the rocks at Hermanus in 1928 by Bill Selkirk with rod and reel and 18-cord line—"certainly the biggest fish ever caught by man on rod and line from the rocks." Reg Harrison of Durban is also credited with a blue pointer (white) of 752.7 kilograms in July, 1953.

New Zealand anglers appreciated the mako long before it became popular in other areas, and Zane Grey wrote about his experiences fishing for them there. Threshers have also long been popular as a gamefish with anglers in that country.

It was Captain Frank Mundus who first popularized sharking in North America, and then Jack Casey who changed the nature of that sport from a "man against beast" killing affair to the largely tag-and-release fishery pursued today.

Mundus developed sportfishing for sharks at Montauk, New York, after World War II and brought public attention to his "monster fishing" by displaying jaws and selling shark teeth while booking charters for his boat *Cricket* from a booth at the New York Sportsmens Show during the 1950s. Mundus was as offbeat as the fish he pursued, sporting port and starboard painted toenails, harpooning porpoises and pilot whales for chum, and berating his customers' skills—all of which brought him a steady supply of business. It was Mundus who provided the inspiration for Peter Benchley's captain in *Jaws,* the book and movie that led to a huge increase in recreational sharking throughout the U.S.

Even before *Jaws,* sharking had already caught on along the south shore of Long Island by the

1960s. The first Bay Shore Tuna Club Shark Tournament resulted in such a massive catch of blue sharks that boats had to wait hours for weigh-ins, and disposal became a significant problem. All sharks were then still regarded as man-eaters to be eliminated from the ocean, but that concept changed within a decade due to the pioneering work of Jack Casey, which started when he was a fisheries scientist at the U.S. Fish and Wildlife Service Marine Fisheries Lab at Sandy Hook, New Jersey.

Casey started studying sharks and one summer took roughly 40 juvenile white sharks from long-lines placed not far off Sandy Hook's beaches. He had to keep that information quiet, however, for fear of starting a panic along the Jersey Shore. He also fished with another sharking pioneer at Montauk, John Walton, an antiques dealer in New York. Not only did they catch and release many sharks, but Casey and his father also caught a great white exceeding 1,000 pounds.

When the National Marine Fisheries Service (NMFS) was formed in the early 1970s, Casey was shifted to the NMFS Lab at Narragansett, Rhode Island, where he established the shark tagging program that continues to this day. Unique among tagging (see) programs at that time, it relied on the volunteer efforts of anglers to place the volume of tags that would paint a picture of the migratory patterns and growth rates of sharks. Anglers responded to Casey's efforts; within a decade, sharking had turned from a killing sport to one in which the vast majority of the catch was released. It soon became almost a disgrace to bring in a blue shark (which aren't highly regarded as food), except for large specimens in tournaments.

That attitude has been further reinforced by declining shark populations in the face of commercial fishing pressures. Many tournaments have eliminated blue sharks altogether, and some don't allow tiger sharks at all. Most U.S. Mid-Atlantic contests are now strictly for the most esteemed of sharks, the mako—although threshers may also be included.

The popularity of sharking spread from Long Island to New Jersey during the 1970s, and some of the largest shark tournaments were held there for two decades before a significant drop in the resource reduced interest somewhat. *Jaws* inspired country-wide interested in sharking, and even many Florida skippers who previously hated sharks found they could improve their business with charters for the fish that created so much interest among the general public.

Another significant recreational shark fishery developed off Virginia, and there is now at least some interest all the way up the Atlantic coast to Maine. The Sarasota area along Florida's Gulf Coast had an active sportfishery for sharks even before *Jaws,* and the California fishery has built up steadily. West Coast fly anglers have realized that they have a unique opportunity to pursue quantities of small

A small bonnethead shark caught on a flat near Big Pine Key, Florida.

blue sharks, which will eat flies just about as readily as anything else. Makos are also a target off California due to a sharp decrease in the thresher population from commercial fishing pressure.

The willingness of the Chinese to pay high prices for fins to be used in shark fin soup put a big dent in North American shark populations during the 1990s, except for blues, which aren't desired for that use. At one point, some commercial fishermen were cutting the fins off sharks and throwing back the live bodies; ultimately, NMFS prohibited this practice.

Because most sharks are slow growing, take a long time to mature, and then produce few young, they can be very easily overfished—after which it can take decades to restore the fishery. Shark populations have crashed in every area, no matter how remote, where commercial shark fisheries have been established—and usually within a few years after the fishery was established. This fact was well known even during the first half of the twentieth century, but the same practices were allowed when the Chinese market for fins developed; species such as the sandbar (brown) and dusky may remain scarce for many years.

NMFS belatedly protected the extremely vulnerable sand tiger, which sports jutting teeth like a mako but is actually a lazy ground shark (making them a favorite species for aquariums) and lives in shallow waters. Also placed on the protected list were the white and basking sharks.

S

What used to be a wide-open sportfishery along the Atlantic coast and in the Gulf of Mexico with no restrictions has become a tightly controlled situation with a limit of two fish per boat as recently as 1998 for all except the small coastal species—and a prohibition on the sale of these fish by anglers and even most captains.

Techniques/Tackle.   One of the attractions of fishing for the poor man's big-game fish is that almost any tackle will do the job under most circumstances. The vast majority of sharks are caught in open waters, where even large specimens can be handled on relatively light tackle if the angler exercises patience. Light big-game tackle, such as 20- and 30-pound-class outfits, are perfect for most sharks caught offshore. Anglers specifically seeking makos usually opt for 50-pound gear, and 80-pound tackle can be used during tournaments or when tigers, whites, and the largest of makos are sought. Modern standup rods, belts, and harnesses can entirely eliminate the need to sit in a chair to fight even the largest of sharks.

Blue sharks are usually pushovers on heavy gear but can be lots of fun on light tackle. This is especially true when they can be chummed to boatside, making it possible to select individuals of suitable size for spinning, baitcasting, or flycasting tackle. That same light tackle is standard for sharks caught on Florida Keys flats, where there is no deep water available. The sporty blacktip, which also jumps, is a favorite of flats anglers who cast lures and flies to them. Blacktips have poor eyesight, so lures must be placed close to these sharks and drawn right in front of their mouths. Lemon sharks also hit lures on the flats, but the largest sharks that wander into that area are primarily tempted with baits.

Terminal tackle for sharks is important. Their teeth make wire leaders a must; 15 feet of No. 12 to 15 single-strand wire is the usual choice for large sharks, so even if they spin in the leader they may not reach the main line. Kinking is also a problem due to a shark's tendency to spin in the leader, but braided wire presents another problem in that very large sharks can chew through it. Some skippers create leaders using very heavy monofilament attached to a large swivel, to which they add several feet of wire at the terminal end.

Sharks of one species or another may be encountered almost anywhere, from rivers and bays out to midocean. Indeed, shore and small-boat anglers catch some of the largest sharks, particularly in warm waters, where some species even enter areas barely deep enough to cover their bodies. Sharks on the Florida Keys or Bahamas flats can be as spooky as bonefish, although it's hard to imagine what they might fear.

The vast majority of sharking occurs in ocean areas, but sharks are scattered over wide areas. Unlike other fish, which tend to swarm over wrecks or dropoffs, most migratory sharks aren't tied to a particular area. Anglers usually select structure

(such as a dropoff) at a likely depth to start their drift, but a means of attracting sharks to the boat is important.

By far the most common and productive method of accomplishing that is chumming *(see)*. Any oily fish can be ground up for chum, which may be mixed with water and ladled over the side to create a steady slick, or frozen in a bucket that is turned over in a net or a crate with holes so it can automatically create a slick as it gradually thaws. The most common fish used for shark chum along the east coast of the U.S. is the menhaden (bunker or pogy), although mackerel and bluefish also work well.

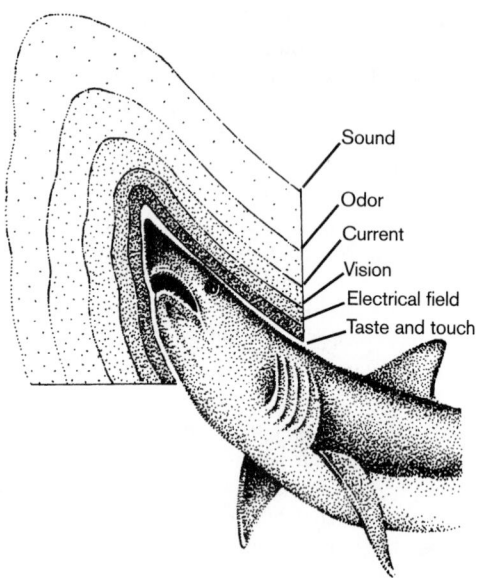

Sound
Odor
Current
Vision
Electrical field
Taste and touch

The extraordinary sensory abilities of sharks allow them to detect sounds generated miles away and to detect odor, current, and pressure at a distance of hundreds of yards. They can also see 30 to 60 or more feet away, detect electrical fields that are within inches, and utilize both taste and contact by touching.

Because sharks have an extremely fine sense of smell, they can zero in on that slick from great distances. This enables boaters to make long drifts that provide an ever-greater attraction as the slick gets longer during the day. Any sharks intersecting that aroma should follow it to its source and find the baits, which are usually distributed from just below the surface down to at least half the water depth. Floats or balloons are used to hold baits at the desired depths, and sinkers are normally required to hold the baits down.

Almost any kind of hooked bait will work at times, with the same fish used for chum being ideal. Natural baits can be fished whole or as fillets. Mackerel are most commonly used along the northeastern U.S., but fresh bluefish are even better, especially when caught on the spot as is common during the prime spring season. Any member of the tuna family is probably the best shark bait of all, as sharks can't seem to resist the smell of tuna blood.

Live baits are typically productive; small bottom fish such as silver and red hake are good choices. Live bluefish are also effective, but those caught while sharking tend to be large, and sharks often play with them and don't get hooked.

Because the vast majority of sharks are now released by anglers, it's best to use just one hook and to strike after allowing only a short run on freespool in order not too hook the prey deeply. Fillets are preferable to whole baits in that regard, as hooking is easier and quicker.

Whole and strip baits are combined on a shark hook attached to a wire leader.

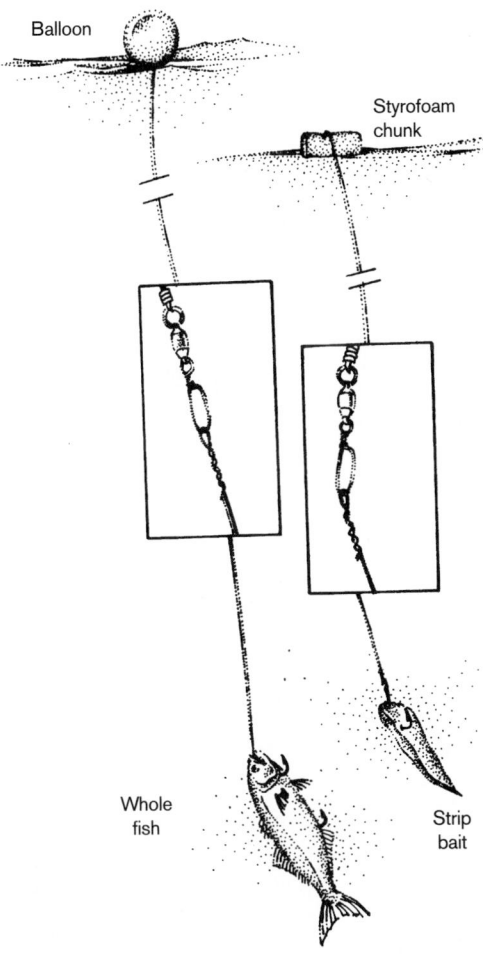
Shark fishing rigs for use offshore and when chumming include a heavy-leader rig with whole bait (left) and a light-leader rig with strip bait (right).

Some sharks, especially makos and threshers, can be trolled, although unadorned lures don't work well. California anglers add a baitfish to a heavy lure, however, which can be slow-trolled below the surface. These connect with makos regularly.

A few large sharks, such as tigers and duskys, tend to fight straight down and are no fun to catch on light tackle. Most sharks will return to the surface even if they do take a dive during the fight.

This tendency permits the use of relatively light tackle and makes sharks an ideal target for standup fishing. They'll usually tow a small boat after sufficient pressure is applied, and larger boats can follow them if necessary, although the vast majority of sharks can be caught from a dead boat.

Landing care.   Needless to say, sharks must be handled very carefully at boatside. Not only are the teeth a threat, but in the case of an active shark like the mako, there's always a chance that the fish could jump into the boat. A live shark in a cockpit can be a disaster for anyone trapped there and certainly for equipment and the boat itself. Tiring sharks out before bringing them alongside is the best way to avoid such scenarios.

Whereas ordinary gaffs are fine for tuna, flying gaffs are the usual choice by sharkers because those fish tend to spin when gaffed rather than run straight ahead. Secure the tail with tail ropes as soon as possible after gaffing. Some anglers use a gaffless method that involves a coated wire tail rope with a clip, which is looped around the line and slipped over the shark's body before being cinched at the tail.

Most sharkers carry firearms or a bang stick with which to dispatch sharks that are to be boated. The alternative is to hang the shark upside down, which usually kills the fish within an hour or so. As mentioned earlier, once the fish is out of the water, its skeleton isn't strong enough to support its body adequately; the shark soon dies, crushed under its

The business end of a great white shark.

poles are ideal for raising sharks and keeping them away from people.

Shark teeth are a threat at all times. Even "dead" sharks may have active nerves that can cause the jaws to clamp down. More people have probably been cut by dead sharks than by live ones for this reason. Simple carelessness on the boat or at the dock is all it takes. Makos are particularly dangerous, as their sharp teeth protrude and can cut like razors.

Sharks to be kept for food should be bled, and smaller specimens can be completely gutted and packed in ice for prime eating. Makos are an exception to the rule, but, as noted previously, most sharks have urea in their blood and will develop an ammonia smell and tainted taste in their flesh if not bled when caught.

A tagging stick and a supply of tags is of more use these days than the gaff because the vast majority of sharks are released. Free tags are available at no charge to legitimate taggers in the Atlantic from NMFS Cooperative Shark Tagging Program, 28 Tarzwell Drive, Narragansett, RI 02882. For the Pacific, from Cabo San Lucas to Monteray Bay, those tags come from California Pelagic Shark Tagging Program, California Department of Fish and Game, Marine Resources Division, Southern Operations, 330 Golden Shore, Suite 50, Long Beach, CA 90802.

Species of Note

Atlantic angel shark *(Squatina dumeril).* Also called sand devil, the Atlantic angel shark is frequently mistaken for a ray because of its flattened, triangular body.

This fish is unlike a ray, however, as its gill slits are lateral and create a deep indentation between its head and pectoral fin. The Atlantic angel is brownish to bluish gray on the back and whitish on the belly, and it has a mid-dorsal row of

own weight. This lack of rigidity is also the reason why it can be very hard to boat if you're trying to pull it over the side or stern—the weight shifts away from you regardless which end you pull on. It's important to stay away from shark teeth, but pulling from the tail creates a great deal of friction due to the sandpaperlike skin and fins, which catch on everything. It's easy to drag a shark forward because the skin is smooth in that direction. Gin

Atlantic Angel Shark

Basking Shark

denticles. The large mouth is terminal, and the teeth have a broad base with a long, pointed central cusp. The pectoral fins are not attached to the body at the rear, and Atlantic angels swim without making much use of them. Growing to 5 feet long, Atlantic angels will bite when captured and can inflict vicious wounds. In the western Atlantic, they range from southern New England to the Gulf of Mexico, also occurring around Jamaica, Nicaragua, and Venezuela; they are rarer off southern Florida and in the Gulf of Mexico. They are common during the summer along the Mid-Atlantic states.

Basking shark *(Cetorhinus maximus).* The second largest shark in existence today, growing to 45 feet, the basking shark is a member of the mackerel shark family and is basically harmless to humans.

A dark-gray or slate-gray fish fading to a paler shade on its belly, the basking shark gets its name from its habit of swimming slowly at the surface. As a plankton feeder, it will not take bait, being too large for sportfishing anyway. Long gill slits span the sides and nearly meet below, with long, closely set gill rakers that it uses to strain zooplankton; the rakers are shed during the winter, and the basking shark fasts on the bottom while it grows new ones. Pelagic in cool, temperate waters nearly worldwide, its three-year gestation period is the longest of any shark's. Once extensively fished commercially and valued for its liver for oil, the basking shark may be a potential source of anticarcinoma drugs and is used in Chinese medicine.

Blacktip shark *(Carcharhinus limbatus).* Sometimes called blacktip whaler, common blacktip shark, or small blacktipped shark, this shark reaches just over 8 feet in length; the all-tackle world record is a 270-pound, 9-ounce fish taken off Kenya in 1995.

It is dark bluish gray on the back and whitish below, with a distinctive silver white stripe on its flank; young fish are generally paler. As the name implies, it is black-tipped on the inside of the pectoral fin, as well as on the dorsal, anal, and lower lobe of the caudal fins in young fish. This shading may be faint, especially on the first dorsal fin, and it fades with growth. The blacktip shark has a long, almost V-shaped snout and serrated, nearly symmetrical teeth. It often forms large surface schools and is an active hunter in midwater, responsible for very few attacks on humans but dangerous when provoked.

A wide-ranging species, the blacktip extends along the western Atlantic from Massachusetts to Brazil, and in the east from Senegal to Zaire,

Blacktip Shark

Blue Shark

Madeira, the Canaries, and the Mediterranean. In the Indo–West Pacific, they occur from South Africa, Madagascar, and the Red Sea to Australia, as well as from China to Australia and also around Hawaii, Tahiti, and the Marquesas. In the eastern Pacific, it occurs from southern Baja California to Peru and the Galápagos Islands.

Blue shark *(Prionace glauca).* This shark is also called bluedog, great blue shark, and blue whaler, the last because of its habit of trailing whaling ships and feeding off whale carcasses and ship garbage.

A member of the requiem shark family, the blue shark is very slender and streamlined, with a long and pointed snout that is much longer than the width of its mouth. Appropriately, it is a deep, brilliant blue or a dark cobalt to indigo blue above, fading gradually to white below. With up to three rows of functional teeth in each jaw, the larger teeth in the upper jaw are "saber shaped," or broadly convex on one side and concave on the other; the teeth are serrated along the edges, and those in the lower jaw are narrower.

Circumglobal in temperate and tropical waters, blue sharks hardly rate as fighters in comparison to makos and threshers, but they are much more abundant and provide fine sport on appropriate tackle in cooler temperate waters off the northeastern United States, England, and California, where there are large sportfisheries for them. They usually swim slowly, and yet they can be one of the swiftest sharks. The largest fish exceed 400 pounds and are fairly strong fighters when taken from cool waters. Viviparous, blue sharks bear live young in large litters, up to 54 at one time (135 have been recorded); they mature at a length of 7 or 8 feet but can reach upward of 13 feet. The all-tackle world record is a 454-pound fish taken off Massachusetts in 1996. Blue sharks are potentially dangerous to humans because they are related to unprovoked attacks on both humans and boats, especially during accidents and disasters at sea when injured people are in the water.

Bonnethead shark *(Sphyrna tiburo).* Occasionally referred to simply as bonnet, the bonnethead shark is the smallest member of the hammerhead sharks, the family characterized by having eyes located at the far ends of extended lateral lobes.

The bonnethead is particularly distinctive in appearance because it has a smooth, broadly widened head, frequently described as "spade shaped," which has more curve to it than do the heads of any other hammerheads. Also, the front of the head is lacking a median groove, which is present in other hammerheads. Gray to grayish brown in color, the bonnethead shark seldom exceeds 3 feet in length, maturing at about that length to bear 6 to 12 live young at one time.

Bonnethead Shark

Bull Shark

Bonnetheads, particularly young fish, are often found over flats, where they can be taken on flies and ultralight tackle. The all-tackle world record is a 23-pound, 11-ounce fish taken off Georgia in 1994. These fish occur in the western Atlantic from North Carolina (occasionally Rhode Island) to southern Brazil, as well as around Cuba and the Bahamas, and in the eastern Pacific from Southern California to Ecuador.

Bull shark *(Carcharhinus leucas).* A large member of the requiem shark family, the bull shark is also called freshwater whaler and river whaler because it is most common inshore around river mouths and can adapt to life in freshwater.

This is the species that is landlocked in Lake Nicaragua in Nicaragua and has gained fame as a man-eater because it has been repeatedly implicated in attacks on humans. Also known as the Zambezi shark in southern African waters, the bull shark is one of the three most dangerous sharks in that area, along with great white and tiger sharks, due to its relative abundance in inshore habitats where people are more likely to be attacked.

The bull shark gets its name from its bull-like head and is known for its heavy body and short snout, the latter of which appears very broad and rounded from below. Gray to dull brown above and growing pale below, the bull shark has a large first dorsal fin that begins above the midpectoral fin, and the upper lobe of the tail is much larger than the lower.

The bull shark can be sluggish and unwilling to strike a fly or crankbait, but it will hit natural baits readily; unlike other sharks that rise to the surface, the bull shark often stays deep and fights hard. Like the hammerhead, it will frequently attack hooked tarpon. Usually growing to a length of 6 to 9 feet, the bull shark can reach 12 feet and more 500 pounds. The all-tackle world record is a 490-pounder taken off Alabama in 1986. Bull sharks are widespread; they inhabit the western Atlantic from Massachusetts to southern Brazil, and the eastern Atlantic from Morocco and Senegal to Angola. In the Indo–West Pacific, they occur from South Africa to India and Vietnam to Australia, and in the eastern Pacific from southern Baja California, Mexico, to Ecuador and possibly Peru.

Hammerhead sharks *(Sphyrna species).* Hammerhead sharks occur worldwide; the most prominent species include the great hammerhead *(S. mokarran),* the smooth hammerhead *(S. zygaena),* the scalloped hammerhead *(S. lewini),* and the bonnethead shark *(see previous heading).*

Hammerhead Shark

S

Lemon Shark

Hammerheads are easy for even a novice to identify, with eyes located at the ends of two thin lobes and the overall structure resembling a hammer. One possible reason why the head takes on a hammer shape may be that the shape is ideal for turning and locating odors, making the best use of the electroreceptors present in all sharks, which in turn makes detecting food an easier chore.

The largest species is the great hammerhead, which can reach a length of 20 feet and a weight of 1,000 pounds. This shark prefers warm waters and is rarely found outside tropical areas. The most widely distributed hammerhead is most likely the smooth hammerhead, which grows to 14 feet. The front edge of its head is rounded and unnotched at the center, or smooth, and it inhabits shallow, calm coastal waters of bays and harbors. The scalloped hammerhead is a gray brown to olive shark that generally grows 5 to 7 feet, usually smaller than the smooth hammerhead but sometimes reaching 15 feet. The front edge of its head is rounded and notched, or scalloped. Both smooth and scalloped hammerheads occasionally school in large numbers. Some lesser-known hammerheads include *S. couardi,* a large West African shark that bears a resemblance to the scalloped hammerhead, and *S. blochii,* whose strange appearance is due to head lobes, which often measure 50 percent of the body length and are swept back like the wings of an airplane.

Stingrays are thought to be the favored food of many hammerheads, and all species are viviparous and prolific, giving birth to many live young at a time. These sharks are exceptionally strong and can make fast, long surface and midwater runs when hooked, fighting hard and thrashing about with a great deal of excitement.

Lemon shark *(Negaprion brevirostris).* A requiem family shark, the lemon shark grows to 11 feet at maximum, although it is usually between 5 and 8 feet long.

A potentially dangerous shark, it may rest on the bottom in coastal waters in groups of 4 to 6 and become aggressive when in the vicinity of spearfishing. It is commonly yellow brown, although it can also be muddy dark brown or dark gray with olive sides and a paler belly. It has a blunt and broad snout that appears rounded from below. The second dorsal fin is almost equal in size to the large first dorsal fin, and the upper lobe of the tail is much larger than the lower.

Lemon sharks are good inshore, light-tackle sportfish that inhabit western Atlantic waters from New Jersey to Brazil, including the Gulf of Mexico, the Bahamas, and the Caribbean, and eastern Atlantic waters from Senegal and the Ivory Coast possibly down the African continent; in the eastern Pacific they extend from southern Baja California, Mexico, and the Gulf of California to Ecuador.

Leopard shark *(Triakis semifasciata).* Sometimes called cat shark, the leopard shark is a striking fish, so named for its leopardlike black spots, which run in crossbars across its back and sides over a lighter gray background.

It has an elongate body and a short snout that is bluntly rounded. Attaining lengths of up to 7 feet, the leopard shark inhabits inshore sand flats and

Leopard Shark

Porbeagle Shark

rocky areas, often in schools with smoothhound sharks. As a smaller, less-aggressive species of shark, it is not considered dangerous. Female bear live young in moderate numbers, between 4 and 29 at each birth. Found in the eastern Pacific from Oregon to the Gulf of California, the leopard shark is good light-tackle game and very good table fare. It is often sought by commercial fishermen.

Porbeagle shark *(Lamna nasus).*   The porbeagle shark is recognized by many different names, among them beaumaris shark, blue dog, bonito shark, herring shark, mackerel shark, porbeagle, and salmon shark.

It is a member of the mackerel shark family, as are the great white and the mako sharks, and bears a resemblance to both species. The porbeagle has a robust, cobalt blue body with a perfectly conical snout that ends in a point. It is easily identified by its teeth, which are smooth and have little cusps on each side of the base. It often has a distinctive white area at the base portion of the first dorsal fin; this fin is farther forward than it is on mako or white sharks. There is a large, particularly prominent flattened keel

on both sides of the caudal peduncle, and beneath that but farther back on the tail is a small secondary keel, which mako and white sharks also lack. Its anal fin is directly aligned with the second dorsal fin.

The flesh of the porbeagle is of good quality and texture and is said to taste something like swordfish. Excellent sportfish, porbeagles occur in colder waters than makos or whites, which may explain why they are not implicated in attacks on humans. A widespread species, they exist in the western Atlantic from Newfoundland to New Jersey, although they rarely venture south of New England, and probably range from southern Brazil through Argentina. In the eastern Atlantic, porbeagles range from Iceland and the western Barents Sea to South Africa, being present as well in the Mediterranean; in the South Pacific, they inhabit waters around Australia, New Zealand, and Chile. They are also known in the Antarctic and in the South Indian Ocean.

Sandbar shark *(Carcharhinus plumbeus).*   The sandbar shark is an inshore fish and a good light-tackle fighter, growing usually to between 5 and 7 feet long. A relatively heavy-bodied fish, it is dark

Sandbar Shark

Sand Tiger Shark

bluish gray to brownish gray and has a pale or white belly.

There is a distinct ridge on the back between the first and second dorsal fins, and the first fin is large and pointed, starting over the middle of the pectoral fin. Its snout is shorter than the width of its mouth, appearing rounded from below.

Sandbar and dusky *(Carcharhinus obscurus)* sharks are coastal migrants that have taken a particularly hard hit from longlining for both their fins and flesh. Sandbars are usually called browns by anglers along the east coast of the U.S., where they commonly migrate into large bays to spawn. Although basically ground sharks, they are extremely strong fighters. The dusky is almost indistinguishable from the sandbar but grows to more than 700 pounds; the brown never exceeds much more than 200 pounds. The most common gray shark along the coast of the Middle Atlantic states, sandbars extend in the western Atlantic from southern Massachusetts to southern Brazil, and in the east from Portugal to Zaire, including the Mediterranean. In the western Indian Ocean, they occur in the Red Sea, the Gulf of Oman, eastern Africa, Madagascar, Mauritius, and the Seychelles. In the Pacific, they occur in the west from Japan to Australia and in the east around the Hawaiian, Galápagos, and Revillagigedo Islands.

Sand tiger shark *(Carcharias taurus).* Previously called *Odontaspis taurus,* the sand tiger shark is the most common shark sighted along Atlantic beaches. It grows to about 9 feet and is grayish brown or tan with dark brown spots along the sides that grow more numerous toward the tail; although it bears a resemblance to the tiger shark, it has a larger second dorsal fin, a longer snout, and strongly projecting teeth.

Usually caught accidentally by surf casters fishing for other fish, sand tigers are sluggish and offer little resistance when hooked. In the western Atlantic, they occur from the Gulf of Maine to Argentina, and in the east from the Mediterranean to Cameroon. In the western Indian Ocean, sand tigers extend from the Red Sea to South Africa, Pakistan, and possibly India; in the western Pacific, they extend from Japan to Australia, possibly including waters around Vietnam and Indonesia.

Sharpnose sharks *(Rhizoprionodon species).* There are six sharpnose sharks in the *Rhizoprionodon* genus of the requiem shark family, all sharing a similar external appearance that is characterized by a long flattened snout. The best-known member of the family is the Atlantic sharpnose, which is a very popular small species as an inshore food and a small gamefish in the Gulf of Mexico.

It grows to between 2 and 4 feet in length and has the characteristic long and flattened snout, as well as a slender, brown to olive gray body with a pale belly. The dorsal and caudal fins may be edged in black, especially in the young, and often there are small, scattered whitish spots on the sides. The Atlantic sharpnose is further distinguished by well-developed furrows in the lips at the corners of the mouth, and by the second dorsal fin, which begins over the middle of the anal fin. This sharpnose

Atlantic Sharpnose Shark

Shortfin Mako Shark

S

ranges as far north as New Brunswick but is rarely found north of North Carolina. The Caribbean sharpnose *(R. porosus)* may actually be a subspecies of the Atlantic sharpnose but is found in mostly Caribbean waters. The Brazilian sharpnose *(R. lalandii)* is confined to Brazilian waters.

The Australian sharpnose *(R. taylori)* and gray sharpnose *(R. oligolinx)* sharks are nearly identical in appearance but are easy to distinguish because of their different ranges, the former being a western Pacific species and the latter inhabiting Indo–West Pacific waters. The Pacific sharpnose is fairly common in the Gulf of California and a frequent catch of the shark fisheries there, extending as far south as Peru.

Shortfin mako shark *(Isurus oxyrinchus).* Also called blue pointer, bonito shark, dog shark, and short-nosed mackerel shark, the shortfin mako is by far the most popular of angling sharks, exceeding 1,000 pounds in weight and 13 feet in length.

It is widely distributed throughout the oceans, ranging in the western Atlantic from the Gulf of Maine to southern Brazil, in the eastern Atlantic from Norway to South Africa, and in the Indo–West Pacific from South Africa to Australia, Russia to New Zealand, south of the Aleutian Islands to Hawaii, and Southern California to Chile. Although most abundant in temperate waters (64° to 70°F is considered ideal), some large makos adapt to temperatures in the upper 50s, and smaller makos often prefer waters in the 70s. A similar species, the longfin mako *(I. paucus),* is encountered mainly at night by anglers fishing great depths well offshore.

The shortfin mako has a streamlined, well-proportioned body that is most striking for a vivid blue gray or cobalt blue coloring on its back, which changes to a lighter blue on the sides and a snowy white on the belly; this brilliant coloring fades after death to a grayish brown. Other characteristic features are a conical, sharply pointed snout, a large flattened keel on either side of the caudal peduncle, and a lunate (crescent-shaped) tail with lobes of nearly equal size. The large, first dorsal fin begins just behind the base of the pectoral fins. The shortfin mako can be easily distinguished from all other

sharks by its teeth, which are slender and curved and lack cusps or serrations.

Makos have all the characteristics of gamefish in that they fight hard, have good endurance, and are fast, active, strong swimmers that jump. Indeed, their jumps are possibly the most spectacular of all, as they may suddenly appear 20 feet in the air while the line is still pointing at another angle. At the top of their leap, makos typically turn over and reenter the water where they exited. Some makos never jump, and those that do rarely jump more than two or three times. They are also potentially dangerous, known to bite or otherwise attack boats by leaping into them, causing severe injuries and damage.

Unfortunately for makos, they are also very good food fish—a quality that has endeared them to longliners and led to a sharp decline in abundance. Mako steaks command a good price under their own name, but they used to be a cheap substitute for swordfish steaks, which they resemble in both texture and taste. Ironically, makos love to eat swordfish, which they attack by chopping their tails off while the swordfish are dozing on the surface.

Because female makos weigh more than 600 pounds before becoming mature, and only a few pregnant specimens have ever been recorded, it's something of a miracle that there are any makos left in the oceans at all. The warm-blooded mako is ovoviviparous, which means the eggs hatch inside the mother and the young are born alive; while in the uterus, the unborn young often resort to cannibalism until just one remains for birth. The all-tackle world record is a 1,115-pound fish taken off Mauritius in 1988.

Thresher sharks *(Alopias species).* Known by a variety of names, among them fox shark, longtail thresher, pelagic thresher, sea fox, swiveltail, thintail thresher, and thrasher shark, a thresher shark is characterized by its well-muscled tail, the upper lobe of which is usually as long as the rest of the body.

These sharks use their tails to herd baitfish into a mass by slapping or thrashing the water, then stunning or injuring fish before swallowing them. There are four species, including the pelagic thresher

Thresher Shark

(*A. pelagicus*) and the Pacific bigeye thresher (*A. profundis*), which occur in the northwestern Pacific, and the Atlantic bigeye thresher shark (*A. superciliosus*), which occurs in the Atlantic. The longtail thresher (*A. vulpinus*) is cosmopolitan in temperate and tropical waters. All threshers are fundamentally pelagic but will occasionally move in close to shore.

Grayish to dark charcoal in color, thresher sharks turn abruptly white on the belly and may be mottled on the lower half of the body. Threshers are further identified by the absence of a keel on the caudal peduncle; by their small, pointed and broad-based teeth; and by their comparatively smooth skin. Longtail and pelagic threshers have moderate-size eyes, and the first dorsal fin is set almost directly in the middle of the back and far ahead of the beginning of the pelvic fins. The Atlantic and Pacific bigeye threshers have much larger eyes, and the rear margin of the dorsal fin is located at least as far back as the origin of the pelvic fins.

Threshers are excellent food fish, comparable to mako and swordfish, and they are outstanding fighters (the longtail has been known to leap out of the water). They are often hooked in the tail because of their habit of using their tail to herd potential prey. Thresher sharks were more popular than makos off California until recently and are a relatively rare catch along the U.S. Atlantic coast, although specimens in the 300- to 600-pound class are the most common size encountered from New Jersey to Massachusetts. The largest threshers have come from New Zealand, where they've been boated in excess of 800 pounds; in general they are said to reach 20 feet and 1,000 pounds, but are usually much smaller. The all-tackle world record for *A. vulpinus* is a 767-pound, 3-ounce fish taken off New Zealand in 1983.

Tiger shark *(Galeocerdo cuvier)*. One of the largest of the requiem sharks, the tiger shark grows to 24 feet. It is infamous as one of the most dangerous sharks.

Although some sharks will attack and kill humans without necessarily eating them, the tiger shark is especially fearsome because it is well-known as a man-eater, often devouring the remains of its victims. The tiger shark frequents shallow waters where people swim and is circumglobal in tropical and temperate waters. One study has shown that the tiger shark can travel more than 30 miles within a 24-hour period, and that, although tiger sharks do revisit the same coastal areas, the time elapsed between visits can vary from a few days to many months.

Dark bluish gray to brownish gray above and whitish below, the tiger shark is so called because of its prominent dark brown blotches and bars, or "tiger stripes and leopard spots"; these are especially evident in juveniles and small adults but fade with age. This fish has an extremely blunt snout that appears broadly rounded from below, and a mid-dorsal ridge is present. The tiger shark is also distinguished by its broad and coarsely serrated

Tiger Shark

teeth, which have deep notches and are the same in both jaws. The first two of five gill slits are located above the pectoral fin, and there is a long, prominent keel on either side of the caudal peduncle, as well as a long upper lobe on the tail.

The tiger shark is an important species for anglers only because it is commonly in the 300- to 800-pound class when encountered, and can grow much larger. The long-standing all-tackle record of 1,780 pounds was caught from a pier at Cherry Grove, South Carolina, in 1964. Tigers are famed for eating virtually anything, including metal objects, and are generally poor fighters.

Tope (*Galeorhinus galeus*). One of the smallest members of the requiem shark family, the tope is an active and highly sought species within its extensive range.

Tope

It is also known throughout that range by various names, including flake, greyboy, greyshark, hundshai, school shark, snapper shark, soupfin shark, and vitamin shark.

The tope has a slender body; a prominent, long, pointed snout; long pectoral fins; and a large and strong tail fin with a large lower lobe. It is a bottom-roaming inhabitant of inshore environs that commonly weighs from 20 to 40 pounds but may grow as large as 75 pounds and exceed 5 feet in length. It is reported to live as long as 55 years. Despite its size, it is favorably regarded by anglers for its vigorous fight.

Tope occur in all oceans. In the western Atlantic, they are found in southern Brazil and Argentina; in the eastern Atlantic, they range from Iceland to South Africa, including the Mediterranean Sea. In the western Indian Ocean, tope are found in South Africa; in the western Pacific, they are found in Australia and New Zealand; in the eastern Pacific, they range from British Columbia to southern Baja California, Mexico, including the Gulf of California, and also Peru and Chile.

White shark (*Carcharodon carcharias*). The white shark goes by a few different names, such as white pointer, white death, man-eater, and great white shark, the last two of which hint at both the deadly habits and threatening size of this mackerel shark.

Although a relatively uncommon deep-water fish, the white shark occasionally enters shallow waters and will attack, without provocation, humans and small boats alike; because it often lingers near islands and offshore colonies of seals and sea lions, which are some of its preferred foods, it is thought that some attacks on humans occur because the white shark mistakes divers or surfers in wet suits for seals. It is undoubtedly the most dangerous shark due to a combination of size, strength, ability, and disposition to attack, and because of the many recorded attacks that have taken place in the twentieth century.

Growing to 26 feet but usually less than 16 feet in length, the white shark has a stout, heavy body that may be a dull slate blue, grayish brown, or almost black above, turning dirty white below. There are black edges on the pectoral fins, and often there is a black oval blotch on the body just above or behind the fins. The large head ends in a point at the conical snout, which accounts for the name "white pointer." There is a large, distinct, flattened keel on either side of the caudal peduncle and a greatly reduced second dorsal fin. A distinguishing feature of the white shark is its teeth, which are large and triangular with sharp, serrated cutting edges.

Sportfishing for whites has virtually come to an end as a result of conservation efforts aimed at preserving the greatest of the predators, which were never especially abundant in any case. Most whites

White Shark

S

S

are found in temperate or even cool waters worldwide, and close to a source of the marine mammals they prefer to eat after growing to large sizes. Actually, there are two much larger sharks, the basking shark of the North Atlantic and the whale shark of the tropics, but these are harmless plankton feeders.

Though Alf Dean's white shark record—2,664 pounds off South Australia in 1959—continues to be recognized by the IGFA, a much larger 17-foot specimen of 3,427 pounds was caught on August 6, 1986, on legitimate tackle by Donnie Braddick out of Montauk, New York. Captain Frank Mundus had found a dead whale floating offshore, a sure attraction for the huge whites and tigers that seem to appear out of nowhere for such a feast. Although sharks feeding on blubber have no interest in fish, Mundus (who had harpooned several great whites over the years) managed to slip a string of baitfish into a white's mouth to get the hookup. After much controversy, the IGFA decided not to accept the catch because the dead whale was, in effect, the forbidden mammal chum.

SHARPENER
See: Hook Sharpening.

SHEEFISH
A common term in North America for inconnu *(see)*.

SHEEPHEAD, CALIFORNIA   *Semicossyphus pulcher.*
Other names—sheepie, goat, billygoat (large), red fish, humpy, fathead; Spanish: *vieja de California.*

A member of the Labridae family of wrasses *(see)*, the California sheephead is a strong bottom-dwelling fish that is a favorite of spearfishing divers. It has some commercial value, although declining numbers caused it to be supplanted commercially by rockfish. Its flesh is white, firm, and mild, and it is preferred in chowder and in salads.

Identification.   The body of the California sheephead is elongate, robust, and compressed. This species is a hermaphrodite: It begins life as a female and becomes a male later in life. Females mature at about 8 inches in length and four to five years of age. Most females transform to males at a

length of about 12 inches, or seven to eight years of age. This sex change is accompanied by a marked change in appearance. Younger fish (females) are a uniform pinkish red with a white lower jaw. As they age and become males, the head and rear third of the body turn black, the midsection of the body remains red, and the lower jaw remains white. In all stages of their development, sheephead have unusually large doglike teeth.

Size/Age.   The largest sheephead recorded on rod and reel was 36 inches long and weighed $35\frac{1}{2}$ pounds, although the average fish weighs less than 15 pounds. At least two fish of 40 pounds were speared in the past. A 29-pound, 32-inch-long fish was 53 years old.

Distribution.   California sheephead occur from Cabo San Lucas, Baja California, Mexico, to Monterey Bay, California. An isolated population exists in the Gulf of California, but these fish are uncommon north of Point Conception, California

Habitat.   This species is generally taken in rocky kelp areas near shore, in water from 20 to 100 feet deep, although they do occur as deep as 180 feet.

Spawning behavior.   Spawning takes place in early spring and summer.

Food and feeding habits.   Crabs, mussels, various-size snails, squid, sea urchins, sand dollars, and sea cucumbers are typical food items. The large caninelike teeth are used to pry food from rocks. A special plate in the throat crushes shells into small pieces for easy digestion. Occasionally, large adults have been observed out of the water in the intertidal zone, hanging onto mussels after a wave has receded.

Angling.   California sheephead take a variety of live and cut baits, such as anchovies or squid, fished on the bottom. Whole live mackerel fished on the bottom are often good for large specimens. These fish provide a long, determined struggle and must be kept away from kelp and rock ledges to avoid having the line cut.

SHEEPSHEAD
(1) The most commonly used term for freshwater drum.
See: Drum, Freshwater.

(2) *Archosargus probatocephalus.*
Other names—convict fish, sheepshead seabream; Portuguese: *sargo;* Spanish: *sargo chopa.*

This is the most popular member of the Sparidae family of porgies with saltwater anglers in the United States, and a large one that is commonly caught around barnacle-encrusted structures along shorelines. The sheepshead is an excellent food fish and is of commercial value.

Identification.   The basic color of the sheepshead is black, including the fins, but the sides and caudal peduncle are striped alternately with

California Sheephead

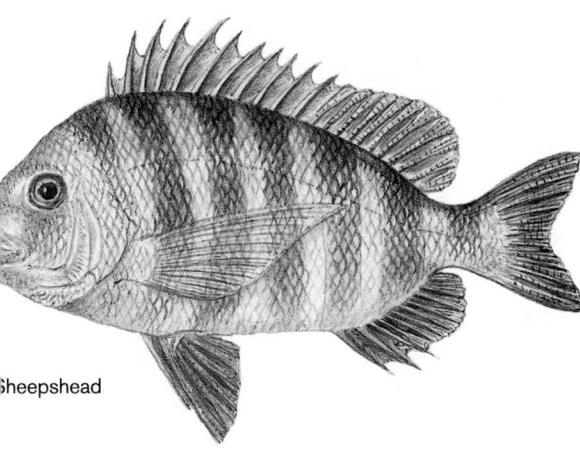

Sheepshead

broad bands of silver and black. The stripes are most prominent in young fish. The mouth is small to medium in size, and the teeth are broad and flat for crushing the shells of crustaceans and mollusks.

Size. Sheepshead average about a pound in weight but may attain a weight of 25 pounds and measure as much as 3 feet in length.

Distribution. This species occurs from Nova Scotia to Florida and the northern Gulf of Mexico and south to Brazil, excluding the Bahamas and West Indies.

Habitat. Sheepshead are found in bays and estuaries and along the shoreline and commonly enter brackish water in coastal rivers.

Food and feeding habits. Sheepshead consume mollusks and crustaceans. Often traveling in schools, they are browsing feeders that forage around the pilings of wharves and docks and may be located around jetties, over rocky bottoms, and in other places where they can find oysters and mussels.

Angling. These game-fighting bottom feeders are primarily caught on bait and bottom or float rigs, usually with light or medium tackle as necessary for the depths fished and weights used. Assorted crabs, clams, mussels, shrimp, or cut baits are the primary natural baits, sometimes used with sliding sinker rigs, although small jigs may also catch fish. Because these fish are wary, chumming is popular. Although most fishing occurs around objects and structures near shore, the possibilities for stalking fewer and warier fish also exist in some backwater marsh areas. In winter, deeper artificial reefs (in 35 to 60 feet of water) in Southern waters may be the best place to find these fish, as they congregate here where the water temperature is relatively stable.

Sheepshead bite lightly, sometimes remaining undetected and stealing baits. They can be tough and frustrating fish to hook. Furthermore, the hook must be set firmly because of the fish's hard mouth.
See: Inshore Fishing; Porgies.

SHEET BEND
See: Knots, Boating.

SHELLFISH
A popular general term for crustaceans and mollusks, but not including finfish. Shellfish may be used as bait when angling, but they are not targeted by anglers, or deliberately sought with sporting equipment.

SHELL LURE
A lure made with pearl shell inserts, devised by Polynesians for tuna fishing.

SHINER
Shiners are members of the minnow, or Cyprinidae, family of freshwater fish. A number of minnows are called "shiners" because their shimmering silvery sides flash as the little fish turn in the water. There are well over a hundred species in North America. All are relatively slender fish, and their fins are relatively large compared to the size of their body. They are prominent forage species for predator fish, are used frequently as baits, and are often imitated with lures and flies.

Typical of the group is the common shiner *(Luxilus cornutus)*, which is olive green above and silvery on its sides and belly. At spawning time in spring, the male's body takes on a pinkish tinge, and the tail and fins become bright orange or red, particularly at the base. Hard bumps, or tubercles, develop on the top of the head and on the fins. Males are larger than females, sometimes attaining a length of 8 inches, although they are usually sold for bait when they are half this size or smaller. The common shiner is widely distributed, inhabiting small streams from southern Canada southward over much of the northern United States east of the Rockies.

Another widely distributed minnow of this group is the emerald shiner *(Notropis atherinoides)*, which often travels in tremendously large schools. It is smaller than the common shiner, rarely exceeding 3 inches in length, and has a proportionately shorter snout. The striped shiner *(Luxilus chrysocephalus)* is also common and widespread, and is similar in size to the common shiner.

Some of the more attractive and hardy shiners are kept in aquariums. Among these is the sailfin shiner *(Pteronotropis hypselopterus)*, which has exceptionally high fins. The males' fins are streaked handsomely with red during the spawning season.

The golden shiner *(Notemigonus crysoleucas)* rates as one of the best bait minnows and is commonly reared specifically for this market. Unlike most members of the minnow family, the golden shiner has a scaleless keel on the midline of its belly. The lateral line bows sharply downward, and the mouth angles upward. When young, these minnows are silvery; as adults, they become a bright metallic or brassy gold. The average size varies with the environment, but in some large lakes the golden shiner attains a length of 10 inches or more; in Florida, large shiners are commonly used as live baits for largemouth bass. Found throughout eastern Canada and in the U.S. east of the Rockies, the golden shiner is adaptable to a wide range of water conditions and temperatures, from cool and swift-flowing, which it cohabits with trout, to warm and weedy sluggish streams and ponds.

See: Minnow; Shiner, Common; Shiner, Emerald; Shiner, Golden; Shiner, Striped.

SHINER, COMMON   *Luxilus cornutus.*
Other names—shiner.

The common shiner is an abundant minnow of the Cyprinidae family that is commonly used as a baitfish. It has been known to hybridize with striped shiners *(see: shiner, striped)*.

Identification.   The common shiner is silvery with a deep compressed body, a dusky dorsal stripe, large eyes, diamond-shaped scales that flake off easily, and nine anal rays. It has no barbels, and no dark lateral stripe, but there is a dark stripe along the middle of the generally olive-colored back. During the spawning season, males develop blue backs and red or pink bodies, with pinkish fins, and display large tubercles on the head, pectoral fins, and anterior parts of the body.

Size.   Common shiners are usually 3 to 4 inches long but can grow to 8 inches.

Distribution.   This species occurs throughout the Mississippi River, Hudson Bay, Great Lakes, and Atlantic basins from Nova Scotia to Saskatchewan south to Missouri and Virginia.

Habitat.   Common shiners are most prevalent in small to moderate-size streams, preferring areas that are clear and without fast-moving water. They will tolerate a small amount of silt, but not muddy water.

Spawning behavior.   Common shiners spawn in late spring in water temperatures ranging from 60° to 65°F. They are diverse spawners, preferring to use the nests of other minnows such as chub and fallfish, but they also spawn over gravel or in excavated depressions in gravel or sand. Groups of males gather at the spawning sight and vie for position at the upstream end of the nesting area. Spawning occurs when the male wraps his body around a female and drives her toward the nest. Because they often spawn in nests constructed by other minnow species, hybridization is common.

Food.   Common shiners feed mainly on insects and insect larvae, but their diet may also include plant material, fish eggs, and small fish.

Angling.   Common shiners have no angling value, but they are one of many shiners that are important forage for larger predators and are often used as baitfish by anglers.

See: Minnow; Shiner.

SHINER, EMERALD   *Notropis atherinoides.*
Other names—buckeye, shiner, lake shiner, lake emerald shiner, common emerald shiner; French: *mémé émeraude.*

The emerald shiner is one of many shiners that are members of the minnow, or Cyprinidae, family. These fish are important forage for predator species and are frequently used as bait by anglers. Unlike most minnows, however, the emerald shiner is a pelagic big-water species and is abundant in large rivers and in lakes within its range.

Identification.   The emerald shiner is a slender, elongated fish with a pale and silvery slab-sided body; it is faintly iridescent green on the top, fading to silver or white on the belly. Juveniles appear semitransparent. Other characteristics include a faint lateral band, a short and fairly pointed snout, large eyes, and usually 11 anal fin rays. It has no barbels. During the spawning season, males develop very small tubercles on the fins but have no breeding colors.

Size/Age.   Emerald shiners are commonly 3 to 4 inches long, and seldom grow to more than 5 inches long. They typically living for only three years.

Distribution.   This species has a wide range, from the St. Lawrence and Hudson River basins west to the Mackenzie River drainage of the Northwest Territories and south throughout the Great Lakes and Mississippi River drainages to the Gulf Coast from Texas to Alabama. It is probably the most abundant fish in the Mississippi River and other large rivers, and is also prominent in the Great Lakes as well as other large lakes.

Habitat.   Emerald shiners travel in large schools in midwater and near-surface areas. They roam in large lakes and are common in the pools of big rivers. They are known to move vertically toward the surface at night, and to deeper water in daylight.

Spawning behavior.   Spawning occurs when water temperatures reach about 75°F and may be

Common Shiner

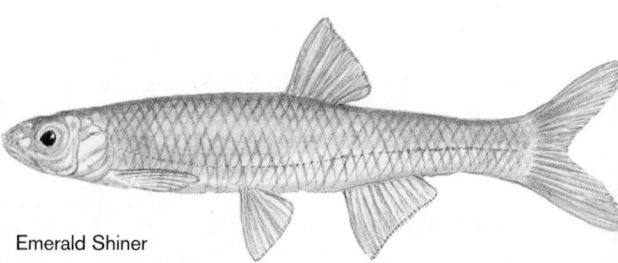

Emerald Shiner

continued over an extended period, lasting from late spring through midsummer in some places. Unlike many other shiners, this species spawns in midwater in groups. It is also prone to cyclical abundance.

Food. A pelagic species, emerald shiners feed on plankton, zooplankton, blue-green algae, diatoms, and insect larvae.

Angling. Emerald shiners have no angling value, but they are one of many shiners that are important forage for larger predators, and are often used as bait by anglers.

See: Minnow; Shiner.

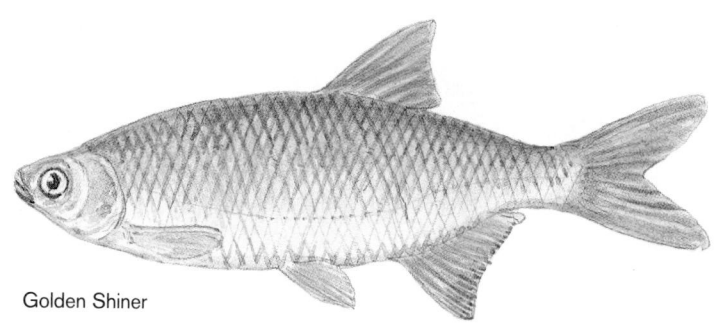

Golden Shiner

SHINER, GOLDEN   *Notemigonus crysoleucas.*
Other names—roach, shad roach, shiner, pond shiner.

The golden shiner is a prominent and widespread minnow of the Cyprinidae family. These fish are important forage species for predators and are widely used in various sizes as baits by anglers.

Identification. The golden shiner has a deep, compressed body that is generally golden yellow or brass colored in turbid water, varying to more silvery in clear water. The fins are yellow green but become reddish in large spawning adults. The mouth is small and upturned with a slightly pointed snout, and there is a distinctive fleshy scaleless keel along the belly from the pelvic to anal fin. This keel distinguishes the golden shiner from other similar species, especially the European rudd (*see: rudd*), which is an introduced species in the native North American range of the golden shiner. The dusky lateral line of the golden shiner noticeably dips down in the middle of the body, and the caudal fin is moderately forked. The color of the fins is more pronounced during breeding season; breeding males develop fine tubercles on the dorsal surface of the head and body. The golden shiner has 7 to 9 dorsal rays, and 8 to 19 anal rays.

Size/Age. Golden shiners can grow to $10^{1}/_{2}$ to 12 inches in length, although the average size varies with the environment. Many northerly waters are likely to produce smaller fish on average, and 3 to 5 inches is the norm in many places. These fish reportedly live for up to 10 years.

Distribution. This species is widely distributed east of the Rockies in the central and eastern United States, ranging from Quebec to Saskatchewan in the north, and to Florida, Texas, and Mexico in the south. It has been introduced elsewhere, including Arizona, California, and Washington.

Habitat. Slow-water fish, golden shiners are prevalent in lakes, ponds, and backwaters, and in the slower parts of streams and small to medium rivers. They are common in weedy, clean, quiet, and shallow waters.

Spawning behavior. Golden shiners reach sexual maturity in their second year when they are usually $2^{1}/_{2}$ to $3^{1}/_{2}$ inches long, and spawn over an extended period, commencing in spring when water temperatures exceed 68°F. They do not prepare a nest as many other shiners and minnows do; rather, they scatter adhesive eggs over algae and other aquatic vegetation and do not exhibit parental care. Large females reportedly lay more than 200,000 eggs in a spawning season.

Food. The food of golden shiners consists of plankton, algae, insects, and small fish; they feed in midwater and at or near the surface.

Angling. The primary interest of anglers in golden shiners is as baits, and the species is widely cultured in ponds, as well as in large tanks, for distribution to bait shops. In some places, most notably large Florida waters, commercial bait netters (and some energetic and devoted anglers) use chum or groundbait to attract and concentrate large (7- to 10-inch) golden shiners, which are caught by throwing cast nets over the shallow baited area. These are purchased in bait shops at a premium price and used for live-bait fishing for big largemouth bass, or for striped bass. Elsewhere, smaller sizes are preferred for the majority of species.

Golden shiners can be caught on hook and line, although relatively few anglers deliberately do so, as there is little merit to them from a consumptive standpoint. They are caught incidentally, however, by anglers using small hooks and natural baits, as well as flies or tiny jigs, in shallow vegetated areas. European methods of coarse fishing, which employs fine hooks and baits and prebaiting tactics, would likely be effective, although with many other species options there is little incentive for North American anglers to pursue golden shiners as sport.

See: Minnow; Shiner.

SHINER, STRIPED   *Luxilus chrysocephalus.*
Other names—shiner.

The striped shiner is a common and widespread minnow of the Cyprinidae family that is familiar to anglers who use it as bait or observe it spawning over the gravel nests built by other minnows. Two subspecies are recognized: *Luxilus chrysocephalus chrysocephalus* and *L. c. isolepis.*

Identification. The striped shiner is a silvery, laterally compressed minnow with large eyes and a terminal mouth. As in other species of *Luxilus,* the

S

Striped Shiner

exposed portion of its scales near the anterior lateral line is much more deep than it is wide. Anterior portions of scales are darkly pigmented, giving a crescent shaped appearance to the sides of striped shiners. Its common name stems from several parallel stripes that run along each side of the upper body and converge posterior to the dorsal fin. The convergence of these lines appears as large Vs when viewed from above.

The two subspecies can be separated by the appearance of the lateral stripes; *L. c. chrysocephalus* has wavy stripes, whereas *L. c. isolepis* has straight stripes. Other characteristics of striped shiners are 8 to 10 anal fin rays, a complete lateral line with 36 to 42 scales, and a pharyngeal tooth count formula of 2-4-4-2. Nuptial males possess striking coloration, developing a rosy pink color on their head, body, and the margins of all fins. Tubercles occur on the head, snout, lower jaw, and pectoral fins of nuptial males.

Size/Age. Adults can exceed 8 inches in length, but most are less than 5 inches long; they can live up to six years.

Distribution. The subspecies *L. c. chrysocephalus* extends throughout drainages of the lower Mississippi River and Gulf Coast; *L. c. isolepis* occurs in drainages of the Great Lakes and Mississippi River basins north of the Red River in Arkansas.

Habitat. Striped shiners occur in water bodies ranging from small streams to small rivers but are most abundant in small to medium streams. Their preferred habitats are pools, runs, and backwaters of flowing streams. They are more common in free-flowing streams with clear or slightly turbid water.

Spawning behavior. Striped shiners reach sexual maturity in their second year. Adult males are larger than females. Spawning occurs from late spring to early summer in water temperatures ranging from 16° to 27°C. Striped shiners are classified as pit spawners. Males excavate small pits on the top of chub nests or directly on the stream bottom and aggressively defend these pits while attempting to secure females for spawning. Spawning occurs when the male wraps his body around a female and drives her toward the pit. Females probably release less than 50 eggs during a single spawning event. Because of their tendency to spawn over chub nests, striped shiners often hybridize with chub and with other minnows that use nests.

Food. Striped shiners feed mainly on insects, but their diet may also include detritus, algae, fish eggs, crayfish, and small fish.

Angling. Although striped shiners have no angling value, they are one of many shiners that are important forage for larger predators, and may be used as baitfish by anglers.
See: Minnow; Shiner.

SHOAL
(1) A shallow part of a body of water representing a submerged ridge, bar, or bank that consists of, or is covered by, unconsolidated sediment (mud, sand, gravel) and that rises near enough to the water surface to be a danger to navigation. A shoal is usually visible during low water and in the right daylight conditions and, if deep enough for a boat to pass over, can be observed on sonar. The area adjacent to a shoal may at times be attractive to fish.

(2) A school of fish, usually at the surface or in shallow water (a term used in Europe and sometimes in South America).
See: School; Schooling.

SHOCKING
A term for electrofishing *(see)*.

SHOCK TIPPET
A short length of heavy monofilament or wire that is added to the end of a fly fishing leader.
See: Tippet.

SHOES, WADING
See: Waders.

SHOOTING HEAD
See: Flycasting Tackle; Shooting Line.

SHOOTING LINE
A type of weight-forward fly line that is attached to a long, thin-diameter running line.
See: Flycasting Tackle.

SHORT STRIKE
When a fish strikes at a lure but misses it without contacting the lure, the fish has made a short strike. This often happens because fish are swiping at a lure to stun or cripple it, rather than to instantly consume it. A short strike may be due to frenzied activity, cold water temperatures that make a particular species only moderately aggressive, or other factors. Using a trailer hook *(see)* with some lures will help catch such fish; making quick repeat

presentations with the same lure or (often better) a different lure may get a hookup; and slowing the speed of retrieve may get a more solid strike.

SHORT STROKING

A term for the method of fighting big-game species used primarily in standup fishing *(see)*.

SHOT

A small round fishing weight.
See: Bulk Shot; Sinker.

SHOTTING

Balancing a float *(see)* with split shot.

SIDE CAST

See: Casting.

SIDECAST REEL

Similar in appearance to a fly reel, a sidecast reel is a revolving spool reel with adjustable spool positioning. The spool is turned perpendicular to the rod for casting and the line flows outward on a cast as it does on a spinning reel. The spool is turned parallel to the rod for retrieving line, and the line is wound on just as it is for a fly rod. Primarily made and used in Australia, this reel has such limited popularity that few anglers around the world are familiar with it or have seen one. Although it has good direct winching power, it has a very low retrieve ratio and thus slow line take-up.

SIDEPLANER

See: Planer Boards.

SIERRA LEONE

Situated roughly 7° north of the equator on the western coast of the African continent, Sierra Leone lies between Guinea to the north and Liberia to the southeast. Its coastal region faces the Atlantic Ocean. The country has a tropical climate, with a yearly average temperature between 82° and 90°F, and English is the official language.

Sierra Leone is renowned for exceptional tarpon fishing. Anglers fishing out of the Sherbro Fishing Club on Sherbro Island, approximately 100 miles south of the capital city of Freetown, have set many of the most significant world records for this species. Since 1991, 15 world records have been set in the Sherbro Island vicinity, and many of these fish weighed more than 240 pounds. The largest among them tied the all-tackle world record of 283 pounds. World records notwithstanding, fish in excess of 200 pounds are more than the rule here,

and the first 300-pound tarpon ever known was caught in Sierra Leone waters. It's no wonder that Sierra Leone is known as "Tarpon Capital of the World."

The club at Sherbro opened in 1990 and accommodates 14 anglers. It has a small fleet of skiffs and provides tackle, although many anglers bring their own equipment, especially fly tackle.

The estuary at Sherbro opens out on the Atlantic Ocean, and the mouth of the Sherbro River constitutes a "pass" that funnels many smaller rivers into one big estuary. Drift fishing with rigged baits (mullet and bongas) is the principal technique, and tarpon are active throughout the area on favorable tides. Depths range from 12 to 25 feet in the Sherbro River, and at the end of low tide—weather permitting—it is possible to fish for tarpon out in deeper ocean waters.

The daily average tarpon strike ratio is around six, and all tarpon—except possible records—are released. The best fishing is from January through June, but February through May are peak.

Tarpon are not the only gamefish here; big snapper, barracuda, jacks, sharks, bream, and grouper are easily caught by anglers trolling up and down the river and the sea banks. As most of the coastal region is swampy, a number of short rivers drain Sierra Leone, most navigable only in the rainy season, which is primarily from May to October. These rivers are inhabited by crocodiles and hippos.

SIGHT FISHING

Some elements of sportfishing require a good deal of observation on the part of anglers. This takes the form of actually looking for fish and either stalking or hunting visible fish (almost always in shallow water), or looking for telltale signs of fish that cannot actually be seen.

General observation. Many anglers don't notice the little things that sometimes make a big difference in sportfishing. They don't see fish swirl after a lure. They don't see that quick moment when a fish spooks a bunch of bait and gives its presence away. They don't notice characteristics of the water that attract fish or stimulate activity.

Often this inattention is a matter of not being observant or of not knowing what some signs may mean. Observation is an important factor in fishing success. To some extent, on-the-water angling observation is a function of frequent fishing, but it is also a function of being in the right frame of mind and applying yourself to finding fish and thinking about what you're doing. This is especially so when the action is not fast and easy. Some anglers are simply not observant enough of natural signs because they rely on various gadgets, such as sonar and temperature gauges, a bit too heavily, forgetting that there are other aspects to fishing success besides the information gleaned from instrumentation.

S

Watching the water, for example, is very important in many ways, and helpful when pursuing many species of fish. Watching the water includes watching for reefs, rips, near-surface vegetation, current flows, shade, and water color.

Water color is an especially good example. The clarity of the water can be important to fish movement and/or location as well as to lure selection. If the water always looks the same to you in all places, you may not be looking closely enough at it.

Some species of fish are more likely to be in clear water (or the clearest possible) or are more prone to strike lures in clear water (because they can locate them better), and it would behoove you to look for such. The places where clear and turbid water mix—runoffs, creek mouths, tidal influxes, wind-affected edges, etc.—and the immediate environs around them, are sometimes the best locales to fish.

In certain instances, where dirty water, such as from a creek, enters a clearer body of water, the dirty water is carrying nutrients or small forage that attracts bait, and the bait in turn attract predators. Another good place to put a lure is where there are a lot of baitfish (or perhaps a place to not put a lure if there are none). When fishing for some species of fish at certain times of the year, especially in unfamiliar waters, it can be disconcerting if there is little or no sign of bait. That doesn't mean you won't catch fish; however, when you see bait flitting on or near the surface or in the shallows, that is often a sign directing you to the kinds of places to fish.

When the water is calm, you can spot bait or baitfish movement without much trouble by being attentive. When the water is roiled by wind and waves, it is much more difficult to make visual observations. The presence of some species of birds (see), incidentally, such as a shorebird like heron, can indicate an abundance of bait or small fish in an area.

When bait are schooled and being pushed aggressively by predators, it is quite easy to spot the action. Other times, just one fish is pursuing a single prey or a few fish, and the action is less obvious and perhaps more likely to be missed. Probably every angler has noticed a fish swirling and creating a commotion when it captured or chased some type of prey in either open water or the shallows; occasionally this activity results in a strike and hookup, although a gamefish may not even be responsible for the activity; people confuse the splash of a jumping mullet, for example, with feeding gamefish activity.

Nevertheless, fish that are stalking shallow water, that spook bait, or that capture some prey item on or near the surface, usually give away their presence and often are aggressive fish highly susceptible to capture at that moment. If you look for the signs of the presence of such fish, you'll probably be disappointed; but if you keep your eyes open and (just as important) listen while fishing, you will become aware of gamefish movement. This is especially true when casting and when fishing for most warmwater species of freshwater fish.

It is also true when fishing in coldwater streams. Both Atlantic and Pacific salmon, for example, will roll occasionally on or near the surface, sometimes in a very subtle manner. If you are unfamiliar with the water that you're fishing, this movement, though unrelated to feeding activity, will give you an indication of a fish lie and will point you toward an appropriate place to direct your efforts. Noticing a fish that jumps or rolls is obvious to many anglers, but not to all, especially when there is merely a rise on the surface that can be confused with the swirl of current.

Noticing bait that is in an agitated state is a subtlety that few anglers possess. Avid anglers describe this phenomenon as "nervous water," which is quite accurate although hard to convey. Nervous water is a surface patch, usually just a few yards across, where there is some slight rippling on the surface, distinctly different from that caused by current or light breezes. It happens when a pod of small baitfish is balled up and flitting about, neither feeding nor fleeing, but disturbed—usually because something is lurking nearby that means to maraud them shortly. If you see this action, work the area hard, keeping a lure handy that might imitate a small fish that is injured or struggling.

One of the easiest and best ways to enjoy more success through being observant is to watch your lures when you retrieve them, especially as they near the boat. Some fish are prone to swirl after shallow-running or surface lures and create a sizable boil in the water after they miss the lure in an apparent attempt to stun it. Anglers who aren't watching closely don't see those occasions when a fish strikes and misses the lure, and they cast elsewhere, though they might have been able to catch that particular fish or at least note its location for a later visit.

Stalking shallow fish. On some occasions, you're able to see fish in shallow water that are not actually in the process of chasing bait but are foraging below the surface, or merely taking a feeding or

Wading the flats to cast to wary species is a game of spotting and stalking; this angler and guide are fishing on the south coast of Cuba.

resting position. Spotting such fish is certainly helpful for making the best presentation in the proper locale. Obviously some species of fish actively feed in shallow water, and they are primarily caught in those environs by stalking and sight-casting to them, often by intercepting them. This is the basis of most flats fishing.

The most common fish that are stalked by sight fishing in shallow water include tarpon, permit, bonefish, and redfish in saltwater, as well as other species, like sharks, cobia, and mutton snapper. In freshwater, various trout and Atlantic salmon are objects of stalking, as are certain members of the sunfish family—largemouth bass, smallmouth bass, and bluegills—especially in springtime when they are spawning. Other stalked freshwater fish include northern pike and, very rarely, lake trout in far northern areas when they are feeding in shallows.

When trying to spot shallow-water fish, look not at the surface but below the surface and at the bottom. Look for something that stands out as being different, whose movement contrasts with the bottom locale enough for you to detect it. Don't stare at one spot for long, especially when you're searching for fish, and try to bring your peripheral vision into play. When you see the wake of a moving fish, realize that the forward edge of the wake is behind the fish and take this into account when making a cast that is intended to intercept it.

Sometimes it's important to be able to see fish before you cast to them because you have to be able to approach them without alarming them. Other times, it's important to see certain objects that might be harboring fish. Polarized sunglasses are a big help here; those with wraparound side-view protection are best. A cap with a wide bill and dark underside is also a good aid. For difficult viewing, even with a cap or sunglasses, put your hands around the corners of your glasses and cup them to reduce side glare.

If you're fishing with someone else who sees a fish that you do not, use the clock system (the bow of the boat is 12 o'clock and the stern is 6 o'clock) to figure out the specific location of the fish by having your companion give you specific directions; if your companion says a fish is at 2 o'clock and about 60 feet away, you know where to be looking. These directions can be accompanied by rod pointing to help narrow down the positioning; you can point to the spot where you think the fish is, and your companion can tell you to point more to the left or right to zero in on it.

Remember that visibility is improved from high vantage points. Wading anglers (and those sitting in a kayak or canoe) rarely can see into the water the way someone fishing from a boat can. However, in freshwater, especially on salmon rivers, anglers will walk high banks to get a viewing vantage, and some have been known to climb trees (watching from bridges is also common).

A person sitting in a boat cannot see as well as someone standing, and a person standing in the well of a boat has inferior vision compared with someone standing on a deck. The best vision comes from standing on platforms (see) or towers (see). Many flats guides, especially those who carry fly anglers, have transom platforms from which they pole, and these offer good visibility. Some flats boats have mini-towers over a center console; these are even better for visibility but are less conducive to fly casting, though fine for those using other types of tackle.
See: Finding Fish; Flat.

SIGHT INDICATOR

A visible lightweight object on the line used to detect subsurface strikes and monitor the position of the angler's offering (usually a nymph).
See: Strike Indicator.

SILICON CARBIDE GUIDE

Silicon carbide (SiC) is a material popularly used to form the ring in many fishing rod guides. Often called a ceramic, it is a hard material that resists abrasion well, although it can be brittle.
See: Rod, Fishing.

SILVERSIDES

Silversides are members of the Atherinidae family and occur throughout the world. Some are valued as food fish, and a few are caught for keeping in aquariums. They are important forage for larger predatory species, especially alongshore, in bays, and in estuaries.

All silversides lack a lateral line and have small, almost useless teeth. Their pelvic fins are located well behind the pectoral fins, and the small, spiny dorsal is well separated from the soft dorsal. The body is typically elongated. Some silversides live in freshwater; others are marine, found near shore. They are often called shiners but are more commonly referred to as "smelt," although they are not related to the true osmerid smelt (see).

One of the most prominent silversides is the California grunion (*Leuresthes tenuis*; see: grunion, California), which grows to 7$^1/_2$ inches in length and is famous for moonlight spawning runs and remarkable beach spawning. A similar fish is the gulf grunion (*L. sardina*), which is restricted to the Gulf of California.

Also prominent and frequently caught along Pacific piers is the larger (to 17$^1/_2$ inches) jacksmelt

California Grunion

Brook Silverside

(Atherinopsis californiensis; see: jacksmelt), which have small, unforked teeth in bands. This characteristic differentiates the jacksmelt from the California grunion and also from the topsmelt *(Atherinops affinis),* which grows to 12 inches but generally is in the same range as the jacksmelt. The topsmelt is most easily distinguished from the jacksmelt by its forked teeth set in a single row rather than in bands. These species constitute a sizable portion of the Pacific coast "smelt" catch.

Along the Atlantic coast, the tidewater silverside *(Menidia beryllina),* which grows to only 3 inches long, ranges from Massachusetts southward to the Gulf of Mexico. Although it is predominantly a saltwater species, it is also found in brackish water and freshwater. Other names frequently used for this species are whitebait and spearing. Several similar species occur in the same general range. These include the Atlantic silverside *(M. menidia)* and the Mississippi silverside *(M. audens),* a freshwater species.

The brook silverside *(Labidesthes sicculus),* which is 2 to 4 inches long, is also found only in freshwater, from the St. Lawrence River southward throughout the southeastern United States. Brook silverside schools are often observed skipping along the surface. This behavior has earned them the nickname skipjacks. Olive green above and silvery below, this species has a prominent silver stripe down each side. The snout is projected into a short beak, and the first dorsal fin is so small that it may go unnoticed. The brook silverside is sometimes used for bait but is not hardy.

SINGLE-ACTION REEL

A revolving spool reel whose spool revolves one time for every turn of the handle, resulting in a 1:1 retrieve ratio. The single-action reel, which is primarily used to store line, and which has been predominant in fly fishing, was the forerunner of all fishing reels, having been the only type of reel in existence until around the turn of the nineteenth century, when the multiplying reel came into existence.
See: Antique Fishing Tackle; Baitcasting Tackle; Flycasting Tackle.

SINGLE-FOOT GUIDE

A guide with a single attachment point to the blank of a fishing rod. A single-foot guide is advantageous for casting, and is primarily found on spinning rods, where it is placed on the underside of the rod.
See: Rod, Fishing.

SINGLE HAUL

Accelerating a fly line to load the rod either to help pick the line up off the water or to shoot out a greater length of it in the forward cast. Doing both of these during a cast is called a double haul.
See: Flycasting Tackle.

SINGLE HOOK

A hook with one point.
See: Hook.

SINKER

A metal fishing weight used to sink a lure or bait. There are many different shapes, sizes, and applications of sinkers. They are employed in freshwater and saltwater and primarily used for fishing with lightweight objects, especially natural bait.

Sinkers are made from a number of metals. They were once virtually all made of lead, and most sinkers in North America still are lead; however, an increasing number are being made from other materials due to toxicity concerns. Lead sinkers were banned years ago in Great Britain because it was believed that small sinkers (actually shot) were being swallowed by swans and killing them. This has led to the use of nontoxic metals, including brass, steel, tin, and tungsten, in small sinkers, although these were in somewhat scarce supply in the United States as of early 1999.

In North America, there has been a growing concern by environmental agencies about lead fishing sinkers (lead in shotgun loads was banned around water in the 1980s), and at least one state has enacted a ban on certain size lead sinkers and jigs due to loon mortality, while others have recommended that anglers voluntarily cease using small lead (in sinkers, jigs, and flies). This is likely to be a more widespread issue in the future, especially if the U.S. Environmental Protection Agency enacts regulations.

Naturally, these materials all differ in various ways, and both anglers and manufacturers are still adjusting to differences in densities, durability, cost, and other factors. Tin, for example, which is softer than other nonlead metals, is mainly being used in removable split shot. Steel, which is expensive but the most durable and noisiest metal, is being used in sliding and fixed sinkers. Brass is harder and noisier than lead but less so than steel; hard brass weights are less likely to be deformed, but poor quality control standards in production can lead to abrasive surfaces that will cut line.

Using sinkers. In an overall sense, there are fixed and free-sliding sinkers. Fixed versions attach directly to a fishing line or leader (dropper line) by being pinched, twisted, or tied; they move whenever the bait or lure moves and when a fish takes the bait or lure. Free-sliding, or slip, sinkers ride along the line; they are used almost exclusively with bait and allow the line to move when a fish takes the bait without moving the sinker, which provides less resistance than a fixed sinker and may be preferable for shy or light-biting fish.

Split shot, which are small pinch-on spheres that are commonly used in freshwater fishing, are usually attached firmly ahead of a hook and used with light line for suspending natural bait or drifting it along a stream bottom. Very light shot is also used with flies in trout fishing and with processed baits for coarse fishing. A rubber core sinker is fastened by turning the rubber core around the line ahead of the hook or lure; it is often used in trolling. Clinch sinkers are affixed like split shot. Split shot, egg, and pencil sinkers can be fixed to a dropper leader via a three-way swivel, which lessens hangups when fishing bait in fast water and facilitates unsnagging without losing the entire rig.

Obviously, heavier sinkers are needed the deeper you fish, the greater the wind pushes you while drifting, the faster you troll, or the faster the current. A golden rule for using sinkers is to use the lightest sinker that you can get away with and still fish in the necessary manner or place.

In addition to weight, sinker shape has an effect on casting, sink rate, and ability to hold bottom. Bulky sinkers are least castable and offer most air resistance; bottom-heavy sinkers offer the most

Sinkers used in trolling include: torpedo (1), torpedo-style bead chain (2), keel-style bead chain (3), bottom-walking (4 and 8), planing (5), clinch (6), rubber-core (7), and bottom-bouncing (9).

accuracy because they don't roll over in the air. Streamlined and compact sinkers have the best sink rate, which is of special interest in current and partially explains why split shot is so popular in rivers and streams. Split shot is also good for resisting snagging in current, because it rolls over rocky bottoms. In stillwater or where there is a soft bottom with light current, a sinker with a rounded bottom is adequate, but where there is heavier current or surf action, an angled sinker that digs into the bottom is necessary.

Trolling sinkers. Trolling sinkers include the torpedo sinker, which has minimal drag or water resistance because of shape; a torpedo-style bead chain sinker, which swivels and prevents line twist; a keel style, which tracks well with little swaying motion; a planing sinker, which dives to achieve depth; a clinch sinker, which is simple to add to or remove from fishing line; and a rubber core sinker, which is simple to use and has no abrasion. Many sizes and weights are available. These are all fastened in line, either being affixed on the main fishing line or tied to a leader. The bead chain styles are especially good for preventing line twist and, with a snap, aid leader and lure changing.

Slip sinkers. Sliding or slip sinkers include ball, egg or barrel, cone or bullet, and walking versions. Egg and ball sinkers slide freely on the line, are often stopped by a small split shot or a barrel swivel, and are preferred for open water. Cone shaped sinkers provide minimal drag, are relatively weedless, and are used with plastic worms. They may be pegged with a toothpick to keep them from sliding in heavy cover; some feature a corkscrewed stem that grabs the head of the worm and keeps the sinker and worm together. Walking sinkers are used with a stopper when casting or trolling with bait along the bottom; they remain upright when a fish runs with the bait.

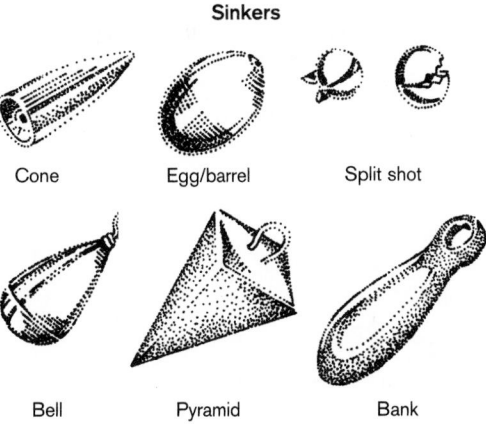
Sinkers

Cone   Egg/barrel   Split shot

Bell   Pyramid   Bank

Bottom sinkers. Bottom fishing sinkers include pyramid, bank, bell, and split shot. Choice depends on fishing conditions, including the species you seek, the depth to be fished, and such factors as current and wave action. Pyramid sinkers hold bottom especially well where there is much current or wave action and are especially useful where there is an undertow current. Bank sinkers are good in deep water and cast well. Split shot are preferred for light tackle. Dipsey sinkers are also used with light to medium tackle and where bait is suspended off the bottom above the sinker.

SINKING LINE

A fly line weighted to sink below the surface; there are full-sink lines and partial-sink lines, the latter sinking only at the tip.
See: Flycasting Tackle.

SINKING PLUG

See: Plug.

SINK-TIP LINE

A fly line with a floating body and a sinking tip section, also known as a floating/sinking line.
See: Flycasting Tackle.

SISCOWET

The siscowet, also known as siscoet, is a variety of lake trout (see: trout, lake) found in Lake Superior. It once existed in Lakes Huron and Michigan as well. It dwells at depths of up to 600 feet and was known to commercial fishermen as "fat trout" because of its high (70 to 90 percent) oil content, which made it mostly of value when salted or smoked. This fish lives and spawns deeper than other lake trout (which are referred to by some taxonomists as "lean" trout, in order to differentiate them from the siscowet) and may be genetically different or evolving. It is not a sport-caught fish.

Lake Superior also has a variety of lake trout known as the humper (also bumper, paperbelly, and bank trout), found on isolated offshore humps and reefs. It has a larger eye than the siscowet or the lake trout, a thin abdominal wall, a low fat content, and is small and long-lived.

SKAMANIA

A summer-run strain of steelhead (see).

SKATE

See: Rays and Skates.

SKATER

A high-floating dry fly, created with thick, long hackle. It is fished in a gliding (skating) manner in a river or stream. A skater is primarily used on Atlantic salmon but may also be effective on trout.
See: Fly.

SKEG

The lowest projecting part of an outboard or inboard/outboard motor, also known as the fin.

SKI BOAT

In North America a ski boat is any motorboat used to tow water-skiers. However, in South Africa, a ski boat is a small boat that is launched with great struggle and nerve from the beach to get through and fish beyond the surf line. Once very primitive, these boats, now equipped with two outboard motors and well-outfitted for angling, are launched from the beach as a necessity due to a lack of harbors and formal access sites. Up to four anglers may fish in ski boats, and they are used for inshore and offshore angling, sometimes for pursuing large pelagic species. Ski-boat anglers are numerous, and many ski-boat clubs exist.
See: South Africa.

SKIFF

This is a catch-all boating term, now used less frequently and primarily with regard to saltwater, which refers to small boats, usually not more than 16 feet in length, that are meant for all-purpose use, often in shallow and/or quiet waters. It may refer to a dory or small craft used as a tender to larger, moored boats, or a utility jonboat, or a small runabout. Generally, a skiff has a flat or slightly round hull and a pointed bow. It may be propelled by oars or a small outboard motor. Public rental boats at marinas are often referred to as skiffs.
See: Boat; Flats Boat; Jonboat.

SKIN CARE

See: First Aid.

SKINNING

See: Fish Preparation—Cleaning/Dressing.

SKIP CAST

A bounce cast (see).

SKIPJACK, BLACK   Euthynnus lineatus.
Other names—little tuna, false albacore, spotted tuna, mackerel tuna, skipjack; Spanish: barrilete negro, bonito negro, pataseca.

A member of the Scombridae family of mackerel, bonito, and tuna, the black skipjack is commonly caught by anglers, usually while trolling or casting for other pelagic species. It is often used as a bait for big-game fish. Its food value has mixed ratings, although it is of some commercial importance. Its flesh is dark red and the taste is strong.

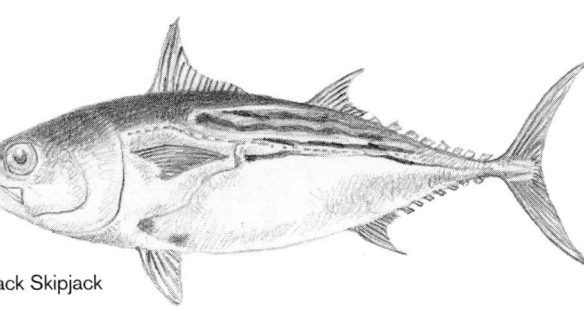

ack Skipjack

Identification. The dorsal fin of the black skipjack has 13 to 15 spines and is high anteriorly. This distinguishes it from bonito *(Sarda)*, which have a relatively long and low first dorsal fin. The anal fin, which has 11 to 13 rays, is similar to the second dorsal fin in size and shape. The body lacks scales, except on the anterior corselet and along the lateral line. This is the only species of *Euthynnus* with 37, instead of the usual 39, vertebrae. Each jaw has 20 to 40 small, conical teeth. Bonito have fewer and larger conical teeth. Mackerel have flat, triangular teeth.

The black skipjack is distinguished from similar species by the four or five broad, straight, black stripes that run horizontally along the back and by its dark spots between the pectoral and ventral fins. In live specimens, stripes may be visible on the venter as well as on the back, which has frequently led to confusion with the skipjack tuna *(Katsuwonus pelamis)*. The stripes on the belly rarely persist long after death in the black skipjack, however, whereas they remain prominent in the skipjack tuna *(see: tuna, skipjack)*.

Size. Black skipjack are reported to attain a maximum length of 33 inches and a weight of 20 pounds, although they are usually encountered weighing several pounds. The all-tackle world record is a 26-pound specimen.

Distribution. This species occurs in tropical and warm temperate waters of the eastern Pacific Ocean from California to northern Peru, including the Galápagos Islands, and rarely the central Pacific.

Habitat. Like other pelagic and migratory species, the black skipjack occurs in schools near the surface of coastal and offshore waters. It sometimes forms multispecies schools with other scombrids.

Food. Black skipjack feed predominantly on small surface fish, squid, and crustaceans.

Angling. These fish can be hooked by trolling or casting small whole baits or strip baits, or small lures such as spoons, plugs, jigs, and feathers. They reportedly will strike lures trolled at speeds of up to 8 or 10 mph. Skipjack are usually caught deliberately for use as whole or cut baits, and fish caught incidental to other angling efforts are often kept for use as baits. Whole live skipjacks of several pounds are rigged and live-lined in some areas for marlin.

See: Bonito, Pacific; Mackerel; Tuna.

SKIRT

A dressing of synthetic material, hair, or rubber attached to a hook shank or lure body. Skirts are commonly made of silicone and Mylar, but may be rubber, vinyl, bucktail hair, squirrel hair, and other materials; they give body to a lure as well as action when retrieved. These may be used in some fashion and in varying lengths on most types of lures, but are especially common on spinnerbaits *(see)*, buzzbaits *(see)*, and jigs *(see)*.

SLAB

(1) A term for large panfish, usually crappie and occasionally bluegills.

See: Bluegill; Crappie, Black; Crappie, White.

(2) A flat wide-bodied lead spoon used by freshwater anglers for deep jigging.

See: Jigging; Spoon.

SLACK LINE CAST

An in-air flycasting maneuver that places slack in a fly line as it is laid on the water.

See: Mending.

SLACK TIDE

The state of the tide when tidal current velocity is near zero.

See: Tides.

SLEEPERS

Of little angling interest, sleepers are distributed in tropical and subtropical waters throughout the world. They are so called because of their habit of resting on the bottom as though "sleeping," rarely moving unless disturbed. If not resting on the bottom, they often remain suspended and motionless in the water, diving down to hide when frightened or in danger. Sleepers are closely related to gobies, although they lack the sucking disk that is customary in gobies and instead have separated ventral and pelvic fins. Most sleepers are fairly small, although the larger species have some food value. Sleepers are predatory in their feeding, hiding in weeds and crevices in wait for fish; they will strike live baits and are occasionally attracted by spinners, flies, and small plugs.

Bigmouth Sleeper

The fat sleeper *(Dormitator maculatus)* can reach 2 feet in length but is usually less than a foot long. It inhabits brackish waters and freshwaters through the Caribbean and the warm Atlantic northward to the Carolinas. Usually dark brown and mottled, it has a bluntly rounded head, a large mouth, no visible lateral line, and a rounded caudal fin. It bears a resemblance to a fat mullet, but its second dorsal and anal fins are large and of equal size. It makes a good aquarium pet because it can tolerate a wide range of water conditions.

The bigmouth sleeper *(Gobiomorus dormitor)* occurs along the Florida coasts, in the Caribbean, and also in freshwater. It can exceed 2 feet in length and is much thinner than the fat sleeper. It has a large, pikelike mouth and obliquely squared-off second dorsal and anal fins. The bigmouth sleeper has an olive green body and its first dorsal fin is outlined in black.

A 4-inch species, the blue sleeper *(Isoglossus calliurus)* inhabits the deep waters of the Gulf of Mexico; a 6-inch species, the emerald sleeper *(Erotelis smaragdus),* lives off the southern coasts of Florida and in the Caribbean, where it blends with bright green algae. The blackfin dartfish *(Ptereleotris tricolor)* is also striking in color, with light green blue in front, purple blue from the second dorsal fins to the caudal fin, and a tail that is bright yellow in the center.

SLICK

An oily section of the water's surface, caused by oil seeping from chum *(see)* or by the residue of game-fish feeding on schools of bait.

SLIDER RIG

A slider rig is a lure that is affixed to a short leader and run down a fishing line while trolling. Also known as a "cheater," it's a means of fishing more than one lure on a single line attached to a downrigger *(see).* This does not involve using two rods *(see: stacking).*

To rig it, tie a snap swivel to one end of a 3-foot length of line and attach a lure, preferably a spoon, to the snap swivel. Tie a snap to the other end of the leader, then clip it to the line that is already connected to a downrigger release below the boat. With the boat moving forward, carefully toss the lure into the water behind the main fishing line and watch to make sure it isn't fouled. The slider rig will drift out of sight and ultimately stop well above the downrigger weight at a point where the main line is bowed most sharply in the water.

When a fish strikes the slider lure, it pulls back on the main fishing line and pops the release to which that line is attached. The rig slides down the main fishing line and stops at the snap or lure there (use a bead to keep the upper snap from

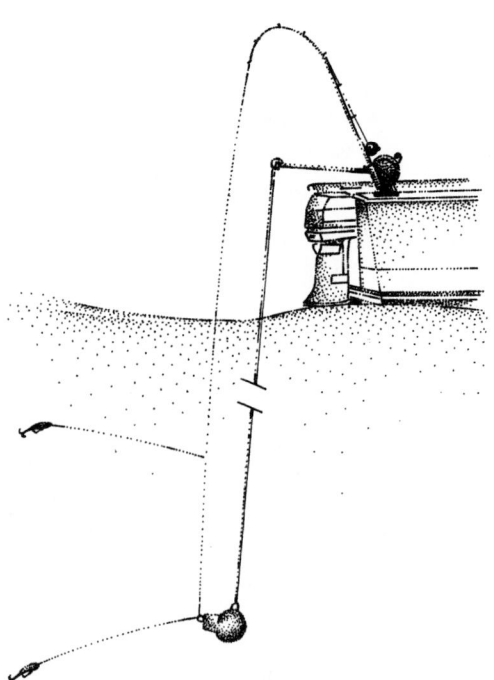

This depiction of a slider rig shows how it is possible to place the main lure at the same level as the downrigger weight, while placing a slider along the fishing line at a higher level; when a fish takes either lure, the fishing line detaches from the release clip at the weight.

marring the lower snap, knot, or line-tie area). The exact depth of the slider rig will be unknown, but you'll have two lures on one line and one downrigger.

Slider rigs probably are of little value when the main, or lower, lure is fished less than 20 feet down. If you drop the main lure down 12 feet and put a slider rig on, you'll see that the slider runs just below the surface; so at 20 feet, you might be getting the slider down only 8 feet or less, and there may be little reason to expect to get a fish on such a short line so close to the boat.

One drawback to slider rigs is that you lose a lot of fish that strike them because the hook doesn't get set into the mouth of the fish very forcefully. On the other hand, sliders give you the opportunity to put a different type and color of lure out. If a slider gets a strike or catches a fish, this may convince you to change the other lures or the depth at which you're trolling. Sliders are particularly useful when trolling deep, when fish may be scattered at all levels, when you are unsure of what depth to fish but need to scour a lot of water, or when you have no idea what color lure to use and need to try many different patterns.

There are some devices available that accomplish the same thing, but can be located more precisely on the fishing line, sliding down once a fish is on.

When using slider rigs it's possible to get double hookups (doubleheaders). This is interesting from both a fish playing and fish netting standpoint, especially when the catch is of decent size. Netting a double can be troublesome, because the fish caught on a slider rig will be several feet behind the fish on the main line. Once you net the lead fish, it's hard to get the trailing one; it's best to get the trailing one first, though this isn't always possible. Such problems aren't encountered that often, so it's something you can happily endure.

When using any type of slider rig, be careful not to exceed the number of lures, hooks, or hook points legally allowed per rod or per angler in the waters you're fishing. Be aware also of the number of rods allowed per angler. In Canada, only one rod is allowed per angler; in most states each angler can troll with two rods. American charter captains, many of whom fish out of 25- to 35-foot boats capable of holding five anglers plus the captain and mate, technically can fish two rods per person. Big-boat trollers may have as many as six downriggers; lines can be stacked on several of them to get eight or nine lures deep, and several of these will be equipped with sliders as well, so a veritable school of lures is swimming beneath the boat. Couple all of this with one or two rods on diving planers and/or flatlines, and you can see why it takes a good crew and a good boat handler to work all this without major problems.
See: Downrigger Fishing.

SLIP
A place at a marina where a boat is moored, usually between sets of pilings, piers, or floats; also referred to as a stall or berth.

SLIP BOBBER/FLOAT
Known as a slip bobber or slip float, this is a light-weight float *(see)* that slides along the fishing line, and is used in conjunction with some type of stop (a bead or thin line knot) on the line to position a bait at a certain level. This is usually used when the depth to be fished is greater than the length of the fishing rod (which is equal to the maximum that can be cast). In use, fishing line slips through or along the float until the stop halts the bait (or sometimes light jig) at the right depth.

SLIP CLUTCH
The drag mechanism on a fishing reel.
See: Drag.

SLIPPING
See: Backtrolling.

SLIP SINKER
A sinker *(see)* that slides freely on a line; this term is mostly associated with cone-shaped products used with soft worms *(see)*.

SLOT LIMIT
A restriction pertaining to the size of fish that may be kept, a slot limit prohibits anglers from keeping fish that are either outside of a specified range or within the specified range. If a slot limit is meant to protect fish of a certain size, then fish within that range have to be released, and fish outside that range may be kept. If a slot limit is meant to encourage harvesting fish of a certain size, then fish within that range may be kept, while fish outside that range have to be released.

Slot limits may be established for various species but are especially implemented for controlling largemouth bass populations. It is common for a slot limit to be established to protect fish of a certain size. For example, if a slot limit on bass prohibits keeping fish between 14 and 18 inches in size, then the effect is to aid the survival of fish in that range (presumably because there is a lack of such fish) in order to produce more large specimens; the larger fish will be effective predators and theoretically help control forage fish populations, including such species as shad and sunfish.

A slot limit, like a minimum length limit, must be tailored to a specific environment in order to respond to existing conditions. It is seldom a universally applicable regulation, and in order for it to be effective on a designated water, there must be angler compliance. For example, if there are few large bass in a given body of water as a result of high angling mortality, then a slot limit should help foster more big bass by protecting fish in the slot range and causing more mortality of smaller fish. However, if anglers treat the slot limit as a minimum length limit (for example, if a minimum length limit of 12 inches in a lake is changed to a slot of 14 to 18 inches because the lake has too many small fish and no large ones), the eventual result is a lot of small, medium, and large fish; and the impact on the forage base may be such that food becomes scarcer and growth rates decline, and the quality of the fish suffers. Therefore, anglers must keep fish that are under the size of this slot limit in order for the slot limit to achieve the desired goal, and especially for there to be a wide size range of fish that grow at desirable and sustainable levels.

A slot limit is seldom a permanent measure and usually changes over time to adapt to the changing status of both the gamefish and the forage species that they eat. It is a legal game regulation established by the fisheries agency that has jurisdiction over the location being fished, and enforced by fish and wildlife conservation officers.
See: Fisheries Management; Minimum Length Limit; Regulations.

SLOUGH
A marshy backwater; a small, fingerlike dead-end channel off a river or lake that often contains warmwater species, especially largemouth bass.

S

SLOVENIA

The southeastern republic of Slovenia, formerly a province of Yugoslavia, is a small country with an area of just 20,253 square kilometers. Mountainous and heavily forested, however, Slovenia offers among Europe's best trout and grayling fishing.

Slovenia is bounded by Austria on the north, Hungary on the northeast, Croatia on the southeast, Italy on the west, and 47 kilometers of Adriatic coastline on the west. The best fishing is in the main rivers and tributaries of the Julian Alps in the northwestern part of the country.

Rivers and streams such as the Obra, Unec, Sava Bohinjka, Krka, Soca, and Iscica, and their tributaries, contain sizable populations of brown trout (locally called *poto na postrv*), rainbow trout *(arenka)*, and European grayling *(lipan)*; also present, in streams that flow to the Adriatic Sea, is the rare marble trout *(Salmo mormoratus)*, and softmouth trout *(S. obtusirostris)*, and huchen, which are found in streams that flow to the Danube River and eventually the Black Sea.

Snowcapped peaks and verdant valleys characterize Slovenia, and the rivers and scenery draw not only anglers but also rafters, kayakers, and others. All this attention makes some waters more difficult to fish in summer. April, September, and October are preferred for less crowded conditions, but summer fishing can be productive, especially for those who hike away from the more accessible areas. Snow runoff may prevent any fishing on some waters in spring. Nonetheless, most streams have good populations of fish, which are wary but beautifully colored and well marked.

The Obra is a meadow stream with beautifully marked brown trout and grayling; it is accessed about 10 miles from Postojna. The Unec is a spring creek also located near Postojna and is known for large grayling as well as brown trout. The Sava Bohinjka is a large, quick-flowing stream offering brown trout, rainbow trout, and grayling. The Krka, 25 miles south of the capital city of Ljubljana, flows through the village of Krka and has browns, rainbows, and grayling. The Soca has good numbers of these species, as well as marble trout; it flows from high peaks through gorges and villages and into the Adriatic. Its tributaries, the Tolminka and Idrijca, are also notable. The Iscica is a weedy, marshy stream about 6 miles from Ljubljana and harbors grayling and brown trout.

Fly fishing is the primary legal method for pursuing trout and grayling. Restrictions pertaining to barbless hooks, fish size, creel limits, and open seasons vary according to location along each river and from river to river. Fishing permits are necessary and can be obtained at tourist offices and major hotels.

SMELT

Smelt are small, silvery anadromous fish of the Osmeridae family that live primarily in the sea but

European Smelt

make spawning runs into freshwater streams, as salmons do. A few smelt are strictly marine; others live only in large freshwater lakes and spawn in tributary brooks and streams. Some are marine by origin but have adapted to a strictly freshwater environment; populations of some species live both in the sea and in freshwater. In all environments they are extremely important as forage for predators, including many game species.

All smelt inhabit the cool waters of the Northern Hemisphere in the Atlantic, Arctic, and Pacific Oceans and their drainages. The family is related to salmonids and contains 11 species in six genera, and is most generously represented in Pacific waters; many smelt species are so similar in appearance that they are difficult to distinguish. Most are harvested commercially. Smelt are among the top commercial fish exports of Canada, most of this going to markets in the United States. They are seldom pursued or captured on rod and reel by anglers but may be harvested recreationally in the winter and during spawning runs, often with a dipnet *(see)*.

Like salmon and trout, smelt have a stubby adipose fin just in front of the tail. The lower jaw projects slightly beyond the tip of the snout. A lateral line is prominent, and there are no scales on the head. They are generally small (most growing to no more than 8 inches), schooling fish, often found in enormous numbers; in spring, great numbers move from their marine or freshwater habitats to tributary waters to spawn. Only one species, the anadromous Pacific longfin smelt *(Spirinchus thaleichthys)*, spawns in late fall and early winter. All species spawn at night. In North America, the pond smelt *(Hypomesus olidus)* and the rainbow smelt *(Osmerus mordax)* are considered excellent food fish. In quantity, freshly caught smelt have an odor more nearly like cucumbers than fish.

The rainbow smelt, which is also commonly known as the American smelt, is the species most familiar to anglers and most common in North American fish markets. It ranges from Nova Scotia southward to Virginia along the Atlantic coast and also occurs in inland lakes. In the early 1900s, the rainbow smelt was introduced to the Great Lakes and other large, cold bodies of water to serve as forage fish. In nearly all instances, the smelt prospered, although the freshwater variety do not grow as large on average as the marine variety. This species is commonly caught by dipnetting in streams. The European smelt *(Osmerus eperlanus)* is similar in size and habits to the rainbow smelt. It is harvested in large numbers in northern European waters.

Among the other smelt species are the surf smelt *(Hypomesus pretiosus)*, which, as its name suggests, spends most of its life in the surf and also spawns there. The closely related pond smelt *(H. olidus)* lives wholly in freshwater ponds along the west coast of North America, apparently having become landlocked in the geologic past. The same species occurs also in Japan, where it is marine but enters freshwater streams to spawn. The delta smelt *(H. transpacificus)* is a species from both Japan and the eastern Pacific in California, where it lives in freshwater and brackish water. The whitebait smelt *(Allosmerus elongatus)*, the smaller night smelt *(Spirinchus starksi)*, and the longfin smelt *(S. thaleichthys)* are other Pacific species that are commercially fished to a limited extent and are used also as baits. The capelin *(Mallotus villosus)*, which is circumpolar in arctic seas, is another prominent smelt, as is the eulachon *(Thaleichthys pacificus)*, an oily fish found throughout northern Pacific waters.
See: Capelin; Eulachon; Smelt, Rainbow.

SMELT, RAINBOW   *Osmerus mordax.*

Other names—American smelt, frostfish, leefish, toothed smelt, freshwater smelt; French: *éperlan du nord.*

One of the most prominent members of the Osmeridae family of smelt, the rainbow smelt is an important forage species for predatory fish and a principal target for inland and coastal commercial fishing. It is the subject of some recreational activity, particularly via dipnetting in the spring during spawning runs and ice fishing for land-locked populations in some lakes.

The rainbow smelt is a close relative of the eulachon *(see)* of the Pacific, the pond smelt *(Hypomesus olidus)* of the western Arctic, the capelin *(see)* of the Atlantic, and the European smelt *(Osmerus eperlanus).*

Originally an anadromous coastal species, rainbow smelt were first stocked inland in 1906, in streams and lakes feeding Lake Michigan in order to provide forage for salmonids. Eventually large rainbow smelt populations were found in all the Great Lakes, especially Lake Erie. There is some evidence that the rainbow smelt inhabiting Lake Ontario were not a result of these stockings but of an independent movement from Lake Champlain stocks.

Commercial fishing for rainbow smelt was primarily centered on the Atlantic coast until the middle of the twentieth century; in 1948, an experimental gillnet fishery was established in the Great Lakes and became increasingly successful. Gradually, the Great Lakes fishery exceeded Atlantic coast ventures in terms of the weight of total landings and their market value. Coastal anadromous rainbow smelt, however, are more highly valued—fetching more than twice the price—than inland smelt and are considered to be

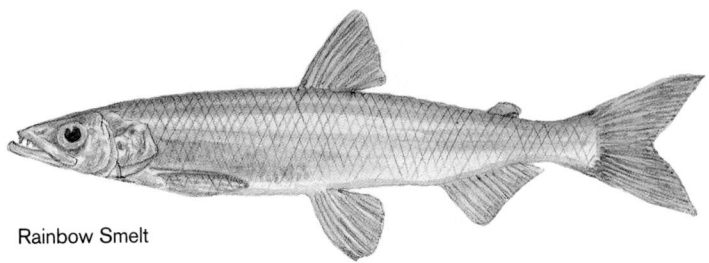

Rainbow Smelt

of superior food quality. Anglers target rainbow smelt strictly as a food fish, and this species generates extensive efforts in the Great Lakes and the coastal areas of the Maritime Provinces and the northeastern U.S.

Identification.   The rainbow smelt is a slender, silver fish, with a pale green or olive green back. Fresh from the water, the sides of the fish take on a purple, blue, or pink iridescent hue. The scales on the rainbow smelt are large and easily detached, and at spawning time those on the males develop small tubercles, resembling tiny buttons that serve as a mark of their sex. The lower jaw of the fish projects beyond the upper one, and the entire mouth extends beyond the middle of the eye. On the tip of the tongue are large teeth. One large dorsal fin is located about halfway along the back, and behind that is a small adipose fin.

Size/Age.   Most rainbow smelt are less than 8 inches long, although some coastal specimens measuring 14 inches have been found in the coastal waters of the Maritimes and in Lake Ontario. They may live for at least six years.

Distribution.   The rainbow smelt is widely distributed throughout eastern and western North America, inhabiting coastal waters as well as countless inland freshwater lakes. On the Atlantic coast they range from New Jersey in the south to Hamilton Inlet, Labrador, in the north. Their inland habitats include lakes in northeastern states and provinces, as well as throughout the Great Lakes from the St. Lawrence River to Lake Superior.

Populations of rainbow smelt also exist on the Pacific coast from Vancouver Island northward around Alaska and eastward along the Arctic coast at least as far as the Mackenzie River. The same species also ranges westward along the Arctic coast of Russia to the North Sea, including the White Sea. These westerly fish are identified by some taxonomists as arctic rainbow smelt *(O. mordax dentex)*, whereas the easterly species is identified by those taxonomists as *O. mordax mordax.*

Habitat.   The rainbow smelt is a pelagic schooling species, inhabiting inshore coastal regions and the midwaters of lakes. Because it is sensitive to both light and warmer temperatures, schools of rainbow smelt tend to concentrate near the bottom of lakes and coastal waters during daylight hours.

Life history.   In the spring, both anadromous and landlocked adult rainbow smelt migrate

S

upstream to freshwater spawning grounds. In some rivers, rainbow smelt begin their upstream migration before the spring thaw has begun. Spawners reach the tide head in the main tributaries when the water temperature is only 4° to 5°C. In the Great Lakes, migration begins shortly after ice out, when the water temperature is at least 8°C. They enter smaller streams when the temperature is 6° to 7°C. Anadromous rainbow smelt in the Gaspé Peninsula spawn in similar temperatures, although some land-locked populations in Lake Champlain and lakes in New Hampshire may spawn in temperatures as low as 2°C.

Rainbow smelt remain at spawning sites for a number of days. Larger smelt of all ages spawn first, and the average size of rainbow smelt on the spawning grounds decreases as the season advances. Shortly after spawning, many males die. Surviving males and females remain for about 5 to 10 days before migrating downstream.

Some rainbow smelt are mature at two years of age and all are mature at age 3. Fecundity varies from one area to another, and anadromous populations are more fecund than landlocked populations. A fully grown female rainbow smelt from the Miramichi River in New Brunswick will produce roughly 70,000 eggs, whereas a similar-size female from Lake Superior will produce roughly 31,000 eggs.

Spawning occurs mainly at night, typically over a gravelly bottom. The eggs are adhesive and stick to the gravel or other bottom objects. The time required for the eggs to hatch depends on the water temperature and can vary from 20 to 50 days. Female rainbow smelt grow more quickly than males, attain a larger size, and live longer. Rainbow smelt restricted to small inland lakes are usually smaller than they are elsewhere, and often do not exceed 4 inches in length.

Food. Zooplankton, insect larvae, aquatic worms, and small fish constitute the diet of rainbow smelt, with zooplankton being predominant.

Angling. In some places, including northeastern Canada, rainbow smelt are fished with hook and line from docks during summer months. Fly anglers sometimes take smelt on artificial flies in summer, although these fish generally stay in deep, cool water. In winter, landlocked rainbow smelt in lakes are caught on hook and line through the ice. Thousands of people use dipnets and seines to capture rainbow smelt when they are abundant in spring, and regulations for this activity exist in all parts of their range.

Rainbow smelt dipping can be an extremely social activity and is usually done at night, wearing hip boots and carrying a lantern, a fine-meshed dipnet, and a bucket. Dipping usually commences once the first warm rain raises the water temperature above 39°F and continues for roughly two- to three weeks. Some people stalk rainbow smelt in the shallows and scoop them up one or two at a time as they see them in the light of their lantern. Others dip blindly in the deeper part of a stream, which can be arm-wearying when there are few or no fish but highly productive during peak run times (one to many dozen may be netted). Most dipping occurs in tributary streams, but in some places, especially the Great Lakes, it also occurs along the lakeshore and around sheltered points.

Rainbow smelt must be kept on ice and cleaned quickly to preserve their flavor; this is sometimes difficult in the middle of the night when you're tired and have a few quarts of fish to clean.
See: Smelt.

SMOKING

A term for the creation of a frothy, misty turbulence and silvery trail of bubbles, accompanied by an occasional roostertail, on the surface of the water as made by certain offshore trolling lures and teasers when running properly at a high speed.
See: Trolling Lures, Saltwater.

SMOLT

A young silvery salmon migrating from freshwater to the sea.
See: Salmon, Atlantic.

SNAG

(1) An obstruction on which a lure is likely to get stuck, especially a conglomeration of debris such as tree branches and brush.
See: Unsnagging.

(2) To deliberately hook a fish in any part of its body other than the inside of its mouth.
See: Snagging.

SNAGGING

Technically, snagging is the hooking of a fish in any part of its body other than the inside of its mouth. It may be called snatching and is also referred to as foul hooking, but, in a practical sense, foul hooking is considered an accidental or incidental hooking of a fish at a site other than in the mouth, whereas snagging has the connotation of being done deliberately. Snagging is commonly done by a rapid drawing motion, using a handheld rod and attached line with single or multiple fish hooks. Often the hook is weighted on the shank for casting and sinking purposes, and the gap of the hook is wide enough to permit the hook to sink more readily into the flesh of a fish. One of the reasons for regulations that set a maximum hook gap is to inhibit the ability to snag, usually in places where this activity has occurred frequently or was once permissible.

Fish that are the target of snagging may or may not be visible. It is not always necessary to use a rapid drawing motion to snag fish. Some snagging occurs when fish are crowded and a hook is retrieved slowly until it bumps a fish; then the fisherman instantly sets the hook as if responding to a strike. Also, fish that are crowded may be snagged while trolling with a multihooked lure, although this is usually an accidental occurrence.

Whether accidental or deliberate, snagging is generally prohibited except for certain nongame species, such as paddlefish, and for some Great Lakes fish, such as salmon, during their spawning runs. Fish that are accidentally snagged or foulhooked by law must be returned unharmed to the water. In some places, it is legal to gather baitfish for personal use by snagging; small herring, bunkers, and other baitfish are sometimes snagged with small hooks and put in an aerated well for later use as live bait, especially for stripers.

Legal snagging of gamefish has generated controversy among anglers and nonanglers alike. It has been a hotly debated topic in places bordering the Great Lakes for many years. Some state fisheries agencies, responding to outcries, have outlawed snagging for salmon and trout in tributaries, although they once encouraged the practice to provide support for fledgling fisheries programs and as a means of harvesting fish that would die and be wasted. New York encouraged and permitted this practice as recently as the mid 1990s, at one time erroneously claiming that the migrating salmon could not be caught by means other than snagging. In Great Lakes tributaries, the crowding of rivers by people acting like game hogs and slinging leaded hooks in an attempt to snag big salmon brought out the very worst behavior and created a repugnant social fishing spectacle. Gradually this inappropriate activity has been curtailed and is less prevalent (legally) than it was in the 1970s and 1980s.

Snagging is still practiced in specific places and for certain species, and where legal it is considered a form of recreational fishing. However, snagging is not treated as sportfishing by the general angling community and is widely considered unethical and unsportsmanlike.
See: Foul Hook; Regulations.

SNAKE
A term, often derogatory, used for chain pickerel and small northern pike.

SNAKE GUIDE
The upper light-wire guides on a fly rod that aid the passage of fly line during casting and retrieval.
See: Flycasting Tackle.

SNAP
A metal connector between fishing line and a lure. Snaps are knotted to the fishing line and connected to the wire line-tie loop of a lure or to a split ring (see) that is connected to that loop.

In many cases, fishing line is tied directly to a lure. Lures that spin or roll when retrieved or trolled cause twist in the fishing line; twisting is countered by using some type of swivel (see). Lures that do not twist, which includes some spoons (see) and virtually all floating/diving plugs, do not need a swivel; they can be fished with a snap for two reasons, the most important of which is to enhance lure action. This is usually done with lures that do not have a split ring attached to the line-tie area. You can put a split ring there and tie the line directly to this, or you can use a snap; the snap should have a rounded bend to facilitate lure movement. The second, and subordinate, reason for using a snap is simply for convenience sake. A snap makes it easy to change lures quickly without having to retie knots. This may be especially useful with some lines that are difficult to tie knots in, such as thin-diameter microfilament lines (see: line).

Though convenient, snaps lead to problems and should only be used if really necessary. Poor quality snaps, or light snaps used with too heavy tackle, are the main causes of problems. They can be the weakest link in the angler-to-fish scenario due to their strength. If the rated breaking strength of a snap is 10 pounds, for example, and you're using 20-pound line, it's very possible that you could force the snap open, and lose the lure and/or fish, when maximum pressure is applied. It is unlikely that you'll know what the breaking strength of most snaps is when they are preattached to a lure or when buying them in bulk (though some have the strength noted on the packaging), but you can test the lighter ones with a heavy-duty spring scale.

Snaps

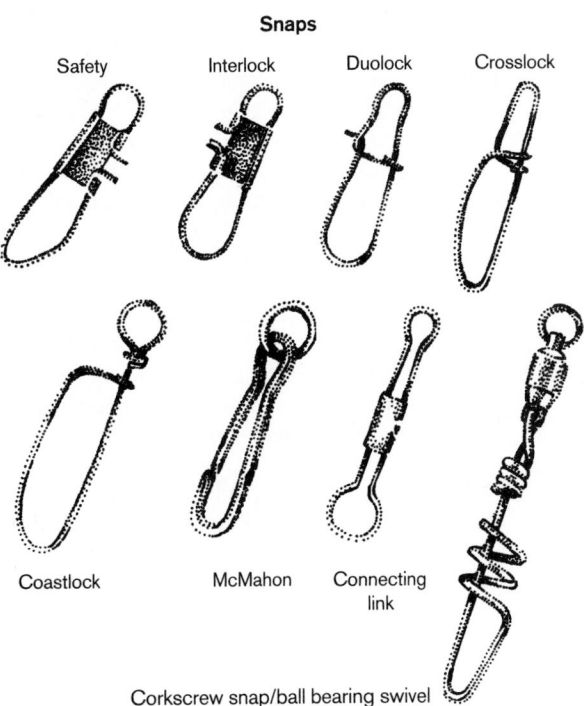

Safety   Interlock   Duolock   Crosslock

Coastlock   McMahon   Connecting link

Corkscrew snap/ball bearing swivel

S

It would be worthwhile to clip a few different snaps around a firm object, attach a reliable scale to the clips, and then pull on them until the clip breaks, noting how much pressure it takes to do so. The amount of force that it takes to open, straighten, or collapse a snap is a key to its usage.

Though you should generally use the size of snap that complements the lure and line diameter, strength is a function of size and thickness of the metal, so take this into consideration. It is misguided economy to use thin metal snaps—especially the common two-piece safety snaps that are cheap and popularly used in freshwater—so avoid these or replace them on lures or rigs that come equipped with them.

Strength and ease of use are also functions of the locking design. The safety snap model, which has a sharp bend and doesn't really lock (the tag end sits in a guarded channel), is one of the poorest snaps but cheap and commonly used. A similar two-piece snap is the interlock (or lock snap) model, which is only slightly better because the tag end rests in a guarded channel and tucks around the edge for more holding power. Both of these are subject to failure after repeated opening and closing.

One-piece all-wire snaps in which the tempered wire wraps around itself are better than the previous items. The common duolock model has a double-end opening that allows attachment to two items with closed eye rings; this is a good, moderately priced, easy-to-use connector that is also found as part of light- to medium-duty snap-swivels. This snap is used by many freshwater anglers when tied to spoons and plugs, and is favored because of its rounded bend. Another popular and strong model is the crosslock, which has double ends that meet on the same plane and abut each other; the bend is less rounded, however, so it does not maximize action for some lures. Other types that are especially popular in saltwater include the coastlock snap, which has a single-opening end that is especially strong and common on many big-game swivels; the tournament snap, which is similar to but stronger than the coastlock; the heavy-duty corkscrew snap; and the McMahon snap, a dual grip model.

Other types of connectors that can loosely be considered snaps include a variety of lightweight light-wire models for fly fishing, some of which are really spring clips, and connecting links, which are double-looped wire with a sliding sleeve.

As for color or finish, some anglers prefer flat black; others silver and gold. The silver and gold colors sometimes help attract fish, which is viewed positively by many freshwater anglers and negatively by most saltwater anglers. Fish attracted to the snap may strike ahead of the lure instead of at the body of the lure where the hooks are; in bigger and toothier saltwater species, this may result in cutoffs.

SNAPPER

Snapper are members of the large Lutjanidae family of fish, which includes more than 100 species. These fish inhabit tropical or subtropical waters in the Atlantic, Indian, and Pacific Oceans. Most are schooling species, although sizes vary widely. Likewise they range by species from shallow near-shore and inshore waters to deeper shelf environs. They seldom inhabit estuaries and are generally demersal. Some snapper, especially larger-growing species, may be confused with grouper; however, they can be readily distinguished from grouper by one or two large canine teeth at the front of the upper jaw. Also, the rear end of the upper jaw slides under the suborbital rim instead of outside it. Snapper have a moderately large mouth and their dorsal fin is continuous or slightly notched.

Many snapper species are important commercial fish and high-quality food fish. Some, particularly reef-dwelling species, are popular with anglers. A few, notably dog snapper and cubera snapper, have been known to cause ciguatera poisoning.
See: Snapper; Snapper, Cubera; Snapper, Gray; Snapper, Lane; Snapper, Mutton; Snapper, Pacific Cubera; Snapper, Red; Snapper, Yellowtail.

SNAPPER, CUBERA   *Lutjanus cyanopterus.*
Other names—Cuban snapper; Spanish: *cubera, guasinuco, pargo cabalo, pargo cubera.*

The largest of all the snapper and a member of the Lutjanidae family, the cubera is a hard-fighting gamefish as well as a fine food fish, although larger specimens may have coarse meat.

Identification.   The head, body, and fins of the cubera snapper are silver or steely gray to dark brown with an occasional reddish tinge; the body is darker above than below, sometimes with a purplish sheen. Most young fish and some adults have irregular pale bands on the upper body. The cubera snapper has dark red eyes, thick lips, and a rounded anal fin. It also has connected dorsal fins that consist of 10 spines and 14 rays, and pectoral fins that do not extend as far as the start of the anal fin. The cubera snapper is often confused with the gray or "mangrove" snapper, although they can be differentiated by the number of gill rakers present on the lower limb of the first branchial arch; there are an average of seven to nine gill rakers on the gray snapper in contrast to five to seven on the cubera snapper. They can also be distinguished by the tooth patch on the roof of the mouth; the gray snapper has an anchor-shaped patch, whereas the cubera snapper has a triangular one that does not extend back as the anchor-shaped one does. In general, the canine teeth of the cubera snapper are enlarged and noticeable even when the mouth is closed. The cubera can lighten or darken dramatically in color.

Size.   Although the cubera snapper commonly weighs up to 40 pounds, it can weigh more than

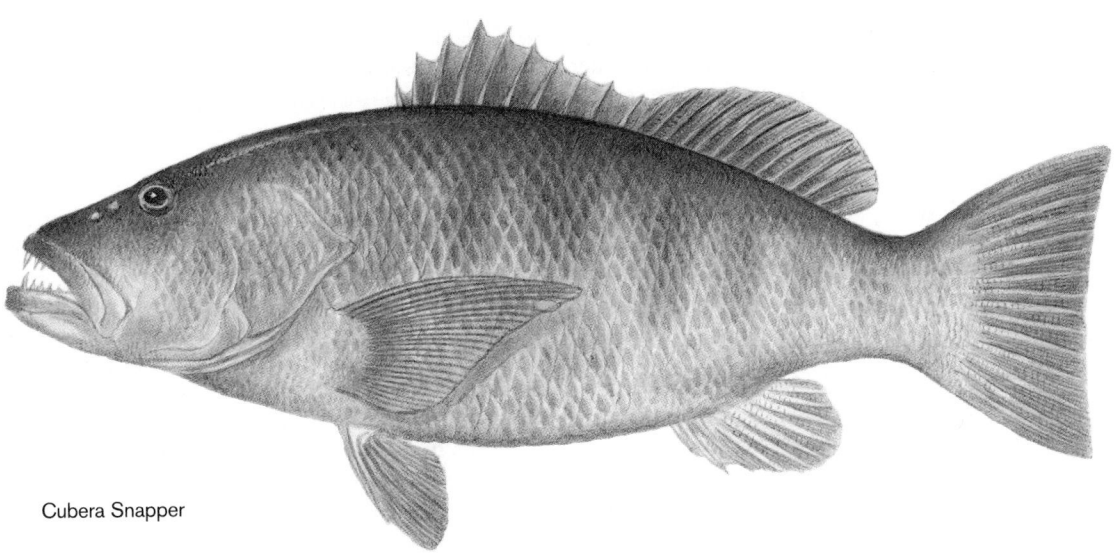

Cubera Snapper

S

100 pounds and reach lengths of 4 or more feet. The all-tackle world record is a 121-pound, 8-ounce Louisiana fish.

Distribution.   In the western Atlantic, cubera snapper occur from Florida and Cuba southward to the mouth of the Amazon in Brazil. They are very occasionally found north of Florida to New Jersey, are rare in the Gulf of Mexico, and are generally scarce in most of their range.

Habitat.   Adult fish are found offshore over wrecks, reefs, ledges, and rocky bottoms; young fish sometimes enter freshwater or inhabit mangrove areas and grassbeds. Cubera snapper are solitary and are usually found in 60 feet of water or deeper.

Spawning behavior.   In the Florida Keys, cubera snapper spawn during late summer and early fall during full moon phases.

Food.   Cubera snapper feed primarily on fish, shrimp, and crabs.

Angling.   Like grouper and other deep reef fish, the cubera snapper is primarily caught by bottom fishing methods at the right depth over irregular terrain. Off Florida, anglers catch them on wrecks with heavy tackle (50- and 80-pound two-speed outfits, as fish of 40 to 60 pounds are likely), using lobsters for baits on bottom rigs and often spotting moving fish on sonar while drifting. Strikes may be rather light, but the fish bulldoze to the wreck or reef quickly and must be outmuscled. See: **Grouper; Inshore Fishing; Snapper.**

SNAPPER, GRAY   *Lutjanus griseus.*

Other names—mangrove snapper; French: *sarde grise, vivaneau sarde grise;* Portuguese: *caranha, castanhola, luciano;* Spanish: *caballerote, pargo manglero, pargo prieto.*

A member of the Lutjanidae family of snapper and important commercially, the gray snapper is a good gamefish and also an excellent food fish. It is commonly referred to as the mangrove snapper and

has white, flaky meat that is easily filleted and is marketed fresh or frozen.

Identification.   The coloring of the gray snapper is variable, from dark gray or dark brown to gray green. The belly is grayish tinged with olive, bronze, or red, sometimes described as reddish or orange spots running in rows on the lower sides. A dark horizontal band occasionally runs from the lip through the eye, and some fish are said to have dark vertical bars or blotches along the sides. The tail may also have a dark margin, and the anal fin is rounded. There are two conspicuous canine teeth at the front of the upper jaw. The gray snapper can be distinguished from the cubera snapper by the shape of the tooth patch in the mouth, which is triangular in the cubera snapper and anchor shaped in the gray snapper. In general, the gray snapper resembles other snapper except that it lacks a distinct spot on the sides.

Size/Age.   The gray snapper averages only about a pound in weight, although offshore catches commonly weigh 8 to 10 pounds; it reportedly may grow to 35 inches and a weight of 25 pounds, although fish exceeding 15 pounds are rare. The all-tackle world record is a 17-pound Florida fish. The gray snapper may live up to 21 years.

Distribution.   In the western Atlantic, gray snapper extend from Massachusetts to Rio de

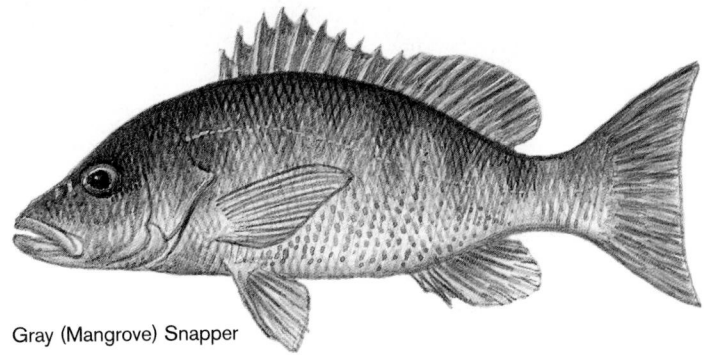

Gray (Mangrove) Snapper

Janeiro, occurring throughout the Caribbean Sea, the Gulf of Mexico, and Bermuda. Although rare north of Florida, they are common off southeastern Florida and around the Antilles. In the eastern Atlantic, gray snapper extend from Senegal to the Congo, including the Cape Verde Islands.

Habitat.   Young gray snapper are mostly found inshore over smooth bottom in such places as estuaries, the lower reaches of tidal creeks, mangroves, and seagrass meadows; adult fish generally range offshore over irregular bottom in such places as coral or rocky reefs, rock outcroppings, and shipwrecks, to depths of about 300 feet.

Life history/Behavior.   When gray snapper reach age 3 or older and a length of about 9 inches, they begin to spawn, usually at dusk in shallow water during full moon phases and between June and August. The female is courted by one or many males, and fertilized eggs settle to the bottom and remain unattended until they hatch. Gray snapper drift in small schools.

Food and feeding habits.   Gray snapper feed primarily at night, leaving reefs late in the day for grassflats, where they consume plankton, small fish, shrimp, and crabs.

Angling.   This species is particularly popular in Florida and around the Antilles, where it is caught by hook and line, by beach and boat seines, and in traps. Like other bottom and reef fish, the gray snapper is primarily caught by bottom fishing methods at the right depth over irregular terrain. Anglers fish for these and other reef fish from head boats and smaller private boats using manual and electric reels, sturdy boat rods, heavy monofilament line, and two-hook bottom rigs baited with squid and cut fish. In addition to fishing offshore, anglers also catch gray snapper in mangrove- and seagrass-dominated estuaries, using shrimp, clams, bloodworms, and occasionally artificial lures, especially small jigs.

See: Inshore Fishing; Snapper.

SNAPPER, LANE   *Lutjanus synagris.*

Other names—Portuguese: *areocó;* Spanish: *biajaiba, chino, machego, pargo biajaiba, pargo guanapo, rayado, villajaiba.*

A member of the Lutjanidae family of snapper and highly regarded as a food fish, the lane snapper is caught commercially throughout its range and is marketed fresh and frozen.

Identification.   The lane snapper is silvery pink to reddish with short, somewhat parallel pink and yellow stripes on its sides; there is often a faint greenish cast to the back and upper sides, which sometimes highlights a few light olive bands. The pectoral, pelvic, and anal fins are often yellowish, and the dorsal and tail fins are often reddish. The outer margin of the tail is black, particularly toward the center. A black spot about as large as the eye is present just below the rear dorsal fin and just above the lateral line, although it may be missing in rare cases; this spot is what distinguishes the lane from other snapper, in addition to an anchor-shaped tooth patch on the roof of the mouth, 18 to 22 gill rakers on the first arch, and a round anal fin.

Size.   Usually weighing less than a pound, the lane snapper is ordinarily 8 to 12 inches long, sometimes reaching a maximum of 15 inches in length. The all-tackle world record is a 7-pound Alabama fish.

Distribution.   In the tropical western Atlantic, lane snapper range from North Carolina to southeastern Brazil, including the Caribbean Sea and the Gulf of Mexico. They are most abundant around the Antilles, on the Campeche Bank off eastern

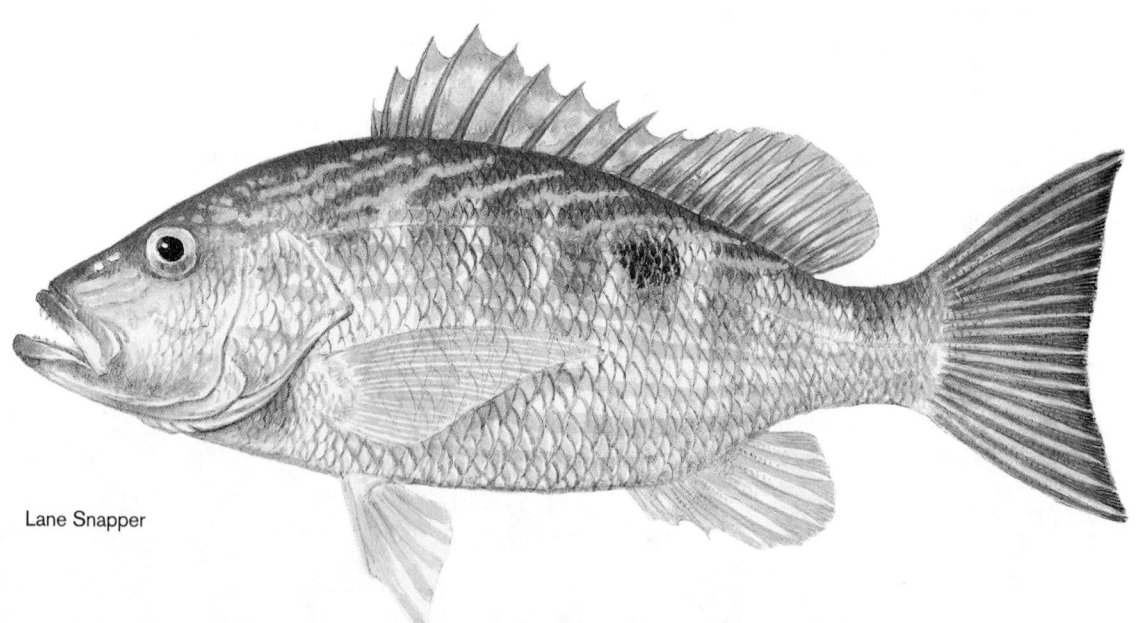

Lane Snapper

Panama, and on the northern coast of South America. They are commonly found in Florida and only occasionally inhabit waters of the Bahamas and the Caribbean.

Habitat. Ranging from depths of 5 to 130 feet, lane snapper are found over all types of bottom, although they prefer coral reefs and sandy areas with vegetation; young fish stay inshore over grassbeds or shallow reefs, whereas adults move offshore, where they explore deeper reefs. Occurring in turbid as well as clear water, lane snapper often drift in schools, especially during the breeding season.

Spawning behavior. Becoming sexually mature when they are one year old and 6 to 7 inches long, lane snapper spawn from March through September. Spawning activity peaks from June through August. Depending on size, a female may lay 300,000 to more than 1 million pelagic eggs; young fish stay in grassbeds in estuaries, which serve as nursery areas until they reach 5 or 6 inches in length, when they migrate offshore.

Food and feeding habits. Lane snapper are opportunistic carnivores and primarily consume forage that is near or on the bottom, including anchovies and other small fish, crabs, shrimp, worms, and mollusks. They are fast enough to pursue and capture their prey, and they feed at night, moving off of reefs and onto grassbeds.

Angling. Because the lane snapper is small and occurs in shallow water, it is caught in baited traps and beach seines, as well as by hook and line. It is an excellent and fierce fighter on light tackle. See: Inshore Fishing; Snapper.

SNAPPER, MANGROVE
See: Snapper, Gray.

SNAPPER, MUTTON *Lutjanus analis.*
Other names—Portuguese: *cioba;* Spanish: *pargo cebalo, pargo cebal, pargo colorado, pargo criollo, pargo mulato.*

Often marketed as "red snapper," the flesh of the mutton snapper is firm, white, and is an excellent food fish. It is a member of the Lutjanidae family of snapper.

Identification. The mutton snapper can be striking in appearance, varying from orangish to reddish yellow or reddish brown, or from silver gray to olive green on the back and upper sides. All the fins below the lateral line have a reddish cast, and the larger mutton snapper takes on an overall reddish color, which causes it to be confused with the red snapper. Young fish are often olive colored and may display dark bars. There is a distinct black spot about the size of the eye on the mid-body line below the rear dorsal fin, and of all the snapper with this type of dark spot, the mutton snapper is the only one with a V-shaped tooth patch in the roof of the mouth rather than an anchor-shaped one. There are also small blue lines below and near the eye, and the dorsal fin has 10 spines and 14 rays. Adults tend to develop a high back, and all fish have pointed anal fins.

The lane snapper *(see: snapper, lane)* is somewhat similar in coloring except that it has yellow streaks, and the mutton snapper has small blue streaks on a yellowish background, although these usually disappear with age. Another difference is that the lane snapper has squarish or even rounded anal and dorsal fins, whereas the mutton snapper has pointed anal and dorsal fins.

Size. Ordinarily 1 to 2 feet in length and 15 pounds in weight, the mutton snapper can reach weights of 25 to 30 pounds and lengths of 30 inches.

S

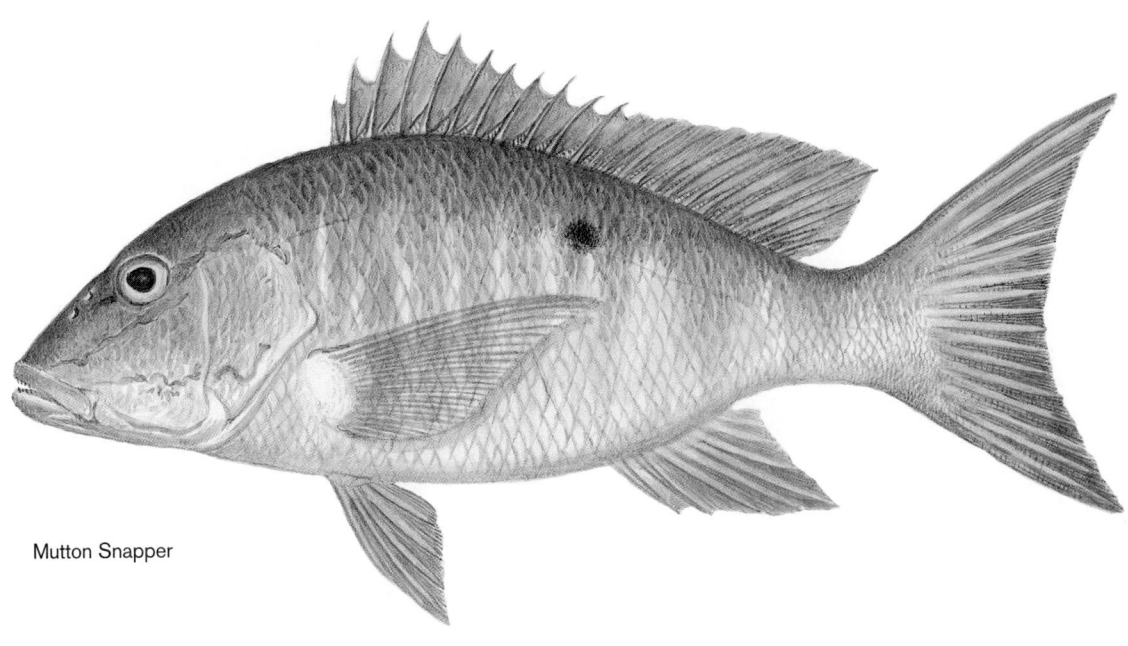

Mutton Snapper

The all-tackle world record is a 28-pound, 5-ounce Florida fish.

Distribution.   In the western Atlantic, mutton snapper extend from Massachusetts to southeastern Brazil, including the Caribbean Sea and the northern Gulf of Mexico. They are most abundant around the Antilles, the Bahamas, and off southern Florida, and have been introduced into Bermuda waters.

Habitat.   Young fish occur over soft bottoms such as seagrass beds, whereas adults are found over hard bottoms around rocky and coral reefs, as well as in bays and estuaries. They drift above the bottom at depths of 5 to 60 feet.

Spawning behavior.   Spawning takes place from May through October with a peak of activity in July and August. Mutton snapper form small groups that disperse during the night.

Food and feeding habits.   Mutton snapper feed both day and night on shrimp, fish, snails, crabs, and plankton.

Angling.   Mutton snapper are strong fighters on light tackle and can be taken on natural baits or small lures fished vertically or slowly trolled near the bottom. They are primarily caught by bottom fishing methods at the right depth over irregular terrain but are sometimes taken on flats or lured to the surface and caught on a fly.

See: Inshore Fishing; Snapper.

SNAPPER, PACIFIC CUBERA   *Lutjanus novemfasciatus.*

Other names—dog snapper, Pacific dog snapper; Spanish: *boca fuerte, huachinango, panza prieta, pargo jilguero, pargo moreno, pargo negro.*

The Pacific cubera snapper closely resembles the cubera snapper, the "river" or "mangrove red" snapper, and an African snapper; this resemblance involves habitat and behavior but extends as well to a similar appearance; they share deep reddish bodies, four large canine teeth, stubby gill rakers, and almost identical body and fin shapes. This seems to suggest that large cubera-type snappers may be more closely related to each other than are other members of the Lutjanidae (snapper) family. Marketed fresh and frozen, the Pacific cubera snapper is an excellent food fish and is greatly prized as a sport catch.

Identification.   The young Pacific cubera snapper is purplish brown with a light spot in the center of each scale, whereas adults and older fish are almost a deep red. Occasionally a blue streak is evident under the eye, as are roughly nine shaded bars on the flanks. The tail is very slightly forked or lunate (crescent shaped), the dorsal fin is made up of 10 spines and 14 soft rays, and the anal fin is rounded and has 3 spines and 8 rays. The pectoral fins do not extend to the anal fin or even as far as the vent in adults. The most distinctive feature of the Pacific cubera snapper is four uncommonly large canine teeth, two in the upper jaw and two in the lower, which are somewhat larger than the pupil of the eye. There is also a crescent-shaped tooth patch in the roof of the mouth.

Size.   The Pacific cubera snapper is the largest of nine snapper occurring in its range, growing to at least 80 pounds. The all-tackle world record is a 78-pound, 12-ounce fish taken off Costa Rica.

Distribution.   Pacific cubera inhabit the eastern Pacific from northern Mexico to northern Peru.

Habitat.   Pacific cubera snapper are an inshore species, preferring rocky and coral reefs and caves in shallow waters with depths of 100 feet and possibly deeper. Young fish are found in estuaries near mangroves and the mouths of rivers.

Food and feeding habits.   Carnivorous, Pacific cubera snapper prey at night on big invertebrates such as crabs, prawns, and shrimp, as well as fish.

Angling.   This species is a strong fighter and a tough sportfish that can be caught on live baits, jigs, spoons, feathers, plugs, or pork rind fished or trolled at up to 5 mph. Where there are plenty of rocky pinnacles, reefs, and islands, anglers can land these fish by casting diving plugs and surface plugs, the latter creating some terrific explosions.

See: Inshore Fishing; Snapper.

SNAPPER (SQUIREFISH)   *Pagrus auratus.*

Other names—cockney bream (up to 13 centimeters), red bream (at about 450 grams), squire (up to about 1.5 kilograms), old man snapper, pink snapper, tamure, squirefish (U.S.).

An Australian and New Zealand member of the Sparidae family of sea bream (formerly known as *Chrysophrys auratus*), the snapper is a highly valued food and sport species targeted by both recreational anglers and commercial fishermen.

Identification.   Snapper are a handsome fish with a deep, elongate body that is strongly compressed. Some older fish (usually females) have a prominent bump on the head and a bulge on the snout, both thought to be developed as a result of nudging into reefs in order to obtain food. The mouth is of moderate size, and the teeth are large and peglike in front and molarlike on the sides.

Pacific Cubera Snapper

Their body coloring can vary, but is generally reddish pink with many bright blue spots on the sides. The fins are reddish or pink. The caudal fin is forked, and the single dorsal fin is not notched.

Size. Snapper are known to reach a weight of 19.5 kilograms and a length of 1.3 meters. An Australian record, taken at Whyalla, South Australia, in 1990, is listed at 16.4 kilograms; a 17.2-kilogram fish from New Zealand is the all-tackle world record. Most big snapper are taken close inshore, and the Spencer Gulf and Gulf of St. Vincent waters in South Australia are famous for large individuals. Large specimens have also been taken from the waters off Lord Howe Island, to the east of New South Wales.

Distribution. Snapper are found across the northern two-thirds of New Zealand, and in Australia from Barrow Island off the central coast of Western Australia, across the bottom of Australia, occasionally along the northern coastline of Tasmania, and up the East Coast as far north as Hinchinbrook Island in North Queensland. The predominant Australian angling areas are the inshore waters of Shark Bay in Western Australia, Spencer Gulf and the Gulf of St. Vincent in South Australia, and Port Phillip and Westernport Bays in Victoria. New South Wales anglers take fish along the entire coastline, whereas offshore reefs of southern Queensland appear to take precedence over other areas.

Habitat. Juvenile snapper, called cockney bream, inhabit estuaries and bays, where they live in and around seagrass beds, over sandy bottoms, and around any man-made or natural structures. Mature fish move out of the estuaries into offshore waters, where they stay close to both deep- and shallow-water reefs, bomboras, gravel beds, rocky headlands, and offshore islands. In South Australian waters, many snapper tend to remain within Spencer Gulf and the Gulf of St. Vincent.

Life history/Behavior. During the spawning season, which can vary with geographic location, snapper may spawn several times, usually well out to sea and when water temperatures range from 18° to 21°C. As young juveniles, they move close inshore and eventually make their way into the sheltered waters of bays, inlets, and estuaries. As they mature, they leave these waters and make their way to the open sea, where they find sustenance around islands and reefs, and along the rocky coastline. They are known to migrate for long distances, that is from the southern state of Victoria to the northern state of Queensland. Big snapper often seek the shelter of estuarine waters following coastal storms.

Food and feeding habits. The diet of the snapper is varied and includes small fish, mollusks, blue crabs, sand crabs, soldier crabs, squid, and prawns. It will also take strip baits of tuna, bonito, mackerel, mullet, octopus or squid tentacles, whole blue pilchards, and garfish. It tends to forage in

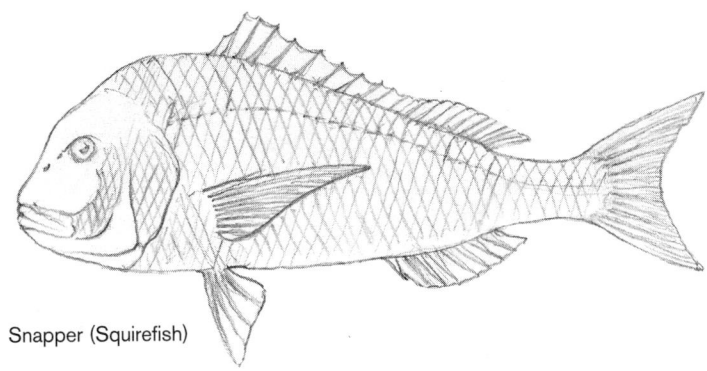

Snapper (Squirefish)

deep water during daylight hours but will move into shallow water after dark.

Angling. A big old man snapper is a prize that many anglers strive for, yet the capture of any adult snapper from the red bream stage upward makes for a successful day. Tackle varies from 2-meter boat rods and reels spooled with 7-kilogram line to 3.5-meter rods and reels with 10- to 12-kilogram lines used by shore-based rock anglers. Long-handled gaffs to 6 meters are essential in shore-based situations, where anglers, perched high on a rock ledge, can be in danger from waves and swells if they clamber down to land a fish.

Heavy handlines (15 kilograms) are frequently used by Australian boat anglers, and jetty fishing is popular with shore-based anglers confined to bays and inlets. Most shore-based angling occurs at night.

Hook sizes vary from 3/0 to 7/0; ganged hooks (a series of four or five hooks joined eye to bend) to 5/0 are suitable for most baits. Chumming is commonly used and may consist of a mix of fish scraps, prawns, chicken pellets, and soaked bread sparingly distributed so as not to overfeed the fish. Baits are fished on bottom rigs with heavy sinkers for fixed positions, or allowed to sink naturally and drift. This latter method is popular with rock anglers using ganged hooks and unweighted baits. Boat anglers either drift over reefs or anchor upcurrent of a known reef and rely on chum to bring the fish around. Where snapper are attracted to the surface by chum, they can sometimes be tempted into taking a lure such as a soft plastic, feathered leadhead jig, or streamer fly.

Snapper are a favorite species for charter boat anglers. These craft leave for known snapper reefs early in the morning and can accommodate 20 or more anglers, who use rail-mounted winches or handlines. Charter boat skippers usually demand that rigs be identical in order to prevent entanglement, and sinkers to 500 grams are not uncommon where ocean currents are strong.

SNAPPER, RED   *Lutjanus campechanus.*
Other names—American red snapper, northern red snapper, mutton snapper; Portuguese: *vermelho;* Spanish: *guachinango del Golfo, pargo colorado, pargo de Golfo.*

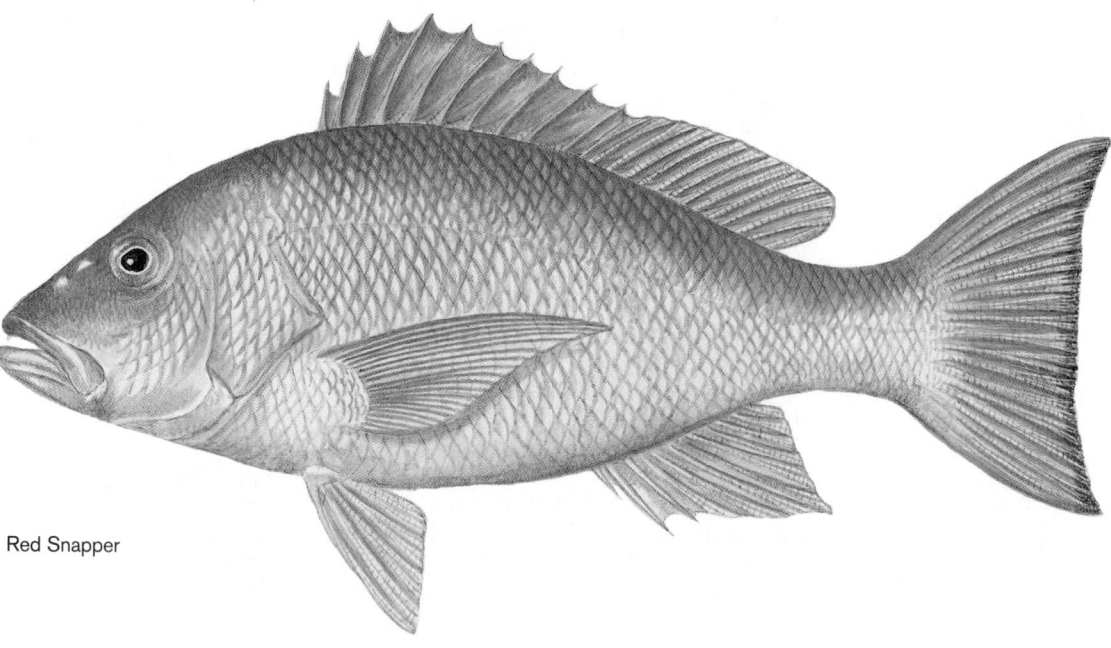

Red Snapper

S

The red snapper is one of the most valuable snapper for anglers and commercial fishermen; as a result, it has been severely overfished in American waters and is now closely protected. A member of the Lutjanidae family of snapper, it is one of the most highly coveted of all reef fish and is almost always the most expensive fish per pound on the market. The white meat of the red snapper is superb and is marketed fresh.

Identification. The red snapper is pinkish, scarlet, or brick red on its head and upper body, and silvery whitish below. It has a long triangular snout, a sharply pointed anal fin, and a distinctively red iris. Young fish of under 10 inches in length have a dusky spot below the soft dorsal fin at and above the midline, and the tail sometimes has a dark edge. Although the adult resembles the Caribbean red snapper, there are differences in ray and scale counts; the Caribbean snapper has eight soft rays in the anal fin, 50 to 51 scales in a row along the flank, and 10 to 11 scales between the beginning of the dorsal fin and the lateral line. The red snapper has nine soft rays, 47 to 49 flank scales, and 8 to 9 scales between the dorsal fin and the lateral line.

Size/Age. Commonly growing to between 1 and 2 feet in length, the red snapper can reach 3 feet and weigh more than 35 pounds. The all-tackle world record is a 50-pound, 4-ounce Louisiana fish. Adults can live for more than 20 years.

Distribution. Red snapper occur in the Gulf of Mexico and along the entire Atlantic coast of the United States as far north as Massachusetts but rarely north of the Carolinas. They are occasionally found in Florida but are absent from the Bahamas and the Caribbean.

Habitat. Adult fish are usually found over rocky bottom at depths of 60 to 400 feet, whereas young fish inhabit shallow waters over sandy or muddy bottoms.

Life history/Behavior. Red snapper spawn from June through October, and sometimes as early as April. They often intermingle with grunts and other snapper in schools. It takes three to four years for these fish to reach their spawning size of 15 to 16 inches.

Food and feeding habits. Red snapper are opportunistic bottom feeders that prey on fish, shrimp, crabs, and worms.

Angling. This species is caught commercially throughout its range, primarily with handlines, but also by using large electrically and manually powered reels to haul up line that has multiple-hook rigs.

Anglers use bottom fishing tactics over reefs, wrecks, oil rigs, and the like, usually fishing with stout tackle and lines in the 50-pound class. Consistently catching red snapper by hook and line is an art. Not only must one know where the best fishing grounds are, but also the bait must be presented in a manner that entices the snapper to bite. Although multiple-hook rigs similar to those used for other reef fish are effective, a favorite rig for large red snapper is a single 7/0 hook fastened to a 4- to 5-foot dropper off the main leader, which ends with an 8- to 16-ounce sinker. Selection of baits is critical. Squid heads with long tentacles, whole medium-size fish, and fresh bloody strips of little tunny or greater amberjack catch big red snapper. The fish seem to prefer a still or very slowly moving bait. Fishing from an anchored boat is productive, but when drifting, it can be beneficial to freespool the line for a few minutes before slowly retrieving the slack. As with many big snapper and grouper, gaining line quickly in the first few moments after the strike is critical. A hard strike and feverish winding is necessary.

Although many red snapper are caught right on the bottom, in some situations the larger fish are suspended off the bottom. These may be caught on heavy jigs, often tipped with a strip of bait, or by freelining baits at the proper upper level.

Artificial reefs have been built in the Gulf of Mexico to attract this species for sportfishing. Commercial shrimp fishing operations, accused of destroying young snapper through bycatch, is currently restricted.

See: Inshore Fishing; Snapper.

SNAPPER, YELLOWTAIL   *Ocyrus chrysurus.*
Other names—Creole: *colas;* French: *sarde queue jaune;* Portuguese: *cioba, mulata;* Spanish: *rabirrubia.*

The yellowtail snapper is a member of the Lutjanidae family of snapper, a colorful tropical reef fish, and an excellent sportfish with superb meat that is marketed fresh and frozen.

Identification. The yellowtail snapper has a streamlined body that is olive or bluish gray above and silver to white below. It has fine yellowish stripes on the belly. Most striking is the prominent mid-body yellow stripe, which runs from the tip of the snout through the eye to the tail, widening as it extends past the dorsal fins. The tail is bright yellow and deeply forked, and the dorsal fins are mostly yellowish. There is no dark lateral spot, and the eye is red.

Size/Age. The yellowtail snapper usually grows 1 to 2 feet long and commonly weighs up to 3 pounds, although it rarely exceeds 5 pounds. It can reach 30 inches and 7 pounds, and a Florida fish that weighed 8 pounds, 8 ounces is the all-tackle world record. The yellowtail snapper can live for 14 years.

Distribution. In the tropical western Atlantic, yellowtail snapper range from Massachusetts and Bermuda to southeastern Brazil, including the Gulf of Mexico. They are abundant in the Bahamas, southern Florida, and throughout the Caribbean but are rare north of the Carolinas. They have also been found in the eastern Atlantic at the Cape Verde Islands.

Habitat. Inhabiting tropical coastal waters with depths of 10 to 300 feet, yellowtail snapper occur around coral reefs, either alone or in loose schools, and are usually seen well above the bottom. Young fish typically dwell inshore over grassbeds.

Life history/Behavior. Some yellowtail snapper are sexually mature at age 2; all are mature at age 4. Spawning occurs from April through August, and activity peaks in June and July. Yellowtail snapper move into deeper water, where they will produce from 11,000 to more than 1.5 million pelagic eggs.

Food and feeding habits. Yellowtail snapper feed mainly at night on benthic and pelagic animals, including fish, crustaceans, and worms. Young fish feed primarily on plankton.

Angling. Anglers use cut fish and squid to catch yellowtail inshore by fishing on the bottom from bridges and piers, and they catch them offshore by fishing over reefs from small private boats and party boats. These fish are attracted to chum and can be caught higher in the water column when they come into an established chum slick. They often do not take baits as aggressively as some other snapper or grouper do, however, and many are not hooked due to their small mouth (or too large a hook). They put a good bend in a light to medium-action spinning rod and make an excellent meal.

See: Inshore Fishing; Snapper.

SNAP-SWIVEL
A terminal connection that combines a snap *(see)* and a swivel *(see).*

S

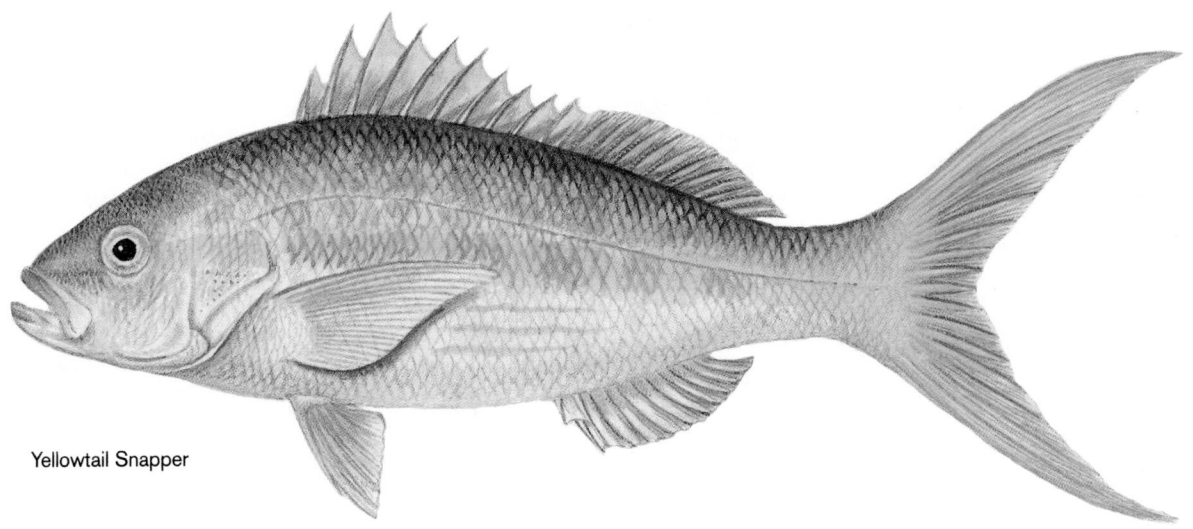
Yellowtail Snapper

SNELLED HOOK

A bait hook with an angled eye that is attached to the line by making a snell knot on the shank.
See: Hook; Knots, Fishing.

SNELL KNOT

A fishing knot for terminal connections.
See: Knots, Fishing.

SNOOK

Fat Snook   *Centropomus parallelus.*
   Other names—Portuguese: *robalo;* Spanish: *robalo chucumite.*

Swordspine Snook   *Centropomus ensiferus.*

Tarpon Snook   *Centropomus pectinatus.*
   Other names—Spanish: *constantino, robalito, róbalos, robalos prieto.*

These three species of snook are all small, similar-looking fish with almost identical ranges and habits but are less prominent than their larger relative the common snook *(see: snook, common).* As members of the Centropomidae family, which includes the Nile perch *(see: perch, Nile)* and barramundi *(see),* they are excellent table fish with delicate, white, flaky meat, and are good gamefish despite their small size.

There are believed to be 12 species of snook, 6 of which occur in the western Atlantic and 6 in the eastern Pacific, although no single species occurs in both oceans. A good deal is known about these three smaller Atlantic-occurring species, and about the common snook, but not about the others, especially those in the Pacific, which include such large-growing species as the Pacific black snook (*C. nigrescens;* commonly called black snook) and the Pacific white snook (*C. viridis*), as well as the smaller Pacific blackfin snook (*C. medius*).

Identification.   Snook in general are distinctive in appearance, with a characteristic protruding lower jaw and a particularly prominent black lateral line running from the gill cover to the tail.

The fat snook has a deeper body than the other snook, although it is not strongly compressed. Coloration varies depending on the area the fish inhabits, but the fat snook is frequently yellow

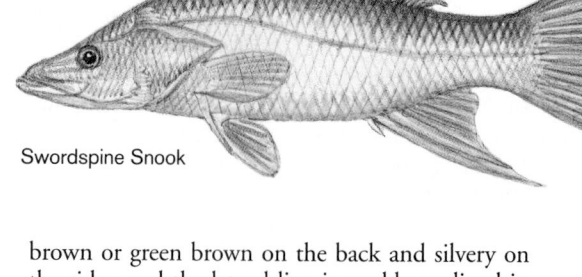

Swordspine Snook

brown or green brown on the back and silvery on the sides, and the lateral line is weakly outlined in black. The mouth reaches to or beyond the center of the eye, and it has the smallest scales of all the snook. There are 15 to 16 rays in the pectoral fin, 6 soft rays in the anal fin, and 10 to 13 gill rakers.

The swordspine snook is the smallest snook and is named for its very long second anal spine, which usually extends to or farther than the area below the base of the tail. With a slightly concave profile, it is yellow green or brown green on the back and silvery on the belly, and it has a prominent lateral line outlined in black. It has the largest scales of all the snook, as well as 15 to 16 rays in the pectoral fin, 6 soft rays in the anal fin, and 13 to 16 gill rakers.

The tarpon snook is distinctive, having 7 anal fin rays, when all other snook have 6. It also has a distinguishing upturned or tarponlike snout and a compressed, flat-sided body. The prominent black lateral line extends through the tail. The pelvic fin is orange yellow with a blackish edge, and the tips of the pelvic fins reach past the anus. There are 14 rays in the pectoral fin, 7 soft rays in the anal fin, and 15 to 18 gill rakers.

Size/Age.   The fat snook rarely reaches more than 20 inches in length, although it is said to attain a length of $2^1/_2$ feet. The swordspine and tarpon snook are usually less than 1 pound in weight or 12 inches in length. The all-tackle world records for the fat and tarpon snook are, respectively, 7 pounds, 4 ounces and 3 pounds, 2 ounces, both taken in Florida. Snook have a life span of at least seven years.

Distribution.   In the western Atlantic, all three species are present and are most abundant in southern Florida, although swordspine and tarpon snook are rare on Florida's west coast. Fat and swordspine snook occur around the Greater and Lesser Antilles,

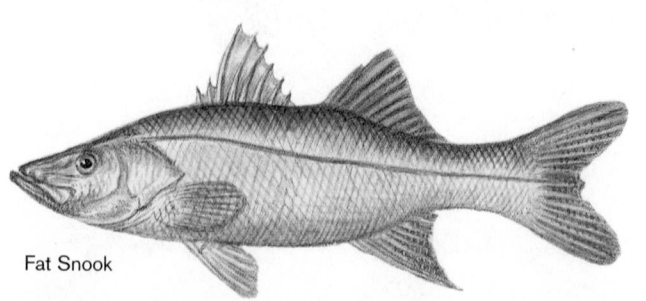

Fat Snook

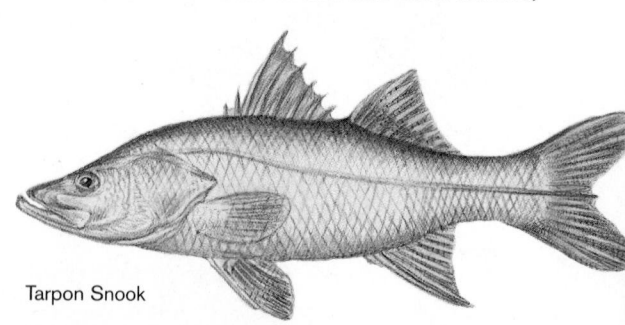

Tarpon Snook

A common snook from the surf near the Parismina River, Costa Rica.

after because of its strength and acrobatics when hooked. It is a member of the Centropomidae family, which also includes such prized species as the Nile perch *(see: perch, Nile)*, although it is superior to the former as a sportfish, even though it doesn't reach the same monstrous proportions. It is also related to the barramundi *(see)*, with which it shares some appearance and behavioral traits.

In all there are believed to be 12 species of snook, 6 of which occur in the western Atlantic and 6 in the eastern Pacific, although no single species occurs in both oceans. Large-growing Pacific species with similar traits, although less common, include the Pacific black snook *(C. nigrescens;* commonly known as the black snook) and the Pacific white snook *(C. viridis).*

The common snook was once a favored commercial species in Florida; it is now strictly a gamefish there but may be taken commercially in other parts of its range (Pacific snook are also commercially harvested). In the late 1970s and early 1980s, a severe decline in the Florida snook population occurred due to overfishing, loss of habitat, and pollution. Numbers have increased to safe levels, however, since the fish was given protected status in Florida in 1982. This effort established a legal size, a bag limit, and a closed season during the summer spawning period,.

Identification.   A silvery fish with a yellow green or olive tint, the common snook has a body that is streamlined and slender with a distinct black lateral line running from the top of its gills to the end of its forked tail. It has a sloping forehead, a long, concave snout, and a large mouth with brush-like teeth and a protruding lower jaw. The fins are occasionally bright yellow, although the pelvic fin is usually pale, unlike the orange yellow, black-tipped pelvic fin of the tarpon snook *(see: snook)*. The common snook has a high, divided dorsal fin, as well as small scales that run from about 70 to 77 along the lateral line to the base of the tail. It has relatively short anal spines that do not reach the base of the tail when pressed against the body; there are usually 6 soft rays in the anal fin. There are also 15 to 16 rays in the pectoral fins and 7 to 9 gill rakers on the first arch.

Size/Age.   The common snook grows much larger than other Atlantic-range snook, averaging $1^1/_2$ to $2^1/_2$ feet or 5 to 8 pounds, although it can reach 4 feet and 50 pounds. Females are almost always larger than males, although growth rates are variable. The all-tackle world record is a 53-pound, 10-ounce fish taken off eastern Costa Rica in 1978. Common snook can live for more than 20 years.

The Pacific black snook attains similar sizes and is believed to reach 60 pounds; a 57-pound, 12-ounce fish from western Costa Rica is the all-tackle world record for this species. The Pacific white snook also grows large, and a $39^1/_2$-pound specimen from Cabo San Lucas, Mexico, is the all-tackle world record.

whereas fat snook also extend down the southeastern coast of the Gulf of Mexico and the continental Caribbean coasts to Santos, Brazil. Swordspine snook occur down the continental Caribbean coasts of Central and South America to Rio de Janeiro, Brazil. Tarpon snook are found in the West Indies, and from Mexico to Brazil. They are also reported on the Pacific coast from Mexico to Colombia.

Habitat/Behavior.   Snook inhabit the coastal waters of estuaries and lagoons, moving between freshwater and saltwater seasonally but always remaining close to shore and to estuaries. Fat and swordspine snook prefer very low salinity water or freshwater, whereas the tarpon snook is most common in shaded lakes with brackish waters. Fat snook occur more often in interior waters than other snook (instead of estuarine waters), and all three species use mangrove shorelines as nursery grounds. Snook are usually sexually mature by their third year.

Food.   These species feed on fish and crustaceans.

Angling.   *See: Snook, Common.*

SNOOK, COMMON
Centropomus undecimalis.

Other names—linesider, robalo, sergeant fish, snook; Portuguese: *robalo;* Spanish: *robalo, robalito.*

The common snook is the most abundant and wide-ranging of the snook and is highly sought

Common Snook

Distribution. In the western Atlantic, common snook are found primarily in southern Florida, as well as off the southeastern coast of the Gulf of Mexico, around most of the Antilles, and off the Caribbean coast of Central and South America extending southward to Rio de Janeiro, Brazil. They are also occasionally encountered off North Carolina and Texas. The largest snook in Florida, exceeding 30 pounds, are caught chiefly in east coast bays and inlets from Vero Beach south to Miami, but their most abundant populations are on the west coast from Boca Grande south throughout the Everglades region, including Florida Bay.

The range of the Pacific black snook is in the eastern Pacific, primarily from Baja California, Mexico, to Colombia, although it has also been reported from Ecuador and Peru. It is most common in Costa Rica and Panama. The range of the Pacific white snook is similar, extending from Baja California to Peru, including the Galápagos Islands.

Habitat. Snook inhabit warm, shallow coastal waters and are able to tolerate freshwater and saltwater. They are most common along continental shores, preferring fast-moving tides and relying on the shelter of estuaries, lagoons, mangrove areas, and brackish streams, as well as freshwater canals and rivers, usually at depths of less than 65 feet. Occasionally they occur in small groups over grassy flats and shallow patch reefs, and may be found at the mouths of tributaries and along the ocean side of shores near tributaries. Snook cannot tolerate water temperatures below 60°F; in winter, they stay in protected, stable-temperature areas such as those under bridges, in ship channels, turning basins, warmwater outflows near power plants, and the upper reaches of estuaries.

Life history/Behavior. Common snook congregate at mouths of passes and rivers during the spawning season, returning to the same spawning sites each summer. Spawning grounds include significant passes and inlets of the Atlantic Ocean and the Gulf of Mexico, such as Sebastian, Ft. Pierce, St. Lucie, Jupiter, and Lake Worth inlets on the east coast and Hurricane, Clearwater, and John's passes

on the west coast. Common snook also spawn inside Tampa Bay around passes to the secondary embankments of Miquel Bay, Terra Ceia Bay, and Riviera Bay. The season extends from April through November but activity peaks between May and July; more intense spawning occurs during new or full moon phases. Females may spawn more than 1.5 million eggs every day in the early part of the season, with larvae drifting for 15 to 20 days after hatching. Young fish remain in the quiet, secluded upper reaches of estuaries until they reach sexual maturity, which males attain after two to three years and females after three to four years.

Common snook are protandric hermaphrodites—they can change their sex from male to female; this change usually happens between the ages of 2 and 7 and between the lengths of 17 to 30 inches. Within a group of common snook, sex reversal is brought about by a change in the size of individuals; that is, if a group that loses its largest fish has lost females, some males may undergo sex reversal to fill the absence, a process that takes from 60 to 90 days.

Food and feeding habits. Carnivorous predators that ambush their prey as currents sweep food into their vicinity, snook feed on both freshwater and saltwater fish, shrimp, crabs, and larger crustaceans.

Angling. Commonly caught in brackish water, snook are often found in the far reaches of freshwater rivers, as well as in lagoons and canals, often in the same cover-laden areas inhabited by largemouth bass where these species overlap. Their most common habitat, however, is inshore saltwater areas, particularly along mangrove-lined banks, as well as around such objects as bridges, docks, pilings, oyster bars and sandbars, along dropoffs and island edges, and in deep holes.

Renowned fighters, snook jump, run, dive deep, pull very hard, and are generally tough to land, especially in larger sizes. Many snook are lost by anglers. These fish have a penchant for heavy cover; when hooked, they repeatedly try to reach cover and get free by cutting the line, and they are often successful.

Although anglers must have a good reel drag, they also must be able to apply pressure to the fish to turn it and force it away from objects. The bigger the snook, the more of a challenge this becomes.

Casting or live-bait fishing are the primary means of pursuing snook. With the latter method, a small bait, such as a mullet, is livelined by anglers who stillfish or drift. Casters primarily work shallow nearshore areas, often casting into thick mangrove stands and up under the bank. Accurate casters who can pitch a plug into an opening or back under the brush will usually fare better than those whose casts repeatedly land on the edge of the cover and are always working away from, rather than through, it.

Although small spoons and flies or poppers are used, the favored snook lures are walking plugs worked rapidly on the surface, or darting shallow-running plugs worked in jerky, erratic motions just under the surface. A moving tide, usually the high ebb, produces well. Some sight fishing is done by anglers drifting and looking for cruising fish on cover laden flats or shores, but most angling is blind prospecting in likely places. Fly fishing is most prudent when the fish are visible, but it is also practiced in known snook-holding cover where fish aren't visible. Popping bugs and streamer flies are popular terminal items.

Snook are found singly or in groups, and the larger fish tend to be loners. Some fishing is done in deep holes with jigs or by trolling, too, although this is often in the winter when cold water makes snook sluggish. The better fishing time is during the spawning period. Some night fishing, primarily around bridges and piers, is also done for snook in the summer.

Although anglers need a stiff-tipped rod to properly work snook plugs, the tackle may be similar to that used in largemouth bass fishing. Baitcasting gear is better for accuracy and fish control, and 12- to 17-pound line is the norm.
See: Snook.

SOFT LURE

This is a catch-all term for a lure or body component of a lure that is made of a soft substance, as opposed to a lure made of metal (like a spoon or spinner), wood, or hard plastic (like a plug). Also called soft baits (as in artificial bait), these are primarily fashioned from soft plastic, but some are produced from soft processed natural food or a combination of both, and a few products are rubber.

Soft lures are not a category of lure per se; they are mostly found as artificial worms, as various body shapes for leadhead jigs, and as trailers or add-ons for a variety of other lures. Some plugs and surface lures have soft bodies as well.

Most soft lures exactly or closely represent some type of natural food. The list is headed by various kinds of worms and small baitfish, and includes

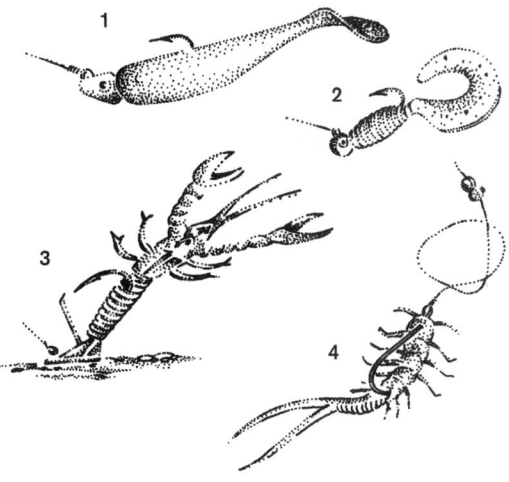

Popular soft lures include a so-called "shad" or fish-shaped body used on jigs (1), a curl-tail grub body (2), a crayfish imitation (3), and a hellgrammite imitation (4).

eels, leeches, salamanders (often called lizards), frogs, crayfish, hellgrammites, and mice. These are used in freshwater and saltwater; in the latter, most soft lures are used as jig bodies.

Soft lures have a feel that is unmatched by hard lures; in many cases, this means that they may be held by a striking fish for a moment or two longer than a hard lure. Since the strike and rejection of some lures happens in an instant, this extra holding ability can make a difference in catching fish. The use of scents with some soft bodies might have an added measure of appeal to certain fish. They also have the advantage of being relatively inexpensive and easily replaced; changing to a different color or style, or simply replacing a soft body, is easy and cheap. Some bodies also have a swimming action that is not only different, but better than that of most hard lures, and often can be fished effectively at a slower pace than hard lures.

There are various rigging methods for soft lures or soft bodies on lures. Methods of rigging worms or wormlike lures are described elsewhere *(see: soft worm)*. Standard means of rigging soft bodies on jigs follow, as well as a method of rigging an imitation hellgrammite for stream fishing.

Shad/Fish body on a jig. Fish-shaped soft baits, particularly those with a broad tail that shimmies widely, are often called shad baits and are fished on various styles of leadhead jig, with the larger bodies being used with blunt-end versions. The point and shank of the hook must be threaded through the middle of the soft bait to a location where, when the point is pushed out, the gap is about halfway exposed and the body of the bait is aligned with the leadhead and not bunched.

Grub on a jig.   There are all kinds of soft-bait bodies, lumped under the category of grub, for use with leadhead jigs. The most common, used in various sizes for diverse species, is a curl-tail model. Rig this so the curled tail rides up vertically in the same direction as the hook, with the gap in the hook

S

point halfway exposed and the body of the grub aligned and not bunched along the hook shank. Flat-tailed grubs should be rigged so that the tail is horizontal.

Crayfish standup jig. Some types of soft baits, especially the many-tentacled versions that might represent crayfish and those models that closely imitate these crustaceans, are effectively fished with a leadhead jig that allows them to either stand up or have a higher profile on the bottom. The hook is usually exposed on such a bait, although it may have a weedguard, and the extremities of the lure are free to move actively with every twitch of the rod tip.

Split shot bottom rig. When fishing in current, light round clamp-on split shot provides better movement through riffles and shallow runs than other types of weights. These can be fished at various distances, usually 8 to 18 inches, ahead of the soft lure. The lure body can be one of many different soft styles; it is fished with the hook point buried or exposed, the latter producing quick hookups but also more rock snags. A hellgrammite imitation, or something similar, is especially good in creeks and streams when bottom drifting for smallmouth bass.

See: Jerkbait; Jig; Lure.

SOFT WORM

An artificial wormlike lure made of supple synthetic material. Artificial worms are mostly made of soft plastic and commonly called plastic worms, but they may be made from other substances as well as imitate other food, such as leeches, snakes, eels, or salamanders.

Soft worms are perhaps the most productive of all artificial lures for freshwater bass; they are primarily used in fishing for largemouth bass but will catch other species, such as northern pike and pickerel, and are frequently used as components of jigs

Tackle shops in largemouth bass country offer a huge variety of types, sizes, and colors of soft worms.

(see), spinnerbaits *(see),* and other lures. So popular are soft worms for bass fishing, it is possible that more of them are sold each year than all other bass lures combined.

What a soft worm specifically represents— earthworm, eel, leech, salamander, and so on—may be speculative, but there is no guessing about why it is successful. It looks like a fairly substantial morsel; it has a realistic feel; it has good action and moves enticingly and relatively naturally through cover; and, perhaps most importantly, it is worked effectively down at the level of the bass, which is to say the bottom and in protected hideaways. Moreover, one of the pleasant effects of successful soft worm fishing is a sense of accomplishment. Some lures require little more than accurate casting and routine retrieval to be effective, particularly when bass are active. But an artificial worm must be worked with your brain as well as your wrists; how you give it action, detect strikes, and react reflexively are major factors in its effectiveness.

Features

There are relatively soft worms and truly soft worms, versions that float and others that sink, and worms with all types of tail designs. They come in a whole spectrum of colors, and may sport light tails, light heads, light bellies, stripes, and polka dots. They are made in small, medium, large, and huge sizes. Some are scented, some are oiled, some come prerigged. In short, there is a veritable smorgasbord of soft worms.

The most important features of a worm, in descending order, are softness, buoyancy, size, body and tail shape, color, and scent.

Softness. Worms were once all made of rubber and very tough. Today, very few artificial worms are made of rubber (though some exist as prerigged worms on snelled hooks and leaders). The vast majority are made entirely of soft plastic. An increasing number are made of an amalgamation of soft plastic and processed natural foods that provide scent and flavor; these processed natural foods may be fish, crayfish, and other organisms and proteins. Thus, this category of lure transcends the use of plastic, and is chiefly categorized by its soft nature. In addition, advances in the chemical composition of certain plasticizing agents allow for manufacturing control over the suppleness of a worm, enabling some designs to deliberately be harder or softer in character than others.

Softness is a vital feature. A soft worm feels more lifelike and aids the angler in setting the hook. An artificial worm that is too soft is also fragile; it will tear when it comes into contact with objects and will barely hold a hook. A worm that is too hard feels unnatural and offers more resistance to hook point penetration, which at times is crucial in the timing of hooksetting. Most worm manufacturers try to make worms that are tough enough to withstand reasonable use, but soft enough to aid fish catching, although for Carolina rigging, which will be explained shortly, worms should be a little tougher than the norm.

Buoyancy. Another prominent feature of worms is their degree of buoyancy. Better worms have a light enough density to float on the surface of the water without a hook in them. Some will even float with a 1/0 or 2/0 hook in them, which is useful for fishing a completely unweighted worm on the surface over thick cover.

A worm that floats has a better appearance in the water because when it rests on the bottom, the tail section rides up. This accentuates both the behavior of the moving worm and its stationary appearance. Some specialty worms, such as very large and pre-rigged versions, understandably do not float and are not meant to float.

Size. The size of worm to use can vary with fishing conditions and the size of bass that you expect to take in any particular water. There is often a corollary between the size of the worm and the size of the bass that are caught. However, large bass are caught on small worms and small bass on big worms, including some bass that are shorter than the length of the worm.

Choice of worm size also depends on what you're seeking. If you're expressly interested in a trophy-size bass, then you should fish with nothing less than a 7-inch worm. In places where 10-pound bass are possible, an 8- to 12-inch worm is usually the best bet; where bass over 6 pounds are caught infrequently, a 7-inch worm is usually as large as you need.

Most bass fishing is done with 6-inch worms. All but the largest bass are good candidates for this bait, and in waters that are heavily fished, this size worm is relatively unobtrusive and unalarming to fish that are probably well conditioned to the presence of artificial lures. In some places, like heavily fished, clear-water lakes, it's necessary to use 4- and 5-inch worms for regular success.

Body/Tail shape. The basic body shape of most worms is round and moderately tapered from head to tail. Some worms are flat on one side, which is not as appealing as fully round models and which doesn't produce as good an action or object resistance. (Some soft lures that suspend or sink slowly are vaguely wormlike in appearance but shaped more like fish and fished differently; *see: jerkbait*).

Most worms have circularly molded indented impressions along their length, much like an earthworm, though a few are completely smooth. It probably doesn't make much difference to a bass or to the action of the worm whether it is smooth or slightly rippled. Some worms have a series of raised rings along their body, which trap air between them and release bubbles as the worm is retrieved. These worms have a tendency to grab onto grass, pads, rocks, and limbs more so than other worms, which hampers their action and restricts their ability to freely move over objects.

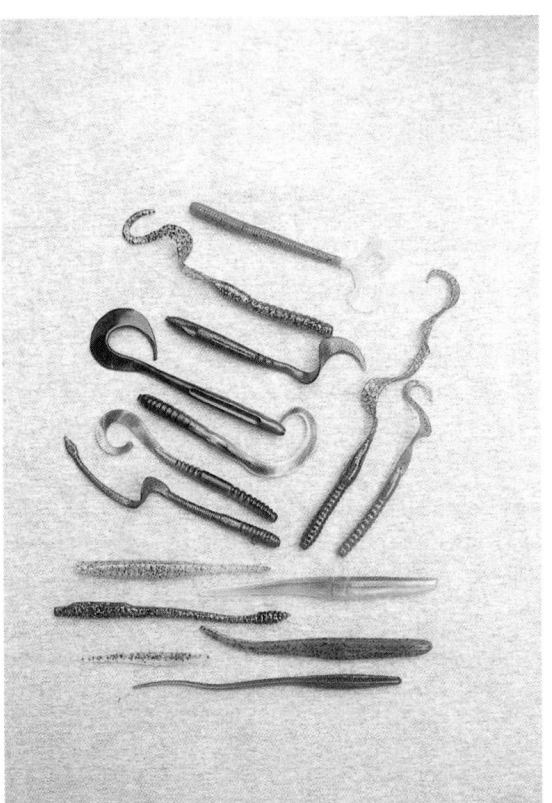

In this assortment of soft worms, the horizontal group includes various jerk worms.

Many worms are designed with straight tails, and an equal or greater number sport some type of curl tail. A few have beaver or paddle tails. Beaver-tailed models are bulkier than other worms, and you have to get used to the different feel of fishing them. They produce more action and vibration than a straight-tailed worm, and are effective in murky water, where added vibration for the large tail helps a fish locate the lure. They also make a nice trailer behind a jig, especially when flipping.

Curl tail worms include those with a simple J bend at the end as well as those with opposite curl features either at the end or two-thirds of the way through the body. Curl tails produce a nice swimming action with only the slightest assistance on the part of the angler.

It's worthwhile to experiment with different designs, just as it's desirable to have an assortment of different size and color worms. Many anglers eventually develop the most confidence in one particular design and use it for 90 percent of their worm fishing.

Scent/Color. Scent is also a matter of choice and personal confidence. Many worms are coated with some type of oil-like covering, which may or may not be scented; many others are imbedded with scents or derive scent from the processed natural materials they are made from. It is arguable what the value of this is and the extent to which it either attracts fish or makes them hold onto a lure. Scents may help mask human odors that are imprinted on soft plastic worms through hand contact, but it's hard to say that they contribute to the attraction of fish.

It is possible that fish will hold onto soft worms that are made with processed food a bit longer before rejecting them, providing a little more time to detect a strike and set the hook. Nevertheless, the most important factors for success are using a soft floating worm in the appropriate size and color and fishing it well.

Dark-colored worms are far more popular and successful than light ones, but there isn't a color or variation on color that hasn't been tried in soft worms. Some anglers are still partial to black and purple worms, and others to red, blue, grape, and motor oil, plus the two-toned shad colors and metal-flecked varieties. Many newer combination colors, like Fire and Ice, Junebug, tequila, electric blue, and red shad are also good.

Water color and visibility play a part in worm color determination, and at times one color outperforms another because it stands out better in a particular type of water. At other times, several colors are equally productive. More important than color, perhaps, is having confidence in your lure, fishing in the right places, and utilizing proper technique.

Some worms are better known by flavors than by colors. There is nothing to the flavor gimmick other than the fact that the impregnated smells help mask human odors, which may be imparted to worms when touched. Most worms are coated or otherwise treated with anise oil or some similar licorice-like smelling agent that keeps them moist and soft. Salt worms, which are impregnated with salt, are popular in some areas and are thought to induce bass to retain them longer than they might otherwise, but this advantage may be only psychological.

Firetail worms have merit when success is slow. Firetail worms are merely those with a light color blended into the tail section. Black, grape, blue, and purple worms with either a light pink or lime green tail are traditionally productive. Unfortunately, firetail worms also attract other species, including pickerel, bluegill, and rock bass, even more so than one-color worms. These fish can be a nuisance at times when you're seeking only bass.

Rigging

Texas rig. The Texas rig has been the standard worm-rigging method since suppliers stopped making worms out of hard rubber in preference for soft plastic. It can be used in almost any bass habitat, though it has limited value in really deep water and with heavy weights.

The Texas rig incorporates nothing more than a worm, slip sinker, and hook, with the hook point turned back and imbedded in the neck area of the worm so that it is essentially snag free. To accomplish this, put a cone shaped slip sinker onto your line, narrow end first, then tie the line to your hook.

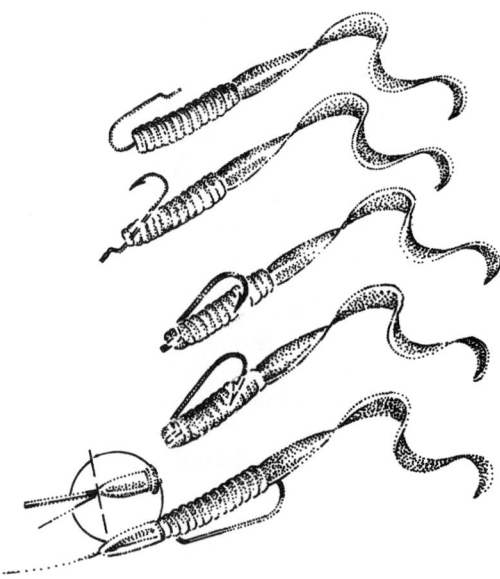

Shown from top to bottom are the steps for creating a Texas-rigged soft worm. If necessary when fishing in cover, a slip sinker can be pegged with the tip of a toothpick (inset) to keep it from moving.

Take the point of the hook and imbed it into the center of the head of the worm up past the barb, then bring the point out the side of the worm. Pull the shank of the hook through this passage and rotate it 180 degrees. Bring the shank all the way out until the eye of the hook is secured in the worm head. Slide the point into the body of the worm so that it is firmly imbedded in it, yet has not pierced through it. Do not curl or rotate the worm but be sure that the hook and worm are aligned and that the worm is straight and not bunched up.

The slip sinker will slide freely on this rig, but there are times, such as when fishing in thick cover, when it is advantageous to prevent the sinker from sliding freely (and getting hung up). To do this, jam one end of a toothpick in the head of a sinker as far as it will go, and then break it off. Jam the other end into the back of the cone, and break it off. An alternative way of accomplishing the same thing is to use a slip sinker with a corkscrew stem, which holds the worm in place.

To use the Texas rigging style to place the hook further along the body of the worm, carefully thread the point and shank of the hook through it to near the midsection. This rig can be fished with either a very light slip sinker or without a sinker, and is employed when bass are taking a worm in the middle rather than head first. It is often used when bass are spawning, and thus called a bed, or spawning, rig.

The biggest problem experienced by users of the Texas rig is getting the worm curled or bunched up. This causes the worm to spin when it is retrieved, producing an unnatural, unappealing action and contributing to line twist.

The theory behind the unpegged Texas rig is that when a bass grabs the worm, it does not feel the hook and does not detect the weight, which slides up the line. Theoretically, this gives the angler an extra moment in which to react and set the hook. When the hook is set, it should freely pierce the worm, which is another reason why the worm should be relatively soft.

The size of slip sinker, which is also called a worm weight, varies from $1/16$-ounce to $1/2$-ounce and depends on depth, wind, and the general activity of the fish. They are still primarily lead, but that could change in the future to brass or stainless steel alloys. Some anglers like painted sinkers, but unpainted weights are overwhelmingly popular.

The lighter the sinker's weight, the more likely you are to have success. Sinker weight must be matched to the terrain and fishing conditions, but using the lightest sinker possible while still correctly fishing under those conditions brings the best results.

The primary reason for this is that the heavier the sinker, the larger it is and the more detectable it may be to a bass. This is particularly true when fishing pressure is intense or when the bass are sluggish. Another important reason is that the worm is moved more naturally with a light sinker than with a heavy one, where its actions are more dramatic and pronounced. A worm with a light weight swims more convincingly than one with a heavy sinker. Light weights don't hang up as much as heavy ones, and they aid in detecting strikes, so it's best to use the lightest slip sinker possible for the conditions.

Sometimes, strong winds or current make worm fishing very difficult, and you have to use a larger than customary weight to gain casting accuracy and to maintain a feel for the bottom. In shallow water you can usually get away with a light sinker, but as you fish deep, you may need to increase the weight of the sinker. You can cast small worms and light weights more effectively with spinning tackle than with baitcasting equipment. Light line is conducive to light sinker use, since it does not offer as much resistance as the larger diameter, heavier line.

Hooks vary from 1/0 to 6/0, depending on the length of the worm. A general guideline is: 1/0 or 2/0 with 4-inch worms; 3/0 with 6-inchers; 4/0 with 7-inchers, 5/0 with 8-inchers; and 6/0 with larger worms.

A number of worm hook styles are popular, and there's a dizzying array to select from now. Many anglers prefer a keel, or offset, hook shank with a wide, or so-called Southern, sproat. The offset shank retains the worm pretty well, and the wide gap gives plenty of room for hooking. You might try experimenting with various hooks that turn when you strike a fish, and also with hooks that have outside edge barbs. Make sure that the hook point is as sharp as it possibly can be.

Carolina rig.　The Texas rig may be the most popular plastic worm rigging method, but it is not the only one. The Carolina rig, especially good for deep-water bottom fishing, features a floating worm that rises up unweighted. This rig sports a medium-weight sinker, followed by a barrel swivel, an 18- to 36-inch leader, and a hooked worm. The hook is generally no more than 1/0 size to give greater buoyancy to the worm and is usually exposed, though it can be imbedded into the worm Texas rig style when there are obstructions present. The sinker, which can be barrel-, egg-, or cone-shaped, weighs $3/4$-ounce to 1 ounce and slides freely to the swivel, so a fish can take the worm and move off without feeling resistance. The length of line between barrel and worm is somewhat arbitrary; 18 to 24 inches is the norm, but some anglers like to go with as little as 8 inches for swimming the worm through weed beds.

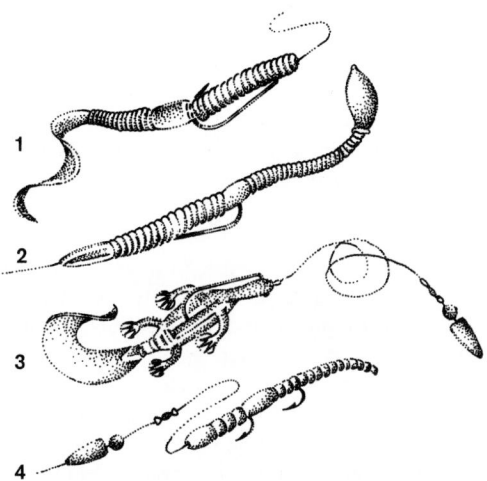

Soft worm rigs include: weightless floating Texas rig (1), mid-body Texas rig (2), Carolina rig (3), and an exposed-hook do-nothing rig (4).

Other rigs.　Another variation on this rigging method that is useful for unobstructed open-water fishing is the so-called Do Nothing rig. It features a heavy ($1/2$-to $1^1/2$-ounce) sliding slip sinker ahead of a barrel swivel, 3 to 5 feet of line between the swivel and worm, two panfish-size hooks, and a short straight worm. The hooks are rigged in tandem and are exposed; the worm is roughly 4 inches long. Some anglers use a small plastic bead between the sinker and swivel to prevent knot abrasion. A little tough to cast, this rig is fished in a slow, reel-cranking manner without any special rod or retrieval action. Despite its name, it is good enough to interest reluctant, bottom-dwelling bass.

The manner of hooking worms is often subject to experimentation. Setting the hook into the bony jaw of a bass is often difficult, especially if the hook point must first pierce the worm body; that's one reason super-soft worms are preferred by Texas rig users. Hooking variations, therefore, are usually directed at improving hooking efficiency. Some anglers put the hook through the head and leave the point exposed for fishing on the surface (without a weight), or they hook it in the collar or near the midsection for weightless, extremely slow, free-swimming simulation. A variation on the latter, with Texas-style hooking, is to thread the hook from the top of the worm down near the midsection, then bring the point out and imbed it into the worm. This is fished without a weight and has been called a spawning rig for bedding bass, which normally take a worm in the middle and swim off to remove it from the nest area.

Multiple hooking is another possibility, especially for short striking fish. Small worms can be rigged with one hook toward the rear by using a long, thin sewing needle to bring the line through the body, then tying it to the hook and inserting the shank of the hook in the worm. The hook can be exposed or it can be imbedded to make it weedless. A two-hook rig, in tandem and using snelled hooks, is a little tougher to execute, but many anglers prefer this. Such a rig enables anglers to catch bass that strike either the head or the tail of the worm. Worms can also be attached to jig hooks. Many anglers have summer bass success with 4-inch worms behind small jigs, fished on light line.

Fishing

When/Where.   Bass are receptive to worms in relatively warm water. In warm water, worms are softer and feel more natural. In cold water, plastic worms harden and are more quickly rejected by bass. In temperatures below 55°F or so, worms don't seem to appeal to bass; from temperatures in the mid-50s to the mid-60s, they have some appeal; they are in their best range from the mid-60's on up.

When you want to cover a lot of territory fairly rapidly, a worm is not the best bait to use. If, however, in doing this while using another lure, you catch a couple of fish in one area, it may pay to switch to a worm in order to work that area more thoroughly and more productively.

Worms work well at any given time of the day, particularly during the summer, and at night. Summer is traditionally the best time to fish a worm, when the bass are well secured in or near some type of cover, and you need a worm to work that cover extensively. This is one of the true benefits of worm fishing: You cover the area well, and you fish it on the bottom, where the bass are. Though swimming a worm over cover may at times have merit, primarily you fish it on the bottom.

A plastic worm rigged in weedless fashion is at its best when used around typical bass holding objects like stumps, fallen trees, grass, pads, hyacinths, hydrilla, docks, milfoil, and the like. When making a cast to a particular object, such as a stump, for example, cast beyond and to one side of that stump (such as the shaded side) initially, working the worm slowly up alongside and then past the stump. Baitcasters should take care to cast beyond the area they want to fish a worm, as the worm does not drop straight downward, but

usually falls on an angle toward the caster due to tension on the line. With a spinning reel, keep the bail open to allow the worm to fall relatively straight down from the place where it hits the water.

Retrieval.   The strike of a bass on a worm has often been related as feeling like a double tapping at the end of the line; the first tap is what you detect when the bass makes the motion to inhale it, and the second is what you detect as it enters the fish's mouth. If you feel a third tap, the bass is probably expelling it.

Learning to detect a strike or to differentiate a strike from contact with underwater objects is the most difficult aspect of worm fishing. There is no shortcut to learning this. An ability to detect strikes and learn the "feel" of a worm comes through experience. The more you fish with a worm, the quicker you'll develop this feel.

Beginning worm anglers might try practicing in their backyard or in shallow water where they can see the worm. Drag it over rocks and logs and tree limbs. Crawl it on gravel surfaces. Watch it work in a clear pool. Simulate fishing conditions.

Another key to detecting strikes is closely watching your line. In the most radical instances, an eager bass may pick up a worm and immediately run with it, in which case the line noticeably moves off to the side or away. Sometimes you'll see the line move like this before you feel the strike. Usually, however, there is a barely perceptible flickering of the line, particularly the section nearest to the water, which is a result of the bass inhaling the worm and drawing it (and the line) inward. In time, you'll come to see and feel the strike at the same instant.

When rigged to be snag-free, soft worms are great bass producers, fished in and around cover and on the bottom. They should be retrieved slowly, crawled along the bottom, and lifted and dropped over stumps, limbs, and other cover.

To retrieve a plastic worm, begin with the rod butt and your arms close to your body, with the rod held perpendicular to you and parallel to the water. Raise the rod from this position (we'll call it 9 o'clock) upward, extending it between a 45 and 60 degree angle, which would mean moving it from 9:00 to 10:30 or 11:00. As you raise the rod, the worm is lifted up off the bottom and swims forward, falling to a new position. Make this motion slowly, so the worm does not hop too far off the bottom and swims slowly. When your rod reaches that upward position, drop it back to its original position while at the same time retrieving slack line. Keep your motions slow. When you encounter some resistance, as would happen when crawling it over a log or through a bush, first gently try to work the worm along; if this fails, try to hop the worm along with short flickers of the rod tip.

Sometimes the slip sinker gets hung up under rocks, and if you jiggle your line, the sinker falls back and becomes free. Other times, the sinker will fall over a limb and slide down the line, while the worm stays back behind that limb. This makes detection and retrieval difficult and can be solved by pegging the slip sinker with a toothpick and breaking it off, thus preventing the sinker from sliding up the line. The sinker remains directly in front of the worm.

Pegging a worm is useful for fishing brushy areas, lily pads, hyacinths, moss, and grass as well as amidst stumps and trees, and it makes retrieval and strike detection easier. It goes against the theory of having a freely sliding slip sinker so a fish can pick up the lure and run off with it without detecting the weight, but this is minimized by a quick hook-setting reaction, a sensitive rod, and a sensitive line to detect strikes more readily.

Set the hook as soon as you can after detecting a strike. Remember that because the worm is rigged weedless with the hook imbedded in it, you can't simply rear back when you feel a strike, as you might when fishing a lure with exposed hooks. As soon as you detect a strike, lower the rod tip and extend it out and point it toward the fish. This momentarily gives the bass slack line. Quickly reel up the slack, and as the line draws tight, set the hook. Continue to reel in line to counteract the effect of stretch and to ensure that no slack is present. The whole maneuver is accomplished in an instant and appears to be one fluid motion. Removing slack line is critical, because your hook must penetrate not only the balled-up worm, but the cartilaginous mouth of the fish as well.

It is very difficult to fish a worm properly in wind. If you have a specific place that you wish to fish and it is buffeted by wind, you might anchor your boat in such a way that you can fish directly upwind or downwind of that spot. At other times you may elect to drift and fish, using an electric motor to either slow the drift speed or keep a desired position. If you have to drift, fishing in the direction the boat is headed is difficult, but may work because it allows you to fish a spot before the boat drifts over it. Where deep water is worked, it only makes sense to drift behind the boat.

Fishing against the wind can almost be like trolling and can be effective provided your boat is not moving too fast and your sinker is heavy enough to keep the worm down. One trouble with trolling a sinker-rigged worm is that bass strike and reject it quickly, but if you slow-troll it without a weight, it can be a different story; you might try this on shallow weedy lakes.

Occasionally, you may find it beneficial to swim the worm slowly just off the bottom. This works best in lily pads, in moderately thin grassy areas, and in similar spots. It's difficult to cast an unweighted worm with most baitcasting equipment, though not too difficult with spinning tackle.

Tackle. For worm fishing, use a good quality rod that has an even taper, with a strong butt and backbone and a "fast" or relatively limber tip. The disadvantage of a rod with a stiff tip is that it casts a worm poorly and is not sensitive enough for detecting strikes. Having a special "worm" rod to fish plastic worms isn't necessary. A graphite or good composite rod is strong and sensitive and is an advantage to an angler skilled at detecting pickups. The most popular rod choice is a $5^1/_2$-foot baitcasting model, but many anglers like 6-footers.

Spinning rods are not used as much for worm fishing as are baitcasting and spincasting rods, but they are perfectly acceptable if you have a fast-action rod that allows you to detect even faint strikes and to set the hook. Most people who fish worms on spinning rods use a rod that is too limber, and they are unable to set the hook.

There are no special criteria for reels where worm fishing is concerned. Line choice runs to the intermediate and heavy side, but 10- to 14-pound line is generally adequate for most situations, although it is worth noting that worms are fished in all manner of cover, so the line you use should be high quality and particularly resistant to abrasion and able to withstand sudden shock loading.

See: Jerkbait; Lure; Soft Lure.

SOLE

(1) Sole are flatfish *(see)* that typically have an extremely rounded to oval body. Their small eyes are close together, and most are right-eyed; like other flatfish, they undergo a unique maturation from egg to adult in which one eye migrates to the opposite side of the head. They live mainly in warm or temperate waters, and some species migrate into freshwater.

True sole are members of the Soleidae family of flatfish, but the word "sole" has been widely used to refer to some flatfish that actually belong to other

European Sole

families. Species referred to as sole in North America are rarely seen by the recreational angler and are more common in cold European waters, where they are taken by both commercial and recreational anglers. European sole have been heavily marketed, and the term "fillet of sole," which was once specific to the common or European sole *(Solea solea),* is now applied to many other sole and indeed for many non-sole flatfish.

(2) Common Sole   *Solea solea.*
Other names—European sole, black sole, Dover sole, parkgate sole, river sole, sea partridge, slip, tounge, true sole; Danish: *søtunge, tunge;* Dutch: *tong;* Finnish: *kielikampela;* French: *sole commune;* Icelandic: *sóikoli, sölflúra;* Italian: *sogliola;* Norwegian: *tunge;* Portuguese: *linguado legitimo;* Spanish: *lenguado común;* Swedish: *akta tunga, tunga, tungor, sjötunga;* Turkish: *dil, dil baligi.*

The common, or European, sole is a right-eyed member of the Soleidae family of flatfish *(see)* that has been commercially significant for European markets, where it is mainly caught by commercial trawlers.

Identification.   The body of the common sole is oval; the eyed side is uniformly yellowish brown with dark blotches, and the blind side is creamy white. Distinguishing characteristics include a downward-curved mouth and a small caudal fin. The pectoral fins are well developed on both sides, and the anal and dorsal fins are tinged with white.

Size/Age.   This species grows to 27 inches and 7 pounds but is commonly caught at 12 to 14 inches in length. It reportedly can live for 20 years.

Distribution.   The common sole occurs in the eastern Atlantic southward from Trondheim Fjord, including the North Sea and western Baltic, and the Mediterranean Sea, including the Sea of Marmara, Bosphorus, and the southwestern Black Sea. Elsewhere, it occurs southward to Senegal, including the Cape Verde Islands.

Habitat.   Common sole prefer water temperature ranging from 8 to 24°C and are located over sand and mud bottoms in varying depths, from near shore to 200 feet; they migrate to deeper water in winter.

Spawning behavior.   Spawning occurs in spring and early summer in shallow water.

Food.   The diet of sole consists of worms, mollusks, and small crustaceans. This fish is primarily a night feeder.

Angling.   Bottom fishing with natural baits and metal jigs is the primary method of catching sole. Angling techniques are discussed in greater detail under other entries *(see: drift fishing; inshore fishing).*

SOLE, GRAY
A common name for witch flounder.
See: Flounder, Witch.

Petrale Sole

SOLE, PETRALE   *Eopsetta jordani.*
Other names—sole, round-nosed sole, Jordan's flounder, California sole, brill.

A member of the Pleuronectidae family of right-eyed flatfish *(see),* the petrale sole is an occasional catch by anglers and a good sportfish, in part owing to its moderate size. It is an excellent food fish and is highly sought commercially, primarily by trawlers, and is marketed fresh or as frozen fillets. The liver of large specimens is known to be rich in vitamin A.

Identification.   The body of the petrale sole is elongate, moderately slender, and compressed. The head is deep and the mouth large. The eyes are large, and the color on the eyed side is uniformly dark to light brown with dusky blotches on the dorsal and anal fins. It is white on the blind side.

The petrale sole are often confused with California halibut *(see: halibut, California)* because these species have a similar color and large mouths. Petrale sole, however, have an even, brown coloration and do not have a high arch in their lateral line.

Size.   The average commercial catch is between 1 and 2 pounds, but this species can attain lengths to 28 inches and a weight of 8 pounds.

Distribution.   The petrale sole ranges from the Bering Sea and Aleutian Islands throughout the Gulf of Alaska to the Coronado Islands of northern Baja California, Mexico.

Habitat.   Petrale sole occur on sand and mud bottoms in waters from 60 to 1,500 feet deep, although they are most commonly found between 180 and 400 feet from April through October, and deeper in winter. Anglers on party boats are likely to encounter them at such depths on sand bottoms near rocky reefs.

Food.   The diet of petrale sole includes crabs, shrimp, and fish such as anchovies, hake, small rockfish, and other flatfish.

Angling.   In California, most of the petrale sole catch is made by anglers pursuing deep rockfish on party boats. Angling techniques for flatfish are discussed in greater detail under other entries *(see: drift fishing; inshore fishing).*

SOLUNAR TABLES *(Fish Activity Charts)*
Tables and charts that forecast periods of fish and game activity are commonly and generically

referred to as solunar tables, partly because they are based on the location of the sun and moon in relation to the earth, but mostly because the first and most well-known of these was named and registered under the trademark of the Solunar Tables by its creator, John Alden Knight, in 1926. For decades, these solunar tables were the most prominently used forecasters of fish and game activity.

Today a number of fish and game activity forecasting tables (also called charts or calendars) are available. Magazines and newspapers publish various ones on a regular basis, including the original by Knight. Some people have a lot of faith in forecasting tables and use them to plan their local outings and major fishing trips; these tables are often popular with readers of outdoor publications, as publishers found out when the tables were stopped and protests poured in. On the other hand, many people think that forecasting fish and game activity is psychic babble, and never pay attention to the tables. Still others take the position that this business is like UFOs; maybe they exist and maybe they don't; neither side can unequivocally prove or disprove their validity.

Without getting into a long and tedious lesson in astronomy and related sciences, the nature of these tables can be summarized by saying that they are based upon the phase of the moon and the proximity of the sun and the moon to the earth on any given day. In most tables, the periods of peak activity, or "best" times to be afield, are forecast to occur during the full and new moon phases, and other, lesser periods of activity are forecast at times that coincide with quarter-moon phases and peak times of daylight or darkness daily. Activity periods are forecast to the exact minute of the day and are claimed (or implied) to be valid for all creatures, with appropriate time factoring for different geographic locations.

Some of the activity periods forecast by these tables coincide with tidal movement, and it is well-known to anglers that tide (see) has a significant bearing on fish activity in areas where it exists. It is also well-known to many serious anglers that low levels of light are prime for fish activity and fishing success, either because the predators that anglers seek can see their prey better or because they are simply more stimulated by the changing conditions.

Some producers of various forecasting tables make far-reaching claims about the validity of their information, even stating that it is based on proven scientific theories or facts, but there is no scientific proof that this information is correct. It's a theory. Nevertheless, some people who use activity periods to pick the times that they go fishing report dependability. Such a result is not scientifically valid, since the predetermined times influence when to focus efforts.

Many unbiased observers and anglers have looked at these tables after they have fished, or after compiling an array of detailed information about their own efforts, and have found that there were correlations between their better fishing results and the times that were forecast to be productive. Others have concluded that there was not enough of a correlation to be important.

Logically, one has to wonder how any fish and game activity forecasting table can be applicable for all species of fish (and game) in all habitats at all times and under all circumstances. So many intangible factors influence sportfishing that it is not only skeptical but reasonable to wonder how all fish activity can be pegged in such a way. Certainly the sun and moon do play a role in tides and in spawning for some species, and they are known to influence some insect hatches. But there is such great diversity in the rhythmic behavior of all fish, and especially the top predators that are sought by anglers, that forecasting, at least on an all-for-one basis, remains clouded in skepticism.

SONAR

Most anglers simply use the term "depthfinder" or "depth sounder" when referring to what is actually sonar equipment. At one time, sonar devices were also called fish locators, and are still sometimes called fishfinders. To much of the rest of the world, they are echo sounders.

The word sonar is an acronym for sound navigation and ranging equipment. This was applied by the military in World Wars I and II. Today's electronic depth finding and fish locating equipment helps anglers enjoy their sport and become more learned and proficient. Sonar is the boat angler's underwater eyes, and in some circumstances is viewed as being virtually indispensable. With it, the angler can find concentrations of migratory, suspended, schooling, and nomadic fish, and locate submerged habitat that may be attractive to particular species. With sportfishing sonar, an angler can become accurately acquainted with the beneath-the-surface environment of any body of water in significantly less time than without it. Additionally, the use of sportfishing sonar allows an angler to navigate more safely and quickly than he might otherwise, although it is not actually a navigational tool.

Locating fish with sonar is no guarantee that they are the kind of fish being sought. Sonar also can't ensure that you'll be able to catch the fish, regardless of the extent of your knowledge and experience. There is still no substitute for angling savvy, skillful presentation, and knowledge of fish behavior and habits. This notwithstanding, there are many times when even the most skillful anglers can find fish but not catch them.

While locating fish is an important usage of sonar (more for some species than others), transmitting depth information is its predominant function. Depth information is used consistently as an

S

Although many people think that the primary usefulness of sonar is for finding fish, it is even more important for determining depth, finding contours and structures, and in general locating places that are likely to contain specific kinds of fish.

aid to determining where and how to fish, allowing more precise, and thus more effective, presentation of lures or bait than might be possible if the depth, bottom contours, and underwater habitat were unknown and constantly changing.

A basic key to catching fish is locating them or their preferred habitat and fishing appropriate lures or bait at the proper depths. If you're not familiar with the place you're fishing, chances are that without sonar you'll be largely unaware of the depths of the various areas, or would repeatedly have to drop a weighted line down to determine depth. This does not mean that you can't or won't catch fish. However, you may not be aware of certain characteristics of that body of water which might greatly aid your fish finding and fish catching efforts. If you learn to interpret the information that it provides, sonar can be one of the most important pieces of angling equipment. Skilled sonar users can predict with startling accuracy what species of gamefish are below and how catchable they are simply by noting how they relate to each other, to schools of baitfish, and to the bottom.

How Sonar Works

Sonar is essentially made up of a display unit and a transducer, which are connected by coaxial cable to each other. The display unit indicates the information that the transducer has provided by issuing signals through the water. Sound travels at about 4,800 feet per second through the water, which is

four times faster than it travels through air. Sonar instruments issue signals (pulses or sound waves) from the transducer at extremely swift rates, actually many times per second. The greater the distance between transducer (the system component that sends the pulses out and receives echoes back from them) and bottom, the longer it takes for the pulses to reach bottom, and return echoes. Nonetheless, the speed of operation is amazingly swift, so swift that it is unlikely that a boat can outrun the signal. By measuring the time from the transmission of the signals until their reflected echoes are received, the sonar can determine the depth of underwater objects as well as the bottom.

Although, as previously noted, most anglers use the terms depthfinder, depthsounder, and fishfinder interchangeably when referring to sonar equipment, there is technically a difference. Most sonar used by anglers is very functional for determining depth and for determining the location of fish; however, there is some sonar, primarily digital numerical display units, that only provide depth information. These are primarily used by sailboaters and cruisers, and by design, they do not provide information about fish, suspended objects, and type of bottom. These are strictly depth-finding sonar, not sportfishing sonar. A digital depth readout is often included as a secondary feature on more sophisticated sonar units.

The two most popular operating frequencies for sportfishing sonar are 50kHz and 200kHz, although 120kHz, 455kHz, and other frequencies are also used. The lower frequency is meant for very deep water (beyond 300 feet) while the higher frequency is meant for shallower use, and some sonar features dual-frequency operation with corresponding transducers. Most anglers, especially freshwater anglers, use 200kHz units, or dual-frequency units that are primarily set for the higher frequency mode. Some dual-frequency models can display simultaneous information from both frequencies on the same screen or in a split screen presentation, enabling them to display and compare information.

The signal echoes that are returned to sonar instruments are presented via a liquid crystal display (LCD), cathode-ray tube (CRT), or light-emitting diodes (LED). The former provide picturelike representations on small rectangular screens while the latter appears as a flashing light on a circular calibrated dial. At least two manufacturers offer LCD screens that mimic the readouts of circular LED dial displays. Most sonar units used by anglers are of the LCD variety.

Transducers come in various sizes, mounts, and frequencies, and send out pulses in a three-dimensional cone-shaped wave. Cone angles range from narrow to extremely wide. The diameter of these cones influences how much detail will be seen. Unfortunately, there is no universally accepted "standard" method for measuring and rating cone angles in the sportfishing sonar industry. One

manufacturer's 8-degree transducer may be the equivalent of another's 16-degree model, and so on. Generally speaking, high frequency (more than 100kHz) transducers come in "wide" and "narrow" cone angle versions. As a rule of thumb, you can quickly find the diameter of a transducer's coverage at any depth by dividing that depth by 7 for a narrow cone or by 3 for a wide cone. A narrow cone angle has about a 2-foot diameter at a depth of 15 feet; it has about a 4-foot diameter at a depth of 30 feet. A wide cone angle has a 5-foot diameter in 15 feet of water and 10-foot in 30. Most low frequency transducers have a cone angle of about 45 degrees, which covers a diameter about equal to the depth. Its diameter is about 15 feet at a depth of 15 feet and about 30 feet at a depth of 30 feet. As with all rules of thumb, there are exceptions and a given unit's cone angle can be verified by checking the owner's manual.

it details are directly below the boat when they may be well off to the side. Some sonar sports dual transducer or single transducer housings with dual cone angle capability, so that you can switch back and forth.

Generally speaking, searching for fish with a wide cone cuts search time because a wider swath of water is scanned as the boat moves along. Once fish are spotted, switching to a narrow cone helps pinpoint their location. It's like searching for something in the dark. A floodlight will help you find something faster than a spotlight; switching to the more concentrated power of a spotlight lets you examine it in better detail.

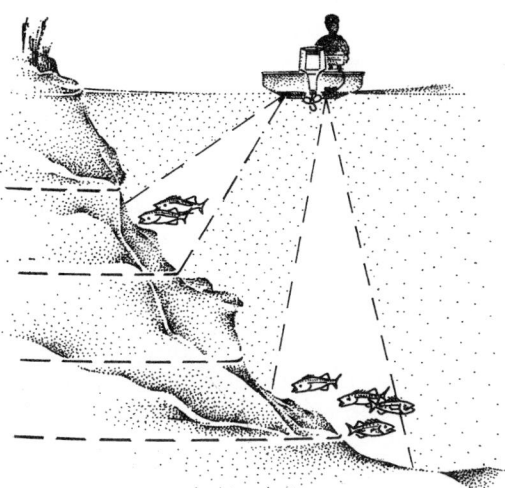

The majority of sonar devices only view what is directly below the boat, but some are designed to view out to the side, and a few can do both.

In addition to looking down, some units look to the side, either via a rotating transducer or a fixed mount, side-viewing transducer. The advantages of side-viewing are obvious: finding fish that are not below the boat, looking along a bank for fish to cast to, scanning through a river pool to see if it holds fish, and so on. Some anglers report success with side-viewing sonar and express confidence in it, but many anglers are not convinced that they reliably detect fish. Within the industry, there has been debate over the technological ability of sonar to reliably locate fish past the distance at which the upper edge of the horizontally aimed cone strikes the water's surface or the lower edge hits the bottom. Both the surface and bottom solidly reflect the transducer's sound signal and their massive echoes may mask the much weaker echoes from fish.

Nevertheless, more manufacturers are offering side-looking equipment each year. And many engineers, particularly those who in the past have worked on the design of anti-submarine, mine detection, and torpedo guidance systems are now working at sportfishing sonar development. This is an area in which there will likely be technological advances in the future.

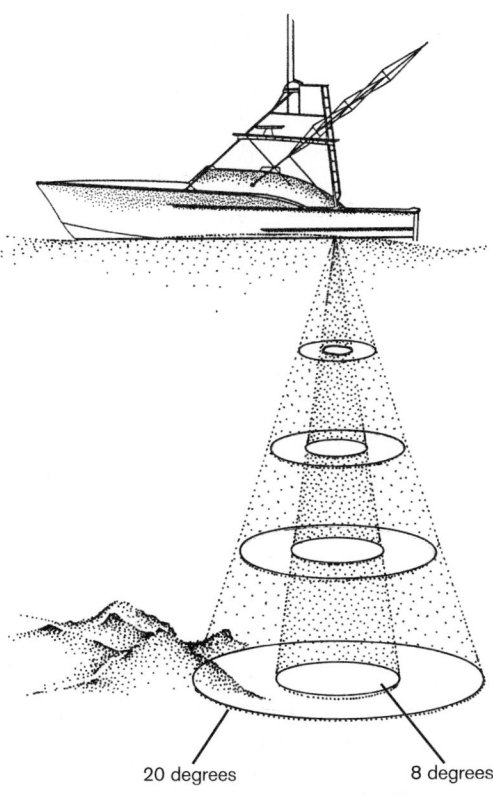

20 degrees   8 degrees

The diameter of the transducer cone angle affects coverage area.

The narrowest cone angles are most useful in extremely deep water, such as 150 feet or more. The widest cones enable you to see a lot more of what's beneath you, are especially useful for downrigger trolling and fishing directly below the boat, and work best at slow boat speeds. The medium-range cones are less specialized, have all-around functionality, and are best used in less than 100 feet of water. The only drawback to the super-wide cone angle is that it takes in so much information that you may trick yourself into thinking that fish

Incidentally, some manufacturers offer an alternative for viewing areas away from the angler or the boat. This is a floating device that cradles the transducer, and which can be used to scan selected areas without the user being on top of them. The device, loaded with a transducer and connected to a read-out unit via a long cable, can be tossed Frisbee-style into the water, or allowed to float downstream or offshore. This makes it possible for boat, bank, bridge, or pier anglers to scout an area within casting distance.

Another area ripe for improvement will be sonar that can unerringly determine the size of individual fish and distinguish between species. Manufacturers have made such claims in regard to existing equipment, but that era has not yet arrived. When sonar can truly indicate size and species (not leaving it up to individual interpretation and speculation), a whole new world will open up. Because anglers are frequently unable to determine the direction that deep fish are headed, as well as the distance they may be from the boat (at the speed traveled in passing over and beyond them), these issues, too, will change.

Types of Sonar

The sportfishing sonar field has changed radically since computer chips were integrated into marine electronics. Sonar today is incredibly sophisticated, with phenomenal abilities and incredible options.

Sonar evolved from flashers (LEDs) to paper chart recorders to LCDs and video sonar using cathode-ray tubes (CRTs). Chart recorders were once the premium sonar and the equipment that provided the best underwater detail; they are now obsolete and flashers are practically so, although some veteran sonar users still prefer flashers, which have enjoyed a minor resurgence, primarily among some bass and walleye anglers. Most sonar today features a liquid crystal display, and many people now use the terms sonar and LCD virtually synonymously. The better LCD sonar today gives as good detail as the premium paper chart sonar of old, and it's better in many ways than a flasher. Depending on the unit and optional accessories, sonar can also provide boat speed, distance traveled, and water temperature information, and can be integrated into other electronics, especially global positioning systems (see: GPS).

Sonar is available in portable as well as permanent mount versions. Portable models work on almost any boat but are primarily used on small craft. The transducer is generally attached to a bracket and clamped to the gunwale or transom, or to a suction cup placed on the transom.

A fixed bow-mounted sonar is particularly helpful for freshwater anglers who spend much of their angling time in the bow, casting and running the electric motor to maneuver along likely fishing areas. Ideally, the transducer for this unit should be located on the bottom of the bow-mounted electric motor to give readings directly below the front of the boat. Remember that in water shallower than 15 feet a transducer's cone angle scans an area that may not be as wide as the boat. A trolling-motor-mounted transducer shows what's under the forward part of the boat, not what's under the transom 15 to 20 feet behind it.

A fixed console-mounted sonar is used by many boaters, sometimes as their only type of sonar, sometimes in conjunction with a bow-mounted unit. When it's the only sonar aboard, an accessory swivel bracket can let it be turned as necessary to be seen from anywhere in the boat. The transducer for console-mounted sonar (as well as for sonar located near the stern on a tiller-steered boat) is located on the transom, or, in a few cases, mounted in the sump or integrated into the hull during construction.

The basic types of sonar include the following.

Flasher. A flasher is an LED device with a flashing light on a circular calibrated dial. Flashers indicate everything that other types of sonar do, but they require extensive experience to interpret, especially in regard to the characteristics of the bottom. Although they depict the location of fish, that depiction is fleeting; thus, this type of sonar, less common than in previous years, is most useful in determining depth and bottom contour.

Flashers are simple units and deliver instantaneous readings without computer filtering or averaging. For this reason some experienced users who have multiple sonar on their boats still prefer flashers for tracking depth and spotting suspended fish at high boat speeds. When the flasher shows a string of blips, the user slows the boat, turns around, and reexamines the area with an LCD or video unit to identify what the flasher spotted.

Chart recorder. Also known as a graph recorder, this device uses a roll of paper upon which the images of fish, objects, and underwater terrain are displayed and permanently printed. These units have been made obsolete by liquid crystal displays and are no longer in production outside of the commercial arena, although some guides, charter boat captains, and avid anglers still retain and use them. Chart recorders are large and heavy, take up a lot space, and require some maintenance; however, they have excellent (some would say unmatched) detail and provide a permanent record for later review. They are most useful in shallow and moderate depths.

Video sonar. This device uses a cathode-ray tube (CRT) and displays images on a screen that looks much like a video monitor or television. Different colors are used to represent fish by size and distinguish objects and the bottom on color units. Monochrome units make these distinctions by displaying objects with different levels of image brightness rather than in different colors. They offer more screen detail and better visibility in sunlight than color units. Video sonar comprises a minor portion of the sportfishing sonar market, being used primarily on large sportfishing boats on the Great Lakes and in saltwater. A current a trend is toward increased use of monochrome video sonar by professional walleye tournament anglers. CRTs are also known as video sounders. They are generally more expensive, larger, heavier, and more fragile than other types. They are also harder to read in direct sunlight and use more battery power. However, some monochrome units offer excellent detail and target separation. They can be hard to match for spotting fish on the bottom or in weeds.

Liquid crystal displays. These units, known by the acronym LCD, are by far the most prominent sonar for anglers; they are also, but less commonly, referred to as liquid crystal recorders (LCR). There are digital readout models that only display numerical depth information and are of most use for routine boating. Most LCDs display fish, objects, and bottom information in a scrolling videolike manner via a grid of dots called pixels. The number of pixels in each vertical column on a screen determines its ability to display detail while the number of pixels in each horizontal row determines how long information stays on the screen before it scrolls off the edge. The greater the number of vertical pixels, the better the resolution or screen detail. The deeper the water you fish and the more screen detail you desire, the more vertical pixels you need for better images. The same is true for power; for deep water you need units with greater wattage.

The visibility of LCDs varies between products and in general has improved over the years, but is still an area of dissatisfaction for some users. Though easily read in some light conditions and from a position immediately in front of the unit, liquid crystal displays have been difficult to read from other angles, by viewers using polarized sunglasses, and in the dark with side- or backlighting.

Some LCDs have large screens and a split-screen zoom feature. This allows you to split the screen and show the normal image of everything in the water from surface to bottom on one side and a magnified portion of the water column on the other side. The zoom feature can be adjusted in size and magnification on better units. Some LCDs also have a three-dimensional viewing feature; however, many users may find this confusing and difficult to relate to for fishing applications. Three-dimensional viewing is offered as an option on some sonar, subordinate to conventional chart-style display.

LCDs do not produce paper records. Some have memory capabilities and can be linked to a home personal computer so that information can be stored and retrieved. This is undoubtedly an area that will become more prominent in the future. More technical information about the characteristics of LCDs and other sonar are contained in the following section.

More Technical Points

Although many advances are being made in sportfishing sonar, there are some underlying and unchanging fundamentals of sonar that affect performance no matter what new features may be added to this equipment. The technical information in literature provided by manufacturers includes a listing of operating frequencies, power, transducer cone angle, display resolution, and receiver sensitivity, all of which have an effect on the performance of sonar. If you were able to put sonar units side by side on the water and evaluate them, you'd see that some sonar units have better display capabilities than others, some can find and depict fish better than others, and some are easier to use than others. The following review of technical matters puts some of these performance aspects into perspective.

Frequency. Which frequency to use or which frequency sonar to purchase is one of the key issues that face anglers, and the choice depends on the application. There are advantages and disadvantages to both high- and low-frequency sonars for different applications.

The higher the frequency of the sound waves, the more quickly they fade and the shorter their useful range; low frequency sound waves don't fade as quickly as high frequency waves, and have a deeper useful range. Knowing a sonar unit's frequency, you can determine its useful range with any given output power and transducer cone angle.

High frequency sound waves have a shorter wavelength than low frequency waves; therefore, there are more cycles in a high frequency pulse than in a low frequency pulse of the same width or duration. The more cycles there are, the stronger the signal and the stronger the echoes. Therefore, a high frequency echo from a small object is stronger than a low frequency echo from the same object, and is more likely to be received by the sonar. This is relative only to the high frequency sonar's useful range.

The shorter pulse length of the high frequency can also be used for better target separation. From the instant a sound pulse begins to leave the

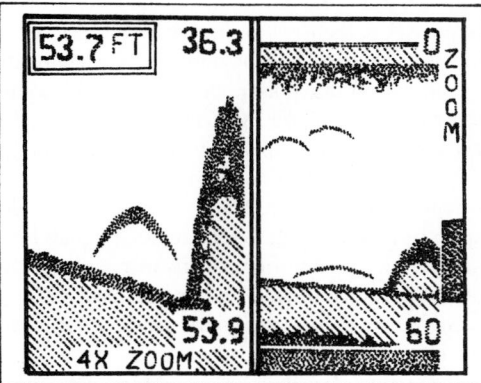

Split-screen sonar views, as depicted here, are very useful, allowing you to focus on a specific area in more detail.

S

transducer, it travels downward at the speed of sound through water. From the beginning to the end, the pulse takes up an area of depth measured in inches or feet. A pulse has a vertical thickness of about 1 inch for each 30 microseconds (millionths of a second) that the pulse lasts. The length of time a pulse lasts is usually computer controlled and varies with the depth range selected and the amount of filtering currently engaged. The deeper the depth range or the higher the level of filtering, the longer the pulse length. The thickness or width of this pulse determines how far apart objects must be before the sonar unit can see them as separate entities.

Sonar can see objects individually only if they are vertically separated by enough distance. Imagine a pulse that is 6 inches thick traveling downward toward two fish that are only 2 vertical inches apart. The leading edge of the pulse strikes the deeper fish before the trailing edge of the pulse clears the shallower fish. The transducer receives the sound reflected by both fish as a single, unbroken echo. As far as the unit is concerned there is only one fish. If the fish are 7 inches apart, the trailing edge of the pulse leaves the first fish, ending its echo, before the leading edge of the pulse strikes the deeper fish and begins returning its echo. Now, the transducer hears two consecutive shorter echoes instead of a single longer echo and the unit recognizes the fish as two separate objects.

The same is true for fish holding close to the bottom. If a fish is so close to the bottom that a pulse begins sending back a bottom echo before it stops sending the fish echo, the unit thinks the fish is a high spot on the bottom and blends it into the bottom reading.

The shorter the pulse length, the thinner the physical width of the pulse, and the closer things can be to each other on a vertical plane and still be seen by sonar as separate objects. High frequency sonar is capable of superior target separation and general screen detail because it can transmit short pulses with better results than low frequency sonar.

Whether high frequency sonar does detect smaller objects and have better target separation than low frequency sonar depends on other factors, such as receiver sensitivity and display resolution, and whether the sonar is capable of transmitting a short pulse. If the sonar doesn't have a highly sensitive receiver, it won't be able to receive the weak echoes from small objects. And if it doesn't have a good quality high-resolution display, or if you are not zoomed in very closely, it won't be able to show good target separation. If each pixel represents 12 inches of depth, for instance, two fish that are 6 inches apart can't be displayed separately regardless of the unit's pulse length.

The real benefit of low frequency sonar is that it has a deeper useful range. It can penetrate to deeper depths than high frequency sonar with the same amount of power. Imagine listening to an approaching band during a parade. The first instrument you hear is the low frequency sound of the bass drum. As the band gets closer, the last thing you hear is the high frequency notes of the flutes. Low frequency sound simply carries farther. Also, low frequency sonar has a wider coverage area than high frequency sonar. One of the main uses of the low frequency, wide-cone angle is tracking downriggers while trolling and being able to adjust their depth in relation to the depth of the fish that are also observed on the sonar. With high frequency sonar, the cone angle may be too small to see the downrigger weights because they do not drop directly beneath the boat. They usually swing out behind the boat and may swing out of the high frequency sonar's cone angle.

The difference between the two frequencies is most evident in different applications. One place where high frequency sonar would be preferable is in a lake where there is a lot of weeds or brush. In this situation, the longer pulse and broader cone angle of low frequency sonar would pick up so much of the brush or weeds that anything else in the area would blend into the echoes from the weeds. The shorter pulses and narrower cone angle of the high frequency would focus on a smaller area and be more likely to see a fish at or near the top of the weeds, possibly even allowing you to locate a fish in the weeds. If there is a lot of debris and turbidity in the water, the low frequency sonar will not pick up all the small particles in the water and can provide better information.

Power and sensitivity. Output power is a measurement of the strength of a sonar's transmitted signal, usually expressed as watts peak-to-peak, or as watts RMS. This can be confusing, but the peak-to-peak rating equals the RMS rating multiplied by 8. For instance, a transmitter rated at 400 watts RMS would have a peak-to-peak output of 3200 watts. Output power is usually constant at all depth-range settings and at all receiver sensitivity settings, although some units turn the output power down at shallower range settings.

Turning up the sensitivity doesn't increase the output power, as some think. Like the volume control on a radio, it simply makes the receiver more sensitive. The higher the sensitivity level, the weaker echoes can be and still be detected. Generally, the higher the output power, the stronger the sound waves transmitted and the deeper the sound waves will go; thus, the deeper the sonar's useful range. However, high power doesn't necessarily guarantee extreme depth readings. The receiver sensitivity also has to be good enough to receive weak signals from great depths. A low frequency sonar with low to medium power can read deeper and have a deeper useful range than a high frequency, high-power sonar.

Generally, the more levels of adjustment a receiver has, the more sensitive a unit is and/or the more it can be fine-tuned. Receivers with fewer levels of adjustment cannot be fine-tuned as well as those with more levels of adjustment. They can offer either too much or not enough sensitivity for present conditions and leave you wishing for an adjustment increment between the closest two that are available.

When trying to judge the effectiveness of a sonar's output power in terms of ability to detect fish, look at the maximum depth capability listed in the specifications. A good rule of thumb for judging how deep a sonar device will show you fish is to cut the maximum depth capability in half. The strongest echo will always be from the bottom. It is many times stronger than anything else. If a unit says that its maximum depth capability is 500 feet, you can trust it to depict fish that are as deep as 250 feet.

Whether it offers good performance in this area or not also depends on the cone angle of the transducer. A transducer is basically the sonar's antenna, and most are made up of crystals sealed inside a watertight plastic or bronze housing. The size and shape of the transducer crystal determines the pattern of sound waves the crystal will transmit. In each case, the pattern consists of one main teardrop-shaped lobe formed by most of the signal, and several smaller side lobes with small amounts of signal. Most manufacturers measure their cone angle at the minus 3dB or half-power point. Imagine measuring the sound volume directly below the transducer at a given depth, then moving horizontally in any direction until the sound volume decreases 50 percent. If you could mark that point in all directions, your marks would form a rough circle that indicates the area of sonar coverage for that depth. Some manufacturers may include the side lobes in their cone angle measurement and/or go far beyond the half-power point to measure the edge of the cone. This results in general confusion, and can make transducers appear to have greater effective coverage than they actually do, which means that in use the products do not provide the performance that is expected.

To further confuse matters, a transducer's effective cone angle is influenced by the sensitivity setting. The more you increase sensitivity, the farther off to the side fish and other objects can be and still be displayed. The more you decrease sensitivity, the closer to the center of the cone (where the sound power is strongest) these same objects have to be to appear on the display.

Display resolution.   The resolution capability is one of the most important features of sonar. Liquid crystal displays are made up of a matrix of vertical and horizontal pixels; this provides resolution and is directly related to the detail that is displayed. The more vertical pixels there are, the better the resolution and the more detail that is provided. The more detail you see, the more you know about what is below and the better you're equipped to adjust fishing techniques. In a sense, it's like driving a car in the rain without windshield wipers: The poorer that you see, the less able you are to drive.

Each of the pixels in a vertical column represents a certain portion of the total depth. The more vertical pixels there are, the smaller portion of depth that each will represent, and the more detailed the picture. For instance, for a sonar with 100 vertical pixels set on the 100-foot range, each vertical pixel is covering 1 foot of water. In 200 feet of water, each pixel would be covering 2 feet of water. The 25th pixel down on the 200-foot range is covering from 50 to 52 feet. If a fish is at 51 feet, the corresponding pixel turns on to tell you there is an echo somewhere between 50 and 52 feet.

If a sonar had 100 vertical pixels and was used on a depth scale setting of 0 to 50 feet, it would provide a resolution of 6 inches per pixel. Yet, if there were two fish below and they were vertically less than 12 inches apart, they might be displayed as only one fish. The unit must be able to show a blank pixel between two darkened pixels in a vertical column to separately display targets. Depending upon how the unit's computer software fits each fish into the pixel grid, there might not be enough separation. If that sonar had 200 vertical pixels, then the resolution would be 3 inches per pixel, and two fish that were less than 12 inches apart could easily be displayed as two separate fish.

When the sonar transmits a sound pulse and receives echoes, it turns on the pixels in the vertical column at the right-hand edge of the display that correspond to the depth of the object returning the echoes. Then it moves that information one column to the left. It again transmits and listens for echoes and again darkens the pixels in the right-hand vertical column that correspond to the depth of the new echoes it receives. By doing this, the sonar screen constantly scrolls from right to left.

Many anglers mistakenly think that the whole screen renews with each sounding and shows a real-time picture of the underwater world, but the screen image is really built one vertical column at a time. What's happening right now between your boat and the bottom is shown at the far right edge of the screen and everything to the left is a screen history of past soundings.

In many LCD units, resolution can be enhanced further by using the zoom feature. Zoom allows you to magnify a small segment of the depth range currently on the display by applying the screen's full vertical pixel count to it. If, for instance, an entire 0 to 50–foot depth range is viewed on a display with 200 vertical pixels, there are four pixels for each foot of depth and each pixel represents about 3 inches. Zoom in on the depth segment from 40 to 50 feet and you apply all 200 pixels to only 10 feet of depth. Now, there are 20 pixels in each foot of depth and each pixel represents slightly more than half an inch. Since $1^1/_2$ inches of target separation is about the best that is claimed for an LCD sonar at this writing, that's better screen resolution than the unit's electronics are capable of using, so you'll get all of the detail the unit can produce.

Some of the confusion with regard to resolution centers on the manner of advertising the number of pixels. Some manufacturers talk about the number of pixels per square inch while others talk about the number of vertical pixels. These are not comparable figures, and a high pixels-per-square-inch count could mask a low vertical-pixels-per-column count, meaning that the unit may actually have less resolution than you think.

If you have a display grid that is 240 pixels tall and 100 pixels wide, you'll have great resolution because the vertical count is very high. A screen that is 100 pixels tall by 240 pixels wide has the same number of pixels per square inch but less than half the vertical resolution. Remember, the vertical columns of pixels represent the vertical water column between the boat and the bottom, and the higher the number of pixels in each column, the finer the detail it can display. The horizontal pixel count only determines how many vertical columns of screen history a display can show, and tells you how long information will stay on the screen before it scrolls off the left-hand edge.

Transducer Installation

Getting good readings from sonar is important to interpretation. Unfortunately, improper transducer installation leads to many problems and can hamper fishing efforts; it is the most common cause of poor sonar performance. Whether the transducer is mounted inside or outside the hull, it must be placed in a position that receives a smooth flow of water at all speeds. If it doesn't have a smooth flow of water, interference from turbulence can cause poor sonar readings or intermittent readings when the boat is under power. If you don't want to make the installation yourself, take the sonar and transducer to a boat dealer who has experience in rigging fishing boats.

If you're purchasing a new fiberglass boat, the absolute best thing to do is purchase the sonar before the boat is manufactured, send the transducer to the factory, and have them hand-lay it into the fiberglass when they build the hull. Some transducers installed by boat manufacturers and dealers shoot through the hull (but performance can suffer if there is air in the fiberglass or resin). Some boat builders mount the transducer face flush with the hull and you can't even tell where it's located. With some manufacturers, different transducers are required for different applications. In some boats, usually single-thickness fiberglass models, a shoot-through-hull transducer can be installed after the boat is built, but it may require a bit of experimentation to locate the best position. In any event, some signal loss is likely to occur. Generally, the faster a boat can travel, the further aft and closer to the centerline the installation location should be, so that it stays in the water at high speeds.

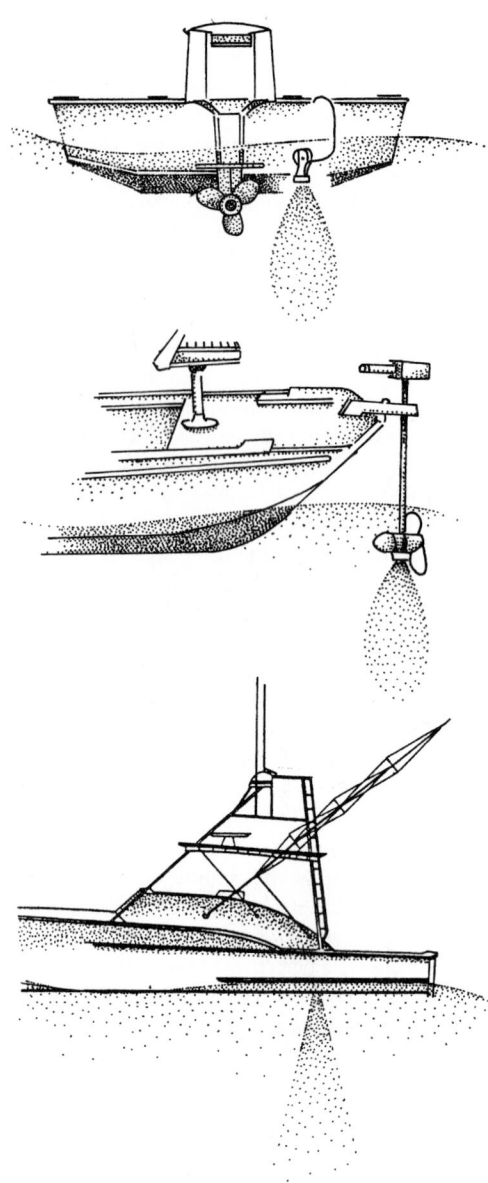

Depending on boat and fishing needs, sonar transducers are located on the transom (top), beneath an electric motor (middle), and in the sump (bottom).

If you can't install a shoot-through-hull type of transducer, you'll have to mount the transducer to the transom exterior. This is done for the vast majority of small and medium-size fishing boats and for virtually all aluminum boats. An outside transom mounting is difficult or impossible with high-performance fiberglass hulls that have stepped transoms or narrow pads. Be sure to read and closely follow the manufacturer's instructions pertaining to installation. On aluminum boats, be sure to install a transom mount transducer midway between the hull strakes to minimize the effects of turbulence when the boat is underway, and don't tighten the kickup bracket so much that it will not push back if you strike an obstruction.

If the bracket mounting holes are slotted for vertical adjustment, position the bracket according to the manufacturer's instructions, and then drill the mounting holes near the bottom of the slots. This leaves room to slide the transducer deeper than normal if necessary to get below turbulence. The more flexible or uneven the bottom of an aluminum hull is (or gets with age), the deeper a transducer needs to run to reach smooth water.

Position a transom-mount transducer so that no air bubbles will trail below it. Strakes, weld lines, and rivets, among other things, give off a bubble trail, especially at high speed. Find a location that permits clear water to flow below the face of the transducer, such as between strakes on an aluminum hull. Don't get so far from the centerline of the hull that the transducer might be out of water under certain conditions. If you get it too close to the propeller, it could cause prop cavitation. If there are heavy bubbles below a transducer, you'll get no readings.

Generally, however, to get the best readings of fish, the transducer should be level, on a horizontal plane, with its face looking straight down. Units capable of displaying fish as arches will only display a partial arch when going over fish if the transducer isn't facing straight down, and units that display fish as fish symbols or as pixel clusters will show small or

Shown is a transducer installation on a boat with a flat hull (top) and one with a modified-V hull (bottom); it is important with transom installation to get the transducer as shown, and situated between hull strakes and away from rivets.

weak signals. Transom mounting allows you to make adjustments to correct these errors. It should also be noted that sensors for speed and surface temperature readouts must be mounted outside in order to work, and they are sometimes available only as snap-on accessories for transom-mounted transducers.

The location and installation of the actual sonar unit and electrical and transducer wires should be well thought out. Other wiring and electronics may interfere with sonar and result in dots or lines appearing on the sonar screen. It may be necessary to keep the wiring from other electrical accessories away from the wires of your sonar to avoid interference. Rerouting wires may be necessary if you're experiencing problems caused by other electrical equipment.

There is one other location for mounting transducers: on the lower unit of an electric motor. This provides excellent and turbulence-free reading, but electrical interference from a trolling motor's pulse-modulated speed controller may cause interference at speed settings below wide-open. Don't worry about this unless you see interference spikes on your screen when the motor is operated. If you do have this problem, the customer service departments of your sonar and motor manufacturers can help you minimize or eliminate it.

Using Sonar

Many people have difficulty getting optimum results from their sonar, and a lot of units are returned for service when there is really nothing wrong with them. Most operator problems result from improper transducer installation and general misuse.

Today's electronics are so sophisticated and the operations manuals are so thick, they can be intimidating. Most people want to simply turn the device on and let it run, as if it were television. Thus, many people simply run their units in automatic mode and never get into the finer points of operation. Take the time to read every page of your manual. The place to do this is out on the water (not while fishing), so that you can go through the operations step by step, gain confidence in the unit, and actually see the machine do what it's supposed to do. It's a good idea as well to bring your boat over shallow water near shore, where you know the depth, and check to see that the sonar reads accurately. Find a stump several feet down, and see how it registers on your machine. Go over a sandy bottom, a mud bottom, a rocky bottom, and so on.

Sonar should be relatively easy to use, especially if you are already familiar with sonar in general and have used these devices before. Many better models of LCDs have on-screen menus and can guide you through their operation, letting you learn to use them without feeling like you need to enroll in an engineering course.

Most anglers use sonar, especially LCDs, in the automatic mode. Although many units work

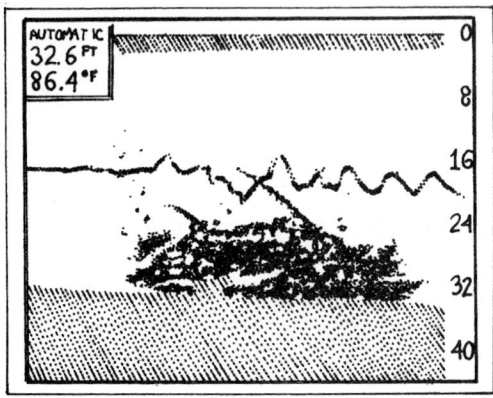

A huge school of baitfish is displayed on sportfishing sonar.

adequately in automatic mode, you may get much better performance in the manual mode, where you control the sensitivity and range settings to get much finer detail. However, when most units are used in manual mode, the bottom setting does not change automatically, and it is a minor nuisance to have to do this whenever you move into deeper or shallower water. Depending on the unit, you may be able to work around this in automatic mode by zooming or by splitting the screen for two different views. In automatic mode, some units keep the bottom contour displayed in the lower third of the screen no matter how the bottom depth changes.

A lot of operational troubles center around the control functions, particularly sensitivity and suppression. The sensitivity control, which used to be called gain, is akin to the volume control on a radio. Many inexperienced sonar users keep this turned down too low, either because they are experiencing electrical interference or because they think a low setting is adequate. When the sensitivity is too low, sonar may fail to register key bait, fish, or bottom readings. Modern units run on automatic don't usually have this problem. However, more detail can be observed from higher sensitivity settings. Some cannot be adjusted in the auto mode, but if they can, turn up the sensitivity for trolling and fast moving. On the other hand, if you are merely looking for big fish and don't want to see every detail, you might want to lower sensitivity.

If you turn sensitivity too high, you might clutter the screen with a lot of nonfish debris. The best marriage is a high enough sensitivity to get a solid bottom reading with a distinguished bottom differentiation, some surface clutter (minute "scatter" near the surface), and a lot of detail in between. A good rule of thumb is to turn sensitivity up until you begin to see random dots of interference on the screen, then turn it down until they disappear.

Some sonars have a feature called grayline (or whiteline on some units) to help identify

bottom hardness and to separate bottom-hugging fish from the bottom contour. It appears as a gray shading below a dark, sharply defined bottom contour line. Again, you may want to run sonar in the manual mode to get the best detail. If fish are holding tight to structures or the bottom, especially mud, the manual mode provides a better view. Some sonars also have advanced filtering features that clear out all or some of the clutter while having little or no influence on the fish and bottom readings.

If it's possible to adjust the scroll rate of your screen, crank that up, too, especially when you're on the move or when trolling. For many sonar instruments, there's a corollary between detail and a fast screen. A slow speed compresses readings horizontally, which hides important details. When you know what to expect, are continuously going over the same ground, or are interested only in depth, a slow speed might be adequate.

Many anglers want to see as much on screen as possible, including the latest split-screen features, which is why the narrow-screen sonars that were once prevalent have faded from popularity. By the time you studied the sonar, the information was off the screen. Units with wide screens (actual viewing area) and clear pictures are optimum. Sonar can be critical to fishing success, so the better you see below, the better you fish.

Illustrated is how a sonar unit might show a dense school of fish, a jigging spoon being fished above the school (the ragged line at 18 to 20 feet), and a fish that comes out of the middle of the school (the forward-slanting line) to look at the lure.

Most sonar today can show fish symbols in a so-called Fish I.D. mode. In standard mode (Fish I.D. turned off), sonar identifies fish as a series of dots (pixels) in a line or arch. It also displays surface clutter, temperature variations, minute particles, and thoroughly indistinguishable "stuff." Standard mode is preferable for serious fishing efforts because the sophisticated level of detail allows you to make your own determination of what you're seeing. However, many operators prefer the Fish I.D. mode in which only fish (in theory) are targeted; all other information is filtered out by the machine, and several sizes of symbols are used to correspond to the size of fish. Although Fish I.D. has some entertainment value, especially for youngsters and novice anglers, it is really not helpful. In fact, this feature may do more harm than good by blocking the display of scattered baitfish, downrigger weights, jigged lures, thermoclines, and other important information. Anglers should turn this feature off in deference to the more detailed hard-core view.

Most sonars also have fish and bottom alarms, and although these features may be useful, they are mostly regarded as an annoyance by avid anglers. The bottom alarm, however, can be very practical for high-speed navigation, boat operation in unfamiliar areas, and certain precise fishing methods (such as downrigger trolling).

Interpreting what you see on sonar is the million-dollar question. What signals are fish, what kind of fish they are, how big they are, what kind of bottom is below—these are the foremost puzzles.

Bottom characteristics are not as easy to distinguish as some anglers would like, perhaps in part due to the deficiencies of the unit or perhaps because of the settings employed. In manual mode, it is possible to fine-tune settings in order to get a clearer idea of bottom features. With LCD sonar, a hard bottom returns a strong signal, which on the display is seen as a dense, thick band.

If grayline is engaged, a hard bottom is shown as a thin black line with a wide gray band beneath. The harder the bottom, the wider the gray band. A soft or muddy bottom returns a weaker signal, and is displayed as a thinner, less dense band. With grayline on, it will appear as a dark band with little or no gray area beneath it. A rocky bottom produces a hard, thick signal with a ragged band. This is different with color video sonar, however, because different colors are used to indicate different echo strengths. Thus, on a color video sonar, a hard bottom appears as a wide band in the color reserved for the strongest echoes (red in some units), a mud bottom appears as a narrow band in a "weaker" color, and a sand bottom will be somewhere in between. On monochrome video sonars, the harder the bottom or the stronger an echo from suspended objects, the wider (top-to-bottom) and brighter the mark on the screen.

Fish signals often appear as arches on better units unless the fish are very small, the scroll speed is very slow, or the boat is moving very fast. This is because a fish is first picked up on the outer edge of the cone where it is farthest from the transducer; then, as the fish passes directly underneath the transducer, it gets closer so its reading curves upward. Because the sound is strongest in the center of the cone, the arch also gets thicker from top to bottom in the middle. The fish then gets farther away again as it passes through the opposite outer edge of the cone, causing its screen reading to curve downward again. A partial arch or diagonal line means that a fish was moving either into or out of the cone when you passed by. A fish that swims along under the boat prints as a solid horizontal line until it swims out of the cone. A school of bait shows up as a big pod, which may be vertical or horizontal depending on the school's orientation. Not all units depict fish in arches, however, and fish will not always appear as arches on any unit.

It is very difficult to tell the specific size of fish detected with sonar because this varies according to the species, the speed of the boat, the scroll speed, the sensitivity setting, and even where the fish is within the transducer's cone. If you catch a fish out of a school that you've just marked, you may have some idea how fish size compares to signal size, but if any of these factors change as you continue fishing, it's a new ballgame. Determining size of fish is somewhat possible but determining species is not, although educated guesses based on extensive experience and knowledge of individual species behavior and certain environments can be accurate.

Troubleshooting

It is common for the service departments of sonar manufacturers to receive units for repair that do not actually need repair. Therefore, it pays to consult your manual or call the customer service department of the manufacturer if you're experiencing difficulties. Poor operation often has to do with poor electrical connections, improper transducer installation, or interference due to other devices or other installation deficiencies. Here are a few tips on common problems:

If the unit does not turn on, check the power cable connections at the battery and at the unit, the in-line fuse, and the battery voltage to be sure it is above 10 volts.

If the unit freezes or operates erratically, it may be caused by electrical noise from the boat's outboard motor, electric trolling motor, an accessory, a cable connection to the back of the unit or to the battery, or a broken or pinched transducer cable.

If there's a weak bottom echo, erratic digital readings, or no fish signals, make sure the transducer is shooting straight down. If the transducer is shooting through the hull, be sure it is shooting through only one layer of solid fiberglass, and is bonded to the hull with hard two-part epoxy only. Never install a shoot-through-hull transducer with a flexible epoxy or spongy material like silicone sealant, because it can absorb up to half of the transducer's transmit power. Electrical noise from the boat's motor, trolling motor, or an accessory may be interfering with the sonar's electronics. The water may be deeper than the unit's limits with the transducer it is using. After a severe storm or flood, there may be enough debris in the water to mimic severe random interference until the junk settles to the bottom. Also check battery voltage; if the battery voltage drops, the unit's transmit power is reduced as well. Be sure that control settings are proper.

If you're not getting proper fish readings, electrical noise from the boat's motor, trolling motor, or an accessory may be interfering. Also, the transducer may be cavitating; it has to be mounted where it has a smooth flow of water at all speeds. Cavitation or turbulence around the transducer will reduce the unit's ability to receive echoes from the bottom and other objects below the transducer.

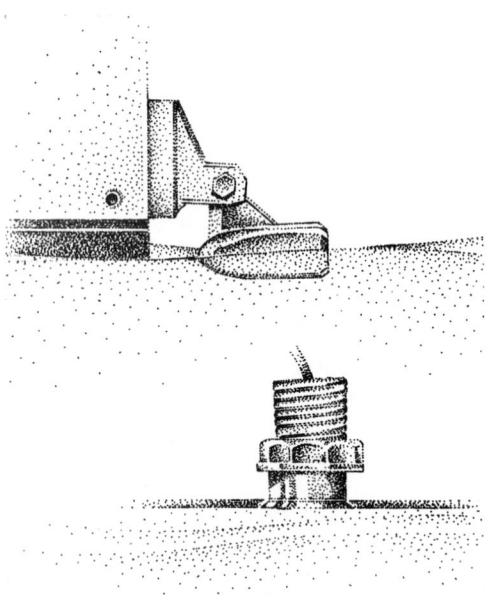

Shown is a transom installation for a high-speed transducer (top) and a through-hull installation (bottom) of a transducer as it would appear in the sump of a boat.

If there are gaps in the display reading when running at high speed, the transducer mount needs adjustment. Either the height or the angle needs correction. Gaps in the bottom reading on an aluminum boat may call for a deeper transducer running depth. If a transom-mounted transducer loses the bottom only at high speed, try tilting the rear end of the transducer's face 3 to 5 degrees downward. Make sure the adjustment doesn't cause the leading edge of the face to rise out of the water where it will catch air.

SORUBIM

A shovelnose catfish of South America, also known as tiger catfish and frequently misspelled "surubim."
See: Catfish.

SOUNDER

See: Sonar.

SOUTH AFRICA

South Africa sprawls over the southernmost tip of the African continent, covering a landmass that is greater than that of Great Britain, France, and Italy combined, and one-eighth the size of the United States. It takes in part of the Kalahari and Namib Deserts, has high peaks and expansive plateaus, and is swept by the cool waters of the South Atlantic and the warm waters of the Indian Ocean.

South Africa lacks any huge natural or man-made lakes, but it has many rivers and numerous impoundments. More freshwater fishing effort is expended on imported species—carp, trout, and largemouth bass—than on indigenous fish. The highland interior of the country, with its lofty altitude and numbers of fast-flowing rivers, provides excellent trout fishing. Significant trout fisheries range from the southern mountains of the Western Cape through the Cathcart and Hoggsback Districts of the Eastern Cape, and along the full range of the Drakensberg Mountains in Natal, with special emphasis on the southern Berg at Bergville to Himeville.

The country is blessed with 2,670 kilometers (1,725 miles) of coastline, yet that coastline has few bays or coves or natural harbors, and access to the sea is poor despite such length. Coastal fisheries are numerous, ranging from billfish and pelagic species offshore to a surfeit of species inshore, yet contrary currents on each side of the continent make the type and availability of species different, and far less numerous in the west than in the east. The warm Agulhas Current sweeping southward along the eastern coast provides different opportunities from those offered by the cool Benguela Current sweeping northward along the western coast. Nevertheless, saltwater fishing is well developed and avidly pursued, and South Africans as a whole are likely the most avid anglers on this continent.

Saltwater

The following review of the long South African coastline begins at the Mozambique border on the northeastern seaboard and follows the shoreline around the Cape of Good Hope.

Kwa-Zulu Natal. This rugged area is not only noted for its fishing opportunities, but for the adventure that is required just to get out on the water.

Northern coast. South Africa's only claim to tropical seas is the short segment of eastern coast nearest to southern Mozambique in the regions formerly known as Zululand. The clear blue waters here wash over coral reefs and into vast offshore trenches, drawing not only a good concentration of pelagic species, including billfish, but also the cream of South Africa's big-game anglers.

A vast section of the northern 120-mile-long coastline is a marine sanctuary. Anglers fishing from the beach and from boats, however, are permitted to target the abundant pelagic fish that migrate southward from the warmer northern tropical waters.

To access these waters, anglers use high-speed ski boats capable of being launched from the beach, as the only harbor is Richard's Bay at the southern extremity of the region. Launching through the surf line very often terrorizes the crew while exciting those watching from the beach, but these boats do allow anglers access to known fishing spots.

As this region falls within a wildlife conservation area, the only development surrounds the port of Richard's Bay and the tiny fishing hamlet of St. Lucia. Accommodations are in short supply, apart from these two venues, where hotels, lodges, and apartments are available. Most South Africans visiting this part of the Kwa-Zulu Natal coast prefer either caravans or tents for their coastal vacations. The board that manages the wildlife conservation area oversees numerous comfortable log chalets at selected venues, including Kosi Bay, Sodwana Bay, Cape Vidal, St. Lucia, and Mapelane. Restricted entrepreneurial development has taken place at Sodwana Bay.

Fish that predominate in this area are all tropical water species of the Indian Ocean, headed by the billfish family, of which the black and striped marlin are most common. Sailfish and an occasional (Pacific) blue marlin are also captured in these waters.

The biggest black marlin caught in South African waters was captured in December 1984 at Sodwana Bay and weighed 938 pounds. The second largest fish, caught from a 20-foot boat at Sodwana in November 1981, was a 927-pounder. Many marlin of 900 pounds or more have been caught since then, and there's little doubt that a grander is waiting.

The marlin season commences in early November and peaks in late November, then tapers off to a conclusion at the end of April. Pacific sailfish are also captured in fair numbers, often by anglers targeting king mackerel. Sailfish visit these shores from October through April and range from 45 to 150 pounds. Releasing these and other billfish has become much more commonplace.

The main attraction is not billfish, however, but a plethora of other species that provide good light-tackle sport, especially king mackerel, and also queen mackerel, yellowfin tuna, bonito, dorado, and wahoo. Surf casting and fishing from rocky ledges also provide exciting catches, ranging from small bream to large sharks. Two tidal lake/estuary systems are found in the area. Anglers working from small craft and with light tackle are assured of good sport.

Southern coast. This stretch of coastline has fostered a fishing passion in many South Africans, as it is a holiday playground for most residents of the hinterland cities in the Pretoria-Witwatersrand region.

There is much diversity among the opportunities along the eastern seaboard in what was formerly

A view of the coast along Sodwana Bay, where anglers launch boats directly into the surf.

the Natal region, from small species in a rock pool to 400-pound marlin. Anglers pursue their sport from the protection of estuaries and bays, at rocky gullies, on ledges and high rock promontories, from long white beaches, and beyond the surf line in the deep sea.

The annual migration of vast shoals of sardines (pilchards) up the coast heralds the beginning of another fishing year. During June and July, these little fish make their yearly appearance along the shore where the Natal coast stretches from the Umtamvuna River in the south to the Tugela River and the former Zululand boundary in the north.

The sardine run here is a fantastic annual phenomenon that brings gamefish in, and because this usually occurs during one of the premium holiday periods, many people are attracted to picking up rod and reel. The elf (bluefish) then makes an appearance and falls easy prey to the countless anglers who pursue these fish until August 31 each year. They are protected for spawning until November 30.

Surf and estuary fishing here is about as old as the Port of Natal, Durban. Historical records reflect that early settlers soon realized the potential of these waters to produce a harvest of fine table fare. It wasn't until just prior to World War II, however, that beach anglers—continually tempted by splashing and boiling shoals of fish just beyond casting range—effected an improvisation and paddled out beyond the big surf line aboard upgraded surfboards to catch these fish.

As the original surfboard was called a "crocker ski," the new craft is colloquially called a "ski boat"—a name that has been retained even for today's vastly different high-powered, sophisticated offshore fishing craft.

From this humble beginning, a new vista opened. Catches multiplied as king mackerel, Natal snoek (a barracuda-like fish), dorado, and a vast variety of reef fish added a new dimension to the

S

sport of angling. Today, offshore angling is practiced extensively from this section of the South African seaboard. Ski-boat clubs have been formed from nearly every rocky promontory that affords some protection from the relentless surf line.

It is from these little bays, as well as from open river mouths, that ski boats negotiate the surf, permitting anglers to fish beyond the surf line. The port of Durban is the only deep-water harbor along this 250-mile coastline. Therefore, it is the intrepid ski-boat skippers who break the barriers of the heavy surf who enable this sport to be enjoyed.

In summer, warm current makes its way close to shore and brings with it a concentration of various pelagic gamefish, including king mackerel, tuna, bonito, and dorado, as well as a fair number of sailfish and black, blue, and striped marlin. Reef fishing for species such as black and red steenbras, "kob" (kabeljou), yellowtail, and rock cod is a winter sport when the colder green water pushes in from the south.

Durban supports a fair number of offshore charter craft and private sportfishing vessels. Together with the high-class hotels, these operations offer visitors an opportunity to experience offshore fishing along this coast.

This area used to support a unique opportunity to fish for sharks off the southern breakwater of Durban Harbour, which was a whaling port until the early 1960s. A large number of sharks used to follow the whale carcasses as they were towed into port by whaleboats. These sharks were sought by a select band of anglers using heavy surf rods, wooden Scarborough reels, and 2,000 yards of 18-cord flex line and a chunk of whale meat as bait, to land numerous sharks exceeding 1,000 pounds. The heaviest recorded was a great white of 1,660 pounds in 1953. The end of whaling virtually put an end to this type of angling, and today it is only the odd shark that is caught.

Wild Coast and border. The lack of coastal development and beautiful but rugged nature of this 300-mile stretch of oceanfront gave it the name "Wild Coast." Extending roughly from west of Port Edward to just east of Port Alfred, this area features varied species and angling conditions.

From the northeast corner and down the coast past the port city of East London to the Great Fish River, there's an abundance of estuaries, rarely more than 5 or 6 miles apart. For the first hundred miles, the green rolling hills slope steeply from 300 or 400 feet down to the sea and are interspersed with short stretches of sheer cliffs, sandy beaches, and estuaries. At one beautiful spot near Msikaba, a waterfall tumbles over the cliff face and into the sea.

From the central Transkei region southward, the high green hills make way for heavily wooded sand dunes and long stretches of beach again broken by the estuaries, some of which are open to the sea only for short periods in the rainy season. Nevertheless, they harbor many saltwater fish and

prawns. Several of the estuaries feature hotels that cater to visiting anglers, whereas other estuaries lack facilities and are accessed only via four-wheel-drive vehicles. The steep banks of the estuaries are heavily forested and are home to an incredible array of birds. This backdrop makes fishing here an unforgettable experience.

The warm Agulhas Current (up to 26°C in summer) sweeps down the length of this coastline. Close to shore in the north, it meanders as it nears East London, sometimes moving in close, sometimes moving 12 miles offshore, depending on the prevailing winds. At its strongest near the continental shelf, the current allows little sand and silt to settle, which results in large areas of prime reef fishing.

The Agulhas brings pelagic fish south almost year-round. Regular catches include black and striped marlin, yellowfin tuna, record-size kawakawa, skipjack tuna, king mackerel, queenfish, kingfish, dorado, and wahoo.

A prime attraction for reef anglers on this 300-mile stretch is the giant, endemic snapperlike fish called the red, or copper, steenbras. These magnificent fish grow to 130 pounds, and strict management measures have been implemented to limit the catch, as their numbers have been reduced. Numerous other reef species here make bottom fishing attractive.

The Agulhas also provides shore anglers with a variety of warmwater fish interspersed with cooler-water fish when the current meanders offshore. Garrick are prized targets at some deeper-water shore spots like Brazen Head, Poenskop, Mbolompo, Mazeppa Bay, the East London Harbour breakwater, and Cove Rock. Tuna are sometimes taken from these ledges. Some marlin have also been hooked and lost. Yellowtail, elf, and kob constitute the bulk of the catches.

A variety of breamlike fish are still reasonably abundant, as are sharks and rays, which, on a tag-and-release basis, make up the bulk of the catches in competitions. Estuarine angling is good for kob (which grow to more than 100 pounds), spotted grunter, river snapper, garrick, and small kingfish. A popular light-tackle fish is the tarpon relative called the skipjack, which performs spectacular aerobatics when hooked. Although saltwater fly fishing is still in its infancy in South Africa, many anglers have recorded good catches of all these fish in the estuaries.

With the exception of the East London Harbour, all boats launch through the surf from estuaries, semi-sheltered bays, or open beaches. This coast is extremely popular with South African anglers, and a growing number of visitors are sampling its unspoiled beauty and variety of fish.

Eastern Cape. The Eastern Cape has a well-deserved reputation for exceptionally varied and versatile angling. The offshore grounds are a short distance away, bottom fish are plentiful, rock and surf angling exist along many miles of unspoiled and uninhabited beaches, and opportunities to cruise up one of numerous rivers or estuaries are also available. Many angling clubs exist in this region, and given the area's well-controlled launching areas, much of the excellent fishing is accessible.

Most anglers work the inshore reefs and target bottom fish, which include kob reaching 60 kilograms, and black and red steenbras, among many other species. The region is of foremost renown for garrick, a great gamefish prized for its excellent displays on light tackle. The Eastern Cape boasts what is likely the best garrick angling in the world, and many world records have been captured here.

Yellowtail inhabit the inshore reefs, and shoals half the size of a football field are not uncommon. The banks at Struisbaai are especially known for such shoals. The winter run of yellowfin tuna, following the sardine migration northward to Natal, can provide outstanding action. Sometimes fast-moving fish, ranging from 15 to 50 kilograms, are observed chasing food. Masses of birds mill overhead, forming the backdrop to a spectacle that can produce scores of tuna.

The Eastern Cape has a high success ratio for the popular, speedy, and powerful mako shark. Although makos here are usually small, ranging from 30 to 100 kilograms, an angler is virtually assured of catching one on the offshore reefs with relatively light tackle when the water is clean. The far offshore environs also produce hammerhead sharks, some large, and occasionally broadbill swordfish. The largest broadbill docked at the capital city of Port Elizabeth was caught accidentally by a commercial boat more than a decade ago and weighed an incredible 650 kilograms.

The Eastern Cape has spectacular and extensive unspoiled beaches and cliffs. One can travel for miles up the beach in a four-wheel-drive vehicle, meeting only the occasional angler. The Tsitsikama coastline, which stretches from Port Elizabeth to Knysna, has breathtaking and untouched rock angling. Tsitsikama forest reaches the cliff face, and the ocean melts to incredible depths at one's feet. As a result, large black and red steenbras, which are traditionally caught only out at sea, are landed from these rocks.

With numerous rivers and estuaries entering the sea here, excellent light-tackle angling is available amidst tranquil and varied settings. A wide variety of fish thrive in these rivers and estuaries, and excellent catches of kob, grunter, steenbras, skipjacks, and other species are the norm. Some rivers stretch inland for up to 30 kilometers, and, when venturing by boat (the only method), an angler can be virtually guaranteed of memorable exclusivity. It is not uncommon to stop the boat to view wildlife in or near the water. The flats and inaccessible dense bush are home to a multitude of birds and game. Many upriver trips have been rewarded with glimpses of the shy and elusive bushbuck ram and other seldom-seen animals.

Western/Southern Cape. This vast region has an incredibly diverse array of sportfish.

Cape Agulhas to Cape Point. Just east of Cape Agulhas, Africa's southernmost point, lies the small coastal town of Stiruisbaai, arguably the capital of nearshore boat angling in the region known as the Western Cape. This is served by a small but functional harbor that is home to a sizable commercial fleet and is frequented in season by many recreational ski-boat anglers. The huge shelf of nearby Agulhas Bank supports a variety of bottom-feeding as well as pelagic species, desirable both as sport and food fish.

Fed from the east by the tropical Agulhas Current and the nutrient-rich cool Benguela system in the west, this continental shelf area extends as far as 120 miles offshore, in places, to the dropoff. The bank is home to many sought-after species, most prominently the southern yellowtail. Present year-round but most abundant in summer and autumn when they average 6 to 15 pounds, the strikingly hued yellowtail offers a combination of dogged fighting spirit, attractive appearance, and excellent edibility that encourages many here to consider it the prince of ocean pelagic species.

A productive method of capture includes drifting over pinnacles with weighted lines placed between midwater and the bottom, and baited with squid, sardines, or Japanese sauries. Another successful procedure is to cast metal spoons (called spinners) at shoals of yellowtail feeding on the surface with birds, usually terns, overhead.

Another favorite species here, the kob is similar to the red drum. Favoring reefs surrounded by sand, this species is generally similar in size to yellowtail, but 100-pounders are fairly common. The South African record weighed more than 150 pounds. Sometimes occurring in large shoals, the bottom-feeding kob is most abundant from December through June and feeds during dark hours, particularly at dusk and dawn.

Similar at first glance to the kob but sleeker and more sporty is the geelbek (Cape salmon), primarily a night feeder. Reaching 40 pounds but averaging about 10 pounds, this species is a relative of the American white seabass and is an excellent gamefish. Although normally caught near the bottom, geelbek often come to within a few yards of the surface, particularly at night.

A number of bottom-feeding redfish species also occur in this area. The largest is the famous red steenbras, which attains 150 pounds but is commonly around 30 pounds. This species is a powerful and aggressive member of the snapper family, sometimes occurring in schools. With its large canine teeth, it is striking in appearance; the pinkish blue of the juveniles changes to an orange yellow to copper coloration, sometimes with dark markings, in the adults.

Other popular redfish include the red stumpnose and the red roman, reaching 20 and 10

Sharks are said to have existed 200 million years before dinosaurs; the power of a 6$\frac{1}{2}$-foot dusky shark at the tip of its teeth was measured at 22 tons per square inch.

S

S

pounds respectively. As with most redfish, these species are all prized table fare. Another common fish is the elf, which averages about 2 pounds and rarely exceeds 10 pounds. This species never reaches the size of its North American equivalent, although it is an esteemed food fish.

Occurring occasionally along the surf line and over reefs is the garrick, also known locally as the leervis. Although never common, this hard-fighting gamefish is highly sought by a select band of anglers and is most often caught in the summer.

Rock and surf angling are popular and rewarding pastimes here. Anglers land numerous species of sharks from these sites, and they take kob and elf regularly. White steenbras are also targeted.

Huge shark specimens thrive in this region, among them duskies, ragged-tooth, mako, and the occasional hammerhead, but the most impressive is the great white. This species is at times abundant on the reefs and is a bait-stealing nuisance to anglers. Always commanding respect when encountered, the great white is occasionally caught by recreational anglers, mainly for tagging and release.

Moving west from Cape Agulhas toward Cape Point, the coastline consists of rocky sections interspersed by long, white sandy beaches. Gansbaai and Hermanus are the only two harbors of note in this area. Although mainly used by the commercial fishing sector, these harbors do have some facilities for the recreational angler. Recreational-boat angling in this area is not common, but rock and surf angling are popular.

Species encountered along this coast are the same as those in the Cape Agulhas area, both at sea and from the shore. Another species that shows itself at certain times of the year, mainly in winter, is the snoek. This barracuda-like fish has a vicious set of teeth; although normally caught commercially, it is a popular recreational catch. Averaging 5 to 9 pounds and growing to 20 pounds, the snoek offers excellent sport on light tackle.

At the western end of this section of coastline is the large, shallow, semi-enclosed body of water known as False Bay, which is up to 30 miles long and 35 miles wide and hosts a variety of species. The more common are yellowtail, kob, geelbek, elf, and snoek, and bottom-feeding redfish also occur regularly. This bay was famous for summer catches of bluefin tuna in the 1960s, but these fish were heavily depleted and have not been encountered in this location for many years.

False Bay is serviced by two excellent harbors, Gordon's Bay on the eastern side and Simonstown on the western side. A number of excellent slipways for trailer-borne craft are located here. Because of its sheltered waters and variety of fish, False Bay is an excellent and popular boating venue, with hundreds of boats at sea on good days.

Cape Point to Table Bay. Although not the southernmost point of Africa, Cape Point is generally accepted as a meeting place of the warm,

sub-tropical Agulhas Current and the cold, Antarctic-influenced Benguela Current. Consequently, the inshore waters of the coastline between Cape Point and Table Bay are cool, averaging 12°C, but the Agulhas Current has a continuing effect as one moves farther offshore, where the water reaches 22°C in summer.

Due to the mixing of currents and the presence of two large undersea canyons in this area, conditions are often ideal for big-game species, particularly tuna. Albacore, or longfin tuna as the fish is known off the Cape, are at times extremely abundant and support a large commercial fishery. Cape Point is famous for producing big catches of this species and for having large specimens, many of which have made the record books over the years.

Albacore are abundant off the Cape in spring (September and October) and in autumn (April and May); shoals normally move north with the prevailing southeast drift in the hot summer months, when the water temperature climbs to more than 20°C. With the onset of northwesterly winds in autumn, the cool subtropical water is displaced by warmer, temperate water, and the albacore return.

Another common tuna species here is the yellowfin. These fish are caught up to 200 pounds, and the average catch off Cape Town runs between 80 and 120 pounds. Often occurring in great shoals, this fish is an exciting quarry. Trolling plastic lures and diving plugs is the common method of catching tuna off the Cape, but chunking and drifting with bait is also popular and effective. Anglers often use the latter technique in conjunction with casting a metal spoon.

Many large offshore sportfishing vessels operate in this area and are berthed either at Simonstown in False Bay or at Hout Bay on the western coast of the Cape Peninsula. In addition, many trailered boats launch from Hout Bay or False Bay and make daily runs to the tuna grounds anywhere from 10 to 50 miles offshore.

Other area species include skipjack tuna, yellowtail, dorado, bigeye tuna, striped and black marlin, and swordfish. Also common but not normally fished for are a number of shark species, including makos, blues, duskies, and great whites.

Marlin are rare visitors to Cape waters and are normally found during summer, when water temperatures are highest. Although rarely deliberately fished for by anglers because of their scarcity, some large specimens have been landed, mainly by commercial vessels. The largest of these was a 1,338-pound black marlin. Swordfish have been more abundant than previously estimated, and some Cape anglers have caught them using night fishing techniques.

Inshore angling in the cooler waters is confined mainly to snoek in autumn and winter. No other significant sportfish are caught with rod and reel, but a popular fishery using ring nets exists for the delicious Cape rock lobster.

Pearl essence is the silvery substance in the skin of herring and other fishes, and it is essential to the manufacture of lipstick, nail polish, paints, ceramics, and costume jewelry.

West coast.   Due to the influence of the cool Benguela Current, recreational angling off the west coast of the Cape and farther north is limited and consists mainly of snoek. A commercial fishery exists for this species, particularly around Dassen Island and St. Helenabaai.

The Cape rock lobster is also abundant and provides a substantial recreational fishery. Tuna are prolific off the west coast of the Cape Peninsula but are normally encountered too far offshore for recreational boats to reach. At times, however, shoals move to within striking distance of small boats, and some good catches have been made during the summer.

A large estuary known as the Langebaan Lagoon at Saldanha Bay is a popular area for water sports. Again due to low water temperatures, the variety of fish in this area is restricted. Anglers use light tackle to land kob, elf, and yellowtail, as well as a number of bottom-feeding species, plus sharks and rays. Leaping thresher sharks are much sought after, as are tope, duskies, and cow sharks, and the occasional great white. Large skates are also landed.

Freshwater

South Africa has few natural lakes but numerous small to midsize impoundments and many rivers. A few of the rivers are large, many are shorter tributaries to the larger flows, and some are intermittent. Angling for coarse species is popular in warmwater rivers and lakes, and in lakes for bass, whereas trout fishing in the scenic mountainous regions is excellent, unsung, and lightly publicized.

For the traveling angler, the tourism infrastructure in South Africa is excellent. Numerous dams have been built in nearly every river system, and resorts offer accommodations ranging from well-appointed chalets and rondavels to high-grade caravan and camping parks.

Because of its year-round mild climate, the region east of Pretoria offers traveling anglers good fishing during summer and winter, with mid- to late summer possibly the best time.

South Africa has only three natural lakes that offer sportfishing: Barberspan in the Western Transvaal, Groenvlei in the Southern Cape, and Zeekoeivlei in the Western Cape. The more famous dams (reservoirs) visited by thousands of anglers every year include Loskop in the southeastern Transvaal, Fanie Botha near Tzaneen in the northeastern Transvaal, Hartebeespoort near Pretoria, Vaal Dam south of Johannesburg, Koppies in the Orange Free State, Chelmsford in Natal, and Sterkfontein near Harrismith in the eastern Free State.

In total, more than 130 dams are under the control of the Department of Water Affairs, and all are open to anglers, although the directorates of nature conservation in each district provide fisheries control and management.

The biggest man-made lake, with some 130 kilometers of navigable water, is Hendrik Verwoerd on the Orange River. This impoundment holds significant populations of enormous yellowfish and catfish, and has become more popular in recent years; previously it was regarded as too far from either the Cape or the huge Pretoria-Witwatersrand-Vereeniging area (which holds some 70 percent of the country's population). It is, however, just about in the center of the country.

Anglers take a limited number of tigerfish from the eastward flowing rivers of Mpumalanga Lowveld and northern Kwa-Zulu Natal. The fish are rather small, but a few impoundments do contain larger fish. The Pongola Dam in northern Kwa-Zulu Natal, for example, has produced tigerfish up to 8.3 kilograms.

Coarse species, especially carp and catfish, are the primary freshwater fishing interests of South Africans. Freshwater coarse fishing is a large industry in its own right, and because most of the dams are within nature reserves, anglers have the opportunity to get close to nature on every outing.

Bass and coarse species.   In terms of hours spent in pursuit of various fish, carp are the most heavily favored freshwater species. Introduced here by British colonials evidently as early as 1859, they have thrived throughout the land and been widely distributed. The generally warm and discolored rivers and dams, as well as abundant natural vegetation, have contributed greatly to their success. The most popular angling technique for carp is similar to that for coarse fish in Europe: using long, supple rods and mushy corn baits that are cast great distances from shore. The rods are then set in rod rests to await a bite. This activity attracts tens of thousands of anglers to riverbanks and dams every weekend. At Hartebeespoort Dam, for instance, some 7,000 to 10,000 people congregate on its banks during summer weekends, nearly all in search of a big carp.

The current South African all-tackle carp record is a 21.98-kilogram fish, caught in 1988 in the Transvaal Lowveld. The previous record was a specimen of 21.85 kilograms, caught at Hartebeespoort. Carp fishing throughout South Africa is very good, and anglers have also perfected techniques for catching carp from boats, which has generated a healthy inland fishing industry among boaters.

The second most popularly targeted fish is the sharptoothed catfish *(Clarius gariepinus),* popularly (but incorrectly) termed "barbel." These are South Africa's largest indigenous sportfish and grow to large sizes; the current South African all-tackle record stands at 31.805 kilograms. Catfish occur throughout the region, with the exception of the southern Cape Province.

The third most popular fish is the blue kurper (called bream in Zimbabwe). These are known elsewhere as tilapia and are excellent table and sportfish, occurring mostly in the warmer regions. They are a particular target of boat anglers.

Highly regarded indigenous sportfish also include the largemouth yellowfish *(Barbus kimberleyensis),* with a record of 22.20 kilograms, and the smallmouth yellowfish *(Barbus aeneus),* with a record of 7.837 kilograms. The big yellows are most often caught during cold winter months on the Transvaal and Orange Free State Highveld and, according to popular legend, bite best "at 2 o'clock on a winter's night with a rising moon and the temperature below freezing."

Many of the dams in South Africa, particularly in the Transvaal, Kwa-Zulu Natal, and Cape Provinces, have populations of black bass. Largemouth and smallmouth bass are found here, as is the occasional spotted bass. Largemouth bass were imported to South Africa in 1928 and smallmouth bass in 1937; these species, as well as the less common spotted bass, have been transplanted extensively. The Natal Parks Board began experimenting with Florida-strain largemouth bass in the early 1980s, and these fish were also stocked in many waters.

Largemouths seldom exceed 10 pounds in South African waters, but they have been caught in the 12- to 13-pound range, usually those of the Florida strain. Waters in Mpumalanga produced a 13-pound, 6-ounce bass in 1997. A catch of five bass weighing a total of 52 pounds was made in Kwa-Zulu Natal.

Anglers have organized bass fishing clubs, which have been very active in recent decades, holding competitions on various waters. Much more water for bass fishing is being developed as a result. The best angling times are from late winter to midspring during the spawning period, but bass are caught year-round. Catch-and-release is particularly popular for this exotic species.

Trout. South Africa has an underestimated trout fishery. Rainbow and brown trout are underutilized resources here, and competition for these fish is generally light. This fishery consists of miles of rivers, and plenty of small still waters, many of them in beautifully scenic country.

Eastern South Africa is divided from its vast interior by the Drakensberg Mountain range, which stretches from the Eastern Cape in the south to the Transvaal in the north. To the trout angler, the mountains are a godsend. Close to the coastal plains these mountains rise steeply to more than 10,000 feet, causing a massive upwelling of moist air and heavy rain on the eastern slopes in summer (December and January). Thus, they are the birthplace of countless trout streams flowing east into three prime trout areas: the midlands of Kwa-Zulu Natal, the Eastern Transvaal, and the Eastern Cape around the towns of Barkly East and Lady Grey. At the farthest tip of Africa in the Western Cape, trout thrive in the high mountains a short distance inland of Cape Town, where the climate is Mediterranean and offers clear sun-filled days in summer.

Fishing for trout on the Holsloot River in the South African mountains.

Apart from these main locations, there is good trout fishing in the independent Kingdom of Lesotho, a landlocked mountainous country crisscrossed by bright, clear streams, most of them rising more than 8,000 feet above sea level. Food is more abundant in these high streams, and the mayfly populations are particularly dense. The condition and average size of the trout are exceptional. The area is accessible with four-wheel-drive vehicles, but travel by plane or helicopter makes the trip much more comfortable. Lesotho is unlike most of South Africa, where rivers and lakes can be reached with ease.

Trout were first introduced to South Africa in the late 1890s, coming from Loch Leven brown trout stock imported from Scotland. These browns did well in their environment, and rainbows were introduced a decade or so later to complement them. Still, most of the rivers today retain a clear one-species identity, rarely holding both species simultaneously. South African trout waters are small by international standards, more like streams than rivers, yet the average size of the trout caught is large. Most of the rivers produce fish of up to 4 or 5 pounds, and in the Barkly East area, river fish up to 9 pounds are encountered.

Trout proliferate in the upland sections of most rivers, and the waters tend to become overpopulated. Natural predation is fairly significant, especially from otters and white-breasted cormorants, but, as with most exotic species, the trout generally has an easy passage in this country's waters. High midsummer water temperatures, hail storms, flash floods, extended periods of drought, siltation, and the predations of humans do more damage to the trout populations than their rivals in the animal kingdom. Because trout were once alien to South Africa, some naturalists think trout should be outlawed. Fortunately, most conservationists have decided that trout play an important role in recreation and tourism.

If Africa in general, and African trout fishing in particular, has an Achilles heel, it is drought. Good trout fishing is dependent on good rainfall, and a season or two of poor rains sets the sport back a notch or two. Although South Africa is a dry country, droughts are less common in the eastern highlands than in the interior, and often less devastating. Equally problematic are flash flooding and siltation. On the other hand, given a spell of good rainfall, such as might happen over a several-year period, the country is a veritable trout fishing paradise.

South African trout water is largely in the hands of private riparian owners. Public fishing is available, primarily in the Western Cape and in Kwa-Zulu Natal, but as the sport has grown in popularity, more water has been reserved for private use. Farmers owning stretches of the famous rivers guard their asset jealously, and syndication of fishing rights to groups of anglers, once a rarity, is now the norm. A few commercial operations make excellent fishing available to visitors, arranging safaris to some of the best trout rivers and still waters in South Africa and Lesotho. Most anglers fish these rivers by wading.

To compensate for the relative uncertainty of river water and the fact that rivers are not always easy to access, South African trout anglers have taken to stillwater fly fishing in a big way. All of these stillwaters are man-made impoundments, and they average 10 to 20 acres. Most are remarkably fertile, and the growth rate of the fish in them is phenomenal. Trout up to 10 pounds have become commonplace, and the best exceed 14 pounds.

Most stillwater anglers fish from float tubes, using floating lines with nymphs and dry flies. The rewards are great catches of rainbows and browns. The sport is exciting and all but totally independent of the vagaries of the weather.

The trout season generally starts in September and runs through the end of May. Many stillwaters, however, have no closed season. The best fishing is in spring (September and October) and in autumn (from late March through May). During these months, the water is cooler and the trout feed more actively.

Although these waters are fertile, hatches are not predictable. In fact, most are sporadic, so dry flies are not used as extensively as they are overseas. The fish are consequently less likely to be selective feeders, and, in the main, nymph anglers do best. Most fly anglers fishing on stillwaters and in rivers use 4- or 5-weight outfits, with 8- to 9-foot rods. The fish are hardly ever consistent surface feeders.

The mountain streams of the Western Cape are a notable exception, where free-rising trout come to the dry fly smartly, just as they do in the upland streams in Lesotho.

SOUTH CAROLINA

Thanks to geographical diversity, a comparatively small population density, a long coastline, and an abundance of streams, lakes, and ponds, South Carolina has a great deal to offer anglers. The variety of fish, the types of fishing available, and a plethora of easily accessible destinations make South Carolina angling broadly appealing to residents and visitors alike.

The Palmetto State is home to a dozen large man-made lakes with a total surface area of some 463,000 acres. In addition, 16 state-owned lakes are intensively managed for angling. Many public and private waters offer angling opportunities in all of South Carolina's 46 counties. Altogether, some 1,400 such small lakes and ponds—all larger than 10 acres—offer a total surface area of almost 500,000 acres. Thousands of miles of free-flowing streams, ranging from Appalachian trout streams to coastal blackwater rivers, add to the delightful mix, as does a hefty chunk of Atlantic coast.

The state's freshwater lakes and streams offer a smorgasbord of species. Rainbow, brown, and brook trout exist in a handful of counties; all three species reproduce naturally in some streams and are stocked in others. Trout grow fairly large in the cold, clear waters of Lake Jocassee, which is also home to smallmouth bass. For the most part, though, the state's featured freshwater species are of the warmwater variety. These include largemouth, hybrid, and striped bass; various panfish, including bluegills, shellcrackers, redbreasts, warmouth, and perch; black crappie; white crappie; channel, blue, and flathead catfish; pickerel; and nongamefish species like gar and mudfish. Popular saltwater species include seatrout, redfish, amberjack, grouper, sea bass, sea bream, cobia, and tarpon.

Freshwater

South Carolina's inland topography falls into three distinct regions—the Upcountry, the Piedmont, and the Lowcountry—and each has its own distinctive features. The state's large lakes, with the noteworthy exceptions of Lakes Marion and Moultrie (often called Santee-Cooper after the rivers impounded to create them), are all in the Upcountry and Piedmont regions. In addition to the major waters noted in these areas, South Carolina has plenty of small and generally unpublicized bodies of water, many of which offer exceptional fishing opportunities.

S

S

Upcountry. The northwesternmost portion of South Carolina, a sort of rough triangle formed by the state's borders with North Carolina and Georgia, is locally known as the Upcountry. It is home to a number of trout streams and three large lakes—Jocassee, Keowee, and Hartwell. Although South Carolina's stream fishing for trout cannot rival that found in neighboring North Carolina, the Department of Natural Resources (DNR) does stock large numbers of fish each year; these are raised at a hatchery in Walhalla.

There is limited natural reproduction in several remote streams, most notably those flowing into Lake Jocassee. The best trout streams include the upper reaches of the Chattooga and its East Fork, plus the Chauga, Whitewater, Eastatoe, and Saluda Rivers. For those who enjoy getting back of beyond, some of the feeder streams, along with creeks that can be reached by hiking the Foothills Trail, are inviting destinations.

The tactics that take trout in this area range from dry-fly fishing to the plying the waters with natural baits. For fly anglers, the emphasis is on good presentation rather than selecting the best fly pattern. Streams are relatively low in fertility, so the trout are opportunistic feeders. Among consistently productive dry-fly patterns are the Adams, Royal Wulff, Thunderhead, Elk-Hair Caddis, Adams Variant, and Yellow and Royal Humpies. In late summer, flies that imitate beetles, jassids, and hoppers are productive. The nymph angler will score well with bead-head versions of Tellico, Gold-Ribbed Hare's Ear, and Prince patterns, whereas favored streamers include Muddler Minnows, Matukas, and Black-Nosed Dace. For those using ultralight spinning gear, the smallest spinners are effective, as are such live baits as crickets, spring lizards, red worms, and nightcrawlers.

For the stillwater angler, all three of the area's large lakes have much to offer. Keowee, and particularly Jocassee, have good populations of brown trout. These stay mostly quite deep; in warmer weather, trolling with downriggers is effective. Jigging with large spoons, or using threadfin shad or blueback herring, both of which inhabit the reservoirs, are other favored techniques.

Some smallmouth bass live in these lakes, and largemouth bass are plentiful. Panfishing for black crappie and various species of bream is also available, although lakes with warmer water elsewhere in the state are better.

Although located in the Upcountry region, sprawling Lake Hartwell's 56,000 acres (shared with Georgia) offer fishing similar to that found in the Piedmont. The northernmost impoundment in a chain of dams on the Savannah River, Hartwell is one of the state's better crappie lakes. It has plenty of largemouth bass as well, although they tend to run smaller on average than those in South Carolina's favorite bass fishing destinations. Spotted bass are nearly as abundant here as largemouths.

Hybrid striped bass, and—to a lesser degree—pure-strain stripers, are Hartwell's featured species, and the lake is generally lightly fished.

Piedmont region. Overall, the Piedmont region of South Carolina offers the state's finest fishing. This is due in large part to the area's seven major lakes: Thurmond and Russell on the Savannah River, Wylie and Wateree on the Catawba River, and Greenwood, Monticello, and Murray.

Lake Wylie splits the North Carolina–South Carolina border. It's a prime crappie and largemouth reservoir, and an overlooked hotspot for bullhead and channel cats. Large catches of crappie are regularly taken using small minnows or jigs, and most of the fish linger around numerous brush piles placed by anglers around docks and piers. Largemouth bass get a lot of pressure, but the lake is sufficiently fertile to withstand constant attention. Both crappie and bass fishing are best in spring and fall, although mild temperatures here as well as in the Lowcountry mean viable fishing throughout the year.

The height of summer is prime time for Wylie's plentiful catfish, most of which are in the 1- to 5-pound class. Stinkbaits, including a local favorite, "aged" mussels taken from the lake's sandy shorelines, can be fished off gradually sloping points. There are some white bass in Lake Wylie as well, and bluegills are exceptionally plentiful.

Lake Wateree is very similar, with the one notable difference that the reservoir has striped bass. These do not normally run as large as in other lakes where size limits are in effect, but the fish are plentiful. Crappie in Wateree run large, and in the lake's long, straight main channel, anglers troll with several rods using jigs to catch this species in great numbers.

Lake Murray has long enjoyed a richly deserved reputation as a hotspot for big largemouth bass. This fame was at least in part a product of the reservoir's having extensive areas of grass. The grass was killed in the late 1990s, however, so this fishery is likely to experience some decline. On the other hand, thanks to the implementation of a 21-inch minimum size limit for stripers and the presence of plenty of the baitfish favored by rockfish, action for this species improves a bit every year. A return to the glory days of the late 1960s (stripers were first stocked here in 1961, after South Carolina biologists became the first to determine how to raise and stock them in landlocked situations) is a distinct possibility. With 525 miles of shoreline and extensive development, including the construction of numerous docks and piers, Murray has plenty of the shallow-water structure and cover in which crappie and bream thrive. Both are here in great numbers.

Lakes Russell and Thurmond (also known as Clarks Hill Lake) are shared with Georgia, and the two states enjoy a reciprocal licensing agreement. Russell is a sprawling reservoir of some 27,000 acres, 1,500 of which were left with standing timber when the gates on the dam first closed. Buoys mark this prime fish-attracting cover. The lake's most popular species is white bass, although it is also noted for yellow perch, catfish, and rainbow trout.

Thurmond Lake, with its 71,000 acres, 1,200 miles of shoreline, and scores of islands, is one of the largest man-made bodies of water in the country. The lake is renowned for its striper and hybrid bass fishing, and blueback herring are the natural baits of choice. The humble but popular crappie is this reservoir's number one fish; anglers creel between 200,000 and 300,000 pounds of slabs in an average year. An ideal way to access this impoundment—also true of most other large lakes in South Carolina—is via one of the state parks located on its shores. Here, as elsewhere, these parks normally include camping areas, launch sites, bait and tackle stores, and other facilities.

Like Thurmond, Lake Greenwood is considered a crappie hotspot. In most years it ranks tops in South Carolina for the number of this species caught per acre. It is also known as one of the state's better largemouth bass lakes, and the nature and configuration of its many fingers and small side channels make Greenwood a structure-fishing dream.

Monticello is relatively small at just under 7,000 acres, but in quantity, it ranks as South Carolina's top catfishing destination. It features a 300-acre sub-impoundment (also called Monticello) that is intensively managed. This sub-impoundment is but one of a number of state-managed lakes in the Piedmont. Most have stricter creel limits and more rigid size restrictions than do waters open to the general public, and they also are restricted to electric (or in some cases, small gasoline) motors on boats.

The Piedmont region has fine moving-water fishing in larger rivers (mostly navigable with jonboats and canoes) and medium-size streams that are easily waded. Many of these waterways are underutilized because they're not suitable for modern, high-powered boats—the choice of anglers who fish the state's larger waters. Yet rivers such as the Catawba, Broad, and Wateree hold good populations of bass, channel cats, and panfish. They also feature false springtime spawning runs by stripers. The Saluda River tailrace near Columbia offers all these species as well as trout.

Lowcountry.   The Palmetto Lowcountry is an area rich in history, with stately homes sitting atop river bluffs, and remainders of rice dikes dotting the landscape. Much of the finest fishing here is a throwback to yesteryear, when large impoundments and powerful boats were unknown. Blackwater rivers weave their way seaward like so many laughter lines on an old man's face, and their inky waters, stained dark by decomposing leaves and other vegetation, are as rich in fish as they seem steeped in mystery.

Santee Cooper is South Carolina's most prominent place for stripers and big catfish.

The best way to fish most of these streams, especially over the many miles between the fall line and the high-tide mark, is by drifting. Jonboats, canoes, and tiny one- or two-person craft—manufactured locally and known as strip boats—are ideal for this type of fishing. Bigger boats can be used on the lower reaches of some of the larger blackwater rivers. Largemouth bass, redbreasts, crappie, and catfish inhabit these streams, and some local anglers concentrate on less-esteemed species such as bowfin, gar, and grinnel (technically, bowfin and locally known as "swamp lawyers").

Among the better blackwater rivers are the Black, Edisto (famed for its redbreast fishery, although monster catfish have made inroads on the populations of this popular panfish), Ashepoo, Santee, Ashley, Combahee, Lumber, Waccamaw, and Pee Dee. Also deserving of angling attention is storied Wambaw Creek, which figured prominently in the tales of the late and renowned writer Archibald Rutledge, and Four Holes Swamp, which links a number of natural lakes before eventually emptying into the Edisto River.

The most noted angling destination in the Lowcountry is the vast, interlocking complex formed by Lakes Marion and Moultrie and their connecting diversion canal. Commonly known as Santee-Cooper, this vast inland sea of 171,000 acres features a mixture of flooded timber, cypress swamps, and huge stretches of open water. Over the years, world records for several species of fish, including striped bass, channel catfish, blue catfish, and warmouth, have been produced here.

That in part explains the presence of dozens of marinas around the lake. In addition to offering record-breaking fish, Marion and Moultrie are also first-rate largemouth bass and crappie lakes. When it comes to big catfish, Santee-Cooper may be in a class by itself. It takes specimens above 50 pounds even to raise eyebrows, and every year whiskered giants in the 80-pound range are landed. In winter, smaller cats—mostly channels and blues—are caught in large numbers around the riprap at the base of the dam.

For largemouth anglers, vast areas of flooded timber and cypress swamps offer ideal topwater or shallow-running lure fishing in the spring and fall. The plentiful structure also lends itself to prime bream and crappie fishing; the latter usually spawn in late March and April, whereas bream go on the beds in May. Striped bass fishing peaks in the spring when the linesiders head to the diversion canal in spawning runs, but action can also be fast and furious in late fall and winter, when schooling fish "herd" baitfish to the surface and then smash them in savage flurries of feeding. Circling sea gulls are a visual index to such frenzies.

Saltwater

Saltwater fishing in South Carolina has many faces. Inshore, surf casting and pier fishing have long been popular, and public beaches, state-operated piers, and daily-fee fishing piers line the coast. In recent years, fly anglers have discovered that coastal waters offer action on redfish (usually called spottail bass, or just spots, in South Carolina), trout, and channel bass, among other species. Fly fishing has become particularly popular in and around Charleston Harbor. There is less sight casting than one encounters in crystal clear flats—thanks to waters that are normally murky—but shrimp, minnow, or crab patterns can be effective.

Snapper, sea bass, sea bream, cobia, grouper, and sharks, among other species, are the available inshore species. A recent angling dimension of recent vintage is spadefishing with jellyfish as baits. Mullet, spots, and sheepshead are regularly caught from the many piers that dot the more developed portions of the coastline; flounder, croaker, and whiting are the favored species. The most popular enticements for inshore species are live shrimp or shrimp-imitating jigs, but fiddler crabs are the offering of choice for the shell-cracking sheepshead. Minnows (or minnow-imitating streamers for fly anglers) are preferred for flounder.

In the northern coastal area, where the Gulf Stream comes a bit closer to shore, regular charter and head boats sail out of Myrtle Beach and Little River for mackerel, bluefish, tuna, and billfish. In recent years, increasing numbers of tarpon have shown up during the summer. Farther south, numerous wrecks and some jetties were built specifically with the angler in mind. Among the fish regularly taken on the wrecks are Spanish and king mackerel, albacore, false albacore, amberjack, bluefish, cobia, and bonito. Sharks can be caught almost anywhere if you can find a deep hole not too distant from shore.

SOUTH DAKOTA

Most people don't know that more cattle than people live in South Dakota. Nor do they know that you can cast flies on a mountain stream for wild trout in the western region, fish for bass on nearly every body of water in the central region, catch jumbo yellow perch well over 2 pounds through the ice in the eastern region, and catch many (and large) walleye along the vast stretches of the Missouri River. And all of these activities can be enjoyed without seeing very many cattle or people.

The most prominent angling attention in South Dakota is garnered by the Missouri River system, which in this state encompasses four large dams that were built between the late 1940s and early 1960s. These dams have spread water over 900 square miles and have divided the system into four reservoirs that range from large to enormous.

Beginning at the North Dakota border and ending at Nebraska, the South Dakota's fisheries are home to walleye, chinook salmon, northern pike, rainbow trout, brown trout, lake trout, smallmouth bass, largemouth bass, blue catfish, channel catfish, flathead catfish, white bass, crappie, tiger muskies, paddlefish, and sturgeon. The northernmost and largest reservoir, Lake Oahe is also the most attractive body of water and produces football-shaped walleye that are esteemed by even the most well-versed walleye anglers throughout North America. Because Oahe is so popular for producing sizable and numerous walleye, the other reservoirs in the system receive comparatively less pressure, even though they potentially host equal fishing opportunity.

The Black Hills region in the far western part of the state is South Dakota's taste of Montana. Full of trout fishing possibilities in countless streams surrounded by scenic landscape, it is also the home of three large reservoirs that offer a diversity of species and fishing prospects.

The Glacial Lakes region, in the eastern part of the state, consists of a series of relatively small and shallow lakes that are similar to a dishpan in structure. Good walleye, northern pike, and perch fishing is present in nearly every body of water. Anglers enjoy stable and sometimes abundant fishing opportunities when water levels are high due to above-normal precipitation. The glacial lakes are famous for producing abnormally large perch, and ice fishing here draws anglers from afar. In winter, it's not uncommon for more than 500 vehicles to be parked on one body of water when there is a good perch bite on.

There are several public and private stock ponds that start near the Missouri River in the central part of the state and spread west, some of which have not been tested with a lure in years. Top-quality bluegill and largemouth bass fishing are available for those who know where fish have been stocked, and for those who are willing to find out.

Missouri River System

One hundred years ago, the Missouri River flowed almost uninterrupted through South Dakota. Paddlefish, catfish, sauger, and sturgeon were among the most abundant native fish that survived in the flowage of the muddy Missouri. But today, four dams block the flow of water and have created four impressive reservoirs, often referred to as the "Great Lakes of South Dakota," that provide superb sportfishing.

Lake Oahe.   Covering 256,000 acres in South Dakota and stretching 232 miles from Bismark, North Dakota, to the dam near Pierre, Lake Oahe (pronounced oh-wha-hee) is by far the largest and most prominent reservoir in the system. In terms of size and population of walleye that live in a reservoir, Oahe is among the best in the nation. The mother reservoir is also home to chinook salmon, northern pike, rainbow trout, brown trout, lake trout, smallmouth bass, catfish, white bass, yellow perch, and crappie.

Walleye move into the larger creek arms and rivers in the spring to spawn. The Grand River near Mobridge and the Moreau River near Akaska are two significant tributaries on the upper reservoir, and these are prominent spawning areas for walleye. Anglers fish light jigs tipped with a minnow, keying on points, flats, and dropoffs near these large creek arms. It is difficult to catch pre-spawning walleye on Oahe; however, after spawning, walleye will hold in spawning areas and can be caught in relatively shallow water. On warmer spring days, anglers work fairly shallow waters, ranging from 1 to 15 feet deep, casting a light jig tipped with a minnow or chub up into shallow dirty water. By late April, walleye begin moving back downstream.

Summer is also a good time on Lake Oahe for walleye. As the water temperature increases, fish can generally be found anywhere from 15 to 25 feet deep. Most anglers switch to fishing live nightcrawlers or leeches behind a bottom-bouncing rig on points, colored water, flats, and dropoffs near the main river channel. Generally the lower third of the lake, from the Cheyenne River area to the dam, produces the biggest fish. Eight- to 10-pounders are more likely there than in the upper reaches, although numerous fish frequent the upper two-thirds of the lake.

Anglers in the northern reaches of the lake continue to take walleye through the ice during the winter. A cold winter is needed to freeze the lower end of the lake, but anglers can have success ice-fishing for salmon, walleye, pike, and smelt when ice is present.

A fall fishing scene on Lake Oahe.

The smallmouth population at Oahe is very respectable but underfished, because walleye receive most of the attention. Smallmouths are fairly predictable and easy to find here; the action center predominantly on rocky points, sunken islands, submerged vegetation, and dropoffs. With roughly 2,251 miles of shoreline, Oahe offers many locations to seek smallmouths.

Lake Oahe has produced healthy populations of large northern pike over the years, some of which have weighed in at over 30 pounds. Fifteen- to 20-pound fish are common. However, consistent availability of quality spawning cover necessary for natural reproduction causes the pike population to be cyclic. Anglers can expect good pike fishing when the water levels at Oahe are high enough in the spring to flood vegetation near the edges of the reservoir.

Most anglers fish for pike during the spring, when they move into the creek arms to feed and spawn, often spawning under the ice-covered bays. Most pike are taken using a stationary dead smelt rig. Casting spoons and assorted plugs will produce fish on warmer spring days. Shore-based anglers often do better than boaters in the spring, although the latter can reach bays that are harder to access by land. Some of the better pike locales on the lake are Cow and Spring Creeks near Pierre, West Whitlock near Gettysburg, and Blue Blanket and Swan Creeks near Mobridge. Fishing is also productive from mid-October through the fall.

Chinook salmon were introduced to Oahe in 1982. These powerhouse fighters can grow at a rate of 5 pounds a year here, feeding mainly on rainbow smelt and lake herring. Lake herring were stocked in Oahe in an attempt to take pressure off the smelt, an important forage base for walleye. Much like chinooks introduced into the Great Lakes, Oahe salmon have failed to prove they are an easy fish population to manage, even when conditions appear to be in their favor. The Oahe salmon population is cyclic and cannot be considered a

dependable fishery. When all the pieces fall into place, however, anglers can enjoy reeling in a fish that never would have survived in the middle of South Dakota without the construction of the dams. Salmon exist throughout the lake, but most angling occurs near Oahe Dam and north from Spring Creek to the Cheyenne River.

Lake Sharpe.   Lake Sharpe is an 80-mile-long 55,000-acre reservoir between the towns of Pierre and Chamberlain. Although it is not likely to raise a big population of large fish, such as the state-record 15.3-ounce walleye that was pulled from its waters, Sharpe is unique its consistent spawning success. Walleye, catfish, northern pike, crappie, white bass, perch, and large- and smallmouth bass are other gamefish available in the lake.

A large portion of the lake's walleye population winters in the tailwaters below Pierre down to the Antelope Creek area. Following an upstream migration of walleye that begins in September, most anglers do well in late fall and early winter below Oahe Dam in the tailrace. Walleye fishing is best from late April through roughly mid-June, when the fish are in a serious feeding mode following the spawn. Walleye inhabit the West Bend and Joe Creek areas around Memorial Day, and most are caught by anglers drifting with nightcrawlers.

Trout are stocked below Oahe Dam, where fly anglers find the fish in slack water. Three- to 9-pound rainbows are common in the spring. White bass are also caught in abundance as they make their way upriver in the spring to spawn.

Lake Francis Case.   The next reservoir in the system, and second largest at 100,000 acres and 107 miles long, is Lake Francis Case. Several catchable species exist in the lake, along with a few that may accidentally show up on the end of the line. With a lake of such large proportions and connected to other large bodies of water, there is always a chance of catching the unexpected, such as a shortnose gar. More likely angling targets, however, are catfish, northern pike, crappie, white bass, perch, large- and smallmouth bass, and tiger muskellunge.

Anglers can catch good numbers of walleye and consistent sizes year-round; the average walleye is 14 to 17 inches. The forage for walleye primarily consists of emerald shiners and gizzard shad; neither of these are comparable to the high-energy rainbow smelt forage in Lake Oahe, which prevents the fish in Francis Case from growing as large as the walleye in Oahe.

Walleye are caught at the upper end of the lake near Ft. Thompson in coldwater conditions in January. Anglers then use light line and a jig tipped with a minnow to catch sluggish fish. This pre-spawn bite will usually run from January through April, weather permitting.

When a lake is capable of producing smallmouth in the 5- to 6-pound class, it is destined to develop a reputation, and this has happened to some degree at Lake Francis Case. Smallmouth

fishing, however, is overshadowed by the interest in walleye. Points, dropoffs, and rocky areas are key places to locate smallmouth.

The northern pike in this lake do not hold a strong tradition, but they do in other reservoirs along the river system. Catfish are caught throughout the reservoir and can grow to fairly good size. Using a stationary bait rig to catch cats is the most popular and successful technique. Francis Case produced the state's 54-pound flathead catfish record, and also the 33-pound tiger muskellunge record.

Lewis and Clark.   The smallest of the four main-stem Missouri reservoirs, Lewis and Clark covers 32,000 acres and is probably the most under-fished reservoir in the state. It is the only one, however, that boasts smallmouth bass as its prime fishing attraction. This lake produces top-quality small-mouth angling, with a high average daily catch. The upper section of the lake, along with that portion of the Missouri River between Springfield and Fort Randall, has good largemouth fishing and the best smallmouth action in the state. Large stands of bulrushes and winding sandbars create a series of chutes and back bays that harbor plentiful bass.

There's also a good population of walleye and sauger. Because of its smaller size, relatively shallow depths, and high water-exchange rate, the reservoir has had fishery problems, and fish populations fluctuate.

Below Gavins Point Dam is the only place in South Dakota where you can legally take paddle-fish. Anglers are required to apply for a tag for this activity, which takes place during a set season.

Glacial Lakes Region

The Glacial Lakes Region stretches from the town of Aberdeen in northeastern South Dakota over to Watertown and down past Sioux Falls. Glaciers carved out roughly 200 lakes here thousands of years ago. The lakes range in size from a few acres to several that cover 16,000 acres (including Thompson, Poinsett, and Waubay Lakes).

Three relatively small rivers drain much of the eastern part of the state. The James River runs a course through both North Dakota and South Dakota and eventually feeds into the Missouri near the southern part of the state. Any fish found in the Missouri are also found in the James.

Most of the lakes provide walleye and saugeye. Saugeye, which are the offspring of a female walleye and male sauger, grow larger than pure sauger; they reach an average size of 5 pounds and inhabit turbid waters.

Many anglers wear waders to cast the shorelines in the spring and fall. When water temperatures are cold enough, walleye cruise and feed in the shallows during the morning, evening, and at night. The best action for wade fishing is usually during May.

Opportunity exists to catch yellow perch that average over a pound in size; some are in the 2-pound class and a few push the 3-pound barrier during a good cycle. Excellent water conditions and a broad-based forage cycle contribute to the abnormal size.

The quality of the Glacial Lakes' yellow perch fishery, and the overall fisheries, is directly related to high-quality water that provides excellent breeding conditions. A low water level and declining water quality will take their toll on these relatively shallow lakes. Lakes Waubay, Thompson, Henry, Whitewood, Preston, and Cattail are a few of the jumbo perch producers.

Northern pike also exist in many of the lakes, but Waubay has the most noted fishery for this species. In early spring, once the ice starts to leave the lakes, anglers can catch pre- and post-spawn pike with spoons and quick-strike dead smelt rigs.

Smallmouth bass were stocked in many eastern South Dakota lakes during the 1980s, and self-sustaining populations are found throughout the region. Popular smallmouth lakes are Clear, Enemy Swim, Pickerel, Poinsett, Kampeska, and Amsden. Amsden is also the only lake in South Dakota that possesses pure-strain muskellunge.

Ice fishing. A particular fishing activity in the Glacial Lakes region happens during the winter after the lakes ice over. Excellent walleye, pike, perch, and crappie angling attract people who might not fish at all during the open-water season. Once the ice is roughly 12 inches thick, anglers drive vehicles onto the frozen lakes, punching holes and searching for fish. A few vehicles fall through the ice nearly every year, and some fatalities occur because of accidents. Ice fishing requires prudence.

As to fishing tactics, anglers use stationary live-bait setups tipped with a minnow, chub, or wax worm, depending on the species they seek. Jigging is also a popular method, used to both attract and trigger fish into hitting the jig or a nearby baited line.

Black Hills Region

The Black Hills region, where roughly 400 miles of streams are actively managed for trout, holds trout promise for South Dakota anglers. Wild brook and brown trout, plus a few rainbows, have acclimated and maintained a self-sustaining population in some streams, although these species were not native to the area. Gold miners brought the fish to the Black Hills from Colorado in 1886.

Castle, Spring, Rapid, and Box Elder Creeks are the principal coldwater streams that not only feed the large lakes but also provide outstanding stream trout fishing. Two stretches of Rapid Creek, one in Rapid City, receive special management and are maintained as "blue-ribbon" fly fishing areas.

Beaver ponds in many of the tributaries in the Black Hills region provide additional remote fishing opportunities for anglers wishing to be absolutely alone. Immeasurable miles of streams run through the Black Hills, where stream anglers can fish for brookies and rainbows away from popular access areas.

The major mountain lakes provide opportunities for trout fishing as well, especially in Pactola, Sheridan, and Deerfield Lakes. Rainbows are a top attraction at Deerfield, which is near Hill City. The dam face and deep channel running parallel to it offer the best shot at splake. Most splake and rainbows in Deerfield average 12 inches long, although there's always a shot at a big splake. Pactola offers excellent opportunity for cutthroat fishing. Sheridan Lake has superb angling for northern pike, yellow perch, and largemouth bass, in addition to trout. For a measure of seclusion, anglers can ply the smaller trout lakes, such as Mitchell Lake, Horsethief Lake, and Slate Creek Dam.

West River Dams

Publicly owned dams on the West River prairie are managed for largemouth bass and panfish. West River stock dams (farm ponds) have produced South Dakota's biggest largemouth bass. The main problem with catching them is finding the waters and the people that own the water. Most of western South Dakota is privately owned. Bass in the 3- to 5-pound class are common, however. Privately owned waters here can sometimes be accessed simply by driving up and asking area ranchers if they have any ponds with fish in them and if they would allow you to wet a line.

Numerous small stock dams on private land throughout the state have been stocked by the Game, Fish and Parks Department under Fish Management Agreements. Permission must be obtained from the private property owner to fish such waters.

Dams also exist on the various National Grasslands, and some hold fishing opportunities; there are several on the Fort Pierre National Grassland. A float tube or small boat has become a common way to fish these small waters.

SOWBUG

Sowbugs are small freshwater crustaceans of the order Isopoda that are a favorite food of trout and other fish. Also known as pillbugs, they are mostly terrestrial or marine. Approximately 130 freshwater species occur in North America. Large numbers of sowbugs are often an indication of organic enrichment.

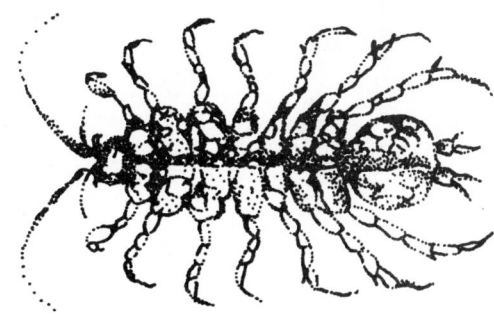

Sowbug, greatly enlarged.

S

Sowbugs are dark brown to gray in color and up to ³/₄-inch long. They are flattened dorsally and much wider than they are high, with seven pairs of legs and two pairs of antennae, one of which is usually much longer. They move by slowly crawling over surfaces and are sometimes confused with scuds, but they are wider than scuds and walk instead of swim.

SPADEFISH

Spadefish are distinctively shaped members of the Ephippidae family of mainly tropical and subtropical species. Their bodies are very flattened and nearly as deep as they are long. The first, or spiny, dorsal fin is separate from the second, or soft-rayed, dorsal, which has exceptionally long rays at the front and is matched in size and shape by the anal fin directly beneath it. The body is silvery and has four to six black bands that may be absent in older fish. The broad caudal fin has long rays at the tips of the upper and lower lobes so that the fin is concave. The mouth is small. Juvenile spadefish are black and are known to lie on their side to mimic floating debris.

Species that occur in North American waters and are occasionally encountered by anglers include the Pacific spadefish (*Chaetodipterus zonatus*), which ranges from Southern California to Mexico in the eastern Pacific, and the similar Atlantic spadefish (*C. faber*), which ranges from Massachusetts to Brazil in the western Atlantic and is more abundant in the Caribbean and Florida. The latter is sometimes mistakenly called angelfish; they are also known in Portuguese as *enxada* and in Spanish as *paguara*.

Spadefish travel in large schools, spawn in spring and summer, feed on shrimp and crustaceans, and are found inshore or in nearshore environs, especially around navigational markers, along sandy beaches, in harbors, or over wrecks. They may grow to 15 pounds but usually weigh less than 2 pounds. These fish are good table fare.

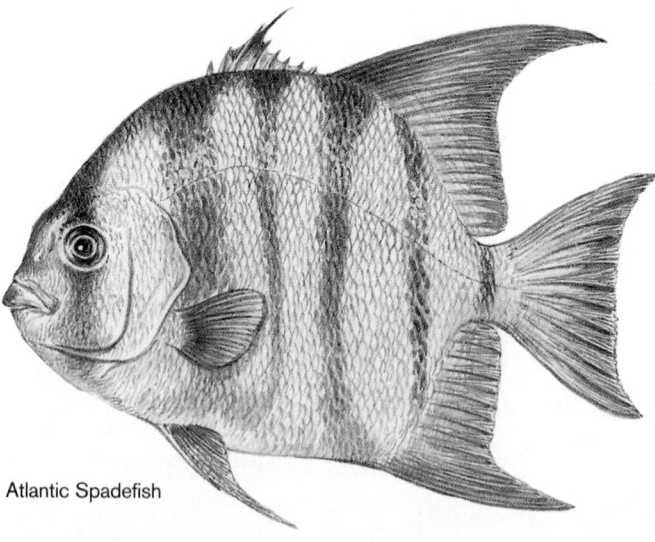

Atlantic Spadefish

SPAIN

Some of Europe's most diverse fishing exists in the southwest, in Spain, where anglers will find a good array of trout fishing in the mountains, some salmon and sea-run trout, and a potpourri of coarse species in many river systems. These offerings are rounded out by opportunities to catch black bass, zander, and pike. In addition, the Canary Islands are home to perhaps the most internationally renowned fishery for big-game species.

With a richly varied topography among its 194,885 square miles, Spain offers more freshwater fishing opportunities than most nonresidents realize. Some 76,000 kilometers of river water courses through Iberia, and many of the waterways have been impounded for hydroelectric purposes, creating large reservoirs. The primary freshwater fish for anglers is brown trout *(trucha común)*, but others include Atlantic salmon *(salmón)*; sea-run brown trout *(reo)*; rainbow trout *(trucha carco iris)*; largemouth bass *(perca negra)*; pike *(lucio)*; zander, or pike-perch *(lucioperca)*; carp *(carpa)*; tench *(tenca)*; barbel *(barbo)*; and chub *(cacho)*.

Salmon numbers and runs are modest and are concentrated in the Asturias region in the north, fronting the Atlantic. The Eo, Porcia, Esta, Narcea, Sella, Cares, Deva, and Piloña Rivers contain salmon and are accessed through specific reserves, where beats are controlled and hard to access. The season varies according to location but generally runs from early or mid-March through early July.

Sea-run trout are also modest in numbers and found in the northeast in a few rivers in the Galicia region. The Mandeo, Tambre, Sar, Mero, Jubia, and Sor Rivers are most notable; the season is generally from early March through mid-August.

Although trout are the main angling attraction, their populations are widespread. Rainbow trout have been introduced in various waters, but brown trout are more numerous. Most rivers and streams across the northern section of the country, including the Galicia, Asturias, Castilla, Pais Vasco, Navarra, Aragon, and Cataluna regions, support trout. These regions encompass many mountainous areas, including the Cordillera and Cantabrica ranges of the Pyrenees, which extend for some 270 miles and also form Spain's northeastern border with France.

Although the entire northern region is the most prominent brown trout area, two other regions host significant populations of these fish. One is in the middle of the country in rivers and streams emanating from the Sierra de Gredos, Sierra de Guadaramma, and Sierra de Albarracin ranges, respectively northwest, north, and northeast of the capital city of Madrid. Most of these flow to the Duero River, a large waterway that flows westerly to the Atlantic. The second region is in the mountainous area of southern Spain, especially in the many flows between the cities of Granada and Albacete in the Sierra de Segura range.

Fishing for coarse species is particularly popular among Spaniards and occurs especially in the central tableland in slower rivers and stillwaters. Waters in the vicinity of Madrid, south of Cuenca, north of Granada, near Linares, and north and west of Ciudad Real are the focal points.

Spaniards are showing a growing interest in largemouth bass, which were introduced to Spain and have flourished in many impoundments. Large lakes with bass include Ricobayo north of the city of Zamora, Almendra northeast of Salamanca, Alcántara north of Caceres, Orellana west of Ciudad Real, the backwaters of the Rio Guadalquivir southwest of Sevilla, Mequinenza and Ribarroja south of Lerida, Alarcón and Contreras south of Cuenca, and Entrepeñas and Buendía east of Guadalajara. Numerous smaller bass waters exist, including some near Madrid and Granada.

Roughly 88 percent of Spain is bordered by saltwater. This includes the Bay of Biscay on the north, some 770 kilometers of the Atlantic on the west and south, and some 1,660 kilometers of the Mediterranean on the south and west. Although opportunities for sportfishing exist, there is little to attract the visiting angler. The narrow coastal plain has many rocky headlands and few good harbors, the exceptions being Barcelona along the Mediterranean and several places along the Galician coast on the Atlantic. Thus saltwater angling efforts are directed primarily at the Canary Islands.

Canary Islands

The Canary Islands are situated roughly 80 miles off the northwest coast of Africa in the Canary basin of the eastern Atlantic, which is at roughly the same latitude as Daytona Beach, Florida, in the western Atlantic. There are seven islands in all, and they aren't far from the Madeiras and the Azores, which have produced monster blue marlin, yellowfin tuna, and bigeye tuna throughout the 1990s.

The Canaries, of course, are better known for sun, fun, and frolicking than they are for fishing. They do not offer a large fleet of modern sportfishing boats, but they do have some of the large blue marlin (and blues of a large average size), for which this region of the North Atlantic is noted. This is because the Canaries are situated on a shelf where the water drops off to awe-inspiring depths. The drop is steep not far from shore—there's a 1,200-foot dropoff about 5 miles out—and creates an upwelling. These shelves and the upwelling, coupled with the Canarian Current, attract pelagic species to these waters. June through October is the preferred fishing period, and the island of Lanzarote provides chartering opportunities.

As with other places in the eastern waters of the North and South Atlantic, where local fisheries concentrate on inshore waters and traditional commercial pursuits focused on sustenance, there is much less effort devoted to rod-and-reel clashes with the big, speedy, powerful denizens of the deep than there is in many other waters. But these trends have slowly been changing, and big-game sportfishing is on the rise here.

The record books show that the Canary Islands currently possess three line-class bigeye tuna records. The largest is a 363-pounder taken on 130-pound tackle. In addition, the waters have produced a record 897-pound bluefin tuna on 50-pound line, one Atlantic blue marlin line-class record, and five Atlantic bonito and two albacore records (including the all-tackle record-holding 88-pound albacore).

How big the marlin actually get is anyone's guess, but reports say that blues of 1,300 and 1,600 pounds have been registered by commercial fishermen, as well as bluefin to 1,200 pounds and a broadbill swordfish of 691 pounds. Anglers do encounter yellowfin and bigeye tuna in the 200-pound class, sometimes in schools, and some success has been registered with smaller swordfish at night, although the angling is often spotty, with streaks of activity for both tuna and billfish.

In September 1987, the Canaries produced their first 1,000-pound blue marlin on rod and reel, and since then numerous 800- to 1,000-pounders have been tagged and released, and a few granders landed. The average size of these blues approaches the 500-pound range.

SPAWN BAG

A mesh enclosure for a small group of fish eggs. Also known as a spawn sack, it is commonly used in river fishing for coho and chinook salmon and steelhead.

See: Natural Bait.

SPAWNING

The reproduction activities of fish.

See: Fish.

SPAWNING RUN

The migratory movement of fish related to spawning, mostly used with reference to fish that move up rivers and streams.

See: Fish.

SPEARFISH

Longbill Spearfish *Tetrapturus pfluegeri.*

Other names—longnose spearfish, Atlantic longbill spearfish; French: *makaire becune;* Japanese: *kuchinaga, kuchinagafuura;* Portuguese: *espadim bicudo;* Spanish: *aguja picuda.*

Shortbill Spearfish *Tetrapturus angustirostris.*

Other names—shortnose spearfish; Arabic: *kheil;* Hawaiian: *a'u;* Japanese: *furaikajiki.*

Longbill Spearfish

Mediterranean Spearfish *Tetrapturus belone.*
Other names—French: *aguglia impériale;* Italian: *acura imperiale, aguglia pelerana.*

These species are lesser-known and small members of the Istiophoridae family of billfish that are also referred to as slender spearfish. They are pelagic, offshore, deep-water fish that appear to be available all year in small numbers but are infrequently encountered by anglers in most parts of their range. They are of some commercial value, usually as incidental catch, and are fairly good eating, although the flesh is dark.

Identification.   Spearfish can be distinguished from other billfish by a slender, lightweight body, short bill, and a dorsal fin that is highest anteriorly (higher than in marlin and lower than in the sailfish). The vent is located well in front of the anal fin; in all other billfish, the vent is located close to the anal fin. The bill of the shortbill spearfish is barely longer than its lower jaw, whereas in the longbill spearfish it is about twice as long, but it is still noticeably short when compared to that in other billfish. The pectoral fins of the shortbill and Mediterranean spearfish barely reach to the curve of the lateral line. In the longbill spearfish, they extend beyond the curve. The longbill spearfish has more elements (45 to 53) in the first dorsal fin than any other Atlantic billfish, although it may appear similar to the white marlin *(see: marlin, white).* The shortbill spearfish of the Pacific has approximately the same count (47 to 50 elements), but the Mediterranean spearfish has fewer (39 to 46). The lateral line is single and arches above the pectoral fins. The dorsal fin is bright blue and has no spots. The vertical bars on the body are never as prominent as in other billfish and may show only slightly or not at all.

Some scientists believe that a fourth species of spearfish *(Tetrapturus georgei)* exists. Called the roundscale spearfish *(marlin peto* in Spanish), it occurs around Sicily, Portugal, and Spain and is said to resemble the so-called hatchet marlin. The hatchet marlin, which has not been named scientifically, has not yet been proven to be a separate species and is presently considered a variation of the white marlin, which may also be the fate of the roundscale spearfish.

Size/Age.   Available data indicate that the longbill spearfish matures by the age of 2 and rarely lives past age 3. Its maximum longevity may be age 4 to 5. The all-tackle world record for the longbill spearfish is a fish of 94 pounds, 12 ounces, and for the Mediterranean spearfish is 90 pounds, 13 ounces.

Distribution.   Spearfish are cosmopolitan but nowhere are they abundant. The longbill spearfish is known to occur in the northwest Atlantic from New Jersey to Venezuela, including the Gulf of Mexico. Japanese longliners have also recorded its occurrence in the north-central Atlantic, in the south Atlantic, and off South Africa. The shortbill spearfish is known in the Pacific and Indian Oceans. It is not reported to occur in the Mediterranean but has been captured in the Atlantic Ocean west of the Cape of Good Hope, South Africa. The Mediterranean spearfish is known to occur only in the Mediterranean Sea. The Canary Islands and Hawaii have produced a number of record-setting specimens.

Food and feeding habits.   Spearfish feed at or near the surface, mainly on small and medium-size fish and squid, including dolphin, sauries, flyingfish, and needlefish.

Angling.   The fishing methods to use for these species are the same as for other billfish, although lighter tackle, as would be used for white marlin or sailfish, is more appropriate. Most catches are incidental.

See: Big-Game Fishing; Billfish; Offshore Fishing.

SPEARFISHING

(1) The taking of fish with a handheld spear or spear gun by a snorkeler or diver while swimming in the water. Spearfishing is generally legal in saltwater; the legality varies in freshwater. Where allowed, spearfishing is regulated by fisheries agencies, usually requires a fishing license, is subject to seasons, and is usually restricted to certain species. Although spearfishing is popular with some snorkelers and divers and, where legal, is considered a form of recreational fishing, it is not widely practiced and is not treated as sportfishing by the general angling community.

(2) An alternate term for spearing *(see)*, the taking of fish with a handheld prong, harpoonlike device, or spear.

SPEARING

Taking fish with a handheld prong, harpoonlike device, or spear, any of which may also be known as a gig. These devices are meant to spear or impale fish by means of a pronged or barbed instrument, which is attached to a rigid object such as a pole. Also known in some places as gigging, spearing is primarily a freshwater activity and one that has been practiced traditionally to procure food. The legality today varies in freshwater and is regulated by fisheries agencies; it usually requires a fishing license, is subject to seasons, and may be restricted to certain species. In some locales, a spear must be attached to a tethered line.

Eels and suckers are among the fish subject to spearing in streams and creeks, but spearing is also practiced for other species, especially rough fish such as carp, buffalo, and bullhead. It is also practiced in northern locales during the winter, usually on frozen lakes in small shanties (fish houses or dark houses) that have been darkened to enhance visibility through the water. Although spearing is still practiced and, where legal, is considered a form of recreational fishing, it is not widely employed and is not treated as sportfishing by the general angling community.
See: **Spearfishing.**

SPEARING

A term for silversides *(see)* of the Atlantic coast.

SPECIES

A group of similar fish that can freely interbreed; similar species make up a genus.
See: **Fish; Fisheries Management.**

SPECIMEN

A term predominantly used by British coarse anglers to refer to a large or trophy-size representative of a particular species. Specimens are fish that are above average in size, and people who specialize in pursuing such individual fish are called specimen hunters.

SPECK

A term primarily used in southern parts of the United States for crappie *(see)*, which are often also called speckled perch, although they are not a true perch.

SPECKLED PERCH

A term primarily used in southern parts of the United States for crappie *(see)*, which are not a true perch. They may also be called specks.

SPECKLED TROUT

(1) A term primarily used in northeastern parts of the United States and eastern Canada for brook trout. They may also be called squaretails.
See: **Trout, Brook.**

(2) A common alternative term for spotted seatrout.
See: **Seatrout, Spotted.**

SPEED GAUGE

Although a speedometer measures the velocity of a moving boat, it is often not precise enough for fishing usage, especially trolling, or not capable of depicting slow-speed measurements. Anglers who troll use various instruments, referred to as speed gauges, speed sensors, or speed indicators, to accomplish this. These include electronic instruments fitted with a paddlewheel, which is secured to the boat transom flush to the hull; global positioning (GPS) navigational devices, which measure speed via distance traveled over time; and by non-electronic drag-weight gauges, which measure speed relative to markings on a plate. They may also include a standard tachometer, which measures engine rpm, and which can be used to gauge relative speed, although this is very imprecise. Additionally, there are devices, attached to downrigger weights, which measure via paddlewheel the speed of the lure at the depth of the downrigger weight. This is sometimes different than surface speed.

The most common dedicated speed gauges are electronic models that measure surface speed; these are either stand-alone products or accessory elements incorporated into sonar instruments. They are not generally accurate above about 50 mph but are excellent for measuring trolling speed. As a boat moves over the water's surface, the drag of the water turns the unit's paddlewheel, which is mounted on the transom of the boat. One of the wheel's paddles contains a piece of magnetic metal that triggers a sensor on the wheel's stationary frame with each revolution of the wheel. The electronic speedometer simply counts the number of times its sensor is triggered and uses the wheel's rpm to calculate speed.

The mounting position of the paddlewheel sensor is critical. Like a sonar transducer, it must receive an uninterrupted flow of smooth water, free of turbulence and air bubble streams at all speeds. Don't mount it behind hull strakes or ribs, or directly in front of the engine's lower unit. The prop may pull extra water past the wheel giving an artificially high speed reading. Mounting the wheel's bracket too high or low will also cause inaccurate readings.

Maintaining a consistent boat speed can be critical to trolling success, and even with these potential problems, the electronic speedometer is hard to

beat. Conventional boat speedometers measure water pressure picked up by a tube mounted on the transom or built into an engine's lower unit. They don't generally work below 5 to 10 mph and are useless for trolling. Even the speed-over-ground readings of nondifferential GPS may not be as accurate as a paddlewheel-driven electronic speedometer at trolling speed. If, for instance, you're trolling north at $1\frac{1}{2}$ mph and the GPS system's selective availability feature is falsely moving your position south at 2 mph, speed accuracy is out the window *(see: GPS).*

Nevertheless, dedicated paddlewheel speed gauges vary from one brand to the next, although some can be calibrated. Boat speed is influenced by a host of factors, making exact speed comparisons between boats with paddlewheel speed gauges difficult, no matter which gauge is used. Incidentally, since accuracy is dependent upon the speed differential between the boat's hull and the surface of the water, things that make the surface of the water move can cause erroneous speed readings. Wind actually moves the surface of the water and a boat traveling with the wind will show a slower speed than a boat moving against it at the same true speed over the bottom. A boat moving with a river's current will also have a slower speed reading than when moving against it. It is possible to be moving with a swift current downriver and yet show no reading on the speed gauge because the paddle is either not turning forward or barely turning.
See: Trolling.

SPENTWING

A dry fly that imitates a mayfly spinner that has fallen on the water with its wings outstretched.

SPEY ROD

A long, two-handed fly rod, named after Scotland's River Spey, preferred by some European casters; this type of rod may also be called a Euro rod or salmon rod.
See: Flycasting Tackle.

SPIDER HITCH KNOT

A double-line knot primarily associated with saltwater fishing, especially the use of heavy leaders and big-game angling, and used as a quick-tie replacement for the Bimini Twist.
See: Knots, Fishing.

SPIKE

A rod-holding tube, also known as a sand spike *(see)* and pointed at one end for insertion into the sand, used by surf anglers to secure a rod.
See: Surf Fishing.

SPINCASTING REEL
See: Spinning Tackle.

SPINCASTING ROD
See: Rod, Fishing; Spincasting Tackle.

SPINCASTING TACKLE

Spincasting tackle is arguably the easiest type of fishing tackle to learn to master. While suited to a variety of light- to medium-duty fishing applications, sizing practicalities of the spincasting reel ultimately limit the application of the tackle due to line capacity constraints and mechanical disadvantages.

Spincasting tackle, which is often referred to as spincast tackle, is characterized by a front-cover reel with a hole or opening through which line passes. Line is wound on a stationary spool under the cover or hood, and a button is used to release the line. This is distinctive from other tackle forms, whose reel design and geometry overcome the line capacity restraints characteristic of spincasting products. Those forms include baitcasting tackle *(see)* and conventional tackle *(see),* both of which recover line via a revolving spool; spinning tackle *(see),* which features a stationary spool and a revolving line winding bail; and flycasting tackle *(see),* which has a revolving spool but a much narrower application. The spincasting reel is also distinctive from other tackle forms in that its design and geometry inherently lacks cranking power, although this limitation is not serious for the typical light- to medium-duty applications for which this style of reel is intended.

This is reflected in the fact that spincasting tackle is widely used across North America, and ranks first in total number of units sold annually, Nevertheless, it is the stepchild of fishing equipment. It is seldom given serious consideration in popular publications and virtually overlooked by avid or broadly experienced anglers, some of whom have never used it. Yet beginning anglers of all ages, as well as casual anglers, are drawn to spincasting tackle, largely because it is the simplest of all tackle types to use. A five-year-old can learn to use spincasting tackle in a short time but would have problems with another type of tackle. People are also drawn to it because it is durable, adequate for the majority of their angling activities, and relatively inexpensive. The fact that most spincasting reels come pre-spooled with line eliminates the most basic rigging problem.

Mostly employed in light freshwater fishing applications, spincasting tackle, to many people, is associated with less arduous and less intense fishing activities, particularly stillfishing *(see)*. Some people believe—erroneously—that this gear is only meant for panfish and catfish angling, or for fishing with bait and a float. Usage really depends on the individual's abilities and preferences, and on the grade of equipment.

Despite their popularity for freshwater fishing, very few spincasting reels are used in saltwater. Spincasting reels targeted for saltwater applications are really high line capacity freshwater reels whose metal components have been replaced with stainless steel components to prevent corrosion. The fact that most spincasting reel components are enclosed makes cleaning the reel with freshwater a challenging task. Additionally, relatively low line capacities and reduced crank power make them a rarity for saltwater applications.

In part, the lesser esteem that has befallen spincasting tackle is due to the fact that the spincasting reel of the past had modest to poor cranking power, inferior drag capability, and perceived limited casting accuracy and range. That has changed somewhat with today's higher-end products. Many of the elements of today's better spincasting reels now rival spinning and baitcasting reels in the quality of features and in their applicability to varied freshwater fishing activities.

Nevertheless, a primary constraint to the spincasting reel category is relatively low line capacity. Spincasting tackle is limited to reels that hold less than 150 yards of 25-pound line; most, in fact, hold far less line of much lighter strength, and their limits in this regard in part explain why spincasting reels are typically pre-spooled by the manufacturer. Baitcasting and spinning reels are available that operate with much greater line capacities. Additionally, the spool of a spincasting reel, which is enclosed by the front cover, makes the reel easier to use but also creates a misperception that the line cannot be easily feathered on the cast to control accuracy. Furthermore, because the line on the spool is not in constant view of the angler, several line-related functional problems can unknowingly develop. Too much line, too little line, tangled, frayed, or twisted line are more difficult to detect with spincasting reels than in reel types with open spools.

The gearing system on spincasting reels is similar to the gearing system on spinning reels. Both transfer crank handle rotational forces through a 90-degree bend to the reel's mechanism that wraps line on the spool. This is accomplished through a gear system capable of converting motion between two 90-degree shafts. In comparison, baitcasting reels transfer motion from the crank handle directly to the revolving spool through two parallel shafts. Of the three categories of fishing equipment, spincasting reels display the most inherent limitations in gearing efficiency, and many anglers feel that it is more difficult to retrieve identical weights with a spincasting reel than with a spinning or baitcasting reel. These constraints are further explored in the gearing section that follows.

There are some other limitations to spincasting reels. Spincasting reels have more areas that come in contact with the line during casting than spinning or baitcasting reels. These contact areas impart friction to the line, thus reducing the potential casting distance. Line flows freely off the end of a spinning reel, only hitting the front flange of the spool before reaching the first line guide (stripper guide) on the rod. In contrast, line on a spincasting reel comes in contact with similar components, plus the inside surface of the front cover and the edges of the protective front cover line guide as it exits the reel. This friction reduces casting distance and cranking power. Thus, casting distance is generally greater on spinning reels than spincasting reels. Spincasting and spinning reels both inherently have the capability to cast further distances than baitcasting reels—compliments of a stationary spool versus the revolving spool on baitcasting reels.

There is a perception among anglers that accuracy with spincasting tackle is not very good, but this is often a function of poor casting technique, mismatched tackle, or both.

Some exhibition casters are remarkably accurate with conventional spincasting tackle, more so than they would be with other equipment, simply because they've mastered all of the elements of the spincasting game and have properly matched gear. And some of the best European match tournament anglers use specialized spincasting reels with rods worth thousands of dollars, because of the ease with which the reel can be controlled. The typical angler, however, uses spincasting tackle primarily in situations where accuracy and distance are not critical, and where the species of fish sought are usually small, which tends to reinforce the perception that accuracy is not an attribute of this equipment.

As with any type of tackle, accuracy is really a function of practice and using the right technique. In theory, baitcasting reels are the most accurate because the angler can easily be in constant contact with the revolving spool which controls the line. The spool can be slowed or stopped at any point. The spincasting reel has the capability of being the next most accurate—by using the forefinger to contact the line as it exits the front cover, an angler is in almost constant contact with the line. Because the line is making a loop as it exits the front cover, in theory, the angler may not be in constant contact with the line as would be possible when using a baitcasting reel. In addition, hand position on most spincasting reels is the same as it is on baitcasting reels, making the transition from using spincasting tackle to baitcasting tackle easier. The third most accurate gear, in theory, is the spinning reel. Although the line departing a spinning reel can be feathered with the angler's forefinger, that line is traveling in a larger loop than on a spincasting reel, therefore, the angler is not in contact with the line as continuously as on spincasting reels, which have a much smaller line loop.

Rods play an important part in matching fishing application. Given a proper matching of rod, reel, and line diameter for the intended lure size,

Some prehistoric sharks had bizarre features; *Stethacantus* had a brush of external teeth on a rigid massive dorsal fin, while *Damocles serratus* had a rigid, serrated, forward-pointing dorsal spine.

spincasting anglers have the equipment to rival even the most skilled baitcasting angler in casting accuracy, and they have little difficulty casting ultralight lures for trout and panfish.

As with most other tackle types, spincasting gear varies widely in quality; some models are better suited to certain fishing activity than others. Some reels sport features that make them suitable to achieving casting distance, reducing line twist, making fast or slow (power) retrieves, instantly engaging the anti-reverse, back-reeling, being able to indicate strikes, and having interchangeable right or left retrieves. Some hybrid models even reside under the rod, featuring a casting trigger instead of a button, making them more like a spinning reel. These products are used on spinning rods instead of spincasting rods.

A product of the mid-twentieth century, spincasting gear is the youngest of all types of tackle. It fills an important role in the marketplace, and deserves more respect than it is usually accorded.

It was fisherman R. D. Hull who, in the fall of 1947, convinced the Oklahoma-based Zero Hour Bomb Company, a firm that was in need of new direction after World War II and which manufactured explosive timing devices used in oil production, to tool up to produce his new type of fishing reel. A west Texas watchmaker, Hull was said to be frustrated with backlash problems in baitcasting reels, and allegedly got the idea for the prototype of

a spincasting reel while in a grocery store, observing a clerk wrapping a meat package. The string for wrapping the package was pulled from a stationary spool. Hull created a contraption that looked like a tin can with a hole in both ends.

The contraption was designed with a fixed spool in mind, so that line would come off it much the way that the wrapping string came off its spool in the grocery store, and, most importantly, wouldn't backlash.

It is not known whether officials at the Zero Hour Bomb Company were anglers, but they decided to produce Hull's new reel under the acronym ZEBCO. In June of 1949, 25 handmade Zebco Standards—the first spincasting reels—were built on the first day of production. The manufacturer ceased building explosive timing devices and concentrated on fishing reels.

With a good deal of promotional help over the following decade, the spincasting reel surged in popularity. In 1955, Zebco began production of their now infamous 33 model spincasting reel (then called a closed-face spinning reel). It was priced at $19.95, a hefty sum at a time when gasoline was about 25 cents a gallon and soda pop was 5 cents a bottle. That model reel is still in production today, and still costs under $20. In 1961, Zebco produced one of its other infamous spincasting models, the 202, which is also still in production and believed to be the largest selling reel in the history of fishing, with over 50 million sold. The company that allied itself with R. D. Hull and the contraption that would be known as a spincasting reel was turning into one of the giants in the world of sportfishing tackle.

The spincasting reel, which did not use a revolving spool for casting or line retrieval, came along at the same time that the previously invented European spinning reel was emerging in North America, and concurrent with the development of nylon monofilament fishing line *(see: line)* and the evolution of fiberglass fishing rods. It offered easier use for casters than the baitcasting (levelwind) reels then available, which at that time caused an annoying and frustrating backlash (line tangling) for most anglers on every fourth or fifth cast.

At the time of the emergence of both spinning and spincasting tackle, anglers primarily used levelwind or baitcasting gear, flycasting tackle, and conventional or big-game tackle for respective applications. But there was a lack of equipment that was easy for anyone to use and which could handle varied angling activity, especially the casting of various weighted objects. Both spinning and spincasting reels filled that void, and eventually played a huge role in a fishing participation boom that has extended to the present day.

In the early 1950s, the reels that are presently referred to as spinning models were then called open-faced spinning or, less often, open-faced reels. The reels that are referred to today as spincasting

The contraption nailed to this board in 1947 was the prototype of the first production spincasting reel, which is shown in the lower right and was made in 1949.

were then called closed-faced spinning, or closed-faced reels. This terminology has caused some confusions in literature, although the intentions are understandable; the early nomenclature was arguably more appropriate than what is used in today's parlance.

Spinning reels all feature an exposed stationary spool and an exposed line pickup and line-winding bail arm; thus, it was common in the early days of their existence for these to be called open-faced reels. Spincasting reels all feature a stationary spool, a line pickup, and a line-winding mechanism that are covered by a cone or hood; thus, it was common for these to initially be called closed-face reels. Both types of reel feature a spool that remains stationary when line is wound, or spun, around it, and when it is unwound during casting. However, during the operation of the drag, the spools on both categories of reels generally rotate. This is different than baitcasting and conventional reels, whose spools turn and cause the line to wind and unwind. Essentially, any reel with an exposed stationary spool is a spinning reel, and any reel with a covered stationary spool is a spincasting reel.

Over the years, covered stationary spool reels became predominantly known and categorized simply as spincasting (or spincast) reels. Perhaps this was an outgrowth of the use of the word baitcasting to describe levelwind revolving spool reels. If this seems confusing, it is.

This Zebco reel is typical of spincasting reels; note the star drag on the handle shaft, the conelike hood, and the pushbutton line release.

At the risk of further confusion, it should be pointed out that another distinguishing difference between spinning and spincasting reels is that the former always sit underneath the rod seat, while the latter usually sit atop the rod seat. Some hybrid spincasting reels sit underneath the rod handle, but they have a covered stationary spool, and otherwise basically function like a conventional spincasting reel. These may actually be easier for many people to use than the conventional spincasting reels, and are similar in operation to spinning reels.

Finally, it is worth noting that a major difference between spincasting and other reel types is the ability to change line. Although changing line on a spincasting reel is not actually difficult, it is less easy with this reel than with spinning or baitcasting products because the others have easier access to the spool. On spincasting reels, the spool is shrouded by a spinner head and both are underneath a front cover. To get to the spool you have to remove the cover and raise the spinner head (which might also be referred to as an internal rotor). This is one reason all spincasting reels come from the manufacturer pre-spooled with an appropriate strength and length of line. Another reason is that performance is greatly affected by line limpness and diameter. The spincasting reel is the least tolerant of all reel types in this regard and can fail to function with improper line. Yet another reason for pre-spooling, and one that plays to the greatest strength of spincasting reels in the marketplace, is that it makes them more appealing to the less experienced angler. There are virtually no spinning or baitcasting reels pre-spooled with line by the manufacturer. This interesting difference says a lot.

General Operation

Spincasting reels range from ultralight models weighing a few ounces and used with 4-pound line, to heavy freshwater and light saltwater models weighing between 15 and 17 ounces and used with 20- to 25-pound line; they generally work best when the terminal gear weighs between $1/4$ and $3/4$ ounce. They are also known as American spinning reels, spincasting reels, spincast reels, spin-cast reels, and closed-face spinning reels, and they generally mount on top of the rod handle (rod seat), similar to baitcasting reels. This is evidently due to the fact that when spincasting reels were first created, most nonfly and nonconventional casting rod handles were of the recessed-seat type suitable for use with revolving spool reels. Those reels sat atop the rod and had a right-handed retrieve. Spincasting reels followed suit.

The spincasting reel usually has a pushbutton that controls the release of line, a stationary spool that line is wound around by a spinner head with a line pickup pin, and a round or cone-shaped cover with an opening for line to pass through. It also has an adjustable drag that is controlled mostly by a thumb wheel or star wheel, and either a single or dual grip handle.

In use, with the back of the reel facing the angler, the pushbutton is depressed by the thumb, which releases the line for casting yet holds it in place until the thumb is removed from the button. When the button is released, line flows off the spool, through the opening in the reel hood, or cover, and out through the guides, carried by the weight of the object at the terminal end of the line. To retrieve the line, the handle is rotated forward, which causes the pickup pin to turn and catch the

line under the hood, winding it around the concealed spool.

These are the basic elements of operating a spincasting reel, although drag and anti-reverse features come into play as well, and the general design, style, and feel of each product has relevance to its use.

Casting/Line Release Features

Pushbutton. The operation of a spincasting reel essentially starts with depressing the pushbutton, a component that is usually touched with the thumb and frequently called the thumb button. This releases the line and allows it to come off the spool. As long as the pushbutton is fully depressed, it acts as a brake and keeps the line in place. When tension on the button is released, the line flows unimpeded off the spool, through the opening in the cover, and out the line guides of the rod. A pushbutton should be easy to activate, with little force necessary, and virtually all of them are.

In spincasting reels, when you press the pushbutton, the line is compressed between the inside of the cover and the external surface of the rotor (spinner head). The line is sandwiched between these two components until the pushbutton is released. On some higher quality reels, a brake ring is located on the external surface of the rotor or spinner head. On these models, the brake ring holds the line against the front cover instead of the surface of the spinner head itself. The brake ring is typically molded from a softer rubber or plastic material. Material selection for this component is very critical. A soft material is best so that the line is not damaged when it is pressed against the front cover, yet the material must also resist being cut or permanently deformed by the line. Those spincasting reels without a brake ring have metal to metal contact between the spinner head and front cover, which compresses the line and has the potential to damage it.

When the pushbutton is pressed, it also causes a line pickup pin to drop out of the way. The pickup pin winds line onto the spool. As long as the pin is extended in the retrieve position, it holds line in place and you can't cast or let line out (except when the drag functions). Thus, pressing the pushbutton causes the pickup pin to drop out of the way, moves the spinner head forward, and sandwiches the line between the spinner head and the inside cover, so that in the casting motion the lure doesn't drop to the ground. When you release the pushbutton, the spinner head drops back, which allows the line to flow freely off the spool. Naturally, this works the same when you are simply releasing line rather than casting, as might be done when lowering bait or a jig; you just press the pushbutton and let go of it to let line flow from the reel. At this point, and until you turn the handle, line is free to flow off the spool, and the reel is said to be in freespool.

Freespool is a term commonly used to refer to that state when line is able to freely unwind from the spool; it does not literally mean that the spool of the reel can freely rotate. The term is something of a carryover from the use of baitcasting and conventional tackle. In these types of tackle, the spool does revolve to release line, and freespool really does indicate that the spool is free to rotate to easily release line. With spincasting reels, in freespool the gears are engaged and the pickup pin has just been moved out of the way so that line can flow off the spool. In some of the very early model spincasting reels, the gears actually did separate or disengage from each other in the cast position.

Although the pushbutton is by far the typical means of changing the reel from the retrieve to the cast position, there are some variations. A common one in use today is a trigger release, which is used on spincasting reels that mount under the rod handle, facing away from the angler, and are cast more like a spinning reel than a conventional spincasting reel. These operate somewhat like pushbuttons, except that a trigger, which is pulled by the index finger, performs the function of a button. Pulling the trigger up is like pushing a thumb button in. This variation makes a spincasting reel with a trigger release something of a crossover between a spinning reel and a spincasting reel. Although most of this type of tackle is very good quality and very easy to use, there is not a big market demand for it.

Another version of spincasting reel, virtually unknown in North America but used by expert match tournament anglers in Europe, also mounts under the rod handle and has a button on the front nose that releases the line; the button is touched by the forefinger. Old spincasting reels had a post on top of the reel that you pushed down to disengage the gear set (this post, or button, really did disengage the gear sets; thumb buttons and triggers today do not); when you cast the reel, the center shaft gear still rotated. Instead of line just coming off the spool, the center shaft gear rotated and there was a flywheel on the back of the reel so you could feather the flywheel. To engage it, you pushed the handle in toward the reel. The thumb button is a little bit different than the original approach to line release in spincasting reels, but an easier one.

Cover/Hood. When making a cast with a spincasting reel, it is important that as the line comes off the spool and heads out the rod, it does not touch very many components. Each component it touches adds friction and decreases distance.

Most spincasting reels feature a rounded or cone-shaped hood or front cover that encloses the line spool and other parts. When the line comes off the fairly narrow spool, it forms a loop. Most rounded and cone-shaped front covers have a hole at the front of the reel for line passage. It is important that as the line comes off the spool the loop is necked down quickly to form a straight or nearly straight stream as it goes through this hole and out to the first rod guide. The large first guide on a spinning rod serves this necking-down function, and the design of most spincasting reel covers does the same thing.

Some spincasting reels have a rounded cover with a large open area at the front of the reel. This allows the line to come off the spool without encountering the inside of the cover. The larger coils of line that flow off the reel have to be necked down at the first rod guide, much like a spinning reel. If the line is properly controlled between the reel exit and the first rod guide, this system has the potential to generate longer casts than other types of front covers. However, to realize this increased casting distance, the rod line guides would have to be of the large variety associated with those found on spinning rods. If they are not, having a large line exit on the cover is counterproductive. In reality, properly shaped front covers, with small holes for the line to exit, work best with today's casting rods, which sport smaller line guides.

Spool size/Capacity. The amount of line on a reel spool, in addition to the size of the spool, are also key factors in casting. Spool size on spincasting reels is primarily governed by line capacity and practicality of the overall reel size. As line capacity is increased, the reel becomes longer to compensate for a wider spool, or bigger in diameter to compensate for a bigger diameter spool. If a longer spool is used, a spool oscillation system is required—like spinning reels—to evenly lay the line across the width of the spool. An oscillation system makes the reel even longer. Additionally, the bigger diameter spools have a limitation. Line must travel from the center hub of the spool over the front flange of the spool and out the reel. As this distance increases, friction on the line increases, dramatically decreasing casting distance.

Overall reel sizing is more a concern with spincasting reels than spinning reels because of the balance issue. With a spincasting reel perched on top of a rod, gravity causes the reel and rod to naturally rotate so that the reel is upside down. The larger and heavier the reel, the more difficult it is to comfortably balance the reel right side up. Spinning reels are naturally positioned underneath the rod, so that this tendency to rotate is avoided.

Spincasting reels generally have less line capacity than spinning reels for the reasons already listed. Most spincasting reels hold a maximum of 100 yards of the recommended line diameter. Typically, a spincasting reel user does not cast a distance of more than 30 yards, and more frequently only 15 to 20 yards. However, when the line gets low on a spincasting reel, which happens through regular use (breaking some off, retying knots, and so on), an angler may not realize it as readily as when using other types of tackle with constantly visible spools. Obviously, the cover can be removed to readily check line capacity, but many people just don't do this and can suddenly discover that they are so low on line that they cannot cast a proper distance (or would be subject to a crisis if they caught a large fish that took line off the drag).

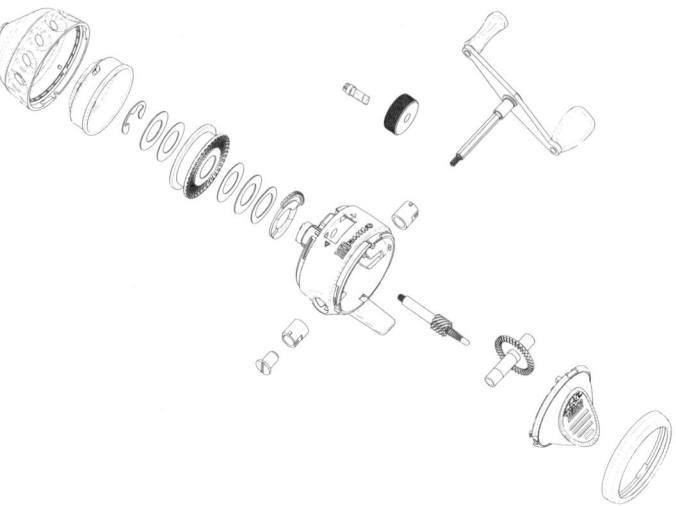

All of the parts of a Zebco Red Rhino spincasting reel are shown here; this product features a soft-touch thumb pad release, large helical gears, and continuous anti-reverse.

Spincasting reel spools are narrow and shallow, and the line lays fairly uniformly on them. A few spincasting reels have over-wrapping or oscillating line-winding to keep more line on the top surface near the edge of the spool. European match reels are almost always of this variety, as are some of the higher quality spincasting reels in the North American market.

When a spool is wider, which means that more line is near the surface, it casts better, because the line won't have to make as sharp an angle as it comes off the spool. If you have a thin, deep spool, and you cast 30 yards off the spool, the line pulls down deeper as it comes off the spool than it would with a wider spool. Naturally, this is compensated to some extent by how full the spool is with line to start. Some spincasting reels oscillate the spool to lay line more evenly, as is done on spinning reels, but the value of this is dubious in spincasting reels due to their generally shallow and narrow spools. It does put more cost into the reel, and the gain in casting distance is not likely to be that significant or of that much value to spincasting tackle users.

Retrieving/Line Recovery Features

Line pickup. When you turn the handle on a spincasting reel, the gears rotate and cause the internal rotor, or spinner head, to revolve. This allows a line pickup pin to wind line on the stationary spool. Some reels have multiple pins to hasten pickup.

The pickup pins on some reels are ceramic, and on others stainless steel. Ceramic (the same type of material used for most rod guides) has a low friction surface and does not get cut by line. Fishing line can pick up assorted matter on its surface and is extremely abrasive. Held under tension, and pulled back and forth across a surface, it can cut a groove in brass, soft steels, and other materials. Some stainless steel holds up pretty well, although it is not as smooth as ceramic. Some manufacturers use hard chrome-plated spinner heads and ceramic pickup pins to help prevent the line from cutting those mechanisms and to help reduce some of the friction in the retrieve.

One of the things that is important in the start of the retrieval motion is how fast the pickup pin engages. This is generally measured by the degrees of rotation the handle must be rotated through before the reel reengages and line starts wrapping on the spool. A faster engagement is an advantage in certain fishing situations. If a fish strikes when the reel is not in the retrieve mode, the speed at which it can be converted to the retrieve mode may be the difference between catching and missing the fish. The less rotation there is before engagement, the better.

Engagement speed is partly affected by numerical gear ratio. The faster the gear ratio, the faster the pickup pin is going to reengage. It is also affected by the number of cams on the top surface of the spool boss. In spincasting reels, there is a cammed surface on the end of the spool boss (a cylindrical extension of the body around which the spool rotates). One surface of the pickup arm is in continuous contact with the outer surface of the spool boss. When this surface of the pickup arm is in contact with the outer surface of the body's spool boss, the pickup pin (connected to the end of the pickup arm) is positioned to wrap line on the spool. In the cast position, this surface of the pickup arm is pushed above the spool boss, allowing the pickup pin to retract within the outside diameter of the reel's internal rotor. As the rotor is turned, the critical surface of the pickup arm engages cammed surfaces on the end of the body's spool boss. These surfaces direct the pickup arm back to the outer surface of the spool boss, and thus position the pickup pin in the retrieve position. Hence, the more cam surfaces on the end of the spool boss or the more pickup arms in the reel, the faster the reel will convert from the cast position to the retrieve position. Having only one cam or only one pickup pin isn't bad, just slower to convert the reel from the cast to retrieve position.

If you must retrieve a lure the minute it hits the water, pickup speed can be very important. Ditto for striking a fish that hits the moment a lure or bait lands down. For many people, however, line pickup speed is not much of a factor. In baitcasting reels, this is more of an issue. Flipping switches were designed for these products specifically for this reason. Anglers can flip or short-cast a lure and have the reel gears engaged the moment the lure hits the water, without having to manually make this adjustment.

Gears.   The gear set in a spincasting reel is less efficient than in a baitcasting reel, but comparable to that in a spinning reel. Both spincasting and spinning reels have a right-angled gear set, which means that the equipment is trying to transfer the rotation force input at the crank knob through a 90-degree bend to the shaft that rotates the spinner head or rotor. Baitcasting reel gears, by contrast, simply transfer rotation force between two parallel shafts, having the advantage of no lateral forces like a right-angled gear set.

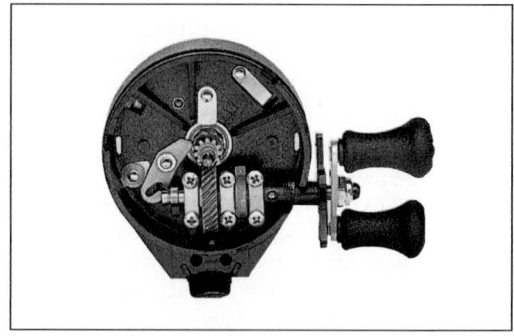

This internal view of a spincasting reel reveals the connection from handle to gear shaft, as well as this product's brass worm gears.

In spincasting reels, the gear sets are composed of a small pinion gear on the center shaft (connected to the spinner head) and a drive gear on the drive shaft (connected to the handle). These gear sets can be on-center or off-center gears. Most spincasting reels, and especially the less expensive models, have on-center gears. This means that if the shafts were extended, they would eventually intersect inside the back of the reel. In off-center gears, the crank shaft is "off-center" from the center shaft. The shafts can be extended inside the back of the reel without intersecting. The pinion, or small gear, is always located on the center shaft. The drive gear is always located on the drive shaft, which attaches to the handle.

It should be noted that in most gearing applications, gears are used to allow a small force to move a big object (for instance, as in a winch). In these applications, gears act as speed reducers, reducing the speed and increasing the torque. In most fishing reels, this function is reversed. It is speed of retrieve that the gears are used to maximize, not torque. Thus, the drive gear is on the crank shaft and the pinion on the center shaft. Winches have the opposite approach.

The better quality, and more expensive, reels often have off-center gears. In these higher quality reels, the gear teeth are cut at an angle, called a helix angle. Helix angles for spincasting reels can range from around 20 degrees to 45 degrees. Helical gears permit higher gear ratios in smaller spaces. Additionally, helix angles on gears allow more of the drive gear tooth's surface to remain in contact with the pinion gear tooth's surface. The more area of the teeth that remain in contact, the quieter, smoother, and more durable the gear set.

One of the advantages to off-center gears is that the crank shaft can be run all the way through the reel and be supported on both ends. This is not possible with an on-center gear set because the crank shaft is blocked by the center shaft. With the off-center gear supported at both ends, it is much more solid and durable and can support heavier loads. This type of gear support typically results in a sturdier feel for the user. With an on-center gear set, the drive gear is only supported on the handle side. Putting a heavy force on the crank handle can tend to cause the drive shaft to twist, putting undo wear on gear support components. This condition is eliminated by supporting the drive shaft on both ends.

Another advantage to the off-center gear design is that it permits higher helical angles, therefore higher gear ratios and smoother and quieter gears. This is a price-driven aspect to spincasting reels from the standpoint of the manufacturers; off-center gear systems are more expensive but meant for those who expect more and are willing to pay for it.

The material of the gears, incidentally, is extremely important. The drive gear in spincasting reels can be created from a die cast or powder metal process. Most are die cast of zinc or aluminum alloy materials. Some stainless steel powder metal spincasting drive gears are also used. In some spinning reels, the drive gear may also be forged. Die casting is a process used to form molten metal into complex, predetermined shapes. Powder metal is a process that starts with very small particles of a metal, forms them to a predetermined shape under pressure, then sinters the particles together so that a solid component is formed. The pinion gear can be die cast, machined, or powdered metal. The same materials are used if the pinion is die cast or powdered metal. Brass is typically used if the gear is machined. Machining (gear hobbing) creates a more precise gear, yet is also more expensive. Proper material selection between the gears results in a gear set that exhibits even wear. Due to the gear ratio, the pinion gear rotates more times in one revolution of the crank handle than the drive gear. For this reason, it is generally important to make the pinion gear of a more durable material than the drive gear. So the gear sets on more expensive spincasting reels will be offset, usually with high helix angles and brass pinions.

The average spincasting reel user has little understanding of this. Most people don't relate to what mechanisms in a reel make up their fishing experience. Manufacturers feel that the average spincasting reel user is looking for reliability, durability, and ease of use, all at an attractive price level. But if you have the opportunity to use spincasting reels of different quality, you will quickly see the difference. The question is whether the differences are important for your fishing experiences and expectations.

Left/Right retrieve. This is not generally an element of spincasting reels because of the dominance of on-center gear sets, which by their nature prohibit convertibility. Therefore, the majority of spincasting reels are set up for right-handed cranking. However, spincasting reels with off-center gears can have convertible right or left retrieves. These are always the higher end products, and include models that sport line-release triggers and sit under the rod handle.

Gear ratio/Cranking power. Engineers can talk in technical terms about the cranking power of a reel, about torque, and about how you can theoretically convert the force at the handle knob to the force on the line. But what anglers relate to in the simplest terms is how fast the reel is (retrieve speed) and how easy or difficult it is to retrieve a set weight (including an object that offers a lot of resistance). There are various factors that come into play to optimize both areas.

The components that directly relate to the retrieve speed of the reel are the reel's gear ratio and the diameter of the spool. Any reel's gear ratio can be exactly determined by dividing the number of gear teeth located on the drive gear by the number of gear teeth located on the pinion gear. With everything else being the same (handle length, spool diameter, number of ball bearings, and so on), a reel with a gear ratio of 3:1 (read three to one), can more easily retrieve a set weight than a reel with a 6:1 gear ratio. However, the reel with the 3:1 ratio will retrieve less line with one revolution of the crank handle than the reel with the 6:1 gear ratio.

While many anglers look for reels with specific gear ratios, their desire is really to optimize retrieve speed and crank power. A lower retrieve speed is typically optimal for crankbaits, while a faster retrieve speed is typically required for buzzbaits. Numerical gear ratio is an indication of retrieve speed, but the spool diameter is just as important. The larger the spool diameter, the more line that is wrapped on it for each turn of the crank handle. The larger the gear ratio, the more revolutions of the spinner head (spincasting reels), rotor (spinning reels), and spool (baitcasting and conventional tackle), thus the more line that is wrapped on the spool.

Because both factors are important for retrieve speed, it is possible for a large spincasting reel with a 3.5:1 gear ratio to have a faster line retrieval than a baitcasting reel with a gear ratio of 6:1. This really describes the number of inches of line that is retrieved for one revolution of the crank handle. This is typically measured as IPT (inches per turn). Because anglers can obviously rotate the crank handle at different speeds, manufacturers utilize IPT to distinguish between slow, cranking reels and faster reels.

Many spincasting reels have a low gear ratio, ranging from 2.5:1 to about 4:1. Some of the models intended for use with artificial lures have a higher gear ratio. The gear ratio is usually marked on the reel packaging, but may not be noted at all. In comparison to the gear ratios on other types of tackle, spincasting reel gear ratios are generally numerically low. However, spool diameters are typically larger. Therefore, manufacturers tend to optimize gear ratios and spool diameters to produce products for specific fishing conditions. In reality, it is not fair to compare the performance of a spincasting reel sto that of other types of tackle based solely on respective gear ratios.

Anglers can't quickly determine line recovery when evaluating a reel they might purchase because specifications on the circumference of the spincasting spool aren't provided on the reel or in the packaging materials. Although with a 4:1 ratio reel, for example, you know that one revolution of the handle wraps four revolutions of line on the spool, if you don't know how much line is gained with each complete wrap, then you don't know the actual recovery. (Of course, in a reel that you own, you can determine the gain by marking the line and measuring it.) For a greater discussion of this subject, *see: Gear Ratio and Line Recovery.*

Although line recovery is not quite as big an issue in spincasting reels as it is in spinning reels, it is nevertheless a factor that anglers should be aware of. The generally low rate of line recovery of spincasting reels, particularly less expensive models, is one of the reasons that some anglers do not use them, or don't use them for certain species of fish or methods of fishing (like trolling). While most consumers have a notion that gear ratio is of primary importance, there are other factors that go into this, and line recovery is a major one. Remember, however, that reels with low gear ratio do better the greater the load and the more resistance offered by lure or fish. Many components affect the relative ease or difficulty with which a reel retrieves a set load. These include easily measured items such as gear ratio, spool diameter, and handle length, as well as less tangible items that tend to reduce frictional loss in the gearing system (efficiency of gear sets, ball bearings, and lubrication).

The length of the handle has a bearing on this issue because that length controls the leverage that you can put on the handle. The longer the handle, the more leverage and the easier it is to retrieve a set load. It is essentially the same principle used in wrenches; it's easier to loosen nuts with a long-handled wrench than with a short-handled one. Spinning reels, because their handles are very long, tend to have a better advantage in terms of cranking power than spincasting reels. Because spinning reels hang underneath the rod and have a long stem, there is room to put a long handle on them, which adds more leverage advantage than can be obtained with most spincasting reels. Long handles on a spincasting reel tend to interfere with the rod. You can replace a short handle on a spincasting reel with a longer one, but it will look a little funny, and it may interfere with the gripping of the rod.

Ball bearings/Bushings. Ball bearings and bushings provide a way to minimize friction on rotating shafts. There are well-engineered plastics today that provide very low friction. If there is a very good surface finish on these, and close tolerance between the bushings and the shafts, the reel will perform well.

Ball bearings are typically viewed as more durable and more reliable products, and usually employed in higher end reels, although there are different grades of ball bearings. There is a performance difference in these grades, although the average consumer does not know which grade is in the reel.

Spincasting reels usually have either no ball bearings or one, typically on the center shaft. Some may have three, but it is doubtful that there is much performance gain from the extra ball bearings. Spincasting reels with three ball bearings usually have one on either side of the crank shaft and one on the center shaft. For a more detailed review of ball bearings and bushings, *see: Reel, Fishing.*

Depth locator. Some spincasting reels have a depth locating feature that is meant to allow an angler to repeatedly let out the same amount of line, usually in order to lower a bait or lure to the same depth. This is often used in panfishing, especially for crappies, and may be known as a crappie locator or crappie finder.

Usually this feature is activated by a lever on top of the reel. The lever is attached to a pin, which is pushed forward by the lever and which lays across the spool. When you start retrieving, the recovered line goes over the pin. When you release the line, it goes out until it reaches the pin and then stops; line cannot be pulled from under the bottom of the pin with ordinary tension (although in some models the depth locating selector switch automatically releases when there is heavy pressure, as might be applied suddenly by a large fish). Now you have a preselected depth to fish or the amount of line to set out. This is most commonly used in crappie fishing for returning to the same depth, and the lever can be pressed either when you're fishing at a certain depth, or at the exact moment that you receive a strike at a given depth. This feature has a niche application and performs the same purpose as using a tiny stopper on the line of a spinning reel, which some anglers employ for selecting depth. However, in spinning reels, a tiny stopper can travel onto the reel without much problem, whereas such a stopper is likely to catch on the pickup pin of a spincasting reel.

Strike detector. A few spincasting reels have an audible clicking mechanism, which may be known as a strike detector or bait clicker, to alert you to activity when the reel is in the cast or freespool mode. This can be important when a rod is left unattended or out of reach, usually when fishing with bait and when the reel is in freespool (anti-reverse off). If this feature is activated, it will produce an audible clicking sound when a fish strikes and the line starts running. Then you can pick up the reel, convert it from the cast to the retrieve mode, and set the hook. A selectable anti-reverse is important here; you should disengage the anti-reverse so that the line will come freely off the reel and the clicker will sound.

Drag Features

Common drag factors.   As with the gear sets, the drag systems in spinning and spincasting reels are also similar. Most spincasting and spinning reel drag systems operate on the same principle. When tension on the fishing line exceeds a preset limit, the spool slips (rotates counterclockwise) and allows additional line to unwrap off the spool. When that tension drops below the preset drag level, the spool stops rotating counterclockwise.

In most of these products, there are drag washers on either side of the spool. Compressing the drag washers against the spool makes the spool more difficult to rotate, resulting in stronger drag tension. Decreasing pressure on the drag washers makes the spool easier to rotate, resulting in lighter drag tension. However, it is the mechanism that controls pressure on the spool that is the significant difference between the drag on a spincasting versus a spinning reel. In most spinning reels, there is more uniform pressure on the spool than there is in a spincasting reel. Additionally, multiple drag washers may be used on either side of the spool in spinning reel drag systems. Nevertheless, there are certain things to look for when evaluating the drag systems of these, as well as other, reels.

The measure of a drag system is determined by smoothness and adjustment range. Technically, smoothness is a measure of line tension variation measured at the reel. If the desired line tension is 4 pounds, the drag should allow additional line to be released from the spool when line tension immediately reaches exactly 4 pounds. In actual practice, additional line can be released from the spool when line tension is less than or more than 4 pounds. Typically, this is measured by manufacturers as percent of drag variation. With the drag set at 4 pounds, the drag may actually release line when line tension reaches 10 percent above or below the actual setting, or 20 percent, or 30 percent, and so on. The lower the drag variation number (percent), the smoother the drag.

Variations to this include the "breakaway" force, which is the force required to start the drag releasing line. In some reels, with the drag set at 4 pounds, a higher line tension is required to get the drag started. Once started, it may release line at 4 pounds. In some reels, this breakaway force is close to the original drag setting. In other reels, this breakaway force might be twice as high as the original drag setting, or even higher. Drag variation may also be influenced by the speed at which line is pulled from the reel. On some reels, allowable line tension may vary, depending on whether line is pulled rapidly or slowly from the reel. Drag

variation differs with the drag setting. It is easier to achieve a low drag variation at a low drag setting (1 or 2 pounds). Generally speaking, as the drag setting is increased, most drag systems are not as smooth. The best reels display a breakaway force equivalent to the drag setting, a consistent line tension at all speeds, and drag settings within 10 percent to 20 percent of the actual drag setting.

It should be noted that in fishing conditions there are many variables that affect the smoothness of a drag system: those mentioned here that apply directly to the performance of the reel, plus other variables, such as the stretch in the line, the amount of line out, the limberness of the rod, the type of line guides used, and so on. Another variable obviously is the friction material; for example, Teflon is often used in light-duty drags because it has the same static and kinetic friction coefficient, which means that it takes the same force to start it moving as to keep it moving. In other materials, it takes more force to start movement than to maintain it.

Adjustment range is the second measure of a drag system's performance. In spincasting reels, there are two basic types of actuators used to increase or decrease the drag setting. Drag stars are typically located near the reel handle. Drag wheels typically extend through the body of the reel. Both are rotated clockwise to increase drag force and counterclockwise to decrease drag force. In theory, anglers desire great flexibility in adjusting the drag setting. The best drag systems allow some type of correlation between the degree of rotation of the drag actuator and the increased or decreased line tension. For instance, 90-degree drag actuator rotation may equate to a $1/4$-pound increase in allowable line tension. Ideally, drag actuators should be limited to between two and three complete revolutions. Additional revolutions become somewhat cumbersome. Fewer revolutions provide an inadequate

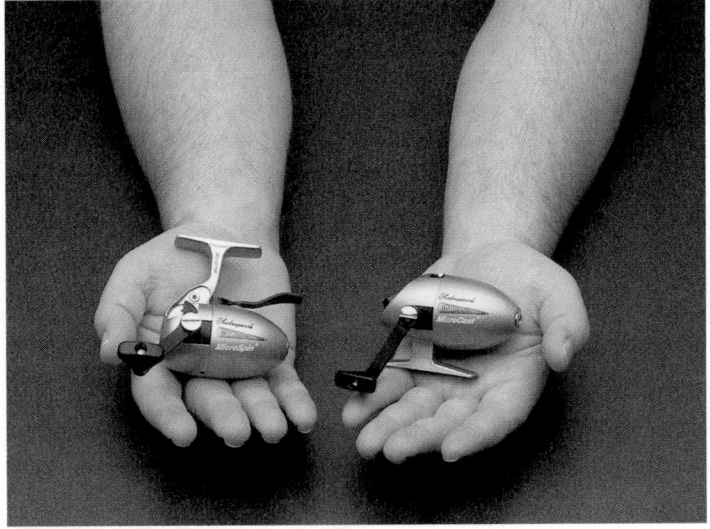

These two diminutive Shakespeare spincasting reels exemplify a trigger-release model (left), which mounts under the rod, and a pushbutton-release model (right), which mounts atop the rod.

amount of flexibility in drag settings. The drag actuator should be easy to rotate to its maximum setting; at this setting, the drag force should be adequate to break the recommended line weight for the reel.

In typical freshwater fishing situations, anglers set the drag at 30 to 50 percent of the breaking strength of their line; most, if they have a 10-pound line, for example, set the drag by feel at between 3 to 5 pounds, meaning that it will take 3 to 5 pounds of tension to cause line to slip (5 pounds may actually be too much for some situations). This is measured with a short length of line on a straight pull off the reel.

To optimize ease of use, manufacturers should strive to allow plenty of adjustment for the drag setting in this range. If you consider line tension in terms of revolutions of the thumb wheel or the star wheel, you'll see that it is desirable to ramp up the drag very rapidly to get to 30 percent of the line's breaking strength. Few people are going to set their drag tension at less than 30 percent of the line strength. Ideally, the first quarter-revolution should get you up to that 30 percent number. Then, for the 30 to 50 percent breaking strength range, there should be a lot of adjustment; it may take two revolutions to cover that range and fine-tune the drag. Then, after reaching 50 percent of the breaking strength, the drag should ramp up very quickly to a full lock-down position with a short revolution of the control wheel; this is in case you have to break off, pull on a snag, or have more tension for a strike in heavy cover. Thus, the important aspect of drag range is how many rotations it takes to get to the lock-down point, and where is the most adjustment range for fine tuning.

Some of the greatest interest among anglers comes from being able to readily get maximum force, which locks the reel down and completely prevents the drag from slipping. This maximum force is seldom beneficial for most fishing activities, including playing large or strong fish, unless you are using very heavy line. Where it is most likely to be useful, however, is when a lure or hook gets snagged and cannot be freed; this situation may require you to lock the reel down, point the rod directly at the snag, and pull back to free the hook or break the line *(see: unsnagging)*. However, this may bury the line on the spool and put a severe strain on the reel. It might be better to wrap the line around another object before pulling on it. If the drag cannot be locked down completely, line will slip off, and it may be harder to free the hook.

Many people mistakenly think that they need to set the drag very tight for effective hooksetting. Once you have 20 yards of line out and you have rod flex, line stretch, and the dampening effect of the water to contend with, you don't need very much drag force at the reel. You cannot exert the maximum pressure when you set the hook. But when you set the drag pressure at or near maximum force, when the fish is close to the boat and less contribution is made by line stretch, rod flex, and water, having the drag locked down may mean that the line cannot absorb the sudden shock of a quick run, even from a fish whose weight is less than the breaking strength of the line. People are often amazed that a 5-pound fish can break 14-pound line, but that does not happen if the drag is set properly and the washers are allowed to slip freely when necessary.

Drag systems.   The purpose of the drag function on any reel is to let line slip from the reel at varying pressures when force is applied to the line. It serves as a sort of clutch, or shock absorber. It is especially important when using light line, when playing large and strong fish, and when fish make strong and sudden surges while being landed. If an angler never catches large fish, only uses heavy strength line, and is content to wind fish in, then it is conceivable that his drag will never be used. But heavy line is not suitable for many species and many methods of fishing, and it is practically inevitable that at some time, even with moderate-strength line, an angler will catch a fish that weighs more than the actual breaking strength of his line, and which requires some finesse, rather than brute strength, to land. This means that the drag will come into play, because if it doesn't, the force will exceed the strength of the line and the line will break.

When the drag comes into play, it allows the fish to continue applying force, but at a pressure that is less than the breaking strength of the line, because when the force reaches a certain level (usually less than 50 percent of the line's breaking strength), a properly set drag mechanism allows line to slip from the reel.

Understanding how to use drag, and how to set drag, is one of the most important aspects of sportfishing, and is reviewed in detail elsewhere *(see: drag)*. Clearly, however, the functioning of a drag is a critical element of every reel, and the quality of reel drags vary considerably.

The drag mechanism on spincasting reels, as on most smaller reels for various fishing applications, used to be fair to poor at best, but these systems have changed markedly since anglers started using all of the various equipment types for more challenging fishing, and placed greater demands on the rod, reel, and line. While the lowest priced spincasting reels (toddler or kiddie versions) do not have sophisticated drags, most medium and higher quality models have reasonably good drags, and a few excellent ones.

Approximately three types of drag systems are used in spincasting reels today. The most simple is one that uses a drag wheel and features a spring arm that puts pressure on the edge of the spool. As the drag wheel (commonly called a thumb wheel and located on the body of the reel) is rotated, it puts more or less pressure on the edges of the spool. This system is composed of the spool, the spring arm, and the adjustment wheel, and is reasonably effective for modest fishing applications.

The more common system has a threaded shaft that, when rotated by means of the drag wheel, puts pressure on the clutch plate. The clutch plate is located between the spool and the body of the reel. As pressure is applied to the clutch plate, it exerts pressure on the drag washers, thus making the spool more difficult to rotate. This type of drag system has the ability to produce extremely smooth drags at low tension settings. One variation of this type of drag is when the clutch plate is raised or lowered by means of a drag star instead of a drag wheel.

In another variation, the clutch plate rotates instead of being pushed forward when the drag wheel rotates. This features a drag wheel and a clutch plate with cams. As the wheel is rotated, it turns a little gear that is keyed to a clutch plate that has cams on its bottom surface. These cams are like small opposing ramps, and they start to engage when the drag wheel is rotated. This pushes the clutch plate forward. As more pressure is applied to the spool, it becomes harder for the spool to rotate. This method provides more uniform pressure against the drag washers and against the spool than the previously mentioned systems. Those systems produce side load, whereas this system moves the entire clutch plate forward, resulting in a more uniform center loading of the drag washers and spool. The result is a drag that is smoother at higher loads, puts less wear on the other parts, and produces less stress on the other components of the reel.

These drag systems rely on the spinner head remaining stationary and the spool rotating to release line. An advantage of this is that line exits the spool in a fixed location; it comes off the spool at the position of the pickup pin and flows through the front cover. Because the line is not traveling around the spool, as it would if the spinner head rotated, a loop, such as the one generated in the casting mode, is not produced. The absence of this loop contributes to reduced drag variation, and thus, a smoother drag.

A disadvantage of a stationary spinner head and rotating spool is that if the reel handle is rotated when the drag is slipping, line twist is introduced into the reel. If not remedied, this line twist can cause line tangling problems on subsequent casts. For this reason, many spincasting reels have a spool clicker built into the reel. When the spool turns backward, releasing line, a clicking sound is heard, indicating that the drag is functioning. This is an audible reminder not to rotate the reels handle until the drag stops slipping. Unfortunately, many people (using this type of reel as well as others, especially spinning reels) inadvertently put twist in their line by continuing to reel when the line is slipping via the drag. This is especially likely to be done by inexperienced anglers.

Finally, another unique type of drag system found in spincasting reels functions with a slipping gear instead of a slipping spool and has the advantage of producing less twist in the line, regardless of the level of expertise of the angler. In this type of reel, the spinner head is allowed to rotate backward, unwrapping line from the spool much like back-reeling. This is accomplished by a floating drive gear. The drive gear is not rigidly attached to the drive shaft, but is actually sandwiched between drag washers. This type of system is only actuated with a drag star. As the drag star is rotated, additional pressure is applied to the drive gear. When line tension exceeds the drag setting, the spinner head rotates backward, causing the center shaft to rotate backward, which, in turn, causes the drive gear to slip. Because the drive gear slips on the drive shaft, the reel handle does not rotate backward.

In this system, rotating the handle while the drag is slipping has no effect on line twist. It is the drive gear that slips, not the spool. However, because the spinner head unwraps line from the spool, a loop (like that generated when casting) is formed. This loop results in drag variations much higher than that found in other spincasting reel drag systems. Additionally, the anti-reverse mechanism on this type of reel must be between the reel handle and the drive gear. Shock loads imparted by fish or other solid objects are transmitted through the gear set to the anti-reverse device. Thus, the gear set is more exposed to damage in such a system. In drag systems characterized by a slipping spool, anti-reverse mechanisms can be located between the spinner head and the pinion gear. Shock loads are absorbed by the anti-reverse, instead of being transmitted through the gear set, thus protecting the gear set from potential damage.

Drag washers.   Ideally the drag in any reel operates smoothly, without hesitation. In other words, it starts immediately when needed and maintains a constant rate of tension as line flows continuously off, and it keeps the same level of tension as it is periodically called upon during the time it takes to play and land a strong fish. The less variation in the performance of the drag, the better. Some of this performance is affected by the type of drag system and the range of adjustment it is capable of, as well as the amount of force it can apply. Some of this is affected by the number and material of the washers.

Drag washer material is really most critical in the setup stage of drag usage. One of the problems with drags and the materials from which they are made is that they are being asked to do something very difficult. It is desirable to have a drag that slips freely yet creates a high amount of pressure. It has to be able to slip, yet sustain a high load, perhaps even a compete no-slip lockdown load. Thus, you're looking for two opposite attributes in a washer to accomplish these needs.

S

Drag washer materials in spincasting reels, like those in other reel types, have evolved over the years. Phenolic washers were used in the past, as were various fibrous washers, and some people replaced their washers with leather versions. Today, the primary drag washer material in better quality spincasting reels is Teflon or polyethylene (specifically, ultra-high molecular weight polyethylene). In spincasting reels, these materials do a reasonable job of satisfying the two opposite demands.

There is a correlation between the size and the surface area of the drag washers and their ability to function at higher forces. The total force is more a function of the maximum diameter of the washers instead of the total surface area. A large diameter washer, even if it covers only a small surface area, can produce a greater force than a small diameter washer with a lot of surface area.

Anti-Reverse Features

When the handle of a spincasting reel is turned forward, line is wound onto the spool. If the handle can be wound backward, in reverse, line unwinds from the spool. Some reel handles cannot be turned in reverse. Most, however, can be turned in reverse by the operation of a switch on the outside of the reel. This switch, known as the anti-reverse, allows anglers to put the reel in reverse by turning it to the off position, or to keep the anti-reverse constantly out of use by turning it to the on position.

When the anti-reverse switch is in the off position, the handle and the rotor can be moved forward and backward; line can come off the spool when the handle is turned backward and also when the drag slips. When the anti-reverse switch is in the on position, the handle and rotor can be turned forward but cannot be turned backward; line can only come off the spool when the drag slips. A reel with this switch is said to have selectable, or selective, anti-reverse, while one without it is said to have nonselectable anti-reverse.

At one time when reel drags were poor and often unreliable, it was useful to have a reel with a selective anti-reverse feature. Anglers felt more comfortable when playing a strong fish if they could reel backward to let line out to play the fish. Many were accustomed to doing this with baitcasting, or levelwind, reels, which initially had direct drive, and had to be back-reeled, or wound backward, when a strong fish put a lot of pressure on it. The trouble with back-reeling is that it is rare to be able to reel backward quickly enough to keep up with a rapidly turning handle when a fish speeds off; therefore, you have to let go of the handle, which usually spins wildly and which may cause a snarl, backlash, or overrun upon completion of the swift back-reeling. When an angler tries to grab the rapidly turning handle, it often smacks his fingers, which caused the old reels to be called knuckle busters.

Today, reel drags are quite reliable and efficient, especially when properly set, and there is no reason to back-reel, even if a reel has the ability to do so. Today's reels do not need selective anti-reverse, but most of them have it to give anglers the option of using it. Probably the only time that the average angler uses this feature is when line is accidentally wound around inner or outer parts of the reel and needs to be worked free.

What is more important for anglers, however, is how the reel operates when the forward-turning motion is stopped. There is a natural tendency to pull up on the handle when not reeling, whether to set the hook or to momentarily stop while retrieving. In older models of reels, and in some lesser quality current models, there is considerable play in the handle and rotor when the reel stops, and the handle may actually turn backward slightly before engaging. This tendency produces a feeling of sloppiness or instability, and if there is too much backward movement of the handle, it may adversely affect hooksetting and may allow a loop of slack line to appear on the spool in some retrieval motions, which may eventually impair casting. Ideally, the reel should engage instantly and firmly, and the better spincasting reels have features that provide this. It is usually called continuous anti-reverse or infinite anti-reverse and should keep the drive gear from moving even the slightest bit backward.

One thing that governs how quickly the drive gear engages is how many ratchets there are in the system. The ratchets are little stops for a pawl; when the pawl hits a ratchet, it causes engagement. The more stops there are, the quicker it engages.

Most anti-reverse systems in spincasting reels are built into the drive gear. One method of doing this is with a walking pawl system. As the drive gear turns forward, a small pointed pawl slides over the ratchets, creating a clicking sound, but does not engage them; as the gear tries to rotate backward, the point catches the ratchets and stops the gear from turning in reverse. This is a two-piece system, and the most simple one.

Another anti-reverse system features a little actuating piece on the crank shaft with a small pawl that engages the ratchets on the back side of the drag. As the handle rotates forward, the actuator keeps the pawl out of the way. The pawl sits up at an angle, so that, as the actuating piece starts to rotate backward, it kicks the pawl up to engage the ratchets. There is no clicking sound in this reel because the pawl is always disengaged completely, and the anti-reverse is considered silent. When the anti-reverse is in the off position, it keeps the pawl out of the way and the crank shaft can always turn backward.

Both of these systems are located on the drive gear. A disadvantage to this is that when there is a shock load on the line, that shock load gets transferred through the gear set to the anti-reverse, which can be damaging to the gear set. If the anti-reverse system were in front of the gear set, between the shock load and the gear set, then the anti-reverse system would absorb the load before it got to the gear set.

In a few high quality spincasting reels as well as some spinning reels, the anti-reverse system is in front of the gear set. This may be accomplished with a one-way clutch, or a more conventional pawl and ratchet setup. It should also be noted that, with the anti-reverse located on the center shaft, a five-tooth ratchet will engage much faster than a five-tooth ratchet located on the drive shaft. The center shaft rotates much faster than the drive shaft due to the gear ratio; therefore, a much smaller amount of rotational motion is required to engage the anti-reverse located on the center shaft than is required if it is located on the drive shaft.

The one-way clutch device is a part that came from printers, where it is used to control the location of print on paper and the rotation of parts. In reels, its job is to completely prohibit backward travel of the shaft. It does this very well on most reels, and if it doesn't do it as well on some as on others, it is because of different tolerances in the other components. This system results in a (silent) continuous or infinite anti-reverse.

Ergonomics and Appearance

Shape. In a sense, many spincasting reels today are very similar in outward appearance to the early versions, particularly with respect to the cone-shaped covers. Reels with these and similar large covers are adequate for people who hold a spincasting outfit with their hand on the rod itself, and mainly touch the reel when they grab the handle or press the pushbutton. For such users, the pushbutton must be located low and close to the rod for easy use. Some people wrap their hand around the rod and reel, in effect palming it. For these users, a low-profile reel that sits closer to the rod is more desirable. Some spincasting reels have a pushbutton that extends off the right side of the reel; these are very easy for palming and pushbutton actuation, but they are far less common than those with centrally located buttons. The smaller housing and less boxy contour of most spincasting reels are more conducive to a wraparound hand grip. Whichever system is preferred, the reel should have a smooth design and surface on the side that is held with the hand or in the palm. Any projections will cause discomfort.

Naturally, the pushbutton (or trigger) should be easy to depress, and a thumb wheel drag should be easy to reach and finger. Reels with convertible left or right retrieve need a large drag wheel that is centered so it can be easily reached no matter which hand is used. The more casting the user does, the more important are ergonomic matters. A person who mostly stillfishes and places the rod in a holder is less concerned about this than someone who will be holding and casting the reel continuously.

Handles. Handles and knobs are largely a matter of personal preference. There is no benefit in terms of reel function or technical performance for having a dual-knob rather than single-knob handle, but some people prefer two knobs, in part because they feel that it is easier to grab one of them quickly, as when they aren't looking at the reel. There is no strength advantage to having dual knobs because, as noted earlier, strength and cranking power are governed by the distance from the crank shaft hole to the knob, not from the distance between two knobs. But for many people there seems to be a better balance to spincasting reels with dual-knob handles.

Many spincasting reels, especially in the lower price range, feature a single-knob handle, while many of the more expensive reels feature a dual-knob handle. It is interesting to note that virtually no baitcasting reels with a single-knob handle are sold in North America, while nearly all spinning reels have a single-knob handle, and some have a counterbalanced handle.

Handles are mostly made from stamped aircraft-grade aluminum. Some are made from plastic to achieve better aesthetics and to reduce cost. The knobs vary in material, although most anglers prefer a soft material that is easy to grip, especially when wet, and that may be contoured for comfort. On higher end reels a soft rubber is used on the knobs rather than hard plastic. If the handle and the knobs are not large and comfortable enough for the user, they will be fatiguing and perhaps counterproductive.

Appearance. Overall appearance is largely a subjective matter. Manufacturers feel that the average spincasting reel user needs a reliable and durable product. They may use metal on higher end products to convey a tough image, but this is not necessarily a performance factor or an ergonomic one. Weight may be a factor to some people but not to others, and the materials used will have some impact on that. Size should be relative to application. Color is trend driven and tends to parallel what is popular in the automotive industry, because it is industrial designers who pick colors. In spincasting reels, there are colored plastics, metals, painted plastics, and a variety of decoration approaches, none of which have functional significance and are mainly geared toward aesthetics.

The materials used on spincasting reel parts vary. Metal exteriors are stainless steel or aluminum. Stainless steel is strong and forms easily; aluminum is softer and bends easily and is not as tough as stainless steel. The spinner heads are typically plated brass or stainless steel. Various plastics are used for different parts, primarily glass-reinforced nylon, ABS, polystyrene, or polycarbonate. The reel foot may be glass-filled nylon because this material is very stiff and very strong. ABS and polystyrene are typically used for covers; these are lower cost materials and not as stiff or strong as others, but in many spincasting reels those values aren't needed in that component.

Scientists say that sharks have changed little in the past 360 million years; the first shark-like scales were discovered in Mongolia and aged at 420 million years.

S

Rods

Spincasting rods are mostly similar to those used in baitcasting and fairly uncomplicated. The guides are mainly mounted atop the rod, and guide rings are generally small, unlike those used with spinning tackle, because lines come straight out of the nose cone of the spincasting reel. (An exception to this is the hybrid spincasting reel sporting a trigger release, which mounts under the rod rather than on top of it, and is used with a spinning rods.)

Reels mount a little higher on top of the rod's reel seat and above the rod, which used to be facilitated by a handle with an offset seat (when the rod blank fit into the handle as a separate, rather than integral, component), providing more comfortable use. However, refinements in reel design, including the placement of the release button, and rods featuring blank-through handle construction, have virtually done away with this offset design, meaning that spincasting reels today are used with rods having standard straight and pistol grip (especially popular) styles of handle. Pistol grip handles, and some straight grip handles, have a trigger grip on the underside of the rod opposite and at the lower end of the reel seat.

Spincasting rods usually aren't as stiff as baitcasting rods, having generally lighter action for use with light lines and lures. They are made in one- and two-piece models, and a few are telescopic. Lengths are shorter than most baitcasting and spinning rods; they range from $4^1/_2$ feet to 6 feet, with 5- and $5^1/_2$-footers the norm, and some shorter rods available for youngsters. Most rods marketed specifically for spincasting use are made of fiberglass, usually E-glass (see), but a few feature composite construction, with graphite used in the material or the resin.

Unlike reels, many of the issues pertaining to spincasting rods—functions, materials, components, and so on—are similar to those of other rods, and these are more fully detailed elsewhere (see: rod, fishing).

Using Spincasting Tackle

Line.   Six- to 10-pound nylon monofilament line is most commonly used on spincasting tackle and is the choice of many anglers who do varied and general fishing, although some models handle line up to 25-pound strength. Whatever the strength, line is pre-spooled on spincasting reels by the manufacturer. It is possible to use lighter line, such as 2- through 4-pound test, on ultralight models, but few people use 2-pound on spincasting tackle, and a minority use 4. When you change the line, it is best to use the same strength of line if it is of the same or similar diameter, although you can make some changes. If you go to lighter line, you may find that the finer diameter is so thin that it gets hung up because the reel tolerances are not adequate for that diameter. On the other hand, you can go up in strength but keep a similar diameter. For example, if you had a spincasting reel spooled with conventional diameter 8-pound line, you might replace this with a 12-pound line of thin diameter. This could give you a line with a diameter equivalent to a 6- or 8-pound conventional nylon monofilament line, but with the strength of 12-pound line, and offer some species and condition advantages that you might not have had with the original line (see: line).

Although it is possible to use other types of line with some spincasting reels, nylon monofilament is the best choice. A good monofilament with controlled stretch to help buffer the drag, the actions of the angler, and the actions of the fish, is more forgiving and less prone to problems than a braided or microfilament product.

Refilling the spool.   The various aspects of properly filling a reel spool are detailed elsewhere (see: line). Putting line on a spincasting reel spool is slightly more complicated than other reel types only because the spool is under the cover. To get to it, remove the cover, and take off whatever old line remains on the spool. Because spincasting reels do not have large line capacities, it is usually best to refill the entire spool so that you have a continuous unknotted section of line. If you choose, you can tie a line-to-line knot and replace only that portion of the spool that is missing. However, there's a good chance that this knot will catch on the pickup pin or the inner edge of the front cover opening, and cause some difficulty, unless it is very small and the ends are clipped off perfectly. It is generally best to replace all of the line rather than put a knot in it that may cause trouble.

When you refill the spool, start by putting the tag end of the line from the filler spool through the rod guides and then through the front cover opening, and tie it to the spincasting reel spool. It has to come through the reel cover opening for you to put the cover back in place and then wind line on. Make sure that you wind the new line on under tension, and fill the reel spool to within $1/_8$-inch of the top of the reel spool lip.

If you overfill the spool, or have excessive line slack, you may encounter a situation when the line gets under the spinner head. You'll know when this happens because the line will stop dead right in the middle of a cast. This is an infrequent occurrence, especially in better quality spincasting reels, but when it does occur you can fix it simply by removing the front cover of the reel, pressing the pushbutton or trigger, and removing line from underneath the spinner head. The line usually comes free by unwinding it several turns. If this does not work, you will have to take the spinner head off to get the line out. Check to see that the line is not frayed before reusing.

Line twist.   Line twist is commonly associated with the use of both spinning and spincasting tackle. This issue is discussed in greater detail under other entries (see: line; spinning tackle). However, some general observations are in order here.

As twist accumulates in nylon monofilament line, it causes damage by building up ever greater stresses. Under load, as when fighting a fish, these stresses may weaken the structure of the line and can lead to breakoffs. A twisted line is like a loaded spring. When tension is released on a cast, the line tends to balloon outward from the axis of the line flow. This increases line-to-guide friction and reduces casting distance. It is also why some line twist disasters (a wad of mangled line) tend to wrap around the first rod guide. Twist causes almost no problem when line is kept under tension. The stored spring energy due to twist is evident only when tension is released. Then, a snarl can almost instantly appear.

Twisted line is not difficult to cure if you're in a boat or near running water. Line will untwist itself if you let a long length of it out behind your boat, with nothing attached to the end of it (no snap, swivel, split shot, hook, or lure), and drag it along for a few minutes. The faster your boat travels, the faster the line unravels. Reel the line back in and you're ready to attach terminal gear and fish. You can achieve the same effect on moderate to fast flowing water by letting the unweighted line float downstream and then holding it in the current for several minutes. This has the same effect as dragging it behind the boat.

Line twist can occur when using spincasting (as well as spinning) reels, and it may cost valuable angling time, cause otherwise unnecessary replacement of line, and contribute to lost lures and breakoffs. To a large extent, it can be overcome or prevented by putting line on correctly, reeling it in under tension, using a swivel with lures that are likely to spin in the water, playing large fish properly, and, especially, by not reeling against a slipping drag.

As previously explained, some spincasting reels have a drag system that is built into the drive shaft; in this configuration, reeling against the drag does not twist the line. However, for all other types, when the handle is turned as the drag slips, line twist occurs.

One of the absolute worst causes of line twist is turning the reel handle while the drag is releasing line. Excited anglers continue to quickly crank the handle, typically against a drag that is set too light, while no line is retrieved. Each turn of the handle puts multiple twists in the line in a direct relationship to the gear ratio of the reel. High gear ratio reels add more twists than low gear ratio reels. You can minimize this by being conscious of what the drag is doing at all times while fighting a fish, or using a slightly tighter drag. If the reel has a drag clicker, whenever it starts to sound, you should stop reeling, and learn to pump-and-reel, which requires proper rod manipulation (see: *playing fish*), rather than to crank and crank and crank. Some drag types are better at reducing or preventing twist than others, and while some do a good job of eliminating twist even when an angler reels against a slipping drag, the best solution is not to reel when this is happening, and to take measures to reduce other means of creating twist.

This includes trying to maintain some tension on the line when you are reeling in under ordinary circumstances, as when retrieving a light-tension object. This tension can be applied by letting the line flow through the thumb and forefinger of the hand that holds the rod and reel. This may require holding the outfit slightly forward of the top of the reel and/or in the back of your palm, which may feel slightly awkward or uncomfortable to people with small hands and no wrist strength. Using your fingers for moderate tension should only be done when retrieving lures or hooks that offer little or no tension; it should not be done when playing a fish. Remember that the purpose of this is to try to control slack line and keep whatever spring may have built up in the line from unloading.

Matching and selecting. As with any type of fishing tackle, the issue of matching the right reel to the right rod is an important one, but in these times, it is a relatively easy one. A lot of spincasting tackle is sold in matched combinations of rods and reels, and the manufacturers have already done the job of putting the right reel with the right rod. Naturally, many of these items, and especially the upper end products, are also sold separately. Fishing rods are virtually all labeled by line classifications and by weight of objects to be used, which practically assures that you don't put a light-duty spincasting reel, for example, loaded with 6-pound line, on a medium-heavy rod that is rated for 10- to 14-pound line use. What you might do is look for a rod with a specific type of action, say one that had a fast taper for casting light lures, and look for this in the length that you prefer for your most frequent tackle use.

When selecting tackle, as well as matching a rod and reel, you have to take into consideration the kinds of fishing that you expect to do. A beginning angler may be unsure what to select without any prior fishing experience. Guidance from a knowledgeable salesperson could be very helpful; such a person is more likely to be found in a specialized store (a sporting goods dealer or bait and tackle shop). You might also seek guidance from an acquaintance or relative who has experience with this type of equipment and some knowledge of the fishing that a beginner is likely to do. Some manufacturers provide equipment guidelines on their packaging or display materials to provide general direction for appropriate usage, and this can be helpful.

In a general sense, selecting tackle starts with a determination of the size of fish that you are likely to catch and evaluating the conditions under which you will be fishing. The larger and stronger the fish, the stronger the tackle necessary for beginners, until you get the experience to use lighter gear. Fishing where there are a lot of obstructions usually requires medium or heavy grades of tackle. Small fish, fewer obstructions, and clearer water usually are suitable for lighter tackle. Most selection thus starts with a determination of the line strength necessary for the conditions, and having the appropriate rod and reel. You should also give some attention to line capacity. If you will be fishing in a way or under circumstances that require a lot of line, then you will need an appropriate amount of line on the reel. Spincasting reels seldom have more than 100 yards of line capacity, and many smaller models have only 60 or 70 yards. This is significantly less than the capacity of spinning reels. If you expect to go trolling, for example, the smaller line capacities will not be adequate.

Again, in a general sense, spincasting tackle in the 4- to 8-pound class is suitable for all types of panfish (including crappie, bluegills, and yellow perch) as well as small trout, small bass, and small catfish or bullheads. Tackle in the 8- to 14-pound range is heavy for most panfish, but adequate for bass, walleye, pickerel, some trout fishing, and some pike and catfish angling. Heavier tackle is suited to fishing for larger fish (trout, pike, catfish, bass, and stripers) and in places where there are a lot of obstructions. Six- to 10-pound line is most commonly used on spincasting tackle and is the choice of many anglers who do varied and general fishing.

It is commonly believed by manufacturers that spincasting tackle is purchased largely according to price, and evidently sales patterns bear this out. Generally, spincasting tackle is less expensive than other comparable types of tackle, and it represents a good value for the expense. For a little more money, you usually can step up to better equipment, especially a better reel, and the kind of features that the best spincasting reels have (ceramic pickup pins, dual-grip handles, helical gears, continuous anti-reverse, and so on) certainly provide elevated performance and, in most cases, greater useful life.

When purchasing spincasting tackle, you should obviously take into consideration the species that you will be targeting, the places that you will fish, and your own level of experience. If you purchase the tackle from a store, you will have an idea of how well it fits your hand, how comfortable it is, and whether the weight and general feel are to your liking. It's a good idea to mount it on the rod that you intend to use with it, to make sure that it sits securely in the reel seat and that it is at the proper height for comfortable handle turning as well as line flow to the guides.

Setting up.   Prior to making that first cast, you must set up the rod and reel. Attaching the reel to the rod is a simple and straightforward matter of placing the reel so that the cover opening is facing the first rod guide (otherwise it would be backwards!), nestling it in the reel seat of the handle, and tightening it so that the reel is firmly in place. Ideally, it should be snug and have no wobble.

Tighten the retaining mechanism by hand so that it is snug but not so tight that you can't undo it by hand.

On a new reel with pre-spooled line, the tag end of the line is attached to a ring that is outside the front cover opening, which is there to keep the line from slipping under the front cover. Put the reel in freespool (press the pushbutton or trigger), clip the ring off, run the line through the rod guides, and attach it to a lure or, preferably, a practice casting weight. If the line is not attached to a ring but inside the cover, take the cover off (usually by unscrewing it or twisting and lifting), place the end of the line through the opening in the cover, put the cover back on, and feed the line through the rod guides with the reel in freespool.

Holding the rod and reel.   Most spincasting reels have only right-handed retrieve. This means that regardless of which hand you prefer to reel with, with a right-hand-retrieve model you hold the rod and reel with your left hand and reel with your right hand. In those models that have convertible retrieve systems, you can set the handle up to retrieve from whichever side you prefer. Normally, it is beneficial for people who are right-handed to reel with their left hand and for lefties to reel with their right hand, so that the dominant hand is the one that holds the rod and is used to play the fish or direct the retrieve. Because the dominant hand is used to cast the rod, there is no need to take further action after casting to start using the reel; the other hand is immediately placed on the reel handle grip and it starts turning the handle. This is how most people use a spinning reel, the difference being that a spinning reel is under the rod handle instead of on top of it. This is also how most people use a trigger-release spincasting reel, which also mounts under the rod.

Whether out of habit or because it feels better, most right-handed anglers who use mount-on-top spincasting (and baitcasting) reels, cast with the reel in their right hand, then switch the reel over to their left hand and grab the handle (located on the right side of the reel) with their right hand. This means that they have their dominant hand reeling and subordinate hand holding the rod, and they must make the extra step of switching the rod and reel from one hand to the other every time they cast. By contrast, using a mount-on-top spincasting reel with a right-sided cranking handle, a left-handed person would cast with the rod in their left hand and then simply grab the reel handle with their right hand. Thus, the rod is in the dominant hand, the reel handle is in the subordinate hand, and there is no switching of rod and reel from one hand to the other. This is clearly the proper way to do things for most anglers, and yet, most do it backward, perhaps because of custom or habit, or because they have a right-hand-retrieve model that requires them to cast with their right hand and reel with their right hand.

Spincasting tackle is easy enough for young children to use.

If you do this, and are happy and comfortable with it, fine. But if you are a beginning spincasting reel user, you should learn to cast and hold the reel in your dominant hand, and reel with your subordinate hand. This will soon feel completely natural and comfortable to you, and you'll wonder how anyone could do it otherwise. Because many spincasting reels have only right-handed retrieve, a beginning angler who is right-handed should consider a trigger-release model with left retrieve, or a pushbutton model with convertible retrieve.

No matter which hand you use to hold the reel, two-handed casting is best for the sake of both learning and accuracy. The preferred hand holds the reel with the thumb actuating the pushbutton; the other hand is wrapped around the reel cover with the thumb and forefinger properly positioned to feather the line. This is an important point for people who are learning to use this tackle, as it will lead to greater accuracy with practice.

You may choose to palm the reel and rod handle in your hand, or you may hold the rod handle without palming the reel. Whatever feels best for you is right, provided that you are comfortable casting and holding it that way for long periods, and can readily access the pushbutton or trigger with the same hand that holds the rod for easy one-handed operation.

Casting technique. The actual method of casting is accomplished by pressing the pushbutton with your thumb (or the trigger with your forefinger) and holding it throughout the backcast, then releasing it at the optimum point of rod flex in the forward motion of the cast. When the button is released, line flows off the spool, through the opening in the reel cover, and out through the guides, carried by the weight of the object at the terminal end of the line. When you are not casting, but simply letting line out, as might be done when lowering a weighted bait or lure directly below, you simply press the button or trigger and let go of it to release the line. The released line can be stopped altogether by pressing it firmly. To convert the reel to the retrieve position, turn the handle, and the pickup pin will gather the line and begin to wind it on the spool.

Before making a cast for on-the-water fishing, you should set the drag to the proper amount of tension, and then adjust the position of the lure at the rod tip. The lure should hang a few inches below the rod tip. You can get it to this position by reeling in the line until the lure is a few inches from the tip guide; if the reel is right at the tip, pull a few inches of line off the reel drag, which will cause the lure to hang a few inches below the tip.

Assuming that you are right-handed, place the rod and reel in the palm of your left hand so that the handle of the reel is up and facing you. Extend the left forefinger to trap the line against the opening of the spool. Depress the pushbutton with your right thumb and point the rod tip at your intended target. Lift the rod back toward you swiftly, using your wrist and forearm (not the whole arm), and allow the weight of the plug to flex the rod. In a continuous and unhesitating motion, still using the wrist and forearm, bring the rod forward in an accelerated motion. Release the line and the push-button at the same instant during the forward stroke to cast the plug toward the target. While the casting plug is in the air, the line should flow across the tip of your left forefinger. To put the plug right where you want it, increase upward pressure with the left forefinger. With a bit of practice, you will learn at exactly what point in the forward stroke to release the line and the pushbutton, which is a major element in attaining the proper trajectory for accurate placement.

Although explaining this belabors the act of casting, it is really a simple technique that almost anybody can master in a short period of time. You'll quickly learn to feather the line with your left forefinger to drop the plug right where it needs to be. This does involve the use of both hands, but for most people that shouldn't be an issue. Your right hand still executes the casting stroke. The only function of the left hand is to get your left forefinger out where it needs to be to control the line.

When you are learning, and whenever striving for accuracy, get the rod and reel out in front of your body with both hands and make the rod follow an imaginary line from your nose to the target. Always remember the most important single phase of the spincasting technique is to have the line flowing over your left forefinger while the plug is in the air. Once you get the feel for the control you have over the lure by simply lifting the forefinger slightly up against the line, you're on your way.

Although most people do not rate spincasting tackle very highly in the accuracy department, some of the best exhibition and trick casters can do things with spincasting tackle that are truly amazing, so obtaining accuracy is partly a matter of how far you are willing to take the practice element, and using the right rod and weight of lure. It is true, however, that when using lures and fishing in cover, baitcasting tackle (once you have mastered spool control) is an easier type of tackle to consistently obtain accuracy with. For many spincasting tackle users, achieving casting accuracy is not a big issue. A lot of spincasting reel users do not need accuracy in their fishing, because they primarily employ this tackle while using bait and bait rigs, especially from a dock or shore, and in relatively open water. For more information on all aspects of casting, *see: Casting.*

Setting/Checking drag. The drag on a spincasting reel is adjusted by turning the drag wheel or star wheel. When either of these wheels is facing you, turning them to the right increases tension, and turning to the left decreases it. If a reel is used infrequently, it is a good idea at the end of each outing to back the drag tension off to relieve pressure on the drag washers. Before starting a day of fishing, you should check and adjust the drag tension setting before making a cast. Many an angler has neglected this and found upon hooking the first fish of the day that the drag was so weak it impaired hooksetting, or so tight that it adversely affected fish playing.

To test the drag on a spincasting reel, pull line off it at various drag tension settings. Most people, especially if they have fishing experience, test the drag by pulling the line by hand directly ahead of the reel, and making necessary adjustments by feel, starting with a light drag setting and testing and adjusting until they reach a tension setting that feels right. For most fishing situations, especially in freshwater, this is adequate, and anglers wind up putting somewhere in the neighborhood of 30 to 50 percent of the maximum breaking tension on the line. This "by feel" adjustment is a somewhat imprecise method of doing things, but adequate for the vast majority of spincasting reel users. Using and setting drag is covered in more detail elsewhere *(see: drag).*

If you want a general evaluation of how smooth the drag on a given reel is, run the line from the reel through the rod guides and attach it to a scale. Angle the rod tip up and pull on the line while you check what happens to the rod tip. If the tip remains in place, the drag is smooth, which is good. If it moves up and down, the drag is erratic, which may cause problems.

Maintenance and repair. Many people do very little, if anything, to maintain their spincasting reels other than removing tangled line from them. This may be all right if the reel is only used occasionally. Common sense dictates that if the reel has any loose part, which is most likely to be the retaining nut on the handle, it should be tightened as soon as you notice it, and that you should rinse any reel that has encountered sand, dirt, mud, or saltwater. Use a fine spray of freshwater, rather that a hard stream, to clean the reel and do so as soon as possible after use. Cleanse it of dirt or sand whenever it gets dirty, and give the reel a chance to dry out completely when it gets wet. It's a good practice to reapply lubricant to the areas recommended by the manufacturer's literature after cleaning a reel, subjecting it to a lot of moisture, or submersing it.

Details on reel maintenance are discussed elsewhere *(see: tackle care/maintenance/repair).* Manufacturers recommend that infrequently used reels be cleaned and relubricated annually, and that reels that are used several times a week be attended to monthly. Periodic maintenance means lightly oiling and greasing accessible parts. Some reels come with small oil or grease tubes, and these can be purchased from tackle suppliers or obtained from the manufacturer. A thorough cleaning requires disassembling most of the reel, scrubbing or rinsing most of the gunk from the parts, drying, and then relubricating.

SPINNER

(1) A term for the sexually mature, or imago, stage of an adult mayfly *(see)*. Spinners sometimes appear in great numbers over the water; they mate in the air and females fly down to the water's surface to lay their eggs.

(2) A metal lure with a blade that revolves around a central shaft and spins when retrieved.

Probably no type of lure is sold in such quantity and with such international reception as the spinner. Its origins in history are uncertain, and what it represents is more the suggestion of something to eat rather than a duplication of it, but through its flashy appearance and movement, and in a variety of models and sizes, the spinner has been a perennially popular freshwater lure. It is seldom used in saltwater (due mainly to strength and corrosion concerns), and would be a rare sight among the tackle of a veteran saltwater angler, even though some models will surely catch certain marine species.

A spinner may not be the best lure to use for all freshwater fish, or to use in every possible circumstance, but in the right size and fished in the appropriate place, it is a lure that will catch most species of freshwater fish. The basic small to intermediate size spinner is of foremost appeal in angling for stream trout and salmon, which probably see more spinners (in $1/30$- to $1/4$-ounce sizes) than all other species of fish combined. Smallmouth bass, panfish, pickerel, pike, and muskies (large bucktail versions for the latter) are also favorite targets.

Most spinners are used for casting, but some are trolled. They are relatively uncomplicated to use and, in most sizes, hook fish fairly readily. The blade is central to the effectiveness of the spinner, not only because of the visual appearance it has when moving, but because it generates a good deal of vibration, which can be detected by fish in murky water where visibility is limited. The blade vibrates differently from one style to another.

There are essentially two types of lures that fit this well-established lure category: in-line spinners, and weight-forward spinners. A spinning blade of some type is also used in combination with a variety of lures, including spinnerbaits *(see)*, buzzbaits *(see)*, and tailspinners *(see)*, although usually not in an in-line fashion, and may be an add-on to plugs, plastic worms, and jigs.

In-Line Spinners

In-line spinners feature a freely rotating blade (or blades), mounted on a single straight (in-line) shaft. Behind the blades are beads or bodies of lead or metal, which provide the lure's basic weight and make it castable. Skirts of feather, hair, or plastic tubing, may be added to the hook to increase the spinner's appeal, but many hooks are unadorned.

Assorted spinners, from top to bottom, include small versions for trout and panfish, midsize versions for bass and walleye, and bucktail spinners for larger fish, including pike and muskies.

These lures are available in weights from $1/32$ ounce to several ounces; with single, double, and treble hooks; with blade lengths from $1/2$ inch to several inches; and with assorted types of tail material. Squirrel and bucktail hair are traditionally favorite hook garnishes, but soft plastic bodies are increasingly used on single-hooked spinners, and some feature rubber or plastic minnow bodies.

A majority of spinners are equipped by manufacturers with a treble hook, but some have single hooks, and a few feature an interchangeable hook (others are not interchangeable, meaning that when you must use a single hook, two points of the treble have to be snipped off). The $1/16$-, $3/8$-, and $1/4$-ounce sizes are best for bass fishing; the smaller sizes are used in panfishing; and the biggest models are fished for large pike, muskies, and possibly striped bass.

The blade design controls the action and the angle of blade revolution. Blades that are attached to the shaft via a clevis are mainly of Colorado, Indiana, French, or willowleaf shape, although there are variations on these and some nonconformist styles as well. The willowleaf, which is the narrowest blade, has less water resistance, so it rotates closest to the shaft, and thus, spins faster. The Colorado is the broadest blade and has the most water resistance, so it rotates farthest from the shaft and spins slowest. The others are in between these two. Another style, the so-called sonic blade, is somewhat like a broad willowleaf; it is concave at one end and convex at the other, mounts directly on the shaft (which runs through the lure), and has a narrow rotation to make it work well in fast current. In a properly designed spinner, the blade spins even at a slow retrieval speed, so water conditions and current flow, if present, help determine which style to use.

The actual spinner blade is available in many colors, but the blade's color is not nearly as important as its visibility under fishing conditions. A good reflective quality is desired. Spinners also give some vibration when retrieved, a fact that is important to the fish and which probably accounts for the success of spinners when used at night and under very poor water clarity conditions.

Factors like blade design, weight, and surface area are related to how the lure is retrieved. A spinner does not begin working until it is being retrieved. The blade does not spin when the lure is falling, meaning that this is not a lure for jigging. If a spinner is fished too slowly, the blade may not spin or may spin erratically, but if it is retrieved too quickly, the blade cannot catch the water, and it will fall flat against the lure's body, keeping the blade from rotating and probably causing the whole lure to spin, which will not catch fish. Therefore, it's important to get the right speed to work the blade properly; this is usually not much of a problem because these lures generally accommodate a range of normal swimming speeds.

In moving water, you generally don't fish a spinner directly downstream, but cast it upstream at a quartering angle. The lure is tumbled by the swift water and also reeled forward at the same time, or it is fished like a spoon (see) with rod tip held high and the lure retrieved just slowly enough to let the blade turn while the spinner swings downstream. Fish a spinner as slowly as you can under the circumstances; you should be able to feel the blade revolve with a sensitive rod. The depth of retrieve can be altered by raising or lowering the rod, or changing the speed of retrieval. Hanging the spinner directly downstream in the current can also be effective, as long as the current has enough force to turn the blade freely.

Though spinners may often hang up, this may be due to poor use. In streams, it's important to get the lure working the moment it hits the water. Hesitation often means hung spinners, particularly when casting across a stream in a fast flow. Matching the size and weight to the water is also important.

In lakes and ponds, small and intermediate size spinners are mostly fished fairly close to the surface or relatively shallow and on a straight retrieve. In deeper water, they are worked by counting the lure down to a specific level (you must predetermine the sink rate) and retrieving slowly. Because lighter spinners don't have the weight or lure action to stay at one level, they angle upward on the retrieve; a long cast, an unimpeded freefall to deeper levels (keep an open bail on a spinning reel), and a low-angled rod help lengthen the time that the lure is in the right zone. Although a steady retrieve is often productive, it pays to vary a straight retrieve occasionally by hesitating the lure, twitching it quickly, and otherwise briefly altering its movement, which may cause a following fish to pounce.

Large spinners with bucktail hair dressing are known as bucktails and stand out from all other spinners in terms of their application, although they're fished similarly to smaller spinners in most respects. These weighted spinners sink quickly and are strictly cast for muskies and pike, generally being fished over the top of submerged grass (in which case you can't let the lure sink too far on the initial drop), along weedlines, and around cover or structure.

Spinning tackle and light lines are best for most in-line spinner use, although baitcasting tackle is preferable with large bucktail spinners. The majority of spinners are fished with light line, usually in the 2- to 6-pound range, and sometimes from 8- to 12-pound line. For stream fishing, light tackle, light line, and small spinners are the rule. Heavier line is used with the largest spinners.

It is always necessary to use a swivel or snap-swivel with these lures to counter the tendency of the rotating blade to turn the lure over repeatedly and cause line twist. A few spinners are very good at resisting line twist, and bending the upper shaft may help avoid it, but line twist is such a serious problem with spinners that you should not take a chance in going without a good quality swivel or snap-swivel.

Twist can also be caused by debris on the lure, especially on the clevis. Debris tends to get on spinners fairly readily, as these are not very weed-free lures. This or anything else that causes the blade not to spin freely deserves attention.

Weight-Forward Spinners

Weight-forward spinners are long-shanked lures with a lead weight molded to the shaft ahead of a spinner blade, which in turn is ahead of a single hook. The hook is primarily supplied bare and impaled with a live worm. Some have a single or treble hook that is dressed with hair, fur, or a soft plastic body such as a grub.

These spinners are used for slow trolling, drifting, and casting in freshwater, and are mainly popular for smallmouth bass and walleye fishing on northern lakes, especially when garnished with a live worm and drifted across rocky reefs. Simpler versions, which feature a long-shanked hook and a single rotating blade with beads along the shaft, have long been known as June Bug spinners.

Weight-forward spinners exist in small to intermediate sizes and with a variety of weight and blade shapes. The positioning of the weight on the lure causes it to sink headfirst, meaning that, unlike in-line spinners, the blade can spin on the descent and possibly catch fish. Narrow weight shapes allow a weight-forward spinner to sink quickly, and are good for fishing in current and deep water. Wider weights have more water resistance, and are preferred for shallow-water use. The head is usually preceded by a long wire shaft (sometimes removable), to foil bite-offs from sharp-toothed fish, and the twist-free nature of the lure allows usage without a swivel or snap-swivel.

Unlike in-line spinners, weight-forward spinners stay at a deep level when retrieved slowly. They should be counted down to the proper level when fished high in the water column, and allowed to reach bottom when it's necessary to crawl deep. To start the retrieve, snap the rod tip up to help get the blade turning. These lures catch fish on both a routine uninterrupted retrieve, and when the lure is hesitated and jerked occasionally during a normal retrieve However, they are prone to fouling when cast. To minimize this, bring the rod tip back gently and lob the lure forward instead of making a standard rod-loading cast; also, pull the rod tip in as the lure hits the water to turn it toward you and straighten it out. Avoid a snap-swivel or snap to further decrease fouling.

SPINNERBAIT

A spinnerbait is an unusual looking lure in a V-like configuration if viewed from the side. The lower arm of V-shaped wire sports a tapered lead headed hook usually garnished with a skirt or soft-bodied grub, and the upper arm features one or two freely revolving spinner blades. When the lure is retrieved steadily, the blades and upper arm run vertically above the bottom part of the lure. Viewed from the side, the ensemble resembles an open safety pin, which prompted some early users to dub it a safety pin spinner. It is not a true spinner (see), in the on-line sense of that lure, but is referred to as a spinner by some anglers, and an overhead spinner by others.

A spinnerbait is one of the favorite lures of bass anglers and one of their most popular offerings for springtime and shallow-water angling. Although it is thought of almost exclusively as a freshwater lure for bass fishing, and is primarily available in sizes appropriate for largemouth and smallmouth bass, a spinnerbait can be very effective for chain pickerel and northern pike, and may be useful for catching some panfish and the occasional muskie. Strictly a casting lure that is primarily used on largemouth bass and secondarily on smallmouth and spotted bass, a spinnerbait is seldom deliberately employed for, or effective on, such species as trout, salmon, or striped bass, although it will catch peacock bass.

A relatively easy lure to fish, the spinnerbait is remarkably weed- and tangle-free when fished around cover and obstructions. It can be an exciting lure to retrieve in shallow water and in water that is clear near the surface, because it's possible to watch

Spinnerbaits come in a variety of configurations, with differing blades, lead heads, and body colors.

fish rush after it and strike. Because they are fairly large and bulky lures, spinnerbaits cast very well, although models with large blades and with tandem blades can be more air-resistant and are subject to swaying from the intended trajectory or target; this may be countered by making low-angle presentations, such as casting underhanded or side-armed.

What a spinnerbait is supposed to look like is uncertain. Obviously, its shape does not imitate a particular natural food, yet it possesses certain qualities that attract fish, especially bass in the spring and fall. Through blade color and movement, a spinnerbait certainly offers visual flash and auditory vibration. Fish can both see and hear it well. With a good skirt on the hook shaft, a spinnerbait also offers pulsating movement and the impression of having plenty of substance. Add to this the fact that it can be effectively fished in all but the thickest cover and can be fished in intermediate and deep water, and you have the elements of a unique but effective type of lure.

Sizes, Bodies, Colors

Spinnerbaits are available in a wide range of sizes, from micro to maxi models. The lightest ones, in $1/16$- to $3/16$-ounce sizes, are used with light line and light spinning tackle, primarily for bluegills and crappie, but also for smaller specimens of largemouth and smallmouth bass, plus white bass. Small spinnerbaits usually feature a single blade on the overhead shaft and a soft grub-shaped body rather than a multi-tentacled skirt. For the most part, these are fished in shallow areas and near the surface.

The largest versions, which weigh in the $1^1/2$- to 2-ounce range and sport thick gauge wire and huge blades, can be employed in muskie and northern pike fishing, but are not heavily favored for the former, where in-line bucktail spinners predominate. These lures must be used with heavy-action tackle and rods whose tip can respond quickly and with authority to punch a lure home.

S

Bass-sized spinnerbaits primarily range from $^1/_4$- to 1-ounce, with $^1/_2$- and $^5/_8$-ounce models being especially popular. Many bass anglers seldom use less than a $^1/_2$-ounce spinnerbait, and a few may use magnum models (up to $1^1/_2$ ounces) for deep-water work. Though by many standards these are large lures, such sizes are readily accepted by largemouth bass, although the smaller models are usually more appropriate for smallmouths; the intermediate sizes are so favored by bass anglers that they constitute the bulk of the spinnerbait market.

The weight of a spinnerbait is, in large part, determined by the size of the head on the lower shaft. This is essentially a lead jig head, and is usually tapered to facilitate swimming. On small spinnerbaits, that head may be rounded, like a ball-head jig, but for most bass models, it is shaped more like a cone or bullet. Some heads may be turned up slightly to resist diving and enhance upward or shallow movement, especially on a fast retrieve.

The main part of all spinnerbaits is the wire used to form the upper and lower arms. The thickness of the wire in these arms has some bearing on how the lure fishes and how durable it is. Thin wire produces a good feel and good lure action but can snap under the strain of a big fish, and, in general, will not withstand as much use as thicker arms. Yet, wire arms that are too thick detract substantially from lure action and feel, and are thus undesirable for most fishing. When using a good spinnerbait, the angler can usually feel the vibration of the turning blade, which produces a thumping sensation. When a spinnerbait is not visible, strikes are often detected when that thumping ceases. If the wire arm on a spinnerbait is too thick, the angler cannot constantly feel the lure working, and is thus more likely to not detect some strikes, or to be delayed in setting the hook upon receiving some strikes. But if the wire is too thin, the angler may not be able to drive the hook well enough when he gets a strike, or the lure will be easily deformed after a bit of use.

Spinnerbaits that are used for pike fishing, however, should be made of a heavier gauge wire to take the extra twisting, thrashing, and strain that pike inflict on a lure. Most spinnerbaits designed for bass fishing do not hold up well to repeated northern pike catching. Also, spinnerbaits used for pike fishing are better if they have a fixed line-tie point rather than an open one. Most spinnerbaits have an open crook at the tip of the lure where the upper and lower arms converge, which is where the fishing line is directly tied with a nonslip knot. However, in pike fishing, wire leaders are often employed, and a snap is used at the front end of that leader to connect to a lure. When a snap is connected to a standard spinnerbait, there is nothing to prevent that snap from sliding along either shaft, which it will do when cast, when fluttered into deep water, or sometimes during the fight with a fish. This can cause you to lose a fish, to lose the lure, or to damage the lure. A better style for this

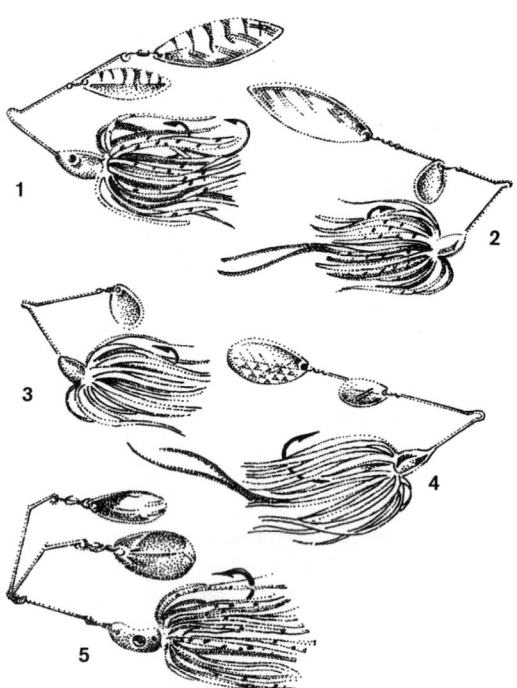

Spinnerbait styles are numerous and generally defined by their blade configurations, arm length, and arm number. Popular single-arm arrangements include twin willowleaf (1), willowleaf and Colorado (2), single Colorado on a short arm (3), and twin Indiana (4); the twin spin (5) is distinguished by its double overhead arms, usually with Colorado or Indiana blades.

usage is a spinnerbait with a circular loop bend at the line-tie point; a snap cannot wander from that type of connection.

Some spinnerbaits feature overhead blade arms that extend well beyond the hook on the bottom arm. This is of some help in preventing hangups, but it sometimes hampers hooksetting. Spinnerbaits with a long arm and a jumbo willowleaf trailing blade are used to create a large look when targeting big fish. The majority of spinnerbaits primarily have a medium-length overhead arm in which the blade assembly is directly above the hook, which is thus unobstructed, or which extends just a tad past the hook but no further than the end of the skirt. A combination of blade types and sizes is used on these. Some spinnerbaits have short arms and usually a single Colorado or Indiana style blade. These produce a lot of vibration and are good for deep fishing.

Arm length can be a two-edged sword. Short-armed spinnerbaits hang up frequently in thick brush and stumps and timber. If you need to roll such a lure over a log, it often won't make it, because the overhead shaft is too short to afford any protection. If you take a short-armed spinnerbait that is attached to fishing line and gently try to pull it over your arm, you'll get the picture; if the hook pricks your arm, it will stick in a log. For such times, a longer-armed spinnerbait is best.

Incidentally, there is a now relatively obscure type of spinnerbait called a twin spinner that features two overhead arms instead of the normal one, with each possessing a single blade. The overhead arms are fairly short and lay off to an angle instead of being directly in line with the lower arm, so that the blades on each (Indiana or Colorado versions) can spin freely. These are very snag-resistant lures, and they can be worked well at slow speeds, which may be good for inactive fish. Also, the larger models with smaller blades can be good for deep-water probing.

Spinnerbaits have to be periodically tuned to keep running properly. When retrieved at a normal pace, a good spinnerbait runs straight, without twisting 360 degrees or leaning off to the side. It should be able to do this at slow as well as high speeds. You can adjust a spinnerbait so that the blades and hook run vertically in the water by bending the entire overhead shaft arm in the opposite direction from which it is running astray. Bend the arm slightly, and then test the lure; keep adjusting in increments until you get it right.

The primary aspect of a spinnerbait's body is its type and color. Although soft plastics and bucktail hair may be used on the shank of the hook for body, greater bulk and action is had with other materials, so soft bodies and bucktails are not that prominent on spinnerbaits. Most bodies feature a skirt that has been evolving over the past few decades in material from vinyl to rubber to synthetics and in appearance from monochrome to multicolor to an ultra snazzy potpourri of colors and enhancements.

White has long been a preferred skirt color, especially for the early season and in murky water; all chartreuse and chartreuse/blue (or black) combinations have been preferred in clearer water. Variations of these, with sparkle or iridescent enhancements, are still very popular, but you can find a host of colors and local preferences now, just as you can for fishing other types of lures, and opinions on skirt and overall lure color vary widely.

On many occasions, the color of skirt makes no difference in the number or size of fish caught. This is especially true when the lure is fished in water that is extremely turbid, at night in the dark, and in very deep water. There are many contradicting beliefs among anglers as to body color, just as there are as to blade color, blade size, and even the number of blades.

Most spinnerbaits today are equipped with silicone skirts, but they used to be primarily dressed with vinyl, hair, or rubber skirts, and some are still available in these materials, particularly rubber. The newer synthetics hold up well in cold water and offer good body swimming action. The disadvantage with rubber is that the tentacles have a tendency to stick together in the tackle box; you can avoid this by sprinkling some talcum powder in the compartments that house your spinnerbaits and by using trays that allow you to store spinnerbaits with

the skirts hanging loosely rather than bunched up. If the legs melt together, pull the skirt off and replace it with a fresh one. Synthetic skirts, some with elaborate colors and designs, have become much more prevalent, and it's now possible to create a pop art look with spinnerbaits. Metal flake and iridescent skirts make the older types and colors look especially drab. By changing skirts, you can readily mix and match body and head colors. Most anglers believe that the jig head and body should complement each other in color, but that is not an absolute necessity.

To apply a skirt, hold it up so that the tentacles hang straight down, then turn it upside down so that the tentacles come out and over the stem of the skirt, resembling small streams of water being shot out of a fountain; thread the stem over the hook point and the shank until it fits snugly on the base of the lead head. This backward skirt produces far more pulsating action than a straight-back skirt would.

It's a good idea to dress up spinnerbaits still further, especially large ones, by adding a curl-tailed soft worm, grub, or pork chunk to the main hook. Some anglers are partial to 3-inch, twin-tailed, soft plastic trailers, which swim feverishly just behind the skirt, and give a valuable extra dimension to the look of the lure. A short plastic worm with a twisted or curled tail is also good, and provides nice additional motion. Slender pork rind or other materials are also possibilities. Remember that many of these add a little more weight as well as bulk. Keep long plastic trailers from extending too far behind the lure in pike and pickerel country or they will be snipped off.

A trailer hook is a good idea for bass fishing, except when the cover is so thick that the extra hook causes hangups. Spinnerbaits account for a lot of fish and one of the beneficial aspects about using them is that their single main-body hook permits relatively quick unhooking and near zero chance of hurting yourself (similar to jigs but unlike multi-hooked plugs). However, they are often subject to swiping or short-striking by bass, and a trailer hook can account for many bass that would otherwise be lost. It is not necessary to use a trailer hook all the time, but it doesn't hurt, especially if the fish are visibly striking short or hitting merely to stun. The trailer hook should ride up like the spinnerbait hook, and should not be imbedded in any skirt or body material. To keep the trailer hook from sliding off, block it with a small piece of surgical tubing. Place a small ring of this material over the eye of the trailer hook, then bring the point of the spinnerbait hook through the eye and tubing, and secure it.

Another addition sometimes made to a spinnerbait is a small rattle. Some lures have a receptacle for a rattle that is on the hook shank underneath the forward part of the skirt. A rattle may be added using pieces of surgical tubing as well, usually on the hook shank but sometimes in front of the head

A bathyscape 7 miles deep in the ocean receives more than 8 tons of weight per square inch, yet there are various fish at this level that live in equilibrium by equalizing internal and external pressure.

S

on the lower wire arm. The purpose of this obviously is to add more noise to the lure, which may be most appropriate in spinnerbaits that do not produce a lot of vibration, like a smaller lure with a short willowleaf blade.

Blades

Spinnerbaits are available in single and tandem blade versions. Tandem blades on the overhead arm of the spinnerbait usually feature a small spinner followed by a larger one. These are predominantly for shallow fishing, but this is just a generality. Single blade spinnerbaits can also be effective when fished shallow, although they are thought to be a better lure style for deeper retrieves. In actuality, although some anglers have strong preferences for when and where to use single or tandem blade spinnerbaits, they can be used in a broad range of conditions that are equally affected by the overall weight of the lure and the size and shape of the blades.

Spinnerbait Blades

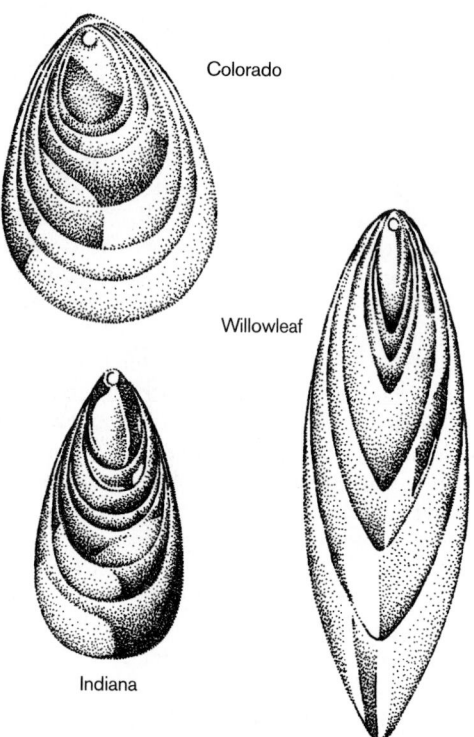

Colorado

Willowleaf

Indiana

Spinnerbaits principally feature Colorado, Indiana, and willowleaf design blades, or hybrid versions of these basic styles. The Colorado is between round and pear-shaped and is generally believed to produce the most vibration, although this is a function of how much it is cupped. The more cupping there is to the blade, the greater the vibration. The common size is No. 4, which is roughly the size of a quarter, but the range is from No. 2 to the magnum No. 8. Colorado blades are often found on single blade spinnerbaits. They are good for slow retrieves, murky water, and dark

conditions. A small Colorado may precede a larger willowleaf blade on a tandem spinnerbait.

Indiana blades are teardrop-shaped and produce good vibration, too, though they spin faster, and work well on tandem blade lures. They, too, are used in combination with other blade types, either in front of a willowleaf or behind a Colorado. Willowleaf blades, shaped as the name implies and coming to a sharply tapered tail point, were less commonly used in the past but are now extremely popular. These long blades are mainly used on a tandem rig with a big No. 4 or 5 willowleaf, usually in silver or copper, behind a smaller Indiana blade; however, willowleaf blades can be used in tandem, or as a single, and are preferred in the magnum sizes (up to No. 8) for big fish. The willowleaf doesn't offer as much vibration as other types of blades, but it revolves freely and produces a lot of flash. It is an attention getter, especially when hammered or fluted or spiced with light-bouncing colors.

Spinnerbaits with big blades are generally reserved for waters with distinct big-fish potential. This is not to say you won't catch big bass on smaller lures, but the probability is that you'll catch fewer small bass with an oversized bait. They are also used for deep-water fishing, where flash may not be a factor, but where a heavy dose of vibration is essential. Smaller blade sizes, especially the willowleaf, are necessary when the primary forage is small, and it may be necessary to try to match the size of blade to the size of baitfish currently available where you're fishing.

There are also hybrid blade styles that don't fit generic descriptions. The most prominent of these are jointed oval-shaped blades, which wave rather than spin and are usually found on short-armed spinnerbaits. There are also winged blades, spiral blades, and blades with various intentional deformations that change or exaggerate a basic shape. Additionally, there may be a difference in action as well as vibration among blades of the same overall design due to the amount of cupping in the blade. The greater the cupping, the more the blade pulls water. With a pair of pliers you can increase the cupping or decrease it, even flattening it in the latter case.

Spinnerbait blades come in different colors and impressions. Nickel (silver) and copper have traditionally been most popular, followed by gold, and painted white, chartreuse, and orange. However, multicolored blades and paintings have made great inroads, and the standard metal finishes may now be much more diverse than polished older versions, including hammered design, horizontal bars, fluted patterns, diamond patterns, and more. Most are intended to reflect light rays and create flash.

Copper, which historically has been the favorite of most anglers, is good for slightly turbid and off color water. Silver works well for most of the year, especially in the spring and in clear water. Painted blades, most notably chartreuse, work well when murky green water conditions are present, and are preferred by some anglers in clear water because they are more subtle overall, do not produce as much flash, and provide something of a three-dimensional appearance. Many newer blades are painted with various patterns and with sparkling, flashy designs. They look great, but it is unclear whether this produces a practical effective advantage, although there may be a psychological benefit if the appearance causes the user to retrieve it more attentively. Some anglers believe that painted blades, combined with reflective painted skirts, many of which are garnished with sparkles or a prismatic finish, imitate a school of baitfish and appear more attractive to fish than more traditional looking spinnerbaits.

Because spinnerbaits are very popular lures, and used in common bass haunts on many heavily pressured waters, it is reasonable to wonder if bass do not become accustomed to seeing certain colors of these lures and thus more wary of them, which leads to a rise in the usage of newer and formerly less popular colors. To some extent, this may be true with all types of lures. The point is that colors on all lures, especially spinnerbaits, run in fads among anglers, and it may well be worthwhile to use colors that differ from the norm on heavily pressured lakes, or to return to colors that were once popular but which have fallen out of favor, and thus are no longer being seen so often by the fish.

The style or combination of blades you use may be a reflection of where and how you fish. Tandem spinnerbaits are generally meant for speedy retrieval. A twin willowleaf combination is the best for pure quick retrieving, and a willowleaf-Colorado combination is for more intermediate retrieval. To get a slow retrieve, especially in shallow water, you need a blade that grabs a lot of water and spins well. This might be a Colorado combination, or more likely a single Colorado blade, perhaps of large size. Although some anglers use tandem blades for deep fishing, their effectiveness there is primarily when being retrieved rather than when falling, because the blades usually get tangled on the drop and don't rotate. If you consider this issue in terms of water condition, try spinnerbaits that produce more vibration when the water is turbid (fish rely more on sound than sight) or when it is cold (sound coaxes better than flash), and spinnerbaits that produce more flash when the water is clear (sight is most important) or when it is warm (the fish are active and more aggressive).

Spinnerbait Fishing for Bass

A spinnerbait evidently appeals to the predatory, reflexive instincts of bass as much as to its hunger instincts. A bass must strike a spinnerbait because it grabs its eye and looks like something vulnerable, or because it produces vibrations that sound like something it ordinarily eats or might eat.

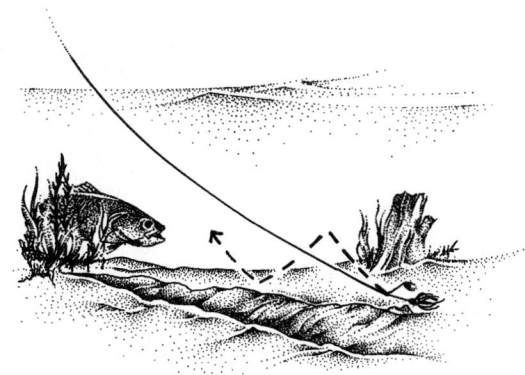

Although most anglers retrieve spinnerbaits shallow, these lures can be very effective when crawled across the bottom, and fished in a slow, deep, lift-and-drop manner.

Spinnerbaits are versatile lures, as might be inferred from the wide assortment of blades, colors, and sizes available. A spinnerbait is a good lure for fishing in and around cover; lily pads, grass, stumps, brush, treetops, boat docks, rock piles, logs, and similar fish holding places can all be effectively worked. A spinnerbait is primarily fished on a standard cast-and-retrieve, usually in shallow or intermediate depths, where it is most productive for the average angler. But it can also be fished in deep water, although the methods in each case are quite different.

The most common technique of fishing a spinnerbait is to retrieve it from within a few inches to several feet beneath the surface; if the water is clear enough, you can see and watch the lure coming through the water on the retrieve. It is not only beneficial, but highly enjoyable, to watch a spinnerbait when it is being retrieved this shallow. Nearly every time, if you can see the lure, you will see the fish strike it. Sometimes, a bass seems to dart out of nowhere. Other times, it comes from right where expected. This is very much like surface fishing; the excitement of anticipating and seeing the strike is always present. Even when the water is murky and you can't see the lure, you usually know about where it is located as it swims, and the strike may create a splash or boil on the surface. Spinnerbaits are usually struck from the side, suddenly forcing the lure sideways as if it were hit by a gust of wind. When this happens, jam the hook home fast. Another distinct advantage of this technique is that you can see the fish that attempt to strike the bait. You can often see if a bass misses the lure, hits short, or is merely taking a close look. Sometimes, these fish can be caught with another cast of that spinnerbait in the same area, or with an alternative lure that works more slowly.

It is also beneficial to watch the lure as it is retrieved right to the boat. Sometimes, particularly on shallow, stumpy flats, a fish may come from almost under the boat after the lure, yet turn away at the last second as the lure nears the boat. Chain pickerel and northern pike characteristically follow this lure right up to the boat, sometimes striking at boatside. If you see this, you can be prepared.

It is important to begin retrieving a spinnerbait the moment it hits the water for maximum effectiveness when working the shallows. With spinning tackle, this is no problem, but right-handed baitcasters will have to switch the rod to their left hand during the cast so they can engage the reel as the lure hits the water, or their lure may get fouled initially or fall too deep to fish the nearby cover.

Sometimes, bass are holding by objects at a level deeper than your lure is being retrieved and will not come up for it, even though you're fishing in what is generally considered shallow water. If you're fishing a spinnerbait close to the surface with poor results, try letting it sink out of sight to a depth of between 4 and 8 feet, and retrieve it steadily at that depth. Occasionally, you'll have to fish a spinnerbait out of sight right along the bottom like this, in intermediate or greater depths.

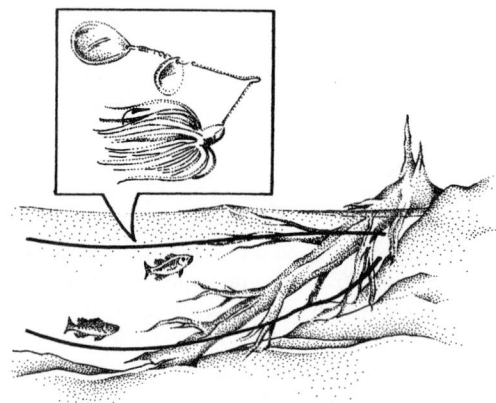

When cast into cover along the bank, a spinnerbait can be retrieved shallow at a moderate pace (upper dark line) through the top layer of water, or more slowly and deeper (lower dark line) through the lower layer.

The shallow cover places where most anglers successfully use a spinnerbait necessitate getting as close to the particular object as possible. Do this by casting the lure beyond the target and bringing it back into contact with it, then continuing on. Make several casts to each object, from every angle, paying particular attention to the deep and shady sides.

An effective method for working weed beds and weedlines is to crawl a spinnerbait slowly over the top of grass that is submerged a few feet. For grass beds with definable weedlines, however, it may be better to cast parallel to the edge or bring the lure over the top and let it flutter down the edge. For lily pads, it's best to work the channel-like openings, but don't be afraid to throw into thick clusters and far back into pockets, then ease it over the pads and drop it in another pocket.

Perhaps the most reliable pattern for spinnerbait fishing, especially in the spring, is working the wood. This includes stumps, logs, and stickups. Make sure your spinnerbait is close to these objects; in fact, bump them with the lure at times. The momentary fluttering of the bait's blades and the object contact seem to produce strikes. Stickup trees, bushes, and floating logjams (as often found in coves) also are productive for spinnerbait users. In these locales, you should get your bait as far back in them as possible before commencing the retrieve. Boat docks and houses, too, fit in this category.

Spring and early summer are prime times for spinnerbait use. In spring and early summer, spinnerbaits allow you to cover a lot of ground effectively and quickly, while you watch your lure work and see strikes. Midsummer is generally not considered a very good spinnerbait time, but this is all relative. Smallmouths in deep water are very susceptible to spinnerbaits fished at night in the summer, and many northern waters, where the water stays warm and fish are relatively shallow, can provide spinnerbait action that rivals that of early season. In some well timbered lakes where bass remain in shallow to intermediate depths through summer, spinnerbaits are quite effective. As the water cools in early fall, spinnerbaits again become primary bass lures, and when fished slowly and deep in the winter or early spring, they are also productive.

Although it has been long taken for gospel that spinnerbaits are only for fishing in water that is as deep as your fishing rod is long, or where you can see the lure from the time it hits the water until the time it gets back to the boat, this is not the case, as some savvy anglers have discovered. Deep fishing with spinnerbaits is something that many anglers have overlooked in the past, preferring to use a deep-diving plug or a Carolina rig worm for probing the nether regions of bass lakes and reservoirs. However, the vibration of big-bladed spinnerbaits in deep water can be enticing to larger bass. Spinnerbaits do indeed have merit for fishing along sharply sloping shorelines, dropoffs, rocky ledges,

Shallow grass and bushes are excellent places to fish a spinnerbait for largemouth bass.

and among deep timber, whether on a lift-and-drop motion, in a series of short hops, or on a straight retrieve at a deeper than normal level.

Where there is submerged cover in deeper water—points, open-water humps, stumpy flats or ridges near deep water, ledges, and assorted vegetation—you can make a long cast and either let the lure fall to the bottom, or count it down to the proper level, before beginning the retrieve. Watch the line for indications of a strike as the lure is falling, and after it reaches the desired level, start a slow steady retrieve. If you crank the reel handle too fast, the lure will rise and lift away from the bottom of the desired zone, so be sure to reel slowly to keep the spinnerbait in the right place.

You may need a very heavy spinnerbait for this, one in the 1-ounce range, to get and keep it at the right level. This is harder to cast than smaller spinnerbaits and may require the use of a two-handed rod, both for casting and retrieving comfort. If you can't find such a heavy spinnerbait, or are pressed to use a lighter one, then try putting a rubber-core sinker onto the shaft of a lighter lure, camouflaged by the skirt.

There are different opinions about using single or tandem blades in deep water. Most people are likely to find a single large Colorado blade very effective, especially in the dark and dirty depths. In addition to producing a lot of vibration, the single Colorado also spins when the lure is on the descent, which can provoke strikes on a falling spinnerbait (say one that is dropped off a deep ledge), or when it is retrieved in a short-hopping motion rather than on a steady retrieve. When short-hopped, a deep spinnerbait is worked more or less like a jig, but if the blade doesn't spin on the descent as well as on the ascent, then it's not that effective. Tandem blades often do not do that.

Keep in mind when fishing a spinnerbait deep that the size of your line may be an important factor. In shallow water, line diameter is not that critical to spinnerbait success or to effective action, but in deep water, a line with a heavier diameter may not fall as well as one with a smaller diameter, and thus tends to ride up. Also, using a short-armed spinnerbait has an advantage for blade action as well, again especially on the drop.

Because heavy spinnerbaits are required for deep water, a fishing rod should be stout enough to make long casts, set the hook when a long length of line is out, and move a good-size fish off or out of cover if necessary. A 7-foot medium-heavy action rod fills that bill, provided it can also transmit the feel of the lure working.

In general, baitcasting tackle is best for spinnerbait use, except when using the lightest versions for small fish. A baitcasting reel does not need a lot of line capacity for spinnerbait use, but it should be filled to capacity for the sake of casting efficiency as well as retrieval. Because it is common to fish a spinnerbait at a fast retrieve, especially in shallow water, reels with a medium or fast retrieval ratio work fine; however, a high-speed reel can lead to fishing a spinnerbait too fast on those occasions when it is necessary to fish a spinnerbait slowly. For really slow fishing, a slower retrieval ratio is advantageous, as it is difficult to deliberately fish a high-speed reel in a slow mode for long periods.

There are a lot of good spinnerbaits on the market, including many that are made and sold within a localized area, so you shouldn't have to look far to find variety. If you keep a supply of extra blades, barrel swivels, trailer hooks, and skirts to be able to modify your spinnerbaits as necessary, you'll be able to enhance the lure's effectiveness and increase your angling success.

SPINNER-JIG
A spinner with a small spinner blade on it.
See: Spinner.

SPINNER RIG
A slow-trolling device, also called a nightcrawler harness, comprised of a Colorado or Indiana spinner, five or six plastic beads, and two short-shanked snelled bait hooks that are impaled in a whole live nightcrawler. This rig is used in freshwater for catching walleye, perch, and smallmouth bass.

SPINNING REEL
See: Spinning Tackle.

SPINNING ROD
See: Spinning Tackle.

SPINNING TACKLE
Spinning tackle is a type of multipurpose fishing equipment characterized by a reel with a stationary spool around which line is wound. This is distinctive from other multipurpose tackle forms, which feature a reel with some type of revolving spool, particularly baitcasting (see) and conventional tackle (see), and from flycasting tackle (see), which has a much narrower purpose.

Spinning tackle is related to spincasting tackle (see), which has a stationary spool and is the easiest type of tackle to learn to use. Spincasting reels have a housing over the spool that caused them to be known at one time as closed-face spinning. The reels that are now known simply as spinning were once called open-faced spinning. These terms are used with decreasing frequency in North America today.

Spinning tackle is extremely popular and widespread in use across North America and Europe. Spinning reels have long ranked second among the various reel categories both in terms of the value of the units sold (behind baitcasting) and total number of units sold (behind spincasting). There is some irony to this because the stationary-spool spinning reel is the second most recent tackle type to be developed and to become widely available (spincasting is even more recent). In North America, spinning began its ascendancy after World War II; it exploded as a popular tool for casting small- to medium-size lures and fishing with bait in freshwater when nylon monofilament line was introduced. At that time, revolving spool reels were widely employed but difficult to cast and use with small or light terminal gear, and flycasting tackle was (and essentially still is) being used strictly for casting super-lightweight objects.

Today, the boundaries between application by type of tackle have blurred due to improvements in all categories of reels, rods, and line. Baitcasting and conventional tackle, for example, have progressed markedly, and some of this equipment is today suitable for use with small terminal gear. Yet spinning has retained a strong following because there is a fairly short learning curve for using it, it is economically priced, and it is suitable for a diverse range of species and angling techniques, particularly in freshwater. Spinning tackle has become a preferred equipment choice for young anglers and one that anglers continue to employ to some degree as they progress from novice through more experienced stages and expand their interests and activities.

Spinning tackle has had a greater following in freshwater than in saltwater, in part because of the differences in conditions, techniques, and size of fish. Spinning gear was once relegated to specific applications, but refinements in equipment have resulted in models of spinning tackle that can be used in applications ranging from ultralight pan-fishing to offshore billfishing (as in sailfish and white marlin). Appropriate models of spinning reels with corresponding rods can be used for virtually all fishing methods, including casting, trolling, and fishing with bait, but not all spinning reels are up to all tasks, and the factors that go into the selection and use of this or any type of fishing tackle are many and varied.

Reels

The development of the spinning reel is generally credited to British caster Alfred Holden Illingworth, who may have taken a cue from the loom spindles and bobbins used in the cotton mills owned by his family. In 1905, he designed and patented a mechanical means of retrieving line and rotating it around a handheld stationary spool. Anglers had previously hand-wound fishing line around stationary objects and used a weight to propel them. There were earlier attempts at achieving what Illingworth perfected, but none offered the advantages of his device.

In the March 21, 1908, edition of the British publication *Fishing Gazette,* an advertisement by

The Light Casting Reel Company for the Illingworth Casting Reel depicted the product mounted underneath the rod, with a left-retrieve handle and looking like a husky flycasting reel. The advertising copy listed among the reel's advantages: "extremely simple in use; no over-running; will cast the lightest bait; does not kink the line; the speed of winding is rapid; the line needs no guiding when winding in as it is automatically spread with precision; proficiency is rapidly acquired . . ." To prove at least one of his points, Illingworth used his invention to take first place in the 3-gram ($1/10$-ounce) distance casting competition at the International Casting Tournament of 1908.

Although Illingworth's reel could cast light objects ($1/16$- to $3/8$-ounce in particular), it was not as proficient at casting heavy objects as the American multiplier, or baitcasting, reel. Yet it was ahead of its time. The rods of that day were ill-suited to casting lightweight lures. There wasn't enough interest yet in lightweight lures for many to be produced, and the gut or braided silk lines of the day were woefully inadequate. These factors combined to make the early spinning reel more novel than utilitarian.

The first spinning reel to be commercially distributed in the United States was the French-made Luxor, which was introduced by New York importer Bache Brown in 1938. Like Illingworth's reel, and unlike other types of fishing reels of the day, it did not use a revolving spool for casting or retrieving line. Yet that reel, and the principle behind it, went virtually unnoticed until 1944, when Brown used the Luxor patent to design a new model named Airex and built in the U.S. Nylon line (braided at first) was just becoming available; rods, mostly made from bamboo, tubular steel, or tubular aluminum, were getting better. Many more lightweight lures were being made, and the public was hungry for an alternative to the stiff and difficult-to-use baitcasting tackle and the flies-only capability of flycasting gear. Six million Airex reels were reportedly sold by 1950, and many other companies joined in the manufacture of what was then called a fixed-spool reel. In the 1950s, fiberglass rods and nylon monofilament line became available, and spinning was on a fast track to increased sportfishing interest.

Although created decades earlier, the spinning reel burst into popularity just ahead of the spincasting reel. Until both spinning and spincasting tackle emerged, anglers primarily used levelwind or baitcasting gear, flycasting tackle, and conventional or big-game tackle for respective, and at that time somewhat specialized, applications. There was a lack of easy-to-use equipment for varied angling activity, especially the casting of different weight objects. As Illingworth's invention promised in 1908, the new fixed-spool, or spinning, reel offered easier casting than the baitcasting (levelwind) reels then available, which at that time generated an annoying and frustrating backlash for most anglers on every fourth or fifth cast. The spinning reel was also capable of casting lightweight lures (which eventually led to casting a range of lure weights).

Both spinning and spincasting reels eventually played a huge role in a fishing participation boom that has extended to the present day, and spilled over into the improvement of all other tackle types.

In the early 1950s, with the emergence of spincasting reels, which also had a stationary rather than revolving spool, the terminology used to describe these products was slightly different. Reels that are presently referred to as spinning models were then called open-faced spinning or, less often, open-faced reels. The reels that are referred to today as spincasting were then called closed-face spinning, or closed-face reels. This terminology has caused some confusion in literature, although the intentions are understandable; the early nomenclature was arguably more appropriate than what is used in today's parlance.

Spinning reels all feature an exposed spool that is stationary during the casting and retrieving processes; thus, it was common to call these open-faced reels in the early days of their existence. Spincasting reels all feature a stationary spool, a line pickup, and a line-winding mechanism that are covered by a cone or hood; thus, it was common for these to initially be called closed-face reels. Both feature a spool that remains stationary (fixed) when line is wound, or spun, around it, and when it is unwound, although the spool does revolve when the drag feature is called upon. This is different from other reel types, whose spool revolves and in so doing causes the line to wind and unwind. Essentially, in the modern vernacular, any reel with an exposed stationary spool is a spinning reel, and any reel with a covered stationary spool is a spincasting reel.

At the risk of further confusion, it should be pointed out that another distinguishing difference between spinning and spincasting reels is that the former always sit underneath the reel handle, while the latter usually sit atop the reel handle. Likewise, baitcasting reels are always mounted on top of the rod handle.

The fact that spinning reels are mounted underneath the rod handle no doubt contributes greatly to their prominence. To most people, especially those who have never used fishing equipment before, it seems natural, and feels more comfortable and balanced, to hold a fishing outfit in which the reel is positioned underneath the rod rather than one in which the reel is atop the rod. This placement reduces the type of arm fatigue that is associated with frequent, if not constant, casting, and the fact that spinning reels are convertible to either right- or left-handed retrieve assures that the rod is held in the dominant hand, which is often not the case when using spincasting or baitcasting tackle.

Spinning reels today are used in freshwater and saltwater, although more commonly in the former,

There are many spinning reels with various features available.

primarily because freshwater anglers outnumber saltwater anglers, freshwater fish are smaller and less punishing on tackle, and more casting is generally done in freshwater. They range from small-profile ultralight models for use with 2-pound-test line to large-profile saltwater heavyweights for use with up to 30-pound line. Despite the improvements that have been made to other equipment, spinning reels are generally considered the most versatile reels.

Spinning reels have undergone many changes over the years, perhaps the most significant being in drag and casting features, as well as in line twist reduction aspects. Spinning (and spincasting) reels have long been products that were conducive to producing line twist through angler misuse or through the activation of the reels themselves. Twisted line hampers casting and general fishing effectiveness and may result in damaged line, so it is a problem to be avoided and corrected. Therefore, reducing or eliminating twist, from whatever source, has been a major focus of spinning reel manufacturers, and continues to be a work-in-progress, notwithstanding advertising claims to the contrary.

General Operation

In the most basic sense, spinning equipment works much like all other tackle except flycasting in that a weighted object, when cast, pulls line from the spool. The spool of a spinning reel is stationary during the cast, which means that there is little chance of a backlash *(see)* forming, as happens when a

moving spool turns faster than the line is carried off that spool.

The spinning reel has a line roller that controls the release and retrieval of line. The line is guided by the bail to the line roller. When the handle is rotated, the line roller wraps line around the stationary spool. It also has an adjustable drag mechanism and usually a single-grip handle. When the bail is opened, line may flow freely off the spool.

In use, with the reel under the rod handle and facing away from the angler, the bail is opened and the line is held, usually by the index finger of the hand that holds the rod handle, to prevent the line from coming freely off the spool until released by the finger. When the finger is removed, released line flows off the spool and out through the rod guides, carried by the weight of the object at the terminal end of the line.

To retrieve line, the gears are engaged by rotating the handle clockwise (forward). This rotational movement is transferred to the rotor, with a simultaneous axial movement (forward and backward motion) transferred to the spool of better quality reels. As the line roller, which is connected to the rotor, rotates around the spool, line is wrapped on the spool. The spool's axial motion causes it to move toward the front of the reel and then toward the back of the reel. This motion, coupled with the rotor motion, causes line to wrap onto the spool in an equal layer instead of piling up in one place.

These are the basic elements of operating a spinning reel. Some models have different bail-opening, line-holding, drag, anti-reverse, spool oscillation, and other features. The general design, style, feature selection, and feel of each product also has relevance to its intended use.

Casting/Line Release Features

Bail.   The bail on a spinning reel is an important component of both line release and line pickup, and is a standard feature on virtually all present-day reels.

Early spinning reels did not possess a bail as such. These models all featured a roller mounted to a bracket on the edge of a revolving housing. The line was directed to the roller by finger so that it could be captured for spool winding. The angler used the tip of the index finger to lift line off the roller preparatory to making a cast; to retrieve, the line was caught at the spool lip by the tip of the index finger and placed on the roller. This system was referred to at the time as a manual pickup. Because there were no moving parts, it was mechanically reliable, but becoming adept with it took practice.

Some adroit anglers, who found this system quick and certain if the line was kept under tension, stayed with it even when a quasi-pickup bail, in the form of a metal finger, evolved. This bail forerunner was a short outward curved arm that cocked open for casting and tripped closed for retrieval and automatically caught and secured the line. Known at the time as an automatic pickup, it was easier to use than the manual version, but did not always catch the line instantly.

That lead to the development of a more efficient auto-pickup system that featured a curved and longer wire arm hoop fixed to opposite sides of the housing. When tripped over the top of a reel, this arm always scooped in the line and became known as the pickup bail, or simply the bail. The bail and its anchor points to the rotor became known as the bail assembly.

Naturally, the functioning of a pickup bail today is more elaborate than it used to be, and so reliable that it is a rarity to find an angler who uses a spinning reel without a bail (the metal arm can be removed from some bails, however, to permit manual finger pickup, and a bail-less reel is favored by a small number of surf anglers). Virtually all spinning reels feature a bail, and the process of opening it in modern reels is accomplished either by manual or automatic means.

Bail opening systems.   Because the bail holds line in place, it must be opened to cast or to allow line to flow off the reel without casting. There are several bail opening systems in spinning reels. No matter which system is used, the lure must first be placed in the proper casting position relative to the rod tip before the bail is opened.

For conventional spinning reels the best way to do this is to turn the handle and reel the line in until the lure is near the rod tip and the line roller is just under the index finger so that it is convenient to grab the line. With the lure in proper casting position, generally 3 to 6 inches below the tip of the rod, and the line roller correctly positioned directly below the rod, the line can be grabbed. If the line roller is not correctly positioned, strip line off the reel by pulling on it above the reel (which uses the drag to allow the spool to slip backward). Pull just enough off the spool so that the lure is the right distance below the rod tip. Once the lure and line roller are at the proper casting point, the bail is opened and the line held.

The manual and customary manner of opening the bail is to grab the line by the roller with the tip of the rod-holding forefinger, then flip up the bail with your other hand. Keep tension on the line with your finger until the cast is made. This is how the vast majority of reel bails are opened.

As inventors improved the original spinning reels by adding a bail to automatically direct the line to the line roller, improvements were also made in the line pickup area. Most of these improvements were intended to make it easier and faster to open the bail and capture the line before casting. The vast majority of these systems still require that the line roller be positioned directly in line between the spool and the rod.

Automatic bail opening is another system that has evolved as a means of simplifying basic spinning reel operation. This was first manifested in line pickup via a trigger positioned directly above or beside the line roller. Early trigger systems simply opened the bail as the trigger was pulled by the index finger, with the line being captured by that finger as it pulled the trigger.

In this system, positioning of the trigger in relation to the line roller was critical so that the index finger captured the line and pulled the bail-opening trigger at the same time. As the trigger is pulled and the bail opens, the index finger continues its upward motion to capture the line against the rod. The reel can then be cast in the customary manner. This mechanism made for a little faster casting, and eliminated the need for the user's free hand to open the bail.

A major improvement in automatic bail opening occurred in the early 1980s with a system that used a pin to capture the line. In this system, as the trigger is pulled by the index finger, the bail opens and a special "firing pin" simultaneously captures the line. The line is firmly held by the pin until the trigger is released. With this more user-friendly system, the index finger simply pulled the trigger to open the bail and capture the line during the back cast. As the rod is brought forward through the casting motion, the trigger is released, causing the pin to release the line and the line to freely flow off the end of the spool. The caster never has to touch the line.

This Zebco reel has an automatic bail-opening feature in which a pin captures the line when the trigger opens the bail; the empty spool helps illustrate this process.

A drawback, however, is that the line roller has to be positioned directly underneath the index finger before the trigger can be actuated. This problem was overcome in the early 1990s with the development of a reel with a trigger that extends from the base of the reel stem instead of being attached to the rotor. Because the trigger is not attached to the rotor, it can be actuated regardless of the position of the line roller relative to the user's index finger. As the trigger is pulled—even if the line roller is directly beneath the reel, instead of being positioned between the spool and rod—the casting mechanism still functions. In this system, the bail opens, and the firing pin captures the line until the trigger is released. When the trigger is released, the firing pin drops the line, which flows freely off the end of the spool. This system is currently the ultimate evolution of "one-handed" casting systems for spinning reels.

While changes were evolving in casting systems, they were also evolving in the anti-reverse area. In conventional spinning reels without a trigger bail, the user rotates the handle until the line roller is visually in the correct casting position. This requires taking your eye off the surrounding fishing area for a few moments and takes a few seconds longer to correctly position the line roller.

To address this, manufacturers developed anti-reverse systems with on-, off-, and self-center positions. With the reel in the self-center setting, the spinning reel handle can be rotated in reverse for up to one full revolution. The internal anti-reverse mechanism engages, thus stopping the counter-clockwise revolution of the handle exactly at the point where the line roller is located in the proper casting position.

With this self-centering anti-reverse system, you can turn the handle backward, and when it stops, the line roller—and optional trigger system—is always correctly positioned for casting. Visual alignment of the line roller is not required. While this is an advantage in casting, it is something of a hindrance when setting the hook on a big fish because the line roller can travel up to one complete revolution before encountering the anti-reverse stop. Not only does this allow excess line to play out while trying to secure a big fish, it creates a significant amount of shock loading on the anti-reverse single stop. Most, if not all, reels that utilize a self-centering bail anti-reverse system, also have a full on setting for the anti-reverse. From a mechanical point of view, the best operating condition is to turn the anti-reverse setting to the self-centering position immediately prior to casting, and switch it to the full on position as soon as the cast is completed. Obviously, this is not convenient.

While there is a more in-depth discussion of anti-reverse systems later in this text, it should be noted that continuous anti-reverse mechanisms, which are very popular in better quality baitcasting reels, are also employed in better quality spinning reels. However, only one series of spinning reels currently on the market incorporates the advantages of a fully functional continuous anti-reverse system with a casting mechanism that is always correctly positioned for the next cast.

Spinning reels that have bail triggers can definitely make it easier and faster to cast. If time and number of casts are an important element of an angler's fishing activity, a bail trigger should be beneficial. While the species pursued and the angling circumstances are critical factors, the result of being able to cast quickly can be greater or more

S

efficient water coverage, and more opportunities to catch fish.

For most people, making more casts in a shorter time is less significant than ease of use. Reels that automatically align the line roller with the stem of the reel certainly facilitate line pickup, and grabbing a bail trigger is indeed simple.

Although automatic bail-opening reels do enable one-handed operation, they have been modestly received by anglers. This may be due to the fact that many spinning reel users have been accustomed to manual bail operation for so long that they do not view that method as being difficult, and are reluctant to change.

Another factor is that many trigger-equipped reels have a somewhat narrow area between the rotor housing and the stem, which people with large fingers find problematic. A thick-fingered person may get knuckles wrapped by a spinning trigger or find that there isn't enough area for the trigger to open because it pinches against the fingers when pressed. These are ergonomic design issues that may be flaws for some, but insignificant to others. It is possible to remove the trigger assembly on some reels without adversely affecting other aspects of performance.

The repeated opening of a spinning reel bail is something that frequently used to cause trouble. A lot of that had to do with broken springs, a problem that has been virtually eliminated today with over-center design. The modern bail spring, which may be called a lever spring or an arm lever spring, works in a simple in-and-out mode that helps flip the arm open and, in most models, allows the bail to be closed manually as well if desired, in lieu of closure by turning the handle. Bails may still be problematic if they are damaged in such a way that the inner surface area is made coarse and causes line to snare, which is uncommon, or if they are bent or broken as the result of a mishap, which is fairly common. Occasionally, a bail will fail to close when the rotor is turned, and if this begins to happen frequently, the reel should be serviced.

The unplanned and unanticipated closure of a bail when casting is occasionally a problem. Older spinning reel bails locked in place, but lever spring bails do not. Stronger springs have largely eliminated that, but when a spring goes bad, it is possible for a bail to close unexpectedly, often when a forceful long-distance heave is made.

Spool type.   Another aspect of spools that has a bearing on casting, and is today mostly an historical footnote, pertains to the design of the rotor and position relative to the spool. Until the 1960s, spinning reels all featured a rotor that moved around the outside of a spool; the lower portion of the spool moved back and forth inside the rotor. This was standard operating procedure for many years; today, a spool that moves within the rotor is known as a cupped or internal spool. This design produced a reel with a somewhat large diameter frame or

Most spinning reel spools are easily removed and feature a skirt that covers internal components; the majority, including this one, are aluminum.

housing, which did nothing for comfort or performance. More significantly, however, was the irritating fact that line frequently got caught between the lower portion of the spool and the interior of the rotor, and was swept under the spool, causing it to be wrapped around the gears or the gear shaft. Most of the time, the spool had to be removed to get to the trapped line, which had to be unwound and usually had gear grease on it or was damaged. This process required unscrewing the drag retaining knob, which may have caused the loss of washers in some products, and always required the resetting of drag tension later.

This issue was changed by skirted spool reels, which became popular in the mid-1970s. In these, the rotor revolves around the inside of the lower portion of the spool; in effect, the lower portion of the spool is like a flange and shrouds the moving rotor like a skirt. This virtually eliminates the problem of line slipping under the spool and wrapping around the shaft, and it helps reduce the overall profile and bulk of a reel. The net result is more trouble-free casting.

Such a spool is now predominantly called a skirted spool, also known as an external spool. Skirted spools are found on nearly all modern spinning reels. Some anglers continue to use older reels with internal spools, and a few internal-spool reels are still being produced, but they make up a small percentage of the spinning reels in current use. Modern reels with internal spools generally have tight machined tolerances to minimize the line-under-spool problem, and they also have a pop-off spool button that makes it possible to remove the spool without altering the drag setting or losing parts, so they are not quite as problematic as in the past.

Spool flange and material.   Factors affecting casting efficiency include the design and material of the front spool flange (lip), the material of the spool, its diameter, and the ratio of the front spool flange diameter to the spool hub diameter.

The flange obviously has to help retain or catch line when tension is momentarily relaxed, but it cannot impede the flow of line off the inner spool when a cast is made. When line is low on the spool, it is more likely to contact that flange, which increases friction and reduces distance, so the problem becomes amplified. Therefore, the design of the spool flange can have a significant influence on casting distance.

Spinning reels that have a big, broad radius on the lip certainly hold the line against the spool as you cast, but they also funnel the line down into a small cone pattern, which constricts the line coming off the spool. A very sharp radius on the edge of the spool tends to explode the line off the spool. It will actually make the line blow off as it heads toward the first rod guide. Some manufacturers say that the sharp edge can provide 10 to 15 percent additional distance. This is not something that you can see very well with your eye by watching repetitive casts, although it can be revealed by high-speed photography.

The material of the front spool flange also has some influence on casting distance or casting ease, and this boils down to friction. Aluminum and stainless steel spools produce less line friction and are preferable for top performance. Spools made of synthetic materials, including graphite, composites, or different plastics, are usually found on lower priced reels. These materials are used primarily for economic reasons. Such spools are easily made, but the material has a relatively high coefficient of friction in relation to nylon monofilament line, so it causes a noticeable loss in casting distance. A lot of manufacturers upgrade synthetic material spools by putting a metal rim, mainly aluminum, stainless steel, or even titanium, over the flange.

Spool width and diameter.   The size of the spool is an element of casting, especially with regard to the width relative to the depth of the spool. Many spinning reels now have relatively large width-to-depth ratio spools, much more so than spincasting reels. In a very narrow spool (small width-to-depth ratio), line pulls from deeper in the spool and makes a sharper angle as it comes off. On a wider spool (large width-to-depth ratio), referred to by marketers as longer and resulting in the term "long-cast" spools, more of the line remains closer to the top of the spool flanges. When casting, the line doesn't make as dramatic an angle as it passes over the spool flange as it does on a narrower spool. This is the premise behind long-cast or long-stroke reels. Such spools also usually have a fairly large arbor diameter, which cuts back on total line capacity, but also means that there is less deep line to flow off a reel. Naturally, this is compensated to some

extent by how full the spool is with line to start, and it reinforces the point that a filled spool aids casting.

Overall, spool diameter has an influence on casting distance also, not to mention its effect on line retrieval. In the distant past, spinning reel spools had a larger overall diameter than they do today. In broad terms, the larger the diameter of the spool, the better the casting distance. If you had a spool that released line at a rate of one wrap per foot instead of at a rate of three or four wraps per foot, there would theoretically be much less friction per wrap from the spool and, therefore, greater distance achieved.

However, it is rather unwieldy to have a light-action reel with a very large spool diameter, say one of 3 to 4 inches. To get this, you would have to compromise weight and styling. Designers have moved toward lighter and more streamlined spinning reels for many years, and this styling is not conducive to overly large diameter spools. In fact, spool diameters have shrunk on all but heavy-duty models (mostly for surf and other saltwater fishing applications). Although these reels represent a numerically small portion of the total spinning reel market, line capacity as well as extreme casting distance are important issues for the saltwater market. With the majority of spinning reels used in freshwater, and in circumstances where casting a normal distance is acceptable, manufacturers have enhanced casting distance with spool lip design, optimized spool width-to-depth ratio, and especially the method of winding line on the spool.

Line winding.   While line winding is an aspect of reel operation accomplished during retrieval, it directly affects casting performance. The more even the winding lay, the better the line comes off the spool when cast. The ideal is a system that puts line on a spool as evenly as possible and allows line to come off the spool as cleanly as possible. The methods of moving the spool back and forth to get an even line lay are generally called line winding, and, in the case of spinning reels, oscillation. There are four oscillation systems or methods of line winding, and each as described here provides progressively better performance. These systems relate to the gears, which will be reviewed in more depth shortly, but this information will explain the relationship of line winding to casting function.

In general terms, the line winding operation is accomplished by turning the rotor, which drives the spool back and forth, revolves the bail assembly around the spool, brings line across the line roller, and lays it on the spool.

The most basic line winding method is a locomotive system, which operates on the same principle as a steam locomotive. The gear has an eccentric cam, and as it turns, the yoke moves back and forth. The yoke is attached to the center shaft, which in turn is attached to the spool. As the yoke moves back and forth, the center shaft and spool duplicate the motion. This is normally used on inexpensive reels, and it does not provide a very even line lay.

The Scotch yoke system is a variation of the locomotive; it utilizes an off-center pin on the backside of the crank gear, which rides in a groove on the yoke that is attached to the center shaft. As the crank gear turns, the pin moves up and down the groove in an eccentric circle and pushes the center shaft back and forth.

These systems simply move the spool back and forth and put parallel wraps of line on the spool. The wraps often bury themselves amongst each other so they do not come off the spool as easily as do better systems, and when they are put on the spool under intense pressure, they may become so deep-seated that the line jams and will not freely come off the spool under a cast, or experiences distance inhibiting pinching. If light line is employed, this pinched wrapping could lead to snapping off a lure during a cast, or it could mean that the line doesn't flow off the spool when the drag is needed for fighting a strong fish, causing the fish to be lost. In addition, these systems have a tendency to pile line up in the middle of the spool, which also impairs casting.

A variation of the Scotch yoke is the S-curve system, which provides a longer stroke (the spool travels forward and backward over a longer distance). This type of oscillating system is an integral part of achieving spools with larger width-to-depth ratios that hold a significant amount of line and cast smoothly. This oscillating method features an S-shaped groove in the yoke, and there is a pause at each end of the stroke so that the line will lay on the edges of the spool as well as in the middle. The S-curve system reduces midspool bunching and produces more even line distribution than the previously noted systems, but with some reels, there is a tendency for line to bunch at the top or (most likely) the bottom edge of the spool.

Currently, the most efficient line lay system features a helical gear or worm gear system, similar to what exists in baitcasting reels. Oscillation is achieved by a pawl connected to the center shaft that follows a groove cut in the worm gear. This method permits smooth line lay without dwelling at each end of the stroke, and permits an even longer stroke than the S-curve system. This system is more efficient at distributing line and preventing both line bunching and parallel wrapping.

Unfortunately for new reel buyers, when you look at a spinning reel in a store, it is difficult to tell which line winding system the reel utilizes. The information provided with higher priced reels usually contains some descriptive information; in the case of worm gears, this is almost always pointed out. If you compare two reels of similar size, the main difference will be in the width of the line-holding area of the spool. A greater gap indicates a long stroke and either an S-curve or worm gear system. If you turn the handle of a reel, you should notice a difference in smoothness, with worm gears having the smoothest operation. A reel with a locomotive system is fairly apparent because this produces a pretty rapid back and forth movement of the spool, and it is fairly jerky.

Retrieving/Line Recovery Features

Line is retrieved by rotating the handle, which in turn rotates the rotor and drives the spool back and forth. As the rotor rotates, the bail assembly revolves around the spool, brings line across the line roller, and lays it on the spool. The process of retrieving begins with closing the bail, and performance is greatly affected by how the line moves over the roller and is wound onto the spool, as well as by the gear type and operation.

Line pickup/Bail closure. There are manual and automatic means of closing the bail to begin picking up line. Manual closure is possible due to a reliable lever spring in the bail assembly; it exists on many reels in conjunction with automatic closure, but allows you to close the bail without turning the handle. To manually close the bail, you simply flip it down by hand. This feature is often used in live-bait fishing when it is necessary to let a fish move off before setting the hook; the angler opens the bail after detecting pickup of the bait, waits for the fish to move off, then, at the appropriate time, closes the bail manually and sets the hook when the line draws tight.

Automatic bail closure is found on all spinning reels and is activated by turning the handle, which instantly flips the bail down. To automatically pick up line when the bail of a spinning reel is open, move the handle forward, which turns the rotor and causes the bail to trip closed and directs the line to the line roller.

There are internal and external bail trip mechanisms. Internal trip bails are more common and work inside the reel so that you don't see any of the mechanism. When the bail is opened, it moves an internal pawl into a position where it will strike a ramp inside; when the rotor is turned, the pawl strikes the ramp and forces the bail to close.

External trip mechanisms operate by having some part of the open bail strike a ramp or plate on the stem of the reel handle. It may be a pawl or the back of the arm lever that makes contact; when the rotor is turned, the pawl or lever strikes the ramp or plate and forces the bail to close. In effect, this system knocks the bail down; some operate fairly noisily and with varying degrees of jarring. Various shapes and surfaces are used at the stem contact point to aid smooth operation; some, like a plastic roller, work better than others.

Although mechanically there is no advantage to either method, as a general rule the internal trip operates a little more easily and quietly than the external trip, which is why it is preferred by most anglers. However, an external trip provides more internal room for design freedom; for example, it permits the use of a larger clutch mechanism.

In practical use, the bail closure needs to operate as smoothly, quickly, and effortlessly as possible. The greatest irritation with automatic bail closures is tight operation, which for many spinning reels is the result of the positioning of the trip mechanism relative to the striking ramp or plate.

When the bail is open, the farther the strike mechanism is from the ramp or plate, the more momentum is built up when the handle is first turned and the more force is generated as that mechanism hits the ramp or plate. But if the strike mechanism is close to the ramp or plate when the handle is first turned, there is little or no momentum in the rotor, so the trip mechanism binds at the ramp or plate, particularly the latter, and more force has to be applied to turn the handle and move the rotor in order to trip the bail. The design of the part that actually causes the bail to trip, whether internal or external, has some bearing on the fluidity of this operation. Some (like the roller part on the stem) make it easier to force the handle than others.

Many high-end internal trip spinning reels have a smooth closing reel because of the location of the internal trip in relation to the normal position of the bail roller when the line is picked up. Line is usually picked up when the bail roller is close and slightly to the right of the reel stem; this provides more than 180 degrees of rotor revolution before the bail trips, which generally makes for consistent performance. Ironically, although there are disadvantages to reels with self-centering bail triggers, these have a fairly trouble-free internal trip bail closing, also because the rotor makes half of a rotation before striking the ramp that closes the bail.

Naturally, the ease or difficulty of bail closure is related to speed of overall operation. If you have to fight with the reel to close the bail, you may lose precious seconds, like when you're trying to keep your eyes on the fishing action but have to look down at the reel, or when you have to retrieve a lure the minute it hits the water.

Some people manually close the bail with their hand not holding the rod at the end of a cast. With practice, this becomes a very natural motion, avoiding the inconvenience of trying to rotate the handle to close the bail.

Because a reel is likely to be cast many times in the course of a day, this most basic aspect of spinning reel usage is very important. When purchasing a reel in a store, you can assess this feature by holding the reel and repeatedly opening and closing the bail, alternating the location of the bail each time it is opened to simulate in-field use. This is one aspect of a reel that you can seriously evaluate and compare before buying; you can assure yourself beforehand if bail closure on a given reel operates smoothly, quickly, and effortlessly, or at least more so than other products.

Left/Right retrieve. Although there are a few exceptions, virtually all spinning reels today have convertible retrieve systems, so you can set the handle up to retrieve from whichever side you prefer. Normally, it is beneficial for people who are right-handed to reel with their left hand and for lefties to reel with their right hand, so that the dominant hand is the one that holds the rod and is used to play the fish or direct the retrieve. Because the dominant hand is used to cast the rod, there is no need to take further action after casting to start using the reel; the other hand is immediately placed on the reel handle grip, and it starts turning the handle. However, anglers who are used to fishing with baitcasting or spincasting tackle may wish to maintain the same standard by placing the spinning reel handle on the right side.

This retrieval convertibility is made possible by the type of gears in spinning reels, and separates them from most spincasting and baitcasting products, which are primarily designed for right-handed cranking, or in a few cases left-handed cranking, but not convertible cranking.

Gears. The most basic part of the operation of a reel is the gear set, which in a spinning reel is less efficient than in a baitcasting reel, but better than that of most spincasting reels. Both spinning and spincasting reels have a face or right-angled gear set. The drive gear shaft is at a right angle to the pinion gear shaft. Rotational motion at the handle is transferred through a 90-degree angle by means of the gear set to the pinion or center shaft. Baitcasting reel gears, by contrast, are in-line and have parallel gear sets, which has the advantage of no lateral thrust forces on the right-angled gear set.

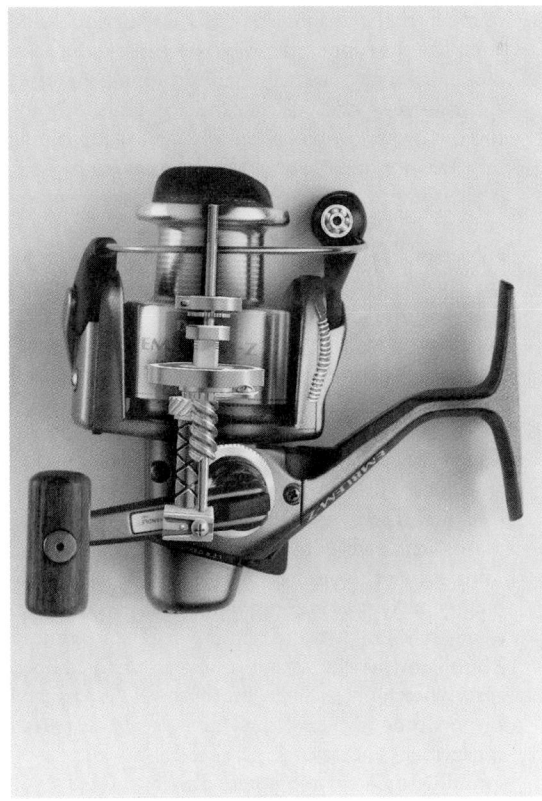

This composite image reveals the gears and some internal components of a Daiwa spinning reel.

Spinning reels may have on-center or off-center gears. Whereas most spincasting reel gears are on-center, the vast majority of spinning reel gears are off-center, which means that the axis of the crank shaft is above or below the axis of the center shaft. Because spinning reels have off-center gears, the crank shaft runs all the way through the reel and is supported on both sides. This gear set allows for convertible right- or left-hand cranking, and is durable with less motion, or play, in the operation of the reel. It also produces a much sturdier feel than on-center gears.

The least expensive spinning reels use a zinc diecast face gear and a straight-tooth zinc diecast pinion gear. The next step up is a zinc diecast face gear and a diecast helical pinion with a fairly low helix angle. There is a limit to how high a helix angle can be diecast, but this does provide a better gear feeling. The next grade up is a zinc diecast face gear and brass pinion, which is by far the most universally used combination. This provides strength and durability as well as smooth gear meshing. Most of the better reels that have a reputation for being smooth use this system. For other applications, like heavy-duty saltwater, the gears are made out of stainless steel. The face gear is powdered metal (processed into a die and pressed under extreme pressures), and the pinion is a cut gear. Aluminum forged gears are also used in some of the more expensive reels in freshwater applications, primarily for longevity and strength.

In almost any simple gear set, one gear material is normally harder than the other. This both directs and controls the action of the two parts throughout their life and actually keeps the gears running smoothly for a longer period. Two hardened gears running together would amplify even the smallest machining imperfection or piece of grit on the gear teeth.

It is common in spinning reels for the pinion gear to be brass. This is a hard material, and it allows for the more intricate machining required in this smaller part as well as absorbs the greater anticipated wear in this gear with its fewer teeth. The corresponding drive gear is most often made of aluminum in quality reels, and is sometimes made of easily diecast zinc. In either case the gear teeth should be machined as precisely as possible to assure smooth operation and long life.

Almost all reel gears in better quality spinning reels are fabricated with helical gear teeth. This means that each gear tooth is curved, rather than straight, on the gear circumference. Helical hobbing results in greater strength, thicker cross section, and a high degree of inherent smoothness. The major benefit is that, unlike straight-hobbed gears where only a single gear tooth is fully engaged at one time, helical gears allow at least partial engagement of several gear teeth at all times, spreading the load and potential wear.

Very few of the spinning reels constructed today don't use the face gear system mentioned earlier.

Some older reels (especially Zebco's Cardinal models) in the past used a cross-helical gear system (which was erroneously called a worm gear) and were widely considered to be the smoothest reels ever made. Both gears in those reels were cut gears similar to the gearing in a baitcasting reel; having a perfect tolerance was critical. This method is not nearly as forgiving as the other systems, and everything has to be aligned very precisely. Such a system is expensive to manufacture, however, and reels that had it have been out of production for a long time. Those reels were prized by many avid anglers and are still in use by owners who have taken good care of them. Despite their smoothness, however, they had relatively slow gear ratios as compared to today's reels.

Gear ratio/Cranking power. Engineers can talk in technical terms about the cranking power of a reel, about torque, and about how you can theoretically convert the force at the handle knob to the force on the line and the center shaft. But what anglers relate to in the simplest terms is how easy or difficult it is to retrieve a heavy weight, or an object that offers a lot of resistance. Reels that can easily handle a heavy load are said to have a lot of cranking power. Various factors come into play here.

The length of the handle has a bearing because that length has to do with the leverage that you can put on the handle. The longer the handle, the more leverage and the easier it is to retrieve a set load. If you make a handle longer, you reduce the force at the crank knob. It is essentially the same principle seen in wrenches; it's easier to loosen nuts with a long-handled wrench than one with a short handle. Spinning reels tend to have a better advantage than spincasting reels in terms of cranking power because their handles are very long. Because spinning reels hang underneath the rod and have a long stem, there is room to put a long handle on them, which adds more leverage advantage.

The gear set itself is also a big factor with regard to cranking power. If you have a reel with a gear ratio of 4:1 (read four to one), it's easier to retrieve a load because this is a low gear ratio. If you have a reel with a gear ratio of 6:1, which is considered high, it's a lot more difficult to retrieve a load, although you get more speed. If you're retrieving something that offers very little resistance, the high gear ratio is okay. But you need a lower gear ratio for something that offers more resistance. Thus, the lowest gear ratio reels have the greatest cranking power and the highest gear ratio reels have the least cranking power.

There is a wide range of gear ratios in spinning reels. Many have a high gear ratio in the 6:1 to 7:1 range. The gear ratio is usually marked on the reel packaging and sometimes on a sideplate decal, but may not be noted on some at all. Gear ratios are much higher on spinning reels than they are on spincasting reels, which average below 4:1. Manufacturers tend to refer to a reel with an upper-end gear ratio as a "high gear ratio" or a "fast-retrieve" reel, but this is all relative. A 5:1 reel might be called high, and in comparison to a 4:1 spincasting reel, it would be high, but it is clearly lower than some other spinning reels. And in any event, gear ratio does nothing more than designate the mechanical gear action of the reel, which is not the whole story about true speed.

No matter what the gear ratio is, the evaluation of a reel's ability to retrieve line should boil down to something engineers call Inches Per Turn of the handle, or IPT. This is the amount of line recovered per turn of the handle, or, simply, line recovery. That is a better measurement of retrieval ability than gear ratio. Line recovery is determined by spool diameter, which is a key dimension for any reel and which sets the circumference of the line level on the spool and the amount of line wound onto the spool with each turn of the reel handle. A 6.2:1 ratio reel with a 1.5-inch diameter spool, for example, will recover about 11 inches of line per handle turn. A 6.2:1 gear ratio reel with a 2-inch diameter spool will recover almost 19.5 inches of line per handle turn. This is the true measurement for anglers interested in retrieve speed.

Anglers cannot quickly determine line recovery when evaluating a reel they might purchase because specifications on the circumference of the spool aren't provided on the reel or in the packaging materials. In a 6:1 ratio reel, for example, you know that one revolution of the handle puts six wraps of line on the spool, but if you don't know how much line is gained with each complete wrap, you don't know the actual recovery. (Of course in a reel that you own, you can determine the gain by marking the line and measuring it.)

For a greater discussion of this subject, *see: Gear Ratio and Line Recovery.* While most consumers have a notion that gear ratio is of primary importance in retrieval, and some think that the higher the ratio the better, there are other factors that go into this, and line recovery is a major one. Remember, however, that reels with low gear ratio do better the greater the load and the more resistance offered by lure or fish.

Line winding/Twist reduction. The impact of line winding on casting as well as its relationship to the gears was previously detailed, but in terms of retrieval and overall fishing performance, line winding is equally important, especially with regard to its affect on line twist, which is the most common difficulty incurred with this type of tackle. Although improper use of fishing equipment is the major cause of line twist *(see: line)*, the normal operation of a spinning reel may promote line twisting.

In an effort to reduce line twist when winding line, much attention has been paid to the bail roller. Rollers used to be primarily ceramic; most today are made of chrome plated brass and some have a tungsten coating. An important aspect of the line roller mechanism is dissipating the heat to prevent the line from breaking down. A line roller that actually rolls is important for this. Some bails have either no

This is a magnified view of a twist-reducing line roller on the bail of a Daiwa spinning reel.

roller or a stationary roller. Most line rollers actually turn as the line comes in to reduce friction on the line.

Some higher priced reels have a ball bearing in the roller to help make it turn easier. The downside to this is that grit and water can get to this spot, so it requires regular lubrication to prevent destruction of the ball bearing. Most ball bearings aren't designed for use in places where there is a lot of water, as happens on the bail roller when line constantly pulls water across it.

The size and shape of the line roller are factors that affect twisting. Although line rollers have to move the line from the bail to the spool, the problem is that twist can occur if the line turns over on itself while moving from the bail to the spool. The different systems in use now have sharp roller slopes and grooves in the roller to help prevent twist. They are built to even larger diameters, they keep the line in one spot on the roller and prevent it from moving around, and they eliminate slack line movement on the roller surface. These components by themselves do not prevent twist, but they do help keep the line in such a position that it does not spin over.

Another key to preventing twist is the proper alignment of the line roller and the spool. If the system is aligned properly, there won't be line twist that is attributable to the line roller. In order to put line on a spool in a controlled even manner and to eliminate line twist, the line roller and the bail arm have to be positioned precisely in relation to the spool. The manufacturer has to design the reel so that the line roller is perpendicular with the axis of the spool, which allows for proper line placement. Another factor is the distance between the line roller and the surface of the spool. Rollers mounted close to the spool form sharper angles at extreme oscillation points and contribute to rollover twist formation.

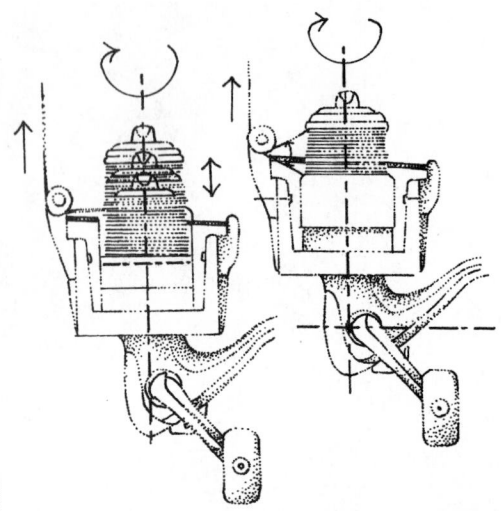

In most spinning reels, when line is pulled off the spool and across the roller, the spool simply turns clockwise without the spool moving up and down (right); this repeatedly changes the angle of line from spool to line roller and increases its tendency to twist. In an oscillating spool reel (left), in addition to turning clockwise the spool moves up and down on the shaft when line is pulled off the reel; this provides a constant angle from spool to line roller, thereby helping to prevent twist.

A recent innovative reel system eliminates critical angles and prevents twist by oscillating the spool both during the retrieve and when releasing line under drag. It moves the mechanism that drives the spool oscillation from the body of the reel up, under the spool itself. Here, a worm drive, similar to the levelwind on a baitcasting reel, is connected to the pinion gear/rotor assembly and oscillates the spool. It allows the spool to rise and fall as a pawl travels through the endless worm track. This true spool

This computer-generated illustration represents the interior of the unique Marado Helix spinning reel, in which a worm drive, connected to the pinion gear/rotor assembly, oscillates the spool both during the retrieve and when the spool is releasing line via the drag.

oscillation design permits the spool to oscillate during the retrieve and, unlike other reels, also when the spool is releasing line via the drag.

With this design, the line is continuously fed straight from the spool to the roller guide at all times, no matter how far a fish runs or what the line level on the spool is. Critical angles are completely eliminated. This means that the drag force on the line does not vary due to changing line feed angles. This prevents twist caused by line rollover when the line feeds from the spool to the roller, and eliminates line damaging friction.

Handle/Rotor. As previously noted the length of the handle affects cranking power, and longer handles provide more cranking power than shorter handles. Some handles seem longer than they actually are because they have a counterbalance on the nongrip side, but this is simply an optical illusion. Length is really measured from the handle grip to the crank shaft. Obviously, handles that are too short decrease leverage, and those that are too long are awkward.

Nearly all spinning reel handles have a single grip, but there has been a trend toward adding a counterbalanced extension to them. Although found on higher priced reels, the value of this is arbitrary, especially in lightweight reels. Admittedly, a counterbalanced handle feels good in a store when a person takes a reel and gives the handle a wild spin. Likewise, a balanced rotor gives the reel a stable feeling, too. When you spin such a reel in a store, and it has no wobble whatsoever, you'll likely say it "feels good." However, an angler never spins the handle wildly like this when fishing, and seldom turns the handle this fast when retrieving or fighting a fish, particularly when using the smaller models and angling for the average freshwater fish. You can't make your hand turn the handle this fast. When you're cranking at most normal rates of retrieve, you will never notice whether the spinning reel handle is balanced or not.

There is more merit to having a balanced rotor than a counterbalanced handle, as sensitivity is enhanced with a waver-free action. Theoretically, a smoother working reel with less wobble or vibration makes it easier to detect a light strike. Conventionally designed spinning reels are somewhat unbalanced because the rotor has a heavy bail mechanism on one side. If the weight of the entire rotor is balanced, you get a smoother retrieve, and it feels better when you're cranking it.

Manufacturers of better spinning reels use computers and design software to balance by weight, adding or adjusting weight in the required spots when they are designing the reels to get the rotors perfectly balanced. Rotors balanced in this fashion use the required functional components placed at the proper positions of the correct mass to cause the rotor to be "balanced" while it is rotated. This is a relatively new technique, one that was developed as a result of new computer-aided design (CAD) technology utilized by engineers. Some manufacturers still rely on balancing rotors by adding counterweights at the appropriate location, much as car tires are balanced today.

Ball bearings/Bushings.   Bearings and bushings provide a way to minimize friction on rotating shafts. Bushings don't spin as freely as ball bearings, which are typically viewed as durable and reliable and a way to add rotational freeness to the system. They are usually employed to differing degrees in medium- and high-end reels; they may also appear in some lower priced reels, but keep in mind that there are different grades and materials of ball bearings. There is a performance difference in these grades, although the average consumer doesn't know which grade is in a given reel. Some lower grades of ball bearing actually add noise to a reel.

Spinning reels may have from one to nine ball bearings, although it is debatable as to whether having more than four or five of these adds significant performance advantages. What the added ones seem to be is a marketing ploy, and a supplemental cost factor.

The most important place to have a ball bearing is under the pinion gear. When a reel is advertised as having one ball bearing, it will always be under the pinion. The second most important spot is behind the crank, or drive, gear. On a two–ball bearing reel, the second ball bearing is usually on the left side of the crank gear, because most people reel with their left hand, and this side experiences the most load. A reel with three ball bearings often has a bearing on the other side of the crank shaft as well so that both ends of the main gear are supported with a ball bearing. On an oscillating worm gear system, a ball bearing may be placed on each end of the worm shaft.

These are all useful bearings and do improve performance of the system. The continuous anti-reverse clutch is counted as a bearing by some manufacturers, and this feature is seldom found on a reel with less than two ball bearings.

When you add more ball bearings than these you have to look for creative places to put them, and most of these are of dubious value, like on the handle knob, in the bail assembly, in the drag system (front and/or rear), and possibly in the line

Bearings in a top-quality spinning reel may include, clockwise from top: a continuous anti-reverse clutch bearing, a bail roller ball bearing, and five standard ball bearings.

roller. A ball bearing on the line roller is even of dubious value because it is exposed and potentially subject to fouling. In the primary places, however, ball bearings do result in smoother operation and greater reel longevity. For a more detailed review of ball bearings and bushings, *see: Reel, Fishing.*

Drag Features

The purpose of the drag function on any reel is to let line slip from the reel at varying pressures when force is applied to the line. It serves as a sort of clutch, or shock absorber, and only works when the anti-reverse mechanism, which will be explained shortly, is employed (which it is virtually all the time). A properly set drag is especially important when using light line, when playing large and strong fish, and when fish make strong and sudden surges while being landed. If an angler never catches large fish, only uses heavy strength line, and is content to wind fish in, then it is conceivable that his drag will never be used. But heavy line is not suitable for many species and many methods of fishing, and it is practically inevitable that at some time, even with moderate strength line, an angler will catch a fish that weighs more than the actual breaking strength of his line, and which requires some finesse, rather than sheer strength, to land. This means that the drag will come into play, because if it doesn't, the force will exceed the strength of the line and the line will break.

When the drag comes into play, it allows the fish to continue applying force, but at a pressure that is less than the breaking strength of the line, because when the force reaches a certain level (usually less than 50 percent of the line's breaking strength), a properly set drag mechanism will allow line to slip from the reel. The way it allows line to slip from the spool is by turning or revolving the spool. A spinning reel spool (as well as a spincasting reel spool) is stationary when the line is cast and when it is retrieved; the spool moves back and forth when line is retrieved, but it does not turn. However, when there is sufficient force to activate the drag, the spool turns in a clockwise rotation, which allows line to come off under tension. Thus, although spinning reels are said to have a stationary spool, that spool will revolve when the drag is employed.

Understanding how to use and set drag is one of the most important aspects of sportfishing and is reviewed in detail elsewhere *(see: drag)*. Clearly, however, the functioning of a drag is a critical element of every reel, and the quality of reel drags varies considerably.

The drag mechanism on spinning reels, as on most smaller reels for various fishing applications, used to be fair to poor at best, but these systems have changed markedly since anglers started using all of the various equipment types for more challenging fishing, and placed greater demands on the rod, reel, and line. While low-end spinning reels do not have sophisticated drags, most medium and higher quality models have reasonably good drags, and many of the higher priced ones have very good drag systems.

Common drag factors. While the gear sets in spinning and spincasting reels are comparable, the drag systems are a little bit different. They basically work off the same principle in that they're adding pressure to, compressing, and causing resistance on, the spool. In most spinning reels, there is more uniform pressure on the spool than there is in a spincasting reel, perhaps making some of the drags a little bit smoother as well as more controllable. There are certain things to look for when evaluating the drag systems of these, as well as other, reels, and although this information is supplied elsewhere in slightly different form, it bears inclusion here because of the great importance that the drag feature has in practical fishing.

The first item to look for in a good reel drag is variation. If you set the drag to create 4 pounds of tension on the line, you want it to stay at 4 pounds. If it varies to 5 and 6 pounds, that is not particularly good. Influencing factors include how fast you pull on the line, and where you set the drag. If you have 10-pound line and you set the drag at 2 pounds, you'll have less variation than if you set it at 8 pounds. With lower force, it is easier to control variation.

Another aspect is maximum drag force. Ideally, you should try to set the drag at 30 to 50 percent of breaking strength. If you could only set it at 4 pounds for a 10-pound line, that's probably not enough for some fishing situations. So you should check the maximum force you can obtain on the reel before using it to make sure that it will be adequate for your needs. However, achieving absolute maximum drag force—where the drag doesn't slip at all—is not as important for actual fishing as many anglers believe.

Some anglers are very interested in being able to readily get maximum force, which locks the reel down and completely prevents the drag from slipping. This maximum force is seldom beneficial for most fishing activities, including playing large or strong fish, unless you're using very heavy line. Where it is most likely to be useful, however, is when a lure or hook gets snagged and cannot be freed; this situation may require you to lock the reel down, point the rod directly at the snag, and pull back to free the hook or break the line *(see: unsnagging)*. If the drag cannot be locked down completely, then line will slip off, and it may be harder to free the hook.

Many people mistakenly think that they need to set the drag very tight for effective hooksetting. When you have 20 yards of line out, and you have rod flex, line stretch, and the dampening effect of the water to contend with, you don't need very much drag force at the reel. You cannot exert the maximum pressure when you set the hook. But when you set the drag pressure at or near maximum

force, when the fish is close to the boat and there is less contribution made by line stretch, rod flex, and water, having the drag locked down may mean that the line cannot absorb the sudden shock of a quick run, even from a fish whose weight is less than the breaking strength of the line. People are often amazed that a 5-pound fish can break 14-pound line, but that does not happen if the drag is set properly and the washers are allowed to slip freely when necessary.

In typical fishing, anglers set the drag at 30 to 50 percent of the breaking strength of their line; most, if they have a 10-pound line, for example, set the drag by feel at between 3 to 5 pounds, meaning that it will take 3 to 5 pounds of tension to cause line to slip. This is measured with a short length of line on a straight pull off the reel.

Another important aspect of drag is range of adjustment, or how many revolutions you can turn the control mechanism on the reel. If you consider line tension in terms of revolutions of the drag knob, you'll see that it is desirable to ramp up the drag very rapidly to get to 30 percent of the line's breaking strength. Few people are going to set their drag tension at less than 30 percent of the line strength. Ideally, you should get up to that 30 percent number with just a short revolution of the knob. Then, for the 30 to 50 percent breaking strength range, there should be a lot of adjustment available to cover that range and fine-tune the drag. After reaching 50 percent of the breaking strength, the drag should ramp up very quickly to a full lockdown position; this is in case you have to break off, pull on a snag, or have more tension for a strike in heavy cover.

Thus, the important aspect of drag range is how many rotations it takes to get to the lockdown point, and where is the most adjustment range for fine-tuning. Some spinning reel drags, usually on the lowest-end models, have a small rotation from no drag to maximum drag. That might encompass one full, 360-degree, rotation of the adjustment knob. The best drags allow more than two, and usually up to three, full rotations of the drag knob, meaning that they will rotate 720 degrees or more. This maximum adjustment range is accomplished through the spring system that applies the load to the drag stack.

The problem with adjustment range comes from conflicting demands. Some anglers want a wide range of adjustment while others want to get maximum force. These differences require tradeoffs in design elements. There's a point where smoothness versus lockdown just aren't compatible.

Normally a reel is designed for an average weight of line. If, for example, a reel is designed for 10-pound line, a normal drag setting for that would be about a third of the line weight to prevent line breakage. So 3 to 4 pounds would be the medium range. But it still has to be able to achieve lockdown pressure while maintaining a smooth drag. For anglers who need a range of adjustments, the best system for this 10-pound-rated reel is one that can actually break 10-pound line yet have a smooth range of adjustment and smooth drag performance throughout that range.

Another element of drag performance is the amount of force required to start the drag slipping. On some drag systems, this force (called breakaway force) can be significantly higher than the actual drag setting. This condition is especially found in reels where the drag has been tightened and left to sit for several days. The drag washers and drag lubrication tends to take a "set." The next time the drag is called on, additional line tension is required to overcome this "set" before line tension returns to the intended setting. Many a big fish has been lost by the angler who forgot to loosen the drag before storing equipment for the next trip, or who didn't check the drag setting before beginning to fish.

Drag systems.   Spinning reels have either front or rear mounted drag systems. Front mounted drags were the norm for many years, then rear mounted drags became overwhelmingly popular, and then there was a move back to front drags in better quality reels and virtually all saltwater models. Today there is a mix of both in the marketplace, with many experienced anglers preferring front drag because of smoother performance.

Both systems feature one or more discs or washers that direct adjustable tension on the spool shaft by turning an adjustment knob. Generally, both systems include hard metal washers on the extremity of a stack or series, and soft or nonmetallic friction washers on the inside of the series. Tension on the main shaft is increased by turning the knob clockwise and decreased by turning it counterclockwise.

On a front mounted drag the adjustment knob is at the very top of the spool, and for many such reels, the spool is actually removed by turning the knob counterclockwise until it is completely free of the center shaft. On some of these reels, there is a pop-off button in the middle of the knob, which is pressed to free the spool from the shaft, allowing the drag adjustment to be unaltered when the spool is removed.

On a rear mounted drag, the adjustment knob is at the very bottom of the reel and is generally circular. A screw in the middle of the knob holds it fast to the center shaft so that the knob cannot accidentally be removed. Turning this knob completely counterclockwise does not remove the knob and has no bearing on spool removal. The spool on such a reel is simply removed by pressing a pop-off button at the top of the spool, regardless of the drag tension setting. Such easy spool removal is an advantage to rear mounted drag reels, although spool removal is not a frequent necessity for many anglers.

There are other advantages and disadvantages to both systems. It is possible, for example, that the drag control knob on some front mounted drag reels will become so loose that the knob will fall off and be lost, which ends fishing with that reel until a new knob is obtained. That cannot happen with a rear mounted drag reel.

Rear mounts are also somewhat easier to adjust during the act of fishing because they keep hands away from the line. Adjusting drag tension on a front mounted drag while playing a fish means that your hand may get in the way of the line. On a reel with top mounted drag, the line extending from the bail roller, which is usually under a lot of tension, is often in the way when a quick adjustment is necessary. This is generally viewed as a disadvantage to top mounted drags, although for many anglers it is seldom necessary to increase or decrease drag tension during the act of fighting a fish, and, in fact it should not be adjusted if it has been set properly.

Drag tension should be checked and adjusted before using a reel for the first time, at the beginning of each new fishing session, after a spool has been removed, and whenever the tension setting has been increased or decreased while the reel is in use. In theory, the majority of tension setting adjustment takes place when the reel is not actually being fished, and seldom when a fish is being played, so the location of the drag adjustment knob may not be that critical.

What is most critical, in fact, is the smoothness of the drag, or its ability to perform without erratic motion over a wide range of adjustment. The smoothness of a drag is controlled by the materials, the way they are assembled, and the size of the washers. Front drags are thought to be smoother than rear drags. Many, although not all, are smoother, mostly as a result of larger components in the drag system.

This exposed view of a Fin-Nor Ahab spinning reel reveals a very large drag disc in a front-drag system that allows two-way access to the drag; the spool can be rotated counterclockwise and removed without affecting the preset drag setting.

S

It is important for drag washers to dissipate heat, which builds up rapidly in a reel when the drag is under a lot of pressure. The size of the washers is a major element of this, with spool material also being a contributing factor. Aluminum dissipates heat more efficiently than synthetic spools. Therefore, aluminum spools are a better choice for reels expected to handle long runs by strong fish. Smaller washers build up heat more quickly and dissipate it less efficiently than larger washers. Poor dissipation causes erratic drag performance. The design and placement of front mounted drags allow for the use of larger washers, which is one reason they perform well. A rear drag can be every bit as smooth as a front drag but has difficulty maintaining that smoothness at higher line tension settings unless it uses the same size drag washers as the front drags. When large washers are used in a rear drag reel, the body starts getting bigger, which to some people is less aesthetically attractive. Because the trend in most reels has been to smaller overall size, rear drags have had correspondingly sized washers. Front drags, however, allow for small overall body size but larger washers. In comparable quality front and rear drag reels, the washers are of similar quality, but the size differs. So many, if not most, rear drags aren't as smooth as front drags because of design constraints.

Incidentally, research and development personnel say that it is not the overall size, or outside diameter, of a drag washer that is critical to obtain maximum line tension, but the mean diameter. That is a calculation of the inside diameter and the outside diameter. If you take a large outside diameter and a small inside diameter, the mean diameter is actually closer to the inside than it is to the outside, so in order for drag washers to be more efficient, they should have a large inside diameter as well as a large outside diameter to obtain maximum drag lockdown.

Naturally, the washers in a stack or series should be as close as possible to each other in size. Large diameter front and rear washers promote smoothness. Some reels have large diameter washers in the front of the stack and smaller washers in the rear of the stack. It's best if the stack is tailored front and back on the spool to make it efficient.

Drag washers.   Ideally, the drag in any reel will operate smoothly, without hesitation. In other words, it will start immediately when needed and maintain a constant rate of tension as line flows continuously off, as well as keep the same level of tension as it is periodically called upon during the time it takes to play and land a strong fish. The less variation that there is in the performance of the drag, the better. Some of this performance is affected by the type of drag system and the range of adjustment it is capable of, as previously noted. Some of this is affected by the number and material of the washers.

Drag washer material, which is usually the same whether in front or rear drag systems, is really most critical in the setup stage of usage. One of the problems with drags and materials is that they are asked to do something that is very difficult. It is desirable to have a drag that slips freely and yet can create a high amount of pressure. It has to be able to slip, yet sustain a high load, perhaps even a complete no-slip lockdown load. Thus, you're looking for two opposite attributes in a washer to accomplish these needs.

Drag washer materials in spinning reels, like those in other reel types, have evolved over the years. Phenolic washers were used in the past, as were various fibrous washers, and some people replaced manufacturer-supplied washers with oil-soaked leather, composition cork, and other materials. Felt, nylon, cork, and metal have been common in many spinning reel drag washers. The primary material in modern high-end spinning reels, most of which have very smooth drags, is Teflon or a proprietary synthetic composite, including a material called TDM, which is a mix of fiberglass, graphite, and Teflon; in spinning reels, these materials do a reasonable job of satisfying the two opposite demands. Teflon, for example, has a very low coefficient of friction, which allows the spool to turn while providing a smooth slip surface; it has the same static and kinetic friction coefficient, which means that it takes the same force to start it moving as it takes to keep it moving. In other materials, it takes more force to start movement than to maintain it. A material that does not have a low coefficient of friction produces a jerk or spurt in spool momentum as the line pays off. This smoothness, incidentally, can be aided by lubricants. Many of the lubricants used by manufacturers are also proprietary, and some are Teflon impregnated greases; they help considerably to smooth the drags out.

There is a co-mingling of different material washers in many drags. Because heat dissipation is one of the most important elements to deal with, metal washers, which dissipate heat well, are used in conjunction with washers made from other materials, which provide the smooth slip surface. In better quality reels, for example, Teflon may be used with stainless steel.

The drag system in most midpriced spinning reels is generally of fairly good quality while the drag in most high priced models is good to excellent. The majority of spinning reels sold are used for light and medium-light applications in freshwater and, for the majority of users, the drags are actually overbuilt. Freshwater anglers, for the most part, do not require exceptional drag performance unless they use the reels for such species as steelhead, salmon, striper, and big trout. Many freshwater anglers catch relatively small species on average, and fish that do not require a lot of drag usage except during extraordinary circumstances. Then there is the average bass angler, who wants to lock the drag knob down so that a fish can't run into cover. As a result, many freshwater anglers do not appreciate or understand the drag function, and barely pay attention to it, even if they have a spinning reel with a good drag. That is why the drag is overbuilt for them.

Saltwater anglers, on the other hand, frequently need and really test the performance of a spinning reel drag. Thus, drag performance and drag components are mainly significant to people who catch fish that will put some pressure on a reel. The irony is that in freshwater or saltwater, you never know when a fish will come along that does just that, so if you do understand drag and prepare for fighting a strong fish, you'll be covered.

Combinations/Levers. Some spinning reels have sported combined drag systems in which there are both front and rear drags, the front drag being the primary one for fish fighting and the rear drag being a means of releasing tension on the line while the bail is closed. The rear drag is small and has a very light setting, so if a fish takes live bait, for example, it can move off under minimal resistance. When ready, the angler engages the main system and uses it to play the fish. Generally, there is a lever to engage or disengage the main drag; in some systems, the main gear is engaged automatically when the handle is turned. The idea is to have a preset main drag as well as a lightly adjustable secondary drag so that it's possible to quickly switch between them. It is primarily an advantage in fishing with bait; if you tried to accomplish the same thing with an open-bail reel, extra line could wind off the reel (especially if drift fishing in current) and possibly delay hooksetting.

There have also been some spinning reels that featured a lever or trigger that was used to apply supplemental pressure to a spool. The lever is mounted on the stem and activated by the index finger; this is similar in location to, but different in operation from, a bail trigger, which opens the bail. In operation, when the spool is turning under preset drag tension, additional pressure is applied to the revolving spool by pulling the lever. Theoretically, this allows you to have a light preset drag, yet provides additional pressure if needed when fighting a fish.

This feature is one that has not caught on with anglers and which has some serious practical drawbacks. Gauging the right amount of supplemental pressure to apply via the lever is probably the biggest problem, because you must use an appropriate amount of pressure to correspond to the strength of the line and the circumstances, and it is easy to apply too much additional pressure. The possibility of grabbing the trigger accidentally and applying unnecessary additional pressure exists, as does the possibility of inadvertently holding onto the lever for too long a time when you really need to completely let go.

Anti-Reverse Features

When the handle of a spinning reel is turned forward, line is wound onto the spool. If the handle can be wound backward, in reverse, line unwinds from the spool provided that there is tension on the outgoing line. Some reel handles cannot be turned in reverse. Most, however, can be turned in reverse by the operation of a switch on the outside of the reel. This switch, known as the anti-reverse, allows anglers to put the reel in reverse by turning it to the off position, or to keep the anti-reverse constantly out of use by turning it to the on position.

When the anti-reverse switch is in the off position, the handle and the rotor can be moved forward and backward; line can come off the spool when the handle is turned backward and also when the drag slips. When the anti-reverse switch is in the on position, the handle and rotor can be turned forward but cannot be turned backward; line can only come off the spool when the drag slips. A reel with this switch is said to have selectable, or selective, anti-reverse, while one without it is said to have nonselectable anti-reverse.

At one time when reel drags were poor and often unreliable, it was useful to have a reel with a selective anti-reverse feature. Anglers felt more comfortable when playing a strong fish if they could reel backward to let line out to play the fish. Many were accustomed to doing this with baitcasting, or levelwind, reels, which initially had direct drive, and had to be back-reeled, or wound backward, when a strong fish put a lot of pressure on it.

There are some anglers who back-reel for freshwater fish and advocate this on its own or in conjunction with using the drag. Many do so because they do not want to rely on the drag, or have a reel with a poor drag system, or simply do not set the drag properly (usually they tighten it too far). The trouble with back-reeling is that it is hard for many people to reel backward quickly enough to keep up with a rapidly turning handle when a strong fish speeds off; therefore, they have to let go of the handle, which usually spins wildly, and which may cause a snarl, backlash, or overrun upon completion of the swift back-reeling. When anglers try to grab the rapidly turning handles, they often smack their fingers, which caused the old reels to be called knuckle busters. Another problem is that you have to gauge the action of the fish in order to reel quickly to keep up with it. It is possible to back-reel small fish, like 2-pound bass, as long as the drag is a good one and properly set, but it is better to keep the anti-reverse engaged, especially for stronger and harder-fighting fish.

Today, reel drags are quite reliable and efficient, especially when properly set, and there is no reason to back-wind, even if a reel has the ability to do so. Today's spinning reels do not really need selective anti-reverse, but most of them have it in order to give anglers—especially competitive bass anglers

Think paddlefish are bizarre? The prehistoric shark *Helicoprian* had a coiled lower jaw known as a tooth whorl, which coiled springlike back on itself and hung below the head.

S

who insist on cranking the drag tension up high—the option of using it. Probably the only time that the average angler uses this feature is when line is accidentally wound around inner or outer parts of the reel and needs to be worked free.

What is more important for anglers, however, is how the reel operates when the forward turning motion is stopped. There is a natural tendency to pull up on the handle when not reeling, whether to set the hook or to momentarily stop while retrieving. In older models of reels, and in some lesser quality current models, there is considerable play in the handle and rotor when the reel stops, and the handle may actually turn backward slightly before engaging. This tendency produces a feeling of sloppiness or instability, and if there is too much backward movement of the handle, it may adversely affect hooksetting and may allow a loop of slack line to appear on the spool in some retrieval motions, which may eventually impair casting. Ideally, the reel should engage instantly and firmly, and better spincasting reels have features that allow this, which are usually called continuous anti-reverse or infinite anti-reverse reels. These should keep the drive gear from moving even the slightest bit backward.

In today's spinning reels, there are two major variations on spinning reel anti-reverse systems. The continuous anti-reverse system, or one-way clutch, as some people call it, is used in most higher end spinning reels. This system provides seemingly immediate engagement of the anti-reverse system, allowing instantaneous bone-jarring hooksets. This system is composed of a device underneath the pinion, which looks like a roller bearing (it may be called a one-way roller bearing and really is a bearing, except its configuration allows it to only turn in one direction). This is a part that is most commonly used in the printer industry to control the location of ink on paper and the rotation of parts. In reels its job is to completely prohibit backward travel of the shaft. It does this very well on most reels, and if it doesn't do it as well on some reels as on others, it is because of different tolerances in the other components. This system results in a continuous or infinite anti-reverse.

The second type of anti-reverse system is the pawl and ratchet system. This system is similar to the anti-reverse system on winches on the front of a boat trailer. A metal pawl engages gear teeth or ratchets to prevent backward rotation of the rotor. A finite number of teeth or ratchets translate to some backward rotation of the rotor before the pawl engages. The number of teeth on the ratchet plate really determine how fast the anti-reverse system will engage. The more teeth, the faster the system will engage. As with all things, optimizing one feature often creates other problem areas. To add more teeth, either the ratchet plate has to become bigger in diameter, or the teeth must become smaller. Obviously, with a bigger diameter plate, the reel itself must become larger. And with smaller teeth, the anti-reverse system becomes weaker.

Actuating the ratchet plate can be accomplished in several different manners. One of the most common is to utilize a small slider or actuator (generally plastic) on the crank gear shaft. The actuator contacts a pawl in such a fashion that when the crank shaft is rotated forward, the actuator keeps the pawl from contacting the ratchet gear located on the center or pinion shaft. When the reel is cranked backward, or when the rotor rotates backward, the slider actuator forces the anti-reverse pawl into the anti-reverse ratchets, thus preventing backward rotation of the system. This system does not produce a "clicking" sound, because the slider actuator keeps the pawl away from the ratchet teeth, except when the rotor turns backwards. When the anti-reverse is in the off position, the selector switch prevents the slider actuator from forcing the pawl into contact with the anti-reverse ratchets. In this condition, the rotor is allowed to freely turn forward or backward.

Manufacturers have compensated for the inherent limitations of the typical pawl and ratchet system in better spinning reels by installing continuous anti-reverse devices or moving the anti-reverse into the rotor itself. Most anti-reverse systems are located on the gear shafts inside the body of the reel. Recently, manufacturers have found a way to move the pawl and ratchet anti-reverse system to the rotor of the reel. In this position, a bigger diameter is available for the ratchet plate. In some reels, ratchet teeth are actually located on the inner diameter of the rotor. As noted, this bigger diameter ratchet plate allows more teeth on the ratchet, providing a more immediate stop on pawl and ratchet systems. Some reels actually have 60-point anti-reverse systems, which is a tremendous improvement from the less than 20-point systems obtained when the anti-reverse is in the reel's body.

In considering these anti-reverse systems for speed of engagement, it is also important to consider where the anti-reverse mechanism is located in reference to the gear set itself. In spinning and spincasting reels, the gear ratios are arranged so that the pinion gear, and thus the center shaft, rotate faster

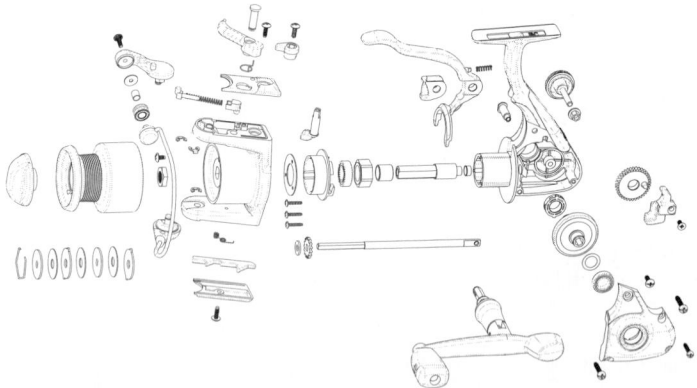

Shown are all of the parts of a Quantum Hypercast spinning reel, which includes a bail trigger, counterbalanced handle, front drag system, and continuous anti-reverse.

than the drive shaft. A low speed rotation at the reel handle is translated to a faster speed at the device that winds line on the spool. This is important to note, because it requires more efficient anti-reverse mechanisms, whether pawl and ratchet or continuous anti-reverse, to be placed on the center or pinion shaft. A more immediate stop is achieved when the anti-reverse is actuated from this shaft instead of the drive shaft. An additional advantage is that the jarring forces producing a radical hookset are absorbed in the anti-reverse mechanism instead of being transmitted through the gear set before the anti-reverse engages. In the latter condition, more wear and tear is passed on to the gear teeth, potentially causing preliminary gear roughness, and perhaps even broken gear teeth.

As discussed earlier with regard to bail opening systems, there can be several settings for anti-reverse systems. These settings are generally selectable by means of a lever or sliding switch at the rear or along the bottom side of the reel. If the reel is equipped with a selectable anti-reverse system, it will have a combination of either an on-off setting, or an on-off–self center setting. In the on setting, the anti-reverse system is in fully functional mode. In the off setting, the anti-reverse is turned off and the reel handle will freely rotate backward to release line from the spool with the bail closed. The self-center position allows the angler to rotate the handle backward to a degree. Backward rotation will stop when the line roller, and in most cases casting trigger, are positioned correctly directly underneath the rod for the next cast.

Most modern spinning reels have silent anti-reverse, which means that when the anti-reverse is engaged, there is no noise in the system. Some low-end units, and much older reels, have an audible anti-reverse, so there is a constant clicking sound when you turn the handle, which is due to the fact that the pawl is forced into the ratchet constantly, and as you turn the handle, the pawl bounces up and down on the ratchet. The same thing happens when the drag is used and the spool revolves to let out line under tension, which, incidentally, is what used to produce the phenomenon of "screaming reels" that some writers prosaically described. Now when the drag is used on most reels, there is no sound.

Ergonomics/Convenience Features

Weight/Body materials. The issue of ergonomics is fairly simple in a spinning reel, and boils down to a comfortable fit in the hands, easy access to features, and overall weight.

Spinning reels sit under the rod handle; the stem of the reel has a foot that is seated in the handle so the outfit is held by wrapping your fingers around the reel foot, with the stem laying between the fingers. Most people place the stem between their middle and third finger. A minority place it between their third finger and little finger. In each case, it is held close to the base of the fingers, and

this contact with the stem, as well as the separation between the fingers and the weight that sits there, may be uncomfortable, especially if the reel is held for long continuous periods.

Obviously, this part of the reel needs to be as comfortable to hold as possible. The thickness and width of stems vary on reels, and preferences among anglers do as well. A thin stem is generally viewed as being more comfortable, as is a perpendicular stem in the area where it is held, but to some people, a wider stem, which puts more surface area between the fingers, provides greater support than one that is thinner and narrower. Some reel stems have been padded for cushioning or contoured to relieve pressure points. The design of the stem becomes more important as the weight and the amount of continuous use increase.

Another factor, especially for cold weather anglers, is how the stem feels when the reel is cold and handled with bare hands. Metal is colder than composite materials, so the latter feels better in cold weather and a padded area may offer some warmth. A bit of electrician's tape or some type of padded tape wrapped tightly and evenly around the handle stem can help ward off the cold contact. There are a lot of good lightweight gloves that can be worn without sacrificing finger movement, so this may be the best route to take, especially if you need the strength of a metal frame and stem for the type of fishing done.

An especially important practical and ergonomic issue is that the distance from the foot to the spool or bail roller has to be such that the line or bail trigger can be readily grabbed with your index finger. For people with small hands, including children, this may be a problem, especially with larger reels. People who have large hands or thick fingers often have a problem with lighter spinning reels, which seem to have a clearance between the foot and bail assembly or trigger that was designed for small or thinner fingers. Thus, when they press the bail trigger, it pinches against their fingers, or when they turn the handle, the bail assembly smacks their knuckles. This may not only occur to people with large hands or thick fingers, but to others with normal size hands who hold the reel between their third and little fingers, primarily when using bail triggers. That type of hold, while it is comfortable to those who prefer it, places two fingers above the stem, so that when the trigger is pressed by the forefinger, there is less room for it to lever back, meaning that it pinches against the middle finger and may not open. This requires people to change their hold, which can be disrupting, sort of like having to hold your pencil differently than you've always been accustomed.

Weight, of course, has an influence on comfort for nearly everyone except those with the strongest hands and wrists. While both anglers and manufacturers would like reels to be as light as possible—after all, rods are much lighter than reels—there are

S

trade-offs to going light. Lighter reels are comfortable to hold, but they cannot be so light that they lose durability and strength. Reels can be punished not only through the torque and pressures of playing a fish or unsnagging, but also from abuse, like being dropped or banged or stepped on.

Spinning reel housings used to be made solely out of diecast aluminum, which provided plenty of strength but was heavy. When plastics and various composite synthetic materials became available, people didn't trust them, and only the cheaper reels used them.

It should be noted that plastics can offer significant advantages, not only in the tackle industry but many other places. Complete experimental car engines are currently being produced from plastic resins. Proper selection of engineering grade resins today for fishing reel components provides a combination of strength, durability, corrosion resistance, and economic price unparalleled by any other class of materials. In fact, design engineers claim gear sets could be made of plastic resins that would be quieter, smoother, and more durable than conventional diecast or brass gear sets. Yet, would the public be willing to take a chance on these gears? Many gear sets in handheld portable power drills, and screwdrivers are molded from plastic today.

Eventually more expensive reels used the better synthetic components and they became much more accepted. Then aluminum bodies became preferred again on better reels because of their durability. Mostly these changes evolved because of marketing and an understanding of the demands that tough fishing placed on reels.

Certainly aluminum didn't get any lighter, although some synthetics did get better. Nevertheless, even with the advanced state of synthetics today, aluminum is more durable. It moves less and is less prone to allowing misalignments in the system under pressure. A strong reel has a stable mounting system, so gears maintain their strength and don't wear out as fast. The stronger the housing, the more stability for the gears.

A lot of force is applied to a reel under heavy use, and in a spinning reel, it is applied to the gears in a manner that is opposite to the norm. A small gear normally drives a large gear, so you put a small force in and get a large force out. In a spinning reel, however, a large gear drives a small gear, so the forces are reversed, and it takes a lot more pressure on the crank gear to turn it under a load. This is why higher gear ratios have less cranking power. There is a speed increase instead of a power increase. Consequently, the forces generated in the gear teeth are substantial and resistance to turning in the rotor forces the gear teeth apart. If the housing or frame is made of stiff materials to back the gears up, spreading can be kept to a minimum and the system lasts longer.

Most freshwater anglers don't put substantial force on their reel when retrieving or playing a fish,

but they do when they are snagged on some object. Wrestling a hook or lure off the bottom is typically how the average freshwater angler generates a lot of force. In saltwater, where more large fish are caught, it is more likely that an angler will put substantial force on a reel when retrieving or playing a fish.

Handles.	Handles and knobs are largely a matter of personal preference. Nearly all spinning reels have a single-knob handle, and some have a counterbalanced handle. Strength and cranking power are governed by the distance from the crank shaft hole to the knob, not from the end of the counterbalance to the knob or, in the case of two-knob handles, the distance between the knobs.

There is no benefit in terms of reel function or technical performance for having a dual-knob rather than single-knob handle, yet dual-knob handles are popular on mid- and top-range spincasting reels and on virtually all baitcasting reels, in part because people feel that it is easier to grab either one of them quickly, as when they aren't looking at the reel. There is no strength advantage to dual knobs, and since spinning reels are mounted under the rod rather than on top of it, most people are happy to do without the extra weight and awkward look of a dual-knob handle.

Handles on spinning reels are made from engineering grade plastic resins, zinc, and aluminum diecast alloys. The knobs vary in material, although most anglers prefer a soft material that is easy to grip, especially when wet, and that may be contoured for comfort. On higher end reels, a soft rubber is often used on the knobs rather than hard plastic, and they are more flat and paddle shaped than round. If the handle and the knobs are not large and comfortable enough for the user, they will be fatiguing and perhaps counterproductive.

Appearance.	Overall appearance is largely a subjective matter with no practical bearing on performance. Spinning reel design has steadily favored smaller and more streamlined bodies, and the styling (and color) follows automotive trends with rounded smooth contours, which are more pleasing to the eye than the shapes that used to prevail. Some popular reels get a body face-lift after a few years to keep up with trends, but they may not be much different internally.

Spool features.	Being able to change a spool quickly is a nice feature for those who might use a supplemental spool filled with a different type or strength of line. Spool removal is easy on rear drag reels, all of which have a front pushbutton spool release. Some front drag reels also have a push-button release, but most feature a drag adjustment knob that must be wound off to release the spool, which is a bit less convenient. One of the newer innovations in top saltwater spinning reels is a spool that can be removed simply by pushing down on the spool and rotating it counterclockwise. This is done without touching the drag adjustment knob, so the drag tension remains where it was.

Some spinning reels come with a spare spool, and if they don't, a spare can readily be purchased from the manufacturer. Spares are generally the same size as the original spool, but there may be some that have a smaller or larger arbor diameter, or it may be possible to get an arbor spacer, which snaps around the spool arbor and decreases line capacity. It is seldom possible to mix and match spools from various reels, although it would be nice to put a larger diameter (outside diameter, not arbor) spool on a reel whose original spool diameter was small. This is not possible on current reels, but there was once a product that sported different screw-on rotors with different diameter spools. It never caught on, probably because people decided that they could just as well buy another reel with a larger diameter spool, if they could find one.

Many spinning reel spools, especially smaller models for freshwater use, sport a tab or clip that can hold line when the terminal tackle has been removed and the reel is being stored. This keeps loose line from spiraling off the spool and is a nice feature, provided that the tab is slightly recessed on the spool exterior. If the line keeper tab is not recessed, and protrudes just a smidgen past the spool surface, it will occasionally catch a spiral of line and the tab will have to be cut off.

Other convenience features on some spinning reels include: a switch on the rotor or bail assembly that allows the bail to collapse for compact storage; a lever, button, or other means of folding the handle easily for storage; line size and capacity information on the surface of the spool.

Saltwater features. Although most of the issues previously reviewed are relevant to any spinning reel, the products that are intended for saltwater use have a few different elements that are worth mentioning. This is not to infer that a spinning reel that is primarily used in freshwater cannot also be used in saltwater, provided that it has an appropriate drag mechanism and line capacity; it certainly can, but the reel will need daily and careful washdown maintenance to help avoid corrosion, and it must be very sturdy if it will be used on really tough fish.

Reels that are going to be used regularly in saltwater need to have more built-in corrosion resistance, very sturdy components, and a top quality drag. Most saltwater angling entails encounters with larger and tougher fish than found in freshwater, and the environment is far more punishing, so reels that will be used regularly in saltwater have to withstand the environment and the application. These are built heavier, with more substantial components, including beefier drags and more corrosion protection through the use of stainless steel and/or anodized coatings. Naturally, they are heavier reels, and they often have large spools to accommodate 200 to 300 yards of line. These spools should be forged rather than diecast and the spools should preferably be made from a high grade of

stainless steel. Graphite spools may do for light saltwater fishing, but not where heavier lines and intense pressure are involved. Super-heavy pressure on a graphite spool will break it, especially if a person puts stronger line on the reel than what it is designed for.

Virtually all saltwater spinning reels have a multi-element top mounted drag system and most have large drag washers, at least two or three stainless steel aircraft grade ball bearings, and a very sturdy handle; there are no bail opening triggers and few folding bails. The retrieve ratio is usually in the 4.5:1 to 5.1:1 range, with a few slightly higher, but not in the ultrahigh ranges that are found in many freshwater spinning reels. The reason—lower gear ratio for cranking power—is obvious and especially acute for saltwater fish. Even reels that are designed for saltwater need to be properly cleaned after each use and periodically maintained.

Rods

Spinning rods are different in one important and distinguishing respect from baitcasting rods and most spincasting rods: The guides mount under the axis of the rod and thus are placed under it, and the reel sits under the handle rather than on top of it. This also occurs with flycasting tackle *(see)* because these products are theoretically geared more to casting functions than to fish fighting functions. This doesn't mean that they do not fight fish well if properly designed, just that casting is generally their greatest attribute.

The rings on spinning rod guides are also larger than they are with other tackle, in order to accommodate the large spirals of line that come off the spinning reel spool when casting, and to minimize the effects of coiled or possibly twisted line rapidly funneling through the guides. A single foot is standard for the guides, meaning that there is just one attachment point for the rod to the blank, which improves rod action. In addition, spinning rod guides are designed so that they extend a greater distance from the rod shaft than with other types of rods in order to help reduce line slap, which is the tendency of line that is cast from a spinning reel to strike the rod shaft, thereby increasing friction and reducing casting distance.

Spinning rod handles are straight, with fixed or adjustable (ring) reel seats, and both one- and two-piece models are common. Handle length and overall rod length vary widely according to application, ranging from 4-foot ultralight models to some surf fishing versions in the 14-foot class. Shorter models exist for ice fishing (jigging).

Action, taper, and material construction vary considerably. Spinning rods are commonly made of graphite and a mix of graphite and other materials, and many models are specifically tailored to special uses and styles of fishing.

Unlike reels, many of the issues pertaining to spinning rods—functions, materials, and components—

China's Fan Li is believed to be the first person to breed and raise fish (reportedly common carp); he wrote the first known document on fish culture, a book entitled *Fish Breeding,* in 473 B.C.

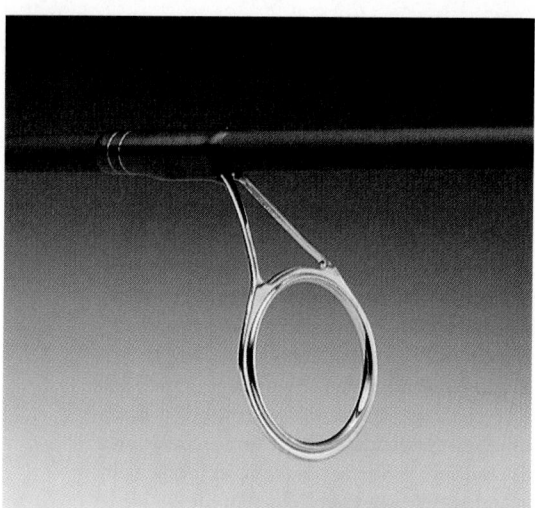
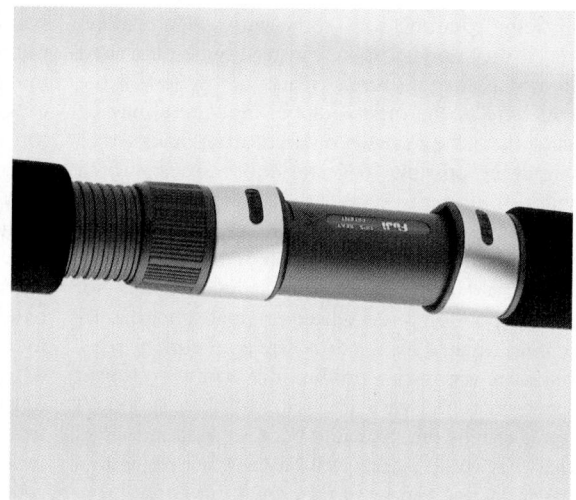

The single-foot guide (left) and fixed reel seat (right) are common on spinning rods.

are similar to those of other rods, and these are more fully detailed elsewhere *(see: rod, fishing).*

Using Spinning Tackle

Line. Although all of the various line strengths from 2 through 30 pounds are employed with spinning gear, 6, 8, and 10 pounds are certainly the most commonly used strengths and are a choice of many anglers who do varied and general fishing. For light-tackle fishing 4- to 6-pound line is popular, although 8 pounds might be light for some circumstances and species; 2- and 4-pound strengths are ultralight for most circumstances, with more people using 4 than 2. Exceeding 12-pound strength is less common in freshwater and more common in saltwater, and the heaviest strengths are seldom used in freshwater but often in saltwater, especially for surf fishing and offshore use.

Fishing line is rarely pre-spooled onto a spinning reel, although with some lower priced models and some start-up combinations, it may be. Users make their own selection of line type, strength, and brand, usually purchasing it separately and either spooling it on the reel themselves or having it done by a tackle dealer.

Nylon monofilament is the overwhelming choice of line type for spinning reels, and there is some usage of microfilament line for freshwater use. Lead core, wire, and braided Dacron lines are more suitable for levelwind or baitcasting reels, and are seldom employed on spinning reels of any size. The better nylon monofilaments for spinning reel use are those that are supple rather than stiff. Stiff, wiry lines tend to coil more and spring off the spool. Lines with low memory cast better on spinning reels. Some nylon monofilaments have less memory than others. Braided and fused microfilament lines, which have very low memory as well as little stretch, cast well on spinning reels and are compatible with both wide and narrow spools.

Spinning reels are designated for certain line strengths or diameters. Most reels indicate the strength of line they are intended for, and some also give a diameter. Diameter is as important as strength (or more so); there are many lines with a thin diameter but conventional strength. Thus, if a spinning reel holds 150 yards of conventional diameter 8-pound line, it will take much more yardage of an 8-pound line with a 4-pound diameter. The labeling on a box or spool of a good quality line should not only denote strength, but also diameter, and if you know the diameter, you will have a clearer picture of how much line to put on the spool.

Generally, it is best to keep within the recommended line strengths when filling a spinning reel. If the manufacturer recommends using 6- and 8-pound line with the reel, that recommendation is based upon a standard 6- or 8-pound line with a conventional diameter. You can probably use conventional diameter 4- and 10-pound line as well, but it would not be worthwhile to use much higher line. Not only are spool size and capacity issues, but this reel is not meant to handle the greater stresses that might be generated with much heavier line. So, for example, putting 15-pound line on that reel could be problematic.

However, and this is where things get tricky, there are 15-pound lines that have the diameter of a conventional 8-pound line, so you can get it to lay on the spool quite nicely. Nevertheless, it is still line with a 15-pound breaking strength (and some 15s actually break much higher); this may be capable of overpowering the reel. If the rod is up to handling a lot of stress, and the line is rated to break at a minimum of 15 (often more) pounds, and the reel is meant for up to 8-pound line, then the forces generated on the reel by maximum pressures could be harmful to some parts (handle, gears, crank shaft, bail) of the reel.

On the other hand, you might use an 8-pound line with a diameter of conventional 4, and achieve much greater line capacity on the reel at a line strength that the reel is rated for. Or, you could "cheat" a little bit and use 10-pound line that has a diameter of conventional 6-pound line, if that benefited your fishing situation (see: line).

This is a grossly misunderstood aspect of spinning reel usage that has largely been brought about by the emergence of thin diameter lines (nylon monofilaments, braids, and microfilaments). Remember that, although reels are primarily designated according to line strength and general application, many good reels also bear line diameter ratings.

Filling/Refilling the spool. The various aspects of properly filling a reel spool are detailed elsewhere (see: line). Putting line on a spinning reel spool is less complicated than putting it on a spincasting reel because the spool is open and accessible whereas the spool on a spincasting reel is under the cover.

If you are a new angler or new to the use of spinning reels, the fastest and easiest way to fill a reel is to have it wound on by a linewinder, which is a professional machine. Many tackle dealers offer this service to their customers, although it is seldom available from a mail order supplier or mass merchant.

In brief, the spooling process entails mounting the reel on the rod and running line from a service spool through the rod guides beginning at the top of the rod. Open the bail and tie the line to the arbor of the spool, snip off the tag end excess, close the bail, and reel the line on under tension. It is important to avoid or at least minimize twisting of the line during the spooling process, as detailed elsewhere (see: line). Fill the spool to within $1/8$-inch of the lip, but do not overfill, which may cause line to coil off the spool and tangle.

When the line gets low on the spool, or when it is old and needs replacement, you have the option of completely refilling the spool, or refilling only part of the spool. If a spinning reel holds 150 yards of line, economically it makes sense to refill with just 60 or 80 yards of line rather than the full 150, depending on a number of factors.

When you partially refill the spool, you have to tie a line-to-line knot (see: knots, fishing). The weakest portion of a line is usually the knot, so this connection must be a good one to maintain the basic strength of the line, should that knotted section come under pressure. If you never use more than the first 30 or 40 yards of line on a reel, then such a knot is unlikely to come under pressure. If you tie a perfect line-to-line knot, it shouldn't matter if and when it does come under pressure.

The line-to-line knot must be small and smooth, however, for it to lay on the reel without interference, and to minimize friction when it comes off the spool lip and through the rod guides. Some people tie a bulky line-to-line knot that gets in the way.

Of course, the line that stays on the back of the spool, to which the newer line is connected, must be in a usable condition and of the requisite strength for your fishing needs. That line, which is usually referred to as backing when another section is tied to it, has to hold up to the demands of the fishing situation when put under pressure. If it does not have the proper strength, it needs to be replaced, and the entire spool should be refilled.

Line twist and its prevention. Line twist has been an inherent problem in spinning reels since they were introduced and is somewhat analogous to the problem of backlash in baitcasting tackle in terms of causing line tangles and irritation. There is no spinning reel user who has not experienced some degree of line-twisting trouble when using either their own or someone else's spinning gear, and, unfortunately, some anglers experience far more line twisting than others. There are anglers who have given up on this tackle because of line twisting trouble, but there are ways to deal with twist, and manufacturers have in recent times produced spinning reels that are much less likely to instill twist than older products. Giving up on spinning gear because you've experienced twist is not a good idea, as this tackle serves a useful purpose and can perform some functions better than any other tackle type when used properly.

Although twist can occur when using other types of tackle, it is more prevalent with spinning gear, and line twist does cost spinning tackle users valuable angling time, induces frustration and

Twisted loops often form on the spool of a spinning reel and generally cause further problems; a loop like this should be removed as soon as possible.

irritation, and may cause otherwise unnecessary replacement of line. It may also contribute to lost lures and breakoffs. Therefore, spinning tackle users need to know what causes line twist and how to avoid as well as cure it. The general phenomenon of line twist has been addressed elsewhere *(see: line),* so this section will address specific issues relative to spinning reels because of the significance this issue has with these products.

Line twist damages nylon monofilament line by building ever greater stresses as it accumulates in the line due to a variety of causes. Under load, as when fighting a fish, these stresses may weaken the structure of the line and can lead to break-offs. A twisted line is like a loaded spring. When tension is released on a cast the line tends to balloon outward from the axis of the line flow. This increases line-to-guide friction and reduces casting distance. It is also why some line twist disasters (a wad of mangled line) tend to wrap around a spinning rod's gathering guide. Twist is of little problem when line is kept under tension. The stored spring energy due to twist is evident only when tension is released. Then, a snarl can almost instantly appear.

Technique is one of the agents of these snarls. A semi-slack slow-retrieve application with lures that have minimal water resistance, for example, does not provide constant tension, and if a line is predisposed to twisting due to other factors, such tackle usage may foster twist and line snarls, which they would not in applications with more water resistant lures and under constant retrieve speeds that maintain tension on the line. But, if you need to use a semi-slack retrieve, then that's what you have to do, and because that does not cause line twist in itself, you have to address the root problems.

No matter what steps you take, however, you must realize that most spinning reels, especially older models, actually put a twist in the line just by virtue of their design, which is a root problem that is not experienced with revolving spool tackle.

Reel manufacturers have devoted a great deal of effort and research time to analyzing and attempting to eliminate line twist from spinning tackle. Among the many discoveries made by the best known producers of quality spinning reels is the fact that it is impossible to totally eliminate all of the causes that contribute to line twist in spinning reels. Some advertising claims would lead you to believe that certain reels eliminate twist; actually they may minimize twist (in some cases to a significant degree), but they do not entirely eliminate it, and they cannot eliminate twist that is caused by improper angling use.

As previously noted in the review of spinning reel components, some twists are caused by the physical design factors built into the reel. For example, as the rotor and bail of a spinning reel rotate, line is put under tension that draws it to the low point of the typical roller on the bail arm. This line movement happens when the line rolls over the

guide surface until it reaches the low point. The rolling action causes the line to twist. Each time slack is allowed to form in the line, through rod action, for instance, the line can move on the roller. When tension is reapplied, the line can again roll and twist. These many small twists are cumulative and eventually become a problem, especially when combined with other causes.

The twist problem is compounded by nylon monofilament line, which has a memory and tends to retain its coiled shape after it has remained on the spool for a while. These coils can help twist-induced spring to tangle the line more easily. Luckily, after several casts the line absorbs some water, softens, and loses some or all of the coil. This is why some spinning reel users soak their line, preferably in warm water, to relax the memory before starting to fish with it.

One of the absolute worst causes of line twist is turning the spinning reel handle while the drag is releasing line. Excited anglers continue to quickly crank the handle, typically against a drag that is set too light, while no line is retrieved. Each turn of the handle puts multiple twists in the line in a direct relationship to the gear ratio of the reel. A 4.4:1 ratio reel puts over four twists into the line per turn of the handle. High-ratio reels add even more twists. Being conscious of what the drag is doing at all times while fighting a fish, or using a slightly tighter drag, can minimize this.

Wide- or long-spool reels that increase distance between the front and rear spool flanges have also contributed to line twist. Through spool oscillation on the retrieve, the line is wound onto the spool in a straight line from the line guide to the spool. But when the drag is employed, and line is taken off under tension, for example with the spool at the full extension of its oscillation stroke, the line wound onto the top of the spool forms a sharp, critical angle on its travel to the line guide on the bail. Tension on the line pulls the line downward along the spool and causes it to roll over the surface of the remaining line. This rolling action creates twist in the line and under tension creates friction that can result in damage and wear. While this phenomenon is at its worst in long-spool reels, it does occur to a lesser degree in traditional size spools.

Another factor that adds to this problem is the distance between the line roller on the bail and the line surface on the spool. This distance has an effect on the angle formed in the line at extreme oscillation points and contributes to roll-over twist formation. Rollers mounted close to the spool form sharper angles and can add to the twist problem.

Designers and engineers over the years have provided partial solutions to the overall problem through new mechanisms and parts refinements. Some of the early successes were the introduction of the roller line guide, which lowered friction and strain and increased the diameter of the guide. Reels were even designed to allow the entire rotor and bail to rotate backward when line was released to the drag. This had the same effect as the back-reeling technique, which literally unwinds and untwists the line as it is released. This design proved to prematurely wear out drag parts and caused the occasional knuckle smacking. Another manufacturer deliberately created a very wide diameter spool with a short distance between the spool flanges to minimize oscillation induced twist under drag release.

More recently, reel makers have concentrated on the line twist induced by the line roller. These parts are now built to even larger diameters with integral ball bearings. This reduces friction and stress on the line. It also allows the more important design addition of a narrow slot that instantly captures the line and eliminates the possibility of twist caused by the line rolling over the surface of the roller, as well as eliminates slack line movement on the roller surface. Removal of this almost unnoticed contribution to line twist has been a remarkable improvement.

Spools are also reaching a realistic compromise in geometry. Extremely long flange to flange distances have been reduced while spool diameters have increased to the point where oscillation strokes are shorter and line memory is reduced. This, in turn, decreases the critical angles formed under drag release and reduces the tendency of the line to roll over itself, inducing twist. Some reels help prevent line twist by eliminating critical angles as a result of oscillating the spool not only during the retrieve, but also when the spool is releasing line through the drag. The line is continuously fed straight from the spool to the roller guide at all times, no matter how far a fish runs or what the line level on the spool is. Therefore, there is no twist from line roll-over when the line feeds from the spool to the roller.

Obviously some degree of line twist may be inevitable when using spinning reels, but a great deal can be done to reduce it to acceptable levels. As noted elsewhere *(see: line)*, among the root problems, or contributing to them, is the way that your equipment has been used. Line twist can be reduced by using a good quality ball bearing swivel with lures that rotate or spin in the water. Incorrectly filling the reel from a bulk line spool can result in a tremendous amount of line twist even before the first cast is made. These are basic line-use issues that you can control.

You can also control how you play fish when using spinning gear. Try to fight all fish with the spinning reel spool in the center of its oscillation stroke. In this way, when the drag releases line, feed angles are reduced and so is twist. Try to maintain some tension on the line at all times to control slack line situations and keep the spring from unloading. If there is any twist in your line at the end of a day's fishing, cut off the lure and hardware and trail an empty line through the water to remove the twist, then reel it back on the spool under moderate finger tension.

Untangling line. There are two types of tangles that occur with spinning reels when a loose coil or loop of line is covered by a tight wrap of line. One is the obvious snarl that catches in the rod guides or slips through the rod guides. The severity of this varies, and most can be untangled by patient manipulation and reverse picking of the various coils and strands. In bad cases, the line will have to be cut, which means that the lure or hook has to be retied and also that a certain amount of line will be lost on the edge of the spool. If this happens a couple of times, the line level on the spool may be reduced to the point where casting performance is adversely affected.

The other type is the obvious appearance of a loose coil on the spool itself. This loose coil is what leads to the bird's nest tangle that comes off a reel, and if you notice this, you should address the problem by removing the spool rather than by casting the line again or pulling it off the top of the spool. If you remove the spool from the reel, you can pull line off from the back of the spool, over the skirt or flange, until you get to the problem loop or coil. Wind the line back onto the spool and then put it back on the reel. This is more easily accomplished on reels where the spool can be removed without unwinding the drag adjustment knob.

Try to address what causes these snarls or loops in order to prevent their occurrence. The problem occurs when line is retrieved on little or no tension, and gets placed onto the spool in a loose loop, which is then covered by other loops. Often a stop-and-go type of retrieve, such as the motion used in slowly working a jig, causes this. Make sure that line retrieval is accomplished under tension, and keep an eye on the spool to spot a loose loop before it becomes a major snarl.

Matching and selecting. As with any type of fishing tackle, the issue of matching the right reel to the right rod is an important one, but in these times, it is a relatively easy one. Some spinning reels and rods are sold in combination, although these are usually of lesser quality with minimal features, and more geared to light and beginning usage. Most of the time, a reel is purchased separately from a rod. Matching these up used to be referred to as balancing, and properly paired outfits were referred to as "balanced tackle." This simply meant that the rod and reel felt right when used together; the outfit was not overly butt heavy due to a large reel paired with a lightweight rod, or tip heavy due to a small reel paired with a medium or heavy action rod.

Fishing rods are virtually all labeled by line classifications and by weight of objects to be used, which practically assures that you don't put a light-duty spinning reel, for example, loaded with 6-pound line, on a medium-heavy rod that is rated for 10- to 14-pound line use. What you might do is look for a rod with a specific type of action, say one that has a fast taper for casting light lures, and look for this in the length that you prefer for the most frequent uses that you'll put the tackle to.

Spinning tackle is often classified by the manufacturers as being in a certain category and for a certain type or range of usage. Reels, for example, might be classified as ultralight, light, medium-light, medium, medium-heavy, and heavy, but the exact definition of this can range from one manufacturer to the next and, in any event, is most likely to be found by the line capacity information on the reel or in the packaging literature. A reel that is designated as medium freshwater/light saltwater is pretty self-explanatory. Anglers, of course, have different definitions of what a light, medium, or heavy rod is, too, and so there is often some confusion in terminology. A rod and reel for use with 6-pound line, for example, is light to most people, yet classified as medium by others. Like describing the weather as partly cloudy or partly sunny, it all depends on your point of view, and, of course, conforms to the size of the species you'll catch and the conditions you'll face.

When selecting tackle, as well as matching a rod and reel, you must take into consideration the kinds of fishing that you expect to do. A beginning angler may be unsure what to select without any prior fishing experience. Guidance from a knowledgeable

salesperson could be very helpful; such a person is more likely to be found in a specialized store (a sporting goods dealer or bait and tackle shop). You might also seek guidance from an acquaintance or relative who has experience with this type of equipment and some knowledge of the fishing that a beginner is likely to do. Some manufacturers provide equipment guidelines on their packaging or display materials to provide general direction for appropriate usage, and this can be helpful.

In a general sense, selecting spinning tackle starts with a determination of the size of fish that you will be likely to catch an evaluation of the conditions under which you will be fishing. The larger and stronger the fish, the stronger the tackle necessary for beginners, until you get the experience to use lighter gear. Fishing where there are a lot of obstructions usually requires medium or heavy grades of tackle. Small fish, fewer obstructions, and clearer water usually are suitable for lighter tackle. Most selection thus starts with a determination of the line strength necessary for the conditions, and having the rod and reel appropriate for this. You should also give some attention to line capacity. If you will be fishing in a way or under circumstances that

General Guidelines for Matching Spinning Tackle

Line Strength	Lure Weight	Reel Type	Rod Type	Fish Species
2–4 lbs.	$1/16$–$1/4$ oz.	ultralight	ultralight; 4–$6^1/2$ ft.	stream trout, small bass, panfish, white bass
4–8 lbs.	$1/4$–$3/8$ oz.	light	light; 5–7 ft.	freshwater: panfish, trout, largemouth and smallmouth bass, white bass, pickerel, shad, walleye, small catfish; saltwater: small bonefish, redfish, striped bass, other inshore species
8–12 lbs.	$3/8$–$5/8$ oz.	medium	medium; 6–$7^1/2$ ft.	freshwater: catfish, walleye, pike, salmon, striped bass, large bass and trout; saltwater: most small to midsize bay and inshore species, smaller offshore species
14–17 lbs.	$1/2$–$1^1/2$ oz.	medium-heavy	medium-heavy to heavy; $6^1/2$–9 ft.	freshwater: large catfish/salmon/striped bass/pike/muskie/lake trout; saltwater: tarpon, striped bass, larger inshore species, midsize offshore species
20–30 lbs.	1–3+ oz.	heavy	heavy and ultraheavy; 9–13 ft.	freshwater: very largest species; saltwater: surf fishing, largest inshore species, offshore species

require a lot of line, then you'll need an appropriate amount of line on the reel. The preceding table provides a general guide to matching fishing tackle, but is by no means an absolute definition.

For some people, spinning gear is purchased strictly according to price; in other words, you have a certain amount of money to allocate to the purchase. Generally, spinning tackle is less expensive than baitcasting tackle but a bit more expensive than spincasting tackle, and the lower-end items have fewer features and a lower performance factor. For undemanding fishing activities, and as an entree into the game, these rods and reels are fine. You get more features, better materials, and improved performance as you move up in price, especially in regard to reels. Higher priced reels should provide not only elevated performance, but also greater useful life if you take care of them.

If you purchase the tackle from a store, you'll have an idea how comfortable it is between your fingers, and whether the weight, general feel, handle knob, and general operation are to your liking. Make sure that there is enough room for your fingers between the handle and the bail or bail trigger; you don't want to find out later that either of these smacks your fingers. It's a good idea to mount the reel on the rod that you intend to use with it, to make sure that it sits securely in the reel seat; this is seldom a problem, but it could be, especially if you're using it with an older rod.

The purchase of fishing equipment relies a lot on word-of-mouth or the advice of in-store sales personnel, who are expected to know the value of certain features or the differences among various products. This is a problem, because many such personnel do not know enough about these matters to be really helpful. Also, manufacturers generally do a mediocre job of fully explaining features in their own literature and ads. While they are quick to point out benefits or claims, such as that a certain reel casts further, they seldom explain exactly how this is accomplished, or how much further it will cast. Many of the points that were reviewed earlier have emphasized issues that a prospective purchaser should be aware of and should consider in the selection process.

Holding the rod and reel.   Most spinning reels have a convertible retrieve system, so you can set the handle up to retrieve from whichever side that you prefer. Normally, it is beneficial for right-handed people to reel with their left hand and for lefties to reel with their right hand, so that the dominant hand is the one that holds the rod and is used to play the fish or direct the retrieve. Because the dominant hand is used to cast the rod, there is no need to take further action after casting to start using the reel; the other hand is immediately placed on the reel handle grip and starts turning the handle. This is how most people use a spinning reel.

The most common means of holding a spinning outfit is by wrapping the middle fingers around the reel foot and stem, as shown; some people prefer to hold it between the middle finger and forefinger. The reel is always underneath the axis of the rod, never on top of it.

As for the actual grip on the rod and reel, this is again personal preference. Because spinning reels sit under the rod handle and the stem of the reel has a foot that is seated in the handle, the outfit is held by wrapping your fingers around the reel foot, with the stem laying between and close to the base of the fingers. Most people place the stem between their middle and third finger. A minority place it between their third finger and little finger. Whatever feels best for you is right, provided that you're comfortable casting and holding it that way for long periods, and can readily access the bail roller or trigger.

Casting technique.   The actual method of casting is accomplished in the following manner.

Begin with the reel under the handle and facing away from you. Adjust the drag to the proper tension level. Hang the casting plug (or lure or weight when fishing) from 3 to 6 inches below the tip of the rod and turn the handle to bring the bail roller close to the reel stem. If the lure is not in this position, reel it up to the tip and strip line off the reel by pulling on the line above the reel. Pull just enough off the spool so the lure is the right distance below the rod tip, while at the same time bringing the bail roller close to the reel stem and extended index finger. The bail roller must be properly positioned to allow the finger to easily grab the line and to touch the lip of the spool.

To open the bail manually, grab the line at the roller with the tip of your forefinger and flip up the bail with your other hand. To open the bail automatically, depending on the reel, either extend your forefinger over the roller and grab both the line and the trigger, or simply grab the trigger.

Keep tension on the line with your finger; this will be released at the optimum point of rod flex in the forward motion of the cast. When this tension is released, line flows off the spool and out through the guides, carried by the weight of the object at the terminal end of the line.

To execute the cast, the reel should face away from you and you should be looking at the back of your hand. Point the rod tip at and slightly above your intended target. When you are learning, and whenever striving for accuracy, get the rod and reel

S

out in front of your body and make the rod follow an imaginary line from your nose to the target. Bring the rod back sharply, using your wrist and forearm (not the whole arm), and allowing the weight of the lure to flex the rod. In a continuous and unhesitating motion, and still using the wrist and forearm, bring the rod forward in an accelerated motion, releasing the line with your forefinger during the forward stroke when the rod tip is pointing above the target.

The amount of flex in the rod depends on the rod design and material, with pure graphite rods only requiring a short hammering type of stroke, and more parabolic composite or fiberglass rods requiring more of a back-and-forth motion. With a bit of practice, you'll learn what adjustment to make for the rod action as well as for different lure weights, and you'll learn at exactly what point in the forward stroke to release the line, which is a major element in attaining the proper trajectory for accurate placement. If the lure goes too high in the air, the line was released prematurely; if the lure lands a short distance in front of you, the line was released too late. It shouldn't take too long to get the hang of it, which is one of the key benefits of using this type of tackle.

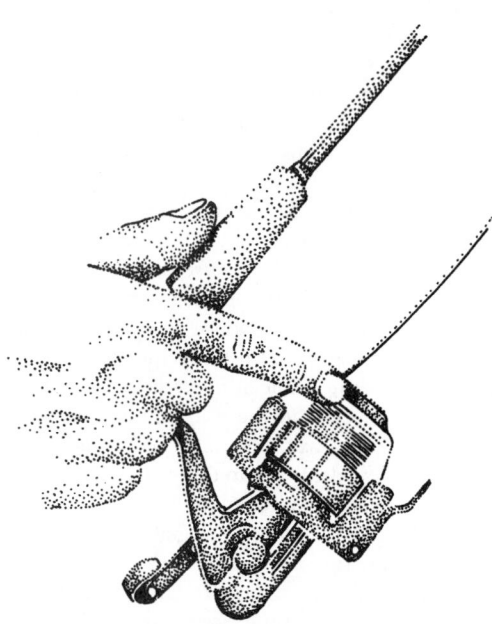

To feather line for accuracy when casting with spinning tackle, place your forefinger near the lip of the spool to contact outgoing line.

The released line can be moderately controlled during a cast by allowing it to brush against an extended index finger from the rod-holding hand; the finger should be held near the spool lip. This is called feathering and is the most common method of controlling line that is cast from a spinning reel, although it is only moderately effective at achieving accuracy. Better accuracy can be obtained by allowing the outgoing line to brush against the forefinger

of the noncasting hand, although the open bail wire may make this difficult. To do this, the front of the reel has to be in the palm of the other (usually left) hand; extend the left forefinger out and press it against the lip of the reel's spool, keeping it there during the casting motions. When the cast is made and the weight released, keep the left hand in place and control the line by applying slight pressure on it with the left forefinger. This method puts your left forefinger on top of your line as it peels off the spool during the cast.

On some reels, the location of the open bail arm sometimes makes this two-handed method of line control a little difficult, but it can nevertheless be done. An improvement upon this is removing the bail arm, as described later.

In lieu of feathering the line in either of these manners, many spinning reel users simply stop the cast altogether by pressing the extended index finger against the spool; by closing the bail; and by the end of forward momentum when the lure or weight reaches its target. Abruptly pressing a finger against the spool and closing the bail may cause the plug to stop abruptly and even lurch back toward you; allowing the lure to stop when it loses its own momentum is only suitable for open-water situations and cannot be used when obstructions are present or when pinpoint accuracy is necessary. These acts are not conducive to pinpoint casting, although they may be acceptable in situations where it is not necessary to place a lure or bait in an exact spot.

Achieving accuracy is largely a matter of practice, reflex, and timing. This is greatly aided by feathering the line to control speed and distance, although it is still necessary to have the right rod speed and lure trajectory. Mastering this takes times and practice.

Although most people do not rate spinning tackle very highly in the accuracy department, some anglers are able to be extremely accurate, so obtaining accuracy is partly a matter of how far you are willing to take the practice element, and using the right rod and weight of lure. It is true, however, that when using lures and fishing in cover, baitcasting tackle (once you have mastered spool control) is easier for most people to consistently obtain accuracy with. For some spinning tackle users, achieving casting accuracy is not a big issue because they do a lot of open-water casting with this equipment.

Achieving distance is an issue that many spinning tackle users dwell on, and which is repeatedly emphasized by reel manufacturers in touting the benefits of their products. This deserves a thorough review, since it has relevance to other tackle and fishing techniques as well. For more information on this and all aspects of casting, including other methods of achieving accuracy, *see: Casting*.

Setting/Checking drag.   Before making a cast for on-the-water fishing, it is vital to set the drag to the proper amount of tension. Issues pertaining to drag in spinning reels were reviewed earlier in this section, and using and setting drag is covered in more detail elsewhere *(see: drag)*. Briefly, however, the drag on a spinning reel is adjusted by turning the front- or rear-mounted drag knob. Turning this clockwise increases tension, and counterclockwise decreases it. If a reel is used infrequently, it is a good idea at the end of each outing to back the drag tension off to relieve pressure on the drag washers. When starting a day of fishing, you should check and adjust the drag tension setting before making a cast. Many an angler has neglected this and found upon hooking the first fish of the day that the drag was so weak that it impaired hooksetting, or so tight that it adversely affected fish playing.

To test the drag on a spinning reel, pull line off it at various drag tension settings. Most people, especially if they have fishing experience, test the drag by pulling the line by hand directly ahead of the reel, and making necessary adjustments by feel, starting with a light drag setting and testing and adjusting until they reach a tension setting that feels right. For most fishing situations, especially in freshwater, this is adequate, and anglers wind up putting somewhere in the neighborhood of 25 to 30 percent breaking tension on the line. This "by feel" adjustment is a somewhat imprecise method of doing things, but adequate for the vast majority of spinning reel users.

If you want a general evaluation of how smooth the drag on a given reel is, run the line from the reel through the rod guides and attach it to a scale. Angle the rod tip up and pull on the line while you check what happens to the rod tip. If the tip remains in place, the drag is smooth, which is good. If it moves up and down, the drag is erratic, which may cause problems.

Maintenance and repair. Many people do very little, if anything, to maintain their spinning reels. This may be all right if the reel is only used occasionally. Common sense dictates that if the reel has any loose part, which is most likely to be a sideplate screw, it should be tightened as soon as you notice it, and that you should rinse any reel that has encountered sand, dirt, mud, or saltwater. Use a fine spray of freshwater, rather that a hard stream, to clean the reel and do so as soon as possible after use. There is nothing wrong with dipping a reel in freshwater if you have to cleanse it of dirt or sand, since it is likely to be exposed to wet and rainy conditions while fishing; just don't make a habit of it, give the reel a chance to dry out completely, and keep it lubricated.

Details on reel maintenance are discussed elsewhere *(see: tackle care/maintenance/repair)*. Manufacturers recommend that infrequently used reels be cleaned and relubricated annually, and that reels that are used several times a week be attended to monthly. Periodic maintenance means lightly oiling and greasing accessible parts. Some reels come with small oil or grease tubes, and these can be purchased from tackle suppliers or obtained from the manufacturer. A thorough cleaning requires disassembling most of the reel, scrubbing or rinsing most of the gunk from the parts, drying, and then relubricating.

See: Baitcasting Tackle; Reel, Fishing; Spincasting Tackle.

SPINY WATER FLEA
Bythotrephes cederstroemi.

An exotic species in North America, the so-called spiny water flea is not an insect but a tiny crustacean with a long, sharp, barbed tail spine. A native of Great Britain and northern Europe east to the Caspian Sea, the spiny water flea was first found in Lake Huron in December 1984. It is believed to have arrived in freshwater or mud in the ballast of ocean-going freighters, similar to the manner in which other exotics, particularly zebra mussels, were inadvertently imported. By 1985, it had spread to Lakes Erie and Ontario, by 1986 to Lake Michigan, and by 1987 to Lake Superior. It has since spread throughout the Great Lakes and into some inland waters, and has evidently established itself as a permanent part of the North American ecosystem, carving out a niche for itself at the expense of existing lake fisheries.

The quick success of the spiny water flea in colonizing all of the Great Lakes raises the possibility that it may become even more widespread over the years. Because these animals compete with native organisms, including young perch and other small fish, for food, and because they reproduce rapidly, they pose a threat to native species that is not yet fully understood and may become more significant in the future.

Unique body. The spiny water flea is easily recognized by its unique body shape. As an adult, the spiny water flea is no longer than $3/8$ inch. The tail spine is its distinguishing feature and separates it from all other free-swimming lake invertebrate animals, or zooplankton. That spine is proportionately long, often comprising more than 70 percent of the animal's length, and contains from one to four pairs of thornlike barbs. The head consists

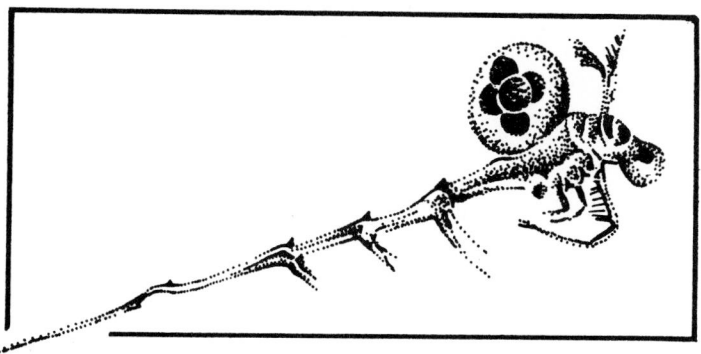

These tiny crustaceans (adults are $3/8$ inch long) exist in clusters that look like bristly gobs of jelly with black spots.

S

primarily of a single large eye filled with black pigment. Also present are a pair of sickle-shaped mandibles, or jaws, used to pierce and shred prey. These animals possess four pairs of legs; the first pair is much longer than the others and is used for catching prey, whereas the other pairs are designed for grasping prey to be consumed. Just behind the head is a pair of swimming antennae, which propel the animal through the water. Spiny water fleas are good swimmers, moving several times their body length in a second. The ability to swim, as opposed to merely drifting with the current, helps them encounter prey and to move between shallow and deeper lake waters.

Like all other crustaceans, its outer shell is molted during growth phases. The spiny water flea is unique because it sheds only the outer shell that covers the tail spine. The animal is never without its long stout spine; this fact suggests to biologists that the tail serves a vital protective function.

Unusual reproduction.   The spiny water flea has a remarkable influence on biological communities in large part due to its rapid reproduction. Reproductive females carry their offspring on their backs in a balloonlike brood pouch, which can be filled either with developing embryos or resting eggs. Most of the time, females exhibit a rapid and unusual method of reproduction known as parthenogenesis, or asexual reproduction. By this method, females produce from 1 to 10 eggs that are able to develop into new females in the absence of mating or fertilization. The new females are genetic replicas, or clones, of the mother.

The generation time of this life cycle (embryo to adult females) varies with water temperature, because rates of metabolism rise and fall with temperature. During the summer when the surface water of the lake is warm, spiny water fleas can produce a new generation without fertilization in less than two weeks. Since males are not needed for this method, they are rarely found when food is plentiful, or when environmental conditions favor rapid population growth.

In spiny water fleas, the sex of offspring is not determined genetically but by environmental factors. So, when food becomes limited or when the lake cools in the fall, males begin to appear. Declining environmental quality can be sensed by adult females, who respond by producing male rather than female offspring. These males are able to mate with surviving females, producing resting eggs. The resting eggs are first carried as orange brown spheres in the female brood pouch. They are later released and fall to the lake bottom, where they can survive the cold winter. In spring or early summer, these eggs hatch into juvenile females that begin parthenogenic reproduction again. Resting eggs can remain dormant for long period, which may explain their arrival in North America and which may be indicative of their ability to be spread through innocent means to other waters via such carriers as boat wells and wet grass on boat trailers.

Disrupting the balance.   Spiny water fleas eat smaller herbivorous crustaceans, including the common zooplankton, Daphnia, which is an important food item for small, juvenile fish. Thus, they compete directly with young fish for food. Because of their unique reproductive pattern, spiny water fleas can reproduce many times faster than fish. Rapid population growth enables them to monopolize the food supply at times, to the eventual detriment of other species.

Although the spiny water flea can fall prey to fish, its spine seems to frustrate most small fish, which tend to experience great difficulty in swallowing the animal. Fish usually manipulate food in their mouths before they swallow it, but the awkwardly shaped spiny water flea is difficult for small fish to ingest, although they have no trouble capturing it. Laboratory experiments show that small fish spend 8 to 10 percent more time eating spiny water fleas than other prey, and eventually learn to avoid it.

In Lake Michigan, spiny water fleas have rarely been found in stomachs of fish less than 2 inches in length, although fish of that size avidly consume Daphnia when that food item is available. There are indications that the growth rates and survival of these young fish may be adversely affected by the presence of spiny water fleas in the ecosystem, owing to competition for food. In general, the more abundant the spiny water flea becomes, the less food remains available for juvenile fish.

In European lakes, populations of spiny water fleas are often suppressed as the result of predation by larger fish. The large black eye and full brood pouches make adult females fully visible to fish, and fish prefer them over smaller species of zooplankton. In addition, because of their size, they provide more protein. Scientists have found large numbers of spiny water fleas in the stomachs of adult fish in the Great Lakes, but the benefits of this food to older fish may be outweighed by the tendency of small fish to avoid it, and by the fact that it competes for the food eaten by small fish.

Faced with possible predation by fish, the spiny water flea has been found to adopt a behavior called diel (daily) vertical migration. Adult females move deeper in the water during daylight hours, where less light penetrates and visibility to fish is reduced. At night, they move closer to the surface, where there is abundant food and the warmer water helps to quicken metabolism and growth.

Studies of the offshore waters of Lake Michigan found that spiny water fleas were mainly found in depths of 33 to 66 feet during the day, while at night the majority of the population occupied the water from the surface to 33 feet.

Avoid spreading.   Spiny water flea adults as well as their eggs may wind up unseen in the bilge water or well water of boats, as well as in bait buckets. In areas of high infestation, fishing lines and downrigger cables may become coated with both eggs and adults. To avoid spreading these animals, precautionary steps should be taken while fishing and after fishing, especially when a boat or bait container is transported from one place to another. Therefore, it is important to remove any aquatic hitchhikers from your boat, boat trailer, fishing tackle, and accessory equipment before leaving the water, and to clean all equipment with hot water and dry it later on.

Drain all water from the boat (bilge and livewells or baitwells) before leaving the area. Do not transport water, fish, or baits from one place to another. Empty a bait container on the land, not in the water. Wash your boat, trailer, and gear with hot water if possible at home and flush the engine with water. Let everything dry for three days. Be advised that in many places it is illegal to transport exotic species. **See: Exotic Species.**

SPLAKE *Salvelinus namaycush x Salvelinus fontinalis.*

Other names—wendigo.

A member of the charr group of the Salmonidae family, the splake is a distinctively marked hybrid fish produced in a hatchery by crossing a true lake trout female *(S. Namaycush)* and a true brook trout male *(S. fontinalis).* This interbreeding does not occur in nature but is initiated by humans, and results in a fertile hybrid species capable of reproducing. The name "splake" is a combination of the words "speckled" from speckled trout, which is an alternate common name for brook trout *(see: trout, brook)*, and "lake" from lake trout *(see: trout, lake)*.

The splake has been stocked in various lakes across the northern United States and Canada. Because of the splake's fast growth rate, resiliency, and adaptability, it has viewed as an excellent candidate for restocking waters where lake trout have been decimated by the sea lamprey, or for providing trophy fish potential in waters that cannot support lake trout. Splake are aggressive fish and excellent to eat. They are a popular ice fishing target in lakes that contain them.

Identification. The splake is difficult to identify externally because it resembles different aspects of both parents. The body shape is intermediate between the heavier lake trout and the slimmer brook trout. The shape of the tail is also intermediate. It is not as deeply forked as that of the lake trout, and more closely resembles the slightly indented tail of the brook trout. In coloration and markings, the splake more closely resembles the brook trout. It has vermiculations like brook trout, red orange ventral fins, and yellowish spots along its flanks. Dead specimens can be positively identified by the number of pyloric caeca, the wormlike appendages on the intestinal tract right after the stomach. The brook trout, which is the

Splake

smaller parent, has only 23 to 55 (usually less than 50) pyloric caeca, whereas the intermediate-size hybrid has 65 to 85, and the lake trout, the larger parent, has 93 to 208 (usually 120 to 180) pyloric caeca.

Size. Splake do not grow as large as lake trout, but they do grow larger than brook trout. Most splake weigh a few pounds, although those from bigger waters with a large forage base may be in the 8- to 12-pound class. The all-tackle world record is a fish from Ontario's Georgian Bay on Lake Huron; it weighed 20 pounds, 11 ounces and was caught in 1987.

Distribution. Splake inhabit Lakes Superior and Huron in the Great Lakes, and various midsize lakes in selected states from Colorado, Utah, and Idaho in the western U.S., to northern New York and Maine in the east.

Life history/Behavior. Although they can reproduce, not all splake do, and some populations lack suitable habitat for spawning, which is generally rocky reefs near deep water. They also are capable of back-crossing (hybrids mating with parent species), which has occurred in hatcheries but evidently not in the wild. Spawning occurs in fall, usually in October, on rocky reefs. In spring, splake are often near tributaries or on gravel shoals, and in summer they seek deep water.

Food. This omnivorous species eats smelt, white perch, yellow perch, crayfish, insects, sculpin, and other fish.

Angling. Due to its initial fast growth rate and game nature, the splake is highly regarded by anglers, who pursue these fish by using shallow and deep lake techniques similar to those employed for its parents, especially lake trout. Spring, when the fish are shallow, is generally best for open-water success, but fall fishing on reefs, when the fish are spawning, can also be good. Working near bottom along the edges of dropoffs while ice fishing is most popular in many splake waters.

See: Charr.

SPLIT RING

A small steel ring with two spiral turns. Similar to a key ring but smaller, split rings are primarily used to connect the closed eye of hooks to a closed wire loop on a lure and to serve as a line-tie connector to certain lures. In the latter capacity, split rings are used with many spoons *(see)*, being connected to the line tie hole at the head of the lure, and with most floating/diving plugs *(see: plug)*, being connected to the wire loop at the head or on the lip. Split rings are used in place of open rings, where a gap in the ends can allow a hook eye to slip out, and in place of solid rings, which prohibit easy hook changing.

Anglers often add split rings to some lures that don't have them in the line-tie area to improve their action; this is best for lures that don't incur twist and for which the line can be directly knotted to the split ring. Split rings are also changed when lure hooks are changed or if the ring spirals spread apart under pressure. To give added action to a lure or to move the hook a little farther away, you can add one or two split rings between the hook eye and the body wire loop.

When the spirals on a split ring are out of alignment, the ring has lost its strength and should be replaced; you're likely to lose the lure to a strong fish or a snag unless you change the ring. Split rings are available in a range of sizes and should be used in a size that complements the lure and hook. However, a split ring can be the weakest link in the angler-to-fish scenario due to its strength. If the rated breaking strength of a split ring is 12 pounds, for example, and you're using 20-pound line, it's possible that you could open up the spirals of the ring, and lose the lure and/or fish, when maximum pressure is applied. It is unlikely that you will know the breaking strength of most split rings when they are pre-attached to a lure or when buying them in bulk, but you can test them with a heavy-duty spring scale.

Changing split rings can be difficult with standard pliers that have a large grip area. Needle-nose pliers with a good tip grip work well for intermediate and large split rings, but split ring pliers, which have a beaklike tip to separate the spirals, are best, and eliminate the chance of weakening a ring by spreading the spirals, which is especially likely in smaller split rings.
See: Snap.

SPLIT SHOT
A small round fishing weight split in the middle.
See: Sinker.

SPOOL
(1) The part of a reel that holds fishing line.

(2) A manufacturer's storage device (usually round and with a large arbor) that holds fresh line for use on a fishing reel. The capacity and purpose depend on whether such a spool is classified as a tippet or leader spool, a reel-filler spool, or a bulk spool.

(3) The act of putting line on a fishing reel; one might say, "the dealer spooled my new reel with 6-pound line."

(4) Depleting line on a reel when accomplished by the actions of a large and powerful fish; one might say, "the fish spooled all of the line off the reel and just kept going."
See: Line.

SPOON
A sinking, wobbling lure, primarily made of hard metal. Spoons are used for casting, trolling, and jigging in freshwater and saltwater; they can be fished with many types of tackle and are used at all levels in the water column, from just under the surface to the bottom.

Julio T. Buel of Whitehall, New York, is credited with inventing the fishing spoon; he fished with his own creation as early as 1821, reportedly was issued a patent in 1834, and began the commercial manufacture of spoons in 1848. Whether it was derived from an actual utensil or merely had a vague resemblance to one, the lure he created did prove attractive to gamefish, imitating through its action, flash, and size the movement and appearance of prey fish. This, plus being relatively simple to fish, is still the main attribute of a spoon, although it is available in a multitude of shapes and styles to suit particular applications.

Spoons are unlike other lure forms in that the bladelike metal body wobbles but doesn't spin, is not attached to a center shaft, and generally suggests an injured or fleeing baitfish through a range of retrieval speeds. These are popular lures that have international appeal and at some time or another will likely catch nearly any species of fish, although they are more preferable for some species than for others, predominantly employed in freshwater, and most useful in clear water due to their visual appeal.

Trout, salmon, and charr species are the primary targets for spoon use, but northern pike, largemouth bass, smallmouth bass, striped bass, and walleye are also susceptible to specific types of spoons. Smaller predators are generally not good targets for these active lures, except for the smaller jigging versions.

Most spoons are metal and generally slender, with a slight curvature that provides swimming action when retrieved and a flashy appearance that complements its movement. There are wide-body models, flat-sided models, a few plastic spoons, and in general greater diversity in appearance and application than most people realize.

Spoons can be divided into two basic yet vastly different categories. The first and foremost are casting and trolling spoons, all of which have a curved body; the second is jigging spoons, which generally have a flatter and thicker body and a more focused application.

Casting and Trolling Spoons
This is the standard category of spoons, and it includes a wide array of lures, some of which are used

strictly for trolling, some strictly for casting, and some for both. Those used strictly for casting can be subdivided into weedless and nonweedless models.

The design of the metal body and the overall weight govern what can and cannot be cast, as well as the overall action and working speed. In a general sense, these can be separated into thin- or thick-bodied lures. An assortment of thick-bodied spoons are used in both casting and trolling. These range from tiny $\frac{1}{32}$-ounce versions used for panfish and trout to objects 9 inches long weighing several ounces and used for large lake trout and muskies. Wafer-thin spoons, which are too light and too air-resistant to be cast, are used in trolling, where a weighted line, a sinker, a downrigger, or some other device is employed to get the lure down to the desired fishing depth.

No matter what the application, casting and trolling spoons are made of hard metal, usually brass or steel, and have a curved body (one side is concave). This curvature causes the lure to drag and wobble as it moves through the water. Generally, the longer the lure, the wider and slower the wobbling action; the shorter the lure, the narrower and quicker the action. Likewise, the more pronounced the curvature, the more resistance the lure has and the more accentuated its action; spoons with little curvature have less water resistance and a narrower and less pronounced action.

Thick-bodied spoons have more weight and cast better than lighter and thinner models, provided they aren't too heavy. Some compact aerodynamic models can be cast a country mile on light line and long rods, which is very beneficial for shore-based anglers. This distance cannot be achieved with most other lures, especially air-resistant plugs. However, because long, wide-bodied spoons have more air resistance, it's harder to achieve distance and accuracy with them.

A thick body also has the advantage of sinking faster, which is a factor in both open water and river fishing. In a slow moving river, a thick body might sink too fast and invite snagging on the river bottom; however, in deep and swift flows, a thick-bodied spoon is better for getting down in the water as soon as it lands and staying deeper and closer to the fish upon retrieval.

The surface of the spoon has a lot to do with its effectiveness and complements its action. This is more than a matter of mere color, although all types of colors and combinations (sometimes with prism tape in dots, stripes, and other patterns) are used. Most casting and trolling spoons have an unpainted polished side, which reflects light and helps make the lure, or at least the flash from it, visible from a good distance. Others have a plated or hammered surface that also has good reflection qualities. Lesser quality spoons have a duller and less reflective surface, and older tarnished or scarred spoons are less effective (they can be restored with polish and spruced up with prism tape).

Spoon types, from top to bottom, include weedless, jigging, casting, and trolling versions.

Spoons always have a hole at their front end for attachment to the fishing line. Line should never be tied directly to this hole but instead to a snap or, preferably, a snap-swivel; the latter will minimize or prevent line twist. Some spoons are preassembled with a swivel, snap, or metal split ring. Line can be tied directly to the swivel, but a snap-swivel should be used with the others.

Virtually all spoons have one hook, a single or treble version, on their back end. Trebles are more common than singles, especially on lightweight spoons; most hooks are attached via a split ring to the back of the lure, but a few (weedless versions) have single hooks that are integral to the metal body. It is generally the manufacturing norm that spoons intended mainly or solely for casting have treble hooks, and that lightweight trolling spoons have single hooks, but there are exceptions, and many anglers replace the treble hooks on their spoons with singles; this usually doesn't impair action (it may improve it) and aids hook removal (it may be mandated in some places).

Incidentally, spoons are generally fished far enough off the bottom in lakes that they don't get snagged, although they often get snagged in rivers. Single hooks help avoid snagging and, on spoons, are equally effective at hooking fish (which often hook themselves when they strike a trolled lure).

The most important factor in using casting and trolling spoons is achieving the right retrieve or trolling speed to get the proper action out of a particular spoon. Some spoons swim lazily and sink too deep when worked too slowly; or they swim too rapidly and rise too high when worked too fast. You should always swim a spoon near you and observe it to determine the best speed for using it.

In trolling, there are two main approaches to fishing a spoon. Lightweight spoons are used with some device for getting deep. Heavier spoons are generally flatlined, mostly on nylon monofilament but also on lead-core and wire lines. Determining

S

S

the depth of flatlined spoons is critical to fishing at the right level. Trolling is discussed in greater detail in a separate entry *(see: trolling)*. Remember to alter the behavior of a spoon when trolling; this can be done by letting it flutter down when the boat slows or rise briefly when the boat speeds up, and by jerking the rod tip periodically to dart the spoon forward like a struggling or fleeing baitfish. This tactic is highly effective when trolling a spoon.

When casting in current, you normally cast up and across stream or directly across stream, reel in slack line, keep the rod tip angled up, and allow the spoon to drift downstream with the current (sometimes reeling it very lightly), then lower the rod tip and reel it in with a slow, steady retrieve, a jerk-reel motion, or a combination of both. You can also fish it directly downstream for a sustained period, keeping the rod tip high and allowing the movement of the water to activate the lure; this is best with a thin or intermediate thickness spoon.

When casting in lakes, let the lure sink after it enters the water, perhaps counting it down to a certain level (you have to predetermine sink rate) to reach the desired depth before beginning the retrieve. A straightforward retrieve sometimes does the job, especially if fish are numerous and aggressive, or a stop-and-go or jerking retrieve may be better. It usually pays to put a twitch or jerk into a straight retrieve to stimulate a strike.

Spincasting, spinning, and baitcasting tackle are appropriate for casting with spoons, depending on the weight of the lure used. Spinning, baitcasting, and light conventional tackle are better for trolling, also depending on lure weight as well as other factors. Thin diameter lines bring out the best action in casting and trolling spoons because they have less water resistance.

Weedless models. Weedless spoons are used for bass, pike, and pickerel fishing in and around thick vegetation, such as lily pads, bulrushes, sawgrass, and milfoil. They are generally not 100 percent snag-free, but will usually get through most vegetation with the aid of their incorporated wire hook guard. These lures are best used with a rippled pork rind, soft plastic curl tail, or rubber skirt trailer to spice up their swimming action, and some anglers like to garnish this with a pork chunk. Good colors vary with species, but silver is a perennial favorite for bass, pike, and pickerel. Orange with red diamonds (the five of diamonds), red-and-white, and chartreuse-and-red are very popular for pike. Gold, black, chartreuse, and frog green are good for bass as well. Sizes range from $1/4$ ounce to 1 ounce, with the largest models intended for pike fishing.

The basic technique for fishing a weedless spoon is to cast it far back into the vegetation and work the lure slowly over and through it, allowing it to ease into and flutter down every little opening possible. When fishing thick lily pads, for example, you would cast back into the pads and slowly reel the lure up to an opening, let it slither off a pad into a pocket, and ever so slowly bring it through that pocket and then over or through more pads to the next pocket.

The important point about weedless spoons is that you must fish them slowly and pick your way through the vegetation. Also, you must delay a moment in setting the hook when a fish strikes. Numerous missed strikes or "boils," especially by bass, on these lures are due to the nature of the cover, so you must be sure a fish has your lure before you try to hook it.

A sometimes useful modification of this type of lure for bass is the placement of a spinner blade in front. This is accomplished through a short wire shaft ahead of the basic lure, around which a small silver or gold blade revolves. This combination provides added flash and attraction that will bring the lure to the attention of reluctant bass when the lure appears in holes or openings of thick grass or lily pad clusters.

Jigging Spoons

Jigging spoons are thick-bodied lures made of hard metal or lead that lack a curved profile. Though somewhat spoonlike in appearance, they don't have a distinctive wobble when retrieved, which makes them suitable for vertical jigging. Their action is essentially one of darting upward and fluttering backward. Most jigging spoons, especially those used in freshwater, have a flat, compressed, two-sided body, but others, especially large versions used in saltwater, have a three- or four-sided profile that tapers at either end; the so-called diamond jig of saltwater prominence has four sides and is wide at the middle and tapered to a point at either end.

Jigging spoons used in freshwater vary in shape and size; they are commonly used in $1/4$- to $1/2$-ounce sizes for black bass, white bass, and stripers, and mainly employed for vertical jigging in situations where fish may be schooled or suspended. However, smaller models are used to catch panfish and for ice fishing, and larger models (up to 2 ounces) are occasionally used for striped bass and deep bottom fishing for lake trout. Many versions are long, narrow, and tapered, but others are wide and squat (called slabs or slab spoons). The former usually have a plain or hammered plated finish while the latter are painted, generally in white, yellow, silver, or gold. In saltwater, jigging spoons are usually larger and commonly fished up to several ounces in inshore waters, though versions up to 16 ounces (more of a lead lure with a hook than a spoon) are used on appropriately heavy tackle for the greatest depths.

Jigging spoons have an integral line-tie ring or hole at the head, and some are equipped with a split ring. Nearly all have a treble hook attached to the rear via a split ring. The trebles are likely to get hung up a good deal, but their weight helps unsnag them fairly easily if you have a direct line of pull

How did we get the term *blue ribbon* trout streams? Perhaps from the use of the color blue to depict the best trout streams in a Montana survey report, akin to the first-place ribbons awarded at country fairs.

overhead. Fishing line should be tied directly to the lure or to a split ring; avoid using a snap or snap-swivel, which increase hook fouling.

In vertical jigging look for fish that are near or on the bottom around specific structure, or for suspended fish that are at various levels in the water column. To use these jigs, lower them either to the bottom or to a specific depth, jerk your rod up, and let the lure flutter down. Repeat this procedure for a while at the same depth. The lure jerks up and flutters back, and should rise a foot to a foot and a half with each upward motion, then be allowed to sink back slowly as you keep gentle contact with it (if the line is tight on the fall the lure will not flutter properly). Most strikes come on the fall back, and feel like a faint tap or simply stopping of the lure. Microfilament or other low-stretch lines are especially good for this work because of their high sensitivity, which telegraphs a strike. Spinning and baitcasting tackle (or conventional tackle for heavyweight jigging spoons in saltwater) are good, and rods should have a stiff butt section and fast taper; a limber tip decreases sensitivity and makes both strike detection and hooksetting more difficult.

Jigging spoons can also be used for casting to (and rapidly retrieving through) schools of surface-breaking fish because great casting distance can be achieved. Their main attribute is that they can be cast a long distance, and vaguely look like fleeing baitfish. Jigging spoons lack wobbling action on a straight retrieve, so they should be retrieved in a quick jerk-and-reel manner for schooling fish.

Other jigging lures. A few lures are a cross between a spoon and a leadhead jig, and are mainly used for vertical jigging, though they are sometimes cast. A few of these are primarily thin metal bodies, and called blade baits by some anglers; they may be vertically jigged or fished on a cast-settle-jig-settle-jig manner for white bass, smallmouth bass, largemouth bass, and panfish. Likewise, some lures, called tailspinners (see), have a rounded lead body and a spinning blade on the tail; they are fished similarly to the thin-bodied baits. As a group, these lures are sometimes called jump baits, meaning that they are primarily used in quick-casting to schools of surface-feeding white bass, largemouth bass, and striped bass, although the same can be said for various spinners, casting spoons, and vertical jigging spoons.

There are also some balanced jigging lures, made of metal and used for vertical fishing in a different manner than jigging spoons. The lead bodies of these lie horizontally instead of vertically in the water when fished. One type is a heavy lead body mainly used in saltwater with treble hooks on the tail and under the belly and a forward slanting head; the line tie is on top just behind the head, and the lure is weighted so that the tail sits slightly down and the lure darts upward when jigged.

Another type that is favored in freshwater for ice fishing (see), but sometimes used for open-water deep jigging, is a balanced lead minnowlike lure that has a single hook at each end, a treble hook under its belly (in larger models), a small plastic lip on the tail, and a centered topside line-tie. This lure swings out and up to either side of a vertical position when jigged, always with the body staying horizontal.

See: Inshore Fishing; Jig; Jigging.

SPOONPLUG

Spoonplugs are specialized metal lures used occasionally in flatline trolling in freshwater. These uncommon lures are stamped from brass into a slightly arched position with upsweeping sides, and are generally used on a low-stretch line. There used to be seven models, all used solely for bottom bumping. Spoonplugs can take a lot of abuse; they can be run into all kinds of objects but still hold their form without needing tuning adjustments.

As with other trolling baits, the size of the lure and the length and strength (diameter) of line out determine how deep it will run. Spoonplugs are intended for relatively high speed trolling, particularly by anglers who are new to a lake and are both scouting for fish and trying to learn the bottom contours and structures.

There are very few practitioners of spoonplugging today outside of the upper Midwest, in part because of the evolution of deep-diving plugs, thin diameter low-stretch lines, and other methods of getting deep.

See: Flatlining.

SPORTFISH

In the broadest sense, sportfish refers to freshwater and saltwater fish sought by recreational anglers using sporting equipment. In some quarters, "sportfish" is used interchangeably and synonymously with the term "gamefish" (see), although there is a subtle difference. In a sense, the sportfish could be narrowed to species with characteristics that are especially favored by anglers, such as size, strength, ability to sustain resistance to capture, feeding methods, jumping ability, etc. However, that would leave out many species that are very popular with anglers and caught for recreational enjoyment and/or for food, some of which do not have much fighting endurance or have good endurance but are not as exciting to catch as others. Certainly some sportfish are more flamboyant or more vigorous than others, but sporting virtue is in the eye and definition of the beholder; some of the most difficult fish to entice, such as carp, are highly prized by one segment of the angling population yet disdained by another segment, even though they are tenacious fighters.

See: Sportfishing.

SPORTFISHERMAN

(1) A person who catches or tries to catch fish for personal use, fun, challenge, and leisure by using sporting methods and sporting equipment, essentially some type of rod, usually but not always equipped with a reel, to which a line and a hook or lure are attached. "Sportfisherman" is used interchangeably with "angler." It has a more specific meaning than "fisherman," although both words may connote the same thing when used in reference to the employment of sporting equipment.

Although sportfisherman has a masculine gender, it is often used in a generic sense throughout the recreational and fisheries management communities, the sportfishing equipment industries, and the boat and motor manufacturing industries to imply female as well as male anglers. That generic usage appears often because of its overwhelming dominance in everyday language and also because the alternative, "fisher," which is an archaic although non-gender-specific version of "fisherman" *(see)*, may also refer to an individual engaged in commercial or recreational activity.

See: **Angler; Angling; Commercial Fisherman; Fishing; Recreational Fisherman; Sportfishing.**

(2) A large boat, also referred to as a sportfishing boat or offshore boat, that is usually over 35 feet long, outfitted with big-game fishing equipment and set up for angling, and capable of cruising many miles offshore in the primary pursuit of pelagic species. Such a boat is designed with accessories and an interior layout that facilitate sportfishing activities and needs; it would be used to fish off all coastal areas and far from the coastline, as well as in such big bodies of freshwater as the Great Lakes.

See: **Sportfishing Boat.**

SPORTFISHERY

All aspects of catching or trying to catch fish for personal use, fun, challenge, and leisure by using sporting equipment; the proceeds are released or kept for personal use and not sold. This term includes fisheries resources, anglers, and businesses providing goods and services.

See: **Sportfisherman.**

SPORTFISHING

The act of catching or trying to catch fish for personal use, fun, challenge, and leisure by using sporting methods and sporting equipment, essentially some type of rod, usually but not always equipped with a reel, to which a line and a hook or lure are attached. "Sportfishing" is used interchangeably with "angling" but is more often associated with saltwater angling, especially the type of offshore activities characterized by the use of a vessel, called a sportfisherman *(see)*, outfitted for big-game fishing.

"Sportfishing" has a more specific meaning than "fishing," although both may connote the same thing when used in reference to the employment of sporting equipment. It is distinguished from commercial or recreational fishing by virtue of the equipment employed, an implicit understanding of fair chase, and the exercise of sportsmanship. Sportfishing also implies the intent to keep fish (if fish are kept) for personal use rather than for sale or trade, although some saltwater fish that are caught by sporting means may legally be sold.

What constitutes sport or sporting equipment is open to individual interpretation and encompasses a wide range of equipment and circumstances. Even anglers disagree as to whether certain tactics, tackle, and techniques exclusively used in sportfishing actually qualify as "sport." This is a debate grounded, in part, in attitudes and ethical considerations that defy settlement and muddy any attempt at strict definition.

See: **Angler; Angling; Commercial Fisherman; Fishing; Recreational Fisherman; Sportfish.**

SPORTFISHING BOAT

The term "sportfishing boat" is used in the angling and recreational boat manufacturing world synonymously for midsize to large boats used for inshore and offshore fishing in saltwater, or in large bodies of freshwater, and specifically outfitted for fishing applications as opposed to general-purpose use or recreational cruising. Technically, any boat that is designed precisely for fishing (as opposed to cruising, water-skiing, or running about), with accessories and interior layout that exclusively accommodate angling activities and needs, is a "sportfishing" boat, but in common parlance, this term has become associated with the type of craft (a minority of which are trailerable) that might be used to fish off all coastal areas and far from the coastline, as well as in such big bodies of freshwater as the Great Lakes.

Sportfishing boats can be loosely grouped into offshore and inshore categories, although there is much that is common between the two, and considered in terms of outboard, inboard, and inboard/outboard power, as well as by interior and hull configuration.

Offshore Boats

Modern offshore boats provide more speed, comfort, and standard fishing features than ever before. The higher speeds are made possible through the use of high-tech coring materials that reduce weight, and also due to the revolution in marine power. Engines produce more horsepower with less weight these days, providing more speed.

The comfort aspect came about as boat builders discovered that women fish and boat, too, and so the Spartan finishing work of yesteryear has given way to fishing boats that can be downright plush.

And fishing features have grown as competition for sales has intensified and features were added to enhance sales. Yesterday's option is often today's standard equipment.

There are more types of boats available to the consumer, too. A walk down the aisle of a boat show will expose you to a dizzying variety of sizes, hull types, construction materials, power options, and, of course, prices. But even with all of the evolution in the boat marketplace, there are still some basic choices that must be made when considering a sportfishing boat.

The first is a major choice of power options: inboard, outboard, or inboard/outboard, the latter being a hybrid of the others. In the past, any boat over about 30 feet was sure to be built around inboard power, but that's no longer true. Modern outboards, with their vastly improved reliability and economy, are now commonly found on the transoms of boats up to 35 feet long.

Outboard models. Outboard-powered fishing boats come in several different configurations. The center console is arguably the most common, and it's easy to see why. With the helm located roughly amidships, the center console design offers unparalleled fishing room and access, with a spacious cockpit and an open bow. You can generally fight a fish 360 degrees around the boat without running into an obstacle, and that can come in handy when the fishing action is fast and furious.

Some people prefer the cuddy cabin design, with a spacious cockpit aft and an enclosed cabin forward. Cuddy designs offer at least minimal bunk space so you can spend the night aboard, but most people use the cuddy for lockable storage and for temporary shelter in inclement weather. Lockable storage can be very important when you have lots of tackle aboard and you have to leave the boat unattended in remote or unfamiliar areas.

The third design type combines some of the best features of center console and cuddy cabin boats; this is the walkaround, and it's a style that seems to be growing in popularity. The walkaround has a cabin forward, but, like the center console, it generally also has some space forward, at the bow. This space is accessed via walkways between the cabin sides and the gunwales. You give up a little bit of cabin area with the walkaround, but you get easier access to the bow for fishing, anchoring, docking, sunbathing, or whatever.

Another major choice involves hull design. Offshore boats generally have either a modified-V or a deep-V hull. Modified-V hulls have less than 18 degrees of transom deadrise and tend to be more stable while at rest or when trolling. The downside to the modified-V is that it tends to pound more in a head sea.

The deep-V hull has 18 degrees or more of transom deadrise and usually a sharper entry at the bow. Deep-V hulls were developed for the offshore racing circuit and slice through waves better than their

This 27-foot sportfishing boat has twin outboard motors mounted on a transom bracket.

flatter counterparts, enabling higher speeds in choppy conditions. However, deep-V hulls tend to roll more at rest (a phenomenon known as being "tender").

All of the aforementioned boats are mono-hull designs. Perhaps the hottest trend in outboard-powered boats is the rise in popularity of the catamaran. Cats, as they are known, have two hulls connected by a deck. They ride very differently from a mono-hull because most cats use semi-displacement rather than planing hulls. It should be noted, however, that several builders do use twin planing hulls for their cats.

Either way, the cats offer a substantially smoother ride in choppy conditions. The twin hulls have much less forward surface than mono-hulls, so when they meet the face of an oncoming wave, they cut through it rather than slamming into it. A cat's bow rises gently with the waves rather than reacting quickly. This gentle motion is preferred by many people who are tired of being pounded in a chop. Cats also ride level at virtually any speed, so when things get really rough, you can throttle back and still maintain decent headway and not worry about the boat's trim. Mono-hulls often struggle at slow speeds in rough water conditions, as they fall on and off plane.

You also must consider power requirements when choosing a hull type. Deep-V hulls have more wet surface than modified Vs, and therefore require more power to push them. They are also somewhat harder to get onto plane. Catamarans also require quite a bit of power to push them through the water. In the old days, offshore boats all had flat bottoms so they would run well with the relatively weak engines that were then available. In the 1950s and '60s, boats were slow, so they didn't need deep-V hulls to cut waves.

That's no longer the case. Modern outboards (and inboards) have improved radically and can push most any kind of hull with ease, so the choice really gets narrowed down to one of personal preference based on how the boat will be used. If you tend to make long runs in rough water, a deep-V or catamaran will most likely be necessary. If you don't often run in rough stuff, however, or if you anchor or drift a lot, a modified-V may be the ticket.

In mono-hull designs, a sturdy and well designed offshore boat should have a wide chine area for a dry ride. The chine is where the hullside meets the bottom of the boat. Sportfishing boat builders usually put in a flat chine section of a few inches to throw spray out and away from the boat, rather than allowing it to travel up the hullsides, where it will most likely blow in your face. Many builders utilize a reverse chine design which actually angles downward to deflect spray even further.

Most offshore hulls (especially deep-V hulls) also use lifting strakes to get the boat out of the water at speed. Strakes are the lengthwise ridges molded into the bottom of the hull. They force water down and out, creating lift and helping to throw water out to the side where the chines will theoretically knock it down. Too many strakes, however, adds even more wet surface and slows the boat down. This was a problem with older hulls that had strakes placed all over the place in the days when designers were experimenting with different designs.

Today's designers, of course, benefit from the wonderful world of computers. CAD (computer-assisted design) systems enable naval architects to study hydrodynamics in much more detail, and everyone benefits from this as hulls evolve and become much more suited to specific tasks. Furthermore, computerized manufacturing systems let boat builders (at least the bigger ones) turn out well-fitted boats with tight manufacturing tolerances, boats that should provide many years of reliable service.

Having said all of that, it should be pointed out that many, if not most, boat companies do not have such computer systems, and simply make it up as they go along. This isn't necessarily bad, but the point is that you should do your homework when looking at sportfishing boats and know how the boat you are looking at was designed and built.

As mentioned, modern outboard sportfishing boats are finished to a much higher standard than they were 20 years ago. Sub-console head compartments, freshwater showers, tackle storage lockers, livewell systems, and other goodies are now standard on many boats. That was unheard of even a few years ago. Fishing features have proliferated as well.

Rod storage used to be a problem on outboard-powered sportfishing boats, but there are well thought-out storage solutions on lots of boats these days. Livewell systems are now ubiquitous, and come in a wide variety of configurations and sizes. No matter what your live-bait needs, you can certainly find a boat with a well that suits you.

Modern sportfishing boat builders have also finally gotten around to dealing with the issue of fish boxes. It used to be that if you caught a lot of fish, or a few big ones, you had no choice but to store them in large coolers on the deck, and that took up a lot of precious fishing room. Nowadays, however, boat builders have devised some clever ways to build in fish boxes beneath the cockpit sole of many boats. Just be sure that these boxes drain overboard either directly or through a macerator pump, because many builders drain their boxes into the bilge. That transforms a fish box into a mere storage compartment.

Another modern trend in outboard sportfishing boats is the transom configuration. The outboard sportfishing boat building world has almost completely switched over to a modification of the transom bracket known throughout the industry as the integrated transom system, or the "Euro transom." This design places a transom wall between the cockpit and the engines, creating an engine platform. Livewells, fish boxes, sinks, and bait rigging trays are often built into this transom wall, providing a convenient location for them right in the middle of the fishing action.

Other builders utilize actual engine brackets that are bolted onto a flat transom. One of the advantages of these transom styles is safety; a full transom effectively prevents waves from sloshing into the cockpit and increases performance. Another advantage is that by mounting the engine(s) farther aft and slightly higher, there is less drag in the water, and the boat runs faster. It also gets weight farther aft, which increases performance as well.

Some hard-core anglers, however, still prefer the old notched transom design in which the outboards are simply bolted to the back of the boat with some sort of splashwell or transom gate in front of them. These people feel that the integrated transom system places the engines too far aft, making it difficult to fight a fish around the engines. With the notched transom, you generally can walk right up to the front of the engines and fight the fish around the lower units without being cut off by having the line nick the skeg or propeller. Once again, the choice comes down to personal preference.

Indeed, preference means a lot in the sportfishing boat market. Modern outboard sportfishing boats have the fuel capacity, construction integrity, and enough comfort features to make them viable for serious duty far from the sight of land. They are the boat of choice for many offshore anglers because of their speed, maneuverability, and relatively low initial cost. That's also why you see more and more outboard sportfishing boats at major offshore tournaments these days.

Inboard models.   There are circumstances where only an inboard boat will suffice, however, and once again, technology has provided a tremendous range of options. Inboard-powered boats have benefited from major advancements in engine technology, primarily in the development of high horsepower, low weight diesel engines. Gasoline inboard power has improved rapidly, too, with the development of sophisticated new fuel injection systems that have remarkably improved both efficiency and reliability.

For sportfishing boats over 35 feet (often called "sportfishermen"), inboard engines are still the standard. The same hull considerations discussed with outboard boats also hold true with inboards, and again you must weigh modified-V versus deep-V considerations. But with the wider beams normally found in inboard boats, tenderness can be less of a problem, as beam adds stability.

In days gone by, almost all inboard boats were made of wood; indeed, many of the super expensive custom sportfishermen still are. Wood is still one of the lightest, yet strongest, materials available, but building a wooden boat is obviously labor intensive and therefore expensive. Aluminum boats can still be found offshore, but fiberglass boats are far and away the most common.

Inboard boats come in two basic configurations: flybridge and express. Flybridge boats have the helm placed on top of a salon area, where it is normally accessed by either a ladder or steps. Flybridge boats are often referred to as "convertibles," an archaic term meaning they can do double duty as both cruising and fishing boats. Flybridge boats do offer more comfort amenities on the whole when compared to express boats. The salons they provide often are a combination living room, dining area, and galley, and there are usually additional staterooms below.

Express boats have the helm on a raised bridge deck, forward of and just slightly higher than the cockpit. The bridge deck is where the salon would be on a flybridge boat. Express boats can be fished with a smaller crew than flybridge boats because the captain is just a few steps away from the action and can help wire, tag, or gaff a fish at boatside. Whereas you may need a crew of at least three to effectively fish a flybridge boat, an owner can fish with one other person or even alone on an express boat.

While the high-tech construction methods briefly mentioned earlier are important with smaller outboard boats, inboard boats have benefited the most from the use of new and lighter materials. Solid fiberglass hulls were once the norm, but they were heavy, hard to push, and therefore usually slow. Lightweight materials began showing up in the 1980s as core materials in decks, hullsides, bulkheads, and even stringers. Nowadays, lightweight coring is standard all over inboard boats, even in many hull bottoms. This has allowed larger boats to shed thousands of unnecessary pounds and helped bring about much higher speeds.

New high-power diesel engines have helped push the speed envelope, too. New turbocharging technology has allowed engine manufacturers to squeeze more and more power out of smaller blocks than ever before. This has caused many boat builders to offer inboard diesel power as an option

A 40-plus-foot sportfisherman, with a 12- to 14-foot beam, is capable of taking large parties offshore.

in smaller and smaller boats. It's sort of the opposite of the trend toward outboards on larger boats, but, once again, it's indicative of the amount of choice available.

Inboard sportfishing boats, whether of the express or flybridge design, should have a large cockpit, although one regrettable trend these days involves sacrificing cockpit space in some flybridge boats for the sake of enlarging the salon. All things are tradeoffs on boats, and if you make one thing bigger you must take away from something else. To many serious offshore anglers, lots of cockpit space is important.

Cockpits should provide an uncluttered working area, with storage for gaffs, tag sticks, mops, shore power cords, and so forth. There should be ample fish box volume, and if you normally boat big fish, some sort of transom gate is nice, too. Padded cockpit coaming is great on any size boat. A sportfisherman shouldn't have too much freeboard at the cockpit; it should be easy to reach the water's surface when leaning over the side.

Fighting chairs are mounted in the center on many cockpits. These specialized chairs have a rod gimbal that receives the butt of a rod and allows it to pivot freely in a fore-and-aft motion while fighting a fish. The chair is mounted on some sort of pedestal, or it can be freestanding, but it must be able to rotate so you can follow a fish with the rod tip during a fight. Some chairs have a footrest that gives the angler leverage during the fight.

Chairs on a centerline pedestal should be mounted so that there is plenty of room for the mate to walk between the footrest and the transom, and chairs must be securely fastened to the deck. Several unlucky anglers doing battle with a huge marlin or tuna have suddenly found themselves in the water when their fighting chair ripped loose and went overboard! Chairs should ideally be mounted with the pedestal securely bolted to the keel, but oftentimes that's not possible because fuel tanks are under the cockpit sole. In that case, a large backing plate should be used to spread out the load.

Inboard sportfishermen, with either gas or diesel power, are sensitive to loads, and ideally should be designed with a specific table of weights and balances. In smaller inboards, it's hard to get enough weight aft, especially on flybridge boats with their forward superstructure. That's why fuel tanks are placed as far aft as possible. It is wise to pay close attention to how a boat rides at cruising speeds. It should ride proud, with the bow high, but without squatting at the stern. Beware of a boat that runs bow down, even with a full load of fuel. It is bow-heavy and may have handling difficulties, especially in a low fuel situation.

Inboard/Outboard models. Inboard/outboard sportfishing boats, or simply "I/Os," have been around for a long time, but they never really took off with the fishing crowd. I/Os are a combination of inboard and outboard technology, with a lower unit like an outboard, coupled to an inboard engine. The engine sat under a hood right in front of the transom, where many anglers perceived it was in the way.

Things are changing with this system too, though. The explosion of new high-horsepower, lightweight diesel engines has caused many people to reconsider I/Os. Builders are now experimenting with jackshaft technology, placing the engines forward where they would normally sit in an inboard application, and connecting them to the drive unit via a long drive shaft. This gets weight forward and frees up the cockpit area for fishing.

I/O boats offer several major advantages over both outboard and inboard versions. They offer competitive performance with outboards but much better efficiency, especially when diesels are used. The longevity of these engines is better as well. Because all of the underwater running gear associated with a straight inboard is eliminated, drag is reduced substantially with an I/O too, and performance is greatly enhanced. For some people, I/Os may truly offer the best of both worlds.

Inshore Boats

General-purpose inshore boats may be the most popular type of fishing boat available because of their versatility. As opposed to flats boats *(see)* or skiffs, which are designed and built for a very specific purpose, inshore boats can be fished in a wide variety of situations.

Inshore boats typically have more freeboard than flats boats, so they can be used in rougher waters. This makes them perfect for bays, rivers, and limited coastal use, all of which are situations where running across open water is always a possibility. And even though the higher hullsides add weight, these skiffs still have relatively shallow drafts, with either modified-V or flat bottoms.

Most inshore boats are laid out in some variation of the center console design. Again, this provides optimum fishing space and room to move around, and lets you carry lots of gear. A well-designed inshore boat should have lots of rod storage, including extended tubes for fly rods, as well as plentiful dry storage.

These boats usually lack big fish boxes, but they often come with large livewells. The livewells are usually placed aft, but sometimes builders will put a smaller well forward for storage of "pitch baits." These are baits that are kept handy to pitch to a passing fish. Just note that wells placed forward bounce more than wells placed aft and will be pretty hard on the bait.

A rugged nonskid surface on all walking areas is a must, especially on raised casting decks. These decks can be found both at the bow and the stern of many boats, both with and without toe rails that help keep you from sliding overboard. Hand rails should be placed in strategic locations, too.

Because almost all of these boats are outboard powered, it really comes down to a choice of style and options. Inshore boats can probably be considered to be 22 feet or less, but most will probably be 18 to 19 feet long. Hull styles include V-hulls and cathedral hulls, with V-hulls riding better in a chop, but cathedral hulls providing better stability and a wider bow.

Some inshore boats are of the rolled-edge skiff design, basically a one-piece boat where the tops of the gunwales roll outward. Others are conventional hull-and-cap designs, with a separate molded hull and cap that are bonded and screwed together. The one-piece rolled-edge design is light and very cost-effective, but many people prefer the additional fit-and-finish to be found only with the two-piece design.

Inshore boats are pretty simple, and by carefully analyzing your individual needs, you'll soon find a style that fits your fishing requirements like a hand in a glove.

See: **Bass Boat; Boat; Inshore Fishing; Jonboat; Navigation; Offshore Fishing; Trailer; Walleye Boat.**

SPOT *Leiostomus xanthurus.*

Other names—Norfolk spot, spot croaker; French: *tambour croca;* Spanish: *verrugato croca.*

A member of the Sciaenidae family, the spot is an important commercial fish. Its migration habits bring it to shore in schools, enabling both recreational anglers and commercial fishermen to catch

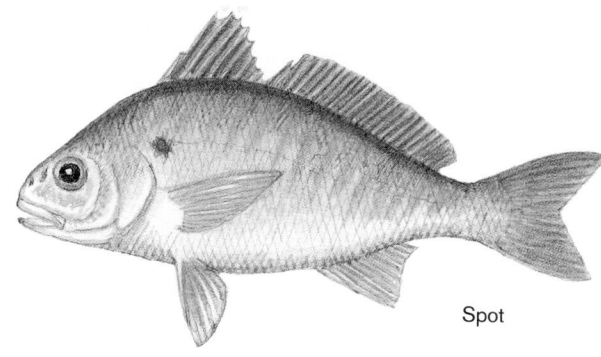

Spot

spot in large numbers. Much like its cousin, the Atlantic croaker *(see: croaker, Atlantic)*, the spot is a small and flavorful fish.

Identification. The body of the spot is deep and stout, and the tail is slightly forked. The soft dorsal fin has more than 30 rays, and the anal fin has more than 12 rays. Its coloring is gray to silver with a gold tint on the sides and 12 to 15 dark lines extending from the dorsal fins to the lateral line. There is a round black spot about the same size as the eye above each pectoral fin. The fins are pale yellow, except the dorsal and caudal fins, which are milky. The spot's color and lack of chin barbels distinguish it from other sciaenids.

Size/Age. The average spot weighs a ¹/₂ pound, and these fish rarely reach 2 pounds, making them the proverbial saltwater panfish. They can live for five years.

Distribution. Spot occur from Massachusetts to Mexico, inhabiting roughly the same range as the Atlantic croaker. Although a western Atlantic fish, at least one spot was discovered in Tokyo Bay, Japan, in the late 1980s, although it is believed that it was transported in the ballast water of a ship.

Habitat. Spot inhabit estuaries and coastal saltwaters, generally roaming over sandy and muddy bottoms. They may frequent waters as deep as 60 meters but usually remain much shallower.

Life history/Behavior. Spawning occurs at sea in the fall and winter, in water temperatures of 59° to 79°F. The spot is capable of producing as many eggs as the Atlantic croaker, nearly 1 million. The eggs are pelagic and carried shoreward by wind and currents. Juveniles move into less saline estuary areas, sometimes even to freshwater, until they are old enough to return to saltwater. Growth is rapid for the first few years, due to the abundance of food in estuaries. They reach maturity at age 3. The spot is a schooling fish and travels in groups of 100 or more.

Food and feeding habits. Spot consume small crustaceans, detritus, worms, and small fish.

Angling. Spot are found over mud and sand bottoms, and shell reefs. They are often caught accidentally by anglers pursuing other species, but they are best deliberately pursued with light line, small hooks, and pieces of clams and cut fish, or worms,

presented on the bottom. Spot are not viewed with great enthusiasm by anglers but can be a fortuitous catch on days when nothing else is happening and some food is expected.

SPREADER BAR
A stainless steel bar, also called a spreader rig, that contains a number of teasers mounted in a pattern and trolled either alongside or directly in front of flatlined baits or lures to resemble a large school of baitfish. A spreader bar is used in offshore fishing, especially for marlin and tuna.
See: Trolling Lures, Saltwater.

SPREADER RIG
To flounder anglers, a spreader rig is a wire bar used for fishing two baits on the bottom. It consists of a coat hanger–like wire with two loops in the middle, the upper of which is attached to the fishing line, and the lower of which supports a bank sinker, and two short leaders at either end, both attached to snelled bait hooks. It is hard to detect light strikes with this rig, and many anglers prefer to fish their line direct to a sinker, without the spreader, using one or more hooks up above.

This term is also used by offshore anglers for a spreader bar *(see)* for trolling multiple teasers.
See: Inshore Fishing.

SPRING TIDE
See: Tides.

SPUD
A heavy long-handled metal bar with a chisel blade for chopping holes in ice for fishing.
See: Ice Fishing.

SQUARETAIL
A term primarily used in northeastern parts of the United States and eastern Canada for brook trout *(see)*, which may also be called speckled trout.

SQUAWFISH, NORTHERN *Ptychocheilus oregonensis.*
Other names—squawfish, Columbia River dace, Columbia squawfish; French: *sauvagesse du nord.*

The northern squawfish is a large-growing member of the Cyprinidae family of minnows that is often caught in northwestern North America trout and salmon waters. Yet it is not actively sought and is viewed as a threat to more popular species. Related fish include the Colorado squawfish *(P. lucius)*, the Sacramento squawfish *(P. grandis)*, and the Umpqua squawfish *(P. umpquae)*, which have limited distribution in their respective river

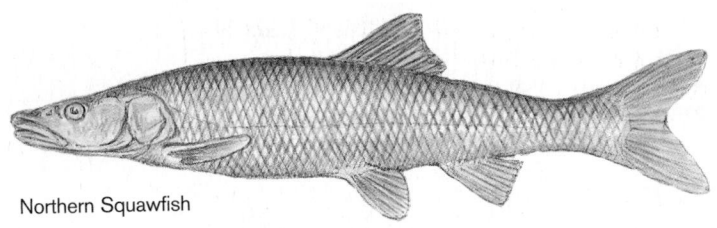

Northern Squawfish

systems. The Colorado squawfish, which is endangered, is North America's largest native minnow and can grow to 6 feet.

Identification. The northern squawfish's mouth is terminal and large, extending back past the front edge of the eye. The head is somewhat conical and flattened between the eyes, and the body is slender and barely compressed. All fins are clear, with no spots or coloration, and there are 9 to 10 rays in the dorsal fin and 8 rays in the anal fin. The caudal fin is deeply forked. Its coloring is usually dark green or greenish brown above and lighter and often silvery on the sides, and it has a whitish belly. Spawning males take on a yellowish or yellow orange color and develop tubercles on the head, back, and some fins.

Size/Age. This species can live 10 years and grow to 25 inches, although it has been reported to attain lengths between 3 and 4 feet. Common sizes are in the 7- to 10-inch range.

Distribution. Northern squawfish occur in North America in the Pacific drainages from the Nass River in British Columbia to the Columbia River in Nevada, in the Harney River basin in Oregon, and in the Peace River system (Arctic basin) in British Columbia and Alberta.

Habitat. Northern squawfish inhabit lakes, ponds, and runs of small to large rivers.

Food. The diet of northern squawfish is terrestrial insects, aquatic insect larvae, plankton, crustaceans, small fish, and fish eggs. Large individuals especially prey on small fish and are considered serious predators of juvenile salmonids. In the Columbia River, fisheries managers undertake efforts to control squawfish numbers to minimize this problem.

Angling. This and other squawfish species are generally viewed with disdain or at least dissatisfaction by anglers, in part because of their threat to trout and salmon, although larger specimens can be extremely sporty on light tackle and are readily caught on small lures and flies. Squawfish are edible and may be smoked, although their (bony) flesh is not especially sought after.

See: Minnow.

SRI LANKA

A pear-shaped island approximately 45 kilometers from the southeast tip of India, Sri Lanka is engulfed by the vast Indian Ocean on the south and the Bay of Bengal on the east. It is separated from India by the Palk Strait and the Gulf of Mannar.

Covering an area of 65,663 square kilometers, Sri Lanka boasts a coastline that features lagoons, inlets, and sandy beaches. The central region is covered with hills that spew 16 rivers into the broad plains of the north and the narrow plains of the south. The largest of these is the 333-kilometer Mahaweli Ganga, which enters the Indian Ocean south of Trincomalee; the smallest is the 107-kilometer Gal Oya. The rivers tumble over rocks in the hilly section, forming waterfalls, and are broken by rapids. Other prominent rivers include the Kelani, which reaches the sea near Colombo; the Kalu, which reaches the sea near Kalutara; and the Aruvi Aru, which reaches the sea near Mannar.

The climate of Sri Lanka is equatorial and tropical; thus it is mostly hot and wet. Temperatures vary by region; when it is 37°C or higher in the northwest, it can be around 10°C in the hills. Days are unpleasant because of high humidity, but evenings are cool. The cooler months of December and January are best for outdoor activity; March and April are the hottest months, and May through August are wet due to monsoons. These storms bring very heavy rains, although the monsoon season varies by region.

There is much commercial fishing along the coastlines, but very little sportfishing. The successive Portuguese, Dutch, and British dominance over this land for 500 years left no mark on the local population with respect to inducing interest in angling as a hobby. As such, very few people in Sri Lanka fish for pleasure. Fishing is predominantly a matter of subsistence, and commercial fishing is an important industry. Freshwater fisheries have started recently with the help of Japanese experts, but local anglers are poor and generally use crude equipment. Nevertheless, the freshwater, brackish, and marine habitats in the country support quite a few good gamefish.

The major rivers of Sri Lanka host appreciable stocks of the khudchee mahseer *(Tor khudree)* of the family Cyprinidae, which attains a length of 1,447 millimeters; the mulley *(Wallago attu),* a catfish of the family Siluridae that grows to a length of 1,828 millimeters; and several murrel (snakehead catfish), of the family Channidae, including ara *(Channa marulius),* which grows to 1,219 millimeters, *C. punctatus,* which grows to 304 millimeters, and *C. striatus,* which grows to 914 millimeters; and rainbow trout, which were introduced and attain a length of 381 millimeters.

The khudchee mahseer is taken on spoons or paste baits, and is a noted fighter. The mulley is caught on live ground bait, whereas murrel are caught on natural baits like live frogs or small fish. The trout are caught on flies and various lures. Local anglers are known to uniformly use gram-flour paste as bait for most of the fish they target.

The brackish waters of Sri Lanka support two members of the family Plotosidae, the keengar *(Plotosus canius),* a gray eel-catfish that grows to

914 millimeters, and the striped eel–catfish *(Plotosus lineatus)*, which attains a length of 304 millimeters; as well as the ilish *(Tenualosa ilisha)*, an anadromous fish of the family Clupeidae and also known as Hilsa shad, which grows to 457 millimeters.

Marine anglers target several sea catfish of the family Ariidae, including soldier catfish *(Osteogeneiosus militaris)*, which grows to a length of 355 millimeters, and *Hemipimelosus jatius,* which grow to a length of 304 millimeters; ladyfish of the family Elopidae *(Elops machnata)*, which grow to a length of 457 millimeters; Indo-Pacific tarpon *(Megalops cyprinoides)*, which grow to a maximum size of 457 millimeters; whitings *(Sillago sihama)* of the family Sillaginidae, which grow to 304 millimeters; threadfins *(Eleutheronema tetradactylum)* of the family Polynemidae, which grow to 1,828 millimeters; and the most relished silver pomfret *(Pampus aregenteus)*, which grow to 304 millimeters, and black pomfrets *(Parastromateus niger)*, which grow to 609 millimeters. Both are in the family Stromateidae.

In addition to these species, the offshore and inshore waters are also known to host wahoo, trevally, pompano, dolphin, grouper, snapper, croaker, barramundi, cobia, mackerel, amberjack, albacore, yellowfin tuna, marlin, and sailfish.

There are very few anglers in the open seas because Sri Lankans cannot afford to own or use seaworthy boats. A small number of anglers, who fish from the beach, land only small-size fish. The rugged northeastern coast contains Trincomalee Harbor, which is an excellent natural harbor and provides some opportunity for offshore and inshore boat fishing. Other harbors of prominence are at Colombo and Galle on the southwestern coast.

(*Note:* many of the species mentioned here are not listed individually in this book because very little information about them is available.)
See: India.

STACKING

This is a means of fishing with multiple rods on a downrigger *(see)*. It is especially useful on boats equipped with just one or two downriggers and allows you to control the depth at which two lures are fished.

To employ a stacked system, set the first line as you would conventionally. Once the first line has been placed in the release next to the weight, lower the weight 10 feet and attach a stacker release to the downrigger cable. Put the second lure out the desired distance, and set the line in the stacker release. Place both reels in rod holders, and leave on the freespool clickers; then place the boom in the proper position (if applicable), and lower the weight to the desired depth. The two lines are now spaced 10 to 12 feet apart.

Be sure to place the rods in holders so that the lower line will not tangle with the upper line if a

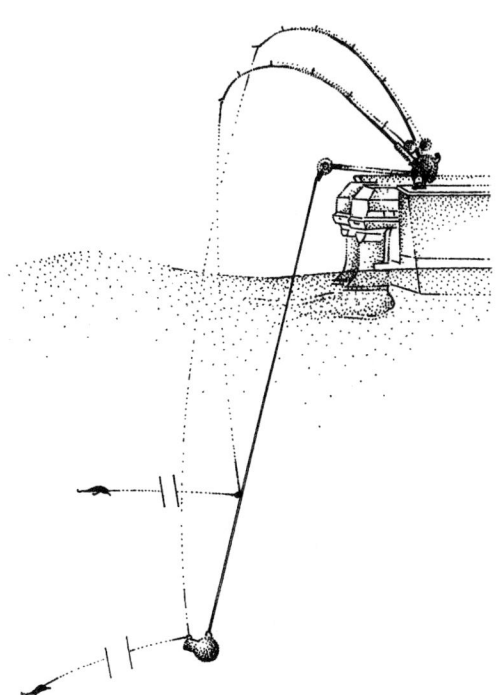

Two rods can be fished off one downrigger by stacking as shown, resulting in two lures being placed at different depths.

fish strikes and immediately comes toward the surface. The setback for the upper line should be shorter than for the lower line to minimize interference if a fish strikes the lower line.

The vertical distance between the two lines is optional, although it shouldn't be less than 10 feet to avoid tangling from erratic action or turns. Where very deep water is fished or where you're scouting at various depths, a difference of 30 to 50 feet may be useful. You might encounter this situation when trolling near the bottom for one species of fish (lake trout, for example) while running a second line off the same downrigger for a different species (such as chinook salmon) that might be considerably higher in the water column and near the thermocline.
See: Downrigger Fishing.

STAMP

(1) Used and issued by fisheries management agencies, a stamp is a form of fee-based permit (usually in freshwater) supplemental to a resident or nonresident fishing license. It allows the holder to angle for, and possess, a particular species or group of (usually related) species. The revenue derived from the sale of a stamp is directed to a specific program and used for purposes that are specific to the management of that specie(s), instead of being put into general fisheries management coffers.
See: Regulations.

(2) Issued by government postal services, stamps depicting fish have been used to reflect art, history,

and prominent natural resources, as well to document the payment of a postal fee. Because fish have been important natural resources in numerous countries, and in some cases are very colorful, they have graced stamps in many countries. A stamplike article that depicted cod was issued in 1755 in the then-colony of Massachusetts, and the first gummed stamp depicting a fish, again cod, was issued in 1865 in Newfoundland. Today there are many colorful stamps of fish issued by countries around the world, and tropical philatelists have devised a system of classifying postal fish stamps based upon their prominence in the design of the stamp.

STANDARD LENGTH

The length of a fish as measured from the tip of its snout to the hidden base of the tail fin rays.

See: Measuring Fish; Regulations.

STANDUP FISHING

Standup fishing is a saltwater angling technique in which anglers stand up while utilizing relatively short rods and repeated short-pumping strokes to fight offshore fish. It is differentiated from standard big-game or offshore fishing in which conventional rods are longer and the angler sits in a fighting chair equipped with a between-the-legs gimbal.

Standup tackle and fish-fighting methods evolved in the 1980s in response to the needs of Southern California offshore anglers who were primarily tangling with monstrous yellowfin tuna on long range party boats. These boats were not equipped with fighting chairs, and dozens of anglers on a single long-range boat at anchor labored with heavy conventional big-game tackle and long rods while standing up to fight tuna and, occasionally, billfish. With their knees locked against the railings, and their backs and shoulders under a lot of strain, they struggled to maintain their balance and keep from joining their quarry in the briny far below their high deck perch.

An entire tackle and fishing system for these anglers emerged. Short, sturdy rods with short butts were rediscovered and further developed to provide incredible leverage when nestled in low rise, custom gimbal belts. As rod butts were shortened, fore grips were lengthened. Matching kidney harnesses in a variety of sizes and shapes to match the range of body shapes and sizes of the anglers soon followed. A multitude of modifications to fine-tune the system appeared next, and short, powerful, "Stroker" rods were soon joined by equally short graphite composite rods with excellent recovery power.

Because much of the success of the standup system depended on the fit of the harness employed, harness systems were the next component to upgrade. Borrowing from improvements in sit-down harnesses, more comfortable standup harnesses with sophisticated padding and bracing appeared. Nylon and space-age plastic replaced the old canvas and leather contrivances from the early days when anglers did battle with giant Nova Scotia tuna from makeshift barber chairs. Strap lengths were altered to accommodate the special needs of the standing position, and then harnesses that allowed the gimbal belt to be clipped onto the harness itself developed, thus reducing the number of belts encircling the angler.

Standup systems spread east, and Northeastern tuna anglers began to adopt the San Diego gear on forays to far off canyons of the Western Atlantic. In many situations, especially on smaller skiffs, the California tackle seemed custom designed for their needs as well, and bigeye, bluefin, and yellowfin tuna fell to standup anglers in yet another ocean.

Standup systems offer several advantages not afforded big-game anglers anchored to a chair. The most significant of these is mobility. The standup angler is able to rove about the cockpit whenever the fish surges or changes direction, which in turn increases the odds for successfully landing a powerful fish. This is especially true near the end of the fight. When a large billfish or tuna is brought to the boat, the seated angler can do little to prevent a cutoff if his quarry suddenly charges beneath the boat. The mobile angler can more easily handle any situation by following the fish around the cockpit, can keep the rod tip pointed at the fish more easily, and can often prevent catastrophe when a green fish is brought to the boat.

Many people feel that greater pressure can be exerted on a gamefish with a short standup rod and a quick pumping action, which in turn reduces the fighting time. Marlin experts have tallied innumerable marlin catches using the standup "short stroke" technique to support such a contention, while many California tuna anglers fighting straight down monsters from high decks certainly concur. However, this is not necessarily the case; in some instances, using standup tackle to land big fish may take longer. This depends upon the physical condition of the angler, having the appropriate tackle, and properly employing effective technique.

Many anglers find greater satisfaction in fighting a big fish while standing up than while seated in a large chair that has to be moved by an accomplice. They feel that they get to see more of the action, especially right after the hookup, when their seated counterparts are busy settling into fighting chairs and adjusting seat harnesses. Some even consider the standup catch a greater accomplishment than catching the same fish from a fighting chair.

There is yet another advantage offered by standup systems. The small-boat angler with a limited budget quickly discovers the difference in cost between an expensive fighting chair and a standup harness. The harness doesn't deflate the tackle budget the way a fighting chair does.

himself at all with standup gear. Multiple hookups, which can often occur when seeking sailfish, are more easily handled by the standup angler, especially if the boat is equipped with a rocket launcher. This multiple rod holder can actually provide the standup angler an advantage over his compatriot who chooses to fish from a fighting chair, and multiple hookups can more often result in multiple catches.

Indeed, most billfish that can be handled on tackle up to and including 50-pound class, can be taken standing up with the right rod and fitted harness system, and some practice. Although the amount of pressure that can be applied to the fish is limited by the drag setting of the reel commensurate with the line class (whether standing or sitting), many offshore anglers feel that they can more easily apply maximum pressure with a good standup system. In either case, the experienced angler usually adds additional pressure on the line or spool with a gloved hand when the situation calls for it.

There is no doubt that fighting a large gamefish from a standing position can sometimes offer advantages and thrills not possible for the seated angler. However, this has to be put into perspective as an option.

The angler fishing from a skiff or sportfishing cruiser replete with a fighting chair has choices. The advantages of fighting a truly large billfish or shark, or a giant bluefin tuna with a longer conventional trolling rod from a fighting chair give the seated angler a decided edge. Such fish require 80- and 130-pound class tackle, which is just too heavy in the true conventional design for standup fishing. It isn't possible for most people to exert enough pressure while standing up with such tackle to wear out monster fish. However, standup tackle is often used to take yellowfin tuna as large as 400 pounds on long-range boats, as well as giant bluefin tuna in the 200- to 500-pound range; the tackle employed for this is generally 50-pound class (the wide-spool models for greater capacity) and sometimes 80-pound class, equipped with 100- to 130-pound line.

However, those fish that are not truly monstrous in size are certainly fair game for standup fishing, and this tackle is preferred by many people over heavier conventional gear used in fighting chairs. Thus, standup tackle has become popular not only for midsize tuna and billfish, but sharks, wahoo, amberjack, yellowtail, and large bottom fish, including halibut and lingcod.

Tackle

The rod and the gimbal harness are at the heart of the standup system. Most standup fishing, especially for deep and hard-fighting species, is done with big-game reels and special standup rods, although some standup spinning tackle is available for lighter work. Standup rods are made by most leading rod makers and are generally 5 to 6 feet in length. Some

With a short standup rod and quick-pumping motion, an angler can catch large fish without an overly long endurance contest.

As the early enthusiasm for standup fishing spread from West Coast tuna anglers to Northeast tuna anglers and marlin anglers in the Atlantic and Caribbean, it was unfortunately not accompanied by a clear understanding of either its practical applicability or of the necessity for proper choice and fitting of rods and accessories. Even now, many newcomers to standup fishing do not realize the tremendous force that can be generated by the leverage of short rods, and are not setting the drags on their reels accordingly. In short, they are not considering their own physical limitations or even those of their gear. They run the risk of placing themselves in jeopardy of either being pulled overboard or hurled backwards if the hook pulls.

There's a big difference between a fish simulating machine at a sport show, which is where many anglers get their first exposure to standup gear, and the tossing deck of a sportfishing cruiser. The machine doesn't always surge and run like a real life giant gamefish, and the line never seems to break on a simulator. It's an interesting exercise, but there's more to preparing for standup fishing.

Although standup tackle was geared originally at tuna anglers, it has broadened to a base that includes billfish and shark anglers as well, plus any small-skiff anglers without a chair. An angler fishing from a small skiff without a chair is in much the same position as the angler in the party boat: He can't sit down. When fishing for billfish with 20- to 50-pound class tackle, he is not handicapping are lighter than others, with graphite offering the most strength per weight. Many standup rods are made from fiberglass, but some are made from graphite or from composites. Although graphite offers the advantage of lighter weight without a commensurate sacrifice of strength, the advantage of its greater recovery power is lost when fishing from a standing position because standup anglers depend less on the tip of the rod to fight their fish than do seated anglers. The pumping strokes (called short stroking or short pumping) that are most effective when standing, are short and rely little on the recovery power of the rod. They need the strength of a strong butt. Short stroke pumping gains line a little at a time; this, not the gradual recovery of the rod itself, is what whips the fish.

Anglers should follow a number of simple, mostly common sense, guidelines when shopping for their own standup system.

Because people are built differently, not every standup rod or rod butt length fits every angler. Choose a rod with enough backbone to handle about 18 to 22 pounds of drag without exploding. There are a multitude of short rods available that have been developed specifically for standup fishing pressures. Avoid simply a short blank; most standup rods are 5 to 6 feet long with $5^1/_2$ feet a favorite, and whatever you select should have been specifically designed for the rigors of standup fishing. An aluminum butt and full set of roller guides are favored for the most arduous work, but some standup rods combine roller and stainless steel ring guides. The overall length as well as butt length should be matched to your stature. The fore grip should be long and extend well up the rod from the reel seat, but how far can only be determined by trying on the whole system. An extra long fore grip is essential because it provides the angler with greater leverage if you hold it as far forward on the grip as possible. A long fore grip also allows you to fully extend your arms in comfort, so you don't tire as quickly.

Most standup rods are rated by line class, but this is not as closely followed when matching reels and line as it is in conventional offshore fishing. For example, a rod might be rated as 80-pound class, but used with a 50-pound class reel spooled with 50- or 80-pound line. One hundred and 130-pound line is used on some outfits.

The harness system is every bit as important in standup fishing as the rod and reel. Much of the advantage of the short rod is lost if the harness and gimbal belt do not fit properly. When fighting a large fish with standup tackle, one is constantly on the edge of a fine balance. If the reel drag should grab, or if the harness straps are not adjusted properly, you may find yourself on the verge of going overboard as you rock back and forth to pump your fish. The harness must allow your center of gravity to be precisely where it should be, tipping you neither too far forward nor backward. If you have to lean forward all the time, you're in trouble.

Just any old harness with a high riding gimbal belt will not do. Ideally, you should shop for the entire system—harness, gimbal belt, and rod—at the same time.

The padded harness should fit snugly across your hips, not above the hip bones. This is most important. It should definitely not be situated beneath your buttocks or across the back of your legs where it would force your center of gravity, under load, much too far back for safety.

The gimbal belt, either attached to the harness by clips or snaps, or belted separately around your body, should be situated across the top of your legs. It should not be down around your knees or up around your belt line. For comfort, its width should be dictated by the width of your upper legs. If it's too narrow, you'll realize your error 5 minutes into a tussle with your first large fish, and then it's too late for exchanges.

Once you've taken these factors into consideration, hook up everything together: rod and reel, harness, and gimbal belt. Adjust the straps so that your arms reach well up on the fore grip with the harness and gimbal belt placed as previously noted. Break your knees only enough to settle your weight onto your heels. Your body should be leaning slightly forward, much like the posture of a skier. A skier (like a standup angler) must maintain balance without either pitching forward or falling backward, especially when encountering bumps and holes in the surface of the snow (analogous to a pitching deck or surging gamefish). Neither skier nor standup angler should hold his shoulders back or settle into a seated position with his center of gravity behind his heels. Nor should he force himself into a weight-forward position, where a sudden bump could pitch him face first into the snow (or a surging fish yank the angler headfirst over the transom and into the ocean).

The triangle formed between the point where your outstretched hand grasps the rod high on the fore grip, your armpit, and the end of the gimbal rod butt where it rests in the gimbal belt, should be equilateral and each of these three angles should approximate 60 degrees. The dimensions of rod and rod butt, along with the fit of the harness and gimbal belt, should allow you to assume such a posture comfortably. If it doesn't feel right, try a longer or shorter butt, or look for a longer fore grip until you find what fits your height, weight, and torso and arm length.

Next, try an exercise that will confirm that the entire system fits you, and allow you to make a dry run to make sure that the system is adjusted according to your own physical limitations. First, tie the end of the line to an immovable object. Then, assume the position outlined above with your weight on your heels and your body in the "skiing position." Tilt back a bit, lowering your center of gravity and applying pressure on the bent rod. While in that position, set the strike drag on the reel to a comfortable point. Regardless of the line test, set it so that you pull line off the reel against the drag at a point that is both comfortable and realistic for your own strength and balance. You should not be able to lean backward with all your weight without pulling line against the drag. For the average angler, the reel's strike drag setting should probably never exceed 18 to 22 pounds. This is no time for machismo. To be on the safe side, try maintaining the pressure on the bent rod for at least 15 or 20 minutes, and then see how you feel. You may decide to lighten the drag still further.

That "safe" drag setting, which you can record afterwards using a hand scale, should be your reference point for your standup tackle system. It becomes your safety factor and helps prevent accidents. Remember, the breaking strength of your line is a consideration secondary to your own physical capacity and safety. While heavier line provides more abrasion resistance, line diameter must also be considered in terms of reel capacity. If you're after trophy gamefish you must first match your choice of reels (including considerations of line capacities and drag systems) to your chosen line test, always remembering the drag setting limit imposed by your physical capacity. As a standup angler, you're operating under a whole new set of rules from the seated angler, whose chair takes much of the heavy pressure. Your personally fitted harness system, along with a sensible drag setting and a balanced, rather than exaggerated, stance will help prevent a nasty accident should you pop the line or pull the hook on a large fish.

Little has been said here about reels, but that's because special types of reels expressly for standup fishing are unnecessary. Most standup anglers after big game prefer lever drag reels, and many use models with two-speed features. Star drag reels are still widely used and can do the job, but have the disadvantage of not being able to be readjusted accurately during the fight. The drag on lever reels, however, can be preset so that the angler can always return to his preset strike position and know how many pounds of drag his reel is exerting at a variety of settings. Drag is an important element of this system, however, for obvious reasons. There is a lot of pressure applied on big fish, and when they surge, it's essential that the drag not only be properly set, but smooth. If it surges, the angler can lose balance and be in danger of falling. At the very least, it will hamper fishing efforts and increase the length of the fight.

Line capacity, of course, is a factor when fighting big fish in a broad offshore ocean, but all of the common big-game reels (see: big-game tackle) have plenty of capacity, especially if used with thinner diameter line. A full reel is important, however, as it means that more line is recovered with each turn of the handle. Many anglers fill their reels with a greater line strength than the customary rating for the reel (for instance, filling a 50-pound IGFA-class reel with 80-pound line).

Standup fishing is a necessity on long-range boats.

Accessory tackle items that many standup anglers employ, especially those on long-range party boats where they fish over railings, is a forearm pad and knee pads. The forearm pad protects the arm when it brushes against the rail, and the knee pads protect the knees against railings and gunwales. On boats with high gunwales or rails, many anglers plant their feet squarely on the deck with their knees against these objects, so the pads provide some comfort.

Technique

When using standup tackle on a deep fish, begin with your left hand on the rod near the top of the fore grip and right hand on the reel handle, and lift up. Some anglers lift up with their arms, but many prefer leg-hip-pelvis action in conjunction with the harness. When you use your arms you're putting a lot of stress on back and shoulder muscles; there is more power in your legs. Therefore, you should stand with your feet well apart for comfort and stability, then make a dipping and pumping motion by bending your knees and thrusting the gimbal on your pelvis forward as you pump the rod upward. This is followed quickly by using your legs to rise up while lowering the rod a short distance and winding a few inches of line rapidly and evenly onto the reel spool. Lowering the rod only a short distance produces just a few inches of line at a time, but the idea is to keep this up and make many line-gaining strokes per minute, giving the fish no chance to get its head or have a moment of recovery.

In the real world of pitching decks and surging big gamefish, much has been made of this standup fishing technique, referred to by some as a "pump and grind" burlesque motion. No matter how it looks, when used sensibly it allows the angler to apply maximum pressure on a fish, especially when the fight is straight up and down (and close to that), or when the boat is backing down. If the feet are planted too far apart, or the angler exaggerates the pumping action to the point of leaning too far forward or backward at either end of the stroke, the angler can place himself in jeopardy.

This can be especially true when a fish is pulling hard far from the boat horizontally. At such times, the rod is bent less than when the fight is more up and down, and the chances of pitching forward when the boat rolls or the fish suddenly surges harder, or of crashing backwards if the line snaps or the hook pulls, are greater. When a fish is close to the boat, with the rod sharply bent by a fish bulldogging below, you can maintain better balance while at the same time applying greater pressure. The leverage becomes greater because the fore grip-to-rod-tip distance is shorter when the rod takes a deep bend. It's also easier to maintain a steady balance when the pressure of the fish is down, rather than out.

At such times, there is little doubt that a short stroke pumping action, with only a quick turn of the reel handle at each short stroke, applies maximum pressure on a fish. This technique was developed many years ago by anglers fighting giant bluefin tuna in the Bahamas, who used a short stroke, even though fishing from a fighting chair using long trolling rods, to land many giant tuna in a day. But the average angler is often unable to do that, especially with long rods, and he has a tendency to tire himself out and give the fish too much opportunity to recoup some energy.

When standup fishing, the same principal can work as well, the difference being that the short rod aids pumping and pressuring, enhances mobility, and can be employed more effectively by more anglers. It is important to realize that this short-rod/short-pumping technique avoids the long strokes from conventional tackle that often permit a fish to get its head on a downstroke even though it appears that the angler is making progress.

There are some formulas that explain the difference in mechanical advantage of a long rod versus a short rod when fighting fish that are deep, but the bottom line is that there is a mechanical advantage to the shorter rod and more efficient use of the angler's energy because he can handle the pressure more easily.

The basic method of fighting a large fish on standup tackle, called short stroking, is more than just a continuous series of short rod jerks. However, it does involve short rod lifts followed by rapid cranking of the handle, with attention paid to maximizing effort in the power zone and being careful not to lift the rod too high. Bringing the rod tip up high (above horizontal in the case of standup fishing) places too much pressure on the rod tip and not enough on the butt. Properly designed standup rods have a fast rod tip recovery, but gain most of

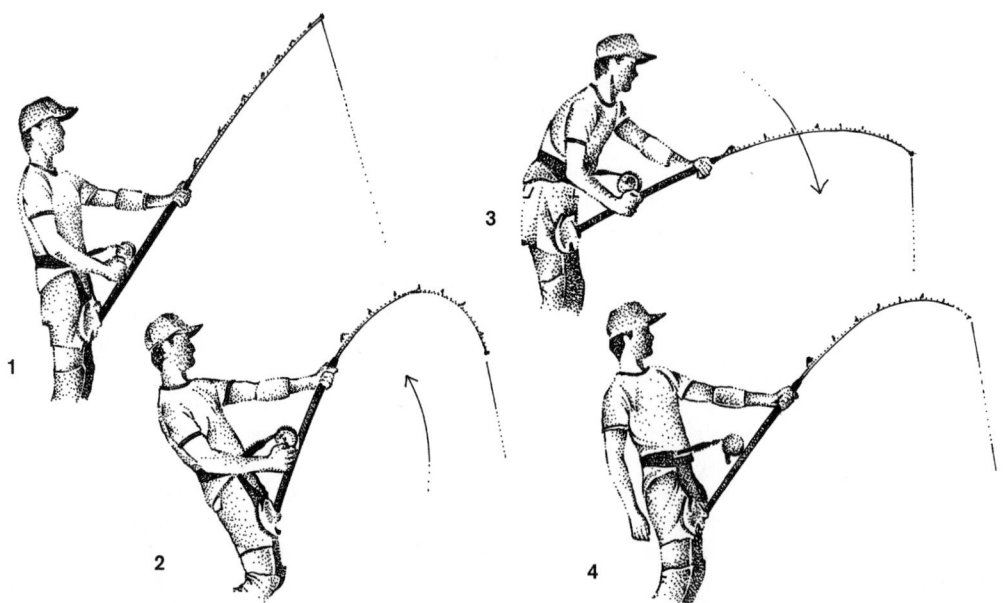

This angler is using standup tackle with a properly adjusted rod belt and harness, and knee pads for bracing. Playing a fish begins with the left hand gripping the rod near the top of the fore grip (1). Working a deep fish requires lifting, which is best done by dipping the knees and hips and leaning back (2), then simultaneously lowering the rod and turning the handle to recover line (3). Continue this until the fish is brought to landing position. When a fish runs off and takes line during a battle, or when you need to rest briefly, maintain pressure by leaning slightly back to keep the rod tip up, and hold the rod in hand without pulling on it (4). Alternate hands for holding the rod if necessary, but recover line whenever the opportunity exists.

their muscling ability from a powerful butt; the lower two-thirds of the rod provide great lifting ability, and this is diminished when the rod is raised above the horizontal level. Therefore, the correct technique is nonstop short cycles of lifting and retrieving.

With the knees bent, the reel in low gear (assuming a two-speed reel), and the rod doubled over to the water, begin by raising the rod up to horizontal position; this is called the upstroke. You should start cranking the reel handle a fraction of a second before lowering the rod and continue until the downstroke is completed. The distance move may be so slight that only a fraction of a turn of the handle is completed. As soon as the downstroke is completed, the upstroke begins, and the cycle is repeated. Most of the time, you make progress in short increments, but it is important with large fish that you keep it up. Keeping the short-stroking action up does not allow a fish to rest for a second, and directs its head upward.

Remember that the greatest advantage is for fish that are not close to the surface, and that the best scenario is not when a fish is directly below your boat at a 90-degree angle, but out a bit so that the line points to the fish at a lesser angle. When a hooked fish is far from a dead boat and the angle of the line is shallow or closer to horizontal, be careful not to exaggerate the pumping motion. Although short pumping works here, it is in such situations that the beginning standup angler must remember the guidelines on drag setting and stance. When the pull is nearly horizontal, the risk of pitching forward or backward are greatest, and an exaggerated short stroke can get you into trouble. Also note that the motion of some standup experts, when tested against a machine, produces a pull that exceeds the preset drag setting of the reel. Although this translates into greater pressure on a fish, it also carries implications in terms of the safety factor of drags set according to the physical limitations of the individual angler.

It is generally helpful if anglers maintain a steady rhythm when pumping fish using standup tackle and are careful not to overdo it. Some anglers get excited and forget about their own comfort and safety, which they will likely pay for later. Rest when the fish is taking line, and cradle the rod in your hand rather than wrapping your thumb around it; this avoids the "death" grip and lessens hand cramping and fatigue. When there are swells, you can also use the motion of the sea to your benefit, pulling on a fish as the boat lifts upward, and reeling in line as the boat descends.

Although standup fishing has become a popular technique for big-game anglers, and has actually prevented many of the aches and pains that were incurred by anglers who fought large tough species while standing up with older gear, there are some physical limitations to it and not everyone can do this. This technique is not recommended for children or for adults with a bad back or in a physical condition that would prevent them from maintaining their balance and strength during the course of a fight.

This does not mean that standup fishing is only for athletic muscle-bound gym rats. On the contrary, proper technique rather than plenty of muscle is the key, provided that you have the right equipment.

Incidentally, this system of equipment and technique is still evolving, and anglers are finding ways to merge the best aspects of standup fishing with the virtues of a fighting chair. Remember that standup tackle has limitations when the fish are too large and heavier equipment than can be held is necessary. What if you're using standup tackle for midsize fish and along comes a monster? Suddenly it's obvious that the fish on the other end of the string should best be fought from a fighting chair. To address this, some chairs now have a double-ended gimbal; turned one way the gimbal fits long butt conventional trolling rods and turned over it accommodates short standup rod butts in such a position that the reel handle can be cranked without banging your thighs. There are also rod holder inserts designed specifically to handle standup rod butts.

Short standup rods, when placed in conventionally situated fighting chairs, have the disadvantage of being too short for the line to clear the gunwale or covering board, and the angler in a chair with a short rod runs a great risk of abrading his line during the fight. However, if the chair is mounted on a platform high above the covering board, where the line could clear either corner of the boat, the angler could gain tremendous leverage advantage from the short rod with its long fore grip. At the same time, the pressures normally absorbed by his body when standing would be transferred to the gimbal in the chair itself when seated. This could be the best of both worlds.
See: **Big-Game Fishing.**

STARBOARD
The right side of a boat facing the bow.

STAR DRAG
A mechanism for adjusting the spool tension on certain types of fishing reels. Also known as a star wheel, this multispoked wheel is located at the handle, and is rotated to increase or decrease drag tension.
See: **Baitcasting Tackle; Conventional Tackle; Spincasting Tackle.**

STEAKING
The cutting of large fish into steak-size portions.
See: **Fish Preparation—Cleaning/Dressing.**

STEELHEAD   *Oncorhynchus mykiss.*
Other names—steelhead trout, steelie, sea-run rainbow.

There is a lot of confusion among the non-angling public about this fish. The term "steelhead" refers to the anadromous form of rainbow trout *(see: trout, rainbow),* and the fish known as steelhead bears the same scientific name as rainbow trout. Most scientific evaluations of rainbow trout list the steelhead as a form of rainbow trout. There are no major physical differences between a steelhead and rainbow trout, although the nature of their differing lifestyles results in subtle differences in shape and general appearance and a greater difference in color. Technically, the steelhead is a rainbow trout that migrates to sea as a juvenile and returns to freshwater as an adult to spawn, a process known as anadromy. Pacific salmon *(see: salmon, Pacific)* do this too, although steelhead (and rainbow trout) are positively separated from the various Pacific salmon species by having 8 to 12 rays in the anal fin.

"Anadromous" refers to fish that live a good portion of their lives in saltwater and spawn in freshwater; steelhead, which are endemic to the Pacific coasts of North America and Asia, have been successfully transplanted to inland environments, especially the Great Lakes. They live their entire lives in freshwater, residing in the lake but migrating up tributaries to spawn (which they accomplish more successfully than other introduced trout or salmon). Thus, steelhead may exist both in coastal environments and in large inland lake-river systems. The appearance and behavior of both forms of steelhead is largely the same.

The scientific classification of steelhead/rainbow trout, and the terminology that has been used for decades by the public, also led to confusion. Anglers view steelhead/rainbow trout as a type of "trout," as that is how scientists viewed them for more than two centuries. Steelhead/rainbow trout were placed in the trout genus and called *Salmo gairdneri* until late in the twentieth century, when both were reclassified and incorporated into the genus of Pacific salmon. This change resulted in the current scientific name, *Oncorhynchus mykiss.* Unlike Pacific salmon, the steelhead/rainbow trout has 8 to 12 rays in the anal fin, does not always die following spawning, may spawn more than once, and returns to the sea after each spawning.

No matter what it is called or where it is found, the steelhead is one of the most coveted fish for anglers, both in freshwater lakes and in rivers or streams. It is frequently acrobatic, grows to large and challenging sizes, and is a strong battler. Some anglers consider it the best of all freshwater sportfish, and most would rank it among the top three or five.

The coastal steelhead is also a target of commercial fishing. Its flesh is bright orange or red, delicious, and marketed both fresh and frozen.

Identification.   Generally speaking, steelhead are more slender and streamlined than rainbow trout. As with rainbow trout, the coloration on the back is basically a blue green shading to olive with black, regularly spaced spots. The black spots also cover both lobes of the tail. The black coloration fades over the lateral line to a silver white coloration that blends more toward white on the stomach. Steelhead fresh from the ocean or an inland lake are much more silvery than the resident rainbow. On steelhead, the typical colors and spots of the trout appear to be coming from beneath a dominant silvery sheen. This sheen gradually fades when the fish are in rivers, and steelhead become difficult to differentiate from resident rainbow trout as the spawning period approaches.

Steelhead and rainbow trout lack the red slash on the underjaw characteristic of cutthroat trout, but they do have white leading edges on the anal, pectoral, and pelvic fins. Spawning steelhead and rainbow develop a distinct pink to red striplike coloration that blends along the side, both above and below the lateral line. On steelhead, the rainbow trout coloration gradually fades following spawning to the more characteristic silvery color that the fish display during their ocean and lake journey. The distinct and beautiful coloration of steelhead during the spawning period is apparently important for mating and reproductive process. The silvery sheen and streamlined shape of ocean- or lake-bright steelhead is essential to survival in the large-water environment.

Steelhead

Juvenile steelhead trout are identical to rainbow trout until the period prior to their ocean migrations. Young trout and stunted adults have 8 to 13 parr marks on their sides. There are 5 to 10 parr marks between the head and dorsal fin. Prior to migrating to the sea, juvenile steelhead become very silvery and resemble miniature adults. They are called smolts during this life phase.

Size/Age. Steelhead grow much larger on average than rainbow trout and are capable of exceeding 40 pounds. The all-tackle world record is for a 42-pound, 2-ounce Alaskan fish caught in 1970. Steelhead are typically caught from 5 to 12 pounds, and fish exceeding 15 pounds are not uncommon in some waters. Most fish returning to rivers are five to six years old, and they can live for eight years.

Distribution. The original steelhead range in North America extended from Alaska's Kenai Peninsula to the Baja Peninsula in Mexico, and far inland in coastal rivers. Northern California, Oregon, Washington, southern Alaska, and especially British Columbia have had significant steelhead populations. Overfishing, pollution, dams, other habitat alteration, and additional factors have adversely affected many native runs of steelhead, as they have impacted Pacific salmon stocks. Some coastal runs are depressed if not threatened. Steelhead are also native to the eastern Pacific and portions of Asia, and have been widely introduced throughout the Great Lakes in North America, where they are primarily supported through hatchery production, as well as to other waters in North America and on other continents.

Life history/Behavior. When compared to the mundane habits of rainbow trout that spend their entire lives in streams and lakes, steelhead lead a complicated and dangerous life. Each spring thousands of 6-inch steelhead smolts leave the streams to begin their ocean journeys. Few survive to return; in Alaska, for every 100 smolts that reach the sea, only 5 to 10 return as a first-spawning adult.

Over a period of one to three years, steelhead move hundreds of miles or more from their parent stream. Many steelhead from Washington and Oregon are known to migrate far at sea to areas off the Alaskan Peninsula. A steelhead tagged south of Kiska Island in the western Aleutians was recovered roughly six months and 2,200 miles later in the Wynoochee River, Washington. Some fish from Alaska migrate to areas west of the Aleutian Islands and are routinely caught in net fisheries off the coast of Japan. Large numbers are intercepted in high-seas fisheries.

Most populations of steelhead appear in rivers in the fall; called fall-run steelhead, they enter freshwater systems as adults from August into the winter. Some river systems have spring-run steelhead, which end their ocean journeys in mid-April, May, and June; bright, shiny spring-run fish may be

A steelhead from the North Fork of the Lewis River, Washington.

mixed with well-marked resident rainbows that have spent the entire winter waiting for the spring spawning period. Still other populations return to their home stream in July and are known as summer steelhead. Spring and summer runs are much less common.

Spawning takes places in winter and spring. A male may spawn with several females, and more males than females die during the spawning period. Unlike salmon, steelhead commonly spawn more than once, and fish exceeding 28 inches are almost always repeat spawners. The ragged and spent spawners move slowly downstream to the sea, and their spawning, rainbow colors of spring return to a bright silvery hue. Lost fats are restored and adults again visit the feeding regions of their first ocean migration. On rare occasions, a fish will return to the stream within a few months, but most repeat spawners spend at least one winter in the sea between spawning migrations.

Generally, juvenile steelhead remain in the parent stream for roughly three years before migrating out to saltwater. If all steelhead left the stream at the same age, returned after the same length of time in the ocean, and died after spawning, the adults in a given stream would be of similar age. But they don't. In some Pacific coast rivers, summer-run, spring-run, and fall-run fish appear at the same time, greatly complicating matters.

Steelhead of the Great Lakes and inland systems have a similar life history, although their appearance in or near tributaries varies depending on their origins. Most migrate into tributaries from late fall through early spring, spawning in late winter or early spring. Summer-run fish, called Skamania steelhead, appear near shore and in tributaries in summer months.

Food and feeding habits. Steelhead in the ocean consume squid, crustaceans, and small fish. In large lakes, they primarily consume pelagic baitfish such as alewives and smelt. When making spawning runs in rivers and streams, they do not feed.

S

Angling. Steelhead in the ocean are seldom deliberately pursued by anglers; most of those taken are caught incidental to salmon fishing efforts, and are spawning or post-spawning migrants. There is a significant fishery for lake-dwelling steelhead in the Great Lakes, which are caught in a manner similar to salmon and brown trout, primarily by trolling. Spawning-run steelhead in rivers and streams are eagerly pursued throughout winter and spring by anglers using flies, spinners, spoons, diving plugs, and natural baits, especially salmon or trout roe and crayfish tails; they like fast, deep, running water, often gathering in deep holes, in fast whitewater areas, and behind rocks and logjams. Angling techniques in general are similar to those for chinook salmon (*see: salmon, chinook*).
See: Trout.

STEEL ROD

A fishing rod made from solid or tubular steel, and mounted with a handle, reel seat, and guides. Steel and split-cane bamboo were the primary rod materials until the development of fiberglass and the perfection of rods manufactured from those materials.

Now antiquated, steel rods are no longer used for either mass or custom rod construction. Some older versions may be collectibles.
See: Antique Fishing Tackle; Rod, Fishing.

STEERING DEVICE, REMOTE

For big-boat skippers, particularly those who spend a lot of time at the stern tending rigs and lines, who frequently fish alone, or who don't have a mate, remote control steering is very helpful. There are two ways to accomplish this, the most common being an autopilot, which works on a preselected course bearing and maintains a specific heading. This is primarily used for navigation as opposed to boat handling while rigging lines or fighting fish. A better way is with a wired or wireless control that allows for remote and constant positioning and repositioning as circumstances dictate. These help maintain boat control and are especially useful for keeping the boat straight when you set lines, fish alone, fight a big fish, or when you maneuver to adjust lines. Remote control steering doesn't work as well in rough water, in saltwater (due to corrosion of electronic parts), or when you're headed into the wind because many small steering adjustments must be made constantly.

STERN

The rear part of a boat.

STERN DRIVE

A term for inboard/outboard motor and the boats powered with such a motor.
See: Boat; Sportfishing Boat.

STICKBAIT

A long, generally slender, plug without a lip or concave head, used for surface fishing.
See: Plug; Surface Lure.

STICKLEBACKS

Sticklebacks are small, slim members of the Gasterosteidae family that are rarely more than 3 inches long and are confined to the Northern Hemisphere, occurring most abundantly in North America. They are primarily freshwater fish, but some occur also in brackish or shallow inshore waters of seas. The family contains seven genera, nine species, and several subspecies; they are of minimal forage value for predatory fish and little used as baits, but they have a distinctive appearance and unusual courtship and spawning behaviors.

Sticklebacks get their name from the short, stout spines in their first dorsal fin, the number of spines generally identifying the species. Family members have from 3 to 26 well-developed isolated dorsal spines preceding a normal dorsal fin having 6 to 14 rays. Most also have a spine at the leading edge of the anal fin and each pelvic fin. The body lacks scales, but in most species it is armored along the sides with bony plates.

Several species of sticklebacks are kept in aquariums. They swim with short spurts of speed, then pause. This makes them interesting to watch, as does their spawning ritual, which people are unlikely to observe in the wild. At spawning time, the males adopt courtship colors, with the belly bright red in some and velvety black in others. Each male builds a nest among the stems of aquatic plants; the nest is hollow inside but completely covered on the top, bottom, and sides with stems held together with a secretion of sticky threads. Once the nest has been built, the male searches for a female and drives her toward the nest, nipping at her fins and chasing after her if she turns the wrong way.

As soon as the female has laid her eggs, she leaves the nest, sometimes squirming out through the bottom. The male enters the nest immediately and fertilizes the eggs. Often he may go out again and get one or two other females to lay eggs in the nest. Some males build several nests at the same time. The eggs hatch in a week or less. While the eggs are incubating, the males of most species aerate them by fanning currents of water through the nest (the male of one species builds a nest with two holes in the top, and sucks water from one of the holes to cause circulation over the eggs). After the eggs hatch, the male tends the fry

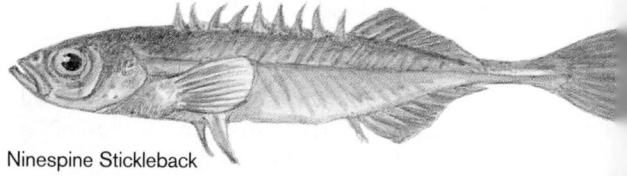

Ninespine Stickleback

for several days, generally trying to keep them near the nest.

One of the common species in North America is the brook stickleback *(Culaea inconstans),* found in streams from southern Ohio westward to Montana and northward, and throughout southern Canada from Nova Scotia to eastern British Columbia. It is generally less than $3^{1}/_{2}$ inches long. The five or six spines on its back are completely separate from one another rather than joined by a membrane, and the caudal peduncle is especially slender. Like most sticklebacks, it is quarrelsome and guards its territory, particularly its nest, from intruders.

The three-spine stickleback *(Gasterosteus aculeatus)* occurs in northern Eurasia and North America, living in both brackish water and freshwater. A number of subspecies are recognized. The ninespine stickleback *(Pungitius pungitius),* found in northern Europe, China, Japan, and northern North America, is dark brown, and the male becomes a rich black during the courtship and spawning periods. The fifteen spine stickleback *(Spinachia spinachia)* is a Euro-pean saltwater species restricted to northwestern Europe. The fourspine stickleback *(Apeltes quadracus)* is found only along the eastern coast of North America, from North Carolina to the Gulf of St. Lawrence. The blackspotted or two-spine stickleback *(G. wheatlandi)* is another western Atlantic species.

STILLFISHING

A somewhat antiquated term for any activity in which the angler fishes from a stationary position, usually with bait and float or bobber. This term commonly refers to a person in a boat that is anchored or otherwise stationed in a fixed place, but it may also refer to fishing from a fixed shore or bank position.
See: Float.

STILLWATER

A broadly used term, more prevalent in the United Kingdom, to classify and include any body of water that is not a river, stream, or tributary. To the British, stillwaters include a lake, reservoir, pond, or canal. To North Americans, they mainly refer to small lakes or ponds.

In a technical sense, stillwater means a body of water without current; however, many reservoirs, and some lakes, can have movement, either as a result of wind, inlets and outlets, or, in the case of man-made sites, as the result of water being used for irrigation or water supply or power generation.

STINGER HOOK
See: Trailer Hook.

STINGRAY
See: Rays and Skates.

STINKBAIT

A dough, paste, dip, or other prepared and foul smelling product that is applied to a hook and used for catfishing. Stinkbaits may be commercially manufactured or devised in home kitchen or home workshop experiments.

For more details and fishing information, *see: Catfish.*

STOCK

(1) A grouping of fish usually based on genetic relationship, geographic distribution, and movement patterns. This term is used more often with respect to saltwater species, especially in regard to a harvested or managed unit of fish. It is slightly different from a "population" of fish, a term that is used more commonly with respect to freshwater species and in regard to a group of individuals of the same species living in a specified area.
See: Fisheries Management.

(2) To place into a waterway fish that have been raised in a hatchery or other breeding area or that have been captured from some other location.
See: Hatchery.

STOCK DAM

A small pond, often called a tank or stock tank, possibly used for watering farm animals.

STOCKING

The introduction of fish (and other organisms) into a body of water. Stocking is usually considered to be an activity carried out deliberately or inadvertently by humans, although it can occur through natural means. With regard to fish, stocking may refer to the transfer of naturally grown specimens from one body of water into another, or it may refer to the introduction of hatchery-reared fish, in either case to introduce a new species or to supplement an existing population of that species.

The deliberate transfer of naturally grown fish is generally a prohibited activity, or one that can be done only with a permit from an appropriate management agency. The purpose of such a restriction is to prevent the spread of undesirable species, to control fish populations, to protect existing strains of fish, and in general to leave the management of aquatic resources to professionals. Anglers can inadvertently spread game and non-gamefish species, as well as aquatic plants and other animals, via the water in their boats and bait containers. The introduction of some species into a new environment can have adverse impacts upon fish populations and other resources.

The stocking of hatchery-reared fish occurs on several levels. A small number of federal hatcheries exist, usually for the purpose of helping to restore

native fish populations (such as naturally spawning lake trout in the Great Lakes) by raising and stocking native species. There are many privately owned and operated fish hatcheries, some of which are now also called fish farms, that supply fish for stocking purposes, primarily to individuals and groups with private waters. This is almost entirely freshwater fish, particularly bass, trout, catfish, and panfish.

Most stocking of fish into public waters is carried out by state fisheries agencies, primarily for freshwater fish. The majority of their stocking effort is focused on popular and prominent species, some of which have been depressed in number on specific waters because of overfishing, pollution, environmental changes, or other reasons. Various species of trout and salmon, plus striped bass, are among the most commonly stocked fish, but bass, walleye, and muskellunge are stocked as well.

Stocking is one of the tools that may be used by fishery biologists to manage fisheries. Stocking is subject to controversy and expectation; the rearing and stocking of some species of fish (like striped bass and chinook salmon) have provided enormous sportfishing opportunity, but the introduction of others (like various species of carp) has been ill advised and detrimental in assorted ways.
See: Exotic Species; Fisheries Management; Hatchery.

STOCKING FOOT WADERS
See: Waders.

STONECAT   *Noturus flavus.*
The stonecat is a widely distributed and relatively common member of the madtoms *(see).* It represents one extreme of madtom life histories, including the largest madtom in body size, the species with the longest life span, and a lower relative fecundity than other madtoms. It may be used for bait, especially in bass fishing.

Identification.   Stonecats are olive, yellowish, or slate colored on the upper half of their bodies and are the only madtoms that exceed 7 inches in total length. As a member of the *Noturus* subgenus, the stonecat has backward extensions from the sides of the toothpatch on the roof of its mouth.

The stonecat has two forms. In the Cumberland drainage in Tennessee, a scientifically undescribed form of the stonecat possesses two light bars (perpendicular to body length) on its nape. In other areas, there exists a patch in place of the bars. In both forms, the stonecat has a white spot at the rear of the dorsal fin base and one on the upper edge of the caudal fin. There are either no or a few weak teeth on the rear of the pectoral spine.

Size/Age.   Of 261 specimens collected from Missouri and Illinois streams, the largest specimens were a male 7.0 inches and a female that was 6.4 inches. Growth is fastest in the first year of life. Individuals up to 5.3 inches are at least three years of age. Individuals greater than 6.5 inches are four years and older. One-year-old specimens average 2.0 inches. The largest and oldest stonecat ever collected was 12.25 inches in total length and nine years old.

Distribution.   The stonecat has a widespread distribution. It exists in the Great Lakes, the St. Lawrence River, drainages of Hudson Bay, and the Mississippi River basin. It can be found from the Hudson River drainage of New York west to the Red River drainage of Hudson Bay. It is found in drainages of the Mississippi River basin from Quebec to Alberta, southerly to northern Alabama and Mississippi, and westerly to northeastern Oklahoma.

Habitat.   Generally, the stonecat inhabits riffles of medium to large rivers in places with many large rocks. It also occurs in lakes where currents or wave action produce streamlike conditions. In the main channels of large rivers, it has been found in swift water over sand substrate.

Food.   Mayfly larvae is an important food item for all sizes of stonecat. Excluding those specimens greater than 4.7 inches in standard length, all stonecats consume stonefly, caddisfly, and midge larvae. Stonecats less than 3.1 inches in standard length consume blackfly larvae, whereas larger stonecats consume more crayfish. Like most typical madtoms, stonecats consume a variety of organisms that are only infrequent prey, including fish eggs, worms, amphipods, and chilopods.

Spawning behavior.   Females mature at three to fours years of age and a mean standard length of 4.7 inches. Clutches are guarded by males under large, flat rocks in pools or crests of riffles. Rocks used as spawning cover averaged 200 square inches and were found in water averaging 34 inches deep. Nest-guarding males were a minimum of three years of age. Clutches contained 104 to more than 306 eggs.
See: Catfish.

STONEFLIES
Stoneflies belong to the scientific order Plecoptera, a term derived from *pleco,* meaning folded, and *ptera,* meaning wing, owing to the fact that their wings are folded down along the back when at rest. They are well-known aquatic insects *(see),* some species of which are also called salmonflies, and they include nearly 500 species in North America, all of which

Stonecat

Stonefly

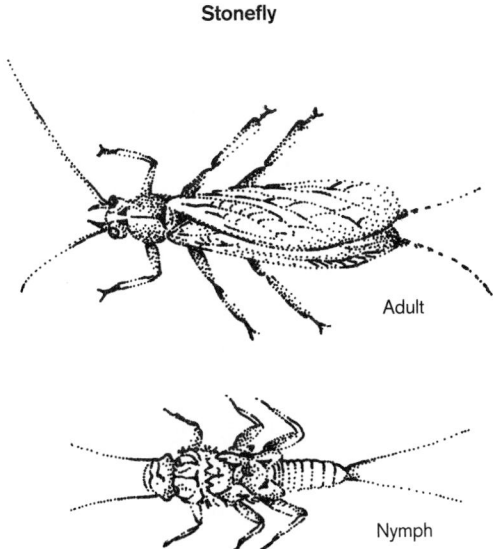

Adult

Nymph

have aquatic larvae and all but one of which are terrestrial (nonaquatic) as adults. Their life cycle consists of egg, nymph, and adult stages, with most of this being in the nymph, or immature, form.

The larval development period depends on species and local climate but can last underwater from three months to three years. During a given year, the larvae of different stonefly species hatch into adults at different times. Stonefly larvae are either predators or they feed on fungi and bacteria associated with leaf debris.

Generally, stoneflies are flattened and have legs that end with two hooks which allow them to maintain themselves in fast-moving current. Typically, stonefly larvae are found in cool clean streams with high levels of dissolved oxygen, and are very sensitive to pollution.

The life cycle of stoneflies is very similar to that of mayflies (see). Nymphs are timid and become active upon maturity. Unlike mayflies, when stoneflies are ready to hatch, they crawl out of the water onto the streamside and shed their nymphal skin out of the water on logs, stones, or tree branches. Although they are food for fish in the nymph form, they become especially significant food when migrating to the shoreline to hatch.

Some adult stoneflies fall or are blown into the water after hatching, and some fall in while flying, because they are awkward and weak in flight. They mate in flight, and females deposit their eggs on the water, bouncing like bombers along the surface. Both sexes fall spent to the water after. This mating stage is when stoneflies are most available to fish; they may be present in great numbers, which is referred to as a hatch and which may provide spectacular surface feeding by trout.

Stonefly larvae are mostly distinguished by these characteristics: two long antennae, much longer than the head; two hairlike tails; gill filaments that are often located on or behind each leg; three pairs of segmented legs (six legs total) on the middle

section of the body that each end in two hooks; and four wings that are folded back and flat on top of each other when the insect is at rest.

Stonefly larvae are similar to mayfly larvae; however, mayflies have platelike or feathery gill tufts along the sides of their abdomen, and stoneflies have none (rarely, stonefly larvae have fine gill filaments on some of the abdominal segments). Mayfly larvae usually have three tails (although some have two), whereas stonefly larvae have only two hairlike tails. Also, the antennae of mayfly larvae are much shorter than those of stonefly larvae. Further, mayfly larvae have only one hook at the end of each leg and stonefly larvae have two hooks.

Damselfly larvae can also superficially look like stoneflies, but damselfly larvae have three (not two) oar-shaped tails and short antennae.

STONEROLLER, CENTRAL   *Campostoma anomalum.*

Other names—stoneroller, minnow, hornyhead, knottyhead.

The central stoneroller is a member of the Cyprinidae family of minnows. It is a hardy species that provides important forage for gamefish and is commonly used as bait.

Identification.   The central stoneroller has a thick and barely compressed torpedo-shaped body that is dull gray with a brassy tint and a pale golden stripe along the upper side. It has an unusual appearance due its subterminal mouth and a hard cartilaginous ridge on the lower jaw. The mouth formation and lower ridge enable the central stoneroller to scrape algae and other minute organisms off rocks. There are dark brown to black blotches on the back and side of large specimens, the caudal fin is moderately forked, and the lateral line is nearly straight. Breeding males exhibit large tubercles on the top of the head and the upper scales almost to the base of the tail, and there are small tubercles on the pectoral rays and the first dorsal ray; they also have an orange cast, with orange and black anal and dorsal fins.

Size.   This species grows to $8^1/_2$ inches but is usually 4 to 6 inches long.

Distribution.   The central stoneroller ranges widely in the eastern and central United States and southern Canada in the Atlantic, Great Lakes, Hudson Bay, and Mississippi River basins, from

Central Stoneroller

New York to North Dakota and south to Georgia and Texas and northern Mexico. It is least common in the Great Plains.

Habitat. Central stonerollers prefer clean riffles, runs, and pools with current in streams, creeks, and small to medium rivers.

Spawning behavior. The male central stoneroller primarily builds pit nests by carrying pebbles in its mouth or disturbing the upstream gravel to float pebbles downstream. Nests are communal and constructed in gravel areas at the top of riffles. They are relatively shallow and are built in quiet areas or those with moderate current or where there is overhanging protection. Spawning occurs in spring, and males defend their territories and aggressively challenge other males.

Food. The diet of central stonerollers is algae, insect larvae, and other bottom organisms. This fish has an unusually elongated gut that winds around the swim bladder to facilitate the digestion of algae.

Angling. Because it is hardy and lively on a hook, the central stoneroller is often used as bait.
See: Minnow.

STRAKE
Longitudinal ridge along the bottom of a boat hull that ends at the stern. These are usually multiple strakes on either side of the centerline, and they help lift the boat when running.
See: Boat.

STRATIFICATION
The temperature layering of lakes in temperate climates. The water temperature in shallow lakes is generally the same, or not very different, from top to bottom, through the season. However, deep lakes stratify because the density of water changes as its temperature changes.

Water is most dense at 39°F. Above and below that temperature, water expands and becomes less dense. This means that in the spring, just before the ice melts, the water near the bottom will be at 39°. Water above that layer will be cooler, approaching 32° just under the ice. As the air temperature rises, the ice melts and the surface waters begin to heat up. Wind action and increasing density cause this surface water to sink and mix with the deeper water; this process is called spring turnover, and the entire lake is essentially a uniform 39°.

As long as the weather remains windy, the lake will continue to mix. When a calm period occurs, the lake water will stratify thermally, separating into layers of different temperature. The warmer, lighter surface water becomes segregated from the colder, heavier bottom water.

As summer progresses and the temperature difference between top and bottom increases, stratification becomes more stable, and water layers are isolated from each other. The surface layer, or epilimnion, is well mixed and of nearly uniform temperature. Below that is a transition layer, called the thermocline or metalimnion, where the temperature drops at least a degree per meter. The bottom layer, containing the coldest water, is the hypolimnion. Significant differences may exist in the water chemistry between the three layers and are most pronounced by mid- to late-summer. One of the most important things that also happens at this stage is that new oxygen *(see)* usually remains in the upper layers, being prevented by the thermocline from reaching the deeper levels; oxygen is not replenished in the deeper cold levels, and the lack of replenishment can be a problem in some waters.

Seasonal Water Conditions

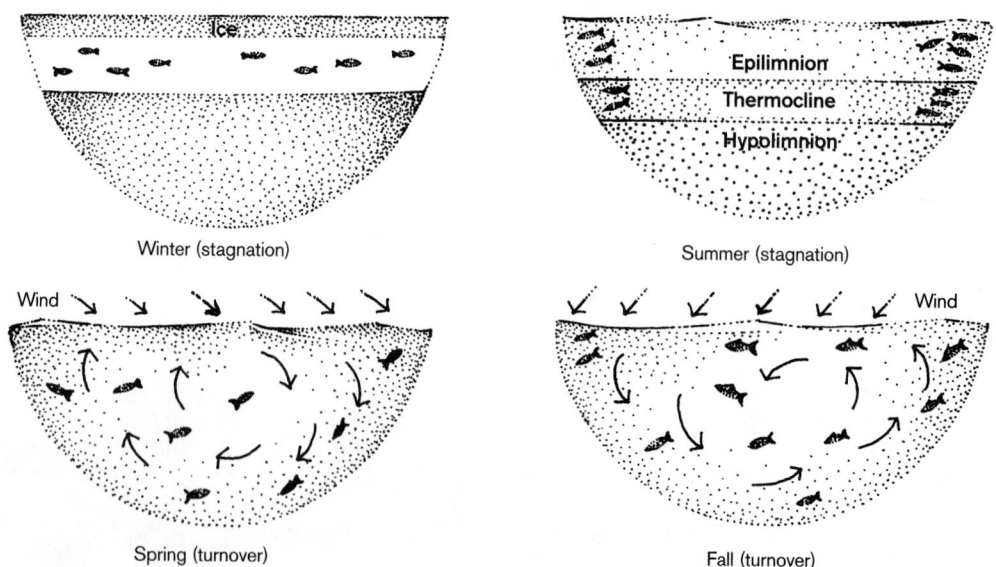

The turnover phenomenon occurs twice yearly after periods of stagnation.

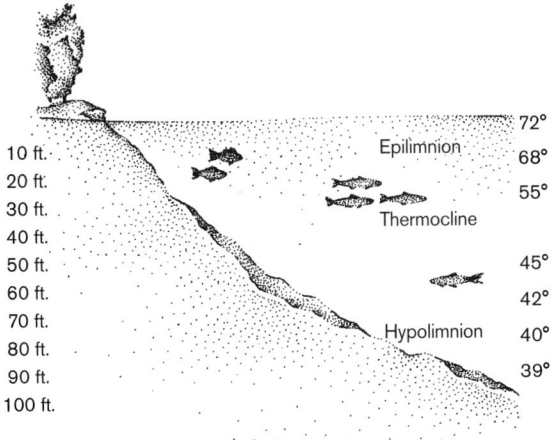

10 ft.
20 ft.
30 ft.
40 ft.
50 ft.
60 ft.
70 ft.
80 ft.
90 ft.
100 ft.

Epilimnion 72°
68°
55°
Thermocline
45°
42°
Hypolimnion 40°
39°

In lakes where a thermocline is established, that zone is usually rich with oxygen and fish.

As air temperature drops in the fall, the surface water temperature declines. Gradually the thermal gradient is broken down and the lake water again becomes all the same temperature; this process is called the fall turnover. As water temperature continues to drop, the lake mixes until it reaches a uniform 39°. Once the lake surface has reached 32°, a cold, calm night can leave a sheet of ice on the surface, leading to increasing ice thickness.

The stratification of a lake has important implications for anglers from spring through fall, especially those who seek coldwater species. Early in the season, the warming upper layers become most attractive for the widest variety of species and are most accessible to anglers, which in part explains why spring fishing is very popular. In the warmer weather when the upper layers have warmed, coldwater fish will generally be in the deeper levels that correspond to their preferred temperature zone, which is usually also the same zone that their primary forage inhabits. This is usually just above, in, or just below the thermocline, the depth of which varies depending on the body of water. In the fall, the reverse scenario occurs, although the location of coldwater fish may now also be influenced by spawning (and movement to tributaries).

Gamefish that do not prefer colder water are generally in the upper layer of a lake and along the margins throughout the seasons, and in the warmest water available in winter.

STREAMER FLY
A sinking artificial fly with feathers that represents specific or generic baitfish as well as such assorted prey as leeches, worms, eels, and so forth.
See: Fly.

STRIKE
(1) The actual, or attempted, assault of a lure, fly, or hooked natural bait by a fish; also called a "bite" with reference to natural bait.

(2) The reaction of an angler when a fish takes the lure, fly, or bait, generally known as "setting the hook" (see) but also referred to as striking the fish.

(3) A preset drag position on a lever drag reel (see).

STRIKE DRAG
The basic drag position on lever drag (big-game) reels used for most fish fighting activities. This is preset to desired levels of tension, usually 25 percent and sometimes up to 33 percent of the wet breaking strength of the line.
See: Big-Game Tackle; Line.

STRIKE INDICATOR
(1) Also known as a bite indicator, a strike indicator is any small object, usually one that floats, which is used to indicate a bite, or strike, by a fish on some form of natural bait. All floats and bobbers are types of strike indicators, although not actually called such.
See: Bite Indicator; Bobber; Float.

(2) A visible object that is attached to the leader when fly fishing to help show leader movement when a fly has been taken by a fish in moving water. By watching this object, which is primarily used in nymph fishing, the angler knows when to react quickly to a strike. A strike indicator may be a white swatch of deer hair, a colorful adhesive-backed piece of foam, or floatant-dressed yarn, and is attached to the leader an appropriate distance above the fly in accordance with the depth of water to be fished.
See: Fly.

STRINGER
A rope, chain, cord, line, or similar device for tethering fish. Fish may be retained on the main strand of the stringer, or on plastic or metal clips that are spaced along the stringer. A stringer is usually placed in the water to prevent exposure to sun, wind, dirt, and other elements, and is intended for retaining fish that will be kept, not later released. Further information about stringers and the proper care and storage of fish is contained in other entries.
See: Catch-and-Release; Fish Preparation—Care.

STRIP BAIT
A strip of meat from a fish, clam, squid, or other bait impaled on a fish hook.

STRIPPING
The act of manipulating a fly and retrieving line and fly by pulling on the fly line.
See: Fly; Flycasting Tackle.

STRIPPING BASKET

A basketlike container, also called a shooting basket, for holding fly line that is retrieved (stripped) after a cast. The basket, which may be fastened to the waist of an angler by a belt, or placed on the ground or boat floor, should be completely smooth inside and with rounded edges. In addition to being a convenient place to stow fly line, it keeps that line from getting tangled on loose objects so that it can flow readily (shoot) through the rod guides when executing a cast.

STRIPPING GUIDE

The lowest guide or guides, closest to the reel on a fly rod.
See: Flycasting Tackle.

STRIPPING LINE

An important element of fly fishing and flycasting in which a fly is retrieved or manipulated by stripping it in with your free hand; fish may also be played by stripping line in, as opposed to reeling it onto the spool of the fly reel.
See: Flycasting Tackle.

STRUCTURE

In the broadest sense, structure is any object that provides shelter or feeding opportunity to gamefish; this term is especially used by bass anglers in freshwater and covers a wide array of natural and man-made objects where bass are caught. In coastal waters, a structure is a man-made object, primarily a gas or oil rig or platform, which tends to concentrate species much like a natural or artificial reef *(see)*.

STURGEON

Sturgeon are large, slow-maturing, long-lived, and primitive fish found in large inland and coastal rivers, as well as in some lakes. They are contemporary species of ancient lineages; fossil remains of sturgeon and related paddlefish *(see)* have been dated to early in the Triassic Period of the Mesozoic Era (230 to 265 million years ago), making them contemporaries of dinosaurs and causing them to be referred to as "living fossils." Of the relatively few bony fish that can be characterized as living fossils, such as the coelacanth *(see)*, only sturgeon and paddlefish are represented by more than one or two living species.

Best known for the black caviar made from their eggs, sturgeon and paddlefish are members of the order Acipenseriformes, but at some distant point they separated from a common ancestor. As a result, sturgeon are members of the family Acipenseridae, and paddlefish are members of Polyodontidae. Both are considered bony fish; however, they have a mostly cartilaginous skeleton. Their closest living relatives are gar *(see)* and bowfin *(see)*.

Like paddlefish, sturgeon are distinctive in appearance. Both possess a heterocercal tail (the upper lobe is larger than the lower), a spiral valve intestine, a spiracle (aperture for breathing), an upper jaw that is not fused with the cranium, and a cartilaginous backbone as adults. Sturgeon have five rows of bony scutes (scalelike plates), a bottom-oriented extendible hoselike mouth with fleshy lips, four barbels; an extended snout, and a teardrop-shaped body.

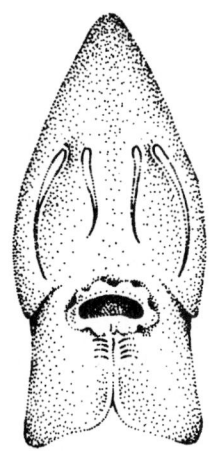

The mouth and barbels of a shovelnose sturgeon.

Most sturgeon are good to eat, although many people have never had the opportunity to taste them, or only associate them with their roe, which is the only true form of caviar (because paddlefish are related to sturgeon, there is some debate over whether their roe can be called caviar; but all other fish eggs are simply fish eggs, even if creative marketers call them caviar). In North America, in their days of abundance, sturgeon were highly marketable, particularly the flesh of the white, lake, and Atlantic sturgeon. Sturgeon is compared to beef or veal (the flesh of Atlantic sturgeon from New York's Hudson River was called "Albany beef"), and there was once a booming market for it when smoked. Smoked lake sturgeon helped fuel the economy of some Ohio towns along Lake Erie in the late 1800s.

Sturgeon have been steadily declining in numbers due to overexploitation; habitat changes, especially the construction of dams; and pollution, especially from chemicals that threaten the viability of eggs. In North America, a federally threatened or endangered sturgeon occurs on every coast and in the Mississippi River drainage. Populations of North American sturgeon that can sustain fishing pressure exist in only a few localities.

Green Sturgeon

The situation is even more critical in Eurasia, where poaching has augmented the problems caused by dams, pollution, and overfishing. Several species are on the verge of extinction, several are unofficially endangered, and all of the rest are threatened or virtually endangered.

Species

Estimates of the number of sturgeon species worldwide range from 23 to 30. Ichthyologists generally recognize four genera of sturgeon: *Acipenser, Scaphirhynchus, Huso,* and *Pseudoscaphirhynchus.* All are found only in the Northern Hemisphere, throughout Eurasia and North America, and they are remarkably similar across this range.

In North America, there are nine recognized species in two genera, *Acipenser* and the endemic genus *Scaphirhynchus.* White sturgeon *(Acipenser transmontanus)* and green sturgeon *(A. medirostris)* occur on the West Coast of North America. White sturgeon occur in lower and upper waters, sometimes hundreds of miles inland. Green sturgeon are usually found in the lower areas of estuaries (this species is also found in China, Japan, Korea, and Russia). Atlantic sturgeon *(A. oxyrinchus oxyrinchus)* and shortnose sturgeon *(A. brevirostrum)* live on the East Coast. The lake sturgeon *(A. fulvescens),* occurs in the Great Lakes and the upper Mississippi river system. Shovelnose sturgeon *(Scaphirhynchus platorhynchus)* and pallid sturgeon *(S. albus)* are found in the Mississippi River system. The Alabama sturgeon *(S. suttkusi)* is endemic to the Mobile River drainage in Alabama. The gulf sturgeon *(A. oxyrinchus desotoi),* a subspecies of the Atlantic sturgeon, occurs frequently in all gulf drainages from Tampa Bay, Florida, west to Mermantau River, Louisiana.

The best-known North American sturgeon are the Atlantic, lake, and white species. The white is most popular with anglers, largely due to its size and greater abundance within its range. Accounts of historic landings of white sturgeon report maximum weights between 1,300 and 2,000 pounds, and lengths of 20 feet. At least three white sturgeon caught in the nineteenth century reportedly weighed more than 1,500 pounds, and the largest-known rod-and-reel catch was a Columbia River specimen of 1,285 pounds. They are not known to attain such sizes today.

Sturgeon have historically been especially prevalent in the territories of the former Soviet Union, especially in the Volga River and the Caspian Sea into which it drains, as well as the Black and Adriatic Seas. The best known of the Eurasian species are the endangered beluga sturgeon *(Huso huso),* which produces beluga caviar; the endangered stellate or starry sturgeon *(A. stellatus),* which produces sevruga caviar; and the critically endangered European, or osetr, sturgeon *(A. sturio),* which produces golden brown osetr (or ossetra) caviar.

The beluga sturgeon is the largest fish known to inhabit freshwater, although accounts of its enormity vary widely; it has been reported to grow to lengths up to 20 feet and possibly 28 feet, and to reach a maximum weight of $1^{1}/_{2}$ tons. Reportedly a 3,359-pound beluga sturgeon was at one time captured; a 2,707-pound female caught in 1924 reportedly yielded 542 pounds of roe. A 2,645-pounder was reportedly netted in the Ural River in 1986. Another species, the sterlet sturgeon *(A. ruthenus),* which is near extinction, produces a legendary roe described as the "gold caviar of the Czars."

Life History

Members of the genus *Scaphirhynchus,* and the lake sturgeon, are potamodromous. They live in rivers or lakes, respectively, and migrate upstream into smaller tributaries or rivers to spawn. Their migratory patterns are similar to those of paddlefish.

Adult sturgeon of the genus *Acipenser,* with the lone exception of lake sturgeon, are anadromous. They typically winter in the ocean, migrating into coastal rivers as the water warms above 12°C. Sturgeon also use peak river discharge in the spring as a cue for migratory behavior. Most sturgeon stage in brackish water for a few days before migrating upstream, or out to the ocean. Staging in brackish water allows their body to adjust to the difficulties of regulating mineral concentrations in saltwater to the often extreme opposite problems of attaining balance in freshwater. They then migrate hundreds of miles upstream to reach gravel bars and spawn in high-velocity currents. Several males spawn with each female, and the eggs adhere to the gravel. The eggs hatch and the fry are carried downstream to areas with slower water velocity. Adults then move downstream to summer habitats where they remain until the fall. For many sturgeon species, summer habitat may be a refuge from high water temperatures.

In the fall, adults migrate downstream, stage in brackish water, and then migrate out to the ocean. Juvenile sturgeon remain in freshwater for several years. During the fall, they may migrate downstream until they reach brackish water, overwinter there, and migrate upstream in the spring.

Early growth is rapid, and juveniles may reach their adult size in as few as 3 years. Sturgeon often do not mature until 6 years of age, and in some areas they do not mature until age 10 or 12. Sturgeon spawn intermittently, every 2 to 6 years depending on the species.

The longevity and maximum size of sturgeon vary with local conditions and according to large-scale geographic patterns. Members of *Acipenser* are the largest and longest-living North American sturgeon, easily reaching a length of 4 feet and a weight of 100 or more pounds. Most species frequently will live 30 years and have been aged at more than 100 years. *Scaphirhynchus* are smaller (slightly

S

under 3 feet), sometimes reaching a weight of 70 pounds, and, typically, older individuals have been aged at 25 to 30 years old. All North American sturgeon species have been overfished, however, and it is likely that the oldest and largest individuals may have been removed and that, for various reasons, the individual species do not attain weights approaching their historic highs.

Most sturgeon are opportunistic feeders. Juveniles primarily eat aquatic invertebrates, whereas sub-adults may also consume mollusks, fish, and crayfish. Some species such as white sturgeon are good predators and willingly prey on other fish. Migrating adults of *Acipenser* typically do not feed while in freshwater, except white and lake sturgeon. Feeding occurs year-round in saline waters, but diets are relatively undescribed for most species.

Sturgeon are benthic and are most often found on or near the bottom. They are typically concentrated in deep pools that occur in river bends. During migration (spring and fall), juveniles and adults inhabit deep pools that occur in brackish water along the freshwater-saltwater interface of coastal rivers.

Threats

North American sturgeon were commercially important in the nineteenth and early twentieth centuries for caviar, oil, and food. These products were largely exported to Europe. Overfishing and pollution led to rapid population declines by the early 1900s. The construction of dams and the loss or alteration of habitat throughout the twentieth century, as well as increased and different types of pollution, contributed to further decline.

The slow growth, long periods of sexual immaturity, and intermittent spawning of sturgeon exacerbates recovery of their populations, as does the continued effects of habitat alteration, pollution, and locks and dams that prevent access to spawning sites. Consequently, most sturgeon are rare throughout their range, and either declining or holding at current levels, although at one time they were all common and abundant.

Currently, shortnose sturgeon, white sturgeon in the Kootenai River, and pallid sturgeon are federally listed as endangered species. The gulf sturgeon is federally protected as a threatened species. Federal protection has been proposed for the Alabama sturgeon. Every sturgeon, except for the green sturgeon, is protected by state laws in at least one state within its distribution. Because shovelnose sturgeon are nearly identical to pallid sturgeon, a federally endangered species, some localities do not allow commercial or recreational fishing for shovelnose.

Although many states have limited the commercial and recreational harvest of their respective sturgeon species, because these fish cross so many jurisdictional boundaries, including the U.S.–Canada border, a coordinated management and recovery effort is difficult and is further hindered by a lack of awareness among the general public regarding the history and status of these species.

Sportfishing

In the United States, anglers can potentially participate in three fisheries for sturgeon. In the Northwest and in Northern California, anglers can catch white sturgeon, and deliberate efforts at catching this species on rod and reel occur mostly in the Columbia and Snake Rivers as well as in San Francisco Bay. Lake sturgeon are caught in Wisconsin and Michigan; an ice fishing spear fishery for lake sturgeon exists in Lake Winnebago. In the Mississippi River drainage, it may be legal to catch shovelnose sturgeon in some areas.

Sturgeon are an infrequent accidental catch for anglers fishing for other species. Unlike paddlefish, it is illegal to snag them in most areas where they occur. Anglers should check regulations regarding these species; you may be required to release any sturgeon caught. Large fish that may legally be kept are best released to help benefit the recovery of the species. Because of their bottom-feeding habits and due to pollution (especially chemical) in some bodies of water inhabited by sturgeon, there are often health advisories about consuming these species.

Sturgeon are still part of legal commercial fisheries in some states, and they were once important, and in some cases still are important, components of indigenous fisheries.

See: Sturgeon, Atlantic; Sturgeon, Lake; Sturgeon, Shovelnose; Sturgeon, White.

STURGEON, ATLANTIC   *Acipenser oxyrinchus.*
Other names—sturgeon, common sturgeon, sea sturgeon, Albany beef; French: *esturgeon noir d'Amerique.*

The Atlantic sturgeon is a member of the Acipenseridae family of sturgeon and primarily a fish of the East Coast of North America. It has been used as a high-quality food fish and as a source of caviar since colonial days; it was so abundant in portions of its range that, in 1675, canoeists in Delaware Bay were warned to beware of 14- to 18-foot sturgeon that floated like submerged logs in tidal tributaries.

Although of traditional value to aboriginal people, Atlantic and other sturgeon primarily became highly prized in the nineteenth century for meat and roe, and as a source of isinglass, a gelatin obtained from the lining of the swim bladder and used as a clarifying agent and as an adhesive in glue. Caviar and smoked meat from Atlantic sturgeon were important exports (if processed correctly, the caviar from Atlantic sturgeon can be equal to that from Eurasian sturgeon), and restaurants characterized the meat of Atlantic sturgeon from the Hudson River as "Albany beef." The head, skin, and

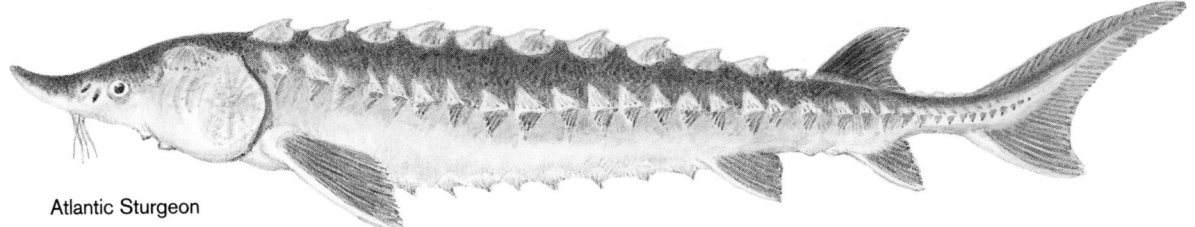

Atlantic Sturgeon

backbone were boiled for oil. By the late nineteenth century, the numbers of Atlantic sturgeon, as well as those of shortnose sturgeon (*A. brevirostrum*), a smaller species that shares much of the same range, had dramatically declined. Near the end of the nineteenth century, commercial landings of East Coast sturgeon, believed to be a mix of Atlantic and shortnose, were in excess of 7 million pounds a year. Landings throughout the twentieth century were only incidental.

Like many other sturgeon, the Atlantic is anadromous, living much of its life in brackish or saltwater and spawning in freshwater rivers. This species, and other sturgeon, are relatively slow growing and mature late in life, making them vulnerable to overexploitation. Dam construction, water pollution, and other changes in habitat, in addition to commercial overfishing, caused continued declines throughout the twentieth century. The Atlantic sturgeon is a threatened species today, and the shortnose is federally listed as endangered.

The decline of both species has left only remnant populations. Today, the lack of fish-passage facilities at dams, as well as poor habitat conditions, continues to impede the reestablishment of many sturgeon populations.

There is virtually no sportfishery for Atlantic sturgeon, due to their low numbers and harvest restrictions. If populations were high, a recreational fishery would undoubtedly exist, similar to that for the white sturgeon (*see: sturgeon, white*) in the Pacific Northwest, as catching hard-fighting specimens of the largest species in freshwater would appeal to many anglers. A limited directed commercial fishery still occurs for them, however, and a large portion of the landings are bycatch due to developing ocean fisheries. These practices continue to threaten recovery efforts.

Most fisheries are now closed in compliance with the Atlantic sturgeon management plan of the Atlantic States Marine Fisheries Commission, but the outlook is still poor, and much needs to be done to bring about even a modest growth in populations. Minimum size limits, harvest restrictions, and closed seasons exist in some states.

Identification. The Atlantic sturgeon is dark brown or olive green with a white belly. The head is protractile and has a long flat snout with four barbels on the underside. Five rows of scutes (bony scalelike plates) extend along the length of the body; one is along the back, and two each are along the sides and belly. The centers of the scutes along the back and sides are light, making them stand out in contrast to the darker surrounding color. These scutes are set extremely close together, and the bases of most overlap. The Atlantic sturgeon is distinguished from the similar shortnose by a longer snout.

Size/Age. Atlantic sturgeon may live as long as 60 years. They can attain a size of 14 feet and weigh more than 800 pounds. An 811-pounder is the largest known specimen. Fish exceeding 200 pounds, however, are rare today.

Distribution. This species ranges along the northwestern and western Atlantic coast in North America from the Hamilton River in Labrador, Canada, to northeastern Florida. It is currently more populous in the Hudson River, New York, than in other parts of its range, although it is not abundant there.

Habitat. The habitat of Atlantic sturgeon is primarily the estuaries and bays of large rivers, and deep pools of rivers when inland; in the ocean it inhabits shallow waters of the continental shelf.

Life history/Behavior. Spawning migrations to freshwater last from late winter through early summer, occurring later in the year at higher latitudes. Although it matures late in life, the Atlantic sturgeon is highly fecund, with total egg production proportional to its body size (a 9-foot, 245-pound female, about 30 years old, produced 61 pounds of roe). Nevertheless, it has a low reproduction rate, as females spawn only once every 3 to 5 years, and juvenile mortality is high. Furthermore, females do not mature until ages 7 to 10 in the southern part of their range, and ages 22 to 28 in the most northern part of their range; these late maturations complicate management efforts, especially because the fish are at sea for long periods, until they return to natal waters to spawn.

Juvenile sturgeon remain in freshwater for their first summer of life and then migrate to deeper more brackish water in winter. The juveniles migrate to and from freshwater for a number of years before joining the adult migration pattern. Tagging studies have demonstrated that Atlantic sturgeon migrate extensively both north and south of their natal river systems.

Food and feeding habits. Juveniles and adults are bottom-feeding scavengers, consuming a variety of crustaceans, bivalves, and worm prey, as well as insect larvae and small fish.

See: Sturgeon.

STURGEON, LAKE   *Acipenser fulvescens.*

Other names—sturgeon, red sturgeon, rock sturgeon; Cree: *nameo, nemeo.*

A member of the Acipenseridae family of sturgeon, the lake sturgeon was an important part of aboriginal culture in North America. In some cultures, spring ceremonial festivities were held at lake sturgeon spawning sites. In the early 1800s, lake sturgeon (and other sturgeon) were important as a source of isinglass, a gelatin obtained from the lining of the swim bladder, which was used as a clarifying agent in wine, beer, and jelly and as an adhesive in glue. Around 1855, a market for caviar was developed that in turn spurred a market for smoked fish around 1860. Caviar and smoked meat from lake sturgeon were also important exports to Europe. By 1910, however, lake sturgeon fisheries had been overexploited through the Great Lakes region. Overfishing, coupled with dams, habitation alteration, and pollution have since impeded the lake sturgeon's recovery in most areas.

Currently, there are minor sport fisheries (hook and line and spear fishing) for lake sturgeon in Wisconsin and Michigan, including Lake Winnebago, the Menominee River, and other areas. Recent commercial fisheries existed in the Moose River, Ontario, and St. Lawrence and Ottawa River systems in Quebec. In some fisheries, research indicated that stocks were experiencing too much fishing pressure, and new regulations to prevent damage to these self-sustaining populations were suggested.

For waterways with declining or extirpated populations (that is, Lake Winnipeg, Lake Erie, and Lake Ontario), lake sturgeon are being successfully raised in hatcheries for stocking. Current research shows, however, that brood stock should be taken from the water body where hatchery raised fish will be released; yet brood stock is also rare in areas where stocking may be helpful. These populations will require a great deal of time and improved conditions before they can recover fully. Lake sturgeon have responded positively to changes in dam discharges that facilitate or imitate run of river conditions. Signs of this include increased spawning activity.

Identification.   The somewhat torpedo-shaped lake sturgeon has a spiracle, and the upper lobe of the caudal fin is longer than the lower lobe. The anal fin origin is behind the dorsal fin origin. The fish exhibits an olive brown coloring, and the scutes (bony scalelike plates) on the back and along the side are the same color as the skin. There are 9 to 17 scutes on the back, 29 to 42 scutes along the sides, and 25 to 30 anal rays. There are 4 barbels on the underside of the mouth.

Size/Age.   Lake sturgeon may reach 9 feet in length and have been reported to weigh between 200 and 300 pounds, although fish of 100 pounds are extremely large today, and most are in the 40-pound range and about 4 feet long. The life expectancy of lake sturgeon varies according to different reports, but at one time it was believed to be 80 to 100 years or more. A specimen caught in 1952 was reputed to have been 152 years old, but older specimens of the modern era have only ranged to 38 years old.

Distribution.   Lake sturgeon occur in the St. Lawrence waterway and the Great Lakes. They are found in the Hudson Bay and Mississippi River basins from Quebec to Alberta and southward to Alabama and Louisiana, including Lake Winnipeg, Manitoba, and its tributaries. They are rare in the Ohio and middle Mississippi River basins. Lake sturgeon numbers are a fraction of what they once were throughout this range, and the species does not occur in some parts of its former range; some stocking efforts are undertaken.

Habitat.   Lake sturgeon are primarily freshwater fish, occurring in large lakes and rivers, usually 15 to 30 feet deep. They are found over mud, sand, or gravel bottoms but may (rarely) occur in brackish water.

Life history/Behavior.   Males mature around 14 to 16 years of age and females near 24 to 26 years of age. As adults, lake sturgeon migrate as far as 125 miles to spawn. They sometimes leap out of the water during spawning, and fall with a loud splash.

Spawning sturgeon migrate in the fall and then overwinter at the spawning sites. Spawning peaks in April at temperatures of 48° to 58°F; a secondary spawning probably follows in May. They spawn on gravel bars, or below dams or other obstructions, in swift, shallow water, sometimes in a spectacular commotion of thrashing, rolling, and leaping. Six to eight males spawn with each female. They broadcast their eggs and sperm over large substrate such as boulders, and the eggs adhere to the substrate. Eggs hatch at 8 to 14 days of fertilization and drift downstream to more placid waters during the night. As is typical for most sturgeon, early growth

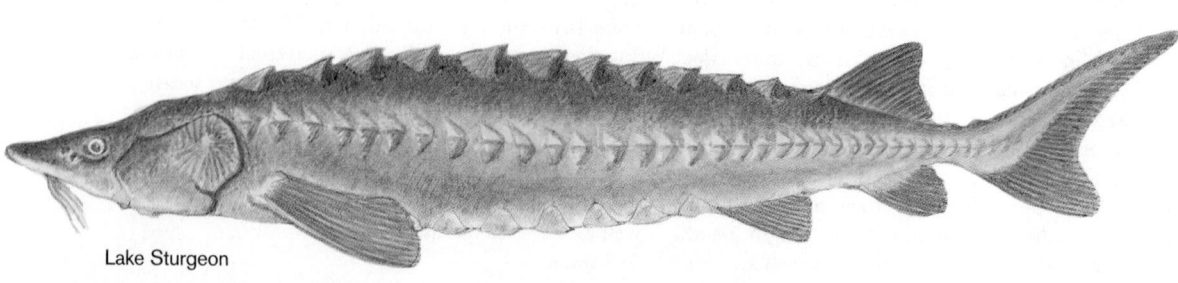

Lake Sturgeon

is rapid. Mature females spawn only once every several years.

Food and feeding habits.   Lake sturgeon feed in freshwater, typically on the bottom. In Lake Winnebago, young lake sturgeon feed primarily on midge larvae, larvae of some moths with aquatic life phases, and water fleas. Mayfly nymphs and mollusks are also important components of the lake sturgeon's diet. The amount of fish consumed by lake sturgeon varies by location, ranging from little or none to 25 percent of the diet. In some areas, small fish are a preferred bait.

Angling.   *See: Sturgeon, White.*

STURGEON, SHOVELNOSE

Scaphirhynchus platorinchus.
Other names—sturgeon, hackleback sturgeon.

A member of the Acipenseridae family of sturgeon, the shovelnose is a small species and the most abundant sturgeon in the Mississippi and Missouri Rivers and tributaries. The shovelnose is rarely encountered by anglers but has historically had commercial value. Because shovelnose sturgeon are nearly identical to pallid sturgeon (*S. albus*), a federally endangered species, some localities do not allow commercial or recreational fishing for shovelnose.

Identification.   Shovelnose sturgeon have a broad, flat head with an extended spadelike snout. There are four barbels under the snout, the two middle ones being almost as long as the outside barbels. All four are located in a straight line in front of the mouth. The body is brown to gray in color, with five rows of scutes (bony scalelike plates). The upper lobe of the caudal fin is longer than the lower lobe and has a threadlike extension, which may be worn off in older individuals. There are scales under the body and also on the caudal peduncle.

Size/Age.   The average size of adult shovelnose sturgeon is about 20 inches and $1^1/_2$ pounds. A large specimen is about 5 pounds; they rarely exceed 3 feet or 6 pounds in weight but reportedly may grow to 10 pounds. The shovelnose is smaller than the pallid sturgeon, which is also found in the Mississippi River system.

Distribution.   The shovelnose occurs in much the same range as the lake sturgeon *(see),* although not in the Great Lakes. Its range is the Mississippi River basin from western Pennsylvania to Montana and south to Louisiana; the Mobile Bay drainage in Alabama and Mississippi; and the upper Rio Grande in New Mexico.

Habitat.   This species prefers the fast currents of large rivers with sand or gravel bottoms but can live in muddy waters.

Spawning behavior.   Spawning begins at five to seven years of age and occurs over sand and gravel in large channels with fast currents.

Food.   The shovelnose feeds entirely on the bottom on the larvae of aquatic insects, which constitute the bulk of its diet. It may occasionally eat small fish.

STURGEON, WHITE   *Acipenser transmontanus.*
Other names—sturgeon, Columbia sturgeon, Oregon sturgeon, Pacific sturgeon, Sacramento sturgeon; French: *esturgeon blanc.*

A member of the Acipenseridae family of sturgeon, the white sturgeon is the largest fish occurring in freshwater in North America. In some areas, populations have recovered sufficiently since their decline in the early 1900s to support important recreational and commercial fisheries. Fisheries for white sturgeon occur in California, Washington, Oregon, and Idaho. Regulations vary from catch-and-release to slot limits. Peak fishing seasons vary among locations and span the entire calendar year. White sturgeon are listed as federally endangered in the Kootenai River, where the population has declined to critical levels due to dam operations and poor water quality from mining operations. Recent improvements in dam operations and water quality have allowed white sturgeon to begin spawning again in that river, and it is hoped that this population will not be extirpated.

Identification.   White sturgeon have a moderately blunt snout as adults, barbels closer to the snout tip than to the mouth, and no obvious scutes (bony scalelike plates behind the dorsal and anal fins. The fish is gray to pale olive on its upper body and white to pale gray on its ventral side. It has 28 to 30 anal rays, 11 to 14 scutes on its back, and 38 to 48 scutes along the sides.

Size/Age.   White sturgeon have been reported at more than 100 years old; most of the oldest individuals of the current era are roughly 40 to 60 years old. Accounts of historic landings of white sturgeon report maximum weights of between 1,300 and 2,000 pounds, and a length of 20 feet. At least three white sturgeon caught in the nineteenth century reportedly exceeded 1,500 pounds, and the largest-known rod-and-reel catch was a Columbia River specimen of 1,285 pounds. Fish under 6 feet long

Shovelnose Sturgeon

White Sturgeon

and weighing 60 to 70 pounds are commonly caught today, and fish from 6 to 9 feet long and weighing 200 to 500 pounds are possible, certainly in the Hell's Canyon section of the Snake River.

Distribution. White sturgeon are limited to the Pacific shores of North America from the Aleutian Islands, Alaska, to Monterey Bay, California, although they move far inland to spawn. In Canada, this fish is found in the Fraser River system; the Columbia River above Revelstoke, British Columbia; Duncan Lake, Vancouver Island; and possibly Okanagan Lake and other coastal drainages. The white sturgeon is landlocked in the upper Columbia River drainage and Montana. In Idaho, the white sturgeon occurs in the Snake River downstream from Shoshone Falls and in the Clearwater and Salmon Rivers. An isolated stock occurs in the Kootenai River drainage. In Montana, the white sturgeon appears in the Kootenai River. Genetic studies of Northwest populations have suggested that distinct subpopulations may be present within the species range. Some of the most reliable sportfisheries occur in the lower Columbia River, in the Snake River in Idaho, and in California's San Francisco Bay.

Habitat. The habitat of white sturgeon is primarily the estuaries and bays of large rivers, and the deep pools of rivers when inland.

Life history/Behavior. White sturgeon are anadromous, migrating from the ocean into freshwater to spawn; populations that are landlocked due to dams also show seasonal movements. Spawning typically occurs from April through early July, when water temperatures are 50° to 64°F, during the highest daily flows of the river. Spawning occurs in swift water. When hatched, yolk-sac larvae drift to deep water with slower currents where they grow rapidly, sometimes 15 inches or more in the first year. Females typically mature when 16 to 35 years of age, at roughly 47 inches in fork length.

Food and feeding habits. Young-of-year fish prey on amphipods, chironomid larvae, eulachon eggs, and other benthic organisms. Juveniles additionally consume bivalves. Adults are piscivorous and do feed in freshwater. Common baits include pile worms, ghost shrimp, grass shrimp, squawfish, and carp.

Angling. Sportfishing for white sturgeon (and other sturgeon for that matter) is strictly a bottom-working proposition, often with heavy tackle. The tackle must be matched to the water conditions and potential size of fish to be encountered. Light levelwind outfits and 17- or 20-pound line, for example, might be used for 60-pounders in the relatively slow and open water of San Francisco Bay, but heavy-duty lever-drag ocean reels with 40- to 80-pound line or more, and a capacity of 200 to 300 yards, might be used in the swift water of upper rivers where much bigger fish are a possibility.

Contrary to some beliefs, sturgeon are not idle squatters waiting for the current to bring them food; they meander about using their sensory abilities to locate prey or a scent trail that leads them to food. As a consequence, bait is the ticket to catching fish, and the possibilities are broad, depending on circumstances. Favorites include assorted fish (carp, squawfish, whitefish, herring, shad, and the like), both whole and cut in halves or chunks, as well as roe or spawn in bags, nightcrawlers, eels, and scented bait concoctions.

Hooks need not be especially large for smaller fish; 1/0 to 4/0 short-shanked models do the job, although larger versions, like 8/0 or 10/0 sizes, are necessary where big fish are likely. Sinkers are heavy, however, as most sturgeon fishing is done below high falls and dams, with slip, three-way, or walking sinkers in 3- to 10-ounce sizes, and sometimes a pound or more in serious current. Recently, white sturgeon anglers have taken to using microfilament line for its sensitivity, as the take of a sturgeon is extremely subtle. Sturgeon don't grab and run, so you look for a slight tap and then wait for the fish to steadily move off with the bait before setting the hook sharply.

When seeking sturgeon, fish large, deep holes directly below dams and falls, downstream from rapids, along the outside edge of a bend, and in the main channel. They also hold directly downstream from areas where the river bottom shallows up and there is a hard rock area. In smaller rivers, if the shallows are 2 to 4 feet deep, fast, and running over rock and gravel, look for sturgeon to hold about 50 yards downstream from structure, where the surface water visibly smoothes out. Here, the water should be about 8 to 10 feet deep.

When fishing a slow-moving, mud-bottom river that has a number of slowly twisting turns, look for sturgeon to hold along the outside edge of a bend. Investigate places that are at least 2 feet deeper than other areas in the river channel. Stick

A white sturgeon from the Columbia River, Washington.

to the center of the river channel if the river has few or no bends.

Where the river bottom consists of mud and loam, keep your bait slightly above bottom by using a floating jig tipped with a leech or nightcrawler or a tiny crappie float tied between sinker and bait. In fast rivers, fish channel areas with deep drops.

In tidal bays, either side of a tide change is good for fishing along dropoffs and by bridge abutments, on points, at bay mouths, and along breakwalls with baits, using a bottom rig with plenty of weight.

Sturgeon look like plodders, but they are strong, fast swimmers when hooked, and the battle can last a long time. They can provide exhilarating moments, sometimes leaping out of the water.
See: Sturgeon.

SUBSPECIES
A recognizable subpopulation of a single species (see), usually with a particular geographic distribution.

SUBSTRATE
The base on which an organism lives or grows; the sea or lake bed.
See: Bottom.

SUCKER
Suckers are medium-size fish that are well known to many anglers for their large lips. They belong to the family Catostomidae, which is closely related to the minnows. Their closest relatives are actually a group of fish from Southeast Asian rivers known as loaches. Suckers and related groups belong to the Ostariophysi order, a successful group with several physiological advancements for life in freshwater.

Suckers are widespread, distributed all across North America and into Russia and southern Asia. In North America, they occur from the Arctic Circle down well into Mexico and from the East Coast to the West Coast. The white sucker (Catostomus commersoni) is one of the most widely distributed fish in North America.

There are 75 species in the family Catostomidae, and they are distributed among three subfamilies:

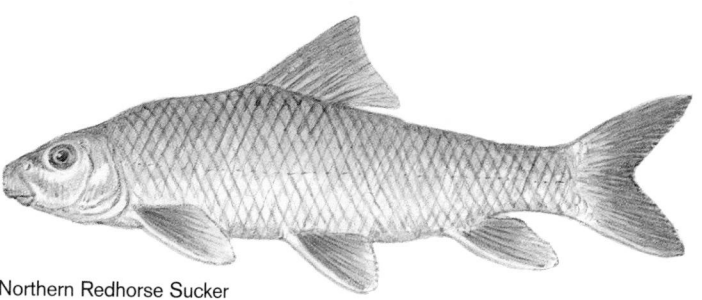

Northern Redhorse Sucker

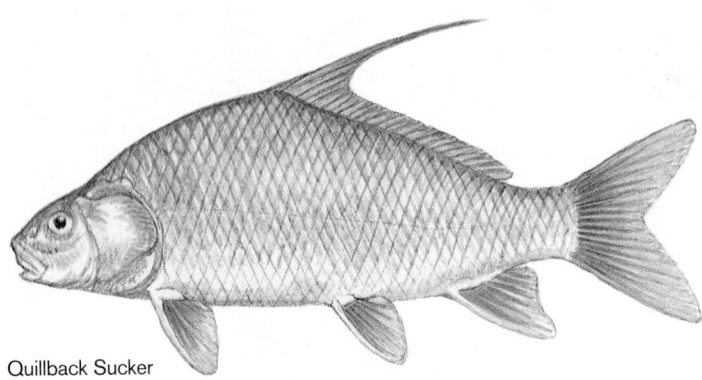

Quillback Sucker

Ictiobinae, Cycleptinae, and Catostominae. Ictiobinae, the buffalofish, are the biggest suckers and are widely distributed across the Great Plains, the Mississippi Valley, and the Gulf Coast of North America. They are distinguished from other suckers in North America by their very long dorsal and anal fins *(see: buffalo, bigmouth; buffalo, smallmouth).* The subfamily Cycleptinae has two members; one is in Southeast Asia, and the other, the blue sucker *(Cycleptus elongatus),* is in North America. Catostominae is the most wide-ranging of the three subfamilies. This group, primarily inhabiting North America, is composed of two tribes, Catostomini (the fine-scaled suckers) and Moxostomatini (the redhorses). Representative of the latter is the northern redhorse *(Moxostoma macrolepidotum),* which ranges across most of the northern United States and is characterized by red fins, especially the tail fin.

Suckers are most easily distinguished by their inferior mouths and large fleshy lips. They have no barbels like catfish, no hardened spines in their dorsal or anal fins like perch and sunfish, and no adipose fin like trout. Suckers are robust fish, slightly laterally compressed. Most suckers are medium-size fish, but they range in adult size from only 6 inches (Roanoke hogsucker, *Hypentelium roanokense*) to more than 33 pounds (buffalo).

Most suckers are not bright or distinctive in color. Many have an almost metallic sheen in shades of gold, green, purple, or white. Their coloration becomes more intense during reproduction, when many species darken in color and develop lateral stripes. Reproductive adults also develop hardened tubercles on their anal and caudal fins and heads. Young suckers typically have a more distinct color pattern, with several saddles on their backs and dark blotches on their sides for camouflage.

Many suckers get their names from their appearance, behavior, or habitat. The hogsuckers (genus *Hypentelium*) are named for their piglike heads and snouts. The quillback sucker *(Carpiodes cyprinus)* has extended narrow fin rays in its dorsal fin that are similar in appearance to porcupine quills. Buffalofish are named for their thick heads and steep foreheads that liken them in appearance to the American bison. The jumprocks (genus

Scartomyzon) are so named because some species jump out of the water while spawning. The torrent sucker *(Thoburnia rhothoeca)* is named for the fast-moving, turbulent riffles that it inhabits in Appalachian mountain streams.

Life history.   Suckers inhabit all types of freshwater habitats, including rivers, lakes, and small streams. Most river species live in moderately fast-run habitats with moderate depths. The biggest suckers live in large lakes and deep pools in larger rivers. Among the three subfamilies, Ictiobines and Cycleptines are specialized for life in large rivers and lakes, whereas the Catostomines inhabit a wide range of habitats. Most suckers live in waters with moderate velocity, although some mountain suckers in the Appalachian region inhabit very fast riffles. Because of their large size, suckers do not need to seek cover from predators, so they often coexist with bass and trout in deep pools. Despite popular belief, suckers are not fish that inhabit dirty, silty waters. In fact, most suckers require very clean substrate and are not tolerant of low dissolved oxygen.

With inferior mouths and large, fleshy lips, suckers are well adapted to feeding on the bottom of streams or lakes. Most species suck up substrate and sift out small invertebrates and other organic materials. The most common foods are insects and worms, although some suckers are specialized for feeding on snails, vegetation, or crustaceans. Several species will also feed on detritus, and scrape algae from rocks. Suckers that feed on detritus, like the white sucker *(see: sucker, white),* are the most widespread and abundant. Chubsuckers (genus *Erimyzon*) are midwater plankton feeders.

Many sucker species congregate in schools in deep habitats. Most of these species are large, and it is not believed that the schooling behavior is a mechanism for avoiding predators, but for feeding and reproducing. Many sucker species are thought to be nocturnal, feeding on other organisms that are most active at night. Their fleshy lips have sensory organs that allow them to seek out food at night.

Most suckers are moderately long lived; most species average a life span of 8 to 15 years. They become sexually mature at 2 to 3 years.

Spawning behavior.   A majority of suckers spawn in early spring, although some species continue into early summer. Many larger species make long migrations to the headwaters of rivers to spawn. They may come from farther down in the river or from adjacent lakes. These species spawn upstream, then the larvae hatch and drift downstream to recolonize lower stream reaches. Suckers typically need clean gravel substrate in which to spawn. This type of habitat usually occurs at the tail ends of pools, in riffles, and in gravel bars.

Most sucker species spawn in large aggregations. Several males may spawn with the same female at the same time. Many suckers spawn in a trio, with a female flanked by two smaller males. The males align next to the female in a suitable location in a riffle or pool tail. Then all three individuals shake violently as sperm and eggs are released. This shaking allows the fish to dig down into the substrate and bury the newly deposited eggs. Only one species of sucker, the river redhorse *(Moxostoma carinatum)*, actually prepares a redd like trout, but many do move around much gravel as they dig into the stream bottom. Suckers produce many small eggs and provide little or no parental care.

Value. Suckers are often labeled as trash fish and are badly maligned by many anglers. This most likely results from a misunderstanding of their life history and value. It is thought by some that suckers feed on trout eggs and pose a threat to trout populations. This is not true, as most suckers and trout that live in the same streams are adapted to living with each other and trout reproduction is not hindered. They certainly do not specialize on trout eggs, and there is little evidence that they regularly feed on trout eggs at all.

Suckers are also not commonly thought of as gamefish, although there are substantial commercial and recreational fisheries for them in certain regions of the country. Large species are often snagged or dipnetted as they make their large spawning runs in early spring. Also contrary to popular belief, suckers have very tasty flesh, although it is somewhat bony.

The real value of suckers is in their ecological role. They utilize food resources such as snails, detritus, and algae that would otherwise go largely unused. This gives them an important role in the ecosystems in which they live, processing nutrients and resources that benefit other species. Their usefulness as pike and muskellunge bait is also a testament to their value as prey for these large gamefish.

Angling. Although not a gamefish per se, suckers are pursued by a small number of anglers every year, especially in the spring when these fish ascend tributaries and rivers to spawn.

Suckers are found in most watersheds in creeks, streams, rivers, lakes, reservoirs, clear backwaters, and ponds. They will eat just about any fresh, natural baits found in their locale, but they aren't crazy about artificial lures and are not prone to chase after lures, although they may occasionally be caught on a slowly worked spinner or a jig tipped with bait, usually by an angler fishing for some other species. They are bottom feeders, and offerings should be presented on bottom or within a few inches of bottom. A host of sinker styles do the job, and the desired sinker weight varies according to depth and current.

Garden worms and bits of nightcrawlers work on suckers better than anything else. Don't put an entire nightcrawler on the hook when fishing for suckers; this is simply a way to feed these hard-to-hook creatures. Use about a third of a worm at a time and bunch it on the hook. A single, No. 2, turned-up-eye hook with a short shank is good for sucker fishing. There should be at least 24 inches between the hook and the sinker. In slow water, or no current, the length may be shortened.

Avoid setting the hook prematurely. Most anglers set the hook when they feel the initial tap of a sucker, but they miss the fish. Let the fish tap your bait about three times. After the third time, point the rod tip directly at the fish, pick up slack line, and then set the hook hard; in this way you'll hook about 85 percent of your strikes.

When fishing rivers, work the flats where current flows over rocks and gravel. It is the same structure where you might find catfish or walleye. Try eddies, small pools below islands, currents behind stumps, pockets downstream from large rocks, holes below bridge abutments, and small-stream channel areas where there is a gradual slope into deeper water. Cast bait downstream and allow it to rest directly below you.

See: Hogsucker, Northern.

SUCKER, WHITE   *Catostomus commersoni.*

Other names—black sucker, black mullet, brook sucker, carp, common sucker, common white sucker, eastern sucker, mud sucker, fine scaled sucker, grey sucker, mullet; French: *meunier noir, cyprin-sucet.*

This is one of the most widespread and abundant suckers, found only in North America.

Identification. White suckers are inconspicuously colored, usually in drab hues of white, yellow, and pink. The upper half of the fish is typically more darkly colored than the lower half. Although adults have little dark pigmentation, juveniles have three lateral black blotches halfway up the side of the body: one between the dorsal fin and opercle, one below the dorsal fin, and one on the caudal peduncle. The body is elongate and nearly circular in cross section. They have rather small scales that get larger near the posterior.

Age/Size. The white sucker is a medium-size fish reaching up to 18 inches or more in length and up to 8 pounds in weight. The largest individuals may be as old as 17 years, but the normal life expectancy is between 12 and 15 years. Sexual maturity is reached at about the same time in both sexes. The first spawning occurs between 3 and 5 years of age, depending on the region.

Distribution. The white sucker is one of the most widely distributed suckers in North America.

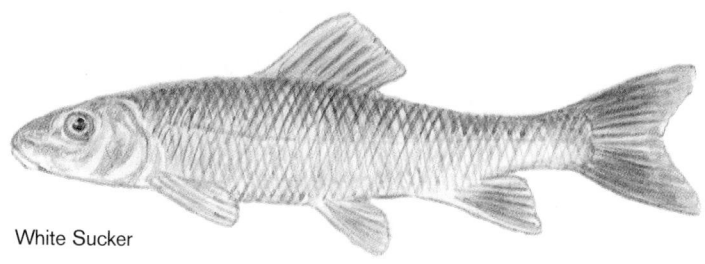

White Sucker

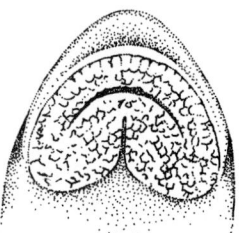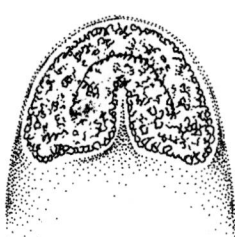

Sensory pores around the mouths of suckers, including the white sucker (left) and northern sucker (right), help these bottom scroungers find food.

It ranges from Canada south to the southern Appalachian Mountains and west into Utah and Idaho. Its range has expanded from bait bucket transfers when anglers release unused baitfish.

Habitat.   The white sucker is a habitat generalist, living in all types of freshwater environs. It occurs in lakes, rivers, ponds, reservoirs, and even some small streams. It can exist in fairly degraded systems, being tolerant of some turbidity, pollution, siltation, and eutrophication. In rivers, adults frequently inhabit deep pools, whereas juveniles live in stream margins and backwaters.

Life history/Spawning behavior.   White suckers make long upstream spawning migrations in early spring. The spawning season may extend from late March into early July in some areas. Upstream migration may be triggered by increasing water temperature or stream flow that occurs during this time of year. The suckers move into deep pools and congregate before spawning. They then gather and spawn in areas of clean gravel substrate. Males and females line up next to each other on the bottom of the stream, then shake violently, releasing eggs and sperm as they bury the eggs in the substrate. In lakes, they perform this activity in shallow shoals or may move upstream into rivers. White suckers darken in coloration during spawning. The males become olive colored on the upper portion of the body and may develop a pinkish lateral stripe.

Food and feeding behavior.   Like most suckers, this species feeds on a variety of benthic organisms and organic nutrients. Its primary diet includes burrowing insect larvae that are sucked up and sifted in its gill rakers. Midge larvae, small crustaceans, algae, and detritus are the most common foods.

Angling.   The white sucker is not a commonly sought after gamefish, though it is occasionally taken with spears and snags during its spawning runs. It is not a common commercial fish either because of its soft and bony flesh. It is, however, widely utilized as bait. The value of white suckers as bait for large muskellunge and pike is well known. See: **Sucker.**

SUMMERKILL
See: **Fishkill.**

SUNFISH

Scientifically, sunfish are members of the Centrarchidae (meaning nest building) family. Although this family is typically categorized as including sunfish only, some scientists include sunfish and bass. The terminology and cross-usage of some words attributed to the various species has made for a good deal of confusion among nonscientists.

Centrarchids number some 30 strictly freshwater species of North America and include three generalized subdivisions: black bass, crappie, and true sunfish. All of these are warmwater species with similar or overlapping habitats. They have rough scales and two dorsal fins that are united, the first of which is heavily spined. Their anal fins all have three or more spines, and their tail is typically broad. Nearly all are nest spawners, with nests built by the males, who also guard the nest and the young briefly. All are carnivorous, and the larger members prey on small fish.

Black bass *(see: bass, black)* belong to the genus *Micropterus;* they have more elongated bodies than other centrarchids and include the largest and most famous family member, the largemouth bass *(see: bass, largemouth).* Crappie belong to the genus *Pomoxis;* they have a longer anal fin, generally equal in length at the base to their dorsal fin, than any of the other centrarchids, and are capable of larger growth than most of the sunfish. There are two species of crappie;

Bluegill

Pumpkinseed Sunfish

On sunfish, the markings and shape of the gill covers are key identifiers.

A float-fished cricket nabbed this bluegill at Lake Okeechobee, Florida.

however, a smaller crappielike species, the flier *(Centrarchus macropterus),* is sometimes lumped with crappie by ichthyologists even though it is generally grouped with sunfish by the public.

The largest group of centrachids is the true sunfish. Most of the species are small and not of much angling interest, although they are of great importance in their respective environments as forage for larger predators and for the foraging they do themselves. True sunfish do not include the pygmy sunfish of the Elassomatidae family.

The larger-growing and more widely distributed sunfish are extremely popular with anglers throughout the United States, and provide countless hours of angling enjoyment. They are widely valued for their excellent, white flaky flesh. Their abundance and high rates of reproduction generally allow for liberal recreational harvest; commercial fishing for these species is illegal in all places where they are found.

The various sunfish and crappie are all considered panfish *(see),* which is a nontechnical generic group term for small freshwater fish that are widely utilized for food as well as sport.

The most wide-ranging and best known true sunfish is the bluegill *(see);* it and many others species of sunfish are colloquially known as "bream." Other popular species of sunfish are the green *(see: sunfish, green),* pumpkinseed *(see: sunfish, pumpkinseed),* redbreast *(see: sunfish, redbreast),* and redear *(see: sunfish, redear);* the warmouth *(see);* and the rock bass *(see: bass, rock).* In some

places, anglers may encounter such sunfish as the Sacramento perch *(Archoplites interruptus);* the Roanoke bass *(see: bass, Roanoke);* the orangespotted sunfish *(Lepomis humilis);* the mud sunfish *(see: sunfish, mud);* and the spotted sunfish *(Lepomis punctatus).*

Sunfish are tolerant of diverse and warm environments, and have proven very adaptable. They have been widely introduced elsewhere in North America, sometimes deliberately and others by accident, and have also been introduced to Europe and Africa. In some places they are kept in balance by angling and natural predation, but in others they become overpopulated, resulting in stunting.

The generally shallow nature of true sunfish permits angling by shore-based anglers, making them collectively the number-one warmwater pursuit of nonboating anglers. They are characteristically strong, although not flashy, fighters for their size, making them a pleasing catch on light spinning, spincasting, and fly tackle, as well as with reel-less poles.

SUNFISH, GREEN   *Lepomis cyanellus.*

Other names—green perch, black perch, pond perch, creek perch, sand bass, blue-spotted sunfish, rubbertail.

The green sunfish is a widespread and commonly caught member of the Centrarchidae family. It has white, flaky flesh like other sunfish, and is a good food fish.

Identification.   The green sunfish has a slender, thick body, a fairly long snout, and a large mouth with the upper jaw extending beneath the pupil of the eye; it has a larger mouth and a thicker, longer body than most sunfish of the genus *Lepomis,* thus resembling the warmouth *(see)* and the smallmouth bass *(see: bass, smallmouth).* It has short, rounded pectoral fins and, like other sunfish, it has connected dorsal fins and an extended gill cover flap, or "ear lobe." This lobe is black and has a light red, pink, or yellow edge, and the body is usually brown to olive or bluish green with a bronze to emerald green sheen, fading to yellow green on the lower sides and yellow or white on the belly. Adult fish have a large black spot at the rear of the second

Green Sunfish

dorsal and anal fin bases, and breeding males have yellow or orange edges on the second dorsal, caudal, and anal fins. There are also emerald or bluish spots on the head, and sometimes 7 to 12 indistinct dark bars on the back; these are especially visible when the fish is excited or stressed.

Size.   The average length is 4 inches, ranging usually from 2 to 8 inches and reaching a maximum of 12 inches, which is extremely rare. Most weigh less than a half pound. The all-tackle world record is a 2-pound, 2-ounce fish taken in Missouri in 1971.

Distribution.   In North America, green sunfish occur from New York and Ontario through the Great Lakes and the Hudson Bay and Mississippi River basins to Minnesota and South Dakota, and south to the Gulf of Mexico. They also occur from the Escambia River in Florida and Mobile Bay in Georgia and Alabama to the Rio Grande in Texas, as well as in northern Mexico.

Habitat.   Green sunfish prefer warm, still pools and backwaters of sluggish streams as well as ponds and small shallow lakes. Often found near vegetation, they are known to establish territory near the water's edge under brush, rocks, or exposed roots. They often become stunted in ponds.

Spawning behavior.   This species becomes sexually mature at two years old or as small as 2 to 3 inches long, spawning from April through August, when water temperatures range from 68° to 84°F. Males build saucer-shaped nests in water usually less than 1 foot deep, and often in areas sheltered by rocks or logs. The yellow, adhesive eggs are guarded by the male until they hatch in three to five days. Green sunfish spawn simultaneously with other species of *Lepomis,* and hybridization is not uncommon; crosses between bluegills and green sunfish occur most frequently, producing sterile offspring.

Food.   Green sunfish prefer dragonfly and mayfly nymphs, caddisfly larvae, midges, freshwater shrimp, and beetles, and will occasionally eat small fish such as mosquitofish.

Angling.   These fish are a common catch, taken with standard panfishing methods.
See: **Panfish; Sunfish.**

SUNFISH, LONGEAR   *Lepomis megalotis.*
Other names—longear.

Similar in size and general appearance to the pumpkinseed *(see: sunfish, pumpkinseed)* and a member of the Centrarchidae family of sunfish, the longear sunfish is a small, excellent gamefish on light tackle, although in many places it is generally too small to be avidly sought. The white and sweet flesh is excellent to eat.

Identification.   With a stout body, the longear sunfish is not as compressed as the bluegill *(see)* or the pumpkinseed, its close relatives. It is one of the most colorful sunfish, particularly the breeding male, which is dark red above and bright orange below, marbled, and spotted with blue. The longear

Longear Sunfish

generally has a red eye, orange to red median fins, and a blue black pelvic fin. There are wavy blue lines on the cheek and opercle, and the long, flexible, black ear flap is generally edged with a light blue, white, or orange line. The longear sunfish has a short and rounded pectoral fin, which usually does not reach past the eye when it is bent forward. It has a fairly large mouth, and the upper jaw extends under the eye pupil.

Size.   The longear sunfish may grow to $9\frac{1}{2}$ inches, averaging 3 to 4 inches and just a few ounces. The all-tackle world record is a 1-pound, 12-ounce fish taken in New Mexico in 1985. Males grow faster and live longer than females.

Distribution.   Similar in range to the green sunfish *(see: sunfish, green),* the longear sunfish occurs in east-central North America, west of the Appalachian Mountains from southern Quebec and western New York throughout the Mississippi Valley and westward through Minnesota and Nebraska and south into Texas, as well as along Gulf Coast drainages to western Florida.

Habitat.   This species inhabits rocky and sandy pools of headwaters, creeks, and small to medium rivers, as well as ponds, bays, lakes, and reservoirs; it is usually found near vegetation and is generally absent from downstream and lowland waters.

Spawning behavior.   Spawning takes place from late May to mid-August, when water temperatures range in the upper 70s and lower 80s, with longear sunfish that are at least one to two years old moving to gravel bottoms. Males build shallow, saucer-shaped nests in water 8 inches to 2 feet in depth, guarding the eggs until they hatch about a week after being deposited. Many nests are usually found close together, and the number of eggs laid during the season by one fish ranges from the hundreds to thousands depending on the size of the fish.

Food.   Longear sunfish feed primarily on aquatic insects, but also on worms, crayfish, and fish eggs off the bottom.

Angling.   Longears are caught with standard panfishing methods, and are especially caught on live worms and crickets.
See: **Panfish; Sunfish.**

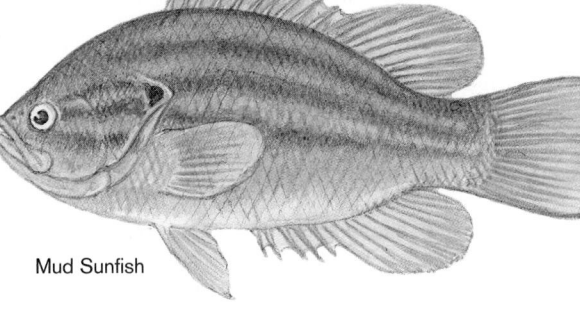

Mud Sunfish

SUNFISH, MUD *Acantharchus pomotis.*

Strongly resembling the rock bass *(see: bass, rock)* in general color and shape, the mud sunfish is not actually a member of the *Lepomis* sunfish family, although it is called a sunfish. It has a rectangular, compressed body that is dusky reddish brown on the back and pale brownish underneath. The lateral-line scales are pale, and along the arch of the lateral line is a broad irregular stripe of dark scales about three scale rows wide. Below the lateral line are two straight dark bands, each two scale rows wide, and an incomplete third, lower stripe one scale wide. It is distinguished from the similar rock bass by the shape of the tail, which is round in the mud sunfish and forked in the rock bass. Also, young mud sunfish have wavy dark lines along the sides, whereas young rock bass have a checkerboard pattern of squarish blotches. The mud sunfish may reach a maximum of 6$\frac{1}{2}$ inches.

In North America, mud sunfish are widely distributed in the Atlantic Coastal Plain and lower Piedmont drainages from the Hudson River in New York to the St. Johns River in Florida, and in Gulf Coastal Plain drainages of northern Florida and southern Georgia from the Suwanee River to the St. Marks River. They usually occur over mud or silt in vegetated lakes, pools, and backwaters of creeks and in small to medium rivers. Adult fish are frequently seen resting head down in vegetation.

This species is generally an incidental catch for anglers.

See: Panfish.

SUNFISH, OCEAN *Mola mola.*

Other names—headfish, moonfish; Danish/Swedish: *klumpfisk;* Dutch: *maanvis;* Finnish: *m hk kala;* French: *môle commun, poisson-lune;* German: *mondfisch;* Greek: *fegaró psaro;* Icelandic: *tunglfiskur;* Italian: *pesce luna;* Norwegian: *månefisk;* Polish: *samoglów;* Portuguese: *lua, peixe-lua;* Spanish: *mola, pez cabeza, pez luna, pez sol;* Turkish: *pervane.*

A relative of the puffers, triggerfish, and porcupinefish, the giant ocean sunfish is listed in the *Guinness Book of World Records* as the heaviest bony fish and the one with the most eggs. Ocean sunfish are exceptionally strong swimmers, and most records of this fish are based on sick specimens, which are easily captured. Occasionally caught with harpoons, ocean sunfish are utilized fresh and in Chinese medicine.

Identification. Appearing to be all head, the ocean sunfish is characterized by its much-reduced and rudderlike caudal fin, which is gently curved and sturdy; it also has a high soft dorsal fin and anal fin that it swims with by sculling. It lacks a spinous dorsal fin or pelvic fins, and it is dark brownish gray or gray blue. It has no scales, a small terminal mouth, leathery skin, and a poorly developed skeleton.

Size. The ocean sunfish can grow to 10 feet long and 11 feet high (including dorsal and anal fins) and weigh up to 4,400 pounds.

Distribution. Found in all oceans except polar seas, the ocean sunfish ranges in the eastern Pacific from British Columbia to Peru and Chile. In the eastern Atlantic, it occurs from Scandinavia to South Africa (occasionally in the western Baltic and Mediterranean), and in the western Atlantic from Canada to northern South America.

Habitat. Often drifting at the surface while lying on their sides, ocean sunfish may also swim upright and close to the surface with their dorsal fin projecting above the water. They are sluggish in cold water.

Food. Ocean sunfish feed on zooplankton, eel larvae, small deep-sea fish, as well as on jellyfish, crustaceans, mollusks, and brittle stars.

S

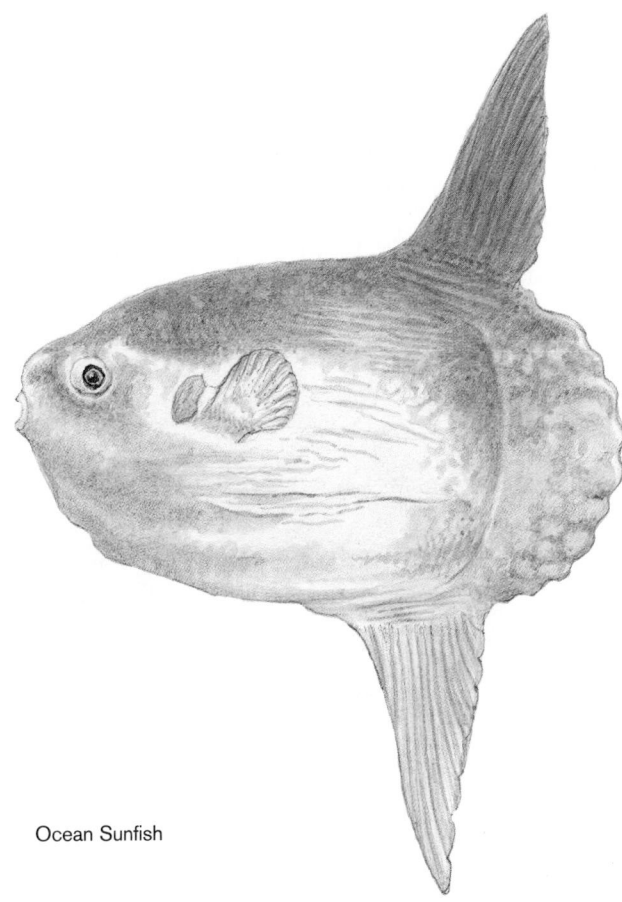

Ocean Sunfish

Angling.   The ocean sunfish is not an angling target, but it may occasionally be observed by off-shore anglers.

SUNFISH, PUMPKINSEED   *Lepomis gibbosus.*

Other names—bream, common sunfish, round sunfish, pond perch, pumpkinseed, punky, speckled perch, sun bass, sunfish, sunny, yellow sunfish.

The pumpkinseed is one of the most common and brightly colored members of the Centrarchidae family of sunfish. Although small on average, it is especially popular with young anglers because of its willingness to bite on worms, its wide distribution and abundance, and its close proximity to shore. Its flaky white flesh is also good eat.

Identification.   A brilliantly colored fish, the adult pumpkinseed is olive green, spotted with blue and orange as well as streaked with gold along the lower sides; there are dusky chainlike bars on the side of juveniles and adult females. A bright red or orange spot is located on the back edge of the short, black ear flap. Many bold dark brown wavy lines or orange spots cover the second dorsal, caudal, and anal fins, and there are wavy blue lines on the cheek. The pumpkinseed sunfish has a long, pointed pectoral fin that usually extends far past the eye when bent forward. It has a small mouth, with the upper jaw not extending under the pupil of the eye. There is a stiff rear edge on the gill cover and short thick rakers on the first gill arch.

Size/Age.   Although most pumpkinseed sunfish are small, about 4 to 6 inches, some reach a length of 12 inches and are believed to live to age 10. The all-tackle world record is a 1-pound, 6-ounce fish taken in new York in 1985.

Distribution.   Although pumpkinseeds occur from Washington and Oregon in western North America to New Brunswick, Canada, they are most abundant in the northeastern United States. Their range extends as far south as Georgia on the east, and includes most of the United States except for the south-central and southwestern regions. It includes Ontario and southern Quebec. They have been introduced to Europe but are considered a nuisance there.

Habitat.   Pumpkinseed sunfish inhabit quiet and vegetated lakes, ponds, and pools of creeks and small rivers, with a preference for weed patches, docks, logs, and other cover close to shore.

Spawning behavior.   Males and females reach sexual maturity during the second year of life, spawning during the spring and summer when waters are in the mid-60°F range. The males construct nests in water of less than 5-foot depths, often near shore and aquatic vegetation; the circular nests are 4 to 16 inches in diameter and are built separately or in small groups. The number of eggs produced by a female varies with age and size, and they hatch in about three days, the male guarding the young for a week or more. After the young leave the nest, the male often clears it in preparation for a second spawning. More than one female may lay eggs in a single nest, and because several species of sunfish often spawn in the same area at the same time, there is frequent hybridization between this and other fish in the genus *Lepomis*.

Food.   Pumpkinseed sunfish feed on a variety of small foods, including crustaceans, dragonfly and mayfly nymphs, ants, small salamanders, mollusks, midge larvae, snails, water beetles, and small fish.

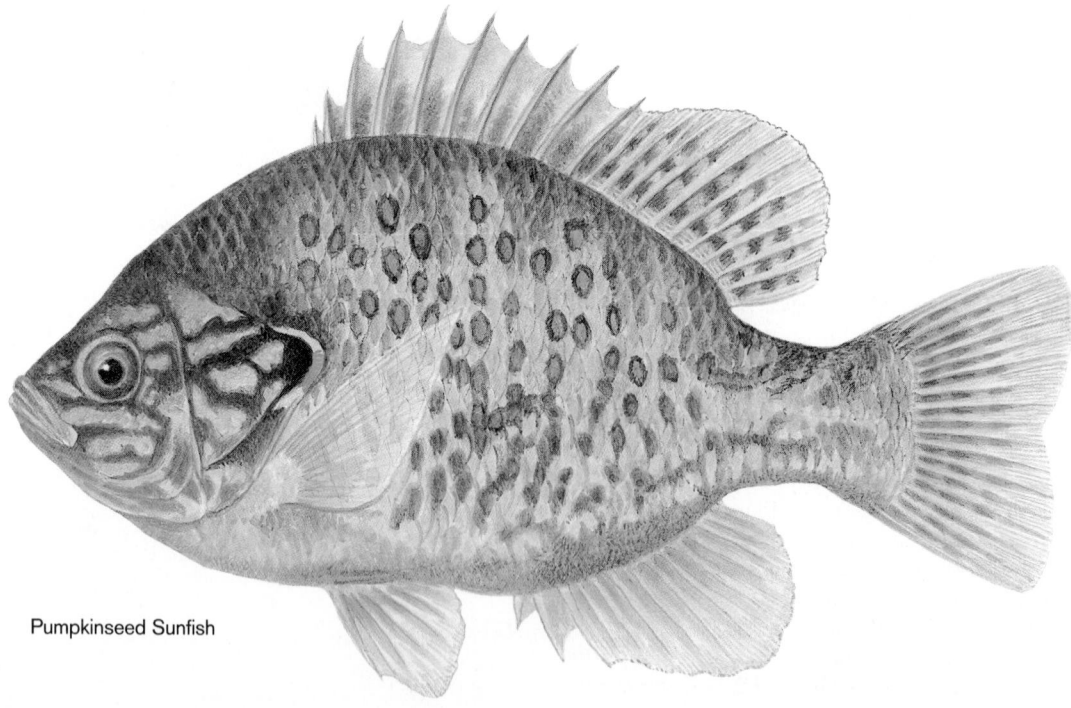

Pumpkinseed Sunfish

A pumpkinseed sunfish from a New York reservoir.

Angling. These fish are a common catch, taken with standard panfishing methods, although their small mouths make them nibblers, requiring small hooks and baits.
See: **Panfish; Sunfish.**

SUNFISH, REDBREAST   *Lepomis auritus.*

Other names—longear sunfish, redbreast bream, robin, redbelly, sun perch, yellowbelly sunfish.

The redbreast sunfish is the most abundant sunfish in Atlantic Coastal Plain streams. Like other members of the Centrarchidae family of sunfish, it is a good fighter for its size and excellent to eat.

Identification. The body of the redbreast sunfish is deep and compressed but rather elongate for a sunfish. It is olive above, fading to bluish bronze below; in the spawning season, males have bright orange red bellies while females are pale orange underneath. There are several light blue streaks radiating from the mouth, and the gill rakers are short and stiff. The lobe or flap on the gill cover is usually long and narrow in adult males, actually longer than in the so-called longear sunfish *(see: sunfish, longear).* The two species are easily distinguished because the lobe of the redbreast is blue black or completely black all the way to the tip and is narrower than the eyes, whereas the lobe of the longear is much wider and is bordered by a thin margin of pale red or yellow around the black. The pectoral fins of both species are short and roundish

in contrast to the longer, pointed pectoral fins of the redear sunfish *(see: sunfish, redear),* and the opercular flaps are softer and more flexible than the rigid flaps of the pumpkinseed sunfish *(see: sunfish, pumpkinseed).*

Size. Redbreast sunfish grow at a slow rate and may reach lengths of 6 to 8 inches, although they can attain 11 to 12 inches and weigh about a pound. The all-tackle world record is a 1-pound, 12-ounce fish from Florida in 1984.

Distribution. Generally occurring in rivers across the United States and Canada, the original distribution of redbreast sunfish is the Atlantic slope of North America from New Brunswick, Canada, to central Florida, and westward to the Appalachian Mountains; the range now extends to parts of Texas, Oklahoma, Arkansas, and Kentucky. They have been introduced to waters in Mexico, Puerto Rico, and Italy, where they are considered a nuisance due to stunting.

Habitat. Redbreast sunfish inhabit rocky and sandy pools of creeks and small to medium rivers. They prefer the deeper sections of streams and vegetated lake margins.

Spawning behavior. Redbreasts spawn in spring and summer when they are two to three years old and as small as 4 inches long; this may occur as early as April in the southern part of their range. Spawning peaks in June or when water temperatures range from 68° to 82°F. Males build nests in water 1 to 2 feet deep near stumps, logs, rocks, or other protected areas over sand or gravel bottom; the nests are 30 to 36 inches in diameter and 6 to 8 inches deep. Redbreast sunfish often occupy nests that have been abandoned by other sunfish. The number of eggs laid ranges in the thousands to tens of thousands, varying with the age and size of the female.

Food. Their primary food is aquatic insects, but redbreasts also feed on snails, crayfish, small fish, and occasionally on organic matter from the bottom.

Angling. These fish are a common catch, taken with standard panfishing methods.
See: **Panfish; Sunfish.**

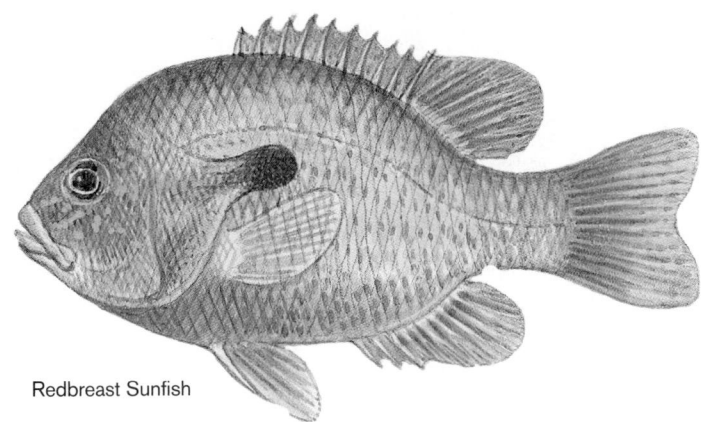
Redbreast Sunfish

SUNFISH, REDEAR   *Lepomis microlophus.*

Other names—shellcracker, stumpknocker, yellow bream, bream.

The redear sunfish is a popular sportfish because it fights hard on light tackle, reaches a relatively large size for a sunfish, and can be caught in large numbers. Like other members of the Centrarchidae family of sunfish it is an excellent panfish, with white, flaky meat.

Identification.   Light golden green above, the redear sunfish is roundish and laterally compressed; adults have dusky gray spots on the sides, whereas juveniles have bars. It is white to yellow on the belly, with mostly clear fins, and the breeding male is brassy gold with dusky pelvic fins. The redear sunfish has a fairly pointed snout and a small mouth, with blunted molaform teeth that make shell cracking possible. It has connected dorsal fins and long, pointed pectoral fins that extend far beyond the eye when bent forward; the latter distinguish it from both the longear *(see: sunfish, longear)* and redbreast *(see: sunfish, redbreast)* sunfish, which have short, roundish pectoral fins. The ear flap is also much shorter than in the other two species and is black, with a bright red or orange spot or a light margin at the edge.

It can also be distinguished from the pumpkinseed sunfish *(see: sunfish, pumpkinseed)* by its gill cover flap, which is relatively flexible and can be bent at least to right angles, whereas the flap on the pumpkinseed is rigid. The redear sunfish is somewhat less compressed than the bluegill *(see),* which contrasts with the redear sunfish by having an entirely black ear flap without any spot or light edge.

Size/Age.   The redear sunfish can become rather large, reaching weights of more than $4^1/_2$ pounds, although it averages under a half pound and about 9 inches. The all-tackle world record is a 5-pound, 3-ounce fish taken in California in 1994. It can live up to eight years.

Distribution.   Native to North America, redear sunfish are found from about the Savannah River in South Carolina to the Nueces River in Texas north toward the Mississippi River basin to southern Indiana and Illinois, with some populations in western states. They have been introduced to waters in Africa and Latin America.

Habitat.   Redear sunfish inhabit ponds, swamps, lakes, and vegetated pools of small to medium rivers; they prefer warm, clear, and quiet waters.

Spawning behavior.   Some redear sunfish are able to spawn when they are only 5 inches long and one year old, although most do so after they are age 2 or older. Spawning occurs when waters reach 70°F, which may be as early as March in Florida, and extends through early fall. Males build and guard shallow circular nests, which hold tens of thousands of eggs; nests are often built in colonies near vegetation, in 2- to 8-foot depths.

Food.   An opportunistic bottom feeder, the redear sunfish forages mostly during the day on aquatic snails, which gives it its common name, "shellcracker." These fish also feed on midge larvae, amphipods, mayfly and dragonfly nymphs, clams, fish eggs, and crayfish.

Angling.   Shellcrackers are taken with standard panfishing methods.

See: Panfish; Sunfish.

SUNGLASSES

Sunglasses are one of the most important accessories that any angler can have for two important reasons: eye protection from sun and wind, and improved visibility.

From a medical standpoint, protecting your eyes takes precedence over other concerns, and in this regard, it is necessary to wear sunglasses that block 99 to 100 percent of ultraviolet radiation to reduce sun exposure that can lead to cataracts and other eye damage. Because exposure to ultraviolet radiation can occur even when the sun is not shining, it's a good idea to wear sunglasses even on cloudy days; as a general rule, if you can see any shadow, then wear sunglasses. For maximum protection, sunglasses that offer side shielding are even better, and because they block out light just as if you cupped your hands around the edges of your face, they also improve visibility.

From an angling standpoint, improved visibility is an important reason to wear sunglasses. Visibility can be improved in a number of ways, the most important of which is reducing glare. This is reflected light that occurs from all directions and is present even on cloudy or hazy days and can be very uncomfortable and fatiguing to the eyes as well as a reason for preventing visibility into or through the water.

Another aspect of improving visibility by wearing sunglasses is enhancing depth of field to see close and distant objects better, distinguishing colors in the environment (a contrast issue), and being able to look into the water to see fish and objects. Seeing fish is especially important in sight

Redear Sunfish

fishing activities where you must see a fish in order to be able to make a proper presentation to it, but also in other activities, such as wading to see objects that should be avoided, and when fishing in clear offshore waters to spot either gamefish or baitfish that are attracted to your boat. Sunglasses should be polarized to reduce glare and improve through-water vision; side shielding is also very helpful.

Polarized lenses are a necessity for fishing and boating activities because they are the most effective means of eliminating glare and preventing light absorption, meaning that they allow your eyes to be more comfortable and more contracted, which means greater distant vision. To make sure that sunglasses you are considering purchasing are, in fact, polarized, you can take two pairs of sunglasses that are believed to be polarized and hold them parallel to each other (one in front of the other) and then rotate one lens 90 degrees; if they are polarized the lenses will become dark.

Many different lens colors are available. Dark gray and dark brown lenses are preferred by most anglers, although not all are the same or of equal quality; dark gray lenses are considered best for very bright conditions, although dark brown is generally more versatile. Light brown or nearly amber lenses are also popular and provide very good contrast, and are also helpful for spotting fish. The wild colors, including mirror lenses, may look cool, but they are not a benefit for fishing.

Anglers who do not wear glasses, or who wear contact lenses, have an extensive array of good sunglass choices, but eyeglass wearers have a much greater problem. Some eyeglass wearers have polarized prescription lenses, which are costly; many use polarized clip-ons, which are cheap, do not offer side protection, and may not fit all eyeglass frames or thickness of lens. Some eyeglass wearers prefer lightweight, polarized, supplemental sunglasses that fits over their prescription lens; these are economical and moderately priced, and many offer full wraparound protection as well.
See: First Aid.

SUNSCREEN
See: First Aid.

SURFACE
The uppermost part of a body of water. The most favored manner of fishing is probably fishing with lures or flies that float on the surface (also referred to by some anglers as topwater fishing) or that are trolled across the surface (standard big-game procedure) in order to receive visible strikes, although this method is not suitable to all conditions or all species.
See: Dry Fly; Surface Lure.

SURFACE FILM
See: Surface Tension.

SURFACE TENSION
A skin of hydrogen-bonded molecules formed on the surface of a liquid over the freer-moving molecules within the liquid. Because of this bonding, the surface of water has a tendency to contract, drawing taut like the rubber of an inflated balloon and being much like a skin. When observed under calm conditions, it may be referred to as the surface film. Surface tension may cause a free-floating object on the surface to move in a different manner or speed than if it were below the surface.

The surface of water is able to support small objects and organisms; this is how water spiders are able to run across the surface of a pond. Surface tension is a barrier to some organisms, namely insects, some of which want to pass into the water below it and some of which want to pass into the air above. The surface tension is too great for some insects to break, and it is an element for others to avoid; they can become trapped while gliding across the surface to lay eggs or to feed. When an insect is caught in the surface tension, it may struggle and become easy prey for fish, especially trout. The imagoes (sexually mature adults, or spinners) of mayflies and caddisflies struggle to escape the surface tension and emerge from the water. These elements are all at work on artificial flies, and all have a bearing on angling activities.

SURF CART
A manufactured or homemade device, often with low-pressure balloon tires for wheels, used by surf anglers for toting equipment.
See: Surf Fishing.

SURF CASTING
See: Casting; Surf Fishing.

SURF FISHING
Fishing from the beach—minus the pier or bridge—is the saltwater angler's answer to freshwater fishing from the bank. Known as surf fishing, it brings forth a vision of an angler with a long rod, braving large breaking waves and casting a heavily weighted bait great distances over the roiled and foamy water, mostly on a deserted stretch of beach, at dawn or at night. However, angling in or from the surf not only refers to this conventional view, but also to fishing accessible coastal beaches, in protected backwaters or in locations where the surf ripples instead of pounds, with a variety of fishing equipment for any number of inshore species, at all times of the day.

S

Fishing from the surf may be the venue of choice for anglers without boats or for those who prefer to be on *terra firma* (sometimes not so *firma,* however, along the beach). It may be preferred by those who simply like the sights, sounds, challenges, and camaraderie provided, notwithstanding some disadvantages in mobility. And surf fishing has been an angling mode since before there were boats with motors; in the United States, it really blossomed after World War II, when new rods, reels, and lines made casting easier and when surplus Army Jeeps made it possible to access then undeveloped beach areas.

Surf fishing has experienced some cyclic levels of activity, particularly along the Atlantic seaboard where landforms make it a readily available angling option in virtually every coastal state. Relatively high fish population levels generated a lot of surf fishing activity from the 1950s through the 1980s. Striped bass, bluefish, and weakfish were the mainstays along the Northeast and Mid-Atlantic states. Red drum, channel bass, spottail bass, puppy drum, and redfish had a large following along southeastern and Gulf Coast states. And on the West Coast, the previously transplanted striped bass drew many anglers to the rocky shoreline.

But surf fishing fortunes took a nosedive in the late 1980s as striped bass, weakfish, bluefish, and red drum populations suffered because of commercial overfishing, poor reproductive rates, and myriad environmental problems. These fisheries reemerged in the mid- to late 1990s, and the number of surf anglers concurrently blossomed.

All surf anglers aspire to the lofty goal of catching a trophy specimen of one of these popular species, but most are happy with a bucketful of spot, croaker, trout, flounder, perch, or any of the various small species that are common along the surf line. And although specialized attention is devoted to some species, especially when fishing with lures, a majority of the effort is directed at catching anything that is available.

Certainly the tackle and the techniques that are devoted to surf fishing for particular species vary according to the habits of the fish as well as the conditions, but certain similarities are evident no matter where it is enjoyed.

Surf fishing pits angler against fish in a place where almost everything favors the fish. It is an act that requires total confidence in the ability to pick the exact spot along thousands of miles of coastline where a fish will find the angler's single offering. More often than not, the choice is wrong, but it is a tremendous thrill to stand in the surf with spray on your face and a big fish on the line, knowing you did it all by yourself.

Basic Outfits

Surf anglers are often pictured as lone wolves patrolling the high surf with long rods, tossing heavy baits or lures and landing 50-pound stripers or drum through the breakers. Indeed, that is how most surf anglers picture themselves. In reality they spend most of their angling time pursuing much smaller fish with much lighter tackle. The average surf caster will carry some heavy artillery but will also have a variety of smaller outfits that in some cases are light enough to be at home on freshwater trout streams.

Selecting a surf fishing outfit, particularly the magnum versions, requires an examination of several factors, beginning with the size and strength of the individual. A big person can usually handle a much heavier outfit than someone small in stature. This does not mean that these two people couldn't fish side by side and have an equal chance of success; they just need tackle to match their physical capabilities.

Heavy gear. The heaviest outfit in common use by today's surf caster is one called the Hatteras Heaver. Developed along the Outer Banks of North Carolina, this rod-and-reel combination is designed to toss a 6- to 12-ounce sinker and a big chunk of cut mullet or menhaden into the teeth of a gale.

The rod will be 10 to 12 feet long with a heavy action and will have a tip whose diameter is equivalent to the business end of a pool cue. Most Hatteras Heavers are made of graphite, but some anglers prefer heavier fiberglass models that are less likely to be damaged by rough handling. Such big rods call for big reels and heavy line. Conventional reels having a capacity of at least 300 yards of 20-pound line or 200 yards of 30-pound, and sporting ball bearings on the drive shaft, are very popular. These are filled with 20- to 30-pound line (primarily conventional-diameter nylon monofilament) that is usually knotted to a 50- to 80-pound shock leader. Spinning reels are not as common on heavy-duty rods as they are on lighter gear, but some mega spinning reels, which hold a similar amount of line and have high-strength gears, will handle the load. Spinning tackle users may fill up with 30-pound line, but 25 is more common, again tied to a 50- to 80-pound shock leader.

Hatteras Heavers generally find limited use, although fishing a drum run on a place like Hatteras Point without one puts the angler at a great disadvantage.

Medium and light gear. A more practical outfit that will serve all but the most severe fishing operations is a 10- to 12-foot medium-action rod that will handle 4 to 6 ounces of weight. A conventional reel, or a spinning reel, filled with 15- to 20-pound line and matched to the rod, completes the package.

Fiberglass, graphite, and a blend of both fibers are currently used for these rods. A fiberglass surf casting rod is heavier and less expensive than graphite, although the latter is more powerful, meaning that it transfers more energy from the rod to the object being cast. A rod made with both fiberglass and graphite combines the best properties of both and has more durability than an all-graphite product.

Most rods used by surf anglers are longer than those used by saltwater anglers who fish from boats. Long rods are needed to overcome the height of the waves and to attain greater casting distance. While long is good, longer is not necessarily better. Once a rod surpasses 12 to 13 feet in length, effectiveness drops off dramatically. Long-distance tournament casters use 12- to 13-foot rods, and if they could get another inch of distance out of a longer stick, they would use 30-footers. Even 12-footers may be too much for some people, so this is where you need to evaluate rod length in relation to your own stature and strength.

Older two-piece surf rods were made of fiberglass and had metal ferrules. These behaved like two separate rods, one short stiff piece that held the reel

An angler fishes a nearly calm surf at sunset.

and one long thin piece running out from the ferrule to the tip. The metal ferrule not only made an unyielding connection but also had an annoying habit of becoming a permanent connection. Dissatisfied with these, hard-core surf casters turned to one-piece rods that were lighter and more powerful but created serious storage problems. Eventually rod designers began to build two-piece rods that behaved like one-piece models by making the ferrule part of the rod blank; this has made storage and transportation of rods much easier for surf anglers.

Although this is the conventional medium-weight tackle for surf fishing, some situations require slightly different approaches. For example, anglers who fish for snook in the surf in some parts of their range may use 7- to 9-foot rods equipped with medium-weight baitcasting reels and spooled with 12- to 17-pound line. To the hard-core surf-caster, this is a lightweight rig, one that would not do for heaving heavy weights with bait; but these anglers are more concerned with getting some distance on their casts to get lures out into the proper depth of water and portion of the surf, as well as having some leverage for playing fish. They may use the same tackle inland or inshore for non–surf fishing activities. So surf tackle is relative to the situation, and some situations may dictate still lighter tackle yet.

In addition to the standard medium-action outfit, most surf anglers will also have at least one smaller setup. This will be used, for example, when working a slough for small bottom feeders or when tossing light lures for trout, blues, and drum.

A 7-foot rod matched to a reel holding 10- to 15-pound line will handle bottom fishing and will cast all but the smallest lures. Speckled trout anglers and anglers fishing for small stripers often toss small jigs or lightweight plugs, and they will step down to much lighter rods and reels using 6- to 8-pound line. These smaller outfits are also utilized by pompano anglers who cast light weights and small baits just beyond the surf line.

The choice between a spinning or conventional reel for medium or light surf gear is primarily decided by personal preference and experience. Many anglers like the ease of operation provided by a spinning reel, whereas others feel they have more control with the revolving spool on a conventional reel (see: baitcasting tackle; conventional tackle; spinning tackle). In the hands of a good caster, the modern conventional reel works well and offers less line-twisting trouble.

Nylon monofilament remains the line of choice for the vast majority of surf fishing situations. Braided and fused multifilament lines with a thin diameter aid casting and reel capacity, but their low abrasion resistance can cause problems in the tough conditions of surf fishing.

Shock leaders.   Shock leaders are required in most surf fishing situations. A shock leader absorbs the wear on the line created by constant casting with heavy weights or lures. It should be long enough to wrap two or three times around the spool while the lure or bait rig hangs close to the first guide up from the reel. This heavy leader also comes in handy when trying to pull a big fish in through the breakers. As a general rule the shock leader should be twice as heavy as the running line. Use a Blood Knot for tying a 50- to 80-pound leader to 20- or 30-pound fishing line, and an Albright Knot for a heavier leader (see: knots, fishing). The knot is the weak link in the entire rig, so it must be properly tied, trimmed off as closely as possible, and regularly checked for wear.

Accessories

Surf fishing can be a very simple sport requiring only rod, reel, line, hook, sinker, and bait. But surf anglers, like most other anglers, are drawn to accessories; some may be as simple as a canvas bag to carry spare tackle or as elaborate as a four-wheel-drive truck with a fully equipped slide-in camper.

One thing that most dedicated surf anglers agree on is that it is false economy to go fishing with only one rig or lure. Even the most experienced surf caster will snap off the occasional rig, and it may take only one nasty bluefish to render that lure inoperable. You need to be prepared.

Transporting gear.   Since you need more than just one easily carried outfit, the problem becomes transporting extra gear from the point of departure to the surf line. Certainly the most convenient and comfortable method of conveyance is a four-wheel-drive vehicle, but many beaches are closed to vehicles and many surf anglers are not willing to devote a considerable amount of capital to the sport. Enter the 5-gallon bucket. A surf angler can pack everything needed for a day at the beach in a 5-gallon spackle bucket, which is readily available at many construction sites.

Clean the bucket and modify it as necessary. Holes drilled around the lip will serve as places to store lures and will prevent horrible tangles on the bottom of the bucket. An old bicycle tire stretched around the outside will keep exposed hooks from finding waders or body parts. Small tackle boxes filled with hooks, snaps, and various hardware can be placed inside, along with bait, bait knife, cutting board, sand spikes, and something to eat and drink. Expeditions of more than a few hours require a small cooler to keep bait fresh, and this means more to carry; if you're planning to keep some of your catch, consider that you will be more burdened on the return trip.

Although most surf anglers set up shop and stay in one place, others prefer to walk the beach, fishing as they go. These anglers must travel light but still have the tackle they need. A surf bag made from canvas or nylon, carried on a shoulder strap or wader belt, becomes the tackle box. The interior of the bag is divided into compartments that hold lures or rigs, and the outside has small pockets that separate the snaps, swivels, and leaders.

A surf cart is a device that makes life much easier for the walk-on angler. Carts are made from a variety of materials including wood, plastic, and aluminum. Style and design reflect the builder's personal choice and encompass everything from a flat piece of plywood to an elaborate cart complete with rod holders and tackle drawers. Some manufactured carts use low-pressure balloon tires for wheels, similar to those used for beach wheelchairs, with rod holders along the sides and enough storage to accommodate an extended stay.

At the optimum end of the transportation scene is the convenience offered by a four-wheel-drive vehicle, traditionally called a beach buggy by surf fishing enthusiasts. Many people who live near the beach or who fish the surf regularly have four-wheel-drive trucks or sport utilities that they use for getting to a parking place close to the fishing spot; in a few cases, it is possible to actually drive onto the beach, but this is now becoming less of an option. Naturally, such transportation is expensive, especially when the vehicle is new and deluxe. Used four-wheel-drives can be found, but careful inspection is needed to weed out the ones that have led a rough life.

These vehicles are usually outfitted to varying degrees to facilitate hauling tackle and accessories. Most beach buggy owners will add a rod-holding

Accessories for surf fishing are very popular in places where vehicles can access the beach; this is a scene from Montauk, New York.

rack on the front to store rods, with reels on them, in a vertical position; a front cooler rack can hold waders, rods, sand spikes, buckets, and other items.

The interior of some beach buggies can be customized with tackle lockers, coolers, rod holders, stoves, bunks, portable toilets, and any number of other accessories to make life and fishing more convenient while on the beach.

It would be nice to have a vehicle just for surf fishing, but most anglers must use their beach-access vehicle for everyday driving as well, so the surf fishing accessories should be removable when not in use.

Waders and wet suits. Fishing the surf without getting into the water is almost impossible. In areas where the weather and the water are warm, anglers may wade in shorts or a bathing suit. Northern climates require more protection from the elements, except during midsummer.

A set of good-quality chest waders *(see)* is the best protection from cold water. Some are made from rubber, and the newer models are constructed from neoprene and are preferred by many surf anglers. Inexpensive and poor-quality waders will not hold up under the constant abuse delivered by pounding waves and abrasive sand, so it's smart to get a good pair from the start.

Chest waders must be worn with a tightened belt to seal off the top in case the angler takes a tumble in the surf. Without this protection, the waders can fill up, pulling the angler under the water. As an added precaution, and for additional protection against rain and surf spray, a foul weather jacket is worn over the waders and is also belted at the waist.

A few surf anglers in certain places are not satisfied with casting from shore and feel compelled to swim to an offshore rock or sandbar in an effort to reach fish feeding beyond the range of shore-bound casters. These anglers are in the water for long periods of time and require the protection of a wet suit. They may find themselves exposed to stinging jellyfish, curious and possibly hungry sharks, and strong currents. Their rods and reels are designed to operate under water. Most use spinning reels with holes drilled in the back plates so that the water pressure doesn't pop off the spools. The rods are graphite to save weight, and other tackle is kept to a waterproof minimum. Obviously this activity is not for the average person and doesn't appeal to everyone, but in certain locations it can be the means to success.

Footwear. When fishing warmwater areas where waders and wet suits are not required, the surf caster should always have some type of footwear protection. "Wet shoes" (shoes made to be worn in water), an old pair of canvas deck shoes, or even a pair of high-sided rubber boots will work. It's important to protect your feet from the many sharp objects found in the sand. A cut on the bottom of the foot may end a day at the beach, and a severe cut may be an inconvenience for many days to come.

In many areas, jellyfish are common in the surf, and they will make it very uncomfortable for the unprotected wading angler. A pair of long pants provides some protection, but stings may still occur. Meat tenderizer, incidentally, is the best remedy for jellyfish stings. Rub a liberal amount of tenderizer on the injured area to relieve the pain.

Many surf anglers not only fish from the beach proper, but also walk the beach and stop to fish from jetties *(see)*. Because jetties are wet and often moss-coated, they are slippery, and firm-gripping soles are a must. Standard rubber soles and felt soles will not suffice unless the jetty is dry. Many jetty anglers use manufactured creepers, which are devices that strap on over other footwear (they must be sized accordingly) and have spikes on the soles for gripping. The creepers can be slipped over canvas boat shoes in warm climates or over waders in cold areas. A more expensive solution is a pair of creepers custom-made from stainless steel or aluminum. On the less expensive but temporary side, a pair of discarded golf shoes will work; however, they soon fall apart under the ravages of saltwater, sand, and rocks.

Sand spikes. Sand spikes are devices employed by surf anglers to hold their rods while baiting up or changing rigs. They also hold the rod as the angler waits for a fish to take the bait. Most sand spikes are made from plastic pipe, but a few are constructed from aluminum tubing. Aluminum sand spikes are custom-made by shops that specialize in cooler racks and other accessories for surf fishing vehicles.

Plastic sand spikes may be 3 to 5 feet long and made from heavy PVC pipe or very light plastic tubes. A 3-footer is well suited for the walk-on angler because of its light weight. Longer and heavier sand spikes made from schedule 40 PVC are used when the surf is high. They may be hand carried, but the extra weight and length make this a burden.

Other gear. For the angler who is wading in the surf or standing on a jetty, landing a big fish can be difficult, and a gaff *(see)* is often indispensable. Beach anglers can use a short-handled or release gaff placed under the fish's lower jaw, but jetty jockeys need a longer tool and placement is not always as accurate. Jetty gaffs are normally custom-made from 5- to 6-foot rod blanks. The gaff is epoxied into the small end, and the butt is wrapped with cork tape. A bungee strap is used to hold the gaff across the angler's back until needed.

Many surf anglers patrol the beach at night, which is sometimes a delicate and dangerous job, complicated by the fact that any light shown on the water will probably spook the fish. Most after-dark surf anglers carry a small flashlight with a narrow beam that is usually held in the mouth when a light is needed to tie on new rigs or untangle lines. A miner's light worn around the head is another option.

Several tools should be a part of every surf angler's kit; the most important tool is a pair of high-quality fishing pliers. These are invaluable for cutting line and leader, removing hooks, crimping wire leader sleeves, and many other uses. A multipurpose tool is equally valuable for a variety of purposes, many of which cannot be anticipated. A knife for cutting bait or cleaning and filleting fish is also necessary.

Like all other anglers, those plying the surf should have raingear (at least a jacket for rain, surf spray, and wind), polarized sunglasses, a long-billed hat, sunscreen, and possibly insect repellent.

Bait

In most surf fishing situations, bait will outproduce artificial lures, but there is more to bait fishing than simply tossing a hunk of meat into the ocean. The angler who presents the proper bait in a natural manner will consistently bring fish to the beach. An effective presentation requires consideration of both the proper bait to use and the way to use it, as well as the bait rigs.

Bait rigs. A typical surf bait rig consists of a hook and sinker held together by a section of monofilament leader material. For big fish, such as trophy-size red drum or striped bass, you need 50- to 100-pound leaders. Small bottom fish, however, can be taken on leaders as light as 10 pounds.

Rigs can be purchased in local tackle shops, and these shops usually stock all the various types of rigs popular in the area. Tackle shops also carry the locally favored baits. When fishing an unfamiliar area, you should begin by purchasing local rigs to match whatever has been catching fish in that location even if you prefer to make up your own rig, as many surf anglers do.

Effective bait rigs do vary from one location to another, but most fall into one of three categories: top/bottom, single hook, and fishfinder.

Top/Bottom Rig

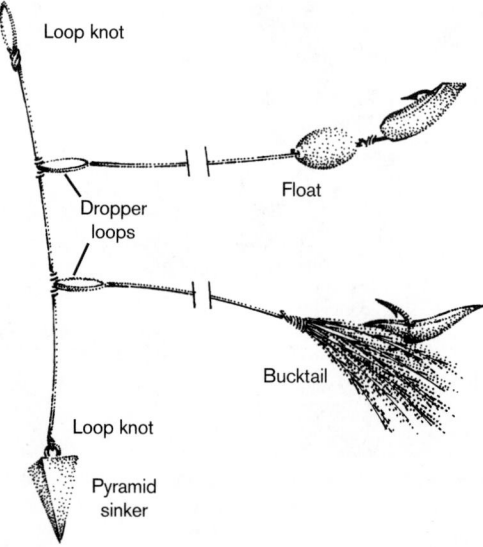

Loop knot

Dropper loops

Float

Bucktail

Loop knot

Pyramid sinker

The top/bottom rig, which is primarily used for small bottom fish, features a sinker and two hooks, spaced 5 to 12 inches apart, decorated with beads, spinner blades, bucktail hair, soft grubs, floats, or any other device that you believe will attract fish. Some species, such as pompano, prefer to take their bait from a plain hook.

In most applications, the drop from the leader to the hook will be quite short. Long leaders will foul when they're cast or as they're tossed about in the surf. Short leaders keep the hook close to the line for a better hookset. A top/bottom rig made from wire with 3- to 4-inch standoffs is popular in a few areas. Snelled hooks are looped over the ends of the standoffs.

Single-hook rigs are used when bigger fish are sought. Leaders may be 12 inches or longer and are made from heavy nylon monofilament or braided wire; the latter is reserved for such toothy critters as big bluefish, and the monofilament is used in all other cases.

Single-Hook Rig

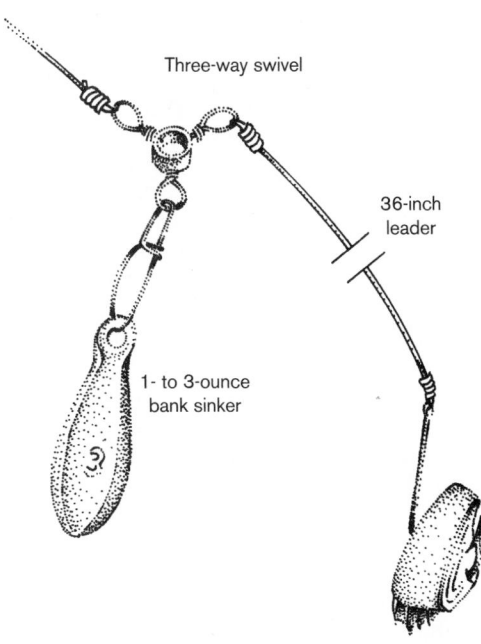

Three-way swivel

36-inch leader

1- to 3-ounce bank sinker

The heart of the single-hook rig is a three-way swivel. The leader is attached to one eye, a sinker snap to the second eye, and the running line to the third eye. In most cases, the hook is left undecorated, but a large cork float, known as a fireball, may be added when sight feeders are the target.

A fishfinder rig is a single-hook rig that moves along the line. The running line or shock leader is threaded through a sleeve, usually made from plastic, and then tied to a large swivel. The leader is tied to the other end of the swivel. A sinker snap is attached to the plastic sleeve to secure the sinker, which will rest on the bottom. When a fish picks up the bait, it can move away without feeling the weight of the sinker. This is important

when using live baits or when the target species needs a bit of time to get the bait well into its mouth.

Fishfinder Rig

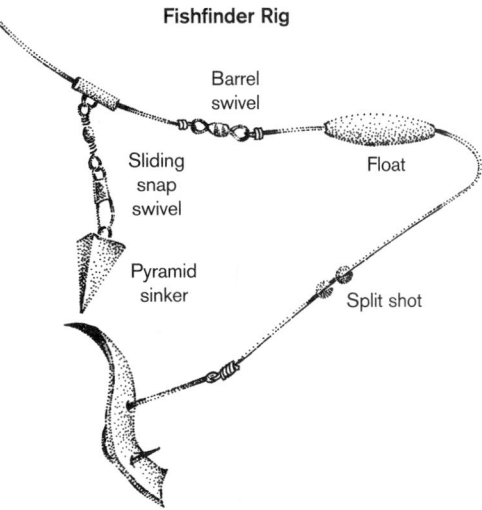

Barrel swivel

Sliding snap swivel

Float

Pyramid sinker

Split shot

Known as a fishfinder rig, this is a basic setup for surf fishing.

The length of the leader on a fishfinder rig is a matter of some disagreement among anglers. A long leader, up to 36 inches, is favored by some, but it is very difficult to cast. Short leaders of 12 inches or less are easier to cast but provide little protection to the running line or shock leader. One variation is to put the plastic sleeve on the leader; this restricts the amount of line a fish can take but allows the sinker to slide down within 6 inches of the hook when casting.

Surf anglers seek all types and sizes of fish and utilize all types and sizes of hooks. The Chestertown is popular for small bottom feeders; the wide-gap Siwash works well on larger fish such as trout or flounder; and the offset Beak is often used for big drum or striped bass. In recent years, the Tuna Circle hook has gained popularity as catch-and-release (see) fishing has become more common. The Tuna Circle usually hooks a fish in the corner of the mouth, causing little if any injury to the victim. It is easy to remove once the fish is landed but has excellent holding power while the fish is being played.

Sinkers are needed to anchor each of these rigs to the bottom. They basically are found in pyramid and bank styles, with the former more common along the beach. A pyramid sinker has four angled sides that meet in a point. The eye is on the flat base, causing the sinker to dig into the sand and hold the rig. A bank sinker is shaped like a teardrop and will not dig into the sand or hold a rig in one location. It is used when the angler wants the bait to move across the bottom as the angler slowly cranks the rig back to the beach.

Various modifications have been made by anglers in an effort to build a better sinker for surf fishing. The Hurricane sinker is a pyramid with rounded sides that is supposed to cast well into a wind. A bank sinker with stiff wires molded into the end has less wind resistance than a pyramid. The wires turn over and dig into the bottom to hold better than the standard bank sinker.

Modifications are common not only on sinkers but on every aspect of surf fishing tackle. Surf anglers are an inventive lot. Many make their own rigs, build their own rods, and pour their own sinkers. Some create new products, but very few of these inventions make their creators rich.

Surf bait basics. The most important consideration when using bait is its condition. Fresh bait is vital to success and must be selected with the same care used to buy fish for the table. Look at the gills of prospective baitfish; they should be red, and the eyes should be clear, not pink. The flesh should not be soft, and the fish should have a clean smell. Frozen fish will work as bait, but fresh (unfrozen) is preferable. Frozen shrimp and crabs are useless. Frozen squid, however, seems to work as well as the fresh product.

Buying good bait is the first step, but it must be properly stored to keep it in prime condition. A cooler should be dedicated just for bait and set up to keep bait and ice separated. Most bait will lose color and turn to mush when submerged in ice water. Plastic containers that seal out air and water are excellent for keeping bait in a cooler. They also separate the different types of bait you might use, making it convenient to find what you want in the bottom of a crowded cooler.

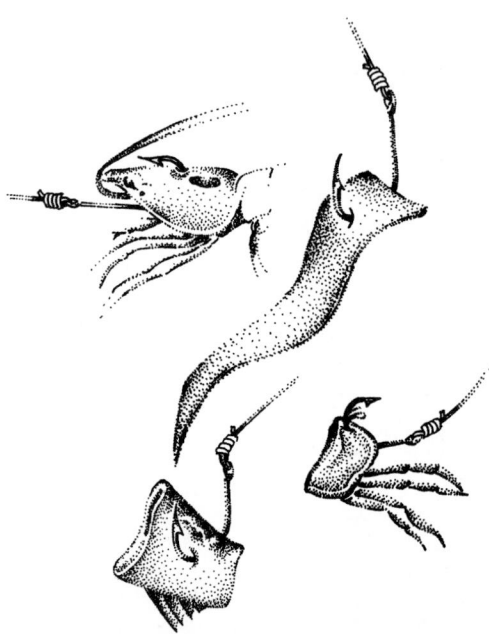

Shrimp, strips of fish or squid, crabs, and chunks of fish are among the top baits for surf fishing.

All efforts to keep bait fresh will be wasted if it is cut up and left out for sea gulls, flies, and hot sun to spoil. Cut the bait into whatever size is appropriate, take what you need to put on the hook, and return the rest to the cooler.

Fish used for bait in surf angling come in all shapes and sizes. In most cases, fish will be cut into pieces, but small specimens such as finger mullet may be used whole. Depending on the target species, fish bait is cut into fillets or chunks. Chunks are used when you need a tougher bait for long casts or bigger fish. Fillets are used when you want a thin bait that will move in current. Fillets may be whole or cut into strips. Strip baits are effective when trying to imitate small thin baitfish, whereas whole fillets imitate larger species.

Fish baits should be cut with care. Try to make strips wide at the hook end tapering down to a point. Fillets should be cut to the shape of a fish; a sharp knife will split the tail for a very lifelike presentation. Chunks should be cut from the back of the head to the tail. The size of the target species determines the size of the chunk. For some reason, many anglers discard the head and tail, forgetting that fish eat the whole thing. In all cases it's a good idea to remove the scales from fish bait; this is easy to do and makes hook insertion much easier.

Baits should be hooked through the thickest part, chunks through the back, fillets and strip baits through the wide end. Put the hook all the way through the bait, and leave the point exposed. It is hard enough to drive a hook into the fish's mouth; you don't want to be driving it through the bait as well.

Squid is cut into strips or small pieces. The strips work well when small, thin baitfish are in the surf. Pieces are just right for bottom feeders that prey on small invertebrates. The head of a squid makes an excellent bait for larger gamefish, and the tentacles can be threaded onto a Chestertown hook in place of a worm.

Sea worms are great baits for a surprising number of fish. Striped bass and weakfish are very fond of worms, especially in the spring. Sea mullet and spot will take a worm in place of anything else. Whole worms are hooked through the head or tail and allowed to stream out in the current. At times you may need several worms on the same hook to attract attention. Worms cut into bite-size pieces and threaded onto the hook are the ticket for bottom feeders who suck the bait into their mouths. A bit of worm left dangling from the end of the hook will add some moving enticement to the bait.

Fresh shrimp may be fished whole or cut into small pieces. They are very expensive bait and are saved for situations where only shrimp are effective. Pompano and speckled trout do show a definite preference for shrimp, but both will often take less-expensive offerings.

Crabs come in two stages: hard and peeler. A hard crab has a hard outer shell; a peeler crab has a soft shell under a hard outer shell. A peeler, which is also called a shedder, is getting ready to shed the outer shell and emerge as a soft-shelled crab. The soft shell variety is defenseless and is easy prey for all types of eager predators.

When fishing with either type of crab, remove the hard outer shell and cut the crab into sections with a pair of heavy-duty shears. Place the hook through a leg hole, not through the shell. Crabs do not stay on the hook very well and are often secured with rubber bands or dental floss.

Red drum are very fond of peeler crabs, especially in the spring when crabs are shedding. Unfortunately, every other fish in the ocean shares this craving for peeler crabs, and baits do not last long in the water.

Peelers can be expensive bait. Try to get the largest peelers you can, and cut them into as many pieces as possible. Trout will take a single section, but red drum require at least a quarter of a crab to attract their attention. A small piece of peeler on a bucktail will give the appearance of a larger bait.

Hard crab is a poor substitute when fish are feeding on peelers. The two baits evidently smell and taste different because fish can certainly tell them apart. Hard crabs become more acceptable later in the season when peelers are scarce. Cut hard crabs in small sections for big fall-run spot and croaker, and use half of a crab for drum and striped bass.

Live bait is used by surf anglers, but it does require a special container to keep the bait alive. Carrying a large container full of water and bait is not practical for a walk-on angler. A four-wheel-drive vehicle is needed to move a heavy livewell and provide the power to aerate it.

An angler prepares a bait rig for surf fishing off of a Virginia barrier beach.

A large cooler can be converted into a portable livewell (see) or bait tank. A 30- to 50-quart cooler will suffice, but some anglers use a big 120-quart cooler. Obviously the larger the cooler, the more baitfish it will support, but a 120-quart cooler full of water weighs about 240 pounds and requires a big pump to keep it properly aerated.

A 50-quart cooler and a bilge pump that moves 800 gallons per hour will keep three or four dozen baits alive all day. Mount the pump in the bottom of the cooler, and run a hose up to a piece of PVC pipe hanging just below the hinge. The pipe should be between 18 and 24 inches long with $1/2$-inch holes drilled at 1-inch intervals. A cap seals one end with a 90-degree elbow on the other end. The hose from the pump attaches to this elbow.

The pump and the pipe can be permanently attached to the cooler with clamps and screws, although this will make it difficult to use the cooler for anything but a live bait tank. If the pipe hangs down from the hinges on heavy monofilament and the pump just sits on the bottom, the whole rig can be removed when not in use.

Live baitfish are deployed with a fishfinder rig. When live bait is taken, the fish will swim off while turning the bait around to swallow it head first. This procedure takes a few seconds, and the fish may drop the bait if it feels the weight of the sinker. Exactly how much time you should allow for the fish to have the bait before you take up the slack and set the hook depends on the size of the bait, the species of fish, and your own judgment, keeping in mind that a longer wait usually means a more deeply hooked fish, which is more difficult to release unharmed.

Fish used as bait are best hooked through the lips or eye sockets. This allows them to swim in a somewhat natural manner while anchored to the bottom or while being slowly retrieved. Eels are also fished alive but require different treatment and handling. Store eels in a small cooler with a mixture of ice and water. By keeping the eels as cold as possible, they will be much easier to handle when the time comes to put them on a hook. A damp rag will allow the eel to be handled without getting slime on the angler and the tackle.

Hook the eel through the lips or the eyes. Use a single-hook rig with a 3-foot leader tied to a drail heavy enough to cast the bait beyond the breakers. A slow retrieve back to the beach keeps the eel moving and prevents a seriously tangled leader. Eels that are cast out and allowed to sit on the bottom will get into all sorts of curled and line-wrapped mischief.

Salted eels are fished with a swimming lip. Although technically they are dead baits, rigged eels are worked like a lure. Cast them out and retrieve them so that they swim just above the bottom. A rigged eel is deadly on striped bass, especially at night or on overcast days.

S

In most coastal areas, there is a favorite bait and favorite way of fishing it. If you are a traveling angler, check with local tackle shops and follow local guidance until you find something that works better.

Sitting versus fishing. Most surf anglers leave their rods in a sand spike while their bait soaks somewhere offshore. Spiking the rod and soaking bait allows the angler to enjoy the social side of surf fishing while still catching the occasional fish. In some cases, you want the bait to stay in one place, such as at the edge of a bar when you're waiting for a big drum to pass by. Nearly all surf anglers in drum country, while sitting in a beach chair with rod securely spiked and a cooler of refreshment nearby, will assure you that they really are drum fishing. But if you want to catch more than the occasional fish, you need to work at it. Get your rod out of the sand spike, and tend to business by replacing old bait with fresh bait, repositioning the bait, and covering various areas of the surf.

Certain situations clearly dictate a more active approach to surf angling than the chair and cooler method. Flounder, for instance, prefer a moving target, so you must keep the bait moving over the bottom. Several fish species cruise the inshore side of an outer bar looking for food washed over by the wave action. The best way to capitalize on this is to cast a bait onto the bar and allow it to wash down the dropoff. It takes some practice to reel in just enough line to keep in touch with the rig while letting it drop in a natural manner. You don't do this once and then stop; you keep trying.

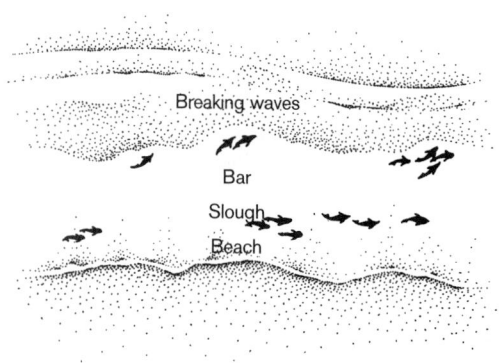

Where there is an outer bar that receives breaking waves, fish hold close to the inner side of the bar and also lurk in the deeper water of the slough.

Using very light tackle and small rigs for pompano requires similar techniques. The small sinker will not hold bottom and will be swept along the beach. You must watch the angle of your line, moving it inshore while the current takes it parallel to the shore. The strike will come just beyond the breaker or in the white water after the wave breaks. Once the rig has passed these spots without notice, slowly reel in and try again.

Lures

The successful surf angler will choose the appropriate bait or lure to match current conditions. Although fishing with bait is generally preferred in the surf, lures are used in many locations on a wide variety of fish, and at certain times they will outproduce live or dead baits. Certain species, like Spanish mackerel, for example, are seldom taken on bait but will hit a well-placed metal lure. When bluefish are blitzing the beach, a surf bait will work, but a big surface popper provides more exciting action.

Three basic types of lures are used in the surf: metal lures, plugs, and leadhead jigs. Each has a specific use, but most fish will take all three under varying conditions.

Metal lures. Because surf angling requires casting a good distance and letting a sinking lure settle into and work through roiling water, surf anglers often prefer a thick-bodied metal lure. Metal lures for taking fish from the surf began with the heavy-bodied and so-called tin squids (see) that were hand-cast on tarred line coiled at the angler's feet. Now metal lures are made from lead or stainless steel and are tossed by rods and reels. These are straight, heavy-bodied products that are primarily used for casting.

There are several well-known brands of stainless steel models that cast like a bullet and work with either a fast or a slow retrieve. Thin and thick versions are used when you're matching thin or fat baitfish, respectively. Lead models also come in various sizes, with smaller ones working on Spanish mackerel and small bluefish, and larger ones on trout and striped bass.

Smaller metal lures are cast to breaking fish and retrieved rather quickly. The strike often comes as soon as the lure hits the water, so the reel must be engaged upon impact. If the fish fails to make contact immediately, you must crank the lure quickly to keep it working close to the surface. At times a slight pause to let the lure drop a bit may induce a strike. Larger, heavier lures are fished along the bottom with a hopping, jigging action to imitate a sand eel. Sometimes it's good to let lure sink into the sand and then jerk it out by quickly raising the rod tip.

Spoons are sometimes also used in the surf, but their wide surface area and generally light weight make them less aerodynamic and more difficult to cast. Under favorable conditions, the heavier, thicker metal spoons can be employed as is. Lightweight spoons can be effective when accompanied by a drail, which is tied 12 to 18 inches above the spoon to add the weight necessary to cast beyond the breakers. Allow the rig to sink; then use a moderate retrieve to keep the spoon just above the bottom. Trout, stripers, drum, and other bottom feeders may find this technique irresistible.

A few manufacturers still produce lures made from tin, and more may do so if regulations prohibit lead lures. Tin is more expensive than other metals, but it does have a special glow when polished in the wet sand.

Plugs.   Saltwater surf plugs had their roots in freshwater and really got started in the 1940s with models that were introduced and used successfully for stripers on Cape Cod. Then, as now, a surf fishing plug must be heavy enough and have the proper shape to cast well, plus have a slow to moderate swimming action. Most surf plugs are shallow-swimming models; deep divers have little merit in the shallow intertidal zone of the surf.

Swimming plugs for surf use come in various styles. The most popular plugs have a slow side-to-side action and can be worked in different sea conditions. Darting versions have a long, angled face and will swim in a wide side-to-side motion. They can be very effective in a rip at the mouth of an inlet or at the end of a point or bar. Cast the plug upcurrent, and allow it to sweep past with little or no retrieve. The force of the current will cause the plug to work.

The breaking waves and cross currents will contribute to the action of most swimming lures, and you must adjust the retrieve to compensate for these factors. Plugs should be cast just beyond a wave that is about to break. As the wave rolls toward the beach, the plug is retrieved at the proper speed to keep it working in the whitewater but ahead of the next wave that would tumble it head over tail. The plug should give the impression of a baitfish caught up in, or struggling against, the waves and thus be easy prey.

An exception to this retrieval tactic are needle-fishlike plugs that are long and thin and without inherent action. These are slowly retrieved without any movement of the rod tip so that they come through the water in a straight line. These plugs are basically like a stick with hooks, but they have accounted for many big stripers. Some other straight-running plugs are used in the surf with a bit of rod-tip movement.

Surf anglers can also double-up when using a plug by placing a second lure on a dropper line ahead of the plug. This second lure may be a small fly, a soft grub, or a small bucktail jig, each of which acts like a baitfish trying to avoid a predator (the plug). Quite often a strike will come on the dropper lure.

Cross currents or rips at the end of points leave eddies of slower-moving water where gamefish wait for bait to tumble past. A plug cast up and across the current will sweep by this eddy and may attract a strike. Slow-swimming lures that will work with little more than the pressure of the current are particularly effective in these rips. Plugs worked in the roiled surf along jetties, causeways, and pilings are also likely to bring strikes, since the flash of these lures where waves wash up and roil can be an attractant.

Occasionally a surface plug has merit in the surf, although this is usually when a school of gamefish

Not all surf fishing occurs along open beach, as this scene at an old gun-mount structure in Cape May, New Jersey, attests.

has pinned a school of bait against the beach or is chasing bait to the surface. At such times, almost any lure that will reach the fracas will be effective, but a surface lure that pops, chugs, and spits water is most exciting to fish.

Many topwater surf plugs are weighted for long casts but sit very low once they are in the water. A constant, fast retrieve is needed to keep them working on the surface. Plugs that float high can be retrieved slowly; allow them to rest a bit between pops. This style of plug can be effective at night on calm waters.

The pencil-style popper has a unique design and action. Weighted at the stern, it rides in the water with the top pointed up and the rear pointed down. Work the popper with a slow retrieve combined with a fast and furious action from the rod tip. This is best accomplished with the rod butt placed between your legs while you work the tip with your hand placed above the reel. This position is rather awkward looking but very effective when you want the plug to jump up and down in one place like an injured baitfish.

Leadhead jigs.   The most versatile weapon in the surf angler's arsenal is the leadhead jig, known to many simply as a leadhead. Dressed with bucktail hair, a soft-bait tail, or a strip of bait, this lure will imitate the food of most gamefish.

Leadheads come in a variety of head shapes, with the rounded, bullet, and Upperman styles very popular with surf casters. A surf jig must cast well and sink fast, and these particular shapes have low resistance to both air and water.

Larger jigs are usually shaped like a bullet and may be adorned with glass eyes or a smiling face. A few leadheads are shaped to impart a swimming action. The lip used ahead of a rubber or plastic eel is an example of this style of leadhead. The boxing glove style makes the jig wobble slowly from side to side as it falls through the water column. Most strikes occur when a jig is dropping, so this style can attract more fish. It does have a higher wind resistance than most jig heads but can still be effective when worked along the beach on a still, warm summer evening. Turbulent waters in the surf make it difficult to maintain control of a jig. Light line will aid in both casting distance and control, with the jig tied directly to the main line without benefit of leader or hardware.

Bucktail jigs will catch just about anything that swims in the ocean at one time or another, and they are the preferred surf jig. The hollow deer hair of a bucktail adds buoyancy and a breathing action unlike any other lure. Worked with a jigging motion that allows the bucktail to rise and fall, the hair will compress and expand, imparting a lifelike action.

Select the size and color of the bucktail to match the size and color of local baitfish. Also consider contrast. A dark lure works better against a light background like sand, and a light color stands out more against a dark background like rocks. A bucktail with white hair and a red head is a popular all-around pattern.

Tie a bucktail directly to the line or leader with an Improved Clinch or Loop Knot. The Improved Clinch keeps the jig working in a vertical direction, and a loop allows it to swing from side to side. Bucktails can be worked fast, slow, shallow, and deep. A fast retrieve just below the surface can be deadly on Spanish mackerel or bluefish. Working it slowly along the bottom is good for speckled trout, flounder, or striped bass.

Threading a soft-tail bait onto the hook shank makes a leadhead jig even more versatile. Large soft-tail leadheads are deadly on drum, striped bass, and flounder. Smaller versions are used for speckled trout, puppy drum, and a wide variety of other small bottom feeders. Some have a curled tail and a swimming action; others impart little motion or only a small wag. The speed of retrieve is generally slower for soft-tailed jigs. A straight retrieve works best on swimming models, whereas a hop-and-skip action can make the straight runners come alive. Tying two jigs 8 to 10 inches apart improves casting distance and may make the lure more appealing.

In all cases, a jig should be worked all the way through the surf line. Gamefish may follow a jig to the water's edge before deciding to eat, so an early end to the retrieve may take the bait out of the water too soon.

Sweetening a jig with some sort of natural bait is a common practice along the surf. Tough baits such as squid or shark belly hold up well and may be added to a naked jig or one dressed with bucktail hair or a soft tail. Pork rind can add life to any leadhead; the long, thin strips imitate such natural food as spearing, and they are deadly on flounder and trout. They also work for bluefish and hold up against their sharp teeth. White seems to be the favorite and most productive color in the surf, but pork rind is available in many hues.

The prudent angler will carry a selection of lead-head jigs in a wide variety of colors. The same is true of soft tails. Surf fish can be finicky, and the angler who can present the lure *du jour* will look like an expert angler.

Casting

Obviously, surf fishing is dependent on casting to get the bait or lure into the strike zone. The angler who can cast the farthest will often, but not always, catch the most fish. However, this is all relative. Casting far does not usually mean launching a lure or bait more than 150 feet. This distance may seem extreme to some anglers, particularly those used to fishing in freshwater, but it is not that far by saltwater standards, and some anglers are able to cast several times that distance at the beach. Fortunately, most fish feed close to the beach, and a super long heave is not required. A simple overhead cast will put the bait in the strike zone most of the time. Try to place such a cast just beyond the breakers or just inside the outer bar.

Proper tackle selection goes a long way toward making a good surf cast, especially one of moderate to long distances. A graphite rod combined with a conventional reel is a good beginning. Using the lightest line practical, in combination with a shock leader tied with a low-friction knot, also aids distance. Although thick-bodied metal lures and weighted surface plugs produce long casts, they may not always produce fish. Sometimes only a big hunk of cut bait will catch a fish. The problem with casting a heavy sinker and a big hunk of bait is trying to move two different objects in the same direction at the same time. The sinker sits at the very end of the line and by itself would be easy to cast. Add a second weight that has completely different aerodynamic properties and is dangling from a leader offset from the main line, and you encounter a problem.

Technique. To begin the most basic cast, start with the bait and sinker lying on the beach behind you. While facing the ocean, point the tip of the rod directly at the rig, take out all line slack, and then bring the rod tip up sharply over your head, stopping at an imaginary 10 o'clock position as you release the line. Many beginners have a problem releasing the line at the proper time. Releasing it too early will cause the rig to fall behind you; releasing too late will cause it to fall short and the line may cut your finger. Practice will overcome this problem.

Small rigs with one or two hooks are much easier to cast. Some rigs currently on the market have a release system that holds the hook tight to the line but lets it swing free when the rig hits the water. This produces an aerodynamic packet that should go farther toward the horizon.

For extreme distances, you might try the pendulum cast, which was introduced to American surf anglers by John Holden in the 1970s. This technique is a bit complicated and involves swinging a single weight around, behind, and over your head to load the rod with the maximum amount of energy. Long-distance casters can exceed 700 feet in competition, using special equipment and this technique. Beach casters may top 600 feet with outfits capable of bringing in a fish. To practice this cast, you will need a very long practice field with plenty of room on all sides because a breakoff will often travel to the right or left of the caster.

A modified version of the pendulum cast will do the job in most fishing situations. Hold the rod over your shoulder, and let the rig swing just above the ground. Push the rod back until the rig swings straight out, loading the rod. Come around in a side-arm fashion, and release the line when you feel maximum load. For more information, *see: Casting.*

Conventional reels permit longer casts than spinning reels because their revolving spools actually push the line off the reel, and there is less coiling and friction from the departing line. If left uncontrolled, the line will overrun the spool and create a backlash *(see).* Expert casters control the line with light thumb pressure on the spool; most people rely on counterweights or magnets to do this job, in some cases with a moderate amount of thumb pressure. These cast control mechanisms cut down on maximum casting distance, however, especially when dealing with such forces and distances as are required for surf fishing.

Remember that a longer rod does not always result in a longer cast. A 7- to 10-foot rod will work well up to 150 feet. An 11- to 13-foot rod will cast as far as anyone needs to go if it is well matched to the angler. Anything over 13 feet will only get in the way.

Be practical and safe. When trying to get a lure or bait into distant water, you do not need to start running from the base of the dunes to just short of the water's edge before making a cast. Forward body speed is not carried over to the cast. This is not javelin throwing. Stay in one spot and concentrate on making a good casting motion, using the rod to maximize leverage.

Also, it does little good to wade out up to your armpits, make a cast, lock the reel in gear, and drag your rig back to the beach. Leave the reel out of gear until you're back on dry land; then lock it down and crank out the slack.

Always look behind you before making a cast. Fellow anglers, children, bathers, and pets may stroll behind you, and they may take exception to being hooked or whacked with a bait or heavy sinker. You should also be mindful of your own safety. If waves are crashing over the jetty, for example, wait for the tide to subside so you don't take an unnecessary risk.

Picking a Spot

The surf line is a constantly changing mix of sand, mud, rock, or any combination of materials. Surf anglers must use experience and knowledge to pick a spot where the fish will be active during their time on the beach. Anglers working from boats not only have greater mobility, but also have electronic aids, which are of no value to surf casters. Most surf anglers are on foot and thus have limited mobility. While it is always possible that the inexperienced angler may stumble onto a fishing hotspot, those who study the surf and learn about tides and currents will know where to be and at what preferred times, and will do better over the long haul.

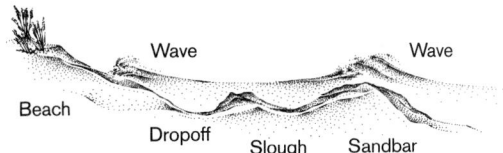

This cross-sectional view of the beach and surf helps to illustrate the features that impact on site selection and fish presence.

Sand makes up most of the beaches where surf anglers congregate, and it moves about with the tides and currents. This movement creates bars, sloughs, washouts, runouts, holes, channels, and other formations that may combine some or all of the above. The surf angler must look at the surface of the water and figure out exactly what lies underneath, be aware of the present stage of the tide and current, and have some knowledge of what the existing or predicted winds will do to the waves. It is also helpful to know when the target species is likely to stop by for a meal. This sounds like finding a needle in a haystack, but it is not that complicated.

According to oceanographers, a wave will break when the water below it is twice as deep as the wave is high. In other words, a 1-foot wave will break in 2 feet of water. Thus, waves break in shallow water but hold together over deep water.

A natural beach allows the wave to break gradually, dissipating its energy over some distance. As the wave rolls in, it begins to break offshore on the outer bar, churning sand from the bottom and pushing it back to the bar. A smaller wave now rides across the deeper water of the slough before breaking onshore. As this wave breaks on the beach, it scours out a dropoff at the edge of the white water. This dropoff moves in and out with the tide, but the outer bar remains somewhat stationary.

The distance from where the surf caster stands to the outer bar can vary considerably. In some places the bar will come to the beach forming a point, but a little farther up or down the shoreline the bar will be a distance of at least two and a half casting lengths offshore.

Because of varying combinations of wind, tide, and current, deep holes form along the beach. Some may come and go on a single tide, and others stay around until the next big storm. Washouts, runouts, and breaks in the outer bar are channels created by currents moving back and forth on the tides. Not only are these channels deeper than the surrounding water, but they act as highways for fish and bait to move from offshore to inshore and back offshore.

Low tide is the best time to figure out what type of structure lies below the water. When the depth of the water is at its lowest point, the difference between shallow and deep water is apparent. Waves will be breaking on the shallow areas, some of which may be completely exposed. Deeper water will be calm and should appear blue or green rather than white.

An offshore wind will create problems as it pushes more water toward the beach and increases the size of the waves. Deeper water and higher waves can disguise bottom structure; if the wind increases to more than 15 knots, the entire ocean may turn white.

Winds blowing offshore have a different effect. They push water away from land, exposing structure not seen on normal low tides. These winds also push the warm surface water offshore and can drop surf temperatures by 10° to 15°F. This sudden temperature drop is seldom beneficial to surf fishing.

If you crest the top of the dune line at low tide, you can survey a considerable stretch of beach. Look for waves breaking on an offshore bar that is close enough to be in casting range. A break in the bar or a place where the bar comes to the beach will funnel fish to you.

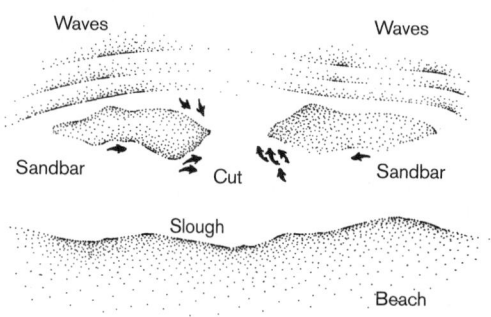

Although waves will break on sandbars, there will be no waves in the cut between the bars, and fish will be located as shown here.

Set up a station close to the break or the point, and you will be in position for some action on the rising tide. Walk-on anglers will stay in one area, but those with four-wheel-drive vehicles can move about looking for the best action. Drive slowly and stop often to watch wave action and water color. Birds feeding close to shore are a positive sign, especially if big fish are observed breaking under the birds.

Watch not only the water, birds, and fish, but other anglers. When everyone is sitting in chairs or leaning on their vehicles talking, the action is pretty slow. A tight group of anglers standing at the water's edge, holding rods without a sand spike in sight, indicates that someone recently caught something. If most of the rods are bent, you've found a good place to fish, and you better get started.

Every beach is a separate entity. Some are similar but none are exactly the same. A rocky coast in Maine or California fishes completely different from a sandy beach in North Carolina. The only way to learn how to read the beach where you fish is experience. The more time you put in on the beach, the more knowledge you'll gain. For example, you should learn when stripers stage on the end of a certain bar, or when pompano move over an outer bar, or at what stage of the tide you can expect to find flounder in a particular slough. No matter how much you read or how many old salts you talk to, the only way to learn how to read the beach is to get out there and fish.

Night Fishing

Many fish species move into the surf at night to feed when they feel safer in the shallow water. Striped bass, weakfish, and red drum are among the fish that are taken regularly after dark.

Fishing the surf at night is similar to fishing in daylight but does require a few modifications. Avoid bright lights at all cost. Fish have very sensitive eyes, and the beam from a flashlight, headlights, or searchlight will send them to deeper, darker water. Never approach a fishing site with the headlights on or scan the water with a flashlight or searchlight. Should you violate this rule, those anglers who were catching fish before your arrival will do things to hasten your departure.

It's a good idea to arrive at the beach before dark to scout the waters and allow your eyes to adjust. Scouting out the situation in daylight will make the return trip easier and safer because you will have seen the territory earlier in the light. You should always be careful when wading in the surf but especially so after dark. An angler who is knocked down by a wave or who steps into a deep hole may go unnoticed until it is too late. A miner's light worn around the neck or on a hat helps surf anglers keep track of one another without shedding enough light on the water to spook the fish. The same light is also handy for close work when tying knots or unhooking fish.

Dress appropriately for night fishing because even the warmest summer day can turn into a chilly night on the beach. This is amplified when water temperatures are cold and the wind is blowing in.

Casting into a totally dark ocean using the sound of breaking waves as a guide takes a bit of getting used to. Any available moonlight helps, as do permanent shore lights. Fortunately, the tops of breaking waves are white and reflect even the smallest amount of available light.

Surf casters who work the night tides are a pretty dedicated bunch. Usually standoffish at first, they will come around when a newcomer demonstrates that he or she is capable and as dedicated as they are. Of course, it may take 15 to 20 years, but they will come around.

Playing/Landing Fish

Surf anglers face several obstacles when playing and landing fish. The quarry is quite a distance from the angler, which allows wind, tide, current and seaweed to play havoc with the fishing line. The long line gives a big fish plenty of room to swim up or down the beach, picking up the lines of neighboring anglers and creating quite a mess.

In almost every surf fishing situation, the angler will use heavy tackle and put as much pressure as possible on the fish. Heavy is relative, since 10-pound test may be fine for small fish in calm water but 50-pound may not be heavy enough for a big fish in heavy seas with crowded anglers.

It is seldom necessary to set the hook when fishing with bait. The fish hooks itself when it moves away with the bait and tries to pull the sinker out of the sand. Live or dead baits on fishfinder rigs are an exception, since the fish is allowed to run with the bait before the angler takes up all the slack and sets the hook.

Lures, of course, require some hooksetting, but they are generally fished on a shorter line than bait, and the angler will be aware of the strike. A quick upward sweep of the rod tip is enough to set the hook. Continued hooksetting is unnecessary and may pull the hook out of the fish.

Once hooked, the fish should be brought to the beach as quickly as possible. Keep the rod tip high, and crank in the line at a steady pace. If you crank too fast, the fish may come to the top, tumbling head over tail until the hook is free. A slow retrieve allows the fish too much time to figure out how to get away. Fish with a soft mouth do require a bit of finesse; a slow but steady retrieve will keep pressure on the hook and hold the fish on the line.

The real problem with landing a fish from the beach occurs at the surf line. Breaking waves tumble fish, which allows the line to go slack and gives the hook an opportunity to come out. Watch the waves and time your retrieve so that the fish rides the back of the wave without going over the top. The bigger the waves and the bigger the fish, the harder the job.

Once through the waves, the fish will be pulled back to sea by the undertow. Be careful not to exert much pressure on the fish, holding it in place until the undertow subsides. At this point, the prize should be lying on wet sand, waiting for you to pick it up.

Fish weighing up to 20 pounds can be landed with relative ease. Those over 20 are more difficult. Big fish are going to take line, but drag tension must be high. Fish usually run toward deeper water, but some will go up and down the beach instead of heading offshore. In either case, try to get as close to the water's edge as possible to shorten the distance between you and the fish.

Keep the rod tip as high as possible when the fish is taking line; then drop down and crank before lifting up again to gain line. Always apply maximum

Snook are sought in the frothy Caribbean surf of Costa Rica, where warm water makes wet wading practical.

pressure to tire the fish as quickly as possible. The longer the fight, the better the odds the fish will win.

Using quality tackle and tying good knots is the most important aspect of landing a big fish in the surf. Cheap rods, reels with jerky drags, rusty hooks, and weak knots will work on small fish; but when that trophy of a lifetime is finally hooked, everything had better be first-rate.

For more information on this topic, *see: Playing Fish.*

Access and Responsibility

For the most part, coastal beaches are controlled by federal, state, and municipal governments, as well as by private individuals, organizations, and corporations. In most cases, you must have permission to access a particular portion of beach. Many government agencies have established access points for a good deal of oceanfront. Most charge a fee to use a four-wheel-drive vehicle, if that is allowed at all (a special permit is usually issued, and it may require the holder to have a pail, tow rope or chain, shovel, fishing rod, and other items in the vehicle while on the beach). A few beaches are free for walk-on anglers, but very few have free and unrestricted access to the ocean for beach buggies.

As coastal areas become more populated and increasingly utilized, fishing space becomes a rarer commodity. The fate of all beaches is susceptible to many influences, and anglers may find it increasingly difficult to gain access to beaches or to convince policymakers that they are entitled to recreate there as well. Some angling organizations and surf fishing clubs have been able to hold their ground, but pressure to ban access has grown and is likely to continue.

Surf anglers must be aware of this problem and do what they can to establish and maintain a good image and a good rapport with others. Exercising common sense is important. Always leaving the beach as clean as, or cleaner than, you found it, even if this involves cleaning up someone else's mess, is a good way to start. Dispose of unused or discarded bait properly. Take off cleats or creepers when walking on wooden boardwalks or access lanes. Do not cross a strip of private property without permission simply because it is the easy way to get to a desirable fishing spot. If someone is swimming or surfing right in the middle of your favorite fishing spot, leave it and come back later. Beach buggy owners must be particularly careful. Stay in designated areas, do not drive on or even near the dunes, and avoid nesting bird habitat, especially that of piping plovers. Don't take an unnecessary risk. If the sand looks a little soft, get out of the vehicle and walk across; if you sink, your beach buggy will go down to the axles, and it may put one more nail in the coffin of other vehicular users.

Fishing when less people are present will help avoid user conflicts. The best surf fishing is often at dawn, at dusk, at night, in poor weather, and in the fall, all of which are times when there are few others on the beach. Nevertheless, you shouldn't crowd in on another angler's spot, or put out more than two rods.

Surf anglers seldom make a significant dent in fish populations, but they must be mindful of the need to conserve. As is also true for other fishing, surf anglers must obey all regulations, keep only the fish they plan to eat, and never kill unwanted fish or leave them to die on the beach.

SURFACE LURE
An artificial lure that is strictly, or primarily, retrieved on the water's surface.

Surface lures, which are also known as topwater lures, are almost exclusively fished by casting and retrieving, and many require proper manipulation to be effective. As a category, surface lures are the most presumptuous of all lure types because they must draw fish to a place where they spend the least amount of their time—the surface. Thus, surface lures appeal to highly aggressive fish and to species that attack from hiding places or gang up on prey and "corner" them at the surface, but not to bottom-dwelling species, true deep-water denizens, and fish that don't hunt near the surface in packs.

Salmon, for example, though aggressive fish in open water, do not find any of their prey on the surface; likewise, walleyes prowl deep water, often near the bottom. However, largemouth bass, smallmouth bass, northern pike, and striped bass are freshwater species that sometimes feed on or close to the surface. In saltwater, species that maraud baitfish schools (like bluefish) and pin them near the surface, and those that use and feed near cover (like snook), are also candidates for surface fishing, while those that feed deep (like groupers) or mainly pick shrimp off the bottom (like bonefish), are not.

Without question, surface fishing is highly appealing to anglers. Ask trout anglers if they prefer to catch a fish on a dry fly or on a subsurface fly, and they will certainly vote for the former, even though the vast majority of trout feed and are caught beneath the surface. The extra visual stimulus to every kind of surface fishing is of exceptional entertainment value, and can be exciting no matter when or where it is experienced.

Because surface fishing requires aggressive fish behavior, it is more of a warmwater phenomenon than a coldwater one, which also restricts its suitability in many places (summertime for most species, especially in temperate climates). For some species—freshwater bass, for example—surface lures are more effective in shallow water and places with cover than in open deep-water environs. But that depends on the nature of the fish. Some saltwater species may be taken on the surface miles from the nearest shore, when they happen to be feeding on baitfish that have been pushed to the surface.

For the most part, however, because more surface fishing is done in freshwater (for bass) and near some form of cover, being an accurate caster and having full mastery over the workings of these lures is important in surface fishing. The keys to successful surface fishing include knowing when, and when not, to use them; knowing what type to use and how; knowing where to use them; knowing when to stop fishing on the surface (a common mistake for many anglers is staying with surface fishing long after the surface activity has petered out); and being able to put those lures in the position where they will be most productive.

Basically, any lure that is worked on the surface or is fished both on the surface or within the first 1 to 3 feet of the surface, is part of this category. There are basically four types of surface lures: popping and wobbling plugs, floating/diving plugs and darters, propellered lures, and stickbaits. There is also, in the broadest sense, the dry fly, which is detailed separately because it is vastly different in principle and application from other lures, as is the fly rod popper or bug *(see: fly)*.

Poppers and Wobblers
There are two distinct lures in this category: plugs that pop or chug and those that wobble. Some poppers are also called chuggers and they are also known as popping plugs; they come in small sizes for light-tackle casting in freshwater to long heavy versions used in surf casting. Many are short and squat, some are long and slender, and the rear treble hook on many is dressed with bucktail or synthetic material for extra pizzazz. Wobblers are strictly a freshwater lure for bass fishing, and less numerous than poppers. All these plugs are strictly fished on top of the water.

A popper doesn't actually resemble the actions of any prevalent form of fish food, since nothing deliberately calls attention to itself or makes popping or chugging sounds. It is possible, however, that the noise generated by these lures is construed by fish as the surface feeding activity of other fish. More likely, this sound simply attracts feeding fish or calls some out of hiding for curiosity's sake. Poppers are most effective on largemouth and smallmouth bass in freshwater, particularly the former, and on striped bass and bluefish in saltwater.

Nearly all poppers have a concave, scooped out mouth. They function mainly as a noisemaker and attractor. They may be worked in a continuous retrieve manner in locations where fish feed on schools of bait, but otherwise they should be fished with pauses of varying duration during the retrieve. The actual popping or forward chugging motion is made by jerking the rod up or back, not by reeling line in, to achieve the proper movement.

In freshwater, in generally close quarters fishing, it's best to keep the rod low and pointed toward the lure; this helps avoid slack to work the lure well and puts the rod in the best possible position to react to a strike. In saltwater, where casting long distances may be common, it is often necessary to keep the rod tip up to help work the lure properly, especially when there is much wave action; when a strike occurs, drop the rod tip while reeling up slack, and quickly set the hook.

Popping plugs should be worked with varying degrees of emphasis. Seldom is it worthwhile to jerk the rod hard to create a loud commotion. This can occasionally be effective for schooling striped bass, but seldom is it warranted for other fish, especially largemouth bass, and even then when they're schooling and chasing baitfish pods near the surface. Usually when the surface is calm, you need only to effect a mild popping noise; a loud noise under this condition is alarming. When the surface is disturbed by a mild chop, make a slightly noisier retrieve.

If it appears that fish are feeding fairly actively, you can shorten the time between retrieval strokes, but in nonfrenzied situations it's usually best to maintain pauses of several seconds' duration. When worked slowly and enticingly in places with good concentrations of fish, especially largemouth bass, they can be dynamically effective. A good tactic is to let a popper lie motionless awhile after splashdown, then reel up all slack line and gently jiggle the rod just enough to impart the slightest sign of life to the lure. This tactic works well for just about all surface lures and sometimes makes a striker out of a fish, usually bass, that has been attracted to the landing of the plug in the water but might be spooked by the first quick motion. In situations where there is plenty of bait or where there is surface-feeding commotion, however, work the popper with a quicker motion.

Poppers are obviously time-consuming lures to use, and do not cover a lot of area very well. They work best near cover and in water that is not too deep, roughly to 12 feet in freshwater. Early and late in the day (particularly in the summer), night, and

A frog-patterned popper is eyed by a largemouth bass.

cloudy days are the best fishing times for this lure. Don't use a popper continuously unless you're having exceptionally good success. Poppers are good for spot fishing, that is, making a few casts in selected areas and then switching to another, different type of lure.

Wobbling plugs are used much in the manner of poppers. They are more effective for largemouths, but can produce some dandy smallmouths at night, and are probably more effective in the dark than at dusk, daylight, or dawn.

Wobblers are characterized by their to and fro undulating action, resulting in large part from a wide, spoonlike metal lip or metal side "wings" that rock the lure from side to side. The common retrieval method is a straight, continuous motion. At times, though, a worthwhile technique is to make the lure stop and go, or to give it a pull-pause motion, particularly as it swims next to an object like a stump or dock support. As long as there is some cover present or the water is not excessively deep under the boat, it's wise to work these lures all the way back to you; they may be struck at any point along the retrieve, especially at night.

Keep your rod tip low and resist the urge to reel too fast. Wobblers don't have as good an action when retrieved quickly as they do when worked slowly. Moreover, a fast retrieve is more conducive to missed strikes. Many bass strike and miss wobbling surface lures. This may be because they have difficulty pinpointing the lure's location or more often because they're intending to stun this surface swimming creature. Try a more frequent stop-and-go retrieval cadence if the fish keep missing it.

For some reason, many fish that strike and miss fail to hit the lure when you toss it out a second time. Resist the urge to set the hook the instant a fish slashes at the lure, and momentarily wait to feel the fish take your plug before setting the hook sharply. This hard to master delay is very effective in fishing weedless spoons in the grass, and works well with wobbling surface plugs too. If the fish misses altogether, try stopping the lure in its tracks and twitching it a little, then moving it a few inches and stopping it. Repeat this before resuming the retrieve.

Very light or very dark colors are preferred in poppers and wobblers by many anglers. Black is especially favored in freshwater, but chrome, clear, and frog-patterned models are also effective; in saltwater, silver and blue-and-white are popular.

Floating/Diving Lures

Probably the most universally applied method of surface or near surface fishing involves the use of floating/diving plugs. These lures are made either of plastic or wood and are generally minnow-shaped, which cause them to be generically called minnow plugs by some anglers. They have a small lip that serves to bring the lure beneath the surface at a maximum of about 3 feet on a conventional cast and retrieve. (These same minnow plugs, incidentally, will get down to a depth of 6 or 7 feet when trolled slowly and when using at least 150 feet of light line.) This type of lure is manufactured in sizes from 2 inches up to 8 inches; the most practical size for bass fishing is the 4- to 6-inch model, and larger versions are used for pike, muskie, and striped bass.

These lures are most effectively worked in a deliberately erratic fashion to imitate a crippled baitfish. A small dying fish lies on its side, wiggles its tail fin occasionally, goes around in circles, and sometimes gets up enough energy to swim a few inches underwater before bobbing to the surface. This is essentially the activity to mimic in the retrieval of a floating/diving lure. Opportunistic gamefish are likely to charge such a defenseless morsel with gusto, creating an electrifying strike.

To get the most out of this lure, it has to be fished convincingly. Results are directly proportional to the action put into it. Start a retrieve by reeling in all slack line, and keep the rod pointed low in case a fish strikes a well-cast surface lure shortly after it hits the water or has been retrieved a few feet. If a fish hits that lure while it's first sitting still in the water and you have either slack line or a sky busting rod, it's very hard to set the hook.

The objective with a floater/diver is to make it gyrate as enticingly as possible in a stationary position. Keep the rod tip pointed low toward the water and use your wrist to move the rod. Jiggle the rod tip in a controlled, not frantic, fashion. Then jerk the lure back toward you a few inches. Then gyrate it some more, all the time reeling in an appropriate amount of line to keep the slack to a minimum. This is not very difficult to accomplish, particularly if you have a rod with a fairly limber tip; stiff-tipped rods don't allow for soft lure movement.

Another way to use this lure type is on a straight retrieve, allowing it to run a foot or two beneath the surface. This is more like using it as a crankbait, and sometimes fish strike it this way. But a better technique, especially when fish won't hit this plug on top of the water, is to make it run just below the surface in a series of short jerk-pause movements, running it forward half a foot with each motion. This retrieve is more in the style of darters, those plugs that float but have no significant surface action and are used solely just below the surface. Some lures that are fished this way, incidentally, are called "jerkbaits" by bass anglers, and some manufacturers use the words jerking or ripping in labeling such lures that they make for stop-and-go retrieves.

There are good floating/diving plugs made from wood (usually balsa) or plastic. The balsa lures do not seem to rise as quickly to the surface after being pulled under as do many of the plastic products; however, some of these lures have neutral buoyancy and suspend when they're pulled under the surface, or can be made to do so with adhesive weight add-ons. A host of colors have merit in both freshwater and saltwater, although the silver (gray) version with black back probably out catches all the others combined.

In freshwater, perhaps the best location for the use of a floating/diving plug is over submerged grass that comes to within a few feet of the surface. This lure is not only good for catching bass in such a locale, but also for locating possible concentrations of fish, which may then be tapped by the use of a plastic worm. Any type of relatively shallow cover can be a target for this lure. In less covered locations, it can be quite effective as well, including spots such as long, shallow points; the backs of bays; and rocky shorelines. Smallmouth bass are particularly receptive to this lure in late spring and early summer when they're in shallow water. Look for every sizable rock or boulder and toss a floating/diving minnow plug to it.

Propellered Lures

Plugs.   Propellered surface plugs catch pickerel, pike, inland stripers, and some saltwater fish, but are mostly associated with largemouth and smallmouth bass. These lures, in 2- to 6-inch sizes, are basically shaped like small cigars or torpedoes; they may feature propeller-like blades both fore and aft, or have one or two blades at the rear. Smaller sizes are better for smallmouths, but all sizes are productive for largemouth bass, and it is likely that the larger plugs account for the larger fish, too.

The basic retrieval technique is similar to the surface retrieve of floating/diving minnow plugs, which was outlined previously. The retrieve constitutes an erratic jiggling-jerking-pausing motion that represents a struggling or crippled baitfish. As in fishing with floating/diving lures, you need to keep the rod down, utilize the rod tip to effectively impart action, and make your wrist do the rod-manipulating work.

You can retrieve a propellered plug either quickly or slowly. The slow retrieve is good when prospecting for unseen fish, using a deliberate, convincing action. The propellers will make a loud churning noise with some bubbly effect, and this may aid in attracting the attention of bass in the vicinity. A rapid, ripping retrieve is warranted for schooling largemouths, and the noise thereby created seems to imitate the slashing surface breaking feeding activity common to this situation. At this time, if you can keep with the school and if they stay near the surface, it is possible to have a lot of action on a propellered plug. This generally occurs (with varying degrees of frequency) in southern impoundments with abundant concentrations of threadfin shad, where bass have gathered to chase and feed on these baitfish. Summer and fall are productive fishing times for this lure, usually early and late in the day. Areas with heavy cover are prime; in northern waters especially, shore hugging weedlines before a gradual dropoff are quite productive. These lures do not work well in deeper water, other than for school-feeding situations.

Buzzbaits. Another type of propellered lure is a buzzbait, which is not a plug but a sinking spinnerbait-like lure that is fished strictly on the surface. It is solely used in freshwater and almost entirely for largemouth bass, although it does catch pike and occasionally muskie, and has been known to catch the occasional peacock bass. In warm water, it especially appeals to the aggressive nature of largemouths.

Buzzbaits have either in-line or overhead configuration. The overhead version resembles a spinnerbait (*see*) in its construction—an overhead arm with a blade and a lower arm with a lead head and single skirted hook—while the in-line version features a weedless spoon or a bucktail or rubber skirt behind the blade. The revolving "buzz" blade itself is of unique design, vaguely resembling an airplane propeller, and having cupped ends that give the lure a clicking, chop-chop-chop sound that accounts for the name of the lure.

The noise of a buzzbait is not only attractive to feeding bass, but also to shallow nonfeeding bass. Its effectiveness is not limited to one time of the day, to one season, or to a specific geographic locale. Moreover, this lure is an excellent producer of big fish, and certainly of larger than average bass. It works well in spring, summer, and fall, under most weather conditions, and during the day as well as at night. It is generally not very productive in bright sunlight, but good for warm water and hot weather conditions.

A buzzbait is at its very best in areas with thick cover. It is deadly in emergent vegetation that is not too thick to prevent free lure passage and over submerged vegetation that comes fairly close to the surface. It is also highly effective around brush, in timber, and around any fallen wood that might conceal a bass. The closer you can work a buzzbait to such cover, the better.

A well designed buzzbait is reasonably weed-free and can be fished effectively in all but dense concentrations of matted vegetation. Even in fairly thick areas, with accurate casting and a little side-to-side rod manipulation, you can pick your spots and work a buzzer. Mid- to late spring, when lily pads and grass have not fully grown up, is an excellent buzzbait season, provided the water is warm enough.

Bass don't seem to mind how warm the water is in order to hit a buzzer, but they won't come up for it if the water is too cold. The upper 60s is the lower water temperature range for buzzbait action. The summer and early fall are consistently productive buzzbait times, usually in the first few hours of the morning, in late evening, and at night.

Like all surface lures, buzzbaits are basically shallow water products. They seldom produce fish in water over 12 feet deep, even if the vegetation comes to the surface. Furthermore, they allow anglers to cover a lot of water in search of feeding fish.

When bass strike a buzzer, they usually crush it. There are times, however, when they either miss (this happens a lot at night) or strike short. A lot of short strikers can be caught by placing a trailer hook on the bend of the lure's main hook. This is rigged the same as a spinnerbait trailer.

There are many buzzbaits available. In selecting, look for a lure that can be worked effectively at a slow retrieval speed, a bullet-shaped lead head that can cut through the water and ride over vegetation neatly, heavy duty gauge shaft arms, an overall slim profile for lightweight lures to permit easy casting with baitcasting tackle, and large hooks, generally in the 4/0 or 5/0 sizes. Triple-cupped plastic blades are favored by some people for their subtlety rather than a clanking metal blade, but various blade styles and combinations exist. Black, white, and chartreuse are good skirt or body colors, as are combinations, but selection depends on the color and clarity of the water and the relative lightness of the day. Sometimes, color makes no difference.

Stickbaits

Resembling a cigar or tapered broom handle in basic shape, the unimaginatively named stickbait is the antithesis of the natural shape and imitation design of many lures. An artsy paint job may dress up this lure, but essentially it's still a torpedo in costume. Most of the lures that fit into this category of surface plug are similar in size and conformation to propellered plugs, except that they don't have propellers or a lip. They are retrieved much like, and are fished in the same areas as, propellered plugs and to a lesser extent floating/diving lures. However, they have a more pronounced walking or wide swimming action than other surface plugs, and this can be very seductive when done in a slow and deliberate manner or in a fast and frantic manner.

S

A stickbait is "walked" around a flooded bush; the low rod position is necessary to effect the right lure action.

Stickbaits do not have a lip or concave mouth, but a rounded head. They're weighted in the tail so the head sits off the water and the tail rests slightly under the surface. Stickbaits are also known as "splash" baits, "jumpers," and "walkers" because of their darting activity on the surface and the way they splash and seem to be lurching in and out of the water.

Although appearance has little to do with a stickbait's fish catching appeal, its activity when retrieved has everything to do with it. A stickbait can't be tossed out with abandon and then cranked back in. The secret of its effectiveness lies in a masterful retrieval technique. All of the action must be supplied by the angler, making the stickbait foremost among lures for which retrieval skill is of paramount importance.

Many anglers find stickbait retrieval difficult to master. Perhaps this difficulty has been a factor in the relatively lower popularity of these lures compared to other surface plugs. Stickbaits are effective for largemouth, smallmouth, and spotted bass, and also productive at times in angling for stripers, muskies, pike, pickerel, peacock bass, snook, tarpon, and an assortment of other saltwater fish.

Stickbaits come and go among manufacturers, but the one standard of this field is Heddon's Zara Spook, which is widely known and even revered in some circles. The largest and most productive of the Spooks are the $^3/_4$- and $^7/_8$-ounce versions, which are $4^1/_2$ inches long.

Learning to retrieve stickbaits comes easily to anglers who are familiar with techniques for fishing floating/diving minnow plugs. The principal stickbait retrieve causes the lure to step from side to side. This side-stepping technique for stickbaits is called "walking the dog," a term that originated with the Zara Spook; this, and an advanced technique known as "half stepping," is described and illustrated under that entry (see: walking the dog).

A propensity to attract big fish, incidentally, is one of the prime virtues of stickbaits. On the average, these lures produce bigger fish than most other types, and it seems that the larger the plug, the larger the fish.

One difficulty with these lures is that they are hard to fish from a sitting position, especially from a low seat. Sitting on a pedestal seat or, preferably standing, improves retrieval ability. Also, a relatively limber tipped rod is preferable to a stiff tipped one.

Using a snap or a loop knot with a stickbait is especially important; it allows the line to go back and forth quickly and unimpeded. Tying a conventional knot snug to the eye of the lure definitely hinders the action. Also, using thinner diameter line enhances the movement of these lures (less drag).

Stickbaits can be productive in all cover situations where you'd expect to find fish that ambush their prey. You can work specific objects or fish blindly. These lures are especially effective, however, around wood, particularly stumps, logs, and fallen trees, and for calling up bass from submerged timber. They should be worked along the full length of logs and as close to stumps and bushes as possible. When casting to a specific object, land the lure well past your target. Slow walk the lure up to the object, then fast walk it past. Vary retrieval speeds. A moderate retrieve is often best, though there are times when the best approach is to work the lure slowly and seductively, or with a very quick, constant retrieval speed (this is when there is very active fish feeding).

Wind and wave action is a prohibiting factor in working stickbaits because they affect the line and impede retrieval. A light wind that ripples the surface is sometimes desirable, and cloudy, overcast, drizzly conditions are good. Bright sun can be inhibiting. When the angle of the sun is low, retrieve the lure toward the sun, rather than away from it.

A lot of fish strike or boil after a stickbait and miss it. Many of these fish can be enticed to strike again if you can control your reflexes. When fish strike a stickbait, the over anxious angler often rears back to set the hook and jerks the lure away from the fish. Try to hold back your reaction until the fish has clearly taken the lure. If the fish misses the plug and you don't jerk it away but keep it walking along, there's a good chance it will strike again. If you jerk the lure clear away from the fish, you probably won't get a second hit. Then it pays to toss out a different lure to the same spot immediately if another one is handy.

It's important to cast a stickbait very accurately. In thick cover, you'll need to lay the line in such a way that you help direct a clear path of travel for the lure. If you've been fishing another type of lure for some time and then switch to a stickbait, you'll find it hard to cast precisely in close quarters until you get accustomed to the larger, heavier lure.

Pay close attention to the working action of every stickbait you fish. These are critically balanced lures, and though they may come from the same manufacturer, they are not identical. Some lures may need smaller treble hooks to perform well; with others you may have to fiddle with the line-tie screw to lower the angle. It's not uncommon to find one stickbait that works better than an identical one from the same manufacturer. Out of a dozen, it's a fair bet that one or two will have superior action.

As with other lures, colors run the full gamut, and there are many opinions on what to use. The species and clarity of the water will have a lot to do with selection. Try clear (transparent) models if you can find them, as well as Walkers and frog-, perch-, and shad-colored models for bass. Silver, chrome, blue and white, and red and white are among the good saltwater choices. Try dark models on dark days and light colors in clear water.

Specialty Surface Lures

There are a few surface lures that do not quite fit into the standard categories previously mentioned. The soft plastic frog or mouse is such a lure, as are other styles of soft and hard plastic lures that are meant to swim through and over heavy cover in fishing for freshwater bass. These lures are generally preferred in natural colors, with white or yellow bellies, and in all green and all black versions.

These lures are strictly for fishing the vegetation—the thicker the better. Some can be retrieved steadily along while others, like frogs, must be fished extremely slowly and deliberately and with a delay in setting the hook. The latter requires a lot of patience on the angler's part, and with soft plastic lures, it's best to work two on separate rods at the same time, in different locations, alternating between retrieving them.

When a fish hits, delay your hook setting momentarily until you actually feel the fish with the lure. This is less of a problem with soft lures than others because of their consistency, which makes it feel more natural to the fish and results in the bass holding it a bit longer than it might otherwise. When you do set the hook, it must be done hard.

See: Lure; Plug.

SURFPERCH

Also called seaperch and surffish, this group of 21 members of the Embiotocidae family is abundant along the eastern Pacific and is rare among marine fish for being viviparous, or producing live offspring. This characteristic was first noticed at Sausalito, California, in 1853, when an angler

Barred Surfperch

named A. C. Jackson discovered a number of small fish swimming in a pail into which he had just placed some recently caught adult black surfperch. This led to the discovery and naming of the surfperch family by Louis Agassiz.

Unlike most other fish, female surfperch do not scatter eggs outside their body but nourish young fish internally and then spawn them live into the surf. Just as remarkably, these young fish are sexually mature at or before their birth, and infant males can inseminate infant females soon after birth.

Two members of this family occur off Japan and Korea, and the remainder occur along the Pacific coast of North America from Alaska to Baja California, Mexico. All are marine with the exception of the small tule perch (Hysterocarpus traski), which is found in California's Sacramento and Russian Rivers.

None of the species in the family is large; their maximum size ranges from 4 to 18 inches. They have compressed bodies, more or less oval in shape and generally silvery, and large fleshy lips. The spiny and soft-rayed dorsal fins are joined. Most species inhabit the surf along both sandy and rocky coasts, but several species live mainly in bays or in similar shallow inshore waters. One species occurs in relatively deep water (to more than 700 feet), and two smaller species inhabit only tidal pools. They primarily consume small crustaceans, but some also feed on worms, small crabs, shrimp, and mussels. The larger species are popular with anglers and are caught year-round from docks, piers, kelp, the surf line, tidepools, and a variety of other sites. They contribute to the commercial catch but not to a significant extent.

The shiner surfperch (Cymatogaster aggregata) is probably the number one fish caught by youngsters along the California coast. They range from Baja California, Mexico, to Wrangell, Alaska, and are most abundant around bays and eelgrass beds and the pilings of wharves and piers. They grow to a maximum of only 8 inches and are generally greenish or silvery but may be reddish.

The barred surfperch (Amphistichus argenteus) is one of the larger members of the group, growing to a maximum of 17 inches and $4^1/_2$ pounds, although it is usually much smaller. It occurs along sandy

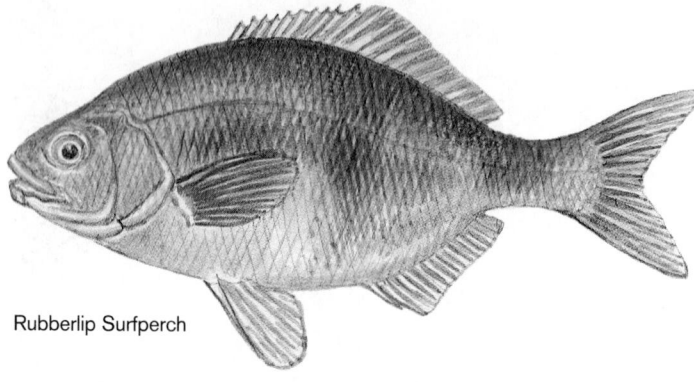

Rubberlip Surfperch

coasts from central California to Baja California. Its sides are marked with a series of dusky, brassy vertical bars with spots between them. The back and sides are gray to olive, and the belly is white. This is among the most popular surfperch with anglers.

The redtail surfperch (*A. rhodoterus*) is more northern in range than the barred species; it ranges from Vancouver Island, British Columbia, to central California. Its vertical bars and the pelvic and caudal fins are usually reddish; it may grow to 16 inches.

The calico surfperch (*A. koeizi*) occurs from Cape Flattery, Washington, to Northern California and grows to 12 inches. It is similar to the redtail, but has a deeper body. It is also similar to the barred, but its lower jaw projects slightly beyond the upper; in the barred surfperch, the lower jaw is shorter than the upper jaw.

The walleye surfperch (*Hyperprosopon argenteum*), occurring from British Columbia to Baja California, is another surfperch that is highly popular with anglers, and the most frequent catch from piers. It grows to about 11 inches and is distinguished by its large eyes and by the black tips on its pelvic, anal, and caudal fins. The back and sides are bluish, the belly is white or silvery. The last spiny rays of the dorsal fin are higher than any of the rays of the soft dorsal.

Relatives of the walleye surfperch include the spotfin surfperch (*H. anale*), found from central California to Baja California; it has no black tips on its fins but does have a distinctive black spot on its spiny dorsal fin and sometimes a black blotch on the anal fin. The silver surfperch (*H. ellipticum*) ranges from Vancouver, British Columbia, to Baja California and is one of the most frequently caught surfperch. It has no black markings on its body and grows to a maximum of $10^1/_2$ inches. All three of these species are found mostly along sandy shores.

The rainbow surfperch (*Hypsurus caryi*) grows to 12 inches and lives principally along rocky shores from northern California to northern Baja California. Somewhat less oval in shape than other surfperch, its silvery body is striped horizontally with blue, orange, and red. The fins are generally orange, and a large black blotch appears on both the soft dorsal and the anal fins.

The white surfperch (*Phanerodon furcatus*) is distinguished by its deeply forked tail and has a rather slim body compared to other surfperch. Growing to 12 inches long, it ranges from Vancouver Island, British Columbia, to northern Baja California, occurring mainly off sandy coasts. There is usually a black spot on the anal fin. This is the species most commonly caught by commercial fishermen due to its schooling tendencies.

Largest in the surfperch family is the rubberlip seaperch (*Rhacocilus toxotes*), which reaches 18 inches in length. Occurring from central to Southern California, it is distinguished by thick white to pinkish lips, so large in some individuals that they droop. The whitish background color is usually tinged with a smoky or blackish color, and the pectoral fins are yellow.

Closely related to the rubberlip is the pile surfperch (*R. vacca*), which ranges from Alaska to Baja California. It is only slightly smaller and is distinguished by a deeply forked tail and very high first rays in the second dorsal fin. The color is silvery, with a blackish or brownish cast on the back, and it has dark fins.

The black surfperch (*Embiotoca jacksoni*) reaches a length of 15 inches. Found from Northern California to central Baja California, it is dark brownish black and often tinged with blue or yellow. It has thick reddish lips. A group of scales between the pectoral and pelvic fins are exceptionally large, and the spiny rays of the dorsal fin are all shorter than the soft rays. The tail is slightly forked.

The striped surfperch (*E. lateralis*) ranges from Baja California to Alaska and is most abundant in the cooler waters north of Point Conception. It has a less forked tail than the black surfperch, and its coppery body is striped horizontally with orange and blue. The scales are spotted with black above the lateral line.

SURGEON'S KNOT
A fishing knot for line-to-line connections.
See: Knots, Fishing.

SURGEON'S LOOP
A fishing knot for line-to-line connections, primarily used in fly fishing for loop-to-loop leaders.
See: Knots, Fishing.

SURGICAL TUBE LURE
A long, slender, hollow trolling lure fashioned from rubber tubing; many are now made from plastic.
See: Trolling Lures, Saltwater; Umbrella Rig.

SURVEY
A tool used by fisheries managers to determine the needs and desires of anglers, the extent of the fish

harvest, methods of angling, and the condition of fish populations. Multiple surveys are used in fisheries management and can include angler surveys, biological surveys, and tagging surveys.
See: Fisheries Management.

SURVIVAL

Most anglers find it hard to imagine themselves in a survival situation. This is something that most people associate with extremely remote areas and extraordinary weather conditions. Given the state of sophisticated communications and population density, some people cannot imagine being in a situation where survival is really an issue. Yet, every angler is exposed to the elements, and one can easily imagine scenarios in which people can be suddenly and unexpectedly placed into a situation that is, or can become, life threatening.

A capsized boat, a flash flood, a breakaway ice floe are just some of the things that can happen to anglers. What if you're deep in the Everglades, lose all electric power, and can't get your motor started? What if you're on a big lake in the Far North, 20 miles from camp, and you damage the lower unit of the motor on a reef and have to spend the night ashore with the black flies and without any wood? What if one evening you're on a trout stream just a half mile from the nearest house and you fall and break your leg? What if a storm rises, the waves pitch into your boat, the bilge pump fails, and you find yourself capsized miles from shore?

These are not far-fetched what-ifs. These and a lot more unexpected circumstances affect anglers every year whether they fish big water in a boat, hike into mountain lakes, or take a snowmobile for miles across a frozen lake. Some circumstances obviously have the potential for danger, but many do not. Storms and heavy winds often are the cause of unexpected events, and anglers should realize that even in routine activities they may sometime face a short- or long-term survival predicament. Even though the odds are against your being in a life or death situation, it is foolish to think that you're immune from it, and practical to be aware of and prepared for it.

In essence, survival is the art of making efficient use of any available resource for sustenance. If individuals are able to think clearly and objectively about an emergency situation—usually because they have prepared for it—they are far more likely to survive than those who panic and are unable to take full advantage of resources that may be at hand.

In a survival situation, there are five basic needs: sustenance, medical, fire, shelter, and rescue. Few survival situations are identical, and some needs are more urgent than others. However, when thinking about and planning for survival, you must prepare for emergencies in a way that will meet all of these needs. Equally important is thinking about these

Strong wind, as experienced on this remote Ontario lake, can be especially dangerous for small boats.

needs in the context of the environment that you'll be in. The following basic information pertains to these needs within the context of the angling world, although it is apropos of other outdoor enthusiasts as well. There is also a review of water safety issues, since anglers are more likely to encounter such issues than others.

Planning Ahead

Survival situations often strike unexpectedly, and they strike the ill-prepared. The angler with only light clothing invariably is the one caught in the "unexpected" late spring snowstorm. Boats never seem to sink when there are enough life jackets to go around.

Planning and preparing for emergencies is more than proper clothing or PFDs, and it is more than carrying a Swiss army knife with you. Preparation requires investing time so that you are physically and mentally fit; it requires thoughtful planning and intelligent selection of resources so that they will be available when you need them. Since you are unlikely to remember all this information (and this is just a primer on survival), it would be a good idea to copy it, laminate it, or otherwise make it waterproof, so you can keep it with you should you ever be in an emergency situation.

Angler's survival kit. It's a smart idea to assemble into a kit all the items necessary for a survival situation; then you can tote the kit wherever you go. Far more is involved than simply buying a prepackaged "survival kit," and it is unlikely that any single kit will meet your specific needs.

Select the items for your survival kit based on their versatility, multifunctionality, and practicality. Although the ability to improvise is not one of the five basic needs of survival, it is an important process in bringing all these needs together. The surgical tubing that you selected as a tourniquet for the first aid kit, for example, can be used to collect water from an improvised solar still; the tubing also makes a straw for drinking out of your water container, or even a slingshot.

The following items are recommended for day or weekend anglers and are versatile for all survival-related emergencies. However, no kit can be entirely right for every situation. These items form a foundation to build upon depending on your activity and the environment. Although the list may seem long, many items are small and light, and some are tools you may want along anyway for everyday use. The GPS navigational unit is optional, but handheld versions are becoming more of a staple for backcountry travelers.

- ❏ One-gallon water bag or container (collapsible or folded)
- ❏ Water purification tablets
- ❏ Nonperishable food ration, 3,600 calories
- ❏ Hard candy
- ❏ Container for boiling water
- ❏ Large fixed-blade knife
- ❏ Pocket knife, with locking blade
- ❏ Flint-and-steel fire starter
- ❏ Tinder for lighting a fire
- ❏ Windproof and waterproof matches (strike-anywhere versions are best)
- ❏ Waterproof match case
- ❏ Lighter
- ❏ Flashlight with spare batteries
- ❏ Three 12-hour high-intensity cyalume light sticks (activated by snapping and shaking)
- ❏ Signal mirror
- ❏ Whistle
- ❏ Compass
- ❏ Compact strobe light
- ❏ First aid kit (should be adequate for environment and include prescription medicines and large compresses)
- ❏ Saw
- ❏ Multiperson emergency tube shelter
- ❏ Survival bag
- ❏ Mylar space blanket sleeping bag
- ❏ Space blanket
- ❏ Wool gloves
- ❏ Wool hat
- ❏ Dry socks
- ❏ Emergency poncho or rain jacket
- ❏ Cord or rope
- ❏ Sewing kit
- ❏ Fishing line and hooks (and also perhaps a few sinkers, small jigs, and streamers)
- ❏ Multifunction tool
- ❏ Sharpening stone
- ❏ Carry/storage bag (sealed for pilfer resistance)
- ❏ Handheld GPS *(see)* navigational unit

Vehicle survival kit.   Like the survival kit for anglers, a survival kit for a vehicle is something that few people assemble, whether they are anglers or not. If you travel off the beaten path, in places where help may be hard to get, and in places subject to extreme weather, then a vehicle survival kit is especially important. Savvy north-country drivers have some or all of these items in their vehicle in case they get stuck on the road in a snowstorm; this kind of situation can happen to people who are simply driving home from work.

The following products are recommended for a complete vehicle survival kit. They include some of the items in the angler's traveling survival kit; you might be wise to have both, since a situation may occur when you have access to one kit but not the other. Items like jumper cables, tire chains, and road flares are normally considered safety items rather than part of a vehicle survival kit, but many survival situations have started along the side of the road because these items were not present. Be ready to improvise. For example, if your vehicle overheats because of a ruptured hose, wait for the car to cool and fix the rupture with duct tape. This may not be the perfect fix but it will probably get you to the next town or nearest phone.

- ❏ Cellular phone
- ❏ Spare tire
- ❏ Flashlight
- ❏ Vehicle jack
- ❏ Gas can
- ❏ Spool of 20-gauge wire
- ❏ Tire chains
- ❏ Flat tire repair items
- ❏ Ground tarp
- ❏ Jumper cables
- ❏ Tool kit
- ❏ Tow rope
- ❏ Road flares (or red light sticks)
- ❏ Shovel
- ❏ Duct tape
- ❏ One gallon of water
- ❏ Blanket
- ❏ Saw
- ❏ Emergency poncho or rain jacket
- ❏ Wool gloves
- ❏ Wool hat
- ❏ Multifunction tool
- ❏ Strapping cord or rope
- ❏ Large emergency tube shelter/tarp
- ❏ Water storage container
- ❏ Water purification tablets
- ❏ Six red, 12-hour Cyalume light sticks
- ❏ Six 12-hour high-intensity yellow cyalume light sticks
- ❏ Nonperishable food ration, 3,600 calories
- ❏ Signal mirror
- ❏ Whistle
- ❏ Compact strobe light
- ❏ First aid kit (should include prescription medicines, trauma dressings, and other large bandages)
- ❏ Surgical tubing
- ❏ Large fixed-blade survival knife
- ❏ Pocket knife with locking blade

- ❏ Flint-and-steel fire starter
- ❏ Tinder for lighting a fire
- ❏ Windproof and waterproof matches (strike-anywhere version)
- ❏ Waterproof match case
- ❏ Lighter
- ❏ Compact sewing kit
- ❏ Handheld GPS navigational unit

Sustenance

Sustenance is providing food and water to supply energy, increase metabolism, regulate temperature, and allow the mind to work rationally. Most healthy adults can miss a few meals without significant distress. However, even the healthiest adults can go no longer than a few days without water before they become delirious and lose vital body functions. Although ready-to-eat low-water rations make an excellent addition to many survival kits, far too much emphasis is placed on food and not nearly enough on water, water storage, and water purification. The following information assumes that you are in a pure survival situation without food or water/beverage and without a means of catching fish or hunting game.

Making potable water. Rainwater collected in clean containers or from plants is generally safe for drinking. However, you must purify water from lakes, ponds, swamps, springs, or streams, especially those near human habitation. When at all possible, disinfect all water obtained from vegetation or from the ground by using iodine or chlorine or by boiling it.

You can purify water by using one of the following methods:

- Use water purification tablets.
- Pour 5 drops of 2 percent tincture of iodine in a canteen full of clear water, and 10 drops in a canteen full of cloudy or cold water. Let the canteen of water stand for 30 minutes before drinking.
- Boil water for 1 minute at sea level, adding 1 minute for each additional 1,000 feet above sea level, or boil for 10 minutes no matter where you are.
- Use a commercial water purification device.

Potable drinking-water system devices. Having to purify water is a bother. The only reason to carry any drinking water purifier at all is to protect your health against microbiological and chemical contaminants. Water-related health threats can occur anytime you're in contact with water: drinking it directly, using it as a food or beverage ingredient, using it for bathing or for brushing teeth, and using it to clean cookware.

Primary exposure to drinking-water contaminants occurs at various times. It can happen when you are collecting raw water for purification: Use a separate container, whenever possible, for raw water supply; be selective and choose a source least likely to be badly polluted. Other situations inviting exposure to contamination can occur: during purification (don't let dirty water drip or flow into purified water); during storage of the purifier (at meal and campsites); and during handling of the unit while placing it in a pack or performing maintenance tasks.

The micro-organisms of concern in most wilderness recreation areas are tough, hardy cystic parasites that resist heat, freezing cold, drought, chlorine, iodine, and just about everything else. Although bacteria are relatively fragile and have very short life cycles, often less than a day, cysts can exist for months. All micro-organisms of chief concern are invisibly small, and they cannot be seen, smelled, or detected in any quick and easy manner. Accordingly, you must rely on knowledge of the area and on common sense.

It is widely known today that Giardia and/or Cryptosporidia have been found in water supplies in almost every country in the world. Therefore, you should always protect against parasitic cysts, and you should insist on 100 percent reduction. Since one cyst is enough to infect, 99.9 percent reduction may not be good enough, especially when there is no known treatment for some cysts.

Pesticides, herbicides, and other chemicals can be present anywhere downwind or downstream from major agricultural and industrial areas, and perhaps hundreds of miles away. These contaminants concentrate in streams, rivers, and lakes. Asbestos fibers can be found in very high numbers of more than a million fibers per liter in most western and some eastern wilderness waters. Even though trace amounts of these chemicals won't make you ill, no one wants to drink such fibers if they can easily be avoided.

Micron ratings from potable drinking-water treatment systems must be absolute to be meaningful, and precise measurements are essentially impossible to make. Micron ratings pertain only to physical removal or straining of particles, so absolute micron ratings are only one means of evaluating effectiveness. Removal of pesticides, herbicides, tastes, odors, and most colors and solvents requires other purification (separation) mechanisms. Many units, even those with very low micron ratings, have little or no ability to remove anything other than particles.

According to United States federal regulations, all water purification devices are defined as being either pesticide or device products. Pesticide products rely on chemically poisoning organisms (pests), and devices rely on physically removing them. It's easy to tell whether a product is categorized as a pesticide or a device. All products must carry an EPA Establishment Regulation Number; pesticide products must carry two EPA registration numbers, one for the manufacturing establishment and one for

Some common expressions with fish-related origins include: loan shark; fluke; red herring; fish or cut bait; swallow hook, line, and sinker; and stewed to the gills.

S

the pesticide being used. So, decide on a device or a pesticide product for water purification needs, and check the label to choose the right type. In certain applications, it may be desirable to use a pesticide to pretest water. Complete removal of the pesticide is very desirable after enough kill time is allowed. Iodine resins are not effective against cysts.

Solar still for safe water. No matter how fresh and clean water may appear to be, even in a wild stream or creek, you can never be sure that it isn't contaminated with chemicals and bacteria that make it unsafe for drinking. It is good common sense to always carry a safe container of water with your gear, especially in warm climates where dehydration is a danger.

In a survival situation, you can get safe drinking water by building a solar still, which will usually provide at least a pint of water every 24 hours. Here's how to use the sun to get safe drinking water:

1. Dig a hole in the ground about 2 feet deep and 3 feet across.
2. Place a clean bucket or pan at the bottom of the hole.
3. Set a plastic sheet over the hole, and hold it in place by piling stones or dirt around the edges.
4. Place a small stone in the center of the plastic sheet, so that the water formed by condensation on the sheet's sides is funneled into the catch container.

The sun causes condensation to form on the sides of the plastic sheet. As the water collects at the bottom of the sheet, it drips into the bucket. As an extra precaution, boil the water for 10 minutes or add a commercial water treatment tablet.

Wild plants for food. After water, food is your most urgent need. In a survival situation, you should always be on the lookout for wild foods and live off the land whenever possible. Plants are a valuable food source. Although they may not offer a balanced diet, they will sustain you. Many plant foods, such as nuts and seeds, will provide enough protein for normal efficiency. Roots, green vegetables, and plant food containing natural sugar will provide calories and carbohydrates that will give your body energy.

Being able to recognize wild edible plants is important in a survival situation. There are certain factors you should keep in mind when collecting edible plants:

- Cultivated plants and wild plants growing in or near cultivated plants may have been sprayed with pesticides. Thoroughly wash whatever plants you collect.
- The surface of any plant food that grows on, or is washed in, contaminated water is also contaminated. To eat the plant raw, wash it in water suitable for drinking.

- Some plants may have fungal toxins that are extremely poisonous. To lessen the chances that these toxins are present, collect fresh seeds, fruit, or leaves, but not those that have fallen to the ground.
- Plants of the same species may differ in the amount of toxic or subtoxic compounds they contain because of different environmental and genetic factors. One example is the foliage of the common chokeberry. Some chokeberry plants have high concentrations of cyanide compounds, other plants low concentrations.
- Some people are more susceptible than others to gastric upset from plants. Those who are sensitive this way should avoid unknown wild plants. If you are extremely sensitive to poison ivy, avoid products from this family, including drinks made from sumacs, mangos, and cashews.
- There are some edible wild plants, such as acorns and water lily rhizomes, that are bitter. These bitter substances (usually tannin compounds) make them unpalatable. Boiling in several changes of water will help remove these substances.
- Many valuable wild plants have high concentrations of oxalate compounds. Oxalates usually produce a sharp burning sensation in your mouth. And they are bad for the kidneys. Boiling usually destroys these oxalates.
- The only way to tell if a mushroom is edible is by proper examination. Even then, some species are questionable, so do not eat mushrooms.

There are many, many plants throughout the world. Tasting or swallowing even a small portion of some can cause severe discomfort, extreme internal disorders, or even death. Therefore, if you have the slightest doubt about the edibility of a plant, apply the Universal Edibility Test (which follows) before eating any part of it.

Before testing a plant for edibility, make sure that there are a sufficient number of the plants to make testing worth your time and effort. You need more than 24 hours to apply the edibility test. Keep in mind that eating large amounts of plant food on an empty stomach may cause diarrhea or cramps. Familiar foods that cause this problem are green apples and too many fresh berries. Even if you've tested plant food and found it safe, eat it in moderation with other foods. You can see from the steps and time involved in testing edibility just how important it is to be able to identify edible plants.

Universal Edibility Test

1. Test only one part of a potential food plant at a time.
2. Break the plant into its basic components: leaves, stems, roots, buds, and flowers.

3. Smell the food for strong or acidic odors. Smell alone is not an indication of edibility.

4. Do not eat for eight hours before starting the test.

5. During the eight hours you are abstaining from eating, test for contact poisoning by placing on the inside of your elbow or wrist a piece of the plant part being tested. Usually 15 minutes is enough time to allow for a reaction.

6. During the test period, take nothing by mouth except purified water and the plant part being tested.

7. Select a small portion of a single component and prepare it the way you plan to eat it.

8. Before putting the prepared plant part in your mouth, touch a small portion (a pinch) to the outer surface of the lip to test for burning or itching.

9. If after 3 minutes there is no reaction on your lip, place the plant part on your tongue, holding it there for 15 minutes.

10. If there is no reaction, thoroughly chew a pinch and hold it in your mouth for 15 minutes. *Do not swallow.*

11. If no burning, itching, numbing, stinging, or other irritation occurs during the 15 minutes, swallow the food.

12. Wait eight hours. If any ill effects occur during this period, induce vomiting and drink a lot of water.

13. If no ill effects occur, eat one-half cup of the same plant part prepared the same way. Wait another eight hours. If no ill effects occur, the plant part as prepared is safe for eating.

Caution: Test all parts of the plant for edibility, since some plants have both edible and inedible parts. Also, do not assume that a part that proved edible when cooked is also edible when raw. Test the part raw to ensure edibility before eating raw.

Do not eat unknown plants that:

- Have a milky sap or a sap that turns black when exposed to air.
- Are mushroomlike.
- Resemble onion or garlic.
- Resemble parsley, parsnip, or dill.
- Have carrotlike leaves, roots, or tubers.

Preparation of plant food. Although some plants or plant parts are edible raw, others must be cooked to be edible or palatable. Some methods of improving the taste of plant food are soaking, parboiling, cooking, or leaching. (Leaching is done by crushing food, placing it in some sort of strainer, and pouring boiling water through it.)

Leaves, stems, and buds should be boiled until tender; several changes of water help to eliminate bitterness.

Roots and tubers can be boiled, baked, or roasted. Boiling removes harmful substances such as oxalic acid crystals.

Nuts can be leached or soaked in water to remove the bitterness. Although chestnuts are edible raw, they are tastier roasted or steamed.

Grains and seeds may be parched to improve the taste, or ground into meal to use as a thickener with soups or stews or to use as flour to make bread.

To get sugar, sap is dehydrated by boiling until the water is gone.

Fruit is baked or roasted if it is tough with heavy skin. Boil juicy fruit.

Medical

You need not be a member of the medical profession to be prepared to meet basic medical and health needs. Good outdoor first aid kits are available, but be sure to take your specific circumstances into account and supplement any kit with items you will need. This means taking sufficient quantities of any prescribed medicines, bringing extra contact lenses or pairs of glasses, and taking additional supplies (bug spray, antivenin, seasickness medication) that are appropriate for the environment. A separate entry on first aid has more information on medical and health issues.
See: First Aid.

Fire

It is often said that the presence of a fire means that a person is going to survive. Although this is not an absolute truth, it is true that in a survival situation nothing can warm the soul, calm fear, and bring hope more than a warm fire. Fire is a versatile and often essential survival resource. Cold weather, wind, and moisture are three impediments to survival. A good fire can help fight and prevail against them all. Fire also helps meet other needs, like purifying water, sterilizing bandages, signaling, etc.

Unfortunately, most survival kits offer only mediocre fire-making implements, and fire is seldom given the attention it deserves in survival guides. It takes skill to build a warming fire in the pouring rain. For a small investment of time, learning this skill can help save your life.

Use good judgment when selecting fire-making implements for your own survival kit, and think about how the tools you're selecting might fail under various conditions. For example, most lighters work poorly in extreme cold temperatures, can blow out in the wind, and last only as long as the butane fuel source. Most waterproof matches are waterproof only at the striking head and will stay lit for only four to five seconds.

In the hands of someone who has practiced with it, there is no better all-purpose fire-starting device than a large piece of flint and something to scrape it. Flints work effectively in the wind or rain and last a long time. Commercially made flint-based fire-starter tools are excellent choices for a survival kit.

The Queensland lungfish, genera *Neoceratodus* from Australia, is one of the world's most primitive fish and has changed little in 100 million years.

Commercial fire starters or fuels should be chosen with care to ensure that they will work in wet weather. For those wanting to save a few pennies, a good homemade tinder is a 100 percent cotton ball saturated with Vaseline. Ten to 20 of these can be crammed into a waterproof match case or empty film canister.

Of course, good cutting tools can help immeasurably when you're preparing to make a fire. First, it makes sense to carry both a fixed-blade and a folding knife. A large fixed-blade knife is great for cutting into the heart of dry wood. A smaller folding locking-blade knife is good for preparing shavings and fire-starting materials.

Rescue

The chances of being rescued can be dramatically improved if you know and can use basic signaling skills. Being seen or heard is the key. No one should ever venture far afield or go anywhere in a car, boat, or plane, without a signal mirror and a whistle.

You can't outscream a good whistle, and you can't sustain the effort of screaming or hollering. But you can blow a good whistle long and often. A signal mirror is second only to electronic communication devices (radios, phone, e-mail–capable GPS, etc.) for conveying the need for help. When those other devices are unavailable, it may be your only means. Except for military personnel, who have a signal mirror in their survival kit and who use this device religiously, the general public has only limited knowledge of the value of the signal mirror. The key is having a targetable signal mirror, such as the official Air Force Star Flash, so that the signal flash can be aimed.

Other widely available signaling devices include flashlights, strobe lights, and chemical lights. High-intensity 12-hour chemical lights are a better choice in most instances than a flashlight because they're lighter in weight and don't require batteries. A small string tied to the end of a chem light and spun in a circle overhead makes an excellent night signal that can be seen from a great distance. Anglers who venture offshore in large boats should have a flare gun for signaling.

With signaling and rescue devices, the key is to be seen. Bigger, louder, and more is better. A recognized international distress call is a series of three signals: three blasts of your whistle, three long honks of your car horn, three shots of a flare, or three small fires (smoke or flame), etc.

Shelter and Personal Protection

The need for shelter encompasses all aspects of covering or protecting the human body according to the circumstances and with regard to facing wind, sun, heat, cold, rain, snow, insects, snakebite, and more.

Clothing is the most obvious element of protection and one that sometimes gets little attention. People tend to dress for the conditions that exist at the moment they leave their home, RV, camp, etc., and not for what might be encountered. While appropriate clothing should be worn according to the weather, workload, and activity, you must take into account possible extremes and worst-case scenarios. When venturing on the water, always ask yourself if your clothes would be sufficient to spend the night in them if you had to.

Personal survival protection items like space blankets, emergency tube shelters, and others lead many people to a false sense of security. Most space blankets claim to reflect up to 90 percent of your body heat back to you. This might be true when used in perfect conditions, but these blankets can tear in the wind and are open at the end. The best lightweight shelters are Mylar (or equivalent-film) sleeping bags. This is because you can get inside them and trap the heat while minimizing the loss of heat through convection. Bodily heat transfer in cold weather is done by evaporation, radiation, convection, conduction, and respiration. Fifty percent of all body heat can be lost through the head alone.

The better reflective-type blankets are reinforced by polyethylene or polypropylene materials. These resist tearing and damage. Survival bags (oversize and double strength garbage bags that go from head to toe) are widely available. This item should be part of a survival kit and makes an excellent emergency shelter to climb into, especially when used in conjunction with a Mylar space blanket sleeping bag. It is important to recognize, however, that these emergency shelters are not self-regulating and that they can become exceptionally hot and wet inside when moisture is not allowed to escape.

Sheltering not only affects the body directly but is important in meeting other survival needs. It is very difficult to build a fire in the pouring rain if you cannot keep the material you're preparing dry or, for that matter, your hands.

If these Nunavut Territory anglers all suddenly lean to the same side when landing their fish, one or more could wind up in the frigid water and suddenly be in a survival situation.

Combating cold.   You can't beat the cold, but you can learn how to survive in it. Modern clothing is insulated, waterproof, and windproof, but you can still get into trouble. Hypothermia is the cold-weather killer, and it is caused by exposure to wind, rain, snow, or wet clothing. If the body's core temperature drops below 98.6°, you'll start to shiver and stamp your feet to keep warm. If these early signs are ignored, the next symptoms will be slurred speech, memory lapses, fumbling hands, and drowsiness. If not treated quickly, hypothermia can kill its victim when body temperature drops below 78°, and this can happen within 90 minutes after shivering begins.

If you detect these symptoms in yourself or a friend, start treatment immediately. Get to shelter and warmth as soon as possible. If no shelter is available, build a fire. Get out of wet clothing and apply heat to head, neck, chest, and groin. Use body heat from another person. Give the victim warm liquids, chocolate, or any food with a high sugar content. Never give a victim alcohol; this will impair judgment, dilate blood vessels, and prevent shivering, which is the body's way of producing needed heat.

You'll be better prepared to survive the cold if you've stayed in shape and have had a good night's sleep before going outdoors. Carrying candy, mixed nuts, raisins, and other high-energy food helps. To avoid hypothermia in a survival situation, stay as dry as possible and avoid overheating your body, which produces perspiration and damp clothes. Most importantly, dress properly. This means several layers of clothing and rain gear. Wear a wool hat with ear protection. An uncovered head can lose up to 50 percent of the body's heat. If you are thrust into a situation without proper clothing protection, you must seek shelter and find a way to stay warm. It is very dangerous to risk cold elements when you don't have the right clothing. Anglers should keep in mind that going out on a large body of cold water can be greatly different than being onshore at the same time. A moderate breeze coming across a cold body of water mandates heavy clothing, even though people on land may be dressed much lighter.

Combating heat.   To survive in extreme heat, you must understand how heat affects the human body, and you must be prepared for it. You have to determine what you need, how you can combat the heat, and what impact the environment will have on you.

The body's normal temperature is 98.6°, and the body gets rid of excess heat by sweating. The warmer the body becomes, the more it sweats and thus the more moisture it loses. Sweating is the principal cause of water loss. A person who stops sweating during periods of high air temperature and heavy work or exercise could have a heat stroke, which is an emergency that requires immediate medical attention.

Understanding how the air temperature and your physical activity affect your water requirements allows you to take measures to get the most from your water supply. These measures include:

- Find shade. Get out of the sun. Place something between you and the hot ground. Limit your movements.
- Conserve your sweat. Wear all your clothes, including tee shirt; roll the sleeves down, cover your head, and protect your neck with a scarf or similar item. This will protect your body from hot blowing winds and the direct rays of the sun. Your clothing will absorb your sweat, keeping it against your skin so you gain its full cooling effect. By staying in the shade quietly, fully clothed, not talking, keeping your mouth closed and breathing through your nose, your water requirement for survival drops dramatically.
- If water is scarce, do not eat. Food requires water for digestion. Eating food will use water that you need for cooling.

Thirst is not a reliable guide for your need for water. A person who uses thirst as a guide will drink only two-thirds of the daily requirement. To prevent this "voluntary" dehydration, use this guide: at temperatures below 100°, drink 1 pint of water every hour; at temperatures above 100°, drink 1 quart of water every hour.

Drinking water at regular intervals helps the body to remain cool, thus decreasing sweating. Even when your water supply is low, sipping water constantly will keep your body cooler and will reduce water loss through sweating. Conserve water by reducing activity during the heat of the day; this minimizes perspiration. Do not ration your water, or you stand a good chance of becoming a heat casualty.

Intense sunlight/heat.   Intense sunlight and heat are present in all arid areas. Air temperature can rise as high as 140°F during the day. Heat gain results from direct sunlight, hot blowing winds, reflective heat (the sun's rays bouncing off the sand), and conductive heat from direct contact with sand and rock. The temperature of sand and rock averages 30 to 40° more than that of the air. For instance, when the air temperature is 110°F, the sand temperature may be 140°. Intense sunlight and heat increase the body's need for water. To conserve your body sweat and energy, you need a shelter that will reduce your exposure to the heat of the day.

Temperatures may get as high as 130°F during the day and as low as 50° at night in arid areas. The drop in temperature at night occurs rapidly and will chill a person who lacks warm clothing and is unable to move about. At night you'll find a wool sweater, long underwear, and a wool stocking cap very helpful.

Sunburn results from overexposing skin to ultraviolet rays, so in extreme situations try to keep your body completely clothed, including gloves on your hands and a scarf around your neck. Use sunscreen *(see)* liberally on all exposed areas. Sun poisoning equals nausea and dehydration. In addition, burns may become infected, causing more problems. So you must protect yourself from overexposure. There is as much danger of sunburn on cloudy days as on sunny days, especially at high altitudes. Most sunscreens do not give complete protection against excessive exposure.

The glare on sand causes eyestrain, and wind-blown, fine sand particles can irritate the eyes and cause inflammation. Wear goggles and use eye ointments to protect your eyes. The combination of wind and sand or dust can cause your lips and other exposed skin to chap. Use lip and skin balms or ointments to prevent or overcome this problem. Rest is essential in this environment. You need 20 minutes of rest for each hour in the heat, and a minimum of six hours of sleep each day.
See: Safety.

Water Safety

For anglers, some survival circumstances occur as the result of mishaps on the water, such as a boat capsizing. Dealing with such an event is covered in greater detail in other entries *(see: boat; safety)*. Finding yourself in the water, especially if that water is cold (and essentially anything under normal body temperature is cold) presents an immediate survival concern due to the potential for hypothermia, and the colder the water the greater the concern. Anglers who find themselves having to fend for survival on the land, as wilderness travelers might, will also have to deal with water, probably in terms of crossing or traveling along it, so it's worth reviewing both of these matters.

Surviving in cold water. If you are suddenly the victim of a capsizing, you can survive if you follow a few important rules.

First, don't panic. Clothing will trap body heat, so don't remove your clothes. If you're wearing a life jacket (PFD), restrict your body movements and draw your knees up to your body, which is a position that will reduce heat loss.

Don't try to swim or tread water. That will just pump out warm water between your body and clothing. Get into a protective posture and wait for a rescue. There are body positions that will minimize heat loss and increase your chances for survival. For solo survival, H.E.L.P. (Heat Escape Lessening Posture) is the body position that will best minimize heat loss. If you're wearing waders, keep them on, and assume a sitting position. The trapped air in the waders will help keep you afloat. Cover head and neck if possible. Two or more persons in cold water should huddle together to conserve body heat. A small group in this position can extend survival time 50 percent longer than by swimming.

To survive in cold water when alone and wearing a PFD, draw your knees up to your chest and hold them there with locked arms; this is the Heat Escape Lessening Posture. Two or three people should huddle together to conserve body heat.

Crossing rivers and streams. In a wilderness survival situation, you'll likely encounter some type of water that needs crossing when you are finding your way through the country. Rivers and streams are the most tempting, since the distance across is less than it is in a pond or lake. A river or stream may be narrow or wide, shallow or deep, slow or fast, and fed by ice or snow, making it colder than would be comfortable or wise to cross.

The first thing to do is find a place where the river is basically safe for crossing. Look for a high vantage point to scout the water and find a place for crossing. Check the river carefully for the following:

1. A level stretch where it breaks into a number of channels. Two or three narrow channels are usually easier to cross than a single wide section.
2. Obstacles on the opposite side of the river that might hinder travel. Try to select the spot from which your exit will be safest and easiest.
3. A ledge of rocks that crosses the river. This often indicates dangerous rapids or canyons.
4. A deep or rapid waterfall or a deep channel. Never attempt to ford a stream directly above or even close to such spots.
5. Rocky places. Avoid these; you can be seriously injured from falling on rocks. An occasional rock that breaks the current, however, may assist you.
6. A shallow bank or sandbar. If possible, select a point upstream from a shallow bank or sandbar so that the current will carry you to it if you lose your footing.
7. A course across the river that leads downstream so that you will cross the current at about a 45-degree angle.

Crossing rapids. Crossing a deep, swift river or rapids is not as dangerous as it looks. If you must swim across, swim with the current. Never fight it. Try to keep your body horizontal to the water to reduce the danger of being pulled under.

In fast, shallow rapids, float on your back, feet first; fin your hands alongside your hips to add buoyancy and to fend away from submerged rocks. Keep your feet up to avoid getting them bruised or pinned by rocks, and also to fend off any objects.

In deep rapids, float on your belly, head first; angle toward shore whenever you can. Breathe between wave troughs. Be careful of backwater eddies and converging currents as they often contain dangerous swirls. Avoid bubbly water under falls; it has little buoyancy.

When fording a swift, treacherous stream, remove your pants and underpants so that the water will have less grip on your legs. Keep your shoes on to protect your feet and ankles from rocks and to provide firmer footing. Tie your pants and important articles securely to the top of your pack. If you have to release the pack, all of your articles will be together. It is easier to find one large pack than to find several small items.

Carry your pack well up on your shoulders so you can release it quickly if you are swept off your feet. Not being able to get a pack off quickly enough can drag even the strongest of swimmers under.

Find a strong pole about 5 inches in diameter and 7 to 8 feet long to help you ford the stream. Grasp the pole and plant it firmly on your upstream side to break the current. Plant your feet firmly with each step, and move the pole forward a little downstream from its previous position, but still upstream from you. With your next step, place your foot below the pole. Keep the pole well slanted so that the force of the current keeps the pole against your shoulder.

If there are other people with you, cross the stream together. Make sure that everyone has prepared a pack and clothing as above. The heaviest person should be downstream of the pole and the lightest person at the end of the group. This way, the upstream person breaks the current, and the persons below can move with comparative ease in the eddy formed by the upstream person. If the upstream person is temporarily swept off his or her feet, the others can hold steady while that wader regains footing.

As in all fording, move so that you will cross the downstream current at a 45-degree angle. Currents too strong for one person to stand against can usually be crossed safely in this manner. Do not be concerned about the weight of your pack because the weight will help rather than hinder you in fording the stream. Just make sure you can release the pack quickly if necessary.
See: Boat; Compass; First Aid; Navigation; Safety.

SURVIVAL SUIT

A name for a full-body garment with maximum flotation capability, usually classified as a Type V flotation device. It is designed to provide upright flotation, with face and head out of the water, and to provide longer protection in life-threatening cold water than other devices or garments. It is worn by some anglers who boat in cold weather for both personal comfort as well as for lifesaving values in case they get wet or wind up in cold water and have a chance of developing hypothermia (see).

Many survival suits have hoods and inflatable collars or head rests. They are often brightly colored or have patches of reflective material to aid in spotting for rescue purposes, although some that are used for hunting may be in camouflage patterns. Anglers who venture onto cold water should consider wearing a U.S. Coast Guard–approved and rated survival suit in lieu of a PFD because of the increased chances of quickly developing hypothermia in cold water.
See: Personal Flotation Device; Safety.

SUSPENDING

The habit of some fish, mainly freshwater species, to hold steady in midwater; this is distinguished from species that normally live in midwater levels, cruising in pursuit of baitfish. A fish that is located 10 feet off the bottom in 40 feet of water is often said to be suspended. Certain lures that float on the surface but dive on retrieve have the ability to suspend by virtue of neutral buoyancy; when the retrieval action is stopped, the lure stays where it is in the water column, neither rising nor sinking. This most accurately mimics the behavior of fish and may be useful in some angling situations.
See: Plug.

SUSTAINABLE FISHERIES ACT

See: Fishery Conservation Act.

SWAYBACK

The distance that a trolled line and weight, especially downrigger weight, inclines back from a perpendicular position beneath a boat, caused by current or speed.
See: Downrigger Fishing.

SWEDEN

Spanning more than 2,000 kilometers from north to south, Sweden is blessed with tens of thousands of lakes and roughly the same number of rivers and streams, as well as a lengthy coastline along the Gulf of Bothnia, the Baltic Sea, and the North Sea. Small wonder that it is a nation with plenty of angling opportunity and a diversity of fish species.

Sweden's western saltwaters have such typical northern species as cod, lire (pollack), and mackerel, and its eastern and more brackish waters contain mostly pike (big ones), zander (pike-perch), and perch. The rivers and small streams host Atlantic salmon, brown trout, pike, perch, carp, and various coarse species. With the exception of salmon, these species are present in an almost uncountable number of big and small lakes (about 100,000).

Diversity is also found in the country's climate, thanks to the distance between north and south. In January, the temperature can be above 0°C with no snow or ice in southernmost Sweden, but it may be 20° to 30° below zero with several meters of ice and snow on the lakes in the northern region of Lapland. Spring normally begins in March or April in the south, but it may not arrive until June in the north, when the snow and ice begin to melt.

As a result, the waters in the north are ice-free for only three or four months per year, whereas some are ice-free year-round in most places in the south, especially on the coasts. Seasonal activity, therefore, varies according to latitude; for instance, April is normally a very good month for pike and brown trout in the south, but in the north April is a prime period for ice fishing.

Methods and Tackle

Casting with spinning and fly tackle is most common in Sweden's lakes, although coarse fishing and trolling can also produce good results for certain species, and ice fishing is popular.

Fishing with spinning tackle is the most common, and often the most effective, method of pursuing predator species. Sinking and floating plugs are common lures for pike, zander, salmon, and brown trout, but standard spinners and different kinds of spoons can produce good catches. Long, slender spoons, often combined with a dropper fly, can be rewarding for sea trout along the coast. Heavy diamond jigs (100 to 300 grams) are used for heavy-tackle coastal fishing, including deep jigging for cod and coalfish (pollock).

Fly fishing is very common in Sweden, mainly for trout and grayling, but good opportunities also exist to catch arctic charr, salmon, and sea trout on fly tackle. Perch and pike can be pursued with fly tackle, and, along the coast—especially in the south—fly fishing for sea trout has grown in popularity.

Coarse fishing techniques are favored for perch, pike, and zander, especially by those who prefer live or dead baits. Opportunities to catch big roach, tench, bream, ide, and coarse species are extremely good, perhaps because relatively few Swedes practice this kind of fishing. Many waters contain especially good stocks of coarse species.

A particularly popular method for catching salmon and trout is trolling, especially in southern Sweden and in Lakes Vänern and Vättern. The boats for this type of fishing are normally well equipped with downriggers, sonar, GPS navigational units, and the like. It is also common to troll the old and original way—by towing a couple of wobblers (plugs) behind a small boat.

Ice fishing, of course, is a very common activity in northern Sweden, where the ice is thick for six to eight months per year. A popular and exciting local ice fishing tactic has anglers lie belly down on a reindeer skin placed on the ice, then shade their eyes with their hands while looking through a hole and watching their bait until a fish takes it. The equipment for northern ice fishing in Sweden includes an ice drill, an ice fishing rod about 30 centimeters long, a line that doesn't freeze, and special jigging spoons that are often baited with maggots.

Lakes and Tarns

In southern Sweden there are mostly lowland lakes, which especially hold pike, zander, perch, and coarse species. As one heads northward, the landscape changes and becomes more hilly and covered with large, forested areas that have many fish-rich lakes. Pike, perch, and carp species are dominant, but many lakes have brown trout.

Massive forests cover the middle part of Sweden, and these contain a good number of lakes, primarily containing pike, perch, and carp species, as well as brown trout, grayling, and zander. Zander become increasingly scarce in this region, whereas trout, grayling, and arctic charr become more prevalent. In the lightly populated northern region, the landscape opens up and becomes more rugged, and huge spruce forests dominate up to the tree line. There are many lakes here, and brown trout (known as "lake" trout when inhabiting Swedish lakes), grayling, pike, and perch are the predominant species.

In the lakes and tarns (small mountain lakes or ponds) of southern Sweden, fishing for brown trout and pike is normally best in spring and autumn. In summer, zander and coarse species are extremely active. In the middle region of Sweden the fishing season on open water is a little shorter. Generally, pike and brown trout fishing begins later and finishes earlier than in the southern part of the country. On the other hand, lower water temperature makes summer fishing better in the middle region. In northern Sweden, all fishing in open water occurs from May through October. The best time here is from June through August.

The Great Lakes

With a surface area of 5,600 square kilometers, Lake Vänern is one of Europe's largest lakes. It includes more than 20,000 islands, and 35 species of fish live in this gigantic lake. This combination naturally creates fantastic angling possibilities. A large population of landlocked Atlantic salmon provides excellent trolling, which is also a good method for pike and zander. Pike fishing is usually best after spawning in the spring, and salmon fishing can be good from spring through autumn.

Lake Vättern is also large at 130 kilometers long and 30 kilometers wide. This deep-water lake has big pike, as well as brown trout, salmon, and grayling, but the main attraction is large arctic charr that reach weights over 10 kilograms. These charr lie in deep water, and trolling with downriggers is the best method of catching them.

Mälaren is yet a another big lake with many islands and bays. The common game here are perch, pike, and zander, and the population of coarse species is good. Casting from shore is common, but trolling also produces big pike and zander. The best times for pike are spring and autumn. Zander, perch, and coarse anglers are most successful during the summer.

The West Coast

Warm northerly flowing current from the Atlantic Ocean brings a good supply of saltwater to the west coast of Sweden, providing good fishing. On the northern part of this coast, many areas offer relatively deep water close to shore, making it possible for anglers to cast lures and baits from the cliffs. Cod, mackerel, pollack, garfish, and sea trout are all caught this way. Even anglers in small boats can have rewarding fishing without venturing into the open sea. Deep-sea fishing farther offshore, however, is possible, and mackerel, cod, ling, pollock, and pollack are the targets of a great number of charter boats with experienced skippers.

In some places along the coast, the water is shallow and there are almost no skerries (a group of small rocky islands or reefs) at all. Here it is possible to wade and catch sea trout, flatfish, cod, and—during late spring—garfish. Anglers also fish from piers and breakwaters for mackerel and eels. In the south, the Öresund Strait is well known for its excellent cod fishing during winter, especially in January and February.

Cod fishing along the west coast is best during spring and autumn. Sea trout fishing peaks in April. Garfish arrive along the coast at the end of May, closely followed by mackerel; these species are caught throughout the summer. Autumn is also a productive time, offering good catches both from the coast and farther offshore.

The South Coast

Since the salt content of the Baltic water along the South Coast is lower than that on the west coast, fewer species thrive here, although cod and garfish are present. The brackish water of the Baltic Sea, however, provides good conditions for pike fishing. Angling from shore or small boats can produce big pike and sea trout. One of the best areas for these species is Hanöbukten, where it is also possible to troll for heavy salmon on their way to entering the Mörrumsån. Salmon over 25 kilograms have been caught on rod and reel here, and many anglers believe that Hanöbukten offers one of the world's best salmon fisheries.

Fishing for sea trout along the South Coast starts as early as January but reaches its peak during April, when pike fishing also begins to be good. In May, big salmon arrive, and trolling continues throughout the summer and into autumn, although the size of salmon drops as the season progresses. The autumn months offer good sea trout fishing all season long. Pike fishing run through late autumn as well, with good chances then of catching fish over 10 kilograms.

The East Coast

This coast stretches all the way from southern Sweden to the border with Finland and has a wide variety of environments, climate, and fish species. Large areas of the East Coast are scattered with skerries and, unlike the West Coast, are rich in vegetation and protected.

Fishing for sea trout and pike is the favorite activity along the southern part of this coast up to the Swedish capital of Stockholm. Fishing from the shore or small boats provides an excellent chance of catching big specimens. Every year, pike of 10 to 15 kilograms are caught here. The large Öland and Gotland Islands also have coasts that offer good fishing for pike and sea trout.

As one moves north, the salinity weakens, and only freshwater species—such as perch, zander, and coarse fish—continue to thrive. Pike and sea trout fishing are still interesting, and along the northern region there are good populations of coarse species and grayling. The main angling methods along the entire East Coast are spinning, fly fishing, and coarse fishing, from shore or small boats.

In the southern section of this coast, fishing for pike and sea trout is usually best during spring and autumn (April through May, and September through October). The season begins later farther north, because melting ice in the Baltic keeps the water cooler. In the very north in Bottenviken, it is usually possible to fish in open water only from the end of May through September.

Coastal Rivers

A large number of rivers along the East Coast host Atlantic salmon and sea trout. The best-known river here is the Mörrumsån, which is about 500 kilometers south of Stockholm. Due to increasing numbers of salmon and sea trout, it attracts thousands of anglers every year.

Even along the western side of Sweden there are 10 rivers with salmon. A few of them also offer sea trout. These rivers are slow-flowing and are situated in rich countryside. A few hundred salmon are typically taken from each western river, but some yield more than 1,000 salmon per river in a season. Fishing for Atlantic salmon usually starts in May or June, but the best chance to catch them is in autumn, although this is dependent on rainfall and water temperature.

The angler who wishes to fish for wild salmon on the eastern side of Sweden should go north of Stockholm. One of the best rivers there is Nedre

S

An angler casts in a remote, wild site in Lapland.

Dalälven, where the fishing begins in January and continues into the autumn. Heavy fly and spinning tackle are recommended, since this is a big, deep river, and the fish often lie on the bottom.

North of this river are several other salmon rivers, but the catches in these large waters are varied, and the angler often needs local knowledge in the form of a guide to ensure success. In recent years these rivers have become increasingly more productive. Summer and autumn are the best fishing periods.

Inland Rivers

The rivers in southern and middle Sweden have pike, perch, and coarse species, and sometimes brown trout, whereas rivers and brooks in the northern area contain brown trout, grayling, and arctic charr. Many of the rivers in southern and middle Sweden can sometimes have good fishing for eels and zander.

Casting with spinning tackle, and coarse fishing, are the most common fishing methods in southern Sweden. In the middle and northern regions, fly and spinning tackle are both popular. Even in flowing water, the season stretches from spring through autumn. Farther north, the fishing season concentrates around the summer months.

For the versatile angler, there are good opportunities for diverse and exciting river fishing throughout the season. During spring and autumn, for example, pike fishing can be excellent in southern Sweden; in May, when the mayflies are hatching, the fly angler goes into action for brown trout; spinning, coarse, and fly anglers have all summer in different parts of the country to experience good fishing for pike, perch, bream, ide, tench, trout, grayling, and eels.

Large Northern Rivers

With a few exceptions, the really big river systems are in the northern part of Sweden. These are up to 200 kilometers long and extremely powerful as they rush through the wild landscape. Fishing possibilities in these huge waters are normally especially good, and they provide an unforgettable experience. All of the big northern rivers flow out into the upper parts of the Baltic Sea and run through big valleys from east to west.

These big river systems have many slow pools, rapids, and waterfalls, and a local guide is advisable to improve your chances. Furthermore, in the thinly populated areas of this region, where there are large areas of true wilderness, you might have to walk long distances to reach the fishing spots, although in some places there are roads to and along the rivers.

Brown trout, grayling, and arctic charr are the main species, although you might find good pike fishing on the slower stretches. Very large trout sometimes linger in the deep pools, but you must fish for them selectively with relatively heavy tackle.

Both spinning and fly fishing are effective. The season stretches from May through October depending on northern latitude. Generally, June through August are good months; during this period, daylight lasts nearly 24 hours a day, although the mosquitoes can be bad.

Lapland's Mountain Fishing
Mountain fishing in Lapland is probably the most exotic angling sport Sweden can offer. Midnight sun, northern lights, vast open spaces, unpopulated mountain plateaus, snow-covered peaks, and top-class fishing are a few benefits you can expect. Unexplored and road-free mountain and forest areas here offer many lakes, brooks, and rivers.

Lapland is often described as Europe's last wilderness and is only sparsely populated. In this vast area there are countless rivers and lakes, most of which contain brown trout, arctic charr, and grayling, and many of which have pike and perch. The large river systems are generally best, as spawning areas are large and fishing pressure is low.

Although the wild natural habitat of northern Sweden is alluring, it can be dangerous. Roads are few, the weather can change very fast, and a long walk to comfort and rest may await you. The angler who isn't familiar with mountain travel but who wishes to experience fishing north of the Arctic Circle has the option of staying at a fishing camp. Small aircraft and helicopters transport anglers to many such camps, which have comfortable cabins and often have a service shop and boats for hire, in some cases even a restaurant. With a fishing camp as a base, it is possible to safely experience the north and to enjoy fine fishing for trout, grayling, and charr.

The two main fishing seasons in Lapland are the short summer and long winter. July and August are the peak months for fly and spinning tackle in open water. March, April, and sometimes even the first half of May are the best times for ice fishing for trout and charr.

Licenses and Regulations
All waters in Sweden are private and may be administered by the owner or a fishing club. Every angler needs a license to fish in all lakes and rivers, except for the four biggest lakes (Vänern, Vättern, Hjälmaren, and Storsjön), where it is free to fish with a rod and reel. Private water may be accessed for a fee, which is nominal in most cases. Salmon rivers are the exception. Fishing from or along the coast is also free. Some areas and/or species may be protected, however. In some places, restrictions pertaining to a minimum size for certain species, angling methods, or seasons may apply. Anglers should check the regulations, which are printed (in Swedish) on the back of licenses. Licenses are obtainable at tourist centers, tackle shops, and guest houses.

SWEETFISH
See: Ayu.

SWELL
A long, huge free ocean wave that moves away from its origin, releasing its energy along the continental margins; a long-crested wave that moves steadily without breaking.
See: Waves.

SWIM
A term predominantly used by British coarse anglers to refer to a particular spot that is fished from the bank; anglers fishing a swim do not rove but remain stationary, working one location and usually baiting and/or prebaiting that spot.

SWIMFEEDER
A perforated cylinder containing chum (see), used for coarse species (see: coarse fish). Swimfeeders are weighted to facilitate casting, and they remain on the bottom where their contents are dispersed.

SWITZERLAND
If any European country is predetermined to become a country of anglers, Switzerland certainly qualifies. The most mountainous country in Europe, with 70 percent of its landmass covered by the Alps in the central and southern sections, and the Jura in the northwest, Switzerland is the source of many of Europe's greatest rivers. The Rhône and Rhine Rivers emerge from the very heart of this country in the mountain massif of Saint Gotthard. The origin of the Ticino River is also nearby. The Ticino becomes a main tributary of the big Italian river, the Po. From the Alpine Engadine Valley in the south of the canton (state or province) of Graubünden, the River Inn flows down to Austria and gives its name to the famous town of Innsbruck before reaching Germany and finally flowing into the Danube.

Water from the Swiss Alps therefore feeds the Atlantic Ocean as well as the Mediterranean, Adriatic, and Black Seas. One can easily understand the pride with which the Swiss call their country the "Aquatic Heart of Europe." This bounty also attracts some nonresident visitors.

Within Switzerland's 41,293 square kilometers are many large and small rivers with a total length of roughly 50,000 kilometers, as well as roughly 2,000 lakes and reservoirs. Switzerland is well known for its lakes, especially those in the Alpine region, which are oft-visited for their scenic beauty. Covering roughly 4 percent of the highly structured Alpine topography, these inland waters—surpassed in quantity, in Europe, only by some Nordic and eastern countries—represent a great variety of aquatic habitats.

One measure of the fisheries resources of Switzerland can be gleaned from its commercial fishery: The 14 largest lakes provide approximately

300 professional (commercial) fishermen with a full-time living from netting fish, and another 200 with a part-time living. The total number of annual or seasonal angling permits issued by the cantonal fishery offices is about 200,000, not including the countless people who acquire private angling permits or profit from the right to fish free of charge from the banks and shores of some of the bigger rivers and lakes.

The Swiss lakes and rivers are populated by 58 species of fish, of which 45 are indigenous and 13 have been introduced. The latter originated mainly from North America and include rainbow trout, arctic charr, and lake trout (which are called namaycush), and from Asia, from which originated fish of the carp family.

Brown trout are the foremost game species for Swiss anglers. A native fish, they are primarily pursued in rivers (where they are called *bachforelle*) but are also found in lakes (where they are called *seeforelle*, which literally means "lake trout" but refers to lake-resident brown trout). Rainbow trout *(regenbogenforelle)* have become a favorite of many anglers, and exist in numerous rivers and lakes. Grayling *(äsche)*, lake trout *(kanadische seeforelle)*, and arctic charr *(saibling)* have more limited distribution and following among the coldwater species, whereas pike *(hecht)*, perch *(barsch)*, zander (called pike-perch), carp, and various coarse species are among the warmwater interests.

Large catches of some of these are possible, including pike over 20 pounds, zander over 10 pounds, and brown trout over 3 pounds, all in the midlands, plus namaycush over 10 pounds in the mountain lakes. Trolling in the big lakes is very popular for trout as well as for pike, and the latter are also caught on dead or live bait. Fly fishing in rivers has an enthusiastic following, but the majority of anglers use spinning tackle and assorted lures.

Eight other species—among them Atlantic salmon and sea trout—died out between 50 and 150 years ago. Numerous hydroelectric dams and pollution on the Rhine River stopped these fish from swimming upstream to their traditional spawning grounds in the pre-Alpine freshwater rivers. Since the late 1980s, however, the water quality has improved significantly, and it is hoped that a new salmon restoration program will be a complete success in the early twenty-first century.

The program, initiated by a group of Swiss anglers from the Basle area with the support of fishing authorities and angler associations, has been rearing salmon smolts in local tributaries of the Rhine and then releasing them to swim downstream to the Atlantic Ocean, anticipating that they will come back to their native waters to spawn. Atlantic salmon have been seen as far upstream as the lowest of the barrier dams near the German city of Freiburg. Because hydroelectric power companies have committed themselves to construct fish passages on the dams after the year 2000, there is real hope that the Swiss will see Atlantic salmon return to their river systems in the very near future.

Lake Fishing

In 1995 the total catch of fish on the 14 largest Swiss lakes (Lakes Geneva, Neuchâtel, Konstanz, Lucerne, Zurich, Thun, Locarno, Biel, Zug, Lugano, Brienz, Walenstadt, Murten, and Sempach) was approximately 1.8 million kilograms, of which 1.5 million, or 85 percent, was netted by professional fishermen and the remainder caught by recreational anglers. Although these numbers might seem alarming, they beg comparison by the percentage of different species of fish.

Professional fishermen mainly fish for different species of whitefish and perch. In these big lakes (they no longer fish in the smaller lakes), they account for 97 percent of all whitefish caught and 73 percent of all perch, which together represent more than 90 percent of their income. Natural reproduction of perch is fully guaranteed in all the bigger lakes, although this is not the case with whitefish. In the big cantons (Bern, Zurich, St. Gall, among others) and in the smaller cantons (such as Lucerne), the professional fishermen operate special fish nurseries for the breeding of whitefish fry.

Professional fishermen also have a bycatch of many other species in large quantities, especially roach (97 percent of the total catch), zander (96 percent), eels (89 percent), and burbot (76 percent). Although recreational anglers may be as keen as professionals to catch lake whitefish, their chances are greatly diminished because the professionals are more efficient at netting. This is also true in the big lakes for recreational perch anglers; in addition, perch are subject to restricted bag limits, as these are particularly valuable to professionals and are highly desired as table fare. The professional fishermen, in protecting their income, have arranged for legal restriction on the numbers of perch taken by anglers.

In addition to perch and whitefish, the lake angler pursues other species, and records indicate that recreational anglers in the 14 largest lakes catch 57 percent of all arctic charr, 51 percent of northern pike, and 48 percent of lake-resident brown trout. In the 1990s, in some lakes in the west of Switzerland, zander stocks have increased phenomenally for unknown reasons, becoming a favorite catch of local anglers.

Bream, dace, carp, perch, pike, roach, rudd, and tench exist in great numbers in the big lakes, as well as in ponds and smaller lakes, and most of these species are favorite catches of many coarse anglers. Burbot live in the deep waters of numerous pre-Alpine lakes but are pursued only by keen specialists. European catfish live in the restricted area of only two western lakes (Lake Murten and Lake Neuchâtel), and in the Broye and Zihl Canals that link them.

In small Alpine lakes, anglers often find good stocks of arctic charr, brown trout, and namaycush. A species of shad that lives in the Adriatic Sea and once came up the Po and Ticino Rivers for spawning in Lakes Lugano and Maggiore (which is located at Locarno and is Switzerland's lowest point at 636 feet above sea level) before returning to the sea, became resident in these lakes about 100 years ago and has lived there ever since in great quantities; these fish are caught by local anglers who preserve them in salt, as is usual with fish of the herring family. In the same southern lakes, as well as in some lakes in the Swiss midland, anglers also land pumpkinseed panfish, and there is some angling for these.

River Fishing

Brown trout is the predominant species in many of the bigger and all of the smaller Swiss rivers, as well as in mountain lakes and reservoirs, which are subject to the same fishing regulations as are applied to the rivers. This species is the favorite catch of Swiss anglers because of its table value and the sport it provides. Due to the popularity of brown trout and the ensuing pressure on population levels, an annual stocking program is applied to waterways. The application of this program is controlled by the cantonal fishery offices. Depending on the area, the raising and stocking of brown trout is either carried out by cantonal or commercial nurseries or by individual groups of anglers with their own facilities.

Also found in the Alpine lakes are arctic charr and/or namaycush. Namaycush were introduced in the 1880s by the Federal Fishery Inspectorate because of their suitability as a stocked fish for lakes in the cold mountainous regions.

At the same time the inspectorate initiated a similar program of stocking rainbow trout in closed water systems and especially in commercial fish farms. Over the years, rainbow trout have become more widespread and are nowadays found in many rivers and lakes. Despite the fact that this fish adapted exceptionally well to its Swiss habitat and was recognized as a native fish by the average person, recent federal legislation has reclassified it as a foreign species. Hence, stocking of rainbow trout is again restricted to closed water systems. Numerous anglers and their clubs disagree wholeheartedly with this federal finding because in some areas where pollution and modern technology and construction work has tipped the natural balance of the waterways, brown trout have declined while rainbow trout have survived such adverse conditions.

The elusive grayling exists for the dedicated angler in such diverse locations as the River Inn in the Engadine Valley, located at 1,700 meters above sea level; the Doubs River in the Jura Mountains on the Swiss-French border; the Aare River between Thun and Berne; the Reuss River not far from the outflow of Lake of Lucerne; the Linth Canal, which links the lakes of Walenstadt and Zurich; and the Rhine River between Lake Konstanz (Bodensee) and the famous Rhein Falls.

Below the Alpine areas the variety of fish species increases in the larger rivers, which course through to the flatland. Depending on such factors as river size and depth, height above sea level, and the regions through which they flow, there will be species like barbel, nose, carp, chub, dace, bream, carp, roach, rudd, tench, perch, and pike, and in the last few years an increasing number of zander. Some small species of fish, such as European minnows and bleak, are caught by anglers for use as baitfish.

A Regulation Jungle

Fishing and angling practices in Switzerland are mainly regulated by the laws and decrees of the 26 cantons. The regulations can therefore be very diverse. The cantons decide such practical matters as the permitted equipment, tackle and methods of angling, and the compulsory restocking of rivers with brown trout.

The Federal Fishery Act of 1994 declares the main objectives of fishery policies and lists all native and introduced species of fish and crayfish that exist in Swiss waters. In the interest of preserving certain species, the act also regulates some basic fishing practices, such as the closed season for catching trout, charr, whitefish, grayling, pike, and native crayfish, and the minimum catch size for the same species and for perch. The cantons can apply stricter size limits and closed seasons, however, to guarantee the perpetuation of certain fish species.

The professional fishermen and most of the lake anglers who fish the 14 largest lakes of Switzerland are legally obliged to register their catches and report the annual results to their cantonal fishery office. Therefore, the total weight of fish caught in general and per species every year in these lakes is known.

For the rivers, smaller lakes, and Alpine reservoirs there are no catch figures available because in a number of the Swiss cantons—among them three of the biggest, Graubünden, Tessin, and Wallis, which cover two-fifths of the country—such registering and reporting is not compulsory. This situation may change, and catch results may become compulsory in the future.

The issue of fishing permits is a complex matter because each of the 26 cantons has its own rules and regulations. There are mainly three different systems operated by the cantons, however. Some cantons (like Appenzell Innerrhoden, Freiburg, Geneva, Graubünden, Ticino, Waadt, and Wallis) use a general cantonal permit, which is known as a patent, for all the public waters within their territory. Other cantons (Aargau, Appenzell, Ausserrhoden, and Solothurn, among others) close the general access to their public waterways and apply a method of leasing, whereby fishing is restricted to certain stretches of water for a limited number of

The largest predatory shark that ever lived was *Carcharocles megalodon;* it was up to 15 meters long and had teeth that were 15 centimeters long.

anglers. A third group of cantons (including Berne, Lucerne, St. Gall, and Zurich) combine the patent and leasing systems, opening the bigger lakes and rivers with a general permit to everyone, and closing general access to the smaller ones by leasing them to restricted groups of anglers.

For the visiting angler it is worth bearing in mind that there are several inland lakes and waterways surrounded by more that one canton; therefore, special fishing regulations have been reached by mutual agreement between the cantons. A similar situation applies to some lakes and rivers that border Switzerland and surrounding countries, whereby fishing regulations are mutually agreed.

Outside the cantonal jurisdiction there still exist a few very old, private-family or corporate fishery rights. A permit to angle these private waters is usually obtainable locally through tackle shops, tourist offices, and the like.

The visiting angler faced with such a convoluted cocktail of different laws, rules, and systems may feel the need for guidance out of this labyrinth. One channel leading to all the necessary information (in the German language only) is the office of the Swiss angling magazine *Petri-Heil*, Readers Services, P.O. Box CH-8645, Jona (phone: 055225-5030; fax: 055225-5039). Also available from the same address is the annually issued Swiss Fishing Calendar, which provides a concise source of all the current rules and regulations.

SWIVEL

A freely turning metal connector that is meant to prevent twist in fishing line that would otherwise be caused by the action of a lure, bait, or sinker *(see)*. Swivels are used by themselves in connecting two lines or a line and one or more leaders, or used in conjunction with a snap *(see)*, in which case the combined entity is known as a snap-swivel. They are not attached directly to a hook.

Like some other types of terminal tackle, swivels can lead to problems by breaking or by failing to actually swivel, and should only be used if really necessary. Poor quality swivels, or light swivels used with too heavy tackle, are the main causes of problems. They can be the weakest link in the angler-to-fish scenario due to their strength. If the rated breaking strength of a swivel is less than the fishing line, it's possible that you could break the swivel and lose the lure and/or fish when maximum pressure is applied. Most swivels are relatively strong, so this is less likely to be a problem with them than with snaps or split rings *(see)*.

Swivels used without a snap technically belong in one of two categories: slide bearing and ball bearing. Most slide-bearing swivels are of the two-way barrel, the chain, or the three-way dropper variety. The bearing surface of these types of swivels—the strand and curved barrel or ring body—slide against each other and, when subjected to linear

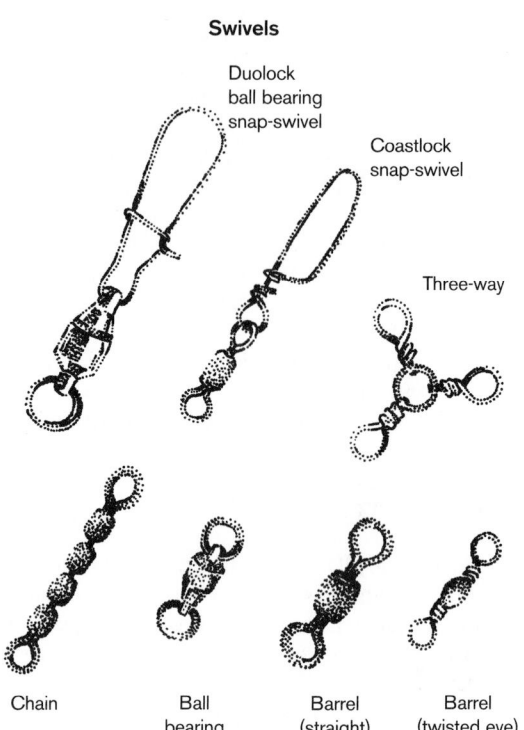

Swivels

Duolock ball bearing snap-swivel

Coastlock snap-swivel

Three-way

Chain   Ball bearing   Barrel (straight)   Barrel (twisted eye)

tension and torque, become deformed and bind, thereby negating their effectiveness.

Barrel swivels that have a twisted and single-strand head are the cheapest and poorest style available, and often unreliable. A little better in performance, because they're less prone to binding, are barrel swivels that have a straight and double-strand head; these are sometimes called crane swivels. Both of these styles are made of brass, and are used singly or as part of a snap-swivel. Three-way swivels are made of brass and feature three twisted and single-strand rings equally spaced on a ring. These are used to separate bait or lure from sinker via separate leaders. They are even more subject to binding than similar quality barrel swivels and rarely swivel well.

A chain swivel is a series of barrel-like swivels with an eye at each end; the better ones are made of stainless steel, are less prone to binding than barrel swivels, and are mainly used in conjunction with trolling sinkers. A dropper-line arrangement exists with some models that have a second chain attached to the middle of them, forming a T-shaped setup.

Although brass barrel swivels are by far the most commonly used swivels, especially among freshwater anglers, they are not nearly as functional as ball bearing swivels, which are much more expensive but greatly superior in operation and reliability. The rings of the best quality ball bearing swivels rotate freely due to highly polished stainless steel ball bearings and tapered design. These may be solid rings or split rings.

Swivels are often used when they don't have to be. For example, some anglers use barrel swivels as stops on a line to halt the movement of a slip sinker, even though a simpler device like a small split shot pinched on the line would do better and pose less trouble. As with other terminal tackle, it is best to use the smallest size that is compatible with the size of lure, strength of line, and type of fishing to be done.

Snap-swivels. A snap-swivel is strictly intended for attaching an artificial lure directly to a line, or leader to an artificial lure. It is only used with some spoons, and with spinners (especially when trolling or when retrieving these lures in current), and is unnecessary with other lures. Snap-swivels are distinct from snaps *(see)* in function, even though they may be used together. Swivels used with a snap are always barrel-shaped, with closed-eye rings at both ends; snaps may be of various design.

The same issues that apply to swivels and to snaps apply to the combined product. Preventing twist is their primary purpose, and providing a convenient means of quick attachment and detachment is their secondary purpose. Lures that do not need both of these (which is the majority of them) should not be fished with a snap-swivel. It is one more piece of equipment that can cause a problem, and may be the weakest part of the terminal tackle. Moreover, it can inhibit the action of some lures.

It's best to tie your line directly to a lure whenever you can, and to change knots when putting new lures on. However, some situations demand the use of snap-swivels, and these should be of the highest quality in terms of strength and durability in both the snap and the swivel.

SWORDFISH *Xiphias gladius.*

Other names—broadbill, broadbill swordfish; Arabic: *kheil al bahar;* French: *espadon;* Hawaiian, *a'u ku;* Italian, *pesce sapda;* Japanese: *dakuda, medara, meka, mekaiiki;* Norwegian: *sverdfisk;* Portuguese: *agulha, espadarte;* Spanish: *aja para, aibacora, espada.*

The only member of the Xiphidae family, the swordfish is one of the most highly regarded big-game species in the ocean, yet one that has been caught by relatively few anglers in modern times. Thus, any rod-and-reel catch today is a notable distinction regardless of size. Big-game fishing for swordfish was pioneered by author Zane Grey a century ago, and in the 1940s and 1950s it was popularly sought by other pioneering anglers who had the means and equipment to best these giants in their offshore haunts. Then the average catch well exceeded 200 pounds, and much larger monsters were often lost. Today, fish under 100 pounds—which have likely never had the opportunity to spawn once—are primarily encountered, and in some places only rarely, and too few are released alive (this is hard to do with larger specimens).

Unfortunately, swordfish have been especially coveted in world seafood markets—the meat of the swordfish is excellent—making this fish the object of large commercial fisheries and resulting in overexploitation virtually worldwide, as well as contributing to a demise in large specimens. Commercial fishermen take them in gillnets, with harpoons, and, most successfully, on longlines. Approximately 95 percent of swordfish harvested by U.S. commercial fishermen in the Atlantic are caught on longline gear.

Once almost unsalable, swordfish meat gained popularity following World War II and continuing through the early 1970s, when the U.S. and Canadian swordfish fishery was essentially terminated following restrictions imposed on the sale of swordfish found to contain certain levels of mercury. The acceptable level of mercury was raised in 1979, and then changed again in 1984, when it was determined that methyl mercury was the toxic component of the total mercury concentration and a test specific for methyl mercury became available. Since then, both the commercial catch and fishing effort have been exceedingly high in the Atlantic Ocean, with swordfish meat commanding top prices in the marketplace. An increasing amount of swordfish is now harvested from the South Atlantic and the Pacific, much of it destined for North American consumption.

Because these fish cross international boundaries, multination cooperation is critical to achieve effective swordfish management, but this has been painfully slow in occurring, and many countries have not complied with international catch reduction efforts. The body responsible for the multilateral coordination of Atlantic swordfish management is the International Commission for the Conservation of Atlantic Tunas (ICCAT), and most anglers have been dissatisfied with their management efforts for this species.

The countries that have the highest swordfish catches in the North Atlantic are Spain, the United States, Canada, Portugal, and Japan. In the South Atlantic, Brazil, Japan, Spain, Taiwan, and Uruguay dominate the swordfish fisheries. In the mid-1990s, approximately 50 percent of the world's total swordfish catch came from the Atlantic Ocean, with the Indian Ocean producing 15 percent and the Pacific Ocean 35 percent of the total. Recreational catches have been insignificant in the total harvest, in part because recreational catch numbers are low, the fish are found far offshore and are not often encountered, and they are not caught by the same water-covering methods used for other billfish.

Adult swordfish have few natural enemies, with the exceptions of large sharks and sperm and killer whales. They are easily frightened by small boats, yet, paradoxically, large craft are often able to draw very near without scaring them. This makes swordfish easy to harpoon, although that once-prominent commercial-capture method is rarely used today.

S

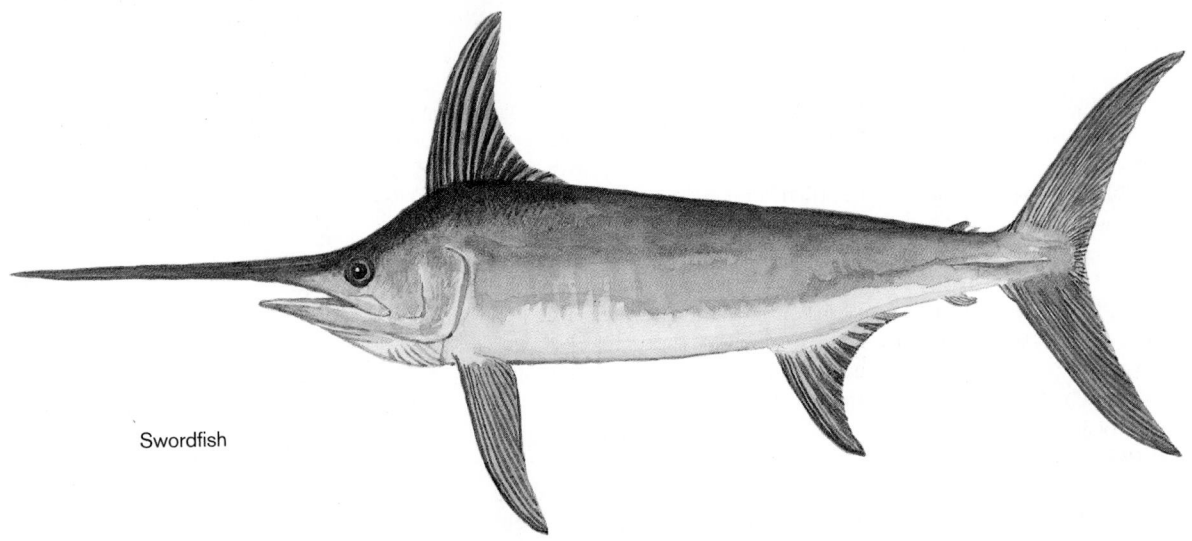

Swordfish

Identification. The swordfish has a stout, fairly rounded body and large eyes. The first dorsal fin is tall, nonretractable, and crescent-shaped. The second dorsal fin is widely separated from the first and very small. Both are soft rayed, having thin, bony rods that extend from the base of the fin and support the fin membrane. The anal fins approximate the shape of the dorsal fins but are noticeably smaller. Ventral fins, on the underside of the fish, are absent. There is a strong longitudinal keel, or ridge, on either side of the caudal peduncle, which leads to a broad, crescent-shaped tail. Adult swordfish have neither teeth nor scales.

The back may be dark brown, bronze, dark metallic purple, grayish blue, or black. The sides may be dark like the back or dusky. The belly and lower sides of the head are dirty white or light brown.

The swordfish snout elongates into a true sword shape. Measuring at least one-third the length of the body, it is long, flat, pointed, and very sharp (especially on smaller fish), and significantly longer and wider than the bill of any other billfish. The lower jaw is much smaller, although just as pointed, ending in a very wide mouth.

The bodies of swordfish fry are quite different from those of adults. Their upper and lower jaws are equally prolonged; the bodies are long, thin, and snakelike; and they are covered with rough, spiny scales and plates, are rounded, and have just one long dorsal and anal fin.

Although they are distinctive fish, they do bear some resemblance to the spearfish *(see)*, which is distinguished from the swordfish by its rounded sword, small teeth, a long continuous dorsal fin, and ventral fins.

Size/Age. Swordfish are capable of growing well over a thousand pounds, although fish of this size are unheard of in modern times. In the North Atlantic, a fish weighing more than 400 pounds is extremely unusual, and the average fish caught in the commercial fishery there weighs less than half of that amount; reports vary from under 90 pounds to under 200

pounds. The National Marine Fisheries Service reports that the largest swordfish ever caught in the North Atlantic weighed 1,210 pounds—more than double the size of the largest known in that region on rod and reel. The all-tackle world record for the species was caught in 1953 in Chile and weighed 1,182 pounds. The larger fish measure approximately 15 feet in length and have a 10-foot-long body and a 5-foot-long sword. Female swordfish grow faster, live longer, and are proportionally heavier than their male counterparts. Very large swordfish are always females; males seldom exceed 200 pounds.

The maximum longevity of swordfish is unknown, but they do live for at least nine years. The majority of swordfish caught in the North Atlantic sportfishery are thought to be immature fish only up to two years old.

Distribution. Swordfish occur in tropical, temperate, and occasionally cold waters of the Atlantic, Pacific, and Indian Oceans. They generally migrate between cooler waters in the summer to warmer waters in the winter for spawning. In the Atlantic Ocean, swordfish range from Canada to Argentina in the west, and from Ireland to South Africa in the east, including the Mediterranean and Black Seas. Swordfish are also found in the Indian and Pacific Oceans.

Habitat. These are pelagic fish living within the water column rather than on the bottom or in coastal areas. They typically inhabit waters from 600 to 2,000 feet deep and are believed to prefer waters where the surface temperature is above 58°F, although they can tolerate temperatures as low as 50°F. There seems to be some correlation between larger size and the ability to tolerate cooler temperatures. Few fish under 200 pounds are found in waters with temperatures less than 64°F.

In the western Atlantic, swordfish are summer and fall visitors to New England waters, entering the warming Atlantic coastal waters from far offshore in the Gulf Stream around June and departing in late October. Evidence suggests that such onshore-offshore seasonal migrations are more prevalent than are migrations between the northern feeding areas off Cape Hatteras and the southern spawning grounds off Florida and the Caribbean.

Life history/Behavior. Swordfish are not schooling fish. They swim alone or in loose aggregations, separated by as much as 10 meters from a neighboring swordfish. They are frequently found basking at the surface, airing their first dorsal fin. Boaters report this to be a beautiful sight, as is the powerful free jumping for which the species is known. This free jumping, also called breaching, is thought by some researchers to be an effort to dislodge pests, such as remoras or lampreys. It could also be a way of surface feeding by stunning small fish. They reach sexual maturity at about two to three years of age.

Food and feeding habits. Swordfish feed daily, most often at night. They may rise to surface and near-surface waters in search of smaller fish, or prey upon abundant forage at depths to 1,200 feet. They have been observed moving through schools of fish, thrashing their swords to kill or stun their prey and then quickly turning to consume their catch. Squid is the most popular food item, but many species of midwater and deep-sea pelagic fish, such as menhaden, mackerel, bluefish, silver hake, butterfish, herring, dolphin, and others are part of their diet.

This fish also uses its sword for defense. Occasional attacks on boats have been authenticated by the recovery of swords found broken off in wooden hulls. One swordfish attacked *Alvin,* the Woods Hole Oceanographic Institute submarine, at a depth of 330 fathoms, and wedged its sword so tightly into a seam that it could not be withdrawn.

Angling. Swordfish are vigorous, powerful fighters and impressive jumpers. When hooked or harpooned, they have been known to dive so quickly that they have impaled their swords up to their eyes in the ocean bottom. Anglers normally fish for them by trolling and drift fishing, and have had a slightly increased catch rate since the mid-1970s, when night drifting with squid for bait was adopted.

As mentioned, swordfish often bask on the surface with their dorsal and tail fins protruding from the water, so anglers intent on fishing during daylight will actually scan the water looking for a fish to present a trolled bait to. Swordfish are finicky, however, and are easily frightened by an approaching boat. They rarely strike blindly; typically, the bait must be presented carefully and repeatedly before the swordfish will take it. Once a swordfish has been spotted, the speed of the boat should not be changed appreciably and the bait should be eased quietly and gently in front of the fish. Squid is the most popular bait, although Spanish mackerel, eel, mullet, herring, tuna, and live or dead bonito are also used.

The soft mouth makes hookup uncertain, and the slashing bill can make short work of an angler's line or leader. Sighted swordfish are most often attracted by a trolled, rigged squid or baitfish on a long line. This must be done in such a manner as to

A 200-pound-class swordfish is about to be released (note the tag below its dorsal fin) at La Guaira, Venezuela.

keep the boat from spooking the finning fish but still bring the offering in front of it. This often results in avoidance by the swordfish. When it does attract the sword's attention, a strike can result, but the slashing fish often does not inhale the bait and is frequently not hooked. Casting live bait to surface-finning swords is also practiced.

One reason why swordfish are not actively pursued in daytime is that they rarely feed actively during daylight, and thus are not often interested in anglers' offerings. Because this sport usually takes many sightings and presentations—which is not common in some places but is more common in others—the odds are not especially good.

The odds of catching swordfish are generally better for nighttime anglers, although the option of fishing at night far offshore does not appeal to many anglers and probably restricts greater angling activity. Depths run a wide gamut, from 60 to 80 feet below the surface to 1,200 feet and much more, depending on geographical location, water temperature, and moon phase. Often, baits are staggered at various levels, and light sticks are employed at least 6 feet above the baits to call attention to them, with balloons attached to the line with rubber bands to help indicate pickups.

Tackle for swordfish can be as light as 30- to 50-pound outfits with lever-drag reels, primarily in shallow water, but ranges up to 130-pound tackle for deeper water and larger fish. Line capacity is of great concern, as swordfish may be hooked exceptionally deep and run a long way. In their fight they may also rush the surface at any time and leap out of the water, then continue with blistering runs. Some of the most epic angling battles have occurred with swordfish, which fortifies their reputation as the "Gladiator of the Sea," which is the translation of their Latin name. Although the average swordfish caught today is small, landing one is considered by many to be the highest achievement in angling.

See: Big-Game Tackle; Billfish; Offshore Fishing.

TACKLE

A generic term for the man-made equipment used almost exclusively for sportfishing; also commonly referred to as fishing tackle. In prevailing use, tackle fundamentally refers to rods, reels, lines, leaders, and assorted terminal gear. The term "tackle box" is derived from this, obviously because it refers to a compact portable means of storing the assorted small items that comprise terminal gear: hooks, weights, lures, connectors, and so forth. Natural bait is not considered tackle, hence the common term "bait and tackle" shop.

In an extended sense today, tackle also refers to accessory equipment used in sportfishing, such as a landing net, a bait container, or a downrigger. Clothing items are not considered tackle, although waders and wading footwear blur this distinction, as do such items as electric motors and sonar; these and other products are often included in the broad designation "tackle," although they may be used for other purposes besides fishing. As time advances, most gear that is used in sportfishing, whether exclusively or not, is considered an item of tackle, especially by manufacturers and merchants.

Although rods and reels are considered intrinsic to fishing tackle, they are not absolutely necessary to the act of fishing. The most basic fishing tackle consists of a line with a weight and a baited hook, which is cast and retrieved by hand. This is the basis of handline fishing. Handlines today are primarily used in underdeveloped regions, primarily with a baited hook and sometimes with a (baited or unbaited) jig or jigging spoon, and predominately as a means of procuring food rather than providing sport. This is how most people fished throughout history for subsistence purposes.

Another basic item of fishing tackle is a line connected to a reel-less pole (see). That line may feature a baited hook or a lure, but it cannot be cast or retrieved as the line is fixed to the end of the pole. A line attached to a pole is usually no longer than the length of the pole and therefore a bait or lure can be placed up to twice the length of the pole away from the angler. Such a pole may be made of cane or synthetic material, and it may be of one length or telescopic, but there is no reel for the storage of line.

Other than these basic forms, fishing tackle for practical sportfishing purposes includes a rod, reel, line, and terminal tackle. These items are reviewed in detail as individual entries elsewhere in this book.

(Some of those individual entries are listed at the end of this entry.)

The major components of fishing tackle—rods and reels—were once easily categorized as being freshwater tackle or saltwater tackle. But as the world of sportfishing changes, it has become less and less appropriate to make this type of designation. With the advancements made in materials and features, many products can be used in both freshwater and saltwater. Granted, an outfit that is classified as medium-heavy for freshwater (say for Great Lakes chinook salmon trolling) would probably be classified as light for saltwater (and used by the inshore casting/trolling/bottom fishing crowd), but it would definitely be appropriate. And a light spinning outfit suited with 6-pound line, which might be employed for some types of freshwater trout or bass fishing, could be very useful for casting small jigs to bonefish or redfish in saltwater.

Clearly some tackle, such as big-game tackle and certain types of conventional tackle, are used only in saltwater. Otherwise, it is not the type of tackle that dictates usage; that is dictated by two factors: individual models and their features, and/or the type of fishing being done and the size and behavior of the quarry. Because there are so many variables in fishing for all species, such as the places that anglers fish, the size and strength of the fish they catch, the techniques used, and the circumstances under which they are caught (depth, current, and so forth), it is difficult to categorize tackle as being just for freshwater, just for saltwater, just for trolling, or just for bottom fishing. At the extremes of the fishing tackle spectrum, this may be so, but the vast middle ground is more of a gray area.

What often happens with tackle is that the length and action of a rod is the major factor in determining the preferred or predominant use of that rod and an appropriately matched reel. In some cases, the strength of line, or line-test, further refines the use of a rod and reel. The size of a reel is usually a factor in line capacity and in the range of line strengths that are used.

This does not stop the manufacturers of fishing tackle from marketing products for specific uses, however. Just as there are a dozen kinds of fishing boats and a slew of lure types, so, too, are there reels and rods, especially the latter, marketed and promoted for specific (and in some cases niche) applications. To those unfamiliar with sportfishing, this is indeed a confusing potpourri. In an effort to make this less confusing, this book reviews the rod and reel components of fishing tackle in detail in the following categories, which readers are urged to reference.

See: Baitcasting Tackle; Big-Game Tackle; Conventional Tackle; Flycasting Tackle; Reel, Fishing; Rod, Fishing; Spincasting Tackle; Spinning Tackle; Tackle Care/Maintenance/Repair.

Because there are so many aspects to consider for the other elements of fishing tackle, these, too, have been treated in detail under their respective entries See: Hook; Line; Lure; Terminal Tackle; Weighted Line; Wire Line.

TACKLE BOX
See: Lure Storage.

TACKLE CARE/MAINTENANCE/REPAIR

Contemporary fishing tackle is a high-tech wonder of engineering, manufacturing, and design. Rods and reels use materials that evolved from aerospace applications, and they benefit from refined and sophisticated manufacturing techniques. Whether simple or complex instruments, they have the ability to last for years with a reasonable amount of care and maintenance, and sometimes even repair or refurbishing.

Fishing tackle requires care during use and storage. Maintenance should be performed on a regular basis, and repairs should be made when something starts to go wrong or breaks. Proper care and maintenance often mitigate a need for repair. It's a smart move to look after your rods and reels so that they aren't mistreated and don't malfunction (and a malfunction will always occur when you need your equipment the most). Some tackle represents a significant economic investment, which is another reason to care and maintain equipment. It is possible to send rods and reels to service centers for repair, but many repairs can be made easily and economically in your workshop or in the field.

Tools

Tools for maintenance and repair vary with the extent of service necessary. For basic maintenance, almost no tools are needed other than perhaps those supplied with a reel for the purpose of taking it apart to check on lubrication and excessive wear. For repair, you may need glues, small screwdrivers, wrenches, rod wrapping devices, finishing brushes, polishing rags, etc. Some possibilities and their uses with tackle include the following.

Manufacturer's reel tool. This small tool will vary with the manufacturer but typically comes with the reel. Usually made from flat plate steel, with one or more screwdriver ends and an expanded center with hex holes to act as wrenches, it is designed for simple take-down of a reel, often in the field, for basic repairs.

Small screwdrivers and screwdriver sets. Since reels possess bantam parts and screws, small sets of a half dozen or more screwdrivers are ideal. They are usually available in hobby shops or through tool mail-order outlets.

Small wrench sets. These consist of sets of standard wrenches, Allen wrenches, and Torx wrenches for various reel fasteners.

Oil and grease. Tubes of oil and grease are often supplied with reels; if they are not supplied, or are misplaced, they can be obtained from hardware, hobby, and automotive stores. You'll need a light oil (like a sewing machine oil) for most parts and a medium grease for gears and shafts. It's best if the tubes have small, tapered applicator tips for reaching the small spots and crevices found on most reels. Make sure that you have the right oil for the right application, however, as will be discussed later. Read the manual that comes with the reel for the manufacturer's recommendations.

Compartmented box. This can be nothing more than an egg carton or biscuit tin for separating reel parts. Place parts in order in the compartments as you remove them from the reel to make reassembly easier.

Old toothbrush. These are ideal for cleaning around the crevices of reels and removing grime during regular care and maintenance sessions. To avoid scratching the reel, use with liquid soap in a soapy water solution.

Heat source. This can be an alcohol lamp, cigarette lighter, or similar flame source. These devices are ideal for heating the ferrule cement or heat-set cement that is used to secure a tiptop onto a rod.

Razor blades. These are necessary for cutting thread, removing old and damaged rod wraps, and doing similar tasks when you are working on rods.

Emery board. Use an emery board to smooth rough spots on a rod and to remove old epoxy rod finish at the edges of a wrap after removing the old thread and before making the new wrap.

Rasps and files. These smoothing tools are a must for shaping and rounding cork grips when you must repair or replace rod handle grips.

Sandpaper. Sandpaper is necessary for final shaping of a cork rod grip. Use several grades, finishing with the finest grade available to smooth the grip surface.

Rod-wrapping jig. Rod-wrapping stands or jigs allow the fishing rod to be held horizontally while at the same time supporting the thread spool and creating tension on the thread for wrapping new guides on a repaired rod. However, for repairs you do not need a commercially made rod-wrapping jig. (They are nice, though, if you do a lot of repairs. A fishing club might consider buying one to loan to members.) A simple substitute is a large cardboard box, about 1 foot high, 1 foot deep, and 2 feet wide, with the top and front side removed. With the open front facing you, cut notches in the top of both sides. Cut out the bottom of the back panel to hold a book. In back of the book, place a cup to hold the thread, and then run the thread between two sheets of clean paper held in the pages of the book. Place the rod in the notches, the thread in the cup (which keeps it from rolling around), and adjust the thread through the book to control the tension on the thread as you rotate the rod and wrap on new guides. This is a simple, no-cost, disposable method for easy rod wrapping.

Burnisher. This is available from rod component supply catalogs, but an easy substitute is a round-shaft plastic pen or pencil. Use the pen or pencil to smooth and burnish thread wraps and to close up any slight gaps in the thread that would otherwise occur.

Rodcuring motor. A rodcuring motor is nothing more than a slow rpm motor capable of holding a rod by the butt cap and slowly rotating the rod while the epoxy finish is curing; the slow rotation prevents sags and runs. The middle of the rod has a simple support. Such devices are available commercially, but often substitutes can be made by using a slow rpm rotisserie motor from a barbecue grill and fitting it with a rod to which a butt cap can be taped in place.

Field kit. You can add some of the items already mentioned to a kit that travels with you or is kept in your boat. An assortment of tools and reel parts is mandatory; the latter should include the extra parts that come with some reels, especially screws, nuts, bail springs, and reel oil. Other items could include a razor blade, rod-wrapping thread, matches, rasp, quick-setting epoxy, candle wax, and wire for temporary guides.

Basic Tackle Care

Rods and reels are not unduly fragile, but they still should be used, handled, and stored with care.

Storing. The best ways to store rods are to stand them vertically in a rod rack, support them horizontally on shelving or with several cup-type hooks, or place them in bags and cases designed for storage. Some rods are supplied with protective storage cases, and rod storage racks and systems are available from tackle suppliers or through catalogs.

Do not store a rod by leaning it against the wall; this will cause a permanent set or bend in the rod blank that will damage the rod over time. Adding the weight of an attached reel makes the matter worse. Also, do not run the line through the guides and place a hook or snap in a butt guide in a way that makes the rod curve; in time, this can cause a permanent bend. It is equally bad to hang up a rod by the tiptop, since some tiptops are glued on with a heat-set cement and may be pulled off. This problem is exacerbated with heavy rods or rods with reels still attached.

While traveling, keep rods in their cases or otherwise protected from bending. If carrying several rods, bundle and tape them together for added strength and security. On boats, store rods flat or in horizontal or vertical rod racks. For detailed information on transporting and caring for tackle when traveling, *see: Travel.*

A drying motor board is used to create a glasslike finish on rods.

Never store a rod in a bag or closed case when it is wet from fishing. To do so can cause damage to the finish and possibly corrosion to metal parts, such as reel seats and guides.

Reels should be stored apart from rods, if only to protect from corrosion or electrolysis that can occur when dissimilar metals of the reel foot and the reel seat become wet while fishing. When reels are not in use, reduce the drag tension to a loose setting so that pressure on the soft drag washers is eliminated. Pressure over time can make an impression on the soft washers and cause sticking and erratic drags, which might later cost you a fish.

While you are fishing, protect reels on rods by covering them with a reel case. Many such cases for casting, spinning, and flycasting reels are made to fit onto a reel, even when it is mounted on a rod. If you don't have a case, use an old sock.

Washing. Rods and reels often require a little extra care after a fishing trip, particularly if they've been used in saltwater or in dirty, muddy, or algae-filled water where tackle is likely to pick up line-damaging grit and grime. Through repeated casting and retrieving, the grime builds up on guide rings, and over time it also damages reel parts and wire guides, such as snake guides on a fly rod.

Be especially concerned with salt because of the corrosive effect that it has on tackle. This is true even for reels with components that are meant to combat saltwater. Plastics and graphites are impervious to corrosion, but aluminum and stainless steel only resist corrosion; they are not impervious to it. And the biggest concern is the interior components, the inner workings of a reel that are not as accessible as the exterior for cleaning. Of equal concern is caring for reels that have been submerged in saltwater, especially the surf where there is a lot of sand in the mix,

T

and reels that have been dropped in the dirt or sand. Simply rinsing reels that have been exposed to salt is not enough to remove the little crystals of salt. Many crystals will still remain after a freshwater rinse, so you need to use soap or detergent with warm water to help remove all of the crystals.

Ideally you should wash rods and reels after each trip of a day or longer if they have been used in any of the aforementioned circumstances. An easy way to do this is to first separate the rods and reels and then wash the rods in the shower. An ideal time to do this is when you are also taking a shower, since you can easily scrub and rinse each rod. Use a sudsy washcloth and scrub the entire rod. Run a corner of the washcloth through the guide rings and around the guide feet, or use an old toothbrush for extra cleaning. Use a toothbrush on the collet nuts and threads of the reel seat, and move the nuts so that you wash all parts of each reel seat.

Separate two-piece rods, but try to keep water from getting into either ferrule end. Most male ends have a plug, and most female ends are at the lower end of the tip section and thus not subject to water when the tiptop is pointed up. Once the rods are completely clean, rinse thoroughly and allow to air dry in the shower or out of the way in a corner. They can be stored after they are completely dry.

Reels should be similarly washed to remove any salt or grime. First, remove spools from those reels where this is easy: flycasting reels, spinning reels, and a few baitcasting reels. A few baitcasting reels have easy-access ports on the palming sideplate (opposite the handle) by which the spool can be removed. In addition, most have thumbscrews on the handle sideplate that are easily unscrewed without tools to remove the spool. Take care that small parts are not dislodged; if the reel has centrifugal cast control, make sure that you do not lose any brake blocks.

Place the spools in a warm sudsy bath to soak for a while. Do the same with reel bodies, soaking them in warm water to help soften any grime or salt. To remove the salt or grime (soaking won't accomplish this), use a soft scrub brush or old toothbrush for crevices and corners. After the spools and reels are washed completely, rinse thoroughly and place on an old towel to dry. Flycasting reels are easy to dry this way by placing them open and face down to drain off any water. Spinning and baitcasting reels are best dried by shaking out any water that might have entered the gear casing or sideplates and then air drying, turning occasionally to allow drying or draining of any water puddles on the interior or exterior.

If you have access to clean freshwater at the dock or launch site, you can use it to clean your tackle. But don't spray the reels with a sharp stream of water from a hose; you may actually drive salt into important areas. A fine spray is better, and using warm water with soap is best. Fill a bucket with warm soapy water; then use a brush or sponge to go over the reels.

This combination washes salt away, but on many reels there is still reason to be concerned about getting anything into the critical drag washers. Therefore, you can tighten down the drag tension, wash the reels with warm soapy water and a brush or sponge, rinse with a fine spray, wipe dry, and then loosen the drag tension.

If a reel has been completely submerged in saltwater or exposed to the sandy surf wash, you should take the reel apart to get to the inner mechanisms. How quickly you do this depends on when you will be fishing next. If you'll be fishing with that item for the next few days, then you can probably wait a few days before giving it a thorough cleaning and possibly a relubrication. But if you will not be using the reel for a while, then you should clean it thoroughly soon after. At the very least, give it the regular soap and water treatment at the end of each day.

Another step that you can take after washing and drying is to apply an anticorrosion product. There are a number of rust-inhibiting liquids available; some can be sprayed, but you need to be careful about getting the product on the fishing line, because it could impact the strength of the line or at least impregnate the line with scent. Using a cloth to wipe all the metal parts will alleviate any concerns.

Practicalities.   The aforementioned care recommendations are the ideal, and they are the highest standards that can be followed. Within reason, some lesser attention to these details will likely not harm your equipment. Obviously, saltwater anglers need to rinse, if not wash, their rods and reels after every single outing; most freshwater anglers do not need to do this on a daily basis, although it is a good idea to rinse them with clean fresh water occasionally and to give them a more thorough soapy cleaning once in a while. Clearly, it is a burden to remove reels from rods after every outing, especially if you finish angling late one day and start early the next with the same tackle. Many people clean their reels without removing them from the rods; this is generally okay, but remember that the connection between reel foot and reel seat is an area that is likely to retain moisture and that is especially subject to corrosion.

Use common sense about this, remembering that even if you do not feel obliged to take the maximum cleaning measures each time, you should at least do so periodically, and more frequently when circumstances warrant.

Tackle Maintenance

All anglers should check their tackle periodically to avoid later repairs or to catch problems while they are small and more easily corrected. A careful visual inspection is ideal for this, and for reels should include trying and testing all functions to make sure that they work properly. For rods and reels, the best time to check them is after cleaning them, although a thorough inspection isn't necessary after each trip unless you think that you might have damaged the rod or reel while fishing or you suspect problems. Inspect your tackle on a regular basis, according to how often and how hard you fish. Do so at least once a year, preferably soon after ending the season so that you have plenty of time for repairs or adjustments.

Rods.   Begin to visually inspect the rod by using a bright light. Check the entire blank, turning the rod as you examine it from tip to butt for possible dings or cracks. Often you can do little about severe problems, other than to be aware of them in case they cause later rod breakage—and carry a backup rod for the one that is susceptible to breakage. Evidence of possible damage to a rod blank would be areas where the finish is separated from the blank itself, where the finish or underlying rod blank has a bruised look, where there is a noticeable visual crack, or where you can feel something in the blank surface.

If you do find obvious damage, you may want to notify the manufacturer or check your rod warranty. Your rod may be under limited warranty, although the warranty may not cover the specific problem. A few rods, primarily expensive products (often fly rods), have unlimited warranties that cover almost anything that might happen.

Check the wraps on each guide, at the tiptop, at the ferrules, and immediately above the rod grip. The wraps at the tiptop and above the grip are decorative but still must be protected, and they are indicative of wrap condition in general. All the wraps should be protected by a rod finish, preferably epoxy. Wraps in good condition will show no signs of fraying, damage, bruising, or color fading. The protective finish should be intact, without blistering, peeling, or flaking. Assuming that you use and store your rod carefully, such wraps and finishes should last for many years without requiring refinishing or rewrapping. The topics of refinishing and rewrapping are both reviewed here later under "Repairing Rods."

Take the rod apart if not already disassembled, and check the condition of the ferrules. Make sure that the ferrule wraps are intact and in good condition, since they provide a protective hoop strength to the rod at this critical junction point. If the male ferrule is soiled, clean it with lighter fluid to remove any grime, dirt, or wax. Use a cotton-tipped applicator dipped in lighter fluid to clean the inside of the female ferrule. Candle wax is often used to help ferrules grip tightly and work smoothly, but it can also attract dirt. Once the ferrules are clean and dry, reapply candle wax to help the ferrules work smoothly.

Check each guide frame and ring. Guide frames that are bent can often be returned to original shape by using flat-nose pliers. Use care to avoid pulling them free from the thread wraps. Most guides today are made of some form of ceramic: aluminum oxide, Hardloy, silicone carbide, silicone nitride, etc. They are well protected in a wire frame with a plastic (nylon) shock ring, but the internal rings are very hard and can crack with a sharp blow. Check visually for cracks, or run a piece of old hosiery through each ring to check for damage. The hosiery will usually catch on any slight crack or damage.

Check the grip next. Grips are made of cork or synthetic foams, usually EVA or PVC types of cushiony foam. Often both types of grip become dirty with use, but they are easily cleaned with a scrub brush and suds. This often takes extra work and may not have been completely accomplished with the normal cleaning. Any dirt left after this second thorough cleaning is best removed using a very fine sandpaper on cork grips and a medium sandpaper on the foam grips. If cleaning this way, protect the blank and the reel seat with several layers of masking tape to prevent scratches.

Check the reel seat for damage or wear. Reel seats are made of chrome (plating over brass on saltwater trolling rods), aluminum (saltwater and freshwater rods of all types), and graphite (all types of rods and is really a graphite-filled plastic). Slide the hood, which holds one end of the reel foot, up and down the reel seat to make sure that it works smoothly. Check for hairline cracks in the corners of the hood, which is the most common place that they occur. Turn and move the collet nuts up and down the threaded portion to check for function and any wear or damage. With some spinning and casting rods, the foregrip is built on the forward collet nuts. In these cases, unthread the foregrip completely and slide it up the blank to examine the underlying threads. For saltwater tackle, check for corrosion on the reel, especially if the reel is always kept on the rod. Treat this area with corrosion-resistant liquid; applying a light coat of grease can help prevent corrosive buildup.

Some fly rod reel seats have wood inserts, or barrels, between the threaded portion holding the sliding hood and the fixed hood. Check these for cracks and splintering, and protect them by regularly polishing them with a wood furniture polish.

Some saltwater rod butt sections, mainly in big-game versions, separate from the rod blank (tip) at the upper part of the reel seat, using a separate locking, keyed collet nut system that holds the metal ferrule on the butt end of the rod into the upper end of the reel seat. Check these and wash carefully if this has not already been done.

Reels.   Maintenance of all reels is simple and basically involves periodic checking, oiling, and greasing. Ideally, you've saved the manual that came with your reel; it will suggest how to take care of the reel and will explain which parts you should regularly oil and grease, as well as recommended timetables for doing so. The latter is important, because overlubrication can be a problem, especially if it causes oil or grease to get onto parts that shouldn't have it. If you don't have the reel manual, you may

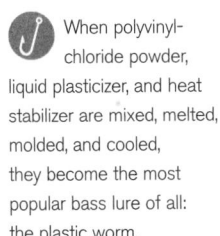

When polyvinyl-chloride powder, liquid plasticizer, and heat stabilizer are mixed, melted, molded, and cooled, they become the most popular bass lure of all: the plastic worm.

be able to get another from the manufacturer, especially if it is a fairly recent model.

Usually you'll notice if something is amiss with a reel while you're using it. If the drag sticks, a moving part binds, or there is a grinding sound, you'll know. However, if a reel hasn't been used in a while, if someone else has been using it, or if some of the features haven't been used recently, you may not be aware of any difficulties. In such case, you should check the operation of the reel before using it. Since the drag is a critical element for landing strong fish, and an improperly functioning drag is a common problem, this feature should be carefully inspected on all types of reels.

Check drag operation by running line off the spool and through the rod guides; have someone stand a short distance away, wrap line around a gloved or towel-covered hand, and pull line from the reel while the rod is at a 45-degree angle. Repeat this a few times while you check and adjust the drag tension setting through its full range to make sure it's working properly. Pull the line rapidly and evenly. If constant, even pressure is applied to pull line from the reel, the rod tip should not jump or move much, indicating an even, smooth drag. If the drag is erratic, you may need to replace the tension washers. Some spinning reels have a standard front drag but also have a lighter secondary rear drag for fishing with bait. If so, test both drags through their full range, realizing that the secondary drag will not be as resistant to line pull as the primary drag.

When testing the spinning reel drag, make sure that the line roller on the bail assembly is turning at the same speed as the line going out. If it doesn't, it will wear the line in time. Turn the handle to regain line, and make sure that the line lies down properly on the spool. Don't turn against the reel drag, since this will cause line twist.

With a spinning reel, you should begin maintenance efforts by removing the reel spool. Check the rim of the spool for any nicks or roughness. If the rim is rough, you have no choice but to discard it and replace with another spool. (This would probably indicate that the reel hasn't been properly cared for, so you should determine why this has happened and avoid it for the future.) Some reels are supplied with a spare spool when new, and spare spools are also available from your tackle dealer. Check the frame to make sure that nothing is twisted, broken, chipped, or otherwise damaged in a way that affects performance. Turn the handle to make sure that the gears are smooth. Move the antireverse switch back and forth several times to make sure that it is working. If it has a bail trigger, see if this works smoothly and opens the bail easily and completely.

Oil the handle nut, handle shaft, handle knob, line roller, ends of the level bail arms or fittings, drag knob nut and spring, antireverse lever or switch, the arm joint for the bail trigger, and the main shaft (remove the spool for this). Periodically remove the sideplate, using the right type and size of screwdriver

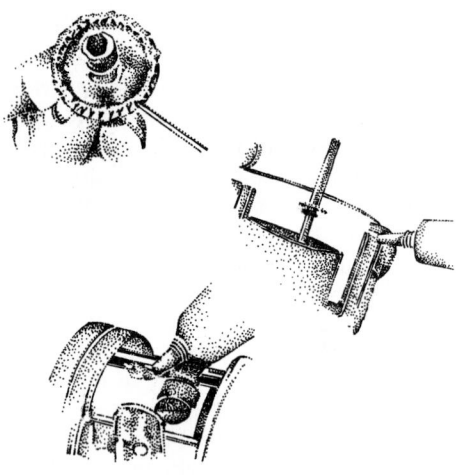

When lubricating a reel, apply a judicious amount of grease to the gears (top), oil to the bail of a spinning reel (middle), and oil to the levelwind pawl on a baitcasting reel (bottom).

for the job. Check the gear box for wear and proper grease on the gears. If necessary, grease the main gears. To do this properly, don't smear a dollop of grease into the gear box and close it up; use a toothpick to deposit a tiny dot of grease on each and every gear tooth, because this will distribute the grease better. Once greased properly, reassemble the reel and tighten all the screws. Gear systems and types will vary with the reel model and manufacturer, but this basic lubrication is easy to apply to every reel.

For spincasting reels, check the exterior for any damage, particularly the hood or nose cone for any cracks or dents that might interfere with line flow. Remove the nose cone, and push down on the line-release button (or trigger in some models), and make sure that the line becomes free (the pin drops on the rotor pickup) and that the spool or a bumper pushes forward to hold the line against the nose cone for casting. Check the antireverse switch if there is one, and make sure that the handle and gears turn smoothly.

Oil the rotary pin and spring (remove the cone or hood for this), the pushbutton line release, the handle knob and shaft, the knob or star drag adjustment mechanism, the antireverse switch or lever, and the main shaft (in back of or under the spool). Periodically remove the sideplate and check the gears, greasing the same as with spinning reels.

With a baitcasting reel, turn the handle to make sure that the levelwind runs smoothly back and forth on the worm gear and in the track. Make sure that the levelwind disengages when the reel is in freespool for casting. The same thing applies, and should be checked, with the drag engaged and line being pulled from the reel, as happens when a fish is taking line. Depress the freespool button or bar to place the reel in freespool; then turn the handle to make sure it pops out of freespool easily. Do this several times. Using a practice casting weight, make a few casts with the cast control at several different settings to check performance. If the reel has a flipping switch, make sure that this works properly.

Oil the handle fitting, shaft, and knob, the rack for the levelwind guide (not the worm gear or pawl), the shaft bearings on both sides of the reel (remove the sideplate and spool to do this), the drag controls, the flipping switch, and the antireverse switch if there is one. Grease the gears after removing the sideplate. Baitcasting reels typically have a small pinion gear and a larger main gear, so add small dots of grease to each gear tooth, as with spinning reels. Unscrew the cap to remove the pawl from the levelwind and check for wear, since this part wears most rapidly. Replacements should have been included with the reel, so replace with a new one if necessary. Grease the pawl housing and pawl at the same time, along with the worm gear in which the pawl rides.

The same things apply to conventional and big-game reels, which are larger and heavier. Putting a conventional reel into freespool means moving a lever rather than depressing a button, and most lack a levelwind feature. Big-game reels feature lever drag operation instead of star drag. Both types have a click alarm. Check this to make sure that it is fully on or fully off when switched back and forth; on older conventional reels, these often wear out. A few conventional reels have line counters, which are easily checked for accuracy by pulling measured amounts of line from the reel.

Oil the handle knob, handle shaft, star or lever drag, antireverse switch, and spool shafts (some reels have oiling ports for this and other parts). If greasing the main gears, use the reel manual for directions in disassembly, and use extreme care. Lever drag reels and many conventional reels are very complex internally, and they can be damaged by inappropriate care. Grease the gears as noted for other reels, one drop at a time on each tooth.

Flycasting reels are basically simple frames to hold a spool, the handle being mounted on the spool on direct drive reels. Antireverse reels (in which the handle will not turn when line goes out against the drag) have a separate plate or arm on which the handle is mounted. Multiplier reels are few, but they have additional gearing and a separate arm for the handle so that one turn of the handle makes more than one turn of the spool. Most flycasting reels have drags, but these can vary from a simple click, made by a pawl striking a gear tooth, to more-complex disk or caliper drag systems that are simple variations of car brakes. As with other reels, check the drag system through the range of settings. Note that fly line is thick and will be more erratic in coming off the spool, so that the drag will not initially appear to be as smooth as on other reels. To check for smoothness, pull out all the fly line and check the drag against the backing line, or pull off the front part of weight-forward lines to check the drag against the thinner section of the rear running line.

For direct drive, antireverse, and multiplier reels, remove the spool and arms and oil the moving parts such as click pawls, handle knobs, main shaft, drag adjustment controls, and spool locking catch. Use a very small amount of grease on each gear tooth of multipliers. For automatic flycasting reels, follow the reel manual for instructions, oiling the moving parts such as the spring control lever and spring ratchet. Because a spring is involved, follow the manufacturer's instructions as to any further disassembly.

The following precautions apply to all reels. Avoid oiling or greasing them excessively, and do not lubricate drags or use demoisturizers. Avoid excessive grease or oil on the internal parts of antireverse mechanisms, flipping switches, click pawls, antireverse pawls, etc. Too much oil or grease on these mechanisms might slow their operating time or prevent them from working completely. Use light oil in all oiling procedures, and use it only very lightly and sparingly, especially in these areas.

Drag care and lubrication *must* be performed following the manufacturer's instructions. Some drag washer materials should not receive any lubrication, and if lubricated they will not perform properly. Some drags can be ruined by the application of greases or silicones to the drag plates and washers. Friction drag materials (usually as washers) used in reels today include cork, cork composite, graphite, graphite composite, Teflon, various other plastics, smooth metal washers (in disk drags), asbestos-like materials, carbon, etc. There is no general rule for all of them; some benefit from the use of pure neat's-foot oil (don't use a compound meant for waterproofing footwear on some cork drags), whereas others may need cleaning and light sanding only, silicone lubes, no oil at all, etc. Follow the manufacturer's instructions for each reel and drag system. The way to apply grease has been described, but it is also worth mentioning that you should not add more grease if enough already exists in a reel. If there is an insufficient amount of grease, then you can add more judiciously; it's better to clean off the old grease (it may have particles of grit in it that have gotten inside the reel) and reapply fresh grease.

De-moisturizers will help to repel moisture and "dry" reels after use and cleaning. Used selectively and with care, they can help keep reels in good shape. They should be applied to metal parts and are unnecessary on plastic, resin, or graphite. Be aware that de-moisturizers may damage the PVC coating on fly lines and may damage some of the plastics used in many reel parts today. They will not harm monofilament lines but may impart a scent to the line. However, some anglers have used these products as a fish attractant on lures, so such a scent may or may not be detrimental.

Repairing Rods

Rod repairs may involve only a few minutes to glue on a new tiptop or a full evening to replace all the guides. Many rod repairs are easy, even fun, to make, and don't require any special talents or tools. Some examples of easy repairs follow.

Trophy lake trout in the Far North are older than most anglers; 40 years old is common, and up to 62 has been recorded.

Replacing the tiptop. Tiptop repair on a rod involves replacing the tiptop either because it is broken or worn, or because the blank has broken right at the end of the tiptop. In both cases, the repair is similar. If the tiptop is broken, the simple solution is to replace it with a new tiptop of the same style, finish, and tube size; you don't need to remove the wraps at all, since they are only decorative and don't cover the tiptop tube.

To replace the tiptop, cover the thread wraps with several layers of masking tape to provide insulation over the wraps. With the wraps protected, use heat on the tip-top tube and then remove it with pliers. Heat the tube only, using an alcohol lamp, cigarette lighter, or a hair dryer held close to the tube. In all cases, heat will break down the cement, including epoxy. Test frequently with pliers, since you don't want to overheat the area and possibly damage the blank. If the blank becomes damaged, then you'll have to cut back the blank at this point, remove the thread wraps, replace with a larger tube-size tiptop, and finally rewrap and refinish the thread wrap.

If the blank is not damaged after removing the tiptop, allow it to cool and then clean with an emery board or by scraping with a razor blade. Do *not* cut into the blank or reduce its diameter.

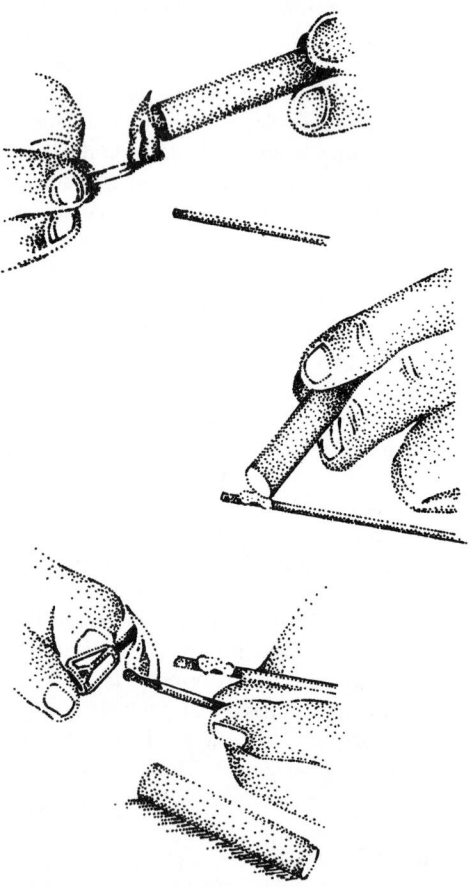

To put a new tip guide on a rod in the field, heat ferrule cement (top) and apply the cement to the rod shaft (middle); then heat the tip guide (bottom) and align it in position on the rod.

Use either heat-set cement (ferrule cement) or epoxy to glue the new tiptop in place. With heat-set cement, use a flame to heat it; smear it rapidly onto the blank, and just as rapidly slide the new tiptop in place. Immediately line up the tiptop with the guide rings. Do *not* try to remove any excess cement; you will be able to remove it easily after it sets and cools. Once the cement cools, peel off the excess with your thumbnail and then remove the protective masking tape.

An alternative method is to shave off splinters of the heat-set cement, place them in the tube of the tiptop, and heat the tube to melt the cement. Immediately slide the tiptop in place and line it up; remove the excess cement as described above. *Never* heat the blank when using heat-set cement.

If using epoxy glue, mix thoroughly; then use a toothpick to insert some glue into the tip-top tube. Smear more on the end of the blank, and slide the tiptop in place. Use a rag to remove any excess glue, line up the tiptop with the guides, and allow it to set. Keep the rod horizontal or at an angle while the glue cures, with the guides facing down to prevent gravity from moving the tiptop out of alignment. In both gluing methods, glue will sometimes ooze through a small opening in the end of the tube. Should this happen, remove it with a rag or toothpick.

If the blank is broken, remove the tiptop and then remove the thread wraps. An easy way to do this is to use a razor blade, scraping through the finish and wrap (using the razor like a carpenter's plane). After you've scraped away one side of the thread wrap, remove the wrap as if peeling the shell from a steamed shrimp. Lightly clean the area with an emery board. Measure for a new tiptop, and buy the right size. (Tip-top gauges are available from mail-order houses, and many tackle shops will have one to aid you in determining the right size of tube for your rod.) Then glue on as already described, using heat-set or epoxy glue. Finish with thread wraps and a protective finish as later described.

Replacing and rewrapping a guide. To remove a guide, use a razor blade to cut through the wrap along the foot; then pull the remaining thread to remove all of the guide wrap, or peel it off the blank. When the guide wrap is removed, use an emery board to sand down any excess finish at the ends of each wrap. Once the blank is clean, you're ready to rewrap. Make sure that you have guides of the same ring size and style as those being replaced, unless for some reason you wish to change them or upgrade them. Prepare each guide by filing the end of the guide foot for an easy, smooth transition of the thread from the blank and up onto the guide foot. Lightly file the underside of the feet to remove any metal spurs that could damage the rod blank.

Guides are best replaced in the same spot from which they were removed. If you're adjusting the position or number of guides on a rod, realize that, even when cleaned and refinished, the old wrap areas will likely be a different color (often lighter)

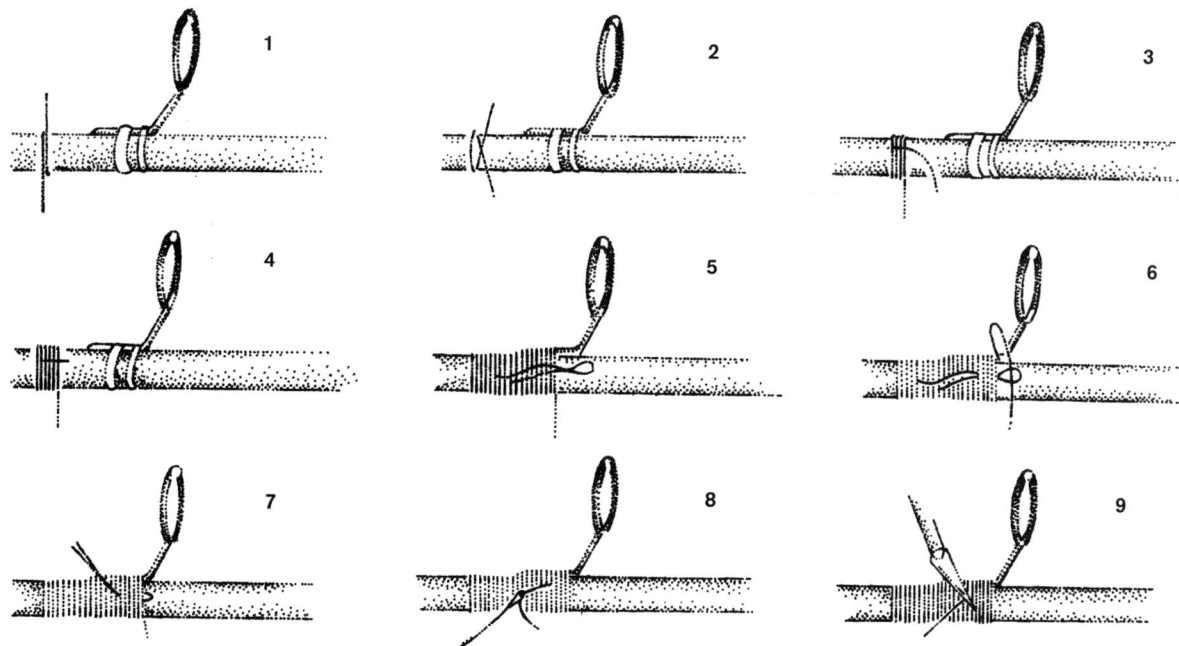

Depicted are the steps for wrapping a guide on a rod blank. In this case, a single-foot guide is shown. Note that in step 5 a loop of line is wrapped in, and in step 6 the tag end of the wrapping thread is run through the loop; this end is pulled through and then trimmed.

than the rest of the rod. This is due to the sun fading the blank and cannot be corrected.

Prepare the blank by taping the guide in place on the blank; make sure that it is lined up with the other guides, the tiptop, and the reel seat hoods. Use thin strips of masking tape, which can be cut from a standard-width spool or are available in narrow-width spools from arts and crafts stores; 1/4-inch is best. Place tape in the middle of the foot, not the end; if you put it on the end, you won't be able to wrap the end with thread. Use masking tape also to mark the beginning of the rod wrap on the blank. (Note: all wraps begin on the blank and progress up onto the foot, ending at the frame.)

Thread for wrapping guides is available in different sizes (diameters). The 2/0 size is best for most fly rods. Size A is best for heavy fly rods and all freshwater spinning, spincasting, and baitcasting rods, and most light saltwater rods. Size D is best for heavy saltwater rods, and size E is used only on the heaviest saltwater trolling rods.

Use a rod-wrapping jig, or rig a modified cardboard box (described earlier in the tools section). Before starting, cut a 1-foot-long piece of wrapping thread, fold it over, and tie a knot to make a loop. This will be used to finish the wrap.

Most rod wrappers work from left to right, but either direction is all right provided that you wrap from the blank up onto the guide foot. Begin by bringing the thread over the rod blank and around it, wrapping over the thread by turning the rod while holding or pulling on the end of the thread. Make sure that the wraps are tight, and after a few turns clip any excess thread, since there will then be enough friction to hold the thread. Continue wrapping by turning the blank. Make sure that there are

no gaps, and work slowly and carefully as the thread begins to cover the guide foot.

When you're about six to eight wraps from the end, lay down the previously prepared loop, with the loop toward the center of the guide. Continue wrapping over the loop until reaching the end of the foot (where the frame rises from the foot). At this point, hold the thread to prevent unraveling, clip the end, and tuck the end into the loop. Pull the loop tight, then under the wraps, which pulls the end of the thread with it and provides a neat, secure finish. With a razor blade, cut the excess flush with the wrap or open a gap and cut straight down to sever the excess thread. Reverse the rod on the wrapping jig, and make the other wrap on the other side of the guide (assuming it's a double-foot guide).

There are plenty of supplies for building and repairing rods, especially with regard to guides; shown here is a variety of wrapping threads.

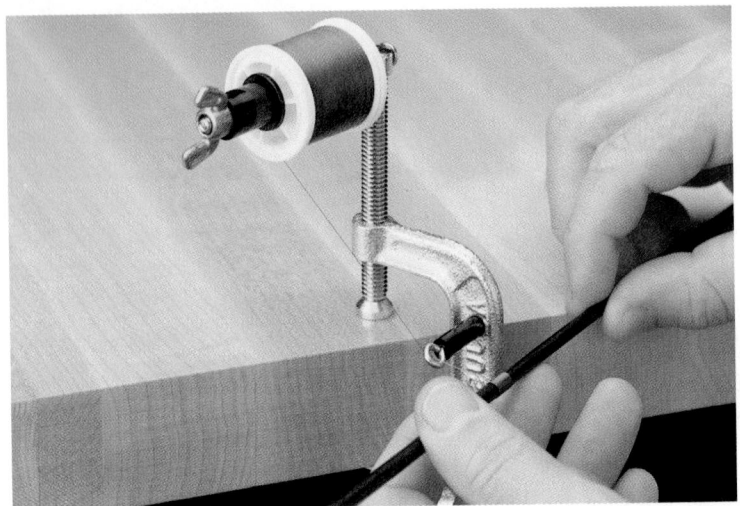

This simple device is used for rod wrapping.

If you're redoing only one guide, try to match the thread color, although age and sun will make an exact match impossible. If rewrapping the entire rod or replacing all the guides, use whatever color you desire. Additional wraps are also necessary at the tiptop, at the junction of the blank with the rod grip, and at the ferrules. Those at the ferrules are necessary for hoop strength; those at the grip and tiptop are only decorative.

Emergency guide replacement.   If you break a guide in the field, especially a tip-top guide, it could be a detriment to casting and to playing fish. You can make a temporary replacement guide out of stainless steel wire if you have some with you. Number 12 or 14 wire is good for this, and it can be rolled and formed into an appropriate ring shape with double feet. Take the straight piece of wire and wrap it twice over a round object of an appropriate size (about $1/4$-inch in diameter will do for tip-top guides). Bend the ends so that they are at right angles to the doubled wire and are parallel to each other; these will become the "feet" for securing the replacement guide to the rod. Align the replacement guide, and make several wraps over the feet with electrical tape (or better, use thread and epoxy if you happen to have them). Make a permanent replacement as soon as you can, since line will cut through the wire eventually.

Finishing or refinishing wraps.   Once a wrap has been replaced on an existing guide or has been put on a new guide, the wrap should be protected with a sealer and finish. Most are epoxy finishes and very durable, clear, and flexible. If you choose, you can add color preserver, which will retain the existing spooled color of the thread. Without color preserver, dark thread colors will become darker, light thread colors will become lighter, and all will become somewhat translucent. If using color preserver, use the same brand as the rod finish; apply two coats, waiting 24 hours between each coat and before applying the rod finish. Add the color preserver with a disposable brush, liberally coating the

wraps; after a few minutes blot any excess with a paper towel.

After applying the epoxy finish, the rod has to be slowly rotated for a few hours. You can rotate it yourself (maybe while watching a movie), or use a slow rpm motor made for the purpose and available commercially. You can also rig such a device using a slow rpm rotisserie motor from an electric grill.

Follow the rod finish manufacturer's directions, but a general procedure is to mix two equal parts of the two-part mix, stir thoroughly, then pour out on a flat surface; pouring on a flat surface helps dissipate bubbles and extends the working life of the mix. Any slight bubbles are easily dissipated by breathing on the mix. Using a small disposable brush, first wrap around the end of each wrap and then fill in the middle area. Use a bright overhead light to help detect missed spots or bubbles. Once all the wraps are coated with rod finish, rotate the rod to prevent the finish from dripping and sagging. Try to apply the finish in a clean environment so that dust, dirt, and pet hair don't soil the finish.

In some situations, the existing wraps on a rod are okay, but the original finish is starting to peel and flake. In this case, you can simply add an additional coating of protective finish. For best results, wrap the blank with masking tape at the end of each wrap that is to be refinished. Then lightly abrade with steel wool, and clean completely. Remove any loose or peeling finish. Remove the masking tape. Mix new rod finish and apply.

Regluing a reel seat.   Rarely does the reel seat on a rod become loose, but when it does, repairing may be difficult. There are several possible solutions. If the reel seat is a skeletal type with the blank exposed in several areas, you can often wiggle the reel seat completely loose and then apply epoxy glue to the blank to reglue the reel seat in place. Tubular-type reel seats are more difficult to repair, since they are glued to a bushing or shim material, which in turn is glued to the blank. On a fly-rod reel seat, it is often possible to slide the reel seat completely off, clean the bushing and reel seat, and reglue.

Tubular reel seats on spinning and baitcasting rods can usually be repaired only by drilling holes through the reel seat (taking care to avoid hitting the blank), or you can drill holes at an angle from the rear or the fore grips. Then mix epoxy glue, and use a syringe to force glue through the holes to reglue the reel seat. This doesn't always work, but it's usually worth a try. The only other alternative with cork-grip rods is to cut off and remove the fore or rear cork grip, slide the reel seat up for cleaning and regluing onto the blank, and then rebuild the cork grip.

Replacing part of a cork grip.   Badly damaged cork grips, and difficult reel seat repair problems, can be fixed by completely removing the old grip or a major part of it and replacing with a new grip, without removing the reel seat or guides. This method is appropriate when the damage to the grip is such that you could not effectively fill in a gouge with cork/glue filler. To make this major repair to the cork grips, you need a flexible waterproof cork glue (such as Ultra Flex, Pliobond, various cork glues, or others) and enough cork rings to fill in the gap you will create. Cork rings are usually $1/2$ inch thick and come in $1^1/8$-, $1^1/4$-, and $1^1/2$-inch diameters. Make sure that you pick rings larger in diameter than the grip, since some filing and sanding to shape will be necessary.

To make this repair, remove the old damaged cork by rasping down to the rod blank. Do not rasp or damage the rod blank. Remove all the cork in $1/2$-inch increments. Make sure that the resultant gap is squared off and even, so that the $1/2$-inch-thick cork rings will fit in precisely. If necessary, enlarge the hole in each ring to the diameter of the rod blank. Then cut each cork ring in half, numbering each half with the same number on the same side of the cork ring face so that the matching halves can be easily identified. Place the matching halves into the cut gap to check for fit.

Remove the halves; add glue to the rod blank, the facing cork halves, and the facing corks in the cut gap. Replace the cork halves into the gap on the rod blank, making sure that the halves match and face the right way. Fit them securely; then wrap with tape or cord to bind while curing. Once the cork is cured, remove the binding material; file, sand, and then polish with fine sandpaper to match the previous grip shape and diameter. Other than being a slightly lighter color than the handled portion of the grip, it will not be noticeable as a repair.

Repairing cork gouges. Small gouges and nicks in cork grips are easier to repair than large parts. The simple solution is to fill in these gouges with a glue/cork mix, overfill, and then sand after curing. To repair a gouge, first rasp and file some cork to make a cork dust. Cork rings are best to maintain quality, but bottle corks will also work. Then mix the dust into a thick paste with flexible, waterproof glue such as Pliobond or Elmer's Carpenter's Glue. Remove all loose cork from the gouged area, and coat with glue. Then fill with the cork/glue mix, overfill, and allow to cure overnight or longer until hard. (A prolonged curing time is often a must because of the high percentage of glue in the mix.) Then file and sand the excess, finally sanding with fine paper to polish the repair to a finish like that of the original.

Replacing a butt cap. Butt caps sometimes fall off or become damaged. If damaged, obtain a new one; reapply with a flexible glue such as Pliobond or Ultra Flex.

Repairing blanks. Cracked, broken, or damaged blanks are usually difficult to repair. One option for tip sections that are broken about an inch or two from the end is to clean the break and replace with a new tiptop (a larger tube size than the existing tiptop will be required). For this, follow the tip replacement, wrapping, and finishing instructions previously given.

Other breaks and damage are more difficult to repair. The only way to repair them is to smooth the cracks, breaks, and splintered edges as much as possible; insert an internal sleeve of blank under the broken area; and finally bind the outside of the rod with a long thread wrap. Unfortunately, the nature of the repair precludes repairs to the tip sections of all but the largest rods for three reasons: It's difficult to find thin scrap-blank sections that are strong enough and that will fit into the thin cores of tip sections; the repair makes the rod stiff in an area where you want it to be flexible; and the repair makes the tip feel heavy. This repair can be done, although it is chiefly recommended for the butt section of those rods for which flexibility and sensitivity are less important and additional weight is a secondary concern. Any repairs like this require access to the butt end of the rod, which requires removal of the butt cap. If the cap is rubber or plastic, often the best way is to cut it off and replace with a new cap. If it is metal, insulate the grip with several layers of masking tape and heat the butt cap to break the glue bond; then remove and replace it later.

It is important to be extremely careful when handling a broken rod, especially one with splintered ends. The sharp microfilament-like slivers, especially if they are graphite, can easily pierce your skin; so do not grab the broken area and be careful not to poke yourself with it.

To make this type of repair, you must find a scrap blank section in which the outside diameter matches the inside diameter of the broken area of the rod. To accomplish this, first clean and restore the broken splintered sections as much as possible; then insert the scrap blank section to check for proper length. Ideally, the insert blank should be 2 to 3 inches longer on each side of the broken area. Thus, if the break is sharp—almost like a transverse cut—the reinforcing insert might be no longer than 6 inches. If the break is splintered and about 6 inches long, then the total insert must be 10 to 12 inches long to overlap the end of the break.

Once the insert is sized and cut, roughen it with a light sanding, smear it with epoxy glue, and insert it into the rod. Since the glue will cause it to bind on the blank, use a thin dowel to push the insert into position. Use some glue in the splintered exterior area, and spiral wrap with cord to bind the glued areas together. Do not wrap too tightly, since the pressure can compress the rod and force the insert section out of position. When the glued area has cured for about 24 hours, remove the binding cord and use a file, followed by an emery board and then fine sandpaper, to smooth the repaired break area. Once smooth, add hoop strength with a thread wrap that completely covers and overlaps the ends of the break area. To blend the wrap with the blank, use a color closely matching the blank color and do not use color preserver before sealing with a protective finish.

Repairing Reels

Repairing a reel usually involves replacing one or more individual broken parts. If the necessary parts can be obtained, any angler can make the repairs; you simply need to follow instructions exactly, have a basic understanding of the mechanics of the reel, and use the schematic drawings provided with the reel. Some small tools, in addition to the one sometimes provided with the reel, are needed or useful for making certain repairs; these include needle-nose pliers, a small adjustable wrench or set of small wrenches, and a set of small Phillips and standard screwdrivers. It's a good idea to have oil and grease handy to lube the repaired reel.

A vital aspect of reel repair is using the manual or instruction sheet that comes with each reel when purchased new. These usually have schematic drawings to show how parts are assembled, a list of parts and ordering instructions, lubricating instructions, and suggestions for simple part replacements and adjustments. Some basic repairs to major reel categories follow. Keep in mind that most repairs are simply replacement of worn or broken parts and are not difficult to accomplish.

Also note that for anglers who put their reels to hard use in fighting strong fish, the friction drag washers on their reels need to be in top shape for maximum performance. These may need to be changed if the drag is not operating well. One of the major causes of poor drag performance is keeping tension on the drag washers for extended periods when the reel is not in use. Many drag-related problems could be avoided by getting into the habit of backing off the tension completely at the end of every fishing day so that there is no undue and prolonged tension on the drag washers; over time, the prolonged tension unnecessarily compresses the washers. If you don't back off the tension like this, you may need to service the drag washers more often than you otherwise should.

Spinning Tackle

Bail arm.   Should the bail arm on a spinning reel become bent, it will need to be returned to its original shape; otherwise, you will not get the proper line pickup. Sometimes the repair can be done while the bail arm is still on the reel. If not, the bail arm has to be removed. In most cases, the line roller is part of the arm, so the bail arm is detached by removing screws from both ends of the bail assembly; it may also be detached by removing screws at the assembly point opposite the line roller and then removing the other end from the line roller. The latter method also facilitates checking the line roller and lubricating at the same time, and it lessens the chance of losing springs. Springs are used in one or both ends of the bail arm, so be careful that you don't dislodge or lose them. Once the arm is removed, bend the bail to reshape it to fit onto the reel; to avoid binding, make sure that the ends or end brackets are parallel to the body part on which they fit.

Line roller.   The line roller is held in place on the side of the bail assembly by a bracket attached to the skirted spool or rotor. You can easily remove it with the appropriate tool. As you remove the line roller from the pin on which it turns, take care not to lose any washers, sleeves, or bearings that are part of this mechanism. Pay attention to any distinguishing marks that will indicate proper reassembly. Clean thoroughly, oil and replace, or replace with a new line roller if the original one is damaged.

Drag washers.   Drag washers in spinning reels are located in the spool, in the rear part of the gear box (rear drag), or in the main part of the gear box (no-twist drag systems). Those in the gear box or under the sideplate are well protected and usually don't require replacement or care other than an annual check when the gears are greased, as previously outlined. Those in the spool are subject to more environmental damage through water and possible corrosion, and should be checked periodically. Most of these are multidisk drags and consist of metal washers alternately keyed to the spool or the rotor shaft, in between which are soft composition or cork washers. They are held in place by a spring that fits into the top of the drag stack. To check the drag washers, carefully remove the spring and then remove the washers, one at a time. Keep them in order so that you can replace them in the same order. Check for damage or wear on the washers. Sometimes the metal washers will become slightly rough or corroded. If necessary, polish the metal washers with steel wool, followed by abrasive cleanser; replace them if they cannot be restored to original smoothness. Grease or lube drag washers only if suggested by the manufacturer. Many are designed to run dry. If they are worn or are indented from compression, replace them.

Other repairs.   Other repairs will be rare but could involve replacing gears or replacing the antireverse switch. Replacing gears can be time-consuming, since you will have to dismantle the reel almost completely to remove the main shaft (the reciprocating shaft that moves the spool in and out to put on line evenly). Usually, the drive gear is attached to the handle, and the main gear to the main shaft and rotor. Refer to the reel manual to remove the rotor, spool, and main shaft to replace the gears. To make reassembly easy, keep parts in order in a compartmented box.

The antireverse switch usually consists of a switch or lever that moves a pawl; the pawl catches a tooth to prevent the rotor from turning backward. These parts are easy to replace but are not always easily accessible on the sideplate or at the rear of the gear housing.

Bent or broken handles are easily replaced, since virtually all spinning reels have convertible left/right retrieve and, as a result, have easy attachment to the gear set. Most either are screwed into a shaft or have a hex or square shaft, which slips through a similar

Proper storage of rods and reels, especially in boats where they can be accidentally damaged, helps prevent the need for repairs.

sleeve to be held in place by a machine screw on the opposite side of the reel.

Spincasting Tackle

Handle. Handles on spincasting reels also become broken, but they are generally screwed in place on the shaft, similarly to the attachment used with baitcasting reels. No tools are needed to replace a handle; unscrew the old handle and replace it with a new one.

Spools. Damaged spools are easily replaced by first removing the hood or nose cone (usually twisted off), then removing (unscrewing counterclockwise) the winding cup that holds the line pickup pin, and slipping off the old damaged spool. Replace with a new one, reversing the procedure to reassemble.

Pickup pin and snubber. The pickup pin and snubber are easy to check and replace when you are removing the spool. The pin operates on a cam or spring system on the winding cup. Metal and even ceramic pickup pins may become worn and should be checked periodically. The plastic or rubber line snubber on the forward inside of the hood can become worn or sometimes separated from the hood. If separated, it can usually be glued back into place by using epoxy or rubber cement. If worn, pry off and replace with a new one, also glued in place.

Washers and gears. The drag tension adjustment mechanism on most spincasting reels is located under the handle, in the same place as on baitcasting reels. To check or replace washers, remove the handle nut or screw, slip the handle off, unscrew the star drag wheel, and then remove the washers for examination or replacement. Follow the same instructions as those given for the washers on spinning reels.

Access to the gears on some spincasting reels is gained by removing the sideplate, the same as with spinning reels; on others, access is gained when the hood is removed. Replacing gears can be a little involved, as it is with spinning reels. Use the reel manual for guidance in removing the rotor, spool, and main shaft. To facilitate reassembly, keep parts in order in a compartmented box.

Baitcasting Tackle

Levelwind pawl. The levelwind pawl is the small-toothed pin that travels in the levelwind gear to spool the line evenly. To check or replace the pawl (spares are usually included in a small container of parts with each baitcasting reel), remove the small cap that holds the pawl in place and slide out the pawl. Check to see whether the pawl is worn or has become pinlike, in which case it needs to be replaced. Replace by sliding a new pawl into the housing; make sure that the tooth engages the worm gear, and replace the cap.

Levelwind worm gear. Levelwind worm gears seldom wear enough to require replacement; but if they do, they can be easily replaced by removing the handle sideplate, loosening and removing some retainer rings or screws and the levelwind pawl, and sliding out the worm gear. Replace and reassemble; then grease both the worm gear and the pawl housing.

Drag washers and gears. Drag washers and gears on baitcasting reels are both in the same location; the drag washer is usually mounted on the face of the main gear. To check or replace any of these parts, first remove the handle-side sideplate. Then remove the handle and unscrew the star drag wheel, following the manufacturer's instructions. Most require first unscrewing a small locking plate and then using a wrench to remove a handle nut, followed by spinning off the star drag wheel. With the handle removed, use a small screwdriver to remove the internal plate that holds the gears. This separates the external sideplate from the plate holding the gears and drag washers, and allows examination of the gears and drag washers. If the gear teeth have been stripped, then one or both gears in the set should be replaced.

Check for damage or wear on the washers. Sometimes the metal washers will become slightly rough or corroded. If necessary, polish the metal washers with steel wool, followed by abrasive cleanser; replace them if they cannot be restored to original smoothness. Lubricate drag washers only if suggested by the manufacturer. Many are designed to run dry. If they are worn or are indented from compression, replace them.

Handle. Sometimes the handle of a baitcasting reel becomes bent; more likely one of the knobs breaks. In both cases it's a good idea to replace the handle entirely. It is generally tightened in place on the shaft by a covering nut. The small tool supplied with the reel can be used to remove the nut. Make sure that you make the repair in a location where the nut can be recovered if you drop it. Some anglers have done this on a boat or dock and watched their retaining nut fall into the water, rendering the reel useless until a new nut is obtained.

Flycasting Tackle

Flycasting reels are simple and require little in repairs, provided that they are kept clean and maintained as previously outlined. In some cases, a reel foot or line guard, if these are separate from the reel frame, will become corroded or worn. For those that are separate from the frame, replacement is easy through the screws that hold these parts in place. Pawls that become worn as a click drag are easily replaced, often by just removing the spool and gently holding the spring apart to lift the pawl free and then replacing with a new one.

Drag components must be cared for on flycasting reels that feature disk or caliper drags; follow the manufacturer's instructions for care, cleaning, and any lubrication.

Conventional and Lever Drag Tackle

Making repairs to conventional reels and lever drag reels is something that must be done very carefully, since these products are put under tremendous strains and torque in some fishing situations. These products are meant for rugged use and are built accordingly, but you need to be careful when tinkering with them, especially if you take them apart and reassemble them. If you don't feel confident about doing this, have a repair shop or the manufacturer do the work.

Simple things like replacing handles or clickers or the levelwind pawl (in some models) are easy to do, and such repairs are accomplished as already noted for other products. Handles on conventional reels are held in place similarly to those on baitcasting reels, since they both have star drag operation. Thus, unscrew and remove the nut-locking plate, then use a wrench to loosen the nut and slip off the handle. Some conventional reels have multiple attachment for power or leverage advantages, so they may be frequently changed. Just be sure to use the right tool so that you don't strip the handle-fastening screw or nut.

It is unlikely that you will have to replace either the pinion or the main gear in these heavy-duty products, although such a repair can certainly be made if needed. These parts are typically located under the handle. To get to them, remove the handle and then spin off the star drag wheel. Remove the screws around the perimeter of the sideplate; for easy reassembly, remove them in order. After the sideplate has been removed, additional bracketing might have to be removed to expose the gearing. Once this is done, access to the gears and drag washers is similar to that of baitcasting reels, and they are relatively easily replaced.

The drag washers on conventional reels are critical to their performance, and all points that have previously been made about washers apply even more so

to conventional reels. Lever drag reels are a distinctive product, operating differently, and they do not have a stack of washers. Nevertheless, the friction drag material that they use and the drag plate need to be inspected, and obviously replaced if they are worn. For some older reels, this material can be replaced with a better friction material supplied by the manufacturer. **See: Baitcasting Tackle; Big-Game Tackle; Conventional Tackle; Flycasting Tackle; Spincasting Tackle; Spinning Tackle.**

TACKLE STORAGE
See: Lure Storage.

TAG
A mark on a fish made for identification purposes; also a physical device attached to a fish for this purpose.
See: Tagging.

TAG-AND-RELEASE
A term for placing a tag in fish that are captured by sportfishing and released unharmed.
See: Catch-and-Release; Tagging.

TAGGING
Tagging is a method of marking fish for identification purposes. In a very few cases, a visible tag is placed on a dead fish (such as Atlantic salmon in some Canadian provinces), much the same way that hunters place a tag on game animals or birds they have taken. Tagging is done when a limited number of fish are allowed to be harvested, and a tag (provided with fishing license) must legally be placed on harvested fish. Most of the time, however, visible tags are used to identify live fish that are returned to the water for the purpose of providing information about individual fish or particular species.

Tagging is commonly used by biologists for specific research and management purposes, and it has become an increasingly common voluntary practice by anglers, especially for pelagic and migratory species. Although tagging is generally viewed as the placement of visible objects on or in the bodies of fish, it is actually a method of marking, which also includes such practices as clipping the fins, coloring with long-lasting fluorescent pigment or short-term dye, tattooing, branding, and outfitting with electronic devices that transmit detectable signals. The most common item to anglers, however, is a visible exterior tag; anglers occasionally catch fish that possess such objects, and many actually place tags in fish that they release, especially saltwater anglers.

The Scientific Side
Biologists mark fish with visible exterior tags and hidden body cavity tags, usually after weighing

Scientists say that most fish are color blind but can see color shadings, reflected light, shape, and movement.

and measuring them. The tags usually contain an identification number and often a phone number or other information so that recaptured fish can be evaluated. Anglers are asked to return the tag to a sponsoring agency or organization and to provide information on when and where the fish was caught, as well as its measurements and weight upon capture. In some cases, there are rewards for returning the tag and/or providing necessary information.

Several things can be learned by biologists from a tagging program. The movement of a species, for example, is known if the release and recapture points are known. The rate of movement may be determined if the time between release and recapture is recorded.

Often the goal of a tagging program is estimating the size of a fish population, determining the rate at which fish are being caught, and verifying growth rates. A tagging program that records the size at the date of tagging and at the date of recapture provides an independent measure of the growth rate. When biologists tag a specific number of fish and later recapture a portion of them (through netting or other means), they can estimate the number of fish in that population. Likewise, when a biologist knows the number of tagged fish in a population, the death rate through angling can be determined when tags are returned for fish that have been kept.

Biologists conduct tagging activities for a wide range of fish in freshwater and saltwater; in North America, there is a distinct difference in the way programs are carried out within those environments, owing to the fact that many saltwater species cross state and even international boundaries.

In freshwater, the majority of tagging is done by technicians and biologists representing individual state fisheries agencies. Many tagged fish are ones raised in hatcheries and tagged prior to release in the wild, and others are fish that are caught in their natural environments, usually via netting and sometimes via electrofishing (see). In a few cases, state agencies use angler volunteers to assist in getting wild-caught fish tagged more widely over a given time period, but these individuals are trained and provided with equipment. Most agency-related tagging efforts are locally targeted, geared to specific water bodies and certain species.

In saltwater, few states conduct tagging activities other than for inshore species and resident populations of fish, and then usually only for short periods and specific management purposes. However, private groups sponsor extensive tagging programs coordinated with federal agencies, especially the National Marine Fisheries Service (see). Some mass tagging is done by federal fisheries managers in places where numbers of fish are available seasonally (such as anadromous species like shad in coastal rivers). However, limited resources and wide-ranging fish make it impractical for federal fisheries managers to tag marine species in quantity over a

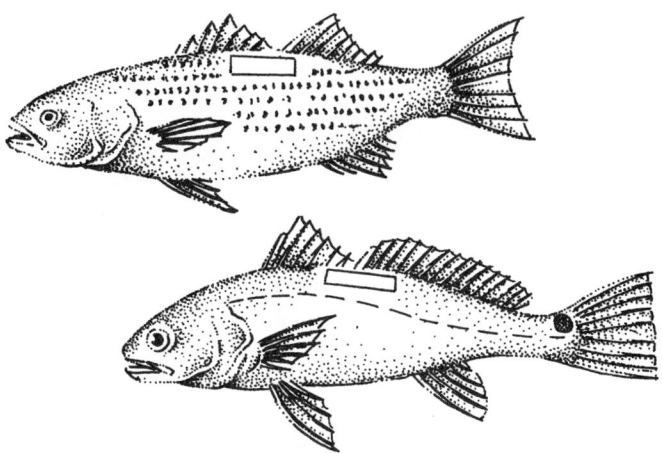

The bandagelike boxes on this striped bass (top) and red drum indicate optimal tag location.

reasonable period of time; therefore, they rely on angler volunteers to report taggings and recaptures to appropriate agencies.

Some of the more interesting and technologically advanced activities recently conducted by federal fisheries biologists are harness tags that send data to satellites, and in-body archival tags used with pelagic fish. The latter tags cost over a thousand dollars and are implanted by scientists in the body of a fish to record its swimming depth, water temperature, body temperature, and location by means of a sensor. A two-tone green alert tag, which is meant to bring attention to the presence of the archival tag, is also placed on the fish.

The National Marine Fisheries Service (NMFS) has placed these archival tags in a number of billfish, and in hundreds of Atlantic bluefin tuna. The tagging has particular value because it provides information about all the places that the fish visits between the point of tagging and recapture. Substantial rewards are offered for the return of an undamaged tag, and fish that are caught out of season or without the proper permit may be kept if they have such a tag. The most sophisticated and expensive of archival tags may be the pop-up variety, which are attached to the base of the fish's dorsal fin and detach after time, emerging on the surface and relaying data to a satellite.

Tagging by Anglers

As mentioned, the differences between tagging activities in freshwater and saltwater are extensive. Most freshwater fisheries managers discourage and do not favor tagging by the public because they feel that improper handling of fish and misguided tagging efforts are likely to be harmful to fish and because there is a chance (usually remote) that private tagging activities might interfere with agency efforts. Freshwater biologists note that tagging produces more stress on a fish than it would already receive through the process of hooking, landing, and handling for release, not to mention the possibility of in some way hurting the fish. Tagging in

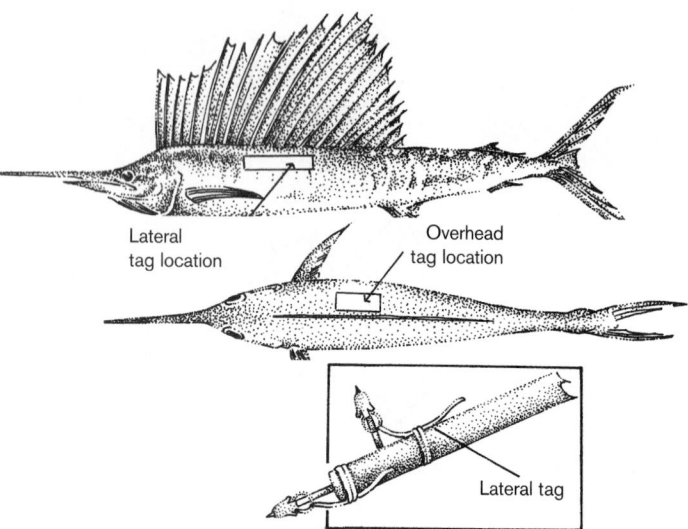

Lateral
tag location

Overhead
tag location

Lateral tag

Patched areas show where a tag should be placed when a big fish, such as a sail-fish, is approached from lateral and overhead vantages. A tagging stick (inset) rigged with two tags—one on the end for overhead tagging and the other on the side for lateral tagging—will permit tagging in either instance.

Tagging information. There are a number of different tag types, and suppliers provide information on the best method of tagging, angle of tag insertion, and placement location, depending on the tag type and target species. The Littoral Society, for example, which uses so-called spaghetti tags, recommends tag insertion behind the dorsal fin near the tail. Suppliers of barbed tags generally recommend placing it near the middle of the dorsal fin, well above the lateral line, with single-barbed tags at a 45-degree angle and double-barbed tags at a 90-degree angle. Some species have to be captured and handled for tagging; others (including billfish and large tuna) are tagged in the water with the use of tagging sticks (sticks to which tags are attached).

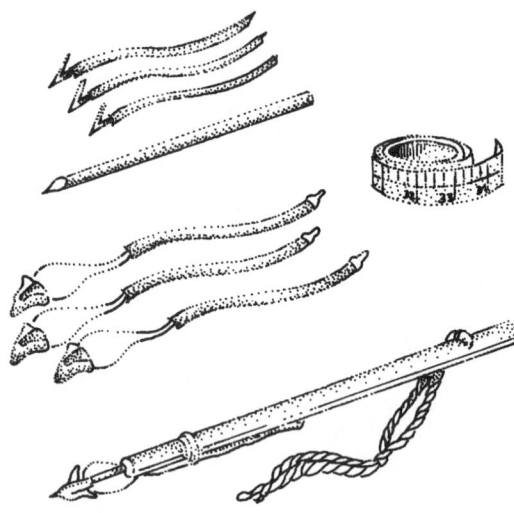

The tagging tools shown here, from top to bottom, include single-barb tags, hollow stainless steel small-tag applicator, double-barb tags, measuring tape, and solid stainless steel large-tag applicator.

public waters may be illegal in some places, and anglers should check on this.

In a practical sense, freshwater anglers have little reason to tag fish unless there is a coordinated research or management program associated with tagging, even though some companies have made fish tagging tools or kits available to the public. The end result of tagging should be to advance information that has scientific value, but without a program to use the information derived from tagging, there is little use for it other than curiosity. Even tagging anadromous fish is of little value without a program to utilize the information. However, tagging on private bodies of water (small lakes and ponds in particular) may have merit, even if just for personal reasons and curiosity, since these are closed environments.

In the marine environment, however, there is no private water, there are few public agencies that tag fish, and those that do are under severe budget constraints. Tagging and releasing fish has become increasingly popular here and is conducted under the auspices of a number of private organizations, which supply tags (for a fee) to the public or to members, as well as extensive tagging information. These organizations also report recaptures to participants, and they supply data to public agencies, such as NMFS or the Fish and Wildlife Service, for research and management efforts. The oldest such program was started in 1965 at Sandy Hook in Highlands, New Jersey, by the American Littoral Society, and tens of thousands of fish annually are entered into the database by volunteer taggers. Another organization, the Billfish Foundation of Miami, Florida, has reported over 40,000 billfish tagged since its program was initiated in 1990. The Cooperative Shark Tagging Program run by NMFS has over 6,000 participants and has been responsible for tagging over 125,000 sharks. And there are other programs as well.

Anglers who intend to tag fish need to keep the well-being of the fish foremost in mind. This means following all procedures for quickly playing and landing the fish *(see: landing fish; playing fish)*, as well as following the proper procedures for catch-and-release *(see)*. Fish that will be handled during tagging will benefit from having extra water poured over them and from having a wet towel placed over their heads while they are being held. With the proper tools already available, experienced taggers can accomplish the tagging very quickly and with no harm to the fish. The pertinent information should be supplied to the appropriate organization promptly. There is a lot of satisfaction in tagging and releasing a fish for science, and even more in recapturing one or in having one that you tagged be recaptured later at some distant place.

Proper tagging does reveal recaptures, although the overall percentage of recaptured fish is quite small. Some tagged fish have been recaptured many years after their initial tagging, and great distances from their original site. Some have been recaptured only minutes after first being tagged, some tagged fish are recaptured by their original captors, and some have been recaught numerous times.

If you catch a tagged fish. Although some tags are immediately obvious on fish, some are not. You should check both sides of a fish that you catch to see whether it has a tag, and check out any growths or trailing objects. A piece of "seaweed" could be the extension of an algae-covered tag.

If you're keeping the fish, then information can be obtained at your convenience. Otherwise, you'll have to act quickly. Copy down the serial number of the tag, and record the measurements of the fish, the location, and any other information, including the program to be contacted. If you keep the fish, clip and send the tag to the appropriate program.

TAGLINE

A heavy cord fixed either to an outrigger *(see)* or to a transom cleat and connected to a fishing line to provide hooksetting tension when a fish strikes. A tagline is used to help spread out offshore trolling lures *(see: trolling lures, saltwater)* behind the boat and adjust their angle of entry into the water for better running. It is used with lures and fishing methods that do not require a dropback for striking a fish when it attacks a fast-trolled lure.

The tagline consists of a short length of heavy, no-stretch line or cord (offshore trollers use 500-pound-test braided cord) connected to a cleat or clipped to the outrigger line. The business end sports a nonrelease clip or waxed line-tie. A rubber band (No. 64 is the preferred size for 50- to 130-pound-class line) is wrapped at least five times around the fishing line, then the two end loops of the rubber band are snapped into the clip, or secured to the waxed line-ties by a quick-release loop. When a fish strikes, the rubber band stretches considerably before breaking, providing some initial give, which helps in setting the hook.

Some offshore anglers attach the tagline to the fishing line via a slipknot in the rubber band, which is easily freed by yanking the cord when changing lures. Be careful that your knot doesn't bind onto the fishing line under tension; if it does, it will usually remain attached to the line even after breaking free of the tagline when a fish strikes. As the fish is subsequently fought to the boat, the rubber band, now knotted to the fishing line, will eventually arrive at the rod's tiptop, and unless the tip-top and lower guides are oversized, won't pass through them, which could prove to be an impediment to landing the fish. You can avoid this by wrapping the rubber band around the line at least five times, then securing the two free end loops of the rubber band to the tagline. This way, when the rubber band breaks, it flies off the line.

Incidentally, a similar system can be used for trolling spoons and plugs on flatlines, in both

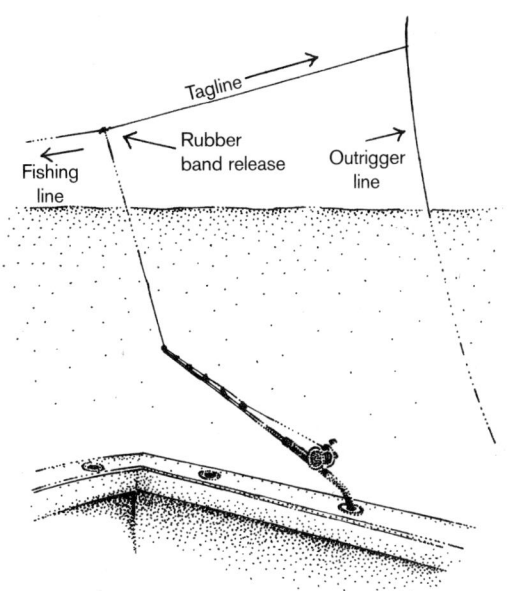

As shown, a tagline is a length of heavy cord or line between outrigger line and fishing line (or between boat and fishing line). A rubber band release, or spring tension release, is used to free the fishing line when a fish strikes the trolled lure or bait.

freshwater and saltwater, as a means of lowering the angle of line entry into the water and also as a means of helping to set the hook. Some trout, salmon, and striped bass trollers attach a heavy (200-pound) 2- to 4-foot length of monofilament or microfilament line to a transom cleat and use a standard commercial release *(see)*, with tension tightened, to hold the fishing line. This is primarily used to hold a flatlined lure in a center position in the boat wake and keep it away from lures spread to the sides.

See: **Big-Game Fishing.**

TAHITI

See: **French Polynesia.**

TAILER

Also called a tail rope or loop, a tailer is a nooselike device that slips over the fish and cinches down on the caudal peduncle for landing. It is best for fish with a stiff rather than flexible caudal peduncle.

Hand tailers are used in freshwater, primarily for Atlantic salmon. Tail ropes and mechanical tailing loops are used in saltwater, primarily for large fish, especially sharks, that are hard to subdue, and they are sometimes used in conjunction with gaffing. A tail rope is usually slid down the fishing line and headfirst over the body of a fish, then drawn tight as it nears the caudal peduncle. The mechanical loop is attached to a long pole to reach out over the gunwale, and it is slipped onto the fish tailfirst.

See: **Landing Fish.**

T

TAILING

(1) A method of landing a fish by grabbing it around the caudal peduncle, either by hand or with a tailer.

See: Landing Fish.

(2) A term used to describe the observation of a fish's fins sticking above the surface of the water. It is sometimes used to refer to large fish in saltwater that are swimming along the surface, whose dorsal and tail fins are out of the water *(see: finning)*, but it is more commonly associated with shallow water feeding by fish, especially in saltwater. A bonefish, for example, when on a shallow tidal flat, may feed on the bottom at such an angle as to leave the upper tip of its tail fin exposed. Likewise, a redfish in shallow water may also expose its upper tail fin while feeding in the shallows.

TAILRACE

The disturbed and often turbulent section of river directly below a large dam, where water from the upstream impoundment is released. This term is often used interchangeably with tailwater *(see),* which is actually the entire section of river below a dam whose flows are dependent upon dam releases. The tailrace is the section closest to the dam.

Tailraces often have varied fishing opportunities, even if one species usually dominates; catches may include a number of species. This section of water is often very good for fishing because of cooler and well-oxygenated water, an abundance of food, turbulent water conditions that are conducive to aggressive feeding, and the concentration of upstream-migrating fish, which can go no farther than the dam.

When the water is moving swiftly, which often depends on releases for power generation or flood control, fishing is likely to be prime. This is not

Turbulent water in tailraces can attract large fish; this angler is fishing the Red River at Selkirk, Manitoba.

unlike the movement of tides *(see)* in coastal rivers and their influence on fish activity.

In swift tailraces, much fishing is done from boats, since shore fishing limits effectiveness; and being situated on the bank has inherent danger when rising water levels are prevalent. Anglers in boats cast with lures or drift bait, both while anchored or while drifting. Fishing with live bait, especially shad that have been caught by dipping or using a cast net, is highly popular.

One of the often overlooked benefits of tailrace fishing is that the swift and well-oxygenated water here lends itself very well to releasing fish unharmed. This is especially true for striped bass, which are often difficult to revive and release in good condition, especially in summer months.

A drawback, however, is the extra safety precautions that must be taken in the turbulent below-dam environment. Rising water levels can sink improperly anchored boats, and extreme currents and roiling water can make boat operation very tricky.

See: Boat; Currents; Safety.

TAIL ROPE

See: Tailer.

TAILSPINNER

A small lead-bodied lure with a treble hook under its belly and a revolving spinner blade at its tail.

Tailspinners are used in freshwater fishing, primarily for largemouth bass and white bass in schooling situations, when the fish are near the surface and feeding frenziedly. These lures are aerodynamically shaped and can be cast a great distance, particularly with spinning gear and light to medium line. They're worked in a quick pump-and-go style, just under the surface in such a situation, always retrieving at a rate that keeps the blade turning.

Tailspinners can also be fished deep, in vertical jigging style, for suspended bass in deep water near some particular structure, or they can be hopped off the bottom in fishing submerged islands, rocky points, and such. Effective colors are white, silver, and gray.

TAILWATER

The entire section of river below a dam whose flows are dependent upon dam releases. A tailwater is sometimes also called a tailrace *(see),* which is actually a component of the tailwater, being the often turbulent section of river directly below a large dam, where water spews from the upstream impoundment.

Tailwaters exist wherever rivers have been impounded, and they flow for varied distances. Some flow from one reservoir to another, which may be just a short distance or a dozen or more miles. Some flow to their merger with other rivers, which may or may not be tailwaters themselves.

In North America, tailwaters offer excellent fishing opportunities for a host of species, although most species that exist in these places aren't native. Many tailwaters exist, and have the environment that they do, because natural rivers and their habitats and native species were flooded by environmentally destructive dams. Those dams primarily support hydroelectric power generation, and downstream flows are dependent on water releases, which means that the species and fishing are likewise dependent on them. In some tailwaters, erratic release schedules, meager flows, and warm water from reservoir surface discharges adversely impact the fisheries, and there have been long ongoing struggles with water regulators to achieve sustained flows of proper temperature to benefit fish and other downstream aquatic life.

In the southern United States, the most prominent tailwater species is striped bass, but significant fisheries exist in many tailwaters for trout, catfish, walleye, smallmouth bass, and white bass. In western states, trout are the primary fish, and tailwaters there provide some of the best and most popular trout fishing that is known. Many of these species, particularly trout, feed well and grow to good, if not large, sizes but don't manage natural reproduction; their populations are supported through regular plantings in the river itself or in a downstream impoundment.

The type of fishery in tailraces is dependent on the temperature of the water that is released, especially during summer, and this is a function of the thermal stratification *(see)* characteristics of the reservoir and the location of the outlet in the dam. On many large dams, the outlet portals are located at or near the bottom of the dam, and this position ensures a constant flow of cold water. This water usually has good oxygen levels for most of the year, but may have poor oxygen during summer when the cold, deep waters of the reservoir become oxygen-deficient. However, in many tailraces, the discharge of great volumes of water creates enough turbulence to highly oxygenate the water in that area. In most tailwaters, discharge levels vary annually as well as seasonally; there may be shutdown periods, and water levels may be subject to extreme fluctuations. These conditions pose good fishing opportunities when current is strong but also present boating and wading dangers. However, a generally cool or cold water temperature year-round, often without much summer and winter fluctuation, makes them fishable all season and keeps fish active all year.

Boating and fishing in the actual tailrace section of a tailwater is a bit different than through the rest of the river because of its turbulence. Farther downriver, the tailwater becomes more like a normal river, except that water temperatures usually are constant, and there are often sudden increases in

The long, shallow runs of the White River in Arkansas provide some of North America's best tailwater trout fishing.

water level. In rivers that are waded, such increases can be especially dangerous; an unobservant angler may be quickly stranded on a rock with swift and rising cold water closing in.

The methods for fishing tailwaters vary with species and the rivers. In larger, heavier flows, a lot of fishing is done from boats, often power boats, some having jet drive *(see)* motors. Fishing is also is carried out by floating in inflatable rafts, canoes, jonboats, or drift boats *(see)*. Wading is prominent also, especially by trout anglers, and occurs whenever and wherever shallow water and pools or runs can feasibly be approached by a wading angler—obviously in the smaller and shallow systems but also in the downstream reaches of larger tailwaters. Anglers who float down tailwaters often get out of their craft to fish some runs and pools.

For various species, a lot of fishing is done with bait. This includes live or cut shad or herring for stripers, assorted baits for catfish, minnows for walleye, and eggs and various processed baits for trout. Where stripers are found, live bait is best, but it usually has to be gathered, often by cast netting, and must be well cared for in proper wells. Jigs, assorted swimming plugs, jigging spoons, and bottom-bouncing bait rigs are among the mix as well.

Miles and miles of prime trout habitat exist in many tailwaters, and this opens up a range of fishing possibilities for primarily rainbow and brown trout. Bait is popular in many waters, but casting with spinners, small jigs, and small minnow plugs can be effective. Fly fishing is highly effective in many tailwater trout fisheries, and more common in western than southern rivers. The variety of food in downstream tailwaters—various types of baitfish, aquatic insects, terrestrial insects, aquatic worms, and crustaceans—means that a fly angler has a bulging vest in order to imitate everything that tailwater trout might feed upon.

For trout fishing, streamer flies are good when the water level is rising or falling, and baitfish may be a more prominent food item. The rising water will often bring fair numbers of terrestrial insects into the water, making it good for fishing with hoppers, beetles, crickets, and the like. Day in and day out fly fishing in tailwaters, however, sees the use of mayfly and caddisfly imitations, various nymphs, and a variety of flies that imitate scuds, worms, and the like.

See: Boat; Currents; Safety.

TAIMEN   *Hucho hucho taimen.*

Other names—taimen salmon, Siberian taimen.

A member of the Salmonidae family, which includes salmon and trout, taimen are closely related to *Hucho hucho,* the huchen *(see),* and one of evidently four species in the same genus. These two fish cannot be separated by conventional scientific analyses but are distinguished by virtue of Asian versus European geographical location. Taimen have become a fish of greater interest to traveling anglers in recent years but are largely unknown to most and have been caught by relatively few Europeans and even fewer Westerners. They have white, sweet-tasting meat.

Identification.   Taimen physically resemble northern pike or muskies. The body is round and elongated, and the head is flattened and has an enormous terminal mouth, which is equipped with small sharp teeth. Like huchen, taimen are specked with dark spots over the entire body, predominating on the upper portions, including the head and fins. The tail and anal fins are a crimson red. During the spawning period, most of the body becomes copper red.

Size/Age.   Taimen evidently are capable of attaining the largest maximum size of any salmonid, as befits a fish of large rivers. An 1871 Russian report noted that taimen can reach 175 pounds in the Yenisei, Pyasina, and Khatanga Rivers in Siberia. A report exists of a 231-pound specimen taken in a commercial net in the Kotui River in 1943, but the largest authenticated record is a 123-pounder, which is slightly less than a commercially caught 126-pound chinook salmon, the largest of that salmonid species. The all-tackle world record is a $92^1/_2$-pounder. They are also evidently long-lived fish, as a 65-pounder was estimated at more than 50 years of age.

Distribution.   The taimen is restricted to the Ural-Siberian-Amur drainages of Asia, most of which flow into the Arctic Ocean; it is reportedly found as far west as the Pechora River. This range is similar to that of another exotic salmonid, the lenok *(see).* The huchen, in contrast, is restricted to the Danube River drainage of Europe. The taimen and huchen ranges do not overlap and are separated by the eastern European flatland.

Habitat/Spawning behavior.   The taimen inhabits large rivers with fast currents, especially the large lower reaches and often travels into their estuaries, although it is strictly a freshwater fish. It also occurs in lakes. In spring, it ascends rivers and enters shallow creeks, spawning in May in some Russian waters.

Food and feeding habits.   As voracious feeders, taimen have a wide-ranging diet of other fish; smaller taimen, pike, salmon, and especially grayling are part of their diet. They are also reported to consume small mammals and birds. Lemmings are a staple during migratory periods, and this explains why they are attracted to mouselike offerings. They have been noted by observers to hunt in groups, and also to attract smaller fish into range through a tail-waving action that raises bottom sediment.

Angling.   Taimen inhabit remote areas that have experienced little to no sportfishing until recently, and they are of no commercial fishing interest. Both factors contribute to a general paucity of information, especially scientific reports on life history.

Taimen fishing is accomplished with large streamer flies, surface and swimming plugs, spoons, and spinners. Live baits are used by native fishermen. These offerings run to large sizes and include fish and mammals (which may be attached to rope-like line and tied to a tree overnight). The voracious taimen reportedly will strike at anything resembling wounded prey, and in the remote Mongolian reaches of their range, they are pursued with huge natural baits, flies, and lures. "Huge" is not an exaggeration, as fly anglers have discovered that the biggest streamers primarily attracted only smaller fish.

TAKE
A strike by a fish.

TANK
A small pond, often called a stock tank, possibly used for watering farm animals.

TANZANIA
The land of Mount Kilimanjaro, Zanzibar, Ngorongoro Crater, and the Serengeti Plain, Tanzania is mostly associated with great wildlife viewing and stupendous natural beauty. Four times the size of Great Britain, its Selous Game Reserve is one of the last great wildernesses on earth, and its 938,000 square kilometers contains a significant part of the Great Rift Valley.

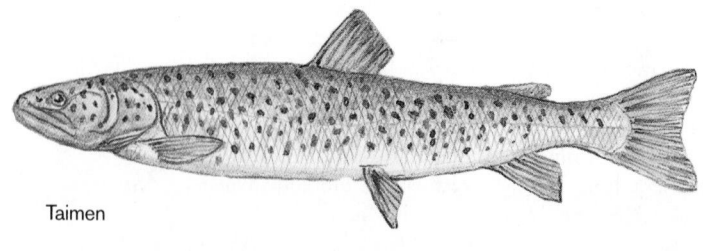

Taimen

International visitors to Tanzania tend to focus on Africa's highest mountain and tremendous game, leaving sportfishing opportunities lightly explored. This is especially so in freshwater, even though Tanzania possesses several rivers and borders on Africa's three largest lakes. Tanzania shares Lake Victoria with Kenya (see) and Uganda (see), Lake Tanganyika with the Democratic Republic of the Congo (formerly Zaire) and a small portion of Zambia (see), and Lake Malaŵi (also known as Nyasa) with Malaŵi (see). Its several large rivers flow eastward into the Indian Ocean, and its watershed feeds the great Nile, Zambezi, and Congo Rivers, all of which course through other countries.

In Tanzania, the focus is on saltwater angling along the country's 800 kilometers of coastline, which borders the Indian Ocean between Kenya to the north and Mozambique to the south. This coastline embraces the romantic islands of the Zanzibar archipelago, and the best sportfishing facilities are strategically situated in this region.

North of the capital city of Dar es Salaam, Zanzibar Island is separated from the mainland by a 40-kilometer-wide channel. Covering an area of more than 2,000 square kilometers, Zanzibar is a large coral island off the coast of Africa. Lying to its north and close to Kenya is 1,600-square-kilometer Pemba, and to the south of Dar es Salaam is Mafia. The banks to the east of Dar es Salaam and south of Zanzibar are known for excellent fishing. Still, many of the fishing opportunities in this area are hard to access and are lightly explored, but their potential is likely quite good. The most prevalent gamefish are marlin, sailfish, yellowfin tuna, shark, wahoo, dolphin, trevally, and rainbow runners.

Billfish are present year-round, but the two prime periods are during the Kusi and Kaskasi monsoon seasons. Kusi is the southeast monsoon, occurring from May through September. From August into September is the best period during Kusi for billfish, as blue marlin, black marlin, and sailfish are available in good numbers. Large schools of yellowfin tuna and wahoo dominate the action in October and November.

Kaskasi, the northeast monsoon, blows from November through March. This is the primary billfish season of the year. Striped marlin are present in vast numbers, black marlin move close to shore, and sailfish are most abundant. A grand slam of these species is a strong possibility during Kaskasi.

The billfish here have not been very large, but their plentiful numbers make the region a good light-tackle destination. Larger fish are in the area, but their precise locations have yet to be discovered.

Sportfishing in this region is primarily conducted out of two fishing lodges, one on Zanzibar Island and the other at Pangani Bay, about 200 miles north of the capital city. Both are located close to the most productive hotspots.

Situated high on a cliff overlooking Pangani Bay, Mashado Lodge has a stunning panorama across the sparkling blue waters of the Indian Ocean. Opened in 1996, and offering the comfort and feeling of an East African plantation home, Mashado provides boat access to the nearby Maziwi sandbank and reef, and to Pemba Channel and the northern reaches of Zanzibar Channel.

On the reef, anglers cast with spinning and fly tackle, surrounded by an exotic and private sand island. Big-game enthusiasts ply the channels for black marlin, blue marlin, striped marlin, swordfish, sailfish, sharks, wahoo, and yellowfin tuna, among other species. Anglers have access to modern equipment on large offshore charter boats, and inshore and river fishing are also offered.

Northwest of Pemba, Ras Kigomasha (Cape Kigomasha) and Pemba Channel are well-known gamefishing areas favored by Kenyan anglers since 1960. Most of Africa's billfish records are registered in this area, especially for striped marlin. Sailfish, giant trevally, wahoo, and yellowfin tuna are all excellent here. Pemba's best fishing is on its east and south, where swells and current action are prevalent. As one nears the reef, the bottom slopes quickly in deep water.

Zanzibar Island offers the only hotel accommodations on the archipelago; some of these are rated with four and five stars and provide other amenities and attractions. This island has good gamefishing opportunity, especially on the northeast at Leven Bank, Mnemba Atoll, and the south side of Pemba Channel. South of Zanzibar, at Ras (Cape) Makunduki and Kizimkazi, the fishing is also good. The Zanzibar Channel, which flows between the island and the mainland, is a known spot for sailfish, small tuna, and dorado—especially at Bumbwini, Bosa, and north of Tumbatu Island.

Zanzibar Fishing Club, situated on the island, can be reached from Dar es Salaam or Nairobi, Kenya, via a brief flight. The marine habitat around Zanzibar hosts many fascinating creatures, including the rare green turtle, and the offshore species caught here are the same as those previously mentioned. The club has one charter boat for fishing the nearly untouched waters of the Zanzibar Channel on the west and the dropoff shelf of the Indian Ocean on the east.

Anglers enjoy sensational gamefishing around submerged Latham Bank, which is 13 miles long and 6 miles wide. It is situated in the middle of the Indian Ocean, about 40 miles east of Dar es Salaam and 35 miles south of Zanzibar. The top of the bank rises out of the water only a few meters and drops off to 300 meters and more. All of the gamefish that populate the Indian Ocean are present here in big numbers and good sizes. In a good day of fishing many tuna are caught, and three to five marlin strikes are routine. Great white, mako, and hammerhead sharks are also present.

When lake sturgeon were abundant, their skin was sometimes tanned for leather, and their swim bladders were used as a component for pottery cement and waterproofing.

TAPER

The shape and diameter of a fly line, and a fishing rod blank, throughout its length.
See: Flycasting Tackle; Rod, Fishing.

TAPERED LEADER

The nylon monofilament line, tapering to a fine diameter and lighter strength, that connects fly line and artificial fly.
See: Flycasting Tackle; Leader.

TARPON   *Megalops atlanticus.*

Other names—silver king, Atlantic tarpon, cuffum; French: *tarpon argenté;* Italian: *tarpone;* Portuguese: *camurupi, peixe-prata-do-atlântico, tarpao;* Spanish: *pez lagarto.*

The largest member of the small Elopidae family, the tarpon is one of the world's premier saltwater gamefish. A species of warm tropical waters, it would probably be recognized as the greatest gamefish in the world if it also occurred in temperate waters and was available to all anglers. It presents the foremost qualities that anglers seek in sportfish—it is very large, very strong, challenging to hook and land, often a target of sight fishing and casting in shallow water, and a spectacular leaper when hooked.

Also known as Atlantic tarpon, this species is sometimes scientifically identified as *Tarpon atlanticus;* it is a relative of ladyfish *(see)* and of a similar but much smaller species, the Indo-Pacific tarpon *(Megalops cyprinoides),* also known as oxeye tarpon or oxeye herring. In prehistoric times, there were many more species of tarpon; today, there are just these two.

A hardy giant that can survive in a variety of habitats and salinities, the tarpon can even gulp air for extended periods when not enough oxygen is present in the water to sustain it. Despite its popularity among anglers, many aspects of this extremely long-lived fish's life cycle and behavior remain a mystery. This especially includes its migratory habits.

Tarpon are edible but not rated high as table fare, although there is some commercial interest in them in parts of their range outside North America. In Florida, where tarpon sportfishing is a popular business, the sale of this species has been prohibited since it was declared a gamefish in 1953. There, a permit must be purchased to legally kill and keep a tarpon. Fewer than 100 tarpon a year meet this fate, and the fishery is almost entirely a catch-and-release endeavor.

Identification.   The tarpon's body is compressed and covered with extremely large platelike scales and a deeply forked tail fin. Its back is greenish or bluish, varying in darkness from silvery to almost black. The sides and belly are brilliant silver. Underwater, they appear to shimmer like huge gray ghosts as they swim sedately by. This appearance, along with their impressive size, is likely responsible for their nickname, "silver king." Inland, brackish-water tarpon frequently have a golden or brownish color because of tannic acid.

The huge mouth of the tarpon has a projecting, upturned lower law that contains an elongated bony plate. A single, short dorsal fin originates just behind the origin of the pelvic fin and consists of 12 to 16 soft rays (no spines), the last of which is greatly elongated. The anal fin has 19 to 25 soft rays. The lateral line is straight, even along the anterior portion, with a scale count of 41 to 48.

Size/Age.   Most angler-caught Atlantic tarpon are in the range of 40 to 50 pounds, but many from 60 to 100 pounds are encountered. Fish exceeding 150 pounds are rare in the western Atlantic, but western Africa, especially Sierra Leone and Gabon, have consistently produced heavyweights exceeding 200 pounds, including a reported 300-pounder that is believed to be the maximum size of the species, as is a length of 8 feet. The all-tackle world record is shared by two 283-pound fish, one caught in 1956 at Lake Maracaibo, Venezuela, and the

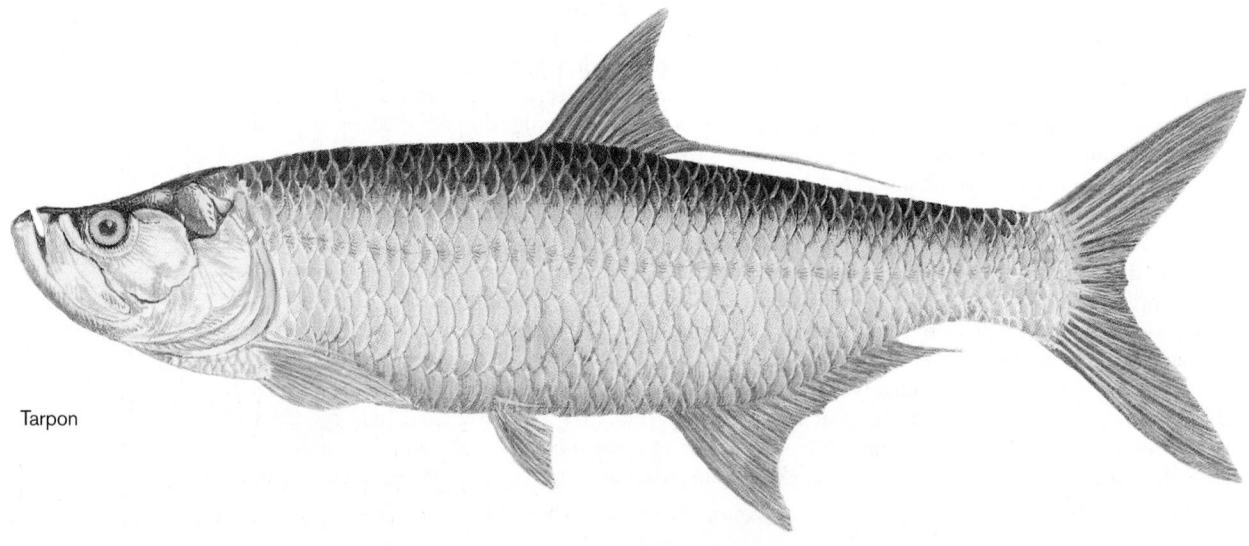

Tarpon

other in 1991 at Sherbro Island, Sierra Leone. The Florida record for tarpon caught with conventional tackle was a 243-pounder from Key West in 1975.

Some Atlantic tarpon live as long as 55 years. Most of the tarpon caught in the Florida fishery are 15 to 30 years old.

The Indo-Pacific tarpon is reported to attain a maximum length of 60 inches and a weight of between 32 and 40 pounds.

Distribution.   Because tarpon are sensitive to cold water, their range is generally limited to temperate climates. Atlantic tarpon have been reported as far north as Nova Scotia and also off the coast of Ireland, although they prefer tropical and subtropical waters. In the eastern Atlantic, they are most common off western Africa, from Mauritania to Angola. In the western Atlantic, they are most common from Virginia to central Brazil and throughout the Caribbean Sea and Gulf of Mexico. Atlantic tarpon from the western Atlantic have also emigrated through the Panama Canal and become established in the eastern Pacific; large specimens have been caught along the western Panamanian coast and in the vicinity of some rivers.

Although scientists believe the western Atlantic stock is genetically uniform, they have observed regional differences in behavior and size. Tarpon in Costa Rica, for example, are generally smaller than Florida tarpon, and Costa Rica tarpon spawn throughout the year rather than seasonally as Florida tarpon do.

The Indo-Pacific tarpon occurs in the western Indian Ocean from the Red Sea to South Africa and eastward to the Society Islands, northward to southern Korea, and southward to the Arafura Sea and New South Wales. It is restricted to high islands in Micronesia, and reported as far inland as the lower Shire River in Malawi and the Save-Runde junction in Zimbabwe.

Habitat.   Tarpon are most abundant in estuaries and coastal waters but also occur in freshwater lakes and rivers, offshore marine waters, and occasionally on coral reefs. Adults often patrol the coral reefs of the Florida Keys. In Costa Rica and Nicaragua, anglers frequently catch tarpon in freshwater lakes and rivers miles from the coast. Although tarpon do migrate, little is known about the frequency or extent of their travels. Tarpon captured in Florida have later been recaptured as far west as Louisiana and as far north as South Carolina.

Life history/Behavior.   In May and June, Atlantic tarpon in the western Atlantic begin gathering together in staging areas near the coast in preparation for the journey to their offshore spawning grounds. Here, schools of tarpon may be observed swimming in a circular, rotating motion. This behavior, known as a "daisy chain," may be prenuptial activity that prepares the fish for spawning. The actual exodus to the offshore spawning areas is probably triggered by lunar phases and tides.

During each spawning season, each female produces from 4.5 to 20.7 million eggs. The heavier the fish, the more eggs she is likely to shed. Scientists have never observed tarpon spawning or collected their fertilized eggs. Although no one knows exactly where tarpon spawn, tarpon larvae only a few days old have been collected as far as 125 miles offshore in the Gulf of Mexico. Spawning in Florida occurs mainly in May, June, and July.

The eggs hatch into larvae called leptocephali. These bizarre-looking creatures have a transparent, ribbonlike body and slender, fanglike teeth. The leptocephali drift with the currents toward the shore, reaching estuarine areas within about 30 days. Storms may assist in pushing the larvae toward their inshore nurseries.

By the time the larvae reach these inshore areas, they are about an inch long. At this point, they begin an amazing transformation in which they lose their teeth and begin shrinking in length, winding up as miniature versions of the behemoths they will eventually become. Scientists don't know how long this metamorphosis takes. Tarpon, bonefish (see), ladyfish, and eels (see) all undergo a similar leptocephalus stage, but the first three fish all have forked tails even at the larval state, whereas the eel does not.

Juvenile tarpon make their way into marshes and mangrove swamps, where they will spend the remainder of the first year of their life, often showing a preference for stagnant pools. They grow rapidly and are roughly a foot long within one to two years. Females usually grow more quickly and are larger than males, and both reach sexual maturity around age 10. The sex of a tarpon cannot reliably be determined until their second or third year and then only by an internal examination.

One particularly remarkable facet of tarpon physiology is the fish's ability to breathe both underwater and out of the water. When dissolved oxygen levels in the water are adequate, tarpon breathe like most fish, through their gills. When oxygen levels are depleted, however, they can also breathe by gulping air, which is then passed along to their highly specialized swim bladder. The swim bladder functions as an accessory lung and even resembles that organ, with its spongy, highly vascular tissue. The swim bladder can also be filled with air as needed to help the fish maintain its desired depth in the water. Scientists believe the tarpon's ability to breathe air is a nifty adaptation that allows it to survive in the stagnant, oxygen-poor pools and ditches it frequents.

Although tarpon can tolerate water of various salinities, they are vulnerable to cold snaps and become stressed when water temperatures fall below 55°F. Although adults can often seek refuge from the cold in deep holes and channels, young fish are less able to escape cold waters.

Food.   Tarpon often travel in schools with other tarpon and are opportunistic eaters that feed on a variety of fish and crabs.

T

A tarpon clears the surface near Sugarloaf Key, Florida.

Angling. The tarpon's powerful leaps, sometimes up to 10 feet out of the water, and bone-jarring bursts of speed test the skill and fortitude of even the most experienced angler. The nature of their high and often frequent jumps is such that many anglers are happy simply to get a few jumps out of a tarpon before it shakes the hook.

The better fishing is in spring and fall, but they are caught in all months in some locales. Prominent fishing sites include rivers, bays, lagoons, shallow flats, passes between islands, mangrove-lined banks, and the like. Small, or "baby" tarpon, those up to 20 pounds or so, are usually located in estuaries and river mouths, even considerable distances up fresh-water rivers and in sloughs and canals.

Fishing methods include drifting or stillfishing with live mullet, pinfish, crabs, shrimp, or other natural baits, or casting or trolling with spoons, plugs, or other artificial lures and flies. Trolling is generally the least-practiced method; casting is generally most favored, as it involves stalking, spotting, and skillful bait or lure presentations. It may not be appropriate, however, when the fish are deep or unaggressive. The best fishing can be at night when tarpon are feeding.

When casting, anglers usually sight-fish for tarpon, staking out a shallow-draft boat near a channel or hole or moving along shallow grassy flats, usually by poling. They wait for tarpon to come within casting range, or try to spot cruising fish and then move to intercept them. A variety of plugs are cast for

tarpon, with shallow runners fished in a whip or jerky pull-pause retrieve being most effective. Surface plugs are also fished, and flycasters mainly employ large streamers. Lures and flies are cast just ahead of a passing fish. Often, casters get only one chance at a cruising fish or school, and poor placement of the offering can spook the fish. Sometimes tarpon strike readily, even turning and moving a short distance to take a lure or fly, although it is usually necessary to have the item right in front of the fish, in its path of travel. Tarpon seldom take a lure or bait with great authority, however. Sometimes they are quite finicky and ignore even a perfect presentation.

Live-bait fishing occurs with anglers drifting or anchored and stillfishing with a float. Such live baits as mullet, pinfish, crabs, and shrimp are used, usually in deep areas or in channels where the fish cruise through. Some anglers jig in deep-water holes and passes; others slow-troll along the edges of flats near deep water with big spoons, plugs, and feathers. Although tarpon appear to be sensitive to noise and boat traffic and may become skittish and reluctant to take baits when the waters are crowded with boaters, tarpon are unlike many other fish in that they are frequently found in highly urbanized areas with poor water quality.

Sharp hooks are an absolute necessity for tarpon fishing; these silvery fish have a tough, bony mouth that is hard to penetrate, and it is usually necessary to set the hook firmly several times in order to make a good connection. Even so, many tarpon are lost during one of their many jumps. They also have a tough gill plate that can cut the fishing line readily, so strong leaders are routinely used.

Standard tackle is a 7-foot baitcasting rod and reel filled with at least 200 yards of between 12- and 20-pound line. The heavier strengths are used most often, especially where landing large fish is a possibility. Flycasters use a 9- to 10-foot rod with plenty of backbone for 10- to 12-weight line, and a fly reel that has plenty of strong backing line.

Tarpon have to be thoroughly played out before being landed, although they revive well for release. Many are lip-gaffed for hook removal, a process that doesn't cause harm if done properly. Fish that are close to the boat and still green can be very dangerous, however. Some have leaped into a boat when the gaff was placed into the lower jaw; some have pulled the gaffer overboard; and some have jumped into the boat without being touched. A big, heavy fish with a wildly flapping body and tail, not to mention hooks and other paraphernalia lying about, can be enormously dangerous inside a boat, so it behooves anglers to be careful and observant at all times.
See: Flats Fishing.

TAUTOG   *Tautoga onitis.*
Other names—blackfish, tog, Molly George, chub, oysterfish; French: *tautogue noir.*

Primarily known as blackfish, the tautog is a member of the Labridae family of wrasses *(see),* which includes some 500 species in 57 known genera. It one of the largest families of fish. The tautog is not a fast or extremely active species, but it puts up a stubborn fight, and its flesh is edible and of good quality. These factors, plus year-round availability and good size, make it a popular inshore sportfish.

Identification.   Blunt-nosed and thick-lipped, the tautog has a high forehead and a heavy body. It is brownish on the back and sides and lighter below, and it has blackish mottling over the entire body. Tautogs are darker over a dark bottom background and lighter over a light bottom background. The belly and chin are white or gray, and there may be spots on the chin. Females develop a white saddle down the middle of each side during spawning. The caudal fin is rounded on the corners and squared across the tip; the soft-rayed dorsal and anal fins are rounded.

The first dorsal fin has 16 to 17 spines of almost equal length. The short second dorsal fin consists of 10 somewhat longer soft rays. The anal fin has 3 spines and 7 to 8 soft rays. There is a detached area of small scales behind and beneath the eye, but none on the opercle. The lateral line is arched more or less following the contour of the back and has a scale count of 69 to 73. There are 9 gill rakers on the first branchial arch, 3 on the upper limb, and 6 on the lower limb. A number of small teeth are present along the sides of the jaws, and there are two to three large canine teeth in the tips.

Size.   This fish averages 3 pounds or less in weight. Specimens weighing 6 to 10 pounds are caught with some regularity, however, and the all-tackle world record is a Virginia fish that was caught in 1988 and weighed 24 pounds.

Distribution.   The tautog occurs in the western Atlantic from Nova Scotia to South Carolina, and the greatest abundance is between Cape Cod, Massachusetts, and Delaware Bay. It overlaps in range with the smaller and more northerly relative, the cunner *(see).*

Habitat.   Tautog are known to move in and out of bays or inshore and offshore according to the water temperature, but they do not make extensive

T

Tautog

migrations up and down the coast. Preferred environs include shallow waters over rocky bottoms, shell beds, inshore wrecks, and the like, which it often inhabits year-round.

Food and feeding habits. The diet of tautog is mainly mollusks and crustaceans, with blue mussels being especially favored where abundant. It uses the flat, rounded, stout teeth located in the rear of its mouth to crush the shells of mollusks or crustaceans. The front teeth do the picking.

Angling. The place to look for tautog is around rocks. These fish are almost always found on a rocky bottom, and on or within a foot of it. Key areas include reefs, jetties, breakwaters, and boulders. The more extensive the area, the better. Shellfish beds are a popular locale, too. The edges of these structures are often the focal points, and early morning is a particularly good time of day to catch these fish.

Tautog don't school as such, but they will cluster in small areas. It's important to note the location of fish when they're caught, so you can place your baits back in the same spot. Being off a few feet may result in not catching anymore fish.

As with most bottom feeders, it is common to use baits with tautog. Crabs, mussels, and soft-shelled clams are mostly preferred, although worms are sometimes used. Tautog normally feed on hard-shelled food, and they have tough mouths for crushing it. Well-sharpened hooks are necessary as a result, and a quick, hard hooksetting action is also needed. A two-hook rig is commonly fished.

Tautog are stubborn battlers that often dive for rocks when they have been hooked. Although the average fish weighs only a few pounds, fairly stout boat rods are used to keep them from digging in behind a rock. That tackle is also employed because heavy weights are used to get and keep baits down near bottom, sometimes in heavy current. Tautog anglers lose a lot of terminal tackle, however, hanging it in the rocks, but that is to be expected.

These fish seldom exist in more than 60 feet of water, and they may remain much shallower and close to shore if the right bottom terrain is available. In shallow water, they are wary fish, and keeping the bait away from the boat, instead of directly below it, is a better presentation. They also do more nibbling than hard striking in shallow water, and you may have to give them a little time to move off with the bait before setting the hook. Sometimes, however, tautog move in with the incoming tide to feed on mussels that are normally above the low-tide level.
See: Inshore Fishing; Jetty Fishing.

TAXIDERMY

The field of taxidermy is probably one of the least understood aspects of outdoor recreation and one that is rarely discussed in popular periodicals, despite the fact that thousands of people every year hire the services of a professional taxidermist, and many people, especially youngsters, are taxidermy hobbyists. Fish taxidermy is more difficult than game and bird taxidermy, in part because it requires different methods, not to mention painting, and the field has greatly advanced in the past three decades because of new processes and changing public interests.

History

There is no clear record of when the practice of taxidermy began. The sixteenth century is the earliest period with records of animals preserved in a lifelike manner. Some writings on the history of taxidermy incorrectly associate the embalming of animals by ancient Egyptians as one of the earliest records of taxidermy. Embalming and taxidermy are two different techniques. Embalming refers to the preservation of skin and flesh with chemicals and/or herbs to protect it from decay. The Egyptians did this because of religious beliefs (they felt the soul would one day return to the body), not because of aesthetics and beauty. Embalming is not an appropriate method for longtime preservation of animals in a lifelike form.

Technically, taxidermy is the arrangement of a preserved or tanned skin over a sculpted form. The purpose of taxidermy is to reproduce the anatomy, attitude, and expressions of animals as they appear in life. However, there are many variations as to how taxidermy is performed, and this term, and the field, have become broader with time.

The first publication to offer information on fish taxidermy was a 1752 French manual by M. B. Stollas, *Instructions on the Manner of Preparing Objects of Natural History.* The main subject was birds, but it established the fact that fish taxidermy was being performed at that time.

The methods used to mount fish from the mid-1700s until 1900 were very inadequate. Most taxidermists employed a stuffing technique that made it difficult to portray anatomy correctly. It was during this early period of taxidermy when people began to refer to works of taxidermy as "stuffed" animals. In most cases, the term was appropriate a hundred years ago, but today it is very rare for a stuffing technique to be used. A more appropriate, modern term is "mounted," and modern works of taxidermy are referred to as mounts.

During those early days, it was not uncommon for natural oils to ooze from a mount because of improper degreasing. Fins were weak and fragile, shrinkage around the head and fin bases distorted the anatomy, and proper paints for restoring colors were lacking. Fish were much more difficult to work with than mammals and birds, so most people avoided them; thus, few advancements were made in fish taxidermy.

It was not until the early 1900s, with the increasing popularity of natural history museums, that fish taxidermy began to catch up with progress in mammal and bird taxidermy. It was museum curators, not commercial taxidermists, who found a better way than stuffing to prepare each animal in museum exhibits for longevity and a natural, lifelike appearance.

Several leading natural history museums had already begun reproducing reptiles for exhibits, using new, plasticlike or synthetic materials that were being developed, notably, celluloid acetate. The practice was soon applied to fish, and a new era for fish taxidermy began. The reproduction method is not true to the Greek derivations of the word "taxidermy," which comes from *taxi*, meaning movement, and *dermy*, meaning skin. There is no movement of the skin in the reproduction process. However, even though the skin is not removed and rearranged over a form or filled and reshaped, the reproduction process for fish is an accepted taxidermy procedure.

One of the early pioneers of reptile and fish reproductions was Leon L. Walters of the Field Museum of Natural History in Chicago, Illinois. In 1925, the Field Museum published Walters' manuscript, *New Uses of Celluloid and Similar Materials Used in Taxidermy.* This manuscript is considered by many to be one of the important turning points leading to the modern era of taxidermy.

An even earlier publication (1894), *Methods in the Art of Taxidermy,* by Oliver Davie, cited a brief mention of reproducing fish. It stated, "Stuffed fishes are not always a triumphant success. In many cases, it is better to cast them in plaster and paint them." This 360-page book was considered at that time to be the most complete book ever published on taxidermy. The method it promoted for mounting fish was the sawdust-fill method, which is still considered an adequate method for panfish such as bluegills and redear sunfish.

Museum taxidermists proved that reproduction processes were more permanent and exact processes for lifelike renderings of most saltwater fish and many freshwater species. Nonetheless, commercial taxidermists stayed with skin-mounting processes for virtually all fish. The main reason for this was that anglers wanted their real fish hanging on their walls, not copies of what resembled their prized trophies. Another reason was the extra time required to individually custom-cast and reproduce each fish. This lengthy process required a higher price, almost triple the cost of a skin mount. In museums, higher price was not a deterrent.

To avoid confusion, it must be noted that making reproductions is not the answer for all fish species, from a purely academic point of view. Many freshwater species of fish are very adaptable to skin mounting. Some of the popular fish acceptable for skin mounts are largemouth and smallmouth bass, walleye, crappie, and most members of the sunfish family. Trout and salmon are also skin-mount candidates, but in modern taxidermy a combination of skin and reproduction parts mounted on artificial bodies is the most popular method used for these species.

In the early 1900s, many improvements were still needed to produce skin mounts with a lifelike appearance and permanency. However, taxidermists continued to use skin-mounting methods in futile attempts at preserving fish trophies for their customers. After several decades of receiving and seeing aging, poor fish taxidermy, people began putting their prize catches in the frying pan more often than bringing them to taxidermists.

By the 1940s, the basic methods for skin mounting and reproducing fish had been further developed, but the refinements of these processes had a long way to go. This was especially true in smaller, commercial taxidermy shops. Taxidermy was a very secretive profession in the first half of the twentieth century. After museums completed their natural history exhibits, highly trained and knowledgeable museum taxidermists started their own studios or went to work for a few large, established taxidermy studios. Their wealth of new, proven techniques would rarely be shared with the smaller commercial shops, which were, for the most part, still using the techniques described by Davie in 1894.

It was not until the 1960s and early 1970s that advancements began to take place on an industry-wide basis. Taxidermy trade publications started, as did state and national associations, and this promoted sharing ideas and new developments. Taxidermy supply companies formed research departments and expanded their search for new products. Seminars and competitions offered incentives and stirred the imagination of gifted artists, who are today producing commercial fish taxidermy that equals or surpasses the best museum work of the previous 60 years. The process of taxidermy, which for many years was practiced more as a craft, now incorporates innovative compositions, design, accuracy, and permanency, and can truly be called an art. Today, fish taxidermy is alive and well, and people are having their trophies mounted and re-created in record numbers.

Creative displays are increasingly popular; this largemouth bass spawning scene by noted taxidermist Ron Kelly uses replicas.

T

Skin Mounts vs. Cast Reproductions

Skin mounting is the most popular means of preserving fish. With modern taxidermy techniques, skin mounts of the highest quality can be produced from many fish. Some fish are poor candidates for skin mounts, however, because of their structure and chemical makeup. And others that would be good candidates for skin mounting legally cannot be kept or are voluntarily released. Additionally, in certain instances, transportation and/or storage may be a problem. In these cases, a skin mount is not an option, so a reproduction is done.

It is faster and easier for a taxidermist to complete a realistic skin mount than to make a reproduction. First of all, a taxidermist is working with a real skin. Even though this real skin will lose its colors as the skin dries, the natural markings of the fish will remain and can be used as patterns when painting the fish. The natural teeth, gills, and fins of a real fish add to the realism of a skin mount. The same holds true when the real scales are retained and the real inner mouth details remain as part of the mount. Because a skin mount takes less time and is easier to do than a reproduction, the cost will be less.

A reproduction is much like a blank canvas, with no patterns or natural markings to follow when painting. Without these natural markings to follow, it will take more time and skill for a taxidermist to realistically paint a fish. Some taxidermists can produce outstanding paint jobs on skin mounts, yet lack the artistic ability to realistically paint a blank fish reproduction. This is one reason some completed fish reproductions look fake. Most fish have variations of color tones and markings on each scale, and there are hundreds of scales on each fish. Painting techniques can reproduce this natural appearance, but many hours of practice and a thorough knowledge of paints and their properties are needed.

Many fish blanks available to taxidermists are molded in action positions, but with the gill covers closed. Since most fish in action have open gill covers with the gills exposed, even more work is required to achieve a realistic-looking reproduction.

Some fish species lend themselves to quality skin mounts more than others. Most warmwater fish such as bass, crappie, walleye, and many smaller panfish are ideal candidates for skin mounts. Coldwater species such as trout, whitefish, and charr, can also be successfully skin mounted but are more difficult and time-consuming to skin mount than the warmwater fish mentioned. Trout and charr are oily and have more delicate skins and fleshier heads, which have a high degree of shrinkage after drying. This shrinkage requires more work and time for a taxidermist to repair. Many taxidermists prefer to skin-mount the bodies of trout and charr and use reproduction heads in place of the real heads. In comparing the same size warmwater and coldwater fish, coldwater fish, on the average, will cost more to mount than warmwater fish.

Salmon and trout over 12 pounds are more difficult to mount and offer more problems when it comes to producing skin mounts that will hold up. The reason is the older (and bigger) these fish become, the higher the oil content of the skin. A skilled, professional taxidermist can produce a quality mount on these larger coldwater fish, but do not be surprised if a taxidermist recommends a reproduction.

Freshwater catfish are extremely poor candidates for skin mounting. A taxidermist who accepts one for a skin mount is asking for trouble. Reproductions are the only way to go for this family of fish.

The majority of saltwater fish are considered reproduction candidates. There are some exceptions, and there is one marine studio that still offers skin mounts on fish such as marlin and sailfish. This studio developed special methods many years ago when reproductions were a taboo subject with many commercial taxidermists. Even after fiberglass reproductions became the standard for most of the big coastal marine studios, this studio continued to be competitive and financially successful with its process.

The process was simple. Various sizes of hollow, molded paper forms (mannikins) were made for the many varieties of fish they accepted. As an example, a marlin form would have the body and head shape, but no tail, fins, or bill. The skin on each side of the real fish was removed separately from the fins, tail, and bill. The skin went through a secret degreasing and tanning formula and, when cured, was glued to the sides of the artificial mannikin. The bill, tail, and fins were degreased and reattached to the artificial form. Once the finishing work was completed, the fish was painted in the conventional manner.

Even though longevity has always been a problem with large marine species that are skin-mounted, this company has proven their process as one of the best. Nonetheless, specialists in saltwater marine taxidermy contend that fiberglass reproductions are the only viable means of properly displaying the beauty and action of big, blue-water gamefish.

Some saltwater fish that can be skin-mounted are the coastal species such as red drum, spotted seatrout, and sheepshead. For deep-water or bottom-dwelling fish like red snappers and groupers, reproductions are again the best alternatives.

Opinions differ on which fish are acceptable for skin mounts and which should be reproduced. If you select an established taxidermist with a reputation for quality work, it is best to go by his or her recommendation. The most important consideration should be the quality and realistic appearance of the finished work. After all, you have your trophies mounted, or in some cases reproduced, to admire and to beautify your home. How they were done is incidental if the results are beautiful.

Fish Reproductions and Replicas

In taxidermy, the terms "reproduction" and "replica" are both used when referring to any fish that are not skin mounts. Taxidermists also use the term "fish blanks." A fish reproduction is a cast copy of a real fish. A mold is made from a real fish. This mold is called the negative. From the negative, a positive is made by using any of a variety of plastic resin materials. The most common materials used for making reproductions are casting resins with fiberglass reinforcement. To have a reproduction made of an actual fish, the fish must be supplied in good condition to a taxidermist. Custom reproductions of an actual fish will be more expensive because of the molding process that must take place before the reproduction can be made.

The alternative is to request a reproduction positive of the same species that closely matches the size. These matching reproductions are made from molds already available to taxidermists; thus, they are less expensive than having a particular fish custom-reproduced. Using reproduction copies for many offshore saltwater species has been an option for years. Today this option is also becoming a popular practice for freshwater trophy fish. The catch-and-release practice established in many leading freshwater lakes has brought a new demand for freshwater fish reproductions. The big difference being noticed with freshwater reproductions is improved mold-making, giving even more realistic reproductions, and the capabilities of customizing the reproductions in more exact sizes. First of all, freshwater fish are much smaller specimens to work with than larger saltwater billfish. This smaller size has allowed taxidermists to use flexible mold-making materials and two-part epoxy resins that pick up exceptionally greater details than the traditional fiberglass and resins. These highly developed epoxies are also flexible and transparent, which, more than ever before, adds more realism and an appearance of fleshy depth to the painting.

Today, the term "replica" in taxidermy usually means a customized reproduction. Some taxidermists may describe an unaltered reproduction as a replica, but replica usually means an altered version of a reproduction to more closely match the particular measurements of a fish. A fish replica can also be a sculpted or carved likeness of a particular fish, which is not really the work of a taxidermist, although some excellent taxidermists have become outstanding fish carvers *(see: fish carving)*. Understandably, custom-made sculptures or carved wood replicas of a particular fish are extremely expensive. For this reason, it is more common and less expensive to have a replica custom-made from reproductions of the species of fish you have caught.

Another means of re-creating a trophy fish is with a painting, and there are traditional canvas artists who do this. These paintings demand rather healthy prices, especially if a recognized artist is commissioned for the job. Original paintings that

Taxidermists compare a 20-pound peacock bass in the flesh and in unpainted fiberglass form.

replicate the dimensions, colors of the fish, and story of the catch can range from $800 to $2,500. This would certainly be a collector's item, but it still gives only a two-dimensional effect as compared with a three-dimensional fish reproduction.

Artificial fish reproductions are here to stay; they've been increasing in popularity and will be playing a bigger role in fish taxidermy in the future. Catch-and-release *(see)* is the main reason for this increase. Voluntary release of fish, even trophy specimens, has become very popular and an accepted practice by many fishing clubs and individuals. In some places, certain fish cannot be kept no matter what size they are. Also, some people find it politically correct to have a reproduction or replica, especially if the original fish was released, instead of the skin-mounted original.

Other reasons may enter into the decision to choose a replica over a skin mount. The difficulty of properly transporting the fish when long distance travel is involved makes replicas a logical choice; this is especially true for anglers who travel to northernmost Canada and to South America, where a lot of travel time is involved, and transporting fish in a frozen state is difficult (and maybe impossible or illegal). The popularity of fishing for peacock bass in South America, for example, has made some excellent lines of peacock bass reproductions available to taxidermists.

For anglers who caught that special fish in their youth but could not afford to mount their trophies at the time, replicas become a nice way to commemorate youthful achievements. Also, old trophy mounts that were not up to par or have been damaged beyond repair are being replaced with realistic reproductions.

Skin Mounts

Skinning a fish for the purpose of mounting it is no easy task. Special care must be taken to prevent scale loss and to avoid cutting through the skin; there are no feathers or fur to cover mistakes. Each fin must be cut free from the body without tearing the skin, and the head must be detached with the gills in place and throat skin remaining. Once the body is removed, the tedious work remains of scraping flesh from the fragile skin, removing flesh and excess bone from the fin bases, and cleaning the cheeks and skull. All of these processes are vitally important in order to eliminate decay and shrinkage during the drying process.

Fish skins are not tanned like mammal skins. Some taxidermists will soak fish skins in a mild pickle (an acidic preserving solution) and degreaser. A full pickling and/or tanning process, like that used on mammal skins, will produce a very rubbery fish skin that cannot be mounted. Different fish will also require different treatments. This is especially true for skin-degreasing procedures. If this important process is not properly completed, a mounted fish can begin to leach grease from its skin anywhere from 1 to 10 years later, destroying the appearance of the mount.

The filler method and the artificial fish body method are two primary means of skin mounting fish, and there are many variations of both. The filler method is a holdover from the early days of taxidermy, and, until about 1980, it was very popular. It has declined in popularity with the emergence of accurate and fairly inexpensive artificial fish bodies made from polyurethane plastic. Today the filler method is used mainly for some smaller species of fish, such as bluegills, for which choices

It's getting hard to tell skin mounts from replicas.

of artificial bodies are few. The filler material can be as simple as sawdust, or it can be a mixture of ground, low-density plastic foam mixed with a binder, such as plaster of Paris.

For best results with the filler method, a plaster cast must be made of the side of the fish that has been selected as the outer or "show" side. Once a mold is made, an incision is made on the other side in order to skin the fish. After the skin has been fleshed and prepared, the incision is partially sewn, leaving an opening large enough to insert filler material. The skin is laid in the half-mold, and the fish is filled with an appropriate amount of filler. As the fish is filled, it is gently pressed into the shape of the mold so that the skin regains the correct anatomical shape. A small piece of wood is sewn into the back of the fish for future attachment to an appropriate base. The fish is then removed from the mold and cleaned of any filler residue. The fins are positioned between cardboard or plastic splints to hold them open, and the fish is put aside to dry for a minimum of two weeks.

The more popular artificial body method utilizes artificial bodies that are sculpted to simulate the shape and musculature of the fish (minus the skin and head). Many taxidermy supply houses offer hundreds of sizes and poses for all species that are normally skin-mounted.

Before skinning a fish that is to be mounted over an artificial body, the taxidermist takes measurements of girth (circumference at the middle or largest area of the fish) and length (from the base of the tail to the "collar bone" behind the gill plate) so that the appropriate size body can be ordered. If the right size body has been selected, the skin of the fish should fit correctly around the artificial body and will meet on the back side.

Many steps in the mounting process must be followed to mount a fish accurately. Skin glues and a maché mixture that is the consistency of soft clay are used as a transition between the artificial body and the skin. Good live-fish references (photography and study casts) should be used to study the correct position for the head, how the mouth is opened, how the fins are flared, etc., all of which must be correctly done before the drying process begins. Drying can take from a few days to several weeks, depending on the size of the fish and the drying conditions.

Once a mounted fish is dry, glass eyes are properly positioned, fins are reinforced, and all other necessary finishing work is completed. The final step is painting the fish. Although all the mounting steps are important, it is the painting that will make the biggest impact when a completed mount is viewed. If the fish isn't painted realistically, a customer will never be happy.

The entire process can take as long as six weeks from start to finish. The actual hours involved will vary, depending on the kind of fish and its size. For a 6-pound largemouth bass, for example, the actual work time for skinning, mounting, finishing, and painting for a professional taxidermist will be around 4 hours. In between are three to four weeks for drying. The steps for finishing and painting require another one to two weeks.

Selecting a Taxidermist

For years it has been debated whether taxidermy is an art or a craft. The answer is both, and much more. The processes and steps in performing taxidermy demand skilled craftsmanship. The composition and design of a mount involve art and creativity. A thorough working knowledge of paint types, their applications, and color blending is necessary. A taxidermist must be aware of chemical properties in order to tan and preserve skins properly, as well as know how to mix and use compounds to re-create and repair natural surface textures. A complete understanding of species anatomy, as well as species behavior and natural attitudes, is needed to re-create natural lifelike mounts. When artistic and mechanical talents have been combined and merged with a knowledge of nature and its properties, the foundation is there to be a competent taxidermist.

The old, musty unnatural-looking gameheads, discolored fish on boards, or distorted bird mounts that still exist in some older gas stations, bars, and clubhouses are things of the past. These old treasured antiques still have nostalgic value, but today you should expect much, much more. The taxidermy profession has made tremendous advances in education, professionalism, procedures, and products.

Selecting a top professional is crucial to getting a mount that will bring beauty to a home or office. Today there are hundreds of good taxidermists in every state, but, as in all professions, there are also those who lack ethics and a desire to produce quality work. Almost every community will have several taxidermists, and quite often there will be a wide range in the quality of work they offer. It is also very common to find taxidermists who excel in certain areas of taxidermy. Professional taxidermists often specialize in their favorite areas of taxidermy.

Choosing a taxidermist can be a perplexing task unless you know what to look for and what questions to ask. Two important qualities are honesty and competence. The best way to select someone is to check references and examine the person's work.

The first problem most people confront is time. Most trophy fish (and animals) will be taken unexpectedly, causing a person to make a rushed decision. It is therefore best to look for a taxidermist before you actually need one. Another way to eliminate a rushed judgment is to know how to handle and preserve a fish after catching it. This will be explained shortly.

A good way to start searching for a taxidermist is to ask friends, co-workers, and relatives if they've used a taxidermist recently and if they were satisfied with the service and quality of work. Sporting goods stores, bait shops, marinas, and professional fishing guides will often recommend taxidermists; however, you should not necessarily accept their opinions as fact. Sometimes friendships and/or personal feelings can cause misleading information about quality and service. Boat captains, guides, lodges, and sporting goods stores may also be on commission for referrals. Most established lodges in Canada, for example, work this way. That should not keep you from using a taxidermist they recommend, but it certainly can cause favoritism from the source.

Talking to personal contacts should produce several names to follow up on. If not, there is always the telephone book. In the United States, an effective way to get names of taxidermists is through a state taxidermist association. Call the state president or secretary and ask if a list of members in your area is available. You should be able to get the phone number for an association by contacting the National Taxidermists Association (NTA). The NTA has a national certification program that recognizes taxidermists who have proven their skills by winning taxidermy competitions. A list of taxidermists who have received certification in your state can be requested by contacting the NTA.

Instead of just dropping in on a taxidermist, call and arrange an appointment to view finished works. If the taxidermist has no work to view, you should wonder why. All busy, professional taxidermists have showrooms or at least displays. Usually you will see work on display that has been recently completed for customers. If a shop is empty, it could be a sign that business is bad or this taxidermist has little experience.

If you have never visited a taxidermy studio before, you are in for a real treat. First, you will be seeing the best trophies that have been taken by area hunters and anglers. Enjoy the display, but do not let yourself be overwhelmed by exceptionally large, trophy-class fish. You are there to check out the quality and service being offered. As an angler, your interest must be focused on the aquatic species on display. Here are some of the things you should look for and ask about:

Examine a mounted fish closely, looking at the base of the tail and along the edges of all fins for shrinkage. If these areas show evidence of shrinkage, it means meat or flesh was not properly cleaned from these areas, which will cause them to be distorted. The cheek area of the head and the throat below the gills should also be checked for shrinkage.

The body shape of the fish should have a smooth, clean flow and exhibit the proper contours and silhouette of the species. Check to see whether there are any lumps under the skin. All scales should be flat and not raised. If the gills are exposed, they should each be separated and symmetrically displayed. Check to see whether the dorsal fins are centered along the top of the body. The same should be noticed with the fins on the bottom of the fish. Are they located along the bottom center line? If they are off to one side, the skin is not properly aligned and the fish will have a distorted appearance. Compare all of these features to what you see when you catch a fresh fish. The best taxidermists will duplicate what is seen in nature. The prime objective is to complete a mount that mimics a live fish.

The paint job will be the most telling element of a taxidermist's ability. Even a fish that exhibits some of the above flaws will look outstanding with a quality paint job. Examine some of the mounted fish that you're familiar with. Do they have the natural colors and markings that you see in a freshly caught fish? The colors should have a blended, translucent appearance with proper shimmers and iridescence for that species of fish. Study the fish closely. A taxidermist should be able to answer any questions you may have about the fish.

It's also a good idea to ask how a fish is tagged so that you are assured of having your own fish returned. Most taxidermists will attach a tag to the back side of the gill cover, which will remain on the fish during the entire mounting process.

After you've visited several taxidermists, you'll see differences in the style and quality of their work. Like most artists, taxidermists tend to develop their own styles in mounting fish and will favor a certain color pattern for each species of fish. The more mounted fish you look at, the more you'll begin to see, and you'll likely become more conscious and aware of the anatomy and colors of the fish you catch. Anglers who begin a collection of trophy fish often develop a much deeper appreciation for the skill and artistic values needed to perform quality taxidermy.

Most of these evaluation tips can be used for inspecting both skin and reproduction fish taxidermy, but there are some additional elements that should be looked at when checking out reproduction taxidermy. If a taxidermist does not have any reproductions for you to see, ask if repros are finished with closed or open gills. Many freshwater replicas are available with transparent flexible fins that are difficult to tell from the real thing. Either look for or ask about this. Also look along the top and bottom lines of a reproduction to see if a seam is evident. A quality reproduction that has been properly finished should show no seams. Look inside the mouth to see if it exhibits detail. Detail in the mouth of a reproduction indicates quality workmanship.

Ask the taxidermist how long it will take to get your fish back. The average turnaround time for most shops will be three to six months, but some taxidermists require a year. The wait will be worth it for a taxidermist who produces top-quality work.

Last but not least is the question of cost. Ask what is included with the price, such as open gills/closed gills, panel, driftwood, or nameplate.

You'll also want to know what sort of guarantee comes with the work. Good quality taxidermy will last a lifetime, and reputable taxidermists should stand behind their work. Do not let the price be the determining factor in whom you select, unless all things are equal. If you find a taxidermist whose work you like and you have confidence in his or her business practices, price should not be a deterrent. You usually get what you pay for. You will be admiring your trophy on a daily basis for many years, and it will be a symbol of good times and great memories. Cost should be secondary to selecting quality taxidermy.

According to a 1997 national survey of taxidermists in the United States, the majority of fish taxidermists charge by the inch. Taxidermists also have a minimum charge for fish skin mounts, which then averaged $100. Minimum charges for replicas were $150. The national average for skin mounts was $9.30 per inch, and for reproductions it was $13.65 per inch. Thus, for a 6-pound bass, which will have an average length of 22 inches, the average cost for skin mounting would be $205, and for a replica it would be $300.

Replicas averaged one-third more than skin mounts. The cost of fish replicas or reproductions can range from $12 to $20 per inch. The lower price range would be for stock reproductions with no alterations. The upper price range would be for custom replicas made to meet the exact dimensions of a fish with a lot of attention to realistic details, such as opening the gill covers and installing artificial gills. Prices will also vary in different regions of the United States. Taxidermists who have established national reputations for exceptional quality will get higher fees.

The survey revealed some extreme variations in pricing, due mainly to the types of fish most commonly mounted in various sections of the United States. In the South, bass, bream, and crappie are more commonly mounted, while in the North, trout, northern pike, walleye, and muskies are common. The southern fish mentioned are easier to mount because of a heavier skin texture. This is one of the reasons why southern prices per inch were a little less than the national average.

Anglers who have a trout mounted can expect to pay more than for bass of equal size. Since saltwater fish are more commonly completed as reproductions, they cost more.

Care in the Field

To get the best mount of a fish, you'll need to do some important things in the field. Proper care of a fish that will be skin-mounted should begin while you are still on or near the water. If you release the fish but desire a replica, you still need to do a few things before you return the fish to the water. With cellular phones being readily at hand, some anglers are calling in their orders for replica fish within minutes of the catch!

It is estimated that 75 percent of the United States' population lives within 50 miles of a coastline.

Skin mounts. If you intend to have a trophy fish skin-mounted, it's best to keep it alive as long as possible. Care should be taken to prevent scale loss due to flopping in the boat or rough handling. If you have already selected a taxidermist, the fish should be delivered to the studio as soon as possible. If the fish cannot be taken to a taxidermist while it is still alive, immediately place the fish in an ice chest with plenty of ice. A fish begins decomposing as soon as it dies, so care for it in the same way you would if you were going to eat it *(see: fish preparation—care)*. Before you place the fish on ice, however, take good photographs of it in its natural colors; these will be useful to the taxidermist later.

Never eviscerate or scale a fish that you wish to have mounted! If you cannot take the fish to a taxidermist the day it is caught, it is best to freeze it. Prepare the fish for freezing by wrapping it in a damp terry cloth towel. Fold all fins close to the body before wrapping it. If an old bath towel isn't available, wrap the fish in good-quality white paper towels. After the fish is wrapped in at least three layers of paper towels, saturate the towels with water and place the wrapped fish into a plastic bag. The damp cloth or paper towels will form a layer of ice around the entire fish. This protects the fins, which become very susceptible to breakage once frozen. The layer of ice will also prevent freezer dehydration.

If you're away on a trip and freezing isn't an option, follow the same procedure of wrapping the fish, but place it on ice in an ice chest. Try not to let the fish float in ice water, which will bleach out and reduce the intensity of the fish's natural markings. These natural markings will aid a taxidermist in re-creating natural colors and details.

When placing a fish into a freezer, lay it on a flat surface and don't put anything on top of it until it is completely frozen. The fish will be fine in a freezer for several weeks, but it is always best to get it to a taxidermist as soon as possible.

In some situations, it is very difficult to save a trophy fish. If you are fortunate enough to have ice along or have some snow or ice packs in the area, you can follow the same procedures previously mentioned. If you'll be getting back to refrigeration within 24 hours and the air temperature is cool, you can possibly save a fish by packing it in powdered borax and wrapping it in damp towels. Place the fish in insulated storage to keep it cool. You'll have a fifty-fifty chance of getting it to a taxidermist in mounting condition. If you wish to give this a try, you'll have to bring along a box of borax. Chances are, however, that you will be better off just releasing the fish and having a replica made.

Replicas. If you catch a fish you want replicated, you need to be prepared to do one, and preferably all, of the following: Take measurements, weigh it, and photograph it. Of course, the greatest priority is minimizing the time a fish is kept out of the water so that you can release it unharmed; thus, you need to take these steps quickly and with proper care of the fish. Length and girth measurements are the most accurate means of ensuring a close replica to the body of the fish. The length should be taken from the tip of the tail to the tip of the lip, or jaw. Girth is determined by measuring around the largest circumference of the fish. If you don't have a measuring tape on the boat, monofilament line can be cut to record these measurements, then kept in your wallet for safekeeping. Weighing the fish is very helpful, since most reproduction bodies available to taxidermists from supply sources are listed according to the length, girth, and weight of the original fish from which the reproduction was cast, so the taxidermist who does your mount will try to obtain a reproduction body that matches, or very nearly matches, your fish. A good photograph not only will help a taxidermist select the closest replica available, but will be a color reference for your fish.

Care at Home

A professionally mounted fish will last a lifetime if it is properly cared for. The same precautions should be followed for protecting any medium of artwork. The elements of nature that promote aging are heat and cold, especially repeated extremes of each, plus humidity. Fortunately, in homes with central air and heat, these environmental conditions are controlled.

Rapid and frequent changes in temperature can eventually cause cracking in skin mounts. This occurrence is less likely in reproductions because the epoxy polymers used to make them are very durable. Even in homes with central air and heat, heat sources should be avoided. Hanging mounted fish over a fireplace has always been popular, but it is a bad location for all mounts if the fireplace is used during the winter. Avoid hanging a mounted fish in any heat source location, such as where air vents will blow directly on it. Another source of heat is direct sunlight. Sunlight can also cause bleaching after prolonged exposure.

Some other conditions can change the original beauty of a fish mount. Exposure to daily cigarette smoke, for example, will yellow a mount in only a few years. The same will happen if a mount is near a kitchen. Grease from frying or broiling meats is especially damaging. If a fish is displayed in a restaurant or tavern where these problems are apparent, it should be cleaned weekly with a soft cotton cloth dampened with a small amount of glass cleaner. The mild cleaning agents will clean the fish and should not harm the protective gloss surface. As a precaution, try the cleaning agent on the back of the fish first to make sure it will not mar the finish on the show side. Anytime a fish is being cleaned with a cloth towel, always wipe in the direction that the fins flow. The sharp points of the dorsal (top) fins can catch the towel and cause the fish to be pulled off a wall, or cause a portion of the fin to be bent or broken.

For normal cleaning, a feather duster works fine. A furniture oil cloth should not be used to wipe the surface of a fish mount. The oil tends to dull the gloss finish; this finish is very important because it enhances and amplifies the pigments and iridescent reflectors used to give a fish its lifelike colors.

If a fish mount is damaged through handling or shipping, it should be taken to a professional taxidermist for repairs. A damaged fish mount can be compared to a damaged car. After the repairs are made, a new or partial paint job will be needed to cover the repaired area.

After 10 or more years, the surface of a fish mount may dull. The gloss can be easily and inexpensively restored by a taxidermist, or you can take the fish to the taxidermist who mounted it, who will probably resurface it for nothing. Do not try this yourself because many different paints are used in painting and glossing a fish mount. Using a gloss that is not compatible with the original paints will cause big problems.

Taxidermy as a Hobby

If you're interested in taxidermy as a hobby or as a part-time or full-time profession, begin slowly to see if it is really something you want to pursue. There is no need to enroll in a school or spend hundreds of dollars on equipment, books, supplies, and video instructions before you're sure taxidermy is for you. You will soon find out that doing taxidermy may not be as simple as it appears, or as rewarding as you had hoped.

There are many inexpensive sources for information on taxidermy. Check with a local library for books or taxidermy trade journals. The classified section in the back of outdoor magazines will usually contain several vendors that offer catalogs with a wealth of information. Taxidermy trade magazines are probably the definitive source for general information. There you can find articles with step-by-step instructions, as well as information about association meetings, suppliers, schools, workshops, and additional resources covering every aspect of taxidermy.

If your interest is strictly fish, order a video on mounting and painting a largemouth or smallmouth bass. If you still feel like trying, save a bass from your next fishing trip and order the supplies as instructed in the video. A bass is a great fish to start with because it is easier to skin and mount than trout and many of the other gamefish that have more delicate skins. Mount the fish and set it up to dry. If you enjoyed the first part, then it is probably safe to invest in an airbrush, air compressor, and the paints you'll need to paint the fish. This is the area of fish taxidermy that is most costly, and there is no need to invest money in painting equipment if you did not enjoy skinning and mounting the fish.

If skinning and mounting a fish is not what you expected, but you're interested in painting, you have the option of finishing and painting replica fish. Some excellent videos on the market show these procedures. If you find an area of fish taxidermy that you would like to pursue, check out the many fine books, schools, and workshops that offer advanced training. One of the less expensive ways of learning more about fish taxidermy is to join a state taxidermy association and attend meetings and seminars. There you will also find many professional taxidermists who can offer advice on how you can learn more about this fascinating art.

For more information contact the following taxidermy trade magazines: *Breakthrough,* P.O. Box 2945, Ham-mond, LA 70404 (800-783-7266); *Taxidermy Today,* 119 Gadsden St., Chester, SC 29706 (803-377-7211); and *American Taxidermist,* P.O. Box 93476, Albuquerque, NM 87199 (505-771-1828). *Breakthrough* sponsors the World Taxidermy and Fish Carving Championships, held every other year in Springfield, Illinois. Over 1,000 taxidermists and carvers from around the world attend this prestigious event.

To get information about a state taxidermist association, contact the National Taxidermist Association, 108 Branch Drive, Slidell, Louisiana, 70461 (504-641-4NTA) for a list of affiliated state associations.

TAXONOMIST

A person involved in the science of classifying fish, animals, and other organisms according to resemblances and differences.

TEASER

A general term for several types of attractors used on the surface in offshore trolling. These include plastic teasers, trolling birds, and daisy chains.
See: Big-Game Fishing; Trolling Lures, Saltwater.

TEMPERATURE

Water temperature is an important element of all aquatic habitats and is relevant to the habits and habitat of baitfish and predators. A fish's body temperature approximates that of its surrounding medium, and its lateral line helps the fish to determine water temperature. Most species have preferred comfort zones as well as upper, lower, or upper and lower temperature thresholds. Spawning is related to water temperatures for many fish, and the hatching of eggs and the success of fry is dependent on suitable water temperatures for most species. In addition, feeding is related to temperature, especially for fish that live in a temperate zone, where seasons are well defined; these species eat more during warm months than during cold months, and their metabolism slows down greatly during winter.

Temperature is one of the many factors that anglers consider, consciously or unconsciously, when seeking gamefish in both freshwater and saltwater.

In the extreme, some offshore big-game anglers rely on ocean surface temperature data provided by satellites to guide them to billfish and tuna hotspots. In the more commonplace, big-lake anglers in early spring use surface temperature gauges to find pockets of warm, nearshore water that are likely to hold trout.

Big-river anglers know that the upper region near the headwaters is colder and more conducive to trout, whereas the middle region is often more temperate and conducive to bass and walleye. Panfish that make nests in spring along the shores of lakes and ponds do so because the water temperature has reached a certain level and their eggs and milt are almost ready to be discharged.

The warming and cooling of water bodies, and especially the influence of tributaries in the spring (which bring warm water to cold lakes), are important factors in the presence of many fish species. Throughout the season, both surface and deep temperatures influence where to fish.

See: Anatomy; Finding Fish; Stratification; Thermal Bar.

TEMPERATURE GAUGE

For boaters.   One of the most important aids for anglers who fish out of a boat is a temperature gauge. For many types of fishing, including shallow spring angling in freshwater, deep-water fishing, big-lake trolling for salmon and trout, and offshore fishing for pelagic saltwater species, the ability to find preferred temperature levels is a big help in catching fish. Some anglers believe in the importance of temperature so much that they seldom fish for any species without having some means of taking water temperature.

Fish are cold-blooded and their metabolism is keyed to the temperature of their environment. Knowing the temperature of the water can help you find fish and then determine how fast to move a lure to catch them. Ripping a lure through water cold enough to make a fish lethargic, for instance, isn't going to increase your fishing success.

Surface water temperature is a strong indication of where you might find certain fish and under what conditions the fish might become more active. In winter, surface temperature instruments can help find the warmest water available in hopes of locating the most active or most concentrated fish. In spring, these devices help identify the places where the water warms first. During the summer on freshwater lakes when the water can get too hot, temperature gauges can guide you to the coolest water available. Saltwater species often locate along temperature shears at the edges of ocean currents where warmer and colder water meet; these are often small variations and finding them is difficult without a temperature gauge.

You can use a stand-alone surface temperature gauge on a boat, with the sensor mounted on the transom, or you can use a handheld pool thermometer, or a combination temp/sonar or temp/speed electronic instrument. Many sonar devices have optional temperature and speed sensors, and the unit displays these measurements whenever the sonar is on. These devices read only surface temperature, but they are particularly valuable in the spring and fall when water temperature is changing on a daily basis. Some sonars have the sensing device built into their transducers, and some use optional, separate pickups that mount on the transom. Models have even been offered with the capability to display air, livewell, and water surface temperature readings.

To check temperature at greater depths, tie a pool thermometer to a snap, lower it to a specific depth on fishing line, leave it for a few minutes, then reel it up quickly. Or, tie it to a downrigger weight and lower it with the weight to a known depth, let it stay for a few minutes, then raise it quickly.

For some deep water trolling, it is helpful to constantly check deep water temperature. This has been done using probes attached to coaxial cable, but the coaxial cable has always broken down and generally not proven reliable for constant use. A better method of obtaining continuous deep-water temperature readings is to use a large, torpedo-like probe that attaches to the downrigger cable just above the weight. The unit has a 9-volt battery inside the probe, and sends temperature readings up to a meter without using the downrigger cable as a signal conduit. If it works right, it provides both temperature and speed data at the downrigger weight.

Temperature sensors on cables let anglers probe vertically for differences in water temperature. They can be used to confirm the depth of a thermocline (the boundary between the sun-warmed upper layer of water and the cooler layer below, where the water temperature changes the greatest number of degrees in the shortest span of depth) that is spotted on sonar, or to locate a thermocline if your sonar isn't capable of spotting one. If you believe that fish seek out their "ideal" temperature, you can find the depth at which that temperature occurs. If a thermocline was present yesterday in a freshwater lake, but no temperature stratification of any kind is apparent today, a lake turnover is indicated. When you find fish at a certain depth, a probe lets you check the temperature and record it. Over time, a pattern may emerge on a certain body of water that helps you locate fish on future trips.

For nonboaters.   Small clip-on thermometers are available for anglers who wish to check the surface water temperature. Waders, tubers, shore anglers, and small-boat anglers use these, or a simple pool thermometer, especially in the spring and when looking for warm pockets of water. They can be tied to a weight or other device for checking subsurface temperatures, although it should be recognized that in flowing water, there is usually little variance in temperature from top to bottom.

See: Thermal Bar; Thermocline; Trolling.

In Minnesota, using leeches for walleye bait is a big business; one survey stated that more than $2 million was spent on these slippery critters, most of which are ribbon leeches.

T

TENCH   *Tinca tinca.*

Other names—golden tench; French: *tanche;* German: *alia, schleie;* Italian and Portuguese: *tinca;* Spanish, *tenca.*

Tench are among the more popular coarse fish *(see)* of Europe, inhabiting many waters and providing a large measure of summer fishing interest. These members of the Cyprinidae family are relatives of carp *(see)* and are like these species in some ways. They are a popular food fish, widely sought for food and also raised commercially.

Identification.   The back of the tench is dark green or olive, and the sides are greenish to coppery, often with an orange or yellow orange belly. Its color varies and may be darker in some locations. It has a thick caudal stem; a broad, rounded tail fin; and a rounded, erect dorsal fin. Small scales are set flat against its chunky body and are covered with a thick coat of mucus, making the fish appear scaleless. There is one barbel on each side of the mouth.

Size.   Tench are common in the 1- to 4-pound class and are occasionally caught at 6 pounds; their reported maximum size is 18 pounds, although the all-tackle world record is a Swedish fish of 10 pounds, 3 ounces caught in 1985.

Distribution.   With the exception of northern Scandinavia, the tench ranges throughout Europe, including the British Isles. It is also native in Asia in the Arctic Ocean drainage, the Ob and Yenisei basins, and rarely in Lake Baikal. It has been introduced into Australia and North America.

Habitat.   Warm lakes and ponds with weeds and a muddy bottom are the primary environs of tench; they also inhabit sluggish rivers and occasionally hold in swifter flows, as well as over hard sand or gravel bottoms. They tolerate low oxygen levels, are known to bury into the mud, and are often found amid vegetation.

Life history/Behavior.   These fish spawn in late spring and early summer, usually in weedy shallows, broadcasting numerous adhesive eggs rather than constructing a nest. The fry stay in schools and eventually gather in loose congregations. Adult tench form small groups rather than large close schools, but they are also sometimes encountered in an assembly of groups and caught in numbers in a given location.

Food and feeding habits.   Tench are omnivorous and feed mostly, although not exclusively, on the bottom. When feeding on the bottom, tench assume a more angular, rather than horizontal, position, and their tail is pointed up as the mouth is positioned to pick food off the bottom. Their diet includes various invertebrates, snails, mussels, aquatic insect larvae, leeches, and bloodworms. They are renowned low-light feeders, and are especially pursued at daybreak by anglers, although evening, night, and overcast conditions are also favorable. They favor warm water and are more active when the water temperature exceeds 55°F; they are relatively inactive in cold water and hold fast to muddy bottoms in the winter.

Angling.   Tench provide a dogged fight with persistent runs, although without aerial maneuvers, and are regarded very favorably by light-tackle anglers.

Feeding tench often send up a stream of small bubbles, which is the result of trapped gases escaping from soft bottom sediment as this fish roots while feeding. They may also roll at the surface, and both incidents are a sign of the fish's presence in a given location because tench do not stir up the water as carp do and are identified by means of disturbed water.

They tend to move shallower as light decreases, and deeper as it increases. In bright midday, they seek a cooler, deeper comfort zone, although there are occasional exceptions to this behavior.

Bottom fishing with assorted baits is almost exclusively the technique for tench fishing, and this usually involves prebaiting or chumming *(see)*, using groundbait *(see)*, and an assortment of prepared, processed, and natural baits. Maggots, corn, worms, cheese, bread, meat cubes, pastes, and other items are popular; anglers primarily bait hooks with those commodities that have been employed in prebaiting or chumming and which the fish have been conditioned to.

Hooked baits may be fished with a float or without one, but many tench anglers prefer a fixed bolt rig *(see)* and a bottom feeder (a device for precise-location chumming). Anglers use rods up to 12 feet in length, line from 6 to 10 pounds in strength, and No. 6 to 12 bait hooks.

TENNESSEE

Tennessee is best known for country music and the Smoky Mountains, but it also boasts superb freshwater opportunities—among the best in the United States. This is not a secret to resident and nearby anglers, and the news is beginning to spread far beyond the state's borders.

Home to more than 300 species of fish, Tennessee is among the most ichthyologically diverse of any state in the country. From the sandy-bottomed ponds and creeks of the coastal plains of western Tennessee, to the cold tumbling streams and large man-made reservoirs of the east, anglers have access to a multitude of environments that

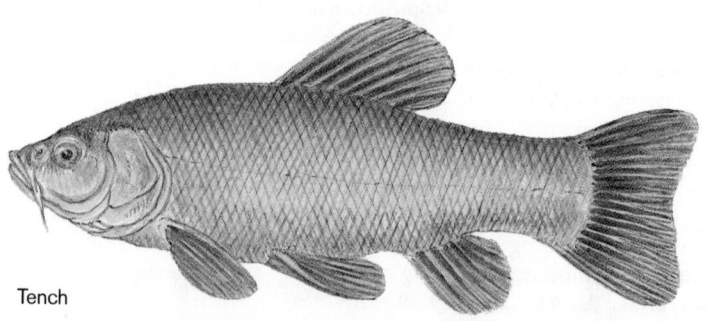

Tench

support gamefish. As a result of the federal government's attempts to control flooding and create inexpensive electricity, the Tennessee and Cumberland Rivers were converted into a series of lakes that step-stone from one end of the state to another. The 24 major reservoirs along these rivers attract the bulk of the angling interest in the state. In total, Tennessee has 29 large lakes that contain more than 500,000 surface acres of water; this is complemented by more than 2,000 miles of coldwater streams, 19,000 miles of warmwater streams, and more than a dozen family fishing lakes created by the Tennessee Wildlife Resources Agency (TWRA).

All of this water, matched with ample rainfall and a mild climate, makes Tennessee an angler's paradise. East Tennessee is home to some of the South's best trout fishing; here, stocked rainbows and browns offer a larger, more plentiful, and easier-to-find alternative to native brook trout. Since the 1960s, striped bass have been aggressively stocked statewide and are now the predominant fishery on some lakes. Largemouth bass thrive statewide in every significant reservoir and river, and they are usually the dominant species in thousands of farm ponds. In the clearer, cooler waters, largemouth are often joined by smallmouth and spotted bass. Smallmouths are also abundant in the many smaller rivers that have not been dammed or otherwise altered.

Reservoirs are the most popular angling destinations in the state, and some 440,000 individuals participate in these fisheries in any given year. Seventy-five percent of them pursue a particular species; largemouth bass are the most popular species by far and attract roughly half that number of anglers annually. In a recent Tennessee Valley Authority (TVA) rating of lakes according to angler success, fish quantity, and fish quality, Chickamauga in the eastern end of the state, Percy Priest in the middle, and Barkley in the west ranked as the best places to fish for Tennessee largemouths. Barkley, which gets surprisingly little fishing pressure, produced the most consistent angling across the state.

The TWRA manages a group of family fishing lakes in middle and west Tennessee, and another group is under construction. Some of these small lakes are operated by private concessionaires and offer everything from boats to baitfish; most require a daily angling permit.

Species Overview

Bass, crappie, and catfish. Quality largemouth bass fishing isn't limited to any one region of the state, and anglers can expect the same angling quality in the foothills of the Smoky Mountains as on the plains of the Mississippi River. Reelfoot Lake lies a stone's throw from the Mississippi, and, although it is best known for an outstanding crappie population, it also harbors fine largemouths. East Tennessee's Tellico and Douglas Lakes are

gaining a reputation for springtime catches of largemouths weighing up to 12 pounds. Most of the largemouths taken from Tennessee reservoirs have a mean harvested size of about 15 inches. Although more Tennessee largemouths are caught in the spring than at any other time, bass are readily available year-round across the state.

The smallmouth bass is native to Tennessee but is not found in great numbers in the western third of the state. A fish of cool, clear waters, it has gained a reputation as a tough fighter, often pleasing the angler with its aerial displays. The best Tennessee lakes to fish for smallmouth bass are Watauga, Dale Hollow, Center Hill, Percy Priest, Boone, South Holston, and Norris. Dale Hollow is a designated trophy smallmouth lake and has special size regulations. The present world-record smallmouth bass—at 11 pounds, 15 ounces—came from Dale Hollow Lake in 1955. At one time smallmouths were more plentiful in Tennessee, but reservoir building by the TVA and the U.S. Army Corps of Engineers destroyed much of their prime habitat. In recent years, the fish has made a bit of a comeback and is again showing up in some of its old, but now impounded, haunts.

Black crappie and white crappie inhabit streams and reservoirs across Tennessee. Reelfoot Lake is by far the best crappie lake in the Volunteer State and even has a commercial fishery for panfish. Other good crappie lakes are Douglas, Percy Priest, Kentucky, Barkley, and Cherokee. Of the 22 catfish species found in Tennessee, the most popular are the blue, channel, and the flathead. In some locations—such as the tailwaters below hydroelectric dams and in the warm discharge canals of power plants—the majority of angling interest is often for catfish. Blues and flatheads are most often caught on live bait; the channels fall for a wider variety of natural bait—including nightcrawlers, chicken livers, and cut shad—as well as lures.

Stripers and walleye. Since the 1960s, striped bass have made a significant impact in Tennessee, but public opinion is still split over whether this is for the better. Norris and Melton Hill Lakes have produced freshwater world-record stripers, the latter having yielded two state-record specimens—one $60^1/_2$ pounds, the other $63^3/_4$ pounds. Each year both lakes produce several stripers weighing in excess of 50 pounds. Biologists in Tennessee developed many of the procedures currently used in many states for stocking striped bass. Although the fish is both popular and abundant in Tennessee, some anglers blame the striped bass for the decline of other species. Not only do the big fish compete for food with the likes of walleye, bass, and crappie, it is widely believed they often eat these gamefish. Studies are currently underway across the state to determine the impact stripers have on native species, although in the past there has been no scientific confirmation of stripers eating largemouth bass in any quantity. If new studies find that striped bass are detrimental to populations of native game-fish and panfish, however, it is possible that the stocking of striped bass will be halted.

Also not well known outside the state are Tennessee's healthy walleye and sauger fisheries. middle and east Tennessee are home to the South's best walleye and sauger fishing, and both species are actively managed by biologists. Old Hickory and Norris are probably the state's top walleye lakes; the former is home to the long-standing world-record catch, and Douglas Lake is tops for sauger. Kentucky and Pickwick Lakes also provide prime sauger fishing opportunities. The best time to fish for sauger and walleye is late winter and early spring, when the fish make spawning runs upriver.

Trout. Trout fishing is among the fastest-growing outdoor sports in Tennessee. Be it fishing for native brook trout in the mountains or for stocked rainbows and browns in the tailwaters of many dams in middle and east Tennessee, the state's trout fishing has never been better.

Tennessee's only native trout, the brookie, rarely reaches 12 inches in length, and even 6-inch specimens are hard to come by. Although their status seems to have stabilized, until recently brook trout were considered threatened by loss of habitat, acid rain, and competition from rainbow trout. Brookies are probably the most studied fish in Tennessee. Their populations are on the rise in some areas and declining in others.

Rainbow trout were introduced into Tennessee waters a century ago, and they have flourished in many streams where there is little fishing pressure, reproducing naturally in their adopted environments. Most of the rainbow trout caught in Tennessee waters, however, are stocked fish in put-and-take streams. The state-record rainbow trout is a 15$\frac{1}{4}$-pound fish caught in 1994 at Boone Lake, and it was undoubtedly a stocked fish. The same goes for the record brown, a 28-pound, 12-ounce individual caught in the Norris tailwater in 1988. Although brown trout have not been stocked as extensively as rainbows, they, too, have been very successful. Probably the most difficult to catch of Tennessee's trout species, browns are found mostly in the tailwater fisheries.

In the east are roughly 250 miles of small head-water streams that are not stocked. Brook trout dominate nearly 95 miles of these streams, and rainbows dominate almost all the rest. Another 245 miles of small headwater streams flow through the Tennessee portion of the Great Smoky Mountains National Park, which is governed by a different set of regulations. These wild streams are preferred by growing legions of fly anglers, not only because these enthusiasts favor wild trout over stocked fish, but also because just getting to the fish often provides as big a challenge as catching them.

Another 1,000 miles of streams are managed by the TWRA and are stocked with adult fish on a regular basis. Of these waters, the Tellico River and

Citico Creek in the Cherokee National Forest are among the South's most popular and intensively fished trout streams. Both waters receive weekly stockings of rainbows in the spring, summer, and fall.

Roughly 135 miles of water have been classified as tailwater trout fisheries, and these are also popular with anglers. Tailwaters receive regular stockings of adult fish, as well as thousands of fingerlings in the fall. With the cooperation of the Corps of Engineers and the TVA, minimum flow levels are now maintained below nine dams to help ensure the quality of trout fishing. Research in the 1980s showed the tailwater fisheries were often too warm or did not have enough oxygen to maintain viable year-round trout populations. The minimum flow agreements, along with many varied aeration projects, have helped make tailwater trout fishing the best it has been. The Clinch River below Norris Dam, and the Watauga River below Watauga Dam, are prime examples of tailwater trout fisheries that are thriving under intensive management. Watauga is best known for its rainbows, and the Clinch has produced many brown trout in excess of 12 pounds.

West Tennessee

Reelfoot Lake. By Tennessee standards, Reelfoot Lake is on the small side, but it is probably the best-known body of water in Tennessee. Unlike its dam-formed cousins, 12,000-acre Reelfoot is a natural lake that was created when an earthquake forced the Mississippi River to change its course. Crappie fishing in the saw grass and among the cypress trees is so good that the lake supports the United State's only commercial fishery for panfish, making these fish a popular menu item at local restaurants. And although Tennessee anglers often turn their noses up at bluegill fishing, at Reelfoot, the bluegills are almost as big a draw as the crappie. That leaves the state's most popular gamefish, largemouth bass, a distant third at Reelfoot, but that doesn't mean the fishery should be overlooked. Acre for acre, Reelfoot probably produces as many trophy large-mouth bass as any lake in the state.

Kentucky Lake. At 158,000 acres, Kentucky Lake is the largest in the TVA chain and possibly the most productive. It has gained a national reputation for the quality of its crappie fishing and is also known as a top producer of largemouth bass. Although the best fishing for crappie and bass is in spring, the lake consistently produces both species year-round. Summertime night fishing on the lake is particularly popular. Kentucky Lake is also home to a superb sauger fishery, and the southern portion of the lake provides some of the state's best sauger, a fact overlooked by many anglers.

Barkley Lake. Running parallel to Kentucky Lake, Barkley has the same quality of fishing but receives hardly one-tenth the pressure. Considered Tennessee's "sleeper lake" by biologists, Barkley

Crustaceans, which are segmented hard-shelled invertebrates such as crayfish, shrimp, and crabs, are a major food source for fish; there are about 30,000 crustacean species, most of them marine.

supports a better fishery than does Kentucky Lake—according to data collected by the TWRA. Good for all species, Barkley offers crappie fishing that ranks with Douglas, which is widely considered the best of the man-made reservoirs. Although the lake is large at 57,920 acres (some of which is in Kentucky), 90 percent of the fishing occurs on only 10 percent of the water.

Pickwick Lake. With 43,100 acres to choose from, anglers on Pickwick usually head to the same place: the tailwaters. Tailwater fishing at Pickwick has always been popular, but it became more so when the TVA made several enhancements that provided more water, more oxygen, and cooler temperatures. Most of the state's species thrive in these tailwaters, but white bass, crappie, and sauger are probably the most popular. Although the sauger fishing is best in the late winter, crappie and white bass are caught year-round, and smallmouth bass fishing has been popular as well.

Family fishing lakes. Diverse opportunities exist at Browns Creek, Carroll, Glenn Springs, Herb Parsons, Humboldt, Graham, Maples Creek, Garrett, and Whitesville Lakes. These range in size from 87 to 500 acres, and most have good catfish and panfish populations. Browns Creek is noted for large bass as well.

Middle Tennessee

Center Hill. A top crappie lake from March through May, Center Hill receives much less pressure than some of its counterparts in the region, and it is the source of the state-record spotted bass, a 5-pound, 8-ounce specimen. The 23,060-acre lake also has excellent smallmouth fishing; March through May, and November through December, are the best months. Nighttime fishing for smallmouth is also exceptionally good in late May and June. Walleye fishing on the upper end of the lake is good from March through May. Fishing for paddlefish is popular from February through April.

Cheatham Lake. At 7,450 acres, Cheatham is small, but it produces decent seasonal fishing. Crappie are probably the lake's top draw in both spring and fall. Striper fishing in the tailwaters is popular from January through March. The lake suffers from fluctuating water levels, which impact angling results.

Cordell Hull. At full pool, Cordell Hull covers 11,960 acres and offers excellent year-round largemouth bass fishing. In August and September sauger are popular, making an annual run into the headwaters in late winter and early spring. Bream and catfish are favored targets as well.

Dale Hollow. At 30,990-acres, Dale Hollow is best known for its smallmouth fishing, which includes the recently disputed state- and world-record specimen caught in 1955. March through May provides the best smallmouth fishing, although nighttime fishing in June is also excellent. Good smallmouth fishing can be had during the winter months, but the action is considerably slower than in the spring. Largemouth bass and white bass are good in the spring, and crappie are also abundant in the lake. Muskie fishing provides an unusual December and January diversion for Tennesseans.

Lake Normandy. Lake Normandy is one of the state's better lakes for spotted bass, yet smallmouth bass and largemouth bass are also big draws. Crappie fishing at 3,160-acre Normandy is good in the spring, and walleye fishing is popular on the lake's upper end from February through April. Trout fishing in the tailwaters is good in spring but falls off in summer.

Old Hickory. Located just outside Nashville, 22,550-acre Old Hickory receives inordinate year-round fishing pressure, but it continues to produce good numbers of bass, crappie, stripers, and sauger. The lake is well known for its sauger and striper fishing from December through April, and each year the sauger run up the lake's headwaters, making for excellent early-spring fishing. Walleye are a top attraction at Old Hickory, too, although anglers cannot expect the likes of the state- and world-record specimen—a 25-pounder caught here in 1960.

Percy Priest. A Corps of Engineers impoundment on the Stones River, Percy Priest is a 14,200-acre lake that lies minutes east of Nashville. A deep, clear reservoir with an annual fluctuation of about 20 feet, it supports one of the better largemouth and smallmouth fisheries in the state, and a good crappie population. Smallmouths linger along the rocky outcroppings of the main channel and on clay and rock points lakewide, but the better fishing is closer to the dam. In late winter and early spring, the lower half of the lake has good crappie fishing.

Tims Ford. Probably best known for trout fishing in its tailwaters, Tims Ford is a 10,600-acre impoundment. It is also home to good bass, crappie, stripers, and walleye. Although striped bass stay deep in the summer and winter, during their run up the Elk River in early spring they are caught in the shallows. Walleye fishing in the Elk is also popular in the early spring.

Woods Reservoir. One of the states' smaller lakes, Wood Reservoir covers 3,910 acres. Its top attraction is smallmouth bass from March through May, and again in October and November. Among locals the lake is well known for its early-spring and late-fall crappie fishing. Despite its size, the lake does not receive inordinate fishing pressure.

Family fishing lakes. Diverse opportunities exist at Marrowbone, Laurel Hill, VFW, Williamsport, and Gaither/Bedford Lakes. These range up to 325 acres in size, and have bluegills, catfish, and bass.

East Tennessee

Chickamauga Lake. Chickamauga's bass fishing has become a lot more difficult since the TVA

Though small compared to other Tennessee waters, Boone Lake has a notable striper fishery.

T

destroyed much of the aquatic vegetation. The lake was once renowned for its bass fishing in stands of milfoil, spinyleaf naiad, and hydrilla, but today's anglers have been forced to change tactics. Those wanting to catch bass from this old 34,500-acre reservoir should target brushpiles placed by the TWRA or local anglers. Creek channels and old ditches hold bass in summer. Winter sauger are caught on small jigs and on minnows at the Watts Bar dam tailwaters on the upper end.

Cherokee Lake. Located amidst rolling farmland, 30,300-acre Cherokee Lake boasts good fishing for a variety of species. Striped bass abound near the dam in summer months. In fall and spring, stripers run upstream to the John Sevier steam plant discharge. Jigs and crankbaits take largemouth bass from rock outcroppings during the winter, when the water level drops as much as 28 feet. Crappie fishing is excellent in the large creek embayments; these fish strike small jigs or minnows on the flats in spring, and trolled grubs or jigs in deep creek channels in summer.

Douglas Lake. Nourished by three rivers, Douglas Lake is a 30,400-acre reservoir that has become the premier crappie lake in East Tennessee. It is considered second only to Reelfoot Lake. Despite an average 48-foot annual drawdown, fertile creek hollows and an ample supply of stump beds provide hot crappie fishing year-round. Successful anglers tight-line small minnows in the hollows during the spring spawn, and switch to deep trolling with small plugs, grubs, or small flies during the fall and winter. Bass fishing is best on the lake during the spring, but it is consistently good most of the time. Although anglers can catch a few bass here in the 8-pound range, the lake suffers from an overpopulation of largemouths, and most of the fish are small.

Nickajack Lake. At 10,900 acres and mostly river channel, Nickajack is a small lake with little seasonal fluctuation. During the summer months,

spinnerbaits and buzzbaits take largemouth bass from stands of milfoil and around the many areas of shoreline riprap. Crappie concentrate near milfoil and woody structure, and the best crappie fishing is in the coves and around the islands on the lower end.

Watauga and South Holston. Although the total surface area of these two northeast Tennessee reservoirs is less than 13,000 acres, Watauga and South Holston nevertheless support a substantial two-story fishery. The most commonly caught species are smallmouth and largemouth bass, bluegills, walleye, and rainbow trout. The smallmouth fishery is one of the best in the state. The lower end of South Holston is better for smallmouth, and the upper end for largemouth. Watauga has an excellent walleye population.

Boone Lake. Tiny (4,300 acres) Boone Lake, near Johnson City and Kingsport, supports a tremendous variety of gamefish. Largemouth bass constitute the bulk of the annual catch, but smallmouths, striped bass, Cherokee bass (hybrid stripers), and panfish abound. In spring and early summer, largemouths stage at the mouths of the hollows and creeks, and on the dropoffs. The stump beds in Boone Creek and on the upper end of the lake are good locations for casting topwater plugs to largemouths. The best smallmouth fishing is on the South Fork of the Holston river arm of the lake, where 17-inch or better specimens are abundant. Try for stripers in the headwaters in the late fall and early spring. Drifting or slow trolling with live baits is favored, and there are some big individuals here. Boone produced the state-record hybrid—a 23-pounder—in 1994, and contains 40-pound pure-strain stripers.

Norris Lake. Norris is the oldest of the TVA reservoirs. An impoundment of the Powell and Clinch Rivers, it was completed in 1936, creating a lake of 34,200 acres. The annual fluctuation can exceed 45 feet, which doesn't allow shoreline vegetation to become established. In the winter, its clear, cool water provides excellent smallmouth fishing. Striped bass exceeding 50 pounds lurk here, making fall and spring runs far into the headwaters. The lower half of the lake is best for winter and summer striped bass fishing. Walleye are stocked annually and are caught by anglers trolling deep-running crankbaits. Bottom trolling with a spinner and worm combo is another favored technique.

Melton Hill Lake. Wedged between Knoxville and Oak Ridge, Melton Hill Lake gets surprisingly little fishing pressure, especially when you consider its propensity for producing record fish. The lake yielded a state-record 63-pound, 12-ounce striped bass in February 1998 and formerly held the world freshwater striper record. This big striper was caught from the warmwater discharge at Bull Run Steam Plant, which is probably the most intensely fished section of the lake for all species. The tailwaters below the dam are also productive and popular, but anglers would be remiss to fish just those two areas. Both largemouths and smallmouths are abundant throughout the lake. Spring and fall crappie fishing on Melton Hill is one of east Tennessee's better-kept fishing secrets.

Fort Loudon-Tellico. Located near Knoxville, Fort Loudon and Tellico are reservoirs joined by a canal near the dams. Tellico is a deeper, clear-water reservoir fed by mountain streams via the Tellico and Little Tennessee Rivers. The French, Broad, and Holston Rivers supply warmer, more turbid water to Fort Loudon. Every spring, several huge largemouths are caught on Tellico above the Highway 411 bridge, most falling to spinnerbaits or crankbaits. Bat, Clear, and Island Creeks provide excellent pre-spawn bass fishing. On Fort Loudon, white bass and crappie are caught in the springtime in Little Turkey, Sinking, and Ish Creeks, and near Louisville Point Park. Catfishing is excellent at Fort Loudon.

Watts Bar Lake. Probably the finest lake in east Tennessee, 38,000-acre Watts Bar has the best of just about everything. Largemouths and smallmouths are the big draws. April through June provide peak fishing for largemouths, and October through December offer the best fishing for smallmouths. Although the lake experiences the same summer doldrums as other Tennessee reservoirs, the nighttime bass fishing in July and August ranks with the best in the state. Crappie fishing in the spring is also exceptionally good on Watts Bar, as is the sauger fishing. October and November are the best times for striped bass, but big stripers are caught year-round. In August and September the lake's white bass fishing is second to none in the state.

TERMINAL RIG

An arrangement of terminal tackle items as a fishing unit; this usually involves some type of sinker, swivel, and hook or lure, plus a leader.

TERMINAL TACKLE

The individual and collective equipment used at the end of a fishing line.

See: Bait; Hook; Knots, Fishing; Leader; Lure; Natural Bait; Sinker; Snap; Split Ring; Swivel.

TERRESTRIAL INSECTS

Terrestrial insects spend all of their nymphal and adult stages on land. Like aquatic insects *(see)*, they are very diverse and abundant, especially in warm latitudes and during the summer in cold latitudes. Most occur near the banks of waterways, except in periods of high wind. These insects accidentally fall into the water for various reasons and become prey for fish, especially trout in streams during the latter part of the summer;

many terrestrial insects struggle noticeably when they land in the water. Thus, they are also the imitation object of many artificial flies.

Terrestrial insects most likely to be found in the water are ants, beetles, crickets, grasshoppers, leafhoppers (jassids), caterpillars, moths, and spiders. Generally the most important terrestrial insects to fish and to anglers are ants, grasshoppers, and leafhoppers. The life cycle of these insects is not a factor in imitation, although close resemblance of body forms is. Most float on the water, though some sink slowly. Artificial flies that imitate terrestrial insects are usually floaters and may float high or low depending on the type of insect and circumstances.

TEST LINE
See: Line.

TEXAS

For many Americans, Texas retains its old western movie image of a barren desert. In truth, Texas is a watery wonderland featuring 1.5 million acres of lakes; 80,000 miles of rivers, streams, and bayous; and 624 miles of beaches and shoreline on the Gulf of Mexico. From blue marlin in the offshore waters to bluegills in the Panhandle, Texas is an angler's dream.

Since the 1970s, a progressive fisheries division at Texas Parks and Wildlife Department (TPWD) has enhanced the natural bounty with cutting-edge limits and stocking programs. Texas was the first state to ban commercial fishing for saltwater spotted seatrout and red drum (redfish), a measure that has subsequently been adopted by other Gulf Coast states and has led to a resurgence of inshore fishing. Texas built the first saltwater fish hatchery and continues to stock millions of redfish and seatrout (known locally as speckled trout).

Texas likewise led the charge of progressive bag limits for largemouth bass and has a worldwide reputation for great bass fishing. In the 1970s, TPWD recognized the genetic superiority of Florida-strain largemouth bass and began stocking that subspecies in Texas waters. Florida bass genes plus restrictive limits pushed the envelope on what is considered a big bass in Texas. Where an 8-pounder was once considered huge, hundreds of lakes have produced bass bigger than 10 pounds, and 15- to 18-pounders have been caught.

The state agency also recognized the sporting potential of gamefish species that are not native to the Lone Star State. Stocking programs continue for striped bass, smallmouth bass, coppernose bluegills, walleye, and hybrid striped bass.

Freshwater
The opportunities for fishing in Texas vary widely, from huge lakes shared with neighboring states, to

T

small lakes in or near municipalities, to many small and privately managed waters. Largemouth bass are the primary angling interest, but stripers have a strong following, as do catfish and panfish species. The majority of opportunity exists in large lakes, which are profiled here.

East Texas.   The climate and habitat of East Texas more closely resemble those of states in the southeastern United States. Thanks to the U.S. Army Corps of Engineers and other lake-building authorities, the region is dotted with more good lakes than can be mentioned in this space. Fishing in most of East Texas is acceptable if not downright good.

Lake Fork.   A 27,000-acre impoundment, Lake Fork has redefined big-bass fishing in Texas. Fork dominates the state's big-bass records and attracts anglers from as far away as Japan. One economic study done in the early 1990s estimated the value of Lake Fork's sportfishing at $27.5 million per year.

A number of factors—some intentional, others accidental—make Fork so productive. Lake Fork was built by the Sabine River Authority, which left most of the lake's abundant timber in place. The lake filled in three stages. Each stage inundated many more acres of thick cover that was inaccessible to fishing boats, thereby protecting the fish.

When the lake opened to fishing in 1980, it did so under the state's first restrictive bag limit. The limit has since been fine-tuned to accommodate changes in the fishery. A catch-and-release following developed at Fork and has matured with the lake's big bass. Most fishing guides discourage their clients from killing big bass. Instead, they push replica mounts. One of North America's top replica taxidermists has a shop 10 miles from the lake and does a booming business.

An additional study indicated that Fork may well profit from the abundance of dairy farms around the lake. Cow manure that leeches into the water with rains may increase the lake's fertility. Finally, Fork has one of the most constant water

levels among Texas lakes. This combination of factors is responsible for Fork's phenomenal bass fishery.

Late winter and early spring are the best times to catch a Lake Fork bass weighing 13 pounds or more, but the most consistent angling occurs during the hot summer months. Carolina-rigged plastic worms fished on submerged roadbeds, points, humps, ridges, and other structure may yield as many as 50 bass per day during the summer. Fish weighing 8 to 10 pounds are common at this time of year.

Sam Rayburn Reservoir.   At 114,000 acres, Sam Rayburn is the largest lake totally within Texas boundaries. Rayburn and its nearby cousins, Toledo Bend Reservoir and Lake Livingston, put Texas on the national bass fishing map in the 1960s. Rayburn fell on hard times but has since enjoyed a renaissance of sorts, partly because of state stocking programs and restrictive bag limits, and partly because of fluctuating water levels.

Sam Rayburn has endured regular cycles of low and high water. When water levels drop 10 to 20 feet below normal, new vegetation grows along the exposed shorelines. When water levels rise, the new growth is inundated, creating a stimulant that is almost like a new lake effect.

Largemouth bass are the big draw at Rayburn, although the lake also produces excellent crappie and catfish action. An abundance of hydrilla is another factor that seems to have helped Rayburn's bass population. Hydrilla creates excellent bass cover that frustrates the efforts of most anglers. To tempt bass from the hydrilla, anglers will fish the edges of the plant beds with topwater plugs or buzzbaits. A heavy jig pitched into hydrilla will crash down through the growth and draw reaction strikes as it sinks. Jig fishing in hydrilla requires heavy tackle and a deft touch to determine strikes.

Although a popular lake among anglers, Rayburn's sheer size tends to disperse the crowds. Camping facilities and boat ramps are abundant at this Corps of Engineers lake, and an angler wishing to escape the crowds can usually find a secluded cove.

Toledo Bend Reservoir.   Texas shares Toledo Bend with the neighboring state of Louisiana. Since it was impounded in 1967, T-Bend has sustained its reputation as a great all-around fishing lake. Toledo is great for largemouth bass, crappie, bluegills, and catfish, as well as for striped bass stocked by Louisiana.

At 185,000 acres, the lake is huge. It stretches 65 miles and includes 1,200 miles of shoreline. In fact, Toledo Bend is so big that it fishes more like three lakes than one.

Toledo Bend veterans enjoy a lengthy spawning season for largemouth bass by first concentrating on the upper reaches of the lake, which warm before the more southern waters. Spawning action begins as early as February in T-Bend's northern end and

Sam Rayburn Reservoir is one of Texas's best largemouth bass fisheries.

continues through April in waters near the dam. Big fish are possible in this period; a 14-pound lake-record largemouth was caught in March of 1998.

A little-known fishery occurs in the Sabine River below Toledo Bend Dam, where huge striped bass fatten on baitfish in the swift tailrace waters. Tailrace anglers who fish from the banks and use saltwater tackle regularly tie into stripers weighing 20 to 30 pounds. The best fishing in the tailrace waters generally occurs during cold winter months and continues through April.

The coldest winter months are also when crappie in huge numbers suspend over the Sabine River channel above the Pendleton Bridge at midlake. In January and February, the hotspot is obvious from the boats positioned over the fish. Most anglers use live minnows to tempt the succulent panfish, which will readily strike light jigs.

Caddo Lake. One of the most hauntingly beautiful lakes in Texas, Caddo is the Lone Star State's only large natural lake. It was apparently formed more than 200 years ago when a huge earthquake created a logjam that diverted water from the Red River into the Big Cypress Basin. A dam later increased the lake's size to 25,400 acres.

Caddo is a shallow, blackwater labyrinth of channels and bayous winding through huge cypress brakes. Newcomers should make certain they have a good map and pay attention to navigational markers in the channels. It's easy to get lost at Caddo.

The most unusual gamefish common to Caddo is the chain pickerel, a long, toothy fish that readily strikes bass lures. Pickerel seem especially fascinated by spinnerbaits. They're most readily caught during the coldest weather by anglers casting near weedbeds or lily pads. Unlike other fish, chain pickerel seem to favor a lure that's moving fast.

Caddo is a good lake for largemouth bass, but it's best known for panfish. Crappie, bluegills, and warmouth bass (locally called goggle-eye perch) are favorites. Panfishing is great in the spring, when locals often use cane poles or fly rods with earthworms or crickets for bait. With an electric motor or sculling paddle, they move from one cypress tree to the next, dunking the bait around the base of the tree until they locate a customer.

Lake Texoma. A sprawling 88,000-acre impoundment on the Texas-Oklahoma border, Lake Texoma is the most prolific inland fishery for striped bass in North America. Stripers were stocked in Texoma in 1965 and soon began to reproduce naturally. Texoma is fed by the Red and the Washita Rivers. The Red River, in particular, is high in dissolved salts and perfectly suited to spring spawning runs by Texoma stripers.

Although anglers remove thousands of striped bass from Texoma each year, the fish remain incredibly plentiful. Some of the most reliable fishing occurs during the summer months, when anglers using a vast array of tactics land stripers in most parts of the lake. Using live shad fished deep is a common method, as is flatline trolling with crankbaits and plugs in 10 to 30 feet of water. Others use downriggers for fish that suspend in deep water off points and creek channels.

Summer also offers some of the most exciting topwater action of the year. Stripers often break the surface of the water, particularly on calm days. Popping plugs are local favorites, but anything that splashes on the surface is apt to draw a bone-jarring strike. In fall and winter, the fish often school on the surface and will readily strike plugs or jigs. Fishing under flocks of circling sea gulls is a popular tactic for pursuing surfacing fish. The sharp-eyed birds can spot feeding fish from a long distance and dive to attack the hapless shad from above.

Probably because the fish are so numerous and the fishing pressure is so relentless, Texoma stripers tend to be small. A 10-pounder is a nice fish, and a 20-pounder is considered a trophy. Bigger stripers are frequently caught in the tailrace waters below Denison Dam, and the fishing is good for several miles downstream from the dam. Free-lining live bait is an effective tactic, but many large fish are caught on jigs and topwater plugs.

Texoma probably has more active fishing guides than any Texas lake. It's less crowded in the Red River below the dam, where a handful of guides use air boats to negotiate the fluctuating river levels.

Striped bass dominate the fishing at Texoma, but it's also a good lake for catfish, largemouth bass, crappie, and smallmouth bass; some smallmouths between 5 and 7 pounds have been caught here. February and March are best for big smallmouths; late spring through early summer is tops for overall action.

In winter, big blue catfish are often caught on natural baits fished on submerged river ledges. The blues average more than 20 pounds. Blue and channel catfish are numerous here, and many successful anglers drift with live or cut shad, concentrating on middepth flats, the shoreline, and deeper creek channels. Platter Flats, Willafa Wood, and Willow Springs are prime spots.

Richland Chambers Reservoir. At nearly 45,000 acres, this lake near Corsicana is one of the best all-around fishing lakes in Texas. Richland Chambers is excellent for largemouth bass, crappie, white bass, and catfish. When the lake was filling in 1987, anglers caught tremendous numbers of channel catfish by simply fishing with natural bait along inundated roadbeds. Richland Chambers remains a exceptionally productive catfish lake.

It's also an excellent lake for crappie, which spend most of their year suspended next to submerged trees on main lake points. For an angler unfamiliar with Richland Chambers, the best time to catch crappie is during the spring spawn, which generally peaks in April. During this period, you can find crappie around shallow spawning areas in

T

virtually every part of the lake. Dabble for them with live minnows or jigs. Bona fide 2-pounders are common in this lake.

Also common are 2-pound white bass. From spring through fall, Richland Chambers is an excellent white bass lake. These fish hang out on main-lake structure most of the time and can usually be caught on jigging spoons or grubs bounced off the bottom. When white bass school on the surface, catching a mess of them is an absolute given.

The lake's Richland Creek arm contains an abundance of standing timber and is a favorite haunt for largemouth bass anglers. Richland Chambers has earned a deserved reputation for high-quality bass. The best action occurs during the spring spawn from March through April, and during the consistent dog days of summer.

Lake Ray Roberts. About an hour's drive north of Dallas, Ray Roberts, at 29,350 acres, is an excellent fishery for largemouth bass, white bass, and crappie. The best structure occurs in the lake's easternmost arm, which features numerous feeder creeks with abundant timber and brush. Emergent vegetation, including hydrilla, also provides good cover, particularly for bass.

A good bet for oversize bass at Lake Ray Roberts is to fish the shallow flats and coves in the backs of creeks when the early-spring water temperature creeps into the high 50s. That's when bigger bass stage near spawning areas and are often caught on big spinnerbaits, jigs, or soft-plastic lizards.

Crappie fishing is good most of the year around standing timber or submerged brushpiles in 15 to 30 feet of water. The lower end of the lake is mostly open water, but an abundance of humps and ridges hold concentrations of white bass. Whites often school on the surface during warm months.

Ray Roberts State Park is one of the most fully developed Texas state parks. It surrounds the lake in several different units, offering good camping facilities and lake access.

Cooper Lake. East of Dallas, Cooper Lake lies north of Sulphur Springs, about equidistant from that small town as Lake Fork is located south of Sulphur Springs. Cooper was supposed to become another Lake Fork, but this hasn't happened yet. Cooper is, however, a solid bass fishery in its own right.

Half of Cooper consists of flooded timber with occasional boat rows cut through the thickets. That's where most bass anglers concentrate their efforts, particularly during spring spawning season. The open-water portion of Cooper also contains interesting structure, however. Summer fishing is particularly good on humps and submerged pond dams in the main portion of the lake.

At 22,740 acres, Cooper is an excellent crappie lake and also very good for catfish. There's a particularly productive fishery for virtually all species in the Cooper Dam tailrace. Fishing for a variety of species, including catfish, crappie, and white bass, is best in late winter and early spring.

Cooper Lake has an excellent state park complex that provides good boat ramp access to all areas of the lake. The park also has excellent camping facilities and even has fully furnished cabins for rent.

Lake Livingston. One of the "Big Three" East Texas lakes that put Texas on the national fishing map decades ago, Livingston remains a good fishery. Livingston was originally known for largemouth bass but the emphasis has shifted to striped bass, white bass, crappie, and catfish.

Interestingly, top striper fishing occurs in the Trinity River tailrace below the lake, and superb white bass fishing happens during the spring spawning run in the Trinity River above Lake Livingston. Striper angling below the dam requires specialized equipment: rods capable of long casts, and reels that hold enough line to handle sustained, current-aided runs from a powerful fish. This tailrace fishery is likewise great for big catfish.

The white bass run above Livingston is historically one of the strongest spawning runs in the state. When water flows are good, the best spawning runs occur from late January through March. It's possible to catch hundreds of big whites (up to 3 pounds) per day. The best lures are light jigs with a spinner attached for added flash. The water usually ranges from murky to downright muddy. When water is muddy in the river proper, the fish move up various tributary creeks and often congregate in unbelievable numbers.

Fairfield Lake. Covering just 2,353 acres, this power plant cooling reservoir between Dallas and Houston is an unusual fishery. Fairfield is an excellent lake for largemouth bass, but it's also a literal hotspot for big red drum and hybrid stripers.

Like other power plant lakes, Fairfield uses its water to cool an electrical generating plant. The plant releases warm water into the lake. The outlet canal is a coldwater gathering place for an unlikely assortment of tackle-wrecking gamefish, the toughest being red drum.

These are the same redfish caught on the coast, but they seem particularly strong in the forage-rich waters of Fairfield and several other power plant lakes around Texas. The power plant reds also take on an incredible color, like the copper shine of a new penny. Reds take live bait, but they'll readily smash just about any swimming plug that resembles a baitfish.

Redfish gather in schools over humps and creek channels. For those unfamiliar with the lake, trolling is a good way to locate fish. Fairfield reds commonly weigh 10 to 15 pounds; you won't catch many on light tackle. The same techniques that yield redfish will also tempt the lake's abundant hybrid stripers.

Fairfield Lake is surrounded by an excellent state park with good camping facilities and hiking trails. The lake has become a hotspot for wintering bald

Collect Pond in lower New York City was once one-fourth of a mile long and contained a good population of brook trout; Federal Plaza now sits on the site of that pond, which was filled in by 1803.

eagles. They're visible from the hiking trails, but you'll get a better look from a boat or from the eagle tours run by park personnel.

Lake Tawakoni. A venerable 36,700-acre lake east of Dallas, Lake Tawakoni was impounded in 1960 and was originally known for largemouth bass. Tawakoni has developed into more of an open-water fishery, however. It may be the top white bass lake in the state.

When the whites, locally called sand bass or sandies, are feeding from spring through fall, you can catch them literally by the hundreds. Two basic fishing patterns yield huge catches. The fish often feed on the bottom, attacking shad as the hapless baitfish cross submerged humps or main-lake points. Use sonar to locate the structure and the fish. Sand bass often show up as giant schools on the sonar. At such times, any kind of small jigging spoon will catch them. A solid chunk of brightly painted lead called a slab spoon is most commonly used to jig the fish.

You may also see white bass schooling on the surface. When the fish are in a surface feeding frenzy, they'll strike just about anything that vaguely resembles a shad. Everything from slabs reeled like mad to keep them in the strike zone to buzzbaits and small topwaters will work. Fly anglers can catch these fish on nearly every cast by using a small white streamer.

Striped bass often mix in with the white bass and are caught with the same techniques. The best fishing for both white and striped bass usually occurs from the FM 35 bridge south to the dam.

Other notable East Texas lakes in this region include Cypress Springs, Conroe, Cedar Creek, Lewisville, Lake Ray Hubbard, Murvaul, Lake O' the Pines, Palestine, Monticello, and Nacogdoches.

Central Texas. The waters of Central Texas are not as large or well-known as those in East Texas, but they still draw many anglers. Some have excellent bass fishing, and the larger ones are briefly profiled here.

Guadalupe River. The scenic Guadalupe River below Canyon Dam is the state's only rainbow trout fishery where fish survive during the brutal summers. Water coming from the bottom of Canyon Lake maintains the same temperature, roughly 50°F, year-round. Thus, trout are present in the river for at least 10 miles below the dam. These are stocked trout, but a few fish do survive from year to year, so a fair number of 16- to 20-inch rainbows can be caught along with the typical hatchery 10-inchers.

The best fishing occurs during cold months, when hatchery trout are released on a regular basis. Guadalupe trout take a variety of dry and wet flies. Top dry-fly patterns include Adams on Nos. 14 to 22, Light Cahill No. 14, and Blue-Winged Olive in Nos. 18 to 20. Productive wet flies include San Juan Worm No. 8, Quill Gordon in Nos. 14 to 16, and Black Gnat in Nos. 12 to 14. Top streamers are a No. 6 Woolly Bugger in olive, black, or olive; a black Clouser Minnow No. 10; and an olive Clouser Crayfish.

Although the Guadalupe is best known for cold-weather rainbows, it is an excellent fly fishing stream for smallmouth bass and sunfish. Giant striped bass also prowl deep pools below the tailrace, fattening on trout. The big stripers aren't plentiful and are difficult to catch, but the river has yielded 50-pounders.

Lake Whitney. A scenic 23,000-acre impoundment on the Brazos and Nolan Rivers north of Waco, Whitney is arguably the best all-around fishing lake in Texas. It has excellent angling for striped bass, smallmouth bass, white bass, and largemouth bass, and is also a good catfish and crappie lake.

The lake's rocky substrata has made it the top smallmouth bass lake in Texas. Smallmouths aren't native to the state, but they've been stocked in several impoundments. Whitney dominates the state's smallmouth bass records. Five-pounders are caught here year-round.

The best time to catch a big smallmouth is in fall and winter. The fish readily strike crankbaits and spinnerbaits cast along rocky points and dropoffs in the lower end of the lake. Any submerged tree line will likely hold smallmouth as well as largemouth bass. For the best odds on a big smallmouth, try night fishing at Whitney for several nights before and after a full moon. That's when the biggest fish are historically caught.

Winter months also produce the best action at Whitney for big striped bass. Use sonar to locate schools of stripers, which like to feed on humps or points from midlake south. Live shad or large white jigs dropped into the feeding fish will draw strikes. Fifteen-pound stripers are common here, and 20-pounders are caught on a regular basis. There's also a scenic fishery for stripers, smallmouth bass, and largemouth bass in the Brazos River below the dam. The river is ideal for float fishing either with a canoe or an aluminum jonboat.

Fayette Power Project Lake. This is one of several very good power plant lakes scattered around Texas. Fayette Power Project (FPP) Lake's fame is based on surface schooling largemouth bass. This may be the best school bass lake in the nation and is certainly the best 2,400-acre school bass lake anywhere.

Surface activity is best from early summer through fall, with the peak occurring in September or October. During calm days this time of year, you may see 10 different schools of bass simultaneously murdering shad on the surface. Many of the schoolies weigh 3 to 5 pounds.

Because the water is clear and the fishing pressure is heavy, FPP schoolies are very sophisticated. It's best to experiment with different sizes and styles of topwater plugs, small crankbaits, or plastic grubs to find the most productive lure. Locate the right offering and you'll catch a bass on nearly every cast.

T

Other notable Central Texas lakes include Possum Kingdom, Buchanan, Belton, Brownwood, Aquilla, and Proctor.

West Texas. This region is characterized by arid country and fewer impoundments, but its major waters are very popular fisheries.

Lake Amistad. Situated in West Texas on the Texas-Mexico border near Del Rio, Amistad is known as "Big Friendly," but it could easily be called "Big Windy." When full, the lake covers 67,000 acres of open river canyons at the confluence of the Rio Grande, Pecos, and Devil's Rivers. The wind blows in this part of the world, and the water gets rough.

Amistad is an excellent lake for largemouth bass and a top Texas lake for channel catfish. Anglers using soured maize to bait catfish to their anchored boat will often catch a pile of channel cats. A good method for Amistad's bass is to fish Texas-rigged plastic worms along ledges on the river channels.

Other notable West Texas lakes include O. H. Ivie, O. C. Fisher, and E. V. Spence.

South Texas. *Falcon Lake.* Probably because of its location in South Texas and fluctuating water levels, Falcon Lake is one of the unsung fisheries in Texas. When full, Falcon covers nearly 80,000 acres. It's seldom full, but low water in these parts tends to congregate fish into a smaller space.

Falcon lies on the Rio Grande, 75 miles south of Laredo. It receives light fishing pressure for such a good lake. Five-bass catches totaling 30 pounds are common during the spawning season, which tends to peak in February because of Falcon's location. The weather is often pleasant early in the year when conditions are blustery elsewhere. Like many Texas lakes, Falcon is prime water for fishing spinnerbaits.

Choke Canyon Reservoir. An unstable lake level has caused problems for Choke Canyon, which appeared destined to be the Lake Fork of South Texas. Choke Canyon produced, and continues to produce, many bass weighing 10 pounds or more. The lake is cursed by a small watershed, however. Combined with an arid location 75 miles south of San Antonio, Choke Canyon has experienced a roller-coaster cycle of high and low water.

Fishing is dramatic during the spring, when spinnerbaits cast beside brushy or grassy cover are a good bet for big fish. Although bass fishing is the big draw at Choke Canyon, this is also an excellent year-round lake for crappie and catfish. An interesting sidelight is the abundance of wildlife viewing. The Calliham Unit of Choke Canyon State Park offers some of the best public-area wildlife viewing in the entire state.

An offbeat fishery at Choke Canyon revolves around alligator gar. The big, prehistoric-looking fish are incredibly plentiful. In summer, they surface to gulp air, and it's possible to sight cast to these rising fish, some of which top 100 pounds.

Other notable South Texas lakes include Texana and Corpus Christi.

Saltwater

Upper coast. From the Louisiana border to Matagorda, inshore waters of the upper coast consist of Sabine Lake, Trinity Bay, Galveston Bay, East Bay, West Bay, and East Matagorda Bay. Despite the proximity to Houston and the resulting fishing pressure, the upper coast is very productive for a wide variety of species.

Inflow from several large river systems keeps the water turbid and, during heavy rainfall periods, brackish. Eastern Texas receives more rainfall than the remainder of the state. This portion of the coast also features boggy bottoms and deeper water than most Texas bay systems.

Fishing is nonetheless good, and most of the pressure is directed toward trout and redfish. Both species are abundant year-round.

The upper coast is also good for flounder. Flounder in other Texas waters are seldom the target species for rod-and-reel anglers. Along the upper coast, particularly around Sabine Lake, anglers use live bait to tempt flatfish. The preferred baits are live gulf killifish, locally called marsh minnows or mud minnows. Marsh minnows are hooked through the lips on a light wire hook. The rigging includes a short leader about 6 inches long attached to the fishing line via a barrel swivel. A slip sinker just heavy enough to keep the bait on bottom is placed above the swivel. Fishing in this fashion for flounder is like fishing a plastic worm for bass. Flatfish often strike tentatively. Veteran anglers wait 5 to 10 seconds after the strike before setting the hook.

When water temperatures cool in the fall, flounder move out of the bays and head for the gulf. This creates a fall flounder run along jetties leading from the bays. Rollover Pass, a narrow cut that connects East Bay to the gulf on the Bolivar Peninsula, is a historic spot for fishing the fall flounder run.

Another major event that lures anglers to beachfront piers and the surf itself is the late summer run of bull reds. Big redfish spend their adult lives in deep waters of the gulf and move into the surf to spawn in August and September. Spawning runs are generally triggered by stormy weather. Redfish eggs must suspend in the turbulent water until they hatch. Bull reds are caught by anglers fishing cut mullet on the bottom. These fish typically weigh 20 to 40 pounds. Anglers can keep only one big redfish per year, but there's no limit on how many fish they can catch and release.

Middle coast. From Port O'Connor to Baffin Bay, Texas inshore waters take on a different personality. With more sand bottom and less freshwater inflow, the middle coast features clear, shallow water. It also contains one of the least-crowded and little-known coastal fishing destinations: Port O'Connor. From Port O'Connor, anglers have access to hundreds of square miles of shallow, clear water, much of which is well suited to wade fishing.

Just offshore of Port O'Connor lies Matagorda Island State Park. The island is 38 miles long and virtually undeveloped. Access is by boat only. Primitive camping is permitted along 2 miles of beach and also in the bay-side dock area. No motorized vehicles are allowed on the island, but anglers who bring their own bicycles can have miles of pristine beachfront to themselves. Surf fishing is best during summer months, when schools of trout, redfish, ladyfish, and Spanish mackerel are common.

Just down the coast from Port O'Connor, Rockport is a more popular sportfishing destination. A booming guide business takes clients after trout and redfish. Fishing can be good during any month, but summer and fall yield the most dependable weather and the most consistent fishing. Trout fishing is best on live shrimp, generally fished 2 to 3 feet beneath a popping cork. The popping cork has a concave head and, when jerked through the water, makes a slurping sound that imitates feeding fish. Live croaker are a favorite bait for tempting oversize trout.

Corpus Christi is the biggest city on the middle coast, and it's the jumping off place for Padre Island, the longest barrier island in North America. Adventurous anglers with 4-wheel-drive vehicles can explore more than 40 miles down the beach through Padre Island National Seashore. When conditions are right, dozens of fish species cruise within casting range of shore. The best conditions occur in the summer and fall; action peaks around September, when a migration of offshore baitfish usually comes in proximity of the island and triggers a feeding frenzy that includes everything from tiger sharks to ladyfish.

The southernmost extremity of the middle coast is Baffin Bay, an isolated area known for big speckled trout. Two Texas trout records have come from Baffin Bay. Spring is the best time for a shot at a Baffin Bay trout weighing 10 pounds or more. Local pros cast shallow-diving jointed plugs and concentrate on ancient rock formations scattered around the shallow bay system. The rocks aren't rocks at all; these formations were excreted by marine worms and exist nowhere else in Texas.

Lower coast.   Inland waters of the lower coast consist almost entirely of the Laguna Madre—the mother lagoon—which spreads over hundreds of square miles of clear, shallow water covering turtle grass and other vegetation from Baffin Bay to Boca Chica. The Laguna Madre incorporates among the best sight fishing for trout and redfish in the state. The habitat is more akin to the Florida Keys than the opposite end of Texas.

Although fly fishing is a favorite sport throughout the middle coast, the lower coast is perfectly suited to flycasting from the raised platform of a shallow-draft boat or by wading. Redfish are ideally suited to being stalked by anglers, especially flycasters. The copper-colored reds are easy to see in the clear, shallow water. Fish sometimes feed with

Redfish, being held by the middle angler here, are a primary draw in the shallow waters of Aransas Bay near Rockport.

their noses rooting on the bottom and their tails literally out of the water (tailing). Moreover, the fish are nearsighted and not particularly spooky. Fly fishing on the middle and lower coast is perfectly suited to floating fly lines. Best flies include shrimp and crab patterns, and small baitfish patterns in yellow and green.

Snook have made a comeback in the Lower Laguna Madre, an area that features subtropical weather. Although snook are caught on the shallow flats, the deep waters of the Brownsville Ship Channel are more consistent for this species. During summer and fall, topwater lures fished along the edges of the ship channel draw enough strikes to make an interesting day.

Port Isabel is the best-known spot for catching Texas tarpon. Luckily, tarpon have also made a comeback in Texas and are more prevalent all along the coast.

Offshore.   Texas offshore fishing is good from one end of the coast to the other. The best fishing generally begins in May, with the arrival of migrant species that spend the warm months in Texas waters. Fishing remains good through October.

Offshore fishing along the upper coast is good out of Sabine Pass, Galveston, and Freeport. Freshwater outflows, shallow inshore water, and general offshore currents combine for murky water conditions along this stretch. In May, you might not hit clear water until you're 40 miles offshore. By midsummer, the calm winds and favorable currents often push blue water very near the beaches.

Offshore favorites include king and Spanish mackerel, cobia (called ling here), dolphin (dorado), amberjack, red snapper, bluefish, and a variety of large and small sharks. Along the upper coast, angling concentrates around offshore oil rigs; these towering structures represent irresistible structure to migrant gamefish. The oil rigs are attractive to anglers because they are visible for miles across the open water and are thus easy to locate.

T

T

Anglers either troll around the rigs or tie up to the downcurrent side of the structure and put out lines baited with natural baits like sandtrout, cigar minnows, or menhaden. Good combination fishing is available by allowing unweighted or lightly weighted baits to drift downcurrent while you probe the bottom with jigs or heavily weighted squid or other baits. It's possible to catch an amazing assortment of fish using these techniques.

Veteran offshore anglers generally include light tackle in their arsenal. When the big fish are not cooperative, there are always spadefish, bluefish, and other small denizens that can be tempted to bite small lures.

During the shrimping season, working the shrimp fleet is another productive fishing style. Shrimp boats pull their nets all night, then anchor at daylight to cull the catch. The bycatch consists mostly of small fish that are shoveled into the water, creating a huge chum line that attracts predators. Kingfish, sharks, and other gamefish eat their fill and lounge in the shade of the anchored boat, where they can be tempted by lures or natural baits. Shrimp boat crews may be enticed to trade several pounds of fresh baitfish for beverages.

Although billfishing in Texas is a low-percentage sport, sailfish, white marlin, and blue marlin are caught on a regular basis, mostly from ports along the middle and lower coasts.

TEXAS RIG
See: **Soft Worm.**

THERMAL BAR
A sharp distinction between temperatures offshore, primarily a phenomenon of large lakes, including the Great Lakes of North America, that exists in mid- to late spring. A thermal bar is a mixing of water temperatures leading to the development of a thermocline *(see)*. A thermal bar may establish many miles offshore on huge lakes, starting at the edge of a mass of 39°F water.

Cooler offshore water on a distinct surface thermal break is a prime place to be looking for big-lake

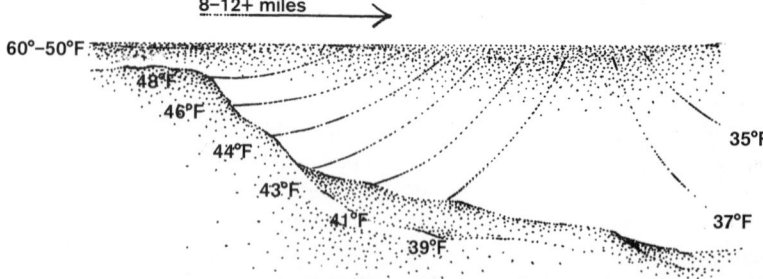

A thermal bar may form several miles offshore on huge lakes, starting at the edge of a mass of 39°F water. Fishing takes place on the edges where the temperature jumps several degrees, such as the area between 48° and 44°F illustrated here.

fish such as salmon and steelhead. Such an area is prime for trollers but may offer rare opportunities for casting to cruising steelhead or salmon.

A thermal bar does not form in some years and may last for only a few weeks at most when it does. The interface between differing temperatures may trap insects and small aquatic organisms, and provide feeding opportunities.
See: **Finding Fish; Temperature.**

THERMAL STRATIFICATION
See: **Stratification.**

THERMOCLINE
The layer of water with rapid temperature change in a lake or pond that is stratified; the layer above is the epilimnion, and the layer below is the hypolimnion.
See: **Stratification.**

THERMOMETER
See: **Temperature Gauge.**

THREADFIN, KING   *Polynemus sheridani.*
Other names—Threadfin salmon, Burnett salmon, king salmon, Sheridan's threadfin, gold threadfin.

The king threadfin, along with the four-fingered or blue threadfin (*Eleutheronema tetradactylum;* also called blue salmon, Cooktown salmon, Rockhampton salmon, giant threadfin, colonial salmon, blind tassel fish, and blunt-nosed salmon), make up a commercially viable fishery and are of considerable interest to recreational anglers in the northern half of Australia. Fast and sometimes spectacular fighters, they are also excellent table fish, preferred by many over barramundi, and their fillets have been substituted for barramundi by unscrupulous commercial fishermen, the difference being detectable only by scientific methods. Of the two species, the king threadfin is the more popular commercially, and in Australia is taken in gillnets used in the barramundi fishery. Anglers favor the king threadfin because of its larger size, although many anglers tend to ignore the distinction between the two species and characterize both as king threadfin or threadfin salmon.

Identification. Both species are similar in general appearance. The principal and definite identification characteristics, however, are the long filaments or rays located in the pectoral area, sometimes known as "fingers." There are five in the king threadfin and three or four in the blue threadfin. These are thought to be used for finding food and, possibly, for detecting obstructions invisible in the muddy water in which they are frequently found. Each has an adipose eyelid that is a thin membrane over the eye. Body coloring is bluish gray or bluish green above, shading to silver in the belly area. Yellowish pectoral fins and a deeply forked caudal fin are other features of both species. They lack real teeth.

Size. In northern Australian waters, king threadfin have been known to grow to at least 32 kilograms with a fork length of 140 centimeters, whereas the blue threadfin appears to maximize at a fork length of 82 centimeters and 18 kilograms. An Australian sportfishing record has been listed as 16.35 kilograms for the king threadfin, and 9.64 kilograms for the blue threadfin.

Distribution. King threadfin range over the top half of Australia from the Exmouth Gulf in Western Australia to the Mary River in southern Queensland.

Habitat. These fish are found in shallow and often muddy waters over sandbars and mud bottoms, although the blue threadfin is sometimes taken in clear, offshore waters and along ocean beaches. They mostly live in tidal streams, especially those places where feeder creeks enter the main stream and where runoff from mangrove areas brings food. They also favor tidal mud flats and feed on a rising tide there, and they are not averse to journeying far upstream into freshwater during the wet season.

Life history/Behavior. The king threadfin and the blue threadfin both appear to spawn during the summer months from October through March, and the most active month is December. The eggs are planktonic, and the nursery areas are known to be in shallow inshore waters of low salinity. The larval stage is not well documented, but it is known that specimens with a 3-centimeter fork length are present over tidal flats and in the lower estuaries from October through May. Fecundity is high; ripe blue threadfin contain more than 681,000 eggs. Like barramundi, mature threadfin exist as males for several years, then become females.

Food and feeding habits. Threadfin are carnivorous feeders that find the bulk of their food in surface waters. In some areas they hunt for crabs, prawns, and shellfish, but their main food consists of small fish such as herring, mullet, whiting, pilchards, garfish, small flathead, jewfish, squid, and octopus.

Angling. Whether specifically targeted, or fortuitously taken by the angler chasing barramundi, threadfin are highly respected for their fighting qualities. Fast moving, tackle testing, unforgiving, ornery, and as spectacular as any barramundi, they are a high priority among Australian anglers.

Because they are frequently found in turbid water, such areas are best fished using live or dead baits. Favorite items are crabs, live fish, pilchards, garfish, and whiting. The bait angler's tackle is generally a 2- to 3-meter rod, 10-kilogram line, and 4/0 to 6/0 hooks. Baits are fished near the bottom and under a float. Wire leaders may be necessary to avoid cutting on the threadfin's powerful jaws, and also because of the ever-present possibility of

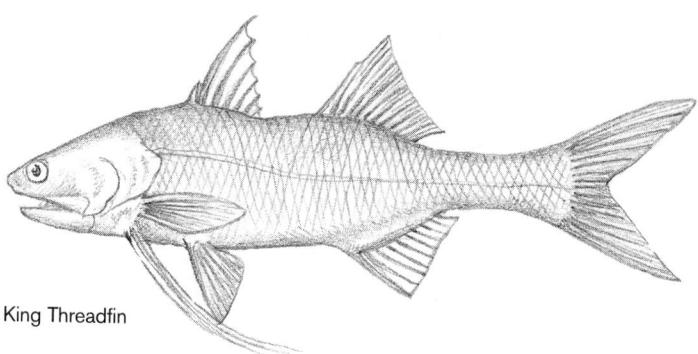

King Threadfin

hooking a barramundi. Most fishing is from a boat due to the difficulties of shoreline access.

Lure fishing is increasingly seen as the most exciting threadfin fishing method. Both baitcasting and spinning outfits are used, similar to that for taking barramundi. Lures vary from diving minnow plugs to surface poppers. A common technique is to identify where the fish are feeding (surface activity can be frantic) and to cast a surface popper to the edges of the school of baitfish. Noisy swimming lures are worth trying, particularly where the water is clouded.

The best angling times are late afternoons on a rising tide, when threadfin move in over flats to feed. A falling tide can also be productive, especially in the vicinity of gutters that are draining water from mangrove areas and are carrying food.

THREADLINE

An uncommon term referring to light- or ultra-light-strength fishing line.
See: Line.

THREATENED SPECIES

In the United States, a species is classified as threatened if it is likely to become endangered within the foreseeable future throughout all or a significant portion of its range. Elsewhere, a species is classified as vulnerable rather than threatened, according to the International Union for the Conservation of Nature and Natural Resources (IUCN).
See: Endangered Species.

THUNDERSTORM
See: Safety; Weather.

TIDAL CURRENT

Horizontal movement of water in response to tide.
See: Tides.

TIDAL RIP

A spot where two or more currents collide or where a swift deep current confronts a shoal. Also known

T

as a tide line, tide rip, rip tide, or rip, it is common in coastal waters in sounds, bays, estuaries, and inlets; the disturbed water that is generated here is often conducive to foraging for top predatory species, especially striped bass, bluefish, red drum, and snook as forage fish become trapped or disoriented in the strong flow. Some sportfish can be caught on or near the surface in a tidal rip, especially coho salmon, but most are caught by getting lures or bait close to the bottom. Drift fishing is popular, as is trolling.

Tidal rips result from the movement of currents rather than the movement of tides as the name suggests. Usually when two currents converge, one is stronger than the other, creating a seam or wall, often accompanied by debris at the surface, which is called a tide line and forms along the edge of the currents. Tidal rips are often visible from the surface, as currents push upward and disturb the surface, especially when the water is calm or nearly calm. Churned surface water is one indicator, as are surface debris and feeding birds. In rougher water a large tidal rip can be felt because boats require more power to maintain speed through the turbulent water, similar to running up a swift river. Disturbance through the entire water column also has a tendency to confuse sonar, which may not operate properly. Some tidal rips are smaller and less obvious, however. A small rip may be distinguished only by a short length of "nervous," rippled, or choppy water that fronts against calm or calmer water.

When tides are strong, as in spring tides, when a strong wind drives waves counter to the tidal rip, and when ocean swells are large, tidal rips can be dangerous, and boaters have to be careful and maintain constant control.

See: Currents; Tides.

TIDE LINE

The line of debris that often collects along the edge of a tidal rip.

See: Tidal Rip.

TIDES

A tide is the change in water level, at a given point on the earth, due to the revolution of the moon around the earth and to the rotation of the earth along its axis; these forces result in gravitational pull by the moon and the sun. This pull causes the water in the oceans to bulge on both sides of the earth, alternately raising and lowering the water level along coastlines, completing the cycle twice each day in most locales (some places experience one high and one low daily, and some have two of each that vary in range). Since the moon does not follow exactly the same path around the earth every day, tide frequency varies slightly. Usually, based on average time, the frequency between high tides is approximately 12 hours and 25 minutes, and each

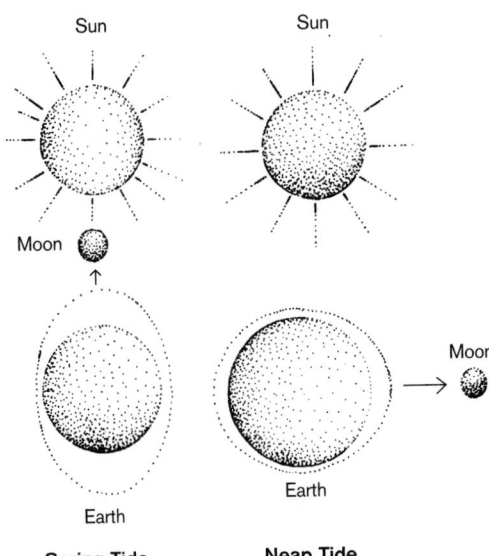

Spring Tide   **Neap Tide**

Spring tides occur when the sun and the moon lie in a direct line with the earth at full moon and new moon. Neap tides occur when the sun and the moon pull at right angles at first quarter and last quarter. Spring tides are more extreme than normal tides, being very high and very low, whereas neap tides are less extreme.

day the high tide will be approximately 50 minutes later than it was the day before; the same is true for low tides.

The lowest level of water is the low tidewater mark, also called the low water level; the highest level of water is the high tidewater mark, or high water level. The distance between these is the tidal range, or amplitude.

Because the tidal range depends on the basin containing the water and the contour of the coastline, tidal ranges vary widely around the world. Where the coastline provides open access to the sea or to larger bodies of water (such as rivers), the tidal range may be less than 1 foot. In the Gulf of Mexico along Texas, for example, the tidal range is 1 to 2 feet. Where an irregular coastline forms an inlet, the tidal range can be as much as 40 feet, as occurs in the Bay of Fundy in Nova Scotia.

When the sun and the moon lie in a direct line with the earth at full moon and new moon, their combined gravitational pull causes high tides to be very high and low tides to be very low. These are called spring tides. At first quarter and last quarter, when the sun and moon pull at right angles, tides are less extreme than usual. These are known as neap tides.

Since the moon rotates around the earth in an elliptical orbit, it is not always the same distance from the earth and it is not always directly over the same part of the earth's surface. The point of the orbit closest to earth is the perigee. The point of the orbit farthest from earth is the apogee. When the moon is in perigee, its gravitational pull affects the earth more and the tidal range is greater. When it is in apogee, the opposite is true.

Tides are predictable because the orbits of the earth and moon are predictable and the slope of the ocean basins is known. Tide charts or tables for specific areas are published for shipping purposes, and the tides for other nearby areas can be calculated by adding or subtracting correction factors. These tables provide daily high and low tide information, as well as the time at which the tide is going out or coming in. The incoming portion of a high tide is commonly known as a rising tide or a flood tide; the outgoing portion is known as the falling tide or ebb tide. The tide is said to be slack when tidal current velocity is near zero.

Tide levels or heights are measured in reference to a fixed point called "mean low tide," which is the average level of low tides in that location. If a tide height is listed as $2^1/_2$, for example, it will be $2^1/_2$ feet above mean low tide. These predictions are generally quite accurate, but they can be greater or less than predicted because of storms or strong wind.

Tides and fishing.   In many aspects of sportfishing, there is a clear relevance between tidal activity and fish feeding activity. Tidal effects and tidal influences are visually most obvious in estuaries *(see)* and along the coastline by the shore and surf, rather than in the open ocean, except for tidal rips; they are especially obvious in rivers and marshes. In a salt marsh *(see)*, for example, with the incoming and high tide, large fish enter the marsh in search of small fish, crabs, or other food, and they depart when the tide gets to a certain ebb point. The incoming tide can present more food, and the outgoing tide can flush food out with it, making the activity of gamefish most likely at certain stages of the tide.

In this situation, and in most coastal fishing, anglers experience better angling at certain times of tidal movement. Many anglers find that the hour or so of flood tide before high slack, and the hour or so of ebb tide after it, tend to generate the most fish activity, with best results during the latter. This depends to some extent on species as well; fish that utilize cover, like largemouth bass in tidal portions of rivers, may be most receptive to angling at the opposite period; the last hour or two of the outgoing tide before low slack and the same period after it are good for bass action because the fish are more restricted in location. The high water period for this species scatters baitfish.

The change in tide movement, no matter whether it is changing to or from high or low tide, is generally a preferred time to fish; slack tides are often unproductive. Keep in mind what the current direction is and use it to proper advantage when presenting your lures, flies, or bait. Fish face into the current, which is moving in different directions when it is incoming or outgoing, so you need to present your offering so that it comes to the fish rather than from behind it.

See: Currents.

TIGERFISH

Tigerfish are members of the characin subfamily Alestiidae and endemic to Africa. A relative of African tetras of aquarium popularity, and of such South American predators as piranhas *(see)* and payara *(see)*, they are equipped with a massive and fearsome set of canine teeth and are one of the leading freshwater sportfish on the African continent. They are also valued as a food fish for native people, and are harvested commercially in some areas. Excessive fishing by commercial interests and, in some cases, poaching, have caused population declines in certain waters. Sportfishing for tigerfish has increased in popularity since the 1980s, and in some areas, especially Zimbabwe, catch-and-release has been widely adopted.

The most widespread and most frequently referenced species is the common tigerfish *(Hydrocynus vittatus)*. It is also known as *tiervis* in the Afrikaans language, *nsanga* in Zambia, and in other native languages as *ndweshi, maluvali, mcheni, muvanga, manga, shabani, simu-kuta, uthlangi, uluthlangi.*

The larger but less well-known species is the giant tigerfish *(Hydrocynus goliath)*. It is also known as goliath tigerfish.

Identification.   Tigerfish have long conical teeth that overlap the outside of the jaws when the mouth is shut. They have an elongated compressed body with a raised dorsal fin, a deeply forked caudal fin, and an adipose fin. The body is silvery overall and dark on the back. The common tigerfish has a series of dashlike horizontal stripes that extend the

A tigerfish from Lake Kariba, Zimbabwe.

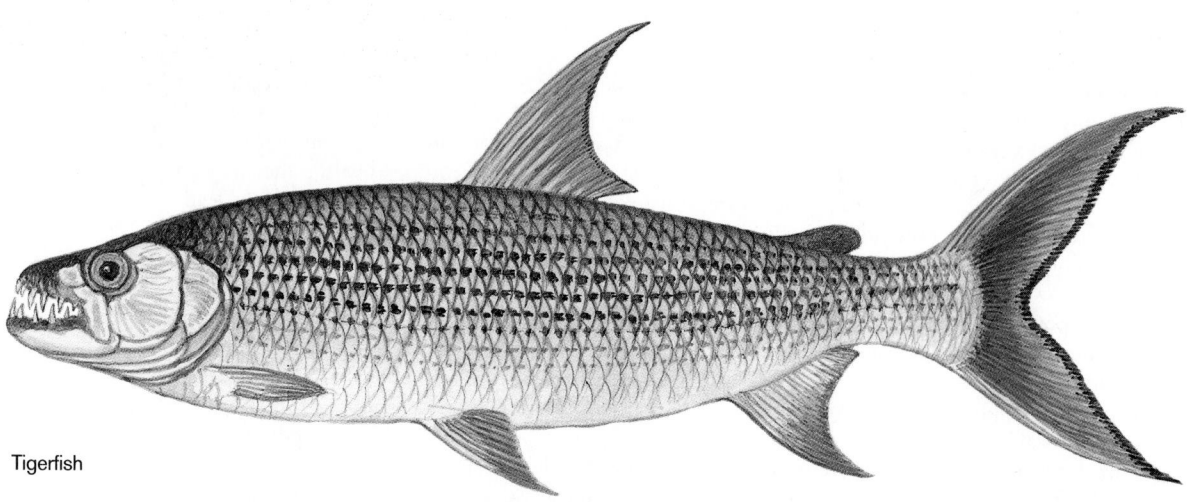

Tigerfish

lengthy of the body; actually, its heavy scales are blackened on the posterior, creating a continuous stripelike appearance from a distance. Its pelvic and pectoral fins, as well as the anterior part of the anal fin, are reddish orange; the caudal fin is also tinged with red or orange and fringed with black. Striping is absent on the giant tigerfish.

The common tigerfish has long gill rakers, which are approximately equal to the filaments, whereas the giant tigerfish has short gill rakers, which are less than one-third the length of the filaments.

Size.   The common tigerfish can grow to 34 pounds; the Zimbabwean record is a Lake Kariba fish of 34 pounds, 4 ounces. The all-tackle world record is a 21-pound, 13-ounce fish from the Zambezi River in Zimbabwe. In most areas the normal catch is in the 1- to 4-pound range, although larger fish are common in some waters. The giant tigerfish is the largest characin, growing to more than 5 feet long and possibly weighing more than 100 pounds; the all-tackle world record is a 97-pounder caught in the Zaire River in Zaire in 1988.

Distribution.   The common tigerfish occurs widely in rivers and lakes from West Africa to the Nile and southward to the Zaire, Zambezi, and Limpopo systems, as well as lowveld coastal systems to Pongola. It is present in Kenya's Lakes Victoria and Turkana, Malawi's Lake Nyasa and Shire River, Zimbabwe's Zambezi River and Lake Kariba, Uganda's Lake Victoria, Botswana's Okavanago Swamp, Mozambique's Zambezi and Shire Rivers, South Africa's Pongola Dam, Zambia's Lake Tanganyika and Zambezi River, Namibia's Caprivi Strip, and possibly in Angolan rivers, as well as other sites.

The giant tigerfish is more limited in range. It occurs in the Zaire River system, the Lualaba River, Lake Upemba, and Lake Tanganyika.

Habitat.   Tigerfish occur in warm, well-oxygenated waters—mainly larger rivers and lakes. In rivers they are commonly found on the edges of fast-flowing water, and occupy channel edges and eddies. With the exception of large specimens,

common tigerfish form roving schools of similar-size individuals.

Food and feeding habits.   Tigerfish have terrific appetites and consume a wide range of fish in their respective habitats. Small bream are one of their favorite foods. They are capable of consuming fish that are up to 40 percent of their own body length. These are fit, strong, almost muscular fish, and they are quick to strike, which makes them especially interesting to anglers.

Obviously their formidable dentition allows them to be rapacious, but it also presents an unusual facet of their life history. Tigerfish naturally lose and regrow their teeth. New teeth are always present in the gum just below the functional teeth; these quickly rotate into position to replace the lost teeth. In 1972, biologists observed that dozens of teeth were discovered on the bottom of a tank that held eight large tigerfish, yet the captive fish had full dentition; it was assumed that the fish all shed their teeth and replaced them with new ones without anyone noticing. Anglers have (although rarely) caught toothless tigerfish, which is a stage of several days' duration. The temporary absence of teeth obviously does not hinder this fish's rapaciousness.

Angling.   Although a vicious predator, the tigerfish does not attack humans as has been reported. It will strike readily at a variety of spoons, spinners, flies, and plugs, as well as live or cut baits, and it is caught by casting lures or flies, trolling, and drifting or stillfishing. The strike is strong and vicious and is followed by a series of spectacular leaps. The fish battles right up until boated. Many are lost because the line is cut, or because the teeth prevent the hook from imbedding. Tigerfish caught in fast water are even more tenacious than those in lakes, as they are more vigorous in fast water. The tendency of these fish to strike hard, leap when hooked, and fight aggressively, as well as to be caught by a variety of conventional angling methods, is what makes them such prized sportfish.

Medium-action rods of $6^1/_2$ to 7 feet are generally preferred, as is line of about 12-pound strength (although greater strength may be appropriate in heavily obstructed areas and where large individuals are possible). Terminal tackle should be protected by a wire leader to prevent the fish from severing the line with its sharp teeth.

Tigerfish schools vary in size from a pair of fish to 20 or more. In some waters, these schools become active, biting suddenly and for a period lasting up to 30 minutes. This activity ceases suddenly.

Many visiting anglers use small to medium spoons, spinners, and assorted swimming and diving plugs, as well as streamer flies. Local anglers in tigerfish waters are also fond of using live or dead baits.

A unique tigerfishing method, practiced on sections of some rivers, is fishing slightly downstream of a herd of wallowing hippos, where small bream are attracted by stirred-up detritus and can be easy pickings for tigerfish. Anglers need to stay a safe distance from the hippos, however.

See: Botswana; Zimbabwe.

TILAPIA

Tilapia are members of the Cichlidae family, which is well known to aquarium hobbyists and numbers approximately 1,300 species and 105 genera. Possibly 900 cichlid species occur in Africa, including the native tilapia, which number approximately 100 species in two genera. Tilapia are native to that continent and to the Middle East, and have been widely introduced around the world for food production.

It is believed that the fish that fed the biblical 5,000 was the tilapia. Even before that, some 4,000 years ago, the first identifiable fish ponds built by Egyptians contained tilapia (and Nile perch). Perhaps the most well-known member of this group, the Mozambique tilapia *(Oreochromis mossambicus),* was transplanted to the Indonesian island of Java and eventually also became widely known as the Java tilapia; it has been widely cultivated in fish ponds.

Tilapia are generally small with a moderately deep and compressed body. They are characterized by the presence of a long dorsal fin, the anterior of which is spiny; a single nostril on each side of the snout; and an interrupted lateral line, which may be in either two or three parts. In North America, they may be confused with bluegills but can easily be distinguished from that species by the absence of a dark blue or black opercular flap.

Tilapia are common to the warm, weedy waters of sluggish streams, canals, irrigation ditches, ponds, and small lakes. Most tilapia are strictly freshwater fish, but some have adapted to brackish or saltwater environments, and some can tolerate environments with an extremely high temperature and very low oxygen. In freshwater, they are primarily algae and plant feeders. Many are

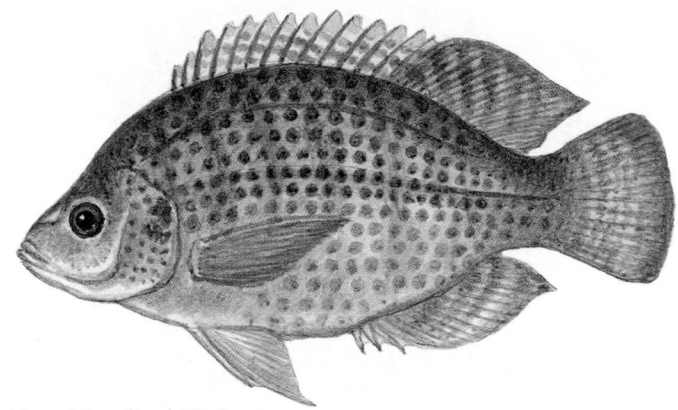

Mozambique (Java) Tilapia

mouthbrooders, although some build spawning nests, which they guard after the eggs hatch. Most are small, although some reportedly can grow as large as 20 pounds, and they are schooling species.

Despite their abundance, tilapia have little to no sportfishing value in some areas where they have been introduced, including North America, but some species are pursued by anglers in their native range, especially in southern Africa. As non-predatory fish, they do not respond to most lures and casting presentations but are caught with coarse fishing methods.

Tilapia have had mixed value in some areas where they have been introduced, crowding out some native species, stunting and breeding rapidly, and sometimes producing large crops of very small individuals, but also providing forage for larger predators, especially largemouth bass. They are important food fish that are harvested from cultured ponds and the wild for human consumption; tilapia are netted, for example, in Mexican lakes where they were introduced, and sold in U.S. markets.

TILEFISH

Tilefish are members of the Branchiostegidae and Malacanthidae families, which include roughly 50 species that are distributed worldwide. Most have little to no significance to anglers but are popular food fish, with firm white flesh, and are found in fish markets.

Most tilefish are less than 2 feet long and slender. The anal and dorsal fins are long and low; the pelvic fins are located far forward, directly under the pectorals. Some exist in temperate waters, but most are tropical.

A well-known species is the great northern tilefish *(Lopholatilus chamaeleonticeps),* which inhabits the outer continental shelf from Nova Scotia to northern South America (including the eastern Gulf of Mexico, Venezuela, Guyana, and Suriname) and is relatively abundant from southern New England to the mid-Atlantic coast of the United States at depths of 44 to 240 fathoms. They are generally

Sand Tilefish

found in and around submarine canyons, where they occupy burrows in the sedimentary substrate and feed on crustaceans, shrimp, squid, and small fish.

This species is relatively slow growing and long lived, with a maximum age and length of 35 years and 43 inches in females, and 26 years and 44 inches in males. At lengths exceeding 27 inches, the predorsal adipose flap, characteristic of this species, is larger in males and can be used to distinguish the sexes. Tilefish of both sexes are mature at ages 5 to 7. The back and sides are bluish or greenish gray, sprinkled with yellow spots. The belly and cheeks are rose, grading into white at the midline. The dorsal fin is marked with yellow spots. The pectoral fins are dark and margined with black, as is the anal fin.

A mass die-off of this species occurred in 1882, after which it was rare for decades. A small recreational fishery for tilefish developed during the late 1960s in New York and New Jersey, but recent recreational catches have been virtually nonexistent; some are caught occasionally by deep-fishing party boat anglers. Commercial longlining efforts have resulted in overexploitation of this species in its northern range.

The sand tilefish *(Malacanthus plumieri),* averaging 12 inches in length and occasionally reaching 24 inches, is a slim, almost eel-like fish found in reefs and sandy areas of warm Caribbean and Florida waters, rarely deeper than 50 feet. Like the tilefish, it has low, long dorsal and anal fins. The upper and lower lobes of the caudal fin are extended almost into filaments, and are more prominent than in the tilefish. The sand tilefish is light brown above and silvery below, marked with vertical bluish bars, the last of which forms a distinct blotch in front of the caudal fin.

A similar species to the sand tilefish is *M. hoedtii* of the western Pacific. Its tail, squared across the end, is white in the middle and has black upper and lower lobes. Another similar species, *M. latovittatus,* occurs in the Indo-Pacific region.

The ocean whitefish *(Caulolatilus princeps),* found from British Columbia to Peru (including the Galápagos but rare north of California) is a relative found in eastern Pacific waters. It is known in Spanish as *blanquillo* and *peje blanco.* Reaching a length of about $3^1/_2$ feet, it provides some angling sport and is caught commercially and sold in markets. The ocean whitefish has a comparatively small mouth. The back and sides are usually brown, the belly light. The fins are yellowish, tinged or streaked with blue or green.

TIMBER
Flooded timber is a form of natural cover that exists in many impoundments and in the flooded backwater of river systems. It can be important in fishing for largemouth bass, striped bass, and crappie, and sometimes important for such different species as walleye and peacock bass. Fields of standing timber in relatively shallow water, or the remnant stumps that remain, are very obvious to anglers, but in many reservoirs timber is covered by water and not obvious to the eye. The latter occurs when the flooded land is left uncleared, so that live trees are flooded when the impoundment fills with water. They have a long life when submerged in the water, and though hazards to navigation, they can provide shelter and ambush feeding opportunities for some gamefish.

Fishing. Timber can be intimidating to anglers, especially those who haven't encountered it before. Many anglers take a pretty haphazard approach to timber, but not every tree is the same.

Where timber sticks out of the water, there can be visible clues to good places to fish. The most conspicuous is the leading edge of the timber, which many anglers treat like a shoreline, keeping their boat out from it and casting lures to the edge or just beyond the edge and by it. In young reservoirs, where fish may be highly mobile and schools of wandering fish are likely to swim along this edge in search of bait, particularly shad, it may be good to spend a lot of time in such places, using relatively noisy, vibrating lures and covering a lot of territory. This tactic is not as reliable in lakes where timber has stood for a long time and fish behavior is relatively stabilized, although it may be more likely at times for striped bass than for largemouth bass.

Almost as obvious, and for similar reasons, are timbered points. If a timbered point is being washed by wind, it could have a concentration of bait on it, so that would be a good spot to fish.

Fishing among treetops is common in some reservoirs and in the backwaters of large rivers; this scene is at El Salto Lake, Mexico.

Another prominent place in a stand of trees might be the edge of a clearing, which could be where an old pond existed. In many flooded timber environments, farmlands were inundated, and old ponds or lakes with fish were important to early angling.

Where largemouth bass are the quarry, you frequently need to get into the trees and maneuver around, fishing deliberately in those places that are just a little different. This might be as simple as finding leaning trees rather than perpendicular ones. Leaning trees offer more shade and are more conducive to hiding than straight ones. It might mean looking for the largest, widest trees, again for shade, but also because of the underwater protection they might afford. Large multi-limbed trees eventually lose their limbs, which usually fall around the base of the tree. If enough fall and get stuck on lower below-water limbs, they form a canopy, which is a great hiding place.

Watch for different species of trees, too. Pines among hardwood usually signal a change in bottom depth. Pines usually grow on higher ground, such as a ridge; in the water this would be like a hump, and that might be the best place to fish. Tight clumps of smaller trees can provide protection and may be the ticket as well. A clump of trees on the edge of a creek channel is a particularly good spot. Some channels through timber are fairly obvious and can visually be followed through the trees, but in some flooded timber it is easy to lose the channel visually, in part because trees have fallen or are leaning or have disintegrated at the water line. That is when sonar equipment becomes important.

A channel is one of the most important underwater terrain features to look for with sonar, with special emphasis on the outside bends, where it comes near a point or shore, and especially where two channels meet. A roadbed, a dropoff, and other features are worth looking for as well.

Sonar is absolutely invaluable for fishing completely submerged timber, where there are seldom visual clues to depth or tree conformations. In deep, submerged timber, fish are usually suspended, sometimes at the treetops and sometimes among the branches. To prevent fishing haphazardly, you have to know where you are and where your lure is. With a good sonar, some anglers are able to troll with downriggers over the tops of deep submerged timber to catch stripers.

You can vertically jig deep timber, too. The way to do this is to use a fairly heavy lead jig or preferably a jigging spoon. Spoons have treble hooks, whereas jigs have a single hook. Single hooks get hung up less so you might try replacing trebles with singles.

Spoons have an O-ring between the body and the hook, and this allows for a bit of swiveling, which facilitates de-snagging. In any event, lower the lure through the limbs, and retrieve by slowly jigging it; when it hits a limb, drop it down and then bring it back up over the limb. Keep jigging.

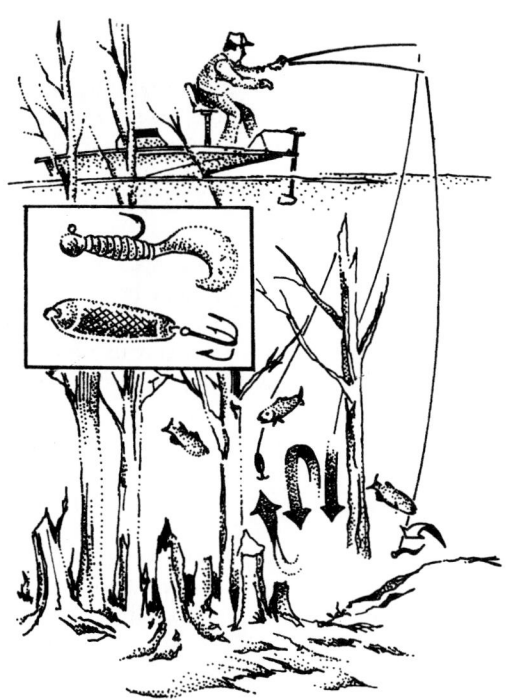

To fish deep in timber with minimal snagging, get directly over the tops of trees and fish vertically with jigs and jigging spoons (inset).

As long as you haven't buried the hook, it will usually come free when the weight of the lure falls back on it. When it gets wedged in a crotch, however, you may not get it free.

This tactic is most effective when you use an electric motor for positioning (or are tied to a tree) and where there is no breeze. You have to be able to jig vertically, and when you move off the vertical line, you greatly increase the chance of hanging up the jig. Doing this jigging gently and using heavy line with a fairly stiff-tipped rod, you can have a lot of excitement in the treetops with striped bass, hybrid stripers, or largemouths. Obviously, you need to be able to muscle a fish out of the branches and limbs very quickly.

Most of the angling done in trees is by casting, however, especially for largemouth bass and active schooling fish. Surface lures, when appropriate, are very productive. Because the water is usually stained or turbid in flooded timber, noise and action are important, so walking stick baits, poppers, and buzzbaits are good choices.

A rattling, vibrating crankbait is also a good lure choice, worked just below the surface. So is a spinnerbait. Floating-diving crankbaits have merit at times as well, although there is a knack to working these just right; don't set the hook when you tick a limb, and let the plug float up to get over obstructions.

For conventional casting as well as flipping, a plastic worm (use a pegged slip sinker) is a prime lure for largemouths in timber, as is a weedguard-protected jig with rubber tentacles and pork chunk.

The latter is used for flipping in shallow to mid-depth water.

One thing about conventional casting in the trees is certain: you'll fine-tune your casting abilities. Spend enough time in the flooded timber and your accuracy will be sharp.

Be sure to follow some common-sense precautions while fishing in flooded trees. Watch where you put your hands, for example; ants, bees, snakes, tarantulas, and other creatures may be about. Tilt the outboard motor up when in use, and run only at low-throttle speed. When standing in a boat, be aware of bumping into trees and be careful not to fall out.
See: Finding Fish.

TIN SQUID

An older style of metal spoonlike lure molded from block tin (and also called block tin squid), with a flat top and round or square keel, and used in saltwater fishing.
See: Spoon.

TIPPET

The terminal section of a fly fishing leader that is tied to the fly. Generally made of nylon monofilament like the leader, a tippet may be heavier and stiffer than the remainder of the leader, in which case it is called a shock tippet, or lighter

Shock tippets attached to tarpon flies are stretched on this board so that they're ready for instant, and natural-looking, use.

and softer, which is necessary for most fly fishing presentations.

A tippet is a standard and especially important component of a tapered leader, which is used in most fly fishing. It may be the final link in a personally constructed knotted compound tapered leader, or a section that is added to a commercially manufactured knotless tapered leader. For most freshwater fishing, and especially when angling for trout, a tippet is the lightest and thinnest in diameter portion of a fly fishing leader, and thus the weakest link in the chain from fly line to fly, as well as the section most easily cut or broken. For most freshwater fly fishing, especially for trout and salmon, it is important to match the size of the tippet to the hook size of the fly.

The normal length is about 15 inches for most fishing, but may be several feet long, especially when a supple tippet is necessary to make a delicate presentation, to turn the entire leader and fly over properly, and to enhance the drag-free float of the fly. Less delicate and shorter tippets, however, are more useful where large flies (and poppers or bugs) are fished. A fly fishing tippet is frequently replaced as the length diminishes due to breakoffs and shortening from replacing and retying flies.

The strength of the tippet or tip section of a leader is characterized in a system that derived from European watchmakers hundreds of years ago and was used to draw silkworm gut for nineteenth-century leader construction. Thus, gradations are based on sizes that each vary by .001-inch starting at size 1/5, which is equivalent to a diameter of .021-inch, down to 10/5, which is .012-inch, and continuing from 0X, which is .011-inch, down to 7X, which is .004-inch. These categorizations identify the diameter, not the strength. Strength is somewhat related to diameter, but different products with different tensile strengths make for varying strengths in products of identical diameter (see: line). Line spools and packaging, however, denote size, strength, and diameter. When in doubt, you can determine the classification in lighter tippet categories if you know the diameter; to do this, subtract the diameter from 11; for example, .004 subtracted from 11 is 4X, .011 subtracted from 11 is 0X, and .021 subtracted from 11 is (minus) 10, which translates into the 10/5 designation.

In some circumstances it is necessary to protect the end of the leader from being cut by the teeth, jaws, or gill covers of a fish. This is when a shock tippet, which is a short length of heavy monofilament or wire, is added to the end of the fly fishing leader. The breaking strength and diameter of the shock tippet exceed the breaking strength of the rest of the leader, sometimes by a great deal (often being from 30- to 100-pound strength). Shock tippets are generally no more than 12 inches long, especially to conform to world record specifications.

A tippet might also be identified as a class tippet. This is of primary concern to anglers trying to

establish world records on flycasting tackle. According to International Game Fish Association *(see)* regulations, a class tippet must be made of nonmetallic material and either attached directly to the fly or to the shock tippet, and at least 15 inches long. The 15-inch shock tippet, whether part of a knotted tapered leader or the last 15 inches of a knotless tapered leader, must conform to exact breaking strength specifications (the "class"), and it is this portion that is tested and judged according to the tippet-strength categories of records that exist.
See: Leader; Line.

TIPPING

Placing live or dead natural bait on the hook of a lure, primarily a jig. In freshwater, a live minnow or a whole worm or piece of worm is often placed either on the bare hook of a jig or on a jig hook that is already adorned with a soft artificial bait. In saltwater, tipping is typically done with a strip of fish flesh, which may or may not be used in conjunction with a soft artificial bait.
See: Jig.

TIP-UP

A device for ice fishing with bait.
See: Ice Fishing.

TOMCOD, ATLANTIC   *Microgadus tomcod.*
Other names—tomcod; French: *poulamon atlantique;* Spanish: *microgado.*

A member of the Gadidae family (codfish), the Atlantic tomcod is a small, hardy fish, resembling its relative the Atlantic cod *(see: cod, Atlantic).* Able to adapt to salinity changes and sudden cold spells, the tomcod can survive in both saltwater and freshwater. It is a delicious fish sometimes taken in large quantities by anglers and is caught commercially in small numbers due to its size.

Identification.   Characteristic of the cod family, the Atlantic tomcod has three dorsal and two anal fins, which are rounded, as is the caudal fin. The body is heavy and has a large, subterminal mouth. Its eyes are small. The coloring is olive brown on the back, fading lighter below, and the sides are heavily blotched with black. The fins have wavy or mottled designs.

The Atlantic tomcod can be distinguished from the Atlantic cod by its long, tapering ventral fins and smaller body.

Size/Age.   A generally small species that might be considered a saltwater panfish, the Atlantic tomcod averages 6 to 12 inches in length. It can weigh up to 1 pound.

Distribution.   The Atlantic tomcod inhabits waters along the North American coast from Labrador and the Gulf of St. Lawrence south to

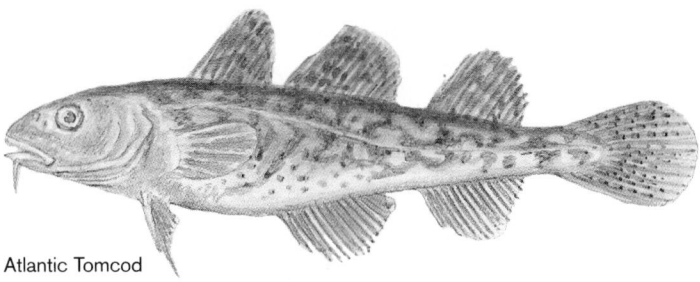

Atlantic Tomcod

Virginia. It is common locally north from Long Island.

Habitat.   Primarily dwelling along the coast, the Atlantic tomcod is known to enter freshwater rivers during winter. It is also landlocked in some Canadian lakes. The tomcod lives close to the bottom and is usually found in depths of 2 to 3 fathoms.

Spawning behavior.   The spawning season of Atlantic tomcod is from November through February. It spawns in brackish water or saltwater. The eggs sink to the bottom and attach to algae and rocks.

Food.   The Atlantic tomcod uses its chin barbel and ventral fins to detect and inspect food. It consumes small shrimp, amphipods, worms, clams, squid, and small fish.

Angling.   Tomcod are primarily taken on light line and while bottom fishing for other species, usually with small pieces of cut bait, shrimp, or worms.
See: Cod and Hake; Tomcod, Pacific.

TOMCOD, PACIFIC   *Microgadus proximus.*
Other names—tomcod, piciata, California tomcod.

A member of the Gadidae family, the Pacific tomcod is a small fish with minor commercial importance due to its small average size. In central California, it is a popular recreational sportfish, usually taken incidentally by anglers pursuing larger-growing species. Its flesh is tasty, and it might be considered a saltwater panfish.

Identification.   The body of the Pacific tomcod is elongated and slender. It has a small barbel on the chin. Characteristic of the cod family, the Pacific tomcod has three dorsal fins, two anal fins, a large head, and a large mouth with fine teeth. The body is covered with small, thin scales. Its coloring is olive green above and creamy white below, and the fins have dusky tips.

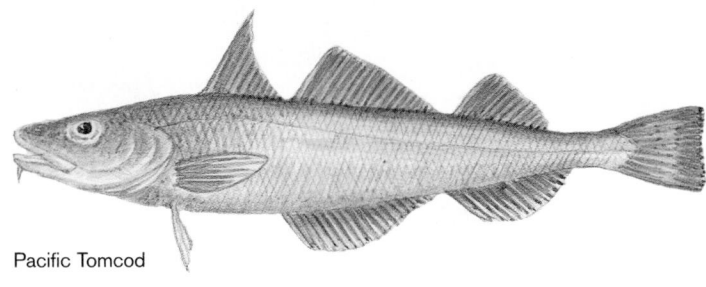

Pacific Tomcod

Three spineless dorsal fins and the small chin barbel separate the Pacific tomcod from any similar-appearing fish, except its cousin, the Pacific cod *(see: cod, Pacific)*. The Pacific cod has a barbel as long as the diameter of the eye, whereas the Pacific tomcod has a barbel less than one half the diameter of the eye.

Size.   The Pacific tomcod can reach up to 1 foot in length.

Distribution.   It occurs from central California, at roughly Point Sal, to Unalaska Island, Alaska.

Habitat.   Inhabiting depths from 60 to 720 feet, the Pacific tomcod prefers the shallower end of this range, and locations with a sandy bottom.

Food.   The Pacific tomcod primarily consumes anchovies, shrimp, and worms.

Angling.   Like Atlantic tomcod *(see: tomcod, Atlantic)*, these fish are primarily taken on light line and while bottom fishing for other species, usually with small pieces of cut bait, shrimp, or worms.
See: **Cod and Hake.**

TOMTATE   *Haemulon aurolineatum*

Other names—tomtate grunt; Spanish: *ronco jeníguano.*

The tomtate is the widest-ranging member of the grunts, a small species and one that is fairly tolerant of colder water. It is not often caught by anglers, but it is important as a forage fish for larger species and may be used as bait.

Identification.   Slim-bodied and silvery, the tomtate is silver white overall and has a yellow brown stripe along the length of its body, ending in a dark blotch on the caudal peduncle. The pelvic and anal fins are yellowish. The inside of the mouth is red. It has 13 dorsal spines and 14 to 15 dorsal rays, 9 anal rays, and 17 to 18 pectoral rays.

Age/Size.   The maximum length is 10 inches but seldom exceeds 8 inches. Tomtate are reported to live up to nine years.

Distribution.   The tomtate exists in the Western Atlantic from Massachusetts and Bermuda to Brazil, including the Caribbean and Gulf of Mexico.

Habitat.   Tomtate prefer shallower water from nearshore to outer reef areas, and rocky and sandy

bottoms. Schools are commonly seen congregated around piers or docks.

Behavior.   Like other grunts, this species is a schooling fish often found in large groups around natural and artificial reefs. Fish are sexually mature at about $5^1/_2$ inches, and spawning takes place in the southeastern United States in spring.

Food and feeding habits.   Tomtate are bottom feeders that forage on worms, snails, shrimp, crabs, and amphipods; they are in turn food for various snapper, grouper, and mackerel.

Angling.   Tomtate may be cut on small pieces of cut baits.
See: **Grunt.**

TONGA

The only remaining Polynesian monarchy, the Kingdom of Tonga is located in the South Pacific Ocean about 650 kilometers southeast of Fiji. It has never been subject to a colonial power, which is unusual in this region, but it was visited by early European explorers. The famed "Mutiny on the Bounty" took place in Tongan waters.

Tonga is a chain of 170 islands, seamounts, and reefs that consists of three major groups: the Tongatapu Group, which is southerly and includes the capital and chief port of Nuku'alofa; the thinly populated Ha'apai Group to the north of Tongatapu; and the northernmost Vava'u Group. Roughly 40 islands are inhabited, and there is daily air service among the groups by the domestic carrier Royal Tongan Airlines.

The coral islands in the east are low, fertile, and more heavily populated than the more volcanic islands in the west, which include active volcanoes. The city of Nuku'alofa on the large island of Tongatapu is the site of Tonga's international airport, which is a three-hour flight northeast from New Zealand. Roughly 105,000 people live throughout Tonga; they are Polynesians who speak Tongan as a first language, but nearly all understand and speak English as a second language.

Most of the approximately 20,000 tourists who visit this island kingdom do so from June through October, when the weather is most settled and temperatures average an agreeable 20°C. December through April is the hottest period, averaging around 30°C. It is also the wettest period, although rainfall does not reach monsoon proportions, as it does at some island groups in the western Pacific. This is also the cyclone (hurricane) season. Consequently, tourist traffic is light at this time, and some facilities shut down for the off-season. Paradoxically, fishing can be excellent at this time, although few anglers are around to take advantage of it.

Domestic fishing pressure is light; this, coupled with a complex volcanic history that has produced a large number of reefs and offshore seamounts, produces the basis for an exciting sportfishery, the

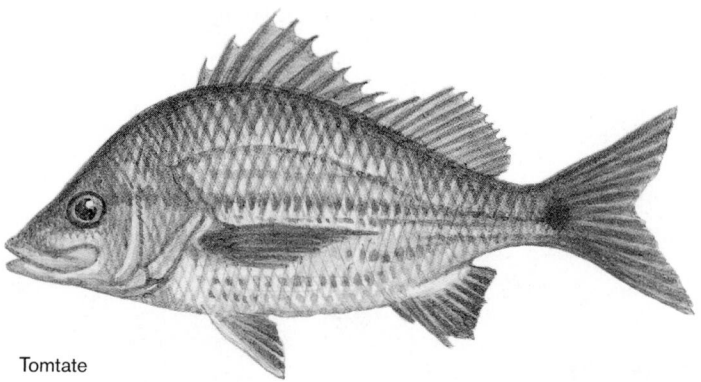

Tomtate

parameters of which are still being explored. Tonga is a popular destination for New Zealand anglers during their own winter off-season, and for some Australians and Americans. Sportfishing is administered by the Tongan International Game Fishing Association, which is affiliated with the International Game Fish Association (IGFA).

Sportfish taken in Tongan waters include blue marlin, sailfish, striped and black marlin, shortbill spearfish, mahimahi (dolphin), wahoo, dogtooth tuna, sharks, queenfish, yellowfin tuna, great barracuda, bluefin and giant trevally, shark mackerel, skipjack tuna, coral trout, red bass, bonefish, and a wide range of light-tackle and bottom fish.

Bonefish are present in lagoons from January through March, but this is the cyclone season, when tourist anglers are largely absent, so there is little angling effort for them. In addition, bonefish are not a popular eating species with village fishermen (they are known as "wire-fish" locally, for the large number of bones in their flesh) and are usually taken incidentally when netting for mullet. The extent of this fishery is consequently unknown.

Pacific sailfish in this region are present in moderate numbers but are of excellent quality. They average around 45 kilograms, and a 95.5-kilogram line-class world record was caught here in 1990.

Blue marlin make up roughly 70 percent of the marlin fishery, and striped and black marlin are also present. Several blues over 390 kilograms have been captured; the largest, a Tongan all-tackle record of 394 kilograms, was taken single-handed from a tiny 4.5-meter powerboat. A number of fish over 1,000 pounds have been hooked by anglers, but all have broken off. The average blue marlin captured weighs around 120 kilograms, but weights vary widely.

Another feature of Tongan fishing is the occasional appearance of schools of very large skipjack tuna, in the 13- to 15-kilogram range, which produced at least one (since defeated) IGFA line-class record.

Several fishing charters have recently been available out of Tongatapu, and include at least four modern, well-equipped boats in the 6- to 9-meter range. Most of these work out of the boat harbor on the Nuku'alofa waterfront, or from resorts on small islands a few miles offshore.

A number of seamounts, many reefs, and several fish aggregation devices (FADs) can be fished by the day from Tongatapu. Mahimahi are the most regular catch. Most of these fish weigh from 10 to 20 kilograms, and occasional catches reach 25 kilograms. Most Pacific sportfish are encountered in Tongatapu waters, however, including marlin, sailfish, tuna, and wahoo.

North of Tongatapu, the complex of atolls, reefs, shoals, and seamounts that constitutes the Ha'apai islands is an exciting proposition to explore. One charter operator works from the town of Lifuka, which is reached by air from Tongatapu. Another option is to access the area in a live-aboard charter boat from Vava'u. The fishery in these waters is very much a mixed bag, and all of the fish species previously mentioned are caught here.

North of the Ha'apai islands, the Vava'u group is a magnificent cluster of islands and has the second largest population after the capital of Tongatapu. This is a well-established fishing destination, and most Tongan big-game charter boats operate out of sheltered Neiafu Harbour; this recently included three modern game boats run by New Zealand skippers, and some smaller craft aimed at light-tackle fishing.

The picturesque Vava'u Group has produced exciting fishing action for visiting anglers, especially for billfish and mahimahi, and is the base for an annual international billfish tournament, normally held around September.

Commercial fishing pressure around Tonga is mostly from a small domestic fleet that targets red snapper using deep drop lines. As yet, there is no large-scale surface longlining or purse seining.

Blue-water trolling with lures and baits produces marlin, sailfish, mahimahi, wahoo, and tuna. Trolling the reef edges and passes with rigged baits or diving plugs can produce a wide range of predators, including wahoo, dogtooth tuna, jobfish, sailfish, and great barracuda. Downriggers are effective.

Offshore seamounts can rise steeply from over 1,000 meters deep to within 40 meters of the surface. These hold a variety of pelagic and reef predators. Baits, although effective, will often draw the attention of sharks over these structures. Dropping a large metal jig or heavy spoon to the bottom, then either jigging it up and down or retrieving it at high speed, is a good way to fish here. This technique can produce various species, but the powerful dogtooth tuna is a regular customer in lightly fished regions.

Casting surface lures, especially popping plugs, onto the reefs is an effective way to target giant and bluefin trevally, and is most productive in the northern island groups, especially in the hottest months, from December through April.

Light-tackle lure casting from the shore with small metal jigs, soft-plastic lures, and tiny bucktails also produces good sport with small trevally, longtoms (needlefish or houndfish), and various reef snapper and small grouper.

Most charter boats are equipped with good-quality modern trolling tackle, but anglers wishing to cast lures or flies or to use light tackle are advised to bring their own equipment. Tackle stores in Nuku'alofa and Neiafu have a limited selection of line, lures, and terminal tackle.

As in many parts of the Pacific, any fish caught on charters belong to the boat, although most captains are happy to release billfish at the angler's request. This should be discussed with the captain before fishing starts. Other species are usually kept for local consumption, and most skippers are happy when anglers take a share for their own table.

Visiting anglers should be aware that most Tongans are deeply religious and that fishing on Sundays is prohibited. Fishing is not considered a sport; it is work, intended to provide food. Other local customs to be aware of include dress standards. It is considered offensive and provocative for men to appear in public without a shirt. Traditionally, only warriors about to enter into battle go bare-chested. Likewise, women should not wear skimpy clothing or swimwear in public but may do so at the pool or beach.

TONKIN CANE
Raw bamboo cane used in bamboo fishing rod construction.
See: Bamboo Rod; Rod, Fishing.

TOPE
See: Shark.

TOPMINNOW
See: Killifish.

TOPWATER
A term for the surface of a water body, usually a pond or lake; for lures fished on the surface; and for surface fishing tactics (*see: surface lure*).

TOPWATER LURE
See: Surface Lure.

TORPEDO, ATLANTIC   *Torpedo nobiliana.*
Other names—torpedo, electric ray, dark electric ray; French: *torpille noire;* Spanish: *tremolina negra.*

A member of the electric ray family, the Atlantic torpedo can generate a shock between 170 to 220 volts. The electricity-generating organs are located in the front half of the body, one on each side, making up about one-sixth of the fish's total weight. The Atlantic torpedo may use these to stun prey, to protect themselves from predators, and to identify or attract members of the opposite sex.

Identification.   The Atlantic torpedo has a broad disk squared off in front and a short snout. It is uniformly dark olive to brown or black, occasionally with black blotches and small white spots, and whitish underneath. The Atlantic torpedo can be distinguished from its relatives by its large size.

Size.   The average fish weighs roughly 30 pounds and has been known to reach 200 pounds in weight and 6 feet in length.

Distribution.   Strictly an Atlantic Ocean species, it ranges from Nova Scotia and the Bay of Fundy to the Florida Keys and Cuba, but is absent from the Gulf of Mexico. In the eastern Atlantic, it ranges from Scotland to West Africa and the Azores.

Habitat.   Atlantic torpedoes live on sandy or rubble bottoms, ranging from beaches to sounds, and appear to be more common in the cooler parts of their range. They are believed to be most common in waters 60 to 240 feet deep.

Life history.   Reproduction takes place in deeper waters in warm areas, and the young are born alive.

Food.   Atlantic torpedoes are sluggish bottom dwellers and feed on such fish as flounders and eels, although they are able to capture fast-swimming prey such as sharks and salmon.

Angling.   There is little to no angling interest in Atlantic torpedoes.
See: Rays and Skates.

TOTAL ALLOWABLE CATCH
The annual recommended catch in saltwater for a species or species group set by a regional fisheries management council. This applies to both recreational anglers and commercial fishermen.
See: Fisheries Management; Fisheries Management Council.

TOTAL LENGTH
The length of a fish as measured from the tip of its snout to the tip of its tail.
See: Measuring Fish; Regulations.

TOTUAVA   *Totoaba macdonaldi.*
See: Corvina.

TOURNAMENTS
See: Competitive Fishing.

TOWER
Originally called a "tuna tower," this is an elevated platform designed to give the captain a better view,

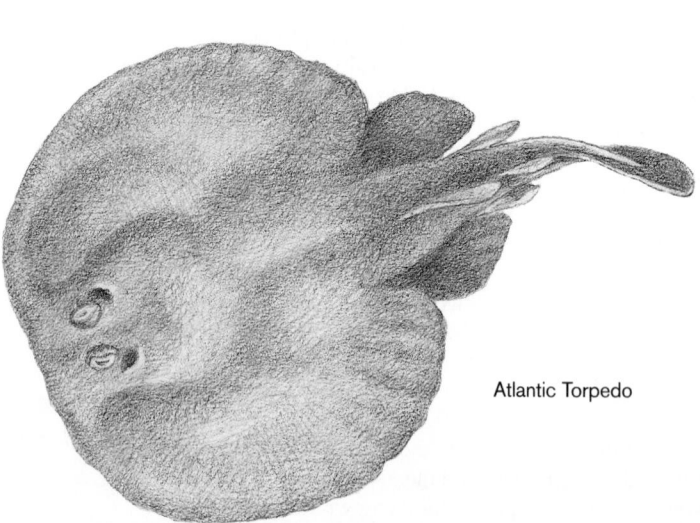
Atlantic Torpedo

enabling visibility at a much greater distance. Towers were developed for captains spotting bluefin tuna in the Bahamas, but have been adapted to most sportfishing boats and virtually all large offshore cruisers. Their purpose is not only to see farther on the horizon, but also to see down into the water. Seeing into the water is very helpful at times, such as when landing big fish, identifying fish that come into a chum slick, and spotting fish that casters can toss a lure or live bait to; in these circumstances, a guide or boat captain can direct the anglers or mates to action that cannot be as readily observed from deck level.

Towers these days come in many different shapes and sizes, but all accomplish basically the same thing: better visibility. They are made almost exclusively of aluminum to save weight, and can be rigged either with or without a remote helm station.

Though towers are primarily found on boats that are 25 feet or longer, mini-towers have been created for use on some smaller craft, including trailerable boats in the 18- to 25-foot range. Deck or console towers, mounted on the deck of center console boats so that anglers can walk around them easily, have become more popular in certain areas. Some, used on larger boats, have upper control stations while others are merely higher platforms without controls.

These small towers were created primarily for shallow fishing in calm inshore waters. Small towers improve visibility in small boats, just as poling platforms do, but they also come with some disadvantages, including safety concerns when used in rough water, and the possibility of altering performance, if added to an existing boat. On some boats, these small towers can, and must, be folded down for trailering.

See: Boat; Sportfishing Boat.

TRACE
A wire leader.
See: Leader.

TRACK PLOTTER
A display method used on electronic navigational equipment, particularly GPS, that presents a bird's-eye view of a boat and the surrounding area, and marks a trail to show the complete path that the moving boat has traveled. It is one of the most important features of GPS units and is used for practical fishing application as well as navigation.
See: GPS.

TRAHIRA *Hoplias malabaricus.*
Other names—guabine, haimara, tararura, tiger characin; Portuguese: *traíra, trairão;* Spanish: *guabina, tararira.*

An unknown number of trahiras are widely scattered throughout Central and South America; some

A large trahira, or *trairão*, from Brazil.

reports mention 13, and most are undescribed. These are members of the Erythrinidae family of fish in the genus *Hoplias.* They are voracious, prehistoric-looking species that are unfamiliar to most anglers.

The trahira commonly caught by anglers in the backwaters of Amazon tributaries in Brazil is called *traíra (H. malabaricus)* by Brazilians and references a fish weighing up to 3 kilograms; the *trairão (H. lacerdae)* is a larger, darker, but otherwise similar specimen.

Identification. Trahiras are cylindrical-bodied fish with a blunt head and a mouth full of canine teeth. They are partly air-breathing fish, and look somewhat like a bowfin *(see).* Most *traíra* and *trairão* are a mottled dark brown color. Their fins, with the exception of the dorsal fins, are rounded.

Size. *Traíra* are said to attain a maximum length of 60 centimeters and a weight of 3 kilograms; *trairão* reportedly grow to 1 meter and 20 kilograms.

Distribution. The range of *traíra* is from Costa Rica and Trinidad to Argentina and Ecuador, including the tributaries of the Amazon. Among anglers, they are most known in Brazil. This species was introduced into the United States in 1977 but was later eliminated.

Habitat. Trahiras inhabit rivers, streams, swamps, and lakes. They are encountered in backwaters, in slower sections of rivers, and around cover, especially fallen trees. They are usually found alone but sometimes travel in small groups.

Food. The specific diet of trahiras is unknown, although from their behavior toward lures and their dental structure, it is apparent that they feed voraciously on other fish. Their preference for lurking near cover-providing structure indicates that they are accomplished ambush feeders.

Angling. *Traíra* and *trairão* strike lures aggressively and provide a strong battle on appropriate tackle, although most specimens do not make long runs and seldom jump. They will make explosive strikes on various surface plugs, and also take shallow-running crankbaits; other lures, including large streamer flies, will likely be effective in the right circumstances. Wire leaders are useful, if not necessary, particularly if large fish are likely. Sturdy bait-casting tackle with 15- to 20-pound line is advisable.

Neither of these fish seems to stalk and follow a lure from afar, but they strike at objects placed fairly close to their ambush spot. In slow-moving rivers, they are mostly found along the banks by fallen trees, logs, and similar cover, requiring pin-point casting, often to tight spots. Sluggish near-shore backwaters are other locations favored by these fish, although they are usually taken by surprise rather than being deliberately targeted.

Trahiras require careful handling when landed. Their jaws are very powerful and sometimes have to be pried apart for hook removal. A lip-gripping tool, and possibly a jaw spreader, such as that used for pike, may be useful.

TRAILER, BOAT

Boat trailers run nearly as wide a gamut as do boats. Anglers are among the biggest consumers for boat trailers because they frequently fish in different waters and want the mobility, as well as the convenience of home storage, that is provided by keeping a fishing boat on a trailer. If you didn't keep a boat on a trailer, you would have to leave it permanently moored at a marina, incurring dockage, storage, and bottom-cleaning maintenance costs. The advantages of trailering come with a lot of considerations, however, from vehicular towing to insurance to proper support for the boat.

The vast majority of boats used for fishing can be towed, and a very high percentage are. It is generally accepted that boats in the 14- to 25-foot length are suitable for trailering. Boats under and over that length are sometimes trailered, and light-weight boats in the 14- to 16-foot range are even placed atop cars and trucks (by two or three sturdy anglers) with the right type of roof supports.

At the lower end of the spectrum, no matter what size the boat is, if you want to pre-rig it for convenience with various accessories, including motor(s), and you want to be able to put it in the water and quickly be on your way rather than assembling gear prior to fishing and then disassembling it later, you probably should consider putting it on a trailer rather than car topping. That is a matter of choice. Most fishing boats are too heavy for car topping and have to be towed if you are to fish in varied and distant places.

At the upper end of the spectrum, boats in excess of 25 feet are sometimes towed, but usually with custom-made trailers and special heavy-duty tow vehicles. Otherwise, it takes a professional transport service to "tow" the boat somewhere other than its home mooring. There can, in fact, be unanticipated problems with towing some boats in the 20- to 25-foot range if they are too wide for state and federal highway width requirements ($8^1/_2$ feet). Then, permits or special arrangements may be required.

The majority of fishing boat trailers fall in the middle ground, and most are acquired with a boat rather than separately, especially when a boat is purchased new. The packaging of boats, motors, equipment, and trailers today usually assures that a proper trailer is matched to the boat by the boat manufacturer and/or the dealer. But not always. Problems especially occur when people buy used boats and trailers, or replace the old trailer with a new or used trailer.

Some people who do a minimal amount of trailering, especially limited driving locally, opt for a cheaper and lighter-duty trailer, but this is penny-wise and pound-foolish unless you will only use that trailer to take a boat to a marina in the spring and then haul it out before winter. Even then, you have to figure that the boat may get weighted with rainwater or snow, and could incur damage while sitting on the trailer if the hull is not evenly supported. Many anglers who skimp on a trailer eventually want to take their boat someplace they hadn't originally planned on, like a 500-mile trip on their vacation, or they miscalculate the effect that bad roads or even limited bumping and bouncing can have, or they don't take into account the times they

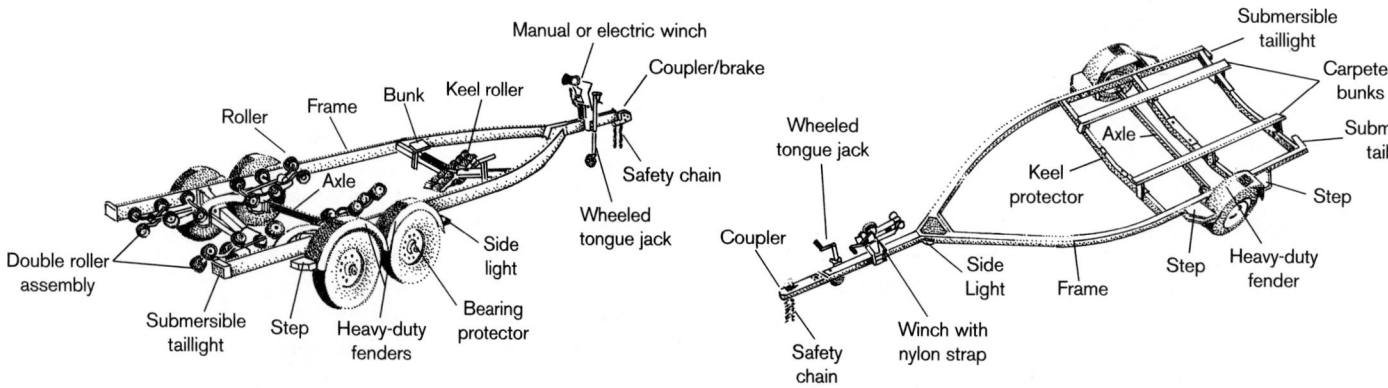

Large-boat Winch-on Trailer

Manual or electric winch · Coupler/brake · Keel roller · Bunk · Frame · Roller · Axle · Safety chain · Wheeled tongue jack · Side light · Double roller assembly · Submersible taillight · Step · Heavy-duty fenders · Bearing protector

Small-boat Drive-on Trailer

Submersible taillight · Carpeted bunks · Submersible taillight · Wheeled tongue jack · Axle · Keel protector · Coupler · Side Light · Winch with nylon strap · Safety chain · Frame · Step · Step · Heavy-duty fender decide to put a lot of gear into the boat to make space in their vehicle. So it is generally not a good idea to skimp.

Indeed, if you'll be putting a lot of miles on a trailer, and under all kinds of conditions in all types of places, then you may want to explore heavy-duty options or at least acquire the best you can for your budget.

Selecting a Boat Trailer

The right boat trailer permits smoother towing, easier launching and loading, lower maintenance, and better appearance than the wrong trailer. It also makes for safer towing and optimum physical support for your boat. The best thing you can do when selecting a boat trailer is to get one that was made for your boat. Trailer manufacturers can figure out what trailer is best for your boat if they know the make, model, and year the boat was manufactured, or can determine it if they know the technical specifications (deadrise, transom width, and so on). The job of choosing a trailer is often made for you when purchasing a new boat as part of a preassembled package. However, you may want to opt for a different trailer, especially one size larger, as dealers will sometimes offer a trailer that is marginally appropriate in order to shave the package price. In the long run, that may not turn out to be a bargain.

There are many things to consider when selecting a trailer, but weight capacity and length are two of the most prominent. Boats are often toted with full gas tanks, assorted accessories, coolers full of beverages (or fish), and other gear that all adds up. It's a good rule of thumb, therefore, to consider a trailer that exceeds by 20 percent the gross weight of the boat and motor. You can do some simple arithmetic on this issue by looking at the manufacturer's weight of the unladen boat and the unladen motor, then add in the things that would normally be toted all the time, such as batteries, electric motor, miscellaneous electronics, storage boxes full of goodies, plus a full tank of gas (gas weighs roughly 6 pounds per gallon). This is what your rig might ordinarily weigh day in and day out. For extreme conditions, figure in other items. You need to have a trailer with the capacity to handle the extreme conditions.

Length is important both in regard to achieving desirable tongue weight (trailer weight as measured on the tongue) on your tow vehicle, and for getting the proper support for the boat, especially in the transom. A boat should fit on a trailer so that the transom is directly supported; the transom should not hang over the back of the trailer, which causes too much stress. However, if the bow is too far forward on a trailer, there will be excessive tongue weight, which is not good for the tow vehicle, and if it is not forward enough, there will be too little tongue weight, which can cause fishtailing (the swaying motion of a trailer behind a tow vehicle at highway speed). Most of the time you'll need a

Mobility is the prime asset of having a boat on a trailer.

trailer that is a little longer than the boat. Although you need the right length of trailer, you may have some options in length (and width) between different models and different brands. This can be an important consideration for those who store their boats in home garages. Premeasure all your clearances to know what you'll need to fit a trailer and boat in your available space.

A trailer not only enables transportation, but it takes the place of water as the means of support. Whereas a boat in water is supported equally, that is not the case on a trailer, so support for the boat is an important consideration, and it should conform to the contour of the hull. Carpeted bunks, padded bars, and rubber rollers are the primary hull supports on a trailer, and they have advantages and disadvantages. The size and type of the boat and how it will be launched and loaded have a large influence on desirable supports.

Rollers are used on trailers that tilt, as well as those that do not, but their primary purpose is to allow boats to ease into the water by gravity. They are good on steep boat ramps, places where you cannot back far into the water, and unimproved launch sites. Most trailers with rollers sit a little higher than trailers with bunks, so they can be better in off-road and unimproved locations. Rollers apply pressure to the hull of a boat, however, at specific places, which means that the pressure is not evenly distributed. The more rollers there are, the better this distribution is. If the rollers are designed to limit lateral movement, this is good, as they hold the boat in wind and current for easier loading. Some roller-support trailers also feature a self-centering keel cradle, which makes loading a boat under some conditions much easier than it would be otherwise.

Trailers with carpeted bunks distribute pressure more evenly. They provide more friction, so they can be harder to launch from the trailer by hand (pushing into the water) if it is necessary to do so (super shallow spots and places where the trailer cannot be backed far into the water). However, where launch sites are improved and with moderate inclines, a bunk trailer can be backed into the water until the boat floats off, and with the bunks partially submerged, the boat can be easily driven back on for loading. Many freshwater boat trailers, especially those for bass boats, have bunks; the boats are easily driven on and off the trailers, which also offer a low profile for easier towing.

Boat trailers are made of aluminum or either galvanized or ungalvanized carbon steel. Because most anglers have a tendency to put their trailers well into the water (although you should never submerge the hubs unless they have grease-fitted end caps and waterproof spindle seals), as well as travel over all types of trailer-wetting conditions, it is best to go with a material that resists corrosion. This is especially so if the trailer will be used in or around saltwater. The frame should be of welded construction, which is stronger than bolted construction and less likely to wear or rust.

When selecting a trailer, you also have to consider the size and quality of the tires. Small tires offer a low profile, but they turn faster than the larger tires on the tow vehicle, so they do not last as long and are best suited for light loads and short trips. Ideally, tires should be the same, or close to, the size of the tires on the tow vehicle. Some heavy-duty trailers have twin or triple axles and four or six tires, to distribute the load as well as to provide better tracking; these are harder to turn and tougher to maneuver in tight places. It's prudent to have a spare tire for your boat trailer, and to lock it to the frame. It's also good to have a fold-up jack for supporting the tongue when the trailer is off the hitch and also to help maneuver it around.

Brakes and Lights

Brake and lighting considerations are determined by vehicle laws. Lighter loads, usually those up to 3,000 pounds, can legally be handled by the brakes of most tow vehicles without additional help in many states, although you should drive with caution and realize that you don't have the stopping range and power with a trailer as you do without it. Laws aside, manufacturers recommend that you consider trailer brakes if the weight of the towing rig exceeds 40 percent of the gross vehicle weight of the tow vehicle. For heavy rigs, you may be required to have a trailer with hydraulic surge brakes, or you may opt for this even if it isn't required if you regularly tow in places where it is best to give the tow vehicle's brakes some help (steep terrain and wet roads are tough to brake on).

Trailers almost always come with sufficient lights, located on the frame, but anglers sometimes add lights onto trailer uprights. These should not replace frame lights. Remember to disconnect the trailer light wiring harness from the main vehicle before backing the trailer into the water. Lights are more likely to be inoperative on a boat trailer than

any other element, so carry replacements. Putting some reflective tape on the back and side frame of the trailer could be helpful. Check for corrosion, bare wires, and cracked insulation, and put waterproof grease on plug and bulb contacts.

Wheel Bearings

One of the most likely problem areas for a boat trailer is the wheel bearings, which are subject to failure through overheating when a trailer is towed at high speeds and then taken to the water. If the wheels are submerged, there is a likelihood of water getting into the bearings and causing damage that will eventually lead to a breakdown, usually on the road and possibly at a high speed of travel, posing serious danger. Taking care of the bearings is essential for safety and for convenience.

Nowadays many boat trailers come with wheel end caps that have grease fittings (Buddy Bearings) to protect those bearings. If your trailer doesn't have them, they're easy and inexpensive to add. *Never* submerge a trailer that does not have this type fitting as well as waterproof spindle seals. These devices make it simple to pump a little grease into the bearings every two to three months, but don't pump too much, which could push the spindle seals out of place, allowing water and road dirt to get inside. Just add grease until the spring on the end cap barely begins to compress. Even if the hubs have grease fittings, the bearings should be removed, cleaned, and completely regreased every three years, more often if you submerge the wheels. Replace the spindle seals if they show signs of leakage.

Consider buying a complete hub with bearings already in place (and prepacked in grease), double-bagging it in big sealable bags, and always keeping it with you; if a bearing should fail while on the road, simply replace the complete hub with your spare. Have the old hub thoroughly cleaned and the bearings replaced at a service station to ensure there are no metal fragments left inside that could quickly destroy the new bearings, then keep it as a spare.

Winches and Tongue Weight

All trailers have a bow chock, which keeps the boat from moving farther forward. The location of this is relative to the position of the transom on the trailer and to the tongue weight. They also have a winch of some type. For smaller rigs, use a nylon-web strap instead of rope, and on larger boats, consider having a braided steel winch cable. The winch itself should not be high speed if you have a heavy load to pull up; some winches have dual speeds, using the lower gear for taking up slack and the higher one for the hard work. An electric winch is just about mandatory for the largest boats and for people who have physical impairments that make strenuous winching unacceptable.

The tongue weight should be between 6 and 10 percent of the gross weight of the objects in tow (boat, motor, trailer, etc.). You can determine tongue weight by placing the tongue on a bathroom scale covered by a piece of 2 × 4. Move the winch stand and bow chock assembly forward or backward, and reposition the boat, until you achieve the right weight. Too much tongue weight will cause the rear wheels of the tow vehicle to drag and may make steering more difficult. Too little tongue weight means that there is too much weight on the rear of the trailer; this will cause the trailer to fishtail at high speeds and may reduce traction or even lift the rear wheels of the tow vehicle off the ground. So get it right before you ever start towing.

Towing and Security

When towing a trailer and boat, it takes longer to accelerate, pass other vehicles, slow down, and stop. Keep this in mind at all times, as you have to drive more cautiously than you do when not towing. Remember that the turning radius is greater for vehicles towing a trailer; you may have to give curbs, vehicles, barriers, and other items a much wider berth when cornering. At highway speeds, be careful not to make sudden movements, which may cause the trailer to fishtail; keep a steady hand and foot. The speed limit for vehicles with trailers may be different than for those without, and there may be restricted access on some highways, so be observant. Be aware that you will have to get into cash lanes at toll booths and pay a higher fee (usually per axle).

Take it very slow over bumpy roads and in places where the angle between trailer and vehicle is great; you can scrape the trailer frame, axle, jack, spare tire, or other parts in severe spots if you don't proceed slowly. And remember that no one should be towed in a boat, except at slow speed while launching or loading at an access site. If you are completely new to towing a trailer, you should take it first to an uncongested level area (like a mall parking lot in off hours) and practice backing up, turning, and parking. Some strategically placed cardboard boxes will help greatly as you practice.

With the proper tongue weight and proper tow vehicle, you should be able to tow a boat trailer safely. However, the weight of the boat and trailer determine what kind of vehicle you can tow with. You should check your owner's manual and speak to an auto dealer regarding towing specifics for your vehicle, but keep in mind that different circumstances create different needs. Towing in flat terrain is easier than towing in hill country. Launching at paved improved access sites is easier than at unimproved ones.

The majority of anglers who trailer boats use heavier-duty vehicles, including trucks, vans, and sport utilities, many equipped with four-wheel-drive, to handle the varied demands of towing. For serious towing and long distances, it is advisable to have a towing package installed by the manufacturer. Heavy-duty cooling for the engine and transmission, as well as heavy-duty brakes, turn signals, and shocks are among the necessities. While recommendations vary, it is generally wise to use Class II or III hitches for heavier loads. A load-bearing hitch attached to the frame, not the bumper, is best unless you will only be towing a light weight for short distances. Always use two safety chains to secure the trailer to the hitch of the tow vehicle so that it cannot run away from you if the coupler or stem of the ball breaks; cross the safety chains to keep the trailer following you. Put a lock onto the tongue hitch to ensure that it stays locked and does not pop free.

It is important to make sure that the tow ball (on the hitch) is the same size as the coupler, and that bolts with washers are tightly secured. Vibration during road travel may loosen them, so check them before you get on the road. The coupler should be completely over the ball and latched down firmly on it.

Lock the trailer when it is parked by itself or attached to your vehicle. There are various locking mechanisms for boat trailers. The best are those that immobilize the trailer and keep the wheel from turning. Others, which are padlocks or hitch coupler locks, can be cut with good bolt cutters or, in some cases, bypassed, and are lightweight short-term measures.

Make sure to properly tie the boat to the trailer before towing. Some boaters employ a single long nylon web strap that crosses the gunwales near the stern and attaches to the side frame of the trailer. Others prefer two separate straps that attach from port and starboard transom bolts to the trailer frame. Make sure that they are tight. Also use a safety chain from the winch stand to the bow eyebolt or a rope from the frame to the eyebolt. On bigger boats a turnbuckle may be necessary. The connection from winch to bolt should be firm as well.

When leaving the water to head home, drain all unnecessary water out of the boat. That includes the sump and unused wells. Water weighs 8 pounds per gallon, and if there is a lot of water in your boat, it can add significant weight to the towing package, perhaps producing a greater load than the trailer should handle, or perhaps changing the stress points on the trailer, particularly if the water shifts (as it might in the sump) with trailer movement. Besides lightening your load, this action will keep you from transferring any exotic or nuisance organisms from one place to another.

Maintenance

There is a small amount of maintenance required for trailer owners, especially those who launch in saltwater.

Washdown.   There are two important reasons for cleaning your trailer down after every use just as you would clean your boat. The first reason is less obvious: to keep from bringing unwanted elements from one place to another. In fact, before leaving

Published reports indicate that the industrial freezing of food was begun by Clarence Birdseye, prompted by a 1912 ice fishing expedition in −20°F weather in Labrador.

T

the launching site, make sure that there are no aquatic plants clinging to the trailer, and when at home, use hot water if possible to clean it. Taking steps to insure against the spread of exotic and/or undesirable plants and organisms is becoming more important than ever (see: exotic species; zebra mussel).

Trailers that are exposed to saltwater are especially in need of cleaning for the sake of removing the salt and preventing corrosion. Salt is like an acid bath; it can eventually eat away just about any metal. Even stainless steel will eventually develop small rust spots and pits if constantly exposed to it. It's also tough to wash off your boat and trailer unless you use soap. That's important because, unless all traces of salt are removed, it will constantly attract moisture and continue uninterrupted with its dirty work, even if you're far from the nearest ocean.

One way to wash the trailer is to stop by a coin-operated car wash and use the soapy water cycle followed by a rinse cycle. Another way is to buy a sprayer attachment for your garden hose and use that. Get one that can spray both soapy water and rinse water under very high pressure.

Lubricate and tighten. It's a good idea to periodically tighten all nuts and bolts and spot-coat them as well as other parts. If you even occasionally submerge your trailer in either fresh or saltwater, at least once a year remove all lug bolts or nuts, one at a time, and coat them with a thin layer of anti-seize grease. Otherwise, if you manage to go several years without a flat or other reason to change a tire, you might find it impossible to get that wheel off.

Also, check and oil every roller and replace those that are worn. A little oil on the roller spindles every few months will keep them turning easily and add years to their usable life. The time to do this is just before you put the boat back on the trailer.

Just like rollers, hull bunkers should be adjusted so that they support the boat evenly, thereby distributing the load over as much area as possible. Give these a quick visual check; look for supports that need attention, and rollers that might need to be replaced. Some trailers have carpeted bunkers. You can make the hull slide on them a lot easier by coating the carpet with silicone, which comes in pressurized spray cans.

Boat trailer springs should be kept out of water while launching if at all possible, especially around saltwater. In any case you can also protect them with a corrosion-resistant coating at the start of every season. One way is to apply a mix of 70 percent STP oil and 30 percent mineral oil (to enhance penetration within layers of the spring). A quicker way is to spray them with a heavy-duty corrosion protection, available at automotive supply stores. Spray this on nuts and bolts, too.

Inspect bearings. Check the bearings and replace corroding parts. Pump grease into the bearings periodically and repack them once in a while because water seepage and poor lubrication are the chief causes of bearing failure.

It's a good idea once a year to jack up each wheel, one at a time, and spin them by hand. Listen for grinding noises. Check for looseness (wobble), and tighten the spindle nut carefully if needed. You can do that by tightening as far as it will go without excess force, then backing it off just enough so that the wheel spins freely. Visually inspect the spindle seal on the inside of the tire for grease leaks. If there is any leakage, replace the seal. If you have hubs with grease fittings on them, add a little more grease and then check to make sure you didn't overfill enough to force the spindle seals out of their seats. These steps take only a few minutes. If you find anything suspicious and you're not absolutely sure how to fix it, play it safe and let a pro do it.

If you have a dry, squeaky bearing while on the road miles from a service station, remove the cap that covers the bearings and squirt a generous amount of outboard motor lower unit oil into the bearing chamber. Replace the cap, and proceed slowly (45 mph or less) to the nearest service station where the proper grease can be added.

Tire check. Check the tires periodically. Improper inflation can cause steering trouble and tire failure. Under-inflation ruins most tires; it causes more flex in the sidewalls, allowing for a very high heat buildup, which leads the plies to delaminate and cause a blowout. Sometimes you can see a warning sign of this before it happens in the form of a large bubble in the side of the tire. But, if that bubble happens to form on the side of the tire where it isn't readily visible, you might not see it in time.

Check for proper inflation with a tire gauge when the tire is cool, before the start of a trip, and add the necessary air when you get to the nearest gas station. Make sure that the spare tire is properly inflated as well. Inspect tires periodically for uneven wear that could indicate a bent axle or balance problem. If you tow in the boondocks a lot, consider getting a 12-volt inflation kit or a tire repair kit.

Light check. Lights, of course, need to be checked for proper operation and appropriate steps taken to remedy problems for safety's sake and to avoid a traffic summons. Spray the connectors regularly with a moisture-displacing lubricant to ensure good contacts. The bulbs in the trailer lights themselves should be checked regularly to make sure that one of their filaments hasn't burned out. The housing for each light should be monitored to make sure it isn't collecting and trapping water. It's also a good idea to apply a light layer of grease to the base of each light bulb so there's no chance it can freeze in the socket because of rust.
See: Boat; Boat Launch; Launching.

TRAILER HOOK

An auxiliary hook attached to the main hook of a lure; this is primarily used with a spinnerbait (see), but may be employed with other single-hook lures and with some bait rigs.

TRANSDUCER

The object that sends and receives sonar pulses.
See: Sonar.

TRANSOM

The furthest portion of the stern of a boat extending from port to starboard.

TRANSOM DOOR/GATE

A part of the transom on some sportfishing boats *(see)* that can be opened to facilitate bringing large fish into the cockpit. Very large fish (primarily billfish, sharks, and tunas), when kept, are difficult even for several people to bring into a boat due to the weight and length of the fish and the boat's freeboard. A latched gate that can be opened permits pulling and sliding a big fish into the boat instead of lifting it over the side.

TRAP

A device for capturing live fish or crustaceans for consumption or use as bait. Traps have been used for ages in procuring many animals from freshwater and saltwater, both for commercial and recreational purposes. The most popular trapping targets for anglers are minnows, crayfish, crabs, and eels. The use of traps for any of these or other purposes is subject to local regulations, so you should check on the legality of trap use before using any trap; placing a label on a trap, or otherwise identifying it, may be necessary, and there may be other regulations that pertain to their use.

Minnow/eel trap. When used properly a minnow trap is an easy and inexpensive way to catch fish for bait. The standard modern minnow trap is a wire mesh product that has been around for almost a century, and features two identical baskets of $1/4$-inch galvanized wire mesh that snap together at their large end and feature a cone-shaped opposite end with a 1-inch-diameter opening. In use the trap is baited with any number of items, but primarily with dry bread, crackers, dough balls, and meat. It is attached via cord or chain to some anchoring point, and positioned lengthwise in the water, and always with an opening facing upcurrent wherever there is a flow. In a good location, a minnow trap will produce results in a half hour or less. It can be left as long as overnight.

Some people like to paint a new minnow trap a dull color to make it less visible to detection (and pilferage or theft), and this is the only modification that might be considered. Such a trap can be converted into an eel trap by adding a separate cylindrical extension piece that connects to the two halves.

Traps

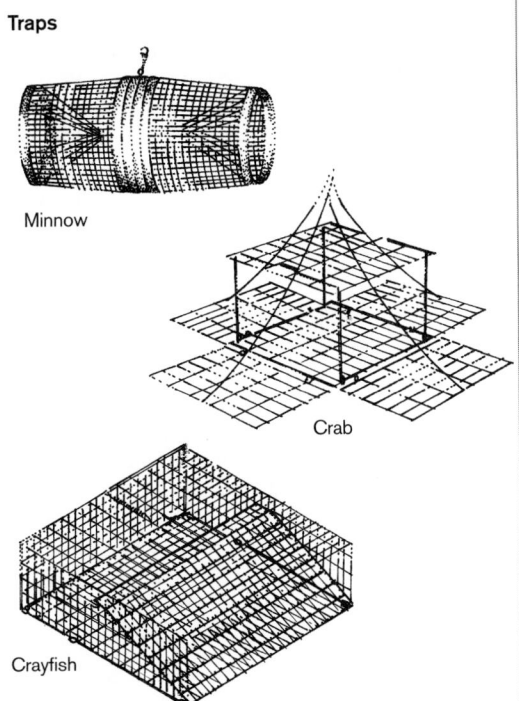

Minnow

Crab

Crayfish

These traps can be placed near shore in a lake or stream if there is sufficient depth to cover the trap, and if it is a location likely to yield results, or it can be tossed up to 20 feet away via rope, provided that there is not too much current to sweep it sideways (the cone has to face into the current). Placing a trap by an undercut bank in a stream, near fallen trees and logs, and by other cover is usually best.

Crab trap. Although crabs may be caught on handlines or trotlines, they are able to escape those devices by letting go of them; traps have the advantage of not allowing a crab to escape, do not entangle crabs as nets do, and are more durable and longer lasting.

Crab traps are either of the box or pyramid variety. Both work the same way in that they have four folding sides that lie flat when lowered to the bottom of the water and close when the trap is raised to the surface via rope. Both are made of wire mesh; the box version has a fixed top and bottom whereas the triangular sides of the pyramid version preclude a top.

A crab trap should be baited with fish heads, pieces of eel, chicken necks or wings, or other meat that will not disintegrate too quickly. The bait is tied to the bottom of the trap, which has to be checked periodically. It is placed along a shoreline, fished underneath an anchored boat, and attached to a bridge or pier. When a trap is checked, it should be raised quickly to make sure that the crab is well enclosed. In time, an experienced user can lift the trap and feel by weight if it contains a crab, rather than pulling it completely to the surface.

Crayfish trap. A number of traps can be used to capture crayfish, and some people make their own. One commercial version is the same extended minnow trap that is used for catching eels. Another is a squared, galvanized wire model that lies flat on the bottom and has a rear section that opens to empty the trap; this type also keeps minnows.

A crayfish trap should be baited with fish heads, entrails, meat, or a can of cat food with holes punched in it. The trap is attached via cord or chain to some anchoring point when placed in the water. It may catch crayfish in a short time, but is best left overnight, especially since crayfish are most active after dark.

All of these traps should be rinsed with freshwater, especially if used in saltwater.

TRAVEL

Anglers have as big a yen to travel, probably more so, than other sports-minded people or hobbyists. The reasons are simple: to catch species not available where they live and to visit places where the angling is better, the fish larger or more plentiful, or the experience just different from what they're accustomed to. So they travel by auto, train, bus, horse, commercial airline, charter plane, floatplane, and even helicopter to reach near, far, or extremely remote destinations. Agents, outfitters, guides, captains, lodges, hotels, and many others cater to the traveling angler.

Fishing travel is big business. The livelihood of hundreds of thousands of people is all or partly dependent on fishing tourism. In some areas, small communities are completely dependent on visiting anglers for their survival. Some people have no other means of making the same amount of money in their community as they do from a sportfishing-related job; in one day, for example, a Mexican bass fishing guide earns what would take about a week and a half to earn in another job.

Fishing trips may be as mundane as toting a rod and tackle box during the family's car-camping vacation or as exotic as flying to an inaccessible spot for a rare and seldom encountered species. The more

distant and involved, the more expensive the trips are, with far-flung international destinations costing thousands of dollars for a five- or seven-day excursion, plus airfare and incidental expenses. Spending five grand on a weeklong fishing adventure is not uncommon, and a few cost twice that amount. Getting to many places is not quite the ordeal that it used be; some prime fishing destinations that were once difficult to access can be reached in just a day of travel. Yet there are still places that take a lot of time, and possibly circuitous travel, to reach, depending upon where your journey starts from.

The following information pertains to fishing travel, especially that requiring air transportation and access to distant places. The needs for those who travel by auto or camper are more obvious and less involved than for those who trek to distant places on a tighter time schedule, although there is some overlap in considerations that need to be made. Since the issues of selecting a guide or a charter boat are detailed elsewhere *(see: guide boat),* this information focuses on selecting destinations, trip planning, equipment considerations, and practical related aspects. There is also a special section devoted to major Canadian travel issues, since Canada is an enormously popular fishing travel destination in North America. Information about specific provinces and territories in Canada, and about issues for other countries, is contained in those entries.

Selecting

Every traveling angler is interested in having quality fishing and being in a quality facility. Quality is a nebulous thing and identified in different ways. The best fishing isn't all in the most remote or most costly places or, for that matter, accessed from the most deluxe facilities. Some remote Alaskan and Canadian salmon rivers, for example, are fished out of tent camp operations, with no running water and primitive showers, but they provide a great experience. Ditto for wilderness float fishing trips. Some terrific Amazonian fishing is accessed out of African Queen–style boats. Then, of course, there are places with five star lodges providing trained chefs, first-rate boats, and wonderful fishing. Great fishing spots and great facilities run the gamut.

One thing that has changed somewhat in recent years is that many top outfitters and lodge owners have upgraded facilities and put more emphasis on comfort. This is partly to attract the more pampered traveler, partly to attract corporate business, partly to keep up with competitors, and partly to be more amenable to women.

For a long time the traveling angler was almost exclusively male. Today that person is still most likely to be male, but in some camps the ratio of male to female in a given week might be 3:2 or 3:1; and many women accompany their spouse, boyfriend, or father, and they want better lodges and facilities. Fewer people are willing to put up

Some angling travel takes people far up jungle or rain forest rivers, such as this one in Brazil.

with dubious sanitary conditions and "roughing it," even in many isolated and remote places. You pay for better facilities, of course, but you can find diverse creature comforts. The majority of angling destinations are not deluxe but are very good for all but the most fastidious person; they meet the major requirements of good (and ample) food, a comfortable bed, sanitary facilities, warm lodging, and the obvious fishing and boating necessities.

Naturally, your own requirements need to be focused a bit before you begin searching or selecting destinations, lodges, agents, outfitters, and the like. This is certainly the most obvious element of travel. The number of people in your group, the level of comfort you (and others) require, your willingness to share accommodations/boats/etc. if traveling solo (few people go solo, however), preferred methods of fishing, length of time and season you have available, budget, personal angling skills, personal fitness level, and personal expectations (how big a fish or how many?) are among the obvious issues that you have to confront before anything else begins. Be honest with yourself and your companions when it comes to what you can and cannot do. Your preferred method of fishing and personal abilities are probably foremost among these considerations.

Learning about locations, services, and sport-fishing opportunities primarily comes from communicating directly with lodges and outfitters or their representatives, reading travel articles that appear in magazines and newspapers, and speaking to others who have been there. Having happy clients who provide repeat business is the most significant element in successful guiding businesses, lodges, outfitting operations, and travel agencies. Brochures, publicity, and appearances at shows have some value, and all have a part in the marketing of a site or service.

Shows. Sport shows include many exhibits by lodges and outfitters whose booths are generally staffed by owners and/or their families and employees. Speaking with these people is the best possible way to get direct answers to specific questions, as many as you care to ask. If you're seriously interested in visiting a particular place, a sport show is a prime opportunity to go beyond the obvious questions (When is the best time to visit? What lures should I bring?) to the most intricate matters (Are there reefs and shoals in the lake, how deep are they found, do you need sonar to locate them, and do they hold walleye throughout the summer?). Answers to such specifics will help an ardent angler make up his or her mind, as well as plan ahead.

Sometimes, booths are staffed by people who are filling in for the lodge owner and who cannot answer the most detailed angling questions; that doesn't mean the place is unsuitable, but you'll have to dig deeper for information. The person who digs deep and asks pointed questions is usually considered a more serious prospective client than someone

Many people get fishing destination information at sport shows.

who is collecting brochures and just kicking the tires, so the serious questioner usually gets detailed answers.

Many good operators do not have the time or interest to exhibit at shows. Shows are expensive and generally do not produce a lot of business for many lodges, particularly the pricier and more upscale ones. Shows have their pitfalls. Beware of people who use negative selling; be suspicious of those who criticize and downgrade their competitors. New lodges and new owners of existing businesses often exhibit at shows, and they may still be pulling their operation together. Shows are just a starting point, but if they provide an opportunity to interact personally with the owner or manager, then they can be very worthwhile.

Publicity. Articles in newspapers and magazines reflect the experiences of someone who has been there. They are relied upon for credibility by the average reader and, in general, are second in importance to repeat customers and word-of-mouth for helping to attract new clients. There are some pitfalls and problems associated with publicity but usually nothing that cannot be overcome by an astute angler/reader.

Seldom are articles published about places that you should not visit, nor are negative comments about places that are otherwise commendable. Sportswriters who review angling destinations nearly always focus on the positive. Keep in mind that they usually receive red carpet treatment, visit at optimum times, and may be hosted to some extent by the lodge; so it is easy to accentuate positives and bypass the less notable things. Some destination articles focus so much on the angling action, especially the number and size of fish caught, that you get little feel for other aspects. This is not always the case, although often some of the most important issues are addressed only in small print in sidebars.

Nevertheless, an article should help focus your interest and questions. Also, when photographs accompany an article, they can help establish the setting and the kind of place it is. Unfortunately, the photos are often too few or are of people holding fish, and little is seen of the other aspects of the lodge/locale/body of water.

One of the drawbacks of most articles is that they emphasize too much the exceptional catches and outstanding days, failing to note that every day was not fabulous and did not produce a monstrous fish, or that only one behemoth was caught all week even though 15 people were at the lodge, or that it took a particularly skillful angler to really do well.

The result can be that expectations are raised too high, and when people do not attain the same level of achievement as that described in the article, they feel that the author lied or that some special circumstances were at work. And they are disappointed when they do not experience what the author experienced. This is even more acute with television fishing shows; most people fail to realize that 23 minutes of constant video fishing action may have taken a week to actually experience and film (it may also take only half a day, but you can bet that the production value of such shows is very low). Seldom do all those TV lunkers fall cast after cast in real life, although it seems like they do on the screen. And the great shallow fishing or surface action depicted in a spring visit to a place shown on television will not necessarily be the experience from a fall or winter visit.

Many lodge owners say that television shows depicting far-off hotspots seldom bring clients to them, although they may be useful for helping to raise awareness. If the cameras do not spend all the time focused on the show host and his or her fish, this medium may provide a better visual feel for the camp facilities, the location, and the overall experience than an article with limited photographs. But if you haven't recorded the program, it's gone quickly from the screen. Many television fishing shows seem more inclined to depict a constant stream of fish catching rather than present a full view of the experience; granted the foremost purpose of fishing travel is fishing, but there are so many other issues influencing the selection of a place to visit, or a determination of what is a good place for you or what is not, that televised shows are of marginal value. Many issues are ones that you will want to learn about before placing a reservation, and they are discussed here.

It is important to realize that the skill level of many anglers and the skill level of the author of an encouraging article (or television show host) about a good fishing locale are often quite different. Some readers or viewers are better anglers than the author/host, and they may find even better fishing. That is not usually the case, but it happens. Many readers or viewers are much less proficient and may inadvertently be set up for disappointment. For example, just because an author caught a lot of bass at a great new lake by fishing heavy jigs in thick tree cover at 20 feet doesn't mean that you can do the same or that you will enjoy that.

By the same token, the fishing experiences of people at a camp at the same time are very different owing to their own skills (or lack thereof), so that while one person has a lot of success, another does not. Consider any article (or show), therefore, not as the last word but as something that motivates you to look further into the matter.

Finally, it is worth pointing out that savvy fishing travel marketers tend to get a lot of publicity, and the media tends to flock to the places that have good access, cheap access, a newly discovered fishery, and angling that provides good photo or video opportunities in a somewhat disproportionate manner. A review of fishing destination articles in major magazines, for example, will show far more attention to Costa Rican fishing or a hot new bass lake in Mexico, than to a lot of other equally deserving places. The Florida Keys, certainly one of the top angling destinations in the world, receives tarpon fishing publicity that is disproportionate to the number of people who can, or want to, fish for tarpon. Tarpon are more glamorous than walleye, to be sure, but the outdoor press and others who write about angling destinations often have a bias toward the more glamorous or renowned species, certain methods of fishing (have you noticed that most articles about bonefish emphasize fly fishing and almost never light-tackle spinning, which is just as much fun and equally demanding?), and some destinations.

This is not a recent phenomenon; it has been going on for over a century and is even more true where television shows are concerned; in this visual medium, producers and show hosts cater to activities that have more visible action and obvious drama. They would much rather show bass striking surface lures than being caught deep on jigs; if you can't see the strike or film the fish underwater, you wind up with more-than-the-usual amount of talking heads and after-the-hookset action. How many times do you see people on television trolling, unless it is for offshore saltwater species that will jump and look big in the camera?

As with anything else, you should approach all media attention with your eyes wide open and your brain thinking, and recognize that there are many excellent facilities and destinations that get very little, or no, popular press.

Literature.   One of your first tasks is to look over the lodge's literature, usually a brochure, obtained from the lodge or its agent. This will range from a black-and-white photocopy to a glossy color folder. Be wary of the former and of literature that appears to have been hastily slapped together; that may reflect on the rest of the operation as well. Don't be too expectant based on the photos either. In the best brochures, the boats, rooms, facilities, and scenes usually look more impressive in photographs taken from the best possible angle, in the best possible light, with a telephoto or wide-angle lens, and under the best of circumstances, than they do in person. Of course, that is also true of most advertising photos, magazine pictures, and videos (some lodges now offer videos for prospective clients to review).

Most brochures depict large fish, especially camp record fish, but sometimes these are very old photos, of fish taken years ago. What have you done lately? is a good question to ask. Be wary of photos that show strings or piles of dead fish; lodges that appeal to meat hogs tend to emphasize that aspect more than others. The days of keeping limits has yielded to catch-and-release *(see)*, and the best camps advocate and practice catch-and-release. Many people are not pleased to be in a camp where the major interest of the staff and guests is in poundage and full coolers.

Look in the printed literature for a commitment to resource conservation and to the continuation of quality fishing. Far more lodges and outfitters are interested in advocating these issues today than in the past because the clientele has matured into one that recognizes the value of sportsmanship and conservation. A lodge whose policy allows keeping only one trophy fish of a particular species is one that is not attracting the meat hog element and is interested in having quality angling for the future. That means it plans to be around in the future rather than trying to make a quick buck now (if the fishing is lousy through overfishing, then the value of the business is hurt) and that it will be a place worth returning to. The merits of this have already been proven, especially in northern Canada, where most of the top lodges have had strict conservation policies that go way beyond the mandates of regulations established by fisheries agencies. The angling at these places continues to get better. But there are still operators—especially those whose facilities are accessible by driving—that emphasize limits and numbers and taking fish home.

Many lodge brochures give good details about accommodations, food, and services but are less specific about actual fishing information, which is described in general and glowing terms (perhaps because these places are leery of making promises that may not be fulfilled), although there are certainly exceptions. Ardent anglers usually want as many particulars as possible about the fishing (boats, angling styles, equipment needs, etc.). Some places provide detailed fishing information bulletins. This is very helpful and shows the commitment of

A boat drifts the flats of the Florida Keys at sunset.

the lodge to ensuring that clients experience good fishing.

The more traveling and fishing experiences that you have, the better you'll be able to satisfy yourself when selecting a fishing lodge. Astute lodge owners and their representatives make this chore a little easier by anticipating the kinds of things that you might want to know about (and anglers want to know different things than general tourists) and by providing you with those particulars to help make a decision.

Speaking to others. Speaking to someone who has been to the lodge or waters in question is an excellent idea, and some places encourage this and will gladly supply a few references. If a lodge doesn't volunteer this, ask. Certainly a lodge is going to refer you only to someone who has had a positive experience, but in speaking to such a person, especially one who has recently visited that destination, you can learn some valuable things.

When you call someone to talk about their experience and recommendations, have a prepared list of specific questions in hand. Ask what they would do differently if they were to return (time of the season that they would go, gear they would bring, things they wouldn't do, etc.). Ask for a guide, cabin, or room recommendation, as well as a suggestion on specific places to fish (a certain pool, bay, flat, etc.). Be sure to talk about tackle requirements, especially productive types and colors of lures or flies. Find out if they paid for their trip, and make sure they aren't a relative of the owner or an old

T

college roommate. Be sure to phone on your nickel, or if the person isn't home, leave a message to call you collect; don't expect someone who is doing you a favor to return your long distance call and help you at their expense. It is probably better to call someone than to write, but if you do write a letter, enclose a stamped self-addressed envelope to facilitate reply. Communication via e-mail may bring a quick response, but speaking one-on-one is still the best approach for getting detailed information as well as a sense of satisfaction that only the nuances of the spoken word can provide.

One of the best ways to find out about places that you might like to visit is by talking with other clients at a given camp or lodge when you are there. Many visitors to remote lodges and camps are experienced traveling anglers. For example, you might be visiting a bass lake in Mexico for the first time, but you find out that two of the people in camp have been to this place once before, to three other bass fishing lodges in Mexico, to two peacock bass fishing camps in Brazil, and to Alaska twice for salmon. Those people are likely to be excellent sources of information, and if they do not recommend a place, you can be sure they will say so.

Agents.   Many people represent lodges, camps, and outfitters as agents. For some of these representatives, the world "agent" has a loose definition, although a small group of others offer all or most of the services that could be expected from a traditional travel agency, the difference being that these people specialize in outdoor (and maybe just fishing) travel. An agent who not only provides good information about prospective sites, but can also advise on scheduling and transportation issues and book air travel and lodging (if necessary) is very helpful. The cost of using an agent should be no more than if you dealt directly with the actual service provider; agents receive a commission from the service provider, so it does not cost extra to use an agent. And, you may get more and better information, especially if the agent has done a lot of the legwork. Some agents have newsletters that regular clients find very useful.

In fact, using an established full-service fishing travel agent has benefits that you cannot get elsewhere. The agent can often save you money on airline travel and can suggest or arrange the most advantageous travel routes. Although a regular travel counselor could do this, the regular travel counselor has not been to the off-the-beaten-path places that many anglers visit. More importantly, an established fishing travel agent who represents many clients is able to direct you to the place that is best for what you want. An agent usually is current on the places that he or she represents, so it is in the agent's best interests to look out for your interests so that you will be back for other trips.

If, for example, you ask an agent for a recommendation on where to go for the first-time experience of catching Arctic charr, the agent should be able to determine which site is best for you; he might suggest that instead of a location known for big charr, but tough fishing and less guarantee of success, you try another that has reliable action but nothing larger than mid-size char. Maybe after experiencing the thrill of catching small- to medium-size charr, you'll feel that you know that game better and next year will be ready for the big bruisers; the agent can work with you to accomplish this.

Furthermore, a fishing travel agent should know if a place that fits your interests is not suitable at the present time because of circumstances you would not be aware of (high or low water, unreliable transportation services, political or governmental concerns, etc.). The agent can steer you away from there until the situation improves. If something happens between the time that you booked a trip and your departure date, the agent can let you know and possibly change your reservation to another time. Would the lodge owner or outfitter call you if this was the case? Maybe, maybe not. Unfortunately, a lot wouldn't because they hope right up to the last minute that things will change, whereas a good agent will advise not taking the chance.

Usually agents have been to the places that they represent, or to most of them, and can give you a first-hand evaluation of a facility that interests you; or they can direct you to another place that is more within your means, interests, and abilities. The best agents try to visit every place that they represent to be sure that they are up to their own standards. This helps when they talk to a client who has specific interests and questions.

A final reason to use an established travel agent is that if the agent books a number of people to a given facility, the outfitter or camp manager will try to do his or her best for those clients and perhaps give them a little preferential treatment because the agent will not send people there if things go wrong. An agent who gets feedback from clients about the sites visited and the angling experiences is able to pass this information along to prospective clients, which provides a wider pool of information than what any individual could obtain on his or her own without a lot of time and effort.

Not all agents are equal, however, and not all provide a full range of services. Many so-called agents appear and disappear each year. Some are almost totally inexperienced at being an agent, even though they might be capable anglers. A few are totally inexperienced at fishing and thus are unable to evaluate a destination based upon what traveling anglers need or want. You are better off having a capable agent who is an adequate angler or has adequate knowledge of fishing than one who is a talented angler but has no skills at handling the varied tasks of being an agent.

An agent who has been in business for a while, probably five years or more, is likely to be reasonably good. An agent who has airline accreditation is probably financially responsible because the agent has to post bonds in order to work with the airlines, and this accreditation will be revoked if there are financial difficulties. Not all good agents have airline accreditation; some have an alliance with regular travel agencies to do their airline and hotel bookings. You could ask an agent for a bank reference and check it out if you are concerned; this is not a bad idea given the sums of money that can be involved, especially if you're taking family, business associates, or a group of friends on an excursion.

Bear in mind that many agents today are specialized. Some deal with fly anglers only, or fly fishing for trout only, or just largemouth bass and peacock bass adventures, or just remote Canadian and Alaskan operations, etc. It is getting harder to find a single agent who really can do it all, although the larger fishing travel agencies employ a number of people who collectively have diverse experience.

Liabilities. For the most part, dealings with well-established and reputable lodges, outfitters, agents, and the like go without incident. Everything doesn't always happen as planned, though, whether the mishap occurs through the actions of the operator or the people the operator has engaged, or the actions of a client or some other party. Planes have crashed, vehicles have been in accidents, boats have sunk, people have been thrown out of moving boats and injured, and so forth. Angling adventures are not without an element of risk. In a well-known incident in Costa Rica, a small boat capsized and the guide and at least one client were killed. Some people in Mexico have been robbed at gunpoint in their camp. A well-known South American outfitter was kidnapped. People at a Russian river salmon camp were simply thrown out. These are unusual and extreme cases, and not necessarily indicative of the ordinary perils of adventurous angling.

Disagreements or troubles with certain operators have prompted necessary lawsuits by clients; however, disgruntled clients have filed frivolous lawsuits as well. The byword in all of this is *caveat emptor.* Read the fine print in any literature, and be attentive to liability issues. Some agents and operators require that clients sign a total-liability release in order to be booked for a site. Some people balk at this, and you might want to have an attorney review any such release before you sign.

Keep in mind that there are many things that are not within the control of agents, lodge owners, or outfitters, no matter how reputable or attentive they are. Even though royal service is found at a select few deluxe lodges around the world, it is not possible in every phase of a fishing trip. If you aren't flexible, practical, and patient within reason, not to mention a little self-reliant, then exotic or distant international angling adventures are not for you.

Access to wild waters by floatplane is the dream of many an angler.

Preplanning Issues

When selecting a lodge or service, you will be asking many questions of friends, lodge owners, references, and agents. Here are some thoughts on specific topics that will be a concern to many people and that may have some bearing on whether you visit a particular place or choose one site over another even though they access the same waters. Keep in mind that it is customary that all things except fishing tackle and personal incidentals are supplied at a site, especially when visiting a lodge or using an outfitter.

Distance to fishing grounds. Here is a subject many people don't think to inquire about. Great Bear and Great Slave Lakes in the Northwest Territories are excellent examples of this issue because they have good fishing, but much of it takes place considerable distances from the lodges. It is not uncommon to boat daily between one and two hours each way to get to the favored spots on these huge lakes. A lot of potential fishing time is spent riding. If you're assured of catching a big lake trout, you may find the long distances worthwhile; but since such assurances cannot realistically be made, long boat rides may be unappealing to you. These are extreme examples, but the issue of distance is pertinent to Caribbean saltwater or South American jungle fishing just as much as to big lakes in the far north. In a nutshell, the thing to determine is how long, on average, it takes to get from the lodge to the usual fishing sites.

A long boat ride may be worth taking once in a week, and then only if you pick the right day. When it's calm, this can be quite nice; but when the wind picks up and you have to venture out in rough open water for a great distance in a small boat with aluminum seats, little or no derriere padding, and no back support, it can be uncomfortable (and wet) for many, and intolerable for older anglers and those with back problems.

The distance issue is also relative to nonboat fishing and to getting to the boats. In some places,

Great moments to remember occur even when the big ones get away, as happened to these tarpon anglers in Costa Rica.

you may have to be almost a mountain goat to get from lodge to water, and bringing your gear back and forth each day is a real chore. In such cases, for older anglers, poorly conditioned anglers, and the clumsy, there is ample opportunity to twist an ankle while teetering from rock to rock. If you don't ask how far it is to the fishing or to the boats (especially important in periods of low water), you could be unpleasantly surprised.

Fitness and health concerns. It is a fact that many people visiting a fishing destination for the first time, especially if it is remote, have little or no idea what they are getting into from a physical standpoint. How rigorous will the activities be? If you're on an exploratory or pure adventure trip, you could spend many days bouncing in and out of boats, freighter canoes, and floatplanes, and walking through the bush. You might have to climb up and down banks to get to prime river pools, or you might have to negotiate a boulder-studded shoreline to get into casting position on a wild river, or help a guide pull a heavy boat from a cached shore spot. Climbing in and out of a floatplane is a chore for some people, especially when you're in a pair of chest waders. If you have a weak or bad back, consider bringing a brace along.

Such adventures have obvious fitness and medical implications and may be only for those who are up to the rigors. Some lodges and outfitters will properly detail the nature of things and forewarn clients. But this is not always true. When asked by a client, "Why didn't you tell me?" the response may be, "You didn't ask." So ask.

Guides. A guide can make or break a trip. Not all guides are good, not all guides have been guiding very long, and in some places anyone can hang out a "guide shingle." What makes a good guide? Ability to interact well with clients is foremost. That is closely followed by knowledge of the waters and fishing experience but also includes boat-handling ability and willingness to work to achieve success.

A guide who takes you to one place and has no interest in going elsewhere, especially when the fishing slows, is a lazy guide.

The level of guide knowledge varies greatly, and expectations among clients vary greatly. Some people simply want a guide who will get them to and from the better fishing sites; some need expert tutelage in various aspects of angling or in presentation for the peculiarities of the situation. The range is as variable as the fish species and angling conditions.

Here is a general list of attributes of the absolute best guides: They carry themselves and behave as professionals; they will not violate game laws or allow clients to do so; they are courteous and helpful; they can communicate well; they can instruct a client on any element of the skills necessary for success at the particular type of fishing to be done; they have good equipment in good condition (important if you will be using the equipment supplied by a guide); they have safety equipment appropriate to the circumstances; they can provide accurate information about other elements of the experience (the place, the water, other species, etc.); they do not fish unless asked or invited to do so or unless they have to demonstrate something; and they have basic first aid and emergency skills. Very few guides have all of these, and many who don't are still very good guides. A great deal of variability exists here.

Likewise, the skills, personalities, and interests of the people who hire guides are varied. Some are unpleasant, unreasonable, overly expectant, and maybe not very capable anglers, and they may not treat a guide with courtesy or behave properly.

Every angler wants to get the lodge's top guide, which is impossible. It is reasonable to ask how many guides there are, how many years they have guided on the waters you will be fishing, if some specialize in certain areas (fly fishing, trolling, etc.), and other questions. You might ask if they are certified or receive any training. Some guides simply learn as they go, some are taught quite ably by camp managers, and some go through a formal training program.

Generally it is best to be with someone who has a few years of experience on that water, rather than with someone who is guiding for the first time as a summer job. Someone who is inexperienced on that water might be fine, however, if the person has had guiding experience elsewhere or if the lodge owner assures you that the person is a skillful angler. The concern here is not just being able to navigate properly in tricky places, but knowing where to fish when the obvious spots are not producing. If you especially want to learn about fishing techniques, ask if you can be placed with a good guide who is able and willing to communicate and show you how things are done.

If you are a well-traveled angler, and if you have experience in the kind of fishing that is done at a given site, then a guide need only be a boat driver. The guide should be able to navigate safely, get you back to camp at the end of the day from wherever you wind up, and be willing to position the boat however is necessary. You can pick the spots to fish and decide when and where to move and what to do from a technique standpoint.

For most people, a good guide is one who can suggest places, suggest or demonstrate technique, suggest lures or flies, and do the usual boat-handling and fish-unhooking activities. In Third World countries, in places where a foreign language is spoken, and in situations where the turnover of guides is high, such an individual is hard to come by, let alone a full squadron of them in a camp. You should give thought to what you need and what you expect out of a guide, and talk to the agent or lodge manager about this. Fishing on your own without a guide may not be an option because of laws or liability concerns. The more angling travel experience you have, the more you understand guide concerns and can discuss these issues up front when selecting a destination. The entry for guides has more information about guides and being guided.
See: Guide.

Boats and motors. Although this maxim is not carved in stone, it is usually best to be in a place where the motors and perhaps the boats are replaced fairly often. In some places, the whole fleet of boats and motors is replaced annually, which impresses a lot of people. Most lodges replace their motors on a two-year cycle, sometimes a one-year. Motors are the lifeblood of many remote fishing experiences, and they have to work like a clock. In many places, they are put through their paces all season, being run a lot and also abused (striking rocks and such), so it is a good investment for a lodge to change them frequently. Few anglers think to ask about such matters, but it reflects well on the lodge when such matters receive attention.

Boats don't need replacing as frequently as motors, but it is not reassuring to arrive at a lodge where the boats are obviously old and battered. However, this is a variable issue; on the White River in Arkansas, for example, you will see a lot of older flat-bottomed boats in guide use, but these are specialized craft and well cared for, so a newer boat is not always a necessity. A good or new motor is more critical than a new boat.

Electric motors have become much more common, even in distant places, and especially where people fish for largemouth bass. Bass anglers are so accustomed to using electric motors (and sonar) for positioning and effective fishing that even camps in remote parts of Mexico and Brazil have electric-motor boats so that anglers can fish in their customary style. However, having an electric motor may not mean that the guide is skilled at using it for positioning. Not having an electric motor means that the guide has to pole (*see: pushpole*) or paddle to keep you in position. But poling is possible only in the shallows, and constant paddling just does not happen, and is ineffective in the wind.

If an electric motor is advantageous for the type of fishing being done (especially casting along shorelines and cover), then it should be on a guide boat. Make sure that you ask about this, and also inquire as to whether sufficient power is available to recharge electric motor batteries on a daily basis (this is hard to do in some remote places). Many Canadian lodges that offer pike fishing could benefit from having electric motors on the boats, but only a few enlightened lodges provide them; this is not quite as bad as it might seem, since the fishing is usually very good even without using an electric motor.

Safety equipment is a necessity, however, and life jackets are the foremost concern. It is dismaying to be out on a large lake in a 16-foot aluminum boat when the water is 40° and find no life jacket in the boat and perhaps not even a floating cushion. The orange kapok preserver that many lodges place in their boats is abhorred by most anglers, but it is better than a cushion—or nothing—when the chips are down. Almost no one wears life jackets, however, so when an accident happens, no one is prepared.

Lodges or outfitters should have Type III flotation vests (*see: personal flotation device*) in every boat if they want to be considered a top-quality operation. Ideally there is an assortment to choose from. Many of the life jackets provided in remote fishing camps are so small that a large, fully clothed person cannot get one on or cannot buckle it up.

Some anglers bring their own personal flotation device (PFD) to counter such issues. Compact inflatables now available make it easier to do this without taking up a lot of precious baggage space.

There is no harm in asking about the age of any lodge's boats and motors and about the availability of electric motors and life preservers. Your life could depend on the preserver, and possibly on the boat and motor.

Clothing and gear needs. Most lodges will advise clients what to bring; some provide more detailed and specific advice than others. It is more than a shame if you arrive at a choice fishing locale and are inconvenienced or severely hampered by not having things you need. This especially includes warm clothing; "warm" to a lifelong resident of Minnesota doesn't mean the same thing to a lifelong resident of Arizona. Foul weather gear is always important but often underappreciated by novice travelers, who don't know what good rain gear and truly nasty weather are. On the other hand, tropical climates demand clothing that is light and action friendly. Make sure you understand what is appropriate for the time of year that you'll be there. What is true for July may not be true for October.

Specific points about tackle needs (fly-rod length and fly-line size, for example, or baitcasting rod power) are useful. Experienced anglers can give themselves latitude, but the inexperienced need explicit instructions. A lodge that will provide you with such is one that is looking out for your best interests in all aspects of the experience. Invariably, a person who has not been to a specific place or has not obtained detailed advice from the lodge or from someone who has been there, will not have the full complement of tackle that may be needed. The more that you can narrow this down, and the more specific the information you receive, the better you can prepare and plan.

The best-time dilemma. The best times (or those perceived to be the best) are usually booked first by anglers-in-the-know, many of whom are repeat clients. How honestly a lodge owner or agent deals with this issue will tell you a lot about how he or she conducts business and whether you want to do business with that person.

Ideally, any time in a given season is a good time to visit, and in a few cases this may be true, but usually it is not unless there are overlapping seasons for three or four principal species. The best operators will tell you whether this is so, and they will squarely lay out your options and explain how things differ at nonprime times. They will also tell you that conditions may not be the same from year to year on given dates and that weather (cold, excessive rain, excessive heat, storms) and other forces beyond their control (such as drawing down a reservoir to repair a dam or prepare for anticipated heavy rains) can affect your success.

It is not uncommon to be at a fishing hotspot at what is ordinarily the "best" time, only to find the fishing uncharacteristically poor. Experienced anglers know this happens. But a lot of people who visit good fishing spots are not skillful or experienced anglers, and they do not understand this point. Many lodges do not warn people, perhaps because they fear losing a prospective customer, but it is better to be forewarned than to learn after the fact when disappointment and frustration have set in. Lodge owners and outfitters who are honest about varying conditions and can get this idea

across to people, verbally or in their literature, deserve praise, and are likely to give you the straight scoop about all aspects of their operation.

What is "poor," of course, is also subjective. If you go to a Mexican bass reservoir that is renowned for plentiful shallow and surface action and find that, due to a cold front and/or dropping water, the fish are deep and being caught only on plastic worms or jigging spoons, you may consider your experience poor, even if you personally catch 20 fish a day. If you go fly fishing on tropical saltwater flats and find that, because of the conditions, regular success requires longer casts and more skillful presentations than you can make, you'll probably be disappointed. At times, the best fishing is experienced by only the most skillful anglers.

Occasionally the best spot in the world is a bust for everyone. Usually the reason is weather, especially cold fronts and high winds, but it could be drought, floods, or even commercial fishing. Anglers who have visited some prime salmon waters have been virtually shut out by commercial fishing activities. Sometimes these things are avoidable, but sometimes not. The troubles afflicting a remote region or fisheries are seldom newsworthy at home. However, thanks to satellites and world weather coverage through the media and the Internet, it is possible to get information about issues that might affect either your fishing or travel plans, even in remote places, so that at least you are forewarned and can plan or strategize accordingly.

Outposts. One of the options available at some lodges, primarily in northern Canada where outfitters are granted exclusive or near-exclusive rights to a certain territorial area, is staying at what are called outpost camps. The difference between outpost camps and established lodges is that the lodges supply almost everything, including guides. Not everyone wants or can afford this, however, so many places offer outpost camps; these can be as enjoyable as an established lodge, but they take an economical do-it-yourself approach.

Outfitters offer various kinds of outpost packages. The camp itself is usually a log or plywood cabin on a remote lake reached by floatplane. You bring your own sleeping bag and fishing equipment. Food supplies may be included, or you may bring your own. Boats, outboard motors, and gas are provided, and sometimes a guide or outpost camp manager/cook. Some outpost facilities are large enough to handle six to eight people, and they have a husband and wife team serving as camp managers and cooks, in charge of keeping things in order, providing firewood, and assisting guests with problems. In Canada, pike, walleye, and lake trout are the main species sought by outpost camp anglers. Some outpost sites provide opportunities to catch grayling.

If you're a reasonably able angler, if you don't need to be pampered, if you can unhook your own fish, if you want to *really* get away, and if you want

A well-outfitted facility at Campbell River, British Columbia.

to economize, then you should try the outpost experience. Envision a rustic cabin with bunks, a propane tank and cookstove, a wood-burning heat stove, an aluminum boat and working motor, a few housekeeping rules, and a lake or river with cooperative fish.

In most outpost waters, whether or not the fish are cooperative depends on your ability to find and catch them. There is pleasure in exploring wild and unfamiliar water, but the more you know about techniques and tackle for the species sought, as well as the places they're found, the better your angling experience will likely be. With few others to compete for the fish, however, it is possible to find good angling and a completely secluded wilderness fishing experience by going the outpost route.

Other matters. Of course, you will have other concerns regarding the selection of a destination or service. Ask about extra costs (such as fly-out trips); travel routing (including overnight stays); special food concerns (almost every lodge that caters to Americans expects them to eat like Paul Bunyan, so quantity is seldom a problem; although when it is, it will override the good fishing for many people); language barriers, particularly with guides (a primary concern when English-language anglers fish in Spanish- and Portuguese-speaking countries); availability and cost (usually high) of tackle at the lodge; and so forth. If you have any special concerns or needs, be sure to bring them up. Many remote facilities are not conducive to people who are mobility impaired. However, there are exceptions to this. Some lodges exist in settings that permit easy access to boats from the camp, and they are able to accommodate people with special needs.

Few people think of everything to inquire about, and some of the final decision making rests on impressions and an intuitive "feel" for the people you are dealing with. You should go into the selection process with your eyes wide open and ask about anything. Naturally some things will escape you. You might not think to ask if a certain outpost camp has recently had bear problems, for example. And what about the wildlife? A place may have grizzly bears, crocodiles, lions, or snakes. Few people ever think about these matters.

Payments. Everyone understands the purpose of a deposit. Before making a deposit, however, find out the cancellation policy, the amount of time allowed for a refund, and whether deposits can be applied to a new date and a different booking. A cancellation fee may apply. Most cancellations made after a prescribed time period are subject to complete forfeiture. If you are a steady client with an agent or outfitter, you may be given some leeway.

Prepayment is usually required before the trip. This policy is no different from that of most general tourism operators and is meant to help ensure that you will be coming and to give the operator time to fill your slot if you must cancel. Many, though not all, lodges and outfitters will refund the cost of the trip minus deposit if you have to suddenly cancel and if you do so early enough. It is difficult, however, for many outfitters and lodge owners to fill a slot or two when there are last-minute cancellations. Find out beforehand what the cancellation policy is; if it is not clearly stated in the literature, get it in writing.

Most of the time a fishing trip to an international destination is priced to be all-inclusive beginning after your airport arrival. For example, if you're going to a northern Manitoba lodge, you are responsible for getting yourself to Winnipeg by a certain time; from there, the operator will take care of getting you to the camp, usually by charter plane. There are many exceptions and variations to this general rule, so you should have a clear idea of costs above and beyond the package price and of what services you are paying for.

You will probably be responsible for round-trip airfare from your home airport to that international airport. You may or may not be responsible for ground transportation to/from a charter plane, floatplane, hotel, etc. At the fishing site, all expenses, including food, lodging, boat, motor, guide, and gas, are usually included. In some cases, having a guide is optional, and an additional fee is required to reserve a guide in advance for select days or for the entire trip. Fly-outs are usually extra and optional, although some facilities include one or two days of fly-out fishing as part of the package. You pay for that at camp. Gratuities are usually extra, but a few outfitters include them. At some camps alcoholic beverages are extra, but increasingly these are simply included with the package.

At some camps you pay nothing extra except gratuities; others have lures and clothing and odds and ends to offer in camp, and you may have some incidentals to settle up at the end of the visit. For Americans, expenses are usually figured in U.S. currency.

Some operators make it easy for clients by including everything except gratuities in the prepaid package, which means that you don't need to carry a lot of cash. At certain sites, or at stopping points between an airport and the final fishing destination, there is more concern about cash and valuables than at others, so reducing exposure to theft or loss makes sense. Using traveler's checks (not for gratuities, however) further lightens concerns. In any event, be prepared with a good amount of money in ones, fives, and tens, for tipping porters, van or bus drivers, expediters, and the like.

Itinerary. In making plans for your transportation from home to your angling destination, you will need to pay special attention to the air travel arrangements, whether you make them or whether a fishing travel agent, outfitter, or general travel agent makes them. Missing a flight, or not allowing enough time for connections and delays, means extra expense, conceivably a ruined trip, and possibly arriving without your necessary clothes and/or fishing equipment.

Make sure that you have sufficient time between connections, particularly in case delays (due to weather or unforeseen circumstances) occur. Two hours connecting time between international flights (when making an international connection in Los Angeles or Miami, for example) is more than what the airlines require, but a good safety hedge. Remember that you will have to clear Customs upon return, so you may need more time, even though the minimum requirement is an hour and a half.

You should have a clear itinerary with dates, flight numbers, departure and arrival times, and the names and hopefully phone numbers of people or services that will provide ground transport or expediting when you arrive at a transfer point. It's a good idea to check on the flights and confirm your status and departure dates and times; occasionally departure times are changed. If your agent has not already gotten assigned seating, you can do this at that time if possible (there may not be assigned seating or you may have to wait until you arrive at the airport).

Many lodges use expediters who meet arriving flights and shuttle clients and their baggage to a hotel if an overnight stay is required, or to another terminal for a charter flight, or to the lodge itself. Make sure that you know who is doing this or where you need to go if you're responsible for getting yourself and baggage to a transfer point.

Packing and Preparing

The needs of traveling anglers are different from those of regular tourists. Seldom is tackle provided at fishing destinations, unless you'll be hiring a fully equipped sportfishing boat for big-game fishing, and even then experienced offshore anglers are likely to bring some of their own equipment. Most of the time, you have to arrive at a destination with the rods and reels that you expect to use, as well as the lures or flies and some ancillary equipment (scale, gripping tool, waders, etc.). For some places, and for extended stays, this amounts to a lot of gear; and it's hard to properly pack it all, plus appropriate clothes, and still be within weight limitations. This is especially true if your destination requires cold weather garb.

If you travel often for angling, it is helpful to prepare a standard list of things to consider bringing (some trips require things that others do not, so the list ensures that you review all possible choices). A comprehensive checklist is contained here, but a little commentary is required about certain items.

Lures/tackle. Ask well beforehand which lures work best at your destination, and purchase what you'll need before leaving home if possible. If you can't find what you need, some tackle shops cater to international angling travel, and they may have specialty items (especially offbeat lures) that your local shop doesn't carry. The agent or outfitter may be able to recommend these to you.

Your final destination may not have a supply of lures, or the camp may have a good but expensive selection. Don't count on the lodge or camp having what you'll need when you arrive (and there is always a run on hot lures/flies). It should be obvious that this also applies to rods and reels. Some people arrive at distant camps with rods and reels that are unsuitable for the angling conditions; some places have tackle that you can use, but most do not.

Trying to plan for all eventualities at a place you've never visited is difficult. Listen to the advice given by the outfitter, the agent, and people who have visited. The more specific they can be, the better. Once you've obtained the suggested equipment, you can consider bringing other items that have similar attributes or applications.

Whether you carry your lures/flies with you or pack them in checked baggage is up to you. A box or satchel full of hooks and metal sometimes requires close scrutiny by inspectors when it is carried onboard a plane; pack any knives in your checked luggage. Bringing these items as carry-ons could be useful if your luggage is lost or delayed. If you do carry them on, or if you check them as baggage, put duct tape around the latches and draws to prevent pilferage as well as to keep the contents secure in case the container breaks or inadvertently opens. Some boxes can also be locked.

There are all kinds of ways to handle the tackle storage issue. Some people use a bunch of individual plastic containers, stored in some type of bag; others use one multicompartmented flat-sided box that can also fit reels in it and some incidentals, plus a lot of lures. If you don't carry tackle onboard with you, it's best to put it in the same duffle that contains your clothing, and pack the clothing around the tackle for protection *(see: tackle storage)*.

Rod cases.   Traveling with rods is a burden but a necessary evil, and there are two main issues to deal with: making sure that they arrive with you and making sure they are not damaged in transit.

The only way to be sure that your rods make it to your fishing spot with you is to personally carry them all the way. Occasionally you will see a traveler get onto a plane with one or two rods, without reels, banded together and carried in hand, to be stowed overhead. Airlines often do not allow this, and you cannot be sure that it will permitted. Furthermore, you don't want valuable unprotected rods exposed to overhead storage problems, like crushing and shifting. Even if you can get away with this for one flight, you have no guarantee that the rods will not get damaged when you have to stow them elsewhere, such as in a pickup truck, the back of a floatplane, or other place.

Rods should be placed in a protective case for all-around travel purposes. In theory, the best way to travel with fishing rods to distant places is to use breakdown rods that can be stored in a case and that are small enough to be hand-carried everywhere. The overhead storage compartments of some planes are so small that long tubes (3 or 4 feet might be a long tube) cannot fit in them. Airline personnel might require that these be checked as baggage, although you may be able to put a tube of such length under your seat. Three- and four-piece travel (or pack) rods break down into a smaller overall length that, inside a small-diameter tube, is small enough to be carried on any plane or even placed inside some duffel bags. Some companies make travel rods that are every bit the equal of two- or one-piece rods, but they are expensive, and they are limited to certain models.

Travel or two-piece rods that can be carried on planes are preferred by many fly anglers, particularly those who will mainly be fishing for one or two species that permit limited rod choices. A padded tube or carrying case for the rods is best; if not padded throughout, then it should be padded at least at the ends. The case should also be rigid enough to prevent bending and compressing and have a strap for easy handling. If you can carry one or more rods while traveling and pack your reels and essential tackle items in carry-on luggage, you will be ready to fish when you get to your destination, even if the rest of your luggage doesn't arrive with you.

This is the ideal way to travel with rods, but it is not possible, or practical, for the majority of traveling anglers. The limitation is that if the rod you bring (maybe two rods can be carried this way) breaks or is inadequate for the conditions, you're in trouble. Furthermore, not many high-quality travel rods are suitable for really demanding fishing, such as casting heavy lures, or for diverse use. For bait-casting and spinning tackle users, the choices are few (and the demand not that great); the choice is nonexistent for conventional and big-game fishing use. So, most people who travel and who are not fly fishing must bring longer rods, often one-piece, that must be stored as cargo for airline travel. This brings up a dimension of travel that is not encountered by many people other than golfers and skiers—checking oversize rod cases and tubes as luggage. (Incidentally, you might consider bringing a travel rod as a carry-on item strictly as a backup, and putting your other rods in a large case. This way, if the case gets lost, at least you have one rod that you can fish with at your destination.)

Thinking that you can bring just one or two fishing rods to a destination is optimistic but not realistic. A very short trip might permit this, but generally only the most seasoned travelers, repeat visitors to the same location, and veteran anglers who are very focused on one species or type of fishing, can do this.

Most traveling anglers realize that they have to be adaptable to the conditions that may exist (or change) at their destination, and the situation might require different methods of fishing that in turn require different tackle. Ditto for catching varied species of fish; at a northern Canada lake, for

Rugged duffel bags and sturdy rod tubes are essential for traveling anglers; this is a scene at Scott Lake in northern Saskatchewan.

example, you might need one outfit for lake trout trolling, another for northern pike casting, and a third for light-tackle grayling fishing. Furthermore, extended trips and varied circumstances mandate that you have some type of backup, at least for the primary angling that you expect to do. Many rods have been broken on fishing trips, and since the main objective is catching fish, you don't want to be caught without your main equipment.

Carrying a selection of rods is accomplished by using some type of case (see: rod storage). There are many commercial rod cases, and the majority of traveling anglers use a commercial case. A few are sturdy products that provide good protection under all but the most extreme circumstances; most commercial cases, however, are suitable only for light applications and should be avoided.

Lockable flat-sided cases are available; these are similar to gun cases, with ample interior padding, and can be used for some rod storage but aren't long enough for one-piece rods. They are used mostly by people with multipiece rods, usually someone who is going both hunting and fishing at a destination (with fishing secondary) and needs maximum gun protection but cannot carry another case for rods.

Most commercial cases are tubular and adjustable. They are made out of fairly rigid material, but seldom out of a material rigid enough to withstand a heavy weight. You can test a rod case when empty by laying it on the ground and standing on it. If the sidewall flexes deeply, the product is inadequate. It should not flex at all, or just barely under heavy weight. Many commercial models have top and bottom sections that adjust for different rod lengths. At short lengths the cases seem very rigid; when extended to accommodate long rods, though, they are weak. Furthermore, the latch is likely to be a problem. Any case or tube that flexes is highly suspect, not only when weight is piled on it, but also when negotiating the corners and turns of a luggage conveyor belt.

Many people who use commercial cases do little to secure their rods; they simply lay the rods in the case and close it up. You can tell just by picking the case up and shaking it; you hear a bunch of rods rattling around. Do not pack rods this way. The rods should be wrapped, banded, or taped together; padding should be added to the top and bottom of the case so that the rods cannot move up and down; and the rods should be wrapped to prevent side-to-side movement inside the case. These measures should keep the rods (usually the tips and sometimes the guides) from being damaged.

Keep in mind that a rod case is likely to be subjected to all kinds of adventures depending on where you go and what you do. It might wind up being strapped to the struts of a floatplane or a helicopter; it might fall off the back of a truck and bounce down a hillside; it might get run over. When packing your rods in a case (tube), your mission is to make sure that the tube can survive the most severe punishment possible so that the contents are kept safe. Five premium rods in one case can be worth over $1,500. That is worth protecting, and since the airlines mainly treat rods as fragile merchandise not subject to damage claims, you had better protect them well. Imagine that a gorilla will be giving your rod tube the bash-and-thrash test.

The best solution for toting multiple one-piece rods is to protect them in a homemade PVC tube and to pack them with utmost care. You can construct such a tube yourself out of 4-inch (inside diameter) Schedule 40 PVC tubing. The overall length of the finished tube should be a few inches over 7 feet to accommodate one-piece 7-foot rods easily, or a few inches over $6^{1}/_{2}$ feet or 6 feet if that corresponds to the length of rod you use most often. You might make two, one shorter and one longer, for different needs. Shorter tubes travel easier and fit into more places (including vehicles). Do not go over 7 feet plus a few inches, or you will find situations where the tube doesn't fit.

You can use screw-on end caps if you like, but these tend to lengthen the tube and can be hard to get off if they crack or if the grooves fill with grit. Better to use flush end caps. You may only be able to find 4-inch diameter caps, which will not fit over the PVC pipe. The way to fix this is to apply heat to the end of the tube until the material is pliable; if you have a wood-burning stove, you can briefly rotate the end of the tube at the mouth of the stove. When the PVC becomes pliable, push the end cap over it fully; then let the tube cool to shape. You will now have a snug fit for the cap. Do this to both tube ends. Take one end cap and fill it with a foam pad that is several inches thick (you can cut the pad to shape from an old foam mattress); then epoxy the end cap permanently in place. You need a similar pad for the other end cap, but that cap will be secured to the tube with ample duct tape. To remove the rods at your destination, carefully unwrap the duct tape and save it for rewrapping the end cap on the return trip.

The case needs a handle, which is really the tricky part and should be done prior to putting the permanent end cap on. Without the end cap, you have more light to see by. A metal handle, like those used on storm doors, is cheap and adequate. Don't pick the largest handle, but something that your hand can grip with a glove on. The handle has to be secured with rounded Phillips-head screws that come from the inside out, so the nut is on the outside and only a small bit of rounded head is inside. This is tricky. One way to do it is to drill two facing holes on the opposite side of the tube that are large enough to accommodate a long-stemmed screwdriver; the screw can be gripped by the screwdriver and, working from underneath the tube to the top, you can then push the screw through the handle holes on the other side of the tube. Having two people makes this job easier.

Before the nut is tightened down, put epoxy on the screw stem; then tighten the nut fully and saw off the top of the screw stem. Do the same for the other screw, and fill the two screwdriver holes with silicone sealant, which should be trimmed flush when dry. Use a permanent marking pen to write your name and address on the tube.

Now you have a cheap, indestructible fishing rod tube that can hold 8 to 10 rods—more than enough for two people for even a two-week fishing trip. The absolute best way to pack the rods in it is as follows: Lay the rods alternately tip to butt (if you have six rods, for example, three should face in one direction and three in the other). Make sure that no rod tip extends beyond opposing rod handles and that the overall length is shorter than the rod tube; don't jam them in a tight fit. With the rods grouped and facing in opposite directions, bundle them close by wrapping in four or five places with masking tape or rubber bands. The rods should be firmly in place, not loose.

Take a bath-size towel and spread it out on the floor. Place one end of the bundled rods on the towel and near the end of the towel, but not extending beyond it. Roll the rods up in the towel and secure it with rubber bands. Take a second bath-size towel and do the same thing with the other end of the rod bundle. Make sure that both ends are covered with the wrapped towels. Now put the towel-protected rods inside the tube. Put the foam end protector into the tube; then put the end cap fully over the tube and wrap it securely with duct tape.

The contents should be very secure, with no forward, backward, or sideways movement inside. Packed like this, in such a container, the best rods in the world can endure the harshest treatment. Some anglers have not broken a rod through travel in over 20 years of using the same tube and the same packing method. A bonus: you have two towels to use at camp.

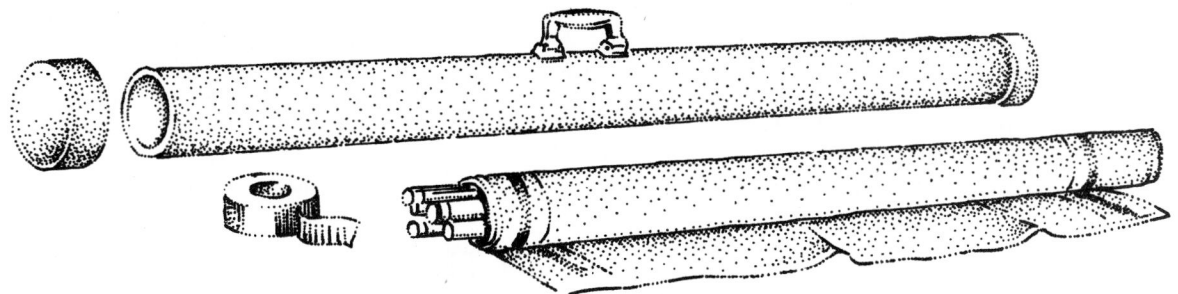

A cylindrical heavy-duty traveling case for rod protection can be made or purchased. It's essential to wrap fishing rods securely and fully before placing them inside the case. Towels make good wrapping material and should cover the entire rod bundle; in the illustration, one end of the rod bundle has been left uncovered to depict the rods, although in actuality one or more towels should cover the rods completely. The ends of the case should be padded.

Duffels, not suitcases. Angling travel is much easier if you use duffel bags rather than hard- or soft-sided suitcases, because duffels can be stuffed almost anywhere. A large heavy-duty duffel without exterior or side compartments is best, and the better versions have rugged leather handles, twin zippers, and a full leather bottom that extends partway up the sides. The twin zippers can be fastened together with a small but reliable lock, although many people don't bother to lock them. Such a bag can store a lot of gear, handle plenty of weight, and be subjected to rough handling with relative impunity.

It's a good idea to treat the bag with a waterproofing agent, and especially to line the bottom and the top of the duffel with your rain gear (pants on bottom, jacket on top) for protection; a plastic garbage bag will also work and can be useful for other things during a trip. Outdoor travel often includes transport of gear in open trucks, wagons, boats, and the like, as well as temporary storage outside. A duffel may be exposed to the rain or sit on wet turf or airport pavement, and this protection could keep your clothes from arriving wet at camp.

Clothing. Clothing considerations are fairly obvious; expect to be cold whenever you head north, and pack for the worst-case scenario by including things you can layer up. You need to be flexible, but in a remote place you don't need a complete change of clothing for every day of the trip. Remember that you can always take clothes off if it's too hot, but you can't warm up with clothes that you don't have. Include a set of thermal underwear for north-country trips, even when you think it's silly; you'll be surprised how often this becomes practical. Several changes of socks and underwear are mandatory.

Consider carefully what you wear en route to your destination. It could be all that you have for a while if your bags are waylaid. Also, your baggage may not be accessible to you when you arrive at your final airport if it is being transferred to the camp. What if the weather is colder there than it was when you left home (which is almost always the case in northern Canada)? What if it's raining (maybe you should wear a waterproof jacket or windbreaker)? Could you go fishing for a day or two with what you're wearing if your luggage doesn't arrive with you?

Some lodges and camps are able to provide laundry service, which cuts down on your clothing needs. You should inquire about this beforehand. Many places do not offer laundry service; however, the creative traveler can bring some cold water detergent in a resealable plastic bag and hand-soak shirts and light pants in a tub or sink one evening, hanging them to dry in the sun or breeze the next day. You must be able to dry them in one day, however, for this method to be effective because if your other clothing gets wet, you might not have any dry clothes.

Some anglers who go to tropical climes wear short pants and short sleeve shirts only when in camp in the coolness of the evening, but not while out in the elements during the day. During the daytime they wear long pants and shirts to minimize sun exposure. Good-quality, supple, breathable clothing tailored for active people (casting all day and catching and releasing plenty of fish is active) is readily available today, so long pants and shirts need not be burdensome.

Footwear varies with the situation. Sneakers are useful almost anywhere, and sneakers or boat shoes with proper soles are best in many situations. In the north, you will need more rugged footwear, such as waterproof or water-resistant ankle-high boots with good-gripping soles. For warmth and all-around use, these are more practical than sneakers. To reduce baggage weight, you can wear the boots to and from the destination. For wet wading in warm locales, you can use old lightweight sneakers or wading booties that protect the ankle and help keep muck out of the shoe.

Waders and wading boots may be necessary at some locations and unnecessary at others. They certainly take up a lot of space in baggage, so you don't want to bring them if you don't have to. Hip boots are sometimes recommended, but you're better off with chest waders most of the time. Find out whether you need insulated or neoprene waders.

Lightweight waders will not do in cold water and can lead to frostbite if you're exposed to the water for too long. Neoprene waders are great for cold water, but brutal if a lot of land walking is necessary. Ask whether felt-soled bottoms are adequate or whether you need grippers. Also, don't break in a new pair of waders on an adventure fishing trip; make sure that the waders fit comfortably and suit you before your trip. And bring some patching material with you just in case.

Necessities and desirables. Make absolutely certain that you have polarized sunglasses, a hat, and sunscreen with you. The benefits of these items have been discussed in detail elsewhere. Another must-have item in many places is insect repellent *(see: repellents)*. Keep insect repellent handy at all times, from the moment you deplane at a distant airport to the moment you leave for a scheduled flight back home. A small, full, screw-top lotion container that fits into a pants pocket will last you for a week. Use something that you know to be effective, not a product you're trying for the first time.

Other good items to tote include aspirin (or the equivalent), lip balm, bandages, and triple antibiotic ointment (for your wounded fingers after you catch and unhook a lot of fish). It's a good idea to have cortisone-type ointment for relieving itches from bites, needle-nosed pliers for unhooking fish, a pocket knife or multi-use tool), and possibly a small compass. Do not carry a pocket knife or fillet knife on your person or in your carry-on luggage if you're traveling by air through major airports; pack it into your checked luggage. A handheld GPS unit is a great addition to an exotic trip, provided you have room for it. It's best to carry this with you rather than check it with your luggage.

Keep in mind that if you're traveling with another person, you can probably pool your gear and bring less than if you both packed separately. You might be able to pack all your rods in one rod case, for example, thus freeing up another baggage allotment. Doubling up may allow you to tote something that might have otherwise been a burden, such as a portable sonar, an insulated float suit, a life preserver, or a camcorder (never check cameras as baggage).

Boat comfort. Travel by small boat for any distance on large waters can get very rough and can be hard on tackle as well as hard on your buttocks and back. Before you go, find out what kind of boats you'll be fishing out of and whether they have padded seats with back support (the best, but also the least common) or whether you will be sitting on the flat wooden or aluminum seats with no support (the worst and most common situation). If you have a bad back and will be traveling in unprotected waters that could get rough, you may want to think twice about your plans, or bring your own seat. Some anglers tote a stadium seat with them.

Ditto for life jackets. Every boat should be equipped with a Type III PFD for each occupant;

nevertheless, you might find that there are no life preservers in your boat. Ask, and consider bringing your own. U.S. Coast Guard–approved Type III inflatables are compact and easy to tote if you have room in your luggage.

Some boats are liable to get wet or have puddles of water, so you should consider which footwear would be appropriate. In the north, where the water is cold, a leaky aluminum boat will puddle water on the bottom and you could wind up with wet, cold feet unless you have waterproof footwear. Remember that even a little puddle (like the kind that happens when everyone leans to one side looking at a fish) is enough to soak your feet.

Papers. For international travel, a passport and a visa may be necessary. American visitors to Canada technically do not need a passport, but it's a good idea to have it anyway. A passport is a must for visiting Mexico and for many other countries, some of which also require a visa. It takes time to acquire a visa, so plan accordingly. There are some services that can obtain a visa on short notice—they walk it through the embassy approval process—for a fee, and your agent or outfitter may be able to recommend them. This is necessary only when travel arrangements have been made on short notice. If you do not have a passport, or if it will be expiring within the next six months, allow plenty of time to get a new or renewed one before a trip; the process takes time when handled by mail. You might speed up this process by personally appearing at the nearest issuing office, but you can be sure that it will be an all-day sit-and-wait affair.

Make sure that you have your passport and visa handy at all times when traveling, and do not let them out of your sight. Do not tuck them in baggage that will be stowed away, since you will have to show them to Customs officials and airline agents, and possibly to others depending on where you travel; if they are stowed in a bag that is under a cart full of baggage, you'll delay everybody by having to dig them out, and if something happens to the bag, there go your important papers. If security is a concern when you are at your final destination, do not leave your passport in your room. Take it with you or store it in a secure place.

It may be necessary, or at least a good idea, to register items of value (cameras, personal computer, etc.) when headed to certain countries or when returning to the United States. This is to make sure that valuables that would be subject to taxes and import duties are not purchased elsewhere and brought back without payment, or sold while en route without payment of taxes. You might make up a list of these items, with date of purchase, cost or value, and serial numbers; the list can be kept with your passport and used to fill out any necessary declaration forms. The list might be notarized beforehand, or it might be stamped by a Customs official at a U.S. international airport. Check with the Customs offices of respective countries to see if

Eighty-five percent of the salmon streams that existed in California in 1850 have been degraded to such an extent that they no longer provide spawning and rearing habitat for salmon.

T

this is necessary. If you have to fill out declaration forms or get a list stamped at an airport Customs office, recognize that this will add some time to your itinerary and plan accordingly. Customs officials usually don't check these items very closely, but if they do, and they have reason to be suspicious about valuable goods, you'll need some proof of prior ownership or proof that you had this merchandise with you when you departed on your trip. A copy of the purchase receipt would likely suffice as well as the registered list.

As for insurance, check to see what your personal insurance covers with regard to loss, theft, breakage, or damage of personal items when traveling abroad. There is no reason to bring valuable jewelry with you when traveling for fishing, so leave that items at home. If you will be driving your own car in a foreign country, you may need a proof of insurance card or statement from your carrier or agent. There are special considerations for driving to Canada and Mexico, and you should check on these with regard to your own vehicle and to any boat and trailer that you might be towing. If you'll be renting a car in a foreign country, check with your carrier to see what provisions are made for this. It may differ depending on the country.

No matter what papers you have, you may get hassled in some places for no obvious reason. Mexico is notorious for unexplainable difficulties that are usually eased by greasing someone's palm. Having smaller bills on hand for this can smooth things along.

Last-minute check.   The night before departing from home, make a quick check of your things to be sure that you have everything that you'll need, starting with necessary papers and then going through your entire checklist. Make sure that all baggage, including carry-ons and rod case, is tagged with personal identification. Some people like to use their business address instead of personal address on their luggage; others prefer just the opposite. It's a good idea to have identification both inside and outside the baggage. Some agents suggest including a copy of your itinerary, with destination phone numbers, in your luggage ID tags, so that your luggage can be forwarded if lost.

Consider marking the bags and tube with some common item (colorful tape, red cloth ribbon, decal, etc.) that makes your items stand out and easily identified. Make sure you include some reading material (a paperback book is good) with your carry-ons, since you will surely be waiting several times during the trip under ordinary circumstances, and even longer if there are transportation delays. Hurry up, then wait, is a common part of the itinerary when going or coming from many foreign destinations, especially in Central and South America.

The following is an all-purpose checklist that will cover just about all general travel as well as fishing travel (including auto travel) and that can be modified to suit your own needs. It's a good idea to print up two copies of your list on index cards; keep one at home and stick the other in your toiletries kit. By looking over the list before leaving home, and again before leaving the lodge or camp, you can be sure you haven't left anything behind.

Traveler's Checklist

- ❏ Underwear: pants, shirts, thermal
- ❏ Pants: work, dress, suit (and tie), sweat
- ❏ Shirts: long, short, tee
- ❏ Shoes: sneakers, dress, deck or boat, boots
- ❏ Socks: white, color, thermal
- ❏ Outer: sweatshirt, jacket, hat, rainsuit, snowsuit
- ❏ Bathing suit, gloves, goggles, belts, clock, pocket knife/tool, sunglasses, sunscreen, insect repellent
- ❏ House/car keys, watch, camera, batteries, film, cash, traveler's checks, personal checks, airline tickets, pad, pen, book
- ❏ Razor, soap, toothbrush, toothpaste, hairbrush, makeup, lip balm, deodorant, Q-tips, moleskin
- ❏ Lozenges, anti-diarrhea medicine, cold tablets, cortisone ointment, aspirin/ibuprofen
- ❏ Prescription medicine, anti-inflammatory drug, seasick tablets, Bacitracin, bandages
- ❏ Shampoo, towel, cloth, hand lotion, hair dryer, Walkman-type radio
- ❏ Rods, reels, line, lures, waders, wading shoes, sonar, compass, GPS, pliers and sheath
- ❏ Boat battery, battery charger, rod holder, downriggers and weights, fly tying gear
- ❏ Cooler, extension cord, thermos, large tools, weather radio, repair kit
- ❏ Rope, tie-downs, spotlight, tackle boxes, net, float tube, fins, scale, measuring tape
- ❏ Duct tape, electric tape, fillet knife, flashlight, lock and keys, fish-gripping tool
- ❏ Small duffel for boat, hook sharpener, binoculars, plastic bags

En route

Baggage considerations.   Many frequent travelers prefer to use curbside check-in whenever possible, so they can avoid toting a lot of stuff any distance and shuffling a rod tube and luggage through waiting lines at the ticket counter. Technically there are weight limitations to all baggage; since porters seldom weigh baggage, it is to your advantage to use them when you have weight concerns. Be sure to tip the curbside porter and see that the routing tags are placed on your luggage. Unfortunately, for security reasons, international travelers cannot check luggage at the curb; it has to be personally checked in at the ticket counter. At U.S. airports, you are less likely to have your baggage weighed, and to be assessed if you are overweight. In a foreign airport, expect your luggage to be weighed at the ticket counter when you're returning home, and to be assessed if you are overweight.

Whenever an agent or porter checks your luggage, always be sure that the person has put the right flights and routing on the tags. Check your luggage receipt. It helps when heading home if you know the airport code for your home airport and can verify that.

For convenience, most travelers check their luggage all the way through to their final destination. However, if you have to board a connecting flight on a different carrier, you may have a problem if your luggage is lost, since the carriers always blame each other. Some people who have domestic travel connections to catch before they board their international flight (flying one airline to Miami, for example, then another from Miami to Manaus, Brazil) check their luggage from their starting point as far as the international departure point; then they claim their baggage and take it to the international carrier for check-in. This way they know where their luggage is and who lost it.

For international destinations, the ticket agent may ask to look in your bags; this should not be a problem, except for your rod cases with their carefully wrapped contents. Suggest that the rod case be run through the passenger carry-on X-ray machine and then hand-carried to the gate for baggage loading by the attendants. It will save having to unwrap and rewrap the case and contents in what is likely to be a cramped area in full view of the public, something that is not easily done with a 7-foot tube at a crowded, bustling ticket counter.

If you're worried about your baggage making a tight connection (and you know that if it doesn't, it will be hard to catch up with you at your remote destination), you can sometimes get peace of mind by watching the on-plane baggage-loading operations (either from the right side of the airplane or from the gate area) to see if your items come along. You might politely express your concern to the attendants and see if anything can be done to wait a moment longer or encourage that baggage transfer. Be pleasant about it.

Losing baggage containing fishing tackle and/or a rod case occasionally happens and is probably the number one worry of travelers. The more remote your final destination, the less likely it is that your bags will catch up to you if they don't arrive with you. It sometimes takes great luck, or exceptional effort on the part of the outfitter, to get delayed or waylaid baggage to you. If you're visiting a lot of places, or have several legs to your itinerary, the lost bags may reach you somewhere along the line. If other anglers are coming to the camp a day or two after you, it is possible that your items can tag along with them. But, in many cases, no one is coming to camp shortly after, and no flights are available to the area in question for several days. If you're headed to a destination that is serviced by a carrier with more than one flight per day, it's a good idea to book an earlier flight in case your baggage gets misplaced. It might come on the later flight, which you can wait for. However, if you're on the last flight to a destination, and your bags don't make it, then they will not be there until the following day at best, by which time you may well be in the hinterland.

You might consider purchasing optional trip insurance that covers lost baggage and/or trip cancellation or accidents.

When you and your bags have reached the final commercial airport before heading to the lodge or camp, continue to be vigilant about your luggage and carry-on bags. Watch your luggage at all times to make sure that it goes where you want it to. When your luggage is unloaded at any destination, especially at far northern transfer points, check immediately to see that all of your pieces are there, and do your best to facilitate their arrival. Even if you're with a group and someone else is looking after the baggage transfers, keep an eye on your gear, not so much for pilferage, but to be sure that it gets from commercial airliner to transportation vehicle to floatplane to camp. Keep an eye on it whenever it is handled; you would hate to lose a bag that made it all the way to the hotel, only to have it placed off to the side during unloading of the vehicle, then be inadvertently overlooked, and subsequently found to have disappeared.

Customs.   Most of the time you will have no problem when entering other countries and going through either foreign or U.S. Customs and immigration checkpoints. This is especially true for passengers on regularly scheduled airline flights; more attention may be paid to those arriving via private aircraft and small charter flights, particularly in Mexico. If you don't have the required papers, however, especially passport and visa, you could be denied entry, so be especially careful to bring, and not lose, these items. If you have a problem with a customs inspector, be courteous, patient, and cooperative. Try to avoid an argument or an unpleasant scene.

If you have to clear Customs before heading onto a connecting flight, you'll have to bring your bags through the inspection area and then take them to another dropoff point after clearing Customs so that they can be sent on. Time may be of the essence here, so don't delay, and be absolutely sure that the bags are left in the right place for continuing travel. Unfortunately, this is often where a duffel and rod tube part company. Tubes are oversized luggage, and in some places they will not be placed on a con-veyor belt to the baggage holding site. They may get placed to the side to be hand-carried to that site, which might not happen expeditiously. Even if you have plenty of time between flights, a tube that gets placed off to the side can be overlooked for a long time, and you may find that when you arrive at your destination airport, your duffel is there but the tube isn't. Do what you can to see that it gets taken to the right place and is not neglected, even if that means waiting awhile to see it get picked up and carted off.

Reconfirmation. On international flights, it is a good idea (and may be required by the carrier) to reconfirm your return departure flights. You may have to reconfirm at least 72 hours in advance, which could be impossible for anglers headed to the boondocks. Reconfirming return flights might be possible when you arrive at a takeoff airport and have a little time to kill prior to moving on. A camp or lodge representative might be able to do this for you during your stay. If you reconfirm a flight on your own at an airport, go to the ticket counter and explain to the agent that you will be out of touch at a fishing camp for an extended period and ask the agent to immediately reconfirm your flight and place his or her initials on the ticket next to the outbound flight.

Exchanging money. Exchange some money at the first possible location (often the airport) to be sure that you have what you need. Local currency is especially useful if you will need to take a taxi somewhere. Some hotels will exchange money for you. In most countries, American paper money (no need for coins) is readily accepted; in a few, you need the local currency. American currency is more likely to be accepted at popular tourist stops than deep in the interior, and it doesn't hurt to have both your own currency and the local currency with you. Check with your agent or outfitter for suggestions. If you are paying a bill at the lodge or camp, make sure you know what currency is accepted. The pricing at many Canadian lodges is based on American currency. Know before you go.

At the Site

Guide matters. Most guides are excellent for navigating on local waters, and this is important because many remote locales are tricky. In some places, if you fish without a guide, and damage a motor or boat, you will likely be responsible for the damage.

When you use a guide, establish immediately what you want and how you care to fish, but accept the guide's suggestions and recommendations, especially at the beginning of the trip. If you are a knowledgeable and experienced angler, so much the better. Not all guides are professional anglers, and if you have enough experience, you can make a valuable contribution to the effort of finding and catching fish. Don't be afraid to experiment with lures and places to fish or to make suggestions to your guide regarding a place to fish and boat speed. The more that you and your guide communicate with each other, the better. Just do it without being obnoxious.

When there are language differences, communicating can be a struggle, and sometimes frustrating. Some agents and lodge owners have prepared a small translation list of useful terms in actual and phonetic pronunciation, so that clients can relay some basic fishing and personal interests to a guide in the guide's language. Knowing how to tell a guide to get closer to or farther from the bank, to put the boat in shallower or deeper water, to go to another place, etc., is very useful and will help both you and the guide (the guide always looks good when customers have had success).

It's a good idea to establish a rapport with your guide, especially those in Third World countries who speak a different language. Respect the guide's ways and culture, and give praise when it is due, especially when a big fish is caught. The large fish may be a moment of pride or even reward for the guide (some camps have big fish pools for the guides), and in any event let the guide know you are happy. If you remain positive and enthusiastic, even when the going is slow, the guide probably will, too. And if the guide is working hard, respect this; don't take advantage of the person, and don't expect the guide to paddle all day against the wind.

Treat your guide well, but don't spoil the person. If you take over the boat and run it, land the fish, unhook them, and leave the guide with nothing to do, the guide will be bored and probably lazy when you do want him or her to do something, not to mention that this treatment may be what the guide will expect of other clients. Guides should not fish unless they are asked or invited to, and you'll spoil a guide by having the guide do what you're there to do, not to mention adding additional pressure to the resource. You fish, your guide guides.

Talk to the head guide, camp manager, or owner, if you have a problem with a guide. They may be able to resolve it without problems or resentment on either side. Do not give a guide alcohol at any time, especially when running the boat, which could be dangerous if not illegal. Do not give a guide alcoholic beverages as a tip, and do not give the guide your alcoholic leftovers prior to your departure. This might send the guide on a bender that will cause problems for the next party in camp, or for the manager or owner.

Boating matters. You should check out your boat prior to departing the dock every day of a trip. Although it is the guide's business to see that everything needed is onboard, make it your business as well. This is especially true for the first day, when everyone in camp is eager to get headed to the fishing grounds. Take a moment to look over things and check that life preservers are available, that an adequate supply of beverages and ice is onboard (this is especially important in the tropics), that the boat has a net or gaff as necessary, that the seats are set up properly for you, that the lunch box is onboard, and so forth.

Stainless steel hooks will not corrode or break down in freshwater; they'll start to corrode after 7 to 10 days in saltwater and will take several months to break down.

Before you start off, make sure that your gear is properly stowed and secured so that it doesn't get damaged while running across the water. An unexpected wave or boat wake, or some rough water, can smack a boat hard and send equipment flying. You don't want your rod left where something like an anchor might bounce onto it. Also, do whatever you can to keep your expensive graphite rods from being banged about on the seats, gunwale, or struts of an aluminum boat. Some guides have absolutely no concern for the value or condition of your fishing equipment, so it's your responsibility to keep it safe. Repeated banging will scrape the protective finish off rods and damage them, resulting in weak spots that may lead to breakage. Rod covers may help with this. Be especially careful when your rod tips extend overboard in brushy and weedy places; they could be snagged and pulled overboard or broken, or the hooks could get stuck in someone.

Tipping.   It is common to give the guide a tip for daily or weekly services and also to tip the camp or lodge staff. The dock manager and the transporter, as well as some others, might also be tipped, although a lesser amount. Check with the camp manager, who is seldom tipped, for customary policies. Many places ask you to tip the guides separately and to make a collective tip to the staff; the staff tip is pooled by all staff members, from the kitchen help to the workers around camp. In many distant places, a tip of $10 per angler per day to the guide is standard. A larger tip, however, is usually warranted, and a $25 daily tip is more likely in some places and situations. A similar amount is provided to the camp staff. An extra amount is warranted for exceptional performance and extra services, and a lesser amount is suitable for inferior service.

Keep in mind that the activities of a guide at one location may basically amount to being a boat driver, whereas at another place they may include being a full-fledged fishing advisor, shore lunch chef, the person who hauls the boat or motor around, and an indispensable factotum who assists with myriad chores. Even when both types of guides do their job well, the tip for the former should not equal the tip for the latter.

Many clients give guides a cash tip plus some equipment or give them some useful or valuable equipment in lieu of a tip. The equipment might be a rod, reel, some lures, or other merchandise. At many destinations, this is not a problem, but you may want to check with the manager about it. Some Mexican outfitters recommend not giving fishing tackle to guides because it may well be used by them or others for commercial fishing activities (legal or illegal) and contribute to depleting the resource. As mentioned before, do not give alcohol to a guide, as a tip or otherwise.

Incidentally, some camps will allow you to fish extra hours (in the evening perhaps for several hours) by private arrangement with the guide.

Food and water concerns.   In some places you will have few if any concerns about the food, water, ice, or beverages; and the biggest problem is not stuffing yourself with all the breakfast, lunch, and dinner items that are made available. In tropical locations, where the heat can be intense, the quantity of food consumed may well be an issue. It is best to eat moderately and to drink a lot in such locations.

Where the quality of water is of concern, be careful about what you eat and about any contact that you might have with water. This could include the water that you use to brush your teeth, the ice cubes in your drink, and the salad that was washed in suspect water. Drink only pure bottled water, or bottled or canned soda or juice while you're out fishing, and recognize that the ice cubes that keep the beverages cold may come from suspect water, so you may want to clean the top of the beverage container before drinking from it. Some camps make ice cubes from pure water, so be sure to ask before using any ice cubes in your drink; likewise ask about any beverages (like lemonade or iced tea) that are mostly made from water. At the main camp, these matters should be less of a concern than while on the water, but find out about them when you first arrive in camp.

If you get diarrhea (Montezuma's revenge), the cause may be drinking the water, overeating fresh tropical fruit, or simply undergoing a change in diet. If the problem persists, you should take an anti-diarrhea medicine; Immodium works well for many travelers, and it's a good idea to carry a supply of this or something similar in your toiletry kit. You might want to put a few tablets in with your fishing tackle (you might do this for bandages and aspirin/ibuprofen, too). Don't wait too long to take remedial action, as you risk making the fishing uncomfortable as well as becoming dehydrated and invoking other medical concerns.

No garbage or fires.   One of the things that makes remote fishing an enjoyable experience is the fact that relatively few others are able to do the same thing and visit the distant and (usually) pristine places that offer good fishing. Therefore, every effort should be made not to despoil these areas. There is no excuse for allowing garbage to fly out of the boat or for not properly disposing of refuse, including bottles, cans, old fishing line, etc. Pick up after yourself and encourage the guide to do likewise. Be attentive to fire concerns, especially in the wilderness; make sure that any fire is completely doused and that cigarettes and cigars are extinguished and then field-stripped. You don't want to be the cause of a forest fire. Finally, try to "tread lightly" in sensitive areas.

Be patient.   Bring some patience and understanding with you. Be aware that no one can control the weather or unforeseen difficulties, such as a plane breaking down. In some far northern locales, floatplanes arrive or depart late because of

---

There are 10 known living fossils in the world; 2 are fish: the Australian lungfish and the coelacanth, a deep dweller found off eastern Africa.

a complicated chain of events; you may get fogged in at camp or at an airport, and you may have to stay somewhere for an extra day(s). Things don't always happen as planned, so leave time in your itinerary, be flexible, and maintain a good spirit. It will all work out eventually.

Canadian Issues

The stereotypical view of a Canadian wilderness fishing experience is more or less like this: postcard-quality scenery; dark, clean water; fragrant Jackie and birch; a rich and spongy undergrowth; deep-blue skies with marvelous cloud patterns; a star-studded night sky like what you'd see at a planetarium; possibly a view of the *aurora borealis;* maybe a loon, moose, or bald eagle sighting; maybe the discovery of old Indian camp ruins; fish that practically flop from the water into the frying pan; and fast angling action, big fish, not-too-sophisticated techniques.

Of course, the fish are not everywhere in Canada. And they're not always easy. Some of Canada's good fishing waters actually have cottages on them. Some virgin-looking lakes have previously been netted. Even in remote Canada, the inhabitants have discovered propane stoves, fast food, and satellite television. When the fish do flop into the shore lunch frying pan, they land too often in a pound of artery-hardening lard. And it's a fact that beautiful secluded places can be hazardous or hostile when misfortune or bad weather occurs.

But if the fishing wasn't good for the most part, hundreds of thousands of anglers wouldn't be visiting the land of the maple leaf every year. The main focus of this attention throughout central Canada is northern pike, lake trout, and walleye. On the west coast, Pacific salmon and steelhead draw many people to British Columbia; back east, trout and Atlantic salmon hold sway. There is some fine but geographically limited fishing for bass and muskie, as well as grayling and charr, but it is fair to say that the greatest overall interest by far is for pike, walleye, lake trout, and Pacific salmon, so some specific information about planning to tackle these species will follow after these general observations.

Trophies versus action. Anglers want to visit a good lodge, fish in an attractive place, and have lots of action, but you can bet that they also want a chance to catch a trophy fish. Don't believe all the stories you hear about 20-pound Canadian fish. Who know what makes anglers stretch 15-pounders into 20-pounders, but it happens a lot in regard to Canada's plentiful pike and lake trout resources. Twenty is a magic number, and, to hear some returning anglers tell it, they caught that size pike or lake trout until their arms fell off.

While stupendous fishing does happen from time to time, be wary of so many grand claims. On the other hand, you could follow one pundit's whimsical assessment of this situation by deducting 25 percent from the size and number of the stated catch; hooking a lot of 15-pounders, by that standard, is still some mighty fine fishing. Indeed, simply having a lot of action is exciting.

Size notwithstanding, you simply cannot do as well in the states for northern pike or lake trout as in Canada. You cannot find consistently fast pike action in most of the United States, and trophy pike are increasingly rare. In the states, a 15-pound pike or lake trout is a darned good fish, but not one found regularly or with much certainty. Not so in these provinces.

Pike are as plentiful in Saskatchewan, Manitoba, and Ontario waters as bluegills are in American lakes. In many of the former, you can count on having lots of action, and in some of the more conservation-oriented waters you can catch and release your personal best. Any cast could do it. It is primarily this attraction, this abundance of riches, that brings anglers north.

The pursuit of trophy fish is an obsession for some anglers, but a steady dose of action is usually what turns on people the most. When you get into that kind of pike fishing, there are many thrills to enjoy: sudden strikes near the boat, fish that you see but that don't strike, fish that you can stalk, fish on odd lures, and opportunities to experiment with different tackle (the popularity of light spinning gear and fly tackle for pike has grown). If ever there was a cast-and-retrieve angler's fish, a pike is it.

The lake trout game is a bit different, however. Casting is a great deal of fun, but seldom the norm for these fish. You can cast for lakers with spoons, plugs, flies, and jigs early in the season, the time when lakers cruise shorelines and stack up below heavy-flowing tributaries to ambush suckers. You can cast around reefs at other times of the year, but seldom are the bigger fish caught this way. You can also jig for lakers through the year, but this doesn't seem to produce giants either. Trolling, therefore, makes up the majority of lake trout effort, whether fishing deep in midsummer, or shallow early and late in the season.

Whether you catch them by casting or trolling, Canadian lake trout are a different fish than their southern brethren. They have a fighting attitude. Southern lake trout are usually caught on heavy tackle at great depths; it's a tepid tussle. And in the Great Lakes, the fish are bleached-gray. To experience the other lake trout, you must go where there is perpetually cold water, brief summers, shallow angling, and old fish that are dark and richly vermiculated. No one experiencing the vigorous fight of a large Canadian laker, or the tenacious battling of smaller northern-water lake trout, would dispute their sportiveness or the enjoyability of catching them. But you have to experience it to believe it.

Where walleye are concerned, be advised that plenty of this species is available to catch across the heartland, but trophy specimens are not as abundant as they are proportionately for pike or lake trout. If size is your standard for walleye, then you'd better not go too deep into the bush. Yes, a big (7 to 9 pound) walleye can be had occasionally in some remote waters, but think more in terms of near-border waters and the Great Lakes if you want giants. Smaller walleye, however, are abundant in many interior lakes.

Timing. Interest in fishing for the various species at prime time is always immense. Heavy outfitter bookings for the opening of the season confirm the most popular time. Many anglers want to be first, or among the first, to visit a lake each season. And some regulars book the same early week year after year. These anglers feel that the fish are shallow and most accessible then because the fish have had a long winter's respite from lures and boats and motors, they are more vulnerable to deception (although some anglers book the first week because the bugs are not yet bad). For anglers of moderate ability or skill, this may be true. And no doubt some fish, especially pike, are abundant in the shallows early in the season and you stand the best chance then for continuous action.

But first isn't always best. Sometimes, early-season anglers outfox themselves when a tenacious winter causes a lake to be mostly frozen when the camp opens. Then, everyone fishes in the same limited area, even on a huge lake. You could do that at home. And yet, a lot depends upon your skills no matter what time of the season you visit.

If you want fast lake trout action, for example, but are ill-equipped or inexperienced at fishing deep for them in the middle of the summer, then you probably shouldn't be there at that time. A good lodge owner/manager will be honest about season-long prospects. Nevertheless, it's a fact that some people will have terrific fishing on a mid-season week, while other people will have poor success at the same place at the same time. That is not necessarily attributable to luck, although it could be attributable to the guide, if one is used. The bottom line: Don't assume the fish will jump into your boat.

Weather. No matter where you go or what species you pursue, weather *(see: weather)* can be a factor, and there is nothing that you, a guide, or an outfitter can do about it. Virtually all the photos in advertisements, magazines, brochures, and tourism literature show moderately dressed anglers in idyllic lake settings on bluebird days. But it doesn't always happen like this, a fact that lodge owners, writers, and veteran travelers take for granted, but many other folks don't. You could be stuck in camp for a day or two in midsummer because of horrendous weather. And even when you can fish, it may not always be pleasant. Don't underestimate how cold it can be in mid-July when the clouds roll in, the wind blows, and the surface temperature on the lake you're fishing is much lower than you'd have back home. If you're not prepared, the fishing will have to be awfully good for you to forget your discomfort.

In the far north, weather can change quickly and frequently. Many days start with bluebird skies and budding warmth, and turn wet, windy, and miserable a few hours later. While fishing in locales far from camp, and where big expanses of open water are encountered, be attentive to increasing wind speed and changes in direction, so you can head back before conditions get unsafe. Your guide, if you have one, should be attuned to this, but may not be. You should assume this responsibility if the guide doesn't.

When you can see white on the tops of a few waves, you've already lingered too long in a small boat. Put rain gear and/or flotation equipment on before making a run across wind-whipped water. The person sitting on the windward side of the boat and those in the stern will get the wettest from spray. If you have inadequate rain gear, it is possible to get completely soaked and frozen on an otherwise clear sunny day while running across a wind-whipped coldwater lake.

Clothing, rain gear. Dress for cold weather, and use the layered approach. You can always take off clothes to get cooler. Bring thermal underwear as a precaution, plus two pairs of thermal socks (one in case the first gets wet). Bring waterproof pack boots (or wear them to your destination to save weight and space). You may need them for warmth, for hiking to hotspots, for getting out of the boat in shallow water when you can't step right onshore, for keeping your feet dry when it rains, and/or when there is water in the bottom of your boat, etc. A pair of shin-high rubber boots might do as well. Check with your outfitter, booking agent, or lodge operator to see if hip or chest waders will be helpful or necessary, and if the water will be cold enough to justify insulated rubber or neoprene waders.

Bring rain gear that will meet the toughest tests (most rainwear failures occur at the jacket collar and in the crotch or lower back) for water repellency, comfort while fishing, and wind protection (warmth). Bring a suit, preferably one with bib overalls, and make sure it will fit over all other clothes. Carry that rain gear whenever you go fishing or when you go somewhere for a day trip. Few lodges or camps supply rain gear; although on the British Columbia coast, most camps provide their guests with rain suits and rubber footwear.

Bugs. One positive side to cold weather and wind is that it keeps bugs at bay. Canada has black flies and mosquitoes like the ocean has salt. Fortunately, in Canada the wind is usually blowing, warm from the south and southwest till midsummer, and later cool from the northwest and north. As long as the wind is blowing and you're not in the lee, all will be well. It is back in camp, when someone has left the cabin door open for more than a nanosecond, that the invasion starts; when you get firmly tucked into bed or sleeping bag, visions of ferocious fish swirling in your mind, the critters divebomb your head. Be forewarned and prepared.

As a general rule, the fishing is best when the bugs bite the most. That may mean black flies in

June in northern Manitoba or Saskatchewan, or mosquitoes in July in the Northwest Territories. Expect to have to deal with mosquitoes or flies, and be happy if they are not present or are less of a nuisance than you expected.

Keep insect repellent *(see: repellents)* handy at all times, from the moment you deplane at a distant airport to the moment you leave for a scheduled flight back home. If heavy concentrations of mosquitoes and/or black flies are a possibility, you might want to tote a headnet and bug jacket. Remember that some bugs will bite through a light shirt, so simply covering exposed flesh may not be enough. You can douse your clothes with repellent (although this could be harmful to the material), wear a treated bug jacket, or you can wear a light windbreaker that doubles as a rain jacket.

If you are allergic to bug bites, bring appropriate medication with you and advise your companions and outfitter.

Catch-and-release.   Anglers with mostly meat on their minds have become increasingly less welcome in most of the Canadian provinces and territories. In the southern part of all of the provinces, drive-in access has resulted in extraordinary fishing pressure. The existence of more logging roads has meant access to places few could previously reach in the summer, and these sites have been hammered.

Overfishing is one of the reasons why travelers who can forgo the convenience of having their own boat will journey to fly-in locations, whether main lodge or outpost, to be assured of a Canadian experience that more closely resembles the stereotype. Such places have a growing emphasis on catch-and-release *(see)*, including trophy specimens (though small fish for your lunch can be kept); they also emphasize using barbless or de-barbed hooks, using single-hooked lures, and fishing without bait in order to minimize injuries to fish.

What is making this accepted policy are new owners, new customers, and a quality resource. Younger and progressive owners have stepped in at many lodges across Canada, especially in Manitoba, Saskatchewan, and Ontario. They have refurbished or newly built deluxe or near-deluxe accommodations and have made an enormous investment in the resource, most of which they have exclusive access to. Aside from offering a good service, they must sink or swim with that resource, which they, and most of their customers, recognize is finite. It used to be thought that the number and the size of fish that could be kept were unlimited, even in lightly angled wilderness waters, and that fishing pressure wasn't harmful. Now we know better.

Although resource-protection changes have met with resistance from a few anglers, these measures have been well received by most conservation-oriented visitors. Considering the cost of such trips, no amount of killing fish, trophies or otherwise, would be of comparable worth, so quality of experience becomes the real issue. The quality of experience is surely enhanced where there is enjoyable fishing opportunity.

Hot lure pattern.   Certainly many different types of lures and color patterns catch Canadian fish. For pike and lake trout in far northern waters, however, you'd be remiss not to have a Five of Diamonds pattern spoon, which has been called the Lure of the North. It is arguably responsible for catching more modern-era Maple Leaf trout and pike than any other lure. So respected is it that you need but say the words and anyone who knows north country fishing is on your wavelength.

Although people speak about the Five of Diamonds as if it were a lure, it is really a pattern: five red diamond-shaped marks on a yellow background. In recent years, this pattern has become increasingly better known and more popular. In any article about fishing in the north, especially about lake trout, the Five of Diamonds is almost always the first lure mentioned. The effectiveness of this lure may be due to the fact that many far north waters are tannin-stained; this pattern shows up especially well in such water and in the depths of clearer water. The key to effectiveness could be the ratio of red to yellow on the lure, combined with a brass back; this pattern is not nearly as effective with a nickel back.

Guides and lodge managers can attest to the effectiveness of the Five of Diamonds, whether cast in its weedless mode for pike or trolled in dessert-plate-size versions for lake trout. It is heavily stocked and touted at camps and lodges, and many people say that if you had to bet the farm on one lure pattern to catch a fish, especially a lake trout, this is it. You can modify single-color lures and put the Five of Diamonds pattern on them with a waterproof marking pen. Keep in mind that using these colors or this pattern is in itself not a miracle solution. You still have to use a spoon with the right action, and you still have to troll or retrieve it in the proper manner.

Lake trout.   Some anglers have no interest in going anywhere to fish for lake trout, even in the deep, remote, and fish-abundant waters of northern Canada. They don't like trolling; they don't want to endure long boat rides in small aluminum boats; and they have no appreciation for a fish that is known to be a deep-dweller and reputedly a sluggish fighter. But there are still plenty of anglers who prefer lake trout to Canada's other main attractions and who make a trip to one or more distant locales every year or two.

It is true that most Canadian lake trout fishing is trolling, but not all of it; many fish, including some over 30 pounds, can be caught by casting or jigging in the right circumstances. It is not true that these fish are sluggish. They can be sluggish if they are small and caught on heavy gear from deep water, but a lot of Canadian lake trout fishing is done in the upper 30 feet of water and these fish are scrappy. The smaller ones, which sometimes thrash

Of the major oceans, the North Atlantic is the saltiest, averaging 37.8 parts per thousand of salinity; the Sargasso Sea is the saltiest part of that ocean.

and roll wildly near the boat, can be a spunky nuisance. And more than one angler, fishing in prime waters, has hooked and played a tenacious and drag-pulling laker for an hour or more, sometimes catching the monster, sometimes not.

In those far north places where the water stays cold all season, you can catch lake trout in the upper strata all year long. In places that warm up in the summer and where the surface water reaches the 60s, the trout will positively go deep. If you expect to fish shallow and use light tackle, and you arrive in the middle of the season, then you'll probably be disappointed.

The busiest time for most lake trout lodges is the first few weeks of the season. Camps are usually full. Most bookings are made 8 to 12 months in advance, prior to knowing what the winter will serve up. A severe winter and/or a long cold spring will delay ice out and possibly limit the places where you can fish if you're scheduled for a lodge on the first or second week. But many anglers take that chance. Right after ice out, and for the first few weeks of the season while the thaw continues and lakes remain cold, is the best time for light-tackle fishing and shallow trolling. It's a good time for catching big trout, as well as many trout. It's also a good time for casting plugs, spoons, flies, and jigs around reefs, at tributaries (a big fish hotspot), and along shorelines. As the season progresses, casting becomes less practical in lakes, and trolling the norm. Don't overlook late in the season when some of the heaviest fish are caught. Not all lodges stay open late in August or into September, because of hostile weather and airplane delays, but those who do, cater to knowledgeable, hearty anglers searching for trophy fish.

The better lake trout angling is usually found in the upper half or upper third of the southern provinces, as well as throughout the Northwest Territories. Northern Manitoba and northern Saskatchewan provide some of the best opportunities for big fish, but the tundra waters of eastern and central Northwest Territories, as well as Victoria Island, are equally notable.

In the far north, rivers offer exciting lake trout fishing by casting but seldom are the fish big; however, larger fish will prowl the turbulent inlet. In lakes, trout are often structure oriented, and they migrate to reefs, shoals, and islands to feed. They also cruise the shorelines. In lakes that warm up and create a thermocline, lakers will go to cool water below the thermocline in large open-water bowls. This is where their primary food, ciscoes and other lake trout, is found.

Most veteran Canadian lake trout trollers use stout rods and 20-pound (minimum) line and large spoons (sometimes plugs). Big trout can be caught, however, on lighter tackle, including 12-pound line and conventional baitcasting tackle. In some places you can catch small trout on streamers, dry flies, and light spinning tackle with small spoons, spinners, and plugs.

Alberta's Bow River, one of North America's great rainbow trout waters, was stocked with these fish accidentally in 1905 because a fisheries wagon bound for Banff broke down.

The old standard technique in the far north is flatline trolling with a big spoon that gets down 20 to 25 feet when trolled behind about 120 feet of line. When fish are shallow or relatively near the surface, flatline trolling with various spoons and plugs is effective. When they're deep, you can use a diving in-line planer, weighted line, wire line, or a downrigger (a minority of lodges have these) to get down, primarily with spoons (big flutter spoons work well).

Wherever you're headed, find out what kinds of boats and equipment are available. Bring portable sonar if it isn't provided. Ask how long you'll spend, on average, to get to the prime laker grounds (on some big lakes you spend hours every day just traveling). Check on the camp's conservation policy. Many of the best lake trout lodges have strict catch-and-release/single-barbless-hooks-only provisions; they'll probably have good fishing for years to come.

Northern pike. Many people love to fish Canada for northern pike but wouldn't spend five minutes fishing for lake trout, and vice versa. For the most part, pike fishing is a different situation.

Pike fishing is almost always a casting fishery rather than a trolling one. You seldom fish in big open-water areas, although you may have to cross large expanses of lake (which can sometimes be rough) to go from place to place. Pike fishing often takes you to some of the northern lakes prettier locations: weedy back bays, meandering marshes, nooks and crannies that no self-respecting lake trout would ever visit.

This kind of fishing has a more visual element to it. You see a lot of pike, whether they're cruising the shallows or chasing a lure. And, because the fish are pretty voracious, you sometimes get to see a cavernous mouth open and inhale your lure. It's an active game.

As with lake trout, you can have some great action early in the season, especially for lots of fish. When northern lakes melt, the shallow bays and backwaters are the first to open and warm up, and pike get into these places big-time, sometimes resting in water barely deep enough to cover their backs. You can do a lot of sight casting then. Weeds are sparse at best, and the water is ultraclear. You can also catch large fish, but since pike spawn in late winter or early spring, the big pike now are not as hefty as they will be later, and the real monsters seem to be elusive.

Good pike lakes usually have no bad time. Later in the season, when the weeds are thick, most pike will be off the shoreline and in the weeds, and sight fishing opportunities are greatly reduced. Pike will have been feeding well and many will have better girth.

Except for the Maritime provinces and British Columbia, all of Canada has pike fishing to enjoy. The bigger fish seem to come from the remote northern lakes in the heartland provinces of

Manitoba, Saskatchewan, Ontario, and, to a lesser degree, northern Quebec.

The pike action is good in some of the bigger rivers and lakes within big river systems, but the majority of the best fishing is in lakes, especially big lakes and places that aren't readily accessible from roads.

Pike are an ambush fish and in many ways are like largemouth bass in their habitat preferences. They aren't fond of current, but they'll hide in eddies and backwaters on rivers. They like wood and vegetative cover, especially if it's thick, and they can be caught in that cover and induced out of it to chase a lure.

Pike fishing tackle is very similar to bass fishing tackle. You can use baitcasting, spinning, or fly gear, and an assortment of lures. Line needn't be ultra-heavy, but you should use a short wire leader or heavy monofilament shock leader in case you hook a big fish that gets the lure inside of its mouth, or crosses the line on its sharp teeth. Experienced anglers can use an 8-pound outfit for spinning and 12-pound for baitcasting, although some use heavier-duty gear.

Some of the better pike lures are large and thus require at least a medium-action rod for casting. Line capacity on reels is seldom an issue. Drags should function well, but they come into play only for big fish or when using light tackle. Weedless spoons tipped with a plastic trailer, super-shallow-running plugs, and spinnerbaits with bright-colored blades are top lures but jigs, buzzbaits, bucktail spinners, and plastic worms are also effective.

Cruising and casting shallow backwaters in the early part of the season is the best bet. Shallow-running snagless lures are a hot item then, and so are many flashy plugs. As the season progresses, weed cover grows and lakes warm. Pike move into deeper cover, and lure selection changes to items with more vibration, more color, and more flash for active fish, and to jigs and plastic worms for inactive fish. Deeper running lures (heavy spinnerbaits, bucktail spinners, and diving plugs) may be necessary. Move away from shorelines unless they're steep and have ambush cover along them; cast around the mouths of bays, points, and where there is a tributary. Pike can move into deep water if there is ample food, but they are seldom deliberately sought in deep open areas.

Be extremely careful when using multihooked lures for pike. Try to avoid them if possible, not only for the sake of the person handling and unhooking fish, but also for the sake of the fish. Barbless hooks are the way to go; better yet, replace trebles with appropriate single hooks for lures that will still work well in this fashion.

Pike are mean and tough looking, but they aren't invincible and shouldn't be manhandled. Don't grab them by the eyes or the gills, and don't keep them out of the water for long. On many of the better pike waters, lodges practice catch-and-release; with the great replica taxidermy available today, anglers have no good reason to keep these fish. Some of the better lodges use a fish cradle to immobilize pike in the water for safe unhooking and release.

Walleye. From big fish to lots of action, Canada's got whatever suits your walleye interests, and the best part is that you don't necessarily have to go to remote waters to find it. Sure some distant spots have some fine walleye angling, but seldom are the biggest fish found in those places. A 6-pounder, which is a good-size walleye, is pretty rare in most northern waters. But get closer to the border, and include such havens for 8- to 10-pound walleye as Lake of the Woods, Rainy Lake, the Detroit River, Lake Erie, the St. Lawrence River, and the Bay of Quinte on northeastern Lake Ontario, and you can see that the biggest fish may be the closest ones.

Lots of people fish walleye in near and far Canadian waters, from Labrador to Saskatchewan, and much of it is fish-on-your-own angling, either piloting a boat by yourself at a resort or towing your own fish-catching machine to the designated site. The entire gamut of walleye tackle and techniques is employed, with fishing ranging from difficult to find in hard-fished waters to cast-after-cast easy in some remote fly-in lakes. The latter usually also offer good pike fishing, so there's combo angling available.

A big rush in Canada starts when the spring walleye season opens, a time that varies by province and by district within provinces. Walleye have usually spawned by the time that the opener occurs, but not necessarily. The people rush subsides after the walleye disperse and migrate to summer grounds and become temporarily harder to locate. Fishing early in the season can mean enduring some fickle weather and having plenty of company for the walleye's attention, especially in the more popular and heavy publicized places. It's not so frenetic yet very enjoyable in June, but when school is out and summer vacations have started, popular walleye waters see a lot of traffic.

Big and small lakes and big and small rivers, of which there are plenty in southern Canada, provide ample angling opportunity. Quebec, Ontario, Manitoba, and Saskatchewan lead the field, particularly the mid to southern regions of those provinces. Some of the finest small-walleye waters have been hit hard over the years by increasing accessibility; for bigger fish, the largest lake and river systems hold the most promise. But smaller waters have more charm and interest, and walleye eat well no matter where they come from.

For most of the season, from late spring through summer and into fall, walleye are located on rock reefs, sandbars, points, weed edges, and the like. In big lakes, some walleye suspend in open water where there are schools of baitfish.

Tackle for Canadian walleye fishing is no different than that elsewhere. Spinning rods with a medium action and sensitive tip for detecting jig strikes are common, usually with 8-pound line. Longer rods are necessary for trolling, where baitcasting gear is preferable. Jigs, bottom-walking rigs, in-line spinners, and assorted minnow-style plugs are the mainstays.

Bait is especially important in using bottom-walking rigs and for tipping jigs, but it is illegal to bring bait into Canada. You have to buy what you need there; plan ahead and make sure that what you want will be available where you're headed or en route there.

Drifting, stillfishing, jigging, slip-bobbering, and various forms of trolling are employed as conditions warrant. Casting with plugs or spinners is possible in some remote places where the fish are stacked up and not terribly sophisticated, but that isn't the norm.

Walleye are called pickerel in many parts of Canada and usually referenced that way in fishing regulations literature. But everyone knows what you're talking about when you say "walleye." People who keep walleye and return to the United States with them should check those regulations and be sure that their fish are readily identifiable as walleye to anyone who checks (that may mean leaving some skin on a fillet). Remember that in Canada you can fish only with one rod per angler, not two, no matter where or how you pursue walleye.

TRAVEL ROD

A multi-piece fishing rod whose sections are of small enough length to be packed inside a protective tube and easily transported for travel purposes, especially airline travel. Travel rods are usually three- or four-piece models whose individual sections are of equal length, and may be from 18 to 24 inches long; some models, especially pack rods meant for campers, may have more sections of shorter length, and others may be just two sections, which include a telescoping butt.

The purpose of a travel rod is to make the transportation of a rod for fishing practical in situations where longer rods can be problematic. They are especially designed for international travel via air. Longer rods, especially one-piece 6- and 7-footers, would have to be secured in a rigid and heavy tube of appropriate length, which provides ample protection but which becomes checked baggage and is subject to loss. When travel is to distant and obscure places, losing fishing rods can ruin a trip, so some anglers hand-carry one or more travel rods in a tube aboard an airplane, either as a backup in case their other rods are lost, or as the sole fishing implements.

Although some multi-piece travel rods are of mediocre fishability, high-end three- and four-piece travel products are eminently fishable. These can be found in 6- to 9-foot spinning, baitcasting, and fly-casting versions, and are the equal of similar one- or two-piece rods in performance. The majority of these travel rods are fly models; spinning models are fairly common, but only a few baitcasting travel rods exist, in part because many baitcasters tend to use numerous rods while fishing.

Standard two-piece fly rods, which can be stowed into 44- to 50-inch tubes, are often carried onboard airplanes by traveling anglers, but these are not travel rods per se. They may be subject to luggage checking, but may also be permitted in the cabin; this may differ with airlines and also be dependent upon the storage capabilities of the specific plane.
See: Pack Rod; Rod, Fishing; Travel.

TREBLE HOOK
A hook with three points.
See: Hook.

TREVALLY
Trevally are members of the Carangidae family of jacks and are numerous in worldwide tropical, subtropical, and temperate oceans. Reportedly, more than 25 species of trevally inhabit Australian waters. Species of most importance to anglers include the giant trevally *(Caranx caranx ignobilis),* golden trevally *(Gnathanodon speciosus),* bigeye trevally *(Caranx caranx sexfasciatus),* silver trevally *(Pseudocaranx dentex),* and bluefin trevally *(Caranx caranx melampygus).* All are excellent sportfish whose strength, power, and stamina is esteemed, and their flesh is very good table fare.

Identification.   All these trevally have moderately elongated and compressed bodies, deeply forked caudal fins, and pectoral fins that are long and sickle shaped (falcate). With the exception of the silver trevally, the soft dorsal and anal fins have a prominent anterior lobe. A row of scutes (varying from 25 to 38 in number) along the posterior section of the lateral line serves as a basis for identification. The anterior section of the lateral line has a pronounced upward curve. Of the aforementioned species, only the golden trevally has no teeth.

The silver trevally (also known as white trevally, silver bream, skippy, skipjack trevally, blurter, and ranger) has a black spot on the trailing margin of the operculum. Its body color shades from bluish green on the back to silvery yellow to silvery white on the belly.

Juvenile golden trevally are striped vertically (the first stripe is oblique and passes through the eye) and have a golden body coloring. As the fish matures, the stripes fade, and the gold changes to canary yellow, with a bluish tinge along the back. These colors also fade over time.

The giant trevally (also called turrum, ulua, and previously by the misnomer, lowly or lesser trevally)

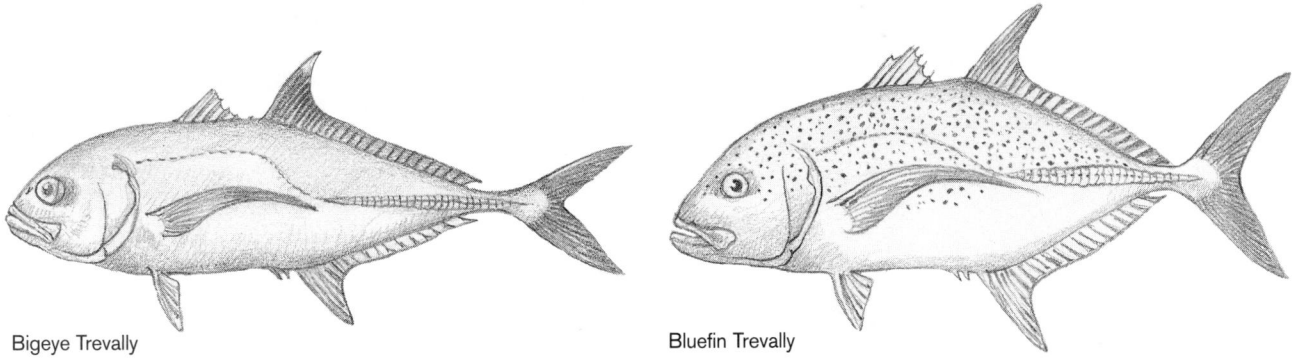

Bigeye Trevally

Bluefin Trevally

is identifiable by a small, oval patch of small scales within a larger scaleless area located on the breast immediately in front of the ventral fins. The breasts of other trevally are fully scaled. There is no opercular spot.

The bigeye trevally (also called turrum, ulua, and previously by the misnomer, giant or great trevally) has a body color that ranges from dusky above to silvery below, and eyes that are comparatively large. There is a black spot on the upper edge of the operculum. Its body is more elongated.

The back and flanks of the adult bluefin trevally (also called blue-spotted jack, starry jack, blue crevally, omilu, and bluefin kingfish) are a brilliant turquoise blue, silvery blue, or greenish blue, generously covered with small black or blue spots. The tail and other fins may be even more striking in color. The anal and dorsal fin lobes are often white tipped and the tail black edged.

Size.   The silver trevally can grow to 15 kilograms, but specimens to 2 kilograms are the norm; the all-tackle world record is a 15.25-kilogram specimen caught in Japan in 1998. The golden trevally can grow to a weight of 37 kilograms. The giant trevally is the largest of the species, growing to 65 kilograms. The bigeye trevally is generally smaller, with fish from 7 to 9 kilograms being large, although a record of more than 14 kilograms was established in the Seychelles. The bluefin trevally grows to at least 10 kilograms.

Distribution.   Bigeye trevally range in the Indian and Pacific Oceans from east Africa to western America. Giant trevally are common in Hawaiian and Kenyan waters, and range from eastern Africa throughout the Philippines and to the Marquesas, as well as down to Australia and New Zealand. The bluefin trevally ranges from Japan and the Philippines south to Australia, west to eastern Africa, and east through Hawaii and to Baja, Mexico.

All of these species are encountered in Australia. There, silver trevally are found around the bottom half of Australia from Rockhampton in the east to the North West Cape in the west. The other species are mostly taken from subtropical to tropical waters from northern New South Wales in the east, across the top of Australia, to the central coast of Western Australia.

Habitat.   Young silver trevally are found in estuaries, bays, and shallow offshore waters, whereas adults range from offshore waters around inshore reefs to the deep waters of the continental shelf. Giant, golden, and bigeye trevally are pursued near rocky headlands, in estuaries, around outer reefs and within tropical lagoons, and from ocean beaches; the bluefin is found in similar locations, in lagoons and outer reefs during the day, and in harbors, channels, and shallow reef areas in the evening.

Life history/Behavior.   Little is known about the history or spawning behavior of the tropical species. Silver trevally spawn during the summer months, roughly from October through March, releasing their eggs in batches over a period of several weeks. Specimens in spawning condition have been found in both estuaries and offshore waters.

Food and feeding habits.   All these trevally are carnivores. The golden trevally tends to prefer crabs and shellfish, whereas the bigeye, giant, and bluefin trevally prefer small fish but also eat crustaceans. The latter three species are often more active feeders at night. Silver trevally feed on crustaceans, small fish, worms, and mollusks at all times of the day or night.

Angling.   Trevally are tough, powerful fish that fight tenaciously, characteristics that endear them to anglers. Baitfishing methods for the large tropical species depend on the use of live baits, or strip baits of mullet, garfish, pilchards, squid, and herring, and even prawns and worms (also fish liver if it can be kept on the hook). Hook sizes to 9/0 2X strong, and lines to 10 kilograms are in order, as are stout boat rods in the 6- to 10-kilogram class, and reels to match.

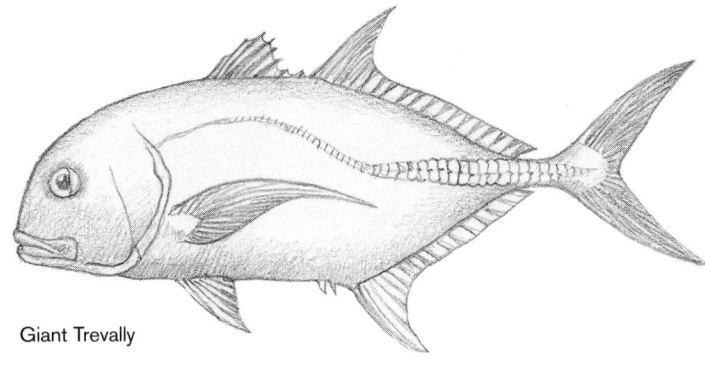

Giant Trevally

A giant trevally from the Arafura Sea near the Cobourg Peninsula, Australia.

The smaller silver trevally feeds more on worms, prawns, and small shellfish but will not hesitate to take small fish baits. Hooks to 3/0 are usual, combined with lines to 7 kilograms on spinning or baitcasting gear.

Lures can be trolled along the edges of coral reefs or cast to surface-feeding fish. Feathered and plastic offshore trolling lures, metal spoons, plastic jigs, minnow-type plugs, and surface poppers will all interest the tropical trevally. Fly fishing, using up to 10-weight outfits, is popular for these species. Rock and surf anglers can choose between bait and lures.

The body shape of trevally gives them tremendous resistance in the water; this attribute, combined with powerful muscles, has an effect of sheer strength that can humble the most confident of anglers. Add to this their disconcerting habit of heading for the nearest reef in an effort to cut the line, and these characteristics quickly earn the respect of all trevally anglers. It's best not to exert too much pressure on a hooked fish; gentler tactics tend to contain the fish to the upper layers, where it can be handled without the worry of underwater obstructions.

TRIGGER

A lever that permits one-handed disengagement of reel gears or opening of a spinning reel bail. On spincasting reels, a trigger performs the same function as a pushbutton, although it is used on a product that mounts underneath the rod instead of on top of it. On spinning reels, a trigger is an automatic bail opening mechanism. On baitcasting reels the finger grip located on the back of the handle is known as a "trigger grip."

See: Baitcasting Tackle; Spincasting Tackle; Spinning Tackle.

TRIGGERFISH

Triggerfish are members of the Balistidae family, which includes 40 species in 11 genera that inhabit coral reefs in the Atlantic, Indian, and Pacific Oceans. They are more common to divers than to anglers, although some are occasionally caught incidentally.

These fish have compressed bodies, and the stout first spine of the dorsal fin is locked into place when erect by the much shorter second dorsal spine, which slides forward. The long first spine can be lowered again only by sliding the second spine back. This can be done by depressing the third spine—the "trigger"—which is attached by a bony base to the second spine. By erecting the first spine and locking it in place, triggerfish can lodge themselves immovably in crevices.

The second dorsal and the anal fins are the same size and shape. Pelvic fins are lacking, and the belly has a sharp-edged outline, with its greatest depth just in front of the anal fin. Triggerfish are covered with an armor of bony plates. Their leathery skin lacks the slime or mucus usually found on fish, and they are capable of rotating each eyeball independently. They normally swim by undulating their second dorsal and anal fins but will use their tail for rapid bursts.

The queen triggerfish *(Balistes vetula)* occurs in warm western Atlantic waters northward to the Carolinas and also in the Caribbean, as well as in the western Atlantic from Ascension and Cape Verde Islands and the Azores south to Angola. It usually travels alone or in pairs but is occasionally seen in small groups. It has been caught to 12 pounds. Although its color varies considerably with its background, the queen triggerfish always has an iridescent bluish purple stripe circling the mouth

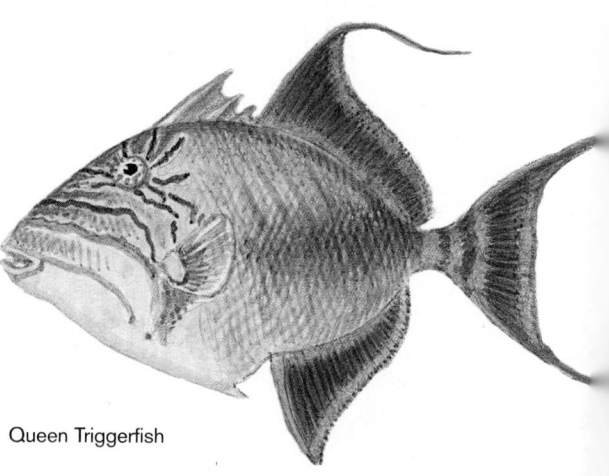

Queen Triggerfish

and extending back on each side to beneath the pectoral fin. A second stripe crosses the snout and runs along the cheeks to the base of the pectoral fin. The base of the caudal fin is also bluish purple. The back is generally greenish, whereas the throat and belly are orange. The front of the dorsal fin and both lobes of the caudal fin are elongated.

The gray triggerfish *(B. capriscus)* is widely distributed in the warm Atlantic, Gulf of Mexico, and Mediterranean, ranging farther north than most triggerfish. It has been caught at more than 13 pounds. In the open water it is a dull gray color, but when swimming near seaweeds or over rocks it is usually mottled.

The ocean triggerfish *(Canthidermis sufflamen)* may also weigh more than 13 pounds and is found off the Florida coasts and in the Caribbean. It is dark brown to gray, with black spots at the base of the caudal fin. Like some other triggerfish, it emits noises, made either by grinding its pharyngeal teeth or by vibrating the muscles attached to the swim bladder.

Triggerfish can be eaten, but they have been associated with poisoning.

TRIM TABS

Small platelike devices on the port and starboard sides of the lower transom that adjust a boat's attitude when operated at planing speeds, producing a more stable and comfortable ride. Trim tabs, which operate like the wing flaps on an airplane, once were solely used for correcting hull performance deficiencies that caused porpoising, a rhythmic and uncomfortable rise and fall of the bow while underway at planing speed. The usual cause was too much fore-and-aft rocker in the bottom; trim tabs provided enough adjustable "hook" to correct or offset that.

Now they are commonly used on otherwise good-running boats for several reasons. Perhaps most importantly, they can control a boat's fore-and-aft, as well as side-to-side, attitude. This means lowering the bow in choppy seas to soften the ride and preventing the tendency to lean into the wind (lowering the upwind gunwale, which often makes for a miserably wet ride). The upwind gunwale can actually be raised higher than the opposite gunwale for a pleasantly dry ride. Trim tabs also allow a boat to stay on plane at much lower speeds, and they improve fuel economy throughout most of the planing speed range.

Using remote-adjusting trim tabs in conjunction with the engine's power trim also improves overall performance. For example, trimming the lower unit all the way forward and setting the tabs in the full down position allows most planing hulls to stay on plane comfortably in rough seas at speeds as low as 12 mph. By comparison, without tabs and with the lower unit all the way forward, minimum planing speed would typically be 16 to 18 mph, producing a much rougher ride. While the difference in miles per hour may not sound great, maintaining 12 mph in a subplaning attitude (if it could be done at all) requires a great deal more horsepower and burns 30 to 60 percent more fuel as compared to holding the same speed while on plane.

Even in a relatively small chop a light boat without trim tabs would require significant forward lower unit trim to ride comfortably. And as the lower unit is trimmed forward, the propeller shaft is no longer in its attitude of maximum efficiency, which is horizontal (parallel to the surface of the water). Part of the propeller's thrust is then wasted on pushing the bow down into the water. If the boat has tabs, the lower unit can be left with the prop shaft in its most efficient position, while the tabs do the work of keeping the bow lower. So although there is a slight amount of drag from the tabs, this is more than offset by greater propeller efficiency.

Trim tabs come in manual and electric versions. The least costly are the manually adjusted models, depending upon size and materials. Their disadvantage is that the boat has to be stopped while adjustments are made, and often tools are required to do this. Electric remote-controlled tabs allow precise adjustment while on the fly. They're operated from the dashboard by a lever or buttons. The tabs are moved up and down via an electric motor.
See: Boat.

TRINIDAD AND TOBAGO
See: Lesser Antilles.

TRIPLETAIL   *Lobotes surinamensis.*
Other names—Atlantic tripletail, brown tripletail, dusky tripletail, sleepfish, buoy fish, buoy bass, chobie, triplefin, flasher; Afrikaans: *driestert;* Bengali: *samudra koi;* French: *croupia roche;* Japanese: *matsudai;* Malay/Indonesian: *ikan tidur, kakapbato, pelayak, sekusong;* Portuguese: *furriel, prejereba;* Spanish: *dormilona.*

The tripletail gets its name from its second dorsal and anal fins, which extend far back on the body

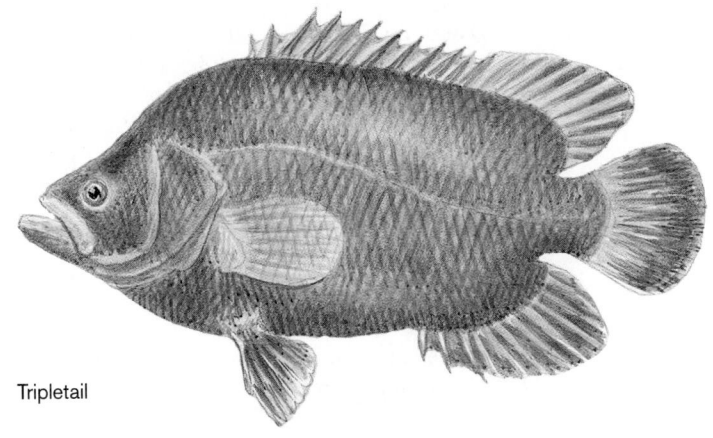

Tripletail

T

so that the fish appears to have three tails. A member of the Lobotidae family, it is an excellent food fish with white, sweet, flaky meat. There is relatively little commercial fishing for this species.

Identification. The tripletail is characterized by its rounded dorsal and anal fins, which reach backward along the caudal peduncle, giving the fish the appearance of having a three-lobed, or triple, tail. It has a deep, compressed body that resembles the body shape of the freshwater crappie, and it has a concave profile. The eyes are far forward on the snout, and the edge of the preopercle is strongly serrated.

Compared with other saltwater fish, tripletail probably most resemble grouper but lack teeth on the roof of the mouth. The color is drab, various shades of yellow brown to dark brown, with obscure spots and mottling on the sides.

Size/Age. The tripletail may reach a length of $3^1/_2$ feet and weigh as much as 50 pounds, although $1^1/_2$- to $2^1/_2$-foot lengths and weights of less than 20 pounds are more common. The all-tackle world record is for a 42-pound, 5-ounce fish taken off South Africa in 1989. The tripletail may live as long as 7 to 10 years.

Distribution. Inhabiting tropical and subtropical waters of all oceans, tripletail are found in the western Atlantic from Massachusetts and Bermuda to Argentina. In the eastern Atlantic, they are found from Madeira to the Gulf of Guinea, as well as along the southern coasts of Europe and in South African waters. In the eastern Pacific they occur from Costa Rica to Peru, in the western Pacific from Japan to Fiji and Tuvalu.

Habitat. Tripletail occur in coastal waters and enter muddy estuaries, commonly in depths of up to 20 feet. There is some suggestion of a northerly and inshore migration into warm waters in the spring and summer.

Life history/Behavior. Although little is known about their spawning behavior, tripletail are believed to be sexually mature by the end of their first year. Spawning occurs in the spring and summer, and although some fish may move inshore to spawn, young tripletails have been found in estuaries and in patches of offshore sargassum. Tripletail swim or float on their side in the company of floating objects.

Food and feeding habits. Tripletail feed almost exclusively on other fish, such as herring, menhaden, and anchovies, as well as on eels and benthic crustaceans like shrimp, crabs, and squid.

Angling. Anglers usually catch tripletail around wrecks, buoys, and offshore pilings and markers from May through October. They are generally ignored, however, either because they are viewed as an oddity, or because anglers don't notice them. Ironically, this species, which looks like it would fight like a bath towel, is a strong and determined battler, one that light-tackle anglers really enjoy catching, and also one that leaps. A 10- or 15-pound tripletail is a handful on a fly rod or spinning rod with 8- or 10-pound line.

Most tripletail are caught by sight fishing. Anglers observe surface-floating specimens, often near weeds, and pitch bait to them. Shrimp works especially well. Small jigs, tipped with baits or equipped with a soft grub body, and streamer flies, also catch these fish, as do small plugs on occasion. Lures and flies should be worked near the surface, usually with a pausing, twitching motion.

Anglers sight cast around floating debris in open and unobstructed water, typically for isolated cruising fish, and also near shore in shallow water, and sometimes on bottom near cover. In Mississippi and other Gulf States, some anglers place pine trees in the bottom to attract fish, somewhat like a brushpile *(see)* in freshwater, and cast a live shrimp or fish toward these trees.

Tripletail usually are best netted rather than gaffed, as they have tough scales. Anglers should use gloves when handling this species, as their gill covers can cause painful cuts.

TROLLING

Trolling is a commonly practiced method of fishing in both freshwater and saltwater for a wide range of species. In simplest terms, it is a method of presenting a lure or bait behind a power-driven boat. In a general sense, it is especially popular in wide-open waters, where it is used for fish that are deep and/or nomadic and where there are few underwater obstructions.

Despite the fact that it is a widely used technique, trolling is underappreciated both in popular angling literature and among anglers who primarily cast for presentation rather than use a boat. There is an image problem associated with an activity in which the angler doesn't cast and retrieve, and in which unseen fish are attracted to, and hooked by, lures pulled by a moving boat—television producers say that the action lacks drama. In many quarters, a myth has long been perpetuated that trolling is easy or too effective or less sporting than other techniques.

Trolling is an important means of searching conscientiously for fish that anglers rarely see until they are brought to the side of a boat. Trolling appeals to anglers who want to know more about the fish that live in wide open water and about the environment they inhabit. Modern trolling attracts those who want to master the challenge of catching fish—especially big fish—that are often far out of the reach of people using other methods. Trolling with proper tackle can be as sporting and enjoyable as fishing by any other method.

Many anglers troll for some or most of their fish. Trolling is *the* way to catch trout and salmon on lakes and reservoirs; it is *the* method on some muskie waters. It is a valued technique for walleye, an overlooked method for black bass, and an important means of catching striped bass. In saltwater, trolling is a critical method for catching many pelagic species, especially billfish, and important for pursuing many inshore species, including kingfish, bluefish, and various jacks. There is plenty of science and drama involved, whether the quarry is blue marlin, chinook salmon, walleye, or dolphin.

Knowledgeable anglers know that trolling does not entail dragging any old lure or bait an indeterminate distance behind a boat at an unknown depth, in an unplanned fashion. Successful trollers must know exactly where their lures are and how those lures are acting, and they must make a calculated, determined effort to entice a fish. That means being able to do many things well, including rigging lines, reading sonar, setting lures, judging when to change lures or locations, knowing the proper speed at which to fish, and understanding how to manipulate a boat to effect the kind of presentation that attracts fish.

General methods. Trolling can be broken down into the following basic methods:

Flatline trolling for muskellunge on the French River, Ontario.

1. Fishing an object on an unweighted monofilament, braided, or fly line.

    This method, known as flatlining *(see)*, is popular for relatively shallow fishing in freshwater and saltwater because the depth achieved is entirely dependent on the weight or diving ability of the object being trolled. To know how deep you're fishing, you must know the depth that object will attain given boat speed, line size, current, trolling-line length, etc. To avoid haphazard effort and sporadic success, you must learn to evaluate the depth that the trolled lures or baits actually attain.

    High-speed surface flatlining is also practiced in some situations, primarily in saltwater for billfish. Here, lures are trolled quickly on top of the water or through the surface foam.

2. Fishing an object on a weighted line.

    Fishing an object on a weighted line involves using a weight *(see)*—drail, split shot, keel, bell, bead chain, or other type of sinker—to get a lure or bait deeper than it could be presented unaided. The problem of knowing the actual depth being fished is the same as with unweighted lines.

3. Fishing an object behind a lead core or wire line.

    Here, the weight of the line causes the object being trolled to sink. The depth of the lure or bait depends on how much line is let out. This can be a more precise method of fishing than flatlining when it is important to achieve a specific depth. To gauge distance, lead core line *(see)* is marked by different colors at intervals, and wire line *(see)* is usually marked with tape by anglers. Although stronger than nylon or braided line, lead core line is bulkier, and it dampens the fight of a fish. Wire, which has

to be used on stout tackle, is subject to kinking, crimping, and spooling difficulties; although it transmits the actions of the fish well to the angler, wire line and the corresponding tackle also blunt the fight.

4. Fishing an object behind a diving planer.

    A diving planer *(see)* is a device used on a fishing line for the purpose of getting lures deep without weight or other attachments. Because it pulls so hard when trolled, a diving planer is fished off a very stout rod and is used with fairly heavy line. Diving planers run deep on a relatively short line; the length of line trolled determines how deep the planer will dive. A planer releases when a fish strikes, so you don't have to fight it along with the fish; nevertheless, the planer may impede the fight and activity of the fish, and its size or presence may deter some fish from striking. You have to set the lure no more than 5 feet behind the planer in order to land a fish.

5. Fishing an object behind a releasable cannonball sinker.

    This is a deep-trolling system traditionally used for Pacific salmon fishing. A large, cannonball-shaped sinker *(see: weight)* gets the line down deep; the sinker is released and drops to the bottom when a fish strikes. You lose a lot of lead weight in this system, and you need stout, heavy tackle. Also, you don't often know the depth at which you're fishing when you're off the bottom. Present and future restrictions on lead usage and disposal may preclude this approach.

6. Fishing an object behind a downrigger.

    A downrigger *(see)* takes the burden of getting a line to a specific depth away from the fishing line. A lure attached to your fishing line is placed in the water and set at the desired distance to run behind your boat. The fishing line is placed in the release attached to the downrigger cable; the release frees the line

Deep trollers fish for salmon in the coastal waters of northern British Columbia near Dundas Island.

T

when a fish strikes, and the angler plays the fish unencumbered. This affords the most controlled-depth presentation possible, plus the use of lighter and more sporting tackle. It has relegated wire and lead core line to near-antique status among regular and accomplished trollers, except in places where the lake or ocean floor is full of rocks and radical changes in depth. Downrigger trolling originated on the Great Lakes for trout and salmon fishing; it spread inland for muskies, stripers, and walleye, then to saltwater for inshore and offshore fishing.

Trolling speed.   Most anglers are unaware of the vital role that speed plays in trolling, which perhaps explains why trolling is such a hit-and-miss proposition for so many. Routinely successful trollers have a special understanding of the behavior of the fish they seek; of the size, color, and style of lure that appeals to those fish under various conditions; and of boat maneuvering techniques for proper presentation. They also have a keen awareness of how speed relates to these other elements. The better guides and charter boat captains have a sixth sense about speed; they intuitively know if they are at the right speed, or they rely on an instrument to gauge it. Many anglers, however, fail to recognize that boat and lure speed (there can be a difference) is an integral aspect of trolling and that they must be attentive to it. No matter what

kind of fish you troll for, or what tackle and type of boat you use, you'll get more out of your lures by paying close attention to the speed at which they are working.

The key point about trolling speed is not speed for speed's sake: You don't necessarily go fast because your quarry is accustomed to out-hustling its prey, or slow because the target species won't run down an object moving quickly. The correct speed is the one that gets the right action out of your lures *and* is correct for the fish you seek.

The swimming action of a lure, perhaps more than shape or color, causes fish to strike. If it didn't, anglers might as well troll treble-hooked pencils. Action is the key. It is determined by lure design and the speed with which the lure is pulled. Complexity arises when you consider all the variables that affect trolling speed and lure action, including current, waves, wind velocity and direction, type and weight of boat, power of the engine, type of lure, and so forth.

One of the greatest mistakes made by trollers is to fish at the same boat speed when heading into the wind as when moving with the wind. On an otherwise still body of water, you will obviously go faster with the wind than against it, assuming you never reposition the throttle. The same is true of current. As an example, suppose you maintain a boat speed of 2 miles per hour (mph) downstream and then turn upstream at the same throttle setting; depending on the strength of the current, you may head upstream at only 1 mph, make no headway at all, or lose ground. Add varying wave heights, and think about the effect they would have. These factors affect the way your lure works and may explain why, on a particular day, you catch fish trolling in one direction but not in the other.

Boat speed, however, must be compatible with the lures fished. Trolling lures are designed to be fished within a certain range of speeds; there is a particular speed at which each lure exhibits its maximum action. Some lures work tolerably at slow or fast speeds, some can sustain action in a wide range of speeds, and others have a narrow range of workability.

Plugs that don't wobble, don't have a natural swimming action, or don't track true, or that run on their sides, roll, or skip out of the water, either need to be tuned to work properly or are being run too slow or too fast. Spoons that lie flat as they're trolled, have a lazy wobble, hang more vertically than horizontally, or spin furiously, aren't working right. You may find that a spoon will swim perfectly at a certain boat speed, whereas a plug will hardly wobble at the same speed. The two should not be fished together.

Most trollers have experienced occasions when one rod out of several consistently caught fish while the others had no action. Maybe the lure on that rod was at the magic depth or had the hot color, so you put other lures of that color out and/or more lures at the same depth. But the one rod still outproduced the others. Often the reason is that the lure on the productive rod was perfectly matched to the speed of the boat and exhibited the action the fish wanted or that it most accurately mimicked the movement of prey. The other lures may not have been swimming correctly because the boat was going too slow or too fast.

Trollers should check the swimming action of every lure before it is put into the water, even a lure that they have recently fished successfully. Put the lure in the water, point the rod tip at the water or lower it into the water with the lure several feet behind the tip, and watch the lure swim at the boat's current speed. You can alter boat speed to get the lure to run well, but this might adversely affect the action of other lures that you already have out.

Focus on the speeds that work well for the lures in your boat. If you do a lot of trolling, it is an excellent idea to make up a lure speed chart. Use a tachometer, an electronic speedometer, an incremental indicator, or whatever reference device you have. Spend the time to run all of your different lures in the water beside the boat to determine their ideal speed, and observe the range of speed they will tolerate. It may not be fun, but that information will be valuable, especially when you want to mix lures or change boat speed.

Knowing the range of speed your lures will tolerate is very helpful when you want to find out which lure speed is preferred by fish on a given day.

It is no accident that many fish are caught when boaters speed up or slow down and when they make turns. On a turn, the lure on the outside of the turn speeds up and the lure on the inside slows down, unless the turn is very long and gradual. These changes in lure behavior often trigger strikes and may indicate that your speed was previously incorrect for the lure to be successful or that you needed a change in speed to trigger a strike from a curious fish. Making frequent alterations in speed, either by decreasing or advancing the throttle or by turning, is a valuable tactic—but you'll need to know whether your lures will work properly at the different speeds.

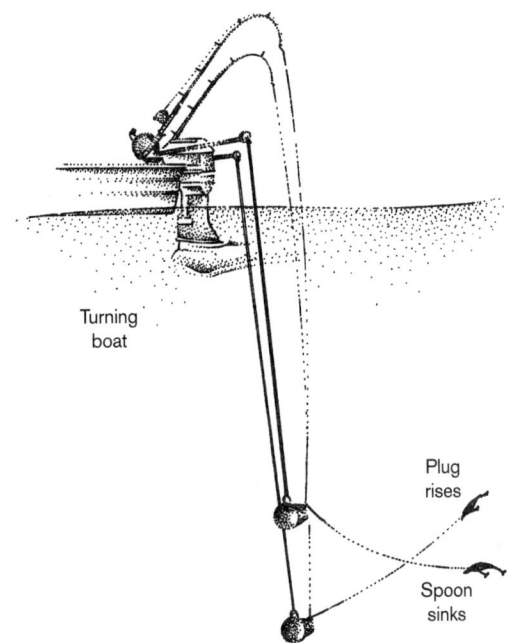

Turns are an important trolling maneuver because they change lure behavior and can trigger strikes. When a boat makes a sharp turn, a floating/diving plug rises momentarily in the water whereas a spoon sinks. Lures return to normal positions shortly afterward.

Even though you may achieve the proper speed and action for a particular lure, that speed may be inappropriate for the fish you seek. Thus, you have to experiment with different lures and different trolling speeds. Effective trolling speed varies according to species and season. Few anglers have the problem of not being able to troll fast enough (except rowers and electric-motor trollers headed into a wind), but some encounter situations when they cannot troll slowly enough. Some boats simply cannot troll slowly enough even at the lowest throttle setting, particularly if they're headed downwind. A light boat with a moderate-size engine will troll faster than many larger, heavier boats with powerful stern-drives or inboards. Some large outboard motors will not run below 600 rpm and, on a moderate-size craft, will push that vessel along at a speed greater than is practical. Consider using an auxiliary motor (9.9 or 15 horsepower) if you have a big boat, or use a trolling plate *(see),* which baffles the prop thrust and stymies forward propulsion, or a sea anchor *(see),* a bag that is dragged alongside or behind the boat, to slow it down.

Boat speed. To determine boat speed, you need some reference point. A tachometer shows engine revolutions per minute (rpm). Although rmp is not a perfect gauge of boat speed, lacking other references, you can use it to estimate speed when conditions are relatively calm. Stick with a certain setting if you're catching fish. You have to alter the rpm, however, when wind, waves, or current impedes your forward movement. If you're using a lure that has caught fish at a certain rpm setting, and if you encounter current or wind that is affecting your headway at that setting, run the lure alongside the boat and watch how it behaves. Increase the throttle until you get the lure to run perfectly; then note the new rpm and try to maintain it.

Small-boat trollers, including those with tiller steering, may not have a tachometer, so they have to guess at relative speeds or use some type of measuring device. Some boaters fashion a speed indicator by attaching one end of a 3-foot wire or heavy monofilament leader to a l-pound lead weight and the other end to an arrowlike indicator, which pivots along a plate that has incremental measuring units marked on it. The weight is dropped in the water, and the arrow points to a spot on the plate; the arrow's position changes as boat speed is altered. Commercially made speed indicators work similarly.

The units of measurement on these devices do not correlate to actual speed in miles per hour or knots, but simply to relative speed. When you put a lure in the water and get it to work properly, note the position of the arrow and run the boat at a speed that keeps it there.

Precise indications of knots or miles per hour are obtained by using relatively sophisticated, battery-operated electronic instruments. These sport paddlewheels are mounted on the transom; the paddle spins as the boat moves, relaying speed on a digital display. These units may read differently from each other, but they can be calibrated. Once you get accustomed to a particular unit, you'll learn to correlate what it reveals to fishing conditions. Another electronic device for calculating boat speed, and one with exceptional reliability and accuracy, is a GPS, which calculates distance moved over time and should be used in the fastest update mode.

The speed recorded on one boat may not be comparable with the speed recorded on another boat. You may be catching fish while motoring at 550 rpms, for example, yet friends in another boat are not catching anything despite the fact that their tachometer has the same reading. Or, you may be catching fish while traveling at 2.25 mph while someone else is catching fish at 2.50 mph using the same lures. Gauges do vary slightly, and boat speed is influenced by a host of factors, making exact speed comparisons between boats difficult.

How should you gauge speed if you don't have some type of indicating device? Become a rod-tip watcher when you flatline (this is a good flatline practice at all times because you can often tell whether your lure has picked up some debris that impedes its success). Listen carefully to the sound of your engine, and watch the action of your lures. Watch other anglers; come up alongside a boat that has recently caught a fish, duplicate the speed of the other boat, and then check your tachometer.

Lure speed. Most speedometers measure boat and lure speed at or near the surface. In many trolling situations, this speed will be the same, or nearly the same, as the speed of the lure at the level you are trolling. There are times, however, when surface speed has no relation to lure speed. If you have ever anchored your boat in a river and fished a lure on a fixed length of line behind the boat, you can readily appreciate this. This is how steelhead anglers work downriver with plugs; it is also how shad anglers use jigs or darts. The boat may be stationary, but the force of the current makes the lure swim. In effect, it's like trolling in place; the lure actually is going nowhere, but the speed of the current gives it action.

Imagine now that you are trolling upriver. The force of the current, in addition to the pressure of the forward movement of your boat, could be making your lure swim wildly instead of working naturally. How do you know? If the water is fairly shallow, you can watch your lure swim beside the boat and be fairly certain that it will swim the same when you drop it a little deeper. But in a deep river, or where there may be back currents or varying flow patterns, the lure may not swim at the same speed down deep as it does on the surface. What if you are trolling up a tidal river when the tide is coming in? Does that negate the force of the current, and if so, how does that affect your lure? If you are slow-trolling downriver when the tide is going out, it's conceivable that your lure might be hanging listlessly below your boat instead of swimming provocatively behind it.

These problems are not restricted to rivers and obvious current or tidal environments. There are currents in the ocean; there are also currents in open-water portions of the Great Lakes and in many large inland lakes. Few big-water anglers understand current's effect on lure presentation.

Current in lakes and reservoirs can be caused by tributaries entering the lake, by dam releases ("pulling water") or other outlets, and by wind and wave action. The presence of current may be obvious, but it is usually so subtle that a visual inspection of the surface and measurements of speed at that level give no indication of the presence of current. In some places, there is such a strong current at 50 feet or deeper that it is detectable by watching the action of downrigger weights and cables: With the boat at a slow speed heading into the current, the weights and cables sway back; going with the current, the weights and cables hang nearly vertically.

Below-surface or deep-water currents affect the speed and action of trolling lures. It is possible for a boat to be moving at 2 mph while the lure is acting as if it were running faster. You can troll all day, change colors over the entire spectral range, have no success whatsoever, and have no idea why. If you're flatlining under such circumstances, you may be able to detect the influence of current by watching your lines and rod tips, but most of the time this will not be an indicator. You can determine the presence of strong current by watching a downrigger, but even then you won't know how it is influencing your lures.

Electronic speed indicators can relay the speed of your lure or downrigger via sensors that attach to the downrigger cable above the weight and electrically transmit that speed to a readout. They also can indicate temperature at the depth of the sensor and at the water surface.

See: Backtrolling; Big-Game Fishing; Downrigger Fishing; Flatlining; Mooching.

TROLLING BOARD

A trolling board is a wooden or aluminum slat that extends from gunwale to gunwale and either mounts onto a boat or, in smaller boats, slides under the rear handrails, and is used to hold various trolling accessories. Rod holders and mounting plates for downriggers are attached to the board so that downriggers can be readily detached from the board. On roomier boats, boards are easily acces-sible in the back, may also be fitted with sonar or speed indicators, and don't interfere with other types of fishing even when the board is permanently mounted. Most are homemade, although you can buy board installation systems.

On some small boats, the trolling board or downriggers might be mounted directly in front of the console. It's not bad for solo fishing, but the downrigger weights are close together due to the narrow beam of the boat, and this causes the fishing lines to be directly under the boat. When fishing near the surface, you may cut a line on the propeller if you turn too sharply.

See: Downrigger Fishing.

TROLLING JIG

See: Trolling Lures, Saltwater.

TROLLING LURES, SALTWATER

Most of the lures that are trolled in freshwater are also capable of being cast, and for this reason, there is no special category of freshwater trolling lures. Lures that can be trolled as well as cast, be that in freshwater or saltwater, are covered under their

An offshore trolling lure is unhooked from a Pacific sailfish.

respective categories (*see: fly; jig; plug; spinner; spoon; trolling*). The situation is different in saltwater, however, where there are many lures that are of use for trolling and which only have application for trolling. They are not designed to be cast, or jigged, or retrieved by some combination of rod movement and wrist action. They're too large, too hard-pulling, or too cumbersome for anything but trolling, and they often must be worked faster than would be prudent for any caster. The action they exhibit, the noise they produce, the water disturbance they make, and their passing resemblance to squid and flyingfish are important and intertwined elements—all of which are best accentuated when traveling at high rates of speed. Thus, special trolling lures have evolved for roaming the vast ocean expanses and, in some cases, for use with the heavier tackle that is often demanded for saltwater bruisers.

The category of saltwater trolling lures includes a number of distinctive items and some that are closely related or fished in conjunction with others. Teasers, for example, can be fished hookless as an attractor ahead of a hard-headed offshore lure or can be fished as lures when rigged with hooks. While teasers are primarily used as attention getting devices, similar to cowbells, flashers, and dodgers, which are all deep-trolling attractors (*see*) in freshwater, they are relatively unique in fishing because they are only used in saltwater, only used on the surface, and only used for trolling.

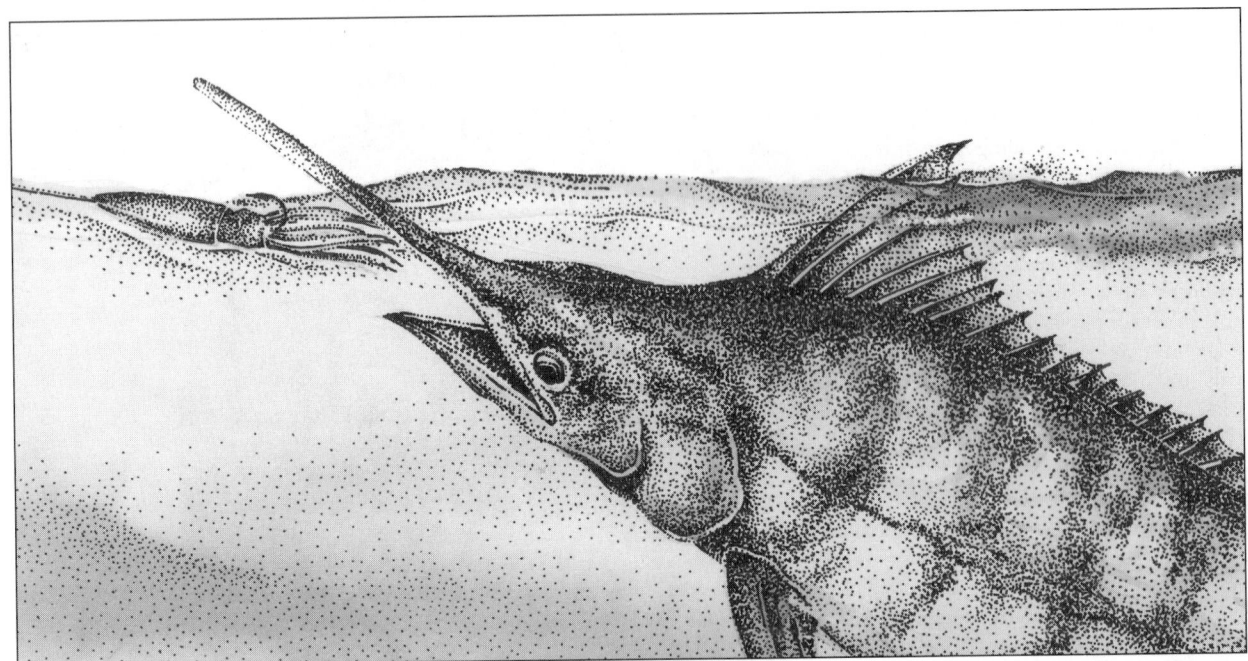

T

Offshore lures, teasers, and feathers are essentially big-game products primarily targeted at pelagic species. Tubes, on the other hand, are an inshore trolling lure and about as unsophisticated as you can get.

Offshore Lures

Also called blue-water lures, big-game lures, and trolling lures, the category of saltwater trolling products known collectively as offshore lures are at the pinnacle of manufactured fish catchers and are specialized trolling items meant strictly for such dynamic offshore species as billfish, tuna, wahoo, and dolphin, usually at speeds that no other lure is capable of handling and under a wide range of sea conditions.

Offshore lures are fished either on the surface or under but fairly close to the surface, and though they look dazzling and sophisticated today, they evolved from fairly recent and humble origins. In part, their relatively recent evolvement is due to traditional and successful reliance on using live or dead natural baits for big-game species. Different types of dead bait have long been rigged for offshore trolling but these have always required brining, storing, freezing, thawing, and rigging, as well as repeated rerigging when the baits caught fish or were dragged to the point of no longer being serviceable. And, of course, if availability became a problem, or you used up your supply of bait while fishing offshore, then you had a dilemma. Artificials avoided these problems, required one-time rigging, and were always on call to catch fish; they offered a sensible substitute or option, and savvy anglers wisely broadened their outlook.

The earliest offshore lures were reportedly fashioned in the Pacific and their faces were either slanted or dished to provide maximum swimming action at the displacement speeds of the fishing boats of the time. The erratic pushing action of slant-faced lures and the darting actions of dish-faced lures swimming beneath the surface served to effectively attract attention at what were very slow trolling speeds by today's standards.

After World War II, when boat designs and more powerful marine engines allowed faster trolling speeds, lures were designed more to create commotion than to simulate swimming baitfish. "Smoking" bubble trails and occasional roostertails of water became the criteria for proper action, and trolling speeds increased to enhance the commotion of the lures. As sportfishing boats became faster and more sophisticated, anglers realized the value of covering as much blue water as possible during the fishing day, and modified their lures to work at faster speeds, resulting in flat-faced offshore versions. Broad, flat-faced lures that tracked straight at high speeds created impressive fish-attracting turbulence. Their intermittent but frequent trips to the surface to gulp air and create a solid bubble trail ("smoke"), along with an occasional roostertail, became favored actions for offshore trolling lures.

Then anglers started employing straight-running lures with concave faces (sometimes called chuggers), and slowed down a bit. The lure face here was not slanted, and the hole for the leader was still centered, but the scooped-out face provided bubble trails and roostertails over a wider range of speeds. The diameter of the concave head and the depth of the concavity determined the maximum speeds at which each lure performed best. Such lures that featured an up-front placement of the lead hook, combined with a short lure head, helped increase hookups and influenced future lure designs. Ever since, there has been a continuous refinement and hybridization of head styles, plus development of a potpourri of weights and a plethora of colors.

With increased use, anglers figured that if they could cover a great expanse of water at high trolling speeds, they might as well cover a still greater area by dragging lures while traveling to and from the fishing grounds. Doorknob-style lures (a patented shape with a narrowed neck, good high-speed tracking, and extreme turbulence) were designed to troll at the ultra-high cruising speeds of modern sportfishing boats, and anglers suddenly became aware of the incredible speeds at which blue marlin could spurt after a plastic meal. The weighted and aerodynamic offshore lures, when dragged far behind a speeding boat, resisted the tendency of more traditional shapes to "fly" and caught blue marlin at speeds from 10 to 20 knots.

A distinguishing characteristic of offshore lures is their ability and effectiveness—some would call it necessity—to be trolled at high speeds. High speeds in offshore fishing go way beyond the higher speeds that are used in most other forms of trolling, being on average in the 8 to 10 knots range, but on the low end starting at 5 knots and on the high end going into the upper teens (with some reports of offshore trolling lures catching fish up to 24 knots).

Despite the fact that offshore lures have proven effective for aggressive fish and in high-speed trolling, like any other lure, they are only effective when a combination of factors are at play; above all else, for a lure to be effective it has to "look right" in the water. The right look is a result of many variables, including the shape, weight, and color of the lure itself; the hull design and speed of the boat; the wake pattern of the boat; the position of the trolled lures behind the boat; and the sea conditions. Each can play a part in whether a marlin notices, and then strikes, a trolled plastic offering.

Types. Offshore lures consist for the most part of a weighted head and a synthetic tail or skirt. Most heads are made of durable hard plastic, and the skirts from soft plastic or vinyl. There are also soft-headed lures that are meant to feel more natural to a fish. There are a number of guidelines for choosing lures from among the plethora of head shapes and sizes available. Offshore lures can be divided into several categories, and each is designed to provide maximum visibility in a different manner and under different conditions.

In some cases, your choice depends on the habits of the species you're after. In the broadest sense, offshore lures either run on the surface or just beneath it. Surface runners create a silvery trail of bubbles (called "smoke") and produce a lot of surface commotion. They especially appeal to fish that strike from the side, like marlin. Underwater runners generally swim in a straight or near-straight manner, not far under the surface, and especially appeal to fish that strike from beneath, such as tuna or wahoo.

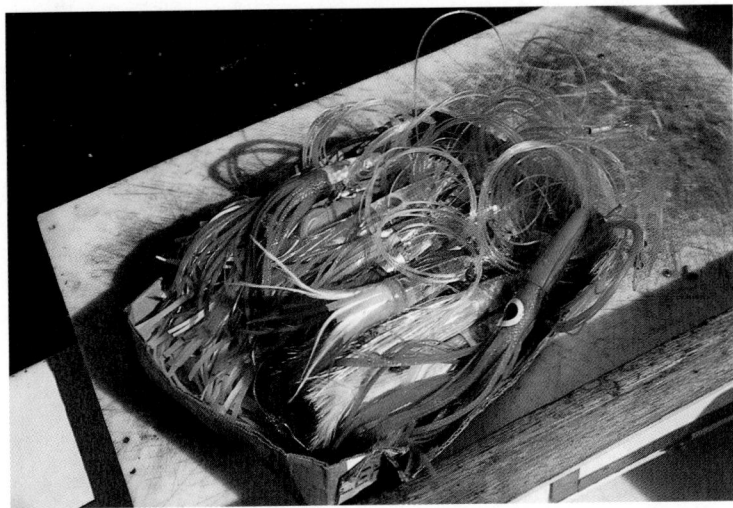
Assorted offshore trolling lures.

Some general rules of thumb can help reduce the amount of trial and error to achieve the right look. With surface lures, the desired effect is the densest possible stream of bubbles. The lure should make intermittent but frequent trips to the surface creating a solid bubble trail after each gulp of air, with an occasional roostertail of water pushed up by the lure on its forays to the surface. The lure should make a definite commotion.

Lures designed to stay continuously beneath the surface should swim fast enough to simulate a fast-swimming baitfish. Those with concave faces should be trolled fast enough to create a zigzagging, swimming action. It is their erratic, swimming action that is designed to attract attention, in addition to surface commotion and bubble trails.

At a given speed, most straight runners smoke more effectively when the angle between line and water is increased. Similarly, if they tend to fly at a given speed, or in rough seas, they are more likely to stay in the water if that angle is reduced. This can be accomplished by lowering the outrigger clip or outrigger tagline closer to water level, or in the case of flatlines, taglining them at the transom. This reduces the angle from that of simply trolling the line directly from the rod tip, and reduces the chafing of the line at the tiptop. When limited by a slow boat speed, action can be improved by bringing both flat and outrigger lures closer to the boat. This serves to increase the line-to-water angle and raise the head of the lure where it can gather more air and produce more bubbling action. When seas are up, this effect can be reversed, and the lures kept from flying by letting them out farther from the boat. The reduced angle thus produced helps keep them in the water. Of course, in really rough seas, other options include switching to weighted lures, slowing the boat speed, and trolling the lures still farther back.

Although the different head faces of trolling lures get a lot of attention, this plus the length and weight contribute to performance. Some heads are

Head Types

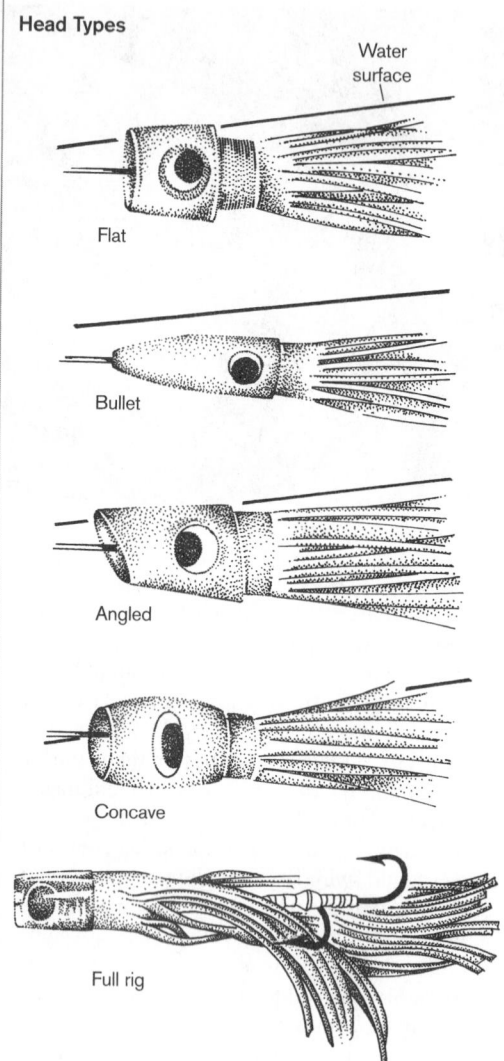

Water surface

Flat

Bullet

Angled

Concave

Full rig

T

short and some long, some are narrow and others wide. The face style is of special importance when the head is short; this contributes most to the action. When the head is long, the face style, plus the whole body design, contribute to the action. Weight may be added to any lures, and may be less necessary with heavier long-head lures.

Although they are described in various ways, there are basically four types of faces: cone, slanted, flat, and concave.

Cone-shaped faces are also called bullet faces and swimmers, and they have a narrow point to provide minimal water resistance. These run underwater and are usually weighted; they primarily run straight, but some versions swim from side to side. They are particularly effective when trolled short and flat, somewhat like teasers with hooks in them. They also serve well on boats that cannot get up to speeds normally considered minimal for artificial lure trolling. Swimmers tend to fly, however, and often become too active and erratic when trolled above 6 or 8 knots.

Slanted or angled faces provide a moderate amount of water resistance, less than flat models

but more than cone-shaped faces. Although the angle of the slant can often vary widely from one brand to another, these lures track straight when trolled fast, and create quite a commotion in the water, moving up and down as well as diving. The roostertail raised by these lures is impressive, but you must be careful when setting out a full spread of these. Slight differences in slant angle can result in markedly different actions from the lures in the spread. At a given trolling speed, the different lures in the spread may be tracking in dissimilar fashion, and when trolled too fast, slant-head lures tend to track erratically. This is sometimes rectified by arranging the two hooks 180 degrees from each other (rather than at the more traditional 90-degree-angle alignment), so that they act somewhat like a rudder or keel.

A flat-faced lure provides a lot of water resistance and a big bubble trail but without the motion of other lures. This style of surface lure handles a wide range of speeds, although it can fly out of the water in rough seas. Concave-faced lures, also called chuggers, track well and are designed for rough water; the cupped or dished face digs into the water so that it doesn't fly out. It pulls the water so well that it is also useful in calm or light sea conditions. Flat- and concave-faced straight runners bubble well at slower trolling speeds, and some models, which are hybrids with holes in the face and also called jets, are especially effective at both slow and fast speeds because their light weight, flat face, and holes serve to create long, sinewy smoke trails. Heavy lures with large-diameter concave faces troll best at slower speeds, while their flat-faced counterparts track well at considerably higher speeds. Concave-faced lures with small-diameter faces also track well at high speeds.

There are, of course, variations and hybrids of these that have created trolling lures that are hard to categorize. These include so-called jetheads and doorknobs, as well as shorter stubbier versions of conventional lures, and various designs with channels in them.

Size has become an aspect of change in modern trolling lures. Big lures in the 12-inch range used to be the norm, and they were fished off heavy tackle and from big boats, but the growth in small-boat offshore fishing and interest in lighter tackle has lead to many trolling lures that are suitable for use with 20- to 50-pound tackle, and which, perhaps most importantly, can be trolled more slowly. Smaller lures, including those from 6 to 9 inches in overall length, have been successful with various species, and have a greater tendency to be eaten rather than swatted.

Colors. The color scheme for offshore trolling lures varies widely and this is an area of much debate and little consensus among participants. Many offshore lure color preferences are regional, and sometimes based upon imprecise reasoning. When a particularly noteworthy blue marlin, for example, is caught on a particular color at a particular location, everyone in the area begins to troll the same lure and color thereafter. Because everyone is soon trolling the same color, it stands to reason that later catches are all made on that color lure. Soon, the word spreads that the particular color is the only one that produces in that area.

The compulsive use of green lures in the northeastern U.S., especially off New Jersey, is an excellent example of such a phenomenon, as perhaps may be the preference in Baja, Mexico, for green or orange and yellow. When the majority of anglers in an area predominantly troll one color, the majority of fish are caught on that color. Who's to say that another color combination might not produce just as well on any given day?

In Florida, the Bahamas, and much of the Caribbean, darker colors have been preferred in lure skirts. A majority of giant fish and tournament winners have been caught on combinations of black with (in approximate order of preference) purple, orange, dark blue, red, pink, and, especially in the northern Bahamas, green. All show a flash of light color beneath the predominant dark outside skirt, or consist of two dark shades. Some offbeat colors that have been favored by certain anglers include blue and white (or silver), pink and white, and blue over pink over yellow (which simulates dolphin).

Those few anglers who fish white marlin with lures instead of natural baits seem to prefer blue and white, as do the few Ecuadorian anglers who choose lures over giant ballyhoo for big black marlin.

This confusing potpourri does little to help the angler starting out. If you're on a limited budget, try a selection of darker colors, with a couple of light colors thrown in. You'll gather a personal list of preferred colors as soon as you catch some fish and get talking with other anglers.

Technique.   The principal key to success with offshore lures is that they must "look right." They must create maximum visibility while still tracking straight and not flying, and to do this it may be necessary to make numerous adjustments when first setting them out. If you are new to the game, this requires some experimentation and experience to accomplish. There is a difference between looking good and looking perfect, and you really want them to be perfect. It's worth remembering that fish feed in certain ways and that their common foods behave in certain ways. Flyingfish, for example, exit the water sharply, and after gliding they dive back into the water and swim, but they don't skip. This is the action you want to imitate.

First, the boat speed must be adjusted to your choice of lures, or vice versa in the case of a boat with limited power, keeping in mind that you shouldn't mix lures that run best at different speeds. When the boat speed is limited by power or design or by sea conditions, the choice of lure design must be made accordingly. Flat- and slant-faced lures (with a shallow angle) have the widest range of application, while swimming lures are limited to slower trolling speeds. Concave straight runners work well over a broad range of boat speeds but tend to fly at the upper end or when seas are up. Weighted lures, pointy-headed styles, and doorknob styles can handle the highest speeds.

When seas are up, you must adjust, and your options include switching to weighted lures, slowing the boat speed and switching to lures that either swim erratically or create turbulence and smoke at slower speeds, or dropping the lures farther back behind the boat to keep them from flying.

In all cases, lures should ride the face of the wave for best action. Although there are many theories on placement, most pros prefer to set large lures out flat on the second to fourth wake wave behind the boat, and smaller lures on the fifth to seventh wave. Some put out a fifth line (called a "shotgun"), which is placed very short and center or very far back and center. Wherever you place them, make sure that they are getting the proper action. Many people new to this activity tend to troll at too slow a speed, and the lure action suffers. Remember that most offshore lures are designed to run best at 8 to 10 knots, and some even higher; 8 to 10 knots is generally considered an optimum range for marlin, tuna, and wahoo.

Because action, as well as a tendency to fly, increases when the angle of the line where it hits the water increases, many experts use a tagline on their flatlines. The angle of entry of the long lines can usually be lowered by running the outrigger tagline lower. Reducing this angle can also help prevent lures from flying out of the water in rough seas.

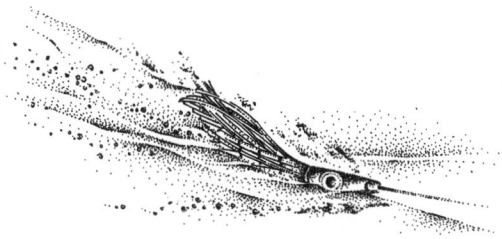

Offshore trolling lures are meant to create an attractive commotion on top of the water, as depicted here, just beneath the surface, or both, depending on design.

A tagline is nothing more than a heavy cord fixed either to the outrigger poles or to a cleat at the transom. Fixed, nonrelease clips or waxed line-ties are secured to the end of the cord. A rubber band (No. 64 is the preferred size) is wrapped at least five times around the fishing line, then the two end loops in the rubber band are snapped into the clip or secured to the waxed-line ties by a quick-release loop. When a fish strikes, the rubber band stretches considerably before breaking, providing some initial give, and helping to set the hook.

The size of the lure hook should be determined by the breaking strength of the line employed, and

Nile perch are the largest strictly freshwater gamefish; the best officially recorded on rod and reel was a 213-pounder, but this species reportedly is capable of attaining 500 pounds.

T

T

if possible, the distance between barb and shank should be greater than the diameter of the lure head. Remember that heavy, thick hooks require heavier strike drags and, hence, heavier line.

Most pros rig two hooks with artificial lures, connecting them with a variety of materials from heavy monofilament (usually snelled), to heavy wire or cable. Even the experts argue between using stiff rigs versus loose swinging "gaffer" rigs, but the beginner would do well to start with ready-made rigs. Many tackle shops sell pre-rigged lures, and that's a good way to start.

The second most important axiom for successful marlin fishing with artificial lures is paying close attention. When fishing offshore lures with tackle up to and including 50-pound-test class, the angler must set the hook and do so quickly. To accomplish this, he must be within a short step or two of the rods and watching the lures at all times. Besides, it's more fun to see the fish approach and strike the lure. Although a good captain will hit the throttle the instant the rod bends and line begins to spill against the drag of the reel, the function of his action is simply to keep slack out of the line if the fish should charge toward the boat. With line of 50-pound test or less, this added momentum of the boat is not guaranteed to set the hooks for the inattentive angler. The angler must take the rod in hand and haul back hard and repeatedly to set the hook; failure to do so is the most frequent cause of "pulled hooks" and lost fish when using offshore lures, especially for big fish.

When fishing 80- to 130-pound-test tackle for marlin, the greater strike drag setting of the reel made possible by the heavier line does make it possible for the captain to set the hook by advancing the throttle. Although not foolproof, the inattentive heavy-tackle angler can count on a high degree of success as long as he has a capable and attentive helmsman.

Spread. There is a lot of discussion among big-game anglers about offshore trolling lure spreads. A commonly employed standard marlin spread is as follows: Two giant concave-face lures are fished flat and very close to the boat, within 30 to 40 feet behind the transom. These lines are rubber banded to taglines tied off at each corner of the transom. The outrigger-connected lines are either held directly by the outrigger clips, or taglined with rubber bands and trolled about 150 feet out, no farther from the boat than dead baits would be trolled. A fifth line is trolled either just behind the flat lines, dead center, or far away down the middle. The three farthest lures are either small teardrops or all-eyes with concave faces.

In all cases the lure distance from the boat is adjusted so that each lure rides on the face of one of the boat's wake waves. It's easy to tell when the placement is correct. The air gathering action is considerably greater when the placement is just right; you can see the difference as you let out or

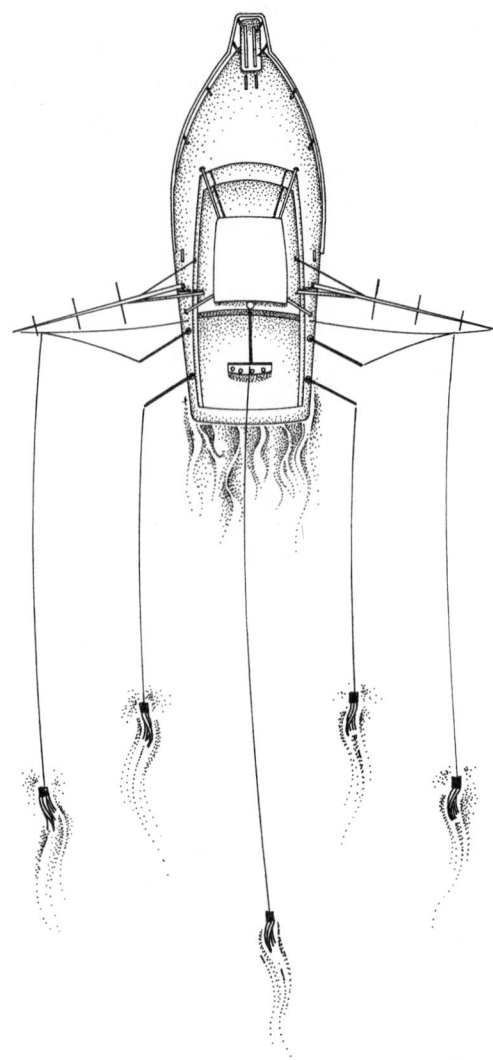

In a common spread for trolling offshore lures, the longest line is set down the middle off a rod placed in a holder on the flying bridge. The outrigger lines are about equal in length and deeper than the inside flatlines. The distance of lures relative to each other is proportionally greater than shown in this compressed depiction.

bring in the lure ever so slightly, seeking just the right spot on the wave. Here again, standard placement on this wave or that is nothing more than a guideline: flatlines on third and fourth, outrigger lures on fifth and sixth, and so on. What matters most is that the lures look right, that is, they are smoking maximally, tracking well, and not flying.

Once a spread is set and looks just right, it's best to resist the urge to keep changing things simply because no fish has risen immediately. Offshore trolling is a waiting game, and once you have confidence in the spread, stick with it. Troll up-sea, then down-sea, preferably with slight S-curve course variations. By not always trolling in dead-straight lines, you will alternately speed up and slow down the port and starboard lures. This slight alteration in lure speed is more natural than constant throttle changes, and often incites fish interest.

Soft Lures. It is reasonable to assume that a fish can distinguish between something the consistency of food it normally consumes and something that is the consistency of a chunk of granite, like the hard head of standard offshore trolling lures. Long ago, anglers made the reasonable assumption that if a billfish mouthed a soft lure once (like mouthing a natural bait), it might not be deterred from returning for a second try and chances for a hookup would increase, but that if the same fish mouthed a rock-hard acrylic lure, it was far less likely to try again. This assumption led to the creation of soft offshore lures, and their use has proven that many species, and especially billfish, do seem more inclined to try again when they hit and miss a soft lure.

The use of soft trolling lures prompted anglers to use them in much the same way they fished rigged dead baits: freespooling the line the minute a fish strikes, then dropping the lure back as if it were a stunned baitfish before setting the hook. Now many anglers who use soft-headed offshore lures leave their rods in holders with the reels set at just enough drag to prevent line spilling from the pull of the lure being trolled through the water. Then, when a big fish strikes, it feels little or no tension on the "meal" it has just mouthed, and swims away with it. The angler has time to pull the rod from the holder and either adjust a stand-up harness or settle into a fighting chair before setting the hook. When the angler is ready, the drag lever is advanced to strike position, slack is quickly cranked back onto the reel, the rod tip is raised, and the hook is set hard. When done right, the technique delivers a high hookup percentage. There can be little doubt that this success is made possible in large measure by the more realistic feel of soft lures.

Because most soft lures are light in weight, they may tend to fly when trolled at high speeds or in particularly rough seas. The problem can usually be solved quite easily. When seas are up, simply reduce trolling speed until the lures track properly. This points out an important attribute of soft lures: They can be trolled a bit slower than hard, heavier lures and still create a splashing, bubbling commotion at the surface. Cup-faced (chugger-style) soft lures in particular smoke effectively at fuel efficient speeds as slow as 5 to 6 knots.

Feathers and trolling jigs. Known as trolling feathers, Japanese feathers, and feather jigs, the offshore lures commonly referred to as feathers are weighted trolling lures that can be fished hookless as single teasers or part of a daisy chain, or they can be run with hooks as a lure unto itself. The heads are either metal or plastic covering lead and the skirts are made of colorful feathers. Trolling feathers are perhaps the single most used type of offshore trolling lure, and are a key element in survival fishing packs. They are seldom used for really big gamefish, including billfish, because they don't travel right at the surface or make much of a surface commotion; rather, they are trolled for a variety of smaller species, such as dolphin, tunas, and wahoo, which often rise from the depths to feed just below the surface.

Feathers with a hook superficially resemble a jig, but they differ in that no hook is incorporated into the lure itself. They consist of a head, often weighted, in front of a binding over feathers as a skirt, all holed to allow the leader to pass through to rigged hooks, which nestle within the trailing end of the feathers. There are other lures that are similar to feathers, sporting soft plastic bodies and streamer-like skirts, and which are fished in a similar manner.

Feathers and similar lures differ in size and weight. They are trolled on or close to the surface, although the heavier versions run slightly deeper. Hookless heavy feathers are often fished in combination with a hooked natural bait, either a whole rigged bait or a strip. Those with heavily weighted heads are often slow-trolled deep or on wire line or downriggers for deep dwellers such as grouper.

Trolling jigs are lures with cone-, bullet-, or torpedo-head shapes, usually dressed with feather skirts or hooks, some of which have little or no practical value for vertical or deep jigging. They include cedar jigs and leadheads, and their single hook, which is part of the body or attached to it, may be adorned with a strip of pork rind or leathery fish flesh. A cedar jig is an old-time saltwater trolling lure made of rounded $^3/_4$-inch light or dark cedar about 4 to 5 inches long with a tapered lead head molded to it. A hole is drilled through the center of both and a leader is passed through the hole, then tied to a large hook, whose shank is drawn up into the hole. The lure may be fished in natural color or painted, and it is especially used for schools of small tuna, bonito, and albacore.

Both feathers and trolling jigs are smaller, on average, than other trolling lures, but move on and through the water easily and with an intrinsic action that appeals to some schooling species. They may also be effective at slower speeds when an angler works them occasionally with a quick, jerking rod action.

Teasers

Teasers are attractors designed to be trolled and create commotion in the water to attract gamefish to rigged baits or lures. Essentially, a teaser is a hookless lurelike device that is used ahead of a hooked lure or hooked baitfish, primarily while trolling. It's purpose is to draw the attention of fish by making a commotion in the water that imitates natural forage; it is followed by a lure or bait, rigged with one or more hooks, that may also look like the imitated forage (often a squid or flyingfish) or like a predator in pursuit. The following lure or bait is the item that is actually struck by the fish attracted to it and to the teaser, although there are times when the hookless teaser is struck first (which may or may not result in the fish striking a following hooked lure).

Inventors first created lures with soft bodies early in the twentieth century; in the 1950s the emergence of soft plastic lures resulted in an unprecedented array of food imitations.

T

Teasers are essentially offshore fishing devices used (like offshore lures) for pelagic species, particularly billfish and, to a lesser extent, tuna. Tuna do not feed the same way as billfish, so they do not look at a teaser and than hang around to grab another lure. Similarly, dolphin and wahoo are species that use quickness and stealth to feed, so they are likely to attack a teaser but not likely to continue attacking the other lures in the trolled spread.

Remember that the ocean is vast and that it is usually necessary when roaming offshore waters to get your lures or baits noticed in order to be effective. No matter how big those lures or baits look to people, in the big water of the ocean, they are really small. The objective narrows to the task of making your offerings as visible as possible, especially from a distance. Visibility is the key to the trolling game, so the angler must do everything possible to draw attention to his small lures as they track across the boundless sea. That's what various types of teasers do.

It is well known that the vibrations produced by a boat in offshore waters—from the noise of the motor(s), the flash of the propeller(s), and the splashing sounds of the hull as it courses through the water—are considerable and attractive to fish. Likewise, the churning wake created by the boat's propellers attracts attention and raises saltwater gamefish. Whether or not fish confuse the frothy white water behind a boat at trolling speed for a school of baitfish is a debatable point. It seems clearer, however, that the more attention that is drawn to the area directly behind the moving boat, the more likely it will be that gamefish will find and strike the relatively small baits and lures that are dragged there. Then, the action and appearance of the baits or lures can do their job of drawing a strike. So teasers are an important part of the attraction element of offshore fishing.

There are numerous kinds of commonly recognized teasers, made from assorted materials and in varied shapes; and although there are exceptions to all categorizations, in general such devices can be considered as one of several types: hard or soft conventional single teasers, trolling birds, and daisy chains. However, the entire category of lures known as teasers is rather broad and ill-defined. Some anglers refer to slender wooden popping plugs, for example, as teasers, and many items are used as a teaser when fished without a hook as well as a fish-catching lure when they have a hook. Conventional teasers are analogous to hard- and soft-headed offshore lures, which themselves can be used as teasers when run without a hook. Most devices that are used as both lures or teasers are best suited to heavier tackle because of the extreme tension they exert. The weight of water pressure on them as they swim or churn is considerable. When fishing light line, a teaser should be dragged separately, and strictly to draw attention to the other baits or lures behind

your boat. And the lighter line can be directly attached to an appropriate size bait or lure. When fishing heavy tackle, a teaser can be employed with a lure or bait, or it can also be dragged separately.

Teasers can be employed at any time when trolling offshore. There's nothing to lose, and little doubt that anything you can add to your spread of hooked baits or lures that may attract gamefish is worth setting out. That teasers attract gamefish is born out by the fact that gamefish often attack the teaser first, proving that this device is what attracted their attention in the first place.

Single teasers.   Fixed by heavy cord to a stern cleat, large single teasers crash and dive in the boat's wake directly behind the transom. There is little doubt that they effectively mimic a single large baitfish in apparent trouble.

These come in a wide array of sizes and shapes. The most common are simply large chunks of wood or plastic that dive and dart, occasionally rising to the surface to grab air and smoke a churning bubble trail in their wake. They may be nothing more than giant Kona head lures, or chuggers with broad faces, or they may be fancy affairs with air-grabbing holes drilled in their faces or flashing mirrors glued to their flanks.

Most single teasers were originally carved of wood and painted to resemble members of the tuna family. Now, molded bodies of plastic or hardened foam have replaced wood, but the effect is the same. The leading edges of these creations may be flat or scooped, holed or dished, depending on the amount of swimming or darting action desired. Those with dished faces can swing too widely if trolled at fast speeds, and may gather up the two flatlines trolled just behind them. Teasers with flat faces work well at higher speeds, while those with concave faces provide attractive turbulence even at slower trolling speeds. Both create sinewy bubble trails in addition to periodic roostertails when they rise to the surface.

You need only to inspect the teaser drawer of any busy sportfishing cruiser to find out if they work. Teasers that have been trolled for any length of time look like they've been through a threshing machine. Billfish leave broad scrapes from their filelike bills, while such toothy critters as wahoo or barracuda leave deep cuts and gashes from their attacks.

When such attacks occur, the trick is to move a hooked bait or lure into the vicinity of the teaser, while at the same time removing the hookless attractor from the spot. To facilitate this action, some people simply drag the teaser from a long heavy rod, rather than from a heavy cord fixed to a cleat. The fish's attention must be drawn away from the teaser and toward the bait with the hook in it. It's often not as difficult as it sounds. Indeed, the attacking or inspecting fish often will first strike the teaser, and then dart away and strike one of the other trolled offerings without any action on the part of the angler. The fish may simply be

Naturalist Louis Agassiz described and cataloged New Hampshire's silver trout in 1884; this fish was common in the early twentieth century but is thought to be extinct today.

drawn within sight of the other baits or lures by the teaser itself, and, once in the spread, may decide to inspect each of them. To cover both situations, troll at least one flatlined lure or bait just behind the churning teaser.

If the fish doesn't attack the nearby lure, you can take matters into your own hands by reeling the hooked lure or bait to a position in front of the fish, diverting its attention. Then "feed" the fish the armed bait or lure, preferably with a rod-tip dropback when fishing lures. The rod-tip dropback is simply a maneuver in which the rod is held high above and behind the angler's head with a firm two-handed grip. When the fish grabs the bait or lure, the rod tip is instantly lowered to a position pointing at the fish, thus feeding the bait into his mouth. Then, the rod tip is immediately raised hard several times in a stabbing motion to set the hook. If the hook pulls free, the lure is rapidly reeled back to the surface and the procedure is repeated.

An alternative move, used more often with baits than with lures, is to raise the rod tip with the reel in freespool mode and the spool held firmly by the thumb. When the fish strikes, thumb tension is eased and the line is freespooled briefly to allow the fish to swallow the bait, taking care not to allow the spool to overrun and create a bird's nest. Then the reel is shifted back into gear, and when the line comes taut, the fish is struck by repeatedly and forcefully raising the rod tip.

Incidentally, bizarre makeshift teasers made from soda cans or plastic bottles have been improvised by clever anglers, and have done the job in emergency situations as effectively as expensive manufactured models. So it is not always necessary to use manufactured and pre-rigged models, although they certainly look more dazzling than most improvisations.

It is also not always necessary to use artificials as single teasers. Using hookless natural baits as teasers, is nothing new. Single split-tail mullet and other baitfish, or strips cut from the shiny bellies of tuna or dolphin, have long been dragged in the wake of trollers. The manner of using them is usually to yank them away from an inspecting gamefish at the same instant that rigged baits, flies, or castable lures are presented. Attracted by the natural teaser and then subsequently angered by its sudden disappearance, the gamefish is more likely to cast caution to the wind and strike the new offering with reckless abandon. Such teasers are preferred to artificial ones in many parts of the world and are the teasers of choice for many fly anglers, although categorically speaking, they are not, in fact, lures.

For billfishing, a majority of today's experienced trollers favor soft teasers because the fish seem to hold onto them longer and are more likely to return to them because they feel like natural bait. While the objective is not to catch fish on these hookless teasers, the fact that they are soft is more likely to cause a fish that strikes one to return to take a

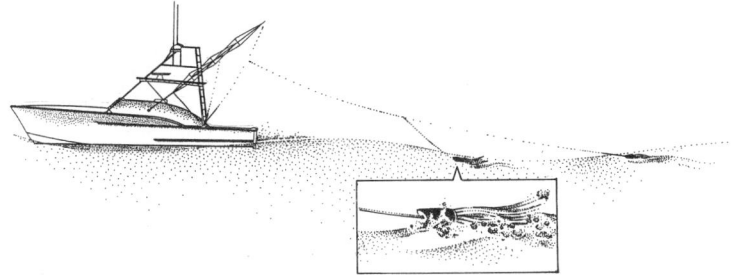

It's possible to run a commotion-making teaser ahead of a trolling lure as shown. The teaser (inset) is attached to a leader and snap, which in turn is connected to a snap swivel on the main line. The same connection is used for the trolling lure.

hooked lure that is following in the spread. This is less of an issue with blue marlin, and more of one with white marlin and sailfish.

Teasers are usually attached to a flatline that is tied to the stern cleat; this is especially common on smaller boats. On larger boats, especially offshore charter boats, teasers are attached to lines that connect to reels mounted up on the bridge; this allows the captain to manipulate or retrieve them when necessary. Some of these are attached to electric reels or winches for fast retrieval; the line for these is run through glass eyes or locked-down release clips that are positioned low on the outriggers. Teasers can also be deployed via a rod and reel that is secured in a recessed gunwale or transom rod holder.

Large teasers are usually fixed close to the transom under the theory that they are easier to see in the frothy wake than smaller teasers, and that they are most likely to be the first thing that a billfish sees after it comes up to inspect a moving boat. This is especially so when trolling at fast speeds, such as 7 to 10 knots, for marlin. When fishing slower, smaller teasers can be fished close to the transom, and are more visible then because the area behind the boat is less disturbed.

Often billfish move away from the teaser and then inspect or strike one or more of the hooked lures that are pulled a few waves back. When they hit big teasers, the lures are pulled away from them by virtue of the motion of the boat or the action of the angler or mate, and this tends to make the fish mad and ready to pounce on the trailing lure.

Trolling birds. These are most commonly referred to simply as "birds," but they are in reality bird- or airplane-shaped trolling teasers. These specialized teasers are designed to be used either in the conventional manner (dragged hookless behind the boat), or rigged in-line on the fishing line itself, and placed one leader length in front of the lure.

Developed originally by Japanese commercial tuna fishermen, and also called airplane teasers, birds gained rapid acceptance first among recreational tuna anglers and then among billfish anglers. Made of wood, hard plastic, or dense urethane foam, birds come in a variety of sizes for sportfishing, primarily from $4^1/_2$ to 13 inches long.

T

They attract attention by creating a unique splashing action on the surface of the water with their fluttering and splashing "wings." In fact, birds produce more splashing, skittering, and spraying commotion than any other teaser.

Evidently, birds resemble baitfish (especially flyingfish) fleeing frantically from some predator. When rigged in-line, especially in front of a lure rather than a rigged bait, a bird unquestionably mimics a baitfish fleeing the smoking lure behind it, which itself might appear to be a small predator, like a bonito. Used singly or rigged as a group, birds add splashing flutter and very effectively draw attention to the spread of baits and lures. A chain of birds closely resembles showering ballyhoo or flyingfish, and fairly shouts to a gamefish to come and investigate. Some anglers, especially those in the Pacific, prefer to use them on calm days, but they can be used in rougher water.

Many people rig single bird teasers directly in line with leaders and artificial lures at the snap swivel, or, when trolling at slightly slower speeds, rigged on a separate trailer line attached to the swivel in front of the leader. The hooked bait or lure appears to be chasing the bird, or it may look like two fleeing baitfish. Both billfish and tuna react to bird teasers, whichever way they are rigged.

Several versions of birds are available, including some that are soft, and the design contributes to their action. Birds with more of a keel tend to track better, while others meander from side to side. Soft birds can also be rigged with hooks and fished as a lure, which may be advantageous if fish are striking the bird instead of the trailed offering. The size of the bird to use is generally dependent upon the tackle being fished: smaller birds for lighter tackle and bigger birds for heavier tackle. While small birds can also be fished on heavy tackle, large birds should not be fished on light tackle.

The number of birds and the pattern, or spread, will vary with sea conditions and fishing tactics. Yellowfin tuna anglers in Hawaii, who make tight turns when following schools of surface tuna, run just one bird on a long center line, to keep it from tangling with other lines. If you turn sharply and in any direction, you always have to be careful of crossing lines of dissimilar lengths or with differently behaving lures, so a single long-lined bird eliminates this problem.

Many anglers elsewhere, however, fish in wider turning or straight running patterns that allow them to fish from two to four or five birds, at staggered lengths and off outriggers as well as on flatlines. These are used ahead of the lures, with the main consideration being proper placement of the lures to get the best action out of them.

Some anglers prefer not to use birds when the water is really rough, while others merely lengthen their trolling line in rough water to get their lures to work most effectively. However, birds may flip in rough water. When birds attached to outriggers flip over, they cause a false strike by pulling out of the release, and may careen into other lines.

There has been concern in the past about the acceptability of birds for record-setting purposes due to a perceived problem with the drag created by a bird when a fish pulled it backward through the water and jumped with it in-line. The question was if this fit sporting definitions for record-setting purposes *(see: records)*. However, many anglers, as well as the record-tending International Game Fish Association *(see)*, determined that this is not so where standard sportfishing-size birds (as opposed to huge homemade versions) are concerned. The angler is virtually unaware of any added drag on his line as he fights a big fish that is also tethered to a bird. In the case of billfish, he is only reminded of the bird when a hooked specimen leaps clear of the water and the brightly colored bird can be seen flying behind the leaping fish, looking as if it's trying to catch up.

This is a typical setup for using four bird teasers (followed by plastic squid), all trolled off outriggers, with inside lines shorter than outside lines.

One word of caution needs to be sounded about using birds. When a large fish is brought to the boat and someone wires the fish (grabs the leader), an in-line bird can get in the way. This is generally no problem in the case of birds with wooden or plastic wings that have been sanded smooth at their edges. However, birds with sharp-edged aluminum wings have the potential to seriously cut the arms or hands in this situation and should be avoided.

Daisy chains and spreaders. A daisy chain is a combination of natural or artificial teasers rigged together in-line and trolled separately or on a fishing line. Born in the early days of giant tuna fishing off the Canadian Maritimes, daisy chains originally consisted of strings of dead herring dragged behind the boat while attached to the fishing line and meant to simulate a school of live fish. The last herring on the string hid a large tuna hook. Similarly, many Florida Keys skippers make natural bait daisy chains by stringing a succession of snap swivels on the line and then fastening ballyhoo to each snap through the lower jaw. The last ballyhoo is often rigged with a hook. This natural daisy chain works very effectively for everything from kingfish to sailfish, and often the angler is treated to the sight of gamefish violently eating their way down the string of baits before finally nailing the one with the hook in it.

Artificial daisy chains mainly consist of a string of lures, birds, or soft plastic baits (usually squid but sometimes other body types), and occasionally natural bait. Daisy chains made of artificials are primarily dragged hook-less behind the boat on a heavy cord exactly like a standard single teaser.

Although ready-made daisy chains are available, especially those made up of four or five plastic squid, many anglers simply string together a collection of old lures that have been irreparably damaged in the offshore trolling wars. The lures are held in place about 3 or 4 feet apart on heavy cord or monofilament by crimping small egg sinkers or sleeves onto the line. The daisy chain string of lures trails behind the boat on the second or third wake wave between the boat and the nearest lures and undoubtedly mimics a whole school of fleeing baitfish.

Although standard teasers and plastic squid are most commonly used on in-line daisy chains, trolling birds may also be rigged this way. Several birds (or small, plastic flyingfish) can be strung

right on the leader in front of the lure to attract marlin. In the water they give the appearance of a small school of flyingfish being pursued by a larger predator, and marlin attack the lure perhaps as much out of a competitive urge as out of hunger.

Just as tuna anglers used to arm the tail-end bait of their daisy chain string of herring with a giant tuna hook, so, too, are modern anglers sometimes placing a stinger at the end of their daisy chain of artificial lures, rather than drag an unhooked daisy chain simply as an attractor. So the option exists to fish a daisy chain with a hook in it as well as strictly an attractor. By placing a hooked lure or bait behind, you can give the impression of perhaps a small school with the weakest member straggling behind, or of a small school being chased by something slightly larger.

The concept of daisy chains and imitating a group of baitfish may be expanded through the use of a spreader bar. Also known as a spreader rig, this is made up of a number of teasers mounted in a pattern behind a stainless steel bar, and instead of just imitating a straight-line formation, it broadens and increases it.

Egg-sinker stoppers or crimps squashed to the cord keep each component lure or plastic squid in place, and the rigs are dragged either alongside or directly in front of flatlined baits or lures. Some anglers, especially those after tuna, prefer to troll them farther back, in front of the trolled outrigger baits. Tuna anglers have been known to drag a large number of spreader rigs at the same time, presenting a pattern of teasers that resembles a large school of fleeing baitfish. The baits or lures with hooks in them probably resemble stragglers or larger predators that are chasing the pack.

In a pinch you can make your own daisy chain teasers by simply digging into your old tackle box and gathering a variety of offshore trolling lures, preferably about the same length. Old battered lures are fine. Then, all you need is a length of heavy monofilament leader and a bunch of small egg sinkers. By squashing the sinkers between the lures at intervals to keep them separated, and tying a large swivel at the end, you have made yourself a daisy chain. The fact that not one lure in the chain resembles another in either shape or color doesn't seem to affect their attracting ability.

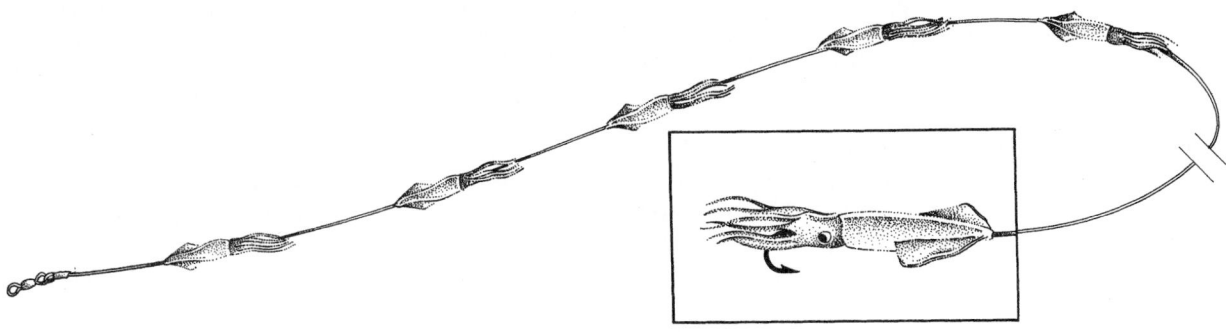

A daisy chain rig features a series of synthetic squid without hooks followed by one that is hooked.

This spreader bar is deploying soft teasers, the last of which is rigged with a hook.

Tubes

Tubes are long, slender, hollow trolling lures fashioned from rubber or plastic tubing. Most are made from pliable plastic and some from rubber; rubber versions were derived from surgical tubes and are also known as surgical tube lures. They feature a lead head, which may or may not have eyes, and two hooks that are attached to a wire leader that runs through the tubing; one hook is placed midway along the tube body and the other is at the tail. The tail is usually split or cut on an angle to taper to a point. The lure is fished with a ball bearing swivel and is trolled by itself on wire line or behind a downrigger weight, or with others on an umbrella rig *(see)*.

Trolling tube lures are available in sizes from 5 inches to 18 inches and in a variety of colors, with red and black being top preferences. Meant to imitate an eel or long sandworm, they are a top trolling lure for striped bass in saltwater, and also effective on bluefish and barracuda.

See: Offshore Fishing

TROLLING MOTOR

(1) A fuel-powered motor, usually of low horsepower, used for slow movement in trolling *(see)*. It is often an auxiliary means of propulsion, and is available as an emergency backup.

(2) Commonly used term for electric motor. In a strict sense, any motor can be used for the act of trolling. However, electric outboard motors are routinely referred to by many anglers and by the general boating industry as "trolling motors," even though many people who own them never actually troll, but use them for positioning while casting or bottom fishing.

See: Motor, Electric.

TROLLING PLATE

A trolling plate is a boating accessory that baffles propeller thrust, and which is used by trollers who need to move slowly but whose big engines don't allow them to. With the plate up, the boat can be run at high speed without impairment; when down, the plate acts as a door behind the propeller and slows boat speed without sacrificing maneuverability.

Trolling plates are spring-loaded and flip down by pulling a cord. Some plates don't lock into position easily, so it may be necessary to put your engine in reverse momentarily to lock the plate down. Use super-heavy monofilament line or a length of low-stretch braided line to work the plate. A trolling plate is needed when headed downwind but not when headed upwind on very windy days. Be careful that you don't bang the plate on an underwater obstruction, and don't leave the plate down when you plane out, which can damage it.

TROLLING REEL/ROD

Anglers sometimes refer to a "trolling rod" or "trolling reel" when describing tackle used for that technique. No rods and reels are suitable for every type of trolling in freshwater or every type in saltwater, and some rods and many reels can be used for casting as well as for trolling. Whether a rod or reel is suitable for trolling depends to some extent on the type of trolling being done, the weight or pull of the objects being trolled, and the size of the fish to be encountered. Rods designed for downrigger fishing for trout and salmon, for example, are long and parabolic, and are not very useful in other fishing applications. Muskie trolling rods, by comparison, are shorter and stiffer than those used for downrigger trolling. Saltwater rods used for offshore big-game trolling tend to be of medium length and stout, while those for inshore fishing are longer and have more action, largely due to the type of lures and weights trolled.

Reel needs, too, vary widely, even among anglers trolling for the same type of fish. For instance, one could use a light-duty spinning reel that holds over 200 yards of 8-pound-test line for brown trout trolling, a narrow-spooled baitcasting reel (as employed when casting for bass) that holds 180 yards of 8-pound-test line, or a large capacity levelwind reel that holds over 300 yards of 14-pound-test line.

Line capacity and drag are the key factors to consider when selecting a reel to be used in trolling, matching them to the angler's abilities and the size of the quarry. Many reels used in trolling have a clicker to help alert anglers to a strike. In some freshwater trolling, reels with a line counter are preferred to regularly and reliably set lures at specific distances behind the boat.

See: Reel, Fishing; Rod, Fishing.

TROPHY FISH

A large specimen of gamefish, usually above an arbitrary size deemed notable by common consensus or one that exceeds the minimum requirements of an award or recognition program. Trophy fish are often candidates for replica or skin-mount taxidermy *(see)*.

TROTLINE

A main line, usually of braided nylon, with drop lines to which hooks are attached and baited in order to catch fish. Trotlines are attached at one or both ends to a fixed object, often a stump or tree on the bank or shore at one end and a heavy weight or anchor at the other end; they are meant to catch nongamefish species and are especially used for catfish. They may be sunk to any depth, or they may be near the surface and have floats attached. Commercial trotlines are used by licensed commercial fishermen. So-called recreational trotlines are used by holders of a general fishing license who fish for personal consumption. Regulations govern the length of trotlines, the number of hooks, the spacing of hooks, and other issues. Trotlines are illegal in some places; where legal, they usually must be tagged or marked with the owner's identifying information.

Trotlines are not under the direct view and control of the person placing the line; however, they must be checked periodically, in some cases daily. Although using a trotline may be called fishing, and such usage may be covered under established regulations, a trotline is not a sportfishing instrument, and trotline fishing is not sportfishing.

TROUT

The word "trout" is used to describe various related members of the Salmonidae family, which also includes salmon, charr, whitefish, and grayling. As a group, these fish are endemic to freshwaters of the temperate and cool regions of the Northern Hemisphere but have been introduced widely outside their native range. Species that are commonly referred to as trout occur not only in the true trout genus *Salmo,* but also in the Pacific salmon genus *Oncorhynchus* and the charr genus *Salvelinus,* which complicates both a definition and an explanation of what a trout is.

Species

Among the most popular and widely known species of fish that are called trout are brook trout *(see: trout, brook),* brown trout *(see: trout, brown),* cutthroat trout *(see: trout, cutthroat),* rainbow trout *(see: trout, rainbow),* and lake trout *(see: trout, lake);* these have many strains, sea-run forms, and hybrid versions.

Some taxonomists would argue that the brown trout is the only true trout, as it was the first of its kind described by Linnaeus, the father of modern taxonomy, and that other fish species have been labeled as trout (especially in North America) largely because of their similar body form. This issue is best left to scientists, but from a technical standpoint it should be noted that such commonly known species as lake trout and brook trout are actually members of the charr group. So is the lesser-known bull trout *(see: trout, bull).* Likewise, the rainbow trout and its anadromous steelhead *(see)* variation, which was once placed in the trout genus, is now a member of the Pacific salmon group, as are the cutthroat trout, the lesser-known golden trout *(see: trout, golden),* and the Apache trout *(see: trout, Apache).*

Identification

In any event, true trout and would-be trout, as well as other members of the Salmonidae family, are primitive fish, with fossil remains dating to more than 100 million years ago. Evidence indicates that many of the more advanced or specialized families of modern-day bony fish have ancestral stocks closely resembling these primitive fish.

The most clearly evident primitive feature of the group is the lack of spines in the fins. Most of the soft rays in the fins are branched. The pelvic fins are situated far back on the body—in the "hip" region, where the legs of amphibians articulate with the body. This placement contrasts with the location of the pelvic fins in many other species, like largemouth bass, for example, whose pelvic fins are so far forward they are almost directly beneath the pectoral fins *(see: anatomy).* Other indications of their primitive nature are the possession of an adipose fin and a primitive air bladder.

Trout as a group are among the most distinguished-looking and prettiest freshwater fish. Some are especially colorful, particularly in spawning mode, and most have distinctive body markings, although there are great variations depending on the environment. Within each species there is considerable variation in color and markings from one river to another, as well as between river and lake populations. The brown trout found deep in a lake, for example, are more silvery and rather bland compared to brown trout caught in a rich limestone stream; so great is the difference that the casual observer would not assume that the two were the same species.

Gulf Coast marshes are home to mosquitoes termed Galinippers, so named by sailors who would see insect clouds so large that they were called "gallon-nippers"—a gallon of blood to the bite.

T

Habitat/Distribution

Like most members of the Salmonidae family, trout are in some way associated with cold, often rushing waters and high oxygen demands. Some—including the brown trout, cutthroat, and rainbow—have forms that are also tied to the sea and spend a portion of their lives there. The Pacific salmon, Atlantic salmon *(see: salmon, Atlantic)*, and arctic charr *(see: charr, arctic)* are all examples of this. All trout spawn in freshwater and most require cold running water.

Some trout, especially the brown, have a lineage of historical, cultural, and angling significance, especially in Europe. All are good table fare and esteemed sportfish. They include species with limited range, especially various strains and isolated populations that are little known to most people, and species that have been distributed virtually around the world. Rainbow trout are likely the most widely spread gamefish worldwide, and have become important food fish through aquaculture production. As a group, trout are among the most widely cultivated fish, perhaps second only to carp *(see)*, which are the mainstay of fish farming in China. Trout have been widely planted to supplement existing stocks, reintroduce species to waters where natural populations were extirpated, or introduce them to waters where they did not previously exist.

Like nearly all members of the Salmonidae family, trout have suffered from changes wrought by humans. These include overfishing, pollution, habitat alteration, factors that have caused a warming of waters, hatchery impacts, and competition from exotic species.

Some native populations of the various trout and their subspecies or strains have declined dramatically or have even been extirpated, although others have declined and recovered or expanded. Competition between species, especially between native and introduced trout, or trout and other introduced species, has often been a great problem. Unlike some other salmonids, trout (except steelhead and lake trout) are generally not a target of commercial fishing, or are a minor target, and recreational harvest regulations are well established.

Each of the major trout species is of great interest to anglers, although rainbow trout and brown trout have the greatest following because of their suitability to diverse habitats and wide international distribution. Trout are generally associated with rivers and stream fishing, especially wading and casting activities, although a great many anglers pursue these fish from various types of boats in large rivers and lakes, making it possible to fish for them in a multitude of ways. Because most trout are entirely freshwater in their existence, fishing methods are not centered exclusively around individuals that are preparing to spawn and undertaking migrations, as it true for sea-run salmon, and some species are available year-round.

Angling

Angling techniques for trout vary widely according to their environment; flowing water requires a different approach from that used in lakes, reservoirs, and ponds. The following information is a general overview and applies to the various trout except for lakers.

Rivers.   To some anglers, the thought of fishing for river trout brings to mind a gentle flowage and small fish dimpling the surface during a profuse insect hatch, and using a light fly rod and fine-tippet leader to daintily drop a tiny imitation fly among the rising fish. To others it means tossing a flashy spinner in a roily cold flow and prospecting for an intermediate-size fish that will mistake the lure for a darting minnow. And to still others it means flipping a gob of fish eggs into a deep pool with a long rod and setting the hook into a 30-inch-long ball of silver fury that rockets out of the water and heads for the next area code.

Each of these is a classic view of river trout fishing, and this range of experiences highlights the extremes of this facet of angling. Fishing for trout in rivers—and, for simplicity, here "river" refers to all forms of flowing water—is a diverse activity, one that, in order to be consistently successful, requires proper presentation, a knowledge of the species' habits, and an ability to analyze the water and determine what places will likely hold fish.

Brook, brown, cutthroat, and rainbow trout, as well as steelhead, exist in a number of different-size flowages, and portions of these can be extremely fast or dramatically slow. Excellent trout-holding areas are available in nearly any flowage, however, and all of these fish are found in some of the same waters.

Brown trout tend to lie in slower and warmer waters than brookies and cutthroats, yet they will all inhabit pools and slicks in rapid-flowing waters. They primarily feed on various stages of aquatic insects but also on small minnows. Rainbows and steelhead tend to stay in deep main-flow water, and feed on aquatic insects as well as fish eggs and small fish. Yet all of these trout are often found in some similar locations, such as pockets behind rocks; fishing the so-called "pocket water" is a standard river fishing ploy, especially in low water and where smaller fish exist. Other such places include the slick water downstream from an eddy or pool; dark, swift water just above a falls or rapids drop; the sanctuary beneath a falls; and spring holes.

A great many river trout are caught by fly anglers, who typically use a light outfit (7- or 8-foot rod and 4- to 7-weight line) to fish small streams. They might use an outfit on the upper end of this range for larger or more open waters and/or places where big fish might linger.

Leader length should be about 7 feet long for small waters, slightly longer elsewhere (equal to the length of the rod is often a normal measurement), tapering to a 2X or 3X tippet. Flies must be selected according to the type of minnow or aquatic insect prevalent at the time. An enormous assortment of dry and wet flies, nymphs, and streamers are presented to these fish, depending on the circumstances.

Spring and summer insect hatches particularly attract river trout. In the spring these hatches may occur during the day, but later in the season they may be most evident around sundown and last long into the night. Trout, especially browns, will feed on meatier forage in the night as well. Small fish are often preyed upon in a long, shallow, gravel flat above a deep pool.

Fly fishing tactics vary, of course. Nymphs must be retrieved in short jerking movements, and at an angle downstream. Streamer flies, which primarily represent minnows, are retrieved at a steady pace across or upstream in rivers. Dry flies are cast upstream and float naturally downstream while the angler gathers line rapidly or mends line in order to get a natural, drag-free drift. To work a fly across stream or retrieve upstream causes your offering to drag or move in an unnatural fashion, and fish will seldom strike a fly presented this way. In a very slow pool or a midstream beaver pond, a dry fly should sit motionless and drift with a breeze if there is one. Give the dry fly enough slack by mending line so it drifts without line pull.

Spinning tackle users have a lot of success with river trout also, employing small spinners, small spoons, occasionally a light jig, and sometimes minnow-imitation plugs, as well as live worms and salmon eggs where baitfishing is legal, and large spoons and spinners in big, swift-flowing waters. Spinning equipment should be light or ultralight, with lines ranging from 4- to 8-pound test. In some smaller streams it's possible to use 2-pound line and a 5-foot ultralight rod. Line capacity and drag are seldom factors with reels used in spinning for trout. Where big steelhead are likely, line capacity and drag are more crucial.

Steelhead, rainbow, and brown trout are sometimes targets for big-river drifting, backtrolling, or back bouncing presentations, too, which are described elsewhere. Most of this is done with diving plugs or baits; winter-run steelhead, for example, are caught with pencil-lead-weighted spawn sacks or single-hook salmon eggs. Many different attractions, including plugs, spoons, spinners, flies, and bait, are used.

Lakes. Angling for trout in lakes—including in this term not only lakes but also reservoirs and ponds—is a completely different sport than angling for trout in flowages, not only because lakes usually harbor larger fish, but because such waters often provide suitable year-round water temperatures and have abundant forage fish opportunities, and their trout aren't readily accessible.

Trout in lakes move a lot and aren't always confined to readily identifiable terrain. Primarily they move in search of food, which is not made up principally of aquatic insects but such forage as alewives,

Most anglers associate trout fishing with clear cold flows, such as the Blackwater River, British Columbia.

smelt, cisco, chub, sculpin, assorted species of shiners and darters, and even yellow perch and crayfish. It is usually a certainty that the prominent forage species in any environment constitutes the major element in the trout's diet.

After ice out, or in late winter and early spring, trout lakes begin to warm on the surface. Trout are found at any level at this time, and are often within the upper strata (20 feet or less) of a lake or in shallow water close to shore. Thermal discharges, tributaries, rocky shorelines, and the like contribute to warmer water locales. In large lakes, a vertical surface distinction between water temperatures may exist until the weather warms. Known as a thermal bar, and found offshore in the spring, it is particularly attractive to steelhead.

As lakes get warmer, trout seek preferred temperature zones. Brown and rainbow trout prefer water in the upper 50s and low 60s, and once the water warms on the surface, they usually are found in waters of these temperatures, at whatever depth they may exist, provided that there is ample oxygen at that level. Often, their forage exists at or close to the same level. With brown and rainbow trout, the place where those temperatures meet with the bottom of the lake can be a productive locale for catching fish, especially if it is a prominent aspect of underwater terrain, such as a point or nearshore ledge.

An ideal situation in large lakes is to find a place where temperature, forage, and shore structure coincide. If you are looking for schools of baitfish, and monitoring preferred water temperature, try to find both of these where the thermocline intersects the bottom. This would be a prime place to begin looking for trout in the summer on large lakes. Trout may be more concentrated, incidentally, along a sharply sloped shoreline than a moderately sloped one.

Trout orient to objects and edges. By identifying physical terrain, from depth contours to irregularities in the shore or bottom, you can discern which places attract baitfish as well as trout and pinpoint possible ways to fish them. A good locale is where baitfish get funneled, or where they might routinely pass by. The deep-water/shallow-water interface near islands can be equally productive. The edges of long underwater bars or shoals are places where baits migrate naturally, and logically present feeding opportunities for trout. In midsummer, deep trout may cruise over a large area, so in big lakes you may have a lot of scouring to do.

Fishing for trout in lakes is like blind prospecting. To have regular success means covering a lot of water. When trout are shallow and near the surface, trolling, casting from shore or from a float tube, or drifting with baits are all productive angling methods. Although casting is the most fun, trolling is often more popular because anglers can cover a large area in search of active, aggressive fish, particularly trout that perhaps have not been spooked or otherwise bothered by other anglers and boaters. Drift fishing with a boat usually is a live-bait proposition, but it is slow and, where motors are permitted on lakes, often less productive than lure trolling. If you cast from shore, you may simply be limited to one spot, such as a pier or breakwall, and must cast repeatedly in the hope of attracting a moving, incoming fish to strike your lure. This can pay off in tributary areas in spring when warm river water attracts a significant number of fish, or when fish are attracted here prior to upstream spawning migration. In most lakes, however, it is better to be mobile, concentrating shore casting efforts near prominent points, inlets, steep banks, rock- and boulder-studded shores, shorelines with sharp dropoffs to deep water, and warm bay and cove areas. Try casting spoons and plugs (crankbaits or sinking minnow-style lures) from shore.

Once the trout are deep, it becomes tough, if not impossible, to catch them from shore, and here the boater with the ability to get lures down, to scout for fish with some type of sonar, and with the ability to ply a lot of water by trolling, has a distinct advantage.

In fishing for trout in lakes, once you have established roughly where and how deep to fish, the next consideration becomes what type of lure to fish, what color, and at what speed. Spoons, plugs, and spinners all catch trout, as do jigs at times. Many flatline trollers use fairly heavy spoons to get these offerings down to appropriate depths, but light spoons are preferred on downriggers. Fly fishing is predominantly done in small, shallow lakes and ponds, to rising fish with dry flies or to nearshore fish with streamers and wet flies and sinking lines.

There is seldom any reason to use extremely heavy tackle for trout in lakes, although large browns and steelhead can be powerful fish, and line capacity may be a factor. Spinning and baitcasting tackle is used for trolling, and spinning and fly equipment for casting. Rods are usually long, in the 7- to 9-foot range for all but brook trout and cutthroat fishing, and line strengths from 4- to 10-pound test are usually adequate, although big-water anglers who troll simultaneously for trout and chinook or coho salmon may use heavier line.

In many northern lakes, trout are a favorite target for ice fishing.

See: Charr; Salmon, Atlantic; Salmon, Pacific.

TROUT, APACHE　　*Oncorhynchus apache.*

Other names—Arizona trout.

The Apache trout is Arizona's state fish and was once so abundant that early pioneers caught and salted large numbers of them as a winter meat source. Since those times, a 95 percent reduction in range has resulted from hybridization with rainbow trout, brook trout, and other trout; in the early 1900s, nonnative trout species were stocked in the streams and lakes of Arizona's White Mountains to increase fishing opportunities, but they preyed upon Apache trout and out-competed them for limited food supplies. By the mid-1950s, pure Apache trout populations occurred primarily on the White Mountain Apache Reservation; in 1969, the Apache trout became one of the first species to be listed under the Endangered Species Conservation Act, and it was among the first fish species protected when the Endangered Species Act of 1973 was enacted.

This member of the Salmonidae family is currently listed as "threatened," or "likely to become endangered in the near future." The Apache Trout Recovery Team was eventually established with the goal of ensuring that healthy, self-sustaining populations of Apache trout exist in their White Mountain stream habitat. Currently, the Apache trout range is increasing due to joint conservation efforts by state and federal agencies and private organizations. These efforts have centered around reintroductions into streams where barriers have been constructed to prevent upstream immigration of nonnative trout species, and where "renovation" programs are in place to remove nonnative fish.

Identification.　　The Apache trout is a striking fish, with yellow to golden sides, an adipose fin, and a large dark spot behind the eye. The head, dorsum, sides, and fins have evenly spaced dark spots, and the dorsal, pelvic, and anal fins are white tipped. The underside of the head is orange to yellowish orange, with a complete lateral line of 112 to 124 scales.

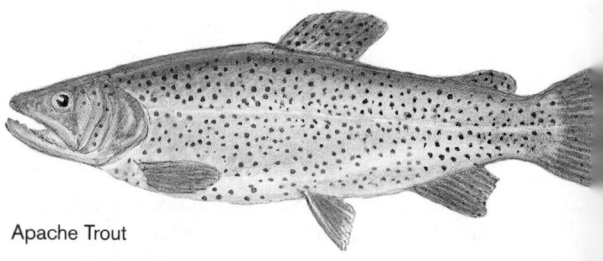

Apache Trout

Blueback Trout

Size. Adult fish usually range from 8 to 15 inches in length, although they can reach 18 inches. The all-tackle world record is a 5-pound, 3-ounce fish taken in Arizona in 1991.

Distribution. The Apache trout occurs in the upper Salt River and Little Colorado River systems (the Colorado River drainage) in Arizona. It exists in the West Fork of the Black River and a few small impoundments, such as Lee Valley Lake, and the largest population is on the Fort Apache Indian Reservation.

Habitat. Apache trout inhabit clear, cool mountain headwaters of streams and creeks above 7,500 feet and mountain lakes. They are dependent on pool development, shade-giving streamside vegetation, and undercut banks for cover, and are capable of tolerating a range of temperatures.

Life history/Behavior. Depending on the geographic elevation, spawning occurs between March and mid-June; the higher the elevation, the later spawning occurs, beginning when water temperatures reach 46°F. Females lay between 100 and 4,000 eggs in nests (called redds) at the downstream ends of pools; the lower egg counts occur in wild stream populations and the higher counts in hatcheries.

Food. As with other trout that live in flowing water, Apache trout eat both aquatic and terrestrial insects such as mayflies, caddisflies, and grasshoppers.

Angling. Fishing tactics are similar to those for other stream- and small lake-dwelling trout. See: **Trout.**

TROUT, AURORA

The aurora trout is a form of brook trout *(see: trout, brook),* that has been considered extinct in its original form since 1971. The aurora trout was native to several lakes in the Timiskaming region of northeastern Ontario, Canada. Designated as *Salvelinus fontinalis timagamiensis* by some tax-onomists, it was considered either a strain, color variation, or subspecies of brook trout by different scientists; it was distinguished by a lack of vermiculations or spots.

TROUT, BLUEBACK

This member of the charr *(see)* was once classified as a separate species with the scientific name *Salvelinus oquassa.* A landlocked, or nonanadromous, charr, it was reclassified as a subspecies of the arctic charr *(S. alpinus oquassa; see: charr, arctic)* along with its close relatives the Sunapee trout *(see: trout, Sunapee)* and the Quebec red trout *(see: trout, Quebec red).* The blueback trout of Rangeley Lakes, Maine, were once extremely abundant but are now extinct; however, bluebacks are abundant in a few other waters of this state, and there is open-water fishing for them.

TROUT, BROOK   *Salvelinus fontinalis.*

Other names—Eastern brook trout, speckled trout, native, spotted trout, speckled charr, brook charr, salter, coaster, squaretail, brookie, aurora trout, and mountain trout; French: *truite mouchetée.*

Brook trout are technically not true trout but are closely related to trout; they are charr and members of a family composed of lake trout, bull trout, blue-backed trout, Dolly Varden, and arctic charr. All of these species are members of an ancient order of fish that had their beginnings more than 100 million years ago in the Oligocene Epoch—a time period that is characterized by the development of higher forms of animals and today is represented by salmon, trout, charr, whitefish, and cisco.

As a native North American fish, and a sensitive one that has been displaced in some habitats as the result of fish stocking or water degradation, brook trout have long been a favorite of stream and pond anglers, especially in the northeastern region of North America. The transplanting and stocking of hatchery-reared brook trout, as well as brown trout, have been subjects of controversy both among anglers and members of the scientific community for more than a century.

Brook trout are, in general, more eager to come to the hook than brown trout, with whom they cross range and share some common waters. Today, large brook trout are fairly uncommon, except in some of the lake and river systems in Canada, particularly Quebec and Labrador, and in some locations where they have access to big-water forage, such as in certain Great Lakes tributaries. Native brook trout are virtually a delicacy, with bright orange flesh that is best sampled as soon as possible after a specimen has been taken. Commercially raised individuals are important to the restaurant trade.

Identification. Brook trout are among the prettiest fish in the world, both in color and body form. Their coloration and patterns are so unique that there is seldom any confusion with other fish, especially when one is looking at a native specimen (which will be richer and more brightly marked and colored than a hatchery specimen). Three external features allow immediate separation of brook trout from either brown or rainbow trout, or other charr. White pipings on the outer edges of all but the caudal (tail) fin identify it as a charr. On the interior of the white leading edges on the fins is a narrow black stripe. Body spots of true trout are on a light background but reversed in all charr. Trout have large

T

Brook Trout

scales easily seen by the eye, whereas charr have very small scales. The feature that is wholly unique to brook trout is the wormlike wavy lines, called vermiculations, on the back and head. These appear on the dorsal, adipose, and caudal fins like a series of tiger stripes.

Like all salmonids, brook trout sport a vestigial adipose fin on their back, located closer to the caudal than the dorsal fin. They also have paired pectoral and pelvic fins and a singular anal fin, just posterior of the vent. The body is generally fusiform (torpedo-like) in shape. It is slightly laterally compressed in young fish, but this becomes more noticeable in both sexes as fish age, especially older males.

Coloration can vary greatly depending on the environment; ranging from a light, metallic blue in fish that enter saltwater (which are called salters) or in fish that leave natal streams and spend part of the year in large, deep, clear lakes (which are called coasters), to dark brown and yellowish bodies in trout trapped behind beaver dams or in high mountain ponds whose streams drain leachates from surrounding conifer forest.

In general, its back coloration is olive drab or greenish brown, which fades down the sides into a light brown and somewhat yellowish color below the lateral line. On the abdomen, it merges into a pearly white that during spawning phases is replaced by roseate, then red and orange hues with a black swath along the very bottom. Upon this pallet, vermiculations are just a bit lighter green phasing into yellow; as these run down the sides, they break into pale yellow irregularly shaped dots and eventually become blotches. Over this collage are dispersed small, vermillion-colored dots surrounded by powder blue halos.

Body dots do not appear on the head or the gill covers, but green vermiculations from the back run forward onto the head and snout. Ventral (bottom) fins are red and almost transparent, whereas dorsal and caudal fins are dark and patterned. Both male and female brook trout undergo color changes as spawning approaches. In both sexes, all the colors intensify, but this is more pronounced in males.

Young brook trout have 8 to 12 wide, vertical parr markings along the length of their body and usually a few red, yellow, and blue spots.

The head of a brook trout is large, encompassing nearly a quarter of its total length. The eyes are large and the snout is long compared to that of other charr (except lake trout) and true trout. In other charr, the maxillary jaw ends forward under the eye; in brook trout, it extends rearward for a longer distance and gives the appearance of a large mouth.

Size/Age.   Brook trout are not a long-lived fish, generally surviving into their fourth or fifth year, although some fish have lived to at least 10 years of age. In most environs, the average brook trout caught is between 7 and 10 inches long and weighs considerably less than a pound. In many of their small-water natural habitats, the conditions do not exist to foster large sizes. A brook trout exceeding 12 inches in most Northeastern waters is a sizable fish, and one exceeding 2 pounds is uncommon. Nevertheless, brook trout are capable of reaching larger sizes; a 14-pound, 8-ounce brook trout caught in 1916 is the all-tackle world record for the species, and that individual measured 31 inches in length. It is the second-oldest all-tackle freshwater record chronicled, and in modern times, any brook trout exceeding 5 pounds is indeed a large fish. Few exceeding 7 pounds are caught in current times, and in those places where big brookies exist, the majority of anglers release them in any event.

Distribution.   Brook trout populations still exist over much of the species' original distribution. Their range covers all of New York, New England, the Canadian Maritimes, Labrador, and Newfoundland. Brook trout exist in all the Quebec and On-tario rivers and streams that enter Hudson and James Bays. In Manitoba, brook trout are spread along all the streams that enter James and Hudson Bays. In all of Manitoba's east- and northeast-flowing rivers, brook trout do not appear, or are not significant, west of the 96° longitude. This longitudinal line, where it crosses into Minnesota, is also the natural western limit of brook trout in the United States, although they have been introduced elsewhere and as far west as California. In Minnesota, brook trout are found in the watershed that forms the beginning of the Mississippi River, but below its junction with the Minnesota River they appear only in the waters east of the Mississippi as far south as its junction with the Wisconsin River. They are spread throughout Wisconsin but not much farther south into Illinois. Brook trout are widely distributed on both Michigan peninsulas.

Brook trout range over all of Pennsylvania, but here their numbers are greatest on the eastern slopes of the Appalachians (Alleghenies), in the northeastern part of the state. Farther south, they spread into the eastern half of West Virginia and extreme western parts of Virginia, North and South Carolina, and the extreme northern part of Georgia. The most southerly brook trout distribution is the headwaters of the Chattahoochee River in Georgia. Brook trout also inhabit extreme eastern parts of Tennessee and Kentucky. Along the eastern slopes of the Alleghenies, they are native to Maryland north and west of the Chesapeake Bay. In New Jersey, the best brook trout fishing today is in the very northwest corner of the state.

Habitat. Compared to all other charr, as well as salmon and trout, brook trout are the least specialized in their habitat demands. This allows them to live in a great variety of environments with a wide range of tolerances. They inhabit small trickles, rivulets, creeks, and beaver ponds. They live in larger streams and any lake, from the Great Lakes to little lakes and ponds, to small rivers and big rivers with tumbling falls and rapids. Because of a unique organ (the glomerulus) in their kidney, they are anadromous and can move into riverine estuaries and are at home in brackish streams that feel the surge of tides, in a purely saline bay, or even the oceans themselves. They are, however, the classic example of a coldwater species, and thrive best in the northern half of the Northern Hemisphere.

The rate of water flow in a river or stream habitat is a factor in where brook trout are located. Slow, sluggish streams, or streams with plenty of backwater and pockets of little or no movement, are not brook trout waters. These fish are primarily "drift" feeders and prefer to lie in wait for food to come to them. But too fast a flow has a negative effect. In such a flow, fish must exert more energy to stay in place than can be replaced by the amount of food that moving water brings them. They cannot operate at a net loss for long, and seek out environments where the food en route is more than equal to the energy they burn to stay behind a boulder or even in midstream. In streams, brook trout are territorial and will defend their feeding station against other brook trout or fish. They give way only to larger brook trout or other, bigger fish.

Life history/Behavior. Brook trout spawn in late fall and early winter. The eggs grow throughout winter, remaining in the protection of the redd's gravel from 23 to as many as 80 days, depending on their latitude. They become free swimming at about $1\frac{1}{2}$ inches, and scales begin forming when they are 2 inches long. As they grow, they abandon the redd and work their way to the edges of the stream or, in a lake, into shallow water were aquatic vegetation provides protection from predators. Growth rates vary greatly over their range and depend on local conditions, that is food and competition with other larvae or fry, often of the same species. First-year growth depends on several factors, the most immediate of which is the length of the growing season. Other factors include water temperature, population density, and availability of food. Brook trout reach sexual maturity at ages 2 or 3.

Movements of brook trout in a stream are localized and especially likely during daytime hours, as indicated by their activity cycle. Biologists concluded that they are habitually inactive during the normal hours of darkness. During the day, they avoid being active during full-noon sunlight. Their activities are also controlled by the length of the day and even the time of day. Most food searches take place in early morning and again in late afternoon. When they aren't hunting, brook trout situate themselves out of main currents and find protected areas behind large rocks, under overhanging bushes and undercut banks. When rivers are up, the fish still maintain their general place in a stream. When temperatures rise or fall, they still like the place they chose.

Stocked brook trout undergo an immediate downstream movement when water temperatures are less than 50°F. When water temperatures are above 50°F at stocking, they show little or no movement. Limited movement by wild brook trout demonstrates the species' tendency toward a degree of territoriality. This is lacking in stocked fish because they are not born in the locale. Brook trout are a solitary fish, but, if alarmed or frightened, they will exhibit schooling tendencies.

Lake or pond habitat offers brook trout another set of living challenges. Immature and small, adult brook trout are likely to stay in a stream even when access to a lake or pond is nearby because stream habitats offer more protection from predators, especially larger brook trout. During summer months, larger brook trout typically inhabit the lake and move to rivers or streams only to spawn.

Big brook trout are also more likely to inhabit lakes and ponds in the summer because these environments usually produce more food, especially small fish upon which bigger trout prefer to feed as their size increases. In a lake, brook trout are more prone to inhabit the periphery, between 20 feet of depth and the shore, and in shoals in the lake where water depths are 30 feet or less. During summers with high temperatures, brook trout might be on the shoals that contain springs, where they can remain cool. During especially warm periods, they may be restricted from feeding in shoal waters until late in the night or early the next morning. In lake

T

A brook trout from the English River, Labrador.

and pond habitats, brook trout cruise the lake, feeding individually or in loosely connected schools. Brook trout in a lake environment gather in more defined schools only when water temperatures are high and the fish find a source of cooler water on the bottom.

Some populations of brook trout migrate to sea for short periods. They move downstream and upstream in the spring or early summer and remain in estuaries and ocean areas where food is plentiful. After roughly two months, they return to freshwater. This migration may be in response to crowded conditions, low food supplies, or unfavorable temperatures in their home waters. Some overwinter in estuaries (in Nova Scotia, shore movements have been observed along the coast). Not all fish in a population migrate, nor do they necessarily do so every year. Sea-run brook trout live longer and grow larger than strictly freshwater brook trout.

Food and feeding habits.   There isn't much living in the brook trout's world upon which this fish won't feed. They are predacious animals and need light to find their prey, and they feed as long as there is sufficient light. On evenings when there is sufficient moonlight, they feed into the night. There's a recognizable feeding pattern in both juveniles and adults. They feed best in early morning and late afternoon, when insect hatches are most likely to occur. They will be "off their feed," however, when water temperatures become too warm, such as during midday, especially in midsummer.

Brook trout are omnivorous, carnivorous, piscivorous, and even cannibalistic, and they occasionally feed on plants. Fry feed primarily on macroscopic crustaceans. At 1 to $1^1/_2$ inches, fry abandon crustaceans for insect larvae. They also begin taking their first terrestrial insects. At $1^1/_2$ to 4 inches, they shift to nymphs. Fish from 4 to 8 inches long feed mainly on aquatic and terrestrial insects. Between 8 and 12 inches, they begin feeding on small fish. Large trout, particularly in northern waters during summer, are known to eat small mammals (mice, voles, shrews, and lemmings) that find their way into the water.

Angling.   Brook trout readily take various lures, flies, and baits and generally provide a showy fight. The larger fish put up a particularly good fight. Their free-wheeling appetite and spunky disposition make them susceptible to a variety of tackle types and methods, although fly fishing and spinning are the primary means of catching these fish, essentially by casting, but also by trolling.

Unlike the rainbow trout, a brookie seldom jumps. This fish is a stubborn fighter, preferring to dig down and bore into the deeper, heavier water, employing a series of twisting, running rolls. It is during these heavy rolls that an angler with a limber, forgiving fly rod has an advantage over another angler with a shorter, stiffer rod. A fly rod, or a limber spinning rod, gives and provides leverage and constant pressure on a hooked trout.

Brookies are a terrific species for fly anglers, in part because of their nature but also because many of their habitats suit fly fishing's advantages, especially in rivers and streams. In those waters, brook trout hole up in some nearly impenetrable places, like an undercut bank, beneath a watery tree thicket, in a deep dark hole, and the like, where they wait for meals to come to them rather than chasing after the meal. When the waterway is narrow with overgrown banks, and the water is fairly shallow, a fly can be roll cast efficiently and quietly.

A 6-weight flycasting outfit will handle most brook trout that one can expect to catch in the United States on a small stream or river, as well as on a pond or lake. A $7^1/_2$- to $8^1/_2$-foot rod with a single-action reel, spare spool, and two 6-weight lines will do. You'll need a weight-forward floating line for use with dry flies, and either a sinking line, which is difficult to handle, or a floating line with only a sinking tip. The sinking tip is used to fish nymphs, wet flies, and streamers.

For those occasions when you might seek bigger fish, a heavier outfit is necessary, partly to play heftier fish, which are easier to land on a heavier rod, and partly to make longer casts and to deal with wind, but primarily to work lines deeper in heavier current, especially with all-sink lines. An 8-weight outfit will do the job. If most of your fishing is for small brook trout on small streams or with minimal room for backcasting, then you can try a lighter 4- or 5-weight outfit.

As with most aspects of fishing, the appropriate flies to use run a wide gamut. Time-proven flies that imitate natural forage and that are still effective include White Hackle or White Miller, March Brown, Pale Yellow Dun, Orange Dun, Royal Coachman, Hare's Ear Dun, Black Gnat, Red Ant, Stone Fly, Green and Gray Drakes, Black Palmer, Ginger Hackle, and Cinnamon Fly. More colorful and suggestive patterns include the No Name, Montreal, Silver Doctor, Grizzly King, Yellow Professor, Brown Hackle, Parmachene Belle, and Mickey Finn flies.

Fly fishing tactics vary, of course. Nymphs must be retrieved in short jerking movements at a steady pace across stream or upstream in rivers. Dry flies are cast upstream and float naturally downstream while the angler gathers line rapidly. To work a fly across stream or retrieve upstream causes it to drag or move in an unnatural fashion, and fish will seldom strike a fly presented this way. In a very slow pool or a midstream beaver pond, a dry fly should sit motionless and drift with a breeze, if there is one. Give the dry fly enough slack by mending line so it drifts without line pull. Pick an open area for your fly when a hatch is on.

One unusual aspect of note is the phenomenon of large flies for brook trout in northern waters, especially in Canada. Big deer-hair surface flies such as Bombers and assorted mouse imitations are effective for brook trout in places where rodents, lemmings in particular, occasionally are waterbound. These large offerings are dead-drifted on a slack line, skittered across the surface at a pace that will produce a slight wake, or floated in a drift-and-twitch manner. This produces fish of various sizes but can be especially productive for fish exceeding 3 pounds. The chase and capture of such offerings runs contrary to the usual stealth and ambush behavior of brookies, but large surface flies bring fish after them, and their take is usually explosive and exciting.

Spinners, spoons, and small plugs are the primary nonfly hardware used by casters, and a variety of these are effective. Large lures, however, are seldom of great value in brook trout fishing, except where trophy fish and the aforementioned surface flies are concerned. Lure sizes are common in the $1/4$- to $1/8$-ounce range, seldom larger, and often smaller for low-water situations and shallow streams.

Lures and baits are fished across stream and downstream. It is almost always necessary to drift a lure or bait from above and let the current carry it, both to effect a natural look and also to induce the lures to swim, wobble, or waver as designed. Larger trout are likely to have a partial minnow diet and are susceptible to lures (including minnow-shaped plugs), although these usually have to be fished slowly and deep. Smaller trout are really more inclined toward flies and baits (worms in particular), with baits also fished slowly and close to the bottom. Because brook trout often lie in slack water and then dart out for a morsel as it goes by, be on the lookout for strikes during the drift rather than when the lure is swimming.

Spinning tackle users need different outfits for the entire brook trout fishing spectrum. The standard is an ultralight outfit, with a rod 4- to 6-feet long and a reel that handles 2- through 6-pound line and has an easy-starting drag that will cope with the fish's first lunge and remain uniform throughout the fight. An option is another spinning outfit that is a slightly larger version of the first: a rod between 7-and 8-feet long with a medium- to stiff-action tip and a proportionately larger reel equipped with a spare spool; this way the line size can be quickly changed if necessary. Terminal tackle, other than a bait hook, is small spoons and spinners, especially sizes 0 and 1, and small plugs. Weighting such lines with lead when using live baits (worms, minnows, grubs, grasshoppers, crickets, and the like) can be a problem if it is crimped so tightly that it reduces the line's strength.

Fishing for trophy brook trout, such as Canadian fish 5 pounds or heavier, may require a longer rod, especially for big, fast-flowing rivers. The rod should be between 8 and $9^1/2$ feet long and have a long-handled grip. This heavier rod is not meant to overpower a trout; it simply leaves you prepared for an incidental catch of lake trout, or in some waters, northern pike or landlocked salmon. They live well in rivers and can grow to larger sizes, perhaps 20 pounds in the case of lakers and pike.

There are occasions, incidentally, both in ponds and small lakes, when trolling is the technique to employ, although trolling is not often associated with brook trout today, except on large bodies of water. However, washing a lure, fly, or bait behind a slowly rowed boat or paddled canoe is an old fishing technique. The most efficient method is to row or use an electric motor while trolling a large chub or minnow, although anglers intent on releasing fish should consider a small minnow plug or spoon, perhaps garnishing the spoon with a leech or worm. Trolling wet flies and streamers from a slowly paddled canoe is another possibility. Usually, a very slow troll is required, and it's important not to collect debris on the lure or line near the lure. In big bodies of water, deeper and more precise methods of trolling are sometimes employed.
See: Trout

TROUT, BROWN   *Salmo trutta.*

Other names for brown trout (all forms): German brown, German trout, German brown trout, Loch Leven trout, European brown trout, English trout, von Behr trout, brownie, sea trout, lake trout, brook trout, river trout.

Other names for river and stream brown trout: Danish: *baekørred;* Finnish: *tammukka, purotaimen;* French: *truite commune;* German: *bachforelle;* Norwegian: *bekkaure;* Polish: *pstrag potokowy;* Russian: *forel strumkova;* Swedish: *bäcköring.*

Other names for brown trout in lakes: Danish: *søørred;* Finnish: *jarvitaimen;* French: *truite de lac;* German: *seeforelle;* Polish: *troc jeziorowa;* Russian: *forel ozernaya.*

Other names for sea trout, or sea-run brown trout: Danish: *havørred;* Dutch: *zeeforel;* French: *truite de mer;* Gaelic: *breac;* German: *meerforelle;* Italian: *salmo trota;* Norwegian: *aure orret;* Russian: *losos taimen;* Spanish: *trucha marina;* Swedish: *öring.*

One of the most adaptable members of the Salmonidae family, the brown trout was the first species of trout described by Linnaeus, the father of modern taxonomy, in his 1758 book *The System of Nature.* It was the foremost species of interest to Izaak Walton in *The Compleat Angler.* And it has been the darling of stream and river anglers over an expanding range for centuries.

The species called *Salmo trutta* (meaning respectively "salmon" and "trout") is the backbone of natural and hatchery-maintained trout fisheries on six continents, and is one of the world's premier sportfish, but it takes on many forms—river, lake, and sea-run—in many diverse environments, and is so varied in its appearance that it has been classified as scores of different species and subspecies over the years by scientists. This complexity has produced controversy, confusion, and many different scientific as well as common names. Some scientists have opined that there is one common ancestor for the various brown trout forms, and thus the brown trout of river or stream origin, the brown trout of lake origin, and the brown trout of sea-run disposition are specializations that have evolved. Throughout most of their range, brown trout are primarily thought of as residents of flowing water; therefore, those originating from lake environments—some capable of enormous sizes—are viewed as variations, whereas sea-run brown trout, which are anadromous and generically called sea trout (which differ from seatrout; *see*), are likewise a different form, also capable of growing very large, and obviously limited to coastal regions.

There are many populations (also referred to as strains or stocks) of brown trout that might well be individual races or subspecies; these are especially evident in the native European and Asian ranges of brown trout, although some have greatly diminished or disappeared for various human-induced reasons, including interbreeding with other races of brown trout. One of the more well-known strains is the *seeforelle;* this is a lake-dwelling brown trout indigenous to western Europe, which in the past has been scientifically designated as *S. trutta lacustris.* It has grown to huge sizes in its native waters and has been introduced to some waters in the United States.

The British were so enamored with brown trout that they introduced them widely. The Australian island of Tasmania, for example, received its first brown trout eggs in 1864. In North America, the brown trout is one of the few examples of an exotic species that was introduced with great success and general public approval, as it was not native to this continent until eggs from Germany arrived in February 1883, and fish were stocked that year in Michigan and New York. This was followed by eggs from Loch Leven, Scotland, introduced to Newfoundland in 1884 and then to the U.S. a year later; Canada received its first stocking of German brown trout in 1889. The brown trout eventually replaced native salmonids, however, like grayling, cutthroat trout, and brook trout, in some places, and would eventually become widespread. The North American brown trout came to represent what some scientists view as a mix of various different forms, resulting in a "melting pot" heredity, and a derivative form that was fashioned by its adaptation to a wholly new environment.

Although the brown trout is a true trout, its closest relative and a member of the same genus is the Atlantic salmon *(see: salmon, Atlantic).* Like that anadromous species, regardless of its environment or geographical location, the brown trout is a challenge to anglers, a strong fighter occasionally prone to jumping when hooked, and a fish that can be caught using varied tackle and techniques.

The flesh of the brown trout is good, although not as esteemed as that of Atlantic salmon; native or

Brown Trout

A distinctively marked brown trout from the Rangitaiki River, New Zealand.

along the back, and rusty red spots also occur on the sides. There is a small adipose fin, sometimes with a reddish hue, ahead of the tail. Sea-run brown trout have a more silvery coloration, and the spotting is less visible. Residents of large lake systems, especially the Great Lakes of North America, have a silvery coloration as well, dark spots without halos, and no colored spots.

Although the brown trout is a salmonid, it differs from Pacific salmon (see: salmon, Pacific) in having fewer than 13 rays in the anal fin. It differs from charr (see) in having larger scales and a pattern of dark spots on a light background (instead of light spots on a dark background). Stream-dwelling browns differ from stream-dwelling rainbow trout (see: trout, rainbow) in having red spots on the sides, larger spots on the head, fewer spots on the body, and few or no spots on the tail.

The brown trout is sometimes confused with the similar-looking Atlantic salmon; both have black spots on the back, upper sides, and gill cover, and sometimes have red spots. In freshwater, especially near spawning time, both species are bronze to dark brown in general coloration, with black and (usually) red spots on the body and head. In saltwater, both species tend to become silvery with fewer black spots and no red spots.

Although both brown trout and Atlantic salmon often occur in the same areas, they can usually be distinguished without laboratory analysis, although lake-dwelling specimens of both are much harder to distinguish. In freshwater as a rule, brown trout are more heavily spotted than Atlantic salmon, and usually a good number of these spots are surrounded by lighter halos. The spots on the Atlantic salmon have no halos and usually some take the shape of Xs or Ys, which is not usually the case in the brown trout. The brown trout also has dark spots on the dorsal and adipose fins and vague or no spots on the tail, although nothing like the prominent radiating spots on the tail of the rainbow trout.

sea-run specimens are gastronomically best. It is not sought commercially in most places, but it is intensively reared in public and private hatcheries to augment naturally spawning populations or to artificially sustain fisheries.

Identification. Brown trout get their common name from the typical olive green, brown, or golden brown hue of their body. The belly is white or yellowish, and dark spots, sometimes encircled by a pale halo, are plentiful on the back and sides. Spotting also can be found on the head and the fins

T

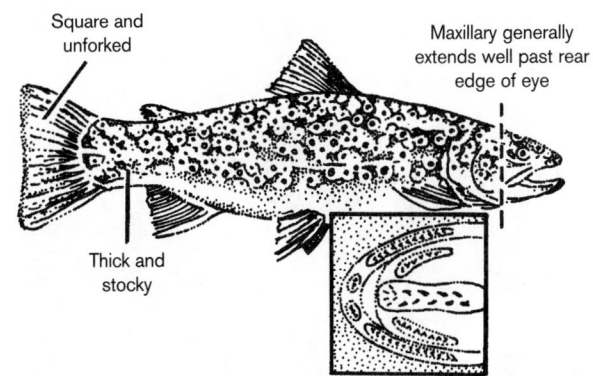

Atlantic Salmon

Slightly forked

Maxillary usually extends to rear edge of eye or slightly beyond

Narrow and tapered

Brown Trout

Square and unforked

Maxillary generally extends well past rear edge of eye

Thick and stocky

The most obvious differences between adult Atlantic salmon and brown trout are apparent in the head and tail areas. The vomerine teeth, which are inside the upper jaw, are depicted in the insets. On the salmon, these teeth are small and extremely sparse and appear in a straight row on the shaft; on the brown trout, they are well developed and form a zigzag on the shaft.

The Atlantic salmon has no clear spots on any of these fins. Also, the brown trout's tail is squarish or very slightly concave or convex, whereas the Atlantic salmon's tail is slightly forked or indented.

In juveniles, the tail of the brown trout is slightly forked and the tail of the Atlantic salmon is deeply forked. Otherwise, these parr (young salmonids) look very much alike with small exceptions. A positive distinction between these two species, usually observed in the laboratory, is that the brown trout has well-developed vomerine teeth in a double zigzag row, whereas the Atlantic salmon has only a single row of poorly developed vomerine teeth.

Brown trout sometimes hybridize with brook trout (see: trout, brook) in the wild, and are also manipulated in hatcheries; the pairing of a brown trout female and brook trout male produces a deeply vermiculated fish called a tiger trout. Few of the eggs or hatchlings of this hybrid survive due to genetic differences between the two genera, and the offspring are unable to reproduce. The anadromous brown trout can also be successfully crossed with the Atlantic salmon to produce a fertile hybrid, sometimes called a "trousal."

Size/Age.   Brown trout are capable of living up to 18 years, but most live no more than 12 years; sea trout can spend as long as 9 years in the sea. Technically, the brown trout is one of the larger salmonids, although growth and maximum size are especially relative to the particular environment. Most river and stream fish are only 9 to 14 inches long and weigh up to 4 or 5 pounds, rarely growing more than double that weight, although there are some notable exceptions. The White River in Arkansas has produced line-class world records exceeding 30 pounds, and the Little Red River, also in Arkansas, yielded the current all-tackle world record, a 40-pound, 4-ounce brown trout, in 1992.

Most large brown trout come from big lakes or from the sea-run form. Numerous brown trout exceeding 20 pounds have come from the Great Lakes, including record-setting 34-pounders from

A huge brown trout from Lake Ontario, New York.

Lakes Michigan and Ontario (respectively in 1984 and 1994), and a 37-pounder from Lake Strosjon in Sweden (in 1991). The large Alpine lakes of central Europe and the Caspian Sea drainage held fish exceeding 50 pounds in the past; Germany's Lake Wolfgang yielded a 68-pounder to a commercial handline fisherman in 1934, and a 60-pounder was caught in a net in an unidentified German lake in 1976. Sea-run browns, especially from the native range of the Caspian Sea, evidently grew even larger, and sea trout from Russia's Kura River have been reported to 72 pounds.

Distribution.   The brown trout is native to Europe and parts of Asia, from Afghanistan and the Aral Sea across Europe to the British Isles and Iceland, and back across Scandinavia to Cape Kanin, Russia, on the Barents Sea. It is also native to the Atlas Mountains of North Africa. It has been introduced into all other suitable waters of the world, including Canada and the United States in North America, as well as South America, New Zealand, Australia, and other parts of the African continent.

It is now found in rivers and lakes in much of North America, with the exception of the most southerly American states, the most northerly Canadian regions, and Alaska. It is also found in some coastal rivers from Long Island, New York, to the Maritime Provinces and Quebec.

Habitat.   Brown trout prefer cool, clear rivers and lakes with temperatures of 54° to 65°F. They can survive and thrive in 65° to 75°F conditions, which are warmer than most other trout can tolerate, but in streams they do best where the summer temperature is less than 68°F. In streams and rivers, they are wary and elusive fish that look for cover more than any other salmonid, hiding in undercut banks, in stream debris, surface turbulence, rocks, and deep pools. They also take shelter under overhanging vegetation.

Life history/Behavior.   Brown trout spawn in the fall and early winter (October through February) in rivers or tributaries of lakes or large rivers. They return to the stream where they were born, choosing spawning sites that are spring-fed headwaters, the head of a riffle, or the tail of a pool. Selected sites have good water flows through the gravel bottom. The female uses her body to excavate a nest (redd) in the gravel. She and the male may spawn there several times. Females cover their eggs with gravel after spawning, and the adults return downstream. The eggs develop slowly over the winter, hatching in the spring. A good flow of clean, well-oxygenated water is necessary for successful egg development.

Brown trout fry are aggressive and establish territories soon after they emerge. They are found in quiet pools or shallow, slow-flowing waters where older trout are absent. They grow rapidly and can reach a size of $6^1/_2$ inches in their first year. Yearling brown trout move into cobble and riffle areas. Adults are found in still deeper waters and are most active at night. They mature in their third to fifth year and many become repeat spawners. Apart from moving upstream to spawn, adults tend to stay in the same place in a river with very little movement to other stream areas. They can be found at these stations day after day, even year after year. Others move to or from estuaries in the spring or fall.

In sea-run populations, brown trout spend two to three years in freshwater, then migrate downstream to spend one or two growing seasons in coastal waters near river mouths and estuaries, where they feed on small fish and crustaceans. Most return to their home streams to spawn, but some straying occurs. In lakes, brown trout seek out levels of preferred temperature, and are deep during summer months and shallower in spring and fall when the water is cooler. After ice out, they are in shallow and nearshore areas, often around warmer tributaries, but move deeper as the surface level warms.

Food.   Brown trout are carnivores and consume aquatic and terrestrial insects, worms, crustaceans, mollusks, fish, salamanders, and even tadpoles or frogs. In small streams their diet may be largely insects; but in larger flows or where there is plenty of baitfish, it also includes assorted small fish. In large lakes, the primary diet is other fish, especially abundant pelagic schooling species, such as alewives; small fish are a primary food for sea trout.

Angling.   Brown trout are a selective sportfish and challenging at times, no matter what environment they inhabit. Angling methods differ depending on whether the fish are found in rivers or lakes, and are similar to the methods used to pursue other trout species.

See: Trout.

TROUT, BULL   *Salvelinus confluentus.*
A member of the charr group of the Salmonidae family, the bull trout is nearly identical to the Dolly Varden, and these fish have many overlapping traits. It is therefore detailed under the entry for Dolly Varden *(see).*

TROUT, CUTTHROAT   *Oncorhynchus clarki.*
Other names—cut, native trout, coastal cutthroat, Clark's trout, red-throated trout, short-tailed trout, lake trout, sea trout, brook trout, native trout, Yellowstone cutthroat, Snake River cutthroat, Lahontan cutthroat, Rio Grande cutthroat, Colorado cutthroat, Utah cutthroat, Paiute cutthroat, harvest trout, blackspotted trout; French: *truite fardée.*

The term "cutthroat throat" and its scientific designation *O. clarki*—the species name in honor of Captain Clark of the Lewis and Clark expedition—is more like a name for a family tree than for a single species of fish. According to some scientific estimates, there are 14 subspecies, hybrids, and variations, forming what has been called an ichthyological jigsaw puzzle of fish that are endemic to western North America. All of these are members of the Salmonidae family of salmon, trout, whitefish, and grayling, and were reclassified from the trout genus *Salmo* to the Pacific salmon genus *Oncorhynchus.*

Of the 14 species, all but one inhabit only freshwater rivers, lakes, and streams; the exception is the coastal cutthroat trout *(O. clarki clarki),* which has both freshwater and anadromous forms; for unknown reasons, some fish migrate to sea, whereas others stay in freshwater. The coastal cutthroat is fairly well distributed and available to anglers, and is one of the more prominent cutthroat species, in addition to the West Slope (intermountain) cutthroat *(O. clarki lewisi),* the Yellowstone cutthroat *(O. clarki bouvieri),* and the Lahontan cutthroat *(O. clarki henshawi).* Others species include the Bonneville cutthroat, blackspotted cutthroat, greenback cutthroat, and Rio Grande cutthroat.

Cutthroats are popular with anglers and are generally not as selective as other trout species. They are not as acrobatic as rainbow trout *(see: trout, rainbow),* but they are strong fighters. Their flesh, which can range from white to red, has an excellent flavor. They hybridize freely in nature with rainbow trout (which are called a cutbows), golden trout, and other close relatives.

Perhaps as much or more than other trout species, all cutthroat species and populations are sensitive to overharvest, pollution, stream warming,

A cutthroat trout from the Elk River, Colorado.

Cutthroat Trout

and habitat alteration. Some strains have been greatly diminished and others extirpated.

Identification. This is a highly variable fish, in coloration and size. The characteristic that gives the inland cutthroat its name is the yellow, orange, or red streak or slash mark in the skin fold on each side under the lower jaw. The color of the body ranges from cadmium blue and silvery (sea-run) to olive green or yellowish green. There may be red on the sides of the head, front part of the body, and the belly. In some specimens there may be a narrow pink streak along the sides, but not as broad as in the rainbow trout *(see: trout, rainbow)*. The body is covered with black spots, which extend onto the dorsal, adipose, and tail fins. Some are literally covered with spots, whereas in others the spots are sparse and larger, being more numerous on the posterior part of the body. On the tail, the spots radiate evenly outward, as they do in such species as the rainbow trout, golden trout *(see: trout, golden),* and Apache trout *(see: trout, Apache)*. Although all these species are similar and closely related, only the cutthroat trout has hyoid teeth (teeth located on the back of the tongue). These may be difficult to see or are obsolete in some specimens. The tail of the cutthroat is slightly forked, and all the fins are soft rayed.

Coastal cutthroat coloration also varies with habitat and life history. Resident fish living in bog ponds are typically from 6 to 16 inches long; are golden yellow with dark spots on the body, dorsal, and caudal fin; and have a vivid red slash mark under the jaw. Free-swimming residents in large landlocked lakes can exceed 24 inches. They are uniformly silver with black spots and have rosy gill covers and a faint slash mark. Sea-run cutthroats are smaller, seldom more than 18 inches long. They are bluish silver with dark or olive backs and less conspicuous black spots; the characteristic slash is a faint yellow. Lack of a distinct slash mark in sea-run and resident forms has led anglers to confuse the fish with rainbow trout, but a sure identification of the cutthroat is its hyoid teeth.

Size/Age. The largest form (or subspecies) of *O. clarki* was once the Lahontan cutthroat, which was native to the Lahontan drainage system of Nevada and California, including Lake Tahoe,

Pyramid Lake, and the Truckee River. These specimens weighed roughly 20 pounds on average; a 41-pound Lahontan cutthroat caught in Pyramid Lake in 1925 is the all-tackle world record for cutthroats. In 1938, water was diverted from the Truckee River, and the Lahontan became extinct except for populations maintained by stocking, none of which attain the large sizes they once did. Yet a number of fish from there have become line-class world records in the 1980s and 1990s.

The smallest cutthroat occurs only in upper Silver King Creek, California, and does not exceed 12 inches. Coastal anadromous cutthroats have been recorded to 17 pounds but average under 5 pounds, whereas most inland specimens seldom exceed 5 pounds. Most cutthroats live 4 to 7 years, and they can have a maximum life span of at least 12 years.

Distribution. Cutthroat trout are the most widely distributed of all the western trout of North America, which is proven by the many names that refer to rivers, states, or drainages where unique forms occur. The coastal cutthroat trout normally does not exist more than 100 miles inland. They are known from the Eel River, California, north to Prince William Sound, Alaska. Inland nonanadromous forms occur from southern Alberta, Canada, to as far south as New Mexico, as far east as Colorado and most of Montana, and west as far as Alberta and eastern California. A small, disjunct population that may have been transplanted occurs in northern Baja California, Mexico. The species has been transplanted to other locations, including the east coast of Quebec, Canada, and Europe.

Habitat. Inland cutthroat and resident (nonanadromous) coastal cutthroat live in a wide variety of coldwater habitats, from small headwater tributaries, mountain streams, and bog ponds to large lakes and rivers. During their spawning migration, sea-run cutthroat are usually found in river or stream systems with accessible lakes; otherwise, they stay in saltwater near shore and their natal tributaries. In some watersheds, both anadromous and resident coastal cutthroats occur together.

Life history/Behavior. Cutthroat trout are late-winter or early-spring spawners, although sea-run fish typically ascend rivers from late summer through fall of the year prior to spawning. They spawn in small, isolated headwater streams; for anadromous coastal cutthroat, the selection of isolated spawning areas is thought to reduce interaction of young cutthroat with more aggressive juvenile steelhead and coho salmon. The female makes one or more nests; eggs hatch in six to seven weeks and, by the time they become parr, are difficult to distinguish from rainbow trout. Later, the young occupy beaver ponds, sloughs, or lakes. In lakes, smaller inland and nonanadromous coastal cutthroat trout hide among lily pads, sunken logs, or rubble from which they dart out and seize insects and small fish. Some fish abandon this "sit and wait" feeding strategy when they reach about 14 inches and become cruisers, pursuing and eating other fish. Cutthroat that adapt this feeding strategy can grow from 24 to 28 inches, weigh 8 pounds, and live to be more than 12 years old. These trophy-class cutthroat are always found in large landlocked lakes with populations of kokanee (see) salmon.

Sea-run juveniles can be displaced to downstream main-stem and estuarine areas where they reside for the summer, then migrate back upstream with the onset of winter floods. Sea-run cutthroat rear for three to four years in freshwater and migrate to sea in spring when they are about 8 inches long. Time at sea varies from a few days to more than 100 days before they return to their natal stream. During their migration, they follow the shoreline and do not cross open bodies of water, seldom venturing farther than 30 to 45 miles from their home stream. In the fall they return to their home stream, where they mature during the winter months. Homing is extremely precise; cutthroat can return to the same tributary stream from where they emerged and were reared. Fish mature at five to seven years. The rate of survival through the winter and return to saltwater is about 40 percent. About 60 percent of the migrants are sexually mature, a characteristic that tends to limit egg deposition and reproductive potential.

Food. Inland cutthroats mostly consume insects and small fish. Coastal cutthroats eat various small fish, shrimp, sandworms, and squid.

Angling. Angling techniques vary with the stream, river, pond, or lake environment, as also occurs with other species. These methods are similar to those used in fishing for other trout, and light tackle is generally appropriate for the smaller inland cutthroats. Cutthroats are aggressive fish, and a wide variety of flies, spoons, spinners, and other lures can be effective.

Sea-run coastal cutthroat can be taken in freshwater in the spring, or during the fall when they enter freshwater to overwinter. They are often caught by anglers fishing for steelhead (see). They stay close to the bottom of deep pools or sloughs, and must be fished close to the bottom. During their migrations, they are caught in their home stream estuary or bays and salt chucks in the vicinity.

Because sea-run coastal cutthroat smolt are large, they are often confused with mature, catchable fish, and some runs have been depleted by overfishing the smolt run. Resident coastal cutthroats can be caught with spinners, spoons, flies, and baits fished deep in pools or along lake shorelines, especially where submerged debris is abundant. Dry or wet flies fished off inlet streams work well. A Muddler Minnow on a fast-sinking line fished along shores with submerged cover is often the best bet. Large trophy-class coastal cutthroat are best caught by trolling hardware or baits off steep shorelines of landlocked lakes.
See: Trout.

Gila Trout

TROUT, GILA *Oncorhynchus gilae.*
Along with the Apache trout (see: trout, Apache), the Gila is one of two native trout in Arizona, both severely threatened. Because of interbreeding with rainbow trout (see: trout, rainbow) and a similarity in appearance to cutthroat trout (see: trout, cutthroat), it wasn't identified as a separate species until 1950.

A member of the Salmonidae family, the Gila trout is an olive yellow to brassy fish with small irregular black spots across its upper body, head, dorsal, and caudal fins. These markings protect the fish from predators. There is an indistinct rose stripe along the side, as well as a yellow "cutthroat" mark under the lower jaw and white or yellow tips on the dorsal, anal, and pelvic fins.

Growing to 18 inches, the Gila trout was originally found in tributaries of the Verde River in Arizona and still lives in small numbers in the headwaters of the Gila River in New Mexico. It prefers clear, cool mountain creeks above 2,000 meters in elevation and feeds on both aquatic and terrestrial invertebrates.
See: Trout.

TROUT, GOLDEN *Oncorhynchus aguabonita.*
Other names—French: *truite dorée.*
California's state fish, the golden trout is classified as two recognizable subspecies, *O. aguabonita aguabonita* of California's South Fork of the Kern River and Golden Trout Creek, and *O. aguabonita gilberti* of the main Kern and Little Kern Rivers; an area of warm water where the South Fork joins the Kern apparently serves as a natural barrier separating the two subspecies. This attractive member of

Golden Trout

the Salmonidae family is highly desirable to anglers; its pinkish flesh is somewhat oily in comparison to that of other trout, but it is firm, finely textured, and delicious, especially when fresh or smoked. The meat does not keep for extended periods and should be cooked soon after capture or well iced and properly packed.

Identification.   The golden trout is considered one of the most beautiful of freshwater gamefish because of its striking coloration and markings; it has a bright red to red orange belly and cheeks, with golden lower sides, a red orange lateral streak, and a deep olive green back. The sides have 10 parr marks centered on the lateral line, and the golden trout is the only salmonid in which these marks remain prominent throughout life. The tail is a brilliant golden yellow and is covered with large black spots that are also scattered across the back and upper sides as well as on the dorsal fins; the front part of the body may have spots above the lateral line on the back and top of the head, but not always. The lower fins are orange to red with no spots, and the dorsal, ventral, and anal fins often have white tips that are sometimes preceded by a broad black band. The golden trout loses its brilliant colors and becomes steely blue when at lower altitudes than its normal habitat. The lateral line has 175 to 210 scales, and there are 17 to 21 gill rakers and an adipose fin.

Size/Age.   The golden trout grows slowly, usually weighing less than a pound, and is capable of reaching seven years of age. The all-tackle world record is an 11-pound Wyoming fish taken in 1948.

Distribution.   In North America, golden trout occur in the upper Kern River basin in Tulare and Kern Counties in California, and has been introduced into Canada as well as the states of Washington, Idaho, and Wyoming, which have developed self-sustaining populations.

Habitat.   Golden trout inhabit clear, cool headwaters, creeks, and lakes at elevations above 6,890 feet.

Life history/Behavior.   Spawning takes place when water temperatures reach about 50°F in early to midsummer. Stream dwellers spawn in their native streams or small tributaries, and lake dwellers spawn in inlets or outlets. Females dig several nests (redds), generally at the tail of a pool, depositing eggs in each and returning to their home pools or lakes afterward.

Many populations are believed to hybridize with cutthroat and rainbow trout, and apparently most trout in the Kern River basin are hybrids of recent origin. The only pure populations of golden trout are those limited to headwater areas.

Food and feeding habits.   Golden trout feed primarily on small crustaceans and adult and immature insects, especially caddisflies and midges.

Angling.   Fishing tactics are similar to those for other trout.
See: Trout.

TROUT, KAMLOOPS
See: Trout, Rainbow.

TROUT, LAKE   *Salvelinus namaycush.*
Other names—laker, mackinaw, Great Lakes trout or charr, salmon trout, landlocked salmon, gray trout, great gray trout, mountain trout, tongue, togue, namaycush or masamaycush, siscowet, fat trout, paperbelly, bank trout, bumper, humper; Cree: *namekus, nemakos, nemeks;* French: *touladi;* Inuit: *iluuraq, isuuraq.*

The lake trout is one of the largest members of the Salmonidae family, which encompasses salmon, trout, charr, and whitefish. This fish is not actually a "trout" but a charr *(see),* and thus a close relative of the brook trout *(see: trout, brook)* and the Arctic charr *(see: charr, Arctic).* It probably should be known as "lake charr," but the whole name game is already confused, and, indeed, some scientists have placed it in a genus of its own *(Cristivomer).*

The lake trout was once associated with many variations, some of which have been termed subspecies or strains; some of these no longer exist, and others are deep dwellers that are not commonly known to anglers. The siscowet *(see)* or siscoet (which has been listed by some sources as *S. siscoet)* is one of these; a deep-dwelling (reportedly from 300 to 600 feet) fish of Lake Superior, it is known as the fat lake trout to commercial fishermen because of its extremely oily flesh.

Of all the charr, the lake trout is the least tolerant of saltwater and is the only freshwater fish ranging into the far north of Canada and Alaska that has apparently not crossed the Bering Strait. There are some northernmost stocks that evidently appear in brackish water, although the brackish water above the Arctic Circle is of low salinity.

Lakers are generally one of the least-accessible freshwater gamefish to most North Americans because of their preference for cold, dark, and mysterious nether depths, or because the greatest numbers exist in far-off or hard-to-access regions of northern Canada. Most of the fish that are geographically available to anglers are deep dwellers and are not regarded as exciting sportfish, at least not in comparison to salmon or stream trout species. This characterization is ill-deserved, however, and is

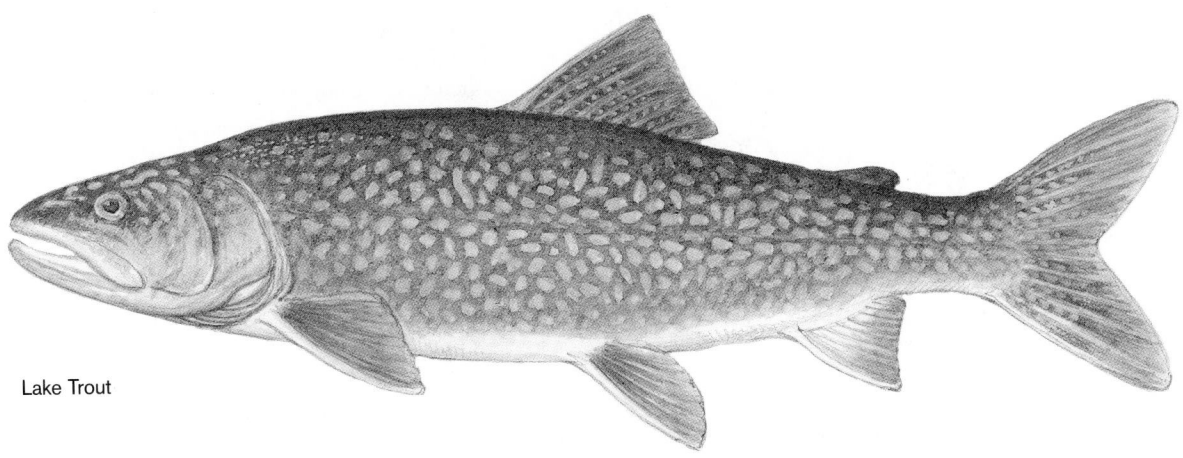

Lake Trout

partially a result of the heavy tackle many anglers traditionally use, the depths from which southerly lakers are often dredged, and the nature of the lakes in which they are found. There is a distinct difference between north-country lakers, which reside in waters that seldom warm up enough to establish a thermocline, and those that live in lakes where the upper strata become quite warm. Fish in the former are strong-pulling, head-shaking runners that give a fine account of themselves in all sizes, and are readily taken on all types of fishing tackle by versatile and accomplished anglers.

The flesh of lake trout varies from creamy white to deep orange and is excellent eating; the more colorful and flavorful fish come from the year-round cold waters of the far north. Historically, the lake has been eagerly sought by commercial fishermen, anglers, and subsistence fishermen. Some subsistence fishing still exists among northern native peoples. Commercial production via gillnetting occurs in winter and summer in northern Saskatchewan and the Northwest Territories. Lake trout flesh has a high fat content and is especially good when smoked. It is principally marketed fresh, or frozen as whole dressed fish and as fillets.

It is extremely vulnerable to pollution, however; this trait, combined with the introduction of the sea lamprey into the Great Lakes through the Welland Canal, had a devastating effect on natural populations. A campaign to control the sea lamprey and the level of pollution has helped restore the stocks in more recent years. Natural mortality is low in most lake trout populations; however, slow growth, alternate-year spawning, and older ages at maturity combine to make lake trout populations susceptible to overharvest by commercial and recreational fisheries. The number of large fish from the far north was severely hurt by overfishing from the 1950s through the early 1970s, and the lakers started to rebound only after conservation measures were enacted. Most of the larger specimens in northern Canada are now fished with single, barbless hooks and are released alive.

Identification. Lake trout have the same moderately elongated shape as trout and salmon, as well as other charr, although they grow much larger than other charr. Extremely heavy specimens have a distended belly and a less elongated shape. Their tail is moderately forked (most people describe it as deeply forked, but in comparison to saltwater fish with truly deeply forked tails, this is incorrect, and certainly incorrect for large specimens), more so than other charr, their scales are minute, and they have several rows of strong teeth, which are weak, less numerous, or absent in other charr. Their head is generally large, although fast-growing stocked fish will have small heads in relation to body size, and there is an adipose fin.

Like other charr the lake trout has white leading edges on all its lower fins and light colored spots on a dark background, instead of the dark spots on a light background which is characteristic of salmon and trout. The body is typically grayish to brownish, with white or nearly white spots which extend onto the dorsal, adipose, and caudal fins. There are no red, black, or haloed spots of any kind.

Coloration is highly variable, depending as it does on seasons and specific populations, and is susceptible to much lighter and much darker variations from the norm. Lighter specimens are often the deep-dwelling fish of light-colored southerly lakes with alewife and smelt forage bases; darker specimens, including some with reddish and orange tones, come from less-fertile, tannin-colored shallow northern lakes. Males and females are similar, but males have a slightly longer, more pointed snout.

The lake trout has been crossed with the brook trout to produce a hybrid known as a splake *(see)*. The hybrid's tail is less deeply forked, and its body markings more closely resemble those of the brook trout.

Size/Age. The lake trout is evidently the second-largest of the salmonids (after chinook salmon), both in a historical and a modern sense (as more large lake trout than large Atlantic salmon exist today). Although the all-tackle world record for lake trout is a 66-pound, 8-ounce fish caught in 1991 at Great Bear Lake, Northwest Territories, larger fish have been caught in that lake since (including a 72-pounder in 1995) that have not

T

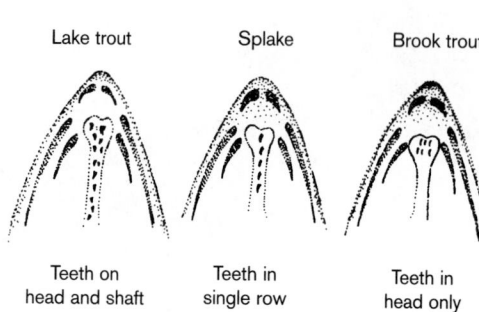

Teeth on Roof of Mouth

Lake trout   Splake   Brook trout

Teeth on   Teeth in   Teeth in
head and shaft   single row   head only

met record-recognition standards. A 102-pound lake trout was netted in Lake Athabasca, Northwest Territories, in 1961, and was 50 inches long; according to legend, a 120-pounder was caught in 1818 in the Great Lakes, although this may not have validity.

In most of its range, a 20-pound lake trout is a very large specimen and is considered a trophy catch; fish from 30 to 45 pounds are caught every season in a few far-northern waters, most of them being released. The average angler catch in most places weighs 4 to 10 pounds.

Lake trout growth and age vary from place to place depending on diet, water temperature, altitude, and genetics. Lake trout in the cold, deep, infertile waters of the north are capable of long life spans. Some grow to 40 to 50 years of age and reportedly can live to age 62. In the more southerly portions of their range, however, they grow more quickly but do not live as long, and in most places they do not live longer than 20 years.

Distribution.   The natural range of the lake trout is across the northern region of North America. It occurs from Quebec, the Maritime Provinces, and Labrador in the east, southerly through New York, and west across the north-central United States and all of Canada to British Columbia and Alaska in the west. It is widely distributed in the Nunavut, Yukon, and Northwest Territories, and in the northern sections of other Canadian provinces, including arctic islands. It has been introduced to northern deep lakes elsewhere in the U.S., as well as in Europe, New Zealand, and South America, and reintroduced to some parts of its native range, including the Great Lakes in North America.

Habitat.   Overall, and especially in the southern portions of its range, or where introduced south of its native range, the lake trout is an inhabitant of cool waters of large, deep lakes. In far-northern regions it may occur in lakes that are generally shallow and that remain cold all season long, and it may occur in either the shallow or deep portions of lakes that have large expanses of deep water. It is also found in large deep rivers, or in the lower reaches of rivers, especially in the far north, although it may also move into the tributaries of large southerly lakes to forage. They rarely inhabit brackish water.

Life history/Behavior.   Lake trout generally spend their entire lives in lakes, staying deep and often near the bottom at cool levels; in some places, including the Great Lakes, this level may exceed 100 feet. In far-northern waters, they may not be very deep even in midsummer, staying from 10 to 30 or 40 feet deep because of cool upper-level temperatures. They often orient to structure, cluster at tributaries, and wander in search of food; and although they are not school species like some of their forage, they are usually found in groups, often of like-size individuals.

Spawning takes place in late summer or early fall over clean, rocky lake bottoms. Rocky shoals or reefs, where they exist, are prominent spawning sites. Males reach the spawning sites several days before the females and use their snouts and fins to clean the substrate. Unlike other salmonids, lake trout do not make nests. Spawning usually takes place at night, with peak activity occurring after dusk. Females release from 400 to 1,200 eggs per pound of body weight, and the eggs hatch early in the following spring. In some populations, spawning occurs every year, whereas in others spawning may occur every other year or less frequently.

Food.   As with other predacious fish, the diet of lake trout varies with the age and size of the fish, locality, and the food available. Food items commonly include zooplankton, insect larvae, small crustaceans, clams, snails, leeches, and various species of fish, including their own kind. Lake trout feed extensively on such other fish such as whitefish, grayling, sticklebacks, suckers, and sculpin in the far north, or cisco, smelt, and alewives elsewhere.

Angling.   In spring, when lake waters are cold, trout are found near the surface and along the shoreline. As the season progresses, lakers go deeper; in waters where the surface temperatures warm considerably, they finally reside beneath the thermocline.

Some early coldwater lake trout fishing is done by casting from shore with spoons, spinners, plugs, and flies, especially along rocky shorelines and around tributaries. Most anglers then and throughout the season fish from a boat, occasionally by casting and jigging, but primarily by trolling. In the winter, ice anglers use jigs, live baits, and dead cut baits.

In most large waters, lakers are predominantly caught by anglers trolling slowly with flashy spoons and diving plugs. Jigging for lake trout is possible, as is casting with spoons, spinners, and flies in northerly locales.

In most places in the southern part of the lake trout's range, trolling for these fish is done at relatively deep levels, below the thermocline, and often near bottom and some form of hard structure (primarily shoals or reefs) from late spring through early fall, especially along dropoffs, around reefs and rocky structures, and along steep rock walls.

Not all trolling for lakers is done at decompression depths. Shallower rocky islands and reefs are prime foraging grounds for lake trout, which move into such spots to feed (even in the summer and even if the water temperature is higher than they generally prefer), then retreat to deep water. Also, early and late in the year are good times to find lake trout in the upper 20 feet of a lake or reservoir if the water temperature is favorable.

Lake trout are one of the most curious of freshwater fish, a fact that can make you more successful at catching them when you know how to appeal to this trait. Lakers may follow a lure a considerable distance, sometimes nudging the lure and sometimes staying just behind it for a long while, like a bird dog. When holding a rod, jerking or pumping the rod tip periodically, as well as dropping it back a few feet or speeding it up momentarily, are tactics that provoke these fish into striking. When rods are set in holders, changes in boat speed, turns, and manipulative boat operation momentarily affect the swimming pattern of a lure, and these are often factors that cause a lake trout to strike. It isn't the faster or slower speed of the lure that draws strikes so much as the change in behavior. Lakers basically like a slow presentation, quite slow, in fact, compared to salmon and other trout.

It is because of the laker's preference for slow-moving lures that the most successful lake trout tactic on the Great Lakes is to run a small plastic wobbling bait (called a Peanut by some) about 12 to 18 inches behind a dodger or cowbell attractor. Some spoons and small diving plugs are also worked in this fashion. In areas where there is a sandy bottom and when fish presumed to be lakers are spotted via sonar on the bottom in deep water (maybe 100 to 150 feet in summer), you can literally set your line by dropping the downrigger weight until it hits bottom, then raise it up a turn. The lead from weight to lure can be very short. Some bottom trollers like to use a banana-shaped downrigger weight for this, incidentally, dragging it right on the bottom.

Although trolling is the foremost method of lake trout fishing, jigging is also effective. Light jigs can provide exciting small lake trout action in north-country rivers, and for schools of small fish that prowl the shorelines of lakes in the evening. Large jigs are occasionally more effective than trolling spoons or plugs where lake trout are abundant. But it is best to limit jigging activities to known lake trout reefs, fishing for bottom-hugging trout that are spotted on sonar, or fishing where you've recently caught lakers. In north-country locales, it's worth jigging at river mouths, to the side of heavy current where a major tributary dumps into a large lake. You can also catch lake trout by casting and retrieving small spinners and spoons, streamer flies, and plugs, primarily in northern locales. In flies, try streamers when fishing in current and in the shallows, and possibly dry flies when small lakers are observed cruising shorelines for mosquitoes in the far north.

A lake trout from Kaminuriak Lake, Nunavut Territory.

Tackle runs the gamut, from deep-trolling hardware to fly, spinning, and baitcasting equipment. Lakers give the best account of themselves on light line, which, because they inhabit open water, is feasible provided you don't need heavy weight to get down to the fish.
See: Charr.

TROUT, QUEBEC RED

This member of the charr (see) was once classified as a separate species with the scientific name *Salvelinus marstoni*. A landlocked, or nonanadromous, charr, and also known as Marston's trout, it was reclassified as a subspecies of the arctic charr (*S. alpinus oquassa*; see: charr, arctic) along with its close relatives the blueback trout (see: trout, blueback) and Sunapee trout (see: trout, Sunapee). The Quebec red trout exists as a remnant population in some waters of eastern Quebec.

TROUT, RAINBOW   *Oncorhynchus mykiss.*

Other names—steelhead, rainbow, 'bow, redsides, Kamloops, redband trout, Eagle Lake trout, Kern River trout, Shasta trout, San Gorgonio trout, Nelson trout, Whitney trout, silver trout; Danish: *regnbueørred;* Finnish: *kirjolohi;* French: *truite-arc-en-ciel;* German: *regenbogenforelle;* Italian: *trota iridea;* Japanese: *nijimasu;* Russian: *forel raduzhnaya;* Spanish: *trucha arco iris;* Swedish: *regnbåge;* Turkish: *alabalik türü.*

Rainbow Trout

The rainbow trout is one of the most widely distributed freshwater fish, and the one member of the Salmonidae family of salmon, trout, whitefish, and grayling that presently has global distribution. Endemic to western North America and now found on six continents, it was reclassified from the trout genus *Salmo* to the Pacific salmon genus *Oncorhynchus* (it was formerly identified as *Salmo gairdneri*), and occurs in both freshwater resident and anadromous, or sea-run, races. Seagoing rainbows, known as steelhead or steelhead trout, are briefly noted here but are reviewed in greater detail under a separate entry *(see: steelhead)*. One landlocked variety of rainbow trout from the interior of British Columbia is called the Kamloops trout, a genetically large strain called Gerrard trout exists in British Columbia's Kootenay Lake and its Lardeau River tributary, and there are many other variations (as well as hatchery created hybrids) of rainbows known.

One of the top freshwater sportfish, the rainbow is tolerant of moderate temperatures, which has allowed it to become available to many anglers around the world; this, plus its beautiful coloration and acrobatic tendencies when hooked, have helped make it a favorite in streams, rivers, and lakes.

The rainbow trout is one of the most heavily cultured species of freshwater fish, both for recreational use and for food production. Although natural populations of rainbows are not commercially fished, the species is pond-reared in North America, Europe, and Asia and sold as frozen whole fish. The flesh ranges from bright red in small lake and stream populations to pink or white in large lake and river populations in which the diet is largely piscivorous, and it has an excellent flavor. Commercial fishing for ocean steelhead, however, which have bright orange red flesh, is of significance, resulting in fresh and frozen market sale.

Identification. Rainbow trout possess the typical elongated and streamlined salmonid form, although body shape and coloration vary widely and reflect habitat, age, sex, and degree of maturity. The body shape may range from slender to thick.

The back may shade from blue green to olive. There is a reddish pink band along each side about the midline that may range from faint to radiant. The lower sides are usually silver, fading to pure white beneath.

Small black spots are present over the back above the lateral line, as well as on the upper fins and tail. In some locations, the black spots of adults may extend well below the lateral line and even cover the entire lower side. The rainbow and its closest relatives in the Pacific salmon group (cutthroat, golden, Apache, and Gila trout) are known as the "blackspotted" trout because they are covered with numerous prominent black spots. These spots may cover the entire body or may be more abundant near the tail. The spots characteristically extend onto the dorsal fin, the adipose fin, and the tail. Those on the tail radiate outward in an even, orderly pattern. Spots may be present on any of the lower fins, and there are never any red spots such as occur on freshwater and spawning specimens of brown trout *(see: trout, brown)* and Atlantic salmon *(see: salmon, Atlantic)*. Rainbow trout are positively identified by the 8 to 12 rays in the anal fin, a mouth that does not extend past the back of the eye, and the lack of teeth at the base of the tongue.

The rainbow trout's coloration varies greatly with size, habitat, and spawning periods. Stream dwellers and spawners usually show the darkest and most vivid colors and markings. River or stream residents normally display the most intense pink stripe coloration and heaviest spotting, followed by rainbows from lake and lake-stream systems. By contrast, the steelhead is silvery and may not have a pink stripe along the middle of its sides.

The rainbow trout readily hybridizes with other "blackspotted" trout, especially with the cutthroat and golden trout, producing fertile offspring with all manner of confusing color combinations and intermediate characteristics. A short-lived but colorful (orange) hatchery-reared rainbow hybrid, crossed with a mutant albino form of golden trout, is called a Palomino trout, and has been widely stocked in Pennsylvania.

The absence of orange red slash marks on the underside of the jaw, and the lack of teeth near the base of the tongue, are good keys for distinguishing rainbows from inland or nonanadromous cutthroat trout *(see: trout, cutthroat)*.

Size/Age. In general, large rainbows are caught in large bodies of water and small ones in streams and ponds. Stream-caught fish commonly weigh a pound or so, whereas fish from larger rivers and lakes commonly weigh between 2 and 4 pounds. Rainbows that have migrated to a large inland lake (called steelhead), such as one of the Great Lakes, may attain double-digit weights, although most weigh 7 to 10 pounds, and sea-run fish likewise become heavyweights. The largest nonanadromous rainbow trout in North America presently come from Alaska and British Columbia waters. World records are kept for all varieties of rainbow trout as one species, meaning that the anadromous form dominates the record books. Rainbows from 20 pounds to more than 30 pounds have been caught, however, and Lake Pend Oreille in Idaho produced a 37-pounder in 1947. Rainbows can live for 11 years but typically have a 4- to 6-year life span.

Distribution. The rainbow trout is native to the West Coast of North America from southern Alaska to Durango, Mexico, and inland as far as central Alberta in Canada and Idaho and Nevada in the United States. It has been extensively introduced across the lower Canadian provinces, throughout the Great Lakes region and the northeastern U.S. to the Atlantic coast and south through the Appalachians to northern Georgia and Alabama, in the western U.S. easterly to western Texas, and sporadically in the central U.S. south of the Great Lakes. It has been transplanted to New Zealand, Australia, South America, Africa, Japan, southern Asia, Europe, and Hawaii. An Asian species known as the Kamchatka trout is believed to be a form of the rainbow trout. It is native to the Amur River in the eastern part of Russia as well as the Kamchatka Peninsula and the Commander Islands.

Habitat. Although rainbows do well in large lakes with cool, deep waters, they prefer moderately flowing streams with abundant cover and deep pools. In most streams they are found in stretches of swift-flowing water, at the edge of strong currents, and at the head of rapids or strong riffles. They prefer water temperatures of 55° to 64°F but can tolerate water to 70°F.

Life history/Behavior. Most varieties of rainbow trout spawn in the spring in small tributaries of rivers, or in inlets or outlets of lakes, but some strains spawn at other times. Rainbow trout usually return to the streams where they hatched.

During late winter or early spring, when water temperatures are on the rise, maturing adult rainbows usually seek out the shallow gravel riffles in

A close look at a rainbow trout from a Colorado pond.

their stream or a suitable clear-water stream that enters their lake. Spawning takes place from late winter or early spring through early summer, depending on the specific location and the severity of the winter. The female uses her tail to prepare a nest (redd) 4 to 12 inches deep and 10 to 15 inches in diameter. From 200 to 8,000 eggs are deposited in the redd, fertilized by a male, and covered with gravel.

Hatching normally occurs from a few weeks to as much as four months after spawning, depending on the water temperature. The tiny fry emerge from the gravel in a week or up to several weeks, again depending on the temperature. On emerging, the small trout assemble in groups and seek shelter along the stream margins or protected lakeshore, feeding on crustaceans, plant material, and aquatic insects and their larvae. Rainbow trout rear in similar habitat for the first two or three years then move into the larger water of lakes and streams and turn more to a diet of fish, salmon carcasses, eggs, and even small mammals.

Age of onset of sexual maturity varies markedly among individuals due primarily to such factors as population density, productivity of the aquatic environment, and genetic makeup. In the wild, male and female spawners as young as ages 3 and 5, respectively, have been found, but a majority of both sexes matures at ages 6 to 7. Spawning frequency ranges from annually to once every three years. Fish that live in large productive lakes generally grow largest and live longer than those of river, stream, or pond environs. In Alaska, rainbow trout that live in or migrate to large lakes with sockeye salmon runs generally grow faster and larger than fish that remain year-round in streams.

Food. Rainbows feed on a variety of food, mainly insects, crustaceans, snails, leeches, and other fish if available. Some studies have shown that they feed less often on the surface than brown trout.

T

Angling. The beauty, strength, endurance, and spectacular leaps of the rainbow trout and all of its variations and strains have endeared it to anglers. It takes lures, flies, and baits well, leaps often, and fights hard no matter what its size, although larger individuals are especially exciting. In rivers that also contain salmon runs, rainbow fishing success is typically greatest in the spring and fall before and after the large salmon runs. Angling methods differ depending on whether the fish are found in rivers or lakes, and are similar to fishing for other trout species. Weighted spinners, wobbling spoons, streamer flies, Muddlers Minnows, and egg-imitation flies fished near the bottom are especially preferred in river and stream habitats.
See: Trout.

Sunapee Trout

TROUT, SUNAPEE

This member of the charr *(see)* was once classified as a separate species with the scientific name *Salvelinus aureolus.* A landlocked, or nonanadromous, charr, it was reclassified as a subspecies of the arctic charr *(S. alpinus oquassa; see: charr, arctic)* along with its close relatives the blueback trout *(see: trout, blueback)* and Quebec red trout *(see: trout, Quebec red).* The common name is derived from a native population of Sunapee Lake in New Hampshire; Sunapee trout there hybridized with lake trout and are no longer believed to exist, and the species is not currently documented in that state. Sunapees do exist in Maine, where there is a remnant population in Flood's Pond, and reintroductions have been made into some other waters.

TROUT, TIGER

A hybrid trout resulting from crossing a female brown trout with a male brook trout.
See: Trout, Brown.

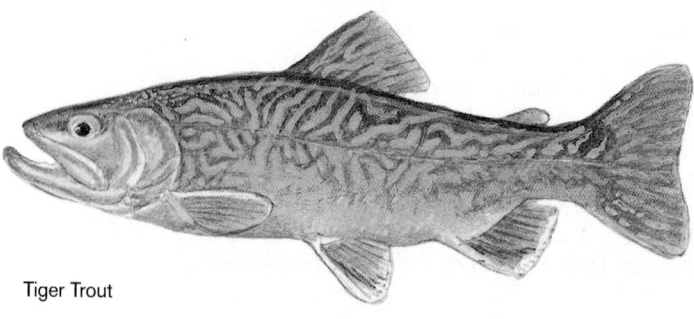

Tiger Trout

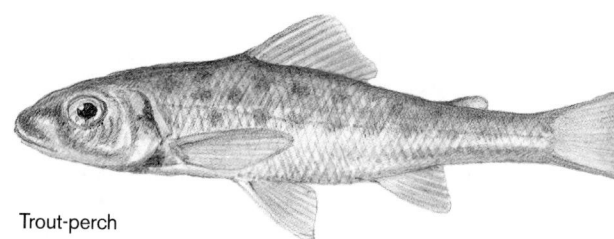

Trout-perch

TROUT-PERCH   *Percopsis omiscomaycus.*
Other names—troutperch, silver chub; French: *omisco.*

A member of the small Percopsidae family, the confusingly named trout-perch is neither a trout nor a perch, nor is it of angling significance, although it is an important forage species for predators.

Identification. The trout-perch derives its name from a superficial resemblance to trout by virtue of having an adipose fin, and to yellow perch or juvenile walleye by its body configuration. It has a fairly deep cylindrical body with a narrow caudal peduncle, large eyes, and a large unscaled head that is flattened on the underside. Its color is transparent yellow olive with silver flecks above, and rows of dusky spots appear along the back and sides. A related species, the sandroller *(P. transmontana),* is smaller and slightly darker, with a more arched back.

Size. This species reaches a maximum length of 6 to 8 inches; 3 to 5 inches is common.

Distribution. The trout-perch ranges from Hudson Bay to the Yukon Territory and from the Potomac River west to Kansas. The sandroller is found in the Columbia River drainage.

Habitat. The trout-perch occurs in lakes, and in the backwaters and pool margins of midsize to large streams. It is primarily a deep-water resident.

Spawning behavior. This species spawns in late spring, usually on sand and gravel sections of tributaries and occasionally on lake sandbars. Most trout-perch die after spawning, although a few fish live to spawn twice.

Food and feeding habits. Trout-perch feed on aquatic insects and small crustaceans, and generally move from deeper water to shallower nearshore areas at night to feed.

Angling. These fish are an important food item for many larger predator fish, but not a source of angler attention. Trout-perch may be used as bait by some anglers, including those pursuing lake trout, although they are not a hardy species and do not keep well in bait buckets. In the northeastern U.S., people dipping for smelt sometimes capture trout-perch.

T-TOP

Center console boats often have no overhead shading or storage feature; the first ones to do so had a console-shading option that was known as a Bimini top. Then someone invented the so-called T-Top. Shaped like the letter "T," T-Tops feature aluminum frames that mount either to the deck or to the console itself, and have an overhead top made of either soft (canvas or polyester material similar to boat covers) or hard (primarily fiberglass) material. The primary purpose of the top is to provide at least minimal protection from the sun and the rain.

T-Tops, especially the hard material models, have become much more functional, and designs exist that also provide a handy spot for mounting antennas, rod holders, spreader lights, and outriggers. Many of these items used to be mounted on the gunwales of a center console, compromising the T-Tops effectiveness as a fishing platform.

Some T-Tops can incorporate a lockable electronics box on the underside, which allows some or all electronics to be positioned away from the console. They can be fitted with weather enclosures, and some models allow vertical rod holding alongside the console.

See: Sportfishing Boat.

TUBE KNOT
A fishing knot for line-to-line connections.
See: Knots, Fishing.

TUBE LURE
(1) A hollow soft plastic body covering a jig.
See: Jig.

(2) A long, slender, hollow trolling lure fashioned from plastic or rubber tubing (once surgical tubing).
See: Trolling Lures, Saltwater; Umbrella Rig.

TUBERCLE
A small hard knob on the skin that appears seasonally on some breeding male fish.

TUCUNARÉ
The Brazilian/Portuguese word for peacock bass *(see: bass, peacock).*

TULLIBEE
A name for cisco *(see),* perhaps derived from the Cree Indian language.

TUNA
Tuna are members of the Scombridae family, which includes mackerel *(see)* and numbers some 50 species in 15 genera. They are schooling fish found throughout the open waters of most of the world's temperate and tropical seas, and are among the most commercially important fish, as they are all good to eat.

Tuna are also great gamefish. Anglers consider them the most powerful gamefish of all, and the largest members of the bluefin tuna species are the strongest of all fish pursued with rod and reel. They are also among the fastest; schools of these swift swimmers may cruise at 30 miles per hour.

All tuna have an especially streamlined body shape, with a pointed head and a much-tapered tail. The large caudal fin is lunate (crescent shaped). The spiny and soft-rayed dorsal fins are separate, the soft-rayed dorsal matched in size and shape by the anal fin directly beneath it. Following each fin is a series of finlets, the number varying with the species. In all species, the scales are extremely small or lacking. Most tuna and mackerel are ocean blue or greenish on the back, grading into silvery on the sides and the belly, but some notable exceptions occur.

Whereas fish are generally cold-blooded, tuna expert and biologist Frank Carey of Woods Hole Oceanographic Institution in Massachusetts determined that tuna are able to maintain a body temperature up to 18°F above that of the surrounding water. Carey concluded that a rise in body temperature effectively triples the power and response of a muscle mass, and explains not only the ability of tuna to seemingly fight forever on light tackle but also their adaptability to both Gulf Stream waters off the Bahamas and frigid Nova Scotian waters.

The unique physiology of tuna is such that they must consume great amounts of food to maintain their constant-swimming lifestyle and fuel the rapid growth characteristic of the tuna. Thus, tuna are likely to be encountered where massive quantities of schooling baitfish are located and feeding can be accomplished with a minimum expenditure of energy. For instance, giant bluefin tuna tend to stay with schools of herring, mackerel, and squid during summer visits to cool northern areas, whereas school bluefins may hang around shoals of sand launce (sand eels), anchovies, and other smaller baitfish off the Mid-Atlantic States. Yet, these eating machines are often no pushovers, as they can also be surprisingly fussy about baits and very line shy.

Angling for tuna is fairly similar throughout most of their range, as they are seldom encountered anywhere but in open water. Trolling with rigged baits and lures, and fishing bait from a drifting or anchored boat, are the major angling methods. A minor amount of casting is done, usually when fish are attracted close to a boat via chumming.

Prominent Species
There are 13 species of tuna, 6 of which are intensively exploited by commercial interests. Most are considered overexploited, and some—especially both species of bluefin tuna—have declined dramatically. The bluefins are relatively slow to mature and are especially vulnerable to overfishing. Albacore and skipjack tuna are the species most frequently sold in cans in the United States; the

T

yellowfin tuna fishery in the eastern Pacific is best known for causing the deaths of porpoises (a k a "dolphins"), which are encircled and then become trapped in the purse seining nets.

Most popular among anglers are members of the *Thunnus* genus, which includes the largest of the true tuna—the bluefin and southern bluefin, yellowfin, and bigeye—as well as the smaller albacore, longtail, and blackfin. The dogtooth tuna grows to about 300 pounds, but this relatively scarce Indo-Pacific species is actually part of the closely related bonito tribe and the only one with an air bladder.

Bluefin tuna.   Perhaps more than any other species, bluefin tuna are categorized in terms of their size, but, unlike most other fish, there is a definite understanding of what these terms mean. The National Marine Fisheries Service (NMFS) has changed what used to be commonly accepted angler definitions of school (under 100 pounds), medium (100 to 400 pounds) and giant (400 pounds up) bluefins. The definitions they now use for management purposes are definitive. Small school bluefins are those under 27 inches curved fork length; these can never be retained. School bluefins are from 27 to 47 inches (about 14 to 66 pounds). Large schoolies range from 47 to 59 inches (66 to 135 pounds), and small mediums from 59 to 73 inches (135 to 235 pounds). All bluefin of these sizes in the U.S. are reserved for angling and cannot be sold. Large medium bluefins are from 73 to 81 inches (235 to 310 pounds), and giants are from 81 inches up. Large medium and giant bluefin can be sold.

Fishing for giant bluefins is fundamentally different from fishing for all other tuna in that the sheer size and power of the fish dictate the use of very heavy tackle. The International Game Fish Association (IGFA) limits sportfishing tackle to 130-pound line, and this was traditionally the standard for giant tuna sportfishing. Some anglers also used 80-pound tackle, but only those seeking records dropped to 50-pound, and they found it almost impossible to boat giants until the IGFA extended the allowable length of double line and leader.

Tackle got much heavier when Japanese fish buyers began paying big money for giants starting in the mid-1970s. Most giant tuna anglers from New Jersey through Maine now use lines even heavier than 130 pounds and "fight" their quarry out of pivoting rod holders by just cranking on the handle of a two-speed lever-drag 130-pound reel. Hardly any of the giants boated during the spring to fall northeastern U.S. season are caught in sporting fashion, as the objective is getting a valuable fish in quickly.

Sporting tackle still prevails during the winter fishery off Hatteras and Morehead City, North Carolina, and will as long as the NMFS continues to prohibit the sale of those fish, which are almost exclusively released. Most winter bluefins are also tagged and provide a wealth of information for scientists. Because those fish are encountered in relatively shallow waters, sometimes less than 90 feet, it's possible to not only fight them on standard 130-pound gear, but also for experienced anglers to release most in 5 to 15 minutes by using heavy drags.

Unlike most other members of the genus, bluefins are basically inshore fish that at times even enter the mouths of large bays, such as Rhode Island's Narragansett Bay. When much more abundant, giant tuna were even regularly caught in ocean fish traps along the northern New Jersey shore. Many popular fishing areas for bluefins, such as the Mud Hole in the New York/New Jersey Bight and Stellwagen Bight in Cape Cod Bay, are within 20 miles of shore. Boats out of North Lake in Prince Edward Island and in the Canso Causeway area of Nova Scotia can start trolling daisy chains of mackerel almost as soon as they leave their docks.

Bluefins are important to anglers along the U.S. Atlantic Coast from North Carolina to the Canadian Maritimes. Many spawning bluefins are encountered by longliners in the Gulf of Mexico during the winter, but few are caught by anglers in those waters. However, there is a traditional trolling fishery for giants off Bimini and Cat Cay in the Bahamas, as those giants head north in the spring. Bluefins also provide a major fishery in the Mediterranean Sea and in the Atlantic around

A giant bluefin comes through the transom door off Provincetown, Cape Cod, Massachusetts.

Spain, although the formerly strong North Sea fisheries have long been depleted.

This fishery is managed by the International Commission for the Conservation of Atlantic Tunas (ICCAT), which has imposed severe restrictions on the depleted western Atlantic bluefin stocks but provides much more liberal regulations on the European and African fisheries, which harvest vast numbers of tiny bluefins as well as giants. Management has been based on a two-stock theory that assumes there is only occasional interchange across the ocean. Extensive tagging, however, now indicates there may be a much more regular interchange, which would dictate a change in regulations.

The same species occurs in the North Pacific Ocean, although it never seems to grow to much more than 500 pounds—as compared to a maximum of about 1,500 pounds in the Atlantic. Sportfishing for tuna started when Charles Holder subdued a 183-pound bluefin off Santa Catalina Island in Southern California in 1898, and the Tuna Club of Avalon record was pushed to 251$\frac{1}{2}$ pounds the next year despite the primitive tackle used during the infancy of big-game fishing. Commercial fishing pressure severely reduced that fishery within a few decades, and bluefins were eventually all but wiped out by purse seiners along the coasts of California and Mexico's Baja California, as the last significant sportfishing catches of even small schoolies by the wide-ranging California sportfishing fleet were made in 1956. The decline of the San Pedro purse seining fleet, however, permitted a return of fair numbers of school bluefins in 1992, and they've built up since then, and ever-larger fish are now encountered.

School bluefins provided a consistent trolling fishery for slow private and charter boats along the mid-Atlantic coast from at least the 1920s, as they rarely had to run more than 20 miles offshore in order to fill their boxes. Large charter fleets developed in such ports as Beach Haven, New Jersey, and Freeport, New York, but most of those boats disappeared after tuna stocks were decimated by purse seining in the 1960s and 1970s, plus an extensive Japanese longlining effort on spawning giants in the Gulf of Mexico during a portion of the same period. Regulations adopted during the 1990s prohibit the sale of bluefins under 225 pounds and impose severe catch limitations on anglers but have failed to return that fishery to even a fraction of the early-1970s level, which was already only a shadow of what existed prior to the 1960s.

The southern bluefin is found worldwide from about 30° to 50° south latitude. It is distinguished from the bluefin only by a difference in the number of gill rakers and by being the only species of *Thunnus* in which the caudal keels are bright yellow. It is most commonly caught in Australia and New Zealand, and doesn't appear to achieve true "giant" sizes of 400 pounds or more.

Yellowfin tuna.   Yellowfins are the most common warmwater tuna, and the most colorful. Indeed, many large yellowfins become particularly distinguished as they grow extremely long second dorsal and anal fins. These fish are often referred to as Allisons and were once thought to be a separate species. Although heavily pursued by purse seiners and longliners, yellowfins have managed to remain reasonably abundant in their ocean haunts. Although not strictly committed to the depths, yellowfins only occasionally wander relatively close to shore. One such exception occurred during the mid-1980s when vast quantities of sand launce (sand eels) lured yellowfins to banks and sloughs within 12 miles of northern New Jersey and Montauk, New York, for several summers. The only area along the U.S. Atlantic coast where they're regularly caught within 30 miles of shore is off the Outer Banks of North Carolina due to the proximity of the Gulf Stream.

A surface fish, yellowfins are a good target for trollers. Canyon anglers usually make their biggest catches by chunking for yellowfins at night and are often able to spot them racing through the slick to pick up chunks.

Most yellowfins are caught in sizes under 100 pounds, but they are common up to 200 pounds and can grow to 400 or more pounds. The largest yellowfins have been encountered by San Diego long-range party boats fishing in the Revillagigedo Islands off the coast of Baja California, Mexico. Specimens exceeding 200 pounds are common during many winter trips, and some in the 300- to 400-pound class are boated.

Bigeye tuna.   Bigeyes are found in warm temperate waters of the Atlantic, Pacific, and Indian Oceans. Although the IGFA maintains separate records for the Atlantic and Pacific, the species is the same. They frequent the depths, particularly during the day, and, unlike other tuna, are rarely seen chasing baits at the surface.

Bigeyes are very strong fighters caught on baits primarily set at depths of 100 feet or more during the night and are irregularly caught by trolling, even at night around a full moon. They are just about as highly regarded as fresh fish by sophisticated Japanese food purveyors, as are medium and giant bluefins.

Anglers tend to troll for them with heavy tackle, such as 80-pound outfits, although most caught in mid-Atlantic canyons are only in the 100- to 250-pound class; any exceeding 300 pounds are exceptional. The maximum size of these fish in the Atlantic appears to be around 400 pounds. A Pacific fishery off Ecuador and Cabo Blanco, Peru, has produced bigeyes exceeding 400 pounds, although the once-large runs in that area have been depleted by commercial fishing.

Its large eyes, which probably facilitate feeding activities in low light deep below the surface, aren't sufficient to differentiate this species from yellowfins in smaller sizes, especially after the fish are dead. Sure identification involves the liver, as there are striations on the margin of the bigeye's liver, and the right and left lobes are about the same size. The yellowfin's liver is smooth, and its right lobe is longer than the middle or left.

Albacore.   Albacore are the only white meat tuna and as such are highly valued by Americans as the finest canned tuna, but Japanese fish processors downgrade them for the same reason. Although much smaller than other members of their genus, these fish are good sport on lighter tackle. Often referred to as longfins, they are easily distinguished by pectoral fins that extend beyond the anal fin and by their somewhat slimmer form.

These oceanic wanderers are most important to anglers in the Pacific, and their summer appearances well off California lure thousands of anglers to the docks. Although Southern California is the focal point for that summer fishery, the migration takes them far north, and they are frequently found within range of boats from Northern California to Washington. El Niño years provide much warmer waters that bring albacore even closer, and can provide an unusual tropical fishery in British Columbia. Not only did that occur in 1997, but much larger than normal albacore were caught, and the 90-pound mark was finally broached off California when those fish should have been long gone, in January 1998. Anglers could thank El Niño for this.

Albacore are also important to canyon anglers in the western North Atlantic. Only a scattered few are normally caught from the more southerly canyons, but large schools tend to show during late summer into early fall from Hudson Canyon east. Anglers also enjoy good fishing for albacore across the Atlantic in the Azores, Canary Islands, and Madeira.

Longtail tuna.   The longtail tuna is more elongated than the southern bluefin and much smaller, with a maximum size possibly around 80 pounds. It is an inshore species of the tropical and subtropical Pacific and the eastern Indian Ocean, and is caught in large schools off the western and northeastern coasts of Australia.

Blackfin tuna.   The blackfin only runs up to about 50 pounds and is most common in the 10- to 30-pound range. It is Florida's primary tuna, and is most abundant from there south to Brazil and also in the Gulf of Mexico and Caribbean Sea. Blackfins are fine light-tackle fish, especially when chummed to the boat with live baits. Charter captains at Islamorada, Florida, specialize in that sport, cast netting hundreds of pilchards that are then distributed on The Hump (a mountain peak in the Gulf Stream) to attract blackfins, which can be hooked on the live baits or sometimes even by flycasters. Another popular but more complicated method involves rigging the wings of dead flyingfish to hold them straight out and then bouncing those baits in and out of the water from outriggers.

Little tunny.   The genus *Euthynnus* includes three tuna species that tend to live closer to shore and are highly regarded as baitfish, although they are generally considered the least palatable of the tuna. The coarse red flesh of the Atlantic's little tunny results in its being looked down on, although it may well be one of the world's finest small gamefish. Indeed, they frequently fight so hard on light tackle that anglers find themselves boating dead or almost dead fish. Little tunny are almost never referred to by their correct name, instead being called false albacore in the northeastern U.S. and "bonito" (confusing them with Atlantic bonito) from Virginia south to the Gulf of Mexico. Identification is never a problem due to the several black spots always present under the pectoral fin.

Although they spread themselves out over the continental shelf, little tunny are most abundant within 30 miles of shore during a late-summer to early-fall run along the mid-Atlantic and southern New England coasts, when they average 5 to 15 pounds. Unlike the other tuna, the little tunny commonly chases baits into the surf and can be caught by surf casters retrieving small metal lures and jigs at high speed. Many are also caught by trollers seeking school tuna and in chum lines intended for bluefish. The same species is encountered south to Brazil and across the Atlantic to Europe and the Mediterranean and down to South Africa.

Black skipjack.   The black skipjack is the eastern Pacific version of the little tunny. Primarily found from California to Peru, it is often conveniently available in large schools at black marlin hotspots such as Hannibal Bank and Piñas Reef in Panama, where ideal-size live baits in the 2- to 4-pound class will swim for hours when rigged Australian-style. The third very similar member of the genus is the kawakawa, which is primarily found in the western Pacific and Oceania. All three species would be considered large when weighing in the midteens, and they grow to a maximum of about 35 pounds in the case of the little tunny.

Skipjack tuna.   The skipjack tuna (not to be confused with the black skipjack) is the lone member of the genus *Katsuwonus,* and has also suffered from name misidentification over the years with such misnomers as arctic bonito and oceanic bonito—even though it's a tuna, not a bonito. It is readily identified by the stripes along its belly, which are unique in the clan. This fine gamefish is widely distributed in temperate and tropical seas, and often travels in huge schools, making it a favorite of purse seiners, who capture it for cannery conversion into chunk light tuna. Despite that, many anglers turn their noses up at the softer skipjacks as being less desirable than most other tuna. Anglers catch skipjacks primarily while trolling. They are quite common from 5 to 15 pounds but may run as large as 50 pounds.

Sportfishing Techniques

Anglers pursue tuna by many means around the globe, but their basic physical characteristics largely determine the methodology. For instance, trolling occurs almost invariably at as high a speed as will work the lures or baits correctly. An exception involves the spreader bar rigs that have become popular for medium and giant bluefins in the northeast U.S. They're trolled somewhat slower than other tuna lures due to the action provided by multiple mackerel or artificial squid splashing on the surface. Live baits also can be trolled as slowly as necessary to keep them alive, and the same applies to live or dead baits fished from downriggers.

The vast majority of tuna trolling, however, involves rigged baits or lures being trolled at speeds of 6 to 8 knots or more. It's probably impossible to run away from a tuna that wants to eat at any speed at which that bait or lure can be kept in the water. High-speed trolling is particularly effective, as most species of tuna seem to be attracted by wakes and possibly engine noise. Some lures should always be placed in the whitewater very close to the boat and pinned down to stay there. Feathers and cedar jigs are ideal for that purpose. The wakes created by some boats seem to produce more tuna than others, and theories abound as to what the reason might be.

Trolling can be "blind" in areas where tuna should be present, or directed to surface schooling fish. Most of the yellowfin, bigeye, and albacore tuna trolled in U.S. East Coast canyons (100-fathom dropoffs at the edge of the continental shelf far offshore) are caught by blind trolling, especially where baits are marked and around temperature breaks. The arrival of a Gulf Stream eddy usually ensures a tuna bite.

In areas without such "structure," trollers often depend on sightings in order to focus their efforts. This is particularly the case with yellowfin tuna in the Pacific, as those fish associate with porpoises, a fact purse seiners learned long ago. Invariably, those feeding tuna are moving at a high rate of speed, and boaters may have a hard time keeping up with them.

Balao and large squid make good natural trolling baits. Straight-running high-speed offshore trolling lures work well for larger tuna; jethead versions are particularly favored for bigeyes. Lure sizes are scaled down for smaller specimens of large tuna as well as the smaller species, but even the largest tuna sometimes prefer short lures if they're feeding on similar-looking baits. Plugs that can be run at relatively high trolling speeds are also effective.

The lack of an air bladder is also a clue to hooking on bait. Anyone who has watched tuna feeding alongside understands that no matter how much bait is provided, tuna always move through at a steady swimming pace. There is no such thing as a tuna "nibble." They either suck in or reject a bait as they swim through. Thus, it's possible to

Swirls and boils in the water off this boat's transom are made by frenzied school tuna ripping through bait and chum.

instantly hook a tuna by coming tight when it hits. Dropping back to those fish may result in deeper hooking, if that's the object, provided that the tuna doesn't spit the bait first if it feels something is wrong.

Chumming (see) is a popular method of attracting tuna in many areas. In some cases it's accomplished with ground-up fish that forms a slick. Tuna seem to be more attracted to meat than scent, however, so chunking with pieces of baitfish tends to be more effective. Chunking is the primary means of catching bluefins in the northeast U.S., from schoolies, which are sought primarily for sport and food in the Mid-Atlantic States, to giants, which are big business in New England for shipment at very high prices to Japan.

Chumming is also the basic method of yellowfin tuna fishing on Challenger and Argus Banks off Bermuda. Long-range party boat anglers from San Diego who used to fish yellowfins exclusively with live baits, found during the 1990s that chunking was sometimes more effective, particularly for the largest fish.

At first it would seem that tuna would be reluctant to eat dead baits in a chum line. But these fish have learned to adapt and frequently are found feeding on fish spilling out of trawler nets or being thrown overboard by commercial vessels as unmarketable. Bluefins are particularly noted for this tendency, and they rarely display any selectivity in eating everything provided free. It's only when a heavy hook and leader are attached to one of those baits that tuna become selective. Frequently they'll run through the chum line picking up every scrap of even old rotten fish while leaving the freshest item in the selection—the one with a hook in it that isn't drifting down at the correct rate.

The general rule in tuna chunking is to drop over just a few chunks and wait until the current carries them out of sight before repeating the procedure. Baited lines may be worked in the chum line by being dropped back with the chunks and fed out for a couple of hundred feet, after which it will be well below the chunks. Other lines are set at various depths with the aid of sinkers and held in place with floats. The depth selected may be based on recent experience, or by viewing marks on sonar. Many professionals use scanning sonar as well as conventional recorders in order to pinpoint tuna movements and bait placement. In earlier days, this was accomplished with a spool of 4-pound monofilament line tied to a bait and fed back into the slick where a tuna would surely grab it on such light line and give away its presence.

Anglers use a great variety of dead baits. Butterfish and menhaden are the most likely choices in the Mid-Atlantic, whereas New England anglers use mostly the herring and mackerel that attract giants to that area during the summer. These baits may be used whole or cut. When giant tuna are fussy, anglers often resort to a mousetrap rig in which a cable leader is bundled up on a short-shanked hook and secured with a rubber band or shrink tape before being sewn into the bait. The small teeth of tuna wear down leaders during the course of a long fight, but the cable eliminates that problem, and the mousetrap rig permits elimination of a heavy leader that could spook fish. Most tuna anglers are turning to fluorocarbon leaders in order to overcome the visibility factor with 300-pound mono leaders.

Any sort of small live bait found in the area is desirable. Mackerel, harbor pollock, silver hake (whiting), red hake (ling), menhaden (bunker), and bluefish are most commonly used in the northeastern U.S. Live baits are also used as chum in situations where large quantities can be obtained and kept. For instance, anglers fishing out of Southern California have long gone to sea with livewells full of anchovies to be tossed at schools of yellowfin tuna. Long-range party boats from San Diego also jig up quantities of mackerel and scad, which may be used in smaller quantities as chum in addition to live baits. Commercial fishermen at Madeira net mackerel at night and then chum with them during the day to raise bigeye tuna to their live mackerel offerings.

Relatively few tuna are caught on lures that are cast, but that method is very exciting and seems to be gaining popularity. Casting usually involves spotting surfacing schools of tuna and getting ahead of them to make a cast. Popping and swimming plugs that can be retrieved at a rapid pace are ideal for this method, which is becoming more common off Virginia and North Carolina. Watching a school of tuna attack a popper is among the greatest thrills in fishing. When tuna are feeding in chum lines, it's often possible to stir them up with a popping or darting plug, and that is frequently done with yellowfins in Bermuda.

Various types of jigs can also be worked effectively for tuna. Anglers in the northeastern U.S.

catch many school and medium bluefins on diamond jigs. The usual method involves a fast retrieve, but the flutter of a falling diamond jig is often sufficient to attract tuna strikes when the lure is simply moved up and down in long sweeps at a level where the depth recorder indicates the fish are coming through.

Tackle for tuna fishing runs the gamut, from the heaviest gear to almost ultralight. Sportfishing for giant tuna almost invariably involves fighting them out of a fighting chair with 130-pound tackle, but a few have been caught when the angler was standing up—particularly during the winter fishery at Hatteras, where the abundance of tuna and relatively shallow water create a perfect opportunity for such an achievement.

Stand-up tackle (see: stand-up fishing) suitable to handle all but the largest of tuna was developed aboard San Diego long-range party boats, where anglers often fight yellowfins well over 200 pounds at anchor. The long, parabolic trolling rods that were once pressed into service for stand-up fishing worked against the angler, creating lots of back strain without putting enough pressure on the fish. Those Californians created short rods ($5\frac{1}{2}$ to 6 feet) with extended foregrips and tip action. This innovation brought the bend of the flexed rod almost back to the upper hand, putting leverage in the angler's favor. These rods, combined with dual-gear-ratio reels and rod belts and harnesses that are worn low and transfer pressure to the thighs, have made it possible for stand-up anglers to battle tuna to well over 300 pounds with fair success and a good chance of staying out of the hospital.

Trolling tackle for large tuna other than giants usually involves 50- and 80-pound outfits. That gear may be too heavy for the average catch, but most anglers want to be ready for the occasional large yellowfin or bigeye. In areas closer to shore, it's much sportier to troll with 20- and 30-pound outfits for smaller tuna such as school bluefins and yellowfins or blackfins, which may be mixed with such species as little tunny, skipjacks, bonito, dolphin, and king mackerel.

Light spinning and baitcasting tackle is perfect for chumming little tunny and skipjacks, and is still sufficient for handling most school tuna. Those fish are often leader shy, and it may be necessary to drop to 20-pound leaders to get strikes.

Tuna are difficult to catch on fly tackle due to their high-speed lifestyle. Even when it's possible to cast to moving tuna, it's hard to strip fast enough to interest them. The best bet for hooking up is in chum slicks, as the fish are then concentrated for each cast and they can occasionally be worked into such a competitive feeding frenzy with chunks that just about any fly flipped out to them will be inhaled immediately.

It is frequently necessary to run after large tuna to prevent reels from being stripped. Skippers fishing at anchor, particularly for giants, utilize an

T

One of the earliest laws regulating the taking of fish was the 1678 Virginia regulation that banned the attraction of fish with lights.

anchor ball that permits them to cast off their anchor within seconds in order to both follow the fish and avoid getting cut off or tangled in their own anchor line. Anglers who try to fight giants with their arms rarely last long. The technique from a chair uses the legs and lower back in a seat harness with a sliding motion across the chair to retrieve line.

The stand-up technique for large tuna works best with a short stroke, raising the rod only a few inches to gain line rather than lifting it overhead. The idea is to keep the tuna's head up and coming steadily, whereas the long stroke allows the tuna to get his head down no matter how fast the angler thinks he's reeling. Mastering the short-stroke technique can change excruciatingly long, painful battles with tuna into relatively short, pleasant ones.

Unless tuna are to be released, they are normally gaffed. As tuna don't jump or do anything unusual except continue to forge ahead when wired alongside, straight gaffs work well on them. Some anglers do prefer flying gaffs for large tuna, and most giant tuna pros now use cockpit harpoons (which aren't legal under IGFA standards) to ensure their capture.

Although the tuna remains a fish that is sought as much for its flesh as for sport, release fishing is increasing steadily in popularity even for this species. Tagging makes releasing fish even more worthwhile, and anglers are urged to participate in U.S. government programs that provide free tags. For Atlantic waters, contact Cooperative Tagging Center, NMFS/NOAA, Southeast Fisheries Center, 75 Virginia Beach Dr., Miami, FL 33149. For Pacific waters, contact Cooperative Marine Gamefish Tagging Program, NMFS/NOAA, Southwest Fisheries Center, P.O. Box 271, La Jolla, CA 92038.

Other Issues

Identifying tuna. There is often confusion about tuna species, especially those of small to intermediate size. Some external clues do exist that aid in making a quick identification, which may be necessary to enable the release of specific species and to comply with existing regulations. Most external clues involve fin length.

If the pectoral fin, when held flush to the side of the tuna's body, ends well before the origin of the second dorsal fin, the fish is probably a bluefin tuna. If the pectoral fin extends to or past the origin of the second dorsal fin, it is likely either a bigeye or yellowfin. A tuna with extremely long pectoral fins, extending beyond the origin of the anal fin, is most likely an albacore. A tuna exceeding 40 pounds with extremely long anal and second dorsal fins is most likely a yellowfin.

Other clues are useful only after the species has been landed and is dead. This includes counting the gill rakers on the first gill arch and observing the liver for its shape and presence of striations. Headed and gutted yellowfin tuna have a distinct, white, fleshy round node (like a fleshy cord) that runs along the top of the body cavity from front to rear. This is absent in bigeye and bluefin.

Headed and gutted bluefin tuna have a distinct pocket that can be felt by running a hand along the inside of the body cavity underneath the insertion of the pectoral fin. Yellowfin and bigeye tuna do not have this indentation in their body cavity.

Measurements. For some regions where tuna are found (especially the western Atlantic), total curved fork length is the sole criterion for determining the size class of whole (head on) tuna for regulatory purposes. Curved fork length means a measurement of the length of a tuna taken in a line tracing the contour of the body from the tip of the upper jaw to the fork of the tail, which abuts the upper side of the pectoral fin and the upper side of the caudal keel. When determining this length, the measuring tape must pass over (and touch) the pectoral fin and the caudal keel.

Atlantic tuna permits. Bluefin, bigeye, yellowfin, skipjack, albacore, and blackfin tuna, as well as bonito, are all regulated in U.S. waters of the western Atlantic. All owners/operators of commercial, charter, head boat, and recreational vessels harvesting regulated Atlantic tuna must obtain an Atlantic Tunas Permit issued by NMFS. These permits are issued in six categories, five of which are assigned as "commercial" permits: General, Charter/Head Boat, Harpoon Boat, Purse Seine, and Incidental Catch. The remaining permit category, Angling, is for recreational catches.

Only one category is assigned to a vessel. Atlantic tuna may be sold only by those permitted in commercial categories and may be sold only to permitted dealers. Atlantic tuna taken by persons aboard Angling category vessels may not be sold. Thus, charter boats may fish in a "recreational manner" for tuna, but they are classified as commercial vessels if it is their intent (which it is for many) to sell their catch. The propriety of doing this, of course, is questionable, especially when it is the angling community that clamors most for management of the fisheries and restrictions that would help rebuild stocks.

See: Albacore; Big-Game Fishing; Offshore Fishing; Skipjack, Black; Tuna, Bigeye; Tuna, Blackfin; Tuna, Bluefin; Tuna, Dogtooth; Tuna, Longtail; Tuna, Skipjack; Tuna, Southern Bluefin; Tuna, Yellowfin; Tunny, Little.

TUNA, BIGEYE *Thunnus obesus.*
Other names—bigeyed tuna, bigeye tunny; French: *patudo, thon obèse;* Hawaiian: *ahi;* Indonesian: *taguw, tongkol;* Italian: *tonno obeso;* Japanese: *mebachi, mebuto;* Portuguese: *albacora bandolim, atum patudo, patudo;* Spanish: *albacora, atún ojo grande, patudo.*

Like other tuna, the bigeye is a member of the Scombridae family and a strong-fighting species

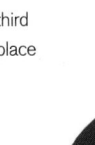 Ninety-seven percent of the earth's supply of water is contained in the oceans; in North America, approximately one third of all fishing takes place in saltwater.

Bigeye Tuna

that is equally revered for sport as for its flesh. The meat of large bigeyes is as favored as that of medium and giant bluefin tuna.

Identification. A stocky body and large eyes characterize this species. Generally, there are no special markings on the body, but some specimens may have vertical rows of whitish spots on the venter. The first dorsal fin is deep yellow. The second dorsal fin and the anal fin are blackish brown or yellow and may be edged with black. The finlets are bright yellow with narrow black edges. The tail does not have a white trailing edge like that of the albacore.

The pectoral fins may reach to the second dorsal fin. The second dorsal and anal fins never reach back as far as those of large yellowfin tuna (see: tuna, yellowfin). It has a total of 23 to 31 gill rakers on the first arch. The margin of the liver is striated. The two dorsal fins are close-set, the first having 13 to 14 spines and the second 14 to 16 rays. The anal fin has 11 to 15 rays. On either side of the caudal peduncle is a strong lateral keel between two small keels that are located slightly farther back on the tail. The scales are small except on the anterior corselet. The vent is oval or teardrop shaped, not round as in the albacore.

At one time the bigeye was not recognized as a separate species but considered a variation of the yellowfin tuna. They are similar in many respects, but the bigeye's second dorsal and anal fins never grow as long as those of the yellowfin. In the bigeye tuna, the margin of the liver is striated and the right lobe is about the same size as the left lobe; in the yellowfin tuna, the liver is smooth and the right lobe is clearly longer than either the left or the middle lobe.

Size. Bigeyes are normally found from 16 to 67 inches in length but may attain 75 inches. They usually exceed 100 pounds in weight in U.S. waters. The all-tackle world record is a 435-pound

fish caught off Peru in 1957. Although separate angling records are kept for bigeyes occurring in the Atlantic and Pacific, they are the same species.

Distribution/Habitat. Found in warm temperate waters of the Atlantic, Indian, and Pacific Oceans, this schooling, pelagic, seasonally migratory species is suspected of making rather extensive migrations. Schools of bigeye tuna generally run deep during the day, whereas schools of bluefin, yellowfin, and some other tuna are known to occasionally swim at the surface, especially in warm water.

Spawning behavior. Bigeye tuna reach sexual maturity at about 40 to 50 inches in length and spawn at least twice a year. This occurs throughout the year in tropical waters, peaking during summer months.

Food. The diet of bigeyes includes squid, crustaceans, mullet, sardines, small mackerel, and some deep-water species. They frequent the depths, particularly during the day, and, unlike other tuna, are rarely seen chasing baitfish at the surface.

Angling. Bigeyes are strong fighters and are caught on baits primarily set at depths of 100 feet or more during the night. Anglers irregularly catch them by trolling, even at night around a full moon. Fishing methods include trolling deep with squid, mullet, or other small baits, plus artificial lures, and live-bait fishing in deep water.

See: Big-Game Fishing; Offshore Fishing; Tuna.

TUNA, BLACKFIN   *Thunnus atlanticus.*

Other names—Bermuda tuna, blackfinned albacore, deep-bodied tunny; French: *bonite, giromon, thon nuit;* Japanese: *mini maguro, monte maguro, taiseiyo maguro;* Spanish: *albacora, atún aleta negra.*

A member of the Scomberidae family and one of the smaller tuna, the blackfin is primarily a sportfish with minor commercial interest. Found

Blackfin Tuna

on or near the surface, it is readily caught on light tackle and is a strong fighter whose flesh is of good quality and flavor.

Identification. The pectoral fins of the blackfin tuna reach to somewhere between the twelfth dorsal spine and the origin of the second dorsal fin, but they never extend beyond the second dorsal fin as in the albacore *(see)*. There is a total of 19 to 25 (usually 21 to 23) gill rakers on the first arch (15 to 19 are on the lower limb), which is fewer than in any other species of *Thunnus*. The finlets are uniformly dark, without a touch of the bright lemon yellow usually present in those of other tuna, and they may have white edges. Light bars alternate with light spots on the lower flanks. The first dorsal fin is dusky; the second dorsal and anal fins are also dusky with a silvery luster. The back of the fish is bluish black, the sides are silvery gray, and the belly is milky white. A small swim bladder is present. The ventral surface of the liver is without striations, and the right lobe is longer than the left and center lobes.

Size. Blackfin tuna may attain a maximum length of 40 inches, although they are common at about 28 inches and weigh in the 10- to 30-pound range. The all-tackle world record is a 45-pound, 8-ounce Florida fish.

Distribution/Habitat. Blackfin are a pelagic, schooling fish that occurs in the tropical and warm temperate waters of the western Atlantic from Brazil to Cape Cod, including the Caribbean and the Gulf of Mexico. They are most common from North Carolina south, and are Florida's most abundant tuna.

Spawning behavior. The blackfin's spawning grounds are believed to be well offshore. Off Florida, the spawning season extends from April through November with a peak in May; in the Gulf of Mexico, it lasts from June through September.

Food and feeding habits. The diet of blackfin tuna consists of small fish, squid, crustaceans, and plankton. Blackfin often feed near the surface, and they frequently form large mixed schools with skipjacks.

Angling. An excellent light-tackle species, the blackfin can be taken by trolling or casting small lures, flies, or natural baits, including ballyhoo, mullet, and other small fish, as well as strip baits, spoons, feathers, jigs, or plugs. They are also pursued by chumming or live-bait fishing from boats at the surface of deep waters 1 to 2 miles offshore. A popular method employed in the Florida Keys involves rigging the wings of dead flyingfish to hold them straight out and then bouncing those baits in and out of the water from outriggers.

See: **Big-Game Fishing; Offshore Fishing; Tuna.**

TUNA, BLUEFIN   *Thunnus thynnus.*

Other names—Atlantic bluefin tuna, northern bluefin tuna, tunny fish, horse-mackerel; Arabic: *tunna;* Chinese: *cá chan, thu;* French: *thon rouge;* Italian: *tonno;* Japanese: *kuromaguro;* Norwegian: *sjorjf, thunfisk;* Portuguese: *atum, rabilha;* Spanish: *atún aleta azul, atun rojo;* Turkish: *orkinos.*

The bluefin tuna is the largest member of the Scombridae family and one of the largest true bony fish. A pelagic, schooling, highly migratory species, it has enormous commercial value, especially in large sizes. It is of great recreational interest, albeit only to the relative few who have the means and equipment to venture to appropriate offshore environs.

The red flesh of the bluefin has made the species coveted for food, especially in Japan, where giant specimens are sold at daily auction for prices far greater than those demanded for other species, especially late in the season when the meat contains the most fat. To date, the largest price paid for a single Atlantic bluefin was U.S. $90,000 at the Tokyo market, making this species the most economically

T

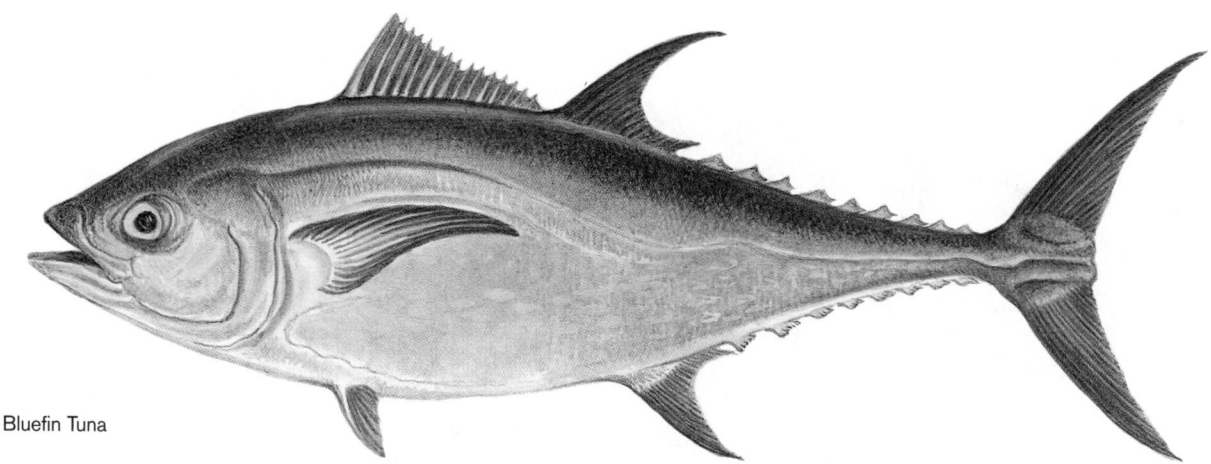

Bluefin Tuna

T

valuable wild animal on the planet. Bluefin tuna are prepared for consumption in many ways but are most commonly associated with sushi and sashimi.

High demand for its dark red flesh has made the bluefin tuna the object of intense commercial and recreational fishing efforts and has resulted in a dwindling population of adult fish. This species, as well as its cousin the southern bluefin tuna *(see: tuna, southern bluefin),* is gravely overfished, and its numbers have declined dramatically in the western Atlantic, the eastern Atlantic, and the Pacific. According to some estimates, the population of the species in the western Atlantic has declined by roughly 87 percent since 1970. The southern bluefin tuna population may have declined by as much as 90 percent. Commercial fisheries continue to be active in the Bay of Biscay, off the Iberian Peninsula, in the Mediterranean, and off North America. Fisheries in the North Sea and off South America have collapsed.

Because both species are slow to mature, they are especially vulnerable to overexploitation. Although some catch quotas have been established, the continued landing of small bluefins as well

as large ones (called giants) in some regions, the failure to restrict harvest in others, the ignorance of restrictions by commercial fishermen of some countries, the lack of punishment or enforcement, and the managerial treatment of bluefins on a separate two-stock basis instead of one interpolar migratory one are leading reasons for both species of bluefin tuna to be further troubled if not endangered. In 1996, scientists warned that existing worldwide catch quotas would have to be cut by 80 percent for populations to recover in 20 years, but they were raised instead.

Identification. The bluefin tuna has a fusiform body, compressed and stocky in front. It can be distinguished from almost all other tuna by its rather short pectoral fins, which extend only as far back as the eleventh or twelfth spine in the first dorsal fin. There are 12 to 14 spines in the first dorsal fin and 13 to 15 rays in the second. The anal fin has 11 to 15 rays. It has the highest gill raker count of any species of *Thunnus,* with 34 to 43 on the first arch. The ventral surface of the liver is striated, and the middle lobe is usually the largest.

The back and upper sides are dark blue to black with a gray or green iridescence. The lower sides are silvery, marked with gray spots and bands. The anal fin is dusky and has some yellow. The finlets are yellow and edged with black. The caudal keel is black at the adult stage but is semitransparent when immature.

Size/Age. Bluefin tuna can grow to more than 10 feet and are commonly found at lengths from 16 to 79 inches. Adults weigh from 300 to 1,500 pounds, although fish exceeding 1,000 pounds are rare. The all-tackle world record is a fish from Nova Scotia that weighed 1,496 pounds when caught in 1979. The species reportedly can live for 40 years.

Distribution/Habitat. Bluefin tuna occur in subtropical and temperate waters of the north Pacific Ocean, the North Atlantic Ocean, and in the Mediterranean and Black Seas. They are widely distributed throughout the Atlantic. Distribution

A small bluefin tuna from the offshore waters of Montauk, New York.

in the western Atlantic occurs along Labrador and Newfoundland southward to Tobago, Trinidad, Venezuela, and the Brazilian coast; they are especially encountered by anglers off Nova Scotia and Prince Edward Island; Cape Cod; Montauk, New York; the canyons offshore of New York and New Jersey; the North Carolina region; and the Bahamas. Distribution in the eastern Atlantic extends as far north as Norway and Iceland, and as far south as northern West Africa. Atlantic bluefin tuna spawn in the Gulf of Mexico between April and June and in the Mediterranean Sea in June and July.

Life history/Behavior. Bluefin tuna are warm blooded and able to maintain their body temperatures up to 18°F above the surrounding water, which makes them superbly adapted to temperate and cold waters. They retain 98 percent of muscular heat, may have the highest metabolism of any known fish, and are among the fastest and most wide-ranging animals on earth. When hunted or hunting, they can accelerate to 35 miles per hour.

Bluefins are schooling fish and do congregate by size, although the largest schools are formed by the smallest individuals, and the smallest schools are composed of the largest fish. They swim in a single file, side by side (soldier formation), or in an arc (hunter formation). Sometimes bluefins swim below a school of yellowfin tuna, relying on the skittish yellowfin to alert them of predators.

Extensive migrations appear to be tied to water temperature, spawning habits, and the seasonal movements of forage species. Specimens tagged in the Bahamas have been recaptured as far north as Newfoundland and Norway and as far south as Uruguay. In some cases, the recaptured fish had traveled 5,000 miles in 50 days. The giants of the species make the longest migrations.

During spawning, a giant female may shed 25 million or more eggs. Larvae have one chance in 40 million of reaching adulthood eight years later, but the survivors grow rapidly and may be 2-feet long and weigh 9 pounds by the end of their first year. By age 14 they may be more than 8-feet long and weigh 700 pounds.

Bluefins in the western Atlantic are sexually mature at approximately age 8 (80 inches curved fork length), and in the eastern Atlantic at about age 5 (60 inches).

Food. The diet of bluefin tuna consists of squid, eels, and crustaceans, as well as pelagic schooling fish such as mackerel, flyingfish, herring, whiting, and mullet.

Angling. Bluefins are not flashy fighters that jump out of the water like other highly prized species; however, they are tractor-pull strong and capable of great speeds. Fishing methods include stillfishing or trolling with live or dead baits such as mackerel, herring, mullet, or squid; and trolling with artificial lures, including spoons, plugs, or feathers.

See: **Big-Game Fishing; Offshore Fishing; Tuna.**

TUNA, DOGTOOTH *Gymnosarda unicolor.*
Other names—white tuna, scaleless tuna, lizard-mouth tuna, jackass, pegtooth tuna; Arabic: *moak-aba, tomad;* French: *bonite à gros yeux, thon blanc;* Japanese: *isomaguro, tokakin;* Spanish: *casarte ojón;* various South Pacific Islands: *vau, atu, kidukidu, dadori.*

This generally lesser-known member of the Scombridae family has minor commercial value and is often an incidental catch for anglers. It is good table fare and has white flesh, which causes it to be named "white tuna" in some places.

Identification. The dogtooth tuna is noted for its lack of scales (except on the corselet and along either side of the lateral line) and for its large conical teeth—features that have earned it the names "scaleless tuna" and "dogtooth tuna" respectively, although it is actually a bonito. The first dorsal fin has 13 to 15 spines; the second is higher and has 12 to 14 rays followed by 6 to 7 dorsal finlets. The anal fin has 12 to 13 rays. There are 11 to 14 gill rakers on the first arch. The lateral line is prominent and wavy, ending in a keel on the caudal peduncle.

The dogtooth is the only bonito that has a swim bladder and a large, single interpelvic process. It is similar to the Australian *Cybiosarda* in having two patches of teeth on the tongue. There are no dark stripes or spots on the body. The second dorsal and anal fins are tipped with white.

Size. The all-tackle world record is a fish that weighed 288 pounds, 12 ounces and was taken off Korea in 1982.

Distribution/Habitat. The dogtooth tuna inhabits tropical and subtropical areas of the Indian and western Pacific Oceans around coral reefs. It occurs from East Africa through the Red Sea to the Philippines and sporadically in southern Japanese waters, as well as around Australia, New Guinea, the Marshall Islands, the Society Islands, the Marquesas, Fiji, and other islands in the South Pacific. It is a pelagic and migratory species but is known to enter inshore waters during the warm season. It may be solitary or travel in small groups of six or less individuals.

Food. This species is usually found around coral reefs, channels, passes, or rocky areas, where it feeds extensively on reef fish. It also consumes mackerel, squid, and various pelagic schooling fish.

Angling. Like many of its relatives, the dogtooth makes a searing, long, fast run when first hooked, followed by a deep, circling, tough fight. It

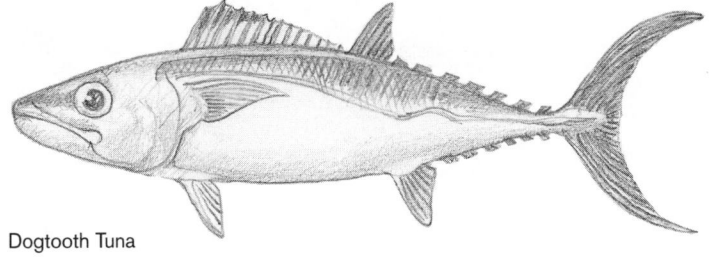
Dogtooth Tuna

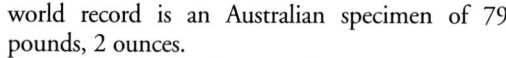

A dogtooth tuna from Ujong Kulong, Indonesia.

world record is an Australian specimen of 79 pounds, 2 ounces.

Distribution/Habitat.   This species occurs in the tropical and subtropical central Pacific Ocean, and in the Indo-west Pacific region. Although largely coastal, it avoids low-salinity areas near the mouths of rivers. It is also seasonally migratory, occurring in large feeding schools off the western and northeastern coasts of Australia. Smaller schools occur off the coasts of India.

Food and feeding behavior.   The diet of longtail tuna consists of a wide variety of crustaceans, squid, and fish, including hardyheads and garfish. Longtail tuna are often observed making dashing bursts through dense shoals of baitfish, showering spray as they do so.

Angling.   Longtails are sometimes extremely aggressive and at other times frustratingly difficult to catch. Large schools are sometimes prevalent, and they may appear from nowhere to strike baits and lures. The fight is a tough one, both on the surface and deep down.

Anglers can work concentrations of fish by casting with lures or flies, and chumming helps brings boiling masses of fish to the surface. Trolling with live or dead baits and with lures over deep pockets and between coral reefs at high tide produces strikes. Live baits include small whiting, mullet, yellowtail, mackerel, crabs, and squid.

See: Big-Game Fishing; Offshore Fishing; Tuna.

is usually taken incidentally by anglers deep trolling or fishing deep with live or dead baits for other species in the vicinity of an offshore reef, although some are caught on rigs trolled on or near the surface. It has been known to take mackerel, mullet, squid, strip baits, spoons, plugs, feathers, and plastic lures. **See: Big-Game Fishing; Offshore Fishing; Tuna.**

TUNA, LONGTAIL   *Thunnus tonggol.*

Other names—northern bluefin tuna, oriental bonito; Arabic: *gebab, sahwa;* French: *thon mignon;* Indonesian: *aya, bakulan, kayu;* Italian: *tonno indiano;* Japanese: *koshinaga;* Spanish: *atún tongol.*

This member of the Scombridae family of tuna and mackerel occurs inshore in large schools. It is of some commercial importance, having good-quality pink flesh.

Identification.   The longtail is more elongated and smaller than the southern bluefin tuna *(see: tuna, southern bluefin).* Other traits that separate this species from the southern bluefin are colorless oval spots on the belly, the absence of a swim bladder, the lack of striations on the liver surface, and the lower gill raker count (20 to 23 mean total). The ventral surface from about the pectoral fin to the anal fin is covered with colorless elongated spots. The tips of the second dorsal and anal fins are yellow. The finlets are yellow and edged with gray.

Size.   The longtail tuna has a maximum size of possibly 80 pounds and 53 inches. The all-tackle

TUNA, SKIPJACK   *Katsuwonus pelamis.*

Other names—skipjack, ocean bonito, arctic bonito, striped tuna, watermelon tuna; French: *benite à ventre raye;* Hawaiian: *aku;* Italian: *tonnetto striato;* Japanese: *katsuo;* Portuguese: *gaiado, listão, listado;* Spanish: *bonito ártico, barrilete, listado.*

Although commonly called arctic bonito, the skipjack tuna is not a bonito and does not venture into arctic waters. This member of the Scombridae family of tuna and mackerel (which includes bonito) is an esteemed light-tackle species and has great commercial value. It is a mainstay of the California tuna fishery and is of tremendous importance in Japan, Hawaii, Cuba, and other areas. It is marketed canned, frozen, smoked, fresh, and dried/salted. In the United States, it is canned with yellowfin and bigeye tuna and sold as light meat or chunk light tuna.

Identification.   The presence of stripes on the belly and the absence of markings on the back are sufficient to distinguish the skipjack tuna from all similar species. The lower flanks and belly are silvery and have four to six prominent, dark, longitudinal stripes running from just behind the corselet back toward the tail, ending when they come into contact with the lateral line. Although some other species do have stripes on the belly, they have markings on the back as well, and the latter remain the most prominent after death.

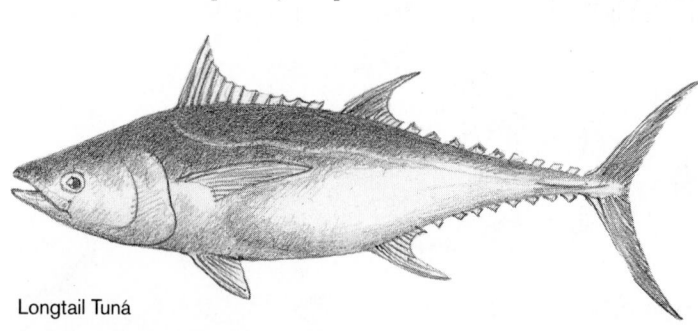

Longtail Tuna

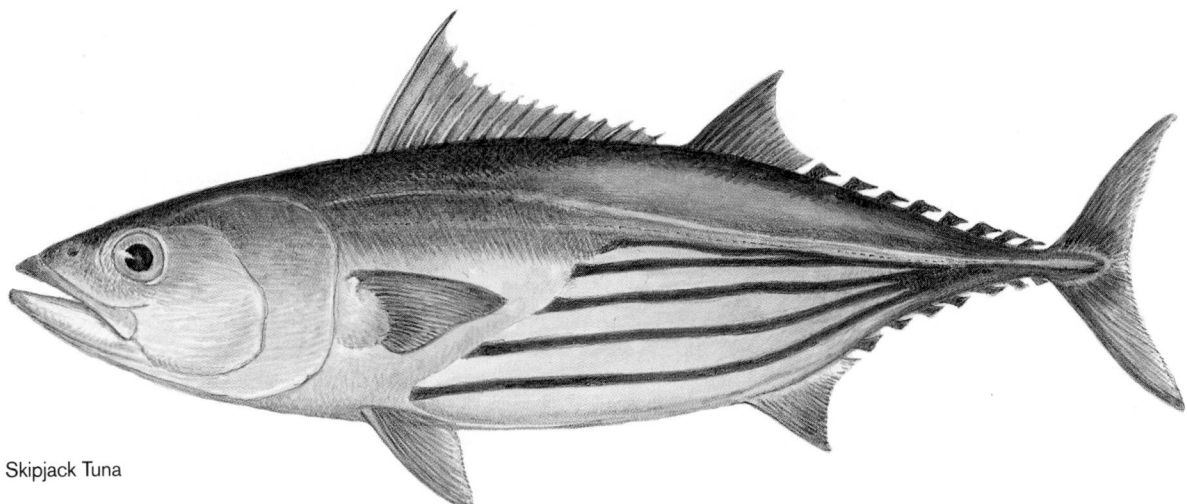

Skipjack Tuna

The top of the fish is a dark purplish blue, and the lower flanks and belly are silvery. The first dorsal fin has 14 to 16 spines, and the pectoral and ventral fins are short. The body is scaleless except on the corselet and along the lateral line. This fish has no swim bladder. On each side of the caudal peduncle is a strong lateral keel. There are roughly 30 to 40 small conical teeth in each jaw. The teeth are smaller and more numerous than those of bonito and are unlike the triangular, compressed teeth of mackerel. There are 53 to 63 gill rakers on the first arch, which is more than in any other species of tuna except the slender tuna (Allothunnus).

Size/Age. Skipjack tuna can attain a maximum of 40 to 45 inches in length but are commonly between 16 and 28 long and weigh from 5 to 15 pounds. The all-tackle world record is a 45-pound, 4-ounce from Baja California, Mexico, but they are believed to grow larger. They may live for 12 years.

Distribution/Habitat. Skipjack tuna are cosmopolitan in tropical and subtropical seas, usually in deep coastal and oceanic waters. They are common throughout the tropical Atlantic south to Argentina, and may range as far north as Cape Cod, Massachusetts, in the summer months. A pelagic, migratory, deep-water species, it may form schools composed of 50,000 or more individuals, which makes it a prime target for commercial fishermen using purse seines.

Life history/Behavior. In the western Atlantic, skipjack tuna frequently school with blackfin tuna (see: tuna, blackfin); in the Pacific and Indian Oceans they often school with yellowfin tuna (see: tuna, yellowfin). Skipjack tuna reach sexual maturity at about 18 to 20 inches in length. Spawning occurs in spurts throughout the year in tropical waters, and from spring to early fall in subtropical waters, with the spawning season becoming shorter with increased distance from the equator.

Food and feeding habits. This is a gregarious fish and a fast swimmer. It feeds near the surface, and its diet consists of herring, squid, small mackerel and bonito, lanternfish, shrimp, and crustaceans.

Angling. The skipjack tuna is a fine gamefish caught by a variety of means. It will strike trolled strip baits, feathers, spoons, plugs, or small whole baits, and most are taken via trolling. Some anglers catch them by casting, jigging, or live-bait fishing offshore. Their soft meat causes them to be less favored by anglers than most other tuna.

See: **Big-Game Fishing; Offshore Fishing; Tuna.**

TUNA, SOUTHERN BLUEFIN

Thunnus maccoyi.

Other names—Japanese Central Pacific bluefin tuna, southern tunny, tunny; Japanese: *bachimaguro, indo (goshu) maguro, minami maguro.*

A member of the Scombridae family of tuna, the pelagic and seasonally migratory southern bluefin is an apparently smaller-growing cousin to the more widely dispersed Atlantic bluefin tuna (see: tuna, bluefin). It is an important commercial species as well as a powerful, hard-fighting gamefish, but its population is estimated to be reduced to 90 percent of historic levels as a result of overfishing. Its red meat is excellent table fare; the raw flesh is prized for sashimi and draws a high price on the commercial market.

Identification. The southern bluefin tuna closely resembles the Atlantic bluefin and was once thought to be the same species. The primary difference is the number of gill rakers. The southern bluefin has a total of 31 to 40 on the first arch, whereas the Atlantic bluefin has a total of 34 to 43 gill rakers. Both have in common striations on the ventral surface of the liver, short pectoral fins that do not reach to the space between the first and second dorsal fins, and moderate second dorsal and anal fins that are never elongated like those of the yellowfin tuna (see: tuna, yellowfin). The finlets are dusky yellow and edged with black. This is the only species of *Thunnus* in which the caudal keel is bright yellow, except in fish larger than 150 pounds, where the caudal keel tends to be darker.

Size/Age. The southern bluefin doesn't appear to achieve weights exceeding 400 pounds. The all-tackle world record is a 348-pound New Zealand specimen caught in 1981. It is believed to attain an age of at least 20 years.

Distribution/Habitat. A species of the southern oceans, the southern bluefin occurs worldwide from 30° to about 50° south latitude in oceanic to coastal waters. It is commonly found off the southern and eastern coasts of Australia and New Zealand.

Life history/Behavior. This species spawns in the eastern Indian Ocean, with one- and two-year-olds appearing off Western Australia in summer. Fish three and four years of age appear off Southern Australia in summer and New South Wales in winter. The migratory route from the Indian Ocean to the Pacific splits into two paths off southern Tasmania. Fish move either to northern New Zealand via South Island or up the Australian coast. They travel in schools of similar-size fish and are relatively slow to mature. This occurs at roughly ages 8 to 9.

Food. The southern bluefin's diet consists of a variety of crustaceans, squid, and fish, including anchovies and pilchards.

Angling. The most popular method of catching this species is via trolling with assorted offshore lures. It can also be taken from boats or from the shore using live mackerel and little tuna for baits. It is rarely taken on dead baits, although very large specimens have been landed by this method. Hooked fish are prone to fast surface runs and deep sounding, like their bluefin relatives.

See: **Big-Game Fishing; Offshore Fishing; Tuna.**

TUNA TOWER

A term for elevated platforms on large sportfishing boats *(see)* designed to give the captain a better view, enabling visibility at a much greater distance. The name derives from the fact that they were developed in 1952 as lookout towers in the Bahamas for captains spotting bluefin tuna, but they have been adapted for wider use.

See: **Tower.**

A small yellowfin tuna caught off Virginia Beach, Virginia.

TUNA, YELLOWFIN   *Thunnus albacares.*

Other names—Allison tuna, albacore, autumn albacore, yellow-finned albacore; French: *albacore, thon à nageoires jaunes;* Hawaiian: *ahi, ahimalailena;* Italian: *albacore, tonno albacora;* Japanese: *kihada, kiwade, kiwada maguro;* Portuguese: *albacora, atum amarello;* Spanish: *atún de aleta amarilla, atún de Allison, rabil.*

Preferring warm waters, the yellowfin is the most tropical species of tuna in the Scombridae family. It is highly esteemed both as a sportfish and as table fare. Anglers throughout the world are familiar with the yellowfin, and they are heavily targeted commercially; hundreds of thousands of tons are taken worldwide annually by longliners and purse seiners. The meat of the yellowfin is light in color compared to that of most other tuna, with the exception of the albacore *(see)* and dogtooth tuna *(see: tuna, dogtooth),* which have white meat.

Identification. This is probably the most colorful of all the tuna. The back is blue black, fading to silver on the lower flanks and belly. A golden yellow or iridescent blue stripe runs from the eye to the tail, although this is not always prominent. All the fins and finlets are golden yellow, although in some very large specimens the elongated dorsal and anal fins may be silver edged with yellow. The finlets have black edges. The belly frequently shows as many as 20 vertical rows of whitish spots. Many large yellowfins become particularly distinguished, as they grow very long second dorsal and anal fins.

Overall, the body shape is streamlined and more slender than that of bluefin or bigeye tuna. The eyes and head are comparatively small. Just as the albacore has characteristically overextended pectoral fins, the yellowfin has overextended second dorsal and anal fins that may reach more than halfway back to the tail base in some large specimens. In smaller specimens under about 60 pounds, and in some very large specimens as well, this may not be an accurate distinguishing factor, as the fins do not appear to be as long in all specimens. The pectoral fins in adults reach to the origin of the second dorsal fin but never beyond the second dorsal fin to the finlets, as in the albacore. The bigeye tuna *(see: tuna, bigeye)* and the blackfin tuna *(see: tuna, blackfin)* may have pectoral fins similar in length to those of the yellowfin. The yellowfin can be distinguished from the blackfin by the black margins on its finlets; blackfin tuna, like albacore, have white margins on the finlets. It can be distinguished from the bigeye tuna by the lack of striations on the ventral surface of the liver. The yellowfin tuna has a total of 25 to 35 gill rakers on the first arch, and it has an air bladder, as do all species of *Thunnus* except the longtail tuna *(see: tuna, longtail).* There is no white, trailing margin on the tail.

Previously, large yellowfins with long second dorsal and anal fins were called Allison tuna or

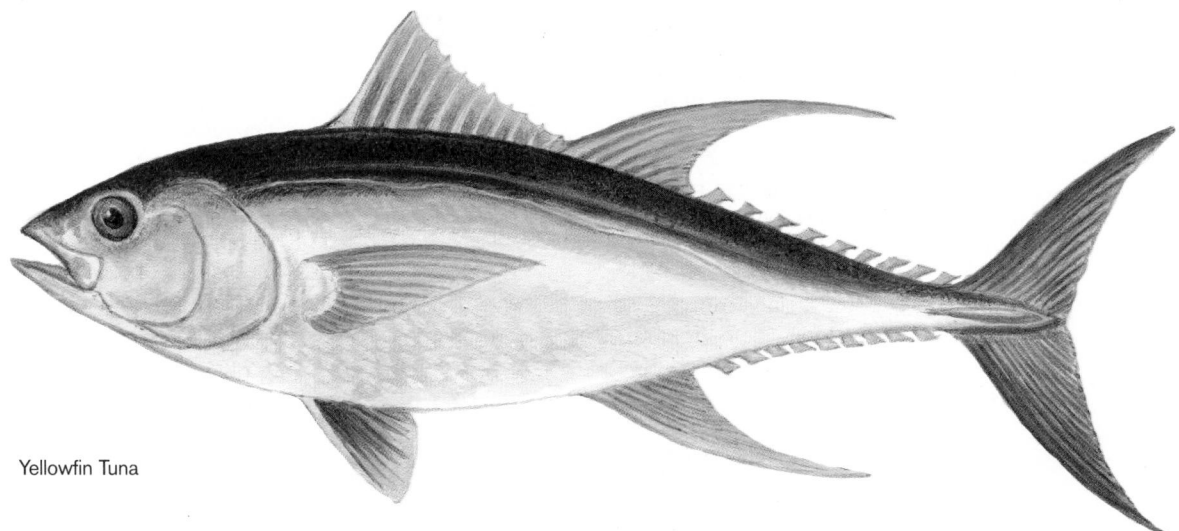

Yellowfin Tuna

long-finned yellowfin tuna, and the smaller specimens were called short-finned yellowfin tuna in the
mistaken belief that they were a separate species. It
is now the general consensus that there is only one
species of yellowfin tuna.

Size/Age.   Yellowfins are commonly caught
under 100 pounds in size but may grow to more
than 400 pounds. Their maximum length is 75
inches, and the all-tackle world record is a 388-
pound, 12-ounce Mexican fish.

Distribution/Habitat.   This species occurs
worldwide in deep, warm, temperate oceanic
waters. It is both pelagic and seasonally migratory
but has been known to come fairly close to shore
where there are warm currents. The largest yellowfins have been encountered by long-range party
boats fishing in the Revillagigedo Islands off the
coast of Baja California, Mexico. Specimens
exceeding 200 pounds are common during many
winter trips, and some in the 300-plus-pound class
are boated.

Life history/Behavior.   Yellowfins are fairly abundant in tropical waters. Young fish are known to
form large schools near the surface. Adults inhabit
fairly deep water but also live near the surface, and
are caught close to the surface by anglers. They often
mix with other species, especially skipjack and bigeye
tuna. Yellowfin are sexually mature when they reach
a length of approximately 40 inches, and spawn
throughout the year in the core areas of their distribution, with peaks occurring in summer months.

Food.   The diet depends largely on local abundance, and includes flyingfish, other small fish,
squid, and crustaceans.

Angling.   Yellowfins are a good target for
trollers and also for bait anglers. Trolling with small
fish, squid, strip baits, and artificial lures, as well as
chumming and live-bait fishing are primary methods.
Offshore anglers do especially well with this species
by chumming with chunk baits at night.

**See: Big-Game Fishing; Chumming; Chunking;
Offshore Fishing; Tuna.**

TUNING LURES

All lures must swim true to be effective. If they don't
have the right action, they will probably not be as
effective as they were designed to be—in fact, they
may be totally ineffective. Plugs, for example, must
run straight on the retrieve, not lay on their side or
run off at an angle; spoons must have the right
wobble and should not lay flat or skip.

Some anglers take already serviceable lures and
make minor adjustments—such as bending the lip
or changing the hooks—that make the lures work
exceptionally well, and it can be worthwhile to tinker with some lures to see whether they can be
improved through modification. Tuning, however,
means more than modifying a lure that already
works; it's making minor adjustments to lures that
are not swimming properly. Lures don't always
work just right, or as well as they could. Some that
have been working properly may run awry after you
catch fish on them, someone steps on them, or they
get bashed against a hard object. Some lures work
perfectly right out of the box, but others, especially
diving plugs, do not. Moreover, you can buy a
dozen identical lures and find that several need tuning to work right.

There are ways to tune lures to make them run
true. Tuning is not difficult, but it does take a few
minutes to accomplish, and it takes observation to
know when to work on a lure to make it run better.
Some plugs seem to need more frequent tuning
than others, and some small lures need more frequent tuning than large ones. Others never get
tuned exactly right. It is not uncommon to make
many attempts to modify a new lure before you get
it running to your satisfaction.

The majority of plugs have clear plastic bills of
various lengths and shapes designed to make them
dive. Into these bills are attached line-tie screws,
and virtually all running problems involve the
position of these little screws. When a plug runs
awry, it is usually the fault of the line tie. The line-
tie screw must be placed perpendicularly to the

T

plane of the bill of the lure. Because this screw eye is partially positioned by hand at the manufacturing plant, human error can be introduced. If the screw is placed a fraction of an inch out of position, the lure will not run true.

Besides the line tie, other factors are at work as well. Plastic lures are molded in two halves that are joined and glued, and sometimes a change in the sealing of those halves, or some other aspect of mold design or construction, can affect a lure's performance. A few manufacturers tank-test each lure before they package it to ensure that it runs properly; however, most do not perform this labor-intensive activity.

A well-designed plug, with or without a lip, should have a good wiggling action. Some lures have a tight action, and some have more of a wide wobble. Whatever its action, a lure should come back in a straight line while swimming or diving. The body of a plug should swim on a vertical axis, like a real baitfish, not be canted off to either side; if it runs even a little bit off, it will have an unnatural action that will likely cost you fish. (This is not necessarily true for erratic-swimming and darting

running to left

bend eye slightly to right

running to right

bend eye slightly to left

true runner

To tune a plug to run properly, bend the line-tie screw in the opposite direction from which the lure is running astray. Do this incrementally until the plug runs straight ahead with a good side-to-side wobble.

cut-plug lures that have no lip or bill. These lures appeal to fish, especially salmon, precisely because of their erratic movement.)

It is a good idea to check each plug before you fish it. Tie it on your line, drop a few feet of line from the tip of the rod to the lure, and then run the lure through the water next to your boat. If the lure does not run properly, adjust it immediately. If you can't tell by doing this, then cast the lure about 30 feet away, hold the rod tip out straight, and watch to see whether the lure runs off an imaginary straight line to either the right or the left

To adjust a plug, you need a pair of pliers to bend the line-tie screw. Watch the lure swim. If the lure runs off to the right, bend the line-tie screw to the left; and if the lure runs left, bend the screw right. Tweak the screw in small steps, bending it slightly and checking its action in the water to see the change. Keep adjusting and checking until the lure runs perfectly. (In serious cases, you may have to bend the line-tie screw far from its original position.) When bending the line-tie screw, be careful not to loosen it; the screw is epoxied in place, and loosening it may render the plug unusable. Sometimes you can take out the screw and reglue it, using clear, quick-setting epoxy. Also, make sure that you bend the eye, not twist it.

Before you tune a lure that seems to run awry, make sure you're not retrieving or trolling it too fast. All plugs have a top working speed beyond which they will not run properly. This speed is not the same for all lures. Some lures that run well at slower speeds will run awry at faster speeds, yet can be tuned to swim properly anyway.

Generally, most plugs will not run very well if a tight knot is tied directly to the screw eye. For this reason, it is best to use a split ring or rounded snap—not a snap swivel—for connection. Most plugs are supplied with split rings or snaps, and your knot should be tied to this. Snap swivels may alter the action of these plugs, making tuning difficult. A lure that is tuned to work without a snap swivel may have to be retuned to work with one. Moreover, a snap swivel poses a possible problem when you are fighting fish, and the fewer things that can go wrong the better. The only advantages to using a snap swivel are that it facilitates lure changing and prevents line twist, but diving plugs don't induce twist.

A new knot on a lure that was running fine may change the action because of the position of the knot. This is corrected by changing the position and alignment of the knot, or by retying the knot and snugging it tight. You may find that some plugs work best if you use a loop knot. With some deep-diving minnow plugs, tie a loop knot directly to the line-tie screw or the split ring.

Some of these comments about plugs and line ties apply to other lures. Spinners usually don't pose much of a problem except for the occasional bent shaft, which can be corrected easily if not too severe.

Streamers need to swim upright, and usually you simply adjust the knot location on the eye of the fly to achieve this. Heavy spoons don't usually get bent out of shape, but wafer-thin spoons do, and this sometimes requires adroit remodeling. A few thin flutter spoons can be bent at the tip and base, to the left or right, to modify their action.

It pays to experiment with such tuning, if for no other reason than to compare actions. Remember to watch for line twist with these lures; in the case of spoons or spinners, use a good-quality snap swivel to eliminate twist. In addition, be aware of the small things that might affect the way your lure swims. Sometimes plugs can be sensitive to the slightest adornment. If you pull a lure through weeds and get a tiny confetti trailer on your hooks or line tie, you'll feel the action of the lure change if you have the rod in your hand, or you may notice a change in the movement of your rod tip.

TUNNEL HULL

A term for a shallow-water style of boat hull with a raised center section that is flat and ductlike. This permits high-mounting of a transom engine to allow the boat to jump quickly on plane in bare inches of water.

See: Boat.

TUNNY, LITTLE   *Euthynnus alletteratus.*

Other names—little tuna, Atlantic little tunny, false albacore, bonito; French: *thonine de l'Atlantique;* Italian: *tonnetto dell' Atlantico, tonnella sanguinaccio, alletterato;* Japanese: *yaito, suma-rui;* Portuguese: *merma;* Spanish: *bacoreta del Atlántico, merma, barrilete, carachana pintada.*

Although not part of the *Thunnus* genus like many tuna, the little tunny is a member of the same Scombridae family and one of the finest small game-fish available. Frequently misnamed as false albacore and bonito, this species fights so hard on light tackle that anglers are likely to boat dead or near-dead

A little tunny from Montauk, New York.

individuals. It has coarse red flesh, however, which does not endear it to many anglers as food, although it does attract some commercial interest.

Identification.   The little tunny is most easily distinguished from similar species by its markings. It has a scattering of dark spots resembling finger-prints between the pectoral and ventral fins that are not present on any related Atlantic species. It also has wavy, "wormlike" markings on the back. These markings are above the lateral line within a well-marked border and never extend farther forward than about the middle of the first dorsal fin. The markings are the same as in the closely related kawakawa *(see)* but are unlike those of any other Atlantic species. The pectoral and ventral fins are short and broad, and the two dorsal fins are sepa-rated at the base by a small space. The body has no scales except on the corselet and along the lateral line, and there is no air bladder. Unlike its close Pacific relatives the kawakawa and black skipjack *(see: skipjack, black),* it has no teeth on the vomer.

The little tunny is often confused with the Atlantic bonito *(see: bonito, Atlantic),* the skipjack tuna *(see: tuna, skipjack),* and the frigate mackerel *(see: mackerel, frigate)* and bullet mackerel (genus

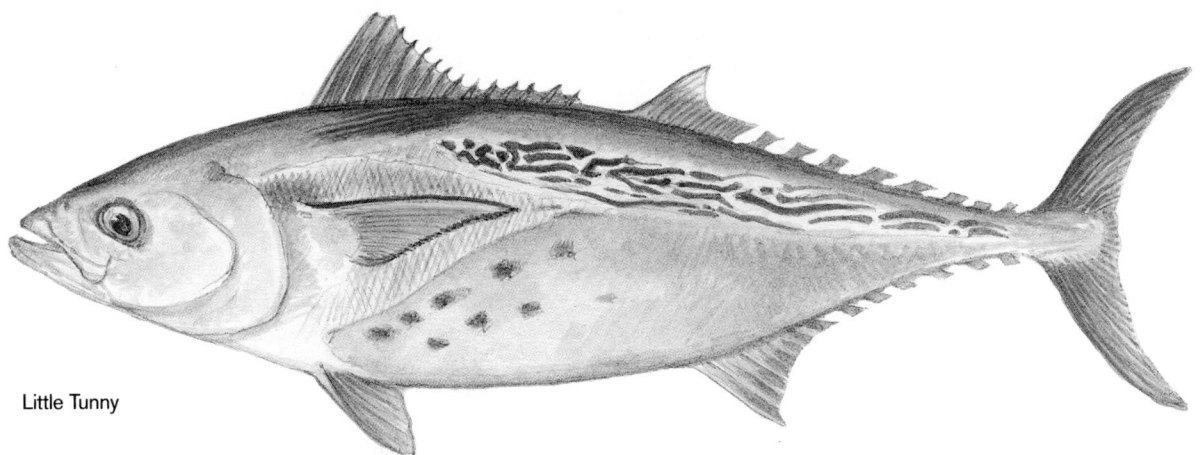

Little Tunny

Auxis). There are, however, differences among these species. The Atlantic bonito has a lower, sloping first dorsal fin. The frigate and bullet mackerel have the dorsal fins set apart. The skipjack tuna has broad, straight stripes on the belly and lacks markings on the back.

Size. Little tunny may attain a length of 40 inches but are most common to 25 inches. The all-tackle world record is an Algerian fish that weighed 35 pounds, 2 ounces.

Distribution/Habitat. This species occurs in tropical and warm temperate waters of the Atlantic Ocean; in the western Atlantic, it ranges from the New England states and Bermuda south to Brazil, and in the eastern Atlantic from Great Britain to South Africa, including the Mediterranean. It is not as migratory as other tuna species and is found regularly in inshore waters, as well as offshore, usually in large schools.

Spawning behavior. Little tunny reach sexual maturity at approximately 15 inches in length. Spawning occurs from about April through November in both the western and eastern Atlantic.

Food and feeding habits. Little tunny are common in inshore waters near the surface where they feed on squid, crustaceans, fish larvae, and large numbers of smaller pelagic fish, especially herring.

Angling. Flocks of diving seabirds often indicate the presence of a school of little tunny. Because this species feeds on small pelagic fish near the surface, any school feeding action tends to attract and excite birds looking for a meal. Fishing methods include trolling or casting from a boat and offering small whole baits, strip baits, or small spoons, plugs, jigs, and feathers.

These fish spread out over the continental shelf and are most abundant within 30 miles of shore during a late-summer to early-fall run along the Mid-Atlantic and southern New England coasts, when they average 5 to 15 pounds. Unlike the other tuna, the little tunny commonly chases baitfish into the surf and can be caught by surf casters retrieving small metal lures and jigs at high speed. Many are also caught by trollers seeking school tuna, and in chum lines intended for bluefish.

See: **Big-Game Fishing; Offshore Fishing; Tuna.**

TURBIDITY

The amount of suspended particles in the water column. Turbid water is clouded with sediment and in extreme cases may be muddy.

See: **Water Clarity.**

TURBOT   *Scophthalmus maxima (also Psetta maxima).*

Other names—breet, britt, butt; Danish: *pigh-varre;* Dutch: *tarbot;* Finnish: *piikkikampela;* French: *turbot;* Italian: *rombo chiodat;* Norwegian

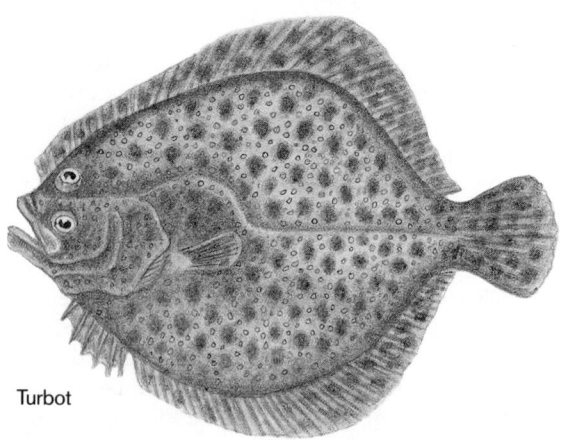

Turbot

and Swedish: *piggvar;* Portuguese: *pregado;* Russian: *azovskii kalkan;* Spanish: *rodaballo.*

The turbot is a left-eyed member of the Scophthalmidae family of flatfish *(see)* that has long been commercially significant for European markets, and is mainly caught by commercial trawlers. Like other flatfish, it undergoes a unique maturation from egg to adult in which one eye migrates to the opposite side of the head.

Identification. The body of the turbot is diamond shaped. The eyed side is grayish brown with darker speckles and blotches, and the blind side is white. Although similar in appearance to the more oval brill *(see)*, the turbot grows larger and lacks scales.

Size/Age. This species grows to 39 inches in length and is reported to reach a maximum weight of 55 pounds, but it commonly grows to 17 inches in length.

Distribution. The turbot occurs in the northeastern Atlantic throughout the Mediterranean Sea and along the European coast to the Arctic Circle; it is also found in most of the Baltic Sea.

Habitat. Turbot are located over sandy, rocky, and mixed bottoms in depths of up to 500 feet, but they normally range from the shore to a depth of 260 feet. They also commonly occur in brackish water.

Spawning behavior. Spawning occurs between April and August.

Food. The diet of turbot is mainly various fish and, to a lesser extent, larger crustaceans and bivalves.

Angling. Turbot are caught on standard, deep, bottom fishing methods, using heavy weights and natural baits, or heavy metal jigs.

See: **Drift Fishing; Inshore Fishing.**

TURKEY

Situated in southeastern Europe and southwestern Asia, the Republic of Turkey is seldom the focus of sportfishing interest by globe-trotting anglers. This is largely because its varied fisheries resources—found in mountain streams, rivers, freshwater lakes, and especially in four warm seas—are largely unknown outside its borders. It is also because

Turkey has a scarcity of modern tackle, boats, and facilities for the visiting angler.

Situated centrally in the Northern Hemisphere, Turkey is both a Mediterranean and Middle Eastern country. Technically, 97 percent of its surface area of 814,578 square kilometers is situated in Asia and the remainder in Europe. Much of this generally east-west landmass is surrounded by warm saltwater: the Black Sea in the north, the Marmara Sea in the northwest, the Aegean Sea in the west, and the Mediterranean Sea in the south. As a result, Turkey has 8,333 kilometers of coastline. Most of it is in the Anatolia region (between the Mediterranean and Black Seas) and includes 1,067 kilometers of island coastline.

Surface formations in Turkey show a wide variety due to high altitude. These include mountains in parallel ranges, a single or linear lineup of extinguished volcanoes, flat plateaus that are covered with lava or small rocks and that once belonged to ancient lakes, and plains with alluvial beds widening at river deltas.

Turkey is rich in rivers, and these flow to the Black, Mediterranean, Aegean, Marmara, and Caspian Seas, and to the Persian Gulf. Most contain rapids and are not suited to navigation, and some are important for hydroelectric and irrigation purposes. The amount of water flowing from the rivers, however, varies greatly during the year. In summer, nearly all the rivers are at their lowest, and some completely dry up. With the beginning of autumn rains and decreased evaporation, flows increase and continue during the winter, becoming highest during the spring.

In addition to its rivers, Turkey possesses more than 200 natural lakes. These cover nearly 9,000 square kilometers, although they are more abundant in some areas and nonexistent in others. In the Thrace (the small portion of Turkey in Europe) and Black Sea regions, for example, there are practically no lakes; the regions of Marmara, Central Anatolia, Eastern Anatolia, and especially the Mediterranean contain areas with an accumulation of lakes.

Turkey has three distinct climates. The climate of the Mediterranean region is dry and hot in summer, with mild rainy winters; this climate is also experienced in Western Anatolia and in the Aegean and Marmara regions. The Black Sea coast has a temperate climate, and it is rainy there throughout the year. The steppe, or plains, climate dominates Eastern and Central Anatolia; here the winter is cold with little rain, and the summer is dry.

Abundant water results in a rich overall harvest of fish for the people of Turkey, who number about 64 million. According to government statistics, the amount of combined saltwater and freshwater fish produced per person per year in the country is 11.4 kilograms. This includes mussels and shrimp, but of the saltwater finfish harvested commercially, the anchovy represents 55 percent of the catch, followed by horse mackerel (19 percent), chub mackerel (6 percent), and bonito (3 percent). The saltwater catch comes primarily from the Black Sea, which produces 87 percent of the harvest. Among freshwater fish, 46 percent of the commercial production is carp, followed by trout and chub.

Saltwater species caught by recreational anglers, which in Turkey includes the vast majority of people who use handlines and the lesser number who use rod and reel, are garrick, red mullet, sole, horse mackerel, Black Sea turbot, two-banded bream, comber, gray mullet, red gurnard, chub mackerel, European sea bass, bluefish, red bream, whiting, picarel, bluefin tuna, albacore, bonito, pilchards, mackerel, sturgeon, blue marlin, shad, lizardfish, moray eels, conger eels, sailfish, garfish (a type of needlefish), hake, Mediterranean ling, three-bearded rockling, John Dory, barracuda, stone bass (wreckfish), grouper, dentex, shortbill spearfish, gilt-head bream, bogue, salema, saddled bream, black bream, meagre, amberjack, pompano, dolphin (mahimahi), little tunny, frigate mackerel, swordfish, scorpionfish, brill, flounder, anglerfish, porbeagle sharks, hammerhead sharks, blue sharks, thresher sharks, spiny dogfish, smoothhound sharks, angel sharks, ray, and skate.

Freshwater species include river charr, lake trout, rainbow trout, brook trout, sea trout, perch, carp, roach, tench, chub, barbel, pike, eels, grayling, white bass, and wels catfish.

There are no fishing prohibitions for anglers in Turkey, a sportfishing license is not required anywhere, and there is no requirement to belong to a club or group in order to obtain permission to fish at particular sites. There are no overall limits and no size limits. Recreational anglers can use all kinds of natural baits and artificial lures, and they can fish at any time of the day or night.

In Turkey, a handline is generally used by resident anglers. The effectiveness of this method, as well as using rod and reel, varies according to the species, region, environment, type of boat, currents, and season. The type of natural and artificial baits used, and techniques employed, also varies according to region and environment; people who use fly-casting tackle are extremely scarce.

In saltwater, such live baits as pilchards, garfish, scorpionfish, gray mullet, horse mackerel, chub mackerel, and small bream are commonly used. Other natural baits include crabs, squid, octopus, shrimp, mussels, clams, scallops, and pieces of fish. Artificial lures include spoons, plugs, and jigs. Fishing is primarily done from an anchored boat, by drifting in a boat, or by trolling.

The most productive fishing season in saltwater is from late summer until early winter, although this varies according to region. In summer, saltwater fish approach the shores; in winter, they retreat to open and deep waters.

The favored natural baits used in Turkish lakes and rivers are worms, frogs, rodents, certain flies,

T

and insects. Some anglers use different shapes of spoons and plugs.

There are no specially designed open-sea fishing boats for hire in Turkey. At practically every saltwater fishing site, however, it is possible to fish with local fishermen and use their methods and tackle. For freshwater fishing, it is best to use a guide who knows the region being fished, although guides are not numerous.

Black Sea

The Black Sea is an inland body of saltwater bordered in the east by Russia and Georgia, in the north by Ukraine, in the west by Romania and Bulgaria, and in the south by Turkey. This huge sea covers 436,400 square kilometers, and its size impacts the nearby climate by making it milder; in winter it is noticeably milder along the Black Sea coast than inland.

With an average depth of 1,272 meters, the Black Sea is the deepest of the seas surrounding Turkey. Its deepest point, 2,234 meters, is north of the Turkish city of Sinop. There are shallow waters, less than 200 meters, in the northwestern region where the Danube enters, but apart from that area the entire coastline is very narrow, and the continental shelf drops off extremely sharply. The continental shelf between Giresun and the Strait of Istanbul (Bosphorus) widens somewhat following the Turkish coast toward the west, and is intersected by valleys of ancient rivers reaching a depth of 200 to 220 meters.

The Black Sea consists of two basins and has both surface and subsurface currents. The surface, or upper, current runs counterclockwise along the Anatolian coast toward the east, continuing along the northern and western shores eventually to the Strait of Istanbul. In general, the strength of this current diminishes the farther one gets from shore, but the coastal current is still felt 15 to 19 miles from shore. The complex current system in the southeastern region can be extremely strong, many times greater than the norm elsewhere. Along the coastal strip between the entrance to the strait and the Bay of Burgaz there are opposite currents.

In addition to this current flow, the Black Sea has low salinity, especially at the surface and near river deltas, and a rich upper water zone. The surface waters create a thin layer over the more salty and heavier water underneath. The differences in density created by the changes in salinity cause the surface and deep waters to remain in two separate, unmixed layers. This situation prevents oxygen from mixing into deep waters, so that no fish can thrive at the greater depths. Yet the area where these two layers meet, whether by virtue of temperature or salinity, provides an ideal living environment for many species of migratory fish. Thanks to the rivers that enter the Black Sea, which occurs primarily along the north shores, the upper layer of water is rich in oxygen, alimentary salts, and plankton, and this creates a productive environment for fish.

The surface waters of the Black Sea reach 20° to 26°C in the summer. The warmest waters are in the southeast and the coolest in the northwest. The difference in temperature is more evident in winter, when the temperature in the southeastern region is 13°C, and in the northwest it drops to 2°C.

Black Sea fish consist of permanent and migratory species. Permanent residents include horse mackerel, Black Sea bass, whiting, garfish, shad, silversides, anchovies, turbot, gray mullet, skate, spiny dogfish, and smoothhound. Perhaps most prized are sturgeon and herring; these anadromous fish are famous for their roe (caviar, in the case of sturgeon) but have decreased in abundance due to pollution.

Migratory fish that originate from the Mediterranean Sea include bonito, mackerel, bluefish, bluefin tuna, swordfish, sole, and red mullet. These species migrate in spring to the Black Sea to feed, and leave between the end of August and January. Their passage back to the Mediterranean is by way of the Strait of Istanbul into the Marmara Sea, then through the Dardanelles Strait into the Aegean Sea, and from there into the Mediterranean. Seventy-five percent of the fish fauna of the Black Sea originates from the Mediterranean. If the winter is mild, migrating fish stay longer in the Bosphorus area and in the Marmara Sea, and can be caught in large quantities.

Bluefin tuna and swordfish are among the premier fish that can be caught from a boat by drifting or trolling with live bait in the open waters of the Black Sea. They are caught respectively up to maximum weights of 360 kilograms and 110 kilograms; however, both have decreased in number due to extensive and uncontrolled fishing.

On the other hand, trolling with many feathered hooks for bonito is highly productive in August and September. Fishing for bluefish is done from a boat with handlines and live baits, or with spoons and jigs by trolling. August and September produce good-eating, fat bluefish. Bluefish are also taken from shore by anglers casting with lures.

Flatfish are found near sandy shores and can be caught on bottom bait rigs. The prime season for these fish is April and May. Fishing for mackerel is also done from boats by drifting and using handlines with many feathered hooks; the most productive fishing seasons for mackerel are August through November, and April through June. Sea bass are caught along the coasts with live baits or artificial lures in November, February, and May, where the rivers flow into the Black Sea.

As in every part of Turkey, local anglers plying the Black Sea fish primarily with handlines. In recent years, rods and reels have been used to fish from shore. Samsun, Ordu (Fatsa Bay and its coast), Giresun (around the small islands across the city), and Trabzon are all noted for their fishing. Visitors here are advised to fish with locals, and to realize that there are very few ports to take shelter in when sudden storms or strong winds break out. Winter is noted for being windy and rough.

A number of small lakes exist in the Turkish Black Sea region. Carp, whitefish, pike, and wels inhabit the lakes of Abant and Yedigöller (Seven Lakes area). Also, several species of trout exist in the Yesilirmak, Kizilirmak, and Sakarya Rivers and their branches. The Kizilirmak is 1,150 kilometers in length and is the longest river that flows entirely within Turkey, originating in the mountains east of Sivas.

Trout fishing occurs in every season in the high plateaus of the Black Sea region. In general, Turkish anglers fish for these species with rod and reel, using natural baits. It is advisable to hire a local guide for freshwater fishing.

Strait of Istanbul

The Strait of Istanbul, also known as the Bosphorus and sometimes called the Black Sea Strait, joins the Black and Marmara Seas. Along with the Dardanelles Strait, it separates Asia from Europe. The waters of the Bosphorus are rich in oxygen and provide a positive environment for sportfish, as well as tricky currents and challenging fishing.

This sharply bending strait is approximately 30 kilometers long. It is wide at the north and south entrances, and narrow in the middle. The widest point is 3.6 kilometers, and the narrowest 700 meters.

Two differing current systems provide an exchange of water between the Black and Marmara Seas, and these are related to differences in level and density. The less dense and less saline waters of the Black Sea, which is 25 centimeters higher than the Marmara Sea, flow from north to south on the upper level of the Bosphorus into the Marmara Sea. Underneath this, another current carries the more saline and more dense waters of the Marmara from south to north into the Black Sea. The boundary between the upper and lower currents in the southern Bosphorus is 20 meters deep, and in the north 40 meters deep.

The speed of the upper current increases in front of the capes and in areas where the strait narrows. Although its average speed is approximately 3.2 kilometers per hour, it reaches 5.2 kilometers per hour and may attain 9 to 10 kilometers per hour when aided by strong winds. The upper current also creates eddies in the small bays when it hits the capes.

The amount of water transferred into the Marmara Sea via the upper current is estimated to be double that of the water transferred into the Black Sea via the slower lower current. Sometimes important changes are observed in the currents. When strong and constant north winds blow, the speed of the upper current increases, and the waters of the Black Sea rise and overflow to fill in completely the strait channel, thus blocking the lower current. In contrast, when strong southwest winds blow constantly, the rising waters of the Marmara Sea enter the southern mouth of the strait and push

A fishing scene from the Strait of Istanbul.

harder against the upper current; as a result, the large water mass entering from the south joins with the lower current and fills in the strait channel, causing the upper current to flow from the south to the north.

Fishing is very productive during the period when the speed of the upper current increases. From September through December, migratory fish move from the Black Sea to the Mediterranean, and, with the help of the fast current, large masses of fish enter the strait and provide good fishing. Fishing is poor when southwest winds create a stronger lower current, as the fish are more dispersed.

Depending on the species and their temperature preferences, migrating fish start leaving the Black Sea for the Marmara at the end of August, heading to the Aegean Sea and sometimes into the Mediterranean. This migration continues until the middle of January. In the spring, these species migrate from the Mediterranean, Aegean, and Marmara Seas beginning in April and continuing until early June, spending their summer in the Black Sea.

The direction of the winds and the currents plays an important role in the beginning of the migration. Bonito, bluefish, and bluefin tuna are the primary migratory gamefish. High numbers of bonito and bluefish begin to appear around the last week of August at the northern entrance of the Bosphorus and in the nearby waters. These species are present in the Bosphorus and in the Marmara Sea from the end of September until December. Bluefin tuna are in both areas in January and February.

Bonito can be fished from boats in the Bosphorus during the day with artificial lures and with multiple feathered hooks, and at night with pieces of bait. During the day, bluefish are caught from drifting boats with live bait, and with jigs and spoons. The favorite natural baits for these species are sliced or live horse mackerel, picarel, anchovies, and garfish.

Fishing for bluefish in the Bosphorus has an important place in Turkish sportfishing and is

T

marked with traditional activities. These include the formation of special lures, as well as the preparation of tackle and attaching pressurized kerosene lamps on boats for night fishing. During the nineteenth century, master fishermen reportedly used to cast jigs out of pure silver. These were used only once, on the first day, to catch the first bluefish of the season.

When fishing at night for bluefish, the boat's motor is shut off and the anchor is not employed because the rope leaves a phosphorescent trail in the water. The boat is maneuvered with oars in the strong current, and the person doing the rowing also throws a handline and tries to hold it in a straight position.

Bluefish caught in September and October are juveniles, but larger fish appear in following months. Sometimes small coal grills are placed in the boats, and the fish caught are immediately cleaned and cooked.

The bluefish approach the shores following horse mackerel and are caught on rod and reel either with natural bait or lures. It is always useful to keep large amounts of live baitfish in the boat.

There are many villages on both shores of the Bosphorus, and it is possible to fish with local fishermen in a rented boat either during the day or at night. The best hours for fishing are generally from sunrise till 9 A.M., and from evening throughout the night.

Marmara Sea

The Marmara region covers just 8.5 percent of Turkey but includes the entire coast around the Marmara Sea, which joins the Black and Aegean Seas via straits in the northeast and southwest that are 290 kilometers apart. It also encompasses the city of Istanbul, and its 16 million inhabitants, and is the most populated region in the country.

Marmara is an inland sea completely contained within Turkey. The Bosphorus connects the Marmara to the Black Sea, and the Dardanelles Strait connects it to the Aegean Sea. It spans 76 kilometers at its widest point, and at its narrowest, 9 kilometers.

The European and Asian coasts of the Marmara Sea differ in shape. The Bays of Tekirdag and Silivri on the coasts of Thrace have suitable boat shelters. The major inlets on the Anatolian coast are Izmit, Gemlik, Erdek, and Bandirma Bays. The principal islands are the Marmara, Imrali, and Princess Islands.

The coasts and open seas of these islands are suitable for fishing. The continental shelf area is not particularly deep and takes up a wide portion of the Marmara Sea. All of the islands are located on this continental shelf. There are very deep places in the Marmara Sea, however, which is uncommon for small seas. One of the deepest spots is just south of Princess Island and reaches 1,238 meters. Another area over 1,000 meters deep is situated in the middle of the Marmara, and still farther west is a pit that reaches 1,112 meters. Large schools of fish typ-

ically gather around these regions, including bluefin tuna and bonito, which follow horse mackerel and anchovies.

The surface waters of the Marmara Sea are generally not very salty. The less saline surface layer ranges from the surface down to 15 to 20 meters. As depth increases, so does salinity. Mackerel and bonito prefer to live in more saline waters and can be found between 30 and 40 meters.

The Marmara's surface temperature reaches 24° to 26°C in summer and 7° to 9°C in winter. There is an upper (surface) current and an opposite lower current in the Marmara Sea, too. The surface current is caused by the difference in water level between the Black and Marmara Seas. The surface current leaves the Bosphorus and spreads out like a fan on the Marmara Sea, then accumulates in the west and, with increasing speed, enters the Dardanelles Strait.

The Marmara Sea, along with the Bosphorus and the Dardanelles Strait, is one of the most important waterways of the world and is subject to heavy traffic. Due to pollution created by large cities around the Marmara Sea, and excessive uncontrolled commercial fishing, aquatic life here has become much more scarce. There is still a local fish population, but pelagic species such as swordfish, mackerel, and bluefin tuna do not stay in the Marmara Sea, although these species do migrate through the Marmara from the Mediterranean and Aegean Seas.

Resident species include sea bass, red bream, dentex, comber, and striped bream. Fish like red mullet, sole, red gurnard, whiting, John Dory, flounder, ray, and skate prefer sandy bottoms. Migrating fish like horse mackerel, gray mullet, chub mackerel, bluefish, and bonito appear in April, May, October, and November.

Turkish anglers usually fish in the Marmara from a moving or anchored boat with a handline, primarily fishing at sunrise and sunset. The major baits used for bottom fishing are mussels, shrimp, crabs, and small live or sliced baitfish. Plugs and spoons are used to fish for dentex and sea bass.

In the deep waters around the Princess Islands, fishing occurs for mackerel and bonito from April through June, and October through December, with multiple feathered hooks and handlines. Live or cut bait are used for bluefish, and the most productive months for this species are October and November.

Even though they are near extinction in the Marmara Sea, bluefin tuna are still caught in December and January. Some specimens over 300 kilograms are taken on live bonito, bluefish, horse mackerel, and garfish. The prime area is off the Kumkapi and Princess Islands. It is possible to find 8- to 12-meter boats for rent from local fishermen, either from the islands or from Istanbul.

The Marmara region is rich in lakes and rivers. River charr, lake trout, brook trout, perch, carp,

Some of the earliest bamboo fly rods were round instead of polygonal; cork was not used as handgrip material until the 1890s.

roach, tench, chub, pike, and wels are found in the Meriç River, which borders Turkey and Greece, and in Manyas, Ulubat, Iznik, Sapanca, and Terkos Lakes. Anglers here favor rod and reel, and use live baitfish or artificial lures. Wels over 100 kilograms are caught in the Meriç River. The carp in Iznik Lake are very large and delicious. Pike over 4 kilograms can be caught on spoons in Terkos Lake, where it is possible to rent boats.

The Çanakkale Strait

The Çanakkale Strait joins the Marmara and Aegean Seas and is known in the west by the name Dardanelles, which is derived from the ancient city of Dardanos, 10 kilometers south of the city of Çanakkale. In the Ottoman era this was also known as the Mediterranean Strait.

Compared with the Bosphorus, this strait is straighter and longer at 94 kilometers, and its narrowest point is 1.2 kilometers wide. The Anatolian coastline is sharp, but there are many delta valleys where rivers enter. The current changes direction in the northern and central parts of the strait due to the narrowness of the coasts. The deepest spot is 109 meters, between Çanakkale and Kilitbahir, and the area experiences hot, dry summers and cold, windy winters.

As in the Bosphorus, there are two current systems—an upper surface current and a lower current. The waters of the Black Sea pass through the Marmara Sea and approach the Çanakkale Strait in a 25- to 30-meter-wide surface current. This current extends to depths of between 25 and 30 meters, where the more saline waters of the Aegean Sea (with a constant temperature of 14° to 16°C) flow toward the Marmara Sea. The upper and lower currents are rich in oxygen and organic matter. The nutrients found here, and the funneling of many fish species through this area on their migration routes, makes the Çanakkale Strait one of Turkey's most productive fishing sites.

Species that migrate through the strait include chub mackerel, horse mackerel, gray mullet, spiny dogfish, smoothhound, sea bass, bluefish, bluefin tuna, albacore, little tunny, bonito, and garfish. Resident species include garrick, red mullet, sole, comber, red gurnard, assorted sea bream, dentex, pilchards, picarel, moray eels, conger eels, John Dory, stone bass, grouper, solema, scorpionfish, and angel sharks.

Saroz Bay, reached by passing through the Gallipoli Peninsula from Koru Mountain in the northeast, hosts one of the richest fish areas in Turkey. In the center of this bay are Büyükada, Ortaada, and Küçükada Islands. Saroz is the spawning ground for many species of fish, and mackerel are seen in shoals here. Closer to the stony shores are sea bream. Sea bass and dentex are close to shore between the Büyük Kemikli and Küçük Kemikli Capes. Around the islands and in the depths are grouper. Moray eels lie in their holes, keeping a sharp watch for fish swimming too close. At nighttime, conger eels search for prey, and octopus watch from their holes, sometimes grabbing fishing lines.

Past Anafartalar is the island of Gökçeada, which is known for its fishing. The Mehmetçik headland has many garfish and produces garrick, which range up to 60 kilograms.

Southwest of this is the wreck of the battleship *Majestic* in Ertugrul Bay, and farther along is Morto Bay, whose western end marks the entrance to Çanakkale Strait. This area produces some 30 species of fish. Occasionally, a shoal of tuna weighing from 60 to 100 kilograms makes a foray into the bay. The waters that open onto the Aegean Sea at the end of Çanakkale Strait are very rich in variety of fish.

As the water warms during August, the fish approach the shore, and angling action increases. Bottom species are caught on mussels, shrimp, squid, pieces of octopus, and other items. Locals fishing for large species like garrick and dentex primarily use a handline. Live mackerel, scorpionfish, and garfish are the favored baits. Trolling is also popular. Plugs and spoons are sometimes used for dentex, which can weigh up to 12 kilograms. The garrick range between 35 and 60 kilograms.

The prime times for sea bass are November, February, and May. Fishing is done by drifting near the coast before sunrise, using shrimp or live small gray mullet. Anglers troll using small spoons to pursue sea bass, which sometimes reach 10 kilograms in November. When chasing smaller fish into the shallows, sea bass can be caught from shore on rod and reel, with spoons or plugs.

While it is possible to rent a boat from local fishermen for personal use, it is best to hire and fish with them in their boat.

Aegean Sea

The Aegean region, which encompasses 11 percent of Turkey, is in western Anatolia and abuts the Aegean Sea. The climate is usually hot, with dry summers and mild, rainy winters. The most populated area is around the large city of Izmir.

The Aegean Sea is situated between Turkey and Greece and is part of the Mediterranean, extending about 660 kilometers from north to south. It was once called the "Sea of Islands," due to the hundreds of islands here, most of which belong to Greece. Its coastline features many inlets, bays, straits, and peninsulas.

The temperature of the Aegean Sea is higher in the south than in the north, a difference that is most evident in winter. In most areas of the Aegean, the salinity of the surface waters is at conventional levels, although waters with higher salinity exist in the open areas of the west along the Anatolian shores. This is because the less saline surface current from the Black Sea, after passing through the Çanakkale Strait, moves close to the shores of

T

Greece and spreads out, whereas the more saline waters of the Mediterranean pass close by these shores while moving toward that strait and then to the Marmara Sea.

The Turkish waters of the Aegean Sea, especially in the northern region, harbor red mullet, gray mullet, frigate mackerel, sea bass, dentex, red bream, grouper, gilt-head bream, little tunny, and stone bass, among others. Karaburun, Balçova, Çesç me, and Ilica are the main fishing areas, and most fish are caught in waters within the continental shelf. Fishing in the southern Aegean Sea is poor.

It is possible to rent boats from local fishermen in fishing villages along the Turkish coast. Often these boats are 6 to 7 meters in length, with an inboard or outboard motor, and are not suitable for open-sea fishing. Turkish fishermen in this region strictly use handlines.

Mediterranean Sea

This region of southern Anatolia extends along the Mediterranean Sea and encompasses 14 percent of Turkey. It includes 1,542 kilometers of coastline. The most populated areas are around the cities of Adana and Antalya.

The coast of this region is less indented than that along the Aegean Sea and forms wide arcs that bear resemblance to the Black Sea coast. Summers are hot and dry, and the winters mild and rainy. Temperatures in the hottest month average 27° to 28°C along the coast, and 23° to 25°C inland. In summer, western and southern winds are dominant; in winter, the dominant wind is northern.

The Mediterranean Sea is a deep sea that extends from the western Atlantic Ocean to eastern Asia and separates the continents of Europe and Africa. It is joined in the northwest by the Çanakkale Strait to the Marmara Sea and thence to the Bosphorus and the Black Sea. Its deepest point, at 5,121 meters, is south of Greece in the Ion Basin.

In most places the Mediterranean coastline of Turkey is steep, with mountains rising immediately from the shore. These mountains create two big inlets in the bays of Antalya and Iskenderun.

In the eastern Mediterranean, a particular current moves along the Turkish coast from east to west. The origin of this current is the great southern current moving through the Aegean Sea along the western Anatolian coast toward Çanakkale Strait.

In winter, the temperature of the surface waters along the Turkish coast averages between 15° and 16°C, and in summer it averages 26°C in the western region and 28°C in the eastern region. Winter in the Mediterranean Sea is mild, rainy, and windy; in the summer it is hot, dry, and calm. Springtime is a rather changeable season, and autumn a short one.

Most fish species of the Mediterranean live in the upper layers and roam widely. These include bonito, mackerel, gray mullet, garrick, albacore, and dolphin. Some bottom-feeding species include plaice,

sole, whiting, conger eels, stone bass, grouper, red gurnard, red mullet, comber, ray, and skate.

The major shark species that prowl deep waters are hammerhead, blue, thresher, and porbeagle sharks. These species follow shoals of bonito and albacore and enter shallow waters or sometimes follow the fish shoals up into the northern Aegean Sea. Sometimes they are caught in the nets of commercial fishermen, but they are not specifically pursued by anglers. No shark attacks on humans have been reported in Turkish waters.

A number of swordfish, blue marlin, sailfish, and spearfish are caught with longlines and nets by commercial fishermen in May, but there is little angling effort for these species. It is possible to rent boats from local fishermen in Antalya, and, using rod and reel and artificial lures or chub mackerel and garfish, to try for these species. Amberjack, garrick, pompano, and dolphin enter shallower waters in June and July and can be caught with live baits or spoons.

Turkey's largest freshwater lakes (some saline lakes have no sportfish) are in this region, and such locations as Beyşehir and Eǵridir Lakes are important for freshwater fishing. Freshwater fish here include lake trout, perch, carp, roach, chub, barbel, pike, eels, and wels. Rods and reels are used with natural baits.

Central and Eastern Anatolia

Eastern Anatolia is a region with high mountains, crater lakes, and many rivers. Some of those lakes, however, including Turkey's largest—Lake Van—are saline. This highland region is the most rugged and mountainous area of Turkey, and includes Mount Ararat, which is cited in the Bible as the place where Noah's Ark came to rest. It is Turkey's highest peak at 5,137 meters (16,854 feet). Lake trout and rainbow trout are found in the eastern highlands. Trout up to 10 kilograms exist in the Ardahan area in northeastern Turkey, which is north of Ararat. This area is also the headwaters for the Tigris and Euphrates Rivers, which flow through Syria and Iraq to the Persian Gulf.

The lakes and rivers of central and eastern Anatolia also contain carp; these grow large, sometimes reaching 20 to 25 kilograms. Wels are also found here, and most anglers pursue them at dawn, dusk, and throughout the night, using frogs as bait. Pike, too, exist in the reservoirs of central and eastern Anatolia. They are fished with spoons and live baits.

TURKS AND CAICOS ISLANDS

The Turks and Caicos are a British dependency that are geologically part of the Bahamas, situated roughly 30 miles southeast of that island archipelago and 100 miles northwest of the Dominican Republic. There are two island groups here. The smaller Turks encompass six uninhabited cays, the inhabited islands of Grand Turk and Salt Cay,

Scientists calculate that there are about 23,000 different fish in the world; 40 percent inhabit freshwater and 60 percent inhabit saltwater.

and numerous small rocky islands; the Caicos encompass numerous islets and six principal islands, which include Providenciales, and West, North, Grand, East, and South Caicos, the largest of which is Grand Caicos.

With an awe-inspiring dropoff close to the reef edge, the Turks and Caicos offer excellent fishing for pelagic species, as well as lightly tapped reef fishing and hordes of small bonefish on flats. Miles of coral reefs make the islands a popular destination for divers. Established tourist facilities and resorts are available on the main islands, and airports exist on Providenciales, South Caicos, and Grand Turk.

Pelagic species are caught along the dropoff at the edges of these reefs, as well as farther offshore and at an impressive seamount that rises to 130 feet from the surface out of a depth of 7,000 feet. That great depth is part of the Turks Island Passage, and from Providenciales, which draws many big-game anglers and hosts a popular billfish tournament each summer, the deep-water fishing grounds are just a 15-minute run.

Blue marlin are the prime attraction here, and they are available year-round. The peak period is from June through August, when there's a good run of spawning fish and several blues a day can be raised. Most blue marlin are small, in the 100- to 200-pound range, and this provides good light-tackle fishing opportunities, including blues on a fly rod; indeed, the first blue marlin caught on a fly rod by a woman was taken here in 1994.

White marlin and sailfish are present from November through April. Wahoo are also available then but are especially abundant in November. Yellowfin and blackfin tuna are caught from December through June, and prime yellowfin action is in the spring.

Reef and flats fishing offer opportunities year-round. The reefs hold the typical array of snapper, grouper, jacks, and big barracuda. The flats reportedly have small tarpon, but they are mainly blessed with relatively unmolested schools of small bonefish. Large schools of 1- to 2-pound bones allow opportunities for catching good numbers in a given day.

The islands have an average annual temperature of 85°F, and the hottest months are September and October. Easterly trade winds help abate the heat, and the islands are subject to frequent hurricanes.

TURLE KNOT

A fishing knot for terminal connections, primarily used by fly anglers to tie a tippet to a fly.
See: Knots, Fishing.

TURNOVER

The complete mixing of all the water in a lake. Turnover occurs when a lake's temperature is essentially the same from the surface to the bottom, a process accomplished through water movement and wind. In deep lakes, this occurs twice a year, in the spring and fall, and is referred to as spring and fall turnover, respectively. In the spring, after turnover, the upper waters start to warm and eventually will stratify. In the fall, the upper waters cool and in some places will eventually freeze.
See: Stratification.

TWO-HANDED ROD

A loosely used term for any long-handled rod designed to be used with two hands when casting. These may be equipped with spinning, baitcasting, or conventional reels. A two-handed fly rod has a long butt section as well as long foregrip.
See: Casting; Flycasting Tackle.

TYEE

A chinook salmon (see) that is 35 pounds or larger. This Indian term, as well as the term "tyee salmon," is primarily used in British Columbia, but it may refer to large chinook, or king, salmon wherever they are found.

Lake Chargogagogmanchogagogcharbunagungamog is said to be the longest place name in North America. Massachusetts anglers call it Webster Lake and know it for bass, pickerel, and yellow perch.

UGANDA

Sandwiched between the Democratic Republic of the Congo on the west and Kenya on the east, Uganda is a relatively small east-central African country with diverse topography and plenty of water. Elevated plains, low-lying swamps, broad forests, arid basins, and snow-capped mountain peaks all exist amidst Uganda's 93,104 square miles. The southern portion of the country, which borders on Lake Victoria, Tanzania, and Rwanda, is largely forested; the north is largely savanna. Although Uganda straddles the equator, its climate is relatively mild due to its generally high altitude.

Along its borders or contained within the interior are Lakes Albert, Edward, George, Kyoga, and a significant northern portion of the largest lake on the African continent, Lake Victoria, as well as the Nile River between Lakes Victoria and Kyoga, between Kyoga and Lake Albert, and below Albert to Sudan. The section of the Nile River below the dam at Lake Albert is referred to as the Albert Nile, and the section from Lake Albert to the Owen Falls Dam at Lake Victoria is referred to as the Victoria Nile.

As with other countries in the region, various game and coarse species exist in Uganda's waters, but tigerfish and Nile perch (locally called *emputa*) are the fish of most interest to anglers. Most of the waterways in Uganda have seen little or no sportfishing since the early 1970s, and the full extent of its angling opportunities for tigerfish and Nile perch in its rivers and lakes is generally unknown.

Nile perch originally inhabited rivers and lakes of the Rift Valley, mainly the Nile and its tributaries, Kenya's Lake Turkana, and Tanzania's Lake Tanganyika. They did not inhabit Lakes Kyoga and Victoria, or the waters above the renowned Murchison Falls (upstream a short distance from Lake Albert), which is also known as Kabalega Falls and resides within Uganda's 1,500-square-mile Murchison Falls National Park. Fossilized remains of both Nile perch and tigerfish were discovered in and around Lake Victoria, and were dated back to the great upheavals of the ice age, when the upper waters of the Nile had become shallow and deoxygenated.

In the 1950s, Major Bruce Kinloch, a keen and dedicated angler who was deputy head of the Uganda Game and Fisheries Department, undertook to revitalize Lake Victoria, which was then the least productive lake in Africa, and at that time contained no trace of predatory fish species. During that decade, Nile perch were introduced above Murchison Falls into the Victoria Nile and Lake Kyoga. In the 1960s, they were introduced into Lake Victoria above the Owen Falls Dam.

In 1967, anglers started landing large catches of Nile perch in Lake Kyoga, at Namasagali where the river enters the lake, and along the Victoria Nile upstream to the Owen Falls Dam. This included some specimens weighing up to 72 kilograms. Anglers from East Africa and Europe fished these waters—which are swifter upriver and broader and slower near Kyoga—mostly from the bank, and many stayed at Chobe Lodge (which was destroyed in 1979). This area has been seldom fished since Uganda gained independence from Britain in 1962, and hardly at all in the 1980s and 1990s.

Today Nile perch are well established throughout this system and in Lake Victoria. All 15 line-class, fly-rod, and all-tackle world records for the species have been caught in Lake Victoria—some in Tanzania, some in Kenya, and some in Uganda. The all-tackle record, and largest ever certified on rod and reel, was an 87-kilogram ($191\frac{1}{2}$ pounds) fish landed in 1991. An 84-kilogram fish caught in 1995 became a line-class record. Specimens of more than 150 kilograms reportedly have been landed with

This large Nile perch was caught by trolling (note the heavy tackle) on Lake Victoria.

nets and longlines around Jinja; the largest specimen was a 160-kilogram fish taken from Lake Albert (still larger Nile perch have been reported in Egypt).

The phenomenal spread and growth of the Nile perch throughout Lake Victoria has occurred at the expense of indigenous species, and this has concerned ecologists. On balance, however, the outcome has been beneficial in terms of increased production of fish for the local market and export, and for anglers. More than 12 fish factories have mushroomed in each of the three East African nations, and exports of perch fillets earn valuable foreign exchange for them. Charter boat companies have recently been started, and this development is expected to attract anglers and tourists.

Although some huge Nile perch were landed in the lake in the early to mid-1990s, these days it takes a lot of luck to come by a big one. The fish factories do keep to the law and catch a certain size fish, but local fishermen break the law by fishing close to shore and catching small breeding fish. The water hyacinth has also spread rapidly in the late 1990s, and at times blankets Ugandan bays, making navigation and fishing difficult.

In Uganda, most access to Lake Victoria originates at Entebbe. Fishing is still productive around the Ssese Islands, but getting there can be difficult. A new boat service from Entebbe has improved transportation to the islands, however. The main fishing method there is trolling with plugs around rocky bays and inlets, where big fish lurk in pursuit of tilapia. Although tilapia are their main food source, Nile perch will also eat fellow perch and live bait. In the late 1990s, a small lodge opened on one of the Ssese islands.

Tanzanian authorities have banned commercial and local subsistence fishing around Rubondo Island, and this conservation effort has attracted many anglers from Africa and Europe, who are able to catch Nile perch there on large flies.

Little fishing has been done in the Victoria Nile in recent decades, although some anglers have made visits, no doubt seeking one of the larger Nile perch this area was known for decades ago (at least 10 fish between 54 and 72 kilograms were recorded between 1957 and 1966). An exploratory expedition below Murchison Falls in late 1997 revealed the presence of Nile perch in various sizes, including some monsters that were observed but not landed. The river perch are much more challenging to land than those in the lakes, as the swift currents and eddies, and the lack of accessibility by boats, mean that shore-based anglers struggle to handle behemoths that may take hundreds of yards of line from a reel on a downstream run. Heavy concentrations of water hyacinths increase the level of difficulty, making lures hard—if not impossible—to use in the areas that are accessible. Many anglers thus rely on live bait. Large catfish, incidentally, as well as tigerfish, exist in the turbulent river below these thundering falls.

ULTRALIGHT FISHING
See: Light-Tackle Fishing.

ULTRALIGHT TACKLE
See: Light-Tackle Fishing.

UMBRELLA RIG
A heavy wire multi-lure saltwater trolling rig used predominantly in the northeastern United States for striped bass and bluefish. The umbrella rig is one of the oddest and most effective saltwater trolling lures ever created. It started as the brainchild of a veteran Montauk, New York, skipper, who got the idea for trolling a school of lures while visiting his commercial fishing relatives in Nova Scotia and watching them troll with strips of beer cans rigged off a metal bar.

The original rigs were three-armed devices made with great difficulty by twisting three stands of relatively stiff No. 15 wire (a size used for sharks and giant tuna) with a trolling sinker at the head of the contraption. Attached to the arms were monofilament leaders, each with a plastic tube rigged with a bent hook, the same type of tube that had become popular as cod and pollock lures when rigged above a diamond jig. Small tubes without hooks were added in the middle of each arm to make the "school" look larger.

Others copied the concept with light single metal bars joined with a sinker in the middle, creating a four-armed trolling rig, which proved more effective even if drag through the water increased. As use of the deadly setup spread, a variation was created in New Jersey called the gorilla rig, in which tubes were hung directly from the ends of multiple bars.

Umbrella rigs are primarily used with tubes and are most effective when schooling bait such as sand eels (sand launce) are present because the tubes

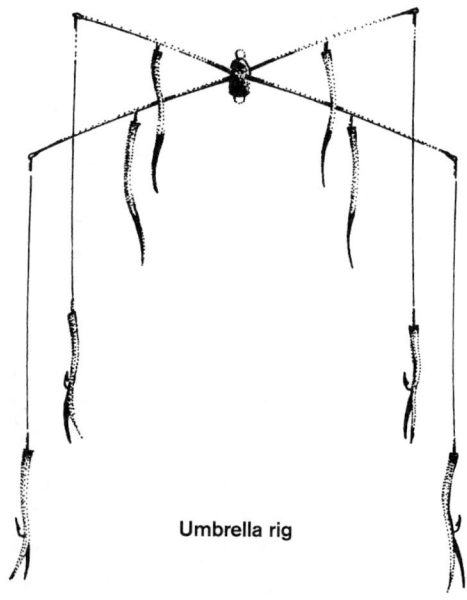

Umbrella rig

closely resemble those slim fish. However, just about any lure that doesn't create excessive drag (such as small spoons or soft plastics) can be hung on umbrellas. In a standard setup, an umbrella rig has four teaser tubes, one each midway on the wire arm, and four hooked tubes, one each on a leader tied to the end of each arm. A larger lure, such as a longer unweighted tube or a plug, is often fished from the middle of these rigs on a long leader to create the impression of a predator chasing a school of baitfish.

There are variations, of course, and rigs of different size with different size lures. Fishing with these takes some practice. You can't just drop an umbrella rig in the water and keep trolling. You have to ease it over the side of the boat and make sure that the lures swim properly without tangling, then slowly drop it back while the boat is moving forward. Fish it uptide (moving against the tide) and be careful not to let it out so fast that it sinks to the bottom, where it will get snagged. Long lines are often employed with umbrella rigs, so sharp turns should be avoided.

Because of their size and the drag they exert, umbrella rigs are almost invariably trolled on wire line for striped bass and bluefish, although they also attract many other mid-Atlantic species such as bonito, weakfish, and even little tunny. They've never caught on in other areas, though such species as barracuda, king mackerel, and yellowtail snappers have fallen for them, even when trolled in shallow waters on monofilament line.
See: Trolling Lures, Saltwater.

UNDERHAND CAST
See: Casting.

UNDERWATER VIDEO
A system utilizing a video camera attached to a cable to view underwater activity. Underwater video systems (known as UVS) have become more prominent, particularly aboard charter boats used in clear-water environments, as a means of studying fish and lure activity.

UVS systems are primarily used in trolling applications. They consist of a low-light, wide-angle camera installed in a hermetically sealed waterproof hydrodynamic housing attached to a downrigger cable both inline and ahead of the downrigger weight. Some units feature coaxial-like cable, which provides a lot of water resistance; better ones have a thin-diameter stainless steel–jacketed cable, which offers less water resistance and acts as a conduit for the signal to a video monitor above on the boat.

Underwater video systems can be used in depths up to 200 feet, although this is dependent upon water clarity. Greater depths do not allow for much distance visibility, primarily allowing for seeing lures and fish that are within 6 to 8 feet of the camera. Watching fish come into the viewing area to inspect or take a lure provides interest to some anglers, and has entertainment value, which is why some charter boat captains are using them.

This is a fairly new phenomenon in sportfishing, and one primarily used for trout and salmon trolling, in part because of the clarity of the habitat of these fish and also because it is often feasible with these fish to run a lure a short distance behind the downrigger weight. However, there are other practical applications that do not have to be associated with trolling, although they do need relatively clear water. Ice fishing, for example, is a possible application (for those who have shanties and a source of power). Searching for weeds, surveying wrecks, monitoring lure and bait behavior, locating fish, viewing under objects and structures, and other actions are all possible. UVS systems can also be hooked up to a VCR for recording.

Although underwater video systems are unknown, expensive, and seemingly frivolous pieces of equipment to some people, they are likely to become more popular in the future.
See: Downrigger; Downrigger Fishing.

UNI KNOT
A versatile fishing knot that can be used for terminal and line-to-line connections.
See: Knots, Fishing.

UNITED STATES
Note: Specific fisheries and angling opportunities in the United States are detailed under individual state listings. This entry provides an overview of sportfishing in the U.S.

No matter how you measure it, as a country the United States has the greatest sportfishing in the world. Blessed with water throughout most of its landmass, and abutting two oceans with powerful currents, the U.S. has an incomparable variety of esteemed freshwater and saltwater gamefish, from trout to tuna, bass to bonefish, salmon to sailfish, bluegills to bluefish, and pike to permit.

America's abundant opportunities range from the pine-studded wilderness lakes of northern Minnesota to the mangrove-flooded backwaters of the Everglades, from fishing under the Golden Gate Bridge in San Francisco to alongside the Chesapeake Bay Bridge in Virginia, and from wading Rocky Mountain coldwater streams to using jonboats in Florida's reclaimed sea-level phosphate pits. These venues provide many great, almost-great, and just-plain-good angling—from inlet to ocean, river to lake, highlands to lowlands, and region to region.

U.S. fisheries are, remarkably, publicly accessible with very few exceptions, although some excellent American waters—Alaska's in particular—are difficult, and relatively expensive, to reach because of their remoteness.

The 25-foot-long *Alvin*, a submersible belonging to the Woods Hole Oceanographic Institution, was once attacked at 1,700 feet by a swordfish, which left 2 1/2 feet of bill in the vessel's seam.

U

The United States has an enormous amount of public fishing opportunity and access.

Abundant waters, diverse species, and easy access put sportfishing into the category of third most popular recreational activity in the U.S., surpassed only by the number of people who annually swim or ride a bicycle. A federal government survey in 1996 indicated that 35.6 million Americans over the age of 16 fished annually, and the value of their purchases relative to sportfishing—equipment, travel, jobs, wages, taxes, and the like—exceeded $108 billion. It is no accident that 75 percent of all people vacationing in the U.S. head for the water, and that two out of every five Americans on vacation will do some sportfishing.

A great deal of that angling is done from boats, perhaps more so in the U.S. than in any other country. It is estimated that more than 16 million recreational boats are in use by Americans, and more than 12 million of these are large enough to be powered and/or to require state registration. Many recreational boat owners trailer their boats, and many of these are anglers for whom being mobile and sampling different places are especially important.

Freshwater

In the U.S., anglers focus their effort predominantly on freshwater fishing, in part due to geography; most states are far from marine environments. In freshwater, bass—specifically largemouth and smallmouth varieties—are the most popular species.

The largemouth is a highly adaptable fish, one that is widely available in large and small bodies of water alike, including lakes, reservoirs, ponds, rivers, and streams, as well as in some low-saline tidewater environments. They are found in 49 of 50 states, the lone exception being Alaska. Texas, Florida, and California are especially noted for bass, in part because they have in the recent past produced, or currently produce, the larger specimens. Many states, however—especially in the central and eastern portions of the U.S.—have excellent largemouth bass populations and fish of good proportions.

Almost all sportfishing for bass is done by casting with lures, the vast majority of that from boats. The wide array of bass habitats and cover preferences, as well as the species' predatory ambush nature, lend themselves to virtually all types of lures and diverse presentations.

Smallmouth bass, which inhabit cooler and rockier environs than largemouths, are less widely distributed and on average smaller in size; they predominantly range from the southerly regions of Canada to the middle of the U.S. but are absent in warmer latitudes. A belt running from southwestern Ontario and Minnesota eastward to New Brunswick and Maine has long held the premier smallmouth fisheries, but some rivers and impoundments in the central U.S., including Tennessee and Alabama, are notable for big specimens.

A similar overall range exists for walleye, a species highly coveted for its flesh and one that attracts legions of anglers with the beginning of the open-water season each spring. Walleye have expanded westward to develop significant fisheries in some waters, however, including the mighty Columbia River in Washington State. In recent years, the emphasis in walleye fishing has shifted to the largest lakes and river systems. These tend to produce the bigger fish and abundant numbers of this species, which take advantage of prolific baitfish populations in large waters. Little directed casting is done for walleye; the main emphasis is on trolling, jigging, and presentation of natural bait.

Northern pike have a good following but are less widely available than the foregoing species, and muskellunge attract a small but ardent coterie of anglers who devote much effort to what are generally modest catch results. Other than Atlantic salmon, muskies are the least widely available established freshwater gamefish in the U.S., and they are considered difficult to catch with consistency. As with bass, the majority of muskies today are released. Muskies are most prominent in and around the states bordering the Great Lakes. They receive special attention in Minnesota and Wisconsin. Pike overlap muskies in many of the same waters and do not grow as large on average, but they are much more numerous and are susceptible to a variety of lures. Truly large pike are not common in the U.S., although the opposite is true in northern Canada.

It is the various species of panfish—crappie, bluegills, sunfish, perch, white bass, and the like—as well as assorted catfish and bullhead species, that collectively rank second to bass in total angling interest. Panfish provide much satisfaction (as well as good eating) to many anglers but lack the glamour and publicity associated with other species. However, these fish are generally abundant and widely available, and they are accessible to people of all skill levels. Panfish anglers use spinning and spincasting tackle almost exclusively, and they place great emphasis on angling with small natural baits and jigs.

All of the species previously mentioned are largely self-sustaining in their respective environments, although some supplemental or introductory stocking by government agencies does occur.

Trout are widely available in the U.S., with a great deal of variety in both species and habitats. Brook trout, native to North America, are favored by many small-stream and high-pond aficionados, especially in the midwestern and northeastern regions, although they are rarely large specimens.

These fish are actually charr, and their family relatives—lake trout—do grow to large sizes, although they exclusively inhabit the cold waters of northern lakes, especially those that are large and deep. The object of many outings on the Great Lakes, lake trout are primarily caught by anglers trolling with medium- to medium-heavy tackle—shallow when the water is cold early in the season, then deep as it warms. Within the U.S., the Great Lakes offer the best opportunities for great numbers and large sizes of lake trout, although good fishing is available on smaller inland waters in a few states.

Rainbow and brown trout, which are more tolerant of warmer and less pristine waters than both brook and lake trout, are more widespread and thus a greater part of the American angler's catch. They are the primary river and stream trout species, although circumstances, sizes, and fishing methods vary widely. Small specimens, the product of regular stockings, inhabit waters where these fish cannot sustain themselves. The largest specimens, some over 20 pounds, exist in large lakes and rivers, and may also be the product of stocking.

Excellent fishing for rainbow trout and/or brown trout (and in some places cutthroat trout) exist in the highlands of various regions. This includes Northern California, the Rocky Mountain states, the Ozarks of Arkansas and Missouri, the Catskill and Adirondack Mountains of New York, and the southern Appalachian Mountains; but very good fishing also exists in Michigan, Pennsylvania, Washington, Idaho, Vermont, and elsewhere. Big rainbow (or steelhead) and brown trout also inhabit some waters scattered around the continent, most notably in the Great Lakes, where trolling in spring and summer, and bank or wade fishing in tributaries from fall through winter, are the favored methods. Some inhabit rivers in the Ozarks.

Salmon are intensely popular in the regions where they occur, but, as anadromous coldwater species, they are not available to the vast majority of Americans, who must devote substantial travel time and expense to access them. They are restricted geographically to naturally occurring Pacific stocks, and the greatest populations exist in Alaska. In New England, there is virtually no viable Atlantic salmon fishery, although fishable populations do exist in the Maritime Provinces of Canada.

With the exception of Pacific salmon (coho, chinook, sockeye, and chum salmon) in Alaska, native North American salmon have been under tremendous pressures due to environmental changes, especially damming of rivers and poor water quality, and to excessive commercial harvest in the oceans. Thriving fisheries for transplanted salmon in the Great Lakes, however, have provided exceptional angling in both lakes and major tributaries; this is sustained by extraordinary levels of stocking and is not subject to commercial fishing pressures.

Saltwater

Saltwater fishing in the U.S. varies considerably between the West and East Coasts, the Gulf of Mexico, and the Caribbean, where the Bahamas, although not technically part of the continental landmass, are a substantial light-tackle fishing destination for American anglers.

Along the East Coast, anadromous species such as shad and striped bass are popular attractions in large coastal rivers, and striped bass are among the most important coastal species from the Carolinas to Maine. Although striped bass were imperiled as recently as the mid-1980s due to commercial fishing and water pollution, stiff commercial controls and improved water quality have allowed their numbers to rebound dramatically. They have regained their place as the primary sportfish in the cooler middle and northern Atlantic waters, where they are caught on various tackle, with both bait and lures, and most fish are released due to regulations.

Stripers, incidentally, although naturally a saltwater species, have been widely transplanted into freshwater rivers and lakes, and huge landlocked populations of these fish occur in many impoundments throughout the middle and southern regions of the U.S.; few are naturally self-sustaining. In many locations, hybrid striped bass—the result of crossbreeding a pure-strain striped bass with a pure-strain white bass—are stocked by state fisheries managers and provide a fast-growing and aggressive sportfish that can be completely managed, as they are sterile.

Bluefish, weakfish, spotted seatrout, flounder, and assorted bottom fish are important species that thrive in the same inshore region as striped bass and, to some extent, drum; these are all suitable to presentations using lighter tackle. The upper East Coast offers offshore opportunities for big-game species, including marlin, tuna, dolphin, and sharks, although this is a more specialized and expensive endeavor involving heavier tackle. Blue marlin are caught off New York, New Jersey, and North Carolina, although not in great numbers, and white marlin are taken off Maryland. Bluefin tuna are sometimes caught in these regions, especially and most recently off North Carolina in the winter, but yellowfins are more likely targets.

Farther south, the emphasis is on a different mix of species, as the warmer climate leads to somewhat tropical conditions and the coastal sweep of the warm Gulf Stream current moves closer to the shoreline. This is why sailfish and dolphin are caught not far from the South Florida coast, as are king mackerel and other species. Some marlin and yellowfin tuna are likely catches, but these fish, and other pelagic species, are more prominent in the deep, blue water off various Bahamian islands.

Inshore, however, attention turns to drum (redfish), seatrout, snook, tarpon, and bonefish, as well as the occasional permit. Wading and casting for redfish and seatrout along the Gulf of Mexico is very popular, as are poling and stalking fish along shallow grassflats. Snook are probably the least abundant of these species and are mainly found in the brackish backwaters of the Sunshine State. Premier light-tackle fish, tarpon are extremely abundant, both on the flats and in passes and inlets, and are eagerly pursued and almost universally released after capture.

Bonefish are a glamour species, hotly pursued by anglers fishing from flats skiffs. In Florida waters, bonefish can run to large sizes but are solitary and skittish; in some parts of the Bahamas, they frequently travel in schools and tend to be less wary than they are elsewhere.

Coho and chinook salmon have long been the premier catches in the Pacific Northwest. These fisheries have been depressed in recent years, however, due to low populations. Their plight has drawn much attention in Northern California, Oregon, and Washington, although Alaska has good inland and coastal salmon fisheries as well as excellent angling for deep-dwelling halibut.

California is a hotbed for saltwater fishing, and its opportunities range from imported striped bass and shad fisheries in northerly coastal rivers, to offshore pelagic species, to the ever popular yellowtail and albacore, and a great diversity of surf and bottom-dwelling species. In Southern California, assorted rockfish, lingcod, and other species are always popular and available, whereas warm, bait-laden currents are necessary to produce good catches of bonito, barracuda, yellowtail, albacore, and tuna. Long-range fishing trips, some lasting up to several weeks, explore distant waters, especially off Mexico. Albacore and yellowfin tuna are the primary pursuits.

Possessing a considerably different topography than that of the East Coast, the West Coast does not offer the shallow flats found in the southeastern U.S. and thus has none of the East's inshore species; however, there is no lack of challenging opportunity for light-tackle enthusiasts.

It is easy to forget that Hawaii is part of the American fishing scene, too, because it is so distant from the mainland. Hawaii is in a league of its own for saltwater angling, however, and is certainly a hotspot in American saltwater fishing. The main emphasis is on pelagic species, especially yellowfin tuna and blue marlin.

General Information

Visitors to the U.S. will find no lack of guides, charter boats, and services catering to anglers, especially in the more well known and publicized areas. In freshwater, important lakes and rivers, and areas with abundant opportunities, have many guides, with and without boats. Charter boats are plentiful on the largest waters (restricted to four to six anglers with reservations only). Major coastal ports have fleets of party boats, capable of accommodating a large number of anglers for bottom fishing, and charter boats for inshore and offshore forays. Smaller guide boats—usually taking no more than three anglers and primarily used for near-shore, estuary, and flats fishing—are available as well and are especially numerous in southern regions. Lodges, camps, and other facilities dedicated to serving anglers are plentiful and are widely advertised in major outdoor publications. Outfitters exist who cater to canoe camping/fishing trips, houseboat vacations/fishing trips, horse or foot pack trips, and so forth.

If anything, the U.S. is so large and has such a plethora of angling opportunities that it can be a bit bewildering for the visitor from another country who aspires to do some fishing. Therefore, a prospective angler needs to focus either on the region that he or she is planning to visit (perhaps on vacation) and discovering both the opportunities available and the common means of angling, or on the species that he or she wishes to catch and then decide what place(s) to visit in order to catch either many of that species or large specimens (at some places it may be possible to do both).

Sportfishing in the U.S. is most popularly pursued from early spring through fall. Far fewer people fish during the cold weather months, although ice fishing is extremely popular in northerly regions, and the most southerly areas (especially Southern California, South Texas, and Florida) provide the most comfortable winter fishing due to a normally mild winter climate.

There are regulations that restrict sportfishing by season, usually to protect spawning fish or fragile populations; these are more prominent in freshwater than in saltwater. During a limited time frame, the season will be "closed" for a particular species. This is especially prevalent for trout and salmon species; it also occurs for bass, walleye, pike, and muskies, especially in northern states.

For the most part, regulations regarding seasons, methods of fishing, catch limits, and licensing are determined by state governments. There is no national or federal sportfishing license in the U.S., although each of the 50 American states requires a license issued by its government to fish in freshwater. In some places, the same license also applies to saltwater fishing in the state's marine waters; in some places there is a separate license required for saltwater fishing; and in a few places there is no license requirement for saltwater fishing.

A fishing license issued by a state is valid only in waters within that state (although some states with shared water boundaries do cooperate), and in none is there a test or examination required to obtain a sportfishing license. Any person, whether resident or nonresident, can purchase a fishing license, although the nonresident fee is higher. Licenses can usually be purchased for varying time periods (a full year, a week, three days, and, in some cases, daily); they are most commonly acquired at stores selling fishing tackle but are also obtained at some government offices, marinas, lodges, and the like. Licenses are becoming increasingly available by telephone purchase with a credit card.

A license is valid for both public and private waters within a state. Most waters are publicly accessible, but a license does not grant permission to cross private property to reach or leave the water. Ingress and egress must be accomplished at places provided for such purposes. In privately owned waters—or in waters that are inaccessible because all the land around them is in private ownership—permission must be received to fish. There is no private licensing arrangement as exists in Europe, although an access fee may be charged by the owners of private land or waters who run a commercial business (such as a private marina or boat dock where people launch a boat, or a pay-to-fish facility).

There may be regulations pertaining to the manner of fishing; examples include a waterway where only barbless hooks are permitted, or where the use of live or dead baits is prohibited. These and other issues are addressed in a brochure or booklet provided with the purchase of a fishing license.

Although from afar it may seem that there is a complicated maze of regulations, species, waters, and opportunities associated with American sportfishing, a newcomer can obtain guidance at a local bait and tackle shop (which are sadly fewer in number these days), or from organized clubs, or while attending one of numerous regional outdoor shows that are held all around the country during winter months.

Although fishing in the U.S. is good to excellent by most standards, it is generally not as good as it was in the middle of the twentieth century, or even as recently as the 1970s. Pollution, habitat destruction and alteration, and commercial fishing are the biggest culprits. In saltwater, increasingly sophisticated and numerous commercial efforts have led to the overharvesting of many food fish as well as forage fish. This has directly or indirectly impacted gamefish species. The effects have been particularly evident with marlin, swordfish, tuna, salmon, cod, and haddock, but also with many other species, including redfish and striped bass. The latter two species rebounded after reaching near-catastrophic population lows and were subjected to long-term harvest moratoriums.

Recreational angling has played a role in diminished populations and/or fishing success, if not as a result of overharvesting, then as a result of intense pressure. This is especially so in freshwater, where water quality took a nose dive for decades before experiencing a reverse trend, years after passage of the federal Clean Water Act. Some fisheries are still recovering from excessive angling-related fish mortality in the 1950s and 1960s, when it was erroneously believed that angling effort could not wipe out or severely depress populations of fish in large bodies of water.

Fisheries management efforts have sometimes helped and sometimes hindered the situation. Attempts to propagate some species have resulted in successful stocking, transplanting, and fish restoration. Trout and salmon introduction into the Great Lakes is one of the greatest fisheries success stories of all time. Striped bass have been successfully introduced to freshwater, and management of bass has brought huge specimens of Florida strain largemouths to various states. The widespread introduction of carp, however, is recognized as a mistake, and these fish are greatly ignored or denigrated, although they are widespread and numerous and harmful to many environs.

Although many species of fish are retained by anglers for consumption (especially panfish, catfish, walleye, chinook and coho salmon, and stocked trout in freshwater; plus dolphin, yellowtail, bluefish, flounder, snapper, grouper, and other species in saltwater), the past 20 years have seen an evolution in attitudes toward preservation and a much greater inclination to voluntarily release fish. Catch-and-release fishing is not only common, it is accepted for some species in certain areas, no matter what the size.

This fact notwithstanding, fishing pressure is intense on many popular bodies of water, especially seasonally (for example, the opening of the season, in early spring, during the spawning run), and crowding is possible at the most popular waters. Much of this pressure is driven by media and marketing attention, which tends to be overly skewed toward a select few highly marketable species in both freshwater and saltwater. As a result, some species, some waters, and some seasons are neglected. Because of the many waters that exist in America, it is possible to find underutilized fisheries populations and locations that can be enjoyed in solitude.

A review of the species and opportunities in each of the states indicates that high-quality fishing can still be enjoyed; but sportfishing, and management of American fisheries resources, is still a relatively new phenomenon in the overall scheme of things, and thus a work-in-progress.

UNSNAGGING

Getting snagged—having your lure stuck on some object in, on, under, or near the water—is part of the fishing game. Many species of fish orient to bottom and to different types of structural cover, and, as the saying goes, if you aren't getting snagged occasionally, you're probably not angling where the fish are. Therefore, getting unsnagged is a practice you'll have to master unless you don't mind losing lures and breaking your line a lot.

An important point to realize about retrieving a snagged lure is that it doesn't pay to use brute strength and yank on a stuck lure unless you have very heavy line (and then you may straighten the hook) or you are stuck on something flimsy. You usually can't muscle that lure free. Moreover, in so doing you probably will sink the hook deeper into the snagged object; or you may break your line, meaning that you've probably lost the plug altogether, or you may free the bait but send it speeding perilously back to you.

Many lures will come free if you simply jiggle your rod a bit. Another tactic is to take line from the rod between the reel and first guide, pull back on the rod to get the line very taut, and then snap free the line in the other hand; this action may jolt the lure free, especially if it is a jig or single-hooked lure. This technique sometimes works when you are a distance away from an object that is fairly shallow and don't want to go into the shallow to retrieve it. It is especially worth trying on a snagged lure that is deeper than the length of your rod, in which case you position your boat directly over it.

Sometimes it pays to give the stuck lure slack line. A floating plug may float free, or another bait might fall back from the object it was hung on. In current, you can often free a lightly snagged lure by paying out 20 to 30 feet of line so that it drifts down current, and then retrieve the slack line slowly. The force of the downstream current provides a different angle of pull that frequently frees the lure.

Generally, you need to change the angle of pull to retrieve many snagged lures, which simply hang up by the lip or bill or head, usually by wedging into something. Changing position, whether that means walking down the bank or moving your boat so that you get a different angle of pull, usually does the job. In deeper water, position yourself 180 degrees from where you were when you got stuck and simply pull.

If your lure is stuck in water that is no deeper than the length of your rod, and will not come free by any other means, position your boat over the location, stick your rod tip into the water, reel up the slack line until the tip of the rod hits the lure, and then gently push or wiggle it free. You must be gentle when doing this so that you don't break the tip of the rod or jam the guide ring out of its retainer. Be especially careful when you're doing this around rocks. This technique is very effective when a lure is stuck on vegetation, dock pilings, or wood.

You might try using a long pole to poke a stuck lure free or to pull the lure free. Some of the push-poles used in freshwater, which telescope to 12 feet, have a ring eye on one foot and a bent metal piece on the other. These are meant for reaching up to a stuck lure (tree limbs but no power lines, please) or for sliding down a fishing line to get to where a lure is snagged, and they are almost 100 percent effective for anything that can be reached within 10 to 15 feet.

For lures that are snagged deeper and can't be reached or snapped or jiggled free, you'll have to employ some type of retriever or knocker, which is a weight that slides down the fishing line and dislodges the stuck lure. This technique is most commonly used for plugs, which is why the knocker is often called a plug knocker, and also for jigging spoons. The knocker may be homemade or commercially manufactured. Sometimes an old spark-plug is used as a knocker by putting a split ring over the gap arm and pinching the arm to a closed position. The trouble with these free-falling devices is that they sometimes don't work, especially if a lure has been pulled hard into an object (a deep stump, for example); later, when the line gets broken, you lose both the lure and the knocker. Leaving large weights (often lead) and spark plugs on the bottom is really akin to littering, and not environmentally sensitive.

There are, however, string- or cord-fastened retrievers, which are meant either to dislodge the snagged lure or to tangle around the hooks. When the lure is freed, you simply pull on the string to retrieve everything. These attach to the fishing line and slide down it also. They usually take some time to use, but if you have to retrieve a lure that is catching fish, or the last of its kind, or one that you paid premium dollars for, then it's probably worth the time. With either kind of device, you should position yourself over the top of it for best results.

Before applying direct, hard-pulling pressure in an attempt to free a snagged lure, first try taking the line ahead of the rod tip, bringing it taut (top), and then making a snap release (bottom).

When you can't get free by any of these means, then you have to try pulling up on the lure as a last resort. For last-chance unsnagging, try tightening the drag and pointing the rod directly at the lure while reeling up all slack and pulling back. When a lure is deep, because of the distance of water between you and the lure, you don't have to worry about it rocketing back at you if you are successful in freeing it. But beware of pulling on a lure that is stuck out of the water (on a dock or limb, for example) or close to the surface. Many people have been hit by multi-hooked lures, lead sinkers, and hard objects that suddenly pull free under great tension and fly back at them at the speed of light. It can be dangerous. Warn others in your boat to watch out before you pull on the lure if there is a chance of it coming back to the boat.

This direct pulling might break the line if it doesn't free the lure. If the line doesn't break, usually because it is very strong, then you should wrap the line over a short- or jacket-covered elbow and pull on it. Do not wrap the line around your hand, especially if the line is a slick, thin-diameter type, because it can slice right through the flesh.

After you've been stuck on an object, check the first few feet of line to make sure it isn't abraded. If it is, cut off the damaged section and tie a new knot.

UPSTREAM FISHING

Facing, casting, and fishing upstream in flowing water. This is the typical, and normally advantageous, presentation mode for fly anglers who wade and fish dry flies in rivers and streams, since the angler needs to face upstream and cast up, or up and across, and allow the fly to drift back to the angler. This means that the fly is likely to float most naturally with the current (there are exceptions), and the angler will be below and out of the sight of a fish that is ahead of the angler and facing the current.

A direct upstream presentation is suitable for an angler using spinning tackle when floating lures are fished, but generally not with any lure that sinks and requires retrieval and manipulation to give it life. Casting moderately up and across is better with lures, and requires retrieving, but casting down and across may be necessary.

See: Downstream Fishing.

UPWELLING

A rise in water from a lower level to a higher level, usually induced by current and wind. Upwelling is most prevalent in the ocean and may occur when current pushes water up and over a prominent seafloor structure. Upwelling may have sportfishing implications when it occurs over canyons, seamounts, humps, reefs, or other major irregularities. It can cause a temperature change and stir up water in the vicinity of these structures, and through effects on the food chain it can produce more forage and be attractive to predators.

U-TUBE

A term for a self-propelled float tube shaped like a U with one open end to improve entry and exit.
See: Float Tubes.

UTAH

About one in every four Utah residents goes fishing at least once a year. Big waters such as Lake Powell, Flaming Gorge, the Green River, and Strawberry Reservoir draw close to 200,000 people from outside the state annually.

There was a time in the not-so-distant past when most Utah residents considered trout the only fish worthy of pursuit. Most young Beehive State anglers grow up learning to fish by catching trout on a small High Uintas lake or a local pond.

These days, fish managers use an extensive hatchery system to raise hundreds of thousands of trout each year, which enables Utah's growing population to enjoy fishing. Because Utah is one of the driest states in the country, few waters exist in which enough sportfish can reproduce naturally to satisfy angling needs. Thus, most of the state's lakes, streams, and reservoirs are managed by planting either catchable-size or fingerling trout raised at hatcheries.

Although the emphasis remains on trout, a new generation of anglers fed by newcomers to the state has discovered the joys of warmwater fishing. The impoundment of huge Lake Powell in southeastern Utah in the middle 1960s created more interest. And, because warmwater species such as striped bass, largemouth bass, smallmouth bass, perch, crappie, and bluegills tend to be more self-sustaining, managers have diversified Utah fishing in recent years. Many "two-tiered" fisheries have been developed since 1980, catering to those who enjoy trout fishing and those who enjoy catching bass or other species.

The most difficult thing for a Utah angler is to find a stretch of blue-ribbon trout stream, a reflection of the emphasis on damming nearly every possible stream for culinary or irrigation purposes. But the tailwater fishery on the Green River below Flaming Gorge Dam is premier North American trout waters. And the close-to-the-Wasatch Front Provo River below Deer Creek Dam provides hundreds of hours of fly fishing pleasure for those seeking wild brown trout.

Northern Region
Bear Lake. Large, turquoise blue Bear Lake straddles the Utah-Idaho border. Although intensive management has improved the cutthroat trout fishery in recent years, Bear Lake is largely known for three unique species of fish believed to be

Small black spots on the outer skin of fish are parasites; they're harmless to humans, and the fish are safe to eat.

U

remnants of ancient Lake Bonneville, a huge freshwater lake that once covered much of the Great Basin.

Although few anglers fish for Bear Lake or Bonneville whitefish, the Bonneville cisco is another story. These sardinelike 6-inch fish school by the thousands from mid- to late January each year during their spawning run. Anglers are allowed to use dipnets with long handles to scoop the minnowlike fish from the water. Dipnetting is best during the years when Bear Lake freezes over. A few anglers like to jig for the tiny fish. Although cisco can be eaten (they are best deep-fried whole), many Bear Lake anglers like to freeze them and use them later in the year as bait for the large lake and cutthroat trout that cruise these waters. Although cisco spawn throughout Bear Lake, the east shoreline tends to be most productive.

The Bear Lake cutthroat trout is a hard-fighting, voracious fish eater that the DWR is utilizing in many other reservoirs around Utah because it competes better than do rainbows with nongamefish such as chub. Managers have planted thousands of cutthroat in Bear Lake in recent years, greatly improving the fishing. Due to boating pressure in the summer, however, October through April is prime for angling. Trolling deep, jigging flashy spoons, and using cisco as bait are all common methods of catching trout, some of which weigh 5 or 6 pounds.

Willard Bay. A relatively shallow and somewhat barren reservoir, Willard Bay was created by diking a corner of the Great Salt Lake. Located just off Interstate 15 north of Ogden, Willard Bay had been known more as a close-to-home water-skiing area than as a fishery, but that image began to change in the late 1990s. Biologists have found several forage fish that could survive and serve as feed for the channel catfish, crappie, and walleye that traditionally inhabited the reservoir.

Biologists also introduced another popular gamefish, hybrid striped bass, known locally as wipers, to Willard Bay with good results. These hard fighters are popular with trollers.

Perhaps the best time to fish Willard Bay is in the spring during the walleye spawning run. Always a challenge to catch in Utah, walleye spawn along rocky shorelines, where anglers bounce jigs off the bottom for them. When the crappie cycle ends, Willard Bay is also popular with ice anglers. Because of its heavy boating activity, Willard Bay can be a difficult water to fish in the summer.

Pineview Reservoir. Located up Ogden Canyon, Pineview declined steadily as a trout fishery in the 1970s and 1980s as its waters warmed. But this is good news for panfish enthusiasts because Pineview might be northern Utah's most prolific producer of yellow perch, crappie, and bluegills.

Pineview is the place to take the kids to teach them to fish. On most days, the action is fast and furious. Just attach a piece of wax worm or night-crawler to a small chartreuse-colored jig and cast along the shallow shorelines, or use a worm dangled below a float or bobber. Pineview also might be the best place in Utah for ice fishing, consistently yielding large numbers of panfish.

Because the panfish were stunting, biologists have added a new, interesting twist to Pineview fishing in recent years by planting limited numbers of fish-eating tiger muskies. The muskies have done their job, thinning the stunted populations of panfish. They also provide a thrilling trophy fish that is among the hardest fighting anywhere in the state. Young anglers targeting panfish are often surprised when a tiger muskie takes their bait and bolts off, stripping most of their light tackle with it.

Rockport Reservoir. Located between the tiny towns of Wanship and Peoa and near the thriving ski town of Park City, Rockport Reservoir is one of those frustrating waters that never managed to cut it as a rainbow trout fishery. But the addition of yellow perch and smallmouth bass actually seems to have helped trout fishing a bit. Trolling is best, although ice anglers enjoy sporadic success. Fishing with nightcrawlers near the rocky dam can be especially productive for yellow perch. Summer fishing is sometimes difficult due to heavy boat traffic.

East Canyon Reservoir. Located close to the town of Henefer, East Canyon Reservoir is among the nearest fishing and boating reservoirs to Salt Lake City. It is a put-and-take managed resource for catchable rainbows. Fishing is best when the ice leaves in late April, and bait angling is best near the dam. Trollers enjoying success lakewide. Late fall fishing can be fruitful as well. Heavy boating pressure in the summer can make trolling difficult, although many try.

Logan River. The Logan flows through Logan Canyon and is a good place to fly fish for wild cutthroat and brown trout. The fast-flowing upper stretches are particularly fertile. Three small impoundments grace the lower part of the canyon closer to the town of Logan, and these might be better suited to families using bait to land the rainbow trout planted there on a regular basis. But the edges of those impoundments can be good for fly anglers using No. 18 or 22 patterns and a light leader. This type of fishing, on the right day, can produce excellent results for enthusiasts of hard-fighting brown trout, which inhabit the upper edges of the impoundments or some of the deeper pools. The Logan is one of northern Utah's best river fisheries.

Blacksmith Fork River. Flowing through the Blacksmith Fork Canyon above the town of Hyrum, and located near the Hardware Ranch where the Division of Wildlife Resources (DWR) feeds hundreds of elk each winter, the Blacksmith Fork River is a classic wild brown trout fishery. Fly anglers look at its deep, green holes and know there has to be a lunker lurking down there somewhere. They often find one. This river receives less pressure than almost any other northern Utah river. Don't ignore the large schools of mountain whitefish, especially in the winter, when they are especially vulnerable to nymph anglers. In fact, fishing for these whitefish is a good way to introduce novice anglers to fly fishing.

Weber River. The Weber River is one of northern Utah's longest, flowing from the Uintas all the way through the urban environment of Ogden. A variety of trout coupled with many whitefish makes this a good, close-to-home river fishery, although much of the land along its banks is private. Anglers must know they are not trespassing, or have permission to fish the better stretches. The tailwater fisheries of both Echo and Rockport Reservoirs are open to the public and can generate good fishing. Angling for whitefish and trout near Morgan and the Devil's Slide area can also be worthwhile, especially in the winter months.

Ogden River. The Ogden River flows from Pineview Dam through Ogden all the way to the waterfowl management area at Ogden Bay. Biologists say it hosts a surprising number of trout throughout its length. In the 1990s, the advent of the Ogden River Parkway turned the Ogden River into Utah's best urban fishery. Try fishing with flies or spinners near Dinosaur Park at the mouth of the canyon, or well into town. Some trophy wild brown trout have been caught along this stretch. Avoid the river during the spring runoff, when the high water can be dangerous and difficult to fish.

Central Region

Strawberry Reservoir. Located on U.S. 40 east of Heber City, Strawberry Reservoir is certainly Utah's most fertile trout water and may rank with Yellowstone Lake as the West's greatest cutthroat fishery. This is a big reservoir, surrounded by marinas, boat ramps, and campgrounds, that yields prodigious numbers of 3- to 5-pound cutthroat or rainbow trout. Well over 1 million angler days are spent on this water, largely because it produces bigger trout faster than nearly any place in the world. From the time the ice leaves in mid-May until it returns in late November, fishing at Strawberry seldom slows. For the hardy few who can stand the cold and the deep, slushy snow, it even produces some good ice fishing.

Although shore fishing with bait can yield good numbers of trout after ice out and in the fall, especially near inlets, the best success at Strawberry comes to boaters. Trollers use weighted line and a variety of lures; most groups start with each angler trolling at a different depth with a different lure. Once the right depth, spot, and lure are found, fishing can be fast.

Strawberry also earns high marks from float-tube anglers who like to use dry flies in the early morning and late evening, or Woolly Buggers any time of the year. Where tributaries flow into the main reservoir are especially popular places with tubers.

Fisheries managers hope that one day Strawberry's many tributaries will be capable of naturally reproducing sufficient wild Bear Lake cutthroat trout and kokanee salmon that they will no longer have to plant fish. The tributaries are becoming more productive all the time, especially since the U.S. Forest Service bought the land around the lake and moved cattle out of much of the valley, improving the riparian areas. Sterile rainbow trout and thousands of Bear Lake cutts are planted each year to keep up with the high pressure Strawberry receives. But the reservoir is rich in insect life and seems capable of sustaining trout at an amazing rate. The size of the average fish is consistently bigger than in any water in Utah, and probably than any in the West.

Jordanelle Reservoir. One of the newest Central Utah Project reservoirs, Jordanelle opened with a flurry in the early 1990s. Fishing may have been too good and limits too liberal because trout angling quickly slowed after the first year, only to slowly build up again. Because of its proximity to Salt Lake City on U.S. 40 near the ski town of Park City and to some of Utah's best state park camping facilities, Jordanelle receives heavy boating and fishing pressure. Brown and rainbow trout fishing for bait anglers, trollers, and float tubers is best on the upper arm where the Provo River flows into the reservoir. Fishing can be quite good.

As of the late 1990s, the up-and-coming gamefish at Jordanelle has been smallmouth bass, which seem to be growing at a faster rate than was expected. Smallmouth anglers casting traditional bass lures along the rocky shoreline or the deep area near the dam can expect to enjoy good success, especially in the middle of the summer, when the trout fishing tails off.

Utah Lake. Many Utah anglers don't know that this shallow and muddy-colored reservoir, which has probably been hurt more than any single body of water by the industrialization of the Wasatch Front, was once a cutthroat fishery. But the warming, muddy water drove the trout away years ago, leaving a good place to catch channel catfish, walleye in the spring, an occasional black bass, and plenty of white bass.

Much of Utah Lake's fishing interest and pressure is centered around the walleye spawning run, which begins in mid- to late March. This brings dozens of lantern-carrying walleye anglers who bounce plugs and jigs off the bottom of the rocky shorelines at places such as Lincoln Beach, the Provo Boat Harbor, and the area just west of the Geneva steel plant. Some of the boat harbors are good places to fish through the ice for white bass in the winter. And stinkbait fishing for channel catfish and bullhead can be productive most of the year,

 The fat content of fish, 2.5 milligrams per 100 grams on average, is lower than that of beef, pork, or lamb.

U

especially near the structure found at the boat harbors around the lake, at Lincoln Beach, and near where tributaries flow into the Provo.

Northeastern Region

Flaming Gorge–Green River.   It may be difficult to decide whether the 91-mile-long Flaming Gorge Reservoir, or the Green River below the Flaming Gorge Dam, ranks as Utah's most famous fishery. A case can be made for both of these waters inside the Flaming Gorge National Recreation Area.

The reservoir, which straddles the Utah-Wyoming border, became world famous in the late 1970s for producing lunker specimens of both lake trout and brown trout, which approached world-record status on occasion. Although the trophy brown trout fishery has all but died out, the big reservoir still produces 20-plus-pound lake trout on a surprisingly regular basis.

Of course, anglers must work to catch those trophies. Whereas lake trout are caught in the deeper areas of the reservoir year-round, the trophies are not plentiful and require hours and sometimes days of trolling or jigging before that one memorable fish is landed. But the big fish are there, and they certainly are a draw.

Other types of gamefish are easier to catch at Flaming Gorge Reservoir. Rainbow trout are stocked regularly and provide fair shore fishing and trolling, although trollers often have more success landing kokanee salmon. Shore anglers seeking rainbows do well fishing the lower part of the reservoir.

In spring and early summer, smallmouth bass are plentiful along the rocky shorelines, especially on the Utah side of the reservoir near Mustang Ridge and Antelope Flat. It's possible to catch smallmouths from shore as well; traditional bass plugs and small spinners provide some of the best fishing.

The Green River below Flaming Gorge Dam ranks among the West's top fly fishing rivers, drawing anglers from around the world. There may be more trout per mile in the stretch of river from the dam to Brown's Park than in almost any river in America. Wild brown trout and rainbows are the main species caught. Most are fat and healthy. More than one angler has been overcome by the river's beauty and clarity and decided to pass the time simply floating downriver, watching the 4- and 5-pound trout feed.

Dories operated by professional guides have become a popular way for first-time Green River anglers to learn the river. But several shops in nearby Dutch John rent rafts, and a 7-mile National Recreation Trail, which stretches from the dam down to the Little Hole take-out point, offers good access for wading anglers.

Scuds rank among the best patterns to use on the Green, although regular hatches send dry fly enthusiasts into ecstasy throughout the year. Good

anglers can experience 100-fish days when they hit the river just right.

High Uintas.   A 460,000-acre wilderness area with peaks exceeding heights of 12,000 feet, remote drainages, and gorgeous alpine scenery, the High Uintas region is the 17th largest wilderness in the U.S.

Although its season is short, usually from early July until late September, the area's 650 managed lakes and dozens of small streams consistently yield among Utah's best fishing for cutthroat, brook, and rainbow trout, as well as a few grayling. The DWR stocks many of the lakes from the air.

Wilderness anglers would do well to avoid more crowded drainages such as Henry's Fork, Naturalist Basin, and the Granddaddy Lakes and head into some of the less well-known drainages. The DWR publishes and sells a series of 12 inexpensive pamphlets called "The Lakes of the High Uintas," which indicate the species available in area lakes and streams and offer tips on avoiding crowds. Backpacking or horsepacking into the Uintas to fish for small, hungry trout is a delight.

Not everyone has to be a backpacker to enjoy the Uintas, however. This wilderness area is surrounded by lakes and rivers that can be reached by automobile. Although put-and-take rainbow trout are the focus, most of the waters are stocked two to three times a month, which keeps the fishing lively. The most popular campgrounds adjacent to alpine lakes are along Utah Highway 150—known locally as the Mirror Lake Highway—which connects Kamas, Utah, with Evanston, Wyoming. Don't ignore the Upper Provo River and Beaver Creek in that area as well.

Southern Region

Lake Powell.   Although the Glen Canyon Dam is located in Arizona, most of 186-mile-long Lake Powell is in Utah. With 1,960 miles of shoreline cutting into twisting red-rock canyons, this designated National Recreation Area managed by the National Park Service has more nooks and crannies than a person could explore in several lifetimes.

This is good news for anglers in search of stripers, smallmouth and largemouth bass, crappie, walleye, catfish, and bluegills, which favor the shoreline. The frequent fluctuations of the huge lake actually improve the fishing by continually flooding new areas, giving fish fresh cover.

Stripers were planted as a trophy fish with the idea that they would not spawn. But the stripers fooled the biologists, creating a feast-and-famine fishery based on the number of forage fish available. As a result, biologists have lifted the limit on stripers and encourage anglers to bring home as many as they can keep. The stripers gather near the Glen Canyon Dam in the spring to spawn, and in the fall, when they "boil" on the surface during feeding frenzies, creating fast and fun angling.

Lake Powell draws bass anglers from throughout the West.

Although largemouth bass were the primary gamefish in the early days of Lake Powell, the relatively recent addition of smallmouth to the mix has been successful. Other than the thousands of catfish, bluegills, or crappie that often cruise under the big houseboats found all over Lake Powell, smallmouths are the easiest of the gamefish to catch. This is especially true in the spring, when they head to their shallow spawning beds at the first hint of approaching hot weather.

Newcomers to Lake Powell can be intimidated by its sheer size. Don't be afraid to ask marina operators at Bullfrog, Hite, Wahweap, or Hall's Crossing for advice on what to use and where to fish. This is, after all, one of the world's largest man-made reservoirs.

Fish Lake.   Located near Richfield in south-central Utah, pine-shrouded Fish Lake has lived up to its name for generations, developing a local lore built up around the occasional trophy lake trout pulled from its depths by trollers and jiggers. Although not as common as the lunkers at Flaming Gorge, 10-plus-pound lake trout succumb to several lucky anglers every year. A few old-timers still troll deep with steel line wrapped around paddles instead of using poles.

Anglers more interested in catching good numbers of trout usually head for the east shoreline of the lake, where rainbow trout are plentiful along the weedbeds. Some like to troll, some fish with bait, and a few even toss flies. Splake are also caught.

There has been a new wrinkle to Fish Lake angling in recent years in the form of plentiful yellow perch. Those who simply dangle a worm over the side of the bank in the upper part of this beautiful, natural lake surrounded by pleasant U.S. Forest Service campgrounds are usually rewarded by catching dozens of this species.

Ice fishing has also become popular in recent years, and at least one of the three lodges on the lake usually stays open, providing lodging and access in the winter months.

Scofield Reservoir/Electric Lake/Joe's Valley Reservoir.   Located in southeastern Utah within an hour's drive of each other, Scofield, Electric, and Joe's Valley are the most popular trout fisheries in the Price area.

Scofield, which is surrounded by two state park camping and boat launching areas as well as some private land, is the most productive of the three, primarily offering large numbers of 10- to 16-inch rainbow trout to trollers, shore anglers using bait, and ice anglers in the winter. Although it can be plagued by invasions of Utah chub and is treated to remove these nongamefish every decade or so, Scofield ranks with Strawberry Reservoir in its ability to produce fast-growing fish quickly.

Electric Lake, with limited facilities and usually restrictive regulations, is primarily a cutthroat trout fishery. It supplies the cutthroat egg needs for many Utah hatcheries, so anglers should study regulations closely. Those seeking large cutthroats find success by casting flies or spinners from the shoreline or by trolling.

Joe's Valley can be spotty but does yield good splake and rainbow trout. Anglers should check out many of the smaller lakes and reservoirs on either side of the Wasatch Plateau that runs down the central part of the state. Some of these smaller waters produce good summer fishing, and the alpine scenery is spectacular.

Boulder Mountain.   An alpine area full of small lakes known for their trophy-size brook trout, Boulder Mountain sits between Capitol Reef National Park and the Grand Staircase National Monument. This location attracted heavy pressure during the 1990s that has hurt the fishery, but numerous remote area lakes are still capable of providing good catches of trout in a scenic environment. Check with the U.S. Forest Service ranger station in the tiny town of Teasdale, or in Escalante, for maps and information.

Unlike the Uintas, Boulder Mountain is not a federally designated wilderness area, so some of the lakes can be reached by four-wheel-drive vehicles. Others require a short hike.

Southwestern reservoirs.   Panguitch Lake, Otter Creek, and Minersville and Quail Creek Reservoirs rank as the top fishing waters in southwestern Utah. All are capable of growing fish fast, and—with the exception of Quail Creek, which has bass and trout—most feature nice-size rainbow trout.

Panguitch Lake has the most developed facilities. It is surrounded by private lodges offering boat rentals and places to spend the night. A couple of nice U.S. Forest Service campgrounds are on one end. Boat fishing is best for trout, usually between 10 and 16 inches.

Otter Creek typically yields the biggest trout. Although trolling is probably the preferred angling option, shore fishing can be good. There is a small lodge that rents boats, and a state park campground and boat launching facility. Infestations of Utah chub can slow fishing at times, but Otter Creek is a consistent trout producer most years.

Minersville is a state park that has been managed as a trophy trout fishery in recent years, largely due to problems with fish-eating birds and Utah chub. Because pressure is usually light, it's a great place for float tubers. Trout exceeding 20 inches in length are common. Expect to find restrictive limits.

Quail Creek is a few miles from the entrance to Zion National Park in the midst of southern Utah's red-rock country. It features open water year-round, and good trout fishing most of the year. Largemouth angling is excellent in the early spring.

U

VANUATU

Formerly the New Hebrides Islands, Vanuatu comprises a group of 82 coral and volcanic islands that runs roughly northwest-southeast over 1,300 kilometers of the Pacific Ocean. The group is roughly 1,000 kilometers west of Fiji.

Only 12 of the islands are of a significant size. Espiritu Santo (called Santo locally) and Malekula are the largest. The most developed is Efate, where the international airport and the capital city of Port Vila are located. Port Vila is one of the prettiest tropical towns on these Pacific islands. It is clean, with low crime rates, and has a wide range of shops and services.

Rainfall and temperatures increase to the north of the group. July through September are the wettest, and also the coolest, months. November through April is the cyclone (hurricane) season.

Vanuatu was jointly run by the French and British from 1906 until its independence in 1980. American influence was felt during World War II, and James Michener's book *Tales of the South Pacific* was set in these islands.

Outside influences are evident from Vanuatu's cosmopolitan atmosphere, one seldom encountered on other Pacific islands. For example, in Port Vila there are Chinese, French, Italian, Japanese, Mexican, Spanish, Thai, Indonesian, and Vietnamese restaurants, and others serve a variety of seafood dishes and European cuisine.

The local people are of Melanesian stock and are called "Ni-Vanuatu." They make up 90 percent of the population, which numbers roughly 200,000. The main languages are Bislama pidgin (which bridges the gulf formed by 105 indigenous languages), English, and French.

The main fishing base is Port Vila, where there's a wide range of quality accommodations and a handful of modern, quality charter boats equipped with good tackle. This includes two Australian-made 34-foot sportfishing boats and several smaller day boats. Many of these are based at the yacht club in downtown Port Vila.

Fishing can be excellent out of Port Vila. Besides fish attraction devices (FADs), the Erromango Seamounts are a hotspot, as is "marlin alley"—a stretch of water where the coastal shelf falls away into deep water; a parallel chain of seamounts exists out in the depths. During peak season, this area is hot! Regular pelagic captures are wahoo, yellowfin tuna, mahimahi (dolphin), Pacific sailfish, black marlin, and blue marlin.

Although yellowfin are available all year, the peak season runs from January through May. Fish average 40 to 60 kilograms, but 90-kilogram specimens are caught regularly. Mahimahi are best from June through October.

Peak marlin season runs from October through February, when there are good numbers of blue marlin about. There's also a run of striped marlin in October, as these fish head into the Coral Sea to spawn. Black marlin peak from January through May, but lesser numbers of blues and blacks are encountered throughout the year, along with sailfish.

Blue and black marlin in excess of 300 kilograms have been captured here on rod and reel, but the average is closer to 130 kilograms. Striped marlin are large and average around 100 kilograms. Skippers may release billfish on request, but this issue should be discussed before fishing starts. Custom dictates that the catch belongs to the boat, and most species are kept for sale on the domestic market. Lure trolling is favored for offshore fishing, as baits tend to produce sharks.

Big dogtooth tuna have been captured in this region, usually on the dropoffs around reefs and islands. These are taken on jigs, baits, and sometimes on trolled lures. Reef trolling with minnow-type diving lures and rigged baits, as well as casting surface lures and metal jigs, are ways to produce a mixed bag of tropical species that includes barracuda, rainbow runners, coral trout, red bass, and both bluefin and giant trevally.

Shore casting with lures can provide excellent fishing, although access is not open to all areas; visitors should check before starting to fish. Small lures and light tackle catch a wide range of reef fish, many of which have anglers running for fish identification books. Larger lures on more sturdy equipment will see hookups on larger reef predators such as coral trout, red bass, barracuda, and several species of trevally.

Anglers heading into the northern islands of Vanuatu will find frequent access by small aircraft. The most regular destinations are Espiritu Santo, Malekula, Tanna, and Pentecost.

Pentecost is known for its tower divers; at an annual festival, local men jump off high towers with vines attached to their ankles that stop their fall just above the ground—a primitive form of bungee jumping.

Varying levels of accommodation are available, including resorts on Espiritu Santo and Tanna. Although fully equipped charter boats are not available, dive operators and local fishermen can often be persuaded to take adventurous anglers out on the water. Such boats are minimally outfitted for angling, and it's necessary to supply your own tackle.

North of Efate, malaria becomes a more common concern. Visitors should take antimalarial medication if venturing into this area.

V-BOTTOM

A term loosely used to describe a boat with a planing hull, and separated into modified-V or deep-V categories.

See: Boat.

VEER

To change direction or swerve; also, when the wind changes direction in a clockwise direction, it veers.

VEGETATION

See: Aquatic Plants.

VENEZUELA

It stands to reason that Venezuela is well endowed with fisheries resources. The country boasts more than 1,700 miles of coastline and in excess of 1,000 streams, and it possesses one of the greatest rivers in the world—not to mention the world's tallest waterfall (Angel Falls). With its huge peacock bass and payara far inland, tarpon on the coast, bonefish on island flats, and marlin in blue water, Venezuela is one of South America's most diversified, high-quality sportfishing destinations.

Freshwater

Six navigable rivers course through Venezuela, but the most significant one, the Orinoco, drains and influences nearly 80 percent of the country. One arm branches off into Brazil and heads to the Río Negro and eventually the Amazon River. The highland plains rivers, as well as the impoundments that have been formed on some of the major tributaries, provide excellent fishing for the likes of peacock bass, payara, piranha, and other highly prized warmwater species. The many rivers and fishing opportunities here are described in the Orinoco and Amazon watersheds review under Brazil (see).

Saltwater

Inshore fishing. The Los Roques, Río Chico, and Río Aruca areas of Venezuela are relatively recent discoveries that rate highly for bonefish, tarpon, and snook, and provide good opportunities for light-tackle fishing.

Bonefish are plentiful and cruise the flats of some 20 islands that constitute Islas Los Roques ("Island of Rocks"), which lies almost 80 miles north of Caracas at approximately 12° latitude. To its north is the 2,000-fathom-deep water of the eastern Caribbean Sea; the next land to sight north of Los Roques is Puerto Rico, hundreds of miles distant.

Las Roques is one of Venezuela's national parks; further development is prohibited, and commercial fishing is tightly controlled. Out on the 30-mile-long Los Roques atoll are all manner of easily waded coral, sand, and grassflats. Tidal fluctuation is not great, so shallow water bonefishing is virtually always possible, and anglers encounter nearly every type of feeding situation.

Most bonefish here are caught on falling water, which is a bit unusual (rising water floods the flats and brings fish in to feed in most locations), and are found in classic tailing situations. Although singles and small fish are available, bonefish travel in large schools, sometimes numbering many hundred individuals and covering large expanses of the flats. The average bonefish here is small, in the 2- to 3-pound range, but 5- to 10-pounders exist.

The beautiful flats and reef edges provide opportunities for other quarries as well. Permit are scarce, but limited fishing for snook and small tarpon exists in lagoons and near mangroves in the summer. Of course, barracuda are often seen on the flats, and various snapper are taken as well. Few people bother with the reef edges, where action with a host of species is likely.

Although Los Roques is frequently windy, the area provides sufficient protected water to enable anglers to escape the brunt of the wind. With a water temperature that seldom varies from 80°F, the Los Roques flats are otherwise comfortable, with generally hard bottoms. Cold fronts and muddy water are not the problems here that they pose at other bonefishing sites.

Dirty water is another matter along the mainland coast, however, in the back bays, lagoons, and creeks that support hot fishing for snook and tarpon. A notable eastern site for this is in the Gulf of Paria, which is between Trinidad and the Venezuelan mainland, and several hours from Caracas. There, the Aruca River and assorted tributaries feed a brackish-water jungle-like estuary that hosts snook up to 20 pounds and tarpon up to 50 pounds. Anglers have reportedly seen larger tarpon here, but the average fish is in the 20-pound class. Snook are abundant in the mangrove- and deadfall-lined areas, and average several pounds.

The stained, milk chocolate water prevalent in these areas during the rainy season doesn't produce nearly as well as the darker, cleaner water, which one has to look for. The dry season, from November through April, produces cleaner water and good tarpon action. Schools of sardines are said to come into these waters beginning in September, followed by mullet in November, enhancing the tarpon prospects.

Light-tackle snook and tarpon fishing are equally productive in mangrove-lined Tacariqua Lagoon, a national park and wildlife refuge near Río Chico. Excellent small tarpon (up to 50 pounds) angling can be had here amidst small mangrove islands and in backwater bays and creeks.

The tarpon of Tacariqua are mostly under 15 pounds, and the snook average 2 to 4 pounds. Larger snook in the 6- to 8-pound class are caught as well, and some have been reported to 20 pounds. Casting tight to the edge of the mangroves is the norm in these dark, tannin-stained waters, with streamer flies and an assortment of surface and shallow-running plugs. Bigger fish are reported in the channels and in the open lagoon waters, however. As often happens in such places, early and late in the day are favored times for the bigger fish.

The absence of giant fish in these and other places may deter trophy seekers, but it's worth noting that Venezuela's Lake Maracaibo once produced a 283-pound tarpon. And the Boca Grande area of the Orinoco Delta, which is expansive by any measure, is mostly covered with mangrove swamps, but little has been reported about sportfishing there.

Offshore fishing. The North Equatorial Current sweeps westward from the northwest coast of Africa, coursing over 3,000 miles of the Atlantic and sweeping into the Caribbean Sea below Barbados and Grenada, striking the northern coast of Venezuela. There, just north of the coastal town of La Guaira, an eddy current works counter to the main flow. Added to this is the steady contribution of nutrients from the Orinoco River, one of South America's most prominent watersheds. Together, these natural circumstances create an environment that brings baitfish and large predators into the area and holds them there. The fish arrive in great quantities, quantities that at times produce fabulous action, especially for billfish, which are attracted by the abundance of baitfish along the dropoffs washed by the current. In the peak of their availability, these fish provide world-famous big-game fishing.

The tales of marlin and sailfish action off La Guaira Bank, although stupendous to anglers of today, are barely half what was experienced several decades ago, when the first anglers pioneered offshore fishing here. In intervening years, there was little exploration or exploitation of the area with sportfishing craft. It came as a surprise to many anglers when they ventured to La Guaira in the early to mid-1980s with better boats and equipment and raised 20 to 40 fish per day per boat.

Today the numbers aren't that high, but they are exceptionally good, and the variety is unmatched. Where captains in most other ports are glad to talk of hooking or catching a couple of sailfish and perhaps a single marlin in a day, success off Venezuela is measured in slightly better form.

There are many popular big-game fishing destinations that offer concentrations of particular species within a tight season, but few have excellent potential for catching a variety of billfish, and fewer

Peacock bass anglers ply the flooded backwaters of Venezuela's Guri Lake.

still provide that potential at virtually any time of the year. The waters offshore of the north coast of Venezuela are perhaps unique in that they support year-round populations of a wide variety of pelagic fish, especially sailfish, blue marlin, white marlin, and swordfish. These species are augmented by wahoo, yellowfin tuna, and dolphin, which occur seasonally but are still found in varying numbers over much of the year.

Certainly there may be day-to-day and week-to-week variations in the numbers and cooperation of offshore species, but Venezuela's food-rich waters come close to predictability, and the notion of good or better seasons has less meaning when billfish are present in significant numbers year-round, and when a blue marlin, white marlin, or sailfish is a possible catch on any given day of the year. Indeed, a grand slam catch—a sailfish, a blue marlin, and a white marlin—is possible every day. Not many places can make such a claim.

The Venezuela recreational fishing fleet is headquartered in Caraballeda and generally fishes over La Guaira Bank or closer to shore off the power plant west of Maiquetia. Lines are usually in the water within 45 minutes after the boat leaves the inlet—sooner if you troll an artificial lure at high speed on the way out.

La Guaira Bank is a broad underwater plateau that rises to within about 350 feet of the surface a scant dozen miles from shore (a few miles farther out is a deeper bank, Playa Grande, but few boats venture there). The swift currents that sweep along the northern coastline of South America create tremendous upwellings around the banks, and the full range of the marine food chain is found in the area.

Squadrons of flyingfish, legions of bullet bonito, and clouds of seabirds overhead signal the richness of these waters. Southwest of the bank and slightly inland, an occasional whale blows a plume of spray, and vast schools of leaping porpoises often stretch almost as far as the eye can see. In the spring, great

schools of yellowfin tuna skirt the northernmost edges of the bank and beyond, under the traveling umbrella of screaming, feeding seabirds.

In spring and summer, pods of dorado feed over the bank. These schooling fish are not the ubiquitous "chicken" dolphin of Florida waters, but rather weigh between 20 and 50 pounds.

The constant trade winds and powerful currents responsible for the upwellings and concentrations of baitfish, however, also bring alpine seas. Although the bank can look like a millpond at times, it is more likely to have heavy swells rolling in from the east, accompanied by a sharp chop on top of the swells. This explains why most of the boats here measure 35 feet or more, and are of rough-water design. During the summer months, mornings may dawn clear and calm, but such blessings are rare and not dependable. October's popularity with anglers has nothing to do with calmer seas or greater comforts.

Seas notwithstanding, the abundance and variety of billfish is primarily what draws anglers from around the world. An ever-present possibility of trophy specimens makes every day on La Guaira still more exciting. Venezuela, in fact, has produced a number of blue marlin in the 850- to over 1,000-pound range in the last decade. Huge blues have come during such diverse months as April, July, September, and October.

The fall months have long been regarded as the premier billfish time here, especially September for sailfish and October and November for white marlin. In recent times, anglers have discovered that opportunities from February through June probably exceed those in the fall, if not for big fish then for quantity. And fishing during the summer can also be excellent. For swordfishing, the lighter summer breezes offer the most comfortable night angling; the winds and seas are far more likely to be calmer in June, July, and August than in the spring and fall. Three-hundred-fathom depths scant miles offshore provide good odds for swordfish success, even on a one-night trip. Conservation efforts make angling for swordfish generally less popular, however. A few charter boats still pursue swords here, but most leave the species alone.

In the past, white marlin fishing in the fall has been so productive that anglers often raised as many as 20 to 30 in a day. Although such banner days occur less frequently, undoubtedly because of commercial longline fishing pressures in the Caribbean, it is still common to raise a dozen whites in a day, and not only in the fall. If the number of whites raised is not as consistently high as it once was, it is still excellent when compared with any other locale.

As is true elsewhere, the presence and number of Venezuelan billfish are subject to various factors, not the least of which is excessive commercial fishing exploitation. Although many billfish off Venezuela are resident, others are migratory; some billfish from La Guaira Bank travel to and from the

Cozumel/Cancún area of the Yucatán, and there is some white marlin movement between Venezuela and the mid-Atlantic coast in North America. What happens in one area or between areas can affect all of them. Local conservation efforts in U.S. waters, for example, afford protection to billfish populations only during that portion of their yearly wanderings when they fall within U.S. jurisdiction; elsewhere, they may be subject to less-restrictive commercial exploitation (something to keep in mind when you see billfish offered in a restaurant or fish market).

La Guaira Bank and surrounding waters also offer marvelous opportunities for other gamefish. Wahoo are frequent visitors and provide action for the angler willing to switch from monofilament to wire leaders. Although the wire may spook white marlin, it's a necessity for landing toothy wahoo. No such sacrifice needs to be made for dolphin or yellowfin tuna, and both are frequently caught here by anglers seeking billfish.

The dolphin (dorado), caught off Venezuela's verdant coast are larger on average than the schoolies familiar to most anglers. Schools of fish in which each specimen exceeds 20 pounds are common; 35- to 50-pound fish are taken with surprising regularity. Landed on the same rigged ballyhoo that produce sailfish and white marlin, giant bull dolphin provide an exciting diversion, even for the obsessive billfish addict.

Yellowfins are something else again, and for some anglers here, they may not be as welcome as wahoo or dorado due to their indefatigable nature. From 30 to 50 miles north of the coastal mountains, great clouds of screaming, diving seabirds commonly feed over schools of tuna. This is where commercial netters ply their trade. Tuna schools range far inshore to feed on swarms of baitfish, however, and billfish-seeking anglers are occasionally interrupted by crashing strikes, often in multiples, from feeding yellowfins. Averaging from 160 to 190 pounds, these tuna are often hooked on light lines intended for white marlin or sailfish, and anglers often are leashed to a seemingly inexhaustible monster by slim 20- or 30-pound-test line. One such angler, trolling close to shore on the way in from fishing on the bank one March day, latched onto a 245-pound yellowfin.

Not everyone fishes with conventional and big-game tackle here, of course. The bank attracts a growing number of anglers eager to tangle with billfish on fly tackle. Sailfish and white marlin are especially popular fly fishing targets, and some also pursue blue marlin. The smaller 100- to 200-pound fish that occur in incredible numbers over La Guaira Bank from April through June provide the most appropriate and realistic fly-tackle opportunities.

One of the joys of offshore fishing in Venezuela is its accessibility. Caracas is a $2^1/_2$-hour flight from Miami, and a few anglers head there on Friday, fish for two days, and return on Monday morning. Although many of the available charter boats are booked months in advance, it's sometimes possible to slip in a brief, spur-of-the-moment trip.

As a bonus to the visiting angler, Venezuela adds aesthetic factors to the bare fishing statistics. These include shoreside comforts, delicious local delicacies, great shopping opportunities, and the awe-inspiring beauty of Venezuela's northern coastline, especially when viewed from offshore.

The offshore fleet originates at Caraballeda, a small town about a half-hour from the Caracas airport, which is actually in Maiquetia on the coast north of Caracas. Visiting anglers take a taxi from the airport to Caraballeda, a ride that leads through a succession of small towns nestled along a narrow strip of land beneath towering 7,500-foot-high mountains that separate the sea from the city of Caracas beyond. Visible from far offshore, these velvet-green peaks topped with whipped cream clouds serve as a constant reference point during the day's fishing, and as a magnificent backdrop for evening shoreside activities.

Most Venezuelan charter boats supply modern tackle from 20- through 80-pound class, but those who prefer to gamble with lighter lines are advised to bring their own tackle. Similarly, those who wish to do battle with stand-up gear would do well to bring their own fitted harnesses. Since many anglers seeking blue marlin prefer to troll artificial lures, they may wish to bring along a few proven favorites, although most boats carry a supply of rigged artificials. Everything else is supplied. The common fishing routine for charter boats is to start on or near La Guaira Bank, working the peak and the adjacent vicinity. If action slows, or for variety, the boats head southwest and inland.

VENTILATED-SPOOL REEL
A reel with perforations on the spool, also known as a perforated spool reel; this is an increasingly popular item in fly fishing for lightness and line drying; it has appeared recently on a few baitcasting reel spools, where it is mainly intended to reduce weight.
See: Baitcasting Tackle; Flycasting Tackle.

VENUE
A term predominantly used by British anglers to refer to a particular fishing site or location, be that a river, lake, reservoir, canal, etc. For example, an angler might say, "River fishing in the north has declined in recent years; previously the venues there produced excellent numbers of fish."

VERMICULATIONS
Short, wavy wormlike lines on the back and sides of some fish.

VERMONT
Vermont is a small state, but it offers greater variety in fish species and angling opportunity than much larger states. With 280 lakes and ponds that exceed 20 acres each, and 5,000 miles of fishable streams, good fishing locations are not lacking.

Among these possibilities is 110-mile-long Lake Champlain, one of the most formidable natural lakes in North America, and more than 200 miles of New England's most prominent river, the Connecticut. About half of Vermont's waters drain into Champlain, and about 40 percent drain into the Connecticut River, eventually reaching Long Island Sound.

The Green Mountain State's excellent offerings vary from big lakes and rivers to remote mountain trout streams and tiny beaver ponds. Almost every significant freshwater fish thrives in this state. Species of prominence in various waters include brook trout, brown trout, rainbow trout, lake trout, landlocked salmon, steelhead, largemouth bass, smallmouth bass, walleye, northern pike, pickerel, muskellunge, yellow perch, white perch, smelt, and several species of catfish.

Although Vermont is the only New England state that doesn't have a seacoast, it does offer anadromous fishing. The Connecticut River, which forms the state's eastern border, provides a good spring fishery for shad in its lower reaches. Time will tell if Atlantic salmon runs will be restored and with enough abundance to permit angling.

Access is rarely a problem in the state, as the Vermont Fish and Wildlife Department has been aggressive in purchasing land and building parking areas and boat ramps. Those who want to get away should look to the Northeast Kingdom or the Green Mountain National Forest. Lake Champlain in the west and the Connecticut River in the east offer great variety. In between is more good fishing than most people realize, and it all comes with beautiful scenery.

Lake Champlain
Lake Champlain is often referred to as the Sixth Great Lake and occupies much of Vermont's western boundary, or coast, as some call it. At 120 miles long, with 587 miles of shoreline and 435 square miles of surface, Lake Champlain is truly a great lake. Shared with New York and Quebec, its waters drain to the north through the Richelieu River into the St. Lawrence, and its fisheries are jointly managed.

Champlain's coldwater fishery consists primarily of lake trout, landlocked salmon, brown trout, and steelhead trout. The main warmwater species are large- and smallmouth bass, walleye, northern pike, and pickerel. Yellow perch are the species taken in greatest numbers throughout the length and breadth of the lake, although white perch are also popular.

In addition to these prominent and sought-after species, however, there are channel catfish, crappie, bluegills, rock bass, brown bullhead, whitefish, and

smelt in Champlain, as well as cisco, burbot, bowfin, carp, gar, suckers, eels, freshwater drum, and mooneye. If this potpourri isn't satisfactory, you can try for the occasional muskie that lurks near river mouths.

Lake sturgeon are also present, incidentally; this is one species that anglers should not be fishing for, although occasionally one is caught. The lake sturgeon grows to impressive lengths here, but it is an endangered species and protected by law. Release of accidental catch is mandatory.

Lake Champlain is divided into five sections for purposes of fishery management and assessment. From north to south the divisions are: Missisquoi Bay, Inland Sea, Mallets Bay, Broad Lake, and South Lake.

Missisquoi Bay is the northernmost part of the lake and extends into Canada. The Missisquoi River forms a delta that divides the bay, which is quite shallow and home to good populations of walleye, largemouth bass, northern pike, and perch. Along the delta is the Missisquoi National Wildlife Refuge.

The Inland Sea is the area from the causeway at Sandbar north, and is bounded on the west by the islands that form Grand Isle County. There are both deep water and shallow bays here, as well as a variety of guts around and between the many islands. The main species are landlocked salmon, northern pike, largemouth and smallmouth bass, walleye, and yellow perch.

Mallets Bay is south of Sandbar and north of the old railroad bed that connected Colchester Point and South Hero. Water depths exceed 100 feet in several places, yet there's a long, shallow flat along the causeway at Sandbar. Anglers do well here with largemouth and smallmouth bass, landlocked salmon, northern pike, walleye, and yellow perch.

The Broad Lake area is the biggest section and, at 12 miles, is the widest part of the lake. It is bounded on the south by the Champlain Bridge at Addison and on the north by the railroad bed, the Champlain Islands, and Quebec. Most of this section is deep and cold and naturally holds big lake trout and salmon, plus good populations of walleye, smallmouth bass, and smelt.

The South Lake sector extends from the Champlain Bridge to the Champlain Canal at Whitehall, New York. This section is shallow and apt to be turbid. Walleye, channel catfish, white perch, largemouth bass, sauger, and northern pike are the primary species.

Connecticut River

At 410 miles long, the Connecticut is New England's longest river, running the length of Vermont and forming its eastern border. From high in the New Hampshire mountains within sight of the Canadian border, the Connecticut flows south to Long Island Sound. Some 235 miles of its length abuts the Green Mountain State.

The big river offers excellent fishing and a greater variety of species than any other body of water in Vermont, with the possible exception of Lake Champlain. There is no better way to fish the river and enjoy its tranquillity and natural beauty than by floating it.

This great river was once an industrial and municipal sewer in Vermont but is now very clean and provides a variety of angling opportunities, from strictly trout waters in the north to the warmwater fishery in the south. Year after year the New Hampshire and Vermont annual records for several species of fish are taken from the Connecticut River.

The upper river holds brookies, browns, and rainbows. Much of the river between the upper and lower sections has a mix of species, including trout, largemouth and smallmouth bass, walleye, pickerel, northern pike, yellow perch, white perch, bluegills, hornpout, and the occasional tiger muskie.

The upper sections of the river from Beecher Falls to Guildhall are mostly easy to wade. From Guildhall south to Gilman there are plenty of trout, but smallmouth bass also thrive here.

Many anglers concentrate on a particular section of trout water in the upper river. From a point 250 feet below the Lyman Dam to a point 1,600 feet upstream of the Bloomfield/North Stratford Bridge, fishing is restricted to catch and release by flies or artificial lures with barbless hooks.

The Fifteen Mile Falls hydroelectric complex, which extends from Gilman to McIndoes, consists of three dams: Moore, Comerford, and McIndoes. The big reservoirs hold brook, brown, and rainbow trout, large- and smallmouth bass, and yellow perch. Many anglers consider Comerford one of the best smallmouth bass fisheries in the region. The tailraces of the three dams hold lunker brown and rainbow trout and can be productive year-round.

From McIndoes south to Wilder Dam, the fishery is mostly for warmwater species, but trout linger

Lake trout are a staple catch in Lake Champlain; note the lamprey attached to the flank of this trout.

near the mouths of tributaries. This section of river holds both large- and smallmouth bass, pickerel, northern pike, walleye, and perch. Many anglers devote most of their time on this section to fishing for walleye. Also popular are perch, which are plentiful, or the monster pike that feed on them.

The lower river has anadromous fish, including American shad and Atlantic salmon. Shad arrive in late May and provide a particularly exciting and popular fishery below the dams at Bellows Falls and Vernon. These areas offer good walleye fishing, as do Sumner Falls and Wilder Dam farther upstream.

Those who fish the lower river for largemouth bass should concentrate on the many setbacks, such as those at Herricks Cove and at Retreat Meadows in Brattleboro. The mouths of the larger tributaries are good bets for both walleye and northern pike.

Northeast Kingdom

Rivers.   The Northeast Kingdom consists of Essex, Orleans, and Caledonia Counties. A fabled region that offers excellent trout waters, it also provides as much seclusion as anyone could want. Much of the area is commercial forest owned by large forest-products companies. These large landowners have been exceptionally generous in keeping their lands open to the public free of charge.

The upper reaches of the Kingdom are referred to as the place "where the rivers flow north" because the Barton, Black, Clyde, Johns, and Coaticook Rivers do just that, as do their smaller tributaries, ultimately flowing into in the mighty St. Lawrence. The remainder of the Kingdom's rivers, however, empty into the Connecticut and drain south into Long Island Sound.

If there is one stream in Vermont as famous as the Battenkill, it is the Willoughby. This river, and its annual run of large rainbows, attracts shoulder-to-shoulder fishing in the spring. The Willoughby drains the picturesque glacial lake of the same name and empties into the Barton River in the village of Orleans. It also has a good population of brook trout. The main stem of the Barton between Orleans and Glover holds both rainbows and browns.

The Black River rises in the hill town of Albany and winds its way north to Lake Memphremagog. It is best known as a premier brown trout fishery but holds brookies and rainbows in many sections.

Nature took charge of the lower Clyde River in the mid-1990s, breaching a dam that had ended a once-heralded spring run of landlocked salmon. The Federal Regulatory Energy Commission ordered the permanent removal of the remaining dam, and the salmon have returned in increasing numbers, attracting anglers from afar.

Although less than 6 miles long, Johns River serves as an important spawning area for brown and rainbow trout from Lake Memphremagog. It starts and ends in Derby but swings into Canada for a short distance before emptying into the big lake.

The Nulhegan River and its tributaries drain one of Vermont's most remote and least-populated areas. Exploring the watershed is possible due to a network of private logging roads. Most of the watershed is populated with native brook trout, and the lower reaches of the main stem hold brown trout as well.

The Moose and Passumpsic Rivers and their tributaries drain southern Essex and northern Caledonia Counties. Both are good trout waters holding mostly brook trout in the upper sections and browns lower down. On the southern edge of the Kingdom, the Wells River is also a good trout stream, with browns in the lower reaches and brookies upstream.

Lakes and ponds.   The Northeast Kingdom is dotted with clear, cold lakes and ponds holding trout and landlocked salmon. Anglers have so many options for trout and salmon that it is often difficult to choose a lake. Lake Willoughby in Westmore is the best known of these, and it produces the largest lake trout in the region. It is also one of the most picturesque lakes in the state. Lake Memphremagog is an international body of water that straddles the border at Newport. Until the water warms in early summer, the portion in Vermont provides good fishing for salmon, lake trout, browns, rainbows, and brookies. When the water temperature climbs, the trout tend to head across the border to deeper water. Another international lake is Wallace Pond in Canaan, which has rainbow, brown, and lake trout.

Great Averill and Little Averill Lakes are located in the border town of Averill and, along with good fishing, offer seclusion. Seymour Lake, and its neighbor Echo Lake, as well as Island Pond just down the road in the village of the same name, are all good bets for trout. On the east side of the Kingdom is Maidstone Lake, a beautiful trout water adjacent to Maidstone Lake State Park.

Shadow Lake in Glover, Crystal Lake in Barton, Caspian Lake in Greensboro, Harveys Lake in Barnet, and Joe's Pond in Danville are all easily accessed trout waters offering a variety of fishing opportunities.

Trout ponds are numerous, and two groups are especially worth noting. Newark, Bald Hill, Center, Long, and Jobs are located within minutes of each other in Westmore and Newark. To the south in Groton State Forest are Peacham, Martins, Osmore, Levi, Kettle, and Noyes.

Of special note is Noyes Pond in Groton, which is controlled by the Forests, Parks and Recreation Department and restricted to fly fishing only. The pond covers only 39 acres, but the restrictive regulations imposed on it for years make the brook trout fishing very popular.

Exploring the remote Kingdom in search of trout ponds is best accomplished with a good topographic map. Many ponds, such as Lewis, South America, Notch, and West Mountain, lie far up paper-company roads that have no road signs and

where visitors are guests who must give way to logging trucks.

Although best known for its trout and salmon, the Kingdom has some good bass fishing. Lake Memphremagog, the big lake that straddles the Vermont/Quebec border in Newport and Derby, has a sizable smallmouth bass population, as does Seymour Lake in Morgan. The Connecticut River in this region also offers both small- and largemouth bass fishing.

Northwestern Region

The Lamoille and Missisquoi Rivers are two good-size northwestern trout rivers that flow west into Lake Champlain, cutting deep valleys across the Green Mountains.

Approximately 85 miles long, the Lamoille holds browns, rainbows, and brookies in its various reaches. Perhaps the most productive section is between Morrisville and Wolcott, where trophy rainbows and browns await the dedicated angler.

The Missisquoi River winds back and forth across the border between Vermont and Quebec. Those who float it in canoes have to deal with Customs in both the U.S. and Canada. The availability of brook trout, rainbows, and browns varies according to the section of the river.

The northwestern region of the state isn't known for trout, but worthwhile trout waters do exist here. Good bets for brookies are Enosburg Reservoir in Berkshire, Kings Hill Pond in Bakersfield, and Adams Pond in Enosburg. At 2,920 feet in elevation, tiny Sterling Pond is Vermont's highest trout pond. A pleasant hike up the Long Trail from Route 108 leads to scenic book trout fishing.

A wide variety of warmwater fishing is available in Arrowhead Mountain Lake, Lake Carmi, Lake Iroquois, Shelburne Pond, and Green River Reservoir.

Central Region

Central Vermont extends from the Connecticut river on the east to Lake Champlain on the west. Consisting of lowlands on both sides and encompassing the backbone of the Green Mountains, this region includes high, fast-flowing mountain streams and meandering lowland rivers.

On the east there are three important rivers: the Waits, the Ompompanoosuc, and the White. Starting high in the mountains of Orange, Waits River flows eastward to empty into the Connecticut in Bradford. It is trout water all the way and holds brookies, browns, and rainbows. The Ompompanoosuc is best fished in its upper reaches, where water temperatures are more conducive to trout.

The White River and its many branches have a popular trout fishery. The river is very accessible and easily fished, and excellent trout populations draw anglers from afar. In the lower reaches, the trout share habitat with smallmouth bass, which are much sought after by local anglers.

The White also holds the hopes of those working to reestablish Atlantic salmon. The White River National Fish Hatchery was erected in Bethel to help meet the needs of the anadromous fish stocking program for the many tributaries of the Connecticut River. The goal here and throughout the Connecticut is to establish a self-sustaining Atlantic salmon fishery similar to what once spawned in the river before the first dam was built on it during the eighteenth century.

In central Vermont, the western trout flowages that empty into Lake Champlain consist of Poultney River, Otter Creek, and Winooski River.

The Winooski and its many tributaries offer excellent trout fishing throughout the central and western portion of this region. Brook, brown, and rainbow trout are found throughout the watershed, and the lower Winooski has an extremely popular steelhead fishery. Much of the Poultney River serves as the boundary between Vermont and New York. The Poultney is a good wild trout stream, offering angling for brookies and browns.

The Washington County towns of Calais and Woodbury have four rainbow trout waters in close proximity. Nelson Pond, Lake Greenwood, Mirror Lake, and Sabin Pond are all very accessible and have good fishing. Nelson Pond also has big lake trout.

To the west in Essex, Indian Brook Reservoir holds rainbows and browns, as does Waterbury Reservoir in Waterbury and Stowe. A short drive north of the state capitol in Montpelier is Wrightsville Reservoir, which boasts brown trout. To the south in Addison County, Lake Dunmore possesses lake trout, rainbows, and landlocked salmon, and there are rainbow and brown trout in Silver Lake nearby. Lake Fairlee in Thetford is well known for rainbow trout as well as for a winter smelt fishery.

Bass are not without some presence in this region. Buck Lake in Woodbury and Green River Reservoir in Hyde Park are notable sites, and the premier bass water is Lake Morey, located in the town of Fairlee on the east side of the state. Fairfield Pond in Fairfield, Arrowhead Mountain Lake in Georgia, Waterbury Reservoir in Waterbury, and Salisbury's Lake in Dunmore are prime bass waters.

Southern Region

The southern four counties of Windsor, Rutland, Windham, and Bennington are like those of the central region in that they encompass low-lying agricultural lands and high-mountain terrain along the north-south Green Mountain range.

Rising high in Sherburne, the Ottauquechee River meanders south and east to the Connecticut River and holds rainbow trout throughout its length, plus brookies in some areas. The river runs through Quechee Gorge, a picturesque natural attraction that holds large brown trout. Most of the smaller tributaries possess brook trout.

As one moves south, the next major trout streams are the Black, Williams, Saxtons, and West

Rivers. Trout fishing in the West River consists mainly of brookies and browns. The section of this stream below Ball Mountain Dam is a whitewater course used for Olympic trials.

The Deerfield River flows south from its start on Stratton Mountain through a high basin between ridges of the Green Mountains until it enters Massachusetts. The upper reaches are scenic and remote, and hold brown trout and brookies.

The region's southwestern trout rivers drain into the Hudson, and the three most important are the Hoosic, Battenkill, and Mettawee.

The Battenkill is easily Vermont's best-known and most-fished trout stream. Its brook and brown trout are very wary and challenge the best anglers. Manchester, through which the Battenkill flows, is home to the world-renowned fishing gear supplier Orvis and the American Museum of Fly Fishing. Anglers flock to both just as they do to the river itself.

The waters of the Mettawee flow northwest from Dorset to the New York line in Wells, and are conducive to an especially good natural trout fishery.

Lake Bomoseen in Castleton is the largest body of water entirely in Vermont, and one of its best southern bass waters. It also has brook and brown trout. A bit farther south in Poultney and Wells is Lake St. Catherine, which is known for brown trout, lake trout, and a good warmwater fishery. Also in Castleton is Glen Lake, a favorite rainbow trout spot for local anglers.

The mountain towns of Chittenden, Mendon, and Sherburne are home to several good brook trout ponds. These include Lefferts, North, South, Colton, and Kent Ponds. Chittenden Reservoir also has brookies, as well as rainbows, browns, and salmon.

Vermont's scenic Route 100 runs the length of the state along the Green Mountains; a series of trout waters abut the highway between Ludlow and Plymouth. They include Woodward Reservoir, Amherst Lake, and Echo Lake. In the southwestern corner of the state, Lake Paran and Lake Shaftsbury, both in the town of Shaftsbury, offer rainbow trout.

High up along Route 9 are Searsburg and Harriman Reservoirs, which are part of the Deerfield River hydro system. Searsburg is known for its brook trout fishery, and the much bigger Harriman holds brook, brown, and rainbow trout, plus perch, pickerel, and smallmouth bass. Somerset Reservoir, which is a few miles up a road that follows the Deerfield River, is a remote lake that offers secluded brook trout angling.

The big Green Mountain National Forest has many trout ponds, most of which require a hike to get to. Bourn, Branch, and Beebe Ponds in Sunderland, and nearby Stratton Pond in Stratton, are among the notable sites here, and all possess brook trout.

VERTICAL JIGGING
See: Jigging.

VEST, FISHING

A compartmented sleeveless garment for storing terminal fishing tackle, including flies and lures, plus other accessories. Designed primarily for stowing readily accessible tackle while wading, and mostly used by stream and river fly anglers, a fishing vest is equally useful for anglers who hike a fair distance into fishing waters, for those who are mobile when fishing from shore, and for those who use spinning and baitcasting tackle.

Fishing vests are characterized by numerous pockets, which anglers, being tackle junkies, commonly fill to overflowing. Many also attach various tools to the exterior, so that they appear to be walking tackle shops. Vests for some anglers are so pregnant with supplies that a lot of weight is carried for long periods on the shoulders and back, which may be uncomfortable, and may even interfere with ordinary angling activities. Veteran anglers have learned to pare their streamside tackle down and carry in their vest what is most useful for the task at hand on a given day. This has also given rise to alternative carrying systems, some of which appeal to the go-light angler who does not need a great deal of equipment.

Vest features. Although there are vests with many pockets that may be fine for general outdoor or photographic use, fishing vests have a very specific design that is tailored to angling needs, and the various features are intended to accommodate specific types of equipment and have assorted angler-friendly virtues.

Fishing vests are categorized as standard or short length, the former extending to the waist and the latter to the chest. A chest-high vest, commonly called a shorty, is intended to permit wading in deep water with chest-high waders *(see)* without dunking the vest and its contents, which can happen anyway if you fall.

Among the most important items to stow in a vest are small boxes with flies or lures, and better vests have many deep-bellowed pockets to specifically accommodate these. Some are sized to accommodate the larger boxes that are used for streamer flies or lures, while others, both on the exterior and interior of the vest, accommodate other styles. Many of the pockets or compartments are suited to holding such objects as a penlight, stream thermometer, hook sharpener, sunglasses, sunscreen, fly floatant, leader-dispensing spools, and so forth. Back pockets accommodate a light rain jacket and possibly a camera or extra reel or reel spool, and interior pockets are intended for keys, wallet, map, and the like.

Better vests are now made of quick-drying ripstop nylon, have stretchable mesh shoulder construction to help spread the weight load, sport a comfortable rib-net collar, and have noncorroding zippers. A good feature on some is exterior loops, D-rings, or tubes for retractable tool holders, and Velcro loops for temporary rod holding.

 The ridges and spaces on some types of fish scales can be counted like the rings on a tree to determine a fish's age, and can be read to provide other information, such as the times it has spawned.

While you can really stuff a vest, most of the contents go unused from day to day. This behooves you to cut out some of the items previously mentioned for comfort and practicality. Whether you really need a net, a compass, first aid items, a scale, a host of tools instead of one multi-purpose tool, six or more boxes of flies or lures instead of two or three, and food and water, among many other possible items, is up to you, your back, and the distance you'll be from the car, where you can stow everything that really doesn't have to be toted in the vest. However, you will definitely want to have a place to store insect repellent (it should not contact other items, which it can harm), fly line dressing, a split shot container or lead wrap, and a small knife.

Incidentally, some short-length wading-style rain jackets are designed for holding tackle boxes and a few accessories, and some personal flotation vests do likewise. Neither is as comfortable or functional as a fishing vest, however.

Alternatives.   Other means of carrying gear for wading and mobile anglers include a wide array of rigid chest boxes, soft chest packs, and soft fanny packs. Non of these store the full range of items that a vest can, but they do offer short-trip, grab-and-go options, plus lightweight freedom, and may be very useful if you put the right things inside.

Rigid metal or plastic chest boxes have trays for fly storage, which is good for organization, and some offer quick-change options to suit the day's needs. Some also have a light, magnifier, tippet dispenser, and other elements. The box, which has shoulder and chest straps and is worn conveniently in front of the angler, is readily accessible, but its rigidity can be a disadvantage for travel, making it susceptible to breakage.

Soft chest packs are also convenient to use and available in a wide range of styles, from simple one-pocket items more like a small pouch to multi-compartmented products that are a step short of being a mini-vest. Many of these feature mesh or see-through material so you can view a pocket's contents without opening it. Soft fanny packs, too, range from single-pocket models to versions that can hold a few small fly boxes and several accessories.
See: Tackle Storage.

VHF RADIO
Acronym for Very High Frequency radio.
See: Communications.

VIDEO SOUNDER
A type of sonar using a cathode-ray tube.
See: Sonar.

VIRGIN ISLANDS
The Virgin Islands lie east of Puerto Rico between the Atlantic Ocean and the Caribbean Sea.

Fish names are not always what they seem. For instance, the dogfish is actually a shark, the buffalo is actually a sucker, and the sea robin is actually a sculpin.

Forming part of the Lesser Antilles chain in the West Indies, the British Virgins consist of 36 small islands, the largest being Tortola and Virgin Gorda; and the U.S. Virgins consist of the three small islands of St. Croix, St. Thomas, and St. John, as well as 50 islets. The U.S. Virgins are the easternmost portion of that country. Tourism is important to all of the Virgin Islands but especially to the U.S. islands. St. Thomas lays claim to being one of the world's foremost blue marlin fishing centers.

For some big-game anglers, if you say "St. Thomas, blue marlin, North Drop, summer, and full moon" all in the same breath, you've hit the proverbial nail on the head. Look no farther. It's not quite that simple, actually, but for many marlin buffs, St. Thomas is a great place to hook up with a marlin. It is probably the premier location for this species in the western Atlantic.

The record books back this up. St. Thomas has produced more than its share of officially recorded sport-caught 1,000-pound Atlantic blue marlin (four) than any other location, certainly in the western Atlantic. Numerous line-class (and at least one fly-rod) world records for Atlantic blue marlin have been established in St. Thomas as well. And for many years it owned the one that all big-game anglers set their sights on, the former all-tackle and 130-pound line-class world-record catch of 1,282 pounds, which was established in August of 1977 and stood for 15 years.

Records aside, the hallowed billfish grounds are relatively near St. Thomas (and the other islands) and are uniquely situated to provide excellent opportunities and plenty of action. Relatively inexperienced anglers on a boat that sees (or raises) from one to three marlin in a day think that's pretty good. Regulars here call it slow.

On a good day, during the best of times, an angler will see six to eight fish raised, and two or three hooked. This kind of action doesn't happen just anywhere, and it has attracted sophisticated anglers and top boats from around the world, particularly in August for major tournaments, but throughout the summer as well.

The main reason for this highly productive fishery is St. Thomas's location in the Caribbean and the effects of currents and winds on the local environs. The deepest water in the Atlantic Ocean is directly offshore from the Virgin Islands, in the Puerto Rican Trench. Its depths plunge more than 6 miles. But within 10 to 12 miles of the Virgin Islands, the ocean floor slopes up to a bank that ranges from 140 fathoms up to 40 fathoms.

This is the site of the North Drop, and this is also where an upwelling of current and a prodigious amount of baitfish occur, due in part to the prevailing easterly trade winds. Bonito, tuna, and various predators routinely feed here. The marlin are primarily caught in an area that extends for nearly 10 miles and is about 2 miles wide, although anglers work the entire dropoff, from in front of

St. Thomas to the island of Anegada. The so-called Corner, a section where the dropoff doglegs easterly, also causes marlin to congregate in the area.

The North Drop is between 10 and 12 miles from St. Thomas. In the peak of the season (July, August, and September, especially around the full moon) many boats descend on the dropoff. Deep water and dropoffs exist off each of the major islands, including off St. Croix in the Caribbean.

Anglers encounter white marlin and sailfish in area waters, although not as regularly as blue marlin. Other typical Caribbean offshore creatures also in the catch include wahoo (St. Thomas holds one long-standing line-class world record for this species), dolphin, yellowfin tuna, blackfin tuna, and various sharks. Lang Bank, east of St. Croix, is a place frequented for dolphin, king mackerel, and wahoo.

Although blue marlin are caught year-round, the prime time, as previously noted, is from July through September for the big fish. White marlin are most abundant in spring. Dolphin and king mackerel are best in spring, tuna in fall and winter, and wahoo through the winter.

Sharks sometimes pose a problem because of their relative abundance, and they have attacked many hooked marlin. Such an occurrence disqualifies a fish from record consideration and is especially hard to avoid when light tackle is employed. With the number of marlin to be raised out here, light-tackle fishing has grown in popularity, so sharks are a concern. Most of the marlin are released, and if they are too weak when freed, they can be vulnerable.

Some inshore fishing also takes place in and around the various Virgin Islands, especially around the reefs and on the flats. King mackerel, barracuda, and various jacks, snapper, and grouper are among the reef catch. These fish provide excitement for those not interested in the muscle fishing of offshore waters.

Tarpon prowl these islands, too, mostly off the northern shore of St. Thomas and along St. Croix, but also in the British Virgins. St. Croix provides bonefishing, incidentally, on flats along the southern shore, but the rest of the U.S. islands, with their steeper terrain, do not possess the flats and typical habitat that harbor this species. The British island of Anegada, however, is low lying, and it possesses shallows that have in the past been abundant with this species.

Permit are plentiful around these islands, especially St. Croix, and they are a lightly pursued fishery. Fifteen- to 30-pound fish are caught here by relatively few anglers, as the interest lies predominantly with offshore locations. Some visitors, however, have reported sighting high numbers of permit in a day, some actually in schools, on flats that surround St. Croix. The more reliable permit fishing is reportedly on the island's southern coral flats; the permit come into these areas from deeper water to feed, and winter is the prime season.

Subject to easterly winds, the Virgin Islands are also subject to rough water at times, especially in winter, although the prime billfishing period of midsummer is usually fairly calm. Late summer can bring hurricanes; St. Croix was nearly destroyed by Hurricane Hugo in September 1989. Well-equipped and experienced charter boats are available, especially in St. Thomas, and facilities are plentiful. The Virgin Islands draw many visitors for reef diving, and the local waters are rated among the best in the world for this activity. A favored spot is Buck Island Reef National Monument at St. Croix.

VIRGINIA

Not too many states can say that they offer anglers the opportunity to catch native brook trout from small mountain streams and also giant blue marlin from the vast waters of the Atlantic Ocean's Gulf Stream. The Commonwealth of Virginia can boast this and much more because in between these extremes are ponds, reservoirs, streams, rivers, and the Chesapeake Bay, all with varied species and multiple angling possibilities.

This may be a surprise to those unfamiliar with the Old Dominion state, but it shouldn't be when you consider that Virginia has 2,800 miles of trout streams, 112 miles of coastline, more than 1,500 square miles of the Chesapeake Bay, several major rivers, and loads of ponds, lakes, and small to medium reservoirs.

For freshwater devotees, some of Virginia's lakes and reservoirs offer first-class angling for various species, especially largemouth bass and striped bass, and the rivers and streams have terrific opportunities for trout and smallmouths. For saltwater enthusiasts, Virginia could be as good as it gets, with striped bass, bluefish, speckled trout, and drum heading a long list of highly desirable species that are often found in good abundance.

Freshwater

Virginia's varied topography ranges from the coastal plain to the Piedmont Plateau to the Blue Ridge, and the result is a plethora of creeks, rivers, ponds, lakes, and reservoirs. Largemouth bass, smallmouth bass, various panfish, and catfish anchor the warmwater scene, with some opportunity for striped bass, muskies, and walleye as well. Brook, rainbow, and brown trout are staples in many locations, and having the brook trout as a state fish is perhaps indicative of how Virginians view their freshwater fisheries, particularly when there are 2,200 miles of wild trout streams in the state.

Notable small waters. One of the more noteworthy trout fisheries in Virginia is Whitetop Laurel Creek in the Mount Rogers National Recreational Area. Located near the appropriately named town of Troutville, this beautiful stream is filled with native rainbows and browns. The water

cascades over huge boulders, forming deep pools where rainbows grow to 14 inches and a few brown trout reach trophy size. The trout here have seen every fly tied by anglers, however, so a delicate presentation is required. Dry flies will work during a hatch, and nymphs are the most consistent producers.

An old railroad bed follows Whitetop Laurel Creek, providing access to the water. The streambed is covered with loose and slippery rocks, making for some treacherous footing; felt-soled shoes or waders and a walking staff should be used here to prevent a nasty spill.

Those looking for slightly less challenge in their trout fishing but not wanting to give up beautiful scenery can drive a few miles north and west to the Clinch Mountain Fee Fishing Area. Roughly 7 miles from Saltville, this area is controlled by the Virginia Department of Natural Resources, which provides campsites and a small convenience store on the property.

At Clinch Mountain, Big Tumbling Creek and Laurel Bed Lake hold good numbers of rainbow trout. Fish are stocked in the creek every day during the season, providing good, and consistent, opportunities for success. Two launch sites on the lake can be used for small, shallow-draft boats. The lake covers 300 acres, and its usually smooth, quiet surface stands in sharp contrast to the roaring waters of Big Tumbling Creek. It takes the abilities of a mountain goat to reach the deep pools below the falls and rapids, but the fishing is worth the effort. The lower part of the creek near the checking station is easier to access and holds an equal number of trout.

Not far away, bass anglers find good smallmouth action along the North Fork of the Holston River in Saltville. At one time, this river was a mess, but efforts to remove the pollution have brought improvements, and fishing here is very good. Smallmouths are caught from shore, from a small boat, or by wading. Plugs and plastic grubs that imitate small minnows or crayfish work best.

Hungry Mother State Park near Marion is close to Mt. Rogers and Clinch Mountain, and contains a small lake with walleye, largemouth bass, bluegills, crappie, and muskellunge. The park has campgrounds and various facilities, and the lake has a small-boat launch site and a fishing pier.

Another site noted for diverse species is Lake Moomaw in the George Washington National Forest. Formed in 1981 with the completion of the Gathright Dam on the Jackson River, this 2,530-acre reservoir lies between Bath and Allegheny Counties near Hot Springs and Covington. Boats can be launched at Bolar Flat and at Fortney Branch.

Smallmouth bass have thrived in the lower part of this lake and in the headwaters; 3- to 4-pounders are common. Largemouths average 13 to 15 inches, and a few 3- to 5-pounders are taken each year. Local fishing clubs and the Department of Game and Inland Fisheries have improved fish habitat to benefit the crappie population, which is considered one of the best in the state. Crappie in the 1- to 1^1/$_2$-pound range are taken here in the spring.

Trout fishing at lake Moomaw is good for rainbows and browns. Anglers do not need a state trout stamp or a national forest stamp to possess trout from this lake. Shad are the primary forage species here and are fished live for bass and trout; crankbaits that imitate shad are cast or trolled.

Although small at just 118 acres, Skidmore Reservoir, which provides water for the city of Harrisonburg, has great fishing for trout and bass. West of Harrisonburg, the lake is clear and deep, offering excellent habitat for brook trout, some of which grow to 3 pounds. Brown and tiger trout have been stocked in Skidmore, and these fish grow to 4 pounds or more. Warmwater species in the lake include largemouth bass, crappie, and sunfish, but most are small. Access is via a primitive boat ramp and adjoining parking lot off the forest road. The shoreline is open to fishing on the west side and the upper end of the lake.

James and Rappahannock Rivers. Two bodies of water that flow through a good part of Virginia are the James and the Rappahannock Rivers. The upper parts of both rivers contain good numbers of smallmouth bass and can be fished from shore, by boat, or by wading. These are peaceful and pretty fisheries as the rivers flow through farmland and the foothills of the Appalachian Mountains.

Below the cities of Fredericksburg on the Rappahannock and Richmond on the James, the fishing takes a decided turn. The rivers here are swift and deep and provide excellent habitat for big blue and channel catfish. Channel cats over 20 pounds and blues approaching 50 pounds are taken out of both rivers each year. This is not a fancy fishery with lots of special tackle and equipment; most practitioners here use a stout rod with 20- to 30-pound line, and fish a big hunk of shad, herring, or eel in a deep hole or eddy.

Numerous access points and launch ramps are located along the banks of both rivers. Some of the best catfish action is in or close to Richmond and Fredricksburg.

Big waters. Virginia is home to big-water fishing on several lakes that have received national attention for their resources.

The biggest of these is Buggs Island Lake, which is also known as Kerr Reservoir. It covers 48,900 acres in Mecklenburg County and is the largest body of freshwater in Virginia. In addition to having an excellent largemouth bass population, the lake holds good numbers of big crappie, white perch, and striped bass.

Bass fishing is especially good in the spring, when the lake rises to its highest level, flooding trees and underbrush along the shoreline. Soft worms and lizards, and pork rind–decorated jigs, tossed to the base of this vegetation usually produce excellent

An ancient Chinese and Japanese method of catching fish is using tethered cormorants; this is still practiced today, and some birds are also used to catch turtles.

results. Big crappie are caught here in the spring, when they school over submerged structure. A small jig tipped with a minnow is the favored offering.

Stripers spawn naturally in Buggs Island Lake, and the state stocks them to keep the population level in years of poor reproduction. Striper fishing has become more popular as the size and number of these fish increase. Live shad or crankbaits that imitate them are the most common offerings.

Lake Gaston is a 20,300-acre reservoir located in Brunswick County just below Buggs Island Lake. Largemouth bass draw most anglers here, but trophy striped bass have been vying for attention. Walleye are available in Lake Gaston, as are good-size black crappie and white crappie. The usual assortment of warmwater panfish, including sunfish, perch, and catfish, show up in the creel.

Access to both Lake Gaston and Buggs Island Lake is easy and convenient. Numerous boat ramps are available at both, and the nearby area offers every service necessary. Both lakes cross the Virginia–North Carolina border, and a license for either state will be honored throughout the waterway, although regulations may differ.

Smith Mountain Lake in Bedford County is the top place in the state to fish for big inland striped bass. A state freshwater record—45 pounds, 10 ounces—was established at this 20,600-acre reservoir in 1995, and stripers exceeding 30 pounds are caught each year. Stocking of 300,000 fingerling stripers every year helps to maintain a stable population. Live shad make the best bait, but various fishing methods are applicable.

The variety of species available at Smith Mountain Lake is excellent. Largemouth bass and muskies also get a lot of attention, and big flathead catfish, crappie, white bass, smallmouth bass, and walleye are caught regularly.

Largemouth bass are a good bet at Smith Mountain in cover and around boat docks. Pitching a jig-and-pork combo is particularly effective on largemouths. Spinnerbaits, plastic worms, and crankbaits all take their share of fish. Muskies are stocked each year, and most are caught incidentally by anglers pursuing bass and stripers. With fish to 20 pounds available, especially in the Roanoke River arm, a more directed fishery is developing. Flathead catfish have been strong in the Blackwater arm in recent years, and crappie fishing has been best in the upper ends, where there is structure. Smith Mountain has plenty of access, as well as many nearby facilities.

Lake Anna is the smallest of the big reservoirs at 9,600 acres, but it manages to flow over into three counties: Spotsylvania, Louisa, and Orange. It contains largemouth bass, walleye, striped bass, perch, pickerel, sunfish, crappie, and catfish. Numerous private marinas line the lake, and there's a public boat ramp near the Spotsylvania–Orange County line.

This lake supplies water to a nuclear power plant, and the warmwater discharge can create good wintertime fishing. Dike No. 3 is a good spot when the water temperature on the main lake drops. The warm discharge water attracts striped bass, walleye, and catfish; live shad, jigs, or chunks of cut baits are preferred choices for catching them.

Suffolk chain. A number of small water supply lakes are found in Suffolk, and, although their size may be dwarfed by the bigger reservoirs, the quality of the fishing stands up to any comparison.

Known as the Suffolk chain of lakes, they supply drinking water to the communities of Norfolk, Portsmouth, and Suffolk. These cities take every precaution to keep the lakes clean, including preventing the cutting of timber that surrounds each body of water. The result is excellent fishing in a beautiful setting.

Western Branch Reservoir, at 1,597 acres, is the largest of the seven lakes in the chain. The others range in size from 777-acre Lake Prince to 197-acre Speight's Run. Each lake has its own personality, but all hold a variety of angling opportunities. Bass, stripers, perch, pickerel, and catfish are taken in numbers each year; but redear sunfish, known locally as shellcrackers, draw the most attention. More citation-size shellcrackers are caught here than anywhere else in Virginia, and a few anglers are lucky enough to catch more than a dozen exceeding the 1-pound minimum weight. Special permits are required to launch a private boat, but rental boats and electric motors are available at a reasonable rate.

Saltwater

Virginia has one of the longest tidal coastlines of any state due to the many creeks and rivers that flow into the Chesapeake Bay, plus the barrier islands that line its Atlantic Ocean front. In all, this amounts to some 3,315 miles of tidal shoreline. All of this means good access to what many people consider the finest saltwater fishing available.

Chesapeake Bay and vicinity. The boats running out of Smith Point at the mouth of the Potomac River spend most of their time chumming for blues, striped bass, and weakfish. Trolling with spoons, bucktails, and tubes is common for the same species in the spring and fall. Bottom fishing produces spot and croaker along with flounder and weakfish; squid and peeler crabs are the most popular baits.

Trolling and chumming are practiced over the Middle Grounds to the north in Maryland waters, and over the Cabbage Patch and the wrecks southeast of Smith Point Light. Bottom fishing occurs closer to shore as well as along the shoals, wrecks, and channel edges.

A small charter fleet runs out of the Little Wicomico River, and there is a launch ramp at Kanyan. Several marinas in the area can service larger boats, and campgrounds are available on the south side of the river.

Anglers running out of the Great Wicomico River will chum and troll the same general area as

those working out of Smith Point. They may fish a bit farther south around the Tangier Lumps or the Davidson Wreck, and travel north to Maryland only when all else fails.

A fair number of charter boats operate out of Reedville. They specialize in chumming or trolling for blues, stripers, and gray trout (weakfish). Bottom fishing for flounder, spot, croaker, and weakfish is the primary summertime activity.

Boat launch ramps are found at Glebe Point, Shell Landing, and Crane's Creek Landing. Fishing is possible from the shore in these locations, but parking is limited. Several marinas in the area can accommodate larger boats.

The coastline from the Great Wicomico to the Rappahannock River is populated by small creeks, bays, and marshland, giving the angler several choices of species and techniques. Speckled trout inhabit the shallow waters of the creeks, whereas bluefish and weakfish stage along the creek mouths and in the bays. Flounder, croaker, spot, and weakfish hold in the deeper water where the creeks and bays meet the Chesapeake.

Deltaville on the Rappahannock River is a center for recreational anglers fishing the river and the nearby waters of the Chesapeake Bay. A charter fleet runs out of here, and there are boat ramps at Kruses Wharf and Upper Mill Creek Landing.

Trolling for blues and stripers is the top activity in the spring and fall. Trollers here pull bucktail jigs, spoons, tubes, and plugs over shallow areas around Windmill Point Light, as well as in the deeper

Striped bass are a staple in Chesapeake Bay; this one was caught near the Bay Bridge Tunnel.

waters of the Cut Channel. The Cut Channel produced a state record 61-pound, 12-ounce striper in 1996; this early December fish was caught by trolling a spoon. When fishing solely for stripers, trollers continue up the river to the White Stone Bridge.

Bottom fishing takes over in the summer, when flounder, weakfish, spot, and croaker are the most popular species. These are caught throughout the river and over shoals, channel edges, and rocks in the bay. The Cell on the Eastern Shore side of the bay is a hotspot for big flounder, croaker, stripers, and spadefish. A relic of World War II, the degaussing cell was used to demagnetize ships and was blown up when the war was over. The remains litter the ocean bottom, attracting all types of marine life.

One of the better known speckled trout hotspots is just south of Gwynn Island at the Hole in the Wall. This narrow outlet to the bay is surrounded by sandbars and marsh—perfect speckled trout habitat. Small, shallow-draft boats are required to access this area, where small jigs and plugs take the majority of fish.

Hallieford Public landing on Gwynn Island provides access to the Hole in the Wall as well as the Piankatank River. Anglers take speckled trout from the river, along with weakfish, croaker, spot, and small blues.

Mobjack Bay and the rivers that feeds it are rich in fishing opportunities. Speckled trout attract most of the attention in the spring and fall. Croaker, spot, weakfish, small blues, and flounder take center stage in the summer. Specks are usually taken near the shore over grassbeds. Peeler crabs are the top baitfish in the spring, and live pinfish are a good bet in the fall. Plugs and jigs are effective throughout the year.

Warehouse Landing near Gloucester has a boat ramp and fishing pier with limited parking. One of the better speckled trout areas is at Ware Point, just a short run down the Ware River from the ramp.

The York River from West Point to the Chesapeake Bay offers various fishing opportunities for croaker, spot, striped bass, flounder, and bluefish. The shoreline along the Colonial Parkway from Yorktown to Williamsburg slopes gradually to the river, forming a large flat that is especially popular with light-tackle and fly anglers. Many people wade while casting small jigs, plugs, or flies. Others fish from small flats-style boats. Their efforts are rewarded with speckled trout, weakfish, striped bass, flounder, and bluefish. A boat ramp at Gloucester Point is the closest access. A fishing pier is located in the same area and is very popular with croaker and spot fanciers.

The Poquoson River also holds good fishing opportunities for spot, croaker, small blues, striped bass, and weakfish. Boat ramps are available on Back Creek and the Tide Mill Landing in York.

Bluefish Rock just outside the mouth of the Back River draws legions of cobia anglers each summer. They anchor up and chum with ground menhaden while soaking chunks of menhaden on the bottom. This area sees lots of trolling for striped bass and bluefish in the spring and fall. Drifting cut bait, squid, and shrimp produces spot, croaker, and flounder during the summer. Wallace's Marina and the nearby boat ramp are the center of fishing activity in this region; they are located at the end of Dandy Point Road in Hampton.

Hampton Roads is the junction of the James and Elizabeth Rivers before they fan out into the Chesapeake Bay. The entire area is heavily developed, but fishing is very good. The charter and head boats sailing from here seek spot, croaker, and weakfish from the Hampton Bar out to Thimble Shoal. In the fall, charter boats find striped bass in the same area.

The urban fishing available from shore, bridges, piers, and old boat docks can be good even if not aesthetically pleasing. Spot and croaker provide most of the activity, but stripers are taken in the spring and fall.

Little Creek and Lynnhaven Inlets are found between Hampton Roads and Cape Henry. Several marinas and boat ramps inside these inlets support a large fleet of private boats. Depending on the size of the boat and the preference of the owner, anglers can fish anywhere from inside the inlets out to the canyons.

A great deal of fishing activity in the lower bay is centered around the three bridge tunnels. The Monitor Merrimack, Hampton Roads, and the Chesapeake Bay Bridge Tunnel each act as artificial reefs and attract and hold a wide variety of fish species.

The Chesapeake Bay Bridge Tunnel is the longest of these spans, running 17 miles across the mouth of the bay, and it holds the greatest number of fish. Each year striped bass, bluefish, cobia, gray trout, speckled trout, croaker, spot, tautog, and flounder are taken along with such locally exotic species as jack crevalle, houndfish, spadefish, and mackerel. This is a true cornucopia.

Fishing piers are scattered from Hampton to Virginia Beach, and they produce good fishing from spring through fall. Small species like spot and croaker are the basis of pier fishing, but each year cobia, mackerel, bluefish, weakfish, and striped bass are caught from the piers. Grandview and Buckroe Piers are in Hampton, Harrison's Pier is in Norfolk, and Lynnhaven and Sea Gull Piers are in Virginia Beach. The Sea Gull Pier is located on the first island of the Chesapeake Bay Bridge Tunnel.

Small boat anglers and those who fish from shore will find good action inside Lynnhaven Inlet. The base of the Lessner Bridge over the inlet is a good bet for flounder, speckled trout, and striped bass. The sheltered waters inside the inlet hold the same species plus croaker and spot. Launch ramps at Bubba's Marina on the east side of the bridge and at First Landing State Park at the end of 65th Street in Virginia Beach provide access.

Rudee Inlet in Virginia Beach is the only direct outlet to the ocean between Cape Henry and Oregon Inlet. A large offshore charter fleet heads out to the Norfolk Canyon or the Cigar in pursuit of marlin, tuna, dolphin, and wahoo. Blue marlin are sometimes caught, but whites are the mainstays; white marlin action can be hot in some years. Inshore fishing is good for bluefish, mackerel, and striped bass.

The head boat fleet out of here and out of Lynnhaven Inlet fish for sea bass and tautog over inshore wrecks and reefs, as well as spot, croaker, and weakfish around the mouth of the Chesapeake Bay.

The two fishing piers in Virginia Beach are at 14th Street and in Sandbridge, and they attract spot, croaker, flounder, bluefish, striped bass, and mackerel. Surf casters along the beach can expect the same mixed bag. A boat ramp on Owl's Creek adjacent to the Virginia Marine Science Museum off of General Booth Boulevard provides access to Rudee Inlet.

The Eastern Shore. No single area in the United States and possibly the world offers as many fishing possibilities as the Eastern Shore of Virginia. The season runs all year, and the variety of species available is overwhelming.

The Eastern Shore of Virginia is divided into the ocean side and the bay side. Fishermen can troll for tuna on the ocean side in the morning and cast for speckled trout on the bay side in the afternoon.

Accomac and Northampton Counties divide the narrow tip of the Delmarva Peninsula, which is Virginia's Eastern Shore. Both counties and the state have built numerous boat ramps on both the bay and ocean sides, so access to this good fishing is never a problem. Finding a way across the shallow waters on either side is a dilemma solved only by experience.

Beginning on the bay side, Saxis is the jumping-off point for fishing in Pocomoke Sound. Anglers find weakfish, flounder, croaker, spot, and striped bass over the numerous rocks in the sound. Bottom fishing with peeler crabs or squid is the most popular activity, but trolling bucktails, plugs, and spoons occurs in the spring and fall.

Onancock, at the head of Onancock Creek, is close to the good fishing in the lower part of Pocomoke Sound and the open waters of the Chesapeake Bay. In the spring, anglers soak peeler crabs on night tides near Half Moon Island between Saxis and Onancock. At times, the mosquito bites are more frequent than the fish bites, but when a speck is caught it is usually a big one. Pungoteague and Nandua Creeks below Onancock also hold good numbers of speckled trout in the spring and fall.

Nassawadox Creek is also known for speckled trout, but the channel edge that lies just offshore between Buoys C20 and CB is a good location for channel bass in late summer and early fall. A good

tactic is to anchor along the dropoff and soak chunks of spot, croaker, or menhaden about a hour or two before dark.

The junction of Hungars and Mahawoman Creeks forms a shallow grassbed surrounded by sandbars. Many speckled trout anglers feel this is the best area for their favorite quarry. Casting jigs and plugs begins in the spring and peaks in late fall. A light rain on an east wind is considered ideal weather for speckled trout.

Cape Charles is the last town on the bay side, and it is a center for fishing in the lower bay. Black drum draw the first anglers here each spring, and striped bass keep them coming into December. Old Plantation Light, the Cabbage Patch, the Concrete Ships, and Latimer Shoal are a few of the good fishing spots located just a short run from Cape Charles Harbor.

The cobia run on Latimer Shoal has been spectacular. Fish approaching 100 pounds are caught from June through September. Hundreds of boats anchor up and chum, creating a slick that goes on for miles. Cobia follow the slick and may or may not eat the baits waiting for them on the bottom.

Kiptopeke State Park on the bay side south of Cape Charles offers excellent camping facilities, a boat ramp, and a fishing pier. Cherrystone Campground just above Cape Charles has year-round camping, a fishing pier, a marina, and many family activities.

As one moves over to the ocean side, Oyster is the first town with access to the sea. As with all ocean-side access points, the run to the sea from here can be a challenge. Channels are marked, but they are narrow and subject to change without notice. Study the latest charts before departure, and do not stray from the channel until you know where you're headed.

The outlet from Oyster is Sand Shoal Inlet, where flounder, weakfish, and blues are caught throughout the spring, summer, and fall. The dropoff next to the 224 Day Marker is a great location to drift minnows, squid strips, or cut bait.

The marshes and channels between the mainland and the barrier islands produce several big tarpon each summer. All are taken on chunks of cut spot or menhaden, and the best action is during the hottest days of summer.

Quinby and Wachapreague are famous for spectacular flounder fishing, especially in the spring, when big doormats enter the channels between these two ports and the ocean. Drifting along the edge of the channels with live minnows is the best way to find a big flounder.

Wachapreague has a charter fleet that specializes in flounder fishing as well as working the offshore grounds for tuna, king mackerel, and big bluefish. Chunking with cut-up butterfish has become a popular technique for catching tuna. Most of the action occurs on the 26 Mile Hill or the Parking Lot.

Chincoteague lies just below the Maryland line and is the largest town along the sea side. It offers numerous motels and restaurants as well as several campgrounds. Rental boats, charter boats, marinas, and launch ramps provide access to every type of angler.

A lack of motorized transportation does not prevent folks from fishing the rest of Virginia's beautiful coastline. Most of the barrier islands from Assawoman down to Smith are owned by the Virginia Coast Preserve, a division of the Nature Conservancy. They are open to the public for surf fishing, but overnight camping is prohibited.

The best surf action takes place in the spring and fall, when big red drum move close to the beach. Peeler crabs are the top bait in the spring, and cut mullet or menhaden are preferred in the fall. Access is by small boat, and the islands are undeveloped.

VISE

A tool, also known as a fly tying vise, with adjustable clamping jaws to secure a hook for dressing with fly tying materials.
See: Fly.

VOMERINE TEETH

Teeth located on the vomer, a median bone in the front of the roof of the mouth of fish.
See: Anatomy.

WADE FISHING

Fishing by means of wading in the water.
See: Waders.

WADERS

Anglers who fish from the bank, who wade, or who get in and out of boats during the course of fishing (such as river drifters), often need to cover that portion of the body that will be in the water. Such a covering is generically called waders, which are chest- or hip-high products with connected or separate boots that keep anglers dry and sometimes warm, and which also help provide good footing. Waders also may serve a subordinate function as protection from such natural, and sometimes problematic, elements as leeches, bugs, snakes, prickly bushes, and poisonous plants along the waterway.

Some warmwater fishing situations permit anglers to "wade wet" by walking in the water in their clothes or bare-legged; however, this generally occurs when both the water and air temperatures are sufficiently warm, or when the angler will be wading for a relatively short period. In cool or cold water, when the air temperature is cool or cold, when a cool breeze is blowing, and when the angler must spend a long time in the water, it is usually appropriate, if not absolutely necessary, to wear some type of waders. In these circumstances, few pieces of equipment can be as valuable as a pair of warm, dry waders. For anglers who get into the water, waders are literally one of the most important pieces of fishing equipment that they own, and they will likely own many pairs during a lifetime of fishing, especially if they are guides, or have the enviable ability to fish on a very frequent basis.

The ideal wader has several obvious features: It should be totally waterproof, warm in cold water yet cool in hot weather, durable or long-lived, lightweight, supple and stretchable, tear- and puncture-proof, not bulky, not damp inside when worn, and low in cost. No wader achieves all of this, but in order to achieve these features, waders have been evolving since the late nineteenth century. Due to modern technology, they have taken quantum leaps since the late 1970s, and great strides have been made in most of these features. As a result, today's waders are extremely functional products, and there are waders now to suit nearly all angling situations; some anglers have two or three pairs of waders to use for different conditions.

History

In 1839, Charles Goodyear stumbled on a rubber treatment process he named vulcanization. Vulcanization is the combination of heat and pressure over time combined with ammonia, and in some cases sulfur, to create rubber products that are completely stable. Before vulcanization, rubber products would melt on a hot day and crack on a cold one.

Until the development of vulcanization, there was no reliably waterproof footwear. Thus, when the first vulcanized rubber boot was created, a revolutionary product was born. The success of waterproof rubber footwear eventually lead to the development of rubber waders, which were made by the Uniroyal Company in 1896. They were stiff and heavy, but waterproof. At the beginning of the twentieth century, a lighter, more comfortable wader was created by combining cotton canvas with rubber.

Few changes occurred in waders until manufacturing technology improved in the mid-1960s, and makers used extrusion laminates to produce far more supple and forgiving products that were much more comfortable to wear. In the extrusion process, materials are heated until their molecules change, and they are bonded completely together without depending on adhesives. Shortly after this improvement came the use of polyvinyl chloride (PVC) materials in boot bottoms, which made this component of waders lighter and less expensive.

A complete rethinking of wader materials and construction was reflected in the 1978 introduction of chest-high stocking foot waders made from nylon that weighed only 10 ounces. They had stocking-style feet and were meant to be worn with separate wading shoes or boots. These featherweight waders proved to be durable and far more comfortable to wear than pre-existing waders, and created a whole new category of wader, as well as opened the doors to achieving products that made wader-wearing anglers much less stiff-legged and encumbered.

The advent of neoprene, and its use in wetsuits, started a demand for neoprene waders, and the first national distribution of neoprene waders occurred in 1981. Neoprene wader manufacture—all of the stocking foot variety, which had to be worn with separate boots—rapidly advanced thereafter with lighter, less absorbent closed cell fabrics.

Early neoprene waders were tight fitting and had to be rolled down instead of pulled off. There was little room for wearing extra clothing underneath, but they were eagerly embraced by the coldest water waders. Neoprene waders are the warmest waders for severe cold because this material not only keeps water out but body heat in.

In just a few years, wader manufacturers quickly moved into neoprene production to meet growing demand. The greatest improvement for severe cold weather anglers was the development of boot foot neoprene waders, which featured a traditional insulated rubber boot bottom attached to upper full-cut neoprene.

Releasing body heat but still keeping dry and reasonably warm in appropriate conditions became the next goal of wader manufacturers, and in 1993 the first breathable wader, made of Gore-Tex, became available. This product allowed human body heat to be released through the material, even while standing in the water. Like most truly new designs, the first year of production saw many returns and field problems that were quickly resolved, and today this type of product is well accepted, without the flaws that marked the first items, and it is likely the wave of the future for wader manufacturing technology.

Waders are now made from even newer high-tech materials, and by using complex adhesives. Anglers today have a far greater choice in wader wear as a result of these developments, and can find a good product to meet virtually any use and season. Rubber hip waders for shallow stream wading, lightweight breathable chest waders for warm or cool water wading, rubber chest waders for general purpose wading, and neoprene chest waders for the coldest water fishing, are among the major possibilities.

Types

Chest and hip. Irrespective of the material they are made from, there are two general types of waders: chest and hip.

Chest waders are similar to pants in that the material extends from the legs up over the hips and waist to the upper part of the chest. Chest-high waders have straps or suspenders that loop over the user's shoulders, but they should also be worn with a waist-level outer belt to help keep water out and trap air inside in the event of a spill. Quite simply, chest waders are meant to be worn in water that is too deep for the use of hip waders—large rivers or ocean surf—and for extra water and weather protection in cold weather.

The biggest advantage of chest waders is that they get you to deeper fishing holes, either by allowing you to wade deeper to cast or to ford deep places to get to locales that can't be accessed otherwise. They are a bit heavy and bulky, however, which provides more warmth but makes for more difficult distance walking or climbing. A modified version, referred to as a waist-high wader because it extends only to the waist, is made for anglers who get in and out of boats frequently (especially guides), wading in cold water but otherwise being in warm air temperatures.

Hip waders are all that are necessary for many fishing situations.

Most chest waders actually do extend to the breast area of the chest, but some extend to the upper chest and armpits for the deepest possible wading.

Hip waders are short and more like boots, and are also called hip boots, or hippers. They are fitted to each leg, with the material of each leg extending up to the hips and held up by a strap that loops onto the wearer's belt. Though they are often synonymously referred to as hip boots, they are technically slightly different; hip boots cover the same area, but technically they are made from heavier material from top to bottom.

Hip waders are meant for wading in relatively shallow water. It is easier to get in and out of a boat or car in them, and they are easiest to take off or put on. They are also cool to wear in warm weather, and, if fitted properly, good for long distance walking on land.

Boot and stocking foot. Both basic wader types can be further categorized by the nature of their bottom, or foot section. Those with integral boots are known as boot foot models. The boot section of the wader, usually a heavy-soled boot, is part of the legs and permanently attached to a chest- or hip-high upper section (called uppers), forming a single unit. Boot foot waders are generally popular with anglers who do a moderate amount of wading and are found on virtually all rubber chest and hip waders and on many neoprene chest waders. They are easier to take off or put on than stocking foot waders because of their one-piece construction, and are warmer in the coldest water. They generally are not as comfortable as, and are heavier than, stocking foot waders with wading shoes. The ankle portion of the boot provides support as good as that of a wading shoe. The ridge where the stiffer boot area joins the upper wader material can be a source of leaks, as well as of chafing to the angler who has to walk considerable distances.

Those waders that require separate boots are called stocking foot models, or sometimes pants. The actual wader itself is a separate component from the boot, and features an integral stocking-style foot section that is worn inside a pair of wading boots or shoes; these may be chest- or hip-high products, mostly the former. Stocking foot waders fit the lower body closer, which can mean less drag in the water and easier climbing; the wading shoes worn with them often provide better ankle and foot support and traction; the soft ankle and calf section of the wader provides for more comfortable walking over distances. They take more time to get on or off, there is a greater chance of grit working into the boot, and they are not as warm in extreme cold water wading.

Materials and Styles

Rubber. With the exception of soles, rubber waders are much like they were a hundred years ago. They are generally stiff, bulky, and relatively heavy. Their greatest benefit is the sturdy construction of their integrated boot, and the capability of the boot to provide warmth in severe cold conditions. Lug-soled rubber boots are very durable, offering excellent support and protection from rocks. Rubber waders are also economical, which, coupled with durable boots, is why people who do construction and hard labor around docks and the like often use rubber waders, especially hip models.

In recent years, better quality rubber waders have added hi-tech tennis shoe–style air insole and air grip outsoles for better traction. These innovations have made the boots much more comfortable to walk and stand in. There is no getting around the fact that they are heavy, however, and it is also difficult to repair large tears in the rubber. Despite being low in cost, they do not tend to last long (especially the upper section), and they do not breathe, making them clammy inside.

Rubber hip waders and chest waders, as well as knee-high boots, are common in stores and economically priced. Each can be obtained in either full-cut boot bottoms for warmth or ankle-fit boot bottoms for walking support, both of which are available in insulated and non-insulated varieties. Some brands also have models that are factory-equipped with felt soles.

Canvas. The canvas wader is still readily available in the extrusion form that is lighter and more supple than rubber-canvas combination waders. However, some traditional rubber-canvas combination waders can still be purchased. Most extrusion canvas waders have PVC boot foot bottoms that make them lighter and less expensive than waders with rubber bottoms. Unfortunately, they do not offer the same support that traditional rubber boots offer. The modern canvas wader is very supple and light compared to full-rubber waders.

Canvas waders can be purchased in both insulated and non-insulated hip and chest models, Some brands offer felt-soled versions.

Nylon ultralights. Nylon stocking foot models make up the majority of ultralight waders. A few manufacturers make ultralight waders with PVC boot foot bottoms. Both configurations can be found in hip and chest waders with or without felt soles, but generally non-insulated.

Nylon waders are comfortable in warmer weather and are the lightest waders an angler can purchase, which is especially good for travel purposes. They are also comparatively low in cost, and durable enough to provide long life. They have no insulating properties, however, are not stretchable or breathable, and can be difficult to repair.

PVC. The PVC wader is usually less expensive than ultralight models and is sold primarily as a stocking foot wader. It is not very durable and is often used as a backup wader or for first-time anglers looking for an inexpensive solution to a day's wading.

Neoprene. Stocking foot and boot foot neoprene waders make up a significant portion of wader sales, despite the fact that they are more expensive than all other wader styles except breathables. They are commonly offered in 2 mil. (millimeter), 3.5 mil., and 5 mil. thicknesses. Many manufacturers offer models with felt soles. Most waders made from neoprene are chest-high models, and in stocking foot style.

Neoprene stretches in a 360-degree radius that substantially reduces fatigue and increases the angler's mobility. Bending, casting, and moving in general is essentially unimpeded in well-made products. Neoprene chest waders are generally form fitting, which is also comfortable and reduces drag in the water; more neoprene waders are currently available in wider cuts, the lack of which used to be a problem for larger-bodied anglers.

The greatest benefit of this material is its ability to keep an angler warm in cold conditions. Furthermore, neoprene is resistant to punctures, and repairs are easily accomplished even when the repair is over a large area. Neoprene itself, though bulky, has some flotation value. Existing mil thicknesses continue to become lighter and less absorbent.

Neoprene waders, such as the chest-high model worn by this steelhead angler, are invaluable for cold-weather fishing.

The very attribute that makes neoprene warm also contributes to its greatest drawback. Because this material does not disperse heat outwardly, it produces interior wetness or dampness from perspiration; it is common for a neoprene chest wader wearer to be damp from waist to feet at the end of a day's use in anything but cold weather, and especially if exertion is required. Some brands have pile linings for displacing perspiration. Many brands also offer waist-high models that are ideal for anglers getting in and out of boats in cold water, but facing warmer air temperature when out of the water.

Neoprene waders can therefore be very uncomfortable in warm weather wading, or if significant walking is required. This is especially a problem when fishing where the air temperature is warm but the water cold. In heavy use, stocking foot neoprene can develop compression leaks in the bottoms of the foot portion of the wader.

Breathable. Breathable waders are heavier than ultralights, and a relatively new wader category that is likely to be the wave of the future as manufacturers perfect them and overcome some of the present disadvantages, which include being baggy, not stretchable, and easy to puncture.

The big advantage of breathable waders is that they disperse body heat, leaving the wearer much drier (no clamminess from condensation) than when wearing other types of waders. Most anglers can walk and fish all day with little condensation in their clothes.

This so-called "breathability" is derived from sophisticated breathable-membrane and breathable-coating products that allow water vapor (perspiration) to migrate outward from the interior of the garment but prevent water molecules (H_2O) from migrating inward from the exterior of the garment. The result, simply put, is that perspiration goes out and external water stays out.

For summer fishing, which is obviously when the majority of anglers are astream, these waders are very comfortable. They do not in themselves have any insulating property (more like nylon ultralights and less so than rubber). Because breathable waders are not form fitting, however, there is room for wearing warm clothes underneath, and it's possible to gain warmth for cool and cold water fishing, up to a point. For the coldest conditions, breathables do not compare in warmth to neoprene waders.

Breathable waders are expensive and can be difficult to repair (in fact, self-repair may void the warranty), which is a problem as these items have not proven to be very puncture-proof to date. The outer shell provides puncture resistance, and this material varies with different manufacturers.

A number of companies manufacture breathable waders in chest- and waist-high stocking foot models; there is little advantage to having these in hip waders. A few boot foot versions are available. Some stocking-foot models feature neoprene feet and are primarily found in fly fishing shops and specialty mail-order catalogs.

Other Gear

Soles. The purpose of the soles on a pair of waders or wading shoes is to provide stable nonslip footing. However, each sole type has limited application and will not function efficiently in every situation.

Traditional hard rubber-bottomed soles with lug-like gripping tread are best suited to traversing soft bottoms and gravel. Soft felt soles and similar woven polypropylene soles are a vast improvement for boulders and slick rocks, though not a help on wet shore grass or icy banks; felt wears out, however, and has to be replaced or at least reglued from time to time. Applying felt to rubber soles may require grinding down the rubber lugs and strapping or clamping replacement felt down until the cement cures, and the job is difficult on PVC soles because they don't mix well with many cements. Nevertheless, it's best to get boots with felt soles rather than to apply them yourself, even though you may need to replace the felt in time.

A recent option to smooth felt, though presently of limited availability, is a flat compressible soft rubber sole that is akin to rock-climbing shoe soles and grips as well or better than felt on slippery stream bottoms and better on other surfaces, and is far more durable. These are worth trying as resoling options, and are available on select wading shoes.

Metal gripping cleats, or creepers, which are either permanent attachments or strap-on metal studs of various shapes, provide the most stable walking on boulders and slick rocks, but are cumbersome to walk in and not welcomed in some situations (fiberglass boats, dune boardwalks, and so on). Metal cleats are absolutely essential for jetty fishing, where jetty rocks are moss covered and extremely slippery. They are also vital where wading anglers have to engage ice along rocky banks.

Some jetty anglers have a shoemaker cement golf shoe soles to the bottom of waders. Golf shoe spikes do not last long, but they can be replaced; always lubricate the threads of the cleats when inserting them; this prevents them from becoming corroded and makes replacement easier.

Wading boots/shoes. Wading boots (worn with stocking foot waders), which are often called wading shoes, should always be a consideration for fishing that requires wading in large, turbulent, or fast waters. They provide hiking boot–like support for walking on unstable ground, and superior protection from falls and below-ankle collisions. It is much easier to walk longer distances in wading boots (than in boot foot waders or booties), and they come in a varied selection of soles, making it possible to choose the best sole for the best application.

Wading boots are fairly heavy and rugged products; most are of high quality and truly boot-like, made from leather or synthetic materials.

Using cormorants to fetch fish—a collar around the neck keeps the bird from swallowing its catch—is still done today and was practiced by Chinese fishermen back in 902 A.D.

W
X
Y
Z

Leather versions are becoming less popular because they absorb water and become heavier, are subject to rotting and cracking, shrink, and can be difficult to put on when dry.

There are various grades of wading boots, and you should choose one based upon the degree of wading difficulty that you will most likely encounter. An angler who has one pair of stocking foot waders and fishes easy wading streams most of the time can get a lightweight boot for everyday fishing, and also have a more solid and heavier boot for occasional fishing on swifter rivers and where there is more slippery and rugged bottom terrain. Obviously, outer sole considerations apply to wading boots, as previously discussed.

When wading wet in warm waters, including beaches, flats, and streams, special booty-style wading shoes are available that provide a tight ankle fit to keep gravel and sediment out, and offer overall foot protection. Many are made of neoprene, are calf-high in design, and have sturdy rubber composition bottoms. Wet-wading shoes with hard, ridged soles are good for varying applications, while those with felt bottoms are best for stream usage. Some have a zippered entry, which can be annoying when fine grit lodges in the zipper teeth. Most also have a heel bump that helps secure swim fins, which are used when fishing from float tubes *(see)*. Dark colored booties work fine for continuous wading, but not for saltwater flats fishing where you may spend a lot of time in a boat, subject to the sun heating the dark boots.

Accessories.   Additional items that are useful if not necessary for waders include wading belts, staffs, PFDs, and gravel guards.

Wading belts keep chest waders from filling with water if you take a spill. Any belt that is large enough and which you don't mind getting wet can do, although easily adjustable synthetic belts with snap closures are excellent for this purpose. Some premium chest waders have lever or pinch latches in lieu of belts, and some have belt channels for handy enclosure of belts (auxiliary belts tend to get mislaid), but are also an added stress and point-prone to leaking.

Wading staffs, which allow an angler to be more sure-footed in fast water, are very helpful. A staff can be simply a sturdy green stick found at streamside, although finding a good stick isn't always possible. Multi-sectioned folding staffs are available, and many anglers make their own out of old ski poles (with the basket taken off).

Light inflatable personal flotation devices *(see)*, which do not hinder wading or casting, are good options for some people and in some circumstances. If worn (they are no good in the back of your vest), they can be instantly inflated in an emergency and will keep your head above water.

Gravel guards or cuffs (also called gaiters) are worn by some users of stocking foot waders or booties to help keep sand and gravel out of the boots, which can abrade the bottoms of the waders and cause water seepage. If long enough, the guards can also cover boot laces, which might catch loose fly line.

Selecting Waders
Just because you're a person of medium-average build who wears a size 9 shoe doesn't mean that a pair of medium waders will fit you. The best way to get proper fitting waders is to try them on to see how they fit. Mail-order catalogs offer extensive product lines, but even within the same brand, fit and last sizes (shoe sizes) will vary from product line to product line, so choosing by mail may be difficult.

Always try waders on with the clothing you will wade in. Make sure they are comfortable in all respects and you have enough room. Try bending over, squatting, sitting, and raising your leg as if you were climbing up a bank or out of a boat. Pay special attention to the boot and its fit; use the same sock(s) that you will wear when wading to determine proper fit. When you try on the waders make sure that your feet slip in the boots easily without a struggle, and that there's enough room to wiggle your toes. If not, you probably should go up to the next size. If you use stocking foot waders in extreme cold, consider a larger size wading shoe to accommodate the need for extra room.

If you order from a mail-order catalog, make sure you can return or exchange the wader if it doesn't fit you properly. If you absolutely cannot find a pair that fits properly (which especially happens to large individuals), check with manufacturers directly. A select few manufacturers offer custom waders at 40 to 60 percent above the retail price.

When buying waders, always keep your intended use in mind, and look for features that benefit your most common applications. If durability is an issue, for example, then you may want to consider models that are reinforced in the knees.

Ladies' waders.   Women have been challenged to find waders that are made specifically for them, since the majority of anglers are male, and manufacturers have generally taken a one-size-fits-all design approach.

Some waders are cut for women, however. These are generally made in neoprene, ultralight, and breathable styles. The best place for women to be fitted is in a fly fishing shop; the selection and service is worth it.

Children's waders.   Buying waders for children can be both challenging and expensive. The greatest frustration is that they will change sizes so quickly that they'll outgrow a good and otherwise usable pair of waders.

A few companies manufacture sizes as small as a children's size 1, but the most common sizes start at a children's size 3. One option is to purchase a size small nylon stocking foot wader that a child could wear with old tennis shoes as an alternative to an

expensive wading shoe; this would allow the wader to last through several size changes in the child.

Consider chest waders instead of hippers for children, since children are shorter to start out with and are prone to stumbling into the water with hippers on and likely to get wet enough to spoil the outing. If they're wearing chest waders, they stand a substantial chance of staying dry. Children should always wear a wader belt and a proper personal flotation device when wading, and they should avoid swift current.

Care and Repair

It's a good idea to clean and properly dry your waders after each use; many freshwater anglers do not need to clean their waders, but saltwater anglers should give them a freshwater rinse. Don't walk in stocking foot waders without boots on, as this is guaranteed to abrade them and diminish their life.

Storage. Taking good care of a pair of waders will pay you back in years of service. The first consideration in all wader care and storage is drying your waders by hanging them or otherwise storing them in an unfolded position. Always try to dry both the inside and the outside before storing for long periods of time. Except for short-term drying, keep waders out of direct sunlight. Do not store them where they will be under direct fluorescent lighting. Never fold waders for long-term storage. If you must fold them, try not to do so the same way each time. This will prevent permanent crease marks that can weaken the wader over many years.

Boot foot waders and wading boots should be dried as much as possible before long-term storage. If the boot has a removable insole, lift it up and set it sideways in the boot so air can circulate. Store boot foot waders hanging upside down with commercial boot hangers so the weight of the boot is supported by the hanger and not the wader. If hung by their suspenders, most boot foot waders will weaken at the suspender connections due to their heavy weight. Rinse wading boots to remove any grit or dirt inside, tie them together by their laces, and hang them where they can air dry. Short-term storage of wet boots, as when traveling, is best in a ventilated bag.

Stocking foot waders can be hung on a regular heavy duty plastic hanger by their suspenders. They are much lighter in weight and will not stress the suspender areas. Instead of folding stocking foots, roll them whenever possible to relieve stress cracks.

Finding leaks. With a little practice repairing waders can be efficient and easy. The key is finding the leak. Whether working with neoprene, nylon, or rubber, the leak can be found no matter how small. Holding the wader up to a light or using a flashlight will work for an easy leak, but seepage leaks demand more careful testing to ensure a quality permanent repair. When using the light methods, it is possible to miss the area entirely, and these may not show additional small leaks.

The trick to clearly identifying a leak is to fill the suspect section of the wader from the inside with water. This creates the same or greater pressure that is happening when they are being worn. One of the best places to do this is in a bath tub. Make sure that the bath tub is bone dry. Even the slightest moisture in the tub will leave a small damp mark on the outside of the wader creating the impression that the wet spot is a leak. Put the wader up to the spigot and begin to fill the inside of the wader with cold or barely warm water. Do not use hot water. Again, you must not spill any water while completing this procedure.

If the leak is in the right foot, direct all the water down the right leg filling the inside of the wader several inches above the estimated area that the leak is in. Stop the water flow and squeeze the area until water starts to seep outside. In most cases, the pressure created by the volume of water instantly shows the leak without any pressure being applied. Use a waterproof marker to draw a circle around the area so it will be easy to find during the repair process. This test often shows more than one culprit causing moisture to enter your waders.

Off-site repair. Make sure you save the kit that comes from the manufacturer and refer to it before repairing. In the case of breathable waders, making your own repair can invalidate the warranty and also create an area that will not breathe, but condensate. This may give the angler the impression that there is a small leak even after the repair is complete. Refer to the manufacturer for instructions.

For all other types of waders, an efficient repair can be easily made that will last the life of the wader. When making a repair it is important to determine whether or not the repair requires an added piece of material. Adhesives that work well and with all types of wader materials include GOOP, which can be purchased in a hardware or sporting goods store, and Aquaseal, which can be purchased in a sporting goods store. Both adhesives dry flexible and, if properly cured, will repair areas that might otherwise require a small piece of material.

When making the repair, make sure you mark the inside of the wader so the same repair can be made inside as well as outside. Be sure you're in a well-ventilated area and that the wader is completely dry and turned inside out. When the wader is ready, complete the inside repair first, using as little adhesive as necessary. If the wader has to be turned right-side out before the adhesive is dry, put a block of wood inside to keep the sides separate and apart. You don't want to glue the inside of the waders shut. Make sure you follow the curing instructions, which can be an hour to 24 hours depending on the formula. Follow the same procedure on the outside of the repair.

On-site repair. Depending on the adhesive formula, an emergency streamside repair can be made by drying the wader as much as possible and using a quick dry formula from GOOP. In most cases the repair will set immediately from the cold temperatures of the water. However, it is best to repair the site again for a long-term permanent solution.

Rubber sticks that can be lit by a match to melt over the needed area are another option. If done properly, this method can work efficiently if the area is small and has little stress from movement.

Tears.   In the case of larger tears, repairs can be made with the same adhesives used for small repairs. Tears can be repaired effectively on neoprene, nylon, and some canvas waders. Rubber waders are most difficult and not always salvageable. The longer-curing formulas are recommended. The other challenge is to find the same material that the wader is manufactured from. If you can't find the extra piece the manufacturer gave you, most waders have an internal pocket that could be cut for the material required to make the repair.

For larger tears (1 to 3 inches), find a well-ventilated area with a clean, flat working surface. Turn the wader inside out, completing the inside repair first. Carefully rough up the area with 100 grit or finer sandpaper, just enough to raise the grain of the material. Precut the selected repair patch, making sure to generously cover the tear, and round the edges.

Clean the surface and apply a light coating of adhesive using a Popsicle stick or similar tool. Make sure not to get any of the glue inside the wader, risking gluing it together. Allow it to dry until tacky (see adhesive instructions), then firmly apply the patch material to the repair area, working the excess adhesive away. Wait 10 minutes and apply the outside final layer of adhesive. Let dry for 24 hours.

Wading Issues

Most anglers give little thought to safety while wading, until they fall when they least expect to or when they're washed down a turbulent stream with their waders perilously filling up with frigid water. The latter can be a frightening and possibly fatal experience, which most anglers can avoid through common sense and the correct equipment. By learning to read and judge waters, you'll become adept at sensing when to move forward and when to step back.

Swift flowage poses the most obvious difficulty, of course, and rivers that have steep drops and whitewater are most dangerous and allow only edge wading (and maybe not even that). Likewise, some flows may have objects floating down them, such as ice chunks or logs, that you need to look out for, especially if you are not facing upstream (keep looking behind you). Many rivers have sections that are easy to wade, and sections that are difficult, and some that look easy are actually not because their bottoms are slippery and put a lot of pressure on your feet. Surf anglers generally need waders so they can stand on the surf edge and gain extra casting distance without getting wet, but sometimes they need to wade out in the surf and have to beware of underwater tow. So, wading is different depending

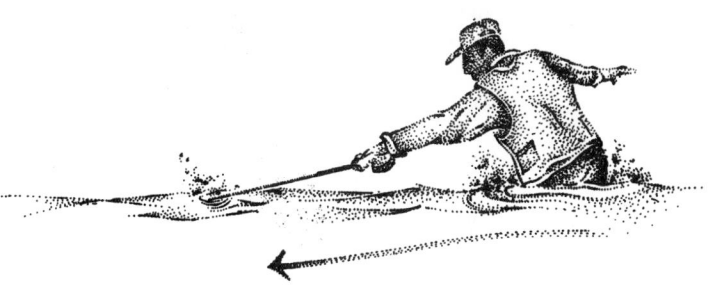

When wading across a river, to help maintain balance when footing is uncertain or the current is swift, lay the tip of your fishing rod into the water directly downstream of your position, and keep the rod in the water while wading across the flow.

on the circumstances. Nevertheless, there are some general guidelines to follow.

Techniques.   Wading is a skill. The more you do it, the better you become. Consideration should always be given to depth, water speed, bottom configuration, and whether it is prudent to wade through the fast or deep areas at all. Many anglers have taken one step too many and found themselves slipping into deeper water over the top of their waders; in rivers, this may result in a floating trip though the rapids or pool, which is not worth the fish you might have caught.

Always respect water. Go slowly. Make sure that your foot is firmly planted and stable before taking the next step. Crablike steps are much better than reaching strides. Concentrate on the task at hand. Wearing polarized sunglasses helps make the trail under the water more visible, although the deeper you wade and the murkier the water, the less this helps. In clear water, polarized sunglasses are a great aid.

Scout an area that you intend to wade across before starting to do so. Often, you will find a better route, usually shallower, a little distance upstream or downstream; often, the tail of a pool is best to cross because the water is shallower at the bottom lip and the velocity is less. Do not cast and wade at the same time; better to get into position and then cast. Don't walk or leap from one large rock to another, which is asking for trouble; don't wade in the turbulent water upstream of a large rock; and beware of deep holes below large rocks. In tailwater rivers, beware of rising water; dam releases can suddenly raise the water level, and if you notice the water coming up, waste no time in getting to shore.

In swift, deep, or unfamiliar water, you should plan every step, and take slow steps by sliding your foot along, rather than lifting it. If you lift your feet in swift water, the current can push your leg away and throw you off balance. Also, place your feet between rocks instead of on top of them, which is an invitation to slipping or moving too deep with the next step.

In rivers, you should wade with your body and feet sideways to the flow. Even a slight turn in fast water can spin you or knock you over. Wade across at an angle, preferably slightly quartered upstream. Remember that the more you weigh, the easier it is

W
X
Y
Z

to wade fast water; the lighter you are, the harder. A light person should draft below a heavier one if the two can cross swift water together; a better idea for two people in swift water may be to link elbows and cross slowly, having the stability of four feet on the bottom.

Using a wading staff or stick can be very helpful. It acts as a stabilizing third leg, and is also valuable for probing depth and poking for rocks. Most people find that it's best to place the staff upstream.

Using a staff is a good way to maintain balance when wading in swift flows; place the staff on your upstream side and don't extend it too far from your body.

Without a stick, you can use your fishing rod to help stabilize you in deep swift current, especially when you start to feel unbalanced or are about to stumble or fall. Hold the rod in your downstream hand and keep it pointed directly downstream. Place the tip section in the current to act as a stabilizer. Obviously, you need to have the rod in the proper hand to start with, so when you don't have a staff, start wading with the rod in your downstream hand. In the worst cases, use both a staff in your upstream hand and the rod in your downstream hand.

Once you get across a rough spot, or are about to leave the water, don't let up your concentration. Many people fall on their way out of the water by taking their last steps for granted. High and slippery stream banks are also a problem.

When you're getting out of a boat to wade, especially if you're not right on shore in shallow water,

If you fall into a swift flow, get your feet headed downstream and float with the current so you can fend off objects and see where you're headed; work toward the shallows or light-current areas where you can get your footing and leave the water.

don't be fooled by the illusion of depth that comes with clear water. The water is often deeper than it looks, and many people have gotten out of boats to find that they are over the top of their waders, or sometimes their heads.

If you start heading into soft-bottomed areas, which may happen in stillwater, do not keep going forward, as you may find your feet so deeply buried in muck that suction keeps your feet mired. If you start sinking into soft bottoms, retreat to firmer ground and find a better route.

When you hook a strong fish, gradually retreat from deep water and get to shore. You can follow a fish easier, if necessary, from the shallows, where you have more maneuverability, and also can effect a higher rod angle.

If you do find yourself floating downriver in current while wearing chest waders, don't panic. Get your feet pointed downstream so they can be used to deflect your body, and especially head, from objects, and go with the flow on your back with your head up. Use your arms to try to maneuver toward the bank and water that is calm and shallow enough for you stand up in. Do not float head first or try to fight the current.

It is a good idea to test your waders sometime in a swimming pool or warm safe stream or lake to see what happens to them when they fill with water, and how you are able (or not able) to maneuver. A wet, fully clothed person in waders full of water is very heavy, barely able to move, and a candidate for drowning, so this is a matter to be taken very seriously.

Staying warm. Staying warm has never been easier. Tremendous strides in wader manufacturing and clothing have made it possible to stay out in weather that your fishing gear won't even work in.

Anglers who venture out when the air temperature is subfreezing and water temperature is at the freezing mark must take special precautions and wear specialized equipment. Waders must be open cut, allowing the angler to comfortably wear clothing made of noncotton-based polypropylenes, piles, or their equivalents.

The foot is the most important design feature of a wader. A full-cut rubber boot foot bottom on any wader is superior to even heavy stocking foot neoprene waders for warmth and comfort in severe cold. Boot foot bottoms offer superior insulation and, most importantly, open space for your toes and feet to move. Stocking foots tend to constrict blood flow from the tight "walking fit" that happens when you lace your wading shoes. Even full-cut rubber and canvas waders can provide adequate warmth if the angler has enough room to wear the proper clothing.

Most people can stay warm all day if they can keep their feet warm. To make sure that your feet stay warm, wear a light polypropylene liner sock with a heavy poly or wool sock over it. This combination will keep you much warmer than two heavy wool socks, which will most likely fit your feet too tightly, constricting blood flow. Do not wear cotton socks, which absorb perspiration and make feet damp and cold. When you put the waders on, your feet should slip into the boots easily without a struggle, and there should be enough room to wiggle your toes. If you use stocking foot waders in extreme cold, consider a larger size wading shoe to accommodate the need for extra room.

Even the warmest waders will not keep you dry if you sweat and soak your cotton-based underclothes. This is a common mistake that can ruin a day of fishing quickly. Always wear an undergarment made from polypropylene or other micro fibers. Expedition-weight underwear can even substitute for pants if worn with thin poly liner underwear. The same is true for the upper half of your body. Wear layered poly or other micro fibers, and never wear cotton. When taking long walks, remove as much upper clothing as possible to let hot air escape to keep you from perspiring.

It is true that most of your body heat can be lost through your head. Always wear warm hats in the winter. If it's a long walk to your destination, take the hat off while walking to release more heat and to keep you from perspiring.

WADING BOOTS
See: Waders.

WADING STAFF
See: Waders.

WAGGLER
A float attached to fishing line by its bottom only, used with a rod and reel for stillwater angling.
See: Float.

WAHOO *Acanthocybium solandri.*
Other names—barracuda, oahu fish, ocean barracuda, Pacific kingfish, pride of Bermuda, queenfish, tigerfish; Arabic: *kanaad znjebari;* Creole: *bécune grosse race, kin fis, thazard raité;* French: *paere;* Hawaiian: *ono;* Japanese: *kamasu-sawara;* Portuguese: *cavala gigante, cavala-da-India, cavala empinge;* Spanish: *guacho, peto, sierra;* Tuvaluan: *tepala.*

The wahoo is a popular gamefish and a close relative of the king mackerel. It is reputedly one of the fastest fish in the sea, attaining speeds of 50 miles per hour and more, and no angler who has hooked a large wahoo and watched it sizzle a hundred yards of line off the reel in a few seconds will dispute this.

The wahoo was originally plentiful off the Hawaiian island of Oahu, once commonly spelled "Wahoo," and this accounts for the fish's name. The Hawaiian word for this fish, *ono,* meaning "good to eat," is an appropriate description of the wahoo's sweet, white, flaky flesh. It has a more delicate texture than the meat of other fast-swimming pelagic species, as it contains less of the strong-tasting "blood meat" muscle—used for long-distance swimming—found in tuna and marlin. The wahoo has commercial importance in some countries and is marketed fresh, salted, spice-cured, or frozen.

Identification. A long, slender, cigar-shaped mackerel with a sharply pointed head and widely forked tail, the wahoo is a brilliant or dark blue color along its back. It has 25 to 30 bright or dusky blue vertical bands, or "tiger stripes" that extend down the bright silver to silvery gray sides and sometimes join into pairs below. The stripes are not always prominent or even apparent in large specimens, although they may become more noticeable when the fish is excited. A distinguishing feature is the movable upper jaw, which has 45 to 64 teeth, of which 32 to 50 are on the lower jaw; these teeth are large, strong, and laterally compressed. The gill structure resembles that of the marlin more than it does those of the tuna or mackerel, and it lacks the characteristic gill rakers of the latter fish. The lateral line is well defined and drops significantly at the middle of the first dorsal fin and extends in a wavy line back to the tail. The first dorsal fin is long and low and has 21 to 27 spines. It is separated from the second dorsal fin, which has 13 to 15 rays; the anal fin has 12 to 14 very small rays. There are a series of 9 dorsal finlets both above and below the caudal peduncle.

Size. The wahoo grows rapidly, reaching on average 10 to 30 pounds, and 4- to 5-foot lengths are not uncommon. Its maximum size is 7 feet in

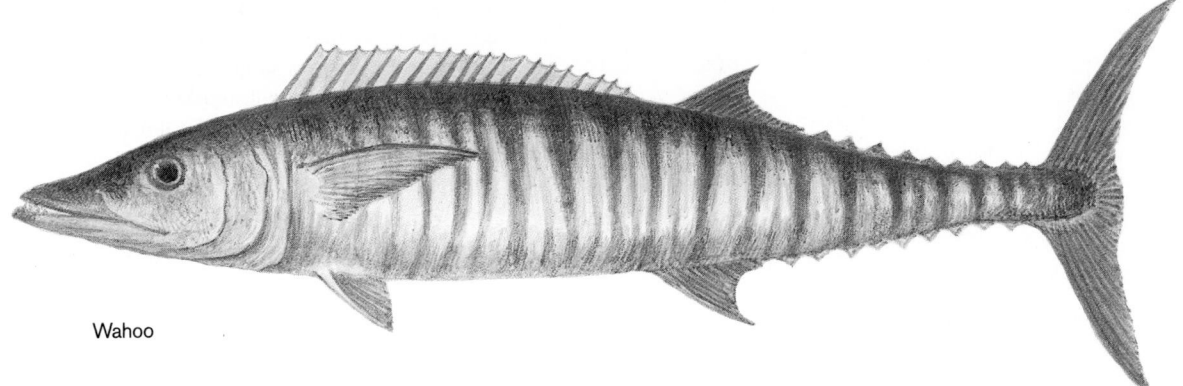

Wahoo

length and more than 180 pounds in weight. The all-tackle world record is a 158-pound, 8-ounce fish taken off Baja California, Mexico, in 1996.

Distribution. Wahoo occur in the Atlantic, Pacific, and Indian Oceans in tropical and subtropical waters, including the Caribbean and Mediterranean Seas. Seasonal concentrations are thought to exist off the Pacific coasts of Panama, Costa Rica, and Baja California during the summer, off Grand Cayman in the Atlantic during the winter and spring, and off the western Bahamas and Bermuda during the spring and fall. Some of the best sportfishing and largest specimens occur off San Salvador in the Bahamas, and off Baja California, Mexico.

Habitat. An oceanic species, wahoo are pelagic and seasonally migratory. They are frequently solitary or form small, loose groupings of two to seven fish rather than large compact schools. They are known to associate around banks, pinnacles, and even flotsam. They are occasionally found around wrecks and deeper reefs where smaller fish are abundant.

Life history. Both sexes reach sexual maturity during the first year of life. Depending on their size, females may discharge from hundreds of thousands to tens of millions of eggs.

Food. Wahoo feed on such pelagic species as porcupinefish, flyingfish, herring, pilchards, scad, lanternfish, and small mackerel and tuna, as well as on squid.

Angling. This speedy member of the mackerel family is caught in a variety of ways, although trolling is by far the number one activity. A great many fish are caught incidental to other fishing activities, although they can be targeted specifically where they are abundant. As mentioned, wahoo are often solitary but may travel in small groups in some areas, especially in hard-fished waters where they can be less numerous and wary.

Wahoo are mostly caught in waters that range from 72° to 77°F. They are located over or along humps, ledges, seamounts, and other structure that causes current to well up and provide good feeding opportunities, as well as along current edges and around floating objects and sargassum. Near-surface trolling at high speeds is a standard ploy for wahoo-seeking anglers, as is deeper trolling via planers, downriggers, and wire line. Because wahoo are seldom found in the concentrations typical of other mackerel and tuna, trolling is a good way to cover a lot of territory. In addition, the fast swimming ability of this species allows for speedy boat travel; wahoo are typically caught at boat speeds of 6 to 10 knots, and a few anglers troll at up to 14 knots.

Trolled offerings include whole, rigged Spanish mackerel; mullet, ballyhoo, squid, or other small baits; strip baits and diving plugs; or heavy bullet-head trolling lures and other assorted offshore trolling lures. Live-bait fishing and kite fishing are less practiced but sometimes productive, and on occasion opportunities for casting with plugs, spoons, metal jigs, and flies exist. In the Pacific, long-range anglers use heavy plastic- or vinyl-skirted trolling or casting heads—called bombs—for trolling and for casting to secondary-strike fish; these usually feature a spinning willowleaf blade on the main hook, and sometimes a trailer hook, and weigh 3 to 8 ounces.

Wahoo are most likely to be active early in the day, so anglers who specialize in wahoo like to beat the competition to productive spots and commence fishing at dawn. Although wahoo are caught by trolling in the upper levels, trolling at deeper levels is the way to target larger fish. Appropriate depths range from just under the surface to 120 or more feet, and anglers use varied approaches to cover different depths. Weighted natural baits, deep-running plugs, and spoons are favored. Some anglers prefer wire line (60-pound) for this deep work, whereas others use planers that can take fast trolling as well as downriggers.

Other anglers use 50- to 60-pound nylon monofilament, although lighter line can be employed off downriggers. Reels must have an excellent drag and plenty of line capacity; 4/0 to 6/0 conventional reels and comparable lever drags are standard. Where the fish may not be really deep, spreading the lures horizontally in a trolling pattern is necessary; in a four-line setup, two center lines are fished at a shorter distance in the boat wake (which often attracts fish), and the two outside lines are fished twice that distance back in the wake.

Dark lure colors—especially green, mackerel patterns, purple and black bodies, and dark-combo bodies—are effective on these fish. Deep-running plugs must be capable of tracking straight at high speeds, which limits the possibilities. Heavy-duty wire leaders are a necessity owing to the toothy mouths of these fish.

Where there are groups of wahoo, continued trolling over likely structure is a good tactic, and when a fish is hooked, it may be possible to get a second hookup by casting out a metal jig after the other trolling lines have been cleared.

The first scorching run of a wahoo may peel off at least a hundred yards of line in seconds, and the heat generated by the friction has been known to burn out the drag on some reels. Keep your hands off the spool. Occasionally these fish jump on the strike and often shake their head violently when hooked in an effort to free themselves. Be careful when handling these fish, as you may otherwise put your fingers in jeopardy.

See: Mackerel; Offshore Fishing.

WAKE

The waves created by a passing boat; the visible track or trail behind a moving boat.

WALES
Gamefishing

Trout. The mountains of Wales give rise to dozens of rivers and streams holding brown trout, and many of these also have a sea trout and salmon run. Fishing for brown trout is relatively inexpensive, and permits are available locally. It is also possible to enjoy good salmon and sea trout (often called sewin) fishing at a reasonable cost, and assistance is available on some beats from a local gillie (guide) or fishing instructor.

In the 1980s, the trend to start up commercially stocked put-and-take stillwaters (in a broad sense, a stillwater is anything that is not a river, stream, or tributary) fisheries spread from England to Wales, and the south in particular now has a proliferation of these waters, some holding rainbows in excess of 20 pounds. Big brown trout are more expensive, because they take twice as long as rainbows to grow to any given weight and are therefore in shorter supply. It's difficult to land and return these big fish alive, so captured fish are seldom allowed to be released.

Of the biggest rivers, the Teifi holds wild brownies, and the Towy, Welsh Dee, Wye, and the upper reaches of the Severn are among the best-known rivers inhabited by wild browns and grayling. Day tickets are available on most at a very reasonable cost, usually from a local shop. Much of this fishery is fly angling only.

Salmon and sea trout. The best Welsh rivers for sea trout and salmon are the Towy, Conwy, Mawddach, Wnion (pronounced Oonion), Usk, Teifi, Welsh Dee, Wye, and Dovey. Three good smaller rivers are the Seiont, Gwyrfai, and Llyfni, near the Menai Straits, for which day tickets are easily available.

Welsh rivers tend to be shorter and faster than many English game rivers, and more of them have pools. It is easier to obtain fishing tickets here than on rivers in either England or Scotland. Some have private and expensive beats, however, including the Towy, which is reputed to be the best sea trout river in the UK; individual specimens run as big as the salmon and approach 20 pounds. Also worth trying is the Taf in South Wales. This venue was badly polluted, but a dedicated restocking policy has resulted in the return of salmon and the development of a good run.

Coarse Fishing

Coarse fishing in Wales plays second fiddle to gamefishing, but excellent venues do exist. The River Wye in particular can produce spectacular fishing for barbel, chub, and dace, and many experts have predicted that this river will produce a barbel weighing more than 17 pounds. The stretch below Symonds Yat has reportedly yielded such fish to salmon anglers, and there are loads of barbel from Hereford downward. The Wye is also famous for big catches of one of Britain's smallest fish, the bleak. It weighs only a couple of ounces on average but is present in such numbers that 50-pound catches have been taken in five-hour matches.

When the River Wye floods, tributaries such as the Rivers Lugg and Monnow become productive for dace, chub, and barbel. The nearby River Usk is dominated by gamefishing concerns, but where coarse fishing is allowed, the action is spectacular. Usk town center and Newbridge produce 100-plus-pound catches of dace and chub regularly, and roach exceeding 3 pounds are present. The river holds many specimen (large or trophy) dace, and the fish average nearly 1 pound in places.

The River Severn rises in Wales before making its way into England above Shrewsbury. The Welsh section is mainly fast and clear, but if you can find the slower, deeper stretches, you can enjoy great sport for medium-size barbel, chub, grayling, and roach. Welshpool and Newton are good spots. Farther north, the River Dee is full of chub, but this river has been hit hard by cormorant predation, and local knowledge is needed for success. These fish do tend to congregate near bridges.

Probably the most famous coarse fishing venue in Wales is not a coarse venue at all, but a trout reservoir. When a pike fishing trial was first held at Llandegfedd Reservoir in South Wales in the 1980s, it became known that these waters held big pike, but few people could have guessed what would follow. The venue yielded more 40-plus-pound pike than any other in UK history. The British record fell several times in quick succession and finally settled at a massive 46 pounds, 13 ounces. The pike at Llandegfedd Reservoir grow incredibly fast on a diet of stocked trout, and the big catches sparked the opening of a string of trout venues and changed the face of pike fishing for good.

Another worthwhile venue in South Wales is the Monmouthshire and Brecon Canal in Cwmbran, which is known to hold huge chub and carp. For big roach, pike, eels, and perch, giant Bala Lake near Oswestry is a hard stillwater to better. This ancient, deep glacial lake is also home to the rare gwyniad, a protected fish from the days when the country was dominated by glaciers and snowdrifts.

In Cardiff, the mile-long East Bute Dock is well worth a visit. This site holds an enormous number of small roach and bream (called skimmers), and 20-plus-pound catches are easily taken. It's also home to specimen eels weighing more than 5 pounds; these are taken at night. Other stillwaters worth mentioning are Ponsticill Reservoir in the Brecon Beacons, home to some enormous perch, including a rumored fish of 7 pounds; Llangorse Lake, where second-to-none bream and pike fishing can be enjoyed with stunning scenery as a backdrop; and Roath Park Lake in Cardiff, for summer roach fishing.

Coarse fishing in Wales is covered by the same national license as in England.

Sea Fishing

The south coast of Wales has a considerable number of charter ports, whose boats fish the Bristol

In Botswana, the climbing perch can breathe atmospheric air, crawl out of the water, and "walk" across muddy and moist land to find suitable spawning grounds; it has traveled as far as 9.4 kilometers.

W
X
Y
Z

Channel and regularly make the trip south to fish off the Devon coast. The ray fishing is exceptionally good from spring to midwinter, and anglers regularly land big cod as well. Other main species include conger, ling, and bass, which are usually taken inshore. The main ports are Penarth, Swansea, Tenby, and Pembroke.

Shore fishing from Penarth around the peninsula to Fishguard is especially productive, offering bass and flounder in summer and great numbers of codling (small cod) in winter. Mullet favor the waters around the many marinas. Anglers can avail themselves of a variety of sites, ranging from sandy beaches to rocky headlands, and many local clubs exist should the visitor need help.

Curiously, the west coast is little fished when compared with the rest of Wales, although some well-known storm beaches produce bass, as well as flounder in the estuaries. The long sweep of Cardigan Bay, however, is open to the prevailing westerly winds, at times rendering most of it almost unfishable. The main charter ports are Newquay, Aberystwyth, Barmouth, and Pwhelli; they get fantastic catches of rays, tope, cod, black bream, sharks, and other species from the Gulf Stream, rivaling most other areas of the UK on their best day.

To the north is the Lleyn Peninsula, known in particular for bull bass in spring, when pregnant females come close to shore and near-record fish are taken every year. Some of the marks are especially dangerous, and anglers fishing here should always be accompanied by a companion who has local knowledge. On the north coast, flounder, codling, and bass are the main species, and the established charter ports are Bangor, Conway, Colwyn Bay, Rhyl, and Rhos.

The island of Anglesey, off the northwest tip of Wales, offers exceptional fishing from its rocky shoreline all around the island. Species include pollack, rays, codling, whiting, and conger. Conger and bass are plentiful from the narrow, fast-running Menai Straits. Local knowledge is essential here. The main ports are Amlwch and Holyhead. There's year-round fishing from Anglesey, which is easily reached by road across one of two bridges. No license is required for saltwater angling.

See: England; Scotland.

WALKING THE DOG

One of the few lure retrieval techniques that actually has a formal name, walking the dog is a slow and tantalizing method of manipulating so-called walking surface plugs or stickbaits *(see: surface lure)*, which are designed to swim from side to side. The term and the method derive from the infamous Heddon Zara Spook plug, and this method is particularly effective at tempting larger-than-average-size bass out of woody cover and thick vegetation, and up from deep clear-water hideouts. However, it is also effective for other freshwater and saltwater fish that may strike a surface lure.

Because of their tail-weighted design, these types of lures are distinctly unimpressive and ineffective if not worked right, and practice is needed to develop the most effective action.

To effect the right retrieval, begin with the rod tip pointed down. It's helpful to stand or be seated high, to have most of your line on the water to help create drag, and to tie the fishing line to the lure with a rounded snap or a loop knot.

To walk the dog, you need to make rhythmic short jerks with the rod tip while simultaneously advancing the reel handle a quarter turn or so with each jerk to take up line. Done slowly, the lure's travel path widens; done quickly, it narrows. The line should lie slightly slack in the water to avoid pulling the lure ahead. The right cadence allows the lure to swim from side to side, but a taut line jerks it ahead. A skilled retriever can slow-fish a walking plug so that it almost stays in place, nodding from left to right, an action that can be highly seductive to otherwise disinterested fish.

"Half-stepping" is an advanced technique for working a walking plug very close to logs, bushes, docks, and so on. Here the plug swims repeatedly to one side instead of from left to right. To do this, you must first get into proper casting position by aligning your line with the object being fished. Walk the lure up to the object so that the plug faces it. Barely nudge the rod tip so that the head of the plug turns away. Now jerk the rod tip; the plug heads inward toward the bush. Nudge again; jerk again. The lure continues to swim toward the bush and actually works around it as if using it for protection. Done right, this tactic is almost irresistible to a bass that is in or under that object.

See: Plug.

Walking the Dog

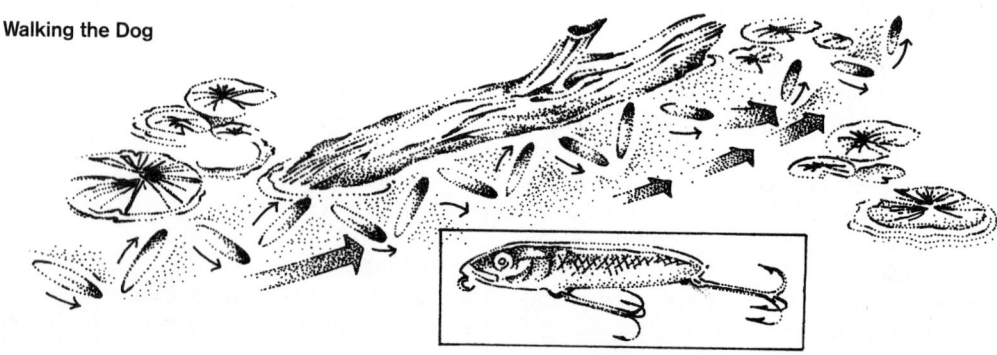

Walleye

WALLEYE *Stizostedion vitreum.*

Other names—pickerel, yellow pickerel, walleyed pike, yellow walleye, jack salmon, jack, pike-perch, walleyed pike-perch, pike, gray pike, green pike, 'eye, marbleye, glass-eye; French: *doré.*

The walleye is the largest member of the Percidae family of perch *(see)* in North America and a close relative of the sauger *(see)*. It is also closely related to the larger-growing zander *(see)* of Europe. A popular freshwater sportfish, the walleye is relatively abundant in many waters, grows to large sizes, and is renowned for its delicious, sweet, and fine-textured meat. As a food fish, the walleye has few peers in freshwater, which helps counterbalance its reputation as a sluggish battler when hooked. It struggles on or near the bottom rather than making long or sustained runs or leaping out of the water.

The walleye has received considerable commercial interest in the past and is still sought commercially in Canada, where Manitoba and Ontario provide the bulk of the commercial harvest. It is also that country's leading inland sportfish, vying with coastal salmon species for overall honors. It is likewise hallowed in upper Midwestern U.S. states. In many parts of Canada, walleye are primarily referred to as "pickerel," which is a misnomer and a source of some confusion. The walleye is sometimes incorrectly associated with the true pickerel *(see: pickerel, chain)*, which, unlike the walleye, is a member of the Esox, or pike, family of fish.

Identification.   The walleye has a slender and cylindrical body with a tapered head. Its first dorsal fin has needle-sharp spiny rays and is separated from the soft-rayed second dorsal fin. The cheeks are sparsely scaled, the gill covers are sharp, and the teeth are sharp. When handling the fish, anglers must take care around the teeth, gill covers, and spiny dorsal fin to avoid cuts and stab wounds.

The walleye has a dark green back, golden yellow sides, and a white belly. The lower lobe of the caudal fin is white, and there is a large black blotch at the rear base of the spinous first dorsal fin. Young walleye usually have dark blotches across their backs and down their sides, but these patterns are absent in adults. As with many fish, the color of the walleye is highly variable depending on habitat, with golden color characteristics in many populations. Typically, fish in turbid or off-color waters are paler with less obvious black markings; clear waters produce more definitively marked specimens.

Perhaps the most prominent feature of a walleye is its large, white, glossy eyes. The special reflective layer in the retina of the eye is a characteristic known as tapetum lucidum; it gathers light that enters the eye, making it extremely sensitive to bright daylight intensities but is conducive to nocturnal vision. This attribute is also present in the sauger. These two species thus have the best night vision among freshwater gamefish, with a light-gathering eyesight similar to that of cats, raccoons, and deer.

Size.   The size of walleye varies with their environment, but anglers commonly encounter fish in the 10- to 18-inch range and weighing about 1 to 3 pounds. Some waters support fish that are larger on average, and it is not uncommon to catch walleye exceeding 5 pounds in many places. Fish exceeding the arbitrary trophy size of 10 pounds are hard to come by in many places, although some waters have an abundance of such fish. Walleye are capable of achieving a maximum size of at least 23 pounds and possibly 25 pounds. The only one known to have exceeded 23 pounds is the Tennessee state record and International Game Fish Association (IGFA) all-tackle world record—a 25-pound fish caught in Old Hickory Lake, Tennessee, in 1960. It has been the subject of revisionist dispute in recent years and is followed in the record annals by a 22-pound, 11-ounce walleye from Greers Ferry Lake, Arkansas, in 1982, and a 22-pound, 4-ounce specimen caught at Fort Erie, Ontario, in 1943.

Distribution.   The walleye is widely distributed in North America. Its native range in the north extended from Great Bear Lake in the Northwest Territories easterly to James Bay and the Gulf of St. Lawrence. In the east it extended southward along the Allegheny Mountains to Georgia and Gulf Coast drainages in Mississippi and Alabama. In the west it extended from Saskatchewan

W
X
Y
Z

throughout the Dakotas to Arkansas. Through some natural expansion and extensive introduction, the range has been extended eastward to Atlantic coast drainages from Vermont to South Carolina and westward to all western states except California, as well as southern Alberta and British Columbia. With few exceptions, the significant walleye fisheries exist in waters within its native range; the walleye forms a dominant part of the fish fauna of central Canada, particularly in the boreal forest zone. In that region, it is clearly the dominant and most popular game species.

Habitat. Walleye are tolerant of a great range of environmental situations but seem to do best in the open water of large lakes and reservoirs, as well as the pools of large rivers. They inhabit many smaller bodies of water but are not typically prolific in the most turbid environs, preferring somewhat clearer water than their sauger cousins. Gravel, rock, and firm sand bottoms are preferred, and they may associate with various weed cover; they will also use sunken trees, standing timber, boulder shoals, and reefs as cover and foraging sites. Although they can survive temperature extremes from 32° to 90°F, they prefer waters with a maximum temperature of roughly 77° and are commonly associated with 65° to 75° water in summer.

In clear lakes, walleye often lie in contact with the bottom during daytime, seemingly resting. In these lakes, they usually feed from top to bottom at night. In turbid water, they are more active during the day, swimming slowly in schools close to the bottom. Walleye frequently are associated with other species such as yellow perch, northern pike, white suckers, and smallmouth bass. During the winter, walleye do not change their habitat except to avoid strong currents. In large water bodies, they will orient to open water in schools that coincide with the presence of baitfish, especially alewives but also shad and perch.

In the spring, the fish have a spawning run to shallow shoals, inshore areas, or tributary rivers; at other times they move up and down in response to light intensity. They also move daily or seasonally in response to water temperature or food availability. For the most part, walleye seem to remain in loose but discrete schools with separate spawning grounds and summer territories.

Life history/Behavior. Spawning occurs in the spring or early summer, depending on latitude and water temperature. Normally, spawning begins shortly after the ice breaks up in lakes that freeze; water temperature is usually in the mid-40s, but spawning may occur at a range between 38° and 50°F.

The males move to the spawning grounds first. These are usually rocky areas in flowing water below impassable falls and dams in rivers and streams, coarse-gravel shoals, or (least common) along rubble shores of lakes at depths of less than 6 feet. Spawning takes place at night, in groups of one large female and one or two smaller males or two females and numerous males.

The male walleye is not territorial and does not build a nest. Prior to spawning, there is a lot of pursuit, pushing, circular swimming, and fin erection. Finally, the spawning group rushes upward into shallow water and stops, the females roll on their sides and release their eggs, and simultaneously, milt is released by the males. Apparently, females deposit most of their eggs in one night of spawning. The fertilized eggs are dispersed at random over rocks and gravel and fall into crevices in the stream or lake bottom where they adhere. Hundreds of thousands of eggs (as many as 600,000) may be dispersed.

The eggs hatch in 12 to 18 days on the spawning grounds, and by 10 to 15 days after hatching the young have dispersed into the upper levels of open water. By the latter part of the summer, young-of-the-year move toward the bottom. Growth is fairly rapid in the south but slower in more northerly latitudes. Females grow more quickly than males.

Juvenile and adult walleye are themselves important food sources for various predatory fish at various stages of their life. The northern pike is probably the dominant predator of the walleye over much of its range, and muskellunge will also consume adults to some degree. Adult perch, other walleye, and sauger prey on young walleye, and yellow perch, sauger, and smallmouth bass are the walleye's main competitors for food.

Food and feeding habits. The walleye can be a voracious feeder and primarily consumes other fish. The wide diet includes alewives, smelt, shad, cisco, shiners, sculpin, suckers, minnows, darters, perch, and crayfish, as well as many other items. Their diet shifts rapidly from invertebrates to fish as walleye increase in size. Some populations, even as adults, feed almost exclusively on emerging larval or adult mayflies for part of the year. The relative amounts of the various species of fish that walleye feed on apparently is determined by their availability. Yellow perch and cyprinids are particularly favored when these species are present.

Angling. In addition to being good food and fairly abundant, the walleye is popular because it is a schooling species often found in concentrations, it does not tend to be an aggressive feeder so it can be challenging to catch, and it is susceptible to a wide range of angling techniques. Although they have light-sensitive eyes that theoretically make them most active in low-light and dark conditions in many environments, they do feed during daylight hours and can be caught during the day.

Walleye abundance relates to baitfish presence and to structure. Their prey varies with the body of water, often being whatever small fish are most prevalent. The activities of the predominant food have a bearing on where walleye are located—suspended in open water, hugging the bottom along sandbars or reefs or points, waiting along weedlines, and so forth. The structure they favor includes rock reefs, sandbars, gravel bars, points, weeds, rocky or riprap causeways or shorelines, and

creek channels. Walleye are particularly known for congregating in or along the edges of vegetation. Walleye weeds, for the most part, are submerged, sometimes slightly visible on or near the surface, especially in shallow water, and often deeper and out of sight. Thick clumps of weeds are preferable to scattered weeds because the former offer more cover. Fishing clumped weeds is easiest. When these are not available, scattered weeds are the second choice. Walleye often prefer shorter weeds in moderately deep water than taller weeds in the same depth. Knowledgeable walleye anglers always look for the weedline and its depth. An excellent situation, although not as readily fished, is where the weeds are thick and the edge is close to a sharp bottom dropoff. Working the edges of the weeds is particularly effective.

In some waters, particularly large lakes, walleye are also found in deep water, suspended or on the bottom where there are open, basinlike flats. Some walleye, especially big specimens and those that are likely to be feeding, do not hold to the traditional bottom and cover-providing structure; instead, they roam open water to take advantage of migratory schools of baitfish—mainly smelt and alewives—prevalent in those waters. Depending on the location of the baitfish, walleye may be in a few feet of water or in 20 to 30 feet, over a bottom that is much deeper.

Fishing presentations for walleye run the gamut, but they largely center on jigging, stillfishing or drifting with live baits, trolling with bait rigs, casting crankbaits, and trolling with plugs. Jigs are typically used with baits (leeches, minnows, and worms), although hair- and grub-bodied jigs are popular as well. Fixed and slip bobbers are used for live-bait fishing, although sometimes a jig and worm is fished below a bobber. Trolling rigs include weight-forward or June-bug–style spinners, as well as spinner-and-worm/leech harnesses, and walking or bottom-bouncing sinkers. Many walleye anglers have employed a controlled wind-drifting and boat-movement technique called backtrolling (see)—using a tiller-steered outboard motor or an electric motor—to keep the boat in proper position. Jigs and rigs are used and almost always fished very slowly.

Walleye anglers on big waters predominantly employ forward trolling, primarily using shallow to deep-diving plugs (and sometimes spoons). They troll them on flatlines, in-line planers, large side-planer boards, and even downriggers. The offerings are presented at precise depths for suspended and mobile walleye; locating the fish, getting to the precise depth, and having good lure action are paramount.

When walleye are spawning in rivers, other tributaries, and in shallow bays, fishing, where legal, is relatively easy. It becomes more difficult after spawning, however, when the fish migrate out of rivers and bays into main-lake structure and disperse. Throughout the summer, anglers work various

A slow-trolled diving minnow plug fooled this walleye.

forms of structure, as well as deep water. In the fall, walleye become more concentrated again and are especially found on main-lake points that are close to deep water. In large lakes, they will migrate toward the upper end where a river comes in, or to a dam end. This is a good time to prospect for bigger fish.

Walleye fishing is different in rivers than in lakes. The fish spawn throughout the same temperature range, and they migrate after spawning, although they may not go particularly far in smaller systems. In both spring and fall they may be located off the mouths of tributaries; in spring, they are drawn by spawning needs; in fall, by baitfish. They do not suspend, however, and almost always respond to bottom-oriented presentations.

In large river systems, anglers land walleye close to dams in winter and spring. At other times, they work the deep water off wing dams, island channel cuts, deep-water bridge abutments, and center-channel edges. Look for walleye along a river channel that has considerable depth as well, especially in midsummer.

Riprap is an especially favored walleye haunt in rivers, particularly in the evening and if there is deep water nearby. Other prominent locales include cuts, where currents meet each other; eddies and slicks; along and behind islands; large rocks; and the head and tail of pools. River walleye feed on assorted forage, including crayfish, hellgrammites, and minnows. They are caught by jigging, casting, and trolling with spoons, spinners, and plugs; and fishing with live baits.

Jigs are the most effective river lure, probably because they are worked close to the bottom and represent minnows or crayfish. Small and shallow rivers generally require $1/8$- to $5/8$-ounce jigs; in fast water, you should increase the weight. Fish jigs with the current; there is no need to actually jig them, and a slow rolling action is best. In spring and fall, use white, yellow, chartreuse, and silver colors; in summer, use brown, black, green, or orange-and-brown.

Live baits are also effective. A live-bait rig, weighing ¹/₄ to 1 ounce and rigged with 20 inches of dropback leader and a No. 2 short-shanked hook, is a popular offering. Minnows, night-crawlers, leeches, salamanders, waterdogs, and cray-fish are used for bait, as are assorted minnows. Sinker style can be split shot, egg, or a different bottom-bouncing type.

Tackle needs for walleye in lakes and rivers are not especially complicated. Medium-action spin-ning rods from 5¹/₂ to 7 feet long, and reels filled with 8- to 12-pound line, are standard. For trolling, especially when planer boards are used, longer rods and stouter gear may be necessary. Baitcasting tackle can be employed but is usually not necessary, except when using long lines off planers in rough water. Fly tackle is seldom appropriate, although fly fishing is possible when the fish are shallow and concentrated.

These anglers, on Lake Erie in Ohio, have a walleye boat that is "dressed to the nines" for big-water fishing.

WALLEYE BOAT

The term "walleye boat" refers to a boat that is sim-ilar in many respects to a bass boat (see). Walleyes can be caught from any type of craft that suits the necessary angling method and the water conditions, but so-called walleye boats are a type of craft that is popular for walleye angling in big lakes and rivers, and has evolved in part due to the wide-ranging demands of fishing tournaments. Walleye boats are not as widespread as bass boats, but are a fishing machine that is particularly functional where a lot of freshwater trolling, stillfishing, jigging, and bot-tom fishing is required; where presentation and boat positioning are especially important; and where fishing is done on large bodies of open water that can get rough. In truth, a so-called walleye boat is really a multi-species freshwater fishing boat that can be useful almost anywhere and used with a

variety of techniques, although it is not as func-tional in shallow rivers.

Walleye or multi-species boats look a bit like bass boats, but they have a deeper design and are better appointed for sustained fishing in wave-whipped water. Generally, they range from 15 to 18 feet in length, with a hull style from semi-V to deep-V, with a deeper interior design and greater freeboard than a bass boat.

Walleye boats are made of both aluminum and fiberglass, and may have tiller or console steering, although bigger versions, suited for large-horsepower motors, employ console steering. With tiller-steered models, 50- to 60-horsepower motors are standard, in part because they gear down and perform well at slow speeds for long periods of time.

Walleye boats sport many of the same features as bass boats, including high-speed bow-mounted electric motor, console and bow sonar devices,

19-ft. Walleye Boat

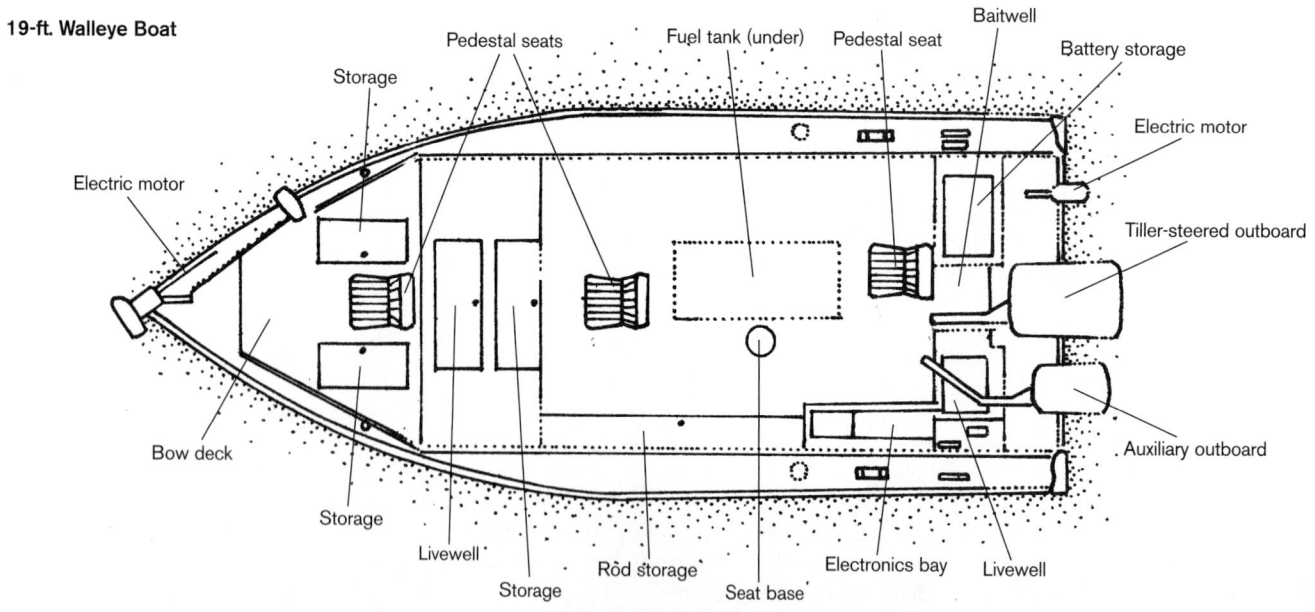

W
X
Y
Z

Warmouth

livewells, and rod and tackle storage. Some models have a baitwell in addition to a livewell, an auxiliary outboard motor on a kick-up transom bracket, a transom-mount electric motor, GPS navigational device, and possibly a platform foredeck with pedestal seating, although this is well below gunwale height. They are usually stored on a trailer for transport to and from the water.

See: Boat; Sonar; Trailer, Boat.

WALLOP-BREAUX AMENDMENT
See: Federal Aid in Sport Fish Restoration Act.

WARMOUTH   *Lepomis gulosus.*
Other names—goggle-eye, openmouth, perch.

The warmouth is a member of the Centrarchidae family of sunfish *(see)* and is typically encountered by anglers fishing for other panfish *(see)* species. It has white, flaky flesh and is good table fare.

Identification. The warmouth has a deep, stout body and is olive brown above and cream to bright yellow below, often with an overall purple luster and a dark brown chainlike mottling on the back and upper sides. Dark, red brown lines extend from the back of the eye. On breeding males, there is a red orange spot on the yellow edge of the short ear flap, and there are dark brown spots and wavy bands on the fins. The warmouth has a large mouth and a patch of teeth on the tongue, and the upper jaw extends under or past the pupil of the eye. It also has a short, rounded pectoral fin and a stiff rear edge on its gill cover.

Size/Age. The warmouth can reach a weight of 1 pound and a length of 12 inches. It is capable of living for six to eight years. The all-tackle world record is a 2-pound, 7-ounce fish taken in Florida in 1985.

Distribution. Originally found in the Great Lakes and Mississippi River basins from western Pennsylvania to Minnesota and south to the Gulf of Mexico, warmouth occur in Atlantic and gulf drainages from the Rappahannock River, Virginia, to the Rio Grande in Texas and New Mexico. They are abundant in lowland areas and less common in the uplands, and they have been introduced in many places, including the lower Colorado River drainage, where they are common.

Habitat. Warmouth inhabit relatively shallow, vegetated, slow-flowing, mud-bottom creeks, ponds, lakes, swamps, and reservoirs. They are often found around weedbeds, snags, hollow trees, or stumps, and under the banks of streams and ponds.

Spawning behavior. Warmouth begin spawning from April through August when they are 3 to 4 inches long and from one to three years old. Spawning peaks in early June, when waters warm to about 70°F. The male builds a shallow, bowl-shaped nest in water less than 5 feet deep, often in the company of others so that a small colony of nests is formed. Preferred nesting sites are in sand or rubble bottom with a thin covering of silt near patches of lily pads, cattails, and grasses, or at the base of trees standing in shallow water.

Food. Because of their large mouths, warmouth have more variety in their diet than do some of their sunfish relatives. They feed on invertebrates, small sunfish, darters, mosquitofish, crayfish, snails, freshwater shrimp, dragonflies, and other insects.

Angling. These fish are caught with standard panfishing methods.

WARMWATER FISH

A term for freshwater species whose optimum environment contains warm water, usually over 70°F, and that can tolerate warm and even turbid or poorly oxygenated water during summer; largemouth bass, various sunfish, crappie, bullhead, and catfish are among this group. They primarily inhabit warm rivers and streams and very fertile lakes and ponds, many of which are shallow.
See: Coldwater Fish; Coolwater Fish.

WASH

The disturbed water close to and immediately behind a moving boat, created by the action of the propeller; often referred to as prop wash.

WASHDOWN

The practice of cleaning fishing equipment, boats, and boat trailers with freshwater after use; this is especially important when this equipment is used in marine environments.
See: Tackle Care/Maintenance/Repair.

WASHINGTON

If angling variety is the deciding factor, then Washington ranks very highly with other states in the U.S. The Evergreen State's list of significant sportfish includes 23 freshwater, 20 saltwater, and 8 anadromous species. Some of these, in fact, have been successfully transplanted to form important fisheries elsewhere. Rainbow trout, for example, flourished in Washington lakes and streams for thousands of years before people transported them to the far corners of the earth. The Skamania steelhead that delights Great Lakes anglers is a Washington native. Chinook and coho salmon from Washington waters have been used to help establish thriving sportfisheries elsewhere as well.

Washington's angling opportunities, on the other hand, have been greatly enhanced by the introduction of several fish species from other parts of the country and the world. Shad were brought from New England in the 1870s and 1880s, largemouth bass came from Ohio and elsewhere a few years later, and smallmouth bass were imported to Washington from various places around the turn of the twentieth century. No one seems to know exactly where Washington's walleye population came from, or when, but anglers have been catching them from the Columbia River since the early 1970s.

As for places to fish, the possibilities are many and varied. As if more than 150 miles of Pacific Ocean coastline weren't enough for saltwater anglers, the 80-mile-long Strait of Juan de Fuca and the inland waterways of Puget Sound offer both marine fishing variety and protection from all but the worst of Northwest storms. Chinook, coho, and pink salmon are among the primary targets of Washington's saltwater fishing fleet, but the possibilities also include Pacific halibut to 100 pounds, ill-tempered lingcod, and many species of rockfish, flounder, sole, and saltwater perch.

Freshwater fishing is virtually unlimited in this state, which has roughly 5,100 lowland lakes and reservoirs, 2,800 high-country lakes, 140 rivers, and more than 1,600 creeks. Rainbow and cutthroat trout inhabit most of these lakes and streams, and a majority of the rivers are home to the big sea-run rainbow trout called steelhead. Anglers searching for warmwater fish don't have to look far, as largemouth and smallmouth bass, walleye, black crappie, yellow perch, brown bullhead, and other species inhabit hundreds of Washington lakes and reservoirs.

Saltwater

Pacific coast.   Nothing better personifies the wild and woolly nature of the rugged northwestern United States than its sometimes stormy, always beautiful, Pacific Ocean coast. From the mouth of the Columbia River at Ilwaco to the Strait of Juan de Fuca entrance near the village of Neah Bay, Washington's 157-mile-long coastline is largely undeveloped and uninhabited, but the angling opportunities are many.

Most of the world knows this area for its salmon fishing, but salmon seasons are shorter, bag limits more conservative, and salmon fishing regulations more restrictive than they were just a few decades ago. Changes in salmon fishing, though, have led to diversification along Washington's coast, and anglers now visit the state's fishing ports in search of many important species. The chinook and coho salmon are still there, along with occasional chum and pink salmon, and anglers also catch good numbers of albacore, Pacific halibut, lingcod, sablefish, and several species of rockfish. Of the rockfish species, the black rockfish is the most abundant and is a mainstay of the coastal charter fishery, but blue, yellowtail, canary, yelloweye, and Boccaccio rockfish also are popular.

Ilwaco, near the mouth of the Columbia River in the extreme southwest corner of the state, is a point of departure for anglers headed for the open Pacific, as well as for those who stay in the Columbia River estuary to try their luck. Both charter and private-boat anglers fish here, but boaters must be alert to the strong currents and tricky bottom contours. Depending on weather and seasons, which vary from year to year, Ilwaco salmon anglers might concentrate their efforts on the open ocean, the Columbia River, or both. Chinook and coho salmon are available, and both are most commonly caught on fresh or frozen herring. August is the prime salmon fishing month in the Ilwaco area.

Interest in bottom fish begins in the spring and runs into early fall, and lingcod and various rockfish species are the most popular targets. Submerged rockpiles and ledges to the south and west of the river mouth are the most productive for bottom fishing. Ilwaco anglers also catch Pacific halibut around off-shore breaklines and underwater plateaus.

The lower Columbia River is the source of spectacular sturgeon fishing, and Ilwaco provides easy access to many good sturgeon holes. White sturgeon can grow to 12 feet or longer, weigh over 500 pounds, and account for a bulk of the catch, but the smaller green sturgeon are also caught from the Columbia estuary. A slot limit protects smaller, immature sturgeon and large females.

Willapa Bay, the large estuary between the Columbia River and Grays Harbor, was long overlooked by Northwest salmon anglers. It has come into its own since the early 1990s, however, thanks to impressive returns of hatchery chinook and coho bound for the Willapa, Nemah, and Naselle Rivers, all of which empty into Willapa Bay. Anglers troll herring or flasher-and-fly combinations throughout the western end of the bay for coho, whereas many of the bigger chinook are taken on herring bounced along the bottom, right up against the beach near the bay's north entrance.

Grays Harbor is home to Westport, Washington's most well-known fishing port. Westport's famous party boat fishery had its start in the 1950s and grew to as many as 400 boats by the mid-1970s. The charter fleet is smaller now, but charter skippers who remain are among the best at what they do. For those who prefer to fish from their own boats, Westport has launch ramps, fuel docks, moorage, and other facilities, but the treacherous Grays Harbor Bar is no place for incompetent or inattentive navigators.

Salmon fishing still is a main attraction here, even though the seasons are now measured in weeks rather than months. July and August are the best months for salmon. The season for bottom fish is open year-round, but winter storms make fishing a tough proposition from October through March. Spring fishing for lingcod of 5 to 30 pounds can be very good around the many rock pinnacles and ledges to the north of Grays Harbor. Deeper waters around those same rockpiles produce yelloweye and canary rockfish, sablefish, and other bottom fish. Large schools of 1- to 3-pound black rockfish provide fast action for Westport anglers from spring through fall.

Albacore tuna cause excitement for Westport anglers nearly every summer, especially when the tuna's northward migration brings them to within 60 or 70 miles of the coast, where party boats and larger private craft can reach them. A typical August or September tuna trip is an overnight affair, and two-day trips are common. Trolling hex-head jigs on heavy tackle helps anglers locate the fish. When a school is found, the anglers swing into action with lighter outfits and single hooks baited with live anchovies. A Westport albacore trip can produce 10 fish or more per rod.

Most people fish Westport-area waters from a boat, but the area also holds a lot of promise for bank anglers. The Grays Harbor South Jetty and the six finger jetties at Westport offer year-round fishing for lingcod, black rockfish, kelp greenling, starry flounder, pike-perch, striped seaperch, and Dungeness crab. The sandy ocean beaches to the south have good numbers of redtail surfperch. The perch, flounder, and crabs will take almost any small bait fished on a No. 4 or 6 hook, but leadhead jigs with plastic grubs work better for rockfish. Larger grub bodies on a leadhead will work for the ling, or try whole herring or a live greenling fished beneath a large foam float.

Once home to several fishing resorts, LaPush is a small Indian village at the mouth of the Quillayute River. It now has only one thing to offer anglers: access to some of the most rugged coastline and most intriguing fishing spots in Washington. Salmon fishing used to be the big draw here, and it still can be very good in August. Rocky ledges and submerged pinnacles are common throughout the area, and they host to some of the largest lingcod remaining in Washington. The area also has several less-severe offshore rockpiles and underwater plateaus that hold good numbers of Pacific halibut. Nearshore coves, boulder piles, and small islands teem with schools of black, blue, and copper rockfish, kelp greenling, small lingcod, and other bottom fish well suited to light-tackle jigging or even fly fishing.

Strait of Juan de Fuca. Connecting Puget Sound to the Pacific Ocean, this 80-mile-long waterway separating the north end of Washington's Olympic Peninsula from British Columbia's Vancouver Island offers great angling variety. At the extreme northwestern tip of the Olympic Peninsula, Neah Bay provides access to excellent fishing both in the Strait of Juan de Fuca and the Pacific Ocean. The summertime fishing for chinook salmon "around the corner" on the Pacific Ocean side is legendary, and such spots as Skagway, Father and Son Rocks, and Spike Rock offer anglers a chance to fish for 40-pound salmon. A little later, usually around Labor Day, large, adult coho become the prime attraction, and they are often caught right on the surface with a fast-trolled streamer fly.

Halibut fishing draws thousands of anglers to Neah Bay every spring and summer. Some fish Swiftsure Bank and Blue Dot, both offshore banks 20 to 30 miles out; some try Garbage Dump and other spots closer to port where halibut are less abundant but where a better chance of hooking a barn-door fish of 100 pounds or larger may exist. Standard baits and lures in both locations include whole herring or squid fished on wire spreaders, homemade pipe jigs or metal slab-type jigs of 12 to 32 ounces, and huge leadhead jigs adorned with 8- or 10-inch plastic grub bodies.

Lingcod are another big Neah Bay attraction, especially during the spring and early summer, when adult ling are still found around the shallow-water rockpiles where they spawned earlier in the

 American fisheries research first began in 1871 at Woods Hole, Massachusetts, with the creation of the U.S. Commission on Fish and Fisheries.

W
X
Y
Z

year. Huge ling of 40 pounds and larger are fairly common, but more and more anglers are releasing the big ones (which are females) to target the 10- to 15-pound males, which are better table fare. A small greenling, worked just off the bottom with a hook through the lips and another near the tail, will coax ling to hit when all else fails.

The waters around the entrance to the Strait of Juan de Fuca are famous for huge populations of black rockfish, which are found at almost any depth, depending on the food supply. When near the surface, they can be caught on light spinning tackle and 4- or 6-pound line, and will take virtually any bait, lure, or fly thrown in their direction.

About 12 miles east of Neah Bay lies Sekiu, pronounced "CQ," which offers a slightly toned-down version of the angling potpourri found farther west. Salmon, halibut, and lingcod are the primary draws, but shoreline kelp beds also hold fair numbers of rockfish, greenling, and various smaller game. In the summer of each odd-numbered year, Sekiu is also a staging area for anglers in search of pink salmon, the smallest of the five Pacific salmon species but the most abundant when it makes its biennial appearance. Trolling near the surface with small wobbling plugs or spoons in pink, orange, or red accounts for the best catches of pink salmon, or humpies, as they're often known.

The odd-year pink salmon runs are also big news farther east, where anglers depart from boat ramps in Freshwater Bay, Port Angeles, and Sequim (pronounced "Skwim"). These areas provide fair fishing for chinook and coho salmon, as well as for halibut. There is good spring fishing for lingcod here. Sequim is also a point of departure for anglers fishing several productive banks near the east end of the Strait of Juan de Fuca. Hein, Middle, and Eastern Banks are the best known, especially for late-winter chinook salmon, and spring lingcod and halibut fishing.

San Juan Islands.   One of the Northwest's most beautiful fishing destinations, the San Juans have been loved to death by anglers in search of bottom fish. Trophy lingcod and yelloweye rockfish, and huge schools of quillback rockfish, once made these islands near the U.S./Canada border a can't-miss destination, but too many people got too good at the game, and fish managers were slow to respond. Now, lingcod regulations are extremely restrictive, and it's a little tough to find an underwater rockpile with a good population of rockfish.

On the bright side, salmon fishing in the San Juans remains good, and the variety is some of the best in Washington. Chinook are available here year-round, and the west side of San Juan Island is one of the state's better summertime spots for kings in the 15- to 30-pound class. Fishing is good for blackmouth (immature, resident chinook) all winter throughout the islands, but the east and west sides of Orcas Island and the east side of Blakely Island are among the favorite spots for blackmouth.

Fishing for coho and odd-year pink salmon is excellent during the summer. Even sockeye salmon pass through the islands on their way to British Columbia's Fraser River, and lucky anglers pick off some of these delicious fish.

Puget Sound.   Salmon fishing is a year-round activity throughout much of this inland waterway, along whose shores more than 60 percent of the state's population lives. From Admiralty Inlet on the north to Hood Canal on the west and down to Anderson Island at the south end, Puget Sound has dozens of productive salmon fishing spots.

Resident chinook salmon—known locally as blackmouth because of the black gumline that helps distinguish them from other salmon species—are especially popular. Among the top blackmouth fishing area in the sound, from north to south, are Port Townsend's Mid-Channel Bank, Possession Point (south end of Whidbey Island), Point No Point (northeast corner of the Kitsap Peninsula), Point Jefferson (east side of the Kitsap Peninsula), Manchester (northeast of Bremerton), Point Defiance/Point Dalco (just north of Tacoma), and Anderson Island and Johnson Point (both near Olympia). Trolling with flasher-and-fly or flasher-and-squid rigs, mooching with whole or plug-cut herring, and jigging with any of several baitfish-imitating metal jigs are productive blackmouth fishing techniques, and the key usually is to fish within a few feet of bottom in 80 to 200 feet of water.

Puget Sound's salmon fishing variety improves in late summer, when adult chinook and coho begin returning from the Pacific. Pink salmon add to the possibilities during odd-numbered years, especially in the northern third of the sound. By mid-October, the chinook and pinks have entered the rivers where they started their lives, but there are still coho to be caught in saltwater. That's when chum salmon, the second largest and hardest-fighting of the five Pacific salmon, make their appearance. Although somewhat difficult to catch in saltwater, chums provide good fishing when they congregate in the estuaries and lower portions of most Puget Sound rivers, where they favor small, sparsely tied green flies or little tufts of green nylon yarn on a No. 2 or 4 hook. The most popular chum fishery of all is near the Hood Canal Salmon Hatchery, at the town of Hoodsport.

Freshwater

Columbia River system.   Draining nearly three-quarters of the state, the Columbia River and its many tributaries constitute not only Washington's largest river system, but the second largest river system in the country. The Columbia flows north to south, to bisect eastern Washington all the way from the British Columbia border to Oregon, then turns west to comprise most of the Washington-Oregon border. All that water provides plenty of angling opportunity for a wide range of freshwater and anadromous species.

W
X
Y
Z

Smallmouth bass fishing on the Columbia River.

The Columbia River system was once the world's top salmon producer, and even though hydroelectric dams, careless agricultural practices, overfishing, and other abuses have taken their toll, at certain times and in certain places salmon fishing can range from good to excellent.

Spring-run chinook salmon return to hatcheries on several lower Columbia tributaries from April through June, and these "springers" are a favorite of Washington anglers. The Cowlitz River from Longview upstream to the salmon hatchery near Salkum has long been a top spring chinook spot, and the North Fork Lewis River is another good bet. Farther up the Columbia, good springer fishing exists around the mouths of the Wind, Little White Salmon, Big White Salmon, and Klickitat Rivers. Trolling various diving plugs and spinners or bouncing large roe clusters along the bottom are the preferred fishing techniques.

Fall-run chinook also inhabit the Columbia, and the techniques that work for springers also are effective for fall fish. Fall chinook anglers congregate in dozens of places along the lower 250 miles of the Columbia, from its mouth to Kennewick. They especially gather around the mouths of major tributary streams, but one of the best fisheries occurs some 300 miles from the ocean, along the last free-flowing section of the river, known as the Hanford Reach. Anglers here commonly catch fall kings of 30 to 50 pounds, and even bigger fish are possible.

The steelhead trout is another sea-run favorite of Columbia River anglers, and there's a steelhead fishery happening somewhere on the main river or several of its tributaries throughout the year. Boaters find good summer and early fall steelheading on the lower Columbia around Camas and Washougal and also in McNary Pool and some of the other reservoirs behind main-stem dams. Bank anglers do well casting from the east side of the Columbia in the Ringold area upstream from Richland. As for the tributaries, the Elochoman, Cowlitz, Lewis, Washougal, Klickitat, Wenatchee, and Methow all are well-known steelhead producers.

White sturgeon thrive throughout the Columbia-Snake River system and have enjoyed increasing popularity over the past decade or two. The lower 200 miles of the Columbia is especially popular with sturgeon anglers. They anchor smelt, shad, shrimp, and other baits to the bottom in areas of moderate current and wait for one of the big bottom feeders to come along. A slot limit protects small and large fish, but many anglers enjoy catching and releasing the bigger females, some of which measure 8 to 12 feet and larger. These large fish often jump when hooked.

American shad were released on the West Coast a century ago, and a shad run of several million fish now occurs in the Columbia every summer. Some of the best shad angling occurs immediately downstream from Bonneville Dam in June.

Walleye began to appear in the Columbia River system around 1970, and now the river and some of its impoundments support good walleye fisheries. Lake Roosevelt (the pool behind Grand Coulee

Dam), nearby Banks Lake, Rufus Woods Lake (behind Chief Joseph Dam), all three lower river reservoirs, and the free-flowing portion of the Columbia below Bonneville Dam are all good walleye fisheries.

The Columbia also offers smallmouth bass, especially in the Hanford Reach, in Lake Celilo (Dalles Dam), and in Lake Wallula (McNary Dam). The Columbia, in fact, produces trophy smallmouths; a state-record 8-pound, 12-ounce bronzeback was caught from the Hanford Reach.

The Snake River, the largest tributary to the Columbia, provides even better smallmouth fishing and is also home to a thriving fall and winter steelhead fishery. Channel catfish also are abundant in the Snake, and the catch-and-release fishery for white sturgeon has been a big draw here for decades.

Another important Columbia tributary, the Yakima River, has a little of everything to offer anglers, from its blue-ribbon trout fishing between the towns of Ellensburg and Yakima to the channel catfish and crappie in the lower reaches. Between the two exists an excellent winter fishery for mountain whitefish, and good smallmouth bass angling.

West-side steelhead streams. Big rainbow trout start their lives in freshwater; migrate to the Pacific to feed, grow, and become belligerent; then return to their natal river as 5- to 25-pound trophies. Such fish are the favorites of about 100,000 Washingtonians as well as visiting anglers from all over the world. Luckily for all those anglers, dozens of rivers here offer opportunities to try their luck whenever the steelhead bug bites them. The best of those steelhead streams are in western Washington, where there is always plenty of rain to keep the rivers flowing and the steelhead runs moving.

The Steelhead rivers flowing into the Pacific from the west side of the Olympic Peninsula are among the most famous in the world. Near the north end of the Peninsula is the Quillayute system, which includes the Bogachiel, Sol Duc, and Calawah Rivers. All three are favorites of river guides, private-boat anglers, and bank anglers alike; and all do well, thanks to generous plants from the system's hatchery facilities. Winter-run steelhead are the big draw, but summer steelies also are available.

It's the same scenario on the Hoh and Queets Rivers to the south, except that the fishing pressure may be a little lighter on these rivers. Even farther down the coast, the Quinault River is perhaps the best of the bunch. Anglers can fish the lower Quinault only with a tribal fishing guide. The Humptulips, Satsop, and Wynoochee Rivers, all of which eventually flow into Grays Harbor, are good possibilities for winter steelhead, and the Wynoochee also offers fair to good summer steelheading.

The crowds are bigger on steelhead streams flowing into Puget Sound, but the fishing, especially for winter-run steelies, can be quite good for hatchery steelhead, especially from December through early February. The Skagit River is the biggest and one of the best known, but good fishing is also available on the (from north to south) Stillaguamish, Skykomish, Snoqualmie, Green, and Puyallup Rivers.

Drift fishing is the most widely practiced steelhead-fishing technique. This entails casting slightly upstream and using just enough weight on the line to bounce a bait or lure along the bottom, moving with the current. Other possibilities include casting weighted spinners and wobbling spoons, working diving plugs along the bottom, and drifting leadhead jigs beneath floats.

Western Washington lakes. A large percentage of the more than 2,000 lakes on the west side of Washington's Cascade Mountains are open to year-round fishing, but that doesn't stop some 300,000 anglers from turning out for the traditional "opening day" on the fourth Saturday of April every year. If you like crowds, that's the day to fish. Otherwise, it's a good idea to check the annual regulations pamphlet and hit the water some other day, either earlier or later in the year, depending on the season details for the particular lake.

Rainbow trout are the biggest draw for western Washington anglers, and the State Department of Fish and Wildlife stocks well over a million hatchery rainbows every year in west-side lakes alone to help meet the demand. Most are pan-size trout, planted in the spring, but a few lakes receive fall plants of fingerlings that tend to provide bigger trout for anglers over the long term.

Some of the top rainbow lakes, in terms of both popularity and catch, are Whatcom County's Padden and Silver Lakes; San Juan County's Cascade and Mountain Lakes; Skagit County's Erie, Pass, and McMurray Lakes; Clallam County's Lake Sutherland; Jefferson County's Anderson Lake; Grays Harbor County's Duck and Failor Lakes; King County's North Lake and Lake Wilderness; Pierce County's Silver and Tanwax Lakes; Thurston County's Clear Lake; Lewis County's Mineral Lake; and Mason County's Phillips, Spencer, and Price's Lakes. More and more west-side lakes also are stocked with hatchery brown trout, and many contain small populations of native cutthroat trout as well.

Although not recognized as a world hotbed of bass fishing action, western Washington does have some good bass lakes, and both largemouth and smallmouth bass are available. Some of the best largemouth waters are Big Lake in Skagit County; Lake Stevens in Snohomish County; King County's Lake Sawyer; Mason Lake in Mason County; Pierce County's Lake Kapowsin; Thurston County's Black Lake; Silver Lake in Cowlitz County; and Lacamas Lake in Clark County. Western Washington's best smallmouth lake is King County's Lake Sammamish.

Anglers willing to hike into the high country of the Cascade Range and the Olympic Mountains may choose from among some 1,500 fishable lakes that most anglers never see. The bulk of these high

The St. Johns River in Florida, long renowned for its largemouth bass, is also one of the few rivers in the United States that flows north.

W
X
Y
Z

lakes (located at 2,500 feet of elevation or higher) hold trout, thanks to the efforts of State Department of Fish and Wildlife personnel and volunteers who pack trout fry and fingerlings on their backs to stock these waters. Some high lakes contain rainbows, some cutthroats, some brookies, and still others golden trout.

Eastern Washington lakes.   Although western Washington hosts lots of trout, the drier two-thirds of the state east of the Cascade Range has some of Washington's best trout waters. Okanogan County's Wannacut, Spectacle, Conconully, and Chopaka Lakes draw rainbow trout anglers from throughout the Pacific Northwest. Douglas County, a little farther south, has only two significant lakes, but both are famous for their trout fishing; Jameson Lake is a top rainbow producer, and Grimes Lake offers excellent fly fishing for Lahontan cutthroats to 8 pounds. Yakima County's Wenas Lake has both husky rainbows and trophy-class browns. Farther east, Waitts Lake in Stevens County, Lincoln County's Fishtrap Lake, and Spokane County's Medical and West Medical Lakes all provide excellent fishing for big rainbows.

The best place to fish for trout in all of Washington, though, might be Grant County, right in the center of the state. Some of that county's prime trout waters include Dry Falls, Blue, Park, Perch, Lenice, Nunnally, and Merry Lakes, all of which have big rainbows, or Lake Lenore, where Lahontan cutthroats grow to 7 or 8 pounds.

Some lakes offer even larger game. Lake trout, known as mackinaws by most Washington anglers, grow to 30 pounds here and are available in several eastern Washington lakes. The best mackinaw lakes include Chelan in Chelan County, Loon and Deer Lakes in Stevens County, and Bead Lake in Pend Oreille County.

Largemouth and smallmouth bass, walleye, crappie, bluegills, and other warmwater fish also inhabit many east-side lakes. Again, Grant County is a leader, offering such possibilities as Banks Lake (largemouth and smallmouth bass and walleye), Potholes Reservoir (largemouths, smallmouths, walleye, black crappie, yellow perch, and bluegills), Moses Lake (largemouths, walleye, and bluegills), and Soda Lake (crappie and perch).

Spokane County's Eloika Lake also offers a mixed bag of warmwater angling ranging from bluegills to largemouths. But for shear variety it's hard to beat Sprague Lake, located near the town of Sprague. Here you'll find largemouth and smallmouth bass, walleye, bluegills, crappie, and channel catfish; their presence is the result of an extensive rehabilitation project that reclaimed the lake from hordes of carp in the mid-1980s.

WATER CLARITY

Water clarity, or transparency, in both freshwater and saltwater ranges from crystal clear to muddy; it is most likely to be turbid in large rivers and in lakes and ponds, where runoff, tributaries, erosion, plankton blooms, and various factors influence the transparency of water.

Biologists measure clarity or transparency by lowering a circular black-and-white plate called a secchi disk into the water to the depth at which the disk just disappears. At this depth, approximately 95 percent of sunlight has been eliminated because of shading from particles in the water; a small amount of light can penetrate two to three times this depth.

Clear water is generally more productive than muddy water for sight-feeding fish and for most aquatic life; muddy water is best suited to species that feed primarily through sense of feel or smell. If clear water is classified (as it is by some biologists) as having visibility over 30 inches, this water may be many times more productive for certain species, such as bass and bluegills, for example, than water with only 5 to 6 inches of visibility.

Water clarity is a factor in angling, both in the sense of where to locate some species as well as how to fish for them. However, the clarity of freshwater varies markedly from one lake to another and even varies in a particular lake through the course of the fishing season. Using largemouth bass in freshwater lakes as an example will illustrate this.

In North America, many of the larger lakes and reservoirs in northern areas are reasonably clear. Light penetrates deep there, and bass either are well secured in what thick cover might exist or are more likely deep enough to avoid the discomfort of light. In such waters, you can see a brightly colored lure 6 or more feet below the surface. Here, bass tend to be spooky, and a refined fishing presentation, using small- to moderate-size lures and light line, is very beneficial. Other waters may be blue-green colored and allow visibility for 3 to 6 feet below the water's surface. Such a condition is considered very clear by many Southern anglers, who never see the ultraclear waters of mountain-region lakes.

Many bass waters are more off-colored, however, allowing limited visibility. This is the only type of condition some anglers see, and it does not require such a stealthy approach or use of light line as clearer waters do. Muddy, milky, slate gray, and tea-colored water is common in many reservoirs after heavy rains; farmland runoff, sediment from tributaries, and bank erosion cause this condition. You may be able to see a light-colored lure if it is only a few inches below the surface. In some large lakes, only the upper ends are affected like this, and the lower ends remain relatively unchanged, or at least unaffected for several days. In still other bass waters, particularly in Florida, the high tannic acid content gives the lake a blackish brown tint.

In highly turbid waters, where visibility is limited, bass are likely to be relatively shallow and holding tight to cover, especially in the early part of the season and when water temperatures are not excessively

high. Turbid water can be good for bass fishing success because of the nature of this fish; certain types of lures, such as big spinnerbaits, crankbaits with good vibration qualities, and noisy surface baits, are well suited to angling under these conditions because they appeal more to the bass's sense of sound than to its vision.

Naturally the clarity of any given water is important to the color of lures that are fished, and this is also intertwined with issues pertaining to depth and the intensity of the light.

See: Finding Fish; Lure.

WATER FLEA

See: Daphnia; Spiny Water Flea.

WATERLINE

(1) That section of the boat's hull that intersects the water's surface; also a painted line separating the hull and topsides of a boat, or a painted line that depicts the point to which a properly loaded boat sinks in the water.

(2) The horizontal line on a shore or bank that reflects maximum high-water level. In areas that are regularly flooded, because of high water or tides, there is an identifiable band on tree trunks, bushes, vegetation, and rocks that serves as a high-water mark. In some places, especially rivers, this line is accompanied by brush and debris in the trees at the waterline. In rivers, periodic water releases from dams may cause sudden fluctuations in water level; anglers wading downstream in such places need to observe this waterline in order to retreat to safety if there is a sudden surge of rising water.

WATERSHED

An area of land from which water drains to a given point, usually a larger body of water. Smaller watersheds make up larger watersheds, creating a series of watersheds, which is known as a drainage basin (see: drainage).

WATERSPOUT

A waterspout is a spinning, funnel-shaped column of water pulled up by a whirling wind from the surface of the ocean, resembling a tornado. Waterspouts are formed in humid, hot, tropical air, though they are sometimes found in more middle latitudes. They do not last long if they move over land.

See: Safety.

WAVES

For the most part, waves are generated by friction created by wind blowing over the water surface. This includes the ripples on a creek or pond, the crests and troughs that run across a lake, the rhythmic pounding of surf against the beach, and the rolling of swells in the open ocean. Generically these are called wind waves. There are other types of waves, such as tsunamis, which are very long waves produced by seismic disturbance, and internal waves, which are waves that occur within the sea rather than at the surface, but these types of waves are seldom encountered by anglers.

Waves are a common fact of life for all open-water anglers. They have a great bearing on boating and boat manipulation in saltwater and freshwater, and they interact with currents and with tidal movement. They can have significance for angling, especially when trolling and drifting activities are influenced by the height or frequency of waves, and especially for those fishing from beach, shore, jetty, or pier. It is therefore useful to understand how waves work, whether for safety, general boating, or varied angling reasons.

Height and length. Wind waves, tsunamis, and internal waves are all considered progressive waves; they appear to progress in a definite direction. The other major wave type is called a standing wave because it appears to oscillate without forward movement. All progressive waves have similar characteristics in form and motion. They have crests and troughs, with the vertical distance between the two called the wave height, and the horizontal distance between crests called the wave length. The wave period is the time it takes for two consecutive wave crests to pass a given point. The speed of a wave's travel can be calculated by dividing the wave length by the wave period.

Wind waves begin as ripples or capillary waves formed as the water surface is deformed by variation in wind pressure. Thus, ripples provide surface roughness necessary for the wind to push the water into larger waves. Ripples disappear almost immediately if the wind dies. However, with continued wind, ripples grow into larger, steeper crested waves. As long as energy is supplied, waves will continue to develop. Once formed, waves persist for a while even after the wind ceases, but the steepness decreases and, in the ocean or large inland lakes, the waves become "swells." Swells can travel thousands of miles without losing much energy.

Speed. The size of waves is dependent on the speed of the wind that formed them, the duration that the wind blew, and the fetch (the length of water surface over which the wind blows in a constant direction). For example, if the wind is blowing across a barrier island toward the mainland at a constant speed, the water in the lee of the island will be relatively free of waves, while that on the opposite side of the sound will have large waves because the winds will have acted across a greater distance of water surface. Given the wind speed, duration, and fetch, it is possible to predict the size of the waves generated by a given storm. Conversely, wind speed at sea can be estimated by the wave conditions

Major fluctuations in sea level and climate eons ago are believed to have been responsible for the extinction of many ancient fish species, as well as the evolution of present fishes

W
X
Y
Z

produced. This relationship is presented in the Beaufort scale, which assigns numbers that correlate to specific wind speeds and sea conditions from calm to hurricane.

A summary of lesser conditions of wind speed in miles per hour and sea conditions is as follows:

Under 1   Calm; mirrorlike sea
1–3   Light air; ripples with scalelike appearance, no foam crests
4–7   Light breeze; small wavelets, crests glassy and not breaking
8–12   Gentle breeze; large wavelets, crests begin to break with scattered whitecaps
13–18   Moderate breeze; small waves (to 4 feet high) becoming longer, more whitecaps
19–24   Fresh breeze; moderate waves (to 8 feet high) taking longer form, many whitecaps and some spray
25–31   Strong breeze; larger waves (to 13 feet high), whitecaps everywhere and more spray.
32–38   Near gale; sea heaps up (to 20 feet), white foam from breaking waves blows in streaks

Most anglers, especially in freshwater, overestimate the height of winds and thus the size of waves that they see or encounter. Nevertheless, most small boaters are off the water when waves are at the 4-foot stage, especially in freshwater, either for personal comfort or for safety, and should not be on the water under fresh breeze conditions. Many large boats do not stay out under the latter conditions. Strong winds have the ability to quickly move sea conditions right up this scale, so anglers in boats should be watching wave and sea conditions for changes, in order to make appropriate moves to shelter in a timely manner. Regardless of wave height, when whitecaps become increasingly prominent, it's time to evaluate the situation. When there's spray on the tops of waves, you probably should be heading for port or not far from it, because the sea will likely keep building. Using a VHF radio *(see)* or weather radio to be forewarned of advancing conditions is a good idea.

Motion. Two types of motion are associated with waves: that of the wave form and that of the water particles. It is important to realize that waves transport only energy, not water. Thus, the wave form moves across miles of sea, but the water does not. Storms make waves of different wave lengths. Since waves travel at different speeds, the longer waves move out ahead of the shorter waves. Long waves may even run ahead of the storm itself. Long, low waves crashing on a beach often warn of approaching storms.

Individual water particles in a wave travel in circular orbits with diameters (at the surface) equal to the wave height. These water particle orbits get smaller with depth but are still measurable at depths of about one-half the wave length.

In deep water, surface waves with long wave lengths travel faster than those with shorter wave lengths. Shorter wave lengths may be encountered in shallow bodies of water and may cause bumpy riding, as boats bounce and plow through them. If large waves with steep troughs are generated in shallow areas, they can be very dangerous for boaters, especially in places with reefs or bars; being in a trough might cause the boat to bottom out.

In water shallower than half the wave length, waves begin to drag along the bottom. The circular motion of the water particles becomes flattened. The bottom of the wave moves more slowly than the top, causing the wave to steepen, become unstable, and eventually "break" on the beach. Water from a breaking wave running up a beach is known as "swash." After dissipating its energy on the beach, the swash runs back down the beach and under the next breaker producing a flow often called "undertow." This back and forth motion of the swash stirs up sand and sediment.

Breakers occur as several types. Spilling breakers are over-steepened waves in which the unstable top spills down the front of the wave as it travels toward the beach. Spilling breakers occur on relatively flat beaches and are good for surfing. Plunging breakers are more spectacular. The wave crest curls over, forming a large air pocket. When the wave breaks, there is usually a large splash of water and foam. These waves are even better for surfing, and they occur on steeper beaches.

In shallow water, long waves travel at the same speed as short waves, but the speed of all waves slows as water depth decreases. If one part of a wave is in deeper water than another part, the shallow water section will slow down and the wave crest will bend. Although most waves approach the beach at an angle, the influence of the bottom causes waves to refract toward the beach. Refraction results in waves with crests almost

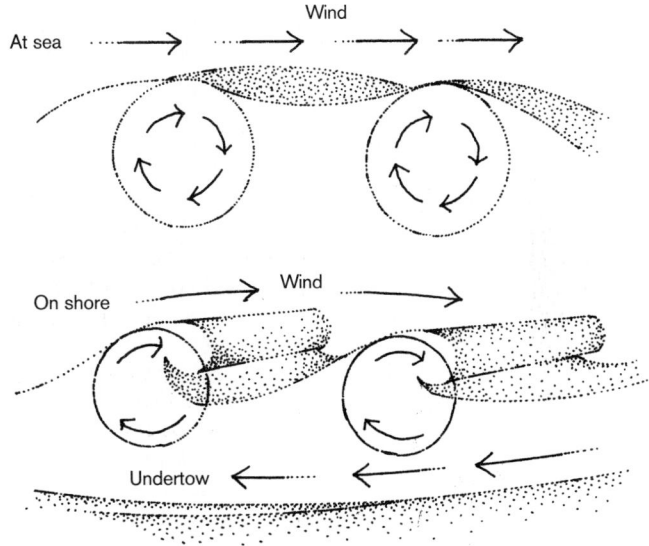

The effect of wind in creating waves is different at sea than on shore.

parallel to the shoreline. Wave refraction causes wave energy to be concentrated on a headland because the crests on either side bend so that the energy of the wave is dissipated along a greater distance of the coast. Wave diffraction occurs when waves bend around objects, such as when they move past a barrier into a harbor; wave reflection occurs when waves strike objects, like a seawall, with the most reflection happening when the wave is at a right angle to the object.

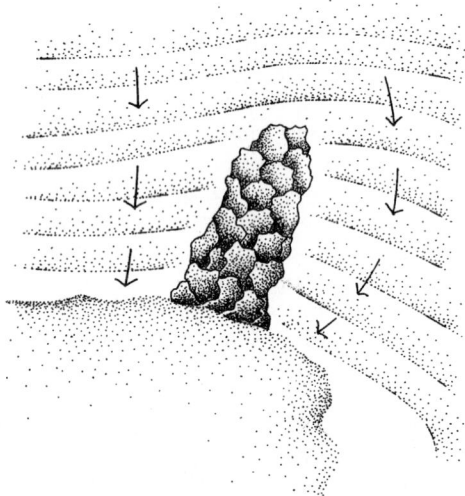

The bending of waves, called diffraction, is evident in this depiction of how waves approach a shoreline at either side of an angled jetty.

Waves are also the originators of two types of currents: the longshore current and the rip current. The longshore current is caused by waves that approach the shore at an angle. As these waves break, they move water and sand grains along the beach in the direction of their travel. This longshore transport exists in the surf zone where waves are breaking. Longshore current is responsible for much of the erosion on barrier islands. Attempts to stop longshore sand transport, such as with jetties and groins, usually result in deposition in one area coupled with increased erosion in another.

Rip currents are localized seaward flows of water from the surf zone. They occur when wave action forces more water into the surf zone than can escape by normal swash run back. As a result, the excess water accumulates and eventually flows seaward in a strong localized current, which can be dangerous to swimmers, who are carried seaward. Such rip currents occur when longshore currents converge in a bay, where water builds up as breakers coming across an underwater sandbar, or where some barrier obstructs longshore currents. Discolored water due to suspended sand, premature steepening of the waves, and accumulation of foam at the head of the rip are signs to watch for.

See: Boat; Jetty Fishing; Surf Fishing.

WAXWORM
See: Maggot.

WAYPOINT
A specific location, as represented by latitude and longitude coordinates, stored in the memory of an electronic navigational device such as GPS or Loran. **See: GPS; Loran.**

WEAKFISH   *Cynoscion regalis.*
Other names—squeteague, common weakfish, northern weakfish, common seatrout, northern seatrout, gray trout, summer trout, tiderunner, yellowfin, weakie; French: *acoupa royal;* Portuguese: *pescada-amarela;* Spanish: *corvinata real.*

The weakfish is a member of the Sciaenidae family (drum and croaker), named for drumming noises made by their swim bladder. The name "weakfish" refers to the tender, easily torn membrane in the fish's mouth, not its fighting ability. It is the gamest of the *Cynoscion* species in North America, striking hard and making one or two strong runs after being hooked.

The weakfish is highly sought, although it experiences dramatic fluctuation in stocks. When abundant, it is a popular gamefish. Commercial overfishing, especially in the Carolinas, however, has had drastic impacts on the overall biomass of this species, and recreational fishing for this species throughout much of the 1990s was extremely poor. Larger fish have been particularly scarce.

The meat of weakfish is white, tender, and moist and has an excellent flavor. The skin is usually left on during cooking to hold the meat together, and the bones are easily removed once the meat is cooked. It does not keep well, so it must be stored properly upon capture and prepared for consumption soon afterward.

Identification.   Weakfish are considered a beautiful fish by many anglers. Their body is slim and shaped somewhat like a trout's. The lower jaw projects beyond the upper jaw. There are two large, protruding canine teeth in the upper jaw, and no chin barbels. The first dorsal fin has 10 spines, and the second has 1 spine and 26 to 29 soft rays. The anal fin has 2 spines and 11 to 12 rays. Its coloring is dark olive or greenish to greenish blue on the dorsal surface, and blue, green, purple, and lavender with a golden tinge on the sides. Numerous small black spots speckle the top, sometimes forming wavy diagonal lines. There is sometimes a black margin on the tip of the tongue.

The weakfish is distinguished from the closely related spotted seatrout *(see: seatrout, spotted)* because its spots do not extend onto the tail or the second dorsal fin, and are not as widely spaced. The scales also do not extend onto the fins on the weakfish.

Size/Age.   This species' average size varies with locale. In southerly U.S. waters, weakfish tend to be smaller on average, generally 1 to 4 pounds. In the upper mid-Atlantic, they typically weigh 4 to 7 pounds on average. Their weight will also vary according to relative abundance. The all-tackle record is 19 pounds, 2 ounces (shared by fish from New York and Delaware), and the maximum possible growth is believed to be higher, as larger fish from commercial catches have been reported. Weakfish of 15 inches in length are between 3 and 5 years old, and those of 24-inch length are 9 to 12 years old. The average life span is roughly 10 years, but some weakfish reportedly live twice that long.

Distribution. Weakfish inhabit the western Atlantic Ocean from Florida to Massachusetts, and records show isolated populations occurring as far north as Nova Scotia. They are most abundant from North Carolina to Florida in the winter, and from Delaware to New York in the summer.

Habitat. Preferring sandy and sometimes grassy bottoms, weakfish are usually found in shallow waters along shores and in large bays and estuaries, including salt marsh creeks and sometimes into river mouths, although they do not enter freshwater. They can be found in depths of up to 55 fathoms in the winter.

Life history/Behavior. Mature weakfish are three to four years old. Spawning occurs in the nearshore and estuarine zones along the coast from May through October. The eggs drift on the surface and hatch within two days. A schooling species, weakfish migrate northward in the spring, spending the summer inshore, then moving southward again in late autumn.

Food and feeding habits. Weakfish are omnivorous and feed on crabs, shrimp, other crustaceans, and mollusks. They also consume small fish like herring, menhaden, silversides, killifish, and butterfish, which are caught in midwater levels or near the surface. Because of their varied diet, weakfish forage at different levels and adapt to local food conditions, feeding at the surface or deeper as necessary. Many anglers believe that weakfish and bluefish cannot share the same habitat, the voracious blues eating the fry and food of the less-aggressive weakfish and driving them out of the

A weakfish from the northern New Jersey shore.

area. Indeed, in past periods of abundance of both these species, the mid- to late-summer arrival of large numbers of bluefish seemed to coincide with a disappearance of weakfish.

Angling. With such a broad diet and feeding range, weakfish are susceptible to an equally wide variety of angling methods, lures, and baits. Drifting or stillfishing with an assortment of live or dead baits is extremely popular. The most common natural baits for weakfish are shrimp, squid, shedder or peeler crabs, worms, eels, mullet, and other small fish, or pieces of such fish as mackerel or bunker. Chumming is also effective, especially with a grass shrimp mix, ground up fish, or conglomerations of fish, shrimp, clams, and the like.

Jigging with metal jigs, grubs, or bucktail jigs garnished with a plastic worm body is also a favorite method, again either drifting in a boat or anchored. Bucktail jigs, usually garnished with a soft-action tail or with a strip of squid or other bait, are highly favored lures, as are leadhead jigs with soft bodies. The latter come in many effective varieties and are also often tipped with a piece of squid or shrimp. Other lures include spoons, tube lures, diamond jigs, and surface and shallow-running plugs.

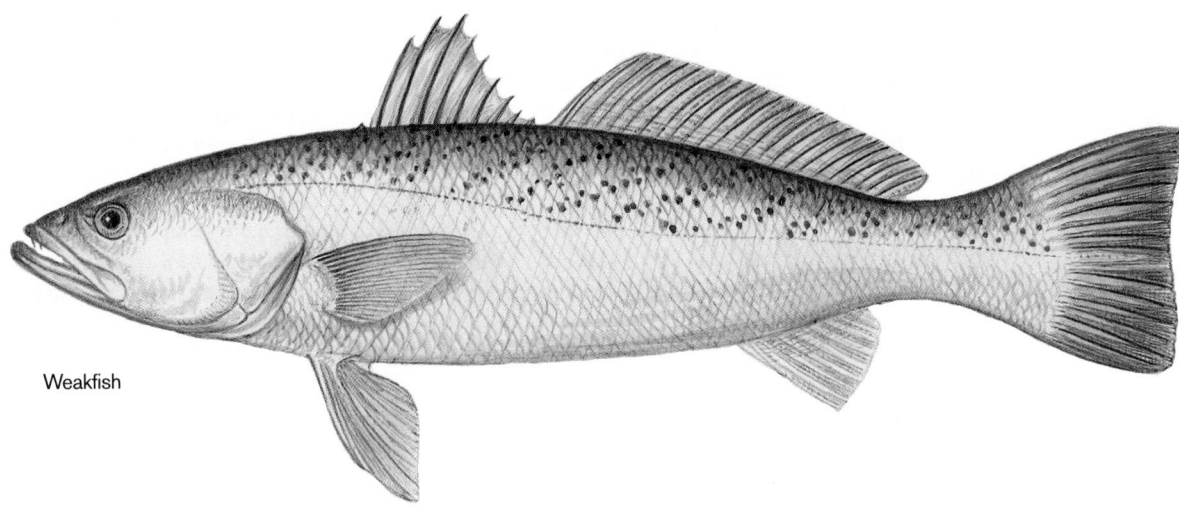

Weakfish

W
X
Y
Z

Trolling with plugs and spoons is another technique, although shore fishing, from the surf and by wading, or by casting from piers and jetties, is just as effective. Casting with plugs or streamer flies is usually done when the fish are fairly shallow, and in bays and estuary environs.

Weakfish will move into brackish water, and the shallow bay areas of estuaries is a common hangout, particularly in brackish rivers or creeks. In the northerly parts of their range, weakfish are seldom taken deeper than 20 feet in bays or open-water areas.

They will move onto shoals in schools to feed, and concentrate around oyster bars, bridges, and inlet jetties. Anglers should especially focus on structure and edges to locate weakfish, including such places as a channel in a shallow bay; a slough, cut, or trough in the surf; the edge of a tide rip, flat, and dropoff; deep holes in a bay; and along a sandbar. In daytime, these fish will usually hold deeper than at night or in low light.

Once weakfish are located in a given spot, it is a good bet that they will be there the following day as well but an hour later, taking into consideration the change in the timing of the tides. Areas that attract weakfish usually continue to do so until a weather change moves the fish, or until something else occurs to affect the site. When the fish are abundant, the same places will produce year after year unless the structures themselves are changed due to some phenomenon.

Light to medium spinning or baitcasting tackle is usually just right; weakfish are able fighters, but a lot of line capacity isn't necessary, and there's fun to be had by using ultralight gear and fine line. Small-boat anglers commonly use 6- to 12-pound line, often on standard freshwater tackle. Slightly heavier gear (15- to 20-pound line and comparable outfits) can be employed for trolling and also for surf fishing. Boat anglers don't need as long a rod as those fishing from shore. Tackle for party boat weakfishing runs to the heavier side, as other species may be encountered, lots of people are on board, and light tackle becomes more problematic in this situation.

WEAKFISH, ACOUPA   *Cynoscion acoupa.*
Other names—French: *acoupa toeroe;* Portuguese: *pescada-amarela, pescada-ticupá;* Spanish: *corvinata amarilla.*

The acoupa weakfish is a member of the Sciaenidae family (drum and croaker), named for drumming noises made by their swim bladder. The name "weakfish" refers to the tender, easily torn membrane in the fish's mouth, not its fighting ability.

It occurs in the western Atlantic from Panama to Argentina and is abundant along the Brazilian coast. It generally inhabits muddy or sand bottoms near river mouths and feeds on shrimp and fish. Juveniles are restricted to brackish- or freshwater environs.

The acoupa weakfish is similar in appearance to the weakfish *(see)* of North America, although found in considerably larger sizes. It is a popular food fish and sportfish, and is highly respected by anglers.

The maximum size of acoupa weakfish has been reported at 43 inches and 29 pounds; the common length is 18 inches. The all-tackle record is a Brazilian fish of 29 pounds, 5 ounces, caught in Guanabara Bay near Río de Janeiro in 1997; in the late 1990s, various specimens exceeding 25 pounds were caught in Brazil.

WEATHER
Obviously anglers are affected by weather every time they go fishing. The extent to which fish are affected by the weather has been a source of uncertainty and speculation for ages. Some elements of weather are known to have certain general effects on fish, but there is no clear scientific proof, nor is there solid evidence that all fish are affected in the same way; if anything, it may be just the opposite. Freshwater species, for example, are more adversely impacted by exceptional weather events than saltwater fish, and deep dwellers seem less affected by most weather than residents of shallow environs.

Certainly some elements of weather are most significant because they impair fishing techniques or angler effectiveness. And some types of weather evidently affect the personal comfort of anglers more than they do the fish, since the majority of fishing is done when conditions are most suitable to humans. Yet, fishing is a four-season sport, and the entire gamut of weather possibilities can come into play for different anglers in different geographical areas.

Weather plays a major role not only in actual fishing activities, but also in boating. This is especially true on large bodies of water, when great distances are traveled by boats, and in places where storms are likely to occur. Weather events can imply safety concerns, which is a far greater issue than how the weather affects fish or fishing conditions.

Most anglers don't know as much as they should about the weather, and even though you can do nothing to change the weather, you can gain basic weather knowledge to understand the significance of cloud patterns, wind direction, barometric pressure, and the like, as well as abnormal events like storms.

There are numerous sources of information about atmospheric conditions and weather events, as well as basic meteorology, not the least of which are various materials provided in the United States by the National Weather Service, which is part of the federal government in the National Oceanic and Atmospheric Administration (NOAA). In addition, much can be learned from professional meteorologists and the weather maps and satellite imagery that are widely televised. Weather forecasting today has greatly improved, and technological advances are taking it to new heights annually.

Watching or listening to standard media weather forecasts, however, is largely of general significance and is often not adequate for boating and fishing activities. For these activities, the best reports are issued by National Weather Radio (NWR), a mariner's service of NOAA on weather band frequencies that is broadcast on VHF radios *(see)*. In the United States, NWR has more than 425 stations; reports are given every four to six minutes and updated every one to six hours, with an excellent warning system for local events; broadcasts are continuous all day all year. In addition to reports about general conditions, NWR gives a synopsis of prevailing regional weather patterns, which can be a clue for the astute listener as to conditions that may affect fishing plans not just for the present time but for a while to come. No big-water boater should be without a means of getting reports from this source.

Reports from any source are just one piece of information, and the wise person is observant of the weather all the time; such observance increases understanding of basic weather patterns and cycles that happen continuously. If you keep in tune with local weather patterns, you'll probably lose less fishing time than the person who doesn't, since you'll understand what the real effect of changing weather means. The important point is to develop your own ability to understand what the best weather forecast information means so that you can assess factors before you go on the water, and also so that you can assess them while you are on the water.

It is beyond the scope of this entry to provide a review of weather development as it pertains to cloud identification, wind *(see)*, barometric pressure changes, and fronts, or to events like thunderstorms, tornadoes, waterspouts, and hurricanes. However, all of these components of weather can have impacts on fishing, boating, and safety. The safety implications of storm events are addressed elsewhere *(see: safety)*, but some general comments can be made about the fishing significance of these factors.

Some marinas provide computerized weather information; this angler is checking a Doppler system at a marina in the Florida Keys.

The presence or absence of sunlight is a basic element of weather. Clear skies and bright sun is indicative of a high pressure system, and it often brings with it a strong wind. Cloudy conditions can cause light-sensitive fish to be more active, especially in shallow freshwater; in freshwater fishing this is generally viewed favorably; in most saltwater fishing it is not as significant. Cloudy cover makes it harder to see shallow saltwater fish that are caught by sight fishing methods, so good light with low wind is preferred. In freshwater, strong overhead light from the sun is often poor for shallow water fishing activities.

Rain or fog is similar in effect to clouds. Light and warm rains are often more conducive to fish activity than heavy or cold rains, although warm heavy rains in the spring in freshwater do a lot to move feeding and spawning activities along.

Wind, or the absence of it, is often the most influential factor in fishing activities. A strong wind makes many presentation methods, particularly casting and drifting, very difficult. If the waves are high enough, wind can make trolling very unpleasant, and proper boat control difficult. The total absence of wind, however, allows light penetration and causes shallow, light-sensitive fish to go deeper or seek shade, and makes many fish more wary. A light breeze, just enough to ripple the surface, can make a positive difference in fishing; moderate winds that chop up the surface are rarely unfavorable.

A cold front is less favorable than a warm front and may be very unfavorable for some fish (shallow water residents in particular). In North America, most cold fronts arrive from the northwest, and most warm fronts arrive from the south and southwest. Severe storms are usually poor for most fishing, because they cause great changes in the environment. It often takes a few days to a week or more to improve fishing after some severe storms. Periods of stable weather tend to produce good fishing, and a continual series of unstable weather and cold fronts, accompanied by high winds, tends to sustain poor or at least sub-par fishing.

WEATHER RADIO

A radio equipped to broadcast weather information issued on three specially designated frequencies by the National Weather Service; also, the system created by the National Weather Service which broadcasts weather information on an all-day, everyday basis. See: Communications; Weather.

WEEDGUARD

A piece of plastic, metal, or rubber that covers a fish hook to help prevent snagging in cover.

WEEDLESS HOOK

A hook with a wire, plastic, or rubber cover over the hook point to keep it from hanging on objects.

WEEDLESS LURE

A lure with some type of a guard covering the hook to help prevent it from getting caught on objects, especially weeds, but other items as well; also, a lure that by its own design and nature is generally free from inadvertent hanging on objects.

WEEDLINE

The edge of aquatic vegetation.
See: Aquatic Plants.

WEEDS

The terms "weeds" is often used to refer to all types of aquatic plants, although technically a weed is a plant that grows where it is not wanted. A native aquatic plant that has spread to an area where it affects navigation or has become so abundant that it hinders fish populations is considered a weed. Any aquatic plant that is not native to a water body is a weed. In North America, such exotic aquatic plants as water hyacinth and hydrilla, which came from other countries, are considered weeds and have become problems because of uncontrolled growth.
See: Aquatic Plants.

WEIGHING FISH

See: Measuring Fish.

WEIGHT

(1) An object used to sink a lure or bait, often referred to as a sinker (see).

(2) A heavy lead object essential to downrigger (see) usage and commonly referred to as a weight or cannonball.

WEIGHTED LINE

Weighted lines are core-heavy products that sink and are used for deep trolling, the objective being to bring a lure or bait (mostly the former) to depths that cannot be reached by flatlining (see), and where other devices are unavailable. Lead core is the foremost type of weighted line, but similar products have a flexible non-toxic lead substitute.

These are not lines to which some external weight has been added. They feature a pliable, dense core that is covered by braided nylon or Dacron. They are available in a somewhat limited range of strengths, from 15- to 60-pound-test, mostly from the upper 20s on up. Weighted lines have the density to sink on their own without the addition of external objects, although the bulky diameter of the line offsets some of the sinking ability at trolling speed, usually meaning that to get very deep, great lengths of line have to be trolled or the boat moved very slowly. In saltwater, and in some freshwater applications, trollers who desire to get lures deep prefer wire line (see).

Weighted lines are not as useful at high speeds and where there is current, but they are much easier to use than wire. They rarely create kinking or jamming problems, and can easily be wound on a reel and set out (they cannot be cast). They are color-coded every 10 yards so you can easily determine how much is out, although this won't necessarily tell you how deep the lure is.

Weighted lines are available in coated and uncoated versions, the former using some type of plastic. Coating may help abrasion, but generally these lines are not very abrasion resistant. They have less stretch than some similar strength nylon monofilaments, but they do stretch. They will corrode in saltwater, and have to be taken off the reel spool and rinsed, in part explaining why wire line is universally preferred in saltwater.

No special tackle is required for weighted lines, although the rod should be relatively stout and the reel large enough to hold this bulky product and some backing. Levelwind reels can be used. A leader of monofilament line is tied to the business end of the weighted line, and then a lure is attached to that.

Weighted-line trolling was a principal means of fishing deep in freshwater but has decreased greatly in popularity with the increased use of downriggers and diving planers, and is primarily employed for lake trout and salmon angling. To many anglers, weighted-line trolling is not as satisfying as other trolling techniques using lighter and more challenging tackle. The problem is that weighted lines make fish landing mostly a reel-cranking, winch-the-fish-up affair. If you catch a really large fish, it will surely fight well enough for you to know it's there. But for every large fish you hook, you'll catch a lot of small- to medium-size fish, which just don't give as good an account of themselves on weighted line as they do on finer line because they must resist the bulky drag of the line in the water.
See: Line; Trolling.

WEIGHT-FORWARD LINE

A fly line that is tapered only at the fishing end.
See: Flycasting Tackle.

WEIGHT-FORWARD SPINNER

See: Spinner.

WELS

A Eurasian catfish and one of the largest of all freshwater fish.
See: Catfish.

WEST INDIES

See: Bahamas; Cayman Islands; Cuba; Jamaica; Lesser Antilles; Puerto Rico; Virgin Islands.

WEST VIRGINIA

Since the early 1970s, West Virginians have proclaimed far and wide the "wild, wonderful" nature of their state. Visitors quickly discover that it's not just a tourism marketing slogan. Pristine trout streams tumble from tall, forested slopes; scenic whitewater rivers cut deep gorges through the mountainous landscape; broad-shouldered waterways meander placidly through farm-dotted valleys.

The rivers' scenic value attracts tens of thousands of tourists each year. Their angling value draws tens of thousands more. Although not widely considered a destination for traveling anglers, the Mountain State nonetheless boasts several national-class, and at least a handful of world-class, fisheries.

Born of the great tectonic collision that formed the Appalachian Mountain chain, West Virginia exhibits all the characteristics of a land squeezed between two continental plates. The rock strata under its highest peaks have been shoved to, and sometimes even past, the vertical. Eons of erosion have carved deep, steep-sided valleys into the sandstone, limestone, and shale. As a whole, the landscape resembles a piece of emerald construction paper that someone wadded up and only haphazardly attempted to straighten.

Like the landscape, West Virginia's rivers and streams vary widely in water quality; quirks of geology render some vastly more fertile than others. The presence or absence of industry plays a significant role in the quality of the rest.

West Virginia has long been known for its natural resources, primarily coal, timber, and natural gas. Where those resources have been heavily exploited, water quality inevitably has suffered. Still, some waters have managed to maintain their fisheries despite decades of industrial degradation. In fact, some of the state's best angling exists in rivers that have been reclaimed through voluntary and government-mandated efforts.

Warmwater Rivers

One need look no farther than West Virginia's western boundary, the Ohio River, to find a sterling example of one of those restored fisheries. Once a troubled waterway that harbored little more than catfish and carp, the Ohio began its comeback after the Clean Water Act of 1970 forced the many heavy industries located along its banks to reduce their pollution levels.

Today, the Ohio ranks as the state's finest mixed-bag fishery. Anglers can fish for largemouth bass, smallmouth bass, spotted bass, white bass, and hybrid striped bass, as well as walleye, sauger, freshwater drum, channel catfish, flathead catfish, and carp.

Anglers familiar with the Ohio tend to concentrate most of their attention at the seven U.S. Army Corps of Engineers navigation locks scattered along the river. Outflows from low-head hydropower plants create ideal fishing conditions in the dams' tailwaters. In addition, most of the power companies have built special piers that bridge the outflows and give anglers access to particularly productive spots. Some angler-access locations even have special parking areas, lights, and fish-cleaning stations.

The Ohio's principal West Virginia tributary, the Kanawha River, boasts a remarkably similar fishery. Once so polluted that carp couldn't even survive in it, the Kanawha now rivals the Ohio in angling variety and productivity.

Fishing began to return to the Kanawha when the many chemical companies located near Charleston started reducing their pollution. Almost instantly, the river recovered. Bass clubs now routinely hold tournaments in areas once devoid of gamefish.

The Kanawha's fishery is even more varied than that of the Ohio. In addition to largemouth, smallmouth, spotted, white, and hybrid striped bass, the Kanawha tosses pure-strain stripers into the mix, plus walleye, sauger, and muskellunge. There aren't many muskies here, but there are enough to pique anglers' interests. Other species of note include freshwater drum, channel catfish, flathead catfish, carp, a rich variety of sunfish, and an occasional crappie.

Three navigation dams interrupt the Kanawha's journey northwest to its junction with the Ohio, and each is home to a first-class angler-access facility. When 3- to 9-pound hybrid stripers begin running in June, it is sometimes difficult to find casting space on the piers.

The Kanawha's main tributary, the New River, easily ranks as the state's most famous warmwater fishery. Although not as varied as either the Ohio or the Kanawha, the New River offers scenic beauty, difficult rapids, and world-class smallmouth bass fishing that make it West Virginia's premier tourist attraction.

Dubbed "River of Death" by Native Americans, the New is a broad, powerful river that roars through a steep-sided gorge for almost its entire journey through the state's southern mountains. From Hinton to Sandstone, its rapids are gentle enough to be navigated by experienced canoeists; from Sandstone to Thurmond, the rapids' size and violence require substantial whitewater skill. From Thurmond to Fayette Station, river navigation is strictly for experts.

Fortunately for anglers, many of the river's whitewater rafting outfitters also offer fishing guide services. With the help of an experienced guide, even novice anglers can experience the thrill of hauling a 3- to 5-pound bronzeback out of a Class IV set of rapids—a double adrenaline rush that shouldn't be missed.

The New River owes a great deal of its water quality to the limestone-rich waters of one of its principal tributaries, the Greenbrier River. As do its larger sister's, the Greenbrier's riches lie in the river's scenic beauty and an abundance of hard-fighting smallmouth bass.

The longest fly-distance double-handed cast in competition is 319 feet 1 inch, set in 1984.

W
X
Y
Z

From Bartow to Hinton, the Greenbrier flows through bucolic farmland bounded on each side by the lofty ridges of the Allegheny Range. For anglers who prefer to float-fish, it is paradise. With the exception of a few minor falls near Talcott on its extreme downstream end, most of the Greenbrier can easily be floated in canoes or jonboats.

The Greenbrier's smallmouth, although not as large as those found in the deep, swirling rapids of the New River, tend to make up in aggressiveness what they lack in size. Rock bass and channel catfish add spice to the fishery.

No description of float fishing in West Virginia would be complete without a mention of three phenomenal sections of the smallmouth-rich South Branch of the Potomac River in the state's Eastern Panhandle.

The first is an 8-mile stretch from the U.S. 220 bridge east of Petersburg to the County Route 13 bridge near Fisher. The second is the most famous: "The Trough." In the Trough, the South Branch tumbles almost straight as a string for 6.5 miles through a road-free, dwelling-free gap where deer, turkeys, and bald eagles appear more often than humans. The third section, nearly 9 miles long, extends from the U.S. 50 bridge west of Romney to the State Route 28 bridge at Blues Beach. All three sections boast some of the state's highest smallmouth catch rates, and all are scenic delights.

Although most productive mainly during early spring, the Elk River in central West Virginia shouldn't be overlooked. Few other rivers offer anglers the chance to catch a trophy smallmouth, a trophy walleye, and a trophy muskellunge from the same pool.

From Sutton Dam downstream to Clendenin, the Elk harbors fine populations of all three of these gamefish. Warmwater discharges from the dam have dramatically improved the river's bass fishing, and 2- to 3-pound bronzebacks have become fairly commonplace. Add to that the potential of catching walleye up to 10 pounds and muskies of 15 to 30 pounds, and one understands why the Elk's live-bait anglers load their minnow buckets with 6-inch chub and suckers during the months of March and April.

Large Impoundments

Since West Virginia's largest and only natural lake measures less than 2 acres in surface area, stillwater anglers must seek recreation at one of the state's many man-made lakes. The U.S. Army Corps of Engineers, through its flood-control system, manages many of the larger impoundments.

Perhaps the best of the lot is 2,500-acre Stonewall Jackson Lake near Weston. Widely acknowledged as West Virginia's finest largemouth bass fishery, Stonewall is a relatively shallow lake with an abundance of flooded timber. In addition to largemouths, the lake also harbors smallmouth bass, muskellunge, walleye, saugeye, and an

The first published description of the use of lures to catch fish appeared in 1496 in Dame Juliana Berners' *The Boke of Saint Albans;* a dozen artificial flies were mentioned.

WXYZ

abundance of crappie, plus channel catfish and other less-desired species.

Located just a few miles northeast of the state's geographic center, and just a stone's throw off Interstate 79, Stonewall is within a single day's drive of every West Virginian. Small wonder that, as its 1988 impoundment, it has become the darling of bass clubs throughout the state.

For sheer scenic splendor, Summersville Lake has no equal within the state. Formed in 1963 when the Corps of Engineers dammed the wild Gauley River near its namesake town, Summersville today is a sprawling complex of quiet coves set in a landscape of sandstone cliffs and thickly forested hillsides.

It is the state's largest, deepest, and clearest lake, and its smallmouth bass and walleye are difficult to locate and to catch. Most of the really productive walleye fishing occurs during the winter, when officials shrink the lake from 2,700 to just 920 acres to catch spring snowmelt from nearby mountains. Smallmouth anglers tend to do better in early fall, when bronzebacks are known to hurtle up through 20 feet of hydrogen-clear water to smash well-presented surface lures.

Most of Summersville's walleye average 18 to 24 inches in length, although larger specimens have been caught. Smallmouths and largemouths of up to 5 pounds are not uncommon. Occasionally, lake anglers catch large brown or rainbow trout; these fish have migrated into the lake from tributary streams and grown large on the impoundment's abundance of forage.

Summertime fishing is difficult at Summersville, mainly because the lake's scenic charms attract so many pleasure boaters and water-skiers. Quiet coves, although abundant, aren't likely to remain secluded for long amid the crowds that flock to Summersville between Memorial Day and Labor Day.

A similar situation, although not quite as severe, exists at Bluestone Lake near Hinton. The 2,040-acre impoundment harbors fine populations of smallmouth, largemouth, and striped bass, but anglers must work hard to find peace amid all the recreational boaters.

Perhaps the best bet for fishing success at Bluestone is to wade into the dam's tailwaters and cast for smallmouth bass. Bronzebacks of up to 4 pounds abound in the rich, highly oxygenated tailrace, and the fishery never seems to become depleted despite heavy pressure. The lake's Bluestone River arm also produces some fine smallmouth fishing, as well as a scenic treat.

One of the state's few major lakes not managed by the Corps of Engineers, 550-acre Stonecoal Lake offers visitors to the Weston area one of the state's most unique fisheries. Deep and unusually cold, Stonecoal is known less for its bass than for its trout and muskellunge. Muskie aficionados consider it West Virginia's finest lake-based fishery, bar none.

Every year, anglers haul muskies in the 45- to 50-inch class from its waters.

Cynics believe the lake's muskies grow so large because fishing clubs continue to stock the lake with trout. But enough 4- to 6-pound trout show up in anglers' creels to make it abundantly clear that not all the stocked rainbows and browns end up in the stomachs of toothy predators.

Despite water quality problems caused by the infertile hills that surround it, Beech Fork Lake near Huntington produces remarkably good catches of hybrid striped bass. This 720-acre impoundment averages less that 20 feet in depth, so its hybrid schools remain within easy reach of anglers regardless of season. Trolled live minnows work remarkably well on schooling fish.

Beech Fork's headwater tributaries harbor most of the lake's largemouth bass. Early evening forays up those thin water tributaries with fly tackle and poppers have been known to bring unforgettable surface action.

Small Impoundments

Lake-based fishing took a sharp turn for the better in West Virginia during the 1980s when local soil-conservation authorities began building small-scale flood-control lakes in the headwaters of flood-prone creeks.

None has captured the public's fancy more than Woodrum Lake, a 240-acre impoundment near Kenna. Only the state's 10-horsepower outboard motor limit for small impoundments keeps Woodrum from being "the" destination for West Virginia's bass clubs.

Built specifically with anglers in mind, Woodrum features dozens of acres of flooded timber. Its deep creek channels, rocky cliffs, and steep hillsides comprise some of the state's most productive bass habitat. Catch rates at Woodrum are among the state's highest, and nowhere in West Virginia do largemouths grow any larger. Fish of 3 to 4 pounds are common, and 6- to 8-pounders show up often enough to keep things interesting.

Just a few miles to the northeast, 217-acre O'Brien Lake boasts a remarkably similar fishery. Although shallower and less clear than Woodrum, it nonetheless harbors a fine largemouth population. O'Brien's fish are a little smaller, on average, and they aren't quite as easy to catch. But they do come often enough to make anglers speak of the two lakes almost as if they were identical twins instead of merely sisters.

The largest of the Mountain State's small impoundments, 300-acre Stephens Lake west of Beckley is home to some of the area's finest fishing for trophy-class tiger muskellunge. For a while in the mid-1980s, Stephens Lake "regulars" swapped the state tiger muskie record back and forth among themselves. The hot streak eventually cooled off, but the lake remains one of the state's three best fisheries for these northern pike/muskie hybrids.

Stephens also produces trophy-class largemouth bass and channel catfish on occasion.

A few miles to the northeast, Plum Orchard Lake offers anglers something they rarely get to experience in West Virginia: the pleasure of casting to lily pad cover. Most Mountain State impoundments simply don't possess the proper habitat for lily pads to grow. Plum Orchard, with its stable lake level and shallow coves, does. The pad-covered coves consistently produce trophy largemouth bass and slab-sided bluegills. Big channel cats lurk in the lake's deeper areas. Unlike most small impoundments, Plum Orchard has no horsepower restrictions for boats.

Trout Streams

West Virginia's higher elevations are home to more than 1,200 miles of trout streams. Nearly half that mileage is composed of tiny native brook trout waters small enough to be jumped across. Mountain State anglers are far more familiar with the other 600 miles, which include many of the state's most storied trout streams and rivers. Of those, none has a more gloried or checkered past than the Cranberry River.

Born amid the soaring 4,000-foot ridges of western Pocahontas County, the Cranberry flows more than 26 miles through some of the state's most remote backcountry. From 1930 to the late 1960s, it harbored self-sustaining populations of brook, rainbow, and brown trout. In the early 1970s, though, the fishery began to decline. Acid rain had soured the waters so badly that trout could no longer survive. The state Division of Natural Resources (DNR) continued to stock trout in the river, even though surveys showed that none of the fish would live through the spring snowmelt.

All that changed in 1988, when the DNR placed an acid-treatment station on Dogway Fork, one of the Cranberry's principal tributaries. A second station, added in 1992 to the river's North Fork, completed the transformation.

Brook and brown trout already have begun to reproduce in the Cranberry, and catches of trophy fish continue to increase. Once insect and baitfish populations expand to their respective carrying capacities, researchers expect the river to match or exceed its former status as the state's finest trout stream.

The current holder of that title, the upper Elk River, won't yield it easily. Nowhere else in the state can an angler legitimately expect to catch an 11-inch native brook trout, a 15-inch stream-spawned rainbow trout, and an 18-inch wild brown trout all in the same day.

Such catches don't often occur, but they could. All three species exist in the Elk watershed, and all three have been known to grow to even larger sizes. From the Elk's birthplace near the little town of Slatyfork, it races 4 miles through a remote canyon, sinks into an underground cavern, runs

underground for nearly 2 miles, then rises as a full-blown river at Elk Springs.

From Elk Springs 20 miles downstream to Webster Springs, the Elk is trophy brown trout water, home to fish that occasionally top 6 pounds. Most of the fish caught, however, are hatchery fish planted during weekly stockings by the DNR.

Shavers Fork of the Cheat River has been described as "the poor man's Madison" because of its strong currents and its boulder-littered bottom. It's an apt description. Like its Montana counterpart, Shavers seldom pauses to rest during its descent from the slopes of Bald Knob to its confluence with the Black Fork at Parsons. For more than 40 miles, it slips straight along the ridge of Cheat Mountain like a needle through the teeth of a saw before it at last tumbles out and assumes a more meandering route.

Recent acid-treatment efforts on its tributaries promise to return Shavers to its once-held status as a top trophy trout producer. For the time being, it will remain one of the state's most popular and productive stocked trout streams.

Anglers might similarly describe the Williams River. A sister to the Cranberry, the Elk, and Shavers Fork, the Williams originates in a portion of western Pocahontas County known locally as the "Birthplace of Rivers." Seven major rivers originate in less than 500 square miles of rugged mountains, and all of those rivers harbor trout.

The Williams might just be the most popular of all. Although it parallels the storied Cranberry for almost its full length, the Williams went unaffected by acid rain because fertile limestone soils underlie its headwaters.

From the Monongahela National Forest's Day Run Campground downstream to Dyer, the Williams harbors both stocked and wild trout. A Forest Service road parallels the stream for almost its entire length, providing easy angler access to every stretch. Anglers can camp at the Day Run or Tea Creek campgrounds, or at any of dozens of designated sites along the stream.

Gandy Creek and the Dry Fork of the Cheat are every bit as accessible as the Williams, and every bit as productive. Practically, the two streams should be considered as one. Gandy forms the drainage's headwaters, although the stream assumes the aptly named Dry Fork's name immediately after the two join together.

Gandy begins as a brook trout limestone stream that actually runs underground for a mile through the famous Sinks of Gandy. Below the Sinks, it assumes a freestone character and harbors native brookies and wild browns as well as stocked rainbows.

After the Gandy's confluence with Dry Fork, browns begin to dominate the species mix. The river's boulder-lined pools produce a few enormous browns each year. Three- to 5-pound fish show up fairly regularly, and 10-pounders have been caught.

Roads parallel the two streams for nearly their entire length, providing easy access.

Just the opposite is true for the Blackwater River, a tannin-stained stream that drains the huge high-altitude wetlands complex known as Canaan Valley. A meandering, slow-paced brown trout stream in its headwaters, the Blackwater picks up speed and difficulty shortly after it vaults over 63-foot-high Blackwater Falls and plunges into the steep-walled Blackwater Canyon.

Anglers who venture into the roadless, nearly trailless canyon often are rewarded with oversize browns and rainbows. The hike out, however, inevitably exacts a toll not many wish to pay. Perhaps more than any other fishery in the state, the Blackwater Canyon stands as the living embodiment of West Virginia's "wild, wonderful" character.

WET FLY

A sinking artificial fly that primarily represents sub-surface forms of aquatic insects in freshwater.
See: Fly.

WETLANDS

Although a wetland is generally thought of as a swamp, the technical definition of a wetland is a debatable one; it is generally viewed as an area between land and water where the water table is at or near the surface, or the land is covered by shallow water. Ponds and lakes less than 6 feet deep may be considered wetlands, as may bogs, swamps, or marshes *(see)*. In the broadest sense, wetlands must have soils that are saturated with water or periodically flooded and have an abundance of plants that can live in wet soils or water. This covers a lot of places along and around freshwater lakes and rivers, and in salt or brackish regions of tidal rivers and estuaries.

Tidal salt marshes are flooded regularly by the rise and fall of tides, but they are not flooded during low tide. They are highly productive ecosystems that support many marine organisms as places for breeding, feeding, and sheltering young. Mangrove *(see)* swamps or forests are also a form of salt marsh in tropical and subtropical areas.

Tidal freshwater marshes are coastal wetlands that maintain freshwater conditions through high amounts of rainwater or because of their location along a river. They also are affected by the tides but are never inundated by saltwater because of their elevation. Tidal freshwater marshes combine the features of salt marshes and inland freshwater marshes. Because they have a concentration of salt lower than tidal salt marshes, there is greater biodiversity. Many species of fish use freshwater tidal marshes to spawn and as a nursery for their young. Anadromous fish, which live their adult lives in the ocean, and fish that spend their adult lives in estuaries, travel through these marshes on their way to freshwater streams to breed.

W
X
Y
Z

An angler fishes near a freshwater marsh in Ontario's Kawartha Lakes.

Nontidal freshwater marshes are of various types. They may be emergent, such as marshes and meadows, and comprised of mostly grasses and sedges, or they may be scrub-shrub wetlands, such as bogs, pocosins, and shrub swamps. Some are small, like a prairie pothole, or large, like the Florida Everglades. Emergent wetlands are thought to be the most diverse of all wetland types. Many insects and animals inhabit these nontidal inland marshes. In general, more fish are found in marsh systems with deeper, open water.

Northern peatlands are wetlands called bogs and fens. Bogs have acidic peat deposits, a high water table, no inlets or outlets, and plants that thrive in acidic soils or water. Fens are fed by groundwater, are dominated by vascular plants, and have grasses, sedges, and reeds as opposed to sphagnum and true mosses. Plants and animals that inhabit bogs and fens have developed some unique characteristics and adaptations. They must deal with many stresses, such as acidic water, low nutrient levels, extreme temperatures, and being waterlogged. Because of low levels of productivity and the apparent unpleasant taste of bog plants, very few wildlife species inhabit the waters of bogs and fens.

Southern deep-water swamps, on the other hand, have a lot of aquatic species, including crayfish, snails, freshwater shrimp, midges, insect larvae, and clams, which use the large amount of detritus found in these swamps. Mayflies, caddisflies, and stoneflies can be found near in-flowing streams in these wetlands. Fish also use these swamps as temporary and permanent residences, where deep-water areas provide optimum habitat. In the southeastern United States, bald cypress, water tupelo, and black gum are the dominant trees in this type of wetland, and there is permanent or almost permanent standing water.

In the aggregate, wetlands are vital resources for a wide array of plant, fish, and animal life. Many prominent species of fish, including bass, trout, stripers, and salmon, need and use wetlands. Most wetlands provide shelter and food for fish species, and some harbor gamefish sought by anglers and thus provide recreation. However, wetlands are equally important as areas that absorb pollutants and filter human sediments and waster, thus maintaining and improving water quality. Some also reduce erosion and flood damage. Many endangered species directly or indirectly rely on wetlands for survival. Wetlands themselves have been threatened or lost because of myriad factors. It has been estimated that more than 100 million acres of wetlands have been destroyed in the United States over the past two centuries, and it is clear that continuing loss or degradation will adversely impact all natural resources, including fish species, as well as angling opportunities.

WET WADING
Fishing by means of wading in the water without the aid of waders (see).

WHIP FINISH
A knot that is used to finish off thread winding and that prevents the thread from unraveling; if done correctly, the whip finish is smooth without bulges or lumps. The whip finish is employed in tying flies, wrapping rod blanks, and tying skirts onto jigs or lure hooks.
See: Fly Tying; Lure Modifying/Repairing.

WHIRLING DISEASE
An infection of young salmonids caused by a microscopic, water-borne, protozoan parasite that attacks the cartilage and causes the fish to chase its own tail. Whirling disease spores (*Myxobolus cerebralis*) are released into the water when infected fish die and decompose, or when the spores are consumed and excreted by predators or scavengers. The parasite has a complex, two-host life cycle that involves a trout or salmon and the bottom-dwelling tubifex worm, which is found in streams, rivers, and lakes.

This parasite is not harmful to humans but has been disastrous on some trout populations, particularly rainbow, and has spread rapidly in northeastern and western North America in the 1990s, although it originated in Europe. It does not directly kill fish, but an infected fish's erratic tail chasing makes it extremely vulnerable to predation. The whirling activity of the fish also makes it unable to feed normally, which eventually results in starvation and death. This disease primarily infects fish smaller than 4 inches long.
See: Diseases and Parasites.

WHITEFISH, LAKE   *Coregonus clupeaformis.*
Other names—high back, bow back, buffalo back, or humpback whitefish; common whitefish; eastern

whitefish; Great Lakes whitefish; inland whitefish; Sault whitefish; gizzard fish; Cree: *atekamek;* French: *grand corégone.*

The lake whitefish is a larger and more widespread fish than are the mountain *(see: whitefish, mountain)* and the round whitefish *(see: whitefish, round),* and it is more highly regarded among anglers. A member of the Salmonidae family, the lake whitefish is a valuable commercial freshwater fish in Canada, although its numbers have declined due to environmental factors and overfishing, especially in the Great Lakes. The flesh—prepared fresh, smoked, and frozen—is considered superb in flavor, and its roe is made into an excellent caviar.

Identification. A slender, elongated species, the lake whitefish is silvery to white with an olive to pale greenish brown back that is dark brown to midnight blue or black in some inland lake specimens; it also has white fins and a dark-edged tail. The mouth is subterminal and the snout protrudes beyond it, with a double flap of skin between the nostrils. The tail is deeply forked, and an adipose fin is present. The lake whitefish is occasionally referred to as "humpback" because the head is small in relation to the length of the body, and older specimens may develop a hump behind the head. It has 10 to 14 anal rays, 70 to 97 scales down the lateral line, and 19 to 33 gill rakers. The body is more laterally compressed than that of the round or mountain whitefish, which belong to a separate genus of "round whitefish."

Size/Age. The lake whitefish is commonly 18 inches long and weigh 2 to 4 pounds. Some are said to reach as much as 31 inches, and the all-tackle world record is a 14-pound, 6-ounce fish caught in Ontario, Canada, in 1984. The average whitefish caught by anglers is in the 1- to 2-pound range. Fish of 4 or 5 pounds, and even larger, are sometimes caught. This species can live for 18 years.

Distribution. Lake whitefish occur throughout Alaska and Canada; in the mainland United States, they occur throughout central Minnesota and the Great Lakes and from New York to Maine. Transplanted populations exist in Washington, Idaho, and Montana. They have been stocked into high Andean lakes in a few countries in South America.

Habitat. Lake whitefish are named for their primary habitat of large, deep lakes, but they are also residents of large rivers. They prefer water temperatures of 50° to 55°F and will enter brackish water.

Life history/Behavior. Spawning occurs in late fall, when fish migrate into shallow areas over sandy bottoms or shoals in large lakes or tributary streams. Eggs are randomly deposited over the bottom by females laying up to 12,000 eggs per pound of body weight. These fish do not build nests, and parents return to deep water after spawning, leaving eggs unprotected on spawning grounds until they hatch the following spring. By early summer, the young move from shallow inshore areas to deeper water.

Food and feeding habits. Mainly bottom feeders, adult lake whitefish feed primarily on aquatic insect larvae, mollusks, and amphipods, but also on other small fish and fish eggs, including their own. Young fish feed on plankton.

Angling. In lakes, whitefish are readily taken when schooled and when rising to flies, but they are often hard to catch otherwise. Although many open-lake anglers catch them accidentally while seeking other game, these fish are successfully pursued through the ice. In rivers where whitefish are abundant, flycasters are routinely successful in landing them; sometimes they are a nuisance rather than a pleasure. They linger in slow pools, beneath waterfalls, and along back-switching bank eddies.

Whitefish are principally an insect feeder, and this is reflected in fishing tactics. They are most likely to be caught on nymphs or dry flies, the latter especially in lakes when these fish rise to the surface in large schools that travel along the shores of a deep-water bay.

Whitefish rise gently when feeding on floating insects, and often one sees the dorsal fin cutting through the surface momentarily. A dry fly presented slightly ahead of the cruising fish will usually be taken, but the hooksetting motion need not be vigorous. The whitefish has a soft mouth, so a smooth rod-lifting action will set the hook without tearing it away from the fish.

Methods other than fly fishing can be productive, but not reliably so. A whitefish will occasionally strike a spoon or small plug, although a jig is far more likely to be effective. A small dark jig is best; it can be fished plain or it can be tipped with a small insect or grub. Grubs are popular for ice fishing, as are small live or salted minnows, and small jigging lures. Chumming is also effective.

Whitefish fight well, occasionally jumping and characteristically making a diving run and shaking near the surface. They are a fine light-tackle fish; light or ultralight spinning rods equipped with 2- to 6-pound line are suitable, as are light, medium-length fly rods for 5- to 7-weight fly lines.

WHITEFISH, MOUNTAIN *Prosopium williamsoni.*

Other names—Rocky mountain whitefish, Williamson's whitefish, grayling; French: *ménomini des montagnes.*

W
X
Y
Z

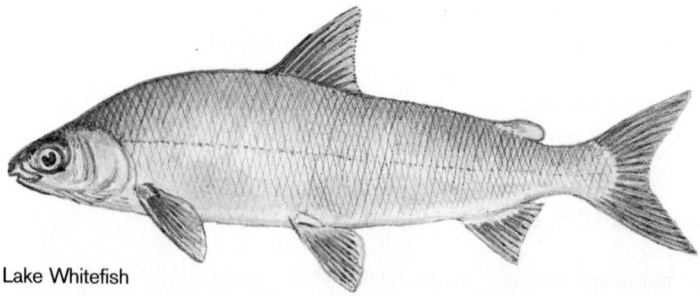

Lake Whitefish

Although not as significant a gamefish as the lake whitefish *(see: whitefish, lake)*, the mountain whitefish has gained popularity and provides an important winter fishery in certain areas, especially where steelhead are absent. A member of the Salmonidae family, it is a very good table fish, particularly when smoked.

Identification. Possessing an adipose fin and an axillary process, the mountain whitefish is long, slender, and nearly cylindrical, although not quite as cylindrical as the round whitefish *(see: whitefish, round)*. It is nevertheless among the species referred to as "round whitefish" and can be distinguished from the lake whitefish, which is more laterally compressed than the mountain whitefish. Silvery overall, it is dark brownish to olive or greenish to blue gray above, with scales that often have dark borders and ventral and pectoral fins that may have an amber shade in adults. The small mouth is slightly subterminal, and the snout extends clearly beyond it. The caudal fin is forked, and there are 74 to 90 scales down the lateral line and 19 to 26 gill rakers. Young fish have 7 to 11 large, oval, dark parr marks.

Size/Age. The mountain whitefish can grow to $22\frac{1}{2}$ inches and 5 pounds. The all-tackle world record is a 1988 5-pound, 6-ounce fish from Saskatchewan. It can live for 18 years.

Distribution. The mountain whitefish is endemic to the lakes and streams of the northwestern United States and southwestern Canada, from the Lahontan basin in Nevada north to the southern border of the Yukon Territory. It occurs inland into Alberta in Canada and Wyoming in the U.S., overlapping the range of the lake whitefish in British Columbia and Alberta, and slightly overlapping that of the round whitefish in extreme northern British Columbia near the Yukon border.

Habitat. Generally inhabiting rivers and fast, clear, or silty areas of larger streams as well as lakes, mountain whitefish usually occur in stream riffles during the summer and in large pools in the winter. They prefer temperatures of 46° to 52°F and are found in the deep water of some lakes, although in northern lakes they usually hold no deeper than 30 feet.

Spawning behavior. Spawning takes place from October through December in shallow, gravelly streams or occasionally in lakes at water temperatures of 42°F or less. Parents do not guard the eggs, which number about 5,000 on average and incubate over winter to hatch in spring.

Food and feeding habits. Mountain whitefish feed primarily on benthic organisms like aquatic insect larvae, mollusks, fish, and fish eggs (including their own), as well as on plankton and surface insects when primary food sources are unavailable.

Angling. Mountain whitefish are underutilized by anglers. Similar to the lake whitefish, they are good fighters and are caught on flies, natural baits, and some artificial lures that they can fit in their small mouths. They bite especially well during the winter months.

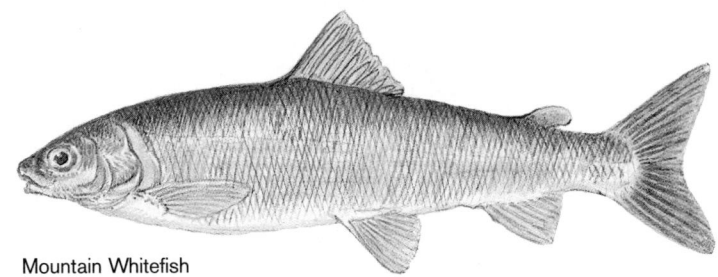

Mountain Whitefish

WHITEFISH, ROUND   *Prosopium cylindraceum.*

Other names—menominee, round fish, frost fish, pilot fish, grayback; French: *ménomini rond.*

A member of the Salmonidae family, the round whitefish seldom exceeds 2 pounds and has considerably less commercial value in Canada than the lake whitefish *(see: whitefish, lake)*, although it is sought to a limited degree by anglers. Its flesh is of good quality.

Identification. The round whitefish is mostly silvery and has a dark brown to almost bronze coloring with a greenish tint on the back. It has black-edged scales, particularly on the back. The lower fins are an amber color, becoming slightly more orange during spawning, and the adipose fin is usually brown spotted. Young fish have two or more rows of black spots on the sides that may merge with a row of black spots on the back. The round whitefish has a small head and a fairly pointed snout, and a single flap of skin between its nostrils. It also has a forked caudal fin, 74 to 108 scales down the lateral line, and 14 to 21 gill rakers. The round and lake whitefish can be easily distinguished because the round whitefish has a very cylindrical body, whereas the body of the lake whitefish is laterally compressed; the mountain whitefish *(see: whitefish, mountain)* is almost cylindrical, although slightly more compressed than the round whitefish.

Size. Usually about 8 to 12 inches long and weighing $\frac{1}{2}$ pound or less, the round whitefish can grow to more than 20 inches long and weigh several pounds. The all-tackle world record is a 6-pounder taken in Manitoba in 1984.

Distribution. The round whitefish occurs in arctic drainages in northeastern Asia from the Yanisea River to Kamchatka and the Bering Sea. A wide-ranging species in the northern portions of North America, it has disjunct populations, one of which is found through the St. Lawrence–Great Lakes basin (with the exception of Lake Erie) north to the Arctic Ocean east of Hudson Bay; the other is found throughout the northern Canadian provinces and Alaska west of Hudson Bay. It also

W
X
Y
Z

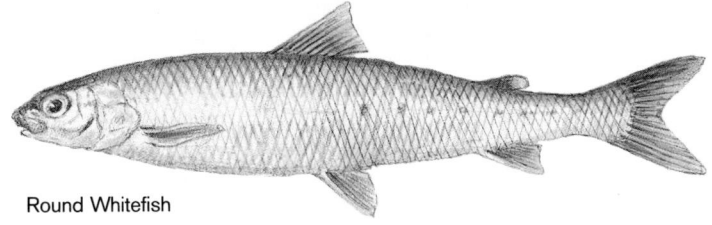

Round Whitefish

occurs in limited areas directly south of Hudson Bay and in East Twin Lake in Connecticut.

Habitat.   Occurring in the shallow areas of lakes and streams, round whitefish may also inhabit rivers with swift current and a stony bottom. They rarely enter brackish water or water more than 150 feet deep.

Spawning behavior.   Spawning takes place during the fall in lakes, tributary mouths, and occasionally in rivers over gravelly shallow areas. Fish spawn in pairs, with females releasing from 2,000 to 12,000 eggs, which are abandoned after spawning and hatch in early spring.

Food.   Round whitefish feed on benthic invertebrates and occasionally on fish and fish eggs.

Angling.   *See: Whitefish, Lake.*

WHITING

(1) A term commonly and primarily used for silver hake *(see: hake, silver).*

(2) A term for members of the *Menticirrhus* genus of the Sciaenidae family of drum *(see)* and croaker *(see).* These include the gulf kingfish *(M. littoralis),* southern kingfish *(M. americanus),* northern kingfish *(M. saxatilis),* and minkfish *(M. focaliger).* These bottom-feeding fish seldom exceed a half pound in weight or more than 10 inches in length and are generally ignored by anglers. They are found close to shore, lack air bladders, and are unable to make the croaking sounds produced by other Sciaenids.

WHITING, KING GEORGE   *Sillaginodes punctata*

Other names—spotted whiting, South Australian whiting, spotted sillago.

One of a number of species of whiting found in Australian waters, and one of the best-known fish along the southern coastline of Australia, the King George whiting is a favorite with anglers. A superb table fish, it is also the target of commercial fisheries in Victoria, South Australia, and Western Australia.

Identification.   This species is readily identified by scattered bronze or brown spots on the back and upper sides that extend to the long dorsal fins. Its body coloring shades from light to dark brown on the back to silvery white on the belly. The body shape is rounded and elongate. The forked caudal fin is yellow, and the pectoral and anal fins are white. This species has a small mouth and extremely small scales.

Size.   King George whiting can exceed 4 kilograms in length and 70 centimeters in length, but the average fish taken by anglers weighs roughly 500 grams.

Distribution.   These fish are an indigenous species confined to temperate waters from Jurien Bay in Western Australia, across the bottom of Australia, including the northern coastline of Tasmania, and along the East Coast to as far north as Sydney, New South Wales.

Habitat.   King George whiting dwell along ocean beaches and in shallow offshore waters, but anglers land greater numbers of them from bays and tidal estuaries, where they live in fairly shallow water (down to 1 or 2 meters) in areas of seagrass beds and sandy bottoms.

Life history/Behavior.   King George whiting are serial spawners. Spawning takes place in offshore waters from May through July, and fecundity can be as high as 800,000 eggs. The eggs float, and the larvae are planktonic until they're about 15 millimeters long; then, they move into sheltered areas where they remain for two to three years. After that, they move to deeper waters where they are targeted by both recreational anglers and commercial fishermen. They reach maturity after three to four years, and are reported to live for 15 years.

Food and feeding habits.   The shape of the King George whiting's mouth identifies it as a bottom feeder. It has a varied diet that includes bivalves, crustaceans, and worms.

Angling.   Recreational anglers of all ages seek the King George whiting because it is relatively easy to hook, provides exciting fishing due to its vigorous attempts to escape, requires the simplest of tackle, and is tasty. Anglers do well with light to medium tackle, light lines to 4 kilograms, and hooks from No. 4 to 1/0, depending on the size of the fish pursued. Handlines are frequently used, especially by boat anglers.

Favorite baits are cockle or mussel flesh, sandworms, and strips of squid. Rigs are either fixed or running; attaching two hooks to leaders is common, and sinker weight varies with conditions but must be enough to take the bait to the bottom, where these fish feed. Boat anglers find that judicious use of chum will attract the fish and hold them in the vicinity of the boat.

Although the shore-based angler is usually limited to a certain area due to the terrain, the boat angler can cover much more of the whiting's territory by drifting over sandy bottom covered in patches of seagrass.

WINCH

A device for helping to load a boat on a trailer and secure it to the trailer for transport. There are single and dual speed manual winches as well as electric winches.

See: Trailer, Boat.

WIND

Without doubt, wind is one of the most significant natural elements that affects sportfishing. No matter which direction it comes from, wind is one of nature's phenomena that can be a blessing or a curse

W
X
Y
Z

to anglers, although usually more of the latter. When there is no wind, anglers usually wish for a light chop on the surface to make it easier to dupe fish. Yet when there is too much wind, boat handling and lure presentation can be so difficult that fishing may be impaired. Wind can direct a cast fly into your hat or your ear. It makes you throw more forcefully with a baitcasting reel, increasing the chance of backlash. It may cause you to troll too fast or too slow, depending on whether you're headed with it or against it. When the temperature is low, wind makes an angler cold and often uncomfortable and less able to fish properly.

Anglers often face the dilemma of whether to get out of the wind or fight it. If the wind is a precursor to a front, changing several days worth of stable weather, it may signal the beginning of fish activity that you don't want to miss because that period before a new frontal system is often a good angling time.

In some places, you have no such choice. In winding or island-studded bodies of water, you often do. However, even though getting in the lee may allow you to fish comfortably, you may not be very successful there or you may have to pursue a species of fish that you were not already after. However, the wind-whipped shore may be, and often is, a good place to be fishing. Small fish and baitfish can be greatly disturbed by hard-driving winds, becoming disoriented or finding it very difficult to move, sometimes even being pinned against wind-driven shores. Wind pushes minute organisms into the windward shore; the organisms attract small fish and in turn larger fish. Oxygen is enhanced on windward shores because of the continued wave-beating. Fish may be facing out toward deep water here, and a controlled drift or troll is a good idea.

Fishing along those shores, or around the sides of wind-driven islands or shoals, may also be a good move. Baitfish may try to move out to deeper water to escape the turbulence, and predators sense this and move from deeper water to shallows to capture their prey. Casting crankbaits and jigs into the shallows and retrieving them outward may be the ticket, provided you can hold boat position. Keeping position is often hard, however, and sometimes impossible.

There will be times when you can't make any headway into the wind or are constantly being blown about, and fishing becomes a hardship. You can't make the right presentation or retrieval, and you can't detect strikes properly. You feel like your efforts are wasted. Dedicated anglers learn to deal with it.

Trolling (see) is one activity that can be done quite well in the wind if your boat is suitable, but you have to be mindful of several factors in order to make an effective trolling presentation. Probably the most important of these is the effect of the wind on speed.

Wind is more of a problem for anglers than for fish, and it can stimulate fish activity.

A boat moving with a motor at a constant engine speed of 500 rpms, for example, will go much faster with the wind than when headed into the wind. Often, fish are caught only when the boat is headed in one direction; this is because the lures being used aren't traveling at a suitable speed in the opposite direction (and don't have the proper action). Traveling into the wind at a moderate speed may bring lures deeper or shallower, depending on the lure, so depth attainment, rather than speed, can be the main factor. The worst thing you can do is troll blindly in one direction, then turn around and head blindly in the other direction, not knowing much about either the real speed or the depth at which your lures are working.

Maintaining a course is another matter that trolling anglers don't anticipate as a problem, but which is affected by wind speed and direction. To counter the tendency of a quartering wind to push a boat forward and away, for example, you must get the boat slightly sideways to the wind. This can be a difficult position to steadily maintain.

Because it helps maintain boat position even in wind, backtrolling is popular with walleye anglers. By using some type of sonar unit, a backtroller can maintain position along specific depths, nearly hover over selected spots, and maneuver the boat to use whatever wind direction is present to position the boat in such a way that a following bait is kept in the proper place and worked very slowly.

Casting is an altogether different story than trolling. Depending on what you are tossing to the fish, the act of casting is itself difficult in a brisk wind; accuracy and distance are often sacrificed. With lures you may have to cast farther upwind, or cast low and sidearm, to be more accurate, or use a heavier lure. You may have to cast only with, or quartering into, the wind instead of directly into it. With flies, you may have to position yourself much closer to your target than you would otherwise, since you may be unable to get the necessary distance.

High winds impact on just about every form of cast-and-retrieve angling, primarily because boat control and lure presentation are made much more difficult the greater the velocity of the wind is. Wind particularly affects jig and plastic worm fishing, which are games of feel and depth attainment. With a bow in your line, you don't have the sensitivity you need, and often your lure spends far too little time in the places it should be.

Anchoring is one way to deal with the wind for casting, but few anglers who are accustomed to positioning with an electric motor and casting to cover a good deal of water are satisfied with repeated anchoring and re-anchoring. Electric motors are certainly very helpful for fishing in the wind and maintaining position, provided the motor is powerful enough to move your particular boat (the more weight the harder) and the battery has enough juice. An electric motor's energy reserves are depleted more quickly in brisk wind because you run the motor more often and at higher speeds. With a bow-mounted electric motor, it may be necessary to have a long shaft to keep the motor in the water as the bow lurches up and down.

These are some of the typical problems to be overcome when the wind is rough. Fishing in heavy winds also raises concerns about safety issues, which are addressed elsewhere.
See: **Safety; Weather.**

WIND KNOT

A simple overhand knot that is inadvertently formed on fly line or (usually) leader while casting. It is attributed to the wind, hence the name, but is likely due to the formation of a loop that causes fly line and leader to cross. Such a knot greatly weakens the breaking strength of the line and should be removed, especially if it occurs in a light tippet.

WINGDAM

In a river, a man-made arrangement of rocks that extends from shore a variable distance perpendicular to the river and is intended to deflect current and prevent bank erosion. A wingdam is often submerged, especially in spring and in periods of high water, and thus a navigation hazard; but in normal to low water levels, it may protrude enough to be visible. It is not actually a dam, since it does not cross a river entirely (although a form of wingdam is an eel weir, which may extend across most of the shallow section of a river), and it may gather tree branches, logs, or other debris for a period of time until swept away.

Where the water is deep enough and current flow great enough, there is likely to be an eddy *(see)* behind the wingdam, and a deep hole alongside or just behind the leading edge that has been scoured out of the bottom. There is also a patch of calmer water on the upstream side of the wingdam. Such species as smallmouth bass, walleye, and catfish will use these key parts of a wingdam for feeding or resting.

Wingdam and Current

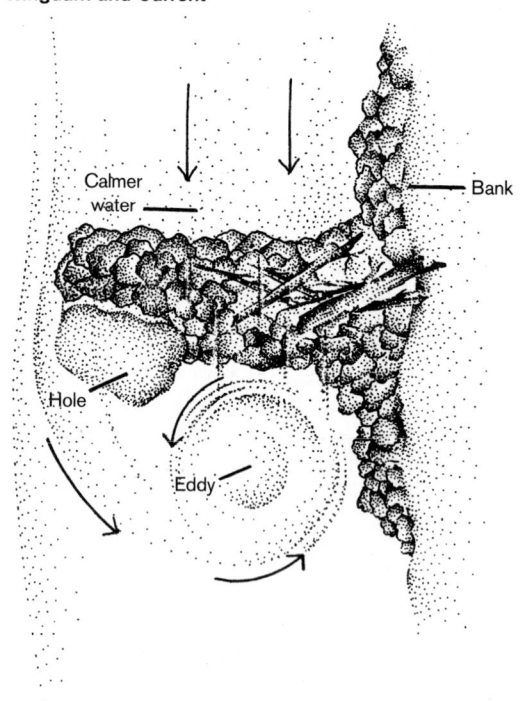

WINTERKILL
See: **Fishkill.**

WIPER
See: **Bass, Whiterock.**

WIRE LEADER
See: **Leader.**

WIRE LINE

Wire line is used by a relatively small but ardent number of both freshwater and saltwater anglers. There is some minor use of it in saltwater for jigging, but it is almost exclusively used for trolling. Wire line trolling is essentially a form of flatlining *(see),* except that the density of wire causes it to sink, bringing a trolled lure or bait down to specific depths. It is used for deep-water probing in freshwater, primarily for lake trout, and for mid- to deep-water bottom probing by inshore saltwater anglers, primarily for striped bass but also for bluefish, wahoo, and king mackerel. Some people do not think there is much sporting virtue in using wire line, and fish caught on wire line are not recognized by the IGFA for world records.

Wire lines are primarily made of single or multiple strands of Monel or stainless steel. Monel is a corrosion-resistant alloy that is more expensive than stainless steel, more pliant, and less prone to kinking. Multiple strand wire is easier to handle but poses difficulties when burrs develop; because it sinks less readily than single-strand wire, it is used

less. It's necessary to use gloves when working with it, because of the possibility of burrs that could slice your flesh.

Wire line doesn't stretch very much and it is very resistant to abrasion; therefore, it makes hookups a little surer and there is less chance of breaking it during a fight with a fish than if you were using other types of line, provided that it doesn't have a kink. Because of low stretch, however, it can contribute to pulling the hooks out of big fish.

Found in various strengths, but primarily used in 30- and 40-pound test, wire line is not as difficult to work with as believed, but it is certainly not as easy as nylon monofilament or weighted line (see) like lead core, and does require some precautions. Wire must be wound on a reel spool under tension, or it will spring off and create a terrible tangle. Tangling, in fact, is possible whenever tension is removed, so when trolling, it's imperative that wire be let out carefully and under controlled tension, usually keeping a thumb on the spool as the line is paid out. You have to get some tension on the lure to be trolled before slowly letting line out. Make sure that the leader, swivel, and any terminal tackle has cleared the rod guides before doing this, or an abrupt stop in the spool will cause an overrun that could be a problem. It helps to hold the rod in your hand and put the tip in the water to get the lure and terminal gear out.

Wire sinks quickly, and if the boat is traveling slowly, it's possible that the wire will sink so fast it gets the lure to the bottom and hangs up. With the boat in forward gear, while letting line out, put your thumb tightly on the spool several times to stop it and to keep the lure from getting hung up. Once underway, on a standard troll, wire will take a lure down 10 feet for every 100 feet let out. To get down 30 feet, therefore, you'd have to let out 300 feet of wire, although you can obtain more depth by using some extra weight and fishing slowly or making turns. Weights up to a pound are used; when using a weight, the length of line out needn't be as great. The tactic here is to troll very slowly and let line out until you feel the sinker hit the bottom. Reel up a turn or two and set the rod in a holder.

One of the benefits of trolling wire is the ability to let out and bring in more as necessary when the bottom depth changes. To know where the lure is you have to know how much line is out. Wire line doesn't hold paint and isn't marked by the manufacturer in lengths, so you have to do this yourself. Because there is no levelwind, you can't count passes to estimate the length of line out, and the pull system isn't practical with such heavy gear, so you'll have to mark wire in specific intervals, usually every 50 feet, to know how much you've set out. One way to do this is to put a short piece of colored adhesive wrap around it.

Some anglers will put a small metal clip on this first wrap to keep leaves, grass, and debris from sliding down the line and fouling the lure. A good

thing about wire line fishing is that, if you have the right kind of rod, you can readily tell if a lure is working properly and when it has gotten some debris on it. It is often not necessary to reel all the line in to remove the debris; jerking the rod back several times may free it. This is one of the big reasons why anglers, especially saltwater anglers, opt for wire over a downrigger. They can tell by watching the rod if a lure is working right, and they can readily adjust for depth and bottom contour changes.

This is heavy-tackle fishing, and big, star-drag reels and stout rods with carbide guides are mandatory. In saltwater, anglers use up to 4/0 to 6/0 reels, in part because they need a lot of winching power to work a fish when a boat keeps moving (if you have a couple of rods out and stop, the wire will take the other lures to the bottom and hang up, or they have to be reeled in). Smaller reels will do the job, however. They needn't be filled entirely with wire line, and usually are filled with 100 yards of wire followed by backing of braided or nylon monofilament. The reel should be nearly full, primarily to let you wind as much as possible on with every turn of the handle. This has to be done under tension. Some tackle shops can wind the line on for you.

Rods need to be equipped with guides that can withstand harsh use. Steel or stainless steel guides will be grooved by wire and can't be used. Silicon and tungsten carbide guides are necessary. Rods must have a lot of power, and actions can charitably

Wire line lays evenly on a conventional reel; it is attached to a nylon leader and a feathered trolling jig.

be described as stiff, although the tips must be limber enough to reflect lure action. Rods specifically meant for wire line trolling are sold by several manufacturers.

Although wire line is very durable, it is subject to kinking and to fatigue. Wire seldom breaks under direct tension but can suddenly break when it is being set out. Kinks are a big problem. If they are severe, the line has to be cut; if they are not too serious, they can be straightened out. If the line is cut, you'll need to use a Haywire Twist (see) to rejoin the sections. Avoid setting the line out in the same spot all the time. Repeated stress (like at the tip guide) in one spot can cause fatigue.

To many anglers, wire line trolling, like trolling with other weighted lines, is not as satisfying as other trolling techniques using lighter and more challenging tackle because fish landing is mostly a reel-cranking, winch-the-fish-up affair. If you catch a giant, it will surely fight well enough for you to know it's there, and you will definitely have a good feel for strikes (although few wire users actually hold the rod when trolling) and for head shakes when a fish is on. But for every giant you hook, you'll catch a lot of smaller fish. On some charter boats, anglers tire quickly of cranking wire lines in. See: Line; Trolling.

WISCONSIN

Few states have the diversity of freshwater habitat that exists in Wisconsin. From the cold depths of Lakes Superior and Michigan to the 231 miles of the Mississippi River to the 15,057 lakes and ponds and 9,560 miles of trout streams, almost every popular species of North American freshwater fish can find a suitable place to thrive. Anglers migrate to Wisconsin like salmon up a river to pursue their sport, and for many years the Badger State has led all other states in the sale of nonresident freshwater fishing licenses and stamps.

Wisconsin straddles the subcontinental divide between the Great Lakes and the Mississippi River drainage basins. Water from the northward-flowing trout streams that enter Lake Superior eventually joins the flow from eastern Wisconsin rivers that drain into Lake Michigan, and exits the Great Lakes via the St. Lawrence River to the Atlantic Ocean. The remaining two-thirds of Wisconsin drains south and west into the Mississippi River and into the Gulf of Mexico. These two great systems each have their own complement of fish species, which contribute to the great variety on the Wisconsin sportfishing menu.

Panfish, which include bluegills, crappie, yellow perch, and white bass, are the most widespread of the angler's quarry, and their tasty fillets make them a perennial favorite. They are found in thousands of lakes and streams and provide both open-water and winter sport.

But it is the large predator fish who live at the top of the aquatic food chain that provide the real excitement. The "big five" in Wisconsin—walleye, muskellunge, northern pike, largemouth bass, and smallmouth bass—steal the spotlight in the cool inland waters.

Walleye have always been extremely popular and inhabit almost all of Wisconsin's 1,107 larger lakes and rivers. Good walleye fishing is available all across the state, led by huge Lake Winnebago, the premier water for this species and home to more than a million adult walleye.

Largemouth bass, smallmouth bass, and northern pike also enjoy a statewide distribution. They thrive in marshy Mississippi River backwaters that are reminiscent of Southern bayous, as well as in crystal-clear lakes of the northern forests that look like the Canadian wilderness.

The muskellunge, however, is the official state fish of Wisconsin. This species is unique to North America, and northern Wisconsin lies in the heart of its original range. For well over 100 years, anglers have pursued these fish, and they have always been viewed as trophies. Wisconsin began propagating and stocking muskellunge fry in 1900, and through stocking has expanded this species' range to more than 700 waters. Nowhere do anglers catch more muskellunge than in Wisconsin.

The inland trout enthusiast has the choice of fishing in 2,674 streams. Brook trout and brown trout are the most common species, and a handful of streams contain rainbow trout. The bulk of these fish are naturally reproducing, and most of the better rivers require no stocking to maintain excellent populations. A few small lakes that are tucked away in the Chequamegon and Nicolet National Forests are stocked annually with trout and offer good fishing.

Wisconsin was one of the first states to protect its most pristine trout streams through the creation of a state wild rivers acquisition program that began in 1965. Almost 50 miles on the Pine, Popple, and Pike Rivers in northeastern Wisconsin have been protected from development and will remain free flowing forever. More than 12,000 acres of adjoining lands are open to the public for fishing and other outdoor recreation.

Across the state, at the western boundary, lies the St. Croix National Scenic Waterway. This wilderness gem was one of the original eight rivers established under the 1968 National Wild and Scenic Rivers Act. The St. Croix flows 25 miles through Wisconsin before it becomes the border river between Minnesota and Wisconsin. The beautiful Namekagon River, which lies completely within Wisconsin, is a part of this system and provides excellent trout fishing. Both rivers have good canoe access sites and offer primitive camping opportunities.

For really large trout and salmon, anglers head to Lakes Superior and Michigan. Lake Superior's waters are best suited for native lake trout, which have rebounded from sea lamprey depredation and overfishing. On Lake Michigan, introduced chinook salmon steal the show, but all the trout species grow

W
X
Y
Z

to mind-boggling sizes in this forage-rich environment. Summer fishing derbies at Lake Michigan ports like Racine, Sheboygan, Manitowoc, Sturgeon Bay, and Marinette attract crowds of onlookers who come to view the trophies as they are registered. It is not uncommon for the winning fish of each species of brown trout, steelhead, and lake trout to all exceed 15 or 20 pounds in a weekend contest. The chinook salmon winners almost always exceed 25 pounds each. Numerous charter boats operate out of these ports, offering a safe and effective way for visiting anglers to sample the fishing on this inland sea.

Although Wisconsin is a relatively small state of 54,000 square miles, it offers great fishing opportunities, and fishing is an important part of its culture. Twenty-five percent of Wisconsin's adult citizens go fishing. They are joined each year by half a million nonresident anglers. The variety of fish available and the excellent access to its lakes and streams fuel Wisconsin's popularity as a fishing destination.

Northern Lakes

State Highway 64 slices across Wisconsin east to west from Marinette to New Richmond. The third of the state that lies north of this road is largely forested and dotted with thousands of inland lakes. Vilas County alone has 1,327 lakes. These lakes are part of the legacy left by the last glacier to cover northern Wisconsin.

Many of the northern lakes appear to be quite similar, but that is not the case. Each has unique qualities, and lakes vary based on physical characteristics like size, depth, and shape. But more important, it's the chemical characteristics of the lake that determine the clarity, productivity, and fishery. Lakes near acidic bogs are stained with natural tannic acid that leaches from surrounding vegetation. The water in these lakes may be as dark as coffee but still harbor a good population of northern pike, yellow perch, crappie, and smallmouth bass.

Just across the ridge from a brown-water lake may be a gin-clear spring lake that gets its water from an underground aquifer. It won't warm up as quickly in the sun as a brown-water lake, and it will probably have a different complement of fish, yet it's just a stone's throw from its neighbor.

When anglers get a hot tip to fish a particular lake in Wisconsin, they had better get an exact location, too, because many bear the same name. There are 116 Mud Lakes, 82 Bass Lakes, 59 Long Lakes, 45 Spring Lakes, and 42 Lost Lakes, plus many that are unnamed.

When the general inland fishing season opens in early May, both northern pike and walleye have usually completed spawning. Water temperatures are still cold, usually near 50°F. Northern pike may remain in shallow waters. When the first warm weather makes its appearance and the water warms up just a bit, these fish feed heavily. Male walleye may still congregate alongshore near spawning grounds. The spent females may be nearby but in deeper water.

By June, muskellunge start to feed aggressively. Panfish move into shallow water in June, and anglers search for their spawning beds in gravel-bottomed areas. Walleye begin to move offshore to deeper rock bars at this time and are predominantly caught on slowly fished nightcrawlers, minnows, and leeches.

Midsummer fishing is never a sure bet anywhere, as northern pike and panfish are tougher to find when they move to deeper water. Two exceptions are muskellunge and smallmouth bass; both species feed heavily during the warmest months. Early morning or late evening is best on lakes with busy boat traffic and water-skiers. In some lakes, walleye move right into the submergent vegetation in 2 to 3 feet of water during the hottest weather, providing fast action on leeches.

Autumn in Wisconsin is not only a beautiful time, but this is also when many of the largest fish of the year are boated. Muskie hunters soak 2-pound suckers trussed up in quick-strike rigs, waiting for that 40-pound fish of a lifetime. Most of the fish species seem to feed heavily in preparation for winter as the days shorten.

Winter fishing can be the most productive of the year for anglers hardy enough to drill through 30 inches of ice and brave the elements. Both walleye and northern pike feed all winter. Live minnows are the most successful bait, but vertically jigging an ice-jig takes plenty of fish. Muskellunge are not legal fare in winter. They are rarely taken through the ice by accident and don't seem to feed in the winter, as do their northern pike cousins. Meanwhile, panfish anglers do well on bluegills, crappie, and perch using light line and tiny, colorful jigs tipped with a tiny grub.

A brief review of the northern counties and opportunities follows.

Oconto County (200 named lakes). The area around Lakewood is famous for clusters of smaller lakes. Many offer excellent northern pike, bass, and panfish angling and are located in the beautiful Nicolet National Forest.

Marinette County (242 named lakes). Big and wild Caldron Falls Reservoir and High Falls Reservoir are angler favorites for walleye and muskies. Lake Noquebay is a well-known panfish lake.

Forest County (194 named lakes). Lake Metonga at Crandon is good for perch and walleye. Beautiful Lake Lucerne and Pine Lake are favorites.

Florence County (101 named lakes). Many of the smaller wildernesslike lakes offer opportunities for northern pike, muskellunge, walleye, bass, and panfish.

Oneida County (428 named lakes). There are many great muskellunge spots among Oneida County's 66,000 acres of water. Excellent fishing abounds for walleye, northern pike, largemouth and smallmouth bass, and panfish.

Why do prey fish school? Individuals are more vulnerable; flash-like escape maneuvers can confuse predators; and usually the slow, sick, or disabled fish become victims.

W
X
Y
Z

Vilas County (561 named lakes). In places, there seems to be more water than land in Vilas County. Many of its lakes are located in the beautiful Northern Highland–American Legion State Forest. All of the popular species are common, including walleye, muskie, northern pike, large- and smallmouth bass, crappie, bluegills, perch, and whitefish.

Iron County (217 named lakes). In Iron County, the sprawling and wild Turtle-Flambeau Flowage covers 14,000 acres. Sixteen natural lakes were flooded when it was created in 1926. It has a super walleye population, but smallmouth bass and muskies are also good. Another wild beauty is the Gile Flowage near Hurley.

Price County (161 named lakes) and **Taylor County** (98 named lakes). Many of the lakes in Price and Taylor Counties are located within the unspoiled Chequamegon National Forest. Anglers willing to carry a canoe can find solitude and great bass fishing on numerous smaller lakes.

Bayfield County (339 named lakes). Best known are Lake Namekagon, Lake Owen, and the Eau Claire Chain, but the whole area is known for walleye fishing.

Ashland County (84 named lakes). Much of this county is wilderness quality with pristine lakes and great trout streams. Day Lake is known to be a good muskellunge water.

Sawyer County (244 named lakes). Most famous is the 15,000-acre Chippewa Flowage, site of the 69-pound, 11-ounce world-record muskellunge. Several other great muskie lakes are Round, Grindstone, Lac Court Oreilles, Chetac, Lost Land, and Teal. Northern pike and walleye are also abundant in these and other waters.

Washburn County (267 named lakes). Excellent fishing for walleye, muskellunge, and northern pike are found here. The bigger lakes like Shell, Long, Spooner, and the Minong Flowage get the most publicity, but knowledgeable anglers explore the lesser-known lakes and do very well.

Burnett County (228 named lakes). Top-notch muskie lakes abound here, but there are good populations of large- and smallmouth bass, and the area is favored by bass anglers.

Polk County (222 named lakes). Many large lakes here provide good action for bass, walleye, and muskies. Best known are Balsam, Deer, Cedar, Wapogasset, and Bone Lakes.

Barron County (124 named lakes). Red Cedar, Bear, Rice, Chetac, and Prairie Lakes offer a wide variety of fish species.

Lake Winnebago

Lake Winnebago is Wisconsin's premier walleye lake and is home to a wide variety of other gamefish, including white bass, sauger, northern pike, smallmouth bass, channel catfish, crappie, and yellow perch. Perhaps its most unusual resident is the lake sturgeon, a freshwater behemoth that can exceed 100 pounds. Although several species of sturgeon are endangered across the United States, Winnebago's lake sturgeon are thriving, and each winter the lake draws thousands of trophy seekers out on the ice for a unique spearing season.

Wisconsin's largest inland lake, at 137,708 acres, measures 28 miles long and 11 miles wide. The average depth is 15 feet, and it doesn't stratify, which makes it good walleye habitat from the surface to the bottom. Being shallow and windswept, Winnebago kicks up rapidly in a wind, so sturdy deep-vee boats are recommended.

Winnebago is not known for producing many huge walleye. Most angler-caught fish are less than 18 inches in length, which is perfect for eating. But 3- to 5-pound fish are common, especially during the spring, when the larger females run the Fox and Wolf Rivers to their spawning grounds. An occasional 10-pound fish is creeled. Although most North American walleye spawn on rocky or gravel shoals and shorelines, Winnebago fish seek out flooded marshes in which to drop their adhesive eggs, sometimes venturing as far as 75 miles upriver from the main lake.

In the spring, some walleye stay in the lake along with the immature fish, but anglers do best when they follow the fish upriver. In April and early May, this means that the best fishing occurs near Oshkosh in and around where the Fox River enters Lake Winnebago. Tens of thousands of spawning-minded walleye and white bass begin to concentrate here in late winter.

A favored fishing technique in the heavy, cold current of April include a three-way swivel rig with live minnows, known locally as a Wolf River rig. A slowly fished jig and a minnow are also popular. As the fish work upstream (the walleye go first and the white bass later in May) to spawn, anglers follow them up the Fox and Wolf Rivers past Winneconne, Fremont, New London, and Shiocton. White bass provide fast and furious action, and crowds of boats get in on the action.

By late May and early June, the walleye are back in Winnebago and feeding actively. Excellent fishing occurs from the many rocky reefs that line the western lakeshore. Trolling works well; wind and rough water will spur a bite. Casting the shallow-water weedbeds is also productive, and a strike could come from not only a walleye but also a smallmouth bass, northern pike, channel catfish, or freshwater drum.

Later in summer, many fish take up a pelagic lifestyle all across the lake. Trolling with bait-imitating plugs and planer boards puts white bass and walleye in the boat. Many freshwater drum are taken this way. Called sheepshead by the locals, most are released, but the skinned fillets are quite good when battered and deep-fried.

Yellow perch are located on the reefs in midsummer. Natural bait work best, followed by nightcrawlers, but local experts use hellgrammites

W
X
Y
Z

(dragonfly nymphs) when the going gets tough. Slip floats work well for perch, as the bait can be suspended near the bottom without its getting hung up on the rocks.

In winter, the lake's frozen surface becomes a playground for anglers and snowmobilers. Thousands of fishing shacks dot the surface, now covered with 2 feet or more of ice. Clubs plow roads so anglers can drive out with their vehicles to fish. Popular spots include Oshkosh, Stockbridge, Brothertown, and Fond du Lac. Tip-ups with minnows fished tight to a silt or clay bottom work well in winter. Jigging also takes many walleye.

Southeastern Lakes

One of the most scenic areas in Wisconsin is the hilly and forested Kettle Moraine region, which was created when the two huge lobes of the last glacier pushed south. Numerous lakes were formed in what is now Manitowoc, Sheboygan, Washington, Waukesha, and Walworth Counties.

Waukesha County has several large and productive lakes with excellent fishing for largemouth bass and panfish. Northern pike are common, walleye are present in some waters, and a few hold muskies. The most popular lakes include Pewaukee, Okauchee, Lac LaBelle, Nagawicka, and Nemahbin. Pewaukee lies just 20 miles due west of downtown Milwaukee. It produces a 40-pound muskie every year or so despite intense fishing pressure.

Farther south in Racine County are Wind, Eagle, and Browns Lakes, all of which have good fishing. Walworth County has two excellent large lakes. One, Delavan Lake, has a thriving walleye population and good numbers of northern pike, largemouth bass, and large bluegills. The other, Lake Geneva, covers 5,262 acres of clear water and is known for smallmouth bass.

To the west, the Yahara Chain of Lakes offers 18,000 acres of highly productive water. Lakes Mendota, Monona, Waubesa, and Kegonsa are most famous for excellent fishing for bluegills, crappie, yellow perch, and white bass. Other species are plentiful, too, and it is not uncommon to hook a 40-inch muskie or a 4-pound largemouth bass with the dome of the state capitol of Wisconsin in downtown Madison in the background.

Big Green Lake near Ripon is Wisconsin's deepest natural lake at 236 feet. Its 7,346 acres of clear, cold water contain an amazing variety of fish. Lake trout provide an excellent trolling fishery in midsummer, plus good ice fishing. A huge population of cisco also provide some unusual action through the ice. These silvery members of the whitefish clan go berserk when hooked, and the fish run from 12 to 18 inches in length. Big Green also contains good numbers of smallmouth bass, northern pike, walleye, yellow perch, white bass, bluegills, and channel catfish. Nearby Lake Puckaway is much shallower and offers largemouth bass along its

Salmon, trout, and walleye draw many boaters to Lake Michigan.

marshy shores; it is a completely different fishery, just 2 miles west of Big Green Lake.

The Wisconsin River and Reservoirs

The Wisconsin River arises in Lac Vieux Desert, a lake straddling the state border with Michigan's Upper Peninsula, and begins its 430-mile journey to the Mississippi River. Smallmouth bass, muskellunge, and walleye are common residents. Huge pines line its banks, and bald eagles nest high in their branches.

The 2,035-acre Rainbow Flowage in Oneida County is the first impoundment of the Wisconsin. This wilderness-type flowage is known for walleye and perch fishing and has excellent boat landings.

Below the dam, the Wisconsin glides around granite boulders on its way south; here it is home to muskellunge, walleye, and smallmouth bass. It passes through the Rhinelander Flowage and bends southwest for about 15 miles over several rapids before it flows through Lake Alice and then Lake Mohawksin in Tomahawk. Both of these flowages have walleye, northern pike, smallmouth bass, muskellunge, and crappie.

From Tomahawk to Wausau are several great areas to float a canoe and fish the river, casting for smallmouth bass that run 12 to 18 inches. The occasional muskie is here, too. Downstream of Wausau lies the Mosinee Flowage, Lake DuBay, and the Wisconsin River Flowage at Stevens Point. Smallmouth bass and walleye are abundant in these reaches.

Below the City of Wisconsin Rapids, the river flows into two of the largest man-made lakes in Wisconsin: 23,000-acre Petenwell Flowage and 14,000-acre Castle Rock Flowage. Both are home to walleye, northern pike, crappie, and muskellunge.

Continuing south, the river is dammed at scenic Wisconsin Dells and again at Prairie du Sac; the latter forms Lake Wisconsin, a popular fishing area for walleye, large- and smallmouth bass, and lake sturgeon. To reach this point, the river has flowed through 21 storage reservoirs.

Downstream of Lake Wisconsin, the river runs free south and west 92 miles to the Mississippi River. The valley along this reach is a scenic marvel of stately bluffs, damp-wooded bottom land, and hundreds of miles of sandy beaches, islands, and sandbars. It will always be permanently preserved in a wild state, because it was established by the state in 1989 as the Lower Wisconsin State Riverway. Plans include the acquisition of 79,000 acres of land to protect the river's environmental corridor.

Fish can and do move all the way from the Mississippi River up to the dam at Prairie du Sac. An amazing 84 species of fish have been recorded in this portion of the river. The angler never knows what may strike here—northern pike, walleye, smallmouth bass, muskellunge, dogfish, drum, longnose gar, carpsuckers, or mooneye. The current can flow upward of 5 miles per hour at times, so the fish usually hide behind the numerous downed trees and in the lee of sandbars. Smallmouth bass will hit within inches of the shore, but for walleye you must fish the bottom. Northern pike like the still backwaters.

Mississippi River

This incredible natural resource defines the boundary between Wisconsin and Minnesota for a distance of 231 miles. The upper Mississippi River is huge, and in most places measures 2 to 3 miles wide.

The Mississippi is much more than a river in this region. It is many rivers, huge riverine lakes, and thousands of potholes, sloughs, and ditches. There are fish everywhere, and more places to fish than an angler could visit in a lifetime. Many of these spots are accessible to the shore angler.

Anglers should become familiar with special features of the river environment that influence the distribution of fish, particularly wing dams and locks. Hundreds of wing dams were constructed during the 1800s to force water to the center of the river to aid navigation. These "piers" of rock rubble were placed perpendicular to the shore and extended out as much as 100 yards.

During the 1930s, the U.S. Army Corps of Engineers constructed a series of locks and dams to create even deeper water for commercial navigation. These dams reconfigured the river into a series of "pools" that lead into one another. The higher water levels now flood over the wing dams, hiding them.

There are 10 locks and dams along the Wisconsin portion of the river; some are only 9 miles apart, whereas the longest span is 44 miles. These are located at or near Red Wing, Minnesota (No. 3); Alma, Wisconsin (No. 4); Buffalo, Wisconsin (No. 5); Winona, Minnesota (No. 5A); Trempealeau, Wisconsin (No. 6); La Crosse, Wisconsin (No. 7); Genoa, Wisconsin (No. 8); Lynxville, Wisconsin (No. 9); Guttenburg, Iowa (No. 10); and Dubuque, Iowa (No. 11).

In essence, the locks and dams modified much of the "wild" or natural appearance of the Mississippi and transformed "Old Man River" into four main types of habitat. Species like largemouth bass and bluegills responded favorably to stillwater, whereas truly riverine fish like paddlefish and sturgeon have suffered.

Tailwaters. Turbulent tailwaters extend about a half mile below each structure. Although fish can migrate upstream through most of the dams during high water, they still temporarily block fish movement, and large numbers of fish build up below all of the structures. This makes for excellent walleye and sauger fishing in late winter. Anglers look for eddies or current breaks where fish are resting in the cold water. These areas, depending on river levels, are good all summer for a host of other species, including channel and flathead catfish, white bass, and freshwater drum.

Backwaters. The upstream sections of each pool look somewhat the same today as they did before the dams. In some instances, there is a maze of sloughs, side channels, flooded forests, and muck-bottomed wetlands. Largemouth bass, bluegills, and northern pike thrive in these stillwaters. Some of the side channels with water flow harbor huge flathead catfish of 25 to 40 pounds. In winter, these backwaters concentrate bluegills, crappie, and yellow perch.

Main channel. Heavy current and copious commercial and recreational boat traffic present challenges to anglers. The navigational channel itself is extremely narrow, and by staying outside the navigational buoys the angler can fish riprap banks for smallmouth bass. The submerged wing dams are the scourge of the boater and ruin hundreds of outboard motor lower units each year because they are unmarked. But walleye and bass anglers love them. As the current slides over the wing dam, some of which are only a foot below the surface, walleye like to lie upstream and bushwhack forage. Crankbaits of all kinds work great along wing dams, and a solid strike could turn out to be any one of a dozen species.

Riverine lakes. Generally, the waters become more open and lakelike as you move downstream toward the dams. There are submerged stump fields out of the channel, which can be great fish habitat for largemouth bass and crappie.

Several of these riverine lakes are so huge they have been given names. Lake Onalaska near La Crosse is a 7,688-acre site and has excellent fishing for largemouth bass and bluegills. Much larger at 25,060 acres, Lake Pepin is of natural origin but is considered part of Pool 4. The Lake Pepin fish community comprises 85 species of fish, including many lesser-known members of the sucker family, such as redhorse and buffalo fish. Dominant gamefish species are sauger, white bass, walleye, northern pike, channel catfish, largemouth bass, and smallmouth bass.

W X Y Z

Stream Trout Fishing

Wisconsin's 2,674 trout streams provide nearly 10,000 miles of trout habitat, and hundreds of miles of top-quality trout fishing water is publicly accessible. These trout streams are found in six general areas.

Northwest forested area. The northwest forest area is wild country for the Midwest. It is home to resident timber wolf packs, deer, elk, and even the occasional moose. Streams in this region drain into the St. Croix and the Chippewa Rivers, and the best-known trout stream is the Namekagon River, a St. Croix National Scenic Riverway. It contains brook, brown, and rainbow trout and has hatches similar to other freestone rivers in Wisconsin. Dozens of tiny native brook trout streams flow through this area and ultimately into the St. Croix and Chippewa Rivers. Many of these sparkling little gems are less than 5 miles in length but contain good numbers of small brook trout. Farther south, other notable streams include the Willow River and the Kinnickinnic near the City of River Falls, and Duncan Creek near the City of Chippewa Falls.

Northeast forested area. The northeast forest area contains big and brawny freestone trout streams that tumble rapidly over large boulders. The streams flow easterly into the Menominee River or into Green Bay of Lake Michigan. The Peshtigo River in Forest and Marinette Counties is big and fast. Its upper watershed is a maze of feeder streams in the nearly wilderness setting of the Nicolet National Forest. Just north lie the drainages of the Pine/Popple and Pike wild rivers, which are fast waters with numerous rapids and waterfalls. Brook trout occupy the headwaters of these rivers, and brown trout predominate in the lower reaches. Anglers who can deal with some brush have no problems finding a place to fish in solitude.

The famous Wolf River is to the west toward Antigo. This is a big, fast, and picturesque freestone river. At 50 yards wide, it rambles through hilly pine forests. The Wolf starts out as a warmwater stream and has numerous whitewater sections in northern Wisconsin. It becomes trout water near Pearson, where the Hunting River joins it. The Wolf offers 34 miles of public trout water. Once it flows into the Menominee Indian Reservation, access is denied. Special regulations protect the river's trout fishery.

Southwestern coulee country. Southwestern Wisconsin is hill country, with steep terrain and almost no lakes. But each valley has a stream, and from Buffalo County all the way south to the Illinois border, there are hundreds of trout streams hidden away in the deep creases of the landscape, all of which drain into the Mississippi River. Brown trout are the most abundant fish in these spring creeks, but both brook and rainbow trout are also present. In the better creeks, the clear but fertile waters support up to 5,000 trout per mile.

In Buffalo and Jackson Counties, the Buffalo River, Elk Creek, the Trempealeau River, and their numerous tributaries are all trout waters. Farther south in Trempealeau and La Crosse Counties, Beaver Creek, the La Crosse River, and Robinson Creek are good streams. Still farther south are the fine waters of the Coon Creek Drainage, Kickapoo, and Bad Axe. Flowing north into the lower Wisconsin River in Grant and Iowa Counties are several popular fly fishing streams: the Big Green River, Crooked Creek, Castle Rock, the Blue River, and Otter Creek.

Central sand country. Glaciers left an indelible imprint in the central sand country. Springs in Portage, Waupaca, Waushara and Marquette Counties are born out of a glacial moraine and flow east into the Fox River or Wolf River drainage basins. Well-known streams like the Tomorrow River, Emmons Creek, the Waupaca, Pine, White, and Mecan Rivers, and Lawrence Creek are like mecca to the trout angler.

Brook, brown, and rainbow trout exist here, and few of these streams require stocking. Much of their required habitat has been permanently preserved through state acquisition, and the trout populations are viable and self-sustaining. Brown trout exceeding 20 inches are caught each year, but the bulk of the fish run from 9 to 15 inches in length. A few sand country streams, like the Mecan and the White River, are famous for large hexagenia hatches in June. Public fishing areas along them provide easy access in many reaches. Warm June evenings find the best spots lined with fly fishers in the twilight, waiting for the hatch.

Lake Superior tributaries. Lake Superior's tributaries are northward-flowing streams with dual personalities. Their upper reaches contain native brook trout and wild brown trout populations, but their lower portions receive migratory runs of steelhead and brown trout, and chinook, coho, and pink salmon.

The most famous is the Bois Brule, a beautiful river almost entirely preserved within the Brule River State Forest. Special early seasons allow the angler to fish the spring run of steelhead, which begins in early April. Steelhead, or migratory rainbow trout, spend the first year or two in the stream and then move to Lake Superior to feed. The males return at 17 inches and larger, but it is common to encounter specimens up to 23 inches in length and an occasional fish to 30 inches and 10 pounds. Large (21 inches) brown trout enter the Brule in August and are soon joined by a fall run of steelhead and the three species of salmon. Hooking a big salmonid in a fast-flowing and often very clear river is hard enough, but landing one among the boulders and fallen logs is a real challenge.

Other streams with Lake Superior runs include the Nemadji, the Flag River, the Cranberry River, Pike's Creek, and the Sioux River. Two systems that are not known for lake-run salmonids are the White

Fossils indicate that over five million years ago the Pacific Ocean contained a giant salmon that was 6 feet long and weighed over 250 pounds.

W
X
Y
Z

Waters throughout Wisconsin are home to muskellunge.

and Marengo Rivers, but their headwaters and upper tributaries are superb water for resident brown and brook trout.

Lake Michigan tributaries.   The rivers that drain eastern Wisconsin's heavily populated regions are too warm to harbor trout populations year-round. Migratory trout and salmon from Lake Michigan, however, are drawn to their temporarily cold waters by the thousands from March through May and again from September through December. Some fish even spend the whole winter in the rivers under the ice.

Three strains of steelhead and both chinook and coho salmon are stocked in Lake Michigan by the Wisconsin Department of Natural Resources (DNR) and by the other states that border Lake Michigan. Most popular of the streams are the Kewaunee, Manitowoc, Sheboygan, Milwaukee, and Root Rivers. Several small tributaries also receive nice runs of fish. The Oconto River, which flows into Green Bay, has a fine run of trout and salmon.

Anglers are surprised to learn that a 10-pound steelhead can be taken on a fly in downtown Milwaukee, literally in the shadow of a freeway overspan or a baseball stadium. These streams have a continuous open season, and a few thousand trophy steelhead and salmon are taken annually. Most of the steelhead run 3 to 7 pounds, but each year several 15-pounders are landed. Spinning gear is popular, and 10- to 15-pound line is a must. Fly anglers use 7- to 9-weight rods with a lot of backing

beneath their fly line. Tippets can be 8 or 10 pounds, as these brawny fish are not leader shy in the often murky waters of April. In autumn, the rivers are low and clear and the fish more skittish.

Lake Michigan

Lake Michigan is the sixth largest lake in the world. Wisconsin occupies 495 miles along its western shore, where 25 permanent streams flow into the lake. The main lake almost never freezes over but can become partially covered with floating pancake ice. Most of Green Bay freezes solidly, depending on the year.

Historically, lake trout and burbot were the top predators of western Lake Michigan. These fish feed mainly on seven species of deep-water cisco and sculpin. The invasion of numerous exotic species changed the mix, and by 1950 the sea lamprey had decimated a lake trout population that was already on the ropes from commercial overharvesting.

The U.S. Fish and Wildlife Service used a selective toxicant to treat the lamprey spawning streams, and federal hatcheries began to restock lake trout in Lake Michigan in 1965.

Wisconsin began its own fisheries rehabilitation program in 1963 by stocking rainbow trout, and then brown trout in 1966, in some of its tributary streams and harbors. Following the State of Michigan's lead, Wisconsin introduced stocks of coho salmon in 1968 and chinook salmon in 1969. With the exotic alewife as forage, the stocked salmon grew rapidly, and a large new sport fishery developed during the 1970s.

Today almost every port has renovated its harbor and launching area. Most provide fish-cleaning facilities and other support services. Hundreds of charter boats are available for those anglers without a boat of their own sturdy enough to tackle a Great Lake.

The fishing season on Lake Michigan is continuous. Even in midwinter, anglers catch brown trout off warmwater discharges such as those at Oak Creek, Port Washington, and the nuclear power plants near Point Beach.

Open-water fishing begins in late March or early April, as trollers dodge icebergs off Door County ports like Baileys Harbor and Sturgeon Bay. Trolling with plugs on light line takes the most browns. The fish average 2 to 3 pounds with an occasional 15- to 20-pound heart stopper. The same technique works well in Green Bay as soon as the ice leaves at Marinette and south.

Coho salmon migrate north from Illinois water in late April or early May. Trolling in the top 30 feet of water with bright-colored flashers and flies produces fast action. The coho average 1 to 3 pounds at this time, and their red orange fillets are excellent table fare.

Anglers land chinook salmon from May through October, but the fastest fishing usually occurs in July. Ports like Kenosha, Racine, Milwaukee,

Sheboygan, Manitowoc, Kewaunee, Algoma, Sturgeon Bay, and Marinette all produce chinook over 20 pounds. Trollers often fish 60 to 100 feet below the surface.

Steelhead are taken all summer almost anywhere out in the open water near the surface. Trolling takes these silvery acrobats, which average 3 to 7 pounds but may approach 20 pounds.

Lake trout remain near bottom in 75 to 150 feet of water for most of the summer and are caught by anglers slow-trolling tight to the bottom. These long-lived fish are getting larger, and each year 30-pounders are landed.

Yellow perch frequent the shallow water of Lake Michigan and are a favorite of the shore angler. Perch have been cyclic in Lake Michigan, and alternate between being extremely abundant to almost rare, depending on their degree of spawning success each June.

Fishing for both yellow perch and salmon is influenced by water temperatures. A strong west wind blows the warm surface water out over the lake, and the cold water upwells along shore; sometimes it is as cold as 46°F in July. This enables salmon to come right into the beach in search of food, so even shore anglers can cast to them. Perch become inactive in this cold water, but a prolonged east wind pushes the warmer water back to shore. This will cause the perch to bite, but it drives the trout and salmon sometimes 8 to 10 miles offshore in search of cooler temperatures.

Door County is the most easterly part of Wisconsin and the peninsula that juts northeast into Lake Michigan. This county alone has 250 miles of shoreline, offering a wide variety of fishing opportunities. Salmon and trout are available, and the shallow, warmer bays of this vacationer's paradise offer superb smallmouth bass fishing. Catches of 30 to 40 bass per day are not uncommon for the experienced angler working out of Sturgeon Bay, Fish Creek, Sister Bay, or Detroit Harbor on Washington Island.

Nearly 100 miles long, Green Bay is the largest bay on Lake Michigan. It behaves differently than the main lake because it is more fertile and shallower. The fish population in southern Green Bay is more typical of the western basin of Lake Erie and contains walleye, yellow perch, white perch, drum, northern pike, carp, white suckers, and channel catfish. In summer, fleets of boats anchor over limestone reefs in search of perch. Farther north at Peshtigo and Marinette, anglers will find excellent fishing for trout, salmon, and smallmouth bass. Brown trout derbies at Marinette in July consistently produce hundreds of huge browns, and it's usually a fish weighing more than 20 pounds that wins.

Lake Superior

Lake Superior is the largest lake on Earth in terms of surface acres (31,800 square miles). It is the deepest, coldest, and most pure of all five of the Great Lakes. Although the 156 miles of its shoreline that lie in Wisconsin are a relatively small part of the lake, it is a very diverse part.

The St. Louis River enters the lake at the extreme western end and forms the border between Minnesota and Wisconsin. A sizable population of the Great Lakes' walleye, nearly 100,000 adults, leave the Wisconsin waters of Lake Superior each April to spawn in the river. The huge St. Louis "estuary" also provides sport for northern pike and yellow perch. It was here that a Wisconsin fisheries biologist discovered the first European ruffe, a small member of the perch family, in 1987. This potential pest continues to expand its range in the Great Lakes.

Fifty miles to the east, the beautiful Bayfield Peninsula juts into the lake, and off its tip lie the spectacular Apostle Islands. This scenic archipelago consists of 22 islands, 20 of which form a national lakeshore managed by the National Park Service. The waters around these islands contain lake trout, brown trout, and steelhead.

The city of Ashland lies at the head of Chequamegon Bay, a large but protected bay that warms up much more than the open lake and is home to a diverse fishery including smallmouth bass, walleye, and perch. Just to the east is the famous Kakagon Slough, a huge maze of wild rice beds and side channels that arise near the entrance of the Bad River. This is part of the Bad River Indian Reservation and is not open to the public without tribal approval.

Much of the Wisconsin portion of Lake Superior freezes over during winter. At ice out in late April, the open-water fishing season begins in Chequamegon Bay, where small coho salmon are caught by trollers. The best fishing is from Washburn to Bayfield, but anglers find coho in many other spots along the shoreline, including the Saxon area and off the city of Superior.

At about the same time, walleye run up the St. Louis River to spawn. These are slow-growing fish, but they can be large and beautiful. The best fishing is in mid-May.

As the water warms up a bit, lake trout move to the surface to feed and are taken high in the water column until mid-July. Trollers must spread out their lines to avoid spooking fish in the crystal clear water. Chinook salmon are taken on spoons in June in many areas, but not in great numbers.

Increasing numbers of siscowet are also taken this way. Siscowet are a subspecies of lake trout found only in Lake Superior that have evolved to survive in its deepest waters, below 55 fathoms. Their extremely high fat content makes them inedible once they exceed about 17 inches in length. It takes experience to identify their slightly rounded snout from that of their close cousin, the lean lake trout, which has excellent flesh.

With the warm weather, a thriving population of smallmouth bass moves into Chequamegon Bay to spawn and spend the summer. This is a trophy

The Pere Marquette River in Michigan was the first stream to be stocked with brown trout in America; the fish were instantly seen as more difficult to catch than native brook trout.

W
X
Y
Z

fishery with some bass over 20 inches in length. Thirty-fish days are common, and many of the smallmouth run 14 to 18 inches.

In September, chinook and coho salmon concentrate off the mouths of rivers like the Brule, Sioux, and Onion.

Water temperatures always greatly influence fishing success in Lake Superior. The open lake rarely warms above 50°F, and when it does, the warm water is just a thin layer on the surface. Strong winds push the water around, so that a fluctuation of 20°F in a day is not unusual. These fluctuations induce the fish to move around. It pays to have a thermometer in the boat.

Ice fishing on Lake Superior is very productive and begins in December, when splake are taken from Washburn to Bayfield in 20 to 50 feet of water. Walleye, northern pike, and perch provide action farther south in Chequamegon Bay. Ice fishing for lake trout, or "bobbing" as the locals call it, starts in late January in water from 70 to 170 feet deep. Ice conditions are often dangerous, and only the experienced or those with a fishing guide should venture out across the numerous cracks and pressure ridges to the bobbing grounds.

Wisconsin Muskellunge

The muskellunge is special in Wisconsin; it has its own following and is the official state fish. Muskie addicts wear T-shirts that proclaim, "To a muskie fisherman, everything else is just bait." Perhaps nowhere else is this species pursued with such fervor.

Although it is closely related to the northern pike in appearance, a muskellunge behaves quite differently. Muskies were never as abundant as pike, and even a good muskie lake today may have only one adult fish for every 2 acres of water. Muskellunge will follow a lure to the boat, often more than once, and sometimes lie on the surface in an unconcerned manner. They are much more inclined to jump than a pike, and grow much larger. Yet, there are plenty of tiger muskies, which are northern pike–muskellunge hybrids. "Natural" tigers are common in Lac Vieux Desert and Big St. Germain in Vilas County, and in several other waters in the upper Wisconsin River drainage.

Wisconsin is the home of the often disputed world-record muskellunge of 69 pounds, 11 ounces, taken in the Chippewa Flowage in 1949. The undisputed world-record tiger muskie was also caught in Wisconsin, a 51-pound, 3-ounce fish that was caught in Lac Vieux Desert in 1919.

Wisconsin lies in the heart of the original range of the muskellunge, and in many lakes here these fish still reproduce naturally. The DNR supplements their populations through stocking. It raises large muskie fingerlings at its two huge fish hatcheries at Spooner and Woodruff. Annual production approaches 100,000 10- to 14-inch fish. These hatcheries also rear the Great Lakes strain of muskellunge, commonly called the spotted muskie. They have been reintroduced into Green Bay waters, where they are becoming a more common catch among anglers.

As a result, Wisconsin leads the world in muskie fishing. These fish are present in 711 lakes and numerous rivers. Anglers land an estimated 100,000 muskellunge a year, 90 percent of which are released. Most fish run between 30 and 40 inches in length, or from 7 to 20 pounds each. A few fish weighing more than 40 pounds are caught each year.

Wisconsin waters receive heavy angling pressure for these fish, and varying length limits have been instituted in an effort to grow more trophy muskies. Some lakes have 45-inch and 50-inch minimum length limits. With these measures, coupled with a growing catch-and-release ethic, the numbers of larger muskies should increase steadily in Wisconsin.

Fishing for muskellunge in Wisconsin begins in late May and runs through November. Smaller baits are preferred in the cold waters of early June, but later, most anglers turn to full-size bucktails and large plugs. Muskie action always picks up in July and August, when anglers use surface lures as well as huge stickbaits or jerkbaits. They take some of the biggest fish in autumn, right until ice-up. Live bait in the form of suckers are preferred, and trophy hunters will use a 17-inch-long sucker in a quick-strike rig.

Although muskies have been known to eat mice, frogs, and even ducks, anglers will do well to remember their preferred foods in Wisconsin are yellow perch, white suckers, and large minnows.

Most anglers use baitcasting reels and stiff rods to handle the heavy baits. Many prefer a nonstretch line to get a better hookset. It is common to see two anglers, each standing in opposite ends of their boat, flinging their lures in an arc over a submerged weedbed. They vigorously work the lure in a figure-eight pattern at the end of each retrieve, hoping to get a strike from this elusive fish.
See: Spoon.

WOBBLER

(1) A generic word for any thin metal spoon, often used for trolling, sometimes for casting; small- and medium-size spoons, especially those used in fishing for lake trout and landlocked salmon, are sometimes referred to as wobblers, especially by anglers in the northeastern U.S., eastern Canada, and in Great Britain.

(2) A generic word for crankbaits or diving plugs, primarily used in Scandinavian countries; plugs that exhibit a strong side-to-side action while diving and swimming may be called wobblers but are distinguished in shape from those with minnowlike bodies.

W
X
Y
Z

WOLFFISH

Eel-like in body shape, wolffish are blenny relatives that live in the cold to arctic waters of the Atlantic and Pacific. They are members of the Anarhichadidae family, which encompasses seven species. Wolffish lack pelvic fins, and the dorsal fin, which begins just behind the head, extends to the caudal fin but is not joined to it. The anal fin extends about half the length of the ventral surface. Wolffish have powerful jaws and numerous broad teeth that are used to crush the shells of mollusks and crustaceans. They also have sharp canine teeth, which makes them dangerous to handle.

The Atlantic wolffish (*Anarhichas lupus*), inhabits the western Atlantic from southern Labrador and western Greenland to Cape Cod, rarely occurring as far south as New Jersey. In the eastern Atlantic, it ranges from Spitsbergen south to the White Sea, along the Scandinavian coasts, into the North Sea, the British Isles, Iceland, and southeastern Greenland. It is also known as, in Danish: *havkat;* Dutch: *zeewolf;* Norwegian: *gråsteinbit;* and Swedish: *havskatt.*

The sides of its brownish gray to purplish body are crossed by as many as a dozen vertical black bars. It is sedentary and rather solitary in habit, and is commonly found at depths of 45 to 65 fathoms. Populations tend to be localized. Although it appears sluggish, it is easily provoked, can move rapidly for short distances, and gives severe bites. Little is known about the biology of this species. Individuals can attain a length of 5 feet and a weight of 40 pounds. They prey on mollusks, crabs, lobster, and sea urchins. The Atlantic wolffish is seldom caught by anglers and is usually taken commercially by otter trawls. It is overexploited and depleted in the western Atlantic.

Also in the North Atlantic and with similar ranges are the spotted wolffish (*A. minor*) and the northern wolffish (*A. denticulatis*). In the North Pacific, the very similar Bering wolffish (*A. orientalis*) occurs in the Sea of Japan and from the Aleutian Islands in Alaska southward to central California. The wolfeel (*Anarrichthys ocellatus*) has a similar range; it reaches a length of 6 feet, 8 inches. These species are also caught by commercial trawlers, as they all make excellent eating despite their ugly appearance.

WOLF RIVER RIG

A bottom fishing bait rig featuring a three-way swivel, weight, and live minnow, derived from anglers fishing for walleyes on the Wolf River in Wisconsin.

WORLD-RECORD FISH

See: Records.

WORM

Any natural earthworm or marine worm; also a soft imitation of the natural object, usually made of plastic. Many types of natural worms exist and are suitable for use as bait, whether whole or in pieces. Imitation worms are primarily used in fishing for largemouth bass, where they are extremely popular and effective, and other soft wormlike lures are used for a variety of fish in freshwater and saltwater.
See: Lure; Natural Bait.

WORM HOOK

A hook for use with various soft lures, especially artificial worms.
See: Hook; Soft Worm.

WRASSES

Wrasses are members of the Labridae family, an extremely varied group of some 500 species that are most abundant in warm seas around the world, although some occur in temperate to cool waters. Projecting canine teeth and thick, protrusible lips give the face a distinctive profile. Many species are brightly colored, and the body is elongated. The spiny and soft dorsal fins are united as one, and the anal fin is the same size and shape as the soft-rayed portion of the dorsal fin. Typically, the pectoral and caudal fins are rounded, and the caudal peduncle is clearly set off from the body.

The color of wrasses varies greatly, often differing from young to mature fish and becoming different during the breeding season, as well as changing with the background over which the fish swim. Most species are greenish, but they may be marked with red, yellow, or blue. Smaller species are

W
X
Y
Z

Atlantic Wolffish

Ballan Wrasse

collected for aquariums. Many smaller wrasses of tropical reefs practice the unusual habit of cleaning parasites from the bodies of larger fish.

Prominent angling wrasses along North American coasts are the California sheephead *(see: sheephead, California)* and the tautog *(see).* Some species are prominent in the warm waters of Florida, the Bahamas, and Bermuda, including the hogfish *(Lachnolaimus maximus),* which is one of the larger-growing members of the clan and has been caught to nearly 20 pounds. The largest of the family is the humphead wrasse *(Cheilinus undualtus),* which is also known as the giant wrasse or giant Maori wrasse; the all-tackle world-record fish weighed 43 pounds, 10 ounces, but these fish can attain much greater weights and have been reported to exceed 6 feet in length. They inhabit Indo-Pacific waters. The ballan wrasse *(Labrus bergylta)* is a common eastern Atlantic species that occurs from Norway and Scotland to northwestern Africa, and grows to roughly 10 pounds.

Wrasses are predominantly reef, rock, and wreck dwellers. Anglers catch them principally by bottom-fishing with baits. They are caught from small boats inshore, from party boats, and from some piers or jetties.
See: Inshore Fishing.

WRECK

Shipwrecks are a type of man-made structure common to the coastal continental shelf waters of many oceans. Resting on the ocean floor, often near bare stretches of mud bottom, they are conspicuous fish attractants and may hold a variety of pelagic as well as bottom species during the season, some offering year-round fishing.

The general location of some wrecks is well known and published on charts and in various publicly available literature. Many are unpublicized, found by luck or by plenty of searching, and their locations are shared with relatively few others. The locations of some are zealously guarded, especially by party boat and charter boat captains.

When the Loran or GPS coordinates of wrecks are known, they are located by using these navigational devices; this is not an automatic thing, because a grid search pattern is usually necessary to pinpoint the exact location of the wreck.

Pinpointing these locations is done in combination with using narrow-cone-angle sonar both to find the main or high point of the wreck as well as to find nearby rubble and baitfish.

Wrecks may be fished via trolling and drifting, but the primary tactic is to anchor and chum. Precise anchoring over the high point of the wreck is essential to properly fishing it. When anchored, some fishing occurs near the surface when fish are attracted to the chum, but most fishing is deep—on or close to the bottom—with bait, baited jigs, or heavy metal jigs, although many of the latter are lost owing to hangups.

Depending on current, fish may be on one side or the other of the wreck, although some species cluster in the wreck and others are found nearby. Some of the best wrecks have large fields of debris within a few hundred feet of the main wreck location.
See: Anchor; Chumming; Drift Fishing; Inshore Fishing; Jigging.

WRECKFISH   *Polyprion americanus.*

Other names—bass, stone bass, wreck bass, hapuku; Afrikaans: *wrakvis;* Danish: *vragfisk;* Dutch: *wrakbaars;* Finnish: *hylkyahven;* French: *chernier commun, mérot gris;* Greek: *vláchos;* Icelandic: *rekaldsfiskur;* Italian: *cherna di fondale;* Norwegian and Swedish: *vrakfisk;* Portuguese: *cherne;* Spanish: *cherna;* Turkish: *iskorpit hanisi.*

A member of the Polyprionidae family and related to the giant sea bass, the wreckfish is a very deep-dwelling and large-growing species occasionally caught by heavy-tackle anglers probing extreme depths. It is marketed fresh or frozen, sometimes as sea bass or stone bass, although it is susceptible to overfishing and is regulated in U.S. federal waters.

Identification.   The wreckfish has a deep, strongly compressed body and a very bumpy head with a ridge and bony protuberances above the eye. Adult fish are uniformly dark brown or bluish gray, and the young are mottled. The second dorsal, as well as the caudal and anal fins, are often edged in black, although the rounded caudal fin is otherwise edged in white, as are the pectoral fins. The spinous and soft parts of the dorsal fins are notched, and the lower jaw projects past the upper jaw.

Size.   The wreckfish grows slowly but can eventually reach 7 feet or more in length and weigh 100 or more pounds. The all-tackle world record is a 106-pound, 14-ounce fish taken off Portugal.

Distribution.   In the eastern Atlantic, the wreckfish is found from Norway to South Africa, including the Madeira, Canary, and Cape Verde Islands, and the Mediterranean. In the western Atlantic, it ranges from Newfoundland to North Carolina. In the western Indian Ocean, it inhabits the St. Paul and Amsterdam Islands and has been reported from New Zealand.

Habitat.   Found in the deep part of the continental shelf, at up to 2,000-foot depths, wreckfish

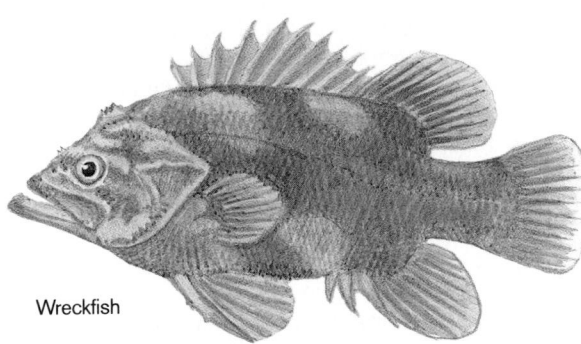

Wreckfish

prefer rocky ledges, pinnacles, and outcroppings around shipwrecks. They are solitary fish and are sometimes found drifting with floating timber or other objects.

Food. Wreckfish feed on crustaceans, mollusks, and deep-dwelling fish found around wrecks or underwater objects.

Angling. Wreckfish are typically caught by anglers using very heavy gear, strong lines, heavy weights, and large hooks baited with fish strips or chunks. They land wreckfish primarily by fishing at the right depth over an irregular bottom. The appropriate depth can vary from 200 feet to 1,000 or more feet; keeping large specimens from cutting the line on bottom obstacles and then winching them to the surface are tough requirements. The amount of weight to use varies with depth, current, and site, but it's important to present the offering right on the bottom.

See: **Inshore Fishing.**

WYOMING

Wyoming is a big place with no large cities, few people, and little industry. This western state has more pronghorn antelope than people and ranks 50th among the states in population. Yet its open spaces and fish and wildlife draw tourists, who flock to such national forests as Shoshone, the first national forest preserve, and Yellowstone National Park, the first national park. People also come to view the unique and spectacular scenery and to participate in the state's phenomenal hunting and fishing opportunities.

Within its 97,809 square miles, Wyoming boasts high plains, mountains, deserts, and badlands. There are many plateaus with elevations between 4,500 and 7,500 feet. In the southeast corner, the Laramie Mountains rise to more than 10,000 feet, and the Medicine Bow Mountains reach 12,005 feet at Medicine Bow Peak. In the north-central area, the Bighorn Mountains jump to 13,165 feet on Cloud Peak. In the northwest corner, Francs Peak in the Absaroka Range rises to 13,140 feet. The Grand Teton in the Teton Range points to 13,766 feet, and Wyoming's highest mountain, Gannett Peak, is in the Wind River Range and rises to 13,785 feet. Many other peaks in the Wind River Range eclipse 13,000 feet.

Just about everything runs downhill out of Wyoming. The state's headwater status provides water for four important drainage systems—the Missouri-Mississippi, the Great Basin, the Columbia, and the Colorado.

Most of Wyoming drains to the north and east into the Missouri-Mississippi system. Tributaries of the Missouri River include the Yellowstone, Clark's Fork, Bighorn, Tongue, and Powder Rivers flowing north, and the Cheyenne, Niobrara, and North Platte Rivers flowing east. The major source of the Colorado River is the Green River. The Snake River and Salt River join and flow into the Columbia system. And the Bear River, part of the Great Basin system, flows along Wyoming's western edge and dumps into the Great Salt Lake in Utah.

Wyoming's fishing bounty derives from hundreds of small, clear mountain streams and lakes. The state's largest freshwater mountain lakes are the Yellowstone, Shoshone, Fremont, and Jackson. Other small bodies of water are man-made due to reclamation projects. The major reservoirs include Seminoe, Pathfinder, Alcova, Glendo, and Guernsey Reservoirs in the North Platte River system, and Boysen Reservoir and Bighorn Lake (Wind River/Big Horn River), Buffalo Bill (Shoshone River), and Flaming Gorge Reservoir (Green River).

Southeast
North Platte River (Colorado line to Seminoe Reservoir). The North Platte River cuts a 300-mile swath through the mountains to the plains and defines fishing in Wyoming's southeast corner. Almost 90 miles of the North Platte are classified by the Wyoming Game and Fish Department as Class I, or blue-ribbon, waters. This classification means that these 90 miles are premium trout waters and fisheries of national importance. Float-fishing for rainbow and brown trout down the undisturbed upper river is one of the most beautiful adventures in the West. The best time for float fishing is from mid-June through July.

Seminoe Reservoir. The first impoundment on the North Platte River system, Seminoe Reservoir spans 21,000 acres and is one of the best fisheries in Wyoming. It produces big rainbow and brown trout, as well as walleye. Spring is a good time for big trout, and walleye fishing improves as the water warms.

Miracle Mile. Two trophy-trout tailwater fisheries draw the most attention from anglers pursuing big rainbow and brown trout: the famous so-called Miracle Mile between Seminoe and Pathfinder Reservoirs, and the Gray Reef area below Alcova Reservoir.

Today, the Mile rarely offers a solitary experience. No matter what Wyoming's weather, a few anglers always seem to be on the Mile, although the fishing can still be very good. The Mile actually

averages 5 to 8 miles in length, from Kortes Dam below Seminoe Reservoir to the backwaters of Pathfinder Reservoir; in drought years, it can be up to 15 miles long.

Pathfinder Reservoir.   You can't see the North Platte River make its big turn to the east anymore, because all 22,000 acres of Pathfinder Reservoir conceal the evidence. That's good news for anglers in search of trophy rainbow trout and big walleye.

Alcova Reservoir.   Good fishing for trout and walleye can be found at 2,260-acre Alcova Reservoir, which produces among the biggest walleyes in the North Platte system. Fishing for brown trout can yield impressive results, especially in the fall. Don't expect a quiet trip to Alcova during the summer; weekends draw Casper-area people who own personal watercraft and speedboats.

Gray Reef.   Some of the state's best year-round trout fishing occurs on the tailwaters of Gray Reef Dam. Large trout are often caught between November and March in the river's warmer waters that don't freeze. Even during high periods, the water below Gray Reef Dam stays clearer and more fishable than in other places on the Platte.

North Platte.   (Alcova to Glendo Reservoir). From Alcova Reservoir to Edness Kimball Wilkins State Park at Casper, the North Platte is one of Wyoming's best stretches of big river. Fishing here is good for rainbow trout, and big browns are sometimes taken. The highest trout densities are in the stretch of river from Lusby public fishing area to Gray Reef, and at The Narrows. Below Casper, the North Platte is a marginal trout fishery because its flow slows and the water warms. Persistent anglers can catch catfish and walleye throughout this stretch.

Glendo Reservoir.   There's good fishing for walleye, catfish, and yellow perch on Glendo Reservoir's 15,000 acres. Most Glendo walleye are taken around islands and rocky points in the upper part of the reservoir, and downstream they're taken near the dam. Catfishing is best near where the North Platte River flows into the reservoir. Yellow perch fishing on Glendo can be good almost anytime or anywhere. Like other Platte reservoirs, Glendo is a busy place on the weekends, so weekdays offer the best fishing.

North Platte below Glendo Reservoir. Between Glendo Dam and Wendover Siding, almost the only fishing pressure is applied by floating anglers. The fishing can be good for rainbow, brown, and cutthroat trout from April through early May, and in September and October. Several miles of publicly accessible water below Glendo Dam can produce good fishing for bank anglers, too.

Encampment River.   For those who are prepared to walk, the Encampment River is a good bet for brown, rainbow, cutthroat, and brook trout. The Encampment begins on the Continental Divide in Colorado and flows north into Wyoming along the eastern flank of the Sierra Madre. It flows gently through Commissary Park to Entrance Falls, where, for the next 18 miles, it drops through a steep, forested canyon known as the Encampment River Wilderness Area. Here, fishing for brown and rainbow trout is best usually in late summer or fall, after the runoff peaks.

The lower part of the Encampment River flows through a series of ranches as it nears its confluence with the North Platte River, and public access is limited.

Hog Park Reservoir.   Above the Encampment River is 695-acre Hog Park Reservoir and the creek bearing its name, Hog Park Creek. The creek merges with the Encampment River near Entrance Falls. Brown, rainbow, and brook trout inhabit the creek and are a challenge to catch. The creek's undercut banks and pools provide refuge for some of its bigger trout. Nearby beaver ponds and other small creeks offer good fishing for brook trout.

Hog Park Reservoir is a popular place for families to fish. Productive angling for cutthroat, rainbow, and brook trout keeps these families coming back year after year.

Little Snake River.   Several branches of the Little Snake River flow off the west slopes of the Sierra Madre. The rare Colorado River cutthroat calls them home, and these colorful trout are protected by catch-and-release regulations. The best fishing is in the higher elevations for cutthroat and brook trout. Rainbow trout are common on the river near the Colorado border. Public access is very limited on the lower stretches of river.

Sweetwater River.   The North Platte's largest tributary, the Sweetwater River, flows into Pathfinder Reservoir. Fishing for rainbow and brown trout is fair to good on the Sweetwater in the late summer and fall, after the runoff ends and the water clears. Be prepared when planning a fishing excursion on the Sweetwater—it's a long way from the Sweetwater to any town. More than 75 miles of public-access fishing is available on the Sweetwater, but these public areas are in some of Wyoming's most remote places. The lower parts of the river, below Sweetwater Station, meander through ranching country. Permission to fish is required in the lower parts of the river.

Laramie Plains lakes.   The Laramie Plains lakes are north, south, and west of Laramie, and they are known for producing fat, fast-growing trout. They are also famous for their winds, and are fished fairly hard all year. They produce nice fish for people with patience, who show up early and stay late in the day.

Lake Alsop is west of Laramie on Herrick Lane. The action is usually slow for rainbow and cutthroat trout, splake, and grayling. Early mornings and late evenings are the best times to fish on points bordered by deep water.

Fishing at Lake Hattie west of Laramie offers particularly diverse fishing. Anglers can catch yellow perch, rainbow, cutthroat, and brown trout, kokanee salmon, and lake trout. The action isn't as good at 1,500-acre Hattie as at other Plains lakes, but the chance of catching a big fish is better. Action is usually best when the wind isn't blowing, making early morning and later afternoon best bets.

Lake Gelatt, west of Laramie, offers fair fishing for rainbow trout and grayling. The lake's bigger fish are generally caught just after the ice melts. Action during the fall is usually fair.

Twin Buttes Reservoir can provide fast action for yellow perch early and late in the day. Fishing for trout is only fair, because the yellow perch are doing so well in the lake.

Spring is usually the best time to fish Sodergreen Lake, west of Laramie. The lake is stocked early each year with rainbow trout. Fishing is best early in the day when the winds are calm.

Pole Mountain beaver ponds. More than 100 beaver ponds dot the Sherman Mountains between Cheyenne and Laramie. Fishing varies depending on water conditions and beaver activity, but where there's a pond, the fishing is usually good for brook trout. Big fish are unusual, but catching lots of little ones is the norm. Fishing is good throughout the season and is best at sunrise, sunset, and after dark.

Snowy Range waters. The Snowy Range is roughly 50 miles west of Laramie. Nearly 100 lakes and several hundred streams are there. Fishing is good for small trout, especially in areas accessed by a considerable hike. Lake Owen and Rob Roy are the largest reservoirs in the Snowy Mountains and provide good seasonal trout fishing.

Laramie Peak country. Wheatland Reservoir No. 3, at 7,600 acres, is one of Wyoming's best reservoirs for big rainbow, brown, and cutthroat trout. The fishing is best in April and early May, and from late September until the lake freezes. Angling pressure is high in the spring.

Toltec Reservoir is north of Wheatland No. 3 in one of Wyoming's most remote areas. Fishing can be good for medium-size rainbow and brook trout. Angling is usually best early and late in the day in spring and fall. Roughly 6 miles of public land allow access to Duck Creek, where there's fair fishing for small rainbow, brown, and brook trout.

Other sites. Hawk Springs Reservoir is southeast of Hawk Springs and the best fishery in the area, boasting good-size walleye, largemouth bass, catfish, yellow perch, and crappie. Anglers sometimes catch nice brown trout as well. Most people fish 1,100-acre Hawk Springs for its walleye, though, either early in the morning or in the evening.

Packers Lake east of Yoder offers fair fishing for walleye, catfish, and rainbow trout. Some bass are also caught. Grayrocks Reservoir east of Wheatland is the best walleye lake in Wyoming. Action for walleye is excellent all over this 3,500-acre lake, which also contains yellow perch, crappie, smallmouth bass, and tiger muskies.

Northeast

Tongue River. The rewards in fishing the Tongue River while viewing the scenery along the way are worth the extra effort required to reach this water. Anglers making the trip can expect to sample classic pocket water for cutthroat, rainbow, and brown trout.

The upper river holds good-size trout, and fall spawning runs bring larger brown trout upriver. Downstream, the river flows through private lands, and permission is required to access this area of good brown trout fishing.

The North Tongue is a gentle stream with a healthy population of Yellowstone cutthroat and smaller numbers of rainbow and brook trout. It receives a lot of pressure, as the size of its fish are steadily increasing due to catch-and-release efforts.

The South Tongue is a small, cascading stream. The best fishing is along the stream's 7-mile descent between Tie Plume and Prune Creeks for rainbow and brook trout.

Northern Bighorns lakes. Sibley Lake is between Dayton and Burgess Junction. It's a popular alpine fishery for cutthroat and brook trout, and requires a short hike to get there. Sawmill and Twin Lakes offer good to fair fishing for cutthroat, rainbow, and brook trout. Cutthroat and rainbow trout are usually part of the creel at Park Reservoir.

Cloud Peak Wilderness. The Cloud Peak Wilderness offers more than 189,000 acres of wilderness land in the Bighorn Mountains, and more than 200 trout-filled lakes are scattered like dots across the range. Hundreds of streams run through the drainages and fill the lakes. Although trout in the lakes are bigger than fish in the streams, the stream fishery is better. Anglers can catch rainbow, brook, and cutthroat trout, as well as grayling and lake trout in the Bighorns.

Among the popular destinations are Seven Brothers Lakes, Lake Angeline, and Willow Park Reservoir. Lake Solitude and West Tensleep

Clear mountain streams, like the Little Laramie River here, provide good trout fishing throughout Wyoming.

Lake are especially scenic. Tensleep Creek and Meadowlark Lake on the west side of the Bighorns are popular, too.

Middle Fork Powder River. Public access to Middle Fork Canyon is southwest of Kaycee. It takes a little extra effort to get there, but it's worth it. Good-size rainbow and brown trout live in the deep canyon pools. Roughly 10 miles of public access water is available to anglers in the canyon.

Sand Creek. Sand Creek is a spring creek that flows through the eastern foothills of Wyoming's Black Hills and is home to a large population of brown trout. These fish, and their creek, pose a challenge. Undercut banks and a summer growth of weedbeds make the fishing tough.

Keyhole Reservoir. Between Sundance and Moorcroft lies Wyoming's premier northern pike fishery, 9,000-acre Keyhole Reservoir. It holds a variety of other warmwater species, including walleye, catfish, crappie, and smallmouth bass.

Fishing for walleye is best in May and June. Northern pike fishing is best early in the spring at Mule Creek Bay on the southeast side of the reservoir, at Eggie Creek Bay on the northern end, or at Cottonwood Bay between the dam and marina.

The reservoir's smallmouth bass are small but fun to catch and are best caught from June through August early and late in the day. The catfishing is good from spring through fall, mainly at night. Keyhole is crowded on summer weekends. Only a few diehard anglers fish the lake during the week.

Prairie reservoirs. Lake DeSmet, north of Buffalo, has a healthy population of Eagle Lake rainbow trout. Yellowstone cutthroat trout and large brown trout are also caught here. The 3,220-acre DeSmet is the most popular lake in the region, and fishes well until the water warms and forces trout deeper. DeSmet fishing is especially good in the fall.

Muddy Guard Reservoir No. 1, southeast of Buffalo, has rainbow and brown trout, as does its twice-larger sibling, Muddy Guard Reservoir No. 2; both fish easier in the spring. Healy Reservoir, east of Buffalo, is a small but popular site and receives significant pressure. Fishing for Healy's rainbow and cutthroat trout is best in the spring.

Northwest

Wind River. The Wind River originates at Wind River Lake at the base of Togwotee Pass northwest of Dubois. By the time it reaches Dubois, it's a good-size stream and the fishing, although challenging, can be good. This is the best stream in central Wyoming.

From Stoney Point northeast of Dubois, the Wind River offers excellent fishing for about 8 miles. Anglers can catch rainbow, brown, and cutthroat trout, plus whitefish. Fishing is best from mid-August through fall, when the water is low and clear.

Below Dubois, the Wind River enters the Wind River Indian Reservation. A special license is required to fish that section. Two miles of the Wind below Boysen is a popular but profitable tailwater fishery. It yields good-size rainbow and brown trout, walleye, and ling. The best time to fish this stretch is from March through early May.

At the end of this 2-mile segment, the Wind River again enters the Wind River Indian Reservation. This 15-mile section is a pocket-water secret, even though a main highway runs beside it through Wind River Canyon. A special permit is required throughout the canyon up to where the river flows under the highway bridge. There, at the Wedding of the Waters, the Wind River's name changes to the Big Horn River.

Big Horn River. The best fishing on the Big Horn River begins south of the town of Thermopolis and extends nearly 20 miles past Wind River Canyon. Fertile waters here produce trophy rainbow, brown, and cutthroat trout. The rest of its 130-mile trek travels north through sagebrush country to Bighorn Lake near the Montana border. The warmer water supports catfish, sauger, and a few brown trout as it nears Bighorn Lake and the Yellowtail Dam in Montana.

The best place to fish for walleye and catfish on Bighorn Lake is generally around Horseshoe Bend. Action is best in May and June.

Wind River Indian Reservation. The 2.3-million-acre Wind River Indian Reservation receives very little angling pressure, but the fishing opportunities are some of the best in the West. The fishery is open during the spring and summer, and special permits are required. Many lowland and alpine venues exist on the reservation, and anglers catch big trout, grayling, and walleye.

Boysen Reservoir. Boysen Reservoir, north of Shoshone, features good rainbow and cutthroat trout fishing in spring. The face of the dam, the bay at the boat ramp, and rocky points along the northeastern shore are productive areas. Fishing for walleye heats up in June. It remains fair or good throughout the summer. The 15,000-acre lake also has ling, crappie, and its perch are particularly sought after. Pressure at Boysen can be heavy on holidays but is moderate the rest of the year.

Foothills fishing. Northwest of Dubois is Brooks Lake, situated in a breathtakingly scenic area. It offers good fishing for rainbow trout, lake trout, and splake. The fishing is best shortly after the ice melts, and in the fall. Upper and Lower Jade Lakes, Upper Brooks Lake, and Rainbow Lake are short hikes from Brooks Lake.

Three popular lakes are east of Dubois: Torrey, Ring, and Trail Lakes. All are home to rainbow, brown, and lake trout, and splake. These lakes fish best in the spring and fall. Near these is Jakey's Fork, a nice trout stream with good summer fishing for browns.

Northwest of Dubois is Horse Creek, which has fair to good fishing for brook, rainbow, and brown trout. The Wiggins Fork River, the East Fork River,

**W
X
Y
Z**

and Bear Creek near Dubois have cutthroat trout, which are caught where there's decent cover.

Ocean Lake, 15 miles northwest of Riverton, is a 6,100-acre reservoir that offers fair walleye fishing from mid-May through June. A few perch, crappie, largemouth bass, and ling are also taken. Pilot Butte Reservoir, west of Kinnear, produces some rainbows as well as big ling.

Local anglers refer to Lake Cameahwait as Bass Lake for its good numbers of largemouth bass. Located near the west shore of Boysen Reservoir, Cameahwait also harbors rainbow trout and perch. The bass fishing is best in June. Middle Depression Reservoir is a rainbow trout fishery west of Lake Cameahwait.

Louis Lake, northeast of Atlantic City, offers fair to good fishing for brook and rainbow trout. Occasionally anglers catch nice-size lake trout. The action is best right after ice out. Northwest of Atlantic City, Rock Creek Reservoir offers good angling for small and medium-size brook and rainbow trout.

Frye and Fiddlers Lakes and Worthen Meadows Reservoir offer fair to good fishing for small and medium trout. The action is best in spring and fall, early and late in the day.

Carmody Lake, Antelope Springs Reservoir, and Silver Creek Reservoir are between Lander and Jeffrey City. All three fisheries produce nice rainbow trout in the spring and fall.

Popo Agie River. The Popo Agie forms at Lander after collecting the flows of its mountain tributaries. The Popo Agie and its tributaries provide good fishing for rainbow and brown trout. Larger brown trout run upstream from Boysen Reservoir to spawn in the fall, and walleye are also present in the river.

The Little Popo Agie—10 miles south of Lander—the North Fork of the Popo Agie, and the Middle Fork of the Popo Agie have good summer and fall fishing for rainbow and brown trout. The Middle Fork also has brook trout.

The high lakes. The waters on the east side of the Wind River Range are known for golden trout and long hikes. This country probably holds the world's best golden trout fishery. Unfortunately, perhaps, a hike of up to 20 miles is required to reach it.

Trips into the wilderness areas above Lander and Dubois probably shouldn't be attempted until after mid-July. Until then, hikers will likely encounter snowdrifts and frozen water. Anglers who make the trip find good fishing for rainbow, brook, lake, and brown trout as well. Fishing is best in August and September.

Clark's Fork River. The Clark's Fork, northwest of Cody, is Wyoming's only Wild and Scenic River. It runs south from Montana into Wyoming from the Absaroka Mountains. Its 66-mile run through Wyoming offers good fishing for Yellowstone cutthroat, rainbow, and brook trout.

Grayling, whitefish, and brown trout add to the selection below Clark's Fork Canyon on the river's desert path back into Montana. The whitefish action is excellent.

Tributaries of the Clark's Fork, such as Sunlight, Crandall, and Dead Indian Creeks, offer good fishing for Yellowstone cutthroat, rainbow, and brook trout. Above Sunlight Creek's headwaters are the three Copper lakes, which harbor golden trout. Swamp Lake is home to some trophy brook trout.

Beartooth Wilderness lakes. More than 100 lakes are fishable in the Beartooths. The fishing is good after the snow and ice melts from the region. Anglers catch Yellowstone cutthroat, brook, rainbow, golden and lake trout, grayling, and splake.

Shoshone River. The North Fork of the Shoshone River and its tributaries offer excellent fishing for Yellowstone cutthroat throughout the year, and the fishing is best from spring through fall. The South Fork of the Shoshone River has good-size brown trout in the summer and fall, when anglers can catch them. Farther upstream, the South Fork has above-average brook and cutthroat trout.

The Shoshone River offers excellent fishing between Buffalo Bill Dam and Willwood Dam between Cody and Powell. This big tailwater river often gives up big brown, cutthroat, and rainbow trout, and the fishing is good throughout the year.

Buffalo Bill Reservoir. Buffalo Bill Reservoir west of Cody is the most popular fishery in the area. Excellent fishing for rainbow and cutthroat is the norm. The 4,900-acre lake also gives up arm-length lake trout. The best fishing times are spring and early summer, and during midweek. The reservoir receives a lot of angling pressure throughout the year.

Other sites. East Newton Lake, north of Cody, is famous for trophy rainbow and golden trout. West Newton Lake offers good fishing for cutthroat and brook trout.

Beck Lake, southeast of Cody, is known for rainbow trout, largemouth bass, yellow perch, and catfish. Fishing pressure is heavy on the weekends, and moderate during the week.

Deaver Reservoir, south of Frannie, has good fishing for small and medium rainbow trout. The reservoir also contains largemouth bass, sunfish, and bluegills.

Upper Sunshine and Lower Sunshine reservoirs are southwest of Meeteetse. Both have fair to good fishing for cutthroat trout and splake.

Luce and Hogan Reservoirs, both north of Cody, are home to good numbers of rainbow, cutthroat, and brook trout. The fishing is fair in spring and fall, and slow in summer.

Renner Reservoir, northeast of Ten Sleep, boasts a good population of largemouth bass. Fishing pressure is heavy on weekends, and angling is best in the mornings and evenings from spring to early summer. Wardell Reservoir, south of Otto, provides good fishing for walleye and crappie.

According to *The Guinness Book of Records,* the longest recorded individual fight with a fish is 37 hours, which occurred in 1989 with a king (chinook) salmon.

W
X
Y
Z

Yellowstone National Park

America's oldest national park offers better fishing than most states. That's because fish harvest is tightly regulated, the park has plenty of water, and it contains arguably the best trout habitat in the lower 48 states.

Yellowstone Lake is the most famous and most fished water in the park. This 87,000-acre lake provides a world-renowned Yellowstone cutthroat trout fishery. It also contains lake trout, and park officials encourage harvesting of this introduced species to minimize predation on cutthroat. Fishing success usually drops off on Yellowstone Lake several days before and after a full moon.

The Yellowstone River flows south to north from its headwaters above Yellowstone Lake until it leaves the park near Gardiner, Montana. This is a big, fast-moving river, so weight is handy in trying to reach the fish. Action is hot for cutthroat trout, usually around mid-July.

The Firehole River flows southwest of Old Faithful geyser until it joins the Gibbon River to form the Madison River at Madison Junction. The Firehole is full of rainbow, brown, and brook trout. Despite this, fishing can be slow. The action is usually best early and late in the season, the best locations are near the mouths of its tributaries, where the water is cooler.

The Madison follows the highway from Madison Junction to the park's boundary north of West Yellowstone, Montana. It's loaded with big trout, but they can be tough to catch. Anglers who avoid midday and midsummer fishing usually have the best success.

Slough Creek is accessible east of Tower Junction. Anglers can find good fishing all along the foot trail. It's easy to see and stalk Slough Creek's big cutthroat trout.

The highway follows Gibbon River east of Norris Junction until it joins the Firehole at Madison Junction. Anglers experience steady fishing along Gibbon for small rainbow and brook trout. Angling for whitefish and brown trout is better near the Firehole confluence.

Lewis Lake is north of the park's south entrance along the main highway. This fishery is good for lake and brown trout. Angling is best early and late in the season.

Gardiner River flows north to south through the park wilderness before joining Obsidian Creek south of Mammoth. The Gardiner is perhaps the park's best brook trout fishery, and some nice browns are caught in its lower section.

The Lamar River flows northwesterly across the northeast corner of the park. It offers almost 50 miles of good fishing for cutthroat and rainbow trout. Much of the good fishing requires a walk-in.

Shoshone Lake is an 8,050-acre backcountry lake that produces big lake and brown trout, plus a few brookies. In July and August, anglers catch more and bigger fish by fishing deep. This can be done from shore by working dropoffs and the mouths of inlets.

Soda Butte Creek, in the northeast corner of the park, offers particularly fast fishing for cutthroat and rainbow trout. The Gallatin River, in the extreme northeast corner of the park, offers good to excellent fishing for rainbow, brown, and cutthroat trout, as well as whitefish. Fishing is best during July and August.

Southwest and West

Jackson Lake. Jackson Lake is 30 miles north of Jackson. This 25,370-acre reservoir produces nice lake and cutthroat trout. Action is best right after the ice melts in late May, and in late September.

Snake River. The Snake River is the common link between Grand Teton National Park and Jackson Hole. It is fished heavily during its 52-mile trek from Jackson Lake Dam through Jackson Hole. It's still one of the top fishing streams in the West.

The Snake River is home to the Snake River fine-spotted cutthroat trout, and anglers enjoy catching a few of these during their trips to the Snake. Besides cutthroat trout, the river's upper section also produces numerous brown trout and whitefish. The middle section, which ends near Jackson, is good for cutthroat trout and whitefish. The lower section has good fishing for bigger cutthroats.

Other waters near Jackson. Pacific Creek crosses the highway between Moran Junction and Jackson Lake. In the Teton National Forest, cutthroat trout fishing is excellent. The Gros Ventre River crosses the highway 6 miles north of Jackson. Its upper stretch, above Kelly in the Teton National Forest, provides good fishing for cutthroat, brook, and rainbow trout. The Hoback River enters the Snake 17 miles south of Jackson. Most of the time, anglers can experience fair fishing here for cutthroat trout and whitefish, and late summer is the best time to pursue these fish. Granite Creek offers fair fishing for small cutthroat trout and whitefish. Flat Creek runs through the National Elk Refuge, and this fishery is good from August through October. The Buffalo Fork River enters the Snake River at Moran Junction. Many sections of the Buffalo Fork offer good fishing for cutthroat, brook, and rainbow trout in late summer and early fall.

Grassy, Leigh, Jenny, Phelps, Lower Slide, and Two Ocean Lakes offer fair to good fishing for brook, cutthroat, and lake trout. At Two Ocean Lake, action is best in spring and late fall. The lake sometimes gives up trophy trout.

Teton high-country waters. The high-country fishing here is good for small brook trout. But even some of the heavily fished waters yield up nice-size trout. It is generally late June before most of the high-country trails open. The best fishing is usually in September.

Green River. Most anglers on the Upper Green River catch good quantities of rainbows, but some catch brook, brown, and cutthroat trout.

Action on the Green River is usually good from spring through fall, and it can be excellent at times. From Fontenelle Reservoir to Flaming Gorge Reservoir, the Green offers fair to good trout fishing; the key is finding good fish habitat. In areas with good habitat, anglers can catch many big rainbow, brown, and cutthroat trout. Float fishing is popular on the Green.

Fontenelle Reservoir. Ten miles south of LaBarge, 7,000-acre Fontenelle Reservoir is one of Wyoming's top lakes for big brown and rainbow trout. On the weekends during the summer, it's a busy place although not usually crowded.

Flaming Gorge Reservoir. Half of Flaming Gorge Reservoir's 42,000 acres is in Wyoming, the other half in Utah. It is famous for its lake trout fishing and produces a tremendous number of 20-plus-pound lake trout. The reservoir also has trophy brown trout, nice-size rainbow trout, kokanee salmon, smallmouth bass, and catfish.

New Fork River. One of the state's best trout streams, the New Fork River yields good numbers of nice-size brown and rainbow trout. The fishing is usually good to excellent following spring runoff. The action is best in the evening.

Lakes near Pinedale. The Finger Lakes near Pinedale all offer good fishing for lake trout. These include the New Fork Lakes 20 miles north of Pinedale, Willow Lake 12 miles north of Pinedale, Fremont Lake 5 miles and Halfmoon Lake 8 miles northeast of Pinedale, Boulder Lake 10 miles east of Pinedale, and Burnt Lake 10 miles east of Pinedale. The action is fastest at Burnt and Willow Lakes, but Fremont and New Fork Lakes have the larger fish. Anglers also catch rainbow and brown trout in the Finger Lakes.

The Green River lakes are roughly 40 miles north of Pinedale. They provide good fishing for big lake trout and rainbow trout. Action is best early and late in the day. Soda Lake, 7 miles north of Pinedale, has brook and brown trout. Mid-May and late September are the best times to fish Soda Lake.

Meadow Lake is the best source of grayling eggs in Wyoming, and it is probably the best grayling fishery in the West. It lies halfway between Halfmoon and Burnt Lakes. Meadow Lake usually loses its ice in mid- or late May, when the fishing is best. Middle Piney Lake, 25 miles west of Big Piney, offers good fishing for rainbow and cutthroat trout and can have good fishing for lake trout. Optimal times to pursue these fish are early and late in the day. Dollar Lake is 10 miles below the Green River lakes and is easy to fish for rainbow trout. The angling is best right before dark.

Bridger Wilderness. There are hundreds of alpine lakes and streams to fish in the Bridger Wilderness and Wind River Range. Anglers can catch plenty of small brook and cutthroat trout, but they have to walk to get there.

Other waters. Lake Viva Naughton, 17 miles northwest of Kemmerer, is usually busy but not too crowded on spring and summer weekends. This 1,375-acre lake holds nice-size rainbow trout. Kemmerer City Reservoir northwest of Kemmerer produces good rainbow trout. About 700 acres of big Palisades Reservoir, 40 miles south of Jackson, spills from Idaho into Wyoming; fishing is best in spring and fall for cutthroat, lake, and brown trout.

The Greys River is one of Wyoming's best-kept secrets, providing good fishing for cutthroat trout below Palisades Reservoir. The Hamms Fork River below Kemmerer City Reservoir has fair to good fishing for rainbow and brown trout. The Salt River produces good-size cutthroat and brown trout near Afton. The Smith's Fork River has fair fishing for brown and cutthroat trout. LaBarge Creek, west of LaBarge, has fair to good fishing for rainbow, brown, cutthroat, and brook trout.

Sulphur Creek Reservoir, 10 miles south of Evanston, spans 699 acres and is known for rainbow, brown, and cutthroat trout. The action is best in May and September. Woodruff Reservoir, north of Evanston, is 1 acre larger and has fair action for rainbow, cutthroat, and brown trout. Anglers also catch a few channel catfish and tiger muskies here. The Bear River is mostly on private land, but it offers fair to good fishing for cutthroat, brown, and rainbow trout.

Y

YARN FLY
An artificial fly tied with yarn, some of which are also called egg flies. See: Fly.

YEAR-CLASS
The fish spawned and hatched in a given year, also referred to as a "generation" of fish.

See: Fisheries Management.

YELLOWTAIL
Other names—kingfish, yellowtail kingfish, king yellowtail, kingie, amberjack.

Yellowtail are members of the Carangidae family and are closely related to amberjack. Although they are commonly referenced by anglers and scientists as three separate species—California yellowtail (*Seriola lalandi dorsalis*), southern yellowtail (*S. lalandi lalandi*), and Asian yellowtail (*S. lalandi aureovittata*)—it is currently believed that the worldwide yellowtail pool

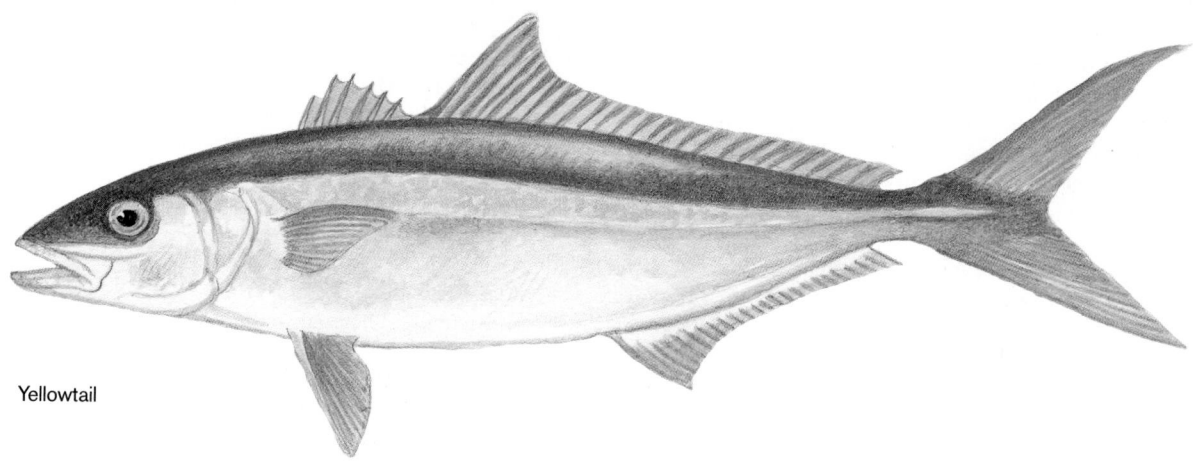

Yellowtail

consists of one species, *S. lalandi*. The three varieties are recognized distinctly, however, because they are isolated from each other and do not appear to interact; there are also size differences with some populations, the southern variety growing larger (especially in New Zealand waters) than the others.

These are fast-swimming, hard-striking, strong-pulling fish that give anglers a great struggle, especially in large sizes, and are a great favorite with shore, boat, and light-tackle big-game anglers. They are a commercially important species and are highly regarded as table fare. The smaller specimens, especially the California population, are preferred, although the flesh of some southern yellowtail has been found to turn milky when cooked.

Identification. Yellowtail are readily identifiable by their deeply forked, bright yellow caudal fins. Their body coloring graduates from a purple blue on the back to a silvery white on the belly. The body is elongate and moderately compressed, and a brass-colored stripe runs the length of the body from mouth to tail. There is a small keel on either side of the caudal peduncle.

Size. The southern yellowtail is believed to grow to a maximum weight of 70 kilograms and a length in excess of 2 meters, although fish of this size are rare. An Australian record, taken off Sydney, New South Wales, stands at 51 kilograms, and a 52-kilogram New Zealand fish holds the all-tackle world record. The world record for the California yellowtail is nearly 36 kilograms, but the average fish is much smaller.

Distribution. The California yellowtail ranges throughout the Gulf of California and along the Pacific coast of North America from Baja California, Mexico, to Los Angeles, California. On occasion, it is found as far north as Washington. The southern yellowtail occurs off southern Brazil and Argentina, South Africa, Australia, and North Island, New Zealand. In Australian waters, it ranges from Perth in Western Australia, around the bottom of Australia, and up the East Coast to North Reef, just North of Brisbane. Lord Howe Island, off the East Coast,

and nearby Elizabeth Reef, hold among the world's largest southern yellowtail.

Habitat. Yellowtail are primarily coastal schooling fish found in inshore waters and out to the continental shelf. In addition to schooling in and around offshore reefs and rocky shores, they frequent deep water around wharves and jetties and man-made structures such as sunken vessels or artificial reefs where baitfish are common. Occasionally they will venture along ocean beaches and into larger estuaries. Large specimens, especially of the southern variety, are encountered in deep water around rocky pinnacles.

Life history/Behavior. Few details of the yellowtail's life history are available. Southern yellowtail are of spawning age at about two to three years. It is known that spawning occurs off eastern Australia from July through February, the occurrence varying with the location. Eggs are pelagic and hatch within two or three days. Juveniles are frequently found around floating objects such as buoys, traps, and channel markers.

Yellowtail can form large schools around reefs and will rise to the surface en masse to feed on schools of baitfish, as well as drive baitfish up against shore. Their migratory habits are not well known, although records tell of southerly moving spawning schools of southern yellowtail covering several square miles. Large individuals are believed to be less migratory.

Food and feeding habits. Yellowtail will eat whatever is available, but they feed predominantly on small fish, squid, and pelagic crustaceans. They are known to herd baitfish into shallow water off beaches, where they are vulnerable to the surf angler. Large specimens will tackle bluefish, salmon, and small tuna.

Angling. Various methods are used to catch yellowtail, including trolling, jigging, casting with lures, rock- and surf fishing, and fishing with baits. Tackle ranges from conventional gamefishing outfits in various classes to roller-tipped boat rods of various configurations to light and medium gear.

W
X
Y
Z

A southern yellowtail from deep water off North Island, New Zealand.

Lures can be large surface poppers, offshore trolling lures, plastic squid, metal spoons, metal jigs, skirted lures, feathered lures, artificial flies, dead fish, casting plugs, among others. Baits can consist of garfish; pilchards; squid; sauries; strips of mullet, tuna, and bonito; and live fish.

Slow to medium-fast trolling is most effective when close to deep-water rocky shores, around bomboras, along the dropoff from reefs, and over and around underwater pinnacles and wrecks. A well-known technique for southern yellowtail is using a flashing device rigged 1 to 2 meters ahead of a trolled bait.

Jigging requires repetitive lifting and dropping of a heavy metal jig and is very effective when used over offshore reefs. Once the school or reef is located by sonar, the jig is dropped over the side of the boat and allowed to sink to the bottom, then raised to the surface in a series of lifts. The procedure is repeated until a fish is hooked. Another strategy is to drop the jig to the bottom, then lift it up and down in one place. Both methods work well, although the former is preferred. Jigging can also be effective when using a strip bait hooked to the jig, or with a whole squid only.

Shore fishing from rocky platforms adjacent to deep water presents a real challenge to the shore-based southern yellowtail angler, as does fishing from man-made structures such as jetties and wharves. In these situations, lure casting with metal spoons or jigs demands physical stamina and finely honed casting skills. Fishing with live baits, using balloons to float the baits out from these areas, is also practiced.

Fly anglers are best served when schools of yellowtail swim close to the surface chasing baitfish. This is also when light-tackle anglers score well by tossing surface poppers. The excitement can be heightened by chumming to keep the fish at the surface, or by tethering a caught yellowtail behind the boat so that its efforts to escape attract the other members of the school and hold them in the vicinity. It's not unusual to see 50 to 100 trophy southern yellowtail swimming within meters of the boat; jigging a feathered lure or strip bait works especially well then.

Yellowtail don't concede easily when hooked. The first lengthy run is followed by several shorter ones, each impressing the angler with the power that this species possesses. In open water, they can usually be played out in a straightforward manner; however, if hooked from a boat over a reef, or from a shore-based location, the southern yellowtail will likely try to head to the nearest obstruction to break the line, often succeeding.

YUGOSLAVIA

The Federal Republic of Yugoslavia covers 102,173 square kilometers of territory and has more than 10 million inhabitants. It is situated in southeastern Europe, and nearly four-fifths of its landmass lies in the central area of the Balkan Peninsula, where the Rodope, Carpathian-Balkan, and Dinaric Mountains meet.

Yugoslavia is bordered on the north by Hungary, on the north and east by Romania, on the east by Bulgaria, on the south by Albania and the former Yugoslav Republic of Macedonia, and on the west by Croatia and Bosnia/Herzegovina. A southwestern strip of 153 kilometers borders the Adriatic Sea. Twenty-one percent of the country is in Middle Europe, that is, north of the Sava and Danube Rivers.

Yugoslavia consists of two republics: Serbia, which accounts for 86 percent of the land, and Montenegro, which is in the southwest facing the Adriatic. There are some 80,000 licensed anglers in the country, but at least twice that number fish without buying a license. There is almost no angling tourism due to water pollution, intensive localized sportfishing, legal and illegal commercial exploitation (on seas, rivers, and lakes), and a lack of angling guides, boat rentals, and other services; recent ethnic conflicts, as well as NATO military activities have obviously precluded visitation in any event. In better times, however, a tourist can still find some interesting fishing in Yugoslavia mainly for grayling, huchen, brown trout, and carp. The key is finding a local angler who is willing to help and with whom you can communicate. The chance of getting information from local tourist boards or angling clubs is slim.

Land, Climate, and Resources

The northern part of Yugoslavia, from its border with Hungary and including the narrow zone to the south of the Sava and Danube Rivers, is part of the Panonian Flat. This area has a height of less then 200 meters and only two small mountains (Fruska Gora and Vrsacke Planine). The Danube, one of Europe's biggest rivers, enters Yugoslavia on the northwest and flows through the country for 588.5 kilometers, collecting 72.3 percent of its water and taking it to the Black Sea. Most of the Danube's big tributaries—the Sava, Tisa, and Tamis—are all slow flowing, with brown and muddy waters that are high in spring and low during summer.

A large network (hundreds of kilometers) of artificial canals connects the Danube and Tisa Rivers in the province of Vojvodina, north of the Sava and Danube. It is used for drainage, agricultural purposes, and water transport.

The climate in this region is continental; the summers are very hot and almost without rain (the daily temperature in July and August can reach 40°C, but is usually 30° to 35°C). Winters are sharp and long, with the lowest temperatures dipping to roughly –20°C. Vojvodina receives 500 to 600 millimeters of rain per year; the southern part of this flat region gets 700 to 900 millimeters of rain, mainly at the end of spring (May through June) and in autumn.

Mountains mainly in the range of 600 to 1,400 meters dominate the rest of Yugoslavia all the way south to the Adriatic coast. The highest mountain peak is Djeravica (2,656 meters) in the Prokletije Mountains in southern Yugoslavia.

Numerous streams, creeks, and medium-size rivers run down the mountains and through the valleys. Waters from this area primarily flow to the Black Sea, connecting to the Velika Morava River and then the Danube, and also via the Drina River to the Sava and the Danube. A few waters (26.6 percent) from this region flow to the Adriatic Sea, and very little (1.1 percent) to the Aegean Sea. All of the rivers get their water from rain and snow; levels are therefore extremely high in spring and extremely low in summer.

The climate of this region is continental; on higher mountains it is sharp, with long and cold winters (temperatures drop to –38°C). Snow is a possibility from 70 to 210 days a year in higher regions, where it can remain for four to five months. Summers are short and fresh. Rainy periods occur in autumn (October and November) and spring (March and April). The mountain area receives 1,000 to 1,500 millimeters of annual rainfall; the Krivosije area north of Boka Kotorska Bay on the Adriatic gets 5,317 millimeters annually.

The biggest Yugoslavian lake, Skadarsko, is located in the far southeast in the Republic of Montenegro. Its surface is 6 meters above sea level, and its bottom is 28 meters below sea level. The lake covers an area of 379 kilometers, 222 of which belong to Yugoslavia and the rest to Albania. It is 55 kilometers long and up to 14 kilometers wide, and has a maximum depth of 44 meters.

Skadarsko (known as Scutari to Italians) is part of a national park and contains many fish. Angling there can be satisfactory to good, especially for wild carp (up to 25 kilograms), eels, and mullet (in the Bojana River, which runs from the lake to the sea). There is a small hotel in the little town of Virpazar, and also private rooms to rent. There is no commercial boat livery, but wherever there are boats it is possible to rent them from the owners along the sea coast (this is true elsewhere in Yugoslavia as well).

The Adriatic coast has a mild Mediterranean climate. Winters are short and mild, and summers are long and hot; temperatures in autumn are 2° to 5°C hotter than in spring. The midsummer temperatures are between 20° and 26°C (July is the hottest month), and in winter the temperature never falls under 7°C.

Yugoslavia has a wide variety of fishing waters: deep, slow-running rivers; fast-running, well-oxygenated brooks and rivers; canals; reservoirs (water dams); small deep lakes; and small, shallow, brown ponds. Nearly all species of native European freshwater fish (some 70 in all) inhabit these waters, as do such introduced species as rainbow trout (generally small and not numerous), Prussian carp (which weigh up to 8 pounds but average well under 1 pound and have suppressed native cyprinids), grass carp, silver carp, bighead carp, largemouth bass, pumpkinseed, and small catfish (brown bullhead).

Largemouth bass probably came from fisheries in Hungary. This species has spread throughout a network of canals in northwestern Vojvodina around the cities of Sombor, Kula, Crvenka, and Vrbas, and is favored by spinning tackle enthusiasts. It is numerous in this area and spawns naturally. The average catch is under 1 pound, and a 4-pounder is rare; the maximum weight of the species in Yugoslavia is thought to be between 6 and 8 pounds.

The brown bullhead, known here as an American catfish, was planted in some waters a few decades ago to make it a sport and food fish. It stays small, however, rarely exceeding 2 pounds. In nearly all the lakes in which it was stocked, it has caused an ecological catastrophe. It commonly grows to 10 centimeters and is so numerous that populations of all other fish in the same waters have sharply decreased, and some domestic species are disappearing.

The most popular species for coarse angling are: carp (saran), Prussian carp (babuska), pike (stuka), pike-perch or zander (smudj), barbel (mrena), nose-carp (skobalj), chub (klen), and catfish (som). Anglers using spinning tackle pursue pike, pike-perch, huchen (mladica), and brown trout (potocna pastrmka). The brown trout is favored by fly anglers, who also pursue grayling (lipljen).

Generally, coarse fishing is more or less satisfactory throughout the country, grayling fishing is good in some areas, and huchen fishing is satisfactory

James Heddon is credited with making the first artificial plug in the early 1900s, yet the first patent for a wooden lure was granted to David Huard and Charles Dunbar in 1874.

W
X
Y
Z

in some areas. Saltwater trolling offers some good sport, especially in the hotter part of the year, around the mouth of the Bojana River (on the Yugoslavia-Albania border), where leerfish (garrick) weighing between 20 and 60 pounds can be numerous.

Except for huchen and grayling in some rivers, the concentration of fish throughout Yugoslavia is lower than it is in many other European countries. Traveling anglers looking for intensive fishing and a lot of trophy catches would be better served elsewhere.

Gamefishing

Yugoslavia offers good grayling fly fishing on the Drina River, especially around the city of Bajina Basta. This is a fast-running river with clear water. A tributary of the Sava, it courses through the mountains between Yugoslavia and the state of Bosnia/Herzegovina. There is a good grayling population here, and the fish average 35 centimeters in length, although some measuring 50 to 53 centimeters (approximately 4 pounds) were caught in the mid- to late 1990s.

The huchen is very popular in this region, too. Anglers who favor spinning tackle pursue it on the Drina and Lim Rivers (the latter being the same type of water as the Drina, shared by Serbia and Montenegro, in the mountainous area), and occasionally produce memorable catches. The visiting angler who hires an experienced local angler to share his spots, lures, and techniques stands a chance of catching a trophy huchen weighing between 10 and 20 kilograms. The largest huchen caught on sportfishing tackle since 1980 have weighed up to 25 kilograms.

The best period for this species is December and January, but autumn can bring good catches, too. The closed season for huchen is from February 1 through June 5 to 15 (depending on local regulations). Fishing with natural baits is prohibited for huchen, brown trout, and grayling on Yugoslavian waters; only lures and flies are allowed.

The Montenegrin mountains contain regions of exceptional scenic beauty that have been proclaimed national parks; these include Durmitor, with 16 lakes, 5 rivers, and 6 canyons, and Biogradska Gora. Some river canyons in Montenegro, namely Tara, Moraca, and Piva, are among the deepest in the world (up to 1,200 meters). These 3 rivers offer brown trout and grayling fishing, and brown trout also inhabit the Mlava, Rzav, Djetinja, Vapa, and Uvac Rivers, as well as numerous small rivers and streams in the mountainous part of Yugoslavia. The average size is well under 2 pounds. In some lakes, however—namely Lake Zavoj near the city of Pirot in southeastern Serbia—there are brown trout weighing 18 kilograms-plus, but such big fish are very rarely caught.

Pike, pike-perch, and wels catfish are caught on lures in slow-flowing rivers (Dunav, Sava, Tisa, and Tamis), but the average pike and pike-perch are small (under 2 pounds). Wels are respectably bigger (from about 4 pounds up to 200 pounds), but fish over 20 pounds are rarely caught.

Coarse Angling

Pike, pike-perch, and wels catfish are all predators favored by Yugoslav coarse anglers on slow-flowing rivers and brown-water lakes and are caught on natural baits as well as artificials. But the number one challenge for most resident anglers in the northern and central parts of the country is hard-fighting wild carp (common carp), which can grow to around 60 pounds, and mirror carp, which can grow to 75 pounds.

With constant feeding of a chosen spot on the river, canal, or natural or artificial lake, and lots of fishing hours, catches of around 10 pounds are possible on nearly all waters. The season for carp lasts from June 1 until winter, and they are caught on natural and processed baits. Generally, catching a trophy carp on Yugoslav waters today requires a lot of luck, as much skill, and weeks or sometimes even months of hard work. A visiting angler ultimately needs the assistance of a good local angler as a guide, just to locate a spot that has any chance of yielding a respectable catch.

Coastal Fishing

Sportfishing in saltwater is not popular with Yugoslavs, but commercial fishing, mainly with nets, is common. It is known, however, that trolling with lures can produce good catches of amberjack, leerfish, mackerel, and bonito. Big-game fishing is popular in the south on the Italian side of the Adriatic, which should mean that the Montenegrin region is worth trying, too. Some catches by Yugoslavian commercial fishermen confirm the presence of swordfish, tuna, and little tunny in local waters. It is also possible to catch seabass while casting (even from the shore), and night anglers have experienced nice catches of hard-fighting conger eels, which favor dead baits. A boat is a must for almost all sea fishing on the Adriatic, and although no charter boats for angling are available, boats can be rented from individuals.

Regulations and Tourist Information

Both Serbia and Montenegro have their own fishing laws and regulations. One license covers fishing in all of Montenegro, with the exception of three national parks, but more than a dozen regional and local licenses are required for fishing on all Serbian waters.

Yearly and daily licenses are sold in fishing clubs and tourist centers, and sometimes in hotels. Prices vary considerably, but generally it is much cheaper to buy a yearlong license for a region than a series of one-day licenses, which are usually site-specific. Prices for residents and nonresidents are the same. The license for fishing on Montenegrin rivers and

W
X
Y
Z

lakes is valid for boat angling on the sea as well. No license is required for saltwater angling from the shore.

Night fishing is illegal on almost all rivers and lakes, and regulations exist that govern size limits, catch limits, seasons, and equipment (mainly regarding the number of hooks). Ask about all of them when buying a license; it's a good idea to check on all regulations before going fishing to avoid difficulties with local authorities. It is not legal to use sonar anywhere in Yugoslavia, but this regulation does not seem to be enforced for those using sonar for sportfishing purposes, as local anglers use it.

All-inclusive angling tours are unavailable in Yugoslavia. Visiting anglers must rely on private contacts with local anglers. Contacting the local, regional, or state tourist boards can only help in making travel plans and reserving accommodations.

YUKON TERRITORY

Located in the northwest corner of Canada and bordering eastern Alaska, the rugged and mountainous Yukon Territory offers good fishing opportunities in a beautiful and pristine wilderness setting. Covering 479,000 square kilometers, the Yukon has a larger landmass than California. Yet it has just 33,000 inhabitants, two-thirds of whom live in the capital city of Whitehorse. It issues only 17,000 fishing licenses annually, to anglers who have approximately 4,500 square kilometers of freshwater to choose from.

Some of that bounty is easily accessed via 4,700 kilometers of roads, but the most notable and exciting opportunities to catch trophy fish are tucked away in remote areas accessible only by boat or plane.

Gamefish primarily inhabit the region's 12 principal lakes and 14 major river systems. These fish include four species of Pacific salmon, lake trout,

Many of the Yukon's top fishing grounds are only accessible by floatplane.

arctic grayling, northern pike, inconnu, lake whitefish, kokanee salmon, arctic charr, bull trout, Dolly Varden, steelhead, and rainbow trout. Grayling, pike, lake trout, rainbow trout, and salmon are the most pursued species, and trophy specimens exist in numerous waters. An active rainbow trout and arctic charr stocking program exists in pothole lakes, most of which are easily accessible by road. A salmon stocking program has enhanced chinook salmon stocks in some tributaries of the Yukon River system.

Waters in the Yukon are generally cool due to the short summers and long ice-covered winters, which last late October into May. These cold waters keep the growth of fish slow and the flesh firm, making them excellent table fare and very active on the end of a fishing line. Due to rapidly changing weather and extremely cold water temperatures, fishing by boat in all Yukon lakes, especially the larger ones, should be approached with caution. It is wise to inquire with government representatives or local inhabitants about water and weather conditions before heading out onto an unfamiliar lake. All waterways are public and are also open to fishing by Yukon-licensed nonresidents.

Commercial airline service is available to Whitehorse from Vancouver, British Columbia, as well as from Anchorage and Fairbanks, Alaska. Primary road access is via the Alaska Highway from northern British Columbia. Many good fishing opportunities exist along this highway, as well as on other road systems within the territory. Guided and fly-in fishing services are also available, and some visitors take advantage of lodge and outfitter opportunities to reach distant waters.

Because much Yukon angling occurs in unspoiled wilderness, the most competition may come from local wildlife, including grizzly bears. During the salmon runs these creatures can add some exciting moments to an angling adventure, so it's important to be alert for bears and give them the right of way.

Catch-and-release fishing is encouraged for conservation throughout the Yukon Territory and is mandated in a few locations for certain species. Barbless single hooks are mandated on some waters as well, and encouraged elsewhere.

Major Species
Arctic grayling. Grayling inhabit most lakes, rivers, and streams of the Yukon. Their abundance, beauty, and fighting qualities on light tackle make them a popular quarry. They may grow as large as 60 centimeters in length and attain a weight of more than 2 kilograms, but the average grayling in the Yukon will be less than 50 centimeters long, with a weight of under 1 kilogram. Grayling are excellent table fare when fresh; these white-fleshed fish lose their taste when frozen for any length of time.

Terrestrial insects form the larger part of their diet, but they also feed on bottom nymphs, snail-

and eggs. One of the more popular times to catch grayling in the Yukon is early spring, when they gather in numbers to spawn in shallow rivers and streams. Flies, spinners, and small spoons are all successfully used by anglers.

Fishing opportunities for arctic grayling exist along the Alaska Highway at the Rancheria, Swift, and Teslin Rivers. The Teslin offers excellent fishing at Johnson's Crossing in early spring. Grayling are caught at Kusawa and Kluane Lakes, as well as at Mendenhall Creek. Notable sites along the Campbell Highway are the Francis and Finlayson Rivers, as well as Frenchman and Francis Lakes. Other good sites are along the Klondike Highway at Fox Creek, the McQuesten River, and the Klondike River.

Lake trout. Lakers are also avidly pursued in the Yukon Territory for their trophy size, bulldog-like fighting abilities, and fine eating qualities. They are found in virtually all Yukon lakes. Ten- to 14-kilogram fish are not uncommon in the larger lakes.

The best time to catch Yukon lake trout is in early spring before the water temperature reaches 9°C. Throughout the month of June, lake trout feed in the shallows before heading to deeper, cooler water in summer. Fishing improves again in the fall, when lake trout move into the shallows to spawn. Methods to catch these fish include trolling and casting lures and flies, and Yukoners also take them through the ice in winter.

Notable lake trout sites along the Alaska Highway are Teslin, Kusawa, Aishihik, and Sekulmun Lakes; along the Campbell Highway are Frances, Little Salmon, and Frenchman Lakes; and along the Klondike Highway are Laberge, Braeburn, and Ethel Lakes.

Northern pike. Pike generally inhabit the shallow waters of lakes and streams in the Yukon, as they tolerate higher water temperatures, lower concentrations of oxygen, and higher concentrations of carbon dioxide than many species of freshwater fish here. Some reach the 12-plus-kilogram category.

Adults spawn in shallow marshy areas of lakes as soon as the ice goes out in the spring. When taken from cold water north of the 60th parallel, the northern pike is an aggressive gamefish and superb table fare. The most popular times to catch northern pike are in the spring and early summer, and a variety of methods are effective.

Good pike lakes along the Alaska Highway include Squanga, Marsh, Kusawa, and Kluane; along the Campbell Highway they include Frances, Finlayson, and Frenchman Lakes; along the Klondike Highway they include Laberge, Fox, Tatchun, and Ethel Lakes.

Probably the most exciting opportunities for Yukon pike exist in lakes and streams away from the beaten track, and these are also likely to yield the bigger fish. Most of those places are accessible only by air via floatplane service available throughout the Yukon. Great fly-in pike fishing exists in

Toobally, Alligator, Tatlmain, Tshawsahmon, Tincup, Wellesley, Wolf, and Big Kalzas Lakes. There is good fishing in the Yukon River for relatively big pike, but except for a few spots it is hard to access, is mainly fished from a boat, and usually requires planning for an extensive trip into the wilderness. More people visit this big river for the unspoiled wilderness travel experience than for the fishing.

Rainbow trout. The Yukon offers opportunities for stocked and native rainbows. A small reproducing population of native rainbow trout inhabits the Kathleen River and McLean Lakes systems. These rainbows generally reach a size of 1.4 kilograms and are all subject to live-release regulations. The Kathleen River is a special site, originating from a deep mountain lake and heading to a chain of shallow nutrient-rich lakes downstream.

Because of an extensive stocking program in pothole lakes, stocked rainbows have reached more than 6 kilograms. These stocked fish can live up to 11 years, although their normal life span is 4 to 6 years. Adults feed mainly on freshwater shrimp, caddisflies, blackflies, mollusks, and occasional small fish. Their flesh ranges from bright salmon orange to pale pink and is very delicious.

Rainbow trout are caught year-round, but spring and summer are most popular. Spinners and dry flies are productive, and some stocked rainbows are taken through the ice during the winter.

Arctic charr. These fish share many of the characteristics that make rainbow trout so popular. Until the arctic charr was included in government stocking programs in the Whitehorse area, however, few Yukoners had had an opportunity to catch this powerful and good-eating fish, as native charr were so remote. Native charr populations are found in the northern part of the territory in the Firth and Blackstone River systems, and there they sometimes weigh up to 9 kilograms. They are caught on streamers and occasionally on dry flies, but a flashy spoon is generally most effective. Ice fishing anglers catch charr on spoons with a small roe bag attached.

There are no outfitters here, however, so this is do-it-yourself fishing. The Firth is very difficult to reach, although the Blackstone can be accessed via the Dempster Highway. You'll need your own river transportation.

Dolly Varden/bull trout. Dolly Varden in the Yukon are recognizable by their dark blue to olive green backs with white or dusky underparts. They have yellow spots on the dorsal surface and orange or red spots on the sides. Stella Lake on the Haines Road contains landlocked Dollies. They're in the Blackstone River along the Dempster Highway in the north, as well as in the southwestern part of the territory.

Bull trout, often confused with Dolly Varden, are aggressive feeders and are easily caught. They inhabit the Liard River basin and tributary lakes and rivers.

Salmon/steelhead. Salmon migrate into two main water systems in the territory, neither of which provides much access. The mighty Yukon River has chinook, coho, and chum salmon. The migration of chinook salmon in the Yukon River system is the longest in the world, extending more than 2,000 kilometers from their home in the Beaufort Sea to their spawning grounds in tributary streams of the Yukon River. The chinook salmon run usually reaches Dawson by mid-July, and Whitehorse by early August. One of the longest fish ladders in North America (1,200 feet) is located at the dam at Whitehorse Rapids, allowing fish to migrate to the headwaters.

Chum salmon are in many Yukon tributaries from August through October. A small number of coho salmon migrate into the Porcupine River tributary system in the northern part of the territory in September and October.

The Alsek-Tatshenshini River system in the southeast corner of the territory holds runs of chinook, coho, and sockeye. The best angling occurs throughout July for chinook, in late September and October for coho, and from late August until October for sockeye.

Adult chinook salmon average 7 to 10 kilograms, but fish up to 30 kilograms have been taken from both river systems. Coho returning from the ocean are in the 5-kilogram category, and sockeye seldom exceed 2 kilograms but are most prized as table fare.

Chum salmon spawn in the major tributaries of the Yukon, White, Stewart, Pelly, and Teslin Rivers. The Porcupine River and its tributary, the Fishing Branch River, contain a sizable spawning population (and also one of the densest grizzly bear populations). This is the least popular salmon species for anglers, and they are generally caught in nets for subsistence purposes. Chum salmon first appear in Dawson City around the middle of August and are still running after freeze-up. Adults average under 2 kilograms in weight.

Kokanee salmon (which are landlocked sockeye) are identical to anadromous sockeye except for their size. They're found only in Kathleen, Frederick, Stella, and Louise Lakes. They seldom exceed .5 kilogram in weight or 42 centimeters in length. During most of the year, kokanee are in deep water; they hold shallow in early June and again in August when they spawn. Flies and small spinners are usually the most successful lures in catching these fighters.

Steelhead are found only in the Alsek-Tatshenshini River system. These are anadromous fish and average better than 2 kilograms.

Other species. Whitefish are abundant in Yukon waters. There are six species here, and lake whitefish are of most interest to anglers (and also commercially). Mature adults average 45 to 50 centimeters long, reach a maximum weight here of 3 to 4 kilograms, and are found in all parts of lakes. From late September to November they move into shallow lake outlets to spawn.

Inconnu, which are also known as coney or sheefish, will take a lure, but they are not often caught by anglers and mostly appear in the gillnets of commercial fishermen. They generally range from 4 to 9 kilograms and are excellent fighters on rod and reel. Inconnu inhabit the Yukon, Pelly, Stewart, and Porcupine Rivers.

Burbot are popular fish with Yukoners for fish and chips, although they're not considered a gamefish. They are voracious, however, feeding mainly at night and primarily on aquatic insects, crustaceans, and fish eggs, and are easily caught on baited lines fished on the bottom. They are popular with ice anglers in early spring, when these fish come into the shallows.

Z

ZAMBIA

Situated in the interior of south-central Africa, Zambia is bounded by several countries with varied angling opportunities (Zimbabwe and Mozambique in particular), and itself has or shares some prominent rivers and lakes. From a sportfishing standpoint, its most significant river is the Zambezi, which flows from Angola in western Zambia and then courses along a shared border with Zimbabwe, forming Lake Kariba in the process. The fisheries of this portion of the Zambezi are detailed elsewhere (see: Namibia; Zimbabwe).

Other important waterways include the Kafue and Luangwa Rivers, which are respectively eastern and western tributaries to the Zambezi; and the Lualaba and Chambeshi Rivers in the north. Other lakes include Mweru, shared with the Democratic Republic of the Congo (Zaire); the southernmost portion of Lake Tanganyika; and Bangweulu, which is surrounded by a vast swampy region. Lake Bangweulu covers more than 1,150 square miles during the dry season, and several times that in full flood, and is one of the headwaters of the Congo River.

Huge Lake Tanganyika is reputedly of great angling interest, but extremely limited information exists on locations, seasons, and, most importantly, availability of true sportfishing services throughout the lake. Several lodges are said to exist at Kasaba Bay in Zambia, and some boats are available for angling. Nile perch, tigerfish (giant catfish) are reportedly the species, but the lake has some 200 sp all. Only a small portion of the southern lake is in Zambia. Tanganyika extends for 420 miles, making it the longest freshwater lake in the world. It has a maximum depth of 4,710 feet, which is second in the world only to Lake Baikal in Siberia. Game viewing is the main attraction for visitors to the area, mostly from Tanzania *(see)*, and the overall lack of knowledge about sportfishing possibilities here (as opposed to Lake Kariba in Zimbabwe, for example) is a cause for wonder.

Sportfishing opportunities throughout Zambia are at best limited and primitive, and primarily relegated to the Zambezi watershed. In addition to the common species of tigerfish, other waters in Zambia are said to contain the giant tigerfish *(Hydrocynus goliath),* as well as vundu.

ZANDER   *Tizostedion lucioperca.*
Other names—pike-perch, pikeperch, pike perch, perch-pike; Danish: *sandart;* Dutch: *snoekbaars;* Finnish: *kuha;* French: *sandre;* German: *schill;* Hungarian: *fogas süllő;* Italian: *sandra;* Norwegian: *gjörs;* Portuguese: *lúcio perca;* Russian: *sudak;* Spanish: *lucioperca;* Swedish: *abborrfisk, gös;* Turkish: *sudak baligi, levrek.*

This is a prominent member of the Percidae family of perch in Europe and an important sportfish. It is commonly known as pike-perch; this is a misnomer, as it is not related to pike nor is it a cross between a pike and a perch. It is very similar and related to the walleye *(see)* of North America, and to a lesser European and western Asian species, the Volga zander *(S. volgense),* which is also known as Volga perch, Volga pike-perch, and *bersh* in Russian.

Identification. The zander's body form and coloration is similar to that of the walleye, although coloration and patterns vary significantly with environment. It has a generally dark greenish back, yellow green sides, and a light belly; the caudal fin is moderately forked; and the spiked first and soft second dorsal fins are separated. There are muted blotches on the back extending down the sides, and the jaws possess large and sharp pikelike canine teeth. The Volga zander is similar but with more distinctive dark markings on its back (somewhat like yellow or European perch) and with smaller teeth.

Size/Age. The zander is commonly found to 20 inches in length but may grow to a maximum of 51 inches and 33 pounds; it can live for 16 years. The Volga zander is much smaller, growing to only 16 inches and 4½ pounds.

Distribution. The zander is native to eastern, northern, and central Europe, including Finland, Sweden, and westernmost Asia; it has been introduced into several western European countries, including England (where it was first introduced in 1878), and has been spreading. The Volga zander occurs in eastern Europe from the Danube River to the Volga and Ural Rivers.

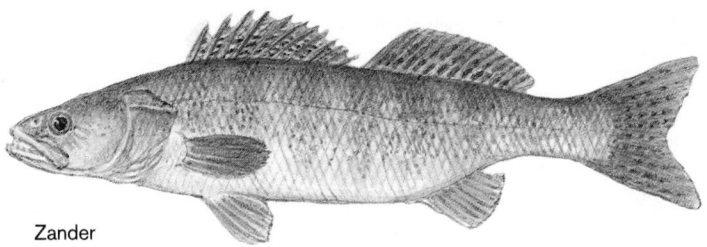
Zander

Habitat/History. Zander are found in rivers, lakes, ponds, and canals, especially in vegetated areas, and they favor larger systems. They spawn between February and July, earliest in southerly areas, and are especially prolific. Their introduction to some nonnative environments has led to a depletion of native fish stocks. Volga zander primarily inhabit deeper nonvegetated areas of rivers but also occur in brackish water near river estuaries.

Food. These carnivorous species consume assorted small fish.

Angling. Although zander have excellent flesh, they are not as widely consumed in Europe as walleye are in North America. As a game species, zander are generally downgraded, falling below the more favored northern pike and above many coarse species, as they are sluggish fighters like walleye.

Sportfishing for zander throughout Europe is largely carried out from shore, although boats may be employed in large waters. Methods are similar to those used for northern pike, the exception being lighter lines and smaller baits and lures; however, zander are susceptible to many of the same tactics used for walleye.

See: Perch.

ZEBRA MUSSEL
The zebra mussel is a small, fingernail-sized mussel native to the Caspian Sea region of Asia. It was discovered in Lake St. Clair near Detroit in 1988. Tolerant of a wide range of environmental conditions, the zebra mussels have spread to parts of all the Great Lakes and the Mississippi River, as well as many other water systems in North America.

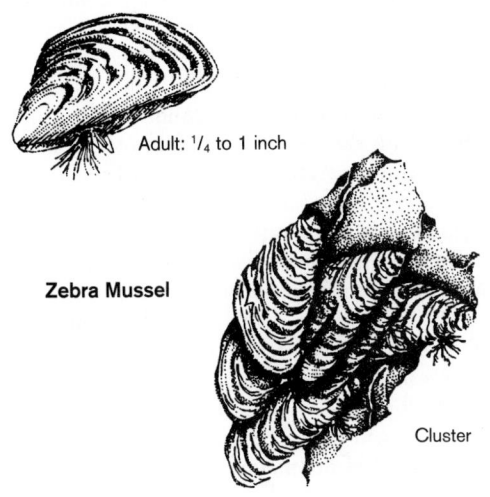
Adult: ¼ to 1 inch
Zebra Mussel
Cluster

W
X
Y
Z

Zebra mussels clog water-intake systems of power plants and water treatment facilities, and the cooling systems of boat engines. They have severely reduced, and may eliminate, native mussel species.

Female zebra mussels can produce as many as 1 million eggs per year. These develop into microscopic, free-swimming larvae called veligers, which quickly begin to form shells. At about three weeks, the sand grain–sized larvae start to settle and attach to any firm surface using "byssal threads." They will cover rock, gravel, metal, rubber, wood, crayfish, native mussels, and each other.

Zebra mussels filter plankton from the surrounding water. Each mussel can filter about 1 quart of lake water per day. However, not all of what they remove is eaten. What they don't eat is combined with mucus as "pseudofeces" and discharged onto the lake bottom where it accumulates. This material may benefit bottom feeders while reducing the plankton food chain for upper water species.

Diving ducks and freshwater drum eat zebra mussels but do not significantly control them. Many methods of control have been tried, and continue to be tried. Minimizing the spread of zebra mussels is important, and anglers and boaters need to make sure they are not part of the problem.
See: Exotic Species.

ZIMBABWE

Described by some Africans as a small country, Zimbabwe is almost the same size as California. Situated in southern Africa and formerly known as Rhodesia, it is one of the most popular tourist destinations in all of Africa. This is not surprising, as Zimbabwe offers tremendous wildlife viewing opportunities, one of the largest waterfalls in the world, and some of the finest freshwater angling available on the continent. Several locations in Zimbabwe have excellent angling for the mighty native tigerfish, dozens of lakes with good populations of introduced largemouth bass, and highland waters with introduced rainbow and brown trout. The country's superb angling is often accompanied by close-up viewing of elephants, buffalo, crocodiles, and other wildlife, which does much to enhance the experience.

Zimbabwe is bordered by Zambia on the north, Botswana on the west, South Africa on the south, and Mozambique on the east. Various rivers span the country, and many of these are dammed to form reservoirs of various sizes.

The most prominent river in the country, which forms the northern boundary with Zambia, is the Zambezi River. The Zambezi winds through the valleys of southern Africa, originating in Angola and coursing through Zambia and the Caprivi Strip of Namibia (see) before entering easternmost Zimbabwe and falling through gorges and chasms to create one of the natural wonders of the world in Victoria Falls. At these dramatic falls, heavily visited but not as developed as Niagara, the Zambezi plunges more than 30 stories before continuing to Lake Kariba, the third largest lake on the continent.

More than 120 indigenous fish species, and nearly a dozen introduced ones, thrive in Zimbabwe. Angling for sport has become more common only in the last few decades of the twentieth century, primarily because equipment was previously difficult and extremely costly to obtain. Sportfishing is gaining significantly here, however, among Zimbabweans as well as among visitors from other African countries, and to some extent among overseas visitors. Visiting anglers have more tourist operators, guides, and—in some places—boats and equipment providers ready to service them in Zimbabwe than in many other countries in southern Africa, although Zimbabwe is still regarded as an emerging market.

Tigerfish are undoubtedly the main attraction for anglers visiting from abroad and from other African countries. Although abundant, these fish have been heavily pressured by angling and poaching (via netting). Zimbabweans have placed greater emphasis on conservation and catch-and-release of this species, following the example set by bass anglers in the country. Largemouth bass have gained a great following with resident anglers since the mid-1980s, whereas trout, which are more limited in distribution, have inspired interest among local and visiting anglers. Popular fish for local and regional anglers also include various coarse species, including bream, barbel, tilapia, and large catfish.

Tigerfish

A number of species of tigerfish inhabit the African continent. The one found in Zimbabwe is *Hydrocynus vittatus,* which is not unique to Zimbabwe but is certainly more prolific here than elsewhere in Africa. The national all-tackle record stands at 34 pounds, 4 ounces. This specimen was taken from Lake Kariba in 1962. Many of these razor-toothed, hard-battling fish are caught in the 5- to 12-pound range; some weigh between 16 and 20 pounds.

The tigerfish is extremely streamlined, predominantly silver in color, with black lateral lines on the body. The fins are a mixture of blending reds and oranges, and these fish have a fine set of razor-sharp, pointed, interlocking teeth similar to the South American piranha. Although a vicious predator, it does not attack humans. It will readily strike at a variety of spoons, spinners, flies, and plugs, as well as at live or cut baitfish.

Tigerfish are found in various lakes and rivers in Zimbabwe. From a sporting perspective, they are most associated with the Zambezi River and its tributaries, and especially with Lake Kariba. Kariba is a man-made lake some 180 miles long and up to 20 miles wide in parts.

W
X
Y
Z

Filled in from 1960 to 1961, Lake Kariba covers 3,750 square miles of water and has an untold amount of shoreline. It is studded with islands and submerged timber. Anyone visiting Zimbabwe for the first time must include a visit to Kariba in their itinerary.

The shores of Kariba, especially along the southern portion in Zimbabwe, have numerous high-quality lodges and hotels. Game viewing is the chief activity. Elephants are commonplace, and there are abundant populations of many game and bird species, including buffaloes and eagles, and some lions. Boats are available for hire here, and numerous angling-oriented safari operators provide extremely worthwhile opportunities in this wild and beautiful country.

In recent years, Kariba has seen a burgeoning houseboat charter industry. Large (60 to 100 feet long) pontoon houseboats, fully equipped with cabins and staff and capable of trips lasting over a week, take out parties for game viewing and/or fishing. At least 100 such boats exist at Kariba. When towing a small fishing boat, the houseboat serves as a mother ship. This setup enables anglers to fish along vast and distant areas of shoreline.

The Kariba International Tigerfishing Tournament is held every October, and in recent years the three-day event has grown to include more than 600 anglers in 4-person teams. Numerous specimens to 13 pounds are landed, and sometimes the largest weighs around 20 pounds.

Nearly all conventional angling methods are successful in landing tigerfish. Medium-action rods of $6^1/_2$ to 7 feet are generally preferred, as is line of about 12-pound test. Terminal tackle must be protected by a wire leader to prevent the fish from severing the line with its sharp teeth. Trolling, casting, and baitfishing are all practiced, and fly fishing is enjoyed as well. Kariba anglers are especially fond of using dead baits, the best of which is the kapenta. This small sardine was introduced into Lake Kariba from Tanzania in the early 1980s for commercial harvesting. Tigerfish like this forage a great deal, and kapenta account for more than half their diet at Kariba.

Tigerfish travel in shoals of varying sizes, from a pair to 20 or more. They start biting suddenly and stay engaged for up to 30 minutes, then cease activity just as suddenly. The strike is strong and vicious and followed by a series of spectacular leaps. Tigerfish are extremely strong fighters, and they battle right up until boated. Many are lost when the line is accidentally cut or the hook simply doesn't get properly imbedded—both because of this species' sharp teeth.

Tigerfish caught in fast water—whether on flies, lures, or baits—are even more tenacious than those taken from lakes, as this species is more vigorous in fast water. The Zambezi River above and below Lake Kariba has excellent opportunities for these fish, and a number of fishing camps line its banks. Some opportunities for self-guided safaris with

Lake Kariba is a premier attraction for angling and wildlife viewing.

4×4 vehicles exist on the Zambian side. More angling is available along the lower river, below 400-foot tall Kariba Dam, and most notably at Mana Pools (and National Park), which is also a noted ornithological area. The middle river, from Victoria Falls to Lake Kariba, is a productive section that also offers whitewater rafting. The upper Zambezi River in Zimbabwe is lush and heavily vegetated; its width varies from 200 yards to a mile or more, and this stretch of river is especially commendable for both beauty and fishing.

Other Species

Both northern-strain and Florida-strain largemouth bass have been introduced into many, if not most, public reservoirs and rivers in Zimbabwe, and they have established self-sustaining populations. They are also present in privately owned ponds. Largemouth bass are believed to have been present here since 1932; Florida-strain bass were introduced in May of 1981. The Zimbabwe record stands at 13 pounds, 13 ounces. A big following for this species exists among organized fishing clubs, and catch-and-release is ardently practiced.

Reservoirs and rivers within 40 to 50 miles of the cities of Bulawayo, Harare, and Masvingo, as well as others at Chinnoyi, Chegutu, the eastern mountains, and elsewhere, provide bass fishing. There may be as many as 60 good bass waters in the country. Near Masvingo, Lake Kyle is one of Zimbabwe's largest reservoirs and most prominent bass waters. Access sites at the lakes are generally poor, and most Zimbabweans must launch their boats along a muddy shoreline. Angling methods are similar to those in North America.

A flourishing bass angling industry since the early 1990s has resulted in a boom in fishing boat manufacture in Zimbabwe, and the country now has suppliers of boats with livewells, electronics, and assorted angling-related features. These are exported regionally in the continent as well.

W
X
Y
Z

Both brown and rainbow trout exist in the mountainous Eastern Highlands region along the Mozambique border. Described as the "Scotland of Africa," this region is a 180-mile-long series of mountain ranges that are representative Zimbabwe's greatest beauty.

Trout were introduced here in 1921 and inhabit various rivers and lakes. Accessibility is best in Nyanga National Park at Nyanga, near 8,500-foot-tall Mt. Inyagani, and at Chimanimani National Park south of Mutare. Clear waters here contrast with the lakes and rivers elsewhere in Zimbabwe. Fly fishing is the rule in the parks, and some hotels may offer private fishing to guests.

Zimbabwe hosts other species, many of which inhabit the same waters as tigerfish and/or large-mouth bass. These include the tackle-busting vundu (giant catfish), which can grow up to 100 pounds but is now rare in the middle Zambezi yet prolific elsewhere, as well as tilapia, bream, barbel, and other coarse species.

ZOOPLANKTON
Minute suspended animals in the water column of seas and lakes.

Conversion Charts

THE SYSTEM OF WEIGHTS AND MEASURES USED IN MOST COUNTRIES AND IN ALL SCIENTIFIC work is the International System of Units (SI), which is commonly referred to as the metric system. A notable and influential exception to this is the United States, where the general public, and non-scientific publications, use the U.S., or U.S. customary, system of weights and measures. Throughout the *Ken Schultz's Fishing Encyclopedia & Worldwide Angling Guide*, there is a liberal use of both metric and U.S. customary weights and measures without parenthetical conversions to equivalent weights or measures. Some anglers, especially those who travel widely and those who pay close attention to world-record fish weights and fishing line classifications, are accustomed to both systems, which are often found mixed at boat docks, fish camps, and tackle shops throughout the world. The following information is provided to help the reader make the conversion from one system to another.

U.S. To Metric Conversion Formulas

When You Know . . .	Multiply By . . .	To Determine . . .
Inches (in)	25.4	Millimeters (mm)
Inches (in)	2.54	Centimeters (cm)
Inches (in)	0.0254	Meters (m)
Square Inches (sq in)	645.0	Square Millimeters (sq mm)
Square Inches (sq in)	6.45	Square Centimeters (sq cm)
Square Inches (sq in)	0.00064	Square Meters(sq m)
Feet (ft)	30.5	Centimeters (cm)
Feet (ft)	0.305	Meters (m)
Feet (ft)	0.0003	Kilometers (km)
Square Feet (sq ft)	0.093	Square Meters (sq m)
Fathoms (fath)	1.827	Meters (m)
Fathoms (fath)	0.0018	Kilometers (km)
Yards (yd)	0.914	Meters (m)
Square Yards (sq yd)	0.836	Square Meters (sq m)
Statute Miles (mi) (5,280 ft)	1.61	Kilometers (km)
Nautical Miles (n mi) (6,020 ft)	1.852	Kilometers (km)
Square Miles (sq mi)	2.56	Square Kilometers (sq km)
Miles per hour (mph)	1.61	Kilometers per hour (kph)
Knots per hour	1.84	Kilometers per hour (kph)
Acres	0.405	Hectares
Ounces of Weight (oz)	28.3	Grams (g)
Ounces of Weight (oz)	0.0283	Kilograms (kg)
Ounces of Fluid (fl oz)	29.6	Milliliters (mL)
Pounds (lb)	454.0	Grams (g)
Pounds (lb)	0.454	Kilograms (kg)
Pints (pt)—U.S.	0.473	Liters (L)
Pints (pt)—Imperial	0.568	Liters (L)
Quarts (qt)—U.S.	0.946	Liters (L)
Quarts (qt)—Imperial	1.14	Liters (L)
Gallons (gal)—U.S.	3.79	Liters (L)
Gallons (gal)—Imperial	4.55	Liters (L)
degrees Fahrenheit (°F)	0.555 (after subtracting 32)	degrees Celsius (°C)

Metric To U.S. Conversion Formulas

When You Know . . .	Multiply By . . .	To Determine . . .
Millimeters (mm)	0.039	Inches (in)
Centimeters (cm)	0.394	Inches (in)
Centimeters (cm)	0.0328	Feet (ft)
Square Centimeters (sq cm)	0.155	Square Inches (sq in)
Meters (m)	39.37	Inches (in)
Meters (m)	3.281	Feet (ft)
Meters (m)	1.09	Yards (yd)
Meters (m)	0.547	Fathoms (fath)
Square Meters (sq m)	1.2	Square Yards (sq yd)
Kilometers (km)	3,279.0	Feet (ft)
Kilometers (km)	1,093.0	Yards (yd)
Kilometers (km)	546.0	Fathoms (fath)
Kilometers (km)	0.621	Statute Miles (mi)
Kilometers (km)	0.545	Nautical Miles (n mi)
Square Kilometers (sq km)	0.386	Square Miles (sq mi)
Kilometers per hour (kph)	0.621	Miles per hour (mph)
Kilometers per hour (kph)	0.545	Knots per hour
Hectares	2.47	Acres
Grams (g)	0.035	Ounces of Weight (oz)
Grams (g)	0.002	Pounds (lb)
Kilograms (kg)	35.2736	Ounces (oz)
Kilograms (kg)	2.2	Pounds (lb)
Milliliter (mL)	0.034	Fluid Ounces (oz)
Liters (L)	2.11	Pints (pt)—U.S.
Liters (L)	1.76	Pints (pt)—Imperial
Liters (L)	1.06	Quarts (qt)—U.S.
Liters (L)	0.880	Quarts (qt)—Imperial
Liters (L)	0.264	Gallons (gal)—U.S.
Liters (L)	0.22	Gallons (gal)—Imperial
degrees Celsius (°C)	1.8 (and add 32)	degrees Fahrenheit (°F)

Table Of Metric and U.S. Equivalent Line Strengths

Metric	U.S. Customary	Metric	U.S. Customary
1 kg	2.2 lb	10 kg	22.0 lb
2 kg	4.4 lb	15 kg	33.0 lb
3 kg	6.6 lb	24 kg	52.8 lb
4 kg	8.8 lb	37 kg	81.4 lb
6 kg	13.2 lb	60 kg	132.0 lb
8 kg	17.6 lb		

Table of Fish Weights

Metric	U.S. Customary	Metric	U.S. Customary
1 kg	2.2 lb	60 kg	132.0 lb
2 kg	4.4 lb	70 kg	154.0 lb
3 kg	6.6 lb	80 kg	176.0 lb
4 kg	8.8 lb	90 kg	198.0 lb
5 kg	11.0 lb	100 kg	220.0 lb
6 kg	13.2 lb	200 kg	440.0 lb
7 kg	15.4 lb	300 kg	660.0 lb
8 kg	17.6 lb	400 kg	880.0 lb
9 kg	19.8 lb	500 kg	1,100.0 lb
10 kg	22.0 lb	600 kg	1,320.0 lb
20 kg	44.0 lb	700 kg	1,540.0 lb
30 kg	66.0 lb	800 kg	1,760.0 lb
40 kg	88.0 lb	900 kg	1,980.0 lb
50 kg	110.0 lb	1,000 kg	2,200.0 lb